FOOTBALL YEARBOOK 2018-2019

IN ASSOCIATION WITH

COMPILED BY JOHN ANDERSON

First published in 2018
by HEADLINE PUBLISHING GROUP

1

Front cover photographs:
(above left) Christian Eriksen (Tottenham Hotspur) – *John Walton/EMPICS Sport*;
(above right) Leroy Sane (Manchester City) – *Mike Hewitt/Getty Images*
(below) Mohamed Salah (Liverpool) – *Simon Stacpoole/Offside/Getty Images*;
Football © *heroman30/Shutterstock*

Spine photograph:
Manchester City manager Pep Guardiola with the Premier League trophy, May 2018 –
Martin Rickett/PA Wire/PA Images

Back cover photographs:
(above) Harry Kane celebrates England's first goal, Columbia v England,
2018 FIFA World Cup Russia Round 16 – *Dan Mullan/Getty Images*;
(below) James Tavernier (Rangers) and Moussa Dembele (Celtic) – *REUTERS/Russell Cheyne*

Cataloguing in Publication Data is available from the British Library

ISBN 9781472261052 (Hardback)
ISBN 9781472261069 (Trade Paperback)

Typeset by Wearset Ltd, Boldon, Tyne and Wear

Printed and bound in the UK by CPI Mackays, Chatham ME5 8TD

HEADLINE PUBLISHING GROUP
An Hachette UK Company
Carmelite House
50 Victoria Embankment
London EC4Y 0DZ

www.headline.co.uk
www.hachette.co.uk

CONTENTS

INTERNATIONAL FOOTBALL

NON-LEAGUE FOOTBALL

INFORMATION AND RECORDS

WELCOME

Welcome to the new edition of *The Football Yearbook*.

John Motson describes this weighty tome as his indispensable bible, a crucial reference throughout his long and distinguished career. That's quite a recommendation, coming as it does from the man who, wrapped in his famous sheepskin coat, evoked the joy of the beautiful game for millions of TV viewers and radio listeners. Copies of every edition of this famous old reference book, stretching back to its inception in the 1970–71 season, sit on John's book shelves. You can bet they are well thumbed. John, after all, has a stat or a fact for every occasion.

Now that line of distinctive fat, blue book spines will be joined by this, the 49th edition, after *The Sun* stepped in to save football's much-loved bible. Last year's *Yearbook* looked to have been the last: but *Sun* readers, who live and breathe football, just wouldn't have forgiven us if we hadn't intervened.

Our readers love football, devouring our football pages, packed with action and analysis from the best writers and pundits in the game: so it was natural that we should want to save such an important and integral part of the fabric of football.

The game is always changing – just look at the introduction of VAR technology – but there's something substantial, authoritative and reliable about *The Football Yearbook*.

The more than a thousand pages that follow this one burst with facts and figures that feed our national obsession, as they have done for nearly five decades.

We football fans are wired up differently from other human beings; our memory banks are packed with images of pain and pleasure, beautiful goals and tragic defeats. As well as the majesty of great players and fine teams, we remember scorelines and team formations, team sheets and tactics. But no brain can process and store every detail thrown up over a season. That's where *The Football Yearbook*, a publication that back in the 1970s set out to be the '*Wisden* of football', comes in.

In the days before the internet, it was the only way to settle a dispute, and the best way to gain authority in a bar-room debate. Even today, when with smartphone in hand you can become an instant expert, there's a gravitas to the facts and figures laid out soberly on these pages.

The 2017–2018 season will be remembered for Pep Guardiola's commanding City team, and their assault on the record books. Whether it was points, wins or passes, City were a symphony in sky blue.

But hidden away in this book is the story of every team's season, the story of *your* team's season. Every page boasts a snippet of information capable of eliciting a smile or a grimace: this book is studded with statistical strikes of beauty and the occasional thudding, two-footed tackle of a reminder, all set out in black and white.

Every summer brings fresh optimism for the football fan – a reason to believe as the new season looms. But before then, lose yourself in the pages of this fine book. Soak up every detail it has to offer. Read the thoughts of *The Sun*'s football experts: England legend Alan Shearer, our Head of Sport Shaun Custis and our Chief Football Reporter Neil Ashton.

Then, like John Motson, place it on the shelf with the others in your collection and brace yourself for another season of passion, pleasure and pain.

Tony Gallagher, Editor-in-Chief, *The Sun*

DREAM TEAM

The 2017–2018 Dream Team season really did belong to one man. Not since Cristiano Ronaldo graced the Premier League nearly a decade ago have we witnessed such a sensational individual campaign. Who are we talking about? Mo Salah, of course.

The 'Egyptian King' emphatically silenced any of the doubters who felt his uninspiring spell at Chelsea before would hamper his impact in the Premier League. Salah racked up a magnificent 412 points – becoming only the second player in Dream Team history after Ronaldo to break that 400-point barrier.

We must admit we were fully subscribed members of the Salah doubting brigade when he first moved to Liverpool last summer, valuing him at just £4m when the season started. But his record-breaking season saw his price rocket to a ridiculous £11.5m by the end of the campaign, by far and away the most expensive player on the game.

Salah smashed 43 goals and 14 assists across all competitions, averaged 7.9 points per game and won that crucial Star Man award a whopping nine times. It meant he finished well clear of nearest points rival Harry Kane, whose score of 376 was no mean feat either.

Despite missing a number of games through injury towards the end of the season, Tottenham's main man kept pace with Salah throughout the campaign but ultimately fell short. Kane hit the 30-goal mark in the Premier League for the first time in his career and, after signing an improved Spurs contract recently, is sure to be a Dream Team favourite again next season.

He was well ahead of Kevin De Bruyne (284 points) in third, with fellow Belgian Eden Hazard (281) and Liverpool forward Roberto Firmino (280) just behind.

Away from the headline names, there was also a lot of success for some of the more bargain options available. Crystal Palace captain Luka Milivojevic was priced at a measly £2.5m when the season started but his set-piece prowess meant he reached double figures for goals. And Burnley stalwart James Tarkowski may have just missed out on the England World Cup squad, but his season performances were stellar throughout on his way to totting up 118 points.

Conversely it was a disappointing season for the 2016–2017 top points scorer Alexis Sanchez, whose form dipped dramatically both at Arsenal and after his move to Manchester United. Sanchez managed just 171 points – just over half his total from the season before – which was only three more than Philippe Coutinho, who left the Premier League for Barcelona in January.

The likes of Wayne Rooney (85 points), Josh King (108) and Gylfi Sigurdsson (81) also had disappointing campaigns when they were tipped to shine at the start.

But their troubles all pale in comparison with Stoke's Kevin Wimmer. The Austrian defender, who moved to the Potteries from Spurs last summer, was officially the worst player on Dream Team after registering a grand total of –12 points. Ouch.

Romelu Lukaku was the most selected player on the game in 2017–2018, feeling the love of 45.3% of managers and just ahead of Salah and Kane.

So what about next season? Well you have to feel like the usual suspects – Salah, Kane, De Bruyne and co. – will all continue to dominate proceedings. We made the bold decision to make Kane the most expensive player in 2017–2018, but Salah's exploits in the last 12 months mean the England captain may have a rival at the top.

One player to monitor may well be Eden Hazard, with lingering doubts over his Chelsea future likely to have an influence over his Dream Team value and impact.

Leroy Sané won PFA Young Player of the Year last season and will look to continue his trail-blazing path towards world domination with Manchester City. Sané hit double figures for both goals and assists in all competitions and is only getting better at the tender age of 22.

His City team-mate Raheem Sterling was equally brilliant, scoring more Dream Team points than household names like Romelu Lukaku, Sadio Mané and Christian Eriksen.

And the new Premier League arrivals so far this summer will also be under the spotlight.

At the time of writing, Liverpool have probably carried out the most impressive business, snapping up one of the Bundesliga's shining lights in Naby Keita as their new midfield enforcer. Manchester United new boy Fred could also be a Dream Team favourite considering his ability from set pieces.

It all makes for a mouth-watering upcoming season which gets under way on 11th August so sign up today at dreamteamfc.com.

Adam Jones

INTRODUCTION

The 49th edition of the Yearbook is our first in association with *The Sun* and includes every game of the European Qualifying campaign for the 2018 World Cup in Russia. Full match line-ups and league tables are included for all of the European qualifiers. Coverage of the qualifying campaign for the rest of the world is also included. The World Cup Finals in Russia are covered in detail. Other international football at various levels is also well catered for in this edition.

The concise feature entitled Cups and Ups and Downs Diary is included with dates of those events affecting cup finals, plus promotion and relegation issues. In a season where again a record number of managerial changes were made, the Managers In and Out section is once again included, with a diary of managerial changes throughout the year. In women's football, the Women's Super League and Premier Leagues are included, together with the UEFA Women's Championship and the UEFA Champions League. England Women's Internationals since 1974 and all of the 2017–18 season's games are covered.

At European level, the Champions League has its usual comprehensive details included, with results, goalscorers, attendances, full line-ups and formations from the qualifying rounds onwards and also including all the league tables from the respective group stages. The Europa League includes full line-ups and formations from the group stages onwards

The 2017–18 season ended as a record-breaking one for Pep Guardiola's Manchester City. Most Premier League points in a season, most Premier League goals in a season, most Premier League wins in a season together with a host of other records. Pep was voted Manager of the Year by his peers at the League Managers Association. Mo Salah of Liverpool was recipient of both the Football Writers' Footballer of the Year award and the PFA Player of the Year award. The Championship season ended with Wolverhampton Wanderers and Cardiff City promoted automatically, and they were joined by Fulham who won the Championship Play-Off 1-0 thanks to a first-half strike by Tom Cairney.

All of these statistics are reproduced in the pages devoted not only to the Premier League, but the three Football League competitions too, as well as all major allied cup competitions.

While transfer fees are invariably those reported at the time and rarely given as official figures, the edition reflects those listed at the time.

In the club-by-club pages that contain the line-ups of all league matches, appearances are split into starting and substitute appearances. In the Players Directory the totals show figures combined.

The Players Directory and its accompanying A to Z index enables the reader to quickly find the club of any specific player.

Throughout the book players sent off are designated with ▪; substitutes in the club pages are 12, 13 and 14. Included again in main cup competitions are the formations for each team.

In addition to competitions already mentioned there is full coverage of Scottish Premiership and Scottish League and cup competitions. There are also sections devoted to Welsh, Irish, Women's football, the Under-21s and various other UEFA youth levels, schools, reserve team, academies, referees and the leading non-league competitions as well as the work of club chaplains. The chief tournaments outside the UK at club and national level are not forgotten. The International Directory itself features Europe in some depth as well as every FIFA-affiliated country's international results for the year since July 2017; every reigning league and cup champion worldwide is listed.

Naturally there are international appearances and goals scored by players for England, Scotland, Northern Ireland, Wales and the Republic. For easy reference, those players making appearances and scoring goals in the season covered are picked out in bold type.

The Yearbook would like to extend its appreciation to the publishers Headline for excellent support in the preparation of this edition, particularly Jonathan Taylor for photographic selection throughout the book and to Graham Green for his continued support.

ACKNOWLEDGEMENTS

In addition the Yearbook is also keen to thank the following individuals and organisations for their co-operation.

Special thanks to Tony Gallagher, Alan Shearer and Shaun Custis from *The Sun* for their contributions, and to Neil Ashton for his Team of the Season.

Thanks are also due to Ian Nannestad for the Obituaries, Did You Know? and Fact File features in the club section. Many thanks also to John English for his conscientious proof reading and compilation of the International Directory.

The Yearbook is grateful to the Football Association, the Scottish Professional Football League, the Football League, Rev. Nigel Sands for his contribution to the Chaplain's page and Bob Bannister, Paul Anderson, Kenny Holmes and Martin Cooper for their help.

Sincere thanks to George Schley and Simon Dunnington for their excellent work on the database, and to Andy Cordiner, Geoff Turner, Brian Tait, Mick Carruthers, Robin Middlemiss and the staff at Wearset for their much appreciated efforts in the production of the book throughout the year.

EDITORIAL

No matter how much money a manager has to spend or how well he has performed in the past, it is no guarantee of success going forward.

Pep Guardiola found English football was no cake-walk in his first year in charge: City finished third, well adrift of champions Chelsea and runners-up Spurs. But last season it all came together.

Guardiola's Manchester City played with a swagger and entertained us all in winning the Premier League title. For that reason, he is my manager of the season. He laid to rest the doubts about whether he could transfer the Barcelona way to the English game and silenced those who suggested he would have to bend to our ways. There were no compromises: Guardiola stuck to his beliefs and got his reward, and lovers of the beautiful game can rest easy that he will never change.

Even if you're not a City fan you have to admire the artistry they produce. But it was hard on their chief architect, Kevin De Bruyne, that he didn't win either of the major individual awards. He had the most assists in the Premier League last season (16) and at one time was my choice for the best player.

You just could not ignore Mo Salah though. Liverpool did not win a trophy but Salah could not have done more. He overtook myself and Cristiano Ronaldo in setting a record of 32 goals for a 38-game Premier League season. Every time Salah went through on goal the odds were on him scoring. He played with such confidence that it came as a real shock if he missed a chance. Salah's ascendancy from a bit-part player at Chelsea to being one of the most feared attackers in world football is a tribute to his hard work and determination to reach the top.

Both Salah and De Bruyne took part in what, for me, was the game of the season when Liverpool beat City 4-3 at Anfield. Salah scored the fourth to put Liverpool 4-1 up but a late rally by City almost rescued a point. Guardiola continued to attack even when City were being picked apart and the game was a wonderful example of the Premier League at its exciting best. It also gave Liverpool the belief that they could take the game to City and come out on top, which stood them in good stead when they overwhelmed City in the Champions League quarter-final.

Mind you, for all the brilliance that both City and Liverpool produced, my goal of the season goes to Chelsea's Willian. The Blues' second goal in the 4-0 win at Brighton showed what that team could do when they put their minds to it. Willian started and finished the move, first firing a pass to Eden Hazard, who flicked it on to Michy Batshuayi. He, in turn, back-heeled a pass to the Brazilian who buried a shot from 18 yards.

When I'm looking for my hero of the season, Sean Dyche gets it hands down. Dyche could easily have been my manager of the season because to get Burnley into Europe was a remarkable achievement on his budget. What a job he has done at a club which are an object lesson to those who panic when things start going wrong and fire the boss. Burnley's strategic long-term planning meant relegation did not cost Dyche his job and instead he was allowed to build and come back stronger.

Finally let's hear it for the three sides promoted from the Championship who all managed to stay up and did so before the last game of the campaign, which was no mean achievement.

A big pat on the back for Rafa Benitez, Chris Hughton and David Wagner, the respective managers of Newcastle, Brighton and Huddersfield.

Many of the players involved in the promotion campaigns were retained for the Premier League battle, in part due to budget restrictions. For clubs like Brighton and Huddersfield, that prudence was understandable.

Newcastle, on the other hand, are one of this country's biggest clubs in terms of fan support and those fans want to see investment in their club. A mid-table finish proved they could be challenging at the top end of the table, not scrapping it out with those at the bottom.

Alan Shearer

TEAM OF THE SEASON 2017–18

NEIL ASHTON, CHIEF FOOTBALL REPORTER, *THE SUN*

David de Gea
(Manchester United)

Kyle Walker   **Nicolás Otamendi**   **Jan Vertonghen**   **Ashley Young**
(Manchester City)   *(Manchester City)*   *(Tottenham Hotspur)*   *(Manchester United)*

Kevin De Bruyne   **Fernandinho**   **David Silva**
(Manchester City)   *(Manchester City)*   *(Manchester City)*

Mo Salah   **Harry Kane**   **Sergio Agüero**
(Liverpool)   *(Tottenham Hotspur)*   *(Manchester City)*

Manager: Pep Guardiola
(Manchester City)

David de Gea: de Gea has been named Manchester United's player of the year in four of the past five seasons. With Bayern Munich keeper Manuel Neuer out for most of the year with an injury, the Spaniard established himself as arguably the best keeper in world football.

Kyle Walker: moved to Manchester City and won his first Premier League title under the guidance and tutelage of Pep Guardiola. In an era when the Premier League is crying out for top-class right-backs, Walker has become one of the very best in the business.

Nicolás Otamendi: overcame a tough start to life in England to become the main man at the heart of Manchester City's title-winning defence. In the absence of captain Vincent Kompany for long periods, the Argentina defender became incredibly influential during City's march towards their first Premier League title under Pep.

Jan Vertonghen: without Toby Alderweireld alongside him, Vertonghen marshalled Tottenham's defence with his customary authority and composure. He has become increasingly assured, establishing himself as one of the best central defenders in the Premier League.

Ashley Young: a right-footed right-winger turned Manchester United's first choice left-back. It sounds crazy, but Young's diligent, disciplined approach under Jose Mourinho was rewarded with a place in England's World Cup squad. Young's performances, keeping Luke Shaw out of the United side for the majority of the season, were rewarded with a one-year contract extension.

Kevin De Bruyne: his sparkling performances for City at the start of the season caught the eye, powering Pep's team on as they set out to win the title. De Bruyne finished the season with 16 assists, one more than his team-mate Leroy Sané.

Fernandinho: stitches it all together in the centre of City's midfield. A combative, driving presence, the Brazilian has cemented his place in the side after Yaya Touré's glorious career at the Etihad started to fade. At 33, he is still going strong and shows no sign of slowing up.

David Silva: regarded by many Manchester City supporters as their greatest player of all time, he had another exceptional season in difficult circumstances. Despite frequent trips back to Spain to be with his wife following a complicated pregnancy, he still finished with 11 assists and nine goals. A first-class footballer.

Mo Salah: the PFA Player of Year and FWA Footballer of the Year, Salah was exceptional. He scored 44 times for Liverpool and made another 10 during this compelling run of form in a red shirt. In a year when Liverpool sold cult hero Philippe Coutinho to Barcelona, Salah has become an Anfield icon.

Harry Kane: despite two spells out through injury, Kane still came up with the goods to score 41 goals in a Tottenham shirt. Despite interest from some of the world's leading football clubs, Kane has committed his future to Spurs by signing a new contract at White Hart Lane. Unquestionably, he has earned it.

Sergio Agüero: not a vintage season in front of goal, but the Argentinian overcame the threat of recent arrival Gabriel Jesus to score another 21 times in the Premier League. Although his relationship with Guardiola appears distant at times, Agüero remains a ruthless finisher.

Manager, Pep Guardiola: Guardiola was heavily criticised when he failed to win the Premier League in his first season, but City became the first side to rack up 100 points when they won it at a canter in his second. They are an exceptional side, perhaps the best in Premier League history after scoring 106 times on the way to claiming the title.

FOOTBALL AWARDS 2017–18

THE FOOTBALL WRITERS' FOOTBALLER OF THE YEAR 2018

The Football Writers' Association Sir Stanley Matthews Trophy for the Footballer of the Year was awarded to Mohamed Salah of Liverpool and Egypt. Kevin De Bruyne (Manchester C and Belgium) was runner-up and Harry Kane (Tottenham H and England) came third.

Past Winners
1947–48 Stanley Matthews (Blackpool), 1948–49 Johnny Carey (Manchester U), 1949–50 Joe Mercer (Arsenal), 1950–51 Harry Johnston (Blackpool), 1951–52 Billy Wright (Wolverhampton W), 1952–53 Nat Lofthouse (Bolton W), 1953–54 Tom Finney (Preston NE), 1954–55 Don Revie (Manchester C), 1955–56 Bert Trautmann (Manchester C), 1956–57 Tom Finney (Preston NE), 1957–58 Danny Blanchflower (Tottenham H), 1958–59 Syd Owen (Luton T), 1959–60 Bill Slater (Wolverhampton W), 1960–61 Danny Blanchflower (Tottenham H), 1961–62 Jimmy Adamson (Burnley), 1962–63 Stanley Matthews (Stoke C), 1963–64 Bobby Moore (West Ham U), 1964–65 Bobby Collins (Leeds U), 1965–66 Bobby Charlton (Manchester U), 1966–67 Jackie Charlton (Leeds U), 1967–68 George Best (Manchester U), 1968–69 Dave Mackay (Derby Co) shared with Tony Book (Manchester C), 1969–70 Billy Bremner (Leeds U), 1970–71 Frank McLintock (Arsenal), 1971–72 Gordon Banks (Stoke C), 1972–73 Pat Jennings (Tottenham H), 1973–74 Ian Callaghan (Liverpool), 1974–75 Alan Mullery (Fulham), 1975–76 Kevin Keegan (Liverpool), 1976–77 Emlyn Hughes (Liverpool), 1977–78 Kenny Burns (Nottingham F), 1978–79 Kenny Dalglish (Liverpool), 1979–80 Terry McDermott (Liverpool), 1980–81 Frans Thijssen (Ipswich T), 1981–82 Steve Perryman (Tottenham H), 1982–83 Kenny Dalglish (Liverpool), 1983–84 Ian Rush (Liverpool), 1984–85 Neville Southall (Everton), 1985–86 Gary Lineker (Everton), 1986–87 Clive Allen (Tottenham H), 1987–88 John Barnes (Liverpool), 1988–89 Steve Nicol (Liverpool), 1989–90 John Barnes (Liverpool), 1990–91 Gordon Strachan (Leeds U), 1991–92 Gary Lineker (Tottenham H), 1992–93 Chris Waddle (Sheffield W), 1993–94 Alan Shearer (Blackburn R), 1994–95 Jurgen Klinsmann (Tottenham H), 1995–96 Eric Cantona (Manchester U), 1996–97 Gianfranco Zola (Chelsea), 1997–98 Dennis Bergkamp (Arsenal), 1998–99 David Ginola (Tottenham H), 1999–2000 Roy Keane (Manchester U), 2000–01 Teddy Sheringham (Manchester U), 2001–02 Robert Pires (Arsenal), 2002–03 Thierry Henry (Arsenal), 2003–04 Thierry Henry (Arsenal), 2004–05 Frank Lampard (Chelsea), 2005–06 Thierry Henry (Arsenal), 2006–07 Cristiano Ronaldo (Manchester U), 2007–08 Cristiano Ronaldo (Manchester U), 2008–09 Ryan Giggs (Manchester U), 2009–10 Wayne Rooney (Manchester U), 2010–11 Scott Parker (West Ham U), 2011–12 Robin van Persie (Arsenal), 2012–13 Gareth Bale (Tottenham H), 2013–14 Luis Suárez (Liverpool), 2014–15 Eden Hazard (Chelsea), 2015–16 Jamie Vardy (Leicester C), 2016–17 N'Golo Kanté (Chelsea and France); 2017–18 Mohamed Salah (Liverpool and Egypt).

THE FOOTBALL WRITERS' WOMEN'S FOOTBALLER OF THE YEAR 2018

Fran Kirby, Chelsea and England

THE PFA AWARDS 2018

Player of the Year: Mohamed Salah, Liverpool and Egypt
Young Player of the Year: Leroy Sané, Manchester C and Germany
Women's Player of the Year: Fran Kirby, Chelsea and England
Women's Young Player of the Year: Lauren Hemp, Bristol C
PFA Merit Award: Cyrille Regis MBE
PFA Special Achievement Award: Casey Stoney MBE

PFA Premier League Team of the Year 2018 sponsored by Panini
David de Gea (Manchester U); Kyle Walker (Manchester C), Jan Vertonghen (Tottenham H), Nicolás Otamendi (Manchester C), Marcos Alonso (Chelsea), David Silva (Manchester C), Kevin De Bruyne (Manchester C), Christian Eriksen (Tottenham H), Harry Kane (Tottenham H), Mohamed Salah (Liverpool), Sergio Agüero (Manchester C).

PFA Championship Team of the Year 2018 sponsored by Panini
John Ruddy (Wolverhampton W); Ryan Fredericks (Fulham), Sol Bamba (Cardiff C), Willy Boly (Wolverhampton W), Ryan Sessegnon (Fulham), James Maddison (Norwich C), Rúben Neves (Wolverhampton W), Tom Cairney (Fulham), Bobby Reid (Bristol C), Leon Clarke (Sheffield U), Matej Vydra (Derby Co).

PFA League One Team of the Year 2018 sponsored by Panini
Dean Henderson (Shrewsbury T); Nathan Byrne (Wigan Ath), Charlie Mulgrew (Blackburn R), Dan Burn (Wigan Ath), Amari'i Bell (Blackburn R), Bradley Dack (Blackburn R), Erhun Oztumer (Walsall), Nick Powell (Wigan Ath), Danny Graham (Blackburn R), Jack Marriott (Peterborough U), Will Grigg (Wigan Ath).

PFA League Two Team of the Year 2018 sponsored by Panini
Marek Štěch (Luton T); Jack Grimmer (Coventry C), Alan Sheehan (Luton T), Mark Hughes (Accrington S), Dan Potts (Luton T), Jorge Grant (Notts Co (on loan from Nottingham F)), Luke Berry (Luton T), Sean McConville (Accrington S), Adebayo Akinfenwa (Wycombe W), Billy Kee (Accrington S), Danny Hylton (Luton T).

SCOTTISH AWARDS 2017–18

SCOTTISH PFA PLAYER OF THE YEAR AWARDS 2018

Player of the Year: Scott Brown, Celtic and Scotland
Young Player of the Year: Kieran Tierney, Celtic and Scotland
Manager of the Year: Jack Ross, St Mirren
Championship Player of the Year: Lewis Morgan, St Mirren (on loan from Celtic) and Scotland U21
League One Player of the Year: Lawrence Shankland, Ayr U and Scotland U21
League Two Player of the Year: Darren Smith, Stirling Alb and Scotland U21
Goal of the Season: Kieran Tierney, Celtic v Kilmarnock, Betfred Scottish League Cup, 8 August 2017

SCOTTISH FOOTBALL WRITERS' ASSOCIATION AWARDS 2018

Player of the Year: Scott Brown, Celtic and Scotland
Young Player of the Year: Kieran Tierney, Celtic and Scotland
International Player of the Year: Leigh Griffiths, Celtic and Scotland
Manager of the Year: Steve Clarke, Kilmarnock

PREMIER LEAGUE AWARDS 2017–18

PLAYER OF THE MONTH AWARDS 2017–18

August	Sadio Mané (Liverpool)
September	Harry Kane (Tottenham H)
October	Leroy Sané (Manchester C)
November	Mohamed Salah (Liverpool)
December	Harry Kane (Tottenham H))
January	Sergio Agüero (Manchester C)
February	Mohamed Salah (Liverpool)
March	Mohamed Salah (Liverpool)
April	Wilfried Zaha (Crystal Palace)

MANAGER OF THE MONTH AWARDS 2017–18

	David Wagner (Huddersfield T)
	Pep Guardiola (Manchester C)
	Pep Guardiola (Manchester C)
	Pep Guardiola (Manchester C)
	Pep Guardiola (Manchester C)
	Eddie Howe (Bournemouth)
	Chris Hughton (Brighton & HA)
	Sean Dyche (Burnley)
	Darren Moore (WBA)

SKY BET LEAGUE AWARDS 2017–18

LEAGUE PLAYER OF THE MONTH AWARDS 2017–18

	Championship	League One	League Two
August	Nathaniel Mendez-Laing (Cardiff C)	Jack Marriott (Peterborough U)	Frank Nouble (Newport Co)
September	Aden Flint (Bristol C)	Brett Pitman (Portsmouth)	Shaquile Coulthirst (Barnet)
October	Leo Bonatini (Wolves)	Graham Carey (Plymouth Arg)	Tom Pope (Port Vale)
November	Leon Clarke (Sheffield U)	Charlie Mulgrew (Blackburn R)	Christian Doige (Forest Green R)
December	Scott Carson (Derby Co)	Dan Burn (Wigan Ath)	Sammie Szmodics (Colchester U)
January	Ryan Sessegnon (Fulham)	John-Joe O'Toole (Northampton T)	Marc McNulty (Coventry C)
February	Oliver McBurnie (Barnsley)	Adam Armstrong (Blackburn R)	Marc Richards (Swindon T)
March	Aleksandar Mitrović (Fulham)	Chey Dunkley (Wigan Ath)	Mohamed Eisa (Cheltenham T)
April	Aleksandar Mitrović (Fulham)	Will Grigg (Wigan Ath)	Mitch Rose (Grimsby T)
Player of the Season			
	Ryan Sessegnon (Fulham)	Bradley Dack (Blackburn R)	Billy Kee (Accrington S)

SKY BET FOOTBALL LEAGUE MANAGER OF THE MONTH AWARDS 2017–18

	Championship	League One	League Two
August	Neil Warnock (Cardiff C)	Grant McCann (Peterborough U)	Paul Tisdale (Exeter C)
September	Lee Johnson (Bristol C)	Paul Hurst (Shrewsbury T)	Kevin Nolan (Notts Co)
October	Gary Rowett (Derby Co)	Paul Cook (Wigan Ath)	Nathan Jones (Luton T)
November	Nuno Espírito Santo (Wolves)	Tony Mowbray (Blackburn R)	Nathan Jones (Luton T)
December	Gary Rowett (Derby Co)	Paul Warne (Rotherham U)	Danny Cowley (Lincoln C)
January	Steve Bruce (Aston Villa)	Steve Lovell (Gillingham)	Gareth Ainsworth (Wycombe W)
February	Neil Warnock (Cardiff C)	Derek Adams (Plymouth Arg)	John Coleman (Accrington S)
March	Neil Warnock (Cardiff C)	Paul Cook (Wigan Ath)	John Coleman (Accrington S)
April	Slavisa Jokanovic (Fulham)	Paul Cook (Wigan Ath)	Nathan Jones (Luton T)
Manager of the Season			
	Neil Warnock (Cardiff C)	Paul Hurst (Shrewsbury T)	John Coleman (Accrington S)

LEAGUE MANAGERS ASSOCIATION AWARDS 2017–18

SIR ALEX FERGUSON TROPHY FOR LMA MANAGER OF THE YEAR SPONSORED BY EVEREST
Pep Guardiola (Manchester C)

PREMIER LEAGUE MANAGER OF THE YEAR SPONSORED BY BARCLAYS
Pep Guardiola (Manchester C)

SKY BET FOOTBALL LEAGUE CHAMPIONSHIP MANAGER OF THE YEAR
Nuno Espírito Santo (Wolverhampton W)

SKY BET FOOTBALL LEAGUE ONE MANAGER OF THE YEAR
Paul Hurst (Shrewsbury T)

SKY BET FOOTBALL LEAGUE TWO MANAGER OF THE YEAR
John Coleman (Accrington S)

FA WOMEN'S SUPER LEAGUE 1 MANAGER OF THE YEAR
Emma Hayes (Chelsea)

FA WOMEN'S SUPER LEAGUE 2 MANAGER OF THE YEAR
Lee Burch (Millwall Lionesses)

LMA SPECIAL ACHIEVEMENT AWARD SPONSORED BY PROSTATE CANCER UK
Steve Cooper (England U17s)
Keith Downing (England U19s)
Paul Simpson (England U20s)
Neil Warnock (Cardiff C)
John Gregory (Chennaiyin FC)

LMA 1000 CLUB AND HALL OF FAME
Sam Allardyce

OTHER AWARDS

EUROPEAN FOOTBALLER OF THE YEAR 2017
Cristiano Ronaldo, Real Madrid and Portugal

EUROPEAN WOMEN'S PLAYER OF THE YEAR 2017
Lieke Martens, Barcelona and Netherlands

FIFA BALLON D'OR PLAYER OF THE YEAR 2017
Cristiano Ronaldo, Real Madrid and Portugal

FIFA BALLON D'OR WOMEN'S PLAYER OF THE YEAR 2017
Lieke Martens, Barcelona and Netherlands

FIFA PUSKAS AWARD GOAL OF THE YEAR 2017
Olivier Giroud, Arsenal v Crystal Palace, Premier League, 1 January 2017

PREMIER LEAGUE 2017–18

(P) *Promoted into division at end of 2016–17 season.*

				Home				Away					Total					
		P	W	D	L	F	A	W	D	L	F	A	W	D	L	F	A	GD	Pts
1	Manchester C	38	16	2	1	61	14	16	2	1	45	13	32	4	2	106	27	79	100
2	Manchester U	38	15	2	2	38	9	10	4	5	30	19	25	6	7	68	28	40	81
3	Tottenham H	38	13	4	2	40	16	10	4	5	34	20	23	8	7	74	36	38	77
4	Liverpool	38	12	7	0	45	10	9	5	5	39	28	21	12	5	84	38	46	75
5	Chelsea	38	11	4	4	30	16	10	3	6	32	22	21	7	10	62	38	24	70
6	Arsenal	38	15	2	2	54	20	4	4	11	20	31	19	6	13	74	51	23	63
7	Burnley	38	7	5	7	16	17	7	7	5	20	22	14	12	12	36	39	−3	54
8	Everton	38	10	4	5	28	22	3	6	10	16	36	13	10	15	44	58	−14	49
9	Leicester C	38	7	6	6	25	22	5	5	9	31	38	12	11	15	56	60	−4	47
10	Newcastle U (P)	38	8	4	7	21	17	4	4	11	18	30	12	8	18	39	47	−8	44
11	Crystal Palace	38	7	5	7	29	27	4	6	9	16	28	11	11	16	45	55	−10	44
12	Bournemouth	38	7	5	7	26	30	4	6	9	19	31	11	11	16	45	61	−16	44
13	West Ham U	38	7	6	6	24	26	3	6	10	24	42	10	12	16	48	68	−20	42
14	Watford	38	7	6	6	27	31	4	2	13	17	33	11	8	19	44	64	−20	41
15	Brighton & HA (P)	38	7	8	4	24	25	2	5	12	10	29	9	13	16	34	54	−20	40
16	Huddersfield T (P)	38	6	5	8	16	25	3	5	11	12	33	9	10	19	28	58	−30	37
17	Southampton	38	4	7	8	20	26	3	8	8	17	30	7	15	16	37	56	−19	36
18	Swansea C	38	6	3	10	17	24	2	6	11	11	32	8	9	21	28	56	−28	33
19	Stoke C	38	5	5	9	20	30	2	7	10	15	38	7	12	19	35	68	−33	33
20	WBA	38	3	9	7	21	29	3	4	12	10	27	6	13	19	31	56	−25	31

PREMIER LEAGUE LEADING GOALSCORERS 2017–18

Qualification 9 league goals	League	FA Cup	EFL Cup	Other	Total
Mohamed Salah (*Liverpool*)	32	1	0	11	44
Harry Kane (*Tottenham H*)	30	4	0	7	41
Sergio Agüero (*Manchester C*)	21	2	3	4	30
Romelu Lukaku (*Manchester U*)	16	5	0	6	27
Roberto Firmino (*Liverpool*)	15	1	0	11	27
Jamie Vardy (*Leicester C*)	20	2	1	0	23
Raheem Sterling (*Manchester C*)	18	1	0	4	23
Sadio Mané (*Liverpool*)	10	0	0	10	20
Heung-Min Son (*Tottenham H*)	12	2	0	4	18
Alexandre Lacazette (*Arsenal*)	14	0	0	3	17
Gabriel Jesus (*Manchester C*)	13	0	0	4	17
Eden Hazard (*Chelsea*)	12	1	1	3	17
Alvaro Morata (*Chelsea*)	11	2	1	1	15
Glenn Murray (*Brighton & HA*)	12	2	0	0	14
Christian Eriksen (*Tottenham H*)	10	2	0	2	14
Leroy Sané (*Manchester C*)	10	1	3	0	14
Dele Alli (*Tottenham H*)	9	1	2	2	14
Riyad Mahrez (*Leicester C*)	12	0	1	0	13
Chris Wood (*Burnley*)	11	0	1	0	12
Includes 1 goal for Leeds U in EFL Championship.					
Marko Arnautovic (*West Ham U*)	11	0	0	0	11
Wayne Rooney (*Everton*)	10	0	0	1	11
Anthony Martial (*Manchester U*)	9	0	1	1	11
Alexis Sanchez (*Manchester U*)	9	1	0	1	11
Includes 7 league goals for Arsenal in Premier League and 1 goal for Arsenal in Europa League.					
Pierre-Emerick Aubameyang (*Arsenal*)	10	0	0	0	10
Luka Milivojevic (*Crystal Palace*)	10	0	0	0	10
Ashley Barnes (*Burnley*)	9	1	0	0	10
David Silva (*Manchester C*)	9	0	1	0	10
Wilfried Zaha (*Crystal Palace*)	9	0	0	0	9

Other matches consist of European games, Community Shield.

SKY BET CHAMPIONSHIP 2017–18

(P) *Promoted into division at end of 2016–17 season.*   (R) *Relegated into division at end of 2016–17 season.*

				Home					Away					Total					
		P	W	D	L	F	A	W	D	L	F	A	W	D	L	F	A	GD	Pts
1	Wolverhampton W	46	16	5	2	47	18	14	4	5	35	21	30	9	7	82	39	43	99
2	Cardiff C	46	16	4	3	40	16	11	5	7	29	23	27	9	10	69	39	30	90
3	Fulham¶	46	13	8	2	40	17	12	5	6	39	29	25	13	8	79	46	33	88
4	Aston Villa	46	14	7	2	42	19	10	4	9	30	23	24	11	11	72	42	30	83
5	Middlesbrough (R)	46	14	3	6	33	17	8	7	8	34	28	22	10	14	67	45	22	76
6	Derby Co	46	12	5	6	41	22	8	10	5	29	26	20	15	11	70	48	22	75
7	Preston NE	46	9	8	6	27	22	10	8	5	30	24	19	16	11	57	46	11	73
8	Millwall (P)	46	12	7	4	33	21	7	8	8	23	24	19	15	12	56	45	11	72
9	Brentford	46	9	11	3	37	24	9	4	10	25	28	18	15	13	62	52	10	69
10	Sheffield U (P)	46	12	5	6	33	20	8	4	11	29	35	20	9	17	62	55	7	69
11	Bristol C	46	11	6	6	41	28	6	10	7	26	30	17	16	13	67	58	9	67
12	Ipswich T	46	9	6	8	29	27	8	3	12	28	33	17	9	20	57	60	–3	60
13	Leeds U	46	10	6	7	32	27	7	3	13	27	37	17	9	20	59	64	–5	60
14	Norwich C	46	8	8	7	25	25	7	7	9	24	35	15	15	16	49	60	–11	60
15	Sheffield W	46	8	7	8	37	31	6	8	9	22	29	14	15	17	59	60	–1	57
16	QPR	46	12	5	6	38	31	3	6	14	20	39	15	11	20	58	70	–12	56
17	Nottingham F	46	10	3	10	25	27	5	5	13	26	38	15	8	23	51	65	–14	53
18	Hull C (R)	46	7	8	8	41	32	4	8	11	29	38	11	16	19	70	70	0	49
19	Birmingham C	46	10	3	10	21	24	3	4	16	17	44	13	7	26	38	68	–30	46
20	Reading	46	5	8	10	25	35	5	6	12	23	35	10	14	22	48	70	–22	44
21	Bolton W (P)	46	9	4	10	25	33	1	9	13	14	41	10	13	23	39	74	–35	43
22	Barnsley	46	5	9	9	25	32	4	5	14	23	40	9	14	23	48	72	–24	41
23	Burton Alb	46	4	5	14	19	43	6	6	11	19	38	10	11	25	38	81	–43	41
24	Sunderland (R)	46	3	7	13	23	39	4	9	10	29	41	7	16	23	52	80	–28	37

¶*Fulham promoted via play-offs.*

SKY BET CHAMPIONSHIP LEADING GOALSCORERS 2017–18

Qualification 10 league goals	League	FA Cup	EFL Cup	Play-offs	Total
Matej Vydra (*Derby Co*)	21	0	1	0	22
Bobby Reid (*Bristol C*)	19	0	2	0	21
Lewis Grabban (*Aston Villa*)	20	0	0	0	20
Includes 12 league goals for Sunderland.					
Leon Clarke (*Sheffield U*)	19	0	0	0	19
Diogo Jota (*Wolverhampton W*)	17	1	0	0	18
Martyn Waghorn (*Ipswich T*)	16	0	0	0	17
Total includes 1 goal for Rangers in Europa League.					
Ryan Sessegnon (*Fulham*)	15	0	0	1	16
Britt Assombalonga (*Middlesbrough*)	15	0	0	0	15
Albert Adomah (*Aston Villa*)	14	0	1	0	15
Jarrod Bowen (*Hull C*)	14	1	0	0	15
James Maddison (*Norwich C*)	14	0	1	0	15
Famara Diedhiou (*Bristol C*)	13	0	1	0	14
Aleksandar Mitrović (*Fulham*)	13	0	1	0	14
Includes 1 league goal for Newcastle U in Premier League and 1 goal for Newcastle U in EFL Cup.					
Billy Sharp (*Sheffield U*)	13	1	0	0	14
Atdhe Nuhiu (*Sheffield W*)	11	3	0	0	14
Kemar Roofe (*Leeds U*)	11	0	3	0	14
Neal Maupay (*Brentford*)	12	0	1	0	13
Patrick Bamford (*Middlesbrough*)	11	0	2	0	13
Sean Maguire (*Preston NE*)	10	0	0	0	13
Total includes 3 goals for Cork C in Europa League.					
Leo Bonatini (*Wolverhampton W*)	12	0	0	0	12
Conor Hourihane (*Aston Villa*)	11	0	0	0	11
Matt Smith (*QPR*)	11	0	0	0	11
Ollie Watkins (*Brentford*)	10	0	1	0	11
Gary Hooper (*Sheffield W*)	10	0	1	0	11
Modou Barrow (*Reading*)	10	0	0	0	10
Joe Garner (*Ipswich T*)	10	0	0	0	10
Lee Gregory (*Millwall*)	10	0	0	0	10
Pierre-Michel Lasogga (*Leeds U*)	10	0	0	0	10
Gary Madine (*Bolton W*)	10	0	0	0	10
Callum Paterson (*Cardiff C*)	10	0	0	0	10
George Saville (*Millwall*)	10	0	0	0	10

SKY BET LEAGUE ONE 2017–18

(P) Promoted into division at end of 2016–17 season.   (R) Relegated into division at end of 2016–17 season.

			Home					Away					Total						
		P	W	D	L	F	A	W	D	L	F	A	W	D	L	F	A	GD	Pts
1	Wigan Ath (R)	46	13	8	2	37	11	16	3	4	52	18	29	11	6	89	29	60	98
2	Blackburn R (R)	46	15	6	2	46	20	13	6	4	36	20	28	12	6	82	40	42	96
3	Shrewsbury T	46	14	4	5	32	17	8	4	28	22		25	12	9	60	39	21	87
4	Rotherham U (R)¶	46	15	3	5	45	23	9	4	10	28	30	24	7	15	73	53	20	79
5	Scunthorpe U	46	9	8	6	28	23	10	9	4	37	27	19	17	10	65	50	15	74
6	Charlton Ath	46	11	6	6	31	24	9	5	9	27	27	20	11	15	58	51	7	71
7	Plymouth Arg (P)	46	13	3	7	37	30	6	8	9	21	29	19	11	16	58	59	–1	68
8	Portsmouth (P)	46	12	3	8	33	21	8	3	12	24	35	20	6	20	57	56	1	66
9	Peterborough U	46	12	4	7	37	26	5	9	9	31	34	17	13	16	68	60	8	64
10	Southend U	46	12	7	4	38	21	5	5	13	20	41	17	12	17	58	62	–4	63
11	Bradford C	46	9	4	10	28	32	9	5	9	29	35	18	9	19	57	67	–10	63
12	Blackpool (P)	46	9	8	6	37	29	6	7	10	23	26	15	15	16	60	55	5	60
13	Bristol R	46	11	6	6	38	30	5	5	13	22	36	16	11	19	60	66	–6	59
14	Fleetwood T	46	7	6	10	32	35	9	3	11	27	33	16	9	21	59	68	–9	57
15	Doncaster R (P)	46	7	9	7	30	25	6	8	9	22	27	13	17	16	52	52	0	56
16	Oxford U	46	9	6	8	34	32	6	5	12	27	34	15	11	20	61	66	–5	56
17	Gillingham	46	5	11	7	26	26	8	6	9	24	29	13	17	16	50	55	–5	56
18	AFC Wimbledon	46	8	6	9	25	30	5	8	10	22	28	13	14	19	47	58	–11	53
19	Walsall	46	9	6	8	30	31	4	7	12	23	35	13	13	20	53	66	–13	52
20	Rochdale	46	6	12	5	24	24	5	6	12	25	33	11	18	17	49	57	–8	51
21	Oldham Ath	46	8	6	9	31	33	3	11	9	27	42	11	17	18	58	75	–17	50
22	Northampton T	46	7	5	11	20	35	5	6	12	23	42	12	11	23	43	77	–34	47
23	Milton Keynes D	46	6	8	9	24	30	5	4	14	19	39	11	12	23	43	69	–26	45
24	Bury	46	7	4	12	20	30	1	8	14	21	41	8	12	26	41	71	–30	36

¶Rotherham U promoted via play-offs.

SKY BET LEAGUE ONE LEADING GOALSCORERS 2017–18

Qualification 10 league goals	League	FA Cup	EFL Cup	EFL Trophy	Play-Offs	Total
Jack Marriott (*Peterborough U*)	27	5	0	1	0	33
Will Grigg (*Wigan Ath*)	19	7	0	0	0	26
Brett Pitman (*Portsmouth*)	24	0	0	1	0	25
Ian Henderson (*Rochdale*)	13	6	0	1	0	20
Bradley Dack (*Blackburn R*)	18	0	0	0	0	18
Tom Eaves (*Gillingham*)	17	1	0	0	0	18
Lyle Taylor (*AFC Wimbledon*)	14	3	0	1	0	18
Kieffer Moore (*Rotherham U*)	17	0	0	0	0	17
Includes 4 league goals for Barnsley in Sky Bet Championship.						
Erhun Oztumer (*Walsall*)	15	0	1	1	0	17
Danny Graham (*Blackburn R*)	14	3	0	0	0	17
Charlie Wyke (*Bradford C*)	15	1	0	0	0	16
Graham Carey (*Plymouth Arg*)	14	2	0	0	0	16
Eoin Doyle (*Oldham Ath*)	14	0	0	2	0	16
Nick Powell (*Wigan Ath*)	15	0	0	0	0	15
John Marquis (*Doncaster R*)	14	1	0	0	0	15
Charlie Mulgrew (*Blackburn R*)	14	0	0	0	0	14
Ellis Harrison (*Bristol R*)	12	0	2	0	0	14
Ivan Toney (*Scunthorpe U*)	12	2	0	0	0	14
Includes 4 league goals and 2 FA Cup goals for Wigan Ath.						
Craig Davies (*Oldham Ath*)	11	0	1	2	0	14
Stefan Payne (*Shrewsbury T*)	11	1	0	1	0	13
Michael Jacobs (*Wigan Ath*)	12	0	0	0	0	12
Josh Morris (*Scunthorpe U*)	11	0	0	1	0	12
Devante Cole (*Fleetwood T*)	10	2	0	0	0	12
Josh Parker (*Gillingham*)	10	1	0	1	0	12
Kyle Vassell (*Blackpool*)	11	0	0	0	0	11
James Henry (*Oxford U*)	10	0	0	1	0	11
Wes Thomas (*Oxford U*)	10	0	0	1	0	11
Simon Cox (*Southend U*)	10	0	0	0	0	10
Josh Magennis (*Charlton Ath*)	10	0	0	0	0	10

SKY BET LEAGUE TWO 2017–18

(P) *Promoted into division at end of 2016–17 season.*   (R) *Relegated into division at end of 2016–17 season.*

			Home					Away					Total					
		P	W	D	L	F	A	W	D	L	F	A	W	D	L	F	A	GD	Pts
1	Accrington S	46	17	3	3	42	19	12	3	8	34	27	29	6	11	76	46	30	93
2	Luton T	46	17	2	4	62	24	8	11	4	32	22	25	13	8	94	46	48	88
3	Wycombe W	46	12	5	6	43	35	12	7	4	36	25	24	12	10	79	60	19	84
4	Exeter C	46	15	4	4	34	19	9	4	10	30	35	24	8	14	64	54	10	80
5	Notts Co	46	14	7	2	43	19	7	7	9	28	29	21	14	11	71	48	23	77
6	Coventry C (R)¶	46	13	4	6	36	24	9	5	9	28	23	22	9	15	64	47	17	75
7	Lincoln C (P)	46	12	8	3	38	23	8	7	8	26	25	20	15	11	64	48	16	75
8	Mansfield T	46	10	10	3	42	26	8	8	7	25	26	18	18	10	67	52	15	72
9	Swindon T (R)	46	9	5	9	29	36	11	3	9	38	29	20	8	18	67	65	2	68
10	Carlisle U	46	7	10	6	31	23	10	6	7	31	31	17	16	13	62	54	8	67
11	Newport Co	46	9	10	4	32	24	7	6	10	24	34	16	16	14	56	58	−2	64
12	Cambridge U	46	13	5	5	38	23	4	8	11	18	37	17	13	16	56	60	−4	64
13	Colchester U	46	9	7	7	30	23	7	7	9	23	29	16	14	16	53	52	1	62
14	Crawley T	46	8	4	11	30	30	8	7	8	28	36	16	11	19	58	66	−8	59
15	Crewe Alex	46	10	4	9	32	32	7	1	15	30	43	17	5	24	62	75	−13	56
16	Stevenage	46	9	9	5	42	27	5	4	14	18	38	14	13	19	60	65	−5	55
17	Cheltenham T	46	8	6	9	31	31	5	6	12	36	42	13	12	21	67	73	−6	51
18	Grimsby T	46	6	9	8	20	26	7	3	13	22	40	13	12	21	42	66	−24	51
19	Yeovil T	46	8	5	10	29	26	4	7	12	30	49	12	12	22	59	75	−16	48
20	Port Vale (R)	46	7	6	10	26	29	4	8	11	23	38	11	14	21	49	67	−18	47
21	Forest Green R (P)	46	10	2	11	35	36	3	6	14	19	41	13	8	25	54	77	−23	47
22	Morecambe	46	6	9	8	22	27	3	10	10	19	29	9	19	18	41	56	−15	46
23	Barnet	46	8	6	9	24	25	4	4	15	22	40	12	10	24	46	65	−19	46
24	Chesterfield (R)	46	8	3	12	27	33	2	5	16	20	50	10	8	28	47	83	−36	38

¶*Coventry C promoted via play-offs.*

SKY BET LEAGUE TWO LEADING GOALSCORERS 2017–18

Qualification 10 league goals	*League*	*FA Cup*	*EFL Cup*	*EFL Trophy*	*Play-Offs*	*Total*
Marc McNulty (*Coventry*)	23	1	0	2	2	28
Billy Kee (*Accrington S*)	25	0	1	0	0	26
Mohamed Eisa (*Cheltenham T*)	23	0	2	0	0	25
Christian Doidge (*Forest Green R*)	20	4	0	1	0	25
Danny Hylton (*Luton T*)	21	2	0	0	0	23
Jayden Stockley (*Exeter C*)	19	3	0	0	1	23
Kristian Dennis (*Chesterfield*)	19	0	1	1	0	21
James Collins (*Luton T*)	19	1	0	0	0	20
Tom Pope (*Port Vale*)	17	2	0	0	0	19
Jorge Grant (*Notts Co*)	15	2	1	0	1	19
Adebayo Akinfenwa (*Wycombe W*)	17	1	0	0	0	18
Danny Rose (*Mansfield T*)	14	3	0	0	0	17
Matt Green (*Lincoln C*)	13	0	0	3	1	17
Kayden Jackson (*Accrington S*)	16	0	0	0	0	16
Danny Newton (*Stevenage*)	14	2	0	0	0	16
Kane Hemmings (*Mansfield T*)	15	0	0	0	0	15
Francois Zoko (*Yeovil T*)	13	1	0	1	0	15
Padraig Amond (*Newport Co*)	13	1	0	0	0	14
Uche Ikpeazu (*Cambridge U*)	13	0	1	0	0	14
Luke Norris (*Swindon T*)	13	0	0	1	0	14
Reuben Reid (*Forest Green R*)	13	0	0	1	0	14
Includes 7 league goals and 1 EFL Trophy goal for Exeter C.						
Matt Godden (*Stevenage*)	10	4	0	0	0	14
Callum Lang (*Morecambe*)	10	1	2	1	0	14
Jordan Bowery (*Crewe Alex*)	12	0	0	1	0	13
Sean McConville (*Accrington S*)	12	1	0	0	0	13
Sammie Szmodics (*Colchester U*)	12	0	0	1	0	13
Marc Richards (*Swindon T*)	12	0	0	0	0	12
Includes 1 league goal for Northampton T in Sky Bet League One.						
Shaq Coulthirst (*Barnet*)	10	0	1	1	0	12
Elliot Lee (*Luton T*)	10	1	0	1	0	12
Jamie Devitt (*Carlisle U*)	11	0	0	0	0	11
Enzio Boldewijn (*Crawley T*)	10	0	0	0	0	10
Mikael Mandron (*Colchester U*)	10	0	0	0	0	10
George Maris (*Cambridge U*)	10	0	0	0	0	10
Jimmy Smith (*Crawley T*)	10	0	0	0	0	10

FOOTBALL LEAGUE PLAY-OFFS 2017–18

᛫ *Denotes player sent off.*

SKY BET CHAMPIONSHIP SEMI-FINALS FIRST LEG

Friday, 11 May 2018
Derby Co (1) 1 *(Jerome 34)*
Fulham (0) 0   27,163
Derby Co: (3421) Carson; Keogh, Davies, Forsyth;
Wisdom, Huddlestone, Johnson, Weimann (Hanson 90);
Vydra (Anya 68), Lawrence; Jerome (Nugent 68).
Fulham: (433) Bettinelli; Fredericks, Odoi, Ream,
Targett; Cairney, McDonald, Johansen (Norwood 88);
Ayite (Piazon 76), Mitrovic, Sessegnon R (Kebano 76).
Referee: Roger East.

Saturday, 12 May 2018
Middlesbrough (0) 0
Aston Villa (1) 1 *(Jedinak 15)*   29,233
Middlesbrough: (433) Randolph; Shotton, Ayala (Da
Silva 64), Gibson, Friend; Howson, Clayton, Besic;
Traore, Assombalonga (Bamford 76), Downing.
Aston Villa: (4141) Johnstone; Elmohamady (Whelan 88),
Chester, Terry, Hutton; Jedinak; Snodgrass, Hourihane,
Grealish, Adomah (Kodjia 71); Grabban (Bjarnason 81).
Referee: Robert Madley.

SKY BET CHAMPIONSHIP SEMI-FINALS SECOND LEG

Monday, 14 May 2018
Fulham (0) 2 *(Sessegnon R 47, Odoi 66)*
Derby Co (0) 0   23,529
Fulham: (433) Bettinelli; Fredericks, Odoi, Ream,
Targett (Kalas 76); Cairney (Norwood 90), McDonald,
Johansen; Kamara, Mitrovic, Sessegnon R.
Derby Co: (3421) Carson; Keogh, Davies, Forsyth;
Wisdom, Huddlestone, Johnson, Anya (Vydra 67);
Lawrence (Palmer 67), Weimann; Jerome (Nugent 75).
Fulham won 2-1 on aggregate. Referee: Chris Kavanagh.

Tuesday, 15 May 2018
Aston Villa (0) 0
Middlesbrough (0) 0   40,505
Aston Villa: (4141) Johnstone; Bree, Chester, Terry,
Hutton; Jedinak; Snodgrass, Hourihane (Whelan 85),
Grealish, Adomah (Bjarnason 90); Grabban (Kodjia 79).
Middlesbrough: (433) Randolph; Shotton (Da Silva 82),
Fry, Gibson, Friend; Howson (Gestede 73), Clayton,
Besic; Traore, Assombalonga (Bamford 68), Downing.
Aston Villa won 1-0 on aggregate. Referee: Mike Dean.

SKY BET CHAMPIONSHIP FINAL

Wembley, Saturday, 26 May 2018
Aston Villa (0) 0
Fulham (1) 1 *(Cairney 23)*   85,243
Aston Villa: (4141) Johnstone; Elmohamady (Kodjia 77),
Chester, Terry, Hutton; Jedinak (Onomah 77); Snodgrass,
Hourihane (Hogan 82), Grealish, Adomah; Grabban.
Fulham: (433) Bettinelli; Fredericks (Christie 83), Odoi᛫,
Ream, Targett; Cairney, McDonald, Johansen (Norwood
72); Kamara (Kalas 77), Mitrovic, Sessegnon R.
Referee: Anthony Taylor.

SKY BET LEAGUE ONE SEMI-FINALS FIRST LEG

Thursday, 10 May 2018
Charlton Ath (0) 0
Shrewsbury T (0) 1 *(Nolan 80)*   14,367
Charlton Ath: (442) Amos; Konsa, Bauer, Pearce,
Dasilva; Reeves (Aribo 77), Kashi, Forster-Caskey,
Mavididi (Fosu 62); Magennis, Ajose (Zyro 90).
Shrewsbury T: (4411) Henderson; Bolton, Nsiala, Sadler,
Beckles; Whalley (Riley 89), Morris B, Godfrey,
Rodman; Nolan (John-Lewis 90); Morris C (Payne 75).
Referee: Simon Hooper.

Saturday, 12 May 2018
Scunthorpe U (1) 2 *(Ihiekwe 18 (og), McGeehan 88)*
Rotherham U (1) 2 *(Taylor 17, Newell 64)*   6591
Scunthorpe U: (4411) Gilks (Watson 62); Clarke,
McArdle, Wallace, Townsend; Adelakun (McGeehan
75), Yates, Ojo, Morris; Holmes; Toney (Hopper 90).
Rotherham U: (4141) Rodak; Emmanuel, Ihiekwe,
Wood, Mattock; Vaulks; Taylor (Newell 63), Towell
(Ajayi 72), Palmer, Williams (Forde 90); Smith.
Referee: Tim Robinson.

SKY BET LEAGUE ONE SEMI-FINALS SECOND LEG

Sunday, 13 May 2018
Shrewsbury T (0) 1 *(Morris C 58)*
Charlton Ath (0) 0   9016
Shrewsbury T: (4411) Henderson; Bolton, Nsiala, Sadler,
Beckles; Whalley (Riley 90), Morris B, Godfrey,
Rodman; Nolan (John-Lewis 90); Morris C (Payne 69).
Charlton Ath: (4312) Amos; Dijksteel (Sarr 86), Bauer,
Pearce, Dasilva; Forster-Caskey, Konsa, Aribo; Fosu
(KaiKai 62); Magennis, Ajose (Mavididi 59).
Shrewsbury T won 2-0 on aggregate.
Referee: Jeremy Simpson.

Tom Cairney scores the only goal of the game as Fulham beat Aston Villa in the Championship Play-off Final at Wembley on 26 May. (Nigel French/PA Wire/PA Images)

The players of Rotherham United celebrate promotion to the Championship after their 2-1 victory over Shrewsbury Town in the League One Play-off Final. (Barrington Coombs/EMPICS Sport)

Wednesday, 16 May 2018

Rotherham U (1) 2 *(Wood 45, Vaulks 63)*

Scunthorpe U (0) 0   11,061

Rotherham U: (4141) Rodak; Emmanuel, Ihiekwe (Ajayi 52), Wood, Mattock; Palmer; Williams (Taylor 68), Towell, Vaulks, Newell (Forde 90); Smith.
Scunthorpe U: (4231) Watson; Vermijl, McArdle■, Wallace, Townsend; Yates (Hopper 83), Ojo; Adelakun (McGeehan 62), Holmes, Morris; Toney (Novak 81).
Rotherham U won 4-2 on aggregate. Referee: Scott Duncan.

SKY BET LEAGUE ONE FINAL

Wembley, Sunday, 27 May 2018

Rotherham U (1) 2 *(Wood 32, 103)*

Shrewsbury T (0) 1 *(Rodman 58)*   26,218

Rotherham U: (4231) Rodak; Emmanuel, Ajayi, Wood, Mattock; Towell, Vaulks; Taylor (Williams 75), David Ball (Lavery 71), Newell (Forde 110); Smith.
Shrewsbury T: (442) Henderson; Bolton (Riley 73), Nsiala, Sadler, Beckles; Whalley, Morris B (Payne 56), Godfrey, Rodman; Nolan, Morris C (John-Lewis 66).
aet. Referee: Robert Jones.

SKY BET LEAGUE TWO SEMI-FINALS FIRST LEG

Saturday, 12 May 2018

Coventry C (0) 1 *(McNulty 87 (pen))*

Notts Co (0) 1 *(Forte 49)*   17,404

Coventry C: (442) Burge; Grimmer, Davies, Hyam, Stokes; Bayliss, Kelly, Doyle, Shipley (Ponticelli 72); Biamou (Clarke-Harris 83), McNulty.
Notts Co: (4222) Collin; Tootle, Duffy, Brisley, Jones; Hewitt, Noble (O'Connor 77), Virtue (Alessandra 58); Grant; Forte (Smith 90), Stead.
Referee: Gavin Ward.

Lincoln C (0) 0

Exeter C (0) 0   9509

Lincoln C: (433) Allsop; Wilson, Waterfall, Wharton (Long 90), Eardley; Woodyard, Bostwick, Whitehouse (Pett 84); Anderson (Palmer 84), Rhead, Green.
Exeter C: (4132) Pym; Sweeney, Storey, Moore-Taylor, Moxey; Tillson; James, Boateng (Simpson 74), Harley (Archibald-Henville 90); Taylor, Stockley.
Referee: Ben Toner.

SKY BET LEAGUE TWO SEMI-FINALS SECOND LEG

Thursday, 17 May 2018

Exeter C (1) 3 *(Stockley 27, Boateng 47, Harley 69)*

Lincoln C (0) 1 *(Green 78)*   5645

Exeter C: (442) Pym; Sweeney, Storey, Moore-Taylor, Moxey; Taylor, Tillson, Boateng (Archibald-Henville 76), Harley; Simpson (James 85), Stockley.
Lincoln C: (4231) Allsop; Wilson, Waterfall, Bostwick, Eardley; Woodyard, Frecklington (Pett 73); Anderson (Palmer 55), Whitehouse, Green; Rhead.
Exeter C won 3-1 on aggregate.
Referee: Darren England.

Friday, 18 May 2018

Notts Co (1) 1 *(Grant 44)*

Coventry C (2) 4 *(Biamou 6, 71, McNulty 37, Bayliss 86)*
                                                                               17,615

Notts Co: (442) Collin; Tootle, Duffy, Brisley, Jones; Alessandra (Ameobi 78), Hewitt, Noble (O'Connor 46), Grant; Forte, Stead.
Coventry C: (442) Burge; Grimmer, Willis, Hyam, Stokes; Bayliss, Kelly, Doyle, Shipley; McNulty (Ponticelli 90); Biamou (Clarke-Harris 74).
Coventry C won 5-2 on aggregate.
Referee: Darren Drysdale.

SKY BET LEAGUE TWO FINAL

Wembley, Monday, 28 May 2018

Coventry C (0) 3 *(Willis 49, Shipley 54, Grimmer 68)*

Exeter C (0) 1 *(Edwards 89)*   50,196

Coventry C: (442) Burge; Grimmer, Willis, Hyam, Stokes; Bayliss, Kelly, Doyle, Shipley (Reid 73); McNulty (Ponticelli 82), Biamou (Clarke-Harris 51).
Exeter C: (4411) Pym; Sweeney, Storey, Moore-Taylor, Woodman (James 63); Taylor, Boateng (Edwards 73), Tillson, Moxey (Jay 63); Harley; Stockley.
Referee: David Webb.

REVIEW OF THE SEASON 2017–18

For Manchester City fans this was one of the greatest seasons of all time even if, as far as the Premier League goes, it wasn't the most competitive.

City seemed to be on a mission to break every record in the book. Pep Guardiola's entertainers, inspired by creative midfielder Kevin De Bruyne, romped to the title setting record after record, including most points in a season (100) and most goals (106).

Their nearest rivals could hardly be called serious challengers as Manchester United finished a distant 19 points behind in second place. United could take little comfort from the fact that a 3-2 win at the Etihad delayed City being crowned champions. That defeat was one of only two City suffered in their League campaign, the other being an eventful 4-3 loss at Liverpool.

Jürgen Klopp's men also inflicted a mortal wound in City's bid for Champions League glory at the quarter-final stage by a surprisingly comfortable 5-1 aggregate over the two legs. There was, too, a shock defeat for City in the FA Cup when they lost to League One Wigan Athletic, the same team which had beaten them in the 2013 FA Cup Final.

City did achieve a trophy double though, lifting the Carabao Cup after a 3-0 thumping of Arsenal, and giving Guardiola his first trophy in England.

Manchester United had little to shout about despite the fact their runners-up position represented positional progress. Manager Jose Mourinho was criticised for his style of play which compared so unfavourably to that of City and produced 38 fewer goals in the Premier League. The FA Cup final offered hope of silverware to wave in front of the critics but United lost to Chelsea to finish the season empty-handed.

Liverpool beat Manchester City 4-3 at Anfield in a thrilling match in January.
Here Sadio Mané scores Liverpool's third goal. (Reuters/Carl Recine)

Romelu Lukaku scored 16 Premier League goals for Manchester United, including this powerful header against West Bromwich Albion at Old Trafford in April. (Reuters/Andrew Yates)

Tottenham found life difficult at first in their adopted home of Wembley. They soon picked up and optimism was again growing that they could challenge for major honours, but they faded away. However, boss Mauricio Pochettino pledged his future to the club, signing a new deal, as did star striker Harry Kane, which sets them up well for when they move in to their brand new stadium which has replaced White Hart Lane.

Liverpool had the star of the season in Mo Salah, who was voted both the FWA and PFA Player of the Year as well as edging out Kane by two goals for the Premier League's golden boot, having netted 32 times.

Klopp may not have threatened City in the title race but his victory over Guardiola in the Champions League showed what his team was capable of. Success against Roma in a remarkable two-legged semi-final took Liverpool to the final in Kiev where they dreamed of adding to their five European Cups.

But they came up short, losing 3-1 to Real Madrid in a game which featured two horrible mistakes by goalkeeper Loris Karius and a sensational overhead kick by Welshman Gareth Bale, who scored twice.

Defending champions Chelsea never seemed happy and there were continuous questions over the future of manager Antonio Conte despite the season ending in that FA Cup final triumph over United thanks to an Eden Hazard penalty.

It was a season in which Arsenal said goodbye to the country's longest serving manager, Arsène Wenger, who was eased out of the hot-seat by a board which eventually decided it was time to take the club in a new direction having been under constant fire from fans who wanted change.

Wenger was in charge of the Gunners for almost 22 years, winning three titles and seven FA Cups and taking his 'Invincibles' through an entire Premier League season unbeaten in 2003–04. But his second decade saw a steady decline

in fortunes and sixth place without a trophy was not the finish to his reign he would have craved.

While Arsenal were seen as failures, Burnley manager Sean Dyche received great plaudits for guiding the small-town club to seventh and into Europe.

Meanwhile Sam Allardyce, who steered Everton away from the relegation zone and into the top half, got only grief for his efforts from supporters who wanted more expansive football. His contract was not renewed.

Leicester fans weren't too enamoured with manager Claude Puel either even though he took them to ninth, while Rafa Benitez fought against the odds to get Newcastle into the top ten against a backdrop of austerity at St James' Park.

For the first time since 2012 all three promoted clubs stayed up: Newcastle, Brighton and Huddersfield. The Terriers performed heroically towards the death to maintain their status, while Swansea fell apart and, along with Stoke and West Brom, were relegated.

West Brom's remarkable late rally under caretaker boss Darren Moore, their fourth manager of the season, was not enough to save them. They were left with far too much to do following the sacking of Alan Pardew.

The Premier League's smallest club, Bournemouth, ensured survival again, along with Watford, while West Ham clinched safety after a tumultuous campaign and fan unrest which resulted in David Moyes leaving at the end of the season.

Former England boss Roy Hodgson did a superb job at Crystal Palace to rescue them from the depths after Frank De Boer was sacked four League games into the season. Palace registered neither a point nor even a goal from their first seven matches.

Manchester City's Kevin De Bruyne blasts one of his eight Premier League goals during the season, this one against Swansea City in April. (Reuters/Phil Noble)

Coventry City's Jordan Shipley scores the Sky Blues' second goal in a 3-1 victory over Exeter City in the League Two Play-off Final at Wembley on 28 May. (Action Images/Andrew Couldridge)

Meanwhile Mark Hughes, so bruised by his dismissal at Stoke, had the last laugh when he took over Southampton and kept them up while his old club went down.

Wolves returned to the big time under Portuguese boss Nuno Espírito Santo whose side were only one point short of three figures in winning the Championship. Neil Warnock worked his promotion magic once more to guide Cardiff City back to the Premier League in second place, and Slavisa Jokanovic's Fulham edged out Aston Villa in the play-off final.

A pitiful Sunderland suffered a second successive relegation and manager Chris Coleman was axed by the new owners. On a dramatic last day, Burton Albion and Barnsley went down too, with Bolton just managing to keep their heads above water along with Reading.

Two famous former top-flight clubs are on the way back: Wigan claimed the League One title while 1995 Premier League champions, Blackburn, were runners-up. Rotherham made it from the play-offs by beating Shrewsbury.

Oldham, Northampton, MK Dons and Bury dropped down to be replaced from League Two by the team synonymous with football history, Accrington Stanley, 1988 League Cup winners Luton, Wycombe and 1987 FA Cup winners Coventry.

Down to the National League went Chesterfield and Barnet swapping places with Macclesfield and Tranmere, who beat Boreham Wood 2-1 in the play-off final. Tranmere played almost the entire game with ten men after having a player sent off in the opening minute. It was a return to League football for the men from the Wirral following three years in the National League wilderness.

Shaun Custis, Head of Sport, *The Sun*

CUPS AND UPS AND DOWNS DIARY

AUGUST 2017
6   FA Community Shield: Arsenal 1 Chelsea 1 (*Arsenal won 4-1 on penalties*).

NOVEMBER 2017
26   Betfred Scottish League Cup Final: Celtic 2 Motherwell 0.

JANUARY 2018
20   Nathaniel MG Welsh League Cup: The New Saints 1 Cardiff Met 0.

FEBRUARY 2018
17   BetMcLean Northern Irish League Cup Final: Dungannon Swifts 3 Ballymena U 1.
25   EFL Cup Final: Manchester C 3 Arsenal 0.

MARCH 2018
14   Women's Continental Cup Final: Arsenal 1 Manchester C 0.
24   Irn-Bru Scottish League Challenge Cup Final: Inverness CT 1 Dumbarton 0.
      Brechin C relegated from Scottish Championship to Scottish League One.

APRIL 2018
7   FAW Trophy Final: Conwy Borough 4 Rhos Aelwyd 1. FC Chester relegated from National League.
8   EFL Trophy Final: Lincoln C 1 Shrewsbury T 0.
14   Wolverhampton W promoted from EFL Championship to.Premier League. Bury relegated from EFL League One to EFL League Two. St Mirren promoted from Scottish Championship to Scottish Premiership. FA County Youth Cup Final: Norfolk 2 Staffordshire 0.
15   Manchester C Champions of Premier League.
17   Accrington S promoted from EFL League Two to EFL League One. Guiseley relegated from National League.
21   Wolverhampton W Champions of EFL Championship. Sunderland relegated from EFL Championship to EFL League One. Wigan Ath promoted from EFL League One to EFL Championship. Luton T promoted from EFL League Two to EFL League One. Macclesfield T promoted from National League to EFL League Two. Torquay U relegated from National League.
24   Blackburn R promoted from EFL League One to EFL Championship. Chesterfield relegated from EFL League Two to National League.
27   FA Youth Cup Final First Leg: Chelsea 3 Arsenal 1.
28   Milton Keynes D relegated from EFL League One to EFL League Two. Accrington S Champions of EFL League Two. Wycombe W promoted from EFL League Two to EFL League One. Ayr U promoted from Scottish League One to Scottish Championship. Montrose promoted from Scottish League Two to Scottish League One. Albion R relegated from Scottish League One to Scottish League Two. Tranmere R, Sutton U, Boreham Wood, Aldershot T, Ebbsfleet U and AFC Fylde into National League play-offs. Woking relegated from National League.
29   Manchester U qualify for Champions League. Celtic Champions of Scottish Premiership. FA Sunday Cup Final: Hardwick Social 2 Gym U 0.
30   FA Youth Cup Final Second Leg: Arsenal 0 Chelsea 4 (*Chelsea won 7-1 on aggregate*).

MAY 2018
5   Burnley qualify for Europa League. Stoke C relegated from Premier League to EFL League One. Wigan Ath Champions of EFL League One. Northampton T and Oldham Ath relegated from EFL League One to EFL League Two. Exeter, Notts Co, Coventry C and Lincoln C qualify for EFL League Two Play-Offs. SSE FA Women's Cup Final: Chelsea 3 Arsenal 1. Tennent's Northern Irish FA Cup Final: Coleraine 3 Cliftonville 1. Barnet relegated from EFL League Two to National League. Queen's Park relegated from Scottish League One to Scottish League Two. Scottish League Two Play-Off Final First Leg: Cove Rangers 0 Cowdenbeath 0.
6   Cardiff C promoted from EFL Championship to Premier League. Fulham, Aston Villa, Middlesbrough and Derby Co qualify for EFL Championship Play-Offs. Barnsley and Burton Alb relegated from EFL Championship to EFL League One. Welsh FA Cup Final: Connah's Quay Nomads 4 Aberystwyth 1. Shrewsbury T, Rotherham U, Scunthorpe U and Charlton Ath qualify for EFL League One Play-Offs.
      FA Inter-League Cup Final: North Riding Football League 4 York Football League 2.
8   WBA relegated from Premier League to EFL Championship.
9   Tottenham H qualify for Champions League. Scottish Championship Play-Off Final First Leg: Alloa Ath 0 Dumbarton 1. Scottish League One Play-Off Final First Leg: Stenhousemuir 2 Peterhead 0.
12   Ross Co relegated from Scottish Premiership to Scottish League Championship.National League Play-Off Final: Tranmere R 2 Boreham Wood 1 (*Tranmere R promoted to EFL League Two*). Scottish Championship Play-Off Second Leg: Dumbarton 0 Alloa Ath 2 (*aet; Alloa Ath won 2-1 on aggregate and promoted from Scottish League One to Scottish Championship, Dumbarton relegated from Scottish Championship to Scottish League One*). Scottish League One Play-Off Second Leg: Peterhead 1 Stenhousemuir 0 (*Stenhousemuir won 2-1 on aggregate and promoted from Scottish League Two to Scottish League One, Peterhead relegated from Scottish League One to Scottish League Two*). Scottish League Two Play-Off Second Leg: Cowdenbeath 3 Cove Rangers 2 (*Cowdenbeath won 3-2 on aggregate and remain in Scottish League Two*).
13   Liverpool qualify for Champions League. Arsenal and Chelsea qualify for Europa League. Aberdeen and Rangers qualify for Europa League. Swansea C relegated from Premier League to EFL Championship.
16   UEFA Europa League Final: Atletico Madrid 3 Marseille 0.
17   Scottish Premiership Play-Off Final First Leg: Livingston 2 Partick Thistle 1.
19   Emirates FA Cup Final: Chelsea 1 Manchester U 0. William Hill Scottish FA Cup Final: Celtic 2 Motherwell 0.
20   Scottish Premiership Play-Off Second Leg: Partick Thistle 0 Livingston 1 (*Livingston won 3-1 on aggregate and promoted to Scottish Premiership, Partick Thistle relegated from Scottish Premiership to Scottish Championship*).
20   FA Trophy Final: Brackley T 1 Bromley 1 (*aet; Brackley T won 5-4 on penalties*). FA Vase Final: Thatcham T 1 Stockton T 0.
24   UEFA Women's Champions League Final: Lyon 4 Wolfsburg 1
26   UEFA Champions League Final: Real Madrid 3 Liverpool 1. EFL Championship Play-Off Final: Fulham 1 Aston Villa 0 (*Fulham promoted to Premier League*).
27   EFL League One Play-Off Final: Rotherham U 2 Shrewsbury T 1 (*aet; Rotherham U promoted to EFL Championship*).
28   EFL League Two Play-Off Final: Coventry C 3 Exeter C 1 (*Coventry C promoted to EFL League One*).

JULY 2018
15   World Cup Final: France 4 Croatia 2.

THE FA COMMUNITY SHIELD WINNERS 1908–2017

CHARITY SHIELD 1908–2001

1908	Manchester U v QPR	1-1
Replay	Manchester U v QPR	4-0
1909	Newcastle U v Northampton T	2-0
1910	Brighton v Aston Villa	1-0
1911	Manchester U v Swindon T	8-4
1912	Blackburn R v QPR	2-1
1913	Professionals v Amateurs	7-2
1920	WBA v Tottenham H	2-0
1921	Tottenham H v Burnley	2-0
1922	Huddersfield T v Liverpool	1-0
1923	Professionals v Amateurs	2-0
1924	Professionals v Amateurs	3-1
1925	Amateurs v Professionals	6-1
1926	Amateurs v Professionals	6-3
1927	Cardiff C v Corinthians	2-1
1928	Everton v Blackburn R	2-1
1929	Professionals v Amateurs	3-0
1930	Arsenal v Sheffield W	2-1
1931	Arsenal v WBA	1-0
1932	Everton v Newcastle U	5-3
1933	Arsenal v Everton	3-0
1934	Arsenal v Manchester C	4-0
1935	Sheffield W v Arsenal	1-0
1936	Sunderland v Arsenal	2-1
1937	Manchester C v Sunderland	2-0
1938	Arsenal v Preston NE	2-1
1948	Arsenal v Manchester U	4-3
1949	Portsmouth v Wolverhampton W	1-1*
1950	English World Cup XI v FA Canadian Touring Team	4-2
1951	Tottenham H v Newcastle U	2-1
1952	Manchester U v Newcastle U	4-2
1953	Arsenal v Blackpool	3-1
1954	Wolverhampton W v WBA	4-4*
1955	Chelsea v Newcastle U	3-0
1956	Manchester U v Manchester C	1-0
1957	Manchester U v Aston Villa	4-0
1958	Bolton W v Wolverhampton W	4-1
1959	Wolverhampton W v Nottingham F	3-1
1960	Burnley v Wolverhampton W	2-2*
1961	Tottenham H v FA XI	3-2
1962	Tottenham H v Ipswich T	5-1
1963	Everton v Manchester U	4-0
1964	Liverpool v West Ham U	2-2*
1965	Manchester U v Liverpool	2-2*
1966	Liverpool v Everton	1-0
1967	Manchester U v Tottenham H	3-3*
1968	Manchester C v WBA	6-1
1969	Leeds U v Manchester C	2-1
1970	Everton v Chelsea	2-1
1971	Leicester C v Liverpool	1-0
1972	Manchester C v Aston Villa	1-0
1973	Burnley v Manchester C	1-0
1974	Liverpool v Leeds U	1-1
	Liverpool won 6-5 on penalties.	
1975	Derby Co v West Ham U	2-0
1976	Liverpool v Southampton	1-0
1977	Liverpool v Manchester U	0-0*
1978	Nottingham F v Ipswich T	5-0
1979	Liverpool v Arsenal	3-1
1980	Liverpool v West Ham U	1-0
1981	Aston Villa v Tottenham H	2-2*
1982	Liverpool v Tottenham H	1-0
1983	Manchester U v Liverpool	2-0
1984	Everton v Liverpool	1-0
1985	Everton v Manchester U	2-0
1986	Everton v Liverpool	1-1*
1987	Everton v Coventry C	1-0
1988	Liverpool v Wimbledon	2-1
1989	Liverpool v Arsenal	1-0
1990	Liverpool v Manchester U	1-1*
1991	Arsenal v Tottenham H	0-0*
1992	Leeds U v Liverpool	4-3
1993	Manchester U v Arsenal	1-1
	Manchester U won 5-4 on penalties.	
1994	Manchester U v Blackburn R	2-0
1995	Everton v Blackburn R	1-0
1996	Manchester U v Newcastle U	4-0
1997	Manchester U v Chelsea	1-1
	Manchester U won 4-2 on penalties.	
1998	Arsenal v Manchester U	3-0
1999	Arsenal v Manchester U	2-1
2000	Chelsea v Manchester U	2-0
2001	Liverpool v Manchester U	2-1

COMMUNITY SHIELD 2002–17

2002	Arsenal v Liverpool	1-0
2003	Manchester U v Arsenal	1-1
	Manchester U won 4-3 on penalties.	
2004	Arsenal v Manchester U	3-1
2005	Chelsea v Arsenal	2-1
2006	Liverpool v Chelsea	2-1
2007	Manchester U v Chelsea	1-1
	Manchester U won 3-0 on penalties.	
2008	Manchester U v Portsmouth	0-0
	Manchester U won 3-1 on penalties.	
2009	Chelsea v Manchester U	2-2
	Chelsea won 4-1 on penalties.	
2010	Manchester U v Chelsea	3-1
2011	Manchester U v Manchester C	3-2
2012	Manchester C v Chelsea	3-2
2013	Manchester U v Wigan Ath	2-0
2014	Arsenal v Manchester C	3-0
2015	Arsenal v Chelsea	1-0
2016	Manchester U v Leicester C	2-1
2017	Arsenal v Chelsea	1-1
	Arsenal won 4-1 on penalties.	

* Each club retained shield for six months. ▪ *Denotes player sent off.*

THE FA COMMUNITY SHIELD 2017

Arsenal (0) 1, Chelsea (0) 1
(Arsenal won 4-1 on penalties)

at Wembley, Sunday 6 August 2017, attendance 83,325

Arsenal: Cech; Bellerin, Mertesacker (Kolasinac 33), Holding, Monreal, Oxlade-Chamberlain, Iwobi (Walcott 67), Elneny, Zhaka, Welbeck (Nelson 87), Lacazette (Giroud 66).
Scorer: Kolasinac 82.

Chelsea: Courtois; Moses, Cahill, Luiz, Azpilicueta, Alonso (Rudiger 79), Fabregas, Kante, Willian (Musonda 82), Batshuayi (Morata 74), Pedro▪.
Scorer: Moses 46.

Referee: Bobby Madley.

ACCRINGTON STANLEY

FOUNDATION

Accrington Football Club, founder members of the Football League in 1888, were not connected with Accrington Stanley. In fact both clubs ran concurrently between 1891 when Stanley were formed and 1895 when Accrington FC folded. Actually Stanley Villa was the original name, those responsible for forming the club living in Stanley Street and using the Stanley Arms as their meeting place. They became Accrington Stanley in 1893. In 1894–95 they joined the Accrington & District League, playing at Moorhead Park. Subsequently they played in the North-East Lancashire Combination and the Lancashire Combination before becoming founder members of the Third Division (North) in 1921, two years after moving to Peel Park. In 1962 they resigned from the Football League, were wound up, re-formed in 1963, disbanded in 1966 only to restart as Accrington Stanley (1968), returning to the Lancashire Combination in 1970.

Wham Stadium, Livingstone Road, Accrington, Lancashire BB5 5BX.
Telephone: (01254) 356 950. *Fax:* (01254) 356 951.
Website: www.accringtonstanley.co.uk
Email: info@accringtonstanley.co.uk
Ground Capacity: 5,254.
Record Attendance: 13,181 v Hull C, Division 3 (N), 28 September 1948 (at Peel Park); 4,753 v Lincoln C, FL 2 28 April 2018 (at Wham Stadium).
Pitch Measurements: 101.5m × 65m (111yd × 71yd).
Chairman: Andy Holt.
Managing Director: David Burgess.
Manager: John Coleman.
Assistant Manager: Jimmy Bell.

HONOURS

League Champions: FL 2 – 2017–18; Conference – 2005–06.
Runners-up: Division 3N – 1954–55, 1957–58.
FA Cup: 4th rd – 1927, 1937, 1959, 2010, 2017.
League Cup: 3rd rd – 2016–17.

Colours: Red shirts with white trim, white shorts with red trim, red socks with white trim.
Year Formed: 1891, reformed 1968.
Turned Professional: 1919.
Club Nickname: 'The Reds', 'Stanley'.
Previous Names: 1891, Stanley Villa; 1893, Accrington Stanley.
Grounds: 1891, Moorhead Park; 1897, Bell's Ground; 1919, Peel Park; 1970, Crown Ground (renamed Interlink Express Stadium, Fraser Eagle Stadium, Store First Stadium 2013, Wham Stadium 2015).
First Football League Game: 27 August 1921, Division 3 (N), v Rochdale (a) L 3-6 – Tattersall; Newton, Baines, Crawshaw, Popplewell, Burkinshaw, Oxley, Makin, Green (1), Hosker (2), Hartles.
Record League Victory: 8–0 v New Brighton, Division 3 (N), 17 March 1934 – Maidment; Armstrong (pen), Price, Dodds, Crawshaw, McCulloch, Wyper, Lennox (2), Cheetham (4), Leedham (1), Watson.
Record Cup Victory: 7–0 v Spennymoor U, FA Cup 2nd rd, 8 December 1938 – Tootill; Armstrong, Whittaker, Latham, Curran, Lee, Parry (2), Chadwick, Jepson (3), McLoughlin (2), Barclay.
Record Defeat: 1–9 v Lincoln C, Division 3 (N), 3 March 1951.

Sᴜn FACT FILE

Accrington Stanley lost their first two games on their return to the Football League in 2006–07. Their first victory came on 12 August when two goals from Benin international Romuald Boco earned a 2-1 win over Barnet.

Most League Points (2 for a win): 61, Division 3 (N), 1954–55.

Most League Points (3 for a win): 93, FL 2, 2017–18.

Most League Goals: 96, Division 3 (N), 1954–55.

Highest League Scorer in Season: George Stewart, 35, Division 3 (N), 1955–56; George Hudson, 35, Division 4, 1960–61.

Most League Goals in Total Aggregate: George Stewart, 136, 1954–58.

Most League Goals in One Match: 5, Billy Harker v Gateshead, Division 3 (N), 16 November 1935; George Stewart v Gateshead, Division 3 (N), 27 November 1954.

Most Capped Player: Romuald Boco, 19 (48), Benin.

Most League Appearances: Andy Procter, 275, 2006–12, 2014–16.

Youngest League Player: Ian Gibson, 15 years 358 days, v Norwich C, 23 March 1959.

Record Transfer Fee Received: £260,000 from Scunthorpe U for Bobby Grant, June 2010.

Record Transfer Fee Paid: £85,000 (rising to £150,000) to Swansea C for Ian Craney, January 2008.

Football League Record: 1921 Original Member of Division 3 (N); 1958–60 Division 3; 1960–62 Division 4; 2006–18 FL 2; 2018– FL 1.

LATEST SEQUENCES

Longest Sequence of League Wins: 7, 24.2.2018 – 7.4.2018.

Longest Sequence of League Defeats: 9, 8.3.1930 – 21.4.1930.

Longest Sequence of League Draws: 4, 10.9.1927 – 27.9.1927.

Longest Sequence of Unbeaten League Matches: 15, 3.2.2018 – 21.4.2018.

Longest Sequence Without a League Win: 18, 17.9.1938 – 31.12.1938.

Successive Scoring Runs: 24 from 23.12.2017.

Successive Non-scoring Runs: 5 from 15.3.1930.

MANAGERS

William Cronshaw c.1894
John Haworth 1897–1910
Johnson Haworth c.1916
Sam Pilkingson 1919–24
    (*Tommy Booth p-m 1923–24*)
Ernie Blackburn 1924–32
Amos Wade 1932–35
John Hacking 1935–49
Jimmy Porter 1949–51
Walter Crook 1951–53
Walter Galbraith 1953–58
George Eastham snr 1958–59
Harold Bodle 1959–60
James Harrower 1960–61
Harold Mather 1962–63
Jimmy Hinksman 1963–64
Terry Neville 1964–65
Ian Bryson 1965
Danny Parker 1965–66
Gerry Keenan
Gary Pierce
Dave Thornley
Phil Staley
Eric Whalley
Stan Allen 1995–96
Tony Greenwood 1996–98
Billy Rodaway 1998
Wayne Harrison 1998–99
John Coleman 1999–2012
Paul Cook 2012
Leam Richardson 2012–13
James Beattie 2013–14
John Coleman September 2014–

TEN YEAR LEAGUE RECORD

		P	W	D	L	F	A	Pts	Pos
2008-09	FL 2	46	13	11	22	42	59	50	16
2009-10	FL 2	46	18	7	21	62	74	61	15
2010-11	FL 2	46	18	19	9	73	55	73	5
2011-12	FL 2	46	14	15	17	54	66	57	14
2012-13	FL 2	46	14	12	20	51	68	54	18
2013-14	FL 2	46	14	15	17	54	56	57	15
2014-15	FL 2	46	15	11	20	58	77	56	17
2015-16	FL 2	46	24	13	9	74	48	85	4
2016-17	FL 2	46	17	14	15	59	56	65	13
2017-18	FL 2	46	29	6	11	76	46	93	1

DID YOU KNOW ?

Accrington Stanley have never attracted large crowds throughout their history due to competition from neighbouring clubs. The highest average attendance of 9,766 was achieved in the 1954–55 season when Stanley finished runners-up to Barnsley in Division Three North.

ACCRINGTON STANLEY – SKY BET LEAGUE TWO 2017–18 LEAGUE RECORD

Match No.	Date	Venue	Opponents	Result	H/T Score	Lg Pos.	Goalscorers	Attendance
1	Aug 5	H	Colchester U	W 3-1	2-0	3	Jackson [9], Kee [32], Beckles [64]	1625
2	12	A	Yeovil T	L 2-3	1-3	9	Jackson 2 [12, 53]	2464
3	19	H	Mansfield T	W 2-1	1-1	6	Jackson [10], Kee [90]	1645
4	25	A	Notts Co	D 2-2	0-1	1	Hughes [58], Wilks [90]	6087
5	Sept 2	A	Morecambe	W 2-1	1-0	3	Kee [31], Clark [90]	2059
6	9	H	Carlisle U	W 3-0	2-0	2	Kee [17], McConville 2 [43, 57]	2120
7	12	H	Grimsby T	L 1-2	1-1	3	Jackson [45]	1288
8	16	A	Chesterfield	W 2-1	0-0	3	Kee [68], Wilks [82]	4487
9	23	H	Cheltenham T	D 1-1	1-1	4	Jackson [39]	1321
10	26	H	Port Vale	W 2-1	1-1	3	Kee 2 [36, 62]	3360
11	30	A	Forest Green R	W 1-0	0-0	3	Conneely [56]	2594
12	Oct 7	H	Luton T	L 0-2	0-2	6		2193
13	14	H	Coventry C	W 1-0	1-0	4	McConville [14]	2828
14	17	H	Stevenage	L 2-3	1-0	5	Clark [19], Kee (pen) [64]	1788
15	21	A	Crewe Alex	W 2-0	2-0	3	Kee (pen) [3], Clark [11]	3849
16	28	H	Barnet	W 4-1	1-0	2	McConville [35], Clark [51], Kee [59], Jackson [65]	1485
17	Nov 11	A	Cambridge U	D 0-0	0-0	2		4402
18	18	H	Newport Co	D 1-1	0-0	3	Wilks [88]	1371
19	21	H	Wycombe W	W 1-0	0-0	3	Hughes [70]	1119
20	25	A	Exeter C	L 0-2	0-1	3		3597
21	Dec 16	A	Lincoln C	L 0-2	0-1	5		7696
22	23	H	Crawley T	L 2-3	1-3	7	Kee (pen) [45], Richards-Everton [53]	1295
23	26	H	Carlisle U	L 1-3	0-1	9	Kee (pen) [47]	5404
24	30	A	Grimsby T	W 3-0	0-0	7	Kee (pen) [55], McConville [61], Jackson [77]	4188
25	Jan 6	H	Chesterfield	W 4-0	2-0	4	Hughes [19], McConville [32], Jackson [47], Kee [89]	1655
26	13	A	Cheltenham T	W 2-0	1-0	3	Kee [22], Jackson [62]	2893
27	20	H	Port Vale	W 3-2	0-2	3	McConville 2 [51, 72], Kee [54]	1743
28	27	A	Crawley T	L 1-2	0-2	5	Smith (og) [57]	2153
29	Feb 3	H	Stevenage	W 3-2	1-2	5	McConville 2 [45, 78], Kee [70]	1324
30	6	H	Swindon T	W 2-1	1-0	3	Kee (pen) [25], Jackson [62]	1243
31	10	A	Coventry C	W 2-0	1-0	2	Clark 2 [5, 60]	28,343
32	13	H	Crewe Alex	W 1-0	1-0	2	Jackson [42]	1254
33	17	A	Barnet	D 1-1	0-1	3	Kee (pen) [68]	1501
34	24	A	Cambridge U	W 1-0	0-0	2	Jackson [57]	1819
35	Mar 6	H	Morecambe	W 1-0	1-0	2	Kee (pen) [45]	1769
36	10	A	Luton T	W 2-1	1-0	1	McConville [44], Kee [90]	9503
37	17	H	Forest Green R	W 3-1	1-0	1	Johnson [3], Clark [81], Jackson [90]	2313
38	30	A	Mansfield T	W 1-0	0-0	1	Conneely [60]	5053
39	Apr 2	H	Notts Co	W 1-0	1-0	1	Hughes [9]	3039
40	7	A	Colchester U	W 1-0	0-0	1	Kee [63]	3174
41	14	H	Exeter C	D 1-1	1-1	1	Jackson [38]	3135
42	17	H	Yeovil T	W 2-0	2-0	1	Kee 2 [26, 28]	3176
43	21	A	Wycombe W	W 4-0	2-0	1	Jackson [15], Brown [33], McConville [66], Zanzala (pen) [90]	6178
44	24	A	Newport Co	L 1-2	0-1	1	Kee [90]	2370
45	28	H	Lincoln C	W 1-0	1-0	1	Clark [35]	4753
46	May 5	A	Swindon T	L 0-3	0-2	1		6118

Final League Position: 1

GOALSCORERS

League (76): Kee 25 (8 pens), Jackson 16, McConville 12, Clark 8, Hughes 4, Wilks 3, Conneely 2, Beckles 1, Brown 1, Johnson 1, Richards-Everton 1, Zanzala 1 (1 pen), own goal 1.
FA Cup (1): McConville 1.
Carabao Cup (4): Clark 1, Dallison 1, Kee 1, Richards-Everton 1.
Checkatrade Trophy (10): Sousa 3, Wilks 2, Brown 1, Edwards 1, Leacock-McLeod 1, Nolan 1, own goal 1.

Chapman A 44 + 1	Beckles O 2	Hughes M 46	Richards-Everton B 18 + 4	Donacien J 45	Clark J 43	Nolan L 27 + 2	Conneely S 33	McConville S 43	Jackson K 44	Kee B 46	Hornby-Forbes T 2 + 4	Edwards J 1 + 1	Dallison T 2	Ogle R — + 3	Leacock-McLeod M — + 10	Wilks M 3 + 16	Sykes R — + 2	Stryjek M 1	Rawson F 12	Thornley J 14	Brown S 28 + 8	Sousa E — + 6	Johnson C 29 + 2	Watson N — + 2	Hmami J — + 1	Dunne J 18 + 2	Zanzala O — + 6	Rodgers H 4 + 1	Maxted J 1	Williams D — + 1	Match No.
1	2	3	4	5^1	6	7	8	9	10^1	11	12	13																			1
1		3		5	6	8	7	9	11	10	2^2			4^1	12	13															2
1	5	3	4	2	6	8	7	9	11	10																					3
1		3	4^1	2	6^2	7	8	9	11	10				5^3	12^4	13	14														4
12		4		2	6	8	7	9	11	10^1					14			1^2	13	3^3	5										5
1		4		2	6^2	7	8	9	10^3	11^1	13				12					4	5	14									6
1		3		2	6	8	7^1	9	11	10^3	13				12					4	5^2	14									7
1		3		2	6	7	8	9	10^2	11	12				13					4	5^1										8
1		3		2	6^2	7	8^1	9	10^3	11	2				13	13^2				4		14									9
1		4		2	9^2	7	8	6	10^1	11										3	5	13									10
1		4		2	6	8	7	9		11			10^1							3	5	12									11
1		3		2	6^3	7	9	10^2		11					12	13				4	5	8^1	14								12
1		3	4	2	6	7	8^2	9	10	11											5		13								13
1		3	4	2	9	8	6	7	10	11											5^1										14
1		3	4	2	9	8	6	7^2	10	11											5		13								15
1		3	4	2	6	14		9^2	11	10^1					13	12					5	7^3	8								16
1		4	3	2	9		8	6	10	11											5	12	7^1								17
1		4	3	2	6^2			9	11	10					12	13					5^1	7	8								18
1		3		2	5		8	9	10						12	11^1			4		6	7									19
1		3		2	5		13	8	9^2	10					12^3	11			4		6	7^1	14								20
1		4	12	2	6		8	9^1	10	11					13						3^8	5^2	7								21
1		4	12	2	6^1		7^2	9	10	11					13						3^9		8	14	5						22
1		4	3	2	5	7		8	9	10				12		11^1					6										23
1		3	4	5	6	8		9^2	10	11^3											12	7		2	14	13					24
1		3	4	5^1	6	7		9	11^3	10^2					13		14				8	2				12					25
1		4	3	5	6	7		9		10^2			11								8	2^1				12	13				26
1		4		5	6	8		9	10	11											7	2									27
1	2	7	5	4^1	3			9	8	11					13						6	10^2					12				28
1		4		5		7		9	10	11											8	12	6				2	3^1			29
1		4		5	6	8		9^2	10^1	11											7	2					3	13	12		30
1		4		2	6	8	7		10	11											9						3	5			31
1		3		5	6	7			10	11											8	12	9				4	2^1			32
1		4		5	6	7	8		10	11											13	12^2	9				3	2^1			33
1		3		5	6	7		9	11	10											8	2	4								34
1		3		5	6	7		9	11	10											8	2	4								35
1		4		5	6	7		9	11	10											8	2	3								36
1		3		5	6	8		9	11	10											7	2	4								37
1		3	4		6	7		9	11	10											8	2	5								38
		3		5	6	8		9	10	11											7	2	4						1		39
1		3		5	6	8		9	10	11											7	2	4								40
1		3	12	5^1	6	8		9	11	10											7	2	4								41
1		3		5	6	7		9	11	10											8	2	4								42
1		4	13	5	6	8		9^2	10^1	11^1											7	2	3				12			14	43
1		4		5	6	8		9	11	10											7	2^1	3				12				44
1		3		5	6	7		9	10	11											8	2	4								45
1		4		5	6	8	7^1	9^1	10	11											13	12	2^2				3^4			14	46

AFC WIMBLEDON

FOUNDATION

While the history of AFC Wimbledon is straightforward since it was a new club formed in 2002, there were in effect two clubs operating for two years with Wimbledon connections. The other club was MK Dons, of course. In August 2001, the Football League had rejected the existing Wimbledon's application to move to Milton Keynes. In May 2002, they rejected local sites and were given permission to move by an independent commission set up by the Football League. AFC Wimbledon was founded in the summer of 2002 and held its first trials on Wimbledon Common. In subsequent years, there was considerable debate over the rightful home of the trophies obtained by the former Wimbledon football club. In October 2006, an agreement was reached between Milton Keynes Dons FC, its Supporters Association, the Wimbledon Independent Supporters Association and the Football Supporters Federation to transfer such trophies and honours to the London Borough of Merton.

The Cherry Red Records Stadium, Kingsmeadow, Jack Goodchild Way, 422a Kingston Road, Kingston-upon-Thames, Surrey KT1 3PB.

Telephone: (0208) 547 3528.

Fax: (0808) 2800 816.

Website: www.afcwimbledon.co.uk

Email: info@afcwimbledon.co.uk

Ground Capacity: 5,027.

Record Attendance: 4,870 v Accrington S, FL 2 Play-Offs, 14 May 2016.

Pitch Measurements: 104m × 66m (113.5yd × 72yd).

President: Dickie Guy.

Chief Executive: Erik Samuelson.

Manager: Neal Ardley.

Assistant Manager: Neil Cox.

First-Team Coach: Simon Bassey.

Club Nickname: 'The Dons'.

Colours: Blue shirts with yellow trim, blue shorts with yellow trim, blue socks with yellow trim.

Year Formed: 2002.

Turned Professional: 2002.

HONOURS

League: Runners-up: FL 2 – (7th) 2015–16 *(promoted via play-offs)*; Conference – (2nd) 2010–11 *(promoted via play-offs).*

FA Cup: 3rd rd – 2015, 2017.

League Cup: never past 1st rd.

SUN FACT FILE

AFC Wimbledon hold the record for the longest unbeaten run of league matches in English senior football. Between February 2003 and December 2004 they played 78 games without losing once, remaining unbeaten in 2003–04 when winning the Combined Counties League Premier Division title.

Grounds: 2002, Kingsmeadow (renamed The Cherry Red Records Stadium).

First Football League Game: 6 August 2011, FL 2 v Bristol R (h) L 2–3 – Brown; Hatton, Gwillim (Bush), Porter (Minshull), Stuart (1), Johnson B, Moore L, Wellard, Jolley (Ademeno (1)), Midson, Yussuff.

MANAGERS
Terry Eames 2002–04
Nicky English *(Caretaker)* 2004
Dave Anderson 2004–07
Terry Brown 2007–12
Neal Ardley October 2012–

Record League Victory: 5–1 v Bury, FL 2, 19 November 2016 – Shea; Fuller, Robertson, Robinson (Taylor), Owens, Francomb (2 (1 pen)), Reeves, Parrett, Whelpdale (1), Elliott (1) (Nightingale), Poleon (1), (Barrett).

Record Cup Victory: 5–0 v Bury, FA Cup 1st rd replay, 5 November 2016 – Shea; Fuller (Owens), Robertson, Robinson (1), Francomb. Parrett (1), Reeves, Bulman (Beere), Whelpdale, Barcham (Poleon (2)), Taylor (1).

Record Defeat: 2–6 v Burton Alb, FL 2, 25 August 2012.

Most League Points (3 for a win): 75, FL 2, 2015–16.

Most League Goals: 64, FL 2, 2015–16.

Highest League Scorer in Season: Lyle Taylor, 20, 2015–16.

Most League Goals in Total Aggregate: Kevin Cooper, 107, 2002–04.

Most League Goals in One Match: 3, Lyle Taylor v Rotherham U, FL 1, 17 October 2017.

Most Capped Player: Shane Smeltz, 5 (58), New Zealand.

Most League Appearances: Barry Fuller, 205, 2013–18.

Youngest League Player: Ben Harrison, 17 years 195 days v Accrington S, 13 September 2014.

Record Transfer Fee Received: £150,000 from Bradford C for Jake Reeves, July 2017.

Record Transfer Fee Paid: £25,000 (in excess of) to Stevenage for Byron Harrison, January 2012.

Football League Record: 2011 Promoted from Conference Premier; 2011–16 FL 2; 2016– FL 1.

LATEST SEQUENCES
Longest Sequence of League Wins: 5, 2.4.2016 – 23.4.2016.
Longest Sequence of League Defeats: 6, 26.11.2011 – 2.1.2012.
Longest Sequence of League Draws: 4, 21.4.2018 – 5.5.2018
Longest Sequence of Unbeaten League Matches: 8, 17.9.2016 – 22.10.2016.
Longest Sequence Without a League Win: 12, 15.10.2011 – 2.1.2012.
Successive Scoring Runs: 10 from 28.12.2016.
Successive Non-scoring Runs: 6 from 1.4.2017.

TEN YEAR LEAGUE RECORD

		P	W	D	L	F	A	Pts	Pos
2008-09	Conf S	42	26	10	6	86	36	88	1
2009-10	Conf P	44	18	10	16	61	47	64	8
2010-11	Conf P	46	27	9	10	83	47	90	2
2011-12	FL 2	46	15	9	22	62	78	54	16
2012-13	FL 2	46	14	11	21	54	76	53	20
2013-14	FL 2	46	14	14	18	49	57	53*	20
2014-15	FL 2	46	14	16	16	54	60	58	15
2015-16	FL 2	46	21	12	13	64	50	75	7
2016-17	FL 1	46	13	18	15	52	55	57	15
2017-18	FL 1	46	13	14	19	47	58	53	18

* 3 pts deducted.

DID YOU KNOW ?

AFC Wimbledon have recorded an average home attendance for Football League matches of more than 4,000 for every season since they were promoted in 2011–12. The highest average attendance during this period was 4,477 achieved in 2016–17.

AFC WIMBLEDON – SKY BET LEAGUE ONE 2017–18 LEAGUE RECORD

Match No.	Date	Venue	Opponents	Result		H/T Score	Lg Pos.	Goalscorers	Attendance
1	Aug 5	A	Scunthorpe U	D	1-1	0-1	11	Abdou [67]	4398
2	12	H	Shrewsbury T	L	0-1	0-1	17		3981
3	19	A	Fleetwood T	L	0-2	0-1	22		2730
4	26	H	Doncaster R	W	2-0	0-0	16	Appiah [57], Barcham [59]	4144
5	Sept 2	A	Blackpool	L	0-1	0-0	16		3457
6	9	H	Portsmouth	L	0-2	0-1	18		4585
7	12	H	Gillingham	D	1-1	1-1	20	Barcham [35]	3819
8	16	A	Blackburn R	W	1-0	1-0	16	Appiah [16]	10,833
9	22	H	Milton Keynes D	L	0-2	0-2	16		3973
10	26	A	Southend U	L	0-1	0-0	20		5881
11	30	H	Rochdale	D	0-0	0-0	21		3861
12	Oct 7	A	Oxford U	L	0-3	0-1	21		7241
13	14	A	Northampton T	W	1-0	0-0	21	Forrester [61]	5306
14	17	H	Rotherham U	W	3-1	1-0	18	Taylor 3 [15, 85, 90]	3907
15	21	H	Plymouth Arg	L	0-1	0-0	19		4848
16	28	A	Charlton Ath	L	0-1	0-0	20		12,575
17	Nov 12	H	Peterborough U	D	2-2	2-2	21	Taylor [1], McDonald [45]	4220
18	18	A	Bristol R	W	3-1	2-0	19	Barcham [2], Forrester [45], McDonald [61]	8734
19	21	A	Oldham Ath	D	0-0	0-0	19		3169
20	25	H	Walsall	L	1-2	1-2	20	Taylor [36]	4130
21	Dec 16	H	Wigan Ath	L	0-4	0-0	23		4289
22	23	H	Bradford C	W	2-1	1-0	21	McDonald [7], Taylor [70]	4215
23	26	A	Portsmouth	L	1-2	0-1	21	Taylor (pen) [50]	18,644
24	30	A	Gillingham	D	2-2	0-0	21	Taylor (pen) [67], Forrester [84]	6419
25	Jan 1	H	Southend U	W	2-0	1-0	21	Trotter [27], Soares [46]	4392
26	13	A	Milton Keynes D	D	0-0	0-0	22		9504
27	20	H	Blackpool	W	2-0	0-0	19	Trotter [49], Pigott [77]	4286
28	27	A	Bradford C	W	4-0	1-0	16	Abdou [14], Barcham [59], McDonald 2 [65, 80]	19,103
29	Feb 3	A	Rotherham U	L	0-2	0-1	18		8330
30	6	A	Bury	L	1-2	1-2	19	Trotter [28]	2975
31	10	H	Northampton T	L	1-3	0-1	20	Oshilaja [47]	4485
32	13	A	Plymouth Arg	L	2-4	1-3	21	Taylor 2 [37, 59]	10,671
33	17	H	Bristol R	W	1-0	0-0	18	Pigott [90]	4837
34	24	A	Peterborough U	D	1-1	0-0	18	Taylor [75]	5146
35	27	H	Blackburn R	L	0-3	0-1	18		4401
36	Mar 10	H	Oxford U	W	2-1	1-1	18	Taylor (pen) [32], Meades [71]	4592
37	17	A	Rochdale	D	1-1	1-1	18	Oshilaja [7]	2667
38	24	A	Shrewsbury T	L	0-1	0-0	19		6456
39	30	H	Fleetwood T	L	0-1	0-1	20		4378
40	Apr 7	H	Scunthorpe U	D	1-1	1-0	20	Nightingale [4]	4055
41	10	H	Charlton Ath	W	1-0	1-0	19	Taylor [45]	4457
42	14	A	Walsall	W	3-2	0-2	18	Pigott [48], Taylor [65], Parrett (pen) [90]	4663
43	21	A	Oldham Ath	D	2-2	1-0	18	Meades [10], Pigott [68]	4850
44	28	H	Wigan Ath	D	1-1	1-0	19	Pigott [24]	12,554
45	May 1	A	Doncaster R	D	0-0	0-0	19		7094
46	5	H	Bury	D	2-2	2-0	18	Parrett [12], Appiah [34]	4770

Final League Position: 18

GOALSCORERS

League (47): Taylor 14 (3 pens), McDonald 5, Pigott 5, Barcham 4, Appiah 3, Forrester 3, Trotter 3, Abdou 2, Meades 2, Oshilaja 2, Parrett 2 (1 pen), Nightingale 1, Soares 1.
FA Cup (4): Taylor 3 (1 pen), McDonald 1.
Carabao Cup (1): Robinson 1.
Checkatrade Trophy (9): Kaja 2, Sibbick 2, Hartigan 1, McDonald 1, Parrett 1, Taylor 1, own goal 1.

Long G 45	Fuller B 42	Oshilaja A 41+1	Robinson P 11+4	Kennedy C 11+3	Francomb G 31+6	Abdou N 26+8	Trotter L 41+1	Appiah K 8+6	McDonald C 23+9	Barcham A 38+7	Taylor L 42+4	Nightingale W 15+3	Parrett D 16+7	Egan A —+2	Kaja E 7+12	Hartigan A 6+5	Forrester H 20+16	Charles D 26+5	Soares T 27+4	Meades J 19+7	Sibbick T —+1	McDonnell J 1	Pigott J 10+8	Sam L —+2	Match No.
1	2	3	4	5[1]	6	7	8[2]	9[3]	10	11	12	13	14												1
1	2	4	3	5	6	7[1]		9[1]	10	11[1]	12			8	13	14									2
1	2	4	3	5	6		8	13	12	10[1]	11	9					7[2]								3
1	2	3	4	5[1]	6[3]	7	8		10[2]	12	11	9		14					12						4
1	2	5	4	3[1]	6[2]	8[4]	7	13	10	11	9[3]		14						12						5
1	5		4	2[2]	8		7	10	9	11[1]	14		3	6[2]			12	13							6
1	2	4		5		7	11[2]	12	9[1]	10	3	8[3]		14	6	13									7
1	2	4	14	5		8	11[3]	12	9[2]	10[1]	3	6			7	13									8
1	2	3	4[3]	5		8	11[2]	12	9	10		6[1]			7	13	14								9
1	2	3		5	13	7		10	8[1]	11	4	6[3]			12	14	9[2]								10
1	2	3		5	14	7		10[2]	8[2]	11	4	6[1]			13	12	9								11
1	2	4		5		7		10[2]	8	11	3	6[1]		14		12	13	9[2]							12
1	2	12		7	13	6		14	11	10[1]	5			9[2]	8[3]	4	3								13
1	2	13		5	12	8			11	10	3			9[2]		6[1]	4	7							14
1	2			5[1]	9[2]	8		12	10	11	3			13		6	4	7							15
1	2	3	12	5	9[2]	8		13	10	11				6[1]			4	7							16
1	2	3		5		7		9	11[1]	10				6		4	8	12							17
1	2	3		13	7			10	9[2]	11[1]				12	6[3]	4	8	5	14						18
1	2	4	14	5[1]		7		11[2]	9	10				13	6	3	8[3]	12							19
1	2	3		12				9	11[1]	10				14	8	6[3]	4[2]	13	5						20
1	2	3			7	13		9[1]	11	10				12	6[4]	4	8[5]	5							21
1	2	3		12	6[1]	7		9	11[3]	10[2]	14			13		4	8	5							22
1	2	3			6	8		11	9	10				12		4	7[1]	5							23
1		3	14	2	6	7		10	9[1]	11	13			8[2]	12	4		5[3]							24
1		3	5	2	6	7		13	12	10[1]	4		9	11[2]		8									25
-	2	3		5[2]	6	7		10[1]	9	11				13	4	8	12			1					26
1	2	4		6[3]	5	7		11[2]	9	10[1]				14	3	8	12		13						27
1	2	3		5[3]	7[2]	6		9	11	10[1]				14		4	8	13	12						28
1		3	2[2]	5	7	6		11[1]	9	10				13	4	8[3]	14	12							29
1		4	2[2]	13	8	6		11[3]	5	12				14	3	7[1]	9	10							30
1	2	3		5	12	7			11	10		13		6[2]	4	8[1]			9						31
1	2	3	5		8[2]	9		12		11	13			6	4	7		10[1]							32
1	2	3		5	7	6		10[2]	9[1]	11				12	4[3]	14	8	13							33
1	3	4		2	8	7		6[1]		11	12	13		9				5	10[2]						34
1	2	3	4	6	8	7[1]			10[3]	11[2]	13			9			14	5	12						35
1	2	4		5	7	8		10[3]	9[1]	11				6[2]	3	14	13	12							36
1	2	4		9	8[1]	6			12	11	3			13		7	5	10[2]							37
1	2[3]	3		6	7[2]	9		8	11	4	12	14		10			5	13							38
1	2	3	12		8			13	10	4	6[2]		9	11[1]		7	5								39
1	2	3		13	8			12	10	4	6[2]	9[1]	11[3]		7	5								14	40
1	2	3	14		8			13	9	4[1]	6	10[2]	12	7	5		11[3]								41
1	2[2]	3	14	13	9			12	10	6	8[1]	4	7[3]	5	11										42
1	2	3	12	13	7	8[3]	14	9[1]	11	6	4			5	10[2]										43
1	2	3	5		13			6	10[1]	8	14	12	7[2]	4	9[3]	11									44
1	2	3	5	8		12		6	10	7[1]	13	4	9	11[2]											45
1	2		3	5	6	10[1]		13	11[3]	8	9[2]	4	7		12	14									46

FA Cup

First Round	Lincoln C	(h)	1-0
Second Round	Charlton Ath	(h)	3-1
Third Round	Tottenham H	(a)	0-3

Carabao Cup

First Round	Brentford	(h)	1-3

(aet)

Checkatrade Trophy

Southern Group F	Barnet	(a)	4-3
Southern Group F	Tottenham H U21	(h)	4-3
Southern Group F	Luton T	(h)	1-2
Second Round South	Yeovil T	(a)	0-2

ARSENAL

FOUNDATION

Formed by workers at the Royal Arsenal, Woolwich in 1886, they began as Dial Square (name of one of the workshops), and included two former Nottingham Forest players, Fred Beardsley and Morris Bates. Beardsley wrote to his old club seeking help and they provided the new club with a full set of red jerseys and a ball. The club became known as the 'Woolwich Reds' although their official title soon after formation was Woolwich Arsenal.

Emirates Stadium, Highbury House, 75 Drayton Park, Islington, London N5 1BU.

Telephone: (020) 7619 5003.

Fax: (020) 7704 4001.

Ticket Office: (020) 7619 5000.

Website: www.arsenal.com

Email: info@arsenal.co.uk

Ground Capacity: 59,867.

Record Attendance: 73,295 v Sunderland, Div 1, 9 March 1935 (at Highbury); 73,707 v RC Lens, UEFA Champions League, 25 November 1998 (at Wembley); 60,162 v Manchester U, FA Premier League, 3 November 2007 (at Emirates).

Pitch Measurements: 105m × 68m (114yd × 74yd).

Chairman: Sir John 'Chips' Keswick.

Chief Executive: Ivan Gazidis.

Head Coach: Unai Emery.

Assistant Head Coaches: Steve Bould, Juan Carlos Carcedo.

Colours: Red shirts with white sleeves, white shorts with red trim, white socks with red trim.

Year Formed: 1886.

Turned Professional: 1891.

Previous Names: 1886, Dial Square; 1886, Royal Arsenal; 1891, Woolwich Arsenal; 1914, Arsenal.

Club Nickname: 'The Gunners'.

Grounds: 1886, Plumstead Common; 1887, Sportsman Ground; 1888, Manor Ground; 1890, Invicta Ground; 1893, Manor Ground; 1913, Highbury; 2006, Emirates Stadium.

HONOURS

League Champions: FA Premier League – 1997–98, 2001–02, 2003–04; Division 1 – 1930–31, 1932–33, 1933–34, 1934–35, 1937–38, 1947–48, 1952–53, 1970–71, 1988–89, 1990–91.
Runners-up: FA Premier League – 1998–99, 1999–2000, 2000–01, 2002–03, 2004–05, 2015–16; Division 1 – 1925–26, 1931–32, 1972–73; Division 2 – 1903–04.

FA Cup Winners: 1930, 1936, 1950, 1971, 1979, 1993, 1998, 2002, 2003, 2005, 2014, 2015, 2017.
Runners-up: 1927, 1932, 1952, 1972, 1978, 1980, 2001.

League Cup Winners: 1987, 1993.
Runners-up: 1968, 1969, 1988, 2007, 2011, 2018.

Double performed: 1970–71, 1997–98, 2001–02.

European Competitions
European Cup: 1971–72 *(qf)*, 1991–92.
UEFA Champions League: 1998–99, 1999–2000, 2000–01, 2001–02, 2002–03, 2003–04, 2004–05, 2005–06 *(runners-up)*, 2006–07, 2007–08 *(qf)*, 2008–09 *(sf)*, 2009–10*(qf)*, 2010–11, 2011–12, 2012–13, 2013–14, 2014–15, 2015–16, 2016–17.
Fairs Cup: 1963–64, 1969–70 *(winners)*, 1970–71.
UEFA Cup: 1978–79, 1981–82, 1982–83, 1996–97, 1997–98, 1999–2000 *(runners-up)*.
Europa League: 2017–18 *(sf)*.
European Cup-Winners' Cup: 1979–80 *(runners-up)*, 1993–94 *(winners)*, 1994–95 *(runners-up)*.
Super Cup: 1994 *(runners-up)*.

Sun FACT FILE

Regular live televised coverage of Football League matches began in the 1983–84 season but Arsenal did not feature at all during that campaign. However, they appeared twice in November 1984, with the BBC showing the 4-2 defeat at Old Trafford on 2 November and ITV covering the 2-1 defeat at Sheffield Wednesday on 25 November.

First Football League Game: 2 September 1893, Division 2, v Newcastle U (h) D 2–2 – Williams; Powell, Jeffrey; Devine, Buist, Howat; Gemmell, Henderson, Shaw (1), Elliott (1), Booth.

Record League Victory: 12–0 v Loughborough T, Division 2, 12 March 1900 – Orr; McNichol, Jackson; Moir, Dick (2), Anderson (1); Hunt, Cottrell (2), Main (2), Gaudie (3), Tennant (2).

Record Cup Victory: 11–1 v Darwen, FA Cup 3rd rd, 9 January 1932 – Moss; Parker, Hapgood; Jones, Roberts, John; Hulme (2), Jack (3), Lambert (2), James, Bastin (4).

Record Defeat: 0–8 v Loughborough T, Division 2, 12 December 1896.

Most League Points (2 for a win): 66, Division 1, 1930–31.

Most League Points (3 for a win): 90, FA Premier League, 2003–04.

Most League Goals: 127, Division 1, 1930–31.

Highest League Scorer in Season: Ted Drake, 42, 1934–35.

Most League Goals in Total Aggregate: Thierry Henry, 175, 1999–2007; 2011–12.

Most League Goals in One Match: 7, Ted Drake v Aston Villa, Division 1, 14 December 1935.

Most Capped Player: Thierry Henry, 81 (123), France.

Most League Appearances: David O'Leary, 558, 1975–93.

Youngest League Player: Jack Wilshere, 16 years 256 days v Blackburn R, 13 September 2008.

Record Transfer Fee Received: £40,000,000 from Liverpool for Alex Oxlade-Chamberlain, August 2017.

Record Transfer Fee Paid: £55,000,000 (rising to £60,000,000) to Borussia Dortmund for Pierre-Emerick Aubameyang, January 2018.

Football League Record: 1893 Elected to Division 2; 1904–13 Division 1; 1913–19 Division 2; 1919–92 Division 1; 1992– FA Premier League.

MANAGERS

Sam Hollis 1894–97
Tom Mitchell 1897–98
George Elcoat 1898–99
Harry Bradshaw 1899–1904
Phil Kelso 1904–08
George Morrell 1908–15
Leslie Knighton 1919–25
Herbert Chapman 1925–34
George Allison 1934–47
Tom Whittaker 1947–56
Jack Crayston 1956–58
George Swindin 1958–62
Billy Wright 1962–66
Bertie Mee 1966–76
Terry Neill 1976–83
Don Howe 1984–86
George Graham 1986–95
Bruce Rioch 1995–96
Arsène Wenger 1996–2018
Unai Emery May 2018–

LATEST SEQUENCES

Longest Sequence of League Wins: 14, 10.2.2002 – 18.8.2002.

Longest Sequence of League Defeats: 7, 12.2.1977 – 12.3.1977.

Longest Sequence of League Draws: 6, 4.3.1961 – 1.4.1961.

Longest Sequence of Unbeaten League Matches: 49, 7.5.2003 – 24.10.2004.

Longest Sequence Without a League Win: 23, 28.9.1912 – 1.3.1913.

Successive Scoring Runs: 55 from 19.5.2001.

Successive Non-scoring Runs: 6 from 25.2.1987.

TEN YEAR LEAGUE RECORD

		P	W	D	L	F	A	Pts	Pos
2008-09	PR Lge	38	20	12	6	68	37	72	4
2009-10	PR Lge	38	23	6	9	83	41	75	3
2010-11	PR Lge	38	19	11	8	72	43	68	4
2011-12	PR Lge	38	21	7	10	74	49	70	3
2012-13	PR Lge	38	21	10	7	72	37	73	4
2013-14	PR Lge	38	24	7	7	68	41	79	4
2014-15	PR Lge	38	22	9	7	71	36	75	3
2015-16	PR Lge	38	20	11	7	65	36	71	2
2016-17	PR Lge	38	23	6	9	77	44	75	5
2017-18	PR Lge	38	19	6	13	74	51	63	6

DID YOU KNOW ?

Arsenal full-back Bob McNab once mada a cameo appearance in the television sitcom *On the Buses*. McNab played the role of the bus depot's star footballer in an episode called 'The Football Match', which was shown in the London ITV region on 2 March 1973 and at a later date in other regions.

ARSENAL – PREMIER LEAGUE 2017–18 LEAGUE RECORD

Match No.	Date	Venue	Opponents	Result	H/T Score	Lg Pos.	Goalscorers	Attendance
1	Aug 11	H	Leicester C	W 4-3	2-2	1	Lacazette [2], Welbeck [45], Ramsey [83], Giroud [85]	59,387
2	19	A	Stoke C	L 0-1	0-0	11		29,459
3	27	A	Liverpool	L 0-4	0-2	16		53,206
4	Sept 9	H	Bournemouth	W 3-0	2-0	9	Welbeck 2 [6, 50], Lacazette [27]	59,262
5	17	A	Chelsea	D 0-0	0-0	12		41,478
6	25	H	WBA	W 2-0	1-0	7	Lacazette 2 (1 pen) [20, 67 (p)]	59,134
7	Oct 1	H	Brighton & HA	W 2-0	1-0	5	Monreal [16], Iwobi [56]	59,378
8	14	A	Watford	L 1-2	1-0	6	Mertesacker [39]	20,384
9	22	A	Everton	W 5-2	1-1	5	Monreal [40], Ozil [53], Lacazette [74], Ramsey [90], Sanchez [90]	39,189
10	28	H	Swansea C	W 2-1	0-1	5	Kolasinac [51], Ramsey [58]	59,493
11	Nov 5	A	Manchester C	L 1-3	0-1	6	Lacazette [65]	54,286
12	18	H	Tottenham H	W 2-0	2-0	6	Mustafi [36], Sanchez [41]	59,530
13	26	A	Burnley	W 1-0	0-0	4	Sanchez (pen) [90]	21,722
14	29	H	Huddersfield T	W 5-0	1-0	4	Lacazette [3], Giroud 2 [68, 87], Sanchez [69], Ozil [72]	59,285
15	Dec 2	H	Manchester U	L 1-3	0-2	5	Lacazette [49]	59,547
16	10	A	Southampton	D 1-1	0-1	5	Giroud [88]	31,643
17	13	A	West Ham U	D 0-0	0-0	7		56,921
18	16	H	Newcastle U	W 1-0	1-0	4	Ozil [23]	59,379
19	22	H	Liverpool	D 3-3	0-1	5	Sanchez [53], Xhaka [56], Ozil [58]	59,409
20	28	H	Crystal Palace	W 3-2	1-0	6	Mustafi [25], Sanchez 2 [62, 66]	25,762
21	31	A	WBA	D 1-1	0-0	5	McClean (og) [83]	26,223
22	Jan 3	A	Chelsea	D 2-2	0-0	6	Wilshere [53], Bellerin [90]	59,379
23	14	A	Bournemouth	L 1-2	0-0	6	Bellerin [52]	10,836
24	20	H	Crystal Palace	W 4-1	4-0	6	Monreal [6], Iwobi [10], Koscielny [13], Lacazette [22]	59,386
25	30	A	Swansea C	L 1-3	1-1	6	Monreal [33]	20,819
26	Feb 3	H	Everton	W 5-1	4-0	6	Ramsey 3 [6, 19, 74], Koscielny [14], Aubameyang [37]	59,306
27	10	A	Tottenham H	L 0-1	0-0	6		83,222
28	Mar 1	H	Manchester C	L 0-3	0-3	6		58,420
29	4	A	Brighton & HA	L 1-2	1-2	6	Aubameyang [43]	30,620
30	11	H	Watford	W 3-0	1-0	6	Mustafi [8], Aubameyang [59], Mkhitaryan [77]	59,131
31	Apr 1	H	Stoke C	W 3-0	0-0	6	Aubameyang 2 (1 pen) [75 (p), 86], Lacazette (pen) [89]	59,371
32	8	H	Southampton	W 3-2	2-1	6	Aubameyang [28], Welbeck 2 [38, 81]	59,374
33	15	A	Newcastle U	L 1-2	1-1	6	Lacazette [14]	52,210
34	22	H	West Ham U	W 4-1	0-0	6	Monreal [51], Ramsey [82], Lacazette 2 [85, 89]	59,422
35	29	A	Manchester U	L 1-2	0-1	6	Mkhitaryan [51]	75,035
36	May 6	H	Burnley	W 5-0	2-0	6	Aubameyang 2 [14, 75], Lacazette [45], Kolasinac [54], Iwobi [64]	59,540
37	9	A	Leicester C	L 1-3	0-1	6	Aubameyang [53]	32,095
38	13	A	Huddersfield T	W 1-0	1-0	6	Aubameyang [38]	24,122

Final League Position: 6

GOALSCORERS

League (74): Lacazette 14 (2 pens), Aubameyang 10 (1 pen), Ramsey 7, Sanchez 7 (1 pen), Monreal 5, Welbeck 5, Giroud 4, Ozil 4, Iwobi 3, Mustafi 3, Bellerin 2, Kolasinac 2, Koscielny 2, Mkhitaryan 2, Mertesacker 1, Wilshere 1, Xhaka 1, own goal 1.

FA Cup (2): Mertesacker 1, Welbeck 1.

Carabao Cup (6): Nketiah 2, Walcott 1, Welbeck 1, Xhaka 1, own goal 1.

Europa League (30): Ramsey 4, Giroud 3 (2 pens), Lacazette 3 (1 pen), Walcott 3, Welbeck 3 (1 pen), Kolasinac 2, Bellerin 1, Debuchy 1, Elneny 1, Holding 1, Mkhitaryan 1, Monreal 1, Ozil 1, Sanchez 1, Wilshere 1, Xhaka 1, own goals 2.

Cech P 34	Holding R 9 + 3	Monreal N 26 + 2	Kolasinac S 25 + 2	Bellerin H 34 + 1	Elneny M 11 + 2	Xhaka G 37 + 1	Oxlade-Chamberlain A 3	Ozil M 24 + 2	Welbeck D 12 + 16	Lacazette A 26 + 6	Giroud O 1 + 15	Ramsey A 21 + 3	Walcott T — + 6	Mustafi S 25 + 2	Iwobi A 22 + 4	Koscielny L 25	Sanchez A 17 + 2	Coquelin F 1 + 6	Maitland-Niles A 8 + 7	Mertesacker P 4 + 2	Wilshere J 12 + 8	Chambers C 10 + 2	Nelson R 2 + 1	Mkhitaryan H 9 + 2	Aubameyang P 12 + 1	Ospina D 4 + 1	Nketiah E — + 3	Willock J 1 + 1	Mavropanos K 3	Match No.
1	2^2	3	4	5	6^1	7	8	9	10^3	11	12	13	14																	1
1		3	4^2	8		7^1	5	9	10	11^1	12	6	13	2	14															2
1	2	4		8		7	5^1	9	11	14	13	6^2				3	10^3	12												3
1		4	8	5		7		9	10^2	11^3	13	6^1		3		2	14	12												4
1		4	8	5	14	7			10^1	11^2	13	6		3		9^3	2	12												5
1		4	8	5	6	7		13		11^2	12	9^1		3		2	10^3		14											6
1	2	4	8	5	14	7^1				11^2	12	6	13	3	9^1	10														7
1	14	4	8	5	6	7		12	10^3	11^3	13			9	2^1				3											8
1		4	8	5		7		9^2		11^1		6				2	10	13			3	12								9
1	12	4	8^1	5		7		9		11^2	13	6				2	10				3									10
1		4	8	5		7^2		9		12	13	6				10^3	2	11	3^1		14									11
1		4	8	5		7		9^1		11^2		6		3	13	2	10	12												12
1		4	8	5		7		13		11^1		6		3	9^2	2	10			14										13
1		4	8	5		7		9	13	11^1	12	6^3		3		2	10^2			14										14
1		4	8^3	5		7^2		9	13	11	14	6		3^1	12	2	10													15
1		4	8	5		7^2		9	12	11^3	14	6				2	10		3^1	13										16
1		4		2		7		8	12	13	10					9^2	3	11^1			5	6								17
1		4		2		7		9	12	11^3	13					8^1	3	10^2	14		5	6								18
1		4^1		2		7		9	13	11			14	12	8^3	3	10^2				5	6								19
1		8	5	6^1		9				11^2		3		4	10	12	13		7	2										20
1		8^1	5			7		14	11							3	9^2	4^3	10		12	13	6	2						21
1	4		5		6		9	12	11^1						3		10	8			7	2^2								22
1	4		5		7		10	11	12	13		9^2				3		8			6	2^1								23
1	5^1	14	2	6	9	7^2		11						4	10^1	3	12				8	13								24
1		5		2	7^1	8		9	10	13		6				4	11^2	3						12						25
1^2	5^1	12	2		7		9				6^1			3	8	4					14			10	11	13				26
1		5		2	7^2	8^1		9	14	12				3	13	4			6					11^3	10					27
1		5	2		7		9	10				6		3		4								8	11					28
1		5	13		7		9	12				3			10^3	4					6	2^2		8^1	11	14				29
1	4		5		6	7		9	12					3^1	10^2				2		14	13		8^3	11					30
		5		2	6^2	13		8	10^1	12		7		3							9^3	4		14	11	1				31
1	14		5		2^1	6		7	10	13				3	9						12	4		8^3	11^2					32
1	4	5				6		7	12	10				3	9^3				13			2^1			11		14	8^2		33
		5		2	6^2	7		11	10		8			3	9^3	4			12		14			13		1				34
	13	5^2	2			7			12						9				6			3	10^1	8^1	11		14		4	35
1		5	2		7		12	10^3		13				6		3			14	8^2	3^1			9	11				4	36
1	3	5				7			11^1					8		12	6^2		2					9	10	13		4^a		37
	4	13	5^1	2		7			12	10				8		3	6^3							9	11^2	1	14			38

FA Cup

Third Round	Nottingham F	(a)	2-4

Carabao Cup

Third Round	Doncaster R	(h)	1-0
Fourth Round	Norwich C	(h)	2-1
(aet)			
Quarter-Final	West Ham U	(h)	1-0
Semi-Final 1st leg	Chelsea	(a)	0-0
Semi-Final 2nd leg	Chelsea	(h)	2-1
Final	Manchester C	(Wembley)	0-3

Europa League

Group H	Cologne	(h)	3-1
Group H	BATE Borisov	(a)	4-2
Group H	Red Star Belgrade	(a)	1-0
Group H	Red Star Belgrade	(h)	0-0
Group H	Cologne	(a)	0-1
Group H	BATE Borisov	(h)	6-0
Round of 32 1st leg	Ostersunds	(a)	3-0
Round of 32 2nd leg	Ostersunds	(h)	1-2
Round of 16 1st leg	AC Milan	(a)	2-0
Round of 16 2nd leg	AC Milan	(h)	3-1
Quarter-Final 1st leg	CSKA Moscow	(h)	4-1
Quarter-Final 2nd leg	CSKA Moscow	(a)	2-2
Semi-Final 1st leg	Atletico Madrid	(h)	1-1
Semi-Final 2nd leg	Atletico Madrid	(a)	0-1

ASTON VILLA

FOUNDATION

Cricketing enthusiasts of Villa Cross Wesleyan Chapel, Aston, Birmingham decided to form a football club during the winter of 1874–75. Football clubs were few and far between in the Birmingham area and in their first game against Aston Brook St Mary's rugby team they played one half rugby and the other soccer. In 1876 they were joined by Scottish soccer enthusiast George Ramsay who was immediately appointed captain and went on to lead Aston Villa from obscurity to one of the country's top clubs in a period of less than ten years.

Villa Park, Trinity Road, Birmingham B6 6HE.
Telephone: (0121) 327 2299.
Fax: (0121) 322 2107.
Ticket Office: (0333) 323 1874.
Website: www.avfc.co.uk
Email: postmaster@avfc.co.uk
Ground Capacity: 42,786.
Record Attendance: 76,588 v Derby Co, FA Cup 6th rd, 2 March 1946.
Pitch Measurements: 105m × 68m (114yd × 74yd).
Chairman: Dr Tony Xia.
Chief Executive: Keith Wyness.
Manager: Steve Bruce.
Assistant Manager: Colin Calderwood.
Colours: Claret shirts with sky blue sleeves, white shorts with claret trim, claret socks.
Year Formed: 1874.
Turned Professional: 1885.
Club Nickname: 'The Villans'.
Grounds: 1874, Wilson Road and Aston Park (also used Aston Lower Grounds for some matches); 1876, Wellington Road, Perry Barr; 1897, Villa Park.
First Football League Game: 8 September 1888, Football League, v Wolverhampton W (a) D 1–1 – Warner; Cox, Coulton; Yates, Harry Devey, Dawson; Albert Brown, Green (1), Allen, Garvey, Hodgetts.
Record League Victory: 12–2 v Accrington S, Division 1, 12 March 1892 – Warner; Evans, Cox; Harry Devey, Jimmy Cowan, Baird; Athersmith (1), Dickson (2), John Devey (4), Lewis Campbell (4), Hodgetts (1).

HONOURS

League Champions: Division 1 – 1893–94, 1895–96, 1896–97, 1898–99, 1899–1900, 1909–10, 1980–81; Division 2 – 1937–38, 1959–60; Division 3 – 1971–72.
Runners-up: FA Premier League – 1992–93; Division 1 – 1902–03, 1907–08, 1910–11, 1912–13, 1913–14, 1930–31, 1932–33, 1989–90; Football League 1888–89; Division 2 – 1974–75, 1987–88.
FA Cup Winners: 1887, 1895, 1897, 1905, 1913, 1920, 1957.
Runners-up: 1892, 1924, 2000, 2015.
League Cup Winners: 1961, 1975, 1977, 1994, 1996.
Runners-up: 1963, 1971, 2010.
Double Performed: 1896–97.
European Competitions
European Cup: 1981–82 *(winners)*, 1982–83 *(qf)*.
UEFA Cup: 1975–76, 1977–78 *(qf)*, 1983–84, 1990–91, 1993–94, 1994–95, 1996–97, 1997–98 *(qf)*, 1998–99, 2001–02, 2008–09.
Europa League: 2009–10, 2010–11.
Intertoto Cup: 2000, 2001 *(winners)*, 2002 *(sf)*, 2008 *(qualified for UEFA Cup)*.
Super Cup: 1982 *(winners)*.
World Club Championship: 1982.

THE **Sun** FACT FILE

Aston Villa played West Bromwich Albion in pre-season charity matches in aid of the Football League Jubilee Fund in both 1938 and 1939. Both fixtures were drawn 1-1 with Villa's goals coming from Frank Broome and Eric Houghton.

Record Cup Victory: 13–0 v Wednesbury Old Ath, FA Cup 1st rd, 30 October 1886 – Warner; Coulton, Simmonds; Yates, Robertson, Burton (2); Richard Davis (1), Albert Brown (3), Hunter (3), Loach (2), Hodgetts (2).

Record Defeat: 0–8 v Chelsea, FA Premier League, 23 December 2012.

Most League Points (2 for a win): 70, Division 3, 1971–72.

Most League Points (3 for a win): 83, FL C, 2017–18.

Most League Goals: 128, Division 1, 1930–31.

Highest League Scorer in Season: 'Pongo' Waring, 49, Division 1, 1930–31.

Most League Goals in Total Aggregate: Harry Hampton, 215, 1904–15.

Most League Goals in One Match: 5, Harry Hampton v Sheffield W, Division 1, 5 October 1912; 5, Harold Halse v Derby Co, Division 1, 19 October 1912; 5, Len Capewell v Burnley, Division 1, 29 August 1925; 5, George Brown v Leicester C, Division 1, 2 January 1932; 5, Gerry Hitchens v Charlton Ath, Division 2, 18 November 1959.

Most Capped Player: Steve Staunton, 64 (102), Republic of Ireland.

Most League Appearances: Charlie Aitken, 561, 1961–76.

Youngest League Player: Jimmy Brown, 15 years 349 days v Bolton W, 17 September 1969.

Record Transfer Fee Received: £32,500,000 from Liverpool for Christian Benteke, July 2015.

Record Transfer Fee Paid: £18,000,000 (rising to £24,000,000) to Sunderland for Darren Bent, January 2011.

Football League Record: 1888 Founder Member of the League; 1936–38 Division 2; 1938–59 Division 1; 1959–60 Division 2; 1960–67 Division 1; 1967–70 Division 2; 1970–72 Division 3; 1972–75 Division 2; 1975–87 Division 1; 1987–88 Division 2; 1988–92 Division 1; 1992–2016 FA Premier League; 2016– FL C.

MANAGERS

George Ramsay 1884–1926
(*Secretary-Manager*)
W. J. Smith 1926–34
(*Secretary-Manager*)
Jimmy McMullan 1934–35
Jimmy Hogan 1936–44
Alex Massie 1945–50
George Martin 1950–53
Eric Houghton 1953–58
Joe Mercer 1958–64
Dick Taylor 1964–67
Tommy Cummings 1967–68
Tommy Docherty 1968–70
Vic Crowe 1970–74
Ron Saunders 1974–82
Tony Barton 1982–84
Graham Turner 1984–86
Billy McNeill 1986–87
Graham Taylor 1987–90
Dr Jozef Venglos 1990–91
Ron Atkinson 1991–94
Brian Little 1994–98
John Gregory 1998–2002
Graham Taylor OBE 2002–03
David O'Leary 2003–06
Martin O'Neill 2006–10
Gerard Houllier 2010–11
Alex McLeish 2011–12
Paul Lambert 2012–15
Tim Sherwood 2015
Remi Garde 2015–16
Roberto Di Matteo 2016
Steve Bruce October 2016–

LATEST SEQUENCES

Longest Sequence of League Wins: 9, 15.10.1910 – 10.12.1910.

Longest Sequence of League Defeats: 11, 14.2.2016 – 30.4.2016.

Longest Sequence of League Draws: 6, 12.9.1981 – 10.10.1981.

Longest Sequence of Unbeaten League Matches: 15, 12.3.1949 – 27.8.1949.

Longest Sequence Without a League Win: 19, 14.8.2015 – 2.1.2016.

Successive Scoring Runs: 35 from 10.11.1895.

Successive Non-scoring Runs: 6 from 26.12.2014.

TEN YEAR LEAGUE RECORD

		P	W	D	L	F	A	Pts	Pos
2008-09	PR Lge	38	17	11	10	54	48	62	6
2009-10	PR Lge	38	17	13	8	52	39	64	6
2010-11	PR Lge	38	12	12	14	48	59	48	9
2011-12	PR Lge	38	7	17	14	37	53	38	16
2012-13	PR Lge	38	10	11	17	47	69	41	15
2013-14	PR Lge	38	10	8	20	39	61	38	15
2014-15	PR Lge	38	10	8	20	31	57	38	17
2015-16	PR Lge	38	3	8	27	27	76	17	20
2016-17	FL C	46	16	14	16	47	48	62	13
2017-18	FL C	46	24	11	11	72	42	83	4

DID YOU KNOW ?

When Aston Villa met Everton at Villa Park on 2 May 2015 it was the first time that two clubs had played each other in the Football League on 200 occasions. Villa won 3-2, taking their total of victories in the games to 73. They also won the first encounter back in September 1888 by 2-1.

ASTON VILLA – SKY BET CHAMPIONSHIP 2017–18 LEAGUE RECORD

Match No.	Date	Venue	Opponents	Result	H/T Score	Lg Pos.	Goalscorers	Attendance
1	Aug 5	H	Hull C	D 1-1	1-0	9	Agbonlahor [7]	31,241
2	12	A	Cardiff C	L 0-3	0-1	21		23,899
3	15	A	Reading	L 1-2	0-0	23	Hourihane [87]	20,144
4	19	H	Norwich C	W 4-2	2-0	16	Hourihane 3 [22, 68, 85], Green [42]	29,157
5	25	A	Bristol C	D 1-1	0-0	15	Onomah [64]	21,542
6	Sept 9	H	Brentford	D 0-0	0-0	18		29,799
7	12	H	Middlesbrough	D 0-0	0-0	18		26,631
8	16	A	Barnsley	W 3-0	2-0	13	Adomah 2 (1 pen) [19, 44 (p)], Davis [55]	14,633
9	23	H	Nottingham F	W 2-1	1-0	10	Adomah [15], Hourihane [60]	28,554
10	26	A	Burton Alb	W 4-0	3-0	8	Davis [13], Adomah [16], Snodgrass [32], Onomah [71]	5786
11	30	H	Bolton W	W 1-0	1-0	7	Kodjia (pen) [39]	31,451
12	Oct 14	A	Wolverhampton W	L 0-2	0-0	7		30,239
13	21	H	Fulham	W 2-1	1-1	5	Terry [23], Adomah [49]	30,724
14	29	H	Birmingham C	D 0-0	0-0	6		24,408
15	Nov 1	A	Preston NE	W 2-0	2-0	5	Chester [12], Snodgrass [33]	14,212
16	4	H	Sheffield W	L 1-2	0-2	5	Samba [90]	33,154
17	18	A	QPR	W 2-1	1-1	5	Adomah 2 (1 pen) [45 (p), 58]	16,934
18	21	H	Sunderland	W 2-1	1-0	4	Adomah [10], Onomah [49]	27,662
19	25	H	Ipswich T	W 2-0	1-0	4	Adomah 2 [36, 66]	30,427
20	Dec 1	A	Leeds U	D 1-1	0-1	4	Lansbury [71]	30,547
21	9	H	Millwall	D 0-0	0-0	5		29,628
22	16	A	Derby Co	L 0-2	0-1	5		28,118
23	23	A	Sheffield U	D 2-2	2-2	6	Adomah (pen) [4], Jedinak [9]	35,210
24	26	A	Brentford	L 1-2	1-1	8	Onomah [30]	11,341
25	30	A	Middlesbrough	W 1-0	0-0	7	Snodgrass [75]	29,422
26	Jan 1	H	Bristol C	W 5-0	2-0	5	Hogan [23], Snodgrass 2 [34, 60], Bjarnason [72], Hourihane [85]	32,604
27	13	A	Nottingham F	W 1-0	1-0	4	Hogan [18]	25,433
28	20	H	Barnsley	W 3-1	3-1	4	Hogan 2 [5, 7], Hourihane [19]	31,869
29	30	A	Sheffield U	W 1-0	0-0	3	Snodgrass [90]	26,477
30	Feb 3	H	Burton Alb	W 3-2	1-0	3	Hogan [33], Adomah [65], Grealish [88]	33,022
31	11	H	Birmingham C	W 2-0	0-0	2	Adomah [60], Hourihane [81]	41,233
32	17	A	Fulham	L 0-2	0-0	3		24,547
33	20	H	Preston NE	D 1-1	0-1	3	Grabban (pen) [66]	30,894
34	24	A	Sheffield W	W 4-2	1-2	3	Grabban [21], Whelan [67], Hourihane [87], Snodgrass (pen) [90]	28,604
35	Mar 6	A	Sunderland	W 3-0	2-0	3	Grabban [34], Chester [45], Oviedo (og) [66]	26,081
36	10	H	Wolverhampton W	W 4-1	1-1	3	Adomah [8], Chester [57], Grabban [62], Bjarnason [85]	37,836
37	13	H	QPR	L 1-3	0-2	3	Chester [88]	30,228
38	17	A	Bolton W	L 0-1	0-1	4		19,304
39	31	A	Hull C	D 0-0	0-0	4		16,133
40	Apr 3	H	Reading	W 3-0	0-0	4	Bjarnason [46], Hourihane [63], Hogan [70]	29,223
41	7	A	Norwich C	L 1-3	0-1	4	Grealish [67]	26,278
42	10	H	Cardiff C	W 1-0	0-0	4	Grealish [85]	32,560
43	13	H	Leeds U	W 1-0	1-0	4	Grabban [29]	33,374
44	21	A	Ipswich T	W 4-0	1-0	4	Hourihane [25], Grabban 2 [57, 78], Lansbury [82]	20,034
45	28	H	Derby Co	D 1-1	0-1	4	Grabban [84]	41,745
46	May 6	A	Millwall	L 0-1	0-1	4		17,195

Final League Position: 4

GOALSCORERS

League (72): Adomah 14 (3 pens), Hourihane 11, Grabban 8 (1 pen), Snodgrass 7 (1 pen), Hogan 6, Chester 4, Onomah 4, Bjarnason 3, Grealish 3, Davis 2, Lansbury 2, Agbonlahor 1, Green 1, Jedinak 1, Kodjia 1 (1 pen), Samba 1, Terry 1, Whelan 1, own goal 1.
FA Cup (1): Davis 1.
Carabao Cup (6): Hogan 3, Adomah 1, Bjarnason 1, own goal 1.
Championship Play-Offs (1): Jedinak 1.

Johnstone S 45	Hutton A 26 + 3	Chester J 46	Terry J 46	Taylor N 27 + 2	Elmohamady A 36 + 7	Whelan G 30 + 3	Bacuna L 1	Agbonlahor G 2 + 4	Lansbury H 6 + 4	Hogan S 19 + 18	Green A 4 + 1	Onomah J 20 + 13	Samba C 5 + 7	O'Hare C — + 4	Hourihane C 40 + 1	De Laet R 1 + 4	Bjarnason B 11 + 12	Davis K 17 + 11	Bree J 3 + 3	Snodgrass R 38 + 2	Jedinak M 17 + 8	Kodjia J 9 + 6	Grealish J 19 + 8	Elphick T 3 + 1	Hepburn-Murphy R — + 3	Tuanzebe A 4 + 1	Grabban L 10 + 5	Bunn M 1	Match No.
1	2	3	4	5	6	7	8¹	9	10²	11³	12	13	14																1
1	2	3	4	5	6²	8			10	7³	11		9¹		12	13	14												2
1	13	3	4	5		7			12	11¹	9	10³	14		8	2¹	6												3
1	2²	3	4	5	6	7			12		9	10¹	14		8		11³	13											4
1		2	4	8	5	6				13		10²	9	3³	7		14	11¹	12										5
1		3	4	5	9	7				14		13	11²	6³	8		10¹	2	12										6
1		3	4	5	2				6⁴	13					12		8	11³	10²		9		7¹	14					7
1		3	4	5	2	7				13		12			9		8	14	11¹	6³			10²						8
1	14	3	4	5	2	7				13		12			9		8		11³	6¹			10²						9
1		3	4	5	2	7				13		12			9²		8	14	11³	6			10¹						10
1		3	4	5¹	2	7				12		13	14		9		8		10³	6¹			11²						11
1	5	3	4		2	7				12		13			9¹	14	8		11³	6			10²						12
1	5	3	4		2	7						10			9¹		8	13	14	12			6²	11³					13
1	5	3	4		2	7				14		10			9		8¹		13	6¹	12	11¹							14
1	5	3	4		2	7				13		10¹			9		8	14	11²	6³	12								15
1	5	3	4³		2	7¹				11			12	9	13	8		10		6²			14						16
1	2	3		5		7						10²	4	9⁵	8	13	14	11		6¹									17
1	2	4		5	14	7¹						10	3	9²			11³			6	12		13						18
1	2	3		5¹	13	6						9	12	10	7		11³			8	4²		14						19
1	2	4		5	14	7		13				10²	3	9⁵	8¹		11			6			12						20
1	2²	4		5	13	7		8				10	3³	9			11			6¹			12	14					21
1		3		5	2	7²		13		12		11¹			9		8			6	4		10						22
1		3		5	2³	7		14		13					9		8	12		11¹	6²	4	10						23
1	2	4		5	14	7²				11		12		9²				13		6	8		10	3¹					24
1	5	4			2					11³		8¹			10²	9		14		7	6		12	3	13				25
1	5	4			2					11²					10⁵	13	8	12		7	6		9⁵	3	14				26
1	5	3	4	14	2	6²				11³					10¹		9	12	13	7			8						27
1	5	3	4		2	13				11²		12			10¹		9³		6	7	14		8						28
1	5	3	4		2					11¹		12			10²		8²		6	7	13		9						29
1	5	3	4		2					11		13			10²		8³		6	7¹	14		9				12		30
1	5	3	4		2	14				11²					10¹		8		13	7	6		9³				12		31
1	5	3	4		7¹					11		12			8		9	14		10²	6³				2	13			32
1	5	3	4		14					11		9			8³		10	13		7²	6				2¹	12			33
1	5¹	3	4	12	2	7				11³		9³			8		13			6	14						10		34
1		3	4	5	2	8³				11²			9		7	14				6	12	13					10¹		35
1		3	4	5	2			13	14			10³	9²	12						7	6	8					11¹		36
1		3	4	5¹	2					13		10	8²	14	12					7	6						11¹		37
1		3	4		2					13		10³	8²		6	14	5	7¹				9	12		11			38
1	5	3	4		13			8	14			10¹							7	6²	12	9			2³	11			39
1		3	4	5	2	14				11		13	10³		8		6			7¹		12	9²						40
1		3	4	5	2					11			10²	9	6					7¹		13	8			12			41
1		3			2	6						14	10³	8¹				12	7	4	13	9			5⁵	11			42
1		3			5	2	6			13			9¹	14	12					7	4	11³	8				10²		43
1		3		5¹	2	6				13	12		7		14		9³	8			4		10				11²		44
1	12	3	4	5³	2	6¹						14	10²	8					7		13	9				11			45
	5	3								6	11³		8	7¹	9			2	13	4	10²	14				12	1	46

BARNET

FOUNDATION

Barnet Football Club was formed in 1888 as an amateur organisation and they played at a ground in Queen's Road until they disbanded in 1901. A club known as Alston Works FC was then formed and they played at Totteridge Lane until changing to Barnet Alston FC in 1906. They moved to their present ground a year later, combining with The Avenue to form Barnet and Alston in 1912. The club progressed to senior amateur football by way of the Athenian and Isthmian Leagues, turning professional in 1965. It was as a Southern League and Conference club that they made their name.

The Hive Stadium, Camrose Avenue, Edgware, London HA8 6AG.

Telephone: (020) 8381 3800.

Ticket Office: (020) 8381 3800 (ext. 1027).

Website: www.barnetfc.com

Email: tellus@barnetfc.com

Ground Capacity: 5,454.

Record Attendance: 11,026 v Wycombe Wanderers, FA Amateur Cup 4th rd, 1951–52.

Pitch Measurements: 102m × 65m (111.5yd × 71yd).

Chairman: Anthony Kleanthous.

Manager: John Still.

Colours: Amber shirts with black trim, black shorts, amber socks with black trim.

Year Formed: 1888.

Turned Professional: 1965.

Previous Name: 1906, Barnet Alston FC; 1919, Barnet.

Club Nickname: 'The Bees'.

Grounds: 1888, Queen's Road; 1901, Totteridge Lane; 1907, Barnet Lane; 2013, The Hive.

First Football League Game: 17 August 1991, Division 4, v Crewe Alex (h) L 4–7 – Phillips; Blackford, Cooper (Murphy), Horton, Bodley (Stein), Johnson, Showler, Carter (2), Bull (2), Lowe, Evans.

Record League Victory: 7–0 v Blackpool, Division 3, 11 November 2000 – Naisbitt; Stockley, Sawyers, Niven (Brown), Heald, Arber (1), Currie (3), Doolan, Richards (2) (McGleish), Cottee (1) (Riza), Toms.

Record Cup Victory: 6–1 v Newport Co, FA Cup 1st rd, 21 November 1970 – McClelland; Lye, Jenkins, Ward, Embery, King, Powell (1), Ferry, Adams (1), Gray, George (3), (1 og).

Record Defeat: 1–9 v Peterborough U, Division 3, 5 September 1998.

Most League Points (3 for a win): 79, Division 3, 1992–93.

HONOURS

League Champions: Conference – 1990–91, 2004–05, 2014–15.
Runners-up: Conference – 1986–87, 1987–88, 1989–90. Division 3 – (3rd) 1992–93 *(promoted).*
FA Cup: 4th rd – 2007, 2008.
League Cup: 3rd rd – 2006.
FA Amateur Cup Winners: 1946.

Sun FACT FILE

The first occasion on which Barnet played against a Football League side in the FA Cup was in a sixth qualifying-round tie on 13 December 1924. The Bees visited Exeter City and went down to a 3-0 defeat, although there was some consolation with the West Country press praising their clean play and sportsmanship.

Most League Goals: 81, Division 4, 1991–92.

Highest League Scorer in Season: John Akinde, 26, FL 2, 2016–17.

Most League Goals in Total Aggregate: John Akinde, 56, 2015–18.

Most League Goals in One Match: 4, Dougie Freedman v Rochdale, Division 3, 13 September 1994; 4, Lee Hodges v Rochdale, Division 3, 8 April 1996.

Most Capped Player: Luke Gambin, 7 (16), Malta.

Most League Appearances: Lee Harrison, 270, 1996–2002, 2006–09.

Youngest League Player: Dwight Pascal, 16 years 263 days v Grimsby T, 25 November 2017.

Record Transfer Fee Received: £800,000 from Crystal Palace for Dougie Freedman, September 1995.

Record Transfer Fee Paid: £130,000 to Peterborough U for Greg Heald, August 1997.

Football League Record: 1991 Promoted to Division 4 from Conference; 1991–92 Division 4; 1992–93 Division 3; 1993–94 Division 2; 1994–2001 Division 3; 2001–05 Conference; 2005–13 FL 2; 2013–15 Conference Premier; 2015–18 FL 2; 2018– National League.

LATEST SEQUENCES

Longest Sequence of League Wins: 6, 28.8.1993 – 25.9.1999.

Longest Sequence of League Defeats: 11, 8.5.1993 – 2.10.1993.

Longest Sequence of League Draws: 4, 22.1.1994 – 12.2.1994.

Longest Sequence of Unbeaten League Matches: 12, 5.12.1992 – 2.3.1993.

Longest Sequence Without a League Win: 14, 11.12.1993 – 8.3.1994.

Successive Scoring Runs: 12 from 19.3.1995.

Successive Non-scoring Runs: 5 from 12.2.2000.

MANAGERS

Lester Finch
George Wheeler
Dexter Adams
Tommy Coleman
Gerry Ward
Gordon Ferry
Brian Kelly
Bill Meadows 1976–79
Barry Fry 1979–85
Roger Thompson 1985
Don McAllister 1985–86
Barry Fry 1986–93
Edwin Stein 1993
Gary Phillips (*Player-Manager*) 1993–94
Ray Clemence 1994–96
Alan Mullery (*Director of Football*) 1996–97
Terry Bullivant 1997
John Still 1997–2000
Tony Cottee 2000–01
John Still 2001–02
Peter Shreeves 2002–03
Martin Allen 2003–04
Paul Fairclough 2004–08
Ian Hendon 2008–10
Mark Stimson 2010–11
Martin Allen 2011
Lawrie Sanchez 2011–12
Mark Robson 2012
Edgar Davids 2012–14
Ulrich Landvreugd and Dick Schreuder 2014
Martin Allen 2014–16
Kevin Nugent 2017
Rossi Eames 2017
Mark McGhee 2017–18
Graham Westley 2018
Martin Allen 2018
John Still May 2018–

TEN YEAR LEAGUE RECORD

		P	W	D	L	F	A	Pts	Pos
2008-09	FL 2	46	11	15	20	56	74	48	17
2009-10	FL 2	46	12	12	22	47	63	48	21
2010-11	FL 2	46	12	12	22	58	77	48	22
2011-12	FL 2	46	12	10	24	52	79	46	22
2012-13	FL 2	46	13	12	21	47	59	51	23
2013-14	Conf P	46	19	13	14	58	53	70	8
2014-15	Conf P	46	28	8	10	94	46	92	1
2015-16	FL 2	46	17	11	18	67	68	62	15
2016-17	FL 2	46	14	15	17	57	64	57	15
2017-18	FL 2	46	12	10	24	46	65	46	23

DID YOU KNOW ?

Since turning professional for the 1965–66 season Barnet have attracted an average of more than 3,000 fans on just two occasions – their first two seasons as a Football League club. The Bees' highest average attendance over this period is 3,643 in the 1991–92 season, which was their first as League members.

BARNET – SKY BET LEAGUE TWO 2017–18 LEAGUE RECORD

Match No.	Date	Venue	Opponents	Result	H/T Score	Lg Pos.	Goalscorers	Attendance
1	Aug 5	A	Forest Green R	D 2-2	0-2	11	Akpa Akpro [58], Campbell-Ryce [63]	3171
2	12	H	Luton T	W 1-0	0-0	4	Taylor, J [90]	3555
3	19	A	Crewe Alex	L 0-1	0-0	12		3217
4	26	H	Stevenage	L 0-1	0-1	17		1883
5	Sept 2	A	Swindon T	W 4-1	2-0	9	Coulthirst 3 [10, 65, 69], Campbell-Ryce (pen) [16]	5895
6	9	H	Cambridge U	W 3-1	1-0	7	Vilhete 2 [40, 90], Coulthirst [62]	2031
7	12	A	Exeter C	L 1-2	0-0	12	Coulthirst [48]	1605
8	16	A	Carlisle U	D 1-1	1-0	14	Akpa Akpro [8]	4141
9	23	H	Crawley T	L 1-2	0-0	14	Akinola [65]	1602
10	26	A	Lincoln C	L 1-2	0-2	15	Coulthirst [62]	7320
11	30	A	Wycombe W	L 1-3	0-1	18	Vilhete [78]	4056
12	Oct 7	H	Coventry C	D 0-0	0-0	19		4041
13	14	A	Notts Co	L 1-2	0-1	21	Akinola [81]	5804
14	17	H	Mansfield T	D 1-1	0-1	20	Coulthirst [85]	1262
15	21	H	Yeovil T	D 1-1	1-0	20	Akinola [6]	1751
16	28	A	Accrington S	L 1-4	0-1	21	Campbell-Ryce [54]	1485
17	Nov 11	H	Colchester U	L 0-1	0-0	23		2301
18	18	A	Port Vale	L 0-1	0-0	23		4207
19	21	A	Newport Co	W 2-1	0-0	23	Akinde [88], Coulthirst [90]	2275
20	25	H	Grimsby T	L 0-2	0-1	23		2033
21	Dec 9	A	Chesterfield	L 1-2	1-0	24	Akinde [11]	5272
22	16	H	Morecambe	W 2-1	2-0	22	Campbell-Ryce [30], Taylor, J [34]	1123
23	23	H	Cheltenham T	L 0-2	0-2	22		1487
24	26	A	Cambridge U	L 0-1	0-0	22		4639
25	30	A	Exeter C	L 1-2	0-1	23	Watson [69]	3869
26	Jan 1	H	Swindon T	L 1-2	1-2	23	Akinde [20]	2038
27	13	A	Crawley T	L 0-2	0-0	24		1874
28	20	H	Lincoln C	D 1-1	1-0	24	Akinde [12]	3161
29	27	A	Cheltenham T	D 1-1	1-0	24	Santos [2]	2609
30	Feb 3	A	Mansfield T	L 1-3	0-1	24	Akinola [87]	3795
31	10	H	Notts Co	W 1-0	0-0	24	Nicholls [90]	1752
32	13	H	Yeovil T	L 0-2	0-1	24		2455
33	17	H	Accrington S	D 1-1	1-0	24	Nicholls [18]	1501
34	20	H	Carlisle U	L 1-3	0-0	24	Santos [50]	1151
35	24	A	Colchester U	W 1-0	0-0	24	Nicholls [66]	3121
36	Mar 10	A	Coventry C	L 0-1	0-0	24		7127
37	13	H	Port Vale	D 1-1	1-0	23	Nicholls [4]	1153
38	17	H	Wycombe W	L 0-2	0-0	24		2103
39	24	A	Luton T	L 0-2	0-0	24		8140
40	30	H	Crewe Alex	W 2-1	0-0	24	Akinde 2 (2 pens) [51, 87]	1951
41	Apr 2	A	Stevenage	L 1-4	0-1	24	Coulthirst [82]	3350
42	7	H	Forest Green R	W 1-0	1-0	23	Nicholls [45]	1764
43	14	A	Grimsby T	D 2-2	0-1	23	Akpa Akpro [62], Weston [79]	5416
44	21	H	Newport Co	W 2-0	1-0	23	Coulthirst [10], Santos [82]	1816
45	28	A	Morecambe	W 1-0	0-0	23	Nicholls [79]	2073
46	May 5	H	Chesterfield	W 3-0	1-0	23	Akinde [42], Brindley [81], Nicholls [88]	5539

Final League Position: 23

GOALSCORERS

League (46): Coulthirst 10, Akinde 7 (2 pens), Nicholls 7, Akinola 4, Campbell-Ryce 4 (1 pen), Akpa Akpro 3, Santos 3, Vilhete 3, Taylor, J 2, Brindley 1, Watson 1, Weston 1.
FA Cup (1): Akinola 1.
Carabao Cup (3): Akpa Akpro 1, Coulthirst 1, Vilhete 1.
Checkatrade Trophy (6): Blackman 1, Coulthirst 1, Nicholls 1, Ruben Bover 1, Taylor J 1 (1 pen), own goal 1.

Stephens J 11	Taylor H 14+2	Santos R 42	Clough C 29+7	Johnson E 2	Shomotun F 2+4	Taylor J 27+11	Vilhete M 27+5	Akpa Akpro J 14+12	Campbell-Ryce J 23+1	Coulthirst S 34+6	Tutonda D 35+6	Nelson M 25+2	Amaluzor J —+4	Weston C 22	Fonguck W 10+9	Akinola S 10+19	Ross C 32+1	Reuben Bover 18+5	Blackman A 15+4	Tarpey D 2	Mason-Clark E —+8	Akinde J 30+2	Hinckson-Mars M —+1	Watson R 25+3	Nicholls A 19+6	Sweeney D 20+1	Pascal D 1	Aghadiuno B 1	Brindley R 17+1	Sule F —+1	Kyei N 2+1	Nicholson J 3+5	Plavotic T —+1	Legg G 3	Briggs M —+1	Payne J 1+2	Match No.
1	2	3	4²	5	6³	7*	8	9	10	11¹	12	13	14																								1
1	2²	3	12		6³	13	7	11	8	10	5	4			9¹	14																					2
1	2	5	6			12	7	11	8¹	10²	3	4			9²	13	14																				3
	5³	2	3			6	8	11	9	10²	4	13			7¹	14	1	12																			4
	5	3				7¹	8	12	6	10²	2	4			14		1				9⁴	11³	13														5
	5	2	4			7²	6	12	9	11	8	3			13		1				10²	14															6
	5	2	4			7²	6	10¹	9	11	8	3			13		1				12																7
	5	2	4			8³	6	10	7	11²	9	3			13		1	12			14																8
	8³		4			6²	7	11¹	9	10	2	3			13	12	1				5			14													9
	2		3			7	11¹	8²	6	5	4				9	10³	1	13	14		12																10
	4	2				13	7	6	10¹	11³	5	3			8²	12	1		9		14																11
	2	4	3			14	6	8	11	5					7²	13	1	9³	10¹		12																12
	2²	4	3			14	6		11	9	5	12			7	13	1	8¹	10³																		13
		2	4			6	5	12	9²	10	8	3	14		7	11¹	1				13																14
		2	4			6	5	12	9¹	10²	8	3	14		7	11³	1				13																15
		2	4			6	5	13	9	12		3			10³	1		11¹		14				7	8²												16
1		2	4			7	6	13		9	8¹	3			11³			14				10²			5	12											17
1	2	4	3			7²		14	9¹	10	12				13			5³				11		6	8												18
1	14	4	2			7		9	12	11	5²	3¹						10						6	13	8³											19
1	12	3	4			8²	13		9	5³								14				10		6		7	2⁵	11¹									20
1	2¹	4	3			8	11³	9	13						12	14						13		5	10	7		6²									21
1		3	2			7	8¹		9	11		4				13						5		10²	6	12											22
1		4	2³			7	14		9	11²		3			12				8			10		6	13				5¹								23
1¹		4	3			7			9	14	13						8	11	12			5²		10	6³			2									24
		4	3			8		2	9	10					7²	12	1		5			11¹		6	13			2									25
		3				9	7		10	8	12	4			6¹	13	1		5²			11				2											26
		3	7³			9		10²	8		4			6¹			1		5			11		14				2	12	13							27
		4	14			9			10¹	2		13³	8²					1	12			11		7	6	3		5									28
		4	12			6¹	14		10	5				7³		13	1					11		8	9²	3		2									29
		3	4			14			11²	5				6³	12	1	9					10		7	8¹			2			13					30
		3¹	4				13			5				7			12	1	9³			10		8	11			2			6¹	14				31
		4	3				13			12	5¹			8			9²	1			14	10		7	11			2			6³					32
		3	13				6¹	9²		5				8			12	1				11		7	10	4		2³			14					33
		3	2				12	9³		13	5			7⁴			1	14				10		8	11	4		6¹								34
		4					12	2		9¹	5			7			8²					10		6	11	3		13	1							35
		4					12	2		9¹	5			7	13		8²					10³		6	11	3		14	1							36
		3				8²		2	14	4				7			6¹					11³		5	10	9		12		1	13					37
		4	14				13	2¹		9¹	5			7			1	8²				10		6	11	3		12								38
		4	3				7²	14		13	5			9			12	1			8³	11		10	6		2¹									39
		3					14			13	12	5	4³	10	9¹	1						11		8	6²	7		2									40
		3					13		9	11	14	4¹	7		12	1						10		2	6³	8									5¹		41
		13					10		5	4		8³	14		1			11				7	6²	3	2	9									12		42
		12					13		10	5	4	8			1			11				7	6¹	3	2	9²											43
		3					13		11²	5	4	8			9³	1						10		12	6	7¹		2							14		44
		3					13	6	11¹	5	4³	8			9²	1						10		14	12	7		2									45
		3			13	12		6	11²	5	4²	7				1						10		14	9¹	8		2									46

FA Cup
First Round — Blackburn R (a) 1-3

Carabao Cup
First Round — Peterborough U (a) 3-1
Second Round — Brighton & HA (a) 0-1

Checkatrade Trophy
Southern Group F — AFC Wimbledon (h) 3-4
Southern Group F — Luton T (a) 1-1
(Luton T won 4-3 on penalties)
Southern Group F — Tottenham H U21 (h) 2-1

BARNSLEY

FOUNDATION

Many clubs owe their inception to the Church and Barnsley are among them, for they were formed in 1887 by the Rev. T. T. Preedy, curate of Barnsley St Peter's, and went under that name until it was dropped in 1897 a year before being admitted to the Second Division of the Football League.

Oakwell Stadium, Grove Street, Barnsley, South Yorkshire S71 1ET.

Telephone: (01226) 211 211.

Fax: (01226) 211 444.

Ticket Office: (01226) 211 183.

Website: www.barnsleyfc.co.uk

Email: thereds@barnsleyfc.co.uk

Ground Capacity: 23,287.

Record Attendance: 40,255 v Stoke C, FA Cup 5th rd, 15 February 1936.

Pitch Measurements: 100.5m × 67m (110yd × 73yd).

Co-Chairmen: Chien Lee and Paul Conway.

Chief Executive: Gauthier Ganaye.

Head Coach: Daniel Stendel.

Assistant Head Coach: Andreas Winkler.

Colours: Red shirts with white trim, white shorts with red trim, red socks with white trim.

Year Formed: 1887.

Turned Professional: 1888.

Previous Name: 1887, Barnsley St Peter's; 1897, Barnsley.

Club Nickname: 'The Tykes', 'The Reds', 'The Colliers'.

Ground: 1887, Oakwell.

First Football League Game: 1 September 1898, Division 2, v Lincoln C (a) L 0–1 – Fawcett; McArtney, Nixon; King, Burleigh, Porteous; Davis, Lees, Murray, McCullough, McGee.

Record League Victory: 9–0 v Loughborough T, Division 2, 28 January 1899 – Greaves; McArtney, Nixon; Porteous, Burleigh, Howard; Davis (4), Hepworth (1), Lees (1), McCullough (1), Jones (2). 9–0 v Accrington S, Division 3 (N), 3 February 1934 – Ellis; Cookson, Shotton; Harper, Henderson, Whitworth; Spence (2), Smith (1), Blight (4), Andrews (1), Ashton (1).

Record Cup Victory: 6–0 v Blackpool, FA Cup 1st rd replay, 20 January 1910 – Mearns; Downs, Ness; Glendinning, Boyle (1), Utley; Bartrop, Gadsby (1), Lillycrop (2), Tufnell (2), Forman. 6–0 v Peterborough U, League Cup 1st rd 2nd leg, 15 September 1981 – Horn; Joyce, Chambers, Glavin (2), Banks, McCarthy, Evans, Parker (2), Aylott (1), McHale, Barrowclough (1).

Record Defeat: 0–9 v Notts Co, Division 2, 19 November 1927.

Most League Points (2 for a win): 67, Division 3 (N), 1938–39.

Most League Points (3 for a win): 82, Division 1, 1999–2000.

HONOURS

League Champions: Division 3N – 1933–34, 1938–39, 1954–55.
Runners-up: First Division – 1996–97; Division 3 – 1980–81; Division 3N – 1953–54; Division 4 – 1967–68.
FA Cup Winners: 1912.
Runners-up: 1910.
League Cup: quarter-final – 1982.
League Trophy Winners: 2016.

THE Sun FACT FILE

The last time Barnsley played a home game on Christmas Day was in 1951. On that occasion the Tykes defeated Queens Park Rangers 3-1. The attendance of 15,067 was slightly below the seasonal average of 15,867.

Most League Goals: 118, Division 3 (N), 1933–34.

Highest League Scorer in Season: Cecil McCormack, 33, Division 2, 1950–51.

Most League Goals in Total Aggregate: Ernest Hine, 123, 1921–26 and 1934–38.

Most League Goals in One Match: 5, Frank Eaton v South Shields, Division 3 (N), 9 April 1927; 5, Peter Cunningham v Darlington, Division 3 (N), 4 February 1933; 5, Beau Asquith v Darlington, Division 3 (N), 12 November 1938; 5, Cecil McCormack v Luton T, Division 2, 9 September 1950.

Most Capped Player: Gerry Taggart, 35 (51), Northern Ireland.

Most League Appearances: Barry Murphy, 514, 1962–78.

Youngest League Player: Reuben Noble-Lazarus, 15 years 45 days v Ipswich T, 30 September 2008.

Record Transfer Fee Received: £3,000,000 (rising to £10,125,000) from Everton for John Stones, January 2013.

Record Transfer Fee Paid: £1,500,000 to Partizan Belgrade for Georgi Hristov, July 1997; £1,500,000 to QPR for Mike Sheron, January 1999.

Football League Record: 1898 Elected to Division 2; 1932–34 Division 3 (N); 1934–38 Division 2; 1938–39 Division 3 (N); 1946–53 Division 2; 1953–55 Division 3 (N); 1955–59 Division 2; 1959–65 Division 3; 1965–68 Division 4; 1968–72 Division 3; 1972–79 Division 4; 1979–81 Division 3; 1981–92 Division 2; 1992–97 Division 1; 1997–98 FA Premier League; 1998–2002 Division 1; 2002–04 Division 2; 2004–06 FL 1; 2006–14 FL C; 2014–16 FL 1; 2016–18 FL C; 2018– FL 1.

LATEST SEQUENCES

Longest Sequence of League Wins: 10, 5.3.1955 – 23.4.1955.

Longest Sequence of League Defeats: 9, 14.3.1953 – 25.4.1953.

Longest Sequence of League Draws: 7, 28.3.1911 – 22.4.1911.

Longest Sequence of Unbeaten League Matches: 21, 1.1.1934 – 5.5.1934.

Longest Sequence Without a League Win: 26, 13.12.1952 – 26.8.1953.

Successive Scoring Runs: 44 from 2.10.1926.

Successive Non-scoring Runs: 6 from 27.11.1971.

MANAGERS

Arthur Fairclough 1898–1901
   (*Secretary-Manager*)
John McCartney 1901–04
   (*Secretary-Manager*)
Arthur Fairclough 1904–12
John Hastie 1912–14
Percy Lewis 1914–19
Peter Sant 1919–26
John Commins 1926–29
Arthur Fairclough 1929–30
Brough Fletcher 1930–37
Angus Seed 1937–53
Tim Ward 1953–60
Johnny Steele 1960–71
   (*continued as General Manager*)
John McSeveney 1971–72
Johnny Steele (*General Manager*)
   1972–73
Jim Iley 1973–78
Allan Clarke 1978–80
Norman Hunter 1980–84
Bobby Collins 1984–85
Allan Clarke 1985–89
Mel Machin 1989–93
Viv Anderson 1993–94
Danny Wilson 1994–98
John Hendrie 1998–99
Dave Bassett 1999–2000
Nigel Spackman 2001
Steve Parkin 2001–02
Glyn Hodges 2002–03
Gudjon Thordarson 2003–04
Paul Hart 2004–05
Andy Ritchie 2005–06
Simon Davey 2007–09
   (*Caretaker from November 2006*)
Mark Robins 2009–11
Keith Hill 2011–12
David Flitcroft 2012–13
Danny Wilson 2013–15
Lee Johnson 2015–16
Paul Heckingbottom 2016–18
Jose Morais 2018
Daniel Stendel June 2018–

TEN YEAR LEAGUE RECORD

		P	W	D	L	F	A	Pts	Pos
2008-09	FL C	46	13	13	20	45	58	52	20
2009-10	FL C	46	14	12	20	53	69	54	18
2010-11	FL C	46	14	14	18	55	66	56	17
2011-12	FL C	46	13	9	24	49	74	48	21
2012-13	FL C	46	14	13	19	56	70	55	21
2013-14	FL C	46	9	12	25	44	77	39	23
2014-15	FL 1	46	17	11	18	62	61	62	11
2015-16	FL 1	46	22	8	16	70	54	74	6
2016-17	FL C	46	15	13	18	64	67	58	14
2017-18	FL C	46	9	14	23	48	72	41	22

DID YOU KNOW ?

The first Barnsley game to be shown live on television was the FA Cup sixth-round tie at home to Liverpool on 10 March 1985. Viewers saw the Tykes go down to a 4-0 defeat with Ian Rush netting a hat-trick.

BARNSLEY – SKY BET CHAMPIONSHIP 2017–18 LEAGUE RECORD

Match No.	Date	Venue	Opponents	Result	H/T Score	Lg Pos.	Goalscorers	Attendance
1	Aug 5	A	Bristol C	L 1-3	0-3	23	Hedges [90]	18,742
2	12	H	Ipswich T	L 1-2	1-0	23	Bradshaw [15]	12,009
3	15	H	Nottingham F	W 2-1	1-1	16	Bradshaw [3], Hedges [50]	13,883
4	19	A	Sheffield U	L 0-1	0-1	20		25,482
5	26	H	Sunderland	W 3-0	2-0	15	Ugbo [31], Barnes [35], Moncur [67]	15,697
6	Sept 9	A	Preston NE	D 1-1	1-1	15	Potts [25]	12,813
7	16	H	Aston Villa	L 0-3	0-2	20		14,633
8	23	A	Wolverhampton W	L 1-2	0-0	21	Jackson [90]	28,154
9	26	H	QPR	D 1-1	1-0	21	Barnes [20]	10,920
10	30	A	Millwall	W 3-1	1-1	18	Bradshaw 2 [40, 60], Thiam (pen) [83]	12,147
11	Oct 14	H	Middlesbrough	D 2-2	2-1	19	Bradshaw [2], McGeehan [9]	17,163
12	21	H	Hull C	L 0-1	0-0	19		13,624
13	28	A	Sheffield W	D 1-1	0-1	19	Barnes [67]	27,097
14	31	A	Burton Alb	W 4-2	2-2	19	Isgrove [21], Potts [40], Williams, J [73], Barnes [87]	3761
15	Nov 4	H	Birmingham C	W 2-0	1-0	16	Bradshaw [2], Fryers [68]	12,946
16	18	A	Norwich C	D 1-1	0-1	16	Barnes [47]	25,545
17	21	H	Cardiff C	L 0-1	0-0	17		11,051
18	25	H	Leeds U	L 0-2	0-2	17		16,399
19	28	A	Reading	L 0-3	0-2	18		13,317
20	Dec 2	A	Bolton W	L 1-3	1-2	19	Bradshaw (pen) [22]	14,371
21	9	H	Derby Co	L 0-3	0-2	20		13,973
22	16	A	Brentford	D 0-0	0-0	20		9868
23	23	A	Fulham	L 1-2	0-0	20	Bradshaw [68]	17,308
24	26	H	Preston NE	D 0-0	0-0	20		14,014
25	30	H	Reading	D 1-1	0-0	20	Pinnock [90]	11,945
26	Jan 1	A	Sunderland	W 1-0	0-0	19	Pinnock [47]	28,311
27	13	H	Wolverhampton W	D 0-0	0-0	19		16,050
28	20	A	Aston Villa	L 1-3	1-3	19	Cavare [11]	31,869
29	27	H	Fulham	L 1-3	1-0	19	Lindsay [30]	12,147
30	Feb 3	A	QPR	L 0-1	0-0	21		12,413
31	10	H	Sheffield W	D 1-1	1-1	22	McBurnie [21]	16,858
32	20	H	Burton Alb	L 1-2	0-2	23	Moore [75]	11,774
33	24	A	Birmingham C	W 2-0	2-0	21	McBurnie 2 [12, 36]	19,822
34	27	A	Hull C	D 1-1	1-0	21	McBurnie [22]	14,005
35	Mar 6	A	Cardiff C	L 1-2	0-1	21	McBurnie [60]	16,176
36	10	A	Middlesbrough	L 1-3	0-2	21	Moore [58]	24,917
37	13	H	Norwich C	D 1-1	1-0	21	McBurnie [45]	11,508
38	17	H	Millwall	L 0-2	0-1	21		13,041
39	30	H	Bristol C	D 2-2	1-1	21	Moore [7], Potts [78]	12,236
40	Apr 7	A	Sheffield U	W 3-2	1-0	22	Gardner [25], McBurnie [74], Bradshaw [88]	16,041
41	10	A	Ipswich T	L 0-1	0-0	22		13,271
42	14	H	Bolton W	D 2-2	1-0	22	Gardner [22], McBurnie [90]	14,138
43	21	A	Leeds U	L 1-2	1-1	22	O'Connor (og) [36]	30,451
44	24	A	Nottingham F	L 0-3	0-2	22		23,633
45	28	H	Brentford	W 2-0	1-0	21	Moore [11], McBurnie [51]	13,137
46	May 6	A	Derby Co	L 1-4	0-1	22	Moncur [80]	30,682

Final League Position: 22

GOALSCORERS

League (48): Bradshaw 9 (1 pen), McBurnie 9, Barnes 5, Moore 4, Potts 3, Gardner 2, Hedges 2, Moncur 2, Pinnock 2, Cavare 1, Fryers 1, Isgrove 1, Jackson 1, Lindsay 1, McGeehan 1, Thiam 1 (1 pen), Ugbo 1, Williams, J 1, own goal 1.
FA Cup (1): Potts 1.
Carabao Cup (7): Bradshaw 3, Hammill 1, Hedges 1, Jackson 1, own goal 1.

Davies A 35	McCarthy J 17+4	Jackson A 22	MacDonald A 10+1	Viadom A 31+1	Potts B 35+2	Moncur G 22+12	Williams J 33+1	Mowatt A 1	Ugbo I 7+9	Bradshaw T 26+13	Hammill A 30+8	Hedges R 6+17	Payne S —+2	Pearson M 14+3	Barnes H 18+5	Bird J —+3	Pinnock E 9+3	Thiam M 12+17	Lindsay L 42	Gardner G 28+1	McGeehan C 6+3	Fryers Z 22	Isgrove L 10+6	Mallan S 5+3	Cavare D 7+2	Moore K 16+4	Mottley-Henry D —+1	Pinillos D 7+1	Townsend N 8	Mills M 4	McBurnie O 16+1	Mahoney C 3+5	Knasmuliner C 1+2	Walton J 3	Match No.
1	2	3	4	5	6^2	7	8	9	10^3	11^1	12	13	14																						1
1	2	3	4		8	9	6		12	11^1	7^2	10^3	13	5	14																				2
1	2	3	4		8	9^1	6			11	7^2	10		5	13	12																			3
1	2^1	3	4▪		8	9^3	6		13	11^2	7	10		5			12	14																	4
1	2	3		9	8	6			11^2	13	7^3	12		5	10^1			14	4																5
1	2	3			8	12	7		10	14	9^2	11^3		5	13				4	6^1															6
1	2	3			8	9^2	6		13	11^3	7	12		5	10^1			14	4																7
1	2	3			9^1	8^3	6		14	11	7	12		5	10^2				4		13														8
1	2	3			9^2	8^3	6		11	12	7	14			10^1				4		13	5													9
1	2	3			9		6			11^3	7	12		5	10^1	14	13		4		8^2														10
1		3			9^1		6			11	7	14		2	10^2	13	12		4		8^3	5													11
1	2	3^1	14		8				10^2	11	6	12			9^3			13	4	7		5													12
1	2		3	5	12	14	7		10^2	13				11			9		4		8^3	13													13
1		3	2	6	12	7		10^2	13					11					4	8^1	5	9													14
1		3	2	9	8	6			11^2	12	13			10^3				14	4		5	7^1													15
1	12		3^2	2	8	9	6			11	7^1	13		10					4		5														16
1			2	8	14			13	7	10^2		3	12			11^1	4	6	9^3	5														17
1			3	2	8	9^2	6		13	11	7^3	14		10^1				4	12		5														18
1		3^2	2	6	10	8		11^1	14				13	9			12	4	7^3	5															19
1	2		5	8	9	6^2		11	7^1	13		3	10^3			12	4	14																	20
1	2		5	6^3	13	7		14	11	12		3	9			10^1	4																		21
1	2		5		6	8		13	11	14		3^3	9^2		12	10^1	4	7																	22
1	2		5		6^1	8		14	11	12			9^3		3	10^2	4	7	13																23
1			2		6		11	7			12		3		4	9		5	10^1	8															24
1	12		2^2			7		14	10	6			9^3		3	11	4	8		5	13														25
1	14			8	13	6		12	7^1			3	11^3	4	9^2		5	10		2															26
1			5	9	12		11^1	10			3	14	4	6		7^2	8^3	2	13																27
1	3^2		6	7^1	9		11	12			5	14	4			8	2	10^3	13																28
1			5		8		11^1	9^3	13	3		14	4	7		6	2^1	10^2		12															29
			2		6	8		10	9^2	12			4	7		5^1		11^3																1	30
			2			8		10	9				4	7		6^1		13		5	1	3	11^2	12										31
			2	13		8		11^3	9^1				12	4	7		6^2	14		5	1	3	10											32
	3		2	6		7						14			9^2	4	8^2	5			10		1		11^1	12	13							33
	3^2		13	8	14	7						12			9^3	4	6			2	10		5	1		11^1								34
			2	6^3		7		14		13		3	9^2	4	8^1	5			10		1		11		12									35
	3				6^1					7^3				12	4	9		13	14	2	11		5	1		10		8^2						36
	3		2	6		7^1								9^2	4	8		5	12	13	10		11											37
	3		2	6	8^3	12		13						9	4^2	7		14	6^1	10		5	1		11									38
1	14		3	2	6	8^3	12			13				4	7	5	9^2	10^1		11														39
1			3	2	6	8^1		13	12				4	7	5	9^3	14	10		11^2														40
1			3	2	7				13	9^2	12			4	8	5^3	6^1	14	10		11														41
1	3^1		2	6^2	8			13	9		12			4	7	5^3			10		11	14												42
1			2	9	13		11^3	7	14					4	6	5			12		3^2	10	8^1											43
	3		2	6	8^2				14	9^2				13	4	7			2	10^1	5		11	12									1	44
			2	7	14				9^1				3	12	4	8		5	13	10		11^3	6^2								1			45
			2	7^2	13				9				3	12	4	8		5		10		11	6^1								1			46

FA Cup
| Third Round | Millwall | (a) | 1-4 |

Carabao Cup
First Round	Morecambe	(h)	4-3
Second Round	Derby Co	(h)	3-2
Third Round	Tottenham H	(a)	0-1

BIRMINGHAM CITY

FOUNDATION

In 1875, cricketing enthusiasts who were largely members of Trinity Church, Bordesley, determined to continue their sporting relationships throughout the year by forming a football club which they called Small Heath Alliance. For their earliest games played on waste land in Arthur Street, the team included three Edden brothers and two James brothers.

St Andrew's Stadium, Cattell Road, Birmingham B9 4RL.
Telephone: (0121) 772 0101.
Fax: (0121) 766 7866.
Ticket Office: (0121) 772 0101 (option 2).
Website: www.bcfc.com
Email: reception@bcfc.com
Ground Capacity: 29,409.
Record Attendance: 66,844 v Everton, FA Cup 5th rd, 11 February 1939.
Pitch Measurements: 100m × 67.5m (109.5yd × 74yd).
Directors: Wenqing Zhao, Chun Kong Yiu, Kai Zhu, Gannan Zheng, Yao Weng, Xuandong Ren.
Manager: Garry Monk.
Assistant Manager: Pep Clotet.
Colours: Blue shirts with white trim, white shorts with blue trim, blue socks with white trim.
Year Formed: 1875.
Turned Professional: 1885.
Previous Names: 1875, Small Heath Alliance; 1888, dropped 'Alliance'; 1905, Birmingham; 1945, Birmingham City.
Club Nickname: 'Blues'.
Grounds: 1875, waste ground near Arthur St; 1877, Muntz St, Small Heath; 1906, St Andrew's.
First Football League Game: 3 September 1892, Division 2, v Burslem Port Vale (h) W 5–1 – Charsley; Bayley, Speller; Ollis, Jenkyns, Devey; Hallam (1), Edwards (1), Short (1), Wheldon (2), Hands.
Record League Victory: 12–0 v Walsall T Swifts, Division 2, 17 December 1892 – Charsley; Bayley, Jones; Ollis, Jenkyns, Devey; Hallam (2), Walton (3), Mobley (3), Wheldon (2), Hands (2). 12–0 v Doncaster R, Division 2, 11 April 1903 – Dorrington; Goldie, Wassell; Beer, Dougherty (1), Howard; Athersmith, Leonard (4), McRoberts (1), Wilcox (4), Field (1), (1 og).
Record Cup Victory: 9–2 v Burton W, FA Cup 1st rd, 31 October 1885 – Hedges; Jones, Evetts (1); Fred James, Felton, Arthur James (1); Davenport (2), Stanley (4), Simms, Figures, Morris (1).
Record Defeat: 1–9 v Blackburn R, Division 1, 5 January 1895; 1–9 v Sheffield W, Division 1, 13 December 1930; 0–8 v Bournemouth, FLC, 25 October 2014.

HONOURS

League Champions: Division 2 – 1892–93, 1920–21, 1947–48, 1954–55; Second Division – 1994–95.
Runners-up: FL C – 2006–07, 2008–09; Division 2 – 1893–94, 1900–01, 1902–03; 1971–72, 1984–85; Division 3 – 1991–92.
FA Cup: Runners-up: 1931, 1956.
League Cup Winners: 1963, 2011.
Runners-up: 2001.
League Trophy Winners: 1991, 1995.
European Competitions
Fairs Cup: 1955–58, 1958–60 *(runners-up)*, 1960–61 *(runners-up)*, 1961–62.
Europa League: 2011–12.

Sün FACT FILE

On 15 October 1979 Birmingham City entertained the NASL team Los Angeles Aztecs in a friendly at St Andrews. The visitors included the legendary Dutch player Johan Cruyff in their line-up but he made little impact and was booked. The match finished 1-1 with Terry Lees scoring a second-half penalty for Blues in front of a crowd of 8,317.

Most League Points (2 for a win): 59, Division 2, 1947–48.

Most League Points (3 for a win): 89, Division 2, 1994–95.

Most League Goals: 103, Division 2, 1893–94 (only 28 games).

Highest League Scorer in Season: Walter Abbott, 34, Division 2, 1898–99 (Small Heath); Joe Bradford, 29, Division 1, 1927–28 (Birmingham City).

Most League Goals in Total Aggregate: Joe Bradford, 249, 1920–35.

Most League Goals in One Match: 5, Walter Abbott v Darwen, Division 2, 26 November, 1898; 5, John McMillan v Blackpool, Division 2, 2 March 1901; 5, James Windridge v Glossop, Division 2, 23 January 1915.

Most Capped Player: Maik Taylor, 58 (including 8 on loan at Fulham) (88), Northern Ireland.

Most League Appearances: Frank Womack, 491, 1908–28.

Youngest League Player: Trevor Francis, 16 years 139 days v Cardiff C, 5 September 1970.

Record Transfer Fee Received: £6,700,000 (rising to £8,000,000) from Liverpool for Jermaine Pennant, July 2006.

Record Transfer Fee Paid: £6,250,000 to Brentford for Jota, August 2017.

Football League Record: 1892 Elected to Division 2; 1894–96 Division 1; 1896–1901 Division 2; 1901–02 Division 1; 1902–03 Division 2; 1903–08 Division 1; 1908–21 Division 2; 1921–39 Division 1; 1946–48 Division 2; 1948–50 Division 1; 1950–55 Division 2; 1955–65 Division 1; 1965–72 Division 2; 1972–79 Division 1; 1979–80 Division 2; 1980–84 Division 1; 1984–85 Division 2; 1985–86 Division 1; 1986–89 Division 2; 1989–92 Division 3; 1992–94 Division 1; 1994–95 Division 2; 1995–2002 Division 1; 2002–06 FA Premier League; 2006–07 FL C; 2007–08 FA Premier League; 2008–09 FL C; 2009–11 FA Premier League; 2011– FL C.

LATEST SEQUENCES

Longest Sequence of League Wins: 13, 17.12.1892 – 16.9.1893.

Longest Sequence of League Defeats: 8, 28.9.1985 – 23.11.1985.

Longest Sequence of League Draws: 8, 18.9.1990 – 23.10.1990.

Longest Sequence of Unbeaten League Matches: 20, 3.9.1994 – 2.1.1995.

Longest Sequence Without a League Win: 17, 28.9.1985 – 18.1.1986.

Successive Scoring Runs: 24 from 24.9.1892.

Successive Non-scoring Runs: 6 from 11.2.1989.

MANAGERS

Alfred Jones 1892–1908
(*Secretary-Manager*)
Alec Watson 1908–10
Bob McRoberts 1910–15
Frank Richards 1915–23
Billy Beer 1923–27
William Harvey 1927–28
Leslie Knighton 1928–33
George Liddell 1933–39
William Camkin and Ted Goodier 1939–45
Harry Storer 1945–48
Bob Brocklebank 1949–54
Arthur Turner 1954–58
Pat Beasley 1959–60
Gil Merrick 1960–64
Joe Mallett 1964–65
Stan Cullis 1965–70
Fred Goodwin 1970–75
Willie Bell 1975–77
Sir Alf Ramsay 1977–78
Jim Smith 1978–82
Ron Saunders 1982–86
John Bond 1986–87
Garry Pendrey 1987–89
Dave Mackay 1989–91
Lou Macari 1991
Terry Cooper 1991–93
Barry Fry 1993–96
Trevor Francis 1996–2001
Steve Bruce 2001–07
Alex McLeish 2007–11
Chris Hughton 2011–12
Lee Clark 2012–14
Gary Rowett 2014–16
Gianfranco Zola 2016–17
Harry Redknapp 2017
Steve Cotterill 2017–18
Garry Monk March 2018–

TEN YEAR LEAGUE RECORD

		P	W	D	L	F	A	Pts	Pos
2008-09	FL C	46	23	14	9	54	37	83	2
2009-10	PR Lge	38	13	11	14	38	47	50	9
2010-11	PR Lge	38	8	15	15	37	58	39	18
2011-12	FL C	46	20	16	10	78	51	76	4
2012-13	FL C	46	15	16	15	63	69	61	12
2013-14	FL C	46	11	11	24	58	74	44	21
2014-15	FL C	46	16	15	15	54	64	63	10
2015-16	FL C	46	16	15	15	53	49	63	10
2016-17	FL C	46	13	14	19	45	64	53	19
2017-18	FL C	46	13	7	26	38	68	46	19

DID YOU KNOW ?

Birmingham City failed to score a single goal in their first seven away league games of the 1962–63 season. They had played for 638 minutes before Ken Leek finally netted in the game at Wolverhampton Wanderers on 24 October. Leek scored a second within 10 minutes as Blues went on to win 2-0.

BIRMINGHAM CITY – SKY BET CHAMPIONSHIP 2017–18 LEAGUE RECORD

Match No.	Date	Venue	Opponents	Result		H/T Score	Lg Pos.	Goalscorers	Attendance
1	Aug 5	A	Ipswich T	L	0-1	0-0	17		18,153
2	12	H	Bristol C	W	2-1	1-1	10	Gardner 30, Maghoma 74	21,269
3	15	H	Bolton W	D	0-0	0-0	11		20,215
4	18	A	Burton Alb	L	1-2	1-0	13	Maghoma 29	4948
5	26	H	Reading	L	0-2	0-0	20		19,993
6	Sept 9	A	Norwich C	L	0-1	0-1	21		26,335
7	12	A	Leeds U	L	0-2	0-1	22		31,507
8	16	H	Preston NE	L	1-3	1-0	23	Colin 35	21,168
9	23	A	Derby Co	D	1-1	0-0	23	Jutkiewicz 64	27,392
10	27	H	Sheffield W	W	1-0	0-0	22	Vassell 76	20,365
11	30	A	Hull C	L	1-6	0-3	22	Gallagher 90	15,608
12	Oct 13	H	Cardiff C	W	1-0	1-0	19	Adams 19	19,059
13	21	A	Millwall	L	0-2	0-0	21		14,500
14	29	H	Aston Villa	D	0-0	0-0	21		24,408
15	Nov 1	H	Brentford	L	0-2	0-0	21		19,045
16	4	A	Barnsley	L	0-2	0-1	22		12,946
17	18	H	Nottingham F	W	1-0	1-0	21	Adams 5	21,071
18	22	A	Middlesbrough	L	0-2	0-2	21		22,848
19	25	A	Sheffield U	D	1-1	1-0	21	Boga 38	27,427
20	Dec 4	H	Wolverhampton W	L	0-1	0-1	22		19,641
21	9	A	Fulham	L	0-1	0-1	22		19,644
22	16	H	QPR	L	1-2	0-1	24	Gallagher 57	20,107
23	23	A	Sunderland	D	1-1	1-1	24	Gallagher 16	29,312
24	26	H	Norwich C	L	0-2	0-1	24		19,967
25	30	H	Leeds U	W	1-0	0-0	24	Maghoma 83	21,673
26	Jan 2	A	Reading	W	2-0	1-0	23	Maghoma 24, Gallagher 64	14,491
27	13	H	Derby Co	L	0-3	0-1	23		22,121
28	20	A	Preston NE	D	1-1	0-1	23	Gallagher 63	13,529
29	30	H	Sunderland	W	3-1	2-0	20	Davis 28, Boga 44, Gallagher 54	19,601
30	Feb 3	A	Sheffield W	W	3-3	3-0	19	Davis 8, Jota 2 21, 45	25,648
31	11	A	Aston Villa	L	0-2	0-0	20		41,233
32	17	H	Millwall	L	0-1	0-0	19		19,111
33	20	A	Brentford	L	0-5	0-2	20		9511
34	24	H	Barnsley	L	0-2	0-2	22		19,822
35	Mar 3	A	Nottingham F	L	1-2	0-1	22	Morrison 87	23,296
36	6	H	Middlesbrough	L	0-1	0-1	22		18,301
37	10	A	Cardiff C	L	2-3	0-3	22	Gardner (pen) 54, Colin 90	19,634
38	17	H	Hull C	W	2-0	1-0	22	Jota 2 12, 59, Adams 48	22,970
39	31	H	Ipswich T	W	1-0	1-0	21	Jota (pen) 21	20,555
40	Apr 3	A	Bolton W	W	1-0	1-0	21	Jutkiewicz 40	21,097
41	7	H	Burton Alb	D	1-1	0-0	20	Jutkiewicz 87	22,311
42	10	A	Bristol C	L	1-3	1-2	20	Jutkiewicz 34	20,288
43	15	A	Wolverhampton W	L	0-2	0-1	21		29,536
44	21	H	Sheffield U	W	2-1	1-1	20	Roberts 32, Maghoma 69	23,579
45	28	A	QPR	L	1-3	1-1	20	Adams 27	15,805
46	May 6	H	Fulham	W	3-1	2-0	19	Jutkiewicz 15, Dean 43, Adams 89	27,608

Final League Position: 19

GOALSCORERS

League (38): Gallagher 6, Adams 5, Jota 5 (1 pen), Jutkiewicz 5, Maghoma 5, Boga 2, Colin 2, Davis 2, Gardner 2 (1 pen), Dean 1, Morrison 1, Roberts 1, Vassell 1.
FA Cup (3): Adams 1, Gallagher 1, Jutkiewicz 1.
Carabao Cup (6): Adams 3, Davis 1, Kieftenbeld 1, Tesche 1.

Stockdale D 36	Nsue E 15+3	Morrison M 33	Roberts M 26+4	Grounds J 26	Davis D 33+5	N'Doye C 28+9	Gardner C 20+6	Maghoma J 32+9	Adams C 16+14	Donaldson C 4	Keita C —+1	Kieftenbeld M 33+2	Robinson P —+2	Cotterill D 2+5	Shotton R —+1	Jutkiewicz L 19+16	Vassell 13+6	Gleeson S 3+2	Jenkinson C 7	Bramall C 3+2	Gallagher S 23+10	Colin M 35	Dean H 34	Jota R 24+8	Lowe J 6+3	Boga J 24+7	Walsh L 1+2	Kuszczak T 10	Dacres-Cogley J 1+2	Harding W 9	Lubala B —+1	Match No.
1	2	3	4	5	6	7	8	9¹	10	11		12																				1
1	2	3	4	5¹	6¹	7	8	9	10³	11		12¹	13	14																		2
1	2	3¹	4	5		7²	8		10	11³		9	13	14	6	12																3
1	2	3	4	5	6¹		8	7³	9			11	13			10³	12	14														4
1 12	2	3	4⁴	14	6³		11			8						13		7	5¹	9	10											5
1	4		5	8	14					12						13					10¹	2	3	6	7³	9	11²					6
1	2	4			9¹	8		14	12							13					11²	5	3	7³	6	10	13					7
1	2	4			8	6³		9								14	13				10²	5	3		7¹	11	12					8
	2	3			6	8	7	9								12	13				10²	5	4			11¹			1			9
	2	3	14		6	8	7²	9								10¹	12				13	5	4			11³	1					10
	2	3			6	8	7¹	9²					13			10³	12				14	5	4			11	1					11
		3	4	5	6³	9	13	10¹	8²		7					12	11				14	2						1				12
		3	4	5	6	9³		10²	8¹		7					13	11					2		12		14		1				13
		3	4	5	6	9			10³		7					14	11¹				12	2		8²		13		1				14
		3	4	5	6	9		10	11		7²	12				14					13	2¹		8³				1				15
	2		3	5	6				12		7	8¹				11²					10		4	9		13		1				16
	2		3	5	6	13		12	10³		7					14	8²				11		4	9¹				1				17
	2		3	5	6¹	9		12	11²		7	13	14								10³		4	8				1				18
	5	3	2	8		7		12	13		6					10²					14		4	9¹		11³		1				19
	5	3	2	8	14	7²			13		6					10¹	12						4⁸	11³		9		1				20
	5	3		4	6			13			7					10²	8	9¹	12							11	2	1				21
1		3		5	6¹		7	12			8					13					10	2	4	9²		11						22
1		3		5	13	9²	6	12			7					14					11¹	2	4	8³		10¹						23
1		3		5	13	9²	6	12			7					11						2	4	8¹		10						24
1 14		3		5	9³	13	6	8¹			7										11	2	4	12		10²						25
1 12		3		5	9	13	6¹	8³	14		7										11²	2	4			10¹						26
1		3		5	9²		6	8	12		7										11	2	4	13		10¹						27
1		3		5	9	6		8	12		7										11	2	4			10¹						28
1		3		5	9²	6		8³	13		7					14					11¹	2	4	12		10						29
1		3		5¹	9²	6	13				7¹							12	11	2	4	8	14	10								30
1		3		9¹	6⁸			8³	13		7						2		11	5	4	12		10								31
1		3			9	8³	13				7					14		2		11	5	4	12	6²	10¹							32
1		3			9	7	8²	12									5		11	2	4	13	6	10¹								33
1		3			6²	7	9	10									2¹	13	11	5	4	12		8								34
1	3				9	8¹	10			7						12		2	11	5	4	8		6²	13							35
1	3				6	10	9²			7						11¹		2	12	5	4	8		13								36
1	3	12			8	9¹	13			7						10³		2²	11	5	4	6		14								37
1	3		14	12	7³	9²	10			8						11¹				5	4	6		13			2					38
1	3		7	12	9	11				8³						10²				5	4	6	14			13	2					39
1	3	14	7	8	9³	11⁸		12								10¹				5	4	6²				13	2					40
1	3		6	12	10	7										11				5¹	4	8		9			2					41
1	3		7	13		8⁸										10				5²	4	6	14	11¹		·	2	12				42
1	3	12	5¹	10	7²	14	13			8³						11					6	4⁸	9				2					43
1	3	4	7	14	12	9	11²			8¹						10³				13	5		6				2					44
1	3	4	7	8²	13	9	11¹									10				12	5		6				2					45
1	3			8		13	9¹	12			7	14				11³				10²	5	4	6				2					46

FA Cup

Third Round	Burton Alb	(h)	1-0
Fourth Round	Huddersfield T	(a)	1-1
Replay	Huddersfield T	(h)	1-4
(aet)			

Carabao Cup

First Round	Crawley T	(h)	5-1
Second Round	Bournemouth	(h)	1-2

BLACKBURN ROVERS

FOUNDATION

It was in 1875 that some public school old boys called a meeting at which the Blackburn Rovers club was formed and the colours blue and white adopted. The leading light was John Lewis, later to become a founder of the Lancashire FA, a famous referee who was in charge of two FA Cup finals, and a vice-president of both the FA and the Football League.

Ewood Park, Blackburn, Lancashire BB2 4JF.

Telephone: (01254) 372 001.

Fax: (01254) 671 042.

Ticket Office: (01254) 372 000.

Website: www.rovers.co.uk

Email: enquiries@rovers.co.uk

Ground Capacity: 31,154.

Record Attendance: 62,522 v Bolton W, FA Cup 6th rd, 2 March 1929.

Pitch Measurements: 105m × 66m (115yd × 72yd).

Chief Executive: Steve Waggott.

Manager: Tony Mowbray.

Assistant Manager: Mark Venus.

Colours: Blue and white halved shirts, white shorts, blue socks with white trim.

Year Formed: 1875.

Turned Professional: 1880.

Club Nickname: 'Rovers'.

HONOURS

League Champions: FA Premier League – 1994–95; Division 1 – 1911–12, 1913–14; Division 2 – 1938–39; Division 3 – 1974–75.
Runners-up: FA Premier League – 1993–94; FL 1 – 2017–18; First Division – 2000–01; Division 2 – 1957–58; Division 3 – 1979–80.

FA Cup Winners: 1884, 1885, 1886, 1890, 1891, 1928.
Runners-up: 1882, 1960.

League Cup Winners: 2002.

Full Members' Cup Winners: 1987.

European Competitions
European Cup: 1995–96.
UEFA Cup: 1994–95, 1998–99, 2002–03, 2003–04, 2006–07, 2007–08.
Intertoto Cup: 2007.

Grounds: 1875, all matches played away; 1876, Oozehead Ground; 1877, Pleasington Cricket Ground; 1878, Alexandra Meadows; 1881, Leamington Road; 1890, Ewood Park.

First Football League Game: 15 September 1888, Football League, v Accrington (h) D 5–5 – Arthur; Beverley, James Southworth; Douglas, Almond, Forrest; Beresford (1), Walton, John Southworth (1), Fecitt (1), Townley (2).

Record League Victory: 9–0 v Middlesbrough, Division 2, 6 November 1954 – Elvy; Suart, Eckersley; Clayton, Kelly, Bell; Mooney (3), Crossan (2), Briggs, Quigley (3), Langton (1).

Record Cup Victory: 11–0 v Rossendale, FA Cup 1st rd, 13 October 1884 – Arthur; Hopwood, McIntyre; Forrest, Blenkhorn, Lofthouse; Sowerbutts (2), Jimmy Brown (1), Fecitt (4), Barton (3), Birtwistle (1).

Record Defeat: 0–8 v Arsenal, Division 1, 25 February 1933; 0–8 v Lincoln C, Division 2, 29 August 1953.

Sⁿⁿ FACT FILE

Blackburn Rovers played a charity match at Burton on Trent in aid of the Rawdon Colliery Disaster Fund against Leicester City in October 1908. Rovers won 3-1 with two goals from Ellis Crompton and one from Archie Kyle in front of a crowd of 10,000. The second half of the game was played under electric lighting provided by the local council.

Most League Points (2 for a win): 60, Division 3, 1974–75.

Most League Points (3 for a win): 96, FL 1, 2017–18.

Most League Goals: 114, Division 2, 1954–55.

Highest League Scorer in Season: Ted Harper, 43, Division 1, 1925–26.

Most League Goals in Total Aggregate: Simon Garner, 168, 1978–92.

Most League Goals in One Match: 7, Tommy Briggs v Bristol R, Division 2, 5 February 1955.

Most Capped Player: Morten Gamst Pedersen, 70 (83), Norway.

Most League Appearances: Derek Fazackerley, 596, 1970–86.

Youngest League Player: Harry Dennison, 16 years 155 days v Bristol C, 8 April 1911.

Record Transfer Fee Received: £18,000,000 from Manchester C for Roque Santa Cruz, June 2009.

Record Transfer Fee Paid: £3,000,000 (rising to £10,000,000) to Arsenal for David Bentley, January 2006.

Football League Record: 1888 Founder Member of the League; 1936–39 Division 2; 1946–48 Division 1; 1948–58 Division 2; 1958–66 Division 1; 1966–71 Division 2; 1971–75 Division 3; 1975–79 Division 2; 1979–80 Division 3; 1980–92 Division 2; 1992–99 FA Premier League; 1999–2001 Division 1; 2001–12 FA Premier League; 2012–17 FL C; 2017–18 FL 1; 2018– FL C.

LATEST SEQUENCES

Longest Sequence of League Wins: 8, 1.3.1980 – 7.4.1980.

Longest Sequence of League Defeats: 7, 12.3.1966 – 16.4.1966.

Longest Sequence of League Draws: 5, 11.10.1975 – 1.11.1975.

Longest Sequence of Unbeaten League Matches: 23, 30.9.1987 – 27.2.1988.

Longest Sequence Without a League Win: 16, 11.11.1978 – 24.3.1979.

Successive Scoring Runs: 32 from 24.4.1954.

Successive Non-scoring Runs: 4 from 14.12.2015.

MANAGERS

Thomas Mitchell 1884–96
  (*Secretary-Manager*)
J. Walmsley 1896–1903
  (*Secretary-Manager*)
R. B. Middleton 1903–25
Jack Carr 1922–26
  (*Team Manager under Middleton to 1925*)
Bob Crompton 1926–31
  (*Hon. Team Manager*)
Arthur Barritt 1931–36
  (*had been Secretary from 1927*)
Reg Taylor 1936–38
Bob Crompton 1938–41
Eddie Hapgood 1944–47
Will Scott 1947
Jack Bruton 1947–49
Jackie Bestall 1949–53
Johnny Carey 1953–58
Dally Duncan 1958–60
Jack Marshall 1960–67
Eddie Quigley 1967–70
Johnny Carey 1970–71
Ken Furphy 1971–73
Gordon Lee 1974–75
Jim Smith 1975–78
Jim Iley 1978
John Pickering 1978–79
Howard Kendall 1979–81
Bobby Saxton 1981–86
Don Mackay 1987–91
Kenny Dalglish 1991–95
Ray Harford 1995–96
Roy Hodgson 1997–98
Brian Kidd 1998–99
Graeme Souness 2000–04
Mark Hughes 2004–08
Paul Ince 2008
Sam Allardyce 2008–10
Steve Kean 2010–12
Henning Berg 2012
Michael Appleton 2013
Gary Bowyer 2013–15
Paul Lambert 2015–16
Owen Coyle 2016–17
Tony Mowbray February 2017–

TEN YEAR LEAGUE RECORD

		P	W	D	L	F	A	Pts	Pos
2008-09	PR Lge	38	10	11	17	40	60	41	15
2009-10	PR Lge	38	13	11	14	41	55	50	10
2010-11	PR Lge	38	11	10	17	46	59	43	15
2011-12	PR Lge	38	8	7	23	48	78	31	19
2012-13	FL C	46	14	16	16	55	62	58	17
2013-14	FL C	46	18	16	12	70	62	70	8
2014-15	FL C	46	17	16	13	66	59	67	9
2015-16	FL C	46	13	16	17	46	46	55	15
2016-17	FL C	46	12	15	19	53	65	51	22
2017-18	FL 1	46	28	12	6	82	40	96	2

DID YOU KNOW ?

Blackburn Rovers played their first-ever Sunday Football League match at home to Shrewsbury Town on 27 February 1974. Games could be switched to Sundays due to restrictions on the use of floodlighting during the coal miners' strike. Rovers won 2-0 in front of a season's best crowd of 10,989.

BLACKBURN ROVERS – SKY BET LEAGUE ONE 2017–18 LEAGUE RECORD

Match No.	Date	Venue	Opponents	Result	H/T Score	Lg Pos.	Goalscorers	Attendance
1	Aug 5	A	Southend U	L 1-2	0-2	15	Mulgrew [53]	9257
2	12	H	Doncaster R	L 1-3	0-0	22	Samuel [87]	12,223
3	19	A	Bradford C	W 1-0	0-0	17	Samuel [47]	21,403
4	26	H	Milton Keynes D	W 4-1	2-1	10	Williams [2], Mulgrew 2 [29, 77], Samuel [83]	10,111
5	Sept 9	H	Rochdale	W 3-0	1-0	10	Smallwood [10], Antonsson [57], Graham [79]	6524
6	12	A	Scunthorpe U	W 1-0	0-0	10	Antonsson [58]	4330
7	16	H	AFC Wimbledon	L 0-1	0-1	11		10,833
8	23	A	Shrewsbury T	D 1-1	0-0	9	Dack [85]	8202
9	26	H	Rotherham U	W 2-0	1-0	8	Antonsson [27], Chapman [85]	10,228
10	30	H	Gillingham	W 1-0	1-0	6	Samuel [31]	10,844
11	Oct 14	A	Oldham Ath	L 0-1	0-0	10		7784
12	17	H	Plymouth Arg	D 1-1	1-1	10	Dack [45]	10,011
13	21	H	Portsmouth	W 3-0	1-0	6	Dack [38], Graham [58], Conway [90]	11,673
14	28	A	Wigan Ath	D 0-0	0-0	7		11,211
15	31	H	Fleetwood T	D 2-2	0-0	6	Dack [53], Nuttall [77]	10,399
16	Nov 18	A	Bury	W 3-0	2-0	6	Antonsson 2 [12, 37], Dack [63]	7159
17	21	A	Oxford U	W 4-2	3-1	6	Mulgrew 2 (1 pen) [6, 22 (p)], Antonsson [17], Nuttall [71]	6965
18	25	H	Bristol R	W 2-1	0-0	5	Mulgrew [61], Samuel [67]	11,660
19	28	A	Blackpool	W 4-2	2-1	4	Antonsson [25], Dack [45], Mulgrew [63], Downing [67]	5302
20	Dec 9	A	Peterborough U	W 3-2	0-1	3	Mulgrew [48], Dack 2 [51, 58]	6164
21	16	H	Charlton Ath	W 2-0	1-0	3	Best (og) [30], Graham [90]	10,907
22	23	A	Northampton T	D 1-1	0-1	3	Dack [48]	6541
23	26	H	Rochdale	W 2-0	2-0	3	Ntlhe (og) [35], Mulgrew (pen) [42]	15,115
24	30	H	Scunthorpe U	D 2-2	1-1	3	Graham 2 [6, 47]	12,784
25	Jan 1	A	Rotherham U	D 1-1	0-1	3	Dack [66]	9347
26	13	A	Shrewsbury T	W 3-1	1-1	3	Mulgrew 2 (1 pen) [14, 70 (p)], Graham [60]	13,579
27	20	A	Fleetwood T	W 2-1	1-0	2	Dack [28], Smallwood [83]	4391
28	27	H	Northampton T	D 1-1	0-1	3	Graham [74]	12,555
29	30	H	Walsall	W 3-1	2-1	2	Graham 2 [5, 32], Dack [47]	11,241
30	Feb 3	A	Plymouth Arg	L 0-2	0-2	3		11,801
31	10	H	Oldham Ath	D 2-2	0-2	3	Mulgrew [63], Armstrong [71]	13,665
32	13	A	Portsmouth	W 2-1	1-0	3	Armstrong 2 [21, 87]	18,152
33	19	H	Bury	W 2-0	0-0	1	Graham [51], Armstrong [67]	12,038
34	24	A	Walsall	W 2-1	2-1	1	Graham 2 [17, 26]	6893
35	27	A	AFC Wimbledon	W 3-0	1-0	1	Dack 2 [30, 69], Bennett [64]	4401
36	Mar 4	H	Wigan Ath	D 2-2	2-0	1	Armstrong [6], Bennett [17]	16,142
37	10	H	Blackpool	W 3-0	1-0	1	Dack [45], Armstrong 2 [69, 90]	13,230
38	29	H	Bradford C	W 2-0	0-0	1	Dack [68], Conway [80]	13,443
39	Apr 2	A	Milton Keynes D	W 2-1	2-0	1	Armstrong 2 [12, 45]	11,215
40	7	H	Southend U	W 1-0	0-0	1	Graham [59]	13,186
41	10	A	Gillingham	D 0-0	0-0	2		6361
42	14	A	Bristol R	D 1-1	0-0	2	Mulgrew (pen) [65]	10,029
43	19	H	Peterborough U	W 3-1	0-1	2	Dack 2 [54, 90], Graham [83]	11,679
44	24	A	Doncaster R	W 1-0	0-0	2	Mulgrew [80]	10,443
45	28	A	Charlton Ath	L 0-1	0-1	2		17,310
46	May 5	H	Oxford U	W 2-1	1-0	2	Lenihan [12], Payne [76]	27,600

Final League Position: 2

GOALSCORERS

League (82): Dack 18, Graham 14, Mulgrew 14 (4 pens), Armstrong 9, Antonsson 7, Samuel 5, Bennett 2, Conway 2, Nuttall 2, Smallwood 2, Chapman 1, Downing 1, Lenihan 1, Payne 1, Williams 1, own goals 2.
FA Cup (7): Graham 3, Samuel 2, Antonsson 1, Nuttall 1.
Carabao Cup (3): Evans 1, Samuel 1, Smallwood 1.
Checkatrade Trophy (2): Nuttall 2.

Raya D 45	Nyambe R 27+2	Lenihan D 13+1	Mulgrew C 41	Williams D 45	Samuel D 19+17	Smallwood R 46	Whittingham P 14+6	Bennett E 40+1	Graham D 29+13	Dack B 37+5	Feeney L —+1	Evans C 25+7	Chapman H 1+11	Ward E 9+1	Caddis P 13+1	Gladwin B —+5	Conway C 19+5	Antonsson M 22+9	Downing P 26+2	Harper R 1+3	Hart S —+3	Nuttall J 3+10	Tomlinson W —+4	Armstrong A 17+4	Travis L —+5	Payne J 7+11	Bell A 6+6	Leutwiler J 1	Match No.
1	2	3	4	5	6	7^{3}	8	9^{1}	10	11^{2}	12	13	14																1
1	2		4	8^{1}	12	6	10^{3}	9	11	13		7		3	5^{2}	14													2
1			4	5	11^{3}	6	14	8		9^{2}		7		3	2	12	10^{1}	13											3
1			4	5	10	7		6				8	13	3	2	12	9^{2}	11^{1}											4
1				5	10^{2}	7		6	14	12		8	13	3	2		9^{3}	11^{1}	4										5
1			4	5	10^{2}	6		9	13	12		8	14	3	2			11^{1}		7^{3}									6
1			4	5	10	7^{1}		6	13	12		8	14	3	2		9^{2}	11^{3}											7
1			4	5	10	7	14	6^{2}	11^{3}	9		8^{1}	13	3	2		12												8
1		3		5	10^{2}	8	13	6		9^{3}		7^{1}	12		2		11		4					14					9
1			4	5	11^{1}	6	7	8	13	9^{3}			12		2	14	10^{2}		3										10
1			4	5	11		7^{3}	8	6	13		14	12	3	2		9^{1}	10^{2}											11
1	3		4	5	13	7^{1}	8^{3}	6	11	9^{2}			12		2	14	10												12
1	2		4	5	13	7	8	9	10^{2}	11^{3}		14	6^{1}			12			3										13
1	2	3		5		6	7	8^{4}	13	9^{2}			12		14	10^{1}	11^{3}	4											14
1	2		4	5		7^{1}	9		11^{2}	8		12				6	10^{3}		3					14	13				15
1	2		4	5	13	6	7^{2}	8	14	9							10^{3}		3			12		11^{1}					16
1	2		4	5	13	7		8	14	10^{3}		6^{2}					9^{1}		3			12		11					17
1	2		4	5	12	8	9^{3}	14	13	6^{2}		7					11		3			10^{1}							18
1	2		4	5		6	7^{1}	8	11^{2}	9							10		3			13		12					19
1	2	3		5	10^{1}	7	6^{2}		14	8			12^{4}				9	11	4					13					20
1	2		4	5	9^{2}	6		12	11			7^{3}			8		10^{1}					13		14					21
1	2			5		6	7^{1}		11^{2}	9			4			8	10		3			12		13					22
1	2		4	5		6		8	11^{1}	9		7^{2}				12	10^{4}		3					14	13				23
1	2		4	5	12	7	8	6	11^{2}	9							10^{1}		3			13							24
1	13		4	5	12	6		8	11^{3}	9		7	14	2^{1}			10^{2}		3										25
1	2		4	5	10^{1}	7		6	11^{1}	8							9^{2}		3			13		12		14			26
1	2		4	5	11^{1}	7		6	10^{3}	9							8^{2}		3			14		12		13			27
1	2	4^{1}		5	11	7^{2}		6	10	9							8^{3}		3					13		14	12		28
1	2		4		13	7^{1}		6	10^{2}	11							12		3					9	14	8^{3}	5		29
1	2		4		12	7^{1}		6	11^{2}	9		13				8^{3}			3					14		10	5		30
1	2		4	5		7^{1}		6	10	11									3^{2}					12	13	8	9		31
1	2^{2}	13	3	5	11^{3}	7		6	14	8					4									9	12	10^{1}			32
1	14	2	3	4		6		5	10^{1}	9		7^{3}			12									11	13	8^{2}			33
1	2	3	4	5	12	7		8	10^{3}			6^{1}										13		11		9^{2}	14		34
1	2	3	4	5		6		7	11^{1}	8		12												14	13	10^{3}	9^{2}		35
1	2	3	4	5		7		6	10^{2}	9		8^{3}												13	12	11^{1}	14		36
1	2^{2}	3	4	5		7		6	11	9^{1}		12			13									10		8^{3}	14		37
1	3^{1}		4	10^{3}	6	2		8		7			14	11^{2}	12									9		13	5		38
1			4	5	13	7		2	11^{1}	8^{2}	6			10^{3}	3									9		12	14		39
1			4	5	14	7		2	11^{3}	10^{2}	6			8^{1}	13	3								9		12			40
1		3	4	5	14	7	12	2	11	9^{2}	6			8^{3}										10		13			41
1		3	4	5	13	8		2	11	10^{2}	7^{1}			6^{3}	12									9		14			42
1		2	3	4^{1}	12	6	14	5	10	11	7^{3}			8^{2}										9			13		43
1		3	4	5	12	7		2	11^{3}	9	6			10^{2}	14									8		13			44
	2	3		10	7	14		13			8^{2}		5^{3}		4									9	12	11^{1}	6	1	45
1	2	3	4	5^{2}	11	7^{2}		6	10			8			14									9^{4}		12	13		46

FA Cup

First Round	Barnet	(h)	3-1
Second Round	Crewe Alex	(h)	3-3
Replay	Crewe Alex	(a)	1-0
Third Round	Hull C	(h)	0-1

Carabao Cup

First Round	Coventry C	(a)	3-1
Second Round	Burnley	(h)	0-2

Checkatrade Trophy

Northern Group C	Stoke C U21	(h)	1-0
Northern Group C	Bury	(h)	0-1
Northern Group C	Rochdale	(a)	1-1
(Rochdale won 5-3 on penalties)			

BLACKPOOL

FOUNDATION

Old boys of St John's School, who had formed themselves into a football club, decided to establish a club bearing the name of their town and Blackpool FC came into being at a meeting at the Stanley Arms Hotel in the summer of 1887. In their first season playing at Raikes Hall Gardens, the club won both the Lancashire Junior Cup and the Fylde Cup.

Bloomfield Road, Seasiders Way, Blackpool, Lancashire FY1 6JJ.

Telephone: (01253) 401 953 (option 1).

Fax: (01253) 405 011.

Ticket Office: (0844) 847 1953.

Website: www.blackpoolfc.co.uk

Email: secretary@blackpoolfc.co.uk

Ground Capacity: 16,476.

Record Attendance: 38,098 v Wolverhampton W, Division 1, 17 September 1955.

Pitch Measurements: 100m × 64m (109.5yd × 70yd).

Chairwoman: Natalie Christopher.

Manager: Gary Bowyer.

Assistant Manager: Terry McPhillips.

Colours: Tangerine shirts with white trim, white shorts with tangerine trim, tangerine socks with white hoops.

Year Formed: 1887.

Turned Professional: 1887.

Previous Name: 'South Shore' combined with Blackpool in 1899, twelve years after the latter had been formed on the breaking up of the old 'Blackpool St John's' club.

Club Nickname: 'The Seasiders'.

Grounds: 1887, Raikes Hall Gardens; 1897, Athletic Grounds; 1899, Raikes Hall Gardens; 1899, Bloomfield Road.

First Football League Game: 5 September 1896, Division 2, v Lincoln C (a) L 1–3 – Douglas; Parr, Bowman; Stuart, Stirzaker, Norris; Clarkin, Donnelly, Robert Parkinson, Mount (1), Jack Parkinson.

Record League Victory: 7–0 v Reading, Division 2, 10 November 1928 – Mercer; Gibson, Hamilton, Watson, Wilson, Grant, Ritchie, Oxberry (2), Hampson (5), Tufnell, Neal. 7–0 v Preston NE (away), Division 1, 1 May 1948 – Robinson; Shimwell, Crosland; Buchan, Hayward, Kelly; Hobson, Munro (1), McIntosh (5), McCall, Rickett (1). 7–0 v Sunderland, Division 1, 5 October 1957 – Farm; Armfield, Garrett, Kelly J, Gratrix, Kelly H, Matthews, Taylor (2), Charnley (2), Durie (2), Perry (1).

Record Cup Victory: 7–1 v Charlton Ath, League Cup 2nd rd, 25 September 1963 – Harvey; Armfield, Martin; Crawford, Gratrix, Cranston; Lea, Ball (1), Charnley (4), Durie (1), Oates (1).

HONOURS

League Champions: Division 2 – 1929–30.
Runners-up: Division 1 – 1955–56; Division 2 – 1936–37, 1969–70; Division 4 – 1984–85.
FA Cup Winners: 1953.
Runners-up: 1948, 1951.
League Cup: semi-final – 1962.
League Trophy Winners: 2002, 2004.
Anglo-Italian Cup Winners: 1971.
Runners-up: 1972.

Sun FACT FILE

Blackpool played their home games at the Raikes Hall Pleasure Gardens in their first season as members of the Football League. Raikes Hall had been the Seasiders' home since the club's formation in 1887 and they were the first senior club to play home games at a seaside entertainment complex (New Brighton Tower, Southend United and Leith Athletic all did so, but later).

Record Defeat: 1–10 v Small Heath, Division 2, 2 March 1901 and v Huddersfield T, Division 1, 13 December 1930.

Most League Points (2 for a win): 58, Division 2, 1929–30 and Division 2, 1967–68.

Most League Points (3 for a win): 86, Division 4, 1984–85.

Most League Goals: 98, Division 2, 1929–30.

Highest League Scorer in Season: Jimmy Hampson, 45, Division 2, 1929–30.

Most League Goals in Total Aggregate: Jimmy Hampson, 248, 1927–38.

Most League Goals in One Match: 5, Jimmy Hampson v Reading, Division 2, 10 November 1928; 5, Jimmy McIntosh v Preston NE, Division 1, 1 May 1948.

Most Capped Player: Jimmy Armfield, 43, England.

Most League Appearances: Jimmy Armfield, 568, 1952–71.

Youngest League Player: Matty Kay, 16 years 32 days v Scunthorpe U, 13 November 2005.

Record Transfer Fee Received: £6,750,000 from Liverpool for Charlie Adam, July 2011.

Record Transfer Fee Paid: £1,250,000 to Leicester C for D.J. Campbell, August 2010.

Football League Record: 1896 Elected to Division 2; 1899 Failed re-election; 1900 Re-elected; 1900–30 Division 2; 1930–33 Division 1; 1933–37 Division 2; 1937–67 Division 1; 1967–70 Division 2; 1970–71 Division 1; 1971–78 Division 2; 1978–81 Division 3; 1981–85 Division 4; 1985–90 Division 3; 1990–92 Division 4; 1992–2000 Division 2; 2000–01 Division 3; 2001–04 Division 2; 2004–07 FL 1; 2007–10 FL C; 2010–11 FA Premier League; 2011–15 FL C; 2015–16 FL 1; 2016–17 FL 2; 2017– FL 1.

LATEST SEQUENCES

Longest Sequence of League Wins: 9, 21.11.1936 – 1.1.1937.

Longest Sequence of League Defeats: 8, 26.11.1898 – 7.1.1899.

Longest Sequence of League Draws: 5, 4.12.1976 – 1.1.1977.

Longest Sequence of Unbeaten League Matches: 17, 6.4.1968 – 21.9.1968.

Longest Sequence Without a League Win: 23, 7.2.2015 – 29.8.2015.

Successive Scoring Runs: 33 from 23.2.1929.

Successive Non-scoring Runs: 5 from 25.11.1989.

MANAGERS

Tom Barcroft 1903–33
  (*Secretary-Manager*)
John Cox 1909–11
Bill Norman 1919–23
Maj. Frank Buckley 1923–27
Sid Beaumont 1927–28
Harry Evans 1928–33
  (*Hon. Team Manager*)
Alex 'Sandy' Macfarlane 1933–35
Joe Smith 1935–58
Ronnie Suart 1958–67
Stan Mortensen 1967–69
Les Shannon 1969–70
Bob Stokoe 1970–72
Harry Potts 1972–76
Allan Brown 1976–78
Bob Stokoe 1978–79
Stan Ternent 1979–80
Alan Ball 1980–81
Allan Brown 1981–82
Sam Ellis 1982–89
Jimmy Mullen 1989–90
Graham Carr 1990
Bill Ayre 1990–94
Sam Allardyce 1994–96
Gary Megson 1996–97
Nigel Worthington 1997–99
Steve McMahon 2000–04
Colin Hendry 2004–05
Simon Grayson 2005–08
Ian Holloway 2009–12
Michael Appleton 2012–13
Paul Ince 2013–14
José Riga 2014
Lee Clark 2014–15
Neil McDonald 2015–16
Gary Bowyer June 2016–

TEN YEAR LEAGUE RECORD

		P	W	D	L	F	A	Pts	Pos
2008-09	FL C	46	13	17	16	47	58	56	16
2009-10	FL C	46	19	13	14	74	58	70	6
2010-11	PR Lge	38	10	9	19	55	78	39	19
2011-12	FL C	46	20	15	11	79	59	75	5
2012-13	FL C	46	14	17	15	62	63	59	15
2013-14	FL C	46	11	13	22	38	66	46	20
2014-15	FL C	46	4	14	28	36	91	26	24
2015-16	FL 1	46	12	10	24	40	63	46	22
2016-17	FL 2	46	18	16	12	69	46	70	7
2017-18	FL 1	46	15	15	16	60	55	60	12

DID YOU KNOW ?

On 10 June 1972 Blackpool defeated Lanerossi Vicenza 10-0 at Bloomfield Road in an Anglo-Italian Cup tie. The Seasiders were 4-0 up by half-time and had reached double figures by 71 minutes before relaxing a little. Goalscorers were Micky Burns 4, Mick Hill 2, Alan Ainscow, Alan Suddick, Glynn James and an own goal.

BLACKPOOL – SKY BET LEAGUE ONE 2017–18 LEAGUE RECORD

Match No.	Date	Venue	Opponents	Result		H/T Score	Lg Pos.	Goalscorers	Attendance
1	Aug 5	A	Bradford C	L	1-2	1-1	16	Daniel [43]	20,804
2	12	H	Milton Keynes D	W	1-0	1-0	11	Longstaff [6]	3412
3	19	A	Doncaster R	D	3-3	1-2	11	Longstaff [38], Turton [65], Cooke [76]	7558
4	26	H	Oldham Ath	W	2-1	2-0	8	Longstaff [6], Vassell [15]	4642
5	Sept 2	H	AFC Wimbledon	W	1-0	0-0	7	Longstaff [52]	3457
6	9	A	Scunthorpe U	D	0-0	0-0	7		4290
7	12	A	Plymouth Arg	W	3-1	1-0	5	Daniel [2], Ryan [70], Delfouneso [86]	7411
8	16	H	Oxford U	W	3-1	2-0	4	Vassell 2 [6, 90], Cooke [15]	5274
9	23	A	Bristol R	L	1-3	1-1	6	Vassell [12]	8431
10	26	H	Rochdale	D	0-0	0-0	6		3399
11	30	A	Southend U	L	1-2	0-1	9	Vassell [56]	6688
12	Oct 14	A	Walsall	D	1-1	0-1	11	Solomon-Otabor [65]	4503
13	17	H	Bury	W	2-1	1-0	7	Mellor [38], Tilt [73]	3437
14	21	H	Wigan Ath	L	1-3	1-1	9	Vassell [8]	5817
15	28	A	Northampton T	L	0-1	0-1	12		5213
16	Nov 11	H	Portsmouth	L	2-3	0-0	13	Solomon-Otabor [74], Hawkins (og) [83]	5032
17	18	A	Peterborough U	W	1-0	1-0	12	Vassell [21]	5254
18	21	A	Gillingham	D	1-1	1-0	10	Vassell [41]	2650
19	25	A	Fleetwood T	D	0-0	0-0	10		5035
20	28	H	Blackburn R	L	2-4	1-2	11	Mellor [29], Philliskirk [75]	5302
21	Dec 9	H	Rotherham U	L	1-2	1-0	13	Mellor [21]	3654
22	16	A	Shrewsbury T	L	0-1	0-0	14		5620
23	23	A	Charlton Ath	D	1-1	0-1	12	Robertson [90]	10,172
24	26	H	Scunthorpe U	L	2-3	1-2	15	Philliskirk [25], Longstaff [88]	3446
25	30	H	Plymouth Arg	D	2-2	0-2	15	Daniel [55], Solomon-Otabor [90]	3417
26	Jan 1	A	Rochdale	W	2-1	0-0	13	Delfouneso [54], Mellor [67]	3165
27	6	A	Oxford U	L	0-1	0-0	14		6775
28	13	H	Bristol R	D	0-0	0-0	16		4001
29	20	A	AFC Wimbledon	L	0-2	0-0	17		4286
30	Feb 3	A	Bury	D	1-1	0-0	19	Longstaff [53]	4089
31	10	H	Walsall	D	2-2	1-1	19	Delfouneso [37], Gnanduillet [88]	3404
32	13	A	Wigan Ath	W	2-0	2-0	17	Gnanduillet [3], Mellor [37]	8302
33	18	H	Peterborough U	D	1-1	1-1	17	Delfouneso [45]	3286
34	24	A	Portsmouth	W	2-0	1-0	16	Vassell [41], Robertson [63]	17,895
35	Mar 10	A	Blackburn R	L	0-3	0-1	17		13,230
36	13	H	Charlton Ath	W	1-0	0-0	14	Ryan [90]	3216
37	17	H	Southend U	D	1-1	1-1	14	Robertson [45]	3213
38	24	A	Milton Keynes D	D	0-0	0-0	14		8094
39	30	H	Doncaster R	L	1-2	0-1	16	Daniel [56]	4533
40	Apr 2	A	Oldham Ath	L	1-2	1-0	16	Vassell [37]	4309
41	7	H	Bradford C	W	5-0	3-0	15	Delfouneso 3 [16, 29, 70], Solomon-Otabor [22], Longstaff [80]	5337
42	10	H	Northampton T	W	3-0	1-0	12	Gnanduillet [42], Longstaff [62], Ryan [74]	2964
43	14	H	Fleetwood T	W	2-0	0-0	10	Solomon-Otabor [88], Gnanduillet [90]	7371
44	21	A	Gillingham	W	3-0	2-0	10	Vassell [28], Delfouneso [33], Mellor [83]	5580
45	28	H	Shrewsbury T	D	1-1	0-1	12	Delfouneso [56]	5825
46	May 5	A	Rotherham U	L	0-1	0-0	12		9512

Final League Position: 12

GOALSCORERS

League (60): Vassell 11, Delfouneso 9, Longstaff 8, Mellor 6, Solomon-Otabor 5, Daniel 4, Gnanduillet 4, Robertson 3, Ryan 3, Cooke 2, Philliskirk 2, Tilt 1, Turton 1, own goal 1.
FA Cup (1): Philliskirk 1.
Carabao Cup (1): Gnanduillet 1.
Checkatrade Trophy (8): Philliskirk 3, Clayton 1, D'Almeida 1, Longstaff 1, Mellor 1, Sinclair-Smith 1.

Allsop R 22	Robertson C 39	Tilt C 42	Aimson W 13 + 4	Turton O 41	Daniel C 43 + 1	Ryan J 36	Cooke C 19 + 11	Vassell K 29	Cullen M 3 + 6	Delfouneso N 29 + 11	Samuel B 2 + 2	Solomon-Otabor V 35 + 9	Gnanduillet A 9 + 17	Anderton N 3 + 1	Longstaff S 37 + 5	D'Almeida S 12 + 11	Mellor K 26 + 3	Quigley S — + 9	Spearing J 30 + 3	Clayton M — + 2	Taylor A 4 + 3	Philliskirk D 7 + 12	Menga D — + 8	Williams B 3	Mafoumbi C 4	Lumley J 17	Roache R — + 1	Agyei D 1 + 8	McAlister J — + 1	Match No.
1	2	3	4	5	6	7	8[3]	9	10[2]	11	12	13	14																	1
1	4	3	14	2	8	7			10[1]	13		9[2]	11	12	5	6[3]														2
1	3	4	2	5	8	7		12	10[1]	11[3]		14	13		9[2]	6														3
1	4	3	2	5		7	8[1]		10[3]	12	11[2]	9	14		6	13														4
1	4	3	2	5		7	8		10	11		9			6[1]	12														5
1	4	3	12	2	5	7		9	10	11					8[1]	6														6
1	4	3	2	5		7		9	10[3]	11[1]	13	12			8[2]	6	14													7
1	4	3	2	5		7	8		10[1]	12	11[3]				6[2]	14	9	13												8
1	3	4	2	5	9		8[3]	11	12	10[2]					7[1]	13	6	14												9
1	4	3	13	2	5	6[1]	9[3]	10	12	11					7	8[2]	14													10
1	4	3	12	2	5	6	13	10[1]		11		9[2]			8	7[1]		14												11
1	3	4		5	2	6	9	10[2]		11		12			8[2]	13				7[1]	14									12
1	4	3		2			13	10[1]		11		12			8[2]	7	9	14	6[3]	5										13
1		4	3	7	5				10[1]	9		11	14		13	6[2]	2	8	12[3]											14
1		3	4	2	5[3]		8			10		14	11[2]		7[1]	9		6	12	13										15
1		4	3	2	5	7	9[1]			11		6	13		8				10[2]	12										16
1		4	3	2	5		7	10[2]		12		11[3]	13		6[1]	14	9	8												17
1		3	4	5	11		7[1]	10[3]				9[2]	14		8	13	2	6		12										18
1	3[1]	4	5	10[3]		9	13	11[2]		12		6			7	2	8	14												19
1		3	5	10	6[1]	14		11		8		4[1]	9[3]		2	7						13	12							20
1	4		3	11		7	13	10[2]		12		9			8[3]	2	6[1]		5	14										21
1	3	4			5	8	10	11[2]		6	13	9[3]			2	14	7		12											22
	3	4		9	7	6[2]				13	10	12	8	2	14				5[1]	11[3]		1								23
	4	3		5	7[3]		10[1]			11		8	6[2]	2	12	13		9	14	1										24
	4	3		11			13			12	10[1]	8	6[3]	2	7			5[2]	9	14	1									25
	4	3	5[2]	11	7[4]	6[1]			10	9		13		8		2	14			12		1								26
	3	4	5[2]	11		12			10[3]	9		8	6[1]	2	14		7		13			1								27
	5		4	2	6	8[3]			11[2]		12	10	9[1]	3		7	13							1	14					28
	4		5	2	6		12	11[3]	14	13		7	9[1]	3	8									1	10[2]					29
	3	4		5	13		6	10[1]		11[2]		8			2		7[1]		14					1						30
	3	4		5[3]			6[2]	10[1]		9		11	13		8	14	2		7					1	12					31
	4	3		5	8	6[1]			10	9[2]	11			7	13	2	12							1						32
	4	3		8	5	6			10	9[2]	11			7[1]	13	2			12					1						33
	4	3		2	5[1]	7		9[3]	10	11[2]	13				6		8	14	12					1						34
	3	4		2	5	6	11[3]	8	10[2]	12		9			7[1]				14					1			13			35
	4	3		2	5	7	11[2]	8[3]	10			9[1]	14		6				12					1			13			36
	4	3		2	5	6	11[2]			8	13	9[1]			7		10							1			12			37
	3	4		2	5	6	11[1]	9	10			12			7		8[2]							1			13			38
	3	4	2[2]	5	9	8			11[3]	13	10				7[1]		6		12	14				1						39
	3	4		5	9	7[2]	8[1]	10[3]	14	11	13	12			6		2							1						40
	4	3		2	5	6	14	11[3]	12	8[1]		10			9[2]		7		13					1						41
	3	4		2	5	6	14		12	8		10[2]	11[1]		9[3]		7							1			13			42
	4	3		2	5	6	11[2]	12	8[3]	10		13			9		7		14					1						43
	3	4		2	5	6	11[1]		8[2]	10	13	9[3]	12		7									1				14		44
	4	3		2	5	7		13	8[3]	10	11[2]	9[1]	12		6								1				14			45
	4	3		2	5	8[1]	12		14	10		9[2]	11[3]		6	7							1				13			46

FA Cup
First Round   Boreham Wood   (a)   1-2

Carabao Cup
First Round   Wigan Ath   (a)   1-2

Checkatrade Trophy
Northern Group B   Wigan Ath   (h)   1-1
(Wigan Ath won 5-4 on penalties)
Northern Group B   Accrington S   (a)   2-1
Northern Group B   Middlesbrough U21   (h)   4-1
Second Round North   Mansfield T   (h)   1-1
(Blackpool won 5-4 on penalties)
Third Round   Shrewsbury T   (a)   0-0
(Shrewsbury T won 4-2 on penalties)

BOLTON WANDERERS

FOUNDATION

In 1874 boys of Christ Church Sunday School, Blackburn Street, led by their master Thomas Ogden, established a football club which went under the name of the school and whose president was vicar of Christ Church. Membership was 6d (two and a half pence). When their president began to lay down too many rules about the use of church premises, the club broke away and formed Bolton Wanderers in 1877, holding their earliest meetings at the Gladstone Hotel.

Macron Stadium, Burnden Way, Lostock, Bolton BL6 6JW.

Telephone: (01204) 673 673. *Fax:* (01204) 673 773.

Ticket Office: (0844) 871 2932.

Website: www.bwfc.co.uk

Email: reception@bwfc.co.uk (or via website).

Ground Capacity: 28,018.

Record Attendance: 69,912 v Manchester C, FA Cup 5th rd, 18 February 1933 (at Burnden Park); 28,353 v Leicester C, FA Premier League, 23 December 2003 (at The Reebok Stadium).

Pitch Measurements: 102m × 65m (112yd × 71yd).

Chairman: Ken Anderson.

Manager: Phil Parkinson.

Assistant Manager: Steve Parkin.

HONOURS

League Champions: First Division – 1996–97; Division 2 – 1908–09, 1977–78; Division 3 – 1972–73. *Runners-up:* Division 2 – 1899–1900, 1904–05, 1910–11, 1934–35; Second Division – 1992–93; FL 1 – 2016–17.

FA Cup Winners: 1923, 1926, 1929, 1958. *Runners-up:* 1894, 1904, 1953.

League Cup: Runners-up: 1995, 2004.

League Trophy Winners: 1989. *Runners-up:* 1986.

European Competitions
UEFA Cup: 2005–06, 2007–08.

Colours: White shirts with blue and red trim, blue shorts with white and red trim, blue socks with red trim.

Year Formed: 1874.

Turned Professional: 1880.

Previous Name: 1874, Christ Church FC; 1877, Bolton Wanderers.

Club Nickname: 'The Trotters'.

Grounds: Park Recreation Ground and Cockle's Field before moving to Pike's Lane ground 1881; 1895, Burnden Park; 1997, Reebok Stadium (renamed Macron Stadium 2014).

First Football League Game: 8 September 1888, Football League, v Derby Co (h) L 3–6 – Harrison; Robinson, Mitchell; Roberts, Weir, Bullough, Davenport (2), Milne, Coupar, Barbour, Brogan (1).

Record League Victory: 8–0 v Barnsley, Division 2, 6 October 1934 – Jones; Smith, Finney; Goslin, Atkinson, George Taylor; George T. Taylor (2), Eastham, Milsom (1), Westwood (4), Cook, (1 og).

Record Cup Victory: 13–0 v Sheffield U, FA Cup 2nd rd, 1 February 1890 – Parkinson (1), Jones; Bullough, Davenport, Roberts; Rushton, Brogan (3), Cassidy (5), McNee, Weir (4).

Record Defeat: 1–9 v Preston NE, FA Cup 2nd rd, 5 November 1887.

THE Sun FACT FILE

After finishing fourth from bottom of the Third Division table in 1987, Bolton Wanderers were required to take part in the end-of-season play-offs to avoid relegation. In the semi-final they lost out 3-2 on aggregate to Aldershot, who had finished in sixth place in Division Four, and so were relegated.

Most League Points (2 for a win): 61, Division 3, 1972–73.

Most League Points (3 for a win): 98, Division 1, 1996–97.

Most League Goals: 100, Division 1, 1996–97.

Highest League Scorer in Season: Joe Smith, 38, Division 1, 1920–21.

Most League Goals in Total Aggregate: Nat Lofthouse, 255, 1946–61.

Most League Goals in One Match: 5, Tony Caldwell v Walsall, Division 3, 10 September 1983.

Most Capped Player: Ricardo Gardner, 72 (112), Jamaica.

Most League Appearances: Eddie Hopkinson, 519, 1956–70.

Youngest League Player: Ray Parry, 15 years 267 days v Wolverhampton W, 13 October 1951.

Record Transfer Fee Received: £15,000,000 from Chelsea for Nicolas Anelka, January 2008.

Record Transfer Fee Paid: £8,250,000 to Toulouse for Johan Elmander, June 2008.

Football League Record: 1888 Founder Member of the League; 1899–1900 Division 2; 1900–03 Division 1; 1903–05 Division 2; 1905–08 Division 1; 1908–09 Division 2; 1909–10 Division 1; 1910–11 Division 2; 1911–33 Division 1; 1933–35 Division 2; 1935–64 Division 1; 1964–71 Division 2; 1971–73 Division 3; 1973–78 Division 2; 1978–80 Division 1; 1980–83 Division 2; 1983–87 Division 3; 1987–88 Division 4; 1988–92 Division 3; 1992–93 Division 2; 1993–95 Division 1; 1995–96 FA Premier League; 1996–97 Division 1; 1997–98 FA Premier League; 1998–2001 Division 1; 2001–12 FA Premier League; 2012–16 FL C; 2016–17 FL 1; 2017– FL C.

LATEST SEQUENCES

Longest Sequence of League Wins: 11, 5.11.1904 – 2.1.1905.

Longest Sequence of League Defeats: 11, 7.4.1902 – 18.10.1902.

Longest Sequence of League Draws: 6, 25.1.1913 – 8.3.1913.

Longest Sequence of Unbeaten League Matches: 23, 13.10.1990 – 9.3.1991.

Longest Sequence Without a League Win: 26, 7.4.1902 – 10.1.1903.

Successive Scoring Runs: 24 from 22.11.1996.

Successive Non-scoring Runs: 7 from 25.8.2017.

MANAGERS

Tom Rawthorne 1874–85 (*Secretary*)
J. J. Bentley 1885–86 (*Secretary*)
W. G. Struthers 1886–87 (*Secretary*)
Fitzroy Norris 1887 (*Secretary*)
J. J. Bentley 1887–95 (*Secretary*)
Harry Downs 1895–96 (*Secretary*)
Frank Brettell 1896–98 (*Secretary*)
John Somerville 1898–1910
Will Settle 1910–15
Tom Mather 1915–19
Charles Foweraker 1919–44
Walter Rowley 1944–50
Bill Ridding 1951–68
Nat Lofthouse 1968–70
Jimmy McIlroy 1970
Jimmy Meadows 1971
Nat Lofthouse 1971 (*then Admin. Manager to 1972*)
Jimmy Armfield 1971–74
Ian Greaves 1974–80
Stan Anderson 1980–81
George Mulhall 1981–82
John McGovern 1982–85
Charlie Wright 1985
Phil Neal 1985–92
Bruce Rioch 1992–95
Roy McFarland 1995–96
Colin Todd 1996–99
Roy McFarland and Colin Todd 1995–96
Sam Allardyce 1999–2007
Sammy Lee 2007
Gary Megson 2007–09
Owen Coyle 2010–12
Dougie Freedman 2012–14
Neil Lennon 2014–16
Phil Parkinson June 2016–

TEN YEAR LEAGUE RECORD

		P	W	D	L	F	A	Pts	Pos
2008-09	PR Lge	38	11	8	19	41	53	41	13
2009-10	PR Lge	38	10	9	19	42	67	39	14
2010-11	PR Lge	38	12	10	16	52	56	46	14
2011-12	PR Lge	38	10	6	22	46	77	36	18
2012-13	FL C	46	18	14	14	69	61	68	7
2013-14	FL C	46	14	17	15	59	60	59	14
2014-15	FL C	46	13	12	21	54	67	51	18
2015-16	FL C	46	5	15	26	41	81	30	24
2016-17	FL 1	46	25	11	10	68	36	86	2
2017-18	FL C	46	10	13	23	39	74	43	21

DID YOU KNOW ?

Bolton Wanderers' first experience of competitive European football came in the short-lived Friendship Cup in the 1960–61 season. Wanderers were drawn to play French club Le Havre. The first game finished at 1-1 with Bolton winning the second leg 4-0 at Burnden Park.

BOLTON WANDERERS – SKY BET CHAMPIONSHIP 2017–18 LEAGUE RECORD

Match No.	Date	Venue	Opponents	Result	H/T Score	Lg Pos.	Goalscorers	Attendance
1	Aug 6	H	Leeds U	L 2-3	1-3	16	Madine [39], Le Fondre (pen) [67]	19,857
2	12	A	Millwall	D 1-1	0-0	16	Morais [62]	12,238
3	15	A	Birmingham C	D 0-0	0-0	18		20,215
4	19	H	Derby Co	L 1-2	0-2	22	Madine [90]	15,175
5	25	A	Hull C	L 0-4	0-3	23		16,207
6	Sept 9	H	Middlesbrough	L 0-3	0-1	24		17,385
7	12	H	Sheffield U	L 0-1	0-1	24		14,346
8	16	A	Ipswich T	L 0-2	0-0	24		14,164
9	23	H	Brentford	L 0-3	0-1	24		13,897
10	26	A	Bristol C	L 0-2	0-1	24		17,203
11	30	A	Aston Villa	L 0-1	0-1	24		31,451
12	Oct 14	H	Sheffield W	W 2-1	1-0	24	Ameobi [10], Hutchinson (og) [61]	17,967
13	21	H	QPR	D 1-1	1-0	24	Pratley [22]	14,243
14	28	A	Fulham	D 1-1	1-0	24	Ameobi [28]	18,792
15	31	A	Sunderland	D 3-3	1-1	24	Ameobi [32], Madine [60], Henry [67]	26,395
16	Nov 4	H	Norwich C	W 2-1	2-0	23	Madine [35], Armstrong [40]	14,786
17	17	A	Preston NE	D 0-0	0-0	22		15,213
18	21	H	Reading	D 2-2	2-0	23	Burke [18], Pratley [23]	13,113
19	25	A	Wolverhampton W	L 1-5	0-2	24	Buckley [74]	27,894
20	Dec 2	H	Barnsley	W 3-1	2-1	21	Madine 2 (1 pen) [20, 39 (p)], Little [69]	14,371
21	9	A	Nottingham F	L 2-3	1-1	21	Buckley [45], Worrall (og) [90]	22,882
22	16	A	Burton Alb	L 0-1	0-1	23		13,632
23	23	H	Cardiff C	W 2-0	0-0	23	Madine (pen) [75], Vela [88]	15,344
24	26	A	Middlesbrough	L 0-2	0-0	23		29,443
25	30	A	Sheffield U	W 1-0	1-0	22	Madine [21]	28,387
26	Jan 1	H	Hull C	W 1-0	1-0	20	Madine [20]	14,216
27	13	A	Brentford	L 0-2	0-1	21		9507
28	20	H	Ipswich T	D 1-1	0-0	20	Madine [53]	13,870
29	Feb 2	H	Bristol C	W 1-0	0-0	19	Ameobi [71]	14,172
30	10	H	Fulham	D 1-1	0-1	19	Le Fondre [61]	14,386
31	13	A	Cardiff C	L 0-2	0-2	19		16,013
32	17	A	QPR	L 0-2	0-0	20		12,638
33	20	H	Sunderland	W 1-0	1-0	19	Clough [17]	14,915
34	24	A	Norwich C	D 0-0	0-0	19		25,475
35	Mar 3	H	Preston NE	L 1-3	1-0	19	Beevers [12]	18,141
36	6	A	Reading	D 1-1	1-1	19	Le Fondre [45]	8631
37	10	A	Sheffield W	D 1-1	0-0	20	Wilbraham [90]	26,809
38	17	H	Aston Villa	W 1-0	1-0	19	Le Fondre [19]	19,304
39	30	A	Leeds U	L 1-2	0-1	20	Le Fondre [53]	35,377
40	Apr 3	H	Birmingham C	L 0-1	0-1	20		21,097
41	7	A	Derby Co	L 0-3	0-2	21		25,723
42	10	H	Millwall	L 0-2	0-1	21		13,810
43	14	A	Barnsley	D 2-2	2-1	21	Le Fondre (pen) [82], Noone [85]	14,138
44	21	H	Wolverhampton W	L 0-4	0-2	21		19,092
45	28	A	Burton Alb	L 0-2	0-2	23		6535
46	May 6	H	Nottingham F	W 3-2	0-0	21	Le Fondre [67], Wheater [86], Wilbraham [88]	18,289

Final League Position: 21

GOALSCORERS

League (39): Madine 10 (2 pens), Le Fondre 7 (2 pens), Ameobi 4, Buckley 2, Pratley 2, Wilbraham 2, Armstrong 1, Beevers 1, Burke 1, Clough 1, Henry 1, Little 1, Morais 1, Noone 1, Vela 1, Wheater 1, own goals 2.
FA Cup (1): Osede 1.
Carabao Cup (5): Armstrong 2 (1 pen), Dervite 1, Karacan 1, Osede 1.

Howard M 7+1	Darby S 3	Dervite D 13+1	Wheater D 32+1	Beevers M 44	Taylor A 20	Vela J 26+4	Cullen J 9+3	Karacan J 14+2	Madine G 28	Le Fondre A 15+20	Burke R 22+3	Buckley W 14+10	Armstrong A 14+6	Little M 27+1	Pratley D 31+1	Morais F 17+16	Wilbraham A 3+20	Osede D 13+4	Alnwick B 39	Robinson A 26+4	Noone C 6+18	Henry K 33	King J 1	Ameobi S 33+2	Charsley H 1	Walker T 3+2	Clough 22+7	Flanagan J 8+1	Kirchhoff J 2+2	Match No.
1	2[2]	3	4[3]	5	6	7	8	9[1]	10	11	12	13	14																	1
1		3		5	6		8	9	10[2]	11[3]	4			13	2[1]	7	12	14												2
1	2		4		9	7	8	11[2]	12	3		10[1]			6	5		13												3
1		3		5	6[3]		8	9	11	12	4		13	10[2]	7	2	14													4
1			4	5	6			9[2]	10	14	3	7[1]	11	12	2	13														5
	2[3]	3	4				13	8[2]	11	14		12			9	10	6[1]		1	5	7									6
			4	5			8	9	10	13	3	7[1]	11[3]		2	12	14		1	6[2]										7
			4	5			8	9	11[2]	13	3	12			2[3]	10[1]	14		1	6	7									8
			4	5			8	9	10		12	3[1]	11[3]		2	7	14		1	6[2]	13									9
1		3	4	5						11[1]		13			2	7	14			6[2]		8		9[3]	12					10
1		3	4	5[2]				9[3]	11	13		10			2	8				14	12	6		7[1]						11
		3	4	5	9[1]				14	11		10[1]			2	6	12			1		13		7		8[3]				12
		3	4	5	9[1]				14	11		10[3]			2	6	12			1		13		7		8[2]				13
		3	4	5[2]	9[1]				14	11		10			2	6	13			1	12			7		8[2]				14
		3	4		9					11		10[1]			2	6				1		5	12	7		8				15
		3	4		9					11		12	10[1]		2	6				1		5		7		8				16
		3	4		9[2]					11		12	10[1]		2	6	13			1		5		7		8[3]				17
		3			9[2]					11	14	4	12	10[1]	2	6				1		5	13	7		8[3]				18
		3	4		9					11	14		13	10[2]	2	6[3]				1		5	12	7		8[1]				19
			4		9					11[2]		3	10[3]	12	2	6		14		1		5	13	7		8[1]				20
			4		9					11		3	10[3]	12	2[3]	6[3]		14		1		5	13	7		8				21
	2[2]	3	4		9					11			10		6[3]	12	14		1		5	13	7[1]	8						22
		3	4	5	9					11[1]			10[2]		2	6	13		1			12	7	8						23
		3	4	5[1]	9					11[2]			13		2	6	14		1	12		8[3]	7	10						24
			4	5		14	7[2]		10	11[1]	3		13	12	8	2[3]			1	6			9							25
			4		9		12		11	14	3	10[3]			2	6[1]	13		1	5		7[2]		8						26
		3	4		6					11	13			12		2	10[1]	14	7	1	5			8	9[2]					27
		4	3		9					11[1]			10[3]		2		12	14	6	1	5	13	7	8[2]						28
	2	3	4		8					5[1]			13			6	1	9			7		10		11[2]	12			29
	2	3	4		8					5[2]			13		7	1	9		6		10[3]	14	11[1]						30
	2	12	4		8					10	3[2]				5		6[3]	1	9		11[1]		14	13						31
		3	4		8[2]			12		13	2			5[4]		14		6[1]	1	9		7	11	10[1]						32
5	4	3	6					8[2]		12	14			2	11[3]	13			9	7			10[1]						33
	3	4[3]	5					9	11[1]	8[2]			7	2	12	14	1		6		10			13					34
	3	4	5		9			8[3]	12			7[2]	2	14	1	6			10		11[1]		13						35
			4	5				13		11	3	10[3]		9	8[3]	14	1			12	7			2	6[1]				36
			4	5						11	3	10[2]		9	12	13	7[3]	1			6	8		14	2[1]				37
			4	5	12					11	3	10[2]		9[1]			7	1	13		6	8		2					38
			4	5[2]	9					11	3	10[1]			12	13	6	1			12	7[2]	8	14	2	7[3]			39
			4	5	9					11	3	10[1]					6[3]	1		12	7[2]	8		13	2	14			40
		4	5		7		9		10	3[1]				2		11[2]	14	1	6	12	8[3]	13							41
		3	4	5	14					11					9[1]	13		6[3]	1		8[2]	7	10		12	2			42
	14	4	5							11	3[1]	12		2[3]	8	10[2]		1	6	13	9	7							43
		3	4		12					11[2]		10[3]			6[1]	8		1	5	13	7	9		14	2					44
	3		4	5						11		12			9	13	14	7	1		8	6[1]	10			2[3]				45
12		4	3		9					13					2	6[3]	10[1]	11		1[2]	5	14	7	8						46

FA Cup

Third Round	Huddersfield T	(h)	1-2

Carabao Cup

First Round	Crewe Alex	(a)	2-1
Second Round	Sheffield W	(h)	3-2
Third Round	West Ham U	(a)	0-3

AFC BOURNEMOUTH

FOUNDATION

There was a Bournemouth FC as early as 1875, but the present club arose out of the remnants of the Boscombe St John's club (formed 1890). The meeting at which Boscombe FC came into being was held at a house in Gladstone Road in 1899. They began by playing in the Boscombe and District Junior League.

Vitality Stadium, Dean Court, Kings Park, Bournemouth, Dorset BH7 7AF.

Telephone: (0344) 576 1910.

Fax: (01202) 726 373.

Ticket Office: (0344) 576 1910.

Website: www.afcb.co.uk

Email: enquiries@afcb.co.uk

Ground Capacity: 11,360.

Record Attendance: 28,799 v Manchester U, FA Cup 6th rd, 2 March 1957.

Pitch Measurements: 105m × 68m (115yd × 74.5yd).

Chairman: Jeff Mostyn.

Chief Executive: Neill Blake.

Manager: Eddie Howe.

Assistant Manager: Jason Tindall.

Colours: Red and black striped shirts, black shorts with red trim, black socks with red trim.

Year Formed: 1899.

Turned Professional: 1910.

Previous Names: 1890, Boscombe St John's; 1899, Boscombe FC; 1923, Bournemouth & Boscombe Ath FC; 1972, AFC Bournemouth.

Club Nickname: 'Cherries'.

Grounds: 1899, Castlemain Road, Pokesdown; 1910, Dean Court (renamed Fitness First Stadium 2001, Seward Stadium 2011, Goldsands Stadium 2012, Vitality Stadium 2015).

First Football League Game: 25 August 1923, Division 3 (S), v Swindon T (a) L 1–3 – Heron; Wingham, Lamb; Butt, Charles Smith, Voisey; Miller, Lister (1), Davey, Simpson, Robinson.

Record League Victory: 8–0 v Birmingham C, FL C, 25 October 2014 – Boruc; Francis, Elphick, Cook, Daniels; Ritchie (1), Arter (Gosling), Surman, Pugh (3); Pitman (1) (Rantie 2 (1 pen)), Wilson (1) (Fraser). 10–0 win v Northampton T at start of 1939–40 expunged from the records on outbreak of war.

Record Cup Victory: 11–0 v Margate, FA Cup 1st rd, 20 November 1971 – Davies; Machin (1), Kitchener, Benson, Jones, Powell, Cave (1), Boyer, MacDougall (9 incl. 1p), Miller, Scott (De Garis).

Record Defeat: 0–9 v Lincoln C, Division 3, 18 December 1982.

HONOURS

League Champions: FL C – 2014–15; Division 3 – 1986–87.
Runners-up: FL 1 – 2012–13; Division 3S – 1947–48; FL 2 – 2009–10; Division 4 – 1970–71.
FA Cup: 6th rd – 1957.
League Cup: quarter-final – 2015.
League Trophy Winners: 1984.
Runners-up: 1998.

The Sun FACT FILE

Striker Ted MacDougall was considered so important to Bournemouth's 1970–71 promotion campaign that the club insured him for £85,000 against serious injury (equivalent to around £840,000 today). MacDougall remained injury free and finished the campaign with an all-time club record of 42 League goals.

Most League Points (2 for a win): 62, Division 3, 1971–72.

Most League Points (3 for a win): 97, Division 3, 1986–87.

Most League Goals: 98, FL C, 2014–15.

Highest League Scorer in Season: Ted MacDougall, 42, 1970–71.

Most League Goals in Total Aggregate: Ron Eyre, 202, 1924–33.

Most League Goals in One Match: 4, Jack Russell v Clapton Orient, Division 3 (S), 7 January 1933; 4, Jack Russell v Bristol C, Division 3 (S), 28 January 1933; 4, Harry Mardon v Southend U, Division 3 (S), 1 January 1938; 4, Jack McDonald v Torquay U, Division 3 (S), 8 November 1947; 4, Ted MacDougall v Colchester U, 18 September 1970; 4, Brian Clark v Rotherham U, 10 October 1972; 4, Luther Blissett v Hull C, 29 November 1988; 4, James Hayter v Bury, Division 2, 21 October 2000.

Most Capped Player: Tokelo Rantie, 24 (41), South Africa.

Most League Appearances: Steve Fletcher, 628, 1992–2007; 2008–13.

Youngest League Player: Jimmy White, 15 years 321 days v Brentford, 30 April 1958.

Record Transfer Fee Received: £12,000,000 from Newcastle U for Matt Ritchie, July 2016.

Record Transfer Fee Paid: £20,000,000 to Chelsea for Nathan Ake, June 2017.

Football League Record: 1923 Elected to Division 3 (S) and remained a Third Division club for record number of years until 1970; 1970–71 Division 4; 1971–75 Division 3; 1975–82 Division 4; 1982–87 Division 3; 1987–90 Division 2; 1990–92 Division 3; 1992–2002 Division 3; 2002–03 Division 3; 2003–04 Division 2; 2004–08 FL 1; 2008–10 FL 2; 2010–13 FL 1; 2013–15 FL C; 2015– FA Premier League.

MANAGERS

Vincent Kitcher 1914–23
(*Secretary-Manager*)
Harry Kinghorn 1923–25
Leslie Knighton 1925–28
Frank Richards 1928–30
Billy Birrell 1930–35
Bob Crompton 1935–36
Charlie Bell 1936–39
Harry Kinghorn 1939–47
Harry Lowe 1947–50
Jack Bruton 1950–56
Fred Cox 1956–58
Don Welsh 1958–61
Bill McGarry 1961–63
Reg Flewin 1963–65
Fred Cox 1965–70
John Bond 1970–73
Trevor Hartley 1974–75
John Benson 1975–78
Alec Stock 1979–80
David Webb 1980–82
Don Megson 1983
Harry Redknapp 1983–92
Tony Pulis 1992–94
Mel Machin 1994–2000
Sean O'Driscoll 2000–06
Kevin Bond 2006–08
Jimmy Quinn 2008
Eddie Howe 2008–11
Lee Bradbury 2011–12
Paul Groves 2012
Eddie Howe October 2012–

LATEST SEQUENCES

Longest Sequence of League Wins: 8, 12.3.2013 – 20.4.2013.

Longest Sequence of League Defeats: 7, 13.8.1994 – 13.9.1994.

Longest Sequence of League Draws: 5, 25.4.2000 – 19.8.2000.

Longest Sequence of Unbeaten League Matches: 18, 6.3.1982 – 28.8.1982.

Longest Sequence Without a League Win: 14, 6.3.1974 – 27.4.1974.

Successive Scoring Runs: 31 from 28.10.2000.

Successive Non-scoring Runs: 6 from 1.2.1975.

TEN YEAR LEAGUE RECORD

		P	W	D	L	F	A	Pts	Pos
2008-09	FL 2	46	17	12	17	59	51	46*	21
2009-10	FL 2	46	25	8	13	61	44	83	2
2010-11	FL 1	46	19	14	13	75	54	71	6
2011-12	FL 1	46	15	13	18	48	52	58	11
2012-13	FL 1	46	24	11	11	76	53	83	2
2013-14	FL C	46	18	12	16	67	66	66	10
2014-15	FL C	46	26	12	8	98	45	90	1
2015-16	PR Lge	38	11	9	18	45	67	42	16
2016-17	PR Lge	38	12	10	16	55	67	46	9
2017-18	PR Lge	38	11	11	16	45	61	44	12

17 pts deducted.

DID YOU KNOW ?

Bournemouth played their 3,000th regular season Football League game at Plymouth Argyle on 3 May 1997. The game resulted in a 0-0 draw as the Cherries finished the season with just a single defeat in the last 11 matches.

AFC BOURNEMOUTH – PREMIER LEAGUE 2017–18 LEAGUE RECORD

Match No.	Date	Venue	Opponents	Result	H/T Score	Lg Pos.	Goalscorers	Attendance
1	Aug 12	A	WBA	L	0-1	0-1	17		25,011
2	19	H	Watford	L	0-2	0-0	17		10,501
3	26	H	Manchester C	L	1-2	1-1	18	Daniels [13]	10,419
4	Sept 9	A	Arsenal	L	0-3	0-2	19		59,262
5	15	H	Brighton & HA	W	2-1	0-0	19	Surman [67], Defoe [73]	10,369
6	23	A	Everton	L	1-2	0-0	19	King [49]	38,133
7	30	H	Leicester C	D	0-0	0-0	19		10,444
8	Oct 14	A	Tottenham H	L	0-1	0-0	19		73,502
9	21	A	Stoke C	W	2-1	2-0	19	Surman [16], Stanislas (pen) [18]	29,500
10	28	H	Chelsea	L	0-1	0-0	19		10,998
11	Nov 4	A	Newcastle U	W	1-0	0-0	16	Cook, S [90]	52,237
12	18	H	Huddersfield T	W	4-0	2-0	13	Wilson, C 3 [26, 31, 84], Arter [70]	10,879
13	25	A	Swansea C	D	0-0	0-0	12		20,228
14	29	H	Burnley	L	1-2	0-1	15	King [79]	10,302
15	Dec 3	A	Southampton	D	1-1	1-0	14	Fraser [42]	10,764
16	9	A	Crystal Palace	D	2-2	2-2	14	Defoe 2 [10, 45]	24,823
17	13	A	Manchester U	L	0-1	0-1	14		74,798
18	17	H	Liverpool	L	0-4	0-3	16		10,780
19	23	A	Manchester C	L	0-4	0-1	18		54,270
20	26	H	West Ham U	D	3-3	1-1	18	Gosling [29], Ake [57], Wilson, C [90]	10,596
21	30	H	Everton	W	2-1	1-0	14	Fraser 2 [33, 88]	10,497
22	Jan 1	A	Brighton & HA	D	2-2	1-1	14	Cook, S [33], Wilson, C [79]	30,152
23	14	H	Arsenal	W	2-1	0-0	13	Wilson, C [70], Ibe [74]	10,836
24	20	A	West Ham U	D	1-1	0-0	12	Fraser [71]	56,948
25	31	A	Chelsea	W	3-0	0-0	10	Wilson, C [51], Stanislas [64], Ake [67]	41,464
26	Feb 3	H	Stoke C	W	2-1	0-1	9	King [70], Mousset [79]	10,614
27	11	A	Huddersfield T	L	1-4	1-2	10	Stanislas [13]	23,823
28	24	H	Newcastle U	D	2-2	0-2	11	Smith, A [80], Gosling [89]	10,808
29	Mar 3	A	Leicester C	D	1-1	1-0	11	King (pen) [35]	31,384
30	11	H	Tottenham H	L	1-4	1-1	12	Stanislas [7]	10,623
31	17	H	WBA	W	2-1	0-0	10	Ibe [77], Stanislas [89]	10,242
32	31	A	Watford	D	2-2	1-1	10	King (pen) [43], Defoe [90]	20,393
33	Apr 7	H	Crystal Palace	D	2-2	0-0	11	Mousset [65], King [89]	10,730
34	14	A	Liverpool	L	0-3	0-1	11		52,959
35	18	H	Manchester U	L	0-2	0-1	11		10,952
36	28	A	Southampton	L	1-2	1-1	12	King [45]	31,778
37	May 5	H	Swansea C	W	1-0	1-0	12	Fraser [37]	10,820
38	13	A	Burnley	W	2-1	0-1	12	King [74], Wilson, C [90]	20,720

Final League Position: 12

GOALSCORERS

League (45): King 8 (2 pens), Wilson, C 8, Fraser 5, Stanislas 5 (1 pen), Defoe 4, Ake 2, Cook, S 2, Gosling 2, Ibe 2, Mousset 2, Surman 2, Arter 1, Daniels 1, Smith, A 1.
FA Cup (2): Cook S 1, Mousset 1.
Carabao Cup (7): Afobe 1, Fraser 1, Gosling 1, King 1, Pugh 1, Simpson 1, Wilson C 1 (1 pen).

Begovic A 38	Francis S 31+1	Cook S 31+3	Ake N 37+1	Daniels C 34+1	Fraser R 23+3	Surman A 20+5	Arter H 11+2	Pugh M 11+9	King J 27+6	Afobe B 5+12	Ibe J 11+13	Defoe J 22+10	Smith A 22+5	Mousset L 4+19	Mings T 3+1	Gosling D 21+7	Stanislas J 17+2	Cook L 25+4	Wilson C 23+5	Simpson J 1	Hyndman E 1	Match No.
1	2[1]	3	4	5	6	7	8	9[1]	10	11[2]	12	13	14									1
1		3	4	5	6[2]	7	8	13	10	11[3]		9[1]	12	2	14							2
1		3	4	6		8		9	10		12[2]		11	2	13	5	7					3
1	13	2	3	9	6[1]		8		10		12		11[3]	5	14	4[2]	7					4
1		3	4	5	6[2]	8	7	9	10[3]	13	12	11[1]		2			14					5
1		3	13	4[3]	5		8		10[1]	12	6	11[2]		2	14			7	9			6
1		3	4	5	14		8	9[1]	10	13	12	11[1]		2		6[3]	7					7
1		3	4	5	6		8		11		12	13		2[1]	14	10	9[3]	7[2]				8
1		3	12	4	5		8	13	14	11	6[1]			2		10[3]		9	7[2]			9
1	2	3	4	8		7		13	10[3]	12	11[1]		5			9[2]	6	14				10
1	2	3	4	5		7	8	9	11		6[2]	13	12					10[1]				11
1	2[4]	3	4	5		7	8[2]	9	10[3]		6[1]		12			13	14	11				12
1		3	4	5		7	8[3]	9	10	12	6[1]		2			13		14	11[2]			13
1	2	3	4	5	14	7	8[1]	9[2]	10		6[3]	13						12	11			14
1		3	4	5	9[1]		8		10	14	12	11[3]		2		6[2]	7	13				15
1	2	3	4	5	9[3]		8		10	14	12	11[2]				6[1]	7	13				16
1		3	4	5	9		8	10	12			13	2			7[1]	6[1]	14	11[2]			17
1		3	14	4	5[2]	13	8	9[1]	10[1]	6	11		2				12	7				18
1	2	3			8	7		12	9	14		5	13			6	10[2]	11[1]		4[3]		19
1	2	3	4		9[2]			13	10[1]	12	6		5			8		7	11			20
1	2	3	4		9			13	10[2]	12	6		5	14		8		7[1]	11[3]			21
1		3	4	12	5		8[3]	9[1]	10[3]	6		13	14	2				7	11			22
1	2	3	4	8[3]		10		13	14	9[2]			5			12	7	6	11[1]			23
1	2	3	4	8		11[1]		13		9[2]			5			7	12	6	10			24
1	2	3	4	8	5			13	12	9[1]			14			7	11[2]	6	10[3]			25
1	2	3[1]	4	8	5			14	12	9[3]		13				7	10[2]	6	11			26
1	2	3[2]	4	8	5			12	9[3]	14		13				7	10[1]	6	11			27
1	2	3	4	5[3]	9[1]			10		14	12	13				8	6	7	11[2]			28
1	2	3	4	8				12	9[1]			5	13			7	11	6	10[2]			29
1	2	3	4	5[1]				13	12	14	6	10[2]				8	9[3]	7	11			30
1	2[2]	3	4	12				10		6	14	5[3]	13			8	9	7	11[1]			31
1		3	4	5	2	14		12	10		6[2]	13				8	9[3]	7	11[1]			32
1	2	3	4	5	6	14		9[3]	13	10	12					8		7[1]	11[3]			33
1		3	4	5	6	2	14	7[2]	11[3]	12		9		8[1]	13							34
1	2	3	4	5	9	8[3]		10[2]	6[1]	14	12	13						7	11			35
1	2	3	4	8	5	14		11	12	13		9[3]				7[1]		6	10[2]			36
1	2	3	4	8	5	7	11[2]	9[3]			13	14	12					6	10[1]			37
1		2	3	8	5	7		11	9	14		10[1]	4[2]	13			12				6[3]	38

FA Cup

Third Round	Wigan Ath	(h)	2-2
Replay	Wigan Ath	(a)	0-3

Carabao Cup

Second Round	Birmingham C	(a)	2-1
Third Round *(aet)*	Brighton & HA	(h)	1-0
Fourth Round	Middlesbrough	(h)	3-1
Quarter-Final	Chelsea	(a)	1-2

BRADFORD CITY

FOUNDATION

Bradford was a rugby stronghold around the turn of the 20th century but after Manningham RFC held an archery contest to help them out of financial difficulties in 1903, they were persuaded to give up the handling code and turn to soccer. So they formed Bradford City and continued at Valley Parade. Recognising this as an opportunity to spread the dribbling code in this part of Yorkshire, the Football League immediately accepted the new club's first application for membership of the Second Division.

Northern Commercials Stadium, Valley Parade, Bradford, West Yorkshire BD8 7DY.

Telephone: (01274) 773 355.

Fax: (01274) 773 356.

Ticket Office: (01274) 770 012.

Website: www.bradfordcityfc.co.uk

Email: support@bradfordcityfc.co.uk

Ground Capacity: 25,137.

Record Attendance: 39,146 v Burnley, FA Cup 4th rd, 11 March 1911.

Pitch Measurements: 103.5m × 64m (113yd × 70yd).

Joint Owners: Stefan Rupp and Edin Rahic.

Chief Operating Officer: James Mason.

Manager: Michael Collins.

Assistant Managers: Greg Abbott, Martin Drury.

Colours: Claret and amber striped shirts, claret shorts with amber trim, claret socks with amber trim.

Year Formed: 1903.

Turned Professional: 1903.

Club Nickname: 'The Bantams'.

Ground: 1903, Valley Parade (renamed Bradford & Bingley Stadium 1999, Intersonic Stadium 2007, Coral Windows Stadium 2007, Northern Commercials Stadium 2016).

First Football League Game: 1 September 1903, Division 2, v Grimsby T (a) L 0–2 – Seymour; Wilson, Halliday; Robinson, Millar, Farnall; Guy, Beckram, Forrest, McMillan, Graham.

Record League Victory: 11–1 v Rotherham U, Division 3 (N), 25 August 1928 – Sherlaw; Russell, Watson; Burkinshaw (1), Summers, Bauld; Harvey (2), Edmunds (3), White (3), Cairns, Scriven (2).

Record Cup Victory: 11–3 v Walker Celtic, FA Cup 1st rd (replay), 1 December 1937 – Parker; Rookes, McDermott; Murphy, Mackie, Moore; Bagley (1), Whittingham (1), Deakin (4 incl. 1p), Cooke (1), Bartholomew (4).

Record Defeat: 1–9 v Colchester U, Division 4, 30 December 1961.

HONOURS

League Champions: Division 2 – 1907–08; Division 3 – 1984–85; Division 3N – 1928–29.
Runners-up: First Division – 1998–99; Division 4 – 1981–82.
FA Cup Winners: 1911.
League Cup: Runners-up: 2013.
European Competitions:
Intertoto Cup: 2000.

Sun FACT FILE

Bradford City hosted a major representative game at Valley Parade within a matter of weeks of the club's formation. On 10 October 1903 the Football League defeated the Irish League 2-1 in front of a crowd of 17,000, higher than any Rugby League game played by the club's predecessors Manningham at the ground.

Most League Points (2 for a win): 63, Division 3 (N), 1928–29.

Most League Points (3 for a win): 94, Division 3, 1984–85.

Most League Goals: 128, Division 3 (N), 1928–29.

Highest League Scorer in Season: David Layne, 34, Division 4, 1961–62.

Most League Goals in Total Aggregate: Bobby Campbell, 121, 1981–84, 1984–86.

Most League Goals in One Match: 7, Albert Whitehurst v Tranmere R, Division 3 (N), 6 March 1929.

Most Capped Player: Jamie Lawrence, 19 (24), Jamaica.

Most League Appearances: Cec Podd, 502, 1970–84.

Youngest League Player: Robert Cullingford, 16 years 141 days v Mansfield T, 22 April 1970.

Record Transfer Fee Received: £2,000,000 from Newcastle U for Des Hamilton, March 1997; £2,000,000 from Newcastle U for Andrew O'Brien, March 2001.

Record Transfer Fee Paid: £2,500,000 to Leeds U for David Hopkin, July 2000.

Football League Record: 1903 Elected to Division 2; 1908–22 Division 1; 1922–27 Division 2; 1927–29 Division 3 (N); 1929–37 Division 2; 1937–61 Division 3; 1961–69 Division 4; 1969–72 Division 3; 1972–77 Division 4; 1977–78 Division 3; 1978–82 Division 4; 1982–85 Division 3; 1985–90 Division 2; 1990–92 Division 3; 1992–96 Division 2; 1996–99 Division 1; 1999–2001 FA Premier League; 2001–04 Division 1; 2004–07 FL 1; 2007–13 FL 2; 2013– FL 1.

LATEST SEQUENCES

Longest Sequence of League Wins: 10, 26.11.1983 – 3.2.1984.

Longest Sequence of League Defeats: 8, 21.1.1933 – 11.3.1933.

Longest Sequence of League Draws: 6, 30.1.1976 – 13.3.1976.

Longest Sequence of Unbeaten League Matches: 21, 11.1.1969 – 2.5.1969.

Longest Sequence Without a League Win: 16, 28.8.1948 – 20.11.1948.

Successive Scoring Runs: 30 from 26.12.1961.

Successive Non-scoring Runs: 7 from 18.4.1925.

MANAGERS

Robert Campbell 1903–05
Peter O'Rourke 1905–21
David Menzies 1921–26
Colin Veitch 1926–28
Peter O'Rourke 1928–30
Jack Peart 1930–35
Dick Ray 1935–37
Fred Westgarth 1938–43
Bob Sharp 1943–46
Jack Barker 1946–47
John Milburn 1947–48
David Steele 1948–52
Albert Harris 1952
Ivor Powell 1952–55
Peter Jackson 1955–61
Bob Brocklebank 1961–64
Bill Harris 1965–66
Willie Watson 1966–69
Grenville Hair 1967–68
Jimmy Wheeler 1968–71
Bryan Edwards 1971–75
Bobby Kennedy 1975–78
John Napier 1978
George Mulhall 1978–81
Roy McFarland 1981–82
Trevor Cherry 1982–87
Terry Dolan 1987–89
Terry Yorath 1989–90
John Docherty 1990–91
Frank Stapleton 1991–94
Lennie Lawrence 1994–95
Chris Kamara 1995–98
Paul Jewell 1998–2000
Chris Hutchings 2000
Jim Jefferies 2000–01
Nicky Law 2001–03
Bryan Robson 2003–04
Colin Todd 2004–07
Stuart McCall 2007–10
Peter Taylor 2010–11
Peter Jackson 2011
Phil Parkinson 2011–16
Stuart McCall 2016–18
Simon Grayson 2018
Michael Collins June 2018–

TEN YEAR LEAGUE RECORD

		P	W	D	L	F	A	Pts	Pos
2008-09	FL 2	46	18	13	15	66	55	67	9
2009-10	FL 2	46	16	14	16	59	62	62	14
2010-11	FL 2	46	15	7	24	43	68	52	18
2011-12	FL 2	46	12	14	20	54	59	50	18
2012-13	FL 2	46	18	15	13	63	52	69	7
2013-14	FL 1	46	14	17	15	57	54	59	11
2014-15	FL 1	46	17	14	15	55	55	65	7
2015-16	FL 1	46	23	11	12	55	40	80	5
2016-17	FL 1	46	20	19	7	62	43	79	5
2017-18	FL 1	46	18	9	19	57	67	63	11

DID YOU KNOW ?

Between 1908 and 1970 there were two Bradford clubs in the Football League, Bradford City and Park Avenue. The last of the 'Wool City' derby matches between the two took place at Park Avenue on 25 January 1969. The teams drew 0-0 in front of a crowd of 10,784.

BRADFORD CITY – SKY BET LEAGUE ONE 2017–18 LEAGUE RECORD

Match No.	Date	Venue	Opponents	Result	H/T Score	Lg Pos.	Goalscorers	Attendance
1	Aug 5	H	Blackpool	W 2-1	1-1	4	Knight-Percival [41], Patrick [59]	20,804
2	12	A	Gillingham	W 1-0	1-0	4	Poleon [19]	5267
3	19	H	Blackburn R	L 0-1	0-0	7		21,403
4	26	A	Walsall	D 3-3	2-0	9	McCartan [30], Poleon [38], Leahy (og) [49]	4817
5	Sept 2	H	Bristol R	W 3-1	1-0	6	Wyke 3 [13, 62, 73]	19,284
6	9	A	Peterborough U	W 3-1	3-0	4	Poleon [7], Vincelot [36], Kilgallon [40]	7061
7	12	A	Oxford U	D 2-2	1-0	4	Patrick [30], Vincelot [90]	6658
8	16	H	Rotherham U	W 1-0	1-0	3	Vincelot [21]	20,881
9	23	A	Northampton T	W 1-0	1-0	3	McMahon [34]	6355
10	26	H	Fleetwood T	L 0-3	0-0	4		18,799
11	30	H	Doncaster R	W 2-0	2-0	3	Wyke [18], Knight-Percival [42]	20,430
12	Oct 7	A	Milton Keynes D	W 4-1	2-1	3	Vincelot [11], Wyke 2 [18, 71], Taylor [82]	9106
13	14	A	Bury	L 1-3	1-2	3	Wyke [9]	5514
14	17	H	Oldham Ath	D 1-1	1-1	3	Taylor [3]	19,840
15	21	H	Charlton Ath	L 0-1	0-0	3		20,066
16	28	A	Portsmouth	W 1-0	0-0	3	Kilgallon [80]	18,067
17	Nov 11	A	Plymouth Arg	L 0-1	0-1	4		20,227
18	18	A	Wigan Ath	W 2-1	1-1	3	Wyke [14], Robinson [90]	10,649
19	21	H	Scunthorpe U	L 1-2	1-1	5	Taylor [44]	19,163
20	25	A	Shrewsbury T	W 1-0	0-0	4	Nsiala (og) [55]	7165
21	Dec 9	H	Rochdale	W 4-3	3-2	4	Kilgallon [8], Wyke [40], Poleon [42], Robinson [78]	19,621
22	16	A	Southend U	W 2-1	1-0	4	Poleon [9], Wyke (pen) [90]	6097
23	23	A	AFC Wimbledon	L 1-2	0-1	5	Taylor [47]	4215
24	26	H	Peterborough U	L 1-3	0-2	5	Taylor [83]	21,220
25	30	H	Oxford U	W 3-2	1-0	5	Wyke [2], McCartan [54], Dieng [59]	19,691
26	Jan 1	A	Fleetwood T	W 2-1	0-1	5	Gilliead [56], McCartan [63]	3089
27	13	H	Northampton T	L 1-2	0-1	5	Taylor [90]	19,343
28	20	A	Bristol R	L 1-3	1-0	5	Wyke (pen) [38]	9064
29	23	A	Rotherham U	L 0-2	0-1	5		8904
30	27	H	AFC Wimbledon	L 0-4	0-1	5		19,103
31	Feb 3	A	Oldham Ath	L 1-2	0-1	6	Gibson [88]	5526
32	10	H	Bury	D 2-2	0-0	6	Wyke [58], McCartan [89]	19,476
33	13	A	Charlton Ath	D 1-1	0-1	6	Robinson [80]	10,650
34	24	A	Plymouth Arg	L 0-1	0-1	8		11,113
35	Mar 14	H	Wigan Ath	L 0-1	0-0	10		19,413
36	19	A	Doncaster R	L 0-2	0-0	11		7369
37	24	H	Gillingham	W 1-0	0-0	9	Poleon [48]	19,654
38	29	A	Blackburn R	L 0-2	0-0	10		13,443
39	Apr 7	A	Blackpool	L 0-5	0-3	12		5337
40	12	H	Shrewsbury T	D 0-0	0-0	12		18,997
41	17	H	Portsmouth	W 3-1	1-0	10	Knight-Percival [14], Lund [71], Wyke [90]	19,554
42	21	A	Rochdale	D 1-1	0-1	11	Wyke [90]	4365
43	24	H	Milton Keynes D	W 2-0	1-0	10	Dieng [12], Knight-Percival [80]	19,192
44	28	H	Southend U	L 0-2	0-0	11		19,960
45	May 1	H	Walsall	D 1-1	1-1	11	Lund [45]	18,976
46	5	A	Scunthorpe U	D 1-1	0-0	11	Kilgallon [56]	5452

Final League Position: 11

GOALSCORERS

League (57): Wyke 15 (2 pens), Poleon 6, Taylor 5, Kilgallon 4, Knight-Percival 4, McCartan 4, Vincelot 4, Robinson 3, Dieng 2, Lund 2, Patrick 2, Gibson 1, Gilliead 1, McMahon 1, own goals 2.
FA Cup (5): Gilliead 1, Jones 1, Knight-Percival 1, Vincelot 1, Wyke 1.
Carabao Cup (2): Jones 1, Poleon 1.
Checkatrade Trophy (6): Jones 3, Hanson 1, Patrick 1, Thompson 1.

Doyle C 35	Chicksen A 16+2	Knight-Percival N 40+1	Kilgallon M 42	McMahon T 38	Law N 33+5	Vincelot R 37+1	Reeves J 24+1	Patrick O 8+11	McCartan S 13+11	Jones A 4+3	Dieng T 19+7	Poleon D 16+16	Devine D —+3	Field T 7+1	Gilliead A 36+6	Taylor P 18+9	Wyke C 38+2	Pybus D —+1	Hendrie L 9+4	Barr L —+1	Thompson A 4+5	Hanson J 1+2	Robinson T 13+8	Sattelmaier R 10+1	Raeder L 1	Guy C 15+2	Lund M 7+3	Brunker K 5+4	Gibson J 1+4	McGowan R 3	Warnock S 13	Grodowski J —+1	Hawkes C —+2	Staunton R —+1	Match No.
1	2²	3	4	5	6	7	8	9	10¹	11³	12	13	14																						1
1		4	3	2	6		8	10¹		9²	7	11			5	12	13																		2
1		4	3	2	6		8	10¹		9³	14	7	11²		5	13	12																		3
1		3	4	2	8		7			9³		10		5¹	6²		11		12	13	14														4
1	5	3	4	2	9	8	7	12	13			10¹			6		11²																		5
1	5■	3	4	2	9	8	7	12				10¹			6²	13	11																		6
1		3	4¹	2	9	7	6	10³	13		12			5	8	14	11²																		7
1	5	4	3	2	8¹	7	6	12							9	10	11²						13												8
1	5	3	4	2	8¹	6	7	12							10²	9	11						13												9
1	5²	3	4	2	8	6	7	11³	10¹			14			9	13	12																		10
1	5	3	4	2	12	7	8		13			10¹		6³	9²		11		14																11
1	5	3	4	2²	9	8	7	14	10³					6	13		11¹		12																12
1	5	3	4	2¹	9	8	7²	12			6	13			10		11																		13
1	5	4			6	7¹	8	9³					14	13	12	10	11²				2	3													14
1		4	3		9		6	10¹	14		7²			5³	8		11				2					12	13								15
1		3	2		9	8	7		12					5	6	11¹	10				4														16
1		4	3	2	9	7	8²		10¹		14			5³	13	6	11						12												17
1		4	3	2	9	7	8								6	10¹	11		5				12												18
1¹		3	4	2	9³	7	8					13			6	11	10	5²					14	12											19
		3	4	2	9¹	7	8								6	11²	10		5				13	12	1										20
		4	3	2	8³	7						10²			6	9	11				12		13	14	5¹	1									21
		3¹	4	2	8	7	12		14			10²			6	9³	11						13	5	1										22
			4	2	9¹	7	8²		13	12					6	10	11					3	5	1											23
			4	2	8	7				12	13				6	10	11		5¹		3²		9	1											24
		3	4			7	8	13	9²	6				12	11¹	10■			2				5	1											25
		4			2	8	3		11¹		7		12	6	9	10			5					1											26
		4	3		9	8			11¹		7	13			6	10			2²	5		1	12												27
		2	3		8	4	6¹				7	13			5	10²	11				9		1			12									28
		3	4		9	8¹	6¹		12		7	14			13	10²	11				5		1			2									29
		5	3	4	8³	7	6¹								11²	9	10						1			2	12	13	14						30
1	9		3	5	6²				10³		12	13					11						8			7¹		14	2	4					31
1	5	14	4■	2			8				13				6²	12	10				9¹								3						32
1	9¹	3		5		7			6²						11	12	10				13		8					2	4		5				33
1	9¹	3	4	2		7³						13			6	10²	11■				12		8	14					5						34
1		4	3	2	14	6			11³			8¹	13		10²						5		9	7	12										35
1		4	2	5	6	3			10¹			7²	12		11³				9		8					14			13						36
1	11	2	6	4¹	8		14	7²				10³	13	3							9		12				5								37
1		3	4	5	8	2		13	12		14	10¹		6³		11					7²						9				5				38
1	2		4	7	8³	3		11²	9¹			14			10				13		6		12				5								39
1	12	4	3	2			13				7				6		11		9		8		10²			5¹									40
1		4	3	2	13							7	14		6		11				9³		8²	12	10¹		5								41
1		4	3	2	12	8¹				14		7	13		6		10						9²	11³			5								42
1		4	3	2	12					14		8	13		6³		11				7		9¹	10²			5								43
1		3	4	2	13					14		8¹	12³		6		11				7		9	10²			5								44
1	14	3		2		4						10	8		6³		11				7²		9	12			5¹	13							45
1		3	4	2					13	10		8			6¹		11						7	9³			5²	12	14						46

FA Cup

First Round	Chesterfield	(h)	2-0	
Second Round	Plymouth Arg	(h)	3-1	
Third Round	Yeovil T	(a)	0-2	

Carabao Cup

First Round	Doncaster R	(h)	2-3

Checkatrade Trophy

Northern Group F	Chesterfield	(a)	4-2	
Northern Group F	Manchester C U21	(h)	2-1	
Northern Group F	Rotherham U	(h)	0-3	
Second Round North	Oldham Ath	(h)	0-1	

BRENTFORD

FOUNDATION

Formed as a small amateur concern in 1889 they were very successful in local circles. They won the championship of the West London Alliance in 1893 and a year later the West Middlesex Junior Cup before carrying off the Senior Cup in 1895. After winning both the London Senior Amateur Cup and the Middlesex Senior Cup in 1898 they were admitted to the Second Division of the Southern League.

Griffin Park, Braemar Road, Brentford, Middlesex TW8 0NT.

Telephone: (0208) 847 2511.

Ticket Office: (0208) 847 2511 (option 1).

Website: www.brentfordfc.com

Email: enquiries@brentfordfc.com

Ground Capacity: 12,632.

Record Attendance: 38,678 v Leicester C, FA Cup 6th rd, 26 February 1949.

Pitch Measurements: 100m × 67m (109.5yd × 73yd).

Chairman: Cliff Crown.

Chief Executive: Mark Devlin.

Head Coach: Dean Smith

Assistant Head Coach: Richard O'Kelly.

HONOURS

League Champions: Division 2 – 1934–35; Division 3 – 1991–92; Division 3S – 1932–33; FL 2 – 2008–09; Third Division – 1998–99; Division 4 – 1962–63.
Runners-up: FL 1 – 2013–14; Second Division – 1994–95; Division 3S – 1929–30, 1957–58.
FA Cup: 6th rd – 1938, 1946, 1949, 1989.
League Cup: 4th rd – 1983, 2011.
League Trophy: Runners-up: 1985, 2001, 2011.

Colours: Red and white striped shirts with black trim, black shorts with white trim, black socks with white trim.

Year Formed: 1889.

Turned Professional: 1899.

Club Nickname: 'The Bees'.

Grounds: 1889, Clifden Road; 1891, Benns Fields, Little Ealing; 1895, Shotters Field; 1898, Cross Road, S. Ealing; 1900, Boston Park; 1904, Griffin Park.

First Football League Game: 28 August 1920, Division 3, v Exeter C (a) L 0–3 – Young; Hodson, Rosier, Jimmy Elliott, Levitt, Amos, Smith, Thompson, Spreadbury, Morley, Henery.

Record League Victory: 9–0 v Wrexham, Division 3, 15 October 1963 – Cakebread; Coote, Jones; Slater, Scott, Higginson; Summers (1), Brooks (2), McAdams (2), Ward (2), Hales (1), (1 og).

Record Cup Victory: 7–0 v Windsor & Eton (away), FA Cup 1st rd, 20 November 1982 – Roche; Rowe, Harris (Booker), McNichol (1), Whitehead, Hurlock (2), Kamara, Joseph (1), Mahoney (3), Bowles, Roberts. *N.B.* 8–0 v Uxbridge: Frail, Jock Watson, Caie, Bellingham, Parsonage (1), Jay, Atherton, Leigh (1), Bell (2), Buchanan (2), Underwood (2), FA Cup, 3rd Qual rd, 31 October 1903.

Record Defeat: 0–7 v Swansea T, Division 3 (S), 8 November 1924; v Walsall, Division 3 (S), 19 January 1957; v Peterborough U, 24 November 2007.

Most League Points (2 for a win): 62, Division 3 (S), 1932–33 and Division 4, 1962–63.

Sᴜᴨ FACT FILE

Brentford had one of the earliest independent supporters' organisations. The Brentford Football Club Supporters' League was established around 1910 and organised fund-raising activities and an annual professional athletics event at Griffin Park. After folding during the First World War it was reformed in 1922 and continued to support the club financially until disbanding in 1929.

Most League Points (3 for a win): 94, FL 1, 2013–14.

Most League Goals: 98, Division 4, 1962–63.

Highest League Scorer in Season: Jack Holliday, 38, Division 3 (S), 1932–33.

Most League Goals in Total Aggregate: Jim Towers, 153, 1954–61.

Most League Goals in One Match: 5, Jack Holliday v Luton T, Division 3 (S), 28 January 1933; 5, Billy Scott v Barnsley, Division 2, 15 December 1934; 5, Peter McKennan v Bury, Division 2, 18 February 1949.

Most Capped Player: John Buttigieg, 22 (98), Malta.

Most League Appearances: Ken Coote, 514, 1949–64.

Youngest League Player: Danis Salman, 15 years 248 days v Watford, 15 November 1975.

Record Transfer Fee Received: £12,000,000 from Aston Villa for Scott Hogan, January 2017.

Record Transfer Fee Paid: £750,000 (rising to £4,125,000) to Rochdale for Scott Hogan, July 2014.

Football League Record: 1920 Original Member of Division 3; 1921–33 Division 3 (S); 1933–35 Division 2; 1935–47 Division 1; 1947–54 Division 2; 1954–62 Division 3 (S); 1962–63 Division 4; 1963–66 Division 3; 1966–72 Division 4; 1972–73 Division 3; 1973–78 Division 4; 1978–92 Division 3; 1992–93 Division 1; 1993–98 Division 2; 1998–99 Division 3; 1999–2004 Division 2; 2004–07 FL 1; 2007–09 FL 2; 2009–14 FL 1; 2014– FL C.

LATEST SEQUENCES

Longest Sequence of League Wins: 9, 30.4.1932 – 24.9.1932.

Longest Sequence of League Defeats: 9, 20.10.1928 – 25.12.1928.

Longest Sequence of League Draws: 5, 16.3.1957 – 6.4.1957.

Longest Sequence of Unbeaten League Matches: 26, 20.2.1999 – 16.10.1999.

Longest Sequence Without a League Win: 18, 9.9.2006 – 26.12.2006.

Successive Scoring Runs: 26 from 4.3.1963.

Successive Non-scoring Runs: 7 from 7.3.2000.

MANAGERS

Will Lewis 1900–03
  (*Secretary-Manager*)
Dick Molyneux 1902–06
W. G. Brown 1906–08
Fred Halliday 1908–12, 1915–21, 1924–26
  (*only Secretary to 1922*)
Ephraim Rhodes 1912–15
Archie Mitchell 1921–24
Harry Curtis 1926–49
Jackie Gibbons 1949–52
Jimmy Bain 1952–53
Tommy Lawton 1953
Bill Dodgin Snr 1953–57
Malcolm Macdonald 1957–65
Tommy Cavanagh 1965–66
Billy Gray 1966–67
Jimmy Sirrel 1967–69
Frank Blunstone 1969–73
Mike Everitt 1973–75
John Docherty 1975–76
Bill Dodgin Jnr 1976–80
Fred Callaghan 1980–84
Frank McLintock 1984–87
Steve Perryman 1987–90
Phil Holder 1990–93
David Webb 1993–97
Eddie May 1997
Micky Adams 1997–98
Ron Noades 1998–2000
Ray Lewington 2000–01
Steve Coppell 2001–02
Wally Downes 2002–04
Martin Allen 2004–06
Leroy Rosenior 2006
Scott Fitzgerald 2006–07
Terry Butcher 2007
Andy Scott 2007–11
Nicky Forster 2011
Uwe Rosler 2011–13
Mark Warburton 2013–15
Marinus Dijkhuizen 2015
Dean Smith December 2015–

TEN YEAR LEAGUE RECORD

		P	W	D	L	F	A	Pts	Pos
2008-09	FL 2	46	23	16	7	65	36	85	1
2009-10	FL 1	46	14	20	12	55	52	62	9
2010-11	FL 1	46	17	10	19	55	62	61	11
2011-12	FL 1	46	18	13	15	63	52	67	9
2012-13	FL 1	46	21	16	9	62	47	79	3
2013-14	FL 1	46	28	10	8	72	43	94	2
2014-15	FL C	46	23	9	14	78	59	78	5
2015-16	FL C	46	19	8	19	72	67	65	9
2016-17	FL C	46	18	10	18	75	65	64	10
2017-18	FL C	46	18	15	13	62	52	69	9

DID YOU KNOW ?

Brentford have reached the end-of-season play-offs on eight separate occasions but have yet to be successful once. They have reached the play-off finals three times, most recently in 2012–13 when they lost to Yeovil Town in the League One final at Wembley Stadium. During the same period of time they have gained automatic promotion on four occasions.

BRENTFORD – SKY BET CHAMPIONSHIP 2017–18 LEAGUE RECORD

Match No.	Date	Venue	Opponents		Result	H/T Score	Lg Pos.	Goalscorers	Attendance
1	Aug 5	A	Sheffield U	L	0-1	0-1	18		26,746
2	12	H	Nottingham F	L	3-4	1-2	22	Egan [38], Bjelland [79], Maupay [90]	10,169
3	15	H	Bristol C	D	2-2	0-1	20	Watkins [56], Maupay [77]	9811
4	19	A	Ipswich T	L	0-2	0-1	24		15,348
5	26	H	Wolverhampton W	D	0-0	0-0	23		10,351
6	Sept 9	A	Aston Villa	D	0-0	0-0	23		29,799
7	12	A	Sheffield W	L	1-2	1-1	23	Yennaris [9]	23,536
8	16	H	Reading	D	1-1	1-0	22	Clarke [16]	9739
9	23	A	Bolton W	W	3-0	1-0	20	Barbet [38], Yennaris [62], Watkins [84]	13,897
10	26	H	Derby Co	D	1-1	0-1	20	Watkins [86]	8679
11	30	A	Middlesbrough	D	2-2	1-0	19	Barbet [29], Watkins [72]	24,545
12	Oct 14	H	Millwall	W	1-0	0-0	18	Sawyers [47]	9622
13	21	H	Sunderland	D	3-3	1-3	18	Yennaris [8], Jozefzoon [47], Maupay [78]	10,726
14	28	A	Preston NE	W	3-2	1-1	18	Yennaris [25], Sawyers [56], Watkins [69]	12,005
15	Nov 1	A	Birmingham C	W	2-0	0-0	15	Watkins (pen) [74], Maupay [84]	19,045
16	4	H	Leeds U	W	3-1	1-0	12	Maupay [22], Barbet [85], Woods [90]	11,068
17	18	A	Cardiff C	L	0-2	0-2	13		16,335
18	21	H	Burton Alb	D	1-1	0-0	13	Jozefzoon [54]	7957
19	27	A	QPR	D	2-2	0-0	14	Vibe 2 [52, 81]	13,410
20	Dec 2	H	Fulham	W	3-1	1-1	11	Canos [33], Sawyers [49], Watkins [85]	11,090
21	9	A	Hull C	L	2-3	0-0	13	Meyler (og) [47], Egan [87]	14,620
22	16	H	Barnsley	D	0-0	0-0	13		9868
23	22	A	Norwich C	W	2-1	2-0	11	Vibe 2 [36, 41]	26,725
24	26	H	Aston Villa	W	2-1	1-1	12	Sawyers [22], Vibe [52]	11,341
25	30	H	Sheffield W	W	2-0	1-0	10	Vibe [20], Jozefzoon [83]	10,853
26	Jan 2	A	Wolverhampton W	L	0-3	0-0	11		28,475
27	13	H	Bolton W	W	2-0	1-0	11	Jozefzoon [40], Maupay [90]	9507
28	20	A	Reading	W	1-0	0-0	9	Vibe [74]	17,893
29	27	A	Norwich C	L	0-1	0-1	10		10,252
30	Feb 3	A	Derby Co	L	0-3	0-2	11		25,938
31	10	H	Preston NE	D	1-1	0-0	10	Jozefzoon [62]	9194
32	17	A	Sunderland	W	2-0	2-0	10	Mokotjo [13], Maupay [28]	27,702
33	20	H	Birmingham C	W	5-0	2-0	10	Watkins 2 [31, 81], Jozefzoon [41], Maupay [51], Roberts (og) [54]	9511
34	24	A	Leeds U	L	0-1	0-1	10		28,428
35	Mar 6	A	Burton Alb	W	2-0	0-0	10	McFadzean (og) [60], Watkins [80]	3464
36	10	A	Millwall	L	0-1	0-1	11		13,251
37	13	H	Cardiff C	L	1-3	1-2	11	Maupay [5]	8549
38	17	H	Middlesbrough	D	1-1	1-1	11	Macleod [34]	11,134
39	30	H	Sheffield U	D	1-1	0-0	11	Mepham [88]	11,174
40	Apr 2	A	Bristol C	W	1-0	0-0	11	Maupay [80]	22,049
41	7	H	Ipswich T	W	1-0	0-0	10	Maupay (pen) [72]	10,939
42	10	A	Nottingham F	W	1-0	0-0	10	Dalsgaard [81]	20,596
43	14	A	Fulham	D	1-1	0-0	10	Maupay [90]	20,877
44	21	H	QPR	W	2-1	1-1	8	Canos [16], Jozefzoon [69]	12,367
45	28	A	Barnsley	L	0-2	0-1	9		13,137
46	May 6	H	Hull C	D	1-1	1-1	9	Canos [12]	11,475

Final League Position: 9

GOALSCORERS

League (62): Maupay 12 (1 pen), Watkins 10 (1 pen), Jozefzoon 7, Vibe 7, Sawyers 4, Yennaris 4, Barbet 3, Canos 3, Egan 2, Bjelland 1, Clarke 1, Dalsgaard 1, Macleod 1, Mepham 1, Mokotjo 1, Woods 1, own goals 3.
FA Cup (0).
Carabao Cup (8): Clarke 2, Egan 1, Maupay 1, Sawyers 1, Shaibu 1, Watkins 1, own goal 1.

Bentley D 45	Dalsgaard H 29	Egan J 32 + 1	Bjelland A 32 + 2	Henry R 8	Mokotjo K 25 + 10	Woods R 35 + 4	Jota R 4	McEachran J 14 + 11	Jozefzoon F 31 + 8	Vibe L 14 + 5	Watkins O 39 + 6	Yennaris N 31 + 10	Maupay N 25 + 17	Sawyers R 36 + 6	Dean H 3	Barbet Y 32 + 2	Colin M 3	Archibald T — +2	Clarke J 23 + 5	Canos S 17 + 13	Shaibu J — +2	Mepham C 17 + 4	Macleod L 5 + 5	Judge A 3 + 10	Marcondes E 2 + 10	Ogbene C — +2	Daniels L 1	Match No.
1	2	3	4	5	6²	7	8	8	9³	10¹	11	12	13	14														1
1	2	3	4	5		7		8	9¹	10²	11	13	6¹	14	12													2
1	2		14				8¹	7²	13	11³	10	6	12	9	3	4	5											3
1	2				6			8¹	12³	10	7	11²	9		3	4	5	13	14									4
1	2	14			6²	13	8¹		12		10	7	11	9	3	4¹	5											5
1	2	3	14	5²		7					10	6	11³	9		4			12	8¹	13							6
1	2	3		5		6		13	12		10³	7	11	9²		4			8²	14								7
1		3	4	5	6³	7		12	8¹		10	13	11	9²				14	2									8
1	2	3³	4	5	14	7			13		10	6	11	9²		12			8¹									9
1	2	3²	5			7³			14	13	10	6	11	9		4			8¹			12						10
1	2		5²	6¹		7			14	9		11	8³	10	13	4						3						11
1	2	3	4			7		13	8¹	12	10³	6	11²	9		5				14								12
1	2	3	4			7		12	8	11²	10³	6	13	9¹		5			14									13
1	2	3	4		6	7			9²	10³	11	8	14	12		5			13									14
1	2²	3	4		6	7		8	9¹	11	10	13	9	12		5			14									15
1		3	4¹		13	7			8	14	10	6	11³	9²		5			2			12						16
1		3	4			7¹			14	8³	13	10	6	11²	9	5			2	12								17
1		3	4			6¹			13	8	14	10	7⁴	11³	9	5			2	12								18
1		3	4		6	7				9²	10¹	12	8	14	13	5			2	11³								19
1		3	4		6	7		14		10²	11	8³		12		5			2	9¹		13						20
1		3	4		6³			14	13		8	12	11	9²		5			2	10¹								21
1		3	4			6			7³	13	10	12	11	9		5			2⁵	8¹		14						22
1			4		8³	6		14	7¹	11²	10	2	12	9		5				13	3							23
1			4		12	6		7¹	8	11²		2	13	9		5				10	3							24
1			4		12	6		7¹	8	11²	13	2	14	9		5				10³	3							25
1			4		7	6			12	11³	10	2	13	9		5¹		14	8²	3								26
1			4		7	6			8¹	11²	10	2	13	9		5			12	3								27
1			4		6	7			8¹	11	10²	2		9		5			12	3	13							28
1			4		7³	6		9²	8		10	2	11¹			5			13	3		12	14					29
1	2		4		6¹	7³			8²		11	13		9		5			10¹	3		14	12					30
1	2	3	4					7²	8		10	6	11³	9¹					5			14	12	13				31
1	2	3	4		6³	12		7¹	8		10		11²	9					5				13	14				32
1	2	3	4		6	12		7⁴	8		10		11¹	9²	5								13	14				33
1	2	3	4		9³	6			8		10²		11	7¹	5					12			13	14				34
1	2	3	4		7²	6			8¹		10	14	11³	9	5				13					12				35
1	2	3	4²			6					10	7	13	9	5				8³	12		14	11¹					36
1		3				7					10	6³	11¹	9	5			2	8³	4	13	14	12					37
1	2	3			7²	6			8		10¹		11	13²	5				12	4		9³	14					38
1	2	3			13	6⁴			7³		12	8	11		5				10²	4		9¹	14					39
1	2²	3			7			6¹	8		11	14	13	9	5			12		4		10²						40
1	2	3			6¹			7²			11	13	10	8	5				12	4		9²	14					41
1	2	3	4		14			7			10²	6¹	11	9		5			8³				12	13				42
1	2	12	4³		14	8			6		11	7¹	13	9	5				10²			9³						43
1	2	3			13	6			8		11¹	14	12	7	5				10³	4		9³						44
1	2	3			14	6			7		11	13	12	9¹	5				10³	4		8²						45
	3				9	12		6¹			13	2			4				5	10³				8²	7	11	14	1	46

FA Cup
Third Round   Notts Co   (h)   0-1

Carabao Cup
First Round   AFC Wimbledon   (a)   3-1
(*aet*)
Second Round   QPR   (a)   4-1
Third Round   Norwich C   (h)   1-3

BRIGHTON & HOVE ALBION

FOUNDATION

A professional club Brighton United was formed in November 1897 at the Imperial Hotel, Queen's Road, but folded in March 1900 after less than two seasons in the Southern League at the County Ground. An amateur team Brighton & Hove Rangers was then formed by some prominent United supporters and after one season at Withdean, decided to turn semi-professional and play at the County Ground. Rangers were accepted into the Southern League but folded in June 1901. John Jackson, the former United manager, organised a meeting at the Seven Stars public house, Ship Street on 24 June 1901 at which a new third club Brighton & Hove United was formed. They took over Rangers' place in the Southern League and pitch at County Ground. The name was changed to Brighton & Hove Albion before a match was played because of objections by Hove FC.

American Express Community Stadium, Village Way, Falmer, Brighton BN1 9BL.

Telephone: (01273) 878 288.

Fax: (01273) 878 241.

Ticket Office: (0844) 327 1901.

Website: www.brightonandhovealbion.com

Email: supporter.services@bhafc.co.uk

Ground Capacity: 30,666.

Record Attendance: 36,747 v Fulham, Division 2, 27 December 1958 (at Goldstone Ground); 8,691 v Leeds U, FL 1, 20 October 2007 (at Withdean); 30,338 v Bristol C, FL C, 29 April 2017 (at Amex).

Pitch Measurements: 105m × 68m (115yd × 74.5yd).

Chairman: Tony Bloom.

Chief Executive: Paul Barber.

Manager: Chris Hughton.

Assistant Manager: Paul Trollope.

HONOURS

League Champions: FL 1 – 2010–11; Second Division – 2001–02; Division 3S – 1957–58; Third Division – 2000–01; Division 4 – 1964–65. *Runners-up:* FL C – 2016–17; Division 2 – 1978–79; Division 3 – 1971–72, 1976–77, 1987–88; Division 3S – 1953–54, 1955–56.

FA Cup: Runners-up: 1983.

League Cup: 5th rd – 1979.

Colours: Blue and white striped shirts with blue sleeves, blue shorts with white trim, white socks.

Year Formed: 1901.

Turned Professional: 1901.

Club Nickname: 'The Seagulls'.

Grounds: 1901, County Ground; 1902, Goldstone Ground; 1997, groundshare at Gillingham FC; 1999, Withdean Stadium; 2011, American Express Community Stadium.

First Football League Game: 28 August 1920, Division 3, v Southend U (a) L 0–2 – Hayes; Woodhouse, Little; Hall, Comber, Bentley; Longstaff, Ritchie, Doran, Rodgerson, March.

Record League Victory: 9–1 v Newport Co, Division 3 (S), 18 April 1951 – Ball; Tennant (1p), Mansell (1p); Willard, McCoy, Wilson; Reed, McNichol (4), Garbutt, Bennett (2), Keene (1). 9–1 v Southend U, Division 3, 27 November 1965 – Powney; Magill, Baxter; Leck, Gall, Turner; Gould (1), Collins (1), Livesey (2), Smith (3), Goodchild (2).

S*ü*n FACT FILE

The highest average attendance at Brighton & Hove Albion's former home, the Goldstone Ground, was 25,265 achieved in the 1977–78 season. League attendances at the Amex Stadium have exceeded this every season since 2012–13 with the average achieved in 2017–18 creating an all-time club record of 30,403.

Record Cup Victory: 10–1 v Wisbech, FA Cup 1st rd, 13 November 1965 – Powney; Magill, Baxter; Collins (1), Gall, Turner; Gould, Smith (2), Livesey (3), Cassidy (2), Goodchild (1), (1 og).

Record Defeat: 0–9 v Middlesbrough, Division 2, 23 August 1958.

Most League Points (2 for a win): 65, Division 3 (S), 1955–56 and Division 3, 1971–72.

Most League Points (3 for a win): 95, FL 1, 2010–11.

Most League Goals: 112, Division 3 (S), 1955–56.

Highest League Scorer in Season: Peter Ward, 32, Division 3, 1976–77.

Most League Goals in Total Aggregate: Tommy Cook, 114, 1922–29.

Most League Goals in One Match: 5, Jack Doran v Northampton T, Division 3 (S), 5 November 1921; 5, Adrian Thorne v Watford, Division 3 (S), 30 April 1958.

Most Capped Player: Steve Penney, 17, Northern Ireland.

Most League Appearances: Ernie 'Tug' Wilson, 509, 1922–36.

Youngest League Player: Ian Chapman, 16 years 259 days v Birmingham C, 14 February 1987.

Record Transfer Fee Received: £8,000,000 from Leicester C for Leonardo Ulloa, July 2014.

Record Transfer Fee Paid: £14,000,000 to PSV Eindhoven for Jürgen Locadia, January 2018.

Football League Record: 1920 Original Member of Division 3; 1921–58 Division 3 (S); 1958–62 Division 2; 1962–63 Division 3; 1963–65 Division 4; 1965–72 Division 3; 1972–73 Division 2; 1973–77 Division 3; 1977–79 Division 2; 1979–83 Division 1; 1983–87 Division 2; 1987–88 Division 3; 1988–96 Division 2; 1996–2001 Division 3; 2001–02 Division 2; 2002–03 Division 1; 2003–04 Division 2; 2004–06 FL C; 2006–11 FL 1; 2011–17 FL C; 2017– FA Premier League.

LATEST SEQUENCES

Longest Sequence of League Wins: 9, 2.10.1926 – 20.11.1926.

Longest Sequence of League Defeats: 12, 17.8.2002 – 26.10.2002.

Longest Sequence of League Draws: 6, 16.2.1980 – 15.3.1980.

Longest Sequence of Unbeaten League Matches: 22, 2.5.2015 – 15.12.2015.

Longest Sequence Without a League Win: 15, 21.10.1972 – 27.1.1973.

Successive Scoring Runs: 31 from 4.2.1956.

Successive Non-scoring Runs: 6 from 23.9.1970.

MANAGERS

John Jackson 1901–05
Frank Scott-Walford 1905–08
John Robson 1908–14
Charles Webb 1919–47
Tommy Cook 1947
Don Welsh 1947–51
Billy Lane 1951–61
George Curtis 1961–63
Archie Macaulay 1963–68
Fred Goodwin 1968–70
Pat Saward 1970–73
Brian Clough 1973–74
Peter Taylor 1974–76
Alan Mullery 1976–81
Mike Bailey 1981–82
Jimmy Melia 1982–83
Chris Cattlin 1983–86
Alan Mullery 1986–87
Barry Lloyd 1987–93
Liam Brady 1993–95
Jimmy Case 1995–96
Steve Gritt 1996–98
Brian Horton 1998–99
Jeff Wood 1999
Micky Adams 1999–2001
Peter Taylor 2001–02
Martin Hinshelwood 2002
Steve Coppell 2002–03
Mark McGhee 2003–06
Dean Wilkins 2006–08
Micky Adams 2008–09
Russell Slade 2009
Gus Poyet 2009–13
Óscar Garcia 2013–14
Sammi Hyypia 2014
Chris Hughton December 2014–

TEN YEAR LEAGUE RECORD

		P	W	D	L	F	A	Pts	Pos
2008-09	FL 1	46	13	13	20	55	70	52	16
2009-10	FL 1	46	15	14	17	56	60	59	13
2010-11	FL 1	46	28	11	7	85	40	95	1
2011-12	FL C	46	17	15	14	52	52	66	10
2012-13	FL C	46	19	18	9	69	43	75	4
2013-14	FL C	46	19	15	12	55	40	72	6
2014-15	FL C	46	10	17	19	44	54	47	20
2015-16	FL C	46	24	17	5	72	42	89	3
2016-17	FL C	46	28	9	9	74	40	93	2
2017-18	PR Lge	38	9	13	16	34	54	40	15

DID YOU KNOW ?

Brighton & Hove Albion played their 4,000th League match against Stoke City at home on 20 November 2017, which finished as a 2-2 draw. Albion won 1,564 of those games, drew 1,040 and lost 1,396. The goals tally was for 5,689 and against 5,301.

BRIGHTON & HOVE ALBION – PREMIER LEAGUE 2017–18 LEAGUE RECORD

Match No.	Date	Venue	Opponents	Result		H/T Score	Lg Pos.	Goalscorers	Atten-dance
1	Aug 12	H	Manchester C	L	0-2	0-0	19		30,415
2	19	A	Leicester C	L	0-2	0-1	18		31,902
3	26	A	Watford	D	0-0	0-0	17		20,181
4	Sept 9	H	WBA	W	3-1	1-0	13	Gross 2 [45, 48], Hemed [63]	30,381
5	15	A	Bournemouth	L	1-2	0-0	14	March [55]	10,369
6	24	H	Newcastle U	W	1-0	0-0	13	Hemed [51]	30,468
7	Oct 1	A	Arsenal	L	0-2	0-1	14		59,378
8	15	H	Everton	D	1-1	0-0	14	Knockaert [82]	30,565
9	20	A	West Ham U	W	3-0	2-0	10	Murray 2 (1 pen) [10, 75 (p)], Izquierdo [45]	56,977
10	29	H	Southampton	D	1-1	0-1	12	Murray [52]	30,564
11	Nov 4	A	Swansea C	W	1-0	1-0	8	Murray [29]	20,822
12	20	H	Stoke C	D	2-2	1-2	9	Gross [44], Izquierdo [60]	29,676
13	25	A	Manchester U	L	0-1	0-0	9		75,018
14	28	H	Crystal Palace	D	0-0	0-0	10		29,889
15	Dec 2	H	Liverpool	L	1-5	0-2	11	Murray (pen) [51]	30,634
16	9	A	Huddersfield T	L	0-2	0-2	13		24,018
17	13	A	Tottenham H	L	0-2	0-1	13		55,124
18	16	H	Burnley	D	0-0	0-0	13		29,921
19	23	H	Watford	W	1-0	0-0	12	Gross [64]	30,473
20	26	A	Chelsea	L	0-2	0-0	12		41,568
21	30	A	Newcastle U	D	0-0	0-0	12		52,209
22	Jan 1	H	Bournemouth	D	2-2	1-1	12	Knockaert [5], Murray [48]	30,152
23	13	A	WBA	L	0-2	0-1	15		25,240
24	20	H	Chelsea	L	0-4	0-2	16		30,600
25	31	A	Southampton	D	1-1	1-0	15	Murray (pen) [14]	30,034
26	Feb 3	H	West Ham U	W	3-1	1-0	13	Murray [8], Izquierdo [59], Gross [75]	30,589
27	10	A	Stoke C	D	1-1	1-0	13	Izquierdo [32]	29,876
28	24	H	Swansea C	W	4-1	1-0	12	Murray 2 (1 pen) [18 (p), 69], Knockaert [73], Locadia [90]	30,523
29	Mar 4	H	Arsenal	W	2-1	2-1	10	Dunk [7], Murray [26]	30,620
30	10	A	Everton	L	0-2	0-0	11		39,199
31	31	H	Leicester C	L	0-2	0-0	13		30,629
32	Apr 7	H	Huddersfield T	D	1-1	1-1	13	Lossl (og) [29]	30,501
33	14	A	Crystal Palace	L	2-3	2-3	13	Murray [18], Izquierdo [34]	24,656
34	17	H	Tottenham H	D	1-1	0-0	13	Gross (pen) [50]	30,440
35	28	H	Burnley	D	0-0	0-0	14		19,459
36	May 4	H	Manchester U	W	1-0	0-0	11	Gross [57]	30,611
37	9	A	Manchester C	L	1-3	1-2	14	Ulloa [20]	54,013
38	13	A	Liverpool	L	0-4	0-2	15		50,752

Final League Position: 15

GOALSCORERS

League (34): Murray 12 (4 pens), Gross 7 (1 pen), Izquierdo 5, Knockaert 3, Hemed 2, Dunk 1, Locadia 1, March 1, Ulloa 1, own goal 1.
FA Cup (6): Murray 2, Goldson 1, Locadia 1, Stephens 1, Ulloa 1.
Carabao Cup (1): Tilley 1.
Checkatrade Trophy (3): Mandroiu 1, Murphy 1, Tilley 1.

Ryan M 38	Saltor B 23+2	Duffy S 37	Dunk L 38	Suttner M 13+1	March S 18+18	Stephens D 36	Propper D 35	Brown I 4+9	Gross P 35+3	Hemed T 9+7	Murphy J 1+3	Murray G 25+10	Knockaert A 27+6	Rosenior L 1+2	Izquierdo J 23+9	Bong G 25	Schelotto E 15+5	Hunemeier U —+1	Kayal B 8+11	Goldson C 2+1	Baldock S —+2	Ulloa J 2+8	Locadia J 3+3	Match No.
1	2	3	4	5	6³	7	8	9²	10	11¹	12	13	14											1
1	2	3	4	5	6	7	8		10¹	13	9	11²	12											2
1	2²	3	4	5	9	7	8		10¹	11	14				6³	12	13							3
1	2²	3	4	5	9	7	8		10	11¹		13	6	12										4
1		3	4	5	9	7	8		10²	11		13	6¹	2	12									5
1	2	3	4	5	9	7	8		10	11	12		6¹											6
1	2	3	4		6²	8	7	11¹	9			13	14		10³	5	12							7
1	2	3²	4	5	9³	7	8	14	10			11¹	6		12			13						8
1	2	3	4		12	7	8	13	10³			11	6¹		9²	5	14							9
1	2	3	4		13	7	8	12	10¹			11	6		9²	5								10
1	2	3	4		12	7	8	14	10¹	13		11¹	6		9²	5								11
1	2	3	4		12	7	8	14	10³			11	6¹		9²	5	13							12
1	2	3	4		10³	8	9	14	7¹	12		11²	6		13	5								13
1	2	3	4	5	12	7	8	13	10³	14		11²	6		9¹									14
1	2³	3	4		13	7	8	9¹	10			11	6²		12	5	14							15
1	2	3	4	5	12	7	8	9³	10¹	14		11			13		6²							16
1		3	4		12	8	9		14	11³		13	6		10¹	5	2		7²					17
1	2	3	4		10	7	6	13	9³	12		11¹	8²		14	5								18
1	2		4	5	9³	7	8		10²	11¹		13	6		14				12	3				19
1		3	4	5	6¹	8	9		12	11¹³		13	14		10		2		7²					20
1	2	3	4		9	7	8		10	12		11¹	6			5								21
1	12	3	4	5		7	8	10²				11	6		9		2¹							22
1	2	3	4		12	7	8²	10³				11	6		9¹	5			14	13				23
1		4	5	6	11¹	8	9		7²	10⁹		12			14		2		13	3				24
1		3	4		6	7	8	10¹				11²	6		9	5	2		8			12		25
1		3	4		13	7	8	10²				11	6³		9	5	2		14			12		26
1		3	4		6¹	7	8	10²				11³	14		9	5	2		13			12		27
1		3	4		12	7	8	10¹				11²	6³		9	5	2		14				13	28
1	12	3	4		13	7	8	10¹				11	6³		9	5	2²		14					29
1		3	4	14		8		10				11	6⁸		9	5²	2		7²			13	12	30
1		3	4		12		6		8			11			10	5	2		9²	13		7¹		31
1		3	4		6	7	8⁸	10²				11¹			9	5	2		13			12		32
1		3	4		14	8		6²				10	12		9	5¹	2		7			13	11³	33
1	2	3	4		13	7		10				11²	6		9¹	5			8			12		34
1	2³	3	4		13	8		10				12	6		9¹	5	14		7			11²		35
1	2	3	4		13	7	8	6¹				10³	9		11²	5			12			14		36
1	2	3	4		14	8	7	10¹				6			9³	5			13			11²	12	37
1		3²	4		10	6	7	12				13	8			5	2		9³ 14			11¹		38

FA Cup

Third Round	Crystal Palace	(h)	2-1
Fourth Round	Middlesbrough	(a)	1-0
Fifth Round	Coventry C	(h)	3-1
Sixth Round	Manchester U	(a)	0-2

Carabao Cup

Second Round	Barnet	(h)	1-0
Third Round	Bournemouth	(a)	0-1
(aet)			

Checkatrade Trophy (Brighton & HA U21)

Southern Group G Milton Keynes D	(a)	0-2
Southern Group G Oxford U	(a)	2-2
(Brighton & HA U21 won 5-4 on penalties)		
Southern Group G Stevenage	(a)	1-3

BRISTOL CITY

FOUNDATION

The name Bristol City came into being in 1897 when the Bristol South End club, formed three years earlier, decided to adopt professionalism and apply for admission to the Southern League after competing in the Western League. The historic meeting was held at the Albert Hall, Bedminster. Bristol City employed Sam Hollis from Woolwich Arsenal as manager and gave him £40 to buy players. In 1900 they merged with Bedminster, another leading Bristol club.

Ashton Gate Stadium, Ashton Road, Bristol BS3 2EJ.

Telephone: (0117) 963 0600.

Fax: (0117) 963 0700.

Ticket Office: (0117) 963 0600 (option 1).

Website: www.bcfc.co.uk

Email: supporterservices@bristol-sport.co.uk

Ground Capacity: 26,459.

Record Attendance: 43,335 v Preston NE, FA Cup 5th rd, 16 February 1935.

Pitch Measurements: 105m × 67m (115yd × 73yd).

Chairman: Keith Dawe.

Chief Operating Officer: Mark Ashton.

Head Coach: Lee Johnson.

Assistant Head Coach: Dean Holden.

Colours: Red shirts with thin white stripes, white shorts with red trim, red socks with white trim.

Year Formed: 1894.

Turned Professional: 1897.

Previous Name: 1894, Bristol South End; 1897, Bristol City.

Club Nickname: 'Robins'.

Grounds: 1894, St John's Lane; 1904, Ashton Gate.

First Football League Game: 7 September 1901, Division 2, v Blackpool (a) W 2–0 – Moles; Tuft, Davies; Jones, McLean, Chambers; Bradbury, Connor, Boucher, O'Brien (2), Flynn.

Record League Victory: 9–0 v Aldershot, Division 3 (S), 28 December 1946 – Eddols; Morgan, Fox; Peacock, Roberts, Jones (1); Chilcott, Thomas, Clark (4 incl. 1p), Cyril Williams (1), Hargreaves (3).

Record Cup Victory: 11–0 v Chichester C, FA Cup 1st rd, 5 November 1960 – Cook; Collinson, Thresher; Connor, Alan Williams, Etheridge; Tait (1), Bobby Williams (1), Atyeo (5), Adrian Williams (3), Derrick, (1 og).

Record Defeat: 0–9 v Coventry C, Division 3 (S), 28 April 1934.

HONOURS

League Champions: Division 2 – 1905–06; FL 1 – 2014–15; Division 3S – 1922–23, 1926–27, 1954–55. *Runners-up:* Division 1 – 1906–07; Division 2 – 1975–76; FL 1 – 2006–07; Second Division – 1997–98; Division 3 – 1964–65, 1989–90; Division 3S – 1937–38.
FA Cup: Runners-up: 1909.
League Cup: semi-final – 1971, 1989.
League Trophy Winners: 1986, 2003, 2015. *Runners-up:* 1987, 2000.
Welsh Cup Winners: 1934.
Anglo-Scottish Cup Winners: 1978.

THE **Sun** FACT FILE

Bristol City inaugurated their first set of floodlights with a friendly against Wolverhampton Wanderers on 27 January 1963, going down to a 4-1 defeat in front of 24,319. These lights were eventually sold to Burton Albion and a second set was installed. The grand opening for these was also against Wolves, this time on 28 December 1965. The visitors again won, 1-0, watched by 36,183.

Most League Points (2 for a win): 70, Division 3 (S), 1954–55.

Most League Points (3 for a win): 99, FL 1, 2014–15.

Most League Goals: 104, Division 3 (S), 1926–27.

Highest League Scorer in Season: Don Clark, 36, Division 3 (S), 1946–47.

Most League Goals in Total Aggregate: John Atyeo, 314, 1951–66.

Most League Goals in One Match: 6, Tommy 'Tot' Walsh v Gillingham, Division 3 (S), 15 January 1927.

Most Capped Player: Billy Wedlock, 26, England.

Most League Appearances: John Atyeo, 596, 1951–66.

Youngest League Player: Marvin Brown, 16 years 105 days v Bristol R, 17 October 1999.

Record Transfer Fee Received: £11,000,000 from Aston Villa for Jonathan Kodjia, August 2016.

Record Transfer Fee Paid: £5,300,000 to Angers for Famara Diedhiou, June 2017.

Football League Record: 1901 Elected to Division 2; 1906–11 Division 1; 1911–22 Division 2; 1922–23 Division 3 (S); 1923–24 Division 2; 1924–27 Division 3 (S); 1927–32 Division 2; 1932–55 Division 3 (S); 1955–60 Division 2; 1960–65 Division 3; 1965–76 Division 2; 1976–80 Division 1; 1980–81 Division 2; 1981–82 Division 3; 1982–84 Division 4; 1984–90 Division 3; 1990–92 Division 2; 1992–95 Division 1; 1995–98 Division 2; 1998–99 Division 1; 1999–2004 Division 2; 2004–07 FL 1; 2007–13 FL C; 2013–15 FL 1; 2015– FL C.

LATEST SEQUENCES

Longest Sequence of League Wins: 14, 9.9.1905 – 2.12.1905.

Longest Sequence of League Defeats: 8, 10.12.2016 – 21.1.2017.

Longest Sequence of League Draws: 4, 6.11.1999 – 27.11.1999.

Longest Sequence of Unbeaten League Matches: 24, 9.9.1905 – 10.2.1906.

Longest Sequence Without a League Win: 21, 16.3.2013 – 22.10.2013.

Successive Scoring Runs: 25 from 26.12.1905.

Successive Non-scoring Runs: 6 from 20.12.1980.

MANAGERS

Sam Hollis 1897–99
Bob Campbell 1899–1901
Sam Hollis 1901–05
Harry Thickett 1905–10
Frank Bacon 1910–11
Sam Hollis 1911–13
George Hedley 1913–17
Jack Hamilton 1917–19
Joe Palmer 1919–21
Alex Raisbeck 1921–29
Joe Bradshaw 1929–32
Bob Hewison 1932–49
  (*under suspension 1938–39*)
Bob Wright 1949–50
Pat Beasley 1950–58
Peter Doherty 1958–60
Fred Ford 1960–67
Alan Dicks 1967–80
Bobby Houghton 1980–82
Roy Hodgson 1982
Terry Cooper 1982–88
  (*Director from 1983*)
Joe Jordan 1988–90
Jimmy Lumsden 1990–92
Denis Smith 1992–93
Russell Osman 1993–94
Joe Jordan 1994–97
John Ward 1997–98
Benny Lennartsson 1998–99
Tony Pulis 1999–2000
Tony Fawthrop 2000
Danny Wilson 2000–04
Brian Tinnion 2004–05
Gary Johnson 2005–10
Steve Coppell 2010
Keith Millen 2010–11
Derek McInnes 2011–13
Sean O'Driscoll 2013
Steve Cotterill 2013–16
Lee Johnson February 2016–

TEN YEAR LEAGUE RECORD

		P	W	D	L	F	A	Pts	Pos
2008-09	FL C	46	15	16	15	54	54	61	10
2009-10	FL C	46	15	18	13	56	65	63	10
2010-11	FL C	46	17	9	20	62	65	60	15
2011-12	FL C	46	12	13	21	44	68	49	20
2012-13	FL C	46	11	8	27	59	84	41	24
2013-14	FL 1	46	13	19	14	70	67	58	12
2014-15	FL 1	46	29	12	5	96	38	99	1
2015-16	FL C	46	13	13	20	54	71	52	18
2016-17	FL C	46	15	9	22	60	66	54	17
2017-18	FL C	46	17	16	13	67	58	67	11

DID YOU KNOW ?

Bristol City experienced a very difficult season in 2012–13 when they were relegated from the Championship after finishing bottom of the division. The Supporters' Club and Trust made no Player of the Year award that season but two years later when they topped the League One table with a club-record 99 points the award was given to the whole team.

BRISTOL CITY – SKY BET CHAMPIONSHIP 2017–18 LEAGUE RECORD

Match No.	Date	Venue	Opponents	Result		H/T Score	Lg Pos.	Goalscorers	Atten- dance
1	Aug 5	H	Barnsley	W	3-1	3-0	1	Reid 2 [16, 30], Diedhiou [25]	18,742
2	12	A	Birmingham C	L	1-2	1-1	9	Reid [1]	21,269
3	15	A	Brentford	D	2-2	1-0	10	Brownhill [5], Reid [90]	9811
4	19	H	Millwall	D	0-0	0-0	11		18,230
5	25	A	Aston Villa	D	1-1	0-1	10	Paterson [60]	21,542
6	Sept 9	A	Reading	W	1-0	0-0	9	Flint [84]	18,650
7	12	A	Wolverhampton W	D	3-3	1-1	12	Flint [43], Diedhiou (pen) [58], Reid [82]	23,045
8	16	H	Derby Co	W	4-1	0-1	8	Woodrow [50], Reid (pen) [55], Paterson [83], Diedhiou [90]	19,473
9	23	A	Norwich C	D	0-0	0-0	8		25,715
10	26	H	Bolton W	W	2-0	1-0	7	Diedhiou [39], Flint [77]	17,203
11	30	A	Ipswich T	W	3-1	2-1	5	Brownhill [2], Diedhiou [31], Reid [82]	15,256
12	Oct 13	H	Burton Alb	D	0-0	0-0	3		18,212
13	21	H	Leeds U	L	0-3	0-2	6		24,435
14	28	A	Sunderland	W	2-1	1-1	4	Reid [28], Djuric [73]	27,317
15	31	A	Fulham	W	2-0	2-0	4	Reid [29], Smith [40]	17,634
16	Nov 4	H	Cardiff C	W	2-1	1-1	4	O'Dowda [20], Flint [66]	21,692
17	18	A	Sheffield W	D	0-0	0-0	4		25,916
18	21	H	Preston NE	L	1-2	0-1	5	Woodrow [90]	17,355
19	25	A	Hull C	W	3-2	0-1	5	Flint [68], Reid [79], Brownhill [89]	14,762
20	Dec 2	H	Middlesbrough	W	2-1	0-0	3	Bryan [51], Paterson [54]	18,752
21	8	A	Sheffield U	W	2-1	1-0	3	Paterson [43], Flint [90]	24,409
22	16	H	Nottingham F	W	2-1	2-0	3	Pack [36], Bryan [45]	20,128
23	23	A	QPR	D	1-1	0-1	4	Reid (pen) [81]	13,683
24	26	H	Reading	W	2-0	0-0	2	Paterson [68], Kelly [90]	23,116
25	30	H	Wolverhampton W	L	1-2	0-0	3	Reid [53]	25,540
26	Jan 1	A	Aston Villa	L	0-5	0-2	4		32,604
27	13	H	Norwich C	L	0-1	0-0	5		21,282
28	19	A	Derby Co	D	0-0	0-0	4		26,525
29	27	H	QPR	W	2-0	1-0	4	Diedhiou [45], Bryan [66]	21,492
30	Feb 2	A	Bolton W	L	0-1	0-0	5		14,172
31	10	A	Sunderland	D	3-3	3-0	6	Flint [5], Diedhiou 2 [31, 37]	22,580
32	18	A	Leeds U	D	2-2	2-0	6	Diedhiou [11], Reid [16]	28,004
33	21	H	Fulham	D	1-1	1-1	6	Reid [35]	21,236
34	25	A	Cardiff C	L	0-1	0-0	6		21,018
35	Mar 3	H	Sheffield W	W	4-0	3-0	6	Reid 3 (1 pen) [13, 35, 62 (p)], Brownhill [43]	22,022
36	6	A	Preston NE	L	1-2	0-1	7	Diedhiou [67]	11,264
37	10	A	Burton Alb	D	0-0	0-0	7		4575
38	17	H	Ipswich T	W	1-0	0-0	7	Djuric [64]	21,509
39	30	A	Barnsley	D	2-2	1-1	7	Diedhiou [31], Brownhill [90]	12,236
40	Apr 2	H	Brentford	L	0-1	0-0	7		22,049
41	7	A	Millwall	L	0-2	0-1	8		16,081
42	10	A	Birmingham C	W	3-1	2-1	8	Pack [12], Reid [27], Taylor [84]	20,288
43	14	A	Middlesbrough	L	1-2	1-1	11	Djuric [13]	24,812
44	21	H	Hull C	W	5-5	2-1	10	Pack [37], Diedhiou 2 [40, 53], Reid [64], Bryan [90]	21,136
45	28	A	Nottingham F	D	0-0	0-0	10		24,722
46	May 6	H	Sheffield U	L	2-3	0-3	11	Flint [80], Bryan [75]	23,902

Final League Position: 11

GOALSCORERS

League (67): Reid 19 (3 pens), Diedhiou 13 (1 pen), Flint 8, Brownhill 5, Bryan 5, Paterson 5, Djuric 3, Pack 3, Woodrow 2, Kelly 1, O'Dowda 1, Smith 1, Taylor 1.
FA Cup (0).
Carabao Cup (19): Bryan 2, Hinds 2, Reid 2 (1 pen), Smith 2, Taylor 2, Baker 1, Diedhiou 1, Djuric 1, Eliasson 1, Flint 1, Hegeler 1, O'Dowda 1, Pack 1, Paterson 1.

Fielding F 43	Pisano E 13 + 3	Wright B 36	Hegeler J 3 + 1	Bryan J 42 + 1	Brownhill J 41 + 4	Pack M 36 + 6	Smith K 44 + 1	Paterson J 34 + 7	Diedhiou F 28 + 4	Reid B 46	O'Dowda C 13 + 11	Engvall G — + 2	Flint A 38 + 1	Eliasson N 3 + 10	Baker N 34	O'Neil G — + 4	Hinds F — + 1	Woodrow C 3 + 11	Vyner Z 1	Leko J 5 + 6	Taylor M 4 + 14	Magnusson H 15 + 9	Djuric M 4 + 12	Kelly L 7 + 4	Steele L 3 + 2	Walsh L 3 + 3	Kent R 6 + 4	Diony L 1 + 6	Semenyo A — + 1	Match No.
1	2	3	4³	5	6	7	8	9¹	10	11²	12	13	14																	1
1	2	3	4	5	6²	8	7	9¹	11	10	12			13																2
1	2	3		5	6²	8²	7	9	10³	11	12				4	13	14													3
1	2	3		5	6²	8²	7	9	10¹	11	12				4	13			14											4
1	2	3		5	6	8²	7	9	10³	11	13			14	4			12												5
1				5		7	13	8	9	10²	11	6¹			3	4				2	12									6
1	2			5	8³	14	7	13	10²	11	6				3	4						9¹	12							7
1	2			5	12	8	7	9	13	11¹	14				3	4		10³				6¹								8
1	2			5	8	14	7	9¹	11³	10	12				3	4						6²	13							9
1	2			5		7	8	9²	11³	10¹	6		12		3	4						14	13							10
1	2			5	8	7		9³	11	10¹	6²		13		3	4						12	14							11
1	2			5	7¹	12	8²	9	11	10		6¹			3	4						14	13							12
1	2	4²		5	7	8		12	10	9					3			11³				6²	13⁴	14						13
1	12			5	7	8	14	9²	10	6			4¹		3			11³				13								14
1	2³	4		5	8	6¹	9	10²	11	7					3			13				12	14							15
1			9	7	8²	2		11¹	6				13		3	4						12	5	10						16
1			10¹	6	7	2	13	9	8						3	4						11²	5	12						17
1		5³	7	12	8	9¹		11	6						3	13	4	14					10²							18
1	2		6	8¹	7	12		10	9³						3	13	4	11²					5	14						19
1	2		9³	6	7	8	10²		11¹						3	13	4	14					5	12						20
1	2		5	7	8³	10²	9		11						3	6¹	4	14	13				12							21
1	2		9	6	7	8	10¹		11²						3	4		13				12	5							22
1	2		9	8	12	7		11							3	4		14				6³	10²	13		5¹				23
1	2		9	6	7	8	12⁴		11				4¹		3			13				10²	5	14						24
1¹			9	6³	7	8	10²		11						3	14	4					13	5¹		12					25
	2		9	6	8¹	7	10²		11						3	4		14				12	5¹	13	1					26
1	2		5	8	6	7	10¹		11²						3	4		13	14							9³	12			27
1²	2		9	6	8	7	10	12	11				4¹		3			5						13						28
	2		5	12	7	8	9¹	10²	11				4⁴		3			13				1		6³	14					29
	4		5	7	8²	2	6³	11¹	10	14	3							12				1		9	13					30
1		4	5	2	8	7	9	11³	10²				14					13				6¹	12							31
1	2		5	6¹	7	8	12	11²	10						3		13				4		9							32
1	2		12	7	8	9	10³	11					3	14	4			5²				6¹	13							33
1	2		9	6	8	12	10²	7					3	4¹				5				13	14	11³						34
1	2¹		5	6	8	7	9	11³	10²						3	4			12				13		14					35
1	2		5	6	8	7	9	10	11	3						4¹			12											36
1	2	3			6	7	8	9²	10¹	11						4³			12	14	5					13				37
1	2	3	13		6	7	8	9	11²	10							14		4³	12	5									38
1	2	3			6	7²	8	9	10	11						4			13				12							39
1	2	4¹		5	6		7	12	11³	10		3							14	13		8	9²							40
1	2¹		5	9²	6	8	10	12	11			7³	3	14	4				13											41
1			2	6	7	8		10¹	9³	12	3		4	14					13			11²	5							42
1	12		2	6	7	8		11¹	9	14	3		4¹						13			10²	5²							43
1	2			5	12³	8	7¹	6	10	11	9²	3	4						13				14							44
1	13			9	14	7	2	6	11³	10	12	3	4²										5		8¹					45
1				5	2	7	8	9²	11	10	13	3	6¹								12		4³					14		46

FA Cup
Third Round   Watford   (a)   0-3

Carabao Cup

First Round	Plymouth Arg	(h)	5-0
Second Round	Watford	(a)	3-2
Third Round	Stoke C	(h)	2-0
Fourth Round	Crystal Palace	(h)	4-1
Quarter-Final	Manchester U	(h)	2-1
Semi-Final 1st leg	Manchester C	(a)	1-2
Semi-Final 2nd leg	Manchester C	(h)	2-3

BRISTOL ROVERS

FOUNDATION

Bristol Rovers were formed at a meeting in Stapleton Road, Eastville, in 1883. However, they first went under the name of the Black Arabs (wearing black shirts). Changing their name to Eastville Rovers in their second season in 1888–89, they won the Gloucestershire Senior Cup. Original members of the Bristol & District League in 1892, this eventually became the Western League and Eastville Rovers adopted professionalism in 1897.

The Memorial Stadium, Filton Avenue, Horfield, Bristol BS7 0BF.

Telephone: (0117) 909 6648.

Fax: (0117) 907 4312.

Ticket Office: (0117) 909 6648 (option 1).

Website: www.bristolrovers.co.uk

Email: admin@bristolrovers.co.uk

Ground Capacity: 11,906.

Record Attendance: 38,472 v Preston NE, FA Cup 4th rd, 30 January 1960 (at Eastville); 9,464 v Liverpool, FA Cup 4th rd, 8 February 1992 (at Twerton Park); 12,011 v WBA, FA Cup 6th rd, 9 March 2008 (at Memorial Stadium).

Pitch Measurements: 100m × 64m (109.5yd × 70yd).

Chairman: Steve Hamer.

Manager: Darrell Clarke.

Assistant Manager: Marcus Stewart.

Colours: Blue and white quartered shirts, white shorts with blue trim, white socks with blue trim.

Year Formed: 1883.

Turned Professional: 1897.

Previous Names: 1883, Black Arabs; 1884, Eastville Rovers; 1897, Bristol Eastville Rovers; 1898, Bristol Rovers. *Club Nicknames:* 'The Pirates', 'The Gas'.

Grounds: 1883, Purdown; Three Acres, Ashley Hill; Rudgeway, Fishponds; 1897, Eastville; 1986, Twerton Park; 1996, The Memorial Stadium.

First Football League Game: 28 August 1920, Division 3, v Millwall (a) L 0–2 – Stansfield; Bethune, Panes; Boxley, Kenny, Steele; Chance, Bird, Sims, Bell, Palmer.

Record League Victory: 7–0 v Brighton & HA, Division 3 (S), 29 November 1952 – Hoyle; Bamford, Fox; Pitt, Warren, Sampson; McIlvenny, Roost (2), Lambden (1), Bradford (1), Petherbridge (2), (1 og). 7–0 v Swansea T, Division 2, 2 October 1954 – Radford; Bamford, Watkins; Pitt, Muir, Anderson; Petherbridge, Bradford (2), Meyer, Roost (1), Hooper (2), (2 og). 7–0 v Shrewsbury T, Division 3, 21 March 1964 – Hall; Hillard, Gwyn Jones; Oldfield, Stone (1), Mabbutt; Jarman (2), Brown (1), Biggs (1p), Hamilton, Bobby Jones (2).

Record Cup Victory: 7–1 v Dorchester, FA Cup 4th qualifying rd, 25 October 2014 – Midenhall; Locyer, Trotman (McChrystal), Parkes, Monkhouse (2), Clarke, Mansell (1) (Thomas), Brown, Gosling, Harrison (3), Taylor (1) (White).

Record Defeat: 0–12 v Luton T, Division 3 (S), 13 April 1936.

Most League Points (2 for a win): 64, Division 3 (S), 1952–53.

HONOURS

League Champions: Division 3 – 1989–90; Division 3S – 1952–53.
Runners-up: Division 3 – 1973–74; Conference – (2nd) 2014–15 *(promoted via play-offs).*
FA Cup: 6th rd – 1951, 1958, 2008.
League Cup: 5th rd – 1971, 1972.
League Trophy: Runners-up: 1990, 2007.

THE Sun FACT FILE

When Bristol Rovers entertained Doncaster Rovers on 22 December 1956 they went behind midway through the first half and it was not until the 67th minute that they scored the equaliser. The Pirates went on to score a further five, including four in a six-minute spell during which Dai Ward netted three times, thus recording the club's fastest ever hat-trick.

Most League Points (3 for a win): 93, Division 3, 1989–90.
Most League Goals: 92, Division 3 (S), 1952–53.
Highest League Scorer in Season: Geoff Bradford, 33, Division 3 (S), 1952–53.
Most League Goals in Total Aggregate: Geoff Bradford, 242, 1949–64.
Most League Goals in One Match: 4, Sidney Leigh v Exeter C, Division 3 (S), 2 May 1921; 4, Jonah Wilcox v Bournemouth, Division 3 (S), 12 December 1925; 4, Bill Culley v QPR, Division 3 (S), 5 March 1927; 4, Frank Curran v Swindon T, Division 3 (S), 25 March 1939; 4, Vic Lambden v Aldershot, Division 3 (S), 29 March 1947; 4, George Petherbridge v Torquay U, Division 3 (S), 1 December 1951; 4, Vic Lambden v Colchester U, Division 3 (S), 14 May 1952; 4, Geoff Bradford v Rotherham U, Division 2, 14 March 1959; 4, Robin Stubbs v Gillingham, Division 2, 10 October 1970; 4, Alan Warboys v Brighton & HA, Division 3, 1 December 1973; 4, Jamie Cureton v Reading, Division 2, 16 January 1999; 4, Ellis Harrison v Northampton T, FL 1, 7 January 2017.
Most Capped Player: Vitalijs Astafjevs, 31 (167), Latvia.
Most League Appearances: Stuart Taylor, 546, 1966–80.
Youngest League Player: Ronnie Dix, 15 years 173 days v Charlton Ath, 25 February 1928.
Record Transfer Fee Received: £2,100,000 from Fulham for Barry Hayles, November 1998; £2,100,000 from WBA for Jason Roberts, July 2000.
Record Transfer Fee Paid: £375,000 to QPR for Andy Tillson, November 1992.
Football League Record: 1920 Original Member of Division 3; 1921–53 Division 3 (S); 1953–62 Division 2; 1962–74 Division 3; 1974–81 Division 2; 1981–90 Division 3; 1990–92 Division 2. 1992–93 Division 1; 1993–2001 Division 2; 2001–04 Division 3; 2004–07 FL 2; 2007–11 FL 1; 2011–14 FL 2; 2014–15 Conference Premier; 2015–16 FL 2; 2016– FL 1.

LATEST SEQUENCES

Longest Sequence of League Wins: 12, 18.10.1952 – 17.1.1953.
Longest Sequence of League Defeats: 8, 26.10.2002 – 21.12.2002.
Longest Sequence of League Draws: 6, 4.2.2017 – 28.2.2017.
Longest Sequence of Unbeaten League Matches: 32, 7.4.1973 – 27.1.1974.
Longest Sequence Without a League Win: 20, 5.4.1980 – 1.11.1980.
Successive Scoring Runs: 26 from 26.3.1927.
Successive Non-scoring Runs: 6 from 14.10.1922.

MANAGERS

Alfred Homer 1899–1920
  (continued as Secretary to 1928)
Ben Hall 1920–21
Andy Wilson 1921–26
Joe Palmer 1926–29
Dave McLean 1929–30
Albert Prince-Cox 1930–36
Percy Smith 1936–37
Brough Fletcher 1938–49
Bert Tann 1950–68 *(continued as General Manager to 1972)*
Fred Ford 1968–69
Bill Dodgin Snr 1969–72
Don Megson 1972–77
Bobby Campbell 1978–79
Harold Jarman 1979–80
Terry Cooper 1980–81
Bobby Gould 1981–83
David Williams 1983–85
Bobby Gould 1985–87
Gerry Francis 1987–91
Martin Dobson 1991
Dennis Rofe 1992
Malcolm Allison 1992–93
John Ward 1993–96
Ian Holloway 1996–2001
Garry Thompson 2001
Gerry Francis 2001
Garry Thompson 2001–02
Ray Graydon 2002–04
Ian Atkins 2004–05
Paul Trollope 2005–10
Dave Penney 2011
Paul Buckle 2011–12
Mark McGhee 2012
John Ward 2012–14
Darrell Clarke March 2014–

TEN YEAR LEAGUE RECORD

		P	W	D	L	F	A	Pts	Pos
2008-09	FL 1	46	17	12	17	79	61	63	11
2009-10	FL 1	46	19	5	22	59	70	62	11
2010-11	FL 1	46	11	12	23	48	82	45	22
2011-12	FL 2	46	15	12	19	60	70	57	13
2012-13	FL 2	46	16	12	18	60	69	60	14
2013-14	FL 2	46	12	14	20	43	54	50	23
2014-15	Conf P	46	25	16	5	73	34	91	2
2015-16	FL 2	46	26	7	13	77	46	85	3
2016-17	FL 1	46	18	12	16	68	70	66	10
2017-18	FL 1	46	16	11	19	60	66	59	13

DID YOU KNOW ?

Bristol Rovers attracted an average home attendance of more than 20,000 in every season between 1952–53 and 1957–58. An all-time club-record average of 24,662 was achieved in the 1953–54 season.

BRISTOL ROVERS – SKY BET LEAGUE ONE 2017–18 LEAGUE RECORD

Match No.	Date	Venue	Opponents	Result	H/T Score	Lg Pos.	Goalscorers	Atten- dance
1	Aug 5	A	Charlton Ath	L 0-1	0-1	18		12,968
2	12	H	Peterborough U	L 1-4	0-1	24	Gaffney [85]	9758
3	19	A	Bury	W 3-2	0-0	18	Lockyer [55], Bodin 2 [73, 85]	3402
4	26	H	Fleetwood T	W 3-1	2-0	11	Sinclair [26], Bodin [43], Harrison [79]	8363
5	Sept 2	A	Bradford C	L 1-3	0-1	13	Bodin [81]	19,284
6	9	H	Walsall	W 2-1	1-0	12	Gaffney [5], Clarke, O [86]	8544
7	12	H	Oldham Ath	L 2-3	0-0	12	Gaffney [83], Sweeney [85]	7908
8	16	A	Wigan Ath	L 0-3	0-1	15		8732
9	23	H	Blackpool	W 3-1	1-1	14	Bodin [40], Sweeney [84], Harrison [90]	8431
10	26	A	Portsmouth	L 0-3	0-1	16		17,716
11	30	H	Plymouth Arg	W 2-1	1-0	14	Gaffney [22], Bodin [62]	9879
12	Oct 7	A	Northampton T	W 6-0	1-0	12	Bodin [37], Harrison 2 [56, 61], Gaffney [72], Sercombe [76], Telford [86]	6087
13	14	H	Oxford U	L 0-1	0-0	13		9656
14	17	A	Shrewsbury T	L 0-4	0-4	13		5652
15	21	A	Rochdale	L 0-1	0-1	16		2944
16	28	H	Milton Keynes D	W 2-0	0-0	13	Nichols [65], Gaffney [72]	8701
17	Nov 11	A	Scunthorpe U	L 0-1	0-0	15		4210
18	18	H	AFC Wimbledon	L 1-3	0-2	16	Brown [88]	8734
19	25	H	Blackburn R	L 1-2	0-1	18	Harrison [58]	11,660
20	Dec 2	H	Rotherham U	W 2-1	0-0	15	Harrison [64], Sercombe [75]	7531
21	9	H	Southend U	W 3-0	1-0	15	Bodin [15], Harrison [74], Sercombe [86]	8062
22	16	H	Gillingham	L 1-4	0-2	16	Sercombe [90]	4227
23	23	H	Doncaster R	L 0-1	0-1	17		8300
24	26	A	Walsall	D 0-0	0-0	16		5759
25	30	A	Oldham Ath	D 1-1	0-0	16	Bodin [49]	3928
26	Jan 1	H	Portsmouth	W 2-1	0-0	14	Sinclair [84], Sercombe [90]	10,014
27	13	A	Blackpool	D 0-0	0-0	17		4001
28	20	H	Bradford C	W 3-1	0-1	14	Partington [53], Lines (pen) [84], Sercombe [87]	9064
29	27	A	Doncaster R	W 3-1	1-1	11	Sweeney [24], Gaffney [50], Harrison [85]	8021
30	Feb 3	H	Shrewsbury T	L 1-2	0-0	13	Partington [65]	9380
31	10	A	Oxford U	W 2-1	0-1	11	Bennett [68], Harrison [80]	8471
32	13	H	Rochdale	W 3-2	0-1	11	Sercombe [49], Partington [65], Lines [79]	9219
33	17	A	AFC Wimbledon	L 0-1	0-0	12		4837
34	24	H	Scunthorpe U	D 1-1	0-0	12	Harrison [90]	8346
35	Mar 3	A	Milton Keynes D	W 1-0	0-0	10	Harrison [50]	8240
36	10	H	Northampton T	D 1-1	1-0	9	Bennett [34]	9054
37	17	A	Plymouth Arg	L 2-3	2-1	10	Lines [12], Harrison [36]	13,466
38	24	A	Peterborough U	D 1-1	0-0	11	Craig [55]	5953
39	30	H	Bury	W 2-1	0-0	10	Telford [65], Lines (pen) [85]	9030
40	Apr 2	A	Fleetwood T	L 0-2	0-0	10		2890
41	7	H	Charlton Ath	D 1-1	1-1	10	Bennett [21]	9336
42	14	H	Blackburn R	D 1-1	0-0	11	Lines [90]	10,029
43	21	A	Rotherham U	L 0-2	0-1	12		8579
44	24	H	Wigan Ath	D 1-1	1-0	13	Sercombe [28]	8414
45	28	H	Gillingham	D 1-1	0-0	13	Telford [86]	9715
46	May 5	A	Southend U	D 0-0	0-0	13		8179

Final League Position: 13

GOALSCORERS

League (60): Harrison 12, Bodin 9, Sercombe 8, Gaffney 7, Lines 5 (2 pens), Bennett 3, Partington 3, Sweeney 3, Telford 3, Sinclair 2, Brown 1, Clarke, O 1, Craig 1, Lockyer 1, Nichols 1.
FA Cup (2): Sercombe 1, Sinclair 1.
Carabao Cup (5): Bodin 2, Harrison 2, Sercombe 1.
Checkatrade Trophy (8): Broom 2, Sercombe 2, Telford 2, Nichols 1, Sweeney 1.

Smith A 23	Clarke J 9 + 2	Lockyer T 37	Broadbent T 19 + 3	Brown L 31 + 2	Lines C 36 + 6	Sercombe L 40 + 2	Clarke O 37 + 3	Bodin B 20 + 1	Harrison E 41 + 3	Sinclair S 24 + 5	Nichols T 18 + 21	Broom R — + 3	Gaffney R 21 + 21	Leadbitter D 15 + 2	Sweeney R 17 + 6	Moore B 10 + 10	Slocombe S 23	Partington J 30 + 2	Telford D 1 + 18	Burn J 1	Andre A — + 1	Bola M 15 + 3	Dunnwald K — + 1	Menayese R 2 + 1	Mensah B 3 + 5	Craig T 17	Bennett K 15 + 2	Russe L 1 + 2	Kelly M — + 1	Baghdadi M — + 2	Match No.
1	2²	3	4	5	6	7	8³	9	10¹	11	12	13	14																		1
1		3		5	7¹	8	14	6	10²	9	11		13	2	4	12															2
		3		5	8¹	6	8	7	9	10³	13	11²	12	4				1	2	14											3
		4		5	12	6	8	11	13	7²	9¹	10³		3	14			1	2												4
			4	5	6	7	8	9	10²		12		13	2		11¹	1		3		14										5
	4			5	6³	7	8	9	13		11¹		10²	12	3		1²	2		14											6
1		3		5	12	7	8¹	6	11²		10		13	2	4	9³			14												7
		3	12		8	6	7	9²	11		13		10¹	2	4²		1					5									8
		3		5	7	12	8	6	10		11¹		13	9¹	1	4²	14				2			5							9
	3		13	7	8	6	9	10¹		11³			4²	1	2	12					5	14									10
	4			5	6	7	8	9¹	10		12		11²	3	1	2	13				5										11
	3			6	7	8	9³	11¹	13	12		10²		1	2	14					5	4									12
	4	3			8	6	7¹		9	12	11²		10³		13	1	2	14			5										13
	3			8²	6	7		10	12	11³		9¹	13	4		1	2	14			5										14
1		4	5	6	12	7	9³		11²	8	13		10	2				3¹	14												15
1		3	4	5	6²	9	8			7	11¹		10	2		13		12													16
1			4	5	7	6			11	8	10¹		9	2				12			3										17
1	3	4³	5	8	9	7²	12	10	6	11¹		14	2	13																	18
1	3	12	5		10	8	9²	11	7	13		14	2	4²			6¹														19
1	3		5	12	8	7¹	10	11²	9	14		13	2	4			6³														20
1	3		5	14	6	12	9	11³	8	13		10	2	4			7²														21
1	3		5		6	12	9	11	8¹	13	14	10²	2	4			7³														22
1	3		5	12	6		9	11	8²	13		10³	2¹	4			7	14													23
1	3	4	5	8	9	7	6³	10	14	11¹		13	2²						12												24
1	3		5		11	8	9	10²	6	13		12	4				7¹		2												25
1	4	3²	5	7	14	6¹	9	13	8	11		10³	12				2														26
1	3			6	7²	8		11¹	9	12		10	4				2	13			5										27
1	4	3		6	7	8¹		11²	9	12		10³	14				2				5		13								28
1		4	12	7¹	6	8		11²	10	14		9	3				2³				5	13									29
1		3		6	8	7¹		11	9	14		10³					2				5²		13	4	12						30
1		3	5	6	9	8		10²	7			14	2³		13		12								4	11¹					31
1		3	5¹	6	7	8³			9	10²		11			13		2					12			4	14					32
1	3		7	9³	8¹			10²	6	14		13					12				5				4	11					33
1	3		5	8	6			10	7²			11¹			13		2	12						14	4	9³					34
12	3		5	6	7			10				13	14	9²	1	2									4	11³	8¹				35
12	3		5	7	8			10	6²			11³			14	1	2¹	13							4	9					36
5	3			7	9	6²		10³	8	14		13				1	2¹				12				4	11					37
2		3		8	6²	7		11		14		12				1	5				9³			13	4	10¹					38
	4			8		7		10³	11¹			14		13	1	2	12				5			9²	3	6					39
	4		5	8⁴		7		11				14		12	6²	1	2¹	10²							3	9	13				40
2³	3	12	5		7¹	6		11				13			10	1						8²	4	9				14			41
2³	6	4	5	9		8		11¹				12			10²	1		14					3	7						13	42
2	4			8		7		10³	11²	14						9¹	1		13			5			12	3	6				43
2	4		5	7	8	6¹		11	12							10	1									3	9				44
2	3		5	7	8			11³				10²	14	13		9¹	1		12							4	6				45
2	3	4		8	6¹	7¹		10		14						1									11¹	5	9²	12		13	46

FA Cup

First Round	Notts Co	(a)	2-4

Carabao Cup

First Round	Cambridge U	(h)	4-1
Second Round	Fulham	(a)	1-0
Third Round	Wolverhampton W	(a)	0-1

(*aet*)

Checkatrade Trophy

Southern Group C	Wycombe W	(a)	5-1
Southern Group C	West Ham U U21	(h)	1-3
Southern Group C	Swindon T	(h)	2-4

BURNLEY

FOUNDATION

On 18 May 1882 Burnley (Association) Football Club was still known as Burnley Rovers as members of that rugby club had decided on that date to play Association Football in the future. It was only a matter of days later that the members met again and decided to drop Rovers from the club's name.

Turf Moor, Harry Potts Way, Burnley, Lancashire BB10 4BX.

Telephone: (01282) 446 800.

Fax: (01282) 700 014.

Ticket Office: (0844) 807 1882.

Website: www.burnleyfootballclub.com

Email: info@burnleyfc.com

Ground Capacity: 21,944.

Record Attendance: 54,775 v Huddersfield T, FA Cup 3rd rd, 23 February 1924.

Pitch Measurements: 105m × 68m (115yd × 74.5yd).

Chairman: Mike Garlick.

Chief Executive: Dave Baldwin.

Manager: Sean Dyche.

Assistant Manager: Ian Woan.

Colours: Claret shirts with sky blue trim, sky blue shorts with claret trim, sky blue socks with claret trim.

Year Formed: 1882.

Turned Professional: 1883.

Previous Name: 1882, Burnley Rovers; 1882, Burnley.

Club Nickname: 'The Clarets'.

Grounds: 1882, Calder Vale; 1883, Turf Moor.

First Football League Game: 8 September 1888, Football League, v Preston NE (a) L 2–5 – Smith; Lang, Bury, Abrahams, Friel, Keenan, Brady, Tait, Poland (1), Gallocher (1), Yates.

Record League Victory: 9–0 v Darwen, Division 1, 9 January 1892 – Hillman; Walker, McFettridge, Lang, Matthews, Keenan, Nicol (3), Bowes, Espie (1), McLardie (3), Hill (2).

Record Cup Victory: 9–0 v Crystal Palace, FA Cup 2nd rd (replay), 10 February 1909 – Dawson; Barron, McLean; Cretney (2), Leake, Moffat; Morley, Ogden, Smith (3), Abbott (2), Smethams (1). 9–0 v New Brighton, FA Cup 4th rd, 26 January 1957 – Blacklaw; Angus, Winton; Seith, Adamson, Miller; Newlands (1), McIlroy (3), Lawson (3), Cheesebrough (1), Pilkington (1). 9–0 v Penrith, FA Cup 1st rd, 17 November 1984 – Hansbury; Miller, Hampton, Phelan, Overson (Kennedy), Hird (3 incl. 1p), Grewcock (1), Powell (2), Taylor (3), Biggins, Hutchison.

Record Defeat: 0–11 v Darwen, FA Cup 1st rd, 17 October 1885.

Most League Points (2 for a win): 62, Division 2, 1972–73.

HONOURS

League Champions: Division 1 – 1920–21, 1959–60; FL C – 2015–16; Division 2 – 1897–98, 1972–73; Division 3 – 1981–82; Division 4 – 1991–92.
Runners-up: Division 1 – 1919–20, 1961–62; FL C – 2013–14; Division 2 – 1912–13, 1946–47; Second Division – 1999–2000.

FA Cup Winners: 1914.
Runners-up: 1947, 1962.

League Cup: semi-final – 1961, 1969, 1983, 2009.

League Trophy: Runners-up: 1988.

Anglo–Scottish Cup Winners: 1979.

European Competitions
European Cup: 1960–61 *(qf)*.
Fairs Cup: 1966–67.

☀ THE Sun FACT FILE

Burnley's 5-0 win at Milton Keynes Dons on 12 January 2016 gave the Clarets their first away win in six matches on their way to Championship success and a place in the Premier League. George Boyd's 82nd-minute strike provided a small piece of history in that it was the club's 7,000th goal in Football League matches.

Most League Points (3 for a win): 93, FL C, 2013–14; FL C, 2015–16.

Most League Goals: 102, Division 1, 1960–61.

Highest League Scorer in Season: George Beel, 35, Division 1, 1927–28.

Most League Goals in Total Aggregate: George Beel, 179, 1923–32.

Most League Goals in One Match: 6, Louis Page v Birmingham C, Division 1, 10 April 1926.

Most Capped Player: Jimmy McIlroy, 51 (55), Northern Ireland.

Most League Appearances: Jerry Dawson, 522, 1907–28.

Youngest League Player: Tommy Lawton, 16 years 174 days v Doncaster R, 28 March 1936.

Record Transfer Fee Received: £25,000,000 (rising to £30,000,000) from Everton for Michael Keane, July 2017.

Record Transfer Fee Paid: £15,000,000 to Leeds U for Chris Wood, August 2017.

Football League Record: 1888 Original Member of the Football League; 1897–98 Division 2; 1898–1900 Division 1; 1900–13 Division 2; 1913–30 Division 1; 1930–47 Division 2; 1947–71 Division 1; 1971–73 Division 2; 1973–76 Division 1; 1976–80 Division 2; 1980–82 Division 3; 1982–83 Division 2; 1983–85 Division 3; 1985–92 Division 4; 1992–94 Division 3; 1994–95 Division 1; 1995–2000 Division 2; 2000–04 Division 1; 2004–09 FL C; 2009–10 FA Premier League; 2010–14 FL C; 2014–15 FA Premier League; 2015–16 FL C; 2016– FA Premier League.

LATEST SEQUENCES

Longest Sequence of League Wins: 10, 16.11.1912 – 18.1.1913.

Longest Sequence of League Defeats: 8, 2.1.1995 – 25.2.1995.

Longest Sequence of League Draws: 6, 21.2.1931 – 28.3.1931.

Longest Sequence of Unbeaten League Matches: 30, 6.9.1920 – 25.3.1921.

Longest Sequence Without a League Win: 24, 16.4.1979 – 17.11.1979.

Successive Scoring Runs: 27 from 13.2.1926.

Successive Non-scoring Runs: 6 from 21.3.2015.

MANAGERS

Harry Bradshaw 1894–99
  (*Secretary-Manager from 1897*)
Club Directors 1899–1900
J. Ernest Mangnall 1900–03
  (*Secretary-Manager*)
Spen Whittaker 1903–10
  (*Secretary-Manager*)
John Haworth 1910–24
  (*Secretary-Manager*)
Albert Pickles 1925–31
  (*Secretary-Manager*)
Tom Bromilow 1932–35
Selection Committee 1935–45
Cliff Britton 1945–48
Frank Hill 1948–54
Alan Brown 1954–57
Billy Dougall 1957–58
Harry Potts 1958–70
  (*General Manager to 1972*)
Jimmy Adamson 1970–76
Joe Brown 1976–77
Harry Potts 1977–79
Brian Miller 1979–83
John Bond 1983–84
John Benson 1984–85
Martin Buchan 1985
Tommy Cavanagh 1985–86
Brian Miller 1986–89
Frank Casper 1989–91
Jimmy Mullen 1991–96
Adrian Heath 1996–97
Chris Waddle 1997–98
Stan Ternent 1998–2004
Steve Cotterill 2004–07
Owen Coyle 2007–10
Brian Laws 2010
Eddie Howe 2011–12
Sean Dyche October 2012–

TEN YEAR LEAGUE RECORD

		P	W	D	L	F	A	Pts	Pos
2008-09	FL C	46	21	13	12	72	60	76	5
2009-10	PR Lge	38	8	6	24	42	82	30	18
2010-11	FL C	46	18	14	14	65	61	68	8
2011-12	FL C	46	17	11	18	61	58	62	13
2012-13	FL C	46	16	13	17	62	60	61	11
2013-14	FL C	46	26	15	5	72	37	93	2
2014-15	PR Lge	38	7	12	19	28	53	33	19
2015-16	FL C	46	26	15	5	72	35	93	1
2016-17	PR Lge	38	11	7	20	39	55	40	16
2017-18	PR Lge	38	14	12	12	36	39	54	7

DID YOU KNOW ?

It was not until around 1910 that Burnley switched to their now traditional shirt colours of claret and blue. Prior to this they had played in green shirts for close on a decade and were often referred to in the press as 'the green and whites'.

BURNLEY – PREMIER LEAGUE 2017–18 LEAGUE RECORD

Match No.	Date	Venue	Opponents	Result	H/T Score	Lg Pos.	Goalscorers	Attendance
1	Aug 12	A	Chelsea	W 3-2	3-0	4	Vokes 2 [24, 43], Ward [39]	41,616
2	19	H	WBA	L 0-1	0-0	12		19,619
3	27	A	Tottenham H	D 1-1	0-0	10	Wood [90]	67,862
4	Sept 10	H	Crystal Palace	W 1-0	1-0	7	Wood [3]	18,862
5	16	A	Liverpool	D 1-1	1-1	7	Arfield [27]	53,231
6	23	H	Huddersfield T	D 0-0	0-0	9		20,759
7	Oct 1	A	Everton	W 1-0	1-0	6	Hendrick [21]	38,448
8	14	H	West Ham U	D 1-1	0-1	7	Wood [85]	20,945
9	21	A	Manchester C	L 0-3	0-1	9		54,118
10	30	H	Newcastle U	W 1-0	0-0	7	Hendrick [74]	21,031
11	Nov 4	A	Southampton	W 1-0	0-0	7	Vokes [81]	30,491
12	18	H	Swansea C	W 2-0	2-0	7	Cork [29], Barnes [40]	18,895
13	26	H	Arsenal	L 0-1	0-0	7		21,722
14	29	A	Bournemouth	W 2-1	1-0	6	Wood [37], Brady [65]	10,302
15	Dec 2	A	Leicester C	L 0-1	0-1	7		30,714
16	9	H	Watford	W 1-0	1-0	7	Arfield [45]	19,479
17	12	H	Stoke C	W 1-0	0-0	4	Barnes [89]	19,909
18	16	A	Brighton & HA	D 0-0	0-0	5		29,921
19	23	H	Tottenham H	L 0-3	0-1	7		21,650
20	26	A	Manchester U	D 2-2	2-0	7	Barnes [3], Defour [36]	75,046
21	30	A	Huddersfield T	D 0-0	0-0	7		24,095
22	Jan 1	H	Liverpool	L 1-2	0-0	7	Gudmundsson [87]	21,756
23	13	A	Crystal Palace	L 0-1	0-1	7		24,696
24	20	H	Manchester U	L 0-1	0-0	8		21,841
25	31	A	Newcastle U	D 1-1	0-0	7	Darlow (og) [85]	50,174
26	Feb 3	H	Manchester C	D 1-1	0-1	7	Gudmundsson [82]	21,658
27	10	A	Swansea C	L 0-1	0-0	7		20,179
28	24	H	Southampton	D 1-1	0-0	7	Barnes [67]	20,982
29	Mar 3	H	Everton	W 2-1	0-1	7	Barnes [56], Wood [80]	20,802
30	10	A	West Ham U	W 3-0	0-0	7	Barnes [56], Wood 2 [70, 81]	56,904
31	31	A	WBA	W 2-1	1-0	7	Barnes [22], Wood [73]	23,455
32	Apr 7	A	Watford	W 2-1	0-0	7	Vokes [70], Cork [73]	20,044
33	14	H	Leicester C	W 2-1	2-0	7	Wood [6], Long [9]	21,727
34	19	H	Chelsea	L 1-2	0-1	7	Barnes [64]	21,264
35	22	A	Stoke C	D 1-1	0-1	7	Barnes [62]	29,532
36	28	H	Brighton & HA	D 0-0	0-0	7		19,459
37	May 6	A	Arsenal	L 0-5	0-2	7		59,540
38	13	H	Bournemouth	L 1-2	1-0	7	Wood [39]	20,720

Final League Position: 7

GOALSCORERS
League (36): Wood 10, Barnes 9, Vokes 4, Arfield 2, Cork 2, Gudmundsson 2, Hendrick 2, Brady 1, Defour 1, Long 1, Ward 1, own goal 1.
FA Cup (1): Barnes 1.
Carabao Cup (4): Brady 2, Cork 1, Wood 1 (1 pen).

Heaton T 4	Lowton M 25 + 1	Tarkowski J 31	Mee B 29	Ward S 28	Gudmundsson J 32 + 3	Defour S 24	Cork J 38	Brady R 15	Hendrick J 29 + 5	Vokes S 7 + 23	Walters J — + 3	Arfield S 15 + 3	Barnes A 21 + 15	Wood C 20 + 4	Westwood A 12 + 7	Pope N 34 + 1	Bardsley P 13	Long K 16	Taylor C 10 + 1	Wells N — + 9	Nkoudou G 2 + 6	Lennon A 13 + 1	McNeil D — + 1	Match No.
1	2	3	4	5	6^2	7^1	8	9	10	11	12	13												1
1	2	3	4	5	6^2	8	7	9^1	10	11	12		13											2
1	2	3	4	5	6^1	8^3	7	9			11^2	10	12	13	14									3
1^3	2	3	4	5	6	8^2	7	9			11^1	13	10	14	12									4
	2	3	4	5	6^2	7^3	8	9		13		10	12	11^1	14	1								5
	2	3	4	5	13	9	7	6	8^1			10^2	12	11		1								6
	2	3	4	5		7	8	6	10^1	9			12	11		1								7
	2	3	4	5^3	13	8	7	6	10^1	12		9^1	14	11		1								8
	2	3	4	5	13	7^1	8	6	10^2	9			12	11^3	14	1								9
	2	3	4	5	6	7^1	8	9	10				11		12	1								10
	2	3	4	5	6	7	8	9	10^1	13			12	11^2		1								11
	2	3	4	5	6	7	8	9	10^1				12	11		1								12
	2	3	4	5	6	7^1	8	9	10				11		12	1								13
		3	4	5	6	7^3	8	9	10^2	14			13	11^1	12	1	2							14
		3	4	5	6	7^2	8	9^3	10	14		12	13	11^1		1	2							15
			4	5	8	6^2	7	9^1	10	12			11		13	1	2	3						16
		3		5^2	6	8	7	10^1	14			9	13	11^2		1	2	4	12					17
		3	4		6	8^2	7	10	13			9	12	11^1		1	2	5						18
			4		6	7	8	10^3	13			9^1	12	11^2		1	2	3	5	14				19
			4		6	7	9^2		8	12		13	10	11^1		1	2	3	5					20
			4		6	7	8	10^1	12			9		11^2		1	2	3	5	13				21
		3	4		6	8	7	10^1	12			9^1		11		1	2	5	13					22
		3	4		8^2	7	6	9^1				11		10		1	2	5	13	12				23
		3	4		6	7	8	10^3	13			9^1		11^2		1	2	5	14	12				24
			4		6^1	7	10	13	9^2			11			8^3	1	2	3	5	14	12			25
12			4		6	7	8	10	11							1	2^1	3	5		9			26
	2		4		9^2	7	8	10^1	12			11				1		3	5	13	14	6^3		27
	2		4	5	6	7	10	11	8							1		3				9		28
	2	3	4	5	9	7	10^1	11	12			8				1						6		29
	2	3	4	5	9	7	10^2	13	11^1			12			8	1						6		30
	2	3	4	5	8	12	13	10	11^2			7				1				9^1		6		31
	2		4	5		7	13	12	10			11			8	1		3		9^1		6^2		32
	2		4	5	9	7	12	13	10^2			11^1			8	1		3				6		33
	2		4	5	9	7	12		10			11^1			8	1		3			13	6^2		34
	2		4	5	9	7	13	12	11^1			10			8	1		3				6^2		35
	2		4	5	9	7	14	12	11			10^2			8^1	1		3			13	6^2		36
	2		4	5	9^3	7	10	12	11^1						8	1		3		14	13	6^2		37
	2		4	5	9^3	7	10	12	11^2						8	1		3	13			6^1	14	38

FA Cup
Third Round   Manchester C   (a)   1-4

Carabao Cup
Second Round   Blackburn R   (a)   2-0
Third Round   Leeds U   (h)   2-2
(aet; Leeds U won 5-3 on penalties)

BURTON ALBION

FOUNDATION

Once upon a time there were three Football League clubs bearing the name Burton. Then there was none. In reality it had been two. Originally Burton Swifts and Burton Wanderers competed in it until 1901 when they amalgamated to form Burton United. This club disbanded in 1910. There was no senior club representing the town until 1924 when Burton Town, formerly known as Burton All Saints, played in the Birmingham & District League, subsequently joining the Midland League in 1935–36. When the Second World War broke out the club fielded a team in a truncated version of the Birmingham & District League taking over from the club's reserves. But it was not revived in peacetime. So it was not until a further decade that a club bearing the name of Burton reappeared. Founded in 1950 Burton Albion made progress from the Birmingham & District League, too, then into the Southern League and because of its geographical situation later had spells in the Northern Premier League. In April 2009 Burton Albion restored the name of the town to the Football League competition as champions of the Blue Square Premier League.

Pirelli Stadium, Princess Way, Burton-on-Trent, Staffordshire DE13 0AR.

Telephone: (01283) 565 938.

Fax: (01283) 523 199.

Ticket Office: (01283) 565 938.

Website: www.burtonalbionfc.co.uk

Email: bafc@burtonalbionfc.co.uk

Ground Capactiy: 6,972.

Record Attendance: 5,806 v Weymouth, Southern League Cup final 2nd leg, 1964 (at Eton Park); 6,746 v Derby Co, FL C, 26 August 2016 (at Pirelli Stadium).

Pitch Measurements: 100m × 68.5m (109.5yd × 75yd).

Chairman: Ben Robinson.

Manager: Nigel Clough.

Assistant Manager: Gary Crosby.

Colours: Yellow shirts with black sleeves, black shorts with yellow trim, yellow socks with black trim.

Year Formed: 1950.

Turned Professional: 1950.

Club Nickname: 'The Brewers'.

Grounds: 1950, Eton Park; 2005, Pirelli Stadium.

HONOURS

League Champions: FL 2 – 2014–15; Conference – 2008–09.
Runners-up: FL 1 – 2015–16.
FA Cup: 4th rd – 2011.
League Cup: 3rd rd – 2013, 2015.

Sun FACT FILE

Burton Albion gained their first-ever FA Cup victory over a Football League club with a 1-0 home win over Halifax Town in a second-round replay in December 1955. Jack Barker scored the winning goal from the penalty spot in front of a crowd of 5,127. The Brewers then lost 7-0 at Charlton Athletic in their third-round tie.

First Football League Game: 8 August 2009, FL 2, v Shrewsbury T (a) L 1–3 – Redmond; Edworthy, Boertien, Austin, Branston, McGrath, Maghoma, Penn, Phillips (Stride), Walker, Shroot (Pearson) (1).

Record League Victory: 6-1 v Aldershot T, FL 2, 12 December 2009 – Krysiak; James, Boertien, Stride, Webster, McGrath, Jackson, Penn, Kabba (2), Pearson (3) (Harrad) (1), Gilroy (Maghoma).

Record Cup Victory: 12–1 v Coalville T, Birmingham Senior Cup, 6 September 1954.

Record Defeat: 0–10 v Barnet, Southern League, 7 February 1970.

Most League Points (3 for a win): 94, FL 2, 2014–15.

Most League Goals: 71, FL 2, 2009–10; 2012–13.

Highest League Scorer in Season: Shaun Harrad, 21, 2009–10.

Most League Goals in Total Aggregate: Billy Kee, 39, 2011–15.

Most League Goals in One Match: 3, Greg Pearson v Aldershot T, FL 2, 12 December 2009; 3, Shaun Harrad v Rotherham U, FL 2, 11 September 2010; 3, Lucas Akins v Colchester U, FL 1, 23 April 2016.

Most Capped Player: Jackson, Irvine 9 (22), Australia.

Most League Appearances: Damien McCrory, 181, 2012–18.

Youngest League Player: Sam Austin, 17 years 310 days v Stevenage, 25 October 2014.

Record Transfer Fee Received: £2,000,000 from Hull C for Jackson Irvine, August 2017.

Record Transfer Fee Paid: £500,000 to Ross Co for Liam Boyce, June 2017.

Football League Record: 2009 Promoted from Blue Square Premier; 2009–15 FL 2; 2015–16 FL 1; 2016–18 FL C; 2018– FL 1.

MANAGERS

Reg Weston 1953–57
Sammy Crooks 1957
Eddie Shimwell 1958
Bill Townsend 1959–62
Peter Taylor 1962–65
Alex Tait 1965–70
Richie Norman 1970–73
Ken Gutteridge 1973–74
Harold Bodle 1974–76
Ian Storey-Moore 1978–81
Neil Warnock 1981–86
Brian Fidler 1986–88
Vic Halom 1988
Bobby Hope 1988
Chris Wright 1988–89
Ken Blair 1989–90
Steve Powell 1990–91
Brian Fidler 1991–92
Brian Kenning 1992–94
John Barton 1994–98
Nigel Clough 1998–2009
Roy McFarland 2009
Paul Peschisolido 2009–12
Gary Rowett 2012–14
Jimmy Floyd Hasselbaink 2014–15
Nigel Clough December 2015–

LATEST SEQUENCES

Longest Sequence of League Wins: 4, 24.11.2015 – 12.12.2015.
Longest Sequence of League Defeats: 8, 25.2.2012 – 24.3.2012.
Longest Sequence of League Draws: 6, 25.4.2011 – 16.8.2011.
Longest Sequence of Unbeaten League Matches: 13, 7.3.2015 – 8.8.2015.
Longest Sequence Without a League Win: 16, 31.12.2011 – 24.3.2012.
Successive Scoring Runs: 18 from 16.4.2011 – 8.10.2011.
Successive Non-scoring Runs: 5 from 23.9.2017.

TEN YEAR LEAGUE RECORD

		P	W	D	L	F	A	Pts	Pos
2008-09	Conf P	46	27	7	12	81	52	88	1
2009-10	FL 2	46	17	11	18	71	71	62	13
2010-11	FL 2	46	12	15	19	56	70	51	19
2011-12	FL 2	46	14	12	20	54	81	54	17
2012-13	FL 2	46	22	10	14	71	65	76	4
2013-14	FL 2	46	19	15	12	47	42	72	6
2014-15	FL 2	46	28	10	8	69	39	94	1
2015-16	FL 1	46	25	10	11	57	37	85	2
2016-17	FL C	46	13	13	20	49	63	52	20
2017-18	FL C	46	10	11	25	38	81	41	23

DID YOU KNOW ?

Burton Albion have yet to win a game in the EFL Trophy, despite seven attempts to date. The closest they have come to victory was at Coventry City in the 2012–13 season when they drew 0-0 but then lost out 10-9 on penalties.

BURTON ALBION – SKY BET CHAMPIONSHIP 2017–18 LEAGUE RECORD

Match No.	Date	Venue	Opponents	Result	H/T Score	Lg Pos.	Goalscorers	Attendance
1	Aug 5	H	Cardiff C	L	0-1	0-0	19		5050
2	12	A	Hull C	L	1-4	1-1	24	Irvine [33]	14,882
3	15	A	Middlesbrough	L	0-2	0-1	24		24,522
4	18	H	Birmingham C	W	2-1	0-1	19	Sordell [50], Dyer [66]	4948
5	26	H	Sheffield W	D	1-1	0-1	21	Mason [65]	5084
6	Sept 9	A	Leeds U	L	0-5	0-3	22		33,404
7	12	A	Norwich C	D	0-0	0-0	21		24,841
8	16	H	Fulham	W	2-1	1-1	19	Warnock [12], Akins (pen) [51]	4049
9	23	A	QPR	D	0-0	0-0	19		12,500
10	26	H	Aston Villa	L	0-4	0-3	19		5786
11	30	H	Wolverhampton W	L	0-4	0-3	21		5080
12	Oct 13	A	Bristol C	D	0-0	0-0	20		18,212
13	21	A	Nottingham F	L	0-2	0-0	22		24,686
14	28	H	Ipswich T	L	1-2	0-0	22	Turner [57]	4110
15	31	H	Barnsley	L	2-4	2-2	23	Lund [37], Dyer [45]	3761
16	Nov 4	A	Millwall	W	1-0	0-0	21	Sordell [70]	11,507
17	17	H	Sheffield U	L	1-3	1-2	21	Palmer [31]	5167
18	21	A	Brentford	D	1-1	0-0	22	Turner [78]	7957
19	25	H	Sunderland	L	0-2	0-0	23		4808
20	Dec 2	A	Derby Co	L	0-1	0-0	24		26,761
21	9	H	Preston NE	L	1-2	0-0	24	Akins [90]	3659
22	16	A	Bolton W	W	1-0	1-0	22	Dyer [23]	13,632
23	23	A	Reading	W	2-1	1-0	21	Flanagan [40], Naylor [81]	21,771
24	26	H	Leeds U	L	1-2	1-0	21	Naylor [29]	5612
25	30	H	Norwich C	D	0-0	0-0	23		4565
26	Jan 1	A	Sheffield W	W	3-0	1-0	22	Flanagan [37], Dyer [50], Naylor [89]	25,506
27	13	H	QPR	L	1-3	1-1	22	Dyer [34]	4264
28	20	A	Fulham	L	0-6	0-3	24		19,003
29	30	H	Reading	L	1-3	0-1	24	Akins (pen) [51]	2750
30	Feb 3	A	Aston Villa	L	2-3	0-1	24	Elmohamady (og) [71], Boyce [90]	33,022
31	10	A	Ipswich T	D	0-0	0-0	24		13,815
32	17	H	Nottingham F	D	0-0	0-0	24		5775
33	20	A	Barnsley	W	2-1	2-0	22	Allen [1], Davenport [45]	11,774
34	24	H	Millwall	L	0-1	0-0	23		4105
35	Mar 6	H	Brentford	L	0-2	0-0	23		3464
36	10	H	Bristol C	D	0-0	0-0	23		4575
37	13	A	Sheffield U	L	0-2	0-1	23		24,832
38	17	A	Wolverhampton W	L	1-3	1-2	23	Dyer [44]	29,977
39	30	A	Cardiff C	L	1-3	1-2	24	Bent [21]	21,086
40	Apr 2	H	Middlesbrough	D	1-1	1-0	24	Sordell [6]	4468
41	7	A	Birmingham C	D	1-1	0-0	24	Dyer [48]	22,311
42	10	H	Hull C	L	0-5	0-2	24		3659
43	14	A	Derby Co	W	3-1	2-1	23	Boyce [24], Murphy [44], Akins [68]	5563
44	21	A	Sunderland	W	2-1	0-1	23	Bent [86], Boyce [90]	25,475
45	28	H	Bolton W	W	2-0	2-0	22	Akpan [28], Akins [36]	6535
46	May 6	A	Preston NE	L	1-2	0-1	23	Akpan [63]	17,058

Final League Position: 23

GOALSCORERS

League (38): Dyer 7, Akins 5 (2 pens), Boyce 3, Naylor 3, Sordell 3, Akpan 2, Bent 2, Flanagan 2, Turner 2, Allen 1, Davenport 1, Irvine 1, Lund 1, Mason 1, Murphy 1, Palmer 1, Warnock 1, own goal 1.
FA Cup (0).
Carabao Cup (6): Akins 1 (1 pen), Dyer 1, Fox 1, Lund 1, Naylor 1, Varney 1.

Players (appearances + substitute appearances):

- Bywater S 44
- Mousinho J 1
- McFadzean K 39 + 3
- Buxton J 29 + 3
- Warnock S 13 + 1
- Sordell M 30 + 10
- Murphy L 34 + 4
- Lund M 10 + 2
- Irvine J 3
- Dyer L 30 + 8
- Akins L 39 + 3
- Akpan H 19 + 7
- Varney L 1 + 17
- Sbarra J 4 + 13
- Naylor T 32 + 1
- Flanagan T 20 + 7
- McCrory D 9 + 2
- Palmer M 8 + 3
- Turner B 26 + 4
- Scannell S 13 + 5
- Mason J 3 + 3
- Brayford J 27 + 1
- Allen J 19 + 10
- Ripley C 2
- Miller W 7 + 3
- Samuelsen M 7 + 2
- Bent D 10 + 5
- Davenport J 15 + 2
- Boyce L 12 + 4
- Egert T — + 3
- Barker S — + 1

Bywater	Mousinho	McFadzean	Buxton	Warnock	Sordell	Murphy	Lund	Irvine	Dyer	Akins	Akpan	Varney	Sbarra	Naylor	Flanagan	McCrory	Palmer	Turner	Scannell	Mason	Brayford	Allen	Ripley	Miller	Samuelsen	Bent	Davenport	Boyce	Egert	Barker	Match No.
1	2^2	3	4	5	6^3	7	8	9	10^1	11	12	13	14																		1
1		3	4	9^3	11^1	6	5	8^4	12	10	7^2		14	2	13																2
1		3	4		6^1	8^2	7		10	11^3	12^4	13		14	2	13															3
1		3	4		10	7	6^1	11	9	5		13		2		12	8^2														4
1		7	3		11^2	8			9	10				2	14	5^3	12	4			6^1	13									5
1	6^1	3	5	13		8			12	11						14	4	10^3	7^2	2	9										6
1		3	2		9^3	11^2	7		13	6		12				14		4			10^5	5	8								7
1		3	2		9	11	7	12		6		13						4	10^2			5	8								8
1		3	2		9	11^3	7		12	6	14	13						4	10^1			5	8^2								9
1		3	2		4	13	7		9	10	6^2	14						4^2	10	14	5^3	7									10
1		3	2		4	13	7		9	10	6^2	14		12	5^1			11^3				8									11
1		3	2		9	13	7	12		14	5			6^2	11^1			4				10^3	8								12
1		3	2		8	13	6		11	10^3		14				12		4^1	9		5^2	7									13
1		3	2		9	10^1	7	6		11	5			13				12	4			8^2	1								14
1		3	2		9^1	13	7	8		11	10^2	6^3	14					4	5			12^1	1								15
1		2	3	13	10^3	7	6		11	12		14						5¹	8	4	9^2										16
1		2	3	5^1	10	6	8		11^2	12				9	4	13						7^3	14								17
1		3			11	9	7^2			6				13	2	5	8^3	4	10^1			14	12								18
1	14				11	7				2				10^3	3	5	8	4	6^1	12		13	9^2								19
1		4			11^1	8				7				12	13	3	6	9^2	5		2		10								20
1		3				7^2			10	11		14	13	3	6	5	9	4^1	12		2		8^3								21
1	12	3			11^1	7			10	8				6	5			4	13		2		9^2								22
1	14	4			11^3	9^1			10	2				8	6			5	13		3	12	7^2								23
1		4			11				10	2				8	6			5	7^1		3	9	12								24
1	3				11^2	8			10	2	14			13	7	5		4	6^3		12	9^1									25
1	3	4				9^3			10^2	11	13			8	6	5	14				2	12	7^1								26
1	3^3	4			14	9^1			10	11		12		8	6	5					2	13	7^2								27
1	5	4			11	9^2			10	2	13			14	8	6	3^3	12					7^1								28
1	2	3			13	7			10	12				6	9			4			5			8^2	11^1						29
1	3				7	12^3			10	11	9			8	5^2			4^1			2	13				6	14				30
1	4				13				10^1	2	9			3				5	8						7	11^2	6	12			31
1	4				14				10	2	9^1	12	3					5^2	8^3						7	11	6	13			32
1	4	13							5	2	9	14	10^1	3					8^3						7	12	6	11^2			33
1	4								10	2	9	14		3		12		5^2	8^3						7^1	11	6	13			34
1	4				13	8			10	2				3	6^1	8			9						7^1	14	6	11^2			35
1	4				9	7			12	6^1	8			3	2	5					13	10^2	14	11^3							36
1	4	13			7				10		9	14	12	3	2^1	5			8^2						13	6	11				37
1	5^1	4			7^2				10		9	13	12	3	2	6									8	11³	14				38
1	4				6	8			9			14	3	5				2^3	7						11^1	12	10^3	13			39
1	4^2				6	12			9		8^1			3	5		14				2	13			11	7	10^3				40
1	4				6	14			9	12	8			3	5^2		13				2				11^3	7^1	10				41
1		4			6				9^2	2	8			3	3^3	14					13				5^1	12	11	7	10		42
1	3	4				8				7	9		10^1					5			2	12				6^3	11^2	14	13	43
1	4				14	8^3			7	9			10^1	3	5^2	12					2				13	6	11			44
1	4	12			7	8			10	9				3				5			2				13	6^1	11^3				45
1	4				7	8		13	10	9				3	5^1			2							12	6^2	11				46

FA Cup
Third Round — Birmingham C — (a) 0-1

Carabao Cup
First Round — Oldham Ath — (a) 3-2
Second Round — Cardiff C — (a) 2-1
Third Round — Manchester U — (a) 1-4

BURY

FOUNDATION

A meeting at the Waggon & Horses Hotel, attended largely by members of Bury Wesleyans and Bury Unitarians football clubs, decided to form a new Bury club. This was officially formed at a subsequent gathering at the Old White Horse Hotel, Fleet Street, Bury on 24 April 1885.

The Energy Check Stadium@Gigg Lane, Bury, Lancashire BL9 9HR.

Telephone: (0161) 764 4881.

Fax: (0161) 764 5521.

Ticket Office: (0161) 764 5521 (option 1).

Website: www.buryfc.co.uk

Email: info@buryfc.co.uk

Ground Capacity: 11,376.

Record Attendance: 35,000 v Bolton W, FA Cup 3rd rd, 9 January 1960.

Pitch Measurements: 102.5m × 67m (112yd × 73yd).

Chairman: Stewart Day.

Chief Executive: Karl Evans.

Manager: Ryan Lowe.

First-Team Coach: Steven Schumacher.

Colours: White shirts with blue trim, blue shorts with white trim, blue socks.

Year Formed: 1885.

Turned Professional: 1885.

Club Nickname: 'The Shakers'.

Ground: 1885, Gigg Lane (renamed JD Stadium 2013); 2015 Gigg Lane (renamed The Energy Check Stadium@Gigg Lane 2017).

First Football League Game: 1 September 1894, Division 2, v Manchester C (h) W 4–2 – Lowe; Gillespie, Davies; White, Clegg, Ross; Wylie, Barbour (2), Millar (1), Ostler (1), Plant.

Record League Victory: 8–0 v Tranmere R, Division 3, 10 January 1970 – Forrest; Tinney, Saile; Anderson, Turner, McDermott; Hince (1), Arrowsmith (1), Jones (4), Kerr (1), Grundy, (1 og).

Record Cup Victory: 12–1 v Stockton, FA Cup 1st rd (replay), 2 February 1897 – Montgomery; Darroch, Barbour; Hendry (1), Clegg, Ross (1); Wylie (3), Pangbourn, Millar (4), Henderson (2), Plant, (1 og).

Record Defeat: 0–10 v Blackburn R, FA Cup pr rd, 1 October 1887. 0–10 v West Ham U, Milk Cup 2nd rd 2nd leg, 25 October 1983.

Most League Points (2 for a win): 68, Division 3, 1960–61.

Most League Points (3 for a win): 85, FL 2, 2014–15.

HONOURS

League Champions: Division 2 – 1894–95; Second Division – 1996–97; Division 3 – 1960–61.
Runners-up: Division 2 – 1923–24; Division 3 – 1967–68; FL 2 – 2010–11.
FA Cup Winners: 1900, 1903.
League Cup: semi-final – 1963.

☀THE **Sun** FACT FILE

Bury defeated Chester City 3-1 in an FA Cup second-round replay in December 2006 but were then expelled from the competition for fielding an ineligible player. The Shakers were deemed to have failed to have complied with all regulations before playing loanee Stephen Turnbull of Hartlepool United.

Most League Goals: 108, Division 3, 1960–61.

Highest League Scorer in Season: Craig Madden, 35, Division 4, 1981–82.

Most League Goals in Total Aggregate: Craig Madden, 129, 1978–86.

Most League Goals in One Match: 5, Eddie Quigley v Millwall, Division 2, 15 February 1947; 5, Ray Pointer v Rotherham U, Division 2, 2 October 1965.

Most Capped Player: Bill Gorman, 11 (13), Republic of Ireland and (4), Northern Ireland.

Most League Appearances: Norman Bullock, 505, 1920–35.

Youngest League Player: Brian Williams, 16 years 133 days v Stockport Co, 18 March 1972; Callum Styles, 16 years 41 days v Southend U, 8 May 2016 (later found to be an ineligible player).

Record Transfer Fee Received: £1,100,000 from Ipswich T for David Johnson, November 1997.

Record Transfer Fee Paid: £200,000 to Ipswich T for Chris Swailes, November 1997; £200,000 to Swindon T for Darren Bullock, February 1999.

Football League Record: 1894 Elected to Division 2; 1895–1912 Division 1; 1912–24 Division 2; 1924–29 Division 1; 1929–57 Division 2; 1957–61 Division 3; 1961–67 Division 2; 1967–68 Division 3; 1968–69 Division 2; 1969–71 Division 3; 1971–74 Division 4; 1974–80 Division 3; 1980–85 Division 4; 1985–96 Division 3; 1996–97 Division 2; 1997–99 Division 1; 1999–2002 Division 2; 2002–04 Division 3; 2004–11 FL 2; 2011–13 FL 1; 2013–15 FL 2; 2015–18 FL 1; 2018– FL 2.

LATEST SEQUENCES

Longest Sequence of League Wins: 9, 26.9.1960 – 19.11.1960.

Longest Sequence of League Defeats: 12, 1.10.2016 – 17.12.2016.

Longest Sequence of League Draws: 6, 6.3.1999 – 3.4.1999.

Longest Sequence of Unbeaten League Matches: 18, 4.2.1961 – 29.4.1961.

Longest Sequence Without a League Win: 19, 1.4.1911 – 2.12.1911.

Successive Scoring Runs: 24 from 1.9.1894.

Successive Non-scoring Runs: 8 from 25.11.2017.

MANAGERS

T. Hargreaves 1887
 (*Secretary-Manager*)
H. S. Hamer 1887–1907
 (*Secretary-Manager*)
Archie Montgomery 1907–15
William Cameron 1919–23
James Hunter Thompson 1923–27
Percy Smith 1927–30
Arthur Paine 1930–34
Norman Bullock 1934–38
Charlie Dean 1938–44
Jim Porter 1944–45
Norman Bullock 1945–49
John McNeil 1950–53
Dave Russell 1953–61
Bob Stokoe 1961–65
Bert Head 1965–66
Les Shannon 1966–69
Jack Marshall 1969
Colin McDonald 1970
Les Hart 1970
Tommy McAnearney 1970–72
Alan Brown 1972–73
Bobby Smith 1973–77
Bob Stokoe 1977–78
David Hatton 1978–79
Dave Connor 1979–80
Jim Iley 1980–84
Martin Dobson 1984–89
Sam Ellis 1989–90
Mike Walsh 1990–95
Stan Ternent 1995–98
Neil Warnock 1998–99
Andy Preece 1999–2003
Graham Barrow 2003–05
Chris Casper 2005–08
Alan Knill 2008–11
Richie Barker 2011–12
Kevin Blackwell 2012–13
David Flitcroft 2013–16
Chris Brass 2016–17
Lee Clark 2017
Chris Lucketti 2017–18
Ryan Lowe May 2018–

TEN YEAR LEAGUE RECORD

		P	W	D	L	F	A	Pts	Pos
2008-09	FL 2	46	21	15	10	63	43	78	4
2009-10	FL 2	46	19	12	15	54	59	69	9
2010-11	FL 2	46	23	12	11	82	50	81	2
2011-12	FL 1	46	15	11	20	60	79	56	14
2012-13	FL 1	46	9	14	23	45	73	41	22
2013-14	FL 2	46	13	20	13	59	51	59	12
2014-15	FL 2	46	26	7	13	60	40	85	3
2015-16	FL 1	46	16	12	18	56	73	57*	16
2016-17	FL 1	46	13	11	22	61	73	50	19
2017-18	FL 1	46	8	12	26	41	71	36	24

*3 pts deducted.

DID YOU KNOW ?

Full-back Samuel Wynne collapsed while about to take a free-kick 38 minutes into Bury's away game at Sheffield United on 30 April 1927. He was carried to the dressing rooms but died very shortly afterwards, the game being abandoned. An inquest later found he had been suffering from undiagnosed pneumonia.

BURY – SKY BET LEAGUE ONE 2017–18 LEAGUE RECORD

Match No.	Date	Venue	Opponents	Result	H/T Score	Lg Pos.	Goalscorers	Attendance
1	Aug 5	H	Walsall	W	1-0	1-0	7	Beckford [45]	4240
2	13	A	Wigan Ath	L	1-4	1-1	14	Bruce [15]	9159
3	19	H	Bristol R	L	2-3	0-0	19	Ajose [90], Beckford [90]	3402
4	26	A	Rochdale	D	0-0	0-0	17		4601
5	Sept 2	H	Scunthorpe U	L	0-1	0-0	18		4055
6	9	A	Rotherham U	L	2-3	1-1	19	Beckford [34], Cameron [67]	7848
7	12	A	Fleetwood T	L	2-3	2-2	22	Beckford [31], Laurent [44]	2535
8	16	H	Plymouth Arg	D	0-0	0-0	22		3642
9	23	A	Charlton Ath	D	1-1	1-1	21	Beckford [9]	9895
10	26	H	Oxford U	W	3-0	0-0	19	Maguire (pen) [64], Smith [70], Beckford [72]	2951
11	30	H	Milton Keynes D	L	0-2	0-1	20		3165
12	Oct 14	H	Bradford C	W	3-1	2-1	19	Maguire (pen) [19], Beckford [20], O'Shea [85]	5514
13	17	A	Blackpool	L	1-2	0-1	21	Beckford [58]	3437
14	21	A	Southend U	L	0-1	0-0	21		6787
15	24	A	Oldham Ath	L	1-2	0-1	21	Aldred [47]	5183
16	28	H	Doncaster R	L	0-1	0-0	23		3079
17	Nov 11	A	Gillingham	D	1-1	1-0	24	Danns [39]	4364
18	18	H	Blackburn R	L	0-3	0-2	24		7159
19	21	H	Shrewsbury T	W	1-0	0-0	24	Leigh [56]	3055
20	25	A	Northampton T	D	0-0	0-0	23		4870
21	Dec 16	A	Portsmouth	L	0-1	0-0	24		17,549
22	23	A	Peterborough U	L	0-3	0-1	24		4640
23	26	A	Rotherham U	L	0-3	0-2	24		4630
24	30	H	Fleetwood T	L	0-2	0-1	24		3158
25	Jan 1	A	Scunthorpe U	L	0-1	0-0	24		4270
26	6	A	Plymouth Arg	L	0-3	0-2	24		9139
27	13	H	Charlton Ath	L	0-1	0-0	24		3295
28	20	A	Oxford U	W	2-1	0-1	24	Miller [81], Bunn [84]	6457
29	Feb 3	H	Blackpool	D	1-1	0-0	24	Miller [83]	4089
30	6	H	AFC Wimbledon	W	2-1	2-1	24	Miller [17], Bunn [43]	2975
31	10	A	Bradford C	D	2-2	0-0	24	Cameron [62], Miller [90]	19,476
32	13	H	Southend U	D	0-0	0-0	23		2795
33	19	A	Blackburn R	L	0-2	0-0	23		12,038
34	24	H	Gillingham	W	2-1	2-0	23	Danns [12], Bunn [25]	3004
35	Mar 10	H	Oldham Ath	D	2-2	2-1	24	O'Shea [14], Danns [34]	5904
36	13	A	Peterborough U	L	0-1	0-0	24		2784
37	17	A	Milton Keynes D	L	1-2	0-1	24	Miller [76]	9247
38	24	H	Wigan Ath	L	0-2	0-1	24		5207
39	30	A	Bristol R	L	1-2	0-0	24	Danns [54]	9030
40	Apr 3	H	Rochdale	L	0-2	0-2	24		4628
41	7	A	Walsall	L	0-1	0-0	24		3807
42	14	H	Northampton T	L	2-3	1-2	24	Clarke [11], Mayor [74]	3117
43	17	A	Doncaster R	D	3-3	1-2	24	Mason (og) [38], O'Shea (pen) [51], Miller [60]	7131
44	21	A	Shrewsbury T	D	1-1	0-1	24	O'Shea [66]	5735
45	28	H	Portsmouth	W	1-0	0-0	24	Miller [67]	4575
46	May 5	A	AFC Wimbledon	D	2-2	0-2	24	Danns [66], Miller [85]	4770

Final League Position: 24

GOALSCORERS

League (41): Beckford 8, Miller 8, Danns 5, O'Shea 4 (1 pen), Bunn 3, Cameron 2, Maguire 2 (2 pens), Ajose 1, Aldred 1, Bruce 1, Clarke 1, Laurent 1, Leigh 1, Mayor 1, Smith 1, own goal 1.
FA Cup (1): Smith 1.
Carabao Cup (0).
Checkatrade Trophy (8): Ajose 3, Bunn 2, Dai 1, Leigh 1, Reilly 1.

Murphy J 17	Jones C 6 + 1	Thompson A 13 + 2	Aldred T 18 + 1	Leigh G 40 + 1	Ajose N 8 + 1	Dawson S 9 + 4	Reilly C 15 + 3	O'Shea J 19 + 8	Maguire C 13 + 11	Beckford J 15	Ismail Z 18 + 3	Dai W 2 + 6	Lowe R 2 + 4	Adams J — + 2	Shotton S 4	Bruce A 2	Bunn H 28 + 9	Humphrey C 8 + 2	Whitmore A 7 + 1	Styles C 9 + 2	Williams J 5 + 4	Cameron N 21	Ince R 18 + 4	Edwards P 35 + 2	Fasan L 14 + 1	Cooney R 9 + 3	Laurent J 20 + 2	Smith M 16 + 3	Nyaupembe D — + 1	Dobre M 3 + 7	Skarz J 3 + 1	Danns N 22 + 3	O'Connell E 12	Tutte A 4 + 12	Mayor D 16 + 4	Sang C — + 2	Ripley C 15	Clarke P 16 + 2	Hanson J 8 + 9	Miller G 16 + 3	Match No.
1	2	3	4	5	6^2	7	8	9	10^1	11	12	13	14																												1
1	2	3	4	6	12	7		10^1	11	8^3	14					5^2	9	13																							2
1	2^1		3	5	9		8		10	14	13					7^3	11	12	4	6^2																					3
$1^▪$			5	11^1	12		10		7^2		9		3			2	4	6	8^3	13	14																				4
1	13	5			12	10			11^3	9		3			2	4^1	8	6^2		7	14																			5
1		5				11			10^2	9	4		2^1	3	7	6		8	13	12																				6
1	4	13				7	10			6^2		2^1		8	3	14	12	11	9^3	5																				7
1	3	5			10			13		9^2	6^1			4	8	2		7	11	12																				8
1	3	5	8^3		9^1	10				6	12			4^2		2		7	11	14	13																			9
	5	6	7^3	8	10^1				14	2^2	4				3	1	9	11	13	12																			10
	4^2	6		8	10					2	3^3			13	5	1	7	11	14	12	9^1																			11
	5	6	7	13	8^2	10			12	2^1				3	1		9	11		4																				12
	4^2	2	7	12	8^1	10			11^3		14				5	1	6	9	13		3																			13
1	4	8	7	13	9^3	10			5^2	14		12	2		6^1	11			3																					14
	5	6	7	8	10				2^1			9^3	3	1	13	11^2	12		4	14																				15
1	5	6	7	8^1	12	10^2			2			9^3	3		11				4^1	13	14																				16
	5	6	10	13	8^2			2		7	3	1			11				9^1	4	12																			17
	5	6	10	8	12			11^1	2^1			3	1		13				9^3	4^1	7	14																		18
	2		14	9	12			10^2		13	3	6	5	1	7^1	11^1	8^3		4																					19
	5		9	10^2						12	3	7	2	1	6	11	8^1		4	13																				20
	5	11	8	9	13				13		3	7	2	1		10^2			4	6^1	12																			21
	5	11	12	10	9				13		4	6^1	2	1	7				$3^▪$	8^2																				22
	3	5	11	8^1	6				12	4		9	2	1	7				10																					23
14		4	5		8	9^1	6	13		12		3		2	1			11^3			7	10^2																			24
6^2		3	5		12	7		13		10			2	1	9	11			8^1	4																				25
2^2			5	7				6^1	$12^▪$	10			3	13					8		9		1	4	11															26
			8	6			14	5^3	13	9^1			2					12	7		4^2		11	1	3	10														27
			5	8				10^2		13			3	2		·				7			9	1	4	11	12													28
			5	7				10^1		6^2			3	2						8^3			9	1	4	11	12													29
	4		5	14				8^2		9				2		7				6		12	10^1	1	3	13	11^3													30
			5					8^3		9			4	2						6			7^1	14	10	1	3^2	12	11											31
	3		5	7^2	13			6^1		9				2					8				12	1	4	11	10													32
			5	14				6^1		11			3	2^2					7^3			8	13	9	1	4	12	10												33
	14		5	10^3	8			9^1					3	6	2				7			12	1	4	13	11^2														34
	4		5	9				6^2		10^3			3	7^1	2				8		12	14	1		13	11														35
2^2	3		5	6					10				7	12					8^1			9	1	4	13	11														36
			5	12	8^2	6^1	13			10			3	7^2	2^2				13			8	1	4	9^1	10														37
			5		8^2	6^2	13			10	12		3		2				7			9^1	1	4	14	11														38
	12		5		13	6^2	14			10		8	3^3		2	9			7				1	4^1		11														39
	3			14	8^2			13		6			2		5	7		9^3	10		1	4	12	11^1																40
1	4			14	6^1			10		7		8^3	5		2			9^2			13		3	11	12															41
1	3^1			14	9^2	12		13		6			2	5				8			7		4	10^3	11															42
1	3		8^3			12		11		7		13	4	5				6^2		14	9^1		10																	43
1	4		7			6	3	10^3		9		14	5	2^1				8					13	12	11^2															44
1	3	2		10		8	12	4	9^2	6				5^1				7				14	13		11^3															45
1	2	5		9		14	8	10^1	3				7				4^3	13			6^2	12			11															46

FA Cup

| First Round | Woking | (a) | 1-1 |
| *Replay* | Woking | (h) | 0-3 |

Carabao Cup

| First Round | Sunderland | (h) | 0-1 |

Checkatrade Trophy

Northern Group C	Rochdale	(h)	0-4
Northern Group C	Blackburn R	(a)	1-0
Northern Group C	Stoke C U21	(h)	3-1
Second Round North	Walsall	(a)	2-1
Third Round	Fleetwood T	(h)	2-3

CAMBRIDGE UNITED

FOUNDATION

The football revival in Cambridge began soon after World War II when the Abbey United club (formed 1912) decided to turn professional in 1949. In 1951 they changed their name to Cambridge United. They were competing in the United Counties League before graduating to the Eastern Counties League in 1951 and the Southern League in 1958.

The Abbey Stadium, Newmarket Road, Cambridge CB5 8LN.

Telephone: (01223) 566 500.

Ticket Office: (01223) 566 500 (option 1).

Website: www.cambridge-united.co.uk

Email: info@cambridge-united.co.uk

Ground Capacity: 7,897.

Record Attendance: 14,000 v Chelsea, Friendly, 1 May 1970.

Pitch Measurements: 100.5m × 67.5m (110yd × 74yd).

Vice-Chairman: Eddie Clarke.

Head Coach: Joe Dunne.

Assistant Head Coach: Mark Bonner.

HONOURS

League Champions: Division 3 – 1990–91; Division 4 – 1976–77. *Runners-up:* Division 3 – 1977–78; Fourth Division – (6th) 1989–90 *(promoted via play-offs)*; Third Division – 1998–99; Conference – (2nd) 2013–14 *(promoted via play-offs)*.

FA Cup: 6th rd – 1990, 1991.

League Cup: quarter-final – 1993.

League Trophy: Runners-up: 2002.

Colours: Amber and black striped shirts, black shorts with amber trim, black socks with amber trim.

Year Formed: 1912.

Turned Professional: 1949.

Ltd Co.: 1948.

Previous Name: 1919, Abbey United; 1951, Cambridge United.

Club Nickname: The 'U's'.

Grounds: 1932, Abbey Stadium (renamed R Costings Abbey Stadium 2009, Cambs Glass Stadium 2016, The Abbey Stadium 2017).

First Football League Game: 15 August 1970, Division 4, v Lincoln C (h) D 1–1 – Roberts; Thompson, Meldrum (1), Slack, Eades, Hardy, Leggett, Cassidy, Lindsey, McKinven, Harris.

Record League Victory: 7–0 v Morecambe, FL 2, 19 April 2016 – Norris; Roberts (1), Coulson, Clark, Dunne (Williams), Ismail (1), Berry (2 pens), Ledson (Spencer), Dunk (2), Williamson (1) (Simpson).

Record Cup Victory: 5–1 v Bristol C, FA Cup 5th rd second replay, 27 February 1990 – Vaughan; Fensome, Kimble, Bailie (O'Shea), Chapple, Daish, Cheetham (Robinson), Leadbitter (1), Dublin (2), Taylor (1), Philpott (1).

Record Defeat: 0–7 v Sunderland, League Cup 2nd rd, 1 October 2002; 0–7 v Luton T, FL 2, 18 November 2017.

Most League Points (2 for a win): 65, Division 4, 1976–77.

Sun FACT FILE

United's final game as a Southern League club before their election to the Football League saw them clinch the league title with a 2-0 win over Margate on 2 May 1970. The U's won the game with two goals in the last 10 minutes to ensure they finished above Yeovil Town. At the subsequent Football League annual meeting Cambridge polled 31 votes and were elected in place of Bradford Park Avenue who gained just 17.

Most League Points (3 for a win): 86, Division 3, 1990–91.

Most League Goals: 87, Division 4, 1976–77.

Highest League Scorer in Season: David Crown, 24, Division 4, 1985–86.

Most League Goals in Total Aggregate: John Taylor, 86, 1988–92; 1996–2001.

Most League Goals in One Match: 5, Steve Butler v Exeter C, Division 2, 4 April 1994.

Most Capped Player: Tom Finney, 7 (15), Northern Ireland.

Most League Appearances: Steve Spriggs, 416, 1975–87.

Youngest League Player: Andy Sinton, 16 years 228 days v Wolverhampton W, 2 November 1982.

Record Transfer Fee Received: £1,300,000 from Leicester C for Trevor Benjamin, July 2000.

Record Transfer Fee Paid: £192,000 to Luton T for Steve Claridge, November 1992.

Football League Record: 1970 Elected to Division 4; 1973–74 Division 3; 1974–77 Division 4; 1977–78 Division 3; 1978–84 Division 2; 1984–85 Division 3; 1985–90 Division 4; 1990–91 Division 3; 1991–92 Division 2; 1992–93 Division 1; 1993–95 Division 2; 1995–99 Division 3; 1999–2002 Division 2; 2002–04 Division 3; 2004–05 FL2; 2005–14 Conference Premier; 2014– FL 2.

LATEST SEQUENCES

Longest Sequence of League Wins: 7, 19.2.1977 – 1.4.1977.

Longest Sequence of League Defeats: 7, 8.4.1985 – 30.4.1985.

Longest Sequence of League Draws: 6, 6.9.1986 – 30.9.1986.

Longest Sequence of Unbeaten League Matches: 14, 9.9.1972 – 10.11.1972.

Longest Sequence Without a League Win: 31, 8.10.1983 – 23.4.1984.

Successive Scoring Runs: 26 from 9.4.2002.

Successive Non-scoring Runs: 5 from 29.9.1973.

MANAGERS

Bill Whittaker 1949–55
Gerald Williams 1955
Bert Johnson 1955–59
Bill Craig 1959–60
Alan Moore 1960–63
Roy Kirk 1964–66
Bill Leivers 1967–74
Ron Atkinson 1974–78
John Docherty 1978–83
John Ryan 1984–85
Ken Shellito 1985
Chris Turner 1985–90
John Beck 1990–92
Ian Atkins 1992–93
Gary Johnson 1993–95
Tommy Taylor 1995–96
Roy McFarland 1996–2001
John Beck 2001
John Taylor 2001–04
Claude Le Roy 2004
Herve Renard 2004
Steve Thompson 2004–05
Rob Newman 2005–06
Jimmy Quinn 2006–08
Gary Brabin 2008–09
Martin Ling 2009–11
Jez George 2011–12
Richard Money 2012–15
Shaun Derry 2015–18
Joe Dunne May 2018–

TEN YEAR LEAGUE RECORD

		P	W	D	L	F	A	Pts	Pos
2008-09	Conf P	46	24	14	8	65	39	86	2
2009-10	Conf P	44	15	14	15	65	53	59	10
2010-11	Conf P	46	11	17	18	53	61	50	17
2011-12	Conf P	46	19	14	13	57	41	71	9
2012-13	Conf P	46	15	14	17	68	69	59	14
2013-14	Conf P	46	23	13	10	72	35	82	2
2014-15	FL 2	46	13	12	21	61	66	51	19
2015-16	FL 2	46	18	14	14	66	55	68	9
2016-17	FL 2	46	19	9	18	58	50	66	11
2017-18	FL 2	46	17	13	16	56	60	64	12

DID YOU KNOW ?

Cambridge United featured in the first play-off final to be played at Wembley when they defeated Chesterfield 1-0 on 26 May 1990 to earn promotion from Division Four. Dion Dublin scored the decisive goal in a game that attracted a crowd of 26,404. Previously play-off finals were settled on a two-leg basis with each club playing home and away.

CAMBRIDGE UNITED – SKY BET LEAGUE TWO 2017–18 LEAGUE RECORD

Match No.	Date	Venue	Opponents	Result	H/T Score	Lg Pos.	Goalscorers	Attendance
1	Aug 5	A	Exeter C	L 0-1	0-1	19		4282
2	12	H	Carlisle U	L 1-2	1-2	22	Elito (pen) [14]	4102
3	19	A	Crawley T	W 1-0	0-0	17	Ibehre [63]	2059
4	26	H	Morecambe	D 0-0	0-0	18		4573
5	Sept 2	H	Colchester U	W 1-0	0-0	12	Ikpeazu [64]	4511
6	9	A	Barnet	L 1-3	0-1	15	Legge [71]	2031
7	12	A	Crewe Alex	W 1-0	1-0	13	Ibehre [35]	3042
8	16	H	Coventry C	W 2-1	1-0	7	Ibehre [10], Ikpeazu [76]	5142
9	23	A	Mansfield T	L 1-2	0-0	11	Legge [58]	3814
10	26	H	Forest Green R	W 3-0	1-0	10	Ibehre [15], Ikpeazu 2 [55, 61]	3545
11	30	A	Swindon T	L 0-2	0-1	12		5847
12	Oct 7	H	Wycombe W	L 1-3	0-0	14	Elito (pen) [70]	5365
13	14	A	Lincoln C	D 0-0	0-0	15		8803
14	17	H	Yeovil T	W 2-1	2-0	13	Ikpeazu [20], Maris [26]	4328
15	21	H	Chesterfield	W 2-1	0-0	11	Brown [70], Ikpeazu [78]	4529
16	28	A	Grimsby T	D 0-0	0-0	10		4091
17	Nov 11	H	Accrington S	D 0-0	0-0	12		4402
18	18	A	Luton T	L 0-7	0-4	14		8721
19	21	A	Cheltenham T	D 0-0	0-0	15		2266
20	25	H	Stevenage	W 1-0	0-0	13	Ikpeazu [88]	4039
21	Dec 9	A	Port Vale	L 0-2	0-1	13		3129
22	16	H	Newport Co	L 1-2	0-1	13	Brown [76]	3632
23	23	A	Notts Co	D 3-3	1-0	16	Ikpeazu [40], Brown 2 [49, 68]	6102
24	26	H	Barnet	W 1-0	0-0	14	Maris [62]	4639
25	30	H	Crewe Alex	W 3-1	2-1	12	Maris [1], Amoo [27], Ikpeazu [70]	4165
26	Jan 1	A	Colchester U	D 0-0	0-0	12		4789
27	13	H	Mansfield T	D 0-0	0-0	12		4324
28	20	A	Forest Green R	L 2-5	2-2	13	Maris [3], Elito [25]	2228
29	30	A	Coventry C	L 1-3	0-2	15	Taft [84]	6897
30	Feb 3	A	Yeovil T	L 0-2	0-0	15		2569
31	9	H	Lincoln C	D 0-0	0-0	14		5775
32	13	A	Chesterfield	W 3-2	1-1	14	Ikpeazu 2 (1 pen) [21, 67 (p)], Dunk [90]	4276
33	17	H	Grimsby T	W 3-1	1-0	14	Ikpeazu [19], Waters [67], Maris [71]	4739
34	20	H	Notts Co	W 1-0	1-0	13	Elito [30]	3524
35	24	A	Accrington S	L 0-1	0-0	14		1819
36	Mar 3	H	Luton T	D 1-1	0-1	13	Ibehre [83]	6722
37	10	A	Wycombe W	D 1-1	0-1	14	Lewis [90]	4426
38	17	H	Swindon T	L 1-3	0-1	14	Ikpeazu [73]	5123
39	24	A	Carlisle U	D 1-1	0-0	14	Maris [50]	4652
40	30	H	Crawley T	W 3-1	2-0	13	Ibehre [4], Maris [22], Brown [58]	4131
41	Apr 7	H	Exeter C	L 2-3	1-0	14	Ibehre [42], Maris [67]	4054
42	14	A	Stevenage	W 2-0	0-0	14	Corr 2 [54, 83]	3269
43	21	A	Cheltenham T	W 4-3	1-2	12	Taylor [10], Maris [53], Brown (pen) [60], Corr [81]	3853
44	24	A	Morecambe	D 0-0	0-0	12		992
45	28	A	Newport Co	L 1-2	0-1	13	Maris [81]	3412
46	May 5	H	Port Vale	W 5-0	2-0	12	Amoo [33], Dunk [35], Halliday [68], Corr [74], Waters [78]	4808

Final League Position: 12

GOALSCORERS

League (56): Ikpeazu 13 (1 pen), Maris 10, Ibehre 7, Brown 6 (1 pen), Corr 4, Elito 4 (2 pens), Amoo 2, Dunk 2, Legge 2, Waters 2, Halliday 1, Lewis 1, Taft 1, Taylor 1.
FA Cup (1): Ibehre 1.
Carabao Cup (1): Ikpeazu 1.
Checkatrade Trophy (1): Mingoia 1.

Forde D 43	Davies L 3+1	Legge L 24+3	Taylor G 43	Carroll J 24+9	Deegan G 42	O'Neil L 19+7	Mingoia P 17+5	Berry L 3	Maris G 34+6	Ibehre J 19+8	Ikpeazu U 36+4	Elito M 24+8	Dunk H 28+9	Azeez A 5+8	Lewis P 5+7	Halliday B 43	Brown J 35+6	Osaoabe E —+4	Amoo D 6+18	Taft G 26+2	Howkins K —+2	Darling H 3	Phillips A 4	Waters B 15+3	Corr B 2+8	Mitov D 3	Knowles T —+1	Match No.
1	2	3	4	5	6¹	7	8²	9	10³	11	12	13	14															1
1	2¹	3	4	5		7	8³	12	9	11	10	6²	13	14														2
1	2	3	4	5	6	7²	8¹	9	12³	11	10	13	14															3
1		3	4	8	12		9¹	14	10	6³	5	11²				2	7	13										4
1		3	4	14	6		13		7²	12	10	8³	5	11¹		2	9											5
1		3	4		7		6²		9⁹	10¹	11	12	5	14		2	8	13										6
1		4	3		6	14	7		9³	10	11¹	12	5			2	8²		13									7
1		4	3		8	14	6		9²	11	10	13	5²			2	7¹		12									8
1		4	3³		7		6		9²	11	10	12	5			2	8¹	13	14									9
1		3		12	7	13	6		8¹	11	10	9³	5²			2	14		4									10
1		4		12	8¹		6³		9	11	10	7²	2			5	13	14	3									11
1	3¹	4	12	7			6²		8¹	11	10	9	5			2			13									12
1		4	5	8	9	6			13	11	12	7³	10²			2			3¹	14								13
1		3	4	5	7	13	6		9²	11	10¹	12				2	8											14
1		4	3	5	7		6¹		9²	11	10	12	13			2	8											15
1		3	4	5	7	8	6²		13	12	11	10¹				2	9											16
1		4	3	5	8	7¹	12		11	10	9					2	6											17
1		4	3	5	8	7²	6³		9¹	11		14				2	10	12	13									18
1		4	3	5	7		6¹	8²		11	9	10	12			2	13											19
1		4	3	5		6¹			13	10	11	8	9²	7³		2	12	14										20
1		4	3	5		7	6²		14	11	10⁸	8	9³	12		2	13											21
1		3	5		8²	12		9		6	13	11	7¹			2	10		4									22
1		3	8	5				9¹		10	6		11			2	7		12	4								23
1		3	5		6			7		10	9		11¹			2	8	12	4									24
1		3	5		6	13		7	12⁴	11	10²		14			2	9³		8¹	4								25
1		3	7	5¹	6			8		11	12	14	13			2	9		10²	4¹								26
1		3	5	6				8		11						2	9		12³			4	7²	10¹	14			27
1		4	5	6				8²	10	9		14	13			2	11¹				3	7³		12				28
1			5	6	7²			9		11²		13	12			2	8			3	4	10¹	14					29
1			4	12	8	7²		13		11			5			2	6			3		9¹	10					30
1		3			6	7	6²		10	11			5			2	9		12	4				8²	10¹	11		31
1		3	13		7	6²			10	11			5			2	9		12	4				8¹				32
1		3	13		6	14	7²		10				5			2	8		12	4				9¹	11³			33
1		3	12		6	7			11	10¹			5			2	9		13	4				8²				34
1		3			7	6¹			14	11	9¹		5			2	8		13	4				10²				35
1		3			6	7³		13	14	11	10²		5			2	9		12	4				8¹				36
1		3			6	7³	8²		10	11			5	12		2	14		13	4				9¹				37
1		4			6	7¹		9²	13	11			5			2	10		12	3				8				38
1		3			7	8³	6¹		11	10²			5	13		2	9		12	4				14				39
1		4	5	8	14		7¹		11³	12			9			2	10		6²	3				13				40
1	13	14	4¹	5	8			7	11³				9			2	10		6²	3					12			41
1	14	4	13	6			8³		11⁵		7²		2	9			3				10	12						42
1		3	5	6		7		9³	14		8²	2	11			12	4		10¹	13								43
		3	5	7		8		11	9				2	10		6¹	4							12		1		44
		3	5¹	6		8		10²	13		9³	2	7			14	4							11	12	1		45
	14	3	5	8³		7		9			2	10¹	6²			4								11	12	1	13	46

FA Cup
First Round	Sutton U	(h)	1-0
Second Round	Newport Co	(a)	0-2

Carabao Cup
First Round	Bristol R	(a)	1-4

Checkatrade Trophy
Southern Group H	Northampton T	(a)	1-1
(Northampton T won 5-4 on penalties)			
Southern Group H	Southampton U21	(h)	0-1
Southern Group H	Peterborough U	(h)	0-2

CARDIFF CITY

FOUNDATION

Credit for the establishment of a first class professional football club in such a rugby stronghold as Cardiff is due to members of the Riverside club formed in 1899 out of a cricket club of that name. Cardiff became a city in 1905 and in 1908 the South Wales and Monmouthshire FA granted Riverside permission to call themselves Cardiff City. The club turned professional under that name in 1910.

Cardiff City Stadium, Leckwith Road, Cardiff CF11 8AZ.

Telephone: (0845) 365 1115. *Fax:* (0845) 365 1116.

Ticket Office: (0845) 345 1400.

Website: www.cardiffcityfc.co.uk

Email: club@cardiffcityfc.co.uk

Ground Capacity: 33,280.

Record Attendance: 57,893 v Arsenal, Division 1, 22 April 1953 (at Ninian Park); 32,478 v Reading, FL C, 6 May 2018 (at Cardiff City Stadium).

Ground Record Attendance: 62,634, Wales v England, 17 October 1959 (at Ninian Park); 33,280, Wales v Belgium, 12 June 2013 (at Cardiff City Stadium).

Pitch Measurements: 105m × 68m (115yd × 74.5yd).

Chairman: Mehmet Dalman.

Chief Executive: Ken Choo.

Manager: Neil Warnock.

Assistant Manager: Kevin Blackwell

Colours: Blue shirts with black trim, blue shorts with black trim, blue socks with black trim.

Year Formed: 1899.

Turned Professional: 1910.

Previous Names: 1899, Riverside; 1902, Riverside Albion; 1908, Cardiff City.

Club Nickname: 'The Bluebirds'.

Grounds: Riverside, Sophia Gardens, Old Park and Fir Gardens; 1910, Ninian Park; 2009, Cardiff City Stadium.

First Football League Game: 28 August 1920, Division 2, v Stockport Co (a) W 5–2 – Kneeshaw; Brittan, Leyton; Keenor (1), Smith, Hardy; Grimshaw (1), Gill (2), Cashmore, West, Evans (1).

Record League Victory: 9–2 v Thames, Division 3 (S), 6 February 1932 – Farquharson; Eric Morris, Roberts; Galbraith, Harris, Ronan; Emmerson (1), Keating (1), Jones (1), McCambridge (1), Robbins (5).

Record Cup Victory: 8–0 v Enfield, FA Cup 1st rd, 28 November 1931 – Farquharson; Smith, Roberts; Harris (1), Galbraith, Ronan; Emmerson (2), Keating (3); O'Neill (2), Robbins, McCambridge.

HONOURS

League Champions: FL C – 2012–13; Division 3S – 1946–47; Third Division – 1992–93.

Runners-up: FL C – 2017–18; Division 1 – 1923–24; Division 2 – 1920–21, 1951–52, 1959–60; Division 3 – 1975–76, 1982–83; Third Division – 2000–01; Division 4 – 1987–88.

FA Cup Winners: 1927.
Runners-up: 1925, 2008.

League Cup: Runners-up: 2012.

Welsh Cup Winners: 22 times (joint record).

European Competitions
European Cup-Winners' Cup: 1964–65 *(qf)*, 1965–66, 1967–68 *(sf)*, 1968–69, 1969–70, 1970–71 *(qf)*, 1971–72, 1973–74, 1974–75, 1976–77, 1977–78, 1988–89, 1992–93, 1993–94.

The Sun FACT FILE

George Latham became the oldest Cardiff City debutant when he turned out at inside-right at Blackburn Rovers on 2 January 1922, the day after his 41st birthday. At the time Latham was the Bluebirds' trainer but was required to step in as two men fell ill and there were no further replacements available. It was 14 years since his previous Football League appearance for Liverpool.

Record Defeat: 2–11 v Sheffield U, Division 1, 1 January 1926.

Most League Points (2 for a win): 66, Division 3 (S), 1946–47.

Most League Points (3 for a win): 90, FL C, 2017–18.

Most League Goals: 95, Division 3, 2000–01.

Highest League Scorer in Season: Robert Earnshaw, 31, Division 2, 2002–03.

Most League Goals in Total Aggregate: Len Davies, 128, 1920–31.

Most League Goals in One Match: 5, Hugh Ferguson v Burnley, Division 1, 1 September 1928; 5, Walter Robbins v Thames, Division 3 (S), 6 February 1932; 5, William Henderson v Northampton T, Division 3 (S), 22 April 1933.

Most Capped Player: Aron Gunnarsson, 54 (80), Iceland.

Most League Appearances: Phil Dwyer, 471, 1972–85.

Youngest League Player: Bob Adams, 15 years 355 days v Southend U, 18 February 1933.

Record Transfer Fee Received: £10,000,000 from Internazionale for Gary Medel, August 2014.

Record Transfer Fee Paid: £11,000,000 to Sevilla for Gary Medel, August 2013; £11,000,000 to Norwich C for Josh Murphy, June 2018.

Football League Record: 1920 Elected to Division 2; 1921–29 Division 1; 1929–31 Division 2; 1931–47 Division 3 (S); 1947–52 Division 2; 1952–57 Division 1; 1957–60 Division 2; 1960–62 Division 1; 1962–75 Division 2; 1975–76 Division 3; 1976–82 Division 2; 1982–83 Division 3; 1983–85 Division 2; 1985–86 Division 3; 1986–88 Division 4; 1988–90 Division 3; 1990–92 Division 4; 1992–93 Division 3; 1993–95 Division 2; 1995–99 Division 3; 1999–2000 Division 2; 2000–01 Division 3; 2001–03 Division 2; 2003–04 Division 1; 2004–13 FL C; 2013–14 FA Premier League; 2014–18 FL C; 2018– FA Premier League.

LATEST SEQUENCES

Longest Sequence of League Wins: 9, 26.10.1946 – 28.12.1946.

Longest Sequence of League Defeats: 7, 4.11.1933 – 25.12.1933.

Longest Sequence of League Draws: 6, 29.11.1980 – 17.1.1981.

Longest Sequence of Unbeaten League Matches: 21, 21.9.1946 – 1.3.1947.

Longest Sequence Without a League Win: 15, 21.11.1936 – 6.3.1937.

Successive Scoring Runs: 24 from 25.8.2012.

Successive Non-scoring Runs: 8 from 20.12.1952.

MANAGERS

Davy McDougall 1910–11
Fred Stewart 1911–33
Bartley Wilson 1933–34
B. Watts-Jones 1934–37
Bill Jennings 1937–39
Cyril Spiers 1939–46
Billy McCandless 1946–48
Cyril Spiers 1948–54
Trevor Morris 1954–58
Bill Jones 1958–62
George Swindin 1962–64
Jimmy Scoular 1964–73
Frank O'Farrell 1973–74
Jimmy Andrews 1974–78
Richie Morgan 1978–81
Graham Williams 1981–82
Len Ashurst 1982–84
Jimmy Goodfellow 1984
Alan Durban 1984–86
Frank Burrows 1986–89
Len Ashurst 1989–91
Eddie May 1991–94
Terry Yorath 1994–95
Eddie May 1995
Kenny Hibbitt (*Chief Coach*) 1995–96
Phil Neal 1996
Russell Osman 1996–97
Kenny Hibbitt 1997–98
Frank Burrows 1998–2000
Billy Ayre 2000
Bobby Gould 2000
Alan Cork 2000–02
Lennie Lawrence 2002–05
Dave Jones 2005–11
Malky Mackay 2011–13
Ole Gunnar Solskjaer 2014
Russell Slade 2014–16
Paul Trollope 2016
Neil Warnock October 2016–

TEN YEAR LEAGUE RECORD

		P	W	D	L	F	A	Pts	Pos
2008-09	FL C	46	19	17	10	65	53	74	7
2009-10	FL C	46	22	10	14	73	54	76	4
2010-11	FL C	46	23	11	12	76	54	80	4
2011-12	FL C	46	19	18	9	66	53	75	6
2012-13	FL C	46	25	12	9	72	45	87	1
2013-14	PR Lge	38	7	9	22	32	74	30	20
2014-15	FL C	46	16	14	16	57	61	62	11
2015-16	FL C	46	17	17	12	56	51	68	8
2016-17	FL C	46	17	11	18	60	61	62	12
2017-18	FL C	46	27	9	10	69	39	90	2

DID YOU KNOW ?

Cardiff City achieved their record victory in a competitive match against Knighton in January 1961. The teams met in a fifth-round tie in the Welsh Cup with the Bluebirds winning 16-0. Goalscorers were Derek Tapscott 6, Graham Moore 4, Brian Walsh 2, Peter Donnelly 2, Danny Malloy and Derek Hogg.

CARDIFF CITY – SKY BET CHAMPIONSHIP 2017–18 LEAGUE RECORD

Match No.	Date	Venue	Opponents	Result	H/T Score	Lg Pos.	Goalscorers	Attendance
1	Aug 5	A	Burton Alb	W 1-0	0-0	3	Zohore [87]	5050
2	12	H	Aston Villa	W 3-0	1-0	1	Mendez-Laing 2 [21, 71], Hoilett [60]	23,899
3	15	H	Sheffield U	W 2-0	1-0	1	Morrison [44], Mendez-Laing [55]	17,844
4	19	A	Wolverhampton W	W 2-1	0-0	1	Ralls [54], Mendez-Laing [77]	27,068
5	26	H	QPR	W 2-1	2-1	1	Hoilett [22], Bamba [45]	18,520
6	Sept 9	A	Fulham	D 1-1	0-0	1	Ward, D [83]	20,984
7	12	A	Preston NE	L 0-3	0-1	2		10,796
8	16	H	Sheffield W	D 1-1	0-1	3	Bamba [90]	19,137
9	23	A	Sunderland	W 2-1	1-0	3	Bryson [7], Ralls (pen) [73]	25,733
10	26	H	Leeds U	W 3-1	2-0	1	Zohore 2 [28, 59], Hoilett [37]	27,160
11	30	H	Derby Co	D 0-0	0-0	1		18,480
12	Oct 13	A	Birmingham C	L 0-1	0-1	1		19,059
13	21	A	Middlesbrough	W 1-0	0-0	2	Ralls (pen) [84]	24,806
14	28	A	Millwall	D 0-0	0-0	3		18,496
15	31	H	Ipswich T	W 3-1	1-0	2	Hoilett [12], Bogle [46], Ward, D [90]	15,951
16	Nov 4	A	Bristol C	L 1-2	1-1	3	Bogle [41]	21,692
17	18	H	Brentford	W 2-0	2-0	3	Ralls [8], Ward, D [36]	16,335
18	21	A	Barnsley	W 1-0	0-0	2	Paterson [83]	11,051
19	26	A	Nottingham F	W 2-0	2-0	2	Hoilett [24], Ward, D [38]	25,210
20	Dec 1	H	Norwich C	W 3-1	0-1	2	Ralls (pen) [49], Hoilett [63], Bogle [80]	17,033
21	11	A	Reading	D 2-2	0-2	2	Bennett [63], Tomlin [90]	16,670
22	16	H	Hull C	W 1-0	0-0	2	Bamba [57]	18,049
23	23	A	Bolton W	L 0-2	0-0	2		15,344
24	26	H	Fulham	L 2-4	0-1	3	Zohore [57], Paterson [90]	21,662
25	29	H	Preston NE	L 0-1	0-0	3		17,751
26	Jan 1	A	QPR	L 1-2	0-0	3	Ralls (pen) [54]	13,801
27	13	H	Sunderland	W 4-0	0-0	2	Paterson 2 [46, 80], Ralls [55], Pilkington [90]	17,703
28	20	A	Sheffield W	D 0-0	0-0	3		23,277
29	Feb 3	A	Leeds U	W 4-1	3-0	4	Paterson [9], Hoilett [41], Morrison [45], Pilkington [88]	30,534
30	9	A	Millwall	D 1-1	1-1	4	Hoilett [3]	13,204
31	13	H	Bolton W	W 2-0	2-0	4	Traore [34], Morrison [44]	16,013
32	17	A	Middlesbrough	W 1-0	1-0	2	Morrison [33]	18,720
33	21	A	Ipswich T	W 1-0	0-0	2	Zohore [65]	13,205
34	25	H	Bristol C	W 1-0	0-0	2	Zohore [82]	21,018
35	Mar 6	H	Barnsley	W 2-1	1-0	2	Paterson [31], Grujic [46]	16,176
36	10	H	Birmingham C	W 3-2	3-0	2	Mendez-Laing [12], Bryson [23], Paterson [45]	19,634
37	13	A	Brentford	W 3-1	2-1	2	Bamba [25], Paterson [45], Zohore [58]	8549
38	30	A	Burton Alb	W 3-1	2-1	2	Zohore [16], Mendez-Laing [45], Paterson [64]	21,086
39	Apr 2	A	Sheffield U	D 1-1	0-1	2	Pilkington [90]	25,231
40	6	H	Wolverhampton W	L 0-1	0-0	2		29,317
41	10	A	Aston Villa	L 0-1	0-0	3		32,560
42	14	A	Norwich C	W 2-0	0-0	2	Zohore [86], Hoilett [90]	25,503
43	21	H	Nottingham F	W 2-1	1-0	2	Morrison [35], Gunnarsson [74]	21,310
44	24	A	Derby Co	L 1-3	1-0	2	Paterson [28]	30,294
45	28	A	Hull C	W 2-0	1-0	2	Morrison 2 [32, 80]	17,441
46	May 6	H	Reading	D 0-0	0-0	2		32,478

Final League Position: 2

GOALSCORERS

League (69): Paterson 10, Hoilett 9, Zohore 9, Morrison 7, Ralls 7 (4 pens), Mendez-Laing 6, Bamba 4, Ward, D 4, Bogle 3, Pilkington 3, Bryson 2, Bennett 1, Grujic 1, Gunnarsson 1, Tomlin 1, Traore 1.
FA Cup (4): Hoilett 2, Ecuele Manga 1, Pilkington 1.
Carabao Cup (3): Halford 1, Mendez-Laing 1, Pilkington 1.

Etheridge N 45	Ecuele Manga B 35 + 3	Morrison S 38 + 1	Bamba S 43 + 3	Peltier L 27 + 3	Gunnarsson A 17 + 3	Ralls J 37	Bennett J 38	Tomlin L 5 + 8	Zohore K 30 + 6	Hoilett J 44 + 2	Damour L 18 + 9	Mendez-Laing N 33 + 5	Ward D 6 + 12	Richards A 5 + 1	Kennedy M — + 1	Halford G 2 + 10	Bryson C 19 + 3	Feeney L 4 + 11	Bogle O 4 + 6	Paterson C 23 + 9	Gounonghe F — + 3	Pilkington A 1 + 7	Healey R 1 + 2	Murphy B 1	Connolly M 4	Wildschut Y 3 + 7	Grujic M 12 + 1	Harris K 1 + 2	Traore A 3 + 1	Madine G 5 + 8	Ward J 2 + 2	Match No.
1	2^1	3	4	5	6	7	8	9^3	10	11^2	12	13	14																			1
1		3	4	2	6	8	5^1		10^3	11	7	9	13	12	14																	2
1	2	3	4		6	7		9	11^2	10^3	12	8	13	5		14																3
1	13	3	4	2	6	7			11	10^1	9^2	8	12	5																		4
1	13	3	4	2	6	7	5		11	10^1	9^2	8	12																			5
1		3	4	2	6	7	5		11^2	10^1	9^3	8	13				12	14														6
1		3	4	2	7	6	5	13	11^3	10^1	9^2	8	14				12															7
1		3	4	2	7	6	5	14	11^2	10^1		8	13				9^3	12														8
	4	3	14		6^1	7	5		10^3	12		9		2			8	11^2	13													9
1	4	3	6^3	2			5		11^2	10	8	7^1	12				14	9	13													10
1	4	3	6	2		9	5	12	11	10^1	8^2	7							13													11
1	4	3	6	2	12	9^2	5		11	10^3		7	14				8^1	13														12
1	2	3	4	5		7	8		11			9^1	10^2				6			13	12											13
1	2	3	4	5		7	8^3	14	10			9	11^2				6^1			13	12											14
1	4	3	6	5		9		8^1	10^2	12		7	14				13	11^3	2													15
1	2	3	4	8		7		14	10			9^1	13				6^2	12^3	11^4	5												16
1	2	3	4		12	8	5		11	6^1		10^3					7	9^2		13	14											17
1	2	3	4		7^2	8	5		9	12		11^1					10			6	13	14										18
1	2	3	4^2	12		8	5		10	9		11^3				13	7^1			6	14											19
1	2	3	4			8	5	13	11	6		9^1	10^3				7^2			12	14											20
1	2	3^1	4	12		7	8	13	9	6		10					14			11^3	5^2											21
1	3		4	2^3		7	5	6^2	11	8		9				14	12			13		10^1										22
1	3		4	2		9	5	13^3	12	10	8^1	7				6	14			11^2												23
1	3		4	2		8	5		10	11	6^2	9					7			12			13									24
1	3		4	5		7		6^1	10^1	12	8	11					9^1	14	2				13									25
	2	3	6^2			7	8		11	10	12	13					5			9^1				1	4							26
1	2	3	4			8	9		11^1	10^3							6^2			13						7	14			12		27
1	2	3	4			7	8		11	10^1							12			13						9^2	6^3	14				28
1	2	3	4			7			13	10						14	5			12						9^2	6^1		8	11^3		29
1	2	3	4			8	5		14	11		13	9^2				12			6						7^1	10^3					30
1	4	3	14	2		8			10^3			9^1					6			13						12	7		5	11^2		31
1	2	3	4		12	8	5		10			9	13				6^1			14						7^3				11^2		32
1	2	3^1	4			8			10^3	11		6					9			12			5			7^2				13		33
1		3	4			8	5		12	11		7					9^1			6					2	13				10^2		34
1		3	4			8	5		10	9		13	14				12			6^3					2	7^2				11^1		35
1		3	4	2^3			5		10	11		13				14	12			9^2						8^1	6			7		36
1	2	3	4				5		11^1	10^2	7		8^3							9						13	6	14		12		37
1	2	3	4		12		5		10^3	11		9^1				8^2				6						14	7			13		38
1	2	3	4			8	5		10^1	11^3		9^2								6			13			14	7			12		39
1		3	4	2		8	5		10^2	11	12	9					7^1			14							6^2			13		40
1		3	4	2	6		5		10^1	11^2		9^3					8			14						7				12	13	41
1	12	3	4^1	2	7		5		14	10		6^3					8			9						13				11^2		42
1	4	3	12	2^2	7	6	5		10	11		9^3					8^1			14						13						43
1	2	3	4			8	5		12	10^2		6					13			14						11^3				9^1		44
1		3	4	2	7^1	8	5		10^2	11		9					13			6								12^3		14		45
1		3	4	2		7	5		10^2	11^4		9					8			6										13	12	46

FA Cup

Third Round	Mansfield T	(h)	0-0	
Replay	Mansfield T	(a)	4-1	
Fourth Round	Manchester C	(h)	0-2	

Carabao Cup

First Round	Portsmouth	(h)	2-1	
(aet)				
Second Round	Burton Alb	(h)	1-2	

CARLISLE UNITED

FOUNDATION

Carlisle United came into being when members of Shaddongate United voted to change its name on 17 May 1904. The new club was admitted to the Second Division of the Lancashire Combination in 1905–06, winning promotion the following season. Devonshire Park was officially opened on 2 September 1905, when St Helens Town were the visitors. Despite defeat in a disappointing 3–2 start, a respectable mid-table position was achieved.

Brunton Park, Warwick Road, Carlisle, Cumbria CA1 1LL.

Telephone: (01228) 526 237.

Ticket Office: (0844) 371 1921.

Website: www.carlisleunited.co.uk

Email: enquiries@carlisleunited.co.uk

Ground Capacity: 17,792.

Record Attendance: 27,500 v Birmingham C, FA Cup 3rd rd, 5 January 1957 and v Middlesbrough, FA Cup 5th rd, 7 February 1970.

Pitch Measurements: 102.5m × 67.5m (112yd × 74yd).

Chairman: Andrew Jenkins.

Chief Executive: Nigel Clibbens.

Manager: John Sheridan.

Assistant Manager: Tommy Wright.

Colours: Blue shirts with white and red trim, white shorts with blue and red trim, blue socks with black and white trim.

Year Formed: 1904. *Turned Professional:* 1921.

Previous Name: 1904, Shaddongate United; 1904, Carlisle United.

Club Nicknames: 'The Cumbrians', 'The Blues'.

Grounds: 1904, Milholme Bank; 1905, Devonshire Park; 1909, Brunton Park.

First Football League Game: 25 August 1928, Division 3 (N), v Accrington S (a) W 3–2 – Prout; Coulthard, Cook; Harrison, Ross, Pigg; Agar (1), Hutchison, McConnell (1), Ward (1), Watson.

Record League Victory: 8–0 v Hartlepool U, Division 3 (N), 1 September 1928 – Prout; Smiles, Cook; Robinson (1) Ross, Pigg; Agar (1), Hutchison (1), McConnell (4), Ward (1), Watson. 8–0 v Scunthorpe U, Division 3 (N), 25 December 1952 – MacLaren; Hill, Scott; Stokoe, Twentyman, Waters; Harrison (1), Whitehouse (5), Ashman (2), Duffett, Bond.

Record Cup Victory: 6–0 v Shepshed Dynamo, FA Cup 1st rd, 16 November 1996 – Caig; Hopper, Archdeacon (pen), Walling, Robinson, Pounewatchy, Peacock (1), Conway (1) (Jansen), Smart (McAlindon (1)), Hayward, Aspinall (Thorpe), (2 og). 6–0 v Tipton T, FA Cup 1st rd, 6 November 2010 – Collin; Simek, Murphy, Chester, Cruise, Robson (McKenna), Berrett, Taiwo (Hurst), Marshall, Zoko (Curran) (2), Madine (4).

HONOURS

League Champions: Division 3 – 1964–65; FL 2 – 2005–06; Third Division – 1994–95.
Runners-up: Division 3 – 1981–82; Division 4 – 1963–64; Conference – (3rd) 2004–05 *(promoted via play-offs)*.
FA Cup: 6th rd – 1975.
League Cup: semi-final – 1970.
League Trophy Winners: 1997, 2011.
Runners-up: 1995, 2003, 2006, 2010.

☀️*THE* Sun FACT FILE

Carlisle United have featured in the Football League play-offs on three occasions to date and have yet to win a match, having drawn one and lost five of the six games played. In contrast they featured in the Conference play-offs in 2004–05 when they beat Aldershot Town in the semi-finals and then despatched Stevenage Borough in the final at Stoke to return to the League after 12 months' absence.

Record Defeat: 1–11 v Hull C, Division 3 (N), 14 January 1939.

Most League Points (2 for a win): 62, Division 3 (N), 1950–51.

Most League Points (3 for a win): 91, Division 3, 1994–95.

Most League Goals: 113, Division 4, 1963–64.

Highest League Scorer in Season: Jimmy McConnell, 42, Division 3 (N), 1928–29.

Most League Goals in Total Aggregate: Jimmy McConnell, 124, 1928–32.

Most League Goals in One Match: 5, Hugh Mills v Halifax T, Division 3 (N), 11 September 1937; 5, Jim Whitehouse v Scunthorpe U, Division 3 (N), 25 December 1952.

Most Capped Player: Reggie Lambe, 6 (29), Bermuda.

Most League Appearances: Allan Ross, 466, 1963–79.

Youngest League Player: John Slaven, 16 years 162 days v Scunthorpe U, 16 March 2002.

Record Transfer Fee Received: £1,000,000 from Crystal Palace for Matt Jansen, February 1998.

Record Transfer Fee Paid: £140,000 to Blackburn R for Joe Garner, August 2007.

Football League Record: 1928 Elected to Division 3 (N); 1958–62 Division 4; 1962–63 Division 3; 1963–64 Division 4; 1964–65 Division 3; 1965–74 Division 2; 1974–75 Division 1; 1975–77 Division 2; 1977–82 Division 3; 1982–86 Division 2; 1986–87 Division 3; 1987–92 Division 4; 1992–95 Division 3; 1995–96 Division 2; 1996–97 Division 3; 1997–98 Division 2; 1998–2004 Division 3; 2004–05 Conference; 2005–06 FL 2; 2006–14 FL 1; 2014– FL 2.

LATEST SEQUENCES

Longest Sequence of League Wins: 7, 18.2.2006 – 8.4.2006.

Longest Sequence of League Defeats: 12, 27.9.2003 – 13.12.2003.

Longest Sequence of League Draws: 6, 11.2.1978 – 11.3.1978.

Longest Sequence of Unbeaten League Matches: 19, 1.10.1994 – 11.2.1995.

Longest Sequence Without a League Win: 15, 12.4.2014 – 20.9.2014.

Successive Scoring Runs: 26 from 23.8.1947.

Successive Non-scoring Runs: 7 from 25.2.2017.

MANAGERS

Harry Kirkbride 1904–05
  (*Secretary-Manager*)
McCumiskey 1905–06
  (*Secretary-Manager*)
Jack Houston 1906–08
  (*Secretary-Manager*)
Bert Stansfield 1908–10
Jack Houston 1910–12
Davie Graham 1912–13
George Bristow 1913–30
Billy Hampson 1930–33
Bill Clarke 1933–35
Robert Kelly 1935–36
Fred Westgarth 1936–38
David Taylor 1938–40
Howard Harkness 1940–45
Bill Clark 1945–46
  (*Secretary-Manager*)
Ivor Broadis 1946–49
Bill Shankly 1949–51
Fred Emery 1951–58
Andy Beattie 1958–60
Ivor Powell 1960–63
Alan Ashman 1963–67
Tim Ward 1967–68
Bob Stokoe 1968–70
Ian MacFarlane 1970–72
Alan Ashman 1972–75
Dick Young 1975–76
Bobby Moncur 1976–80
Martin Harvey 1980
Bob Stokoe 1980–85
Bryan 'Pop' Robson 1985
Bob Stokoe 1985–86
Harry Gregg 1986–87
Cliff Middlemass 1987–91
Aidan McCaffery 1991–92
David McCreery 1992–93
Mick Wadsworth (*Director of Coaching*) 1993–96
Mervyn Day 1996–97
David Wilkes and John Halpin (*Directors of Coaching*), and **Michael Knighton** 1997–99
Nigel Pearson 1998–99
Keith Mincher 1999
Martin Wilkinson 1999–2000
Ian Atkins 2000–01
Roddy Collins 2001–02; 2002–03
Paul Simpson 2003–06
Neil McDonald 2006–07
John Ward 2007–08
Greg Abbott 2008–13
Graham Kavanagh 2013–14
Keith Curle 2014–18
John Sheridan June 2018–

TEN YEAR LEAGUE RECORD

		P	W	D	L	F	A	Pts	Pos
2008-09	FL 1	46	12	14	20	56	69	50	20
2009-10	FL 1	46	15	13	18	63	66	58	14
2010-11	FL 1	46	16	11	19	60	62	59	12
2011-12	FL 1	46	18	15	13	65	66	69	8
2012-13	FL 1	46	14	13	19	56	77	55	17
2013-14	FL 1	46	11	12	23	43	76	45	22
2014-15	FL 2	46	14	8	24	56	74	50	20
2015-16	FL 2	46	17	16	13	67	62	67	10
2016-17	FL 2	46	18	17	11	69	68	71	6
2017-18	FL 2	46	17	16	13	62	54	67	10

DID YOU KNOW ?

Carlisle United hold the record for the number of appearances in the EFL Trophy final having reached that stage on six occasions. The Cumbrians were winners in 1996–97 and 2010–11, losing out in the other four finals, including 1995 when the trophy was decided with a 'golden goal' scored by Birmingham City in extra time.

CARLISLE UNITED – SKY BET LEAGUE TWO 2017–18 LEAGUE RECORD

Match No.	Date	Venue	Opponents	Result		H/T Score	Lg Pos.	Goalscorers	Attendance
1	Aug 5	H	Swindon T	L	1-2	0-1	17	Joyce [55]	6036
2	12	A	Cambridge U	W	2-1	2-1	11	Lambe [8], Parkes [39]	4102
3	19	H	Cheltenham T	W	3-0	2-0	5	Pell (og) [5], Lambe [18], Miller, T [60]	4497
4	26	A	Lincoln C	L	1-4	0-1	11	Lambe [75]	8345
5	Sept 2	H	Mansfield T	D	1-1	1-0	11	Hope [15]	4677
6	9	A	Accrington S	L	0-3	0-2	16		2120
7	12	A	Coventry C	L	0-2	0-0	19		6151
8	16	H	Barnet	D	1-1	0-1	18	Miller, S [85]	4141
9	23	A	Crewe Alex	W	5-0	1-0	15	Grainger 2 (1 pen) [13, 48 (p)], Raynes (og) [72], Lambe [75], Hope [90]	4021
10	26	A	Stevenage	L	0-2	0-0	17		3701
11	30	H	Crawley T	W	1-0	0-0	14	Hope [51]	2021
12	Oct 7	H	Exeter C	L	0-1	0-0	16		4677
13	14	A	Colchester U	W	1-0	0-0	14	Devitt [58]	3402
14	17	H	Wycombe W	D	3-3	2-1	15	Lambe 2 [4, 84], Devitt (pen) [38]	3562
15	21	H	Notts Co	D	1-1	1-0	16	Hope [25]	4730
16	28	A	Chesterfield	D	2-2	0-1	16	Grainger [55], Bennett [73]	5102
17	Nov 11	A	Yeovil T	W	4-0	2-0	14	Grainger 2 (1 pen) [7, 75 (p)], Hope [44], Miller, S [90]	4189
18	18	A	Grimsby T	W	1-0	0-0	11	Hill [70]	3753
19	21	A	Luton T	L	0-3	0-2	12		7644
20	25	H	Morecambe	D	1-1	0-0	14	Etuhu [51]	5010
21	Dec 9	A	Newport Co	D	3-3	0-1	14	Joyce [46], Etuhu [52], Miller, T [62]	3176
22	16	H	Port Vale	L	1-2	0-0	14	Bennett [80]	4090
23	23	A	Forest Green R	W	1-0	1-0	13	Bennett [28]	2489
24	26	H	Accrington S	W	3-1	1-0	12	Devitt [11], Miller, S [78], Grainger [83]	5404
25	30	H	Coventry C	L	0-1	0-0	13		5807
26	Jan 1	A	Mansfield T	L	1-3	0-2	13	Devitt (pen) [67]	3632
27	13	H	Crewe Alex	W	1-0	0-0	13	Cosgrove [76]	4467
28	20	A	Stevenage	D	0-0	0-0	12		2476
29	27	H	Forest Green R	W	1-0	1-0	13	Devitt [27]	4176
30	Feb 3	A	Wycombe W	L	3-4	0-2	13	Grainger (pen) [49], Devitt [68], Stockton [70]	4145
31	10	H	Colchester U	D	1-1	0-1	13	Devitt [79]	4006
32	13	H	Notts Co	L	1-2	0-2	13	Devitt [75]	3889
33	17	A	Chesterfield	W	2-0	1-0	13	Etuhu [19], O'Sullivan [81]	4025
34	20	A	Barnet	W	3-1	0-0	12	Nadesan 2 [70, 87], Bennett [82]	1151
35	24	A	Yeovil T	W	1-0	0-0	10	Hope [48]	2688
36	Mar 3	H	Grimsby T	W	2-0	1-0	9	Hope [3], Ellis [73]	4151
37	10	A	Exeter C	D	1-1	0-1	10	Nadesan [64]	3488
38	17	H	Crawley T	D	2-2	1-0	10	Bennett [38], Hope [47]	4097
39	24	H	Cambridge U	D	1-1	0-0	10	Bennett [47]	4652
40	30	A	Cheltenham T	W	1-0	0-0	10	Devitt (pen) [74]	3107
41	Apr 2	H	Lincoln C	L	0-1	0-1	11		5068
42	7	A	Swindon T	D	0-0	0-0	10		5807
43	14	A	Morecambe	D	1-1	0-1	10	Devitt [14]	3319
44	21	H	Luton T	D	1-1	1-0	10	Grainger (pen) [13]	5523
45	28	A	Port Vale	W	2-1	0-1	9	Nadesan [51], Hope [70]	5163
46	May 5	H	Newport Co	D	1-1	1-1	10	Ellis [14]	5311

Final League Position: 10

GOALSCORERS

League (62): Devitt 10 (3 pens), Hope 9, Grainger 8 (4 pens), Bennett 6, Lambe 6, Nadesan 4, Etuhu 3, Miller, S 3, Ellis 2, Joyce 2, Miller, T 2, Cosgrove 1, Hill 1, O'Sullivan 1, Parkes 1, Stockton 1, own goals 2.
FA Cup (7): Hope 3, Bennett 2, Grainger 1 (1 pen), Miller S 1.
Carabao Cup (3): Grainger 1, Miller S 1, Miller T 1.
Checkatrade Trophy (3): Hope 1, Kennedy 1, Miller S 1.

Bonham J 42	Miller T 13+4	Liddle G 37+4	Parkes T 34+3	Grainger D 32+2	Joyce L 35+3	Jones M 39+4	Devitt J 30+10	Lambe R 28+6	Adams N 15+2	Hope H 29+12	Bennett R 24+14	Miller S 11+12	Ellis M 21+2	Cosgrove S 3+5	Kennedy J 1+5	George S 4	Brown J 27	Etuhu K 13+7	Hill C 38	Rigg S —+3	O'Sullivan J 2+16	Stockton C 10+2	Twardek K 5+7	Campbell-Ryce J 4+5	Nadesan A 9+6	Match No.
1	2^1	3	4^2	5	6	7	8	9	10	11^2	12	13	14													1
1	2	3	4	5	6	13	14	8	9^1	11^2	7^3			10	12											2
1	2	14	4	5	8	7^1	12	6	9^3	13	10^2	11	3													3
1	2	8^1	3^2	5		7	6	9	13	11^2	10^3	12	4	14												4
1	2	3		5	8	7		6^1	9	10^2	11^3	13		4	14	12										5
1	2^1	13	4^3	5	8	7		6	9	11	10^2	12	3		14											6
	13	4	5	7		9		10^3	14	12	11	3^1		8	1	2	6^2									7
		4	5	6	8			9^1	13	10^2	12	11	3		14	1	2	7^3								8
	14	4	5	6	10	12	9	8	13			11^1			1	2^2	7^3	3								9
		4	5	8	9	13	6^2	10	14	12	11				1	2^1	7^2	3								10
1	14	4^1	5	7	8	13		9^3	10	12^4		11^1				2	6^2	3								11
1		3		5	8	7^2	12	13	9	10		11			14	2^1	6^2	4								12
1	14	3		5	9	8	12	6	10^1	13		11^2				2	7^2	4								13
1	2	3			8	7	10^1	6	9^3	13		11^2			14	5			4		12					14
1	5	3			9	7	8^1	6	10	11^2	12						2		4		13					15
1	5^3	3	14	10	7	9	8			6^2	11^1	12					2		4		13					16
1		3		5	7	8		6^1	9^2	10^1	11	12					2	14	4		13					17
1		4	13	2	7	8	12	9		11^2	10^3	14					5	6^1	3							18
1	2	8^3	5	7^2	9^1		6			11	13	10		14					$12^?$		4					19
1		3		5	7	8^1	14	6^1		10	11^3	12					2	9	4		13					20
1	5	8	3		7	9		6^2		12	11^1	13					2^3	10	4		14					21
1	5	2	4^2	14	7	8^3	13	9		10	11	12							3		6^1					22
1	13	4	2	9		7	6	8		11^1	10^2	12					5^3	14	3		13					23
1		2	4	9		7	6	8^2		10	11^1	12					5^3	14	3		13					24
1		2	4^3	9		7	8	6^1		10^2	11	13					5	14	3		12					25
1	5	2	4^1		7	6	8^3			13	12	11^2	10				5^1		3		14					26
1		2	4	9	12	7	8	6^2		10^2	14		11				5^1		3		13					27
1		2	4	9	7	8	6	13		12	10^1		11^2				5		3							28
1		2	4	9	7	8	6				12						5^2	14	3		13	10^1	11^3			29
1		5	4	6^2	10	9	8			14							2	12	3^1		11		7^3	13		30
1		3	5			7^3	9	12			13						2	8	4		14	10^2	11	6^1		31
1		3	5			13	9	6		7			12				2^3	8^2	4		11	10^1		14		32
1		2	5			12	7	6		9			3					8^2	4		14	10^2	13	11^1		33
1		2	5		8		7	9^1		11	12		3						4		6^2	10^3	13	14		34
1		2	5		8	12	7			9	10^2		4						3		14	11^3	6^1	13		35
1		2	5		7	8	6^2			9	10^1		3						4		13		12	14	11^3	36
1		2	5		7^3	8	6	13		9	10^2		4						3		11^1	14		12		37
1		2	5		12	8	7^3	6		9	10^2		3						4		13		14	11^1		38
1		2		5	6	7	9			10^1	11		3						4		12			8		39
1	5	2		7^3	8	9^1	14			$13^?$	11		4				6		3		10^1			12		40
1		2	5^1	12	7^3	8^4	6			$9^?$	10		3						4		14		13	11		41
1		5	6	8^3		9	7^2			10^1	14		3				2		4				12	13	11	42
1		5^3	9	12	7	8				10			3				6^2		4		11^1		14	13		43
1	14		5	8	7	6				10			3				2^3		4		12		13	9^1	11^2	44
1		2	9	5^2	7	6	10			13	12		3						4		14			8^3	11^1	45
1		2	12	5^1	7	8	6	14		10			3					4^3			13			9^2	11	46

FA Cup

First Round	Oldham Ath	(h)	3-2
Second Round	Gillingham	(a)	1-1
Replay	Gillingham	(h)	3-1
Third Round	Sheffield W	(h)	0-0
Replay	Sheffield W	(a)	0-2

Carabao Cup

First Round	Fleetwood T	(a)	2-1
(aet)			
Second Round	Sunderland	(h)	1-2

Checkatrade Trophy

Northern Group A	Morecambe	(a)	2-0
Northern Group A	Leicester C U21	(h)	0-1
Northern Group A	Fleetwood T	(h)	1-2

CHARLTON ATHLETIC

FOUNDATION

The club was formed on 9 June 1905, by a group of 14- and 15-year-old youths living in streets by the Thames in the area which now borders the Thames Barrier. The club's progress through local leagues was so rapid that after the First World War they joined the Kent League where they spent a season before turning professional and joining the Southern League in 1920. A year later they were elected to the Football League's Division 3 (South).

The Valley, Floyd Road, Charlton, London SE7 8BL.

Telephone: (020) 8333 4000.

Ticket Office: (03330) 144 444.

Website: www.cafc.co.uk

Email: info@cafc.co.uk

Ground Capacity: 27,111.

Record Attendance: 75,031 v Aston Villa, FA Cup 5th rd, 12 February 1938 (at The Valley).

Pitch Measurements: 102.5m × 66m (112yd × 72yd).

Chairman: Roland Duchatelet.

Manager: Lee Bowyer (caretaker).

Assistant Manager: Johnnie Jackson (caretaker).

Colours: Red shirts with white trim, white shorts with red trim, red socks with white trim.

Year Formed: 1905.

Turned Professional: 1920.

Club Nickname: 'The Addicks'.

HONOURS

League Champions: First Division – 1999–2000; FL 1 – 2011–12; Division 3S – 1928–29, 1934–35.
Runners-up: Division 1 – 1936–37; Division 2 – 1935–36, 1985–86.
FA Cup Winners: 1947.
Runners-up: 1946.
League Cup: quarter-final – 2007.
Full Members' Cup:
Runners-up 1987.

Grounds: 1906, Siemen's Meadow; 1907, Woolwich Common; 1909, Pound Park; 1913, Horn Lane; 1920, The Valley; 1923, Catford (The Mount); 1924, The Valley; 1985, Selhurst Park; 1991, Upton Park; 1992, The Valley.

First Football League Game: 27 August 1921, Division 3 (S), v Exeter C (h) W 1–0 – Hughes; Johnny Mitchell, Goodman; Dowling (1), Hampson, Dunn; Castle, Bailey, Halse, Green, Wilson.

Record League Victory: 8–1 v Middlesbrough, Division 1, 12 September 1953 – Bartram; Campbell, Ellis; Fenton, Ufton, Hammond; Hurst (2), O'Linn (2), Leary (1), Firmani (3), Kiernan.

Record Cup Victory: 7–0 v Burton A, FA Cup 3rd rd, 7 January 1956 – Bartram; Campbell, Townsend; Hewie, Ufton, Hammond; Hurst (1), Gauld (1), Leary (3), White, Kiernan (2).

Record Defeat: 1–11 v Aston Villa, Division 2, 14 November 1959.

Most League Points (2 for a win): 61, Division 3 (S), 1934–35.

Most League Points (3 for a win): 101, FL 1, 2011–12.

Most League Goals: 107, Division 2, 1957–58.

THE Sun FACT FILE

Arthur Horsfield joined Charlton Athletic from Swindon Town in June 1972 and went on to make 156 consecutive League and Cup appearances for the Addicks before losing his place shortly after the start of the 1975–76 season. He made no further appearances before moving on to Watford in September 1975.

Highest League Scorer in Season: Ralph Allen, 32, Division 3 (S), 1934–35.

Most League Goals in Total Aggregate: Stuart Leary, 153, 1953–62.

Most League Goals in One Match: 5, Wilson Lennox v Exeter C, Division 3 (S), 2 February 1929; 5, Eddie Firmani v Aston Villa, Division 1, 5 February 1955; 5, John Summers v Huddersfield T, Division 2, 21 December 1957; 5, John Summers v Portsmouth, Division 2, 1 October 1960.

Most Capped Player: Jonatan Johansson, 42 (106), Finland.

Most League Appearances: Sam Bartram, 579, 1934–56.

Youngest League Player: Jonjo Shelvey, 16 years 59 days v Burnley, 26 April 2008.

Record Transfer Fee Received: £16,500,000 from Tottenham H for Darren Bent, May 2007.

Record Transfer Fee Paid: £4,750,000 to Wimbledon for Jason Euell, January 2001.

Football League Record: 1921 Elected to Division 3 (S); 1929–33 Division 2; 1933–35 Division 3 (S); 1935–36 Division 2; 1936–57 Division 1; 1957–72 Division 2; 1972–75 Division 3; 1975–80 Division 2; 1980–81 Division 3; 1981–86 Division 2; 1986–90 Division 1; 1990–92 Division 2; 1992–98 Division 1; 1998–99 FA Premier League; 1999–2000 Division 1; 2000–07 FA Premier League; 2007–09 FL C; 2009–12 FL 1; 2012–16 FL C; 2016– FL 1.

LATEST SEQUENCES

Longest Sequence of League Wins: 12, 26.12.1999 – 7.3.2000.

Longest Sequence of League Defeats: 10, 11.4.1990 – 15.9.1990.

Longest Sequence of League Draws: 6, 13.12.1992 – 16.1.1993.

Longest Sequence of Unbeaten League Matches: 15, 4.10.1980 – 20.12.1980.

Longest Sequence Without a League Win: 18, 18.10.2008 – 17.1.2009.

Successive Scoring Runs: 25 from 26.12.1935.

Successive Non-scoring Runs: 5 from 17.10.2015.

MANAGERS

Walter Rayner 1920–25
Alex Macfarlane 1925–27
Albert Lindon 1928
Alex Macfarlane 1928–32
Albert Lindon 1932–33
Jimmy Seed 1933–56
Jimmy Trotter 1956–61
Frank Hill 1961–65
Bob Stokoe 1965–67
Eddie Firmani 1967–70
Theo Foley 1970–74
Andy Nelson 1974–79
Mike Bailey 1979–81
Alan Mullery 1981–82
Ken Craggs 1982
Lennie Lawrence 1982–91
Steve Gritt and Alan Curbishley 1991–95
Alan Curbishley 1995–2006
Iain Dowie 2006
Les Reed 2006
Alan Pardew 2006–08
Phil Parkinson 2008–11
Chris Powell 2011–14
José Riga 2014
Bob Peeters 2014–15
Guy Luzon 2015
Karel Fraeye 2015–16
José Riga 2016
Russell Slade 2016
Karl Robinson 2016–18

TEN YEAR LEAGUE RECORD

		P	W	D	L	F	A	Pts	Pos
2008-09	FL C	46	8	15	23	52	74	39	24
2009-10	FL 1	46	23	15	8	71	48	84	4
2010-11	FL 1	46	15	14	17	62	66	59	13
2011-12	FL 1	46	30	11	5	82	36	101	1
2012-13	FL C	46	17	14	15	65	59	65	9
2013-14	FL C	46	13	12	21	41	61	51	18
2014-15	FL C	46	14	18	14	54	60	60	12
2015-16	FL C	46	9	13	24	40	80	40	22
2016-17	FL 1	46	14	18	14	60	53	60	13
2017-18	FL 1	46	20	11	15	58	51	71	6

DID YOU KNOW ?

In 1954 Charlton Athletic were the first-ever winners of the *London Evening Standard* 5-a-side tournament, beating Tottenham Hotspur 3-1 in the final played at the Empress Pool, Earl's Court. They also won the competition in 1968 and 1975 and were runners-up on three occasions.

CHARLTON ATHLETIC – SKY BET LEAGUE ONE 2017–18 LEAGUE RECORD

Match No.	Date	Venue	Opponents	Result	H/T Score	Lg Pos.	Goalscorers	Attendance
1	Aug 5	H	Bristol R	W 1-0	1-0	8	Bauer [38]	12,968
2	12	A	Plymouth Arg	L 0-2	0-0	14		11,178
3	19	H	Northampton T	W 4-1	1-0	6	Magennis [2], Holmes [61], Forster-Caskey 2 [90, 90]	11,289
4	26	A	Rotherham U	W 2-0	1-0	4	Bauer [16], Magennis [66]	7976
5	Sept 2	A	Oldham Ath	W 4-3	2-1	3	Holmes [18], Fosu [21], Clarke [62], Dodoo [72]	3592
6	9	H	Southend U	W 2-1	0-0	2	Magennis [65], Holmes [68]	12,229
7	12	H	Wigan Ath	L 0-3	0-1	3		10,172
8	16	A	Gillingham	L 0-1	0-0	6		7216
9	23	H	Bury	D 1-1	1-1	7	Magennis [39]	9895
10	26	A	Walsall	D 2-2	1-1	7	Fosu [13], Holmes [88]	3712
11	30	A	Fleetwood T	W 3-1	2-1	5	Fosu 3 [13, 39, 71]	3009
12	Oct 14	H	Doncaster R	W 1-0	1-0	5	Fosu [9]	10,917
13	17	A	Oxford U	D 1-1	1-1	5	Fosu [18]	7070
14	21	A	Bradford C	W 1-0	0-0	4	Forster-Caskey [72]	20,066
15	28	H	AFC Wimbledon	W 1-0	0-0	4	Holmes [78]	12,575
16	Nov 18	H	Milton Keynes D	D 2-2	1-0	5	Magennis [6], Golbourne (og) [87]	10,557
17	21	H	Rochdale	W 2-1	1-1	4	Forster-Caskey 2 [35, 60]	8801
18	25	A	Scunthorpe U	L 0-2	0-0	6		4307
19	28	H	Peterborough U	D 2-2	0-1	6	Holmes (pen) [90], Ahearne-Grant [90]	9532
20	Dec 9	H	Portsmouth	L 0-1	0-0	6		16,361
21	16	A	Blackburn R	L 0-2	0-1	6		10,907
22	23	H	Blackpool	D 1-1	1-1	6	Aribo [15]	10,172
23	26	A	Southend U	L 1-3	0-2	9	Reeves [66]	9588
24	29	A	Wigan Ath	D 0-0	0-0	8		9297
25	Jan 1	H	Gillingham	L 1-2	0-2	9	Aribo [83]	11,979
26	6	A	Oldham Ath	W 1-0	1-0	8	Mavididi [27]	9972
27	13	A	Bury	W 1-0	1-0	8	Marshall [63]	3295
28	20	H	Walsall	W 3-1	1-1	6	Aribo [31], Roberts, K (og) [73], Mavididi [89]	10,140
29	Feb 3	H	Oxford U	L 2-3	0-0	7	Kashi [63], Magennis [78]	11,747
30	10	A	Doncaster R	D 1-1	1-0	7	Bauer [18]	7797
31	13	H	Bradford C	D 1-1	1-0	7	Magennis [24]	10,650
32	17	A	Milton Keynes D	W 2-1	1-0	6	Kashi [10], Magennis [60]	8961
33	24	H	Shrewsbury T	L 0-2	0-0	7		17,581
34	Mar 10	A	Peterborough U	L 1-4	0-1	8	Zyro [73]	6337
35	13	A	Blackpool	L 0-1	0-0	8		3216
36	17	H	Fleetwood T	D 0-0	0-0	9		9865
37	24	H	Plymouth Arg	W 2-0	2-0	8	Page [3], Zyro [17]	13,989
38	30	A	Northampton T	W 4-0	2-0	8	Reeves [14], Fosu 2 [19, 51], Magennis [79]	6416
39	Apr 2	H	Rotherham U	W 3-1	0-0	6	Zyro [28], Aribo 2 [54, 65]	11,871
40	7	A	Bristol R	D 1-1	1-1	6	Reeves [45]	9336
41	10	A	AFC Wimbledon	L 0-1	0-1	6		4457
42	14	H	Scunthorpe U	L 0-1	0-1	8		11,877
43	17	H	Shrewsbury T	W 2-0	0-0	5	Pearce [74], Magennis [90]	5838
44	21	A	Portsmouth	W 1-0	1-0	5	Ajose [40]	19,210
45	28	H	Blackburn R	W 1-0	1-0	5	Pearce [19]	17,310
46	May 5	A	Rochdale	L 0-1	0-0	6		5294

Final League Position: 6

GOALSCORERS

League (58): Magennis 10, Fosu 9, Holmes 6 (1 pen), Aribo 5, Forster-Caskey 5, Bauer 3, Reeves 3, Zyro 3, Kashi 2, Mavididi 2, Pearce 2, Ahearne-Grant 1, Ajose 1, Clarke 1, Dodoo 1, Marshall 1, Page 1, own goals 2.
FA Cup (4): Reeves 2, Ahearne-Grant 1, Marshall 1.
Carabao Cup (3): Charles-Cook 1, Clarke 1, Novak 1.
Checkatrade Trophy (9): Ahearne-Grant 2, Hackett-Fairchild 2, Reeves 2, Aribo 1, Dodoo 1, Lapslie 1.
League One Play-Offs (0).

Amos B 46	Solly C 27	Bauer P 33 + 1	Pearce P J 24 + 1	Dasilva J 34 + 4	Kashi A 33 + 1	Holmes R 22 + 1	Forster-Caskey J 40 + 1	Fosu T 26 + 4	Clarke B 16 + 1	Novak L 1 + 1	Watt T — + 1	Ahearne-Grant K 4 + 18	Crofts A — + 1	Magennis J 37 + 5	Hackett-Fairchild R — + 5	Konsa E 32 + 7	Jackson J 4 + 7	Dodoo J — + 5	Sarr N 14 + 4	Marshall M 20 + 7	Reeves B 21 + 8	Aribo J 19 + 7	Best L 2 + 3	Dijksteel A 8 + 2	Lapslie G — + 1	Lennon H 6 + 4	Mavididi S 6 + 6	KaiKai S 8 + 6	Zyro M 8 + 5	Ajose N 7 + 5	Page L 8	Maloney T — + 1	Match No.
1	2	3	4	5	6	7^2	8	9^3	10^1	11*	12	13	14																				1
1	2	3	4	5		7	8	6	10^1	9^2		12		11	13																		2
1	2	3	4	5	6	10^3	7	8^1	9^2		12		11	13	14																		3
1	2	3	4	5		7	9^2	6	8^3	10^1	13	12		11	14																		4
1	2	3	4		7	9	8	10	11^2	6^1	13	5	12																				5
1	2	3	4	5	6	9^1	7	8^2	11	10	13	12																					6
1	2	3	4	5	6^1	8	7	10^2	9^3	12	11	13	14																				7
1	2	3	4	5	8	9	7^3	6^1	11^2	13	10	14	12																				8
1	2	3	4	5	7	6	10	9^1	8^2	11	12	13																					9
1	2		4	5	7	10	6	8	9^1	12	11	3																					10
1	3	10	2	6^3	9	7^1	5^2	4	8	11	12	13	14																				11
1	2	4	5^1	7	10	6	8	9^2	11	3	13	12																					12
1	2	4	5	7	10	6	8^2	12	13	11	3	9^1																					13
1	2	4	12	7	8^1	6	10^2	9^3	11	3	14	5	13																				14
1	2	4	5^1	6	8	7	10^3	9^2	11	3	13	12	14																				15
1	2		5	6	8	7	12	13	11	3	4	10^2	9^1																				16
1	2	13	5^1	6	8	7	12	11	3	4	10^3	9^2	14																				17
1	2	3^2	9	8	10	7	12	11	13	4	5	6^1																					18
1	4^3	3	6^1	8	7	13	11	2	5	10	14	9^2	12																				19
1	2	5	10	6	9^2	12	11	3	4	8^3	14	7^1	13																				20
1	2	3	5	7	8^2	12	11	4	10^1	9	6	12																					21
1	5	14	12	11	4	7	3	8^3	9^1	6	10^2	2	13																				22
1	5	7^1	8	10^2	11	13	4	3	9	6	12																						23
1	5	6	12	8^1	11	14	2	7	3	10^3	9	13	4^2																				24
1	5	6	10	7^1	14	11	3	8	9^2	13	12^3	4																					25
1	3	5	6	10^1	12	11	2	13	8	7	4	9^2																					26
1		5	6	13	11	12	3	14	8	10^2	7^1	2	4	9^3																			27
1	2	5	7	12	13	11	3	14	8^1	9^3	6	4	10^2																				28
1	2	5	6	7	9^1	11	3	8^3	14	4	10^2	12	13																				29
1	2	3	5^1	7	6	10^2	11	4	13	8	9^3	14	12																				30
1	2	4	5	6	7	9	11	3	8^2	10^1	12	13																					31
1	2	4^3	12	5	6	7	11	3	14	9^2	8	13	10^1																				32
1	2	4	5^3	6	7	12	11	3	8^2	9	10^1	14	13																				33
1	2	3	7	10	11^2	4	6^3	5	12	9	8^1	13	14																				34
1	5^3	4	3	7	8	11	6	12	14	9	13	10^2	2^1																				35
1	3	4	7	10	11^3	2	5	8^1	9^2	6	14	12	13																				36
1	3	4	7	10	13	12	9^3	6	2	8	11^1	5^2	14																				37
1	3	4	7	10^3	13	9	6	2	12	14	8^2	11^1	5																				38
1	3	4	5	7	8^2	14	2	9	6	13	12	10^3	11^1																				39
1	4	3	6	13	7	9	2	12	8^1	11	10^2	5																					40
1	4	3	6	12	2	13	7^2	9	10^3	8^1	11	14	5																				41
1	3	4	5	7	13	12	9	6^3	2	14	10^2	8^1	11																				42
1	3	4	13	6	10^2	11	7	8^1	12	2	14	9^3																					43
1	3	4	12	7	8	9^3	11	2	13	6	14	10^2	5^1																				44
1	3	4	12	8	7	10	2	9	6^2	14	13	11^3	5^1																				45
1	4	3	5	8	7^2	2	14	9	12	6^3	13	10^1	11																				46

FA Cup

First Round	Truro C	(h)	3-1
Second Round	AFC Wimbledon	(a)	1-3

Checkatrade Trophy

Southern Group A	Crawley T	(a)	2-0
Southern Group A	Fulham U21	(h)	3-2
Southern Group A	Portsmouth	(h)	0-1
Second Round South	Swansea C U21	(a)	3-2
Third Round	Oxford U	(h)	1-1

(Oxford U won 3-0 on penalties)

Carabao Cup

First Round	Exeter C	(a)	2-1
Second Round	Norwich C	(a)	1-4

League One Play-Offs

Semi-Final 1st leg	Shrewsbury T	(h)	0-1
Semi-Final 2nd leg	Shrewsbury T	(a)	0-1

CHELSEA

FOUNDATION

Chelsea may never have existed but for the fact that Fulham rejected an offer to rent the Stamford Bridge ground from Mr H. A. Mears who had owned it since 1904. Fortunately he was determined to develop it as a football stadium rather than sell it to the Great Western Railway and got together with Frederick Parker, who persuaded Mears of the financial advantages of developing a major sporting venue. Chelsea FC was formed in 1905 and applications made to join both the Southern League and Football League. The latter competition was decided upon because of its comparatively meagre representation in the south of England.

Stamford Bridge, Fulham Road, London SW6 1HS.
Telephone: (0371) 811 1955. *Fax:* (020) 7381 4831.
Ticket Office: (0371) 811 1905.
Website: www.chelseafc.com
Email: enquiries@chelseafc.com
Ground Capacity: 41,631.
Record Attendance: 82,905 v Arsenal, Division 1, 12 October 1935.
Pitch Measurements: 103m × 67.5m (112yd × 74yd).
Chairman: Bruce Buck.
Chief Executive: Marina Granovskaia.
Manager: Antonio Conte.
First-Team Coaches: Angelo Alessio, Gianluca Conte.
Colours: Rush blue shirt with white trim, rush blue shorts with white trim, white socks with rush blue trim.
Year Formed: 1905. *Turned Professional:* 1905.
Club Nickname: 'The Blues'.
Ground: 1905, Stamford Bridge.
First Football League Game: 2 September 1905, Division 2, v Stockport Co (a) L 0–1 – Foulke; Mackie, McEwan; Key, Harris, Miller; Moran, Jack Robertson, Copeland, Windridge, Kirwan.
Record League Victory: 8–0 v Wigan Ath, FA Premier League, 9 May 2010 – Cech; Ivanovic (Belletti), Ashley Cole (1), Ballack (Matic), Terry, Alex, Kalou (1) (Joe Cole), Lampard (pen), Anelka (2), Drogba (3, 1 pen), Malouda; 8–0 v Aston Villa, FA Premier League, 23 December 2012 – Cech; Azpilicueta, Ivanovic (1), Cahill, Cole, Luiz (1), Lampard (1) (Ramirez (2)), Moses, Mata (Piazon), Hazard (1), Torres (1) (Oscar (1)).

THE Sun FACT FILE

On 23 December 2017 Chelsea played their 5,000th competitive fixture, at Goodison Park against Everton. The match ended goalless. Chelsea also failed to score in their first-ever competitive game, losing 1-0 away to Stockport County.

Record Cup Victory: 13–0 v Jeunesse Hautcharage, ECWC, 1st rd 2nd leg, 29 September 1971 – Bonetti; Boyle, Harris (1), Hollins (1p), Webb (1), Hinton, Cooke, Baldwin (3), Osgood (5), Hudson (1), Houseman (1).

Record Defeat: 1–8 v Wolverhampton W, Division 1, 26 September 1953; 0–7 v Nottingham F, Division 1, 20 April 1991.

Most League Points (2 for a win): 57, Division 2, 1906–07.

Most League Points (3 for a win): 99, Division 2, 1988–89.

Most League Goals: 103, FA Premier League, 2009–10.

Highest League Scorer in Season: Jimmy Greaves, 41, 1960–61.

Most League Goals in Total Aggregate: Bobby Tambling, 164, 1958–70.

Most League Goals in One Match: 5, George Hilsdon v Glossop, Division 2, 1 September 1906; 5, Jimmy Greaves v Wolverhampton W, Division 1, 30 August 1958; 5, Jimmy Greaves v Preston NE, Division 1, 19 December 1959; 5, Jimmy Greaves v WBA, Division 1, 3 December 1960; 5, Bobby Tambling v Aston Villa, Division 1, 17 September 1966; 5, Gordon Durie v Walsall, Division 2, 4 February 1989.

Most Capped Player: Frank Lampard, 104 (106), England.

Most League Appearances: Ron Harris, 655, 1962–80.

Youngest League Player: Ian Hamilton, 16 years 138 days v Tottenham H, 18 March 1967.

Record Transfer Fee Received: £60,000,000 from Shanghai SIPG for Oscar, January 2017.

Record Transfer Fee Paid: £60,000,000 to Real Madrid for Alvaro Morata, July 2017.

Football League Record: 1905 Elected to Division 2; 1907–10 Division 1; 1910–12 Division 2; 1912–24 Division 1; 1924–30 Division 2; 1930–62 Division 1; 1962–63 Division 2; 1963–75 Division 1; 1975–77 Division 2; 1977–79 Division 1; 1979–84 Division 2; 1984–88 Division 1; 1988–89 Division 2; 1989–92 Division 1; 1992– FA Premier League.

MANAGERS

John Tait Robertson 1905–07
David Calderhead 1907–33
Leslie Knighton 1933–39
Billy Birrell 1939–52
Ted Drake 1952–61
Tommy Docherty 1961–67
Dave Sexton 1967–74
Ron Suart 1974–75
Eddie McCreadie 1975–77
Ken Shellito 1977–78
Danny Blanchflower 1978–79
Geoff Hurst 1979–81
John Neal 1981–85 (*Director to 1986*)
John Hollins 1985–88
Bobby Campbell 1988–91
Ian Porterfield 1991–93
David Webb 1993
Glenn Hoddle 1993–96
Ruud Gullit 1996–98
Gianluca Vialli 1998–2000
Claudio Ranieri 2000–04
Jose Mourinho 2004–07
Avram Grant 2007–08
Luiz Felipe Scolari 2008–09
Guus Hiddink 2009
Carlo Ancelotti 2009–11
Andre Villas-Boas 2011–12
Roberto Di Matteo 2012
Rafael Benitez 2012–13
Jose Mourinho 2013–15
Guus Hiddink 2015–16
Antonio Conte June 2016–

LATEST SEQUENCES

Longest Sequence of League Wins: 13, 1.10.2016 – 31.12.2016.
Longest Sequence of League Defeats: 7, 1.11.1952 – 20.12.1952.
Longest Sequence of League Draws: 6, 20.8.1969 – 13.9.1969.
Longest Sequence of Unbeaten League Matches: 40, 23.10.2004 – 29.10.2005.
Longest Sequence Without a League Win: 21, 3.11.1987 – 2.4.1988.
Successive Scoring Runs: 27 from 29.10.1988.
Successive Non-scoring Runs: 9 from 14.3.1981.

TEN YEAR LEAGUE RECORD

		P	W	D	L	F	A	Pts	Pos
2008-09	PR Lge	38	25	8	5	68	24	83	3
2009-10	PR Lge	38	27	5	6	103	32	86	1
2010-11	PR Lge	38	21	8	9	69	33	71	2
2011-12	PR Lge	38	18	10	10	65	46	64	6
2012-13	PR Lge	38	22	9	7	75	39	75	3
2013-14	PR Lge	38	25	7	6	71	27	82	3
2014-15	PR Lge	38	26	9	3	73	32	87	1
2015-16	PR Lge	38	12	14	12	59	53	50	10
2016-17	PR Lge	38	30	3	5	85	33	93	1
2017-18	PR Lge	38	21	7	10	62	38	70	5

DID YOU KNOW ?

Chelsea have worn royal blue shirts since switching from a lighter Eton blue shade in 1907. In the 111 years since then the only significant change came in 1964 when they replaced white shorts with royal blue.

CHELSEA – PREMIER LEAGUE 2017–18 LEAGUE RECORD

Match No.	Date	Venue	Opponents	Result	H/T Score	Lg Pos.	Goalscorers	Attendance
1	Aug 12	H	Burnley	L	2-3	0-3	16	Morata [69], Luiz [88]	41,616
2	20	A	Tottenham H	W	2-1	1-0	12	Alonso 2 [24, 88]	73,587
3	27	H	Everton	W	2-0	2-0	6	Fabregas [27], Morata [40]	41,382
4	Sept 9	A	Leicester C	W	2-1	1-0	3	Morata [41], Kante [50]	31,923
5	17	H	Arsenal	D	0-0	0-0	3		41,478
6	23	A	Stoke C	W	4-0	2-0	3	Morata 3 [2, 77, 82], Pedro [30]	29,661
7	30	H	Manchester C	L	0-1	0-0	4		41,530
8	Oct 14	A	Crystal Palace	L	1-2	1-2	5	Bakayoko [18]	25,480
9	21	H	Watford	W	4-2	1-1	4	Pedro [12], Batshuayi 2 [71, 90], Azpilicueta [87]	41,467
10	28	A	Bournemouth	W	1-0	0-0	4	Hazard, E [51]	10,998
11	Nov 5	H	Manchester U	W	1-0	0-0	4	Morata [55]	41,615
12	18	A	WBA	W	4-0	3-0	3	Morata [17], Hazard, E 2 [23, 62], Alonso [38]	23,592
13	25	A	Liverpool	D	1-1	0-0	3	Willian [85]	53,225
14	29	H	Swansea C	W	1-0	0-0	3	Rudiger [55]	41,365
15	Dec 2	H	Newcastle U	W	3-1	2-1	3	Hazard, E 2 (1 pen) [21, 74 (p)], Morata [33]	41,538
16	9	A	West Ham U	L	0-1	0-1	3		56,953
17	12	A	Huddersfield T	W	3-1	2-0	3	Bakayoko [23], Willian [43], Pedro [50]	24,169
18	16	H	Southampton	W	1-0	1-0	3	Alonso [45]	41,562
19	23	A	Everton	D	0-0	0-0	3		39,191
20	26	H	Brighton & HA	W	2-0	0-0	3	Morata [46], Alonso [60]	41,568
21	30	H	Stoke C	W	5-0	3-0	2	Rudiger [3], Drinkwater [9], Pedro [23], Willian (pen) [73], Zappacosta [88]	41,433
22	Jan 3	A	Arsenal	D	2-2	0-0	3	Hazard, E (pen) [67], Alonso [84]	59,379
23	13	H	Leicester C	D	0-0	0-0	3		41,552
24	20	A	Brighton & HA	W	4-0	2-0	3	Hazard, E 2 [3, 77], Willian [6], Moses [89]	30,600
25	31	H	Bournemouth	L	0-3	0-0	4		41,464
26	Feb 5	A	Watford	L	1-4	0-1	4	Hazard, E [82]	20,157
27	12	H	WBA	W	3-0	1-0	4	Hazard, E 2 [25, 71], Moses [63]	41,071
28	25	A	Manchester U	L	1-2	1-1	5	Willian [32]	75,060
29	Mar 4	A	Manchester C	L	0-1	0-0	5		54,328
30	10	H	Crystal Palace	W	2-1	2-0	5	Willian [25], Kelly (og) [32]	40,800
31	Apr 1	H	Tottenham H	L	1-3	1-1	5	Morata [30]	41,364
32	8	H	West Ham U	D	1-1	1-0	5	Azpilicueta [36]	41,324
33	14	A	Southampton	W	3-2	0-1	5	Giroud 2 [70, 78], Hazard, E [75]	31,764
34	19	A	Burnley	W	2-1	1-0	5	Long (og) [20], Moses [69]	21,264
35	28	A	Swansea C	W	1-0	1-0	5	Fabregas [4]	20,900
36	May 6	H	Liverpool	W	1-0	1-0	5	Giroud [32]	41,314
37	9	H	Huddersfield T	D	1-1	0-0	5	Alonso [62]	38,910
38	13	A	Newcastle U	L	0-3	0-1	5		52,294

Final League Position: 5

GOALSCORERS

League (62): Hazard, E 12 (2 pens), Morata 11, Alonso 7, Willian 6 (1 pen), Pedro 4, Giroud 3, Moses 3, Azpilicueta 2, Bakayoko 2, Batshuayi 2, Fabregas 2, Rudiger 2, Drinkwater 1, Kante 1, Luiz 1, Zappacosta 1, own goals 2.
FA Cup (13): Batshuayi 3, Giroud 2, Morata 2, Pedro 2, Willian 2, Alonso 1, Hazard, E 1 (1 pen).
Carabao Cup (10): Batshuayi 3, Willian 2, Hazard, E 1, Kenedy 1, Morata 1, Musonda 1, Rudiger 1.
Checkatrade Trophy (16): Hudson-Odoi 4, Musonda 3, Batshuayi 2, Redan 2, Fanilia-Castilo 1, Grant 1, James 1, McCormick 1, St Clair 1.
Champions League (17): Hazard, E 3 (1 pen), Willian 3, Batshuayi 2, Azpilicueta 1, Bakayoko 1, Fabregas 1 (1 pen), Luiz 1, Morata 1, Pedro 1, Zappacosta 1, own goals 2.

Courtois T 35	Rudiger A 25 + 2	Luiz D 9 + 1	Cahill G 24 + 3	Azpilicueta C 37	Fabregas F 25 + 7	Kante N 34	Alonso M 33	Willian 20 + 16	Boga J 1	Batshuayi M 3 + 9	Christensen A 23 + 4	Morata A 24 + 7	Musonda C — + 3	Moses V 25 + 3	Bakayoko T 24 + 5	Pedro R 17 + 14	Zappacosta D 12 + 10	Hazard E 28 + 6	Drinkwater D 5 + 7	Ampadu E — + 1	Caballero W 3	Barkley R 2	Hudson-Odoi C — + 2	Giroud O 6 + 7	Emerson 3 + 2	Match No.
1	2	3	4*	5	6*	7	8	9	10²	11¹	12³	13	14													1
1	4	7		2		8	9	10²		13	3	11¹		5	6	12										2
1	4	3		2	6	7	8	9		13	14	11¹		5²	12	10³										3
1	4	3		2	10²	6	8	12				11		5¹	7	9³	13	14								4
1		3*	4	2	7	6	8	9²		14	11³			5	12	10¹		13								5
1	4		12	2	13	6	8¹	9¹			3	11		5	7	10²		14								6
1	2		4	5	8	6	9	12		14	3	11³			7¹	13		10²								7
1		3	4	2	6		8	9¹		10³			14	5²	7	13	12	11								8
1	2	3	4	5	6		8²	13		12		10¹		7	9³	14	11									9
1	4	3		2	6		8	14		13		11³		7	9¹	5	10²	12								10
1	12		4	2	7¹	5	9	14			3	10		8			6²	11³	13							11
1			4	2	6³	7²	9	14			3	11		8	13	5	10¹	12								12
1			4	2	12	7	9	14			3	11		8¹	13	5²	10	6³								13
1	2		4		6	7	8	9¹			3	11	12			10²	5³	13	14							14
1	4	14		2	6²	7	9	12			3¹	11		5	13			10³	8							15
1			4	2	6	7	9³	14			3	11		13	8²	12	5¹	10								16
1	4			2		6³	8	9	12	3²				5	7	10		11¹	13	14						17
1			4	2	12	6	8	9		3	13			5²	7	10³	14	11¹								18
1	4			2	12	6	8	9²		13	3			5³	7	10¹	14	11								19
1	4	3	2	6	7²	9	12		13		11¹		5	8			10³	14								20
1	4	3	2		6²	8	9	14			10³		5¹	13	11	12		7								21
1		4	2	8²	7	9	14			3	11		5	6		12	10³	13								22
1	4	3²	2	6¹	7	9	13			12	11		5	8	14		10³								23
	4	12		2		6	8³	9¹	10	3²		14	5	7		13	11				1					24
1	12		4	2	13	6	8			3²				7	9	5³	11					10¹	14			25
1		3	4	2	12	6		9²			5	7*	10¹	8	11								13			26
1	4		13	2	6	7		14			3³	12		5		9²	8	10					11¹			27
1	4			2	14	6	8	9			3	11		5²		12		10¹	7³				13			28
1	4			2	6		8	9¹			3	14		5		10²		11³	7				12	13		29
1			4	2	6³	7	8	9			3	12			14	13	5	10²					11¹			30
	4			2	6	7	8³	9			3	11²		5¹				10			1		14	12	13	31
1	4	3	2	6	7	8	9				11¹		5²		13		10						12			32
1		4	2	6	7	8	9			3	11⁴		14		13	5¹	10³						12			33
1	4	3	2		7						10¹		5	6	9	13	12					11	8²		34
1	4	3	2	6³	7		12				14		5	8	13		10¹					11²	9		35
1	4	3	2	6³	7	9	12				5²	8	14	13	10¹							11			36
	4			2	6	7	8	9			3	11			10¹	5²	13				1		12			37
1		4	2		7		13				3	12		5	8	14		10¹					6³	11²	9	38

FA Cup

Third Round	Norwich C		(a)	0-0
Replay	Norwich C		(h)	1-1

(aet; Chelsea won 5-3 on penalties)

Fourth Round	Newcastle U		(h)	3-0
Fifth Round	Hull C		(h)	4-0
Sixth Round	Leicester C		(a)	2-1

(aet)

Semi-Final	Southampton	(Wembley)		2-0
Final	Manchester U	(Wembley)		1-0

Carabao Cup

Third Round	Nottingham F		(h)	5-1
Fourth Round	Everton		(h)	2-1
Quarter-Final	Bournemouth		(h)	2-1
Semi-Final 1st leg	Arsenal		(h)	0-0
Semi-Final 2nd leg	Arsenal		(a)	1-2

Checkatrade Trophy (Chelsea U21)

Southern Group D	Plymouth Arg	(a)	2-2

(Plymouth Arg won 5-4 on penalties)

Southern Group D	Yeovil T	(a)	1-1

(Yeovil T won 5-3 on penalties)

Southern Group D	Exeter C	(a)	3-1
Second Round South	Milton Keynes D	(a)	4-0
Third Round	Portsmouth	(a)	2-1
Quarter-Final	Oxford U	(h)	3-0
Semi-Final	Lincoln C	(a)	1-1

(Lincoln C won 4-2 on penalties)

Champions League

Group C	Qarabag	(h)	6-0
Group C	Atletico Madrid	(a)	2-1
Group C	Roma	(h)	3-3
Group C	Roma	(a)	0-3
Group C	Qarabag	(a)	4-0
Group C	Atletico Madrid	(h)	1-1
Round of 16 1st leg	Barcelona	(h)	1-1
Round of 16 2nd leg	Barcelona	(a)	0-3

CHELTENHAM TOWN

FOUNDATION

Although a scratch team representing Cheltenham played a match against Gloucester in 1884, the earliest recorded match for Cheltenham Town FC was a friendly against Dean Close School on 12 March 1892. The School won 4–3 and the match was played at Prestbury (half a mile from Whaddon Road). Cheltenham Town played Wednesday afternoon friendlies at a local cricket ground until entering the Mid Gloucester League. In those days the club played in deep red coloured shirts and were nicknamed 'the Rubies'. The club moved to Whaddon Lane for season 1901–02 and changed to red and white colours two years later.

LCI Rail Stadium, Whaddon Road, Cheltenham, Gloucestershire GL52 5NA.

Telephone: (01242) 573 558.

Fax: (01242) 224 675.

Ticket Office: (01242) 573 558 (option 1).

Website: www.ctfc.com

Email: info@ctfc.com

Ground Capacity: 7,027.

HONOURS

League Champions: Conference – 1998–99, 2015–16.
Runners-up: Conference – 1997–98.
FA Cup: 5th rd – 2002.
League Cup: never past 2nd rd.

Record Attendance: 10,389 v Blackpool, FA Cup 3rd rd, 13 January 1934 (at Cheltenham Athletic Ground); 8,326 v Reading, FA Cup 1st rd, 17 November 1956 (at Whaddon Road).

Pitch Measurements: 102.5m × 66m (112yd × 72yd).

Chairman: Paul Baker.

Vice-Chairman: David Bloxham.

Manager: Gary Johnson.

Assistant Manager: Russell Milton.

Colours: Red and white striped shirts, black shorts with white and red trim, black socks with red trim.

Year Formed: 1892.

Turned Professional: 1932.

Club Nickname: 'The Robins'.

Grounds: Pre-1932, Agg-Gardner's Recreation Ground; Whaddon Lane; Carter's Lane; 1932, Whaddon Road (renamed The Abbey Business Stadium 2009, World of Smile Stadium 2015, LCI Rail Stadium 2016).

First Football League Game: 7 August 1999, Division 3, v Rochdale (h) L 0–2 – Book; Griffin, Victory, Banks, Freeman, Brough (Howarth), Howells, Bloomer (Devaney), Grayson, Watkins (McAuley), Yates.

Record League Victory: 5–0 v Mansfield T, FL 2, 6 May 2006 – Higgs; Gallinagh, Bell, McCann (1) (Connolly), Caines, Duff, Wilson, Bird (1p), Gillespie (1) (Spencer), Guinan (Odejayi (1)), Vincent (1).

Record Cup Victory: 12–0 v Chippenham R, FA Cup 3rd qual. rd, 2 November 1935 – Bowles; Whitehouse, Williams; Lang, Devonport (1), Partridge (2); Perkins, Hackett, Jones (4), Black (4), Griffiths (1).

The Sun FACT FILE

Cheltenham Town have made two visits to Wembley Stadium. In May 1998 a crowd of 26,837 saw the Robins defeat Southport 1-0 to win the FA Trophy. They were back again in May 2012 for the League Two Play-Off Final when 24,029 saw them lose out to Crewe Alexandra for a place in League One.

Record Defeat: 1–8 v Crewe Alex, FL 2, 2 April 2011; 0–7 v Crystal Palace, League Cup 2nd rd, 2 October 2002.
N.B. 1–10 v Merthyr T, Southern League, 8 March 1952.

Most League Points (2 for a win): 60, Southern League Division 1, 1963–64.

Most League Points (3 for a win): 78, Division 3, 2001–02.

Most League Goals: 67, FL 2, 2017–18.

Highest League Scorer in Season: Mohamed Eisa, 23, FL 2, 2017–18.

Most League Goals in Total Aggregate: Julian Alsop, 39, 2000–03; 2009–10.

Most League Goals in One Match: 3, Martin Devaney v Plymouth Arg, Division 3, 23 September 2000; 3, Neil Grayson v Cardiff C, Division 3, 1 April 2001; 3, Damien Spencer v Hull C, Division 3, 23 August 2003; 3, Damien Spencer v Milton Keynes D, FL 1, 31 January 2009; 3, Michael Pook v Burton Alb, FL 2, 13 March 2010; 3, Mohamed Eisa v Port Vale, FL 2, 10 February 2017.

Most Capped Player: Grant McCann, 7 (40), Northern Ireland.

Most League Appearances: David Bird, 288, 2001–11.

Youngest League Player: Kyle Haynes, 17 years 85 days v Oldham Ath, 24 March 2009.

Record Transfer Fee Received: £400,000 from Colchester U for Steve Gillespie, July 2008.

Record Transfer Fee Paid: £60,000 to Aldershot T for Jermaine McGlashan, January 2012.

Football League Record: 1999 Promoted to Division 3; 2002 Division 2; 2003–04 Division 3; 2004–06 FL 2; 2006–09 FL 1; 2009–15 FL 2; 2015–16 National League; 2016– FL 2.

LATEST SEQUENCES

Longest Sequence of League Wins: 5, 29.10.2011 – 10.12.2011.

Longest Sequence of League Defeats: 7, 27.1.2009 – 28.2.2009.

Longest Sequence of League Draws: 5, 5.4.2003 – 21.4.2003.

Longest Sequence of Unbeaten League Matches: 16, 1.12.2001 – 12.3.2002.

Longest Sequence Without a League Win: 14, 20.12.2008 – 7.3.2009.

Successive Scoring Runs: 17 from 16.2.2008.

Successive Non-scoring Runs: 5 from 10.3.2012 – 30.3.2012.

MANAGERS

George Blackburn 1932–34
George Carr 1934–37
Jimmy Brain 1937–48
Cyril Dean 1948–50
George Summerbee 1950–52
William Raeside 1952–53
Arch Anderson 1953–58
Ron Lewin 1958–60
Peter Donnelly 1960–61
Tommy Cavanagh 1961
Arch Anderson 1961–65
Harold Fletcher 1965–66
Bob Etheridge 1966–73
Willie Penman 1973–74
Dennis Allen 1974–79
Terry Paine 1979
Alan Grundy 1979–82
Alan Wood 1982–83
John Murphy 1983–88
Jim Barron 1988–90
John Murphy 1990
Dave Lewis 1990–91
Ally Robertson 1991–92
Lindsay Parsons 1992–95
Chris Robinson 1995–97
Steve Cotterill 1997–2002
Graham Allner 2002–03
Bobby Gould 2003
John Ward 2003–07
Keith Downing 2007–08
Martin Allen 2008–09
Mark Yates 2009–14
Paul Buckle 2014–15
Gary Johnson March 2015–

TEN YEAR LEAGUE RECORD

		P	W	D	L	F	A	Pts	Pos
2008-09	FL 1	46	9	12	25	51	91	39	23
2009-10	FL 2	46	10	18	18	54	71	48	22
2010-11	FL 2	46	13	13	20	56	77	52	17
2011-12	FL 2	46	23	8	15	66	50	77	6
2012-13	FL 2	46	20	15	11	58	51	75	5
2013-14	FL 2	46	13	16	17	53	63	55	17
2014-15	FL 2	46	9	14	23	40	67	41	23
2015-16	NL	46	30	11	5	87	30	101	1
2016-17	FL 2	46	12	14	20	49	69	50	21
2017-18	FL 2	46	13	12	21	67	73	51	17

DID YOU KNOW ?

Cheltenham Town AFC was incorporated as a limited company on 27 February 1937. The initial share capital comprised 5,000 shares valued at 10 shillings (50p) each. It was believed that the change in structure would put the club on a better financial footing and also help increase attendances.

CHELTENHAM TOWN – SKY BET LEAGUE TWO 2017–18 LEAGUE RECORD

Match No.	Date	Venue	Opponents	Result	H/T Score	Lg Pos.	Goalscorers	Attendance
1	Aug 5	A	Morecambe	L	1-2	1-0	18	Eisa [43]	1450
2	12	H	Crawley T	W	1-0	1-0	13	Eisa [38]	2834
3	19	A	Carlisle U	L	0-3	0-2	20		4497
4	26	H	Exeter C	L	3-4	2-2	23	Dawson 2 [6, 12], Holman [90]	3168
5	Sept 2	H	Stevenage	L	0-1	0-0	24		2694
6	9	A	Yeovil T	D	0-0	0-0	21		2732
7	12	A	Newport Co	L	0-1	0-1	22		2916
8	16	H	Colchester U	W	3-1	2-1	21	Dawson [10], Eisa [15], Grimes [57]	2718
9	23	A	Accrington S	D	1-1	1-1	21	Eisa [37]	1321
10	26	H	Mansfield T	W	3-0	0-0	16	Graham [51], Morrell [70], Wright [87]	2480
11	30	A	Chesterfield	W	2-0	1-0	13	Eisa 2 [44, 68]	5305
12	Oct 7	H	Swindon T	W	2-1	1-0	12	Graham [20], Wright [90]	5050
13	14	A	Port Vale	L	1-3	0-1	13	Dawson [90]	4277
14	17	H	Grimsby T	L	2-3	1-3	16	Pell [26], Winchester [85]	2469
15	21	H	Lincoln C	W	1-0	1-0	14	Wright [30]	3312
16	28	A	Wycombe W	D	3-3	1-0	15	Graham 2 [22, 89], Winchester [70]	4165
17	Nov 11	H	Luton T	D	2-2	1-1	16	Grimes [37], Boyle [90]	3900
18	18	A	Notts Co	L	1-3	1-1	16	Winchester [35]	5809
19	21	H	Cambridge U	D	0-0	0-0	16		2266
20	25	A	Forest Green R	D	1-1	1-1	16	Eisa [39]	3641
21	Dec 9	H	Crewe Alex	W	1-0	0-0	15	Grimes [52]	2795
22	16	A	Coventry C	L	1-2	1-1	15	Eisa [34]	6457
23	23	A	Barnet	W	2-0	2-0	14	Dawson [32], Winchester [38]	1487
24	26	H	Yeovil T	L	0-2	0-0	15		3484
25	30	H	Newport Co	D	1-1	0-0	16	Eisa [77]	3637
26	Jan 1	A	Stevenage	L	1-4	1-2	17	Eisa [2]	1989
27	6	A	Colchester U	W	4-1	0-1	14	Odelusi [57], Atangana [70], Sellars [79], Eisa [83]	2886
28	13	H	Accrington S	L	0-2	0-1	16		2893
29	20	A	Mansfield T	L	2-3	1-1	17	Pell (pen) [24], Adebayo [74]	3483
30	27	H	Barnet	D	1-1	0-1	16	Eisa [65]	2609
31	Feb 3	A	Grimsby T	D	1-1	0-1	16	Boyle [77]	3352
32	10	H	Port Vale	W	5-1	2-1	14	Eisa 3 [13, 44, 79], Adebayo [66], Boyle [86]	2731
33	13	A	Lincoln C	L	0-1	0-1	15		7891
34	17	H	Wycombe W	L	0-2	0-2	16		3513
35	24	A	Luton T	D	2-2	1-0	16	Morrell [41], Eisa [55]	8453
36	Mar 6	H	Notts Co	D	1-1	0-1	16	Morrell [66]	2273
37	10	A	Swindon T	W	3-0	1-0	15	Andrews [41], Eisa 2 [49, 71]	6658
38	17	H	Chesterfield	D	1-1	0-0	15	Graham [79]	2822
39	24	H	Crawley T	W	5-3	3-0	15	Pell 2 [7, 12], Eisa 2 [36, 47], Boyle [53]	2172
40	30	A	Carlisle U	L	0-1	0-0	15		3107
41	Apr 2	A	Exeter C	L	1-2	1-1	15	Winchester [37]	4420
42	7	H	Morecambe	W	3-0	0-0	15	Sellars [58], Boyle [65], Pell [73]	2420
43	14	H	Forest Green R	L	0-1	0-1	16		4744
44	21	A	Cambridge U	L	3-4	2-1	16	Lloyd [3], Eisa 2 [13, 79]	3853
45	28	H	Coventry C	L	1-6	0-4	17	Eisa [58]	5027
46	May 5	A	Crewe Alex	L	1-2	1-1	17	Lloyd [34]	4350

Final League Position: 17

GOALSCORERS

League (67): Eisa 23, Boyle 5, Dawson 5, Graham 5, Pell 5 (1 pen), Winchester 5, Grimes 3, Morrell 3, Wright 3, Adebayo 2, Lloyd 2, Sellars 2, Andrews 1, Atangana 1, Holman 1, Odelusi 1.
FA Cup (2): Dawson 1, own goal 1.
Carabao Cup (4): Eisa 2, Wright 2.
Checkatrade Trophy (4): Graham 1, Hinds 1, Pell 1, Storer 1.

Flatt J 4	Forster J 4	Boyle W 33 + 1	Grimes J 41 + 2	Winchester C 44	Storer K 17 + 4	Atangana N 23 + 9	Sellars J 21 + 10	Cranston J 17 + 5	Wright D 16 + 17	Holman D — + 2	Pell H 32 + 5	Graham B 15 + 12	Dawson K 32 + 2	Bower M — + 3	O'Shaughnessy D 5 + 5	Flinders S 41	Moore T 35 + 1	Morrell J 38	Hinds F 1 + 11	Gordon J — + 4	Lloyd G 3 + 4	Onariase M 4 + 1	Odelusi S 3 + 6	Adebayo E 2 + 5	Chatzitheodoridis I 18	Rodon J 7 + 5	Andrews J 4 + 3	Lovett R 1	Match No.
1	2	3	4	5	6	7[1]	8	9	10	11	12																		1
1	2	3	4	7	8	12	9[2]	5	11[1]	10		6	13																2
1	6	4[3]	2	9[2]	8	3		5	10	11		7[1]	12	13	14														3
1	3[2]		4[4]	2	7	8		5	12	10	14	9	11[1]	6[3]		13													4
		3[2]	2	8				5	10	11[4]		9	6		13	1	4	7[1]	12	14									5
		4	2	7		14		5	10[1]	11[2]		9	6			1	3	8[3]	13	12									6
		4	2	8		12		5	10[2]	11[3]		9	6			1	3	7[1]	14	13									7
		13	4	2	8[3]			5	14	11		6	10[2]		9[1]	1	3	7	12										8
		3	2	7[2]		14		5	12	11[3]		6	10[1]		9	1	4	8	13										9
		4	2	7		13		5	12	11[3]		6	10[2]		9[1]	1	3	8	14										10
		4	2	7	6	12	13	5[2]	11[3]	8		10[1]				1	3	9	14										11
		4	2	7	9	5	12	11	6	10[1]						1	3	8											12
		3	2	8[3]	6[2]	5	13	10	7	11[1]		12				1	4	9	14										13
		4	2	12	9[1]	5[3]	11	10	8[2]	6		13				1	3	7	14										14
		4	3	7		5	10	11		9	6					1	2	8											15
		2	3	9	14	12	5	8[2]	11	13	10	6[2]				1	4	7[1]											16
		5	4	2	9	7	6[3]	13	10[1]	8	11[3]		12			1	3		14										17
		3	4	6	8[1]	13	12	11	10[2]	7						5	1	2	9										18
		4	3	6[2]	8[1]	13	10	11		7						5	1	2	9	12									19
		4	3	5	12	9		11	10[1]	8		6				1	2	7											20
		3	4	5	12	9[2]		10	11	7		6	13			1	2[1]	8											21
		4	3	2	8	12		10[1]	11	7		6	5			1	9												22
		4	3	5	12	8		13	11	7[1]		6				1	2	9	10[2]										23
		4	3	5		8[2]	9[3]	14	10[1]	11	12	6				1	2	7	13										24
		4	3	5		8	9	12	10	11[1]		6				1	2	7											25
		4[3]	3	5	8[2]	7		12	10	11[1]	6	14				1	2	9	13										26
			4	5	14	7	9[2]	10[3]	11[1]			6				1	2	8		13	3	12							27
			3	5	8	13		14[4]	10[1]	11	12	13	6[2]			1	2[1]	8			4		10[1]						28
			3	8	13		14[4]	10[1]	6	11[3]	5					1	2[4]	7			4		12	9[2]					29
		4	3	7	14	8[3]		11	10	12		5				1		6		2[1]			9[2]						30
		4	3	7	12			11[1]	10	2[2]	5	1					6					13	14	9[1]	8				31
		3	4	5	12			11	6	10[1]	7	1										9[1]	13	8[2]	2	14			32
		3	4	5	7[3]		12	11	8		6	1	14									13	10[1]	9	2[2]				33
		3	4	8	12			10	6[3]	13	5	1					7				11[1]	14	9	2[2]					34
		3	4	8	7	11[2]		10	6[2]	1	2	9								14	13	5[1]	12						35
		3	4	7	8[3]	14		11	12	6	1	2[1]	9										5[2]	13	10				36
		3	4	7	8	14		11	10[2]	1	2	9				13	12						5[1]	6[1]					37
		4	3[3]	8	6	11	12	14	7[1]	1	2	9										5	13	10[2]					38
		4	3	8[2]	6	14	11	9	13	7	1	2				12						5[1]	10[1]						39
		4	3	9	7	10[2]	11	13	12	6	1	2[1]	8									5							40
		3	7[2]	9	10	13	11	12	6[2]	1	2	8										5[1]	4	14					41
		4	3	6[1]	11[2]	13	10	7	14	1	2	8	9							5[3]	12								42
		4	9	8[3]	6[2]	12	11	10[1]	13	1	2	7				5	3	14											43
		3	12	8	7	9	5[3]	13	10	1	2[4]	6	11[1]									4	14						44
		4	12	2	8	9[1]	10	11	6	1	7	13				5	3[2]												45
		3	4[3]	8	12	5[1]	14	11	13	2	7	10[3]	6			9										1			46

FA Cup

First Round	Maidstone U	(h)	2-4

Carabao Cup

First Round (aet)	Oxford U	(a)	4-3
Second Round	West Ham U	(h)	0-2

Checkatrade Trophy

Southern Group E	Swansea C U21	(h)	1-2
Southern Group E	Forest Green R	(h)	1-2
Southern Group E	Newport Co	(a)	2-1

CHESTERFIELD

FOUNDATION

Chesterfield are fourth only to Stoke, Notts County and Nottingham Forest in age for they can trace their existence as far back as 1866, although it is fair to say that they were somewhat casual in the first few years of their history, playing only a few friendlies a year. However, their rules of 1871 are still in existence, showing an annual membership of 2s (10p), but it was not until 1891 that they won a trophy (the Barnes Cup) and followed this a year later by winning the Sheffield Cup, Barnes Cup and the Derbyshire Junior Cup.

The Proact Stadium, 1866 Sheffield Road, Whittington Moor, Chesterfield, Derbyshire S41 8NZ.

Telephone: (01246) 269 300.

Fax: (01246) 556 799.

Ticket Office: (01246) 269 300.

Website: www.chesterfield-fc.co.uk

Email: reception@chesterfield-fc.co.uk

Ground Capacity: 10,379.

Record Attendance: 30,968 v Newcastle U, Division 2, 7 April 1939 (at Saltergate); 10,089 v Rotherham U, FL 2, 18 March 2011 (at b2net Stadium (now called the Proact Stadium)).

Pitch Measurements: 102.5m × 67.5m (112yd × 74yd).

Chairman: Mike Warner.

Chief Executive: Michael Dunford.

Manager: Martin Allen.

Assistant Manager: Adrian Whitbread.

Colours: Blue shirts with white trim, white shorts with blue trim, blue socks with white trim.

Year Formed: 1866.

Turned Professional: 1891.

Previous Name: 1867, Chesterfield Town; 1919, Chesterfield.

Club Nicknames: 'The Blues', 'The Spireites'.

Grounds: 1867, Drill Field; 1871, Recreation Ground, Saltergate; 2010, b2net Stadium (renamed The Proact Stadium 2012).

First Football League Game: 2 September 1899, Division 2, v Sheffield W (a) L 1–5 – Hancock; Pilgrim, Fletcher; Ballantyne, Bell, Downie; Morley, Thacker, Gooing, Munday (1), Geary.

Record League Victory: 10–0 v Glossop NE, Division 2, 17 January 1903 – Clutterbuck; Thorpe, Lerper; Haig, Banner, Thacker; Tomlinson (2), Newton (1), Milward (3), Munday (2), Steel (2).

Record Cup Victory: 6–0 v Braintree T (a), FA Cup 1st rd, 8 November 2014 – Lee; Darikwa, Evatt, Raglan, Jones (Humphreys), Morsy, Ryan, O'Shea (1) (Gardner), Clucas (1), Roberts (1) (Boco), Doyle (2), own goal (1).

Record Defeat: 0–10 v Gillingham, Division 3, 5 September 1987.

HONOURS

League Champions: Division 3N – 1930–31, 1935–36; FL 2 – 2010–11, 2013–14; Division 4 – 1969–70, 1984–85.
Runners-up: Division 3N – 1933–34.
FA Cup: semi-final – 1997.
League Cup: 4th rd – 1965, 2007.
League Trophy Winners: 2012.
Runners-up: 2014.
Anglo-Scottish Cup Winners: 1981.

THE Sun FACT FILE

Jack Lester, who was manager of Chesterfield between October 2017 and April 2018, was the sixth former player to take charge of the club. He followed on from Frank Barlow, Kevin Randall, Nicky Law, Lee Richardson and Danny Wilson. Law was the most successful, leading the team to automatic promotion in 2000–01.

Most League Points (2 for a win): 64, Division 4, 1969–70.

Most League Points (3 for a win): 91, Division 4, 1984–85.

Most League Goals: 102, Division 3 (N), 1930–31.

Highest League Scorer in Season: Jimmy Cookson, 44, Division 3 (N), 1925–26.

Most League Goals in Total Aggregate: Ernie Moss, 162, 1969–76, 1979–81 and 1984–86.

Most League Goals in One Match: 4, Jimmy Cookson v Accrington S, Division 3 (N), 16 January 1926; 4, Jimmy Cookson v Ashington, Division 3 (N), 1 May 1926; 4, Jimmy Cookson v Wigan Borough, Division 3 (N), 4 September 1926; 4, Tommy Lyon v Southampton, Division 2, 3 December 1938.

Most Capped Player: Walter McMillen, 4 (7), Northern Ireland; Mark Williams, 4 (36), Northern Ireland; Liam Graham, 4, New Zealand.

Most League Appearances: Dave Blakey, 617, 1948–67.

Youngest League Player: Dennis Thompson, 16 years 160 days v Notts Co, 26 December 1950.

Record Transfer Fee Received: £1,300,000 from Hull C for Sam Clucas, July 2015.

Record Transfer Fee Paid: £250,000 to Watford for Jason Lee, August 1998.

Football League Record: 1899 Elected to Division 2; 1909 failed re-election; 1921–31 Division 3 (N); 1931–33 Division 2; 1933–36 Division 3 (N); 1936–51 Division 2; 1951–58 Division 3 (N); 1958–61 Division 3; 1961–70 Division 4; 1970–83 Division 3; 1983–85 Division 4; 1985–89 Division 3; 1989–92 Division 4; 1992–95 Division 3; 1995–2000 Division 2; 2000–01 Division 3; 2001–04 Division 2; 2004–07 FL 1; 2007–11 FL 2; 2011–12 FL 1; 2012–14 FL 2; 2014–17 FL 1; 2017–18 FL 2; 2018– National League.

LATEST SEQUENCES

Longest Sequence of League Wins: 10, 6.9.1933 – 4.11.1933.

Longest Sequence of League Defeats: 9, 22.10.1960 – 27.12.1960.

Longest Sequence of League Draws: 8, 26.11.2005 – 2.1.2006.

Longest Sequence of Unbeaten League Matches: 21, 26.12.1994 – 29.4.1995.

Longest Sequence Without a League Win: 18, 11.9.1999 – 3.1.2000.

Successive Scoring Runs: 46 from 25.12.1929.

Successive Non-scoring Runs: 7 from 23.9.1977.

MANAGERS

E. Russell Timmeus 1891–95
(Secretary-Manager)
Gilbert Gillies 1895–1901
E. F. Hind 1901–02
Jack Hoskin 1902–06
W. Furness 1906–07
George Swift 1907–10
G. H. Jones 1911–13
R. L. Weston 1913–17
T. Callaghan 1919
J. J. Caffrey 1920–22
Harry Hadley 1922
Harry Parkes 1922–27
Alec Campbell 1927
Ted Davison 1927–32
Bill Harvey 1932–38
Norman Bullock 1938–45
Bob Brocklebank 1945–48
Bobby Marshall 1948–52
Ted Davison 1952–58
Duggie Livingstone 1958–62
Tony McShane 1962–67
Jimmy McGuigan 1967–73
Joe Shaw 1973–76
Arthur Cox 1976–80
Frank Barlow 1980–83
John Duncan 1983–87
Kevin Randall 1987–88
Paul Hart 1988–91
Chris McMenemy 1991–93
John Duncan 1993–2000
Nicky Law 2000–01
Dave Rushbury 2002–03
Roy McFarland 2003–07
Lee Richardson 2007–09
John Sheridan 2009–12
Paul Cook 2012–15
Dean Saunders 2015
Danny Wilson 2015–17
Gary Caldwell 2017
Jack Lester 2017–18
Martin Allen May 2018–

TEN YEAR LEAGUE RECORD

		P	W	D	L	F	A	Pts	Pos
2008-09	FL 2	46	16	15	15	62	57	63	10
2009-10	FL 2	46	21	7	18	61	62	70	8
2010-11	FL 2	46	24	14	8	85	51	86	1
2011-12	FL 1	46	10	12	24	56	81	42	22
2012-13	FL 2	46	18	13	15	60	45	67	8
2013-14	FL 2	46	23	15	8	71	40	84	1
2014-15	FL 1	46	19	12	15	68	55	69	6
2015-16	FL 1	46	15	8	23	58	70	53	18
2016-17	FL 1	46	9	10	27	43	78	37	24
2017-18	FL 2	46	10	8	28	47	83	38	24

DID YOU KNOW ?

In 1944–45 Chesterfield reached the semi-finals of the wartime League North Cup. They played Manchester United over two legs, drawing the away tie 1-1 before losing 1-0 at Saltergate.

CHESTERFIELD – SKY BET LEAGUE TWO 2017–18 LEAGUE RECORD

Match No.	Date	Venue	Opponents	Result		H/T Score	Lg Pos.	Goalscorers	Attendance
1	Aug 5	H	Grimsby T	L	1-3	0-2	20	Dennis [82]	7925
2	12	A	Notts Co	L	0-2	0-0	24		7021
3	19	H	Port Vale	W	2-0	2-0	19	Dennis [38], Sinnott [43]	5058
4	26	A	Newport Co	L	1-4	1-0	24	O'Grady [37]	4332
5	Sept 2	H	Coventry C	D	0-0	0-0	21		5164
6	9	A	Crewe Alex	L	1-5	0-1	23	Nolan (og) [72]	3513
7	12	A	Colchester U	D	1-1	1-0	21	Reed [43]	2552
8	16	H	Accrington S	L	1-2	0-0	23	Dennis (pen) [77]	4487
9	23	A	Luton T	L	0-1	0-0	23		7575
10	26	H	Yeovil T	L	2-3	0-2	23	Weir [51], Dennis [72]	3955
11	30	H	Cheltenham T	L	0-2	0-1	23		5305
12	Oct 7	A	Lincoln C	L	1-2	0-2	24	Dennis (pen) [82]	9485
13	14	H	Morecambe	L	0-2	0-1	24		4489
14	17	A	Crawley T	W	2-0	0-0	24	Dennis [73], Flores [88]	1516
15	21	A	Cambridge U	L	1-2	0-0	24	Dennis [55]	4529
16	28	H	Carlisle U	D	2-2	1-0	24	McCourt [40], Dennis [84]	5102
17	Nov 11	A	Swindon T	D	2-2	0-0	24	Dennis [56], McCourt [72]	6140
18	18	H	Exeter C	W	1-0	0-0	24	Dennis [50]	5195
19	21	H	Forest Green R	W	3-2	1-0	24	McCourt 2 [22, 54], Dennis [81]	4306
20	25	A	Mansfield T	D	2-2	1-1	24	Rowley [14], Kellett [58]	7525
21	Dec 9	H	Barnet	W	2-1	0-1	21	Clough (og) [66], Weir [90]	5272
22	16	A	Wycombe W	L	0-1	0-0	23		4522
23	23	A	Stevenage	L	1-5	1-3	23	Dennis [42]	2403
24	26	H	Crewe Alex	L	0-2	0-2	23		5904
25	30	H	Colchester U	D	0-0	0-0	22		5537
26	Jan 1	A	Coventry C	L	0-1	0-1	22		7402
27	6	A	Accrington S	L	0-4	0-2	23		1655
28	13	H	Luton T	W	2-0	2-0	22	Rowley [19], McCourt (pen) [25]	5715
29	20	A	Yeovil T	W	2-1	0-0	22	Reed [66], Dennis [90]	3792
30	27	H	Stevenage	L	0-1	0-0	22		4981
31	Feb 3	A	Crawley T	L	1-2	1-0	23	Reed [18]	5159
32	13	H	Cambridge U	L	2-3	1-1	23	Rowley [1], Dennis [55]	4276
33	17	A	Carlisle U	L	0-2	0-1	23		4025
34	24	H	Swindon T	W	2-1	1-0	23	O'Grady [2], Kellett [51]	4668
35	Mar 10	A	Lincoln C	L	1-3	1-1	23	Whitmore [34]	6395
36	17	A	Cheltenham T	D	1-1	0-0	23	Dennis [74]	2822
37	25	H	Notts Co	W	3-1	2-0	23	Nelson, S [16], Hines [39], Dennis (pen) [90]	6005
38	30	A	Port Vale	L	1-2	0-1	23	Reed [56]	5713
39	Apr 7	A	Grimsby T	L	0-1	0-0	24		6780
40	10	A	Morecambe	D	2-2	0-2	24	Dennis [55], Kellett [74]	1042
41	14	H	Mansfield T	L	0-1	0-0	24		7967
42	17	A	Exeter C	L	1-2	0-1	24	Kellett [84]	3560
43	21	A	Forest Green R	L	1-4	1-1	24	Dennis (pen) [36]	3336
44	28	H	Wycombe W	L	1-2	1-1	24	Harriman (og) [39]	5679
45	May 1	H	Newport Co	W	1-0	0-0	24	Dennis [71]	4608
46	5	A	Barnet	L	0-3	0-1	24		5539

Final League Position: 24

GOALSCORERS

League (47): Dennis 19 (4 pens), McCourt 5 (1 pen), Kellett 4, Reed 4, Rowley 3, O'Grady 2, Weir 2, Flores 1, Hines 1, Nelson, S 1, Sinnott 1, Whitmore 1, own goals 3.
FA Cup (0).
Carabao Cup (1): Dennis 1 (1 pen).
Checkatrade Trophy (6): De Girolamo 1, Dennis 1, McCourt 1, O'Grady 1, Rowley 1, Sinnott 1.

Anyon J 14	Wiseman S 23 + 1	Hird S 24	Evatt I 21	Wakefield C 1	Weir R 39 + 2	Reed L 41 + 1	Sinnott J 4 + 4	Donohue D 2	Ugwu C 3 + 9	O'Grady C 20 + 15	Dennis K 38 + 5	Brewster D — + 2	McCourt J 21 + 13	Barry B 29	Maguire L 13 + 5	Mitchell R — + 4	Brown J 8 + 5	Lee T 7	Smith G 6 + 2	Flores J 11 + 2	Kellett A 29 + 7	Rawson L — + 1	Jules Z 6	Briggs M 8 + 3	De Girolamo D 6 + 9	Rowley J 23 + 5	Dimaio C 2 + 8	Williams J 13 + 6	Dawson C 2	German R — + 2	Eastwood J 4	Ramsdale A 19	Talbot D 14	Nelson S 15	Kay J 8 + 3	Hines Z 9 + 2	Whitmore A 14 + 1	Mottley-Henry D 1 + 1	Dodds L 7 + 5	Coke G 1 + 1	Match No.
1	2	3	4^*	5^1	6^2	7	8^3	9	10	11	12	13	14																													1
1	4^*	2	3		7^3	6		8	9^3	11	10^1	13			5	12		14																							2
	2	4	3		6	8	7^1			14	10^3	11		12	5	13		1		9^2																					3
	4	2	3		6	8	7^2			13	11	10		14	5^1			1		9	12^3																				4
	5	3	2		6^8	8				13	11^2	10^5						1		7	12		4	9^1	14																5
	3	2	4			6	14			13	11^2	5						1		7	10^1		8	9^3	12																6
	2	3			7	6^3				14	12	10^1		13	5			1		8			4	9	11^3																7
1	2	3			8^1	7	13			14	12	10			5^8					6	9^3		4^2	11																	8
1	4	3			7	5				14	10^3			12		13				9	2		6	11^2																	9
1	2	3			6	7				5	11^2	13			12					14	8^1		4^3	9	10																10
	2	3	4		6	9^4				13	11	10^2		14			12	1		8^1			5	7																	11
1	2		3		9	12				11	13	10^3		4		14				8	5			7^2	6^1																12
1	3		4		6^2	8				11^1	10	7^3		2				14		5			13	9	12																13
1	2	4	3		7	8					11^1			6						9	5^2		12	14	10^3	13															14
1	2^3	3	4		7^1	8					11			6						9	5^2		12	14	10	13															15
	5	3	4		7					12	11			8	2			1			10^1		9		6																16
1	5	3	4			7					11			6	2	12				9				10^2		8	13														17
1	5^8	4	3		13	6	12			14	11^1			7	2						9^3					8^1		10													18
1		3	4		7	6	12			14	11^2			10^3	2						9^1					8	13	5													19
1		3	4		7	9					11			8	2						10^1					12	6	5													20
14		3	4		6	10				13	11			7	2^1						9^2		12^3		8	5	1														21
	2	3	4		6^1	10				12	11^2			7							9^3					8	14	5	1	13											22
	2	3	4^2			8				10	11			7							9^1					13	6	12	5		1										23
	2	3			6^1	8				10^2	11			7							9					13	5	12	4		1										24
	3	4			6	7					11			2							10					8	9	5			1										25
	4^8	3^2			2	6				13	11^3			7		12					10					14	8	9	5		1										26
					8	7				11				12		3					13					6^2		5^3		14		1	2	4	9^1	10					27
					2	6				11				7^1		4										8	13	12				1	5	3	9	10^2					28
					2	6				11^2	13			7		5					12					8						1		3	9	10^1	4				29
					2	7				13	11			8		4^2					12					6		14				1		3	10^1	9^1	5				30
					2	7				14	11			8		4										13						1		3	6^2	12	5	9^1	10^1		31
					2	8				11	10			14	5	3					6^3											1		13			4	12	9^1	7^2	32
					5	9				11^3	10			7^1	3		14				6^2					13						1	2	8		4					33
					7^1	8				11				12	2						6^2					14	13					1	5^3	4		9	3	10			34
										10^3	11			7	6					5^8	9					14						1	2	3	8^1	12^4	4				35
					7						11				2			6^1		5	10						13					1	8	4	9^2		3	12		36
					7^1	8					10		12	2		11				13	9^3											1	5	4	14	6^2	3			37
					7	8					14^1			2			6^2				10^3											1	5	3	13	9^1	4	12		38
					7^1	6					13	11		12	2		8				9											1	5	3		10^2	4			39
					7^3	9					13	11		6^2	2^4	4	8			12	10											1	5		3		14			40
			4		7^2	8					12	11		14	3	6^3				5	9											1	2		10^1		13			41
					6^3	7					10^2	11^1		5	4	13^3				9^1	12					14						1	3		2^1		8			42
			3^2		7^3	6					14	11		8	2	4	13				9					10^1						1	5				12			43
					6				12		11		13	3	4	14		7								10^3		5^2				1	2	9			8^1			44
					13	8					10			6	4	14		11^1		7^3								5				1	2	3^1		12	9			45
1					8	7^2					11			6	4	9					14					13		5				2^3					3	10^1	12	46

FA Cup
First Round   Bradford C   (a)   0-2

Carabao Cup
First Round   Sheffield W   (a)   1-4

Checkatrade Trophy
Northern Group F   Bradford C   (h)   2-4
Northern Group F   Rotherham U   (a)   2-1
Northern Group F   Manchester C U21   (h)   2-2
(Chesterfield won 4-3 on penalties)
Second Round North Fleetwood T   (a)   0-2

COLCHESTER UNITED

FOUNDATION

Colchester United was formed in 1937 when a number of enthusiasts of the much older Colchester Town club decided to establish a professional concern as a limited liability company. The new club continued at Layer Road which had been the amateur club's home since 1909.

Weston Homes Community Stadium, United Way, Colchester, Essex CO4 5UP.

Telephone: (01206) 755 100.

Ticket Office: (01206) 755 161.

Website: www.cu-fc.com

Email: media@colchesterunited.net

Ground Capacity: 10,105.

Record Attendance: 19,072 v Reading, FA Cup 1st rd, 27 November 1948 (at Layer Road); 10,064 v Norwich C, FL 1, 16 January 2010 (at Community Stadium).

Pitch Measurements: 100.5m × 65m (110yd × 71yd).

Executive Chairman: Robbie Cowling.

Manager: John McGreal.

Assistant Manager: Steve Ball.

Colours: Royal blue and white striped shirts, white shorts with royal blue trim, white socks with royal blue hoops.

Year Formed: 1937.

Turned Professional: 1937.

Club Nickname: 'The U's'.

Grounds: 1937, Layer Road; 2008, Weston Homes Community Stadium.

First Football League Game: 19 August 1950, Division 3 (S), v Gillingham (a) D 0–0 – Wright; Kettle, Allen; Bearryman, Stewart, Elder; Jones, Curry, Turner, McKim, Church.

Record League Victory: 9–1 v Bradford C, Division 4, 30 December 1961 – Ames; Millar, Fowler; Harris, Abrey, Ron Hunt; Foster, Bobby Hunt (4), King (4), Hill (1), Wright.

Record Cup Victory: 9-1 v Leamington, FA Cup 1st rd, 5 November 2005 – Davison; Stockley (Garcia), Duguid, Brown (1), Chilvers, Watson (1), Halford (1), Izzet (Danns) (2), Iwelumo (1) (Williams), Cureton (2), Yeates (1).

Record Defeat: 0–8 v Leyton Orient, Division 4, 15 October 1988.

Most League Points (2 for a win): 60, Division 4, 1973–74.

Most League Points (3 for a win): 81, Division 4, 1982–83.

HONOURS

League Champions: Conference – 1991–92.
Runners-up: FL 1 – 2005–06; Division 4 – 1961–62; Conference – 1990–91.
FA Cup: 6th rd – 1971.
League Cup: 5th rd – 1975.
League Trophy: Runners-up: 1997.

Sun FACT FILE

Colchester United launched their Hall of Fame at the end of the 2006–07 season to mark the club's 70th anniversary as a professional club. The first two inductees, chosen in a poll of fans, were Peter Wright and Micky Cook and they were joined by Brian Hall, Mark Kinsella and Tony English who were selected by a committee.

Most League Goals: 104, Division 4, 1961–62.

Highest League Scorer in Season: Bobby Hunt, 38, Division 4, 1961–62.

Most League Goals in Total Aggregate: Martyn King, 130, 1956–64.

Most League Goals in One Match: 4, Bobby Hunt v Bradford C, Division 4, 30 December 1961; 4, Martyn King v Bradford C, Division 4, 30 December 1961; 4, Bobby Hunt v Doncaster R, Division 4, 30 April 1962.

Most Capped Player: Bela Balogh, 2 (9), Hungary.

Most League Appearances: Micky Cook, 613, 1969–84.

Youngest League Player: Lindsay Smith, 16 years 218 days v Grimsby T, 24 April 1971.

Record Transfer Fee Received: £2,500,000 from Reading for Greg Halford, January 2007.

Record Transfer Fee Paid: £400,000 to Cheltenham T for Steve Gillespie, July 2008.

Football League Record: 1950 Elected to Division 3 (S); 1958–61 Division 3; 1961–62 Division 4; 1962–65 Division 3; 1965–66 Division 4; 1966–68 Division 3; 1968–74 Division 4; 1974–76 Division 3, 1976–77 Division 4; 1977–81 Division 3; 1981–90 Division 4; 1990–92 Conference; 1992–98 Division 3; 1998–2004 Division 2; 2004–06 FL 1; 2006–08 FL C; 2008–16 FL 1; 2016– FL 2.

LATEST SEQUENCES

Longest Sequence of League Wins: 7, 31.12.2005 – 7.2.2006.

Longest Sequence of League Defeats: 9, 31.10.2015 – 28.12.2015.

Longest Sequence of League Draws: 6, 21.3.1977 – 11.4.1977.

Longest Sequence of Unbeaten League Matches: 20, 22.12.1956 – 19.4.1957.

Longest Sequence Without a League Win: 20, 2.3.1968 – 31.8.1968.

Successive Scoring Runs: 24 from 15.9.1962.

Successive Non-scoring Runs: 5 from 11.2.2006.

MANAGERS

Ted Fenton 1946–48
Jimmy Allen 1948–53
Jack Butler 1953–55
Benny Fenton 1955–63
Neil Franklin 1963–68
Dick Graham 1968–72
Jim Smith 1972–75
Bobby Roberts 1975–82
Allan Hunter 1982–83
Cyril Lea 1983–86
Mike Walker 1986–87
Roger Brown 1987–88
Jock Wallace 1989
Mick Mills 1990
Ian Atkins 1990–91
Roy McDonough 1991–94
George Burley 1994
Steve Wignall 1995–99
Mick Wadsworth 1999
Steve Whitton 1999–2003
Phil Parkinson 2003–06
Geraint Williams 2006–08
Paul Lambert 2008–09
Aidy Boothroyd 2009–10
John Ward 2010–12
Joe Dunne 2012–14
Tony Humes 2014–15
Kevin Keen 2015–16
John McGreal May 2016–

TEN YEAR LEAGUE RECORD

		P	W	D	L	F	A	Pts	Pos
2008-09	FL 1	46	18	9	19	58	58	63	12
2009-10	FL 1	46	20	12	14	64	52	72	8
2010-11	FL 1	46	16	14	16	57	63	62	10
2011-12	FL 1	46	13	20	13	61	66	59	10
2012-13	FL 1	46	14	9	23	47	68	51	20
2013-14	FL 1	46	13	14	19	53	61	53	16
2014-15	FL 1	46	14	10	22	58	77	52	19
2015-16	FL 1	46	9	13	24	57	99	40	23
2016-17	FL 2	46	19	12	15	67	57	69	8
2017-18	FL 2	46	16	14	16	53	52	62	13

DID YOU KNOW ?

The first player to score a Football League hat-trick for Colchester United was Vic Keeble who did so in the 3-0 home win over Plymouth Argyle on 17 March 1951. Keeble went on to score 23 goals in 46 games for the U's before being sold to Newcastle United in February 1952.

COLCHESTER UNITED – SKY BET LEAGUE TWO 2017–18 LEAGUE RECORD

Match No.	Date	Venue	Opponents	Result	H/T Score	Lg Pos.	Goalscorers	Attendance
1	Aug 5	A	Accrington S	L	1-3	0-2	21	Szmodics [81]	1625
2	12	H	Stevenage	D	1-1	0-0	20	Mandron [65]	3330
3	19	A	Luton T	L	0-3	0-1	23		7865
4	26	H	Forest Green R	W	5-1	2-1	16	Reid [4], Kent [21], Szmodics [65], Vincent-Young [74], Senior [90]	3047
5	Sept 2	A	Cambridge U	L	0-1	0-0	20		4511
6	9	H	Crawley T	W	3-1	3-0	14	Szmodics [8], Jackson [14], Mandron [38]	2923
7	12	H	Chesterfield	D	1-1	0-1	16	Hanlan [82]	2552
8	16	A	Cheltenham T	L	1-3	1-2	17	Szmodics (pen) [26]	2718
9	23	H	Wycombe W	L	1-2	1-1	20	Hanlan [43]	3562
10	26	A	Grimsby T	D	2-2	1-1	21	Reid 2 [5, 59]	3438
11	30	A	Yeovil T	W	1-0	1-0	16	Murray [43]	2556
12	Oct 7	H	Mansfield T	W	2-0	2-0	15	Murray [29], Mandron [34]	3262
13	14	H	Carlisle U	L	0-1	0-0	16		3402
14	17	A	Newport Co	W	2-1	0-0	14	Jackson [72], Mandron [77]	2704
15	21	A	Coventry C	D	0-0	0-0	15		7149
16	28	H	Crewe Alex	W	3-1	1-1	13	Mandron 2 [39, 71], Eastman [60]	3088
17	Nov 11	H	Barnet	W	1-0	0-0	10	Szmodics [83]	2301
18	18	H	Morecambe	D	0-0	0-0	12		2872
19	21	H	Lincoln C	W	1-0	1-0	9	Szmodics [3]	3102
20	25	A	Notts Co	L	1-2	0-0	11	Odelusi [89]	6770
21	Dec 9	H	Exeter C	W	3-1	3-0	10	James (og) [23], Szmodics 2 (1 pen) [26 (p), 30]	3049
22	15	A	Swindon T	W	3-2	1-1	5	Kent [45], Mandron [63], Szmodics [78]	6020
23	23	H	Port Vale	D	1-1	1-0	8	Szmodics [32]	3485
24	26	A	Crawley T	W	2-0	1-0	5	Mandron [4], Szmodics [57]	2154
25	30	A	Chesterfield	D	0-0	0-0	8		5537
26	Jan 1	H	Cambridge U	D	0-0	0-0	8		4789
27	6	H	Cheltenham T	L	1-4	1-0	9	Guthrie [40]	2886
28	13	A	Wycombe W	L	1-3	0-2	11	Szmodics [78]	4386
29	20	H	Grimsby T	D	1-1	0-1	11	Murray [47]	3016
30	27	A	Port Vale	D	2-2	2-1	11	Senior [12], Drey Wright [45]	4044
31	Feb 3	H	Newport Co	W	2-0	0-0	10	Stevenson [59], Eastman [80]	2874
32	10	A	Carlisle U	D	1-1	1-0	11	Senior [44]	4006
33	13	H	Coventry C	W	2-1	1-0	10	Ogedi-Uzokwe (pen) [27], Mandron [88]	3319
34	17	A	Crewe Alex	L	0-1	0-0	11		3548
35	24	H	Barnet	L	0-1	0-0	12		3121
36	Mar 10	A	Mansfield T	D	1-1	0-1	13	Comley [51]	4050
37	17	H	Yeovil T	L	0-1	0-1	13		2772
38	20	A	Morecambe	D	0-0	0-0	13		893
39	24	A	Stevenage	W	1-0	1-0	11	Mandron [27]	2709
40	30	H	Luton T	W	2-1	2-0	11	Eastman [15], Prosser [27]	5461
41	Apr 2	A	Forest Green R	W	2-1	1-1	10	Drey Wright [1], Stevenson [47]	2869
42	7	H	Accrington S	L	0-1	0-0	11		3174
43	14	H	Notts Co	L	1-3	1-0	11	Drey Wright [9]	3599
44	21	A	Lincoln C	L	1-2	0-0	11	Senior [60]	9211
45	28	H	Swindon T	D	0-0	0-0	12		3687
46	May 5	A	Exeter C	L	0-1	0-0	13		4615

Final League Position: 13

GOALSCORERS

League (53): Szmodics 12 (2 pens), Mandron 10, Senior 4, Eastman 3, Murray 3, Reid 3, Drey Wright 3, Hanlan 2, Jackson 2, Kent 2, Stevenson 2, Comley 1, Guthrie 1, Odelusi 1, Ogedi-Uzokwe 1 (1 pen), Prosser 1, Vincent-Young 1, own goal 1.
FA Cup (0).
Carabao Cup (1): Kent 1.
Checkatrade Trophy (2): Mckeown 1, Szmodics 1.

Walker S 44	Jackson R 41 + 1	Eastman T 41 + 1	Kent F 37	James C 3 + 4	Drey Wright 38 + 6	Lapsie T 27 + 2	Murray S 18 + 19	Slater C 1 + 5	Johnstone D 1 + 1	Mandron M 42 + 2	Kpekawa C 4 + 2	Szmodics S 29 + 8	Kinsella L 4 + 5	Reid K 13 + 4	Loft D 10 + 2	Vincent-Young K 37 + 1	Issa T — + 2	O'Sullivan T — + 1	Senior C 10 + 8	Odelusi S — + 8	Inniss R 18	Comley B 31 + 7	Kabamba N 3 + 5	Hanlan B 10 + 8	Guthrie K 7 + 5	Prosser L 14 + 2	Ogedi-Uzokwe J 3 + 6	Stevenson B 10 + 3	Mandeville L 1 + 6	Dickenson B 4 + 3	Shodipo O 2 + 4	Barnes D 2	Gondoh R 1 + 1	Match No.
1	2	3[1]	4	5	6	7	8	9[1]	10[3]	11	12	13	14																					1
1	5	2	3		10	6	7[2]	13		11		4[3]	9	12	8[1]	14																		2
1		2	3		11[2]	6[1]	12		13	10		4[3]	9	8		7	5	14															3
1		3	4		9[2]	7	6			10		11[3]	5	8[1]		2	12	13	14														4
1	12	3	4	14	9[3]	7	6			10		11	5[1]	8[2]					13															5
1	5	2	3[2]	12	14	6				10		9	8[1]		13					4	7	11[3]												6
1	5	4	2[1]	12	6					10[2]		9[1]			8				14	3	7	11	13											7
1	5	2	4[1]	12	6	14				11[4]		9			8					3	7[3]	10[2]	13											8
1	5	2[1]	4		10	6[1]	14			9					12	7[3]	8			3		13	11											9
1	2		3	12	9		14			10		13[3]		8[1]	6	5				4	7	11[2]												10
1	2		4		9		8			10				7	6[2]	5					3	12		11[1]	13									11
1	2	12	4		6		8			10		9[3]		7	5[1]						3	13	14	11[2]										12
1	2	3	4		6	7	12	10	5			9[1]		8[3]					13			14	11[2]											13
1	5	3	2		13	8				11			12		6[2]	9[3]				14	4	7		10[1]										14
1	5	2	4		8	7[4]	9	12		10[2]											3	6	13	11[1]										15
1	5[3]	2	4		9		12			10		13	8	6[1]							3	7	14	11[2]										16
1	5	2	4		8[1]		11			12		6	9						13	3	7			10[2]										17
1	8	4[1]	2		13	7		12		10		9		14		5					3	6[2]		11[4]										18
1	5	2	4		10	6				11[1]		9[3]		14	7[2]	8					3	12		13										19
1	5	2	4		8[2]	6[1]				10		11	14	13	9[3]						12	3	7											20
1	5	2	4		9	6	12			11		10[1]		8					13		6	3[2]	7											21
1	2	3	4		9	7	12			10		11[1]		8[2]	5						6					7	14							22
1	2	3	4	12	8[1]		6	13		11		9[4]		10[2]	5						7	14												23
1	2	8[3]	4		6	3	12			11		10[3]		9[2]	5						7	14	13											24
1	2	3	4		6	8	12			11[1]		9[2]	10		5						7	13												25
1	5	2	3		9[3]	6	7[2]			11[1]	4	10			8						13	14	12											26
1	2	3	4		6	7		11[3]	12			9[4]	13		5[1]						8[2]	14	10											27
1	2	3	4		6		7	11[1]	8					13	5				5[3]	9[2]	14	10	12											28
1	5	2	4		10	6	7			13		9[2]		8					12		3[3]			11[1]	14									29
1	2	4	3		9[1]	6	7			11[2]		8			5				10[3]		12		14	13										30
1	5	2	3			7[2]				11		13			8				10[1]		6		9[3]	4	14	12								31
1	2	5	4		6		14			10		13		7[1]					8		11[2]	3		9[3]	12									32
1		2	4		5		14			10		12			8[2]				9[3]		7			3	11	6[1]		13						33
1	2	5	4		6		14			10					8[2]				7		6			3	11[3]	9[3]	13	12						34
1	5	2[3]	4		14		7			11					8[2]				9		3	6			10[1]		13	12						35
1	2[2]	4	3		6[3]	7[1]	13			10					5						8			11		14		9	12					36
1		2	4		8	6				13		9			5				12		7[2]			11[1]	3		10[3]	14						37
1	2	3		7	9	14				11		8[3]			5				13		6[1]			4		12		9[3]	14	10[2]				38
1	2	7			6[1]	3	12			11		8			5						13			4			9[3]	14	10[2]					39
1	2	3			6	7[1]	14			11		10			5				13		12			4			8[2]	9[3]						40
1	2	4			6[3]		13			11		10[1]			5				9[2]		8			3			7	14	12					41
1	2	3			8		12			11		9[1]			5				10[3]		6[2]			4			7	14	13					42
1	2	3			6		14			11[3]		10[2]			5				12		7[1]			4	13		8		9					43
1	2	3			6		10[3]			11		13			5				12		7[1]			4	14		8		9[2]					44
	2		3		7[3]		8			11[2]		14			5				10[1]		6			4	12		9					1	13	45
	2		3		13	14	9[2]			11[3]		8			5				10[1]		6			4	12							1	7	46

FA Cup
First Round   Oxford C   (h)   0-1

Carabao Cup
First Round   Aston Villa   (h)   1-2

Checkatrade Trophy
Southern Group B   Reading U21   (h)   2-2
(Colchester U won 6-5 on penalties)
Southern Group B   Gillingham   (h)   0-1
Southern Group B   Southend U   (a)   0-2

COVENTRY CITY

FOUNDATION

Workers at Singers' cycle factory formed a club in 1883. The first success of Singers' FC was to win the Birmingham Junior Cup in 1891 and this led in 1894 to their election to the Birmingham & District League. Four years later they changed their name to Coventry City and joined the Southern League in 1908 at which time they were playing in blue and white quarters.

Ricoh Arena, Judds Lane, Longford, Coventry CV6 6AQ.

Telephone: (02476) 991 987.

Fax: (02476) 303 872.

Ticket Office: (02476) 991 987.

Website: www.ccfc.co.uk

Email: info@ccfc.co.uk

Ground Capacity: 32,609.

Record Attendance: 51,455 v Wolverhampton W, Division 2, 29 April 1967 (at Highfield Road); 31,407 v Chelsea, FA Cup 6th rd, 7 March 2009 (at Ricoh Arena).

Pitch Measurements: 100m × 68m (109.5yd × 74.5yd).

Chairman: Tim Fisher.

Chief Executive: David Boddy.

Manager: Mark Robins.

Assistant Manager: Steve Taylor.

Colours: Sky blue shirts with white trim, sky blue shorts, sky blue socks.

Year Formed: 1883.

Turned Professional: 1893.

Previous Name: 1883, Singers' FC; 1898, Coventry City.

Club Nickname: 'Sky Blues'.

Grounds: 1883, Binley Road; 1887, Stoke Road; 1899, Highfield Road; 2005, Ricoh Arena; 2013, Sixfields Stadium (groundshare with Northampton T); 2014, Ricoh Arena.

First Football League Game: 30 August 1919, Division 2, v Tottenham H (h) L 0–5 – Lindon; Roberts, Chaplin, Allan, Hawley, Clarke, Sheldon, Mercer, Sambrooke, Lowes, Gibson.

Record League Victory: 9–0 v Bristol C, Division 3 (S), 28 April 1934 – Pearson; Brown, Bisby; Perry, Davidson, Frith; White (2), Lauderdale, Bourton (5), Jones (2), Lake.

Record Cup Victory: 8–0 v Rushden & D, League Cup 2nd rd, 2 October 2002 – Debec; Caldwell, Quinn, Betts (1p), Konjic (Shaw), Davenport, Pipe, Safri (Stanford), Mills (2) (Bothroyd (2)), McSheffery (3), Partridge.

Record Defeat: 2–10 v Norwich C, Division 3 (S), 15 March 1930.

HONOURS

League Champions: Division 2 – 1966–67; Division 3 – 1963–64; Division 3S – 1935–36. *Runners-up:* Division 3S – 1933–34; Division 4 – 1958–59. *FA Cup Winners:* 1987. *League Cup:* semi-final – 1981, 1990. *League Trophy Winners:* 2017. **European Competitions** *Fairs Cup:* 1970–71.

Sun FACT FILE

The highest recorded attendance for a Coventry City reserve game is 12,132 for the Football Combination fixture with Queens Park Rangers on 13 April 1965. Estimates suggest there may have been even more at the Boxing Day fixture with Nuneaton Town in 1920 but no accurate figure exists for this occasion.

Most League Points (2 for a win): 60, Division 4, 1958–59 and Division 3, 1963–64.

Most League Points (3 for a win): 75, FL 2, 2017–18.

Most League Goals: 108, Division 3 (S), 1931–32.

Highest League Scorer in Season: Clarrie Bourton, 49, Division 3 (S), 1931–32.

Most League Goals in Total Aggregate: Clarrie Bourton, 173, 1931–37.

Most League Goals in One Match: 5, Clarrie Bourton v Bournemouth, Division 3 (S), 17 October 1931; 5, Arthur Bacon v Gillingham, Division 3 (S), 30 December 1933.

Most Capped Player: Magnus Hedman, 44 (58), Sweden.

Most League Appearances: Steve Ogrizovic, 507, 1984–2000.

Youngest League Player: Ben Mackey, 16 years 167 days v Ipswich T, 12 April 2003.

Record Transfer Fee Received: £13,000,000 from Internazionale for Robbie Keane, July 2000.

Record Transfer Fee Paid: £6,500,000 to Norwich C for Craig Bellamy, August 2000.

Football League Record: 1919 Elected to Division 2; 1925–26 Division 3 (N); 1926–36 Division 3 (S); 1936–52 Division 2; 1952–58 Division 3 (S); 1958–59 Division 4; 1959–64 Division 3; 1964–67 Division 2; 1967–92 Division 1; 1992–2001 FA Premier League; 2001–04 Division 1; 2004–12 FL C; 2012–17 FL 1; 2017–18 FL 2; 2018– FL 1.

LATEST SEQUENCES

Longest Sequence of League Wins: 6, 25.4.1964 – 5.9.1964.

Longest Sequence of League Defeats: 9, 30.8.1919 – 11.10.1919.

Longest Sequence of League Draws: 6, 1.11.2003 – 29.11.2003.

Longest Sequence of Unbeaten League Matches: 25, 26.11.1966 – 13.5.1967.

Longest Sequence Without a League Win: 19, 30.8.1919 – 20.12.1919.

Successive Scoring Runs: 25 from 10.9.1966.

Successive Non-scoring Runs: 11 from 11.10.1919.

MANAGERS

H. R. Buckle 1909–10
Robert Wallace 1910–13
  (*Secretary-Manager*)
Frank Scott-Walford 1913–15
William Clayton 1917–19
H. Pollitt 1919–20
Albert Evans 1920–24
Jimmy Kerr 1924–28
James McIntyre 1928–31
Harry Storer 1931–45
Dick Bayliss 1945–47
Billy Frith 1947–48
Harry Storer 1948–53
Jack Fairbrother 1953–54
Charlie Elliott 1954–55
Jesse Carver 1955–56
George Raynor 1956
Harry Warren 1956–57
Billy Frith 1957–61
Jimmy Hill 1961–67
Noel Cantwell 1967–72
Bob Dennison 1972
Joe Mercer 1972–75
Gordon Milne 1972–81
Dave Sexton 1981–83
Bobby Gould 1983–84
Don Mackay 1985–86
George Curtis 1986–87
  (*became Managing Director*)
John Sillett 1987–90
Terry Butcher 1990–92
Don Howe 1992
Bobby Gould 1992–93
  (*with Don Howe, June 1992*)
Phil Neal 1993–95
Ron Atkinson 1995–96
  (*became Director of Football*)
Gordon Strachan 1996–2001
Roland Nilsson 2001–02
Gary McAllister 2002–04
Eric Black 2004
Peter Reid 2004–05
Micky Adams 2005–07
Iain Dowie 2007–08
Chris Coleman 2008–10
Aidy Boothroyd 2010–11
Andy Thorn 2011–12
Mark Robins 2012–13
Steven Pressley 2013–15
Tony Mowbray 2015–16
Russell Slade 2016–17
Mark Robins March 2017–

TEN YEAR LEAGUE RECORD

		P	W	D	L	F	A	Pts	Pos
2008-09	FL C	46	13	15	18	47	58	54	17
2009-10	FL C	46	13	15	18	47	64	54	19
2010-11	FL C	46	14	13	19	54	58	55	18
2011-12	FL C	46	9	13	24	41	65	40	23
2012-13	FL 1	46	18	11	17	66	59	55*	15
2013-14	FL 1	46	16	13	17	74	77	51*	18
2014-15	FL 1	46	13	16	17	49	60	55	17
2015-16	FL 1	46	19	12	15	67	49	69	8
2016-17	FL 1	46	9	12	25	37	68	39	23
2017-18	FL 2	46	22	9	15	64	47	75	6

* 10 pts deducted.

DID YOU KNOW

Coventry City were the only Third Division club to win the Southern Professional Floodlit Cup, predecessor of the Football League Cup. On 27 April 1960 they defeated West Ham United 2-1 at Highfield Road in front of a crowd of 16,921 with Welsh international Ron Hewitt netting both goals.

COVENTRY CITY – SKY BET LEAGUE TWO 2017–18 LEAGUE RECORD

Match No.	Date	Venue	Opponents	Result	H/T Score	Lg Pos.	Goalscorers	Attendance
1	Aug 5	H	Notts Co	W 3-0	1-0	2	Jones 3 [29, 80, 90]	10,350
2	12	A	Grimsby T	W 2-0	0-0	1	McNulty [62], Grimmer [75]	6767
3	19	H	Newport Co	L 0-1	0-0	4		8745
4	26	A	Yeovil T	L 0-2	0-1	10		3754
5	Sept 2	A	Chesterfield	D 0-0	0-0	10		5164
6	9	H	Port Vale	W 1-0	1-0	8	Jones [24]	6951
7	12	H	Carlisle U	W 2-0	0-0	4	Nazon [48], Vincenti [80]	6151
8	16	A	Cambridge U	L 1-2	1-0	6	Nazon [54]	5142
9	23	H	Exeter C	W 2-0	0-0	6	Brown (og) [58], Devon Kelly-Evans [90]	8340
10	26	A	Swindon T	W 2-1	1-1	4	Doyle [32], Nazon [76]	6340
11	30	H	Crewe Alex	W 1-0	1-0	4	Nazon [9]	7664
12	Oct 7	A	Barnet	D 0-0	0-0	5		4041
13	14	A	Accrington S	L 0-1	0-1	7		2828
14	17	H	Forest Green R	L 0-1	0-1	8		6366
15	21	H	Colchester U	D 0-0	0-0	8		7149
16	28	A	Luton T	W 3-0	1-0	6	McNulty [17], Nazon [90], Shipley [90]	9670
17	Nov 11	H	Mansfield T	L 0-1	0-0	6		8410
18	18	A	Lincoln C	W 2-1	0-1	7	Jones [61], Nazon [70]	9581
19	21	A	Stevenage	D 1-1	1-0	6	McNulty [22]	2544
20	25	H	Crawley T	D 1-1	0-1	6	McNulty [74]	6381
21	Dec 9	A	Morecambe	L 0-2	0-1	7		1773
22	16	H	Cheltenham T	W 2-1	1-1	7	Bayliss [2], McNulty [75]	6457
23	22	H	Wycombe W	W 3-2	2-1	4	Doyle [14], McNulty 2 (1 pen) [41, 55 (p)]	7234
24	26	A	Port Vale	L 0-1	0-0	7		7127
25	30	A	Carlisle U	W 1-0	0-0	5	McNulty [50]	5807
26	Jan 1	H	Chesterfield	W 1-0	1-0	3	McNulty [14]	7402
27	13	A	Exeter C	L 0-1	0-1	8		4219
28	20	H	Swindon T	W 3-1	2-1	6	Biamou [17], McNulty 2 (1 pen) [22 (p), 81]	8643
29	30	A	Cambridge U	W 3-1	2-0	4	McNulty [10], Shipley [30], Doyle [90]	6897
30	Feb 3	A	Forest Green R	L 1-2	0-1	8	McNulty (pen) [59]	3623
31	10	H	Accrington S	L 0-2	0-1	9		28,343
32	13	H	Colchester U	L 1-2	0-1	9	Bayliss [56]	3319
33	24	A	Mansfield T	D 1-1	0-1	9	Clarke-Harris (pen) [71]	6105
34	27	A	Wycombe W	W 1-0	0-0	8	McNulty (pen) [82]	4087
35	Mar 10	H	Barnet	W 1-0	0-0	8	Clarke-Harris [75]	7127
36	13	H	Luton T	D 2-2	2-0	7	Vincenti [3], McNulty [45]	8863
37	17	A	Crewe Alex	W 2-1	2-1	6	Clarke-Harris [5], Bayliss [43]	4666
38	24	H	Grimsby T	W 4-0	1-0	6	Vincenti [38], McNulty 3 [55, 76, 87]	8755
39	30	A	Newport Co	D 1-1	0-1	6	Biamou [79]	4667
40	Apr 2	H	Yeovil T	L 2-6	0-3	7	Biamou 2 [47, 68]	8787
41	7	A	Notts Co	L 1-2	0-0	7	Ponticelli [85]	10,316
42	14	A	Crawley T	W 2-1	1-1	6	Ponticelli 2 [5, 77]	3294
43	20	H	Stevenage	W 3-1	3-1	6	McNulty 2 [2, 6], Kelly [37]	8859
44	24	A	Lincoln C	L 2-4	2-3	7	Bayliss [16], Shipley [39]	13,115
45	28	A	Cheltenham T	W 6-1	4-0	6	Bayliss [12], McNulty 3 [27, 43, 78], Shipley [38], Biamou [74]	5027
46	May 5	H	Morecambe	D 0-0	0-0	6		15,874

Final League Position: 6

GOALSCORERS

League (64): McNulty 23 (4 pens), Nazon 6, Bayliss 5, Biamou 5, Jones 5, Shipley 4, Clarke-Harris 3 (1 pen), Doyle 3, Ponticelli 3, Vincenti 3, Grimmer 1, Devon Kelly-Evans 1, Kelly 1, own goal 1.
FA Cup (9): Ponticelli 2, Biamou 1, Clarke-Harris 1, Grimmer 1, McNulty 1, Nazon 1, Shipley 1, Willis 1.
Carabao Cup (1): Nazon 1.
Checkatrade Trophy (6): McNulty 2 (2 pens), Andreu 1, Biamou 1, Ponticelli 1, Stevenson 1.
League Two Play-Offs (8): Biamou 2, McNulty 2 (1 pen), Bayliss 1, Grimmer 1, Shipley 1, Willis 1.

O'Brien L 6+1	Grimmer J 42	Hyam D 11+3	McDonald R 36+1	Stokes C 28+1	Kelly L 30+3	Doyle M 44	Vincenti P 18+6	McNulty M 40+2	Jones J 19	Beavon S 9+5	Biamou M 20+19	Nazon D 11+10	Willis J 35	Andreu T 2+3	Stevenson B 2+3	Burge L 40	Davies T 15+6	Kelly-Evans Devon 8+6	Shipley J 25+5	Ponticelli J 4+15	Haynes R 18+3	Maycock C —+1	Bayliss T 24	Maguire-Drew J 3	Barrett J 1+5	Kelly-Evans Dion 1+1	Clarke-Harris J 12+5	Reid K 2+11	Match No.
1	2	3	4	5	6	7	8	9^2	10	11^1	12	13																	1
1	2	12	4	5	6	7	8	9	10^3	11^1			14	3^2	13														2
1	2		4	5	6^2	7	10	9	8	11^1			14		3^3	13	12												3
1	2	3		5	6	7		11	10	12	13	8^2		4	9^1														4
	2			5	7	6	10^1	11	8	9^2		13		3	12	1	4												5
	2	4^*	5	6	7	10	11^1	8	12^2			13		3	9^2	1	14												6
	2		5	6	7	8		10	9^1	12	11^1	3				1	4	13											7
	2	4	5	6	7	10^2		8	9^1	12	11	3				1		13											8
	2	4	5	6	7	8^1		10	12	11		3				1		9											9
	2	3	5^1		7	6		13	10^3		11^2	9	4			1	14	8	12										10
	2	4	5	6	7			10	12	11^1	9	3				1		8											11
	2	4	5	6	7			9	10		11	3				1		8^2	12	13									12
	2	4	5		7	14	12	9		11^2	10^3			3	8	1	6^1			13									13
	2	4	5^2	6	7		8	10		11^1		9		3		1			13	12									14
	2	4		6	7	13	9	10^1	11^2		8			3		1		12	5										15
	2^2	4		6	7	6	9^2	10	8^1		13	12		3		1	13		11³	5									16
	2^2	4		6	7	8^1	9	10		12		3				1	13		11	5									17
		4	13	6	7			10^2	8	11	12	2				1	3		9^1	5									18
		3		6^1	7	13	8^3	10^2		11		2				1	4	9	14	5	12								19
5	4			6			9		10^2			11		2	12	1	3^3	14	7^1	13	8								20
	2	4				6	12	11		14	10^1	9^2		3		1	13		7	8^3	5								21
	2	4^2	5			7	8^3	9^1		11	13			3		1	12	14	10		6								22
	2	4	5			7	8^1	9		11^2	13			3		1	14	12	10^3		6								23
	2		5	6		7		11		14	10^3	12		4^1		3	8^2	13	9										24
	2	12	5			7		10		11^2	14	13^3		3^1		1	4	6	8		9								25
	2		5			8		11		10^2				3		1	4	6	9^1	12	13		7						26
	2		5			8		10		11^2				4		14	1	3	9^3	12		7	6^1	13					27
	2		5			8		11		10				3		1	4	9				7	6^1	12					28
	2	3	5			8	12	11		10						1	4	6^1	9^2		13	7							29
2^3	12	5	8	7				11		10^1				3		1	4^2				14	6		9	13				30
1		4	5	8		12	11^1	10						3			9				7^3	6^2		2	14	13			31
	4	3	5	7^2		6	11	10^1						2		1	9				8			12	13				32
	2	12	4			8^1	7	10^3					14	3^*		1		9	13	5	6				11^2				33
	2	4	3			8	7	10					13			1		9^1	5	6					11^2		12		34
	2	3	4			7	8	10					13			1			5	6			12		11^2		9^1		35
	2	3	4			13	8	6^3	10							1		9^2	14	5			7^1		11		12		36
1	2	3	4			12	7	6^2	11							1		9^3	14	5			8^1		10		13		37
	2	3	4			12	8	6^1	10				14			1		9		5			7^2		11³		13		38
	2	4	3			8	6^1	10^3					14			1		9^2	13	5			7		11		12		39
13	2	3	4			8	6^2	10					12			1	1^3			5¹			7		14		11	9	40
	2		3	5	8	7		10				11³				1	4		9^2	13			6^1		14		12		41
	2	4		6	7			10		13				3^3		1	14			11	5		9^1				8^2	12	42
	2	4		6	7			9^1		13				3		1		10	8^2	5					14		11¹	12	43
	2	4		6	7			9		12				3		1		10^2	13	5			8				11¹		44
	2			5	7	8		11¹				10^2	4			1	3		9	13			6^1				14	12	45
	2	3		5	7	8		10				13				1	4		9^2				6				11¹	12	46

FA Cup

First Round	Maidenhead U	(h)	2-0
Second Round	Boreham Wood	(h)	3-0
Third Round	Stoke C	(h)	2-1
Fourth Round	Milton Keynes D	(a)	1-0
Fifth Round	Brighton & HA	(a)	1-3

Carabao Cup

First Round	Blackburn R	(h)	1-3

Checkatrade Trophy

Northern Group E	Shrewsbury T	(h)	2-3
Northern Group E	Walsall	(a)	2-2
(Coventry C won 4-3 on penalties)			
Northern Group E	WBA U21	(h)	2-1

League Two Play-Offs

Semi-Final 1st leg	Notts Co	(h)	1-1
Semi-Final 2nd leg	Notts Co	(a)	4-1
Final	Exeter C	(Wembley)	3-1

CRAWLEY TOWN

FOUNDATION

Formed in 1896, Crawley Town initially entered the West Sussex
League before switching to the mid-Sussex League in 1901,
winning the Second Division in its second season. The club
remained at such level until 1951 when it became members of the
Sussex County League and five years later moved to the
Metropolitan League while remaining as an amateur club. It was
not until 1962 that the club turned semi-professional and a year
later, joined the Southern League. Many honours came the club's
way, but the most successful run was achieved in 2010–11 when
they reached the fifith round of the FA Cup and played before a
crowd of 74,778 spectators at Old Trafford against Manchester
United. Crawley Town spent 48 years at the Town Mead ground
before a new site was occupied at Broadfield in 1997, ideally suited
to access from the neighbouring motorway. History was also made
on 9 April when the team won promotion to the Football League
after beating Tamworth 3-0 to stretch their unbeaten League
record to 26 games. They finished the season with a Conference
record points total of 105 and at the same time, established
another milestone for the longest unbeaten run, having extended it
to 30 matches by the end of the season.

*Checkatrade.com Stadium, Winfield Way, Crawley,
West Sussex RH11 9RX.*

Telephone: (01293) 410 000.

Ticket Office: (01293) 410 005.

Website: www.crawleytownfc.com

Email: feedback@crawleytownfc.com

Ground Capacity: 5,748.

Record Attendance: 5,880 v Reading, FA Cup 3rd rd, 5 January 2013.

Pitch Measurements: 103.5m × 66m (113yd × 72yd).

Chairman: Ziya Eren.

Operations Director: Kelly Derham.

Manager: Harry Kewell.

Assistant Manager: Warren Feeney.

Colours: Red shirts with white trim, red shorts with white trim, red socks.

Year Formed: 1896. *Turned Professional:* 1962.

Club Nickname: 'The Red Devils'.

Grounds: Up to 1997, Town Mead; 1997 Broadfield Stadium (renamed Checkatrade.com Stadium 2013).

HONOURS

League Champions: Conference –
2010–11.
FL 2 – (3rd) 2011–12 *(promoted).*
FA Cup: 5th rd – 2011, 2012.
League Cup: 3rd rd – 2013.

Sun THE FACT FILE

In their days in the Sussex County League in the 1950s Crawley were
run by a management committee who employed a player-coach to look
after team affairs. Among those who held the role were Tom Jarvie,
the former Hamilton Academical player, Reg Swinfin (ex-Queens Park
Rangers), Cyril Newman and Fred Packham.

First Football League Game: 6 August 2011, FL 2 v Port Vale (a) D 2-2 – Shearer; Hunt, Howell, Bulman, McFadzean (1), Dempster (Thomas), Simpson, Torres, Tubbs (Neilson), Barnett (1) (Wassmer), Smith.

Record League Victory: 5–1 v Barnsley, FL 1, 14 February 2015 – Price; Dickson, Bradley (1), Ward, Fowler (Smith); Young, Elliott (1), Edwards, Wordsworth (Morgan), Pogba (Tomlin); McLeod (3).

Record League Defeat: 6-0 v Morecambe, FL 2, 10 September 2011.

Most League Points (3 for a win): 84, FL 2, 2011–12.

Most League Goals: 76, FL 2, 2011–12.

Highest League Scorer in Season: James Collins, 20, FL 2, 2016–17.

Most League Goals in Total Aggregate: Billy Clarke, 20, 2011–14; Matt Tubbs, 20, 2011–12, 2013–14; James Collins, 20, 2016–17.

Most League Goals in One Match: 3, Izale McLeod v Barnsley, FL 1, 14 February 2015; 3, Jimmy Smith v Colchester U, FL 2, 14 February 2017.

Most Capped Player: Dean Morgan, 1 (3), Montserrat.

Most League Appearances: Josh Simpson, 122, 2011–15.

Youngest League Player: Hiram Boateng, 18 years 55 days v Stevenage, 4 March 2014.

Record Transfer Fee Received: £1,100,000 from Peterborough U for Tyrone Barnett, July 2012.

Record Transfer Fee Paid: £220,000 to York C for Richard Brodie, August 2010.

Football League Record: 2011 Promoted from Conference Premier; 2011–12 FL 2; 2012–15 FL 1; 2015–FL 2.

MANAGERS
John Maggs 1978–90
Brian Sparrow 1990–92
Steve Wicks 1992–93
Ted Shepherd 1993–95
Colin Pates 1995–96
Billy Smith 1997–99
Cliff Cant 1999–2000
Billy Smith 2000–03
Francis Vines 2003–05
John Hollins 2005–06
David Woozley, Ben Judge and John Yems 2006–07
Steve Evans 2007–12
Sean O'Driscoll 2012
Richie Barker 2012–13
John Gregory 2013–14
Dean Saunders 2014–15
Mark Yates 2015–16
Dermot Drummy 2016–17
Harry Kewell May 2017–

LATEST SEQUENCES

Longest Sequence of League Wins: 7, 17.9.2011 – 25.10.2011.

Longest Sequence of League Defeats: 8, 28.3.2016 – 7.5.2016.

Longest Sequence of League Draws: 5, 25.10.2014 – 29.11.2014.

Longest Sequence of Unbeaten League Matches: 13, 17.9.2011 – 17.12.2011.

Longest Sequence Without a League Win: 13, 25.10.2014 – 27.1.2015.

Successive Scoring Runs: 16 from 17.9.2011.

Successive Non-scoring Runs: 4 from 14.10.2017.

TEN YEAR LEAGUE RECORD

		P	W	D	L	F	A	Pts	Pos
2008-09	Conf P	46	19	14	13	77	55	70	9
2009-10	Conf P	44	19	9	16	50	57	66	7
2010-11	Conf P	46	31	12	3	93	50	105	1
2011-12	FL 2	46	23	15	8	76	54	84	3
2012-13	FL 1	46	18	14	14	59	58	68	10
2013-14	FL 1	46	14	15	17	48	54	57	14
2014-15	FL 1	46	13	11	22	53	79	50	22
2015-16	FL 2	46	13	8	25	45	78	47	20
2016-17	FL 2	46	13	12	21	53	71	51	19
2017-18	FL 2	46	16	11	19	58	66	59	14

DID YOU KNOW ?

Crawley Town played at the Town Mead Ground until May 1997. The first attendance of any significant size was for the FA Cup fourth qualifying round replay against Wimbledon in November 1969 when 3,256 turned out. The ground record remained unbroken for the next 22 years.

CRAWLEY TOWN – SKY BET LEAGUE TWO 2017–18 LEAGUE RECORD

Match No.	Date	Venue	Opponents	Result	H/T Score	Lg Pos.	Goalscorers	Attendance
1	Aug 5	H	Port Vale	L	1-3	0-2	22	Boldewijn [53]	2270
2	12	A	Cheltenham T	L	0-1	0-1	23		2834
3	19	H	Cambridge U	L	0-1	0-0	24		2059
4	26	A	Swindon T	W	3-0	1-0	20	Lancashire (og) [36], Roberts [79], Smith [85]	6613
5	Sept 2	H	Yeovil T	W	2-0	1-0	16	Roberts 2 [12, 51]	2024
6	9	A	Colchester U	L	1-3	0-3	18	Smith [66]	2923
7	12	A	Stevenage	D	1-1	0-1	18	Meite [49]	1922
8	16	H	Notts Co	L	0-1	0-0	20		2352
9	23	A	Barnet	W	2-1	0-0	17	Smith 2 [63, 89]	1602
10	26	H	Newport Co	L	1-2	1-1	19	Connolly [30]	1455
11	30	H	Carlisle U	L	0-1	0-0	20		2021
12	Oct 7	A	Morecambe	W	1-0	1-0	18	Ellison (og) [18]	1222
13	14	H	Grimsby T	D	0-0	0-0	18		4007
14	17	H	Chesterfield	L	0-2	0-0	19		1516
15	21	H	Luton T	D	0-0	0-0	19		3494
16	28	A	Lincoln C	D	0-0	0-0	19		8038
17	Nov 11	H	Forest Green R	D	1-1	0-0	18	Verheydt [79]	2149
18	18	A	Wycombe W	L	0-4	0-0	21		4494
19	21	H	Exeter C	W	3-1	1-1	17	Payne (pen) [34], Roberts 2 [60, 81]	1580
20	25	A	Coventry C	D	1-1	1-0	17	Roberts [42]	6381
21	Dec 9	H	Mansfield T	W	2-0	0-0	17	McNerney [63], Meite [90]	1791
22	16	A	Crewe Alex	L	0-3	0-2	17		3155
23	23	A	Accrington S	W	3-2	3-1	17	Clark (og) [9], Boldewijn 2 [10, 41]	1295
24	26	H	Colchester U	L	0-2	0-1	18		2154
25	30	H	Stevenage	W	1-0	1-0	18	Boldewijn [33]	2075
26	Jan 1	A	Yeovil T	W	2-1	1-1	16	Randall [44], Verheydt [90]	2635
27	13	H	Barnet	W	2-0	0-0	14	Boldewijn 2 [75, 86]	1874
28	19	A	Newport Co	L	1-2	0-2	14	Smith [48]	5741
29	23	A	Notts Co	W	2-1	1-0	12	Smith [25], Payne (pen) [90]	3738
30	27	H	Accrington S	W	2-1	2-0	12	Boldewijn 2 [15, 33]	2153
31	Feb 3	A	Chesterfield	W	2-1	0-1	12	Ahearne-Grant [57], Young [90]	5159
32	10	H	Grimsby T	W	3-0	1-0	10	Smith (pen) [45], Ahearne-Grant [62], Boldewijn [69]	2055
33	13	A	Luton T	L	1-4	0-2	11	Ahearne-Grant [87]	8020
34	17	H	Lincoln C	W	3-1	1-0	9	Smith [15], Payne (pen) [68], Connolly [72]	2809
35	24	A	Forest Green R	L	0-2	0-2	11		2346
36	Mar 10	H	Morecambe	D	1-1	0-0	12	Ahearne-Grant [90]	1642
37	17	A	Carlisle U	D	2-2	0-1	12	Ahearne-Grant 2 [56, 81]	4097
38	21	H	Wycombe W	L	2-3	1-2	12	Ahearne-Grant [33], Camara [83]	2133
39	24	H	Cheltenham T	L	3-5	0-3	13	Ahearne-Grant [50], Camara [73], Young [84]	2172
40	30	A	Cambridge U	L	1-3	0-2	14	Payne (pen) [49]	4131
41	Apr 2	H	Swindon T	D	1-1	1-0	13	Smith [25]	5008
42	7	A	Port Vale	W	2-1	1-1	12	Payne (pen) [29], Smith (og) [82]	4005
43	14	H	Coventry C	L	1-2	1-1	13	Young [13]	3294
44	21	A	Exeter C	D	2-2	1-1	13	Boldewijn [29], Yorwerth [68]	3998
45	28	H	Crewe Alex	L	1-2	1-1	14	Smith [9]	2089
46	May 5	A	Mansfield T	D	1-1	1-0	14	Ahearne-Grant [7]	4734

Final League Position: 14

GOALSCORERS

League (58): Boldewijn 10, Smith 10 (1 pen), Ahearne-Grant 9, Roberts 6, Payne 5 (5 pens), Young 3, Camara 2, Connolly 2, Meite 2, Verheydt 2, McNerney 1, Randall 1, Yorwerth 1, own goals 4.
FA Cup (1): Roberts 1.
Carabao Cup (1): Camara 1.
Checkatrade Trophy (2): Meite 1, Sanoh 1.

Morris G 44	Lelan J 29+1	Connolly M 40	Yorwerth J 37+2	Young L 41	Bulman D 34+3	Randall M 24+8	Evina C 32+2	Boldewijn E 44+1	Verheydt T 16+4	Roberts J 25+10	Payne J 23+12	Cox D 3+1	Lewis D 3+7	Harrold M —+2	Camara P 14+16	Clifford B 4+3	Smith J 36+1	Meite I 6+13	Doherty J 11+4	Sanoh M 4+8	Tajbakhsh A 8+9	McNerney J 10+6	Djalo K 1+1	Mersin Y 2	Ahearne-Grant K 15	Match No.
1	2	3	4^2	5	6	7	8	9^3	10	11^1	12	13	14													1
1	4	3		2	7	8	5^3	9	10^1	11	6^2			14	12	13										2
1	5	3^3	12	2	7	6^2	4	8	10	11					13	9^1	14									3
1	3		4	2	7		5	8^3		10^1	13		9	14			11^2	6	12							4
1	4		3	2	8		5	11		9^2	14	6^1	13				10^3	7	12							5
1	3		4	2	8	7^2	5^2	6		9	13			11^1			10	12	14							6
1	3		4	2	8	12	5	10			13		6^2				7	11	9^1							7
1	3		4	2	6^2	9^1	5	10		12	7^3			14			8	11		13						8
1	2		4	3	5		12	8	9^1	11	14			13			7	10^2		6^3						9
1	2	4	3	5^2		14	8	9		11	12			13			7	10^3		6^1						10
1	2^1	4	3^4	5	6^2		9^3	11		10	8			13			7	12		14						11
1	3	4		2^2	7^1		5	8		11	13				9^2	6	14		10		12					12
1	2	3			6		5	8		10			12	9^2	7	11^1			13	4						13
1	2	3^3			7^1		5	8		10	12	11^2	13	9	6	14				4						14
1	5	3	4		7			8	11	10					9	6				2						15
1	2	3	7		6^1	12	5	8		10				11	9					4						16
1	2	3	12	5^1	7^3		8	11	10	9	13			14	6^2					4						17
1	2	4	6			14	5^3	10	11	7^2	9	12	13							8^1	3					18
1		3	4	5	6	7^2	8	10^3	11^1	12	2	14	9		13											19
1		3	4	2	8^2	9	5	10^1		11	6			7^3			12				14	13				20
1	2	4^1	3	5	14	7^2	8	11^2		10	6				9	13				12						21
1		3	4	2		8	5^1	9^2	11	10^4	7			6^1	12	13										22
1	10	3	4		2	6	8^1	5	9		7			12	11											23
	2	4	3	6		13	5		10^2	11	14		8		12	9^3			7^1	1						24
1	2	3	4	6	8	9^2		10^1		11	7^4				13	5			12							25
1	2^2	4	3^1	8	9	7	5^3	10	14	11					6	12	13									26
1	2	3	4	5^1	7^2	6^1	8	11		10				14	9			12	13							27
1	2	4	7	5^1		8	11	13	10					14	6			9^3	12	3^2						28
1	2	4	3	6	7^1	12	9	11^{12}		8				13	10	5										29
1	9	8	4	2	12	10^2	6	11		3^1				7	5	13										30
1	12	4^3	3	2	6	9	13	10^1	11		7	5	14									8^2				31
1	2	3	4	6^1	7	12	9	11	13		8^1	5	14									10^3				32
1	3	4	2		10^1	5	6	12	11^2	8				7	13							9				33
1		3	4	2	13	8^1	9	10^2	12	7^3				6	5	14						11				34
1	4	3	2		9^1	12	7	11	6					8	5^2	13						10				35
1	3	4	2	7	8^2	11		6^1		12	9	5			13							10				36
1	4		2	6	11^1	5	10	7^2		12	9				13	3						8				37
1	4^1		2	8	5	11	12	7^1		9	6				3							10				38
1	4^1		2	7	8	5^2	9	12		10	6				13	3						11				39
1	3	4	2	8	7^2	5^3	12	11	6		13	9^1	14									10				40
1	3	4	2	7^1	6^2	9	13	12		10	8				5							11				41
1	3	4	2	9	8^2	13	12	7		11^1	6	14			5							10^3				42
1	4	3	2	6	8	11^2	14	7^1		12	9	13			5^2							10				43
1	3	4	2	7	6^2	8	11	12		10^3	14	13	9^1	5												44
1	3	4	2		6	10^2	12	7		13	8	5	11^1									9				45
	4	3	2	7		8		6^1		11	9	5	12									1	10			46

FA Cup
First Round — Wigan Ath — (a) — 1-2

Carabao Cup
First Round — Birmingham C — (a) — 1-5

Checkatrade Trophy
Southern Group A — Charlton Ath — (h) — 0-2
Southern Group A — Portsmouth — (a) — 1-3
Southern Group A — Fulham U21 — (h) — 1-3

CREWE ALEXANDRA

FOUNDATION

The first match played at Crewe was on 1 December 1877 against Basford, the leading North Staffordshire team of that time. During the club's history they have also played in a number of other leagues including the Football Alliance, Football Combination, Lancashire League, Manchester League, Central League and Lancashire Combination. Two former players, Aaron Scragg in 1899 and Jackie Pearson in 1911, had the distinction of refereeing FA Cup finals. Pearson was also capped for England against Ireland in 1892.

The Alexandra Stadium, Gresty Road, Crewe, Cheshire CW2 6EB.

Telephone: (01270) 213 014.

Fax: (01270) 216 320.

Ticket Office: (01270) 252 610.

Website: www.crewealex.net

Email: info@crewealex.net

Ground Capacity: 10,109.

Record Attendance: 20,000 v Tottenham H, FA Cup 4th rd, 30 January 1960.

Pitch Measurements: 100.5m × 67m (110yd × 73yd).

Chairman: John Bowler MBE.

Vice-Chairman: David Rowlinson.

Manager: David Artell.

Assistant Manager: Kenny Lunt.

Colours: Red shirts with white trim, white shorts with red trim, red socks.

Year Formed: 1877. *Turned Professional:* 1893. *Club Nickname:* 'The Railwaymen'.

Ground: 1898, Gresty Road.

First Football League Game: 3 September 1892, Division 2, v Burton Swifts (a) L 1–7 – Hickton; Moore, Cope; Linnell, Johnson, Osborne; Bennett, Pearson (1), Bailey, Barnett, Roberts.

Record League Victory: 8–0 v Rotherham U, Division 3 (N), 1 October 1932 – Foster; Pringle, Dawson; Ward, Keenor (1), Turner (1); Gillespie, Swindells (1), McConnell (2), Deacon (2), Weale (1).

Record Cup Victory: 8–0 v Hartlepool U, Auto Windscreens Shield 1st rd, 17 October 1995 – Gayle; Collins (1), Booty, Westwood (Unsworth), Macauley (1), Whalley (1), Garvey (1), Murphy (1), Savage (1) (Rivers (1p)), Lennon, Edwards, (1 og). 8–0 v Doncaster R, LDV Vans Trophy 3rd rd, 10 November 2002 – Bankole; Wright, Walker, Foster, Tierney; Lunt (1), Brammer, Sorvel, Vaughan (1) (Bell); Ashton (3) (Miles), Jack (2) (Jones (1)).

Record Defeat: 2–13 v Tottenham H, FA Cup 4th rd replay, 3 February 1960.

Most League Points (2 for a win): 59, Division 4, 1962–63.

HONOURS

League: Runners-up: Second Division – 2002–03.

FA Cup: semi-final – 1888.

League Cup: never past 3rd rd.

League Trophy Winners: 2013.

Welsh Cup Winners: 1936, 1937.

Sun FACT FILE

With just eight games remaining of the 1964–65 season, Terry Harkin had registered 21 goals for Crewe Alexandra. However, he then proceeded to score a further 14 times in the closing fixtures, including four in a 5-0 win over Lincoln City in the season's penultimate game, to establish a new club record of 35 goals in a season, a figure that has yet to be beaten.

Most League Points (3 for a win): 86, Division 2, 2002–03.

Most League Goals: 95, Division 3 (N), 1931–32.

Highest League Scorer in Season: Terry Harkin, 35, Division 4, 1964–65.

Most League Goals in Total Aggregate: Bert Swindells, 126, 1928–37.

Most League Goals in One Match: 5, Tony Naylor v Colchester U, Division 3, 24 April 1993.

Most Capped Player: Clayton Ince, 38 (79), Trinidad & Tobago.

Most League Appearances: Tommy Lowry, 436, 1966–78.

Youngest League Player: Steve Walters, 16 years 119 days v Peterborough U, 6 May 1988.

Record Transfer Fee Received: £3,000,000 (rising to £6,000,000) from Manchester U for Nick Powell, June 2012.

Record Transfer Fee Paid: £650,000 to Torquay U for Rodney Jack, July 1999.

Football League Record: 1892 Original Member of Division 2; 1896 Failed re-election; 1921 Re-entered Division (N); 1958–63 Division 4; 1963–64 Division 3; 1964–68 Division 4; 1968–69 Division 3; 1969–89 Division 4; 1989–91 Division 3; 1991–92 Division 4; 1992–94 Division 3; 1994–97 Division 2; 1997–2002 Division 1; 2002–03 Division 2; 2003–04 Division 1; 2004–06 FL C; 2006–09 FL 1; 2009–12 FL 2; 2012–16 FL 1; 2016– FL 2.

LATEST SEQUENCES

Longest Sequence of League Wins: 7, 30.4.1994 – 3.9.1994.

Longest Sequence of League Defeats: 10, 16.4.1979 – 22.8.1979.

Longest Sequence of League Draws: 5, 18.9.2010 – 9.10.2010.

Longest Sequence of Unbeaten League Matches: 17, 25.3.1995 – 16.9.1995.

Longest Sequence Without a League Win: 30, 22.9.1956 – 6.4.1957.

Successive Scoring Runs: 26 from 7.4.1934.

Successive Non-scoring Runs: 9 from 6.11.1974.

MANAGERS

W. C. McNeill 1892–94
(*Secretary-Manager*)
J. G. Hall 1895–96
(*Secretary-Manager*)
R. Roberts (*1st team Secretary-Manager*) 1897
J. B. Blomerley 1898–1911
(*Secretary-Manager, continued as Hon. Secretary to 1925*)
Tom Bailey (*Secretary only*) 1925–38
George Lillycrop (*Trainer*) 1938–44
Frank Hill 1944–48
Arthur Turner 1948–51
Harry Catterick 1951–53
Ralph Ward 1953–55
Maurice Lindley 1956–57
Willie Cook 1957–58
Harry Ware 1958–60
Jimmy McGuigan 1960–64
Ernie Tagg 1964–71
(*continued as Secretary to 1972*)
Dennis Viollet 1971
Jimmy Melia 1972–74
Ernie Tagg 1974
Harry Gregg 1975–78
Warwick Rimmer 1978–79
Tony Waddington 1979–81
Arfon Griffiths 1981–82
Peter Morris 1982–83
Dario Gradi 1983–2007
Steve Holland 2007–08
Gudjon Thordarson 2008–09
Dario Gradi 2009–11
Steve Davis 2011–17
David Artell January 2017–

TEN YEAR LEAGUE RECORD

		P	W	D	L	F	A	Pts	Pos
2008-09	FL 1	46	12	10	24	59	82	46	22
2009-10	FL 2	46	15	10	21	68	73	55	18
2010-11	FL 2	46	18	11	17	87	65	65	10
2011-12	FL 2	46	20	12	14	67	59	72	7
2012-13	FL 1	46	18	10	18	54	62	64	13
2013-14	FL 1	46	13	12	21	54	80	51	19
2014-15	FL 1	46	14	10	22	43	75	52	20
2015-16	FL 1	46	7	13	26	46	83	34	24
2016-17	FL 2	46	14	13	19	58	67	55	17
2017-18	FL 2	46	17	5	24	62	75	56	15

DID YOU KNOW ?

Centre-forward Frank Lord led the scoring charts for Crewe Alexandra in both 1960–61 and 1961–62, netting a club-record total of eight hat-tricks before being sold to Plymouth Argyle in November 1963.

CREWE ALEXANDRA – SKY BET LEAGUE TWO 2017–18 LEAGUE RECORD

Match No.	Date	Venue	Opponents	Result	H/T Score	Lg Pos.	Goalscorers	Attendance
1	Aug 5	H	Mansfield T	D	2-2	1-0	12	Porter 2 [45, 63]	4933
2	12	H	Newport Co	D	1-1	1-1	18	Dagnall [18]	3400
3	19	H	Barnet	W	1-0	0-0	10	Porter [75]	3217
4	26	A	Port Vale	W	1-0	1-0	4	Dagnall [30]	6299
5	Sept 2	A	Grimsby T	L	0-1	0-1	8		4066
6	9	H	Chesterfield	W	5-1	1-0	4	Porter 2 [6, 47], Ng [54], Cooper [66], Ainley [81]	3513
7	12	H	Cambridge U	L	0-1	0-1	10		3042
8	16	H	Exeter C	L	0-3	0-2	15		4218
9	23	H	Carlisle U	L	0-5	0-1	16		4021
10	26	A	Wycombe W	L	2-3	1-1	18	Dagnall 2 [42, 66]	3295
11	30	A	Coventry C	L	0-1	0-1	19		7664
12	Oct 7	H	Stevenage	W	1-0	0-0	17	Bowery [90]	3679
13	14	A	Yeovil T	L	0-2	0-1	19		2360
14	17	H	Notts Co	W	2-0	1-0	17	Raynes [44], Bowery [66]	3339
15	21	H	Accrington S	L	0-2	0-2	17		3849
16	28	A	Colchester U	L	1-3	1-1	18	Bowery [22]	3088
17	Nov 11	A	Lincoln C	L	1-4	1-0	20	Raynes [8]	4723
18	18	A	Forest Green R	L	2-3	1-1	22	Porter [14], Bowery [54]	2221
19	21	A	Morecambe	W	1-0	0-0	19	Ng [85]	927
20	25	H	Luton T	L	1-2	0-0	19	Mullins (og) [81]	4571
21	Dec 9	A	Cheltenham T	L	0-1	0-0	22		2795
22	16	H	Crawley T	W	3-0	2-0	19	Ainley [40], Dagnall 2 [45, 90]	3155
23	23	H	Swindon T	L	0-3	0-3	20		3736
24	26	A	Chesterfield	W	2-0	2-0	20	Porter [7], Kirk [26]	5904
25	30	A	Cambridge U	L	1-3	1-2	20	Dagnall [30]	4165
26	Jan 1	H	Grimsby T	W	2-0	2-0	19	Porter [12], Walker [34]	3292
27	13	A	Carlisle U	L	0-1	0-0	20		4467
28	20	H	Wycombe W	L	2-3	1-0	20	Porter (pen) [6], McKirdy [88]	3645
29	27	A	Swindon T	L	3-4	2-1	20	Ainley 2 [15, 29], Wintle [51]	5439
30	Feb 3	A	Notts Co	L	1-4	1-2	21	Miller [8]	17,274
31	10	H	Yeovil T	D	0-0	0-0	21		3498
32	13	A	Accrington S	L	0-1	0-1	22		1254
33	17	H	Colchester U	W	1-0	0-0	20	Miller [60]	3548
34	20	H	Exeter C	L	1-2	0-0	20	Miller [88]	3081
35	24	A	Lincoln C	W	4-1	1-1	18	Pickering [45], Bowery 2 [48, 68], Green (pen) [54]	8272
36	Mar 10	A	Stevenage	D	2-2	0-1	18	Ng [80], Kirk [90]	2032
37	17	H	Coventry C	L	1-2	1-2	20	Bowery [33]	4666
38	20	H	Forest Green R	W	3-1	1-0	19	Bowery 2 [44, 61], Kirk [59]	3274
39	24	A	Newport Co	W	2-1	1-0	17	McKirdy [26], Bowery [60]	4638
40	30	A	Barnet	L	1-2	0-0	17	McKirdy [70]	1951
41	Apr 2	H	Port Vale	D	2-2	1-1	18	Wintle [7], Kirk [90]	6680
42	7	A	Mansfield T	W	4-3	4-1	17	Jones [7], Bowery [10], Pickering [25], Kirk [27]	3480
43	14	A	Luton T	L	1-3	1-2	17	Bowery [35]	9202
44	21	H	Morecambe	W	1-0	0-0	17	Miller [88]	3942
45	28	A	Crawley T	W	2-1	1-1	16	Ng [5], Pickering [51]	2089
46	May 5	H	Cheltenham T	W	2-1	1-1	15	Miller 2 [17, 62]	4350

Final League Position: 15

GOALSCORERS

League (62): Bowery 12, Porter 9 (1 pen), Dagnall 7, Miller 6, Kirk 5, Ainley 4, Ng 4, McKirdy 3, Pickering 3, Raynes 2, Wintle 2, Cooper 1, Green 1 (1 pen), Jones 1, Walker 1, own goal 1.
FA Cup (5): Porter 2 (1 pen), Ainley 1, Nolan 1, Walker 1.
Carabao Cup (1): Porter 1.
Checkatrade Trophy (3): Reilly 2, Bowery 1.

Garratt B 35 + 1	Ng P 36 + 2	Walker B 22 + 5	Raynes M 27 + 2	Nolan E 41 + 1	Ainley C 37 + 8	Wintle R 17 + 1	Lowery T 28 + 3	Cooper G 22 + 5	Porter C 23 + 8	Dagnall C 24 + 8	Bowery J 32 + 13	Pickering H 27 + 8	Bakayogo Z 28 + 4	Grant C 13 + 6	Dale O — + 4	Kirk C 15 + 10	Stubbs S 3 + 2	Richards D 11	Reilly L 2 + 3	Green P 19 + 1	Finney O — + 1	McKirdy H 5 + 11	Barlaser D — + 4	Miller S 13 + 2	Sterry J 9	Ray G 12	Jones J 5 + 1	Match No.
1	2	3	4	5	6[1]	7	8	9	10	11	12																	1
1	2*	3	4	5	12	8	11	6[2]	7	10[1]	13	9																2
1		2	3	4	13	8	5	9	11	10	6[2]	7[1]	12															3
1	2	3		4	5	7	6	9[1]	10	11	12			8														4
1	3	7	4	5	2[3]	8		6	10	11	14			12	9[2]	13												5
1	2	7[3]	4	3	12	8	9	6[2]	10[1]	11	14			5		13												6
1	2[2]	7	4	3	12	8	6[1]	11	10	9	13			5														7
1	2[2]	3	4		6[1]	8	7	11	10	9[3]	14			5		13	12											8
1	2[1]	3	4	7	8[3]	6	11	9	10		12			5[2]		13		14										9
1	2	6	3	4	9[1]		7	12	11	8	10			5														10
	2	7[3]	3	4	8[3]		6	12	11	9	10[1]			5	14	13		1										11
	2		4	3	7[2]		8	9	12	11	10	13	5[1]	6				1										12
	2		3	4	6[2]	7	9	10	12	11[1]	13	5[3]	8	14				1										13
	2	12	3	4	6		7[2]	9	10	11	13	5	8	14				1										14
	2	12	3*	4	6[1]		7	9	11	10	13	5[3]	8[2]	14				1										15
	2	3		4	5[1]	6	12	10	9	11	13	8[2]	7					1										16
	2	4	3	14	6[2]	7	9	12	11	10	5[1]	13	8[3]					1										17
	2	4		3	7	8	10	9	11	5	6							1										18
	7	3		2	12		9[1]	10	6	11[2]	8[3]	5	14			4		1		13								19
5	2		4		7[1]		9	10	11	12	8	6[2]				3		1		13								20
1	2	8[1]	4	3	13		6	9	10	7	11[2]	5	12															21
1	2	13	3	4	6[2]		7	9		11	10	8[1]	5	12														22
1	2		3	4	6[3]	7	9[1]	13	11	10[2]	8	5	14							12								23
1	2		3	4	8[2]	7	14	10[1]	11	12	13	5	6							9[3]								24
1	2	3	4		6	7	9	11[1]	10	12	8	5	6							9[1]	2							25
1	2	3	4		6		7	9	11[1]	10	12	5	8							9[1]								26
1	7	3	2	5[2]	6[1]		9	10	11[3]	4				12		14	8			13								27
1	3	4	2	6	7		10[1]	12				5				11[3]	8			9[2]		13	14					28
13		4	3	2	8	6			10	14	5[4]					13				9[2]	1[3]	7		11[1]		12		29
1	4[2]	3	2	9		7[3]			10	5[1]						14						8	13	12		11[1]	6	30
1	2			5	9			7	11	3				4[1]		10						8		12			6	31
1	2		3		9[2]				8	11	5			4								7		12 13 10[1] 6				32
1	2	14		3	9[2]	12			10	7	5			6[1]								8		13 11[3] 4				33
1	2	14	3	4	7[2]	6			12	9	5			13								8		11[1] 10[3]				34
1	7			4	6				10	9	5											8		12 11[1] 2 3				35
1	2			4	6[3]	9[2]			14	10[1]	7	5		13								8		12 11 3				36
1	2			4	12				14	11[2]	7	5[3]		6								8		13 10[1] 9 3				37
1	2			4	6	9			12	11	7			5[1]								8		10[2] 13 3				38
1	2	14		4	6				7[1]	13	11	5		9[2]								8		10[2] 3 12				39
1	2			4	6	12 13			14	10	5			9[2]								8		11[1] 3 7[3]				40
1				4	6[2]	9			12	10	5			14								8		13 11[3] 2 3 7[1]				41
1	14		12	4		8			10	5				9[1]								7		13 11[2] 2[3] 3 6				42
1	2			4	12	8			13 14	10	5			9[1]								7[3]		11[1] 3 6				43
1	2			4	6	8			10[3] 14	11[2]	5			9[1]								7		13 12 3				44
1	3			6[2]	7 14				12	10	9[3]	5		13								8		11[1] 2 4				45
1	2			6[1]	3	7[3]		14		12	5			9		11[2] 13								10 4 8				46

FA Cup

First Round	Rotherham U	(h)	2-1
Second Round	Blackburn R	(a)	3-3
Replay	Blackburn R	(h)	0-1

Carabao Cup

First Round	Bolton W	(h)	1-2

Checkatrade Trophy

Northern Group D	Newcastle U U21	(h)	1-2
Northern Group D	Oldham Ath	(h)	0-1
Northern Group D	Port Vale	(a)	2-4

CRYSTAL PALACE

FOUNDATION

There was a Crystal Palace club as early as 1861 but the present organisation was born in 1905 after the formation of a club by the company that controlled the Crystal Palace (building) had been rejected by the FA, who did not like the idea of the Cup Final hosts running their own club. A separate company had to be formed and they had their home on the old Cup Final ground until 1915.

Selhurst Park Stadium, Whitehorse Lane, London SE25 6PU.

Telephone: (020) 8768 6000.

Fax: (020) 8771 5311.

Ticket Office: (0871) 200 0071.

Website: www.cpfc.co.uk

Email: info@cpfc.co.uk

Ground Capacity: 25,456.

Record Attendance: 51,482 v Burnley, Division 2, 11 May 1979 (at Selhurst Park).

Pitch Measurements: 101m × 68m (109yd × 75yd).

Chairman: Steve Parish.

Chief Executive: Phil Alexander.

Manager: Roy Hodgson.

Assistant Manager: Ray Lewington.

Colours: Red and blue shirts, blue shorts with red trim, blue socks with red trim.

Year Formed: 1905.

Turned Professional: 1905.

Club Nickname: 'The Eagles'.

Grounds: 1905, Crystal Palace; 1915, Herne Hill; 1918, The Nest; 1924, Selhurst Park.

First Football League Game: 28 August 1920, Division 3, v Merthyr T (a) L 1–2 – Alderson; Little, Rhodes; McCracken, Jones, Feebury; Bateman, Conner, Smith, Milligan (1), Whibley.

Record League Victory: 9–0 v Barrow, Division 4, 10 October 1959 – Rouse; Long, Noakes; Truett, Evans, McNichol; Gavin (1), Summersby (4 incl. 1p), Sexton, Byrne (2), Colfar (2).

Record Cup Victory: 8–0 v Southend U, Rumbelows League Cup 2nd rd (1st leg), 25 September 1990 – Martyn; Humphrey (Thompson (1)), Shaw, Pardew, Young, Thorn, McGoldrick, Thomas, Bright (3), Wright (3), Barber (Hodges (1)).

Record Defeat: 0–9 v Burnley, FA Cup 2nd rd replay, 10 February 1909; 0–9 v Liverpool, Division 1, 12 September 1990.

Most League Points (2 for a win): 64, Division 4, 1960–61.

HONOURS

League Champions: First Division – 1993–94; Division 2 – 1978–79; Division 3S – 1920–21.
Runners-up: Division 2 – 1968–69; Division 3 – 1963–64; Division 3S – 1928–29, 1930–31, 1938–39; Division 4 – 1960–61.

FA Cup: Runners-up: 1990, 2016.

League Cup: semi-final – 1993, 1995, 2001, 2012.

Full Members' Cup Winners: 1991.

European Competition
Intertoto Cup: 1998.

Sun FACT FILE

Crystal Palace played in claret shirts with blue sleeves from their formation in 1905 up until the 1937–38 season. This is widely attributed to the fact that assistant-secretary Edmund Goodman, who was in charge of the club's affairs in the early days of their existence, was himself a former Aston Villa player and club official.

Most League Points (3 for a win): 90, Division 1, 1993–94.

Most League Goals: 110, Division 4, 1960–61.

Highest League Scorer in Season: Peter Simpson, 46, Division 3 (S), 1930–31.

Most League Goals in Total Aggregate: Peter Simpson, 153, 1930–36.

Most League Goals in One Match: 6, Peter Simpson v Exeter C, Division 3 (S), 4 October 1930.

Most Capped Player: Mile Jedinak, 37 (79), Australia.

Most League Appearances: Jim Cannon, 571, 1973–88.

Youngest League Player: John Bostock, 15 years 287 days v Watford, 29 October 2007.

Record Transfer Fee Received: £25,000,000 from Everton for Yannick Bolasie, August 2016.

Record Transfer Fee Paid: £27,000,000 to Liverpool for Christian Benteke, August 2016.

Football League Record: 1920 Original Members of Division 3; 1921–25 Division 2; 1925–58 Division 3 (S); 1958–61 Division 4; 1961–64 Division 3; 1964–69 Division 2; 1969–73 Division 1; 1973–74 Division 2; 1974–77 Division 3; 1977–79 Division 2; 1979–81 Division 1; 1981–89 Division 2; 1989–92 Division 1; 1992–93 FA Premier League; 1993–94 Division 1; 1994–95 FA Premier League; 1995–97 Division 1; 1997–98 FA Premier League; 1998–2004 Division 1; 2004–05 FA Premier League; 2005–13 FL C; 2013– FA Premier League.

LATEST SEQUENCES

Longest Sequence of League Wins: 8, 21.5.2017 – 30.9.2017.

Longest Sequence of League Defeats: 8, 10.1.1998 – 14.3.1998.

Longest Sequence of League Draws: 5, 21.9.2002 – 19.10.2002.

Longest Sequence of Unbeaten League Matches: 18, 22.2.1969 – 13.8.1969.

Longest Sequence Without a League Win: 20, 3.3.1962 – 8.9.1962.

Successive Scoring Runs: 24 from 27.4.1929.

Successive Non-scoring Runs: 9 from 19.11.1994.

MANAGERS

John T. Robson 1905–07
Edmund Goodman 1907–25 (*Secretary 1905–33*)
Alex Maley 1925–27
Fred Mavin 1927–30
Jack Tresadern 1930–35
Tom Bromilow 1935–36
R. S. Moyes 1936
Tom Bromilow 1936–39
George Irwin 1939–47
Jack Butler 1947–49
Ronnie Rooke 1949–50
Charlie Slade and Fred Dawes (*Joint Managers*) 1950–51
Laurie Scott 1951–54
Cyril Spiers 1954–58
George Smith 1958–60
Arthur Rowe 1960–62
Dick Graham 1962–66
Bert Head 1966–72 (*continued as General Manager to 1973*)
Malcolm Allison 1973–76
Terry Venables 1976–80
Ernie Walley 1980
Malcolm Allison 1980–81
Dario Gradi 1981
Steve Kember 1981–82
Alan Mullery 1982–84
Steve Coppell 1984–93
Alan Smith 1993–95
Steve Coppell (*Technical Director*) 1995–96
Dave Bassett 1996–97
Steve Coppell 1997–98
Attilio Lombardo 1998
Terry Venables (*Head Coach*) 1998–99
Steve Coppell 1999–2000
Alan Smith 2000–01
Steve Bruce 2001
Trevor Francis 2001–03
Steve Kember 2003
Iain Dowie 2003–06
Peter Taylor 2006–07
Neil Warnock 2007–10
Paul Hart 2010
George Burley 2010–11
Dougie Freedman 2011–12
Ian Holloway 2012–13
Tony Pulis 2013–14
Neil Warnock 2014
Alan Pardew 2015–16
Sam Allardyce 2016–17
Frank de Boer 2017
Roy Hodgson September 2017–

TEN YEAR LEAGUE RECORD

		P	W	D	L	F	A	Pts	Pos
2008-09	FL C	46	15	12	19	52	55	57	15
2009-10	FL C	46	14	17	15	50	53	49*	21
2010-11	FL C	46	12	12	22	44	69	48	20
2011-12	FL C	46	13	17	16	46	51	56	17
2012-13	FL C	46	19	15	12	73	62	72	5
2013-14	PR Lge	38	13	6	19	33	48	45	11
2014-15	PR Lge	38	13	9	16	47	51	48	10
2015-16	PR Lge	38	11	9	18	39	51	42	15
2016-17	PR Lge	38	12	5	21	50	63	41	14
2017-18	PR Lge	38	11	11	16	45	55	44	11

* 10 pts deducted.

DID YOU KNOW ?

Goalkeeper John Jackson was an ever-present for Crystal Palace five seasons in a row (1967–68 to 1971–72). In total he made 222 consecutive League appearances for Palace, a total that has yet to be exceeded. Later in his career he also made more than 200 consecutive appearances for Leyton Orient.

CRYSTAL PALACE – PREMIER LEAGUE 2017–18 LEAGUE RECORD

Match No.	Date	Venue	Opponents	Result	H/T Score	Lg Pos.	Goalscorers	Attendance
1	Aug 12	H	Huddersfield T	L 0-3	0-2	20		25,448
2	19	A	Liverpool	L 0-1	0-0	19		53,138
3	26	H	Swansea C	L 0-2	0-1	19		23,477
4	Sept 10	A	Burnley	L 0-1	0-1	19		18,862
5	16	H	Southampton	L 0-1	0-1	20		24,199
6	23	A	Manchester C	L 0-5	0-1	20		53,526
7	30	A	Manchester U	L 0-4	0-2	20		75,118
8	Oct 14	H	Chelsea	W 2-1	2-1	20	Azpilicueta (og) [11], Zaha [45]	25,480
9	21	A	Newcastle U	L 0-1	0-0	20		52,251
10	28	H	West Ham U	D 2-2	0-2	20	Milivojevic (pen) [50], Zaha [90]	25,242
11	Nov 5	A	Tottenham H	L 0-1	0-0	20		65,270
12	18	H	Everton	D 2-2	2-2	20	McArthur [1], Zaha [35]	25,526
13	25	H	Stoke C	W 2-1	0-0	20	Loftus-Cheek [56], Sakho [90]	23,723
14	28	A	Brighton & HA	D 0-0	0-0	20		29,889
15	Dec 2	A	WBA	D 0-0	0-0	18		23,531
16	9	H	Bournemouth	D 2-2	2-2	20	Milivojevic (pen) [41], Dann [44]	24,823
17	12	H	Watford	W 2-1	0-1	17	Sako [89], McArthur [90]	23,566
18	16	A	Leicester C	W 3-0	2-0	14	Benteke, C [19], Zaha [40], Sako [90]	31,081
19	23	A	Swansea C	D 1-1	0-0	16	Milivojevic (pen) [59]	20,354
20	28	H	Arsenal	L 2-3	0-1	16	Townsend [49], Tomkins [89]	25,762
21	31	H	Manchester C	D 0-0	0-0	17		25,804
22	Jan 2	A	Southampton	W 2-1	0-1	14	McArthur [89], Milivojevic [80]	28,411
23	13	H	Burnley	W 1-0	1-0	12	Sako [21]	24,696
24	20	A	Arsenal	L 1-4	0-4	13	Milivojevic [78]	59,386
25	30	A	West Ham U	D 1-1	1-1	12	Benteke, C [24]	56,911
26	Feb 4	H	Newcastle U	D 1-1	0-0	14	Milivojevic (pen) [55]	25,746
27	10	A	Everton	L 1-3	0-0	14	Milivojevic (pen) [83]	39,139
28	25	H	Tottenham H	L 0-1	0-0	17		25,287
29	Mar 5	H	Manchester U	L 2-3	1-0	18	Townsend [11], Van Aanholt [48]	25,840
30	10	A	Chelsea	L 1-2	0-2	18	Van Aanholt [90]	40,800
31	17	A	Huddersfield T	W 2-0	1-0	16	Tomkins [23], Milivojevic (pen) [68]	23,980
32	31	H	Liverpool	L 1-2	1-0	17	Milivojevic (pen) [13]	25,807
33	Apr 7	A	Bournemouth	D 2-2	0-0	17	Milivojevic [47], Zaha [75]	10,730
34	14	H	Brighton & HA	W 3-2	3-2	16	Zaha 2 [5, 24], Tomkins [14]	24,656
35	21	A	Watford	D 0-0	0-0	15		20,401
36	28	H	Leicester C	W 5-0	2-0	11	Zaha [17], McArthur [38], Loftus-Cheek [81], Van Aanholt [84], Benteke, C (pen) [90]	25,750
37	May 5	A	Stoke C	W 2-1	0-1	11	McArthur [68], Van Aanholt [86]	29,687
38	13	H	WBA	W 2-0	0-0	11	Zaha [70], Van Aanholt [78]	25,357

Final League Position: 11

GOALSCORERS

League (45): Milivojevic 10 (7 pens), Zaha 9, McArthur 5, Van Aanholt 5, Benteke, C 3 (1 pen), Sako 3, Tomkins 3, Loftus-Cheek 2, Townsend 2, Dann 1, Sakho 1, own goal 1.
FA Cup (1): Sako 1.
Carabao Cup (4): McArthur 2, Sako 2.

Hennessey W 27	Fosu-Mensah T 17+4	Dann S 16+1	Riedewald J 4+8	Ward J 19	Milivojevic L 35+1	Puncheon J 6+4	Van Aanholt P 25+3	Loftus-Cheek R 21+3	Zaha W 28+1	Benteke C 24+7	Townsend A 35+1	Tomkins J 27+1	McArthur J 27+6	Kaikai S —+1	Schlupp J 21+3	Kelly M 12+3	Lee C 1+6	Cabaye Y 28+3	Lumeka L —+1	Sako B 4+12	Sakho M 18+1	Delaney D 1+1	Ladapo F —+1	Speroni J 11	Sorloth A 4	Wan Bissaka A 7	Souare P —+1	Match No.
1	2²	3	4	5	6¹	7	8	9	10	11	12	13																1
1	2	3		5	6²	7³	8¹	10		11	9	4	12	13	14													2
1	2	3		5	7²	8	9¹			11	10	4³	6								12	13	14					3
1	3	4	13	2		8			10	9		6¹			5			11²		7	12							4
1	3	4		2	12	9		10¹		11	6		7²		5			8			13							5
1	2	3		6	12	5	9			11²	8		10		7¹			13	4									6
1		13		2	6	9³	5			8		12	10²		7			11¹	3	4	14							7
	13	3	14	2	8	12	5			11	10		6¹		9²			7³		4				1				8
		3		2	8		5			12	11¹		10		6²			9		7	13	4		1				9
12		3		2⁴	8		5¹			6	11		10	4	9			7			13			1				10
	2	3			5¹		8			6	11		10		9			7		12	4			1				11
		3		2	8		13			6	11	12	10		9¹			5		7²	4			1				12
1				2	8					6	11	12	10	3	9¹			5		7	4							13
1				2	8					6	11	10	9	3	12			5		7¹	4							14
				2	7					6	10	11	9¹		8			5	3	12	4			1				15
	2	12			8					9	10	11	6²	3	13			5		7³	14	4¹		1				16
	2¹	4			8			12		9	10	11	6³	3	14			5		7²	13			1				17
		4	12							9	11	10¹	6	3	8			5	2	7²	13			1				18
		4			8			13		9	11	10¹	3	6	5				2	7²	12			1				19
14		4			8					9¹	11	10	6	3	12			5	2²	7²	13			1				20
1	2	4²	8		7	13³	5			11	10	9	3					12	14	6¹								21
1	2				7		12			10	11	8	4	6				5²	3	9¹	13							22
1	2	8			7		5			6	10		4	9				3		11								23
1	2	12			8		5			6	10		4	9				3		7¹	11							24
1	2				8		5			6	10	9	4	7				3		12	11¹							25
1	2				7		5			10	11	6	4	9				3¹		8	12							26
1	3		2		8		5			10	6	4	9					7							11			27
1	3	8			7		5			10	9¹	4²	6			13				12					11		2	28
1		12			7		5			11	6	4	8			9¹	3								10		2	29
1		13			7		5			12	11²	6¹	4	8		9²	3	14							10		2	30
1					7		5	13	11¹	10	9	3	6		8²			12				4					2	31
1	13				7		5	12	11	10	9		8			3		6¹				4				2²		32
1					8		5	9	10	11		3	6		7							4				2		33
1		13	2	8			5	9	10	12	11	3	6		7²							4						34
1				2	7		5	9	11	12	10	3	6¹		8							4						35
1				2	7		5	9¹	11	13	10³	3	6²	12	14	8						4						36
1				2²	8		5	9	11	13	10³	3	6	14	12	7¹						4						37
1					8		5¹	9	11	12	10³	3	6²	14	7							4				2	13	38

FA Cup
Third Round   Brighton & HA   (a)   1-2

Carabao Cup
Second Round   Ipswich T   (h)   2-1
Third Round   Huddersfield T   (h)   1-0
Fourth Round   Bristol C   (a)   1-4

DERBY COUNTY

FOUNDATION

Derby County was formed by members of the Derbyshire County Cricket Club in 1884, when football was booming in the area and the cricketers thought that a football club would help boost finances for the summer game. To begin with, they sported the cricket club's colours of amber, chocolate and pale blue, and went into the game at the top immediately entering the FA Cup.

Pride Park Stadium, Pride Park, Derby DE21 8XL.
Telephone: (0871) 472 1884.

Fax: (0871) 472 1884

Ticket Office: (0871) 472 1884 (option 1).

Website: www.dcfc.co.uk

Email: derby.county@dcfc.co.uk

Ground Capacity: 33,055.

Record Attendance: 41,826 v Tottenham H, Division 1, 20 September 1969 (at Baseball Ground); 33,378 v Liverpool, FA Premier League, 18 March 2000 (at Pride Park).

Stadium Record Attendance: 33,597, England v Mexico, 25 May 2001 (at Pride Park).

Pitch Measurements: 105m × 68m (115yd × 74yd).

Executive Chairman: Mel Morris.

Chief Operating Officer: John Vicars.

Manager: Frank Lampard.

Assistant Manager: Jody Morris.

HONOURS

League Champions: Division 1 – 1971–72, 1974–75; Division 2 – 1911–12, 1914–15, 1968–69, 1986–87; Division 3N – 1956–57.
Runners-up: Division 1 – 1895–96, 1929–30, 1935–36; First Division – 1995–96; Division 2 – 1925–26; Division 3N – 1955–56.

FA Cup Winners: 1946.
Runners-up: 1898, 1899, 1903.

League Cup: semi-final – 1968, 2009.

Texaco Cup Winners: 1972.

Anglo-Italian Cup: Runners-up: 1993–94, 1994–95.

European Competitions
European Cup: 1972–73 *(sf)*, 1975–76.
UEFA Cup: 1974–75, 1976–77.

Colours: White shirts with black trim, black shorts with white trim, white socks with black trim.

Year Formed: 1884.

Turned Professional: 1884.

Club Nickname: 'The Rams'.

Grounds: 1884, Racecourse Ground; 1895, Baseball Ground; 1997, Pride Park (renamed The iPro Stadium 2013; Pride Park Stadium 2016).

First Football League Game: 8 September 1888, Football League, v Bolton W (a) W 6–3 – Marshall; Latham, Ferguson, Williamson; Monks, Walter Roulstone; Bakewell (2), Cooper (2), Higgins, Harry Plackett, Lol Plackett (2).

Record League Victory: 9–0 v Wolverhampton W, Division 1, 10 January 1891 – Bunyan; Archie Goodall, Roberts; Walker, Chalmers, Walter Roulstone (1); Bakewell, McLachlan, Johnny Goodall (1), Holmes (2), McMillan (5). 9–0 v Sheffield W, Division 1, 21 January 1899 – Fryer; Methven, Staley; Cox, Archie Goodall, May; Oakden (1), Bloomer (6), Boag, McDonald (1), Allen, (1 og).

Sün FACT FILE

Derby County took part in European competition for the first time in the 1961–62 season when they were drawn to play Beziers in the Friendship Cup. County won the home leg 1-0 but lost the return 2-1 to leave the scores level. County's goalscorers were Bill Curry and Jack Parry.

Record Cup Victory: 12–0 v Finn Harps, UEFA Cup 1st rd 1st leg, 15 September 1976 – Moseley; Thomas, Nish, Rioch (1), McFarland, Todd (King), Macken, Gemmill, Hector (5), George (3), James (3).

Record Defeat: 2–11 v Everton, FA Cup 1st rd, 1889–90.

Most League Points (2 for a win): 63, Division 2, 1968–69 and Division 3 (N), 1955–56 and 1956–57.

Most League Points (3 for a win): 85, FL C, 2013–14.

Most League Goals: 111, Division 3 (N), 1956–57.

Highest League Scorer in Season: Jack Bowers, 37, Division 1, 1930–31; Ray Straw, 37 Division 3 (N), 1956–57.

Most League Goals in Total Aggregate: Steve Bloomer, 292, 1892–1906 and 1910–14.

Most League Goals in One Match: 6, Steve Bloomer v Sheffield W, Division 1, 2 January 1899.

Most Capped Player: Deon Burton, 42 (59), Jamaica.

Most League Appearances: Kevin Hector, 486, 1966–78 and 1980–82.

Youngest League Player: Mason Bennett, 15 years 99 days v Middlesbrough 22 October 2011.

Record Transfer Fee Received: £10,500,000 from Burnley for Jeff Hendrick, August 2016.

Record Transfer Fee Paid: £8,000,000 to Watford for Matej Vydra, August 2016.

Football League Record: 1888 Founder Member of the Football League; 1907–12 Division 2; 1912–14 Division 1; 1914–15 Division 2; 1915–21 Division 1; 1921–26 Division 2; 1926–53 Division 1; 1953–55 Division 2; 1955–57 Division 3 (N); 1957–69 Division 2; 1969–80 Division 1; 1980–84 Division 2; 1984–86 Division 3; 1986–87 Division 2; 1987–91 Division 1; 1991–92 Division 2; 1992–96 Division 1; 1996–2002 FA Premier League; 2002–04 Division 1; 2004–07 FL C; 2007–08 FA Premier League; 2008– FL C.

LATEST SEQUENCES

Longest Sequence of League Wins: 9, 15.3.1969 – 19.4.1969.

Longest Sequence of League Defeats: 8, 12.12.1987 – 10.2.1988.

Longest Sequence of League Draws: 6, 26.3.1927 – 18.4.1927.

Longest Sequence of Unbeaten League Matches: 22, 8.3.1969 – 20.9.1969.

Longest Sequence Without a League Win: 36, 22.9.2007 – 30.8.2008.

Successive Scoring Runs: 29 from 3.12.1960.

Successive Non-scoring Runs: 8 from 30.10.1920.

MANAGERS

W. D. Clark 1896–1900
Harry Newbould 1900–06
Jimmy Methven 1906–22
Cecil Potter 1922–25
George Jobey 1925–41
Ted Magner 1944–46
Stuart McMillan 1946–53
Jack Barker 1953–55
Harry Storer 1955–62
Tim Ward 1962–67
Brian Clough 1967–73
Dave Mackay 1973–76
Colin Murphy 1977
Tommy Docherty 1977–79
Colin Addison 1979–82
Johnny Newman 1982
Peter Taylor 1982–84
Roy McFarland 1984
Arthur Cox 1984–93
Roy McFarland 1993–95
Jim Smith 1995–2001
Colin Todd 2001–02
John Gregory 2002–03
George Burley 2003–05
Phil Brown 2005–06
Billy Davies 2006–07
Paul Jewell 2007–08
Nigel Clough 2009–13
Steve McClaren 2013–15
Paul Clement 2015–16
Darren Wassall 2016
Nigel Pearson 2016
Steve McClaren 2016–17
Gary Rowett 2017–18
Frank Lampard May 2018–

TEN YEAR LEAGUE RECORD

		P	W	D	L	F	A	Pts	Pos
2008-09	FL C	46	14	12	20	55	67	54	18
2009-10	FL C	46	15	11	20	53	63	56	14
2010-11	FL C	46	13	10	23	58	71	49	19
2011-12	FL C	46	18	10	18	50	58	64	12
2012-13	FL C	46	16	13	17	65	62	61	10
2013-14	FL C	46	25	10	11	84	52	85	3
2014-15	FL C	46	21	14	11	85	56	77	8
2015-16	FL C	46	21	15	10	66	43	78	5
2016-17	FL C	46	18	13	15	54	50	67	9
2017-18	FL C	46	20	15	11	70	48	75	6

DID YOU KNOW ?

Derby County took part in one of the first-ever indoor football tournaments held at Nottingham Mechanics Hall around 1890. The Rams defeated Nottingham Forest in the final and the players were each rewarded with a set of cutlery.

DERBY COUNTY – SKY BET CHAMPIONSHIP 2017–18 LEAGUE RECORD

Match No.	Date	Venue	Opponents	Result		H/T Score	Lg Pos.	Goalscorers	Attendance
1	Aug 4	A	Sunderland	D	1-1	1-1	2	Johnson [11]	29,578
2	12	H	Wolverhampton W	L	0-2	0-1	19		27,757
3	15	H	Preston NE	W	1-0	0-0	14	Vydra (pen) [58]	24,371
4	19	A	Bolton W	W	2-1	2-0	8	Nugent 2 [8, 21]	15,175
5	26	A	Sheffield U	L	1-3	0-2	12	Bryson [90]	26,202
6	Sept 8	H	Hull C	W	5-0	4-0	4	Vydra 2 [15, 34], Davies [38], Johnson 2 [45, 58]	25,107
7	16	A	Bristol C	L	1-4	1-0	15	Vydra (pen) [27]	19,473
8	23	H	Birmingham C	D	1-1	0-0	15	Winnall [67]	27,392
9	26	A	Brentford	D	1-1	1-0	15	Ledley [15]	8679
10	30	A	Cardiff C	D	0-0	0-0	14		18,480
11	Oct 15	H	Nottingham F	W	2-0	1-0	13	Vydra [1], Nugent [50]	31,196
12	21	H	Sheffield W	W	2-0	1-0	8	Vydra (pen) [5], Johnson [86]	27,426
13	28	A	Norwich C	W	2-1	1-0	7	Nugent [45], Winnall [83]	26,048
14	31	A	Leeds U	W	2-1	0-1	5	Winnall 2 (1 pen) [72, 80 (p)]	28,565
15	Nov 4	H	Reading	L	2-4	0-2	6	Russell [71], Martin [90]	25,928
16	18	A	Fulham	D	1-1	0-1	7	Vydra [50]	18,192
17	21	H	QPR	W	2-0	1-0	6	Vydra [45], Lawrence [53]	23,296
18	25	A	Middlesbrough	W	3-0	1-0	6	Vydra 3 (1 pen) [13, 47 (p), 63]	24,607
19	28	H	Ipswich T	L	0-1	0-1	6		24,475
20	Dec 2	H	Burton Alb	W	1-0	0-0	6	Russell [81]	26,761
21	9	A	Barnsley	W	3-0	1-0	4	Lawrence [39], Vydra [44], Weimann [78]	13,973
22	16	H	Aston Villa	W	2-0	1-0	4	Weimann [24], Russell [90]	28,118
23	23	H	Millwall	W	3-0	3-0	3	Nugent 2 [23, 28], Vydra [25]	25,813
24	26	A	Hull C	D	0-0	0-0	4		18,026
25	30	A	Ipswich T	W	2-1	1-0	2	Winnall 2 [13, 49]	17,267
26	Jan 1	H	Sheffield U	D	1-1	1-0	2	Vydra (pen) [24]	30,003
27	13	A	Birmingham C	W	3-0	1-0	2	Russell [19], Vydra [56], Weimann [89]	22,121
28	19	H	Bristol C	D	0-0	0-0	2		26,525
29	30	A	Millwall	D	0-0	0-0	2		10,931
30	Feb 3	H	Brentford	W	3-0	2-0	2	Huddlestone [30], Jerome [34], Vydra (pen) [90]	25,938
31	10	A	Norwich C	D	1-1	1-0	2	Vydra [12]	27,171
32	13	H	Sheffield W	L	0-2	0-1	3		24,180
33	21	H	Leeds U	D	2-2	1-1	4	Weimann [45], Palmer [90]	27,934
34	24	A	Reading	D	3-3	2-2	4	Palmer [6], Keogh [35], Lawrence [46]	17,647
35	Mar 3	H	Fulham	L	1-2	0-2	5	Huddlestone [68]	27,138
36	6	A	QPR	D	1-1	1-0	5	Weimann [38]	11,488
37	11	A	Nottingham F	D	0-0	0-0	5		29,106
38	30	H	Sunderland	L	1-4	1-2	5	Vydra [42]	27,890
39	Apr 2	A	Preston NE	W	1-0	0-0	5	Lawrence [52]	13,520
40	7	H	Bolton W	W	3-0	2-0	5	Pearce [6], Vydra [33], Lawrence [54]	25,723
41	11	A	Wolverhampton W	L	0-2	0-1	5		28,503
42	14	A	Burton Alb	L	1-3	1-2	7	Nugent [29]	5563
43	21	H	Middlesbrough	L	1-2	0-1	7	Nugent (pen) [90]	28,096
44	24	H	Cardiff C	W	3-1	0-1	6	Jerome 2 [69, 90], Vydra [82]	30,294
45	28	A	Aston Villa	D	1-1	1-0	6	Jerome [14]	41,745
46	May 6	H	Barnsley	W	4-1	1-0	6	Jerome [14], Vydra [55], Nugent [68], Lawrence [71]	30,682

Final League Position: 6

GOALSCORERS

League (70): Vydra 21 (6 pens), Nugent 9 (1 pen), Lawrence 6, Winnall 6 (1 pen), Jerome 5, Weimann 5, Johnson 4, Russell 4, Huddlestone 2, Palmer 2, Bryson 1, Davies 1, Keogh 1, Ledley 1, Martin 1, Pearce 1.
FA Cup (0).
Carabao Cup (3): Bennett 1, Russell 1, Vydra 1 (1 pen).
Championship Play-Offs (1): Jerome 1.

Carson S 46	Wisdom A 29+1	Keogh R 42	Davies C 46	Forsyth C 31	Butterfield J 2+1	Huddlestone T 44	Johnson B 25+8	Russell J 13+10	Martin C 5+18	Weimann A 32+8	Vydra M 34+6	Nugent D 29+8	Bryson C —+4	Anya I 3+4	Olsson M 14+1	Bennett M 1+2	Lawrence T 36+3	Baird C 21+1	Winnall S 6+11	Ledley J 23+3	Thorne G 9+11	Pearce A 5+2	Thomas L —+2	Jerome C 8+10	Palmer K 2+13	Hanson J —+6	Match No.
1	2	3	4	5	6	7	8	9³	10¹	11²	12	13	14														1
1	2	3	4	5	6²	7	8	9	10	11³	12	13	14														2
1	2	3	4			7	6	8³	13	10	9¹	11²	12		5	14											3
1	2	3	4	14	6	7	8	13	10²	9¹	11³				5		12										4
1	2	3	4		6	7	8³	13	10¹	9	11¹	14			5		12										5
1		3	4		6	7	13	14	10²	9¹	11³				5		8	2		12							6
1		3	4		6	7	14	12	8¹	9¹	11²				5		10	2		13							7
1		3	4		6	7		12	10¹	9²	11³				5	13	8	2		14							8
1	2	3	4	5	6	9		12	14	13					8¹		10		11³	7²							9
1	2	3	4	5	6	9	8²	12		13							10		11¹	7							10
1	2	3	4	5	6		8	13		9¹	11²						10			7	12						11
1	2	3	4	5	6	13	8	12		9³	11¹						10²			7	14						12
1	2	3	4	5	6	10		12		9¹	11²						8³	13		7	14						13
1	2	3	4	5	6	10		11	12								8		9²	7¹	13						14
1	2	3⁴	4	5	6	7	8	13		9							10		11¹		12						15
1		3	4	5	6	10³	14	12	13	9²	11						8¹	2		7							16
1		3	4	5	6		13	8	9²	11¹							10³	2		7	12	14					17
1		3	4	5	6		14	13	8	9²	11¹						10	2		7³	12						18
1		3	4²	5	6		13	12	8¹	9	11¹						10	2		7	14						19
1		3	4		14	12	11	10	9²					5	8¹	2	13	6	7³								20
1		3	4	5	6	13	12	11²	8	9¹							10³	2	14	7							21
1		3	4	5	6	9	12	13	8¹	10³	11⁴						2			7	14						22
1		3	4	5	6	10	12		8¹	9³	11²						2	13		7	14						23
1		3	4	5	6	10¹	14		8	9³	11						12	2		7²	13						24
1	2	3	4	5	6		8		12	9³		13					10¹	14	11²	7							25
1		3	4	5	6	7³	8	14	10	9²	11¹						2	12		13							26
1	2	3	4	5	6		8	14	13	9¹	12						10³		11²	7							27
1	2	3	4	5	7		8	13	9²	11¹							10³	14	6		12						28
1	2	3	4	5	6		8	9³	11²	14							10¹	13	7		12						29
1	2	3	4		6		9		10¹	5	8	12	13	7²	11²	14											30
1	2	3	4		6	14	13	9³		8	5	10¹		7²		11	12										31
1		3	4	5	6	10		8	9³	11¹	12						2	7²						13	14		32
1		3	4		6	14		8	9	11²	5	10¹	2	7³										12	13		33
1	14	3	4		6	12		8		13	5	10¹	2⁴	7										11²	9³		34
1	2³	3	4	5	6²	14		10	9		13	8		7¹										11	12		35
1	2	3	4	5	6	12		8	14	11³	10			7²										13	9¹		36
1	2	3	4	5	6⁴	7		8		11²	10¹			9³										13	12	14	37
1		3	4	5		7		8	9	13	10³	2		6²										11¹	12		38
1	2		4		6		8	9¹	11³	10²	5	7	3		14	12	13										39
1	2		4		7		8	9¹	11²	10³	5	6	3		14	13	12										40
1	2		4		6		8	9³	11²	10	5	7¹	3		13	12	14										41
1	2		4		6		8	9	11	10	5	7¹	3²		13	12											42
1	5	2	3	4	6¹	7		13	10³	11		8²	9		12	14											43
1	5	2	3	4	6	7		9¹	12		8³	10¹				14					11			13			44
1	5	2	3	8	6	7		9¹	12		10²		4³								11	14		13			45
1	5	2	3	4	6	7		9	12	13	8³	11¹				14					10²						46

FA Cup
Third Round   Manchester U   (a)   0-2

Carabao Cup
First Round   Grimsby T   (a)   1-0
Second Round   Barnsley   (a)   2-3

Championship Play-Offs
Semi-Final 1st leg   Fulham   (h)   1-0
Semi-Final 2nd leg   Fulham   (a)   0-2

DONCASTER ROVERS

FOUNDATION

In 1879, Mr Albert Jenkins assembled a team to play a match against the Yorkshire Institution for the Deaf. The players remained together as Doncaster Rovers, joining the Midland Alliance in 1889 and the Midland Counties League in 1891.

Keepmoat Stadium, Stadium Way, Lakeside, Doncaster, South Yorkshire DN4 5JW.

Telephone: (01302) 764 664.

Ticket Office: (01302) 762 576.

Website: www.doncasterroversfc.co.uk

Email: info@clubdoncaster.co.uk

Ground Capacity: 15,123.

Record Attendance: 37,149 v Hull C, Division 3 (N), 2 October 1948 (at Belle Vue); 15,001 v Leeds U, FL 1, 1 April 2008 (at Keepmoat Stadium).

Pitch Measurements: 100m × 66m (109.5yd × 72yd).

Chairman: David Blunt.

Chief Executive: Gavin Baldwin.

Manager: Grant McCann.

Assistant Manager: Cliff Byrne.

HONOURS

League Champions: FL 1 – 2012–13; Division 3N – 1934–35, 1946–47, 1949–50; Third Division – 2003–04; Division 4 – 1965–66, 1968–69. *Runners-up:* Division 3N – 1937–38, 1938–39; Division 4 – 1983–84; Conference – (3rd) 2002–03 *(promoted via play-offs (and golden goal)).*

FA Cup: 5th rd – 1952, 1954, 1955, 1956.

League Cup: 5th rd – 1976, 2006.

League Trophy Winners: 2007.

Colours: Red and white hooped shirts, red shorts with white and black trim, white socks with red hoops.

Year Formed: 1879.

Turned Professional: 1885.

Club Nickname: 'Rovers', 'Donny'.

Grounds: 1880–1916, Intake Ground; 1920, Benetthorpe Ground; 1922, Low Pasture, Belle Vue; 2007, Keepmoat Stadium.

First Football League Game: 7 September 1901, Division 2, v Burslem Port Vale (h) D 3–3 – Eggett; Simpson, Layton; Longden, Jones, Wright, Langham, Murphy, Price, Goodson (2), Bailey (1).

Record League Victory: 10–0 v Darlington, Division 4, 25 January 1964 – Potter; Raine, Meadows, Windross (1), White, Ripley (2), Robinson, Book (2), Hale (4), Jeffrey, Broadbent (1).

Record Cup Victory: 7–0 v Blyth Spartans, FA Cup 1st rd, 27 November 1937 – Imrie; Shaw, Rodgers, McFarlane, Bycroft, Cyril Smith, Burton (1), Killourhy (4), Morgan (2), Malam, Dutton.

Record Defeat: 0–12 v Small Heath, Division 2, 11 April 1903.

Most League Points (2 for a win): 72, Division 3 (N), 1946–47.

Most League Points (3 for a win): 92, Division 3, 2003–04.

THE **Sun** FACT FILE

Doncaster Rovers were the first team to gain promotion to the Football League through the play-off system. They defeated Dagenham & Redbridge 3-2 at Stoke City's Britannia Stadium in May 2003 in the Conference Play-Off Final. Francis Tierney netted the winning goal in extra time, this being the only occasion that promotion to the League has been decided by the 'golden goal' method.

Most League Goals: 123, Division 3 (N), 1946–47.

Highest League Scorer in Season: Clarrie Jordan, 42, Division 3 (N), 1946–47.

Most League Goals in Total Aggregate: Tom Keetley, 180, 1923–29.

Most League Goals in One Match: 6, Tom Keetley v Ashington, Division 3 (N), 16 February 1929.

Most Capped Player: Len Graham, 14, Northern Ireland.

Most League Appearances: James Coppinger, 510, 2004–18.

Youngest League Player: Alick Jeffrey, 15 years 229 days v Fulham, 15 September 1954.

Record Transfer Fee Received: £2,000,000 from Reading for Matthew Mills, July 2009.

Record Transfer Fee Paid: £1,150,000 to Sheffield U for Billy Sharp, August 2010.

Football League Record: 1901 Elected to Division 2; 1903 Failed re-election; 1904 Re-elected; 1905 Failed re-election; 1923 Re-elected to Division 3 (N); 1935–37 Division 2; 1937–47 Division 3 (N); 1947–48 Division 2; 1948–50 Division 3 (N); 1950–58 Division 2; 1958–59 Division 3; 1959–66 Division 4; 1966–67 Division 3; 1967–69 Division 4; 1969–71 Division 3; 1971–81 Division 4; 1981–83 Division 3; 1983–84 Division 4; 1984–88 Division 3; 1988–92 Division 4; 1992–98 Division 3; 1998–2003 Conference; 2003–04 Division 3; 2004–08 FL 1; 2008–12 FL C; 2012–13 FL 1; 2013–14 FL C; 2014–16 FL 1; 2016–17 FL 2; 2017– FL 1.

LATEST SEQUENCES

Longest Sequence of League Wins: 10, 22.1.1947 – 4.4.1947.

Longest Sequence of League Defeats: 9, 14.1.1905 – 1.4.1905.

Longest Sequence of League Draws: 4, 1.1.2018 – 23.1.2018.

Longest Sequence of Unbeaten League Matches: 20, 26.12.1968 – 12.4.1969.

Longest Sequence Without a League Win: 20, 9.8.1997 – 29.11.1997.

Successive Scoring Runs: 27 from 10.11.1934.

Successive Non-scoring Runs: 7 from 27.9.1947.

MANAGERS

Arthur Porter 1920–21
Harry Tufnell 1921–22
Arthur Porter 1922–23
Dick Ray 1923–27
David Menzies 1928–36
Fred Emery 1936–40
Bill Marsden 1944–46
Jackie Bestall 1946–49
Peter Doherty 1949–58
Jack Hodgson and Sid Bycroft
  (*Joint Managers*) 1958
Jack Crayston 1958–59
  (*continued as Secretary-Manager to 1961*)
Jackie Bestall 1959–60
Norman Curtis 1960–61
Danny Malloy 1961–62
Oscar Hold 1962–64
Bill Leivers 1964–66
Keith Kettleborough 1966–67
George Raynor 1967–68
Lawrie McMenemy 1968–71
Maurice Setters 1971–74
Stan Anderson 1975–78
Billy Bremner 1978–85
Dave Cusack 1985–87
Dave Mackay 1987–89
Billy Bremner 1989–91
Steve Beaglehole 1991–93
Ian Atkins 1994
Sammy Chung 1994–96
Kerry Dixon (*Player-Manager*)
  1996–97
Dave Cowling 1997
Mark Weaver 1997–98
Ian Snodin 1998–99
Steve Wignall 1999–2001
Dave Penney 2002–06
Sean O'Driscoll 2006–11
Dean Saunders 2011–13
Brian Flynn 2013
Paul Dickov 2013–15
Darren Ferguson 2015–18
Grant McCann June 2018–

TEN YEAR LEAGUE RECORD

		P	W	D	L	F	A	Pts	Pos
2008-09	FL C	46	17	7	22	42	53	58	14
2009-10	FL C	46	15	15	16	59	58	60	12
2010-11	FL C	46	11	15	20	55	81	48	21
2011-12	FL C	46	8	12	26	43	80	36	24
2012-13	FL 1	46	25	9	12	62	44	84	1
2013-14	FL C	46	11	11	24	39	70	44	22
2014-15	FL 1	46	16	13	17	58	62	61	13
2015-16	FL 1	46	11	13	22	48	64	46	21
2016-17	FL 2	46	25	10	11	85	55	85	3
2017-18	FL 1	46	13	17	16	52	52	56	15

DID YOU KNOW ?

Centre-half Charlie Williams made over 150 appearances for Doncaster Rovers in the 1950s. When he retired from playing he became a singer and comedian, progressing from working men's clubs to becoming a household name in the 1970s, through television programmes such as *The Golden Shot* for ATV and *The Comedians* (Granada).

DONCASTER ROVERS – SKY BET LEAGUE ONE 2017–18 LEAGUE RECORD

Match No.	Date		Venue	Opponents		Result	H/T Score	Lg Pos.	Goalscorers	Attendance
1	Aug	5	H	Gillingham	D	0-0	0-0	13		7512
2		12	A	Blackburn R	W	3-1	0-0	6	Marquis [46], Coppinger (pen) [67], May [82]	12,223
3		19	H	Blackpool	D	3-3	2-1	8	Allsop (og) [37], Marquis [45], May [75]	7558
4		26	A	AFC Wimbledon	L	0-2	0-0	12		4144
5	Sept	2	H	Peterborough U	D	0-0	0-0	12		8677
6		9	A	Northampton T	L	0-1	0-1	16		5843
7		12	A	Rochdale	L	1-2	0-0	16	Marquis [74]	2371
8		17	H	Scunthorpe U	L	0-1	0-1	19		9227
9		23	A	Plymouth Arg	W	3-0	1-0	17	Butler [19], Marquis [59], May [73]	8510
10		26	H	Shrewsbury T	L	1-2	1-1	18	Rowe [36]	7194
11		30	A	Bradford C	L	0-2	0-2	19		20,430
12	Oct	7	H	Southend U	W	4-1	1-1	17	Marquis [45], Whiteman 3 (1 pen) [47, 50, 57 (p)]	7369
13		14	A	Charlton Ath	L	0-1	0-1	18		10,917
14		17	A	Portsmouth	W	2-1	2-0	17	Mandeville [3], Burgess (og) [5]	7211
15		21	H	Walsall	L	0-3	0-0	18		7391
16		28	A	Bury	W	1-0	0-0	17	Whiteman [78]	3079
17	Nov	11	H	Rotherham U	D	1-1	0-0	16	Wood (og) [62]	12,481
18		18	A	Fleetwood T	D	0-0	0-0	17		3181
19		21	A	Wigan Ath	L	0-3	0-2	18		7966
20		25	H	Milton Keynes D	W	2-1	0-1	16	Marquis [54], Blair [71]	7743
21	Dec	9	A	Oxford U	L	0-1	0-0	18		6711
22		16	H	Oldham Ath	D	1-1	0-0	18	Butler [59]	7831
23		23	A	Bristol R	W	1-0	1-0	14	Mason (pen) [33]	8300
24		26	H	Northampton T	W	3-0	2-0	13	Coppinger [33], Mason (pen) [43], Butler [66]	8032
25		29	H	Rochdale	W	2-0	2-0	10	Whiteman [4], May [27]	7997
26	Jan	1	A	Peterborough U	D	1-1	0-1	11	Whiteman [90]	5173
27		13	H	Plymouth Arg	D	1-1	1-0	12	Beestin [37]	7494
28		20	A	Shrewsbury T	D	2-2	0-1	12	Baudry [62], Henderson (og) [76]	5818
29		23	A	Scunthorpe U	D	1-1	0-1	11	Beestin [90]	5193
30		27	A	Bristol R	L	1-3	1-1	14	Marquis [4]	8021
31	Feb	3	A	Portsmouth	D	2-2	1-1	14	Coppinger [4], Marquis [63]	17,364
32		10	H	Charlton Ath	D	1-1	0-1	15	Blair [90]	7797
33		13	A	Walsall	L	2-4	0-3	16	Rowe [87], Mason (pen) [90]	3514
34		17	H	Fleetwood T	W	3-0	2-0	14	Kiwomya [13], Anderson 2 [27, 55]	7013
35		24	A	Rotherham U	L	1-2	1-0	14	Marquis [39]	11,725
36	Mar	10	A	Southend U	D	0-0	0-0	15		6766
37		19	H	Bradford C	W	2-0	0-0	14	Marquis 2 [75, 90]	7369
38		30	A	Blackpool	W	2-1	1-0	13	Rowe 2 [43, 70]	4533
39	Apr	7	A	Gillingham	D	0-0	0-0	14		4870
40		14	A	Milton Keynes D	W	2-1	0-1	14	Marquis 2 [49, 63]	8954
41		17	H	Bury	D	3-3	2-1	13	Butler [2], Marquis [35], Boyle [65]	7131
42		21	H	Oxford U	L	0-1	0-0	14		8255
43		24	A	Blackburn R	L	0-1	0-0	14		10,443
44		28	A	Oldham Ath	D	0-0	0-0	15		5297
45	May	1	H	AFC Wimbledon	D	0-0	0-0	14		7094
46		5	H	Wigan Ath	L	0-1	0-0	15		12,057

Final League Position: 15

GOALSCORERS

League (52): Marquis 14, Whiteman 6 (1 pen), Butler 4, May 4, Rowe 4, Coppinger 3 (1 pen), Mason 3 (3 pens), Anderson 2, Beestin 2, Blair 2, Baudry 1, Boyle 1, Kiwomya 1, Mandeville 1, own goals 4.
FA Cup (9): Rowe 4, Coppinger 2 (1 pen), Houghton 1, Mandeville 1, Marquis 1.
Carabao Cup (5): May 2, Kongolo 1, Rowe 1, Whiteman 1.
Checkatrade Trophy (4): Mandeville 2, Ben Khemis 1, Williams 1.

Lawlor I 34	Blair M 32 + 8	Wright J 32 + 1	Butler A 34 + 2	Andrew D 4	Mason N 37 + 3	Whiteman B 34 + 8	Rowe T 40	Coppinger J 34 + 4	Marquis J 45	Mandeville L 7 + 10	Kongolo R 17 + 18	May A 13 + 14	Williams A 3 + 6	Garrett T 10 + 3	Houghton J 33 + 4	Toffolo H 11 + 2	Ben Khemis 12 + 1	Marosi M 12 + 1	Fletcher J — + 1	Baudry M 19 + 3	Beestin A 17 + 9	Alcock C 6 + 3	Boyle A 6	Anderson T 7	Kiwomya A 5 + 7	McCullough L 10 + 3	Amos D 2 + 1	Match No.
1	2^2	3	4	5	6	7	8	9	10	11^1	12	13																1
1	6	3	4	5	2	7	9	8^1	10	11^1	13	12																2
1	7	3	4	5	2	6	8	9	11	10^2	13	12																3
1	7	3	4	5	2^3	6	8	9	10^2	13	12	11	14															4
1	7	3	4		2^3	6	8	9	10	13		11^1	14	5	12													5
1	2	3	4			7	8	12	10	11^1	6	13		9^3	14	5^2												6
1	12	3	4		2	8		6	11		13	14	10^3		5	7^1		9^2										7
1	2	3	4	5	6		8	9	10^2	13		7	12	11^1														8
1	5^3	2	3	4	8^2	9	7^1	11	14	12	10			6	13													9
1^1	2	3	4	5^2	12	8	9	10		7	11			6^3	13		14											10
	4	3		2	8	9	12	11	13	7	10			6^2	5^1		1											11
1	12	3	4		2	7	8	9^3	10^2			11		13			6	14										12
1	14	3	4		5	7	8	9^2	10	13	12	11^3		6	2^1													13
1	5^3	2	4		12	8	11			10^1	6		14	7	9					3^1	13							14
1		2	3		5^1	8	6	12	10	11^3	13			7	9					4^2		14						15
1		3	4			12	9	11	10		7		13	8	6					5^1		2^2						16
1	5^1	2	3			8	10^2	11	13	6		7			9					4	12							17
1	5	2	3			12	8	10^1	11		7			6	9					4								18
1	9	7	3			14	6	11^2	5		4		12^3	8	10					2^1	13							19
1	13	3	4		2	6^1	10	9	11	8^2		5		7^1						14^2	12							20
1		3	4		2	6	10	8	9			12		7	5					11^1								21
1		4	3		2	7^1	8		10	12	13	11^2		5^3	6					14	9							22
1		4	3		5	12	8		11		6^2	13		9	7					2	10^1							23
1	12		4		2	6	8	9	10			7^2	11^1	5						3	13							24
1	12		4		2	7	8	9^4	10	13			11^1	5						3								25
1	5	4	2		3	6	9		10	7^3	13	11		8^1							12							26
1	2		4		5	13	8	9	11			7^1	12	6						3	10^2							27
1	2	4	3^2		5	9	10	8	11			7^3		6^1			14			12	13							28
1	2	4			5^2	7	8	9	11			14		13	6^3					3^1	10	12						29
1	2	4^3			12	6	8	9^1	10	14		7^1	13	5						11	3							30
1	2					6	9	8^1	10		14			5^2	7					11^3		3		4	12	13		31
1	2					5^1	7^2	8	9	11				6						10		4		3	13	2^3		32
1	6^1					14	8	9	12	10		7^2		5						11		4		3	13	2^3		33
	13					5		9	8	10			12					1		11^1	2	4		3	7^2	6		34
	13	12				5	9	7	6^1	10				14				1		8^3	2	4		3^2	11			35
	2	4				5		10	9	11			12	6				1		3					8^1	7		36
	2	3				5	13	8	9	10				7				1		4	12				11^1	6^2		37
	2	3				5		8	9	10				7				1		4	11					6		38
	2^1	3	14			5	6	8	9	11		13^1	12					1		4	10^1					7^2		39
	2^1	3^3	14			5	13	9	8	10				6				1		4	12				11	7^4		40
	2^2		4			5	7	8	9^1	10		13		6				1		11		3			12			41
	8		4			5	9		10			7^3	11^1	13	12			1		3		2^2		14	6			42
	7		4			5	6		9^1	11		14		13	8			1		3	10^1	2^2				12		43
1	7^1		3			2	9		10		13	14	11^3	8						4	12				6^3	5		44
1	5		3			2	7		10		12	11^3		6		9^2				8^1			4	13		14		45
	5^1		3			4	6^2		10		12			8					1	11				2^1	13	7	9	46

FA Cup

First Round	Ebbsfleet U	(a)		6-2
Second Round	Scunthorpe U	(h)		3-0
Third Round	Rochdale	(h)		0-1

Carabao Cup

First Round	Bradford C	(a)		3-2
Second Round	Hull C	(h)		2-0
Third Round	Arsenal	(a)		0-1

Checkatrade Trophy

Northern Group H Grimsby T	(a)		1-1
(Doncaster R won 4-3 on penalties)			
Northern Group H Sunderland U21	(h)		1-0
Northern Group H Scunthorpe U	(h)		1-1
(Doncaster R won 3-2 on penalties)			
Second Round North Rochdale	(a)		1-1
(Rochdale won 5-4 on penalties)			

EVERTON

FOUNDATION

St Domingo Church Sunday School formed a football club in 1878 which played at Stanley Park. Enthusiasm was so great that in November 1879 they decided to expand membership and changed the name to Everton, playing in black shirts with a scarlet sash and nicknamed the 'Black Watch'. After wearing several other colours, royal blue was adopted in 1901.

Goodison Park, Goodison Road, Liverpool L4 4EL.

Telephone: (0151) 556 1878.

Fax: (0151) 286 9112.

Ticket Office: (0151) 556 1878.

Website: www.evertonfc.com

Email: everton@evertonfc.com

Ground Capacity: 39,595.

Record Attendance: 78,299 v Liverpool, Division 1, 18 September 1948.

Pitch Measurements: 100.48m × 68m (109yd × 74yd).

Chairman: Bill Kenwright CBE.

Chief Executive: Robert Elstone.

Manager: Marco Silva.

Assistant Manager: Joao Pedro Sousa.

Colours: Blue shirts, white shorts with blue trim, white socks with blue trim.

Year Formed: 1878.

Turned Professional: 1885.

Previous Name: 1878, St Domingo FC; 1879, Everton.

Club Nickname: 'The Toffees'.

Grounds: 1878, Stanley Park; 1882, Priory Road; 1884, Anfield Road; 1892, Goodison Park.

First Football League Game: 8 September 1888, Football League, v Accrington (h) W 2–1 – Smalley; Dick, Ross; Holt, Jones, Dobson; Fleming (2), Waugh, Lewis, Edgar Chadwick, Farmer.

HONOURS

League Champions: Division 1 – 1914–15, 1927–28, 1931–32, 1938–39, 1962–63, 1969–70, 1984–85, 1986–87; Football League 1890–91; Division 2 – 1930–31.
Runners-up: Division 1 – 1894–95, 1901–02, 1904–05, 1908–09, 1911–12, 1985–86; Football League 1889–90; Division 2 – 1953–54.
FA Cup Winners: 1906, 1933, 1966, 1984, 1995.
Runners-up: 1893, 1897, 1907, 1968, 1985, 1986, 1989, 2009.
League Cup: Runners-up: 1977, 1984.
League Super Cup: Runners-up: 1986.
Full Members' Cup: Runners-up: 1989, 1991.
European Competitions
European Cup: 1963–64, 1970–71 *(qf)*.
Champions League: 2005–06.
Fairs Cup: 1962–63, 1964–65, 1965–66.
UEFA Cup: 1975–76, 1978–79, 1979–80, 2005–06, 2007–08, 2008–09.
Europa League: 2009–10, 2014–15, 2017–18.
European Cup-Winners' Cup: 1966–67, 1984–85 *(winners)*, 1995–96.

Record League Victory: 9–1 v Manchester C, Division 1, 3 September 1906 – Scott; Balmer, Crelley; Booth, Taylor (1), Abbott (1); Sharp, Bolton (1), Young (4), Settle (2), George Wilson. 9–1 v Plymouth Arg, Division 2, 27 December 1930 – Coggins; Williams, Cresswell; McPherson, Griffiths, Thomson; Critchley, Dunn, Dean (4), Johnson (1), Stein (4).

Sun FACT FILE

A number of Everton players were caught up in the 'Bogota Affair' of 1951 when a group of English players travelled to Colombia to take part in a lucrative domestic competition outside the jurisdiction of FIFA. Two current players, Billy Higgins and Jack Hedley, travelled to South America although Hedley returned without signing. One of the main agents for the venture was the former Toffees player Jock Dodds.

Record Cup Victory: 11–2 v Derby Co, FA Cup 1st rd, 18 January 1890 – Smalley; Hannah, Doyle (1); Kirkwood, Holt (1), Parry; Latta, Brady (3), Geary (3), Edgar Chadwick, Millward (3).

Record Defeat: 4–10 v Tottenham H, Division 1, 11 October 1958.

Most League Points (2 for a win): 66, Division 1, 1969–70.

Most League Points (3 for a win): 90, Division 1, 1984–85.

Most League Goals: 121, Division 2, 1930–31.

Highest League Scorer in Season: William Ralph 'Dixie' Dean, 60, Division 1, 1927–28 (All-time League record).

Most League Goals in Total Aggregate: William Ralph 'Dixie' Dean, 349, 1925–37.

Most League Goals in One Match: 6, Jack Southworth v WBA, Division 1, 30 December 1893.

Most Capped Player: Tim Howard, 93 (121), USA.

Most League Appearances: Neville Southall, 578, 1981–98.

Youngest League Player: Jose Baxter, 16 years 191 days v Blackburn R, 16 August 2008.

Record Transfer Fee Received: £75,000,000 from Manchester U for Romelu Lukaku, July 2017.

Record Transfer Fee Paid: £40,000,000 (rising to £45,000,000) to Swansea C for Gylfi Sigurdsson, August 2017.

Football League Record: 1888 Founder Member of the Football League; 1930–31 Division 2; 1931–51 Division 1; 1951–54 Division 2; 1954–92 Division 1; 1992– FA Premier League.

MANAGERS

W. E. Barclay 1888–89
(Secretary-Manager)
Dick Molyneux 1889–1901
(Secretary-Manager)
William C. Cuff 1901–18
(Secretary-Manager)
W. J. Sawyer 1918–19
(Secretary-Manager)
Thomas H. McIntosh 1919–35
(Secretary-Manager)
Theo Kelly 1936–48
Cliff Britton 1948–56
Ian Buchan 1956–58
Johnny Carey 1958–61
Harry Catterick 1961–73
Billy Bingham 1973–77
Gordon Lee 1977–81
Howard Kendall 1981–87
Colin Harvey 1987–90
Howard Kendall 1990–93
Mike Walker 1994
Joe Royle 1994–97
Howard Kendall 1997–98
Walter Smith 1998–2002
David Moyes 2002–13
Roberto Martinez 2013–16
Ronald Koeman 2016–17
Sam Allardyce 2017–18
Marco Silva May 2018–

LATEST SEQUENCES

Longest Sequence of League Wins: 12, 24.3.1894 – 13.10.1894.

Longest Sequence of League Defeats: 6, 27.8.2005– 15.10.2005.

Longest Sequence of League Draws: 5, 4.5.1977 – 16.5.1977.

Longest Sequence of Unbeaten League Matches: 20, 29.4.1978 – 16.12.1978.

Longest Sequence Without a League Win: 14, 6.3.1937 – 4.9.1937.

Successive Scoring Runs: 40 from 15.3.1930.

Successive Non-scoring Runs: 6 from 27.8.2005.

TEN YEAR LEAGUE RECORD

		P	W	D	L	F	A	Pts	Pos
2008-09	PR Lge	38	17	12	9	55	37	63	5
2009-10	PR Lge	38	16	13	9	60	49	61	8
2010-11	PR Lge	38	13	15	10	51	45	54	7
2011-12	PR Lge	38	15	11	12	50	40	56	7
2012-13	PR Lge	38	16	15	7	55	40	63	6
2013-14	PR Lge	38	21	9	8	61	39	72	5
2014-15	PR Lge	38	12	11	15	48	50	47	11
2015-16	PR Lge	38	11	14	13	59	55	47	11
2016-17	PR Lge	38	17	10	11	62	44	61	7
2017-18	PR Lge	38	13	10	15	44	58	49	8

DID YOU KNOW ?

The first live televised Football League match involving Everton was the Merseyside derby at Anfield on 6 November 1983, with Liverpool winning 3-0. The first League match screened live from Goodison was the 1-1 draw with Chelsea on 16 March 1985.

EVERTON – PREMIER LEAGUE 2017–18 LEAGUE RECORD

Match No.	Date	Venue	Opponents	Result		H/T Score	Lg Pos.	Goalscorers	Attendance
1	Aug 12	H	Stoke C	W	1-0	1-0	5	Rooney [45]	39,045
2	21	A	Manchester C	D	1-1	1-0	8	Rooney [35]	54,009
3	27	A	Chelsea	L	0-2	0-2	12		41,382
4	Sept 9	H	Tottenham H	L	0-3	0-2	15		38,835
5	17	A	Manchester U	L	0-4	0-1	18		75,042
6	23	H	Bournemouth	W	2-1	0-0	13	Niasse 2 [77, 82]	38,133
7	Oct 1	H	Burnley	L	0-1	0-1	16		38,448
8	15	A	Brighton & HA	D	1-1	0-0	16	Rooney (pen) [90]	30,565
9	22	A	Arsenal	L	2-5	1-1	18	Rooney [12], Niasse [90]	39,189
10	29	A	Leicester C	L	0-2	0-2	18		31,891
11	Nov 5	H	Watford	W	3-2	0-0	15	Niasse [67], Calvert-Lewin [74], Baines (pen) [90]	38,609
12	18	A	Crystal Palace	D	2-2	2-2	16	Baines (pen) [6], Niasse [45]	25,526
13	26	A	Southampton	L	1-4	1-1	16	Sigurdsson [45]	30,461
14	29	H	West Ham U	W	4-0	2-0	13	Rooney 3 [18, 28, 66], Williams [78]	38,242
15	Dec 2	H	Huddersfield T	W	2-0	0-0	10	Sigurdsson [47], Calvert-Lewin [73]	39,167
16	10	A	Liverpool	D	1-1	0-1	10	Rooney (pen) [77]	53,082
17	13	A	Newcastle U	W	1-0	1-0	10	Rooney [27]	51,042
18	18	H	Swansea C	W	3-1	1-1	9	Calvert-Lewin [45], Sigurdsson [64], Rooney (pen) [73]	37,580
19	23	H	Chelsea	D	0-0	0-0	9		39,191
20	26	A	WBA	D	0-0	0-0	9		25,364
21	30	A	Bournemouth	L	1-2	0-1	9	Gana [57]	10,497
22	Jan 1	A	Manchester U	L	0-2	0-0	9		39,188
23	13	A	Tottenham H	L	0-4	0-1	9		76,251
24	20	H	WBA	D	1-1	0-1	9	Niasse [70]	39,061
25	31	H	Leicester C	W	2-1	2-0	9	Walcott 2 [25, 39]	38,390
26	Feb 3	A	Arsenal	L	1-5	0-4	10	Calvert-Lewin [64]	59,306
27	10	H	Crystal Palace	W	3-1	0-0	9	Sigurdsson [46], Niasse [51], Davies [75]	39,139
28	24	A	Watford	L	0-1	0-0	9		20,430
29	Mar 3	A	Burnley	L	1-2	1-0	10	Tosun [20]	20,802
30	10	H	Brighton & HA	W	2-0	0-0	9	Bong (og) [60], Tosun [76]	39,199
31	17	A	Stoke C	W	2-1	0-0	9	Tosun 2 [69, 84]	30,022
32	31	H	Manchester C	L	1-3	0-3	9	Bolasie [63]	39,221
33	Apr 7	H	Liverpool	D	0-0	0-0	9		39,220
34	14	A	Swansea C	D	1-1	1-0	9	Naughton (og) [43]	20,933
35	23	H	Newcastle U	W	1-0	0-0	8	Walcott [51]	39,061
36	28	A	Huddersfield T	W	2-0	1-0	8	Tosun [39], Gana [77]	24,121
37	May 5	H	Southampton	D	1-1	0-0	8	Davies [90]	38,225
38	13	A	West Ham U	L	1-3	0-1	8	Niasse [74]	56,926

Final League Position: 8

GOALSCORERS

League (44): Rooney 10 (3 pens), Niasse 8, Tosun 5, Calvert-Lewin 4, Sigurdsson 4, Walcott 3, Baines 2 (2 pens), Davies 2, Gana 2, Bolasie 1, Williams 1, own goals 2.
FA Cup (1): Sigurdsson 1.
Carabao Cup (4): Calvert-Lewin 3, Niasse 1.
Checkatrade Trophy (2): Adeniran 1, Donkor 1.
Europa League (12): Lookman 2, Vlasic 2, Baines 1, Calvert-Lewin 1, Gueye 1, Keane 1, Rooney 1, Sandro 1, Sigurdsson 1, Williams 1.

Pickford J 38	Keane M 29+1	Williams A 20+4	Jagielka P 23+2	Calvert-Lewin D 18+14	Schneiderlin M 24+6	Gana I 32+1	Baines L 22	Rooney W 27+4	Klaassen D 3+4	Sandro R 3+5	Martina C 20+1	Davies T 20+13	Mirallas K 2+3	Holgate M 13+2	Sigurdsson G 25+2	Besic M —+2	Lennon A 9+6	Vlasic N 7+5	Niasse O 10+12	Kenny J 17+2	Lookman A 1+6	Baningime B 1+7	Bolasie Y 11+5	McCarthy J 3+1	Tosun C 12+2	Walcott T 13+1	Coleman S 12	Mangala E 2	Funes Mori R 1+3	Match No.
1	2	3^3	4	5	6	7	8	9	10^2	11^1	12	13	14																	1
1	2	3^3	4	10	8^4	7	9	11^1	13					6^2	5	12	14													2
1	2	3	4^1	13		7	8	9		11^2				6^3	5		10	12	14											3
1		3	4		13	6	7^2	5	9						10				14											4
1	2	3	4	13	7	6^2	8	11^3		12	5	9^1	14		10															5
1		4		10	7	6	5	9^2	8^3		2^1	12		3	11				13	14										6
1	3	4		9	7^1	6	5	12		14	2	13			11		8^2	10^3												7
1	3	4		10	7	6^2	5^3	11		14	13	2		9	8		12													8
1	3	2^3	4	11^2		6^4	8	9^1				12			10		7	14	5	13										9
1		4	3	11		8	5	10^1				7	9^2		14	6^3		12	2		13									10
1	4		3	13		6	5	11^1				8		9^3		14		10	2	12	7^2									11
1	4		3	13	7^3	6	5			14		12		8	9^2		10	2	11^1											12
1	4^3	12	3	11	8	7	5^2					10^1		9	6	14		2	13											13
1		4	11^1		6		9^3			5	8			3	10		7^2	14		2	13	12								14
1	14	4		11	12	6		9^2						5	8^1		3	10	7^3		2	13								15
1		4	14	10	13	8		6^1				5		7^2	3	9		12	11^3		2									16
1		4	14	11	7	6		9^3				5	13	3	10^2	8^1		12	2											17
1		4	11		7^2	6		9^1	14			5		3	10	8^3			2	13										18
1	4	13	3	11	6	8^2		12		5		9^3			10	7^1			2	14										19
1	4	3	10^3	5				9	7^1		2	8		12		13	6		14	11^3										20
1	3		4	10	7	8^1		12		5		11		9		13	2	14	6^3											21
1	3	4		14	7			9^1		5	6		2		12	8	11^2		10^3	13										22
1		4	13	14	7		9			5		3	10	12			2		8^2	6^1	11^3									23
1		4		7			13			5		3	9		10^3	14	2		12	6^2	11^3	8								24
1	4	14	3	13	12	6		9^2		5	7				10^1				11^3						8	2				25
1	2^2	3		13	6	7		8		12					10^3	5			11		14		9^1			4				26
1	3	12			14	6^3	7			5	9				10			11	13						8	2^1	4^2			27
1	4	3		14		7		8^3		5	6				11^1				10^2	13					12	9	2			28
1	4	3^8		11		7		12		5	6^1					13			14					10^1	9	2				29
1	4		3	12		5	7	14			6^1		13	8							11^3		10		9^2	2				30
1	4		3	12	13	7	5	6^1							9^2	14									10^3	11	8	2		31
1	4		3	9^2	7		5	6^3							12								14		13	10	11^1	8	2	32
1	4		3	13	7	12	5	6^2							8^3										14	11^1	10	9	2	33
1	4		3		6	7^2	5	9^1							14						12	10^2			11	8	2	13		34
1	4		3	13	7^1	6	5	8							12							14			11^2	10^3	9	2		35
1	4		3		7	6	5	9^1				12			8^2	13									11^3	10	2		14	36
1	4		3^9		7	6	5			14		9			10^1	13						8^2			11		2		12	37
1	2		3		5	8	9			12		7^3				11						14			10^2	13	6	4^1		38

FA Cup

Third Round	Liverpool	(a)	1-2

Carabao Cup

Third Round	Sunderland	(h)	3-0
Fourth Round	Chelsea	(a)	1-2

Checkatrade Trophy (Everton U21)

Northern Group G	Notts Co	(a)	1-2
Northern Group G	Lincoln C	(a)	1-2
Northern Group G	Mansfield T	(a)	0-1

Europa League

Third Qualifying Round 1st leg	Ruzomberok	(h)	1-0
Third Qualifying Round 2nd leg	Ruzomberok	(a)	1-0
Play-off Round 1st leg	Hajduk Split	(h)	2-0
Play-off Round 2nd leg	Hajduk Split	(a)	1-1
Group E	Atalanta	(a)	0-3
Group E	Apollon Limassol	(a)	2-2
Group E	Lyon	(h)	1-2
Group E	Lyon	(a)	0-3
Group E	Atalanta	(h)	1-5
Group E	Apollon Limassol	(a)	3-0

EXETER CITY

FOUNDATION

Exeter City was formed in 1904 by the amalgamation of St Sidwell's United and Exeter United. The club first played in the East Devon League and then the Plymouth & District League. After an exhibition match between West Bromwich Albion and Woolwich Arsenal, which was held to test interest as Exeter was then a rugby stronghold, it was decided to form Exeter City. At a meeting at the Red Lion Hotel in 1908, the club turned professional.

St James Park, Stadium Way, Exeter, Devon EX4 6PX.

Telephone: (01392) 411 243.

Fax: (01392) 413 959.

Ticket Office: (01392) 411 243.

Website: www.exetercityfc.co.uk

Email: reception@exetercityfc.co.uk

Ground Capacity: 8,714.

Record Attendance: 20,984 v Sunderland, FA Cup 6th rd (replay), 4 March 1931.

Pitch Measurements: 104m × 64m (113.5yd × 70yd).

Chairman: Julian Tagg.

Trust Board Chairman: Nick Hawker.

Manager: Matt Taylor.

Director of Football: Steve Perryman.

Colours: Red and white striped shirts with red sleeves, black shorts, black socks with white hoops.

Year Formed: 1904.

Turned Professional: 1908.

Club Nickname: 'The Grecians'.

Ground: 1904, St James Park.

HONOURS

League Champions: Division 4 – 1989–90.
Runners-up: Division 3S – 1932–33; FL 2 – 2008–09; Division 4 – 1976–77; Conference – (4th) 2007–08 *(promoted via play-offs).*
FA Cup: 6th rd replay – 1931; 6th rd – 1981.
League Cup: never past 4th rd.

First Football League Game: 28 August 1920, Division 3, v Brentford (h) W 3–0 – Pym; Coleburne, Feebury (1p); Crawshaw, Carrick, Mitton; Appleton, Makin, Wright (1), Vowles (1), Dockray.

Record League Victory: 8–1 v Coventry C, Division 3 (S), 4 December 1926 – Bailey; Pollard, Charlton; Pullen, Pool, Garrett; Purcell (2), McDevitt, Blackmore (2), Dent (2), Compton (2). 8–1 v Aldershot, Division 3 (S), 4 May 1935 – Chesters; Gray, Miller; Risdon, Webb, Angus; Jack Scott (1), Wrightson (1), Poulter (3), McArthur (1), Dryden (1), (1 og).

Record Cup Victory: 14–0 v Weymouth, FA Cup 1st qual rd, 3 October 1908 – Fletcher; Craig, Bulcock; Ambler, Chadwick, Wake; Parnell (1), Watson (1), McGuigan (4), Bell (6), Copestake (2).

Record Defeat: 0–9 v Notts Co, Division 3 (S), 16 October 1948. 0–9 v Northampton T, Division 3 (S), 12 April 1958.

Sun FACT FILE

Exeter City manager Paul Tisdale made his first appearance as a player for over a decade when he came off the bench in added time at Hillsborough during the final game of the 2010–11 season. In August 2014 he was again included on the bench for the home fixture with Portsmouth due to an injury crisis, but was not used on that occasion.

Most League Points (2 for a win): 62, Division 4, 1976–77.

Most League Points (3 for a win): 89, Division 4, 1989–90.

Most League Goals: 88, Division 3 (S), 1932–33.

Highest League Scorer in Season: Fred Whitlow, 33, Division 3 (S), 1932–33.

Most League Goals in Total Aggregate: Tony Kellow, 129, 1976–78, 1980–83, 1985–88.

Most League Goals in One Match: 4, Harold 'Jazzo' Kirk v Portsmouth, Division 3 (S), 3 March 1923; 4, Fred Dent v Bristol R, Division 3 (S), 5 November 1927; 4, Fred Whitlow v Watford, Division 3 (S), 29 October 1932.

Most Capped Player: Joel Grant, 2 (14), Jamaica.

Most League Appearances: Arnold Mitchell, 495, 1952–66.

Youngest League Player: Ethan Ampadu, 15 years 337 days v Crawley T, 16 August 2016.

Record Transfer Fee Received: £1,750,000 from Swansea C for Matt Grimes, January 2015.

Record Transfer Fee Paid: £100,000 to Aberdeen for Jayden Stockley, August 2017.

Football League Record: 1920 Elected to Division 3; 1921–58 Division 3 (S); 1958–64 Division 4; 1964–66 Division 3; 1966–77 Division 4; 1977–84 Division 3; 1984–90 Division 4; 1990–92 Division 3; 1992–94 Division 2; 1994–2003 Division 3; 2003–08 Conference; 2008–09 FL 2; 2009–12 FL 1; 2012– FL 2.

LATEST SEQUENCES

Longest Sequence of League Wins: 7, 31.12.2016 – 4.2.2017.

Longest Sequence of League Defeats: 7, 14.1.1984 – 25.2.1984.

Longest Sequence of League Draws: 6, 13.9.1986 – 4.10.1986.

Longest Sequence of Unbeaten League Matches: 13, 23.8.1986 – 25.10.1986.

Longest Sequence Without a League Win: 18, 21.2.1995 – 19.8.1995.

Successive Scoring Runs: 22 from 15.9.1958.

Successive Non-scoring Runs: 6 from 17.1.1986.

MANAGERS

Arthur Chadwick 1910–22
Fred Mavin 1923–27
Dave Wilson 1928–29
Billy McDevitt 1929–35
Jack English 1935–39
George Roughton 1945–52
Norman Kirkman 1952–53
Norman Dodgin 1953–57
Bill Thompson 1957–58
Frank Broome 1958–60
Glen Wilson 1960–62
Cyril Spiers 1962–63
Jack Edwards 1963–65
Ellis Stuttard 1965–66
Jock Basford 1966–67
Frank Broome 1967–69
Johnny Newman 1969–76
Bobby Saxton 1977–79
Brian Godfrey 1979–83
Gerry Francis 1983–84
Jim Iley 1984–85
Colin Appleton 1985–87
Terry Cooper 1988–91
Alan Ball 1991–94
Terry Cooper 1994–95
Peter Fox 1995–2000
Noel Blake 2000–01
John Cornforth 2001–02
Neil McNab 2002–03
Gary Peters 2003
Eamonn Dolan 2003–04
Alex Inglethorpe 2004–06
Paul Tisdale 2006–18
Matt Taylor June 2018–

TEN YEAR LEAGUE RECORD

		P	W	D	L	F	A	Pts	Pos
2008-09	FL 2	46	22	13	11	65	50	79	2
2009-10	FL 1	46	11	18	17	48	60	51	18
2010-11	FL 1	46	20	10	16	66	73	70	8
2011-12	FL 1	46	10	12	24	46	75	42	23
2012-13	FL 2	46	18	10	18	63	62	64	10
2013-14	FL 2	46	14	13	19	54	57	55	16
2014-15	FL 2	46	17	13	16	61	65	64	10
2015-16	FL 2	46	17	13	16	63	65	64	14
2016-17	FL 2	46	21	8	17	75	56	71	5
2017-18	FL 2	46	24	8	14	64	54	80	4

DID YOU KNOW ❓

Exeter City's penalty shoot-out victory over Colchester United in the FA Cup first-round tie in November 1991 was only the second occasion that spot-kicks had been used in the competition. The Grecians drew the replay at St James Park 0-0 and progressed with a 4-2 win in the shoot-out.

EXETER CITY – SKY BET LEAGUE TWO 2017–18 LEAGUE RECORD

Match No.	Date	Venue	Opponents	Result	H/T Score	Lg Pos.	Goalscorers	Attendance
1	Aug 5	H	Cambridge U	W	1-0	1-0	8	Reid [5]	4282
2	12	A	Swindon T	D	1-1	1-0	7	McAlinden [28]	7795
3	19	H	Lincoln C	W	1-0	1-0	2	Reid [42]	3980
4	26	A	Cheltenham T	W	4-3	2-2	1	Moore-Taylor [39], Reid 2 (1 pen) [45, 77 (p)], Taylor [78]	3168
5	Sept 2	H	Newport Co	W	1-0	0-0	1	Holmes [57]	4193
6	9	A	Forest Green R	W	3-1	2-0	1	Sweeney [4], Reid 2 [18, 53]	2909
7	12	A	Barnet	W	2-1	0-0	1	Reid [78], Stockley [90]	1605
8	16	H	Crewe Alex	W	3-0	2-0	1	Tillson [7], Taylor [38], Stockley [76]	4218
9	23	A	Coventry C	L	0-2	0-0	2		8340
10	26	H	Notts Co	L	0-3	0-1	2		4760
11	30	H	Morecambe	W	4-1	3-1	2	Brown [20], Stockley 2 [24, 45], Moxey [48]	3651
12	Oct 7	A	Carlisle U	W	1-0	0-0	1	Sweeney [49]	4677
13	14	A	Wycombe W	D	0-0	0-0	2		5006
14	17	H	Luton T	L	1-4	1-1	3	Taylor [21]	4209
15	21	H	Port Vale	L	0-1	0-1	4		4258
16	28	A	Mansfield T	D	1-1	0-1	4	Holmes [86]	3608
17	Nov 11	H	Grimsby T	W	2-0	1-0	3	Stockley [29], McAlinden [53]	3854
18	18	A	Chesterfield	L	0-1	0-0	4		5195
19	21	H	Crawley T	L	1-3	1-1	4	Moxey [23]	1580
20	25	H	Accrington S	W	2-0	1-0	4	Boateng [45], Sweeney (pen) [86]	3597
21	Dec 9	A	Colchester U	L	1-3	0-3	4	Stockley [62]	3049
22	16	H	Stevenage	W	2-1	0-0	3	James [53], Sweeney [71]	3448
23	23	A	Yeovil T	L	1-3	0-1	3	Stockley [85]	4834
24	30	H	Barnet	W	2-1	1-0	4	Wilson [30], Taylor [90]	3869
25	Jan 1	A	Newport Co	L	1-2	0-1	7	Stockley [52]	3318
26	13	H	Coventry C	W	1-0	1-0	5	Harley [7]	4219
27	20	A	Notts Co	W	2-1	2-0	5	Taylor [8], Stockley [42]	6677
28	31	H	Forest Green R	W	2-0	0-0	4	Stockley [51], Sweeney (pen) [57]	3382
29	Feb 3	A	Luton T	L	0-1	0-1	6		8788
30	10	H	Wycombe W	D	1-1	1-0	7	James [12]	3956
31	17	H	Mansfield T	L	0-1	0-1	8		3680
32	20	A	Crewe Alex	W	2-1	0-0	7	Moore-Taylor [90], Stockley [90]	3081
33	24	A	Grimsby T	W	1-0	1-0	6	Stockley (pen) [37]	4151
34	Mar 10	A	Carlisle U	D	1-1	1-0	6	Moxey [42]	3488
35	13	H	Yeovil T	D	0-0	0-0	6		3913
36	17	A	Morecambe	L	1-2	1-1	8	Sweeney [37]	1056
37	20	A	Port Vale	W	1-0	1-0	6	Storey [24]	3138
38	24	H	Swindon T	W	3-1	2-1	5	Taylor [33], Sweeney (pen) [44], Stockley [87]	4567
39	30	H	Lincoln C	L	2-3	1-0	5	Stockley [10], Taylor [78]	9785
40	Apr 2	H	Cheltenham T	W	2-1	1-1	4	Simpson [42], Storey [81]	4420
41	7	A	Cambridge U	W	3-2	0-1	4	Stockley [59], Jay [84], Taylor [87]	4054
42	14	A	Accrington S	D	1-1	1-0	5	Stockley [21]	3135
43	17	H	Chesterfield	W	2-1	1-0	4	Stockley [39], Whitmore (og) [74]	3560
44	21	H	Crawley T	D	2-2	1-1	4	Stockley 2 [42, 57]	3998
45	28	A	Stevenage	L	1-3	0-2	4	Sweeney (pen) [78]	3399
46	May 5	H	Colchester U	W	1-0	0-0	4	Simpson [71]	4615

Final League Position: 4

GOALSCORERS

League (64): Stockley 19 (1 pen), Sweeney 8 (4 pens), Taylor 8, Reid 7 (1 pen), Moxey 3, Holmes 2, James 2, McAlinden 2, Moore-Taylor 2, Simpson 2, Storey 2, Boateng 1, Brown 1, Harley 1, Jay 1, Tillson 1, Wilson 1, own goal 1.

FA Cup (8): Stockley 5, McAlinden 1, Moore-Taylor 1, Sweeney 1 (1 pen).

Carabao Cup (1): Holmes 1.

Checkatrade Trophy (4): Edwards 1, McAlinden 1, Reid 1, Sparkes 1.

League Two Play-Offs (4): Boateng 1, Edwards 1, Harley 1, Stockley 1.

Pym C 46	Sweeney P 40	Moore-Taylor J 24	Brown T 25	Woodman C 28+5	Tillson J 35+2	James L 36+4	Taylor J 43+1	Wheeler D 2	Reid R 18+3	McAlinden L 17+12	Harley R 14+5	Brunt R —+1	Holmes L 20+7	Sparkes J —+3	Archibald-Henville T 12+3	Croll L 7+3	Jay M 5+12	Simpson R 5+6	Stockley J 34+7	Boateng H 28+10	Moxey D 30+4	Edwards K 7+16	Wilson K 14+5	Storey J 11+2	Byrne A —+1	Seaborne D 4+1	Loft R 1	Match No.
1	2	3	4	5	6	7	8	9	10^2	11^1	12	13																1
1	2	3	4	5	8	7	12	6^2	11	10^1			9	13														2
1	2		4	6	8	9	7		10^2	11^1			12	13	3^3	5	14											3
1	2	4	3	5	8	7	6		10^1	11^2			9						13	12								4
1	2	4	3	5	8	7	6		10^2	11^1			9						12	13								5
1	2	4	3	5	8	7	6		10^1	11^2			9						12	13								6
1	2	4	3	5^1	8	7	6		10^2	11^3			9						13	12	14							7
1	2	4	3	5^1	8	7	6		10^3	11^2			9						12	13	14							8
1	2	4^2	3	5^1	8	7	6		11	10^3			9						12	14	13							9
1	2		3	5	8^3	7	6		10	14			9		4^2				11	12	13							10
1	2		3	5	8^1	7	6		10^2						4	14			11	12	9^1	13						11
1	2		4	5	13	7	6		10^1	14			9		3^1				11	8^1	12							12
1	2	3	5	4		7	6		10^1	13			12						11	8^1	9							13
1	2	3		5^1	8	7	6		10^1	12			9³					13	11	4	14							14
1	2	4	3			7	6		10^3	12			14						13	11	8	5^1	9^2					15
1		4	3			7^1	6		11^2	13			12						10^3	8	5	9	2^8	14				16
1	2	4	3	5		7			10				6						11	8^1	9			12				17
1	2	3	4			5		12	7	13	11		6^3						10^2	8	9	14						18
1	2	4	3^2	5^1	8	7			11	12									13	9^1	10	6	14					19
1		3	5	4^1		8	7		10					12					11	9	6		2					20
1	2	4				6^2	7		11	14	10^3					3				12	8	9^1	13	5				21
1	2	4		5		7	6^1		10^2	9^3			12		14				11	8		13						22
1	2	3		5		7^1	6		12	11^3			9^2		14			4	10	8		13						23
1		4				7	6		13	12			9^3		14	10^1		11	8^4	5	2			3				24
1	2			5	7	8^1	6		13	14	11		12		4			10^1	9				3^2					25
1	2			12	7	8	10		9		6^1		4						11	13	5		3^3					26
1	2			5	9	8	6^1		7				10^2		3				11	13	4	12						27
1	2			5	6	7	9		8^1				11^2		3				10	4	12	13						28
1				6	7^1	9			13				12					14	10	8	5	11^3	2	3		4^1		29
1	2	4		12	7	8	9		10^1	13			6^3						11	5	14		3^2					30
1		4	3	5	8^1	7^1	6		13										10^2	12	9	14		9^2	2	11^3		31
1		3		5	7				6^1				11		4		12	13	10	8		9^2	2					32
1		3	4		8	12	10		6				9^1						11	7^2	5		2^8	13				33
1	2	4^2	3	12	7		11			8			9^1						10	6	5	13						34
1	2		3	5	7				13	9^2									11^1	10	8	4	12					35
1	2		3	12	7	7^1	9		8^3				4^2		13	14			10	6	5	11						36
1	3			8		6			11^2	9^1					13	12			10	7	5		2	4				37
1	3		5^1	7	14	6									13	10^3		11	8	9	12	2^2	4					38
1		5		13	7	8^1	10								2^1		12	11	6	9		4	3					39
1	2			5	8	7	9										12	10^1	11	6	4		3					40
1	2		5^2	7	6	8			14	12	10^1		11		9^3	3		13	4									41
1	3			7	6	11							12		9^1		10	8	5^2	13	2	4						42
1	3			7	6	8							5		12	11^1	10	9			2	4						43
1	2			7	6	8							4		11^1	13	10	9	5^1	13	12	3						44
1	2			8	7^1	6			14						4		11^2	10	9	5^1	13	12	3					45
1	2	4^1	13	7	14				10^1	9^2					3			11	8	5^3	6					12		46

FLEETWOOD TOWN

FOUNDATION

Originally formed in 1908 as Fleetwood FC, it was liquidated in 1976. Re-formed as Fleetwood Town in 1977, it folded again in 1996. Once again, it was re-formed a year later as Fleetwood Wanderers, but a sponsorship deal saw the club's name immediately changed to Fleetwood Freeport through the local retail outlet centre. This sponsorship ended in 2002, but since then local energy businessman Andy Pilley took charge and the club has risen through the non-league pyramid until finally achieving Football League status in 2012 as Fleetwood Town.

Highbury Stadium, Park Avenue, Fleetwood, Lancashire FY7 6TX.

Telephone: (01253) 775 080.

Ticket Office: (01253) 775 080.

Website: www.fleetwoodtownfc.com

Email: info@fleetwoodtownfc.com

Ground Capacity: 5,133.

Record Attendance: (Before 1997) 6,150 v Rochdale, FA Cup 1st rd, 13 November 1965; (Since 1997) 5,194 v York C, FL 2 Play-Off semi-final 2nd leg, 16 May 2014.

Pitch Measurements: 100.5m × 65m (110yd × 71yd).

Chairman: Andy Pilley.

Chief Executive: Steve Curwood.

Head Coach: Joey Barton.

First-Team Coaches: Barry Nicholson, Clint Hill, Steve Eyre.

Colours: Red shirts with white sleeves and red trim, white shorts with red trim, red socks.

Year Formed: 1908 (re-formed 1997).

Previous Names: 1908, Fleetwood FC; 1977, Fleetwood Town; 1997, Fleetwood Wanderers; 2002 Fleetwood Town.

Club Nicknames: 'The Trawlermen', 'The Cod Army'.

Grounds: 1908, North Euston Hotel; 1934, Memorial Park (now Highbury Stadium).

First Football League Game: 18 August 2012, FL 2, v Torquay U (h) D 0–0 – Davies; Beeley, Mawene, McNulty, Howell, Nicolson, Johnson, McGuire, Ball, Parkin, Mangan.

HONOURS

League Champions: Conference – 2011–12.
FA Cup: 3rd rd – 2012, 2017.
League Cup: never past 1st rd.

Sun FACT FILE

Fleetwood Town's Highbury Stadium has no connection with the former Arsenal ground of the same name and derives its title from its position behind Highbury Avenue in the town. When the club moved there in the summer of 1939 the local council funded the development of the ground including a new grandstand and cover on the popular side.

Record League Victory: 13–0 v Oldham T, North West Counties Div 2, 5 December 1998.

Record Defeat: 0–7 v Billingham T, FA Cup 1st qual'rd, 15 September 2001.

Most League Points (3 for a win): 82, FL 1, 2016–17.

Most League Goals: 66, FL 2, 2013–14.

Highest League Scorer in Season: David Ball, 14, FL 1, 2016–17.

Most League Goals in Total Aggregate: David Ball, 41, 2012–17.

Most League Goals in One Match: 3, Steven Schumacher v Newport Co, FL 2, 2 November 2013.

Most Capped Player: Conor McLaughlin, 26 (33), Northern Ireland.

Most League Appearances: David Ball, 179, 2012–17.

Youngest League Player: Jamie Allen, 17 years 227 days v Northampton T, 5 January 2013.

Record Transfer Fee Received: £1,000,000 (rising to £1,700,000) from Leicester C for Jamie Vardy, May 2012.

Record Transfer Fee Paid: £300,000 to Kidderminster H for Jamille Matt, January 2013.

Football League Record: 2012 Promoted from Conference Premier; 2012–14 FL 2; 2014– FL 1.

MANAGER

Alan Tinsley 1997
Mark Hughes 1998
Brian Wilson 1998–99
Mick Hoyle 1999–2001
Les Attwood 2001
Mark Hughes 2001
Alan Tinsley 2001–02
Mick Hoyle 2002–03
Tony Greenwood 2003–08
Micky Mellon 2008–12
Graham Alexander 2012–15
Steven Pressley 2015–16
Uwe Rosler 2016–18
John Sheridan 2018
Joey Barton June 2018–

LATEST SEQUENCES

Longest Sequence of League Wins: 5, 31.12.2016 – 24.1.2017.

Longest Sequence of League Defeats: 6, 20.1.2018 – 20.2.2018.

Longest Sequence of League Draws: 3, 24.2.2018 – 17.3.2018.

Longest Sequence of Unbeaten League Matches: 18, 19.11.2016 – 4.3.2017.

Longest Sequence Without a League Win: 9, 20.1.2018 – 17.3.2018.

Successive Scoring Runs: 24 from 2.5.2016.

Successive Non-scoring Runs: 4 from 22.2.2014.

TEN YEAR LEAGUE RECORD

		P	W	D	L	F	A	Pts	Pos
2008-09	Conf N	42	17	11	14	70	66	62	8
2009-10	Conf N	42	26	7	7	86	44	85	2
2010-11	Conf P	46	22	12	12	68	42	78	5
2011-12	Conf P	46	31	10	5	102	48	103	1
2012-13	FL 2	46	15	15	16	55	57	60	13
2013-14	FL 2	46	22	10	14	66	52	76	4
2014-15	FL 1	46	17	12	17	49	52	63	10
2015-16	FL 1	46	12	15	19	52	56	51	19
2016-17	FL 1	46	23	13	10	64	43	82	4
2017-18	FL 1	46	16	9	21	59	68	57	14

DID YOU KNOW ?

Devante Cole's goal in added time for Fleetwood Town against Southend United on 23 September 2017 was only a consolation for the home team who went down to a 4-2 defeat. However, it provided Fleetwood with a landmark 300th Football League goal in their 238th match in the competition.

FLEETWOOD TOWN – SKY BET LEAGUE ONE 2017–18 LEAGUE RECORD

Match No.	Date	Venue	Opponents	Result		H/T Score	Lg Pos.	Goalscorers	Attendance
1	Aug 5	H	Rotherham U	W	2-0	1-0	1	McAleny 2 [16, 66]	3623
2	12	A	Northampton T	W	1-0	0-0	3	Cole [75]	5124
3	19	H	AFC Wimbledon	W	2-0	1-0	3	Cole 2 [19, 57]	2730
4	26	A	Bristol R	L	1-3	0-2	5	Cole [60]	8363
5	Sept 9	H	Oldham Ath	D	2-2	1-1	9	Eastham [24], Hunter (pen) [90]	3606
6	12	H	Bury	W	3-2	2-2	7	Hiwula 2 [22, 28], Hunter [66]	2535
7	16	A	Portsmouth	L	1-4	0-1	7	Cole [52]	17,192
8	23	H	Southend U	L	2-4	1-3	10	Bell [4], Cole [90]	2874
9	26	A	Bradford C	W	3-0	0-0	9	Hiwula [51], Cole [56], Hunter [70]	18,799
10	30	H	Charlton Ath	L	1-3	1-2	11	Grant [25]	3009
11	Oct 7	A	Plymouth Arg	W	2-1	0-0	9	Hiwula [64], Bell [90]	8064
12	14	H	Rochdale	D	2-2	1-0	9	Eastham [25], Cole [83]	3260
13	17	A	Scunthorpe U	D	1-1	0-1	9	Hiwula [85]	3120
14	21	A	Shrewsbury T	L	0-1	0-0	11		5989
15	28	H	Oxford U	W	2-0	0-0	9	Grant [88], Ruffels (og) [90]	3261
16	31	A	Blackburn R	D	2-2	0-0	8	O'Neill [64], Burns [82]	10,399
17	Nov 11	A	Milton Keynes D	L	0-1	0-1	8		7827
18	18	H	Doncaster R	D	0-0	0-0	9		3181
19	21	A	Walsall	L	2-4	1-2	12	Hiwula [21], Bell [61]	3225
20	25	H	Blackpool	D	0-0	0-0	11		5035
21	Dec 9	A	Wigan Ath	L	0-2	0-2	14		8879
22	17	H	Peterborough U	L	2-3	0-2	15	Bell [29], Bolger [82]	2273
23	22	A	Gillingham	L	0-2	0-2	15		2088
24	26	A	Oldham Ath	W	2-1	0-0	14	Cole [50], Hunter [67]	4578
25	30	A	Bury	W	2-0	1-0	11	Hunter [24], Cole [47]	3158
26	Jan 1	H	Bradford C	L	1-2	1-0	12	Sowerby [21]	3089
27	13	A	Southend U	W	2-1	0-0	11	Diagouraga [57], Madden [62]	6489
28	20	H	Blackburn R	L	1-2	0-1	13	McAleny [55]	4391
29	27	A	Gillingham	L	1-2	1-0	15	Madden [13]	6332
30	Feb 3	H	Scunthorpe U	L	2-3	1-2	17	Hunter [45], Grant [67]	2901
31	13	A	Shrewsbury T	L	1-2	0-1	18	Madden [59]	2531
32	17	A	Doncaster R	L	0-3	0-2	20		7013
33	20	H	Portsmouth	L	1-2	0-1	20	McAleny [81]	2561
34	24	H	Milton Keynes D	D	1-1	0-1	20	Hunter [54]	2773
35	Mar 10	A	Plymouth Arg	D	1-1	0-1	21	Madden [56]	3079
36	17	A	Charlton Ath	D	0-0	0-0	20		9865
37	20	A	Rochdale	W	2-0	0-0	18	Madden [63], Hiwula [90]	2403
38	24	H	Northampton T	W	2-0	1-0	17	Dempsey [18], Bolger [83]	3049
39	30	A	AFC Wimbledon	W	1-0	1-0	15	Sowerby [22]	4378
40	Apr 2	H	Bristol R	W	2-0	0-0	13	Hunter [78], Hiwula [89]	2890
41	7	A	Rotherham U	L	2-3	1-1	13	Eastham [5], Bolger [54]	7562
42	10	A	Oxford U	W	1-0	0-0	11	McAleny [90]	6337
43	14	A	Blackpool	L	1-2	0-0	12	Burns [75]	7371
44	21	H	Wigan Ath	L	0-4	0-2	15		3836
45	28	A	Peterborough U	L	0-2	0-0	16		4667
46	May 5	H	Walsall	W	2-0	2-0	14	Hunter [31], Madden [45]	3644

Final League Position: 14

GOALSCORERS

League (59): Cole 10, Hunter 9 (1 pen), Hiwula 8, Madden 6, McAleny 5, Bell 4, Bolger 3, Eastham 3, Grant 3, Burns 2, Sowerby 2, Dempsey 1, Diagouraga 1, O'Neill 1, own goal 1.
FA Cup (5): Bolger 2, Cole 2, Sowerby 1.
Carabao Cup (1): Hiwula 1.
Checkatrade Trophy (14): Burns 3, Hiwula 3, Sowerby 2, Bolger 1, Cargill 1, Ekpolo 1, Grant 1 (1 pen), Reid 1, own goal 1.

Cairns A 38	Bolger C 41	Pond N 27 + 3	Eastham A 45	Coyle L 41 + 1	Dempsey K 45	Glendon G 23 + 7	Bell A 27	Grant R 19 + 10	McAleny C 15 + 14	Hiwula J 21 + 22	O'Neill A 13 + 8	Cole D 24 + 4	Hunter A 24 + 20	Burns W 12 + 16	Schwabl M 8 + 2	Nadesan A — + 1	Cargill B 9 + 2	Sowerby J 15 + 7	Ekpolo G 1 + 2	Biggins H 2 + 5	Neal C 8	Diagouraga T 17	Madden P 17 + 3	Jones G 8 + 2	O'Connor K 4	Oliver C — + 1	Maguire J 2	Match No.
1	2	3	4	5	6	7^1	8	9	10^2	11^3	12	13	14															1
1	2	3	4	5	6	7^1	8	9	11^2	10^1	13	14			12													2
1	2	3	4	5	6		8	9		10^1	7^2	11^3	12		13	14												3
1	4	3^1	5	2	8		6	9^2	10^2	7	11	12	13				14											4
1	3		2	5	6	12	8	9^1		10^1	7	11	13	14			4^3											5
1	3		2	5	6	12	8		11^3	7^1	10	13	14				4	9^2										6
1	4^2	3	5	2	8^4	7	6	12	11^3	9^1	10	14					13											7
1	2	3	4^2	5	12	9	8	13	7^1	11	14	10^3	6^1															8
1	2	3	4	5	7	6^2	9	8	10^1	11^3	12	14						13										9
1	9	5	4^1	2^3	7	10^3	3	8	6	13	11	14						12										10
1	2	3	4	5	6	7^1	9	8	10^2	12	11			13														11
1	2	3^1	4	5	6	9	8^3	14	10^2	7	11	13	12^4															12
1	4	3^1	2	5	6	7^1	8	9	12	11	14	10^2	13															13
1	4	3	2	7		6	12	10^1	13	9^3	11	14			8^2		5											14
1	3		2	5	6	7^1	8	9	11^2	12	14	10^1	13				4											15
1	4	3	2	7	9	6	8^1	11^3	12	13	10	14					5^2											16
1	4	3		8	9	6		10	7^3	11	13	2^1						5^2	14	12								17
1	3	2		6	7^1	9		10^1	8^3	11	13	5	14				4			12								18
1	3	2		6	13	9		10	8	12	11^3	14	7^1				4^2			5								19
1	2	3	4		8	7	9	10^1	12	11	13	5						6^2										20
1	8	3	4	2	6^1	10	5	12	11	14	7^3							9^2			13							21
1	4	3^1	2	5	6	7	9	12	8^2	11	14	10^1						13										22
1	3^1	14	2	5	6	7	9	10	8^3	11	13						4^2	12										23
	3	12	2	5	6	8	9	13	11	7^2	10^1	4								1								24
	3		2	5	6	8	9	12	13	11^2	7^1	10^3	4					14		1								25
	4		3	2	7	8	5	13	9^1	11	10^2	12						6		1								26
	3	4		2	2^3	8		5	13	10^2	11	9^1	7							1		6	12	14				27
	4		3	2	8	12		13	10^1	14	9^3	6^2								1		7	11	5				28
	4		3	2	6	8^2		12	11^3	14	9^1	13								1		7	10		5			29
	4	3^1		2	6	7^2		12	11^1	14	9									1		8^2	10		5	13		30
1		3	4	14	8		7	13	12	9								10^1				6^1	11		2^5		5	31
1	4		3	2	6		8^3	13	12	11		9^2										7	10	14	5^1			32
1	4		3	2	5^3	6		8	13		11^1	12						14		7^2			10				9	33
1	4		3	2	6	7		11	13		9							12				8^2	10^1		5			34
1		4	3	2	7	8^1		11^3	13		9	14					6	12					10^2	5				35
1	4	3	2	7				12	13		9	11^1					6					8	10^2	5				36
1	4	6	3	2	9			13	8^2	12	10						5					7	11^1					37
1	2	3	4	5	6	14		12	11^2	13	9						8^3					7	10^1					38
1	4	3	2	5	6			13	10^2	12	9						7					8	11^1					39
1	4	3	2	5	6			13	10^3	12	9	14					8^4					7	11^1					40
1	4	3	2	5	6			12	10^3	13	9	14					8^2					7	11^1					41
1	4		3	2	6^2	14		9^3	13	11^1	10						8					7	12	5				42
1		2	3	5	8			14	10^1	13		9	12				7^3					6	11^2	4				43
1	4		3	2	6			8^1	14	10		11^2	9^1									13	7	12	5			44
	4	3	2	5	6	7		14	10^2	12		9					8^1		13	1			11^3					45
1	4	14	3	2	6			9^3	12	13		11					8					7	10^2	5^1				46

FA Cup

First Round	Chorley		(a)	2-1
Second Round	Hereford		(h)	1-1
Replay	Hereford		(a)	2-0
Third Round	Leicester C		(h)	0-0
Replay	Leicester C		(a)	0-2

Carabao Cup

First Round	Carlisle U		(h)	1-2
(aet)				

Checkatrade Trophy

Northern Group A	Leicester C U21	(h)	3-0
Northern Group A	Morecambe	(h)	2-1
Northern Group A	Carlisle U	(a)	2-1
Second Round North	Chesterfield	(h)	2-0
Third Round	Bury	(a)	3-2
Quarter-Final	Yeovil T	(a)	2-3

FOREST GREEN ROVERS

FOUNDATION

A football club was recorded at Forest Green as early as October 1889, established by Rev Edward Peach, a local Congregationalist minister. This club joined the Mid-Gloucestershire League for 1894–95 but disappeared around 1896 and was reformed as Forest Green Rovers in 1898. Rovers affiliated to the Gloucestershire county FA from 1899–1900 and competed in local leagues, mostly the Stroud & District and Dursley & District Leagues before joining the Gloucestershire Senior League North in 1937, where they remained until 1968. They became founder members of the Gloucestershire County League in 1968 and progressed to the Hellenic League in 1975. Success over Rainworth MW in the 1982 FA Vase final at Wembley was the start of the club's rise up the pyramid, firstly to the Southern League for the 1982–83 season and then the Football Conference from 1998–99. Rovers reached the play-offs in 2014–15 and 2015–16, losing to Bristol Rovers and Grimsby Town respectively, before finally achieving their goal of a place in the Football League with their 3-1 Play-Off victory over Tranmere Rovers on 14 May 2017.

The New Lawn Stadium, Another Way, Nailsworth, GL6 0FG.

Telephone: (01453) 834 860.

Fax: (01453) 835 291.

Ticket Office: (01453) 834 860.

Website: forestgreenroversfc.com

Email: reception@forestgreenroversfc.com

Ground Capacity: 4,803.

Record Attendance: 4,836 v Derby Co, FA Cup 3rd rd, 3 January 2009.

Pitch Measurements: 100m × 65m (109.5yd × 71yd).

Chairman: Dale Vince.

Chief Executive: Helen Taylor.

Manager: Mark Cooper.

Assistant Manager: Scott Lindsey.

Colours: Green and black hooped shirts, green shorts with black trim, green and black hooped socks.

Year Formed: 1889.

Previous Names: 1889, Forest Green; 1898, Forest Green Rovers; 1911, Nailsworth & Forest Green United; 1919 Forest Green Rovers; 1989, Stroud; 1992, Forest Green Rovers.

HONOURS

League Champions: Southern League – 1997–98.

FA Cup: 3rd rd – 2008–09, 2009–10.

FA Trophy: Runners-up: 1998–99, 2000–01.

FA Vase: Winners: 1981–82.

The Sun FACT FILE

The 2017–18 season was not the first occasion that Forest Green Rovers had competed in the EFL Trophy. In the early 2000s the number of entries was supplemented by teams from the Football Conference and in 2003–04 Rovers were drawn away to Brighton & Hove Albion in what was then the LDV Vans Trophy. They lost 2-0 in front of a crowd of 3,969.

Club Nicknames: Rovers, The Green, FGR, The Little Club on the Hill, Green Army, The Green Devils.

Grounds: 1890, The Lawn Ground; 2006, The New Lawn.

Record Victory: 8–0 v Fareham T, Southern League Southern Division, 1996–97; 8–0 v Hyde U, Football Conference, 10 August 2013.

Record Defeat: 0–10 v Gloucester, Mid-Gloucestershire League, 13 January 1900.

Most League Points (3 for a win): 47, FL 2, 2017–18.

Most League Goals: 54, FL 2, 2017–18.

Highest League Scorer in Season: Christian Doidge, 20, FL 2, 2017–18.

Most League Goals in Total Aggregate: Christian Doidge, 20, 2017–18.

Most League Goals in One Match: No more than two by one player.

Most Capped Player: Omar Chaaban, 1, Lebanon.

Most League Appearances: Lee Collins, 43, 2017–18.

Youngest League Player: Jordan Stevens, 17 years 171 days v Lincoln C, 12 September 2017.

Record Transfer Fee Received: £35,000 from Oxford U for Wayne Hatswell, December 2000; £35,000 from Nuneaton Bor for Marc McGregor, June 2000.

Record Transfer Fee Paid: £25,000 to Bury for Adrian Randall, August 1999.

Football League Record: 2017 Promoted from National League; 2017– FL 2.

MANAGERS

Bill Thomas 1955–56
Eddie Cowley 1957–58
Don Cowley 1958–60
Jimmy Sewell 1966–67
Alan Morris 1967–68
Peter Goring 1968–79
Tony Morris 1979–80
Bob Mursell 1980–82
Roy Hillman 1982
Steve Millard 1983–87
John Evans 1987–90
Jeff Evans 1990
Bobby Jones 1990–91
Tim Harris 1991–92
Pat Casey 1992–94
Frank Gregan 1994–2000
Nigel Spink and David Norton 2000–01
Nigel Spink 2001–02
Colin Addison 2002–03
Tim Harris 2003–04
Alan Lewer 2004–05
Gary Owers 2005–06
Jim Harvey 2006–09
Dave Hockaday 2009–13
Adrian Pennock 2013–16
Mark Cooper May 2016–

LATEST SEQUENCES

Longest Sequence of League Wins: 3, 17.10.2017 – 28.10.2017.

Longest Sequence of League Defeats: 5, 9.12.2017 – 1.1.2018.

Longest Sequence of League Draws: no more than 1.

Longest Sequence of Unbeaten League Matches: 5, 3.2.2018 – 6.3.2018.

Longest Sequence Without a League Win: 10, 26.8.2017 – 14.10.2017.

Successive Scoring Runs: 10 from 3.2.2018.

Successive Non-scoring Runs: 3 from 9.12.2017.

TEN YEAR LEAGUE RECORD

		P	W	D	L	F	A	Pts	Pos
2008-09	Conf	46	12	16	18	70	76	52	18
2009-10	Conf	46	12	9	23	50	76	45	21
2010-11	Conf	46	10	16	20	53	72	46	20
2011-12	Conf	46	19	13	14	66	45	70	10
2012-13	Conf	46	18	11	17	63	49	65	10
2013-14	Conf	46	19	10	17	80	66	67	10
2014-15	Conf	46	22	16	8	80	54	79*	5
2015-16	NL	46	26	11	9	69	42	89	2
2016-17	NL	46	25	11	10	88	56	86	3
2017-18	FL 2	46	13	8	25	54	77	47	21

3 pts deducted.

DID YOU KNOW ?

Goalkeeper Jack Brock was one of the first Forest Green Rovers players to go on to play in the Football League. An amateur, Jack played for Forest Green in the Stroud & District League before going on to make five appearances for Swindon Town in the 1936–37 season.

FOREST GREEN ROVERS – SKY BET LEAGUE TWO 2017–18 LEAGUE RECORD

Match No.	Date	Venue	Opponents	Result	H/T Score	Lg Pos.	Goalscorers	Attendance
1	Aug 5	H	Barnet	D	2-2	2-0	13	Doidge 2 [41, 43]	3171
2	12	A	Mansfield T	L	0-2	0-0	21		3826
3	19	H	Yeovil T	W	4-3	2-3	15	Doidge [23], Brown [45], Cooper [49], Bugiel [79]	2615
4	26	A	Colchester U	L	1-5	1-2	19	Noble [23]	3047
5	Sept 2	A	Wycombe W	L	1-3	0-3	22	Doidge [68]	3759
6	9	H	Exeter C	L	1-3	0-2	22	Mullings [75]	2909
7	12	H	Lincoln C	L	0-1	0-0	23		1887
8	16	A	Port Vale	D	1-1	0-1	22	Bugiel [68]	3910
9	22	H	Swindon T	L	0-2	0-0	23		3305
10	26	A	Cambridge U	L	0-3	0-1	24		3545
11	30	H	Accrington S	L	0-1	0-0	24		2594
12	Oct 7	A	Notts Co	D	1-1	1-0	22	Bugiel [30]	13,267
13	14	H	Newport Co	L	0-4	0-2	23		2864
14	17	A	Coventry C	W	1-0	1-0	23	Marsh-Brown [29]	6366
15	21	A	Stevenage	W	2-1	0-1	23	Brown [61], Doidge [73]	2099
16	28	H	Morecambe	W	2-0	1-0	20	Marsh-Brown [30], Laird [64]	2515
17	Nov 11	A	Crawley T	D	1-1	0-0	21	Doidge [67]	2149
18	18	H	Crewe Alex	W	3-2	1-1	18	Doidge 2 [44, 83], Iacovitti [90]	2221
19	21	A	Chesterfield	L	2-3	0-2	20	Doidge 2 [60, 90]	4306
20	25	H	Cheltenham T	D	1-1	1-1	20	Doidge [8]	3641
21	Dec 9	A	Grimsby T	L	0-1	0-1	23		4398
22	16	H	Luton T	L	0-2	0-1	24		2546
23	23	H	Carlisle U	L	0-1	0-1	24		2489
24	30	A	Lincoln C	L	1-2	1-1	24	Doidge [24]	8964
25	Jan 1	H	Wycombe W	L	1-2	0-2	24	Fitzwater [70]	2727
26	6	H	Port Vale	W	1-0	0-0	22	Reid [61]	2437
27	13	A	Swindon T	L	0-1	0-0	23		7062
28	20	H	Cambridge U	W	5-2	2-2	23	Doidge 2 [18, 82], Grubb 2 [43, 74], Campbell [90]	2228
29	27	A	Carlisle U	L	0-1	0-1	23		4176
30	31	A	Exeter C	L	0-2	0-0	23		3382
31	Feb 3	H	Coventry C	W	2-1	1-0	22	Bray [39], Collins, L [64]	3623
32	13	H	Stevenage	W	3-1	1-1	20	Reid [45], Rawson [61], Doidge [81]	1825
33	17	A	Morecambe	D	1-1	1-0	21	Clements [13]	1447
34	24	H	Crawley T	W	2-0	2-0	19	Reid [10], Doidge [24]	2346
35	Mar 6	A	Newport Co	D	3-3	2-3	18	Butler (og) [6], Gunning [30], Collins, L [82]	2862
36	10	H	Notts Co	L	1-2	0-1	19	Campbell [72]	2893
37	17	A	Accrington S	L	1-3	0-1	21	Reid [64]	2313
38	20	A	Crewe Alex	L	1-3	0-1	21	Grubb [64]	3274
39	24	H	Mansfield T	W	2-0	0-0	20	Reid [54], Grubb [78]	2827
40	Apr 2	H	Colchester U	L	1-2	1-1	21	Reid (pen) [37]	2869
41	7	A	Barnet	L	0-1	0-1	22		1764
42	14	A	Cheltenham T	W	1-0	1-0	21	Doidge [43]	4744
43	21	H	Chesterfield	W	4-1	1-1	20	Laird [27], Doidge 2 (1 pen) [78, 90 (p)], Grubb [90]	3336
44	24	H	Yeovil T	D	0-0	0-0	20		2789
45	28	A	Luton T	L	1-3	0-1	21	Doidge [53]	10,029
46	May 5	H	Grimsby T	L	0-3	0-0	21		3880

Final League Position: 21

GOALSCORERS

League (54): Doidge 20 (1 pen), Reid 6 (1 pen), Grubb 5, Bugiel 3, Brown 2, Campbell 2, Collins, L 2, Laird 2, Marsh-Brown 2, Bray 1, Clements 1, Cooper 1, Fitzwater 1, Gunning 1, Iacovitti 1, Mullings 1, Noble 1, Rawson 1, own goal 1.
FA Cup (5): Doidge 4 (1 pen), Laird 1.
Carabao Cup (0).
Checkatrade Trophy (5): Brown 1, Doidge 1, James 1, Stevens 1, Wishart 1.

Collins B 39	Bennett D 33	Collins L 40 + 3	Monthe E 9 + 4	Evans C 2	Laird S 28 + 8	Traore D 17 + 3	Noble L 9	Cooper C 22 + 3	Brown R 23 + 10	Doidge C 41 + 1	Mullings S 2 + 5	Marsh-Brown K 9 + 5	Bugiel O 3 + 16	Fitzwater J 12 + 2	James L 9 + 5	Wishart D 20 + 12	Iacovitti A 10 + 4	Roberts M 11 + 3	Russell S 5	Toni Gomes C 3 + 6	Randall W 5 + 2	Stevens J 2 + 7	Osbourne J 35 + 1	Simpson J 1	Gunning G 21	Rawson F 18	Reid R 20 + 1	Grubb D 16 + 5	Hollis H 19	Whittle A — + 2	Campbell T 3 + 11	Bray A 6 + 5	Clements C 11 + 3	Belford C 2 + 1	Match No.
1	2	3	4		5³	6	7¹	8	9	10²	11	12	13	14																					1
1	2	3	4		6¹	7²	8	9	11³	10	12				5	13	14																		2
1	2	7	3		5		6	8	9¹	11			13		4²	10³	14	12																	3
1	2	6			5	12	8³	7	9¹	10	14	13			11²		4	3																	4
	2		12		5	8³	7	6		10	14		11		9²	3¹	4	1	13																5
1	3	2	4		5	6	7	8³		10²	14	13		12		9¹	11																		6
1	2	4			5		7	8		11	10³	12	6²			3	13	9¹	14																7
1	2	4			5	13	8	7		10	11³	14	9¹			3	12	6²																	8
1	2²	3			5	7³	8	6		10		13			12	4	9¹	11		14															9
	2	3			14	7¹		13	10	11			6²	5³	4	11	12	9		8															10
	2	4			13	8		7	9¹	10	11²		12	5³		3	1		14	6															11
	2	4			6²		7		11		9	10¹	5	13	3	3	1	12		8															12
	2	3			7	6²	8³	10		13	14	11¹	5		4	1	12	9																	13
1	2	3			5	6	8¹	14	11	10³	12	4		13	9²	7																			14
1	5	2			9	7	8	10	11¹	12	4		3		6	7																			15
1	5	3	12		9	8¹	6	11	10²	13	2		4		7																				16
1		3	4²		5	6¹	11³	10	9		2	13	12	8	14	7																			17
1	5	3	14		8¹	7³	9	11	10²	13	2	12	4		6																				18
1	5	3	13⁴		9²	7¹	8	11	10³	2	14	12	4		6																				19
1	5	3			8²	7	10³	11	9	14	2	13	4	12	6¹																				20
1		7			6		8²	10³	11	14	5⁴	2¹	9	4	3	12	13																		21
1		3			2	12	7	10³	11	5¹		4	14	9		13	8²		6																22
1	5²	3			4	9¹	6	11		10³	13	2	8	14		12	7																		23
1		2	4		5		6	9²	11	12		14	8³	10¹	3		13	7																	24
1		2	3	5²	4¹		7⁴	10	11	12	14	13	9			6³	8																		25
1		6	2		5			9¹	10				8				7				3	4	11	12											26
1		8	4		12			11		13		9¹					7				3	2³	10	6²	5	14									27
1	5	2						7	11				9³			14	8				3		10²	6¹		4	12	13							28
1	5³	3						6²	10				12			14	8				2	4	11³	7	9		13								29
1	2	7			12			14	10²				6				8³				3	4	11	9	5¹		13								30
1	2	8						10					13				7³				3	4	11²	9	5		14	6¹	12						31
1	2				12			10					9				7				4	3	11²	6	5		13		8¹						32
1	2					13		10					9²				8				3	4	11	6	5			12	7						33
1	2	13			14			10					12				8				3	4	11	9¹	5			6²	7²						34
1	2	13						14	10¹				12				8				3	4	11	9	5			6²	7³						35
1	2¹	7						12	14				11				8				4	3	10	9³	5		13	6²							36
1		7						2³	12				11¹				6				3	4	10	13	5		9		8						37
	2	7			5			11²	14								6				3	4¹	10	9		12	13		8³	1					38
1	2	8²			12								5				7				3	11	9	4	10	6¹	13								39
1	2	7¹			13			14	12				5				8				4		10	9	3	11¹	6⁴								40
1	2	7³						12	10				14				8				5	4	11	9	3²		6¹	13							41
1		2			5			9²	11								6				8	3	10¹	12	4		14	13	7²						42
1		2			5			9¹	10								6				8	4	11²	12	3		14	13	7³						43
1³		13			6			2	14	10							8				5	4	11²	9¹	3			7	12						44
	2				5			13	10¹	11							7				8	4	12	9²	3		14		6³	1					45
1		2			5			7	9³	10							8¹				6	4	11²	12	3		14	13							46

FA Cup

First Round	Macclesfield T	(h)	1-0	
Second Round	Exeter C	(h)	3-3	
Replay	Exeter C	(a)	1-2	
(aet)				

Carabao Cup

First Round	Milton Keynes D	(h)	0-1
(aet)			

Checkatrade Trophy

Southern Group E	Newport Co	(h)	2-0
Southern Group E	Cheltenham T	(a)	2-1
Southern Group E	Swansea C U21	(h)	0-2
Second Round South	Swindon T	(a)	1-0
Third Round	Yeovil T	(a)	0-2

FULHAM

FOUNDATION

Churchgoers were responsible for the foundation of Fulham, which first saw the light of day as Fulham St Andrew's Church Sunday School FC in 1879. They won the West London Amateur Cup in 1887 and the championship of the West London League in its initial season of 1892–93. The name Fulham had been adopted in 1888.

Craven Cottage, Stevenage Road, London SW6 6HH.
Telephone: (0843) 208 1222.
Fax: (0870) 442 0236.
Ticket Office: (0203) 871 0810.
Website: www.fulhamfc.com
Email: enquiries@fulhamfc.com
Ground Capacity: 25,700.
Record Attendance: 49,335 v Millwall, Division 2, 8 October 1938.
Pitch Measurements: 100m × 65m (109.5yd × 71yd).
Chairman: Shadid Khan.
Chief Executive: Alistair Mackintosh.
Head Coach: Slavisa Jokanovic.
Assistant Head Coach: Javier Pereira.
Colours: White shirts with black trim, black shorts with white trim, white socks with black trim.
Year Formed: 1879.
Turned Professional: 1898.
Reformed: 1987.
Previous Name: 1879, Fulham St Andrew's; 1888, Fulham.
Club Nickname: 'The Cottagers'.

HONOURS

League Champions: First Division – 2000–01; Division 2 – 1948–49; Second Division – 1998–99; Division 3S – 1931–32.
Runners-up: Division 2 – 1958–59; Division 3 – 1970–71; Third Division – 1996–97.
FA Cup: Runners-up: 1975.
League Cup: quarter-final – 1968, 1971, 2000, 2005.
European Competitions
UEFA Cup: 2002–03.
Europa League: 2009–10 *(runners-up)*, 2011–12.
Intertoto Cup: 2002 *(winners)*.

Grounds: 1879, Star Road, Fulham; c.1883, Eel Brook Common, 1884, Lillie Road; 1885, Putney Lower Common; 1886, Ranelagh House, Fulham; 1888, Barn Elms, Castelnau; 1889, Purser's Cross (Roskell's Field), Parsons Green Lane; 1891, Eel Brook Common; 1891, Half Moon, Putney; 1895, Captain James Field, West Brompton; 1896, Craven Cottage.

First Football League Game: 3 September 1907, Division 2, v Hull C (h) L 0–1 – Skene; Ross, Lindsay; Collins, Morrison, Goldie; Dalrymple, Freeman, Bevan, Hubbard, Threlfall.

Record League Victory: 10–1 v Ipswich T, Division 1, 26 December 1963 – Macedo; Cohen, Langley; Mullery (1), Keetch, Robson (1); Key, Cook (1), Leggat (4), Haynes, Howfield (3).

Record Cup Victory: 7–0 v Swansea C, FA Cup 1st rd, 11 November 1995 – Lange; Jupp (1), Herrera, Barkus (Brooker (1)), Moore, Angus, Thomas (1), Morgan, Brazil (Hamill), Conroy (3) (Bolt), Cusack (1).

Record Defeat: 0–10 v Liverpool, League Cup 2nd rd 1st leg, 23 September 1986.

Most League Points (2 for a win): 60, Division 2, 1958–59 and Division 3, 1970–71.

Sun FACT FILE

Craven Cottage staged its first international match in March 1907 when England met Wales. An attendance of 22,000 turned out for a midweek game that saw Wales lead at half-time through a goal from William Jones before Jimmy Stewart equalised for England to leave the final score 1-1. To mark the occasion the referee was presented with a silver whistle.

Most League Points (3 for a win): 101, Division 2, 1998–99. 101, Division 1, 2000–01.

Most League Goals: 111, Division 3 (S), 1931–32.

Highest League Scorer in Season: Frank Newton, 43, Division 3 (S), 1931–32.

Most League Goals in Total Aggregate: Gordon Davies, 159, 1978–84, 1986–91.

Most League Goals in One Match: 5, Fred Harrison v Stockport Co, Division 2, 5 September 1908; 5, Bedford Jezzard v Hull C, Division 2, 8 October 1955; 5, Jimmy Hill v Doncaster R, Division 2, 15 March 1958; 5, Steve Earle v Halifax T, Division 3, 16 September 1969.

Most Capped Player: Johnny Haynes, 56, England.

Most League Appearances: Johnny Haynes, 594, 1952–70.

Youngest League Player: Matthew Briggs, 16 years 65 days v Middlesbrough, 13 May 2007.

Record Transfer Fee Received: £15,000,000 from Tottenham H for Mousa Dembélé, August 2012.

Record Transfer Fee Paid: £12,400,000 to Olympiacos for Konstantinos Mitroglou, January 2014.

Football League Record: 1907 Elected to Division 2; 1928–32 Division 3 (S); 1932–49 Division 2; 1949–52 Division 1; 1952–59 Division 2; 1959–68 Division 1; 1968–69 Division 2; 1969–71 Division 3; 1971–80 Division 2; 1980–82 Division 3; 1982–86 Division 2; 1986–92 Division 3; 1992–94 Division 2; 1994–97 Division 3; 1997–99 Division 2; 1999–2001 Division 1; 2001–14 FA Premier League; 2014–18 FL C; 2018– FA Premier League.

LATEST SEQUENCES

Longest Sequence of League Wins: 12, 7.5.2000 – 18.10.2000.

Longest Sequence of League Defeats: 11, 2.12.1961 – 24.2.1962.

Longest Sequence of League Draws: 6, 23.12.2006 – 20.1.2007.

Longest Sequence of Unbeaten League Matches: 23, 23.12.2017 – 27.4.2018.

Longest Sequence Without a League Win: 15, 25.2.1950 – 23.8.1950.

Successive Scoring Runs: 26 from 28.3.1931.

Successive Non-scoring Runs: 6 from 21.8.1971.

MANAGERS

Harry Bradshaw 1904–09
Phil Kelso 1909–24
Andy Ducat 1924–26
Joe Bradshaw 1926–29
Ned Liddell 1929–31
Jim McIntyre 1931–34
Jimmy Hogan 1934–35
Jack Peart 1935–48
Frank Osborne 1948–64
   (was Secretary-Manager or General Manager for most of this period and Team Manager 1953–56)
Bill Dodgin Snr 1949–53
Duggie Livingstone 1956–58
Bedford Jezzard 1958–64
   (General Manager for last two months)
Vic Buckingham 1965–68
Bobby Robson 1968
Bill Dodgin Jnr 1968–72
Alec Stock 1972–76
Bobby Campbell 1976–80
Malcolm Macdonald 1980–84
Ray Harford 1984–96
Ray Lewington 1986–90
Alan Dicks 1990–91
Don Mackay 1991–94
Ian Branfoot 1994–96
   (continued as General Manager)
Micky Adams 1996–97
Ray Wilkins 1997–98
Kevin Keegan 1998–99
   (Chief Operating Officer)
Paul Bracewell 1999–2000
Jean Tigana 2000–03
Chris Coleman 2003–07
Lawrie Sanchez 2007
Roy Hodgson 2007–10
Mark Hughes 2010–11
Martin Jol 2011–13
Rene Muelenstein 2013–14
Felix Magath 2014
Kit Symons 2014–15
Slavisa Jokanovic December 2015–

TEN YEAR LEAGUE RECORD

		P	W	D	L	F	A	Pts	Pos
2008-09	PR Lge	38	14	11	13	39	34	53	7
2009-10	PR Lge	38	12	10	16	39	46	46	12
2010-11	PR Lge	38	11	16	11	49	43	49	8
2011-12	PR Lge	38	14	10	14	48	51	52	9
2012-13	PR Lge	38	11	10	17	50	60	43	12
2013-14	PR Lge	38	9	5	24	40	85	32	19
2014-15	FL C	46	14	10	22	62	83	52	17
2015-16	FL C	46	12	15	19	66	79	51	20
2016-17	FL C	46	22	14	10	85	57	80	6
2017-18	FL C	46	25	13	8	79	46	88	3

DID YOU KNOW ?

Centre-forward Ronnie Rooke set a club record when he scored all six of Fulham's goals in their FA Cup third-round tie against Bury at Craven Cottage on 7 January 1939. Fulham wore red shirts borrowed from Charlton Athletic for the game because their normal kit clashed with the visitors' shirts.

FULHAM – SKY BET CHAMPIONSHIP 2017–18 LEAGUE RECORD

Match No.	Date	Venue	Opponents	Result	H/T Score	Lg Pos.	Goalscorers	Attendance
1	Aug 5	H	Norwich C	D	1-1	1-0	11	Martin (og) [25]	20,134
2	12	A	Reading	D	1-1	0-0	13	Piazon [82]	17,398
3	15	A	Leeds U	D	0-0	0-0	15		28,918
4	19	H	Sheffield W	L	0-1	0-0	19		20,165
5	26	A	Ipswich T	W	2-0	1-0	14	Kebano [35], Rui Fonte [51]	16,844
6	Sept 9	H	Cardiff C	D	1-1	0-0	13	Sessegnon, R [75]	20,984
7	13	H	Hull C	W	2-1	1-0	13	Ayite [42], Johansen [62]	15,792
8	16	A	Burton Alb	L	1-2	1-1	14	Norwood [31]	4049
9	23	H	Middlesbrough	D	1-1	0-0	14	Kamara [86]	20,718
10	26	A	Nottingham F	W	3-1	1-1	11	Kamara [13], Johansen [72], Kebano [89]	21,208
11	29	A	QPR	W	2-1	1-0	8	Robinson (og) [41], Johansen [85]	16,415
12	Oct 14	H	Preston NE	D	2-2	0-2	9	Norwood (pen) [74], Odoi [90]	18,435
13	21	A	Aston Villa	L	1-2	1-1	11	Johansen [45]	30,724
14	28	H	Bolton W	D	1-1	0-1	13	Cairney [90]	18,792
15	31	H	Bristol C	L	0-2	0-2	15		17,634
16	Nov 3	A	Wolverhampton W	L	0-2	0-2	16		24,388
17	18	H	Derby Co	D	1-1	1-0	17	Norwood [30]	18,192
18	21	A	Sheffield U	W	5-4	3-2	14	Ojo 2 [28, 69], Sessegnon, R 3 [30, 43, 78]	25,445
19	25	H	Millwall	W	1-0	1-0	12	Norwood (pen) [45]	17,984
20	Dec 2	A	Brentford	L	1-3	1-1	15	Kebano [25]	11,090
21	9	H	Birmingham C	W	1-0	1-0	12	Ojo [14]	19,644
22	16	A	Sunderland	L	0-1	0-0	12		25,904
23	23	H	Barnsley	W	2-1	0-0	11	Ayite [54], Ojo [72]	17,308
24	26	A	Cardiff C	W	4-2	1-0	11	Ream [12], Ayite [56], Sessegnon, R [78], Johansen [90]	21,662
25	30	A	Hull C	D	2-2	0-2	12	Kamara 2 (1 pen) [48 (p), 85]	15,701
26	Jan 2	H	Ipswich T	W	4-1	0-1	10	Sessegnon, R 2 [69, 74], Kamara 2 [72, 76]	17,415
27	13	A	Middlesbrough	W	1-0	0-0	8	Norwood (pen) [90]	23,850
28	20	H	Burton Alb	W	6-0	3-0	7	Rui Fonte 2 [18, 38], Piazon [34], Sessegnon, R 2 [72, 79], Kamara [88]	19,003
29	27	A	Barnsley	W	3-1	0-1	6	Sessegnon, R 2 [49, 90], McDonald [90]	12,147
30	Feb 3	H	Nottingham F	W	2-0	0-0	5	Piazon [67], Johansen [90]	22,076
31	10	A	Bolton W	D	1-1	1-0	5	Targett [4]	14,386
32	17	H	Aston Villa	W	2-0	0-0	5	Sessegnon, R [52], Ayite [71]	24,547
33	21	A	Bristol C	D	1-1	1-1	5	Mitrovic [14]	21,236
34	24	A	Wolverhampton W	W	2-0	1-0	5	Sessegnon, R [38], Mitrovic [71]	23,510
35	Mar 3	A	Derby Co	W	2-1	2-0	4	Mitrovic [10], Sessegnon, R [22]	27,138
36	6	H	Sheffield U	W	3-0	2-0	4	Mitrovic 2 [31, 44], Cairney [61]	18,400
37	10	A	Preston NE	W	2-1	0-0	4	Mitrovic 2 [69, 90]	12,970
38	17	H	QPR	D	2-2	2-1	3	Cairney [32], Piazon [45]	23,347
39	30	A	Norwich C	W	2-0	0-0	3	Johansen [66], Cairney [70]	26,750
40	Apr 3	H	Leeds U	W	2-0	1-0	3	McDonald [33], Mitrovic [63]	21,538
41	7	A	Sheffield W	W	1-0	0-0	3	Mitrovic [78]	25,653
42	10	H	Reading	W	1-0	1-0	2	Johansen [25]	19,272
43	14	H	Brentford	D	1-1	0-0	3	Mitrovic [70]	20,877
44	20	A	Millwall	W	3-0	0-0	2	Sessegnon, R [46], McDonald [56], Mitrovic [89]	17,614
45	27	H	Sunderland	W	2-1	1-1	2	Piazon [45], Mitrovic [76]	21,849
46	May 6	A	Birmingham C	L	1-3	0-2	3	Cairney [84]	27,608

Final League Position: 3

GOALSCORERS

League (79): Sessegnon, R 15, Mitrovic 12, Johansen 8, Kamara 7 (1 pen), Cairney 5, Norwood 5 (3 pens), Piazon 5, Ayite 4, Ojo 4, Kebano 3, McDonald 3, Rui Fonte 3, Odoi 1, Ream 1, Targett 1, own goals 2.
FA Cup (0).
Carabao Cup (2): Odoi 1, Piazon 1.
Checkatrade Trophy (8): Adebayo 2, Graham 2, George C Williams 1 (1 pen), Humphrys 1, Thompson 1, Thorsteinsson 1.
Championship Play-Offs (3): Cairney 1, Odoi 1, Sessegnon R 1.

Button D 20	Fredericks R 44	Kalas T 29+4	Ream T 44	Sessegnon R 45+1	Cairney T 30+4	Norwood O 22+14	Johansen S 43+2	Aluko S 4	Ayite F 23+5	Kebano N 10+16	Kamara A 8+22	Cisse I 2+4	Odoi D 30+8	McDonald K 42	Piazon L 14+8	Rui Fonte P 16+11	Ojo S 18+4	Mollo V 2+4	Graham J —+3	De La Torre L —+5	Rafa Soares L —+3	Edun T 1+1	Djalo M —+2	Bettinelli M 26	Targett M 17+1	Mitrovic A 15+2	Christie C 1+4	Match No.
1	2	3	4	5^1	6	7^1	8	9	10^1	11	12	13	14															1
1	2	3^1	4	5		6	8^1	9	10^3	11^2	14		12	7	11^2													2
1	2		4	5	13	8	9		12	10^1	6	3	7	11^2														3
1	2	3	4	11	6	12	8^3	9^2		13	14		5	7^1		10												4
1	2	3	4	5	8	13	9^3		10^1	12			14	6		11^1	7											5
1	2	3	4	10		12	9	11		13	6^1	5	7				8^2											6
1	2^1	3	4	5		6	8		10	11^2	13		14	7			9^3	12										7
1	2	3	4	5		8^1	6		10	11^2				7		12	9	13										8
1	2	3	4	5		6^3	9^2		10^1	12	13	14		7		11	8											9
1	2	3	4	10		12	7			13	11		5^2	6		9^1	8^3	14										10
1	2	3	4	5		6	8			12		14	13	7		10^2	9^3	11^1										11
1		3	4	5	12	6	8^1		11	9^2			2	7		10	13											12
1	2	3	4	5	12	6^5	8^1		11	14	10	13		7		9^3												13
1	2	3^1	4	5	6	8^2	13		11	12	10			7		9^3			14									14
1	5	3^1	4	9	8	13	6^3		10^2	11^1			2	7		12				14								15
1	2		4	5		6	8		9^1	11^2	14		3	7		10^3	12			13								16
1	2	3	4	11	6	7			9		12		5			10^1			13		8^2							17
1	2	3	4	10	9	7	14		11^3		12		5	6^1		13	8^2											18
1	2	3		5		6	7	8^1		11^3	12		4			10^2	9				13	14						19
1	2	3		5		6	8	10^3		11^3			4^1	7		12	9^1		14	13								20
	2	3	4	5	8	6	10^3			11^1	12		7			13	9^2					14	1					21
	2	3^1	4	5	6	8^3	10			13			7			11^2	9	12	14				1					22
	2	3	4	5	8	14	6		11^3	12	10^1			7		13	9^2						1					23
	2	3	4	11^3	6		8		10^2	13			5	7	14	12	9^1						1					24
	2	3	4	11	6		8		10^2	13	12		5^5	7	14		9^1						1					25
	2		4	5^5	6	7	8		11^2	12	10		3		13		9^1			14			1					26
	2	12	4	5		6	8		14	10^2			3	7		9^3	9^3						1					27
	2	3	4	11	12	6^2	8			13			5	7		9^3	10^1			14			1					28
	2	3	4	11		6	8^1		13	14			5^2	7		9^3	10						1		12			29
	2	3	4	10		6	9	13					14	7		8^1	11^3						1	5^2	12			30
	2	3	4	10	14	6^2	9			12			7			8^1	11^3						1	5	13			31
	2	3	4	11	6		8^2		9^1		12		14	7		13							1	5	10^3			32
		4	11	8^3	14	6			12		13		3	7		9							1	5^2	10^1	2		33
	2	3	4	11	6^2		8		9^1				13	7			12						1	5	10			34
	2		4	11	6	12	8^2		9^3				3	7	13		14						1	5	10			35
	2		4	11	6	13	8^2						3	7	12	14	9^3						1	5	10^1			36
	2^1		4	11^3	6		8		9^2				3	7	12		14						1	5	10	13		37
	2		4	11^3	6^2		8		12				3	7	9^1	14	13						1	5	10			38
	2		4	12	8	13	6		11^2		14		3	7^1	9								1	5	10^1			39
	2	13	4	11	8	12	6		9^2				3	7^1									1	5	10			40
	2		4	10	9		7		12^2	13			3	6			8^1						1	5	11			41
	2		4	11	6	13	8^1		12				3	7	9^2								1	5	10			42
	2		4	11	8	14	6^1		12^2				3	7	9^2								1	5	10	13		43
	2^2	12	4	11	6		8						3	7	9^2								1	5	10	13		44
	2	14	4	11	6^1		8			12			3	7	9^2	13							1	5^3	10			45
	2^3		4	11	8		6		13		12		3	7	9^1								1	5^2	10	14		46

FA Cup
Third Round   Southampton   (h)   0-1

Carabao Cup
First Round   Wycombe W   (a)   2-0
Second Round   Bristol R   (h)   0-1

Checkatrade Trophy (Fulham U21)
Southern Group A   Portsmouth   (a)   3-3
(Fulham U21 won 4-2 on penalties)

Southern Group A   Charlton Ath   (a)   2-3
Southern Group A   Crawley T   (a)   3-1

Championship Play-Offs
Semi-Final 1st leg   Derby Co   (a)   0-1
Semi-Final 2nd leg   Derby Co   (h)   2-0
Final   Aston Villa   (Wembley)   1-0

GILLINGHAM

FOUNDATION

The success of the pioneering Royal Engineers of Chatham excited the interest of the residents of the Medway Towns and led to the formation of many clubs including Excelsior. After winning the Kent Junior Cup and the Chatham District League in 1893, Excelsior decided to go for bigger things and it was at a meeting in the Napier Arms, Brompton, in 1893 that New Brompton FC came into being, buying and developing the ground which is now Priestfield Stadium. They changed their name to Gillingham in 1913, when they also changed their strip from black and white stripes to predominantly blue.

MEMS Priestfield Stadium, Redfern Avenue, Gillingham, Kent ME7 4DD.

Telephone: (01634) 300 000.

Fax: (01634) 850 986.

Ticket Office: (01634) 300 000 (option 1).

Website: www.gillinghamfootballclub.com

Email: info@gillinghamfootballclub.com

Ground Capacity: 11,440 (subject to segregation).

Record Attendance: 23,002 v QPR, FA Cup 3rd rd, 10 January 1948.

Pitch Measurements: 100.5m × 64m (110yd × 70yd).

Chairman: Paul D. P. Scally.

Manager: Steve Lovell.

First-Team Coaches: Mark Patterson, Ian Cox.

Colours: Blue shirts with white trim, blue shorts with white trim, white socks with blue trim.

Year Formed: 1893.

Turned Professional: 1894.

Previous Name: 1893, New Brompton; 1913, Gillingham.

Club Nickname: 'The Gills'.

Ground: 1893, Priestfield Stadium (renamed KRBS Priestfield Stadium 2009, MEMS Priestfield Stadium 2011).

First Football League Game: 28 August 1920, Division 3, v Southampton (h) D 1–1 – Branfield; Robertson, Sissons; Battiste, Baxter, Wigmore; Holt, Hall, Gilbey (1), Roe, Gore.

Record League Victory: 10–0 v Chesterfield, Division 3, 5 September 1987 – Kite; Haylock, Pearce, Shipley (2) (Lillis), West, Greenall (1), Pritchard (2), Shearer (2), Lovell, Elsey (2), David Smith (1).

Record Cup Victory: 10–1 v Gorleston, FA Cup 1st rd, 16 November 1957 – Brodie; Parry, Hannaway; Riggs, Boswell, Laing; Payne, Fletcher (2), Saunders (5), Morgan (1), Clark (2).

Record Defeat: 2–9 v Nottingham F, Division 3 (S), 18 November 1950.

Most League Points (2 for a win): 62, Division 4, 1973–74.

HONOURS

League Champions: FL 2 – 2012–13; Division 4 – 1963–64.
Runners-up: Third Division – 1995–96; Division 4 – 1973–74.
FA Cup: 6th rd – 2000.
League Cup: 4th rd – 1964, 1997.

Sun FACT FILE

Gillingham's FA Cup sixth qualifying-round tie with Barrow in 1924–25 took five games and nine hours to resolve. The teams drew 0-0 in Kent then 1-1 in the replay at Barrow after extra time. Further replays took place at Molineux and Highbury before Barrow ran out 2-1 winners in the fourth replay at Millwall.

Most League Points (3 for a win): 85, Division 2, 1999–2000.

Most League Goals: 90, Division 4, 1973–74.

Highest League Scorer in Season: Ernie Morgan, 31, Division 3 (S), 1954–55; Brian Yeo, 31, Division 4, 1973–74.

Most League Goals in Total Aggregate: Brian Yeo, 135, 1963–75.

Most League Goals in One Match: 6, Fred Cheesmur v Merthyr T, Division 3 (S), 26 April 1930.

Most Capped Player: Andrew Crofts, 13 (includes 1 on loan from Brighton & HA) (29), Wales.

Most League Appearances: John Simpson, 571, 1957–72.

Youngest League Player: Luke Freeman, 15 years 247 days v Hartlepool U, 24 November 2007.

Record Transfer Fee Received: £1,500,000 from Manchester C for Robert Taylor, November 1999.

Record Transfer Fee Paid: £600,000 to Reading for Carl Asaba, August 1998.

Football League Record: 1920 Original Member of Division 3; 1921 Division 3 (S); 1938 Failed re-election; Southern League 1938–44; Kent League 1944–46; Southern League 1946–50; 1950 Re-elected to Division 3 (S); 1958–64 Division 4; 1964–71 Division 3; 1971–74 Division 4; 1974–89 Division 3; 1989–92 Division 4; 1992–96; Division 3; 1996–2000 Division 2; 2000–04 Division 1; 2004–05 FL C; 2005–08 FL 1; 2008–09 FL 2; 2009–10 FL 1; 2010–13 FL 2; 2013– FL 1.

LATEST SEQUENCES

Longest Sequence of League Wins: 7, 18.12.1954 – 29.1.1955.

Longest Sequence of League Defeats: 10, 20.9.1988 – 5.11.1988.

Longest Sequence of League Draws: 5, 21.1.2017 – 14.2.2017.

Longest Sequence of Unbeaten League Matches: 20, 13.10.1973 – 10.2.1974.

Longest Sequence Without a League Win: 15, 1.4.1972 – 2.9.1972.

Successive Scoring Runs: 20 from 31.10.1959.

Successive Non-scoring Runs: 6 from 11.2.1961.

MANAGERS

W. Ironside Groombridge 1896–1906 *(Secretary-Manager)* *(previously Financial Secretary)*
Steve Smith 1906–08
W. I. Groombridge 1908–19 *(Secretary-Manager)*
George Collins 1919–20
John McMillan 1920–23
Harry Curtis 1923–26
Albert Hoskins 1926–29
Dick Hendrie 1929–31
Fred Mavin 1932–37
Alan Ure 1937–38
Bill Harvey 1938–39
Archie Clark 1939–58
Harry Barratt 1958–62
Freddie Cox 1962–65
Basil Hayward 1966–71
Andy Nelson 1971–74
Len Ashurst 1974–75
Gerry Summers 1975–81
Keith Peacock 1981–87
Paul Taylor 1988
Keith Burkinshaw 1988–89
Damien Richardson 1989–92
Glenn Roeder 1992–93
Mike Flanagan 1993–95
Neil Smillie 1995
Tony Pulis 1995–99
Peter Taylor 1999–2000
Andy Hessenthaler 2000–04
Stan Ternent 2004–05
Neale Cooper 2005
Ronnie Jepson 2005–07
Mark Stimson 2007–10
Andy Hessenthaler 2010–12
Martin Allen 2012–13
Peter Taylor 2013–14
Justin Edinburgh 2015–17
Adrian Pennock 2017
Steve Lovell November 2017–

TEN YEAR LEAGUE RECORD

		P	W	D	L	F	A	Pts	Pos
2008-09	FL 2	46	21	12	13	58	55	75	5
2009-10	FL 1	46	12	14	20	48	64	50	21
2010-11	FL 2	46	17	17	12	67	57	68	8
2011-12	FL 2	46	20	10	16	79	62	70	8
2012-13	FL 2	46	23	14	9	66	39	83	1
2013-14	FL 1	46	15	8	23	60	79	53	17
2014-15	FL 1	46	16	14	16	65	66	62	12
2015-16	FL 1	46	19	12	15	71	56	69	9
2016-17	FL 1	46	12	14	20	59	79	50	20
2017-18	FL 1	46	13	17	16	50	55	56	17

DID YOU KNOW ?

Gillingham took part in the very first Division Three end-of-season play-offs in May 1987. After seeing off Sunderland in the semi-finals on the away goals rule, they met Swindon in the final over two legs. A 2-2 draw meant the teams had to replay at Selhurst Park and the Gills went down to a 2-0 defeat.

GILLINGHAM – SKY BET LEAGUE ONE 2017–18 LEAGUE RECORD

Match No.	Date	Venue	Opponents	Result	H/T Score	Lg Pos.	Goalscorers	Attendance
1	Aug 5	A	Doncaster R	D	0-0	0-0	14		7512
2	12	H	Bradford C	L	0-1	0-1	18		5267
3	19	A	Milton Keynes D	L	0-1	0-0	20		7901
4	26	H	Southend U	D	3-3	0-1	21	Eaves 3 [56, 63, 80]	5339
5	Sept 2	H	Shrewsbury T	L	1-2	0-2	22	Parker [76]	4080
6	9	A	Oxford U	L	0-3	0-0	23		6730
7	12	A	AFC Wimbledon	D	1-1	1-1	24	Clare [45]	3819
8	16	H	Charlton Ath	W	1-0	0-0	20	Eaves [54]	7216
9	23	A	Rochdale	L	0-3	0-2	22		2793
10	26	H	Scunthorpe U	D	0-0	0-0	22		4002
11	30	A	Blackburn R	L	0-1	0-1	23	O'Neill [55]	10,844
12	Oct 8	H	Portsmouth	L	0-1	0-0	23		8163
13	14	A	Peterborough U	W	1-0	1-0	22	Martin [35]	5257
14	17	H	Wigan Ath	D	1-1	0-0	22	Eaves [55]	4705
15	21	H	Northampton T	L	1-2	0-1	23	Martin [62]	4640
16	28	A	Rotherham U	W	3-1	1-0	22	Parker 2 [2, 86], Eaves [47]	7865
17	Nov 11	H	Bury	D	1-1	0-1	21	Parker [85]	4364
18	18	A	Walsall	W	1-0	1-0	20	Wilkinson [44]	4917
19	21	A	Blackpool	D	1-1	0-1	20	Eaves [90]	2650
20	25	H	Oldham Ath	D	0-0	0-0	21		4364
21	Dec 9	A	Plymouth Arg	L	1-2	0-0	21	Eaves [84]	11,155
22	16	H	Bristol R	W	4-1	2-0	19	Byrne 2 [28, 53], Lacey [37], Parker [47]	4227
23	22	A	Fleetwood T	W	2-0	2-0	17	Parker [2], O'Neill [15]	2088
24	26	A	Oxford U	D	1-1	0-0	17	Wilkinson [87]	5555
25	30	H	AFC Wimbledon	D	2-2	0-0	18	Francomb (og) [62], Ehmer [69]	6419
26	Jan 1	A	Charlton Ath	W	2-1	2-0	15	Parker [11], Eaves [32]	11,979
27	13	H	Rochdale	W	2-1	1-1	14	Garmston [41], Martin [63]	4352
28	20	A	Scunthorpe U	W	3-1	1-0	11	Martin [25], Parker [68], Eaves [73]	4905
29	27	A	Fleetwood T	W	2-1	0-1	10	Eaves 2 (1 pen) [53, 90 (p)]	6332
30	Feb 3	A	Wigan Ath	L	0-2	0-2	12		8384
31	10	H	Peterborough U	D	1-1	0-0	13	Ehmer [90]	7154
32	13	A	Northampton T	W	2-1	2-0	12	Parker [6], Eaves [18]	5123
33	17	H	Walsall	D	0-0	0-0	11		4682
34	20	A	Shrewsbury T	D	1-1	0-1	11	Byrne [82]	4839
35	24	A	Bury	L	1-2	0-2	11	Ogilvie [69]	3004
36	Mar 10	H	Portsmouth	W	3-1	0-1	11	Wilkinson [48], Martin 2 [66, 80]	18,247
37	24	A	Bradford C	L	0-1	0-0	13		19,654
38	29	H	Milton Keynes D	L	1-2	1-1	13	Nasseri [41]	5540
39	Apr 2	A	Southend U	L	0-4	0-4	15		8466
40	7	H	Doncaster R	D	0-0	0-0	16		4870
41	10	H	Blackburn R	D	0-0	0-0	15		6361
42	14	A	Oldham Ath	D	1-1	0-1	16	Eaves (pen) [90]	3850
43	17	H	Rotherham U	L	0-1	0-1	16		4029
44	21	H	Blackpool	L	0-3	0-2	17		5580
45	28	A	Bristol R	D	1-1	0-0	17	List [90]	9715
46	May 5	H	Plymouth Arg	W	5-2	3-1	17	Parker [7], Eaves 3 [30, 36, 51], List [90]	6269

Final League Position: 17

GOALSCORERS

League (50): Eaves 17 (2 pens), Parker 10, Martin 6, Byrne 3, Wilkinson 3, Ehmer 2, List 2, Clare 1, Garmston 1, Lacey 1, Nasseri 1, O'Neill 1, Ogilvie 1, own goal 1.
FA Cup (4): Eaves 1, O'Neill 1, Parker 1, Wagstaff 1.
Carabao Cup (0).
Checkatrade Trophy (11): Oldaker 2, Byrne 1 (1 pen), Cundle 1, Ehmer 1, M'Bo 1, O'Neill 1, Parker 1, Wagstaff 1, Wilkinson 1, own goal 1.

Holy T 45	O'Neill L 36 + 2	Zakuani G 40	Ehmer M 41 + 1	Wagstaff S 19 + 12	Bingham B 9	Martin L 33 + 2	Byrne M 41 + 1	Ogilvie C 28 + 9	Eaves T 34 + 7	Parker J 35 + 7	Wilkinson C 17 + 17	Wright J 2 + 1	Nash L 2 + 10	Lacey A 10 + 1	Oldaker D — + 3	Nugent B 17 + 6	Cundle G 1 + 5	Clare S 20 + 1	Hessenthaler J 33 + 4	List E 7 + 16	Starkey J — + 1	O'Mara F 1 + 1	Tucker J — + 1	Garmston B 16 + 3	Reilly C 15	Moussa F — + 2	Nasseri D 2 + 2	Murphy R 1	Haddler T 1	Match No.
1	2	3	4	5^1	6^1	7	8	9	10^2	11	12	13	14																	1
1	5	3	2	14		7	6^1	9	12	10^3	11■	8	13	4^2																2
1	5	3	2			7	6	9	10	11^2		8	12	4^1	13															3
1	5	4^3	3^2		6	8	7	9	10	12	11^1		2			13	14													4
1	2^1				6	8	9^2	7	5	10	12					11^3	3	4	14	13										5
1	3^1	14	5			7	8	9	10^2	13	11^3	12	2			4			6											6
1	2	3		6		9■	8	5	11	12	10^1					4		7												7
1	2^3	3^2	6	7^1		8	13	10	12	11						4		9	14											8
1	2	3	6^1	8		7	11■	13	10^2	12						5		4	9											9
1	2^3	4	8			9	6	12								3		5	10^2	7	11^1	13								10
1		3	7			10	2^2	5		6	11^3					4	14	9^1	8	13		12								11
1		3	7			9^2	5		6	11			14		4^3	10^1	8	13		2	12									12
1		4	3	13	9	10	8^2	12		6	14					2	7	11^1				5^3								13
1		4	3	12	8	9		5	11^1	6					13	2	7	10^2												14
1		3	2		8	7		4	10^1	9						5	6	11				12								15
1	14	4^2	3	13	6	8		12	11	9						2	7	10^1				5^3								16
1	2	3				7	8	4	10	9	12					5	6	11^1												17
1	5^2	3	7^1	13		6	12	4	11^3	9	10^1			14		2	8													18
1	5	3		12		6	7^2	4	10	9	11^1			14		2	8^3	13												19
1	2	3		12		8	6	5^1	10	11						4	7		12											20
1	2	3		9		8	6	5	10	11						4	7	12												21
1	2	3	6			9^2	8		11	10	14			5^1		4	7^3	12						13						22
1	2	4	3			6^2	9	8	5	10^1	11	13					7	12												23
1	2	4	3			9^3	7^1	5	11^2	10	13					12	8	6	14											24
1	2	4	3			7	5	12	9	10^2				14		11^3	6	8						13						25
1	2	4	3			9^1	6	12	10	11^2	13		14				7	8						5^3						26
1	2	4	3	7^2		9	6	13	10	11							8	12						5^1						27
1	2	4	3			9	7	13	11^2	10	12						8							5^1	6					28
1	2	4^3	3			9	6	12	10	11^1			14				7	13						5^2	8					29
1	2	4	3			7^1	8		10^2	11^3	14						6	12						5	9	13				30
1	2	4	3	12			7	13	10	11	14						6	9^3						5^2	8^1					31
1	5	3	2	13		12	8	9	10	11						4^1	6							7^2						32
1	5^1	3	2	13		7	9	10	11	12						4	6							8^2						33
1	2	4	3			12	8	6	10^2	11	13					5	7							9^1						34
1	9	3^2	2	13		8	7	5	10^1	11	12					4	6													35
1	2	3	4	5^3		7^1	6	10^2	11	12						8	13							9		14				36
1	2	5	4	6		8	11^3	12	13	10		14				7^1								3	9^2					37
1	2	4	3	8^2		7	5	12	11	13						6								10			9^1			38
1	2^3	4	3	6		10■	7	5^2	11	12			14			8^1								9			13			39
1		3	2	5		7	13		10^3							4		6	14		8		12		9^1		11^2			40
1		3	2	5		7			11^2	10^1	13					4		6	12						9^1	8				41
1	13	3	2	5		7		12	11	10^2				4^1		6	14							9■	8					42
1	2	4^1	3	6		8	5^2	13	11	10	12					7								9						43
	2		3	12		9^1	6	5^3	10	11		14				4		7	13					8^2					1	44
1	2	3	4	7		9	6	10^1	11^3	12		13												5	8					45
1	2	4	3	7		9^2	6	10^3	11^1	13		12	14											5	8					46

GRIMSBY TOWN

FOUNDATION

Grimsby Pelham FC, as they were first known, came into being at a meeting held at the Wellington Arms in September 1878. Pelham is the family name of big landowners in the area, the Earls of Yarborough. The receipts for their first game amounted to 6s. 9d. (equivalent to approx. £25 today). After a year, the club name was changed to Grimsby Town.

Blundell Park, Cleethorpes, North East Lincolnshire DN35 7PY.

Telephone: (01472) 605 050.

Ticket Office: (01472) 605 050 (option 4).

Website: www.grimsby-townfc.co.uk

Email: enquiries@gtfc.co.uk

Ground Capacity: 9,052.

Record Attendance: 31,657 v Wolverhampton W, FA Cup 5th rd, 20 February 1937.

Pitch Measurements: 101m × 68m (110yd × 74yd).

Chairman: John Fenty.

Chief Executive: Ian Fleming.

Manager: Michael Jolley.

Assistant Manager: Paul Wilkinson.

HONOURS

League Champions: Division 2 – 1900–01, 1933–34; Division 3 – 1979–80; Division 3N – 1925–26, 1955–56; Division 4 – 1971–72. *Runners-up:* Division 2 – 1928–29; Division 3 – 1961–62; Division 3N – 1951–52; Division 4 – 1978–79, 1989–90. Conference – (4th) 2015–16 *(promoted via play-offs).*
FA Cup: semi-final – 1936, 1939.
League Cup: 5th rd – 1980, 1985.
League Trophy Winners: 1998.
Runners-up: 2008.

Colours: Black and white striped shirts with red trim, black shorts with red trim, red socks with black trim.

Year Formed. 1878. *Turned Professional:* 1890. *Ltd Co.:* 1890.

Previous Name: 1878, Grimsby Pelham; 1879, Grimsby Town.

Club Nickname: 'The Mariners'.

Grounds: 1880, Clee Park; 1889, Abbey Park; 1899, Blundell Park.

First Football League Game: 3 September 1892, Division 2, v Northwich Victoria (h) W 2–1 – Whitehouse; Lundie, T. Frith; C. Frith, Walker, Murrell; Higgins, Henderson, Brayshaw, Riddoch (2), Ackroyd.

Record League Victory: 9–2 v Darwen, Division 2, 15 April 1899 – Bagshaw; Lockie, Nidd; Griffiths, Bell (1), Nelmes; Jenkinson (3), Richards (1), Cockshutt (3), Robinson, Chadburn (1).

Record Cup Victory: 8–0 v Darlington, FA Cup 2nd rd, 21 November 1885 – G. Atkinson; J. H. Taylor, H. Taylor; Hall, Kimpson, Hopewell; H. Atkinson (1), Garnham, Seal (3), Sharman, Monument (4).

Record Defeat: 1–9 v Arsenal, Division 1, 28 January 1931.

Most League Points (2 for a win): 68, Division 3 (N), 1955–56.

Most League Points (3 for a win): 83, Division 3, 1990–91.

Sun FACT FILE

Grimsby Town played in front of the largest-ever attendance at Manchester United's Old Trafford ground. The occasion was the FA Cup semi-final tie against Wolverhampton Wanderers which took place on 25 March 1939 attracting 76,962 fans. The Mariners were without regular keeper George Tweedy through illness and his replacement George Moulson was carried off with concussion after 20 minutes, leading to a 5-0 defeat.

Most League Goals: 103, Division 2, 1933–34.

Highest League Scorer in Season: Pat Glover, 42, Division 2, 1933–34.

Most League Goals in Total Aggregate: Pat Glover, 180, 1930–39.

Most League Goals in One Match: 6, Tommy McCairns v Leicester Fosse, Division 2, 11 April 1896.

Most Capped Player: Pat Glover, 7, Wales.

Most League Appearances: John McDermott, 647, 1987–2007.

Youngest League Player: Tony Ford, 16 years 143 days v Walsall, 4 October 1975.

Record Transfer Fee Received: £1,500,000 from Everton for John Oster, July 1997.

Record Transfer Fee Paid: £500,000 to Preston NE for Lee Ashcroft, August 1998.

Football League Record: 1892 Original Member of Division 2; 1901–03 Division 1; 1903 Division 2; 1910 Failed re-election; 1911 re-elected Division 2; 1920–21 Division 3; 1921–26 Division 3 (N); 1926–29 Division 2; 1929–32 Division 1; 1932–34 Division 2; 1934–48 Division 1; 1948–51 Division 2; 1951–56 Division 3 (N); 1956–59 Division 2; 1959–62 Division 3; 1962–64 Division 2; 1964–68 Division 3; 1968–72 Division 4; 1972–77 Division 3; 1977–79 Division 4; 1979–80 Division 3; 1980–87 Division 2; 1987–88 Division 3; 1988–90 Division 4; 1990–91 Division 3; 1991–92 Division 2; 1992–97 Division 1; 1997–98 Division 2; 1998–2003 Division 1; 2003–04 Division 2; 2004–10 FL 2; 2010–16 Conference/National League; 2016– FL 2.

LATEST SEQUENCES

Longest Sequence of League Wins: 11, 19.1.1952 – 29.3.1952.

Longest Sequence of League Defeats: 9, 30.11.1907 – 18.1.1908.

Longest Sequence of League Draws: 5, 6.2.1965 – 6.3.1965.

Longest Sequence of Unbeaten League Matches: 19, 16.2.1980 – 30.8.1980.

Longest Sequence Without a League Win: 22, 24.3.2008 – 1.11.2008.

Successive Scoring Runs: 33 from 6.10.1928.

Successive Non-scoring Runs: 6 from 11.3.2000.

MANAGERS

H. N. Hickson 1902–20
(Secretary-Manager)
Haydn Price 1920
George Fraser 1921–24
Wilf Gillow 1924–32
Frank Womack 1932–36
Charles Spencer 1937–51
Bill Shankly 1951–53
Billy Walsh 1954–55
Allenby Chilton 1955–59
Tim Ward 1960–62
Tom Johnston 1962–64
Jimmy McGuigan 1964–67
Don McEvoy 1967–68
Bill Harvey 1968–69
Bobby Kennedy 1969–71
Lawrie McMenemy 1971–73
Ron Ashman 1973–75
Tom Casey 1975–76
Johnny Newman 1976–79
George Kerr 1979–82
David Booth 1982–85
Mike Lyons 1985–87
Bobby Roberts 1987–88
Alan Buckley 1988–94
Brian Laws 1994–96
Kenny Swain 1997
Alan Buckley 1997–2000
Lennie Lawrence 2000–01
Paul Groves 2001–04
Nicky Law 2004
Russell Slade 2004–06
Graham Rodger 2006
Alan Buckley 2006–08
Mike Newell 2008–09
Neil Woods 2009–11
Rob Scott and Paul Hurst 2011–13
Paul Hurst 2013–16
Marcus Bignot 2016–17
Russell Slade 2017–18
Michael Jolley March 2018–

TEN YEAR LEAGUE RECORD

		P	W	D	L	F	A	Pts	Pos
2008-09	FL 2	46	9	14	23	51	69	41	22
2009-10	FL 2	46	9	17	20	45	71	44	23
2010-11	Conf	46	15	17	14	72	62	62	11
2011-12	Conf	46	19	13	14	79	60	70	11
2012-13	Conf	46	23	14	9	70	38	83	4
2013-14	Conf	46	22	12	12	65	46	78	4
2014-15	Conf	46	25	11	10	74	40	86	3
2015-16	NL	46	22	14	10	82	45	80	4
2016-17	FL 2	46	17	11	18	59	63	62	14
2017-18	FL 2	46	13	12	21	42	66	51	18

DID YOU KNOW ?

Despite finishing second to bottom of Division Two in 1909–10, Grimsby Town failed to gain re-election at the end of the season and played in the Midland League in 1910–11. They were only away for one season and returned at the expense of Lincoln City for 1911–12, pipping their county rivals by just a single vote.

GRIMSBY TOWN – SKY BET LEAGUE TWO 2017–18 LEAGUE RECORD

Match No.	Date		Venue	Opponents	Result		H/T Score	Lg Pos.	Goalscorers	Atten-dance
1	Aug	5	A	Chesterfield	W	3-1	2-0	4	Clarke [33], Jones [39], Davies, B (pen) [85]	7925
2		12	H	Coventry C	L	0-2	0-0	12		6767
3		19	A	Stevenage	L	1-3	0-2	18	Collins [81]	2793
4		26	H	Wycombe W	L	2-3	0-2	22	Rose (pen) [52], Hooper [65]	4016
5	Sept	2	A	Crewe Alex	W	1-0	1-0	17	Rose [36]	4066
6		9	A	Mansfield T	L	1-4	0-1	19	Jones (pen) [85]	4625
7		12	A	Accrington S	W	2-1	1-1	15	Jones [43], Woolford [47]	1288
8		16	H	Yeovil T	W	2-1	1-1	13	Collins [8], Vernon [71]	3945
9		23	A	Newport Co	L	0-1	0-0	13		3356
10		26	H	Colchester U	D	2-2	1-1	13	Hooper [7], Jones (pen) [89]	3438
11		30	H	Lincoln C	D	0-0	0-0	15		7669
12	Oct	7	A	Port Vale	W	2-1	0-1	13	Jones [51], Dembele [67]	5849
13		14	H	Crawley T	D	0-0	0-0	12		4007
14		17	A	Cheltenham T	W	3-2	3-1	11	Dembele 2 [13, 44], Collins [42]	2469
15		21	A	Morecambe	D	0-0	0-0	12		1525
16		28	H	Cambridge U	D	0-0	0-0	12		4091
17	Nov	11	A	Exeter C	L	0-2	0-1	15		3854
18		18	H	Carlisle U	L	0-1	0-0	15		3753
19		21	H	Swindon T	W	3-2	1-2	14	Matt [11], Dembele [71], Rose [86]	3023
20		25	A	Barnet	W	2-0	1-0	12	Matt [6], Jones [75]	2033
21	Dec	9	H	Forest Green R	W	1-0	1-0	11	Rose [39]	4398
22		16	A	Notts Co	D	0-0	0-0	11		8016
23		23	A	Luton T	L	0-2	0-1	12		9102
24		26	H	Mansfield T	D	1-1	1-0	13	Rose [10]	5704
25		30	H	Accrington S	L	0-3	0-0	14		4188
26	Jan	1	A	Crewe Alex	L	0-2	0-2	14		3292
27		6	H	Morecambe	L	0-2	0-2	15		3104
28		13	H	Newport Co	L	1-2	0-1	17	Matt [80]	3397
29		20	A	Colchester U	D	1-1	1-0	16	Vernam [38]	3016
30		27	H	Luton T	L	0-1	0-0	17		4159
31		30	A	Yeovil T	L	0-3	0-1	17		2330
32	Feb	3	H	Cheltenham T	D	1-1	1-0	17	Jackson [3]	3352
33		10	A	Crawley T	L	0-3	0-1	17		2055
34		17	A	Cambridge U	L	1-3	0-1	18	Hooper (pen) [90]	4739
35		24	H	Exeter C	L	0-1	0-1	20		4151
36	Mar	3	A	Carlisle U	L	0-2	0-1	20		4151
37		10	H	Port Vale	D	1-1	0-1	20	Berrett [90]	5198
38		17	A	Lincoln C	L	1-3	1-3	22	Davies, B (pen) [45]	9774
39		24	A	Coventry C	L	0-4	0-1	22		8755
40		30	H	Stevenage	D	0-0	0-0	22		5368
41	Apr	2	A	Wycombe W	L	1-2	1-0	22	Woolford [15]	5215
42		7	H	Chesterfield	W	1-0	0-0	21	Rose (pen) [88]	6780
43		14	H	Barnet	D	2-2	1-0	22	Collins [6], Rose (pen) [82]	5416
44		21	A	Swindon T	W	1-0	1-0	21	Rose (pen) [45]	6690
45		28	H	Notts Co	W	2-1	1-0	18	Clarke [29], Matt [90]	7133
46	May	5	A	Forest Green R	W	3-0	0-0	18	Hooper 3 [52, 84, 90]	3880

Final League Position: 18

GOALSCORERS

League (42): Rose 8 (4 pens), Hooper 6 (1 pen), Jones 6 (2 pens), Collins 4, Dembele 4, Matt 4, Clarke 2, Davies, B 2 (2 pens), Woolford 2, Berrett 1, Jackson 1, Vernam 1, Vernon 1.
FA Cup (0).
Carabao Cup (0).
Checkatrade Trophy (3): Cardwell 1, Hooper 1 (1 pen), Jaiyesimi 1.

McKeown J 37	Mills Z 24 + 4	Collins D 40	Clarke N 45	Dixon P 26	Dembele S 33 + 3	Kelly S 3 + 5	Berrett J 29 + 3	Rose M 30 + 3	Vernon S 15 + 13	Summerfield L 36 + 3	Davies B 28 + 6	Cardwell H 8 + 8	Hooper J 13 + 18	Jaiyesimi D 10 + 20	Bolarinwa T 1 + 2	Osborne K 9 + 1	Woolford M 26 + 5	Matt J 20 + 14	Osborne J — + 2	Killip B 6 + 1	Kean J 3	Vernam C 7 + 2	Wilks M 4 + 2	Clifton H 7 + 3	Jackson S 3 + 2	Hall-Johnson R 8 + 4	Sutiman E 1 + 1	Fox A 10	McSheffrey G 2 + 4	McAllister S 1	Match No.
1	2*	3	4	5	6²	7³	8	9	10	11⁵	12	13	14																		1
1		4	3	5	11³		6⁵	7		8	9²	2	10¹	12	13	14															2
1	2	4	3	5	6³	11²		7		9⁴	8		12	10¹	14	13															3
1	2	5ⁱ	4	3	11¹	8²	7	6				14	10	12	9³	13															4
1	2		4	5	6¹		8	7	11³			14		10	13		3	9²	12												5
1	2²		3	5	6³		8	7	10	12		13		11¹	14		4	9													6
1		3	4	5	6²		8	7³	14	11	12	2		13				9	10¹												7
1		3	4	5	6³	13	8		12	10¹	7	2	14					9	11²												8
1		4	3	5	6²		8	7³		11	12	2		14	13			9⁵	10												9
1		3	4	5	6		7		11¹	14	8	2		10²	13			9²	12												10
1		4	3	2	6²			7	13	12	10	8³	5			14		9	11¹												11
1	14	4	3	5	6²	11		13	10³	8¹	7	2						9	12												12
1		4	3	5	6		7		11¹	10²	8	2		13				9	12												13
1	12	3	4	5	6²	14			10	11	7	2						9¹	13												14
1		4	3	5	6²		7		11	10¹	8	2		13	12			9													15
1		3	4	5	6¹		7		10	11²	8	2		12	13			9													16
1	14	3	4	5¹	6		7		11¹	10	8	2						9²	13												17
1	5	3	4		6			8	10¹	12	7	2		11²	9³			13	14												18
1	5	4	3		6			7	13	10²	8	2			9¹			11	12												19
1	2	3	4		6³			8	13	10	7	5		12	9²			14	11¹												20
1	2	4	3		9			7³	14	10	8	5		13	6¹			12	11²												21
1	5	3	4		6¹			7	12	11	8	2		14	9³			13	10²												22
1	2	4	3		9³			8	13	10	7	5		12	6¹			14	11²												23
1³	2	4	3		6			8	13	10¹	7	5		14				9	11²	12											24
	2	4	3		9		14	7³		10¹	8	5	12	13	6³			11		1											25
		4	5	9¹		7		11³		8	2	13	14		3	10¹		14		1											26
	2	4	3		6			7²	13	10¹	8	5		12	14			9	11³		1										27
	2		3		6		8		10¹	14	7	5⁴			13		4	9²	12ᵃ			1	11								28
		5	3	6²			7	8	12		9	2		14			4	13	11¹			1	10²								29
	12	5	3	6²	13		8	7¹		9	2³						4		11			1	10	14							30
	5	2	3	9²			6	8⁴		7		12				4⁴	10¹			1		11³	13	14							31
	2	3⁴	4	5	13		6			7		14					10			1		11¹	9³		8	12					32
	2		4	5		12	8			7			13			3	6			1		10¹	9²	11							33
1	4		3	6¹	13	7			8			12	14		5		10		11²			9⁵	2								34
1	2	4	3	5¹	13		7	8		10	11³	9					12					14	6²								35
1	2	4	3	5¹			6²	7		8		10³	14	9			11					13		12							36
1		5	4	10³	14	7		8¹		2	13			11			9					12	3²	6							37
1		4	3			7	13			8	10¹		14			9²	11					6	2³		5	12					38
1	3	4		11		13	12			2			14			8²						10⁵	6		5	9	7¹				39
1	2	4	3	6²			7	13		8			10			11³	12		14			6³		5	9¹						40
1	2	4	3	8²			7	11¹		9			14			10	12					6³		5	13						41
1		4	3	6³			7	10¹		8		13	11²	12		9						2		5	14						42
1		4	3	9³			7			8		10²	11			6						12	13	2	5	14					43
1		4	3			8			7	12	11³	10¹			9	13						6		2²	14	5					44
1		4	3			7			8	12	10²	11			9	13						6³	14	2¹	5						45
1		4	3	14		7³			9	12	11²	8			10	13						6		2¹	5						46

FA Cup
First Round Plymouth Arg (a) 0-1

Carabao Cup
First Round Derby Co (h) 0-1

Checkatrade Trophy
Northern Group H Doncaster R (h) 1-1
(Doncaster R won 4-3 on penalties)
Northern Group H Scunthorpe U (a) 1-2
Northern Group H Sunderland U21 (h) 1-1
(Sunderland U21 won 7-6 on penalties)

HUDDERSFIELD TOWN

FOUNDATION

A meeting, attended largely by members of the Huddersfield & District FA, was held at the Imperial Hotel in 1906 to discuss the feasibility of establishing a football club in this rugby stronghold. However, it was not until a man with both the enthusiasm and the money to back the scheme came on the scene that real progress was made. This benefactor was Mr Hilton Crowther and it was at a meeting at the Albert Hotel in 1908 that the club formally came into existence with an investment of £2,000 and joined the North-Eastern League.

The John Smith's Stadium, Stadium Way, Leeds Road, Huddersfield, West Yorkshire HD1 6PX.

Telephone: (01484) 484 112.

Fax: (01484) 484 101.

Ticket Office: (01484) 484 123.

Website: www.htafc.com

Email: info@htafc.com

Ground Capacity: 24,169.

Record Attendance: 67,037 v Arsenal, FA Cup 6th rd, 27 February 1932 (at Leeds Road); 24,169 v Tottenham H, FA Premier League, 30 September 2017 (at John Smith's Stadium).

Pitch Measurements: 106m × 66.9m (116yd × 73yd).

Chairman: Dean Hoyle.

Chief Executive: Julian Winter.

Head Coach: David Wagner.

Assistant Head Coach: Christoph Buehler.

Colours: Blue and white striped shirts, white shorts with blue trim, white socks.

Year Formed: 1908.

Turned Professional: 1908.

Club Nickname: 'The Terriers'.

HONOURS

League Champions: Division 1 – 1923–24, 1924–25, 1925–26; Division 2 – 1969–70; Division 4 – 1979–80. *Runners-up:* Division 1 – 1926–27, 1927–28, 1933–34; Division 2 – 1919–20, 1952–53.

FA Cup Winners: 1922. *Runners-up:* 1920, 1928, 1930, 1938.

League Cup: semi-final – 1968.

League Trophy: *Runners-up:* 1994.

Grounds: 1908, Leeds Road; 1994, The Alfred McAlpine Stadium (renamed the Galpharm Stadium 2004, John Smith's Stadium 2012).

First Football League Game: 3 September 1910, Division 2, v Bradford PA (a) W 1–0 – Mutch; Taylor, Morris; Beaton, Hall, Bartlett; Blackburn, Wood, Hamilton (1), McCubbin, Jee.

Record League Victory: 10–1 v Blackpool, Division 1, 13 December 1930 – Turner; Goodall, Spencer; Redfern, Wilson, Campbell; Bob Kelly (1), McLean (4), Robson (3), Davies (1), Smailes (1).

Record Cup Victory: 7–0 v Lincoln U, FA Cup 1st rd, 16 November 1991 – Clarke; Trevitt, Charlton, Donovan (2), Mitchell, Doherty, O'Regan (1), Stapleton (1) (Wright), Roberts (2), Onuora (1), Barnett (Ireland). *N.B.* 11–0 v Heckmondwike (a), FA Cup pr rd, 18 September 1909 – Doggart; Roberts, Ewing; Hooton, Stevenson, Randall; Kenworthy (2), McCreadie (1), Foster (4), Stacey (4), Jee.

Record Defeat: 1–10 v Manchester C, Division 2, 7 November 1987.

Most League Points (2 for a win): 66, Division 4, 1979–80.

Sun FACT FILE

Following the collapse of Leeds City in October 1919, J. Hilton Crowther, the major benefactor of Huddersfield Town FC, made a proposal to the Football League to move the club to Elland Road with the aim of making this a permanent change of location. Huddersfield fans organised at short notice to delay the move and after raising £17,500 were able to fight off the proposal.

Most League Points (3 for a win): 87, FL 1, 2010–11.

Most League Goals: 101, Division 4, 1979–80.

Highest League Scorer in Season: Sam Taylor, 35, Division 2, 1919–20; George Brown, 35, Division 1, 1925–26; Jordan Rhodes, 35, 2011–12.

Most League Goals in Total Aggregate: George Brown, 142, 1921–29; Jimmy Glazzard, 142, 1946–56.

Most League Goals in One Match: 5, Dave Mangnall v Derby Co, Division 1, 21 November 1931; 5, Alf Lythgoe v Blackburn R, Division 1, 13 April 1935; 5, Jordan Rhodes v Wycombe W, FL 1, 6 January 2012.

Most Capped Player: Jimmy Nicholson, 31 (41), Northern Ireland.

Most League Appearances: Billy Smith, 521, 1914–34.

Youngest League Player: Denis Law, 16 years 303 days v Notts Co, 24 December 1956.

Record Transfer Fee Received: £8,000,000 from Blackburn R for Jordan Rhodes, August 2012.

Record Transfer Fee Paid: £17,500,000 to Monaco for Terence Kongolo, June 2018.

Football League Record: 1910 Elected to Division 2; 1920–52 Division 1; 1952–53 Division 2; 1953–56 Division 1; 1956–70 Division 2; 1970–72 Division 1; 1972–73 Division 2; 1973–75 Division 3; 1975–80 Division 4; 1980–83 Division 3; 1983–88 Division 3; 1988–92 Division 3; 1992–95 Division 2; 1995–2001 Division 1; 2001–03 Division 2; 2003–04 Division 3; 2004–12 FL 1; 2012–17 FL C; 2017– FA Premier League.

LATEST SEQUENCES

Longest Sequence of League Wins: 11, 5.4.1920 – 4.9.1920.

Longest Sequence of League Defeats: 7, 8.10.1955 – 19.11.1955.

Longest Sequence of League Draws: 6, 3.3.1987 – 3.4.1987.

Longest Sequence of Unbeaten League Matches: 43, 1.1.2011 – 19.11.2011.

Longest Sequence Without a League Win: 22, 4.12.1971 – 29.4.1972.

Successive Scoring Runs: 27 from 12.3.2005.

Successive Non-scoring Runs: 7 from 14.10.2000.

MANAGERS

Fred Walker 1908–10
Richard Pudan 1910–12
Arthur Fairclough 1912–19
Ambrose Langley 1919–21
Herbert Chapman 1921–25
Cecil Potter 1925–26
Jack Chaplin 1926–29
Clem Stephenson 1929–42
Ted Magner 1942–43
David Steele 1943–47
George Stephenson 1947–52
Andy Beattie 1952–56
Bill Shankly 1956–59
Eddie Boot 1960–64
Tom Johnston 1964–68
Ian Greaves 1968–74
Bobby Collins 1974
Tom Johnston 1975–78
    (had been General Manager since 1975)
Mike Buxton 1978–86
Steve Smith 1986–87
Malcolm Macdonald 1987–88
Eoin Hand 1988–92
Ian Ross 1992–93
Neil Warnock 1993–95
Brian Horton 1995–97
Peter Jackson 1997–99
Steve Bruce 1999–2000
Lou Macari 2000–02
Mick Wadsworth 2002–03
Peter Jackson 2003–07
Andy Ritchie 2007–08
Stan Ternent 2008
Lee Clark 2008–12
Simon Grayson 2012–13
Mark Robins 2013–14
Chris Powell 2014–15
David Wagner November 2015–

TEN YEAR LEAGUE RECORD

		P	W	D	L	F	A	Pts	Pos
2008-09	FL 1	46	18	14	14	62	65	68	9
2009-10	FL 1	46	23	11	12	82	56	80	6
2010-11	FL 1	46	25	12	9	77	48	87	3
2011-12	FL 1	46	21	18	7	79	47	81	4
2012-13	FL C	46	15	13	18	53	73	58	19
2013-14	FL C	46	14	11	21	58	65	53	17
2014-15	FL C	46	13	16	17	58	75	55	16
2015-16	FL C	46	13	12	21	59	70	51	19
2016-17	FL C	46	25	6	15	56	58	81	5
2017-18	PR Lge	38	9	10	19	28	58	37	16

DID YOU KNOW

Huddersfield Town have qualified for the end-of season play-offs on eight occasions, and are one of only two clubs to have won each of the three divisional finals. In total they have been successful four times; however, they have yet to win a home game at the semi-final stage in eight attempts.

HUDDERSFIELD TOWN – PREMIER LEAGUE 2017–18 LEAGUE RECORD

Match No.	Date	Venue	Opponents	Result	H/T Score	Lg Pos.	Goalscorers	Atten-dance
1	Aug 12	A	Crystal Palace	W 3-0	2-0	1	Ward (og) [23], Mounie 2 [26, 78]	25,448
2	20	H	Newcastle U	W 1-0	0-0	2	Mooy [50]	24,128
3	26	H	Southampton	D 0-0	0-0	2		23,548
4	Sept 11	A	West Ham U	L 0-2	0-0	6		56,977
5	16	H	Leicester C	D 1-1	0-0	6	Depoitre [46]	24,169
6	23	A	Burnley	D 0-0	0-0	8		20,759
7	30	H	Tottenham H	L 0-4	0-3	11		24,169
8	Oct 14	A	Swansea C	L 0-2	0-1	11		20,657
9	21	H	Manchester U	W 2-1	2-0	11	Mooy [28], Depoitre [33]	24,169
10	28	A	Liverpool	L 0-3	0-0	11		53,268
11	Nov 4	H	WBA	W 1-0	1-0	10	van La Parra [44]	24,169
12	18	A	Bournemouth	L 0-4	0-2	10		10,879
13	26	H	Manchester C	L 1-2	1-0	11	Otamendi (og) [45]	24,121
14	29	A	Arsenal	L 0-5	0-1	14		59,285
15	Dec 2	A	Everton	L 0-2	0-0	15		39,167
16	9	H	Brighton & HA	W 2-0	2-0	11	Mounie 2 [12, 43]	24,018
17	12	H	Chelsea	L 1-3	0-2	12	Depoitre [90]	24,169
18	16	A	Watford	W 4-1	2-0	11	Kachunga [6], Mooy 2 (1 pen) [23, 89 (p)], Depoitre [50]	20,026
19	23	A	Southampton	D 1-1	0-1	11	Depoitre [64]	29,675
20	26	H	Stoke C	D 1-1	1-0	11	Ince [10]	24,047
21	30	H	Burnley	D 0-0	0-0	11		24,095
22	Jan 1	A	Leicester C	L 0-3	0-0	11		31,748
23	13	H	West Ham U	L 1-4	1-1	13	Lolley [40]	24,105
24	20	A	Stoke C	L 0-2	0-0	14		29,785
25	30	H	Liverpool	L 0-3	0-2	14		24,121
26	Feb 3	A	Manchester U	L 0-2	0-0	19		74,742
27	11	A	Bournemouth	W 4-1	2-1	17	Pritchard [7], Mounie [27], Cook, S (og) [66], van La Parra (pen) [90]	23,823
28	24	A	WBA	W 2-1	0-0	14	van La Parra [48], Mounie [56]	25,920
29	Mar 3	H	Tottenham H	L 0-2	0-1	15		68,311
30	10	H	Swansea C	D 0-0	0-0	15		23,567
31	17	H	Crystal Palace	L 0-2	0-1	15		23,980
32	31	A	Newcastle U	L 0-1	0-0	16		52,261
33	Apr 7	A	Brighton & HA	D 1-1	1-1	16	Mounie [32]	30,501
34	14	H	Watford	W 1-0	0-0	14	Ince [90]	23,961
35	28	H	Everton	L 0-2	0-1	16		24,121
36	May 6	A	Manchester C	D 0-0	0-0	16		54,350
37	9	A	Chelsea	D 1-1	0-0	16	Depoitre [50]	38,910
38	13	H	Arsenal	L 0-1	0-1	16		24,122

Final League Position: 16

GOALSCORERS

League (28): Mounie 7, Depoitre 6, Mooy 4 (1 pen), van La Parra 3 (1 pen), Ince 2, Kachunga 1, Lolley 1, Pritchard 1, own goals 3.
FA Cup (7): Mounie 2, van La Parra 2, Ince 1, Williams D 1, own goal 1.
Carabao Cup (2): Billing 1 (1 pen), Lolley 1.

Lossi J 38	Smith T 21+3	Jorgensen M 38	Schindler C 37	Lowe C 19+4	Mooy A 34+2	Billing P 8+8	Kachunga E 17+2	Palmer K 1+3	Ince T 27+6	Mounie S 21+7	Williams D 11+9	Quaner C 13+13	van La Parra R 26+7	Hefele M —+2	Malone S 12+10	Sabiri A 2+3	Depoitre L 18+15	Hogg J 29+1	Hadergjonaj F 19+4	Whitehead D —+4	Cranie M 2+1	Lolley J 2+4	Pritchard A 12+2	Kongolo T 11+2	Match No.
1	2²	3	4	5	6	7	8		9³	10	11¹	12	13	14											1
1	2	3	4	5	6	7	8²	13	9¹	11		12	10³	14											2
1	2	3	4	5	6	7¹	8³	12	9	11	13	14	10²												3
1	2	3	4	5¹	6	7³	8²		9	11				10	12	13	14								4
1	2	3	4	5	7		8²		10		6	12	14				9¹	11³	13						5
1	2	3	4	5	6	13	8¹		10			12					9³	11	7²	14					6
1	2	3	4	5²	7²	13	8		9					10	12			11	6¹	14					7
1	2	3	4	14	12	7¹	8		9		13			10	5²			11	6³						8
1	2	3	4	5	9		8²		10¹	13	7		12		14			11³	6						9
1	2²	3	4	5	9		12		10	14	7³		6¹					11	8	13					10
1		3	4¹	14	8		6³		10		13		9¹		5²		11	7	2		12				11
1		3			6		8¹		9	12	7³	13	10		5	14	11		2		4²				12
1	2	3	4	12	9				6³	14	7	13	10¹		5¹		11	8²							13
1		2	3	8	6³		10			11	13	9					12	7²	5	14	4				14
1	2	3	4		6				10	12	9	13	7	8²	5¹		12	11							15
1	2	3	4	5	6		8¹		9²	11³	14	10					12	7				13			16
1	2	3	4	5²	9		6		10	11¹	7				14		8³	13	12						17
1		3	4	5³	7		10²		12		14	6	9¹	13			11	8⁴	2						18
1	12	3	4		6				9	14	7	8	10²	5			11³		2¹			13			19
1	2	3	4	5³	6				9	11¹		8	10²	14			13	7				12			20
1	12	3	4		6				9²		14	8¹	10	5			11	7	2³			13			21
1	2³	3	4	5²	7				9	11	6	12	8	13			14		10¹						22
1	2²	3	4		7				10			8		5			11	6			9²	12	13		23
1		3	4		7				8²	11		12	10	5	13	14	6¹	2			9¹				24
1		3	4	6²	7¹	9			14	11³		12	13		10	8	2					5			25
1	2	3	4¹		12	9³			14			7	10²	13	11	6	8					5			26
1		3	4		7³	14			8²	11		13	10	5¹		6	2				9	12			27
1	12	3	4						14	11	7	8	10³		13	6	2¹				9²	5			28
1		3	4			13			12	11	6	8²	10		14	7¹	2				9³	5			29
1		3	4	12	7²				8	11	13	12	10³	5	14	6	2				9¹				30
1		3	4	12	7	14			10²	11		8	13	5¹		6	2				9³				31
1	2¹	3	4	8		6²			13		12	9³		14	10	7					11	5			32
1		3	4	8	12				6²	11	13	9¹			14	7²	2				10	5			33
1		3	4	7	14				12	11²	8³	10¹			13	6²	2				9	5			34
1		3	4	7	12				11	8³	10¹			13	14	6²	2				9	5			35
1	2	3	4	6³	9				10²	14	13	12	8	7							11¹	5			36
1	2¹	3	4	6³	7	9			10²	14		11	8	13							12	5			37
1		3	4	6	7	13			9²	11³		12	8¹	2	14						10	5			38

FA Cup

Third Round	Bolton W	(a)	2-1
Fourth Round	Birmingham C	(h)	1-1
Replay	Birmingham C	(a)	4-1
(aet)			
Fifth Round	Manchester U	(h)	0-2

Carabao Cup

Second Round	Rotherham U	(h)	2-1
Third Round	Crystal Palace	(a)	0-1

HULL CITY

FOUNDATION

The enthusiasts who formed Hull City in 1904 were brave men indeed. More than that, they were audacious for they immediately put the club on the map in this Rugby League fortress by obtaining a three-year agreement with the Hull Rugby League club to rent their ground! They had obtained quite a number of conversions to the dribbling code, before the Rugby League forbade the use of any of their club grounds by Association Football clubs. By that time, Hull City were well away, having entered the FA Cup in their initial season and the Football League, Second Division after only a year.

The KCOM Stadium, West Park, Hull, East Yorkshire HU3 6HU.

Telephone: (01482) 504 600.

Ticket Office: (01482) 358 418.

Website: www.hullcitytigers.com

Email: info@hulltigers.com

Ground Capacity: 24,983.

Record Attendance: 55,019 v Manchester U, FA Cup 6th rd, 26 February 1949 (at Boothferry Park); 25,512 v Sunderland, FL C, 28 October 2007 (at KC Stadium).

Pitch Measurements: 105m × 68m (115yd × 74.5yd).

Chairman: Dr Assem Allam.

Vice-Chairman: Ehab Allam.

Manager: Nigel Adkins.

Assistant Manager: Andy Crosby.

Colours: Amber shirts with black stripes, black shorts, amber socks with black trim.

Year Formed: 1904.

Turned Professional: 1905.

Club Nickname: 'The Tigers'.

Grounds: 1904, Boulevard Ground (Hull RFC); 1905, Anlaby Road (Hull CC); 1944, Boulevard Ground; 1946, Boothferry Park; 2002, Kingston Communications Stadium; 2016, renamed KCOM stadium.

First Football League Game: 2 September 1905, Division 2, v Barnsley (h) W 4–1 – Spendiff; Langley, Jones; Martin, Robinson, Gordon (2); Rushton, Spence (1); Wilson (1), Howe, Raisbeck.

Record League Victory: 11–1 v Carlisle U, Division 3 (N), 14 January 1939 – Ellis; Woodhead, Dowen; Robinson (1), Blyth, Hardy; Hubbard (2), Richardson (2), Dickinson (2), Davies (2), Cunliffe (2).

Record Cup Victory: 8–2 v Stalybridge Celtic (a), FA Cup 1st rd, 26 November 1932 – Maddison; Goldsmith, Woodhead; Gardner, Hill (1), Denby; Forward (1), Duncan, McNaughton (1), Wainscoat (4), Sargeant (1).

Record Defeat: 0–8 v Wolverhampton W, Division 2, 4 November 1911.

HONOURS

League Champions: Division 3 – 1965–66; Division 3N – 1932–33, 1948–49.
Runners-up: FL C – 2012–13; FL 1 – 2004–05; Division 3 – 1958–59; Third Division – 2003–04; Division 4 – 1982–83.
FA Cup: Runners-up: 2014.
League Cup: quarter-final – 2016.
League Trophy: Runners-up: 1984.
European Competitions
Europa League: 2014–15.

Sun FACT FILE

Hull City were drawn against Lincoln City over two legs in the first round of the Football League Cup in a run of four seasons out of five in the early 1980s. The only occasion on which the Tigers were successful was in 1983–84 when they won both legs with an aggregate score of 6-1 to set up a second-round tie with Southampton.

Most League Points (2 for a win): 69, Division 3, 1965–66.

Most League Points (3 for a win): 90, Division 4, 1982–83.

Most League Goals: 109, Division 3, 1965–66.

Highest League Scorer in Season: Bill McNaughton, 39, Division 3 (N), 1932–33.

Most League Goals in Total Aggregate: Chris Chilton, 193, 1960–71.

Most League Goals in One Match: 5, Ken McDonald v Bristol C, Division 2, 17 November 1928; 5, Simon 'Slim' Raleigh v Halifax T, Division 3 (N), 26 December 1930.

Most Capped Player: Theo Whitmore, 28 (105), Jamaica.

Most League Appearances: Andy Davidson, 520, 1952–67.

Youngest League Player: Matthew Edeson, 16 years 63 days v Fulham, 10 October 1992.

Record Transfer Fee Received: £12,000,000 (rising to £17,000,000) from Leicester C for Harry Maguire, June 2017.

Record Transfer Fee Paid: £13,000,000 to Tottenham H for Ryan Mason, August 2016.

Football League Record: 1905 Elected to Division 2; 1930–33 Division 3 (N); 1933–36 Division 2; 1936–49 Division 3 (N); 1949–56 Division 2; 1956–58 Division 3 (N); 1958–59 Division 3; 1959–60 Division 2; 1960–66 Division 3; 1966–78 Division 2; 1978–81 Division 3; 1981–83 Division 4; 1983–85 Division 3; 1985–91 Division 2; 1991–92 Division 3; 1992–96 Division 2; 1996–2004 Division 3; 2004–05 FL 1; 2005–08 FL C; 2008–10 FA Premier League; 2010–13 FL C; 2013–15 FA Premier League; 2015–16 FL C; 2016–17 FA Premier League; 2017– FL C.

LATEST SEQUENCES

Longest Sequence of League Wins: 10, 23.2.1966 – 20.4.1966.

Longest Sequence of League Defeats: 8, 7.4.1934 – 8.9.1934.

Longest Sequence of League Draws: 5, 14.2.2012 – 10.3.2012.

Longest Sequence of Unbeaten League Matches: 19, 13.3.2001 – 22.9.2001.

Longest Sequence Without a League Win: 27, 27.3.1989 – 4.11.1989.

Successive Scoring Runs: 26 from 10.4.1990.

Successive Non-scoring Runs: 6 from 13.11.1920.

MANAGERS

James Ramster 1904–05
(Secretary-Manager)
Ambrose Langley 1905–13
Harry Chapman 1913–14
Fred Stringer 1914–16
David Menzies 1916–21
Percy Lewis 1921–23
Bill McCracken 1923–31
Haydn Green 1931–34
John Hill 1934–36
David Menzies 1936
Ernest Blackburn 1936–46
Major Frank Buckley 1946–48
Raich Carter 1948–51
Bob Jackson 1952–55
Bob Brocklebank 1955–61
Cliff Britton 1961–70
(continued as General Manager to 1971)
Terry Neill 1970–74
John Kaye 1974–77
Bobby Collins 1977–78
Ken Houghton 1978–79
Mike Smith 1979–82
Bobby Brown 1982
Colin Appleton 1982–84
Brian Horton 1984–88
Eddie Gray 1988–89
Colin Appleton 1989
Stan Ternent 1989–91
Terry Dolan 1991–97
Mark Hateley 1997–98
Warren Joyce 1998–2000
Brian Little 2000–02
Jan Molby 2002
Peter Taylor 2002–06
Phil Parkinson 2006
Phil Brown *(after caretaker role December 2006)* 2007–10
Ian Dowie *(consultant)* 2010
Nigel Pearson 2010–11
Nick Barmby 2011–12
Steve Bruce 2012–16
Mike Phelan 2016–17
Marco Silva 2017
Leonid Slutsky 2017
Nigel Adkins December 2017–

TEN YEAR LEAGUE RECORD

		P	W	D	L	F	A	Pts	Pos
2008-09	PR Lge	38	8	11	19	39	64	35	17
2009-10	PR Lge	38	6	12	20	34	75	30	19
2010-11	FL C	46	16	17	13	52	51	65	11
2011-12	FL C	46	19	11	16	47	44	68	8
2012-13	FL C	46	24	7	15	61	52	79	2
2013-14	PR Lge	38	10	7	21	38	53	37	16
2014-15	PR Lge	38	8	11	19	33	51	35	18
2015-16	FL C	46	24	11	11	69	35	83	4
2016-17	PR Lge	38	9	7	22	37	80	34	18
2017-18	FL C	46	11	16	19	70	70	49	18

DID YOU KNOW ?

In the period from 1925–26 (when official attendance figures were first held) up to the outbreak of war in 1939, Hull City's average attendance never rose above the 11,302 achieved in 1926–27. However, following the post-war move to Boothferry Park seasonal average attendances were three times those levels by the early 1950s.

HULL CITY – SKY BET CHAMPIONSHIP 2017–18 LEAGUE RECORD

Match No.	Date	Venue	Opponents	Result	H/T Score	Lg Pos.	Goalscorers	Attendance
1	Aug 5	A	Aston Villa	D	1-1	0-1	12	Bowen [62]	31,241
2	12	H	Burton Alb	W	4-1	1-1	5	Hernandez 3 [7, 54, 68], Grosicki [51]	14,882
3	15	H	Wolverhampton W	L	2-3	1-2	7	Dawson [27], Meyler (pen) [90]	17,145
4	19	A	QPR	L	1-2	1-0	14	Bowen [35]	12,609
5	25	H	Bolton W	W	4-0	3-0	6	Diomande [13], Bowen 2 [19, 88], Grosicki [29]	16,207
6	Sept 8	A	Derby Co	L	0-5	0-4	10		25,107
7	13	A	Fulham	L	1-2	0-1	16	Bowen [53]	15,792
8	16	H	Sunderland	D	1-1	0-1	17	Meyler [82]	16,597
9	23	A	Reading	D	1-1	1-0	17	Campbell [28]	15,749
10	26	H	Preston NE	L	1-2	0-1	17	Bowen [50]	15,443
11	30	H	Birmingham C	W	6-1	3-0	17	Campbell [7], Meyler (pen) [11], Bowen [26], Grosicki [72], Henriksen [76], Larsson [87]	15,608
12	Oct 14	A	Norwich C	D	1-1	1-0	15	Dicko [29]	25,666
13	21	A	Barnsley	W	1-0	0-0	14	Campbell [78]	13,624
14	28	H	Nottingham F	L	2-3	0-1	17	Bowen [76], Hector [88]	15,780
15	31	H	Middlesbrough	L	1-3	0-2	17	Grosicki [72]	15,454
16	Nov 4	A	Sheffield U	L	1-4	1-0	20	Grosicki [29]	27,466
17	18	H	Ipswich T	D	2-2	1-1	20	Bowen [34], Dicko [51]	15,516
18	21	A	Millwall	D	0-0	0-0	20		9817
19	25	H	Bristol C	L	2-3	1-0	20	Campbell [33], Bowen [61]	14,762
20	Dec 2	A	Sheffield W	D	2-2	1-0	20	Campbell [21], Dawson [90]	25,412
21	9	H	Brentford	W	3-2	0-0	18	Grosicki [54], Larsson [70], Irvine [75]	14,620
22	16	A	Cardiff C	L	0-1	0-0	19		18,049
23	23	A	Leeds U	L	0-1	0-1	19		35,156
24	26	H	Derby Co	D	0-0	0-0	19		18,026
25	30	H	Fulham	D	2-2	2-0	19	Bowen [32], Dicko [36]	15,701
26	Jan 1	A	Bolton W	L	0-1	0-1	21		14,216
27	13	A	Reading	D	0-0	0-0	20		14,300
28	20	A	Sunderland	L	0-1	0-1	21		27,437
29	30	H	Leeds U	D	0-0	0-0	21		17,237
30	Feb 3	A	Preston NE	L	1-2	1-2	22	Bowen [29]	11,605
31	10	A	Nottingham F	W	2-0	2-0	21	Toral [9], Wilson [38]	23,098
32	20	A	Middlesbrough	L	1-3	1-2	21	Evandro [41]	23,111
33	23	H	Sheffield U	W	1-0	0-0	20	Dicko [55]	15,213
34	27	H	Barnsley	D	1-1	0-1	20	Dawson [73]	14,005
35	Mar 6	H	Millwall	L	1-2	0-2	20	Hernandez [79]	13,524
36	10	H	Norwich C	W	4-3	2-3	18	Irvine [6], Hernandez 2 (2 pens) [41, 48], Wilson [71]	15,120
37	13	A	Ipswich T	W	3-0	2-0	17	Henriksen [18], Wilson [40], Bowen [47]	13,031
38	17	A	Birmingham C	L	0-3	0-1	18		22,970
39	31	H	Aston Villa	D	0-0	0-0	18		16,133
40	Apr 3	A	Wolverhampton W	D	2-2	1-1	18	Meyler (pen) [37], Bennett (og) [78]	29,718
41	7	H	QPR	W	4-0	2-0	18	Wilson [42], Smithies (og) [45], Grosicki [62], Hernandez [69]	14,181
42	10	A	Burton Alb	W	5-0	2-0	16	Wilson [5], Grosicki 2 [33, 86], Meyler (pen) [63], Keane [90]	3659
43	14	H	Sheffield W	L	0-1	0-1	18		16,417
44	21	A	Bristol C	D	5-5	1-2	18	Wilson 2 [16, 72], Fielding (og) [56], Hernandez [80], Campbell [87]	21,136
45	28	H	Cardiff C	L	0-2	0-1	18		17,441
46	May 6	A	Brentford	D	1-1	1-1	18	Bowen [45]	11,475

Final League Position: 18

GOALSCORERS

League (70): Bowen 14, Grosicki 9, Hernandez 8 (2 pens), Wilson 7, Campbell 6, Meyler 5 (4 pens), Dicko 4, Dawson 3, Henriksen 2, Irvine 2, Larsson 2, Diomande 1, Evandro 1, Hector 1, Keane 1, Toral 1, own goals 3.
FA Cup (3): Aina 1, Bowen 1, Dicko 1.
Carabao Cup (0).

McGregor A 44	Aina O 42 + 2	Dawson M 40	Hector M 33 + 3	Clark M 25 + 2	Henriksen M 25 + 6	Clucas S 3	Bowen J 37 + 5	Campbell F 23 + 13	Grosicki K 22 + 15	Hernandez A 8 + 2	Meyler D 17 + 8	Mazuch O 10 + 4	Weir J — + 3	Diomande A 3 + 13	Larsson S 37 + 3	Stewart K 10 + 7	Kingsley S 10 + 1	Toral J 16 + 11	Dicko N 19 + 10	Irvine J 27 + 7	Tomori F 23 + 2	Evandro G 3 + 5	Luer G — + 1	Keane W 3 + 6	MacDonald A 12	Wilson H 11 + 2	Marshall D 2	Batty D 1	Match No.
1	2	3	4	5	6¹	7	8	9³	10²	11	12	13	14																1
1	2	3	4	5		7	8¹	6	11	9³	10²	13			12	14													2
1	2	3	4	5		7	8	6²	11³	9	10¹	14			13	12													3
1	2	3	4	5			8	11¹	10		6	13			12	9	7²												4
1	5	3	4		8³		9		11²		6¹	2	14		10	7	12	13											5
1	2	3	4		6		8		10¹	14		13	7		5	9³	11²	12											6
1	5	3	4				9	13	11	6³			14	7	8¹	12	10²				2								7
1	5	3	4¹		7³		9	14	11		13			6	8	12	10²				2								8
1	5	3	4				9	11²		6		10¹		8	13	12	7	2											9
1	5	3	4		12		9	11²	13	6		10		8¹		14	7	2³											10
1	2	3	4	5	12		8²	11³	10		7		14		6			9¹	13										11
1	2	3	4	5	9		8		10³	6⁴		13	7¹	12		11²		14											12
1	2	3	4	5	9		8	12	10		6	7			11¹	13													13
1	2	3	4	5	9¹		8	11	10²		6				7			12²	14	13									14
1		3	4⁶	5			8	11³	13		6			14	9²	7³		12	10	2									15
1	2	3		5	14		8	11²	10		6				7³	12		13	9¹	4									16
1	5	3	4		9		8		10²			13		14	7³	6		11¹	12	2									17
1	5	3	4		8			6²	11³	12		13		7				10¹	9	2	14								18
1	5		4		9		8³	11¹	14	12	3				6²	7		13	10	2									19
1		3			5		9¹	8²	11³	14	4				6	7		12	13	10	2								20
1	8	3		5²			11¹	10			6³	4			12	14	9	2		13									21
1	5	3	6		12		10				4				13	7	8¹	11²	9	2									22
1	5	3	7		14		13	10					4¹		6	12	8²	11³	9	2									23
1	5	3	4		14		12	10³				13			7	6	8²	11¹	9	2									24
1	5	3	4	14	12		10	13			7				6²		8¹	11¹	9	2									25
1	5	3	4		6³		10	13			12	7¹			8	11²	9	2	14										26
1	5	3	4		14		10	13			6¹				7	8	11³	9²	2	12									27
1	5	3	4		10	11¹		6			7				8²	14	12	2	9³	13									28
1	5	3	13		7¹		6	10	12		4²				8		11³	9	2	14									29
1	2		3	5			6	10³		7²					11¹	9		12		14	4	13							30
1	2		3	5			8	14			13	6	12		9²		7			11¹	4	10³							31
1	9	3	2					10	12		13				7²		8	5¹	6	11	4								32
1	2	3		5			8	13	12		10¹	6	14		11¹	7		9²			4								33
1	2	3		5			8	14	13		10³	6			9²	11¹	7			12	4								34
1	2	3		5	7		8	10¹	14	12				6			11	9³			4²	13							35
	2	3	14	5	7		8²	12	11³	4		6			13	9		10¹								1			36
1	2	3	4	5	7		8	11³	14		13				6²			9¹			12	10							37
1	2	3		5	7		8	12	14	11²	4				6			13	9²			10¹							38
1	2	3	13	5	7		8	14	11			6			12	9³				4²	10¹								39
1	6		3	5	8			14	13	7					9¹	10³	11²	12	2		4								40
1	2	3	4	5	6		8³	14	12	11¹			7			9²	13				10								41
1	14	3		6²			11¹	10	7		12	5³			9	2				13	4	8							42
1	2		3	5	7		12		10¹	11		6			9					4	8								43
1	2³	3		7			8¹	11	13	14		6			5		9²	12			4	10							44
1	2	3		7			13	11	9³		8	12			5	14				10²	4¹	6							45
	12	3			8³	11		4²			7¹	14	5	9			2	13				10	1	6					46

FA Cup
Third Round   Blackburn R   (a)   1-0
Fourth Round   Nottingham F   (h)   2-1
Fifth Round   Chelsea   (a)   0-4

Carabao Cup
Second Round   Doncaster R   (a)   0-2

IPSWICH TOWN

FOUNDATION

Considering that Ipswich Town only reached the Football League in 1938, many people outside of East Anglia may be surprised to learn that this club was formed at a meeting held in the Town Hall as far back as 1878 when Mr T. C. Cobbold, MP, was voted president. Originally it was the Ipswich Association FC to distinguish it from the older Ipswich Football Club which played rugby. These two amalgamated in 1888 and the handling game was dropped in 1893.

Portman Road, Ipswich, Suffolk IP1 2DA.

Telephone: (01473) 400 500.

Fax: (01473) 400 040.

Ticket Office: (03330) 050 503.

Website: www.itfc.co.uk

Email: enquiries@itfc.co.uk

Ground Capacity: 30,311.

Record Attendance: 38,010 v Leeds U, FA Cup 6th rd, 8 March 1975.

Pitch Measurements: 102.5m × 66m (112yd × 72.5yd).

Chairman: Marcus Evans.

Managing Director: Ian Milne.

Manager: Paul Hurst.

Assistant Manager: Chris Doig.

Colours: Blue shirts with white trim, white shorts with blue trim, blue socks with white trim.

Year Formed: 1878.

Turned Professional: 1936.

HONOURS

League Champions: Division 1 – 1961–62; Division 2 – 1960–61, 1967–68, 1991–92; Division 3S – 1953–54, 1956–57.
Runners-up: Division 1 – 1980–81, 1981–82.

FA Cup Winners: 1978.

League Cup: semi-final – 1982, 1985, 2001, 2011.

Texaco Cup Winners: 1973.

European Competitions
European Cup: 1962–63.
UEFA Cup: 1973–74, 1974–75, 1975–76, 1977–78, 1979–80, 1980–81 *(winners)*, 1981–82, 1982–83, 2001–02, 2002–03.
European Cup-Winners' Cup: 1978–79 *(qf)*.

Previous Name: 1878, Ipswich Association FC; 1888, Ipswich Town.

Club Nicknames: 'The Blues', 'Town', 'The Tractor Boys'.

Grounds: 1878, Broom Hill and Brook's Hall; 1884, Portman Road.

First Football League Game: 27 August 1938, Division 3 (S), v Southend U (h) W 4–2 – Burns; Dale, Parry; Perrett, Fillingham, McLuckie; Williams, Davies (1), Jones (2), Alsop (1), Little.

Record League Victory: 7–0 v Portsmouth, Division 2, 7 November 1964 – Thorburn; Smith, McNeil; Baxter, Bolton, Thompson; Broadfoot (1), Hegan (2), Baker (1), Leadbetter, Brogan (3). 7–0 v Southampton, Division 1, 2 February 1974 – Sivell; Burley, Mills (1), Morris, Hunter, Beattie (1), Hamilton (2), Viljoen, Johnson, Whymark (2), Lambert (1) (Woods). 7–0 v WBA, Division 1, 6 November 1976 – Sivell; Burley, Mills, Talbot, Hunter, Beattie (1), Osborne, Wark (1), Mariner (1) (Bertschin), Whymark (4), Woods.

☀️ THE Sun FACT FILE

Ipswich Town's tremendous success in 1980–81 was reflected in their domination of the end-of-season awards. Frans Thijssen was voted as Football Writers' Association Footballer of the Year, with Mick Mills runner-up, John Wark in third place and Arnold Muhren fifth. Wark was voted PFA Player of the Year and was one of three players, along with Thijssen and Russell Osman, to be selected for the PFA Division One Team of the Season.

Record Cup Victory: 10–0 v Floriana, European Cup prel. rd, 25 September 1962 – Bailey; Malcolm, Compton; Baxter, Laurel, Elsworthy (1); Stephenson, Moran (2), Crawford (5), Phillips (2), Blackwood.

Record Defeat: 1–10 v Fulham, Division 1, 26 December 1963.

Most League Points (2 for a win): 64, Division 3 (S), 1953–54 and 1955–56.

Most League Points (3 for a win): 87, Division 1, 1999–2000.

Most League Goals: 106, Division 3 (S), 1955–56.

Highest League Scorer in Season: Ted Phillips, 41, Division 3 (S), 1956–57.

Most League Goals in Total Aggregate: Ray Crawford, 204, 1958–63 and 1966–69.

Most League Goals in One Match: 5, Alan Brazil v Southampton, Division 1, 16 February 1981.

Most Capped Player: Allan Hunter, 47 (53), Northern Ireland.

Most League Appearances: Mick Mills, 591, 1966–82.

Youngest League Player: Conor Wickham, 16 years 11 days, v Doncaster R, 11 April 2009.

Record Transfer Fee Received: £8,000,000 (rising to £12,000,000) from Sunderland for Connor Wickham, June 2011.

Record Transfer Fee Paid: £5,000,000 to Sampdoria for Matteo Sereni, August 2001.

Football League Record: 1938 Elected to Division 3 (S); 1954–55 Division 2; 1955–57 Division 3 (S); 1957–61 Division 2; 1961–64 Division 1; 1964–68 Division 2; 1968–86 Division 1; 1986–92 Division 2; 1992–95 FA Premier League; 1995–2000 Division 1; 2000–02 FA Premier League; 2002–04 Division 1; 2004– FL C.

LATEST SEQUENCES

Longest Sequence of League Wins: 8, 23.9.1953 – 31.10.1953.

Longest Sequence of League Defeats: 10, 4.9.1954 – 16.10.1954.

Longest Sequence of League Draws: 7, 10.11.1990 – 21.12.1990.

Longest Sequence of Unbeaten League Matches: 23, 8.12.1979 – 26.4.1980.

Longest Sequence Without a League Win: 21, 28.8.1963 – 14.12.1963.

Successive Scoring Runs: 31 from 7.3.2004.

Successive Non-scoring Runs: 7 from 28.2.1995.

MANAGERS

Mick O'Brien 1936–37
Scott Duncan 1937–55
(continued as Secretary)
Alf Ramsey 1955–63
Jackie Milburn 1963–64
Bill McGarry 1964–68
Bobby Robson 1969–82
Bobby Ferguson 1982–87
Johnny Duncan 1987–90
John Lyall 1990–94
George Burley 1994–2002
Joe Royle 2002–06
Jim Magilton 2006–09
Roy Keane 2009–11
Paul Jewell 2011–12
Mick McCarthy 2012–18
Paul Hurst May 2018–

TEN YEAR LEAGUE RECORD

		P	W	D	L	F	A	Pts	Pos
2008-09	FL C	46	17	15	14	62	53	66	9
2009-10	FL C	46	12	20	14	50	61	56	15
2010-11	FL C	46	18	8	20	62	68	62	13
2011-12	FL C	46	17	10	19	69	77	61	15
2012-13	FL C	46	16	12	18	48	61	60	14
2013-14	FL C	46	18	14	14	60	54	68	9
2014-15	FL C	46	22	12	12	72	54	78	6
2015-16	FL C	46	18	15	13	53	51	69	7
2016-17	FL C	46	13	16	17	48	58	55	16
2017-18	FL C	46	17	9	20	57	60	60	12

DID YOU KNOW ?

Ipswich Town attracted their best attendances during the 1970s when the average exceeded 20,000 every season. They highest average attendance in the club's history was 26,672 in the 1976–77 season.

IPSWICH TOWN – SKY BET CHAMPIONSHIP 2017–18 LEAGUE RECORD

Match No.	Date	Venue	Opponents	Result		H/T Score	Lg Pos.	Goalscorers	Atten- dance
1	Aug 5	H	Birmingham C	W	1-0	0-0	4	Garner [50]	18,153
2	12	A	Barnsley	W	2-1	0-1	4	McGoldrick [53], Waghorn [70]	12,009
3	15	A	Millwall	W	4-3	3-2	3	Garner [4], Waghorn 2 [34, 45], Spence [88]	11,919
4	19	H	Brentford	W	2-0	1-0	2	Waghorn [35], Garner [51]	15,348
5	26	H	Fulham	L	0-2	0-1	2		16,844
6	Sept 9	A	QPR	L	1-2	0-1	4	Celina [89]	14,060
7	16	H	Bolton W	W	2-0	0-0	5	Skuse [48], McGoldrick [89]	14,164
8	23	A	Leeds U	L	2-3	1-2	6	McGoldrick [30], Garner [71]	34,002
9	26	H	Sunderland	W	5-2	2-1	5	Waghorn [6], Spence [27], Celina [55], McGoldrick [60], Ward [89]	14,907
10	30	H	Bristol C	L	1-3	1-2	8	Waghorn [41]	15,256
11	Oct 14	A	Sheffield U	L	0-1	0-0	10		25,799
12	22	H	Norwich C	L	0-1	0-0	11		24,928
13	28	A	Burton Alb	W	2-1	0-0	10	Waghorn [66], Celina [89]	4110
14	31	A	Cardiff C	L	1-3	0-1	11	Celina [90]	15,951
15	Nov 4	H	Preston NE	W	3-0	1-0	7	Waghorn [45], McGoldrick [49], Celina [64]	14,390
16	18	A	Hull C	D	2-2	1-1	8	McGoldrick [6], Spence [88]	15,516
17	22	H	Sheffield W	D	2-2	0-0	9	Garner [48], Waghorn [70]	15,702
18	25	A	Aston Villa	L	0-2	0-1	10		30,427
19	28	A	Derby Co	W	1-0	1-0	9	Connolly [5]	24,475
20	Dec 2	H	Nottingham F	W	4-2	2-2	7	Connolly [7], Iorfa [37], Waghorn [53], Celina [67]	16,808
21	9	A	Middlesbrough	L	0-2	0-1	9		22,989
22	16	H	Reading	W	2-0	2-0	8	Connolly [3], Garner [27]	13,832
23	23	A	Wolverhampton W	L	0-1	0-1	10		30,218
24	26	H	QPR	D	0-0	0-0	10		18,696
25	30	H	Derby Co	L	1-2	0-1	11	Garner [66]	17,267
26	Jan 2	A	Fulham	L	1-4	1-0	12	Garner [45]	17,415
27	13	H	Leeds U	W	1-0	0-0	12	Celina [67]	18,638
28	20	A	Bolton W	D	1-1	0-0	12	Garner [82]	13,870
29	27	H	Wolverhampton W	L	0-1	0-1	12		15,971
30	Feb 3	A	Sunderland	W	2-0	2-0	12	Garner [35], Matthews (og) [45]	27,909
31	10	H	Burton Alb	D	0-0	0-0	12		13,815
32	18	A	Norwich C	D	1-1	0-0	12	Chambers [89]	27,100
33	21	H	Cardiff C	L	0-1	0-0	14		13,205
34	24	A	Preston NE	W	1-0	1-0	13	Carayol [21]	11,511
35	Mar 6	A	Sheffield W	W	2-1	0-0	12	Waghorn 2 [51, 83]	22,733
36	10	H	Sheffield U	D	0-0	0-0	12		15,152
37	13	H	Hull C	L	0-3	0-2	12		13,031
38	17	A	Bristol C	L	0-1	0-0	12		21,509
39	31	A	Birmingham C	L	0-1	0-1	13		20,555
40	Apr 2	H	Millwall	D	2-2	0-1	13	Waghorn 2 [52, 54]	16,010
41	7	A	Brentford	L	0-1	0-0	14		10,939
42	10	H	Barnsley	W	1-0	0-0	12	Knudsen [64]	13,271
43	14	A	Nottingham F	L	1-2	1-0	12	Ward [38]	25,093
44	21	H	Aston Villa	L	0-4	0-1	14		20,034
45	28	A	Reading	W	4-0	0-0	13	Waghorn [71], Spence [79], Connolly [90], Sears [90]	17,683
46	May 6	H	Middlesbrough	D	2-2	1-0	12	Sears [8], Waghorn (pen) [83]	18,829

Final League Position: 12

GOALSCORERS

League (57): Waghorn 16 (1 pen), Garner 10, Celina 7, McGoldrick 6, Connolly 4, Spence 4, Sears 2, Ward 2, Carayol 1, Chambers 1, Iorfa 1, Knudsen 1, Skuse 1, own goal 1.
FA Cup (0).
Carabao Cup (3): McGoldrick 2, Celina 1.

Bialkowski B 45	Iorfa D 20 + 3	Spence J 37 + 3	Chambers L 37	Smith T 3	Knudsen J 42	Ward G 25 + 12	Skuse C 39	Dozzell A 1	Sears F 15 + 21	Garner J 29 + 3	Downes F 3 + 7	Webster A 25 + 3	Nydam T 12 + 6	Kenlock M 15 + 1	McGoldrick D 18 + 4	Waghorn M 39 + 5	McDonnell A — + 1	Rowe D — + 2	Celina B 23 + 12	Connolly C 29 + 5	Adeyemi T 4 + 1	Bru K 3 + 6	Huws E 3 + 2	Bishop T 1 + 3	Hyam L 6 + 11	Gerken D 1	Carter-Vickers C 17	Gleeson S 5 + 5	Carayol M 5 + 3	Morris B 1 + 2	Folami B 1 + 3	Cotter B 1 + 1	Woolfenden L 1 + 1	McLoughlin S — + 1	Match No.
1	2¹	3	4	5	6	7	8	9²	10	11	12	13																							1
1	5	2	3		4		7		10	11	6¹		8²	9³	12	13	14																		2
1	2	3	4		5	8	7		9	11					10	6¹		12																	3
1	2	3			4	7	8		9³	11	12			13	5	10³	6¹	14																	4
1	2	3			4	7¹	8		9³	11	12			14	5	10	6²		13																5
1	4	3			5	6²	7		13	11		8¹			10	9²			14		2	12													6
1	4	2	3			8¹	7			11	13			14	9	10²			12	5²	6														7
1	2	3	4		5	6³	8		12	11				9¹	10²	14			13			7													8
1	2	3	4		5	13	8		14	10				12	11²	6¹			9¹			7													9
1	2²	3	4		5	14	7		13	11		12	6		9³	8			10¹																10
1	5		3		4	6	7		13			12	2	8¹	9³	11²	10		14																11
	2	3	5				7		14	10¹	12	4	8²		11	9			13			6³													12
	2	3			5	13	6		10²	11		4	7³		9¹	8			14				12												13
1	2		3	4	5	7	6		13	11³		8²				14			10	12		9¹													14
1	2	3			5	13	7³			11		4	14		10	9¹			8	6²		12													15
1	2	3			5	13	6		14	8		4			11²	9¹			10	7³		12													16
1	2¹	3				14			7	12	10	4			5	6³	11¹		9²	8			13												17
1	2¹	3			5	6²	8		9²	11		4				10			13	7			12	14											18
	2	3			5	8	6		12		13	4	14			11			10²	7¹			9³												19
1	2	3			5	8	6		13			4				11²			10	7	12	9¹													20
	2	3			5	8²	6		13	12		4				11			10¹	6		9³	14												21
13	2	3			5	8	6²		14	11¹		4				9			10³	7		12													22
	2	3				8			14	11³		4	5	13	9¹				10	6		7²	12												23
2		3			5	12			10²	11		4			9	8			13	7			6¹												24
13	2	3			5	8						11	4²		12	9			10	6		7¹													25
13	2⁴	3	4		5	8³	7		12	11						9			10¹	6²					14										26
2		3			4				6¹			11		5	8	9			10	7					12	1									27
2		3			5				6¹	13		11			9	8			10²	7³					14		4	12							28
1	2		4		5	14			12	11¹					9²				10	7					13		3	6³							29
1	2		4		5	8¹	6²		10	11³			14			9				7					13		3	12							30
1	2		4		5	8²	6			11						9			10	7¹							3	12	13						31
1	5²	14	3		9		7			11¹		4			12	10			8						13		2	6³							32
1	5²	3			9	6²	7		10			4				13			11	12	14				8¹		2								33
1	5	3			8		6		13	10³		4				9²				7					12		2		11¹						34
1	5	3			9	13	7		12	14		4				11²				8					6³		2		10¹						35
1	2²	12³	4				8			14		5		6		10			11	9¹					13		3	7							36
1		2	4		5	9			10				8²			13			11³	12					7		3	6¹		14					37
1		2	4		6	7¹	8		10²				5			11			12	9					13		3		13						38
1		2	4		6	7²	8		11³				5			10			12	9¹					13		3		14						39
1		5	3		4	13	6¹						2		8¹	10			11						14			7	9³		12				40
1		2	4¹		6	13			10				5		8²	12³			11						9		3								41
1		2			4	12	6								8	10			11	7							14	3		9²	13	5¹			42
1		2			4	5	7							8¹	9	11				13					6²		3		14	12	10³				43
1		2			4	5¹	7		12					8¹	9	11			10³	13					6²		3			14					44
1		5			4				12					3	7¹	8	10			6								13	9²	11³	14	2			45
1		5³			4		7		11					3	8¹	9	10			6²					13		2						14	12	46

FA Cup
Third Round   Sheffield U   (h)   0-1

Carabao Cup
First Round   Luton T   (a)   2-0
Second Round   Crystal Palace   (a)   1-2

LEEDS UNITED

FOUNDATION

Immediately the Leeds City club (founded in 1904) was wound up by the FA in October 1919, following allegations of illegal payments to players, a meeting was called by a Leeds solicitor, Mr Alf Masser, at which Leeds United was formed. They joined the Midland League, playing their first game in that competition in November 1919. It was in this same month that the new club had discussions with the directors of a virtually bankrupt Huddersfield Town who wanted to move to Leeds in an amalgamation. But Huddersfield survived even that crisis.

Elland Road Stadium, Elland Road, Leeds, West Yorkshire LS11 0ES.

Telephone: (0871) 334 1919.

Ticket Office: (0371) 334 1992.

Website: www.leedsunited.com

Email: reception@leedsunited.com

Ground Capacity: 37,890.

Record Attendance: 57,892 v Sunderland, FA Cup 5th rd (replay), 15 March 1967.

Pitch Measurements: 105m × 68m (115yd × 74yd).

Chairman: Andrea Radrizzani.

Chief Executive: Angus Kinnear.

Head Coach: Marcelo Bielsa.

Assistant Head Coaches: Pablo Quiroga, Diego Flores, Diego Reyes.

Colours: White shirts with gold trim, white shorts with gold trim, white socks with gold trim.

Year Formed: 1919, as Leeds United after disbandment (by FA order) of Leeds City (formed in 1904).

Turned Professional: 1920.

Club Nickname: 'The Whites'.

Ground: 1919, Elland Road.

HONOURS

League Champions: Division 1 – 1968–69, 1973–74, 1991–92; Division 2 – 1923–24, 1963–64, 1989–90.
Runners-up: Division 1 – 1964–65, 1965–66, 1969–70, 1970–71, 1971–72; Division 2 – 1927–28, 1931–32, 1955–56; FL 1 – 2009–10.

FA Cup Winners: 1972.
Runners-up: 1965, 1970, 1973.

League Cup Winners: 1968.
Runners-up: 1996.

European Competitions
European Cup: 1969–70 *(sf)*, 1974–75 *(runners-up)*.
Champions League: 1992–93, 2000–01 *(sf)*.
Fairs Cup: 1965–66 *(sf)*, 1966–67 *(runners-up)*, 1967–68 *(winners)*, 1968–69 *(qf)*, 1970–71 *(winners)*.
UEFA Cup: 1971–72, 1973–74, 1979–80, 1995–96, 1998–99, 1999–2000 *(sf)*, 2001–02, 2002–03.
European Cup-Winners' Cup: 1972–73 *(runners-up)*.

First Football League Game: 28 August 1920, Division 2, v Port Vale (a) L 0–2 – Down; Duffield, Tillotson; Musgrove, Baker, Walton; Mason, Goldthorpe, Thompson, Lyon, Best.

Record League Victory: 8–0 v Leicester C, Division 1, 7 April 1934 – Moore; George Milburn, Jack Milburn; Edwards, Hart, Copping; Mahon (2), Firth (2), Duggan (2), Furness (2), Cochrane.

*S*ᵀᴴᴱ*un* FACT FILE

Leeds United were involved in a mammoth FA Cup fourth-round tie against Arsenal in 1990–91, which was only settled after a third replay. The teams drew 0-0 at Highbury and 1-1 in the replay at Elland Road. The next game ended goalless again before Arsenal finally won it 2-1. The four ties attracted a total attendance of 116,281.

Record Cup Victory: 10–0 v Lyn (Oslo), European Cup 1st rd 1st leg, 17 September 1969 – Sprake; Reaney, Cooper, Bremner (2), Charlton, Hunter, Madeley, Clarke (2), Jones (3), Giles (2) (Bates), O'Grady (1).

Record Defeat: 1–8 v Stoke C, Division 1, 27 August 1934.

Most League Points (2 for a win): 67, Division 1, 1968–69.

Most League Points (3 for a win): 86, FL 1, 2009–10.

Most League Goals: 98, Division 2, 1927–28.

Highest League Scorer in Season: John Charles, 42, Division 2, 1953–54.

Most League Goals in Total Aggregate: Peter Lorimer, 168, 1965–79 and 1983–86.

Most League Goals in One Match: 5, Gordon Hodgson v Leicester C, Division 1, 1 October 1938.

Most Capped Player: Lucas Radebe, 58 (70), South Africa.

Most League Appearances: Jack Charlton, 629, 1953–73.

Youngest League Player: Peter Lorimer, 15 years 289 days v Southampton, 29 September 1962.

Record Transfer Fee Received: £30,800,000 from Manchester U for Rio Ferdinand, July 2002.

Record Transfer Fee Paid: £18,000,000 to West Ham U for Rio Ferdinand, November 2000.

Football League Record: 1920 Elected to Division 2; 1924–27 Division 1; 1927–28 Division 2; 1928–31 Division 1; 1931–32 Division 2; 1932–47 Division 1; 1947–56 Division 2; 1956–60 Division 1; 1960–64 Division 2; 1964–82 Division 1; 1982–90 Division 2; 1990–92 Division 1; 1992–2004 FA Premier League; 2004–07 FL C; 2007–10 FL 1; 2010– FL C.

LATEST SEQUENCES

Longest Sequence of League Wins: 9, 18.4.2009 – 5.9.2009.

Longest Sequence of League Defeats: 6, 28.12.2003 – 7.2.2004.

Longest Sequence of League Draws: 5, 2.5.2015 – 22.8.2015.

Longest Sequence of Unbeaten League Matches: 34, 26.10.1968 – 26.8.1969.

Longest Sequence Without a League Win: 17, 1.2.1947 – 26.5.1947.

Successive Scoring Runs: 30 from 27.8.1927.

Successive Non-scoring Runs: 6 from 30.1.1982.

MANAGERS

Dick Ray 1919–20
Arthur Fairclough 1920–27
Dick Ray 1927–35
Bill Hampson 1935–47
Willis Edwards 1947–48
Major Frank Buckley 1948–53
Raich Carter 1953–58
Bill Lambton 1958–59
Jack Taylor 1959–61
Don Revie OBE 1961–74
Brian Clough 1974
Jimmy Armfield 1974–78
Jock Stein CBE 1978
Jimmy Adamson 1978–80
Allan Clarke 1980–82
Eddie Gray MBE 1982–85
Billy Bremner 1985–88
Howard Wilkinson 1988–96
George Graham 1996–98
David O'Leary 1998–2002
Terry Venables 2002–03
Peter Reid 2003
Eddie Gray *(Caretaker)* 2003–04
Kevin Blackwell 2004–06
Dennis Wise 2006–08
Gary McAllister 2008
Simon Grayson 2008–12
Neil Warnock 2012–13
Brian McDermott 2013–14
Dave Hockaday 2014
Darko Milanic 2014
Neil Redfearn 2014–15
Uwe Rosler 2015
Steve Evans 2015–16
Garry Monk 2016–17
Thomas Christiansen 2017–18
Paul Heckingbottom 2018
Marcelo Bielsa June 2018–

TEN YEAR LEAGUE RECORD

		P	W	D	L	F	A	Pts	Pos
2008-09	FL 1	46	26	6	14	77	49	84	4
2009-10	FL 1	46	25	11	10	77	44	86	2
2010-11	FL C	46	19	15	12	81	70	72	7
2011-12	FL C	46	17	10	19	65	68	61	14
2012-13	FL C	46	17	10	19	57	66	61	13
2013-14	FL C	46	16	9	21	59	67	57	15
2014-15	FL C	46	15	11	20	50	61	56	15
2015-16	FL C	46	14	17	15	50	58	59	13
2016-17	FL C	46	22	9	15	61	47	75	7
2017-18	FL C	46	17	9	20	59	64	60	13

DID YOU KNOW

The Leeds United playing squad spent five weeks in the pop charts in 1972 after producing a single titled 'Leeds United' to mark the club reaching the FA Cup final that year. The record entered the *NME* charts on 20 May and peaked at number 15 as United won the Cup for the first time in their history.

LEEDS UNITED – SKY BET CHAMPIONSHIP 2017–18 LEAGUE RECORD

Match No.	Date	Venue	Opponents	Result	H/T Score	Lg Pos.	Goalscorers	Attendance
1	Aug 6	A	Bolton W	W 3-2	3-1	3	Philips 2 [7, 42], Wood [30]	19,857
2	12	H	Preston NE	D 0-0	0-0	7		32,880
3	15	H	Fulham	D 0-0	0-0	6		28,918
4	19	A	Sunderland	W 2-0	1-0	5	Samuel [21], Dallas [76]	31,237
5	26	A	Nottingham F	W 2-0	1-0	3	Roofe [24], Alioski [87]	25,682
6	Sept 9	H	Burton Alb	W 5-0	3-0	2	Lasogga 2 [20, 59], Philips [35], Hernandez (pen) [44], Roofe [54]	33,404
7	12	H	Birmingham C	W 2-0	1-0	1	Samuel [17], Dallas [90]	31,507
8	16	A	Millwall	L 0-1	0-0	1		16,447
9	23	H	Ipswich T	W 3-2	2-1	1	Lasogga [13], Philips [32], Bialkowski (og) [67]	34,002
10	26	H	Cardiff C	L 1-3	0-2	2	Roofe [67]	27,160
11	Oct 1	A	Sheffield W	L 0-3	0-2	5		27,972
12	14	H	Reading	L 0-1	0-0	6		33,900
13	21	A	Bristol C	W 3-0	2-0	4	Samuel 2 [4, 14], Lasogga [67]	24,435
14	27	H	Sheffield U	L 1-2	1-1	4	Philips [34]	34,504
15	31	H	Derby Co	L 1-2	1-0	6	Lasogga [7]	28,565
16	Nov 4	A	Brentford	L 1-3	0-1	10	Alioski [67]	11,068
17	19	H	Middlesbrough	W 2-1	1-0	7	Hernandez [24], Alioski [54]	33,771
18	22	A	Wolverhampton W	L 1-4	0-2	10	Alioski [48]	28,914
19	25	A	Barnsley	W 2-0	2-0	8	Samuel [23], Alioski [45]	16,399
20	Dec 1	H	Aston Villa	D 1-1	1-0	7	Jansson [19]	30,547
21	9	A	QPR	W 3-1	0-0	7	Roofe 3 [63, 68, 90]	15,506
22	16	H	Norwich C	W 1-0	1-0	7	Jansson [41]	30,590
23	23	H	Hull C	W 1-0	1-0	5	Hernandez [29]	35,156
24	26	A	Burton Alb	W 2-1	0-1	5	Hernandez [61], Roofe [64]	5612
25	30	A	Birmingham C	L 0-1	0-0	5		21,673
26	Jan 1	H	Nottingham F	D 0-0	0-0	6		32,426
27	13	A	Ipswich T	L 0-1	0-0	7		18,638
28	20	H	Millwall	L 3-4	0-2	10	Lasogga 2 [46, 62], Roofe [55]	33,564
29	30	A	Hull C	D 0-0	0-0	10		17,237
30	Feb 3	A	Cardiff C	L 1-4	0-3	10	Bamba (og) [54]	30,534
31	10	A	Sheffield U	L 1-2	0-1	11	Lasogga [47]	27,553
32	18	H	Bristol C	D 2-2	0-2	11	Lasogga [72], Roofe [80]	28,004
33	21	A	Derby Co	D 2-2	1-1	11	Lasogga [34], Alioski [79]	27,934
34	24	H	Brentford	W 1-0	1-0	11	Cooper [31]	28,428
35	Mar 2	A	Middlesbrough	L 0-3	0-2	11		27,621
36	7	H	Wolverhampton W	L 0-3	0-2	13		26,434
37	10	A	Reading	D 2-2	1-1	13	Jansson [43], Hernandez [56]	19,770
38	17	H	Sheffield W	L 1-2	0-0	14	Grot [96]	31,638
39	30	H	Bolton W	W 2-1	1-0	12	Ekuban [4], Hernandez [50]	35,377
40	Apr 3	A	Fulham	L 0-2	0-1	13		21,538
41	7	H	Sunderland	D 1-1	0-0	13	Hernandez [72]	30,461
42	10	A	Preston NE	L 1-3	1-0	14	Roofe [13]	14,188
43	13	A	Aston Villa	L 0-1	0-1	14		33,374
44	21	H	Barnsley	W 2-1	1-1	12	Pearce [17], Alioski [50]	30,451
45	28	A	Norwich C	L 1-2	1-1	14	Philips [39]	26,869
46	May 6	H	QPR	W 2-0	1-0	13	Roofe [30], Philips [47]	30,004

Final League Position: 13

GOALSCORERS

League (59): Roofe 11, Lasogga 10, Alioski 7, Hernandez 7 (1 pen), Philips 7, Samuel 5, Jansson 3, Dallas 2, Cooper 1, Ekuban 1, Grot 1, Pearce 1, Wood 1, own goals 2.
FA Cup (1): Berardi 1.
Carabao Cup (12): Samuel 4, Roofe 3, Hernandez 2 (1 pen), Ekuban 1, Sacko 1, Vieira 1.

Wiedwald F 28	Ayling L 27	Pennington M 15+9	Cooper L 30	Berardi G 29+2	O'Kane E 27+5	Phillips K 36+5	Roofe K 27+9	Hernandez P 34+7	Alioski E 40+2	Wood C 3	Anita V 14+4	Shaughnessy C 5+4	Sacko H 1+13	Jansson P 41+1	Borthwick-Jackson C 1	Vieira Ronaldo 23+5	Samuel S 28+6	Dallas S 14+15	Ekuban C 12+8	Klich M 1+3	Grot J 1+19	Lasogga P 21+10	Lonergan A 7	Cibicki P 5+2	De Bock L 7	Forshaw A 9+3	Peacock-Farrell B 11	Pearce T 5	O'Connor P 4	Diaz H —+1	Edmondson R —+1	Match No.
1	2	3¹	4	5	6	7	8	9	10²	11	12	13	14																			1
1	2		4		7	6²	8³	9	10	11				3		5¹	12	13	14													2
1	2			6	7	12	10		8¹	11	5	4		3		9²		13														3
1	2		4		7	6	12	10²	8		5			3		9¹	13	11³	14													4
1	2		4		7	6¹	11³	10¹	8		5			3		14	9	13			12											5
1	2		4		6²	7	8	10			5³			3		9	12		13	14	11¹											6
1	2	4²	13		7	6	12	10³	8¹		5			3		9	14			11												7
1	2				7	6	12	10³	8²		5	3		4		9¹	13		14	11												8
1	2		4	12	7	6		10³	8		5²	3				9	13		14	11¹												9
1	2	12	4⁴	5		7	11	9²	8¹					3		14		10		6²	13											10
1	2	3		5	6	7	8²	13	10¹			12		4³		9	14			11												11
	2		4	5¹	7	6	8²	10				12		3		9	14		13	11³			1									12
	2	3	4	5⁴	7	8			9³		13	12				6	11²		14	10¹			1									13
	2	3	4³		7	6		13	9²			5¹		12		8	11		14	10			1									14
	2	3¹			6		8²	14	10¹				12	4		7	9	5	13	11			1									15
	2		4	5	7³	6	12	13	9¹					3		8	11		14	10²			1									16
	2	14	4	5	13	7	11²	10	8¹					3		6	9³		12				1									17
	2		4	5	13	7	11²	10¹	8					3		6⁴	9	14	12				1									18
1	2		4	5	6¹	7	13	10	8²		12			3		9		11³	14													19
1	2		4	5		7	12	10¹	8³			13		3		6	9	11²	14													20
1	2	14	4	5	13	6	10		8²					3		7³	9	11¹								12						21
1	2	14	4	5		6	11³	12	10					3		7	9²					13				8¹						22
1	2	14	4	5	12	6³	11¹	9²	10					3		7					13				8							23
1	2	14	4	5	6	13	11	9	10²					3		7¹					12				8¹							24
1	2		4	5		7²	11	9	10³		6			3		12		13	14						8¹							25
1	2¹		4	5	7	6	11³	10	8²	12		14	3			9			13													26
1		4	2	6⁴	7	11	9	10¹		5²	13	12	3				14		8³													27
	12	4²	2		7	9¹	8	10			14		3		6³	13		11²				5										28
		2				10²	9	6³			3¹	13	4	8		12		11			14	5	7									29
	3	2⁴			9	10	8					13	4²	7¹		12		14	11³			5	6									30
	4			7	8¹	11²	12	9¹				13	3			2	14		10			5	6									31
	3			8¹	14	12	9		2		13	4			6²	10³		11				5	7									32
		4	2	6	7		13	9³	10²	14			3		7¹	12	8		11			5	6									33
1		4	2	6	7			10	5	13			3		14	9²	8¹	12	11³													34
1		4	2	6²	7¹			8³	5				3	13		9	10	14	11													35
	12	4¹	2		6		13		5	10³	3		9	8	14	11²			7	1												36
		4		2	6			10¹	8			3		9	13	11²	12		5	7	1											37
		4		2	7³	14	9	8				3		10	11²	13	12		6	1	5¹											38
		4		5	8		9	6¹				3		7	12	2	10	13	11²	1												39
		4		5	6²	12		10	8³			3		7	9	2	11¹	13	14	1												40
			5¹		6¹	12	10	8	14			3		7	9³	2	13	11²		1			4									41
					7	9²	10	13	5			3¹		6	14	2	11	8³		1			4	12								42
		4			7	10¹	9	6				8	12	2	11³	13	14		1	5	3											43
		2			6	11	10	8²				3		7	9¹		12	13	1	5³												44
		2	4		7	11	10	8²				3		6¹	9		12	14	13	1	5³											45
2	12	4		14	6	11²		9				3¹		8		10		7³	1	5										13		46

FA Cup
Third Round   Newport Co   (a)   1-2

Carabao Cup
First Round   Port Vale   (h)   4-1
Second Round   Newport Co   (h)   5-1
Third Round   Burnley   (a)   2-2
(aet; Leeds U won 5-3 on penalties)
Fourth Round   Leicester C   (a)   1-3

LEICESTER CITY

FOUNDATION

In 1884 a number of young footballers, who were mostly old boys of Wyggeston School, held a meeting at a house on the Roman Fosse Way and formed Leicester Fosse FC. They collected 9d (less than 4p) towards the cost of a ball, plus the same amount for membership. Their first professional, Harry Webb from Stafford Rangers, was signed in 1888 for 2s 6d (12p) per week, plus travelling expenses.

King Power Stadium, Filbert Way, Leicester LE2 7FL.
Telephone: (0344) 815 5000.
Fax: (0116) 291 5278.
Ticket Office: (0344) 815 5000 (option 1).
Website: www.lcfc.com
Email: lcfchelp@lcfc.co.uk
Ground Capacity: 32,273.
Record Attendance: 47,298 v Tottenham H, FA Cup 5th rd, 18 February 1928 (at Filbert Street); 32,242 v Sunderland, FA Premier League, 8 August 2015 (at King Power Stadium).
Pitch Measurements: 105m × 68m (115yd × 75yd).
Chairman: Khun Vichai Srivaddhanaprabha.
Chief Executive: Susan Whelan.
Manager: Claude Puel.
Assistant Manager: Pascal Plancque.
Colours: Blue shirts with yellow trim, blue shorts with yellow trim, blue socks with yellow trim.
Year Formed: 1884.
Turned Professional: 1888.
Previous Name: 1884, Leicester Fosse; 1919, Leicester City.
Club Nickname: 'The Foxes'.
Grounds: 1884, Victoria Park; 1887, Belgrave Road; 1888, Victoria Park; 1891, Filbert Street; 2002, Walkers Stadium (now known as King Power Stadium from 2011).
First Football League Game: 1 September 1894, Division 2, v Grimsby T (a) L 3–4 – Thraves; Smith, Bailey; Seymour, Brown, Henrys; Hill, Hughes, McArthur (1), Skea (2), Priestman.
Record League Victory: 10–0 v Portsmouth, Division 1, 20 October 1928 – McLaren; Black, Brown; Findlay, Carr, Watson; Adcock, Hine (3), Chandler (6), Lochhead, Barry (1).
Record Cup Victory: 8–1 v Coventry C (a), League Cup 5th rd, 1 December 1964 – Banks; Sjoberg, Norman (2); Roberts, King, McDerment; Hodgson (2), Cross, Goodfellow, Gibson (1), Stringfellow (2), (1 og).
Record Defeat: 0–12 (as Leicester Fosse) v Nottingham F, Division 1, 21 April 1909.

HONOURS

League Champions: FA Premier League – 2015–16; FL C – 2013–14; Division 2 – 1924–25, 1936–37, 1953–54, 1956–57, 1970–71, 1979–80; FL 1 – 2008–09.
Runners-up: Division 1 – 1928–29; First Division – 2002–03; Division 2 – 1907–08.
FA Cup: Runners-up: 1949, 1961, 1963, 1969.
League Cup Winners: 1964, 1997, 2000.
Runners-up: 1965, 1999.
European Competitions
UEFA Champions League: 2016–17 (*qf*).
UEFA Cup: 1997–98, 2000–01.
European Cup-Winners' Cup: 1961–62.

THE Sun FACT FILE

Andy Roxburgh is one of just two players to appear for Leicester City in the Football League and for Leicester rugby club. He spent two seasons as an inside forward for City, appearing as an amateur before switching codes in 1922. He went on to play as a fly-half for the Tigers and also represented Warwickshire but gave up the game due to injury and went back to playing local football.

Most League Points (2 for a win): 61, Division 2, 1956–57.

Most League Points (3 for a win): 102, FL C, 2013–14.

Most League Goals: 109, Division 2, 1956–57.

Highest League Scorer in Season: Arthur Rowley, 44, Division 2, 1956–57.

Most League Goals in Total Aggregate: Arthur Chandler, 259, 1923–35.

Most League Goals in One Match: 6, John Duncan v Port Vale, Division 2, 25 December 1924; 6, Arthur Chandler v Portsmouth, Division 1, 20 October 1928.

Most Capped Player: John O'Neill, 47 , Northern Ireland; Andy King, 47 (includes 3 on loan at Swansea C), Wales.

Most League Appearances: Adam Black, 528, 1920–35.

Youngest League Player: Dave Buchanan, 16 years 192 days v Oldham Ath, 1 January 1979.

Record Transfer Fee Received: £60,000,000 from Manchester C for Riyad Mahrez, July 2018.

Record Transfer Fee Paid: £29,700,000 to Sporting Lisbon for Islam Slimani, August 2016.

Football League Record: 1894 Elected to Division 2; 1908–09 Division 1; 1909–25 Division 2; 1925–35 Division 1; 1935–37 Division 2; 1937–39 Division 1; 1946–54 Division 2; 1954–55 Division 1; 1955–57 Division 2; 1957–69 Division 1; 1969–71 Division 2; 1971–78 Division 1; 1978–80 Division 2; 1980–81 Division 1; 1981–83 Division 2; 1983–87 Division 1; 1987–92 Division 2; 1992–94 Division 1; 1994–95 FA Premier League; 1995–96 Division 1; 1996–2002 FA Premier League; 2002–03 Division 1; 2003–04 FA Premier League; 2004–08 FL C; 2008–09 FL 1; 2009–14 FL C; 2014– FA Premier League.

LATEST SEQUENCES

Longest Sequence of League Wins: 9, 21.12.2013 – 1.2.2014.

Longest Sequence of League Defeats: 8, 17.3.2001 – 28.4.2001.

Longest Sequence of League Draws: 6, 2.10.2004 – 2.11.2004.

Longest Sequence of Unbeaten League Matches: 23, 1.11.2008 – 7.3.2009.

Longest Sequence Without a League Win: 18, 12.4.1975 – 1.11.1975.

Successive Scoring Runs: 32 from 23.11.2013.

Successive Non-scoring Runs: 7 from 21.11.1987.

MANAGERS

Frank Gardner 1884–92
Ernest Marson 1892–94
J. Lee 1894–95
Henry Jackson 1895–97
William Clark 1897–98
George Johnson 1898–1912
Jack Bartlett 1912–14
Louis Ford 1914–15
Harry Linney 1915–19
Peter Hodge 1919–26
Willie Orr 1926–32
Peter Hodge 1932–34
Arthur Lochhead 1934–36
Frank Womack 1936–39
Tom Bromilow 1939–45
Tom Mather 1945–46
John Duncan 1946–49
Norman Bullock 1949–55
David Halliday 1955–58
Matt Gillies 1958–68
Frank O'Farrell 1968–71
Jimmy Bloomfield 1971–77
Frank McLintock 1977–78
Jock Wallace 1978–82
Gordon Milne 1982–86
Bryan Hamilton 1986–87
David Pleat 1987–91
Gordon Lee 1991
Brian Little 1991–94
Mark McGhee 1994–95
Martin O'Neill 1995–2000
Peter Taylor 2000–01
Dave Bassett 2001–02
Micky Adams 2002–04
Craig Levein 2004–06
Robert Kelly 2006–07
Martin Allen 2007
Gary Megson 2007
Ian Holloway 2007–08
Nigel Pearson 2008–10
Paulo Sousa 2010
Sven-Göran Eriksson 2010–11
Nigel Pearson 2011–15
Claudio Ranieri 2015–17
Craig Shakespeare 2017
Claude Puel October 2017–

TEN YEAR LEAGUE RECORD

		P	W	D	L	F	A	Pts	Pos
2008-09	FL 1	46	27	15	4	84	39	96	1
2009-10	FL C	46	21	13	12	61	45	76	5
2010-11	FL C	46	19	10	17	76	71	67	10
2011-12	FL C	46	18	12	16	66	55	66	9
2012-13	FL C	46	19	11	16	71	48	68	6
2013-14	FL C	46	31	9	6	83	43	102	1
2014-15	PR Lge	38	11	8	19	46	55	41	14
2015-16	PR Lge	38	23	12	3	68	36	81	1
2016-17	PR Lge	38	12	8	18	48	63	44	12
2017-18	PR Lge	38	12	11	15	56	60	47	9

DID YOU KNOW ?

Jimmy Goodfellow was the first substitute to be used by Leicester City in a Football League fixture. He replaced the injured Graham Cross 10 minutes from the end of a First Division game against Liverpool at Filbert Street in August 1965 which the visitors won 3-1.

LEICESTER CITY – PREMIER LEAGUE 2017–18 LEAGUE RECORD

Match No.	Date	Venue	Opponents	Result	H/T Score	Lg Pos.	Goalscorers	Attendance
1	Aug 11	A	Arsenal	L 3-4	2-2	20	Okazaki [5], Vardy 2 [29, 56]	59,387
2	19	H	Brighton & HA	W 2-0	1-0	9	Okazaki [1], Maguire [54]	31,902
3	26	A	Manchester U	L 0-2	0-0	16		75,021
4	Sept 9	H	Chelsea	L 1-2	0-1	17	Vardy (pen) [62]	31,923
5	16	A	Huddersfield T	D 1-1	0-0	15	Vardy (pen) [50]	24,169
6	23	H	Liverpool	L 2-3	1-2	16	Okazaki [45], Vardy [69]	32,004
7	30	A	Bournemouth	D 0-0	0-0	17		10,444
8	Oct 16	H	WBA	D 1-1	0-0	18	Mahrez [80]	30,203
9	21	A	Swansea C	W 2-1	1-0	14	Fernandez (og) [24], Okazaki [49]	20,521
10	29	H	Everton	W 2-0	2-0	11	Vardy [18], Gray [29]	31,891
11	Nov 4	A	Stoke C	D 2-2	1-1	12	Iborra [33], Mahrez [60]	29,602
12	18	H	Manchester C	L 0-2	0-1	12		31,908
13	24	A	West Ham U	D 1-1	1-1	11	Albrighton [8]	56,897
14	28	H	Tottenham H	W 2-1	2-0	9	Vardy [13], Mahrez [45]	31,950
15	Dec 2	H	Burnley	W 1-0	1-0	9	Gray [6]	30,714
16	9	A	Newcastle U	W 3-2	1-1	8	Mahrez [20], Gray [60], Perez (og) [86]	52,117
17	13	A	Southampton	W 4-1	3-0	8	Mahrez [11], Okazaki 2 [32, 69], King [38]	27,714
18	16	H	Crystal Palace	L 0-3	0-2	8		31,081
19	23	H	Manchester U	D 2-2	1-1	8	Vardy [27], Maguire [90]	32,202
20	26	A	Watford	L 1-2	1-1	8	Mahrez [37]	20,308
21	30	A	Liverpool	L 1-2	1-0	8	Vardy [3]	53,226
22	Jan 1	H	Huddersfield T	W 3-0	0-0	8	Mahrez [53], Slimani [60], Albrighton [90]	31,748
23	13	A	Chelsea	D 0-0	0-0	8		41,552
24	20	H	Watford	W 2-0	1-0	7	Vardy (pen) [39], Mahrez [90]	31,891
25	31	A	Everton	L 1-2	0-2	8	Vardy (pen) [71]	38,390
26	Feb 3	H	Swansea C	D 1-1	1-0	8	Vardy [17]	31,179
27	10	A	Manchester C	L 1-5	1-1	8	Vardy [24]	54,416
28	24	H	Stoke C	D 1-1	0-1	8	Butland (og) [70]	31,769
29	Mar 3	H	Bournemouth	D 1-1	0-1	8	Mahrez [90]	31,384
30	10	A	WBA	W 4-1	1-1	8	Vardy [21], Mahrez [62], Iheanacho [76], Iborra [90]	23,558
31	31	A	Brighton & HA	W 2-0	0-0	8	Iborra [83], Vardy [90]	30,629
32	Apr 7	H	Newcastle U	L 1-2	0-1	8	Vardy [83]	32,066
33	14	A	Burnley	L 1-2	0-2	8	Vardy [72]	21,727
34	19	H	Southampton	D 0-0	0-0	8		31,160
35	28	A	Crystal Palace	L 0-5	0-2	9		25,750
36	May 5	H	West Ham U	L 0-2	0-1	9		32,013
37	9	H	Arsenal	W 3-1	1-0	9	Iheanacho [14], Vardy (pen) [76], Mahrez [90]	32,095
38	13	A	Tottenham H	L 4-5	2-1	9	Vardy 2 [4, 73], Mahrez [16], Iheanacho [47]	77,841

Final League Position: 9

GOALSCORERS

League (56): Vardy 20 (5 pens), Mahrez 12, Okazaki 6, Gray 3, Iborra 3, Iheanacho 3, Albrighton 2, Maguire 2, King 1, Slimani 1, own goals 3.
FA Cup (9): Iheanacho 4, Diabate 2, Vardy 2, Ndidi 1.
Carabao Cup (10): Slimani 4, Gray 1, Iheanacho 1, Mahrez 1, Musa 1, Okazaki 1, Vardy 1 (1 pen).
Checkatrade Trophy (7): Knight 2, Ndukwu 2, Hughes 1, Musa 1, Thomas 1.

Schmeichel K 33	Simpson D 27 + 1	Morgan W 32	Maguire H 38	Fuchs C 21 + 4	Mahrez R 34 + 2	James M 11 + 2	Ndidi O 33	Albrighton M 30 + 4	Okazaki S 17 + 10	Vardy J 37	Amartey D 6 + 2	Iheanacho K 7 + 14	Gray D 17 + 18	Slimani I 2 + 10	King A 5 + 6	Chilwell B 20 + 4	Iborra V 17 + 2	Choudhury H 4 + 4	Ulloa J — + 4	Dragovic A 7 + 4	Adrien Silva S 9 + 3	Diabate F 5 + 9	Hamer B 3 + 1	Barnes H — + 3	Benalouane Y 1	Jakupovic E 2	Match No.
1	2	3	4	5	6	7^1	8	9^1	10^3	11	12	13	14														1
1	2	3	4	5	6	8	7	9	10^1	11^2		13	12														2
1	2	3	4	5	6	7	8	9	10^3	11^2		13	14	12													3
1	2	3	4	5	6	8^1	7	9^2		11	14	13	10^3	12													4
1	2	3	4		6		7	9	13	11^2		10^3	12	14	8	5											5
1	2	3	4		6^3		7	9	10^2	11		13	12	14	8	5											6
1	2	3	4	5	14		8	6	10^2	11		13	9		7^3	12											7
1	2^1	3	4	5	6		8	9		11		10^3	13	14	12	7^2											8
1	2	3	4	5	6^1		7	9	10^2	11		13	12			8											9
1	2	3	4	5	10^2		7	13	12	11^3	14	6	9^1	8													10
1	2	3	4	5	6		8	14	10^2	11	12	9^1	13			7^3											11
1	2	3	4	5	6^1		7	10^2	14	11	12	9	13			8^3											12
1	2	3	4	5	10^2		7	6		11		9^1	13	12		8											13
1	2	3	4		6^2		7	9	10^1	11^3		12	14		5	8	13										14
1	2	3	4		6		7	9	12	10^1					5	8											15
1	2	3	4	13	6^1		7	9	12	11^2		10^3			5	8	14										16
1	2	3	4	5	8^2		6	12	9	11^3		13		7	10^1	14											17
1	2	3	4		8		6^4	10^1	13	11^3		9	12	5	7^2	14											18
1	2^3	3	4	5	8		6	10	13	11	12^4	9^2		14	7^1												19
1		3	4		8		6	10	9^1	11		13	12	7^3	5		14	2^2									20
1		3	4	5	6^2	14	7	9^1	11^2	2		10	13			8											21
1	3^1	4	5	6^1	8^2	7	9	10		2		13	11						12	14							22
1		4	12	6	8^3	7	9	10^2	11^2	2		13			5^1	14					3						23
1		4		6	8	7	9	10^2	11^1	2		12			5						3	13					24
1		4	13		7	6	8	9^3	11	2^2	14	10^1			5						3	12					25
1	2^2	4	5		12	7	9	14	11	10^1		13			9^1						3	8^3	6				26
1	12	3	4	14	6	7	5		11	13					9^1					2	8^3	10^2					27
1	2^1	3	4		8	7	6	10		11		13	9^2		5							12					28
1		3	5^1	9	6	7	11		10	2^2	13		12								8^1	14					29
1	2	3	4	8^2		7	13	9^1	11	12	10^3				5	6						12					30
1	2	3	4	14	6^2	7^4		9^1	10^3	11		13			5	8						12					31
1	2^2	3	4		8			10	13	11		14			5	7^3	12					6	9^1				32
1^3	2	3	4		6			10^1	11	12	9^2				5	7			8	13	14						33
			4		6		8	2		10^1	9^2				5		14	3	7^1	12	1	13					34
		3	4		6		7^3	2^4		11	10^2	9			5		8^2	14	12	13	1						35
		3	4	5	6			11		13	14				8^1	7^3	12	10	9^2	1		2					36
	2^3	3	4	5	6			10		11^2	12					7	13	8	9^1		14			1			37
	2^1	3	4	5	8			11		9^2	10^3				7	12		6	13		14			1			38

FA Cup

Third Round	Fleetwood T	(a)	0-0	
Replay	Fleetwood T	(h)	2-0	
Fourth Round	Peterborough U	(a)	5-1	
Fifth Round	Sheffield U	(h)	1-0	
Sixth Round	Chelsea	(h)	1-2	
(aet)				

Carabao Cup

Second Round	Sheffield U	(a)	4-1
Third Round	Liverpool	(h)	2-0
Fourth Round	Leeds U	(h)	3-1
Quarter-Final	Manchester C	(h)	1-1
(aet; Manchester C won 4-3 on penalties)			

Checkatrade Trophy (Leicester C U21)

Northern Group A	Fleetwood T	(a)	0-3
Northern Group A	Carlisle U	(a)	1-0
Northern Group A	Morecambe	(a)	2-2
(Morecambe won 4-2 on penalties)			
Second Round North	Scunthorpe U	(a)	2-1
Third Round	Oldham Ath	(a)	2-4

LINCOLN CITY

FOUNDATION

The original Lincoln Football Club was established in the early 1860s and was one of the first provisional clubs to affiliate to the Football Association. In their early years, they regularly played matches against the famous Sheffield Football Club and later became known as Lincoln Lindum. The present organisation was formed at a public meeting held in the Monson Arms Hotel in June 1884 and won the Lincolnshire Cup in only their third season. They were founder members of the Midland League in 1889 and that competition's first champions.

Sincil Bank Stadium, Sincil Bank, Lincoln LN5 8LD.

Telephone: (01522) 880 011.

Fax: (01522) 880 020.

Ticket Office: (01522) 880 011.

Website: www.redimps.com

Email: info@lincolncityfc.co.uk

Ground Capacity: 10,238.

Record Attendance: 23,196 v Derby Co, League Cup 4th rd, 15 November 1967.

Pitch Measurements: 100m × 65m (109.5yd × 71yd).

Chairman: Bob Dorrian.

Managing Director: Kevin Cooke.

Manager: Danny Cowley.

Assistant Manager: Nicky Cowley.

Colours: Red and white striped shirts with black trim, black shorts with white trim, red socks.

Year Formed: 1884.

Turned Professional: 1892.

Ltd Co.: 1895.

Club Nickname: 'The Red Imps'.

Grounds: 1883, John O'Gaunt's; 1894, Sincil Bank.

First Football League Game: 3 September 1892, Division 2, v Sheffield U (a) L 2–4 – William Gresham; Coulton, Neill; Shaw, Mettam, Moore; Smallman, Irving (1), Cameron (1), Kelly, James Gresham.

Record League Victory: 11–1 v Crewe Alex, Division 3 (N), 29 September 1951 – Jones; Green (1p); Varney; Wright, Emery, Grummett (1); Troops (1), Garvey, Graver (6), Whittle (1), Johnson (1).

Record Cup Victory: 8–1 v Bromley, FA Cup 2nd rd, 10 December 1938 – McPhail; Hartshorne, Corbett; Bean, Leach, Whyte (1); Hancock, Wilson (1), Ponting (3), Deacon (1), Clare (2).

Record Defeat: 3–11 v Manchester C, Division 2, 23 March 1895.

Most League Points (2 for a win): 74, Division 4, 1975–76.

Most League Points (3 for a win): 77, Division 3, 1981–82.

HONOURS

League Champions: Division 3 (N) – 1931–32, 1947–48, 1951–52; Division 4 – 1975–76; National League – 1987–88, 2016–17.
Runners-up: Division 3 (N) – 1927–28, 1930–31, 1936–37; Division 4 – 1980–81.

FA Cup: quarter-final – 2017.

League Cup: 4th rd – 1968.

League Trophy: Winners: 2018.

THE Sun FACT FILE

Although Lincoln City's visit to Wembley for the 2017–18 Checkatrade Trophy final against Shrewsbury Town was the first time they had played there, it was not their first appearance at the national stadium complex. In May 1968 they qualified for the national finals of the *Daily Express* 5-a-side tournament which were played at the Empire Pool, Wembley. The Imps lost their first-round tie against Grimsby Town 1-0.

Most League Goals: 121, Division 3 (N), 1951–52.

Highest League Scorer in Season: Allan Hall, 41, Division 3 (N), 1931–32.

Most League Goals in Total Aggregate: Andy Graver, 143, 1950–55 and 1958–61.

Most League Goals in One Match: 6, Frank Keetley v Halifax T, Division 3 (N), 16 January 1932; 6, Andy Graver v Crewe Alex, Division 3 (N), 29 September 1951.

Most Capped Player: Gareth McAuley, 5 (79), Northern Ireland.

Most League Appearances: Grant Brown, 407, 1989–2002.

Youngest League Player: Shane Nicholson, 16 years 172 days v Burnley, 22 November 1986.

Record Transfer Fee Received: £750,000 from Liverpool for Jack Hobbs, August 2005.

Record Transfer Fee Paid: £75,000 to Carlisle U for Dean Walling, October 1997; £75,000 to Bury for Tony Battersby, August 1998.

Football League Record: 1892 Founder member of Division 2. Remained in Division 2 until 1920 when they failed re-election but also missed seasons 1908–09 and 1911–12 when not re-elected. 1921–32 Division 3 (N); 1932–34 Division 2; 1934–48 Division 3 (N); 1948–49 Division 2; 1949–52 Division 3 (N); 1952–61 Division 2; 1961–62 Division 3; 1962–76 Division 4; 1976–79 Division 3; 1979–81 Division 4; 1981–86 Division 3; 1986–87 Division 4; 1987–88 GM Vauxhall Conference; 1988–92 Division 4; 1992–98 Division 3; 1998–99 Division 2; 1999–2004 Division 3; 2004–11 FL 2; 2011–17 Conference National League; 2017– FL 2.

LATEST SEQUENCES

Longest Sequence of League Wins: 10, 1.9.1930 – 18.10.1930.

Longest Sequence of League Defeats: 12, 21.9.1896 – 9.1.1897.

Longest Sequence of League Draws: 5, 21.2.1981 – 7.3.1981.

Longest Sequence of Unbeaten League Matches: 18, 11.3.1980 – 13.9.1980.

Longest Sequence Without a League Win: 19, 22.8.1978 – 23.12.1978.

Successive Scoring Runs: 37 from 1.3.1930.

Successive Non-scoring Runs: 5 from 15.11.1913.

MANAGERS

Alf Martin 1896–97
(Secretary/Manager)
David Calderhead 1900–07
John Henry Strawson 1907–14
(had been Secretary)
George Fraser 1919–21
David Calderhead Jnr. 1921–24
Horace Henshall 1924–27
Harry Parkes 1927–36
Joe McClelland 1936–46
Bill Anderson 1946–65
(General Manager to 1966)
Roy Chapman 1965–66
Ron Gray 1966–70
Bert Loxley 1970–71
David Herd 1971–72
Graham Taylor 1972–77
George Kerr 1977–78
Willie Bell 1977–78
Colin Murphy 1978–85
John Pickering 1985
George Kerr 1985–87
Peter Daniel 1987
Colin Murphy 1987–90
Allan Clarke 1990
Steve Thompson 1990–93
Keith Alexander 1993–94
Sam Ellis 1994–95
Steve Wicks *(Head Coach)* 1995
John Beck 1995–98
Shane Westley 1998
John Reames 1998–2000
Phil Stant 2000–01
Alan Buckley 2001–02
Keith Alexander 2002–06
John Schofield 2006–07
Peter Jackson 2007–09
Chris Sutton 2009–10
Steve Tilson 2010–11
David Holdsworth 2011–13
Gary Simpson 2013–14
Chris Moyses 2014–16
Danny Cowley May 2016–

TEN YEAR LEAGUE RECORD

		P	W	D	L	F	A	Pts	Pos
2008-09	FL 2	46	14	17	15	53	52	59	13
2009-10	FL 2	46	13	11	22	42	65	50	20
2010-11	FL 2	46	13	8	25	45	81	47	23
2011-12	Conf	46	13	10	23	56	66	49	17
2012-13	Conf	46	15	11	20	72	86	54	16
2013-14	Conf	46	17	14	15	60	59	65	14
2014-15	Conf	46	16	10	20	62	71	58	15
2015-16	NL	46	16	13	17	69	68	61	13
2016-17	NL	46	30	9	7	83	40	99	1
2017-18	FL 2	46	20	15	11	64	48	75	7

DID YOU KNOW ?

In the 1963–64 season Lincoln City defeated Hartlepools United on four occasions: 4-2 and 2-1 in Division Four fixtures, 1-0 in the FA Cup and 3-2 in the Football League Cup. They were the first Football League team to achieve this feat since the introduction of the League Cup in 1960–61.

LINCOLN CITY – SKY BET LEAGUE TWO 2017–18 LEAGUE RECORD

Match No.	Date	Venue	Opponents	Result	H/T Score	Lg Pos.	Goalscorers	Attendance
1	Aug 5	A	Wycombe W	D	2-2	1-2	14	Green [31], Ginnelly [49]	5538
2	12	H	Morecambe	D	1-1	0-0	19	Green [70]	8060
3	19	A	Exeter C	L	0-1	0-1	22		3980
4	26	H	Carlisle U	W	4-1	1-0	13	Woodyard 2 [31, 62], Rhead (pen) [67], Knott [87]	8345
5	Sept 2	H	Luton T	D	0-0	0-0	14		9332
6	9	A	Stevenage	W	2-1	0-1	11	Raggett [58], Palmer (pen) [75]	3427
7	12	A	Forest Green R	W	1-0	0-0	5	Anderson [65]	1887
8	16	H	Mansfield T	L	0-1	0-0	10		9563
9	23	A	Notts Co	L	1-4	0-1	12	Anderson [47]	11,672
10	26	H	Barnet	W	2-1	2-0	12	Palmer [7], Anderson [42]	7320
11	30	A	Grimsby T	D	0-0	0-0	11		7669
12	Oct 7	H	Chesterfield	W	2-1	2-0	10	Bostwick [17], Kellett (og) [25]	9485
13	14	H	Cambridge U	D	0-0	0-0	10		8803
14	17	A	Swindon T	W	1-0	0-0	9	Raggett [83]	5864
15	21	A	Cheltenham T	L	0-1	0-1	10		3312
16	28	H	Crawley T	D	0-0	0-0	9		8038
17	Nov 11	A	Crewe Alex	W	4-1	0-1	8	Raynes (og) [70], Anderson 2 [50, 67], Whitehouse [90]	4723
18	18	H	Coventry C	L	1-2	1-0	10	Rhead [28]	9581
19	21	A	Colchester U	L	0-1	0-1	11		3102
20	25	H	Port Vale	W	3-1	1-1	10	Green [10], Bostwick [53], Waterfall [69]	7562
21	Dec 9	A	Yeovil T	W	2-0	0-0	6	Green [50], Rhead [69]	2472
22	16	H	Accrington S	W	2-0	1-0	6	Green (pen) [45], Rhead [56]	7696
23	23	A	Newport Co	D	0-0	0-0	6		3514
24	26	H	Stevenage	W	3-0	1-0	3	Anderson [34], Green [63], Ginnelly [80]	9268
25	30	H	Forest Green R	W	2-1	1-1	3	Rhead 2 [8, 57]	8964
26	Jan 1	A	Luton T	L	2-4	2-2	5	Bostwick [6], Green [34]	9659
27	13	H	Notts Co	D	2-2	1-1	6	Frecklington [37], Green [67]	9603
28	20	A	Barnet	D	1-1	0-1	8	Wilson [47]	3161
29	30	H	Newport Co	W	3-1	1-1	8	Rhead [13], Green [51], Palmer [73]	7567
30	Feb 3	H	Swindon T	D	2-2	1-2	9	Frecklington (pen) [23], Bostwick [90]	8909
31	9	A	Cambridge U	D	0-0	0-0	8		5775
32	13	H	Cheltenham T	W	1-0	1-0	7	Eardley [45]	7891
33	17	A	Crawley T	L	1-3	0-1	7	Green [52]	2809
34	24	H	Crewe Alex	L	1-4	1-1	8	Bostwick [35]	8272
35	Mar 6	A	Mansfield T	D	1-1	0-0	9	Palmer [90]	6091
36	10	A	Chesterfield	W	3-1	1-1	7	Bostwick [45], Wharton [59], Palmer [85]	6395
37	17	H	Grimsby T	W	3-1	3-1	7	Frecklington [31], Green [34], Wharton [39]	9774
38	24	A	Morecambe	D	0-0	0-0	8		1883
39	30	H	Exeter C	W	3-2	0-1	7	Rowe [60], Green [62], Palmer [86]	9785
40	Apr 2	A	Carlisle U	W	1-0	1-0	6	Green [43]	5068
41	14	A	Port Vale	L	0-1	0-0	8		5580
42	17	H	Wycombe W	D	0-0	0-0	6		8948
43	21	A	Colchester U	W	2-1	0-0	6	Whitehouse (pen) [55], Waterfall [90]	9211
44	24	A	Coventry C	W	4-2	3-2	6	Rhead [1], Palmer 2 [38, 44], Frecklington [67]	13,115
45	28	A	Accrington S	L	0-1	0-1	7		4753
46	May 5	H	Yeovil T	D	1-1	0-1	7	Pett [77]	10,004

Final League Position: 7

GOALSCORERS

League (64): Green 13 (1 pen), Palmer 8 (1 pen), Rhead 8 (1 pen), Anderson 6, Bostwick 6, Frecklington 4 (1 pen), Ginnelly 2, Raggett 2, Waterfall 2, Wharton 2, Whitehouse 2 (1 pen), Woodyard 2, Eardley 1, Knott 1, Pett 1, Rowe 1, Wilson 1, own goals 2.
FA Cup (0).
Carabao Cup (1): Knott 1.
Checkatrade Trophy (17): Green 3, Palmer 3, Maguire-Drew 2, Whitehouse 2, Anderson 1, Ginnelly 1, Raggett 1, Rhead 1, Rowe 1, Waterfall 1, own goal 1.
League Two Play-Offs (1): Green 1.

Farman P 13	Long S 13 + 4	Raggett S 25	Dickie R 17 + 1	Eardley N 44	Arnold N 15 + 5	Bostwick M 44	Woodyard A 46	Ginnelly J 8 + 7	Rhead M 35 + 6	Green M 43 + 2	Knott B 9 + 6	Maguire-Drew J 5 + 6	Palmer O 10 + 35	Anderson H 23 + 17	Waterfall L 24 + 6	Whitehouse E 12 + 20	Habergham S 32 + 1	Vickers J 17	Stewart C 2 + 2	Rowe D 9 + 3	Frecklington L 16	Williams J 6 + 5	Wilson J 5 + 3	Pett T 4 + 5	Allsop R 16	Wharton S 13 + 1	Match No.
1	2	3	4	5	6	7	8	9¹	10¹	11²	12	13	14														1
1	2	4		5	9	7	8		11¹²	10				6¹	13	12											2
1	2	4		5	9³	7	8		10¹	11	13			6²	12	14	3										3
1	2	4		5	9	7	8		10¹	11¹³	12			6²	13	14	3										4
1	2	4		5	6	8	7		10²	11¹	9³			13	12	3	14										5
1	2³	4		5		8	7	14	11¹	10⁴	9			13	6²	3	12										6
1		3	4	2	6³		7	8	13	12		10¹		11²	9		14	5									7
1	13	4	3	2			8	7	12	10¹	11	9		14	6³			5¹									8
1	14	4	3	2²			7	8	9¹		11³	10■		13	6		12	5									9
		4	3	2			7	8	9¹		11¹		13	10²	6	14	12	5									10
		4	3	2	6³	8	7		12	13	11		14	10¹	9²			5	1								11
	14	3	4	2			7	8	12		10		9	11³	6¹		13	5	1								12
		3	2	13	7		8	9³	14	11		6²	12	10¹		4		5	1								13
	2	4	3	5	9	7	6	10¹		11³	8²	14	12		13			1									14
	2	3	4	5	6¹		7	9²	14	11	10³	13	12		8			1									15
		4	3	2	9³	7	8		10¹	11	13	6¹	12		14	5		1									16
	2	4	3	5	12	7	6	9¹		13		11³	10²	14	8			1									17
	2	4	3	5	9¹	8	7		10³	11		14	6²		12		1	13									18
	2	4	3	5	9¹		7		12	13	8²		11³	6		10	1	14									19
	14	4		2		8	7	9¹	10²	11		13	6³	3	12	5	1										20
	4		2	14	7	8		11²	10²		13	6	3	12	5	1	9¹										21
	4		2	12	8	7		10¹	11³		14	6	3	13	5	1	9²										22
	4		2	9²	8	7		11¹	10	13		12	6	3	5	1											23
	4	3	2	9¹	8	7	14	10²	11²		13	6		12	5	1											24
	4	3	2	9²	8	7		10³	11¹		12	6	14	13	5	1											25
	2²	4	14		8	7	12	10¹	11³	13		6■	3	9	5	1											26
1			2	12	4	8		10¹	11		13		14		5				6²	7	9³						27
1			2		4	8		10³	11		14	12	3²		5				6	7	9¹	13					28
1			2		3	8		10³	11²		13	9	4		5				6¹	7	14	12					29
1			5		7	6³		12	10		14	9²	4¹		2				11	8		3	13				30
			2		7	8		10³	11		14	9	3		5				13			4²	6¹	1	12		31
			2		7	8		10³	11		13	12	3	14	5				6²			9¹	1	4			32
			2		7	8		10¹	11²		12	6	3	14	5					13		9	1	4³			33
2					4	8		10¹	11		13	12	3	14	5				6	7²		9³	1				34
			2		6	7		10	11¹		14	13	3■		5				12	8	9³		1	4			35
			2		3	7		10²	9³		13	12		6	5					8	11¹	14	1	4			36
			2		3	7		10²	9³		12	13		6	5					8¹	11	14	1	4			37
			2		4	3		10¹	11³		13	12		7	6				14	8	9²		1	5			38
			2		3	7		10³	9		14	12	13	6	5				11²	8¹			1	4			39
			2		6	7		10²	9		12	13	14	4¹	5				11³	8			1	3			40
			2		4	7		10³	9		13	12	3	8	5				11²	6¹	14		1				41
			2		7	6		10¹	11		12	9	3	13	5					8²			1	4			42
			2		3■	7		10	11		12	9	14	6²	5					8		13	1	4³			43
			2		7	6		10³	11³			9	12	3	13					8²	14	4	1	5			44
			2		7	6²		10	11			9³	12	3	13					8¹		4	14	1	5		45
			2¹		7	6		10	11			9³	13	3	8						14	4²	12	1	5		46

FA Cup

First Round	AFC Wimbledon	(a)	0-1

Carabao Cup

First Round	Rotherham U	(a)	1-2

Checkatrade Trophy

Northern Group G	Mansfield T	(a)	3-1
Northern Group G	Everton U21	(h)	2-1
Northern Group G	Notts Co	(h)	2-1
Second Round North	Accrington S	(h)	3-2
Third Round	Rochdale	(a)	1-0
Quarter-Final	Peterborough U	(h)	4-2
Semi-Final	Chelsea U21	(h)	1-1
(aet; Lincoln C won 4-2 on penalties)			
Final	Shrewsbury T	(Wembley)	1-0

League Two Play-Offs

Semi-Final 1st leg	Exeter C	(h)	0-0
Semi-Final 2nd leg	Exeter C	(a)	1-3

LIVERPOOL

FOUNDATION

But for a dispute between Everton FC and their landlord at Anfield in 1892, there may never have been a Liverpool club. This dispute persuaded the majority of Evertonians to quit Anfield for Goodison Park, leaving the landlord, Mr John Houlding, to form a new club. He originally tried to retain the name 'Everton' but when this failed, he founded Liverpool Association FC on 15 March 1892.

Anfield Stadium, Anfield Road, Anfield, Liverpool L4 0TH.

Telephone: (0151) 263 2361.

Fax: (0151) 260 8813.

Ticket Office: (0843) 170 5555.

Website: www.liverpoolfc.com

Email: customerservices@liverpoolfc.com

Ground Capacity: 54,074.

Record Attendance: 61,905 v Wolverhampton W, FA Cup 4th rd, 2 February 1952.

Pitch Measurements: 105m × 68m (115yd × 74yd).

Chairman: Tom Werner.

Chief Executive: Peter Moore.

Manager: Jürgen Klopp.

Assistant Coach: Zeljko Buvac.

Colours: Red shirts with white trim, red shorts, red socks with white trim.

Year Formed: 1892.

Turned Professional: 1892.

Club Nicknames: 'The Reds', 'Pool'.

Ground: 1892, Anfield.

First Football League Game: 2 September 1893, Division 2, v Middlesbrough Ironopolis (a) W 2–0 – McOwen; Hannah, McLean; Henderson, McQue (1), McBride; Gordon, McVean (1), Matt McQueen, Stott, Hugh McQueen.

HONOURS

League Champions: Division 1 – 1900–01, 1905–06, 1921–22, 1922–23, 1946–47, 1963–64, 1965–66, 1972–73, 1975–76, 1976–77, 1978–79, 1979–80, 1981–82, 1982–83, 1983–84, 1985–86, 1987–88, 1989–90; Division 2 – 1893–94, 1895–96, 1904–05, 1961–62.
Runners-up: FA Premier League – 2001–02, 2008–09, 2013–14; Division 1 – 1898–99, 1909–10, 1968–69, 1973–74, 1974–75, 1977–78, 1984–85, 1986–87, 1988–89, 1990–91.

FA Cup Winners: 1965, 1974, 1986, 1989, 1992, 2001, 2006.
Runners-up: 1914, 1950, 1971, 1977, 1988, 1996, 2012.
League Cup Winners: 1981, 1982, 1983, 1984, 1995, 2001, 2003, 2012.
Runners-up: 1978, 1987, 2005, 2016.
League Super Cup Winners: 1986.

European Competitions
European Cup: 1964–65 *(sf)*, 1966–67, 1973–74, 1976–77 *(winners)*, 1977–78 *(winners)*, 1978–79, 1979–80, 1980–81 *(winners)*, 1981–82 *(qf)*, 1982–83 *(qf)*, 1983–84 *(winners)*, 1984–85 *(runners-up)*.
Champions League: 2001–02 *(qf)*, 2002–03, 2004–05 *(winners)*, 2005–06, 2006–07 *(runners-up)*, 2007–08 *(sf)*, 2008–09 *(qf)*, 2009–10, 2014–15, 2017–18 *(runners-up)*.
Fairs Cup: 1967–68, 1968–69, 1969–70, 1970–71 *(sf)*.
UEFA Cup: 1972–73 *(winners)*, 1975–76 *(winners)*, 1991–92 *(qf)*, 1995–96, 1997–98, 1998–99, 2000–01 *(winners)*, 2002–03 *(qf)*, 2003–04.
Europa League: 2009–10 *(sf)*, 2010–11, 2012–13, 2014–15, 2015–16 *(runners-up)*.
European Cup-Winners' Cup: 1965–66 *(runners-up)*, 1971–72, 1974–75, 1992–93, 1996–97 *(sf)*.
Super Cup: 1977 *(winners)*, 1978, 1984, 2001 *(winners)*, 2005 *(winners)*.
World Club Championship: 1981, 1984.
FIFA Club World Cup: 2005.

Sun FACT FILE

Jimmy Jackson, who captained the Liverpool team in the inter-war years, became a clergyman after his playing career came to an end. Jackson, a defender who made over 200 League appearances for the Reds between 1927 and 1933, was ordained as a minister in the Presbyterian Church just 10 weeks after his final game for the club and went on to serve the church for over 25 years.

Record League Victory: 10–1 v Rotherham T, Division 2, 18 February 1896 – Storer; Goldie, Wilkie; McCartney, McQue, Holmes; McVean (3), Ross (2), Allan (4), Becton (1), Bradshaw.

Record Cup Victory: 11–0 v Stromsgodset Drammen, ECWC 1st rd 1st leg, 17 September 1974 – Clemence; Smith (1), Lindsay (1p), Thompson (2), Cormack (1), Hughes (1), Boersma (2), Hall, Heighway (1), Kennedy (1), Callaghan (1).

Record Defeat: 1–9 v Birmingham C, Division 2, 11 December 1954.

Most League Points (2 for a win): 68, Division 1, 1978–79.

Most League Points (3 for a win): 90, Division 1, 1987–88.

Most League Goals: 106, Division 2, 1895–96.

Highest League Scorer in Season: Roger Hunt, 41, Division 2, 1961–62.

Most League Goals in Total Aggregate: Roger Hunt, 245, 1959–69.

Most League Goals in One Match: 5, Andy McGuigan v Stoke C, Division 1, 4 January 1902; 5, John Evans v Bristol R, Division 2, 15 September 1954; 5, Ian Rush v Luton T, Division 1, 29 October 1983.

Most Capped Player: Steven Gerrard, 114, England.

Most League Appearances: Ian Callaghan, 640, 1960–78.

Youngest League Player: Jack Robinson, 16 years 250 days v Hull C, 9 May 2010.

Record Transfer Fee Received: £142,000,000 from Barcelona for Phillippe Coutinho, January 2018.

Record Transfer Fee Paid: £75,000,000 to Southampton for Virgil van Dijk, January 2018.

Football League Record: 1893 Elected to Division 2; 1894–95 Division 1; 1895–96 Division 2; 1896–1904 Division 1; 1904–05 Division 2; 1905–54 Division 1; 1954–62 Division 2; 1962–92 Division 1; 1992– FA Premier League.

MANAGERS

W. E. Barclay 1892–96
Tom Watson 1896–1915
David Ashworth 1920–23
Matt McQueen 1923–28
George Patterson 1928–36
(continued as Secretary)
George Kay 1936–51
Don Welsh 1951–56
Phil Taylor 1956–59
Bill Shankly 1959–74
Bob Paisley 1974–83
Joe Fagan 1983–85
Kenny Dalglish 1985–91
Graeme Souness 1991–94
Roy Evans 1994–98
(then Joint Manager)
Gerard Houllier 1998–2004
Rafael Benitez 2004–10
Roy Hodgson 2010–11
Kenny Dalglish 2011–12
Brendan Rodgers 2012–15
Jürgen Klopp October 2015–

LATEST SEQUENCES

Longest Sequence of League Wins: 12, 21.4.1990 – 6.10.1990.

Longest Sequence of League Defeats: 9, 29.4.1899 – 14.10.1899.

Longest Sequence of League Draws: 6, 19.2.1975 – 19.3.1975.

Longest Sequence of Unbeaten League Matches: 31, 4.5.1987 – 16.3.1988.

Longest Sequence Without a League Win: 14, 12.12.1953 – 20.3.1954.

Successive Scoring Runs: 29 from 27.4.1957.

Successive Non-scoring Runs: 5 from 21.4.2000.

TEN YEAR LEAGUE RECORD

		P	W	D	L	F	A	Pts	Pos
2008-09	PR Lge	38	25	11	2	77	27	86	2
2009-10	PR Lge	38	18	9	11	61	35	63	7
2010-11	PR Lge	38	17	7	14	59	44	58	6
2011-12	PR Lge	38	14	10	14	47	40	52	8
2012-13	PR Lge	38	16	13	9	71	43	61	7
2013-14	PR Lge	38	26	6	6	101	50	84	2
2014-15	PR Lge	38	18	8	12	52	48	62	6
2015-16	PR Lge	38	16	12	10	63	50	60	8
2016-17	PR Lge	38	22	10	6	78	42	76	4
2017-18	PR Lge	38	21	12	5	84	38	75	4

DID YOU KNOW

Liverpool used just 14 players when they won the Football League championship in 1965–66. Nine of the team appeared in 40 or more of their 42 games while Bobby Graham made just a single appearance. The Reds finished the season six points clear of runners-up Leeds United.

LIVERPOOL – PREMIER LEAGUE 2017–18 LEAGUE RECORD

Match No.	Date	Venue	Opponents	Result	H/T Score	Lg Pos.	Goalscorers	Attendance
1	Aug 12	A	Watford	D	3-3	1-2	7	Mane [29], Firmino (pen) [56], Salah [57]	20,407
2	19	H	Crystal Palace	W	1-0	0-0	4	Mane [73]	53,138
3	27	H	Arsenal	W	4-0	2-0	2	Firmino [17], Mane [40], Salah [57], Sturridge [77]	53,206
4	Sept 9	A	Manchester C	L	0-5	0-2	7		54,172
5	16	H	Burnley	D	1-1	1-1	8	Salah [30]	53,231
6	23	A	Leicester C	W	3-2	2-1	5	Salah [15], Coutinho [23], Henderson [68]	32,004
7	Oct 1	A	Newcastle U	D	1-1	1-1	7	Coutinho [29]	52,303
8	14	H	Manchester U	D	0-0	0-0	8		52,912
9	22	A	Tottenham H	L	1-4	1-3	9	Salah [24]	80,827
10	28	H	Huddersfield T	W	3-0	0-0	6	Sturridge [50], Firmino [58], Wijnaldum [75]	53,268
11	Nov 4	A	West Ham U	W	4-1	2-0	6	Salah 2 [21, 75], Matip [24], Oxlade-Chamberlain [56]	56,961
12	18	H	Southampton	W	3-0	2-0	5	Salah 2 [31, 41], Coutinho [68]	53,256
13	25	H	Chelsea	D	1-1	0-0	5	Salah [65]	53,225
14	29	A	Stoke C	W	3-0	1-0	5	Mane [17], Salah 2 [77, 83]	29,423
15	Dec 2	A	Brighton & HA	W	5-1	2-0	4	Can [30], Firmino 2 [31, 48], Coutinho [87], Dunk (og) [89]	30,634
16	10	H	Everton	D	1-1	1-0	4	Salah [42]	53,082
17	13	H	WBA	D	0-0	0-0	5		53,243
18	17	A	Bournemouth	W	4-0	3-0	4	Coutinho [20], Lovren [26], Salah [44], Firmino [66]	10,780
19	22	A	Arsenal	D	3-3	1-1	4	Coutinho [26], Salah [52], Firmino [71]	59,409
20	26	H	Swansea C	W	5-0	1-0	4	Coutinho [6], Firmino 2 [52, 66], Alexander-Arnold [65], Oxlade-Chamberlain [82]	52,850
21	30	H	Leicester C	W	2-1	0-1	4	Salah 2 [52, 76]	53,226
22	Jan 1	A	Burnley	W	2-1	0-0	4	Mane [61], Klavan [90]	21,756
23	14	H	Manchester C	W	4-3	1-1	3	Oxlade-Chamberlain [9], Firmino [59], Mane [61], Salah [68]	53,285
24	22	A	Swansea C	L	0-1	0-1	4		20,886
25	30	A	Huddersfield T	W	3-0	2-0	4	Can [26], Firmino [45], Salah (pen) [78]	24,121
26	Feb 4	H	Tottenham H	D	2-2	1-0	3	Salah 2 [3, 90]	53,213
27	11	A	Southampton	W	2-0	2-0	3	Firmino [6], Salah [42]	31,915
28	24	H	West Ham U	W	4-1	1-0	2	Can [29], Salah [51], Firmino [57], Mane [77]	53,256
29	Mar 3	H	Newcastle U	W	2-0	1-0	2	Salah [40], Mane [55]	53,287
30	10	A	Manchester U	L	1-2	0-2	3	Bailly (og) [66]	74,855
31	17	H	Watford	W	5-0	2-0	3	Salah 4 [4, 43, 77, 85], Firmino [49]	53,287
32	31	A	Crystal Palace	W	2-1	0-1	3	Mane [49], Salah [84]	25,807
33	Apr 7	A	Everton	D	0-0	0-0	3		39,220
34	14	H	Bournemouth	W	3-0	1-0	3	Mane [7], Salah [69], Firmino [90]	52,959
35	21	A	WBA	D	2-2	1-2	3	Ings [4], Salah [72]	24,520
36	28	H	Stoke C	D	0-0	0-0	3		53,255
37	May 6	A	Chelsea	L	0-1	0-1	3		41,314
38	13	H	Brighton & HA	W	4-0	2-0	4	Salah [26], Lovren [40], Solanke [53], Robertson [85]	50,752

Final League Position: 4

GOALSCORERS

League (84): Salah 32 (1 pen), Firmino 15 (1 pen), Mane 10, Coutinho 7, Can 3, Oxlade-Chamberlain 3, Lovren 2, Sturridge 2, Alexander-Arnold 1, Henderson 1, Ings 1, Klavan 1, Matip 1, Robertson 1, Solanke 1, Wijnaldum 1, own goals 2.

FA Cup (4): Firmino 1, Milner 1 (1 pen), Salah 1, van Dijk 1.

Carabao Cup (0).

Champions League (47): Firmino 11, Salah 11, Mane 10, Coutinho 5 (1 pen), Can 3, Alexander-Arnold 2, Oxlade-Chamberlain 2, Sturridge 1, Wijnaldum 1, own goal 1.

Mignolet S 19	Alexander-Arnold T 18+1	Matip J 22+3	Lovren D 24+5	Moreno A 14+2	Can E 24+2	Henderson J 25+2	Wijnaldum G 27+6	Salah M 34+2	Firmino R 32+5	Mane S 28+1	Origi D —+1	Milner J 16+16	Gomez J 21+2	Klavan R 16+3	Robertson A 22	Sturridge D 5+4	Solanke D 5+16	Karius L 19	Grujic M —+3	Oxlade-Chamberlain A 14+18	Coutinho P 13+1	Lallana A 1+11	Ings D 3+5	van Dijk V 14	Clyne N 2+1	Woodburn B —+1	Match No.
1	2^3	3	4	5	6	7	8	9^2	10^1	11	12	13	14														1
1		3	14			7	6^1	12	11^3	9		8	2	4	5	10^2	13										2
		3	4	5	6^1	7	8	9	10^3	11^2		13	2			12		1	14								3
1	2	3		5	8	7	6^2	9	10^1	11^4		13	4			14				12							4
1	2	3				7		9	11^1			6		4	5	10	12			13	8^2						5
1		3	4	5	6^1	7	8	9	10^3			13	2			12				14	11^2						6
1		3	4	5		7	6	9^2	12	11^1		2				10^3	13			14	8						7
1		3	4	5	8	7	6	9^3	10^1			2				13	14			12	11^2						8
1		3	4^2	5	8^3	7		11	10^1			6	2			13				14	12	9					9
1		3		5	13	7	8	9	11^2			6	2	4		10^3	14			12							10
1		3	13	5	7		6	11	10^1	9^3		12	2	4			14			8^2							11
1	2		3	5	12	7	6	9	10	11^3		14		4						13	8^2						12
1		3		5		7	12	9		13		6	2	4		10^2				11^2	8^1	14					13
1		3	4	5	6	14	7	12	9	10^1		13	2				11^3			8^2							14
1	5	3		2	7^3	4	10^2	11^1		6					9	13		14	12	8							15
1		3				7		9	12	11		8	2	4	5	10^3				6^2	13	14					16
	2^2		3		7		6^1	10	11	9^3		14	4	5		12		1		13	8						17
1		3				7	8	9	10^2			2	4	5		13				6	11^3	12	14				18
1		3		7	6^1	13	8	11	10^2		12	2	4	5						14	9^3						19
1	2	3				7		8	9^3	10^2		14		4	5^1	12				6	11	13					20
		3	4		7		13	9^2	10^1	11		8	2	14	5					12	6^3						21
1	2	14	3		6		7		12	8^3		13	5	4		11				10^1	9^2						22
		3	4		7^2		8	9^3	10	11^1		12	2	14	5			1		6	13						23
		3			6		7^1	8	11	10		2		5				1		9^2	12	13	4				24
		3	4		6	7^3	12	9^2	10^2	11		8	2	5		14	1			13							25
2	14	3			6	7^2	12	9	10	11^1		8^1		5				1		13			4				26
2	3	14			7		8	9^2	10^1	11		12		5				1		6^3	13		4				27
2	3		14	7			9	10^2	11^3			8		5			13	1		6	12		4				28
2	14	3		8	7			9	10^1	11^2		13		5				1		6^3	12		4				29
2^2		3		7		13	9	10	11			8		5^3	14			1		6^1	12		4				30
	3			6^1	7	8^3	9	10^2	11			12	2			5		1		13		14	4				31
2	3	14			7	6^1	9	10	11^2			8				5		1		12	13^3		4				32
14		3			7	6		13	11^3	8^1		5				10	1			12		9^2	4	2			33
2		3^2			7	6	9	10^1	11^3			12	13	5		14^1		1		8			4				34
	14	5			7	6	9^1	12	11^3			8	2	4			1			13		10^2	3				35
6^2		5			7	8	9	10				13	2	4				1				11^1	3	12			36
6		3	14		12	7	9	10	11			8^1				5^2	13	1					4	2^2			37
2		3			7	8	6^2	10^3	9^1			5		11	1					12	13	4			14		38

FA Cup

Third Round	Everton	(h)	2-1
Fourth Round	WBA	(h)	2-3

Carabao Cup

Third Round	Leicester C	(a)	0-2

Champions League

Play-off Round 1st leg	TSG Hoffenheim	(a)	2-1
Play-off Round 2nd leg	TSG Hoffenheim	(h)	4-2
Group E	Sevilla	(h)	2-2
Group E	Spartak Moscow	(a)	1-1
Group E	Maribor	(a)	7-0
Group E	Maribor	(h)	3-0
Group E	Sevilla	(a)	3-3
Group E	Spartak Moscow	(h)	7-0
Round of 16 1st leg	Porto	(a)	5-0
Round of 16 2nd leg	Porto	(h)	0-0
Quarter-Final 1st leg	Manchester C	(h)	3-0
Quarter-Final 2nd leg	Manchester C	(a)	2-1
Semi-Final 1st leg	Roma	(h)	5-2
Semi-Final 2nd leg	Roma	(a)	2-4
Final	Real Madrid	(Kiev)	1-3

LUTON TOWN

FOUNDATION

Formed by an amalgamation of two leading local clubs, Wanderers and Excelsior a works team, at a meeting in Luton Town Hall in April 1885. The Wanderers had three months earlier changed their name to Luton Town Wanderers and did not take too kindly to the formation of another Town club but were talked around at this meeting. Wanderers had already appeared in the FA Cup and the new club entered in its inaugural season.

Kenilworth Road Stadium, 1 Maple Road, Luton, Bedfordshire LU4 8AW.

Telephone: (01582) 411 622.

Fax: (01582) 405 070.

Ticket Office: (01582) 416 976.

Website: www.lutontown.co.uk

Email: info@lutontown.co.uk

Ground Capacity: 10,413 (not all available to use).

Record Attendance: 30,069 v Blackpool, FA Cup 6th rd replay, 4 March 1959.

Pitch Measurements: 101m × 66m (110yd × 72yd).

Chairman: David Wilkinson.

Chief Executive: Gary Sweet.

Manager: Nathan Jones.

Assistant Manager: Paul Hart.

HONOURS

League Champions: Division 2 – 1981–82; FL 1 – 2004–05; Division 3S – 1936–37; Division 4 – 1967–68; Conference – 2013–14.
Runners-up: FL 2 – 2017–18; Division 2 – 1954–55, 1973–74; Division 3 – 1969–70; Division 3S – 1935–36; Third Division – 2001–02.
FA Cup: Runners-up: 1959.
League Cup Winners: 1988.
Runners-up: 1989.
League Trophy Winners: 2009.
Full Members' Cup: Runners-up: 1988.

Colours: Orange shirts with white trim, navy blue shorts with orange trim, orange socks with navy blue trim.

Year Formed: 1885.

Turned Professional: 1890.

Ltd Co.: 1897.

Club Nickname: 'The Hatters'.

Grounds: 1885, Excelsior, Dallow Lane; 1897, Dunstable Road; 1905, Kenilworth Road.

First Football League Game: 4 September 1897, Division 2, v Leicester Fosse (a) D 1–1 – Williams; McCartney, McEwen; Davies, Stewart, Docherty; Gallacher, Coupar, Birch, McInnes, Ekins (1).

Record League Victory: 12–0 v Bristol R, Division 3 (S), 13 April 1936 – Dolman; Mackey, Smith; Finlayson, Nelson, Godfrey; Rich, Martin (1), Payne (10), Roberts (1), Stephenson.

Record Cup Victory: 9–0 v Clapton, FA Cup 1st rd (replay after abandoned game), 30 November 1927 – Abbott; Kingham, Graham; Black, Rennie, Fraser; Pointon, Yardley (4), Reid (2), Woods (1), Dennis (2).

Record Defeat: 0–9 v Small Heath, Division 2, 12 November 1898.

Sun FACT FILE

In 1974 the Luton Town players joined with the Barron Knights, who were also from Bedfordshire, to produce a record. The single 'Hatters, Hatters', with a B side of 'We Are Luton Town You Know', was released on the Tavern label but failed to make the UK charts.

Most League Points (2 for a win): 66, Division 4, 1967–68.

Most League Points (3 for a win): 98, FL 1 2004–05.

Most League Goals: 103, Division 3 (S), 1936–37.

Highest League Scorer in Season: Joe Payne, 55, Division 3 (S), 1936–37.

Most League Goals in Total Aggregate: Gordon Turner, 243, 1949–64.

Most League Goals in One Match: 10, Joe Payne v Bristol R, Division 3 (S), 13 April 1936.

Most Capped Player: Mal Donaghy, 58 (91), Northern Ireland.

Most League Appearances: Bob Morton, 495, 1948–64.

Youngest League Player: Mike O'Hara, 16 years 32 days v Stoke C, 1 October 1960.

Record Transfer Fee Received: £3,000,000 from WBA for Curtis Davies, August 2005; £3,000,000 from Birmingham C for Rowan Vine, January 2007.

Record Transfer Fee Paid: £850,000 to Odense for Lars Elstrup, August 1989.

Football League Record: 1897 Elected to Division 2; 1900 Failed re-election; 1920 Division 3; 1921–37 Division 3 (S); 1937–55 Division 2; 1955–60 Division 1; 1960–63 Division 2; 1963–65 Division 3; 1965–68 Division 4; 1968–70 Division 3; 1970–74 Division 2; 1974–75 Division 1; 1975–82 Division 2; 1982–96 Division 1; 1996–2001 Division 2; 2001–02 Division 3; 2002–04 Division 2; 2004–05 FL 1; 2005–07 FL C; 2007–08 FL 1; 2008–09 FL 2; 2009–14 Conference Premier; 2014–18 FL 2; 2018– FL 1.

LATEST SEQUENCES

Longest Sequence of League Wins: 12, 19.2.2002 – 6.4.2002.

Longest Sequence of League Defeats: 8, 11.11.1899 – 6.1.1900.

Longest Sequence of League Draws: 5, 28.8.1971 – 18.9.1971.

Longest Sequence of Unbeaten League Matches: 19, 8.4.1969 – 7.10.1969.

Longest Sequence Without a League Win: 16, 9.9.1964 – 6.11.1964.

Successive Scoring Runs: 25 from 24.10.1931.

Successive Non-scoring Runs: 5 from 10.4.1973.

MANAGERS

Charlie Green 1901–28 (Secretary-Manager)
George Thomson 1925
John McCartney 1927–29
George Kay 1929–31
Harold Wightman 1931–35
Ted Liddell 1936–38
Neil McBain 1938–39
George Martin 1939–47
Dally Duncan 1947–58
Syd Owen 1959–60
Sam Bartram 1960–62
Bill Harvey 1962–64
George Martin 1965–66
Allan Brown 1966–68
Alec Stock 1968–72
Harry Haslam 1972–78
David Pleat 1978–86
John Moore 1986–87
Ray Harford 1987–89
Jim Ryan 1990–91
David Pleat 1991–95
Terry Westley 1995
Lennie Lawrence 1995–2000
Ricky Hill 2000
Lil Fuccillo 2000
Joe Kinnear 2001–03
Mike Newell 2003–07
Kevin Blackwell 2007–08
Mick Harford 2008–09
Richard Money 2009–11
Gary Brabin 2011–12
Paul Buckle 2012–13
John Still 2013–15
Nathan Jones January 2016–

TEN YEAR LEAGUE RECORD

		P	W	D	L	F	A	Pts	Pos
2008-09	FL 2	46	13	17	16	58	65	26*	24
2009-10	Conf P	44	26	10	8	84	40	88	2
2010-11	Conf P	46	23	15	8	85	37	84	3
2011-12	Conf P	46	22	15	9	78	42	81	5
2012-13	Conf P	46	18	13	15	70	62	67	7
2013-14	Conf P	46	30	11	5	102	35	101	1
2014-15	FL 2	46	19	11	16	54	44	68	8
2015-16	FL 2	46	19	9	18	63	61	66	11
2016-17	FL 2	46	20	17	9	70	43	77	4
2017-18	FL 2	46	25	13	8	94	46	88	2

*30 points deducted.

DID YOU KNOW

Luton Town, then in Division Three South, knocked First Division Chelsea out of the FA Cup when they defeated them 2-0 at home in a third-round replay in January 1935. The fixture attracted a new record gate of 23,041 for the club's Kenilworth Road ground.

LUTON TOWN – SKY BET LEAGUE TWO 2017–18 LEAGUE RECORD

Match No.	Date	Venue	Opponents	Result	Score	H/T Score	Lg Pos.	Goalscorers	Attendance
1	Aug 5	H	Yeovil T	W	8-2	5-1	1	Lee, O [12], Collins 3 [19, 58, 66], McCormack [24], Vassell 2 [36, 38], Lee, E [90]	8101
2	12	A	Barnet	L	0-1	0-0	8		3555
3	19	H	Colchester U	W	3-0	1-0	3	Lee, O [45], Collins [52], Potts [83]	7865
4	26	A	Mansfield T	D	2-2	0-1	5	Collins [85], Hylton [89]	4665
5	Sept 2	A	Lincoln C	D	0-0	0-0	6		9332
6	9	H	Swindon T	L	0-3	0-1	13		8455
7	12	H	Port Vale	W	2-0	1-0	9	Whitfield (og) [38], Stacey [50]	7046
8	16	A	Wycombe W	W	2-1	0-1	4	Collins [90], Cuthbert [90]	5512
9	23	H	Chesterfield	W	1-0	0-0	3	Hylton [53]	7575
10	26	A	Morecambe	D	0-0	0-0	5		1354
11	30	H	Newport Co	W	3-1	3-0	5	Sheehan [12], Hylton 2 (1 pen) [22, 35 (p)]	7681
12	Oct 7	A	Accrington S	W	2-0	2-0	3	Collins [22], Hylton (pen) [44]	2193
13	14	H	Stevenage	W	7-1	3-1	3	Berry 3 [3, 21, 62], Hylton 2 (1 pen) [7, 52 (p)], Justin [90], Gambin [90]	9208
14	17	A	Exeter C	W	4-1	1-1	1	Collins [8], Potts [46], Hylton [52], Cornick [55]	4209
15	21	A	Crawley T	D	0-0	0-0	1		3494
16	28	H	Coventry C	L	0-3	0-1	3		9670
17	Nov 11	A	Cheltenham T	D	2-2	1-1	4	Potts [11], Lee, E [86]	3900
18	18	H	Cambridge U	W	7-0	4-0	2	Potts [24], Lee, O [31], Hylton 3 [35, 81, 90], Lee, E 2 [45, 88]	8721
19	21	H	Carlisle U	W	3-0	2-0	1	Shinnie [19], Potts [30], Cornick [76]	7644
20	25	A	Crewe Alex	W	2-1	0-0	1	Hylton [63], Berry [67]	4571
21	Dec 9	H	Notts Co	D	1-1	1-0	1	Mullins [26]	10,063
22	16	A	Forest Green R	W	2-0	1-0	1	Sheehan [45], Hylton [68]	2546
23	23	H	Grimsby T	W	2-0	1-0	1	Berry [40], Collins [61]	9102
24	26	A	Swindon T	W	5-0	0-0	1	Collins [48], Hylton [55], Taylor (og) [66], Cornick [72], Lee, E [84]	8526
25	30	A	Port Vale	L	0-4	0-1	1		5523
26	Jan 1	H	Lincoln C	W	4-2	2-2	1	Collins [32], Justin [43], Hylton [72], Cornick [82]	9659
27	13	A	Chesterfield	L	0-2	0-2	1		5715
28	20	H	Morecambe	W	1-0	0-0	1	Mullins [64]	8476
29	27	A	Grimsby T	W	1-0	0-0	1	Collins [49]	4159
30	30	H	Wycombe W	L	2-3	1-2	1	Lee, E 2 [43, 78]	8564
31	Feb 3	H	Exeter C	W	1-0	1-0	1	Cornick [38]	8788
32	10	A	Stevenage	D	1-1	0-0	1	Collins (pen) [85]	4365
33	13	A	Crawley T	W	4-1	2-0	1	Lee, O [29], Hylton 2 (1 pen) [45, 75 (p)], Berry [55]	8020
34	24	H	Cheltenham T	D	2-2	0-1	1	Berry [58], Sheehan [90]	8453
35	Mar 3	A	Cambridge U	D	1-1	1-0	1	Collins [33]	6722
36	10	H	Accrington S	L	1-2	0-1	2	Lee, E [61]	9503
37	13	A	Coventry C	D	2-2	0-2	2	Cuthbert [55], Collins [88]	8863
38	17	A	Newport Co	D	1-1	1-1	2	Potts [23]	3512
39	24	H	Barnet	W	2-0	0-0	2	Hylton [47], Collins [67]	8140
40	30	A	Colchester U	L	1-2	0-2	2	Hylton (pen) [88]	5461
41	Apr 2	H	Mansfield T	W	2-1	0-1	2	Collins [61], Rea [71]	9592
42	7	A	Yeovil T	W	3-0	0-2	2	Lee, E [4], Hylton 2 (1 pen) [20 (p), 40]	4316
43	14	H	Crewe Alex	W	3-1	2-1	2	Hylton [39], Lee, E [45], Ruddock [51]	9202
44	21	A	Carlisle U	D	1-1	0-1	2	Lee, O [62]	5523
45	28	H	Forest Green R	W	3-1	1-0	2	Hylton [20], Lee, O [86], Ruddock [89]	10,029
46	May 5	A	Notts Co	D	0-0	0-0	2		12,184

Final League Position: 2

GOALSCORERS

League (94): Hylton 21 (5 pens), Collins 19 (2 pens), Lee, E 10, Berry 7, Lee, O 6, Potts 6, Cornick 5, Sheehan 3, Cuthbert 2, Justin 2, Mullins 2, Ruddock 2, Vassell 2, Gambin 1, McCormack 1, Rea 1, Shinnie 1, Stacey 1, own goals 2.
FA Cup (7): Hylton 2, Berry 1, Collins 1, Lee E 1, Lee O 1, Potts 1.
Carabao Cup (0).
Checkatrade Trophy (9): Shinnie 2, Cook 1, Cotter 1, D'Ath 1, Gambin 1, Jarvis 1, Lee E 1, McQuoid 1.

Match No.	Stech M 38	Stacey J 40+1	McCormack A 15+1	Cuthbert S 20+3	Potts D 42	Shinnie A 24+4	Ruddock P 17+11	Lee O 38	Sheehan A 42	Vassell I 2	Collins J 39+3	Rea G 39+7	Lee E 16+16	Mullins J 14+3	Cook J 1+9	Hylton D 37+2	Cornick H 16+21	Berry L 31+3	Gambin L 4+9	Jarvis A —+1	Justin J 10+7	D'Ath L 3+6	Famewo A 1+2	Downes F 7+3	Jervis J 2+8	Jones L —+1	Shea J 8
1	1	2	3^1	4	5	6^2	7	8	9	10	11^3	12	13	14													
2	1	2	3	4^3	5	6^2	8	7	9	10^1	11	12		14	13												
3	1	2	6		5	8^2	9	7	4		10^3	3		14	13	11^1	12										
4	1	2	6^2	3	5	9^1	8	7^3	4		11	12				10	14	13									
5	1	5	7^1	3	9		6		2		11^2	4			13	10	12	8									
6	1	2	6	4^4	5	8^1	9	7^3	3		10	12				11^2	13	14									
7	1	2	6		5	7^2	9		4		11^1	3	13			10	12	8									
8	1	2	6^1	12	5	9^2	8		4		10	3^3	14			11	13	7									
9	1	2		4	5	9^2	8^4	7^3	3		11	13			12	10	14				6^1						
10	1	2		4	5		7		3		11^2	6			12	10	8^1		9	13							
11	1	2	3		5		9		4		11	6			12	10	7^1		8^2	13							
12	1	2	4		5		7		3		11	8				10	6^1	9^2	13	12							
13	1	2	4		12	7			11		8^3	14	3			10^2	6^1	9	13		5						
14	1	2	3	5		14	6	4			10^3	7	13			11	9^1	8^2			12						
15	1	2	3	5		13	7^3	4			11	8	12	14		10^1	6^2	9									
16	1	2	3	5	13	12^7					10^2	8^4	14	4^1		11	6^2	9									
17	1	2	3	5		13	6	4			10^1	7	12			11	9^2	8									
18	1	2	3^3	5^2	9^1	12	6	4			7	10	13^1	11		8				14							
19	1	2		5	9^1	6		4			7	10^2	3^3			11	12	8				13	14				
20	1	2		5	12	13	7^1	4			6	10^3	3			11	9^2	8					14				
21	1	2		5	9^2		7	4			12	6	10^3	3		11		8	13								
22	1	2^4		5	9^2		8^1	4			14	6	10^3	3		11	12	7		13							
23	1			5	9^3		6	4			11^1	7	13	3		10^2	12	8	2	14							
24	1			5	9^1	14	7^2	4			10	6	13	3		11^3	12	8	2								
25	1			5	14	6		4			13	7	11^3	3		10	9^1	12	2	8^2							
26	1	2			9^1		6	4^4			10	7		3		11	12	8	5								
27	1			5	9^3	13	7^2				10^1	6	11	3	14	12	8		2		4						
28	1	2		5	9		6				10	4	12^3	3		11^1	13	8		7^2							
29	1	2		5	9^1			4			11^3	6	14	3^7		10^3	8		13	12							
30	1	2		5	9^1	12	6^2	4			10	7	11	3^3			13	8		14							
31	1	2	3			8	7		9	5						12^{11}	6							4	10^2	13	
32	1	2		5	12	13	8	4			10	3				9	6^2			14				7^1	11^3		
33	1	2			9^1		6	4			11	3				10^2	8	13	5					7	12		
34	1	2			9^3		6^2	4			11	3			13	10	8	14	5					7	12		
35	1	2	14	5			7^1	3			11^4	4				10^2		6	12		9^3			8	13		
36	1	2		5	9^3		6	4				3	11^1			10	12	8	13					7^2	14		
37	1	2	3	5				4			11	7^2	13			10	9^1	8	12			6					
38	1	2	14	3	5			4			10	7	9^2			11^3	12	8	6^1						13		
39		14	7	3	5	9^3		8^1	4		10	12				11^2		6		2					13		1
40			3	5	9^2		7	4			10	6^3	13			11	14	8^{12}		2							1
41		2	7	3^1	5		8	6	4		9	12	11^3			10^2				14					13		1
42		2	7^1		5		8	6	4		9	3	11^2			10^3		14						13	12		1
43		2	7		5		8	6	4		9	3	11^2	13		10^1	12										1
44		2	7^1		5		9	8	4		11	3	6^{12}	10										13			1
45		2	7^2	13	5		9	8	4		10^1	3	6			11	12										1
46		2	7^1		5		9	8	4		10	3	6^2			11^4	12							13			1

FA Cup

First Round	Portsmouth		(h)	1-0
Second Round	Gateshead		(a)	5-0
Third Round	Newcastle U		(a)	1-3

Carabao Cup

First Round	Ipswich T		(h)	0-2

Checkatrade Trophy

Southern Group F	Tottenham H U21	(h)	2-2
(Luton T won 4-2 on penalties)			
Southern Group F	Barnet	(h)	1-1
(Luton T won 4-3 on penalties)			
Southern Group F	AFC Wimbledon	(a)	2-1
Second Round South	West Ham U U21	(h)	4-0
Third Round	Peterborough U	(h)	0-0
(Peterborough U won 7-6 on penalties)			

MACCLESFIELD TOWN

FOUNDATION

From the mid-19th century until 1874, Macclesfield Town FC played under rugby rules. In 1891 they moved to the Moss Rose ground and finished champions of the Manchester & District League in 1906 and 1908. By 1911, they had carried off the Cheshire Senior Cup five times. Macclesfield were founder members of the Cheshire County League in 1919.

Moss Rose Stadium, London Road, Macclesfield, Cheshire SK11 7SP.

Telephone: (01625) 264 686.

Fax: (01625) 264 692.

Ticket Office: (01625) 264 686.

Website: www.mtfc.co.uk

Email: reception@mtfc.co.uk

Ground Capacity: 6,335.

Record Attendance: 9,008 v Winsford U, Cheshire Senior Cup 2nd rd, 4 February 1948.

Pitch Measurements: 100m × 60m.

Chairman: Mark Blower.

Director: Amar Alkadhi.

Manager: Mark Yates.

First-Team Coach: Byron Jenkins.

Colours: Blue shirts with white trim, white shorts, blue socks.

Year Formed: 1874.

Turned Professional: 1886.

Club Nickname: 'The Silkmen'.

Grounds: 1874, Rostron Field; 1891, Moss Rose.

First Football League Game: 9 August 1997, Division 3, v Torquay U (h) W 2–1 – Price; Tinson, Rose, Payne (Edey), Howarth, Sodje (1), Askey, Wood, Landon (1) (Power), Mason, Sorvel.

Record League Victory: 6–0 v Stockport Co, FL 1, 26 December 2005 – Fettis; Harsley, Sandwith, Morley, Swailes (Teague), Navarro, Whitaker (Miles (1)), Bullock (1), Parkin (2), Wijnhard (2) (Townson), McIntyre.

Record Cup Victory: 15–0 v Chester St Mary's, Cheshire Senior Cup 3rd rd, 6 February 1886; 15–0 v Barnton Rovers, Cheshire Senior Cup 1st rd, 12 November 1887.

HONOURS

League Champions: Vauxhall Conference – 1994–95, 1996–97; National League – 2017–18. *Runners-up:* Division 3 – 1997–98. *FA Trophy Winners:* 1969–70, 1995–96. *Runners-up:* 1988–89.

The Sun FACT FILE

Macclesfield Town, then in the Football Conference, knocked out Division Three club Chesterfield from the FA Cup in November 1992 after goalkeeper Steve Farrelly saved three consecutive spot-kicks during a penalty shoot-out. The first-round replay at Saltergate ended 2-2 after extra time and Farrelly's saves meant that Macclesfield won the shoot-out 3-2. Town earned a home tie against local rivals Stockport County in the second round but went down 2-0 in front of a crowd of 5,700.

Record Win: 15–0 v Chester St Marys, Cheshire Senior Cup 2nd rd, 16 February 1886.

Record Defeat: 1–13 v Tranmere R reserves, 3 May 1929.

Most League Points (3 for a win): 82, Division 3, 1997–98.

Most League Goals: 66, Division 3, 1999–2000.

Highest League Scorer in Season: Jon Parkin, 22, FL 2, 2004–05.

Most League Goals in Total Aggregate: Matt Tipton, 50, 2002–05; 2006–07; 2009–10.

Most League Goals in One Match: 3, Ricky Lambert v Luton T, Division 3, 24 November 2001; 3, Jonathan Parkin v Notts Co, FL 2, 25 January 2005; 3, Matt Tipton v Rochdale, FL 2, 19 February 2005.

Most Capped Player: George Abbey, 10 (18), Nigeria.

Most League Appearances: Darren Tinson, 263, 1997–2003.

Youngest League Player: Elliott Hewitt, 16 years 342 days v Hereford U, 7 May 2011.

Record Transfer Fee Received: £300,000 from Stockport Co for Rickie Lambert, April 2002.

Record Transfer Fee Paid: £40,000 to Bury for Danny Swailes, January 2005.

Football League Record: 1997 Promoted to Division 3; 1998–99 Division 2; 1999–2004 Division 3; 2004–12 FL 2; 2012–17 National League; 2018– FL2.

LATEST SEQUENCES

Longest Sequence of League Wins: 6, 25.1.2005 – 26.2.2005.

Longest Sequence of League Defeats: 8, 2.1.2012 – 21.2.2012.

Longest Sequence of League Draws: 5, 5.5.2007 – 1.9.2007.

Longest Sequence of Unbeaten League Matches: 8, 16.10.1999 – 27.11.1999.

Longest Sequence Without a League Win: 23, 2.1.2012 – Season's end.

Successive Scoring Runs: 14 from 11.10.2003.

Successive Non-scoring Runs: 5 from 18.12.1998.

MANAGERS

Since 1967
Keith Goalen 1967–68
Frank Beaumont 1968–72
Billy Haydock 1972–74
Eddie Brown 1974
John Collins 1974
Willie Stevenson 1974
John Collins 1975–76
Tony Coleman 1976
John Barnes 1976
Brian Taylor 1976
Dave Connor 1976–78
Derek Partridge 1978
Phil Staley 1978–80
Jimmy Williams 1980–81
Brian Booth 1981–85
Neil Griffiths 1985–86
Roy Campbell 1986
Peter Wragg 1986–93
Sammy McIlroy 1993–2000
Peter Davenport 2000
Gil Prescott 2000–01
David Moss 2001–03
John Askey 2003–04
Brian Horton 2004–06
Paul Ince 2006–07
Ian Brightwell 2007–08
Keith Alexander 2008–10
Gary Simpson 2010–12
Steve King 2012–13
John Askew 2013–18
Mark Yates June 2018–

TEN YEAR LEAGUE RECORD

		P	W	D	L	F	A	Pts	Pos
2008-09	FL 2	46	13	8	25	45	77	47	20
2009-10	FL 2	46	12	18	16	49	58	54	19
2010-11	FL 2	46	14	13	19	59	73	55	15
2011-12	FL 2	46	8	13	25	39	64	37	24
2012-13	Conf	46	17	12	17	65	70	63	11
2013-14	Conf	46	18	7	21	62	63	61	15
2014-15	Conf	46	21	15	10	60	46	78	6
2015-16	NL	46	19	9	18	60	48	66	10
2016-17	NL	46	20	8	18	64	57	68	9
2017-18	NL	46	27	11	8	67	46	92	1

DID YOU KNOW

Centre-forward John Jepson signed for Macclesfield on New Year's Day 1932 and went on to score in each of his first 12 games for the club. He finished the season as leading scorer with 30 league and cup goals helping the Silkmen win the Cheshire League title for the first time in their history. He failed to score in just four of his 26 appearances for the club.

MANCHESTER CITY

FOUNDATION

Manchester City was formed as a limited company in 1894 after their predecessors Ardwick had been forced into bankruptcy. However, many historians like to trace the club's lineage as far back as 1880 when St Mark's Church, West Gorton added a football section to their cricket club. They amalgamated with Belle Vue for one season before splitting again under the name Gorton Association FC in 1884–85. In 1887 Gorton AFC turned professional and moved ground to Hyde Road under the new name Ardwick AFC.

Etihad Stadium, Etihad Campus, Manchester M11 3FF.
Telephone: (0161) 444 1894.
Fax: (0161) 438 7999.
Ticket Office: (0161) 444 1894.
Website: www.mancity.com
Email: mancity@mancity.com
Ground Capacity: 55,017.
Record Attendance: 84,569 v Stoke C, FA Cup 6th rd, 3 March 1934 (at Maine Road; British record for any game outside London or Glasgow); 54,693 v Leicester C, FA Premier League, 6 February 2016 (at Etihad Stadium).
Pitch Measurements: 105m × 68m (114yd × 74yd).
Chairman: Khaldoon Al Mubarak.
Chief Executive: Ferran Soriano.
Manager: Pep Guardiola.
Assistant Managers: Domene Torrent, Brian Kidd.
Colours: Field blue shirts with white trim, white shorts with field blue trim, field blue socks.
Year Formed: 1887 as Ardwick FC; 1894 as Manchester City.
Turned Professional: 1887 as Ardwick FC.
Previous Names: 1880, St Mark's Church, West Gorton; 1884, Gorton; 1887, Ardwick; 1894, Manchester City.
Club Nicknames: 'The Blues', 'The Citizens'.
Grounds: 1880, Clowes Street; 1881, Kirkmanshulme Cricket Ground; 1882, Queens Road; 1884, Pink Bank Lane; 1887, Hyde Road (1894–1923 as City); 1923, Maine Road; 2003, City of Manchester Stadium (renamed Etihad Stadium 2011).
First Football League Game: 3 September 1892, Division 2, v Bootle (h) W 7–0 – Douglas; McVickers, Robson; Middleton, Russell, Hopkins; Davies (3), Morris (2), Angus (1), Weir (1), Milarvie.
Record League Victory: 10–1 v Huddersfield T, Division 2, 7 November 1987 – Nixon; Gidman, Hinchcliffe, Clements, Lake, Redmond, White (3), Stewart (3), Adcock (3), McNab (1), Simpson.
Record Cup Victory: 10–1 v Swindon T, FA Cup 4th rd, 29 January 1930 – Barber; Felton, McCloy; Barrass, Cowan, Heinemann; Toseland, Marshall (5), Tait (3), Johnson (1), Brook (1).

HONOURS

League Champions: FA Premier League – 2011–12, 2013–14, 2017–18; Division 1 – 1936–37, 1967–68; First Division – 2001–02; Division 2 – 1898–99, 1902–03, 1909–10, 1927–28, 1946–47, 1965–66.
Runners-up: FA Premier League – 2012–13, 2014–15; Division 1 – 1903–04, 1920–21, 1976–77; First Division – 1999–2000; Division 2 – 1895–96, 1950–51, 1988–89.
FA Cup Winners: 1904, 1934, 1956, 1969, 2011.
Runners-up: 1926, 1933, 1955, 1981, 2013.
League Cup Winners: 1970, 1976, 2014, 2016, 2018.
Runners-up: 1974.
Full Members Cup: Runners-up: 1986.
European Competitions
European Cup: 1968–69.
Champions League: 2011–12, 2012–13, 2013–14, 2014–15, 2015–16 *(sf)*, 2016–17, 2017–18 *(qf)*.
UEFA Cup: 1972–73, 1976–77, 1977–78, 1978–79 *(qf)*, 2003–04, 2008–09 *(qf)*.
Europa League: 2010–11, 2011–12.
European Cup-Winners' Cup: 1969–70 *(winners)*, 1970–71 *(sf)*.

THE Sun FACT FILE

In the closing stages of Manchester City's home game with Middlesbrough on 15 May 2005, manager Stuart Pearce brought on goalkeeper Nicky Weaver as a substitute, while sending the incumbent keeper David James up front to play as a striker. James created a certain amount of havoc in the Boro defence but the score remained 1-1 at full time.

Record Defeat: 1–9 v Everton, Division 1, 3 September 1906.

Most League Points (2 for a win): 62, Division 2, 1946–47.

Most League Points (3 for a win): 100, FA Premier League, 2017–18.

Most League Goals: 108, Division 2, 1926–27, 108, Division 1, 2001–02.

Highest League Scorer in Season: Tommy Johnson, 38, Division 1, 1928–29.

Most League Goals in Total Aggregate: Tommy Johnson, 158, 1919–30.

Most League Goals in One Match: 5, Fred Williams v Darwen, Division 2, 18 February 1899; 5, Tom Browell v Burnley, Division 2, 24 October 1925; 5, Tom Johnson v Everton, Division 1, 15 September 1928; 5, George Smith v Newport Co, Division 2, 14 June 1947; 5, Sergio Aguero v Newcastle U, FA Premier League, 3 October 2015.

Most Capped Player: David Silva, 87 (125), Spain.

Most League Appearances: Alan Oakes, 564, 1959–76.

Youngest League Player: Glyn Pardoe, 15 years 314 days v Birmingham C, 11 April 1962.

Record Transfer Fee Received: £25,000,000 from Leicester C for Kelechi Iheanacho, August 2017.

Record Transfer Fee Paid: £60,000,000 to Leicester C for Riyad Mahrez, July 2018.

Football League Record: 1892 Ardwick elected founder member of Division 2; 1894 Newly-formed Manchester C elected to Division 2; Division 1 1899–1902, 1903–09, 1910–26, 1928–38, 1947–50, 1951–63, 1966–83, 1985–87, 1989–92; Division 2 1902–03, 1909–10, 1926–28, 1938–47, 1950–51, 1963–66, 1983–85, 1987–89; 1992–96 FA Premier League; 1996–98 Division 1; 1998–99 Division 2; 1999–2000 Division 1; 2000–01 FA Premier League; 2001–02 Division 1; 2002– FA Premier League.

LATEST SEQUENCES

Longest Sequence of League Wins: 18, 26.8.2017 – 27.12.2017.

Longest Sequence of League Defeats: 8, 23.8.1995 – 14.10.1995.

Longest Sequence of League Draws: 7, 5.10.2009 – 28.11.2009.

Longest Sequence of Unbeaten League Matches: 30, 8.4.2017 – 2.1.2018.

Longest Sequence Without a League Win: 17, 26.12.1979 – 7.4.1980.

Successive Scoring Runs: 44 from 3.10.1936.

Successive Non-scoring Runs: 6 from 30.1.1971.

MANAGERS

Joshua Parlby 1893–95
  (Secretary-Manager)
Sam Omerod 1895–1902
Tom Maley 1902–06
Harry Newbould 1906–12
Ernest Magnall 1912–24
David Ashworth 1924–25
Peter Hodge 1926–32
Wilf Wild 1932–46
  (continued as Secretary to 1950)
Sam Cowan 1946–47
John 'Jock' Thomson 1947–50
Leslie McDowall 1950–63
George Poyser 1963–65
Joe Mercer 1965–71
  (continued as General Manager to 1972)
Malcolm Allison 1972–73
Johnny Hart 1973
Ron Saunders 1973–74
Tony Book 1974–79
Malcolm Allison 1979–80
John Bond 1980–83
John Benson 1983
Billy McNeill 1983–86
Jimmy Frizzell 1986–87
  (continued as General Manager)
Mel Machin 1987–89
Howard Kendall 1989–90
Peter Reid 1990–93
Brian Horton 1993–95
Alan Ball 1995–96
Steve Coppell 1996
Frank Clark 1996–98
Joe Royle 1998–2001
Kevin Keegan 2001–05
Stuart Pearce 2005–07
Sven-Göran Eriksson 2007–08
Mark Hughes 2008–09
Roberto Mancini 2009–13
Manuel Pellegrini 2013–16
Pep Guardiola June 2016–

TEN YEAR LEAGUE RECORD

		P	W	D	L	F	A	Pts	Pos
2008-09	PR Lge	38	15	5	18	58	50	50	10
2009-10	PR Lge	38	18	13	7	73	45	67	5
2010-11	PR Lge	38	21	8	9	60	33	71	3
2011-12	PR Lge	38	28	5	5	93	29	89	1
2012-13	PR Lge	38	23	9	6	66	34	78	2
2013-14	PR Lge	38	27	5	6	102	37	86	1
2014-15	PR Lge	38	24	7	7	83	38	79	2
2015-16	PR Lge	38	19	9	10	71	41	66	4
2016-17	PR Lge	38	23	9	6	80	39	78	3
2017-18	PR Lge	38	32	4	2	106	27	100	1

DID YOU KNOW

Manchester City's home game with Chelsea in the 1983–84 season was switched to a Friday night (4 May) and shown live on BBC television. It was the first live televised Football League match for both clubs and also the first live transmission of a Division Two game.

MANCHESTER CITY – PREMIER LEAGUE 2017–18 LEAGUE RECORD

Match No.	Date	Venue	Opponents	Result	H/T Score	Lg Pos.	Goalscorers	Attendance
1	Aug 12	A	Brighton & HA	W 2-0	0-0	2	Aguero [70], Dunk (og) [75]	55,097
2	21	H	Everton	D 1-1	0-1	5	Sterling [82]	54,009
3	26	A	Bournemouth	W 2-1	1-1	3	Gabriel Jesus [21], Sterling [90]	10,419
4	Sept 9	H	Liverpool	W 5-0	2-0	2	Aguero [24], Gabriel Jesus 2 [45, 53], Sane 2 [77, 90]	54,172
5	16	A	Watford	W 6-0	3-0	1	Aguero 3 [27, 31, 81], Gabriel Jesus [37], Otamendi [63], Sterling (pen) [89]	20,305
6	23	H	Crystal Palace	W 5-0	1-0	1	Sane [44], Sterling 2 [51, 59], Aguero [79], Delph [89]	53,526
7	30	A	Chelsea	W 1-0	0-0	1	De Bruyne [67]	41,530
8	Oct 14	H	Stoke C	W 7-2	3-1	1	Gabriel Jesus 2 [17, 55], Sterling [19], Silva [27], Fernandinho [62], Sane [62], Bernardo Silva [79]	54,128
9	21	H	Burnley	W 3-0	1-0	1	Aguero (pen) [30], Otamendi [73], Sane [75]	54,118
10	28	A	WBA	W 3-2	2-1	1	Sane [10], Fernandinho [15], Sterling [64]	24,003
11	Nov 5	H	Arsenal	W 3-1	1-0	1	De Bruyne [19], Aguero (pen) [50], Gabriel Jesus [74]	54,286
12	18	A	Leicester C	W 2-0	1-0	1	Gabriel Jesus [45], De Bruyne [49]	31,908
13	26	A	Huddersfield T	W 2-1	0-1	1	Aguero (pen) [47], Sterling [84]	24,121
14	29	H	Southampton	W 2-1	0-0	1	De Bruyne [47], Sterling [90]	53,407
15	Dec 3	H	West Ham U	W 2-1	0-1	1	Otamendi [57], Silva [83]	54,203
16	10	A	Manchester U	W 2-1	1-1	1	Silva [43], Otamendi [54]	74,847
17	13	A	Swansea C	W 4-0	2-0	1	Silva 2 [27, 52], De Bruyne [34], Aguero [85]	20,870
18	16	H	Tottenham H	W 4-1	1-0	1	Gundogan [14], De Bruyne [70], Sterling 2 [80, 90]	54,214
19	23	H	Bournemouth	W 4-0	1-0	1	Aguero 2 [27, 79], Sterling [53], Danilo [86]	54,270
20	27	A	Newcastle U	W 1-0	1-0	1	Sterling [31]	52,311
21	31	A	Crystal Palace	D 0-0	0-0	1		25,804
22	Jan 2	H	Watford	W 3-1	1-0	1	Sterling [1], Kabasele (og) [13], Aguero [63]	53,556
23	14	A	Liverpool	L 3-4	1-1	1	Sane [40], Bernardo Silva [84], Gundogan [90]	53,285
24	20	H	Newcastle U	W 3-1	1-0	1	Aguero 3 (1 pen) [34, 63 (pl), 83]	54,452
25	31	H	WBA	W 3-0	1-0	1	Fernandinho [19], De Bruyne [68], Aguero [89]	53,241
26	Feb 3	A	Burnley	D 1-1	1-1	1	Danilo [22]	21,658
27	10	H	Leicester C	W 5-1	1-1	1	Sterling [3], Aguero 4 [48, 53, 77, 90]	54,416
28	Mar 1	A	Arsenal	W 3-0	3-0	1	Bernardo Silva [15], Silva [28], Sane [33]	58,420
29	4	H	Chelsea	W 1-0	0-0	1	Bernardo Silva [46]	54,328
30	12	A	Stoke C	W 2-0	1-0	1	Silva 2 [10, 50]	29,138
31	31	A	Everton	W 3-1	3-0	1	Sane [4], Gabriel Jesus [12], Sterling [37]	39,221
32	Apr 7	H	Manchester U	L 2-3	2-0	1	Kompany [25], Gundogan [30]	54,259
33	14	A	Tottenham H	W 3-1	2-1	1	Gabriel Jesus [22], Gundogan (pen) [25], Sterling [72]	80,811
34	22	H	Swansea C	W 5-0	2-0	1	Silva [12], Sterling [16], De Bruyne [54], Bernardo Silva [64], Gabriel Jesus [88]	54,387
35	29	A	West Ham U	W 4-1	2-1	1	Sane [13], Zabaleta (og) [27], Gabriel Jesus [53], Fernandinho [64]	56,904
36	May 6	H	Huddersfield T	D 0-0	0-0	1		54,350
37	9	H	Brighton & HA	W 3-1	2-1	1	Danilo [16], Bernardo Silva [34], Fernandinho [72]	54,013
38	13	A	Southampton	W 1-0	0-0	1	Gabriel Jesus [90]	31,882

Final League Position: 1

GOALSCORERS

League (106): Aguero 21 (4 pens), Sterling 18 (1 pen), Gabriel Jesus 13, Sane 10, Silva 9, De Bruyne 8, Bernardo Silva 6, Fernandinho 5, Gundogan 4 (1 pen), Otamendi 4, Danilo 3, Delph 1, Kompany 1, own goals 3.
FA Cup (6): Aguero 2, Bernardo Silva 1, De Bruyne 1, Sane 1, Sterling 1.
Carabao Cup (11): Aguero 3, Sane 3, De Bruyne 2, Bernardo Silva 1, Kompany 1, Silva 1.
Checkatrade Trophy (4): Francis 1, Garre 1, Matondo 1, Nmecha 1.
Champions League (20): Aguero 4 (1 pen), Gabriel Jesus 4, Sterling 4, Stones 3, Gundogan 2, Bernardo Silva 1, De Bruyne 1, Otamendi 1.

Ederson 36	Kompany V 17	Stones J 16+2	Otamendi N 33+1	Fernandinho L 33+1	Walker K 32	De Bruyne K 36+1	Silva D 28+1	Danilo 13+10	Aguero S 22+3	Gabriel Jesus F 19+10	Sane L 27+5	Sterling R 29+4	Bernardo Silva M 15+20	Mendy B 4+3	Bravo C 2+1	Mangala E 4+5	Gundogan I 15+15	Delph F 21+1	Toure Y 1+9	Zinchenko A 6+2	Foden P —+5	Diaz B —+5	Laporte A 9	Nmecha L —+2	Match No.
1	2	3	4	5	6	7	8	9²	10³	11¹	12	13	14												1
1	2	3³	4	5	6⁶	8	7	13	10	11²	9¹	12	14												2
1	3	14	4	7		6	8³	2	12	10¹	13	11⁸	9²	5											3
1¹		3	4³	5	6	7	8	2	10	11²	13				9	12	14								4
1		3	4	6	2	8²	9¹		11	10³	14	7	12	5			13								5
1		3²	4	6	2	8	9	12	11		7	10¹	13	5³			14								6
1		3	4	6	2	8¹	9²	14		11	10³	7	12			13	5								7
1		3	4	7¹	2	6³	8		10⁸	11	9	12				13	5	14							8
1		3	4	7³	2	6⁸	8		10²	12	11		9			14	5	13							9
1		3	4	7	2	6	8		10⁸	11	12	9¹				13	5								10
1		3	4	7	2	6	8		10¹	12	11²	9³	14			13	5								11
1	4	3²		7	2	6⁸	8		10	11	9¹	13			12	14	5								12
1	3²		4	7	2	6	8¹		10³	12	11	9			14	13	5								13
1	3		4	7	2	6	12		10	11²		9	13			8¹	5								14
1		3	13		2	6	8	5²	10³	12	11¹	9	14			4		7							15
1	3²		4	7	2	6	8		10³	11¹	9	14			13	12	5								16
1		3	7¹		2	6	8	2	10		11	9			4	14	5³	12	13						17
1		3	7	2		6		10¹	12	11³	9	14			4	8²	5				13				18
1	3		4	7	2	6⁸	8	14	10		11¹	9	12			13	5²								19
1	3³		4	7	2	6		5	10²	12	14	11	9¹			13	8								20
1		3	4	7	2	6		5	12	10⁸	11	13	9¹			4	8³	14							21
1	3¹		4	7²	2	6⁸	8	12	10		11	9	14				5	13							22
1		3	4	7	2	6		12	10		11	9¹	13			8	5²								23
1		3	4	7	2	6	8		10		11²	9¹	12							5	13				24
1		3	7	2	6²	8¹		10		11	9			12					5	13	4				25
1	3		4	7	2	6		5	10		11¹	9				8				12					26
1	14	3²	7¹	2	6		12	10		11	9				8			5³	13	4					27
1	3		4	2¹	6	8³	5	10²	14	11		9			7		13	12							28
1		3		2	6	8¹	13	10³	12	11		9			7		5²	14		4					29
1	3		4	7	2	6		10¹	11	9¹	12				13		5								30
1	4	3	7	2	6²	8	14		10	11	9¹	12				13					5³				31
1	3	4	7		12	8¹	2	14	13	11	10	9²			6³	5									32
1	3	12		2	6³	8		10	11²	9	13				7	5	14				4				33
1	3			6²	8	2		10		11²	9	14			7	5	12			13		4			34
1		3	7	2¹	6		12		10³	11	9				8²	5	13					4	14		35
1	3³	4	7	2	6²	8		10	11	9	14	12			13	5¹									36
	3		6		2			10¹	11		9	12	1		8		7³	5²		13	4	14			37
	3	7		6	2		12	11	9	10³			1		8¹	5²			14	13	4				38

FA Cup

Third Round	Burnley	(h)	4-1
Fourth Round	Cardiff C	(a)	2-0
Fifth Round	Wigan Ath	(a)	0-1

Carabao Cup

Third Round	WBA	(a)	2-1
Fourth Round	Wolverhampton W	(h)	0-0

(aet; Manchester C won 4-1 on penalties)

Quarter-Final	Leicester C	(a)	1-1

(aet; Manchester C won 4-3 on penalties)

Semi-Final 1st leg	Bristol C	(h)	2-1
Semi-Final 2nd leg	Bristol C	(a)	3-2
Final	Arsenal	(Wembley)	3-0

Checkatrade Trophy (Manchester C U21)

Northern Group F	Rotherham U	(a)	1-1

(Manchester C U21 won 4-2 on penalties

Northern Group F	Bradford C	(a)	1-2
Northern Group F	Chesterfield	(a)	2-2

(Chesterfield won 4-3 on penalties)

Champions League

Group F	Feyenoord	(a)	4-0
Group F	Shakhtar Donetsk	(h)	2-0
Group F	Napoli	(h)	2-1
Group F	Napoli	(a)	4-2
Group F	Feyenoord	(h)	1-0
Group F	Shakhtar Donetsk	(a)	1-2
Round of 16 1st leg	FC Basel	(a)	4-0
Round of 16 2nd leg	FC Basel	(h)	1-2
Quarter-Final 1st leg	Liverpool	(a)	0-3
Quarter-Final 2nd leg	Liverpool	(h)	1-2

MANCHESTER UNITED

FOUNDATION

Manchester United was formed as comparatively recently as 1902 after their predecessors, Newton Heath, went bankrupt. However, it is usual to give the date of the club's foundation as 1878 when the dining room committee of the carriage and waggon works of the Lancashire and Yorkshire Railway Company formed Newton Heath L and YR Cricket and Football Club. They won the Manchester Cup in 1886 and as Newton Heath FC were admitted to the Second Division in 1892.

Old Trafford, Sir Matt Busby Way, Manchester M16 0RA.

Telephone: (0161) 868 8000.

Fax: (0161) 868 8804.

Ticket Office: (0161) 868 8000 (option 1).

Website: www.manutd.co.uk

Email: enquiries@manutd.co.uk

Ground Capacity: 74,994.

Record Attendance: 76,098 v Blackburn R, FA Premier League, 31 March 2007. 83,260 v Arsenal, First Division, 17 January 1948 (at Maine Road – United shared City's ground after Old Trafford suffered World War II bomb damage).

Ground Record Attendance: 76,962 Wolverhampton W v Grimsby T, FA Cup semi-final, 25 March 1939.

Pitch Measurements: 105m × 68m (114yd × 74yd).

Co-Chairmen: Joel and Avram Glazer.

Chief Executive: Edward Woodward.

Manager: José Mourinho.

Assistant Manager: Rui Faria.

Colours: Red shirts with white and black trim, white shorts with black trim, black socks with red and white trim.

Year Formed: 1878 as Newton Heath LYR; 1902, Manchester United.

Turned Professional: 1885.

Previous Name: 1880, Newton Heath; 1902, Manchester United.

Club Nickname: 'Red Devils'.

Grounds: 1880, North Road, Monsall Road; 1893, Bank Street; 1910, Old Trafford (played at Maine Road 1941–49).

HONOURS

League Champions: FA Premier League – 1992–93, 1993–94, 1995–96, 1996–97, 1998–99, 1999–2000, 2000–01, 2002–03, 2006–07, 2007–08, 2008–09, 2010–11, 2012–13; Division 1 – 1907–08, 1910–11, 1951–52, 1955–56, 1956–57, 1964–65, 1966–67; Division 2 – 1935–36, 1974–75.
Runners-up: FA Premier League – 1994–95, 1997–98, 2005–06, 2009–10, 2011–12, 2017–18; Division 1 – 1946–47, 1947–48, 1948–49, 1950–51, 1958–59, 1963–64, 1967–68, 1979–80, 1987–88, 1991–92; Division 2 – 1896–97, 1905–06, 1924–25, 1937–38.

FA Cup Winners: 1909, 1948, 1963, 1977, 1983, 1985, 1990, 1994, 1996, 1999, 2004, 2016.
Runners-up: 1957, 1958, 1976, 1979, 1995, 2005, 2007, 2018.

League Cup Winners: 1992, 2006, 2009, 2010, 2017.
Runners-up: 1983, 1991, 1994, 2003.

European Competitions
European Cup: 1956–57 (sf), 1957–58 (sf), 1965–66 (sf), 1967–68 (winners), 1968–69 (sf). *Champions League:* 1993–94, 1994–95, 1996–97 (sf), 1997–98 (qf), 1998–99 (winners), 1999–2000 (qf), 2000–01 (qf), 2001–02 (sf), 2002–03 (qf), 2003–04, 2004–05, 2005–06, 2006–07 (sf), 2007–08 (winners), 2008–09 (runners-up), 2009–10 (qf), 2010–11 (runners-up), 2011–12, 2012–13, 2013–14 (qf), 2015–16, 2017–18.
Fairs Cup: 1964–65.
UEFA Cup: 1976–77, 1980–81, 1982–83, 1984–85 (qf), 1992–93, 1995–96.
Europa League: 2011–12, 2015–16, 2016–17 (winners).
European Cup-Winners' Cup: 1963–64 (qf), 1977–78, 1983–84 (sf), 1990–91 (winners). 1991–92.
Super Cup: 1991 (winners), 1999, 2008.
World Club Championship: 1968, 1999 (winners), 2000.
FIFA Club World Cup: 2008 (winners).
NB: In 1958–59 FA refused permission to compete in European Cup.

Sᵤn FACT FILE

When Manchester United met Bolton Wanderers in a First Division fixture at Old Trafford on 24 August 1949 it was the first time the Reds had played on their own ground since 1941. Old Trafford had been damaged by wartime bombing forcing United to play their home games at Manchester City's Maine Road ground – and pay City £5,000 a year rent. United won their first game back by a 3-0 scoreline.

First Football League Game: 3 September 1892, Division 1, v Blackburn R (a) L 3–4 – Warner; Clements, Brown; Perrins, Stewart, Erentz; Farman (1), Coupar (1), Donaldson (1), Carson, Mathieson.

Record League Victory (as Newton Heath): 10–1 v Wolverhampton W, Division 1, 15 October 1892 – Warner; Mitchell, Clements; Perrins, Stewart (3), Erentz; Farman (1), Hood (1), Donaldson (3), Carson (1), Hendry (1).

Record League Victory (as Manchester U): 9–0 v Ipswich T, FA Premier League, 4 March 1995 – Schmeichel; Keane (1) (Sharpe), Irwin, Bruce (Butt), Kanchelskis, Pallister, Cole (5), Ince (1), McClair, Hughes (2), Giggs.

Record Cup Victory: 10–0 v RSC Anderlecht, European Cup prel. rd 2nd leg, 26 September 1956 – Wood; Foulkes, Byrne; Colman, Jones, Edwards; Berry (1), Whelan (2), Taylor (3), Viollet (4), Pegg.

Record Defeat: 0–7 v Blackburn R, Division 1, 10 April 1926; 0–7 v Aston Villa, Division 1, 27 December 1930; 0–7 v Wolverhampton W, Division 2, 26 December 1931.

Most League Points (2 for a win): 64, Division 1, 1956–57.

Most League Points (3 for a win): 92, FA Premier League, 1993–94.

Most League Goals: 103, Division 1, 1956–57 and 1958–59.

Highest League Scorer in Season: Dennis Viollet, 32, 1959–60.

Most League Goals in Total Aggregate: Bobby Charlton, 199, 1956–73.

Most League Goals in One Match: 5, Andy Cole v Ipswich T, FA Premier League, 3 March 1995; 5, Dimitar Berbatov v Blackburn R, FA Premier League, 27 November 2010.

Most Capped Player: Bobby Charlton, 106, England.

Most League Appearances: Ryan Giggs, 672, 1991–2014.

Youngest League Player: Jeff Whitefoot, 16 years 105 days v Portsmouth, 15 April 1950.

Record Transfer Fee Received: £80,000,000 from Real Madrid for Cristiano Ronaldo, July 2009.

Record Transfer Fee Paid: £89,300,000 to Juventus for Paul Pogba, August 2016.

Football League Record: 1892 Newton Heath elected to Division 1; 1894–1906 Division 2; 1906–22 Division 1; 1922–25 Division 2; 1925–31 Division 1; 1931–36 Division 2; 1936–37 Division 1; 1937–38 Division 2; 1938–74 Division 1; 1974–75 Division 2; 1975–92 Division 1; 1992– FA Premier League.

MANAGERS

J. Ernest Mangnall 1903–12
John Bentley 1912–14
John Robson 1914–21
   (Secretary-Manager from 1916)
John Chapman 1921–26
Clarence Hilditch 1926–27
Herbert Bamlett 1927–31
Walter Crickmer 1931–32
Scott Duncan 1932–37
Walter Crickmer 1937–45
   (Secretary-Manager)
Matt Busby 1945–69
   (continued as General Manager then Director)
Wilf McGuinness 1969–70
Sir Matt Busby 1970–71
Frank O'Farrell 1971–72
Tommy Docherty 1972–77
Dave Sexton 1977–81
Ron Atkinson 1981–86
Sir Alex Ferguson 1986–2013
David Moyes 2013–14
Louis van Gaal 2014–16
Jose Mourinho June 2016–

LATEST SEQUENCES

Longest Sequence of League Wins: 14, 15.10.1904 – 3.1.1905.

Longest Sequence of League Defeats: 14, 26.4.1930 – 25.10.1930.

Longest Sequence of League Draws: 6, 30.10.1988 – 27.11.1988.

Longest Sequence of Unbeaten League Matches: 29, 11.4.2010 – 1.2.2011.

Longest Sequence Without a League Win: 16, 19.4.1930 – 25.10.1930.

Successive Scoring Runs: 36 from 3.12.2007.

Successive Non-scoring Runs: 5 from 7.2.1981.

TEN YEAR LEAGUE RECORD

		P	W	D	L	F	A	Pts	Pos
2008-09	PR Lge	38	28	6	4	68	24	90	1
2009-10	PR Lge	38	27	4	7	86	28	85	2
2010-11	PR Lge	38	23	11	4	78	37	80	1
2011-12	PR Lge	38	28	5	5	89	33	89	2
2012-13	PR Lge	38	28	5	5	86	43	89	1
2013-14	PR Lge	38	19	7	12	64	43	64	7
2014-15	PR Lge	38	20	10	8	62	37	70	4
2015-16	PR Lge	38	19	9	10	49	35	66	5
2016-17	PR Lge	38	18	15	5	54	29	69	6
2017-18	PR Lge	38	25	6	7	68	28	81	2

DID YOU KNOW

Manchester United were the first team to win a domestic cup tie by way of a penalty shoot-out. Their Watney Cup semi-final tie against Hull City in August 1970 finished 1-1 after extra time and under the new rules the game went to penalties. George Best converted the first spot-kick and although Denis Law failed to score with his effort United won the shoot-out 4-3.

MANCHESTER UNITED – PREMIER LEAGUE 2017–18 LEAGUE RECORD

Match No.	Date	Venue	Opponents	Result	H/T Score	Lg Pos.	Goalscorers	Attendance
1	Aug 13	H	West Ham U	W 4-0	1-0	1	Lukaku 2 [33, 52], Martial [87], Pogba [90]	74,928
2	19	A	Swansea C	W 4-0	1-0	1	Bailly [45], Lukaku [80], Pogba [82], Martial [84]	20,862
3	26	H	Leicester C	W 2-0	0-0	1	Rashford [70], Fellaini [82]	75,021
4	Sept 9	A	Stoke C	D 2-2	1-1	1	Rashford [45], Lukaku [57]	29,320
5	17	H	Everton	W 4-0	1-0	2	Valencia [4], Mkhitaryan [83], Lukaku [89], Martial (pen) [90]	75,042
6	23	A	Southampton	W 1-0	1-0	2	Lukaku [20]	31,930
7	30	H	Crystal Palace	W 4-0	2-0	2	Mata [3], Fellaini 2 [35, 49], Lukaku [86]	75,118
8	Oct 14	A	Liverpool	D 0-0	0-0	2		52,912
9	21	A	Huddersfield T	L 1-2	0-2	2	Rashford [78]	24,169
10	28	H	Tottenham H	W 1-0	0-0	2	Martial [81]	75,034
11	Nov 5	A	Chelsea	L 0-1	0-0	2		41,615
12	18	H	Newcastle U	W 4-1	2-1	2	Martial [37], Smalling [45], Pogba [54], Lukaku [70]	75,035
13	25	H	Brighton & HA	W 1-0	0-0	2	Dunk (og) [66]	75,018
14	28	H	Watford	W 4-2	3-0	2	Young 2 [19, 25], Martial [32], Lingard [86]	20,552
15	Dec 2	A	Arsenal	W 3-1	2-0	2	Valencia [4], Lingard 2 [11, 63]	59,547
16	10	H	Manchester C	L 1-2	1-1	2	Rashford [45]	74,847
17	13	H	Bournemouth	W 1-0	0-0	2	Lukaku [25]	74,798
18	17	A	WBA	W 2-1	2-0	2	Lukaku [27], Lingard [35]	24,782
19	23	A	Leicester C	D 2-2	1-1	2	Mata 2 [40, 60]	32,202
20	26	H	Burnley	D 2-2	0-2	2	Lingard 2 [53, 90]	75,046
21	30	H	Southampton	D 0-0	0-0	3		75,051
22	Jan 1	A	Everton	W 2-0	0-0	2	Martial [57], Lingard [81]	39,188
23	15	H	Stoke C	W 3-0	2-0	2	Valencia [9], Martial [38], Lukaku [72]	74,726
24	20	A	Burnley	W 1-0	0-0	2	Martial [54]	21,841
25	31	A	Tottenham H	L 0-2	0-2	2		81,978
26	Feb 3	A	Huddersfield T	W 2-0	0-0	2	Lukaku [55], Sanchez [68]	74,742
27	11	A	Newcastle U	L 0-1	0-0	2		52,309
28	25	H	Chelsea	W 2-1	1-1	2	Lukaku [39], Lingard [75]	75,060
29	Mar 5	A	Crystal Palace	W 3-2	0-1	2	Smalling [55], Lukaku [76], Matic [90]	25,840
30	10	H	Liverpool	W 2-1	2-0	2	Rashford 2 [14, 24]	74,855
31	31	A	Swansea C	W 2-0	2-0	2	Lukaku [5], Sanchez [20]	75,038
32	Apr 7	A	Manchester C	W 3-2	0-2	2	Pogba 2 [53, 55], Smalling [69]	54,259
33	15	H	WBA	L 0-1	0-0	2		75,095
34	18	A	Bournemouth	W 2-0	1-0	2	Smalling [28], Lukaku [70]	10,952
35	29	A	Arsenal	W 2-1	1-0	2	Pogba [16], Fellaini [90]	75,035
36	May 4	A	Brighton & HA	L 0-1	0-0	2		30,611
37	10	A	West Ham U	D 0-0	0-0	2		56,902
38	13	H	Watford	W 1-0	1-0	2	Rashford [34]	75,049

Final League Position: 2

GOALSCORERS

League (68): Lukaku 16, Martial 9 (1 pen), Lingard 8, Rashford 7, Pogba 6, Fellaini 4, Smalling 4, Mata 3, Valencia 3, Sanchez 2, Young 1, Bailly 1, Matic 1, Mkhitaryan 1, own goal 1.
FA Cup (12): Lukaku 5, Ander Herrera 2, Lingard 2, Matic 1, Rashford 1, Sanchez 1.
Carabao Cup (7): Lingard 3, Rashford 2, Ibrahimovic 1, Martial 1.
Champions League (13): Lukaku 5, Rashford 3, Blind 1 (1 pen), Fellaini 1, Martial 1 (1 pen), Mkhitaryan 1, own goal 1.

De Gea D 37	Valencia A 31	Bailly E 11+2	Jones P 23	Blind D 4+3	Matic N 35+1	Pogba P 25+2	Mata J 23+5	Mkhitaryan H 11+4	Rashford M 17+18	Lukaku R 33+1	Fellaini M 5+11	Martial A 18+12	Lingard J 20+13	Ander Herrera A 13+13	Darmian M 5+3	Young A 28+2	Smalling C 28+1	Lindelof V 13+4	Ibrahimovic Z 1+4	Rojo M 8+1	Shaw L 8+3	McTominay S 7+6	Tuanzebe A —+1	Sanchez A 12	Carrick M 1+1	Romero S 1	Match No.
1	2	3	4	5	6	7	8^3	9	10^2	11	12	13	14														1
1	2	3	4	5	7	6	8^1	9	10^2	11	12	13		14													2
1	2	3	4	5	7	6	8^3	9	12	11	13	10^2	14														3
1	2	3	4		7	8	12	9^3	11^2	10		13	14	6^1			5										4
1	2	3	4		7		8^1	9	10^2	11	6	14	12	13			5										5
1	2	3	4	14	7		8^3	9	10^2	11	6			12		5	13										6
1	2		4		6		8^3	9	10^2	11	7	13	12	14		5	3										7
1	2		4		7			9	13	11	10^3	12	6	5	8^3	3	14										8
1	2		4^3		7		8^1	14	13	11	10^2	9	6		5	3	12										9
1	5	2	4		7		9^2	11^3	10	13	12	6	14			8^1	3										10
1	5	2	4^2		7	9	11	10	12	13	14	6				8^1	3										11
1	2				7	6^1	9^2		8	11	12	10^1		14		5	4	3	13								12
1	2				7	6	8^2	13	9^3	11	14	10^1				5	4	3	12								13
1	5				7^1	6		13	11	10^3	9^2	12	14			8	3	2	4								14
1	5				6^4	7		14	10	11^3	9^2	12	13	8^1	3	2		4									15
1	2				7		14		10	11	8	9^2	6^1		5	3	12	13	4^3								16
1	2	4			7		8		12	11		10^2	9^3	13	14	3		5^1	6								17
1	2^2	4			7		8		10^1	11		13	9^0	6		5	3		12	14							18
1		4			7	6	8^2	14	12	11		10^1	9^3	13		5	3	2									19
1		3			7	6	8	12	10	11		13			2					9^1	4^2	5					20
1		4			7	6	8	10^1	12	11^2		13	9		2		3				5						21
1		3	13		7	8	9^2	12			10^3	11^1	6		2					4	5	14					22
1	2		4		7	6	8^3		12	11	13	10^2	9^1		3						5	14					23
1	2		4		7	8	9^2		13	10	12	11^1	6^3	14		5	3										24
1	2		4		7	6^1	13		11	12^3	8	9^2	14		5	3								10			25
1	2				7	12	8^1		13	11^4		9^0			3	4	5	6						10			26
1	2		4		7^3	6^1	13		11		8	9^1			5	3	4					14		10	12		27
1	2	13			7	8			10		11^1	12			5	3	4			6		9^2					28
1	2^3				7	8	13		12	10		9			5^2	3	4		14	6^1		11					29
1	2	3			7		8^2		10^3	11	12		13	14	5	4				6		9^1					30
1	2				6	7	8^3		12	11		9^1	13		5	3	4					14		10^2			31
1	2	3			7	8			12	10		9^0	6^1		5	4	14					13		11^2			32
1	2				7	8^1	9		14	10		13	12	6^3		5^2	3							11			33
1		4	14	13	8^2			10	12	6	11	9^3	7^1	2		3						5					34
1	2				7	8			12	10^2	13	14	9^1	6^1		5	3	4						11			35
1					7	8	9		10		6^2	11	12		2^3	5	3		4^1	13	14						36
1	2^3	14	5		9			12			10^1	8		13	4	3		6	7		11^2						37
		3		8^3		14	9		10				13	2	5^2		4	12	6		11	7^1	1				38

FA Cup

Third Round	Derby Co	(h)	2-0
Fourth Round	Yeovil T	(a)	4-0
Fifth Round	Huddersfield T	(a)	2-0
Sixth Round	Brighton & HA	(h)	2-0
Semi-Final	Tottenham H	(h)	2-1
Final	Chelsea	(a)	0-1

Carabao Cup

Third Round	Burton Alb	(h)	4-1
Fourth Round	Swansea C	(a)	2-0
Quarter-Final	Bristol C	(a)	1-2

Champions League

Group A	FC Basel	(h)	3-0
Group A	CSKA Moscow	(a)	4-1
Group A	Benfica	(a)	1-0
Group A	Benfica	(h)	2-0
Group A	FC Basel	(a)	0-1
Group A	CSKA Moscow	(h)	2-1
Round of 16 1st leg	Sevilla	(a)	0-0
Round of 16 2nd leg	Sevilla	(h)	1-2

MANSFIELD TOWN

FOUNDATION

The club was formed as Mansfield Wesleyans in 1897, and changed their name to Mansfield Wesley in 1906 and Mansfield Town in 1910. This was after the Mansfield Wesleyan Chapel trustees had requested that the club change its name as 'it has no longer had any connection with either the chapel or school'. The new club participated in the Notts and Derby District League, but in the following season 1911–12 joined the Central Alliance.

One Call Stadium, Quarry Lane, Mansfield, Nottinghamshire NG18 5DA.

Telephone: (01623) 482 482.

Fax: (01623) 482 495.

Ticket Office: (01623) 482 482.

Website: www.mansfieldtown.net

Email: info@mansfieldtown.net

Ground Capacity: 9,186.

Record Attendance: 24,467 v Nottingham F, FA Cup 3rd rd, 10 January 1953.

Pitch Measurements: 100.5m × 64m (110yd × 70yd).

Chairman: John Radford.

Chief Executive: Carolyn Radford.

Manager: David Flitcroft.

Assistant Manager: Ben Futcher.

Colours: Yellow and blue shirts, blue shorts, blue socks.

Year Formed: 1897.

Turned Professional: 1906.

Ltd Co.: 1922.

Previous Name: 1897, Mansfield Wesleyans; 1906, Mansfield Wesley; 1910, Mansfield Town.

Grounds: 1897–99, Westfield Lane; 1899–1901, Ratcliffe Gate; 1901–12, Newgate Lane; 1912–16, Ratcliffe Gate; 1916, Field Mill (renamed One Call Stadium 2012).

Club Nickname: 'The Stags'.

First Football League Game: 29 August 1931, Division 3 (S), v Swindon T (h) W 3–2 – Wilson; Clifford, England; Wake, Davis, Blackburn; Gilhespy, Readman (1), Johnson, Broom (2), Baxter.

Record League Victory: 9–2 v Rotherham U, Division 3 (N), 27 December 1932 – Wilson; Anthony, England; Davies, S. Robinson, Slack; Prior, Broom, Readman (3), Hoyland (3), Bowater (3).

Record Cup Victory: 8–0 v Scarborough (a), FA Cup 1st rd, 22 November 1952 – Bramley; Chessell, Bradley; Field, Plummer, Lewis; Scott, Fox (3), Marron (2), Sid Watson (1), Adam (2).

Record Defeat: 1–8 v Walsall, Division 3 (N), 19 January 1933.

Most League Points (2 for a win): 68, Division 4, 1974–75.

HONOURS

League Champions: Division 3 – 1976–77; Division 4 – 1974–75; Conference – 2012–13.
Runners-up: Division 3N – 1950–51, Third Division – (3rd) 2001–02 *(promoted to Second Division).*
FA Cup: 6th rd – 1969.
League Cup: 5th rd – 1976.
League Trophy Winners: 1987.

THE Sun FACT FILE

Mansfield Town, then in the Midland League, had a tricky start to their 1928–29 FA Cup campaign when they were held to a 2-2 draw at Ardsley Athletic of the Barnsley Association League in the final qualifying round. Town won the replay and went on to win away ties at Shirebrook, Barrow and Wolverhampton Wanderers. They went out in the fourth round, losing 2-0 against Arsenal at Highbury in front of an attendance of 44,925.

Most League Points (3 for a win): 81, Division 4, 1985–86.

Most League Goals: 108, Division 4, 1962–63.

Highest League Scorer in Season: Ted Harston, 55, Division 3 (N), 1936–37.

Most League Goals in Total Aggregate: Harry Johnson, 104, 1931–36.

Most League Goals in One Match: 7, Ted Harston v Hartlepools U, Division 3N, 23 January 1937.

Most Capped Player: John McClelland, 6 (53), Northern Ireland; Reggie Lambe, 6 (29), Bermuda.

Most League Appearances: Rod Arnold, 440, 1970–83.

Youngest League Player: Cyril Poole, 15 years 351 days v New Brighton, 27 February 1937.

Record Transfer Fee Received: £500,000 from Manchester C for Lee Peacock, October 1999.

Record Transfer Fee Paid: £125,000 to Wolverhampton W for Colin Larkin, July 2002.

Football League Record: 1931 Elected to Division 3 (S); 1932–37 Division 3 (N); 1937–47 Division 3 (S); 1947–58 Division 3 (N); 1958–60 Division 3; 1960–63 Division 4; 1963–72 Division 3; 1972–75 Division 4; 1975–77 Division 3; 1977–78 Division 2; 1978–80 Division 3; 1980–86 Division 4; 1986–91 Division 3; 1991–92 Division 4; 1992–93 Division 2; 1993–2002 Division 3; 2002–03 Division 2; 2003–04 Division 3; 2004–08 FL 2; 2008–13 Conference Premier; 2013– FL 2.

LATEST SEQUENCES

Longest Sequence of League Wins: 7, 13.9.1991 – 26.10.1991.

Longest Sequence of League Defeats: 7, 18.1.1947 – 15.3.1947.

Longest Sequence of League Draws: 5, 18.10.1986 – 22.11.1986.

Longest Sequence of Unbeaten League Matches: 20, 14.2.1976 – 21.8.1976.

Longest Sequence Without a League Win: 14, 25.3.2000 – 2.9.2000.

Successive Scoring Runs: 27 from 1.10.1962.

Successive Non-scoring Runs: 8 from 25.3.2000.

MANAGERS

John Baynes 1922–25
Ted Davison 1926–28
Jack Hickling 1928–33
Henry Martin 1933–35
Charlie Bell 1935
Harold Wightman 1936
Harold Parkes 1936–38
Jack Poole 1938–44
Lloyd Barke 1944–45
Roy Goodall 1945–49
Freddie Steele 1949–51
George Jobey 1952–53
Stan Mercer 1953–55
Charlie Mitten 1956–58
Sam Weaver 1958–60
Raich Carter 1960–63
Tommy Cummings 1963–67
Tommy Eggleston 1967–70
Jock Basford 1970–71
Danny Williams 1971–74
Dave Smith 1974–76
Peter Morris 1976–78
Billy Bingham 1978–79
Mick Jones 1979–81
Stuart Boam 1981–83
Ian Greaves 1983–89
George Foster 1989–93
Andy King 1993–96
Steve Parkin 1996–99
Billy Dearden 1999–2002
Stuart Watkiss 2002
Keith Curle 2002–04
Carlton Palmer 2004–05
Peter Shirtliff 2005–06
Billy Dearden 2006–08
Paul Holland 2008
Billy McEwan 2008
David Holdsworth 2008–10
Duncan Russell 2010–11
Paul Cox 2011–14
Adam Murray 2014–16
Steve Evans 2016–18
David Flitcroft March 2018–

TEN YEAR LEAGUE RECORD

		P	W	D	L	F	A	Pts	Pos
2008-09	Conf P	46	19	9	18	57	55	62	12
2009-10	Conf P	44	17	11	16	69	60	62	9
2010-11	Conf P	46	17	10	19	73	75	61	13
2011-12	Conf P	46	25	14	7	87	48	89	3
2012-13	Conf P	46	30	5	11	92	52	95	1
2013-14	FL 2	46	15	15	16	49	58	60	11
2014-15	FL 2	46	13	9	24	38	62	48	21
2015-16	FL 2	46	17	13	16	61	53	64	12
2016-17	FL 2	46	17	15	14	54	50	66	12
2017-18	FL 2	46	18	18	10	67	52	72	8

DID YOU KNOW ?

Mansfield Town had a reprieve in 1967–68 when they finished in the Division Three relegation positions at the end of the season. Peterborough United, who ordinarily would have ended up in the top half of the table, were demoted for making irregular payments to players leaving fourth from bottom Mansfield to escape the drop.

MANSFIELD TOWN – SKY BET LEAGUE TWO 2017–18 LEAGUE RECORD

Match No.	Date	Venue	Opponents	Result	H/T Score	Lg Pos.	Goalscorers	Attendance
1	Aug 5	A	Crewe Alex	D	2-2	0-1	15	Rose [55], Mirfin [66]	4933
2	12	H	Forest Green R	W	2-0	0-0	2	Rose [51], Anderson [57]	3826
3	19	A	Accrington S	L	1-2	1-1	11	Angol [25]	1645
4	26	H	Luton T	D	2-2	1-0	14	Bennett [23], Angol [71]	4665
5	Sept 2	A	Carlisle U	D	1-1	0-1	15	Butcher [58]	4677
6	9	H	Grimsby T	W	4-1	1-0	10	Angol 2 (2 pens) [34, 80], Pearce [54], Osborne, K (og) [64]	4625
7	12	A	Wycombe W	D	0-0	0-0	11		2938
8	16	A	Lincoln C	W	1-0	0-0	5	Rose [61]	9563
9	23	H	Cambridge U	W	2-1	0-0	5	Mellis (pen) [65], Rose [87]	3814
10	26	A	Cheltenham T	L	0-3	0-0	9		2480
11	30	H	Notts Co	W	3-1	0-0	8	Rose 2 [47, 59], Duffy (og) [63]	7072
12	Oct 7	A	Colchester U	L	0-2	0-2	9		3262
13	14	H	Swindon T	L	1-3	0-2	11	Rose [90]	4081
14	17	A	Barnet	D	1-1	1-0	12	Hemmings [45]	1262
15	21	A	Newport Co	D	1-1	1-0	13	Rose [22]	3146
16	28	H	Exeter C	D	1-1	1-0	14	Hemmings [18]	3608
17	Nov 11	A	Coventry C	W	1-0	0-0	11	MacDonald [84]	8410
18	18	H	Stevenage	W	1-0	1-0	8	Hemmings [24]	3353
19	21	H	Port Vale	W	4-0	1-0	7	Diamond 2 [43, 52], Rose [54], Hemmings [63]	3878
20	25	H	Chesterfield	D	2-2	1-1	7	White [26], Diamond [88]	7525
21	Dec 9	A	Crawley T	L	0-2	0-0	8		1791
22	16	H	Yeovil T	D	0-0	0-0	10		3032
23	23	H	Morecambe	W	2-1	1-0	9	Hemmings [8], Rose [88]	3058
24	26	A	Grimsby T	D	1-1	0-1	8	Angol [80]	5704
25	30	A	Wycombe W	W	2-1	0-1	9	Potter [52], Angol [81]	4227
26	Jan 1	H	Carlisle U	W	3-1	2-0	6	Hemmings 2 [9, 75], Bennett [31]	3632
27	13	A	Cambridge U	D	0-0	0-0	7		4324
28	20	H	Cheltenham T	W	3-2	1-1	7	Hamilton 2 [35, 90], Hemmings [80]	3483
29	27	A	Morecambe	W	2-1	0-1	3	Rose [70], Spencer [90]	1416
30	Feb 3	H	Barnet	W	3-1	1-0	4	MacDonald [42], Atkinson [55], Rose [70]	3795
31	10	A	Swindon T	L	0-1	0-1	6		6031
32	13	A	Newport Co	W	5-0	4-0	5	Rose [6], Potter 3 [9, 28, 61], MacDonald [34]	2866
33	17	A	Exeter C	W	1-0	1-0	4	Rose [38]	3680
34	24	H	Coventry C	D	1-1	1-0	5	Hemmings [16]	6105
35	Mar 6	H	Lincoln C	D	1-1	0-0	5	Byrom [49]	6091
36	10	A	Colchester U	D	1-1	1-0	5	Hemmings [22]	4050
37	17	A	Notts Co	D	1-1	0-1	5	Hemmings (pen) [90]	12,563
38	24	A	Forest Green R	L	0-2	0-0	7		2827
39	30	H	Accrington S	L	0-1	0-0	8		5053
40	Apr 2	A	Luton T	L	1-2	1-0	8	Hemmings [34]	9592
41	7	H	Crewe Alex	L	3-4	1-4	8	Angol [15], Hemmings [50], Miller [76]	3480
42	10	A	Stevenage	D	1-1	0-1	8	Atkinson [51]	2294
43	14	A	Chesterfield	W	1-0	0-0	7	Benning [67]	7967
44	21	A	Port Vale	D	1-1	0-0	8	Howkins (og) [73]	4210
45	28	A	Yeovil T	W	3-2	0-1	8	Angol 2 [48, 76], Hemmings (pen) [69]	3500
46	May 5	H	Crawley T	D	1-1	0-1	8	Hemmings [64]	4734

Final League Position: 8

GOALSCORERS

League (67): Hemmings 15 (2 pens), Rose 14, Angol 9 (2 pens), Potter 4, Diamond 3, MacDonald 3, Atkinson 2, Bennett 2, Hamilton 2, Anderson 1, Benning 1, Butcher 1, Byrom 1, Mellis 1 (1 pen), Miller 1, Mirfin 1, Pearce 1, Spencer 1, White 1, own goals 3.
FA Cup (7): Rose 3, Spencer 3 (1 pen), Pearce 1.
Carabao Cup (0).
Checkatrade Trophy (5): Angol 1, Butcher 1, Diamond 1, Hamilton 1, Potter 1.

Logan C 45	White H 25 + 3	Diamond Z 18 + 2	Mirfin D 12	Benning M 27 + 1	Atkinson W 24 + 15	Mellis J 22 + 8	Byrom J 18 + 1	Anderson P 24 + 9	Angol L 17 + 12	Rose D 35 + 4	Sterling-James O 2 + 11	Digby P 10 + 5	Hamilton C 28 + 5	Pearce K 36 + 2	Spencer J 3 + 15	Potter A 16 + 11	Bennett R 34 + 4	Hemmings K 36 + 1	Butcher C 10 + 7	Hunt J 18	MacDonald A 40 + 1	Olejnik R 1	Thomas J — + 1	Miller R — + 8	Penney M — + 2	King A 5 + 2	Match No.
1	2	3	4	5	6	7^{1}	8	9	10^{3}	11^{2}	12	13	14														1
1	2	4		5	6^{1}		8	9	11^{2}	10^{3}	12	7		3	13	14											2
1	2	3		5	7	14		6	10^{2}	11^{1}	12	8		9^{3}	4	13											3
1			4	5	6	7^{2}	8	9	10^{1}	13		12		3	14		2	11^{3}									4
1			4	5	9^{2}	7^{1}	8	6	10	14				3		13	2	11	12								5
1			4		13	7^{2}	8	12	10					3		14	2	11	6^{1}	5	9^{3}						6
1			4		13	7^{1}	8	12	11					3		14	2	10	6^{2}	5	9^{3}						7
1	2		4		14			13	11^{1}	12		7		3		6		10^{2}	8	5	9^{3}						8
1	2		4				13		12	14	11		7^{1}	3		6^{3}		10^{1}	8	5	9						9
1			4		6	7		9^{2}	11^{1}	10	14	8^{3}		3		2		12	5	13							10
1			4		7			2	14	11^{1}	12			3	13	9^{2}		10^{3}	8	5	6						11
1			4		8	13		2^{1}	14	10	9^{1}			3		12	11^{2}	7	5	6							12
1	2		3		9^{2}	7			13	10	12			4	11^{1}		8	5	6								13
1	2	4^{1}	5	6				10^{3}	13	7			3	14		12	11^{2}	8		9							14
1	2				8			14		11^{2}	13			3	12	6^{1}	4	10^{3}	7	5	9						15
1			5	13	7^{2}	8	2	14	11^{1}				9	3	12		4	10^{3}		6							16
1	2	4			12		8	6^{2}		11^{1}		14	9			3	10^{2}	13	5	7							17
1	2	4			13	7^{2}	8			12				10^{1}		3	11^{3}	14	5	6							18
1	2	3			12		8^{1}	6		10^{2}			9			13	4	11^{3}	14	5	7						19
1	2	4			13	9^{1}	6^{2}			10	11		8^{1}			14	12^{3}		5	7							20
1	2	4			8			6	12	10			9^{1}	14	11^{3}		3		13	5^{2}	7						21
1	2	5			6	9	8^{3}			12	11^{2}	10	13	4		3^{1}		14	7								22
1	2	3			5	14	13			12		11	6^{2}	8			4	10^{1}	9^{3}	7							23
1	2^{1}	3				7		6	14	10			9	4	13	12	11^{3}		5^{2}	8							24
	3^{1}		13		9		2	12	10^{2}	14	6	4		8	5	11^{1}		7	1								25
1	12				5	13	7^{2}			11^{1}			9	3		6^{2}	4	10	8			14					26
1	12				5	14	8^{2}		2^{3}	10	11	13	9	4		6^{1}	3		7								27
1	2^{4}	13			5		8^{1}	7^{2}		12^{3}	11		9	3		6	4	14	10								28
1	3^{2}				5	13		8	12				9	4	14	6^{2}	2	11^{1}	7								29
1					5	7^{1}		8	2				9^{3}	3	14	4	10^{2}		6	13							30
1					5	7		8^{2}	2				9^{3}	3		14	4	11^{1}	6	12	13						31
1					5			2		11^{3}			9	4	14	7^{2}	3	10^{1}	6	13	12	8					32
1	14				5	12		2		11^{2}			9	4	13	6^{2}	3	10^{3}	8^{1}						7		33
1					5		13			2			9	3		6	4	11^{1}	8	12	7^{2}				8^{1}		34
1	2				5	14		12	6^{2}			10	9	3	13		4^{2}	11^{3}	7					8^{1}			35
1	2	4^{7}			5	12	13	7^{3}	6^{1}		11		14	9	3			10	8								36
1					5	6			2^{2}	12	11	13	9	4			3	10	8		7^{1}						37
1	2				5	6		8^{2}		11^{3}	10^{1}		12	3^{4}	14		4	9	7		13						38
1	2	3			5^{4}	6	7		10				9				4	11^{1}	8	12							39
1	2^{2}	3				8^{1}	7		14	11			9	12		5^{2}	4	10	6	13							40
1	2	3^{3}				7			11^{2}	14			9	12		6^{1}	4	10	5^{2}	8	13						41
1	2				8	12	7^{1}			10			9^{4}	4		13	3	11	5	6							42
1	2^{2}	3			5	9	8^{1}			10			13	4		6	12	11^{1}	7						14		43
1					5	7	12			13	11		4^{2}	9	3		6	2	10^{1}	8							44
1					5	8^{3}	7			13	11		2^{1}	12	4		6^{2}	3	10	9				14			45
1	12				5	6^{1}	8			11			2^{2}	9	3		13	4	10	7							46

FA Cup

First Round	Shaw Lane	(a)	3-1
Second Round	Guiseley	(h)	3-0
Third Round	Cardiff C	(a)	0-0
Replay	Cardiff C	(h)	1-4

Carabao Cup

First Round	Rochdale	(h)	0-1

Checkatrade Trophy

Northern Group G Lincoln C	(h)	1-3
Northern Group G Notts Co	(a)	2-1
Northern Group G Everton U21	(h)	1-0
Second Round North Blackpool	(a)	1-1

(Blackpool won 5-4 on penalties)

MIDDLESBROUGH

FOUNDATION

A previous belief that Middlesbrough Football Club was founded at a tripe supper at the Corporation Hotel has proved to be erroneous. In fact, members of Middlesbrough Cricket Club were responsible for forming it at a meeting in the gymnasium of the Albert Park Hotel in 1875.

Riverside Stadium, Middlehaven Way, Middlesbrough TS3 6RS.

Telephone: (0844) 499 6789.

Ticket Office: (0844) 499 1234.

Website: www.mfc.co.uk

Email: enquiries@mfc.co.uk

Ground Capacity: 34,000.

Record Attendance: 53,536 v Newcastle U, Division 1, 27 December 1949 (at Ayresome Park); 34,814 v Newcastle U, FA Premier League, 5 March 2003 (at Riverside Stadium); 35,000, England v Slovakia, Euro 2004 qualifier, 11 June 2003.

Pitch Measurements: 105m × 68m (115yd × 74.5yd).

Chairman: Steve Gibson.

Chief Executive: Neil Bausor.

Manager: Tony Pulis.

Assistant Manager: Dave Kemp.

Colours: Red shirts with white trim, red shorts with white trim, white socks with red trim.

Year Formed: 1876; re-formed 1986.

Turned Professional: 1889; became amateur 1892, and professional again, 1899.

Club Nickname: 'Boro'.

Grounds: 1877, Old Archery Ground, Albert Park; 1879, Breckon Hill; 1882, Linthorpe Road Ground; 1903, Ayresome Park; 1995, Riverside Stadium.

First Football League Game: 2 September 1899, Division 2, v Lincoln C (a) L 0–3 – Smith; Shaw, Ramsey; Allport, McNally, McCracken; Wanless, Longstaffe, Gettins, Page, Pugh.

Record League Victory: 9–0 v Brighton & HA, Division 2, 23 August 1958 – Taylor; Bilcliff, Robinson; Harris (2p), Phillips, Walley; Day, McLean, Clough (5), Peacock (2), Holliday.

Record Cup Victory: 7–0 v Hereford U, Coca-Cola Cup 2nd rd, 1st leg, 18 September 1996 – Miller; Fleming (1), Branco (1), Whyte, Vickers, Whelan, Emerson (1), Mustoe, Stamp, Juninho, Ravanelli (4).

Record Defeat: 0–9 v Blackburn R, Division 2, 6 November 1954.

HONOURS

League Champions: First Division – 1994–95; Division 2 – 1926–27, 1928–29, 1973–74.
Runners-up: FL C – 2015–16; First Division – 1997–98; Division 2 – 1901–02, 1991–92; Division 3 – 1966–67, 1986–87.

FA Cup: Runners-up: 1997.

League Cup Winners: 2004.
Runners-up: 1997, 1998.

Amateur Cup Winners: 1895, 1898.

Anglo-Scottish Cup Winners: 1976.

Full Members' Cup: Runners-up: 1990.

European Competitions
UEFA Cup: 2004–05, 2005–06 *(runners-up).*

Sᴜn FACT FILE

When Middlesbrough's George Camsell scored twice against Notts County in February 1927 he set a new record for the number of League goals scored by a player. The goals took Camsell's tally to 45, beating the previous highest total set by James Cookson of Chesterfield. Camsell finished the season with a total of 59 League goals.

Most League Points (2 for a win): 65, Division 2, 1973–74.

Most League Points (3 for a win): 94, Division 3, 1986–87.

Most League Goals: 122, Division 2, 1926–27.

Highest League Scorer in Season: George Camsell, 59, Division 2, 1926–27 (Second Division record).

Most League Goals in Total Aggregate: George Camsell, 325, 1925–39.

Most League Goals in One Match: 5, John Wilkie v Gainsborough T, Division 2, 2 March 1901; 5, Andy Wilson v Nottingham F, Division 1, 6 October 1923; 5, George Camsell v Manchester C, Division 2, 25 December 1926; 5, George Camsell v Aston Villa, Division 1, 9 September 1935; 5, Brian Clough v Brighton & HA, Division 2, 22 August 1958.

Most Capped Player: Mark Schwarzer, 52 (109), Australia.

Most League Appearances: Tim Williamson, 563, 1902–23.

Youngest League Player: Luke Williams, 16 years 200 days v Barnsley, 18 December 2009.

Record Transfer Fee Received: £13,000,000 from Atalanta for Marten de Roon, August 2017.

Record Transfer Fee Paid: £15,000,000 to Nottingham F for Britt Assombalonga, July 2017.

Football League Record: 1899 Elected to Division 2; 1902–24 Division 1; 1924–27 Division 2; 1927–28 Division 1; 1928–29 Division 2; 1929–54 Division 1; 1954–66 Division 2; 1966–67 Division 3; 1967–74 Division 2; 1974–82 Division 1; 1982–86 Division 2; 1986–87 Division 3; 1987–88 Division 2; 1988–89 Division 1; 1989–92 Division 2; 1992–93 FA Premier League; 1993–95 Division 1; 1995–97 FA Premier League; 1997–98 Division 1; 1998–2009 FA Premier League; 2009–16 FL C; 2016–17 FA Premier League; 2017– FL C.

MANAGERS

John Robson 1899–1905
Alex Mackie 1905–06
Andy Aitken 1906–09
J. Gunter 1908–10
(Secretary-Manager)
Andy Walker 1910–11
Tom McIntosh 1911–19
Jimmy Howie 1920–23
Herbert Bamlett 1923–26
Peter McWilliam 1927–34
Wilf Gillow 1934–44
David Jack 1944–52
Walter Rowley 1952–54
Bob Dennison 1954–63
Raich Carter 1963–66
Stan Anderson 1966–73
Jack Charlton 1973–77
John Neal 1977–81
Bobby Murdoch 1981–82
Malcolm Allison 1982–84
Willie Maddren 1984–86
Bruce Rioch 1986–90
Colin Todd 1990–91
Lennie Lawrence 1991–94
Bryan Robson 1994–2001
Steve McClaren 2001–06
Gareth Southgate 2006–09
Gordon Strachan 2009–10
Tony Mowbray 2010–13
Aitor Karanka 2013–17
Garry Monk 2017
Tony Pulis December 2017–

LATEST SEQUENCES

Longest Sequence of League Wins: 9, 16.2.1974 – 6.4.1974.

Longest Sequence of League Defeats: 8, 26.12.1995 – 17.2.1996.

Longest Sequence of League Draws: 8, 3.4.1971 – 1.5.1971.

Longest Sequence of Unbeaten League Matches: 24, 8.9.1973 – 19.1.1974.

Longest Sequence Without a League Win: 19, 3.10.1981 – 6.3.1982.

Successive Scoring Runs: 26 from 21.9.1946.

Successive Non-scoring Runs: 7, 25.1.2014 – 1.3.2014.

TEN YEAR LEAGUE RECORD

		P	W	D	L	F	A	Pts	Pos
2008-09	PR Lge	38	7	11	20	28	57	32	19
2009-10	FL C	46	16	14	16	58	50	62	11
2010-11	FL C	46	17	11	18	68	68	62	12
2011-12	FL C	46	18	16	12	52	51	70	7
2012-13	FL C	46	18	5	23	61	70	59	16
2013-14	FL C	46	16	16	14	62	50	64	12
2014-15	FL C	46	25	10	11	68	37	85	4
2015-16	FL C	46	26	11	9	63	31	89	2
2016-17	PR Lge	38	5	13	20	27	53	28	19
2017-18	FL C	46	22	10	14	67	45	76	5

DID YOU KNOW ?

Middlesbrough's final game at Ayresome Park on 30 April 1995 saw them defeat Luton Town 2-1 to all but clinch the then First Division championship. John Hendrie scored twice in front of a season's best attendance of 23,903. Boro drew their final game at Tranmere Rovers to win the title and earn promotion to the top flight.

MIDDLESBROUGH – SKY BET CHAMPIONSHIP 2017–18 LEAGUE RECORD

Match No.	Date		Venue	Opponents	Result		H/T Score	Lg Pos.	Goalscorers	Atten- dance
1	Aug	5	A	Wolverhampton W	L	0-1	0-1	20		29,692
2		12	H	Sheffield U	W	1-0	1-0	11	Gestede [20]	26,876
3		15	H	Burton Alb	W	2-0	1-0	4	Assombalonga 2 [23, 60]	24,522
4		19	A	Nottingham F	L	1-2	0-1	9	Gibson [83]	26,265
5		26	H	Preston NE	D	0-0	0-0	9		25,295
6	Sept	9	A	Bolton W	W	3-0	1-0	6	Assombalonga 2 [13, 71], Johnson [78]	17,385
7		12	A	Aston Villa	D	0-0	0-0	9		26,631
8		16	H	QPR	W	3-2	1-1	7	Baker [36], Fletcher [55], Assombalonga [60]	24,790
9		23	A	Fulham	D	1-1	0-0	5	Christie [88]	20,718
10		26	H	Norwich C	L	0-1	0-1	9		24,084
11		30	H	Brentford	D	2-2	0-1	11	Braithwaite [68], Da Silva [76]	24,545
12	Oct	14	A	Barnsley	D	2-2	1-2	11	Braithwaite [7], Assombalonga [60]	17,163
13		21	H	Cardiff C	L	0-1	0-0	13		24,806
14		28	H	Reading	W	2-0	1-0	12	Leadbitter (pen) [14], Assombalonga [74]	17,928
15		31	H	Hull C	W	3-1	2-0	7	Braithwaite [13], Assombalonga [36], Leadbitter (pen) [85]	15,454
16	Nov	5	H	Sunderland	W	1-0	1-0	5	Tavernier [6]	29,277
17		19	A	Leeds U	L	1-2	0-1	6	Assombalonga (pen) [77]	33,771
18		22	H	Birmingham C	W	2-0	2-0	6	Assombalonga 2 [10, 41]	22,848
19		25	H	Derby Co	L	0-3	0-1	7		24,607
20	Dec	2	A	Bristol C	L	1-2	0-0	9	Magnusson (og) [75]	18,752
21		9	H	Ipswich T	W	2-0	1-0	8	Braithwaite [44], Bamford [51]	22,989
22		16	A	Millwall	L	1-2	0-2	10	Downing [67]	12,026
23		23	A	Sheffield W	W	2-1	0-1	9	Howson [71], Shotton [83]	27,471
24		26	H	Bolton W	W	2-0	0-0	7	Braithwaite [49], Assombalonga [67]	29,443
25		30	H	Aston Villa	L	0-1	0-0	9		29,422
26	Jan	1	A	Preston NE	W	3-2	1-2	8	Ayala 2 [13, 73], Howson [65]	15,101
27		13	H	Fulham	L	0-1	0-0	9		23,850
28		20	A	QPR	W	3-0	2-0	8	Ayala [24], Friend [34], Traore [85]	14,182
29		30	H	Sheffield W	D	0-0	0-0	8		24,120
30	Feb	3	A	Norwich C	L	0-1	0-1	9		25,960
31		10	H	Reading	W	2-1	1-0	9	Traore 2 [44, 49]	23,491
32		17	A	Cardiff C	L	0-1	0-1	9		18,720
33		20	H	Hull C	W	3-1	2-1	8	Gestede 2 [16, 58], Bamford [45]	23,111
34		24	A	Sunderland	D	3-3	0-1	7	Bamford 2 [49, 68], Leadbitter (pen) [53]	29,048
35	Mar	2	H	Leeds U	W	3-0	2-0	6	Bamford 3 [31, 36, 68]	27,621
36		6	A	Birmingham C	W	1-0	1-0	6	Bamford [39]	18,301
37		10	A	Barnsley	W	3-1	2-0	6	Ayala [1], Traore [18], Bamford [53]	24,917
38		17	A	Brentford	D	1-1	1-1	6	Traore [21]	11,134
39		30	H	Wolverhampton W	L	1-2	0-2	6	Bamford [90]	27,658
40	Apr	2	A	Burton Alb	D	1-1	0-1	6	Assombalonga [90]	4468
41		7	H	Nottingham F	W	2-0	2-0	6	Ayala [7], Downing [31]	25,812
42		10	A	Sheffield U	L	1-2	0-2	7	Ayala [48]	26,557
43		14	H	Bristol C	W	2-1	1-1	5	Friend [18], Ayala [68]	24,812
44		21	A	Derby Co	W	2-1	1-0	5	Besic [20], Assombalonga [70]	28,096
45		28	H	Millwall	W	2-0	1-0	5	Assombalonga [11], Howson [66]	28,606
46	May	6	A	Ipswich T	D	2-2	0-1	5	Downing [71], Bamford [90]	18,829

Final League Position: 5

GOALSCORERS

League (67): Assombalonga 15 (1 pen), Bamford 11, Ayala 7, Braithwaite 5, Traore 5, Downing 3, Gestede 3, Howson 3, Leadbitter 3 (3 pens), Friend 2, Baker 1, Besic 1, Christie 1, Da Silva 1, Fletcher 1, Gibson 1, Johnson 1, Shotton 1, Tavernier 1, own goal 1.
FA Cup (2): Braithwaite 1, Gestede 1.
Carabao Cup (6): Bamford 2 (1 pen), Baker 1, Da Silva 1, Fletcher 1, Tavernier 1.
Checkatrade Trophy (4): Armstrong 3, Gibson 1.
Championship Play-Offs (0):

Randolph D 46	Christie C 24 + 1	Ayala D 33	Gibson B 45	Friend G 29 + 4	Howson J 37 + 6	Clayton A 22 + 10	de Roon M 1	Braithwaite M 17 + 2	Assombalonga B 32 + 12	Fletcher A 3 + 13	Bamford P 23 + 16	Forshaw A 5 + 6	Gestede R 10 + 9	Fry D 11 + 2	Baker L 6 + 6	Leadbitter G 29 + 3	Traore A 26 + 8	Da Silva F 18 + 4	Downing S 38 + 2	Johnson M 6 + 11	Shotton R 23 + 1	Tavernier M 4 + 1	Roberts C 1	Guedioura A 1	Cranie M 1 + 8	Besic M 15	Harrison J — + 4	Match No.
1	2	3	4	5	6[3]	7	8[2]	9	10	11[1]	12	13	14															1
1	2		4	5	6	7			10[9]	13	9	8[1]	11[1]			3	12	14										2
1	2		4	5	6	7[1]			10	14	9[3]	8[1]	11[2]			3	12		13									3
1	2		4	5	6	7[1]			10	14	9[3]	8[1]	11			3	13		12									4
1	5		3	4[2]	7	8			11		12		10	2	6[1]					9	13							5
1	2		4			8		11	14	13		3	10[3]	7	6[1]	5	9[2]	12										6
1	2		4		13	8		11[2]	14		3	10	7[3]	6[1]	5	9[2]	12											7
1	2		4	13	7[3]	8		10	12		14	3	8	6[1]	5	9	11											8
1	2		4	13	7	8		11[1]	12	10[2]		3	6		5[1]	14	9											9
1	2		4		6	7[3]		13	11	12	14	3	9		8[1]	5[2]	10											10
1	2		4		7	8		11[3]	10	12	13		14		6[2]	5		9[1]	3									11
1	2	3	4	12		7			9	11	10	13		6		5[1]	8[2]											12
1	2	3	4		7			9	10	11[1]	12	8	13		5	6[2]												13
1	2	3	4		7			9[2]	11	14	13		6[2]	5	8	12			10[1]									14
1	2	3	4	12	6			9	11[1]	14		7		5[2]	8	13		10[3]										15
1	2	3	4	5	7			9	11[2]	13	14	6[3]		8	12		10[1]											16
1		3	4	5[1]	6			9	11	14		7[3]	13		8	12		10[2]	2									17
1	2	3	4		6			9	11		13	12	7[2]	14	5	8[1]	10											18
1	2	3[4]	4		7			9[3]	11		14	6	13	12	5	8[2]	10[1]											19
1	2		4		7			9[2]	11		14	6	12	3	10	5[1]	8[3]	13										20
1	2	3	4		6			9	11		10[2]	14	13	7[1]		5	8[3]	12										21
1	2[2]	3	4		6[3]			10[1]	11		9		12	7	13	5	8	14										22
1	2		4		6			10[3]	11		9[1]		13	7		5	8[2]	12	3	14								23
1	2		4	12	6			10	11[1]		9		13	7		5[2]	8	3										24
1		3	4	5	7			9[3]	10[1]	14	13		11[2]	8	12	6		2										25
1	2[3]	3	4	5	6			10[1]		13	12		10[1]	7		9[3]	8	14	2			8[2]						26
1		3	4	5	6	13		11[2]	12			10[1]		7	9[3]	8	14	2										27
1	14	3	4	5	6	13		11[1]		10[2]	12			7	8	9[3]	2											28
1		3	4	5	6[2]	13		14	10[3]		11[1]	12		7	9	8	2											29
1		3	4	5	12	6[1]			13		11[2]	10[1]		7	9	8	2											30
1		3	4	5	6	12			13		11	10[2]		7	9	8[3]	2					14						31
1		3	4	5	6[1]			12	14		10[3]			7	11	9	2								8[2]	13		32
1		3		5	13	12			11[1]	10	4			7	9	8[3]	2					14	6[2]					33
1		3	4	5	14	13		11[3]	10					7[1]	8[4]	9[2]	2						6	12				34
1		3	4	5	6	12			10[1]					7[2]	9	11	2					13	8					35
1		3	4	5	9	6			13		11[2]			14	8[3]	10	2[1]					12	7					36
1		3	4	5	6	7			14		10[2]			12	9	11[3]	2					13	8[1]					37
1	3[1]		4	5	6[2]				14		10		12		13	9	11	2					8[1]					38
1		3	4	5	12	6[2]			14		10			7[1]	9	11	2[3]					13	8					39
1		3	4	5	6[3]	14			12		10			7[1]	9	11[2]	2		2			8	13					40
1		3	4	5	6	12			13		10[1]			7	9[2]	11	2					14	8[3]					41
1		3	4	5	6	13			14		10[1]			7[4]	9[3]	12	11	2					8[2]					42
1		3	4	5	6	7			12		10[2]				9[3]	13	11[1]	2				14	8					43
1		3	4	5	6	7			10					12	9	13	11[2]	2					8[1]					44
1		3	4	5	6	7			10[1]		12				9	13	11[2]	2					8					45
1		3	4	5	6[2]	7[1]			10		12				9		11	2					8	13				46

FA Cup

Third Round	Sunderland	(h)	2-0
Fourth Round	Brighton & HA	(h)	0-1

Carabao Cup

Second Round	Scunthorpe U	(h)	3-0
Third Round	Aston Villa	(a)	2-0
Fourth Round	Bournemouth	(a)	1-3

Checkatrade Trophy (Middlesbrough U21)

Northern Group B	Accrington S	(a)	2-3
Northern Group B	Wigan Ath	(a)	1-4
Northern Group B	Blackpool	(a)	1-4

Championship Play-Offs

Semi-Final 1st leg	Aston Villa	(h)	0-1
Semi-Final 2nd leg	Aston Villa	(a)	0-0

MILLWALL

FOUNDATION

Formed in 1885 as Millwall Rovers by employees of Morton & Co, a jam and marmalade factory in West Ferry Road. The founders were predominantly Scotsmen. Their first headquarters was The Islanders pub in Tooke Street, Millwall. Their first trophy was the East End Cup in 1887.

The Den, Zampa Road, Bermondsey, London SE16 3LN.

Telephone: (020) 7232 1222.

Ticket Office: (0844) 826 2004.

Website: www.millwallfc.co.uk

Email: questions@millwallplc.com

Ground Capacity: 19,734.

Record Attendance: 48,672 v Derby Co, FA Cup 5th rd, 20 February 1937 (at The Den, Cold Blow Lane); 20,093 v Arsenal, FA Cup 3rd rd, 10 January 1994 (at The Den, Bermondsey).

Pitch Measurements: 106m × 68m (116yd × 74.5yd).

Chairman: John G. Berylson.

Chief Executive: Steve Kavanagh.

Manager: Neil Harris.

Assistant Manager: Dave Livermore.

HONOURS

League Champions: Division 2 – 1987–88; Second Division – 2000–01; Division 3S – 1927–28, 1937–38; Division 4 – 1961–62.
Runners-up: Division 3 – 1965–66, 1984–85; Division 3S – 1952–53; Division 4 – 1964–65.
FA Cup: Runners-up: 2004.
League Cup: 5th rd – 1974, 1977, 1995.
League Trophy: Runners-up: 1999.
European Competitions
UEFA Cup: 2004–05.

Colours: Blue shirts with white trim, white shorts with blue trim, blue socks with white trim.

Year Formed: 1885.

Turned Professional: 1893.

Previous Names: 1885, Millwall Rovers; 1889, Millwall Athletic; 1899, Millwall; 1985, Millwall Football & Athletic Company.

Club Nickname: 'The Lions'.

Grounds: 1885, Glengall Road, Millwall; 1886, Back of 'Lord Nelson'; 1890, East Ferry Road; 1901, North Greenwich; 1910, The Den, Cold Blow Lane; 1993, The Den, Bermondsey.

First Football League Game: 28 August 1920, Division 3, v Bristol R (h) W 2–0 – Lansdale; Fort, Hodge; Voisey (1), Riddell, McAlpine; Waterall, Travers, Broad (1), Sutherland, Dempsey.

Record League Victory: 9–1 v Torquay U, Division 3 (S), 29 August 1927 – Lansdale, Tilling, Hill, Amos, Bryant (3), Graham, Chance, Hawkins (3), Landells (1), Phillips (2), Black. 9–1 v Coventry C, Division 3 (S), 19 November 1927 – Lansdale, Fort, Hill, Amos, Collins (1), Graham, Chance, Landells (4), Cock (2), Phillips (2), Black.

Record Cup Victory: 7–0 v Gateshead, FA Cup 2nd rd, 12 December 1936 – Yuill; Ted Smith, Inns; Brolly, Hancock, Forsyth; Thomas (1), Mangnall (1), Ken Burditt (2), McCartney (2), Thorogood (1).

Record Defeat: 1–9 v Aston Villa, FA Cup 4th rd, 28 January 1946.

Most League Points (2 for a win): 65, Division 3 (S), 1927–28 and Division 3, 1965–66.

THE Sun FACT FILE

In 1936–37 Millwall became the first Third Division side to reach the semi-finals of the FA Cup. They began their campaign with a 6-1 win at Aldershot and followed up with a 7-0 victory over Gateshead in the second round. The Lions went on to defeat Fulham, Chelsea and Derby County before going out of the competition, losing 2-1 to Sunderland.

Most League Points (3 for a win): 93, Division 2, 2000–01.

Most League Goals: 127, Division 3 (S), 1927–28.

Highest League Scorer in Season: Richard Parker, 37, Division 3 (S), 1926–27.

Most League Goals in Total Aggregate: Neil Harris, 124, 1995–2004; 2006–11.

Most League Goals in One Match: 5, Richard Parker v Norwich C, Division 3 (S), 28 August 1926.

Most Capped Player: David Forde, 24, Republic of Ireland.

Most League Appearances: Barry Kitchener, 523, 1967–82.

Youngest League Player: Moses Ashikodi, 15 years 240 days v Brighton & HA, 22 February 2003.

Record Transfer Fee Received: £2,800,000 from Norwich C for Steve Morison, June 2011.

Record Transfer Fee Paid: £800,000 to Derby Co for Paul Goddard, December 1989.

Football League Record: 1920 Original Members of Division 3; 1921 Division 3 (S); 1928–34 Division 2; 1934–38 Division 3 (S); 1938–48 Division 2; 1948–58 Division 3 (S); 1958–62 Division 4; 1962–64 Division 3; 1964–65 Division 4; 1965–66 Division 3; 1966–75 Division 2; 1975–76 Division 3; 1976–79 Division 2; 1979–85 Division 3; 1985–88 Division 2; 1988–90 Division 1; 1990–92 Division 2; 1992–96 Division 1; 1996–2001 Division 2; 2001–04 Division 1; 2004–06 FL C; 2006–10 FL 1; 2010–15 FL C; 2015–17 FL 1; 2017– FL C.

LATEST SEQUENCES

Longest Sequence of League Wins: 10, 10.3.1928 – 25.4.1928.

Longest Sequence of League Defeats: 11, 10.4.1929 – 16.9.1929.

Longest Sequence of League Draws: 5, 22.12.1973 – 12.1.1974.

Longest Sequence of Unbeaten League Matches: 19, 22.8.1959 – 31.10.1959.

Longest Sequence Without a League Win: 20, 26.12.1989 – 5.5.1990.

Successive Scoring Runs: 22 from 27.11.1954.

Successive Non-scoring Runs: 6 from 27.4.2013.

MANAGERS

F. B. Kidd 1894–99
(Hon. Treasurer/Manager)
E. R. Stopher 1899–1900
(Hon. Treasurer/Manager)
George Saunders 1900–11
(Hon. Treasurer/Manager)
Herbert Lipsham 1911–19
Robert Hunter 1919–33
Bill McCracken 1933–36
Charlie Hewitt 1936–40
Bill Voisey 1940–44
Jack Cock 1944–48
Charlie Hewitt 1948–56
Ron Gray 1956–57
Jimmy Seed 1958–59
Reg Smith 1959–61
Ron Gray 1961–63
Billy Gray 1963–66
Benny Fenton 1966–74
Gordon Jago 1974–77
George Petchey 1978–80
Peter Anderson 1980–82
George Graham 1982–86
John Docherty 1986–90
Bob Pearson 1990
Bruce Rioch 1990–92
Mick McCarthy 1992–96
Jimmy Nicholl 1996–97
John Docherty 1997
Billy Bonds 1997–98
Keith Stevens 1998–2000
(then Joint Manager)
(plus **Alan McLeary** 1999–2000*)*
Mark McGhee 2000–03
Dennis Wise 2003–05
Steve Claridge 2005
Colin Lee 2005
David Tuttle 2005–06
Nigel Spackman 2006
Willie Donachie 2006–07
Kenny Jackett 2007–13
Steve Lomas 2013
Ian Holloway 2014–15
Neil Harris March 2015–

TEN YEAR LEAGUE RECORD

		P	W	D	L	F	A	Pts	Pos
2008-09	FL 1	46	25	7	14	63	53	82	5
2009-10	FL 1	46	24	13	9	76	44	85	3
2010-11	FL C	46	18	13	15	62	48	67	9
2011-12	FL C	46	15	12	19	55	57	57	16
2012-13	FL C	46	15	11	20	51	62	56	20
2013-14	FL C	46	11	15	20	46	74	48	19
2014-15	FL C	46	9	14	23	42	76	41	22
2015-16	FL 1	46	24	9	13	73	49	81	4
2016-17	FL 1	46	20	13	13	66	57	73	6
2017-18	FL C	46	19	15	12	56	45	72	8

DID YOU KNOW ?

Millwall equalled a post-war Football League record when they began the 1959–60 season undefeated in their first 19 games. Despite their run they were still three points behind Division Four leaders Walsall and dropped further back when they lost for the first time, going down 2-1 at Notts County on 7 November.

MILLWALL – SKY BET CHAMPIONSHIP 2017–18 LEAGUE RECORD

Match No.	Date	Venue	Opponents	Result	H/T Score	Lg Pos.	Goalscorers	Attendance
1	Aug 4	A	Nottingham F	L	0-1	0-1	24		28,065
2	12	H	Bolton W	D	1-1	0-0	17	Saville [49]	12,238
3	15	H	Ipswich T	L	3-4	2-3	21	Wallace [1], O'Brien [36], Elliott [80]	11,919
4	19	A	Bristol C	D	0-0	0-0	23		18,230
5	26	H	Norwich C	W	4-0	3-0	17	Gregory [15], Saville [17], Wallace [42], Hutchinson [72]	12,671
6	Sept 9	A	Wolverhampton W	L	0-1	0-1	19		24,426
7	12	A	QPR	D	2-2	1-0	19	McLaughlin [6], Wallace [50]	12,600
8	16	H	Leeds U	W	1-0	0-0	16	O'Brien [73]	16,447
9	23	A	Preston NE	D	0-0	0-0	16		12,363
10	26	H	Reading	W	2-1	0-0	12	Saville 2 [80, 85]	10,399
11	30	H	Barnsley	L	1-3	1-1	13	Gregory (pen) [45]	12,147
12	Oct 14	A	Brentford	L	0-1	0-0	16		9622
13	21	H	Birmingham C	W	2-0	0-0	15	Colin (og) [47], Tunnicliffe [78]	14,500
14	28	A	Cardiff C	D	0-0	0-0	15		18,496
15	31	A	Sheffield W	L	1-2	1-2	16	Elliott [13]	23,403
16	Nov 4	H	Burton Alb	L	0-1	0-0	19		11,507
17	18	A	Sunderland	D	2-2	2-1	18	Saville 2 [16, 20]	27,399
18	21	H	Hull C	D	0-0	0-0	18		9817
19	25	A	Fulham	L	0-1	0-1	19		17,984
20	Dec 2	H	Sheffield U	W	3-1	1-1	17	Gregory [14], Romeo [66], Cooper [87]	12,669
21	9	A	Aston Villa	D	0-0	0-0	17		29,628
22	16	H	Middlesbrough	W	2-1	2-0	17	Wallace [31], Saville [37]	12,026
23	23	A	Derby Co	L	0-3	0-3	17		25,813
24	26	H	Wolverhampton W	D	2-2	1-1	16	Gregory [13], Cooper [72]	13,121
25	29	H	QPR	W	1-0	0-0	15	Morison [55]	16,601
26	Jan 1	A	Norwich C	L	1-2	1-0	15	Morison [44]	25,774
27	13	H	Preston NE	D	1-1	1-0	16	O'Brien [43]	11,751
28	20	A	Leeds U	W	4-3	2-0	15	O'Brien [18], Gregory [42], Elliott [87], Wallace [90]	33,564
29	30	H	Derby Co	D	0-0	0-0	14		10,931
30	Feb 3	A	Reading	W	2-0	0-0	14	Bacuna (og) [70], Gregory [73]	17,282
31	9	A	Cardiff C	D	1-1	1-1	14	Gregory [40]	13,204
32	17	A	Birmingham C	W	1-0	0-0	14	Onyedinma [77]	19,111
33	20	H	Sheffield W	W	2-1	0-1	11	Gregory [52], Morison [63]	11,007
34	24	A	Burton Alb	W	1-0	0-0	12	Marshall [61]	4105
35	Mar 3	H	Sunderland	D	1-1	0-1	11	Hutchinson [69]	14,358
36	6	A	Hull C	W	2-1	2-0	11	Saville [1], Cooper [33]	13,524
37	10	H	Brentford	W	1-0	1-0	10	Saville [1]	13,251
38	17	A	Barnsley	W	2-0	1-0	10	Gregory [24], Marshall [63]	13,041
39	30	H	Nottingham F	W	2-0	2-0	8	Williams [1], Gregory [33]	16,004
40	Apr 2	A	Ipswich T	D	2-2	1-0	8	Cooper [27], Saville [60]	16,010
41	7	H	Bristol C	W	2-0	1-0	7	Wallace [11], Morison [52]	16,081
42	10	A	Bolton W	W	2-0	1-0	6	Elliott [34], Marshall [63]	13,810
43	14	A	Sheffield U	D	1-1	0-0	6	Morison [76]	27,454
44	20	H	Fulham	L	0-3	0-0	6		17,614
45	28	A	Middlesbrough	L	0-2	0-1	8		28,606
46	May 6	H	Aston Villa	W	1-0	1-0	8	Williams (pen) [30]	17,195

Final League Position: 8

GOALSCORERS

League (56): Gregory 10 (1 pen), Saville 10, Wallace 6, Morison 5, Cooper 4, Elliott 4, O'Brien 4, Marshall 3, Hutchinson 2, Williams 2 (1 pen), McLaughlin 1, Onyedinma 1, Romeo 1, Tunnicliffe 1, own goals 2.
FA Cup (6): O'Brien 2, Thompson 2, Onyedinma 1, Wallace 1 (1 pen).
Carabao Cup (3): Elliott 2, Ferguson 1.

Archer J 45	McLaughlin C 23 + 1	Hutchinson S 46	Cooper J 35 + 3	Meredith J 46	Wallace J 42 + 1	Williams S 30 + 5	Saville G 44	O'Brien A 23 + 7	Morison S 38 + 6	Gregory J 40 + 3	Onyedinma F 8 + 29	Ferguson S 9 + 15	Elliott T 8 + 16	Webster B 10	Tunnicliffe R 19 + 5	Romeo M 22 + 5	Craig T 1 + 3	Thompson B — + 3	Twardek K — + 2	Martin D 1	Shackell J — + 7	Marshall B 16	Cahill T — + 10	Match No.
1	2	3	4	5	6	7[2]	8	9	10	11[3]	12	13	14											1
1	2	3		5	6	8	7		10	11[2]	12	9[1]	13	4										2
1	2		4	5[1]	6	8	7	9[1]	10[2]	11	14	12	13		3									3
1	2		4	5	6[3]	8	7	9[1]	10	11[2]	12	14	13		3									4
1	2		4	5	6[1]	7	8[3]	9	10	11[2]	14	13			3	12								5
1	2		4	5[2]	6[1]	7	8	9	10	11	12	13			3									6
1	2	4	13	5	6[1]	7	8		10	11		9[2]			3	12								7
1	2	4	14	5	6[1]	7	8	9[2]	11	10[3]	12	13			3									8
1	2		4	5	6[3]	7	8	9[1]	10	11[2]	12	13	14		3									9
1	2	4	13	5	6[1]	7	8	9	10	11[2]	12				3									10
1	2		4	5[2]	6		8	9[1]	11	10	13	12			3	7								11
1	2	3	4	5[1]	6	8			10[2]	11	13	9	12		7									12
1	2	3	4	5	6		8	9[3]	10[2]	11[1]	12	13	14		7			14						13
1	2	3	4	5	6[1]		8	9[3]	11	10[2]	14	13	12		7									14
1	2	3	4	5	6		8	13	14	11[3]	12	9	10[2]		7									15
1	2	3		5[3]	6[1]		8	9[2]	10[1]	11	14	12			7		4	13						16
1	2	3	4	5	6[1]		12	9	10[3]	11[2]	13				7				14					17
1	2	3	4	5	6[2]		12	13	9[3]	11		10[1]			7				14					18
1	2[0]	3	4	5		13	8	9[2]	10	11	12			6[1]	7				14					19
1		3	4	5	6[2]		8	9[1]	10	11[3]	14				7	2	13	12						20
		3	4	5	6	13	8	9[1]	10[2]	11	12				7	2				1				21
1		3	4	5	6	12	8	9[1]	10	11[2]					7	2	13							22
1		3	4	5	6[1]	14	8	9[2]	10	11[3]	13	12			7	2								23
1	2[1]	3	4	5	6	7	8	9[3]	13	11	10[2]				14	12								24
1		3	4	5	6	12	8	9[1]	10	11[2]	13				7	2								25
1		3	4	5	12	7	8[3]	13	10	11[2]		9		6[1]		2			14					26
1		3	4	5	6[2]	13	8	9	10	11[1]	12				7	2								27
1	2[0]	3	4	5[1]	6	7	8	9[2]	10	11	12	13				14								28
1	2	3	4	5	6	7	8	9[1]	10	11	12													29
1	2[2]	3	4	5	6[3]	7	8	9	11	10[1]	13	12										14		30
1		3	4	5	6		8		11	10[1]	12				7	2						9[2]	13	31
1		3	4	5	6		8		11[3]	10[1]	12					2					14	9[2]	13	32
1		3	4	5	6		8		11	10	12					2					13	9[1]		33
1		3	4	5	6		8		11[1]	10[2]	12					2					14	9[2]	13	34
1		3	4	5	6[2]		8		11	10	12					2						9[2]	13	35
1		3	4	5	6		8	10[3]	11[3]		12	13				2						9[2]	14	36
1		3	4	5	6		8		11[3]	10[1]	12	13				2						9[2]	14	37
1		3	4	5	6		8		11[2]	10[1]		13				2					12	9[1]	14	38
1		3	4	5	6[3]	7	8		11	10[2]	13	12				2					14	9[1]		39
1		3	4	5	6	7	8	13	11[2]	10[3]	14		12			2						9[1]		40
1		3	4	5	6	7	8		11[3]	10[2]	12					2					14	9[1]	13	41
1		3	4	5	6	7	8		11[3]	10[2]	12	14			11[3]	2						9[1]	13	42
1		3	4	5	6	7	8		11	10[1]	12	13				2						9[2]		43
1		3	4	5[1]	6	7	8		11	10	14	12				2[3]						9[2]	13	44
1	12	3	4	5[1]	6		8		11	10	14	13			7	2[2]						9[2]		45
1		3	4	5	6		8	9[1]	11	10	12	13			7	2[2]								46

FA Cup

Third Round	Barnsley	(h)	4-1
Fourth Round	Rochdale	(h)	2-2
Replay	Rochdale	(a)	0-1

Carabao Cup

First Round	Stevenage	(h)	2-0
Second Round	Reading	(a)	1-3
(aet)			

MILTON KEYNES DONS

FOUNDATION

In July 2004 Wimbledon became MK Dons and relocated to Milton Keynes. In 2007 it recognised itself as a new club with no connection to the old Wimbledon FC. In August of that year the replica trophies and other Wimbledon FC memorabilia were returned to the London Borough of Merton.

Stadiummk, Stadium Way West, Milton Keynes, Buckinghamshire MK1 1ST.

Telephone: (01908) 622 922.

Fax: (01908) 622 933.

Ticket Office: (0333) 200 5343.

Website: www.mkdons.com

Email: info@mkdons.com

Ground Capacity: 30,690.

Record Attendance: 28,127 v Chelsea, FA Cup 4th rd, 31 January 2016.

Pitch Measurements: 104m × 67.5m (114yd × 74yd).

Chairman: Pete Winkelman.

Executive Director: Andrew Cullen.

Manager: Paul Tisdale.

Assistant Manager: Matt Oakley.

Colours: White shirts with red trim, white shorts with red trim, white socks with red trim.

Year Formed: 2004.

Turned Professional: 2004.

Club Nickname: 'The Dons'.

Grounds: 2004, The National Hockey Stadium; 2007, Stadiummk.

First Football League Game: 7 August 2004, FL 1, v Barnsley (h) D 1–1 – Rachubka; Palmer, Lewington, Harding, Williams, Oyedele, Kamara, Smith, Smart (Herve), McLeod (1) (Hornuss), Small.

Record League Victory: 7–0 v Oldham Ath, FL 1, 20 December 2014 – Martin; Spence, McFadzean, Kay (Baldock), Lewington; Potter (1), Alli (1); Baker C (1), Carruthers (Green), Bowditch (1) (Afobe (1)); Grigg (2).

Record Cup Victory: 6–0 v Nantwich T, FA Cup 1st rd, 12 November 2011 – Martin; Chicksen, Baldock G, Doumbe (1), Flanagan, Williams S, Powell (1) (O'Shea (1), Chadwick (Galloway), Bowditch (2), MacDonald (Williams G (1)), Balanta.

HONOURS

League Champions: FL 2 – 2007–08. *Runners-up:* FL 1 – 2014–15.
FA Cup: 5th rd – 2013.
League Cup: 4th rd – 2015.
League Trophy Winners: 2008.

Sun FACT FILE

Milton Keynes Dons only escaped relegation in their inaugural season of 2004–05 because rivals Wrexham had 10 points deducted for going into administration. The club's finishing total of 51 points put them level with Torquay United but the Dons' better goal difference meant that they escaped the drop from League One.

Record Defeat: 0–6 v Southampton, Capital One Cup 3rd rd, 23 September 2015.

Most League Points (3 for a win): 97, FL 2, 2007–08.

Most League Goals: 101, FL 1, 2014–15.

Highest League Scorer in Season: Izale McLeod, 21, 2006–07.

Most League Goals in Total Aggregate: Izale McLeod, 62, 2004–07; 2012–14.

Most Capped Player: Lee Hodson, 7 (24), Northern Ireland.

MANAGERS
Stuart Murdock 2004
Danny Wilson 2004–06
Martin Allen 2006–07
Paul Ince 2007–08
Roberto Di Matteo 2008–09
Paul Ince 2009–10
Karl Robinson 2010–16
Robbie Neilson 2016–18
Dan Micciche 2018
Paul Tisdale June 2018–

Most League Goals in One Match: 3, Clive Platt v Barnet, FL 2, 20 January 2007; 3, Mark Wright v Bury, FL 2, 2 February 2008; 3, Aaron Wilbraham v Cheltenham T, FL 1, 31 January 2009; 3, Sam Baldock v Colchester U, FL 1, 12 March 2011; 3, Sam Baldock v Chesterfield, FL 1, 20 August 2012; 3, Dean Bowditch v Bury, FL 1, 22 September 2012; 3, Dele Alli v Notts Co, FL 1, 11 March 2014; 3, Dele Alli v Crewe Alex, FL 1, 20 September 2014; 3, Benik Afobe v Colchester U, FL 1, 29 November 2014; 3, Robert Hall v Leyton Orient, FL 1, 18 April 2015; 3, Ryan Colclough v Fleetwood T, FL 1, 9 September 2016.

Most League Appearances: Dean Lewington, 573, 2004–18.

Youngest League Player: Brendon Galloway, 16 years 42 days v Rochdale, 28 April 2012.

Record Transfer Fee Received: £5,000,000 from Tottenham H for Dele Alli, February 2015.

Record Transfer Fee Paid: £400,000 to Bristol C for Kieran Agard, August 2016.

Football League Record: 2004–06 FL 1; 2006–08 FL 2; 2008–15 FL 1; 2015–16 FL C; 2016–18 FL 1; 2018– FL 2.

LATEST SEQUENCES

Longest Sequence of League Wins: 8, 7.9.2007 – 20.10.2007.

Longest Sequence of League Defeats: 6, 2.4.2018 – 28.4.2018.

Longest Sequence of League Draws: 4, 12.2.2013 – 2.3.2013.

Longest Sequence of Unbeaten League Matches: 18, 29.1.2008 – 3.5.2008.

Longest Sequence Without a League Win: 11, 8.3.2016 – 7.5.2016.

Successive Scoring Runs: 18 from 7.4.2007.

Successive Non-scoring Runs: 4, 17.12.2005.

TEN YEAR LEAGUE RECORD

		P	W	D	L	F	A	Pts	Pos
2008-09	FL 1	46	26	9	11	83	47	87	3
2009-10	FL 1	46	17	9	20	60	68	60	12
2010-11	FL 1	46	23	8	15	67	60	77	5
2011-12	FL 1	46	22	14	10	84	47	80	5
2012-13	FL 1	46	19	13	14	62	45	70	8
2013-14	FL 1	46	17	9	20	63	65	60	10
2014-15	FL 1	46	27	10	9	101	44	91	2
2015-16	FL C	46	9	12	25	39	69	39	23
2016-17	FL 1	46	16	13	17	60	58	61	12
2017-18	FL 1	46	11	12	23	43	69	45	23

DID YOU KNOW ?

Milton Keynes Dons' 500th competitive game saw them defeat Northampton Town 2-0 in a Johnstone's Paint Trophy tie on 3 September 2013. The goals came from Patrick Bamford and future England international Dele Alli in front of a crowd of 4,299.

MILTON KEYNES DONS FC – SKY BET LEAGUE ONE 2017–18 LEAGUE RECORD

Match No.	Date	Venue	Opponents	Result	H/T Score	Lg Pos.	Goalscorers	Attendance
1	Aug 5	H	Wigan Ath	L 0-1	0-1	19		9164
2	12	A	Blackpool	L 0-1	0-1	20		3412
3	19	H	Gillingham	W 1-0	0-0	16	Sow [47]	7901
4	26	A	Blackburn R	L 1-4	1-2	20	Upson [25]	10,111
5	Sept 2	H	Oxford U	D 1-1	0-1	19	Brittain [60]	10,746
6	9	A	Plymouth Arg	W 1-0	1-0	15	Nesbitt [8]	8566
7	12	A	Peterborough U	L 0-2	0-0	15		6465
8	16	H	Rochdale	W 3-2	2-2	13	Ariyibi 2 [13, 41], Seager [84]	7670
9	22	A	AFC Wimbledon	W 2-0	2-0	9	Francomb (og) [7], Ariyibi [26]	3973
10	26	H	Northampton T	D 0-0	0-0	12		11,340
11	30	A	Bury	W 2-0	1-0	10	Sow [6], Ebanks-Landell [66]	3165
12	Oct 7	H	Bradford C	L 1-4	1-2	13	Ebanks-Landell [45]	9106
13	14	A	Portsmouth	L 0-2	0-2	14		17,608
14	17	H	Walsall	D 1-1	1-0	14	Aneke [24]	7258
15	21	A	Oldham Ath	D 4-4	1-3	15	Gilbey [17], Upson 2 [56, 89], Nesbitt [82]	9312
16	28	A	Bristol R	L 0-2	0-0	16		8701
17	Nov 11	H	Fleetwood T	W 1-0	1-0	14	Aneke [43]	7827
18	18	A	Charlton Ath	D 2-2	0-1	13	Agard 2 (1 pen) [63, 90 (p)]	10,557
19	21	H	Southend U	D 1-1	0-1	13	Agard (pen) [76]	7521
20	25	A	Doncaster R	L 1-2	1-0	15	Aneke [3]	7743
21	Dec 9	H	Shrewsbury T	D 1-1	0-0	17	Pawlett [56]	8355
22	16	A	Scunthorpe U	D 2-2	1-2	17	Agard [42], Aneke [66]	3569
23	23	A	Rotherham U	L 1-2	1-2	19	Aneke [9]	8333
24	26	H	Plymouth Arg	L 0-1	0-1	20		9268
25	30	H	Peterborough U	W 1-0	1-0	17	Aneke [27]	10,304
26	Jan 1	A	Oxford U	L 1-3	1-2	19	Gilbey [25]	7628
27	13	H	AFC Wimbledon	D 0-0	0-0	19		9504
28	20	A	Northampton T	L 1-2	1-2	21	Gilbey [19]	7231
29	Feb 3	A	Walsall	L 0-1	0-0	22		4009
30	10	H	Portsmouth	L 1-2	1-0	22	Ugbo [21]	14,762
31	13	A	Oldham Ath	L 0-1	0-1	22		3381
32	17	A	Charlton Ath	L 1-2	0-1	22	Agard [62]	8961
33	21	A	Rochdale	D 0-0	0-0	22		2353
34	24	A	Fleetwood T	D 1-1	1-0	22	Muirhead [20]	2773
35	Mar 3	H	Bristol R	L 0-1	0-0	22		8240
36	13	H	Rotherham U	W 3-2	2-1	22	Muirhead 2 [35, 57], Pawlett [41]	7327
37	17	H	Bury	W 2-1	1-0	22	Aneke 2 (2 pens) [11, 57]	9247
38	24	H	Blackpool	D 0-0	0-0	22		8094
39	29	A	Gillingham	W 2-1	1-1	20	Aneke [34], Williams, GB [85]	5540
40	Apr 2	H	Blackburn R	L 1-2	0-2	21	Pawlett [72]	11,215
41	7	A	Wigan Ath	L 1-5	1-2	22	Brittain [35]	8404
42	14	H	Doncaster R	L 1-2	1-0	23	Ugbo [19]	8954
43	21	A	Southend U	L 0-4	0-2	23		7546
44	24	A	Bradford C	L 0-2	0-1	23		19,192
45	28	H	Scunthorpe U	L 0-2	0-2	23		9578
46	May 5	A	Shrewsbury T	W 1-0	0-0	23	Agard (pen) [63]	6516

Final League Position: 23

GOALSCORERS

League (43): Aneke 9 (2 pens), Agard 6 (3 pens), Ariyibi 3, Gilbey 3, Muirhead 3, Pawlett 3, Upson 3, Brittain 2, Ebanks-Landell 2, Nesbitt 2, Sow 2, Ugbo 2, Seager 1, Williams, GB 1, own goal 1.
FA Cup (9): Agard 2, Nesbitt 2, Aneke 1, Cisse 1, Ebanks-Landell 1, Pawlett 1, Upson 1.
Carabao Cup (2): Ariyibi 1, Seager 1.
Checkatrade Trophy (6): Ariyibi 3, Seager 1, Thomas-Asante 1, Tshibola 1 (1 pen).

Nicholls L 41	Williams GB 41+2	Wootton S 37+1	Ebanks-Landell E 25+4	Lewington D 21+1	Upson E 32+5	Cisse O 28+4	Tshibola A 12	Agard K 24+17	Seager R 8+6	Ariyibi G 17+5	Pawlett P 20+4	Muirhead R 13+17	Thomas-Asante B —+15	Nombe S —+6	Walsh J 10	Sow O 17+2	Golbourne S 24+1	Gilbey A 22+1	Britain C 26+3	Nesbitt A 5+14	McGrandles C 13+6	Aneke C 26+5	Tavernier M 5+2	Ugbo I 11+4	Ward E 15	Tymon J 8+1	Rasulo G —+1	Sietsma W 5	Kasumu D —+1	Match No.
1	2	3^4	4	5	6^1	7	8	9^3	10^2	11	12	13	14																	1
1	2	3	4	5	8^1	6	9	10	12	7	11^2				13															2
1	2	3	4		14	8	7	13	10	6^2	12	9^1			5	11^3														3
1	2	4	3	5	7	6	9		11^2	10	8^1	12			13															4
1	2	3	4^2		6		7		11^1	8	10^5	13				5	9	12	14											5
1	4	3		6^1	7		14		8	13						11^3	5	9	2	10^2	12									6
1	2	3	4^2		6	7	10^1	11^3		14						12	9	8	5	13										7
1	3	4		6^2	14	8^1	12	13	10							11	5	9	2	7^3										8
1	3	4	14		6	8^2	13	7^1	10		12					11^3	5	9	2											9
1	3	4			6	8^1	13	7^3	10		14					11^2	5	9	2	12										10
1	13	3	4		6	12	8	7		10^2						11^3	5^1	9	2			14								11
1	2	4	3	5	6		7^4	9^2		11^1		14				10^3		8		13		12								12
1	12	3	4		6	7^3		14		10						11	5	9	2^2	8^1		13								13
1		3	2		6^1	8		10^2		14					4	12^3	9	7	5	13		11								14
1		3^1	2		6	8^2		11^3	12	13					4	9	7	5	14		10									15
1	3	4			7		9^1	13	14	10^3					5		6	8	2^2	12		11								16
1	2	3	4	14	6		11^2	12	8^1	10^3						5	7		13		9									17
1	2	3	4		6^3			12	11^2	8^1	10					5	7		14	13	9									18
1		3						11		8^1	12		13		4		5	7	2	10	6^2	9								19
1	2	3	4		8^1			11^2	12	9		13				5	6		14		7^3	10								20
1	2		4		7			6^1	13	9			12	3	11^3	5				8	10									21
1	2	12	3		7			8	13	10				4	11^2	5^1				6	9									22
1	2	4^3	3		7^2			8	13	10		14			5	11^1	12			6	9									23
1	2		3	13	12			9		5	8				4	10^1		6			7^2	11								24
1	2		3	13	6			14		11^3	12		4^5	9^4	5	8					7^1	10^2								25
1	2	3		6^3	4			11^1		7	10^2	14	13			5	8				9	12								26
1	5	3	4			7		10^3		13	9^1	14	12			8	2		6^1	11										27
1	5	3	4			6^3		14		9^2						10^1	8	2		13	12^4	7	11							28
1	2	3		5	6			11			12					10^1	7				9^3		8^2	13	4	14				29
1	2	3	13	4	6	7^2		10		11^1							5		12			9		8						30
1	5	3^3	2	4	6^2	7		12								14				10^1	13^1	11		8						31
1	2		4	12	7^2			10					9^1				5	13	6^3			11	3	8	14					32
1	5	2		4		7		10					12					9^2	6^1			13	10^1	11	3	8				33
1	5	2		4		7		12					8					6^2			13	10^1		11	3	9				34
1	5	2		3	12	8^2		13					7					6^3	14			10		11	4	9^1				35
1	8	3		4	6	14				9^1	7	13				11^3		5^3			10		12	2						36
1	5	2	14	4	7			9^3	8	12						10^2		6		13	11^1		3							37
1	5	4	2^2	8	6	7^3				10^1	9	12	14			11						13	3							38
1	5	2	13	4	6	7		9^1	8^1	14						12					11		3							39
1	2	3	4	5^3	7	8^2		13		9	11^1	14				12		6			10									40
1	2		3	5	7			11^3		8^1	12	13				9^2		6			10		14	4						41
	5	2		4^1	7			9	13	12			8					6^2			10	14	11^3	3			1			42
	2	4		5	8^3	7		13					12	14				9			6^2	11^1	3				1			43
	2			7	6			14					12	13			4		5^2			10	8^1	11^3	3	9		1		44
	2			6	7			13					12				4		5	14		10	9^2	11^3	3	8^1		1		45
	2	3		5		7		10					11^2	12			6	9		8^1				4					1	46

FA Cup

First Round	Hyde U	(a)	4-0
Second Round	Maidstone U	(h)	4-1
Third Round	QPR	(a)	1-0
Fourth Round	Coventry C	(h)	0-1

Carabao Cup

First Round *(aet)*	Forest Green R	(a)	1-0
Second Round	Swansea C	(h)	1-4

Checkatrade Trophy

Southern Group G	Brighton & HA U21	(h)	2-0
Southern Group G	Stevenage	(h)	0-0
(Milton Keynes D won 5-4 on penalties)			
Southern Group G	Oxford U	(a)	4-3
Second Round South	Chelsea U21	(h)	0-4

MORECAMBE

FOUNDATION

Several attempts to start a senior football club in a rugby stronghold finally succeeded on 7 May 1920 at the West View Hotel, Morecambe and a team competed in the Lancashire Combination for 1920–21. The club shared with a local cricket club at Woodhill Lane for the first season and a crowd of 3,000 watched the first game. The club moved to Roseberry Park, the name of which was changed to Christie Park after J.B. Christie who as President had purchased the ground.

Globe Arena, Christie Way, Westgate, Morecambe, Lancashire LA4 4TB.

Telephone: (01524) 411 797.

Fax: (01524) 832 230.

Ticket Office: (01524) 411 797.

Website: www.morecambefc.com

Email: office@morecambefc.com

Ground Capacity: 6,241.

HONOURS

League: Runners-up: Conference – (3rd) 2006–07 *(promoted via play-offs).*
FA Cup: 3rd rd – 1962, 2001, 2003.
League Cup: 3rd rd – 2008.

Record Attendance: 9,383 v Weymouth, FA Cup 3rd rd, 6 January 1962 (at Christie Park); 5,375 v Newcastle U, League Cup, 28 August 2013 (at Globe Arena).

Pitch Measurements: 103m × 71m (113yd × 78yd).

Chairman: Peter McGuigan.

Manager: Jim Bentley.

Assistant Manager: Ken McKenna.

Colours: Red shirts with black trim, black shorts with red trim, black socks with red trim.

Year Formed: 1920.

Turned Professional: 1920.

Club Nickname: 'The Shrimps'.

Grounds: 1920, Woodhill Lane; 1921, Christie Park; 2010, Globe Arena.

First Football League game: 11 August 2007, FL 2, v Barnet (h) D 0–0 – Lewis; Yates, Adams, Artell, Bentley, Stanley, Baker (Burns), Sorvel, Twiss (Newby), Curtis, Hunter (Thompson).

THE Sun FACT FILE

In 1926–27 centre forward George Grass, in his first full season with Morecambe, set a new club record by scoring 43 goals despite beginning the campaign in the reserves. He was quickly promoted to play for the first team in the Lancashire Combination and scored regularly, including the only goal in the Lancashire Junior Cup final to defeat Lancaster Town. Within days of that victory he was sold to First Division Blackburn Rovers.

Record League Victory: 6–0 v Crawley T, FL 2,
10 September 2011 – Roche; Reid, Wilson (pen),
McCready, Haining (Parrish), Fenton (1), Drummond,
McDonald, Price (Jevons), Carlton (3) (Alessandra),
Ellison (1).

Record Cup Victory: 6–2 v Nelson (a), Lancashire Trophy,
27 January 2004.

Record Defeat: 0–7 v Cambridge U, FL 2, 19 April 2016.

Most League Points (3 for a win): 73, FL 2, 2009–10.

Most League Goals: 73, FL 2, 2009–10.

Highest League Scorer in Season: Phil Jevons, 18, 2009–10.

Most League Goals in Total Aggregate: Kevin Ellison, 73,
2011–18.

Most League Goals in One Match: 3, Jon Newby v
Rotherham U, FL 2, 29 March 2008.

Most League Appearances: Barry Roche, 400, 2008–18.

Youngest League Player: Aaron McGowan, 16 years 263
days, 20 April 2013.

Record Transfer Fee Received: £225,000 from Stockport Co
for Carl Baker, July 2008.

Record Transfer Fee Paid: £50,000 to Southport for Carl
Baker, July 2007.

Football League Record: 2006–07 Promoted from
Conference; 2007– FL 2.

MANAGERS

Jimmy Milne 1947–48
Albert Dainty 1955–56
Ken Horton 1956–61
Joe Dunn 1961–64
Geoff Twentyman 1964–65
Ken Waterhouse 1965–69
Ronnie Clayton 1969–70
Gerry Irving and Ronnie Mitchell
  1970
Ken Waterhouse 1970–72
Dave Roberts 1972–75
Alan Spavin 1975–76
Johnny Johnson 1976–77
Tommy Ferber 1977–78
Mick Hogarth 1978–79
Don Curbage 1979–81
Jim Thompson 1981
Les Rigby 1981–84
Sean Gallagher 1984–85
Joe Wojciechowicz 1985–88
Eric Whalley 1988
Billy Wright 1988–89
Lawrie Milligan 1989
Bryan Griffiths 1989–93
Leighton James 1994
Jim Harvey 1994–2006
Sammy McIlroy 2006–11
Jim Bentley May 2011–

LATEST SEQUENCES

Longest Sequence of League Wins: 7, 31.10.2009 – 12.12.2009.

Longest Sequence of League Defeats: 7, 4.3.2017 – 1.4.2017.

Longest Sequence of League Draws: 5, 3.1.2015 – 31.1.2015.

Longest Sequence of Unbeaten League Matches: 12, 31.1.2009 – 21.3.2009.

Longest Sequence Without a League Win: 10, 20.3.2018 – 5.5.2018.

Successive Scoring Runs: 17 from 13.8.2011.

Successive Non-scoring Runs: 4 from 21.4.2018.

TEN YEAR LEAGUE RECORD

		P	W	D	L	F	A	Pts	Pos
2008-09	FL 2	46	15	18	13	53	56	63	11
2009-10	FL 2	46	20	13	13	73	64	73	4
2010-11	FL 2	46	13	12	21	54	73	51	20
2011-12	FL 2	46	14	14	18	63	57	56	15
2012-13	FL 2	46	15	13	18	55	61	58	16
2013-14	FL 2	46	13	15	18	52	64	54	18
2014-15	FL 2	46	17	12	17	53	52	63	11
2015-16	FL 2	46	12	10	24	69	91	46	21
2016-17	FL 2	46	14	10	22	53	73	52	18
2017-18	FL 2	46	9	19	18	41	56	46	22

DID YOU KNOW ?

Morecambe's 500th game in the
Football League saw them
travel to play Cheltenham
Town on 7 April 2018. The
Shrimps went into the game
with a five-match unbeaten run
behind them but went down to
a 3-0 defeat.

MORECAMBE – SKY BET LEAGUE TWO 2017–18 LEAGUE RECORD

Match No.	Date	Venue	Opponents	Result		H/T Score	Lg Pos.	Goalscorers	Attendance
1	Aug 5	H	Cheltenham T	W	2-1	0-1	6	Thompson 2 [55, 90]	1450
2	12	A	Lincoln C	D	1-1	0-0	5	Wildig [63]	8060
3	19	H	Swindon T	L	0-1	0-1	13		1655
4	26	A	Cambridge U	D	0-0	0-0	15		4573
5	Sept 2	H	Accrington S	L	1-2	0-1	19	Ellison [90]	2059
6	9	A	Notts Co	L	0-2	0-1	20		5305
7	12	A	Yeovil T	D	2-2	0-1	20	McGurk [66], Ellison [77]	2205
8	16	H	Newport Co	W	2-1	1-1	16	Ellison 2 [34, 80]	1189
9	23	A	Stevenage	L	1-2	1-1	18	Old [36]	1996
10	26	H	Luton T	D	0-0	0-0	20		1354
11	30	A	Exeter C	L	1-4	1-3	21	Oliver [38]	3651
12	Oct 7	H	Crawley T	L	0-1	0-1	21		1222
13	14	A	Chesterfield	W	2-0	1-0	20	McGurk 2 [17, 47]	4489
14	17	H	Port Vale	L	0-3	0-1	21		1241
15	21	H	Grimsby T	D	0-0	0-0	22		1525
16	28	A	Forest Green R	L	0-2	0-1	23		2515
17	Nov 11	H	Wycombe W	W	2-1	2-0	19	Old [27], McGurk [43]	1472
18	18	A	Colchester U	D	0-0	0-0	20		2872
19	21	H	Crewe Alex	L	0-1	0-0	22		927
20	25	A	Carlisle U	D	1-1	0-0	21	Old [72]	5010
21	Dec 9	H	Coventry C	W	2-0	1-0	18	Oliver [36], Lang [69]	1773
22	16	A	Barnet	L	1-2	0-2	20	Campbell [72]	1123
23	23	A	Mansfield T	L	1-2	0-1	21	Lang [50]	3058
24	26	H	Notts Co	L	1-4	0-2	21	Lang [89]	1947
25	29	H	Yeovil T	W	4-3	0-2	21	Oliver [72], Lang 2 [79, 85], Ellison [90]	1124
26	Jan 6	A	Grimsby T	W	2-0	2-0	20	Ellison [10], Old [41]	3104
27	13	H	Stevenage	D	1-1	1-0	19	Ellison [23]	1268
28	20	A	Luton T	L	0-1	0-0	19		8476
29	23	A	Newport Co	D	1-1	0-1	19	Rose (pen) [77]	2754
30	27	H	Mansfield T	L	1-2	1-0	19	Lang [31]	1416
31	Feb 3	A	Port Vale	D	0-0	0-0	20		3968
32	17	H	Forest Green R	D	1-1	0-1	22	Wylde [90]	1447
33	24	A	Wycombe W	W	4-2	3-0	21	McGurk [3], Ellison 2 [26, 38], Wylde [52]	4672
34	Mar 6	A	Accrington S	L	0-1	0-1	21		1769
35	10	A	Crawley T	D	1-1	0-0	21	Lang [90]	1642
36	17	H	Exeter C	W	2-1	1-1	18	Lavelle [43], Rose [78]	1056
37	20	H	Colchester U	D	0-0	0-0	18		893
38	24	H	Lincoln C	D	0-0	0-0	19		1883
39	30	A	Swindon T	D	1-1	1-0	19	Lang [43]	6328
40	Apr 7	A	Cheltenham T	L	0-3	0-0	20		2420
41	10	H	Chesterfield	D	2-2	2-0	20	Thompson [16], Lang [33]	1042
42	14	H	Carlisle U	D	1-1	1-1	20	Lang [29]	3319
43	21	A	Crewe Alex	L	0-1	0-0	22		3942
44	24	H	Cambridge U	D	0-0	0-0	21		992
45	28	H	Barnet	L	0-1	0-0	22		2073
46	May 5	A	Coventry C	D	0-0	0-0	22		15,874

Final League Position: 22

GOALSCORERS

League (41): Lang 10, Ellison 9, McGurk 5, Old 4, Oliver 3, Thompson 3, Rose 2 (1 pen), Wylde 2, Campbell 1, Lavelle 1, Wildig 1.
FA Cup (3): Ellison 1, Fleming 1, own goal 1.
Carabao Cup (3): Lavelle 1, Oliver 1, Rose 1 (1 pen).
Checkatrade Trophy (3): Osborne 1, Thompson 1, own goal 1.

Roche B 42	Lund M 8 + 2	Winnard D 20	Kenyon A 33 + 5	Brough P 20	Rose M 38 + 4	Wildig A 22 + 9	Fleming A 23 + 9	Thompson G 26 + 14	Oliver V 24 + 10	Ellison K 27 + 13	Turner R 1 + 5	Campbell A 11 + 14	Lavelle S 26 + 1	McGowan A 38 + 2	Old S 40 + 1	Conlan L 25 + 2	Muller M 19 + 1	McGurk A 29 + 5	Osborne E 6 + 5	Lang C 14 + 16	Nizic D 4 + 3	Jordan L – + 1	Wylde G 10 + 5	Match No.
1	2	3	4	5	6	7[1]	8	9[3]	10	11[2]	12	13	14											1
1		4	5	6	8	7[2]	14	10	11[3]	9[1]	12			3	2	13								2
1	5[2]	2	4	8	7	9	6[1]	10	11	13	12	14			3									3
1	5[1]	4	2	8[2]	7	9	6	10		11					12	3[2]	13	14						4
1		4			9[2]	7			10	11	14	6[2]		5	2		3	8[1]	12	13				5
1		4		5	7[1]	9[2]	8		13	10				2	3	6	11[3]	12	14					6
1		3	14	5	7	9[2]	8		10	13				2	4		11[3]	6[1]	12					7
1			6[2]	5	12	9[1]	14		8	10				13	2	3		4	11	7[3]				8
1			7[2]	5	6	9	8[1]	12	10				14	2	4		3	11[3]		13				9
1	2			5	7	9[3]	13	8	11	12			10[2]		4	3		6[1]	14					10
1[2]	2		13	5	7	6[3]	8	11	10				9		3	4			14	12				11
1	2[1]		12	5	7[3]	9	6	11	10	13	8[2]			14	4	3								12
1		6	13	9[3]	7		8[1]	11		12				2	3	5	4	10[2]	14					13
1		6	13		7[2]	8	11	10[3]	12					2	4	5	3[1]	9	14					14
1	3	8		7	10[2]	5	12	11						2	4	6		9[1]	13					15
1[2]	4[1]		6	9[3]	7	14	11	12						5	3		8	2	10		13			16
1		6	5	13	9[1]	7	8	12	10					3	2	4		11[2]						17
1		7	2		6[2]	8	11	13	9					12	3	5	4	10[1]						18
1	12	6	5		13	7	8[2]	11	10					3	2[2]	4		9[1]	14					19
1	2	8	5		6[2]	7	12	14	9[1]					11	4	3		10[3]	13					20
1			9	7		6	5	10		13				2	3	14	4	11[1]	8[2]	12[3]				21
1		5	9		7	6[2]	11	13		14				2	3		6	10[1]	8[3]	12				22
1		7		6			14	10[1]	13					8[2]	4	5	3	9	2	12	11[3]			23
1	2		6[2]		7		8[2]	11	13					10[1]	3	5	4		9	12		14		24
1		12		7		6[2]	13	10	11					2	5	4	8	3[1]		9				25
1		6		7	12		13	10	11[1]					2	5	4	8	3		9[2]				26
1		6		7[1]	12	13		10[3]	11					2	5	4	8	3	14	9[2]				27
1	14			7		9[2]	6	10		13		12	2	5[4]	4	8	3	11[1]						28
1		6		8			12		10		7[1]	3	5	4	9	2	11[2]		13					29
1		6[1]		7	13	12	14	10	11					3	5	4[3]	8	2		9[2]				30
		4	3	9		8	13	6[2]	7[3]	11[1]	12			2	5				14		1		10	31
	2	6		7			13	11[2]	10					3[1]	5	4	8		12		1		9	32
1	4	7		8	6[2]	13	12		10			14		2	3	5		11[3]					9[1]	33
1	3	7[3]		6	9[2]	13	14		10					2	4	5		11[1]		8				34
1	2			7	11[1]	6	12		8[2]			14	3	4		9		5	13				10[3]	35
1	4	6		7	14		9	13				12	3	2		5	8[2]	11[3]					10[1]	36
1	3	7		6	14		9	12				13	4	2		5	8[9]	11[1]					10[2]	37
1	2	6	8	7				14	10[1]	11[3]			3	5	4			12	9[2]				13	38
1[3]	2	7		6	13			11	14				4	5[1]	3	8		10[2]	12				9	39
	2	7		6[2]	9[1]	14	12		10				3		4	5	11		13		1		8[3]	40
	3	7[3]		6		12	8	14	10[1]				2	4	5	11[2]		9			1		13	41
1	4			7	12	6		9[1]	13	14			2	5	3	8		10[3]	11[2]					42
1		4		7		6	9[3]	14	13				2	5	3	8		10[2]	11[1]		12			43
1		6		7			10			8[1]	3	2	4	5		11		9		12				44
1		6		7			13	10		8[1]	3	2	4	5		11[2]		9		12				45
1		13		7	9[1]	6			10			4	2	3	5		11[12]	12		8				46

FA Cup

First Round	Hartlepool U	(h)	3-0
Second Round	Shrewsbury T	(a)	0-2

Carabao Cup

First Round	Barnsley	(a)	3-4

Checkatrade Trophy

Northern Group A	Carlisle U	(h)	0-2
Northern Group A	Fleetwood T	(a)	1-2
Northern Group A	Leicester C U21	(h)	2-2

(Morecambe won 4-2 on penalties)

NEWCASTLE UNITED

FOUNDATION

In October 1882 a club called Stanley, which had been formed in 1881, changed its name to Newcastle East End to avoid confusion with two other local clubs, Stanley Nops and Stanley Albion. Shortly afterwards another club, Rosewood, merged with them. Newcastle West End had been formed in August 1882 and they played on a pitch which was part of the Town Moor. They moved to Brandling Park in 1885 and St James' Park 1886 (home of Newcastle Rangers). West End went out of existence after a bad run and the remaining committee men invited East End to move to St James' Park. They accepted and, at a meeting in Bath Lane Hall in 1892, changed their name to Newcastle United.

St James' Park, Newcastle-upon-Tyne NE1 4ST.
Telephone: (0844) 372 1892.
Fax: (0191) 201 8600.
Ticket Office: (0844) 372 1892 (option 1).
Website: www.nufc.co.uk
Email: admin@nufc.com
Ground Capacity: 52,354.
Record Attendance: 68,386 v Chelsea, Division 1, 3 September 1930.
Pitch Measurements: 105m × 68m (114yd × 74yd).
Managing Director: Lee Charnley.
Manager: Rafael Benitez.
First-Team Coaches: Mikel Antia, Antonio Gomez Perez, Francisco Moreno, Simon Smith.
Colours: Black and white striped shirts, black shorts, black socks with white trim.
Year Formed: 1881.
Turned Professional: 1889.
Previous Names: 1881, Stanley; 1882, Newcastle East End; 1892, Newcastle United.
Club Nickname: 'The Magpies', 'The Toon'.
Grounds: 1881, South Byker; 1886, Chillingham Road, Heaton; 1892, St James' Park.
First Football League Game: 2 September 1893, Division 2, v Royal Arsenal (a) D 2–2 – Ramsay; Jeffery, Miller; Crielly, Graham, McKane; Bowman, Crate (1), Thompson, Sorley (1), Wallace. Graham not Crate scored according to some reports.
Record League Victory: 13–0 v Newport Co, Division 2, 5 October 1946 – Garbutt; Cowell, Graham; Harvey, Brennan, Wright; Milburn (2), Bentley (1), Wayman (4), Shackleton (6), Pearson.

HONOURS

League Champions: Division 1 – 1904–05, 1906–07, 1908–09, 1926–27; FL C – 2009–10, 2016–17; First Division – 1992–93; Division 2 – 1964–65.
Runners-up: FA Premier League – 1995–96, 1996–97; Division 2 – 1897–98, 1947–48.
FA Cup Winners: 1910, 1924, 1932, 1951, 1952, 1955.
Runners-up: 1905, 1906, 1908, 1911, 1974, 1998, 1999.
League Cup: Runners-up: 1976.
Texaco Cup Winners: 1974, 1975.
Anglo-Italian Cup Winners: 1972–73.
European Competitions
Champions League: 1997–98, 2002–03, 2003–04.
Fairs Cup: 1968–69 *(winners)*, 1969–70 *(qf)*, 1970–71.
UEFA Cup: 1977–78, 1994–95, 1996–97 *(qf)*, 1999–2000, 2003–04 *(sf)*, 2004–05 *(qf)*, 2006–07.
Europa League: 2012–13 *(qf)*.
European Cup Winners' Cup: 1998–99.
Intertoto Cup: 2001 *(runners-up)*, 2005, 2006 *(winners)*.

Sᴜn THE FACT FILE

Newcastle United featured in the first-ever Football League game to be played under floodlights when they won 2-0 against Portsmouth at Fratton Park on 22 February 1956, with goals from Bill Curry and Vic Keeble in front of a crowd of 15,100. The match kicked off six minutes late after a fuse blew, plunging the dressing rooms and spectator areas into darkness. The players changed by candlelight before repairs were carried out to allow the game to go ahead.

Record Cup Victory: 9–0 v Southport (at Hillsborough), FA Cup 4th rd, 1 February 1932 – McInroy; Nelson, Fairhurst; McKenzie, Davidson, Weaver (1); Boyd (1), Jimmy Richardson (3), Cape (2), McMenemy (1), Lang (1).

Record Defeat: 0–9 v Burton Wanderers, Division 2, 15 April 1895.

Most League Points (2 for a win): 57, Division 2, 1964–65.

Most League Points (3 for a win): 102, FL C, 2009–10.

Most League Goals: 98, Division 1, 1951–52.

Highest League Scorer in Season: Hughie Gallacher, 36, Division 1, 1926–27.

Most League Goals in Total Aggregate: Jackie Milburn, 177, 1946–57.

Most League Goals in One Match: 6, Len Shackleton v Newport Co, Division 2, 5 October 1946.

Most Capped Player: Shay Given, 82 (134), Republic of Ireland.

Most League Appearances: Jim Lawrence, 432, 1904–22.

Youngest League Player: Steve Watson, 16 years 223 days v Wolverhampton W, 10 November 1990.

Record Transfer Fee Received: £35,000,000 from Liverpool for Andy Carroll, January 2011.

Record Transfer Fee Paid: £16,000,000 to Real Madrid for Michael Owen, September 2005.

Football League Record: 1893 Elected to Division 2; 1898–1934 Division 1; 1934–48 Division 2; 1948–61 Division 1; 1961–65 Division 2; 1965–78 Division 1; 1978–84 Division 2; 1984–89 Division 1; 1989–92 Division 2; 1992–93 Division 1; 1993–2009 FA Premier League; 2009–10 FL C; 2010–16 FA Premier League; 2016–17 FL C; 2017– FA Premier League.

LATEST SEQUENCES

Longest Sequence of League Wins: 13, 25.4.1992 – 18.10.1992.

Longest Sequence of League Defeats: 10, 23.8.1977 – 15.10.1977.

Longest Sequence of League Draws: 4, 15.11.2008 – 6.12.2008.

Longest Sequence of Unbeaten League Matches: 17, 13.2.2010 – 2.5.2010.

Longest Sequence Without a League Win: 21, 14.1.1978 – 23.8.1978.

Successive Scoring Runs: 25 from 15.4.1939.

Successive Non-scoring Runs: 6 from 29.10.1988.

MANAGERS

Frank Watt 1895–32
(Secretary-Manager)
Andy Cunningham 1930–35
Tom Mather 1935–39
Stan Seymour 1939–47
(Hon. Manager)
George Martin 1947–50
Stan Seymour 1950–54
(Hon. Manager)
Duggie Livingstone 1954–56
Stan Seymour 1956–58
(Hon. Manager)
Charlie Mitten 1958–61
Norman Smith 1961–62
Joe Harvey 1962–75
Gordon Lee 1975–77
Richard Dinnis 1977
Bill McGarry 1977–80
Arthur Cox 1980–84
Jack Charlton 1984
Willie McFaul 1985–88
Jim Smith 1988–91
Ossie Ardiles 1991–92
Kevin Keegan 1992–97
Kenny Dalglish 1997–98
Ruud Gullit 1998–99
Sir Bobby Robson 1999–2004
Graeme Souness 2004–06
Glenn Roeder 2006–07
Sam Allardyce 2007–08
Kevin Keegan 2008
Joe Kinnear 2008–09
Alan Shearer 2009
Chris Hughton 2009–10
Alan Pardew 2010–15
John Carver 2015
Steve McClaren 2015–16
Rafael Benitez March 2016–

TEN YEAR LEAGUE RECORD

		P	W	D	L	F	A	Pts	Pos
2008-09	PR Lge	38	7	13	18	40	59	34	18
2009-10	FL C	46	30	12	4	90	35	102	1
2010-11	PR Lge	38	11	13	14	56	57	46	12
2011-12	PR Lge	38	19	8	11	56	51	65	5
2012-13	PR Lge	38	11	8	19	45	68	41	16
2013-14	PR Lge	38	15	4	19	43	59	49	10
2014-15	PR Lge	38	10	9	19	40	63	39	15
2015-16	PR Lge	38	9	10	19	44	65	37	18
2016-17	FL C	46	29	7	10	85	40	94	1
2017-18	PR Lge	38	12	8	18	39	47	44	10

DID YOU KNOW ?

In 1937–38, Newcastle United were only spared relegation to Division Three North by goal average. The Magpies finished the season level on 36 points with Barnsley and Nottingham Forest after suffering a 4-1 defeat at Luton on the final day of the campaign. Barnsley, who conceded a late equaliser against Forest on the last day, were the team to go down.

NEWCASTLE UNITED – PREMIER LEAGUE 2017–18 LEAGUE RECORD

Match No.	Date	Venue	Opponents	Result	H/T Score	Lg Pos.	Goalscorers	Attendance
1	Aug 13	H	Tottenham H	L	0-2	0-0	18		52,077
2	20	A	Huddersfield T	L	0-1	0-0	17		24,128
3	26	H	West Ham U	W	3-0	1-0	14	Joselu [36], Clark [72], Mitrovic [86]	52,093
4	Sept 10	A	Swansea C	W	1-0	0-0	10	Lascelles [76]	20,872
5	16	H	Stoke C	W	2-1	1-0	4	Atsu [19], Lascelles [68]	51,795
6	24	A	Brighton & HA	L	0-1	0-0	9		30,468
7	Oct 1	H	Liverpool	D	1-1	1-1	9	Joselu [36]	52,303
8	15	A	Southampton	D	2-2	1-0	9	Hayden [20], Perez [51]	31,437
9	21	H	Crystal Palace	W	1-0	0-0	6	Merino [86]	52,251
10	30	A	Burnley	L	0-1	0-0	9		21,031
11	Nov 4	H	Bournemouth	L	0-1	0-0	11		52,237
12	18	A	Manchester U	L	1-4	1-2	11	Gayle [14]	75,035
13	25	H	Watford	L	0-3	0-2	13		52,188
14	28	A	WBA	D	2-2	0-1	12	Clark [59], Evans (og) [83]	25,534
15	Dec 2	A	Chelsea	L	1-3	1-2	14	Gayle [12]	41,538
16	9	H	Leicester C	L	2-3	1-1	16	Joselu [4], Gayle [73]	52,117
17	13	H	Everton	L	0-1	0-1	16		51,042
18	16	A	Arsenal	L	0-1	0-1	18		59,379
19	23	A	West Ham U	W	3-2	1-1	15	Saivet [10], Diame [53], Atsu [61]	56,955
20	27	H	Manchester C	L	0-1	0-1	15		52,311
21	30	H	Brighton & HA	D	0-0	0-0	16		52,209
22	Jan 1	A	Stoke C	W	1-0	0-0	13	Perez [73]	28,471
23	13	H	Swansea C	D	1-1	0-0	14	Joselu [68]	51,444
24	20	A	Manchester C	L	1-3	0-1	15	Murphy [67]	54,452
25	31	H	Burnley	D	1-1	0-0	14	Lascelles [65]	50,174
26	Feb 4	A	Crystal Palace	D	1-1	1-0	16	Diame [22]	25,746
27	11	H	Manchester U	W	1-0	0-0	13	Ritchie [65]	52,309
28	24	A	Bournemouth	D	2-2	2-0	15	Gayle 2 [17, 45]	10,808
29	Mar 3	A	Liverpool	L	0-2	0-1	16		53,287
30	10	H	Southampton	W	3-0	2-0	13	Kenedy 2 [2, 29], Ritchie [57]	52,246
31	31	H	Huddersfield T	W	1-0	0-0	12	Perez [80]	52,261
32	Apr 7	A	Leicester C	W	2-1	1-0	10	Shelvey [18], Perez [75]	32,066
33	15	H	Arsenal	W	2-1	1-1	10	Perez [29], Ritchie [68]	52,210
34	23	A	Everton	L	0-1	0-0	10		39,061
35	28	H	WBA	L	0-1	0-1	10		52,283
36	May 5	A	Watford	L	1-2	0-2	10	Perez [55]	20,375
37	9	A	Tottenham H	L	0-1	0-0	10		54,923
38	13	H	Chelsea	W	3-0	1-0	10	Gayle [23], Perez 2 [59, 63]	52,294

Final League Position: 10

GOALSCORERS

League (39): Perez 8, Gayle 6, Joselu 4, Lascelles 3, Ritchie 3, Atsu 2, Clark 2, Diame 2, Kenedy 2, Hayden 1, Merino 1, Mitrovic 1, Murphy 1, Saivet 1, Shelvey 1, own goal 1.
FA Cup (3): Perez 2, Shelvey 1.
Carabao Cup (2): Aarons 1, Mitrovic 1.
Checkatrade Trophy (3): Aarons 1, Smith L 1, own goal 1.

Elliot R 16	Manquillo J 20 + 1	Lejeune F 24	Clark C 19 + 1	Dummett P 19 + 1	Shelvey J 25 + 5	Hayden I 15 + 11	Ritchie M 32 + 3	Perez A 28 + 8	Atsu C 19 + 9	Gayle D 23 + 12	Lascelles J 32 + 1	Mbemba C 7 + 2	Merino M 14 + 10	Joselu M 19 + 11	Diame M 23 + 8	Murphy J 13 + 12	Mitrovic A — + 6	Jesus Gamez D 1 + 1	Yedlin D 31 + 3	Aarons R 1 + 3	Darlow K 10	Saivet H 1	Kenedy R 13	Dubravka M 12	Slimani I 1 + 3	Haidara M — + 1	Match No.
1	2	3³	4	5²	6⁸	7	8	9	10	11¹	12	13	14														1
1	2		4		6²	10	9¹	8	11³	3	5	7	12	13	14												2
1	2		4			7³	8¹	9	10		3	5	6	11²	13	14	12	5									3
1	2		4			7¹	8	9	12	14		3	6	11³	13	10²		5									4
1			4		12	6²	8	9³	10	13	3	5	7	11¹	14				2								5
1			4		12	6¹	8	9	10	13	3	5¹	11³			14			2								6
1	5	4		6	12	8	9²	10	13	3	7³	11¹	14						2								7
1	5	4		6	7	8	9²	10³	13	3	12	11¹	14						2								8
1	5	4		7	6³	8	9²	10		3	12	11¹	13	14					2								9
1	5	4		6	12	8²	9¹	10	14	3	11	7³	13						2								10
1	5	4	12		8	7	6	13	9³	10	3¹	11²		14					2								11
1	5	3	4		8	7	9²		10³		11¹	14	6	13					2	12							12
1	5	3	4		7		6	14		10	12	11³	8¹	9²	13				2								13
		3	4		14	6³	8	9			5	7	11³	10¹	13				2	12	1						14
	5	3	4	13	12	8	10²		11		2	7¹	6³	9					14		1						15
	5	3	4			7	6²	13	12	11		8	10¹		9³	14			2		1						16
	5	4		7⁸		10²	14	8	11	3		6²	12	9¹					2	13	1						17
1	5	4			8	12	11	9²	13	3	7³	10	14	6¹					2								18
1	5		4			6	12	9³	10¹	3	13		11	8	14				2			7²					19
1	6			5	9			13	12	4	3²	14	11³	8	10				2	7¹							20
	4		5	13	7	6²	12	9	11	3		8²	10¹		14				2		1						21
	5		4	13	6	14	10	11¹	9²	12	3		7	8³					2		1						22
			4	5	6²		8	9	10	11¹	3		13	12	7				2		1						23
	2³		5	6	8	3		12	10¹	14	4		11²	9	7				13		1						24
			4	5			13	10¹	6³	14	3		8	11	7	12			2		1		9²				25
			4	5	7	13	6	10³	12	11	3		14		8²				2		1		9¹				26
		4		5	7	14	6	10	13	11¹	3		12	8					2				9²	1			27
14		4		5	7	13	6³	10	12	11¹	3			8					2				9²	1			28
		2		4		13		14	9	11¹	3		7²	12	6	10³			5				8	1			29
		4		5	7¹		6	10	13	11³	3		14	12	8				2				9²	1			30
		4		5	7	14	6³	10	12	11¹	3		8²						2				9	1	13		31
		4		5	8	14	6	10	12	11¹	3		13	7¹					2				9²	1	12		32
		4		5	8		6¹	10²		11²	3		13	7	14				2				9	1	12		33
		4		5	7²		6³	10		12	3			14	8	13			2				9	1	11¹		34
		4		5⁸	8		6	10¹		11²	3			14	7	12			2				9	1	13		35
	2³	4		5	8		12	10		11	3		14	7¹	6²	13							9	1			36
		4		5	7		8	9		11¹	3		13	6	12				2				10²	1			37
		4		5	6	13	8¹	9		11³	3		12	7²	10				2					1		14	38

FA Cup

Third Round	Luton T	(h)	3-1
Fourth Round	Chelsea	(a)	0-3

Carabao Cup

Second Round (*aet*)	Nottingham F	(h)	2-3

Checkatrade Trophy (Newcastle U 21)

Northern Group D	Crewe Alex	(a)	2-1
Northern Group D	Port Vale	(a)	0-1
Northern Group D	Oldham Ath	(a)	1-4

NEWPORT COUNTY

FOUNDATION

In 1912 Newport County were formed following a meeting at The Tredegar Arms Hotel. A professional football club had existed in the town called Newport FC, but they ceased to exist in 1907. The first season as Newport County was in the second division of the Southern League. They started life playing at Somerton Park where they remained through their League years. They were elected to the Football League for the beginning of the 1920–21 season as founder members of Division 3. At the end of the 1987–88 season, they were relegated from the Football League and replaced by Lincoln City. On February 27 1989, Newport County went out of business and from the ashes Newport AFC was born. Starting down the pyramid in the Hellenic League, they eventually gained promotion to the Conference in 2011 and were promoted to the Football League after a play-off with Wrexham in 2013.

Rodney Parade, Rodney Road, Newport, South Wales NP19 0UU.

Telephone: (01633) 481 896.

Ticket Office: (01633) 481 896.

Website: www.newport-county.co.uk

Email: office@newport-county.co.uk

Ground Capacity: 8,381.

Record Attendance: 24,268 v Cardiff C, Division 3 (S), 16 October 1937 (Somerton Park); 4,660 v Swansea C, FA Cup 1st rd, 11 November 2006 (Newport Stadium); 9,836 v Tottenham H, FA Cup 4th rd, 27 January 2018 (Rodney Parade).

Pitch Measurements: 100.5m × 64m (110yd × 70yd).

Chairmen: Gavin Foxall, Shaun Johnson.

Manager: Michael Flynn.

Assistant Manager: Wayne Hatswell.

Colours: Black shirts with amber trim, black shorts with amber trim, black socks with amber trim.

Year Formed: 1912.

Turned Professional: 1912.

Previous Names: Newport County, 1912; Newport AFC, 1989; Newport County, 1999.

Club Nicknames: 'The Exiles', 'The Ironsides', 'The Port', 'The County'.

Grounds: 1912–89, 1990–92, Somerton Park; 1992–94, Meadow Park Stadium; 1994, Newport Stadium; 2012, Rodney Parade.

First Football League Game: 28 August 1920, Division 3, v Reading (h) L 0–1.

HONOURS

League Champions: Division 3S – 1938–39.
Runners-up: Conference – (3rd) 2012–13 *(promoted via play-offs).*
FA Cup: 5th rd – 1949.
League Cup: never past 3rd rd.
Welsh Cup Winners: 1980.
Runners-up: 1963, 1987.
European Competitions
European Cup Winners' Cup: 1980–81 *(qf).*

The Sun FACT FILE

Newport County won a club record 10 consecutive League games in the second half of the 1979–80 season on their way to promotion to Division Three. County conceded just four goals during the run. The club also won the Welsh Cup, their defeat of Shrewsbury Town 5-1 over two legs in the final earning them entry to the European Cup Winners Cup for 1980–81.

Record League Victory: 10-0 v Merthyr T, Division 3(S), 10 April 1930 – Martin (5), Gittins (2), Thomas (1), Bagley (1), Lawson (1).

Record Cup Victory: 7-0 v Working, FA Cup 1st rd, 24 November 1928 – Young (3), Pugh (2) Gittins (1), Reid (1).

Record Defeat: 0–13 v Newcastle U, Division 2, 5 October 1946.

Most League Points (2 for a win): 61, Division 4, 1979–80.

Most League Points (3 for a win): 78, Division 3, 1982–83.

Most League Goals: 85, Division 4, 1964–65.

Highest League Scorer in Season: Tudor Martin, 34, Division 3 (S), 1929–30.

Most League Goals in Total Aggregate: Reg Parker, 99, 1948–54.

Most League Goals in One Match: 5, Tudor Martin v Merthyr T, Dvision 3 (S), 10 April 1930.

Most Capped Player: Nigel Vaughan, 3 (10), Wales.

Most League Appearances: Len Weare, 527, 1955–70.

Youngest League Player: Regan Poole, 16 years 94 days v Shrewsbury T, 20 September 2014.

Record Transfer Fee Received: £500,000 (rising to £1,000,000) from Peterborough U for Conor Washington, January 2014.

Record Transfer Fee Paid: £80,000 to Swansea C for Alan Waddle, January 1981.

Football League Record: 1920 Original member of Division 3; 1921–31 Division 3 (S) – dropped out of Football League; 1932 Re-elected to Division 3 (S); 1932–39 Division 3 (S); 1946–47 Division 2; 1947–58 Division 3 (S); 1958–62 Division 3; 1962–80 Division 4; 1980–87 Division 3; 1987–88 Division 4 (relegated from Football League); 2011 Promoted to Conference; 2011–13 Conference Premier; 2013– FL 2.

LATEST SEQUENCES

Longest Sequence of League Wins: 4, 26.12.2014 – 10.1.2015.

Longest Sequence of League Defeats: 8, 22.11.2016 – 7.1.2017.

Longest Sequence of League Draws: 4, 31.10.2015 – 24.11.2015.

Longest Sequence of Unbeaten League Matches: 9, 10.11.2014 – 13.12.2014.

Longest Sequence Without a League Win: 12, 15.3.2016 – 6.8.2017.

Successive Scoring Runs: 16 from 11.3.2017.

Successive Non-scoring Runs: 4 from 3.2.2018.

MANAGERS

Davy McDougle 1912–13
(Player-Manager)
Sam Hollis 1913–17
Harry Parkes 1919–22
Jimmy Hindmarsh 1922–35
Louis Page 1935–36
Tom Bromilow 1936–37
Billy McCandless 1937–45
Tom Bromilow 1945–50
Fred Stansfield 1950–53
Billy Lucas 1953–61
Bobby Evans 1961–62
Billy Lucas 1962–67
Leslie Graham 1967–69
Bobby Ferguson 1969–70
(Player-Manager)
Billy Lucas 1970–74
Brian Harris 1974–75
Dave Elliott 1975–76
(Player-Manager)
Jimmy Scoular 1976–77
Colin Addison 1977–78
Len Ashurst 1978–82
Colin Addison 1982–85
Bobby Smith 1985–86
John Relish 1986
Jimmy Mullen 1986–87
John Lewis 1987
Brian Eastick 1987–88
David Williams 1988
Eddie May 1988
John Mahoney 1988–89
John Relish 1989–93
Graham Rogers 1993–96
Chris Price 1997
Tim Harris 1997–2002
Peter Nicholas 2002–04
John Cornforth 2004–05
Peter Beadle 2005–08
Dean Holdsworth 2008–11
Anthony Hudson 2011
Justin Edinburgh 2011–15
Jimmy Dack 2015
Terry Butcher 2015
John Sheridan 2015–16
Warren Feeney 2016
Graham Westley 2016–17
Michael Flynn May 2017–

TEN YEAR LEAGUE RECORD

		P	W	D	L	F	A	Pts	Pos
2008-09	Conf S	42	16	11	15	50	51	59	10
2009-10	Conf S	42	32	7	3	93	26	103	1
2010-11	Conf P	46	18	15	13	78	60	69	9
2011-12	Conf P	46	11	14	21	53	65	47	19
2012-13	Conf P	46	25	10	11	85	60	85	3
2013-14	FL 2	46	14	16	16	56	59	58	14
2014-15	FL 2	46	18	11	17	51	54	65	9
2015-16	FL 2	46	10	13	23	43	64	43	22
2016-17	FL 2	46	12	12	22	51	73	48	22
2017-18	FL 2	46	16	16	14	56	58	64	11

DID YOU KNOW ?

Newport County were expelled from the FA Cup in 1931–32 after the Football Association ruled that they had broken gambling regulations by running a lottery. County offered £1,500 prize money and distributed 50,000 tickets. County, then in the Southern League, should have entered the competition in the fourth qualifying round.

NEWPORT COUNTY – SKY BET LEAGUE TWO 2017–18 LEAGUE RECORD

Match No.	Date		Venue	Opponents	Result	H/T Score	Lg Pos.	Goalscorers	Attendance
1	Aug	5	A	Stevenage	D	3-3	0-1	9	Nouble [55], Demetriou [77], McCoulsky [90]	2650
2		12	A	Crewe Alex	D	1-1	1-1	16	Nouble [13]	3400
3		19	A	Coventry C	W	1-0	0-0	9	Cole [53]	8745
4		26	H	Chesterfield	W	4-1	0-1	2	Nouble 3 [55, 66, 68], Amond [82]	4332
5	Sept	2	A	Exeter C	L	0-1	0-0	7		4193
6		9	H	Wycombe W	D	0-0	0-0	12		3752
7		12	H	Cheltenham T	W	1-0	1-0	6	Amond [35]	2916
8		16	A	Morecambe	L	1-2	1-1	9	Bennett [36]	1189
9		23	H	Grimsby T	W	1-0	0-0	8	Amond [63]	3356
10		26	A	Crawley T	W	2-1	1-1	7	Demetriou 2 [40, 51]	1455
11		30	A	Luton T	L	1-3	0-3	10	Labadie [55]	7681
12	Oct	7	H	Yeovil T	W	2-0	1-0	8	Amond [45], Labadie [55]	3689
13		14	A	Forest Green R	W	4-0	2-0	6	Amond 2 [14, 41], Bennett [78], McCoulsky [86]	2864
14		17	A	Colchester U	L	1-2	0-0	6	McCoulsky [86]	2704
15		21	H	Mansfield T	D	1-1	0-1	6	McCoulsky [69]	3146
16		28	A	Notts Co	L	0-3	0-1	8		6019
17	Nov	10	H	Port Vale	D	1-1	0-0	8	Dolan [54]	2876
18		18	A	Accrington S	D	1-1	0-0	9	Nouble [48]	1371
19		21	H	Barnet	L	1-2	0-0	10	White [73]	2275
20		25	A	Swindon T	W	1-0	0-0	9	Tozer [76]	6764
21	Dec	9	H	Carlisle U	D	3-3	1-0	12	McCoulsky [43], Dolan 2 [56, 69]	3176
22		16	A	Cambridge U	W	2-1	1-0	9	McCoulsky [42], Labadie [90]	3632
23		23	H	Lincoln C	D	0-0	0-0	11		3514
24		26	A	Wycombe W	L	0-2	0-1	10		4629
25		30	A	Cheltenham T	D	1-1	0-0	11	Amond [55]	3637
26	Jan	1	H	Exeter C	W	2-1	1-0	11	Amond [6], Willmott [66]	3318
27		13	A	Grimsby T	W	2-1	1-0	10	Willmott [19], Nouble [56]	3397
28		19	H	Crawley T	W	2-1	2-0	5	Amond [40], Demetriou (pen) [44]	5741
29		23	H	Morecambe	D	1-1	1-0	8	Tozer [14]	2754
30		30	A	Lincoln C	L	1-3	1-1	10	Amond [32]	7567
31	Feb	3	A	Colchester U	L	0-2	0-0	11		2874
32		13	A	Mansfield T	L	0-5	0-4	12		2866
33		17	H	Notts Co	D	0-0	0-0	12		3326
34		24	A	Port Vale	D	0-0	0-0	13		4013
35	Mar	6	H	Forest Green R	D	3-3	3-2	13	Butler [9], Hayes 2 [17, 38]	2862
36		10	A	Yeovil T	W	2-0	0-0	11	Sheehan [57], Hayes [90]	2880
37		17	H	Luton T	D	1-1	1-1	11	Sheehan [2]	3512
38		24	H	Crewe Alex	L	1-2	0-1	12	Demetriou [81]	4638
39		30	H	Coventry C	D	1-1	1-0	12	Demetriou [40]	4667
40	Apr	7	H	Stevenage	L	0-1	0-1	13		4007
41		14	H	Swindon T	W	2-1	2-0	12	Amond [15], Tozer [35]	3911
42		21	A	Barnet	L	0-2	0-1	14		1816
43		24	H	Accrington S	W	2-1	1-0	13	Amond [30], Nouble [85]	2370
44		28	H	Cambridge U	W	2-1	1-0	11	Demetriou [26], Nouble [59]	3412
45	May	1	A	Chesterfield	L	0-1	0-0	11		4608
46		5	A	Carlisle U	D	1-1	1-1	11	Amond [38]	5311

Final League Position: 11

GOALSCORERS

League (56): Amond 13, Nouble 9, Demetriou 7 (1 pen), McCoulsky 6, Dolan 3, Hayes 3, Labadie 3, Tozer 3, Bennett 2, Sheehan 2, Willmott 2, Butler 1, Cole 1, White 1.
FA Cup (7): Labadie 2, McCoulsky 2, Amond 1, Nouble 1, own goal 1.
Carabao Cup (3): McCoulsky 2, Labadie 1.
Checkatrade Trophy (2): McCoulsky 1, Reynolds 1.

Day J 46	Willmott R 36 + 3	Bennett S 21 + 7	O'Brien M 26 + 2	Demetriou M 46	Butler D 40 + 4	Labadie J 24 + 1	Dolan M 39 + 1	Rigg S 9 + 7	Nouble F 38 + 7	Reynolds L 1 + 9	McCoulsky S 8 + 19	Owen-Evans T 3 + 9	Jahraldo-Martin C — + 4	White B 42	Pipe D 33 + 2	Cole R 2 + 2	Quigley J 1 + 1	Amond P 37 + 6	Tozer B 33 + 6	Barnum-Bobb J — + 1	Jackson M — + 6	Reid T 3 + 4	Sheehan J 9 + 4	Hayes P 3 + 10	Osoabe E — + 3	Collins A 6 + 4	Touray M — + 1	Match No.
1	2	3[3]	4	5	6[1]	7[2]	8	9	10	11	12	13	14															1
1	2		4	5	6[2]	7	8	9[1]	10	12	11[3]	13	14	3														2
1	9	12	2	4		7	6		10	13				3	5	8[1]		11[2]										3
1	10	14	3[1]	4	13	6	7	12	8					5	2[2]	9[3]		11										4
1	5[1]		3[3]	2	9	8	6[2]	7	10			13		4			12	11	14									5
1	6[1]		3	5	7[3]	8	9[2]		10				14	4	2		12	11	13									6
1	12	8		3	5		7		9[2]	10			6[1]	4	2			11	13									7
1		3[1]		5	6		7[2]	12	11	13	14	9[3]		4	2			10	8									8
1	6	12	3[1]	4	13		7[3]		8	11			14	5	2			10[2]	9									9
1	6	13	3[3]	4	12		7	14	8	11				5	2[1]			10[4]	9									10
1	6[2]		3	4		7[1]		9		11	12		14	5	2		13	10[3]	8									11
1		3		4	9		6[1]	7[3]	12	11	13		14		2	5		10[1]	8									12
1		12	3	4	9		8[1]	7	11[2]		13		14		2	5[3]		10	6									13
1			3	4	9		6[1]	7[2]	12	11	14	13			2	5		10	8									14
1	7[2]		3	4	9		8		12	11		13			2[1]	5		10	6									15
1	5	7		4	9•		8	3	10[3]	14	13				2			11[2]	6		12							16
1	7		3	4	9		8		11			10[1]			2	5		12	6									17
1	6	7	3[1]	4	9			12	11[2]				14		2	5		10[3]	8	13								18
1	9[3]	7	2[1]	3	12	13	6		10			14		4	5[2]			11	8									19
1	3[2]			4	9		7[3]	8	12	10		11[1]	14		2	5		13	6									20
1	8		3	4	9	7	6		11	12	10[1]			2	5[2]			13										21
1	13	12	4[1]	5	6	7	8		10	11[2]				3	2[3]			14	9									22
1	12		3[4]	4	9	7	8		11	10[2]				2	5			13	6[1]									23
1	12	6[3]		2	9	7•	8		10	13	11[1]			4	5[2]			14	3									24
1	7	4		3	6		8[2]		10[1]	13	9			5	2			11	12									25
1	8	3		4	9	7	6[1]	11[2]	13	12				2	5			10										26
1	11[2]	8		3	5	7[1]	6[3]		9	14				4	2			10	12		13							27
1	9	7		4	5			11[3]	13				3	2			10[1]	8		12	6[2]	14						28
1	8	7	3	4	5			10[2]	13				2			11[1]	6				9[3]	14	12					29
1	9	8		4[1]	5	7	6		11[3]	12		3			10[2]	2		14	13									30
1	9		3	4	5	7	8[3]	11		13					10[1]	6		2[4]	12	14								31
1	9	4[1]	12	3	5	7	8[2]	11[3]						6	2			10	14	13								32
1	9		2	4	8	7		12		11[1]				3	5			10[2]	6	13								33
1	7		3	4	9		6		11[1]	13				2	5			10[2]	8				12					34
1	6[2]		3[1]	4	9		8							2	5			10	7	12		14	11[3]	13				35
1	7[2]	13		4	9	8	6[1]		12					2				10[3]	3			5	11		14			36
1	11		4	3	5		7		12	13				2				10[4]	8			6[1]		9				37
1	5		3	4	9		8		12	14				2				10[1]	6			7[3]	13	11[2]				38
1	6[1]		3	4	9		7		12					2	5			10	8			13	11[2]					39
1	7			4	5		8		9					3	2[3]			10	6[1]	14	13	12		11[2]				40
1	7	3		4	9		8		12					2	5[2]			10	6	13			11[1]					41
1	7	3[2]		4	9		8		12				14	2	5			10	6[1]			13	11[3]					42
1	6		3[2]	4	5		8		11[2]					2				10	7		9[1]	13	12					43
1	6		3[2]	4	5		9[3]	10[1]						2	12			11	7		8	14	13					44
1	6			4	5		7		11[3]			13	3		10			12	2	8[2]	14	9[1]						45
1	6		2[2]	4	5		7		11				14		10[1]	3		9	8[3]			12	13					46

FA Cup

First Round	Walsall	(h)	2-1
Second Round	Cambridge U	(h)	2-0
Third Round	Leeds U	(h)	2-1
Fourth Round	Tottenham H	(h)	1-1
Replay	Tottenham H	(a)	0-2

Carabao Cup

First Round	Southend U	(a)	2-0
Second Round	Leeds U	(a)	1-5

Checkatrade Trophy

Southern Group E	Forest Green R	(a)	0-2
Southern Group E	Swansea C U21	(h)	1-2
Southern Group E	Cheltenham T	(h)	1-2

NORTHAMPTON TOWN

FOUNDATION

Formed in 1897 by schoolteachers connected with the Northampton & District Elementary Schools' Association, they survived a financial crisis at the end of their first year when they were £675 in the red and became members of the Midland League – a fast move indeed for a new club. They achieved Southern League membership in 1901.

Sixfields Stadium, Upton Way, Northampton NN5 5QA.

Telephone: (01604) 683 700.

Fax: (01604) 751 613.

Ticket Office: (01604) 683 777.

Website: www.ntfc.co.uk

Email: secretary@ntfc.co.uk

Ground Capacity: 7,798.

Record Attendance: 24,523 v Fulham, Division 1, 23 April 1966 (at County Ground); 7,798 v Manchester U, EFL Cup 3rd rd, 21 September 2016 (at Sixfields Stadium).

Pitch Measurements: 106m × 66m (116yd × 72yd).

Chairman: Kelvin Thomas.

Chief Executive: James Whiting.

Manager: Dean Austin.

Assistant Manager: Andy Todd.

Colours: Claret shirts with white trim, white shorts, claret socks.

Year Formed: 1897.

Turned Professional: 1901.

Grounds: 1897, County Ground; 1994, Sixfields Stadium.

Club Nickname: 'The Cobblers'.

First Football League Game: 28 August 1920, Division 3, v Grimsby T (a) L 0–2 – Thorpe; Sproston, Hewison; Jobey, Tomkins, Pease; Whitworth, Lockett, Thomas, Freeman, MacKechnie.

Record League Victory: 10–0 v Walsall, Division 3 (S), 5 November 1927 – Hammond; Watson, Jeffs; Allen, Brett, Odell; Daley, Smith (3), Loasby (3), Hoten (1), Wells (3).

Record Cup Victory: 10–0 v Sutton T, FA Cup prel rd, 7 December 1907 – Cooch; Drennan, Lloyd Davies, Tirrell (1), McCartney, Hickleton, Badenock (3), Platt (3), Lowe (1), Chapman (2), McDiarmid.

Record Defeat: 0–11 v Southampton, Southern League, 28 December 1901.

HONOURS

League Champions: Division 3 – 1962–63; FL 2 – 2015–16; Division 4 – 1986–87.
Runners-up: Division 2 – 1964–65; Division 3S – 1927–28, 1949–50; FL 2 – 2005–06; Division 4 – 1975–76.
FA Cup: 5th rd – 1934, 1950, 1970.
League Cup: 5th rd – 1965, 1967.

The Sun FACT FILE

When Sam Hoskins netted a first-half winner for Northampton Town against Blackpool on 28 October 2017 it proved to be an historic occasion. The goal was the 750th Football League goal scored by the Cobblers at their Sixfields Stadium. The club's first League goal at the ground was scored by the late Martin Aldridge against Barnet in October 1994.

Most League Points (2 for a win): 68, Division 4, 1975–76.

Most League Points (3 for a win): 99, Division 4, 1986–87; FL 2, 2015–16.

Most League Goals: 109, Division 3, 1962–63 and Division 3 (S), 1952–53.

Highest League Scorer in Season: Cliff Holton, 36, Division 3, 1961–62.

Most League Goals in Total Aggregate: Jack English, 135, 1947–60.

Most League Goals in One Match: 5, Ralph Hoten v Crystal Palace, Division 3 (S), 27 October 1928.

Most Capped Player: Edwin Lloyd Davies, 12 (16), Wales.

Most League Appearances: Tommy Fowler, 521, 1946–61.

Youngest League Player: Adrian Mann, 16 years 297 days v Bury, 5 May 1984.

Record Transfer Fee Received: £470,000 from Blackburn R for Mark Bunn, September 2008.

Record Transfer Fee Paid: £165,000 to Oldham Ath for Josh Low, July 2003.

Football League Record: 1920 Original Member of Division 3; 1921 Division 3 (S); 1958–61 Division 4; 1961–63 Division 3; 1963–65 Division 2; 1965–66 Division 1; 1966–67 Division 2; 1967–69 Division 3; 1969–76 Division 4; 1976–77 Division 3; 1977–87 Division 4; 1987–90 Division 3; 1990–92 Division 4; 1992–97 Division 3; 1997–99 Division 2; 1999–2000 Division 3; 2000–03 Division 2; 2003–04 Division 3; 2004–06 FL 2; 2006–09 FL 1; 2009–16 FL 2; 2016–18 FL 1; 2018– FL 2.

LATEST SEQUENCES

Longest Sequence of League Wins: 10, 28.12.2015 – 23.2.2016.

Longest Sequence of League Defeats: 8, 26.10.1935 – 21.12.1935.

Longest Sequence of League Draws: 6, 5.2.2011 – 26.2.2011.

Longest Sequence of Unbeaten League Matches: 31, 28.12.2015 – 10.9.2016.

Longest Sequence Without a League Win: 18, 5.2.2011 – 25.4.2011.

Successive Scoring Runs: 28 from 29.8.2015.

Successive Non-scoring Runs: 7 from 7.4.1939.

MANAGERS

Arthur Jones 1897–1907
(Secretary-Manager)
Herbert Chapman 1907–12
Walter Bull 1912–13
Fred Lessons 1913–19
Bob Hewison 1920–25
Jack Tresadern 1925–30
Jack English 1931–35
Syd Puddefoot 1935–37
Warney Cresswell 1937–39
Tom Smith 1939–49
Bob Dennison 1949–54
Dave Smith 1954–59
David Bowen 1959–67
Tony Marchi 1967–68
Ron Flowers 1968–69
Dave Bowen 1969–72
(continued as General Manager and Secretary 1972–85 when joined the board)
Billy Baxter 1972–73
Bill Dodgin Jnr 1973–76
Pat Crerand 1976–77
By committee 1977
Bill Dodgin Jnr 1977
John Petts 1977–78
Mike Keen 1978–79
Clive Walker 1979–80
Bill Dodgin Jnr 1980–82
Clive Walker 1982–84
Tony Barton 1984–85
Graham Carr 1985–90
Theo Foley 1990–92
Phil Chard 1992–93
John Barnwell 1993–94
Ian Atkins 1995–99
Kevin Wilson 1999–2001
Kevan Broadhurst 2001–03
Terry Fenwick 2003
Martin Wilkinson 2003
Colin Calderwood 2003–06
John Gorman 2006
Stuart Gray 2007–09
Ian Sampson 2009–11
Gary Johnson 2011
Aidy Boothroyd 2011–13
Chris Wilder 2014–16
Rob Page 2016–17
Justin Edinburgh 2017
Jimmy Floyd Hasselbaink 2017–18
Dean Austin May 2018–

TEN YEAR LEAGUE RECORD

		P	W	D	L	F	A	Pts	Pos
2008-09	FL 1	46	12	13	21	61	65	49	21
2009-10	FL 2	46	18	13	15	62	53	67	11
2010-11	FL 2	46	11	19	16	63	71	52	16
2011-12	FL 2	46	12	12	22	56	79	48	20
2012-13	FL 2	46	21	10	15	64	55	73	6
2013-14	FL 2	46	13	14	19	42	57	53	21
2014-15	FL 2	46	18	7	21	67	62	61	12
2015-16	FL 2	46	29	12	5	82	46	99	1
2016-17	FL 1	46	14	11	21	60	73	53	16
2017-18	FL 1	46	12	11	23	43	77	47	22

DID YOU KNOW ?

Northampton Town have won three Football League divisional titles and on each occasion the manager was a former Cobblers player. Dave Bowen (1962–63) and Graham Carr (1986–87) were contracted players while Chris Wilder (2015–16) featured as a loanee in the 1998–99 season.

NORTHAMPTON TOWN – SKY BET LEAGUE ONE 2017–18 LEAGUE RECORD

Match No.	Date	Venue	Opponents	Result		H/T Score	Lg Pos.	Goalscorers	Attendance
1	Aug 5	A	Shrewsbury T	L	0-1	0-0	20		5736
2	12	H	Fleetwood T	L	0-1	0-0	21		5124
3	19	A	Charlton Ath	L	1-4	0-1	23	Richards [79]	11,289
4	26	H	Peterborough U	L	1-4	0-2	24	Revell [85]	6685
5	Sept 9	H	Doncaster R	W	1-0	1-0	22	Crooks [1]	5843
6	12	H	Portsmouth	W	3-1	2-0	17	Long 2 [18, 70], Crooks [35]	5855
7	16	A	Southend U	D	2-2	2-0	17	Barnett [20], Crooks [43]	6532
8	19	A	Wigan Ath	L	0-1	0-0	18		7777
9	23	H	Bradford C	L	0-1	0-1	20		6355
10	26	A	Milton Keynes D	D	0-0	0-0	21		11,340
11	30	A	Rotherham U	L	0-1	0-0	22		8073
12	Oct 7	H	Bristol R	L	0-6	0-1	22		6087
13	14	H	AFC Wimbledon	L	0-1	0-0	23		5306
14	17	A	Rochdale	D	2-2	0-1	23	Taylor, A [70], Buchanan [78]	2138
15	21	A	Gillingham	W	2-1	1-0	22	Powell [45], Grimes [73]	4640
16	28	H	Blackpool	W	1-0	1-0	21	Hoskins [21]	5213
17	Nov 11	A	Oxford U	W	2-1	2-1	19	Taylor, A [11], Long [45]	8267
18	18	H	Scunthorpe U	L	0-3	0-0	21		5181
19	21	A	Plymouth Arg	L	0-2	0-1	21		7610
20	25	H	Bury	D	0-0	0-0	22		4870
21	Dec 9	A	Oldham Ath	L	1-5	0-3	23	Foley [47]	3532
22	16	H	Walsall	W	2-1	2-1	20	Long 2 [4, 41]	5055
23	23	H	Blackburn R	D	1-1	1-0	22	Foley [21]	6541
24	26	A	Doncaster R	L	0-3	0-2	22		8032
25	30	A	Portsmouth	L	1-3	1-2	22	Long [36]	18,539
26	Jan 1	H	Wigan Ath	L	0-1	0-1	22		5328
27	6	H	Southend U	W	3-1	1-1	22	O'Toole [19], Grimes (pen) [49], Revell [90]	5267
28	13	A	Bradford C	W	2-1	1-0	21	O'Toole [43], Long [62]	19,343
29	20	A	Milton Keynes D	W	2-1	2-1	18	O'Toole [16], Long [41]	7231
30	27	A	Blackburn R	D	1-1	1-0	20	O'Toole [12]	12,555
31	Feb 3	H	Rochdale	L	0-1	0-0	20		5475
32	10	A	AFC Wimbledon	W	3-1	1-0	18	Grimes (pen) [8], Crooks [62], Powell [72]	4485
33	13	A	Gillingham	L	1-2	0-2	20	Taylor, A [56]	5123
34	17	A	Scunthorpe U	D	2-2	1-1	19	Long [13], O'Toole [57]	4157
35	24	H	Oxford U	D	0-0	0-0	19		7095
36	Mar 10	A	Bristol R	D	1-1	0-1	20	Luckassen [62]	9054
37	17	H	Rotherham U	L	0-3	0-1	21		5882
38	20	H	Shrewsbury T	D	1-1	1-0	21	Facey [45]	4788
39	24	A	Fleetwood T	L	0-2	0-1	21		3049
40	30	H	Charlton Ath	L	0-4	0-2	22		6416
41	Apr 2	A	Peterborough U	L	0-2	0-2	22		8619
42	10	A	Blackpool	L	0-3	0-1	23		2964
43	14	A	Bury	W	3-2	2-1	22	Taylor, A 2 [6, 88], Hoskins [33]	3117
44	21	H	Plymouth Arg	W	2-0	1-0	22	O'Toole [42], Bradley (og) [61]	6868
45	28	A	Walsall	L	0-1	0-0	22		8919
46	May 5	H	Oldham Ath	D	2-2	2-1	22	Grimes (pen) [42], Taylor, A [45]	6511

Final League Position: 22

GOALSCORERS

League (43): Long 9, O'Toole 6, Taylor, A 6, Crooks 4, Grimes 4 (3 pens), Foley 2, Hoskins 2, Powell 2, Revell 2, Barnett 1, Buchanan 1, Facey 1, Luckassen 1, Richards 1, own goal 1.
FA Cup (0).
Carabao Cup (0).
Checkatrade Trophy (5): Foley 1, McGugan 1, Revell 1, Taylor, A 1, own goal 1.

Cornell D 6	Pierre A 19	Barnett L 13 + 2	Taylor A 45	Buchanan D 32	Powell D 21 + 8	Crooks M 29 + 1	Taylor M 1	Bowditch D 3 + 8 / Roberts M — + 1	Richards M 7 + 12	Waters B 9 + 8	Long C 30 + 8	Kasim Y 4 + 2	Revell A 10 + 5	Poole R 18 + 4	Phillips A 2	McWilliams S 15 + 4	Moloney B 31 + 3	Grimes M 43 + 1	Coddington L 1	Ingram M 20	Smith G 5 + 1	Hanley R 3 + 1	Hoskins S 18 + 9	Foley S 15 + 9	McGugan L 7 + 2	O'Toole J 25 + 4	McGivern R — + 1	Facey S 13 + 2	Pereira H 4 + 8	O'Donnell R 19	Turnbull J 14	Bunney J 11 + 1	Ariyibi G 3 + 9	van Veen K 6 + 4	Mathis B 2 + 3	Luckassen K 1 + 3	Bridge J 1 + 3	*Match No.*
1	2	3	4	5	6	7	8^{1}	9	10^{3}	11^{2}	12	13	14																									1
1	4		3	5		7			14	9	10	8^{3}	11	2^{2}	6^{1}	12	13																					2
1	2^{1}	3	4	5	14	7			9	11		8^{2}	10		6^{3}		12	13																				3
	2	4	3^{3}	5	12	7^{1}			10^{2}	14	13		11			8	9	6	1																			4
	4		2	9	14	6^{3}			13	12	10^{1}		11			7	5	8		1	3^{2}																	5
	4		3	5	13	6			14		11	12	10^{1}			7^{3}	2	8		1	9^{2}																	6
		3	4	2	11	8■				12	10^{1}	7	9				5	6		1																		7
		3	4	5	7			14	11^{2}		12	8^{3}	13	6			2	9		1		10^{1}																8
	4		3	5	9^{1}	7			13	12	11^{3}		10	6^{2}			2	8		1			14															9
	4		3	5	9	7^{2}		12	14				10^{3}	6			2	8		1		11^{1}	13															10
	4		3	5	6^{1}			11	13	12			10	7			2	8		1	9^{2}																	11
	4		3	5				6	11				10■	12			2^{2}	8		1		9^{3}	14	7^{1}	13													12
	4		3	5	9			12		10						6^{1}	2	7		1			11^{2}	14	8^{3}	13												13
	4		3	5	11					9	10^{1}			7			2	8		1			13	6^{2}		12												14
	4		3	5	10				14	13	11^{3}			2		7		6		1			8^{2}	12		9^{1}												15
	4		3	5	8			13	12	14	11^{2}			6		2		7		1			10^{3}			9^{1}												16
	4		3	5	6^{3}			12	14	10	11^{1}						2	7		1				13	8	9^{2}												17
	4		3	5		10		13		8^{1}	11						2	6		1				12	7	9^{2}												18
	4^{1}	12	3	5		11		14	13	9^{2}	10			8^{3}			2	6		1					7													19
		3	4	5		9		12	10	13	11^{2}			7		8^{1}	2	6		1																		20
1		4	3	5		10				6^{2}	11			9^{1}			2	7			13			8		12												21
1	4		3	5		10■					11^{2}			12			2	6						9	8^{1}	7	13											22
1	4^{1}		3	5							11			12		14	2	6			10^{3}		13	8	7^{2}	9												23
			4	5					10		11^{2}			3		6^{1}	2	8		1		14	13	9	12	7^{3}												24
			4	5	13	6			14		11^{2}			3			2	7		1			10^{1}	12	8	9^{3}												25
			3		9^{1}	10^{3}			14		11			4		7^{2}	2	8		1	5		13	6		12												26
			4	5		6					11^{1}		13	3			14	7		1			8	10^{3}		9		2^{2}	12									27
			4		12	7					11^{1}		13	3				6					8^{3}	10		9^{2}		2	14	1	5							28
			3			6					11^{1}		14					7					8^{3}	10^{2}		9		2	12	1	4	5	13					29
			3		12	7^{2}					11			4				8					6^{3}	13		10		2		1	5	9^{1}	14					30
			3			6					11			12				7						10		9^{3}		2^{2}	8^{1}	1	4	5	14	13				31
			3		8^{2}	6^{3}					12						2	7					10	13		9			14	1	4	5		11^{1}				32
			3		10^{2}						11						2	7					8^{3}	6^{1}		9			12■	1	4	5	13		14			33
		12	3		9^{2}	7					11						2	8					13	14		10^{3}				1	4	5	6^{1}					34
			3			6					11						2	7					8^{1}			9		13	12	1	4	5	10^{2}					35
			3			7■					11^{2}						2	8					6			10^{3}		14	12	1	4	5	9^{1}			13		36
			3		10												2	7					8^{2}			6^{3}			9	1	4	5	12	13	14	11^{1}		37
			3													14	2	8								7■		6	9^{3}	1	4	5	13	10^{1}	11^{2}	12		38
			3								14					6^{2}	2	8										5	7	1	4	9	13	10^{3}	11^{1}	12		39
			3	8		9					11					6^{1}	2^{3}	7										5	13	1	4		12	10^{2}	14			40
		3	4■		10^{2}	7^{3}					11							9					6	8^{1}				5		1	2	14	13	12				41
		3		5	14						10^{3}			4		12		8					11	6^{2}		7		2^{1}		1				9			13	42
		3	4	5	10	13					14					8^{3}		9					12			6		2		1				11^{2}			7^{1}	43
		3	4	5	10	7^{2}					13					8^{3}		9					11^{1}	12		6		2		1							14	44
		3	4	5	9	6^{1}					12					7^{2}		8					11			10		2		1				13				45
		4	3	5	9			13								7^{2}	2	8					11	6^{1}		10				1							12	46

FA Cup

First Round	Scunthorpe U	(h)	0-0
Replay	Scunthorpe U	(a)	0-1

Carabao Cup

First Round	QPR	(a)	0-1

Checkatrade Trophy

Southern Group H	Cambridge U	(h)	1-1
(Northampton T won 5-4 on penalties)			
Southern Group H	Peterborough U	(a)	1-1
(Northampton T won 4-2 on penalties)			
Southern Group H	Southampton U21	(h)	3-3
(Northampton T won 4-2 on penalties)			
Second Round South	Portsmouth	(a)	0-2

NORWICH CITY

FOUNDATION

Formed in 1902, largely through the initiative of two local schoolmasters who called a meeting at the Criterion Cafe, they were shocked by an FA Commission which in 1904 declared the club professional and ejected them from the FA Amateur Cup. However, this only served to strengthen their determination. New officials were appointed and a professional club established at a meeting in the Agricultural Hall in March 1905.

Carrow Road, Norwich, Norfolk NR1 1JE.

Telephone: (01603) 760 760.

Fax: (01603) 811 815.

Ticket Office: (01603) 721 902.

Website: www.canaries.co.uk

Email: reception@ncfc-canaries.co.uk

Ground Capacity: 27,359.

Record Attendance: 25,037 v Sheffield W, FA Cup 5th rd, 16 February 1935 (at The Nest); 43,984 v Leicester C, FA Cup 6th rd, 30 March 1963 (at Carrow Road).

Pitch Measurements: 105m × 68m (114yd × 74yd).

Chairman: Ed Balls.

Joint Majority Shareholders: Delia Smith and Michael Wynn-Jones.

Managing Director: Steve Stone.

Head Coach: Daniel Farke.

Assistant Head Coach: Edmund Riemer.

Colours: Yellow shirts with green trim, green shorts with yellow trim, yellow socks with green trim.

Year Formed: 1902.

Turned Professional: 1905.

Club Nickname: 'The Canaries'.

HONOURS

League Champions: First Division – 2003–04; Division 2 – 1971–72, 1985–86; FL 1 – 2009–10; Division 3S – 1933–34.
Runners-up: FL C – 2010–11; Division 3 – 1959–60; Division 3S – 1950–51.
FA Cup: semi-final – 1959, 1989, 1992.
League Cup Winners: 1962, 1985.
Runners-up: 1973, 1975.

European Competitions
UEFA Cup: 1993–94.

Grounds: 1902, Newmarket Road; 1908, The Nest, Rosary Road; 1935, Carrow Road.

First Football League Game: 28 August 1920, Division 3, v Plymouth Arg (a) D 1–1 – Skermer; Gray, Gadsden; Wilkinson, Addy, Martin; Laxton, Kidger, Parker, Whitham (1), Dobson.

Record League Victory: 10–2 v Coventry C, Division 3 (S), 15 March 1930 – Jarvie; Hannah, Graham; Brown, O'Brien, Lochhead (1); Porter (1), Anderson, Hunt (5), Scott (2), Slicer (1).

Record Cup Victory: 8–0 v Sutton U, FA Cup 4th rd, 28 January 1989 – Gunn; Culverhouse, Bowen, Butterworth, Linighan, Townsend (Crook), Gordon, Fleck (3), Allen (4), Phelan, Putney (1).

Record Defeat: 2–10 v Swindon T, Southern League, 5 September 1908.

Most League Points (2 for a win): 64, Division 3 (S), 1950–51.

Most League Points (3 for a win): 95, FL 1, 2009–10.

Sun FACT FILE

Centre-half Barry Butler made 349 League and Cup appearances for Norwich City after signing in August 1957 and with his playing career drawing to a close he was appointed as the club's player-coach for 1966–67. Tragically he was killed in a car accident on 9 April 1966. The Barry Butler Memorial Trophy has been awarded to the club's Player of the Year from 1966–67 onwards

Most League Goals: 99, Division 3 (S), 1952–53.

Highest League Scorer in Season: Ralph Hunt, 31, Division 3 (S), 1955–56.

Most League Goals in Total Aggregate: Johnny Gavin, 122, 1945–54, 1955–58.

Most League Goals in One Match: 5, Tommy Hunt v Coventry C, Division 3 (S), 15 March 1930; 5, Roy Hollis v Walsall, Division 3 (S), 29 December 1951.

Most Capped Player: Wes Hoolahan, 42 (43), Republic of Ireland.

Most League Appearances: Ron Ashman, 592, 1947–64.

Youngest League Player: Ryan Jarvis, 16 years 282 days v Walsall, 19 April 2003.

Record Transfer Fee Received: £22,000,000 (rising to £24,000,000) from Leicester C for James Maddison, June 2018.

Record Transfer Fee Paid: £8,500,000 to Sporting Lisbon for Ricky van Wolfswinkel, July 2013; £8,500,000 to Everton for Steven Naismith, January 2016.

Football League Record: 1920 Original Member of Division 3; 1921 Division 3 (S): 1934–39 Division 2; 1946–58 Division 3 (S); 1958–60 Division 3; 1960–72 Division 2; 1972–74 Division 1; 1974–75 Division 2; 1975–81 Division 1; 1981–82 Division 2; 1982–85 Division 1; 1985–86 Division 2; 1986–92 Division 1; 1992–95 FA Premier League; 1995–2004 Division 1; 2004–05 FA Premier League; 2005–09 FL C; 2009–10 FL 1; 2010–11 FL C; 2011–14 FA Premier League; 2014–15 FL C; 2015–16 FA Premier League; 2016– FL C.

LATEST SEQUENCES

Longest Sequence of League Wins: 10, 23.11.1985 – 25.1.1986.

Longest Sequence of League Defeats: 7, 1.4.1995 – 6.5.1995.

Longest Sequence of League Draws: 7, 15.1.1994 – 26.2.1994.

Longest Sequence of Unbeaten League Matches: 20, 31.8.1950 – 30.12.1950.

Longest Sequence Without a League Win: 25, 22.9.1956 – 23.2.1957.

Successive Scoring Runs: 25 from 14.9.2009.

Successive Non-scoring Runs: 5 from 18.9.2007.

MANAGERS

John Bowman 1905–07
James McEwen 1907–08
Arthur Turner 1909–10
Bert Stansfield 1910–15
Major Frank Buckley 1919–20
Charles O'Hagan 1920–21
Albert Gosnell 1921–26
Bert Stansfield 1926
Cecil Potter 1926–29
James Kerr 1929–33
Tom Parker 1933–37
Bob Young 1937–39
Jimmy Jewell 1939
Bob Young 1939–45
Duggie Lochhead 1945–46
Cyril Spiers 1946–47
Duggie Lochhead 1947–50
Norman Low 1950–55
Tom Parker 1955–57
Archie Macaulay 1957–61
Willie Reid 1961–62
George Swindin 1962
Ron Ashman 1962–66
Lol Morgan 1966–69
Ron Saunders 1969–73
John Bond 1973–80
Ken Brown 1980–87
Dave Stringer 1987–92
Mike Walker 1992–94
John Deehan 1994–95
Martin O'Neill 1995
Gary Megson 1995–96
Mike Walker 1996–98
Bruce Rioch 1998–2000
Bryan Hamilton 2000
Nigel Worthington 2000–06
Peter Grant 2006–07
Glenn Roeder 2007–09
Bryan Gunn 2009
Paul Lambert 2009–12
Chris Hughton 2012–14
Neil Adams 2014–15
Alex Neil 2015–17
Daniel Farke May 2017–

TEN YEAR LEAGUE RECORD

		P	W	D	L	F	A	Pts	Pos
2008-09	FL C	46	12	10	24	57	70	46	22
2009-10	FL 1	46	29	8	9	89	47	95	1
2010-11	FL C	46	23	15	8	83	58	84	2
2011-12	PR Lge	38	12	11	15	52	66	47	12
2012-13	PR Lge	38	10	14	14	41	58	44	11
2013-14	PR Lge	38	8	9	21	28	62	33	18
2014-15	FL C	46	25	11	10	88	48	86	3
2015-16	PR Lge	38	9	7	22	39	67	34	19
2016-17	FL C	46	20	10	16	85	69	70	8
2017-18	FL C	46	15	15	16	49	60	60	14

DID YOU KNOW ?

Between 1974–75 and 1995–96 Norwich City played in a total of 20 Football League Cup ties decided over two legs and won every single one of them. The run was eventually broken by Oxford United who defeated the Canaries 4-3 on aggregate in the first-round tie in 1996–97.

NORWICH CITY – SKY BET CHAMPIONSHIP 2017–18 LEAGUE RECORD

Match No.	Date	Venue	Opponents	Result	H/T Score	Lg Pos.	Goalscorers	Attendance
1	Aug 5	A	Fulham	D	1-1	0-1	13	Nelson Oliveira [88]	20,134
2	13	H	Sunderland	L	1-3	0-1	18	Grabban (og) [78]	26,343
3	16	H	QPR	W	2-0	0-0	10	Nelson Oliveira [48], Reed [82]	26,082
4	19	A	Aston Villa	L	2-4	0-2	17	Murphy [60], Nelson Oliveira [79]	29,157
5	26	A	Millwall	L	0-4	0-3	22		12,671
6	Sept 9	H	Birmingham C	W	1-0	1-0	17	Nelson Oliveira [5]	26,335
7	12	H	Burton Alb	D	0-0	0-0	13		24,841
8	16	A	Sheffield U	W	1-0	0-0	12	Wildschut [23]	26,218
9	23	H	Bristol C	D	0-0	0-0	13		25,715
10	26	A	Middlesbrough	W	1-0	1-0	10	Maddison [13]	24,084
11	30	A	Reading	W	2-1	1-1	9	Maddison [10], Jerome [52]	14,226
12	Oct 14	A	Hull C	D	1-1	0-1	8	Nelson Oliveira [90]	25,666
13	22	A	Ipswich T	W	1-0	0-0	6	Maddison [59]	24,928
14	28	H	Derby Co	L	1-2	0-1	8	Klose [71]	26,048
15	31	H	Wolverhampton W	L	0-2	0-1	9		26,554
16	Nov 4	A	Bolton W	L	1-2	0-2	13	Murphy [90]	14,786
17	18	H	Barnsley	D	1-1	1-0	12	Murphy [12]	25,545
18	21	A	Nottingham F	L	0-1	0-0	15		23,831
19	25	H	Preston NE	D	1-1	1-0	14	Maddison [34]	25,167
20	Dec 1	A	Cardiff C	L	1-3	1-0	15	Stiepermann [43]	17,033
21	9	H	Sheffield W	W	3-1	0-1	15	Maddison [55], Klose [68], Nelson Oliveira (pen) [90]	25,561
22	16	A	Leeds U	L	0-1	0-1	16		30,590
23	22	A	Brentford	L	1-2	0-2	16	Nelson Oliveira [90]	26,725
24	26	A	Birmingham C	W	2-0	1-0	15	Pritchard [33], Murphy [71]	19,967
25	30	A	Burton Alb	D	0-0	0-0	13		4565
26	Jan 1	H	Millwall	W	2-1	0-1	13	Trybull [52], Maddison [77]	25,774
27	13	H	Bristol C	W	1-0	0-0	13	Maddison [79]	21,282
28	20	H	Sheffield U	L	1-2	0-1	13	Ivo Pinto [70]	26,486
29	27	H	Brentford	W	1-0	1-0	13	Maddison [5]	10,252
30	Feb 3	H	Middlesbrough	W	1-0	1-0	13	Trybull [44]	25,960
31	10	A	Derby Co	D	1-1	0-1	13	Maddison (pen) [72]	27,171
32	18	H	Ipswich T	D	1-1	0-0	13	Klose [90]	27,100
33	21	A	Wolverhampton W	D	2-2	1-2	12	Zimmermann [27], Nelson Oliveira [90]	29,100
34	24	A	Bolton W	D	0-0	0-0	14		25,475
35	Mar 6	H	Nottingham F	D	0-0	0-0	14		25,184
36	10	A	Hull C	L	3-4	3-2	14	Maddison 3 (2 pens) [18 (p), 19, 39 (p)]	15,120
37	13	A	Barnsley	D	1-1	0-1	14	Murphy [71]	11,506
38	17	A	Reading	W	3-2	3-1	13	Vrancic [14], Hanley [26], Maddison (pen) [37]	25,098
39	30	H	Fulham	L	0-2	0-0	14		26,750
40	Apr 2	A	QPR	L	1-4	1-1	14	Manning (og) [38]	14,053
41	7	A	Aston Villa	W	3-1	1-0	12	Murphy [46], Srbeny [54], Maddison [72]	26,278
42	10	A	Sunderland	D	1-1	0-0	13	Ivo Pinto [89]	24,894
43	14	H	Cardiff C	L	0-2	0-0	13		25,503
44	21	A	Preston NE	D	0-0	0-0	13		13,038
45	28	H	Leeds U	W	2-1	1-1	12	Hoolahan [45], Murphy [69]	26,869
46	May 6	A	Sheffield W	L	1-5	0-2	14	Klose [83]	28,189

Final League Position: 14

GOALSCORERS

League (49): Maddison 14 (4 pens), Nelson Oliveira 8 (1 pen), Murphy 7, Klose 4, Ivo Pinto 2, Trybull 2, Hanley 1, Hoolahan 1, Jerome 1, Pritchard 1, Reed 1, Srbeny 1, Stiepermann 1, Vrancic 1, Wildschut 1, Zimmermann 1, own goals 2.
FA Cup (1): Lewis 1.
Carabao Cup (11): Murphy 4, Vrancic 2 (1 pen), Hoolahan 1, Jerome 1, Maddison 1, Trybull 1, Watkins 1.

Gunn A 46	Martin R 4 + 1	Zimmermann C 30 + 9	Franke M 5	Wildschut Y 7 + 9	Maddison J 42 + 2	Reed H 36 + 3	Vrancic M 29 + 6	Husband J 14 + 4	Watkins M 12 + 12	Jerome C 11 + 4	Murphy J 34 + 7	Nelson Oliveira M 26 + 11	Hoolahan W 14 + 15	Naismith S 2	Ivo Pinto D 31 + 4	Stiepermann M 15 + 8	Tettey A 21 + 2	Klose T 36 + 1	Trybull T 17 + 3	Hanley G 28 + 4	Pritchard A 5 + 3	Lewis J 19 + 3	Raggett S — + 2	Leitner M 10 + 2	Hernandez O 5 + 7	Srbeny D 7 + 7	Edwards M — + 1	Match No.
1	2	3	4	5^1	6	7^3	8	9	10	11^1	12	13	14															1
1	2	3	4	5^1	6	7		9	10	11^3	12	13	14	8^2														2
1	12	3	4		8	6	9	5	13		10^1	11^2	7		2^3	14												3
1	2	3	4	14		6	9	5^2		11^1	10	13	12	8^3		7												4
1		3^3	4		8^1	6^2	9	5		10	11	7			2	12	14											5
1		3	12	9^1		8^3	14			10^2	11				2	5	7	4	6	13								6
1		3	12	13		9	14			10	11^3	8^1			2	5	6	4	7^2									7
1		3		8^1	9^2			12	13	11	10^3				2	5	7	4	6	14								8
1		3	12		6	9^1	14			8^3	11	10^1	13		2	5		4	7									9
1		3		8^2	9^3		5	10		11^1	13				2	12	6	4	7	14								10
1		3	14	9^2	13		5	12^*	11	10^3		8^1			2		6	4	7									11
1		3	10	9	6^2	8	5^2		11		13	12			2	14		4	7^1									12
1		3^3	10	9^2	6	14	13		11				8^1		2	5		4	7	12								13
1		3	13	9	6^4		14	11	10^1	12^3	8				2	5		4	7									14
1	14			9	6	8	5^2	11	12	10^1					2	13		4	7^3	3								15
1		10^1	9	6^2	14		12	11	13		8				2	5		4	7^3									16
1	12	14	10		8	5^3	13			9^2	11				2	6		4	7^1	3								17
1	12		9	6^1	7			10	13		11	12			2	5		4^3		3								18
1		3	12	9	6^2	7				10^1	11	8			2	5		4		3	13							19
1			9	9^1	6	7				10	11	8			2	5		4		3	12							20
1	14		9^1	6	7		12			8^3	11				2	5		4	13	3	10^2							21
1			9	6	7^2			10	13		11	12			2	5^1		4		3	8							22
1	12		9	6	7		10^2			14	11				2	5^1		4		3^3	8	13						23
1		3	14	9^1	13			12		10	11^2				2		6	4	7		8^3	5						24
1		3		13	6^2	9^1	5	10			11	8^3			2	12		7	4	14								25
1		13		9				12		10^2	11				2		6	4	7	3	8^1	5						26
1		3		9^3	14	7				11^2	10^1				5	12	6	4		2		8	13					27
1		3		9	6^3	13				11	10	12			5	14	7^3	4		2^1		8						28
1		3		9^1	5	7^1		13		11^3	10^2					6	4	14	2		8			12				29
1		3		9^3	5	13				11^3	10					6	4	7^2	2		8			12	14			30
1		3		9^3	5					11^2	10^1				14	6^1	4	2		8		7	13	12				31
1		3		9	5	5^3	13			11^2	10					6^1	4	2		8		7	14	12				32
1		3		9	5	7^3		10^2		14	12						4	2		8		6	13	11^1				33
1		3		8	2					10	11	13				6^2		4	5		9	7^1	12					34
1				9	2	14		13		10^1		12				7^3	4	3		5		6	8	11^1				35
1				9	2^2		8			14	11	13		12	6	4		3		5		7^3	10^1					36
1	3^1			9		7	8	10^2		11		13		5	6^3	4		2						12	14			37
1	14			9	6	7		13		10^2		12		2		4		3	5					8^3	11^1			38
1		3		8	7		9^2			10	12	13			6^1	4			5						11^3	14		39
1		3		9	6	-7	5^1			10	11	8		2			4	12										40
1	12			8^2	6^1	9				10	14	13		2		7^1	4	3		5					11^3			41
1	3^3			9	6	7	5^2			10	11	8^1		2		12		4	13						14			42
1				9	2^3	8				11	12	14		13	7^1	4		3		5		6^1				10^2		43
1				9	2	8				11^2	12			14	7^1	4		3		5		6^3	13	10^1				44
1				8^3	2	7				10	11^1	9^2				4	13	3		5		6	14	12				45
1	3^3			9^2	2					10	11^1			12			4	7		5	14	6	8	13				46

FA Cup

Third Round	Chelsea	(h)	0-0
Replay	Chelsea	(a)	1-1
(aet; Chelsea won 5-3 on penalties)			

Carabao Cup

First Round	Swindon T	(h)	3-2
Second Round	Charlton Ath	(h)	4-1
Third Round	Brentford	(a)	3-1
Fourth Round	Arsenal	(a)	1-2
(aet)			

NOTTINGHAM FOREST

FOUNDATION

One of the oldest football clubs in the world, Nottingham Forest was formed at a meeting in the Clinton Arms in 1865. Known originally as the Forest Football Club, the game which first drew the founders together was 'shinney', a form of hockey. When they determined to change to football in 1865, one of their first moves was to buy a set of red caps to wear on the field.

The City Ground, Pavilion Road, Nottingham NG2 5FJ.
Telephone: (0115) 982 4444.
Ticket Office: (0115) 982 4388.
Website: www.nottinghamforest.co.uk
Email: enquiries@nottinghamforest.co.uk
Ground Capacity: 30,445.
Record Attendance: 49,946 v Manchester U, Division 1, 28 October 1967.
Pitch Measurements: 102.5m × 67.5m (112yd × 74yd).
Chairman: Nicholas Randall QC.
Chief Executive: Ioannis Vrentzos.
Manager: Aitor Karanka.
First-Team Coach: Simon Ireland.
Colours: Red shirt with thin white stripes, white shorts with red trim, red socks with white trim.
Year Formed: 1865.
Turned Professional: 1889.
Previous Name: Forest Football Club.
Club Nickname: 'The Reds'.
Grounds: 1865, Forest Racecourse; 1879, The Meadows; 1880, Trent Bridge Cricket Ground; 1882, Parkside, Lenton; 1885, Gregory, Lenton; 1890, Town Ground; 1898, City Ground.

HONOURS

League Champions: Division 1 – 1977–78; First Division – 1997–98; Division 2 – 1906–07, 1921–22; Division 3S – 1950–51.
Runners-up: Division 1 – 1966–67, 1978–79; First Division – 1993–94; Division 2 – 1956–57; FL 1 – 2007–08.
FA Cup Winners: 1898, 1959.
Runners-up: 1991.
League Cup Winners: 1978, 1979, 1989, 1990.
Runners-up: 1980, 1992.
Anglo-Scottish Cup Winners: 1977.
Full Members' Cup Winners: 1989, 1992.

European Competitions
European Cup: 1978–79 *(winners)*, 1979–80 *(winners)*, 1980–81.
Fairs Cup: 1961–62, 1967–68.
UEFA Cup: 1983–84 *(sf)*, 1984–85, 1995–96 *(qf)*.
Super Cup: 1979 *(winners)*, 1980.
World Club Championship: 1980.

First Football League Game: 3 September 1892, Division 1, v Everton (a) D 2–2 – Brown; Earp, Scott; Hamilton, Albert Smith, McCracken; McCallum, 'Tich' Smith, Higgins (2), Pike, McInnes.

Record League Victory: 12–0 v Leicester Fosse, Division 1, 12 April 1909 – Iremonger; Dudley, Maltby; Hughes (1), Needham, Armstrong; Hooper (3), Marrison, West (3), Morris (2), Spouncer (3 incl. 1p).

Record Cup Victory: 14–0 v Clapton (away), FA Cup 1st rd, 17 January 1891 – Brown; Earp, Scott; Albert Smith, Russell, Jeacock; McCallum (2), 'Tich' Smith (1), Higgins (5), Lindley (4), Shaw (2).

Record Defeat: 1–9 v Blackburn R, Division 2, 10 April 1937.

Most League Points (2 for a win): 70, Division 3 (S), 1950–51.

Most League Points (3 for a win): 94, Division 1, 1997–98.

Most League Goals: 110, Division 3 (S), 1950–51.

Highest League Scorer in Season: Wally Ardron, 36, Division 3 (S), 1950–51.

THE Sun FACT FILE

Nottingham Forest have worn predominantly red shirts since the late 1860s, making their colours the oldest continuously worn by any Football League club. According to one source the colours were chosen because several of the early club members were also members of the Robin Hood Rifles Cadet Corps, whose members wore 'Garibaldi red' shirts while on parade.

Most League Goals in Total Aggregate: Grenville Morris, 199, 1898–1913.

Most League Goals in One Match: 4, Enoch West v Sunderland, Division 1, 9 November 1907; 4, Tommy Gibson v Burnley, Division 2, 25 January 1913; 4, Tom Peacock v Port Vale, Division 2, 23 December 1933; 4, Tom Peacock v Barnsley, Division 2, 9 November 1935; 4, Tom Peacock v Port Vale, Division 2, 23 November 1935; 4, Tom Peacock v Doncaster R, Division 2, 26 December 1935; 4, Tommy Capel v Gillingham, Division 3 (S), 18 November 1950; 4, Wally Ardron v Hull C, Division 2, 26 December 1952; 4, Tommy Wilson v Barnsley, Division 2, 9 February 1957; 4, Peter Withe v Ipswich T, Division 1, 4 October 1977; 4, Marlon Harewood v Stoke C, Division 1, 22 February 2003; Gareth McCleary v Leeds U, FL C, 20 March 2012.

Most Capped Player: Stuart Pearce, 76 (78), England.

Most League Appearances: Bob McKinlay, 614, 1951–70.

Youngest League Player: Craig Westcarr, 16 years 257 days v Burnley, 13 October 2001.

Record Transfer Fee Received: £15,000,000 from Middlesbrough for Britt Assombalonga, July 2017.

Record Transfer Fee Paid: £13,200,000 to Benfica for João Carvalho, June 2018.

Football League Record: 1892 Elected to Division 1; 1906–07 Division 2; 1907–11 Division 1; 1911–22 Division 2; 1922–25 Division 1; 1925–49 Division 2; 1949–51 Division 3 (S); 1951–57 Division 2; 1957–72 Division 1; 1972–77 Division 2; 1977–92 Division 1; 1992–93 FA Premier League; 1993–94 Division 1; 1994–97 FA Premier League; 1997–98 Division 1; 1998–99 FA Premier League; 1999–2004 Division 1; 2004–05 FL C; 2005–08 FL 1; 2008– FL C.

LATEST SEQUENCES

Longest Sequence of League Wins: 7, 9.5.1979 – 1.9.1979.

Longest Sequence of League Defeats: 14, 21.3.1913 – 27.9.1913.

Longest Sequence of League Draws: 7, 29.4.1978 – 2.9.1978.

Longest Sequence of Unbeaten League Matches: 42, 26.11.1977 – 25.11.1978.

Longest Sequence Without a League Win: 19, 8.9.1998 – 16.1.1999.

Successive Scoring Runs: 22 from 28.3.1931.

Successive Non-scoring Runs: 7 from 26.11.2011.

MANAGERS

Harry Radford 1889–97
(Secretary-Manager)
Harry Haslam 1897–1909
(Secretary-Manager)
Fred Earp 1909–12
Bob Masters 1912–25
John Baynes 1925–29
Stan Hardy 1930–31
Noel Watson 1931–36
Harold Wightman 1936–39
Billy Walker 1939–60
Andy Beattie 1960–63
Johnny Carey 1963–68
Matt Gillies 1969–72
Dave Mackay 1972
Allan Brown 1973–75
Brian Clough 1975–93
Frank Clark 1993–96
Stuart Pearce 1996–97
Dave Bassett 1997–99
(previously General Manager)
Ron Atkinson 1999
David Platt 1999–2001
Paul Hart 2001–04
Joe Kinnear 2004
Gary Megson 2005–06
Colin Calderwood 2006–08
Billy Davies 2009–11
Steve McClaren 2011
Steve Cotterill 2011–12
Sean O'Driscoll 2012
Alex McLeish 2012–13
Billy Davies 2013–14
Stuart Pearce 2014–15
Dougie Freedman 2015–16
Philippe Montanier 2016–17
Mark Warburton 2017
Aitor Karanka January 2018–

TEN YEAR LEAGUE RECORD

		P	W	D	L	F	A	Pts	Pos
2008-09	FL C	46	13	14	19	50	65	53	19
2009-10	FL C	46	22	13	11	65	40	79	3
2010-11	FL C	46	20	15	11	69	50	75	6
2011-12	FL C	46	14	8	24	48	63	50	19
2012-13	FL C	46	17	16	13	63	59	67	8
2013-14	FL C	46	16	17	13	67	64	65	11
2014-15	FL C	46	15	14	17	71	69	59	14
2015-16	FL C	46	13	16	17	43	47	55	16
2016-17	FL C	46	14	9	23	62	72	51	21
2017-18	FL C	46	15	8	23	51	65	53	17

DID YOU KNOW ?

Live television coverage of League matches in modern times began during the 1983–84 season. The first game shown live was that between Tottenham Hotspur and Nottingham Forest on Sunday 2 October 1983, broadcast on ITV. The attendance of 30,596 was the highest Football League attendance that weekend, suggesting the impact on crowds was minimal.

NOTTINGHAM FOREST – SKY BET CHAMPIONSHIP 2017–18 LEAGUE RECORD

Match No.	Date	Venue	Opponents	Result	H/T Score	Lg Pos.	Goalscorers	Atten-dance
1	Aug 4	H	Millwall	W 1-0	1-0	1	McKay [41]	28,065
2	12	A	Brentford	W 4-3	2-1	3	Bouchalakis 2 [41, 47], Murphy [43], Dowell [83]	10,169
3	15	A	Barnsley	L 1-2	1-1	5	Murphy [26]	13,883
4	19	H	Middlesbrough	W 2-1	1-0	4	McKay [16], Murphy (pen) [79]	26,265
5	26	H	Leeds U	L 0-2	0-1	6		25,682
6	Sept 9	A	Sheffield W	L 1-3	1-1	12	Osborn [29]	25,710
7	12	A	Sunderland	W 1-0	0-0	8	Murphy [86]	26,061
8	16	H	Wolverhampton W	L 1-2	0-0	10	Carayol [75]	25,756
9	23	A	Aston Villa	L 1-2	0-1	12	Murphy [52]	28,554
10	26	H	Fulham	L 1-3	1-1	16	Murphy [33]	21,208
11	30	H	Sheffield U	W 2-1	2-1	12	Cummings [9], Dowell [27]	25,700
12	Oct 15	A	Derby Co	L 0-2	0-1	14		31,196
13	21	H	Burton Alb	W 2-0	0-0	12	McKay [58], Lichaj [78]	24,686
14	28	A	Hull C	W 3-2	1-0	11	Dowell 3 (1 pen) [29, 71, 83 (p)]	15,780
15	31	A	Reading	L 1-3	0-1	13	Osborn [86]	14,868
16	Nov 4	H	QPR	W 4-0	2-0	8	Walker 2 [13, 84], Dowell [44], McKay [52]	24,021
17	18	A	Birmingham C	L 0-1	0-1	10		21,071
18	21	H	Norwich C	W 1-0	0-0	7	Murphy [77]	23,831
19	26	H	Cardiff C	L 0-2	0-2	9		25,210
20	Dec 2	A	Ipswich T	L 2-4	2-2	13	Dowell [29], Walker [43]	16,808
21	9	H	Bolton W	W 3-2	1-1	11	McKay [3], Worrall [60], Brereton [89]	22,882
22	16	A	Bristol C	L 1-2	0-2	11	Dowell [47]	20,128
23	23	A	Preston NE	D 1-1	0-0	13	Brereton [58]	13,481
24	26	H	Sheffield W	L 0-3	0-2	13		28,635
25	30	H	Sunderland	L 0-1	0-1	14		26,830
26	Jan 1	A	Leeds U	D 0-0	0-0	14		32,426
27	13	H	Aston Villa	L 0-1	0-1	15		25,433
28	20	A	Wolverhampton W	W 2-0	2-0	14	Dowell [40], Osborn [43]	29,050
29	30	H	Preston NE	L 0-3	0-1	15		22,044
30	Feb 3	A	Fulham	L 0-2	0-0	16		22,076
31	10	H	Hull C	L 0-2	0-2	16		23,098
32	17	A	Burton Alb	D 0-0	0-0	17		5775
33	20	H	Reading	D 1-1	0-1	17	Tomlin [85]	21,846
34	24	A	QPR	W 5-2	1-0	15	Tomlin 2 [37, 47], Lolley [51], Cash [76], Brereton [90]	13,675
35	Mar 3	H	Birmingham C	W 2-1	1-0	15	Lolley [6], Cash [79]	23,296
36	6	A	Norwich C	D 0-0	0-0	15		25,184
37	11	H	Derby Co	D 0-0	0-0	15		29,106
38	17	A	Sheffield U	D 0-0	0-0	16		28,095
39	30	A	Millwall	L 0-2	0-2	16		16,004
40	Apr 7	A	Middlesbrough	L 0-2	0-2	17		25,812
41	10	H	Brentford	L 0-1	0-0	18		20,596
42	14	H	Ipswich T	W 2-1	0-1	17	Brereton (pen) [89], Lolley [90]	25,093
43	21	A	Cardiff C	L 1-2	0-1	17	Bridcutt [50]	21,310
44	24	H	Barnsley	W 3-0	2-0	17	Tomlin [26], Brereton [36], Vellios [90]	23,633
45	28	H	Bristol C	D 0-0	0-0	17		24,722
46	May 6	A	Bolton W	L 2-3	0-0	17	Osborn [70], Colback [79]	18,289

Final League Position: 17

GOALSCORERS

League (51): Dowell 9 (1 pen), Murphy 7 (1 pen), Brereton 5 (1 pen), McKay 5, Osborn 4, Tomlin 4, Lolley 3, Walker 3, Bouchalakis 2, Cash 2, Bridcutt 1, Carayol 1, Colback 1, Cummings 1, Lichaj 1, Vellios 1, Worrall 1.
FA Cup (5): Lichaj 2, Brereton 1 (1 pen), Dowell 1 (1 pen), Vellios 1.
Carabao Cup (6): Cummings 3, Carayol 1 (1 pen), Darikwa 1, Walker 1.

Smith J 29	Darikwa T 29+1	Worrall B 28+3	Mancienne M 27+2	Traore A 15+3	Vaughan D 14	Brereton B 25+10	Clough Z 4+9	Osborn B 42+4	McKay B 22+4	Murphy D 22+5	Cohen C —+2	Dowell K 31+7	Mills M 11+2	Bouchalakis A 11+10	Carayol M 2+13	Cummings J 7+7	Lichaj E 22+1	Bridcutt L 24+3	Hobbs J 2	Fox D 23	Walker T 7+5	Ward J —+8	Cash M 14+9	Vellios A 4+8	Pantilimon C 13	Guedioura A 6+5	Colback J 16	Tomlin L 12+3	Dejagah A —+1	Lolley J 13+3	Tobias Figueiredo P 12	Watson B 14	Kapino S 4	Fuentes J 1	Match No.
1	2	3	4	5	6	7¹	8	9²	10	11³	12	13	14																						1
1	5	2	4	14	7		9²	8	10¹	11		12	3	6³	13																				2
1	5	2	4²	12	7³			10	8¹	11		9	3	6	13	14																			3
1	2	3	13	5¹	7¹	12		10	8²	11		9	4	6			14																		4
1	2	3		5		12	13	10¹	8	11²		9	4	6¹		14	7																		5
1	6	2				11³	7¹	9	8	13	14	12		10²			5	3	4																6
1	2	3		5		8¹	13	10	12	11		9¹	4	7²	14		6																		7
1	2	3		5		8³	7	10²	11	9¹	4	12	13	6	14																				8
1	2	3		5		8¹	14	13	10³	11		9	4	6²	12		7																		9
1	5	2	4³	8		12	13	7		11		9¹	3	14	10²		6																		10
1	5	2	3	8		13	14	7		11		9²	12	10³			6	4¹																	11
1		3	5			13	8	11¹	10	6³		9²	2	7			4	14	12																12
1	12	3	5²	7¹		10	8	11		13	14	9²	2	6			4																		13
1	2	3	4			7²		10	8³	9		12		11¹	5	6		13	14																14
1	2	3	4			7²		10	8¹	9		14	12	11¹³	5	6		13																	15
1		3	4	5			7	10²	11³	9¹		12	13	2	6		8	14																	16
1	2	3	4			11²	12	7³	10	9			14	5	6		2																		17
1	2³	3	4			7		8	10²	11		9¹	12	14	13		5	6																	18
1		3	4	5	6	13		7¹	10²	11³			12	2			8	14																	19
1		3	4	5	7³			10¹	14	11		9		12	13		2	6					8²												20
1		3	2			14		7²	10³	11¹		9	4	12	13		5	6					8												21
1		3	2			14	13	12		11		9	4²	7³	10¹		5	6					8												22
1		3	4			7²	8¹	5		11		9	14	10³			2	6								12	13								23
1		3	4			8		5	10²	9		7¹		13			2	6					11³	14	12										24
1		3	4	12	7	8		5	10²	11¹		9		6³	13	14	2																		25
1		3	4	5		11¹		7	10²	9			13	2	6			12			8														26
1			4	5	6¹	11	10³	7	12	9	3			2	14						13		8²												27
1	13	3	4			11	12	9				10²		6			2	8¹		5			7												28
1	2	3	4		6	12		7	10²	9				5			13	8	11¹																29
	3	4				11²		9				10¹		2			5				8	14	1	6³		7	12	13							30
	3	4				11²		9				10¹		2²			5				8	11³	1	6¹		7	12		14						31
	2					11¹	12		13			14					5▪			4		8	1			7	9²	10²	3	6					32
	2					11			5			9²								4		12	1	13		7	10¹			3	6				33
	2	13				11			5			12								4		8	1	14		7³	9¹	10²	3	6					34
	2					11²			5		12									4		8	1	13		7	9¹	10	3	6					35
	2					11			5			9¹								4		8	12	1		7		10	3	6					36
	2					11²			5		13	12								4		8	1			7	9	10¹	3	6					37
	2					11			5		10¹	9³								4		6³	14	1		7	13	12	3	8					38
	2¹	14				13			5		10³									4		12	11	1		7	9	8²	3	6					39
	2					12			5		13					8²				4		11¹		1		7	9	10	3	6					40
	2					10			5											4		12	13	1	6¹	7	11¹		9	3	8				41
	2					10			5		13									4		12	14	1	6¹	7	11²		9	3	8²				42
		12				10			5					2	6³					4		9	14			13	7			11¹	3²	8	1		43
		3				10²		12						2	6					4		9	14			8		11³		13		7	1	5¹	44
	2	3							5	10	14			6²			12			4		13				8²	7	11¹		9		8¹	1		45
	2					10			5			6²		3			4			12	14					13		7	11³		9		8¹	1	46

FA Cup

Third Round	Arsenal	(h)	4-2	
Fourth Round	Hull C	(a)	1-2	

Carabao Cup

First Round	Shrewsbury T	(h)	2-1	
Second Round	Newcastle U	(a)	3-2	
(aet)				
Third Round	Chelsea	(a)	1-5	

NOTTS COUNTY

FOUNDATION

According to the official history of Notts County 'the true date of Notts' foundation has to be the meeting at the George Hotel on 7 December 1864'. However, there is documented evidence of continuous play from 1862, when club members played organised matches amongst themselves in The Park in Nottingham. They are the world's oldest professional football club.

Meadow Lane Stadium, Meadow Lane, Nottingham NG2 3HJ.

Telephone: (0115) 952 9000.

Fax: (0115) 955 3994.

Ticket Office: (0115) 955 7210.

Website: www.nottscountyfc.co.uk

Email: office@nottscountyfc.co.uk

Ground Capacity: 19,841.

Record Attendance: 47,310 v York C, FA Cup 6th rd, 12 March 1955.

Pitch Measurements: 100.5m × 66m (110yd × 72yd).

Chairman: Alan Hardy.

Manager: Kevin Nolan.

Assistant Manager: Richard Thomas.

HONOURS

League Champions: Division 2 – 1896–97, 1913–14, 1922–23; Division 3S – 1930–31, 1949–50; FL 2 – 2009–10; Third Division – 1997–98; Division 4 – 1970–71.
Runners-up: Division 2 – 1894–95, 1980–81; Division 3 – 1972–73; Division 3S – 1936–37; Division 4 – 1959–60.

FA Cup Winners: 1894.
Runners-up: 1891.

League Cup: 5th rd – 1964, 1973, 1976.

Anglo-Italian Cup Winners: 1995.
Runners-up: 1994.

Colours: Black and white striped shirts, black shorts with white and yellow trim, black socks.

Year Formed: 1862* (*see Foundation*).

Turned Professional: 1885.

Club Nickname: 'The Magpies'.

Grounds: 1862, The Park; 1864, The Meadows; 1877, Beeston Cricket Ground; 1880, Castle Ground; 1883, Trent Bridge; 1910, Meadow Lane.

First Football League Game: 15 September 1888, Football League, v Everton (a) L 1–2 – Holland; Guttridge, McLean; Brown, Warburton, Shelton; Hodder, Harker, Jardine, Albert Moore (1), Wardle.

Record League Victory: 11–1 v Newport Co, Division 3 (S), 15 January 1949 – Smith; Southwell, Purvis; Gannon, Baxter, Adamson; Houghton (1), Sewell (4), Lawton (4), Pimbley, Johnston (2).

Record Cup Victory: 15–0 v Rotherham T (at Trent Bridge), FA Cup 1st rd, 24 October 1885 – Sherwin; Snook, Henry Thomas Moore; Dobson (1), Emmett (1), Chapman; Gunn (1), Albert Moore (2), Jackson (3), Daft (2), Cursham (4), (1 og).

Record Defeat: 1–9 v Blackburn R, Division 1, 16 November 1889. 1–9 v Aston Villa, Division 1, 29 September 1888. 1–9 v Portsmouth, Division 2, 9 April 1927.

Most League Points (2 for a win): 69, Division 4, 1970–71.

Most League Points (3 for a win): 99, Division 3, 1997–98.

Most League Goals: 107, Division 4, 1959–60.

THE Sun FACT FILE

In the days when teams were allowed only one substitute it was rare for goalkeepers to be listed on the bench. However, when Notts County travelled to play Newport County in February 1970 the nominated 12th man failed to turn up. Reserve goalkeeper Barry Watling sat on the bench and when Don Masson was injured he came on to replace him.

Highest League Scorer in Season: Tom Keetley, 39, Division 3 (S), 1930–31.

Most League Goals in Total Aggregate: Les Bradd, 125, 1967–78.

Most League Goals in One Match: 5, Robert Jardine v Burnley, Division 1, 27 October 1888; 5, Daniel Bruce v Port Vale, Division 2, 26 February 1895; 5, Bertie Mills v Barnsley, Division 2, 19 November 1927.

Most Capped Player: Kevin Wilson, 15 (42), Northern Ireland.

Most League Appearances: Albert Iremonger, 564, 1904–26.

Youngest League Player: Tony Bircumshaw, 16 years 54 days v Brentford, 3 April 1961.

Record Transfer Fee Received: £2,500,000 from Derby Co for Craig Short, September 1992.

Record Transfer Fee Paid: £800,000 to Manchester C for Kasper Schmeichel, July 2009.

Football League Record: 1888 Founder Member of the Football League; 1893–97 Division 2; 1897–1913 Division 1; 1913–14 Division 2; 1914–20 Division 1; 1920–23 Division 2; 1923–26 Division 1; 1926–30 Division 2; 1930–31 Division 3 (S); 1931–35 Division 2; 1935–50 Division 3 (S); 1950–58 Division 2; 1958–59 Division 3; 1959–60 Division 4; 1960–64 Division 3; 1964–71 Division 4; 1971–73 Division 3; 1973–81 Division 2; 1981–84 Division 1; 1984–85 Division 2; 1985–90 Division 3; 1990–91 Division 2; 1991–95 Division 1; 1995–97 Division 2; 1997–98 Division 3; 1998–2004 Division 2; 2004–10 FL 2; 2010–15 FL 1; 2015– FL 2.

LATEST SEQUENCES

Longest Sequence of League Wins: 10, 3.12.1997 – 31.1.1998.

Longest Sequence of League Defeats: 10, 12.11.2016 – 7.1.2017.

Longest Sequence of League Draws: 6, 16.8.2008 – 20.9.2008.

Longest Sequence of Unbeaten League Matches: 19, 26.4.1930 – 6.12.1930.

Longest Sequence Without a League Win: 20, 3.12.1996 – 31.3.1997.

Successive Scoring Runs: 35 from 10.10.1959.

Successive Non-scoring Runs: 5 from 15.3.2011.

MANAGERS

Edwin Browne 1883–93; **Tom Featherstone** 1893; **Tom Harris** 1893–1913; **Albert Fisher** 1913–27; **Horace Henshall** 1927–34; **Charlie Jones** 1934; **David Pratt** 1935; **Percy Smith** 1935–36; **Jimmy McMullan** 1936–37; **Harry Parkes** 1938–39; **Tony Towers** 1939–42; **Frank Womack** 1942–43; **Major Frank Buckley** 1944–46; **Arthur Stollery** 1946–49; **Eric Houghton** 1949–53; **George Poyser** 1953–57; **Tommy Lawton** 1957–58; **Frank Hill** 1958–61; **Tim Coleman** 1961–63; **Eddie Lowe** 1963–65; **Tim Coleman** 1965–66; **Jack Burkitt** 1966–67; **Andy Beattie** *(General Manager)* 1967; **Billy Gray** 1967–68; **Jack Wheeler** *(Caretaker Manager)* 1968–69; **Jimmy Sirrel** 1969–75; **Ron Fenton** 1975–77; **Jimmy Sirrel** 1978–82 *(continued as General Manager to 1984)*; **Howard Wilkinson** 1982–83; **Larry Lloyd** 1983–84; **Richie Barker** 1984–85; **Jimmy Sirrel** 1985–87; **John Barnwell** 1987–88; **Neil Warnock** 1989–93; **Mick Walker** 1993–94; **Russell Slade** 1994–95; **Howard Kendall** 1995; **Colin Murphy** 1995–96 *(General Manager)*; **Steve Thompson** 1995–96; **Sam Allardyce** 1997–99; **Gary Brazil** 1999–2000; **Jocky Scott** 2000–01; **Gary Brazil** 2001–02; **Billy Dearden** 2002–04; **Gary Mills** 2004; **Ian Richardson** 2004–05; **Gudjon Thordarson** 2005–06; **Steve Thompson** 2006–07; **Ian McParland** 2007–09; **Hans Backe** 2009; **Sven-Göran Eriksson** 2009–10 *(Director of Football)*; **Steve Cotterill** 2010; **Craig Short** 2010; **Paul Ince** 2010–11; **Martin Allen** 2011–12; **Keith Curle** 2012–13; **Chris Kiwomya** 2013; **Shaun Derry** 2013–15; **Ricardo Moniz** 2015; **Jamie Fullarton** 2016; **Mark Cooper** 2016; **John Sheridan** 2016–17; **Kevin Nolan** January 2017–

TEN YEAR LEAGUE RECORD

		P	W	D	L	F	A	Pts	Pos
2008-09	FL 2	46	11	14	21	49	69	47	19
2009-10	FL 2	46	27	12	7	96	31	93	1
2010-11	FL 1	46	14	8	24	46	60	50	19
2011-12	FL 1	46	21	10	15	75	63	73	7
2012-13	FL 1	46	16	17	13	61	49	65	12
2013-14	FL 1	46	15	5	26	64	77	50	20
2014-15	FL 1	46	12	14	20	45	63	50	21
2015-16	FL 2	46	14	9	23	54	83	51	17
2016-17	FL 2	46	16	8	22	54	76	56	16
2017-18	FL 2	46	21	14	11	71	48	77	5

DID YOU KNOW ?

The first Player of the Year for Notts County was goalkeeper George Smith in 1964–65. Since then two players have won the award on three occasions: Don Masson (1969, 1974, 1981) and Ian Richardson (jointly in 1999 and outright in 2004 and 2005).

NOTTS COUNTY – SKY BET LEAGUE TWO 2017–18 LEAGUE RECORD

Match No.	Date		Venue	Opponents	Result		H/T Score	Lg Pos.	Goalscorers	Atten- dance
1	Aug	5	A	Coventry C	L	0-3	0-1	23		10,350
2		12	H	Chesterfield	W	2-0	0-0	14	Grant 2 [60, 90]	7021
3		19	A	Wycombe W	W	4-2	2-0	7	Duffy [14], El-Abd (og) [15], Forte [84], Alessandra [89]	3785
4		25	H	Accrington S	D	2-2	1-0	4	Stead (pen) [33], Grant [54]	6087
5	Sept	2	A	Port Vale	W	1-0	0-0	5	Alessandra [67]	4656
6		9	H	Morecambe	W	2-0	1-0	3	Jones [27], Forte [85]	5305
7		12	H	Swindon T	W	1-0	1-0	2	Stead (pen) [32]	5107
8		16	A	Crawley T	W	1-0	0-0	2	Grant [55]	2352
9		23	H	Lincoln C	W	4-1	1-0	1	Stead [39], Tootle [55], Grant [71], Hawkridge [88]	11,672
10		26	A	Exeter C	W	3-0	1-0	1	Alessandra [2], Grant 2 [61, 82]	4760
11		30	A	Mansfield T	L	1-3	0-0	1	Dickinson [90]	7072
12	Oct	7	H	Forest Green R	D	1-1	0-1	2	Milsom [90]	13,267
13		14	H	Barnet	W	2-1	1-0	1	Ameobi [15], Yates [52]	5804
14		17	A	Crewe Alex	L	0-2	0-1	2		3339
15		21	A	Carlisle U	D	1-1	0-1	2	Yates [58]	4730
16		28	H	Newport Co	W	3-0	1-0	2	Grant 2 [36, 55], Ameobi [52]	6019
17	Nov	11	A	Stevenage	D	1-1	0-1	1	Hewitt [58]	2962
18		18	H	Cheltenham T	W	3-1	1-1	1	Grant 2 [30, 52], Brisley [54]	5809
19		21	A	Yeovil T	D	1-1	1-0	2	Forte [41]	2338
20		25	H	Colchester U	W	2-1	0-0	2	Ameobi (pen) [68], Yates [90]	6770
21	Dec	9	A	Luton T	D	1-1	0-1	2	Ameobi [61]	10,063
22		16	H	Grimsby T	D	0-0	0-0	2		8016
23		23	H	Cambridge U	D	3-3	0-1	2	Alessandra [74], Brisley [87], Forte [90]	6102
24		26	A	Morecambe	W	4-1	2-0	2	Grant 2 [13, 59], Alessandra 2 [21, 86]	1947
25		30	A	Swindon T	L	0-1	0-0	2		6247
26	Jan	1	H	Port Vale	W	1-0	0-0	2	Stead (pen) [86]	7241
27		13	A	Lincoln C	D	2-2	1-1	2	Stead [35], Grant [76]	9603
28		20	H	Exeter C	L	1-2	0-2	2	Stead (pen) [73]	6677
29		23	H	Crawley T	L	1-2	0-1	2	Stead (pen) [58]	3738
30	Feb	3	H	Crewe Alex	W	4-1	2-1	3	Husin [15], Hewitt 2 [41, 60], Bennett [89]	17,274
31		10	A	Barnet	L	0-1	0-0	4		1752
32		13	H	Carlisle U	W	2-1	2-0	4	Stead 2 [19, 35]	3889
33		17	A	Newport Co	D	0-0	0-0	5		3326
34		20	A	Cambridge U	L	0-1	0-1	5		3524
35		24	H	Stevenage	W	2-0	0-0	4	Grant [77], Ameobi [80]	5684
36	Mar	6	A	Cheltenham T	D	1-1	1-0	3	Hawkridge [42]	2273
37		10	A	Forest Green R	W	2-1	1-0	3	Noble [34], Tootle [80]	2893
38		17	H	Mansfield T	D	1-1	1-0	3	Hawkridge [35]	12,563
39		25	A	Chesterfield	L	1-3	0-2	4	Jones [85]	6005
40		30	H	Wycombe W	D	0-0	0-0	4		8038
41	Apr	2	A	Accrington S	L	0-1	0-1	5		3039
42		7	A	Coventry C	W	2-1	0-0	5	Forte 2 [60, 86]	10,316
43		14	A	Colchester U	W	3-1	0-1	4	Forte [51], Ameobi [69], Duffy [76]	3599
44		21	H	Yeovil T	W	4-1	1-0	5	Jones [45], James (og) [54], Hewitt [69], Alessandra [73]	7359
45		28	A	Grimsby T	L	1-2	0-1	5	Jones [90]	7133
46	May	5	H	Luton T	D	0-0	0-0	5		12,184

Final League Position: 5

GOALSCORERS

League (71): Grant 15, Stead 9 (5 pens), Alessandra 7, Forte 7, Ameobi 6 (1 pen), Hewitt 4, Jones 4, Hawkridge 3, Yates 3, Brisley 2, Duffy 2, Tootle 2, Bennett 1, Dickinson 1, Husin 1, Milsom 1, Noble 1, own goals 2.
FA Cup (10): Stead 4 (1 pen), Grant 2, Yates 2, Duffy 1, Husin 1.
Carabao Cup (3): Brisley 1, Grant 1, Yates 1.
Checkatrade Trophy (4): Forte 2, Hollis 1, Smith 1.
League Two Play-Offs (2): Forte 1, Grant 1.

Player appearances (shirt number shown per match; superscript in brackets = goals scored):

Collin A 30	Tootle M 36	Duffy R 43	Brisley S 36+1	Jones D 23+4	Hawkridge T 29+2	Hewitt E 35+8	Walker L 6+5	Alessandra L 27+12	Ameobi S 26+8	Stead J 38+5	Milsom R 12+5	Grant J 35+10	Yates R 25	Forte J 13+17	Smith A —+1	Hunt M 10+3	Dickinson C 23+2	Fitzsimons R 16+1	Saunders C —+3	Bird P —+1	Hodge E —+1	Virtue M 9+4	Noble L 13+5	Husin N 10+2	Pindroch B —+1	Bennett M 1+1	Hall B 9+2	O'Connor M 1+5	Match No.
1	2	3	4	5	6	7	8[1]	9	10	11[2]	12	13																	1
1	2[1]	3	4	5	6	7	14	9[3]	10	11[2]				12	8	13													2
1	2	3	4	5	6[1]	7		13	11[3]	10[2]		9	8	12	14														3
1	2[3]	3	4	5	9[3]	8[1]			10	11[2]	13	6	7	12			14												4
1		3	4	5	6[1]	8	14	11[3]	10	12		9	7	13		2[1]													5
1		3	4	5	6	7	14	10[3]	11	13		9[2]	8	12		2[1]													6
1	2	3	4		6[2]	13		9[3]	10[1]	7	12	8	11	14			5												7
1	2	3	4[2]	5	13	12		9[3]		11	7	6	8	10[3]		14													8
1	2	3	4	5[2]	9	13		11[1]	8[3]	6	7	10	14				12												9
1		3			6[2]	4		9[3]	11	10[1]	8	12	7	13	14	2	5												10
1	2	3[1]	4			14	12	6[2]	13	11	8	9	7	10[1]			5												11
1	2	3	4		6[2]	14		12	13	10[1]	8	9	7[3]	11			5												12
1[2]	2	3	4			14		6[3]	10[1]	11	8	9	7	13			5	12											13
1	2	3	6[2]	4	9[1]	11	14	12	8	13	7	10[3]					5	1											14
	2[2]	3	4		6	7		12	10[1]	11[3]		9	8	13	14		5	1											15
	2[1]	3[2]	4		6	8	12	11	10[3]	9	7			14	13		5	1											16
	2	3	4		9	7		6[1]	10	11	8	12					5	1											17
	2	3	4		6[2]	13	14	11[1]	10	8[3]		9	7	12			5	1											18
	2	3	4		6	13		11	10[2]	8[1]		9	7	12			5	1											19
	2	3[2]	4	14	6[3]	8		10[1]	11	12		9	7	13			5	1											20
	2	3	4		6[1]	8		12	10	11[2]		9	7	13			5	1											21
	2	3	4		6[2]	8		13	11	10[1]		9	7	12			5	1											22
	2	3	4	13	6[1]	8		12	11	10[2]		9	7	14			5[3]	1											23
	4[1]	3[2]	5			7	6		10	11[2]				9	8		13	2		1		12	14						24
	2	3	13	6[3]	4	8[1]	10		11			9	7				5[2]	1				12	14						25
	2	3	4	5		8	6	10[1]		9		7		11[2]			13	1	12										26
	2	3[3]	4	5	6[1]	7		11	13	10		9	14									8[2]	12						27
	4[1]	3	13	5	6		12	11	10						2	14		1					8[1]	9	7[3]				28
		3	4[1]	5		13		6	12	11		10			2	1		1				9[4]	8[1]	6[3]	14				29
1		3	4	5		8	6	11[3]	10[1]	9				14	2								13	7[2]		12			30
1	2	3	4	5	6[1]		13		11	8[3]		9		12									14	7[2]			10[2]		31
1	2	3		5		8[2]			9	11[1]	10			13	12								6	7			4		32
1	4					7		11		10		9		13	2	5						12	6[1]	8[2]			3		33
1	2			5		8		11[3]	12	10		9[2]		13								14	6	7[1]			4		34
1	2	3				9	8	6[1]	10[3]	11		12				5							13	7[2]			4		35
1	2	3				6	8		10[3]	11[1]		9		12	14	5							13	7[2]			4		36
1	2	3	14		6[2]	7		10	13	11[3]		9				5						12	8				4[1]		37
1	2	3			6[2]	7		12	11	10		9			13	5							8[1]				4		38
1	2	3	4	14	6[1]	7		9	11	10		12				5[3]						13	8[2]						39
1	2	3	4	5	6[1]	7		9	11	10		12											8						40
1	2	3				7[2]	9[1]		13	11	12	10				5						4	6[3]			8	14		41
1	2	3	4	5		7		10[2]		9		11										8	6[1]				13	12	42
1	2	3	4	5		8		11[2]	12	9[1]		10										6	7[3]				14	13	43
1		3	4	5		7[2]		9	10[2]	12		11			2							6	8[1]	14				13	44
1		3	4	5		7		9	10[2]	12		13		11	2[1]							6[2]	8					14	45
1	2		4	5		7		12		10[3]		9	11									6[1]	13			3	8[1]		46

FA Cup

First Round	Bristol R	(h)	4-2
Second Round	Oxford C	(h)	3-2
Third Round	Brentford	(a)	1-0
Fourth Round	Swansea C	(h)	1-1
Replay	Swansea C	(a)	1-8

Carabao Cup

First Round	Scunthorpe U	(a)	3-3

(aet; Scunthorpe U won 6-5 on penalties)

Checkatrade Trophy

Northern Group G	Everton U21	(h)	2-1
Northern Group G	Mansfield T	(h)	1-2
Northern Group G	Lincoln C	(a)	1-2

League Two Play-Offs

Semi-Final 1st leg	Coventry C	(a)	1-1
Semi-Final 2nd leg	Coventry C	(h)	1-4

OLDHAM ATHLETIC

FOUNDATION

It was in 1895 that John Garland, the landlord of the Featherstall and Junction Hotel, decided to form a football club. As Pine Villa they played in the Oldham Junior League. In 1899 the local professional club, Oldham County, went out of existence and one of the liquidators persuaded Pine Villa to take over their ground at Sheepfoot Lane and change their name to Oldham Athletic.

SportsDirect.com Park, Furtherwood Road, Oldham, Lancashire OL1 2PB.

Telephone: (0161) 624 4972.

Fax: (0161) 627 5915.

Ticket Office: (0161) 785 5150.

Website: www.oldhamathletic.co.uk

Email: enquiries@oldhamathletic.co.uk

Ground Capacity: 13,488.

Record Attendance: 46,471 v Sheffield W, FA Cup 4th rd, 25 January 1930.

Pitch Measurements: 100m × 68m (109yd × 74yd).

Chairman: Simon Corney.

Chief Executive: Mark Moisley.

Manager: Frankie Bunn.

First-Team Coach: Andy Rhodes.

Colours: Blue shirts with white trim, white shorts with blue trim, blue socks with white trim.

Year Formed: 1895.

Turned Professional: 1899.

Previous Name: 1895, Pine Villa; 1899, Oldham Athletic.

Club Nickname: 'The Latics'.

Grounds: 1895, Sheepfoot Lane; 1900, Hudson Field; 1906, Sheepfoot Lane; 1907, Boundary Park (renamed SportsDirect.com Park 2014).

First Football League Game: 9 September 1907, Division 2, v Stoke (a) W 3–1 – Hewitson; Hodson, Hamilton; Fay, Walders, Wilson; Ward, Billy Dodds (1), Newton (1), Hancock, Swarbrick (1).

Record League Victory: 11–0 v Southport, Division 4, 26 December 1962 – Bollands; Branagan, Marshall; McCall, Williams, Scott; Ledger (1), Johnstone, Lister (6), Colquhoun (1), Whitaker (3).

Record Cup Victory: 10–1 v Lytham, FA Cup 1st rd, 28 November 1925 – Gray; Wynne, Grundy; Adlam, Heaton, Naylor (1), Douglas, Pynegar (2), Ormston (2), Barnes (3), Watson (2).

Record Defeat: 4–13 v Tranmere R, Division 3 (N), 26 December 1935.

HONOURS

League Champions: Division 2 – 1990–91; Division 3 – 1973–74; Division 3N – 1952–53.
Runners-up: Division 1 – 1914–15; Division 2 – 1909–10; Division 4 – 1962–63.
FA Cup: semi-final – 1913, 1990, 1994.
League Cup: *Runners-up:* 1990.

Sun FACT FILE

Loanee Danny Lafferty's 78th-minute goal at Scunthorpe on 27 February 2016 gave Oldham Athletic a narrow lead in a match that eventually ended 1-1. The goal had some historical significance as it was the club's 6,000th in the Football League.

Most League Points (2 for a win): 62, Division 3, 1973–74.

Most League Points (3 for a win): 88, Division 2, 1990–91.

Most League Goals: 95, Division 4, 1962–63.

Highest League Scorer in Season: Tom Davis, 33, Division 3 (N), 1936–37.

Most League Goals in Total Aggregate: Roger Palmer, 141, 1980–94.

Most League Goals in One Match: 7, Eric Gemmell v Chester, Division 3 (N), 19 January 1952.

Most Capped Player: Gunnar Halle, 24 (64), Norway.

Most League Appearances: Ian Wood, 525, 1966–80.

Youngest League Player: Wayne Harrison, 16 years 347 days v Notts Co, 27 October 1984.

Record Transfer Fee Received: £1,700,000 from Aston Villa for Earl Barrett, February 1992.

Record Transfer Fee Paid: £750,000 to Aston Villa for Ian Olney, June 1992.

Football League Record: 1907 Elected to Division 2; 1910–23 Division 1; 1923–35 Division 2; 1935–53 Division 3 (N); 1953–54 Division 2; 1954–58 Division 3 (N); 1958–63 Division 4; 1963–69 Division 3; 1969–71 Division 4; 1971–74 Division 3; 1974–91 Division 2; 1991–92 Division 1; 1992–94 FA Premier League; 1994–97 Division 1; 1997–2004 Division 2; 2004–18 FL 1; 2018– FL 2.

LATEST SEQUENCES

Longest Sequence of League Wins: 10, 12.1.1974 – 12.3.1974.

Longest Sequence of League Defeats: 8, 15.12.1934 – 2.2.1935.

Longest Sequence of League Draws: 5, 7.4.2018 – 21.4.2018.

Longest Sequence of Unbeaten League Matches: 20, 1.5.1990 – 10.11.1990.

Longest Sequence Without a League Win: 17, 4.9.1920 – 18.12.1920.

Successive Scoring Runs: 25 from 25.8.1962.

Successive Non-scoring Runs: 6 from 12.2.2011.

MANAGERS

David Ashworth 1906–14
Herbert Bamlett 1914–21
Charlie Roberts 1921–22
David Ashworth 1923–24
Bob Mellor 1924–27
Andy Wilson 1927–32
Bob Mellor 1932–33
Jimmy McMullan 1933–34
Bob Mellor 1934–45
   (continued as Secretary to 1953)
Frank Womack 1945–47
Billy Wootton 1947–50
George Hardwick 1950–56
Ted Goodier 1956–58
Norman Dodgin 1958–60
Danny McLennan 1960
Jack Rowley 1960–63
Les McDowall 1963–65
Gordon Hurst 1965–66
Jimmy McIlroy 1966–68
Jack Rowley 1968–69
Jimmy Frizzell 1970–82
Joe Royle 1982–94
Graeme Sharp 1994–97
Neil Warnock 1997–98
Andy Ritchie 1998–2001
Mick Wadsworth 2001–02
Iain Dowie 2002–03
Brian Talbot 2004–05
Ronnie Moore 2005–06
John Sheridan 2006–09
Joe Royle 2009
Dave Penney 2009–10
Paul Dickov 2010–13
Lee Johnson 2013–15
Dean Holden 2015
Darren Kelly 2015
David Dunn 2015–16
John Sheridan 2016
Stephen Robinson 2016–17
John Sheridan 2017
Richie Wellens 2017–18
Frankie Bunn June 2018–

TEN YEAR LEAGUE RECORD

		P	W	D	L	F	A	Pts	Pos
2008-09	FL 1	46	16	17	13	66	65	65	10
2009-10	FL 1	46	13	13	20	39	57	52	16
2010-11	FL 1	46	13	17	16	53	60	56	17
2011-12	FL 1	46	14	12	20	50	66	54	16
2012-13	FL 1	46	14	9	23	46	59	51	19
2013-14	FL 1	46	14	14	18	50	59	56	15
2014-15	FL 1	46	14	15	17	54	67	57	15
2015-16	FL 1	46	12	18	16	44	58	54	17
2016-17	FL 1	46	12	17	17	31	44	53	17
2017-18	FL 1	46	11	17	18	58	75	50	21

DID YOU KNOW ?

Oldham Athletic have played at Boundary Park since joining the Football League in 1907. It is one of the most exposed of all senior grounds in England and at 509 feet above sea level it is the third-highest League ground in the country, after those of West Bromwich Albion and Port Vale.

OLDHAM ATHLETIC – SKY BET LEAGUE ONE 2017–18 LEAGUE RECORD

Match No.	Date		Venue	Opponents	Result		H/T Score	Lg Pos.	Goalscorers	Attendance
1	Aug	5	H	Oxford U	L	0-2	0-1	22		4874
2		12	A	Walsall	L	1-2	1-0	23	McLaughlin [32]	4419
3		19	H	Wigan Ath	L	0-2	0-2	24		5446
4		26	A	Blackpool	L	1-2	0-2	23	Osei [70]	4642
5	Sept	2	H	Charlton Ath	L	3-4	1-2	23	Davies (pen) [34], Doyle [51], Byrne [82]	3592
6		9	A	Fleetwood T	D	2-2	1-1	24	Davies [18], Bryan [55]	3606
7		12	A	Bristol R	W	3-2	0-0	21	Byrne [49], Davies [71], Doyle [88]	7908
8		16	H	Shrewsbury T	L	1-2	1-1	24	Davies [33]	4150
9		23	H	Rotherham U	L	1-5	1-1	24	Davies [21]	8250
10		26	H	Peterborough U	W	3-2	0-0	23	Doyle 2 [51, 85], Gardner [80]	2975
11		30	A	Portsmouth	W	2-1	1-0	18	Doyle 2 [16, 47]	17,848
12	Oct	14	H	Blackburn R	W	1-0	0-0	17	Menig [90]	7784
13		17	A	Bradford C	D	1-1	1-1	19	Doyle [23]	19,840
14		21	A	Milton Keynes D	D	4-4	3-1	20	Davies [7], Doyle [39], Walsh (og) [45], Clarke [63]	9312
15		24	H	Bury	W	2-1	1-0	17	Doyle [24], Amadi-Holloway [90]	5183
16		28	H	Scunthorpe U	L	2-3	1-2	18	Clarke [45], Davies [81]	4331
17	Nov	18	H	Rochdale	W	3-1	1-1	15	Dummigan [2], Doyle 2 [83, 86]	6129
18		21	H	AFC Wimbledon	D	0-0	0-0	16		3169
19		25	A	Gillingham	D	0-0	0-0	17		4364
20	Dec	2	A	Southend U	L	0-2	0-1	18		5608
21		9	H	Northampton T	W	5-1	3-0	16	Byrne 2 [4, 45], Obadeyi [26], Nepomuceno [60], Davies [90]	3532
22		16	A	Doncaster R	D	1-1	0-0	15	Doyle [88]	7831
23		23	A	Plymouth Arg	L	1-4	0-2	16	Gerrard [56]	10,017
24		26	H	Fleetwood T	L	1-2	0-0	18	Bryan [82]	4578
25		30	H	Bristol R	L	1-1	0-0	19	Davies [72]	3928
26	Jan	1	A	Shrewsbury T	L	0-1	0-1	20		6383
27		6	A	Charlton Ath	L	0-1	0-1	20		9972
28		13	H	Rotherham U	D	1-1	1-1	20	Davies [31]	4775
29		20	A	Peterborough U	L	0-3	0-0	22		5072
30		27	H	Plymouth Arg	L	1-2	0-2	22	Songo'o (og) [54]	4274
31	Feb	3	H	Bradford C	W	2-1	1-0	21	Dummigan [12], Amadi-Holloway [86]	5526
32		10	A	Blackburn R	D	2-2	2-0	21	Nazon 2 [26, 38]	13,665
33		13	H	Milton Keynes D	W	1-0	1-0	19	Gerrard [40]	3381
34	Mar	3	A	Scunthorpe U	W	2-0	0-0	18	McEleney [78], Doyle [82]	3715
35		10	A	Bury	D	2-2	1-2	19	Davies [42], Pringle [77]	5904
36		17	H	Portsmouth	L	0-2	0-2	19		4306
37		30	A	Wigan Ath	L	0-3	0-1	21		10,625
38	Apr	2	H	Blackpool	W	2-1	0-1	19	Byrne [60], Doyle [86]	4309
39		7	A	Oxford U	D	0-0	0-0	19		7096
40		11	H	Walsall	D	1-1	1-1	20	Nazon [45]	3424
41		14	H	Gillingham	D	1-1	1-0	20	Nazon [45]	3850
42		17	A	Rochdale	D	0-0	0-0	20		6261
43		21	A	AFC Wimbledon	D	2-2	0-1	20	Nazon 2 [50, 74]	4850
44		24	H	Southend U	L	0-3	0-1	21		3362
45		28	H	Doncaster R	D	0-0	0-0	20		5297
46	May	5	A	Northampton T	D	2-2	1-2	21	Edmundson [29], Haymer [55]	6511

Final League Position: 21

GOALSCORERS

League (58): Doyle 14, Davies 11 (1 pen), Nazon 6, Byrne 5, Amadi-Holloway 2, Bryan 2, Clarke 2, Dummigan 2, Gerrard 2, Edmundson 1, Gardner 1, Haymer 1, McEleney 1, McLaughlin 1, Menig 1, Nepomuceno 1, Obadeyi 1, Osei 1, Pringle 1, own goals 2.
FA Cup (2): Clarke 1, Holloway 1.
Carabao Cup (2): Davies 1 (1 pen), Green 1.
Checkatrade Trophy (11): Byrne 3, Davies 2, Doyle 2, Obadeyi 2, Gerrard 1, Holloway 1.

Wilson Ben 5	Hunt R 32+1	Clarke P 18+1	Gerrard A 30+1	Wilson Brian 13+6	Banks O 5+2	Fane O 38+3	Green P 3+3	McLaughlin R 10+6	Amadi-Holloway A 7+29	Davies C 34+6	Obadeyi T 10+12	Flynn R 2+5	Duffus C —+6	Dummigan C 28+2	Fawns M 1+3	Gardiner D 42+1	Kyereneh G 1	Osei D 1+2	Mantack K —+1	Bryan K 32	Byrne J 37+3	Doyle E 28+2	Ruddy J 5	Edmundson S 14+1	Nepomuceno G 20+6	Menig Q 4+10	Omrani A 1+7	Placide J 36	Maouche M —+1	Benyu K 3+1	Pringle B 13	Nazon D 13+3	Moimbe W 11	McEleney P 4+5	Haymer T 5+2	Benteke J —+1	Match No.
1	2	3	4	5	6²	7	8³	9	10	11¹	12	13	14																								1
1	7	3	4	13	9	6		8	10³	11²	12		14	2	5¹																						2
1	5	3	4	6	8²	11		9³			12	2	14	7	10¹	13																					3
1	6	4	3¹	5	8	9⁴		10				2	12	7	11	13																					4
1	5	4	3	2	7¹	12⁴		11				13	8	14	6²	9³	10																				5
	3	4						5	12	11¹				6		8	7	10		1	2	9															6
	2	3				12		5	13	10²				7		8	6¹	11		1	4	9															7
	3	4				12		6		10	14			5¹		8²	7	11¹		1	2¹	9	13														8
	3	4						5¹		10	11³			12		8²	9	7		1	2	6	14	13													9
2	4		3⁴	13	8			11³						12		6	7	9²	10			5¹			14	1											10
6	3			13	8			11						2		9²	4	7¹	10			5³	14	12		1											11
5	3	14			7			10						2		6²	4	8	11¹			9²	12	13		1											12
5	3				6			11	14					2		7¹	4	8²	10			9³	12	13		1											13
5	3				7			11¹	13					2		6¹	4	8	10			12	9²	14		1											14
5	4				7	13		14	10³					2		6	3	8²	11				9¹	12		1											15
5¹	3²	13			7			14	10					2		6	4	9	11	1			12	8³													16
5	14	4³			7			12	11¹					2		8	3	6	10			9	13			1											17
5³	3				7	8		13	11¹			14	2			4	6	10				9²	12			1											18
5	3				8	14		12	10⁴					2		7³	4	6	11			9¹	13			1											19
5	3¹	13			8			10	14					2		7	4	6²	11			12	9³			1											20
5	3				7			14	13	11³	12			2		6	4	9	10			8²				1											21
5³	4	2			7		13	14	12		8¹			6		3	9	11				10²				1											22
12	3	4			7¹		5²	13	10	14	11			2		6	9					8³				1											23
5	3³				7			13	10	11	8²		14	2		6¹	4	9				12				1											24
5	3				7			11	14	9	12			2		6²	4	13				10¹	8²			1											25
5	3				7²	14		12	11	10¹	8³			2		6	4	9					13			1											26
5²	3	4		8³	7			11	10	12			14	2		6¹							9				1	13									27
	3	5			8		12	13	10	11				2¹		7²					4	14					1		6³	9							28
	4¹	3			6		13	11	10⁰					2		14				8	7			12⁴		5		1	9³	5							29
	3				7¹		6²	13	11					2		8	4	10				5					1		9	12							30
	3				6		13	12	10	14				2		7²	4	9¹									1		8	11³	5						31
	3	14			7			13	11²	12				2		6	4	8³									1		9	10¹	5⁴						32
	3				8		14	12	10	13				2		6	4	9²				5					1		8³	11¹							33
	3				8			13	10¹					2		7	4	6	14								1		9²	11¹	5	12					34
	3³	12			8			13	10²					2		7	4	6	14								1		9	11¹	5						35
		3			8			9²	13	11¹				2		7	4	6	10								1		14	5³	12						36
2		3			6		14	13	10²					8		4	9⁰	11									1		7¹	5	12						37
2					3			14		13				8		4	12	10		9							1		7²	11	5	6¹					38
2					3			14		11¹				6		4⁴	7	10³	8								1		13	5	9	12					39
2	3				7			12	14	13				6				8¹	10	4		12					1		9²	5	11²						40
2	3				7			13						8				6	10¹	4		12					1		9²	5⁴	11³	14					41
5	3				7			13	14					6				9¹	11	4							1		10³	8²		12	2				42
5	3³	14			8			13	11²	6¹				7				12	10	4							1		9				2				43
5		2			8²			12	10³					7				6	11	3	14						1		9¹				4	13			44
2								12						8				10²	11	4	5						1		6	7¹	9		13	3			45
2								14	12					7²				8	11	4	9³						1		13	6	10¹	5		3			46

FA Cup

First Round	Carlisle U	(a)	2-3

Carabao Cup

First Round	Burton Alb	(h)	2-3

Checkatrade Trophy

Northern Group D	Port Vale	(h)	0-0
(Port Vale won 4-2 on penalties)			
Northern Group D	Crewe Alex	(a)	1-0
Northern Group D	Newcastle U U21	(h)	4-1
Second Round North	Bradford C	(a)	1-0
Third Round	Leicester C U21	(h)	4-2
Quarter-Final	Shrewsbury T	(a)	1-2

OXFORD UNITED

The Kassam Stadium, Grenoble Road, Oxford OX4 4XP.

Telephone: (01865) 337 500.

Ticket Office: (01865) 337 533.

Website: www.oufc.co.uk

Email: admin@oufc.co.uk

Ground Capacity: 12,573.

Record Attendance: 22,730 v Preston NE, FA Cup 6th rd, 29 February 1964 (at Manor Ground); 12,243 v Leyton Orient, FL 2, 6 May 2006 (at The Kassam Stadium).

Pitch Measurements: 100.5m × 64m (110yd × 70yd).

Chairman: Sumrith 'Tiger' Thanakarnjanasuth.

Head Coach: Karl Robinson.

Assistant Head Coach: Derek Fazackerley.

HONOURS

League Champions: Division 2 – 1984–85; Division 3 – 1967–68, 1983–84.

Runners-up: Second Division – 1995–96; FL 2 – 2015–16; Conference – (3rd) 2009–10 *(promoted via play-offs)*.

FA Cup: 6th rd – 1964.

League Cup Winners: 1986.

League Trophy: Runners-up: 2016, 2017.

Colours: Yellow shirts with blue trim, blue shorts with yellow trim, blue socks with yellow trim.

Year Formed: 1893.

Turned Professional: 1949.

Previous Names: 1893, Headington; 1894, Headington United; 1960, Oxford United.

Club Nickname: 'The U's'.

Grounds: 1893, Headington Quarry; 1894, Wootten's Fields; 1898, Sandy Lane Ground; 1902, Britannia Field; 1909, Sandy Lane; 1910, Quarry Recreation Ground; 1914, Sandy Lane; 1922, The Paddock Manor Road; 1925, Manor Ground; 2001, The Kassam Stadium.

First Football League Game: 18 August 1962, Division 4, v Barrow (a) L 2–3 – Medlock; Beavon, Quartermain; Ron Atkinson, Kyle, Jones; Knight, Graham Atkinson (1), Houghton (1), Cornwell, Colfar.

Record League Victory: 7–0 v Barrow, Division 4, 19 December 1964 – Fearnley; Beavon, Quartermain; Ron Atkinson (1), Kyle, Jones; Morris, Booth (3), Willey (1), Graham Atkinson (1), Harrington (1).

Record Cup Victory: 9–1 v Dorchester T, FA Cup 1st rd, 11 November 1995 – Whitehead; Wood (2), Mike Ford (1), Smith, Elliott, Gilchrist, Rush (1), Massey (Murphy), Moody (3), Bobby Ford (1), Angel (Beauchamp (1)).

Record Defeat: 0–7 v Sunderland, Division 1, 19 September 1998; 0–7 v Wigan Ath, FL 1, 23 December 2017.

Most League Points (2 for a win): 61, Division 4, 1964–65.

☀️THE Sun FACT FILE

Headington United were the first British professional club to play a home fixture under floodlights when they faced Birmingham Combination team Banbury Spencer at the Manor Ground on 18 December 1950 – just a week after the Football Association lifted their ban on floodlit football. United won 3-0 in front of a crowd of 2,603.

Most League Points (3 for a win): 95, Division 3, 1983–84.

Most League Goals: 91, Division 3, 1983–84.

Highest League Scorer in Season: John Aldridge, 30, Division 2, 1984–85.

Most League Goals in Total Aggregate: Graham Atkinson, 77, 1962–73.

Most League Goals in One Match: 4, Tony Jones v Newport Co, Division 4, 22 September 1962; 4, Arthur Longbottom v Darlington, Division 4, 26 October 1963; 4, Richard Hill v Walsall, Division 2, 26 December 1988; 4, John Durnin v Luton T, 14 November 1992; 4, Tom Craddock v Accrington S, FL 2, 20 October 2011.

Most Capped Player: Jim Magilton, 18 (52), Northern Ireland.

Most League Appearances: John Shuker, 478, 1962–77.

Youngest League Player: Jason Seacole, 16 years 149 days v Mansfield T, 7 September 1976.

Record Transfer Fee Received: £3,000,000 from Leeds U for Kemar Roofe, July 2016.

Record Transfer Fee Paid: £470,000 to Aberdeen for Dean Windass, July 1998.

Football League Record: 1962 Elected to Division 4; 1965–68 Division 3; 1968–76 Division 2; 1976–84 Division 3; 1984–85 Division 2; 1985–88 Division 1; 1988–92 Division 2; 1992–94 Division 1; 1994–96 Division 2; 1996–99 Division 1; 1999–2001 Division 2; 2001–04 Division 3; 2004–06 FL 2; 2006–10 Conference; 2010–16 FL 2; 2016– FL 1.

LATEST SEQUENCES

Longest Sequence of League Wins: 6, 13.4.2013 – 17.8.2013.

Longest Sequence of League Defeats: 8, 18.4.2014 – 23.8.2014.

Longest Sequence of League Draws: 5, 7.10.1978 – 28.10.1978.

Longest Sequence of Unbeaten League Matches: 20, 17.3.1984 – 29.9.1984.

Longest Sequence Without a League Win: 27, 14.11.1987 – 27.8.1988.

Successive Scoring Runs: 17 from 22.4.2006.

Successive Non-scoring Runs: 6 from 26.3.1988.

MANAGERS

Harry Thompson 1949–58
(Player-Manager) 1949-51
Arthur Turner 1959–69
(continued as General Manager to 1972)
Ron Saunders 1969
Gerry Summers 1969–75
Mick Brown 1975–79
Bill Asprey 1979–80
Ian Greaves 1980–82
Jim Smith 1982–85
Maurice Evans 1985–88
Mark Lawrenson 1988
Brian Horton 1988–93
Denis Smith 1993–97
Malcolm Crosby 1997–98
Malcolm Shotton 1998–99
Micky Lewis 1999–2000
Denis Smith 2000
David Kemp 2000–01
Mark Wright 2001
Ian Atkins 2001–04
Graham Rix 2004
Ramon Diaz 2004–05
Brian Talbot 2005–06
Darren Patterson 2006
Jim Smith 2006–07
Darren Patterson 2007–08
Chris Wilder 2008–14
Gary Waddock 2014
Michael Appleton 2014–17
Pep Clotet 2017–18
Karl Robinson March 2018–

TEN YEAR LEAGUE RECORD

		P	W	D	L	F	A	Pts	Pos
2008-09	Conf P	46	24	10	12	72	51	77*	7
2009-10	Conf P	44	25	11	8	64	31	86	3
2010-11	FL 2	46	17	12	17	58	60	63	12
2011-12	FL 2	46	17	17	12	59	48	68	9
2012-13	FL 2	46	19	8	19	60	61	65	9
2013-14	FL 2	46	16	14	16	53	50	62	8
2014-15	FL 2	46	15	16	15	50	49	61	13
2015-16	FL 2	46	24	14	8	84	41	86	2
2016-17	FL 1	46	20	9	17	65	52	69	8
2017-18	FL 1	46	15	11	20	61	66	56	16

*5 pts deducted.

DID YOU KNOW ❓

Goalkeeper Alan Judge became Oxford United's oldest player when he appeared in a League Two game against Southend United on 6 November 2004. Judge, who was aged 44 years and 176 days, was on Oxford's coaching staff at the time. Southend won the game 4-0.

OXFORD UNITED – SKY BET LEAGUE ONE 2017–18 LEAGUE RECORD

Match No.	Date	Venue	Opponents	Result	H/T Score	Lg Pos.	Goalscorers	Attendance
1	Aug 5	A	Oldham Ath	W 2-0	1-0	2	Thomas [39], Ruffels [71]	4874
2	12	H	Portsmouth	W 3-0	0-0	1	Thomas [47], Novillo [82], Ruffels [90]	9510
3	19	A	Scunthorpe U	L 0-1	0-0	5		4205
4	26	H	Shrewsbury T	D 1-1	0-0	7	Van Kessel [75]	7120
5	Sept 2	A	Milton Keynes D	D 1-1	1-0	9	Hall [8]	10,746
6	9	H	Gillingham	W 3-0	0-0	6	Payne [48], Rothwell [54], Hall [56]	6730
7	12	H	Bradford C	D 2-2	0-1	8	Thomas [74], Rothwell [87]	6658
8	16	A	Blackpool	L 1-3	0-2	9	Henry [90]	5274
9	23	H	Walsall	L 1-2	0-1	12	Ledson (pen) [78]	6895
10	26	A	Bury	L 0-3	0-0	15		2951
11	30	A	Peterborough U	W 4-1	0-1	13	Ruffels [48], Thomas [53], Rothwell [75], Mehmeti [82]	6153
12	Oct 7	H	AFC Wimbledon	W 3-0	1-0	10	Thomas [12], Ricardinho [48], Fernandez Codina [85]	7241
13	14	H	Bristol R	W 1-0	0-0	6	Mowatt [82]	9656
14	17	H	Charlton Ath	D 1-1	1-1	6	Ribeiro [35]	7070
15	21	H	Rotherham U	D 3-3	3-2	7	Payne [21], Ruffels [30], Nelson [40]	7471
16	28	A	Fleetwood T	L 0-2	0-0	10		3261
17	Nov 11	H	Northampton T	L 1-2	1-2	10	Thomas [44]	8267
18	18	A	Plymouth Arg	W 4-0	1-0	7	Ledson (pen) [15], Thomas [52], Henry [68], Obika [77]	10,805
19	21	H	Blackburn R	L 2-4	1-3	8	Payne [45], Obika [85]	6965
20	25	A	Southend U	D 1-1	1-1	9	Thomas [22]	6797
21	Dec 9	H	Doncaster R	W 1-0	0-0	8	Ruffels [90]	6711
22	16	A	Rochdale	D 0-0	0-0	8		2588
23	23	H	Wigan Ath	L 0-7	0-3	10		7957
24	26	A	Gillingham	D 1-1	0-0	10	Ricardinho [52]	5555
25	30	A	Bradford C	L 2-3	0-1	12	Carroll [50], Obika [75]	19,691
26	Jan 1	H	Milton Keynes D	W 3-1	2-1	10	Thomas [15], Van Kessel [45], Obika [59]	7628
27	6	H	Blackpool	W 1-0	0-0	10	Obika [80]	6775
28	13	A	Walsall	L 1-2	0-1	10	Mowatt [70]	4569
29	20	H	Bury	L 1-2	1-0	10	Henry [45]	6457
30	Feb 3	A	Charlton Ath	W 3-2	0-0	10	Henry [76], Kane [89], Ledson [90]	11,747
31	10	H	Bristol R	L 1-2	1-0	12	Rothwell [2]	8471
32	13	H	Rotherham U	L 1-3	1-2	13	Henry [43]	7707
33	17	H	Plymouth Arg	L 0-1	0-1	15		8301
34	24	A	Northampton T	D 0-0	0-0	15		7095
35	Mar 10	A	AFC Wimbledon	L 1-2	1-1	16	Kane [38]	4592
36	17	H	Peterborough U	W 2-1	1-0	15	Dickie [6], Henry [61]	6804
37	25	A	Portsmouth	L 0-3	0-1	16		17,892
38	30	H	Scunthorpe U	D 1-1	0-1	17	Henry (pen) [56]	7479
39	Apr 2	A	Shrewsbury T	L 2-3	0-1	17	Thomas [62], Rothwell [73]	7191
40	7	H	Oldham Ath	D 0-0	0-0	17		7096
41	10	H	Fleetwood T	L 0-1	0-0	17		6337
42	14	H	Southend U	W 2-0	2-0	17	Henry [6], Ricardinho [45]	7332
43	17	A	Wigan Ath	L 0-1	0-0	17		8316
44	21	A	Doncaster R	L 1-0	0-0	16	Henry [63]	8255
45	28	H	Rochdale	W 2-1	0-0	14	Mousinho (pen) [62], Kane (pen) [83]	8375
46	May 5	A	Blackburn R	L 1-2	0-1	16	Henry [66]	27,600

Final League Position: 16

GOALSCORERS

League (61): Henry 10 (1 pen), Thomas 10, Obika 5, Rothwell 5, Ruffels 5, Kane 3 (1 pen), Ledson 3 (2 pens), Payne 3, Ricardinho 3, Hall 2, Mowatt 2, Van Kessel 2, Carroll 1, Dickie 1, Fernandez Codina 1, Mehmeti 1, Mousinho 1 (1 pen), Nelson 1, Novillo 1, Ribeiro 1.
FA Cup (0).
Carabao Cup (3): Fernandez Codina 1, Johnson 1, Obika 1.
Checkatrade Trophy (14): Payne 4 (1 pen), Hall 3, Van Kessel 2, Henry 1, Mowatt 1, Obika 1, Rothwell 1, Thomas 1.

Eastwood S 46	Ribeiro C 10	Nelson C 18+2	Williamson M 13+1	Johnson M 2	Henry J 34+8	Ledson R 37+7	Ruffels J 33+5	Rothwell J 26+10	Payne J 25+3	Thomas W 32+5	Obika J 20+15	Carroll C 10+2	Ricardinho F 29+7	Hall R 10+3	Novillo H —+2	Van Kessel G 8+13	Tiendalli D 12+1	Martin A 10+2	Mousinho J 40	Mowatt A 20+10	Mehmeti A 3+10	Fernandez Codina J 4+6	Roberts J —+1	Napa M 3+11	Buckley-Rickett I 8+3	Kane T 17	Smith-Brown A 9	Dickie R 15	Brannagan C 12	James O —+1	Match No.
1	2	3	4	5	6	7	8	9^2	10	11^1	12	13																			1
1	2	3	4	6^2	9^3	8	7		10	11^2	12		5	13	14																2
1	2	3	4	8^2	6	7	14	9^1	11^3	12			5	10	13																3
1	5	3	4		9^1	7	8	13	10		12		2	6^2		11															4
1		3	4		9^3	8	14	7	10	11			5	6^2	13	2^1	12														5
1		3			6^3	7	8	10^1	14	11^2	2	5	9	12					4	13											6
1		4	3		9^2	8	14	7^2	10^1	11^2		5	6	12					2	13											7
1		4	3		9	8^1	7		10	11^2		5	6	12					2	13											8
1	5	3			12	7	14	9^2	8^1	10^3			2	6		11			4	13											9
1		4	3		6	7^3	8	14	13		2		9	11^1						5	10^2	12									10
1	2^2	3			8	12	7	5	9	11^1					13	6		10^3	4	14											11
1	2	3			6	8	7	9	10^2	11^1			5				12^3		4	13	14										12
1	2		4		6	8	7	9^3	10^1	11^2			5						3	12	13	14									13
1	2	3			6	7	8		10	11^2			5		13				4	9^1	12										14
1		3			6	8	7	12	10	11^3			2		13				5	4	9^2										15
1	2	3			6	7	8	12	10^2	11			5		13				4		9^1										16
1	3^2				9^3	7	8	10^3		11			5	6	13	2	12		4	14											17
1					6	7^3	8	9	10^1	11^2			5		13	2		3	4	12	14										18
1					6^2	7^1	8	9	10	11^3			5		13	2		4	3	12	14										19
1		4			6^1	14	8	9^2	10	11^3			5		13	2			3	12			7								20
1	3				6^1	7	12	10		11^2			5		13	2			4	9			8								21
1	3				8^2	14	7	12	9^3	11			5		13	2			4	10			6^1								22
1		4			8	14	6^1	13	9^3	11	12		5			2			3	10			7^2								23
1	13				8	7	6	12	10^2	11			2	5				9^1	3	4											24
1	12				7	8	9^1	14		11^3	10		2	5		6^2		3	4	13											25
1						7	8	6	10^2	11^3	2	5					9^1	13	4	3				12	14						26
1				12	14	7	8	6^3		11	10		2			9^2	5		4	3^1		13									27
1					6^2	8		9^3	10^1	11	2		14	5		3	4	7		13					12						28
1					6	12	8		9^3	10^1	11		2			5	3	4		7					11^1						29
1	13		3			7	8^1			11^2			14						2	4	6^2				12	10	5	9			30
1	14		3			8	7			11^2			6^1					3	4		10			13	12	9^3	2	5			31
1	10				9	7		6^3		11^1			14						4	12					13	8^2	2	5	3		32
1	9^2				6			10^3		11	12		14						4			7			13	8	2	5^3	3		33
1	9^3				6			12		11^1	10		13						4			7			14	8^2	2	5	3		34
1	14				6	7		12		11^2	10^1		13						4							8^3	2	5	3	9	35
1					6	7				11^1	10^2		14						4	9^2				13		8	2	5	3		36
1					8^2	6		12		11			14					3		7^4	13			9^1			2	5^1	4	10	37
1					8	7	14	9^1		10^2	12								4	11^3				13			2	5	3	6	38
1	10^1				9	5	5	8		13	7^2								4	11^3				12	14		2	3	6		39
1					8	7	9^1	10		13	11		5						4						12^2	2		3	6		40
1					7	13	8^1			10^2	12		5			14			4	9	11^3					2		3	6		41
1	12				6^3	7				10^1	11		5			13			4	9^2	14					2		3	8		42
1	3					13	6	12		8^3		4	10^1						7	14		11^2	2			5	9				43
1	13				12	6	5	8^2		11	10^1			14					4	9^3					2		3	7			44
1					7	5	8^2			10^3	11		14	12					4	9^1		13				2		3	6		45
1	4				10	12	5	9^3			11^1		13						8^2			6				2		3	7	14	46

FA Cup
First Round — Port Vale — (a) — 0-2

Carabao Cup
First Round — Cheltenham T — (h) — 3-4
(aet)

Checkatrade Trophy
Southern Group G — Stevenage — (a) — 6-2
Southern Group G — Brighton & HA U21 — (h) — 2-2
(Brighton & HA U21 won 5-4 on penalties)
Southern Group G — Milton Keynes D — (h) — 3-4
Second Round — South Gillingham — (a) — 2-1
Third Round — Charlton Ath — (a) — 1-1
(Oxford U won 3-0 on penalties)
Quarter-Final — Chelsea U21 — (a) — 0-3

PETERBOROUGH UNITED

FOUNDATION

The old Peterborough & Fletton club, founded in 1923, was suspended by the FA during season 1932–33 and disbanded. Local enthusiasts determined to carry on and in 1934 a new professional club, Peterborough United, was formed and entered the Midland League the following year. Peterborough's first success came in 1939–40, but from 1955–56 to 1959–60 they won five successive titles. During the 1958–59 season they were undefeated in the Midland League. They reached the third round of the FA Cup, won the Northamptonshire Senior Cup, the Maunsell Cup and were runners-up in the East Anglian Cup.

ABAX Stadium, London Road, Peterborough PE2 8AL.
Telephone: (01733) 563 947. *Fax:* (01733) 344 140.
Ticket Office: (0844) 847 1934.
Website: www.theposh.com
Email: info@theposh.com
Ground Capacity: 14,084.
Record Attendance: 30,096 v Swansea T, FA Cup 5th rd, 20 February 1965.
Pitch Measurements: 102.5m × 64m (112yd × 70yd).
Chairman: Darragh MacAnthony.
Chief Executive: Bob Symns.
Manager: Steve Evans.
First-Team Coach: Paul Raynor.
Colours: Blue shirts with dark blue sleeves, blue shorts with white trim, red socks.
Year Formed: 1934.
Turned Professional: 1934.
Club Nickname: 'The Posh'.
Ground: 1934, London Road Stadium (renamed ABAX Stadium 2014).

HONOURS

League Champions: Division 4 – 1960–61, 1973–74.
Runners-up: FL 1 – 2008–09; FL 2 – 2007–08.
FA Cup: 6th rd – 1965.
League Cup: semi-final – 1966.
League Trophy Winners: 2014.

First Football League Game: 20 August 1960, Division 4, v Wrexham (h) W 3–0 – Walls; Stafford, Walker; Rayner, Rigby, Norris; Hails, Emery (1), Bly (1), Smith, McNamee (1).
Record League Victory: 9–1 v Barnet (a) Division 3, 5 September 1998 – Griemink; Hooper (1), Drury (Farell), Gill, Bodley, Edwards, Davies, Payne, Grazioli (5), Quinn (2) (Rowe), Houghton (Etherington) (1).
Record Cup Victory: 9–1 v Rushden T, FA Cup 1st qual rd, 6 October 1945 – Hilliard; Bryan, Parrott, Warner, Hobbs, Woods, Polhill (1), Fairchild, Laxton (6), Tasker (1), Rodgers (1); 9–1 v Kingstonian, FA Cup 1st rd, 25 November 1992. Match ordered to be replayed by FA. Peterborough won replay 1–0.
Record Defeat: 1–8 v Northampton T, FA Cup 2nd rd (2nd replay), 18 December 1946.
Most League Points (2 for a win): 66, Division 4, 1960–61.

Sun FACT FILE

Entering the final day of the 1990–91 season Peterborough United were one of five clubs separated by just a single point, with four automatic promotion places available. Posh took around 5,000 fans to Chesterfield where a 2-2 draw proved sufficient as rivals Blackpool went down to defeat at Walsall.

Most League Points (3 for a win): 92, FL 2, 2007–08.

Most League Goals: 134, Division 4, 1960–61.

Highest League Scorer in Season: Terry Bly, 52, Division 4, 1960–61.

Most League Goals in Total Aggregate: Jim Hall, 122, 1967–75.

Most League Goals in One Match: 5, Guiliano Grazioli v Barnet, Division 3, 5 September 1998.

Most Capped Player: Gabriel Zakuani, 17 (29), DR Congo.

Most League Appearances: Tommy Robson, 482, 1968–81.

Youngest League Player: Matthew Etherington, 15 years 262 days v Brentford, 3 May 1997.

Record Transfer Fee Received: £5,500,000 from Nottingham F for Britt Assombalonga, August 2014.

Record Transfer Fee Paid: £1,250,000 to Watford for Britt Assombalonga, July 2013.

Football League Record: 1960 Elected to Division 4; 1961–68 Division 3, when they were demoted for financial irregularities; 1968–74 Division 4; 1974–79 Division 3; 1979–91 Division 4; 1991–92 Division 3; 1992–94 Division 1; 1994–97 Division 2; 1997–2000 Division 3; 2000–04 Division 2; 2004–05 FL 1; 2005–08 FL 2; 2008–09 FL 1; 2009–10 FL C; 2010–11 FL 1; 2011–13 FL C; 2013– FL 1.

LATEST SEQUENCES

Longest Sequence of League Wins: 9, 1.2.1992 – 14.3.1992.

Longest Sequence of League Defeats: 8, 16.12.2006 – 27.1.2007.

Longest Sequence of League Draws: 8, 18.12.1971 – 12.2.1972.

Longest Sequence of Unbeaten League Matches: 17, 15.1.2008 – 5.4.2008.

Longest Sequence Without a League Win: 17, 23.9.1978 – 30.12.1978.

Successive Scoring Runs: 33 from 20.9.1960.

Successive Non-scoring Runs: 6 from 13.8.2002.

MANAGERS

Jock Porter 1934–36
Fred Taylor 1936–37
Vic Poulter 1937–38
Sam Haden 1938–48
Jack Blood 1948–50
Bob Gurney 1950–52
Jack Fairbrother 1952–54
George Swindin 1954–58
Jimmy Hagan 1958–62
Jack Fairbrother 1962–64
Gordon Clark 1964–67
Norman Rigby 1967–69
Jim Iley 1969–72
Noel Cantwell 1972–77
John Barnwell 1977–78
Billy Hails 1978–79
Peter Morris 1979–82
Martin Wilkinson 1982–83
John Wile 1983–86
Noel Cantwell 1986–88 *(continued as General Manager)*
Mick Jones 1988–89
Mark Lawrenson 1989–90
Dave Booth 1990–91
Chris Turner 1991–92
Lil Fuccillo 1992–93
Chris Turner 1993–94
John Still 1994–95
Mick Halsall 1995–96
Barry Fry 1996–2005
Mark Wright 2005–06
Steve Bleasdale 2006
Keith Alexander 2006–07
Darren Ferguson 2007–09
Mark Cooper 2009–10
Jim Gannon 2010
Gary Johnson 2010–11
Darren Ferguson 2011–15
Dave Robertson 2015
Graham Westley 2015–16
Grant McCann 2016–18
Steve Evans February 2018–

TEN YEAR LEAGUE RECORD

		P	W	D	L	F	A	Pts	Pos
2008-09	FL 1	46	26	11	9	78	54	89	2
2009-10	FL C	46	8	10	28	46	80	34	24
2010-11	FL 1	46	23	10	13	106	75	79	4
2011-12	FL C	46	13	11	22	67	77	50	18
2012-13	FL C	46	15	9	22	66	75	54	22
2013-14	FL 1	46	23	5	18	72	58	74	6
2014-15	FL 1	46	18	9	19	53	56	63	9
2015-16	FL 1	46	19	6	21	82	73	63	13
2016-17	FL 1	46	17	11	18	62	62	62	11
2017-18	FL 1	46	17	13	16	68	60	64	9

DID YOU KNOW ?

Peterborough United played their 2,500th Football League match at home to Scunthorpe United on 1 November 2014. Posh went down to a 2-1 defeat with their consolation goal coming from Conor Washington.

PETERBOROUGH UNITED – SKY BET LEAGUE ONE 2017–18 LEAGUE RECORD

Match No.	Date	Venue	Opponents	Result	H/T Score	Lg Pos.	Goalscorers	Atten- dance
1	Aug 5	H	Plymouth Arg	W	2-1	1-0	5	Sawyer (og) [4], Morias [47]	7622
2	12	A	Bristol R	W	4-1	1-0	2	Marriott 3 [6, 55, 90], Taylor, S [78]	9758
3	19	H	Rotherham U	W	2-1	0-0	2	Marriott 2 [47, 75]	6344
4	26	A	Northampton T	W	4-1	2-0	1	Edwards [32], Morias [41], Marriott [75], Maddison (pen) [90]	6685
5	Sept 2	A	Doncaster R	D	0-0	0-0	1		8677
6	9	H	Bradford C	L	1-3	0-3	3	Baldwin [70]	7061
7	12	H	Milton Keynes D	W	2-0	0-0	2	Tafazolli [47], Maddison [52]	6465
8	16	A	Walsall	D	1-1	0-1	2	Edwards [72]	4453
9	23	H	Wigan Ath	W	3-2	0-1	2	Morias 2 [47, 84], Marriott [90]	6099
10	26	A	Oldham Ath	L	2-3	0-0	3	Maddison (pen) [58], Marriott [90]	2975
11	30	H	Oxford U	L	1-4	1-0	4	Marriott [15]	6153
12	Oct 14	A	Gillingham	L	0-1	0-1	7		5257
13	17	A	Southend U	D	1-1	0-1	8	Marriott [55]	5789
14	21	A	Scunthorpe U	L	1-2	0-0	10	Hughes [51]	4275
15	28	H	Shrewsbury T	W	1-0	1-0	8	Maddison [14]	5606
16	Nov 12	H	AFC Wimbledon	D	2-2	2-2	8	Lloyd [26], Maddison (pen) [38]	4220
17	18	H	Blackpool	L	0-1	0-1	11		5254
18	21	H	Portsmouth	W	2-1	0-0	7	Marriott [58], Clarke (og) [70]	5217
19	25	A	Rochdale	L	0-2	0-2	8		2555
20	28	A	Charlton Ath	D	2-2	1-0	7	Edwards [11], Marriott [58]	9532
21	Dec 9	H	Blackburn R	L	2-3	1-0	10	Taylor, S [11], Marriott [90]	6164
22	17	A	Fleetwood T	W	3-2	0-1	8	Doughty [55], Marriott [88], Lloyd [90]	2273
23	23	H	Bury	W	3-0	1-0	7	Lloyd 2 [3, 71], Marriott [63]	4640
24	26	A	Bradford C	W	3-1	2-0	6	Lloyd [14], Marriott 2 [33, 67]	21,220
25	30	A	Milton Keynes D	L	0-1	0-1	8		10,304
26	Jan 1	H	Doncaster R	D	1-1	1-0	8	Lloyd [14]	5173
27	13	A	Wigan Ath	D	0-0	0-0	9		8602
28	20	H	Oldham Ath	W	3-0	0-0	8	Morias [53], Cooper [84], Marriott (pen) [90]	5072
29	Feb 3	H	Southend U	L	0-1	0-1	8		5114
30	10	A	Gillingham	D	1-1	0-0	9	Lloyd [67]	7154
31	13	H	Scunthorpe U	D	2-2	2-1	10	Maddison [2], Morias [45]	4397
32	18	A	Blackpool	D	1-1	1-1	9	Marriott [21]	3286
33	24	H	AFC Wimbledon	D	1-1	0-0	10	Maddison [79]	5146
34	27	H	Walsall	W	2-1	1-1	8	Bogle [39], Taylor, S [53]	2531
35	Mar 10	A	Charlton Ath	W	4-1	1-0	7	Hughes [44], Maddison (pen) [58], Marriott 2 [81, 84]	6337
36	13	A	Bury	W	1-0	0-0	6	Marriott [90]	2784
37	17	A	Oxford U	L	1-2	0-1	7	Marriott [62]	6804
38	24	H	Bristol R	L	1-1	0-0	6	Lloyd [59]	5953
39	30	A	Rotherham U	D	1-1	0-0	7	Marriott [90]	9573
40	Apr 2	H	Northampton T	W	2-0	2-0	5	Baldwin [12], Marriott [14]	8619
41	7	A	Plymouth Arg	L	1-2	1-1	8	Marriott [9]	10,923
42	14	A	Rochdale	L	0-1	0-1	9		5496
43	19	A	Blackburn R	L	1-3	1-0	9	Mulgrew (og) [44]	11,679
44	24	A	Shrewsbury T	L	1-3	1-0	9	Edwards [14]	4666
45	28	H	Fleetwood T	W	2-0	0-0	8	Marriott [51], Cooper [78]	4667
46	May 5	A	Portsmouth	L	0-2	0-2	9		18,118

Final League Position: 9

GOALSCORERS

League (68): Marriott 27 (1 pen), Lloyd 8, Maddison 8 (4 pens), Morias 6, Edwards 4, Taylor, S 3, Baldwin 2, Cooper 2, Hughes 2, Bogle 1, Doughty 1, Tafazolli 1, own goals 3.
FA Cup (16): Marriott 5, Lloyd 3, Maddison 2 (2 pens), Tafazolli 2, Baldwin 1, Doughty 1, Edwards 1, Hughes 1.
Carabao Cup (1): Edwards 1.
Checkatrade Trophy (9): Lloyd 2, Maddison 2 (1 pen), Edwards 1, Marriott 1, Morias 1, Taylor, S 1, own goal 1.

Bond J 37	Tafazolli R 32 + 1	Baldwin J 32 + 1	Taylor S 43 + 1	De Silva Lopes L 28 + 11	Edwards G 25 + 1	Doughty M 28 + 6	Grant A 37 + 1	Maddison M 41	Marriott J 44	Morias J 12 + 13	Kanu I 1 + 17	Lloyd D 17 + 14	Penny A 6 + 1	Forrester C 22 + 7	Hughes A 35 + 8	Anderson J 7 + 10	Miller R 4 + 6	Shephard L 23 + 1	Chettle C — + 2	O'Malley C 9	Ward J 9 + 8	Cooper G 8 + 5	Bogle O 4 + 5	Freestone L 2 + 2	Match No.
1	2	3	4	5¹	6	7	8	9	10	11¹²	12	13	14												1
1	4	3	2	5	8⁹	6	7	9¹	11	10¹	12			13	14										2
1	2	3	4	8¹	5	7	6	9³	11	10²	12			13	14										3
1	4	3	2	8	5	7¹	6	9	11³	10²	12	14				13									4
1	2	3	4	5²	8	7	6	9	11	10¹	12				13										5
1	2²	3	4	5	8	7¹	6⁸	9	11¹	10				12	13	14									6
1	4		3	12	9²	8		6	11¹	14	13			7	5			10³	2						7
1	3		2	5¹	8	6	7²	9	11	14				13	4			10³	12						8
1	4	12	3			9²	7¹	13	6²	10	11			8	5	14		2							9
1	4	3¹	2	13		7		9	11	10²	12			6	8		14	5²							10
1	4	3	2	7		12	8	6	11			13		5²	9¹	10									11
1		3	4	12	8		6¹	9	11	13	14			7	5	10²	2¹								12
1	4	2	3	6	9		7	11	10					5	8¹		12								13
1		4	3	6²	9		8	10	11					5	7¹	13	2	12							14
1	4	3	2	9	8	7	6	10¹	11²	13				5	12										15
1	2	3	4	8¹	5	7	6	10	11	13	9²			12											16
	2	3⁴	4	5	12	7³	6	8	11	13	10¹			9	14		1								17
4²	2	3	9	5	7	6	8¹	11			10			12	13		1								18
	3	4	2	7⁴	6	9	11	13	10⁹					14	5	8¹	12	1							19
1	4		3	9	10	13	6	8¹	11²				2	7	5		12								20
1	4	3⁴	2		9	13	7³	10	11		14	12		6⁵	5										21
1	3¹		4	9²	8³	7	6	10	11			12	2		5	13	14								22
1	3		4	13		6⁵	8³	9	10		14	11	2	12	5	7¹									23
1	4		3	12		7	6	10	11			8¹	2	9	5										24
1	3		4	13		6³	7	10	11	12		8	2²	9¹	5	14									25
1	3		4	12		7¹	6	9²	11	13		10	2	8	5										26
1	4		3		9¹	6	10	11	13			7²		8	5			2		12					27
1	3		4		7	8¹	10	9³	14	11³				6	5			2		12	13				28
1	4		3	14		7	9	10	13			12		6³	5			2			8¹	11²			29
1	4	2	3			6	7		11	12		9³		14	13			5			8²	10¹			30
1	7	4³	3	14		9²	8	6	11	10		13			12			2			5¹				31
1	6	10		13		9²	4	7	11					8²	3			2			5¹	14	12		32
1	3¹	4	13	8			6³	9	11	14		10		7				2²					12	5	33
1	3	13		8			6	10	12					7	5			2		9¹		11²			34
1		3	4	7¹		12		9	11			13		6	5	14		2		8²		10³			35
1	14	3	4	7				10³	11			9²		6	5			2			8¹	13	12		36
1		3⁵	4	6		7		10	11			14		13³	5	8²		2		9¹		12			37
	3²	4			7	8	10	9¹		11³				7	5			2		1	14	13	12		38
	3³	4			6	8	11	12		10¹				7	5			2		1	13	9²		14	39
	3	4	8	6³	14		10¹	11	13					7²	5			2		1	9	12			40
	3	4⁴	10	9¹	14	8		11				13		7³	5			2¹		1	12	6²			41
	3		8	9¹			10	11³	14	13		7	4		2			1	12	6		5²			42
	3	4	5	8	6³	7		11	13			10²		2	14			1	12	9¹					43
	3	2	5	8	6	7			12			10		4						11	9¹				44
1	3	4	7	9		8	6³	11¹		14	12			5			2			13	10²				45
1	3	4	9	6		8	10			11¹	13			5			2			12	7²				46

FA Cup

First Round	Tranmere R	(h)	1-1
Replay	Tranmere R	(a)	5-0
Second Round	Woking	(a)	1-1
Replay	Woking	(h)	5-2
Third Round	Aston Villa	(a)	3-1
Fourth Round	Leicester C	(h)	1-5

Carabao Cup

First Round	Barnet	(h)	1-3

Checkatrade Trophy

Southern Group H	Southampton U21	(h)	2-0
Southern Group H	Northampton T	(h)	1-1
(Northampton T won 4-2 on penalties)			
Southern Group H	Cambridge U	(a)	2-0
Second Round South	Southend U	(h)	2-0
Third Round	Luton T	(a)	0-0
(Peterborough U won 7-6 on penalties)			
Quarter-Final	Lincoln C	(a)	2-4

PLYMOUTH ARGYLE

Home Park, Plymouth, Devon PL2 3DQ.

Telephone: (01752) 562 561.

Fax: (01752) 606 167.

Ticket Office: (01752) 907 700.

Website: www.pafc.co.uk

Email: argyle@pafc.co.uk

Ground Capacity: 16,388.

Record Attendance: 43,596 v Aston Villa, Division 2, 10 October 1936.

Pitch Measurements: 105m × 68m (115yd × 74yd).

Chairman: James Brent.

Chief Executive: Martyn Starnes.

Manager: Derek Adams.

Assistant Manager: Paul Wotton.

Colours: Dark green shirts with white trim, white shorts with dark green trim, white socks with dark green trim.

Year Formed: 1886.

Turned Professional: 1903.

Previous Name: 1886, Argyle Athletic Club; 1903, Plymouth Argyle.

Club Nickname: 'The Pilgrims'.

Ground: 1886, Home Park.

First Football League Game: 28 August 1920, Division 3, v Norwich C (h) D 1–1 – Craig; Russell, Atterbury; Logan, Dickinson, Forbes; Kirkpatrick, Jack, Bowler, Heeps (1), Dixon.

Record League Victory: 8–1 v Millwall, Division 2, 16 January 1932 – Harper; Roberts, Titmuss; Mackay, Pullan, Reed; Grozier, Bowden (2), Vidler (3), Leslie (1), Black (1), (1 og). 8–1 v Hartlepool U (a), Division 2, 7 May 1994 – Nicholls; Patterson (Naylor), Hill, Burrows, Comyn, McCall (1), Barlow, Castle (1), Landon (3), Marshall (1), Dalton (2).

Record Cup Victory: 6–0 v Corby T, FA Cup 3rd rd, 22 January 1966 – Leiper; Book, Baird; Williams, Nelson, Newman; Jones (1), Jackson (1), Bickle (3), Piper (1), Jennings.

HONOURS

League Champions: Second Division – 2003–04; Division 3 – 1958–59; Division 3S – 1929–30, 1951–52; Third Division – 2001–02.
Runners-up: FL 2 – 2016–17; Division 3 – 1974–75, 1985–86; Division 3S – 1921–22, 1922–23, 1923–24, 1924–25, 1925–26, 1926–27.
FA Cup: semi-final – 1984.
League Cup: semi-final – 1965, 1974.

Sun THE FACT FILE

The highest-ever attendance for a Plymouth Argyle game was 65,386 for the FA Cup fourth-round tie against Arsenal at Highbury in January 1932. The gate was a new ground record for the Gunners at the time. Argyle led with a goal from Jack Vidler but injuries took their toll and they eventually lost 4-2.

Record Defeat: 0–9 v Stoke C, Division 2, 17 December 1960.

Most League Points (2 for a win): 68, Division 3 (S), 1929–30.

Most League Points (3 for a win): 102, Division 3, 2001–02.

Most League Goals: 107, Division 3 (S), 1925–26 and 1951–52.

Highest League Scorer in Season: Jack Cock, 32, Division 3 (S), 1926–27.

Most League Goals in Total Aggregate: Sammy Black, 174, 1924–38.

Most League Goals in One Match: 5, Wilf Carter v Charlton Ath, Division 2, 27 December 1960.

Most Capped Player: Moses Russell, 20 (23), Wales.

Most League Appearances: Kevin Hodges, 530, 1978–92.

Youngest League Player: Lee Phillips, 16 years 43 days v Gillingham, 29 October 1996.

Record Transfer Fee Received: £2,000,000 from Hull C for Peter Halmosi, July 2008.

Record Transfer Fee Paid: £500,000 to Cardiff C for Steve MacLean, January 2008.

Football League Record: 1920 Original Member of Division 3; 1921–30 Division 3 (S); 1930–50 Division 2; 1950–52 Division 3 (S); 1952–56 Division 2; 1956–58 Division 3 (S); 1958–59 Division 3; 1959–68 Division 2; 1968–75 Division 3; 1975–77 Division 2; 1977–86 Division 3; 1986–95 Division 2; 1995–96 Division 3; 1996–98 Division 2; 1998–2002 Division 3; 2002–04 Division 2; 2004–10 FL C; 2010–11 FL 1; 2011–17 FL 2; 2017– FL 1.

LATEST SEQUENCES

Longest Sequence of League Wins: 9, 8.3.1986 – 12.4.1986.

Longest Sequence of League Defeats: 9, 12.10.1963 – 7.12.1963.

Longest Sequence of League Draws: 5, 26.2.2000 – 14.3.2000.

Longest Sequence of Unbeaten League Matches: 22, 20.4.1929 – 21.12.1929.

Longest Sequence Without a League Win: 13, 13.4.2009 – 27.9.2009.

Successive Scoring Runs: 39 from 15.4.1939.

Successive Non-scoring Runs: 5 from 21.11.2009.

MANAGERS

Frank Brettell 1903–05
Bob Jack 1905–06
Bill Fullerton 1906–07
Bob Jack 1910–38
Jack Tresadern 1938–47
Jimmy Rae 1948–55
Jack Rowley 1955–60
Neil Dougall 1961
Ellis Stuttard 1961–63
Andy Beattie 1963–64
Malcolm Allison 1964–65
Derek Ufton 1965–68
Billy Bingham 1968–70
Ellis Stuttard 1970–72
Tony Waiters 1972–77
Mike Kelly 1977–78
Malcolm Allison 1978–79
Bobby Saxton 1979–81
Bobby Moncur 1981–83
Johnny Hore 1983–84
Dave Smith 1984–88
Ken Brown 1988–90
David Kemp 1990–92
Peter Shilton 1992–95
Steve McCall 1995
Neil Warnock 1995–97
Mick Jones 1997–98
Kevin Hodges 1998–2000
Paul Sturrock 2000–04
Bobby Williamson 2004–05
Tony Pulis 2005–06
Ian Holloway 2006–07
Paul Sturrock 2007–09
Paul Mariner 2009–10
Peter Reid 2010–11
Carl Fletcher 2011–13
John Sheridan 2013–15
Derek Adams June 2015–

TEN YEAR LEAGUE RECORD

		P	W	D	L	F	A	Pts	Pos
2008-09	FL C	46	13	12	21	44	57	51	21
2009-10	FL C	46	11	8	27	43	68	41	23
2010-11	FL 1	46	15	7	24	51	74	42*	23
2011-12	FL 2	46	10	16	20	47	64	46	21
2012-13	FL 2	46	13	13	20	46	55	52	21
2013-14	FL 2	46	16	12	18	51	58	60	10
2014-15	FL 2	46	20	11	15	55	37	71	7
2015-16	FL 2	46	24	9	13	72	46	81	5
2016-17	FL 2	46	26	9	11	71	46	87	2
2017-18	FL 1	46	19	11	16	58	59	68	7

* 10 pts deducted.

DID YOU KNOW ?

Left-back Pat Jones was an ever-present for Plymouth Argyle in League games for six seasons in a row. In total he managed 279 consecutive League appearances for Argyle from making his debut in May 1947 through until November 1953 when an injury forced him on the sidelines.

PLYMOUTH ARGYLE – SKY BET LEAGUE ONE 2017–18 LEAGUE RECORD

Match No.	Date	Venue	Opponents	Result	H/T Score	Lg Pos.	Goalscorers	Atten-dance
1	Aug 5	A	Peterborough U	L	1-2	0-1	17	Wylde [76]	7622
2	12	H	Charlton Ath	W	2-0	0-0	8	Jervis 2 [53, 87]	11,178
3	19	A	Southend U	D	1-1	0-1	10	Edwards [61]	7861
4	26	H	Scunthorpe U	L	0-4	0-1	18		9605
5	Sept 2	A	Walsall	L	1-2	0-1	17	Carey (pen) [87]	5495
6	9	H	Milton Keynes D	L	0-1	0-1	20		8566
7	12	H	Blackpool	L	1-3	0-1	23	Bradley [49]	7411
8	16	A	Bury	D	0-0	0-0	23		3642
9	23	H	Doncaster R	L	0-3	0-1	23		8510
10	26	A	Wigan Ath	L	0-1	0-0	24		7868
11	30	A	Bristol R	L	1-2	0-1	24	Blissett [52]	9879
12	Oct 7	H	Fleetwood T	L	1-2	0-0	24	Fletcher [90]	8064
13	14	H	Shrewsbury T	D	1-1	0-0	24	Carey [58]	8280
14	17	A	Blackburn R	D	1-1	1-1	24	Carey [31]	10,011
15	21	A	AFC Wimbledon	W	1-0	0-0	24	Grant [64]	4848
16	28	H	Rochdale	D	1-1	1-1	24	Grant [1]	8805
17	Nov 11	A	Bradford C	W	1-0	1-0	23	Jervis [35]	20,227
18	18	H	Oxford U	L	0-4	0-1	23		10,805
19	21	H	Northampton T	W	2-0	1-0	23	Bradley 2 [30, 52]	7610
20	25	A	Portsmouth	L	0-1	0-1	24		17,923
21	Dec 9	H	Gillingham	W	2-1	0-0	22	Grant [56], Diagouraga [90]	11,155
22	16	A	Rotherham U	D	1-1	0-0	22	Taylor [82]	7562
23	23	H	Oldham Ath	W	4-1	2-0	20	Diagouraga [3], Carey [6], Edwards [59], Jervis [72]	10,017
24	26	A	Milton Keynes D	W	1-0	1-0	19	Sawyer [16]	9268
25	30	A	Blackpool	D	2-2	2-0	20	Lameiras [39], Carey [45]	3417
26	Jan 1	H	Walsall	W	1-0	0-0	16	Taylor [67]	10,432
27	6	H	Bury	W	3-0	2-0	12	Diagouraga [14], Carey [42], Sarcevic [78]	9139
28	13	A	Doncaster R	D	1-1	0-1	13	Edwards [74]	7494
29	20	H	Wigan Ath	L	1-3	1-2	15	Carey (pen) [27]	11,942
30	27	A	Oldham Ath	W	2-1	2-0	13	Sarcevic [17], Lameiras [19]	4274
31	Feb 3	H	Blackburn R	W	2-0	2-0	11	Lameiras [25], Taylor [37]	11,801
32	10	A	Shrewsbury T	W	2-1	1-1	10	Ness [27], Vyner [62]	7036
33	13	H	AFC Wimbledon	W	4-2	3-1	8	Carey [16], Fox [40], Taylor [45], Lameiras [67]	10,671
34	17	A	Oxford U	W	1-0	1-0	7	Bradley [45]	8301
35	24	H	Bradford C	W	1-0	1-0	6	Sarcevic [34]	11,113
36	Mar 10	A	Fleetwood T	D	1-1	1-0	6	Makasi [16]	3079
37	17	H	Bristol R	W	3-2	1-2	6	Ness 2 [34, 48], Carey (pen) [85]	13,466
38	24	A	Charlton Ath	L	0-2	0-2	7		13,989
39	30	H	Southend U	W	4-0	2-0	6	Lameiras 2 [3, 88], Carey 2 [33, 52]	11,965
40	Apr 7	A	Peterborough U	W	2-1	1-1	5	Taylor [27], Carey (pen) [90]	10,923
41	14	H	Portsmouth	D	0-0	0-0	6		14,634
42	21	A	Northampton T	L	0-2	0-1	7		6868
43	24	H	Rochdale	D	1-1	0-0	7	Grant [53]	2760
44	28	H	Rotherham U	W	2-1	0-1	7	Grant [56], Carey (pen) [90]	13,407
45	May 1	A	Scunthorpe U	L	0-2	0-1	7		4712
46	5	A	Gillingham	L	2-5	1-3	7	Grant [23], Carey [77]	6269

Final League Position: 7

GOALSCORERS

League (58): Carey 14 (5 pens), Grant 6, Lameiras 6, Taylor 5, Bradley 4, Jervis 4, Diagouraga 3, Edwards 3, Ness 3, Sarcevic 3, Blissett 1, Fletcher 1, Fox 1, Makasi 1, Sawyer 1, Vyner 1, Wylde 1.
FA Cup (2): Carey 2.
Carabao Cup (0).
Checkatrade Trophy (5): Fletcher 2, Blissett 1, Edwards 1, Taylor 1.

McCormick L 9	Threlkeld O 24	Edwards R 25	Bradley S 39 + 1	Sawyer G 46	Jervis J 17 + 7	Sarcevic A 25 + 5	Fox D 42 + 3	Carey G 42	Taylor R 21	Grant J 24 + 9	Ainsworth L 3 + 16	Wylde G 2 + 7	Lameiras R 25 + 9	Miller G 11 + 4	Blissett N 6 + 7	Ness J 26 + 1	Songo'o Y 24 + 9	Cifci N 6 + 1	Fletcher A 3 + 11	Letheren K 7	Sokolik J — + 2	Taylor-Sinclair A 10 + 14	Diagouraga T 15	Cooper M — + 1	Matthews R 26	Roos K 4	Sangster C — + 2	Vyner Z 17	Church S — + 2	Makasi M 6 + 1	Paton P 1 + 2	Battle A — + 1	Match No.
1	2	3	4	5	6^1	7	8	9	10^3	11^2	12	13	14																				1
1		3	4	5	8^2	6	7	9	10					12	2	11^1	13																2
1		3	4	5	8	6	7^1	9	10^2		12				2	11	13																3
1		3	4	5	9^2	7^4	8^1	11		13			14	2	12	6	10^3																4
1		3	4	5	8^2		6^3	9		10^1			14	2	13	7	12	11															5
1		3	4	5	8^3		6	9^4		10	12		14	2^1		7	11^{12}	13															6
1	3^3		4	5	13		6			11^1	12			2		9^3	8	7	10^2	14													7
1			4	5	14	8	6^1			11	9^3			12	2	2		3^1	7^2	10	9												8
1		3	4^4	5		6	12				13	14	11	2^1				8^3	7^2	10	9												9
	3		5		6	14	7		10	9^1	13		2^2	11^3	8	4			1	12													10
	4		5	9	7	13	8^1			11			2^4	10	6^2	3			1	12													11
2^1	3		5	8^2	6^3		9			10	13		11	7	4	14	1		12														12
	3	13	2	12	6^2	8	9		11^1				14		4		10^3	1		5	7												13
	3	4	2	11^2		9	7		10				13		6			1^1		5	8	12											14
	3	4	5	11^2		9	10		7^1			13	12		6					2	8		1										15
	3	4	2	11^1	13	9^2	7		10^3		14			12	6					5	8		1										16
	2	3	4	11^1	12	9^2			10	7^1			13		6					5	8		1										17
	3^4	4	2	11	14	9	7		10^2			13	12		6					5^3	8^1		1										18
	4	2	11^2	8	9	7^1			10	13					3		12			5	6		1										19
	4	2	10	6^2	7	9^1		11^1	14	13					3	12				5	8		1										20
	3	4	2	8		6	9	11	10^1						12					5	7		1										21
	3	4	2	10^2		7	9	11^1	8^1	12	13				14					5	6		1										22
2	3	4	5	12		8^2	10^3	11	13	7^1				6						9			1	14									23
2	3	4	5	12		8	10^2	11	13	7^1				6						9			1										24
2	3	4	5	13	14	6^2	11	10^1	12				9^3		7					8		1											25
2	3	4	5		6	7	9	10						11						8		1											26
2^2	3	4	5	12	6	7^1	9	10			13	11^3	14							8		1											27
2	3	4	5		8	7	11	10		12		9^1		6								1											28
2		4	5		6	7	9	10^2	14	12		11^3		8^1								1					3	13					29
2		4	5		8	7	9	10				11^2		6	3				12			1					3	13					30
2		4	5		6	7^3	9	10	14			11^2		8	12				13			1					3						31
2		4	5		6	7^1	11	10		13		9^2		8	12				13			1					3						32
2		4	5		6^2	7^3	9	10				11		8	12				13			1					3		14				33
		4	5^1		6	7	9	10	12			11^2		8	3				13			1					2						34
2		4	5		6^1	7	9	10				11^2		8	13				12			1					3						35
2		5^3			7	11	10	14	12			9		8^1	4				13			1					3		6^2				36
2		5			7	9	10			11^1		8	4						13			1					3		6^2	12			37
2		5			7^2	9	10			11^3		8	4^1	12					13			1					3		6	14			38
2		4	5		7^3	9	10^1	12		11		8^2	13						14			1					3		6				39
2		4	5		7	9	10	12		11		8				1											3		6^1				40
2		4	5^1		7	9	10			11^2		8		13	1				12								3		6				41
2		4	5	12	7^1	9		10^2	13	11		8		14								1					3			6^3			42
2		4	5	6^2	7	11		10	12^3	9^1		8			14				13			1					3						43
2		4	5	6^2	7	9		10	12	11^1		8^3	14						13			1					3						44
2^3		4	5		7^1	8	11		10^2	14		9	13		6		12					1					3						45
		3	5		7	8		11^3		9^1	2			6			10^2		13			1			12	4					14		46

FA Cup

First Round	Grimsby T	(h)	1-0
Second Round	Bradford C	(a)	1-3

Carabao Cup

First Round	Bristol C	(a)	0-5

Checkatrade Trophy

Southern Group D	Chelsea U21	(h)	2-2
(Plymouth Arg won 5-4 on penalties)			
Southern Group D	Exeter C	(h)	2-2
(Plymouth Arg won 5-3 on penalties)			
Southern Group D	Yeovil T	(a)	1-2

PORT VALE

FOUNDATION

Port Vale Football Club was formed in 1876 and took its name from the venue of the inaugural meeting at 'Port Vale House' situated in a suburb of Stoke-on-Trent. Upon moving to Burslem in 1884 the club changed its name to 'Burslem Port Vale' and after several seasons in the Midland League became founder members of the Football League Division Two in 1892. The prefix 'Burslem' was dropped from the name as a new ground several miles away was acquired.

Vale Park, Hamil Road, Burslem, Stoke-on-Trent, Staffordshire ST6 1AW.

Telephone: (01782) 655 800.

Ticket Office: (01782) 655 821.

Website: www.port-vale.co.uk

Email: enquiries@port-vale.co.uk

Ground Capacity: 19,148.

Record Attendance: 22,993 v Stoke C, Division 2, 6 March 1920 (at Recreation Ground); 49,768 v Aston Villa, FA Cup 5th rd, 20 February 1960 (at Vale Park).

Pitch Measurements: 104m × 69.5m (114yd × 76yd).

Chairman: Tony Fradley.

Chief Executive: Colin Garlick.

Manager: Neil Aspin.

Assistant Manager: Lee Nogan.

Colours: White shirts with thin black stripes and yellow trim, white shorts with yellow trim, white socks with black and yellow trim.

Year Formed: 1876.

Turned Professional: 1885.

Previous Names: 1876, Port Vale; 1884, Burslem Port Vale; 1909, Port Vale.

Club Nickname: 'Valiants'.

Grounds: 1876, Limekin Lane, Longport; 1881, Westport; 1884, Moorland Road, Burslem; 1886, Athletic Ground, Cobridge; 1913, Recreation Ground, Hanley; 1950, Vale Park.

First Football League Game: 3 September 1892, Division 2, v Small Heath (a) L 1–5 – Frail; Clutton, Elson; Farrington, McCrindle, Delves; Walker, Scarratt, Bliss (1), Jones. (Only 10 men).

Record League Victory: 9–1 v Chesterfield, Division 2, 24 September 1932 – Leckie; Shenton, Poyser; Sherlock, Round, Jones; McGrath, Mills, Littlewood (6), Kirkham (2), Morton (1).

Record Cup Victory: 7–1 v Irthlingborough, FA Cup 1st rd, 12 January 1907 – Matthews; Dunn, Hamilton; Eardley, Baddeley, Holyhead; Carter, Dodds (2), Beats, Mountford (2), Coxon (3).

Record Defeat: 0–10 v Sheffield U, Division 2, 10 December 1892. 0–10 v Notts Co, Division 2, 26 February 1895.

HONOURS

League Champions: Division 3N – 1929–30, 1953–54; Division 4 – 1958–59.
Runners-up: Second Division – 1993–94; Division 3N – 1952–53.
FA Cup: semi-final – 1954.
League Cup: 4th rd – 2007.
League Trophy Winners: 1993, 2001.
Anglo-Italian Cup: Runners-up: 1996.

The Sun FACT FILE

Legendary defender Roy Sproson was the first winner of the Port Vale Player of the Year award in 1967. The player with most wins to date is striker Tom Pope with three (2013, 2014 and 2018), while current manager Neil Aspin (1990 and 1994) is one of several to have won the award twice.

Most League Points (2 for a win): 69, Division 3 (N), 1953–54.

Most League Points (3 for a win): 89, Division 2, 1992–93.

Most League Goals: 110, Division 4, 1958–59.

Highest League Scorer in Season: Wilf Kirkham 38, Division 2, 1926–27.

Most League Goals in Total Aggregate: Wilf Kirkham, 153, 1923–29, 1931–33.

Most League Goals in One Match: 6, Stewart Littlewood v Chesterfield, Division 2, 24 September 1922.

Most Capped Player: Chris Birchall, 24 (43), Trinidad & Tobago.

Most League Appearances: Roy Sproson, 760, 1950–72.

Youngest League Player: Malcolm McKenzie, 15 years 347 days v Newport Co, 12 April 1966.

Record Transfer Fee Received: £2,000,000 from Wimbledon for Gareth Ainsworth, October 1998.

Record Transfer Fee Paid: £500,000 to Lincoln C for Gareth Ainsworth, September 1997.

Football League Record: 1892 Original Member of Division 2. Failed re-election in 1896; Re-elected 1898; Resigned 1907; Returned in Oct, 1919, when they took over the fixtures of Leeds City; 1929–30 Division 3 (N); 1930–36 Division 2; 1936–38 Division 3 (N); 1938–52 Division 3 (S); 1952–54 Division 3 (N); 1954–57 Division 2; 1957–58 Division 3 (S); 1958–59 Division 4; 1959–65 Division 3; 1965–70 Division 4; 1970–78 Division 3; 1978–83 Division 4; 1983–84 Division 3; 1984–86 Division 4; 1986–89 Division 3; 1989–94 Division 2; 1994–2000 Division 1; 2000–04 Division 2; 2004–08 FL 1; 2008–13 FL 2; 2013–17 FL 1; 2017– FL 2.

LATEST SEQUENCES

Longest Sequence of League Wins: 8, 8.4.1893 – 30.9.1893.

Longest Sequence of League Defeats: 9, 9.3.1957 – 20.4.1957.

Longest Sequence of League Draws: 6, 26.4.1981 – 12.9.1981.

Longest Sequence of Unbeaten League Matches: 19, 5.5.1969 – 8.11.1969.

Longest Sequence Without a League Win: 17, 7.12.1991 – 21.3.1992.

Successive Scoring Runs: 22 from 12.9.1992.

Successive Non-scoring Runs: 5 from 19.8.2017.

MANAGERS

Sam Gleaves 1896–1905
   (Secretary-Manager)
Tom Clare 1905–11
A. S. Walker 1911–12
H. Myatt 1912–14
Tom Holford 1919–24
   (continued as Trainer)
Joe Schofield 1924–30
Tom Morgan 1930–32
Tom Holford 1932–35
Warney Cresswell 1936–37
Tom Morgan 1937–38
Billy Frith 1945–46
Gordon Hodgson 1946–51
Ivor Powell 1951
Freddie Steele 1951–57
Norman Low 1957–62
Freddie Steele 1962–65
Jackie Mudie 1965–67
Sir Stanley Matthews
   (General Manager) 1965–68
Gordon Lee 1968–74
Roy Sproson 1974–77
Colin Harper 1977
Bobby Smith 1977–78
Dennis Butler 1978–79
Alan Bloor 1979
John McGrath 1980–83
John Rudge 1983–99
Brian Horton 1999–2004
Martin Foyle 2004–07
Lee Sinnott 2007–08
Dean Glover 2008–09
Micky Adams 2009–10
Jim Gannon 2011
Micky Adams 2011–14
Robert Page 2014–16
Bruno Ribeiro 2016
Michael Brown 2017
Neil Aspin October 2017–

TEN YEAR LEAGUE RECORD

		P	W	D	L	F	A	Pts	Pos
2008-09	FL 2	46	13	9	24	44	66	48	18
2009-10	FL 2	46	17	17	12	61	50	68	10
2010-11	FL 2	46	17	14	15	54	49	65	11
2011-12	FL 2	46	20	9	17	68	60	59*	12
2012-13	FL 2	46	21	15	10	87	52	78	3
2013-14	FL 1	46	18	7	21	59	73	61	9
2014-15	FL 1	46	15	9	22	55	65	54	18
2015-16	FL 1	46	18	11	17	56	58	65	12
2016-17	FL 1	46	12	13	21	45	70	49	21
2017-18	FL 2	46	11	14	21	49	67	47	20

*10 pts deducted.

DID YOU KNOW ?

Fred Perry, a local songwriter, composed 'The Port Vale War Cry', which was introduced at a Supporters' Club social event in November 1920. Copies were sold to raise money for the club, raising around £70, and fans sang the song at matches.

PORT VALE – SKY BET LEAGUE TWO 2017–18 LEAGUE RECORD

Match No.	Date	Venue	Opponents	Result	H/T Score	Lg Pos.	Goalscorers	Atten- dance
1	Aug 5	A	Crawley T	W 3-1	2-0	5	Tonge [9], Kay [26], Turner [82]	2270
2	12	H	Wycombe W	L 2-3	0-3	10	Turner [88], Whitfield [90]	4909
3	19	A	Chesterfield	L 0-2	0-2	16		5058
4	26	H	Crewe Alex	L 0-1	0-1	21		6299
5	Sept 2	H	Notts Co	L 0-1	0-0	23		4656
6	9	A	Coventry C	L 0-1	0-1	24		6951
7	12	A	Luton T	L 0-2	0-1	24		7046
8	16	H	Forest Green R	L 1-1	1-0	24	Turner [21]	3910
9	23	A	Yeovil T	D 1-1	1-0	22	Pope [29]	2614
10	26	H	Accrington S	L 1-2	1-1	22	Worrall [22]	3360
11	30	A	Stevenage	L 0-2	0-1	22		2678
12	Oct 7	H	Grimsby T	L 1-2	1-0	23	Pope [39]	5849
13	14	H	Cheltenham T	W 3-1	1-0	22	Pope 2 [26, 80], Whitfield [61]	4277
14	17	H	Morecambe	W 3-0	1-0	22	Pope 2 [18, 67], Montano [90]	1241
15	21	A	Exeter C	W 1-0	1-0	21	Pope [25]	4258
16	28	H	Swindon T	L 0-3	0-0	22		5071
17	Nov 10	A	Newport Co	D 1-1	0-0	20	Forrester [80]	2876
18	18	H	Barnet	W 1-0	0-0	19	Pope (pen) [80]	4207
19	21	H	Mansfield T	L 0-4	0-1	21		3878
20	25	A	Lincoln C	L 1-3	1-1	22	Pugh [45]	7562
21	Dec 9	H	Cambridge U	W 2-0	1-0	19	Montano 2 [45, 47]	3129
22	16	A	Carlisle U	W 2-1	0-0	18	Barnett [51], Pope [69]	4090
23	23	A	Colchester U	D 1-1	0-1	18	Harness [75]	3485
24	26	H	Coventry C	W 1-0	0-0	17	Smith [79]	7127
25	30	H	Luton T	W 4-0	1-0	16	Mullins (og) [23], Pope 2 [60, 82], Whitfield [70]	5523
26	Jan 1	A	Notts Co	L 0-1	0-0	18		7241
27	6	A	Forest Green R	L 0-1	0-0	18		2437
28	13	H	Yeovil T	D 1-1	0-1	18	Pope (pen) [86]	4120
29	20	A	Accrington S	L 2-3	2-0	18	Pope 3, Tonge [41]	1743
30	27	H	Colchester U	D 2-2	1-2	18	Worrall 2 [33, 87]	4044
31	Feb 3	H	Morecambe	D 0-0	0-0	19		3968
32	10	A	Cheltenham T	L 1-5	1-2	19	Pope (pen) [35]	2731
33	17	A	Swindon T	L 2-3	2-2	19	Tonge [11], Montano [43]	5713
34	24	A	Newport Co	D 0-0	0-0	22		4013
35	Mar 10	A	Grimsby T	D 1-1	1-0	22	Worrall [10]	5198
36	13	A	Barnet	D 1-1	0-1	18	Forrester [51]	1153
37	17	H	Stevenage	D 2-2	0-1	19	Wilson, D [65], Hannant [77]	3462
38	20	A	Exeter C	L 0-1	0-1	20		3138
39	24	A	Wycombe W	D 0-0	0-0	21		4620
40	30	H	Chesterfield	W 2-1	1-0	20	Pugh [45], Whitfield [82]	5713
41	Apr 2	A	Crewe Alex	D 2-2	1-1	19	Pope (pen) [36], Kay [71]	6680
42	7	H	Crawley T	L 1-2	1-1	19	Pope [20]	4005
43	14	A	Lincoln C	W 1-0	0-0	19	Kay [63]	5580
44	21	A	Mansfield T	D 1-1	0-0	18	Pope [89]	4210
45	28	H	Carlisle U	L 1-2	1-0	19	Angus [34]	5163
46	May 5	A	Cambridge U	L 0-5	0-2	20		4808

Final League Position: 20

GOALSCORERS

League (49): Pope 17 (4 pens), Montano 4, Whitfield 4, Worrall 4, Kay 3, Tonge 3, Turner 3, Forrester 2, Pugh 2, Angus 1, Barnett 1, Hannant 1, Harness 1, Smith 1, Wilson, D 1, own goal 1.
FA Cup (5): Pope 2, Gunning 1, Harness 1, Kay 1.
Carabao Cup (1): Tonge 1.
Checkatrade Trophy (6): Montano 2, Barnett 1, Forrester 1, Reeves 1, Regis 1.

Lainton R 6	Wilson L 6 + 1	Kay A 32 + 1	Smith N 46	Gunning G 19	Montano C 21 + 9	Pugh D 31 + 2	Tonge M 30 + 3	Harness M 26 + 9	de-Freitas A 6 + 5	Pope T 41	Turner D 4 + 13	Reeves W 1 + 2	Whitfield B 25 + 12	Hornby S 9 + 2	Denton T 12 + 3	Pyke R 1 + 6	Stobbs J 1 + 4	Davis J 16 + 2	Worrall D 36 + 4	Middleton H 4 + 2	Barnett T 8 + 17	Anderson T 18 + 2	Roos K 8	Gibbons J 24 + 6	Evtimov D 1	Boot R 22	Forrester A 9 + 4	Regis C — + 1	Angus D 2 + 1	Wilson D 1 + 7	Hannant L 18	Jules Z 2	Raglan C 9 + 1	Howe C 1 + 2	Howkins K 10	Calveley M — + 2	Benns H — + 1	Match No.
1	2	3	4	5	6¹	7	8²	9³	10	11	12	13	14																									1
	2	3	4		9²	7¹		6	8	10	13	12	14	1	5	11³																						2
	2	3	4				8	9	12	10	11¹	7²	6³	1	5	13	14																					3
		3	4		13		8⁴	9³		10	14		11	1	5	12	6¹	2	7²																			4
1		3	4	5	10³			6²	13	11	12		9		14	2	7	8¹																				5
1¹		3	4	5			9	14	10		8	12	13		2	7	6¹	11³																				6
		3	5				9	11	12		8	1		14	13	2²	6	7²	10¹	4																		7
	2		4	5		7	12	8	10	11²	13		9¹				6			3	1																	8
	12	3	4			7		8	10¹	11²	13		9¹				6	14		2	1	5⁴																9
	5²	3	4		13		12	10	14	8¹		9				6	7³	11	2	1																		10
	5	3¹	4			7	12	8²	10	13		14	9				6		11²	2	1																	11
		2	3	4		7	6²	9¹	13	10	14		11¹		8		12				1	5																12
		3	4		6		11¹		10	14		9²	8³		7	12	13	2	1	5																		13
		4	5	14	6	12	9¹		11	8²	10³		7		13	3	1	2																				14
	7	4	5	12	6		10²		11	9¹			8		13	3	1	2																				15
	7²	4	5	10¹	6		9		11			13	8	12		3	2	1																				16
	7	4	5	13	6¹		9		11	10²			8³		3		2	1	12	14																		17
	7	4	5	12	8		9²	11	13				6		3		2	1	10¹																			18
		3	5	12	8²	14	7		11	9³	13		6		4		2	1	10¹																			19
	6	3	5	10	7		9¹		11				8		4		2	1	12																			20
	6	3	5	10¹	13	9			11		8²		7		12	4	2	1																				21
	7	2	4		5	6¹	10		11	9²		13	8		12	3	1																					22
	6	3	4	10¹	5		9		11	8²	13		2	7	12		1																					23
	8	3	4	12	5	7	6		11	9¹	13		2		10²		1																					24
	7	4	3¹	11	5	8	9		10¹	6²		2	13	14	12		1																					25
	8	3		10¹	5	7	6		11	9²		2	14		12	4³	13	1																				26
	6¹	3		12	5	7	10²	11		9³		4	8	13		2	1		14																			27
	7	4		9²	5	8	6¹		11	10³		2	14		3	13	1			12																		28
	7	4		14	5	8	13		11	10³			6		3¹	9	1		12	2²																		29
1	3²	2		9¹		6			10	14			7		12	5		13	11²	8	4																	30
1	6³	4			13	7			11	10²			8			2		12	14	9	5¹	3																31
1	7³	4			5	8²			10	12			6			2		11¹	13	9	3	14																32
		3		5	7	8	6²		11				13	10¹	12³		2	1		14	9									4									33
		3		8	7	6³	14		10				12		2	9	13	5²	1		11¹								4										34
		4		5¹	7	6	11		14				2	9	12	13	1	10²		8³								3										35
		4		5	3	10	7²						6¹	11	13		1	8	12	9	2																	36
		4		5	7	8	10²						2¹	6	13		1	11	12	9	3																	37
		4		5	7		8	14		13			6²	10	12		1	11¹		9	2³	3																38
		4		5	7		13			12	8		6²		10	11	1	11¹		9	2	3																39
	12	4		5	6⁴		7¹	14		10			13		6²	11³	1			9	2	3																40
	7	4		5		8³	14			11¹			10	12	6	13		2	1²		9									3									41
	7¹	4		5²		8	13			10			11³	1	12	6	14		2		9	3																	42
	7	4			8					10¹			13	1	5³	6	14		2	11²	9	12								3									43
	6	4			9²	8¹				11	13		12	1	7				5		10	2								3									44
	7⁸	4			5					10	11³		6	1				14		2			9²		8					12	3¹	13							45
		4			7	8				10	13		6²	1				2				5					11¹	9					3³				12	14	46

FA Cup

First Round	Oxford U	(h)	2-0
Second Round	Yeovil T	(h)	1-1
Replay	Yeovil T	(a)	2-3
(aet)			

Carabao Cup

First Round	Leeds U	(a)	1-4

Checkatrade Trophy

Northern Group D	Oldham Ath	(a)	0-0
(Port Vale won 4-2 on penalties)			
Northern Group D	Newcastle U U21	(h)	1-0
Northern Group D	Crewe Alex	(h)	4-2
Second Round North	Shrewsbury T	(h)	1-2

PORTSMOUTH

FOUNDATION

At a meeting held in his High Street, Portsmouth offices in 1898, solicitor Alderman J. E. Pink and five other business and professional men agreed to buy some ground close to Goldsmith Avenue for £4,950 which they developed into Fratton Park in record breaking time. A team of professionals was signed up by manager Frank Brettell and entry to the Southern League obtained for the new club's September 1899 kick-off.

Fratton Park, Frogmore Road, Portsmouth, Hampshire PO4 8RA.

Telephone: (02392) 731 204.

Fax: (02392) 734 129.

Ticket Office: (0345) 646 1898.

Website: www.portsmouthfc.co.uk

Email: info@pompeyfc.co.uk

Ground Capacity: 18,931.

Record Attendance: 51,385 v Derby Co, FA Cup 6th rd, 26 February 1949.

Pitch Measurements: 100m × 66m (109.5yd × 72yd).

Chairman: Michael Eisner.

Chief Executive: Mark Catlin.

Manager: Kenny Jackett.

Assistant Manager: Joe Gallen.

HONOURS

League Champions: Division 1 – 1948–49, 1949–50; First Division – 2002–03; Division 3 – 1961–62, 1982–83; Division 3S – 1923–24; FL 2 – 2016–17.
Runners-up: Division 2 – 1926–27, 1986–87.

FA Cup Winners: 1939, 2008.
Runners-up: 1929, 1934, 2010.

League Cup: 5th rd – 1961, 1986, 1994, 2010.

European Competitions
UEFA Cup: 2008–09.

Colours: Blue shirts with white and red trim, white shorts with blue trim, red socks with white trim.

Year Formed: 1898.

Turned Professional: 1898.

Club Nickname: 'Pompey'.

Ground: 1898, Fratton Park.

First Football League Game: 28 August 1920, Division 3, v Swansea T (h) W 3–0 – Robson; Probert, Potts; Abbott, Harwood, Turner; Thompson, Stringfellow (1), Reid (1), James (1), Beedie.

Record League Victory: 9–1 v Notts Co, Division 2, 9 April 1927 – McPhail; Clifford, Ted Smith; Reg Davies (1), Foxall, Moffat; Forward (1), Mackie (2), Haines (3), Watson, Cook (2).

Record Cup Victory: 7–0 v Stockport Co, FA Cup 3rd rd, 8 January 1949 – Butler; Rookes, Ferrier; Scoular, Flewin, Dickinson; Harris (3), Barlow, Clarke (2), Phillips (2), Froggatt.

Record Defeat: 0–10 v Leicester C, Division 1, 20 October 1928.

Most League Points (2 for a win): 65, Division 3, 1961–62.

Sun FACT FILE

Portsmouth fans' classic song 'The Pompey Chimes' appears to be the oldest surviving football chant still sung today. The song's original association was with the city of Portsmouth and in fact predates the formation of the football club in 1898. It has not, however, been sung at Fratton Park continuously and there were lengthy absences in the 1930s and early 1950s.

Most League Points (3 for a win): 98, Division 1, 2002–03.

Most League Goals: 97, Division 1, 2002–03.

Highest League Scorer in Season: Guy Whittingham, 42, Division 1, 1992–93.

Most League Goals in Total Aggregate: Peter Harris, 194, 1946–60.

Most League Goals in One Match: 5, Alf Strange v Gillingham, Division 3, 27 January 1923; 5, Peter Harris v Aston Villa, Division 1, 3 September 1958.

Most Capped Player: Jimmy Dickinson, 48, England.

Most League Appearances: Jimmy Dickinson, 764, 1946–65.

Youngest League Player: Clive Green, 16 years 259 days v Wrexham, 21 August 1976.

Record Transfer Fee Received: £20,000,000 from Real Madrid for Lassana Diarra, January 2009.

Record Transfer Fee Paid: £9,000,000 (rising to £11,000,000) to Liverpool for Peter Crouch, July 2008.

Football League Record: 1920 Original Member of Division 3; 1921 Division 3 (S); 1924–27 Division 2; 1927–59 Division 1; 1959–61 Division 2; 1961–62 Division 3; 1962–76 Division 2; 1976–78 Division 3; 1978–80 Division 4; 1980–83 Division 3; 1983–87 Division 2; 1987–88 Division 1; 1988–92 Division 2; 1992–2003 Division 1; 2003–10 FA Premier League; 2010–12 FL C; 2012–13 FL 1; 2013–17 FL 2; 2017– FL 1.

LATEST SEQUENCES

Longest Sequence of League Wins: 7, 17.8.2002 – 17.9.2002.

Longest Sequence of League Defeats: 9, 26.12.2012 – 9.2.2013.

Longest Sequence of League Draws: 5, 16.12.2000 – 13.1.2001.

Longest Sequence of Unbeaten League Matches: 15, 18.4.1924 – 18.10.1924.

Longest Sequence Without a League Win: 25, 29.11.1958 – 22.8.1959.

Successive Scoring Runs: 23 from 30.8.1930.

Successive Non-scoring Runs: 6 from 27.12.1993.

MANAGERS

Frank Brettell 1898–1901
Bob Blyth 1901–04
Richard Bonney 1905–08
Bob Brown 1911–20
John McCartney 1920–27
Jack Tinn 1927–47
Bob Jackson 1947–52
Eddie Lever 1952–58
Freddie Cox 1958–61
George Smith 1961–70
Ron Tindall 1970–73
    (General Manager to 1974)
John Mortimore 1973–74
Ian St John 1974–77
Jimmy Dickinson 1977–79
Frank Burrows 1979–82
Bobby Campbell 1982–84
Alan Ball 1984–89
John Gregory 1989–90
Frank Burrows 1990–91
Jim Smith 1991–95
Terry Fenwick 1995–98
Alan Ball 1998–99
Tony Pulis 2000
Steve Claridge 2000–01
Graham Rix 2001–02
Harry Redknapp 2002–04
Velimir Zajec 2004–05
Alain Perrin 2005
Harry Redknapp 2005–08
Tony Adams 2008–09
Paul Hart 2009
Avram Grant 2009–10
Steve Cotterill 2010–11
Michael Appleton 2011–12
Guy Whittingham 2012–13
Richie Barker 2013–14
Andy Awford 2014–15
Paul Cook 2015–17
Kenny Jackett June 2017–

TEN YEAR LEAGUE RECORD

		P	W	D	L	F	A	Pts	Pos
2008-09	PR Lge	38	10	11	17	38	57	41	14
2009-10	PR Lge	38	7	7	24	34	66	19*	20
2010-11	FL C	46	15	13	18	53	60	58	16
2011-12	FL C	46	13	11	22	50	59	40†	22
2012-13	FL 1	46	10	12	24	51	69	32†	24
2013-14	FL 2	46	14	17	15	56	66	59	13
2014-15	FL 2	46	14	15	17	52	54	57	16
2015-16	FL 2	46	21	15	10	75	44	78	6
2016-17	FL 2	46	26	9	11	79	40	87	1
2017-18	FL 1	46	20	6	20	57	56	66	8

*9 pts deducted; †10 pts deducted.

DID YOU KNOW ?

Portsmouth were one of the top teams in the country in the immediate post-war years, winning the Football League title in 1948–49 and 1949–50. In both seasons the club's average attendance topped 37,000 with an all-time record of 37,082 being attracted in 1948–49.

PORTSMOUTH – SKY BET LEAGUE ONE 2017–18 LEAGUE RECORD

Match No.	Date	Venue	Opponents	Result	H/T Score	Lg Pos.	Goalscorers	Attendance
1	Aug 5	H	Rochdale	W 2-0	0-0	3	Pitman 2 [46, 90]	18,009
2	12	A	Oxford U	L 0-3	0-0	13		9510
3	19	H	Walsall	D 1-1	0-0	13	Pitman (pen) [74]	17,198
4	26	A	Wigan Ath	D 1-1	0-1	14	Chaplin [76]	9685
5	Sept 3	H	Rotherham U	L 0-1	0-1	16		17,118
6	9	A	AFC Wimbledon	W 2-0	1-0	14	Pitman (pen) [38], Chaplin [50]	4585
7	12	A	Northampton T	L 1-3	0-2	13	Kennedy [49]	5855
8	16	H	Fleetwood T	W 4-1	1-0	12	Pitman 2 [41, 78], Lowe 2 [57, 70]	17,192
9	23	A	Scunthorpe U	L 0-2	0-2	15		4685
10	26	H	Bristol R	W 3-0	1-0	11	Hawkins [42], Pitman 2 [77, 85]	17,716
11	30	H	Oldham Ath	L 1-2	0-1	15	Pitman [90]	17,848
12	Oct 8	A	Gillingham	W 1-0	0-0	13	Kennedy [46]	8163
13	14	H	Milton Keynes D	W 2-0	2-0	8	Hawkins 2 [14, 45]	17,608
14	17	A	Doncaster R	L 1-2	0-2	11	Baudry (og) [54]	7211
15	21	A	Blackburn R	L 0-3	0-1	12		11,673
16	28	H	Bradford C	L 0-1	0-0	14		18,067
17	Nov 11	A	Blackpool	W 3-2	0-0	11	Pitman 2 [52, 86], Close [80]	5032
18	18	H	Southend U	W 1-0	0-0	10	Pitman [54]	18,431
19	21	A	Peterborough U	L 1-2	0-0	11	Chaplin [78]	5217
20	25	H	Plymouth Arg	W 1-0	1-0	7	Naismith [25]	17,923
21	Dec 9	A	Charlton Ath	W 1-0	0-0	7	Magennis (og) [47]	16,361
22	16	H	Bury	W 1-0	0-0	7	Clarke [62]	17,549
23	23	A	Shrewsbury T	L 0-2	0-0	8		7429
24	26	H	AFC Wimbledon	W 2-1	1-0	7	Close [45], Pitman (pen) [72]	18,644
25	30	H	Northampton T	W 3-1	2-1	6	Kennedy [41], Hawkins 2 [45, 48]	18,539
26	Jan 1	A	Bristol R	L 1-2	0-0	6	Hawkins [64]	10,014
27	13	H	Scunthorpe U	D 1-1	1-0	7	Lowe [15]	17,741
28	20	A	Rotherham U	L 0-1	0-0	9		9129
29	27	H	Shrewsbury T	L 0-1	0-1	9		17,779
30	Feb 3	H	Doncaster R	D 2-2	1-1	9	Walkes [19], Pitman [81]	17,364
31	10	A	Milton Keynes D	W 2-1	0-0	8	Clarke [84], Chaplin [90]	14,762
32	13	H	Blackburn R	L 1-2	0-1	9	Chaplin [50]	18,152
33	17	A	Southend U	L 1-3	1-2	9	Evans [36]	9397
34	20	A	Fleetwood T	W 2-1	1-0	9	Lowe [24], Hawkins [75]	2561
35	24	H	Blackpool	L 0-2	0-1	9		17,895
36	Mar 10	H	Gillingham	L 1-3	1-0	12	Lowe [19]	18,247
37	17	A	Oldham Ath	W 2-0	2-0	8	Pitman 2 [29, 42]	4306
38	25	H	Oxford U	W 3-0	1-0	8	Naismith [5], Pitman 2 [69, 79]	17,892
39	31	A	Walsall	W 1-0	0-0	9	Evans [79]	5159
40	Apr 2	H	Wigan Ath	W 2-1	1-0	7	Pitman (pen) [40], Lowe [55]	17,842
41	7	A	Rochdale	D 3-3	1-1	7	Pitman 2 [26, 62], Done (og) [90]	3781
42	14	A	Plymouth Arg	D 0-0	0-0	7		14,634
43	17	A	Bradford C	L 1-3	0-1	8	Pitman [61]	19,554
44	21	H	Charlton Ath	L 0-1	0-1	8		19,210
45	28	A	Bury	L 0-1	0-0	9		4575
46	May 5	H	Peterborough U	W 2-0	2-0	8	Pitman 2 [13, 25]	18,118

Final League Position: 8

GOALSCORERS

League (57): Pitman 24 (4 pens), Hawkins 7, Lowe 6, Chaplin 5, Kennedy 3, Clarke 2, Close 2, Evans 2, Naismith 2, Walkes 1, own goals 3.
FA Cup (0).
Carabao Cup (1): own goal 1.
Checkatrade Trophy (10): Lowe 2, O'Keefe 2, Clarke 1, Evans 1, Hawkins 1, Main 1, Naismith 1, Pitman 1.

McGee L 44	Talbot D 4	Burgess C 34 + 1	Whatmough J 14	Holmes-Dennis T 1	Evans G 26 + 6	Baker C 1 + 1	Rose D 13 + 2	Bennett K 11 + 7	Chaplin C 11 + 15	Pitman B 35 + 3	Lowe J 39 + 5	Naismith K 19 + 7	Haunstrup B 13 + 3	May A 10 + 3	Lalkovic M 1	Kabamba N — + 1	Main C 2 + 3	Donohue D 29 + 3	Close B 37 + 3	Clarke M 42	O'Keefe S 17 + 4	Hawkins O 22 + 9	Kennedy M 20 + 9	Thompson N 34 + 2	McCrory D 3	Ronan C 8 + 8	Deslandes S 2	Henderson S 1	Walkes A 12	Bass A 1	Match No.
1	2	3	4	5[2]	6	7	8	9	10[1]	11	12	13																			1
1	2[1]	3	4		10	13	6	8	12	9			11[1]	5	7																2
1	2[3]	3	4		8		7	12		11			9[2]	5	6	10[1]	13	14													3
1		3	4		2[4]	6[2]	11[3]	14	10	9	12	5	8						7[1]	13											4
1		3	2[2]						10[3]	11	5	14	9	7						4	6	8[1]	12	13							5
1		4							13	12	11	9	8						3	7	10[3]	6[1]	5	2							6
1		3							11	9	8		6[1]					12	4	7		10	2	5							7
1		4			13		11[1]	10[2]	6	12	8							3	7	14	9	2	5[3]								8
1		3			12		9	8	13									5	6	4	7	11[1]	10[2]	2							9
1		3			12		13	9	8									5	6	4	7	11[1]	10[2]	2							10
1	2[2]				12	14	13	10	6								5	7[1]	4	8	11	9	3[1]								11
1					13	14	9[2]		8	12		11	5[1]	7[3]	3	6	4	10	2												12
1		3			12		9	8					5	7	4	6	11	10[1]	2												13
1		4			8[2]		9[1]	13	12				5[4]	6	3	7	11	10	2												14
1		3			9[1]	13	12	8	14				5	6	4	7	11[1]	10[3]	2												15
1		3			9[2]		12	11	8				5[1]	6	4	7	13	10	2												16
1		4		2	6	9[1]		11	8	10				12	7	5	3														17
1		3		2	7	9[2]		11	8[1]	10				6	5	4	12	13													18
1		3		2	6		12	8	9		11[1]	13	7	5	4	10[2]															19
1		8			7		11[1]	10	9[3]	5	14	6	4	13	3[2]	12	2														20
1		4			10		7	12	9[1]	11	8	5	3	6	2																21
1		3			8		6	9[1]	13	11	10	5	12	4	7[2]																22
1		4			9		7	13	14	11[1]	8[2]	5	6	3	12	10[3]	2														23
1		3			8		6	9[1]	11	10[2]	5	7	4	13	12	2															24
1		3			8[1]	6[2]	14	9[3]	13	12	5	7	4	11	10	2															25
1		4			13		9[1]	8[2]		6	12	5	7	3	11	10	2														26
1		3				10	5	11		13	9[1]	8	4	2	12	6	7[2]														27
1		4			11[1]	8	9		7	6	3	13	10	2			12	5[2]													28
1		3			8		12	10[1]	9[2]		6[4]	5	7	4	11	2	13														29
1		3[4]			10[2]		12	14	13	5	7	4	11[1]	6[1]	8	9	1	2													30
1					8		13	11	12	5	6	4	3	10[1]	7	9[3]	2														31
1		3			6		11[1]	10	9[2]	5	7	4	12	13	8	2															32
1		3			6[2]		11	10[1]	9	5	8	4	13	7[4]	12	2															33
1		3			10[1]		6	8		5	7	4	11	9	12	2															34
1		3			9		8	13	6	5	7	4	11[2]	10[1]	12	2															35
1		3	7[2]				13	8	11	12	10	6	4	9	5[1]	2															36
1		3					11	8	10	5	7	6	4	9	2																37
1		3	12				11	10	8	13	5	7	4	6[2]	9[1]	2															38
1		4	8				11	7	10	5	9[1]	3	6	12	2																39
1		3	9				11	10	8	5	7	4	6	2																	40
1		4	8[3]				11	7	10[2]	5	9	3	13	14	12	2[5]			6												41
1		4	8				11	7	10	5	9	3	6[1]	2	12																42
1		4	8[3]		14	11	7	10[1]	5	9	3	12	13	2	6[2]																43
1	13	4[1]	8			11	7	10	5[3]	9	6	3	12	2[8]	14																44
1		4			14	10	6		13	7[1]	8	3	9	11[2]	12	2	5[3]														45
1		4			7		10	11	9[1]	5	8	3	6	12	2														1		46

FA Cup
First Round   Luton T   (a)   0-1

Carabao Cup
First Round   Cardiff C   (a)   1-2
(aet)

Checkatrade Trophy
Southern Group A   Fulham U21   (h)   3-3
(Fulham U21 won 4-2 on penalties)
Southern Group A   Crawley T   (h)   3-1
Southern Group A   Charlton Ath   (a)   1-0
Second Round South   Northampton T   (h)   2-0
Third Round   Chelsea U21   (h)   1-2

PRESTON NORTH END

FOUNDATION

North End Cricket and Rugby Club, which was formed in 1863, indulged in most sports before taking up soccer in about 1879. In 1881 they decided to stick to football to the exclusion of other sports and even a 16–0 drubbing by Blackburn Rovers in an invitation game at Deepdale, a few weeks after taking this decision, did not deter them for they immediately became affiliated to the Lancashire FA.

Deepdale Stadium, Sir Tom Finney Way, Deepdale, Preston, Lancashire PR1 6RU.

Telephone: (0344) 856 1964.

Ticket Office: (0344) 856 1966.

Website: www.pnefc.net

Email: enquiries@pne.co.uk

Ground Capacity: 23,404.

Record Attendance: 42,684 v Arsenal, Division 1, 23 April 1938.

Pitch Measurements: 100m × 67m (109.5yd × 73.5yd).

Chief Executive: John Kay.

Manager: Alex Neil.

First-Team Coaches: Steve Thompson, Frankie McAvoy.

Colours: White shirts with blue trim, blue shorts, white socks with blue hoops.

Year Formed: 1880.

Turned Professional: 1885.

Club Nicknames: 'The Lilywhites', 'North End'.

Ground: 1881, Deepdale.

First Football League Game: 8 September 1888, Football League, v Burnley (h) W 5–2 – Trainer; Howarth, Holmes; Robertson, William Graham, Johnny Graham; Gordon (1), Jimmy Ross (2), Goodall, Dewhurst (2), Drummond.

Record League Victory: 10–0 v Stoke, Division 1, 14 September 1889 – Trainer; Howarth, Holmes; Kelso, Russell (1), Johnny Graham; Gordon, Jimmy Ross (2), Nick Ross (3), Thomson (2), Drummond (2).

Record Cup Victory: 26–0 v Hyde, FA Cup 1st rd, 15 October 1887 – Addison; Howarth, Nick Ross; Russell (1), Thomson (5), Johnny Graham (1); Gordon (5), Jimmy Ross (8), John Goodall (1), Dewhurst (3), Drummond (3).

Record Defeat: 0–7 v Nottingham F, Division 2, 9 April 1927; 0–7 v Blackpool, Division 1, 1 May 1948.

Most League Points (2 for a win): 61, Division 3, 1970–71.

Most League Points (3 for a win): 95, Division 2, 1999–2000.

Most League Goals: 100, Division 2, 1927–28 and Division 1, 1957–58.

HONOURS

League Champions: Football League 1888–89, 1889–90; Division 2 – 1903–04, 1912–13, 1950–51; Second Division – 1999–2000; Division 3 – 1970–71; Third Division – 1995–96. *Runners-up:* Football League 1890–91, 1891–92; Division 1 – 1892–93, 1905–06, 1952–53, 1957–58; Division 2 – 1914–15, 1933–34; Division 4 – 1986–87.

FA Cup Winners: 1889, 1938. *Runners-up:* 1888, 1922, 1937, 1954, 1964.

League Cup: 4th rd – 1963, 1966, 1972, 1981, 2003, 2017.

Double Performed: 1888–89.

THE Sun FACT FILE

Preston North End had a long-standing policy of not playing home games on Christmas Day and did not do so throughout the period from the end of the First World War through until their last Yuletide game at Blackpool in 1958. The reason for this appears to have been financial rather than religious as North End reserves regularly played home matches on the day.

Highest League Scorer in Season: Ted Harper, 37, Division 2, 1932–33.

Most League Goals in Total Aggregate: Tom Finney, 187, 1946–60.

Most League Goals in One Match: 4, Jimmy Ross v Stoke, Division 1, 6 October 1888; 4, Nick Ross v Derby Co, Division 1, 11 January 1890; 4, George Drummond v Notts Co, Division 1, 12 December 1891; 4, Frank Becton v Notts Co, Division 1, 31 March 1893; 4, George Harrison v Grimsby T, Division 2, 3 November 1928; 4, Alex Reid v Port Vale, Division 2, 23 February 1929; 4, James McClelland v Reading, Division 2, 6 September 1930; 4, Dick Rowley v Notts Co, Division 2, 16 April 1932; 4, Ted Harper v Burnley, Division 2, 29 August 1932; 4, Ted Harper v Lincoln C, Division 2, 11 March 1933; 4, Charlie Wayman v QPR, Division 2, 25 December 1950; 4, Alex Bruce v Colchester U, Division 3, 28 February 1978; 4, Joe Garner v Crewe Alex, FL 1, 14 March 2015.

Most Capped Player: Tom Finney, 76, England.

Most League Appearances: Alan Kelly, 447, 1961–75.

Youngest League Player: Steve Doyle, 16 years 166 days v Tranmere R, 15 November 1974.

Record Transfer Fee Received: £10,000,000 from West Ham U for Jordan Hugill, January 2018.

Record Transfer Fee Paid: £1,500,000 to Manchester U for David Healy, December 2000.

Football League Record: 1888 Founder Member of League; 1901–04 Division 2; 1904–12 Division 1; 1912–13 Division 2; 1913–14 Division 1; 1914–15 Division 2; 1919–25 Division 1; 1925–34 Division 2; 1934–49 Division 1; 1949–51 Division 2; 1951–61 Division 1; 1961–70 Division 2; 1970–71 Division 3; 1971–74 Division 2; 1974–78 Division 3; 1978–81 Division 2; 1981–85 Division 3; 1985–87 Division 4; 1987–92 Division 3; 1992–93 Division 2; 1993–96 Division 3; 1996–2000 Division 2; 2000–04 Division 1; 2004–11 FL C; 2011–15 FL 1; 2015– FL C.

LATEST SEQUENCES

Longest Sequence of League Wins: 14, 25.12.1950 – 27.3.1951.
Longest Sequence of League Defeats: 8, 22.9.1984 – 27.10.1984.
Longest Sequence of League Draws: 6, 24.2.1979 – 20.3.1979.
Longest Sequence of Unbeaten League Matches: 23, 8.9.1888 – 14.9.1889.
Longest Sequence Without a League Win: 15, 14.4.1923 – 20.10.1923.
Successive Scoring Runs: 30 from 15.11.1952.
Successive Non-scoring Runs: 6 from 19.11.1960.

MANAGERS

Charlie Parker 1906–15
Vincent Hayes 1919–23
Jim Lawrence 1923–25
Frank Richards 1925–27
Alex Gibson 1927–31
Lincoln Hayes 1931–32
Run by committee 1932–36
Tommy Muirhead 1936–37
Run by committee 1937–49
Will Scott 1949–53
Scot Symon 1953–54
Frank Hill 1954–56
Cliff Britton 1956–61
Jimmy Milne 1961–68
Bobby Seith 1968–70
Alan Ball Snr 1970–73
Bobby Charlton 1973–75
Harry Catterick 1975–77
Nobby Stiles 1977–81
Tommy Docherty 1981
Gordon Lee 1981–83
Alan Kelly 1983–85
Tommy Booth 1985–86
Brian Kidd 1986
John McGrath 1986–90
Les Chapman 1990–92
Sam Allardyce 1992 (*Caretaker*)
John Beck 1992–94
Gary Peters 1994–98
David Moyes 1998–2002
Kelham O'Hanlon 2002
(*Caretaker*)
Craig Brown 2002–04
Billy Davies 2004–06
Paul Simpson 2006–07
Alan Irvine 2007–09
Darren Ferguson 2010
Phil Brown 2011
Graham Westley 2012–13
Simon Grayson 2013–17
Alex Neil July 2017–

TEN YEAR LEAGUE RECORD

		P	W	D	L	F	A	Pts	Pos
2008-09	FL C	46	21	11	14	66	54	74	6
2009-10	FL C	46	13	15	18	58	73	54	17
2010-11	FL C	46	10	12	24	54	79	42	22
2011-12	FL 1	46	13	15	18	54	68	54	15
2012-13	FL 1	46	14	17	15	54	49	59	14
2013-14	FL 1	46	23	16	7	72	46	85	5
2014-15	FL 1	46	25	14	7	79	40	89	3
2015-16	FL C	46	15	17	14	45	45	62	11
2016-17	FL C	46	16	14	16	64	63	62	11
2017-18	FL C	46	19	16	11	57	46	73	7

DID YOU KNOW

Goalkeeper Alan Kelly was the first recipient of the Preston North End Player of the Year award in 1967–68. The first player to win the award twice was Mike Elwiss (1974–75 and 1977–78) while Tony Ellis is the only player to win the award in successive seasons (1992–93 and 1993–94).

PRESTON NORTH END – SKY BET CHAMPIONSHIP 2017–18 LEAGUE RECORD

Match No.	Date	Venue	Opponents	Result	H/T Score	Lg Pos.	Goalscorers	Attendance
1	Aug 5	H	Sheffield W	W 1-0	0-0	6	Johnson (pen) [79]	18,267
2	12	A	Leeds U	D 0-0	0-0	8		32,880
3	15	A	Derby Co	L 0-1	0-0	12		24,371
4	19	H	Reading	W 1-0	1-0	7	Hugill [22]	11,174
5	26	A	Middlesbrough	D 0-0	0-0	7		25,295
6	Sept 9	H	Barnsley	D 1-1	1-1	11	Maguire [23]	12,813
7	12	H	Cardiff C	W 3-0	1-0	5	Harrop [38], Maguire [70], Browne [78]	10,796
8	16	A	Birmingham C	W 3-1	0-1	4	Johnson [56], Hugill [60], Barkhuizen [67]	21,168
9	23	H	Millwall	D 0-0	0-0	4		12,363
10	26	A	Hull C	W 2-1	1-0	4	Barkhuizen [37], Robinson [88]	15,443
11	30	H	Sunderland	D 2-2	0-1	6	Harrop [55], Hugill [57]	17,621
12	Oct 14	A	Fulham	D 2-2	2-0	5	Hugill [18], Maguire [25]	18,435
13	21	A	Wolverhampton W	L 2-3	0-1	7	Hugill [65], Coady (og) [76]	27,352
14	28	H	Brentford	L 2-3	1-1	9	Maguire [41], Barkhuizen [66]	12,005
15	Nov 1	H	Aston Villa	L 0-2	0-2	10		14,212
16	4	A	Ipswich T	L 0-3	0-1	14		14,390
17	17	H	Bolton W	D 0-0	0-0	13		15,213
18	21	A	Bristol C	W 2-1	1-0	11	Gallagher [44], Robinson [78]	17,355
19	25	A	Norwich C	D 1-1	0-1	13	Barkhuizen [70]	25,167
20	Dec 2	H	QPR	W 1-0	0-0	10	Hugill [88]	11,290
21	9	A	Burton Alb	W 2-1	0-0	10	Clarke [66], Horgan [83]	3659
22	16	H	Sheffield U	W 1-0	0-0	9	Hugill [58]	15,202
23	23	H	Nottingham F	D 1-1	0-0	8	Huntington [75]	13,481
24	26	A	Barnsley	D 0-0	0-0	9		14,014
25	29	A	Cardiff C	W 1-0	0-0	7	Clarke [90]	17,751
26	Jan 1	H	Middlesbrough	L 2-3	2-1	9	Robinson [14], Hugill [40]	15,101
27	13	A	Millwall	D 1-1	0-1	10	Robinson [80]	11,751
28	20	H	Birmingham C	D 1-1	1-0	11	Davies [17]	13,529
29	30	A	Nottingham F	W 3-0	1-0	9	Bodin [35], Barkhuizen [60], Johnson (pen) [83]	22,044
30	Feb 3	H	Hull C	W 2-1	2-0	7	Cunningham [36], Browne (pen) [45]	11,605
31	10	A	Brentford	D 1-1	0-0	7	Barkhuizen [54]	9194
32	17	H	Wolverhampton W	D 1-1	0-0	7	Browne [52]	18,570
33	20	A	Aston Villa	D 1-1	1-0	9	Barkhuizen [37]	30,894
34	24	H	Ipswich T	L 0-1	0-1	9		11,511
35	Mar 3	A	Bolton W	W 3-1	0-1	9	Barkhuizen [53], Maguire 2 [77, 90]	18,141
36	6	H	Bristol C	W 2-1	1-0	8	Browne [20], Maguire [69]	11,264
37	10	H	Fulham	L 1-2	0-0	8	Maguire [76]	12,970
38	17	A	Sunderland	W 2-0	0-0	8	Maguire [50], Robinson [63]	28,543
39	30	A	Sheffield W	L 1-4	0-0	10	Moult [72]	26,588
40	Apr 2	H	Derby Co	L 0-1	0-0	10		13,520
41	7	A	Reading	L 0-1	0-1	11		15,501
42	10	H	Leeds U	W 3-1	0-1	11	Gallagher (pen) [49], Maguire [52], Browne [82]	14,188
43	14	A	QPR	W 2-1	1-1	8	Robinson [45], Browne [74]	13,760
44	21	H	Norwich C	D 0-0	0-0	9		13,038
45	28	A	Sheffield U	W 1-0	0-0	7	Browne [57]	28,568
46	May 6	H	Burton Alb	W 2-1	1-0	7	Robinson [26], Moult [90]	17,058

Final League Position: 7

GOALSCORERS

League (57): Maguire 10, Barkhuizen 8, Hugill 8, Browne 7 (1 pen), Robinson 7, Johnson 3 (2 pens), Clarke 2, Gallagher 2 (1 pen), Harrop 2, Moult 2, Bodin 1, Cunningham 1, Davies 1, Horgan 1, Huntington 1, own goal 1.
FA Cup (5): Browne 2 (1 pen), Harrop 2, Horgan 1.
Carabao Cup (2): Hugill 2.

Maxwell C 30	Fisher D 34	Huntington P 44	Spurr T 5	Cunningham G 20	Pearson B 35	Barkhuizen T 43 + 3	Browne A 38 + 6	Johnson D 25 + 8	Robinson C 30 + 11	Maguire S 19 + 5	Hugill J 26 + 1	Gallagher P 22 + 10	Harrop J 11 + 27	Davies B 33 + 1	Horgan D 2 + 18	Earl J 16 + 3	Mavididi S 3 + 7	Welsh J 5 + 4	Woods C 11 + 5	Vermijl M — + 2	Boyle A 3	O'Connor K 4 + 4	Clarke T 14 + 4	Bodin B 14 + 3	Moult L 3 + 7	Rudd D 16	Simpson C — + 1	Match No.
1	2	3	4	5	6	7	8[2]	9	10	11[1]	12	13																1
1	2	3	4	5	6[4]	10[2]	8[1]	9	7		11	13	12															2
1	5	2	3[1]	9		6[3]	7	10	8[2]	14	11	12			4	13												3
1	2	3			6	10[2]	12	7	13	8[3]	11		9[1]	4		5	14											4
1	2	3			6[3]	10[2]	9	8	14	7[1]	11		12	4		5	13											5
1	2	3	4			9[2]	7		14	10	11	8[3]	13		5	6[1]	12											6
1	2[3]	3				10	6[1]			8[2]	11	13	9	4	14	5		7	12									7
1		3				10	6	7[2]	14	8	11		9[1]	4		5			12			2[3]	13					8
1	2	3				8[1]	12		6[1]	14	9	11		10[2]		5	13	7										9
1	2	3				10[3]	9	6	12	8	11[2]		13	4	14	5		7[1]										10
1	2	3				8[2]	7		6	14	10[3]	11[1]		9	4	12		5	13									11
1		3			6[2]	8[3]	9		7	14	10[1]	11		12	4		5		13	2								12
1	2	3			6	8	9[4]	7			11		10[1]	4		5		12										13
1	2	3			6	8[2]		7		9[3]	10[1]	11		12		13	5		14			4						14
1	2				6	8[3]	9	7		10	11	13		14	5[2]			4[1]			3	12						15
1	2[3]	3			6	8	9	10[1]		11	14	13					7[2]		12	4	5							16
1		3			6	8	9[2]	13	10[3]		7[1]	14		12		11		2		4	5							17
1	2	3			6	8	12	9	13		11[3]	7[2]		4		10[1]		5					14					18
1	2	3[2]				8	9	6	10		11	7[1]	12	4				5					13					19
1	2	4			7	8	9[1]		10		11	6	12	5								13	3[2]					20
1	5	3			6	8	9[1]		10		11[3]	7	12	4	13							14	2[2]					21
1	5[2]	3			7	11	13	8	9[3]		10	6[1]	14	4								12	2					22
1		3			6	8	9[2]		10[1]		11	7	13	4		12						5	2					23
1		3			7	8	14	9		11	6[2]	12	4	10[1]		13		2[3]				5						24
1		3		5[3]	7	8	9		13		11	6[1]	12	4	10[2]			14				2						25
1		3			7	8[2]		6	10		11	12	9	4	13			5				2						26
1				5	6[2]	12	2	14	10		11	7	9[3]	4	13						3	8[1]						27
1		3		5		8	13	7	10[3]		11[2]	6	9	4[1]		12						2		14				28
	2	4			6[2]	10		9	12	11[1]		7[3]		14	5							3	8	13		1		29
	2	4		5	6[1]	10		9	12	11[2]		7[3]	13									3	8	14		1		30
	2	3	4	5[4]		10	7	9	11[3]			6[2]			14				12	13				8[1]		1		31
	2	3				10[2]	9	7	11[3]			13	4	12		5	6[1]						8	14		1		32
	2	4		5	6	10[1]	7	9					14	3		12								8	11[2]	1	13	33
		3		5	6	10	7		9[2]			12	4	14	13		2[3]							8[1]	11	1		34
		3		5	6	10	9		11	12		7[3]	13	4		14	2[1]							8[3]		1		35
	2	3		5	6	10	9	12	11[1]	13		7[2]		4		14								8		1		36
	2	3		5[3]	6	10	9	7[2]	8	11[1]		13	4			12							14			1		37
1	2	3			6	8[1]	9	12	10[3]	11		7[2]	13	4		5							14			1		38
	2[1]	3			6	8	9	12	10	11[2]		7[1]	14	4		5							13			1		39
1	2	3		5	6	8[2]	9[1]	14	10[3]	11		7		4										13	12	1		40
	2	3		5	6	10	7			9[1]	13			14	4[3]								12	8	11[2]	1		41
		3		5	6	10[2]	9		13	11		7[1]	12	4	14							2	8[3]			1		42
	2	4		5	6	10	9	8[1]	11[3]			13	12		14							3	7[1]			1		43
	2	4[1]		5	6	10[2]	9		11	14		7[3]	13	12								3	8			1		44
	2	3		5	6	12	8	7	10	11[3]		14	9[2]	4									13			1		45
	2	4		5	6	12	7[3]		10	11[1]		13	9[2]									3	8[4]	14		1		46

FA Cup
Third Round   Wycombe W   (a)   5-1
Fourth Round   Sheffield U   (a)   0-1

Carabao Cup
First Round   Accrington S   (a)   2-3

QUEENS PARK RANGERS

FOUNDATION

There is an element of doubt about the date of the foundation of this club, but it is believed that in either 1885 or 1886 it was formed through the amalgamation of Christchurch Rangers and St Jude's Institute FC. The leading light was George Wodehouse, whose family maintained a connection with the club until comparatively recent times. Most of the players came from the Queen's Park district so this name was adopted after a year as St Jude's Institute.

Loftus Road Stadium, South Africa Road, Shepherds Bush, London W12 7PJ.

Telephone: (020) 8743 0262.

Fax: (020) 8743 1158.

Ticket Office: (08444) 777 007.

Website: www.qpr.co.uk

Email: boxoffice@qpr.co.uk

Ground Capacity: 18,224.

Record Attendance: 41,097 v Leeds U, FA Cup 3rd rd, 9 January 1932 (at White City); 35,353 v Leeds U, Division 1, 27 April 1974 (at Loftus Road).

Pitch Measurements: 100m × 66m (109yd × 72yd).

Co-Chairmen: Tony Fernandes and Ruben Gnanalingam.

Chief Executive: Lee Hoos.

Manager: Steve McClaren.

Assistant Manager: John Eustace.

Colours: Blue and white hooped shirts, white shorts, white socks with blue hoops.

Year Formed: 1885* (*see Foundation*).

Turned Professional: 1898.

Previous Name: 1885, St Jude's; 1887, Queens Park Rangers. *Club Nicknames:* 'Rangers', 'The Hoops', 'R's'.

Grounds: 1885* (*see Foundation*), Welford's Fields; 1888–99, London Scottish Ground, Brondesbury, Home Farm, Kensal Rise Green, Gun Club Wormwood Scrubs, Kilburn Cricket Ground; 1899, Kensal Rise Athletic Ground; 1901, Latimer Road, Notting Hill; 1904, Agricultural Society, Park Royal; 1907, Park Royal Ground; 1917, Loftus Road; 1931, White City; 1933, Loftus Road; 1962, White City; 1963, Loftus Road.

First Football League Game: 28 August 1920, Division 3, v Watford (h) L 1–2 – Price; Blackman, Wingrove; McGovern, Grant, O'Brien; Faulkner, Birch (1), Smith, Gregory, Middlemiss.

Record League Victory: 9–2 v Tranmere R, Division 3, 3 December 1960 – Drinkwater; Woods, Ingham; Keen, Rutter, Angell; Lazarus (2), Bedford (2), Evans (2), Andrews (1), Clark (2).

Record Cup Victory: 8–1 v Bristol R (a), FA Cup 1st rd, 27 November 1937 – Gilfillan; Smith, Jefferson; Lowe, James, March; Cape, Mallett, Cheetham (3), Fitzgerald (3) Bott (2). 8–1 v Crewe Alex, Milk Cup 1st rd, 3 October 1983 – Hucker; Neill, Dawes, Waddock (1), McDonald (1), Fenwick, Micklewhite (1), Stewart (1), Allen (1), Stainrod (3), Gregory.

HONOURS

League Champions: FL C – 2010–11; Division 2 – 1982–83; Division 3 – 1966–67; Division 3S – 1947–48. *Runners-up:* Division 1 – 1975–76; Division 2 – 1967–68, 1972–73; Second Division – 2003–04; Division 3S – 1946–47.

FA Cup: Runners-up: 1982.

League Cup Winners: 1967. *Runners-up:* 1986.

European Competitions
UEFA Cup: 1976–77 (*qf*), 1984–85.

Sun FACT FILE

Following a disastrous season in 1925–26 when they finished bottom of Division Three South 14 points behind their closest rivals, Queens Park Rangers embarked on a series of changes for the 1926–27 season. Among these was a switch from their traditional green and white hooped shirts to the blue and white hoops they have worn almost continuously since.

Record Defeat: 1–8 v Mansfield T, Division 3, 15 March 1965. 1–8 v Manchester U, Division 1, 19 March 1969.

Most League Points (2 for a win): 67, Division 3, 1966–67.

Most League Points (3 for a win): 88, FL C, 2010–11.

Most League Goals: 111, Division 3, 1961–62.

Highest League Scorer in Season: George Goddard, 37, Division 3 (S), 1929–30.

Most League Goals in Total Aggregate: George Goddard, 174, 1926–34.

Most League Goals in One Match: 4, George Goddard v Merthyr T, Division 3 (S), 9 March 1929; 4, George Goddard v Swindon T, Division 3 (S), 12 April 1930; 4, George Goddard v Exeter C, Division 3 (S), 20 December 1930; 4, George Goddard v Watford, Division 3 (S), 19 September 1931; 4, Tom Cheetham v Aldershot, Division 3 (S), 14 September 1935; 4, Tom Cheetham v Aldershot, Division 3 (S), 12 November 1938.

Most Capped Player: Alan McDonald, 52, Northern Ireland.

Most League Appearances: Tony Ingham, 514, 1950–63.

Youngest League Player: Frank Sibley, 16 years 97 days v Bristol C, 10 March 1964.

Record Transfer Fee Received: £12,000,000 from Anzhi Makhachkala for Chris Samba, July 2013.

Record Transfer Fee Paid: £12,500,000 to Anzhi Makhachkala for Chris Samba, January 2013.

Football League Record: 1920 Original Members of Division 3; 1921–48 Division 3 (S); 1948–52 Division 2; 1952–58 Division 3 (S); 1958–67 Division 3; 1967–68 Division 2; 1968–69 Division 1; 1969–73 Division 2; 1973–79 Division 1; 1979–83 Division 2; 1983–92 Division 1; 1992–96 FA Premier League; 1996–2001 Division 1; 2001–04 Division 2; 2004–11 FL C; 2011–13 FA Premier League; 2013–14 FL C; 2014–15 FA Premier League; 2015– FL C.

LATEST SEQUENCES

Longest Sequence of League Wins: 8, 7.11.1931 – 28.12.1931.

Longest Sequence of League Defeats: 9, 25.2.1969 – 5.4.1969.

Longest Sequence of League Draws: 6, 29.1.2000 – 5.3.2000.

Longest Sequence of Unbeaten League Matches: 20, 11.3.1972 – 23.9.1972.

Longest Sequence Without a League Win: 20, 7.12.1968 – 7.4.1969.

Successive Scoring Runs: 33 from 9.12.1961.

Successive Non-scoring Runs: 6 from 18.3.1939.

MANAGERS

James Cowan 1906–13
Jimmy Howie 1913–20
Ned Liddell 1920–24
Will Wood 1924–25
   (had been Secretary since 1903)
Bob Hewison 1925–31
John Bowman 1931
Archie Mitchell 1931–33
Mick O'Brien 1933–35
Billy Birrell 1935–39
Ted Vizard 1939–44
Dave Mangnall 1944–52
Jack Taylor 1952–59
Alec Stock 1959–65
   (General Manager to 1968)
Bill Dodgin Jnr 1968
Tommy Docherty 1968
Les Allen 1968–71
Gordon Jago 1971–74
Dave Sexton 1974–77
Frank Sibley 1977–78
Steve Burtenshaw 1978–79
Tommy Docherty 1979–80
Terry Venables 1980–84
Gordon Jago 1984
Alan Mullery 1984
Frank Sibley 1984–85
Jim Smith 1985–88
Trevor Francis 1988–89
Don Howe 1989–91
Gerry Francis 1991–94
Ray Wilkins 1994–96
Stewart Houston 1996–97
Ray Harford 1997–98
Gerry Francis 1998–2001
Ian Holloway 2001–06
Gary Waddock 2006
John Gregory 2006–07
Luigi Di Canio 2007–08
Iain Dowie 2008
Paulo Sousa 2008–09
Jim Magilton 2009
Paul Hart 2009–10
Neil Warnock 2010–12
Mark Hughes 2012
Harry Redknapp 2012–15
Chris Ramsey 2015
Jimmy Floyd Hasselbaink 2015–16
Ian Holloway 2016–18
Steve McClaren May 2018–

TEN YEAR LEAGUE RECORD

		P	W	D	L	F	A	Pts	Pos
2008-09	FL C	46	15	16	15	42	44	61	11
2009-10	FL C	46	14	15	17	58	65	57	13
2010-11	FL C	46	24	16	6	71	32	88	1
2011-12	PR Lge	38	10	7	21	43	66	37	17
2012-13	PR Lge	38	4	13	21	30	60	25	20
2013-14	FL C	46	23	11	12	60	44	80	4
2014-15	PR Lge	38	8	6	24	42	73	30	20
2015-16	FL C	46	14	18	14	54	54	60	12
2016-17	FL C	46	15	8	23	52	66	53	18
2017-18	FL C	46	15	11	20	58	70	56	16

DID YOU KNOW ?

Queens Park Rangers won the *London Evening Standard* 5-a-side championships on five occasions, including three times in four years in the 1970s. Their successes came in 1971, 1972, 1974, 1980 and 1985.

QUEENS PARK RANGERS – SKY BET CHAMPIONSHIP 2017–18 LEAGUE RECORD

Match No.	Date	Venue	Opponents	Result	H/T Score	Lg Pos.	Goalscorers	Attendance
1	Aug 5	H	Reading	W 2-0	1-0	2	Washington 2 (1 pen) [22, 59 (p)]	14,460
2	12	A	Sheffield W	D 1-1	1-0	6	Mackie [23]	25,537
3	16	A	Norwich C	L 0-2	0-0	11		26,082
4	19	H	Hull C	W 2-1	0-1	6	Smith [74], Sylla [90]	12,609
5	26	A	Cardiff C	L 1-2	1-2	10	Smith [15]	18,520
6	Sept 9	A	Ipswich T	W 2-1	1-0	8	Mackie [43], Freeman [49]	14,060
7	12	H	Millwall	D 2-2	0-1	10	Luongo [73], Smith [85]	12,600
8	16	A	Middlesbrough	L 2-3	1-1	11	Wheeler [2], Mackie [50]	24,790
9	23	H	Burton Alb	D 0-0	0-0	11		12,500
10	26	A	Barnsley	D 1-1	0-1	14	Freeman [87]	10,920
11	29	H	Fulham	L 1-2	1-2	14	Washington [90]	16,415
12	Oct 14	A	Sunderland	D 1-1	1-0	14	Sylla [37]	26,066
13	21	A	Bolton W	D 1-1	0-1	17	Sylla [78]	14,243
14	28	H	Wolverhampton W	W 2-1	1-1	14	Washington [41], Smith [81]	16,004
15	31	H	Sheffield U	W 1-0	1-0	12	Sylla [4]	13,604
16	Nov 4	A	Nottingham F	L 0-4	0-2	15		24,021
17	18	H	Aston Villa	L 1-2	1-1	15	Mackie [18]	16,934
18	21	A	Derby Co	L 0-2	0-1	16		23,296
19	27	H	Brentford	D 2-2	0-0	16	Freeman [90], Smith [90]	13,410
20	Dec 2	A	Preston NE	L 0-1	0-0	18		11,290
21	9	H	Leeds U	L 1-3	0-0	19	Wszolek [90]	15,506
22	16	A	Birmingham C	W 2-1	1-0	18	Robinson 2 [17, 83]	20,107
23	23	H	Bristol C	D 1-1	1-0	18	Flint (og) [37]	13,683
24	26	A	Ipswich T	D 0-0	0-0	18		18,696
25	29	A	Millwall	L 0-1	0-0	18		16,601
26	Jan 1	H	Cardiff C	W 2-1	0-0	17	Smith [62], Smyth [72]	13,801
27	13	A	Burton Alb	W 3-1	1-1	14	Oteh [32], Washington [74], Luongo [87]	4264
28	20	H	Middlesbrough	L 0-3	0-2	16		14,182
29	27	A	Bristol C	L 0-2	0-1	16		21,492
30	Feb 3	H	Barnsley	W 1-0	0-0	15	Scowen [48]	12,413
31	10	A	Wolverhampton W	L 1-2	0-2	15	Washington [51]	30,168
32	17	H	Bolton W	W 2-0	0-0	15	Lynch [72], Smith [90]	12,638
33	20	A	Sheffield U	L 1-2	0-1	15	Freeman [63]	25,339
34	24	H	Nottingham F	L 2-5	0-1	16	Luongo [68], Smith [78]	13,675
35	Mar 6	H	Derby Co	D 1-1	0-1	16	Luongo [87]	11,488
36	10	H	Sunderland	W 1-0	0-0	16	Eze [62]	14,216
37	13	A	Aston Villa	W 3-1	2-0	15	Manning [12], Bidwell [33], Freeman [82]	30,228
38	17	A	Fulham	D 2-2	1-2	15	Luongo [45], Wszolek [81]	23,347
39	30	A	Reading	L 0-1	0-1	15		20,273
40	Apr 2	H	Norwich C	W 4-1	1-1	15	Manning [80], Luongo [39], Smith [55], Eze [60]	14,053
41	7	A	Hull C	L 0-4	0-2	15		14,181
42	10	H	Sheffield W	W 4-2	3-0	15	Smyth [8], Bidwell [10], Sylla 2 (1 pen) [15, 53 (p)]	12,521
43	14	H	Preston NE	L 1-2	1-1	15	Smith [13]	13,760
44	21	A	Brentford	L 1-2	1-1	16	Sylla [45]	12,367
45	28	H	Birmingham C	W 3-1	1-1	15	Samuel [29], Chair [70], Smith [90]	15,805
46	May 6	A	Leeds U	L 0-2	0-1	16		30,004

Final League Position: 16

GOALSCORERS
League (58): Smith 11, Sylla 7 (1 pen), Luongo 6, Washington 6 (1 pen), Freeman 5, Mackie 4, Bidwell 2, Eze 2, Manning 2, Robinson 2, Smyth 2, Wszolek 2, Chair 1, Lynch 1, Oteh 1, Samuel 1, Scowen 1, Wheeler 1, own goal 1.
FA Cup (0).
Carabao Cup (2): Furlong 1, Ngbakoto 1.

Smithies A 42+1	Perch J 6+1	Onuoha N 28+1	Lynch J 22+3	Wszolek P 28+8	Scowen J 42	Luongo M 38+1	Freeman L 43+2	Bidwell J 45+1	Mackie J 16+4	Washington C 24+9	Sylla I 13+13	Ngbakoto Y 2+3	Robinson J 29+2	LuaLua K 2+6	Manning R 10+9	Furlong D 18+4	Smith M 17+24	Baptiste A 26	Caulker S 2	Wheeler D 5+4	Samuel B 6+12	Cousins J 13+2	Chair 14	Hall G 1+3	Oteh A 3+3	Smyth P 7+6	Eze E 8+8	Ingram M 2	Kakay O 2	Lumley J 2	Match No.
1	2	3	4	5	6	7	8	9[1]	10[2]	11[3]	12	13	14																		1
1	2	3	4	5[2]	7	6	8[3]	9	10[1]	11				12	13	14															2
1	2	3	4[1]	5[2]	7	6	8	9	11[3]	10					12	13	14														3
1	2	3		13	6	8	9	5	10[3]	11	14		7[2]			12	4[1]														4
1		3		14	7	6	8	5	9[3]	11[1]	12	13			2	10	4[2]														5
1		3		5[2]	7	6	8	9	11[1]	10[2]			4	14		13	2	12													6
1		3[3]		5	7	6	8	9	11	10[2]	13		4	14		12	2														7
1				12		6	7	5	13		14		4	11[2]	8	2	10[1]	3		9[3]											8
1				9	7		8	5	11[1]	10	14	6[2]	4			2[1]	13	3			12										9
1				9	7	6	8	5	10[2]	12			4	14		13	2	3[3]		11[1]											10
1			4	7[2]	6	8	9	5	10[3]	13	11[1]		3			12	2	14													11
1			3	5[1]	6	7	10	4	9[2]	12	11			8			2			13											12
1			3	5	6	7	10	4	9[3]	12	11[1]			8[2]		13	2	14													13
1			3	13	7	6	8[2]	9		11	10[3]		4			14	12	2				5[1]									14
1					8	7	9	5	13	11	10[2]		4		14	12		3		6[1]	2[1]										15
1		3			8	7	9[2]	5	13	11	10[3]	14	4			12	2			6[1]											16
1		3			6	7[3]	8	9	11[2]	13	14		4		12		10	2			5[1]										17
1		3[3]	5	6		7	8	9	13		10[2]		4	12		14	2			11[1]											18
1			14	8	7	6	5	11[1]	10	9[3]			4	13		12	3				2[2]										19
1			2	8	7		5	11[4]	10	13			4			12	3[1]		9[3]			6[2]									20
1	3		2	9[3]	6	8	5[1]		10	13			4			11				12		7[2]	14								21
1	3		5	6	7	8[1]	9		10[2]	12			4			11[3]	2			13			14								22
1	3		5	7	6	8[2]	9		12	10[3]			4			13	2			11[1]			14								23
1	3		5	7[4]	6	9	8			11[2]			4			12	2			13	10[1]										24
1	3		6[2]		5	8	9			11[3]						12	2		14	10[1]	7		4	13							25
1	3	13		6	7	8	9[2]			4						11	2			5			12	10[1]						26
1	2	3		7	6	8[2]	9		10	4			13	5	12							11[1]									27
1	2	3		7[2]	6	8	9[3]		11	4			5	13		12					10[1]		14								28
1	3			5	7	8	9		10	4			6[1]	12	2[1]	13					11[3]		14								29
1	2	3	4	5	7		8	14	11[2]				9	12[3]		10[3]				13	6[1]										30
1	4[1]	3	2	5	8		10	9	11				7			13					6[2]					12					31
1		2	4	5	7	6	8	9[2]	11[1]				3			10										12	13				32
1		3	4	5	8	7[2]	6	9	11[1]							10	2[3]			13						12	14				33
1		2	4[1]	5	7	6	8	9[2]	13				3			11										10	12				34
1		3	14	13	7	6	8	5	11[1]				4			12	10[3]										9	12			35
1		3	12		7	6	8	5					4[2]	14	2	10				13						9[1]	11[1]				36
1	12	3	4	9[2]	8	7	14	5						6[2]	2	11				13							10[1]				37
1		3	4	9		7	8	5		13				6[2]	2	11[3]					14					12	10[1]				38
1		3	4	10	7	14	9	5		11[3]					2	12					6[1]					8[2]	13				39
1		3	4	13	7	6	10[2]	5			12			8	2	11[1]										14	9[3]				40
1		3[1]	4[3]	10[1]	7	6	9	5			13	12		8[2]	2					14							11				41
1			14	7[1]		8	5			10[2]			4	12	2	13	3		9[3]	6				11							42
				7	14	5				12			4	8	2	11[3]	3		10[2]	6[1]				13	9	1				43
12			10	7	6	9	5[1]			11				14	3	13	4						8[3]		1[1]	2					44
	12			6		7	4	13		11[3]				5	3	14				8[2]	9			10	2[1]	1					45
				2[3]	7		9	4						5	3	11				12	6	8[1]		14	13	10[2]			1		46

FA Cup
Third Round — Milton Keynes D — (h) — 0-1

Carabao Cup
First Round — Northampton T — (h) — 1-0
Second Round — Brentford — (h) — 1-4

READING

FOUNDATION

Reading was formed as far back as 1871 at a public meeting held at the Bridge Street Rooms. They first entered the FA Cup as early as 1877 when they amalgamated with the Reading Hornets. The club was further strengthened in 1889 when Earley FC joined them. They were the first winners of the Berks & Bucks Cup in 1878–79.

Madejski Stadium, Junction 11, M4, Reading, Berkshire RG2 0FL.

Telephone: (0118) 968 1100.

Fax: (0118) 968 1101.

Ticket Office: (0118) 968 1313.

Website: www.readingfc.co.uk

Email: customerservice@readingfc.co.uk

Ground Capacity: 24,162.

Record Attendance: 33,042 v Brentford, FA Cup 5th rd, 19 February 1927 (at Elm Park); 24,184 v Everton, FA Premier League, 17 November 2012 (at Madejski Stadium).

Pitch Measurements: 105m × 68m (115yd × 74.5yd).

Vice-Chairman: Sir John Madejski.

Chief Executive: Ron Gourlay.

Manager: Paul Clement.

Assistant Managers: Nigel Gibbs and Karl Halabi.

Colours: Blue and white hooped shirts, blue shorts, white socks with blue trim.

Year Formed: 1871.

Turned Professional: 1895.

Club Nickname: 'The Royals'.

Grounds: 1871, Reading Recreation; Reading Cricket Ground; 1882, Coley Park; 1889, Caversham Cricket Ground; 1896, Elm Park; 1998, Madejski Stadium.

First Football League Game: 28 August 1920, Division 3, v Newport Co (a) W 1–0 – Crawford; Smith, Horler; Christie, Mavin, Getgood; Spence, Weston, Yarnell, Bailey (1), Andrews.

Record League Victory: 10–2 v Crystal Palace, Division 3 (S), 4 September 1946 – Groves; Glidden, Gulliver; McKenna, Ratcliffe, Young; Chitty, Maurice Edelston (3), McPhee (4), Barney (1), Deverell (2).

Record Cup Victory: 6–0 v Leyton, FA Cup 2nd rd, 12 December 1925 – Duckworth; Eggo, McConnell; Wilson, Messer, Evans; Smith (2), Braithwaite (1), Davey (1), Tinsley, Robson (2).

Record Defeat: 0–18 v Preston NE, FA Cup 1st rd, 1893–94.

Most League Points (2 for a win): 65, Division 4, 1978–79.

HONOURS

League Champions: FL C – 2005–06, 2011–12; Second Division – 1993–94; Division 3 – 1985–86; Division 3S – 1925–26; Division 4 – 1978–79.
Runners-up: First Division – 1994–95; Second Division – 2001–02; Division 3S – 1931–32, 1934–35, 1948–49, 1951–52.
FA Cup: semi-final – 1927, 2015.
League Cup: 5th rd – 1996, 1998.
Full Members' Cup Winners: 1988.

THE Sun FACT FILE

The highest-ever attendance for a Reading match was for the 2011 Championship play-off final against Swansea City at Wembley Stadium. A total of 86,581 fans turned out to see the Royals go down to a 4-2 defeat. The only other occasion when they have played in front of a similar sized crowd was for the FA Cup semi-final against Arsenal, also at Wembley in April 2015 (84,081).

Most League Points (3 for a win): 106, Championship, 2005–06 (Football League Record).

Most League Goals: 112, Division 3 (S), 1951–52.

Highest League Scorer in Season: Ronnie Blackman, 39, Division 3 (S), 1951–52.

Most League Goals in Total Aggregate: Ronnie Blackman, 158, 1947–54.

Most League Goals in One Match: 6, Arthur Bacon v Stoke C, Division 2, 3 April 1931.

Most Capped Player: Chris Gunter, 51 (88), Wales.

Most League Appearances: Martin Hicks, 500, 1978–91.

Youngest League Player: Peter Castle, 16 years 49 days v Watford, 30 April 2003.

Record Transfer Fee Received: £7,000,000 from TSG 1899 Hoffenheim for Gylfi Sigurdsson, August 2010.

Record Transfer Fee Paid: £6,000,000 (rising to £7,500,000) to Fulham for Sone Aluko, August 2017.

Football League Record: 1920 Original Member of Division 3; 1921–26 Division 3 (S); 1926–31 Division 2; 1931–58 Division 3 (S); 1958–71 Division 3; 1971–76 Division 4; 1976–77 Division 3; 1977–79 Division 4; 1979–83 Division 3; 1983–84 Division 4; 1984–86 Division 3; 1986–88 Division 2; 1988–92 Division 3; 1992–94 Division 2; 1994–98 Division 1; 1998–2002 Division 2; 2002–04 Division 1; 2004–06 FL C; 2006–08 FA Premier League; 2008–12 FL C; 2012–13 FA Premier League; 2013– FL C.

LATEST SEQUENCES

Longest Sequence of League Wins: 13, 17.8.1985 – 19.10.1985.

Longest Sequence of League Defeats: 8, 29.12.2007 – 24.2.2008.

Longest Sequence of League Draws: 6, 23.3.2002 – 20.4.2002.

Longest Sequence of Unbeaten League Matches: 33, 9.8.2005 – 14.2.2006.

Longest Sequence Without a League Win: 14, 30.4.1927 – 29.10.1927.

Successive Scoring Runs: 32 from 1.10.1932.

Successive Non-scoring Runs: 6 from 29.3.2008.

MANAGERS

Thomas Sefton 1897–1901
(Secretary-Manager)
James Sharp 1901–02
Harry Matthews 1902–20
Harry Marshall 1920–22
Arthur Chadwick 1923–25
H. S. Bray 1925–26
(Secretary only since 1922 and 1926–35)
Andrew Wylie 1926–31
Joe Smith 1931–35
Billy Butler 1935–39
John Cochrane 1939
Joe Edelston 1939–47
Ted Drake 1947–52
Jack Smith 1952–55
Harry Johnston 1955–63
Roy Bentley 1963–69
Jack Mansell 1969–71
Charlie Hurley 1972–77
Maurice Evans 1977–84
Ian Branfoot 1984–89
Ian Porterfield 1989–91
Mark McGhee 1991–94
Jimmy Quinn and Mick Gooding 1994–97
Terry Bullivant 1997–98
Tommy Burns 1998–99
Alan Pardew 1999–2003
Steve Coppell 2003–09
Brendan Rodgers 2009
Brian McDermott 2009–13
Nigel Adkins 2013–14
Steve Clarke 2014–15
Brian McDermott 2015–16
Jaap Stam 2016–18
Paul Clement March 2018–

TEN YEAR LEAGUE RECORD

		P	W	D	L	F	A	Pts	Pos
2008-09	FL C	46	21	14	11	72	40	77	4
2009-10	FL C	46	17	12	17	68	63	63	9
2010-11	FL C	46	20	17	9	77	51	77	5
2011-12	FL C	46	27	8	11	69	41	89	1
2012-13	PR Lge	38	6	10	22	43	73	28	19
2013-14	FL C	46	19	14	13	70	56	71	7
2014-15	FL C	46	13	11	22	48	69	50	19
2015-16	FL C	46	13	13	20	52	59	52	17
2016-17	FL C	46	26	7	13	68	64	85	3
2017-18	FL C	46	10	14	22	48	70	44	20

DID YOU KNOW ?

John Swift's 13th-minute goal for Reading against Nottingham Forest on 31 October 2017 helped the Royals on their way to a comfortable 3-1 win over Nottingham Forest. The goal also had a wider historical significance as the 6,000th Football League goal scored by the club since they became members of the competition in 1920.

READING – SKY BET CHAMPIONSHIP 2017–18 LEAGUE RECORD

Match No.	Date	Venue	Opponents	Result		H/T Score	Lg Pos.	Goalscorers	Attendance
1	Aug 5	A	QPR	L	0-2	0-1	24		14,460
2	12	H	Fulham	D	1-1	0-0	20	Kelly [61]	17,398
3	15	H	Aston Villa	W	2-1	0-0	13	Whelan (og) [49], Barrow [55]	20,144
4	19	A	Preston NE	L	0-1	0-1	18		11,174
5	26	A	Birmingham C	W	2-0	0-0	11	Bodvarsson [60], Evans [85]	19,993
6	Sept 9	H	Bristol C	L	0-1	0-0	16		18,650
7	16	A	Brentford	D	1-1	0-1	18	Kelly (pen) [70]	9739
8	23	H	Hull C	D	1-1	0-1	18	Bodvarsson [87]	15,749
9	26	H	Millwall	L	1-2	0-0	18	Edwards [73]	10,399
10	30	H	Norwich C	L	1-2	1-1	20	Moore [13]	14,226
11	Oct 14	A	Leeds U	W	1-0	0-0	20	Barrow [84]	33,900
12	21	A	Sheffield U	L	1-2	0-2	20	Beerens [85]	26,265
13	28	H	Middlesbrough	L	0-2	0-1	20		17,928
14	31	H	Nottingham F	W	3-1	1-0	20	Swift 2 [13, 70], Aluko [78]	14,868
15	Nov 4	A	Derby Co	W	4-2	2-0	18	Moore [9], Aluko [13], Beerens [54], Barrow [75]	25,928
16	18	H	Wolverhampton W	L	0-2	0-1	19		20,708
17	21	A	Bolton W	D	2-2	0-2	19	Moore [76], Bacuna (pen) [83]	13,113
18	25	H	Sheffield W	D	0-0	0-0	18		18,382
19	28	H	Barnsley	W	3-0	2-0	16	Edwards [20], van den Berg [29], Bodvarsson [88]	13,317
20	Dec 2	A	Sunderland	W	3-1	0-0	14	Edwards [53], Barrow 2 [68, 71]	27,386
21	11	H	Cardiff C	D	2-2	2-0	14	Paterson (og) [16], Barrow [41]	16,670
22	16	A	Ipswich T	L	0-2	0-2	14		13,832
23	23	H	Burton Alb	L	1-2	0-1	14	Barrow [76]	21,771
24	26	A	Bristol C	L	0-2	0-0	17		23,116
25	30	A	Barnsley	D	1-1	0-0	17	Kermorgant [68]	11,945
26	Jan 2	H	Birmingham C	L	0-2	0-1	18		14,491
27	13	A	Hull C	D	0-0	0-0	18		14,300
28	20	H	Brentford	L	0-1	0-0	18		17,893
29	30	A	Burton Alb	W	3-1	1-0	18	Bodvarsson 2 [20, 68], Gunter [57]	2750
30	Feb 3	H	Millwall	L	0-2	0-0	18		17,282
31	10	A	Middlesbrough	L	1-2	0-1	18	Martin [78]	23,491
32	20	A	Nottingham F	D	1-1	1-0	18	Richards [35]	21,846
33	24	H	Derby Co	D	3-3	2-2	18	Kelly [16], Barrow [32], Bodvarsson [80]	17,647
34	27	H	Sheffield U	L	1-3	0-2	18	Richards [51]	6769
35	Mar 6	H	Bolton W	D	1-1	1-1	18	Barrow [32]	8631
36	10	H	Leeds U	D	2-2	1-1	19	Bodvarsson [16], O'Kane (og) [58]	19,770
37	13	A	Wolverhampton W	L	0-3	0-1	19		27,341
38	17	A	Norwich C	L	2-3	1-3	20	Kelly [32], Smith [51]	25,098
39	30	H	QPR	W	1-0	1-0	19	Aluko [13]	20,273
40	Apr 3	A	Aston Villa	L	0-3	0-0	19		29,223
41	7	H	Preston NE	W	1-0	1-0	19	Barrow [12]	15,501
42	10	A	Fulham	L	0-1	0-1	19		19,272
43	14	A	Sunderland	D	2-2	1-0	19	Kelly (pen) [20], Kermorgant [79]	17,348
44	21	A	Sheffield W	L	0-3	0-1	19		24,373
45	28	H	Ipswich T	L	0-4	0-0	19		17,683
46	May 6	A	Cardiff C	D	0-0	0-0	20		32,478

Final League Position: 20

GOALSCORERS

League (48): Barrow 10, Bodvarsson 7, Kelly 5 (2 pens), Aluko 3, Edwards 3, Moore 3, Beerens 2, Kermorgant 2, Richards 2, Swift 2, Bacuna 1 (1 pen), Evans 1, Gunter 1, Martin 1, Smith 1, van den Berg 1, own goals 3.
FA Cup (4): Bodvarsson 3, own goal 1.
Carabao Cup (5): Kelly 2, Bacuna 1, Evans 1, Smith 1.
Checkatrade Trophy (7): Popa 2, Barrett 1, House 1, Medford-Smith 1, Rollinson 1, Sheppard 1.

Mannone V 41	Gunter C 46	Moore L 46	Tiago Ilori A 26 + 3	Popa A 3 + 3	Kelly L 28 + 6	Evans G 9 + 9	Blackett T 19 + 6	Swift J 17 + 7	Clement P 10 + 13	Bodvarsson J 20 + 13	Barrow M 37 + 4	Richards O 9 + 4	Mendes J 1 + 2	McShane P 24 + 2	van den Berg J 31 + 2	McCleary G 9 + 9	Beerens R 9 + 8	Bacuna L 29 + 4	Smith S 4 + 4	Aluko S 36 + 3	Edwards D 27 + 5	Obita J — + 2	Kermorgant Y 13 + 12	Jaakkola A 5	Elphick T 2 + 2	Martin C 4 + 6	Holmes T 1	Match No.
1	2	3	4	5	6	7	8	9³	10¹	11²	12	13	14															1
1	5	4	2¹	14	6	7²	8	9	13		10³		11	3	12													2
1	2	4		10²	7	12	5	9	11		8³			3	6¹	13	14	7										3
1	2	4		10	6²	12	5	9³	11¹		8	13		3		14	7											4
1	5	3	4	7	12	9		11³	10²					2	8¹	13		6	14									5
1	2	4		8³	5			10²	9¹					3	7	13	14	6		11	12							6
1	2	4		9³	5¹			11²						3	7	8	12	14		10	6	13						7
1	5¹	3	13	6³		9²		14						2	4	10	7			11	8	12						8
1	5	4	3			8²		13	12					2	6	9¹	10			11	7							9
1	2	4		8	5¹			12	13	14				3	7	11³	10	6		9²								10
1	5	4	3	13				14	10	12				8	6²	9¹	2		11²	7								11
1	2	3	4			9³	13	14		10				12	8		11	5¹		7²	6							12
1	5	4	3²	7³		12	9			13				2	6¹	10		11	8				14					13
1	5	4		9		12	10¹			3	7²			14	2	11³	8	6	13									14
1	2	4		13	9	14	10²	5¹		3				11	7		8¹	6	12									15
1	8	4	3³			7		14	11					2	6	9¹	5	13	12	10²								16
	2	4		5³	7²	12	13	11						3		10¹	8		9	6		1						17
1	8	4	6¹			13	12	11³						2	3	14	5	9	7	10²								18
1	5	4	14	13	9²			12	10					3	6		2		7³	8	11¹							19
1	5	4		9²				13	14	10				3	6	12	2		8³	7	11¹							20
1	5	4	13	9²				12	10					3	6		2		8¹	7	11							21
1	2	4		12	5²			13	11					3	7		6		9¹	8	10							22
1	5	4		8¹		12		13	11					3	7		2		9	6²	10							23
1	2	4		8¹				10²	11					3	7	13	14	2³		9	6	12						24
1	2	4		13	5	9¹		14	10					3	6³		8²		12	7	11							25
1	2	4		14	12	6	9¹		10					3	7²	13		5		8	11							26
1	2	4	13		7		9¹		10	5				3³	6	8²	14		12		11							27
1	2	4	3	9	7	12		11	10	5¹					6³	13		8²		14								28
1	4	3	2		13			11	9					8²			5		7¹	6	10		12					29
1	5	3	2			12³		11	9					7	14	8			6	10¹			4²	13				30
1	2	4	3	9³				13	11²					7	10¹		5		8	6			12					31
1	2	3	4	9²	13				10³	5				7¹	12		6		8	14			11					32
1	2	4	3	7¹		12		9²	11	10³	5				13		6		8	14								33
1	5	3	2³	9	13			7	11		12			4	8³		6¹	14					10					34
	5	4		9	6		13	2	12	10						8²	7					1				11¹	3	35
	5	4	3	7	6¹		12	9²	11	10					2		8	13			1							36
	2	4	3	7²	5		8	10¹	11							12	13	9	6		1							37
	2	4	3	7³		5	12	8		11				13		10	6¹	9²		14	1							38
1	2	4	3	14	5	9³				10				6²		12	8	7	13		11¹							39
1	2	4	3	13	8²	5		12	10							7	11¹	6³	9			14						40
1	2	4	3	7³	14			9	12	11¹	10	5²			6		8				13							41
1	2	3	4	6				12		11²	10	5³			7			8	9¹	13			14					42
1	2	4	3		8²	12	7		10	11	5¹						9	6	13									43
1	2	4	3	7		5▪	9	14	11²	10	13			6³			8¹		12									44
1	2	3	4	7			8	10¹	9	5²						14	6		11³	12	13							45
1	5	4	2³	12				10²	11		14	7			6		9¹	8		13	3							46

FA Cup

Third Round	Stevenage	(a)	0-0	
Replay	Stevenage	(h)	3-0	
Fourth Round	Sheffield W	(a)	1-3	

Carabao Cup

First Round	Gillingham	(h)	2-0
Second Round	Millwall	(h)	3-1
(aet)			
Third Round	Swansea C	(h)	0-2

Checkatrade Trophy (Reading U21)

Southern Group B	Colchester U	(a)	2-2
(Colchester U won 6-5 on penalties)			
Southern Group B	Southend U	(a)	0-1
Southern Group B	Gillingham	(a)	5-7

ROCHDALE

The Crown Oil Arena, Sandy Lane, Rochdale, Lancashire OL11 5DR.

Telephone: (0844) 826 1907.

Fax: (01706) 648 466.

Ticket Office: (0844) 826 1907 (option 8).

Website: www.rochdaleafc.co.uk

Email: admin@rochdaleafc.co.uk

Ground Capacity: 10,037.

Record Attendance: 24,231 v Notts Co, FA Cup 2nd rd, 10 December 1949.

Pitch Measurements: 104m × 69.5m (114yd × 76yd).

Chairman: Chris Dunphy.

Chief Executive: Russ Green.

Manager: Keith Hill.

Assistant Manager: Chris Beech.

Colours: Blue shirts with white and black trim, white shorts with blue and black trim, blue socks with white and black trim.

Year Formed: 1907.

Turned Professional: 1907.

Club Nickname: 'The Dale'.

Ground: 1907, St Clements Playing Fields (renamed Spotland) (renamed The Crown Oil Arena, 2016).

First Football League Game: 27 August 1921, Division 3 (N), v Accrington Stanley (h) W 6–3 – Crabtree; Nuttall, Sheehan; Hill, Farrer, Yarwood; Hoad, Sandiford, Dennison (2), Owens (3), Carney (1).

Record League Victory: 8–1 v Chesterfield, Division 3 (N), 18 December 1926 – Hill; Brown, Ward; Hillhouse, Parkes, Braidwood; Hughes, Bertram, Whitehurst (5), Schofield (2), Martin (1).

Record Cup Victory: 8–2 v Crook T, FA Cup 1st rd, 26 November 1927 – Moody; Hopkins, Ward; Braidwood, Parkes, Barker; Tompkinson, Clennell (3) Whitehurst (4), Hall, Martin (1).

Record Defeat: 1–9 v Tranmere R, Division 3 (N), 25 December 1931.

Most League Points (2 for a win): 62, Division 3 (N), 1923–24.

HONOURS

League: Runners-up: Division 3N – 1923–24, 1926–27.
FA Cup: 5th rd – 1990, 2003.
League Cup: Runners-up: 1962.

THE Sun FACT FILE

Rochdale were one of a number of clubs to experience acute financial problems in the early 1930s. Towards the end of 1931 the club's directors discussed whether they should resign from the League as the situation was so bad. Players were owed wages and the manager resigned but Sunderland loaned two inside-forwards to help out. Results didn't improve as the team finished bottom of Division Three North but the club survived.

Most League Points (3 for a win): 82, FL 2, 2009–10.

Most League Goals: 105, Division 3 (N), 1926–27.

Highest League Scorer in Season: Albert Whitehurst, 44, Division 3 (N), 1926–27.

Most League Goals in Total Aggregate: Reg Jenkins, 119, 1964–73.

Most League Goals in One Match: 6, Tommy Tippett v Hartlepools U, Division 3 (N), 21 April 1930.

Most Capped Player: Leo Bertos, 6 (56), New Zealand.

Most League Appearances: Gary Jones, 470, 1998–2001; 2003–12.

Youngest League Player: Zac Hughes, 16 years 105 days v Exeter C, 19 September 1987.

Record Transfer Fee Received: £750,000 (rising to £4,125,000) from Brentford for Scott Hogan, July 2014.

Record Transfer Fee Paid: £150,000 to Stoke C for Paul Connor, March 2001.

Football League Record: 1921 Elected to Division 3 (N); 1958–59 Division 3; 1959–69 Division 4; 1969–74 Division 3; 1974–92 Division 4; 1992–2004 Division 3; 2004–10 FL 2; 2010–12 FL 1; 2012–14 FL 2; 2014– FL 1.

LATEST SEQUENCES

Longest Sequence of League Wins: 8, 29.9.1969 – 3.11.1969.

Longest Sequence of League Defeats: 17, 14.11.1931 – 12.3.1932.

Longest Sequence of League Draws: 6, 17.8.1968 – 14.9.1968.

Longest Sequence of Unbeaten League Matches: 20, 15.9.1923 – 19.1.1924.

Longest Sequence Without a League Win: 28, 14.11.1931 – 29.8.1932.

Successive Scoring Runs: 29 from 10.10.2008.

Successive Non-scoring Runs: 9 from 14.3.1980.

MANAGERS

Billy Bradshaw 1920
Run by committee 1920–22
Tom Wilson 1922–23
Jack Peart 1923–30
Will Cameron 1930–31
Herbert Hopkinson 1932–34
Billy Smith 1934–35
Ernest Nixon 1935–37
Sam Jennings 1937–38
Ted Goodier 1938–52
Jack Warner 1952–53
Harry Catterick 1953–58
Jack Marshall 1958–60
Tony Collins 1960–68
Bob Stokoe 1967–68
Len Richley 1968–70
Dick Conner 1970–73
Walter Joyce 1973–76
Brian Green 1976–77
Mike Ferguson 1977–78
Doug Collins 1979
Bob Stokoe 1979–80
Peter Madden 1980–83
Jimmy Greenhoff 1983–84
Vic Halom 1984–86
Eddie Gray 1986–88
Danny Bergara 1988–89
Terry Dolan 1989–91
Dave Sutton 1991–94
Mick Docherty 1994–96
Graham Barrow 1996–99
Steve Parkin 1999–2001
John Hollins 2001–02
Paul Simpson 2002–03
Alan Buckley 2003
Steve Parkin 2003–06
Keith Hill 2007–11
   (Caretaker from December 2006)
Steve Eyre 2011
John Coleman 2012–13
Keith Hill January 2013–

TEN YEAR LEAGUE RECORD

		P	W	D	L	F	A	Pts	Pos
2008-09	FL 2	46	19	13	14	70	59	70	6
2009-10	FL 2	46	25	7	14	82	48	82	3
2010-11	FL 1	46	18	14	14	63	55	68	9
2011-12	FL 1	46	8	14	24	47	81	38	24
2012-13	FL 2	46	16	13	17	68	70	61	12
2013-14	FL 2	46	24	9	13	69	48	81	3
2014-15	FL 1	46	19	6	21	72	66	63	8
2015-16	FL 1	46	19	12	15	68	61	69	10
2016-17	FL 1	46	19	12	15	71	62	69	9
2017-18	FL 1	46	11	18	17	49	57	51	20

DID YOU KNOW

The contribution made by Charlie Hurst to the history of English football was considerably greater than the four appearances he made for Rochdale in the 1946–47 season. His son Geoff went on to win 49 England caps and his hat-trick in the 1966 World Cup final provided one of the greatest ever occasions in the nation's football history.

ROCHDALE – SKY BET LEAGUE ONE 2017–18 LEAGUE RECORD

Match No.	Date	Venue	Opponents	Result	H/T Score	Lg Pos.	Goalscorers	Attendance
1	Aug 5	A	Portsmouth	L	0-2	0-0	23		18,009
2	12	H	Scunthorpe U	D	1-1	0-0	19	Davies [55]	3218
3	19	A	Shrewsbury T	L	2-3	1-2	21	Davies 2 (2 pens) [17, 63]	5001
4	26	H	Bury	D	0-0	0-0	22		4601
5	Sept 2	A	Southend U	D	0-0	0-0	21		6208
6	9	H	Blackburn R	L	0-3	0-1	21		6524
7	12	H	Doncaster R	W	2-1	0-0	18	Davies [90], Kitching [90]	2371
8	16	A	Milton Keynes D	L	2-3	2-2	21	Inman [8], Done [42]	7670
9	23	H	Gillingham	W	3-0	2-0	18	Henderson [24], Rafferty [26], Done [90]	2793
10	26	A	Blackpool	D	0-0	0-0	17		3399
11	30	A	AFC Wimbledon	D	0-0	0-0	17		3861
12	Oct 7	H	Rotherham U	L	0-1	0-0	18		4113
13	14	A	Fleetwood T	D	2-2	0-1	20	Inman [48], Henderson [53]	3260
14	17	H	Northampton T	D	2-2	1-0	20	Henderson 2 [25, 62]	2138
15	21	H	Bristol R	W	1-0	1-0	17	Done [7]	2944
16	28	A	Plymouth Arg	D	1-1	1-1	19	Done [33]	8805
17	Nov 18	A	Oldham Ath	L	1-3	1-1	22	Done [16]	6129
18	21	A	Charlton Ath	L	1-2	1-1	22	Gillam [13]	8801
19	25	H	Peterborough U	W	2-0	2-0	19	Andrew [33], Camps [36]	2555
20	Dec 9	A	Bradford C	L	3-4	2-3	19	Henderson 2 [41, 45], Davies [75]	19,621
21	16	H	Oxford U	D	0-0	0-0	21		2588
22	23	H	Walsall	D	1-1	0-0	23	Andrew [63]	2702
23	26	A	Blackburn R	L	0-2	0-2	23		15,115
24	29	A	Doncaster R	L	0-2	0-2	23		7997
25	Jan 1	H	Blackpool	L	1-2	0-0	23	Kitching [90]	3165
26	13	A	Gillingham	L	1-2	1-1	23	Cannon [27]	4352
27	Feb 3	H	Northampton T	W	1-0	0-0	23	Andrew [53]	5475
28	13	A	Bristol R	L	2-3	1-0	24	Henderson 2 [29, 66]	9219
29	21	H	Milton Keynes D	D	0-0	0-0	23		2353
30	24	A	Wigan Ath	L	0-1	0-1	24		8654
31	Mar 6	A	Walsall	W	3-0	1-0	23	McNulty [16], Henderson [71], Dobre [87]	3505
32	10	A	Rotherham U	W	1-0	0-0	22	Humphrys [67]	8418
33	13	H	Southend U	D	0-0	0-0	23		2286
34	17	H	AFC Wimbledon	D	1-1	1-1	23	Cannon [25]	2667
35	20	H	Fleetwood T	L	0-2	0-0	23		2403
36	24	A	Scunthorpe U	D	1-1	1-0	23	Camps [20]	3789
37	30	H	Shrewsbury T	W	3-1	1-1	23	Rathbone [45], Davies [80], Henderson [90]	4098
38	Apr 3	A	Bury	W	2-0	2-0	22	Delaney [30], Henderson [43]	4628
39	7	H	Portsmouth	D	3-3	1-1	21	Inman [13], Humphrys [57], Henderson [71]	3781
40	10	A	Wigan Ath	L	1-4	0-1	21	Davies (pen) [87]	3850
41	14	A	Peterborough U	W	1-0	1-0	21	Henderson [16]	5496
42	17	H	Oldham Ath	D	0-0	0-0	21		6261
43	21	H	Bradford C	D	1-1	1-0	21	Done [41]	4365
44	24	H	Plymouth Arg	D	1-1	0-0	19	Delaney [55]	2760
45	28	A	Oxford U	L	1-2	0-0	21	Inman [59]	8375
46	May 5	H	Charlton Ath	W	1-0	0-0	20	Thompson [69]	5294

Final League Position: 20

GOALSCORERS

League (49): Henderson 13, Davies 7 (3 pens), Done 6, Inman 4, Andrew 3, Camps 2, Cannon 2, Delaney 2, Humphrys 2, Kitching 2, Dobre 1, Gillam 1, McNulty 1, Rafferty 1, Rathbone 1, Thompson 1.
FA Cup (15): Henderson 6 (1 pen), Andrew 2, Done 2, Inman 2, Camps 1, Davies 1, Humphrys 1.
Carabao Cup (1): Camps 1.
Checkatrade Trophy (6): Inman 2, Bunney 1, Gillam 1 (1 pen), Henderson 1, Slew 1.

Lillis J 40	Brown R 2+1	Keane K 3	McNulty J 40	Nthe K 11+9	Cannon A 18+3	Allen J 3+1	Camps C 41+1	Rathbone O 30+3	Andrew C 26+5	Henderson I 39	Done M 40+6	Rafferty J 30+3	Davies S 8+24	Canavan N 3	Moore B 6	McGahey H 41+1	Inman B 25+12	Bunney J 18+2	Williams Jordan LR 6+5	Gillam M 1+7	Williams M Jordan 12	Kitching M 10+3	Daniels D 14+1	Slew J —+5	Thompson J 3+7	Adshead D —+1	Knott B 1+3	Wiseman S 7+6	Delaney R 16+2	Humphrys S 11+5	Hart S 1+2	Dobre M —+5	Match No.
1	2	3⁴	4	5	6³	7	8²	9	10¹	11	12	13	14																				1
1	2		3	5	13		9²	8	7¹	14	10	11³	6	12	4																		2
			3	5²	12		8¹	6			9	14	7		10	4³	1	2	11	13													3
12			3	5³	7	6					9	8	2		10²	1	4	13			11¹	14											4
			5		8³				11⁸	10²	2	13	4	1	3	14			7¹		6	9	12										5
			3		6		12		11		10³	2	13			5	9¹	14	7	8²	4												6
			3		8			7¹			9²	2	11	1		4	10	5		6	12	13											7
			4	12	8³		13	6			11	2	10¹	1	3	9	5²		7			14											8
1			4	13			8	6	12	11	14	2	10²			3	9¹	5³		7													9
1			4				8	6¹	12	10	13		14			3	11³	5	9²	7		2											10
1			4	14			8	6¹	9³	10	12		13			3	11²	5	9²	7		2											11
1			3				7¹	6³	12	10	11²		9			4	13	5		8		2	14										12
1			3				7		10	8	9²	12				4	11	5	13	6		2¹											13
1			4				8		10²	11	6¹	2	12			3	9	5		7		13											14
1			4				7		10²	11	6	2	12			3	9¹	5	13	8													15
1			4	12			6		10	7	9²	2	13			3	11	5¹		8													16
1			4	5¹			7	6²	11	8	10	2	14			3	9²	12		13													17
1			4		13		6²	7	11	8	10¹	2				3	14	5	9¹			2											18
1			5	14			8	7	10	9	11¹	2				3		6²		13		4	12³										19
1		3¹	9	13			6	7	11	8	10³	5¹	14			4			12			2											20
1							7	6	11	8	9¹	2	10²			3	13	5	12			4											21
1							7	6	11	10	9²	2				3	12	5	8¹			4	13										22
1	4¹		5				6	10		9	14		13			2	8²	7	11³			3	12										23
1	7²		4	9			6	8	12	10	11		13³			2		5¹				3		14									24
1			4	8			6	9²	7¹	11	5					2³	12		14			10	3	13									25
1		3	4⁵	5			6		11	9	10³					14	13	8²				7	2		12								26
1			4	8			7¹		10	11	6	2					9					3	5	12			3	5	12				27
1			3		6¹		7			10	9	5				12			8²			13	14	2	4	11³							28
1			3		6		7			10	9	5¹	13			2			8				12	4	11²								29
1		3¹	8		7³		9²		11	6			12			4			10				14	2	5	13							30
1	2		8		6				11	9	5	12				4	7²					3	10¹			13							31
1			3	8			7	13		11	9	5	12			2	6¹						4	10²									32
1			3	8²			7	13		11	9		12			2	6¹						5	4	10³	14							33
1			3	8¹			7			11	9		12			2	6²					13	5	4	10								34
1			3	8²			6			11	9		2			14			12				7¹	5	4¹⁰		13						35
1			4	12			9	8¹	11	7	6	2				3	10¹							13	14	5³							36
1			4	5¹			7	9²	11	8	6	2	13			3	12							14	10³								37
1			4	13			7²	9	10³	8	6	2				3	11¹							12	5	14							38
1			4				7	8	10	11	5	2				3	6¹						12		13	9²							39
1			4²				6	8	10	9	5	2	12			3	7								13	11¹		14					40
1		3	13				9¹	8²	11	7⁸	10	2				4			5²			14		12	6								41
1			3				7	8	10		9	5¹				2	11						6²		13	4	12						42
1			3	12			7	8	10	9	5					2	11²				14		6¹		4	13							43
1				7			8	10¹		5	13	14	3			11	12		6¹				2	4	9²								44
1	2			8³			9	10	6	5	14		3			11¹	12					7²		4					13				45
1	3³			7			8¹	10	11	9	5	13	2			6²						12		4	14								46

FA Cup

First Round	Bromley	(h)	4-0	
Second Round	Slough T	(a)	4-0	
Third Round	Doncaster R	(a)	1-0	
Fourth Round	Millwall	(a)	2-2	
Replay	Millwall	(h)	1-0	
Fifth Round	Tottenham H	(h)	2-2	
Replay	Tottenham H	(a)	1-6	

Carabao Cup

First Round	Mansfield T	(a)	1-0
Second Round	Stoke C	(a)	0-4

Checkatrade Trophy

Northern Group C Bury		(a)	4-0
Northern Group C Stoke C U21		(h)	0-0
(Stoke C U21 won 5-4 on penalties)			
Northern Group C Blackburn R		(h)	1-1
(Rochdale won 5-3 on penalties)			
Second Round North Doncaster R		(h)	1-1
(Rochdale won 5-4 on penalties)			
Third Round Lincoln C		(h)	0-1

ROTHERHAM UNITED

FOUNDATION

Rotherham were formed in 1870 before becoming Town in the late 1880s. Thornhill United were founded in 1877 and changed their name to Rotherham County in 1905. The Town amalgamated with Rotherham County to form Rotherham United in 1925.

The AESSEAL New York Stadium, New York Way, Rotherham, South Yorkshire S60 1AH.

Telephone: (0844) 4140 733.

Fax: (0170) 987 774.

Ticket Office: (0170) 982 7768.

Website: www.themillers.co.uk

Email: office@rotherhamunited.net

Ground Capacity: 12,053.

Record Attendance: 25,170 v Sheffield U, Division 2, 13 December 1952 (at Millmoor); 7,082 v Aldershot T, FL 2 Play-offs semi-final 2nd leg, 19 May 2010 (at Don Valley); 11,758 v Sheffield U, FL 1, 7 September 2013 (at New York Stadium).

Pitch Measurements: 102m × 66m (111.5yd × 72yd).

Chairman: Tony Stewart.

Chief Operating Officer: Paul Douglas.

Manager: Paul Warne.

Assistant Manager: Richie Barker.

HONOURS

League Champions: Division 3 – 1980–81; Division 3N – 1950–51; Division 4 – 1988–89.
Runners-up: Second Division – 2000–01; Division 3N – 1946–47, 1947–48, 1948–49; FL 2 – 2012–13; Third Division – 1999–2000; Division 4 – 1991–92.
FA Cup: 5th rd – 1953, 1968.
League Cup: Runners-up: 1961.
League Trophy Winners: 1996.

Colours: Red shirts with white trim, white shorts with red trim, red socks with white trim.

Year Formed: 1870. *Turned Professional:* 1905. *Club Nickname:* 'The Millers'.

Previous Names: 1877, Thornhill United; 1905, Rotherham County; 1925, amalgamated with Rotherham Town under Rotherham United.

Grounds: 1870, Red House Ground; 1907, Millmoor; 2008, Don Valley Stadium; 2012, New York Stadium (renamed The AESSEAL New York Stadium, 2014).

First Football League Game: 2 September 1893, Division 2, Rotherham T v Lincoln C (a) D 1–1 – McKay; Thickett, Watson; Barr, Brown, Broadhead; Longden, Cutts, Leatherbarrow, McCormick, Pickering, (1 og). 30 August 1919, Division 2, Rotherham Co v Nottingham F (h) W 2–0 – Branston; Alton, Baines; Bailey, Coe, Stanton; Lee (1), Cawley (1), Glennon, Lees, Lamb.

Record League Victory: 8–0 v Oldham Ath, Division 3 (N), 26 May 1947 – Warnes; Selkirk, Ibbotson; Edwards, Horace Williams, Danny Williams; Wilson (2), Shaw (1), Ardron (3), Guest (1), Hainsworth (1).

Record Cup Victory: 6–0 v Spennymoor U, FA Cup 2nd rd, 17 December 1977 – McAlister; Forrest, Breckin, Womble, Stancliffe, Green, Finney, Phillips (3), Gwyther (2) (Smith), Goodfellow, Crawford (1). 6–0 v Wolverhampton W, FA Cup 1st rd, 16 November 1985 – O'Hanlon; Forrest, Dungworth, Gooding (1), Smith (1), Pickering, Birch (2), Emerson, Tynan (1), Simmons (1), Pugh. 6–0 v King's Lynn, FA Cup 2nd rd, 6 December 1997 – Mimms; Clark, Hurst (Goodwin), Garner (1) (Hudson) (1), Warner (Bass), Richardson (1), Berry (1), Thompson, Druce (1), Glover (1), Roscoe.

Record Defeat: 1–11 v Bradford C, Division 3 (N), 25 August 1928.

Sun FACT FILE

Rotherham United were the first team to progress in the FA Cup following a penalty shoot-out. Drawn to play Scunthorpe United in the first round in the 1991–92 season, the Millers drew 1-1 away from home and then 3-3 after extra time in the replay. They were successful by 7-6 in the shoot-out that followed to earn a visit to Burnley in the second round.

Most League Points (2 for a win): 71, Division 3 (N), 1950–51.

Most League Points (3 for a win): 91, Division 2, 2000–01.

Most League Goals: 114, Division 3 (N), 1946–47.

Highest League Scorer in Season: Wally Ardron, 38, Division 3 (N), 1946–47.

Most League Goals in Total Aggregate: Gladstone Guest, 130, 1946–56.

Most League Goals in One Match: 4, Roland Bastow v York C, Division 3 (N), 9 November 1935; 4, Roland Bastow v Rochdale, Division 3 (N), 7 March 1936; 4, Wally Ardron v Crewe Alex, Division 3 (N), 5 October 1946; 4, Wally Ardron v Carlisle U, Division 3 (N), 13 September 1947; 4, Wally Ardron v Hartlepools U, Division 3 (N), 13 October 1948; 4, Ian Wilson v Liverpool, Division 2, 2 May 1955; 4, Carl Gilbert v Swansea C, Division 3, 28 September 1971; 4, Carl Airey v Chester, Division 3, 31 August 1987; 4, Shaun Goater v Hartlepool U, Division 3, 9 April 1994; 4, Lee Glover v Hull C, Division 3, 28 December 1997; 4, Darren Byfield v Millwall, Division 1, 10 August 2002; 4, Adam Le Fondre v Cheltenham T, FL 2, 21 August 2010.

Most Capped Player: Kari Arnason, 20 (69), Iceland.

Most League Appearances: Danny Williams, 461, 1946–62.

Youngest League Player: Kevin Eley, 16 years 72 days v Scunthorpe U, 15 May 1984.

Record Transfer Fee Received: £900,000 from Bristol C for Kieran Agard, August 2014.

Record Transfer Fee Paid: £500,000 to Peterborough U for Jon Taylor, August 2016.

Football League Record: 1893 Rotherham Town elected to Division 2; 1896 Failed re-election; 1919 Rotherham County elected to Division 2; 1923–51 Division 3 (N); 1951–68 Division 2; 1968–73 Division 3; 1973–75 Division 4; 1975–81 Division 3; 1981–83 Division 4; 1983–88 Division 3; 1988–89 Division 4; 1989–91 Division 3; 1991–92 Division 4; 1992–97 Division 2; 1997–2000 Division 3; 2000–01 Division 2; 2001–04 Division 1; 2004–05 FL C; 2005–07 FL 1; 2007–13 FL 2; 2013–14 FL 1; 2014–17 FL C; 2017–18 FL 1; 2018– FL C.

MANAGERS

Billy Heald 1925–29 *(Secretary only for several years)*
Stanley Davies 1929–30
Billy Heald 1930–33
Reg Freeman 1934–52
Andy Smailes 1952–58
Tom Johnston 1958–62
Danny Williams 1962–65
Jack Mansell 1965–67
Tommy Docherty 1967–68
Jimmy McAnearney 1968–73
Jimmy McGuigan 1973–79
Ian Porterfield 1979–81
Emlyn Hughes 1981–83
George Kerr 1983–85
Norman Hunter 1985–87
Dave Cusack 1987–88
Billy McEwan 1988–91
Phil Henson 1991–94
Archie Gemmill and John McGovern 1994–96
Danny Bergara 1996–97
Ronnie Moore 1997–2005
Mick Harford 2005
Alan Knill 2005–07
Mark Robins 2007–09
Ronnie Moore 2009–11
Andy Scott 2011–12
Steve Evans 2012–15
Neil Redfearn 2015–16
Neil Warnock 2016
Alan Stubbs 2016
Kenny Jackett 2016
Paul Warne November 2016–

LATEST SEQUENCES

Longest Sequence of League Wins: 9, 2.2.1982 – 6.3.1982.

Longest Sequence of League Defeats: 10, 14.2.2017 – 8.4.2017.

Longest Sequence of League Draws: 6, 13.10.1969 – 22.11.1969.

Longest Sequence of Unbeaten League Matches: 18, 13.10.1969 – 7.2.1970.

Longest Sequence Without a League Win: 21, 9.5.2004 – 20.11.2004.

Successive Scoring Runs: 30 from 3.4.1954.

Successive Non-scoring Runs: 6 from 21.8.2004.

TEN YEAR LEAGUE RECORD

		P	W	D	L	F	A	Pts	Pos
2008-09	FL 2	46	21	12	13	60	46	58*	14
2009-10	FL 2	46	21	10	15	55	52	73	5
2010-11	FL 2	46	17	15	14	75	60	66	9
2011-12	FL 2	46	18	13	15	67	63	67	10
2012-13	FL 2	46	24	7	15	74	59	79	2
2013-14	FL 1	46	24	14	8	86	58	86	4
2014-15	FL C	46	11	16	19	46	67	46†	21
2015-16	FL C	46	13	10	23	53	71	49	21
2016-17	FL C	46	5	8	33	40	98	23	24
2017-18	FL 1	46	24	7	15	73	53	79	4

17 pts deducted; †3 pts deducted.

DID YOU KNOW ?

Rotherham United gates more than doubled following the appointment of Tommy Docherty as manager in November 1967. However, he was not a great success at Millmoor and the club were relegated at the end of the season. He stayed until shortly before the end of 1968 before moving on to Queens Park Rangers.

ROTHERHAM UNITED – SKY BET LEAGUE ONE 2017–18 LEAGUE RECORD

Match No.	Date	Venue	Opponents	Result	H/T Score	Lg Pos.	Goalscorers	Atten- dance
1	Aug 5	A	Fleetwood T	L	0-2	0-1	24		3623
2	12	H	Southend U	W	5-0	4-0	7	Moore 3 [15, 16, 45], Newell [23], Williams [59]	8004
3	19	A	Peterborough U	L	1-2	0-0	15	Moore [55]	6344
4	26	H	Charlton Ath	L	0-2	0-1	19		7976
5	Sept 3	A	Portsmouth	W	1-0	1-0	12	Taylor [36]	17,118
6	9	H	Bury	W	3-2	1-1	11	Moore 2 [20, 54], Towell [89]	7848
7	12	H	Walsall	W	5-1	4-0	9	Frecklington 3 [13, 31, 88], Taylor 2 [16, 24]	7330
8	16	A	Bradford C	L	0-1	0-1	8		20,881
9	23	H	Oldham Ath	W	5-1	1-1	8	Ihiekwe [8], Moore 2 [73, 78], Forde [87], Yates [89]	8250
10	26	A	Blackburn R	L	0-2	0-1	10		10,228
11	30	H	Northampton T	W	1-0	0-0	8	Moore [52]	8073
12	Oct 7	A	Rochdale	W	1-0	0-0	4	Wood [57]	4113
13	14	H	Scunthorpe U	W	2-0	1-0	4	Vaulks [37], Moore [71]	9167
14	17	A	AFC Wimbledon	L	1-3	0-1	4	Newell [70]	3907
15	21	A	Oxford U	D	3-3	2-3	5	Newell [20], Williams [44], Moore [78]	7471
16	28	H	Gillingham	L	1-3	0-1	6	Moore [56]	7865
17	Nov 11	A	Doncaster R	D	1-1	0-0	6	Moore [90]	12,481
18	18	H	Shrewsbury T	L	1-2	0-1	8	Towell [76]	8184
19	25	H	Wigan Ath	L	1-3	1-2	12	David Ball [16]	8443
20	Dec 2	A	Bristol R	L	1-2	0-0	13	Williams [56]	7531
21	9	A	Blackpool	W	2-1	0-1	9	David Ball 2 [76, 87]	3654
22	16	H	Plymouth Arg	D	1-1	0-0	9	Ajayi [90]	7562
23	23	A	Milton Keynes D	W	2-1	2-1	8	Aneke (og) [21], Vaulks [29]	8333
24	26	A	Bury	W	3-0	2-0	8	David Ball [5], Frecklington [10], Vaulks [83]	4630
25	30	A	Walsall	W	2-1	1-1	7	Ajayi [1], David Ball [58]	4685
26	Jan 1	H	Blackburn R	D	1-1	0-0	7	David Ball [89]	9347
27	13	A	Oldham Ath	D	1-1	1-1	8	Williams [7]	4775
28	20	H	Portsmouth	W	1-0	0-0	7	Mattock [90]	9129
29	23	H	Bradford C	W	2-0	1-0	6	Smith [22], Newell [57]	8904
30	Feb 3	H	AFC Wimbledon	W	2-0	1-0	5	Smith [14], David Ball [90]	8330
31	10	A	Scunthorpe U	W	2-1	1-0	5	Newell [31], Ajayi [70]	6359
32	13	H	Oxford U	W	3-1	2-1	4	Forde [7], Towell [29], Smith [52]	7707
33	17	A	Shrewsbury T	W	1-0	1-0	4	Wood [44]	7007
34	24	H	Doncaster R	W	2-1	0-1	4	Newell (pen) [90], Smith [90]	11,725
35	Mar 10	A	Rochdale	L	0-1	0-0	4		8418
36	13	A	Milton Keynes D	L	2-3	1-2	4	Ajayi [9], Taylor [75]	7327
37	17	A	Northampton T	W	3-0	1-0	4	Smith [17], David Ball [62], Towell [81]	5882
38	24	A	Southend U	L	0-2	0-1	4		7719
39	30	H	Peterborough U	D	1-1	0-0	4	Lavery [68]	9573
40	Apr 2	A	Charlton Ath	L	1-3	0-1	4	Wood [77]	11,871
41	7	H	Fleetwood T	W	3-2	1-1	4	Pond (og) [12], Newell [51], Wood [77]	7562
42	14	A	Wigan Ath	D	0-0	0-0	4		9630
43	17	A	Gillingham	W	1-0	0-0	4	Vaulks [20]	4029
44	21	H	Bristol R	W	2-0	1-0	4	Smith [9], Lavery [90]	8579
45	28	A	Plymouth Arg	L	1-2	1-0	4	Towell [33]	13,407
46	May 5	H	Blackpool	W	1-0	0-0	4	Vaulks [58]	9512

Final League Position: 4

GOALSCORERS

League (73): Moore 13, David Ball 8, Newell 7 (1 pen), Smith 6, Towell 5, Vaulks 5, Ajayi 4, Frecklington 4, Taylor 4, Williams 4, Wood 4, Forde 2, Lavery 2, Ihiekwe 1, Mattock 1, Yates 1, own goals 2.
FA Cup (1): Vaulks 1.
Carabao Cup (3): Ajayi 1, Forde 1, Proctor 1.
Checkatrade Trophy (5): Clarke-Harris 1 (1 pen), David Ball 1, Towell 1, Vaulks 1, Yates 1.
League One Play-Offs (6): Wood 3, Newell 1, Taylor 1, Vaulks 1.

O'Donnell R 10	Emmanuel J 30 + 1	Ajayi S 29 + 6	Ihiekwe M 26 + 5	Mattock J 34 + 1	Taylor J 13 + 12	Vaulks W 38 + 6	Frecklington L 17 + 2	Forde A 27 + 14	Ball David 26 + 6	Proctor J 4	Moore K 19 + 3	Newell J 22 + 17	Williams R 33 + 9	Potter D 16	Clarke-Harris J 1 + 13	Cummings S 11 + 1	Purrington B 10	Wood R 34 + 2	Towell R 34 + 5	Rodak M 35	Yates J 7 + 10	Smith M 18 + 2	Palmer M 10 + 4	Lavery C 1 + 13	Price L 1	Match No.
1	2	3	4	5	6³	7	8	9	10²	11	12	13	14													1
1	2	3	4	5		12	8¹	14	13	11	10²	9	6³	7												2
1	5¹	4	3	2	13		7	14	12	10²	11	6	9³	8												3
1	2²	3	4	5	12	13	7			11¹	10	9	6³	8	14											4
1		3	10¹	8	9²	12		11		13	5³	7				2		4	6		14					5
			4	10	7	9²	13	14		11		6¹	8			2³		5	3	1			12			6
		3	5	10¹	2	9	13	12		11³	14	6	8					4	7²	1						7
		3	5⁴	10¹	2	8	13			11	12	6²	7	14				4	9³	1						8
		3		10¹	2	9	13			11³	12	6	8				5	4	7²	1			14			9
		3	12		2	8	10²			11	9⁴	6	7				5³	4	13	1			14			10
	14	3	5		13	8³				11¹	10	6	7	12	2			4	9²	1						11
1	13	4	5		12	8³	10²			11¹		6	7	14	2			3	9							12
1	13	3	5		7	9²	11¹	10³	12	6			14		2			4	8							13
1	13	3	5²		7	9	10	11	12	6³					2¹			4	8		14					14
	2	3	4	5	12	9		10		11	7	6							8¹	1						15
		3	5⁴	12				10²	13	11	9	6¹	8		2			4	7³	1			14			16
1	2¹	3	5		10²			14		11	9	6	8	13				4³	12							17
1	3		5		7	13	14			11	10	6²	8	12	2¹			4³	9							18
		3	5		13	8	11	9¹		10			12		7³	2		4	6²	1			14			19
	4	3	5		12	7			10⁹	11⁸	9	6	8¹	13	2²					1	14					20
5	2	4³	9²		6		12	10			7		11¹	14				3	8	1	13					21
2²	3		5		7		12	9¹	11			14	6		13			4⁴	8	1			10³			22
2	3	14	5			4	7	6	11¹			12	9²		13				8	1			10³			23
2	4		5			3	7	6	10		14	12	9²					13	8³	1		11¹				24
2	4		5			3	7²	6	11³		14	12	9					13	8	1		10¹				25
2	3	14	5			7		6	11			12	9¹		13			4³	8	1			10²			26
2	3		5			7		6	11			13	9²		14			4	8	1		10³	12			27
2	3		5	14		8		6²	11			12	9³					4	7	1		10¹	13			28
2	3		5	14		8		6	11²			9¹			13			4	7	1	12	10³				29
2	3		5	13		8		6³	11			9²	14					4		1		10	7	12		30
2	3		5			8		6	10¹			9²	12					4	7	1		11		13		31
2	3	12	5¹	14		8		6	11¹			9²						4	7	1		10		13		32
2	3	5				9		6¹	8³			10²	12					4	7	1		11	14	13		33
2	3		5			7		6¹	10²			9	12					4³	8	1		11	14	13		34
2²	3		5			7		6	11³			9	12					4		1		10	14	13		35
	3		5	12	8			6²			9					2		4¹	7	1	13	11	14	10³		36
	2	4	13	5¹	6²	3		12	10³		14	9							8	1		11	7			37
	2¹	4		6³	3			12	10		14	9²							8			13	11	7	1	38
	2	3	13	5²		4		6	11³		9	14							8¹			10	7	12		39
	2	3			12	8		6²			9	11			5¹	4				1		10	7	13		40
12	3¹		13	2				6²	11³		9				5	4		7		1	14	10	8			41
2	4				9	7		12				11			5			3	6¹	1		10	8			42
2	12	4			9¹	7		13				11			5			3	6²	1		10³	8	14		43
2	14	3			9³	6						11	13		5			4	7²	1		10	8¹	12		44
2	3		12		7			6¹	10			14	9³		5			4	8	1		11²		13		45
2	3		5	9	8			13	10²			6¹			4				14	1		11³	7	12		46

FA Cup

First Round	Crewe Alex	(a)	1-2

Carabao Cup

First Round	Lincoln C	(h)	2-1
Second Round	Huddersfield T	(a)	1-2

Checkatrade Trophy
Northern Group F Manchester C U21 (h) 1-1
(Manchester C U21 won 4-2 on penalties.

Northern Group F	Chesterfield	(h)	1-2
Northern Group F	Bradford C	(a)	3-0

League One Play-Offs

Semi-Final 1st leg	Scunthorpe U	(a)	2-2
Semi-Final 2nd leg	Scunthorpe U	(h)	2-0
Final	Shrewsbury T	(Wembley)	2-1
(aet)			

SCUNTHORPE UNITED

FOUNDATION

The year of foundation for Scunthorpe United has often been quoted as 1910, but the club can trace its history back to 1899 when Brumby Hall FC, who played on the Old Showground, consolidated their position by amalgamating with some other clubs and changing their name to Scunthorpe United. The year 1910 was when that club amalgamated with North Lindsey United as Scunthorpe and Lindsey United. The link is Mr W. T. Lockwood whose chairmanship covers both years.

Glanford Park, Jack Brownsword Way, Scunthorpe, North Lincolnshire DN15 8TD.

Telephone: (01724) 840 139.

Fax: (01724) 857 986.

Ticket Office: (01724) 747 670.

Website: www.scunthorpe-united.co.uk

Email: receptionist@scunthorpe-united.co.uk

Ground Capacity: 9,144.

Record Attendance: 23,935 v Portsmouth, FA Cup 4th rd, 30 January 1954 (at Old Showground); 9,077 v Manchester U, League Cup 3rd rd, 22 September 2010 (at Glanford Park).

Pitch Measurements: 102.5m × 66m (112yd × 72yd).

Chairman: Peter Swann.

Chief Executive: James Rodwell.

Manager: Nick Daws.

Assistant Manager: Andy Dawson.

Colours: Claret shirts with thin light blue stripes, light blue shorts with claret trim, claret socks with light blue trim.

Year Formed: 1899.

Turned Professional: 1912.

Previous Names: Amalgamated first with Brumby Hall then North Lindsey United to become Scunthorpe and Lindsey United, 1910; 1958, Scunthorpe United.

Club Nickname: 'The Iron'.

Grounds: 1899, Old Showground; 1988, Glanford Park.

First Football League Game: 19 August 1950, Division 3 (N), v Shrewsbury T (h) D 0–0 – Thompson; Barker, Brownsword; Allen, Taylor, McCormick; Mosby, Payne, Gorin, Rees, Boyes.

Record League Victory: 8–1 v Luton T (h), Division 3, 24 April 1965 – Sidebottom; Horstead, Hemstead; Smith, Neale, Lindsey; Bramley (1), Scott, Thomas (5), Mahy (1), Wilson (1). 8–1 v Torquay U (a), Division 3, 28 October 1995 – Samways; Housham, Wilson, Ford (1), Knill (1), Hope (Nicholson), Thornber, Bullimore (Walsh), McFarlane (4) (Young), Eyre (2), Paterson.

HONOURS

League Champions: FL 1 – 2006–07; Division 3N – 1957–58. *Runners-up:* FL 2 – 2004–05, 2013–14.

FA Cup: 5th rd – 1958, 1970.

League Cup: 4th rd – 2010.

League Trophy: Runners-up: 2009.

Sun FACT FILE

Scunthorpe United's move to Glanford Park in 1988 was the first time a Football League club had moved to a new-build ground since Port Vale had switched to Vale Park some 38 years previously. The Iron enjoyed a good start to their new home, winning the opening game against Hereford United 3-1.

Record Cup Victory: 9–0 v Boston U, FA Cup 1st rd, 21 November 1953 – Malan; Hubbard, Brownsword; Sharpe, White, Bushby; Mosby (1), Haigh (3), Whitfield (2), Gregory (1), Mervyn Jones (2).

Record Defeat: 0–8 v Carlisle U, Division 3 (N), 25 December 1952.

Most League Points (2 for a win): 66, Division 3 (N), 1956–57, 1957–58.

Most League Points (3 for a win): 91, FL 1, 2006–07.

Most League Goals: 88, Division 3 (N), 1957–58.

Highest League Scorer in Season: Barrie Thomas, 31, Division 2, 1961–62.

Most League Goals in Total Aggregate: Steve Cammack, 110, 1979–81, 1981–86.

Most League Goals in One Match: 5, Barrie Thomas v Luton T, Division 3, 24 April 1965.

Most Capped Player: Grant McCann, 12 (40), Northern Ireland.

Most League Appearances: Jack Brownsword, 597, 1950–65.

Youngest League Player: Hakeeb Adelakun, 16 years 201 days v Tranmere R, 29 December 2012.

Record Transfer Fee Received: £2,500,000 from Celtic for Gary Hooper, August 2010.

Record Transfer Fee Paid: £700,000 to Hibernian for Rob Jones, July 2009.

Football League Record: 1950 Elected to Division 3 (N); 1958–64 Division 2; 1964–68 Division 3; 1968–72 Division 4; 1972–73 Division 3; 1973–83 Division 4; 1983–84 Division 3; 1984–92 Division 4; 1992–99 Division 3; 1999–2000 Division 2; 2000–04 Division 3; 2004–05 FL 2; 2005–07 FL 1; 2007–08 FL C; 2008–09 FL 1; 2009–11 FL C; 2011–13 FL 1; 2013–14 FL 2; 2014– FL 1.

MANAGERS

Harry Allcock 1915–53
(Secretary-Manager)
Tom Crilly 1936–37
Bernard Harper 1946–48
Leslie Jones 1950–51
Bill Corkhill 1952–56
Ron Suart 1956–58
Tony McShane 1959
Bill Lambton 1959
Frank Soo 1959–60
Dick Duckworth 1960–64
Fred Goodwin 1964–66
Ron Ashman 1967–73
Ron Bradley 1973–74
Dick Rooks 1974–76
Ron Ashman 1976–81
John Duncan 1981–83
Allan Clarke 1983–84
Frank Barlow 1984–87
Mick Buxton 1987–91
Bill Green 1991–93
Richard Money 1993–94
David Moore 1994–96
Mick Buxton 1996–97
Brian Laws 1997–2004; 2004–06
Nigel Adkins 2006–10
Ian Baraclough 2010–11
Alan Knill 2011–12
Brian Laws 2012–13
Russ Wilcox 2013–14
Mark Robins 2014–16
Nick Daws 2016
Graham Alexander 2016–18
Nick Daws May 2018–

LATEST SEQUENCES

Longest Sequence of League Wins: 7, 9.4.2016 – 6.8.2017.

Longest Sequence of League Defeats: 8, 29.11.1997 – 20.1.1998.

Longest Sequence of League Draws: 6, 2.1.1984 – 25.2.1984.

Longest Sequence of Unbeaten League Matches: 28, 23.11.2013 – 21.4.2014.

Longest Sequence Without a League Win: 14, 22.3.1975 – 6.9.1975.

Successive Scoring Runs: 24 from 13.1.2007.

Successive Non-scoring Runs: 7 from 19.4.1975.

TEN YEAR LEAGUE RECORD

		P	W	D	L	F	A	Pts	Pos
2008-09	FL 1	46	22	10	14	82	63	76	6
2009-10	FL C	46	14	10	22	62	84	52	20
2010-11	FL C	46	12	6	28	43	87	42	24
2011-12	FL 1	46	10	22	14	55	59	52	18
2012-13	FL 1	46	13	9	24	49	73	48	21
2013-14	FL 2	46	20	21	5	68	44	81	2
2014-15	FL 1	46	14	14	18	62	75	56	16
2015-16	FL 1	46	21	11	14	60	47	74	7
2016-17	FL 1	46	24	10	12	80	54	82	3
2017-18	FL 1	46	19	17	10	65	50	74	5

DID YOU KNOW ?

Goalkeeper Geoff Barnard was the first winner of Scunthorpe United's Player of the Year award in 1971–72. Barnard was a near ever-present for the Iron between 1968 and 1972, going on to make over 300 first-team appearances before playing his final match in May 1977.

SCUNTHORPE UNITED – SKY BET LEAGUE ONE 2017–18 LEAGUE RECORD

Match No.	Date	Venue	Opponents	Result	H/T Score	Lg Pos.	Goalscorers	Attendance
1	Aug 5	H	AFC Wimbledon	D	1-1	1-0	12	Townsend [6]	4398
2	12	A	Rochdale	D	1-1	0-0	16	Holmes [63]	3218
3	19	H	Oxford U	W	1-0	0-0	9	Morris [83]	4205
4	26	A	Plymouth Arg	W	4-0	1-0	6	Madden 2 [27, 68], Hopper [77], Morris [90]	9605
5	Sept 2	A	Bury	W	1-0	0-0	4	Morris [86]	4055
6	9	H	Blackpool	D	0-0	0-0	5		4290
7	12	H	Blackburn R	L	0-1	0-0	11		4330
8	17	A	Doncaster R	W	1-0	1-0	6	Novak [10]	9227
9	23	H	Portsmouth	W	2-0	2-0	5	Novak [12], Holmes [33]	4685
10	26	A	Gillingham	D	0-0	0-0	5		4002
11	30	A	Shrewsbury T	L	0-2	0-1	7		5759
12	Oct 7	H	Wigan Ath	L	1-2	0-0	8	Ojo [90]	4480
13	14	A	Rotherham U	L	0-2	0-1	12		9167
14	17	H	Fleetwood T	D	1-1	1-0	12	Novak [18]	3120
15	21	H	Peterborough U	W	2-1	0-0	8	Novak [79], Morris (pen) [87]	4275
16	28	A	Oldham Ath	W	3-2	2-1	5	Hopper [5], Morris [10], Holmes [83]	4331
17	Nov 11	A	Bristol R	W	1-0	0-0	5	Bishop [90]	4210
18	18	A	Northampton T	W	3-0	0-0	4	Burgess [56], Holmes 2 [58, 74]	5181
19	21	A	Bradford C	W	2-1	1-1	3	Burgess [45], Adelakun [69]	19,163
20	25	H	Charlton Ath	W	2-0	0-0	3	Morris 2 [60, 63]	4307
21	Dec 9	A	Walsall	L	0-1	0-1	5		3865
22	16	H	Milton Keynes D	D	2-2	2-1	5	Adelakun [27], van Veen [43]	3569
23	23	H	Southend U	W	3-1	1-1	4	van Veen [32], Townsend [63], Turner (og) [86]	4040
24	26	A	Blackpool	W	3-2	2-1	4	Hopper [2], Holmes [8], Adelakun [46]	3446
25	30	A	Blackburn R	D	2-2	1-1	4	van Veen [12], Townsend [56]	12,784
26	Jan 1	H	Bury	W	1-0	0-0	4	Goode [86]	4270
27	13	A	Portsmouth	D	1-1	0-1	4	van Veen [53]	17,741
28	20	H	Gillingham	L	1-3	0-1	4	Morris [52]	4905
29	23	A	Doncaster R	D	1-1	1-0	4	Hopper [3]	5193
30	27	A	Southend U	L	2-3	1-1	4	Hopper [12], van Veen [56]	6723
31	Feb 3	H	Fleetwood T	W	3-2	2-1	4	Morris 2 (1 pen) [25, 42 (p)], Toney [78]	2901
32	10	H	Rotherham U	L	1-2	0-1	4	Novak [72]	6359
33	13	A	Peterborough U	D	2-2	1-2	5	Toney [34], Yates [60]	4397
34	17	H	Northampton T	D	2-2	1-1	5	Ojo [31], Wallace [77]	4157
35	24	A	Bristol R	D	1-1	0-0	5	Holmes [61]	8346
36	Mar 3	H	Oldham Ath	L	0-2	0-0	5		3715
37	10	A	Wigan Ath	D	3-3	2-2	5	Hopper 2 [16, 45], Toney [53]	8438
38	17	H	Shrewsbury T	L	1-2	1-0	5	Morris [8]	3824
39	24	A	Rochdale	D	1-1	0-0	5	Toney [51]	3789
40	30	A	Oxford U	D	1-1	1-0	5	Toney [12]	7479
41	Apr 7	A	AFC Wimbledon	D	1-1	0-1	9	Novak [84]	4055
42	14	A	Charlton Ath	W	1-0	1-0	5	Toney [31]	11,877
43	21	H	Walsall	W	1-0	0-0	6	Yates [76]	4083
44	28	A	Milton Keynes D	W	2-0	2-0	6	McArdle [20], Toney [35]	9578
45	May 1	H	Plymouth Arg	W	2-0	1-0	5	Adelakun [32], Toney [60]	4712
46	5	H	Bradford C	D	1-1	0-0	5	Townsend [59]	5452

Final League Position: 5

GOALSCORERS

League (65): Morris 11 (2 pens), Toney 8, Holmes 7, Hopper 7, Novak 6, van Veen 5, Adelakun 4, Townsend 4, Burgess 2, Madden 2, Ojo 2, Yates 2, Bishop 1, Goode 1, McArdle 1, Wallace 1, own goal 1.
FA Cup (1): Adelakun 1.
Carabao Cup (3): Madden 2 (1 pen), Holmes 1.
Checkatrade Trophy (7): Hopper 2, van Veen 2, Holmes 1, Lewis 1, Morris 1.
League One Play-Offs (2): McGeehan 1, own goal 1.

Gliks M 42	Burgess C 22 + 3	McArdle R 36	Wallace M 45	Clarke J 20 + 3	Ojo F 40 + 1	Bishop N 33 + 2	Townsend C 24 + 6	Adelakun H 29 + 10	Madden P 15 + 5	Morris J 43 + 1	Manton S 1 + 7	Holmes D 34 + 11	van Veen K 12 + 9	Sutton L 12 + 3	Hopper T 27 + 11	Redmond D — + 1	Novak L 16 + 16	Butroid L 6 + 1	Crofts A 1 + 3	Church S — + 4	Goode C 10 + 3	Lewis C 1 + 3	Watson R 4	Toney I 13 + 3	McGeehan C 3 + 10	Yates R 14 + 2	Vermijl M 3 + 3	Williams L — + 2	Wootton K — + 1	Match No.
1	2	3	4	5	6	7^3	8	9	10^2	11^1	12	13	14																	1
1		4	2		8	6	9	5	11	7^2		13	10^1	3	12															2
1	14	3	4		7	8	5	6^1	10^3	9		13	11^1	2	12															3
1		3	4		7	8^2	5	6^1	10	9		13	12	2	11^3	14														4
1		4	3		7	8	5	6^2	10^1	9		12	14	2	11^3		13													5
1		3	4		8	7	5	6^1	10^2	9		13	14	2	11^3		11													6
1		3	4	13	8	7^1	5	12	10	9		6^2	14	2^3			11													7
1	14	4	3	2	8^3	7	5		10^1	9	12	6^2			13		11													8
1	14	3	4	2	8^2	7		11^1	9	13	6^3			12			10^2	5												9
1		3	4	2	8^2	7	14	11^3	9	13	6^1			12			5													10
1		4	3	2		8	14	13	9	7	6^2	12		11^2			10	5^1												11
1		4	3	2	8	7^1		13	6	14	12	9		10^2			11^3	5												12
1		4	3	2	7		5	12	11	6^2	13	9	14				10^3		8^1											13
1		3	4	2	7	8		12	11	9		6^1					10	5												14
1		3	4	2	7	8		12	10^2	9		6^1	13				11	5^3		14										15
1	4	2	3	5	6	8^2		7^1		9		13			10^1		11		14	12										16
1	4		5	2	7	8		6^1	13	9^2		12	14		10^3		11			3										17
1	4	3	5	2	8	7	13	6	12			9^1			10^3		11^2			14										18
1	5	3	4	2	8	7	13	9^2	12			6^1			10		11^2			14										19
1	4	3	5	2^1	8	7		6^2	11	13		12			10				14			9^2								20
1	4	3	5		7		6	10^3	9			8^1	12	2	11^2					13	14									21
1	3		5		6^1	12	7		8			9^1	11^2	2	10			14	13^3	4										22
1	3		4		7		5	9^2	8			6	10^1		11					12	2	13								23
1	5		3	12		2	9		6			8	10^2	7^1	11		13			4										24
1	3		4		7		9	6^2	8			5	10^1	13^1	11		12			2										25
1	3		4^3		6	14	8	13		7		9^1	10^2	5	12		11			2										26
	3		4		7	6		9	8			5	10		11^1		12			2		1								27
	3		4		7	6^3		9^1	8			5	10		11^2		13			2		1	12	14						28
	4		5		8	7^2		6	9			2	10^3		11^1		13			3		1	14	12						29
	2^1		4		6			9^2	8			5	10^3		11		13			3		1	14	7^1	12					30
1		4	3		8	7	5		9	6		13	11^2	12										10^1		14	2^1			31
	3		4		7	8^1	5^2	13	9	6			11^3	12										10			2	14		32
1		3	4	2		3		5	8^3	9		12		7^2	14	11^1								10^3	13	6				33
1		3	4		7		5	14	9	6		2^2	12	11										10^3	13	8^1				34
1	4	3	2		8	6	12		9	5^1		11										13		10^2	7					35
1	4	3	5^2		8	2	13	10^3	9	6		11^1												14	7	12				36
1	3	4	5		8	2		9	6			11												10	7					37
1	4	3	5	13	7	2^1	12		9	6^2		11												10^2	8		14			38
1	3	4	5	12	8	2^1	13		9	6		10												11	7^2					39
1		4	3	2^3	8		5	11^2	9	6^1					13									10	14	7	12			40
1		4	3	2		8	5	10^3	9^2	7		14	13											11^1	12	6				41
1		4	3	2	8		5	11^2	9	7^1			12											10^3	13	6	14			42
1		4	2	6		5	8^1	10	9^2				13											11^3	12	7	14			43
1		3	4	2	6	12	5	8^2	10^1	9		14	13											11^2		7				44
1		3	4	2	6		5	8	10^2	9^1		13												11	12	7				45
1	4	3			6	5	8^3	10				14	12	11							13			9^2	7	2^1			46

FA Cup

First Round	Northampton T	(a)	0-0
Replay	Northampton T	(h)	1-0
Second Round	Doncaster R	(a)	0-3

Carabao Cup

First Round	Notts Co	(h)	3-3
(aet; Scunthorpe U won 6-5 on penalties)
| Second Round | Middlesbrough | (a) | 0-3 |

Checkatrade Trophy

Northern Group H	Sunderland U21	(h)	3-1
Northern Group H	Grimsby T	(h)	2-1
Northern Group H	Doncaster R	(a)	1-1
(Doncaster R won 3-2 on penalties)
| Second Round North | Leicester C U21 | (h) | 1-2 |

League One Play-Offs

Semi-Final 1st leg	Rotherham U	(h)	2-2
Semi-Final 2nd leg	Rotherham U	(a)	0-2

SHEFFIELD UNITED

FOUNDATION

In March 1889, Yorkshire County Cricket Club formed Sheffield United six days after an FA Cup semi-final between Preston North End and West Bromwich Albion had finally convinced Charles Stokes, a member of the cricket club, that the formation of a professional football club would prove successful at Bramall Lane. The United's first secretary, Mr J. B. Wostinholm, was also secretary of the cricket club.

Bramall Lane Ground, Cherry Street, Bramall Lane, Sheffield, South Yorkshire S2 4SU.

Telephone: (01142) 537 200.

Ticket Office: (01142) 537 200 (option 1).

Website: www.sufc.co.uk

Email: info@sufc.co.uk

Ground Capacity: 32,008.

Record Attendance: 68,287 v Leeds U, FA Cup 5th rd, 15 February 1936.

Pitch Measurements: 100.5m × 67m (110yd × 73yd).

Chairman: Kevin McCabe.

Manager: Chris Wilder.

Assistant Manager: Alan Knill.

HONOURS

League Champions: Division 1 – 1897–98; Division 2 – 1952–53; FL 1 – 2016–17; Division 4 – 1981–82. *Runners-up:* Division 1 – 1896–97, 1899–1900; FL C – 2005–06; Division 2 – 1892–93, 1938–39, 1960–61, 1970–71, 1989–90; Division 3 – 1988–89.
FA Cup Winners: 1899, 1902, 1915, 1925. *Runners-up:* 1901, 1936.
League Cup: semi-final – 2003, 2015.

Colours: Red and white striped shirts with black trim, black shorts with white trim, black socks with white trim.

Year Formed: 1889.

Turned Professional: 1889.

Club Nickname: 'The Blades'.

Ground: 1889, Bramall Lane.

First Football League Game: 3 September 1892, Division 2, v Lincoln C (h) W 4–2 – Lilley; Witham, Cain; Howell, Hendry, Needham (1); Wallace, Dobson, Hammond (3), Davies, Drummond.

Record League Victory: 10–0 v Burslem Port Vale (a), Division 2, 10 December 1892 – Howlett; Witham, Lilley; Howell, Hendry, Needham; Drummond (1), Wallace (1), Hammond (4), Davies (2), Watson (2). 10-0 v Burnley, Division 1 (h), 19 January 1929.

Record Cup Victory: 6–0 v Leyton Orient (h), FA Cup 1st rd, 6 November 2016 – Ramsdale; Basham (1), O'Connell, Wright, Freeman (1), Coutts (Whiteman), Duffy (Brooks), Fleck, Lafferty, Scougall (1) (Lavery), Chapman (3).

Record Defeat: 0–13 v Bolton W, FA Cup 2nd rd, 1 February 1890.

Most League Points (2 for a win): 60, Division 2, 1952–53.

Most League Points (3 for a win): 100, FL 1, 2016–17.

THE Sun FACT FILE

Substitutes were introduced for Football League games for the 1965–66 season. In the opening game at home to Aston Villa, Graham Shaw was sat on the bench although he remained unused. It was not until the sixth game of the season away to Fulham that Tony Wagstaff became the first substitute to be used when he came on to replace Alan Birchenall.

Most League Goals: 102, Division 1, 1925–26.

Highest League Scorer in Season: Jimmy Dunne, 41, Division 1, 1930–31.

Most League Goals in Total Aggregate: Harry Johnson, 201, 1919–30.

Most League Goals in One Match: 5, Harry Hammond v Bootle, Division 2, 26 November 1892; 5, Harry Johnson v West Ham U, Division 1, 26 December 1927.

Most Capped Player: Billy Gillespie, 25, Northern Ireland.

Most League Appearances: Joe Shaw, 632, 1948–66.

Youngest League Player: Louis Reed, 16 years 257 days v Rotherham U, 8 April 2014.

Record Transfer Fee Received: £4,000,000 from Everton for Phil Jagielka, July 2007; £4,000,000 from Tottenham H for Kyle Naughton, July 2009; £4,000,000 from Tottenham H for Kyle Walker, July 2009.

Record Transfer Fee Paid: £4,000,000 to Everton for James Beattie, August 2007.

Football League Record: 1892 Elected to Division 2; 1893–1934 Division 1; 1934–39 Division 2; 1946–49 Division 1; 1949–53 Division 2; 1953–56 Division 1; 1956–61 Division 2; 1961–68 Division 1; 1968–71 Division 2; 1971–76 Division 1; 1976–79 Division 2; 1979–81 Division 3; 1981–82 Division 4; 1982–84 Division 3; 1984–88 Division 2; 1988–89 Division 3; 1989–90 Division 2; 1990–92 Division 1; 1992–94 FA Premier League; 1994–2004 Division 1; 2004–06 FL C; 2006–07 FA Premier League; 2007–11 FL C; 2011–17 FL 1; 2017– FL C.

LATEST SEQUENCES

Longest Sequence of League Wins: 8, 28.3.2017 – 5.8.2017.

Longest Sequence of League Defeats: 7, 19.8.1975 – 20.9.1975.

Longest Sequence of League Draws: 6, 6.5.2001 – 8.9.2001.

Longest Sequence of Unbeaten League Matches: 22, 2.9.1899 – 13.1.1900.

Longest Sequence Without a League Win: 19, 27.9.1975 – 7.2.1976.

Successive Scoring Runs: 34 from 30.3.1956.

Successive Non-scoring Runs: 6 from 4.12.1993.

MANAGERS

J. B. Wostinholm 1889–99
 (Secretary-Manager)
John Nicholson 1899–1932
Ted Davison 1932–52
Reg Freeman 1952–55
Joe Mercer 1955–58
Johnny Harris 1959–68
 (continued as General Manager to 1970)
Arthur Rowley 1968–69
Johnny Harris *(General Manager resumed Team Manager duties)* 1969–73
Ken Furphy 1973–75
Jimmy Sirrel 1975–77
Harry Haslam 1978–81
Martin Peters 1981
Ian Porterfield 1981–86
Billy McEwan 1986–88
Dave Bassett 1988–95
Howard Kendall 1995–97
Nigel Spackman 1997–98
Steve Bruce 1998–99
Adrian Heath 1999
Neil Warnock 1999–2007
Bryan Robson 2007–08
Kevin Blackwell 2008–10
Gary Speed 2010
Micky Adams 2010–11
Danny Wilson 2011–13
David Weir 2013
Nigel Clough 2013–15
Nigel Adkins 2015–16
Chris Wilder May 2016–

TEN YEAR LEAGUE RECORD

		P	W	D	L	F	A	Pts	Pos
2008-09	FL C	46	22	14	10	64	39	80	3
2009-10	FL C	46	17	14	15	62	55	65	8
2010-11	FL C	46	11	9	26	44	79	42	23
2011-12	FL 1	46	27	9	10	92	51	90	3
2012-13	FL 1	46	19	18	9	56	42	75	5
2013-14	FL 1	46	18	13	15	48	46	67	7
2014-15	FL 1	46	19	14	13	66	53	71	5
2015-16	FL 1	46	18	12	16	64	59	66	11
2016-17	FL 1	46	30	10	6	92	47	100	1
2017-18	FL C	46	20	9	17	62	55	69	10

DID YOU KNOW

When Sheffield United visited Yeovil Town on 22 September 2012 they were playing their 4,500th regular-season Football League game. United won 1-0 with a second-half goal from Neill Collins in front of a crowd of 4,117.

SHEFFIELD UNITED – SKY BET CHAMPIONSHIP 2017–18 LEAGUE RECORD

Match No.	Date	Venue	Opponents	Result	H/T Score	Lg Pos.	Goalscorers	Atten-dance
1	Aug 5	H	Brentford	W 1-0	1-0	7	Sharp [39]	26,746
2	12	A	Middlesbrough	L 0-1	0-1	12		26,876
3	15	A	Cardiff C	L 0-2	0-1	17		17,844
4	19	H	Barnsley	W 1-0	1-0	10	Sharp [17]	25,482
5	26	H	Derby Co	W 3-1	2-0	5	Sharp 2 [4, 90], Russell (og) [39]	26,202
6	Sept 9	A	Sunderland	W 2-1	1-0	5	Donaldson 2 [21, 77]	29,579
7	12	A	Bolton W	W 1-0	1-0	3	Carter-Vickers [33]	14,346
8	16	H	Norwich C	L 0-1	0-1	6		26,218
9	24	A	Sheffield W	W 4-2	2-1	4	Fleck [3], Clarke 2 [15, 77], Duffy [67]	32,839
10	27	H	Wolverhampton W	W 2-0	1-0	2	Clarke 2 [39, 58]	25,893
11	30	A	Nottingham F	L 1-2	1-2	3	Lundstram [3]	25,700
12	Oct 14	A	Ipswich T	W 1-0	0-0	3	Basham [49]	25,799
13	21	H	Reading	W 2-1	2-0	3	Coutts [19], Sharp [37]	26,265
14	27	A	Leeds U	W 2-1	1-1	1	Sharp [2], Brooks [81]	34,504
15	31	A	QPR	L 0-1	0-1	3		13,604
16	Nov 4	H	Hull C	W 4-1	0-1	2	Clarke 4 [53, 76, 80, 88]	27,466
17	17	A	Burton Alb	W 3-1	2-1	1	Sharp 2 (1 pen) [10 (p), 34], Clarke [78]	5167
18	21	H	Fulham	L 4-5	2-3	3	Clarke 3 [6, 39, 90], Carruthers [86]	25,445
19	25	H	Birmingham C	D 1-1	0-1	3	Clarke [71]	27,427
20	Dec 2	A	Millwall	L 1-3	1-1	4	Brooks [41]	12,669
21	8	H	Bristol C	L 1-2	0-1	4	Clarke [48]	24,409
22	16	A	Preston NE	L 0-1	0-0	6		15,202
23	23	A	Aston Villa	D 2-2	2-2	7	Donaldson 2 [12, 26]	35,210
24	26	H	Sunderland	W 3-0	1-0	6	Lundstram [36], Stearman [58], Baldock [62]	30,668
25	30	H	Bolton W	L 0-1	0-1	6		28,387
26	Jan 1	A	Derby Co	D 1-1	0-1	7	Clarke [57]	30,003
27	12	H	Sheffield W	D 0-0	0-0	6		31,120
28	20	A	Norwich C	W 2-1	1-0	6	Wilson [6], Donaldson [68]	26,486
29	30	H	Aston Villa	L 0-1	0-0	7		26,477
30	Feb 3	A	Wolverhampton W	L 0-3	0-2	8		29,311
31	10	H	Leeds U	W 2-1	1-0	8	Sharp 2 (1 pen) [2, 73 (p)]	27,553
32	20	H	QPR	W 2-1	1-0	7	Stearman [27], Lundstram [50]	25,339
33	23	A	Hull C	L 0-1	0-0	7		15,213
34	27	A	Reading	W 3-1	2-0	6	Sharp 2 [11, 63], Duffy [44]	6769
35	Mar 6	A	Fulham	L 0-3	0-2	9		18,400
36	10	A	Ipswich T	D 0-0	0-0	9		15,152
37	13	H	Burton Alb	W 2-0	1-0	7	Stevens [29], Brooks [64]	24,832
38	17	H	Nottingham F	D 0-0	0-0	9		28,095
39	30	A	Brentford	D 1-1	0-0	9	Basham [55]	11,174
40	Apr 2	H	Cardiff C	D 1-1	1-0	9	Clarke [28]	25,231
41	7	A	Barnsley	L 2-3	0-1	9	Fleck [57], Clarke [65]	16,041
42	10	H	Middlesbrough	W 2-1	2-0	9	Evans, L 2 [2, 40]	26,557
43	14	H	Millwall	D 1-1	0-0	9	Clarke [74]	27,454
44	21	A	Birmingham C	L 1-2	1-1	11	Duffy [7]	23,579
45	28	H	Preston NE	L 0-1	0-0	11		28,568
46	May 6	A	Bristol C	W 3-2	3-0	10	Clarke [8], Sharp [29], Freeman [34]	23,902

Final League Position: 10

GOALSCORERS

League (62): Clarke 19, Sharp 13 (2 pens), Donaldson 5, Brooks 3, Duffy 3, Lundstram 3, Basham 2, Evans, L 2, Fleck 2, Stearman 2, Baldock 1, Carruthers 1, Carter-Vickers 1, Coutts 1, Freeman 1, Stevens 1, Wilson 1, own goal 1.
FA Cup (2): Sharp 1 (1 pen), Thomas 1.
Carabao Cup (4): Lafferty 1, Lavery 1, Thomas 1, own goal 1.

Blackman J 31	Stearman R 28	Basham C 44+1	O'Connell J 46	Freeman K 10	Coutts P 16	Carruthers S 4+10	Fleck J 41	Stevens E 45	Clarke L 38+1	Sharp B 28+6	Lundstram J 21+15	Lavery C 1+2	Duffy M 28+8	Evans C 2+7	Brooks D 9+21	Wright J 13+4	Donaldson C 9+17	Carter-Vickers C 17	Baldock G 30+4	Lafferty D 1+7	Thomas N —+1	Moore S 15+3	Hanson J —+1	Slater R —+1	Wilson J 4+4	Leonard R 6+7	Evans L 18+1	Holmes R 1+4	Eastwood J —+1	Match No.
1	2	3	4	5	6	7²	8	9	10	11¹	12	13																		1
1	3	2	4	5¹	6	7²	8	9	11	10³		12	13	14																2
1	3³	2	4	5	7	6¹	8	9²	11	10			13	14	12															3
1		2	4	5	6		8	9	10⁴	11			7²	13	12	3														4
1		2	4	5	6	13³	8	9		10	14	11²	7¹	12		3														5
1		2	4	5	6		8	9		11³	13	7¹	14	12		3	10²													6
1	14		4		6		8		10	11²	12		7¹	13	3		2	5³	9											7
1		2	4	5³	6	12	8	9¹				7²	11	10		3		14	13											8
1	7		4		6		8	9¹	11		13	12	10¹		3²		2	5												9
1	6		4		7		8	9¹	11¹		13	14	10		3²		2	5	12											10
1		2	4		7		8	9	13		6¹	10	14	12	11²	3		5³												11
1		2	4	5¹			8	9	10	11²	6				7³	13	12		3			14								12
1		2	4		6		8	9	10	11³	13				7²	12			3	5										13
1		2	4		6		8	9	10	11²	13				7¹	12			3	5										14
1³		2	4		7			9	10	13	6		14		8	11¹	3	5²				12								15
	5	4			6		8	9	10³	11²	13				7¹	12	3	14	2			1								16
1	5	4			6³	14	8	9	10	11²	12				7¹	13	3		2											17
1	5	4				13	8	9	10	11	6				7¹	12	3²	2¹				14								18
1	5	4				13	8	9	10	11²	6				7	12	3	2¹												19
1	3¹	5	4				8	9	11	12	6²				7	10	13		2											20
	3	2¹	4		14		8	9	10	11¹	6				7²	12	13	5				1								21
	3	7	4				8²	9	10	11	6				13			5³	2¹			1			12	14				22
	3	7	4		12		8		10	13	6				9¹	11²		5	2			1								23
	3	7	4		12		8		10³	13	6				9¹	11²		5	2	14		1								24
	3¹	5	4		14		8	9	10	11³	6				7	13	2²		12			1								25
	3	2	4		12		8	9	10		6²				7¹	11		5	13			1								26
	3	2	4				8	9	10		6				7	11¹		5				1								27
	3	2	4				8	9	10		13				12			5				1			11¹	6	7²			28
	3	2	4				8	9	10		12				13			5	14			1			11³	6²	7¹			29
	3	2²	4				8	9	10		13							5	6			1			11¹	12	7³	14		30
1	3	2	4				8	9	10	11³	13				7¹			5							12	6²	14			31
1	3	2	4				8	9	10	11³	6²				7¹	12		5				14			13					32
1	3	2²	4				8	9	10	11	13				12	14		5								6¹	7³			33
1¹	3	2	4				8	9	10³	11	13				7²			5							12	6	14			34
1	3	2²	4				8	9		11¹	13				7	12	10²	5								6	14			35
1	3	2	4				8	9		11¹	13				7³	14	10²	5							12	6				36
1	3	2	4				8	9		11¹	13				7²	12	10³	5							14	6				37
1	3		4				8	9	10	11²					7³	12	14	5	2¹							6	13			38
1¹	3	2	4				8	9	10	11¹	13				7³	14		5							12	6²				39
	3³	2	4				8	9		11	6				10²	12	13	5				1			14		7¹			40
	3³	2	4				8	9		11	6				12	13	10¹	5				1			14		7²			41
	3³	2	4				8	9		11	6¹				12	13	10²	5				1			14		7			42
1	3²	2	4				8	9		11	13				6¹	12	10³	5							14		7			43
1	3	2	4				8	9		12	6¹				13	11³	10²	5							14		7			44
1	3²	2	4	5²			8	9	10	11	13				7	12									14		6¹			45
	3	2	4	5¹			8	9		11	14				10²	12	13					1				6²	7			46

FA Cup

Third Round	Ipswich T	(a)	1-0
Fourth Round	Preston NE	(h)	1-0
Fifth Round	Leicester C	(a)	0-1

Carabao Cup

First Round	Walsall	(h)	3-2
Second Round	Leicester C	(h)	1-4

SHEFFIELD WEDNESDAY

FOUNDATION

Sheffield being one of the principal centres of early Association Football, this club was formed as long ago as 1867 by the Sheffield Wednesday Cricket Club (formed 1825) and their colours from the start were blue and white. The inaugural meeting was held at the Adelphi Hotel and the original committee included Charles Stokes who was subsequently a founder member of Sheffield United.

Hillsborough Stadium, Hillsborough, Sheffield, South Yorkshire S6 1SW.

Telephone: (0370) 020 1867.

Fax: (0114) 221 2122.

Ticket Office: (0370) 020 1867 (option 1).

Website: www.swfc.co.uk

Email: footballenquiries@swfc.co.uk

Ground Capacity: 33,854.

Record Attendance: 72,841 v Manchester C, FA Cup 5th rd, 17 February 1934.

Pitch Measurements: 105m × 68m (115yd × 74yd).

Chairman: Dejphon Chansiri.

Chief Executive: Katrien Meire.

Manager: Jos Luhukay.

Assistant Manager: Remy Reynierse.

Colours: Blue shirts with white sleeves, white shorts, white socks with blue hoops.

Year Formed: 1867 (fifth oldest League club).

Turned Professional: 1887.

Previous Name: The Wednesday until 1929.

Club Nickname: 'The Owls'.

HONOURS

League Champions: Division 1 – 1902–03, 1903–04, 1928–29, 1929–30; Division 2 – 1899–1900, 1925–26, 1951–52, 1955–56, 1958–59.
Runners-up: Division 1 – 1960–61; Division 2 – 1949–50, 1983–84; FL 1 – 2011–12.

FA Cup Winners: 1896, 1907, 1935.
Runners-up: 1890, 1966, 1993.

League Cup Winners: 1991.
Runners-up: 1993.

European Competitions
Fairs Cup: 1961–62 *(qf)*, 1963–64.
UEFA Cup: 1992–93.
Intertoto Cup: 1995.

Grounds: 1867, Highfield; 1869, Myrtle Road; 1877, Sheaf House; 1887, Olive Grove; 1899, Owlerton (since 1912 known as Hillsborough). Some games were played at Endcliffe in the 1880s. Until 1895 Bramall Lane was used for some games.

First Football League Game: 3 September 1892, Division 1, v Notts Co (a) W 1–0 – Allan; Tom Brandon (1), Mumford; Hall, Betts, Harry Brandon; Spiksley, Brady, Davis, Bob Brown, Dunlop.

Record League Victory: 9–1 v Birmingham, Division 1, 13 December 1930 – Brown; Walker, Blenkinsop; Strange, Leach, Wilson; Hooper (3), Seed (2), Ball (2), Burgess (1), Rimmer (1).

Record Cup Victory: 12–0 v Halliwell, FA Cup 1st rd, 17 January 1891 – Smith; Thompson, Brayshaw; Harry Brandon (1), Betts, Cawley (2); Winterbottom, Mumford (2), Bob Brandon (1), Woolhouse (5), Ingram (1).

Record Defeat: 0–10 v Aston Villa, Division 1, 5 October 1912.

Sun FACT FILE

Legendary Brazilian striker Pelé made two appearances for his club side Santos against Sheffield Wednesday at Hillsborough. The first in October 1962 attracted a crowd of 49,058 with Santos winning 4-2. A decade later Santos again won 2-0, this time in front of 36,996. Pelé scored just once in the two games, netting from the penalty spot in the first game.

Most League Points (2 for a win): 62, Division 2, 1958–59.

Most League Points (3 for a win): 93, FL 1, 2011–12.

Most League Goals: 106, Division 2, 1958–59.

Highest League Scorer in Season: Derek Dooley, 46, Division 2, 1951–52.

Most League Goals in Total Aggregate: Andrew Wilson, 199, 1900–20.

Most League Goals in One Match: 6, Doug Hunt v Norwich C, Division 2, 19 November 1938.

Most Capped Player: Nigel Worthington, 50 (66), Northern Ireland.

Most League Appearances: Andrew Wilson, 501, 1900–20.

Youngest League Player: Peter Fox, 15 years 269 days v Orient, 31 March 1973.

Record Transfer Fee Received: £3,000,000 from WBA for Chris Brunt, August 2007.

Record Transfer Fee Paid: £10,000,000 to Middlesbrough for Jordan Rhodes, July 2017.

Football League Record: 1892 Elected to Division 1; 1899–1900 Division 2; 1900–20 Division 1; 1920–26 Division 2; 1926–37 Division 1; 1937–50 Division 2; 1950–51 Division 1; 1951–52 Division 2; 1952–55 Division 1; 1955–56 Division 2; 1956–58 Division 1; 1958–59 Division 2; 1959–70 Division 1; 1970–75 Division 2; 1975–80 Division 3; 1980–84 Division 2; 1984–90 Division 1; 1990–91 Division 2; 1991–92 Division 1; 1992–2000 FA Premier League; 2000–03 Division 1; 2003–04 Division 2; 2004–05 FL 1; 2005–10 FL C; 2010–12 FL 1; 2012– FL C.

LATEST SEQUENCES

Longest Sequence of League Wins: 9, 23.4.1904 – 15.10.1904.

Longest Sequence of League Defeats: 8, 9.9.2000 – 17.10.2000.

Longest Sequence of League Draws: 7, 15.3.2008 – 14.4.2008.

Longest Sequence of Unbeaten League Matches: 19, 10.12.1960 – 8.4.1961.

Longest Sequence Without a League Win: 20, 11.1.1975 – 30.8.1975.

Successive Scoring Runs: 40 from 14.11.1959.

Successive Non-scoring Runs: 8 from 8.3.1975.

MANAGERS

Arthur Dickinson 1891–1920
 (Secretary-Manager)
Robert Brown 1920–33
Billy Walker 1933–37
Jimmy McMullan 1937–42
Eric Taylor 1942–58
 *(continued as General Manager
 to 1974)*
Harry Catterick 1958–61
Vic Buckingham 1961–64
Alan Brown 1964–68
Jack Marshall 1968–69
Danny Williams 1969–71
Derek Dooley 1971–73
Steve Burtenshaw 1974–75
Len Ashurst 1975–77
Jackie Charlton 1977–83
Howard Wilkinson 1983–88
Peter Eustace 1988–89
Ron Atkinson 1989–91
Trevor Francis 1991–95
David Pleat 1995–97
Ron Atkinson 1997–98
Danny Wilson 1998–2000
Peter Shreeves *(Acting)* 2000
Paul Jewell 2000–01
Peter Shreeves 2001
Terry Yorath 2001–02
Chris Turner 2002–04
Paul Sturrock 2004–06
Brian Laws 2006–09
Alan Irvine 2010–11
Gary Megson 2011–12
Dave Jones 2012–13
Stuart Gray 2013–15
Carlos Carvalhal 2015–18
Jos Luhukay January 2018–

TEN YEAR LEAGUE RECORD

		P	W	D	L	F	A	Pts	Pos
2008-09	FL C	46	16	13	17	51	58	61	12
2009-10	FL C	46	11	14	21	49	69	47	22
2010-11	FL 1	46	16	10	20	67	67	58	15
2011-12	FL 1	46	28	9	9	81	48	93	2
2012-13	FL C	46	16	10	20	53	61	58	18
2013-14	FL C	46	13	14	19	63	65	53	16
2014-15	FL C	46	14	18	14	43	49	60	13
2015-16	FL C	46	19	17	10	66	45	74	6
2016-17	FL C	46	24	9	13	60	45	81	4
2017-18	FL C	46	14	15	17	59	60	57	15

DID YOU KNOW ?

Sheffield Wednesday were one of the first clubs to have their own song. 'Play Up, Wednesday Boys' was played by the band before games in the 1890s and was later revived in the 1920s before falling into disuse again.

SHEFFIELD WEDNESDAY – SKY BET CHAMPIONSHIP 2017–18 LEAGUE RECORD

Match No.	Date	Venue	Opponents	Result		H/T Score	Lg Pos.	Goalscorers	Attendance
1	Aug 5	A	Preston NE	L	0-1	0-0	22		18,267
2	12	H	QPR	D	1-1	0-1	18	Winnall [48]	25,537
3	16	H	Sunderland	D	1-1	0-1	20	Jones [70]	27,631
4	19	A	Fulham	W	1-0	0-0	13	Fletcher [64]	20,165
5	26	A	Burton Alb	D	1-1	1-0	16	Hooper [36]	5084
6	Sept 9	H	Nottingham F	W	3-1	1-1	10	Hooper [23], Fletcher [63], Lee [70]	25,710
7	12	H	Brentford	W	2-1	1-1	6	Hooper [45], Wallace [70]	23,536
8	16	A	Cardiff C	D	1-1	1-0	9	Hooper [39]	19,137
9	24	H	Sheffield U	L	2-4	1-2	10	Hooper [45], Lucas Joao [65]	32,839
10	27	A	Birmingham C	L	0-1	0-0	14		20,365
11	Oct 1	H	Leeds U	W	3-0	2-0	12	Hooper 2 [25, 41], Lee [82]	27,972
12	14	A	Bolton W	L	1-2	0-1	12	Lee [68]	17,967
13	21	A	Derby Co	L	0-2	0-1	16		27,426
14	28	H	Barnsley	D	1-1	1-0	16	Reach [34]	27,097
15	31	H	Millwall	W	2-1	2-1	14	Reach [3], Rhodes [43]	23,403
16	Nov 4	A	Aston Villa	W	2-1	2-0	11	Reach [1], Rhodes [23]	33,154
17	18	H	Bristol C	D	0-0	0-0	9		25,916
18	22	A	Ipswich T	D	2-2	0-0	11	Hooper (pen) [64], Nuhiu [90]	15,702
19	25	A	Reading	D	0-0	0-0	11		18,382
20	Dec 2	H	Hull C	D	2-2	0-1	12	Hooper 2 [70, 85]	25,412
21	9	A	Norwich C	L	1-3	1-0	14	Rhodes [18]	25,561
22	15	H	Wolverhampton W	L	0-1	0-1	15		23,809
23	23	H	Middlesbrough	L	1-2	1-0	15	Wallace [30]	27,471
24	26	A	Nottingham F	W	3-0	2-0	14	Reach [5], Rhodes (pen) [45], Lucas Joao [65]	28,635
25	30	A	Brentford	L	0-2	0-0	16		10,853
26	Jan 1	H	Burton Alb	L	0-3	0-1	16		25,506
27	12	A	Sheffield U	D	0-0	0-0	15		31,120
28	20	H	Cardiff C	D	0-0	0-0	17		23,277
29	30	A	Middlesbrough	D	0-0	0-0	16		24,120
30	Feb 3	H	Birmingham C	L	1-3	0-3	17	Lucas Joao [54]	25,648
31	10	A	Barnsley	D	1-1	1-1	17	Nuhiu (pen) [18]	16,858
32	13	H	Derby Co	W	2-0	1-0	15	Lucas Joao 2 [18, 47]	24,180
33	20	A	Millwall	L	1-2	1-0	16	Pelupessy [42]	11,007
34	24	H	Aston Villa	L	2-4	2-1	17	Clare [14], Lucas Joao [45]	28,604
35	Mar 3	A	Bristol C	L	0-4	0-3	17		22,022
36	6	H	Ipswich T	L	1-2	0-0	17	Lucas Joao [69]	22,733
37	10	H	Bolton W	D	1-1	0-0	17	Boyd [78]	26,809
38	17	A	Leeds U	W	2-1	0-0	17	Nuhiu 2 [71, 90]	31,638
39	30	H	Preston NE	W	4-1	0-0	17	Nuhiu 2 [50, 90], Lucas Joao [52], Forestieri [90]	26,588
40	Apr 2	A	Sunderland	W	3-1	0-0	16	Lucas Joao [59], Lees [68], Nuhiu [75]	29,786
41	7	H	Fulham	L	0-1	0-0	16		25,653
42	10	A	QPR	L	2-4	0-3	17	Forestieri [61], Nuhiu [69]	12,521
43	14	A	Hull C	W	1-0	1-0	16	Rhodes [18]	16,417
44	21	H	Reading	W	3-0	1-0	15	Forestieri 2 [34, 73], Boyd [52]	24,373
45	28	A	Wolverhampton W	D	0-0	0-0	16		29,794
46	May 6	H	Norwich C	W	5-1	2-0	15	Nuhiu 3 (1 pen) [14, 60, 90 (p)], Forestieri [30], Frederico Venancio [58]	28,189

Final League Position: 15

GOALSCORERS

League (59): Nuhiu 11 (2 pens), Hooper 10 (1 pen), Lucas Joao 9, Forestieri 5, Rhodes 5 (1 pen), Reach 4, Lee 3, Boyd 2, Fletcher 2, Wallace 2, Clare 1, Frederico Venancio 1, Jones 1, Lees 1, Pelupessy 1, Winnall 1.
FA Cup (5): Nuhiu 3, Boyd 1, Marco Matias 1.
Carabao Cup (6): Rhodes 2, Bannan 1, Fletcher 1, Hooper 1, Hutchinson 1.

Westwood K 18	Hunt J 28+1	Lees T 28+1	Loovens G 20	Pudil D 24+3	Boyd G 13+7	Hutchinson S 7+1	Bannan B 28+1	Reach A 45+1	Forestieri F 6+4	Rhodes J 17+14	Hooper G 22+2	Wallace R 24+3	Jones D 20+7	Winnall S 1+1	Fletcher S 13+6	Abdi A 1+3	Palmer L 16+9	Fox M 26+2	Nuhiu A 15+13	Wildsmith J 25+1	van Aken J 14	Lee K 10+5	Butterfield J 12+8	Lucas Joao E 17+14	Marco Matias A 2+7	Frederico Venancio A 20	Clare S 4+1	Thornliey J 7+4	Pelupessy J 17	Nielsen F —+3	Stobbs J 2+1	Dawson C 3	Kirby C —+1	Baker A 1	Match No.
1	2	3	4	5	6^2	7^1	8	9	10	11^3	12	13	14																						1
1	2	3	4^2	5		7^3	8	9		11^1	10	6	12	13	14																				2
1	2^3	3	4				8	5		13	10	6	7		11^2	12	9^1	14																	3
1	2	3	4	6^1			8	9	12		10^3		7		11^2		14	5	13																4
1^1	2	3	4	6^2			8	9		13	11	14	7		10^3		11^3	5	12																5
1	2	3			12		9	5		14	10^2	6	8		11^3								4	7^1	13										6
1	2	3	14				9^1	5		12	11^3	6	7		10^2								4	8	13										7
1	2	3		5			8^2	9			10^3	12	7		11			14					4	6^1	13										8
1	2	3					8	5		13	10	7^2	6^3		11^1								4	9	14	12									9
	2	3					8	9		12	10				11^1			5^2		1			4	6	7	13									10
	2^3	3					9^2	5		14	10	6	8		11^1		12			1			4	7	13										11
	2	3			12		9	5		13	10	6^2	8^3		11^1					1			4	7		14									12
1	2	3	4				8	9			10	6^1			11^2		5							7	12	13									13
1	2	3	5^2				8	9		13	10	6^1			11^3								4	7	12	14									14
1		3	4				8	9		11^3	10^3	6^2	14		13		2	5					12	7											15
1	2	3	4				8	9		10^3	11^1	6^2	14		13		12	5						7											16
1	2	3	4				8	9		10	11^3	6^2			14			5					13	7^1	12										17
1	2	3	4				8	9		10^2	11^3	6^3			12			5^1	14					13	7										18
1		3					8	9		13	12		7		11^1		2	5	14				4	6		10^2									19
1		3					8	9		12	11				10^3		2	5	14				4	13	7^2	6^1									20
1		3					8	9		10	11	6	7^2				2	5^3	13				4	12											21
		3					8	9		10	11	6					2	5^4	12	1			4	7^2	13										22
		5^1			7			9		14	10	6^3	8				2		11^2	1	4			12	13		3								23
		3	13		7		8	9		11	10^3	9	14		12		2	5		1	4^2			6^1											24
14		3	4		6			9			10		8^1		12		2^2	5	11^3	1				7	13										25
	2^3		4^2	12				9			10	6	8		14			5	13	1				7^1	11		3								26
		3^4	4	12			8				10^2	6^1	7					5	9	13	1			11^3			2	14							27
		3	14				8				10^1	6^3	7					5	9	13	1			11^3	12	2		4							28
		3	12				7				10^2							5	9	13	1			6^1	11^3	2		4	8	14					29
		3^1	4	14			8											5	9	11^3	1			6^2	12	10^1	2		13	7					30
							9						7	4^1				2	6	11	1			10		3		5^4	8	13	12				31
5^5		3^2	4	9			8					10^1					12		13	1				11		2	6	14^1	7		9				32
5		3		11			12				10^3	6^2						8	14	1				13		2		4^3	7			9			33
5			3	9			8											4	10	1				11		2	6		7						34
	12		4	13			8						14				2	5	10	1				11^1		3	6^3		7		9				35
	2	3		9			8				10^1			6			5	4	11	1				7	12										36
5	3		4	9^2			8				12		14				13	11^3	1					10		2	6	7^1							37
2	4		5	6	8^1	12	9										13	11	1					10		3		7^1							38
5^1	3		4		7^2	6^3	10	14					13				13	9^1	11	1				12		2		8							39
5	3		8		7^2	9	14				13						4^3	11^1	1					10^1		2		12	6						40
5	3		4	9^2	7^3	8	13										10	1					12	11^1	14	2			6						41
	3		4	13			9	8^2	14			7					2	10^3	1					11^1	12			5	6						42
5^3	3			9			6	8	10^1	11^2							12							13	2		4	7	14						43
5^3	3		4	9			7	8	10^1	11^1								13						12	2^2			6			1	14		44
	3		4				7	5	11									10						9^1	12	2		8	6		1			45
		3^3	4				7	8^1	11								14	10						9	13	2		12	6		1		5^5	46

FA Cup

Third Round	Carlisle U	(a)	0-0
Replay	Carlisle U	(h)	2-0
Fourth Round	Reading	(h)	3-1
Fifth Round	Swansea C	(h)	0-0
Replay	Swansea C	(a)	0-2

Carabao Cup

First Round	Chesterfield	(h)	4-1
Second Round	Bolton W	(a)	2-3

SHREWSBURY TOWN

FOUNDATION

Shrewsbury School having provided a number of the early England and Wales international players it is not surprising that there was a Town club as early as 1876 which won the Birmingham Senior Cup in 1879. However, the present Shrewsbury Town club was formed in 1886 and won the Welsh FA Cup as early as 1891.

Montgomery Waters Meadow, Oteley Road, Shrewsbury, Shropshire SY2 6ST.

Telephone: (01743) 289 177.

Fax: (01743) 246 942.

Ticket Office: (01743) 273 943.

Website: www.shrewsburytown.com

Email: info@shrewsburytown.co.uk

Ground Capacity: 9,875.

Record Attendance: 18,917 v Walsall, Division 3, 26 April 1961 (at Gay Meadow); 10,210 v Chelsea, League Cup 4th rd, 28 October 2014 (at New Meadow).

Pitch Measurements: 105m × 68.5m (115yd × 75yd).

Chairman: Roland Wycherley.

Chief Executive: Brian Caldwell.

Manager: John Askey.

Assistant Manager: John Filan.

Colours: Blue and yellow striped shirts, blue shorts, yellow socks with blue trim.

Year Formed: 1886.

Turned Professional: 1896.

Club Nicknames: 'Town', 'Blues', 'Salop'. The name 'Salop' is a colloquialism for the county of Shropshire. Since Shrewsbury is the only club in Shropshire, cries of 'Come on Salop' are frequently used!

Grounds: 1886, Old Racecourse Ground; 1889, Ambler's Field; 1893, Sutton Lane; 1895, Barracks Ground; 1910, Gay Meadow; 2007, New Meadow (renamed ProStar Stadium 2008; Greenhous Meadow 2010; Montgomery Waters Meadow 2017).

First Football League Game: 19 August 1950, Division 3 (N), v Scunthorpe U (a) D 0–0 – Eggleston; Fisher, Lewis; Wheatley, Depear, Robinson; Griffin, Hope, Jackson, Brown, Barker.

Record League Victory: 7–0 v Swindon T, Division 3 (S), 6 May 1955 – McBride; Bannister, Skeech; Wallace, Maloney, Candlin; Price, O'Donnell (1), Weigh (4), Russell, McCue (2); 7-0 v Gillingham, FL 2, 13 September 2008 – Daniels; Herd, Tierney, Davies (2), Jackson (1) (Langmead), Coughlan (1), Cansdell-Sherriff (1), Thornton, Hibbert (1) (Hindmarch), Holt (pen), McIntyre (Ashton).

Record Cup Victory: 11–2 v Marine, FA Cup 1st rd, 11 November 1995 – Edwards; Seabury (Dempsey (1)), Withe (1), Evans (1), Whiston (2), Scott (1), Woods, Stevens (1), Spink (3) (Anthrobus), Walton, Berkley, (1 og).

HONOURS

League Champions: Division 3 – 1978–79; Third Division – 1993–94. *Runners-up:* FL 2 – 2011–12, 2014–15; Division 4 – 1974–75; Conference – (3rd) 2003–04 *(promoted via play-offs).*

FA Cup: 6th rd – 1979, 1982.

League Cup: semi-final – 1961.

League Trophy: *Runners-up:* 1996, 2018.

Welsh Cup Winners: 1891, 1938, 1977, 1979, 1984, 1985. *Runners-up:* 1931, 1948, 1980.

THE SUN FACT FILE

Shrewsbury Town experimented with a couple of Saturday evening fixtures in the 1966–67 season in a bid to increase attendances. The first game against Swindon Town on 25 February 1967 was deemed a great success, with the crowd of 5,057 being 1,500 up on the previous game. However, a second fixture against Doncaster attracted less than 5,000 and the idea was dropped.

Record Defeat: 1–8 v Norwich C, Division 3 (S), 13 September 1952; 1–8 v Coventry C, Division 3, 22 October 1963.

Most League Points (2 for a win): 62, Division 4, 1974–75.

Most League Points (3 for a win): 89, FL 2, 2014–15.

Most League Goals: 101, Division 4, 1958–59.

Highest League Scorer in Season: Arthur Rowley, 38, Division 4, 1958–59.

Most League Goals in Total Aggregate: Arthur Rowley, 152, 1958–65 (thus completing his League record of 434 goals).

Most League Goals in One Match: 5, Alf Wood v Blackburn R, Division 3, 2 October 1971.

Most Capped Player: Jimmy McLaughlin, 5 (12), Northern Ireland; Bernard McNally, 5, Northern Ireland.

Most League Appearances: Mickey Brown, 418, 1986–91; 1992–94; 1996–2001.

Youngest League Player: Graham French, 16 years 177 days v Reading, 30 September 1961.

Record Transfer Fee Received: £600,000 (rising to £1,500,000) from Manchester C for Joe Hart, May 2006.

Record Transfer Fee Paid: £170,000 to Nottingham F for Grant Holt, June 2008.

Football League Record: 1950 Elected to Division 3 (N); 1951–58 Division 3 (S); 1958–59 Division 4; 1959–74 Division 3; 1974–75 Division 4; 1975–79 Division 3; 1979–89 Division 2; 1989–94 Division 3; 1994–97 Division 2; 1997–2003 Division 3; 2003–04 Conference; 2004–12 FL 2; 2012–14 FL 1; 2014–15 FL 2; 2015– FL 1.

LATEST SEQUENCES

Longest Sequence of League Wins: 7, 28.10.1995 – 16.12.1995.

Longest Sequence of League Defeats: 11, 9.4.2003 – 14.8.2004. (Spread over 2 periods in Football League. 2003–04 season in Conference.)

Longest Sequence of League Draws: 6, 30.10.1963 – 14.12.1963.

Longest Sequence of Unbeaten League Matches: 16, 30.10.1993 – 26.2.1994.

Longest Sequence Without a League Win: 18, 8.3.2003 – 14.8.2004.

Successive Scoring Runs: 28 from 7.9.1960.

Successive Non-scoring Runs: 6 from 1.1.1991.

MANAGERS

W. Adams 1905–12
(Secretary-Manager)
A. Weston 1912–34
(Secretary-Manager)
Jack Roscamp 1934–35
Sam Ramsey 1935–36
Ted Bousted 1936–40
Leslie Knighton 1945–49
Harry Chapman 1949–50
Sammy Crooks 1950–54
Walter Rowley 1955–57
Harry Potts 1957–58
Johnny Spuhler 1958
Arthur Rowley 1958–68
Harry Gregg 1968–72
Maurice Evans 1972–73
Alan Durban 1974–78
Richie Barker 1978
Graham Turner 1978–84
Chic Bates 1984–87
Ian McNeill 1987–90
Asa Hartford 1990–91
John Bond 1991–93
Fred Davies 1994–97
(previously Caretaker-Manager 1993–94)
Jake King 1997–99
Kevin Ratcliffe 1999–2003
Jimmy Quinn 2003–04
Gary Peters 2004–08
Paul Simpson 2008–10
Graham Turner 2010–14
Mike Jackson 2014
Micky Mellon 2014–16
Paul Hurst 2016–18
John Askey June 2018–

TEN YEAR LEAGUE RECORD

		P	W	D	L	F	A	Pts	Pos
2008-09	FL 2	46	17	18	11	61	44	69	7
2009-10	FL 2	46	17	12	17	55	54	63	12
2010-11	FL 2	46	22	13	11	72	49	79	4
2011-12	FL 2	46	26	10	10	66	41	88	2
2012-13	FL 1	46	13	16	17	54	60	55	16
2013-14	FL 1	46	9	15	22	44	65	42	23
2014-15	FL 2	46	27	8	11	67	31	89	2
2015-16	FL 1	46	13	11	22	58	79	50	20
2016-17	FL 1	46	13	12	21	46	63	51	18
2017-18	FL 1	46	25	12	9	60	39	87	3

DID YOU KNOW ?

Shrewsbury Town played their 3,000th Football League game at home to Wigan Athletic on 9 September 2017. Fittingly Stefan Payne's first-half goal earned them a 1-0 victory and took them to the top of the League One table.

SHREWSBURY TOWN – SKY BET LEAGUE ONE 2017–18 LEAGUE RECORD

Match No.	Date	Venue	Opponents	Result		H/T Score	Lg Pos.	Goalscorers	Attendance
1	Aug 5	H	Northampton T	W	1-0	0-0	9	John-Lewis [90]	5736
2	12	A	AFC Wimbledon	W	1-0	1-0	5	Rodman [8]	3981
3	19	A	Rochdale	W	3-2	2-1	4	Whalley (pen) [30], Morris, C [33], Payne [74]	5001
4	26	A	Oxford U	D	1-1	0-0	3	Payne [83]	7120
5	Sept 2	A	Gillingham	W	2-1	2-0	2	Morris, C [30], Rodman [37]	4080
6	9	H	Wigan Ath	W	1-0	1-0	1	Payne [26]	6929
7	12	H	Southend U	W	1-0	1-0	1	Nolan [23]	5129
8	16	A	Oldham Ath	W	2-1	1-1	1	Payne [19], Nolan [65]	4150
9	23	H	Blackburn R	D	1-1	0-0	1	Nsiala [57]	8202
10	26	A	Doncaster R	W	2-1	1-1	1	Riley [35], Gnahoua [90]	7194
11	30	A	Scunthorpe U	W	2-0	1-0	1	Payne [24], Morris, C [87]	5759
12	Oct 7	A	Walsall	D	1-1	1-1	1	Payne (pen) [20]	5971
13	14	A	Plymouth Arg	D	1-1	0-0	2	Whalley [78]	8280
14	17	H	Bristol R	W	4-0	4-0	1	Rodman [12], Morris, C [24], Nolan [29], Brown [41]	5652
15	21	H	Fleetwood T	W	1-0	1-0	1	Nsiala [89]	5989
16	28	A	Peterborough U	L	0-1	0-1	1		5606
17	Nov 18	A	Rotherham U	W	2-1	1-0	1	Nolan [16], Payne [90]	8184
18	21	A	Bury	L	0-1	0-0	1		3055
19	25	H	Bradford C	L	0-1	0-0	2		7165
20	Dec 9	A	Milton Keynes D	D	1-1	0-0	2	Whalley [86]	8355
21	16	H	Blackpool	W	1-0	0-0	2	Nolan [54]	5620
22	23	H	Portsmouth	W	2-0	0-0	2	Whalley [59], Payne [81]	7429
23	26	A	Wigan Ath	D	0-0	0-0	2		11,115
24	30	A	Southend U	W	2-1	2-0	2	Coker (og) [18], Godfrey [40]	7076
25	Jan 1	H	Oldham Ath	W	1-0	1-0	2	Whalley [16]	6383
26	13	A	Blackburn R	L	1-3	1-1	2	Nolan (pen) [35]	13,579
27	20	H	Doncaster R	D	2-2	1-0	3	Sadler [21], Morris, C [52]	5818
28	27	A	Portsmouth	W	1-0	1-0	2	Bolton [21]	17,779
29	Feb 3	A	Bristol R	W	2-1	0-0	2	Beckles [62], Nsiala [88]	9380
30	10	H	Plymouth Arg	L	1-2	1-1	2	Morris, C [6]	7036
31	13	A	Fleetwood T	W	2-1	1-0	1	Whalley [45], Thomas [82]	2531
32	17	H	Rotherham U	L	0-1	0-1	1		7007
33	20	H	Gillingham	D	1-1	1-0	2	Ogogo [14]	4839
34	24	A	Charlton Ath	W	2-0	0-0	2	Rodman [52], Beckles [67]	17,581
35	Mar 10	H	Walsall	W	2-0	1-0	2	Rodman [6], Ogogo [88]	7633
36	17	A	Scunthorpe U	W	2-1	0-1	2	Nolan [51], Payne (pen) [59]	3824
37	20	A	Northampton T	D	1-1	0-1	2	Nolan [67]	4788
38	24	H	AFC Wimbledon	W	1-0	0-0	1	Payne [54]	6456
39	30	A	Rochdale	L	1-3	1-1	3	Thomas [8]	4098
40	Apr 2	H	Oxford U	W	3-2	1-0	2	Whalley 2 [40, 64], Nolan [47]	7191
41	12	A	Bradford C	D	0-0	0-0	3		18,997
42	17	H	Charlton Ath	L	0-2	0-0	3		5838
43	21	H	Bury	D	1-1	1-0	3	Eisa [13]	5735
44	24	H	Peterborough U	W	3-1	0-1	3	Beckles [59], Payne [73], John-Lewis [90]	4666
45	28	A	Blackpool	W	1-1	1-0	3	Jones [20]	5825
46	May 5	H	Milton Keynes D	L	0-1	0-0	3		6516

Final League Position: 3

GOALSCORERS

League (60): Payne 11 (2 pens), Nolan 9 (1 pen), Whalley 8 (1 pen), Morris, C 6, Rodman 5, Beckles 3, Nsiala 3, John-Lewis 2, Ogogo 2, Thomas 2, Bolton 1, Brown 1, Eisa 1, Gnahoua 1, Godfrey 1, Jones 1, Riley 1, Sadler 1, own goal 1.
FA Cup (7): Rodman 2, Whalley 2 (2 pens), Gnahoua 1, Morris C 1, Payne 1.
Carabao Cup (1): Whalley 1 (1 pen).
Checkatrade Trophy (11): Dodds 2, Morris C 2, Payne 2, Gnahoua 1, John-Lewis 1, Riley 1, Rodman 1, Whalley 1.
League One Play-Offs (3): Morris C 1, Nolan 1, Rodman 1.

Henderson D 38	Bolton J 32 + 1	Nsiala A 44	Sadler M 42	Brown J 15	Whalley S 40 + 4	Ogogo A 35	Nolan J 43	Rodman A 36 + 5	Morris B 13 + 5	Morris C 32 + 10	John-Lewis L — + 34	Gnahoua A 4 + 7	Dodds L 5 + 4	Adams E — + 5	Ennis N — + 1	Payne S 17 + 21	Godfrey B 35 + 5	MacGillivray C 8	Beckles B 29 + 4	Riley J 8 + 2	Lowe M 8 + 4	Hendrie L 9 + 1	Thomas N 7 + 4	Jones S 3 + 2	Elsa A 3 + 2	Match No.
1	2	3	4	5	6^1	7	8	9	10	11^2	12	13														1
1	6	4	3	2	11	8	5	9^3	10^1	12						7^2	13	14								2
1	2	4	3	5	9^1	8	10	7		11^3	14		6^3	13		12										3
1	5	3	4	2	10	8	9	6		11^2	13					12	7^1									4
	2	4	3	5	6^1	9	7	10^2		11^3	13					12	8	1	14							5
1	2	4	3	5	6^2	7	9^3	10		11^1	12	14					8	13								6
1		4	3	5	7	8	9^2	10		12		13				11^1	6		2							7
1		4	3	5	7	8	9	10^1		12				13		11^2	6		2							8
1	2	4	3	5	7^3	8	9	10		12			14	13		11^2	6^1									9
1		4		5	12	7	8	6^3		11			14	9^1		10	13		3	2^2						10
1	2	4	3	5	7^1	8	9^3	10^2		12	14	13				11	6									11
	2	3	4	5	12	8	9	10^2		13		14	7^3			11^1	6	1								12
1	2	3	4	5	7	8	9	12		13	14	10^1				11^2	6^2									13
1	2	4	3	5	7	8^2	9^3	10	14	11^1	13					12	6									14
1	2^1	4	3	5	7	8	9	10		11^3	14					12	6		13							15
1	5^2	4			10	8	7	6	13	11	14					12	9^3		3	2^1						16
1		3	4		7^2	9^3	8	10^1		12	13					11	6		5	2						17
1		3	4		9	7			11^1	12	13	13	10^2			6	8		2	5						18
1	4	2	5^1		7		9	10	8	12	13					11	6^2		3							19
1	2	4	5^2		7	8	9	10		14	13		12			11^1	6^1		3							20
1	2	3	5		7	9	8	10^1	6^3	11^2	14					13	12		4							21
1	2	4	3		7	8	9	10^1	6	11^2						12	13		5							22
1	2	4	3		7	8	9^2	10	13	11^1						12	6		5							23
1	2	3	4		7^1	8	10^3	9	13	11^2	12						6		5	14						24
1	2	4	3		7	6	8		9^2	14	13	10^1				11^3	12		5							25
1	2	3	4		7	8	9	10		11^2	14					13	6		12							26
1		3	4		7	8	9	10^1		11						13	6		12	5	2^1					27
	2	3	4		9^2	6	8	11		10^1	13					12	7	1	5							28
	2	3	4		7^2	8	9	13		11^1						12	6	1	5			10^3	14			29
	2	4	3		12	8	9	10^2		11^1	13					14	6^3	1		5	7					30
1		3	4		6	8	10	9^1	7^2	11	14					13	5			2	12					31
1	2	3	4		6	7	9^3	14		11^2	13					12	8		5		10^1					32
1	2	3			6^1	7		13		11						12	9		4	5	8	10^2				33
1	2^2	3	4		6	7	9	10		11	13					8	5		12							34
1		3	4		7^3	8	9^2	10		11^1	14					12	6		5	2	13					35
1		3	4		7	9	8	10		11^2	13					12	6^1		5	2						36
1		4	3		7	8^4	9	10	6	11^1	13					12			5		2^3					37
	3	4		6^3	8	9	7^4	10^1	14	11^1						1	5	13	2	12						38
1	14	4^3	3		7	9		11			8					13	6		5	12	2^1	10^2				39
1	2	3			7^1	8		6		13						11^3	9		4	5	10^2	14	12			40
1	2	3	4		7	8	10	6^1	12	13						11^2	9		5^3							41
1	2	3^2	4		6^3	8	10	13	11	14						9			5			7^1	12			42
1	6	3	4^3			7^1	9	11	14	13						8	5		2	12	10^2					43
	3							6		13	14					11^2	7^3		4	12	5	2	10	9	8^1	44
	3		12			9	8	6	11	13	10^1						1	4	2	5		7^2				45
1	2	3	4		6		9^1	14		11^2						13	8		5	7	12		10^3			46

FA Cup

First Round	Aldershot T	(h)	5-0
Second Round	Morecambe	(h)	2-0
Third Round	West Ham U	(h)	0-0
Replay (aet)	West Ham U	(a)	0-1

Carabao Cup

First Round	Nottingham F	(a)	1-2

Checkatrade Trophy

Northern Group E	Coventry C	(a)	3-2
Northern Group E	WBA U21	(h)	3-0
Northern Group E	Walsall	(h)	0-1
Second Round North	Port Vale	(a)	2-1
Third Round	Blackpool	(h)	0-0
(Shrewsbury T won 4-2 on penalties)			
Quarter-Final	Oldham Ath	(h)	2-1
Semi-Final	Yeovil T	(h)	1-0
Final	Lincoln C	(Wembley)	0-1

League One Play-Offs

Semi-Final 1st leg	Charlton Ath	(a)	1-0
Semi-Final 2nd leg	Charlton Ath	(h)	1-0
Final (aet)	Rotherham U	(Wembley)	1-2

SOUTHAMPTON

St Mary's Stadium, Britannia Road, Southampton, Hampshire SO14 5FP.

Telephone: (0845) 688 9448.

Fax: (0845) 688 9445.

Ticket Office: (0845) 688 9288.

Website: www.southamptonfc.com

Email: sfc@saintsfc.com

Ground Capacity: 32,384.

Record Attendance: 31,044 v Manchester U, Division 1, 8 October 1969 (at The Dell); 32,363 v Coventry C, FL C, 28 April 2012 (at St Mary's).

Pitch Measurements: 105m × 68m (114yd × 74yd).

Chairman: Ralph Krueger.

Managing Director: Toby Steele.

Manager: Mark Hughes.

Assistant Manager: Mark Bowen.

Colours: Red shirts with white front panel and black trim, black shorts with red trim, white socks with red trim.

Year Formed: 1885. *Turned Professional:* 1894.

Previous Names: 1885, St Mary's Young Men's Association; 1887–88, St Mary's; 1894–95 Southampton St Mary's; 1897, Southampton.

Club Nickname: 'Saints'.

Grounds: 1885, 'The Common' (from 1887 also used the County Cricket Ground and Antelope Cricket Ground); 1889, Antelope Cricket Ground; 1896, The County Cricket Ground; 1898, The Dell; 2001, St Mary's.

First Football League Game: 28 August 1920, Division 3, v Gillingham (a) D 1–1 – Allen; Parker, Titmuss; Shelley, Campbell, Turner; Barratt, Dominy (1), Rawlings, Moore, Foxall.

Record League Victory: 8–0 v Sunderland, FA Premier League, 18 October 2014 – Forster; Clyne, Fonte, Alderweireld, Bertrand; Davis S (Mané), Schneiderlin, Cork (1); Long (Wanyama (1)), Pelle (2) (Mayuka), Tadic (1) (plus 3 Sunderland own goals).

Record Cup Victory: 7–1 v Ipswich T, FA Cup 3rd rd, 7 January 1961 – Reynolds; Davies, Traynor, Conner, Page, Huxford, Paine (1), O'Brien (3 incl. 1p), Reeves, Mulgrew (2), Penk (1).

HONOURS

League Champions: Division 3 – 1959–60; Division 3S – 1921–22. *Runners-up:* Division 1 – 1983–84; FL C – 2011–12; Division 2 – 1965–66, 1977–78; FL 1 – 2010–11; Division 3 – 1920–21.

FA Cup Winners: 1976. *Runners-up:* 1900, 1902, 2003.

League Cup: Runners-up: 1979, 2017.

League Trophy Winners: 2010.

Full Members' Cup: Runners-up: 1992.

European Competitions
Fairs Cup: 1969–70.
UEFA Cup: 1971–72, 1981–82, 1982–83, 1984–85, 2003–04.
Europa League: 2015–16, 2016–17.
European Cup-Winners' Cup: 1976–77 (qf).

Record Defeat: 0–8 v Tottenham H, Division 2, 28 March 1936; 0–8 v Everton, Division 1, 20 November 1971.

Most League Points (2 for a win): 61, Division 3 (S), 1921–22 and Division 3, 1959–60.

Most League Points (3 for a win): 92, FL 1, 2010–11.

Most League Goals: 112, Division 3 (S), 1957–58.

Highest League Scorer in Season: Derek Reeves, 39, Division 3, 1959–60.

Most League Goals in Total Aggregate: Mike Channon, 185, 1966–77, 1979–82.

Most League Goals in One Match: 5, Charlie Wayman v Leicester C, Division 2, 23 October 1948.

Most Capped Player: Maya Yoshida, 69 (86), Japan.

Most League Appearances: Terry Paine, 713, 1956–74.

Youngest League Player: Theo Walcott, 16 years 143 days v Wolverhampton W, 6 August 2005.

Record Transfer Fee Received: £75,000,000 from Liverpool for Virgil van Dijk, January 2018.

Record Transfer Fee Paid: £19,000,000 to Monaco for Guido Carrillo, January 2018.

Football League Record: 1920 Original Member of Division 3; 1921–22 Division 3 (S); 1922–53 Division 2; 1953–58 Division 3 (S); 1958–60 Division 3; 1960–66 Division 2; 1966–74 Division 1; 1974–78 Division 2; 1978–92 Division 1; 1992–2005 FA Premier League; 2005–09 FL C; 2009–11 FL 1; 2011–12 FL C; 2012– FA Premier League.

LATEST SEQUENCES

Longest Sequence of League Wins: 10, 16.4.2011 – 20.8.2011.

Longest Sequence of League Defeats: 5, 16.8.1998 – 12.9.1998.

Longest Sequence of League Draws: 8, 29.8.2005 – 15.10.2005.

Longest Sequence of Unbeaten League Matches: 19, 5.9.1921 – 31.12.1921.

Longest Sequence Without a League Win: 20, 30.8.1969 – 27.12.1969.

Successive Scoring Runs: 28 from 10.2.2008.

Successive Non-scoring Runs: 5 from 2.4.2001.

MANAGERS

Cecil Knight 1894–95
  (Secretary-Manager)
Charles Robson 1895–97
Er Arnfield 1897–1911
  (Secretary-Manager)
  (continued as Secretary)
George Swift 1911–12
Er Arnfield 1912–19
Jimmy McIntyre 1919–24
Arthur Chadwick 1925–31
George Kay 1931–36
George Gross 1936–37
Tom Parker 1937–43
J. R. Sarjantson stepped down
  from the board to act as
  Secretary-Manager 1943–47 with
  the next two listed being Team
  Managers during this period
Arthur Dominy 1943–46
Bill Dodgin Snr 1946–49
Sid Cann 1949–51
George Roughton 1952–55
Ted Bates 1955–73
Lawrie McMenemy 1973–85
Chris Nicholl 1985–91
Ian Branfoot 1991–94
Alan Ball 1994–95
Dave Merrington 1995–96
Graeme Souness 1996–97
Dave Jones 1997–2000
Glenn Hoddle 2000–01
Stuart Gray 2001
Gordon Strachan 2001–04
Paul Sturrock 2004
Steve Wigley 2004
Harry Redknapp 2004–05
George Burley 2005–08
Nigel Pearson 2008
Jan Poortvliet 2008–09
Mark Wotte 2009
Alan Pardew 2009–10
Nigel Adkins 2010–13
Mauricio Pochettino 2013–14
Ronald Koeman 2014–16
Claude Puel 2016–17
Mauricio Pellegrino 2017–18
Mark Hughes March 2018–

TEN YEAR LEAGUE RECORD

		P	W	D	L	F	A	Pts	Pos
2008-09	FL C	46	10	15	21	46	69	45	23
2009-10	FL 1	46	23	14	9	85	47	73*	7
2010-11	FL 1	46	28	8	10	86	38	92	2
2011-12	FL C	46	26	10	10	85	46	88	2
2012-13	PR Lge	38	9	14	15	49	60	41	14
2013-14	PR Lge	38	15	11	12	54	46	56	8
2014-15	PR Lge	38	18	6	14	54	33	60	7
2015-16	PR Lge	38	18	9	11	59	41	63	6
2016-17	PR Lge	38	12	10	16	41	48	46	8
2017-18	PR Lge	38	7	15	16	37	56	36	17

10 pts deducted.

DID YOU KNOW ?

The first live television match broadcast from The Dell was the First Division fixture between Southampton and Liverpool on Friday, 16 March 1984. Saints won the match 2-0 with two goals from Danny Wallace including a spectacular overhead kick.

SOUTHAMPTON – PREMIER LEAGUE 2017–18 LEAGUE RECORD

Match No.	Date	Venue	Opponents	Result	H/T Score	Lg Pos.	Goalscorers	Attendance
1	Aug 12	H	Swansea C	D 0-0	0-0	9		31,447
2	19	H	West Ham U	W 3-2	2-1	5	Gabbiadini [11], Tadic (pen) [38], Austin (pen) [90]	31,424
3	26	A	Huddersfield T	D 0-0	0-0	6		23,548
4	Sept 9	H	Watford	L 0-2	0-1	11		31,435
5	16	A	Crystal Palace	W 1-0	1-0	9	Davis [6]	24,199
6	23	H	Manchester U	L 0-1	0-1	11		31,930
7	30	A	Stoke C	L 1-2	0-1	12	Yoshida [75]	29,285
8	Oct 15	A	Newcastle U	D 2-2	0-1	10	Gabbiadini 2 (1 pen) [49, 75 (p)]	31,437
9	21	H	WBA	W 1-0	0-0	10	Boufal [85]	29,947
10	29	A	Brighton & HA	D 1-1	1-0	9	Davis [7]	30,564
11	Nov 4	H	Burnley	L 0-1	0-0	13		30,491
12	18	A	Liverpool	L 0-3	0-2	14		53,256
13	26	H	Everton	W 4-1	1-1	10	Tadic [18], Austin 2 [52, 58], Davis [87]	30,461
14	29	A	Manchester C	L 1-2	0-0	11	Romeu [75]	53,407
15	Dec 3	A	Bournemouth	D 1-1	0-1	11	Austin [61]	10,764
16	10	H	Arsenal	D 1-1	1-0	11	Austin [3]	31,643
17	13	H	Leicester C	L 1-4	0-3	11	Yoshida [61]	27,714
18	16	A	Chelsea	L 0-1	0-1	12		41,562
19	23	H	Huddersfield T	D 1-1	1-0	13	Austin [24]	29,675
20	26	A	Tottenham H	L 2-5	0-2	14	Boufal [64], Tadic [82]	57,297
21	30	A	Manchester U	D 0-0	0-0	13		75,051
22	Jan 2	H	Crystal Palace	L 1-2	1-0	17	Long [17]	28,411
23	13	A	Watford	D 2-2	2-0	16	Ward-Prowse 2 [20, 44]	20,018
24	21	H	Tottenham H	D 1-1	1-1	18	Sanchez (og) [15]	31,361
25	31	A	Brighton & HA	D 1-1	0-1	18	Stephens [64]	30,034
26	Feb 3	A	WBA	W 3-2	2-1	14	Lemina [40], Stephens [43], Ward-Prowse [55]	25,911
27	11	H	Liverpool	L 0-2	0-2	18		31,915
28	24	A	Burnley	D 1-1	0-0	16	Gabbiadini [90]	20,982
29	Mar 3	H	Stoke C	D 0-0	0-0	17		30,335
30	10	A	Newcastle U	L 0-3	0-2	17		52,246
31	31	A	West Ham U	L 0-3	0-3	18		56,882
32	Apr 8	A	Arsenal	L 2-3	1-2	18	Long [17], Austin [73]	59,374
33	14	H	Chelsea	L 2-3	1-0	18	Tadic [21], Bednarek [60]	31,764
34	19	A	Leicester C	D 0-0	0-0	18		31,160
35	28	H	Bournemouth	W 2-1	1-1	18	Tadic 2 [25, 54]	31,778
36	May 5	A	Everton	D 1-1	0-0	17	Redmond [56]	38,225
37	8	A	Swansea C	W 1-0	0-0	16	Gabbiadini [72]	20,858
38	13	H	Manchester C	L 0-1	0-0	17		31,882

Final League Position: 17

GOALSCORERS

League (37): Austin 7 (1 pen), Tadic 6 (1 pen), Gabbiadini 5 (1 pen), Davis 3, Ward-Prowse 3, Boufal 2, Long 2, Stephens 2, Yoshida 2, Bednarek 1, Lemina 1, Redmond 1, Romeu 1, own goal 1.
FA Cup (6): Cedric 1, Hoedt 1, Hojbjerg 1, Stephens 1, Tadic 1, Ward-Prowse 1.
Carabao Cup (0).
Checkatrade Trophy (4): Hesketh 2, Johnson 1, Jones 1.

Forster F 20	Cedric Soares R 32	Stephens J 22	Yoshida M 23 +1	Bertrand R 35	Romeu O 34	Davis S 17+6	Ward-Prowse J 20+10	Tadic D 34+2	Redmond N 22+9	Gabbiadini M 11+17	Austin C 10+14	Boufal S 11+15	McQueen S 1+6	Lemina M 20+5	Long S 15+15	Hoedt W 28	van Dijk V 11+1	Højbjerg P 19+4	Pied J 2	Target M 2	McCarthy A 18	Sims J 1+5	Obafemi M — +1	Carrillo G 5+2	Bednarek J 5	Match No.
1	2	3	4	5¹	6	7	8²	9	10	11³	12	13	14													1
1	2	3	4	5	6	9¹	12	8	10	11¹	13						7²	14								2
1	2	3	4	5	7	9	13	8²	10	11¹					14		6³	12								3
1	2	3			5	6	7	9²	12	10	11¹	14	8³			13	4									4
1	2		3	5	6	9	12	8¹	10²	14		7			11²		4	13								5
1	2²		3	5	6	9¹	14	8	10	12	13	7			11¹		4									6
1	2		3	5	6	9¹		8	10²	13	14	12		7³	11		4									7
1	2		3	5	7³	13		6	9²	10	14	12		8	11¹		4									8
1	2		3	5	6¹	8		9²	12	11	13	14		7	10³		4									9
1	2			5	6	8	9³	7¹	12	11		10²		14		4	3	13								10
1	2		4	5	6	7	14	8²	10	11³	12	9¹		13		3										11
1	2			5	6	7	13	8³	10	14	12	9²		11¹		4	3									12
1	2	14	5		7	8	9³		11¹	10²		12	13			4	3	6								13
1	2³		3	6	8			10		13	12	14	9	11¹	5	4	7²									14
1			5	6	7³	8²	9	12	14	11	10		13			4	3	2								15
1		2	3	5	6	14	8		9	10³	13	11²	12			4	7									16
1	2		3	5	6²	9	14	8	13	12	11	10³		7			4									17
1	5³	2	3	8	6		9		10	11²	13	14		12		4	7¹									18
	2	3		6¹	8		9²	10	14	11³	13		7		4		12		5							19
1		2	3	6		13	10¹	12		7	14	9⁵	11				4	8	5²							20
	2	3		6		8	9²	14	12	10²		5	13	11¹			4	7			1					21
		3	4	5	6	12	8¹	9¹	14	13		10		11¹				7²			1				2	22
	2	3		5	6	10³	8²	9¹		14	12	11					4	7			1	13				23
	2	3		5	6	13	8	10		11²		12		7¹			4	9³			1	14				24
	2	3		5	6³	9	8	10¹		14		13		11²			4	7			1		12			25
	2	3		5	6	8	9²	14		10²		7	12				4	13			1			11¹		26
	2	3		5	6¹	14	8²	10		12		7³	13				4	9			1			11		27
	2	3		5	6²		8	9¹	10	14		13		7			4				1	12		11		28
	2	3		5	6		9²	10	12		13			7	14		4				1	8²		11¹		29
	2	3		5			8	9¹	10	14		13		7³			4	6			1	12		11²		30
	2	3		5			6	9²	11	10³	13			7	12		4	8			1			14		31
5	2¹	3¹	8	6		9	10			12				11²			4	7			1	13				32
5		3	8	6		9²	10²	14	12	11							4	7			1	13			2¹	33
5		3	8	6	12	9²	10	14	13					11¹			4	7³			1				2	34
5		3	8	6	14	9²	11¹	10²		7				12			4	13			1				2	35
5		3	8	6	13	9²	12	11³	10¹			14					4	7			1				2	36
5		3		8	7		9¹	10³	13	11		14		12			4	6			1				2²	37
2	3	4	6³	9		13	7	10¹		11²			14		12		5	8			1					38

FA Cup

Third Round	Fulham	(a)	1-0
Fourth Round	Watford	(h)	1-0
Fifth Round	WBA	(a)	2-1
Sixth Round	Wigan Ath	(a)	2-0
Semi-Final	Chelsea	(Wembley)	0-2

Carabao Cup

Second Round	Wolverhampton W	(h)	0-2

Checkatrade Trophy (Southampton U21)

Southern Group H	Peterborough U	(a)	0-2
Southern Group H	Cambridge U	(a)	1-0
Southern Group H	Northampton T	(a)	3-3

(Northampton T won 4-2 on penalties)

SOUTHEND UNITED

FOUNDATION

The leading club in Southend around the turn of the 20th century was Southend Athletic, but they were an amateur concern. Southend United was a more ambitious professional club when they were founded in 1906, employing Bob Jack as secretary-manager and immediately joining the Second Division of the Southern League.

Roots Hall Stadium, Victoria Avenue, Southend-on-Sea, Essex SS2 6NQ.

Telephone: (01702) 304 050.

Ticket Office: (08444) 770 077.

Website: www.southendunited.co.uk

Email: info@southend-united.co.uk

Ground Capacity: 12,086.

Record Attendance: 22,862 v Tottenham H, FA Cup 3rd rd replay, 11 January 1936 (at Southend Stadium); 31,090 v Liverpool, FA Cup 3rd rd, 10 January 1979 (at Roots Hall).

Pitch Measurements: 100.5m × 67.5m (110yd × 74yd).

Chairman: Ronald Martin.

Manager: Chris Powell.

Assistant Managers: Damian Matthew and Kevin Keen.

Colours: Navy blue shirts, navy blue shorts, white socks.

Year Formed: 1906.

Turned Professional: 1906.

Club Nicknames: 'The Blues', 'The Shrimpers'.

Grounds: 1906, Roots Hall, Prittlewell; 1920, Kursaal; 1934, Southend Stadium; 1955, Roots Hall Football Ground.

First Football League Game: 28 August 1920, Division 3, v Brighton & HA (a) W 2–0 – Capper; Reid, Newton; Wileman, Henderson, Martin; Nicholls, Nuttall, Fairclough (2), Myers, Dorsett.

Record League Victory: 9–2 v Newport Co, Division 3 (S), 5 September 1936 – McKenzie; Nelson, Everest (1); Deacon, Turner, Carr; Bolan, Lane (1), Goddard (4), Dickinson (2), Oswald (1).

Record Cup Victory: 10–1 v Golders Green, FA Cup 1st rd, 24 November 1934 – Moore; Morfitt, Kelly; Mackay, Joe Wilson, Carr (1); Lane (1), Johnson (5), Cheesmuir (2), Deacon (1), Oswald. 10–1 v Brentwood, FA Cup 2nd rd, 7 December 1968 – Roberts; Bentley, Birks; McMillan (1) Beesley, Kurila; Clayton, Chisnall, Moore (4), Best (5), Hamilton. 10–1 v Aldershot, Leyland DAF Cup prel rd, 6 November 1990 – Sansome; Austin, Powell, Cornwell, Prior (1), Tilson (3), Cawley, Butler, Ansah (1), Benjamin (1), Angell (4).

Record Defeat: 1–9 v Brighton & HA, Division 3, 27 November 1965; 0–8 v Crystal Palace, League Cup 2nd rd (1st leg), 25 September 1990.

Most League Points (2 for a win): 67, Division 4, 1980–81.

HONOURS

League Champions: FL 1 – 2005–06; Division 4 – 1980–81.
Runners-up: Division 3 – 1990–91; Division 4 – 1971–72, 1977–78.
FA Cup: 3rd rd – 1921; 5th rd – 1926, 1952, 1976, 1993.
League Cup: quarter-final – 2007.
League Trophy: *Runners-up:* 2004, 2005, 2013.

THE Sun FACT FILE

The blue shirts worn by Southend United in the 1968–69 season were so dark that referees were often required to change their shirts to avoid a clash of colours. In March 1969 the Football League stepped in and instructed the club to change their colours. As a result the team played in borrowed kit for the closing fixtures.

Most League Points (3 for a win): 85, Division 3, 1990–91.

Most League Goals: 92, Division 3 (S), 1950–51.

Highest League Scorer in Season: Jim Shankly, 31, 1928–29; Sammy McCrory, 1957–58, both in Division 3 (S).

Most League Goals in Total Aggregate: Roy Hollis, 122, 1953–60.

Most League Goals in One Match: 5, Jim Shankly v Merthyr T, Division 3 (S), 1 March 1930.

Most Capped Player: George McKenzie, 9, Republic of Ireland.

Most League Appearances: Sandy Anderson, 452, 1950–63.

Youngest League Player: Phil O'Connor, 16 years 76 days v Lincoln C, 26 December 1969.

Record Transfer Fee Received: £2,000,000 (rising to £2,750,000) from Nottingham F for Stan Collymore, June 1993.

Record Transfer Fee Paid: £500,000 to Galatasaray for Mike Marsh, September 1995.

Football League Record: 1920 Original Member of Division 3; 1921–58 Division 3 (S); 1958–66 Division 3; 1966–72 Division 4; 1972–76 Division 3; 1976–78 Division 4; 1978–80 Division 3; 1980–81 Division 4; 1981–84 Division 3; 1984–87 Division 4; 1987–89 Division 3; 1989–90 Division 4; 1990–91 Division 3; 1991–92 Division 2; 1992–97 Division 1; 1997–98 Division 2; 1998–2004 Division 3; 2004–05 FL 2; 2005–06 FL 1; 2006–07 FL C; 2007–10 FL 1; 2010–15 FL 2; 2015– FL 1.

LATEST SEQUENCES

Longest Sequence of League Wins: 8, 29.8.2005 – 9.10.2005.

Longest Sequence of League Defeats: 7, 16.4.2016 – 13.8.2016.

Longest Sequence of League Draws: 6, 30.1.1982 – 19.2.1982.

Longest Sequence of Unbeaten League Matches: 16, 20.2.1932 – 29.8.1932.

Longest Sequence Without a League Win: 17, 26.8.2006 – 2.12.2006.

Successive Scoring Runs: 24 from 23.3.1929.

Successive Non-scoring Runs: 6 from 6.4.1979.

MANAGERS

Bob Jack 1906–10
George Molyneux 1910–11
O. M. Howard 1911–12
Joe Bradshaw 1912–19
Ned Liddell 1919–20
Tom Mather 1920–21
Ted Birnie 1921–34
David Jack 1934–40
Harry Warren 1946–56
Eddie Perry 1956–60
Frank Broome 1960
Ted Fenton 1961–65
Alvan Williams 1965–67
Ernie Shepherd 1967–69
Geoff Hudson 1969–70
Arthur Rowley 1970–76
Dave Smith 1976–83
Peter Morris 1983–84
Bobby Moore 1984–86
Dave Webb 1986–87
Dick Bate 1987
Paul Clark 1987–88
Dave Webb (*General Manager*) 1988–92
Colin Murphy 1992–93
Barry Fry 1993
Peter Taylor 1993–95
Steve Thompson 1995
Ronnie Whelan 1995–97
Alvin Martin 1997–99
Alan Little 1999–2000
David Webb 2000–01
Rob Newman 2001–03
Steve Wignall 2003
Steve Tilson 2003–10
Paul Sturrock 2010–13
Phil Brown 2013–18
Chris Powell January 2018–

TEN YEAR LEAGUE RECORD

		P	W	D	L	F	A	Pts	Pos
2008-09	FL 1	46	21	8	17	58	61	71	8
2009-10	FL 1	46	10	13	23	51	72	43	23
2010-11	FL 2	46	16	13	17	62	56	61	13
2011-12	FL 2	46	25	8	13	77	48	83	4
2012-13	FL 2	46	16	13	17	61	55	61	11
2013-14	FL 2	46	19	15	12	56	39	72	5
2014-15	FL 2	46	24	12	10	54	38	84	5
2015-16	FL 1	46	16	11	19	58	64	59	14
2016-17	FL 1	46	20	12	14	70	53	72	7
2017-18	FL 1	46	17	12	17	58	62	63	10

DID YOU KNOW ?

Southend United played their 4,000th Football League fixture at Wigan Athletic on 23 April 2016. It was not a particularly memorable occasion, the Shrimpers going down to a 4-1 defeat with their consolation score being an own goal.

SOUTHEND UNITED – SKY BET LEAGUE ONE 2017–18 LEAGUE RECORD

Match No.	Date	Venue	Opponents	Result	H/T Score	Lg Pos.	Goalscorers	Attendance
1	Aug 5	H	Blackburn R	W 2-1	2-0	6	Leonard [27], Kightly [38]	9257
2	12	A	Rotherham U	L 0-5	0-4	15		8004
3	19	H	Plymouth Arg	D 1-1	1-0	14	Bradley (og) [6]	7861
4	26	A	Gillingham	D 3-3	1-0	15	Leonard [20], Kightly [65], Cox [73]	5339
5	Sept 2	H	Rochdale	D 0-0	0-0	14		6208
6	9	A	Charlton Ath	L 1-2	0-0	17	White [78]	12,229
7	12	A	Shrewsbury T	L 0-1	0-1	19		5129
8	16	H	Northampton T	D 2-2	0-2	18	Demetriou [48], Wordsworth [50]	6532
9	23	A	Fleetwood T	W 4-2	3-1	16	Cox [2], McLaughlin [40], Ranger (pen) [45], McGlashan [87]	2874
10	26	H	AFC Wimbledon	W 1-0	0-0	14	Demetriou [60]	5881
11	30	H	Blackpool	W 2-1	1-0	12	Wordsworth [5], Cox [46]	6688
12	Oct 7	A	Doncaster R	L 1-4	1-1	14	Wordsworth [38]	7369
13	14	A	Wigan Ath	L 0-3	0-1	15		8133
14	17	H	Peterborough U	D 1-1	1-0	15	Fortune [10]	5789
15	21	H	Bury	W 1-0	0-0	13	Leonard [84]	6787
16	28	A	Walsall	W 1-0	0-0	11	Cox [17]	4145
17	Nov 18	A	Portsmouth	L 0-1	0-0	14		18,431
18	21	A	Milton Keynes D	D 1-1	1-0	14	McLaughlin [27]	7521
19	25	H	Oxford U	D 1-1	1-1	14	Cox [19]	6797
20	Dec 2	H	Oldham Ath	W 2-0	1-0	9	Demetriou (pen) [17], Wright [54]	5608
21	9	A	Bristol R	L 0-3	0-1	12		8062
22	16	H	Bradford C	L 1-2	0-1	12	Ranger [75]	6097
23	23	A	Scunthorpe U	L 1-3	1-1	13	Demetriou [25]	4040
24	26	H	Charlton Ath	W 3-1	2-0	11	Cox 2 [2, 79], Turner [11]	9588
25	30	H	Shrewsbury T	L 1-2	0-2	13	Leonard [55]	7076
26	Jan 1	A	AFC Wimbledon	L 0-2	0-1	17		4392
27	6	A	Northampton T	L 1-3	1-1	17	Demetriou (pen) [26]	5267
28	13	H	Fleetwood T	L 1-2	0-0	18	Kightly [86]	6489
29	27	H	Scunthorpe U	W 3-2	1-1	17	Kightly [37], McLaughlin [53], Turner [90]	6723
30	Feb 3	A	Peterborough U	W 1-0	1-0	15	Demetriou (pen) [7]	5114
31	10	H	Wigan Ath	W 3-1	2-0	14	Turner [3], Fortune [36], Kightly [83]	7623
32	13	A	Bury	D 0-0	0-0	14		2795
33	17	H	Portsmouth	W 3-1	2-1	13	Clarke (og) [6], Demetriou 2 [12, 84]	9397
34	Mar 3	H	Walsall	L 0-3	0-0	14		6413
35	10	A	Doncaster R	D 0-0	0-0	13		6766
36	13	A	Rochdale	D 0-0	0-0	13		2286
37	17	A	Blackpool	D 1-1	1-1	13	Fortune [11]	3213
38	24	H	Rotherham U	W 2-0	1-0	12	McLaughlin [7], Cox [79]	7719
39	30	A	Plymouth Arg	L 0-4	0-2	12		11,965
40	Apr 2	H	Gillingham	W 4-0	4-0	12	Turner [8], Robinson [11], Kightly [18], McLaughlin [39]	8466
41	7	A	Blackburn R	L 0-1	0-0	11		13,186
42	14	A	Oxford U	L 0-2	0-2	15		7332
43	21	H	Milton Keynes D	W 4-0	2-0	13	Robinson 3 [23, 31, 76], McLaughlin [62]	7546
44	24	A	Oldham Ath	W 3-0	1-0	12	Robinson [5], Cox 2 [52, 56]	3362
45	28	A	Bradford C	W 2-0	0-0	10	White [73], Fortune [78]	19,960
46	May 5	H	Bristol R	D 0-0	0-0	10		8179

Final League Position: 10

GOALSCORERS

League (58): Cox 10, Demetriou 8 (3 pens), Kightly 6, McLaughlin 6, Robinson 5, Fortune 4, Leonard 4, Turner 4, Wordsworth 3, Ranger 2 (1 pen), White 2, McGlashan 1, Wright 1, own goals 2.
FA Cup (0).
Carabao Cup (0).
Checkatrade Trophy (4): Robinson 2, McLaughlin 1, Wright 1.

Oxley M 46	Demetriou J 41 + 1	White J 26 + 5	Ferdinand A 29 + 2	Hendrie S 8 + 4	McGlashan J 9 + 17	Leonard R 25	Timlin M 32 + 2	Kightly M 26 + 3	Cox S 40 + 2	Fortune M 26 + 12	Robinson T 7 + 18	McLaughlin S 35 + 10	Kiernan R — + 1	Bwomono E 9 + 2	Kyprianou H 12 + 1	Ranger N 11 + 7	Yearwood D 24 + 1	Bridge J — + 1	Wordsworth A 21 + 3	Wright J 19 + 4	Turner M 25	Ba A — + 5	Coker B 21 + 1	Bishop N — + 1	Pitoula-Wabo N — + 3	Ladapo F 3 + 7	Harrison S 5 + 8	Manton S 6 + 1	Gard L — + 2	Match No.
1	2	3	4	5	6^1	7	8	9	10^2	11	12	13																		1
1	2	3	4^1	5	6^2	7	8	9	10^3	11	13	14	12																	2
1	2	3	4	5	6^1	7	8	9	10^2	11	12	13																		3
1	2	3	4	5	6	7	8	9	11	10^2	12																			4
1					6^2	7	5	3	8	10	11^1	14	9^1	2	4	12	13													5
1	14	3	4	5^3	6^1	7	8	9	10^2	13	12			2	11															6
1	5	4			9^2	6	7		13	10	12	11^1		2	3		8^3	14												7
1	2	3				13	12	8	5	10		14		9^3	4		11		6^1	7^2										8
1	2	4				14	12	7	5	10		13		9^3	3		11^2		8^1	6										9
1	2	14	3			13	7	5	10^1	12				9^2	4		11		8^2	6										10
1	2	13	3				7	5	10^1	12	14			9^2	4		11^1		8	6										11
1	12	3^*				13	7	5	10^3	9	14			2	4^1		11		8	6^2										12
1	2	3			11^1	4	5	14	13	9^2	12				10^1		6^3		8	7										13
1	2	3				4	5	10	11^1	12				9^2	13	7			8	6										14
1	2	3	4			7	5	9^1	11	10^2	13				12				8	6										15
1	2	4	3			7	5	9^1	11	10^2	13				12				8	6										16
1	2^1	4		14	8	5	9	10	13	6^2	12				11^3		7	3												17
1	2	3	14	13	7	5	6^3	10	11^1						9^2		8	4	12											18
1	2	3	13	8	5	6^2	10^3	11^1	9						12		7	4	14											19
1	2	4	5	7	9^1	11^2	10	6	12						8	3	13													20
1	2	4	5	12	7	11	10^2	9^1	13						8	6^3	3	14												21
1	2	3	13	7^1	8^2	12	9	10^1	11^3						6	11^3	6	4	14	5										22
1^1	6	2	3	11^2	10	9									8	7	4		5	12	13									23
1	2	13	4	12	7	10	14	9^2	11^1						8	6^3	3		5											24
1	2	12	4^1	13	7	10^2	14	9	11						8	6^3	3		5											25
1	2	4		14	7	9^2	10	11^3	13						3	12	6^1	8		5										26
1	2				12	13	6^1	10^2	11					9	4	7^3	8		3	5	14									27
1	6	2	4^1	12	9	7	8	10^3	13			11							3^2	5	14									28
1	2	4				8	9	10	11^1	12	6				7				3	5										29
1	2	4^1	12			7	9	11	10^2	6					8				3	5					13					30
1	2	4	14			8	9^3	10^2	11^1	6					7				3	5						12	13			31
1	2	3	12			7	9^1	13	6					8			7	4	5						10	11^2				32
1	2^1				8	11^2	12	6	14			7				13	3	5					10^3	9						33
1	2	4			8^1	12	10	13	6			7	14			3	5						11^3	9^2						34
1	2	4			9^2	10^3	11^1	6				7	12	8	3	5						14	13							35
1	2	3			8	9	10^1	12				7	8	6	4	5						13	11^2							36
1	2	3			8	11^2	10^1	12	6				9	4	5												13			37
1		4			12	11^3	10^2	6	2			7	9	14	3	5							13	8^1						38
1	2	4			12	10^3	11^1	14	6			7	9^2	13	3	5							12	13						39
1	2	3			8	9	11	10^3	6^1	7^2			14	4	5								13	12						40
1	2	3			9	10^1	11	13	12	7^3		8^2		4	5								14	6						41
1	2	3	13		8	10^1	11		7	12	6	9	4^2	5^3	14															42
1	5	4^3	14	8	9^2	10	11^1	6	2	13	7												12							43
1	2	3	13		9	11^3	8^2	5	4	6													12	10^1	7	14				44
1	2	3	12	9^3	10^2	11^1	8	5	4	6													13	7	14					45
1	2	3	9	11	13	10	6	5^2	4	7^3										12			14	8^1						46

FA Cup

First Round   Yeovil T   (a)   0-1

Carabao Cup

First Round   Newport Co   (h)   0-2

Checkatrade Trophy

Southern Group B Gillingham	(a)	1-2
Southern Group B Reading U21	(h)	1-0
Southern Group B Colchester U	(h)	2-0
Second Round South Peterborough U	(a)	0-2

STEVENAGE

FOUNDATION

There have been several clubs associated with the town of Stevenage. Stevenage Town was formed in 1884. They absorbed Stevenage Rangers in 1955 and later played at Broadhall Way. The club went into liquidation in 1968 and Stevenage Athletic was formed, but they, too, followed a similar path in 1976. Then Stevenage Borough was founded. The Broadhall Way pitch was dug up and remained unused for three years. Thus the new club started its life in the modest surrounds of the King George V playing fields with a roped-off ground in the Chiltern League. A change of competition followed to the Wallspan Southern Combination and by 1980 the club returned to the council-owned Broadhall Way when "Borough" was added to the name. Entry into the United Counties League was so successful the league and cup were won in the first season. On to the Isthmian League Division Two and the climb up the pyramid continued. In 1995–96 Stevenage Borough won the Conference but was denied a place in the Football League as the ground did not measure up to the competition's standards. Subsequent improvements changed this and the 7,100 capacity venue became one of the best appointed grounds in non-league football. After winning elevation to the Football League the club dropped Borough from its title.

Lamex Stadium, Broadhall Way, Stevenage, Hertfordshire SG2 8RH.

Telephone: (01438) 223 223.

Fax: (01438) 743 666.

Ticket Office: (01438) 223 223.

Website: stevenagefc.com

Email: info@stevenagefc.com

Ground Capacity: 6,772.

Record Attendance: 8,040 v Newcastle U, FA Cup 4th rd, 25 January 1998.

Pitch Measurements: 104m × 64m (114yd × 70yd).

Chairman: Phil Wallace.

Manager: Dino Maamria.

Colours: White shirts with red stripes and black trim, red shorts with white trim, red socks with white and black trim.

Nickname: 'The Boro'.

Previous Name: 1976, Stevenage Borough; 2010, Stevenage.

Grounds: 1976, King George V playing fields; 1980, Broadhall Way (renamed Lamex Stadium 2009).

HONOURS

League Champions: Conference – 1995–96, 2009–10.
FA Cup: 5th rd – 2012.
League Cup: 2nd rd – 2012, 2017.

Sun FACT FILE

Between 2000–01 and 2005–06 entries for what is now the EFL Trophy were supplemented by leading teams from the Football Conference. Stevenage Borough, as the club was then known, qualified for the competition in five of those six seasons, achieving their only win when they defeated Swansea City 2-1 at Broadhall Way in the 2002–03 competition in front of a crowd of just 746.

First Football League Game: 7 August 2010, FL 2, v Macclesfield T (h) D 2–2 – Day; Henry, Laird, Bostwick, Roberts, Foster, Wilson (Sinclair), Byrom, Griffin (1), Winn (Odubade), Vincenti (1) (Beardsley).

Year Formed: 1976.

Turned Professional: 1976.

Record League Victory: 6–0 v Yeovil T, FL 2, 14 April 2012 – Day; Lascelles (1), Laird, Roberts (1), Ashton (1), Shroot (Mousinho), Wilson (Myrie-Williams), Long, Agyemang (1), Reid (Slew), Freeman (2).

Record Victory: 11–1 v British Timken Ath 1980–81.

Record Defeat: 0–7 v Southwick 1987–88.

Most League Points (3 for a win): 73, FL 1, 2011–12.

Most League Goals: 69, FL 1, 2011–12.

Highest League Scorer in Season: Matthew Godden, 30, FL 2, 2016–18.

Most League Goals in Total Aggregate: Matthew Godden, 30, 2016–18.

MANAGERS
Derek Montgomery 1976–83
Frank Cornwell 1983–87
John Bailey 1987–88
Brian Wilcox 1988–90
Paul Fairclough 1990–98
Richard Hill 1998–2000
Steve Wignall 2000
Paul Fairclough 2000–02
Wayne Turner 2002–03
Graham Westley 2003–06
Mark Stimson 2006–07
Peter Taylor 2007–08
Graham Westley 2008–12
Gary Smith 2012–13
Graham Westley 2013–15
Teddy Sheringham 2015–16
Darren Sarll 2016–18
Dino Maamria March 2018–

Most League Goals in One Match: 3, Chris Holroyd v Hereford U, FL 2, 28 September 2010; 3, Dani Lopez v Sheffield U, FL 1, 16 March 2013; 3, Chris Whelpdale v Morecambe, FL 2, 28 November 2015; 3, Matthew Godden v Newport Co, FL 2, 7 January 2017; 3, Alex Revell v Exeter C, FL 2, 28 April 2018.

Most Capped Player: Marcus Haber, 5 (including 3 on loan at Notts Co) (27), Canada.

Most League Appearances: Chris Day, 219, 2010–17.

Youngest League Player: Arthur Iontton, 17 years 133 days v Exeter C, 28 April 2018.

Record Transfer Fee Received: £260,000 from Peterborough U for George Boyd, January 2007.

Record Transfer Fee Paid: £125,000 to Exeter C for James Dunne, May 2012.

Football League Record: 2011 Promoted from Conference Premier; 2010–11 FL 2; 2011–14 FL 1; 2014– FL 2.

LATEST SEQUENCES

Longest Sequence of League Wins: 6, 12.3.2011 – 2.4.2011.

Longest Sequence of League Defeats: 6, 13.4.2013 – 17.8.2013.

Longest Sequence of League Draws: 5, 17.3.2012 – 31.3.2012.

Longest Sequence of Unbeaten League Matches: 17, 9.4.2012 – 6.10.2012.

Longest Sequence Without a League Win: 10, 11.3.2014 – 21.4.2014.

Successive Scoring Runs: 17 from 9.4.2012.

Successive Non-scoring Runs: 4 from 20.2.2016.

TEN YEAR LEAGUE RECORD

		P	W	D	L	F	A	Pts	Pos
2008-09	Conf P	46	23	12	11	73	54	81	5
2009-10	Conf P	44	30	9	5	79	24	99	1
2010-11	FL 2	46	18	15	13	62	45	69	6
2011-12	FL 1	46	18	19	9	69	44	73	6
2012-13	FL 1	46	15	9	22	47	64	54	18
2013-14	FL 1	46	11	9	26	46	72	42	24
2014-15	FL 2	46	20	12	14	62	54	72	6
2015-16	FL 2	46	11	15	20	52	67	48	18
2016-17	FL 2	46	20	7	19	67	63	67	10
2017-18	FL 2	46	14	13	19	60	65	55	16

DID YOU KNOW ?

The Stevenage FC Supporters' Association Player of the Year Award was introduced for the 1994–95 season. In the 24 years that have followed only one player has won the award on two occasions. Defender Jason Goodliffe, who spent six seasons with the club, was Player of the Year in both 2002 and 2003.

STEVENAGE – SKY BET LEAGUE TWO 2017–18 LEAGUE RECORD

Match No.	Date	Venue	Opponents	Result	H/T Score	Lg Pos.	Goalscorers	Attendance
1	Aug 5	H	Newport Co	D	3-3	1-0	10	Pett [11], Gorman (pen) [61], Newton [72]	2650
2	12	A	Colchester U	D	1-1	0-0	17	Newton [51]	3330
3	19	H	Grimsby T	W	3-1	2-0	8	Newton [37], Smith [45], Kennedy [65]	2793
4	26	A	Barnet	W	1-0	1-0	3	Pett [27]	1883
5	Sept 2	A	Cheltenham T	W	1-0	0-0	2	Martin [82]	2694
6	9	H	Lincoln C	L	1-2	1-0	5	Godden [26]	3427
7	12	H	Crawley T	D	1-1	1-0	7	Newton [45]	1922
8	16	A	Swindon T	L	2-3	0-2	11	Newton [51], Martin [89]	6022
9	23	H	Morecambe	W	2-1	1-1	9	Godden [27], Wootton [66]	1996
10	26	A	Carlisle U	W	2-0	0-0	6	Kennedy [51], Pett [60]	3701
11	30	H	Port Vale	W	2-0	1-0	6	Newton [22], Smith [54]	2678
12	Oct 7	A	Crewe Alex	L	0-1	0-0	7		3679
13	14	A	Luton T	L	1-7	1-3	9	Kennedy [45]	9208
14	17	H	Accrington S	W	3-2	0-1	7	Godden 2 [61, 83], Kennedy [89]	1788
15	21	H	Forest Green R	L	1-2	1-0	9	Godden [43]	2099
16	28	A	Yeovil T	L	0-3	0-3	11		2439
17	Nov 11	H	Notts Co	D	1-1	1-0	13	Newton [38]	2962
18	18	A	Mansfield T	L	0-1	0-1	13		3353
19	21	H	Coventry C	D	1-1	0-1	13	Pett [76]	2544
20	25	A	Cambridge U	L	0-1	0-0	15		4039
21	Dec 9	H	Wycombe W	D	0-0	0-0	16		2430
22	16	A	Exeter C	L	1-2	0-0	16	Godden [80]	3448
23	23	H	Chesterfield	W	5-1	3-1	15	Newton [13], Gorman [28], McCourt (og) [44], Godden 2 [50, 72]	2403
24	26	A	Lincoln C	L	0-3	0-1	16		9268
25	30	A	Crawley T	L	0-1	0-1	17		2075
26	Jan 1	H	Cheltenham T	W	4-1	2-1	15	Godden [23], Pett 2 [35, 88], Newton [69]	1989
27	13	A	Morecambe	D	1-1	0-1	15	Franks [89]	1268
28	20	H	Carlisle U	D	0-0	0-0	15		2476
29	27	A	Chesterfield	W	1-0	0-0	14	Kennedy [48]	4981
30	30	H	Swindon T	L	0-1	0-1	14		2116
31	Feb 3	A	Accrington S	L	2-3	2-1	14	Godden [14], McKee [38]	1324
32	10	H	Luton T	D	1-1	0-0	15	Newton [88]	4365
33	13	A	Forest Green R	L	1-3	1-1	16	Wilkinson [26]	1825
34	17	H	Yeovil T	W	4-1	2-0	15	Amos [16], Smith [45], Newton [46], Kennedy [58]	2355
35	24	A	Notts Co	L	0-2	0-0	15		5684
36	Mar 10	H	Crewe Alex	D	2-2	1-0	16	Bowditch 2 [14, 50]	2032
37	17	A	Port Vale	D	2-2	1-0	16	Amos [10], Kennedy [48]	3462
38	24	H	Colchester U	L	0-1	0-1	16		2709
39	30	A	Grimsby T	D	0-0	0-0	16		5368
40	Apr 2	H	Barnet	W	4-1	1-0	16	Newton 2 [44, 62], Revell 2 [67, 87]	3350
41	7	A	Newport Co	W	1-0	1-0	16	Whelpdale [43]	4007
42	10	H	Mansfield T	D	1-1	1-0	15	Newton [15]	2294
43	14	H	Cambridge U	L	0-2	0-0	15		3269
44	20	A	Coventry C	L	1-3	1-3	15	Revell [20]	8859
45	28	H	Exeter C	W	3-1	2-0	15	Revell 3 [14, 31, 49]	3399
46	May 5	A	Wycombe W	L	0-1	0-1	16		8802

Final League Position: 16

GOALSCORERS
League (60): Newton 14, Godden 10, Kennedy 7, Pett 6, Revell 6, Smith 3, Amos 2, Bowditch 2, Gorman 2 (1 pen), Martin 2, Franks 1, McKee 1, Whelpdale 1, Wilkinson 1, Wootton 1, own goal 1.
FA Cup (10): Godden 4, Newton 2, Smith 2, Pett 1, Samuel 1.
Carabao Cup (0):
Checkatrade Trophy (5): Samuel 3, Beautyman 1, Wootton 1 (1 pen).

Fryer J 28	Henry R 40	Franks F 22+8	Wilkinson L 23+4	Martin J 39	Pett T 23+4	Beautyman H 8+2	Gorman D 17+7	McKee M 19+5	Samuel A 8+14	Newton D 38+7	Whelpdale C 19+8	Godden M 35+3	King J 29+3	Smith J 34+2	Kennedy B 24+11	Conlon T 1+11	Toner K 2+4	Vancooten T 19+3	Gray J —+8	Wootton K 3+5	Slater L 1+1	Georgiou A —+3	King T 18	Wilmot B 10	Amos L 14+2	Goddard J 9+2	Revell A 12	Bowditch D 1+4	Lokko K —+2	White J —+3	Sheal B 9+1	Ionitton A —+2	O'Donnell D —+2	Johnson R 1	Match No.
1	2	3	4	5	6	7	8^1	9^3	10^2	11	12	13	14																						1
1	2	3	4	5	14	9^2	7		12	11	6^3	10^1		8	13																				2
1	2	4	3	5	9		8	14	6^1	11		10^3			7^2	12	13																		3
1	2	4	3^2	5	9		8^4			11^2	6^1	10			7	12	13	14																	4
1	2	3	4	5		7	9^2	12		11^1	6^3	10		8		14	13																		5
1	2	3	4^4	5^2		7	9^2			11	6^1	10		8	13	12	14																		6
1	2	4^1		5	9		7^2	13	10^3	14	11	8	6	3	12																				7
1	2	3		5	9^1		7^3	14	13	10	12	11	8	6^2	4																				8
1	2		4	5	9		8		13	10^2		11^1		7	6	3	12																		9
1		3^3	13	5	6^1		8		10^2	11		7	9	14	2	12																			10
1	2	3		5	9		8		10^3	11^2	7	6^1	14	4	13	12																			11
1	2	4	3	5		7			10^1		6	11^2	8		9^3		12	13	14																12
1	2	3	4	5	9		8^2	13	14	10^3		11^3		7	6	12																			13
1	2		4	5	9		8		12	14	11	13	7	6^3	3^1	10^2																			14
1	2		4	5	9		8^1		13	12	11	14	7	6^2	3	10^3																			15
1	2	4^2	12	5	9		7		13	10	6	8		14^4	3^1	11^3																			16
1	2		4	5	9	8			12	10	6	11^1	3	7																					17
1	2		4	5	8^2	9^1	12	14	11		7	10^1	3	6	13																				18
1	2		4	5	9^3	7^2	6	12	10	13	11^1	3	8	14																					19
1	2		4	5	9^1	12	7	10	11	6		3	8																						20
1	2		4	5	9^2		8	11	12	6	10	3	7	13																					21
1	2	3	5	9	13		7	11^3	12	6^2	10	4	8^1	14																					22
1	2	14	5		8	6	9^1	11		10^3	4^2	7	12			3	13																		23
1	2	12	5	14	8^2	7	9^1	11	10		3	6				4^1		14																	24
1	2^2	3	5	12	8^1	6	9^3		13	10	4	7	11				14																		25
1	2	3	5	6	13	8^2	12	10^1		11^3	4	7	9				14																		26
	2	14	5	9	8^2			10^1	11	4	7^3	6	12	13									1	3											27
	2	14		5^3	6	8	13	10^1	11	4	7	9^2	12										1	3											28
	2	4	14	12	9		7^3	11^2	3	8	10^1	13	6										1	5											29
	2^3	7			8^2	11^1	10	3	6	9	12				5	14							1	4	13										30
	2			8	12		11^1	3	7^4	13				5									1	4	6	9^2	10	14							31
	2	12		8	14		9^2	3^3	7	13				5									1	4	6^1	11	10								32
	2	3		7	12		10		6^3					5^2									1	4	8	9	11^8	13	14						33
			5					8^3		10^2	4	7	9^1	2									1	3	6	11			13	12	14				34
			5					8		11	4	7^1	10^2	2									1	3	6	9				13	12				35
	14		5					8^4		10	4	13	12	2									1	3	6^1	11		9^3		7					36
12^3	4		5				14			11	13		3	8^2	10		2^1						1		9^2	6				7					37
7	4		5		6					11	8^2	3	2^1	13									1	12	9^1	10			14						38
2^3	12	3	5					14	11^1	9		4	6^2										1	7		10	13			8					39
2		4	5		12					11	6^1	13	3	14	9^2								1	8		10^1				7					40
2	14	3	5		12					11	9	13	4	8^1									1	6		10^3				7^2					41
2		3	5		13					9	6^1	10^3	4		12								1	8	14	11				7^2					42
2	3	4	5		14					11	12	9^3	7^1	8^2									1	6	13	10									43
2	3	3^4	5		12^3	13				9^2	6	11^1	4	14									1	7	10					8					44
1	2									10	6	9^3		8				5			4^2	13			7^1	11				3	12	14			45
1										11^3	8	9	3		7		2	14							6^2	10				4^1	12	13	5		46

FA Cup

First Round	Nantwich T	(h)	5-0	
Second Round	Swindon T	(h)	5-2	
Third Round	Reading	(h)	0-0	
Replay	Reading	(a)	0-3	

Carabao Cup

First Round	Millwall	(a)	0-2

Checkatrade Trophy

Southern Group G	Oxford U	(h)	2-6
Southern Group G	Milton Keynes D	(a)	0-0
(Milton Keynes D won 5-4 on penalties)			
Southern Group G	Brighton & HA U21	(h)	3-1

STOKE CITY

bet365 Stadium, Stanley Matthews Way, Stoke-on-Trent, Staffordshire ST4 4EG.

Telephone: (01782) 367 598.

Fax: (01782) 646 988.

Ticket Office: (01782) 367 599.

Website: www.stokecityfc.com

Email: info@stokecityfc.com

Ground Capacity: 30,089.

Record Attendance: 51,380 v Arsenal, Division 1, 29 March 1937 (at Victoria Ground); 30,022 v Everton, FA Premier League, 17 March 2018 (at bet365 Stadium).

Pitch Measurements: 105m × 68m (115yd × 75yd).

Chairman: Peter Coates.

Chief Executive: Tony Scholes.

Manager: Gary Rowett.

First-Team Coaches: Mark Sale, Kevin Phillips, Callum Davidson, Rory Delap.

Colours: Red and white striped shirts, white shorts with red trim, white socks with red trim.

Year Formed: 1863* (*see Foundation*).

Turned Professional: 1885.

Previous Names: 1868, Stoke Ramblers; 1870, Stoke; 1925, Stoke City.

Club Nickname: 'The Potters'.

Grounds: 1875, Sweeting's Field; 1878, Victoria Ground (previously known as the Athletic Club Ground); 1997, Britannia Stadium (renamed bet365 Stadium, 2016).

First Football League Game: 8 September 1888, Football League, v WBA (h) L 0–2 – Rowley; Clare, Underwood; Ramsey, Shutt, Smith; Sayer, McSkimming, Staton, Edge, Tunnicliffe.

Record League Victory: 10–3 v WBA, Division 1, 4 February 1937 – Doug Westland; Brigham, Harbot; Tutin, Turner (1p), Kirton; Matthews, Antonio (2), Freddie Steele (5), Jimmy Westland, Johnson (2).

Record Cup Victory: 7–1 v Burnley, FA Cup 2nd rd (replay), 20 February 1896 – Clawley; Clare, Eccles; Turner, Grewe, Robertson; Willie Maxwell, Dickson, Alan Maxwell (3), Hyslop (4), Schofield.

Record Defeat: 0–10 v Preston NE, Division 1, 14 September 1889.

Most League Points (2 for a win): 63, Division 3 (N), 1926–27.

HONOURS

League Champions: Division 2 – 1932–33, 1962–63; Second Division – 1992–93; Division 3N – 1926–27. *Runners-up:* FL C – 2007–08; Division 2 – 1921–22.

FA Cup: Runners-up: 2011.

League Cup Winners: 1972. *Runners-up:* 1964.

League Trophy Winners: 1992, 2000.

European Competitions
UEFA Cup: 1972–73, 1974–75. *Europa League:* 2011–12.

Most League Points (3 for a win): 93, Division 2, 1992–93.

Most League Goals: 92, Division 3 (N), 1926–27.

Highest League Scorer in Season: Freddie Steele, 33, Division 1, 1936–37.

Most League Goals in Total Aggregate: Freddie Steele, 142, 1934–49.

Most League Goals in One Match: 7, Neville Coleman v Lincoln C, Division 2, 23 February 1957.

Most Capped Player: Glenn Whelan, 81 (84), Republic of Ireland.

Most League Appearances: Eric Skeels, 507, 1958–76.

Youngest League Player: Peter Bullock, 16 years 163 days v Swansea C, 19 April 1958.

Record Transfer Fee Received: £20,000,000 (rising to £25,000,000) from West Ham U for Marko Arnautovic, July 2017.

Record Transfer Fee Paid: £18,300,000 to Porto for Giannelli Imbula, February 2016.

Football League Record: 1888 Founder Member of Football League; 1890 Not re-elected; 1891 Re-elected; relegated in 1907, and after one year in Division 2, resigned for financial reasons; 1919 re-elected to Division 2; 1922–23 Division 1; 1923–26 Division 2; 1926–27 Division 3 (N); 1927–33 Division 2; 1933–53 Division 1; 1953–63 Division 2; 1963–77 Division 1; 1977–79 Division 2; 1979–85 Division 1; 1985–90 Division 2; 1990–92 Division 3; 1992–93 Division 2; 1993–98 Division 1; 1998–2002 Division 2; 2002–04 Division 1; 2004–08 FL C; 2008–18 FA Premier League; 2018– FL C.

LATEST SEQUENCES

Longest Sequence of League Wins: 8, 30.3.1895 – 21.9.1895.

Longest Sequence of League Defeats: 11, 6.4.1985 – 17.8.1985.

Longest Sequence of League Draws: 5, 13.5.2012 – 15.9.2012.

Longest Sequence of Unbeaten League Matches: 25, 5.9.1992 – 20.2.1993.

Longest Sequence Without a League Win: 17, 22.4.1989 – 14.10.1989.

Successive Scoring Runs: 21 from 24.12.1921.

Successive Non-scoring Runs: 8 from 29.12.1984.

MANAGERS

Tom Slaney 1874–83
(Secretary-Manager)
Walter Cox 1883–84
(Secretary-Manager)
Harry Lockett 1884–90
Joseph Bradshaw 1890–92
Arthur Reeves 1892–95
William Rowley 1895–97
H. D. Austerberry 1897–1908
A. J. Barker 1908–14
Peter Hodge 1914–15
Joe Schofield 1915–19
Arthur Shallcross 1919–23
John 'Jock' Rutherford 1923
Tom Mather 1923–35
Bob McGrory 1935–52
Frank Taylor 1952–60
Tony Waddington 1960–77
George Eastham 1977–78
Alan A'Court 1978
Alan Durban 1978–81
Richie Barker 1981–83
Bill Asprey 1984–85
Mick Mills 1985–89
Alan Ball 1989–91
Lou Macari 1991–93
Joe Jordan 1993–94
Lou Macari 1994–97
Chic Bates 1997–98
Chris Kamara 1998
Brian Little 1998–99
Gary Megson 1999
Gudjon Thordarson 1999–2002
Steve Cotterill 2002
Tony Pulis 2002–05
Johan Boskamp 2005–06
Tony Pulis 2006–13
Mark Hughes 2013–18
Paul Lambert 2018
Gary Rowett May 2018–

TEN YEAR LEAGUE RECORD

		P	W	D	L	F	A	Pts	Pos
2008-09	PR Lge	38	12	9	17	38	55	45	12
2009-10	PR Lge	38	11	14	13	34	48	47	11
2010-11	PR Lge	38	13	7	18	46	48	46	13
2011-12	PR Lge	38	11	12	15	36	53	45	14
2012-13	PR Lge	38	9	15	14	34	45	42	13
2013-14	PR Lge	38	13	11	14	45	52	50	9
2014-15	PR Lge	38	15	9	14	48	45	54	9
2015-16	PR Lge	38	14	9	15	41	55	51	9
2016-17	PR Lge	38	11	11	16	41	56	44	13
2017-18	PR Lge	38	7	12	19	35	68	33	19

DID YOU KNOW ?

Leeds United established a then record of 29 top-flight games without defeat from the start of the 1973–74 season. Their 30th game was at the Victoria Ground against Stoke City and they led 2-0 after 18 minutes before the Potters fought back with goals from Mike Pejic, Alan Hudson and Denis Smith to seal a 3-2 victory and end Leeds' unbeaten run.

STOKE CITY – PREMIER LEAGUE 2017–18 LEAGUE RECORD

Match No.	Date	Venue	Opponents	Result		H/T Score	Lg Pos.	Goalscorers	Attendance
1	Aug 12	A	Everton	L	0-1	0-1	18		39,045
2	19	H	Arsenal	W	1-0	0-0	13	Jese [47]	29,459
3	27	A	WBA	D	1-1	0-0	11	Crouch [77]	22,704
4	Sept 9	H	Manchester U	D	2-2	1-1	10	Choupo-Moting 2 [43, 63]	29,320
5	16	A	Newcastle U	L	1-2	0-1	13	Shaqiri [57]	51,795
6	23	H	Chelsea	L	0-4	0-2	15		29,661
7	30	H	Southampton	W	2-1	1-0	13	Diouf [40], Crouch [85]	29,285
8	Oct 14	A	Manchester C	L	2-7	1-3	15	Diouf [44], Walker (og) [47]	54,128
9	21	A	Bournemouth	L	1-2	0-2	18	Diouf [63]	29,500
10	28	A	Watford	W	1-0	1-0	13	Fletcher [16]	20,087
11	Nov 4	H	Leicester C	D	2-2	1-1	14	Shaqiri [39], Crouch [73]	29,602
12	20	A	Brighton & HA	D	2-2	2-1	15	Choupo-Moting [28], Zouma [45]	29,676
13	25	A	Crystal Palace	L	1-2	0-0	15	Shaqiri [53]	23,723
14	29	H	Liverpool	L	0-3	0-1	16		29,423
15	Dec 2	H	Swansea C	W	2-1	2-1	13	Shaqiri [36], Diouf [40]	28,261
16	9	A	Tottenham H	L	1-5	0-1	15	Shawcross [80]	62,202
17	12	A	Burnley	L	0-1	0-0	15		19,909
18	16	H	West Ham U	L	0-3	0-1	17		29,265
19	23	H	WBA	W	3-1	2-0	14	Allen [19], Choupo-Moting [45], Sobhi [90]	29,057
20	26	A	Huddersfield T	D	1-1	0-1	13	Sobhi [60]	24,047
21	30	A	Chelsea	L	0-5	0-3	15		41,433
22	Jan 1	H	Newcastle U	L	0-1	0-0	16		28,471
23	15	A	Manchester U	L	0-3	0-2	18		74,726
24	20	H	Huddersfield T	W	2-0	0-0	17	Allen [53], Diouf [69]	29,785
25	31	H	Watford	D	0-0	0-0	16		27,458
26	Feb 3	A	Bournemouth	L	1-2	1-0	18	Shaqiri [5]	10,614
27	10	H	Brighton & HA	D	1-1	0-1	18	Shaqiri [68]	29,876
28	24	A	Leicester C	D	1-1	1-0	19	Shaqiri [43]	31,769
29	Mar 3	A	Southampton	D	0-0	0-0	19		30,335
30	12	H	Manchester C	L	0-2	0-1	19		29,138
31	17	H	Everton	L	1-2	0-0	19	Choupo-Moting [77]	30,022
32	Apr 1	A	Arsenal	L	0-3	0-0	19		59,371
33	7	H	Tottenham H	L	1-2	0-0	19	Diouf [57]	29,515
34	16	A	West Ham U	D	1-1	0-0	19	Crouch [79]	56,795
35	22	H	Burnley	D	1-1	1-0	19	Ndiaye [11]	29,532
36	28	A	Liverpool	D	0-0	0-0	19		53,255
37	May 5	H	Crystal Palace	L	1-2	1-0	20	Shaqiri [43]	29,687
38	13	A	Swansea C	W	2-1	2-1	19	Ndiaye [31], Crouch [41]	20,673

Final League Position: 19

GOALSCORERS

League (35): Shaqiri 8, Diouf 6, Choupo-Moting 5, Crouch 5, Allen 2, Ndiaye 2, Sobhi 2, Fletcher 1, Jese 1, Shawcross 1, Zouma 1, own goal 1.
FA Cup (1): Adam 1 (1 pen).
Carabao Cup (4): Allen 2, Crouch 1, Sobhi 1.
Checkatrade Trophy (1): Afellay 1.

Butland J 35	Zouma K 32 + 2	Shawcross R 27	Cameron G 17 + 3	Diouf M 30 + 5	Allen J 36	Fletcher D 25 + 2	Pieters E 30 + 1	Shaqiri X 36	Bojan K 1	Berahino S 3 + 12	Choupo-Moting E 26 + 4	Crouch P 14 + 17	Jese R 8 + 5	Sobhi R 12 + 12	Martins Indi B 14 + 3	Wimmer K 14 + 3	Johnson G 7 + 2	Afellay I 1 + 5	Edwards T 6	Adam C 5 + 6	Grant L 3	Tymon J 2 + 1	Ngoy J — + 1	Bauer M 15	Ireland S 1 + 3	Ndiaye P 13	Stafylidis K 4 + 1	Campbell T — + 4	Sorenson L 1	Match No.
1	2	3	4	5	6	7	8	9	10^{1}	11^{2}	12	13																		1
1	2	3	4	5	7	6	8^{1}	9^{1}		12	11			10^{2}	13	14														2
1	2	3		5^{1}	7	6	8	9			11	12		10^{2}	13	4														3
1	2		3^{2}	5	6	7	8	9		13	10	11^{1}		12		4														4
1	2			5	6^{1}	7	8	9		10	13	11^{2}		12	3	4														5
1				5	6	7	4	9		10	12	11^{1}		8	3^{2}	2	13													6
1	2	3		5^{1}	6	7	8	9^{3}		11^{2}	10	12			4	14	13													7
1		3	8	6		7	5	9		10	11^{1}	14		12	4^{2}	13	2^{3}													8
1	2	3	4	10	7	6	8			13	9	12		11^{2}		5^{1}														9
1	2	3		5	7	6	8	9^{1}		12	11			10^{2}	4	13														10
1	2	3		5^{2}	7	6	8	9		13	11	12		10^{1}	4															11
	2	3		5	7	6	8	9			11	12		10	4						1									12
	2	3		5^{2}	7	6	8	9			11	12	13	10^{1}	4						1									13
	2	3		5	7	6^{1}	8	9		10^{1}	11	12			4				13		1									14
1	2	3		5	6	7^{1}	8	9		11^{2}	10	13			4^{3}	12	14													15
1	2	3	13	10	6^{1}	7	8	9^{2}		11	12				4	14				5^{3}										16
1	4^{2}	3	2	5	7	6	8	9^{1}		13	11	10			12															17
1		3	2	11^{2}	8	7^{1}	5^{1}	6		13	10	9			4	12	14													18
1	4	3	7	12	9	6^{2}	8^{1}	10		11	13				5		2													19
1	4	3^{1}		13	9	6^{3}	8^{2}			10	11	12			5		2	14												20
1		3	8	6						11	13	10				4	9^{1}	2	7^{2}	5		12								21
1		3	7	12	6	5^{2}		9^{1}		13	11	10			4		2			8										22
1		3	14	8	6	7				10^{2}	11^{3}	13			4	12				5^{1}		2		9						23
1	4	3	12	11^{1}	9	6	5	8		10^{2}	13		14							7^{1}				2						24
1	4	3	11^{1}		9	6	5	8		13	10	12								7^{1}				2						25
1	4	3		6	13	9	5	8		14	10^{2}	11^{1}												2		7^{3}		12		26
1	4	3	11	6	7^{1}	5	9			12	10^{3}	13					14							2		8^{2}				27
1		3	6	11^{2}	8	7				10^{3}					4^{1}		14		13					2		9	5	12		28
1		3	6	11^{1}	8	12	7			10^{3}	13			14		4								2		9	5^{2}			29
1		3		7^{1}	6			9		11	12	10^{2}			13	4								2		8	5			30
1	4	3		7		9^{1}				13	12	10	14	11^{2}			2			8^{4}				6		5				31
1		3	10^{2}	7			5			11	12		13	9^{1}	4		2							6		8				32
1	14	3	11	7			5			10	13			9^{2}	4		2^{3}							6^{1}		8	12			33
1	2	3	12	11^{1}	7		5			10	13			9^{2}	4									6^{1}	14	8				34
1	12	3	10^{1}	7		5	6			11					4		2^{3}							9^{1}	13	8	14			35
1	2	3	10	7	13	5	6			11^{1}		12			4^{2}									9		8				36
1	4	3	10	7		5	6			11^{1}		12					2^{2}							9		8	13			37
1	4	3	11	6^{1}	12	5		9			10													2		13	8	7^{2}		38

FA Cup
Third Round   Coventry C   (a)   1-2

Carabao Cup
Second Round   Rochdale   (h)   4-0
Third Round   Bristol C   (a)   0-2

Checkatrade Trophy (Stoke C U21)
Northern Group C   Blackburn R   (a)   0-1
Northern Group C   Rochdale   (a)   0-0
(Stoke C U21 won 5-4 on penalties)
Northern Group C   Bury   (a)   1-3

SUNDERLAND

FOUNDATION

A Scottish schoolmaster named James Allan, working at Hendon Board School, took the initiative in the foundation of Sunderland in 1879 when they were formed as The Sunderland and District Teachers' Association FC at a meeting in the Adults School, Norfolk Street. Due to financial difficulties, they quickly allowed members from outside the teaching profession and so became Sunderland AFC in October 1880.

Stadium of Light, Sunderland, Tyne and Wear SR5 1SU.

Telephone: (0371) 911 1200.

Fax: (0191) 551 5123.

Ticket Office: (0371) 911 1973.

Website: www.safc.com

Email: enquiries@safc.com

Ground Capacity: 48,707.

Record Attendance: 75,118 v Derby Co, FA Cup 6th rd replay, 8 March 1933 (at Roker Park); 48,335 v Liverpool, FA Premier League, 13 April 2002 (at Stadium of Light).

Pitch Measurements: 105m × 68m (114yd × 74yd).

Chairman: Stewart Donald.

Executive Director: Charlie Methven.

Managing Director: Tony Davison.

Manager: Jack Ross.

Assistant Manager: James Fowler.

HONOURS

League Champions: Division 1 – 1892–93, 1894–95, 1901–02, 1912–13, 1935–36; Football League 1891–92; FL C – 2004–05, 2006–07; First Division – 1995–96, 1998–99; Division 2 – 1975–76; Division 3 – 1987–88. *Runners-up:* Division 1 – 1893–94, 1897–98, 1900–01, 1922–23, 1934–35; Division 2 – 1963–64, 1979–80.

FA Cup Winners: 1937, 1973. *Runners-up:* 1913, 1992.

League Cup: Runners-up: 1985, 2014.

European Competitions
European Cup-Winners' Cup: 1973–74.

Colours: Red and white striped shirts with black trim, black shorts with red trim, black socks with red trim.

Year Formed: 1879.

Turned Professional: 1886.

Previous Names: 1879, Sunderland and District Teachers AFC; 1880, Sunderland.

Club Nickname: 'The Black Cats'.

Grounds: 1879, Blue House Field, Hendon; 1882, Groves Field, Ashbrooke; 1883, Horatio Street; 1884, Abbs Field, Fulwell; 1886, Newcastle Road; 1898, Roker Park; 1997, Stadium of Light.

First Football League Game: 13 September 1890, Football League, v Burnley (h) L 2–3 – Kirtley; Porteous, Oliver; Wilson, Auld, Gibson; Spence (1), Miller, Campbell (1), Scott, Davy Hannah.

Record League Victory: 9–1 v Newcastle U (a), Division 1, 5 December 1908 – Roose; Forster, Melton; Daykin, Thomson, Low; Mordue (1), Hogg (3), Brown, Holley (3), Bridgett (2).

Record Cup Victory: 11–1 v Fairfield, FA Cup 1st rd, 2 February 1895 – Doig; McNeill, Johnston; Dunlop, McCreadie (1), Wilson; Gillespie (1), Millar (5), Campbell, Jimmy Hannah (3), Scott (1).

Sun FACT FILE

Sidney Weighell, who was General Secretary of the National Union of Railwaymen from 1975 to 1983, signed for Sunderland in October 1945. He featured regularly at inside-left for the reserves in the North Eastern League but was unable to break into the first team and left football shortly afterwards to focus on his trade union work.

Record Defeat: 0–8 v Sheff Wed, Division 1, 26 December 1911; 0–8 v West Ham U, Division 1, 19 October 1968; 0–8 v Watford, Division 1, 25 September 1982; 0–8 v Southampton, FA Premier League, 18 October 2014.

Most League Points (2 for a win): 61, Division 2, 1963–64.

Most League Points (3 for a win): 105, Division 1, 1998–99.

Most League Goals: 109, Division 1, 1935–36.

Highest League Scorer in Season: Dave Halliday, 43, Division 1, 1928–29.

Most League Goals in Total Aggregate: Charlie Buchan, 209, 1911–25.

Most League Goals in One Match: 5, Charlie Buchan v Liverpool, Division 1, 7 December 1919; 5, Bobby Gurney v Bolton W, Division 1, 7 December 1935; 5, Dominic Sharkey v Norwich C, Division 2, 20 February 1962.

Most Capped Player: Seb Larsson, 59 (104), Sweden.

Most League Appearances: Jim Montgomery, 537, 1962–77.

Youngest League Player: Derek Forster, 15 years 184 days v Leicester C, 22 August 1964.

Record Transfer Fee Received: £25,000,000 (rising to £30,000,000) from Everton for Jordan Pickford, June 2017.

Record Transfer Fee Paid: £13,800,000 (rising to £17,100,000) to FC Lorient for Didier Ndong, August 2016.

Football League Record: 1890 Elected to Division 1; 1958–64 Division 2; 1964–70 Division 1; 1970–76 Division 2; 1976–77 Division 1; 1977–80 Division 2; 1980–85 Division 1; 1985–87 Division 2; 1987–88 Division 3; 1988–90 Division 2; 1990–91 Division 1; 1991–92 Division 2; 1992–96 Division 1; 1996–97 FA Premier League; 1997–99 Division 1; 1999–2003 FA Premier League; 2003–04 Division 1; 2004–05 FL C; 2005–06 FA Premier League; 2006–07 FL C; 2007–17 FA Premier League; 2017–18 FL C: 2018– FL 1.

LATEST SEQUENCES

Longest Sequence of League Wins: 13, 14.11.1891 – 2.4.1892.

Longest Sequence of League Defeats: 17, 18.1.2003 – 16.8.2003.

Longest Sequence of League Draws: 6, 26.3.1949 – 19.4.1949.

Longest Sequence of Unbeaten League Matches: 19, 3.5.1998 – 14.11.1998.

Longest Sequence Without a League Win: 22, 21.12.2002 – 16.8.2003.

Successive Scoring Runs: 29 from 8.11.1997.

Successive Non-scoring Runs: 10 from 27.11.1976.

MANAGERS

Tom Watson 1888–96
Bob Campbell 1896–99
Alex Mackie 1899–1905
Bob Kyle 1905–28
Johnny Cochrane 1928–39
Bill Murray 1939–57
Alan Brown 1957–64
George Hardwick 1964–65
Ian McColl 1965–68
Alan Brown 1968–72
Bob Stokoe 1972–76
Jimmy Adamson 1976–78
Ken Knighton 1979–81
Alan Durban 1981–84
Len Ashurst 1984–85
Lawrie McMenemy 1985–87
Denis Smith 1987–91
Malcolm Crosby 1991–93
Terry Butcher 1993
Mick Buxton 1993–95
Peter Reid 1995–2002
Howard Wilkinson 2002–03
Mick McCarthy 2003–06
Niall Quinn 2006
Roy Keane 2006–08
Ricky Sbragia 2008–09
Steve Bruce 2009–11
Martin O'Neill 2011–13
Paolo Di Canio 2013
Gus Poyet 2013–15
Dick Advocaat 2015
Sam Allardyce 2015–16
David Moyes 2016–17
Simon Grayson 2017
Chris Coleman 2017–18
Jack Ross May 2018–

TEN YEAR LEAGUE RECORD

		P	W	D	L	F	A	Pts	Pos
2008-09	PR Lge	38	9	9	20	34	54	36	16
2009-10	PR Lge	38	11	11	16	48	56	44	13
2010-11	PR Lge	38	12	11	15	45	56	47	10
2011-12	PR Lge	38	11	12	15	45	46	45	13
2012-13	PR Lge	38	9	12	17	41	54	39	17
2013-14	PR Lge	38	10	8	20	41	60	38	14
2014-15	PR Lge	38	7	17	14	31	53	38	16
2015-16	PR Lge	38	9	12	17	48	62	39	17
2016-17	PR Lge	38	6	6	26	29	69	24	20
2017-18	FL C	46	7	16	23	52	80	37	24

DID YOU KNOW ?

When Josh Maja netted for Sunderland against Fulham on 16 December 2017 it provided the Black Cats with their first home win for 364 days. Their previous home win was on 17 December 2016 at home to Watford, with the sequence reaching 20 games, a new record for senior English football.

SUNDERLAND – SKY BET CHAMPIONSHIP 2017–18 LEAGUE RECORD

Match No.	Date	Venue	Opponents	Result	H/T Score	Lg Pos.	Goalscorers	Attendance
1	Aug 4	H	Derby Co	D	1-1	1-1	3	Grabban (pen) [42]	29,578
2	13	A	Norwich C	W	3-1	1-0	6	Grabban 2 [27, 71], McGeady [60]	26,343
3	16	A	Sheffield W	D	1-1	1-0	6	Honeyman [4]	27,631
4	19	H	Leeds U	L	0-2	0-1	12		31,237
5	26	A	Barnsley	L	0-3	0-2	19		15,697
6	Sept 9	A	Sheffield U	L	1-2	0-2	20	Rodwell [90]	29,579
7	12	H	Nottingham F	L	0-1	0-0	20		26,061
8	16	A	Hull C	D	1-1	1-0	21	Vaughan [17]	16,597
9	23	H	Cardiff C	L	1-2	0-1	22	Gooch (pen) [53]	25,733
10	26	A	Ipswich T	L	2-5	1-2	22	Jones [10], McGeady [65]	14,907
11	30	A	Preston NE	D	2-2	1-0	23	Honeyman [28], McGeady [59]	17,621
12	Oct 14	H	QPR	D	1-1	0-1	23	McGeady [61]	26,066
13	21	A	Brentford	D	3-3	3-1	23	Grabban 2 (1 pen) [13, 45 (p)], Bentley (og) [40]	10,726
14	28	A	Bristol C	L	1-2	1-1	23	Grabban [45]	27,317
15	31	H	Bolton W	D	3-3	1-1	22	Grabban 2 [45, 57], McNair [79]	26,395
16	Nov 5	A	Middlesbrough	L	0-1	0-1	24		29,277
17	18	H	Millwall	D	2-2	1-2	24	Grabban [12], Matthews [46]	27,399
18	21	H	Aston Villa	L	1-2	0-1	24	Grabban [72]	27,662
19	25	A	Burton Alb	W	2-0	0-0	22	Vaughan [84], Honeyman [88]	4808
20	Dec 2	H	Reading	L	1-3	0-0	23	Grabban (pen) [76]	27,386
21	9	A	Wolverhampton W	D	0-0	0-0	23		28,488
22	16	H	Fulham	W	1-0	0-0	21	Maja [77]	25,904
23	23	H	Birmingham C	D	1-1	1-1	22	Grabban [21]	29,312
24	26	A	Sheffield U	L	0-3	0-1	22		30,668
25	30	H	Nottingham F	W	1-0	1-0	21	McGeady [40]	26,830
26	Jan 1	A	Barnsley	L	0-1	0-0	23		28,311
27	13	A	Cardiff C	L	0-4	0-0	24		17,703
28	20	H	Hull C	W	1-0	1-0	22	Asoro [20]	27,437
29	30	A	Birmingham C	L	1-3	0-2	23	Oviedo [83]	19,601
30	Feb 3	A	Ipswich T	L	0-2	0-2	23		27,909
31	10	A	Bristol C	D	3-3	0-3	23	Brownhill (og) [70], McGeady [81], Pack (og) [90]	22,580
32	17	H	Brentford	L	0-2	0-2	23		27,702
33	20	A	Bolton W	L	0-1	0-1	24		14,915
34	24	H	Middlesbrough	D	3-3	1-0	24	Asoro [11], Williams [58], McManaman [90]	29,048
35	Mar 3	A	Millwall	D	1-1	1-0	24	Oviedo [29]	14,358
36	6	H	Aston Villa	L	0-3	0-2	24		26,081
37	10	A	QPR	L	0-1	0-0	24		14,216
38	17	H	Preston NE	L	0-2	0-0	24		28,543
39	30	A	Derby Co	W	4-1	2-1	23	Honeyman [10], Fletcher [36], McGeady (pen) [50], O'Shea [76]	27,890
40	Apr 2	H	Sheffield W	L	1-3	0-0	23	Honeyman [61]	29,786
41	7	A	Leeds U	D	1-1	0-0	23	McNair [48]	30,461
42	10	H	Norwich C	D	1-1	0-0	23	Honeyman [63]	24,894
43	14	A	Reading	D	2-2	0-1	24	McNair [47], Cattermole [66]	17,348
44	21	H	Burton Alb	L	1-2	1-0	24	McNair [34]	25,475
45	27	A	Fulham	L	1-2	1-1	24	Asoro [28]	21,849
46	May 6	H	Wolverhampton W	W	3-0	2-0	24	Ejaria [19], Fletcher [45], McNair [66]	28,452

Final League Position: 24

GOALSCORERS

League (52): Grabban 12 (3 pens), McGeady 7 (1 pen), Honeyman 6, McNair 5, Asoro 3, Fletcher 2, Oviedo 2, Vaughan 2, Cattermole 1, Ejaria 1, Gooch 1 (1 pen), Jones 1, Maja 1, Matthews 1, McManaman 1, O'Shea 1, Rodwell 1, Williams 1, own goals 3.
FA Cup (0).
Carabao Cup (3): Gooch 1, Honeyman 1, Love 1.
Checkatrade Trophy (2): Greenwood 1, Love 1.

Steele J 15	Jones B 19+3	Browning T 26+1	Kone L 24	Galloway B 5+2	Honeyman G 37+5	Cattermole L 34+1	Ndong D 16+2	McGeady A 28+7	Vaughan J 15+8	Grabban L 18+1	Gibson D 12+3	Gooch L 12+12	O'Shea J 34+3	Khazri W —+3	Matthews A 25+9	Asoro J 11+15	Ruiter R 20	Oviedo B 31+3	Wilson M 20+1	Rodwell J 1+1	Williams J 7+5	McManaman C 13+11	Robson E 6+3	Watmore D 4+2	McNair P 12+4	Love D 11	Embleton E —+2	Maja J 6+11	Clarke-Salter J 8+3	LuaLua K —+6	Camp L 11+1	Ejaria O 9+2	Fletcher A 15+1	Molyneux L 1	Hume D —+1	Mumba B —+1	Match No.
1	2	3	4	5	6	7	8	9	10	11																											1
1	2	3	4	5	6	8^2	7	9^1	10	11^1	12	13	14																								2
1	2	3	4	5	6	8^1	7	9^1	11	10^1	14	13		12																							3
1	2	3	4	5^1	6	8^1	7	9	10^1	11					13	12	14																				4
	2	3	4		6^2	8	7	9	10^1	11		12	13	14			1	5^1																			5
	2	3^3	8	5^2	6			10^1	11			14	12				1		4		7	9	13														6
14		3			10	6^1	7		12	11^3		13			2		1	5	4			9^1	8^2														7
13		3			10	7	6			11^3			14		2		1	5	4		12	9^1	8^2														8
	2	3			9^3	7	6^2	12	11			10		5	14		1	8^1	4			13															9
1	2	3	14		8			10	11		7	13	12	5								9^3		4^2		6^1											10
1	2^2	3			8^3	7	6	10	11			9^1	4	5	13							14			12												11
1		3			6^2	8	7	9	10^1	12			4	5	13				14			11^3															12
1	2	3			10	8	7	9^3	13	11^2	14		4		5							12				6^1											13
1	2	3			6			10	14	11		7^2			4			8^1				9^3	12	13													14
								7	10	12	11	6^1	3		12		1	5	4			9^2	8^3	13	14												15
	2^2			13	8	6^1		9	11		7		3		12		1	5	4			14				10^3											16
	14			12	6			10	11				3		2		1	5	4^1			9^3	13		8^2	7											17
		4			8			10	12	11		6^2	3		9^1	2	1	5				7^3	14														18
		3			8	6		10^1	13	11	12		4		2	14	1	5				7^1	9^2														19
		3			12	9	6^3	10^2	11		7	14	4		2	13	1	5^1				8^4															20
		3			12	10	8^4	13	11^2		9	7^3	4		6		1	5							2^1	14											21
		3			9	12		11^2	10^3		8	7^1	4		6	14	1	5							2	13											22
		3			9	12		11^3	10^1		8^2	7	4		6	14	1	5							2	13											23
		3			9^3			10	11^2		8	7^1	4		2	12	1	6	5			13			14												24
	2				6	10^2	12	7	13			3	8				1	14	4			9^1			5	11^3											25
	2				6	10	11	7^1				3	4		14		1	8^2				9^3	12		5	13											26
	2	3			10	12	8^4					7^3	4		13		1	6	9^1			14						11^2	5								27
	5^1	2			9	6						13	3		12	11	1	8	7			10^2		4		11^2			5								28
	2	3			9	6		13					14		5	10^1	1	8				7				11^2		4^3	12								29
	2	4			12	7		14					3		5^3	10^1		9				8^2						13		1		6	11				30
	2	3			9	6		13					4		10			6^2				14						5	12	1		9^3	11				31
	2	4^1			10	7		9					3		12	6					13	8^3						14	5	1		11^1	11				32
6^1		2			8	5		12					3		10^3	9					12	13				7^2		11^1	4^2	1		1	11				33
		2			8^3	5		14					3		6	10		9			12	13				7^2		11^1	$4■$	1		1					34
1		4	2		13	7		10^1					3		5	12		8				9^2											6	11			35
1	12	4^2	2			7		10					3^3		13	8		9							5	14							6	11			36
$1■$		3			10	6		12					4		2	7^2		5				8^1					14			13	9	11^3					37
		3			7^3	8							4		2	10		6								14		11^2	5^1	13	1	9^2	12				38
		3			9	6		10				7^1	4		13			5^2	12			8^3	2				14				1	13	11				39
					9^2	6		10				7^1	3		12	14		5^2	4			8	2							14	1	12	11				40
		3			9^3	6^1		10^1				7	4			5		13				8	2							14	1	12	11				41
		3			8	6		10				7^3	4^2		5^1			12					2				13	14		1	9	11					42
		3			9^3	6		10					13		5^1	4		7^2				8	2				14	12		1		11					43
1	2	3^3			9	6		10					4		12	13		5^1				7^2	8					14				11					44
1	2^2	3			10								4		12	8		5				13	7^3		6		14				9^1	11				45
1													3^1		2	7		5^3	4				6			8^2	13				9	11	10	12	14	46

FA Cup
Third Round — Middlesbrough (a) 0-2

Carabao Cup
First Round — Bury (a) 1-0
Second Round — Carlisle U (a) 2-1
Third Round — Everton (a) 0-3

Checkatrade Trophy (Sunderland U21)
Northern Group H — Scunthorpe U (a) 1-3
Northern Group H — Doncaster R (a) 0-1
Northern Group H — Grimsby T (a) 1-1
(Sunderland U21 won 7-6 on penalties)

SWANSEA CITY

FOUNDATION

The earliest Association Football in Wales was played in the northern part of the country and no international took place in the south until 1894, when a local paper still thought it necessary to publish an outline of the rules and an illustration of the pitch markings. There had been an earlier Swansea club, but this has no connection with Swansea Town (now City) formed at a public meeting in June 1912.

Liberty Stadium, Morfa, Landore, Swansea SA1 2FA.
Telephone: (01792) 616 600.
Fax: (01792) 616 606.
Ticket Office: (0844) 815 6665.
Website: www.swanseacity.com
Email: info@swanseacityfc.com
Ground Capacity: 21,088.
Record Attendance: 32,796 v Arsenal, FA Cup 4th rd, 17 February 1968 (at Vetch Field); 20,972 v Liverpool, FA Premier League, 1 May 2016 (at Liberty Stadium).
Pitch Measurements: 105m × 68m (114yd × 74yd).
Chairman: Huw Jenkins.
Chief Operating Officer: Chris Pearlman.
Head Coach: Graham Potter.
Assistant Coach: Billy Reid.
Colours: White shirts with black trim, white shorts with black trim, white socks with black trim.
Year Formed: 1912.
Turned Professional: 1912.
Previous Name: 1912, Swansea Town; 1970, Swansea City.
Club Nicknames: 'The Swans', 'The Jacks'.
Grounds: 1912, Vetch Field; 2005, Liberty Stadium.

HONOURS

League Champions: FL 1 – 2007–08; Division 3S – 1924–25, 1948–49; Third Division – 1999–2000.
FA Cup: semi-final – 1926, 1964.
League Cup Winners: 2013.
League Trophy Winners: 1994, 2006.
Welsh Cup Winners: 11 times; *Runners-up:* 8 times.
European Competitions
Europa League: 2013–14.
European Cup-Winners' Cup: 1961–62, 1966–67, 1981–82, 1982–83, 1983–84, 1989–90, 1991–92.

First Football League Game: 28 August 1920, Division 3, v Portsmouth (a) L 0–3 – Crumley; Robson, Evans; Smith, Holdsworth, Williams; Hole, Ivor Jones, Edmundson, Rigsby, Spottiswood.
Record League Victory: 8–0 v Hartlepool U, Division 4, 1 April 1978 – Barber; Evans, Bartley, Lally (1) (Morris), May, Bruton, Kevin Moore, Robbie James (3 incl. 1p), Curtis (3), Toshack (1), Chappell.
Record Cup Victory: 12–0 v Sliema W (Malta), ECWC 1st rd 1st leg, 15 September 1982 – Davies; Marustik, Hadziabdic (1), Irwin (1), Kennedy, Rajkovic (1), Loveridge (2) (Leighton James), Robbie James, Charles (2), Stevenson (1), Latchford (1) (Walsh (3)).
Record Defeat: 0–8 v Liverpool, FA Cup 3rd rd, 9 January 1990; 0–8 v Monaco, ECWC, 1st rd 2nd leg, 1 October 1991.
Most League Points (2 for a win): 62, Division 3 (S), 1948–49.
Most League Points (3 for a win): 92, FL 1, 2007–08.

Sun FACT FILE

Although Swansea City have regularly attracted average attendances of more than 20,000 to the Liberty Stadium during their recent spell in the Premier League, they drew higher attendances to the Vetch Field in the late 1940s. The record seasonal average attendance is 22,535 for 1948–49 when the Swans won the Division Three South title.

Most League Goals: 90, Division 2, 1956–57.

Highest League Scorer in Season: Cyril Pearce, 35, Division 2, 1931–32.

Most League Goals in Total Aggregate: Ivor Allchurch, 166, 1949–58, 1965–68.

Most League Goals in One Match: 5, Jack Fowler v Charlton Ath, Division 3S, 27 December 1924.

Most Capped Player: Ashley Williams, 64 (79), Wales.

Most League Appearances: Wilfred Milne, 587, 1919–37.

Youngest League Player: Nigel Dalling, 15 years 289 days v Southport, 6 December 1974.

Record Transfer Fee Received: £40,000,000 (rising to £45,000,000) from Everton for Gylfi Sigurdsson, August 2017.

Record Transfer Fee Paid: £18,000,000 to West Ham U for André Ayew, January 2018.

Football League Record: 1920 Original Member of Division 3; 1921–25 Division 3 (S); 1925–47 Division 2; 1947–49 Division 3 (S); 1949–65 Division 2; 1965–67 Division 3; 1967–70 Division 4; 1970–73 Division 3; 1973–78 Division 4; 1978–79 Division 3; 1979–81 Division 2; 1981–83 Division 1; 1983–84 Division 2; 1984–86 Division 3; 1986–88 Division 4; 1988–92 Division 3; 1992–96 Division 2; 1996–2000 Division 3; 2000–01 Division 2; 2001–04 Division 3; 2004–05 FL 2; 2005–08 FL 1; 2008–11 FL C; 2011–18 FA Premier League; 2018– FL C.

LATEST SEQUENCES

Longest Sequence of League Wins: 9, 27.11.1999 – 22.01.2000.

Longest Sequence of League Defeats: 9, 26.1.1991 – 19.3.1991.

Longest Sequence of League Draws: 8, 25.11.2008 – 28.12.2008.

Longest Sequence of Unbeaten League Matches: 19, 19.10.1970 – 9.3.1971.

Longest Sequence Without a League Win: 15, 25.3.1989 – 2.9.1989.

Successive Scoring Runs: 27 from 28.8.1947.

Successive Non-scoring Runs: 6 from 6.2.1996.

MANAGERS

Walter Whittaker 1912–14
William Bartlett 1914–15
Joe Bradshaw 1919–26
Jimmy Thomson 1927–31
Neil Harris 1934–39
Haydn Green 1939–47
Bill McCandless 1947–55
Ron Burgess 1955–58
Trevor Morris 1958–65
Glyn Davies 1965–66
Billy Lucas 1967–69
Roy Bentley 1969–72
Harry Gregg 1972–75
Harry Griffiths 1975–77
John Toshack 1978–83
  (resigned October re-appointed in December) 1983–84
Colin Appleton 1984
John Bond 1984–85
Tommy Hutchison 1985–86
Terry Yorath 1986–89
Ian Evans 1989–90
Terry Yorath 1990–91
Frank Burrows 1991–95
Bobby Smith 1995
Kevin Cullis 1996
Jan Molby 1996–97
Micky Adams 1997
Alan Cork 1997–98
John Hollins 1998–2001
Colin Addison 2001–02
Nick Cusack 2002
Brian Flynn 2002–04
Kenny Jackett 2004–07
Roberto Martinez 2007–09
Paulo Sousa 2009–10
Brendan Rodgers 2010–12
Michael Laudrup 2012–14
Garry Monk 2014–15
Francesco Guidolin 2016
Bob Bradley 2016
Paul Clement 2017
Carlos Carvalhal 2017–18
Graham Potter June 2018–

TEN YEAR LEAGUE RECORD

		P	W	D	L	F	A	Pts	Pos
2008-09	FL C	46	16	20	10	63	50	68	8
2009-10	FL C	46	17	18	11	40	37	69	7
2010-11	FL C	46	24	8	14	69	42	80	3
2011-12	PR Lge	38	12	11	15	44	51	47	11
2012-13	PR Lge	38	11	13	14	47	51	46	9
2013-14	PR Lge	38	11	9	18	54	54	42	12
2014-15	PR Lge	38	16	8	14	46	49	56	8
2015-16	PR Lge	38	12	11	15	42	52	47	12
2016-17	PR Lge	38	12	5	21	45	70	41	15
2017-18	PR Lge	38	8	9	21	28	56	33	18

DID YOU KNOW

Swansea Town fans had their own song written for them in 1913. Published in a local newspaper, *The World of Sport*, 'The Swans' War Song' was written to be sung to the tune of 'Here comes the Chocolate Major', a popular music hall ditty of the time. It is not known whether or not fans actually sang the song at matches.

SWANSEA CITY – PREMIER LEAGUE 2017–18 LEAGUE RECORD

Match No.	Date	Venue	Opponents	Result	H/T Score	Lg Pos.	Goalscorers	Attendance
1	Aug 12	A	Southampton	D 0-0	0-0	10		31,447
2	19	H	Manchester U	L 0-4	0-1	14		20,862
3	26	A	Crystal Palace	W 2-0	1-0	9	Abraham 44, Ayew, J 48	23,477
4	Sept 10	H	Newcastle U	L 0-1	0-0	15		20,872
5	16	A	Tottenham H	D 0-0	0-0	14		65,366
6	23	H	Watford	L 1-2	0-1	14	Abraham 56	20,372
7	30	A	West Ham U	L 0-1	0-0	18		56,922
8	Oct 14	H	Huddersfield T	W 2-0	1-0	13	Abraham 2 42, 48	20,657
9	21	H	Leicester C	L 1-2	0-1	15	Mawson 56	20,521
10	28	A	Arsenal	L 1-2	1-0	17	Clucas 22	59,493
11	Nov 4	H	Brighton & HA	L 0-1	0-1	18		20,822
12	18	A	Burnley	L 0-2	0-2	19		18,895
13	25	H	Bournemouth	D 0-0	0-0	19		20,228
14	29	A	Chelsea	L 0-1	0-0	19		41,365
15	Dec 2	A	Stoke C	L 1-2	1-2	20	Bony 3	28,261
16	9	H	WBA	W 1-0	0-0	19	Bony 81	19,580
17	13	H	Manchester C	L 0-4	0-2	20		20,870
18	18	A	Everton	L 1-3	1-1	20	Fer 35	37,580
19	23	H	Crystal Palace	D 1-1	0-0	20	Ayew, J 77	20,354
20	26	A	Liverpool	L 0-5	0-1	20		52,850
21	30	A	Watford	W 2-1	0-1	19	Ayew, J 86, Narsingh 90	20,002
22	Jan 2	H	Tottenham H	L 0-2	0-1	20		20,615
23	13	A	Newcastle U	D 1-1	0-0	20	Ayew, J 60	51,444
24	22	H	Liverpool	W 1-0	1-0	20	Mawson 40	20,886
25	30	H	Arsenal	W 3-1	1-1	17	Clucas 2 34, 86, Ayew, J 61	20,819
26	Feb 3	A	Leicester C	D 1-1	0-1	17	Fernandez 53	31,179
27	10	H	Burnley	W 1-0	0-0	15	Ki 81	20,179
28	24	A	Brighton & HA	L 1-4	0-1	18	Dunk (og) 85	30,523
29	Mar 3	H	West Ham U	W 4-1	2-0	13	Ki 8, van der Hoorn 32, Andy King 48, Ayew, J (pen) 63	20,829
30	10	A	Huddersfield T	D 0-0	0-0	14		23,567
31	31	A	Manchester U	L 0-2	0-2	15		75,038
32	Apr 7	A	WBA	D 1-1	0-0	15	Abraham 75	23,297
33	14	H	Everton	D 1-1	0-1	17	Ayew, J 71	20,933
34	22	A	Manchester C	L 0-5	0-2	17		54,387
35	28	H	Chelsea	L 0-1	0-1	17		20,900
36	May 5	A	Bournemouth	L 0-1	0-1	18		10,820
37	8	H	Southampton	L 0-1	0-0	18		20,858
38	13	H	Stoke C	L 1-2	1-2	18	Andy King 14	20,673

Final League Position: 18

GOALSCORERS

League (28): Ayew J 7 (1 pen), Abraham 5, Clucas 3, Bony 2, Ki 2, Andy King 2, Mawson 2, Fer 1, Fernandez 1, Narsingh 1, van der Hoorn 1, own goal 1.
FA Cup (13): Dyer 3, Abraham 2, Ayew J 2, Bony 1, Carroll 1, James 1, Narsingh 1, Naughton 1, Routledge 1.
Carabao Cup (6): Ayew J 2, Fer 2, Abraham 1, Mawson 1.
Checkatrade Trophy (8): Gorre 3, Andy King 2, Garrick 1, Lewis 1, own goal 1.

Fabianski L 38	Naughton K 34	Fernandez F 30	Mawson A 38	Olsson M 36	Fer L 15 + 5	Britton L 4 + 1	Carroll T 28 + 9	Routledge W 4 + 11	Ayew J 33 + 3	Abraham T 15 + 16	Fulton J — + 2	Bartley K 2 + 3	McBurnie O 2 + 9	Roque M 9 + 2	Narsingh L 5 + 13	van der Hoorn M 24	Clucas S 23 + 6	Rangel A 2 + 2	Sanches R 9 + 3	Bony W 8 + 7	Ki S 21 + 4	Dyer N 16 + 8	Roberts C 3 + 1	Ayew A 10 + 4	King Andy 9 + 2	Match No.
1	2	3	4	5	6	7²	8	9³	10	11¹	12	13	14													1
1	6	2	4	9	7		8	13	11	10¹		3²	14	5³	12											2
1	5¹	3	4	9	6		8	12	10	11³			13			2²	7	14								3
1	2	3	4	5	9		8²			11	10			13			7	6¹	12							4
1	5	3	4	9	12		8	14	10	11¹						2²	7		6³	13						5
1	5	3	4	9	6		8		10	13			12			2²	7³		14	11¹						6
1	2	3	4	5²	12	7¹	8		9	11		13				14		6	10³							7
1	2	3	4	5	6²	7³	8			10	11			9¹			14					12	13			8
1	2	3	4	5		7³	8	14	11	10				9¹			6²					12	13			9
1	5	3	4		7		8²	10³	11				14		12	2¹	9				6	13				10
1	2	3		4	6		8¹	13	11²	10			14		12	5³					7	9				11
1	2	3	4	5	6²			11³	10¹				14			7	8	12	13	9						12
1	2		4	5	12		8		11²	13		6		3		9¹	10	7								13
1	2		4	5	12		8	14	11²			13	7³		3	8¹		9¹	10	6						14
1	2		4	5	7³		12		9²	10		13		3	8¹		14	11	6							15
1	2		4	5			8²	11¹	12	14			7	13	3		10	6	9³							16
1	2		4	5	14		9¹		10	12			7	13	3		11²	8	6³							17
1	2	3	4	5	6		8¹		13	12			7	9		14		10³		11²						18
1	2³	3	4	5			8		12	10	14		7¹	9²		6	13			11						19
1	2	3	4	5	7¹		9	6	10	12		11²	8³			13	14									20
1	2	3	4	5			8		11	10²		13	7	12		6³	9			14						21
1		4	5	6			9²	14	11			13	12	3	8	2¹	7			10³						22
1		4	5				9		10		3	11²		14	2¹	8		13	6	7³	12					23
1	2	4	5	6	8		12		11²					3	10		13	9	7¹							24
1	2	4	5	6	8		12	14	11³					3	10²		13	9	7¹							25
1	2	4	5	6	7³		12	14	11¹					3	9		13	8	10²							26
1	2	4	5	6²			8		11¹	13				3	10		9	7³		12	14					27
1	2	4	5	6			9³		11	14			13	3²	10		8	7¹		12						28
1	5	3	4	9			13		11	14				2	8³			7	12	10³	6¹					29
1	5	3	4	9			13		10⁸	12				2	8			7²		11¹	6					30
1	5	3	4	9			12	14		13				2	8³			7¹	10²	11	6					31
1	2	4	5	6			9			11	12			3²	10			14	13		7¹	8³				32
1	2	3	4	5			8		11	13			9²				6¹	12			10	7				33
1	2	4³	5	6²			10		11	14	13			3	12			9¹				7	8			34
1	2		4	8²			13	14	11					3	10			6	12	5¹	9	7³				35
1		3	4	8			7		10	12				14	2¹			6³	9²	5	11	13				36
1	2¹	3	4	9²			14		11	12				13			8		6		5	10	7³			37
1			4	5		13	8	9³	11	12					3	14	2				6²		10	7¹		38

FA Cup

Third Round	Wolverhampton W	(a)	0-0
Replay	Wolverhampton W	(h)	2-1
Fourth Round	Notts Co	(a)	1-1
Replay	Notts Co	(h)	8-1
Fifth Round	Sheffield W	(a)	0-0
Replay	Sheffield W	(h)	2-0
Sixth Round	Tottenham H	(h)	0-3

Carabao Cup

Second Round	Milton Keynes D	(a)	4-1
Third Round	Reading	(a)	2-0
Fourth Round	Manchester U	(h)	0-2

Checkatrade Trophy (Swansea C U21)

Southern Group E	Cheltenham T	(a)	2-1
Southern Group E	Newport Co	(a)	2-1
Southern Group E	Forest Green R	(a)	2-0
Second Round South	Charlton Ath	(h)	2-3

SWINDON TOWN

FOUNDATION

It is generally accepted that Swindon Town came into being in 1881, although there is no firm evidence that the club's founder, Rev. William Pitt, captain of the Spartans (an offshoot of a cricket club), changed his club's name to Swindon Town before 1883, when the Spartans amalgamated with St Mark's Young Men's Friendly Society.

The Energy Check County Ground, County Road, Swindon, Wiltshire SN1 2ED.

Telephone: (0871) 876 1879.

Ticket Office: (0871) 876 1993.

Website: www.swindontownfc.co.uk

Email: reception@swindontownfc.co.uk

Ground Capacity: 15,547.

Record Attendance: 32,000 v Arsenal, FA Cup 3rd rd, 15 January 1972.

Pitch Measurements: 100.5m × 68m (110yd × 74.5yd).

Chairman: Lee Power.

Chief Executive: Steve Anderson.

Manager: Phil Brown.

Assistant Manager: Neil McDonald.

Colours: Red shirts with white trim, white shorts with red trim, red socks with white trim.

Year Formed: 1881* (*see Foundation*).

Turned Professional: 1894.

Club Nickname: 'The Robins'.

HONOURS

League Champions: Second Division – 1995–96; FL 2 – 2011–12; Division 4 – 1985–86.
Runners-up: Division 3 – 1962–63, 1968–69.
FA Cup: semi-final – 1910, 1912.
League Cup Winners: 1969.
League Trophy: Runners-up: 2012.
Anglo-Italian Cup Winners: 1970.

Grounds: 1881, The Croft; 1896, County Ground (renamed The Energy Check County Ground 2017).

First Football League Game: 28 August 1920, Division 3, v Luton T (h) W 9–1 – Nash; Kay, Macconachie; Langford, Hawley, Wareing; Jefferson (1), Fleming (4), Rogers, Batty (2), Davies (1), (1 og).

Record League Victory: 9–1 v Luton T, Division 3 (S), 28 August 1920 – Nash; Kay, Macconachie; Langford, Hawley, Wareing; Jefferson (1), Fleming (4), Rogers, Batty (2), Davies (1), (1 og).

Record Cup Victory: 10–1 v Farnham U Breweries (a), FA Cup 1st rd (replay), 28 November 1925 – Nash; Dickenson, Weston, Archer, Bew, Adey; Denyer (2), Wall (1), Richardson (4), Johnson (3), Davies.

Record Defeat: 1–10 v Manchester C, FA Cup 4th rd (replay), 25 January 1930.

Most League Points (2 for a win): 64, Division 3, 1968–69.

The Sun FACT FILE

A total of four players have scored hat-tricks for Swindon Town on their club debut: Harry Morris (1926–27), Maurice Owen (1946–47), Alan Mayes (1978–79) and Sam Parkin (2002–03). Owen achieved the feat on his Football League debut, while Morris scored hat-tricks in his first two appearances for the club.

Most League Points (3 for a win): 102, Division 4, 1985–86.

Most League Goals: 100, Division 3 (S), 1926–27.

Highest League Scorer in Season: Harry Morris, 47, Division 3 (S), 1926–27.

Most League Goals in Total Aggregate: Harry Morris, 216, 1926–33.

Most League Goals in One Match: 5, Harry Morris v QPR, Division 3 (S), 18 December 1926; 5, Harry Morris v Norwich C, Division 3 (S), 26 April 1930; 5, Keith East v Mansfield T, Division 3, 20 November 1965.

Most Capped Player: Rod Thomas, 30 (50), Wales.

Most League Appearances: John Trollope, 770, 1960–80.

Youngest League Player: Paul Rideout, 16 years 107 days v Hull C, 29 November 1980.

Record Transfer Fee Received: A combined £4,000,000 from QPR for Ben Gladwin and Massimo Luongo, May 2015.

Record Transfer Fee Paid: £800,000 to West Ham U for Joey Beauchamp, August 1994.

Football League Record: 1920 Original Member of Division 3; 1921–58 Division 3 (S); 1958–63 Division 3; 1963–65 Division 2; 1965–69 Division 3; 1969–74 Division 2; 1974–82 Division 3; 1982–86 Division 4; 1986–87 Division 3; 1987–92 Division 2; 1992–93 Division 1; 1993–94 FA Premier League; 1994–95 Division 1; 1995–96 Division 2; 1996–2000 Division 1; 2000–04 Division 2; 2004–06 FL 1; 2006–07 FL 2; 2007–11 FL 1; 2011–12 FL 2; 2012–17 FL 1; 2017– FL 2.

LATEST SEQUENCES

Longest Sequence of League Wins: 10, 31.12.2011 – 28.2.2012.

Longest Sequence of League Defeats: 8, 29.8.2005 – 8.10.2005.

Longest Sequence of League Draws: 6, 22.11.1991 – 28.12.1991.

Longest Sequence of Unbeaten League Matches: 22, 12.1.1986 – 23.8.1986.

Longest Sequence Without a League Win: 19, 30.10.1999 – 4.3.2000.

Successive Scoring Runs: 31 from 17.4.1926.

Successive Non-scoring Runs: 5 from 5.4.1997.

MANAGERS

Sam Allen 1902–33
Ted Vizard 1933–39
Neil Harris 1939–41
Louis Page 1945–53
Maurice Lindley 1953–55
Bert Head 1956–65
Danny Williams 1965–69
Fred Ford 1969–71
Dave Mackay 1971–72
Les Allen 1972–74
Danny Williams 1974–78
Bobby Smith 1978–80
John Trollope 1980–83
Ken Beamish 1983–84
Lou Macari 1984–89
Ossie Ardiles 1989–91
Glenn Hoddle 1991–93
John Gorman 1993–94
Steve McMahon 1994–98
Jimmy Quinn 1998–2000
Colin Todd 2000
Andy King 2000–01
Roy Evans 2001
Andy King 2001–05
Iffy Onuora 2005–06
Dennis Wise 2006
Paul Sturrock 2006–07
Maurice Malpas 2008
Danny Wilson 2008–11
Paul Hart 2011
Paolo Di Canio 2011–13
Kevin MacDonald 2013
Mark Cooper 2013–15
Martin Ling 2015
Luke Williams 2015–17
David Flitcroft 2017–18
Phil Brown March 2018–

TEN YEAR LEAGUE RECORD

		P	W	D	L	F	A	Pts	Pos
2008-09	FL 1	46	12	17	17	68	71	53	15
2009-10	FL 1	46	22	16	8	73	57	82	5
2010-11	FL 1	46	9	14	23	50	72	41	24
2011-12	FL 2	46	29	6	11	75	32	93	1
2012-13	FL 1	46	20	14	12	72	39	74	6
2013-14	FL 1	46	19	9	18	63	59	66	8
2014-15	FL 1	46	23	10	13	76	57	79	4
2015-16	FL 1	46	16	11	19	64	71	59	15
2016-17	FL 1	46	11	11	24	44	66	44	22
2017-18	FL 2	46	20	8	18	67	65	68	9

DID YOU KNOW ?

Swindon Town were involved in two games decided by the 'golden goal' method on two occasions, both in the EFL Trophy. In 2000–01 they lost out to Southend United in the Southern Section Final to a goal on 110 minutes while in 2002–03 they went out to Kidderminster Harriers with a decisive goal on 105 minutes.

SWINDON TOWN – SKY BET LEAGUE TWO 2017–18 LEAGUE RECORD

Match No.	Date	Venue	Opponents	Result	H/T Score	Lg Pos.	Goalscorers	Attendance
1	Aug 5	A	Carlisle U	W 2-1	1-0	7	Norris [31], Mullin [48]	6036
2	12	H	Exeter C	D 1-1	0-1	6	Woolery [56]	7795
3	19	A	Morecambe	W 1-0	1-0	1	McDermott [13]	1655
4	26	H	Crawley T	L 0-3	0-1	9		6613
5	Sept 2	H	Barnet	L 1-4	0-2	13	Norris [78]	5895
6	9	A	Luton T	W 3-0	1-0	9	Norris (pen) [32], Hussey [51], Mullin [62]	8455
7	12	A	Notts Co	L 0-1	0-1	14		5107
8	16	H	Stevenage	W 3-2	2-0	8	Norris 2 (1 pen) [9, 62 (p)], Anderson [13]	6022
9	22	A	Forest Green R	W 2-0	0-0	4	Lancashire [86], Taylor [90]	3305
10	26	H	Coventry C	L 1-2	1-1	11	Norris [20]	6340
11	30	H	Cambridge U	W 2-0	1-0	9	Anderson [13], Smith, H [88]	5847
12	Oct 7	A	Cheltenham T	L 1-2	0-1	11	Preston [53]	5050
13	14	A	Mansfield T	W 3-1	2-0	8	Linganzi [4], Goddard [45], Norris (pen) [54]	4081
14	17	H	Lincoln C	L 0-1	0-0	10		5864
15	21	H	Wycombe W	W 1-0	1-0	7	Smith, H [15]	7114
16	28	A	Port Vale	W 3-0	0-0	5	Taylor [51], Mullin [71], Gordon [85]	5071
17	Nov 11	A	Chesterfield	D 2-2	0-0	5	Elsnik [47], Norris (pen) [90]	6140
18	18	H	Yeovil T	W 2-1	0-1	5	Gordon [67], Anderson [89]	3622
19	21	A	Grimsby T	L 2-3	2-1	5	Matt (og) [28], Anderson [26]	3023
20	25	H	Newport Co	L 0-1	0-0	8		6764
21	Dec 15	H	Colchester U	L 2-3	1-1	10	Woolery [36], Gordon [76]	6020
22	23	A	Crewe Alex	W 3-0	3-0	10	Woolery [8], Linganzi [17], Norris (pen) [20]	3736
23	26	H	Luton T	L 0-5	0-0	11		8526
24	30	H	Notts Co	W 1-0	0-0	10	Norris [47]	6247
25	Jan 1	A	Barnet	W 2-1	2-1	9	Iandolo [17], Preston [45]	2038
26	13	H	Forest Green R	W 1-0	0-0	9	Norris [79]	7062
27	20	A	Coventry C	L 1-3	1-2	10	Banks [39]	8643
28	27	H	Crewe Alex	W 4-3	1-2	8	Richards 2 [3, 89], Elsnik 2 [66, 79]	5439
29	30	A	Stevenage	W 1-0	1-0	6	Banks [16]	2116
30	Feb 3	A	Lincoln C	D 2-2	2-1	7	Richards [35], Banks [38]	8909
31	6	A	Accrington S	L 1-2	0-1	7	Richards (pen) [71]	1243
32	10	H	Mansfield T	W 1-0	1-0	5	Taylor [39]	6031
33	13	A	Wycombe W	L 2-3	1-2	6	Richards [2], Taylor [61]	4863
34	17	H	Port Vale	W 3-2	2-2	6	Richards 2 [24, 40], Mullin [88]	5713
35	24	A	Chesterfield	L 1-2	0-1	7	Robertson [75]	4668
36	Mar 10	H	Cheltenham T	L 0-3	0-1	9		6658
37	17	A	Cambridge U	W 3-1	1-0	9	Norris [16], Richards 2 (1 pen) [62, 84 (p)]	5123
38	24	A	Exeter C	L 1-3	1-2	9	Woolery [27]	4567
39	30	H	Morecambe	D 1-1	0-1	9	Norris (pen) [55]	6328
40	Apr 2	A	Crawley T	D 1-1	0-1	9	Richards [85]	5008
41	7	H	Carlisle U	D 0-0	0-0	9		5807
42	10	H	Yeovil T	D 2-2	1-0	9	Taylor 2 [11, 72]	5709
43	14	A	Newport Co	L 1-2	0-2	9	Mullin [62]	3911
44	21	H	Grimsby T	L 0-1	0-1	9		6690
45	28	A	Colchester U	D 0-0	0-0	10		3687
46	May 5	H	Accrington S	W 3-0	2-0	9	Richards [14], Anderson [43], Mullin [55]	6118

Final League Position: 9

GOALSCORERS

League (67): Norris 13 (6 pens), Richards 11 (2 pens), Mullin 6, Taylor 6, Anderson 5, Woolery 4, Banks 3, Elsnik 3, Gordon 3, Linganzi 2, Preston 2, Smith, H 2, Goddard 1, Hussey 1, Iandolo 1, Lancashire 1, McDermott 1, Robertson 1, own goal 1.
FA Cup (7): Elsnik 2, Linganzi 2, Mullin 1, Smith H 1, Taylor 1.
Carabao Cup (2): Lancashire 1, Mullin 1.
Checkatrade Trophy (7): Mullin 2, Goddard 1 (1 pen), Gordon 1, Norris 1 (1 pen), Preston 1, Woolery 1.

Vigouroux L 14	Purkiss B 38 + 3	Lancashire O 35	Conroy D 6 + 1	Hussey C 17 + 1	Goddard J 8 + 5	Linganzi A 19 + 6	Dunne J 37 + 2	Brophy J 2 + 4	Mullin P 20 + 20	Norris L 30 + 5	Smith H 7 + 7	Iandolo E 7 + 5	Thomas C — + 2	Robertson C 13 + 5	McDermott D 7 + 10	Woolery K 21 + 16	Taylor M 34 + 4	Elsnik T 18 + 4	Anderson K 36 + 1	Gordon K 12 + 14	Preston M 21	Charles-Cook R 22	Knoyle K 17 + 1	Banks O 16 + 1	Richards M 18 + 2	Menayese R 13 + 1	Moore S 10	McGivern R 3 + 3	Twine S 3 + 1	Romanski J 1 + 1	Edwards J 1	Match No.
1	2	3	4	5	6	7	8	9¹	10	11²	12	13¹	14																			1
1	2	4		5		7	8	9	10	12	11²		14	3	6³	13																2
1	2	3	4	5		8	7	12	9	10¹			14	13	6³	11²																3
1	2	4	3	5		7¹	8³	12	9	10			14		6	11²	13															4
1	2	3¹	13	5		8		12	10					4	6⁴	14	9³	7	11²													5
1	2	3	4	5	14	7		6	10¹						11²	12	8	9¹	13													6
1	2	4	3	5	14			6¹	11	13					10²	8³	7	9	12													7
1	2	3	4³	5	13	7		8	11		12		14		6²		9	10¹														8
1	2	3		5²		7		9	11³	14				4	12	13	8	10	6¹													9
1	2	4			13	7¹			10¹	11	14			3	12		5	6²	9	8³												10
1	2	3			13	6	7		14	11³	12				10¹		5	9	8¹	4												11
	2	4			12	7	6		14	11					13	10²	5		9¹	8¹	3	1										12
	2	4			7	8	6		10	11²					12	13	5		9¹		3	1										13
	2²	3			9	8	7	6¹	11						12	13	5		10		4	1										14
	2	3			10	7	6		12					11			8¹		5	9	4	1										15
	2	3			10³	7	6		13					11		8²		5	12	9¹	4	1	14									16
	2	4			12	6¹	7		14	13					11³		9²	5	8	10	3	1										17
	2	3			6		7		10¹	11					13		5	8¹	9	12	4	1										18
	2	3			7		6		11	12					10		5		9	8¹	4	1										19
	2	3			7²		6	14	8³	11					9¹		12	5	10	13	4	1										20
1	2¹	3			12	7		6							5		9³	10	8	11³	4		14		13							21
1	2	3			14	8	7	6³	11²						13	10¹	5		9	12	4											22
1	2	3				8	7	6¹	10						13	11	5		9²	12	4											23
12		3				7	8		13	10					6	4	11²		9		5	1	2¹									24
14		4				7¹	8		13	10					6	3	11³		9	12	5	1	2²									25
14	2						6		12	10					9	3	11³		8¹	13	4	1	5²	7								26
	3						7	14	13	10¹					6	4	11³		8	2²	5	1	9	12								27
	2							6³	12						8¹	3	11²	14	13	9	5	4	1	7	10							28
4	3						13		12	10					14		5	6	7³	9¹	2	1	8	11²								29
5	4						13		10¹						14		2	7	6³	9²	3¹	1	8	11	12							30
	2	3					8¹		12	10³					14	9	6		13⁴		1	5²	7	11	4							31
	2								12	10					9	8	6¹		4		1	5	7	11	3							32
	3	4								10					12	6	7	9¹			1	2	8	11	5							33
	2								13	14	11²			3	12	9	8¹	7³			1	5	6	10	4						34
	2	3³							10	13					12	14	8		6²	9¹		1	5	7³	11	4						35
	2						8		14	10²				3	13	9	7		6³	12		5¹		11	4	1						36
	2				5¹		7		6³	10²				3	12	9	8		14			11	4	1	13							37
	2				5		12	7	6²	13				3	10¹	9	8¹		14			11	4	1								38
	3				5²		8		13	10				14	12	9	6¹				2	7	11³	4	1							39
	3				5		8³		12	10¹				14	11	9	6²				2	7	13	4	1							40
	4	3¹		5			6		12	10					9	13	7³				2	8	11²	1			14					41
	3	4¹		5			8		13					10¹	9	14					2	7	11	1	12	6²						42
	3³			5			14	7	13					12	11¹	6					2	8	10	4⁴	1	9²						43
		5				7	8³	11¹	13					9		6²					2	12	10	4	14	3						44
		14				7			13	12	5	6²	9¹				2	8	11	3	1	4	10²									45
						8	7⁴	6		12³				5	14	9			2		10	3²	1	4	13	11¹						46

FA Cup

First Round	Dartford	(a)	5-1
Second Round	Stevenage	(a)	2-5

Carabao Cup

First Round	Norwich C	(a)	2-3

Checkatrade Trophy

Southern Group B	West Ham U U21	(h)	2-3
Southern Group B	Wycombe W	(h)	1-0
Southern Group B	Bristol R	(a)	4-2
Second Round South	Forest Green R	(h)	0-1

TOTTENHAM HOTSPUR

FOUNDATION

The Hotspur Football Club was formed from an older cricket club in 1882. Most of the founders were old boys of St John's Presbyterian School and Tottenham Grammar School. The Casey brothers were well to the fore as the family provided the club's first goalposts (painted blue and white) and their first ball. They soon adopted the local YMCA as their meeting place, but after a couple of moves settled at the Red House.

Tottenham Hotspur Stadium, High Road, Tottenham, London N17 0AP.

Telephone: (0844) 499 5000.

Fax: (020) 3544 8563.

Ticket Office: (0844) 499 5000.

Website: www.tottenhamhotspur.com

Email: email@tottenhamhotspur.com

Ground Capacity: 62,062.

Record Attendance: 75,038 v Sunderland, FA Cup 6th rd, 5 March 1938 (at White Hart Lane); 85,512 v Bayer Leverkusen, UEFA Champions League Group E, 2 November 2016 (at Wembley).

Pitch Measurements: 105m × 68m (114yd × 74yd).

Chairman: Daniel Levy.

Head Coach: Mauricio Pochettino.

Assistant Head Coach: Jesus Perez.

Colours: White shirts with navy blue trim, navy blue shorts with white trim, white socks with navy blue trim.

Year Formed: 1882. *Turned Professional:* 1895.

Previous Names: 1882, Hotspur Football Club; 1884, Tottenham Hotspur.

Club Nickname: 'Spurs'.

Grounds: 1882, Tottenham Marshes; 1888, Northumberland Park; 1899, White Hart Lane; 2018, Tottenham Hotspur Stadium.

First Football League Game: 1 September 1908, Division 2, v Wolverhampton W (h) W 3–0 – Hewitson; Coquet, Burton; Morris (1), Danny Steel, Darnell; Walton, Woodward (2), Macfarlane, Bobby Steel, Middlemiss.

Record League Victory: 9–0 v Bristol R, Division 2, 22 October 1977 – Daines; Naylor, Holmes, Hoddle (1), McAllister, Perryman, Pratt, McNab, Moores (3), Lee (4), Taylor (1).

HONOURS

League Champions: Division 1 – 1950–51, 1960–61; Division 2 – 1919–20, 1949–50.
Runners-up: FA Premier League – 2016–17; Division 1 – 1921–22, 1951–52, 1956–57, 1962–63; Division 2 – 1908–09, 1932–33.
FA Cup Winners: 1901 (as non-league club), 1921, 1961, 1962, 1967, 1981, 1982, 1991.
Runners-up: 1987.
League Cup Winners: 1971, 1973, 1999, 2008.
Runners-up: 1982, 2002, 2009, 2015.
European Competitions
European Cup: 1961–62 (sf).
Champions League: 2010–11 (qf), 2016–17, 2017–18.
UEFA Cup: 1971–72 (winners), 1972–73 (sf), 1973–74 (runners-up), 1983–84 (winners), 1984–85 (qf), 1999–2000, 2006–07 (qf), 2007–08, 2008–09.
Europa League: 2011–12, 2012–13 (qf), 2013–14, 2014–15, 2015–16, 2016–17.
European Cup-Winners' Cup: 1962–63 (winners), 1963–64, 1967–68, 1981–82 (sf), 1982–83, 1991–92 (qf).
Intertoto Cup: 1995.

Sⁱⁱn FACT FILE

Bertie Elkin, who made 28 League and Cup appearances for Tottenham Hotspur, was released at the end of the 1910–11 season and shortly afterwards emigrated to South Africa. He went on to become one of his adopted country's top golfers after the First World War, winning the South African Professional Match Play Championship in 1923 and the South African Open the following year.

Record Cup Victory: 13–2 v Crewe Alex, FA Cup 4th rd (replay), 3 February 1960 – Brown; Hills, Henry; Blanchflower, Norman, Mackay; White, Harmer (1), Smith (4), Allen (5), Jones (3 incl. 1p).

Record Defeat: 0–8 v Cologne, UEFA Intertoto Cup, 22 July 1995.

Most League Points (2 for a win): 70, Division 2, 1919–20.

Most League Points (3 for a win): 86, FA Premier League, 2016–17.

Most League Goals: 115, Division 1, 1960–61.

Highest League Scorer in Season: Jimmy Greaves, 37, Division 1, 1962–63.

Most League Goals in Total Aggregate: Jimmy Greaves, 220, 1961–70.

Most League Goals in One Match: 5, Ted Harper v Reading, Division 2, 30 August 1930; 5, Alf Stokes v Birmingham C, Division 1, 18 September 1957; 5, Bobby Smith v Aston Villa, Division 1, 29 March 1958; 5, Jermain Defoe v Wigan Ath, FA Premier League, 22 November 2009.

Most Capped Player: Pat Jennings, 74 (119), Northern Ireland.

Most League Appearances: Steve Perryman, 655, 1969–86.

Youngest League Player: Ally Dick, 16 years 301 days v Manchester C, 20 February 1982.

Record Transfer Fee Received: £85,300,000 from Real Madrid for Gareth Bale, September 2013.

Record Transfer Fee Paid: £38,000,000 (rising to £42,000,000) to Ajax for Davinson Sánchez, August 2017.

Football League Record: 1908 Elected to Division 2; 1909–15 Division 1; 1919–20 Division 2; 1920–28 Division 1; 1928–33 Division 2; 1933–35 Division 2; 1935–50 Division 2; 1950–77 Division 1; 1977–78 Division 2; 1978–92 Division 1; 1992– FA Premier League.

MANAGERS

Frank Brettell 1898–99
John Cameron 1899–1906
Fred Kirkham 1907–08
Peter McWilliam 1912–27
Billy Minter 1927–29
Percy Smith 1930–35
Jack Tresadern 1935–38
Peter McWilliam 1938–42
Arthur Turner 1942–46
Joe Hulme 1946–49
Arthur Rowe 1949–55
Jimmy Anderson 1955–58
Bill Nicholson 1958–74
Terry Neill 1974–76
Keith Burkinshaw 1976–84
Peter Shreeves 1984–86
David Pleat 1986–87
Terry Venables 1987–91
Peter Shreeves 1991–92
Doug Livermore 1992–93
Ossie Ardiles 1993–94
Gerry Francis 1994–97
Christian Gross *(Head Coach)* 1997–98
George Graham 1998–2001
Glenn Hoddle 2001–03
David Pleat *(Caretaker)* 2003–04
Jacques Santini 2004
Martin Jol 2004–07
Juande Ramos 2007–08
Harry Redknapp 2008–12
Andre Villas-Boas 2012–13
Tim Sherwood 2013–14
Mauricio Pochettino May 2014–

LATEST SEQUENCES

Longest Sequence of League Wins: 13, 23.4.1960 – 1.10.1960.
Longest Sequence of League Defeats: 7, 1.1.1994 – 27.2.1994.
Longest Sequence of League Draws: 6, 9.1.1999 – 27.2.1999.
Longest Sequence of Unbeaten League Matches: 22, 31.8.1949 – 31.12.1949.
Longest Sequence Without a League Win: 16, 29.12.1934 – 13.4.1935.
Successive Scoring Runs: 32 from 24.2.1962.
Successive Non-scoring Runs: 6 from 28.12.1985.

TEN YEAR LEAGUE RECORD

		P	W	D	L	F	A	Pts	Pos
2008-09	PR Lge	38	14	9	15	45	45	51	8
2009-10	PR Lge	38	21	7	10	67	41	70	4
2010-11	PR Lge	38	16	14	8	55	46	62	5
2011-12	PR Lge	38	20	9	9	66	41	69	4
2012-13	PR Lge	38	21	9	8	66	46	72	5
2013-14	PR Lge	38	21	6	11	55	51	69	6
2014-15	PR Lge	38	19	7	12	58	53	64	5
2015-16	PR Lge	38	19	13	6	69	35	70	3
2016-17	PR Lge	38	26	8	4	86	26	86	2
2017-18	PR Lge	38	23	8	7	74	36	77	3

DID YOU KNOW ?

Tottenham Hotspur won two of the first three games they played at Anfield, but then had to wait 73 years and 44 games for their next win at the ground. It was not until March 1985 that they were again successful, a Garth Crooks goal on 70 minutes securing a 1-0 for the North London club.

TOTTENHAM HOTSPUR – PREMIER LEAGUE 2017–18 LEAGUE RECORD

Match No.	Date	Venue	Opponents	Result	H/T Score	Lg Pos.	Goalscorers	Attendance
1	Aug 13	A	Newcastle U	W 2-0	0-0	4	Alli [61], Davies [70]	52,077
2	20	H	Chelsea	L 1-2	0-1	9	Batshuayi (og) [82]	73,587
3	27	H	Burnley	D 1-1	0-0	9	Alli [49]	67,862
4	Sept 9	A	Everton	W 3-0	2-0	5	Kane 2 [28, 46], Eriksen [42]	38,835
5	16	H	Swansea C	D 0-0	0-0	5		65,366
6	23	A	West Ham U	W 3-2	2-0	4	Kane 2 [34, 38], Eriksen [60]	56,988
7	30	A	Huddersfield T	W 4-0	3-0	3	Kane 2 [9, 23], Davies [16], Sissoko [90]	24,169
8	Oct 14	H	Bournemouth	W 1-0	0-0	3	Eriksen [47]	73,502
9	22	H	Liverpool	W 4-1	3-1	3	Kane 2 [4, 56], Son [12], Alli [45]	80,827
10	28	A	Manchester U	L 0-1	0-0	3		75,034
11	Nov 5	H	Crystal Palace	W 1-0	0-0	3	Son [64]	65,270
12	18	A	Arsenal	L 0-2	0-2	4		59,530
13	25	H	WBA	D 1-1	1-1	4	Kane [74]	65,905
14	28	A	Leicester C	L 1-2	0-2	5	Kane [79]	31,950
15	Dec 2	A	Watford	D 1-1	1-1	6	Son [25]	20,278
16	9	H	Stoke C	W 5-1	1-0	5	Shawcross (og) [21], Son [53], Kane 2 [54, 65], Eriksen [74]	62,202
17	13	H	Brighton & HA	W 2-0	1-0	5	Aurier [40], Son [87]	55,124
18	16	A	Manchester C	L 1-4	0-1	7	Eriksen [90]	54,214
19	23	A	Burnley	W 3-0	1-0	5	Kane 3 (1 pen) [7 (p), 69, 79]	21,650
20	26	H	Southampton	W 5-2	2-0	5	Kane 3 [22, 39, 67], Alli [49], Son [51]	57,297
21	Jan 2	A	Swansea C	W 2-0	1-0	5	Llorente [12], Alli [89]	20,615
22	4	H	West Ham U	D 1-1	0-0	5	Son [84]	50,034
23	13	A	Everton	W 4-0	1-0	5	Son [26], Kane 2 [47, 59], Eriksen [81]	76,251
24	21	A	Southampton	D 1-1	1-1	5	Kane [18]	31,361
25	31	H	Manchester U	W 2-0	2-0	5	Eriksen [1], Jones (og) [28]	81,978
26	Feb 4	A	Liverpool	D 2-2	0-1	5	Wanyama [80], Kane (pen) [90]	53,213
27	10	H	Arsenal	W 1-0	0-0	3	Kane [49]	83,222
28	25	A	Crystal Palace	W 1-0	0-0	4	Kane [88]	25,287
29	Mar 3	H	Huddersfield T	W 2-0	1-0	4	Son 2 [27, 54]	68,311
30	11	A	Bournemouth	W 4-1	1-1	3	Alli [35], Son 2 [62, 87], Aurier [90]	10,623
31	Apr 1	A	Chelsea	W 3-1	1-1	4	Eriksen [45], Alli 2 [62, 66]	41,364
32	7	H	Stoke C	W 2-1	0-0	4	Eriksen [52], Kane [63]	29,515
33	14	H	Manchester C	L 1-3	1-2	4	Eriksen [42]	80,811
34	17	A	Brighton & HA	D 1-1	0-0	4	Kane [48]	30,440
35	30	H	Watford	W 2-0	1-0	4	Alli [16], Kane [48]	52,675
36	May 5	A	WBA	L 0-1	0-0	4		23,685
37	9	H	Newcastle U	W 1-0	0-0	3	Kane [50]	54,923
38	13	H	Leicester C	W 5-4	1-2	3	Kane 2 [7, 76], Lamela 2 [49, 60], Fuchs (og) [53]	77,841

Final League Position: 3

GOALSCORERS

League (74): Kane 30 (2 pens), Son 12, Eriksen 10, Alli 9, Aurier 2, Davies 2, Lamela 2, Llorente 1, Sissoko 1, Wanyama 1, own goals 4.
FA Cup (18): Kane 4 (1 pen), Llorente 3, Eriksen 2, Lamela 2, Son 2, Alli 1, Lucas Moura 1, Vertonghen 1, Walker-Peters 1, own goal 1.
Carabao Cup (3): Alli 2, Sissoko 1.
Checkatrade Trophy (6): Harrison 1, Loft 1, Shashoua 1, Sterling 1, Tracey 1, own goal 1.
Champions League (18): Kane 7, Son 4, Alli 2, Eriksen 2, Llorente 1, Nkoudou 1, own goal 1.

Lloris H 36	Walker-Peters K 2+1	Alderweireld T 13+1	Vertonghen J 36	Davies B 26+3	Dier E 32+2	Dembele M 21+7	Sissoko M 15+18	Alli B 34+2	Eriksen C 37	Kane H 35+2	Son H 27+10	Wanyama V 8+10	Winks H 9+7	Trippier K 21+3	Janssen V —+1	Sanchez D 29+2	Aurier S 16+1	Llorente F 1+15	Nkoudou G —+1	Gazzaniga P 1	Rose D 9+1	Lamela E 7+18	Vorm M 1	Lucas Moura R 2+4	Match No.
1	2	3	4	5	6	7²	8¹	9³	10	11	12	13	14												1
1		3	4	8¹	2²	7	13	9	10	11	12	6		5²	14										2
1		3	4	5	6	7³	12	9	10²	11	8¹		13	2		14									3
1	2		4	8	7	12	6²	9	10³	11¹	14		13			5	3								4
1	2		4		7		6¹	10	9	11	8²			5		3	12	13							5
1	2		4	9	7		6¹	10	8³	11²		12	13			3	5⁴	14							6
1	13	2	4	8	7		12	10	9³	11¹	14	6		5²		3									7
1		4	5		6		12	9¹	8	11³	10²		7	2		3		13	14						8
1	2	4		13		12	8	6³	10²	11¹		7	5			3	9	14							9
1	2	4	9	3	12	6²	10	8		11¹	7					5	13								10
1		4	14	3	12	6		8	11¹	10	7³			2		5	13		1	9²					11
1		4	8	3	7³	6	10³	9	11	13		12	5				14								12
1	4²	9	2	13		8	6	10	11		7¹	5		3			12								13
1		4		2	7¹	6²	11	8¹	10	12				3	5	13		9	14						14
1		4	5	6	7	12	9⁶	8³	11	10¹	14	2		3⁴			13								15
1		4	5	3	6	13	9²	8	11	10¹	7³	2					14					12			16
1		4	14	3	12	6	13	9	11	10¹	7²			2							5	8³			17
1		4	14	3	6	13	9²	7	10	11¹	8	2									5³	12			18
1		4	5	7²	12	6	9³	8	11	10¹				3	2	14					5	13			19
1		4		6	7¹	12	9²	8	11	10¹	14			3	2						5	13			20
1		4	5	7		14	9	6	13	10	12		2			3¹	11¹					8²			21
1		4	5¹	7³		6²	9	8	11	10	12			3	2	14						13			22
1		4	5	6³	7¹	13	9	8¹	11	10	12			3	2							14			23
1		4	5	6	7³	8	9		11	10²	14	13		3	2¹							12		1	24
1		4	5	6	7	13	9²	8	11	10³	14			2		3¹						12			25
1		4	5	6	7³		10	9	11	8²	13			2		3¹	14					12			26
1		4	5	6	7		9¹	8	11	10²	13			2		3						12			27
1			5	4	7¹		9	8	11	13	6			3		2						10²	12		28
1		4	5	7	6²	13	9³	8	11	10¹				3	2							12	14		29
1		4			6	14	9¹	8	11³	10	7		13	3	2						5²	12			30
1		4	5	6³	7	14	9	10	12	11²	13			2		3						8¹			31
1		4	13	7	14	9³	8	11	10⁵	6¹				3	2						5	12			32
1		4	5	7	6²	14	10¹	9	11	12				2		3						8³	13		33
1	3	4	5		12	6¹		9	11²	10¹	7			2	14							13	8³		34
1		4	5	6	7³	13	9⁵	8	11	10¹	12			2		3						14			35
1	2	4²					10³	6	11	12	7		5	3		14				8	9¹			13	36
1	13	4	5			6	9	8	11	10¹	7²		2⁸	3						14	12				37
1	2	3		4		6²	12	9	11	14	7			13							5	8¹		10³	38

FA Cup

Third Round	AFC Wimbledon	(h)	3-0
Fourth Round	Newport Co	(a)	1-1
Replay	Newport Co	(h)	2-0
Fifth Round	Rochdale	(a)	2-2
Replay	Rochdale	(h)	6-1
Sixth Round	Swansea C	(a)	3-0
Semi-Final	Manchester U	(Wembley)	1-2

Carabao Cup

Third Round	Barnsley	(h)	1-0
Fourth Round	West Ham U	(h)	2-3

Checkatrade Trophy (Tottenham H U21)

Southern Group F	Luton T	(a)	2-2
(Luton T won 4-2 on penalties)			
Southern Group F	AFC Wimbledon	(a)	3-4
Southern Group F	Barnet	(a)	1-2

Champions League

Group H	Borussia Dortmund	(h)	3-1
Group H	APOEL Nicosia	(a)	3-0
Group H	Real Madrid	(a)	1-1
Group H	Real Madrid	(h)	3-1
Group H	Borussia Dortmund	(a)	2-1
Group H	APOEL Nicosia	(h)	3-0
Round of 16 1st leg	Juventus	(a)	2-2
Round of 16 2nd leg	Juventus	(h)	1-2

TRANMERE ROVERS

FOUNDATION

Formed in 1884 as Belmont they adopted their present title the following year and eventually joined their first league, the West Lancashire League, in 1889–90, the same year as their first success in the Wirral Challenge Cup. The club almost folded in 1899–1900 when all the players left en bloc to join a rival club, but they survived the crisis and went from strength to strength, winning the 'Combination' title in 1907–08 and the Lancashire Combination in 1913–14. They joined the Football League in 1921 from the Central League.

Prenton Park, Prenton Road West, Birkenhead, Merseyside CH42 9PY.

Telephone: (0333) 014 4452.

Ticket Office: (0333) 014 4452.

Website: www.tranmererovers.co.uk

Email: customerservice@tranmererovers.co.uk

Ground Capacity: 16,587.

Record Attendance: 24,424 v Stoke C, FA Cup 4th rd, 5 February 1972.

Pitch Measurements: 100.5m × 64m (110yd × 70yd)

Chairman: Mark Palios.

Vice-Chairman: Nicola Palios.

Manager: Micky Mellon.

Assistant Manager: Mike Jackson.

Colours: White shirts with blue trim, blue shorts with white trim, white socks with blue trim.

Year Formed: 1884.

Turned Professional: 1912.

Previous Name: 1884, Belmont AFC; 1885, Tranmere Rovers.

Club Nickname: 'Rovers'.

Grounds: 1884, Steeles Field; 1887, Ravenshaws Field/Old Prenton Park; 1912, Prenton Park.

First Football League Game: 27 August 1921, Division 3 (N), v Crewe Alex (h) W 4–1 – Bradshaw; Grainger, Stuart (1); Campbell, Milnes (1), Heslop; Moreton, Groves (1), Hyam, Ford (1), Hughes.

Record League Victory: 13–4 v Oldham Ath, Division 3 (N), 26 December 1935 – Gray; Platt, Fairhurst; McLaren, Newton, Spencer; Eden, MacDonald (1), Bell (9), Woodward (2), Urmson (1).

Record Cup Victory: 13–0 v Oswestry U, FA Cup 2nd prel rd, 10 October 1914 – Ashcroft; Stevenson, Bullough, Hancock, Taylor, Holden (1), Moreton (1), Cunningham (2), Smith (5), Leck (3), Gould (1).

HONOURS

League Champions: Division 3 (N) – 1937–38.
Runners-up: Division 4 – 1988–89.
League Cup: Runners-up: 2000; National League – 2017–18.
Welsh Cup Winners: 1935.
Runners-up: 1934.
Leyland DAF Cup Winners: 1990.
Runners-up: 1991.

Sun THE FACT FILE

Tranmere Rovers made their first appearance at Wembley Stadium for the Mercantile Credit Football Festival held in April 1988. Selected as one of just two Fourth Division teams to enter, they defeated Wimbledon and Newcastle United before drawing 2-2 in the semi-final against Nottingham Forest, only to lose the penalty shoot-out that followed 1-0.

Record Defeat: 1–9 v Tottenham H, FA Cup 3rd rd (replay), 14 January 1953.

Most League Points (2 for a win): 60, Division 4, 1964–65.

Most League Points (3 for a win): 80, Division 4, 1988–89; Division 3, 1989–90; Division 2, 2002–03.

Most League Goals: 111, Division 3 (N), 1930–31.

Highest League Scorer in Season: Bunny Bell, 35, Division 3 (N), 1933–34.

Most League Goals in Total Aggregate: Ian Muir, 142, 1985–95.

Most League Goals in One Match: 9, Bunny Bell v Oldham Ath, Division 3 (N), 26 December 1935.

Most Capped Player: John Aldridge, 30 (69), Republic of Ireland.

Most League Appearances: Harold Bell, 595, 1946–64 (incl. League record 401 consecutive appearances).

Youngest League Player: Iain Hume, 16 years 167 days v Swindon T, 15 April 2000.

Record Transfer Fee Received: £2,250,000 from WBA for Jason Koumas, August 2002.

Record Transfer Fee Paid: £450,000 to Aston Villa for Shaun Teale, August 1995.

Football League Record: 1921 Original Member of Division 3 (N): 1938–39 Division 2; 1946–58 Division 3 (N); 1958–61 Division 3; 1961–67 Division 4; 1967–75 Division 3; 1975–76 Division 4; 1976–79 Division 3; 1979–89 Division 4; 1989–91 Division 3; 1991–92 Division 2; 1992–2001 Division 1; 2001–04 Division 2; 2004–14 FL 1; 2014–15 FL 2; 2015–18 National League; 2018– FL 2.

MANAGERS
Bert Cooke 1912–35
Jackie Carr 1935–36
Jim Knowles 1936–39
Bill Ridding 1939–45
Ernie Blackburn 1946–55
Noel Kelly 1955–57
Peter Farrell 1957–60
Walter Galbraith 1961
Dave Russell 1961–69
Jackie Wright 1969–72
Ron Yeats 1972–75
John King 1975–80
Bryan Hamilton 1980–85
Frank Worthington 1985–87
Ronnie Moore 1987
John King 1987–96
John Aldridge 1996–2001
Dave Watson 2001–02
Ray Mathias 2002–03
Brian Little 2003–06
Ronnie Moore 2006–09
John Barnes 2009
Les Parry 2009–12
Ronnie Moore 2012–14
Robert Edwards 2014
Micky Adams 2014–15
Gary Brabin 2015–16
Paul Cardin 2016
Micky Mellon October 2016–

LATEST SEQUENCES

Longest Sequence of League Wins: 9, 9.2.1990 – 19.3.1990.

Longest Sequence of League Defeats: 8, 29.10.1938 – 17.12.1938.

Longest Sequence of League Draws: 5, 26.12.1997 – 31.1.1998.

Longest Sequence of Unbeaten League Matches: 18, 16.3.1970 – 4.9.1970.

Longest Sequence Without a League Win: 16, 8.11.1969 – 14.3.1970.

Successive Scoring Runs: 32 from 24.2.1934.

Successive Non-scoring Runs: 7 from 20.12.1997.

TEN YEAR LEAGUE RECORD

		P	W	D	L	F	A	Pts	Pos
2008-09	FL 1	46	21	11	14	62	49	74	7
2009-10	FL 1	46	14	9	23	45	72	51	19
2010-11	FL 1	46	15	11	20	53	60	56	17
2011-12	FL 1	46	14	14	18	49	53	56	12
2012-13	FL 1	46	19	10	17	58	48	67	11
2013-14	FL 1	46	12	11	23	52	79	47	21
2014-15	FL 2	46	9	12	25	45	67	39	24
2015-16	NL	46	22	12	12	61	44	78	6
2016-17	NL	46	29	8	9	79	39	95	2
2017-18	NL	46	24	10	12	78	46	82	2

DID YOU KNOW ?

Tranmere Rovers reached the fourth round of the FA Cup in 1933–34 where they were drawn at home to play Liverpool. The tie was switched to Anfield and attracted an attendance of 61,036, a new ground record and the highest 'home' gate to watch Rovers. Receipts were £4,006.

WALSALL

FOUNDATION

Two of the leading clubs around Walsall in the 1880s were Walsall Swifts (formed 1877) and Walsall Town (formed 1879). The Swifts were winners of the Birmingham Senior Cup in 1881, while the Town reached the 4th round (5th round modern equivalent) of the FA Cup in 1883. These clubs amalgamated as Walsall Town Swifts in 1888, becoming simply Walsall in 1895.

Banks's Stadium, Bescot Crescent, Walsall WS1 4SA.
Telephone: (01922) 622 791. *Fax:* (01922) 639 202.
Ticket Office: (01922) 651 414 416.
Website: www.saddlers.co.uk
Email: info@walsallfc.co.uk
Ground Capacity: 10,910.
Record Attendance: 25,453 v Newcastle U, Division 2, 29 August 1961 (at Fellows Park); 11,049 v Rotherham U, Division 1, 9 May 2004 (at Bescot Stadium).
Pitch Measurements: 100.5m × 67m (110yd × 73yd).
Chairman: Jeff Bonser.
Chief Executive: Stefan Gamble.
Manager: Dean Keates.
First-Team Coach: Andy Davies.

HONOURS

League Champions: FL 2 – 2006–07; Division 4 – 1959–60.
Runners-up: Second Division – 1998–99; Division 3 – 1960–61; Third Division – 1994–95; Division 4 – 1979–80.
FA Cup: last 16 – 1889; 5th rd – 1939, 1975, 1978, 1987, 2002, 2003.
League Cup: semi-final – 1984.
League Trophy: Runners-up: 2015.

Colours: Red shirts with white and black trim, red shorts with white trim, red socks with black trim.
Year Formed: 1888.
Turned Professional: 1888.
Previous Names: Walsall Swifts (founded 1877) and Walsall Town (founded 1879) amalgamated in 1888 as Walsall Town Swifts; 1895, Walsall.
Club Nickname: 'The Saddlers'.
Grounds: 1888, Fellows Park; 1990, Bescot Stadium (renamed Banks's Stadium 2007).
First Football League Game: 3 September 1892, Division 2, v Darwen (h) L 1–2 – Hawkins; Withington, Pinches; Robinson, Whitrick, Forsyth; Marshall, Holmes, Turner, Gray (1), Pangbourn.
Record League Victory: 10–0 v Darwen, Division 2, 4 March 1899 – Tennent; Ted Peers (1), Davies; Hickinbotham, Jenkyns, Taggart; Dean (3), Vail (2), Aston (4), Martin, Griffin.
Record Cup Victory: 7–0 v Macclesfield T (a), FA Cup 2nd rd, 6 December 1997 – Walker; Evans, Marsh, Viveash (1), Ryder, Peron, Boli (2 incl. 1p) (Ricketts), Porter (2), Keates, Watson (Platt), Hodge (2 incl. 1p).
Record Defeat: 0–12 v Small Heath, 17 December 1892; 0–12 v Darwen, 26 December 1896, both Division 2.
Most League Points (2 for a win): 65, Division 4, 1959–60.
Most League Points (3 for a win): 89, FL 2, 2006–07.
Most League Goals: 102, Division 4, 1959–60.
Highest League Scorer in Season: Gilbert Alsop, 40, Division 3 (N), 1933–34 and 1934–35.

Sun THE FACT FILE

Before Walsall finally made it to Wembley for the Football League Trophy final in 2014–15 they were one of just four Football League clubs never to have played at the national stadium. The Saddlers took over 29,000 fans to the historic match but went down 2-0 to Bristol City in front of a crowd of 72,315.

Most League Goals in Total Aggregate: Tony Richards, 184, 1954–63; Colin Taylor, 184, 1958–63, 1964–68, 1969–73.

Most League Goals in One Match: 5, Gilbert Alsop v Carlisle U, Division 3 (N), 2 February 1935; 5, Bill Evans v Mansfield T, Division 3 (N), 5 October 1935; 5, Johnny Devlin v Torquay U, Division 3 (S), 1 September 1949.

Most Capped Player: Mick Kearns, 15 (18), Republic of Ireland.

Most League Appearances: Colin Harrison, 473, 1964–82.

Youngest League Player: Geoff Morris, 16 years 218 days v Scunthorpe U, 14 September 1965.

Record Transfer Fee Received: £1,500,000 (rising to £5,000,000) from Brentford for Rico Henry, August 2016.

Record Transfer Fee Paid: £300,000 to Anorthosis Famagusta for Andreas Makris, August 2016.

Football League Record: 1892 Elected to Division 2; 1895 Failed re-election; 1896–1901 Division 2; 1901 Failed re-election; 1921 Original Member of Division 3 (N); 1927–31 Division 3 (S); 1931–36 Division 3 (N); 1936–58 Division 3 (S); 1958–60 Division 4; 1960–61 Division 3; 1961–63 Division 2; 1963–79 Division 3; 1979–80 Division 4; 1980–88 Division 3; 1988–89 Division 2; 1989–90 Division 3; 1990–92 Division 4; 1992–95 Division 3; 1995–99 Division 2; 1999–2000 Division 1; 2000–01 Division 2; 2001–04 Division 1; 2004–06 FL 1; 2006–07 FL 2; 2007– FL 1.

LATEST SEQUENCES

Longest Sequence of League Wins: 7, 9.4.2005 – 9.8.2005.

Longest Sequence of League Defeats: 15, 29.10.1988 – 4.2.1989.

Longest Sequence of League Draws: 5, 7.5.1988 – 17.9.1988.

Longest Sequence of Unbeaten League Matches: 21, 6.11.1979 – 22.3.1980.

Longest Sequence Without a League Win: 18, 15.10.1988 – 4.2.1989.

Successive Scoring Runs: 27 from 6.11.1979.

Successive Non-scoring Runs: 5 from 10.4.2004.

MANAGERS

H. Smallwood 1888–91 *(Secretary-Manager)*
A. G. Burton 1891–93
J. H. Robinson 1893–95
C. H. Ailso 1895–96 *(Secretary-Manager)*
A. E. Parsloe 1896–97 *(Secretary-Manager)*
L. Ford 1897–98 *(Secretary-Manager)*
G. Hughes 1898–99 *(Secretary-Manager)*
L. Ford 1899–1901 *(Secretary-Manager)*
J. E. Shutt 1908–13 *(Secretary-Manager)*
Haydn Price 1914–20
Joe Burchell 1920–26
David Ashworth 1926–27
Jack Torrance 1927–28
James Kerr 1928–29
Sid Scholey 1929–30
Peter O'Rourke 1930–32
Bill Slade 1932–34
Andy Wilson 1934–37
Tommy Lowes 1937–44
Harry Hibbs 1944–51
Tony McPhee 1951
Brough Fletcher 1952–53
Major Frank Buckley 1953–55
John Love 1955–57
Billy Moore 1957–64
Alf Wood 1964
Reg Shaw 1964–68
Dick Graham 1968
Ron Lewin 1968–69
Billy Moore 1969–72
John Smith 1972–73
Ronnie Allen 1973
Doug Fraser 1973–77
Dave Mackay 1977–78
Alan Ashman 1978
Frank Sibley 1979
Alan Buckley 1979–86
Neil Martin *(Joint Manager with Buckley)* 1981–82
Tommy Coakley 1986–88
John Barnwell 1989–90
Kenny Hibbitt 1990–94
Chris Nicholl 1994–97
Jan Sorensen 1997–98
Ray Graydon 1998–2002
Colin Lee 2002–04
Paul Merson 2004–06
Kevin Broadhurst 2006
Richard Money 2006–08
Jimmy Mullen 2008–09
Chris Hutchings 2009–11
Dean Smith 2011–15
Sean O'Driscoll 2015–16
Jon Whitney 2016–18
Dean Keates March 2018–

TEN YEAR LEAGUE RECORD

		P	W	D	L	F	A	Pts	Pos
2008-09	FL 1	46	17	10	19	61	66	61	13
2009-10	FL 1	46	16	14	16	60	63	62	10
2010-11	FL 1	46	12	12	22	56	75	48	20
2011-12	FL 1	46	10	20	16	51	57	50	19
2012-13	FL 1	46	17	17	12	65	58	68	9
2013-14	FL 1	46	14	16	16	49	49	58	13
2014-15	FL 1	46	14	17	15	50	54	59	14
2015-16	FL 1	46	24	12	10	71	49	84	3
2016-17	FL 1	46	14	16	16	51	58	58	14
2017-18	FL 1	46	13	13	20	53	66	52	19

DID YOU KNOW ?

Walsall's Player of the Season award dates back to the 1960–61 season when it was first organised by the Supporters' Club. The inaugural winner was Tony Richards who received 35 per cent of the votes. Ken Hill was runner-up and centre-half Albert McPherson was in third place.

WALSALL – SKY BET LEAGUE ONE 2017–18 LEAGUE RECORD

Match No.	Date		Venue	Opponents	Result		H/T Score	Lg Pos.	Goalscorers	Attendance
1	Aug	5	A	Bury	L	0-1	0-1	21		4240
2		12	H	Oldham Ath	W	2-1	0-1	12	Edwards [53], Oztumer [90]	4419
3		19	A	Portsmouth	D	1-1	0-0	12	Leahy [47]	17,198
4		26	H	Bradford C	D	3-3	0-2	13	Leahy [54], Roberts, T [61], Bakayoko [87]	4817
5	Sept	2	H	Plymouth Arg	W	2-1	1-0	10	Agyei [23], Oztumer [81]	5495
6		9	A	Bristol R	L	1-2	0-1	13	Wilson [58]	8544
7		12	A	Rotherham U	L	1-5	0-4	14	Bakayoko [49]	7330
8		16	H	Peterborough U	D	1-1	1-0	14	Oztumer [38]	4453
9		23	A	Oxford U	W	2-1	1-0	13	Edwards [32], Roberts, T [53]	6895
10		26	H	Charlton Ath	D	2-2	1-1	13	Roberts, T [41], Agyei [89]	3712
11		30	A	Wigan Ath	L	0-2	0-1	16		8107
12	Oct	7	H	Shrewsbury T	D	1-1	1-1	16	Agyei [13]	5971
13		14	H	Blackpool	D	1-1	1-0	16	Oztumer [18]	4503
14		17	A	Milton Keynes D	D	1-1	0-1	16	Roberts, T (pen) [58]	7258
15		21	A	Doncaster R	W	3-0	0-0	14	Oztumer 2 [62, 66], Morris [80]	7391
16		28	H	Southend U	L	0-2	0-1	15		4145
17	Nov	18	H	Gillingham	L	0-1	0-1	18		4917
18		21	H	Fleetwood T	W	4-2	2-1	15	Oztumer [26], Ismail [45], Roberts, T [89], Agyei [90]	3225
19		25	A	AFC Wimbledon	W	2-1	2-1	13	Oztumer [15], Bakayoko [31]	4130
20	Dec	9	H	Scunthorpe U	W	1-0	1-0	11	Morris [13]	3865
21		16	A	Northampton T	L	1-2	1-2	11	Oztumer [2]	5055
22		23	A	Rochdale	D	1-1	0-0	11	Kouhyar [90]	2702
23		26	H	Bristol R	D	0-0	0-0	12		5759
24		30	H	Rotherham U	L	1-2	1-1	14	Edwards [12]	4685
25	Jan	1	A	Plymouth Arg	L	0-1	0-0	18		10,432
26		13	H	Oxford U	W	2-1	1-0	15	Bakayoko [33], Oztumer [48]	4569
27		20	A	Charlton Ath	L	1-3	1-1	16	Oztumer [41]	10,140
28		30	A	Blackburn R	L	1-3	1-2	18	Edwards [37]	11,241
29	Feb	3	H	Milton Keynes D	W	1-0	0-0	16	Ngoy [70]	4009
30		10	A	Blackpool	D	2-2	1-1	16	Edwards [28], Guthrie [76]	3404
31		13	A	Doncaster R	W	4-2	3-0	15	Edwards 2 [22, 24], Morris [45], Bakayoko [71]	3514
32		17	A	Gillingham	D	0-0	0-0	16		4682
33		24	H	Blackburn R	L	1-2	1-2	17	Fitzwater [45]	6893
34		27	A	Peterborough U	L	1-2	1-1	17	Ngoy [9]	2531
35	Mar	3	A	Southend U	W	3-0	0-0	13	Oztumer 3 [57, 66, 85]	6413
36		6	H	Rochdale	L	0-3	0-1	13		3505
37		10	A	Shrewsbury T	L	0-2	0-1	14		7633
38		21	H	Wigan Ath	L	0-3	0-3	17		4477
39		31	H	Portsmouth	L	0-1	0-0	18		5159
40	Apr	7	H	Bury	W	1-0	0-0	18	Thompson (og) [89]	3807
41		11	A	Oldham Ath	D	1-1	1-1	17	Fitzwater [34]	3424
42		14	H	AFC Wimbledon	L	2-3	2-0	19	Fitzwater [6], Ngoy [45]	4663
43		21	A	Scunthorpe U	L	0-1	0-0	19		4083
44		28	H	Northampton T	W	1-0	0-0	18	Dobson [90]	8919
45	May	1	A	Bradford C	D	1-1	1-1	18	Oztumer [22]	18,976
46		5	A	Fleetwood T	L	0-2	0-2	19		3644

Final League Position: 19

GOALSCORERS

League (53): Oztumer 15, Edwards 7, Bakayoko 5, Roberts, T 5 (1 pen), Agyei 4, Fitzwater 3, Morris 3, Ngoy 3, Leahy 2, Dobson 1, Guthrie 1, Ismail 1, Kouhyar 1, Wilson 1, own goal 1.
FA Cup (1): Bakayoko 1.
Carabao Cup (2): Bakayoko 1, Oztumer 1 (1 pen).
Checkatrade Trophy (7): Ismail 2 (1 pen), Agyei 1, Bakayoko 1, Flanagan 1, Leahy 1, Oztumer 1.

Gillespie M 23	Kinsella L 17+2	Wilson J 19	Guthrie J 46	Leahy L 46	Morris K 35+7	Cuvelier F 10+13	Chambers A 43	Edwards J 29+1	Oztumer E 41+4	Jackson S 1+7	Kouhyar M 5+10	Bakayoko A 33+8	Candlin M —+3	Devlin N 30+3	Donnellan S 7+3	Roberts T 11+6	Roberts K 18+3	Agyei D 7+11	Ismail Z 12+4	Roberts L 23+1	Flanagan R 3+6	Dobson G 19+2	Shaibu J 3+11	Fitzwater J 15	Ngoy J 9+4	Cockerill-Mollett C 1	Shorrock W —+1	Match No.
1	2	3	4	5	6[1]	7[3]	8	9	10	11[2]	12	13	14															1
1		4	3	5	6		7	9	10[1]	12		11		2	8													2
1		5	3	6	7[2]	12	8	9	11	13		10[1]		2	4													3
1	2	4	9	6[1]			7	8	10			11		5	3		12											4
1		2	4	8	13		7	6	9	12		10[2]		5			3		11[1]									5
1		2	4	8			7	6	9			11		5[1]	3	12		10[2]	13									6
1		3	4	5	13	12	6	8	10[1]			9[3]		2	7[2]	11	14											7
1		2	4	9	13	7[3]	8	6	11[2]			12		5	3	10[1]	14											8
1	13	4	5	3	9		7	2	6			12		8		10[1]		11[2]										9
1		3	4	5[1]	9		7	8	10		12			2	14	11[2]	13	6[1]										10
1[1]		3	4	5	7		6	9	8			14		2		11[2]	13	10[3]	12									11
1		2	4	8			7	6	9			10		5			12	3	11[1]									12
1		2	4	8			7	6	9			10		5			12	3	11[1]									13
1	9	3	4	5	7[2]	8[1]	6							2	14	13	10	11[3]	12									14
1	2	4	3	5	12	8[3]	6	7	9[1]			10				13	11[2]	14										15
1	5	4[2]	2	8	13		6	7	9			11[1]		3		10	12	14										16
	2	4	5	9[1]			8	7[2]	10			11[3]		12	3		14	6		1	13							17
	2	4	5	8			7	10[3]	9			14		11[1]	3	13	6[1]		12	1								18
	2	4	5	8			7	10	9[2]			14		11[3]	3	13	6[1]		12	1								19
1	2	3	4	5	10		7[2]	6	9			11[1]		13	14	8[3]	12											20
1	2[2]	3	4	5	10[3]		7[1]	6	12			9		11[1]	14	13	8											21
1			3	5	10[2]		6	2[1]	9	12		13		7	4	11	8[3]	14										22
1			4	5	9		7	8	10			12		2			3	11[1]	6									23
1			4	5[2]	9[1]		7	8	10	13		12	14	2			3	11[3]	6									24
1	2	3	4	5			7	8[3]	10[1]	12			14	11[2]			13	6	9									25
	2		4	5	12	13	7	10	6[2]			11		14				3		1		9[3]	8[1]					26
	2		4	5			6	7	9			10		11				3		1		8						27
	2		4	5	7[2]		6	10	8[3]			14		11				3[1]		1		13	9		12			28
	2		4	5	9		7	6	10[1]			11[2]						3		1		8	12	13				29
	2		4	5	6[1]		7	8	12			11[2]	14							1		9	13	3	10[3]			30
			4	5	6	14	7	9[3]	10[2]			12		2						1		8	11[1]	3	13			31
			4	5	6[1]	14	8	9	10[3]			13		2				11[2]		1		7	12	3				32
			4	5	10		6	7[1]	9			13		2						1		8	11[2]	3	12			33
			4	5	10[2]	14	6	9	8[1]			12		3[1]						1		7	13	2	11			34
13			4	5	10	14	6	9[1]	8[2]			12		2				3		1		7	11[3]					35
			4	5	6	13	7[3]	10	9[2]			14		2				3		1		8	12		11[1]			36
			4	5	6[1]	12	7	10				11		2				3		1		8	13		9[2]			37
			4	5	8	12	6	9	10			11		2						1		7[1]		3				38
			4	5	9	8[1]	7	6[2]	12			11		2						1		13	14	3	10[3]			39
			4	5	6	8[2]	7	10[1]	9					2				14		1		13	11[3]	3	12			40
9		3	4	5	6		8					11		2						1		7	12		10[1]			41
			4	5		13	8[3]	7	9[2]			11		2				12		1		6	14	3[1]	10			42
	2[1]		4	5	9[2]	14	7	12	10					6						1		8	13	3	11[3]			43
			4	5	9	8	7	12	10[1]			11		2				3		1		6						44
			4	5	9	12	7	6	10[1]			11		2				3		1		8						45
1			4		10[2]	12	6	9[1]				11[3]	13	2								7	8	3		5	14	46

FA Cup

First Round   Newport Co   (a)   1-2

Carabao Cup

First Round   Sheffield U   (a)   2-3

Checkatrade Trophy

Northern Group E	WBA U21	(h)	3-1
Northern Group E	Coventry C	(h)	2-2
(Coventry C won 4-3 on penalties)			
Northern Group E	Shrewsbury T	(a)	1-0
Second Round North	Bury	(h)	1-2

WATFORD

FOUNDATION

The club was formed as Watford Rovers in 1881. The name was changed to West Herts in 1893 and then the name Watford was adopted after rival club Watford St Mary's was absorbed in 1898.

Vicarage Road Stadium, Vicarage Road, Watford, Hertfordshire WD18 0ER.

Telephone: (01923) 496 000.

Fax: (01923) 496 001.

Ticket Office: (01923) 223 023.

Website: www.watfordfc.com

Email: yourvoice@watfordfc.com

Ground Capacity: 21,000.

Record Attendance: 34,099 v Manchester U, FA Cup 4th rd (replay), 3 February 1969.

Pitch Measurements: 105m × 68m (115yd × 74.5yd).

Chairman and Chief Executive: Scott Duxbury.

Head Coach: Javi Gracia.

Assistant Head Coach: Juan Solla.

Colours: Yellow shirts with red trim, black shorts with red trim, black socks with red trim.

Year Formed: 1881.

Turned Professional: 1897.

Previous Names: 1881, Watford Rovers; 1893, West Herts; 1898, Watford.

Club Nickname: 'The Hornets'.

Grounds: 1883, Vicarage Meadow, Rose and Crown Meadow; 1889, Colney Butts; 1890, Cassio Road; 1922, Vicarage Road.

First Football League Game: 28 August 1920, Division 3, v QPR (a) W 2–1 – Williams; Horseman, Fred Gregory; Bacon, Toone, Wilkinson; Bassett, Ronald (1), Hoddinott, White (1), Waterall.

Record League Victory: 8–0 v Sunderland, Division 1, 25 September 1982 – Sherwood; Rice, Rostron, Taylor, Terry, Bolton, Callaghan (2), Blissett (4), Jenkins (2), Jackett, Barnes.

Record Cup Victory: 10–1 v Lowestoft T, FA Cup 1st rd, 27 November 1926 – Yates; Prior, Fletcher (1); Frank Smith, Bert Smith, Strain; Stephenson, Warner (3), Edmonds (3), Swan (1), Daniels (1), (1 og).

Record Defeat: 0–10 v Wolverhampton W, FA Cup 1st rd (replay), 24 January 1912.

Most League Points (2 for a win): 71, Division 4, 1977–78.

Most League Points (3 for a win): 89, FL C, 2014–15.

HONOURS

League Champions: Second Division – 1997–98; Division 3 – 1968–69; Division 4 – 1977–78.
Runners-up: Division 1 – 1982–83; FL C – 2014–15; Division 2 – 1981–82; Division 3 – 1978–79.
FA Cup: Runners-up: 1984.
League Cup: semi-final – 1979, 2005.
European Competitions
UEFA Cup: 1983–84.

Sun FACT FILE

The last Christmas Day game played by Watford was in 1956 when they entertained Ipswich Town at Vicarage Road. The Hornets won 2-1 but only 4,544 fans turned up, well down on the season's average of 9,219, and there were no further games played on the annual holiday in future.

Most League Goals: 92, Division 4, 1959–60.

Highest League Scorer in Season: Cliff Holton, 42, Division 4, 1959–60.

Most League Goals in Total Aggregate: Luther Blissett, 148, 1976–83, 1984–88, 1991–92.

Most League Goals in One Match: 5, Eddie Mummery v Newport Co, Division 3 (S), 5 January 1924.

Most Capped Players: John Barnes, 31 (79), England; Kenny Jackett, 31, Wales.

Most League Appearances: Luther Blissett, 415, 1976–83, 1984–88, 1991–92.

Youngest League Player: Keith Mercer, 16 years 125 days v Tranmere R, 16 February 1973.

Record Transfer Fee Received: £20,000,000 from Changchun Yatai for Odion Ighalo, January 2017.

Record Transfer Fee Paid: £18,500,000 to Burnley for Andre Gray, August 2017.

Football League Record: 1920 Original Member of Division 3; 1921–58 Division 3 (S); 1958–60 Division 4; 1960–69 Division 3; 1969–72 Division 2; 1972–75 Division 3; 1975–78 Division 4; 1978–79 Division 3; 1979–82 Division 2; 1982–88 Division 1; 1988–92 Division 2; 1992–96 Division 1; 1996–98 Division 2; 1998–99 Division 1; 1999–2000 FA Premier League; 2000–04 Division 1; 2004–06 FL C; 2006–07 FA Premier League; 2007–15 FL C; 2015– FA Premier League.

LATEST SEQUENCES

Longest Sequence of League Wins: 7, 28.8.2000 – 14.10.2000.

Longest Sequence of League Defeats: 9, 26.12.1972 – 27.2.1973.

Longest Sequence of League Draws: 7, 16.2.2008 – 22.3.2008.

Longest Sequence of Unbeaten League Matches: 22, 1.10.1996 – 1.3.1997.

Longest Sequence Without a League Win: 19, 27.11.1971 – 8.4.1972.

Successive Scoring Runs: 22 from 20.8.1985.

Successive Non-scoring Runs: 7 from 18.12.1971.

MANAGERS

John Goodall 1903–10
Harry Kent 1910–26
Fred Pagnam 1926–29
Neil McBain 1929–37
Bill Findlay 1938–47
Jack Bray 1947–48
Eddie Hapgood 1948–50
Ron Gray 1950–51
Haydn Green 1951–52
Len Goulden 1952–55
 (General Manager to 1956)
Johnny Paton 1955–56
Neil McBain 1956–59
Ron Burgess 1959–63
Bill McGarry 1963–64
Ken Furphy 1964–71
George Kirby 1971–73
Mike Keen 1973–77
Graham Taylor 1977–87
Dave Bassett 1987–88
Steve Harrison 1988–90
Colin Lee 1990
Steve Perryman 1990–93
Glenn Roeder 1993–96
Graham Taylor 1996
Kenny Jackett 1996–97
Graham Taylor 1997–2001
Gianluca Vialli 2001–02
Ray Lewington 2002–05
Adrian Boothroyd 2005–08
Brendan Rodgers 2008–09
Malky Mackay 2009–11
Sean Dyche 2011–12
Gianfranco Zola 2012–13
Beppe Sannino 2013–14
Oscar Garcia 2014
Billy McKinlay 2014
Slavisa Jokanovic 2014–15
Quique Flores 2015–16
Walter Mazzarri 2016–17
Marco Silva 2017–18
Javi Gracia January 2018–

TEN YEAR LEAGUE RECORD

		P	W	D	L	F	A	Pts	Pos
2008-09	FL C	46	16	10	20	68	72	58	13
2009-10	FL C	46	14	12	20	61	68	54	16
2010-11	FL C	46	16	13	17	77	71	61	14
2011-12	FL C	46	16	16	14	56	64	64	11
2012-13	FL C	46	23	8	15	85	58	77	3
2013-14	FL C	46	15	15	16	74	64	60	13
2014-15	FL C	46	27	8	11	91	50	89	2
2015-16	PR Lge	38	12	9	17	40	50	45	13
2016-17	PR Lge	38	11	7	20	40	68	40	17
2017-18	PR Lge	38	11	8	19	44	64	41	14

DID YOU KNOW ?

Centre-forward Fred Pagnam scored three hat-tricks in a spell of five games for Watford in the 1922–23 season. Two of these were against Gillingham in successive weeks. In total he netted seven hat-tricks for the Hornets in Football League games, a club record.

WATFORD – PREMIER LEAGUE 2017–18 LEAGUE RECORD

Match No.	Date		Venue	Opponents	Result		H/T Score	Lg Pos.	Goalscorers	Attendance
1	Aug	12	H	Liverpool	D	3-3	2-1	8	Okaka [6], Doucoure [32], Britos [90]	20,407
2		19	A	Bournemouth	W	2-0	0-0	3	Richarlison [73], Capoue [86]	10,501
3		26	H	Brighton & HA	D	0-0	0-0	5		20,181
4	Sept	9	A	Southampton	W	2-0	1-0	4	Doucoure [38], Janmaat [66]	31,435
5		16	H	Manchester C	L	0-6	0-3	11		20,305
6		23	A	Swansea C	W	2-1	1-0	6	Gray [13], Richarlison [90]	20,372
7		30	A	WBA	D	2-2	1-2	5	Doucoure [37], Richarlison [90]	24,606
8	Oct	14	A	Arsenal	W	2-1	0-1	4	Deeney (pen) [71], Cleverley [90]	20,384
9		21	A	Chelsea	L	2-4	1-1	5	Doucoure [45], Pereyra [49]	41,467
10		28	H	Stoke C	L	0-1	0-1	7		20,087
11	Nov	5	A	Everton	L	2-3	0-0	9	Richarlison [46], Kabasele [64]	38,609
12		19	H	West Ham U	W	2-0	1-0	8	Hughes [11], Richarlison [64]	20,018
13		25	A	Newcastle U	W	3-0	2-0	8	Hughes [19], Yedlin (og) [45], Gray [62]	52,188
14		28	H	Manchester U	L	2-4	0-3	8	Deeney (pen) [77], Doucoure [84]	20,552
15	Dec	2	H	Tottenham H	D	1-1	1-1	8	Kabasele [13]	20,278
16		9	A	Burnley	L	0-1	0-1	9		19,479
17		12	A	Crystal Palace	L	1-2	1-0	9	Janmaat [3]	23,566
18		16	H	Huddersfield T	L	1-4	0-2	9	Doucoure [68]	20,026
19		23	A	Brighton & HA	L	0-1	0-0	10		30,473
20		26	H	Leicester C	W	2-1	1-1	10	Wague [45], Schmeichel (og) [65]	20,308
21		30	H	Swansea C	L	1-2	1-0	10	Carrillo [11]	20,002
22	Jan	2	A	Manchester C	L	1-3	0-2	10	Gray [82]	53,556
23		13	H	Southampton	D	2-2	0-2	10	Gray [58], Doucoure [90]	20,018
24		20	A	Leicester C	L	0-2	0-1	10		31,891
25		31	A	Stoke C	D	0-0	0-0	11		27,458
26	Feb	5	H	Chelsea	W	4-1	1-0	11	Deeney (pen) [42], Janmaat [84], Deulofeu [88], Pereyra [90]	20,157
27		10	A	West Ham U	L	0-2	0-1	11		56,197
28		24	H	Everton	W	1-0	0-0	10	Deeney [79]	20,430
29	Mar	3	H	WBA	W	1-0	0-0	9	Deeney [77]	20,022
30		11	A	Arsenal	L	0-3	0-1	10		59,131
31		17	A	Liverpool	L	0-5	0-2	11		53,287
32		31	H	Bournemouth	D	2-2	1-1	11	Femenia [13], Pereyra [49]	20,393
33	Apr	7	H	Burnley	L	1-2	0-0	12	Pereyra [61]	20,044
34		14	A	Huddersfield T	L	0-1	0-0	12		23,961
35		21	H	Crystal Palace	D	0-0	0-0	12		20,401
36		30	A	Tottenham H	L	0-2	0-1	13		52,675
37	May	5	H	Newcastle U	W	2-1	2-0	13	Pereyra [2], Gray [28]	20,375
38		12	A	Manchester U	L	0-1	0-1	14		75,049

Final League Position: 14

GOALSCORERS

League (44): Doucoure 7, Deeney 5 (3 pens), Gray 5, Pereyra 5, Richarlison 5, Janmaat 3, Hughes 2, Kabasele 2, Britos 1, Capoue 1, Carrillo 1, Cleverley 1, Deulofeu 1, Femenia 1, Okaka 1, Wague 1, own goals 2.
FA Cup (3): Capoue 1, Carrillo 1, Deeney 1.
Carabao Cup (2): Capoue 1, Mariappa 1.

Gomes H 24	Janmaat D 21 + 2	Kaboul Y 2	Britos M 10 + 2	Holebas J 26 + 2	Cleverley T 22 + 1	Doucoure A 37	Chalobah N 5 + 1	Amrabat N 3	Okaka S 3 + 12	Pereyra R 18 + 14	Femenia K 19 + 4	Richarlison 32 + 6	Gray A 16 + 15	Prodl S 17 + 4	Capoue E 18 + 5	Kabasele C 27 + 1	Watson B 6 + 2	Cathcart C 5 + 2	Carrillo A 16 + 12	Deeney T 20 + 9	Mariappa A 24 + 4	Wague M 5 + 1	Hughes W 11 + 4	Karnezis O 14 + 1	Zeegelaar M 12	Sinclair J — + 4	Deulofeu G 5 + 2	Lukebakio D — + 1	Match No.
1	2²	3	4	5	6	7	8	9	10¹	11³	12	13	14																1
1			4	5	6	7	8¹	9²		2	11²	10	3	12	13	14													2
1		5⁴		7	6	8	9²		2	11	10¹	3	4	12³	13	14													3
1	13	4²		5	9	7	6		2³	10	11¹	3	8	14	12														4
1	2			5	9²	6	7³		12	10	11¹	13	4	8	14	3													5
1			5	9	6		13	2	10	11³	7¹	4	8²	14	3	12													6
1			5	9	6		12	2	10	13	7¹	4	8²	11	3														7
1			4	8	6	7		9³	5	11	10	14	3	12	13	2²													8
1			4	8	6	7		9²	5	11	14	3	13	12	10³	2¹													9
1			4	5	9	7		2	10	12	6¹	3	8²	11	13														10
1¹			4	5	8	7	14	2	11	10	3²	9	13	6³	12														11
1			4	13	6	7		12	5³	10	11¹	3	14	2	9²	8													12
1		4³		8	7		13	5	10¹	11	12	3	14	2	6²	9													13
1			7	6		13	5	11	10³	3¹	4	12	14	2	9²	8													14
1			7¹	6		9³	5	10	14	3	12	4²	13	11	2	8													15
1	2		12	6	7		9²	10	13	4	8¹	11	3	5⁴															16
1	5		8²		7		12	14	10¹	13	3	6¹	4	9²	11³	2													17
1	5		8²		7	14	12	10	13	3	6¹	4	9	11¹	2³														18
1	2		5	6		14	9²	10	11¹	4	13	3	7³	8								12							19
1	2		6	8		12	11³	10		13		4	7²	9¹		3			5	14									20
1	2		9	6		11¹	14	10	13	12		4	7	8³		3²			5										21
1	2		12	7		13		8¹	11		9¹	4	6³	10		3			5	14									22
1	2		9²	6		14	12	10	11³			4	7¹	8	13	3			5										23
	2²			7		14	9	10	12	13		4	6	8	11	3¹	1	5											24
			5	8²	6		13		11¹	12	3	7	4	14	10	2	1					9³							25
	5		4	7		12		10	14	3	6		13	11³	2		1	8		9²									26
	5		4	7		12		11²	14	3	6			10	2		1	8¹		9³	13								27
	2		5	6		9²	13	10¹		3	7		14	11	4		1	8³											28
	2	14	5²	6		12	9	10³		3	7		8¹	11	4	13	1												29
	2²	14	5	6		13	10¹	8³	9	3	7			11	4	12	1												30
	14	4³	8	6		13	9	5	11³	3	7			10¹	2	12	1												31
	2		5	6		13	10	8³	14	3²	7		12	11	4	9¹	1												32
	2¹		5	6²		12	10	8	14	3	7			13	11	4	9²	1											33
	2			7		10	8²	12	13	3	6		4	11³	5	9¹	1				14								34
			5	7		11¹	9³	13	12	14		8	4	3	10	2	6²	1					12						35
			5	7			8³	10	11²	6	4		3	14	12	2	9¹	1					13						36
	2		5	7		9²		14	10³	8	4		3	11	13	6	1					12							37
1	2		5	6	14		9	10	11¹	4³	3			13	12	8					7²								38

FA Cup
Third Round   Bristol C   (h)   3-0
Fourth Round   Southampton   (a)   0-1

Carabao Cup
Second Round   Bristol C   (h)   2-3

WEST BROMWICH ALBION

FOUNDATION

There is a well known story that when employees of Salter's Spring Works in West Bromwich decided to form a football club, they had to send someone to the nearby Association Football stronghold of Wednesbury to purchase a football. A weekly subscription of 2d (less than 1p) was imposed and the name of the new club was West Bromwich Strollers.

The Hawthorns, West Bromwich, West Midlands B71 4LF.

Telephone: (0871) 271 1100.

Fax: (0871) 271 9851.

Ticket Office: (0121) 227 2227.

Website: www.wba.co.uk

Email: enquiries@wbafc.co.uk

Ground Capacity: 26,688.

Record Attendance: 64,815 v Arsenal, FA Cup 6th rd, 6 March 1937.

Pitch Measurements: 105m × 68m (114yd × 74yd).

Chairman: Li Piyue.

Chief Executive: Mark Jenkins.

Head Coach: Darren Moore.

Assistant Head Coach: James Shan.

Colours: Navy blue and white striped shirts, white shorts with navy blue trim, white socks with navy blue trim.

Year Formed: 1878.

Turned Professional: 1885.

Previous Name: 1878, West Bromwich Strollers; 1881, West Bromwich Albion.

Club Nicknames: 'The Throstles', 'The Baggies', 'Albion'.

Grounds: 1878, Coopers Hill; 1879, Dartmouth Park; 1881, Bunns Field, Walsall Street; 1882, Four Acres (Dartmouth Cricket Club); 1885, Stoney Lane; 1900, The Hawthorns.

First Football League Game: 8 September 1888, Football League, v Stoke (a) W 2–0 – Roberts; Jack Horton, Green; Ezra Horton, Perry, Bayliss; Bassett, Woodhall (1), Hendry, Pearson, Wilson (1).

Record League Victory: 12–0 v Darwen, Division 1, 4 April 1892 – Reader; Jack Horton, McCulloch; Reynolds (2), Perry, Groves; Bassett (3), McLeod, Nicholls (1), Pearson (4), Geddes (1), (1 og).

Record Cup Victory: 10–1 v Chatham (away), FA Cup 3rd rd, 2 March 1889 – Roberts; Jack Horton, Green; Timmins (1), Charles Perry, Ezra Horton; Bassett (2), Walter Perry (1), Bayliss (2), Pearson, Wilson (3), (1 og).

League Champions: Division 1 – 1919–20; FL C – 2007–08; Division 2 – 1901–02, 1910–11.
Runners-up: Division 1 – 1924–25, 1953–54; FL C – 2009–10; First Division – 2001–02, 2003–04; Division 2 – 1930–31, 1948–49.
FA Cup Winners: 1888, 1892, 1931, 1954, 1968.
Runners-up: 1886, 1887, 1895, 1912, 1935.
League Cup Winners: 1966.
Runners-up: 1967, 1970.
European Competitions
Fairs Cup: 1966–67.
UEFA Cup: 1978–79 *(qf)*, 1979–80, 1981–82.
European Cup-Winners' Cup: 1968–69 *(qf)*.

THE Sun FACT FILE

West Bromwich Albion's Anglo-Italian Cup tie with Lanerossi Vicenza in May 1970 was abandoned after 75 minutes after players from both sides became involved in violent incidents on the pitch. The match was tied 1-1 at the time and the tournament committee decided the game should not be replayed.

Record Defeat: 3–10 v Stoke C, Division 1, 4 February 1937.

Most League Points (2 for a win): 60, Division 1, 1919–20.

Most League Points (3 for a win): 91, FL C, 2009–10.

Most League Goals: 105, Division 2, 1929–30.

Highest League Scorer in Season: William 'Ginger' Richardson, 39, Division 1, 1935–36.

Most League Goals in Total Aggregate: Tony Brown, 218, 1963–79.

Most League Goals in One Match: 6, Jimmy Cookson v Blackpool, Division 2, 17 September 1927.

Most Capped Player: James Morrison, 46, Scotland.

Most League Appearances: Tony Brown, 574, 1963–80.

Youngest League Player: Charlie Wilson, 16 years 73 days v Oldham Ath, 1 October 1921.

Record Transfer Fee Received: £12,000,000 (rising to £15,000,000) from Stoke C for Saido Berahino, January 2017

Record Transfer Fee Paid: £15,000,000 to RB Leipzig for Oliver Burke, August 2017.

Football League Record: 1888 Founder Member of Football League; 1901–02 Division 2; 1902–04 Division 1; 1904–11 Division 2; 1911–27 Division 1; 1927–31 Division 2; 1931–38 Division 1; 1938–49 Division 2; 1949–73 Division 1; 1973–76 Division 2; 1976–86 Division 1; 1986–91 Division 2; 1991–92 Division 3; 1992–93 Division 2; 1993–2002 Division 1; 2002–03 FA Premier League; 2003–04 Division 1; 2004–06 FA Premier League; 2006–08 FL C; 2008–09 FA Premier League; 2009–10 FL C; 2010–18 FA Premier League; 2018– FL C.

LATEST SEQUENCES

Longest Sequence of League Wins: 11, 5.4.1930 – 8.9.1930.

Longest Sequence of League Defeats: 11, 28.10.1995 – 26.12.1995.

Longest Sequence of League Draws: 5, 30.8.1999 – 3.10.1999.

Longest Sequence of Unbeaten League Matches: 17, 7.9.1957 – 7.12.1957.

Longest Sequence Without a League Win: 20, 27.8.2017 – 2.1.2018.

Successive Scoring Runs: 36 from 26.4.1958.

Successive Non-scoring Runs: 5 from 1.4.2017.

MANAGERS

Louis Ford 1890–92
(Secretary-Manager)
Henry Jackson 1892–94
(Secretary-Manager)
Edward Stephenson 1894–95
(Secretary-Manager)
Clement Keys 1895–96
(Secretary-Manager)
Frank Heaven 1896–1902
(Secretary-Manager)
Fred Everiss 1902–48
Jack Smith 1948–52
Jesse Carver 1952
Vic Buckingham 1953–59
Gordon Clark 1959–61
Archie Macaulay 1961–63
Jimmy Hagan 1963–67
Alan Ashman 1967–71
Don Howe 1971–75
Johnny Giles 1975–77
Ronnie Allen 1977
Ron Atkinson 1978–81
Ronnie Allen 1981–82
Ron Wylie 1982–84
Johnny Giles 1984–85
Nobby Stiles 1985–86
Ron Saunders 1986–87
Ron Atkinson 1987–88
Brian Talbot 1988–91
Bobby Gould 1991–92
Ossie Ardiles 1992–93
Keith Burkinshaw 1993–94
Alan Buckley 1994–97
Ray Harford 1997
Denis Smith 1997–1999
Brian Little 1999–2000
Gary Megson 2000–04
Bryan Robson 2004–06
Tony Mowbray 2006–09
Roberto Di Matteo 2009–11
Roy Hodgson 2011–12
Steve Clarke 2012–13
Pepe Mel 2014
Alan Irvine 2014
Tony Pulis 2015–17
Alan Pardew 2017–18
Darren Moore May 2018–

TEN YEAR LEAGUE RECORD

		P	W	D	L	F	A	Pts	Pos
2008-09	PR Lge	38	8	8	22	36	67	32	20
2009-10	FL C	46	26	13	7	89	48	91	2
2010-11	PR Lge	38	12	11	15	56	71	47	11
2011-12	PR Lge	38	13	8	17	45	52	47	10
2012-13	PR Lge	38	14	7	17	53	57	49	8
2013-14	PR Lge	38	7	15	16	43	59	36	17
2014-15	PR Lge	38	11	11	16	38	51	44	13
2015-16	PR Lge	38	10	13	15	34	48	43	14
2016-17	PR Lge	38	12	9	17	43	51	45	10
2017-18	PR Lge	38	6	13	19	31	56	31	20

DID YOU KNOW ?

West Bromwich Albion regularly attracted crowds of 30,000 or more in the immediate post-war years. An all-time high average attendance of 38,910 was achieved in the 1949–50 season when the Baggies finished in a mid-table position in the First Division.

WEST BROMWICH ALBION – PREMIER LEAGUE 2017–18 LEAGUE RECORD

Match No.	Date	Venue	Opponents	Result	H/T Score	Lg Pos.	Goalscorers	Attendance
1	Aug 12	H	Bournemouth	W 1-0	1-0	6	Hegazi [31]	25,011
2	19	A	Burnley	W 1-0	0-0	2	Robson-Kanu [71]	19,619
3	27	H	Stoke C	D 1-1	0-0	5	Rodriguez [61]	22,704
4	Sept 9	A	Brighton & HA	L 1-3	0-1	8	Morrison [77]	30,381
5	16	A	West Ham U	D 0-0	0-0	10		24,942
6	25	A	Arsenal	L 0-2	0-1	12		59,134
7	30	H	Watford	D 2-2	2-1	10	Rondon [18], Evans [21]	24,606
8	Oct 16	A	Leicester C	D 1-1	1-0	10	Chadli [63]	30,203
9	21	A	Southampton	L 0-1	0-0	13		29,947
10	28	H	Manchester C	L 2-3	1-2	14	Rodriguez [13], Phillips [90]	24,003
11	Nov 4	A	Huddersfield T	L 0-1	0-1	15		24,169
12	18	H	Chelsea	L 0-4	0-3	17		23,592
13	25	A	Tottenham H	D 1-1	1-0	17	Rondon [4]	65,905
14	28	H	Newcastle U	D 2-2	1-0	16	Robson-Kanu [45], Field [56]	25,534
15	Dec 2	H	Crystal Palace	D 0-0	0-0	17		23,531
16	9	A	Swansea C	L 0-1	0-0	17		19,580
17	13	A	Liverpool	D 0-0	0-0	17		53,243
18	17	H	Manchester U	L 1-2	0-2	19	Barry [77]	24,782
19	23	A	Stoke C	L 1-3	0-2	19	Rondon [51]	29,057
20	26	H	Everton	D 0-0	0-0	19		25,364
21	31	H	Arsenal	D 1-1	0-0	19	Rodriguez (pen) [89]	26,223
22	Jan 2	A	West Ham U	L 1-2	1-0	19	McClean [30]	56,888
23	13	H	Brighton & HA	W 2-0	1-0	19	Evans [4], Dawson [55]	25,240
24	20	A	Everton	D 1-1	1-0	19	Rodriguez [7]	39,061
25	31	A	Manchester C	L 0-3	0-1	20		53,241
26	Feb 3	H	Southampton	L 2-3	1-2	20	Hegazi [4], Rondon [72]	25,911
27	12	A	Chelsea	L 0-3	0-1	20		41,071
28	24	H	Huddersfield T	L 1-2	0-0	20	Dawson [64]	25,920
29	Mar 3	A	Watford	L 0-1	0-0	20		20,022
30	10	H	Leicester C	L 1-4	1-1	20	Rondon [8]	23,558
31	17	A	Bournemouth	L 1-2	0-0	20	Rodriguez [49]	10,242
32	31	H	Burnley	L 1-2	0-1	20	Rondon [83]	23,455
33	Apr 7	H	Swansea C	D 1-1	0-0	20	Rodriguez [54]	23,297
34	15	A	Manchester U	W 1-0	0-0	20	Rodriguez [73]	75,095
35	21	H	Liverpool	D 2-2	0-1	20	Livermore [79], Rondon [88]	24,520
36	28	A	Newcastle U	W 1-0	1-0	20	Phillips [29]	52,283
37	May 5	H	Tottenham H	W 1-0	0-0	19	Livermore [90]	23,685
38	13	A	Crystal Palace	L 0-2	0-0	20		25,357

Final League Position: 20

GOALSCORERS

League (31): Rodriguez 7 (1 pen), Rondon 7, Dawson 2, Evans 2, Hegazi 2, Livermore 2, Phillips 2, Robson-Kanu 2, Barry 1, Chadli 1, Field 1, McClean 1, Morrison 1.
FA Cup (6): Rodriguez 3, Rondon 2, own goal 1.
Carabao Cup (4): Phillips 1, Rodriguez 1, Rondon 1, Yacob 1.
Checkatrade Trophy (2): Burke 1, Tulloch 1.

Foster B 37	Nyom A 25 + 4	Dawson C 28	Hegazi A 38	Brunt C 22 + 4	Yacob C 9 + 7	Phillips M 23 + 7	Livermore J 30 + 4	Field S 7 + 3	McClean J 14 + 16	Rodriguez J 31 + 6	Harper R — + 1	Robson-Kanu H 8 + 13	Rondon J 32 + 4	Barry G 22 + 3	Morrison J 2 + 2	Burke O 2 + 13	Evans O 2 + 13	Krychowiak G 20 + 7	Gibbs K 32 + 1	Myhill B 1	Chadli N 2 + 3	McAuley G 5 + 4	Sturridge D 2 + 4	Match No.
1	2	3	4	5	6	7^2	8	9^1	10	11^1	12	13	14											1
1	2	3	4	5		7	9	8^1	10^2	11		12^4	13	6										2
1	2	3	4	5	12	8^3	7		13	10^2			11	6	9^1	14								3
1	5	2	4^2			7	8^1		10			11^3	6	14	13		3	9	12					4
1	14	2	3	8^3		10^2			13	11		12		7	9		4	6	5^1					5
1	5^1	2	3			14	6^2		10			11^3	13	8	12		4	7	9					6
1		2	3	10^2		8^1	13		12	9		14	11^3	7			4	6	5					7
	2	3					6		13	9^1			10	8			4	7	5	1	11^2	12		8
1	12	2	4			14	8			6			11	9^2			3^1	7	5		10^3	13		9
1	5		3			13	8		14	11		12	10^3	7			4	6^2	9			2^1		10
1	5		3			13	8		14	11		10^2	12	7			4	6^2	9			2^1		11
1			4		12	5^3	6		14	11^2		10	7			13	3	8^1	9			2		12
1	2		3		14	6	7	9^2	13	10^1		12	11	8^3			4		5					13
1	2		3		12	6	7	9^1	13			10	11	8^2			4	14	5^2					14
1	2		3		12		6	8	13	11^3		9^1	10	7^2		14	4		5					15
1	2		3	14	7		6	8^1	12	11^2		9^1	10			13	4		5					16
1	2		3	13	7		6		11	12		9^2	10				4	8^1	5					17
1	2		3	14	7^1		6		11	13			10	12		9^2	4	8^1	5					18
1	2		3	8			6		9^2	13		14	10	7		14	4		5^1		12^3			19
1		2	3	9		6^1	7^2		14	10		12	11^3	8		4	13	5						20
1	14	3	4	9^2		2^1	7		12	10		11^3		8		5	13	6						21
1		2	3	6^3		9^2			10	8^1		12	11	14		13	4	7	5					22
1	13	2^1	4	9		6	12			10^1			11	7		3^2	8	5			14			23
1		2	4	9^1		6	12		13	10^2		11	8			3^3	7	5			14			24
1	5	2	4		7	13		6^1	9	10		11^1	12			8^1					3	14		25
1	5^3	2	4	9	7^2	6			14	13		11	8	12				3	10^1					26
1		3	4	9^2	14	2			12			11	8^1	13	5	7	6				10^3			27
1		2	3	12		6^2	13		9^1	10		11	7^3	14	4	8	5							28
1		2	3	8		9	7^3	13	12	11^1		10		14	4	6^4	5							29
1	2	3	4	8		11^1	7	12		13		14	10			9^1		6^2	5					30
1	5	2	4	8^1	7	12	6	13		10^2		14	11			3^3		9						31
1	5	2	4	8	7	12	6			10^1			11	13	3		9^2							32
1	2	3	4	8		6	7		9	11^1		10				12	5							33
1	2	3	4	8	14	6^3	7		9	10		11^2				12	5				13			34
1	2	3	4	8		6	7		9^1	10^2		14	11		13	12	5^3							35
1	2	3	4	8		6	7		9^3	10^1		14	11^1		13	12	5							36
1	2	3	4	8		6	7		9^3	10^1			11^2			14	5				13	12		37
1	2	3	4	8			7		9	6^1		13	11^3			10^2	5				12	14		38

FA Cup

Third Round	Exeter C	(a)	2-0
Fourth Round	Liverpool	(a)	3-2
Fifth Round	Southampton	(h)	1-2

Carabao Cup

Second Round	Accrington S	(a)	3-1
Third Round	Manchester C	(h)	1-2

Checkatrade Trophy (WBA U21)

Northern Group E	Walsall	(a)	1-3
Northern Group E	Shrewsbury T	(a)	0-3
Northern Group E	Coventry C	(a)	1-2

WEST HAM UNITED

FOUNDATION

Thames Ironworks FC was formed by employees of this famous shipbuilding company in 1895 and entered the FA Cup in their initial season at Chatham and the London League in their second. The committee wanted to introduce professional players, so Thames Ironworks was wound up in June 1900 and relaunched a month later as West Ham United.

London Stadium, Queen Elizabeth Olympic Park, London E20 2ST.

Telephone: (020) 8548 2748.

Fax: (020) 8548 2758.

Ticket Office: (0333) 030 1966.

Website: www.whufc.com

Email: supporterservices@westhamunited.co.uk

Ground Capacity: 57,000.

Record Attendance: 42,322 v Tottenham H, Division 1, 17 October 1970 (at Boleyn Ground); 56,996 v Manchester U, FA Premier League, 2 January 2017 (at London Stadium).

Pitch Measurements: 105m × 68m (114yd × 74yd).

Joint Chairmen: David Sullivan and David Gold.

Vice-Chairman: Baroness Karren Brady CBE.

Chief Operating Officer: Ben Illingworth.

Manager: Manuel Pellegrini.

Assistant Manager: Rueben Cousillas.

Colours: Claret shirts with sky blue trim, white shorts, white socks with claret and sky blue and claret trim.

Year Formed: 1895.

Turned Professional: 1900.

Previous Name: 1895, Thames Ironworks FC; 1900, West Ham United.

Club Nicknames: 'The Hammers', 'The Irons'.

Grounds: 1895, Memorial Recreation Ground, Canning Town; 1904, Boleyn Ground; 2016, London Stadium.

First Football League Game: 30 August 1919, Division 2, v Lincoln C (h) D 1–1 – Hufton; Cope, Lee; Lane, Fenwick, McCrae; David Smith, Moyes (1), Puddefoot, Morris, Bradshaw.

Record League Victory: 8–0 v Rotherham U, Division 2, 8 March 1958 – Gregory; Bond, Wright; Malcolm, Brown, Lansdowne; Grice, Smith (2), Keeble (2), Dick (4), Musgrove. 8–0 v Sunderland, Division 1, 19 October 1968 – Ferguson; Bonds, Charles; Peters, Stephenson, Moore (1); Redknapp, Boyce, Brooking (1), Hurst (6), Sissons.

HONOURS

League Champions: Division 2 – 1957–58, 1980–81.
Runners-up: First Division – 1992–93; Division 2 – 1922–23, 1990–91.
FA Cup Winners: 1964, 1975, 1980.
Runners-up: 1923, 2006.
League Cup: Runners-up: 1966, 1981.
European Competitions
UEFA Cup: 1999–2000; 2006–07.
Europa League: 2015–16, 2016–17.
European Cup-Winners' Cup: 1964–65 *(winners)*, 1965–66 *(sf)*, 1975–76 *(runners-up)*, 1980–81 *(qf)*.
Intertoto Cup: 1999 *(winners)*.

The Sun FACT FILE

On 15 December 1999 West Ham United drew their Football League Cup fourth-round tie at Aston Villa 2-2, winning the penalty shoot-out 5-4. However, it was subsequently discovered that one of the Hammers' substitutes, Manny Omoyinmi, had already featured for Gillingham earlier in the competition. The match was ordered to be replayed and Villa went through with a 3-1 victory.

Record Cup Victory: 10–0 v Bury, League Cup 2nd rd
(2nd leg), 25 October 1983 – Parkes; Stewart (1), Walford,
Bonds (Orr), Martin (1), Devonshire (2), Allen, Cottee (4),
Swindlehurst, Brooking (2), Pike.

Record Defeat: 2–8 v Blackburn R, Division 1,
26 December 1963; 0–6 v Oldham Ath, League Cup
semi-final (1st leg), 14 February 1990.

Most League Points (2 for a win): 66, Division 2, 1980–81.

Most League Points (3 for a win): 88, Division 1, 1992–93.

Most League Goals: 101, Division 2, 1957–58.

Highest League Scorer in Season: Vic Watson, 42,
Division 1, 1929–30.

Most League Goals in Total Aggregate: Vic Watson, 298,
1920–35.

Most League Goals in One Match: 6, Vic Watson v
Leeds U, Division 1, 9 February 1929; 6, Geoff Hurst v
Sunderland, Division 1, 19 October 1968.

Most Capped Player: Bobby Moore, 108, England.

Most League Appearances: Billy Bonds, 663, 1967–88.

MANAGERS
Syd King 1902–32
Charlie Paynter 1932–50
Ted Fenton 1950–61
Ron Greenwood 1961–74
(continued as General Manager to 1977)
John Lyall 1974–89
Lou Macari 1989–90
Billy Bonds 1990–94
Harry Redknapp 1994–2001
Glenn Roeder 2001–03
Alan Pardew 2003–06
Alan Curbishley 2006–08
Gianfranco Zola 2008–10
Avram Grant 2010–11
Sam Allardyce 2011–15
Slaven Bilic 2015–17
David Moyes 2017–18
Manuel Pellegrini May 2018–

Youngest League Player: Billy Williams, 16 years 221 days v Blackpool, 6 May 1922.

Record Transfer Fee Received: £25,000,000 from Marseille for Dmitri Payet, January 2017.

Record Transfer Fee Paid: £20,000,000 (rising to £25,000,000) to Stoke C for Marko Arnautovic, July
2017.

Football League Record: 1919 Elected to Division 2; 1923–32 Division 1; 1932–58 Division 2;
1958–78 Division 1; 1978–81 Division 2; 1981–89 Division 1; 1989–91 Division 2; 1991–93 Division 1;
1993–2003 FA Premier League; 2003–04 Division 1; 2004–05 FL C; 2005–11 FA Premier League;
2011–12 FL C; 2012– FA Premier League.

LATEST SEQUENCES

Longest Sequence of League Wins: 9, 19.10.1985 – 14.12.1985.

Longest Sequence of League Defeats: 9, 28.3.1932 – 29.8.1932.

Longest Sequence of League Draws: 5, 29.11.2015 – 26.12.2015.

Longest Sequence of Unbeaten League Matches: 27, 27.12.1980 – 10.10.1981.

Longest Sequence Without a League Win: 17, 31.1.1976 – 21.8.1976.

Successive Scoring Runs: 27 from 5.10.1957.

Successive Non-scoring Runs: 5 from 17.9.2006.

TEN YEAR LEAGUE RECORD								
		P	W	D	L	F	A	Pts	Pos
2008-09	PR Lge	38	14	9	15	42	45	51	9
2009-10	PR Lge	38	8	11	19	47	66	35	17
2010-11	PR Lge	38	7	12	19	43	70	33	20
2011-12	FL C	46	24	14	8	81	48	86	3
2012-13	PR Lge	38	12	10	16	45	53	46	10
2013-14	PR Lge	38	11	7	20	40	51	40	13
2014-15	PR Lge	38	12	11	15	44	47	47	12
2015-16	PR Lge	38	16	14	8	65	51	62	7
2016-17	PR Lge	38	12	9	17	47	64	45	11
2017-18	PR Lge	38	10	12	16	48	68	42	13

DID YOU KNOW ?

West Ham United twice played
Southern League Hereford United
in the FA Cup in the early 1970s
and on both occasions the first
game was drawn. The Hammers
won the replay in 1971–72 but lost
at Edgar Street in 1973–74. This is
the only time since entering the
Football League in 1919 that the
club has been eliminated from the
FA Cup by a non-league side.

WEST HAM UNITED – PREMIER LEAGUE 2017–18 LEAGUE RECORD

Match No.	Date	Venue	Opponents	Result		H/T Score	Lg Pos.	Goalscorers	Attendance
1	Aug 13	A	Manchester U	L	0-4	0-1	20		74,928
2	19	A	Southampton	L	2-3	1-2	20	Hernandez 2 [44, 73]	31,424
3	26	A	Newcastle U	L	0-3	0-1	20		52,093
4	Sept 11	H	Huddersfield T	W	2-0	0-0	18	Obiang [72], Ayew [77]	56,977
5	16	A	WBA	D	0-0	0-0	18		24,942
6	23	H	Tottenham H	L	2-3	0-2	18	Hernandez [65], Kouyate [87]	56,988
7	30	H	Swansea C	W	1-0	0-0	15	Sakho [90]	56,922
8	Oct 14	A	Burnley	D	1-1	1-0	14	Antonio [19]	20,945
9	20	H	Brighton & HA	L	0-3	0-2	17		56,977
10	28	A	Crystal Palace	D	2-2	2-0	16	Hernandez [31], Ayew [43]	25,242
11	Nov 4	H	Liverpool	L	1-4	0-2	17	Lanzini [55]	56,961
12	19	A	Watford	L	0-2	0-1	18		20,018
13	24	H	Leicester C	D	1-1	1-1	18	Kouyate [45]	56,897
14	29	A	Everton	L	0-4	0-2	18		38,242
15	Dec 3	A	Manchester C	L	1-2	1-0	19	Ogbonna [44]	54,203
16	9	H	Chelsea	W	1-0	1-0	18	Arnautovic [6]	56,953
17	13	H	Arsenal	D	0-0	0-0	19		56,921
18	16	A	Stoke C	W	3-0	1-0	15	Noble (pen) [19], Arnautovic [75], Sakho [86]	29,265
19	23	H	Newcastle U	L	2-3	1-1	17	Arnautovic [6], Ayew [69]	56,955
20	26	A	Bournemouth	D	3-3	1-1	17	Collins [7], Arnautovic 2 [81, 89]	10,596
21	Jan 2	A	WBA	W	2-1	0-1	16	Carroll 2 [59, 90]	56,888
22	4	A	Tottenham H	D	1-1	0-0	15	Obiang [70]	50,034
23	13	H	Huddersfield T	W	4-1	1-1	11	Noble [25], Arnautovic [46], Lanzini 2 [56, 61]	24,105
24	20	H	Bournemouth	D	1-1	0-0	11	Hernandez [73]	56,948
25	30	H	Crystal Palace	D	1-1	1-1	10	Noble (pen) [43]	56,911
26	Feb 3	A	Brighton & HA	L	1-3	1-1	12	Hernandez [30]	30,589
27	10	H	Watford	W	2-0	1-0	12	Hernandez [38], Arnautovic [78]	56,197
28	24	A	Liverpool	L	1-4	0-1	13	Antonio [59]	53,256
29	Mar 3	A	Swansea C	L	1-4	0-2	14	Antonio [78]	20,829
30	10	H	Burnley	L	0-3	0-0	16		56,904
31	31	H	Southampton	W	3-0	3-0	14	Joao Mario [13], Arnautovic 2 [17, 45]	56,882
32	Apr 8	A	Chelsea	D	1-1	0-1	14	Hernandez [73]	41,324
33	16	H	Stoke C	D	1-1	0-0	14	Carroll [90]	56,795
34	22	A	Arsenal	L	1-4	0-0	15	Arnautovic [64]	59,422
35	29	H	Manchester C	L	1-4	1-2	15	Cresswell [42]	56,904
36	May 5	A	Leicester C	W	2-0	1-0	15	Joao Mario [34], Noble [64]	32,013
37	10	H	Manchester U	D	0-0	0-0	15		56,902
38	13	H	Everton	W	3-1	1-0	13	Lanzini 2 [39, 82], Arnautovic [63]	56,926

Final League Position: 13

GOALSCORERS

League (48): Arnautovic 11, Hernandez 8, Lanzini 5, Noble 4 (2 pens), Antonio 3, Ayew 3, Carroll 3, Joao Mario 2, Kouyate 2, Obiang 2, Sakho 2, Collins 1, Cresswell 1, Ogbonna 1.
FA Cup (1): Burke 1.
Carabao Cup (8): Ayew 3, Ogbonna 2, Sakho 2, Masuaku 1.
Checkatrade Trophy (6): Martinez 2 (1 pen), Samuelsen 2, Kemp 1, Makasi 1.

Hart J 19	Zabaleta P 37	Reid W 17	Ogbonna A 32	Masuaku A 21+6	Noble M 28+1	Obiang P 18+3	Ayew A 9+9	Fernandes E 9+5	Arnautovic M 28+3	Hernandez J 16+12	Sakho D —+14	Rice D 15+11	Cresswell A 35+1	Fonte J 8	Antonio M 16+5	Collins J 12+1	Lanzini M 23+4	Kouyate C 32+1	Carroll A 7+9	Adrian 19	Byram S 2+3	Joao Mario E 12+1	Oxford R —+1	Hugill J —+3	Evra P 3+2	Cullen J —+2	Match No.
1	2	3	4	5^2	6^1	7	8	9^3	10	11	12	13	14														1
1	2		4		7	14	9^2	12	10^8	11	13	6^3	5	3	8^1												2
1	2		4		7^1		9^2		10	11	13	6^5	5	8	3	12	14										3
1	5	3			7^3	12			11	13	14	8	2	9	4		6	10^2									4
1	5	3			7	13			12	11^2	14	8	2	9	4^3		6	10^1									5
1	5	3	4	14	6		13		11^3	10		8	2^2	9^1			7	12									6
1	2	4		14	7^1		9^3		11^2	13		5	3	6	12	8	10										7
1	2	4		14		12			9^1	11^2	13	5	3	6	7^3	8	10^8										8
1	2	4		5		6	12	13	10^1	11		3	8	9	7^2												9
1	5^3		4	12	8		10	6		11		14	9^1	2^2	13	7	3										10
1		3	4	6^3	7	9	5^1	13	11^2	14		8				10	2	12									11
1	2	3	4	13	7	8		9^2		12		5				11	6	10^1									12
1	2	3	4	10^1	7	12		8^2		13		5				9	6	11									13
1	2	3^2	4	10		6^1	11		7^3		12	14	5		13		9	8									14
	5		3	9		8	14	7	13		12	2	4		11^3		10^1	6^2		1							15
	5	2	3	8	7	6	13		10^2	12		4		11^1		9				1							16
	2	3	4	6	7	8			11	12		5		10^1		9				1							17
	5	3	8	6^3	7		11^1	14	13	12	4		10^2	2	9					1							18
	5	2	3	8	7	10^1	11	13		4		9^2			2	10	6	12		1							19
	5^1	3	8	7^2	9^3	11	13		14	4		2	10	6	12					1							20
	5	2	3	8^2	12	7^3	9	13	14	4^1		10	6	11						1							21
	5	2	3	9	7	8	12			11^1	4	10^2	6	13						1							22
	5	3	9	8	7	12		11^1	13	4		2	10^2	6^3						1	14						23
	6	3	7			11			4	8	2	9^1								1	5	10	12				24
	6	3	7			11			4^8	8	12	2	9							1	5^1	10	13				25
	5	3	6			11^1	10^5	13	4	8	2		7		1	12	9^3	14									26
	5	3	7			11^2	14	13	4		12	2	10^1	6		1	9^2		8								27
	5	3^2		7		11	10		2	4		13		9	6	1	12		8^1								28
1	5	3	7			11	12		4		8	2	10	6			9^1										29
1	5	3	8	7		12	11^1		2	4		9^3			6^2		10	13	14								30
1	5	3	8	7		9^1	11	13	2	4^2					6		10^3	12	14								31
1	5	3	8^1	6		9^2	11	12	2	4		13	7	14			10^1										32
1	5	3	8^3	7		9^2	11	13	2	4		12	6	14			10^1										33
1	5	3	14	7		8^1	11	13	2	9		10^2	6		12			4^3									34
	5	3	8	7		13	11^1		2	4		10^2	6	12	1	9		14									35
	5	3	8^1	7			11		2	4		10	6	12	1	9											36
	5	3	8^2	7	13		12	11	2	4^3		14	10^1	6	1	9											37

FA Cup

Third Round	Shrewsbury T	(a)	0-0
Replay	Shrewsbury T	(h)	1-0
(aet)			
Fourth Round	Wigan Ath	(a)	0-2

Carabao Cup

Second Round	Cheltenham T	(a)	2-0
Third Round	Bolton W	(h)	3-0
Fourth Round	Tottenham H	(a)	3-2
Quarter-Final	Arsenal	(a)	0-1

Checkatrade Trophy (West Ham U U21)

Southern Group B	Swindon T	(a)	3-2
Southern Group B	Bristol R	(a)	3-1
Southern Group B	Wycombe W	(a)	0-2
Second Round South	Luton T	(a)	0-4

WIGAN ATHLETIC

FOUNDATION

Following the demise of Wigan Borough and their resignation from the Football League in 1931, a public meeting was called in Wigan at the Queen's Hall in May 1932 at which a new club, Wigan Athletic, was founded in the hope of carrying on in the Football League. With this in mind, they bought Springfield Park for £2,250, but failed to gain admission to the Football League until 46 years later.

The DW Stadium, Loire Drive, Newtown, Wigan, Lancashire WN5 0UZ.

Telephone: (01942) 774 000.

Fax: (01942) 770 477.

Ticket Office: (0871) 663 3552.

Website: www.wiganathletic.com

Email: feedback@wiganathletic.com

Ground Capacity: 25,138.

Record Attendance: 27,526 v Hereford U, 12 December 1953 (at Springfield Park); 25,133 v Manchester U, FA Premier League, 11 May 2008 (at DW Stadium).

Pitch Measurements: 105m × 68m (115yd × 74.5yd).

Chairman: David Sharpe.

Chief Executive: Jonathan Jackson.

Manager: Paul Cook.

Assistant Manager: Leam Richardson.

HONOURS

League Champions: FL 1 – 2015–16, 2017–18; Second Division – 2002–03; Third Division – 1996–97.
Runners-up: FL C – 2004–05.
FA Cup Winners: 2013.
League Cup: Runners-up: 2006.
League Trophy Winners: 1985, 1999.
European Competitions
Europa League: 2013–14.

Colours: Blue and white striped shirts, blue shorts with white trim, blue socks with gold trim.

Year Formed: 1932.

Turned Professional: 1932.

Club Nickname: 'The Latics'.

Grounds: 1932, Springfield Park; 1999, JJB Stadium (renamed the DW Stadium, 2009).

First Football League Game: 19 August 1978, Division 4, v Hereford U (a) D 0–0 – Brown; Hinnigan, Gore, Gillibrand, Ward, Davids, Corrigan, Purdie, Houghton, Wilkie, Wright.

Record League Victory: 7–0 v Oxford U, FL 1, 23 December 2017 – Walton; Bythe, Dunkley, Burn, Evans, Morsy, Massey (1), Powell (Toney), Jacobs (Robert G), Grigg (3) (Power 2), James.

Record Cup Victory: 6–0 v Carlisle U (a), FA Cup 1st rd, 24 November 1934 – Caunce; Robinson, Talbot; Paterson, Watson, Tufnell; Armes (2), Robson (1), Roberts (2), Felton, Scott (1).

Record Defeat: 1–9 v Tottenham H, FA Premier League, 22 November 2009; 0–8 v Chelsea, FA Premier League, 9 May 2010.

Most League Points (2 for a win): 55, Division 4, 1978–79 and 1979–80.

Most League Points (3 for a win): 100, Division 2, 2002–03.

THE Sun FACT FILE

Wigan Athletic comfortably won the Cheshire League title in 1934–35 scoring 153 goals in the 42 games, an all-time club record total. Leading scorer Jack Roberts netted 46 goals in league games and a further 11 in the FA Cup, also missing a penalty. His total of FA Cup goals remains a seasonal record for the Latics.

Most League Goals: 89, FL 1, 2017–18.

Highest League Scorer in Season: Graeme Jones, 31, Division 3, 1996–97.

Most League Goals in Total Aggregate: Andy Liddell, 70, 1998–2004.

Most League Goals in One Match: Not more than three goals by one player.

Most Capped Players: Kevin Kilbane, 22 (110), Republic of Ireland; Henri Camara, 22 (99), Senegal.

Most League Appearances: Kevin Langley, 317, 1981–86, 1990–94.

Youngest League Player: Steve Nugent, 16 years 132 days v Leyton Orient, 16 September 1989.

Record Transfer Fee Received: £15,250,000 from Manchester U for Antonio Valencia, June 2009.

Record Transfer Fee Paid: £7,000,000 to Newcastle U for Charles N'Zogbia, January 2009.

Football League Record: 1978 Elected to Division 4; 1982–92 Division 3; 1992–93 Division 2; 1993–97 Division 3; 1997–2003 Division 2; 2003–04 Division 1; 2004–05 FL C; 2005–13 FA Premier League; 2013–15 FL C; 2015–16 FL 1; 2016–17 FL C; 2017–18 FL 1; 2018– FL C.

LATEST SEQUENCES

Longest Sequence of League Wins: 11, 2.11.2002 – 18.1.2003.

Longest Sequence of League Defeats: 8, 10.9.2011 – 6.11.2011.

Longest Sequence of League Draws: 6, 11.12.2001 – 5.1.2002.

Longest Sequence of Unbeaten League Matches: 25, 8.5.1999 – 3.1.2000.

Longest Sequence Without a League Win: 14, 9.5.1989 – 17.10.1989.

Successive Scoring Runs: 24 from 27.4.1996.

Successive Non-scoring Runs: 4 from 25.4.2015.

MANAGERS

Charlie Spencer 1932–37
Jimmy Milne 1946–47
Bob Pryde 1949–52
Ted Goodier 1952–54
Walter Crook 1954–55
Ron Suart 1955–56
Billy Cooke 1956
Sam Barkas 1957
Trevor Hitchen 1957–58
Malcolm Barrass 1958–59
Jimmy Shirley 1959
Pat Murphy 1959–60
Allenby Chilton 1960
Johnny Ball 1961–63
Allan Brown 1963–66
Alf Craig 1966–67
Harry Leyland 1967–68
Alan Saunders 1968
Ian McNeill 1968–70
Gordon Milne 1970–72
Les Rigby 1972–74
Brian Tiler 1974–76
Ian McNeill 1976–81
Larry Lloyd 1981–83
Harry McNally 1983–85
Bryan Hamilton 1985–86
Ray Mathias 1986–89
Bryan Hamilton 1989–93
Dave Philpotts 1993
Kenny Swain 1993–94
Graham Barrow 1994–95
John Deehan 1995–98
Ray Mathias 1998–99
John Benson 1999–2000
Bruce Rioch 2000–01
Steve Bruce 2001
Paul Jewell 2001–07
Chris Hutchings 2007
Steve Bruce 2007–09
Roberto Martinez 2009–13
Owen Coyle 2013
Uwe Rosler 2013–14
Malky Mackay 2014–15
Gary Caldwell 2015–16
Warren Joyce 2016–17
Paul Cook May 2017–

TEN YEAR LEAGUE RECORD

		P	W	D	L	F	A	Pts	Pos
2008-09	PR Lge	38	12	9	17	34	45	45	11
2009-10	PR Lge	38	9	9	20	37	79	36	16
2010-11	PR Lge	38	9	15	14	40	61	42	16
2011-12	PR Lge	38	11	10	17	42	62	43	15
2012-13	PR Lge	38	9	9	20	47	73	36	18
2013-14	FL C	46	21	10	15	61	48	73	5
2014-15	FL C	46	9	12	25	39	64	39	23
2015-16	FL 1	46	24	15	7	82	45	87	1
2016-17	FL C	46	10	12	24	40	57	42	23
2017-18	FL 1	46	29	11	6	89	29	98	1

DID YOU KNOW ?

Wigan Athletic created a new club record in the 2017–18 season when they achieved 27 clean sheets in their Football League campaign. This included a run of 700 minutes without conceding at the turn of the year.

WIGAN ATHLETIC – SKY BET LEAGUE ONE 2017–18 LEAGUE RECORD

Match No.	Date		Venue	Opponents	Result	H/T Score	Lg Pos.	Goalscorers	Atten- dance
1	Aug	5	A	Milton Keynes D	W 1-0	1-0	10	Powell [38]	9164
2		13	H	Bury	W 4-1	1-1	3	Jacobs [13], Powell 2 (1 pen) [53, 64 (p)], Evans [90]	9159
3		19	A	Oldham Ath	W 2-0	2-0	1	Toney [8], Jacobs [16]	5446
4		26	H	Portsmouth	D 1-1	1-0	2	Toney [8]	9685
5	Sept	9	A	Shrewsbury T	L 0-1	0-1	8		6929
6		12	H	Charlton Ath	W 3-0	1-0	6	Massey 2 [44, 70], Morsy [87]	10,172
7		16	H	Bristol R	W 3-0	1-0	5	Powell [30], Grigg [49], Massey [90]	8732
8		19	A	Northampton T	W 1-0	0-0	2	Jacobs [56]	7777
9		23	A	Peterborough U	L 2-3	1-0	4	Taylor, S (og) [33], Colclough [87]	6099
10		26	H	Plymouth Arg	W 1-0	0-0	2	Powell (pen) [83]	7868
11		30	H	Walsall	W 2-0	1-0	2	Grigg 2 (1 pen) [30, 54 (p)]	8107
12	Oct	7	A	Scunthorpe U	W 2-1	0-0	2	Burn [51], Powell [74]	4480
13		14	H	Southend U	W 3-0	1-0	1	Jacobs [8], Powell [84], Toney [88]	8133
14		17	A	Gillingham	D 1-1	0-0	2	Morsy [82]	4705
15		21	A	Blackpool	W 3-1	1-1	2	Dunkley 2 [45, 54], Perkins [82]	5817
16		28	H	Blackburn R	D 0-0	0-0	2		11,211
17	Nov	18	H	Bradford C	L 1-2	1-1	2	Dunkley [24]	10,649
18		21	H	Doncaster R	W 3-0	2-0	2	Jacobs [40], Colclough 2 [45, 58]	7966
19		25	A	Rotherham U	W 3-1	2-1	1	Grigg [14], Bruce [28], Jacobs [60]	8443
20	Dec	9	H	Fleetwood T	W 2-0	2-0	1	Powell [7], Burn [38]	8879
21		16	A	AFC Wimbledon	W 4-0	0-0	1	Jacobs [57], Powell [73], Power [80], Toney [90]	4289
22		23	A	Oxford U	W 7-0	3-0	1	Grigg 3 [11, 52, 54], Powell [18], Massey [29], Power 2 [62, 77]	7957
23		26	H	Shrewsbury T	D 0-0	0-0	1		11,115
24		29	H	Charlton Ath	D 0-0	0-0	1		9297
25	Jan	1	A	Northampton T	W 1-0	1-0	1	Powell [5]	5328
26		13	H	Peterborough U	D 0-0	0-0	1		8602
27		20	A	Plymouth Arg	W 3-1	2-1	1	Grigg [29], Massey [45], Burn [69]	11,942
28	Feb	3	H	Gillingham	W 2-0	2-0	1	Grigg [10], Powell [34]	8384
29		10	A	Southend U	L 1-3	0-2	1	Vaughan [67]	7623
30		13	H	Blackpool	L 0-2	0-2	2		8302
31		24	H	Rochdale	W 1-0	1-0	3	Jacobs [12]	8654
32	Mar	4	A	Blackburn R	D 2-2	0-2	3	Grigg [63], Power [73]	16,142
33		10	A	Scunthorpe U	D 3-3	2-2	3	Dunkley [13], Grigg [43], Roberts, G [87]	8438
34		14	A	Bradford C	W 1-0	0-0	2	Jacobs [90]	19,413
35		21	A	Walsall	W 3-0	3-0	3	Jacobs [31], Fulton [35], Dunkley [40]	4477
36		24	A	Bury	W 2-0	1-0	2	Powell [26], Dunkley [50]	5207
37		30	H	Oldham Ath	W 3-0	1-0	1	Grigg [40], Vaughan [48], Powell [66]	10,625
38	Apr	2	A	Portsmouth	L 1-2	0-1	3	Grigg [89]	17,842
39		7	H	Milton Keynes D	W 5-1	2-1	2	Grigg 3 [11, 74, 76], Ebanks-Landell (og) [24], Powell [57]	8404
40		10	A	Rochdale	W 4-1	1-0	1	Burn [17], Vaughan [54], Jacobs [60], Grigg [62]	3850
41		14	H	Rotherham U	D 0-0	0-0	1		9630
42		17	H	Oxford U	W 1-0	1-0	1	Grigg [87]	8316
43		21	H	Fleetwood T	W 4-0	2-0	1	Power [33], Massey [37], Burn [57], Dunkley [66]	3836
44		24	A	Bristol R	D 1-1	0-1	1	Colclough [80]	8414
45		28	H	AFC Wimbledon	D 1-1	0-1	1	Jacobs [69]	12,554
46	May	5	A	Doncaster R	W 1-0	0-0	1	Grigg [75]	12,057

Final League Position: 1

GOALSCORERS

League (89): Grigg 19 (1 pen), Powell 15 (2 pens), Jacobs 12, Dunkley 7, Massey 6, Burn 5, Power 5, Colclough 4, Toney 4, Vaughan 3, Morsy 2, Bruce 1, Evans 1, Fulton 1, Perkins 1, Roberts, G 1, own goals 2.
FA Cup (14): Grigg 7 (1 pen), Toney 2, Burn 1, Elder 1, Evans 1, Morsy 1, own goal 1.
Carabao Cup (3): Colclough 1, Flores 1, Laurent 1.
Checkatrade Trophy (5): Colclough 1, Evans 1 (1 pen), Gilbey 1, Hunt 1, Maffeo 1.

Walton C 31	Byrne N 44	Dunkley C 43	Burn D 45	Elder C 24+3	Evans L 20	Morsy S 41	Massey G 35+7	Powell N 38+1	Jacobs M 44	Toney I 10+14	Thomas T —+3	Grigg W 29+14	Colclough R 11+15	James R 22	Gilbey A —+2	Jones J 15	Bruce A 4+2	Roberts G 6+21	Power M 29+11	Perkins D 2+11	Hunt N —+7	Vaughan J 7+12	Walker J 1+1	Fulton J 4+1	Daniels D 1	Cole D —+6	Match No.
1	2	3	4	5¹	6	7	8¹	9	10	11³	12	13	14														1
1	2	3	4			7	6	11²	9	8	10¹			14	13	5	12										2
1	2	4	3			7	6	9³	11²	8	10¹			13	14	5	12										3
1	2	3¹	4			6	7	11³	10²	8		9	12	13	14	5											4
	2		4			7	6	10¹	9²	8	11³			12	13¹	5		1	3	14							5
	2		4	14		7	6	10	9¹	8²	12			11³		5		1	3	13							6
	2		4			6	8¹	9	10³	7	12			11²		5		1	3	13	14						7
	2	3	4			7	6	9¹		8	12			11²	13	5		1	10³	14							8
	2	3	4		6			9²	10¹	7	11³			14	12	5		1		13	8						9
	2	3	4	12	7	6	9	10³	8	13				11³		5¹		1			14						10
	2	3	4	5	6³	7	9	10¹	8²					11				1		14	13	12					11
	2	3	4	5	7¹		8²	9¹		14	13	11³						1		10	6	12					12
	2	3	4	5		7	8	9²	10¹	12				11³				1		13	6		14				13
	2	3	4	5			6	8¹	9	10	11²			12²				1		13	7		14				14
	2	9	11	3			4	7²	10³	8	6¹							1		13	5	12	14				15
	2	3	4	5		6	7²	9	10	11¹		12						1		13	8						16
	2	4	3	5		7	10¹	9³	6²	11		14						1		12	8	13					17
	2	8	11		5²	3	12		7¹	14		6	10³	9				1			4	13					18
	2	3				7	6	13		8³	12	11²	10¹	5		1	4	14		9							19
1	2	3	4		6	7	12	9¹	10	14		11³	8²	5					13								20
1	2	3	4			7	6	8¹	9	10	14		11²		5				12	13							21
1	2	3	4			7	6	8	9²	10³	13		11¹		5				14	12							22
1	2	3	4			7	6	10²	9¹	8	12		11³		5				13		14						23
1	2	3	4	5	7		6	10³	9¹	8²	12		11						14	13							24
1	2	3	4			7	6	8²	9	10	13		11³		5				12	14							25
1	2	3	4	14			6	10³	9	8¹			11²	13	5				7			12					26
1	2	3	4				6	10³	9¹	8			11²	14	5		13		7			12					27
1	2	3	4			7			9¹	10			11¹	8²	5				6		13	12	14				28
1	2	3	4	5			6	8³	9¹	10²			11	14				12	7		13						29
1	2	3	4				6	10²	9²	8¹			11		5				12	7		13	14				30
1		3	4					13		10			14	8¹	5				9	12		11³	6³	7	2		31
2¹		3	4			6	8²	9¹	10				11						7	14		12	13				32
2¹		3	4			6		9	10				11		5³		13	14	7	8²		12					33
1	2	3	4	5		7	8³	6	10				12	13				9			11²			14			34
1	2	3	4	5			9	10¹					12	8				13	6		11³		7²	14			35
1	2	3	4	5			14	9¹	10				8¹					12	6	13	11		7²				36
1	2	3	4	5		6	13	9¹	10				11¹	8²				14	7		12						37
1	2	3	4	5		7	8¹	9	10³				12	13				14	6		11²						38
1	2	3	4	5		6	10²	9³	8				11¹					14	7		13	12					39
1	2	3	4	5		6	10¹	9³	8				11²					13	7		12	14					40
1	2	3	4	5		6	10³	9²	8				11¹	14				12	7		13						41
1		3	4	5		6	13		10				12	8²				9	2		11³		7¹		14		42
1	2	3	4	5		6	10¹						11³	8²				9	7	14		12		13			43
1	2	3	4	5		7	8¹		10				12	13				9²	6		11³			14			44
1	2	3	4	5		6		12	8				11	10¹				9³	7²		13	14					45
1	2	3	4	5		6	8²	9	10³				11¹					14	7	12					13		46

FA Cup

First Round	Crawley T	(h)	2-1
Second Round	AFC Fylde	(a)	1-1
Replay	AFC Fylde	(h)	3-2
Third Round	Bournemouth	(a)	2-2
Replay	Bournemouth	(h)	3-0
Fourth Round	West Ham U	(h)	2-0
Fifth Round	Manchester C	(h)	1-0
Sixth Round	Southampton	(h)	0-2

Carabao Cup

First Round	Blackpool	(h)	2-1
Second Round	Aston Villa	(a)	1-4

Checkatrade Trophy

Northern Group B	Blackpool	(a)	1-1
(Wigan Ath won 5-4 on penalties)			
Northern Group B	Middlesbrough U21	(h)	4-1
Northern Group B	Accrington S	(h)	0-4

WOLVERHAMPTON WANDERERS

FOUNDATION

Enthusiasts of the game at St Luke's School, Blakenhall formed a club in 1877. In the same neighbourhood a cricket club called Blakenhall Wanderers had a football section. Several St Luke's footballers played cricket for them and shortly before the start of the 1879–80 season the two amalgamated and Wolverhampton Wanderers FC was brought into being.

Molineux Stadium, Waterloo Road, Wolverhampton WV1 4QR.

Telephone: (0871) 222 2220.

Fax: (01902) 687 006.

Ticket Office: (0871) 222 1877.

Website: wolves.co.uk

Email: info@wolves.co.uk

Ground Capacity: 31,700.

Record Attendance: 61,315 v Liverpool, FA Cup 5th rd, 11 February 1939.

Pitch Measurements: 105m × 68m (115yd × 74yd).

Executive Chairman: Jeff Shi.

Managing Director: Laurie Dalrymple.

Head Coach: Nuno Espírito Santo.

Assistant Head Coach: Rui Pedro Silva.

Colours: Gold shirts with black trim, black shorts with gold trim, gold socks with black trim.

Year Formed: 1877* (*see Foundation*).

Turned Professional: 1888.

Previous Names: 1879, St Luke's combined with Wanderers Cricket Club to become Wolverhampton Wanderers (1923) Ltd. New limited companies followed in 1982 and 1986 (current).

Club Nickname: 'Wolves'.

Grounds: 1877, Windmill Field; 1879, John Harper's Field; 1881, Dudley Road; 1889, Molineux.

First Football League Game: 8 September 1888, Football League, v Aston Villa (h) D 1–1 – Baynton; Baugh, Mason; Fletcher, Allen, Lowder; Hunter, Cooper, Anderson, White, Cannon, (1 og).

Record League Victory: 10–1 v Leicester C, Division 1, 15 April 1938 – Sidlow; Morris, Dowen; Galley, Cullis, Gardiner; Maguire (1), Horace Wright, Westcott (4), Jones (1), Dorsett (4).

Record Cup Victory: 14–0 v Crosswell's Brewery, FA Cup 2nd rd, 13 November 1886 – Ike Griffiths; Baugh, Mason; Pearson, Allen (1), Lowder; Hunter (4), Knight (2), Brodie (4), Bernie Griffiths (2), Wood. Plus one goal 'scrambled through'.

HONOURS

League Champions: Division 1 – 1953–54, 1957–58, 1958–59; FL C – 2008–09, 2017–18; Division 2 – 1931–32, 1976–77; FL 1 – 2013–14; Division 3 – 1988–89; Division 3N – 1923–24; Division 4 – 1987–88.
Runners-up: Division 1 – 1937–38, 1938–39, 1949–50, 1954–55, 1959–60; Division 2 – 1966–67, 1982–83.
FA Cup Winners: 1893, 1908, 1949, 1960.
Runners-up: 1889, 1896, 1921, 1939.
League Cup Winners: 1974, 1980.
League Trophy Winners: 1988.
Texaco Cup Winners: 1971.
European Competitions
European Cup: 1958–59, 1959–60 (*qf*).
UEFA Cup: 1971–72 (*runners-up*), 1973–74, 1974–75, 1980–81.
European Cup-Winners' Cup: 1960–61 (*sf*).

Sun FACT FILE

The Boxing Day fixture of 1954 between Everton and Wolverhampton Wanderers attracted a crowd of 75,332, the largest for any Football League game played by the Wolves. The two teams had met at Molineux on Christmas Day when they attracted only 28,494 fans – the club's third-lowest home gate of the season.

Record Defeat: 1–10 v Newton Heath, Division 1, 15 October 1892.

Most League Points (2 for a win): 64, Division 1, 1957–58.

Most League Points (3 for a win): 103, FL 1, 2013–14.

Most League Goals: 115, Division 2, 1931–32.

Highest League Scorer in Season: Dennis Westcott, 38, Division 1, 1946–47.

Most League Goals in Total Aggregate: Steve Bull, 250, 1986–99.

Most League Goals in One Match: 5, Joe Butcher v Accrington, Division 1, 19 November 1892; 5, Tom Phillipson v Barnsley, Division 2, 26 April 1926; 5, Tom Phillipson v Bradford C, Division 2, 25 December 1926; 5, Billy Hartill v Notts Co, Division 2, 12 October 1929; 5, Billy Hartill v Aston Villa, Division 1, 3 September 1934.

Most Capped Player: Billy Wright, 105, England (70 consecutive).

Most League Appearances: Derek Parkin, 501, 1967–82.

Youngest League Player: Jimmy Mullen, 16 years 43 days v Leeds U, 18 February 1939.

Record Transfer Fee Received: £12,000,000 (rising to £14,000,000) from Sunderland for Steven Fletcher, August 2012.

Record Transfer Fee Paid: £15,800,000 to Porto for Ruben Neves, July 2017.

Football League Record: 1888 Founder Member of Football League: 1906–23 Division 2; 1923–24 Division 3 (N); 1924–32 Division 2; 1932–65 Division 1; 1965–67 Division 2; 1967–76 Division 1; 1976–77 Division 2; 1977–82 Division 1; 1982–83 Division 2; 1983–84 Division 1; 1984–85 Division 2; 1985–86 Division 3; 1986–88 Division 4; 1988–89 Division 3; 1989–92 Division 2; 1992–2003 Division 1; 2003–04 FA Premier League; 2004–09 FL C; 2009–12 FA Premier League; 2012–13 FL C; 2013–14 FL 1; 2014–18 FL C; 2018– FA Premier League.

MANAGERS

George Worrall 1877–85
(Secretary-Manager)
John Addenbrooke 1885–1922
George Jobey 1922–24
Albert Hoskins 1924–26
(had been Secretary since 1922)
Fred Scotchbrook 1926–27
Major Frank Buckley 1927–44
Ted Vizard 1944–48
Stan Cullis 1948–64
Andy Beattie 1964–65
Ronnie Allen 1966–68
Bill McGarry 1968–76
Sammy Chung 1976–78
John Barnwell 1978–81
Ian Greaves 1982
Graham Hawkins 1982–84
Tommy Docherty 1984–85
Bill McGarry 1985
Sammy Chapman 1985–86
Brian Little 1986
Graham Turner 1986–94
Graham Taylor 1994–95
Mark McGhee 1995–98
Colin Lee 1998–2000
Dave Jones 2001–04
Glenn Hoddle 2004–06
Mick McCarthy 2006–12
Stale Solbakken 2012–13
Dean Saunders 2013
Kenny Jackett 2013–16
Walter Zenga 2016
Paul Lambert 2016–17
Nuno Espírito Santo May 2017–

LATEST SEQUENCES

Longest Sequence of League Wins: 9, 11.1.2014 – 11.3.2014.

Longest Sequence of League Defeats: 8, 5.12.1981 – 13.2.1982.

Longest Sequence of League Draws: 6, 22.4.1995 – 20.8.1995.

Longest Sequence of Unbeaten League Matches: 21, 15.1.2005 – 13.8.2005.

Longest Sequence Without a League Win: 19, 1.12.1984 – 6.4.1985.

Successive Scoring Runs: 41 from 20.12.1958.

Successive Non-scoring Runs: 7 from 2.2.1985.

TEN YEAR LEAGUE RECORD

		P	W	D	L	F	A	Pts	Pos
2008-09	FL C	46	27	9	10	80	52	90	1
2009-10	PR Lge	38	9	11	18	32	56	38	15
2010-11	PR Lge	38	11	7	20	46	66	40	17
2011-12	PR Lge	38	5	10	23	40	82	25	20
2012-13	FL C	46	14	9	23	55	69	51	23
2013-14	FL 1	46	31	10	5	89	31	103	1
2014-15	FL C	46	22	12	12	70	56	78	7
2015-16	FL C	46	14	16	16	53	58	58	14
2016-17	FL C	46	16	10	20	54	58	58	15
2017-18	FL C	46	30	9	7	82	39	99	1

DID YOU KNOW

Two Wolverhampton Wanderers players have been selected as the Football Writers' Association Footballer of the Year. England skipper Billy Wright was chosen in 1951–52 while Bill Slater received the award in 1959–60.

WOLVERHAMPTON WANDERERS – SKY BET CHAMPIONSHIP 2017–18 LEAGUE RECORD

Match No.	Date	Venue	Opponents	Result	H/T Score	Lg Pos.	Goalscorers	Attendance
1	Aug 5	H	Middlesbrough	W 1-0	1-0	8	Leo Bonatini [33]	29,692
2	12	A	Derby Co	W 2-0	1-0	2	Douglas [32], Ivan Cavaleiro [76]	27,757
3	15	A	Hull C	W 3-2	2-1	2	Neves [6], Jota [43], Dicko [90]	17,145
4	19	H	Cardiff C	L 1-2	0-0	3	Leo Bonatini [67]	27,068
5	26	A	Brentford	D 0-0	0-0	4		10,351
6	Sept 9	H	Millwall	W 1-0	1-0	3	Jota [10]	24,426
7	12	H	Bristol C	D 3-3	1-1	4	Leo Bonatini [28], Jota [54], Batth [85]	23,045
8	16	A	Nottingham F	W 2-1	0-0	2	Jota 2 [47, 81]	25,756
9	23	H	Barnsley	W 2-1	0-0	2	Enobakhare [80], N'Diaye [90]	28,154
10	27	A	Sheffield U	L 0-2	0-1	4		25,893
11	30	A	Burton Alb	W 4-0	3-0	2	Jota [5], Saiss [11], Ruben Vinagre [41], Leo Bonatini [62]	5080
12	Oct 14	H	Aston Villa	W 2-0	0-0	1	Jota [55], Leo Bonatini [71]	30,239
13	21	H	Preston NE	W 3-2	1-0	1	Ivan Cavaleiro [44], Leo Bonatini 2 (1 pen) [59 (p), 63]	27,352
14	28	A	QPR	L 1-2	1-1	2	Leo Bonatini [43]	16,004
15	31	A	Norwich C	W 2-0	1-0	1	Boly [18], Leo Bonatini [72]	26,554
16	Nov 3	H	Fulham	W 2-0	2-0	1	Saiss [9], Leo Bonatini [26]	24,388
17	18	A	Reading	W 2-0	1-0	1	Ivan Cavaleiro [16], Doherty [88]	20,708
18	22	H	Leeds U	W 4-1	2-0	1	Douglas [15], Ivan Cavaleiro [26], Jota [72], Helder Costa (pen) [76]	28,914
19	25	H	Bolton W	W 5-1	2-0	1	Boly [13], Leo Bonatini [25], Ivan Cavaleiro 2 (1 pen) [62 (p), 82], Jota [87]	27,894
20	Dec 4	A	Birmingham C	W 1-0	1-0	1	Leo Bonatini [8]	19,641
21	9	H	Sunderland	D 0-0	0-0	1		28,488
22	15	H	Sheffield W	W 1-0	1-0	1	Neves [34]	23,809
23	23	H	Ipswich T	W 1-0	1-0	1	Ivan Cavaleiro [40]	30,218
24	26	A	Millwall	D 2-2	1-1	1	Jota [45], Saiss [56]	13,121
25	30	A	Bristol C	W 2-1	0-0	1	Douglas [66], Bennett [90]	25,540
26	Jan 2	H	Brentford	W 3-0	0-0	1	Neves [57], Douglas [59], Jota [80]	28,475
27	13	A	Barnsley	D 0-0	0-0	1		16,050
28	20	H	Nottingham F	L 0-2	0-2	1		29,050
29	27	A	Ipswich T	W 1-0	1-0	1	Doherty [15]	15,971
30	Feb 3	H	Sheffield U	W 3-0	2-0	1	Neves [5], Jota [30], Ivan Cavaleiro [76]	29,311
31	10	A	QPR	W 2-1	2-0	1	N'Diaye [12], Helder Costa [21]	30,168
32	17	A	Preston NE	D 1-1	0-0	1	Helder Costa [61]	18,570
33	21	H	Norwich C	D 2-2	2-1	1	Lewis (og) [14], N'Diaye [25]	29,100
34	24	A	Fulham	L 0-2	0-1	1		23,510
35	Mar 7	A	Leeds U	W 3-0	2-0	1	Saiss [28], Boly [45], Afobe [74]	26,434
36	10	A	Aston Villa	L 1-4	1-1	1	Jota [20]	37,836
37	13	H	Reading	W 3-0	1-0	1	Doherty 2 [40, 73], Afobe [58]	27,341
38	17	H	Burton Alb	W 3-1	2-1	1	Helder Costa [15], Afobe 2 [41, 56]	29,977
39	30	A	Middlesbrough	W 2-1	2-0	1	Helder Costa [32], Ivan Cavaleiro [37]	27,658
40	Apr 3	H	Hull C	D 2-2	1-1	1	Jota (pen) [18], Buur [83]	29,718
41	6	A	Cardiff C	W 1-0	0-0	1	Neves [67]	29,317
42	11	H	Derby Co	W 2-0	1-0	1	Jota [6], Neves [51]	28,503
43	15	H	Birmingham C	W 2-0	1-0	1	Jota [21], Afobe [87]	29,536
44	21	A	Bolton W	W 4-0	2-0	1	Douglas [16], Afobe [45], Jota [53], Coady (pen) [66]	19,092
45	28	H	Sheffield W	D 0-0	0-0	1		29,794
46	May 6	A	Sunderland	L 0-3	0-2	1		28,452

Final League Position: 1

GOALSCORERS

League (82): Jota 17 (1 pen), Leo Bonatini 12 (1 pen), Ivan Cavaleiro 9 (1 pen), Afobe 6, Neves 6, Douglas 5, Helder Costa 5 (1 pen), Doherty 4, Saiss 4, Boly 3, N'Diaye 3, Batth 1, Bennett 1, Buur 1, Coady 1 (1 pen), Dicko 1, Enobakhare 1, Ruben Vinagre 1, own goal 1.
FA Cup (1): Jota 1.
Carabao Cup (4): Batth 1, Dicko 1, Enobakhare 1, Wilson 1.

Ruddy John 45	Roderick Miranda J 16 + 1	Coady C 45	Boly W 36	Doherty M 45	Saiss R 37 + 5	Neves R 42	Douglas B 38 + 1	Enobakhare B 5 + 16	Jota D 43 + 1	Lee Bonatini L 29 + 14	Dicko N — + 5	Edwards D — + 1	Graham J — + 1	Ivan Cavaleiro R 31 + 11	Ronan C — + 3	Bennett R 27 + 2	Ruben Vinagre G 8 + 1	Price J — + 5	Bath D 15 + 1	Marshall B 1 + 5	N'Diaye A 13 + 20	Deslandes S — + 1	Helder Costa W 21 + 15	Hause K — + 1	Mir R — + 2	White M 1 + 12	Afobe B 7 + 9	Buur O — + 1	Norris W 1	Burgoyne H — + 1	Match No.
1	2	3	4	5	6	7	8	9	10^2	11^3	12	13	14																		1
1	2	3	4	5	6	7	8	9	11^2	10^3	14			12	13																2
1	2	3	4	5	6	7		9^3	11	10^2	13			12		14															3
1	2	3	4	5	7^1	6	8^3	9^2	11	10	13			12		14															4
1	2	3	4	5	7		6^1		9	11	10^2	13		12		8	14														5
1	4	3		5	6	7^2		12	11^2	10			14	8		2			13				9^1								6
1	4^2	3		5	12	6^1	13		11	10			14	8		2					7		9^3								7
1	4	3		5	6	7			11	10^3	12		14	8		2			13				9^2								8
1	4	3		5	6^2	7	12	13	11	10			14			2							9^2								9
1	4	3^4		5	12	7^3	8	13	11	10^1			14			2					6		9^2								10
1		3	4	5	6^1	7	8	12	10^3	11			14			2			13				9^2								11
1		3	4	5	6	7^2	8	12	10	11^3			14			2			13				9^1								12
1		3	4	5	6	7	8	13	11^1	10^1	12		14			2							9^2								13
1		3	4	5	6	7^1	8	13	11	10	12		14			2							9^3								14
1		3	4	5		7	8	12	11^3	10^1				9^2		2			13		6		14								15
1		3	4^3	5	6	7	8	12	11	10^1				9^3		2			14		13		6								16
1		3	4	5	6	7		12	11^2	10^1				9^3		2			13		8		14								17
1		3	4	5	6^3	7^1	8		11	10				9^2		2			13		14		12								18
1		3	4	5	6	7	8^2		11	10^3				9^1		2			13		14		12								19
1		3	4	5	6^1		8	14	11	10^1				9^2		2			13		7		12								20
1		3	4	5	6^2	7	8^1		11	10				9		2					12		13								21
1		3	4	5	6	7	8^2		11^1	10^3	12			9^3		2			14				13								22
1		3	4	5	6	7	8	12	11^1	10^3				9^2		2					14		13								23
1	13	3	4^1	5	6	7	8	12	10	11^3						2					14		9^2								24
1		3	4	5	6	7	8		11^1	10^2			14	13		12				2^4			9^3								25
1		3	4^2	5	6	7	8	13	11^3	10				12		2					14		9^1								26
1		3	4	5	6	7^2	8		11	10^1				12		2					14		9^2			13					27
1		3	4	5^5	6	7^2	8^1		11	10				9		2					13					14	12				28
1		3	4	5		7	8	13	11	12				10^2		2			6				9^1								29
1		3	4	5		7	8		10^3	12				11^2		2			6				9^1			14	13				30
1		3	4	5	6	7	8		10	11^1						2							9^2			13	12				31
1		3	4	5	13	7	8	14	10	11^1						2					6^1		9^2			12					32
1		3	4	5	12	6	8		10	11^3						2					7^2		9^1			14	13				33
1		3	4	5	6^1		8	13	10	11						2					7^3		9^2			12	14				34
1		3	4	5		7			11^3	10^2				9^1		2					6		13			14	12				35
1		3	4	5	13	7	8		11^1	10				9^3		2^2					6		14			12					36
1		3	4	5	6^3	7	8		11^2	13				12		2					14		9			10^1					37
1		3	4	5	6	7^3	8	13	11^2							2					14		9			12	10^1				38
1		3	4	5^4	6	7^1	8	13	11^1							2					12		9^2			14	10^3				39
1	2^3	3	4		7	8		11^1	10	5				6^2		9										14	12	13			40
1		3	4	5	6	7	8	9^1	11^3					13		2					14		12			10^2					41
1		3	4	5	7	6	8	13	10^1					9^2		2					12		14			11^3					42
1		3	4	5	7	6^2	8	12	10^3					11^1		2					13		9			14					43
1		3	4	5	7^2	6	8	12	11^3							2					14		9			13	10^1				44
1		3	4	5	6	7	8	13	11^2	12						2							9^3			14	10^1				45
	4	3		5	6	7	8	13	11	12						2							9^2			10^1	14		1^3		46

FA Cup

Third Round	Swansea C	(h)	0-0
Replay	Swansea C	(a)	1-2

Carabao Cup

First Round	Yeovil T	(h)	1-0
Second Round	Southampton	(a)	2-0
Third Round *(aet)*	Bristol R	(h)	1-0
Fourth Round	Manchester C	(a)	0-0

(aet; Manchester C won 4-1 on penalties)

WYCOMBE WANDERERS

FOUNDATION

In 1887 a group of young furniture trade workers called a meeting at the Steam Engine public house with the aim of forming a football club and entering junior football. It is thought that they were named after the famous FA Cup winners, The Wanderers, who had visited the town in 1877 for a tie with the original High Wycombe club. It is also possible that they played informally before their formation, although there is no proof of this.

Adams Park, Hillbottom Road, High Wycombe, Buckinghamshire HP12 4HJ.

Telephone: (01494) 472 100.

Ticket Office: (01494) 441 118.

Website: www.wycombewanderers.co.uk

Email: wwfc@wwfc.com

Ground Capacity: 9,552.

Record Attendance: 15,850 v St Albans C, FA Amateur Cup 4th rd, 25 February 1950 (at Loakes Park); 9,921 v Fulham, FA Cup 3rd rd, 9 January 2002 (at Adams Park).

Pitch Measurements: 100.5m × 64m (110yd × 70yd).

Chairman: Trevor Stroud.

Manager: Gareth Ainsworth.

Assistant Manager: Richard Dobson.

Colours: Light blue and dark blue quartered shirts, dark blue shorts with light blue trim, dark blue socks with light blue hoops.

Year Formed: 1887. *Turned Professional:* 1974.

Club Nicknames: 'The Chairboys' (after High Wycombe's tradition of furniture making), 'The Blues'.

Grounds: 1887, The Rye; 1893, Spring Meadow; 1895, Loakes Park; 1899, Daws Hill Park; 1901, Loakes Park; 1990, Adams Park.

First Football League Game: 14 August 1993, Division 3 v Carlisle U (a) D 2–2: Hyde; Cousins, Horton (Langford), Kerr, Crossley, Ryan, Carroll, Stapleton, Thompson, Scott, Guppy (1) (Hutchinson), (1 og).

Record League Victory: 5–0 v Burnley, Division 2, 15 April 1997 – Parkin; Cousins, Bell, Kavanagh, McCarthy, Forsyth, Carroll (2p) (Simpson), Scott (Farrell), Stallard (1), McGavin (1) (Read (1)), Brown. 5–0 v Northampton T, Division 2, 4 January 2003 – Talia; Senda, Ryan, Thomson, McCarthy, Johnson, Bulman, Simpson (1), Faulconbridge (Harris), Dixon (1) (Roberts 3), Brown (Currie). 5–0 v Hartlepool U, FL 1, 25 February 2012 – Bull; McCoy, Basey, Eastmond (Bloomfield), Laing, Doherty (1), Hackett, Lewis, Bevon (2) (Strevons), Hayes (2) (McClure), McNamee.

Record Cup Victory: 5–0 v Hitchin T (a), FA Cup 2nd rd, 3 December 1994 – Hyde; Cousins, Brown, Crossley, Evans, Ryan (1), Carroll, Bell (1), Thompson, Garner (3) (Hemmings), Stapleton (Langford). 5–0 v Chesterfield (a), FA Cup 2nd rd, 3 December 2017 – Blackman; Harriman, Stewart (1), Pierre, Jacobson, Bloomfield (Wood), O'Nien, Gape (Bean), Kashket (3) (Cowan-Hall), Hayes (1), Akinfenwa.

HONOURS

League Champions: Conference – 1992–93.

Runners-up: FL 2 – (3rd) 2008–09, 2010–11 *(promoted to FL 1)*; Conference – 1991–92.

FA Cup: semi-final – 2001.

League Cup: semi-final – 2007.

FA Amateur Cup Winners: 1931.

THE Sun FACT FILE

Wycombe Wanderers won promotion to the Football League after finishing champions of the Football Conference by a 15-point margin over closest rivals Bromsgrove Rovers. For good measure they also won the FA Trophy that season, defeating Runcorn in the final at Wembley in front of an attendance of 32,968.

Record Defeat: 0–7 v Shrewsbury T, Johnstone's Paint Trophy, 7 October 2008.

Most League Points (3 for a win): 84, FL 2, 2014–15; 84, FL 2, 2017–18.

Most League Goals: 79, FL 2, 2017–18.

Highest League Scorer in Season: Scott McGleish, 25, 2007–08.

Most League Goals in Total Aggregate: Nathan Tyson, 50, 2004–06, 2017–18.

Most League Goals in One Match: 3, Miquel Desouza v Bradford C, Division 2, 2 September 1995; 3, John Williams v Stockport Co, Division 2, 24 February 1996; 3, Mark Stallard v Walsall, Division 2, 21 October 1997; 3, Sean Devine v Reading, Division 2, 2 October 1999; 3, Sean Divine v Bury, Division 2, 26 February 2000; 3, Stuart Roberts v Northampton T, Division 2, 4 January 2003; 3, Nathan Tyson v Lincoln C, FL 2, 5 March 2005; 3, Nathan Tyson v Kidderminster H, FL 2, 2 April 2005; 3, Nathan Tyson v Stockport Co, FL 2, 10 September 2005; 3, Kevin Betsy v Mansfield T, FL 2, 24 September 2005; 3, Scott McGleish v Mansfield T, FL 2, 8 January 2008; 3, Stuart Beavon v Bury, FL 1, 17 March 2012; 3, Craig Mackail-Smith v Crawley T, FL 2, 18 November 2017.

Most Capped Player: Mark Rogers, 7, Canada; Marvin McCoy, 7 (8), Antigua and Barbuda.

Most League Appearances: Matt Bloomfield, 379, 2003–17.

Youngest League Player: Jordon Ibe, 15 years 311 days v Hartlepool U, 15 October 2011.

Record Transfer Fee Received: £675,000 from Nottingham F for Nathan Tyson, January 2006.

Record Transfer Fee Paid: £200,000 to Barnet for Sean Devine, April 1999; £200,000 to Barnet for Darren Currie, July 2001.

Football League Record: 1993 Promoted to Division 3 from Conference; 1993–94 Division 3; 1994–2004 Division 2; 2004–09 FL 2; 2009–10 FL 1; 2010–11 FL 2; 2011–12 FL 1; 2012–18 FL 2; 2018– FL 1.

MANAGERS

First coach appointed 1951.
Prior to Brian Lee's appointment in 1969 the team was selected by a Match Committee which met every Monday evening.
James McCormack 1951–52
Sid Cann 1952–61
Graham Adams 1961–62
Don Welsh 1962–64
Barry Darvill 1964–68
Brian Lee 1969–76
Ted Powell 1976–77
John Reardon 1977–78
Andy Williams 1978–80
Mike Keen 1980–84
Paul Bence 1984–86
Alan Gane 1986–87
Peter Suddaby 1987–88
Jim Kelman 1988–90
Martin O'Neill 1990–95
Alan Smith 1995–96
John Gregory 1996–98
Neil Smillie 1998–99
Lawrie Sanchez 1999–2003
Tony Adams 2003–04
John Gorman 2004–06
Paul Lambert 2006–08
Peter Taylor 2008–09
Gary Waddock 2009–12
Gareth Ainsworth November 2012–

LATEST SEQUENCES

Longest Sequence of League Wins: 6, 12.11.2016 – 17.12.2016.
Longest Sequence of League Defeats: 6, 18.3.2006 – 17.4.2006.
Longest Sequence of League Draws: 5, 24.1.2004 – 21.2.2004.
Longest Sequence of Unbeaten League Matches: 21, 6.8.2005 – 10.12.2005.
Longest Sequence Without a League Win: 13, 10.1.2004 – 20.3.2004.
Successive Scoring Runs: 16 from 13.9.2014.
Successive Non-scoring Runs: 5 from 15.10.1996.

TEN YEAR LEAGUE RECORD

		P	W	D	L	F	A	Pts	Pos
2008-09	FL 2	46	20	18	8	54	33	78	3
2009-10	FL 1	46	10	15	21	56	76	45	22
2010-11	FL 2	46	22	14	10	69	50	80	3
2011-12	FL 1	46	11	10	25	65	88	43	21
2012-13	FL 2	46	17	9	20	50	60	60	15
2013-14	FL 2	46	12	14	20	46	54	50	22
2014-15	FL 2	46	23	15	8	67	45	84	4
2015-16	FL 2	46	17	13	16	45	44	64	13
2016-17	FL 2	46	19	12	15	58	53	69	9
2017-18	FL 2	46	24	12	10	79	60	84	3

DID YOU KNOW ?

Wycombe Wanderers goalkeeper Barry Richardson became the third-oldest player to appear in a Football League match when he came off the bench to replace the injured Alex Lynch during the game at Plymouth on 30 January 2016 at the age of 46. He kept a clean sheet as the Chairboys went on to win 1-0.

WYCOMBE WANDERERS – SKY BET LEAGUE TWO 2017–18 LEAGUE RECORD

Match No.	Date	Venue	Opponents	Result	H/T Score	Lg Pos.	Goalscorers	Attendance
1	Aug 5	H	Lincoln C	D	2-2	2-1	16	O'Nien [37], Jacobson [40]	5538
2	12	A	Port Vale	W	3-2	3-0	3	Akinfenwa 2 [2, 25], Cowan-Hall [12]	4909
3	19	H	Notts Co	L	2-4	0-2	14	Freeman [49], Jacobson [68]	3785
4	26	A	Grimsby T	W	3-2	2-0	8	Akinfenwa 2 [28, 75], Jacobson (pen) [43]	4016
5	Sept 2	H	Forest Green R	W	3-1	3-0	4	Cowan-Hall [7], Stewart [22], O'Nien [36]	3759
6	9	A	Newport Co	D	0-0	0-0	6		3752
7	12	A	Mansfield T	D	0-0	0-0	8		2938
8	16	H	Luton T	L	1-2	1-0	12	Akinfenwa [40]	5512
9	23	A	Colchester U	W	2-1	1-1	10	Tyson [32], Mackail-Smith [67]	3562
10	26	H	Crewe Alex	W	3-2	1-1	8	Mackail-Smith [29], Harriman [88], Tyson [90]	3295
11	30	H	Barnet	W	3-1	1-0	7	Akinfenwa [23], Umerah [65], Freeman [76]	4056
12	Oct 7	A	Cambridge U	W	3-1	0-0	4	Eze 2 [48, 57], Umerah [89]	5365
13	14	H	Exeter C	D	0-0	0-0	5		5006
14	17	A	Carlisle U	D	3-3	1-2	4	Saunders [45], Akinfenwa [72], Cowan-Hall [90]	3562
15	21	A	Swindon T	L	0-1	0-1	5		7114
16	28	H	Cheltenham T	D	3-3	0-1	7	Eze [48], Akinfenwa 2 [50, 62]	4165
17	Nov 11	A	Morecambe	L	1-2	0-2	7	Akinfenwa [82]	1472
18	18	H	Crawley T	W	4-0	0-0	6	Eze [50], Mackail-Smith 3 [72, 81, 83]	4494
19	21	A	Accrington S	L	0-1	0-0	8		1119
20	25	H	Yeovil T	W	2-1	2-1	5	Eze [37], Jacobson (pen) [43]	3834
21	Dec 9	A	Stevenage	D	0-0	0-0	5		2430
22	16	H	Chesterfield	W	1-0	0-0	4	O'Nien [54]	4522
23	22	A	Coventry C	L	2-3	1-2	5	Scarr [45], Jacobson (pen) [49]	7234
24	26	H	Newport Co	W	2-0	1-0	4	Tyson [15], Akinfenwa [78]	4629
25	30	H	Mansfield T	L	1-2	1-0	6	Akinfenwa [7]	4227
26	Jan 1	A	Forest Green R	W	2-1	2-0	4	Bloomfield [26], Mackail-Smith [42]	2727
27	13	H	Colchester U	W	3-1	2-0	4	Akinfenwa [14], Cowan-Hall [24], O'Nien [74]	4386
28	20	A	Crewe Alex	W	3-2	0-1	4	Cowan-Hall [61], Tyson [84], Mackail-Smith [90]	3645
29	30	A	Luton T	W	3-2	2-1	2	Cowan-Hall [2], Tyson 2 [39, 70]	8564
30	Feb 3	H	Carlisle U	W	4-3	2-0	2	Bloomfield [28], O'Nien [31], Bean [90], Cowan-Hall [90]	4145
31	10	A	Exeter C	D	1-1	0-1	3	Bean [53]	3956
32	13	H	Swindon T	W	3-2	2-1	3	O'Nien [3], Mackail-Smith [10], Akinfenwa [89]	4863
33	17	A	Cheltenham T	W	2-0	2-0	2	Akinfenwa [40], Cowan-Hall [45]	3513
34	24	H	Morecambe	L	2-4	0-3	3	Freeman [65], O'Nien [84]	4672
35	27	H	Coventry C	L	0-1	0-0	3		4087
36	Mar 10	H	Cambridge U	D	1-1	1-0	4	Akinfenwa [45]	4426
37	17	A	Barnet	W	2-0	0-0	4	Jacobson (pen) [52], Santos (og) [72]	2103
38	21	A	Crawley T	W	3-2	2-1	3	Tyson [25], Akinfenwa [39], Jombati [62]	2133
39	24	H	Port Vale	D	0-0	0-0	3		4620
40	30	A	Notts Co	D	0-0	0-0	3		8038
41	Apr 2	H	Grimsby T	W	2-1	0-1	3	El-Abd [60], Kashket [67]	5215
42	14	A	Yeovil T	W	1-0	0-0	3	Williams, R [79]	3307
43	17	A	Lincoln C	D	0-0	0-0	3		8948
44	21	H	Accrington S	L	0-4	0-2	3		6178
45	28	A	Chesterfield	W	2-1	1-1	3	Tyson [45], Gape [76]	5679
46	May 5	H	Stevenage	W	1-0	1-0	3	Bloomfield [19]	8802

Final League Position: 3

GOALSCORERS

League (79): Akinfenwa 17, Cowan-Hall 8, Mackail-Smith 8, Tyson 8, O'Nien 7, Jacobson 6 (4 pens), Eze 5, Bloomfield 3, Freeman 3, Bean 2, Umerah 2, El-Abd 1, Gape 1, Harriman 1, Jombati 1, Kashket 1, Saunders 1, Scarr 1, Stewart 1, Williams, R 1, own goal 1.
FA Cup (6): Mackail-Smith 2, Akinfenwa 1, Freeman 1, O'Nien 1, Saunders 1.
Carabao Cup (0).
Checkatrade Trophy (3): De Havilland 1, Jombati 1, Southwell 1.

Brown S 46	Harriman M 17 + 1	Jombati S 20	El-Abd A 36	Jacobson J 46	O'Nien L 34 + 1	Gape D 34 + 1	Saunders S 16 + 6	Southwell D 3 + 9	Akinfenwa A 41 + 1	Tyson N 22 + 11	Cowan-Hall P 22 + 12	Bloomfield M 26 + 11	Hayes P 1 + 1	Freeman N 10 + 17	Mackail-Smith C 27 + 14	Williams J — + 1	Stewart A 16 + 1	Bean M 23 + 8	Umerah J 2 + 4	Eze E 16 + 4	Scarr D 19 + 3	De Havilland W 2 + 1	Moore T 13	McGinley N 7 + 4	Kashket S 3 + 6	Thompson C 1 + 6	Williams R 3 + 3	Makabu-Makalamby Y — + 1	Match No.
1	2	3	4	5	6	7	8³	9	10	11²	12	13	14																1
1	2	3	4	5	8	7	6¹	12	10	9³	11³	13		14															2
1	2	3	4	5	7	6		9²	10		8¹	11³	12	13	14														3
1	3		5	2	8	6		13	9		10³	7¹		14	11²		4	12											4
1	2		4	5	6	7		10		9²	8¹			14	11³		3	13	12										5
1	2		4	5	8	7¹			11	6²		9		3	12	10	13												6
1	2		5	8²	6		14			12	13			9³		3	7	10¹	11	4									7
1	2		4	5	8	7³	12		10¹	13	14	9		11²		3	6												8
1	2			5	6			12	10	11		13	9¹		3	7		8²	4										9
1	2		4	5			6²	10	9		14	11¹		12	7	13	8	3³											10
1	2		4	5	14	7		11	8²		13	10³		3	6	12	9¹												11
1		2	4	5		6		10	9²		14	11²		3	7	12	8¹	13											12
1	2¹	5	3		7		13	10		12				9³	11²	4	6			8	14								13
1	2		4	5		7	6²	13	10		12	14		8	11³			9¹											14
1		4	5		7	6³	14	10		11¹	8			9²	12		2	13	3										15
1		4	5		2	8		10		12	13			6²	11¹		7	9		3									16
1		5	12	2¹	8¹		10		13	14		11	9	3	7		6²	4											17
1		4	5	7¹	2	14	13	10²		9³	8		11		3	12													18
1	2³	3¹	5	7			14		10	9	6			11²		4	12			8	13								19
1	2		5	6		12	11	10		9¹	7			13		3				8²	4								20
1	2		4	5	7		13		10	12			8	9¹	11	3				6²									21
1	2		4	5	7		6	14	10	11²	12	13		9³		3				8¹									22
1	2		5	8		6			10	11¹	13	7		9²		3³		14	4	12									23
1	3		5	7	2	6			10	11³	9²	12		14	13					8²	4								24
1	3		5	7	2¹	6			10	11	9³	13		14	12					8¹	4								25
1		5	6	2¹	8			10	13			7²		11	9²		12		14	4	3								26
1		5	7			6²		10	12	11¹	8			9			13			4		2	3						27
1		5	8	7³				11	12	10²	9¹			13			6			4		2	3	14				28
1		3	5	7	6			10	11¹	9³				12			8			4		2²		14	13			29
1		3	5¹	7¹	2²			10	11³	9	8		14				6			4				13	12			30
1		4	5		8			10	11¹	9²	7			14	13		6			3³		2	12					31
1		5	8	7				10²	12	11¹				14	9³		6			3		2	13					32
1		3	5	6	8			10	12	11¹	7²			9			6					2	4		13			33
1		4	5	6	7			10	13	11	8¹			12	9³					3		2²	3		14			34
1		4	5	7	8³			10	11	9¹	14			12	13		6²			3		2						35
1		4	5³	8	7			10	11	9³	6¹			13						3		2	12	14				36
1	4	3	5	8	7			10	12			6³		11¹	9²							2		13	14			37
1	2		4	5	8¹	7		10	11			6²		13			9					3			12			38
1	3		4	5		7		10	11¹		14			9³	12		6					2		13	8²			39
1	12		2	4	5	8		10	11	13	6				9¹		7					3²						40
1	2	3	4	5	8	7		10	12					13			6								11²		9¹	41
1	2		4	5	8³	7		10	14					9³	13		6							3	11²	12		42
1	2	3	5				8³		10²	9	13	7		11¹			6							4		14	12	43
1	2		4	5		7²			9	11³	8			14	13		6							3	10¹	12		44
1	3	2	4	5	6	7	13		9	12	8²			10												11¹		45
1²	2	3	4	5	6	7		14	11	10	8¹				12											9³	13	46

FA Cup

First Round	Solihull Moors	(a)	2-0
Second Round	Leatherhead	(h)	3-1
Third Round	Preston NE	(h)	1-5

Carabao Cup

First Round	Fulham	(h)	0-2

Checkatrade Trophy

Southern Group C	Bristol R	(h)	1-5
Southern Group C	Swindon T	(a)	0-1
Southern Group C	West Ham U U21	(h)	2-0

YEOVIL TOWN

FOUNDATION

One of the prime movers of Yeovil football was Ernest J. Sercombe. His association with the club began in 1895 as a playing member of Yeovil Casuals, of which team he became vice-captain and in his last season 1899–1900, he was chosen to play for Somerset against Devon. Upon the reorganisation of the club, he became secretary of the old Yeovil Town FC and with the amalgamation with Petters United in 1914, he continued to serve until his resignation in 1930.

Huish Park, Lufton Way, Yeovil, Somerset BA22 8YF.

Telephone: (01935) 423 662.

Fax: (01935) 847 886.

Ticket Office: (01935) 847 888.

Website: www.ytfc.net

Email: info@ytfc.net

Ground Capacity: 9,565.

HONOURS

League Champions: FL 2 – 2004–05; Conference – 2002–03. *Runners-up:* Conference – 2000–01. *FA Cup:* 5th rd – 1949. *League Cup:* never past 2nd rd.

Record Attendance: 16,318 v Sunderland, FA Cup 4th rd, 29 January 1949 (at Huish); 9,527 v Leeds U, FL 1, 25 April 2008 (at Huish Park).

Pitch Measurements: 108m × 67m (118yd × 73yd).

Chairman: John R. Fry.

Manager: Darren Way.

Assistant Manager: Terry Skiverton.

Colours: Green and white hooped shirts, white shorts with green trim, white socks with green trim.

Year Formed: 1895.

Turned Professional: 1921.

Previous Names: 1895, Yeovil Casuals; 1907, Yeovil Town; 1915, Yeovil & Petters United; 1946, Yeovil Town.

Club Nickname: 'The Glovers'.

Grounds: 1895, Pen Mill Ground; 1921, Huish; 1990, Huish Park.

First Football League Game: 9 August 2003, Division 3 v Rochdale (a) W 3-1: Weale; Williams (Lindegaard), Crittenden, Lockwood, O'Brien, Pluck (Rodrigues), Gosling (El Kholti), Way, Jackson, Gall (2), Johnson (1).

Record League Victory: 6–1 v Oxford U, FL 2, 18 September 2004 – Weale; Rose, O'Brien, Way, Skiverton, Fontaine, Caceres (Tarachulski), Johnson, Jevons (3), Stoicers (2) (Mirza), Terry (Gall 1).

Record Cup Victory: 12–1 v Westbury United, FA Cup 1st qual rd, 1923–24.

THE Sun FACT FILE

Yeovil Town increased terrace prices for the FA Cup tie with Arsenal in January 1971 from 4s 6d (22½p) to 15s (75p) but there was still a full house to see the Gunners win 3-0. The club reported a profit of approximately £6,000 on the game, significantly reducing their overdraft of around £10,000.

Record Defeat: 0–8 v Manchester United, FA Cup 5th rd, 12 February 1949.

Most League Points (3 for a win): 83, FL 2, 2004–05.

Most League Goals: 90, FL 2, 2004–05.

Highest League Scorer in Season: Phil Jevons, 27, 2004–05.

Most League Goals in Total Aggregate: Phil Jevons, 42, 2004–06.

Most League Goals in One Match: 3, Phil Jevons v Oxford U, FL 2, 18 September 2004; 3, Phil Jevons v Chester C, FL 2, 30 October 2004; 3, Phil Jevons v Bristol R, FL 2, 12 February 2005; 3, Arron Davies v Chesterfield, FL 1, 4 March 2006; 3, Jack Compton v AFC Wimbledon, FL 2, 30 January 2016.

Most Capped Players: Joel Grant, 12 (14), Jamaica.

Most League Appearances: Nathan Smith, 260, 2008–11, 2014–18.

Youngest League Player: Ollie Bassett, 17 years 197 days v Crawley T, 19 September 2015.

Record Transfer Fee Received: A combined £1,000,000 from Nottingham F for Arron Davies and Chris Cohen, July 2007.

Record Transfer Fee Paid: £250,000 to Quilmes for Pablo Bastianini, August 2005.

Football League Record: 2003 Promoted to Division 3 from Conference; 2003–04 Division 3; 2004–05 FL 2; 2005–13 FL 1; 2013–14 FL C; 2014–15 FL 1; 2015– FL 2.

LATEST SEQUENCES

Longest Sequence of League Wins: 8, 29.12.2012 – 16.2.2013.

Longest Sequence of League Defeats: 6, 10.3.2015 – 6.4.2015.

Longest Sequence of League Draws: 3, 15.3.2017 – 25.3.2017.

Longest Sequence of Unbeaten League Matches: 9, 29.12.2012 – 23.2.2013.

Longest Sequence Without a League Win: 16, 26.9.2015 – 28.12.2015.

Successive Scoring Runs: 22 from 30.10.2004.

Successive Non-scoring Runs: 4 from 18.2.2017.

MANAGERS

Jack Gregory 1922–28
Tommy Lawes 1928–29
Dave Pratt 1929–33
Louis Page 1933–35
Dave Halliday 1935–38
Billy Kingdon 1938–46
Alec Stock 1946–49
George Patterson 1949–51
Harry Lowe 1951–53
Ike Clarke 1953–57
Norman Dodgin 1957
Jimmy Baldwin 1957–60
Basil Hayward 1960–64
Glyn Davies 1964–65
Joe McDonald 1965–67
Ron Saunders 1967–69
Mike Hughes 1969–72
Cecil Irwin 1972–75
Stan Harland 1975–81
Barry Lloyd 1978–81
Malcolm Allison 1981
Jimmy Giles 1981–83
Trevor Finnigan and
   Mike Hughes 1983
Steve Coles 1983–84
Ian McFarlane 1984
Gerry Gow 1984–87
Brian Hall 1987–90
Clive Whitehead 1990–91
Steve Rutter 1991–93
Brian Hall 1994–95
Graham Roberts 1995–98
Colin Lippiatt 1998–99
Steve Thompson 1999–2000
Dave Webb 2000
Gary Johnson 2001–05
Steve Thompson 2005–06
Russell Slade 2006–09
Terry Skiverton 2009–12
Gary Johnson 2012–15
Terry Skiverton 2015
Paul Sturrock 2015
Darren Way December 2015–

TEN YEAR LEAGUE RECORD

		P	W	D	L	F	A	Pts	Pos
2008-09	FL 1	46	12	15	19	41	66	51	17
2009-10	FL 1	46	13	14	19	55	59	53	15
2010-11	FL 1	46	16	11	19	56	66	59	14
2011-12	FL 1	46	14	12	20	59	80	54	17
2012-13	FL 1	46	23	8	15	71	56	77	4
2013-14	FL C	46	8	13	25	44	75	37	24
2014-15	FL 1	46	10	10	26	36	75	40	24
2015-16	FL 2	46	11	15	20	43	59	48	19
2016-17	FL 2	46	11	17	18	49	64	50	20
2017-18	FL 2	46	12	12	22	59	75	48	19

DID YOU KNOW ?

Lewis Wing's first-half goal for Yeovil Town against Grimsby Town on 30 January 2018 set the Glovers up for a comfortable 3-0 win. It also provided the club with a landmark 800th Football League goal since promotion in 2003.

YEOVIL TOWN – SKY BET LEAGUE TWO 2017–18 LEAGUE RECORD

Match No.	Date	Venue	Opponents	Result		H/T Score	Lg Pos.	Goalscorers	Attendance
1	Aug 5	A	Luton T	L	2-8	1-5	24	Khan [7], Zoko [67]	8101
2	12	H	Accrington S	W	3-2	3-1	15	Olomola 2 [26, 39], Zoko [38]	2464
3	19	A	Forest Green R	L	3-4	3-2	21	Olomola [9], Khan (pen) [14], Zoko [35]	2615
4	26	H	Coventry C	W	2-0	1-0	12	Browne [27], Olomola [76]	3754
5	Sept 2	A	Crawley T	L	0-2	0-1	18		2024
6	9	H	Cheltenham T	D	0-0	0-0	17		2732
7	12	H	Morecambe	D	2-2	1-0	17	Zoko [37], Surridge [65]	2205
8	16	A	Grimsby T	L	1-2	1-1	19	Zoko [21]	3945
9	23	H	Port Vale	D	1-1	0-1	19	Khan [66]	2614
10	26	A	Chesterfield	W	3-2	2-0	14	Olomola [3], Khan [26], Bailey [90]	3955
11	30	H	Colchester U	L	0-1	0-1	17		2556
12	Oct 7	A	Newport Co	L	0-2	0-1	20		3689
13	14	H	Crewe Alex	W	2-0	1-0	17	Browne [15], Olomola [56]	2360
14	17	H	Cambridge U	L	1-2	0-2	18	Mugabi [60]	4328
15	21	A	Barnet	D	1-1	0-1	18	Khan [81]	1751
16	28	H	Stevenage	W	3-0	3-0	17	Surridge 2 [24, 40], Olomola [27]	2439
17	Nov 11	A	Carlisle U	L	0-4	0-2	17		4189
18	18	H	Swindon T	L	1-2	1-0	17	Browne [4]	3622
19	21	H	Notts Co	D	1-1	0-1	18	Zoko (pen) [80]	2338
20	25	A	Wycombe W	L	1-2	1-2	18	Zoko [44]	3834
21	Dec 9	H	Lincoln C	L	0-2	0-0	20		2472
22	16	A	Mansfield T	D	0-0	0-0	21		3032
23	23	H	Exeter C	W	3-1	1-0	19	Gray [41], Zoko [47], Surridge (pen) [88]	4834
24	26	A	Cheltenham T	W	2-0	0-0	19	Sowunmi [69], Green [85]	3484
25	29	A	Morecambe	L	3-4	2-0	19	Gray [1], Khan [17], Sowunmi [84]	1124
26	Jan 1	H	Crawley T	L	1-2	1-1	20	Surridge [19]	2635
27	13	A	Port Vale	D	1-1	1-0	21	Zoko [11]	4120
28	20	H	Chesterfield	L	1-2	0-0	21	Wing [80]	3792
29	30	H	Grimsby T	W	3-0	1-0	19	Wing [14], Browne [71], Gray [76]	2330
30	Feb 3	A	Cambridge U	W	2-0	0-0	18	Smith, N [54], Fisher [84]	2569
31	10	A	Crewe Alex	D	0-0	0-0	18		3498
32	13	H	Barnet	W	2-0	1-0	17	Surridge (pen) [2], Zoko [90]	2455
33	17	A	Stevenage	L	1-4	0-2	17	Seager [76]	2355
34	24	H	Carlisle U	L	0-1	0-0	17		2688
35	Mar 10	H	Newport Co	L	0-2	0-0	17		2880
36	13	A	Exeter C	D	0-0	0-0	17		3913
37	17	A	Colchester U	W	1-0	1-0	17	Fisher [21]	2772
38	Apr 2	A	Coventry C	W	6-2	3-0	17	Fisher 2 [6, 15], Zoko 2 [11, 55], Surridge 2 [80, 90]	8787
39	7	H	Luton T	L	0-3	0-3	18		4316
40	10	A	Swindon T	D	2-2	0-1	18	Wing [68], Fisher [89]	5709
41	14	H	Wycombe W	L	0-1	0-0	18		3307
42	17	A	Accrington S	L	0-2	0-2	18		3176
43	21	A	Notts Co	L	1-4	0-1	19	Fisher [90]	7359
44	24	H	Forest Green R	D	0-0	0-0	19		2789
45	28	H	Mansfield T	L	2-3	1-0	20	Mugabi [17], Zoko (pen) [57]	3500
46	May 5	A	Lincoln C	D	1-1	1-0	19	Green [10]	10,004

Final League Position: 19

GOALSCORERS

League (59): Zoko 13 (2 pens), Surridge 8 (2 pens), Olomola 7, Fisher 6, Khan 6 (1 pen), Browne 4, Gray 3, Wing 3, Green 2, Mugabi 2, Sowunmi 2, Bailey 1, Seager 1, Smith, N 1.
FA Cup (7): Khan 3 (2 pens), Green 2, Barnes 1, Zoko 1.
Carabao Cup (0).
Checkatrade Trophy (13): Browne 2, Surridge 2, Davies 1, Gray 1, James 1, Khan 1, Smith C 1, Smith N 1, Whelan 1, Zoko 1, own goal 1.

Krysiak A 33	Alfei D 2	Smith N 30+1	Davies K 1+1	Dickson R 35+1	Smith C 15+4	Bailey J 24	Gray J 21+5	Olomola O 18+3	Zoko F 35+2	Khan O 35+3	Sowunmi O 35+1	Santos A 6+8	Surridge S 21+20	Mugabi B 19+3	Browne R 16+19	James T 37+1	Green J 18+19	Nelson Sid 12	Worthington M 13+2	Gobern O 7+4	Bird J 9+2	Barnes M 1+7	Wing L 18+2	Whelan C 6+1	Fisher A 13+4	Seager R 2+5	Maddison J 8+2	Nelson Stuart 5	Donnellan S 11	Match No.
1	2	3	4²	5	6¹	7	8	9³	10	11	12	13	14																	1
1		4		5	8	7			11¹	10	9	3	12	2	6															2
1		4		8	7¹	6		9²	10	11	3⁵		13	2	12	5	14													3
1		4	12	5	8	7		11	10	9			2	6			3¹													4
1	2		5	7²	8	12	11¹	10	6			14	3	9³		13	4													5
1		4		5	7²	8	14	11³	10	9			13	2	6¹	12	3													6
1		4		5		7	8²		10	11¹		6³	9		14	2	12	3	13											7
1		3		5		7	9		10	13		8⁴	11¹	2	14	6³	12	4												8
1	2¹	3		5	8	7	6³	11²	10	9			13		14	4	12													9
1		4		5		8	6¹	10³	11²	9			13		14	2	12	3	7											10
1			5			8	6³	11²	10¹	9	4		13		14	2	12	3	7											11
1		4		5	6³	7		9	10	11¹		14	12		13	2		3	8²											12
1		4		5	8	7		10¹	11	9²	3	13	12	2	6															13
1		3		5	7¹	8²	12	10		6	4	13	11	2	9															14
1		3		5²	8³	7	6	11¹	10	9	4		14	2	13	12														15
1		4			8		6⁸	10⁸	9³			11	2	12	5				7											16
1		3			7	12		9	10			11	4⁸	6²	5¹	13	2	8												17
1		5			7	8		9¹	4	12	11		10	2	13	3¹	6²													18
1		5		14	6²		9	11	8⁴		10³		12	2	13	3⁸		7												19
1		5	8		3	12	6	11		4			10¹		2	9	7													20
1		3		14	7²		11¹	10	6	4	12	13	5		2	9	8¹													21
1		4		5		7	6²	12	10	9	3		11¹		2	13	8													22
1		4		5		8	6		10	9³	3		11		2	12	7													23
1		4		5	12	8¹		6	14	10	9³	3	11		2	13	7													24
1		3			8		6	12	10²	9²	4		11	2		5	13	7												25
1		4		5	8²		6	11¹	14	9²	3²		10³		12	13	7													26
1		4		5			8¹		10	9	3		11³		2	6²				7	12	13	14							27
1		4		5	13		7		11	9⁸			10	3	2	6¹				8²	12									28
1		4		5		6			10³	3	8	11²	13	2	9¹					7		12	14							29
1		4		5		6			10¹	3	7	11²	13	2	9³					8		14	12							30
1¹		4²	12		8		11		3	14	7	5	9			6	2				10³	13								31
		5			6		12		3	14	10	13	4	9²		8¹				7	2	11¹		1						32
		5			6			9¹	3	8²	10	12	4			13				7	2	11²	14	1						33
		5			6¹			12	3		10	9²	4	13		8				7	2	14	11³	1						34
		5	7				11	9¹	3	10³		12	13	4	6²	8	2	14					1							35
		5					10²	9¹	4	14	12	2	6		7	13	8	11³						1	3					36
		5¹					10²	3	13	12	9	2	6		8	14	7	11³						1	4					37
		5					10	14	3	12	9	2	6²		13	7¹	8	11³						1	4					38
		5¹					11⁸	4	13	12	9²	2	6¹		14	8	7	10³						1	3					39
							11	3	7³		2	9²	5	12	8	14	6	10			13	1¹	4							40
		5					9	3	14		10¹	2	6³		8²	12	7	11	13				1		4					41
		5					9¹	3		11	2	6²	7³	14	12	8	10	13					1		4					42
	14	6²						4			3	13	2	12	9³	7	10	8	11			1	1		5¹					43
							11	9	3		13	2	12	5	6¹		8	7	10²				1		4					44
1				8¹			10	9	4⁸		13	2	12	5	6³		14	7	11²						3					45
1							11	9¹			14	2	13	5	6²	12	7	8	4	10³					3					46

FA Cup

First Round	Southend U	(h)	1-0	
Second Round	Port Vale	(a)	1-1	
Replay	Port Vale	(h)	3-2	
(aet)				
Third Round	Bradford C	(h)	2-0	
Fourth Round	Manchester U	(h)	0-4	

Carabao Cup

First Round	Wolverhampton W	(a)	0-1

Checkatrade Trophy

Southern Group D	Exeter C	(a)	3-1
Southern Group D	Chelsea U21	(h)	1-1
(Yeovil T won 5-3 on penalties)			
Southern Group D	Plymouth Arg	(h)	2-1
Second Round South	AFC Wimbledon	(h)	2-0
Third Round	Forest Green R	(h)	2-0
Quarter-Final	Fleetwood T	(h)	3-2
Semi-Final	Shrewsbury T	(a)	0-1

ENGLISH LEAGUE PLAYERS DIRECTORY

Players listed represent those with their clubs during the 2017–18 season.

Players are listed alphabetically on pages 535–541.
The number alongside each player corresponds to the team number heading. (Aarons, Rolando 56 = team 56 (Newcastle U)). Club names in *italic* indicate loans.

ACCRINGTON S (1)

BLOCH JORGENSEN, Simon (G)   0   0
H: 6 11   W: 17 00   b.Flensburg 1-9-92
From Frem, FC Copenhagen, B.93.
2017–18	Accrington S	0	0

BROWN, Scott (M)   215   13
H: 5 9   W: 10 02   b.Runcorn 8-5-85
Internationals: England U17, U18, U19.
2001–02	Everton	0	0
2002–03	Everton	0	0
2003–04	Everton	0	0
2004–05	Bristol C	19	0
2005–06	Bristol C	29	1
2006–07	Bristol C	15 4	63 5
2006–07	Cheltenham T	4	0
2007–08	Cheltenham T	20	0
2008–09	Port Vale	18 1	18 1
2009–10	Cheltenham T	1 0	25 0
2010–11	Morecambe	32 3	32 3

From Fleetwood T, York C, Macclesfield T, Chester FC, Southport, Grimsby T.
2015–16	Accrington S	13 3	
2016–17	Accrington S	28 0	
2017–18	Accrington S	36 1	77 4

CHAPMAN, Aaron (G)   68   0
H: 6 8   W: 14 07   b.Rotherham 29-5-90
2013–14	Chesterfield	0	0
2014–15	Chesterfield	0	0
2014–15	*Accrington S*	3	0
2015–16	Chesterfield	0	0
2015–16	*Bristol R*	5 0	5 0
2016–17	Accrington S	15 0	
2017–18	Accrington S	45 0	63 0

CLARK, Jordan (F)   141   14
H: 6 0   W: 11 07   b.Barnsley 22-9-93
2010–11	Barnsley	4 0	
2011–12	Barnsley	2 0	
2012–13	Barnsley	0 0	
2012–13	*Chesterfield*	2 0	2 0
2013–14	Barnsley	0 0	6 0
2013–14	*Scunthorpe U*	1 0	1 0
2014–15	Shrewsbury T	27 3	
2015–16	Shrewsbury T	20 2	47 5
2016–17	Accrington S	42 1	
2017–18	Accrington S	43 8	85 9

CONNEELY, Seamus (D)   219   11
H: 5 9   W: 10 10   b.Galway 9-7-88
Internationals: Republic of Ireland U21, U23.
2008	Galway U	20 0	
2009	Galway U	34 2	
2010	Galway U	32 0	86 2
2010–11	Sheffield U	0 0	
2011–12	Sheffield U	0 0	
2014–15	Accrington S	16 3	
2015–16	Accrington S	46 3	
2016–17	Accrington S	38 1	
2017–18	Accrington S	33 2	133 9

DONACIEN, Janoi (D)   142   1
H: 6 0   W: 11 11   b.St Lucia 3-11-93
Internationals: St Lucia Full caps.
2011–12	Aston Villa	0 0	
2012–13	Aston Villa	0 0	
2013–14	Aston Villa	0 0	
2014–15	Aston Villa	0 0	
2014–15	*Tranmere R*	31 0	31 0
2015–16	Aston Villa	0 0	
2015–16	*Wycombe W*	2 0	2 0
2015–16	*Newport Co*	29 0	29 0
2016–17	Accrington S	35 1	
2017–18	Accrington S	45 0	80 1

FRANCIS, Akeel (F)   0   0
b.30-3-99
2017–18	Rotherham U	0 0	
2017–18	Accrington S	0 0	

HMAMI, Josh (M)   1   0
b.17-12-99
2017–18	Accrington S	1 0	1 0

HUGHES, Mark (D)   411   26
H: 6 1   W: 13 03   b.Liverpool 9-12-86
2004–05	Everton	0 0	
2005–06	Everton	0 0	
2005–06	*Stockport Co*	3 1	3 1
2006–07	Everton	1 0	1 0
2006–07	Northampton T	17 2	
2007–08	Northampton T	35 1	
2008–09	Northampton T	41 1	93 4
2009–10	Walsall	26 1	26 1
2010–11	N Queensland F	30 4	30 4
2011–12	Bury	25 0	
2012–13	Bury	27 0	52 0
2012–13	*Accrington S*	5 0	
2013–14	Morecambe	44 5	
2014–15	Morecambe	40 3	84 8
2015–16	Stevenage	20 1	20 1
2015–16	Accrington S	15 1	
2016–17	Accrington S	36 2	
2017–18	Accrington S	46 4	102 7

JACKSON, Kayden (F)   64   17
H: 5 11   W: 11 07   b.Bradford 22-2-94
Internationals: England C.
2013–14	Swindon T	0 0	
2014–15	Swindon T	0 0	

From Oxford C, Tamworth, Wrexham.
2016–17	Barnsley	0 0	
2016–17	*Grimsby T*	20 1	20 1
2017–18	Accrington S	44 16	44 16

JOHNSON, Callum (M)   31   1
b. 23-10-97
From Middlesbrough.
2017–18	Accrington S	31 1	31 1

KEE, Billy (F)   335   114
H: 5 9   W: 11 04   b.Loughborough 1-12-90
Internationals: Northern Ireland U19, U21.
2009–10	Leicester C	0 0	
2009–10	*Accrington S*	37 9	
2010–11	Torquay U	40 9	
2011–12	Torquay U	4 0	44 9
2011–12	Burton Alb	20 12	
2012–13	Burton Alb	40 13	
2013–14	Burton Alb	37 12	
2014–15	Burton Alb	2 2	99 39
2014–15	Scunthorpe U	12 0	12 0
2014–15	*Mansfield T*	13 2	13 2
2015–16	Accrington S	45 17	
2016–17	Accrington S	39 13	
2017–18	Accrington S	46 25	167 64

LEACOCK-McLEOD, Mekhi (M)   10   0
b. 15-9-96
2015–16	Wolverhampton W	0 0	

From Eastleigh.
2017–18	Accrington S	10 0	10 0

LITTLE, Jack (G)   0   0
b. 15-2-99
2016–17	Accrington S	0 0	
2017–18	Accrington S	0 0	

MAXTED, Jonathan (G)   1   0
H: 6 0   W: 11 03   b. 26-10-93
2012–13	Doncaster R	0 0	
2013–14	Doncaster R	0 0	
2014–15	Hartlepool U	0 0	
2017–18	Accrington S	1 0	1 0

McCONVILLE, Sean (M)   206   36
H: 5 8   W: 11 07   b.Liverpool 6-3-89
2008–09	Accrington S	5 0	
2009–10	Accrington S	28 1	
2010–11	Accrington S	43 13	
2011–12	Rochdale	4 0	4 0

From Barrow, Stalybridge Celtic, Chester.
2015–16	Accrington S	42 5	
2016–17	Accrington S	41 5	
2017–18	Accrington S	43 12	202 36

MILLS, Joel (M)   0   0
2017–18	Accrington S	0 0	

MOHAMMED, Zehn (D)   0   0
b. 28-2-00
2017–18	Accrington S	0 0	

NOLAN, Liam (D)   55   0
H: 5 9   W: 10 12   b.Liverpool 20-9-94
Internationals: Northern Ireland U21.
2012–13	Crewe Alex	0 0	
2013–14	Crewe Alex	13 0	
2014–15	Crewe Alex	13 0	26 0
2017–18	Accrington S	29 0	29 0

OGLE, Reagan (D)   4   0
H: 5 8   W: 10 06   b. 29-3-99
2016–17	Accrington S	1 0	
2017–18	Accrington S	3 0	4 0

REILLY, Tom (D)   0   0
2017–18	Accrington S	0 0	

RICHARDS-EVERTON, Ben (D)   82   3
H: 6 2   W: 14 00   b.Birmingham 17-10-92
From Hinckley U, Tamworth.
2014–15	Partick Thistle	2 0	2 0
2014–15	*Airdrieonians*	18 0	18 0
2015–16	Dunfermline Ath	34 2	
2016–17	Dunfermline Ath	6 0	40 2
2017–18	Accrington S	22 1	22 1

RODGERS, Harvey (M)   24   1
H: 5 10   W: 12 06   b.York 20-10-96
2016–17	Hull C	0 0	
2016–17	*Accrington S*	19 1	
2017–18	Fleetwood T	0 0	
2017–18	*Accrington S*	5 0	24 1

SAVIN, Toby (G)   0   0
2017–18	Accrington S	0 0	

SOUSA, Erico (M)   6   0
b. 12-3-95
2013–14	Barnsley	0 0	

From Hyde U, Celje, Tadcaster Alb.
2017–18	Accrington S	6 0	6 0

SYKES, Ross (D)   2   0
H: 6 5   W: 11 07   b.Burnley 26-3-99
2016–17	Accrington S	0 0	
2017–18	Accrington S	2 0	2 0

WATSON, Niall (M)   2   0
b. 15-6-00
2017–18	Accrington S	2 0	2 0

WILLIAMS, Danny (M)   112   4
H: 5 9   W: 10 12   b.Wigan 25-1-88
From FC United of Manchester, Clitheroe, Kendal T.
2013–14	Inverness CT	20 1	
2014–15	Inverness CT	34 2	
2015–16	Inverness CT	34 1	88 4
2016–17	Dundee	23 0	
2017–18	Dundee	0 0	23 0
2017–18	*Accrington S*	1 0	1 0

WOLLAND, Nathan (G)   0   0
2017–18	Accrington S	0 0	

Scholars
Burgess, Jack David; Cooper, Adam James Alfred; Cullen, Aspen Shaun; Gilboy, Lewis Anthony; Hmami, Joshua Majid; Mills, Joel William; Morris, John-Jo; O'Neill, Alex James; Perritt, Harrison Joshua; Randell, Jack Andrew; Reilly, Thomas Stephen; Savin, Toby; Shah, Kasom; Waterhouse, Harry; Watson, Niall Robert; Williams, Matthew Charles; Wolland, Nathan David.

AFC WIMBLEDON (2)

APPIAH, Kwesi (F)   66   13
H: 5 11   W: 12 08   b.Thamesmead 12-8-90
Internationals: Ghana Full caps.
2008–09	Peterborough U	0 0	

From Brackley T, Thurrock, Margate.
2011–12	Crystal Palace	4 0	

2012–13	Crystal Palace	2	0		
2012–13	*Aldershot T*	2	0	**2**	**0**
2012–13	*Yeovil T*	5	0	**5**	**0**
2013–14	Crystal Palace	0	0		
2013–14	*Notts Co*	7	0	**7**	**0**
2013–14	*AFC Wimbledon*	7	3		
2014–15	Crystal Palace	0	0		
2014–15	*Cambridge U*	19	6	**19**	**6**
2014–15	*Reading*	6	1	**6**	**1**
2015–16	Crystal Palace	0	0	**6**	**0**
2017–18	Viking FK	0	0		
2017–18	AFC Wimbledon	14	3	**21**	**6**

ASHLEY, Ossama (M) **0** **0**

2017–18	AFC Wimbledon	0	0		

BARCHAM, Andy (F) **359** **47**

H: 5 8 W: 11 10 b.Basildon 16-12-86

Internationals: England U16.

2005–06	Tottenham H	0	0		
2006–07	Tottenham H	0	0		
2007–08	Tottenham H	0	0		
2007–08	*Leyton Orient*	25	1	**25**	**1**
2008–09	Tottenham H	0	0		
2008–09	Gillingham	33	6		
2009–10	Gillingham	42	7		
2010–11	Gillingham	24	6	**99**	**19**
2011–12	Scunthorpe U	41	9		
2012–13	Scunthorpe U	34	0	**75**	**9**
2013–14	Portsmouth	26	3		
2014–15	Portsmouth	19	1	**45**	**4**
2015–16	AFC Wimbledon	33	5		
2016–17	AFC Wimbledon	37	5		
2017–18	AFC Wimbledon	45	4	**115**	**14**

BELLIKLI, Neset (M) **0** **0**

H: 5 10 b.Sutton 9-7-98

2017–18	AFC Wimbledon	0	0		

CHARLES, Darius (M) **255** **16**

H: 6 1 W: 13 05 b.Ealing 10-12-87

Internationals: England C.

2004–05	Brentford	1	0		
2005–06	Brentford	2	0		
2006–07	Brentford	17	1		
2007–08	Brentford	17	0	**37**	**1**
From Ebbsfleet U.					
2010–11	Stevenage	28	2		
2011–12	Stevenage	28	4		
2012–13	Stevenage	37	1		
2013–14	Stevenage	22	4		
2014–15	Stevenage	29	2	**144**	**13**
2015–16	Burton Alb	0	0		
2015–16	*AFC Wimbledon*	9	0		
2016–17	AFC Wimbledon	34	2		
2017–18	AFC Wimbledon	31	0	**74**	**2**

EGAN, Alfie (M) **11** **0**

b. 3-9-97

2016–17	AFC Wimbledon	9	0		
2017–18	AFC Wimbledon	2	0	**11**	**0**

EVANS, Great (F) **0** **0**

b.London

2017–18	AFC Wimbledon	0	0		

FORRESTER, Harry (F) **184** **26**

H: 5 9 W: 11 03 b.Milton Keynes 2-1-91

Internationals: England U16, U17.

2007–08	Aston Villa	0	0		
2008–09	Aston Villa	0	0		
2009–10	Aston Villa	0	0		
2010–11	Aston Villa	0	0		
2010–11	*Kilmarnock*	7	0	**7**	**0**
2011–12	Brentford	19	0		
2012–13	Brentford	36	8	**55**	**8**
2013–14	Doncaster R	7	0		
2014–15	Doncaster R	40	7		
2015–16	Doncaster R	7	1	**54**	**8**
2015–16	Rangers	11	4		
2016–17	Rangers	21	3		
2017–18	Rangers	0	0	**32**	**7**
On loan from Rangers.					
2017–18	AFC Wimbledon	36	3	**36**	**3**

FRANCOMB, George (D) **225** **11**

H: 5 11 W: 11 07 b.Hackney 8-9-91

2009–10	Norwich C	2	0		
2010–11	Norwich C	0	0		
2010–11	*Barnet*	13	0	**13**	**0**
2011–12	Norwich C	0	0		
2011–12	*Hibernian*	14	0	**14**	**0**
2012–13	Norwich C	0	0	**2**	**0**
2012–13	*AFC Wimbledon*	15	0		
2013–14	AFC Wimbledon	33	3		
2014–15	AFC Wimbledon	37	3		
2015–16	AFC Wimbledon	40	3		
2016–17	AFC Wimbledon	34	2		
2017–18	AFC Wimbledon	37	0	**196**	**11**

FULLER, Barry (D) **393** **2**

H: 5 10 W: 11 10 b.Ashford 25-9-84

Internationals: England C.

2004–05	Charlton Ath	0	0		
2005–06	Charlton Ath	0	0		
2005–06	*Barnet*	15	1		
From Stevenage B.					
2007–08	Gillingham	10	0		
2008–09	Gillingham	37	0		
2009–10	Gillingham	36	0		
2010–11	Gillingham	42	0		
2011–12	Gillingham	9	0		
2012–13	Gillingham	0	0	**134**	**0**
2012–13	Barnet	39	0	**54**	**1**
2013–14	AFC Wimbledon	45	0		
2014–15	AFC Wimbledon	45	1		
2015–16	AFC Wimbledon	45	0		
2016–17	AFC Wimbledon	28	0		
2017–18	AFC Wimbledon	42	0	**205**	**1**

HARTIGAN, Anthony (M) **11** **0**

H: 5 10 W: 10 10 b.Kingston upon Thames 27-1-00

2017–18	AFC Wimbledon	11	0	**11**	**0**

KAJA, Egli (M) **22** **0**

H: 5 10 W: 12 04 b. 26-7-97

Internationals: Albania U21.

2015–16	AFC Wimbledon	2	0		
2016–17	AFC Wimbledon	1	0		
2017–18	AFC Wimbledon	19	0	**22**	**0**

KALAMBAYI, Paul (D) **0** **0**

2015–16	AFC Wimbledon	0	0		
2016–17	AFC Wimbledon	0	0		
2017–18	AFC Wimbledon	0	0		

KENNEDY, Callum (D) **171** **3**

H: 6 1 W: 12 10 b.Chertsey 9-11-89

2007–08	Swindon T	0	0		
2008–09	Swindon T	4	0		
2009–10	Swindon T	8	0		
2010–11	Swindon T	3	0		
2010–11	*Gillingham*	3	0	**3**	**0**
2010–11	*Rotherham U*	5	0	**5**	**0**
2011–12	Swindon T	18	1	**33**	**1**
2012–13	Scunthorpe U	17	0	**17**	**0**
2013–14	AFC Wimbledon	22	0		
2014–15	AFC Wimbledon	26	0		
2015–16	AFC Wimbledon	19	1		
2016–17	Leyton Orient	32	1	**32**	**1**
2017–18	AFC Wimbledon	14	0	**81**	**1**

McDONALD, Cody (F) **300** **93**

H: 5 10 W: 11 03 b.Witham 30-5-86

2008–09	Norwich C	7	1		
2009–10	Norwich C	17	3		
2010–11	Norwich C	0	0		
2010–11	*Gillingham*	41	25		
2011–12	Norwich C	0	0	**24**	**4**
2011–12	Coventry C	23	4		
2012–13	Coventry C	20	3	**43**	**7**
2012–13	*Gillingham*	7	4		
2013–14	Gillingham	44	17		
2014–15	Gillingham	43	16		
2015–16	Gillingham	22	5		
2016–17	Gillingham	44	10	**201**	**77**
2017–18	AFC Wimbledon	32	5	**32**	**5**

McDONNELL, Joe (G) **8** **0**

H: 5 10 W: 9 13 b.Basingstoke 19-5-94

2014–15	AFC Wimbledon	4	0		
2015–16	AFC Wimbledon	0	0		
2016–17	AFC Wimbledon	3	0		
2017–18	AFC Wimbledon	1	0	**8**	**0**

MEADES, Jonathan (M) **124** **8**

H: 6 1 W: 13 00 b.Cardiff 2-3-92

Internationals: Wales U17, U21.

2010–11	Cardiff C	0	0		
2011–12	Cardiff C	0	0		
2012–13	Bournemouth	0	0		
2012–13	*AFC Wimbledon*	26	1		
2013–14	Oxford U	0	0		
2014–15	Oxford U	7	0	**7**	**0**
2015–16	AFC Wimbledon	41	3		
2016–17	AFC Wimbledon	24	2		
2017–18	AFC Wimbledon	26	2	**117**	**8**

NELSON-ROBERTS, Ethan (M) **0** **0**

b.London

2017–18	AFC Wimbledon	0	0		

NIGHTINGALE, Will (M) **38** **1**

H: 6 1 W: 13 03 b.Wandsworth 2-7-95

2013–14	AFC Wimbledon	0	0		
2014–15	AFC Wimbledon	4	0		
2015–16	AFC Wimbledon	4	0		
2016–17	AFC Wimbledon	12	0		
2017–18	AFC Wimbledon	18	1	**38**	**1**

OSHILAJA, Adedeji (D) **130** **8**

H: 5 11 W: 11 10 b.Bermondsey 16-7-93

2012–13	Cardiff C	0	0		
2013–14	Cardiff C	0	0		
2013–14	*Newport Co*	8	0	**8**	**0**
2013–14	*Sheffield W*	2	0	**2**	**0**
2014–15	Cardiff C	0	0		
2014–15	*AFC Wimbledon*	23	1		
2015–16	Cardiff C	0	0		
2015–16	*Gillingham*	22	3		
2016–17	Cardiff C	0	0		
2016–17	*Gillingham*	33	2	**55**	**5**
2017–18	AFC Wimbledon	42	2	**65**	**3**

PARRETT, Dean (M) **158** **18**

H: 5 10 W: 11 04 b.Hampstead 16-11-91

Internationals: England U16, U17, U19, U20.

2008–09	Tottenham H	0	0		
2009–10	Tottenham H	0	0		
2009–10	*Aldershot T*	4	0	**4**	**0**
2010–11	Tottenham H	0	0		
2010–11	*Plymouth Arg*	8	1	**8**	**1**
2010–11	*Charlton Ath*	9	1	**9**	**1**
2011–12	Tottenham H	0	0		
2011–12	*Yeovil T*	10	1	**10**	**1**
2012–13	Tottenham H	0	0		
2012–13	*Swindon T*	3	0	**3**	**0**
2013–14	Stevenage	12	1		
2014–15	Stevenage	30	4		
2015–16	Stevenage	27	3	**69**	**8**
2016–17	AFC Wimbledon	32	5		
2017–18	AFC Wimbledon	23	2	**55**	**7**

PIGOTT, Joe (F) **115** **22**

H: 6 0 W: 9 05 b.London 24-11-93

2012–13	Charlton Ath	0	0		
2013–14	Charlton Ath	11	0		
2013–14	*Gillingham*	7	1	**7**	**1**
2014–15	Charlton Ath	1	0		
2014–15	*Newport Co*	10	3	**10**	**3**
2014–15	*Southend U*	20	6		
2015–16	Charlton Ath	0	0	**12**	**0**
2015–16	*Southend U*	23	3	**43**	**9**
2015–16	*Luton T*	15	4	**15**	**4**
2016–17	Cambridge U	10	0	**10**	**0**
From Maidstone U.					
2017–18	AFC Wimbledon	18	5	**18**	**5**

ROBINSON, Paul (D) **451** **23**

H: 6 1 W: 11 09 b.Barnet 7-1-82

2000–01	Millwall	0	0		
2001–02	Millwall	0	0		
2002–03	Millwall	14	0		
2003–04	Millwall	9	0		
2004–05	Millwall	0	0		
2004–05	*Torquay U*	12	0	**12**	**0**
2005–06	Millwall	32	0		
2006–07	Millwall	38	3		
2007–08	Millwall	45	3		
2008–09	Millwall	26	2		
2009–10	Millwall	34	4		
2010–11	Millwall	37	3		
2011–12	Millwall	41	1		
2012–13	Millwall	3	0		
2013–14	Millwall	25	0	**304**	**16**
2014–15	Portsmouth	33	2	**33**	**2**
2015–16	AFC Wimbledon	44	3		
2016–17	AFC Wimbledon	43	2		
2017–18	AFC Wimbledon	15	0	**102**	**5**

SAM, Lloyd (F) **182** **13**

H: 5 10 W: 11 00 b.Leeds 27-9-84

Internationals: England U20. Ghana Full caps.

2002–03	Charlton Ath	0	0		
2003–04	Charlton Ath	0	0		
2003–04	*Leyton Orient*	10	0	**10**	**0**
2004–05	Charlton Ath	1	0		
2005–06	Charlton Ath	2	0		
2006–07	Charlton Ath	7	0		
2006–07	*Sheffield W*	4	0	**4**	**0**
2006–07	*Southend U*	2	0	**2**	**0**
2007–08	Charlton Ath	28	2		
2008–09	Charlton Ath	38	0		
2009–10	Charlton Ath	43	4	**119**	**6**
2010–11	Leeds U	18	2		
2011–12	Leeds U	17	0	**35**	**2**
2011–12	*Notts Co*	10	5	**10**	**5**
2017–18	DC United	0	0		
2017–18	AFC Wimbledon	2	0	**2**	**0**

SIBBICK, Toby (D) **3** **0**

H: 6 0 W: 10 12 b.Isleworth 23-5-99

2016–17	AFC Wimbledon	2	0		
2017–18	AFC Wimbledon	1	0	**3**	**0**

SOARES, Tom (M)   412   39
H: 6 0 W: 11 04 b.Reading 10-7-86
Internationals: England U20, U21.

2003–04	Crystal Palace	3	0		
2004–05	Crystal Palace	22	0		
2005–06	Crystal Palace	44	1		
2006–07	Crystal Palace	37	3		
2007–08	Crystal Palace	39	6		
2008–09	Crystal Palace	4	1	149	11
2008–09	Stoke C	7	0		
2008–09	*Charlton Ath*	11	1	11	1
2009–10	Stoke C	0	0		
2009–10	*Sheffield W*	25	2	25	2
2010–11	Stoke C	0	0		
2011–12	Stoke C	0	0	7	0
2011–12	*Hibernian*	10	2	10	2
2012–13	Bury	23	2		
2013–14	Bury	30	6		
2014–15	Bury	43	8		
2015–16	Bury	42	4		
2016–17	Bury	26	2	164	22
2016–17	AFC Wimbledon	15	0		
2017–18	AFC Wimbledon	31	1	46	1

TAYLOR, Lyle (F)   241   61
H: 6 2 W: 12 00 b.Greenwich 29-3-90
Internationals: Montserrat Full caps.

2007–08	Millwall	0	0		
2008–09	Millwall	0	0		
From Concord R					
2010–11	Bournemouth	11	0		
2011–12	Bournemouth	18	0	29	0
2011–12	*Hereford U*	8	2	8	2
2013–14	Sheffield U	20	2	20	2
2013–14	*Partick Thistle*	20	7		
2014–15	Scunthorpe U	18	3	18	3
2014–15	*Partick Thistle*	15	3	35	10
2015–16	AFC Wimbledon	42	20		
2016–17	AFC Wimbledon	43	10		
2017–18	AFC Wimbledon	46	14	131	44

TROTTER, Liam (M)   311   38
H: 6 2 W: 12 02 b.Ipswich 24-8-88

2005–06	Ipswich T	1	0		
2006–07	Ipswich T	0	0		
2006–07	*Millwall*	2	0		
2007–08	Ipswich T	7	1		
2008–09	Ipswich T	3	0		
2008–09	*Grimsby T*	15	2	15	2
2008–09	*Scunthorpe U*	12	1	12	1
2009–10	Ipswich T	12	0	23	2
2009–10	Millwall	20	1		
2010–11	Millwall	35	7		
2011–12	Millwall	35	7		
2012–13	Millwall	36	6		
2013–14	Millwall	19	3	147	24
2013–14	Bolton W	16	1		
2014–15	Bolton W	14	1		
2015–16	Bolton W	13	1		
2015–16	*Nottingham F*	9	1	9	1
2016–17	Bolton W	30	2	63	5
2017–18	AFC Wimbledon	42	3	42	3

TZANEV, Nikola (G)   0   0
Internationals: New Zealand U20, Full caps.
From Brentford.

2016–17	AFC Wimbledon	0	0
2017–18	AFC Wimbledon	0	0

URHOGHIDE, Osaze (D)   0   0

2017–18	AFC Wimbledon	0	0

Scholars
Ashley, Ossama wassim; Awoyejo, Jamil
Tyrique Daniel; Burey, Tyler David
Sylvester; Carpene, Valentino Enrique
Garcia; Collins, Reuben Alexander; Evans,
Great Nil-Okai; Lodge, Francis Donte
Antonio; Macnab, Finlay Alexander; Mbele,
Richie Bless; Mills, Bobby John Barry;
Nelson-Roberts, Ethan Cameron O'Neil;
Perana, Dean; Rudoni, Jack; Scott, Thomas
Norman; Weekes, Reece Lee Philip.

ARSENAL (3)

AKPOM, Chuba (F)   82   9
H: 6 0 W: 12 02 b.London 9-10-95
Internationals: England U16, U17, U19, U20, U21.

2012–13	Arsenal	0	0		
2013–14	Arsenal	1	0		
2013–14	*Brentford*	4	0	4	0
2013–14	*Coventry C*	6	0	6	0
2014–15	Arsenal	3	0		
2014–15	*Nottingham F*	7	0	7	0
2015–16	Arsenal	0	0		
2015–16	*Hull C*	35	3	35	3
2016–17	Arsenal	0	0		
2016–17	*Brighton & HA*	10	0	10	0
2017–18	Arsenal	0	0	4	0
2017–18	*St. Truidense*	16	6	16	6

AUBAMEYANG, Pierre-Emerick (F)   297   155
H: 6 2 W: 11 09 b.Bitam 18-6-89
Internationals: France U21. Gabon U23, Full caps.

2008–09	AC Milan	0	0		
2008–09	*Dijon*	34	8	34	8
2009–10	AC Milan	0	0		
2009–10	*Lille*	14	2	14	2
2010–11	AC Milan	0	0		
2010–11	*Monaco*	19	2	19	2
2010–11	*Saint-Etienne*	17	10		
2011–12	*Saint-Etienne*	19	6		
2012–13	*Saint-Etienne*	37	19	73	35
2013–14	Borussia Dortmund	32	13		
2014–15	Borussia Dortmund	33	16		
2015–16	Borussia Dortmund	31	25		
2016–17	Borussia Dortmund	32	31		
2017–18	Borussia Dortmund	16	13	144	98
2017–18	Arsenal	13	10	13	10

BELLERIN, Hector (D)   132   6
H: 5 10 W: 11 09 b.Barcelona 19-3-95
Internationals: Spain U16, U17, U19, U21, Full caps.

2012–13	Arsenal	0	0		
2013–14	Arsenal	0	0		
2013–14	*Watford*	8	0	8	0
2014–15	Arsenal	20	2		
2015–16	Arsenal	36	1		
2016–17	Arsenal	33	1		
2017–18	Arsenal	35	2	124	6

BIELIK, Krystian (M)   15   0
H: 5 10 W: 11 00 b.Vrinnevi 4-1-98
Internationals: Poland U16, U17, U18, U19.

2014–15	Legia Warsaw	5	0	5	0
2014–15	Arsenal	0	0		
2015–16	Arsenal	0	0		
2016–17	Arsenal	0	0		
2016–17	*Birmingham C*	10	0	10	0
2017–18	Arsenal	0	0		
2017–18	*Walsall*	0	0		

BOLA, Marc (D)   31   0
H: 6 1 W: 12 04 b.Greenwich 9-12-97

2016–17	Arsenal	0	0		
2016–17	*Notts Co*	13	0	13	0
2017–18	Arsenal	0	0		
2017–18	*Bristol R*	18	0	18	0

BRAMALL, Cohen (D)   5   0
H: 5 9 W: 11 00 b.Crewe 2-4-95
From Hednesford T.

2017–18	Arsenal	0	0		
2017–18	*Birmingham C*	5	0	5	0

CAMPBELL, Joel (F)   159   22
H: 5 10 W: 12 00 b.Costa Rica 26-6-92
Internationals: Costa Rica U17, U20, Full caps.

2009–10	Saprissa	1	0		
2010–11	Saprissa	2	0	3	0
2010–11	*Puntarenas*	5	0	5	0
2011–12	Arsenal	0	0		
2011–12	*Lorient*	25	3	25	3
2012–13	Arsenal	0	0		
2012–13	*Real Betis*	28	2		
2013–14	Arsenal	0	0		
2013–14	*Olympiacos*	32	8	32	8
2014–15	Arsenal	4	0		
2014–15	*Villarreal*	16	1	16	1
2015–16	Arsenal	19	3		
2016–17	Arsenal	0	0		
2016–17	*Sporting Lisbon*	19	3	19	3
2017–18	Arsenal	0	0	23	3
2017–18	*Real Betis*	8	2	36	4

CECH, Petr (G)   564   0
H: 6 5 W: 14 07 b.Plzen 20-5-82
Internationals: Czech Republic U16, U17, U18, U20, U21, Full caps.

1998–99	Viktoria Plzen	1	0		
1999–2000	Chmel	1	0		
2000–01	Chmel	26	0	27	0
2001–02	Sparta Prague	26	0	26	0
2002–03	Rennes	37	0		
2003–04	Rennes	38	0	75	0
2004–05	Chelsea	35	0		
2005–06	Chelsea	34	0		
2006–07	Chelsea	26	0		
2007–08	Chelsea	26	0		
2008–09	Chelsea	35	0		
2009–10	Chelsea	34	0		
2010–11	Chelsea	38	0		
2011–12	Chelsea	34	0		
2012–13	Chelsea	36	0		
2013–14	Chelsea	34	0		
2014–15	Chelsea	7	0	333	0
2015–16	Arsenal	34	0		
2016–17	Arsenal	35	0		
2017–18	Arsenal	34	0	103	0

CHAMBERS, Calum (D)   94   3
H: 6 0 W: 10 05 b.Petersfield 20-1-95
Internationals: England U17, U19, U21, Full caps.

2011–12	Southampton	0	0		
2012–13	Southampton	0	0		
2013–14	Southampton	22	0	22	0
2014–15	Arsenal	23	1		
2015–16	Arsenal	12	0		
2016–17	Arsenal	1	1		
2016–17	*Middlesbrough*	24	1	24	1
2017–18	Arsenal	12	0	48	2

COQUELIN, Francis (M)   180   1
H: 5 10 W: 11 08 b.Laval 13-5-91
Internationals: France U17, U18, U19, U20, U21.

2008–09	Arsenal	0	0		
2009–10	Arsenal	0	0		
2010–11	Arsenal	0	0		
2010–11	*Lorient*	24	1	24	1
2011–12	Arsenal	10	0		
2012–13	Arsenal	11	0		
2013–14	Arsenal	0	0		
2013–14	*SC Freiburg*	16	0	16	0
2014–15	Arsenal	12	0		
2014–15	*Charlton Ath*	5	0	5	0
2015–16	Arsenal	26	0		
2016–17	Arsenal	29	0		
2017–18	Arsenal	7	0	105	0

Transferred to Valencia, January 2018.

DA SILVA, Josh (M)   0   0
b. 23-10-98
Internationals: England U19, U20.

2016–17	Arsenal	0	0
2017–18	Arsenal	0	0

DRAGOMIR, Vlad (M)   2   0
H: 5 10 W: 10 08 b.Timisoara 24-4-99
Internationals: Romania U17, U19, U21.

2014–15	Poli Timisoara	2	0	2	0
2015–16	Arsenal	0	0		
2016–17	Arsenal	0	0		
2017–18	*ACS Poli Timisoara*	0	0		
2017–18	Arsenal	0	0		

ELNENY, Mohamed (M)   164   7
H: 5 11 W: 11 00 b.Al-Mahalla Al-Kubra 11-7-92
Internationals: Egypt U20, U23, Full caps.

2010–11	El Mokawloon	21	2		
2011–12	El Mokawloon	14	0	35	2
2012–13	Basel	15	0		
2013–14	Basel	32	1		
2014–15	Basel	28	2	75	3
2015–16	Basle	16	2	16	2
2015–16	Arsenal	11	0		
2016–17	Arsenal	14	0		
2017–18	Arsenal	13	0	38	0

GILMOUR, Charlie (M)   0   0
b.Brighton 11-2-99
Internationals: England U16, U17. Scotland U16, U17, U19.

2017–18	Arsenal	0	0

HOLDING, Rob (D)   48   1
b.Tameside 20-9-95
Internationals: England U21.

2014–15	Bolton W	0	0		
2014–15	*Bury*	1	0	1	0
2015–16	Bolton W	26	1	26	1
2016–17	Arsenal	9	0		
2017–18	Arsenal	12	0	21	0

ILIEV, Dejan (G)   0   0
H: 6 5 b.Strumica 25-2-95
Internationals: Macedonia U17, U19, U21.

2012–13	Arsenal	0	0
2013–14	Arsenal	0	0
2014–15	Arsenal	0	0
2015–16	Arsenal	0	0
2017–18	Arsenal	0	0

IWOBI, Alex (M)   65   8
H: 5 11 W: 11 11 b.Lagos 3-5-96
Internationals: England U16, U17, U18. Nigeria Full caps.

2012–13	Arsenal	0	0

2013–14 Arsenal 0 0
2014–15 Arsenal 0 0
2015–16 Arsenal 13 2
2016–17 Arsenal 26 3
2017–18 Arsenal 26 3 **65 8**

JENKINSON, Carl (D) **105 3**
H: 6 1 W: 12 02 b.Harlow 8-2-92
Internationals: Finland U19, U21. England U17, U21, Full caps.
2010–11 Charlton Ath 8 0 **8 0**
2010–11 Arsenal 1 0
2011–12 Arsenal 9 0
2012–13 Arsenal 14 0
2013–14 Arsenal 14 1
2014–15 Arsenal 0 0
2014–15 West Ham U 32 0
2015–16 Arsenal 0 0
2015–16 West Ham U 20 2 **52 2**
2016–17 Arsenal 1 0
2017–18 Arsenal 0 0 **38 1**
2017–18 Birmingham C 7 0 **7 0**

KOLASINAC, Sead (D) **121 6**
H: 6 0 W: 12 13 b.Karlsruhe 20-6-93
Internationals: Germany U18, U19, U20. Bosnia and Herzegovina Full caps.
2012–13 Schalke 04 16 0
2013–14 Schalke 04 24 0
2014–15 Schalke 04 6 0
2015–16 Schalke 04 23 1
2016–17 Schalke 04 25 3 **94 4**
2017–18 Arsenal 27 2 **27 2**

KOSCIELNY, Laurent (D) **381 28**
H: 6 1 W: 11 11 b.Tulle 10-9-85
Internationals: France Full caps.
2004–05 Guingamp 11 0
2005–06 Guingamp 9 0
2006–07 Guingamp 21 0 **41 0**
2007–08 Tours 33 1
2008–09 Tours 34 5 **67 6**
2009–10 Lorient 35 3 **35 3**
2010–11 Arsenal 30 2
2011–12 Arsenal 33 2
2012–13 Arsenal 25 2
2013–14 Arsenal 32 2
2014–15 Arsenal 27 3
2015–16 Arsenal 33 4
2016–17 Arsenal 33 2
2017–18 Arsenal 25 2 **238 19**

LACAZETTE, Alexandre (F) **235 114**
H: 5 9 W: 10 12 b.Lyon 28-5-91
Internationals: France U16, U17, U18, U19, U20, U21, Full caps.
2009–10 Lyon 1 0
2010–11 Lyon 9 1
2011–12 Lyon 29 5
2012–13 Lyon 31 3
2013–14 Lyon 36 15
2014–15 Lyon 33 27
2015–16 Lyon 34 21
2016–17 Lyon 30 28 **203 100**
2017–18 Arsenal 32 14 **32 14**

LUCAS PEREZ, Martinez (F) **194 57**
H: 5 11 W: 11 07 b.A Coruna 10-9-88
2009–10 Rayo Vallecano 1 0
2010–11 Rayo Vallecano 5 1 **7 1**
2010–11 Karpaty Lviv 1 0
2011–12 Karpaty Lviv 26 6
2012–13 Karpaty Lviv 17 8 **51 14**
2012–13 Dynamo Kyiv 0 0
2013–14 PAOK 32 9 **32 9**
2014–15 Deportivo La Coruna 21 6
2015–16 Deportivo La Coruna 36 17
2016–17 Deportivo La Coruna 1 1
2016–17 Arsenal 11 1
2017–18 Arsenal 0 0 **11 1**
2017–18 Deportivo La Coruna 35 8 **93 32**

MACEY, Matt (G) **15 0**
H: 6 6 W: 14 05 b.Bristol 9-9-94
2011–12 Bristol R 0 0
2012–13 Bristol R 0 0
2013–14 Arsenal 0 0
2014–15 Arsenal 0 0
2014–15 Accrington S 4 0 **4 0**
2015–16 Arsenal 0 0
2016–17 Arsenal 0 0
2016–17 Luton T 11 0 **11 0**
2017–18 Arsenal 0 0

MAITLAND-NILES, Ainsley (F) **47 1**
H: 5 10 W: 11 05 b.Goodmayes 29-8-97
Internationals: England U17, U18, U19, U20, U21.
2014–15 Arsenal 1 0

2015–16 Arsenal 0 0
2015–16 Ipswich T 30 1 **30 1**
2016–17 Arsenal 1 0
2017–18 Arsenal 15 0 **17 0**

MAVIDIDI, Stephy (F) **27 2**
b.Derby 31-5-98
Internationals: England U17, U18, U19, U20.
2016–17 Arsenal 0 0
2016–17 Charlton Ath 5 0
2017–18 Arsenal 0 0
2017–18 Preston NE 10 0 **10 0**
2017–18 Charlton Ath 12 2 **17 2**

MAVROPANOS, Konstantinos (D) **19 3**
H: 6 4 W: 12 08 b.Athens 11-12-97
Internationals: Greece U21.
2016–17 PAS Giannina 2 0
2017–18 PAS Giannina 14 3 **16 3**
2017–18 Arsenal 3 0 **3 0**

McGUANE, Marcus (M) **0 0**
b.Greenwich 2-2-99
Internationals: Republic of Ireland U17. England U17, U18, U19.
2017–18 Arsenal 0 0
Transferred to Barcelona, January 2018.

MERTESACKER, Per (D) **376 25**
H: 6 6 W: 14 -02 b.Hannover 29-9-84
Internationals: Germany U20, U21, Full caps.
2003–04 Hannover 13 0
2004–05 Hannover 31 2
2005–06 Hannover 30 5 **74 7**
2006–07 Werder Bremen 25 2
2007–08 Werder Bremen 32 1
2008–09 Werder Bremen 23 2
2009–10 Werder Bremen 33 5
2010–11 Werder Bremen 29 2
2011–12 Werder Bremen 4 0 **146 12**
2011–12 Arsenal 21 0
2012–13 Arsenal 34 3
2013–14 Arsenal 35 2
2014–15 Arsenal 35 0
2015–16 Arsenal 24 0
2016–17 Arsenal 1 0
2017–18 Arsenal 6 1 **156 6**

MKHITARYAN, Henrikh (M) **319 110**
H: 5 10 W: 12 00 b.Yerevan 21-1-89
Internationals: Armenia U17, U19, U21, Full caps.
2006 Pyunik 12 1
2007 Pyunik 24 12
2008 Pyunik 24 6
2009 Pyunik 10 11 **70 30**
2009–10 Metalurg Donetsk 29 9
2010–11 Metalurg Donetsk 8 3 **37 12**
2010–11 Shakhtar Donetsk 17 3
2011–12 Shakhtar Donetsk 26 10
2012–13 Shakhtar Donetsk 29 25 **72 38**
2013–14 Borussia Dortmund 31 9
2014–15 Borussia Dortmund 28 3
2015–16 Borussia Dortmund 31 11 **90 23**
2016–17 Manchester U 24 4
2017–18 Manchester U 15 1 **39 5**
2017–18 Arsenal 11 2 **11 2**

MONREAL, Nacho (D) **335 9**
H: 5 10 W: 11 04 b.Pamplona 26-2-86
Internationals: Spain U19, U21, Full caps.
2006–07 Osasuna 11 0
2007–08 Osasuna 27 0
2008–09 Osasuna 28 0
2009–10 Osasuna 31 1
2010–11 Osasuna 31 1 **128 2**
2011–12 Malaga 34 0
2012–13 Malaga 14 1 **45 1**
2012–13 Arsenal 10 1
2013–14 Arsenal 23 0
2014–15 Arsenal 28 0
2015–16 Arsenal 37 0
2016–17 Arsenal 36 0
2017–18 Arsenal 28 5 **162 6**

MOORE, Tafari (D) **13 0**
H: 5 8 b.London 5-7-97
Internationals: England U16, U17, U18, U19, U20.
2015–16 Arsenal 0 0
2016–17 Arsenal 0 0
2017–18 Arsenal 0 0
2017–18 Arsenal 0 0
2017–18 Wycombe W 13 0 **13 0**

MUSTAFI, Shkodran (D) **167 12**
H: 6 0 W: 11 07 b.Bad Hersfeld 17-4-92
Internationals: Germany U16, U17, U18, U19, U20, U21, Full caps.
2009–10 Everton 0 0
2010–11 Everton 0 0
2011–12 Everton 0 0
2011–12 Sampdoria 1 0
2012–13 Sampdoria 17 0
2013–14 Sampdoria 33 1 **51 1**
2014–15 Valencia 33 4
2015–16 Valencia 30 2 **63 6**
2016–17 Arsenal 26 2
2017–18 Arsenal 27 3 **53 5**

NELSON, Reiss (F) **3 0**
H: 5 9 W: 11 00 b.London 10-12-99
Internationals: England U16, U17, U18, U19. From Lewisham Bor.
2017–18 Arsenal 3 0 **3 0**

NKETIAH, Eddie (F) **3 0**
b.Lewisham 30-5-99
Internationals: England U18, U19, U21.
2017–18 Arsenal 3 0 **3 0**

OSEI-TUTU, Jordi (D) **0 0**
b.Slough 2-10-98
2017–18 Arsenal 0 0

OSPINA, David (G) **315 0**
H: 6 0 W: 12 00 b.Medellin 31-8-88
Internationals: Colombia U20, Full caps.
2006 Atletico Nacional 34 0
2007 Atletico Nacional 47 0
2008 Atletico Nacional 16 0 **97 0**
2008–09 Nice 25 0
2009–10 Nice 37 0
2010–11 NIce 35 0
2011–12 Nice 37 0
2012–13 Nice 26 0
2013–14 NIce 29 0 **189 0**
2014–15 Arsenal 18 0
2015–16 Arsenal 4 0
2016–17 Arsenal 2 0
2017–18 Arsenal 5 0 **29 0**

OZIL, Mesut (M) **347 59**
H: 5 11 W: 11 06 b.Gelsenkirchen 15-10-88
Internationals: Germany U19, U21, Full caps.
2005–06 Schalke 04 0 0
2006–07 Schalke 04 19 0
2007–08 Schalke 04 11 0 **30 0**
2007–08 Werder Bremen 12 1
2008–09 Werder Bremen 27 3
2009–10 Werder Bremen 31 9
2010–11 Werder Bremen 0 0 **70 13**
2010–11 Real Madrid 36 6
2011–12 Real Madrid 35 4
2012–13 Real Madrid 32 9
2013–14 Real Madrid 2 0 **105 19**
2013–14 Arsenal 26 5
2014–15 Arsenal 22 4
2015–16 Arsenal 35 6
2016–17 Arsenal 33 8
2017–18 Arsenal 26 4 **142 27**

PLEGUEZUELO, Julio (D) **25 0**
b. 26-1-97
Internationals: Spain U16, U17, U18.
2016–17 Arsenal 0 0
2017–18 Mallorca 15 0 **15 0**
2017–18 Arsenal 0 0
2018 Gimnastic 10 0 **10 0**

RAMSEY, Aaron (M) **261 38**
H: 5 9 W: 10 07 b.Caerphilly 26-12-90
Internationals: Wales U17, U21, Full caps. Great Britain.
2006–07 Cardiff C 1 0
2007–08 Cardiff C 15 1
2008–09 Arsenal 9 0
2009–10 Arsenal 18 3
2010–11 Arsenal 7 1
2010–11 Nottingham F 5 0 **5 0**
2010–11 Cardiff C 6 1 **22 2**
2011–12 Arsenal 34 2
2012–13 Arsenal 36 1
2013–14 Arsenal 23 10
2014–15 Arsenal 29 6
2015–16 Arsenal 31 5
2016–17 Arsenal 23 1
2017–18 Arsenal 24 7 **234 36**

REINE-ADELAIDE, Jeff (M)   **10   0**
H: 6 0   W: 11 11   b.Champigny-sur-Marne 17-1-98
Internationals: France U16, U17, U18, U19, U20.

2014–15	Lens	0	0		
2015–16	Arsenal	0	0		
2016–17	Arsenal	0	0		
2017–18	Arsenal	0	0		
2017–18	*Angers*	10	0	10	0

SHEAF, Ben (M)   **10   0**
H: 5 10   W: 10 01   b.Dartford 5-2-98
Internationals: England U18.

2015–16	Arsenal	0	0		
2016–17	Arsenal	0	0		
2017–18	Arsenal	0	0		
2017–18	*Stevenage*	10	0	10	0

WELBECK, Danny (F)   **206   43**
H: 6 1   W: 11 07   b.Manchester 26-11-90
Internationals: England U17, U18, U19, U21, Full caps.

2007–08	Manchester U	0	0		
2008–09	Manchester U	3	1		
2009–10	Manchester U	5	0		
2009–10	*Preston NE*	8	2	8	2
2010–11	Manchester U	0	0		
2010–11	*Sunderland*	26	6	26	6
2011–12	Manchester U	30	9		
2012–13	Manchester U	27	1		
2013–14	Manchester U	25	9		
2014–15	Manchester U	2	0	92	20
2014–15	Arsenal	25	4		
2015–16	Arsenal	11	4		
2016–17	Arsenal	16	2		
2017–18	Arsenal	28	5	80	15

WILLOCK, Joe (M)   **2   0**
b.Waltham Forest 20-8-99
Internationals: England U16, U19.

2017–18	Arsenal	2	0	2	0

WILSHERE, Jack (M)   **166   8**
H: 5 7   W: 11 03   b.Stevenage 1-1-92
Internationals: England U16, U17, U19, U21, Full caps.

2008–09	Arsenal	1	0		
2009–10	Arsenal	1	0		
2009–10	*Bolton W*	14	1	14	1
2010–11	Arsenal	35	1		
2011–12	Arsenal	0	0		
2012–13	Arsenal	25	0		
2013–14	Arsenal	24	3		
2014–15	Arsenal	14	2		
2015–16	Arsenal	3	0		
2016–17	Arsenal	2	0		
2016–17	*Bournemouth*	27	0	27	0
2017–18	Arsenal	20	1	125	7

Players retained or with offer of contract
Amaechi, Xavier Casmier; Asano, Takuma; Coyle, Trae; Fortune, Yassin Enzo; John-Jules, Tyreece Romayo; Martinez, Damian Emiliano; Medley, Zechariah Joshua Henry; Mustafi, Shkodran; Nwakali, Kelechi; Olowu, Joseph Olugbenga; Pleguezuelo, Julio Jose; Smith Rowe, Emile; Tormey, Nathan Alexander; Virginia, Joao; Zelalem, Gedion.

Scholars
Ballard, Daniel George; Balogun, Folarin Jerry; Barden, Daniel; Burton, Robert; Clarke, Harrison Thomas; Daley-Campbell, Vontae; McEneff, Jordan John; McGuinness, Mark James; Olayinka, Olujimi James Ayodele; Omole, Tobi; Smith, Matthew Gerrard; Spencer-Adams, Bayli Alexander; Swanson, Zak; Thompson, Dominic.

ASTON VILLA (4)

ABDO, Khalid (M)   **0   0**
b.1-9-96

2017–18	Aston Villa	0	0

ADOMAH, Albert (F)   **450   76**
H: 6 1   W: 11 08   b.Lambeth 13-12-87
Internationals: Ghana Full caps.

2007–08	Barnet	22	5		
2008–09	Barnet	45	9		
2009–10	Barnet	45	5	112	19
2010–11	Bristol C	46	5		
2011–12	Bristol C	45	5		
2012–13	Bristol C	40	7	131	17
2013–14	Middlesbrough	42	12		
2014–15	Middlesbrough	43	5		
2015–16	Middlesbrough	43	6		
2016–17	Middlesbrough	2	0	130	23
2016–17	Aston Villa	38	3		
2017–18	Aston Villa	39	14	77	17

AGBONLAHOR, Gabriel (F)   **351   75**
H: 5 11   W: 12 05   b.Birmingham 13-10-86
Internationals: England U21, Full caps.

2005–06	Aston Villa	9	1		
2005–06	*Watford*	2	0	2	0
2005–06	*Sheffield W*	8	0	8	0
2006–07	Aston Villa	38	9		
2007–08	Aston Villa	37	11		
2008–09	Aston Villa	36	11		
2009–10	Aston Villa	36	13		
2010–11	Aston Villa	26	3		
2011–12	Aston Villa	33	5		
2012–13	Aston Villa	28	9		
2013–14	Aston Villa	30	4		
2014–15	Aston Villa	34	6		
2015–16	Aston Villa	15	1		
2016–17	Aston Villa	13	1		
2017–18	Aston Villa	6	1	341	75

AMAVI, Jordan (D)   **126   4**
H: 5 9   W: 11 00   b.Toulon 9-3-94
Internationals: France U18, U20, U21.

2013–14	Nice	19	0		
2014–15	Nice	36	4	55	4
2015–16	Aston Villa	10	0		
2016–17	Aston Villa	34	0		
2017–18	Aston Villa	0	0	44	0
2017–18	*Marseille*	27	0	27	0

BJARNASON, Birkir (M)   **274   46**
H: 6 0   W: 11 07   b.Akureyri 27-5-88
Internationals: Iceland U17, U19, U21, Full caps.

2004	Por Akureyri	0	0		
2005	KA Akureyri	0	0		
2006	Viking Stavanger	16	1		
2007	Viking Stavanger	25	1		
2008	Viking Stavanger	30	1		
2008	*FK Bodo/Glimt*	22	5	22	5
2009	Viking Stavanger	30	7		
2010	Viking Stavanger	25	8		
2011	Viking Stavanger	25	0	102	16
2011–12	Standard Liege	16	0		
2012–13	Standard Liege	0	0	16	0
2012–13	*Pescara Calcio*	24	2		
2013–14	*Pescara Calcio*	1	0		
2013–14	Sampdoria	14	0	14	0
2014–15	*Pescara Calcio*	35	10	60	12
2015–16	Basle	29	10		
2016–17	Basle	0	0	29	10
2016–17	Aston Villa	8	0		
2017–18	Aston Villa	23	3	31	3

BORG, Oscar (M)   **0   0**
From West Ham U.

2017–18	Aston Villa	0	0

BREE, James (D)   **63   0**
H: 5 10   W: 11 09   b.Wakefield 11-10-97

2013–14	Barnsley	1	0		
2014–15	Barnsley	11	0		
2015–16	Barnsley	19	0		
2016–17	Barnsley	19	0	50	0
2016–17	Aston Villa	7	0		
2017–18	Aston Villa	6	0	13	0

BUNN, Mark (G)   **171   0**
H: 6 0   W: 12 02   b.Southgate 16-11-84

2004–05	Northampton T	0	0		
2005–06	Northampton T	0	0		
2006–07	Northampton T	42	0		
2007–08	Northampton T	45	0		
2008–09	Northampton T	3	0	90	0
2008–09	Blackburn R	0	0		
2008–09	*Leicester C*	3	0	3	0
2009–10	Blackburn R	0	0		
2009–10	*Sheffield U*	32	0	32	0
2010–11	Blackburn R	3	0		
2011–12	Blackburn R	3	0		
2012–13	Blackburn R	0	0	6	0
2012–13	Norwich C	23	0		

2013–14	Norwich C	0	0		
2014–15	Norwich C	0	0	23	0
2015–16	Aston Villa	10	0		
2016–17	Aston Villa	6	0		
2017–18	Aston Villa	1	0	17	0

CHESTER, James (D)   **286   16**
H: 5 11   W: 11 04   b.Warrington 23-1-89
Internationals: Wales Full caps.

2007–08	Manchester U	0	0		
2008–09	Manchester U	0	0		
2008–09	*Peterborough U*	5	0	5	0
2009–10	Manchester U	0	0		
2009–10	*Plymouth Arg*	3	0	3	0
2010–11	Manchester U	0	0		
2010–11	*Carlisle U*	18	2	18	2
2010–11	Hull C	21	1		
2011–12	Hull C	44	2		
2012–13	Hull C	44	1		
2013–14	Hull C	24	1		
2014–15	Hull C	23	2	156	7
2015–16	WBA	13	0	13	0
2016–17	Aston Villa	45	3		
2017–18	Aston Villa	46	4	91	7

CLARK, Mitchell (D)   **0   0**
b.Nuneaton 13-3-99
Internationals: Wales U17, U19.

2017–18	Aston Villa	0	0

COX, Jordan (M)   **0   0**
b.Worcester 4-11-98

2017–18	Aston Villa	0	0

DAVIS, Keinan (M)   **34   2**
H: 5 6   W: 10 10   b.Stevenage 13-2-98
Internationals: England U20.

2015–16	Aston Villa	0	0		
2016–17	Aston Villa	6	0		
2017–18	Aston Villa	28	2	34	2

DE LAET, Ritchie (D)   **181   5**
H: 6 1   W: 12 02   b.Antwerp 28-11-88
Internationals: Belgium U21, Full caps.

2007–08	Stoke C	0	0		
2008–09	Stoke C	0	0		
2008–09	Manchester U	1	0		
2009–10	Manchester U	2	0		
2010–11	Manchester U	0	0		
2010–11	*Sheffield U*	6	0	6	0
2010–11	*Preston NE*	5	0	5	0
2010–11	*Portsmouth*	22	0	22	0
2011–12	Manchester U	0	0	3	0
2011–12	*Norwich C*	6	1	6	1
2012–13	Leicester C	41	1		
2013–14	Leicester C	36	2		
2014–15	Leicester C	26	0		
2015–16	Leicester C	12	1	115	4
2015–16	*Middlesbrough*	10	0	10	0
2016–17	Aston Villa	3	0		
2017–18	Aston Villa	5	0	8	0
2017–18	*Royal Antwerp*	6	0	6	0

DOYLE-HAYES, Jake (M)   **0   0**
b.Ballyjamesduff 30-12-98
Internationals: Republic of Ireland U17, U18, U19.

2017–18	Aston Villa	0	0

ELMOHAMADY, Ahmed (M)   **365   25**
H: 5 11   W: 12 10   b.El Mahalla El-Kubra 9-9-87
Internationals: Egypt Full caps.

2003–04	Ghazi Al-Mehalla	0	0		
2004–05	Ghazi Al-Mehalla	14	4		
2005–06	Ghazi Al-Mehalla	3	0	17	4
2006–07	ENPPI	12	2		
2007–08	ENPPI	6	1		
2008–09	ENPPI	28	6		
2009–10	ENPPI	12	1	58	10
2010–11	Sunderland	36	0		
2011–12	Sunderland	18	1		
2012–13	Sunderland	2	0	56	1
2012–13	Hull C	41	3		
2013–14	Hull C	38	2		
2014–15	Hull C	38	2		
2015–16	Hull C	41	3		
2016–17	Hull C	33	0	191	10
2017–18	Aston Villa	43	0	43	0

ELPHICK, Tommy (M)   **317   12**
H: 5 11   W: 11 07   b.Brighton 7-9-87

2005–06	Brighton & HA	1	0
2006–07	Brighton & HA	3	0
2007–08	Brighton & HA	39	2
2008–09	Brighton & HA	39	1
2009–10	Brighton & HA	44	3
2010–11	Brighton & HA	27	1
2011–12	Brighton & HA	0	0

2012–13	Brighton & HA	0	0	**153**	**7**
2012–13	Bournemouth	34	2		
2013–14	Bournemouth	38	1		
2014–15	Bournemouth	46	1		
2015–16	Bournemouth	12	1	**130**	**5**
2016–17	Aston Villa	26	0		
2017–18	Aston Villa	4	0	**30**	**0**
2017–18	*Reading*	4	0	**4**	**0**

GARDNER, Gary (M) **133** **12**
H: 6 2 W: 12 13 b.Solihull 29-6-92
Internationals: England U17, U19, U20, U21.

2009–10	Aston Villa	0	0		
2010–11	Aston Villa	0	0		
2011–12	Aston Villa	14	0		
2011–12	*Coventry C*	4	1	**4**	**1**
2012–13	Aston Villa	2	0		
2013–14	Aston Villa	0	0		
2013–14	*Sheffield W*	3	0	**3**	**0**
2014–15	Aston Villa	0	0		
2014–15	*Brighton & HA*	17	2	**17**	**2**
2014–15	Nottingham F	18	4		
2015–16	Aston Villa	0	0		
2015–16	*Nottingham F*	20	2	**38**	**6**
2016–17	Aston Villa	26	1		
2017–18	Aston Villa	0	0	**42**	**1**
2017–18	*Barnsley*	29	2	**29**	**2**

GREALISH, Jack (M) **129** **14**
H: 5 9 W: 10 10 b.Birmingham 10-9-95
Internationals: Republic of Ireland U17, U18, U21. England U21.

2012–13	Aston Villa	0	0		
2013–14	Aston Villa	1	0		
2013–14	*Notts Co*	37	5	**37**	**5**
2014–15	Aston Villa	17	0		
2015–16	Aston Villa	16	1		
2016–17	Aston Villa	31	5		
2017–18	Aston Villa	27	3	**92**	**9**

GREEN, Andre (F) **22** **1**
H: 5 11 W: 11 03 b.Solihull 2-5-98
Internationals: England U16, U17, U18, U19, U20.

2014–15	Aston Villa	0	0		
2015–16	Aston Villa	2	0		
2016–17	Aston Villa	15	0		
2017–18	Aston Villa	5	1	**22**	**1**

HEPBURN-MURPHY, Rushian (F) **8** **0**
H: 5 8 W: 9 04 b.Birmingham 19-9-98
Internationals: England U16, U17, U18, U19, U20.

2014–15	Aston Villa	1	0		
2015–16	Aston Villa	1	0		
2016–17	Aston Villa	3	0		
2017–18	Aston Villa	3	0	**8**	**0**

HOGAN, Scott (F) **116** **45**
H: 5 11 W: 10 01 b.Salford 13-4-92
Internationals: Republic of Ireland Full caps.

2009–10	Rochdale	0	0		
2013–14	Rochdale	33	17	**33**	**17**
2014–15	Brentford	1	0		
2015–16	Brentford	7	7		
2016–17	Brentford	25	14	**33**	**21**
2016–17	Aston Villa	13	1		
2017–18	Aston Villa	37	6	**50**	**7**

HOURIHANE, Conor (M) **295** **56**
H: 5 11 W: 9 11 b.Cork 2-2-91
Internationals: Republic of Ireland U19, U21, Full caps.

2008–09	Sunderland	0	0		
2009–10	Sunderland	0	0		
2010–11	Ipswich T	0	0		
2011–12	Plymouth Arg	38	2		
2012–13	Plymouth Arg	42	5		
2013–14	Plymouth Arg	45	8	**125**	**15**
2014–15	Barnsley	46	13		
2015–16	Barnsley	41	10		
2016–17	Barnsley	25	6	**112**	**29**
2016–17	Aston Villa	17	1		
2017–18	Aston Villa	41	11	**58**	**12**

HUTTON, Alan (D) **329** **4**
H: 6 1 W: 11 05 b.Glasgow 30-11-84
Internationals: Scotland U21, Full caps.

2004–05	Rangers	10	0		
2005–06	Rangers	19	0		
2006–07	Rangers	33	1		
2007–08	Rangers	20	0	**82**	**1**
2007–08	Tottenham H	14	0		
2008–09	Tottenham H	8	0		
2009–10	Tottenham H	8	0		
2009–10	*Sunderland*	11	0	**11**	**0**
2010–11	Tottenham H	21	2		
2011–12	Tottenham H	0	0	**51**	**2**
2011–12	Aston Villa	31	0		
2012–13	Aston Villa	0	0		
2012–13	*Nottingham F*	7	0	**7**	**0**
2012–13	*Mallorca*	17	0	**17**	**0**
2013–14	Aston Villa	0	0		
2013–14	*Bolton W*	9	0	**9**	**0**
2014–15	Aston Villa	30	1		
2015–16	Aston Villa	28	0		
2016–17	Aston Villa	34	0		
2017–18	Aston Villa	29	0	**152**	**1**

JEDINAK, Mile (M) **413** **40**
H: 6 2 W: 13 12 b.Sydney 3-8-84
Internationals: Australia U20, Full caps.

2000–01	Sydney U	3	0		
2001–02	Sydney U	7	1		
2002–03	Sydney U	18	2		
2003–04	Varteks	0	0		
2004–05	Sydney U	24	3		
2005–06	Sydney U	30	6	**82**	**12**
2006–07	Central Coast M	8	0		
2007–08	Central Coast M	22	2		
2008–09	Central Coast M	15	6	**45**	**8**
2008–09	Genclerbirligi	15	1		
2009–10	Genclerbirligi	2	0		
2009–10	Antalya	28	5	**28**	**5**
2010–11	Genclerbirligi	21	3	**38**	**4**
2011–12	Crystal Palace	31	1		
2012–13	Crystal Palace	41	3		
2013–14	Crystal Palace	38	1		
2014–15	Crystal Palace	24	5		
2015–16	Crystal Palace	27	0		
2016–17	Crystal Palace	1	0	**162**	**10**
2016–17	Aston Villa	33	0		
2017–18	Aston Villa	25	1	**58**	**1**

KODJIA, Jonathan (F) **214** **72**
H: 6 2 W: 12 02 b.Saint-Denis 22-10-89
Internationals: Ivory Coast Full caps.

2008–09	Reims	2	0		
2009–10	Reims	0	0		
2010–11	Reims	5	0		
2011–12	Reims	2	0		
2011–12	*Cherbourg*	16	4	**16**	**4**
2012–13	Reims	0	0		
2012–13	*Amiens SC*	34	9	**34**	**9**
2013–14	Reims	0	0	**9**	**0**
2013–14	*Caen*	27	5	**27**	**5**
2014–15	Angers SCO	28	15	**28**	**15**
2015–16	Bristol C	45	19		
2016–17	Bristol C	4	0	**49**	**19**
2016–17	Aston Villa	36	19		
2017–18	Aston Villa	15	1	**51**	**20**

LANSBURY, Henri (M) **274** **48**
H: 6 0 W: 13 06 b.Enfield 12-10-90
Internationals: England U16, U17, U19, U21.

2007–08	Arsenal	0	0		
2008–09	Arsenal	0	0		
2008–09	*Scunthorpe U*	16	4	**16**	**4**
2009–10	Arsenal	1	0		
2009–10	*Watford*	37	5	**37**	**5**
2010–11	Arsenal	0	0		
2010–11	*Norwich C*	23	4	**23**	**4**
2011–12	Arsenal	2	0		
2011–12	*West Ham U*	22	1	**22**	**1**
2012–13	Arsenal	0	0	**3**	**0**
2012–13	Nottingham F	32	5		
2013–14	Nottingham F	29	7		
2014–15	Nottingham F	39	10		
2015–16	Nottingham F	28	4		
2016–17	Nottingham F	17	6	**145**	**32**
2016–17	Aston Villa	18	0		
2017–18	Aston Villa	10	2	**28**	**2**

LYDEN, Jordan (M) **4** **0**
H: 5 10 W: 11 00 b.Perth 30-1-96
Internationals: Australia U20.

2015–16	Aston Villa	4	0		
2016–17	Aston Villa	0	0		
2017–18	Aston Villa	0	0	**4**	**0**

McCORMACK, Ross (F) **412** **137**
H: 5 9 W: 11 00 b.Glasgow 18-8-86
Internationals: Scotland U21, B, Full caps.

2003–04	Rangers	2	1		
2004–05	Rangers	1	0		
2005–06	Rangers	8	1	**11**	**2**
2005–06	Doncaster R	19	4	**19**	**4**
2006–07	Motherwell	12	2		
2007–08	Motherwell	36	9	**48**	**11**
2008–09	Cardiff C	38	21		
2009–10	Cardiff C	34	4		
2010–11	Cardiff C	2	0	**74**	**25**
2010–11	Leeds U	21	2		
2011–12	Leeds U	45	18		
2012–13	Leeds U	32	5		
2013–14	Leeds U	46	28	**144**	**53**
2014–15	Fulham	44	17		
2015–16	Fulham	45	21	**89**	**38**
2016–17	Aston Villa	20	3		
2016–17	*Nottingham F*	7	1	**7**	**1**
2017–18	Aston Villa	0	0	**20**	**3**
2017–18	*Melbourne City*	0	0		

McKIRDY, Harry (M) **27** **4**
H: 5 9 W: 11 00 b.Stoke-on-Trent 29-3-97
From Stoke C.

2016–17	Aston Villa	0	0		
2016–17	*Stevenage*	11	1	**11**	**1**
2017–18	Aston Villa	0	0		
2017–18	*Crewe Alex*	16	3	**16**	**3**

O'HARE, Callum (F) **4** **0**
b.Solihull 1-5-98
Internationals: England U20.

2016–17	Aston Villa	0	0		
2017–18	Aston Villa	4	0	**4**	**0**

RICHARDS, Micah (D) **215** **8**
H: 5 11 W: 13 00 b.Birmingham 24-6-88
Internationals: England U16, U19, U21, Full caps. Great Britain.

2005–06	Manchester C	13	0		
2006–07	Manchester C	28	1		
2007–08	Manchester C	25	0		
2008–09	Manchester C	34	1		
2009–10	Manchester C	23	3		
2010–11	Manchester C	18	1		
2011–12	Manchester C	29	1		
2012–13	Manchester C	7	0		
2013–14	Manchester C	2	0		
2014–15	Manchester C	0	0	**179**	**7**
2014–15	*Fiorentina*	10	0	**10**	**0**
2015–16	Aston Villa	24	1		
2016–17	Aston Villa	2	0		
2017–18	Aston Villa	0	0	**26**	**1**

SAMBA, Christopher (D) **309** **31**
H: 6 5 W: 13 03 b.Creteil 28-3-84
Internationals: Congo U20, Full caps.

2001–02	Sedan	1	0		
2002–03	Sedan	0	0		
2003–04	Sedan	3	0	**4**	**0**
2004–05	Hertha Berlin	0	0		
2004–05	Hertha Berlin II	16	3		
2005–06	Hertha Berlin	12	0		
2005–06	Hertha Berlin II	12	1		
2006–07	Hertha Berlin	8	0	**20**	**0**
2006–07	Hertha Berlin II	2	0	**30**	**4**
2006–07	Blackburn R	14	2		
2007–08	Blackburn R	33	2		
2008–09	Blackburn R	35	2		
2009–10	Blackburn R	30	4		
2010–11	Blackburn R	33	4		
2011–12	Blackburn R	16	2	**161**	**16**
2012–13	Anzhi Makhachkala	27	3		
2012–13	QPR	10	0	**10**	**0**
2013–14	Anzhi Makhachkala	5	1	**32**	**4**
2013–14	Dinamo Moscow	10	2		
2014–15	Dinamo Moscow	24	4		
2015–16	Dinamo Moscow	4	0	**38**	**6**
2016–17	Panathinaikos	2	0	**2**	**0**
2017–18	Aston Villa	12	1	**12**	**1**

SARKIC, Matija (G) **0** **0**
H: 6 4 W: 11 07 b.Podgorica 23-6-97
Internationals: Montenegro U17, U19, U21.

2014–15	Anderlecht	0	0		
2015–16	Aston Villa	0	0		
2016–17	Aston Villa	0	0		
2017–18	Wigan Ath	0	0		
2017–18	Aston Villa	0	0		

STEER, Jed (G) **76** **0**
H: 6 2 W: 14 00 b.Norwich 23-9-92
Internationals: England U16, U17, U19.

2009–10	Norwich C	0	0		
2010–11	Norwich C	0	0		
2011–12	Norwich C	0	0		
2011–12	*Yeovil T*	12	0		
2012–13	Cambridge U	0	0		
2012–13	Norwich C	0	0		
2013–14	Aston Villa	0	0		
2014–15	Aston Villa	1	0		
2014–15	*Doncaster R*	13	0	**13**	**0**
2014–15	*Yeovil T*	12	0	**24**	**0**
2015–16	Aston Villa	0	0		
2015–16	*Huddersfield T*	38	0	**38**	**0**
2016–17	Aston Villa	0	0		
2017–18	Aston Villa	0	0	**1**	**0**

SULIMAN, Easah (D) **11** **0**
H: 6 2 W: 12 08 b. 26-1-98
Internationals: England U16, U17, U18, U19, U20.

2015–16	Aston Villa	0	0		
2016–17	Aston Villa	0	0		

2016–17	Cheltenham T	9	0	9	0
2017–18	Aston Villa	0	0		
2017–18	Grimsby T	2	0	2	0

TAYLOR, Corey (F)   1   0
b.Erdington 23-9-97
Internationals: England U17.

2015–16	Aston Villa	0	0		
2016–17	Aston Villa	1	0		
2017–18	Aston Villa	0	0	1	0

TAYLOR, Neil (D)   229   0
H: 5 9   W: 10 02   b.Ruthin 7-2-89
Internationals: Wales U17, U19, U21, C, Full caps. Great Britain.

2007–08	Wrexham	26	0	26	0
2010–11	Swansea C	29	0		
2011–12	Swansea C	36	0		
2012–13	Swansea C	6	0		
2013–14	Swansea C	10	0		
2014–15	Swansea C	34	0		
2015–16	Swansea C	34	0		
2016–17	Swansea C	11	0	160	0
2016–17	Aston Villa	14	0		
2017–18	Aston Villa	29	0	43	0

TERRY, John (D)   530   42
H: 6 1   W: 14 02   b.Barking 7-12-80
Internationals: England U21, Full caps.

1997–98	Chelsea	0	0		
1998–99	Chelsea	2	0		
1999–2000	Chelsea	4	0		
1999–2000	Nottingham F	6	0	6	0
2000–01	Chelsea	22	1		
2001–02	Chelsea	33	1		
2002–03	Chelsea	20	3		
2003–04	Chelsea	33	2		
2004–05	Chelsea	36	3		
2005–06	Chelsea	36	4		
2006–07	Chelsea	28	1		
2007–08	Chelsea	23	1		
2008–09	Chelsea	35	1		
2009–10	Chelsea	37	2		
2010–11	Chelsea	33	3		
2011–12	Chelsea	31	6		
2012–13	Chelsea	14	4		
2013–14	Chelsea	34	2		
2014–15	Chelsea	38	5		
2015–16	Chelsea	24	1		
2016–17	Chelsea	9	1	492	41
2017–18	Aston Villa	32	1	32	1

TONER, Kevin (D)   28   1
b. 18-7-96
Internationals: Republic of Ireland U19.

2015–16	Aston Villa	4	0		
2016–17	Aston Villa	0	0		
2016–17	Walsall	16	0	16	0
2016–17	Bradford C	2	1	2	1
2017–18	Aston Villa	0	0	4	0
2017–18	Stevenage	6	0	6	0

Transferred to St Patrick's Athletic December 2017.

TSHIBOLA, Aaron (M)   72   1
H: 6 3   W: 11 01   b.Newham 2-1-95
Internationals: England U18. DR Congo Full caps.

2011–12	Reading	0	0		
2012–13	Reading	0	0		
2013–14	Reading	0	0		
2014–15	Reading	1	0		
2014–15	Hartlepool U	23	0	23	0
2015–16	Reading	12	0	13	0
2016–17	Aston Villa	8	1		
2016–17	Nottingham F	4	0	4	0
2017–18	Aston Villa	0	0	8	1
2017–18	Milton Keynes D	12	0	12	0
2017–18	Kilmarnock	12	0	12	0

WHELAN, Glenn (M)   479   18
H: 5 11   W: 12 07   b.Dublin 13-1-84
Internationals: Republic of Ireland U16, U21, B, Full caps.

2000–01	Manchester C	0	0		
2001–02	Manchester C	0	0		
2002–03	Manchester C	0	0		
2003–04	Manchester C	0	0		
2003–04	Bury	13	0	13	0
2004–05	Sheffield W	36	2		
2005–06	Sheffield W	43	1		
2006–07	Sheffield W	38	7		
2007–08	Sheffield W	25	2	142	12
2007–08	Stoke C	14	1		
2008–09	Stoke C	26	1		
2009–10	Stoke C	33	2		
2010–11	Stoke C	29	0		
2011–12	Stoke C	30	1		
2012–13	Stoke C	32	0		
2013–14	Stoke C	32	0		
2014–15	Stoke C	28	0		
2015–16	Stoke C	37	0		
2016–17	Stoke C	30	0	291	6
2017–18	Aston Villa	33	1	33	1

Players retained or with offer of contract
Adomah, Albert; Bazeley, Isaiah Robert Graham; Bedeau, Jacob Mitchell; Clarke, Jack Aidan; Gil, de Pareja Vicent Carles; Gollini, Pierluigi; Knibbs, Harvey; Mooney, Kelsey; Odutayo, Colin Ladipo; Pastorek, Jozef; Prosser, Alexander; Vassilev, Indiana Denchev.

Scholars
Birch, Jack David; Birch, Mason Lewis; Boucher, Kieran David; Bridge, Mungo Olayipo Oladapo; Brunt, Lewis; Guy, Ben; Hooper, Anton Abeku; Ige, Luke; McConnachie, Charlie; Patterson, Ethan James Alexander; Ramsey, Jacob; Revan, Dominic; Rowe, Callum Miles; Sea, Dimitri Disseka; Stretch, Callum Blu; Tait, Moran Michael; Walker, Jake; Williams, Joshua Arthur.

BARNET (5)

AGHADIUNO, Benjamin (F)   1   0
b. 30-1-00
From Boreham Wood.

| 2017–18 | Barnet | 1 | 0 | 1 | 0 |

AKINDE, John (F)   226   68
H: 6 2   W: 10 01   b.Camberwell 8-7-89

2008–09	Bristol C	7	1		
2008–09	Wycombe W	11	7		
2009–10	Bristol C	7	0		
2009–10	Wycombe W	6	1	17	8
2009–10	Brentford	2	0	2	0
2010–11	Bristol C	2	0	16	1
2010–11	Bristol R	14	0	14	0
2010–11	Dagenham & R	9	2		
2011–12	Crawley T	25	1		
2011–12	Dagenham & R	5	0	14	2
2012–13	Crawley T	6	0	31	1
2012–13	Portsmouth	11	0		
2013–14	Portsmouth	0	0	11	0
2015–16	Barnet	43	23		
2016–17	Barnet	46	26		
2017–18	Barnet	32	7	121	56

AKINOLA, Simeon (F)   48   6
H: 5 10   W: 12 00   b. 6-8-92
From Boreham Wood, Harrow Bor, Braintree T.

| 2016–17 | Barnet | 19 | 2 | | |
| 2017–18 | Barnet | 29 | 4 | 48 | 6 |

AKPA AKPRO, Jean-Louis (F)   382   55
H: 6 0   W: 12 00   b.Toulouse 4-1-85

2004–05	Toulouse	13	0		
2005–06	Toulouse	14	3	27	3
2006–07	Brest	15	2	15	2
2007–08	FC Brussels	3	0	3	0
2008–09	Grimsby T	20	3		
2009–10	Grimsby T	36	5	56	8
2010–11	Rochdale	32	4		
2011–12	Rochdale	41	7	73	11
2012–13	Tranmere R	28	8		
2013–14	Tranmere R	25	2	53	10
2013–14	Bury	10	0	10	0
2014–15	Shrewsbury T	45	9		
2015–16	Shrewsbury T	36	6	83	15
2016–17	Barnet	23	1		
2016–17	Yeovil T	13	2	13	2
2017–18	Barnet	26	3	49	4

AMALUZOR, Justin (F)   15   0
H: 6 0   W: 12 00   b. 17-10-96
From Dartford.

| 2016–17 | Barnet | 11 | 0 | | |
| 2017–18 | Barnet | 4 | 0 | 15 | 0 |

BLACKMAN, Andre (D)   65   0
H: 5 11   W: 11 05   b.Lambeth 10-11-90

2009–10	Bristol C	0	0		
2011–12	Celtic	3	0		
2012–13	Celtic	0	0	3	0
2012–13	Inverness CT	2	0	2	0
2013–14	Plymouth Arg	6	0	6	0
2014–15	Blackpool	3	0	3	0
2016–17	Crawley T	32	0	32	0
2017–18	Barnet	19	0	19	0

BRIGGS, Matthew (D)   109   1
H: 6 1   W: 11 12   b.Wandsworth 6-3-91
Internationals: England U16, U17, U19, U20, U21. Guyana Full caps.

2006–07	Fulham	1	0		
2007–08	Fulham	0	0		
2008–09	Fulham	0	0		
2009–10	Fulham	0	0		
2009–10	Leyton Orient	1	0	1	0
2010–11	Fulham	3	0		
2011–12	Fulham	2	0		
2011–12	Peterborough U	5	0	5	0
2012–13	Fulham	5	0		
2012–13	Bristol C	4	0	4	0
2012–13	Watford	7	1	7	1
2013–14	Fulham	2	0	13	0
2014–15	Millwall	8	0	8	0
2014–15	Colchester U	18	0		
2015–16	Colchester U	26	0		
2016–17	Colchester U	15	0	59	0
2017–18	Chesterfield	11	0	11	0
2017–18	Barnet	1	0	1	0

BRINDLEY, Richard (D)   124   3
H: 5 10   W: 11 09   b.Coventry 30-11-87

2012–13	Chesterfield	12	0	12	0
2013–14	Rotherham U	16	0		
2014–15	Rotherham U	2	0	18	0
2014–15	Scunthorpe U	3	0	3	0
2014–15	Oxford U	3	0	3	0
2014–15	Colchester U	8	0		
2015–16	Colchester U	21	1		
2016–17	Colchester U	41	1	70	2
2017–18	Barnet	18	1	18	1

CLOUGH, Charlie (D)   56   1
H: 6 0   W: 12 04   b.Somerset 3-9-90

2007–08	Bristol R	0	0		
2008–09	Bristol R	0	0		
2009–10	Bristol R	0	0		
2010–11	Bristol R	2	0		
2011–12	Bristol R	0	0	2	0

From Dorchester, Sutton U, Forest Green R.

| 2016–17 | Barnet | 18 | 1 | | |
| 2017–18 | Barnet | 36 | 0 | 54 | 1 |

COKER, Tobi (D)   0   0

| 2016–17 | Barnet | 0 | 0 | | |
| 2017–18 | Barnet | 0 | 0 | | |

COULTHIRST, Shaquile (F)   137   28
H: 5 9   W: 12 02   b.Hackney 2-1-94
Internationals: England U19.

2012–13	Tottenham H	0	0		
2013–14	Tottenham H	0	0		
2013–14	Leyton Orient	1	1	1	1
2013–14	Torquay U	6	2	6	2
2014–15	Tottenham H	0	0		
2014–15	Southend U	22	4	22	4
2014–15	York C	11	2	11	2
2015–16	Tottenham H	0	0		
2015–16	Wigan Ath	2	0	2	0
2015–16	Peterborough U	19	2		
2016–17	Peterborough U	16	2	35	4
2016–17	Mansfield T	20	5	20	5
2017–18	Barnet	40	10	40	10

FONGUCK, Wesley (M)   23   0
H: 6 1   b.16-7-97

2016–17	Barnet	1	0		
2016–17	Barnet	3	0		
2017–18	Barnet	19	0	23	0

HINCKSON-MARS, Malakai (F)   1   0
b. 1-12-98
From Chelsea.

| 2017–18 | Barnet | 1 | 0 | 1 | 0 |

JOHNSON, Elliot (D)   105   2
H: 5 10   W: 12 02   b.Edgeware 17-8-94

2012–13	Barnet	26	1		
2015–16	Barnet	41	1		
2016–17	Barnet	36	0		
2017–18	Barnet	2	0	105	2

KYEI, Nana (M)   16   0
H: 5 11   W: 11 00   b. 10-1-98

2015–16	Barnet	1	0		
2016–17	Barnet	12	0		
2017–18	Barnet	3	0	16	0

MASON-CLARK, Ephron (F)   14   0
H: 5 10   W: 12 00   b.Lambeth 25-8-99

| 2016–17 | Barnet | 6 | 0 | | |
| 2017–18 | Barnet | 8 | 0 | 14 | 0 |

McKENZIE-LYLE, Kai (G)   1   0
H: 6 5   W: 13 08   b. 30-11-97
Internationals: Guyana Full caps.

| 2015–16 | Barnet | 1 | 0 | | |

2016–17 Barnet 0 0
2017–18 Barnet 0 0 1 0

McKENZIE-LYLE, Renell (G) 0 0
2017–18 Barnet 0 0

NELSON, Michael (D) 615 37
H:6 2 W:13 03 b.Gateshead 15-3-82
2000–01 Bury 5 0
2001–02 Bury 31 2
2002–03 Bury 39 5 72 8
2003–04 Hartlepool U 40 3
2004–05 Hartlepool U 43 1
2005–06 Hartlepool U 43 2
2006–07 Hartlepool U 42 1
2007–08 Hartlepool U 45 2
2008–09 Hartlepool U 46 5 259 14
2009–10 Norwich C 31 3
2010–11 Norwich C 8 2 39 5
2010–11 Scunthorpe U 20 0
2011–12 Scunthorpe U 10 1 30 1
2011–12 Kilmarnock 15 1
2012–13 Kilmarnock 21 1 36 2
2012–13 Bradford C 13 0 13 0
2013–14 Hibernian 34 2
2014–15 Hibernian 2 0 36 2
2014–15 Cambridge U 33 3 33 3
2015–16 Barnet 27 1
2016–17 Barnet 43 1
2017–18 Barnet 27 0 97 2

NICHOLLS, Alex (M) 330 51
H:5 10 W:11 00 b.Stourbridge 9-12-87
2005–06 Walsall 8 0
2006–07 Walsall 0 0
2007–08 Walsall 19 2
2008–09 Walsall 45 6
2009–10 Walsall 37 4
2010–11 Walsall 37 3
2011–12 Walsall 45 7 191 24
2012–13 Northampton T 15 7
2013–14 Northampton T 0 0
2014–15 Northampton T 6 1 21 8
2014–15 *Exeter C* 32 5
2015–16 *Exeter C* 35 5 67 10
2016–17 Barnet 17 2
2016–17 *Dundee U* 9 0 9 0
2017–18 Barnet 25 7 42 9

NICHOLSON, Jordan (F) 10 0
b. 29-9-93
From Histon.
2015–16 Peterborough U 2 0
From Nuneaton T.
2017–18 Peterborough U 0 0 2 0
2017–18 Barnet. 8 0 8 0

PASCAL, Dwight (M) 1 0
b.Hackney 7-3-01
2016–17 Barnet 0 0
2017–18 Barnet 1 0 1 0

PAYNE, Joe (D) 3 0
b. 2-4-99
2016–17 Barnet 0 0
2017–18 Barnet 3 0 3 0

ROSS, Craig (G) 33 0
b. 29-1-90
From Hampton & Richmond Bor, Cambridge U, Eastbourne, Farnborough, Whitehawk, Macclesfield T.
2017–18 Barnet 33 0 33 0

RUBEN BOVER, Izquierdo (M) 27 0
H:5 7 W:10 04 b.Majorca 24-6-92
2012–13 Charlton Ath 0 0
2012–13 New York RB 0 0
2016–17 Barnet 14 0
2017–18 Barnet 13 0 27 0

SANTOS, Ricardo (D) 120 6
H:6 5 W:12 02 b.Almada 18-6-95
2012–13 Dagenham & R 0 0
2013–14 Dagenham & R 0 0
2013–14 Peterborough U 1 0
2014–15 Peterborough U 24 0
2015–16 Peterborough U 37 1
2016–17 Peterborough U 1 0 63 1
2016–17 Barnet 15 2
2017–18 Barnet 42 3 57 5

SHOMOTUN, Fumnaya (M) 20 1
H:5 8 W:10 08 b. 29-5-97
2015–16 Barnet 10 1
2016–17 Barnet 4 0
2017–18 Barnet 6 0 20 1

SMITH, Darnell (D) 0 0
2016–17 Barnet 0 0
2017–18 Barnet 0 0

STEPHENS, Jamie (G) 80 0
H:6 1 W:12 04 b.Wotton 24-8-93
2012–13 Liverpool 0 0
2012–13 *Airbus UK* 13 0 13 0
2013–14 Newport Co 2 0
2014–15 Newport Co 7 0 9 0
2015–16 Barnet 29 0
2016–17 Barnet 18 0
2017–18 Barnet 11 0 58 0

SULE, Fuad (M) 26 0
b. 20-1-97
2016 St Patrick's Ath 1 0 1 0
2017 Bohemians 24 0 24 0
2017–18 Barnet 1 0 1 0

SWEENEY, Dan (M) 25 0
H:6 3 W:11 11 b.Kingston upon Thames 25-4-94
Internationals: England C.
From AFC Wimbledon, Kingstonian, Dulwich Hamlet, Maidstone U.
2016–17 Barnet 4 0
2017–18 Barnet 21 0 25 0

TARPEY, Dave (F) 2 0
b. 14-11-88
2017–18 Barnet 2 0 2 0

TAYLOR, Harry (D) 49 0
H:6 2 b.4-5-97
2015–16 Barnet 8 0
2016–17 Barnet 25 0
2017–18 Barnet 16 0 49 0

TAYLOR, Jack (D) 52 2
H:6 1 W:11 00 b. 23-6-98
2016–17 Barnet 14 0
2017–18 Barnet 38 2 52 2

TUTONDA, David (D) 72 3
H:5 11 W:11 00 b.Kinshasa 11-10-95
2014–15 Cardiff C 0 0
2014–15 *Newport Co* 12 2 12 2
2015–16 Cardiff C 0 0
2015–16 *York C* 12 0 12 0
2016–17 Cardiff C 0 0
2016–17 Barnet 7 1
2017–18 Barnet 41 0 48 1

VILHETE, Mauro (M) 117 6
H:5 8 W:11 09 b.Sintra 10-5-93
2009–10 Barnet 2 0
2010–11 Barnet 20 0
2011–12 Barnet 3 0
2012–13 Barnet 5 0
2015–16 Barnet 15 0
2016–17 Barnet 40 3
2017–18 Barnet 32 3 117 6

WATSON, Ryan (M) 63 2
H:6 1 W:11 07 b.Crewe 7-7-93
2011–12 Wigan Ath 0 0
2012–13 Wigan Ath 0 0
2012–13 *Accrington S* 0 0
2013–14 Leicester C 0 0
2014–15 Leicester C 0 0
2014–15 *Northampton T* 5 0
2015–16 Leicester C 0 0
2015–16 *Northampton T* 10 0 16 0
2016–17 Barnet 19 1
2017–18 Barnet 28 1 47 2

WESTON, Curtis (M) 320 27
H:5 11 W:11 09 b.Greenwich 24-1-87
2003–04 Millwall 1 0
2004–05 Millwall 3 0
2005–06 Millwall 0 0 4 0
2006–07 Swindon T 27 1 27 1
2007–08 Leeds U 7 1
2007–08 *Scunthorpe U* 7 0 7 0
2008–09 Leeds U 0 0 7 1
2008–09 Gillingham 45 5
2009–10 Gillingham 39 6
2010–11 Gillingham 33 4
2011–12 Gillingham 30 0 147 15
2012–13 Barnet 29 0
2015–16 Barnet 37 3
2016–17 Barnet 40 6
2017–18 Barnet 22 1 128 10

Scholars
Abbey, Darren; Adinna, Greg; Aghadiuno, Benjamin Okechukwu; Aghayaakwah, Ivan-Kweri; Allen, K-Ci Kane; Busby, Charlie James; Connell, Rio; Francis, Daniel Peter; Hernandez, Loic; Loughney, Kieron; McKenzie-Lyle, Renell Jay; Mohamed, Arale Mohamoud; Pascal, Dwight; Syla, Roy; Vasiliou, Antonis.

BARNSLEY (6)

ADEBOYEJO, Victor (F) 15 1
b. 12-1-98
2014–15 Leyton Orient 1 0
2015–16 Leyton Orient 1 0
2016–17 Leyton Orient 13 1 15 1
2017–18 Barnsley 0 0

BIRD, Jared (M) 14 0
H:5 9 W:9 11 b.Nottingham 21-8-97
From Derby Co.
2016–17 Barnsley 0 0
2017–18 Barnsley 3 0 3 0
2017–18 *Yeovil T* 11 0 11 0

BRADSHAW, Tom (F) 240 68
H:5 5 W:11 02 b.Shrewsbury 27-7-92
Internationals: Wales U19, U21, Full caps.
2009–10 Shrewsbury T 6 3
2010–11 Shrewsbury T 26 6
2011–12 Shrewsbury T 8 1
2012–13 Shrewsbury T 21 0
2013–14 Shrewsbury T 28 7 89 17
2014–15 Walsall 29 17
2015–16 Walsall 41 17 70 34
2016–17 Barnsley 42 8
2017–18 Barnsley 39 9 81 17

BROWN, Jacob (M) 15 0
H:5 10 W:9 11 b. 10-4-98
2014–15 Barnsley 0 0
2015–16 Barnsley 0 0
2016–17 Barnsley 2 0
2017–18 Barnsley 0 0 2 0
2017–18 *Chesterfield* 13 0 13 0

CAVARE, Dimitri (D) 32 1
H:6 1 W:13 03 b.Pointe-‡-Pitre 5-2-95
Internationals: France U20. Guadeloupe Full caps.
2013–14 Lens 1 0
2014–15 Lens 20 0 21 0
2015–16 Rennes 0 0
2016–17 Rennes 2 0
2017–18 Rennes 0 0 2 0
2017–18 Barnsley 9 1 9 1

DAVIES, Adam (G) 142 0
H:6 1 W:11 11 b.Rinteln 17-7-92
2009–10 Everton 0 0
2010–11 Everton 0 0
2011–12 Everton 0 0
2013–14 Sheffield W 0 0
2014–15 Barnsley 23 0
2015–16 Barnsley 38 0
2016–17 Barnsley 46 0
2017–18 Barnsley 35 0 142 0

FRYERS, Zeki (D) 60 1
H:6 0 W:12 00 b.Manchester 9-9-92
Internationals: England U16, U17, U19.
2011–12 Manchester U 2 0 2 0
2012–13 Standard Liege 7 0 7 0
2012–13 Tottenham H 0 0
2013–14 Tottenham H 7 0 7 0
2014–15 Crystal Palace 1 0
2014–15 *Rotherham U* 10 0 10 0
2014–15 *Ipswich T* 3 0 3 0
2015–16 Crystal Palace 0 0
2016–17 Crystal Palace 8 0 9 0
2017–18 Barnsley 22 1 22 1

HAMMILL, Adam (M) 351 28
H:5 11 W:11 07 b.Liverpool 25-1-88
Internationals: England U19, U21.
2005–06 Liverpool 0 0
2006–07 Liverpool 0 0
2006–07 *Dunfermline Ath* 13 1 13 1
2007–08 Liverpool 0 0
2007–08 *Southampton* 25 0 25 0
2008–09 Liverpool 0 0
2008–09 *Blackpool* 22 1 22 1
2008–09 *Barnsley* 14 1
2009–10 Barnsley 39 4
2010–11 Barnsley 25 8
2010–11 Wolverhampton W 10 0
2011–12 Wolverhampton W 9 0
2011–12 *Middlesbrough* 10 0 10 0
2012–13 Wolverhampton W 4 0 23 0
2012–13 *Huddersfield T* 16 2
2013–14 Huddersfield T 44 4
2014–15 Huddersfield T 5 0
2015–16 *Rotherham U* 14 0 14 0
2015–16 Huddersfield T 1 0 66 6
2016–17 Barnsley 25 4
2016–17 Barnsley 37 3
2017–18 Barnsley 38 0 178 20

HEDGES, Ryan (M) 75 8
H: 6 1 W: 10 03 b.Swansea 7-9-95
Internationals: Wales U19, U21, Full caps.

2013–14	Swansea C	0	0	
2014–15	Swansea C	0	0	
2014–15	Leyton Orient	17	2	17 2
2015–16	Swansea C	0	0	
2015–16	Stevenage	6	0	6 0
2016–17	Swansea C	0	0	
2016–17	Yeovil T	21	4	21 4
2016–17	Barnsley	8	0	
2017–18	Barnsley	23	2	31 2

ISGROVE, Lloyd (M) 60 12
H: 5 10 W: 11 05 b.Yeovil 12-1-93
Internationals: Wales U21, Full caps.

2011–12	Southampton	0	0	
2012–13	Southampton	0	0	
2013–14	Southampton	0	0	
2013–14	Peterborough U	8	1	8 1
2014–15	Southampton	1	0	
2014–15	Sheffield W	8	0	8 0
2015–16	Southampton	0	0	
2015–16	*Barnsley*	27	0	
2016–17	Southampton	0	0	1 0
2017–18	Barnsley	16	1	43 1

JACKSON, Adam (D) 61 4
H: 6 2 W: 12 04 b.Darlington 18-5-94
Internationals: England U16, U17, U18, U19.

2011–12	Middlesbrough	0	0	
2012–13	Middlesbrough	0	0	
2013–14	Middlesbrough	0	0	
2014–15	Middlesbrough	0	0	
2015–16	Middlesbrough	0	0	
2015–16	Coventry C	0	0	
2015–16	*Hartlepool U*	29	3	29 3
2016–17	Barnsley	10	0	
2017–18	Barnsley	22	1	32 1

KAY, Josh (M) 12 0
H: 5 5 W: 10 01 b.Blackpool 28-10-96
From AFC Fylde.

2015–16	Barnsley	0	0	
2016–17	Barnsley	1	0	
2017–18	Barnsley	0	0	1 0
2017–18	*Chesterfield*	11	0	11 0

KNASMULLNER, Christoph (M) 112 26
H: 6 0 W: 11 05 b.Vienna 30-4-92
Internationals: Austria U17, U18, U19.

2010–11	Bayern Munich	0	0	
2011–12	Ingolstadt	5	2	
2012–13	Ingolstadt	7	0	
2013–14	Ingolstadt	8	0	20 2
2014–15	Admira	14	0	
2015–16	Admira	22	4	
2016–17	Admira	35	8	
2017–18	Admira	18	12	89 24
2017–18	Barnsley	3	0	3 0

LINDSAY, Liam (D) 129 9
H: 6 4 W: 12 07 b.Paisley 12-10-95

2012–13	Partick Thistle	1	0	
2013–14	*Alloa Ath*	10	0	10 0
2013–14	Partick Thistle	1	0	
2014–15	Partick Thistle	0	0	
2014–15	*Airdrieonians*	13	1	13 1
2015–16	Partick Thistle	25	1	
2016–17	Partick Thistle	36	6	64 7
2017–18	Barnsley	42	1	42 1

MALLAN, Stephen (M) 101 22
H: 5 11 W: 12 04 b.Glasgow 25-3-96
Internationals: Scotland U21.

2014–15	St Mirren	25	4	
2015–16	St Mirren	34	11	
2016–17	St Mirren	34	7	93 22
2017–18	Barnsley	8	0	8 0

McCARTHY, Jason (D) 103 7
H: 6 1 W: 12 08 b.Southampton 7-11-95

2013–14	Southampton	0	0	
2014–15	Southampton	1	0	
2015–16	Southampton	0	0	
2015–16	*Wycombe W*	35	2	35 2
2016–17	Southampton	0	0	1 0
2016–17	*Walsall*	46	5	46 5
2017–18	Barnsley	21	0	21 0

McGEEHAN, Cameron (M) 106 29
H: 5 11 W: 11 03 b.Kingston upon Thames 6-4-95
Internationals: Northern Ireland U17, U19, U21.

2013–14	Norwich C	0	0	
2014–15	Norwich C	0	0	
2014–15	*Luton T*	15	3	
2014–15	*Cambridge U*	4	3	4 3

2015–16	Luton T	41	12	
2016–17	Luton T	24	10	80 25
2017–18	Barnsley	9	1	9 1
2017–18	*Scunthorpe U*	13	0	13 0

MILLS, Matthew (D) 365 23
H: 6 3 W: 12 12 b.Swindon 14-7-86
Internationals: England U19.

2004–05	Southampton	0	0	
2004–05	*Coventry C*	4	0	4 0
2004–05	*Bournemouth*	12	3	12 3
2005–06	Southampton	4	0	4 0
2005–06	Manchester C	1	0	
2006–07	Manchester C	1	0	
2006–07	*Colchester U*	9	0	9 0
2007–08	Manchester C	0	0	2 0
2007–08	Doncaster R	34	3	
2008–09	Doncaster R	41	0	
2009–10	Doncaster R	0	0	75 3
2009–10	Reading	23	2	
2010–11	Reading	38	2	61 4
2011–12	Leicester C	25	1	25 1
2012–13	Bolton W	18	1	
2013–14	Bolton W	32	1	
2014–15	Bolton W	37	4	87 6
2015–16	Nottingham F	42	5	
2016–17	Nottingham F	27	1	
2017–18	Nottingham F	0	0	82 6
2017–18	Barnsley	4	0	4 0

MONCUR, George (M) 167 29
H: 5 9 W: 10 00 b.Swindon 18-8-93
Internationals: England U18.

2010–11	West Ham U	0	0	
2011–12	West Ham U	0	0	
2011–12	*AFC Wimbledon*	20	2	20 2
2012–13	West Ham U	0	0	
2013–14	West Ham U	0	0	
2013–14	*Partick Thistle*	2	1	2 1
2014–15	Colchester U	41	8	
2015–16	Colchester U	45	12	86 20
2016–17	Peterborough U	13	2	13 2
2016–17	Barnsley	12	2	
2017–18	Barnsley	34	2	46 4

MOORE, Kieffer (F) 112 24
H: 6 5 W: 13 01 b.Torquay 8-8-92
Internationals: England C.
From Truro C, Dorchester T.

2013–14	Yeovil T	20	4	
2014–15	Yeovil T	30	3	50 7
2015	*Viking*	9	0	9 0

From Forest Green R, Torquay U.

2016–17	Ipswich T	11	0	
2017–18	Ipswich T	0	0	11 0
2017–18	*Rotherham U*	22	13	22 13
2017–18	Barnsley	20	4	20 4

MOTTLEY-HENRY, Dylan (F) 5 0
b. 2-8-97

2014–15	Bradford C	1	0	
2015–16	Bradford C	1	0	2 0

From Altrincham, Bradford PA, Tranmere R.

2017–18	Barnsley	1	0	1 0
2017–18	*Chesterfield*	2	0	2 0

MOWATT, Alex (M) 158 15
H: 5 10 W: 11 03 b.Doncaster 13-2-95
Internationals: England U19, U20.

2013–14	Leeds U	29	1	
2014–15	Leeds U	38	9	
2015–16	Leeds U	34	2	
2016–17	Leeds U	15	0	116 12
2017–18	Barnsley	11	1	
2017–18	Barnsley	1	0	12 1
2017–18	*Oxford U*	30	2	30 2

PEARSON, Matthew (D) 115 11
H: 6 3 W: 11 05 b.Keighley 3-8-93
Internationals: England U18, C.

2012–13	Rochdale	9	0	
2013–14	Rochdale	0	0	9 0
2015–16	Accrington S	46	3	
2016–17	Accrington S	43	8	89 11
2017–18	Barnsley	17	0	17 0

PINILLOS, Daniel (D) 92 2
H: 6 0 W: 11 09 b.Logrono 22-10-92

2013–14	Ourense	21	0	21 0
2013–14	Cordoba	16	1	
2014–15	Cordoba	12	0	
2015–16	Nottingham F	19	0	
2016–17	Nottingham F	16	1	35 1
2017–18	Cordoba	0	0	28 1
2017–18	Barnsley	8	0	8 0

PINNOCK, Ethan (D) 12 2
H: 6 4 W: 12 06 b.Lambeth 29-5-93
Internationals: England C.
From Dulwich Hamlet.

2017–18	Barnsley	12	2	12 2

POTTS, Brad (M) 227 28
H: 6 2 W: 12 09 b.Carlisle 3-7-94
Internationals: England U19.

2012–13	Carlisle U	27	0	
2013–14	Carlisle U	37	2	
2014–15	Carlisle U	39	7	103 9
2015–16	Blackpool	45	6	
2016–17	Blackpool	42	10	87 16
2017–18	Barnsley	37	3	37 3

SMITH, Will (D) 0 0

2016–17	Barnsley	0	0	
2017–18	Barnsley	0	0	

THIAM, Mamadou (F) 88 12
H: 6 0 W: 12 13 b.Aubervilliers 20-3-95
Internationals: Senegal U20.

2013–14	Dijon	0	0	
2014–15	Dijon	8	0	
2015–16	Dijon	17	3	
2016–17	Dijon	0	0	25 3
2016–17	*Clermont*	34	8	34 8
2017–18	Barnsley	29	1	29 1

TOWNSEND, Nick (G) 16 0
H: 5 11 W: 13 11 b.Solihull 1-11-94

2012–13	Birmingham C	0	0	
2013–14	Birmingham C	0	0	
2014–15	Birmingham C	0	0	
2015–16	Barnsley	8	0	
2016–17	Barnsley	0	0	
2017–18	Barnsley	8	0	16 0

WALTON, Jack (G) 3 0
H: 6 0 W: 12 02 b.Bury 23-4-98

2014–15	Barnsley	0	0	
2015–16	Barnsley	0	0	
2016–17	Barnsley	0	0	
2017–18	Barnsley	3	0	3 0

WILLIAMS, Ben (D) 0 0
H: 5 10 W: 11 00 b. 31-3-99
Internationals: Wales U17.
From Blackburn R.

2017–18	Barnsley	0	0	

WOLFE, Matthew (M) 0 0

2017–18	Barnsley	0	0	

YIADOM, Andy (M) 150 10
H: 5 11 W: 11 11 b.Camden 9-12-91
Internationals: England C. Ghana Full caps.

2011–12	Barnet	7	1	
2012–13	Barnet	39	3	
2015–16	Barnet	40	6	86 10
2016–17	Barnet	32	0	
2017–18	Barnsley	32	0	64 0

Players retained or with offer of contract
Fielding, Samuel Harry; Greatorex, Jake Roy Vincent; Lomax, Samuel James; Palmer, Romal Jordan; Smith, William Owen; Wardle, Louis Aaron.

Scholars
Alderton, William Jack; Berkovits, Amir; Buckwell, Willard Tommy Lee James; Clare, Thomas Patrick; Gagen, Harry; Greenfield, Daniel Christopher James; Kendrick, Henry; Miller, Robbie; Moon, Jasper; Ocran, Wilberforce Paa Kwesi; Rangel, Joao Antonio; Sandhu, Jaydan; Simpson, Cameron Morgan; Swinburn, Kane; Thorpe, Christopher Tevin Johnson; Tingle, Samuel James.

BIRMINGHAM C (7)

ADAMS, Che (F) 117 23
H: 5 10 W: 10 06 b.Leicester 13-7-96
Internationals: England C, U20.

2014–15	Sheffield U	10	0	
2015–16	Sheffield U	36	11	
2016–17	Sheffield U	0	0	47 11
2016–17	Birmingham C	40	7	
2017–18	Birmingham C	30	5	70 12

BAILEY, Odin (M)   0 0
b. 8-12-99
Internationals: England U16.

2017–18	Birmingham C	0	0		

BROCK-MADSEN, Nicolai (F)   130 24
H: 6 4 W: 13 12 b. 9-1-93
Internationals: Denmark U18, U19, U20, U21, Olympic.

2010–11	Randers	0	0		
2011–12	Randers	14	2		
2012–13	Randers	28	5		
2013–14	Randers	27	4		
2014–15	Randers	17	4		
2015–16	Randers	4	1	90	16
2015–16	Birmingham C	6	0		
2016–17	Birmingham C	0	0		
2016–17	*PEC Zwolle*	23	7	23	7
2017–18	Birmingham C	0	0	6	0
2017–18	*Cracovia*	11	1	11	1

COLIN, Maxime (D)   223 7
H: 5 11 W: 12 00 b.Arras 15-11-91
Internationals: France U20.

2010–11	Boulogne	26	0		
2011–12	Boulogne	23	0		
2012–13	Boulogne	4	0	53	0
2012–13	Troyes	18	0		
2013–14	Troyes	35	0		
2014–15	Troyes	2	0	55	0
2014–15	Anderlecht	17	1		
2015–16	Anderlecht	1	0	18	1
2015–16	Brentford	21	0		
2016–17	Brentford	38	4		
2017–18	Brentford	3	0	62	4
2017–18	Birmingham C	35	2	35	2

COTTERILL, David (M)   395 51
H: 5 9 W: 11 02 b.Cardiff 4-12-87
Internationals: Wales U19, U21, Full caps.

2004–05	Bristol C	12	0		
2005–06	Bristol C	45	7		
2006–07	Bristol C	5	1		
2006–07	Wigan Ath	16	1		
2007–08	Wigan Ath	2	0	18	1
2007–08	*Sheffield U*	16	0		
2008–09	Sheffield U	24	4		
2009–10	Sheffield U	14	2	54	6
2009–10	Swansea C	21	3		
2010–11	Swansea C	14	1		
2010–11	Portsmouth	15	1	15	1
2011–12	Swansea C	0	0	35	4
2011–12	Barnsley	11	1	11	1
2012–13	Doncaster R	44	10		
2013–14	Doncaster R	40	4	84	14
2014–15	Birmingham C	42	9		
2015–16	Birmingham C	29	4		
2016–17	Birmingham C	25	1		
2016–17	*Bristol C*	13	2	75	10
2017–18	Birmingham C	7	0	103	14

Transferred to ATK (India) January 2018.

DACRES-COGLEY, Josh (D)   17 0
H: 5 9 W: 10 10 b.Coventry 12-3-96

2016–17	Birmingham C	14	0		
2017–18	Birmingham C	3	0	17	0

DAVIS, David (M)   259 9
H: 5 8 W: 12 03 b.Smethwick 20-2-91

2009–10	Wolverhampton W	0	0		
2009–10	*Darlington*	5	0	5	0
2010–11	Wolverhampton W	0	0		
2010–11	*Walsall*	7	0	7	0
2010–11	*Shrewsbury T*	19	2	19	2
2011–12	Wolverhampton W	7	0		
2011–12	*Chesterfield*	9	0	9	0
2012–13	Wolverhampton W	28	0		
2013–14	Wolverhampton W	18	0	53	0
2014–15	Birmingham C	42	3		
2015–16	Birmingham C	35	1		
2016–17	Birmingham C	41	4		
2017–18	Birmingham C	38	2	156	10

DEAN, Harlee (M)   259 9
H: 6 0 W: 11 10 b.Basingstoke 26-7-91

2008–09	Dagenham & R	0	0		
2009–10	Dagenham & R	1	0	1	0
2010–11	Southampton	0	0		
2011–12	Southampton	0	0		
2011–12	Brentford	26	1		
2012–13	Brentford	44	3		
2013–14	Brentford	32	0		
2014–15	Brentford	35	1		
2015–16	Brentford	42	0		
2016–17	Brentford	42	3		
2017–18	Brentford	3	0	224	8
2017–18	Birmingham C	34	1	34	1

GROUNDS, Jonathan (D)   323 11
H: 6 1 W: 13 10 b.Thornaby 2-2-88

2007–08	Middlesbrough	5	0		
2008–09	Middlesbrough	2	0		
2008–09	*Norwich C*	16	3	16	3
2009–10	Middlesbrough	20	0		
2010–11	Middlesbrough	6	1		
2011–12	Middlesbrough	0	0	33	1
2011–12	*Chesterfield*	13	0	13	0
2011–12	*Yeovil T*	14	0	14	0
2012–13	Oldham Ath	44	1		
2013–14	Oldham Ath	45	2	89	3
2014–15	Birmingham C	45	1		
2015–16	Birmingham C	45	1		
2016–17	Birmingham C	42	2		
2017–18	Birmingham C	26	0	158	4

HARDING, Wes (D)   9 0
H: 5 11 W: 12 06 b.Leicester 20-10-96

2017–18	Birmingham C	9	0	9	0

JOTA, Ramallo (M)   161 39
H: 5 11 W: 10 08 b.A Coruna 16-6-91

2010–11	Celta Vigo	4	0		
2011–12	Celta Vigo	0	0		
2012–13	Celta Vigo	0	0		
2013–14	Celta Vigo	0	0	4	0
2013–14	Eibar	35	11		
2014–15	Brentford	42	11		
2015–16	Brentford	5	0		
2015–16	Eibar	13	0		
2016–17	Brentford	21	12		
2016–17	Eibar	5	0	53	11
2017–18	Brentford	4	0	72	23
2017–18	Birmingham C	32	5	32	5

JUTKIEWICZ, Lucas (F)   339 69
H: 6 1 W: 12 11 b.Southampton 20-3-89

2005–06	Swindon T	5	0		
2006–07	Swindon T	33	5	38	5
2006–07	Everton	0	0		
2007–08	Everton	0	0		
2007–08	*Plymouth Arg*	3	0	3	0
2008–09	Everton	0	0		
2008–09	*Huddersfield T*	7	0	7	0
2009–10	Everton	0	0	1	0
2009–10	*Motherwell*	33	12	33	12
2010–11	Coventry C	42	9		
2011–12	Coventry C	25	9	67	18
2011–12	Middlesbrough	19	2		
2012–13	Middlesbrough	24	8		
2013–14	Middlesbrough	22	1	65	11
2013–14	*Bolton W*	20	7	20	7
2014–15	Burnley	25	0		
2015–16	Burnley	5	0		
2016–17	Burnley	2	0	32	0
2016–17	Birmingham C	38	11		
2017–18	Birmingham C	35	5	73	16

KEITA, Cheick (D)   59 0
H: 5 7 W: 12 00 b.Paris 16-7-96
Internationals: Mali U20.
From Monaco.

2014–15	Virtus Entella	0	0		
2015–16	Virtus Entella	31	0		
2016–17	Virtus Entella	14	0	45	0
2016–17	Birmingham C	10	0		
2017–18	Birmingham C	1	0	11	0
2017–18	*Bologna*	3	0	3	0

KIEFTENBELD, Maikel (M)   331 9
H: 5 10 W: 11 11 b.Lemelerveld 26-6-90
Internationals: Netherlands U21.

2008–09	Go Ahead Eagles	30	1		
2009–10	Go Ahead Eagles	33	2	63	3
2010–11	Groningen	33	0		
2011–12	Groningen	26	1		
2012–13	Groningen	29	1		
2013–14	Groningen	31	0		
2014–15	Groningen	33	0	152	2
2015–16	Birmingham C	42	3		
2016–17	Birmingham C	39	1		
2017–18	Birmingham C	35	0	116	4

KUSZCZAK, Tomasz (G)   262 0
H: 6 3 W: 13 03 b.Krosno Odrzansia 20-3-82
Internationals: Poland U16, U18, U21, Full caps.

2001–02	Hertha Berlin	0	0		
2002–03	Hertha Berlin	0	0		
2003–04	Hertha Berlin	0	0		
2004–05	WBA	3	0		
2005–06	WBA	28	0		
2006–07	WBA	0	0	31	0
2006–07	*Manchester U*	6	0		
2007–08	Manchester U	9	0		
2008–09	Manchester U	4	0		
2009–10	Manchester U	8	0		
2010–11	Manchester U	5	0		
2011–12	Manchester U	0	0	32	0
2011–12	*Watford*	13	0	13	0
2012–13	Brighton & HA	43	0		
2013–14	Brighton & HA	41	0	84	0
2014–15	Wolverhampton W	13	0	13	0
2015–16	Birmingham C	41	0		
2016–17	Birmingham C	38	0		
2017–18	Birmingham C	10	0	89	0

LAKIN, Charlie (M)   0 0
b.Solihull 8-5-99

2017–18	Birmingham C	0	0		

LOWE, Jason (M)   189 3
H: 6 0 W: 12 08 b.Wigan 2-9-91
Internationals: England U20, U21.

2009–10	Blackburn R	0	0		
2010–11	Blackburn R	1	0		
2010–11	*Oldham Ath*	7	2	7	2
2011–12	Blackburn R	32	0		
2012–13	Blackburn R	36	0		
2013–14	Blackburn R	39	1		
2014–15	Blackburn R	12	0		
2015–16	Blackburn R	10	0		
2016–17	Blackburn R	43	0	173	1
2017–18	WBA	0	0		
2017–18	Birmingham C	9	0	9	0

LUBULA, Beryl (F)   1 0
b. 8-1-98

2017–18	Birmingham C	1	0	1	0

MAGHOMA, Jacques (M)   320 41
H: 5 9 W: 11 06 b.Lubumbashi 23-10-87
Internationals: DR Congo Full caps.

2005–06	Tottenham H	0	0		
2006–07	Tottenham H	0	0		
2007–08	Tottenham H	0	0		
2008–09	Tottenham H	0	0		
2009–10	Burton Alb	35	3		
2010–11	Burton Alb	41	4		
2011–12	Burton Alb	36	4		
2012–13	Burton Alb	43	15	155	26
2013–14	Sheffield W	25	2		
2014–15	Sheffield W	32	0	57	2
2015–16	Birmingham C	40	5		
2016–17	Birmingham C	27	3		
2017–18	Birmingham C	41	5	108	13

MORRISON, Michael (D)   356 18
H: 6 0 W: 12 00 b.Bury St Edmunds 3-3-88
Internationals: England U.

2008–09	Leicester C	35	2		
2009–10	Leicester C	31	2		
2010–11	Leicester C	11	0	77	5
2010–11	*Sheffield U*	12	0	12	0
2011–12	Charlton Ath	45	4		
2012–13	Charlton Ath	44	1		
2013–14	Charlton Ath	45	1		
2014–15	Charlton Ath	2	0	136	6
2014–15	Birmingham C	21	0		
2015–16	Birmingham C	46	3		
2016–17	Birmingham C	31	3		
2017–18	Birmingham C	33	1	131	7

N'DOYE, Cheick (M)   281 61
H: 6 3 W: 13 12 b.Rufisque 29-3-86
Internationals: Senegal Full caps.

2009–10	Epinal	7	0		
2010–11	Epinal	30	11		
2011–12	Epinal	35	4	72	15
2012–13	Creteil	34	11		
2013–14	Creteil	36	10		
2014–15	Creteil	37	11	107	32
2015–16	Angers	32	9		
2016–17	Angers	33	5	65	14
2017–18	Angers	37	0	37	0

NSUE, Emilio (F)   319 29
H: 5 10 W: 11 11 b.Palma 30-9-89
Internationals: Spain U16, U17, U19, U20, U21. Equatorial Guinea Full caps.

2007–08	Mallorca	2	0		
2008–09	Mallorca	0	0		
2008–09	*Castellon*	37	7	37	7
2009–10	Mallorca	0	0		
2009–10	*Real Sociedad*	34	5	34	5
2010–11	Mallorca	38	4		
2011–12	Mallorca	30	3		
2012–13	Mallorca	32	2		
2013–14	Mallorca	40	4	142	13
2014–15	Middlesbrough	26	0		
2015–16	Middlesbrough	40	3		
2016–17	Middlesbrough	4	0	70	3
2016–17	Birmingham C	18	1		
2017–18	Birmingham C	18	0	36	1

Transferred to APOEL, January 2018.

O'KEEFFE, Corey (M)   **1 0**
H: 6 1   W: 11 00   b.Birmingham 5-6-88
Internationals: Republic of Ireland U17, U18, U19.

2016–17	Birmingham C	1	0		
2017–18	Birmingham C	0	0	**1**	**0**

ROBERTS, Marc (D)   **102 6**
H: 6 0   W: 12 11   b.Wakefield 26-7-90
Internationals: England C.

2014–15	Barnsley	0	0		
2015–16	Barnsley	32	1		
2016–17	Barnsley	40	4	**72**	**5**
2017–18	Birmingham C	30	1	**30**	**1**

ROBINSON, Paul (D)   **678 15**
H: 5 9   W: 11 12   b.Watford 14-12-78
Internationals: England U21.

1996–97	Watford	12	0		
1997–98	Watford	22	2		
1998–99	Watford	29	0		
1999–2000	Watford	32	0		
2000–01	Watford	39	0		
2001–02	Watford	38	3		
2002–03	Watford	37	3		
2003–04	Watford	10	0	**219**	**8**
2003–04	WBA	31	0		
2004–05	WBA	30	1		
2005–06	WBA	33	0		
2006–07	WBA	42	2		
2007–08	WBA	43	1		
2008–09	WBA	35	0		
2009–10	WBA	0	0	**214**	**4**
2009–10	Bolton W	25	0		
2010–11	Bolton W	35	0		
2011–12	Bolton W	17	0	**77**	**0**
2011–12	Leeds U	10	0	**10**	**0**
2012–13	Birmingham C	35	0		
2013–14	Birmingham C	40	0		
2014–15	Birmingham C	34	0		
2015–16	Birmingham C	25	3		
2016–17	Birmingham C	22	0		
2017–18	Birmingham C	2	0	**158**	**3**

SCARR, Dan (D)   **22 1**
b. 24-12-94
From Reddich U, Stourbridge.

2017–18	Birmingham C	0	0		
2017–18	Wycombe W	22	1	**22**	**1**

SEDDON, Steve (D)   **0 0**
b.Reading 25-12-97

2017–18	Birmingham C	0	0		

SOLOMON-OTABOR, Viv (M)   **73 6**
H: 5 9   W: 12 02   b.London 2-1-96
From Crystal Palace.

2015–16	Birmingham C	22	1		
2016–17	Birmingham C	3	0		
2016–17	*Bolton W*	4	0	**4**	**0**
2017–18	Birmingham C	0	0	**25**	**1**
2017–18	*Blackpool*	44	5	**44**	**5**

STOCKDALE, David (G)   **335 0**
H: 6 3   W: 13 04   b.Leeds 20-9-85
Internationals: England C.

2002–03	York C	1	0		
2003–04	York C	0	0	**1**	**0**
2006–07	Darlington	6	0		
2007–08	Darlington	41	0	**47**	**0**
2008–09	Fulham	0	0		
2008–09	*Rotherham U*	8	0	**8**	**0**
2008–09	*Leicester C*	8	0	**8**	**0**
2009–10	Fulham	1	0		
2009–10	*Plymouth Arg*	21	0	**21**	**0**
2010–11	Fulham	7	0		
2011–12	Fulham	8	0		
2011–12	*Ipswich T*	18	0	**18**	**0**
2012–13	Fulham	2	0		
2012–13	*Hull C*	24	0	**24**	**0**
2013–14	Fulham	21	0	**39**	**0**
2014–15	Brighton & HA	42	0		
2015–16	Brighton & HA	46	0		
2016–17	Brighton & HA	45	0	**133**	**0**
2017–18	Birmingham C	36	0	**36**	**0**

TESCHE, Robert (M)   **225 13**
H: 5 11   W: 11 03   b.Wismar 27-5-87

2006–07	Arminia Bielefeld	7	0		
2007–08	Arminia Bielefeld	15	1	**22**	**1**
2008–09	Arminia Beilefeld	26	2	**26**	**2**
2009–10	Hamburg	16	2		
2010–11	Hamburg	11	0		
2011–12	Hamburg	23	2		
2012–13	Hamburg	9	0		
2012–13	*Fortuna Dusseldorf*	14	0	**14**	**0**
2013–14	Hamburg	9	0	**63**	**4**
2014–15	Nottingham F	22	2		
2014–15	*Birmingham C*	12	2		
2015–16	Nottingham F	24	1	**46**	**3**
2016–17	Birmingham C	24	0		
2017–18	Birmingham C	0	0	**36**	**2**
2017–18	*VfL Bochum*	18	1	**18**	**1**

TRUEMAN, Connal (G)   **0 0**
H: 6 1   W: 11 10   b.Birmingham 26-3-96

2014–15	Birmingham C	0	0
2014–15	*Oldham Ath*	0	0
2015–16	Birmingham C	0	0
2016–17	Birmingham C	0	0
2017–18	Birmingham C	0	0

VASSELL, Isaac (F)   **57 11**
H: 5 7   W: 11 02   b.Newquay 9-9-93

2011–12	Plymouth Arg	6	0		
2012–13	Plymouth Arg	0	0		
2013–14	Plymouth Arg	0	0	**6**	**0**

From Truro C.

2016–17	Luton T	40	8		
2017–18	Luton T	2	2	**42**	**10**
2017–18	Birmingham C	9	1	**9**	**1**

Players retained or with offer of contract
Bernard, Dominic Archie; Chapman, Hale Ronan Aiden Connolly Shea; Fabbrini, Diego; Gardner, Craig; Hutton, Remeao; Lubala, Beryl Logos; Martin, Joshua William; Maxwell, Luke Stephen; McCoy, Oliver John; McFarlane, Raewkon Kyle; Ramallo, Jose Ignacio Peleteiro; Stewart, Greg Alexander James; Stirk, Ryan William; Weaver, Jacob William Robert.

Scholars
Anderson, Tom; Bajrami, Geraldo; Baker, George Nicholas John; Boyd, Munce Caolan Stephen; Brown, Leo Calvin; Burke, Ryan Darren; Chisholm, Tai-Reece D'Mel Amari; Clarke, Jordan Alexander Joseph; Concannon, Jack Paul; Dawes, Kieron Michael; Forrest, Benjamin; Hamilton, Tyrell Anthony; Hilton, Rhys; Jeacock, Zachary Anton John; Landers, Lewis; McLean, Ben Neil; Moore, Ryan; Ngandu, Mayuba Christ Cross; Okoro, Chinedu Nicholas; Redmond, Joseph; Roberts, Mitchell; Siviter, Adam; Thompson-Sommers, Kane Angelis.

BLACKBURN R (8)

BELL, Amari (D)   **145 6**
H: 5 11   W: 12 00   b.Burton-upon-Trent 5-5-94

2012–13	Birmingham C	0	0		
2013–14	Birmingham C	1	0		
2014–15	Birmingham C	0	0	**1**	**0**
2014–15	*Swindon T*	10	0	**10**	**0**
2014–15	*Gillingham*	7	0	**7**	**0**
2015–16	Fleetwood T	44	0		
2016–17	Fleetwood T	44	0		
2017–18	Fleetwood T	27	4	**115**	**6**
2017–18	Blackburn R	12	0	**12**	**0**

BENNETT, Elliott (M)   **340 27**
H: 5 9   W: 10 11   b.Telford 18-12-88

2006–07	Wolverhampton W	0	0		
2007–08	Wolverhampton W	0	0		
2007–08	*Crewe Alex*	9	1	**9**	**1**
2007–08	Bury	19	1		
2008–09	Wolverhampton W	0	0		
2008–09	Bury	46	3	**65**	**4**
2009–10	Wolverhampton W	0	0		
2009–10	Brighton & HA	43	7		
2010–11	Brighton & HA	46	6		
2011–12	Norwich C	33	1		
2012–13	Norwich C	24	1		
2013–14	Norwich C	2	0		
2014–15	Norwich C	9	0		
2014–15	*Brighton & HA*	7	0	**96**	**13**
2015–16	Norwich C	0	0	**68**	**2**
2015–16	*Bristol C*	15	0	**15**	**0**
2015–16	Blackburn R	21	2		
2016–17	Blackburn R	25	3		
2017–18	Blackburn R	41	2	**87**	**7**

BUTTERWORTH, Daniel (F)   **0 0**
H: 5 11   W: 10 12   b.Manchester 14-9-94
From Manchester U.

2017–18	Blackburn R	0	0

CADDIS, Paul (D)   **281 20**
H: 5 7   W: 10 07   b.Irvine 19-4-88
Internationals: Scotland U19, U21, Full caps.

2007–08	Celtic	2	0		
2008–09	Celtic	5	0		
2008–09	*Dundee U*	11	0	**11**	**0**
2009–10	Celtic	10	0	**17**	**0**
2010–11	Swindon T	38	1		
2011–12	Swindon T	39	4		
2012–13	Swindon T	0	0	**77**	**5**
2012–13	Birmingham C	27	0		
2013–14	Birmingham C	38	5		
2014–15	Birmingham C	45	6		
2015–16	Birmingham C	39	4		
2016–17	Birmingham C	0	0	**149**	**15**
2016–17	*Bury*	13	0	**13**	**0**
2017–18	Blackburn R	14	0	**14**	**0**

CONWAY, Craig (M)   **425 44**
H: 5 7   W: 10 07   b.Irvine 2-5-85
Internationals: Scotland Full caps.

2002–03	Ayr U	1	0		
2003–04	Ayr U	6	0		
2004–05	Ayr U	23	3		
2005–06	Ayr U	31	4	**61**	**7**
2006–07	Dundee U	30	0		
2007–08	Dundee U	15	1		
2008–09	Dundee U	36	5		
2009–10	Dundee U	33	4		
2010–11	Dundee U	22	3	**136**	**13**
2011–12	Cardiff C	31	3		
2012–13	Cardiff C	27	2		
2013–14	Cardiff C	0	0	**58**	**5**
2013–14	*Brighton & HA*	13	1	**13**	**1**
2014–15	Blackburn R	18	4		
2015–16	Blackburn R	38	3		
2015–16	Blackburn R	35	3		
2016–17	Blackburn R	42	6		
2017–18	Blackburn R	24	2	**157**	**18**

DACK, Bradley (M)   **202 49**
H: 5 9   b.Greenwich 31-12-93

2012–13	Gillingham	16	1		
2013–14	Gillingham	28	3		
2014–15	Gillingham	42	9		
2015–16	Gillingham	40	13		
2016–17	Gillingham	34	5	**160**	**31**
2017–18	Blackburn R	42	18	**42**	**18**

DOWNING, Paul (D)   **253 7**
H: 6 1   W: 12 06   b.Taunton 26-10-91

2009–10	WBA	0	0		
2009–10	*Hereford U*	6	0		
2010–11	WBA	0	0		
2010–11	*Hereford U*	0	0	**6**	**0**
2010–11	*Swansea U*	0	0		
2011–12	WBA	0	0		
2011–12	*Barnet*	26	0	**26**	**0**
2012–13	Walsall	31	1		
2013–14	Walsall	44	1		
2014–15	Walsall	35	1		
2015–16	Walsall	46	3	**156**	**6**
2016–17	Milton Keynes D	37	0		
2017–18	Milton Keynes D	0	0	**37**	**0**
2017–18	Blackburn R	28	1	**28**	**1**

DOYLE, Jack (D)   **0 0**
H: 5 10   W: 10 01   b. 2-2-97

2015–16	Blackburn R	0	0
2016–17	Blackburn R	0	0
2017–18	Blackburn R	0	0

EVANS, Corry (M)   **234 9**
H: 5 8   W: 10 12   b.Belfast 30-7-90
Internationals: Northern Ireland U16, U17, U19, U21, B, Full caps.

2007–08	Manchester U	0	0		
2008–09	Manchester U	0	0		
2009–10	Manchester U	0	0		
2010–11	Manchester U	0	0		
2010–11	*Carlisle U*	1	0	**1**	**0**
2010–11	Hull C	18	3		
2011–12	Hull C	43	2		
2012–13	Hull C	32	1		
2013–14	Hull C	0	0	**93**	**6**
2013–14	Blackburn R	21	1		
2014–15	Blackburn R	38	1		
2015–16	Blackburn R	30	1		
2016–17	Blackburn R	19	0		
2017–18	Blackburn R	32	0	**140**	**3**

FEENEY, Liam (M)   **330 26**
H: 5 10   W: 12 02   b.Hammersmith 21-1-87

2008–09	Southend U	1	0	**1**	**0**
2008–09	Bournemouth	14	3		
2009–10	Bournemouth	44	5		
2010–11	Bournemouth	46	4		
2011–12	Bournemouth	5	0	**109**	**12**
2011–12	Millwall	34	4		
2012–13	Millwall	22	1		
2013–14	Millwall	17	0	**73**	**5**
2013–14	*Bolton W*	4	0		
2014–15	*Blackburn R*	6	0		
2014–15	Bolton W	41	3		
2015–16	Bolton W	37	5	**82**	**8**

2015–16	*Ipswich T*	9	1	**9**	**1**
2016–17	Blackburn R	34	0		
2017–18	Blackburn R	1	0	**41**	**0**
2017–18	*Cardiff C*	15	0	**15**	**0**

FISHER, Andy (G)   **0**   **0**
b. 12-2-98

2016–17	Blackburn R	0	0		
2017–18	Blackburn R	0	0		

GLADWIN, Ben (D)   **98**   **12**
H: 6 3   b.Reading 8-6-92

2013–14	Swindon T	13	0		
2014–15	Swindon T	34	8		
2015–16	QPR	7	0		
2015–16	*Swindon T*	13	2		
2015–16	*Bristol C*	1	0	**1**	**0**
2016–17	QPR	7	0	**14**	**0**
2016–17	*Swindon T*	18	2	**78**	**12**
2017–18	Blackburn R	5	0	**5**	**0**

GRAHAM, Danny (F)   **463**   **134**
H: 5 11   W: 12 05   b.Gateshead 12-8-85
Internationals: England U20.

2003–04	Middlesbrough	0	0		
2003–04	*Darlington*	9	2	**9**	**2**
2004–05	Middlesbrough	11	1		
2005–06	Middlesbrough	3	0		
2005–06	*Derby Co*	14	0	**14**	**0**
2005–06	*Leeds U*	3	0	**3**	**0**
2006–07	Middlesbrough	1	0		
2006–07	*Blackpool*	4	1	**4**	**1**
2006–07	*Carlisle U*	11	7		
2007–08	Carlisle U	45	14		
2008–09	Carlisle U	44	15	**100**	**36**
2009–10	Watford	46	14		
2010–11	Watford	45	23	**91**	**37**
2011–12	Swansea C	36	12		
2012–13	Swansea C	18	3	**54**	**15**
2012–13	Sunderland	13	0		
2013–14	Sunderland	0	0		
2013–14	*Hull C*	18	1	**18**	**1**
2013–14	*Middlesbrough*	18	6	**33**	**7**
2014–15	Sunderland	14	1		
2014–15	*Wolverhampton W*	5	1	**5**	**1**
2015–16	Sunderland	10	0	**37**	**1**
2015–16	*Blackburn R*	18	7		
2016–17	Blackburn R	35	12		
2017–18	Blackburn R	42	14	**95**	**33**

HARDCASTLE, Lewis (M)   **0**   **0**
H: 5 9   W: 12 00   b.Bolton 4-7-98

2017–18	Blackburn R	0	0		

HART, Sam (D)   **17**   **1**
b. 10-9-96

2016–17	Liverpool	0	0		
2016–17	*Port Vale*	11	1		
2017–18	Port Vale	0	0	**11**	**1**
2017–18	*Blackburn R*	3	0	**3**	**0**
2017–18	*Rochdale*	3	0	**3**	**0**

LENIHAN, Darragh (M)   **97**   **2**
H: 5 10   W: 12 00   b.Dublin 16-3-94
Internationals: Republic of Ireland U17, U19, U21, Full caps.

2011–12	Blackburn R	0	0		
2012–13	Blackburn R	0	0		
2013–14	Blackburn R	0	0		
2014–15	Blackburn R	3	0		
2014–15	*Burton Alb*	17	1	**17**	**1**
2015–16	Blackburn R	23	0		
2016–17	Blackburn R	40	0		
2017–18	Blackburn R	14	1	**80**	**1**

LEUTWILER, Jayson (G)   **122**   **0**
H: 6 3   W: 12 07   b.Basel 25-4-89
Internationals: Switzerland U16, U17, U18, U19, U20, U21. Canada Full caps.

2012–13	Middlesbrough	0	0		
2013–14	Middlesbrough	3	0	**3**	**0**
2014–15	Shrewsbury T	46	0		
2015–16	Shrewsbury T	29	0		
2016–17	Shrewsbury T	43	0	**118**	**0**
2017–18	Blackburn R	1	0	**1**	**0**

MANSELL, Lewis (F)   **0**   **0**
H: 6 2   W: 11 11   b.Burnley 20-9-97

2017–18	Blackburn R	0	0		

MOLS, Stefan (M)   **0**   **0**
H: 5 11   W: 11 11   b. 31-1-99

2017–18	Blackburn R	0	0		

MULGREW, Charlie (D)   **310**   **49**
H: 6 3   W: 13 01   b.Glasgow 6-3-86
Internationals: Scotland U21, Full caps.

2002–03	Celtic	0	0		
2003–04	Celtic	0	0		
2004–05	Celtic	0	0		

2005–06	Celtic	0	0		
2005–06	*Dundee U*	13	2	**13**	**2**
2006–07	Wolverhampton W	6	0		
2007–08	*Southend U*	18	1	**18**	**1**
2007–08	Wolverhampton W	0	0	**6**	**0**
2008–09	Aberdeen	35	5		
2009–10	Aberdeen	37	4	**72**	**9**
2010–11	Celtic	23	0		
2011–12	Celtic	30	8		
2012–13	Celtic	30	5		
2013–14	Celtic	28	6		
2014–15	Celtic	10	0		
2015–16	Celtic	11	1	**132**	**20**
2016–17	Blackburn R	28	3		
2017–18	Blackburn R	41	14	**69**	**17**

NUTTALL, Joe (F)   **26**   **4**
H: 6 0   W: 11 05   b.Bury 27-1-97

2015–16	Aberdeen	0	0		
2016–17	Aberdeen	0	0	**2**	**0**
2016–17	*Stranraer*	9	2	**9**	**2**
2016–17	*Dumbarton*	2	0	**2**	**0**
2017–18	Blackburn R	13	2	**13**	**2**

NYAMBE, Ryan (D)   **54**   **0**
H: 6 0   W: 12 00   b.Katima Mulilo 4-12-97

2014–15	Blackburn R	0	0		
2015–16	Blackburn R	0	0		
2016–17	Blackburn R	25	0		
2017–18	Blackburn R	29	0	**54**	**0**

PLATT, Matt (D)   **0**   **0**
b. 3-10-97

2016–17	Blackburn R	0	0		
2017–18	Blackburn R	0	0		

RANKIN-COSTELLO, Joe (M)   **0**   **0**
H: 5 10   W: 11 00   b.Stockport 26-7-99
From Manchester U.

2017–18	Blackburn R	0	0		

RAYA, David (G)   **57**   **0**
H: 6 0   W: 12 08   b.Barcelona 15-9-95

2013–14	Blackburn R	0	0		
2014–15	Blackburn R	2	0		
2015–16	Blackburn R	5	0		
2016–17	Blackburn R	5	0		
2017–18	Blackburn R	45	0	**57**	**0**

SAMUEL, Dominic (F)   **94**   **20**
H: 6 0   W: 14 00   b.Southwark 1-4-94
Internationals: England U19.

2011–12	Reading	0	0		
2012–13	Reading	1	0		
2012–13	*Colchester U*	2	0	**2**	**0**
2013–14	Reading	0	0		
2013–14	*Dagenham & R*	1	0	**1**	**0**
2014–15	Reading	0	0		
2014–15	*Coventry C*	13	6	**13**	**6**
2015–16	Reading	1	0		
2015–16	Gillingham	25	7	**25**	**7**
2016–17	Reading	9	2	**11**	**2**
2016–17	*Ipswich T*	6	0	**6**	**0**
2017–18	Blackburn R	36	5	**36**	**5**

SMALLWOOD, Richard (M)   **250**   **9**
H: 5 11   W: 11 05   b.Redcar 29-12-90
Internationals: England U18.

2008–09	Middlesbrough	0	0		
2009–10	Middlesbrough	0	0		
2010–11	Middlesbrough	13	1		
2011–12	Middlesbrough	13	0		
2012–13	Middlesbrough	22	2		
2013–14	Middlesbrough	13	0		
2013–14	*Rotherham U*	18	0		
2014–15	Middlesbrough	0	0	**61**	**3**
2014–15	*Rotherham U*	41	1		
2015–16	Rotherham U	13	0		
2016–17	Scunthorpe U	16	1	**16**	**1**
2016–17	Rotherham U	25	1	**127**	**3**
2017–18	Blackburn R	46	2	**46**	**2**

THOMSON, Connor (D)   **0**   **0**
H: 6 3   b. 14-2-96

2013–14	Carlisle U	0	0		
2014–15	Carlisle U	0	0		
2014–15	Blackburn R	0	0		
2015–16	Blackburn R	0	0		
2016–17	Blackburn R	0	0		
2017–18	Blackburn R	0	0		

TOMLINSON, Willem (M)   **5**   **0**
H: 5 10   W: 10 03   b.Burnley 27-1-98

2015–16	Blackburn R	0	0		
2016–17	Blackburn R	1	0		
2017–18	Blackburn R	4	0	**5**	**0**

TRAVIS, Lewis (D)   **5**   **0**
b. 16-10-97

2016–17	Blackburn R	0	0		
2017–18	Blackburn R	5	0	**5**	**0**

WARD, Elliot (D)   **311**   **21**
H: 6 2   W: 13 00   b.Harrow 19-1-85

2001–02	West Ham U	0	0		
2002–03	West Ham U	0	0		
2003–04	West Ham U	0	0		
2004–05	West Ham U	11	0		
2004–05	*Bristol R*	3	0	**3**	**0**
2005–06	West Ham U	4	0	**15**	**0**
2005–06	*Plymouth Arg*	16	1	**16**	**1**
2006–07	Coventry C	39	3		
2007–08	Coventry C	37	6		
2008–09	Coventry C	33	5		
2009–10	Coventry C	8	0	**117**	**14**
2009–10	*Doncaster R*	6	1	**6**	**1**
2009–10	*Preston NE*	4	0	**4**	**0**
2010–11	Norwich C	39	1		
2011–12	Norwich C	12	0		
2012–13	Norwich C	0	0	**51**	**1**
2012–13	*Nottingham F*	31	3	**31**	**3**
2013–14	Bournemouth	23	0		
2014–15	Bournemouth	0	0		
2015–16	Bournemouth	0	0	**25**	**0**
2015–16	*Huddersfield T*	5	0	**5**	**0**
2015–16	Blackburn R	7	1		
2016–17	Blackburn R	6	0		
2017–18	Blackburn R	10	0	**23**	**1**
2017–18	*Milton Keynes D*	15	0	**15**	**0**

WHARTON, Scott (D)   **25**   **3**
b.Blackburn 3-10-97

2015–16	Blackburn R	0	0		
2016–17	Blackburn R	2	0		
2016–17	*Cambridge U*	9	1	**9**	**1**
2017–18	Blackburn R	0	0	**2**	**0**
2017–18	*Lincoln C*	14	2	**14**	**2**

WHITTINGHAM, Peter (M)   **507**   **86**
H: 5 10   W: 9 13   b.Nuneaton 8-9-84
Internationals: England U19, U20, U21.

2002–03	Aston Villa	4	0		
2003–04	Aston Villa	32	0		
2004–05	Aston Villa	13	1		
2004–05	*Burnley*	7	0	**7**	**0**
2005–06	Aston Villa	4	0		
2005–06	*Derby Co*	11	0	**11**	**0**
2006–07	Aston Villa	3	0	**56**	**1**
2006–07	Cardiff C	19	4		
2007–08	Cardiff C	41	5		
2008–09	Cardiff C	33	3		
2009–10	Cardiff C	41	20		
2010–11	Cardiff C	45	11		
2011–12	Cardiff C	46	12		
2012–13	Cardiff C	40	8		
2013–14	Cardiff C	32	3		
2014–15	Cardiff C	43	6		
2015–16	Cardiff C	36	6		
2016–17	Cardiff C	37	7	**413**	**85**
2017–18	Blackburn R	20	0	**20**	**0**

WILLIAMS, Derrick (D)   **196**   **6**
H: 5 11   W: 11 11   b.Waterford 17-1-93
Internationals: Republic of Ireland U19, U21, Full caps.

2009–10	Aston Villa	0	0		
2010–11	Aston Villa	0	0		
2011–12	Aston Villa	0	0		
2012–13	Aston Villa	1	0	**1**	**0**
2013–14	Bristol C	43	1		
2014–15	Bristol C	44	2		
2015–16	Bristol C	24	1	**111**	**4**
2016–17	Blackburn R	39	1		
2017–18	Blackburn R	45	1	**84**	**2**

Players retained or with offer of contract
Albinson, Charlie; Buckley, John Keaton; Byrne, Oliver Joseph; Carter, Hayden James; Doyle, Charley Ian; Evans, Jack Lucas James; Grayson, Joseph Nicholas; Magloire, Tyler Jordan; Paton, Benjamin Alan; Simmonds, Okera.

Scholars
Barnes, Samuel Peter; Campbell, Matthew Scott; Connell, Kyle Edward; Donnelly-Blackburn, Ben Thomas George; Jackson, Andrew Ellis; Jones, Frank Peter; Lynch, Bradley James; Wilson, George Chester; Winterbottom, Benjamin Harry.

BLACKPOOL (9)

AIMSON, Will (D) — 52 0
H: 5 10 W: 11 00 b.Christchurch 1-1-94

Season	Club	A	G		
2013–14	Hull C	0	0		
2014–15	Hull C	0	0		
2014–15	Tranmere R	2	0	2	0
2015–16	Hull C	0	0		
2015–16	Blackpool	15	0		
2016–17	Blackpool	18	0		
2017–18	Blackpool	17	0	50	0

ANDERTON, Nick (D) — 4 0
H: 6 2 W: 12 06 b. 22-4-96

Season	Club	A	G		
2014–15	Preston NE	0	0		
2015–16	Preston NE	0	0		

From Aldershot T, Barrow.

Season	Club	A	G		
2017–18	Blackpool	4	0	4	0

BONEY, Miles (G) — 1 0
H: 5 11 W: 11 09 b.Blackpool 1-2-98

Season	Club	A	G		
2014–15	Blackpool	0	0		
2015–16	Blackpool	0	0		
2016–17	Blackpool	1	0		
2017–18	Blackpool	0	0	1	0

CLAYTON, Max (F) — 103 11
H: 5 9 W: 11 00 b.Crewe 9-8-94
Internationals: England U16, U17, U18, U19.

Season	Club	A	G		
2010–11	Crewe Alex	2	0		
2011–12	Crewe Alex	24	3		
2012–13	Crewe Alex	35	4		
2013–14	Crewe Alex	13	2	74	9
2014–15	Bolton W	9	1		
2015–16	Bolton W	8	0		
2016–17	Bolton W	10	1	27	2
2017–18	Blackpool	2	0	2	0

CORREIA, Raul (F) — 0 0
From Radcliffe Bor.

Season	Club	A	G		
2016–17	Blackpool	0	0		
2017–18	Blackpool	0	0		

CULLEN, Mark (F) — 161 33
H: 5 9 W: 11 11 b.Ashington 21-4-92

Season	Club	A	G		
2009–10	Hull C	3	1		
2010–11	Hull C	17	0		
2010–11	Bradford C	4	0	4	0
2011–12	Hull C	4	0		
2011–12	Bury	4	0		
2012–13	Hull C	0	0		
2012–13	Hull C	0	0	24	1
2012–13	Bury	10	1	14	1
2014–15	Luton T	42	13	42	13
2015–16	Blackpool	41	9		
2016–17	Blackpool	27	9		
2017–18	Blackpool	9	0	77	18

D'ALMEIDA, Sessi (M) — 28 0
H: 5 9 W: 11 09 b.Bordeaux 22-11-95
Internationals: Benin Full caps.

Season	Club	A	G		
2013–14	Bordeaux	0	0		
2014–15	Bordeaux	2	0	2	0
2015–16	Paris Saint-Germain	0	0		
2016–17	Barnsley	3	0	3	0
2017–18	Blackpool	23	0	23	0

DANIEL, Colin (M) — 302 32
H: 5 11 W: 11 06 b.Eastwood 15-2-88

Season	Club	A	G		
2006–07	Crewe Alex	0	0		
2007–08	Crewe Alex	1	0		
2008–09	Crewe Alex	13	1	14	1
2008–09	Macclesfield T	8	0		
2009–10	Macclesfield T	38	3		
2010–11	Macclesfield T	43	8		
2011–12	Macclesfield T	36	2	125	13
2013–14	Mansfield T	28	2		
2014–15	Port Vale	28	4		
2015–16	Port Vale	20	2	48	6
2015–16	Mansfield T	9	2	37	4
2016–17	Blackpool	34	4		
2017–18	Blackpool	44	4	78	8

DELFOUNESO, Nathan (F) — 244 31
H: 6 1 W: 12 04 b.Birmingham 2-2-91
Internationals: England U16, U17, U19, U21.

Season	Club	A	G		
2007–08	Aston Villa	0	0		
2008–09	Aston Villa	4	0		
2009–10	Aston Villa	9	1		
2010–11	Aston Villa	11	1		
2010–11	Burnley	11	1	11	1
2011–12	Aston Villa	6	0		
2011–12	Leicester C	4	0	4	0
2012–13	Blackpool	40	6		
2013–14	Aston Villa	0	0	31	2
2013–14	Blackpool	11	0		
2013–14	Coventry C	14	3	14	3
2014–15	Blackpool	38	3		
2015–16	Blackburn R	15	1	15	1
2015–16	Bury	4	0	4	0
2016–17	Swindon T	18	1	18	1
2016–17	Blackpool	18	5		
2017–18	Blackpool	40	9	147	23

GNANDUILLET, Armand (F) — 167 28
H: 6 4 W: 13 12 b.Angers 13-2-92
Internationals: Ivory Coast U20.

Season	Club	A	G		
2012–13	Chesterfield	13	3		
2013–14	Chesterfield	34	5		
2014–15	Chesterfield	26	2		
2014–15	Tranmere R	4	2	4	2
2014–15	Oxford U	4	0	4	0
2015–16	Chesterfield	9	0	82	10
2015–16	Stevenage	14	5	14	5
2015–16	Leyton Orient	17	4		
2016–17	Leyton Orient	1	0	18	4
2016–17	Blackpool	19	3		
2017–18	Blackpool	26	4	45	7

HARTLEY, Peter (D) — 323 25
H: 6 0 W: 12 06 b.Hartlepool 3-4-88

Season	Club	A	G		
2006–07	Sunderland	1	0		
2007–08	Sunderland	0	0		
2007–08	Chesterfield	12	0	12	0
2008–09	Sunderland	0	0	1	0
2009–10	Hartlepool U	38	2		
2010–11	Hartlepool U	40	2		
2011–12	Hartlepool U	44	4		
2012–13	Hartlepool U	43	2		
2013–14	Hartlepool U	1	0	166	10
2013–14	Stevenage	31	2	31	2
2014–15	Plymouth Arg	39	4		
2015–16	Plymouth Arg	42	2	81	6
2016–17	Bristol R	18	5	18	5
2017–18	Blackpool	14	2		
2017–18	Motherwell	14	2	14	2

Transferred to Motherwell, January 2018.

MAFOUMBI, Christoffer (G) — 23 0
H: 6 5 W: 12 08 b. 3-3-94
Internationals: Congo Full caps.

Season	Club	A	G		
2011–12	Lens	0	0		
2012–13	Lens	0	0		
2013–14	Lens	0	0		
2014–15	Le Ponet	12	0	12	0
2015–16	Vereya Stara Zagora	3	0	3	0
2016–17	Free State Stars	4	0	4	0
2017–18	Blackpool	4	0	4	0

MATT, Jamille (F) — 141 27
H: 6 1 W: 11 11 b.Walsall 20-10-89

Season	Club	A	G		
2012–13	Fleetwood T	14	3		
2013–14	Fleetwood T	25	8		
2014–15	Fleetwood T	0	0		
2015–16	Fleetwood T	17	3	56	14
2015–16	Stevenage	8	1	8	1
2015–16	Plymouth Arg	11	5	11	5
2016–17	Blackpool	32	3		
2017–18	Blackpool	0	0	32	3
2017–18	Grimsby T	34	4	34	4

McALISTER, Jim (M) — 263 11
H: 5 10 W: 13 00 b.Rothesay 2-11-85

Season	Club	A	G		
2009–10	Greenock Morton	30	1	30	1
2010–11	Hamilton A	19	0		
2011–12	Hamilton A	36	1	55	1
2012–13	Dundee	38	3		
2013–14	Dundee	36	4		
2014–15	Dundee	37	2	111	9
2015–16	Blackpool	44	0		
2016–17	Blackpool	22	0		
2017–18	Blackpool	1	0	67	0

MELLOR, Kelvin (D) — 227 14
H: 5 10 W: 11 09 b.Copenhagen 25-1-91

Season	Club	A	G		
2007–08	Crewe Alex	0	0		
2008–09	Crewe Alex	0	0		
2009–10	Crewe Alex	0	0		
2010–11	Crewe Alex	1	0		
2011–12	Crewe Alex	12	1		
2012–13	Crewe Alex	35	0		
2013–14	Crewe Alex	28	1	76	2
2014–15	Plymouth Arg	37	1		
2015–16	Plymouth Arg	41	1	78	2
2016–17	Blackpool	44	4		
2017–18	Blackpool	29	6	73	10

MENGA, Dolly (F) — 111 16
b. 2-5-93
Internationals: Belgium U19, U21. Angola Full caps.

Season	Club	A	G		
2011–12	Standard Liege	0	0	1	0
2011–12	Sint-Truiden	14	2	14	2
2012–13	Lierse	20	2		
2012–13	Torino	1	0	1	0
2013–14	Lierse	17	2	37	4
2014–15	Braga	1	0		
2015–16	Braga	0	0		
2015–16	Tondela	25	0	25	0
2016–17	Braga	0	0		
2016–17	Hapoel Tel Aviv	14	0	14	0
2016–17	FC Ashdod	10	10	10	10
2017–18	Braga	0	0	1	0
2017–18	Blackpool	8	0	8	0

PHILLISKIRK, Daniel (M) — 173 20
H: 5 10 W: 11 05 b.Oldham 10-4-91
Internationals: England U17.

Season	Club	A	G		
2008–09	Chelsea	0	0		
2009–10	Chelsea	0	0		
2010–11	Chelsea	0	0		
2010–11	Oxford U	1	0		
2010–11	Sheffield U	3	0		
2011–12	Sheffield U	0	0		
2011–12	Oxford U	4	0	5	0
2012–13	Sheffield U	1	0	4	0
2012–13	Coventry C	1	0		
2013–14	Coventry C	0	0	1	0
2013–14	Oldham Ath	38	4		
2014–15	Oldham Ath	43	4		
2015–16	Oldham Ath	23	5	104	13
2015–16	Blackpool	22	5		
2016–17	Blackpool	18	0		
2017–18	Blackpool	19	2	59	7

QUIGLEY, Scott (F) — 9 0
H: 6 4 W: 14 02 b. 2-9-92
From The New Saints.

Season	Club	A	G		
2017–18	Blackpool	9	0	9	0

RICHARDS, Caleb (D) — 0 0
b. 8-9-98

Season	Club	A	G		
2017–18	Blackpool	0	0		

ROACHE, Rowan (F) — 1 0
H: 5 10 W: 11 09 b. 9-2-00
Internationals: Republic of Ireland U16, U17.

Season	Club	A	G		
2016–17	Blackpool	0	0		
2017–18	Blackpool	1	0	1	0

ROBERTSON, Clark (D) — 178 4
H: 6 2 W: 12 00 b.Aberdeen 5-9-93
Internationals: Scotland U19, U21.

Season	Club	A	G		
2009–10	Aberdeen	3	0		
2010–11	Aberdeen	13	0		
2011–12	Aberdeen	9	0		
2012–13	Aberdeen	23	0		
2013–14	Aberdeen	8	0		
2014–15	Aberdeen	1	0	57	0
2015–16	Blackpool	38	1		
2016–17	Blackpool	44	0		
2017–18	Blackpool	39	3	121	4

RYAN, James (M) — 380 37
H: 5 8 W: 11 08 b.Maghull 6-9-88
Internationals: Republic of Ireland U21.

Season	Club	A	G		
2006–07	Liverpool	0	0		
2007–08	Liverpool	0	0		
2007–08	Shrewsbury T	4	0	4	0
2008–09	Accrington S	44	10		
2009–10	Accrington S	39	3		
2010–11	Accrington S	46	9	129	22
2011–12	Scunthorpe U	24	2		
2012–13	Scunthorpe U	45	2	69	4
2013–14	Chesterfield	39	2		
2014–15	Chesterfield	44	4	83	6
2015–16	Fleetwood T	43	2		
2016–17	Fleetwood T	16	0	59	2
2017–18	Blackpool	36	3	36	3

SINCLAIR-SMITH, Finlay (M) — 0 0

Season	Club	A	G		
2017–18	Blackpool	0	0		

SPEARING, Jay (M) — 247 12
H: 5 6 W: 11 01 b.Wallasey 25-11-88

Season	Club	A	G		
2006–07	Liverpool	0	0		
2007–08	Liverpool	0	0		
2008–09	Liverpool	0	0		
2009–10	Liverpool	3	0		
2009–10	Leicester C	7	1	7	1
2010–11	Liverpool	11	0		
2011–12	Liverpool	16	0		
2012–13	Liverpool	0	0		
2012–13	Bolton W	37	2		
2013–14	Liverpool	0	0	30	0
2013–14	Bolton W	45	2		
2014–15	Bolton W	21	1		
2014–15	Blackburn R	15	1	15	1
2015–16	Bolton W	22	2		
2016–17	Bolton W	37	3		
2017–18	Bolton W	0	0	162	10
2017–18	Blackpool	33	0	33	0

TAYLOR, Andy (D) 311 9
H: 5 11 W: 11 07 b.Blackburn 14-3-86
Internationals: England U16, U17, U18, U19, U20.

2004–05	Blackburn R	0	0		
2005–06	Blackburn R	0	0		
2005–06	QPR	3	0	3	0
2005–06	Blackpool	3	0		
2006–07	Blackburn R	0	0		
2006–07	Crewe Alex	4	0	4	0
2006–07	Huddersfield T	8	0	8	0
2007–08	Blackburn R	0	0		
2007–08	Tranmere R	30	2		
2008–09	Tranmere R	39	1	69	3
2009–10	Sheffield U	26	0		
2010–11	Sheffield U	9	0		
2011–12	Sheffield U	4	0		
2012–13	Sheffield U	0	0	39	0
2012–13	Nottingham F	0	0		
2012–13	Walsall	34	0		
2013–14	Walsall	33	1		
2014–15	Walsall	39	1		
2015–16	Walsall	34	2	140	4
2016–17	Blackpool	38	2		
2017–18	Blackpool	7	0	48	2

TILT, Curtis (D) 42 1
H: 6 4 W: 11 11 b. 4-8-91
From Halesowen T, Hednesford T, AFC Telford U, Wrexham.

2017–18	Blackpool	42	1	42	1

TURENNE DES PRES, Sebastien (M) 0 0
Internationals: USA U19.

2016–17	Blackpool	0	0		
2017–18	Blackpool	0	0		

TURTON, Oliver (D) 211 5
H: 5 11 W: 11 11 b.Manchester 6-12-92

2010–11	Crewe Alex	1	0		
2011–12	Crewe Alex	2	0		
2012–13	Crewe Alex	20	0		
2013–14	Crewe Alex	12	1		
2014–15	Crewe Alex	44	1		
2015–16	Crewe Alex	46	1		
2016–17	Crewe Alex	45	1	170	4
2017–18	Blackpool	41	1	41	1

VASSELL, Kyle (F) 118 28
H: 6 0 W: 12 04 b.Milton Keynes 7-2-93

2013–14	Peterborough U	6	0		
2014–15	Peterborough U	17	5		
2014–15	Oxford U	6	1	6	1
2015–16	Peterborough U	5	0	28	5
2015–16	Dagenham & R	8	0	8	0
2015–16	Shrewsbury T	13	0	13	0
2016–17	Blackpool	34	11		
2017–18	Blackpool	29	11	63	22

WILLIAMS, Ben (G) 377 0
H: 6 0 W: 13 01 b.Manchester 27-8-82

2001–02	Manchester U	0	0		
2002–03	Manchester U	0	0		
2002–03	Coventry C	0	0		
2002–03	Chesterfield	14	0	14	0
2003–04	Manchester U	0	0		
2003–04	Crewe Alex	10	0		
2004–05	Crewe Alex	23	0		
2005–06	Crewe Alex	17	0		
2006–07	Crewe Alex	39	0		
2007–08	Crewe Alex	46	0	135	0
2008–09	Carlisle U	31	0	31	0
2009–10	Colchester U	46	0		
2010–11	Colchester U	33	0		
2011–12	Colchester U	36	0	115	0
2014–15	Bradford C	14	0		
2015–16	Bradford C	43	0	57	0
2016–17	Bury	22	0	22	0
2017–18	Blackpool	3	0	3	0

Players retained or with offer of contract
Sims, Jack Stephen John.

Scholars
Avon, William Lewis; Dunne, William Joseph; Flynn, Alwyn Michael John; Graham, Sean Malachy Robert; Jaaskelainen, Emil Anton; Jacobson, Ben Aron; Maddox, Samuel William; Newton, Jack Philip; O'Brien, Brendan Sean; Shaw, Nathan Edward; Simson, Harvey; Sinclair-Smith, Finlay; Sumner, Dylan Jack; Thordarson, Craig Raymond; Wainwright, Lewis; Watkinson, Owen Lewis; Williams, Thomas Ellis.

BOLTON W (10)

ALNWICK, Ben (G) 212 0
H: 6 2 W: 13 12 b.Prudhoe 1-1-87
Internationals: England U16, U17, U18, U19, U21.

2003–04	Sunderland	0	0		
2004–05	Sunderland	3	0		
2005–06	Sunderland	5	0		
2006–07	Sunderland	11	0	19	0
2006–07	Tottenham H	0	0		
2007–08	Tottenham H	0	0		
2007–08	Luton T	4	0	4	0
2007–08	Leicester C	8	0	8	0
2008–09	Tottenham H	0	0		
2008–09	Carlisle U	6	0	6	0
2009–10	Tottenham H	1	0		
2009–10	Norwich C	3	0	3	0
2010–11	Tottenham H	0	0		
2010–11	Leeds U	0	0		
2010–11	Doncaster R	0	0		
2011–12	Tottenham H	0	0		
2011–12	Leyton Orient	6	0		
2012–13	Tottenham H	0	0	1	0
2012–13	Barnsley	10	0		
2013–14	Barnsley	0	0	10	0
2013–14	Charlton Ath	10	0	10	0
2013–14	Leyton Orient	1	0	7	0
2014–15	Peterborough U	41	0		
2015–16	Peterborough U	39	0		
2016–17	Peterborough U	4	0	84	0
2016–17	Bolton W	21	0		
2017–18	Bolton W	39	0	60	0

AMEOBI, Sam (F) 158 10
H: 6 3 W: 10 04 b.Newcastle upon Tyne 1-5-92
Internationals: Nigeria U20. England U21.

2010–11	Newcastle U	0	0		
2011–12	Newcastle U	10	0		
2012–13	Newcastle U	8	0		
2012–13	Middlesbrough	9	1	9	1
2013–14	Newcastle U	10	0		
2014–15	Newcastle U	25	2		
2015–16	Newcastle U	0	0		
2015–16	Cardiff C	36	1	36	1
2016–17	Newcastle U	4	0	58	2
2016–17	Bolton W	20	2		
2017–18	Bolton W	35	4	55	6

AMOS, Ben (G) 155 0
H: 6 1 W: 13 00 b.Macclesfield 10-4-90
Internationals: England U16, U17, U18, U19, U20, U21.

2007–08	Manchester U	0	0		
2008–09	Manchester U	0	0		
2009–10	Manchester U	0	0		
2009–10	Peterborough U	1	0	1	0
2010–11	Manchester U	0	0		
2010–11	Oldham Ath	16	0	16	0
2011–12	Manchester U	1	0		
2012–13	Manchester U	0	0		
2012–13	Hull C	17	0	17	0
2013–14	Manchester U	0	0		
2013–14	Carlisle U	9	0	9	0
2014–15	Manchester U	0	0	1	0
2014–15	Bolton W	9	0		
2015–16	Bolton W	40	0		
2016–17	Bolton W	0	0		
2016–17	Cardiff C	16	0	16	0
2017–18	Bolton W	0	0	49	0
2017–18	Charlton Ath	46	0	46	0

BEEVERS, Mark (D) 373 18
H: 6 4 W: 13 00 b.Barnsley 21-11-89
Internationals: England U19.

2006–07	Sheffield W	2	0		
2007–08	Sheffield W	28	0		
2008–09	Sheffield W	34	0		
2009–10	Sheffield W	35	0		
2010–11	Sheffield W	28	2		
2011–12	Sheffield W	7	0		
2011–12	Milton Keynes D	14	1	14	1
2012–13	Sheffield W	6	0	140	2
2012–13	Millwall	35	1		
2013–14	Millwall	28	0		
2014–15	Millwall	25	2		
2015–16	Millwall	42	4	130	7
2016–17	Bolton W	45	7		
2017–18	Bolton W	44	1	89	8

BROCKBANK, Harry (D) 0 0
H: 5 11 W: 12 08 b.Bolton 26-9-98

2017–18	Bolton W	0	0		

BUCKLEY, Will (F) 265 40
H: 6 0 W: 13 00 b.Oldham 12-8-88

2007–08	Rochdale	7	0		
2008–09	Rochdale	37	10		
2009–10	Rochdale	15	3	59	13
2009–10	Watford	6	1		
2010–11	Watford	33	4	39	5
2011–12	Brighton & HA	29	8		
2012–13	Brighton & HA	36	8		
2013–14	Brighton & HA	30	3		
2014–15	Brighton & HA	1	0	96	19
2014–15	Sunderland	22	0		
2015–16	Sunderland	0	0		
2015–16	Leeds U	4	0	4	0
2015–16	Birmingham C	10	1	10	1
2016–17	Sunderland	0	0	22	0
2016–17	Sheffield W	11	0	11	0
2017–18	Bolton W	24	2	24	2

DARBY, Stephen (D) 268 0
H: 5 9 W: 10 00 b.Liverpool 6-10-88
Internationals: England U19.

2006–07	Liverpool	0	0		
2007–08	Liverpool	0	0		
2008–09	Liverpool	0	0		
2009–10	Liverpool	1	0		
2009–10	Swindon T	12	0	12	0
2010–11	Liverpool	0	0		
2010–11	Notts Co	23	0	23	0
2011–12	Liverpool	0	0	1	0
2011–12	Rochdale	35	0	35	0
2012–13	Bradford C	35	0		
2013–14	Bradford C	46	0		
2014–15	Bradford C	45	0		
2015–16	Bradford C	46	0		
2016–17	Bradford C	22	0	194	0
2017–18	Bolton W	3	0	3	0

DERVITE, Dorian (D) 186 6
H: 6 3 W: 13 06 b.Lille 25-7-88
Internationals: France U16, U17, U18, U19, U21.

2008–09	Southend U	18	0	18	0
2010–11	Villarreal B	9	0		
2011–12	Villarreal B	2	0	11	0
2012–13	Villarreal	0	0		
2012–13	Charlton Ath	30	3		
2013–14	Charlton Ath	40	2	70	5
2014–15	Bolton W	37	0		
2015–16	Bolton W	22	1		
2016–17	Bolton W	14	0		
2017–18	Bolton W	14	0	87	1

EARING, Jack (M) 0 0
b.Bury 21-1-99

2016–17	Bolton W	0	0		
2017–18	Bolton W	0	0		

HALL, Connor (F) 0 0
H: 5 11 W: 12 02 b.Slough 18-2-98

2017–18	Bolton W	0	0		

HENRY, Karl (M) 524 11
H: 6 0 W: 12 00 b.Wolverhampton 26-11-82
Internationals: England U18, U20.

1999–2000	Stoke C	0	0		
2000–01	Stoke C	0	0		
2001–02	Stoke C	24	0		
2002–03	Stoke C	18	1		
2003–04	Stoke C	20	0		
2003–04	Cheltenham T	9	1	9	1
2004–05	Stoke C	34	0		
2005–06	Stoke C	24	0	120	1
2006–07	Wolverhampton W	34	3		
2007–08	Wolverhampton W	40	3		
2008–09	Wolverhampton W	43	0		
2009–10	Wolverhampton W	34	0		
2010–11	Wolverhampton W	29	0		
2011–12	Wolverhampton W	31	0		
2012–13	Wolverhampton W	39	0	250	6
2013–14	QPR	27	1		
2014–15	QPR	33	0		
2015–16	QPR	38	1		
2016–17	QPR	14	0	112	2
2017–18	Bolton W	33	1	33	1

HOWARD, Mark (G) 181 0
H: 6 0 W: 11 13 b.Southwark 21-9-86

2005–06	Falkirk	8	0	8	0
2006–07	Cardiff C	0	0		
2006–07	Swansea C	0	0		
2007–08	St Mirren	10	0		
2008–09	St Mirren	33	0		
2009–10	St Mirren	2	0	45	0
2010–11	Aberdeen	9	0	9	0
2011–12	Blackpool	4	0	4	0
2011–12	Sheffield U	0	0		

2012–13	Sheffield U	11	0		
2013–14	Sheffield U	19	0		
2014–15	Sheffield U	35	0		
2015–16	Sheffield U	15	0	80	0
2016–17	Bolton W	27	0		
2017–18	Bolton W	8	0	35	0

KARACAN, Jem (M)   196 13
H: 5 10 W: 11 13 b.Lewisham 21-2-89
Internationals: Turkey U17, U18, U19, U21.

2007–08	Reading	0	0		
2007–08	*Bournemouth*	13	1	13	1
2007–08	*Millwall*	7	0	7	0
2008–09	Reading	15	1		
2009–10	Reading	27	0		
2010–11	Reading	40	3		
2011–12	Reading	37	3		
2012–13	Reading	21	1		
2013–14	Reading	7	2		
2014–15	Reading	8	1		
2015–16	Reading	0	0	155	11
2015–16	Galatasaray	0	0		
2016–17	Galatasaray	0	0		
2017–18	Bolton W	5	1		
2017–18	Bolton W	16	0	21	1

KING, Jeff (M)   1 0
H: 5 10 W: 12 08 b. 19-12-95
From Droylsden.

2017–18	Bolton W	1	0	1	0

KIRCHHOFF, Jan (D)   106 0
H: 6 4 W: 12 04 b.Frankfurt am Main 1-10-90
Internationals: Germany U18, U19, U21.

2010–11	Mainz	10	0		
2011–12	Mainz	29	0		
2012–13	Mainz	18	0	57	0
2013–14	Bayern Munich	7	0		
2013–14	Schalke 04	2	0		
2014–15	Bayern Munich	0	0		
2014–15	*Schalke 04*	14	0	16	0
2015–16	Bayern Munich	0	0	7	0
2015–16	Sunderland	15	0		
2016–17	Sunderland	7	0	22	0
2017–18	Bolton W	4	0	4	0

LE FONDRE, Adam (F)   490 174
H: 5 9 W: 11 04 b.Stockport 2-12-86

2004–05	Stockport Co	20	4		
2005–06	Stockport Co	22	6		
2006–07	Stockport Co	21	7	63	17
2006–07	*Rochdale*	7	4		
2007–08	Rochdale	46	16		
2008–09	Rochdale	44	18		
2009–10	Rochdale	1	0	98	38
2009–10	Rotherham U	44	25		
2010–11	Rotherham U	45	23		
2011–12	Rotherham U	4	4	93	52
2011–12	Reading	32	12		
2012–13	Reading	34	12		
2013–14	Reading	38	15	104	39
2014–15	Cardiff C	23	3		
2014–15	*Bolton W*	17	8		
2015–16	Cardiff C	0	0		
2015–16	*Wolverhampton W*	26	3	26	3
2016–17	Cardiff C	0	0	23	3
2016–17	*Wigan Ath*	12	1	12	1
2016–17	*Bolton W*	19	6		
2017–18	Bolton W	35	7	71	21

LITTLE, Mark (D)   338 5
H: 6 1 W: 12 10 b.Worcester 20-8-88
Internationals: England U19.

2005–06	Wolverhampton W	0	0		
2006–07	Wolverhampton W	26	0		
2007–08	Wolverhampton W	1	0		
2007–08	*Northampton T*	17	0		
2008–09	Wolverhampton W	0	0		
2008–09	*Northampton T*	9	0	26	0
2009–10	Wolverhampton W	0	0	27	0
2009–10	*Chesterfield*	12	0	12	0
2009–10	*Peterborough U*	9	0		
2010–11	Peterborough U	35	0		
2011–12	Peterborough U	35	1		
2012–13	Peterborough U	40	1		
2013–14	Peterborough U	38	1	157	3
2014–15	Bristol C	37	1		
2015–16	Bristol C	23	0		
2016–17	Bristol C	28	0	88	1
2017–18	Bolton W	28	1	28	1

MORAIS, Filipe (M)   330 31
H: 5 9 W: 11 10 b.Lisbon 21-11-85
Internationals: Portugal U21.

2003–04	Chelsea	0	0		
2004–05	Chelsea	0	0		
2005–06	Chelsea	0	0		
2005–06	*Milton Keynes D*	13	0	13	0
2006–07	Millwall	12	1	12	1
2006–07	*St Johnstone*	13	1		
2007–08	Hibernian	28	1		
2008–09	Hibernian	2	0	30	1
2008–09	Inverness CT	12	3	12	3
2009–10	St Johnstone	30	2	43	3
2010–11	Oldham Ath	23	3		
2011–12	Oldham Ath	36	5		
2012–13	Oldham Ath	0	0	59	8
2012–13	Stevenage	28	3		
2013–14	Stevenage	27	4	55	7
2014–15	Bradford C	30	3		
2015–16	Bradford C	7	1		
2016–17	Bradford C	17	1	54	5
2016–17	*Bolton W*	19	2		
2017–18	Bolton W	33	1	52	3

NOONE, Craig (M)   303 28
H: 6 3 W: 12 07 b.Kirkby 17-11-87

2008–09	Plymouth Arg	11	1		
2009–10	Plymouth Arg	17	1		
2009–10	*Exeter C*	7	2	7	2
2010–11	Plymouth Arg	17	3	55	5
2010–11	Brighton & HA	23	2		
2011–12	Brighton & HA	33	2		
2012–13	Brighton & HA	3	0	59	4
2012–13	Cardiff C	32	7		
2013–14	Cardiff C	17	1		
2014–15	Cardiff C	37	1		
2015–16	Cardiff C	38	5		
2016–17	Cardiff C	34	2		
2017–18	Cardiff C	0	0	158	16
2017–18	Bolton W	24	1	24	1

OSEDE, Derik (D)   65 0
H: 5 11 W: 11 09 b.Madrid 21-2-93
Internationals: Spain U16, U17, U18, U19, U20, U21.

2014–15	Real Madrid	0	0		
2015–16	Bolton W	23	0		
2016–17	Bolton W	25	0		
2017–18	Bolton W	17	0	65	0

PRATLEY, Darren (M)   402 43
H: 6 1 W: 11 02 b.Barking 22-4-85

2001–02	Fulham	0	0		
2002–03	Fulham	0	0		
2003–04	Fulham	1	0		
2004–05	Fulham	0	0		
2004–05	*Brentford*	14	1		
2005–06	Fulham	0	0	1	0
2005–06	*Brentford*	32	4	46	5
2006–07	Swansea C	33	2		
2007–08	Swansea C	42	5		
2008–09	Swansea C	37	4		
2009–10	Swansea C	36	7		
2010–11	Swansea C	34	9	177	26
2011–12	Bolton W	25	1		
2012–13	Bolton W	31	2		
2013–14	Bolton W	20	2		
2014–15	Bolton W	22	4		
2015–16	Bolton W	36	1		
2016–17	Bolton W	12	0		
2017–18	Bolton W	32	2	178	12

TAYLOR, Andrew (D)   370 6
H: 5 10 W: 11 04 b.Hartlepool 1-8-86
Internationals: England U16, U17, U18, U19, U20, U21.

2003–04	Middlesbrough	0	0		
2004–05	Middlesbrough	0	0		
2005–06	Middlesbrough	13	0		
2005–06	*Bradford C*	24	0	24	0
2006–07	Middlesbrough	34	0		
2007–08	Middlesbrough	19	0		
2008–09	Middlesbrough	26	0		
2009–10	Middlesbrough	10	0		
2010–11	Middlesbrough	21	3	125	3
2010–11	*Watford*	19	1	19	1
2011–12	Cardiff C	42	1		
2012–13	Cardiff C	43	0		
2013–14	Cardiff C	18	0	103	1
2014–15	Wigan Ath	26	1		
2015–16	*Reading*	19	0	19	0
2016–17	Wigan Ath	0	0	26	1
2016–17	*Bolton W*	34	0		
2017–18	Bolton W	20	0	54	0

TURNER, Jake (G)   0 0
b.Wilmslow 25-2-99
Internationals: England U18, U19.

2016–17	Bolton W	0	0		
2017–18	Bolton W	0	0		

VELA, Joshua (M)   150 12
H: 5 11 W: 11 07 b.Salford 14-12-93

2010–11	Bolton W	0	0		
2011–12	Bolton W	3	0		
2012–13	Bolton W	4	0		
2013–14	Bolton W	0	0		
2013–14	*Notts Co*	7	0	7	0
2014–15	Bolton W	29	0		
2015–16	Bolton W	31	2		
2016–17	Bolton W	46	9		
2017–18	Bolton W	30	1	143	12

WHEATER, David (D)   342 27
H: 6 5 W: 12 12 b.Redcar 14-2-87
Internationals: England U17, U18, U19, U21.

2004–05	Middlesbrough	0	0		
2005–06	Middlesbrough	0	0		
2005–06	*Doncaster R*	7	1	7	1
2006–07	Middlesbrough	2	1		
2006–07	*Wolverhampton W*	1	0	1	0
2006–07	*Darlington*	15	2	15	2
2007–08	Middlesbrough	34	3		
2008–09	Middlesbrough	32	1		
2009–10	Middlesbrough	42	1		
2010–11	Middlesbrough	24	3	140	9
2010–11	Bolton W	7	0		
2011–12	Bolton W	24	2		
2012–13	Bolton W	4	0		
2013–14	Bolton W	23	1		
2014–15	Bolton W	17	1		
2015–16	Bolton W	28	1		
2016–17	Bolton W	43	9		
2017–18	Bolton W	33	1	179	15

WHITE, Ryan (M)   0 0
b. 9-11-98

2017–18	Bolton W	0	0		

WILBRAHAM, Aaron (F)   558 123
H: 6 3 W: 12 04 b.Knutsford 21-10-79

1997–98	Stockport Co	7	1		
1998–99	Stockport Co	26	0		
1999–2000	Stockport Co	26	4		
2000–01	Stockport Co	36	12		
2001–02	Stockport Co	21	3		
2002–03	Stockport Co	15	7		
2003–04	Hull C	41	8	172	35
2004–05	Hull C	19	2	19	2
2004–05	*Oldham Ath*	4	2	4	2
2005–06	Milton Keynes D	31	4		
2005–06	*Bradford C*	5	1	5	1
2006–07	Milton Keynes D	32	7		
2007–08	Milton Keynes D	35	10		
2008–09	Milton Keynes D	33	16		
2009–10	Milton Keynes D	33	16		
2010–11	Milton Keynes D	10	2	176	49
2010–11	Norwich C	12	1		
2011–12	Norwich C	11	1	23	2
2012–13	Crystal Palace	21	0		
2013–14	Crystal Palace	0	4	25	0
2014–15	Bristol C	37	18		
2015–16	Bristol C	43	8		
2016–17	Bristol C	31	4	111	30
2017–18	Bristol C	23	2	23	2

Players retained or with offer of contract
Edwards, Liam John; Obasi, Chinedu Ogbuke.

Scholars
Argent-Barnes, Matthew; Aspinall, James Alexander; Boon, Jordan Mark; Brockbank, Harry William; Broughton, Max Alexander; Brown, Edward James; Connell, Luca John; Darcy, Ronan Thomas; Earing, Jack James; Fearnley, Matthew Neil; Hartshorne, William Lancaster; James, Callum George Lennon; Jones-Griffiths, Shakeel Tyrik Zane; Lonsdale, Cole Stephen; Moore, Cameron James; Moulden, Edward James; Navarro, Luca; Politic, Dennis-Dorian; Preston, Callum Mark; Smith, Laurence Robert; White, Ryan.

BOURNEMOUTH (11)

AFOBE, Benik (F)   215 57
H: 5 10 W: 11 00 b.Leyton 12-2-93
Internationals: England U16, U17, U19, U21. DR Congo Full caps.

2009–10	Arsenal	0	0		
2010–11	Arsenal	0	0		
2010–11	*Huddersfield T*	28	5	28	5
2011–12	Arsenal	0	0		
2011–12	*Reading*	3	0	3	0
2012–13	Arsenal	0	0		
2012–13	*Bolton W*	20	2	20	2
2012–13	*Millwall*	5	0	5	0
2013–14	Arsenal	0	0		
2013–14	*Sheffield W*	12	2	12	2
2014–15	Arsenal	0	0		
2014–15	*Milton Keynes D*	22	10	22	10

2014–15	Wolverhampton W	21	13		
2015–16	Wolverhampton W	25	9		
2015–16	Bournemouth	15	4		
2016–17	Bournemouth	31	6		
2017–18	Bournemouth	17	0	63	10
2017–18	Wolverhampton W	16	6	62	28

AKE, Nathan (M) 84 6
H: 5 11 W: 11 01 b.Den Haag 18-2-95
Internationals: Netherlands U15, U16, U17, U19, U21, Full caps.

2012–13	Chelsea	3	0		
2013–14	Chelsea	1	0		
2014–15	Chelsea	1	0		
2014–15	*Reading*	5	0	5	0
2015–16	Chelsea	0	0		
2015–16	*Watford*	24	1	24	1
2016–17	Chelsea	2	0	7	0
2016–17	*Bournemouth*	10	3		
2017–18	Bournemouth	38	2	48	5

ALLSOP, Ryan (G) 124 0
H: 6 2 W: 12 06 b.Birmingham 17-6-92
Internationals: England U17.

2012–13	Leyton Orient	20	0	20	0
2012–13	Bournemouth	10	0		
2013–14	Bournemouth	12	0		
2014–15	Bournemouth	0	0		
2014–15	*Coventry C*	24	0	24	0
2015–16	Bournemouth	1	0		
2015–16	*Wycombe W*	18	0	18	0
2015–16	Portsmouth	0	0		
2016–17	Bournemouth	1	0		
2017–18	Bournemouth	0	0	24	0
2017–18	*Blackpool*	22	0	22	0
2017–18	*Lincoln C*	16	0	16	0

ARTER, Harry (M) 237 29
H: 5 9 W: 11 07 b.Sidcup 28-12-89
Internationals: Republic of Ireland U17, U19, Full caps.

| 2007–08 | Charlton Ath | 0 | 0 | | |
| 2008–09 | Charlton Ath | 0 | 0 | | |

From Woking.

2010–11	Bournemouth	18	0		
2010–11	*Carlisle U*	5	1	5	1
2011–12	Bournemouth	34	5		
2012–13	Bournemouth	37	8		
2013–14	Bournemouth	31	3		
2014–15	Bournemouth	43	9		
2015–16	Bournemouth	21	1		
2016–17	Bournemouth	35	1		
2017–18	Bournemouth	13	1	232	28

BEGOVIC, Asmir (G) 261 1
H: 6 5 W: 13 01 b.Trebinje 20-6-87
Internationals: Canada U20. Bosnia & Herzegovina Full caps.

2006–07	Portsmouth	0	0		
2006–07	*Macclesfield T*	3	0	3	0
2007–08	Portsmouth	0	0		
2007–08	*Bournemouth*	8	0		
2007–08	*Yeovil T*	2	0		
2008–09	Portsmouth	2	0		
2008–09	*Yeovil T*	14	0	16	0
2009–10	Portsmouth	9	0	11	0
2009–10	*Ipswich T*	6	0	6	0
2009–10	Stoke C	4	0		
2010–11	Stoke C	28	0		
2011–12	Stoke C	23	0		
2012–13	Stoke C	38	0		
2013–14	Stoke C	32	1		
2014–15	Stoke C	35	0	160	0
2015–16	Chelsea	17	0		
2016–17	Chelsea	2	0	19	0
2017–18	Bournemouth	38	0	46	0

BORUC, Artur (G) 377 0
H: 6 4 W: 13 08 b.Siedlce 20-2-80
Internationals: Poland Full caps.

2005–06	Celtic	34	0		
2006–07	Celtic	36	0		
2007–08	Celtic	30	0		
2008–09	Celtic	34	0		
2009–10	Celtic	28	0	162	0
2010–11	Fiorentina	26	0		
2011–12	Fiorentina	36	0	62	0
2012–13	Southampton	20	0		
2013–14	Southampton	29	0		
2014–15	Southampton	0	0	49	0
2014–15	*Bournemouth*	37	0		
2015–16	Bournemouth	32	0		
2016–17	Bournemouth	35	0		
2017–18	Bournemouth	0	0	104	0

BUTCHER, Matt (M) 34 2
H: 6 2 W: 12 13 b.Portsmouth 14-5-97
From Poole T.

2015–16	Bournemouth	0	0		
2016–17	Bournemouth	0	0		
2016–17	*Yeovil T*	34	2	34	2
2017–18	Bournemouth	0	0		

CARGILL, Baily (D) 47 2
H: 6 2 W: 13 10 b.Winchester 13-10-95
Internationals: England U20.

2012–13	Bournemouth	0	0		
2013–14	Bournemouth	0	0		
2013–14	*Torquay U*	5	0	5	0
2014–15	Bournemouth	0	0		
2015–16	Bournemouth	0	0		
2015–16	*Coventry C*	5	1	5	1
2016–17	Bournemouth	1	0		
2016–17	*Gillingham*	9	1	9	1
2017–18	Bournemouth	0	0	1	0
2017–18	*Fleetwood T*	11	0	11	0
2017–18	*Partick Thistle*	16	0	16	0

COOK, Lewis (M) 115 1
H: 5 9 W: 11 03 b.York 3-2-97
Internationals: England U16, U17, U18, U19, U20, U21, Full caps.

2014–15	Leeds U	37	0		
2015–16	Leeds U	43	1	80	1
2016–17	Bournemouth	6	0		
2017–18	Bournemouth	29	0	35	0

COOK, Steve (D) 254 17
H: 6 1 W: 13 03 b.Hastings 19-4-91

2008–09	Brighton & HA	0	0		
2009–10	Brighton & HA	0	0		
2010–11	Brighton & HA	0	0		
2011–12	Brighton & HA	1	0	3	0
2011–12	Bournemouth	26	0		
2012–13	Bournemouth	33	1		
2013–14	Bournemouth	38	3		
2014–15	Bournemouth	46	5		
2015–16	Bournemouth	36	4		
2016–17	Bournemouth	38	2		
2017–18	Bournemouth	34	2	251	17

DANIELS, Charlie (M) 381 20
H: 6 1 W: 12 12 b.Harlow 7-9-86

2005–06	Tottenham H	0	0		
2006–07	Tottenham H	0	0		
2006–07	*Chesterfield*	2	0	2	0
2007–08	Tottenham H	0	0		
2007–08	*Leyton Orient*	31	2		
2008–09	Tottenham H	0	0		
2008–09	*Gillingham*	5	1	5	1
2008–09	*Leyton Orient*	21	2		
2009–10	Leyton Orient	41	0		
2010–11	Leyton Orient	42	0		
2011–12	Leyton Orient	13	0	148	4
2011–12	Bournemouth	21	2		
2012–13	Bournemouth	34	4		
2013–14	Bournemouth	23	0		
2014–15	Bournemouth	42	1		
2015–16	Bournemouth	37	3		
2016–17	Bournemouth	34	4		
2017–18	Bournemouth	35	1	226	15

DEFOE, Jermain (F) 559 202
H: 5 7 W: 10 04 b.Beckton 7-10-82
Internationals: England U16, U18, U21, B, Full caps.

1999–2000	West Ham U	0	0		
2000–01	West Ham U	1	0		
2000–01	*Bournemouth*	29	18		
2001–02	West Ham U	35	10		
2002–03	West Ham U	38	8		
2003–04	West Ham U	19	11	93	29
2003–04	Tottenham H	15	7		
2004–05	Tottenham H	35	13		
2005–06	Tottenham H	36	9		
2006–07	Tottenham H	34	10		
2007–08	Tottenham H	19	4		
2007–08	Portsmouth	12	8		
2008–09	Portsmouth	19	7	31	15
2008–09	Tottenham H	8	3		
2009–10	Tottenham H	34	18		
2010–11	Tottenham H	22	4		
2011–12	Tottenham H	25	11		
2012–13	Tottenham H	33	11		
2013–14	Tottenham H	14	1	276	91
2014	Toronto	19	11	19	11
2014–15	Sunderland	17	4		
2015–16	Sunderland	33	15		
2016–17	Sunderland	37	15	87	34
2017–18	Bournemouth	24	4	53	22

DOBRE, Mihai (M) 15 1
b. 30-8-98
Internationals: Romania U17, U21.

2017–18	Bournemouth	0	0		
2017–18	*Bury*	10	0	10	0
2017–18	*Rochdale*	5	1	5	1

FEDERICI, Adam (G) 227 1
H: 6 2 W: 14 02 b.Nowra 31-1-85
Internationals: Australia U20, U23, Full caps.

2005–06	Reading	0	0		
2006–07	Reading	2	0		
2007–08	Reading	0	0		
2008–09	Reading	15	1		
2008–09	*Southend U*	10	0	10	0
2009–10	Reading	46	0		
2010–11	Reading	34	0		
2011–12	Reading	46	0		
2012–13	Reading	21	0		
2013–14	Reading	2	0		
2014–15	Reading	43	0	209	1
2015–16	Bournemouth	6	0		
2016–17	Bournemouth	2	0		
2017–18	Bournemouth	0	0	8	0
2017–18	*Nottingham F*	0	0		

FRANCIS, Simon (D) 543 9
H: 6 0 W: 12 06 b.Nottingham 16-2-85
Internationals: England U18, U20.

2002–03	Bradford C	25	1		
2003–04	Bradford C	30	0	55	1
2003–04	*Sheffield U*	5	0		
2004–05	Sheffield U	6	0		
2005–06	Sheffield U	1	0	12	0
2005–06	*Grimsby T*	5	0	5	0
2005–06	*Tranmere R*	17	1	17	1
2006–07	Southend U	40	1		
2007–08	Southend U	27	2		
2008–09	Southend U	45	0		
2009–10	Southend U	45	1	157	4
2010–11	Charlton Ath	34	0		
2011–12	Charlton Ath	0	0	34	0
2011–12	Bournemouth	29	0		
2012–13	Bournemouth	42	1		
2013–14	Bournemouth	46	1		
2014–15	Bournemouth	42	1		
2015–16	Bournemouth	38	0		
2016–17	Bournemouth	34	0		
2017–18	Bournemouth	32	0	263	3

FRASER, Ryan (M) 156 16
H: 5 4 W: 10 13 b.Aberdeen 24-2-94
Internationals: Scotland U19, U21, Full caps.

2010–11	Aberdeen	2	0		
2011–12	Aberdeen	3	0		
2012–13	Aberdeen	16	0	21	0
2012–13	*Bournemouth*	5	0		
2013–14	Bournemouth	37	3		
2014–15	Bournemouth	21	1		
2015–16	Bournemouth	0	0		
2015–16	*Ipswich T*	18	4	18	4
2016–17	Bournemouth	28	3		
2017–18	Bournemouth	26	5	117	12

GOSLING, Dan (M) 189 16
H: 6 0 W: 11 00 b.Brixham 2-2-90
Internationals: England U17, U18, U19, U21.

2006–07	Plymouth Arg	12	2		
2007–08	Plymouth Arg	10	0	22	2
2007–08	Everton	0	0		
2008–09	Everton	11	2		
2009–10	Everton	11	2	22	4
2010–11	Newcastle U	1	0		
2011–12	Newcastle U	12	1		
2012–13	Newcastle U	3	0		
2013–14	Newcastle U	8	0	24	1
2014–15	*Blackpool*	14	2	14	2
2014–15	Bournemouth	18	0		
2015–16	Bournemouth	34	3		
2016–17	Bournemouth	27	2		
2017–18	Bournemouth	28	2	107	7

GRABBAN, Lewis (F) 348 106
H: 6 0 W: 11 03 b.Croydon 12-1-88

2005–06	Crystal Palace	0	0		
2006–07	Crystal Palace	8	1		
2006–07	*Oldham Ath*	9	0	9	0
2007–08	Crystal Palace	2	0	10	1
2007–08	*Motherwell*	6	0	6	0
2007–08	*Millwall*	13	3		
2008–09	Millwall	31	6		
2009–10	Millwall	11	0		
2009–10	*Brentford*	7	2		
2010–11	Millwall	1	0	56	9
2010–11	*Brentford*	22	5	29	7
2011–12	Rotherham U	43	18	43	18
2012–13	Bournemouth	42	13		

2013–14	Bournemouth	44	22	
2014–15	Norwich C	35	12	
2015–16	Norwich C	6	1	**41 13**
2015–16	Bournemouth	15	0	
2016–17	Bournemouth	3	0	
2016–17	*Reading*	16	3	**16 3**
2017–18	Bournemouth	0	0	**104 35**
2017–18	*Sunderland*	19	12	**19 12**
2017–18	*Aston Villa*	15	8	**15 8**

GRADEL, Max (M)   **293 75**
H: 5 10   W: 11 00   b.Abidjan 30-11-87
Internationals: Ivory Coast Full caps.

2005–06	Leicester C	0	0	
2006–07	Leicester C	0	0	
2007–08	Leicester C	0	0	
2007–08	Bournemouth	34	9	
2008–09	Leicester C	27	1	
2009–10	Leicester C	0	0	**27 1**
2009–10	Leeds U	32	6	
2010–11	Leeds U	41	18	
2011–12	Leeds U	4	1	**77 25**
2011–12	St Etienne	29	6	
2012–13	St Etienne	23	3	
2013–14	St Etienne	18	5	
2014–15	St Etienne	31	17	**101 31**
2015–16	Bournemouth	14	1	
2016–17	Bournemouth	11	0	
2017–18	Bournemouth	0	0	**59 10**
2017–18	*Toulouse*	29	8	**29 8**

HOBSON, Shaun (D)   **0 0**

2017–18	Bournemouth	0	0

HYNDMAN, Emerson (M)   **39 5**
H: 5 7   W: 9 08   b.Dallas 9-4-96
Internationals: USA U17, U20, U23, Full caps.

2013–14	Fulham	0	0	
2014–15	Fulham	9	0	
2015–16	Fulham	16	1	**25 1**
2016–17	Bournemouth	0	0	
2016–17	*Rangers*	13	4	**13 4**
2017–18	Bournemouth	1	0	**1 0**

IBE, Jordan (F)   **136 10**
H: 5 9   W: 11 00   b.Southwark 8-12-95
Internationals: England U18, U19, U20, U21.

2011–12	Wycombe W	7	1	**7 1**
2011–12	Liverpool	0	0	
2012–13	Liverpool	1	0	
2013–14	Liverpool	0	0	
2013–14	*Birmingham C*	11	1	**11 1**
2014–15	Liverpool	12	0	
2014–15	*Derby Co*	20	5	**20 5**
2015–16	Liverpool	27	1	**41 1**
2016–17	Bournemouth	25	0	
2017–18	Bournemouth	32	2	**57 2**

KING, Josh (F)   **192 36**
H: 5 11   W: 11 09   b.Oslo 15-1-92
Internationals: Norway U15, U16, U18, U19, U21, Full caps.

2008–09	Manchester U	0	0	
2009–10	Manchester U	0	0	
2010–11	Manchester U	0	0	
2010–11	*Preston NE*	8	0	**8 0**
2011–12	Manchester U	0	0	
2011–12	*Borussia M'gladbach*	2	0	**2 0**
2011–12	*Hull C*	18	1	**18 1**
2012–13	Manchester U	0	0	
2012–13	Blackburn R	16	2	
2013–14	Blackburn R	32	2	
2014–15	Blackburn R	16	1	**64 5**
2015–16	Bournemouth	31	6	
2016–17	Bournemouth	36	16	
2017–18	Bournemouth	33	8	**100 30**

MAHONEY, Connor (M)   **28 0**
H: 5 9   W: 10 08   b.Blackburn 12-2-97
Internationals: England U17, U18, U20.

2013–14	*Accrington S*	4	0	**4 0**
2013–14	Blackburn R	0	0	
2014–15	Blackburn R	0	0	
2015–16	Blackburn R	2	0	
2016–17	Blackburn R	14	0	**16 0**
2017–18	Bournemouth	0	0	
2017–18	*Barnsley*	8	0	**8 0**

MINGS, Tyrone (D)   **69 1**
H: 6 3   W: 12 00   b.Bath 19-3-93

2012–13	Ipswich T	1	0	
2013–14	Ipswich T	16	0	
2014–15	Ipswich T	40	1	**57 1**
2015–16	Bournemouth	0	0	
2016–17	Bournemouth	7	0	
2017–18	Bournemouth	4	0	**12 0**

MOUSSET, Lys (M)   **68 16**
H: 6 0   W: 12 08   b.Montvilliers 8-2-96
Internationals: France U20, U21.

2013–14	Le Havre	5	0	
2014–15	Le Havre	1	0	
2015–16	Le Havre	28	14	**34 14**
2016–17	Bournemouth	11	0	
2017–18	Bournemouth	23	2	**34 2**

NDJOLI, Mikael (F)   **0 0**
b.16-12-98

2017–18	Bournemouth	0	0

PUGH, Marc (M)   **412 67**
H: 5 11   W: 11 04   b.Bacup 2-4-87

2005–06	Burnley	0	0	
2005–06	Bury	6	1	
2006–07	Bury	35	3	**41 4**
2007–08	Shrewsbury T	37	4	
2008–09	Shrewsbury T	7	0	**44 4**
2008–09	Luton T	4	0	**4 0**
2008–09	Hereford U	9	1	
2009–10	Hereford U	40	13	**49 14**
2010–11	Bournemouth	41	12	
2011–12	Bournemouth	42	8	
2012–13	Bournemouth	40	6	
2013–14	Bournemouth	42	5	
2014–15	Bournemouth	42	9	
2015–16	Bournemouth	26	3	
2016–17	Bournemouth	21	2	
2017–18	Bournemouth	20	0	**274 45**

QUIGLEY, Joe (F)   **12 1**
H: 6 4   W: 13 01   b.Hayes 12-10-96
Internationals: Republic of Ireland U21.

2016–17	Bournemouth	0	0	
2016–17	*Gillingham*	10	1	**10 1**
2017–18	Bournemouth	0	0	
2017–18	*Newport Co*	2	0	**2 0**

RAMSDALE, Aaron (G)   **19 0**
b. 14-5-98
Internationals: England U18, U19, U20.

2015–16	Sheffield U	0	0	
2016–17	Sheffield U	0	0	
2017–18	Bournemouth	0	0	
2017–18	*Chesterfield*	19	0	**19 0**

SIMPSON, Jack (D)   **1 0**
H: 5 10   W: 13 01   b.8-1-97

2015–16	Bournemouth	0	0	
2016–17	Bournemouth	0	0	
2017–18	Bournemouth	1	0	**1 0**

SMITH, Adam (D)   **239 8**
H: 5 8   W: 10 07   b.Leytonstone 29-4-91
Internationals: England U16, U17, U19, U20, U21.

2007–08	Tottenham H	0	0	
2008–09	Tottenham H	0	0	
2009–10	Tottenham H	0	0	
2009–10	*Wycombe W*	3	0	**3 0**
2009–10	*Torquay U*	16	0	**16 0**
2010–11	Tottenham H	0	0	
2010–11	*Bournemouth*	38	1	
2011–12	Tottenham H	1	0	
2011–12	*Milton Keynes D*	17	2	**17 2**
2011–12	*Leeds U*	3	0	**3 0**
2012–13	Tottenham H	0	0	
2012–13	*Millwall*	25	1	**25 1**
2013–14	Tottenham H	0	0	**1 0**
2013–14	*Derby Co*	8	0	**8 0**
2013–14	Bournemouth	5	0	
2014–15	Bournemouth	29	0	
2015–16	Bournemouth	31	2	
2016–17	Bournemouth	36	1	
2017–18	Bournemouth	27	1	**166 5**

SMITH, Bradley (D)   **17 0**
H: 5 10   W: 11 00   b.New South Wales 9-4-94
Internationals: England U17, U19, U20. Australia U23, Full caps.

2011–12	Liverpool	0	0	
2012–13	Liverpool	0	0	
2013–14	Liverpool	1	0	
2014–15	Liverpool	0	0	
2014–15	*Swindon T*	7	0	**7 0**
2015–16	Liverpool	4	0	**5 0**
2016–17	Bournemouth	5	0	
2017–18	Bournemouth	0	0	**5 0**

STANISLAS, Junior (M)   **215 30**
H: 6 0   W: 12 00   b.Kidbrooke 26-11-89
Internationals: England U20, U21.

2007–08	West Ham U	0	0
2008–09	West Ham U	9	2

2008–09	*Southend U*	6	1	**6 1**
2009–10	West Ham U	26	3	
2010–11	West Ham U	6	1	
2011–12	West Ham U	1	0	**42 6**
2011–12	Burnley	31	0	
2012–13	Burnley	35	5	
2013–14	Burnley	27	2	**93 7**
2014–15	Bournemouth	13	1	
2015–16	Bournemouth	21	3	
2016–17	Bournemouth	21	7	
2017–18	Bournemouth	19	5	**74 16**

SURMAN, Andrew (M)   **391 35**
H: 5 10   W: 11 06   b.Johannesburg 20-8-86
Internationals: England U21.

2003–04	Southampton	0	0	
2004–05	Southampton	0	0	
2004–05	*Walsall*	14	2	**14 2**
2005–06	Southampton	12	2	
2005–06	*Bournemouth*	24	6	
2006–07	Southampton	37	4	
2007–08	Southampton	40	2	
2008–09	Southampton	44	7	
2009–10	Southampton	0	0	**133 15**
2009–10	*Wolverhampton W*	7	0	**7 0**
2010–11	Norwich C	22	3	
2011–12	Norwich C	25	4	
2012–13	Norwich C	4	0	
2013–14	Norwich C	0	0	
2013–14	Bournemouth	35	0	
2014–15	Norwich C	1	0	**52 7**
2014–15	Bournemouth	41	3	
2015–16	Bournemouth	38	0	
2016–17	Bournemouth	22	0	
2017–18	Bournemouth	25	2	**185 11**

SURRIDGE, Sam (F)   **41 8**
b.Wimborne 28-7-98

2015–16	Bournemouth	0	0	
2016–17	Bournemouth	0	0	
2017–18	Bournemouth	0	0	
2017–18	*Yeovil T*	41	8	**41 8**

TAYLOR, Kyle (M)   **0 0**
b. 28-8-99

2017–18	Bournemouth	0	0

WHITFIELD, Ben (M)   **71 6**
H: 5 5   W: 9 11   b.28-2-96

2013–14	Bournemouth	0	0	
2014–15	Bournemouth	0	0	
2015–16	Bournemouth	0	0	
2016–17	Bournemouth	0	0	
2016–17	*Yeovil T*	34	2	**34 2**
2017–18	Bournemouth	0	0	
2017–18	*Port Vale*	37	4	**37 4**

WILSON, Callum (M)   **155 61**
H: 5 11   W: 10 06   b.Coventry 27-2-92
Internationals: England U21.

2009–10	Coventry C	0	0	
2010–11	Coventry C	1	0	
2011–12	Coventry C	0	0	
2012–13	Coventry C	11	1	
2013–14	Coventry C	37	21	**49 22**
2014–15	Bournemouth	45	20	
2015–16	Bournemouth	13	5	
2016–17	Bournemouth	20	6	
2017–18	Bournemouth	28	8	**106 39**

WORTHINGTON, Matt (M)   **16 0**
b.Southampton 18-12-97

2016–17	Bournemouth	1	0	
2017–18	Bournemouth	0	0	**1 0**
2017–18	*Yeovil T*	15	0	**15 0**

Players retained or with offer of contract
Cordner, Tyler Jack; Dennis, William Jonathon; Holmes, Jordan Thomas; Jordan, Corey; O'Connell, Keelan; Ofoborh, Nathan Nnamdi Ugochukwu; Travers, Mark; Vincent, Francis William.

Scholars
Anthony, Jaidon; Boote, James Peter; Camp, Brennan; Clements, Nathan John; Cope, Jake William; Dinsmore, Thomas Jack; Gillela, Dinesh; Glover, Ryan Michael Scott; Hanfrey, Thomas William; Ibsen Rossi, Zeno; Kilkenny, Gavin; Nippard, Luke Ryan; Parker-Trott, Thomas James; Scrimshaw, Jake; Seaman, Charlie; Sherring, Sam; Ward, Calum Brian Joseph.

BRADFORD C (12)

BARR, Lachlan (D)   1 0
b.London 24-9-94
2017–18   Bradford C   1 0   **1 0**

BRUNKER, Kai (F)   9 0
b. 10-6-94
2015–16   Freiburg   0 0
2016–17   Freiburg   0 0
2017–18   Freiburg   0 0
2017–18   Bradford C   9 0   **9 0**

CHICKSEN, Adam (D)   150 3
H: 5 8   W: 11 09   b.Milton Keynes 27-9-91
Internationals: Zimbabwe Full caps.
2008–09   Milton Keynes D   1 0
2009–10   Milton Keynes D   6 0
2010–11   Milton Keynes D   14 0
2011–12   Milton Keynes D   20 0
2011–12   *Leyton Orient*   3 0
2012–13   Milton Keynes D   32 2
2013–14   Milton Keynes D   0 0   **73 2**
2013–14   Brighton & HA   1 0
2014–15   Brighton & HA   5 0
2014–15   *Gillingham*   3 0
2014–15   *Fleetwood T*   13 0   **13 0**
2015–16   Brighton & HA   1 0   **7 0**
2015–16   *Leyton Orient*   6 0   **9 0**
2015–16   *Gillingham*   6 0   **9 0**
2016–17   Charlton Ath   21 1   **21 1**
2017–18   Bradford C   18 0   **18 0**

DEVINE, Daniel (M)   14 0
H: 5 11   W: 12 00   b.Bradford 4-9-97
Internationals: Northern Ireland U21.
2015–16   Bradford C   0 0
2016–17   Bradford C   11 0
2017–18   Bradford C   3 0   **14 0**

DIENG, Timothee (M)   131 6
H: 5 11   W: 12 00   b.Grenoble 9-4-92
2011–12   Brest   0 0
2012–13   Brest   2 0
2013–14   Brest   4 0   **6 0**
2014–15   Oldham Ath   22 0
2015–16   Oldham Ath   38 1   **60 1**
2016–17   Bradford C   39 3
2017–18   Bradford C   26 2   **65 5**

DOYLE, Colin (G)   160 0
H: 6 5   W: 14 05   b.Cork 12-8-85
Internationals: Republic of Ireland U21, B, Full caps.
2004–05   Birmingham C   0 0
2004–05   *Chester C*   0 0
2004–05   *Nottingham F*   3 0   **3 0**
2005–06   Birmingham C   0 0
2005–06   *Millwall*   14 0   **14 0**
2006–07   Birmingham C   19 0
2007–08   Birmingham C   3 0
2008–09   Birmingham C   2 0
2009–10   Birmingham C   0 0
2010–11   Birmingham C   1 0
2011–12   Birmingham C   5 0
2012–13   Birmingham C   0 0
2013–14   Birmingham C   0 0
2014–15   Birmingham C   1 0   **31 0**
2015–16   Blackpool   33 0   **33 0**
2016–17   Bradford C   44 0
2017–18   Bradford C   35 0   **79 0**

GIBSON, Jordan (F)   5 1
b. 26-2-98
From Rangers.
2017–18   Bradford C   5 1   **5 1**

GRODOWSKI, Joel (F)   1 0
b. 30-11-97
2017–18   Bradford C   1 0   **1 0**

GUNNER, Callum (M)   0 0
2016–17   Swindon T   0 0
2017–18   Bradford C   0 0

HANSON, Jacob (D)   3 0
b. 30-11-97
2015–16   Huddersfield T   0 0
2016–17   Bradford C   0 0
2017–18   Bradford C   3 0   **3 0**

HAWKES, Cameron (M)   2 0
b. 15-3-00
From Sheffield U.
2017–18   Bradford C   2 0   **2 0**

HEFELE, Josef (D)   0 0
2017–18   Bradford C   0 0

HUDSON, Ellis (M)   1 0
b.Bradford 14-2-99
2016–17   Bradford C   1 0
2017–18   Bradford C   0 0   **1 0**

JONES, Alex (F)   41 14
b. 28-9-94
From WBA.
2015–16   Birmingham C   0 0
2016–17   Port Vale   19 9   **19 9**
2016–17   Bradford C   15 5
2017–18   Bradford C   7 0   **22 5**

KILGALLON, Matthew (D)   333 13
H: 6 1   W: 12 10   b.York 8-1-84
Internationals: England U18, U19, U20, U21.
2000–01   Leeds U   0 0
2001–02   Leeds U   0 0
2002–03   Leeds U   1 0
2003–04   Leeds U   8 2
2003–04   *West Ham U*   3 0   **3 0**
2004–05   Leeds U   26 0
2005–06   Leeds U   25 1
2006–07   Leeds U   19 0   **80 3**
2006–07   Sheffield U   6 0
2007–08   Sheffield U   40 2
2008–09   Sheffield U   40 1
2009–10   Sheffield U   21 1   **107 4**
2009–10   Sunderland   7 0
2010–11   Sunderland   0 0
2010–11   *Middlesbrough*   2 0   **2 0**
2010–11   *Doncaster R*   12 0   **12 0**
2011–12   Sunderland   0 0
2012–13   Sunderland   6 0   **23 0**
2013–14   Blackburn R   25 1
2014–15   Blackburn R   22 1
2015–16   Blackburn R   10 0   **57 2**
2016–17   Bradford C   7 0
2017–18   Bradford C   42 4   **49 4**

KIRKPATRICK, Oliver (D)   0 0
2017–18   Bradford C   0 0

KNIGHT-PERCIVAL, Nathaniel (M) 192 11
H: 6 0   W: 11 06   b.Cambridge 31-3-87
2012–13   Peterborough U   31 0
2013–14   Peterborough U   15 1   **46 1**
2014–15   Shrewsbury T   28 1
2015–16   Shrewsbury T   35 5   **63 6**
2016–17   Bradford C   42 0
2017–18   Bradford C   41 4   **83 4**

LAIRD, Alex (D)   0 0
2017–18   Bradford C   0 0

LAW, Nicky (M)   380 44
H: 5 10   W: 11 07   b.Nottingham 29-3-88
2005–06   Sheffield U   0 0
2006–07   Sheffield U   4 0
2006–07   *Yeovil T*   6 0   **6 0**
2007–08   Sheffield U   1 0
2007–08   *Bradford C*   10 2
2008–09   Sheffield U   0 0   **5 0**
2008–09   *Bradford C*   33 0
2009–10   Rotherham U   42 4
2010–11   Rotherham U   44 4   **86 8**
2011–12   Motherwell   38 4
2012–13   Motherwell   38 6   **76 10**
2013–14   Rangers   32 9
2014–15   Rangers   36 10
2015–16   Rangers   18 1   **86 20**
2016–17   Bradford C   40 4
2017–18   Bradford C   38 0   **121 6**

MALTBY, Jake (M)   0 0
2017–18   Bradford C   0 0

McCARTAN, Shay (M)   135 29
H: 5 10   W: 11 09   b.Newry 18-5-94
Internationals: Northern Ireland U17, U19, U21, Full caps.
2011–12   Burnley   1 0
2012–13   Burnley   0 0   **1 0**
2013–14   Accrington S   18 1
2014–15   Accrington S   31 6
2015–16   Accrington S   27 7
2016–17   Accrington S   34 11   **110 25**
2017–18   Bradford C   24 4   **24 4**

McGOWAN, Ryan (D)   226 8
H: 6 1   W: 11 09   b.Adelaide 15-8-89
Internationals: Australia U17, U20, U23, Full caps.
2007–08   Hearts   1 0
2008–09   Hearts   0 0
2009–10   Hearts   0 0
2009–10   *Ayr U*   28 1   **28 1**
2010–11   Hearts   8 0
2010–11   *Partick Thistle*   8 0   **8 0**
2011–12   Hearts   28 2
2012–13   Hearts   20 0   **57 2**
2013   Shandong Luneng   29 1
2014   Shandong Luneng   17 1   **46 2**
2014–15   Dundee U   12 1
2015–16   Dundee U   22 0   **34 1**
2016   Henan Jianye   28 2   **28 2**
2017   Guizhou Zhicheng   12 0   **12 0**
2017–18   Al-Sharjah   10 0   **10 0**
2017–18   Bradford C   3 0   **3 0**

McMAHON, Tony (D)   358 19
H: 5 10   W: 11 04   b.Bishop Auckland 24-3-86
Internationals: England U16, U17, U19.
2003–04   Middlesbrough   0 0
2004–05   Middlesbrough   13 0
2005–06   Middlesbrough   3 0
2006–07   Middlesbrough   13 0
2007–08   Middlesbrough   1 0
2007–08   *Blackpool*   2 0
2008–09   Middlesbrough   13 0
2008–09   *Sheffield W*   15 1   **15 1**
2009–10   Middlesbrough   21 0
2010–11   Middlesbrough   34 2
2011–12   Middlesbrough   34 1   **119 3**
2012–13   Sheffield U   38 2
2013–14   Sheffield U   23 0   **61 2**
2013–14   Blackpool   18 0
2014–15   Blackpool   32 1   **52 1**
2014–15   *Bradford C*   8 1
2015–16   Bradford C   40 4
2016–17   Bradford C   25 6
2017–18   Bradford C   38 1   **111 12**

PATRICK, Omari (F)   19 2
H: 6 1   W: 12 08   b. 24-5-96
From Kidderminster H.
2017–18   Bradford C   19 2   **19 2**

POLEON, Dominic (F)   176 27
H: 6 3   W: 12 13   b.Newham 7-9-93
2012–13   Leeds U   6 2
2012–13   *Bury*   7 2   **7 2**
2012–13   *Sheffield U*   7 0   **7 0**
2013–14   Leeds U   19 1
2014–15   Leeds U   4 0   **29 3**
2014–15   Oldham Ath   35 4
2015–16   Oldham Ath   25 4   **60 8**
2016–17   AFC Wimbledon   41 8   **41 8**
2017–18   Bradford C   32 6   **32 6**

POWELL, Reece (F)   0 0
2017–18   Bradford C   0 0

PYBUS, Daniel (M)   2 0
b.South Shields 12-12-97
From Sunderland.
2016–17   Bradford C   1 0
2017–18   Bradford C   1 0   **2 0**

RAEDER, Lukas (G)   30 0
H: 6 4   W: 14 07   b.Essen 30-12-93
2012–13   Bayern Munich   0 0
2013–14   Bayern Munich   2 0   **2 0**
2014–15   Vitoria Setubal   17 0
2015–16   Vitoria Setubal   10 0
2016–17   Vitoria Setubal   0 0
2017–18   Vitoria Setubal   0 0   **27 0**
2017–18   Bradford C   1 0   **1 0**

REEVES, Jake (M)   184 5
H: 5 8   W: 11 11   b.Lewisham 30-6-93
2010–11   Brentford   1 0
2011–12   Brentford   8 0
2012–13   Brentford   6 0
2012–13   *AFC Wimbledon*   5 0
2013–14   Brentford   20 0   **35 0**
2013–14   Swindon T   10 1   **10 1**
2014–15   AFC Wimbledon   23 2
2015–16   AFC Wimbledon   40 1
2016–17   AFC Wimbledon   46 1   **114 4**
2017–18   Bradford C   25 0   **25 0**

ROBINSON, Tyrell (M)   21 3
b. 16-9-97
From Arsenal.
2017–18   Bradford C   21 3   **21 3**

SATTELMAIER, Rouven (G)   112 0
H: 6 1   W: 13 05   b.Ludvigsburg 7-8-87
2007–08   Jahn Regensburg   1 0
2008–09   Jahn Regensburg   0 0
2009–10   Jahn Regensburg   37 0   **65 0**
2010–11   Bayern Munich   0 0
2011–12   Bayern Munich   0 0
2012–13   Heidenheim   2 0
2013–14   Heidenheim   6 0
2014–15   Heidenheim   5 0   **13 0**

2015–16	Stuttgart Kickers	21	0	**21**	**0**
2016–17	Bradford C	2	0		
2017–18	Bradford C	11	0	**13**	**0**

STAUNTON, Reece (D)   **1** **0**
b. 10-12-01

2017–18	Bradford C	1	0	**1**	**0**

SYKES-KENWORTHY, George (G)   **0** **0**

2017–18	Bradford C	0	0

TAYLOR, Paul (F)   **176** **22**
H: 5 9　W: 11 02　b.Liverpool 4-11-87

2008–09	Chester C	9	0	**9**	**0**
2009–10	Montegnee	1	0	**1**	**0**
2009–10	*Charleoi*	3	0	**3**	**0**
2010–11	Anderlecht	0	0		
2010–11	Peterborough U	1	0		
2011–12	Peterborough U	44	12		
2012–13	Peterborough U	3	0		
2012–13	Ipswich T	3	0		
2013–14	Ipswich T	18	1		
2013–14	*Peterborough U*	6	0		
2014–15	Ipswich T	0	0	**21**	**1**
2014–15	*Rotherham U*	17	0	**17**	**0**
2014–15	*Blackburn R*	5	0	**5**	**0**
2016–17	Peterborough U	39	3	**93**	**15**
2017–18	Bradford C	27	6	**27**	**6**

VINCELOT, Romain (M)   **354** **29**
H: 5 11　W: 11 02　b.Poitiers 29-10-85

2004–05	Chamois Niortais	3	0	**3**	**0**
2005–06	Chemois Niortais	28	1		
2006–07	Chemois Niortais	9	0		
2007–08	Chemois Niortais	6	0	**43**	**1**
2008–09	Gueugnon	20	0	**20**	**0**
2009–10	Dagenham & R	9	1		
2010–11	Dagenham & R	46	12	**55**	**13**
2011–12	Brighton & HA	15	1		
2012–13	Brighton & HA	0	0	**15**	**1**
2012–13	*Gillingham*	9	1	**9**	**1**
2012–13	Leyton Orient	15	1		
2013–14	Leyton Orient	39	0		
2014–15	Leyton Orient	27	2	**81**	**3**
2015–16	Coventry U	45	4	**45**	**4**
2016–17	Bradford C	45	2		
2017–18	Bradford C	38	4	**83**	**6**

WYKE, Charlie (F)   **188** **62**
b.Middlesbrough 6-12-92

2011–12	Middlesbrough	0	0		
2012–13	Middlesbrough	0	0		
2012–13	*Hartlepool U*	25	2		
2013–14	Middlesbrough	0	0		
2013–14	*AFC Wimbledon*	17	2	**17**	**2**
2014–15	Middlesbrough	0	0		
2014–15	*Hartlepool U*	13	4	**38**	**6**
2014–15	Carlisle U	17	6		
2015–16	Carlisle U	34	12		
2016–17	Carlisle U	26	14	**77**	**32**
2016–17	Bradford C	16	7		
2017–18	Bradford C	40	15	**56**	**22**

Players retained or with offer of contract
Peters, Curtis Andrew.

Scholars
Adams, Kielen Marcel; Aitken, Daniel Ross; Birchall, Matthew; Darke, Alfie Geoffrey; Drovi, Dyllan Atty Aliby; Ellington, Raeece Abdul-Haq; Farrar, Christian Max; Gardezi, Omed; Kirkpatrick, Oliver James; Maltby, Jake Peter; Milambo, Jeremie Mukanya; Mullett, Ross Peter; Patience, Neil William; Powell, Reece; Taglione, Casey Joe; Warren, Harry Jack; Wright, Sam.

BRENTFORD (13)

ARCHIBALD, Theo (M)   **16** **0**
H: 5 11　W: 9 06　b.Glasgow 5-3-98
Internationals: Scotland U16, U19, U21.

2016–17	Celtic	0	0		
2016–17	*Albion R*	14	0	**14**	**0**
2017–18	Brentford	2	0	**2**	**0**

BALCOMBE, Ellery (G)   **0** **0**
b. 15-10-99
Internationals: England U18, U19, U20.

2016–17	Brentford	0	0
2017–18	Brentford	0	0

BARBET, Yoann (D)   **108** **7**
H: 6 2　W: 12 11　b.Talence 10-5-93
Internationals: France U18.

2014–15	Chamois Niortais	33	2	**33**	**2**
2015–16	Brentford	18	1		
2016–17	Brentford	23	1		
2017–18	Brentford	34	3	**75**	**5**

BENTLEY, Daniel (G)   **231** **0**
H: 6 2　W: 11 05　b.Wickford 13-7-93

2011–12	Southend U	1	0		
2012–13	Southend U	9	0		
2013–14	Southend U	46	0		
2014–15	Southend U	42	0		
2015–16	Southend U	43	0	**141**	**0**
2016–17	Brentford	45	0		
2017–18	Brentford	45	0	**90**	**0**

BJELLAND, Andreas (D)   **240** **8**
H: 6 2　W: 13 05　b.Fredensborg 11-7-88
Internationals: Denmark U16, U18, U19, U21, Full caps.

2007–08	Lyngby	11	0		
2008–09	Lyngby	22	1		
2009–10	Lyngby	4	0	**37**	**1**
2009–10	Nordsjaelland	22	1		
2010–11	Nordsjaelland	24	1		
2011–12	Nordsjaelland	26	1	**72**	**3**
2012–13	FC Twente	10	0		
2013–14	FC Twente	26	3		
2014–15	FC Twente	26	3	**69**	**3**
2015–16	Brentford	0	0		
2016–17	Brentford	28	0		
2017–18	Brentford	34	1	**62**	**1**

BONHAM, Jack (G)   **45** **0**
H: 6 4　W: 14 13　b.Stevenage 14-9-93
Internationals: Republic of Ireland U17.

2010–11	Watford	0	0		
2011–12	Watford	0	0		
2012–13	Watford	1	0	**1**	**0**
2013–14	Brentford	1	0		
2014–15	Brentford	0	0		
2015–16	Brentford	0	0		
2016–17	Brentford	1	0		
2017–18	Brentford	0	0	**2**	**0**
2017–18	*Carlisle U*	42	0	**42**	**0**

CANOS, Sergi (M)   **90** **14**
H: 5 8　W: 11 11　b.Nules 2-2-97
Internationals: Spain U16, U17, U19.

2015–16	Liverpool	1	0	**1**	**0**
2015–16	*Brentford*	38	7		
2016–17	Norwich C	3	0	**3**	**0**
2016–17	Brentford	18	4		
2017–18	Brentford	30	3	**86**	**14**

CHATZITHEODORIDIS, Ilias (D)   **18** **0**
b.Katerini 5-11-97
From Arsenal.

2016–17	Brentford	0	0		
2017–18	Brentford	0	0		
2017–18	*Cheltenham T*	18	0	**18**	**0**

CLARKE, Josh (M)   **81** **6**
H: 5 8　W: 11 00　b.Waltham Forest 5-7-95

2012–13	Brentford	0	0		
2013–14	Brentford	1	0		
2014–15	Brentford	0	0		
2014–15	*Dagenham & R*	0	0		
2014–15	*Stevenage*	1	0	**1**	**0**
2015–16	Brentford	11	0		
2015–16	*Barnet*	10	3	**10**	**3**
2016–17	Brentford	30	2		
2017–18	Brentford	28	1	**70**	**3**

COLE, Reece (M)   **5** **1**
b. 17-2-98

2015–16	Brentford	1	0		
2016–17	Brentford	1	0		
2017–18	Brentford	0	0	**1**	**0**
2017–18	*Newport Co*	4	1	**4**	**1**

DALSGAARD, Henrik (F)   **230** **19**
H: 6 4　W: 12 11　b.Viborg 27-7-89
Internationals: Denmark U20, U21, Full caps.

2008–09	AaB	4	1		
2009–10	AaB	25	0		
2010–11	AaB	15	1		
2011–12	AaB	30	2		
2012–13	AaB	31	2		
2013–14	AaB	18	2		
2014–15	AaB	26	1		
2015–16	AaB	17	0	**166**	**9**
2015–16	Zulte Waregem	19	3		
2016–17	Zulte Waregem	16	6	**35**	**9**
2017–18	Brentford	29	1	**29**	**1**

DANIELS, Luke (G)   **199** **0**
H: 6 1　W: 12 10　b.Bolton 5-1-88
Internationals: England U18, U19.

2006–07	WBA	0	0		
2007–08	*Motherwell*	2	0	**2**	**0**
2007–08	WBA	0	0		
2008–09	WBA	0	0		
2008–09	*Shrewsbury T*	38	0	**38**	**0**
2009–10	WBA	0	0		
2009–10	*Tranmere R*	37	0	**37**	**0**
2010–11	WBA	0	0		
2010–11	*Charlton Ath*	0	0		
2010–11	*Rochdale*	1	0	**1**	**0**
2010–11	*Bristol R*	9	0	**9**	**0**
2011–12	WBA	0	0		
2011–12	*Southend U*	9	0	**9**	**0**
2012–13	WBA	0	0		
2013–14	WBA	1	0		
2014–15	WBA	0	0	**1**	**0**
2014–15	Scunthorpe U	23	0		
2015–16	Scunthorpe U	39	0		
2016–17	Scunthorpe U	39	0	**101**	**0**
2016–17	Brentford	0	0		
2017–18	Brentford	1	0	**1**	**0**

EGAN, John (D)   **167** **17**
H: 6 1　W: 11 11　b.Cork 20-10-92
Internationals: Republic of Ireland U17, U19, U21, Full caps.

2009–10	Sunderland	0	0		
2010–11	Sunderland	0	0		
2011–12	Sunderland	0	0		
2011–12	*Crystal Palace*	1	0	**1**	**0**
2011–12	*Sheffield U*	1	0	**1**	**0**
2012–13	Sunderland	0	0		
2012–13	*Bradford C*	4	0	**4**	**0**
2013–14	Sunderland	0	0		
2013–14	*Southend U*	13	1	**13**	**1**
2014–15	Gillingham	45	4		
2015–16	Gillingham	36	6	**81**	**10**
2016–17	Brentford	34	4		
2017–18	Brentford	33	2	**67**	**6**

FIELD, Tom (D)   **24** **1**
H: 5 10　W: 10 13　b.Kingston upon Thames 2-8-85
Internationals: Republic of Ireland U16.

2013–14	Brentford	0	0		
2014–15	Brentford	0	0		
2015–16	Brentford	1	0		
2016–17	Brentford	15	1		
2017–18	*Bradford C*	8	0	**8**	**0**
2017–18	Brentford	0	0	**16**	**1**

HENRY, Rico (D)   **66** **2**
H: 5 7　W: 10 06　b.Birmingham 8-7-97
Internationals: England U19, U20.

2014–15	Walsall	9	0		
2015–16	Walsall	35	2		
2016–17	Walsall	2	0	**46**	**2**
2016–17	Brentford	12	0		
2017–18	Brentford	8	0	**20**	**0**

JOZEFZOON, Florian (F)   **157** **20**
H: 5 8　W: 11 00　b.Amsterdam 9-2-91
Internationals: Netherlands U19, U21.

2010–11	Ajax	4	0		
2011–12	Ajax	0	0	**4**	**0**
2011–12	NAC Breda	16	0	**16**	**0**
2012–13	RKC Waalwijk	34	7	**34**	**7**
2013–14	PSV Eindhoven	16	2		
2014–15	PSV Eindhoven	15	2		
2015–16	PSV Eindhoven	9	1		
2016–17	PSV Eindhoven	5	0	**45**	**5**
2016–17	Brentford	19	1		
2017–18	Brentford	39	7	**58**	**8**

JUDGE, Alan (F)   **276** **47**
H: 5 6　W: 11 03　b.Dublin 11-11-88
Internationals: Republic of Ireland U17, U8, U19, U21, U23, Full caps.

2006–07	Blackburn R	0	0		
2007–08	Blackburn R	0	0		
2008–09	Blackburn R	0	0		
2008–09	*Plymouth Arg*	17	2		
2009–10	Blackburn R	0	0		
2009–10	*Plymouth Arg*	37	5	**54**	**7**
2010–11	Blackburn R	0	0		
2010–11	*Notts Co*	19	1		
2011–12	*Notts Co*	43	7		
2012–13	*Notts Co*	39	8	**101**	**16**
2013–14	Blackburn R	11	0	**11**	**0**
2013–14	Brentford	22	7		
2014–15	Brentford	37	3		
2015–16	Brentford	38	14		
2017–18	Brentford	13	0	**110**	**24**

MACLEOD, Lewis (M)   **76** **12**
H: 5 9　W: 11 05　b.Law 16-6-94
Internationals: Scotland U16, U17, U18, U19, U21.

2012–13	Rangers	21	3		
2013–14	Rangers	18	5		
2014–15	Rangers	13	3	**52**	**11**
2014–15	Brentford	0	0		
2015–16	Brentford	1	0		
2016–17	Brentford	13	0		
2017–18	Brentford	10	1	**24**	**1**

MARCONDES, Emiliano (M) 124 37
H: 6 0 W: 11 11 b.Hvidovre 9-3-95
Internationals: Denmark U17, U18, U19, U20, U21.

2012–13	Nordsjaelland	3	0		
2013–14	Nordsjaelland	11	1		
2014–15	Nordsjaelland	24	5		
2015–16	Nordsjaelland	30	2		
2016–17	Nordsjaelland	25	12		
2017–18	Nordsjaelland	19	17	112	37
2017–18	Brentford	12	0	12	0

MAUPAY, Neal (F) 129 30
H: 5 7 W: 10 12 b.Versailles 14-8-96
Internationals: France U16, U17, U19, U21.

2012–13	Nice	15	3		
2013–14	Nice	16	2		
2014–15	Nice	13	1	44	6
2015–16	Saint-Etienne	15	1		
2016–17	Saint-Etienne	0	0	15	1
2016–17	*Brest*	28	11	28	11
2017–18	Brentford	42	12	42	12

McEACHRAN, Josh (M) 153 0
H: 5 10 W: 10 03 b.Oxford 1-3-93
Internationals: England U16, U17, U19, U20, U21.

2010–11	Chelsea	9	0		
2011–12	Chelsea	2	0		
2011–12	*Swansea C*	4	0	4	0
2012–13	Chelsea	0	0		
2012–13	*Middlesbrough*	38	0	38	0
2013–14	Chelsea	0	0		
2013–14	*Watford*	7	0	7	0
2013–14	*Wigan Ath*	8	0	8	0
2014–15	Chelsea	0	0	11	0
2014–15	*Vitesse*	19	0	19	0
2015–16	Brentford	14	0		
2016–17	Brentford	27	0		
2017–18	Brentford	25	0	66	0

MEPHAM, Chris (D) 21 1
H: 6 3 W: 11 11 b. 5-11-97
Internationals: Wales U20, U21, Full caps.

| 2016–17 | Brentford | 0 | 0 | | |
| 2017–18 | Brentford | 21 | 1 | 21 | 1 |

MOKOTJO, Kamohelo (M) 220 7
H: 5 6 W: 9 13 b.Odendaalsrus 11-3-91
Internationals: South Africa U20, U23, Full caps.

2008–09	SuperSport U	1	0		
2009–10	SuperSport U	0	0	1	0
2009–10	*Excelsior*	25	1	25	1
2010–11	Feyenoord	14	0		
2011–12	Feyenoord	20	0		
2012–13	Feyenoord	1	0	35	0
2013–14	PEC Zwolle	27	2		
2014–15	PEC Zwolle	0	0	27	2
2014–15	FC Twente	33	1		
2015–16	FC Twente	31	1		
2016–17	FC Twente	33	1	97	3
2017–18	Brentford	35	1	35	1

OGBENE, Chiedozie (M) 2 0
H: 5 9 W: 11 11 b. 1-5-97
From Cork C, Limerick.

| 2017–18 | Brentford | 2 | 0 | 2 | 0 |

SAWYERS, Romaine (M) 229 22
H: 5 9 W: 11 00 b.Birmingham 2-11-91
Internationals: St Kitts and Nevis U23, Full caps.

2009–10	WBA	0	0		
2010–11	WBA	0	0		
2010–11	*Port Vale*	1	0	1	0
2011–12	WBA	0	0		
2011–12	*Shrewsbury T*	7	0	7	0
2012–13	WBA	0	0		
2012–13	Walsall	4	0		
2013–14	Walsall	44	6		
2014–15	Walsall	42	4		
2015–16	Walsall	46	6	136	16
2016–17	Brentford				
2017–18	Brentford	42	4	85	6

SHAIBU, Justin (F) 40 0
H: 5 11 b. 28-10-97
Internationals: Denmark U17, U18, U20.

2014–15	HB Koge	8	0		
2015–16	HB Koge	12	0	20	0
2016–17	Brentford	4	0		
2017–18	Brentford	2	0	6	0
2017–18	*Walsall*	14	0	14	0

SORENSEN, Mads (D) 20 1
H: 6 1 W: 11 07 b. 7-1-99
Internationals: Denmark U18, U19.

2014–15	Horsens	6	0		
2015–16	Horsens	5	0		
2016–17	Horsens	6	0		
2017–18	Horsens	3	1	20	1
2017–18	Brentford				

VIBE, Lasse (F) 284 118
H: 5 11 W: 11 07 b.Tranjberg 22-2-87
Internationals: Denmark Full caps.

2006–07	AGF	1	0		
2007–08	AGF	0	0	1	0
2008–09	Fyn	13	7		
2009–10	Fyn	30	7	43	14
2010–11	Vestsjaelland	29	12		
2011–12	Vestsjaelland	14	6	43	18
2011–12	SonderjyskE	14	6		
2012–13	SonderjyskE	33	13	47	19
2013	Gothenburg	14	2		
2014	Gothenburg	26	23		
2015	Gothenburg	16	6	56	31
2015–16	Brentford	41	14		
2016–17	Brentford	34	15		
2017–18	Brentford	19	7	94	36

Transferred to Changchun Yatai, February 2018.

WATKINS, Ollie (F) 113 31
H: 5 10 W: 11 00 b.Torbay 30-12-95

2013–14	Exeter C	1	0		
2014–15	Exeter C	2	0		
2015–16	Exeter C	20	8		
2016–17	Exeter C	45	13	68	21
2017–18	Brentford	45	10	45	10

WOODS, Ryan (M) 213 4
H: 5 8 W: 13 01 b.Norton Canes 13-12-93

2012–13	Shrewsbury T	2	0		
2013–14	Shrewsbury T	41	1		
2014–15	Shrewsbury T	43	0		
2015–16	Shrewsbury T	5	0	91	1
2015–16	Brentford	41	2		
2016–17	Brentford	42	0		
2017–18	Brentford	39	1	122	3

YENNARIS, Nico (D) 144 13
H: 5 7 W: 10 03 b.Leytonstone 23-5-93
Internationals: England U17, U18, U19.

2010–11	Arsenal	0	0		
2011–12	Arsenal	1	0		
2011–12	*Notts Co*	2	0	2	0
2012–13	Arsenal	0	0		
2013–14	Arsenal	0	0	1	0
2013–14	*Bournemouth*	0	0		
2013–14	Brentford	8	0		
2014–15	Brentford	1	0		
2014–15	*Wycombe W*	14	1	14	1
2015–16	Brentford	31	2		
2016–17	Brentford	46	6		
2017–18	Brentford	41	4	127	12

Players retained or with offer of contract
Coote, Alistair Michael; Edobor, Jarvis
Daniel Osagie Osahon; Forss, Marcus; Hardy,
Joseph Keith; Johansson, Henrik;
Kerschbaumer, Konstantin; Oksanen, Jaakko
Tapio; Talbro, Lukas; Titov, David.

BRIGHTON & HA (14)

AHANNACH, Soufyan (M) 97 29

2012–13	Almere C	2	0		
2013–14	Almere C	6	0		
2014–15	Almere C	13	3		
2015–16	Almere C	26	7		
2016–17	Almere C	38	18	85	28
2017–18	Brighton & HA	0	0		
2017–18	*Sparta Rotterdam*	12	1	12	1

BALDOCK, Sam (F) 287 90
H: 5 7 W: 10 07 b.Buckingham 15-3-89
Internationals: England U20.

2005–06	Milton Keynes D	0	0		
2006–07	Milton Keynes D	0	0		
2007–08	Milton Keynes D	5	0		
2008–09	Milton Keynes D	40	12		
2009–10	Milton Keynes D	20	5		
2010–11	Milton Keynes D	30	12		
2011–12	Milton Keynes D	4	4	100	33
2011–12	West Ham U	23	5		
2012–13	West Ham U	0	0	23	5
2012–13	Bristol C	34	10		
2013–14	Bristol C	45	24		
2014–15	Bristol C	4	0	83	34
2014–15	Brighton & HA	20	3		
2015–16	Brighton & HA	28	4		
2016–17	Brighton & HA	31	11		
2017–18	Brighton & HA	2	0	81	18

BONG, Gaetan (D) 257 3
H: 6 0 W: 11 09 b.Sakbayeme 25-4-88
Internationals: France U21. Cameroon Full caps.

2005–06	Metz	3	0		
2006–07	Metz	2	0		
2007–08	Metz	11	0		
2008–09	Metz	0	0	16	0
2008–09	*Tours*	34	0	34	0
2009–10	Valenciennes	29	2		
2010–11	Valenciennes	22	1		
2011–12	Valenciennes	28	0		
2012–13	Valenciennes	29	0		
2013–14	Valenciennes	1	0	109	3
2013–14	*Olympiacos*	19	0	19	0
2014–15	Wigan Ath	14	0	14	0
2015–16	Brighton & HA	16	0		
2016–17	Brighton & HA	24	0		
2017–18	Brighton & HA	25	0	65	0

CONNOLLY, Aaron (F) 0 0
b. 28-1-00
Internationals: Republic of Ireland U17, U19.

| 2017–18 | Brighton & HA | 0 | 0 | | |

DALLISON, Tom (M) 8 0
H: 5 10 W: 14 01 b. 2-2-96

2012–13	Arsenal	0	0		
2013–14	Brighton & HA	0	0		
2014–15	Brighton & HA	0	0		
2015–16	Brighton & HA	0	0		
2015–16	*Crawley T*	1	0	1	0
2016–17	Brighton & HA	0	0		
2016–17	*Cambridge U*	5	0	5	0
2017–18	Brighton & HA	0	0		
2017–18	*Accrington S*	2	0	2	0

DUFFY, Shane (D) 192 10
H: 6 4 W: 12 00 b.Derry 1-1-92
Internationals: Northern Ireland U16, U17, U19, U21, B. Republic of Ireland U19, U21, Full caps.

2008–09	Everton	0	0		
2009–10	Everton	0	0		
2010–11	Everton	0	0		
2010–11	*Burnley*	1	0	1	0
2011–12	Everton	4	0		
2011–12	*Scunthorpe U*	18	2	18	2
2012–13	Everton	1	0		
2013–14	Everton	0	0		
2013–14	*Yeovil T*	37	1	37	1
2014–15	Everton	0	0	5	0
2014–15	Blackburn R	19	1		
2015–16	Blackburn R	41	4		
2016–17	Blackburn R	3	0	63	5
2016–17	Brighton & HA	31	2		
2017–18	Brighton & HA	37	0	68	2

DUNK, Lewis (D) 210 11
H: 6 3 W: 12 02 b.Brighton 1-12-91

2009–10	Brighton & HA	1	0		
2010–11	Brighton & HA	5	0		
2011–12	Brighton & HA	31	0		
2012–13	Brighton & HA	8	0		
2013–14	Brighton & HA	6	0		
2013–14	*Bristol C*	2	0	2	0
2014–15	Brighton & HA	38	5		
2015–16	Brighton & HA	38	3		
2016–17	Brighton & HA	43	2		
2017–18	Brighton & HA	38	1	208	11

GOLDSON, Connor (D) 142 10
H: 6 3 W: 13 05 b.York 18-12-92

2010–11	Shrewsbury T	3	0		
2011–12	Shrewsbury T	4	0		
2012–13	Shrewsbury T	17	1		
2013–14	Shrewsbury T	36	0		
2013–14	*Cheltenham T*	4	0	4	0
2014–15	Shrewsbury T	44	7		
2015–16	Shrewsbury T	2	0	106	8
2015–16	Brighton & HA	24	2		
2016–17	Brighton & HA	5	0		
2017–18	Brighton & HA	3	0	32	2

GROSS, Pascal (M) 226 27
H: 5 7 W: 10 06 b.Bad Salzungen 15-6-91
Internationals: Germany U18, U19.

2008–09	1899 Hoffenheim	0	0		
2009–10	1899 Hoffenheim	1	0		
2010–11	1899 Hoffenheim	0	0	5	0
2010–11	Karlsruher	3	1		
2011–12	Karlsruher	22	2	25	3
2012–13	Ingolstadt 04	30	2		
2013–14	Ingolstadt 04	29	2		
2014–15	Ingolstadt 04	34	7		
2015–16	Ingolstadt 04	32	1		
2016–17	Ingolstadt 04	33	5	158	17
2017–18	Brighton & HA	38	7	38	7

HALL, Ben (D)   29   1
H: 6 1 W: 12 06 b.Enniskillen 16-1-97
Internationals: Northern Ireland U16, U17, U19, U21.

2015–16	Motherwell	18	1	18	1
2016–17	Brighton & HA	0	0		
2017–18	Brighton & HA	0	0		
2017–18	*Notts Co*	11	0	11	0

HEMED, Tomer (F)   349   87
H: 6 0 W: 12 04 b.Haifa 2-5-87
Internationals: Israel U17, U18, U19, U21, Full caps.

2005–06	Maccabi Haifa	3	1		
2006–07	Maccabi Haifa	8	2		
2007–08	Maccabi Haifa	7	0		
2007–08	*Maccabi Herzliya*	17	3	17	3
2008–09	Maccabi Haifa	0	0		
2008–09	*Bnei Yehuda*	28	1	28	1
2009–10	Maccabi Haifa	0	0		
2009–10	*Maccabi Ahi Nazareth*	33	9	33	9
2010–11	Maccabi Haifa	31	13	49	16
2011–12	Mallorca	29	7		
2012–13	Mallorca	37	11		
2013–14	Mallorca	24	2	90	20
2014–15	Almeria	35	8	35	8
2015–16	Brighton & HA	44	17		
2016–17	Brighton & HA	37	11		
2017–18	Brighton & HA	16	2	97	30

HORNBY-FORBES, Tyler (M)   39   2
b. 8-3-96

2014–15	Fleetwood T	17	0		
2015–16	Fleetwood T	16	2	33	2
2016–17	Brighton & HA	0	0		
2017–18	*Accrington S*	6	0	6	0

HUNEMEIER, Uwe (D)   173   14
H: 6 1 W: 12 06 b.Rietberg 9-1-86
Internationals: Germany U17.

2005–06	Borussia Dortmund	2	0		
2006–07	Borussia Dortmund	0	0		
2007–08	Borussia Dortmund	0	0		
2008–09	Borussia Dortmund	1	0		
2009–10	Borussia Dortmund	0	0	3	0
2010–11	Energie Cottbus	30	9		
2011–12	Energie Cottbus	23	0		
2012–13	Energie Cottbus	23	0	76	9
2013–14	Paderborn	33	2		
2014–15	Paderborn	32	2		
2015–16	Paderborn	2	0	67	4
2015–16	Brighton & HA	5	0		
2016–17	Brighton & HA	11	1		
2017–18	Brighton & HA	1	0	27	1

HUTCHINSON, Des (M)   0   0
b.Waterford 5-12-96
Internationals: Republic of Ireland U19.

2016–17	Brighton & HA	0	0
2017–18	Brighton & HA	0	0

INCE, Rohan (D)   120   4
H: 6 3 W: 12 08 b.Whitechapel 8-11-92

2010–11	Chelsea	0	0		
2011–12	Chelsea	0	0		
2012–13	Chelsea	0	0		
2012–13	*Yeovil T*	2	0	2	0
2013–14	Brighton & HA	28	0		
2014–15	Brighton & HA	32	1		
2015–16	Brighton & HA	12	0		
2015–16	*Fulham*	10	1	10	1
2016–17	Brighton & HA	0	0		
2016–17	*Swindon T*	14	2	14	2
2017–18	Brighton & HA	0	0	72	1
2017–18	*Bury*	22	0	22	0

IZQUIERDO, Jose (D)   225   65
H: 5 7 W: 11 07 b.Pereira 7-7-92
Internationals: Colombia Full caps.

2010	Deportivo Pereira	9	1		
2011	Deportivo Pereira	21	1		
2012	Deportivo Pereira	24	10		
2013	Deportivo Pereira	15	2	69	14
2013	Once Caldas	16	3		
2014	Once Caldas	24	9	40	12
2014–15	Club Brugge	32	13		
2015–16	Club Brugge	24	7		
2016–17	Club Brugge	28	14		
2017–18	Club Brugge	0	0	84	34
2017–18	Brighton & HA	32	5	32	5

KAYAL, Beram (M)   243   7
H: 5 10 W: 11 09 b.Jadeidi 2-5-88
Internationals: Israel U17, U18, U19, U21, Full caps.

2008–09	Maccabi Haifa	30	1		
2009–10	Maccabi Haifa	27	1	57	2
2010–11	Celtic	21	2		
2011–12	Celtic	19	0		
2012–13	Celtic	27	0		
2013–14	Celtic	13	0		
2014–15	Celtic	6	0	86	2
2014–15	Brighton & HA	18	1		
2015–16	Brighton & HA	43	2		
2016–17	Brighton & HA	20	0		
2017–18	Brighton & HA	19	0	100	3

KNOCKAERT, Anthony (M)   244   51
H: 5 8 W: 10 11 b.Lille 20-11-91
Internationals: France U20, U21.

2011–12	Guingamp	34	10	34	10
2012–13	Leicester C	42	8		
2013–14	Leicester C	42	5		
2014–15	Leicester C	9	0	93	13
2015–16	Standard Liege	20	5	20	5
2015–16	Brighton & HA	19	5		
2016–17	Brighton & HA	45	15		
2017–18	Brighton & HA	33	3	97	23

KRUL, Tim (G)   209   0
H: 6 2 W: 11 08 b.Den Haag 3-4-88
Internationals: Netherlands U16, U17, U19, U20, U21, Full caps.

2005–06	Newcastle U	0	0		
2006–07	Newcastle U	0	0		
2007–08	*Falkirk*	22	0	22	0
2007–08	Newcastle U	0	0		
2008–09	Newcastle U	0	0		
2008–09	*Carlisle U*	9	0	9	0
2009–10	Newcastle U	3	0		
2010–11	Newcastle U	21	0		
2011–12	Newcastle U	38	0		
2012–13	Newcastle U	24	0		
2013–14	Newcastle U	36	0		
2014–15	Newcastle U	30	0		
2015–16	Newcastle U	8	0		
2016–17	Newcastle U	0	0		
2016–17	*Ajax*	0	0		
2016–17	*AZ Alkmaar*	18	0	18	0
2017–18	Newcastle U	0	0	160	0
2017–18	Brighton & HA	0	0		

LOCADIA, Jurgen (F)   133   46
H: 6 2 W: 12 04 b.Emmen 7-11-93
Internationals: Netherlands U17, U18, U19, U20, U21.

2011–12	PSV Eindhoven	0	0		
2012–13	PSV Eindhoven	15	6		
2013–14	PSV Eindhoven	31	13		
2014–15	PSV Eindhoven	23	6		
2015–16	PSV Eindhoven	29	8		
2016–17	PSV Eindhoven	14	3		
2017–18	PSV Eindhoven	15	9	127	45
2017–18	Brighton & HA	6	1	6	1

MAENPAA, Niki (G)   187   0
H: 6 3 W: 13 05 b.Espoo 23-1-85
Internationals: Finland U18, U19, U21, Full caps.

2006–07	Den Bosch	27	0		
2007–08	Den Bosch	33	0		
2008–09	Den Bosch	7	0	67	0
2009–10	Willem II	6	0		
2010–11	Willem II	12	0	18	0
2011–12	AZ Alkmaar	0	0		
2012–13	VVV-Venlo	33	0		
2013–14	VVV-Venlo	33	0		
2014–15	VVV-Venlo	35	0	101	0
2015–16	Brighton & HA	0	0		
2016–17	Brighton & HA	1	0		
2017–18	Brighton & HA	0	0	1	0

MAGUIRE-DREW, Jordan (M)   14   0
b. 15-9-97

2017–18	Brighton & HA	0	0		
2017–18	*Lincoln C*	11	0	11	0
2017–18	*Coventry C*	3	0	3	0

MARCH, Solly (M)   111   8
H: 6 1 W: 12 02 b.Lewes 26-7-94
Internationals: England U20, U21.

2012–13	Brighton & HA	0	0		
2013–14	Brighton & HA	23	0		
2014–15	Brighton & HA	11	1		
2015–16	Brighton & HA	16	3		
2016–17	Brighton & HA	25	3		
2017–18	Brighton & HA	36	1	111	8

MATEJU, Ales (D)   50   1
Internationals: Czech Republic U16, U17, U18, U19, U20, U21.

2014–15	Pribram	15	1	15	1
2015–16	Viktoria Plzen	17	0		
2016–17	Viktoria Plzen	18	0	35	0
2017–18	Viktoria Plzen	0	0		
2017–18	Brighton & HA	0	0		

MOLUMBY, Jayson (M)   0   0
b. 6-8-99
Internationals: Republic of Ireland U16, U17, U19.

2017–18	Brighton & HA	0	0

MURPHY, Jamie (F)   363   63
H: 12 00 W: 12 00 b.Glasgow 28-8-89
Internationals: Scotland U19, U21, Full caps.

2006–07	Motherwell	2	0		
2007–08	Motherwell	16	1		
2008–09	Motherwell	30	2		
2009–10	Motherwell	35	6		
2010–11	Motherwell	35	6		
2011–12	Motherwell	36	9		
2012–13	Motherwell	22	10	176	34
2012–13	Sheffield U	17	2		
2013–14	Sheffield U	34	4		
2014–15	Sheffield U	43	11		
2015–16	Sheffield U	1	0	95	17
2015–16	Brighton & HA	37	6		
2016–17	Brighton & HA	35	2		
2017–18	Brighton & HA	4	0	76	8
2017–18	*Rangers*	16	4	16	4

MURRAY, Glenn (F)   440   175
H: 6 1 W: 12 12 b.Maryport 25-9-83

2005–06	Carlisle U	26	3		
2006–07	Carlisle U	1	0	27	3
2006–07	*Stockport Co*	3	3	11	3
2006–07	Rochdale	31	16		
2007–08	Rochdale	23	9	54	25
2007–08	Brighton & HA	21	9		
2008–09	Brighton & HA	23	11		
2009–10	Brighton & HA	32	12		
2010–11	Brighton & HA	42	22		
2011–12	Crystal Palace	38	6		
2012–13	Crystal Palace	42	30		
2013–14	Crystal Palace	14	1		
2014–15	Crystal Palace	17	7		
2014–15	*Reading*	18	8	18	8
2015–16	Crystal Palace	2	0	113	44
2015–16	Bournemouth	19	3	19	3
2016–17	Brighton & HA	45	23		
2017–18	Brighton & HA	35	12	198	89

NORWOOD, Oliver (M)   269   20
H: 5 11 W: 11 13 b.Burnley 12-4-91
Internationals: England U16, U17. Northern Ireland U19, U21, B, Full caps.

2009–10	Manchester U	0	0		
2010–11	Manchester U	0	0		
2010–11	*Carlisle U*	6	0	6	0
2011–12	Manchester U	0	0		
2011–12	*Scunthorpe U*	15	1	15	1
2011–12	*Coventry C*	18	2	18	2
2012–13	Huddersfield	39	3		
2013–14	Huddersfield	40	5		
2014–15	Huddersfield T	1	0	80	8
2014–15	Reading	38	1		
2015–16	Reading	43	3	81	4
2016–17	Brighton & HA	33	0		
2017–18	Brighton & HA	0	0	33	0
2017–18	*Fulham*	36	5	36	5

PROPPER, Davy (M)   244   34
H: 6 1 W: 11 05 b.Arnhem 2-9-91
Internationals: Netherlands U19, U21, Full caps.

2009–10	Vitesse	11	0		
2010–11	Vitesse	29	3		
2011–12	Vitesse	19	1		
2012–13	Vitesse	14	0		
2013–14	Vitesse	35	7		
2014–15	Vitesse	34	7	142	18
2015–16	PSV Eindhoven	33	10		
2016–17	PSV Eindhoven	34	6	67	16
2017–18	PSV	0	0		
2017–18	Brighton & HA	35	0	35	0

ROSENIOR, Liam (D)   392   4
H: 5 10 W: 11 05 b.Wandsworth 9-7-84
Internationals: England U20, U21.

2001–02	Bristol C	1	0		
2002–03	Bristol C	21	2		
2003–04	Bristol C	0	0	22	2
2003–04	Fulham	0	0		
2003–04	*Torquay U*	10	0	10	0
2004–05	Fulham	17	0		
2005–06	Fulham	24	0		
2006–07	Fulham	38	0		
2007–08	Fulham	0	0	79	0
2007–08	Reading	17	0		
2008–09	Reading	42	0		
2009–10	Reading	5	0		
2009–10	*Ipswich T*	29	1	29	1

2010–11	Reading	0	0	64	0
2010–11	Hull C	26	0		
2011–12	Hull C	44	0		
2012–13	Hull C	32	0		
2013–14	Hull C	29	1		
2014–15	Hull C	13	0	144	1
2015–16	Brighton & HA	31	0		
2016–17	Brighton & HA	10	0		
2017–18	Brighton & HA	3	0	44	0

RYAN, Mathew (G)   233 0
H: 6 0   W: 12 13   b.Plumpton 8-4-82
Internationals: Australia U23, Full caps.

2009	Blacktown C	0	0		
2009–10	Central Coast Mariners	0	0		
2010	Blacktown C	11	0	11	0
2010–11	Central Coast Mariners	31	0		
2011–12	Central Coast Mariners	0	0		
2012–13	Central Coast Mariners	25	0	80	0
2013–14	Club Brugge	40	0		
2014–15	Club Brugge	37	0	77	0
2015–16	Valencia	8	0		
2016–17	Valencia	2	0	10	0
2016–17	Genk	17	0	17	0
2017–18	Brighton & HA	38	0	38	0

SALTOR, Bruno (D)   413 7
H: 5 10   W: 11 10   b.Masnou (Barca) 1-10-80

2001–02	Espanyol	1	0	1	0
2001–02	Gimnastic	12	0	12	0
2004–05	Lleida	1	1		
2005–06	Lleida	38	0	39	1
2006–07	Almeria	23	0		
2007–08	Almeria	34	0		
2008–09	Almeria	34	0	91	0
2009–10	Valencia	26	0		
2010–11	Valencia	19	0		
2011–12	Valencia	14	0	59	0
2012–13	Brighton & HA	30	1		
2013–14	Brighton & HA	33	1		
2014–15	Brighton & HA	35	3		
2015–16	Brighton & HA	46	1		
2016–17	Brighton & HA	42	0		
2017–18	Brighton & HA	25	0	211	6

SANDERS, Max (M)   0 0
b. 4-1-99

2017–18	Brighton & HA	0	0

SCHELOTTO, Ezequiel (M)   249 15
H: 6 2   W: 12 00   b.Buenos Aires 23-5-89
Internationals: Italy U21, Full caps.

2008–09	Cesena	0	0		
2009–10	Cesena	40	6		
2010–11	Cesena	17	0		
2010–11	Cesena	14	1	71	7
2011–12	Atalanta	37	2		
2012–13	Atalanta	16	0	53	2
2012–13	Inter Milan	12	1		
2013–14	Inter Milan	0	0		
2013–14	Sassuolo	11	1	11	1
2013–14	Parma	16	4	16	4
2014–15	Inter Milan	0	0	12	1
2014–15	Chievo	29	0	29	0
2015–16	Sporting Lisbon	14	0		
2016–17	Sporting Lisbon	23	0	37	0
2017–18	Sporting	0	0		
2017–18	Brighton & HA	20	0	20	0

SIDWELL, Steve (M)   425 57
H: 5 10   W: 11 00   b.Wandsworth 14-12-82
Internationals: England U20, U21.

2001–02	Arsenal	0	0		
2001–02	Brentford	30	4	30	4
2002–03	Arsenal	0	0		
2002–03	Brighton & HA	12	5		
2002–03	Reading	13	2		
2003–04	Reading	43	8		
2004–05	Reading	44	5		
2005–06	Reading	33	10		
2006–07	Reading	35	4	168	29
2007–08	Chelsea	15	0	15	0
2008–09	Aston Villa	16	3		
2009–10	Aston Villa	25	0		
2010–11	Aston Villa	4	0	45	3
2010–11	Fulham	12	2		
2011–12	Fulham	14	1		
2012–13	Fulham	28	4		
2013–14	Fulham	38	7	92	14
2014–15	Stoke C	12	0		
2015–16	Stoke C	1	0	13	0
2015–16	Brighton & HA	16	1		
2016–17	Brighton & HA	34	1		
2017–18	Brighton & HA	0	0	62	7

SKALAK, Jiri (F)   153 20
H: 5 9   W: 10 10   b.Pardubice 12-3-92
Internationals: Czech Republic U16, U17, U18, U19, U20, U21, Full caps.

2010–11	Sparta Prague	0	0		
2011–12	Sparta Prague	0	0		
2011–12	MFA Ruzomberok	27	3	27	3
2012–13	Sparta Prague	7	0		
2012–13	1.FC Slovacko	9	0	9	0
2013–14	Sparta Prague	3	0		
2013–14	Zbrojovka Brno	24	3	24	3
2014–15	Sparta Prague	0	0	10	0
2014–15	Mlada Boleslav	24	6		
2015–16	Mlada Boleslav	16	6	40	12
2015–16	Brighton & HA	12	2		
2016–17	Brighton & HA	31	0		
2017–18	Brighton & HA	0	0	43	2

STEPHENS, Dale (M)   315 36
H: 5 7   W: 11 04   b.Bolton 12-6-89

2006–07	Bury	3	0		
2007–08	Bury	6	1	9	1
2008–09	Oldham Ath	0	0		
2009–10	Oldham Ath	26	2		
2009–10	Rochdale	6	1	6	1
2010–11	Oldham Ath	34	9	60	11
2010–11	Southampton	6	0	6	0
2011–12	Charlton Ath	30	5		
2012–13	Charlton Ath	28	2		
2013–14	Charlton Ath	26	3	84	10
2013–14	Brighton & HA	14	2		
2014–15	Brighton & HA	16	2		
2015–16	Brighton & HA	45	7		
2016–17	Brighton & HA	39	2		
2017–18	Brighton & HA	36	0	150	13

SUTTNER, Markus (M)   270 13
H: 5 10   W: 11 03   b.Hollabrunn 16-4-87
Internationals: Austria U21, Full caps.

2008–09	Austria Vienna	22	0		
2009–10	Austria Vienna	27	0		
2010–11	Austria Vienna	27	2		
2011–12	Austria Vienna	30	1		
2012–13	Austria Vienna	35	3		
2013–14	Austria Vienna	35	2		
2014–15	Austria Vienna	31	1	207	9
2015–16	Ingolstadt 04	18	0		
2016–17	Ingolstadt 04	31	4	49	4
2017–18	Brighton & HA	14	0	14	0

TILLEY, James (F)   1 0
H: 5 6   W: 9 04   b.Billingshurst 13-6-98

2014–15	Brighton & HA	1	0		
2015–16	Brighton & HA	0	0		
2016–17	Brighton & HA	0	0		
2017–18	Brighton & HA	0	0	1	0

TOWELL, Richie (D)   167 49
H: 5 8   W: 10 06   b.Dublin 17-7-91
Internationals: Republic of Ireland U17, U19, U21.

2010–11	Celtic	1	0		
2011–12	Celtic	0	0		
2011–12	Hibernian	16	0		
2012–13	Celtic	0	0	1	0
2012–13	Hibernian	14	1	30	1
2013	Dundalk	31	7		
2014	Dundalk	33	11		
2015	Dundalk	32	25	96	43
2015–16	Brighton & HA	0	0		
2016–17	Brighton & HA	0	0		
2017–18	Brighton & HA	0	0	1	0
2017–18	Rotherham U	39	5	39	5

WALTON, Christian (G)   76 0
H: 6 0   W: 11 11   b.Wadebridge 9-11-95
Internationals: England U19, U20, U21.

2011–12	Plymouth Arg	0	0		
2012–13	Plymouth Arg	0	0		
2013–14	Brighton & HA	0	0		
2014–15	Brighton & HA	3	0		
2015–16	Brighton & HA	0	0		
2015–16	Bury	4	0	4	0
2015–16	Plymouth Arg	4	0	4	0
2016–17	Brighton & HA	0	0		
2016–17	Luton T	27	0	27	0
2016–17	Southend U	7	0	7	0
2017–18	Brighton & HA	0	0	3	0
2017–18	Wigan Ath	31	0	31	0

WHITE, Ben (D)   42 1
b.Poole 8-11-97

2016–17	Brighton & HA	0	0		
2017–18	Brighton & HA	0	0		
2017–18	Newport Co	42	1	42	1

Players retained or with offer of contract
Alzate, Steven; Araujo, Jordan Nando Marques; Barclay, Benjamin Philip; Bjordal, Henrik Rorvik; Collar, William Guy; Collings, Billy Paul; Cox, George Frederick; Davies, Archie; Davies, Jordan Andrew; Gyokeres, Viktor Einar; Kerr, Joshua Reiss; Ljubicic, Stefan Alexander; Lynch Sanchez, Robert; Mandroiu, Daniel Jordan; McGill, Thomas Peter Wayne; Moore, Owen James; Normann, Mathias Antonsen; O'Hora, Warren Patrick; Radulovic Samoukovic, Bojan; Vose, Bailey Jack.

Scholars
Bentley, George Richard; Cashman, Danny Christopher; Cochrane, Alexander William; Kazukolovas, Kipras; Longman, Ryan James; Onen, Jayden Roy; Shihab, Tareq Shakib; Tutt, Cameron; Weaire, Matthew; Zalewski, Piotr.

BRISTOL C (15)

ANDREWS, Jake (M)   7 1
b. 14-10-97

2017–18	Bristol C	0	0		
2017–18	Cheltenham T	7	1	7	1

BAKER, Nathan (D)   205 2
H: 6 2   W: 11 11   b.Worcester 23-4-91
Internationals: England U19, U20, U21.

2008–09	Aston Villa	0	0		
2009–10	Aston Villa	0	0		
2009–10	Lincoln C	18	0	18	0
2010–11	Aston Villa	4	0		
2011–12	Aston Villa	8	0		
2011–12	Millwall	6	0	6	0
2012–13	Aston Villa	26	0		
2013–14	Aston Villa	30	0		
2014–15	Aston Villa	11	0		
2015–16	Aston Villa	0	0		
2015–16	Bristol C	36	1		
2016–17	Aston Villa	32	1	111	1
2017–18	Bristol C	34	0	70	1

BAKINSON, Tyreeq (M)   1 0
H: 6 1   W: 11 10   b.Camden 8-1-98

2015–16	Luton T	1	0		
2016–17	Luton T	0	0		
2017–18	Luton T	0	0	1	0
2017–18	Bristol C	0	0		

BROWNHILL, Josh (M)   139 13
H: 5 10   W: 10 12   b.Warrington 19-12-95

2013–14	Preston NE	24	3		
2014–15	Preston NE	18	2		
2015–16	Preston NE	3	0	45	5
2015–16	Barnsley	22	2	22	2
2016–17	Bristol C	27	1		
2017–18	Bristol C	45	5	72	6

BRYAN, Joe (D)   212 17
H: 5 7   W: 11 05   b.Bristol 17-9-93

2011–12	Bristol C	1	0		
2012–13	Bristol C	13	0		
2012–13	Plymouth Arg	10	1	10	1
2013–14	Bristol C	21	2		
2014–15	Bristol C	41	6		
2015–16	Bristol C	39	2		
2016–17	Bristol C	44	1		
2017–18	Bristol C	43	5	202	16

DE GIROLAMO, Diago (M)   40 5
H: 5 10   W: 11 00   b.Chesterfield 5-10-95
Internationals: Italy U18, U19, U20.

2012–13	Sheffield U	2	0		
2013–14	Sheffield U	0	0		
2014–15	Sheffield U	0	0		
2014–15	York C	12	4	12	4
2015–16	Northampton T	6	0	6	0
2015–16	Sheffield U	0	0	2	0
2016–17	Bristol C	0	0		
2016–17	Cheltenham T	5	1	5	1
2017–18	Bristol C	0	0		
2017–18	Chesterfield	15	0	15	0

DIEDHIOU, Famara (F)   200 73
H: 6 4   W: 12 08   b.Saint-Louis 15-12-92
Internationals: Senegal Full caps.

2011–12	Belfort	11	3	11	3
2012–13	Epinal	30	12	30	12
2013–14	Ajaccio	33	13	33	13
2014–15	Sochaux	13	1		
2014–15	Clermont	14	2		
2015–16	Sochaux	0	0	13	1
2015–16	Clermont	36	21	50	23
2016–17	Angers	31	8	31	8
2017–18	Bristol C	32	13	32	13

DIONY, Lois (F)   132 28
H: 6 0 W: 12 13 b.Mont-de-Marsan 20-12-92

2012–13	Nantes	2	0	2	0
2013–14	Dijon	10	3		
2014–15	Dijon	33	3		
2015–16	Dijon	29	11		
2016–17	Dijon	35	11	107	28
2017–18	St Etienne	16	0	16	0

On loan from St Etienne.

2017–18	Bristol C	7	0	7	0

DJURIC, Milan (F)   283 46
H: 6 3 W: 13 05 b. 22-5-90
Internationals: Bosnia-Herzegovina U21, Full caps

2007–08	Cesena	24	2		
2008–09	Cesena	21	3		
2009–10	Cesena	28	3		
2010–11	Parma	0	0		
2010–11	Ascoli	17	2	17	2
2010–11	Crotone	16	5		
2011–12	Parma	0	0		
2011–12	Crotone	29	2	45	7
2012–13	Parma	0	0		
2012–13	Cremonese	20	3	20	3
2013–14	Cesena	0	0		
2013–14	Trapani	13	3	13	3
2013–14	Cittadella	15	4	15	4
2014–15	Cesena	28	2		
2015–16	Cesena	26	7		
2016–17	Cesena	19	6	146	23
2016–17	Bristol C	11	1		
2017–18	Bristol C	16	3	27	4

EDWARDS, Opi (M)   0 0
b.Bristol 30-4-99

2017–18	Bristol C	0	0	

ELIASSON, Niclas (M)   103 6
H: 5 9 W: 10 06 b.Varberg 7-12-95
Internationals: Sweden U17, U19, U21.

2012	Falkenberg	0	0		
2013	Falkenberg	29	1	29	1
2014	AIK Solna	16	1		
2015	AIK Solna	10	0		
2016	AIK Solna	5	0	31	1
2016	Norrkoping	13	1		
2017	Norrkoping	17	3	30	4
2017–18	IFK Norrkoping	0	0		
2017–18	Bristol C	13	0	13	0

ENGVALL, Gustav (F)   103 25
H: 6 0 W: 12 11 b.Kalmar 29-4-96
Internationals: Sweden U17, U19, U21, Full caps.

2013	Gothenburg	3	0		
2014	Gothenburg	20	8		
2015	Gothenburg	25	5		
2016	Gothenburg	16	3		
2016–17	Bristol C	2	0		
2017	Djurgarden	25	8	25	8
2017–18	Bristol C	2	0	4	0
2018	Gothenburg	10	1	74	17

FIELDING, Frank (G)   318 0
H: 5 11 W: 12 00 b.Blackburn 4-4-88
Internationals: England U19, U21.

2006–07	Blackburn R	0	0		
2007–08	Blackburn R	0	0		
2007–08	Wycombe W	36	0	36	0
2008–09	Blackburn R	0	0		
2008–09	Northampton T	12	0	12	0
2008–09	Rochdale	23	0		
2009–10	Blackburn R	0	0		
2009–10	Rochdale	18	0	41	0
2010–11	Blackburn R	0	0		
2010–11	Derby Co	16	0		
2011–12	Derby Co	44	0		
2012–13	Derby Co	16	0	76	0
2013–14	Bristol C	16	0		
2014–15	Bristol C	46	0		
2015–16	Bristol C	21	0		
2016–17	Bristol C	27	0		
2017–18	Bristol C	43	0	153	0

FLINT, Aiden (D)   273 40
H: 6 2 W: 12 00 b.Pinxton 11-7-89
Internationals: England C.

2010–11	Swindon T	3	0		
2011–12	Swindon T	32	2		
2012–13	Swindon T	29	2	64	4
2013–14	Bristol C	34	3		
2014–15	Bristol C	46	14		
2015–16	Bristol C	44	6		
2016–17	Bristol C	46	5		
2017–18	Bristol C	39	8	209	36

GARITA, Arnold (M)   43 7
H: 5 10 W: 12 02 b.Douala 18-6-95

2012–13	Chateauroux	3	0		
2013–14	Chateauroux	8	3		
2014–15	Chateauroux	13	1		
2015–16	Chateauroux	5	1	29	5
2015–16	Bristol C	0	0		
2016–17	Bristol C	0	0		
2016–17	Plymouth Arg	14	2	14	2
2017–18	Bristol C	0	0		

GOLBOURNE, Scott (M)   361 6
H: 5 8 W: 11 08 b.Bristol 29-2-88
Internationals: England U17, U19.

2004–05	Bristol C	9	0		
2005–06	Bristol C	5	0		
2005–06	Reading	1	0		
2006–07	Reading	0	0		
2006–07	Wycombe W	34	1	34	1
2007–08	Reading	1	0		
2007–08	Bournemouth	5	0	5	0
2008–09	Reading	0	0	2	0
2008–09	Oldham Ath	8	0	8	0
2009–10	Exeter C	34	0		
2010–11	Exeter C	44	2		
2011–12	Exeter C	26	0	104	2
2011–12	Barnsley	12	1		
2012–13	Barnsley	31	1		
2013–14	Barnsley	4	0	47	2
2013–14	Wolverhampton W	40	1		
2014–15	Wolverhampton W	27	0		
2015–16	Wolverhampton W	20	0	87	1
2015–16	Bristol C	16	0		
2016–17	Bristol C	19	0		
2017–18	Bristol C	0	0	49	0
2017–18	Milton Keynes D	25	0	25	0

HEGELER, Jens (M)   192 12
H: 6 4 W: 12 08 b.Cologne 22-1-88
Internationals: Germany U21.

2007–08	Bayer Leverkusen	1	0		
2008–09	Bayer Leverkusen	6	2		
2008–09	Augsburg	11	0		
2009–10	Bayer Leverkusen	0	0		
2009–10	Augsburg	2	2	13	2
2010–11	Bayer Leverkusen	0	0		
2010–11	Nurembourg	34	3		
2011–12	Bayer Leverkusen	0	0		
2011–12	Nurembourg	31	1	65	4
2012–13	Bayer Leverkusen	27	3		
2013–14	Bayer Leverkusen	18	0	52	5
2014–15	Hertha Berlin	24	1		
2015–16	Hertha Berlin	16	0		
2016–17	Hertha Berlin	6	0	46	1
2016–17	Bristol C	12	0		
2017–18	Bristol C	4	0	16	0

HINDS, Freddy (F)   13 0
H: 5 9 W: 10 08 b.Potton 28-1-99

2016–17	Luton T	0	0		
2017–18	Bristol C	1	0	1	0
2017–18	Cheltenham T	12	0	12	0

HOLDEN, Rory (F)   0 0
H: 5 7 W: 10 10 b.Derry 23-8-97
Internationals: Northern Ireland U21.
From Derry C.

2017–18	Bristol C	0	0	

KELLY, Lloyd (D)   11 1
H: 5 10 W: 11 00 b. 1-10-98
Internationals: England U20.

2016–17	Bristol C	0	0		
2017–18	Bristol C	11	1	11	1

LEMONHEIGH-EVANS, Connor (F)   0 0
b. 24-1-97
Internationals: Wales U17.

2013–14	Bristol C	0	0	
2014–15	Bristol C	0	0	
2015–16	Bristol C	0	0	
2016–17	Bristol C	0	0	
2017–18	Bristol C	0	0	

LUCIC, Ivan (G)   3 0
H: 6 4 W: 14 07 b.Brcko 23-3-95
Internationals: Austria U16, U17, U18, U19, U21.

2012–13	Ried	0	0		
2013–14	Ried	1	0	1	0
2014–15	Bayern Munich	0	0		
2015–16	Bayern Munich	0	0		
2016–17	Bristol C	2	0		
2016–17	Aalborg	0	0		
2017–18	Bristol C	0	0	2	0

MAGNUSSON, Hordur (D)   117 2
H: 6 0 W: 12 02 b.Reykjavik 28-3-86
Internationals: Iceland U17, U19, U21, Full caps.

2009	Fram	3	0		
2010	Fram	3	0	6	0
2011–12	Juventus	0	0		
2012–13	Juventus	0	0		
2013–14	Juventus	0	0		
2013–14	Spezia	20	0	20	0
2014–15	Juventus	0	0		
2014–15	Cesena	12	0		
2015–16	Juventus	0	0		
2015–16	Cesena	27	1	39	1
2016–17	Bristol C	28	1		
2017–18	Bristol C	24	0	52	1

McCOULSKY, Shawn (F)   27 6
b.Lewisham 6-1-97
From Dulwich Hamlet.

2017–18	Bristol C	0	0		
2017–18	Newport Co	27	6	27	6

MOORE, Taylor (D)   69 0
H: 6 0 W: 12 08 b.Walthamstow 12-5-97
Internationals: England U17, U18, U19, U20.
From West Ham U.

2014–15	Lens	4	0		
2015–16	Lens	5	0	9	0
2016–17	Bristol C	5	0		
2016–17	Bury	19	0	19	0
2017–18	Bristol C	0	0	5	0
2017–18	Cheltenham T	36	0	36	0

MORRELL, Joe (M)   38 3
H: 5 3 W: 11 04 b.Ipswich 3-1-97
Internationals: Wales U17, U19, U21.

2013–14	Bristol C	0	0		
2014–15	Bristol C	0	0		
2015–16	Bristol C	0	0		
2016–17	Bristol C	0	0		
2017–18	Cheltenham T	38	3	38	3

O'DOWDA, Callum (M)   145 13
H: 5 11 W: 11 11 b.Oxford 23-4-95
Internationals: Republic of Ireland U21, Full caps.

2012–13	Oxford U	0	0		
2013–14	Oxford U	10	0		
2014–15	Oxford U	39	4		
2015–16	Oxford U	38	8	87	12
2016–17	Bristol C	34	0		
2017–18	Bristol C	24	1	58	1

O'LEARY, Max (G)   0 0
H: 6 1 W: 12 03 b.Bath 10-10-96

2013–14	Bristol C	0	0	
2014–15	Bristol C	0	0	
2015–16	Bristol C	0	0	
2016–17	Bristol C	0	0	
2017–18	Bristol C	0	0	

O'NEIL, Gary (M)   458 30
H: 5 10 W: 11 00 b.Beckenham 18-5-83
Internationals: England U19, U20, U21.

1999–2000	Portsmouth	1	0		
2000–01	Portsmouth	10	1		
2001–02	Portsmouth	33	1		
2002–03	Portsmouth	31	3		
2003–04	Portsmouth	3	2		
2003–04	Walsall	7	0	7	0
2004–05	Portsmouth	24	2		
2004–05	Cardiff C	9	1	9	1
2005–06	Portsmouth	36	6		
2006–07	Portsmouth	35	1		
2007–08	Portsmouth	2	0	175	16
2007–08	Middlesbrough	26	0		
2008–09	Middlesbrough	29	4		
2009–10	Middlesbrough	36	4		
2010–11	Middlesbrough	18	0	109	8
2010–11	West Ham U	16	0		
2011–12	West Ham U	16	2		
2012–13	West Ham U	24	1	48	3
2013–14	QPR	29	1	29	1
2014–15	Norwich C	21	0		
2015–16	Norwich C	27	0	48	0
2016–17	Bristol C	29	1		
2017–18	Bristol C	4	0	33	1

PACK, Marlon (M)   347 24
H: 6 2 W: 11 09 b.Portsmouth 25-3-91

2008–09	Portsmouth	0	0		
2009–10	Portsmouth	0	0		
2009–10	Wycombe W	8	0	8	0
2009–10	Dagenham & R	17	1	17	1
2010–11	Portsmouth	0	0	1	0
2010–11	Cheltenham T	38	2		
2011–12	Cheltenham T	43	5		

2012–13	Cheltenham T	43	7		
2013–14	Cheltenham T	0	0	124	14
2013–14	Bristol C	43	0		
2014–15	Bristol C	34	3		
2015–16	Bristol C	45	1		
2016–17	Bristol C	33	2		
2017–18	Bristol C	42	3	197	9

PATERSON, Jamie (F) 245 39
H: 5 9 W: 10 07 b.Coventry 20-12-91

2010–11	Walsall	14	0		
2011–12	Walsall	34	3		
2012–13	Walsall	46	12	94	15
2013–14	Nottingham F	32	8		
2014–15	Nottingham F	21	1		
2015–16	Nottingham F	1	0	54	9
2015–16	*Huddersfield T*	34	6	34	6
2016–17	Bristol C	22	4		
2017–18	Bristol C	41	5	63	9

PISANO, Eros (D) 339 25
H: 6 1 W: 13 01 b.Butso Arsizio 31-3-87

2004–05	Varese	2	1		
2005–06	Varese	32	2		
2006–07	Varese	22	1		
2007–08	Varese	0	0		
2007–08	*Pisa*	6	0	6	0
2008–09	Varese	28	3		
2009–10	Varese	32	2		
2010–11	Varese	40	5	156	14
2011–12	Palermo	28	0		
2012–13	Palermo	11	0		
2012–13	*Genoa*	10	1	10	1
2013–14	Palermo	34	2		
2014–15	Palermo	4	0	77	2
2014–15	Verona	15	0		
2015–16	Verona	34	5		
2016–17	Verona	25	3	74	8
2017–18	Bristol C	16	0	16	0

PLAVOTIC, Tin (D) 12 1
H: 6 6 W: 15 02 b.Vienna 30-6-97
Internationals: Croatia U19.

2014–15	Admira	0	0		
2015–16	Schalke 04	0	0		
2016–17	Schalke 04	0	0		
2016–17	Bristol C	0	0		
2016–17	*Cheltenham T*	11	1	11	1
2017–18	Bristol C	0	0		
2017–18	*Barnet*	1	0	1	0

REID, Bobby (M) 176 29
H: 5 7 W: 10 10 b.Bristol 1-3-93

2010–11	Bristol C	1	0		
2011–12	Bristol C	0	0		
2011–12	*Cheltenham T*	1	0	1	0
2012–13	Bristol C	4	1		
2012–13	*Oldham Ath*	7	0	7	0
2013–14	Bristol C	24	1		
2014–15	Bristol C	2	0		
2014–15	*Plymouth Arg*	33	3	33	3
2015–16	Bristol C	28	2		
2016–17	Bristol C	30	3		
2017–18	Bristol C	46	19	135	26

SEMENYO, Antoine (F) 1 0
b. 7-1-00

2017–18	Bristol C	1	0	1	0

SMITH, Korey (M) 296 6
H: 5 9 W: 11 01 b.Hatfield 31-1-91

2008–09	Norwich C	2	0		
2009–10	Norwich C	37	4		
2010–11	Norwich C	28	0		
2011–12	Norwich C	0	0		
2011–12	*Barnsley*	12	0	12	0
2012–13	Norwich C	0	0	67	4
2012–13	*Yeovil T*	17	0	17	0
2012–13	*Oldham Ath*	10	0		
2013–14	Oldham Ath	42	1	52	1
2014–15	Bristol C	44	0		
2015–16	Bristol C	36	0		
2016–17	Bristol C	23	0		
2017–18	Bristol C	45	1	148	1

STEELE, Luke (G) 320 0
H: 6 2 W: 12 00 b.Peterborough 24-9-84
Internationals: England U18, U19, U20.

2001–02	Peterborough U	2	0	2	0
2001–02	Manchester U	0	0		
2002–03	Manchester U	0	0		
2003–04	Manchester U	0	0		
2004–05	Manchester U	0	0		
2004–05	*Coventry C*	32	0		
2005–06	Manchester U	0	0		
2006–07	WBA	0	0		
2006–07	*Coventry C*	5	0	37	0
2007–08	WBA	2	0	2	0
2007–08	Barnsley	14	0		

2008–09	Barnsley	10	0		
2009–10	Barnsley	39	0		
2010–11	Barnsley	46	0		
2011–12	Barnsley	36	0		
2012–13	Barnsley	33	0		
2013–14	Barnsley	31	0	209	0
2014–15	Panathinaikos	29	0		
2015–16	Panathinaikos	28	0		
2016–17	Panathinaikos	8	0		
2017–18	Panathinaikos	0	0	65	0
2017–18	Bristol C	5	0	5	0

TAYLOR, Matty (F) 106 46
H: 5 9 W: 11 05 b. 30-3-90
Internationals: England C.
From Oxford U, North Leigh, Forest Green R.

2015–16	Bristol R	46	27		
2016–17	Bristol R	27	16	73	43
2016–17	Bristol C	15	2		
2017–18	Bristol C	18	1	33	3

VYNER, Zak (D) 41 1
H: 5 10 W: 10 10 b.Bath 14-5-97

2015–16	Bristol C	4	0		
2016–17	Bristol C	3	0		
2016–17	*Accrington S*	16	0	16	0
2017–18	Bristol C	1	0	8	0
2017–18	*Plymouth Arg*	17	1	17	1

WALSH, Liam (M) 24 1
b. 15-9-97
Internationals: England U16, U18.

2015–16	Everton	0	0		
2015–16	*Yeovil T*	15	1	15	1
2016–17	Everton	0	0		
2017–18	Everton	0	0		
2017–18	*Birmingham C*	3	0	3	0
2017–18	Bristol C	6	0	6	0

WOLLACOTT, Jojo (G) 0 0
b. 8-9-96

2015–16	Bristol C	0	0		
2016–17	Bristol C	0	0		
2017–18	Bristol C	0	0		

WRIGHT, Bailey (D) 236 9
H: 5 9 W: 13 05 b.Melbourne 28-7-92
Internationals: Australia U17, Full caps.

2010–11	Preston NE	2	0		
2011–12	Preston NE	13	1		
2012–13	Preston NE	38	2		
2013–14	Preston NE	43	4		
2014–15	Preston NE	27	1		
2015–16	Preston NE	38	0		
2016–17	Preston NE	18	0	179	8
2016–17	Bristol C	21	1		
2017–18	Bristol C	36	0	57	1

Players retained or with offer of contract
Baldwin, Aden; Dowling, George Philip Denzil; Harrison, Tom Jack; Janneh, Saikou; Moir-Pring, Cameron Lewis; Morton, James Samuel; Nurse, George Damien; Parsons, Aaron Mathew; Richards, Tom James; Sesay, Alhaji; Smith, Harvey George Charles; Smith, Jonathan Gary.

Scholars
Ali, Jayden Rehman Robert; Allen, Cameron Shaun; Begovic, Denis; Burford, James; Carey, James Dean; Day, Marcus Reece; Hall, Joseph; Harper, Vincent; Mortimore, Joshua Stephen; Rees, Ricardo Estaban; Robertson, Lochlan David William; Sainsbury, Aaron James; Smith, Harry Myles; Smith, Kieran Paul; Smith, Zachary William Pince; Spark, Jack Edward Joseph; Turner, Jack William Peter; Turner, William Christian Michael; Webb, Bradley James.

BRISTOL R (16)

ANDRE, Alexis (G) 1 0
b. 31-5-97

2017–18	Bristol R	1	0	1	0

BAGHDADI, Mohammed (D) 3 0
H: 5 10 W: 11 03 b. 30-10-96

2014–15	Eintracht Braunschweig	0	0		
2015–16	Eintracht Braunschweig	1	0		
2015–16	Eintracht Braunschweig	0	0		
2016–17	Eintracht Braunschweig	0	0	1	0
2017–18	Bristol R	2	0	2	0

BENNETT, Kyle (F) 286 33
H: 5 5 W: 9 08 b.Telford 9-9-90
Internationals: England U18.

2007–08	Wolverhampton W	0	0		
2008–09	Wolverhampton W	0	0		
2009–10	Wolverhampton W	0	0		
2010–11	Bury	32	2	32	2
2011–12	Doncaster R	36	4		
2012–13	Doncaster R	35	3		
2013–14	Doncaster R	3	0		
2013–14	*Crawley T*	4	0	4	0
2013–14	*Bradford C*	18	1	18	1
2014–15	Doncaster R	42	8	116	15
2015–16	Portsmouth	42	6		
2016–17	Portsmouth	39	6		
2017–18	Portsmouth	18	0	99	12
2017–18	Bristol R	17	3	17	3

BROADBENT, Tom (D) 22 0
H: 6 3 W: 14 02 b. 15-2-92
From Farnborough, Petersfield T, Hayes & Yeading U.

2017–18	Bristol R	22	0	22	0

BROOM, Ryan (M) 9 0
H: 5 10 W: 12 08 b.Newport 4-9-96

2015–16	Bristol R	1	0		
2016–17	Bristol R	5	0		
2017–18	Bristol R	3	0	9	0

BROWN, Lee (M) 243 19
H: 6 0 W: 12 06 b.Bromley 10-8-90
Internationals: England C.

2008–09	QPR	0	0		
2009–10	QPR	1	0		
2010–11	QPR	0	0	1	0
2011–12	Bristol R	42	7		
2012–13	Bristol R	39	3		
2013–14	Bristol R	41	2		
2015–16	Bristol R	46	6		
2016–17	Bristol R	41	0		
2017–18	Bristol R	33	1	242	19

BURN, Jonathan (D) 23 1
b. 1-8-95

2014–15	Middlesbrough	0	0		
2015–16	Middlesbrough	0	0		
2015–16	*Oldham Ath*	12	1	12	1
2016–17	Middlesbrough	0	0		
2016–17	*Kilmarnock*	8	0	8	0
2016–17	Bristol R	2	0		
2017–18	Bristol R	1	0	3	0

CLARKE, James (D) 70 0
H: 6 0 W: 13 03 b.Aylesbury 17-11-89
From Watford, Oxford U, Oxford C, Salisbury C, Woking.

2015–16	Bristol R	37	0		
2016–17	Bristol R	22	0		
2017–18	Bristol R	11	0	70	0

CLARKE, Ollie (M) 141 9
H: 5 11 W: 11 11 b.Bristol 29-6-92

2009–10	Bristol R	0	0		
2010–11	Bristol R	1	0		
2011–12	Bristol R	0	0		
2012–13	Bristol R	5	0		
2013–14	Bristol R	32	2		
2015–16	Bristol R	33	2		
2016–17	Bristol R	30	4		
2017–18	Bristol R	40	1	141	9

CRAIG, Tony (D) 429 10
H: 6 0 W: 10 03 b.Greenwich 20-4-85

2002–03	Millwall	2	1		
2003–04	Millwall	9	0		
2004–05	Millwall	10	0		
2004–05	*Wycombe W*	14	0	14	0
2005–06	Millwall	28	0		
2006–07	Millwall	30	1		
2007–08	*Crystal Palace*	13	0	13	0
2007–08	Millwall	5	1		
2008–09	Millwall	44	2		
2009–10	Millwall	30	2		
2010–11	Millwall	24	0		
2011–12	Millwall	23	0		
2011–12	*Leyton Orient*	4	0	4	0
2012–13	Brentford	44	0		
2013–14	Brentford	44	0		
2014–15	Brentford	23	0	111	0
2015–16	Millwall	18	1		
2016–17	Millwall	43	1		
2017–18	Millwall	4	0	270	9
2017–18	Bristol R	17	1	17	1

DUNNWALD, Kenan (F) **1 0**
H: 6 2 W: 12 08 b. 14-11-95
2017–18 Bristol R 1 0 **1 0**

GAFFNEY, Rory (M) **106 23**
H: 6 0 W: 12 04 b.Tuam 23-10-89
2014–15 Cambridge U 0 0
2015–16 Cambridge U 6 2 **6 2**
2015–16 Bristol R 24 8
2016–17 Bristol R 34 6
2017–18 Bristol R 42 7 **100 21**

HARGREAVES, Cameron (D) **0 0**
From Exeter C.
2017–18 Bristol R 0 0

HARRISON, Ellis (F) **152 31**
H: 5 11 W: 12 06 b.Newport 1-2-94
Internationals: Wales U21.
2010–11 Bristol R 1 0
2011–12 Bristol R 0 0
2012–13 Bristol R 13 3
2013–14 Bristol R 25 1
2015–16 Bristol R 30 7
2015–16 *Hartlepool U* 2 0 **2 0**
2016–17 Bristol R 37 8
2017–18 Bristol R 44 12 **150 31**

KAVANAGH, Rhys (F) **0 0**
b. 29-9-98
From Newport Co.
2017–18 Bristol R 0 0

KELLY, Michael (D) **1 0**
H: 5 11 b.Kilmarnock 3-11-97
Internationals: Scotland U16, U17.
2017–18 Bristol R 1 0 **1 0**

KILGOUR, Alfie (D) **0 0**
b. 18-5-98
2015–16 Bristol R 0 0
2016–17 Bristol R 0 0
2017–18 Bristol R 0 0

LEADBITTER, Daniel (D) **95 0**
H: 6 0 W: 11 00 b.Newcastle upon Tyne
17-10-90
2011–12 Torquay U 2 0
2012–13 Torquay U 13 0 **15 0**
2015–16 Bristol R 33 0
2016–17 Bristol R 30 0
2017–18 Bristol R 17 0 **80 0**

LINES, Chris (M) **411 34**
H: 6 2 W: 12 00 b.Bristol 30-11-88
2005–06 Bristol R 4 0
2006–07 Bristol R 7 0
2007–08 Bristol R 27 3
2008–09 Bristol R 45 4
2009–10 Bristol R 42 10
2010–11 Bristol R 42 3
2011–12 Bristol R 1 0
2011–12 Sheffield W 41 3
2012–13 Sheffield W 6 0 **47 3**
2012–13 *Milton Keynes D* 16 0 **16 0**
2013–14 Port Vale 34 1
2014–15 Port Vale 27 2 **61 3**
2015–16 Bristol R 33 0
2016–17 Bristol R 44 3
2017–18 Bristol R 42 5 **287 28**

LOCKYER, Tom (D) **171 2**
H: 6 0 W: 11 05 b.Bristol 30-12-94
Internationals: Wales U21, Full caps.
2012–13 Bristol R 4 0
2013–14 Bristol R 41 1
2015–16 Bristol R 43 0
2016–17 Bristol R 46 0
2017–18 Bristol R 37 1 **171 2**

MENAYESE, Rollin (D) **17 0**
H: 6 3 W: 12 08 b. 4-12-97
Internationals: Wales U17.
From Weston-super-Mare.
2017–18 Bristol R 3 0 **3 0**
2017–18 *Swindon T* 14 0 **14 0**

MENSAH, Bernard (F) **10 0**
H: 5 8 W: 9 04 b.Hounslow 29-12-94
2011–12 Watford 0 0
2012–13 Watford 0 0
2013–14 Watford 1 0
2014–15 Watford 1 0
2015–16 Watford 0 0 **2 0**
From Aldershot T.
2017–18 Bristol R 8 0 **8 0**

MOORE, Byron (M) **360 36**
H: 6 0 W: 10 06 b.Stoke 24-8-88
2006–07 Crewe Alex 0 0
2007–08 Crewe Alex 33 3

2008–09 Crewe Alex 36 3
2009–10 Crewe Alex 32 3
2010–11 Crewe Alex 38 6
2011–12 Crewe Alex 42 8
2012–13 Crewe Alex 41 4
2013–14 Crewe Alex 40 3 **262 30**
2014–15 Port Vale 15 1
2015–16 Port Vale 36 3 **51 4**
2016–17 Bristol R 27 2
2017–18 Bristol R 20 0 **47 2**

NICHOLS, Tom (F) **187 44**
H: 5 10 W: 10 10 b.Wellington 1-9-93
2010–11 Exeter C 1 0
2011–12 Exeter C 7 1
2012–13 Exeter C 3 0
2013–14 Exeter C 28 6
2014–15 Exeter C 36 15
2015–16 Exeter C 23 10 **98 32**
2015–16 Peterborough U 7 1
2016–17 Peterborough U 43 10 **50 11**
2017–18 Bristol R 39 1 **39 1**

OTEDUKO, Kunle (F) **0 0**
2017–18 Bristol R 0 0

PARTINGTON, Joe (M) **91 5**
H: 5 11 W: 11 13 b.Portsmouth 1-4-90
Internationals: Wales U17, U19, U21.
2007–08 Bournemouth 6 1
2008–09 Bournemouth 11 1
2009–10 Bournemouth 11 0
2010–11 Bournemouth 5 0
2011–12 Bournemouth 5 0
2012–13 Bournemouth 14 0
2013–14 Bournemouth 0 0
2014–15 Bournemouth 0 0 **52 2**
2016–17 Bristol R 7 0
2017–18 Bristol R 32 3 **39 3**

RUSSE, Luke (M) **3 0**
b. 19-7-99
2017–18 Bristol R 3 0 **3 0**

SERCOMBE, Liam (M) **353 48**
H: 5 10 W: 10 10 b.Exeter 25-4-90
2008–09 Exeter C 29 2
2009–10 Exeter C 28 1
2010–11 Exeter C 42 3
2011–12 Exeter C 33 7
2012–13 Exeter C 20 1
2013–14 Exeter C 44 5
2014–15 Exeter C 40 4 **236 23**
2015–16 Oxford U 45 14
2016–17 Oxford U 30 3 **75 17**
2017–18 Bristol R 42 8 **42 8**

SINCLAIR, Stuart (M) **97 5**
H: 5 7 W: 10 08 b.Houghton Conquest
9-11-87
From Luton T, Cambridge C, Bedford T,
Dunstable T, Arlesey T, Salisbury C.
2015–16 Bristol R 30 2
2016–17 Bristol R 38 1
2017–18 Bristol R 29 2 **97 5**

SLOCOMBE, Sam (G) **195 0**
H: 6 0 W: 11 11 b.Scunthorpe 5-6-88
2008–09 Scunthorpe U 0 0
2009–10 Scunthorpe U 1 0
2010–11 Scunthorpe U 2 0
2011–12 Scunthorpe U 28 0
2012–13 Scunthorpe U 29 0
2013–14 Scunthorpe U 46 0
2014–15 Scunthorpe U 9 0 **115 0**
2015–16 Oxford U 23 0 **23 0**
2016–17 Blackpool 34 0 **34 0**
2017–18 Bristol R 23 0 **23 0**

SMITH, Adam (G) **113 0**
H: 5 11 W: 11 00 b.Sunderland 23-11-92
2010–11 Leicester C 0 0
2011–12 Leicester C 0 0
2011–12 *Chesterfield* 0 0
2011–12 *Bristol R* 0 0
2012–13 Leicester C 0 0
2013–14 Leicester C 0 0
2013–14 *Stevenage* 0 0
2014–15 Leicester C 0 0
2014–15 *Mansfield T* 4 0 **4 0**
2015–16 Northampton T 46 0
2016–17 Northampton T 40 0 **86 0**
2017–18 Bristol R 23 0 **23 0**

SPRUCE, James (M) **0 0**
Internationals: Wales U19.
2017–18 Bristol R 0 0

Players retained or with offer of contract
Armstrong, Liam James; Ebbutt, Cameron
Ruben; Jones, Connor Stephen Malcom;
Leigh-Gilchrist, Lewis Gordon; Ludford-Ison,
Lewis James; Mansell, Lee Richard Samuel;
Morgan, Ben.

Scholars
Anderson, Graeme James; Bailey, Joshua
Mark; Brace, Joshua Sebastian; Bremner,
James Christopher; Carey, Jordan;
Chamberlain, Harrison David; Clarke, Alfie
Jack; Clutton, Lewis David; Dillon, Osian
Llyr; Isherwood, Scott Benjamin; Mehew,
Thomas Samuel James; Sell, Jack; Spruce,
James Alexander; Swan, Matthew James;
Tomlinson, Lucas George; Warwick, Harry
Joshua.

BURNLEY (17)

AGYEI, Daniel (F) **46 8**
H: 6 0 W: 12 02 b.Dansoman 1-6-97
2014–15 AFC Wimbledon 0 0
2015–16 Burnley 0 0
2016–17 Burnley 3 0
2016–17 *Coventry C* 16 4 **16 4**
2017–18 Burnley 0 0 **3 0**
2017–18 *Walsall* 18 4 **18 4**
2017–18 *Blackpool* 9 0 **9 0**

ANDERSON, Thomas (M) **88 4**
H: 6 4 W: 13 01 b.Burnley 2-9-93
2012–13 Burnley 0 0
2013–14 Burnley 0 0
2014–15 Burnley 0 0
2014–15 *Carlisle U* 8 0 **8 0**
2015–16 Burnley 0 0
2015–16 *Chesterfield* 18 0
2016–17 Burnley 0 0
2016–17 *Chesterfield* 35 2 **53 2**
2017–18 Burnley 0 0
2017–18 *Port Vale* 20 0 **20 0**
2017–18 *Doncaster R* 7 2 **7 2**

ARFIELD, Scott (M) **381 41**
H: 5 10 W: 10 01 b.Livingston 1-11-88
Internationals: Scotland U19, U21, B. Canada
Full caps.
2007–08 Falkirk 35 3
2008–09 Falkirk 37 7
2009–10 Falkirk 36 3 **108 13**
2010–11 Huddersfield T 40 4
2011–12 Huddersfield T 35 2
2012–13 Huddersfield T 21 1 **96 7**
2013–14 Burnley 45 8
2014–15 Burnley 37 2
2015–16 Burnley 46 8
2016–17 Burnley 31 1
2017–18 Burnley 18 2 **177 21**

BARDSLEY, Phillip (D) **286 8**
H: 5 11 W: 11 13 b.Salford 28-6-85
Internationals: Scotland Full caps.
2003–04 Manchester U 0 0
2004–05 Manchester U 0 0
2005–06 Manchester U 0 0
2005–06 *Burnley* 6 0
2006–07 Manchester U 0 0
2006–07 *Rangers* 5 1 **5 1**
2006–07 *Aston Villa* 13 0 **13 0**
2007–08 Manchester U 0 0 **8 0**
2007–08 *Sheffield U* 16 0 **16 0**
2007–08 Sunderland 11 0
2008–09 Sunderland 28 0
2009–10 Sunderland 26 0
2010–11 Sunderland 34 3
2011–12 Sunderland 31 1
2012–13 Sunderland 18 1
2013–14 Sunderland 26 2 **174 7**
2014–15 Stoke C 25 0
2015–16 Stoke C 11 0
2016–17 Stoke C 10 0 **51 0**
2017–18 Burnley 13 0 **19 0**

BARNES, Ashley (F) **305 71**
H: 6 0 W: 12 00 b.Bath 30-10-89
Internationals: Austria U20.
2006–07 Plymouth Arg 0 0
2007–08 Plymouth Arg 0 0
2008–09 Plymouth Arg 15 1
2009–10 Plymouth Arg 7 1 **22 2**
2009–10 *Torquay U* 6 0 **6 0**
2009–10 Brighton & HA 8 4
2010–11 Brighton & HA 42 18
2011–12 Brighton & HA 43 11
2012–13 Brighton & HA 34 8

2013–14	Brighton & HA	22	5	149	46
2013–14	Burnley	21	3		
2014–15	Burnley	35	5		
2015–16	Burnley	8	0		
2016–17	Burnley	28	6		
2017–18	Burnley	36	9	128	23

BRADY, Robert (F) 202 19
H: 5 9 W: 10 12 b.Belfast 14-1-92
Internationals: Republic of Ireland Youth, U21, Full caps.

2008–09	Manchester U	0	0		
2009–10	Manchester U	0	0		
2010–11	Manchester U	0	0		
2011–12	Manchester U	0	0		
2011–12	Hull C	39	3		
2012–13	Manchester U	0	0		
2012–13	Hull C	32	4		
2013–14	Hull C	16	3		
2014–15	Hull C	27	0	114	10
2015–16	Norwich C	36	3		
2016–17	Norwich C	23	4	59	7
2016–17	Burnley	14	1		
2017–18	Burnley	15	1	29	2

CORK, Jack (D) 387 12
H: 6 0 W: 10 12 b.Carshalton 25-6-89
Internationals: England U16, U17, U18, U19, U20, Full caps. Great Britain.

2006–07	Chelsea	0	0		
2006–07	Bournemouth	7	0	7	0
2007–08	Chelsea	0	0		
2007–08	Scunthorpe U	34	2	34	2
2008–09	Chelsea	0	0		
2008–09	Southampton	23	0		
2008–09	Watford	19	0	19	0
2009–10	Chelsea	0	0		
2009–10	Coventry C	21	0	21	0
2009–10	Burnley	11	1		
2010–11	Chelsea	0	0		
2010–11	Burnley	40	3		
2011–12	Southampton	46	0		
2012–13	Southampton	28	0		
2013–14	Southampton	28	0		
2014–15	Southampton	12	2	137	2
2014–15	Swansea C	15	1		
2015–16	Swansea C	35	1		
2016–17	Swansea C	30	0	80	2
2017–18	Burnley	38	2	89	6

DEFOUR, Steven (M) 330 28
H: 5 8 W: 10 03 b.Mechelen 15-4-88
Internationals: Belgium U16, U17, U18, Full caps.

2004–05	Genk	4	0		
2005–06	Genk	26	1	30	1
2006–07	Standard Liege	29	4		
2007–08	Standard Liege	24	1		
2008–09	Standard Liege	33	4		
2009–10	Standard Liege	13	1		
2010–11	Standard Liege	27	3		
2011–12	Standard Liege	1	0	127	13
2011–12	Porto	24	1		
2012–13	Porto	25	2		
2013–14	Porto	16	0	65	3
2014–15	Anderlecht	29	6		
2015–16	Anderlecht	32	2		
2016–17	Anderlecht	2	1	63	9
2016–17	Burnley	21	1		
2017–18	Burnley	24	1	45	2

DUNNE, Jimmy (D) 20 0
b.Drogheda 19-10-97
Internationals: Republic of Ireland U21.

2017–18	Burnley	0	0		
2017–18	Accrington S	20	0	20	0

GINNELLY, Josh (M) 27 2
b.Coventry 24-3-97

2013–14	Shrewsbury T	0	0		
2014–15	Shrewsbury T	3	0	3	0
2015–16	Burnley	0	0		
2016–17	Burnley	0	0		
2016–17	Walsall	9	0	9	0
2017–18	Burnley	0	0		
2017–18	Lincoln C	15	2	15	2

GUDMUNDSSON, Johann Berg (M) 255 28
H: 6 1 W: 12 06 b.Reykjavik 27-10-90
Internationals: Iceland U19, U21, Full caps.

2009–10	AZ	0	0		
2010–11	AZ	23	1		
2011–12	AZ	30	3		
2012–13	AZ	31	2		
2013–14	AZ	35	3	119	9
2014–15	Charlton Ath	41	10		
2015–16	Charlton Ath	40	6	81	16
2016–17	Burnley	20	1		
2017–18	Burnley	35	2	55	3

HEATON, Tom (G) 304 0
H: 6 1 W: 13 12 b.Chester 15-4-86
Internationals: England 16, U17, U18, U19, U21, Full caps.

2003–04	Manchester U	0	0		
2004–05	Manchester U	0	0		
2005–06	Manchester U	0	0		
2005–06	Swindon T	14	0	14	0
2006–07	Manchester U	0	0		
2007–08	Manchester U	0	0		
2008–09	Manchester U	0	0		
2008–09	Cardiff C	21	0		
2009–10	Manchester U	0	0		
2009–10	Rochdale	12	0	12	0
2009–10	Wycombe W	16	0	16	0
2010–11	Cardiff C	27	0		
2011–12	Cardiff C	2	0	50	0
2012–13	Bristol C	43	0	43	0
2013–14	Burnley	46	0		
2014–15	Burnley	38	0		
2015–16	Burnley	46	0		
2016–17	Burnley	35	0		
2017–18	Burnley	4	0	169	0

HENDRICK, Jeff (M) 262 26
H: 6 1 W: 11 11 b.Dublin 31-1-92
Internationals: Republic of Ireland U17, U19, U21, Full caps.

2010–11	Derby Co	4	0		
2011–12	Derby Co	42	3		
2012–13	Derby Co	45	6		
2013–14	Derby Co	30	4		
2014–15	Derby Co	41	7		
2015–16	Derby Co	32	2		
2016–17	Derby Co	2	0	196	22
2016–17	Burnley	32	2		
2017–18	Burnley	34	2	66	4

LEGZDINS, Adam (G) 114 0
H: 6 1 W: 14 02 b.Penkridge 28-11-86

2006–07	Birmingham C	0	0		
2007–08	Birmingham C	0	0		
2008–09	Crewe Alex	0	0		
2009–10	Crewe Alex	6	0	6	0
2010–11	Burton Alb	46	0		
2011–12	Derby Co	4	0		
2011–12	Burton Alb	1	0	47	0
2012–13	Derby Co	31	0		
2013–14	Derby Co	0	0	35	0
2014–15	Leyton Orient	11	0	11	0
2015–16	Birmingham C	5	0		
2016–17	Birmingham C	10	0	15	0
2017–18	Burnley	0	0		

LENNON, Aaron (M) 383 34
H: 5 6 W: 10 03 b.Leeds 16-4-87
Internationals: England U17, U19, U21, B, Full caps.

2003–04	Leeds U	11	0		
2004–05	Leeds U	27	1	38	1
2005–06	Tottenham H	27	2		
2006–07	Tottenham H	26	3		
2007–08	Tottenham H	29	2		
2008–09	Tottenham H	35	5		
2009–10	Tottenham H	22	3		
2010–11	Tottenham H	34	3		
2011–12	Tottenham H	23	3		
2012–13	Tottenham H	34	4		
2013–14	Tottenham H	27	1		
2014–15	Tottenham H	9	0		
2014–15	Everton	14	2		
2015–16	Tottenham H	0	0	266	26
2015–16	Everton	25	5		
2016–17	Everton	11	0		
2017–18	Everton	15	0	65	7
2017–18	Burnley	14	0	14	0

LINDEGAARD, Anders (G) 113 0
H: 6 4 W: 12 08 b.Odense 13-4-84
Internationals: Denmark U19, U20, Full caps.

2003–04	Odense	0	0		
2004–05	Odense	0	0		
2005–06	Odense	0	0		
2006–07	Odense	1	0		
2007–08	Odense	1	0		
2008–09	Kolding	10	0	10	0
2009	Aalesund	26	0		
2009	Odense	4	0	6	0
2010	Aalesund	30	0	56	0
2010–11	Manchester U	7	0		
2011–12	Manchester U	10	0		
2012–13	Manchester U	10	0		
2013–14	Manchester U	1	0		
2014–15	Manchester U	0	0		
2015–16	Manchester U	0	0	19	0
2015–16	WBA	0	0		
2015–16	Preston NE	14	0		

2016–17	Preston NE	8	0	22	0
2017–18	Burnley	0	0		

LONG, Chris (F) 90 19
H: 5 7 W: 12 02 b.Huyton 25-2-95
Internationals: England U16, U17, U18, U19, U20.

2013–14	Everton	0	0		
2013–14	Milton Keynes D	4	1	4	1
2014–15	Everton	0	0		
2014–15	Brentford	10	4	10	4
2015–16	Burnley	10	0		
2016–17	Burnley	0	0		
2016–17	Fleetwood T	18	4	18	4
2016–17	Bolton W	10	1	10	1
2017–18	Burnley	0	0		
2017–18	Northampton T	38	9	38	9

LONG, Kevin (D) 130 7
H: 6 3 W: 13 01 b.Cork 18-8-90
Internationals: Republic of Ireland Full caps.

2009	Cork C	16	0	16	0
2009–10	Burnley	0	0		
2010–11	Burnley	0	0		
2010–11	Accrington S	15	0		
2011–12	Burnley	0	0		
2011–12	Accrington S	24	4	39	4
2011–12	Rochdale	16	0	16	0
2012–13	Burnley	14	0		
2012–13	Portsmouth	5	0	5	0
2013–14	Burnley	7	0		
2014–15	Burnley	1	0		
2015–16	Burnley	0	0		
2015–16	Barnsley	11	2	11	2
2015–16	Milton Keynes D	0	0	2	0
2016–17	Burnley	3	0		
2017–18	Burnley	16	1	41	1

LOWTON, Matt (M) 244 13
H: 5 11 W: 12 04 b.Chesterfield 9-6-89

2008–09	Sheffield U	0	0		
2009–10	Sheffield U	2	0		
2009–10	Ferencvaros	5	0	5	0
2010–11	Sheffield U	32	4		
2011–12	Sheffield U	44	6	78	10
2012–13	Aston Villa	37	2		
2013–14	Aston Villa	23	0		
2014–15	Aston Villa	12	0	72	2
2015–16	Burnley	27	1		
2016–17	Burnley	36	0		
2017–18	Burnley	26	0	89	1

MARNEY, Dean (M) 362 20
H: 5 10 W: 11 09 b.Barking 31-1-84
Internationals: England U21.

2002–03	Tottenham H	0	0		
2002–03	Swindon T	9	0	9	0
2003–04	Tottenham H	3	0		
2003–04	QPR	2	0	2	0
2004–05	Tottenham H	5	2		
2004–05	Gillingham	3	0	3	0
2005–06	Tottenham H	0	0	8	2
2005–06	Norwich C	13	0	13	0
2006–07	Hull C	37	2		
2007–08	Hull C	41	6		
2008–09	Hull C	31	0		
2009–10	Hull C	16	1	125	9
2009–10	Burnley	0	0		
2010–11	Burnley	36	3		
2011–12	Burnley	37	0		
2012–13	Burnley	38	2		
2013–14	Burnley	38	3		
2014–15	Burnley	20	0		
2015–16	Burnley	12	0		
2016–17	Burnley	21	1		
2017–18	Burnley	0	0	202	9

McNEIL, Dwight (F) 1 0
b. 22-11-99

2017–18	Burnley	1	0	1	0

MEE, Ben (D) 245 6
H: 5 11 W: 11 09 b.Sale 21-9-89
Internationals: England U19, U20, U21.

2007–08	Manchester C	0	0		
2008–09	Manchester C	0	0		
2009–10	Manchester C	0	0		
2010–11	Manchester C	0	0		
2010–11	Leicester C	15	0	15	0
2011–12	Manchester C	0	0		
2011–12	Burnley	31	0		
2012–13	Burnley	19	1		
2013–14	Burnley	38	0		
2014–15	Burnley	33	2		
2015–16	Burnley	46	2		
2016–17	Burnley	34	1		
2017–18	Burnley	29	0	230	6

O'NEILL, Aiden (M) 39 1
H: 5 10 W: 11 00 b.Brisbane 4-7-98
Internationals: Australia U23.
From Brisbane Ath.

Season	Club	Apps	Gls	Apps	Gls
2016–17	Burnley	3	0		
2016–17	Oldham Ath	15	0	15	0
2017–18	Burnley	0	0	3	0
2017–18	Fleetwood T	21	1	21	1

POPE, Nick (G) 112 0
H: 6 3 W: 11 13 b.Cambridge 19-4-92
Internationals: England Full caps.

Season	Club	Apps	Gls	Apps	Gls
2011–12	Charlton Ath	0	0		
2012–13	Charlton Ath	1	0		
2013–14	Charlton Ath	0	0		
2013–14	York C	22	0	22	0
2014–15	Charlton Ath	8	0		
2014–15	Bury	22	0	22	0
2015–16	Charlton Ath	24	0	33	0
2016–17	Burnley	0	0		
2017–18	Burnley	35	0	35	0

TARKOWSKI, James (D) 196 9
H: 6 1 W: 12 10 b.Manchester 19-11-92
Internationals: England Full caps.

Season	Club	Apps	Gls	Apps	Gls
2010–11	Oldham Ath	9	0		
2011–12	Oldham Ath	16	1		
2012–13	Oldham Ath	21	2		
2013–14	Oldham Ath	26	2	72	5
2013–14	Brentford	13	2		
2014–15	Brentford	34	1		
2015–16	Brentford	23	1	70	4
2015–16	Burnley	4	0		
2016–17	Burnley	19	0		
2017–18	Burnley	31	0	54	0

TAYLOR, Charlie (D) 150 3
H: 5 9 W: 11 00 b.York 18-9-93
Internationals: England U19.

Season	Club	Apps	Gls	Apps	Gls
2011–12	Leeds U	2	0		
2011–12	Bradford C	3	0	3	0
2012–13	Leeds U	0	0		
2012–13	York C	4	0	4	0
2012–13	Inverness CT	7	0	7	0
2013–14	Leeds U	0	0		
2013–14	Fleetwood T	32	0	32	0
2014–15	Leeds U	23	2		
2015–16	Leeds U	39	1		
2016–17	Leeds U	29	0	93	3
2017–18	Burnley	11	0	11	0

ULVESTAD, Fredrik (M) 140 15
H: 6 0 W: 12 06 b.Alesund 19-5-92
Internationals: Norway U20, U21, U23, Full caps.

Season	Club	Apps	Gls	Apps	Gls
2010	Aalesund	1	0		
2011	Aalesund	24	2		
2012	Aalesund	25	2		
2013	Aalesund	27	7		
2014	Aalesund	29	3	106	14
2014–15	Burnley	2	0		
2015–16	Burnley	5	0		
2016–17	Burnley	0	0		
2016–17	Charlton Ath	27	1	27	1
2017–18	Burnley	0	0	7	0

Transferred to Djurgardens IF, February 2018.

VOKES, Sam (F) 353 83
H: 6 1 W: 13 10 b.Lymington 21-10-89
Internationals: Wales U21, Full caps.

Season	Club	Apps	Gls	Apps	Gls
2006–07	Bournemouth	13	4		
2007–08	Bournemouth	41	12	54	16
2008–09	Wolverhampton W	36	6		
2009–10	Wolverhampton W	5	0		
2009–10	Leeds U	8	1	8	1
2010–11	Bristol C	1	0	1	0
2010–11	Sheffield U	6	1	6	1
2010–11	Norwich C	4	1	4	1
2011–12	Wolverhampton W	4	0		
2011–12	Burnley	0	0		
2011–12	Brighton & HA	14	3	14	3
2012–13	Wolverhampton W	0	0	47	6
2012–13	Burnley	46	4		
2013–14	Burnley	39	20		
2014–15	Burnley	15	0		
2015–16	Burnley	43	15		
2016–17	Burnley	37	10		
2017–18	Burnley	30	4	219	55

WALTERS, Jon (F) 492 94
H: 6 0 W: 12 06 b.Birkenhead 20-9-83
Internationals: Republic of Ireland U21, B, Full caps.

Season	Club	Apps	Gls	Apps	Gls
2001–02	Bolton W	0	0		
2002–03	Bolton W	4	0		
2002–03	Hull C	11	5		
2003–04	Bolton W	0	0	4	0
2003–04	Crewe Alex	0	0		
2003–04	Barnsley	8	0	8	0
2003–04	Hull C	16	1		
2004–05	Hull C	21	1	48	7
2004–05	Scunthorpe U	3	0	3	0
2005–06	Wrexham	38	5	38	5
2006–07	Chester C	26	9	26	9
2006–07	Ipswich T	16	4		
2007–08	Ipswich T	40	13		
2008–09	Ipswich T	36	5		
2009–10	Ipswich T	43	8		
2010–11	Ipswich T	1	0	136	30
2010–11	Stoke C	36	6		
2011–12	Stoke C	38	7		
2012–13	Stoke C	38	8		
2013–14	Stoke C	32	5		
2014–15	Stoke C	32	8		
2015–16	Stoke C	27	5		
2016–17	Stoke C	23	4	226	43
2017–18	Burnley	3	0	3	0

WARD, Stephen (D) 436 27
H: 5 11 W: 12 02 b.Dublin 20-8-85
Internationals: Republic of Ireland U20, U21, B, Full caps.

Season	Club	Apps	Gls	Apps	Gls
2003	Bohemians	6	0		
2004	Bohemians	16	2		
2005	Bohemians	29	7		
2006	Bohemians	21	2	72	11
2006–07	Wolverhampton W	18	3		
2007–08	Wolverhampton W	29	0		
2008–09	Wolverhampton W	42	0		
2009–10	Wolverhampton W	22	0		
2010–11	Wolverhampton W	34	1		
2011–12	Wolverhampton W	38	3		
2012–13	Wolverhampton W	39	2		
2013–14	Wolverhampton W	0	0	222	9
2013–14	Brighton & HA	44	4	44	4
2014–15	Burnley	9	0		
2015–16	Burnley	24	1		
2016–17	Burnley	37	1		
2017–18	Burnley	28	1	98	3

WELLS, Nahki (F) 247 87
H: 5 7 W: 11 00 b.Bermuda 1-6-90
Internationals: Bermuda Full caps.

Season	Club	Apps	Gls	Apps	Gls
2010–11	Carlisle U	3	0	3	0
2011–12	Bradford C	33	10		
2012–13	Bradford C	39	18		
2013–14	Bradford C	19	14	91	42
2013–14	Huddersfield T	22	7		
2014–15	Huddersfield T	35	11		
2015–16	Huddersfield T	44	17		
2016–17	Huddersfield T	43	10		
2017–18	Huddersfield T	0	0	144	45
2017–18	Burnley	9	0	9	0

WESTWOOD, Ashley (M) 303 19
H: 5 10 W: 11 00 b.Nantwich 1-4-90

Season	Club	Apps	Gls	Apps	Gls
2008–09	Crewe Alex	2	0		
2009–10	Crewe Alex	36	6		
2010–11	Crewe Alex	46	5		
2011–12	Crewe Alex	41	3		
2012–13	Crewe Alex	3	0	128	14
2012–13	Aston Villa	30	3		
2013–14	Aston Villa	35	3		
2014–15	Aston Villa	27	0		
2015–16	Aston Villa	32	2		
2016–17	Aston Villa	23	0	147	5
2016–17	Burnley	9	0		
2017–18	Burnley	19	0	28	0

WOOD, Chris (F) 286 97
H: 6 3 W: 12 10 b.Auckland 7-12-91
Internationals: New Zealand U17, U23, Full caps.

Season	Club	Apps	Gls	Apps	Gls
2008–09	WBA	2	0		
2009–10	WBA	18	1		
2010–11	WBA	1	0		
2010–11	Barnsley	7	0	7	0
2010–11	Brighton & HA	29	5	29	8
2011–12	WBA	0	0		
2011–12	Birmingham C	23	9	23	9
2011–12	Bristol C	3	1	9	3
2012–13	WBA	0	0	21	1
2012–13	Millwall	19	11	19	11
2013–14	Leicester C	20	9		
2013–14	Leicester C	26	4		
2014–15	Leicester C	7	1	53	14
2014–15	Ipswich T	8	0	8	0
2015–16	Leeds U	36	13		
2016–17	Leeds U	44	27		
2017–18	Leeds U	3	1	83	41
2017–18	Burnley	24	10	24	10

Players retained or with offer of contract
Bayode, Olatunde Tobias; Blair, Marley Jasiah Kane Noel; Chakwana, Tinashe; Clarke, James Michael Neil; Koiki, Abd-Al-Ali Morakinyo; Massanka, Ntumba; Mitchell, Conor; N'Guessan, Christian Dashiell; Stone, Aiden Thomas; Younger, Oliver.

Scholars
Allan Meredith, Dylon Thomas; Bruce, Adam David; Calderbank-Park, Kai; Cropper, Jordan; Fowler, Michael; Harris, William; Howarth, Mark David; Kershaw, Ethan Samuel; Moss, Daniel Thomas; Mupariwa, Terry Tauyanashe; Taylor, Richard Akinfolarin; Thomas, Bobby Craig; Wilson, Scott John; Yari, Kian.

BURTON ALB (18)

AKINS, Lucas (F) 338 52
H: 5 10 W: 11 07 b.Huddersfield 25-2-89

Season	Club	Apps	Gls	Apps	Gls
2006–07	Huddersfield T	2	0		
2007–08	Huddersfield T	3	0	5	0
2008–09	Hamilton A	11	0		
2008–09	Partick Thistle	9	1	9	1
2009–10	Hamilton A	0	0	11	0
2010–11	Tranmere R	33	2		
2011–12	Tranmere R	44	5	77	7
2012–13	Stevenage	46	10		
2013–14	Stevenage	31	3	77	13
2014–15	Burton Alb	35	9		
2015–16	Burton Alb	44	12		
2016–17	Burton Alb	38	5		
2017–18	Burton Alb	42	5	159	31

AKPAN, Hope (M) 193 12
H: 6 0 W: 10 08 b.Liverpool 14-8-91
Internationals: Nigeria Full caps.

Season	Club	Apps	Gls	Apps	Gls
2007–08	Everton	0	0		
2008–09	Everton	0	0		
2009–10	Everton	0	0		
2010–11	Everton	0	0		
2010–11	Hull C	2	0	2	0
2011–12	Crawley T	26	1		
2012–13	Crawley T	21	4	47	5
2012–13	Reading	9	0		
2013–14	Reading	29	1		
2014–15	Reading	0	0	58	1
2015–16	Blackburn R	35	3		
2016–17	Blackburn R	25	1	60	4
2017–18	Burton Alb	26	2	26	2

ALLEN, Jamie (M) 162 12
H: 5 11 W: 11 05 b.Rochdale 29-1-95

Season	Club	Apps	Gls	Apps	Gls
2012–13	Rochdale	0	0		
2013–14	Rochdale	25	6		
2014–15	Rochdale	35	0		
2015–16	Rochdale	38	3		
2016–17	Rochdale	31	2		
2017–18	Rochdale	4	0	133	11
2017–18	Burton Alb	29	1	29	1

BARKER, Shaun (D) 361 18
H: 6 2 W: 12 08 b.Nottingham 19-9-82

Season	Club	Apps	Gls	Apps	Gls
2002–03	Rotherham U	11	0		
2003–04	Rotherham U	36	2		
2004–05	Rotherham U	33	2		
2005–06	Rotherham U	43	3	123	7
2006–07	Blackpool	45	3		
2007–08	Blackpool	46	2		
2008–09	Blackpool	43	0	134	5
2009–10	Derby Co	35	5		
2010–11	Derby Co	43	1		
2011–12	Derby Co	20	0		
2012–13	Derby Co	0	0		
2013–14	Derby Co	0	0		
2014–15	Derby Co	0	0	98	6
2016–17	Burton Alb	5	0		
2017–18	Burton Alb	1	0	6	0

BOYCE, Liam (F) 115 51
H: 6 0 W: 13 01 b.Belfast 8-4-91
Internationals: Northern Ireland U19, U21, Full caps.
From Cliftonville.

Season	Club	Apps	Gls	Apps	Gls
2014–15	Ross Co	30	10		
2015–16	Ross Co	35	15		
2016–17	Ross Co	34	23	99	48
2017–18	Burton Alb	16	3	16	3

BRAYFORD, John (D) 336 7
H: 5 8 W: 11 02 b.Stoke 29-12-87
Internationals: England C.

Season	Club	Apps	Gls	Apps	Gls
2008–09	Crewe Alex	36	2		
2009–10	Crewe Alex	45	0	81	2
2010–11	Derby Co	46	1		

Season	Club	Apps	Gls	Tot Apps	Tot Gls
2011–12	Derby Co	23	0		
2012–13	Derby Co	40	1	109	2
2013–14	Cardiff C				
2013–14	*Sheffield U*	15	1		
2014–15	Cardiff C	26	0	26	0
2014–15	*Sheffield U*	22	1		
2015–16	*Sheffield U*	19	1		
2016–17	*Sheffield U*	3	0		
2016–17	*Burton Alb*	33	0		
2017–18	*Sheffield U*	0	0	59	3
2017–18	Burton Alb	28	0	61	0

BUXTON, Jake (D)   361 17
H: 6 1 W: 13 05 b.Sutton-in-Ashfield 4-3-85

Season	Club	Apps	Gls	Tot Apps	Tot Gls
2002–03	Mansfield T	3	0		
2003–04	Mansfield T	9	1		
2004–05	Mansfield T	30	1		
2005–06	Mansfield T	39	0		
2006–07	Mansfield T	40	2		
2007–08	Mansfield T	40	2		
2008–09	Mansfield T	0	0	151	5
From Burton Alb.					
2008–09	Derby Co	6	0		
2009–10	Derby Co	19	1		
2010–11	Derby Co	1	0		
2011–12	Derby Co	21	2		
2012–13	Derby Co	31	3		
2013–14	Derby Co	45	2		
2014–15	Derby Co	19	3		
2015–16	Derby Co	3	0	139	11
2016–17	Wigan Ath	39	1	39	1
2017–18	Burton Alb	32	0	32	0

BYWATER, Steve (G)   376 0
H: 6 2 W: 12 10 b.Manchester 7-6-81
Internationals: England U19, U21.

Season	Club	Apps	Gls	Tot Apps	Tot Gls
1997–98	Rochdale	0	0		
1998–99	West Ham U	0	0		
1999–2000	West Ham U	4	0		
1999–2000	*Wycombe W*	2	0	2	0
1999–2000	*Hull C*	4	0	4	0
2000–01	West Ham U	1	0		
2001–02	West Ham U	0	0		
2001–02	*Wolverhampton W*	0	0		
2001–02	*Cardiff C*	0	0		
2002–03	West Ham U	0	0		
2003–04	West Ham U	17	0		
2004–05	West Ham U	36	0		
2005–06	West Ham U	1	0	59	0
2005–06	Coventry C	14	0	14	0
2006–07	Derby Co	37	0		
2007–08	Derby Co	18	0		
2007–08	*Ipswich T*	17	0	17	0
2008–09	Derby Co	31	0		
2009–10	Derby Co	42	0		
2010–11	Derby Co	22	0	150	0
2010–11	Cardiff C	8	0	8	0
2011–12	Sheffield W	32	0		
2012–13	Sheffield W	0	0	32	0
2013–14	Millwall	7	0		
2014–15	Millwall	0	0	7	0
2014–15	*Gillingham*	13	0	13	0
2014–15	*Doncaster R*	21	0	21	0
2015–16	Burton Alb	0	0		
2016–17	Burton Alb	5	0		
2017–18	Burton Alb	44	0	49	0

CAMPBELL, Harry (G)   0 0
H: 6 1 W: 12 02 b.Blackburn 16-11-95

Season	Club	Apps	Gls	Tot Apps	Tot Gls
2015–16	Bolton W	0	0		
2016–17	Burton Alb	0	0		
2017–18	Burton Alb	0	0		

DYER, Lloyd (M)   486 65
H: 5 8 W: 10 03 b.Birmingham 13-9-82

Season	Club	Apps	Gls	Tot Apps	Tot Gls
2001–02	WBA	0	0		
2002–03	WBA	0	0		
2003–04	WBA	17	2		
2003–04	*Kidderminster H*	7	1	7	1
2004–05	WBA	4	0		
2004–05	*Coventry C*	6	0	6	0
2005–06	WBA	0	0	21	2
2005–06	*QPR*	15	0	15	0
2005–06	*Millwall*	6	0	6	0
2006–07	Milton Keynes D	41	5		
2007–08	Milton Keynes D	45	11	86	16
2008–09	Leicester C	44	10		
2009–10	Leicester C	33	3		
2010–11	Leicester C	35	3		
2011–12	Leicester C	36	4		
2012–13	Leicester C	42	3		
2013–14	Leicester C	40	7	230	30
2014–15	Watford	14	1		
2014–15	*Birmingham C*	18	1	18	1
2015–16	Watford	0	0	14	1
2015–16	*Burnley*	3	0	3	0
2016–17	Burton Alb	42	7		
2017–18	Burton Alb	38	7	80	14

EGERT, Tomas (D)   40 1
b. 1-8-94

Season	Club	Apps	Gls	Tot Apps	Tot Gls
2014–15	*Slovan Liberec*	0	0		
2014–15	*Spartak Trnava*	1	0	1	0
2015–16	*Slovan Liberec*	0	0		
2015–16	*Slavoj Vysehrad*	21	0	21	1
2016–17	*Slovan Liberec*	0	0		
2016–17	*Viktoria Zizkov*	15	0	15	0
2017–18	Burton Alb	3	0	3	0

FLANAGAN, Tom (D)   140 6
H: 6 2 W: 11 05 b.Hammersmith 21-10-91
Internationals: Northern Ireland U21, Full caps.

Season	Club	Apps	Gls	Tot Apps	Tot Gls
2009–10	Milton Keynes D	1	0		
2010–11	Milton Keynes D	2	0		
2011–12	Milton Keynes D	21	3		
2012–13	Milton Keynes D	0	0		
2012–13	*Gillingham*	13	1	13	1
2012–13	*Barnet*	9	0	9	0
2013–14	Milton Keynes D	7	0		
2013–14	*Stevenage*	2	0	2	0
2014–15	Milton Keynes D	6	0	37	3
2014–15	*Plymouth Arg*	4	0	4	0
2015–16	Burton Alb	18	0		
2016–17	Burton Alb	30	0		
2017–18	Burton Alb	27	2	75	2

FOX, Ben (M)   1 0
H: 5 11 W: 12 00 b.Burton upon Trent 1-2-98

Season	Club	Apps	Gls	Tot Apps	Tot Gls
2016–17	Burton Alb	1	0		
2017–18	Burton Alb	0	0	1	0

HARNESS, Marcus (M)   71 1
H: 6 0 W: 11 00 b.Coventry 1-8-94

Season	Club	Apps	Gls	Tot Apps	Tot Gls
2013–14	Burton Alb	3	0		
2014–15	Burton Alb	18	0		
2015–16	Burton Alb	5	0		
2016–17	Burton Alb	10	0		
2017–18	Burton Alb	0	0	36	0
2017–18	*Port Vale*	35	1	35	1

HUTCHINSON, Reece (D)

Season	Club	Apps	Gls	Tot Apps	Tot Gls
2017–18	Burton Alb	0	0		

LUND, Matthew (M)   182 28
H: 6 0 W: 11 13 b.Manchester 21-11-90
Internationals: Northern Ireland U21, Full caps.

Season	Club	Apps	Gls	Tot Apps	Tot Gls
2009–10	Stoke C	0	0		
2010–11	Stoke C	0	0		
2010–11	*Hereford U*	2	0	2	0
2011–12	Stoke C	0	0		
2011–12	*Oldham Ath*	3	0	3	0
2011–12	*Bristol R*	13	2		
2012–13	Stoke C	0	0		
2012–13	*Bristol R*	18	2	31	4
2012–13	*Southend U*	12	1	12	1
2013–14	Rochdale	40	8		
2014–15	Rochdale	14	2		
2015–16	Rochdale	29	1		
2016–17	Rochdale	29	9	112	20
2017–18	Burton Alb	0	0		
2017–18	Burton Alb	12	1	12	1
2017–18	*Bradford C*	10	2	10	2

McCRORY, Damien (M)   287 11
H: 6 2 W: 12 10 b.Limerick 22-2-90
Internationals: Republic of Ireland U18, U19.

Season	Club	Apps	Gls	Tot Apps	Tot Gls
2008–09	Plymouth Arg	12	0		
2008–09	*Port Vale*	12	0		
2009–10	Plymouth Arg	12	0		
2009–10	*Port Vale*	5	0	17	0
2009–10	*Grimsby T*	10	0	10	0
2009–10	*Dagenham & R*	20	0		
2010–11	*Dagenham & R*	23	0		
2011–12	*Dagenham & R*	33	1	76	1
2012–13	Burton Alb	42	1		
2013–14	Burton Alb	40	1		
2014–15	Burton Alb	34	5		
2015–16	Burton Alb	38	3		
2016–17	Burton Alb	16	0		
2017–18	Burton Alb	11	0	181	10
2017–18	*Portsmouth*	3	0	3	0

McFADZEAN, Kyle (D)   249 10
H: 6 1 W: 13 04 b.Sheffield 20-2-87
Internationals: England C.

Season	Club	Apps	Gls	Tot Apps	Tot Gls
2004–05	Sheffield U	0	0		
2005–06	Sheffield U	0	0		
2006–07	Sheffield U	0	0		
From Alfreton T					
2011–12	Crawley T	37	2		
2012–13	Crawley T	17	3		
2013–14	Crawley T	42	1	96	6
2014–15	Milton Keynes D	41	3		
2015–16	Milton Keynes D	39	0	80	3
2016–17	Burton Alb	31	1		
2017–18	Burton Alb	42	0	73	1

MILLER, Will (M)   25 1
H: 5 6 W: 10 01 b.London 8-6-96
Internationals: England U18.

Season	Club	Apps	Gls	Tot Apps	Tot Gls
2016–17	Tottenham H	0	0		
2016–17	*Burton Alb*	15	1		
2017–18	Burton Alb	10	0	25	1

NAYLOR, Tom (D)   178 13
H: 5 11 W: 11 05 b.Sutton-in-Ashfield 28-6-91

Season	Club	Apps	Gls	Tot Apps	Tot Gls
2011–12	Derby Co	8	0		
2012–13	Derby Co	0	0		
2012–13	*Bradford C*	5	0	5	0
2013–14	Derby Co	0	0		
2013–14	*Newport Co*	33	1	33	1
2014–15	Derby Co	0	0	8	0
2014–15	*Cambridge U*	8	0	8	0
2014–15	Burton Alb	17	0		
2015–16	Burton Alb	41	6		
2016–17	Burton Alb	33	3		
2017–18	Burton Alb	33	3	124	12

SBARRA, Joe (M)   18 0
H: 5 10 W: 11 00 b.Lichfield 21-12-98

Season	Club	Apps	Gls	Tot Apps	Tot Gls
2016–17	Burton Alb	1	0		
2017–18	Burton Alb	17	0	18	0

SORDELL, Marvin (F)   258 48
H: 5 9 W: 12 06 b.Pinner 17-2-91
Internationals: England U20, U21. Great Britain.

Season	Club	Apps	Gls	Tot Apps	Tot Gls
2009–10	Watford	6	1		
2009–10	*Tranmere R*	8	1	8	1
2010–11	Watford	43	12		
2011–12	Watford	26	8	75	21
2011–12	Bolton W	3	0		
2012–13	Bolton W	22	4		
2013–14	Bolton W	0	0	25	4
2013–14	*Charlton Ath*	31	7	31	7
2014–15	Burnley	14	0		
2015–16	Burnley	3	0	17	0
2015–16	*Colchester U*	21	4	21	4
2016–17	Coventry C	20	4	20	4
2016–17	Burton Alb	21	4		
2017–18	Burton Alb	40	3	61	7

TURNER, Ben (D)   266 11
H: 6 4 W: 14 04 b.Birmingham 21-1-88
Internationals: England U19.

Season	Club	Apps	Gls	Tot Apps	Tot Gls
2005–06	Coventry C	1	0		
2006–07	Coventry C	1	0		
2006–07	*Peterborough U*	8	0	8	0
2006–07	*Oldham Ath*	1	0	1	0
2007–08	Coventry C	19	0		
2008–09	Coventry C	24	0		
2009–10	Coventry C	13	0		
2010–11	Coventry C	14	4		
2011–12	Cardiff C	37	2		
2012–13	Cardiff C	31	1		
2013–14	Cardiff C	31	0		
2014–15	Cardiff C	11	0		
2015–16	Cardiff C	1	0	111	3
2015–16	*Coventry C*	5	1	77	5
2016–17	Burton Alb	39	1		
2017–18	Burton Alb	30	2	69	3

VARNEY, Luke (F)   411 72
H: 5 11 W: 11 00 b.Leicester 28-9-82

Season	Club	Apps	Gls	Tot Apps	Tot Gls
2002–03	Crewe Alex	0	0		
2003–04	Crewe Alex	8	1		
2004–05	Crewe Alex	26	4		
2005–06	Crewe Alex	27	5		
2006–07	Crewe Alex	34	17	95	27
2007–08	Charlton Ath	39	8		
2008–09	Charlton Ath	18	2	57	10
2008–09	*Sheffield W*	4	2		
2008–09	*Derby Co*	10	1		
2009–10	Derby Co	1	0		
2009–10	*Sheffield W*	39	9	43	11
2010–11	Derby Co	1	0	12	1
2010–11	*Blackpool*	30	5	30	5
2011–12	Portsmouth	30	6	30	6
2012–13	Leeds U	34	4		
2013–14	Leeds U	11	2	45	6
2013–14	*Blackburn R*	12	0		
2014–15	*Blackburn R*	11	0	23	0
2014–15	*Ipswich T*	10	1		
2015–16	Ipswich T	18	1		
2016–17	Ipswich T	15	3	43	5
2016–17	Burton Alb	15	1		
2017–18	Burton Alb	18	0	33	1

WARNOCK, Stephen (D) — 457 16
H: 5 7 W: 11 09 b.Ormskirk 12-12-81
Internationals: England Full caps.

1998-99	Liverpool	0	0		
1999-2000	Liverpool	0	0		
2000-01	Liverpool	0	0		
2001-02	Liverpool	0	0		
2002-03	Liverpool	0	0		
2002-03	Bradford C	12	1		
2003-04	Liverpool	0	0		
2003-04	Coventry C	44	3	44	3
2004-05	Liverpool	19	0		
2005-06	Liverpool	20	1		
2006-07	Liverpool	1	0	40	1
2006-07	Blackburn R	13	1		
2007-08	Blackburn R	37	1		
2008-09	Blackburn R	37	3		
2009-10	Blackburn R	1	0	88	5
2009-10	Aston Villa	30	0		
2010-11	Aston Villa	19	0		
2011-12	Aston Villa	35	2		
2012-13	Aston Villa	0	0	84	2
2012-13	Bolton W	15	0	15	0
2012-13	Leeds U	16	1		
2013-14	Leeds U	27	1		
2014-15	Leeds U	21	1	64	3
2014-15	Derby Co	7	0		
2015-16	Derby Co	20	0	27	0
2015-16	Wigan Ath	11	0		
2016-17	Wigan Ath	45	0	56	0
2017-18	Burton Alb	14	1	14	1
2017-18	Bradford C	13	0	25	1

Players retained or with offer of contract
Dinanga, Nyambu Marcus; Livesey, Jack Kinloch.

Scholars
Bromfield, Jack; Brown, Joseph Malcolm Alan; Clamp, Kyle John William; Cooke, Daniel Thomas; Davies, Jake Michael; Dowd, Charlie George; Fairbrother, Oliver Joe; Ganley, Regan Scott; Harrison, James Finley; Hart, Benjamin Ethan; Hawkins, Callum David; Hutchinson, Reece Christopher; Mallass, Noaman; Oddy, Charlie Andrew; Saville, Jacob Malcolm; Smith, Max; Thompson-Matthews, Tristan Luke; Vale, Ethan Peter William.

BURY (19)

ADAMS, Joe (M) — 2 0
b. 13-2-01
Internationals: Wales U17.

2017-18	Bury	2	0	2	0

ALDRED, Tom (D) — 224 12
H: 6 2 W: 13 02 b.Bolton 11-9-90
Internationals: Scotland U19.

2008-09	Carlisle U	0	0		
2009-10	Carlisle U	5	0	5	0
2010-11	Watford	0	0		
2010-11	Stockport Co	7	0	7	0
2011-12	Watford	0	0		
2011-12	Colchester U	0	0		
2011-12	Torquay U	0	0		
2012-13	Colchester U	0	0		
2012-13	Accrington S	13	0		
2013-14	Accrington S	46	2		
2014-15	Accrington S	25	1	84	3
2014-15	Blackpool	6	0		
2015-16	Blackpool	42	5		
2016-17	Blackpool	44	2	92	7
2017-18	Bury	19	1	19	1
2017-18	Motherwell	17	1	17	1

BECKFORD, Jermaine (F) — 358 135
H: 6 2 W: 13 02 b.Ealing 9-12-83
Internationals: Jamaica Full caps.

2005-06	Leeds U	5	0		
2006-07	Leeds U	5	0		
2006-07	Carlisle U	4	1	4	1
2006-07	Scunthorpe U	18	8	18	8
2007-08	Leeds U	40	20		
2008-09	Leeds U	34	26		
2009-10	Leeds U	42	25	126	71
2010-11	Everton	32	8		
2011-12	Everton	2	0	34	8
2011-12	Leicester C	39	9		
2012-13	Leicester C	4	0	43	9
2012-13	Huddersfield T	21	8	21	8
2013-14	Bolton W	33	7		
2014-15	Bolton W	13	0	46	7
2014-15	Preston NE	23	12		
2015-16	Preston NE	10	2		
2016-17	Preston NE	18	1	51	15
2017-18	Bury	15	8	15	8

BUNN, Harry (F) — 152 19
H: 5 9 W: 11 10 b.Oldham 25-11-92

2010-11	Manchester C	0	0		
2011-12	Manchester C	0	0		
2011-12	Rochdale	6	0	6	0
2011-12	Preston NE	1	1	1	1
2011-12	Oldham Ath	11	0	11	0
2012-13	Manchester C	0	0		
2012-13	Crewe Alex	4	0	4	0
2013-14	Manchester C	0	0		
2013-14	Sheffield U	2	0	2	0
2013-14	Huddersfield T	3	0		
2014-15	Manchester C	0	0		
2014-15	Huddersfield T	30	9		
2015-16	Huddersfield T	42	6		
2016-17	Huddersfield T	16	0	91	15
2017-18	Bury	37	3	37	3

CAMERON, Nathan (D) — 177 11
H: 6 2 W: 12 04 b.Birmingham 21-11-91
Internationals: England U20.

2009-10	Coventry C	0	0		
2010-11	Coventry C	25	0		
2011-12	Coventry C	14	0		
2012-13	Coventry C	9	0	48	0
2012-13	Northampton T	3	0	3	0
2013-14	Bury	27	4		
2014-15	Bury	46	2		
2015-16	Bury	28	3		
2016-17	Bury	4	0		
2017-18	Bury	21	2	126	11

COONEY, Ryan (M) — 12 0
b. 26-2-00

2016-17	Bury	0	0		
2017-18	Bury	12	0	12	0

DAI, Wai-Tsun (M) — 8 0
b. 24-7-99
From Reading.

2017-18	Bury	8	0	8	0

DANNS, Neil (M) — 449 70
H: 5 10 W: 10 12 b.Liverpool 23-11-82
Internationals: Guyana Full caps.

2000-01	Blackburn R	0	0		
2001-02	Blackburn R	0	0		
2002-03	Blackburn R	2	0		
2003-04	Blackpool	12	2		
2003-04	Blackburn R	1	0		
2003-04	Hartlepool U	9	1	9	1
2004-05	Blackburn R	0	0		
2004-05	Colchester U	32	11		
2005-06	Colchester U	41	8	73	19
2006-07	Birmingham C	29	3		
2007-08	Birmingham C	2	0	31	3
2007-08	Crystal Palace	4	0		
2008-09	Crystal Palace	20	2		
2009-10	Crystal Palace	42	8		
2010-11	Crystal Palace	37	8	103	18
2011-12	Leicester C	29	5		
2012-13	Leicester C	1	0		
2012-13	Bristol C	9	2	9	2
2012-13	Huddersfield T	17	2	17	2
2013-14	Leicester C	0	0	30	5
2013-14	Bolton W	33	6		
2014-15	Bolton W	41	1		
2015-16	Bolton W	32	2	106	9
2016-17	Bury	18	2		
2016-17	Blackpool	13	2	25	4
2017-18	Bury	25	5	43	7

DAWSON, Stephen (M) — 455 19
H: 5 9 W: 11 09 b.Dublin 4-12-85
Internationals: Republic of Ireland U21.

2003-04	Leicester C	0	0		
2004-05	Leicester C	0	0		
2005-06	Mansfield T	40	1		
2006-07	Mansfield T	34	1		
2007-08	Mansfield T	43	2	117	4
2008-09	Bury	43	2		
2009-10	Bury	45	4		
2010-11	Leyton Orient	40	2		
2011-12	Leyton Orient	20	1	60	3
2011-12	Barnsley	12	0		
2012-13	Barnsley	32	4		
2013-14	Barnsley	37	1	81	5
2014-15	Rochdale	30	0	30	0
2015-16	Scunthorpe U	23	0		
2016-17	Scunthorpe U	43	1	66	1
2016-17	Bury	0	0		
2017-18	Bury	13	0	101	6

EDWARDS, Phil (D) — 476 34
H: 5 8 W: 11 03 b.Bootle 8-11-85

2005-06	Wigan Ath	0	0		
2006-07	Accrington S	33	1		
2007-08	Accrington S	31	1		
2008-09	Accrington S	46	0		
2009-10	Accrington S	46	8		
2010-11	Accrington S	44	13	200	23
2011-12	Stevenage	22	0	22	0
2011-12	Rochdale	3	0		
2012-13	Rochdale	44	0	47	0
2013-14	Burton Alb	41	2		
2014-15	Burton Alb	45	6		
2015-16	Burton Alb	46	0		
2016-17	Burton Alb	0	0	132	8
2016-17	Oxford U	38	3	38	3
2017-18	Bury	37	0	37	0

EDWARDS-WILLIAMS, Mar (G) — 0 0

2017-18	Bury	0	0		

FASAN, Leonardo (G) — 25 0
H: 6 2 W: 12 13 b.San Vito al Tagliamento 4-1-94

2014-15	Celtic	0	0		
2015-16	Celtic	0	0		
2016-17	Celtic	0	0		
2016-17	Port Vale	10	0	10	0
2017-18	Bury	15	0	15	0

Transferred to Kilmarnock, February 2018.

HARKER, Rob (M) — 0 0
b. 6-3-00

2015-16	Bury	0	0		
2016-17	Bury	0	0		
2017-18	Bury	0	0		

HILL, Cameron (M) — 0 0

2017-18	Bury	0	0		

HULME, Callum (M) — 0 0
From Manchester C.

2016-17	Bury	0	0		
2017-18	Bury	0	0		

HUMPHREY, Chris (M) — 328 16
H: 5 11 W: 11 07 b.Walsall 19-9-87
Internationals: Jamaica Full caps.

2006-07	Shrewsbury T	12	0		
2007-08	Shrewsbury T	25	0		
2008-09	Shrewsbury T	37	2	74	2
2009-10	Motherwell	28	0		
2010-11	Motherwell	36	3		
2011-12	Motherwell	35	2		
2012-13	Motherwell	33	3	132	8
2013-14	Preston NE	42	2		
2014-15	Preston NE	44	4		
2015-16	Preston NE	10	0		
2016-17	Preston NE	10	0	106	6
2016-17	Hibernian	6	0	6	0
2017-18	Bury	10	0	10	0

ISMAIL, Zeli (M) — 117 12
H: 5 8 W: 11 12 b.Kukes 12-12-93
Internationals: England U16, U17.

2010-11	Wolverhampton W	0	0		
2011-12	Wolverhampton W	0	0		
2012-13	Wolverhampton W	0	0		
2012-13	Milton Keynes D	7	0	7	0
2013-14	Wolverhampton W	9	0		
2013-14	Burton Alb	15	3		
2014-15	Wolverhampton W	0	0		
2014-15	Notts Co	14	4	14	4
2015-16	Wolverhampton W	0	0	9	0
2015-16	Burton Alb	3	0	18	3
2015-16	Oxford U	5	0	5	0
2015-16	Cambridge U	11	1	11	1
2016-17	Bury	16	3		
2017-18	Bury	21	0	37	3
2017-18	Walsall	16	1	16	1

JONES, Craig (M) — 267 34
H: 5 7 W: 10 13 b.Chester 20-3-87
Internationals: Wales C.

2004-05	Airbus UK	2	2		
2005-06	Airbus UK	7	6	9	8
2007-08	Rhyl	27	8		
2008-09	Rhyl	14	2	41	10
2008-09	Connah's Quay	12	0	12	0
2009-10	New Saints FC	26	7	26	7
2010-11	Port Talbot	14	1		
2011-12	Port Talbot	7	0	21	1
2012-13	Bury	25	1		
2013-14	Bury	37	1		
2014-15	Bury	40	3		
2015-16	Bury	36	3		
2016-17	Bury	13	0		
2017-18	Bury	7	0	158	8

LEIGH, Greg (D) 130 4
H: 5 11 b.Manchester 30-9-94
Internationals: England U19.

2013–14	Manchester C	0	0	
2014–15	Manchester C	0	0	
2014–15	*Crewe Alex*	38	1	38 1
2015–16	Bradford C	6	1	6 1
2016–17	Bury	45	1	
2017–18	Bury	41	1	86 2

LOWE, Ryan (F) 592 175
H: 5 10 W: 12 08 b.Liverpool 18-9-78

2000–01	Shrewsbury T	30	4	
2001–02	Shrewsbury T	38	7	
2002–03	Shrewsbury T	39	9	
2003–04	Shrewsbury T	0	0	
2004–05	Shrewsbury T	30	3	137 23
2004–05	Chester C	8	4	
2005–06	Chester C	32	10	
2005–06	Crewe Alex	0	0	
2006–07	Crewe Alex	37	8	
2007–08	Crewe Alex	27	4	
2007–08	*Stockport Co*	4	0	4 0
2008–09	Chester C	45	16	85 30
2009–10	Bury	39	18	
2010–11	Bury	46	27	
2011–12	Bury	5	4	
2011–12	Sheffield W	26	8	
2012–13	Sheffield W	0	0	26 8
2012–13	Milton Keynes D	42	11	42 11
2013–14	Tranmere R	45	19	45 19
2013–14	Bury	0	0	
2014–15	Bury	34	9	
2015–16	Bury	19	6	
2015–16	Crewe Alex	6	2	
2016–17	Crewe Alex	22	5	92 19
2016–17	Bury	12	1	
2017–18	Bury	6	0	161 65

MAGUIRE, Chris (F) 346 63
H: 5 7 W: 10 05 b.Bellshill 16-1-89
Internationals: Scotland U16, U19, U21, Full caps.

2005–06	Aberdeen	1	0	
2006–07	Aberdeen	19	1	
2007–08	Aberdeen	28	4	
2008–09	Aberdeen	31	3	
2009–10	Aberdeen	17	1	
2009–10	*Kilmarnock*	14	4	14 4
2010–11	Aberdeen	35	7	131 16
2011–12	Derby Co	7	1	7 1
2011–12	Portsmouth	11	3	11 3
2012–13	Sheffield W	10	1	
2013–14	Sheffield W	27	9	
2013–14	Coventry C	3	2	3 2
2014–15	Sheffield W	8	8	79 18
2015–16	Rotherham U	14	0	14 0
2015–16	Oxford U	21	4	
2016–17	Oxford U	42	13	63 17
2017–18	Bury	24	2	24 2

MALONEY, Scott (G) 0 0

2017–18	Bury	0	0

MAYOR, Danny (M) 248 24
H: 6 0 W: 11 12 b.Leyland 18-10-90

2008–09	Preston NE	0	0	
2008–09	*Tranmere R*	3	0	3 0
2009–10	Preston NE	7	0	
2010–11	Preston NE	21	0	
2011–12	Preston NE	36	2	
2012–13	Preston NE	0	0	64 2
2012–13	Sheffield W	8	0	
2012–13	Southend U	5	0	5 0
2013–14	Sheffield W	0	0	8 0
2013–14	Bury	39	5	
2014–15	Bury	44	8	
2015–16	Bury	44	5	
2016–17	Bury	21	3	
2017–18	Bury	20	1	168 22

MURPHY, Joe (G) 487 0
H: 6 2 W: 13 06 b.Dublin 21-8-81
Internationals: Republic of Ireland U21, Full caps.

1999–2000	Tranmere R	21	0	
2000–01	Tranmere R	20	0	
2001–02	Tranmere R	22	0	63 0
2002–03	WBA	2	0	
2003–04	WBA	3	0	
2004–05	WBA	0	0	5 0
2004–05	Walsall	25	0	
2005–06	Sunderland	0	0	
2005–06	Walsall	14	0	39 0
2006–07	Scunthorpe U	45	0	
2007–08	Scunthorpe U	45	0	
2008–09	Scunthorpe U	42	0	
2009–10	Scunthorpe U	40	0	
2010–11	Scunthorpe U	29	0	201 0
2011–12	Coventry C	46	0	
2012–13	Coventry C	45	0	
2013–14	Coventry C	46	0	137 0
2014–15	Huddersfield T	2	0	
2014–15	*Chesterfield*	8	0	
2015–16	Huddersfield T	7	0	
2016–17	Huddersfield T	0	0	9 0
2016–17	Bury	16	0	
2017–18	Bury	17	0	33 0

NYAUPEMBE, Dougie (D) 1 0
H: 5 8 W: 10 10 b. 2-10-99

2017–18	Bury	1	0	1 0

O'CONNELL, Eoghan (D) 45 2
H: 6 1 W: 12 08 b.Cork 13-8-95
Internationals: Republic of Ireland U19, U21.

2013–14	Celtic	1	0	
2014–15	Celtic	3	0	
2015–16	Celtic	1	0	
2015–16	Oldham Ath	2	0	2 0
2016	Cork C	7	1	7 1
2016–17	Celtic	2	0	7 0
2016–17	Walsall	17	1	17 1
2017–18	Bury	12	0	12 0

O'SHEA, Jay (M) 344 67
H: 5 9 W: 12 00 b.Dun Laoghaire 10-8-88
Internationals: Republic of Ireland U19, U21, U23.

2007	Bray Wanderers	27	4	27 4
2008	Galway U	29	8	
2009	Galway U	19	3	48 11
2009–10	Birmingham C	1	0	
2009–10	*Middlesbrough*	2	0	2 0
2010–11	Birmingham C	0	0	1 0
2010–11	*Stevenage*	5	0	5 0
2010–11	*Port Vale*	5	1	5 1
2011–12	Milton Keynes D	28	5	
2012–13	Milton Keynes D	11	1	39 6
2012–13	Chesterfield	26	7	
2013–14	Chesterfield	40	9	
2014–15	Chesterfield	41	7	
2015–16	Chesterfield	46	9	
2016–17	Chesterfield	27	6	180 38
2016–17	*Sheffield U*	10	3	10 3
2017–18	Bury	27	4	27 4

REILLY, Callum (M) 127 2
H: 6 1 W: 12 03 b.Warrington 3-10-93
Internationals: Republic of Ireland U21.

2012–13	Birmingham C	18	1	
2013–14	Birmingham C	25	0	
2014–15	Birmingham C	17	1	60 2
2014–15	*Burton Alb*	2	0	
2015–16	Burton Alb	14	0	
2016–17	Burton Alb	0	0	16 0
2016–17	*Coventry C*	18	0	18 0
2017–18	Bury	18	0	18 0
2017–18	*Gillingham*	15	0	15 0

SANG, Chris (F) 2 0
b. 26-6-98
From Wigan Ath.

2017–18	Bury	2	0	2 0

SHOTTON, Saul (D) 4 0
H: 6 0 W: 11 11 b. 10-11-00

2017–18	Bury	4	0	4 0

SKARZ, Joe (D) 384 7
H: 5 10 W: 11 04 b.Huddersfield 13-7-89

2006–07	Huddersfield T	17	0	
2007–08	Huddersfield T	27	0	
2008–09	Huddersfield T	9	1	
2008–09	*Hartlepool U*	7	0	7 0
2009–10	Huddersfield T	15	0	68 1
2009–10	*Shrewsbury T*	20	0	20 0
2010–11	Bury	46	1	
2011–12	Bury	45	1	
2012–13	Bury	39	2	
2012–13	Rotherham U	8	0	
2013–14	Rotherham U	41	2	
2014–15	Rotherham U	17	0	66 2
2014–15	Oxford U	18	0	
2015–16	Oxford U	41	0	
2016–17	Oxford U	30	0	89 0
2017–18	Bury	4	0	134 4

STYLES, Callum (F) 25 0
b. 28-3-00

2015–16	Bury	1	0	
2016–17	Bury	13	0	
2017–18	Bury	11	0	25 0

THOMPSON, Adam (D) 170 4
H: 6 2 W: 12 10 b.Harlow 28-9-92
Internationals: Northern Ireland U17, U19, U21, Full caps.

2010–11	Watford	10	1	
2011–12	Watford	0	0	
2011–12	*Brentford*	20	0	20 0
2012–13	Watford	4	0	
2012–13	*Wycombe W*	2	0	2 0
2012–13	*Barnet*	1	0	1 0
2013–14	Watford	0	0	14 1
2013–14	Southend U	16	0	
2014–15	Southend U	28	0	
2015–16	Southend U	25	2	
2016–17	Southend U	40	1	109 3
2017–18	Bury	15	0	15 0
2017–18	*Bradford C*	9	0	9 0

TUTTE, Andrew (M) 228 21
H: 5 9 W: 10 10 b.Huyton 21-9-90
Internationals: England U19, U20.

2007–08	Manchester C	0	0	
2008–09	Manchester C	0	0	
2009–10	Manchester C	0	0	
2010–11	Manchester C	0	0	
2010–11	Rochdale	7	0	
2010–11	*Shrewsbury T*	2	0	2 0
2010–11	*Yeovil T*	5	2	15 2
2011–12	Rochdale	40	1	
2012–13	Rochdale	37	7	
2013–14	Rochdale	11	2	95 10
2013–14	Bury	19	1	
2014–15	Bury	42	3	
2015–16	Bury	22	4	
2016–17	Bury	17	1	
2017–18	Bury	16	0	116 9

Players retained or with offer of contract
Burgess, Scott Andrew.

Scholars
Adams, Joseph; Allardyce, Sam Craig; Alli, Millenic Oluwole Sulaiman; Cooney, Ryan Thomas; Dasilva-Olajide, Wealth Abraham; Edwards-Williams, Mark Brendan; Erskine, Calum Andrew; Hatton, Jack Andrew; Hill, Cameron Taylor; Hulme, Callum Jake; Mulgrew, Charlie Dean; Nyaupembe, Douglas Nqobile; Shotton, Saul.

CAMBRIDGE U (20)

AMOO, David (F) 159 21
H: 5 10 W: 12 03 b.Southwark 23-4-91

2007–08	Liverpool	0	0	
2008–09	Liverpool	0	0	
2009–10	Liverpool	0	0	
2010–11	Liverpool	0	0	
2010–11	*Milton Keynes D*	3	0	3 0
2010–11	*Hull C*	7	1	7 1
2011–12	Liverpool	0	0	
2011–12	Bury	27	4	27 4
2012–13	Preston NE	17	0	17 0
2012–13	Tranmere R	11	1	
2013–14	Tranmere R	8	0	11 1
2013–14	Carlisle U	43	8	
2014–15	Carlisle U	27	5	70 13
2017–18	Cambridge U	24	2	24 2

AZEEZ, Adebayo (F) 165 19
H: 6 0 W: 12 07 b.Orpington 8-1-94
Internationals: England U19.

2012–13	Charlton Ath	0	0	
2012–13	*Wycombe W*	4	0	4 0
2012–13	*Leyton Orient*	1	0	1 0
2013–14	Charlton Ath	0	0	
2013–14	*Torquay U*	9	2	9 2
2013–14	*Dagenham & R*	15	3	15 3
2014–15	AFC Wimbledon	43	5	
2015–16	AFC Wimbledon	42	7	85 12
2016–17	Partick Thistle	38	2	38 2
2017–18	Cambridge U	13	0	13 0

BROWN, Jevani (M) 41 6
b. 16-10-94
Internationals: Jamaica U17.

2013–14	Peterborough U	0	0	
2014–15	Peterborough U	0	0	
2017–18	Cambridge U	41	6	41 6

CARROLL, Jake (D) 170 3
H: 6 0 W: 12 03 b.Dublin 11-1-91
Internationals: Republic of Ireland U18.

2011	St Patricks	7	0	
2012	St Patricks	19	1	
2013	St Patricks	7	0	33 1
2013–14	Huddersfield T	4	0	

2013–14	Bury	6	1	6	1
2014–15	Huddersfield T	2	0	6	0
2014–15	*Partick Thistle*	10	0	10	0
2015–16	Hartlepool U	41	1		
2016–17	Hartlepool U	21	0	62	1
2016–17	Cambridge U	20	0		
2017–18	Cambridge U	33	0	53	0

CORR, Barry (F)   284 81
H: 6 3   W: 12 07   b.Co Wicklow 2-4-85

2001–02	Leeds U	0	0		
2002–03	Leeds U	0	0		
2003–04	Leeds U	0	0		
2004–05	Leeds U	0	0		
2005–06	Sheffield W	16	0		
2006–07	Sheffield W	1	0	17	0
2006–07	Bristol C	3	0	3	0
2006–07	Swindon T	8	3		
2007–08	Swindon T	17	5		
2008–09	Swindon T	11	2	36	10
2009–10	Exeter C	34	3	34	3
2010–11	Southend U	41	18		
2011–12	Southend U	0	0		
2012–13	Southend U	32	6		
2013–14	Southend U	43	12		
2014–15	Southend U	39	14	155	50
2015–16	Cambridge U	22	12		
2016–17	Cambridge U	7	2		
2017–18	Cambridge U	10	4	39	18

DARLING, Harry (D)   3 0
H: 5 11   W: 11 11   b. 8-8-99

2016–17	Cambridge U	0	0		
2017–18	Cambridge U	3	0	3	0

DAVIES, Leon (D)   9 0
b. 21-11-99

2015–16	Cambridge U	0	0		
2016–17	Cambridge U	5	0		
2017–18	Cambridge U	4	0	9	0

DEEGAN, Gary (M)   318 18
H: 5 9   W: 11 11   b.Dublin 28-9-87

2005–06	Shelbourne	0	0		
2006	Kilkenny City	18	4	18	4
2007	Longford Town	30	3	30	3
2008	Galway U	17	0	17	0
2008	Bohemians	12	3	12	3
2009	Bohemians	23	2	23	2
2009–10	Coventry C	17	2		
2010–11	Coventry C	1	0		
2011–12	Coventry C	24	3	42	5
2012–13	Hibernian	20	0	20	0
2013–14	Northampton T	27	1	27	1
2014–15	Southend U	22	0		
2015–16	Southend U	25	0	47	0
2016–17	Shrewsbury T	40	0	40	0
2017–18	Cambridge U	42	0	42	0

DUNK, Harrison (M)   152 10
H: 6 0   W: 11 07   b. 25-10-90

2014–15	Cambridge U	32	2		
2015–16	Cambridge U	45	4		
2016–17	Cambridge U	38	2		
2017–18	Cambridge U	37	2	152	10

ELITO, Medy (M)   251 33
H: 6 2   W: 13 00   b.Kinshasa 20-3-90
Internationals: England U17, U18, U19.

2007–08	Colchester U	11	1		
2008–09	Colchester U	5	0		
2009–10	Colchester U	3	0		
2009–10	*Cheltenham T*	12	3		
2010–11	Colchester U	0	0	19	1
2010–11	Dagenham & R	10	2		
2010–11	*Cheltenham T*	2	0	14	3
2011–12	Dagenham & R	24	4		
2012–13	Dagenham & R	46	6		
2013–14	Dagenham & R	45	7	125	19
2015–16	Newport Co	38	1	38	1
2016–17	Cambridge U	23	5		
2017–18	Cambridge U	32	4	55	9

FORDE, David (G)   484 0
H: 6 3   W: 13 06   b.Galway 20-12-79
Internationals: Republic of Ireland Full caps.

2001–02	West Ham U	0	0		
2002–03	West Ham U	0	0		
2003–04	West Ham U	0	0		
2004	Derry C	11	0		
2005	Derry C	33	0		
2006	Derry C	29	0	73	0
2006–07	Cardiff C	7	0		
2007–08	Cardiff C	0	0	7	0
2007–08	*Luton T*	5	0	5	0
2007–08	*Bournemouth*	11	0	11	0
2008–09	Millwall	46	0		
2009–10	Millwall	46	0		
2010–11	Millwall	46	0		

2011–12	Millwall	27	0		
2012–13	Millwall	40	0		
2013–14	Millwall	40	0		
2014–15	Millwall	46	0		
2015–16	Millwall	8	0		
2016–17	Millwall	0	0	299	0
2016–17	Portsmouth	46	0	46	0
2017–18	Cambridge U	43	0	43	0

FOY, Matt (F)   0 0

2014–15	Cambridge U	0	0		
2015–16	Cambridge U	0	0		
2016–17	Cambridge U	0	0		
2017–18	Cambridge U	0	0		

HALLIDAY, Bradley (M)   135 3
H: 5 11   W: 10 10   b.Redcar 10-7-95

2013–14	Middlesbrough	0	0		
2014–15	Middlesbrough	0	0		
2014–15	York C	24	1	24	1
2015–16	Middlesbrough	0	0		
2015–16	Hartlepool U	6	0	6	0
2015–16	Accrington S	32	0	32	0
2016–17	Middlesbrough	0	0		
2016–17	Cambridge U	30	1		
2017–18	Cambridge U	43	1	73	2

IBEHRE, Jabo (F)   559 117
H: 6 3   W: 13 13   b.Islington 28-1-83

1999–2000	Leyton Orient	3	0		
2000–01	Leyton Orient	5	2		
2001–02	Leyton Orient	28	4		
2002–03	Leyton Orient	25	5		
2003–04	Leyton Orient	35	4		
2004–05	Leyton Orient	19	2		
2005–06	Leyton Orient	33	8		
2006–07	Leyton Orient	30	4		
2007–08	Leyton Orient	31	7	209	36
2008–09	Walsall	39	10	39	10
2009–10	Milton Keynes D	10	1		
2009–10	Southend U	4	0	4	0
2009–10	Stockport Co	20	5	20	5
2010–11	Milton Keynes D	42	3		
2011–12	Milton Keynes D	39	8		
2012–13	Milton Keynes D	3	0	94	12
2012–13	Colchester U	30	8		
2013–14	Colchester U	37	8		
2014–15	Colchester U	5	0	72	16
2014–15	Oldham Ath	11	2	11	2
2014–15	Barnsley	9	2	9	2
2015–16	Carlisle U	36	15		
2016–17	Carlisle U	38	12	74	27
2017–18	Cambridge U	27	7	27	7

IKPEAZU, Uche (F)   141 30
H: 6 3   W: 12 04   b.London 28-2-95

2013–14	Watford	0	0		
2013–14	Crewe Alex	15	4		
2014–15	Watford	0	0		
2014–15	Crewe Alex	17	2	32	6
2014–15	Doncaster R	7	0	7	0
2015–16	Watford	0	0		
2015–16	Port Vale	21	5	21	5
2015–16	Blackpool	12	0	12	0
2016–17	Cambridge U	29	6		
2017–18	Cambridge U	40	13	69	19

IRON, Finley (G)   0 0

2016–17	Cambridge U	0	0		
2017–18	Cambridge U	0	0		

KNOWLES, Tom (M)   1 0

2017–18	Cambridge U	1	0	1	0

LEGGE, Leon (D)   285 28
H: 6 1   W: 11 02   b.Bexhill 1-7-85

2009–10	Brentford	29	2		
2010–11	Brentford	30	3		
2011–12	Brentford	28	4		
2012–13	Brentford	7	0	94	9
2012–13	Gillingham	22	2		
2013–14	Gillingham	37	2		
2014–15	Gillingham	22	4	81	8
2015–16	Cambridge U	39	3		
2016–17	Cambridge U	44	5		
2017–18	Cambridge U	27	2	110	11

LEWIS, Paul (M)   25 1
H: 6 1   W: 11 00   b. 17-12-94
Internationals: England C.
From Macclesfield T.

2016–17	Cambridge U	13	0		
2017–18	Cambridge U	12	1	25	1

MARIS, George (F)   66 14
b.Sheffield 6-3-96

2014–15	Barnsley	2	0		
2015–16	Barnsley	1	0	3	0
2016–17	Cambridge U	23	4		
2017–18	Cambridge U	40	10	63	14

MINGOIA, Piero (M)   193 18
H: 5 6   W: 10 12   b.Enfield 20-10-91

2010–11	Watford	5	0		
2011–12	Watford	0	0		
2011–12	*Brentford*	0	0		
2012–13	Watford	0	0		
2012–13	*Accrington S*	7	1		
2013–14	Watford	0	0	5	0
2013–14	Accrington S	37	1		
2014–15	Accrington S	36	8		
2015–16	Accrington S	46	3	126	13
2016–17	Cambridge U	40	5		
2017–18	Cambridge U	22	0	62	5

MITOV, Dimitar (G)   3 0
H: 6 2   W: 12 03   b. 22-1-97
Internationals: Bulgaria U16, U17, U19, U21.

2014–15	Charlton Ath	0	0		
2015–16	Charlton Ath	0	0		
2016–17	Charlton Ath	0	0		
2017–18	Cambridge U	3	0	3	0

NORVILLE-WILLIAMS, Jordan (D)   0 0
From Arsenal.

2017–18	Cambridge U	0	0		

O'NEIL, Liam (D)   121 5
H: 6 0   W: 12 00   b.Cambridge 31-7-93

2011–12	WBA	0	0		
2011–12	*VPS*	14	0	14	0
2012–13	WBA	0	0		
2013–14	WBA	3	0		
2014–15	WBA	0	0	3	0
2014–15	Scunthorpe U	22	2	22	2
2015–16	Chesterfield	26	0		
2016–17	Chesterfield	17	2	43	2
2016–17	Cambridge U	13	1		
2017–18	Cambridge U	26	0	39	1

OSAOABE, Emmanuel (M)   49 3
b.Dundalk 1-10-96

2015–16	Gillingham	18	2		
2016–17	Gillingham	24	1	42	3
2017–18	Cambridge U	4	0	4	0
2017–18	*Newport Co*	3	0	3	0

SQUIRE, Sam (M)   0 0

2017–18	Cambridge U	0	0		

TAYLOR, Greg (D)   138 3
H: 6 1   W: 12 02   b.Bedford 15-1-90
Internationals: England C.

2008–09	Northampton T	0	0		
2014–15	Cambridge U	43	0		
2015–16	Cambridge U	16	0		
2016–17	Cambridge U	36	2		
2017–18	Cambridge U	43	1	138	3

WORMAN, Ben (M)   0 0

2017–18	Cambridge U	0	0		

Players retained or with offer of contract
Watkins, Lee Jacob.

Scholars
Bennett, Sam; Foxall, Craig Thomas; Goode, Samuel Joshua; Hasani, Inglian; Jeche, Joshua Tanatswa; Johnson, Charlie Alexander; Michael, Kaidyn; Mutswunguma, Prince Karikoga; Neal, Joe; Norville-Williams, Jordan Zion Wilford Jr; Shaw, Stevan; Squire, Samuel Joseph; Worman, Ben.

CARDIFF C (21)

BAMBA, Souleymane (D)   318 18
H: 6 3   W: 14 02   b.Ivry-sur-Seine 13-1-85
Internationals: Ivory Coast Full caps.

2004–05	Paris St Germain	1	0		
2005–06	Paris St Germain	0	0	1	0
2006–07	Dunfermline Ath	23	0		
2007–08	Dunfermline Ath	15	0		
2008–09	Dunfermline Ath	1	0	39	0
2008–09	Hibernian	29	0		
2009–10	Hibernian	30	2		
2010–11	Hibernian	16	2	75	4
2010–11	Leicester C	16	2		
2011–12	Leicester C	36	1	52	3
2012–13	Trabzonspor	18	0		
2013–14	Trabzonspor	9	0	27	0
2014–15	Palermo	1	0	1	0
2014–15	*Leeds U*	19	1		
2015–16	Leeds U	30	4		
2016–17	Leeds U	2	0	51	5
2016–17	Cardiff C	26	2		
2017–18	Cardiff C	46	4	72	6

BENNETT, Joe (D) — 221 6
H: 5 10 W: 10 04 b.Rochdale 28-3-90
Internationals: England U19, U20, U21.

2008–09	Middlesbrough	1	0		
2009–10	Middlesbrough	12	0		
2010–11	Middlesbrough	31	0		
2011–12	Middlesbrough	41	1		
2012–13	Middlesbrough	0	0	85	1
2012–13	Aston Villa	25	0		
2013–14	Aston Villa	5	0		
2014–15	Brighton & HA	41	1	41	1
2015–16	Aston Villa	0	0		
2015–16	Bournemouth	0	0		
2015–16	Sheffield W	3	0	3	0
2016–17	Aston Villa	0	0	30	0
2016–17	Cardiff C	24	3		
2017–18	Cardiff C	38	1	62	4

BOGLE, Omar (F) — 60 26
H: 6 3 W: 12 08 b.Birmingham 26-7-92
Internationals: England C
From Hinckley U, Solihull Moors.

2016–17	Grimsby T	27	19	27	19
2016–17	Wigan Ath	14	3	14	3
2017–18	Cardiff C	10	3	10	3
2017–18	Peterborough U	9	1	9	1

CAMP, Lee (G) — 459 0
H: 5 11 W: 11 11 b.Derby 22-8-84
Internationals: England U21. Northern Ireland Full caps.

2002–03	Derby Co	1	0		
2003–04	Derby Co	0	0		
2003–04	QPR	12	0		
2004–05	Derby Co	45	0		
2005–06	Derby Co	40	0		
2006–07	Derby Co	3	0	89	0
2006–07	Norwich C	3	0		
2006–07	QPR	11	0		
2007–08	QPR	46	0		
2008–09	QPR	4	0	73	0
2008–09	Nottingham F	15	0		
2009–10	Nottingham F	45	0		
2010–11	Nottingham F	46	0		
2011–12	Nottingham F	46	0		
2012–13	Nottingham F	26	0	178	0
2012–13	Norwich C	3	0	6	0
2013–14	WBA	0	0		
2013–14	Bournemouth	33	0		
2014–15	Bournemouth	9	0		
2015–16	Bournemouth	0	0	42	0
2015–16	Rotherham U	41	0		
2016–17	Rotherham U	18	0	59	0
2017–18	Cardiff C	0	0		
2017–18	Sunderland	12	0	12	0

CONNOLLY, Matthew (D) — 286 13
H: 6 1 W: 11 03 b.Barnet 24-9-87

2005–06	Arsenal	0	0		
2006–07	Arsenal	0	0		
2006–07	Bournemouth	5	1	5	1
2007–08	Arsenal	0	0		
2007–08	Colchester U	16	2	16	2
2007–08	QPR	20	0		
2008–09	QPR	35	0		
2009–10	QPR	19	2		
2010–11	QPR	36	0		
2011–12	QPR	6	0		
2011–12	Reading	6	0	6	0
2012–13	QPR	0	0	116	2
2012–13	Cardiff C	36	5		
2013–14	Cardiff C	3	0		
2014–15	Cardiff C	23	0		
2014–15	Watford	6	1	6	1
2015–16	Cardiff C	43	1		
2016–17	Cardiff C	28	1		
2017–18	Cardiff C	4	0	137	7

COXE, Cameron (D) — 0 0
b. 18-12-98
Internationals: Wales U17, U19, U20, U21.

2017–18	Cardiff C	0	0		

DAMOUR, Loic (M) — 204 8
H: 5 11 W: 11 09 b.Soissy 8-1-91
Internationals: France U16, U17, U18, U19, U20.

2008–09	Strasbourg	5	0		
2009–10	Strasbourg	5	0		
2010–11	Strasbourg	34	1	44	1
2011–12	Boulogne	17	0		
2012–13	Boulogne	1	0	18	0
2012–13	RWDM Brussels	6	0	6	0
2013–14	White Star Brussels	9	0	9	0
2014–15	Saint-Raphael	31	3	31	3
2015–16	Bourg-en-Bresse	33	2		
2016–17	Bourg-en-Bresse	36	2	69	4
2017–18	Cardiff C	27	0	27	0

ECUELE MANGA, Bruno (D) — 287 13
H: 6 2 W: 11 11 b.Libreville 16-7-88
Internationals: Gabon Full caps.

2008–09	Angers	29	1		
2009–10	Angers	28	3	57	4
2010–11	Lorient	31	1		
2011–12	Lorient	32	2		
2012–13	Lorient	17	0		
2013–14	Lorient	35	1		
2014–15	Lorient	3	0	118	4
2014–15	Cardiff C	29	3		
2015–16	Cardiff C	24	2		
2016–17	Cardiff C	21	0		
2017–18	Cardiff C	38	0	112	5

ETHERIDGE, Neil (G) — 146 0
H: 6 3 W: 14 00 b.Enfield 7-2-90
Internationals: England U16. Philippines Full caps.

2008–09	Fulham	0	0		
2009–10	Fulham	0	0		
2010–11	Fulham	0	0		
2011–12	Fulham	0	0		
2012–13	Fulham	0	0		
2012–13	Bristol R	12	0	12	0
2013–14	Fulham	0	0		
2013–14	Crewe Alex	4	0	4	0
2014–15	Oldham Ath	0	0		
2014–15	Charlton Ath	4	0	4	0
2015–16	Walsall	40	0		
2016–17	Walsall	41	0	81	0
2017–18	Cardiff C	45	0	45	0

GOUNONGBE, Frederic (F) — 176 77
H: 6 3 W: 13 05 b.Brussels 1-5-88
Internationals: Benin Full caps.

2009–10	Woluwe-Aventem	23	10		
2010–11	Woluwe-Aventem	15	6		
2011–12	Woluwe-Aventem	33	19	71	35
2012–13	Zulte-Waregem	0	0		
2012–13	RWDM Brussels	28	9		
2013–14	RWDM Brussels	18	11	46	20
2014–15	Westerlo	17	9		
2015–16	Westerlo	28	13	45	22
2016–17	Cardiff C	11	0		
2017–18	Cardiff C	3	0	14	0

GUNNARSSON, Aron (M) — 366 30
H: 5 9 W: 11 00 b.Akureyri 22-9-89
Internationals: Iceland U17, U19, U21, Full caps.

2007–08	AZ	1	0	1	0
2008–09	Coventry C	40	1		
2009–10	Coventry C	40	1		
2010–11	Coventry C	42	4	122	6
2011–12	Cardiff C	42	5		
2012–13	Cardiff C	45	8		
2013–14	Cardiff C	23	1		
2014–15	Cardiff C	45	4		
2015–16	Cardiff C	28	2		
2016–17	Cardiff C	40	3		
2017–18	Cardiff C	20	1	243	24

HALFORD, Greg (D) — 454 45
H: 6 4 W: 12 10 b.Chelmsford 8-12-84
Internationals: England U20.

2002–03	Colchester U	1	0		
2003–04	Colchester U	18	4		
2004–05	Colchester U	44	4		
2005–06	Colchester U	41	5		
2006–07	Colchester U	28	3	136	18
2006–07	Reading	3	0	3	0
2007–08	Sunderland	8	0		
2007–08	Charlton Ath	16	2	16	2
2008–09	Sunderland	0	0		
2008–09	Sheffield U	41	4	41	4
2009–10	Sunderland	0	0	8	0
2009–10	Wolverhampton W	15	0		
2010–11	Wolverhampton W	2	0	17	0
2010–11	Portsmouth	33	5		
2011–12	Portsmouth	42	7	75	12
2012–13	Nottingham F	3	0		
2013–14	Nottingham F	36	4		
2014–15	Nottingham F	0	0	73	7
2014–15	Brighton & HA	19	0	19	0
2015–16	Rotherham U	21	2		
2015–16	Birmingham C	3	0	3	0
2016–17	Rotherham U	14	0	35	2
2016–17	Cardiff C	16	0		
2017–18	Cardiff C	12	0	28	0

HARRIS, Kedeem (M) — 97 6
H: 5 9 W: 10 08 b.Westminster 8-6-93

2009–10	Wycombe W	2	0		
2010–11	Wycombe W	0	0		
2011–12	Wycombe W	17	0	19	0
2011–12	Cardiff C	0	0		
2012–13	Cardiff C	0	0		
2013–14	Cardiff C	0	0		
2013–14	Brentford	10	1	10	1
2014–15	Cardiff C	14	1		
2015–16	Cardiff C	3	0		
2015–16	Barnsley	11	0	11	0
2016–17	Cardiff C	37	4		
2017–18	Cardiff C	3	0	57	5

HARRIS, Mark (M) — 2 0
b. 29-12-98
Internationals: Wales U17, U19, U20, U21.

2016–17	Cardiff C	2	0		
2017–18	Cardiff C	0	0	2	0

HEALEY, Rhys (M) — 56 12
H: 5 8 W: 10 10 b.Manchester 6-12-94

2012–13	Cardiff C	0	0		
2013–14	Cardiff C	1	0		
2014–15	Cardiff C	0	0		
2014–15	Colchester U	21	4	21	4
2015–16	Cardiff C	0	0		
2015–16	Dundee	7	1	7	1
2016–17	Newport Co	17	6	17	6
2016–17	Cardiff C	7	1		
2017–18	Cardiff C	3	0	11	1

HOILETT, Junior (M) — 305 41
H: 5 8 W: 11 00 b.Ottawa 5-6-90
Internationals: Canada Full caps.

2007–08	Blackburn R	0	0		
2007–08	Paderborn	12	1	12	1
2008–09	Blackburn R	0	0		
2008–09	St Pauli	21	6	21	6
2009–10	Blackburn R	23	0		
2010–11	Blackburn R	24	5		
2011–12	Blackburn R	34	7	81	12
2012–13	QPR	26	1		
2013–14	QPR	35	4		
2014–15	QPR	22	0		
2015–16	QPR	29	6		
2016–17	QPR	0	0	112	11
2016–17	Cardiff C	33	2		
2017–18	Cardiff C	46	9	79	11

KENNEDY, Matthew (M) — 118 9
H: 5 9 W: 10 02 b.Irvine 1-11-94
Internationals: Scotland U16, U17, U18, U19, U21.

2011–12	Kilmarnock	11	0		
2012–13	Kilmarnock	3	0	14	0
2012–13	Everton	0	0		
2013–14	Everton	0	0		
2013–14	Tranmere R	8	0	8	0
2013–14	Milton Keynes D	7	1	7	1
2014–15	Everton	0	0		
2014–15	Hibernian	13	0	13	0
2014–15	Cardiff C	14	0		
2015–16	Cardiff C	1	0		
2015–16	Port Vale	12	0	12	0
2016–17	Cardiff C	2	0		
2016–17	Plymouth Arg	17	5	17	5
2017–18	Cardiff C	1	0	18	0
2017–18	Portsmouth	29	3	29	3

MADINE, Gary (F) — 323 71
H: 6 1 W: 12 00 b.Gateshead 24-8-90

2007–08	Carlisle U	11	0		
2008–09	Carlisle U	14	1		
2008–09	Rochdale	3	0	3	0
2009–10	Carlisle U	20	4		
2009–10	Coventry C	9	0		
2009–10	Chesterfield	4	0	4	0
2010–11	Carlisle U	21	8		
2010–11	Sheffield W	22	5		
2011–12	Sheffield W	38	18		
2012–13	Sheffield W	30	3		
2013–14	Sheffield W	1	0		
2013–14	Carlisle U	5	2	71	15
2014–15	Sheffield W	10	0	101	26
2014–15	Coventry C	11	3	20	3
2014–15	Blackpool	15	3	15	3
2015–16	Bolton W	32	5		
2016–17	Bolton W	36	9		
2017–18	Bolton W	28	10	96	24
2017–18	Cardiff C	13	0	13	0

MEITE, Ibrahim (F) — 20 2
H: 6 1 W: 11 05 b.Wandsworth 1-6-96

2016–17	Cardiff C	1	0		
2017–18	Cardiff C	0	0	1	0
2017–18	Crawley T	19	2	19	2

MENDEZ-LAING, Nathaniel (M) — 227 32
H: 5 10 W: 11 12 b.Birmingham 15-4-92
Internationals: England U16, U17.

2009–10	Wolverhampton W	0	0		
2010–11	Wolverhampton W	0	0		
2010–11	Peterborough U	33	5		
2011–12	Wolverhampton W	0	0		

2011–12	Sheffield U	8	1	8	1
2012–13	Peterborough U	21	3		
2012–13	Portsmouth	8	0	8	0
2013–14	Peterborough U	16	1		
2013–14	Shrewsbury T	6	0	6	0
2014–15	Peterborough U	14	0	84	9
2014–15	Cambridge U	11	1	11	1
2015–16	Rochdale	33	7		
2016–17	Rochdale	39	8	72	15
2017–18	Cardiff C	38	6	38	6

MORRISON, Sean (D)   269 31
H: 6 4   W: 14 00   b.Plymouth 8-1-91

2007–08	Swindon T	2	0		
2008–09	Swindon T	20	1		
2009–10	Swindon T	9	1		
2009–10	Southend U	8	0	8	0
2010–11	Swindon T	19	4	50	6
2010–11	Reading	0	0		
2010–11	Huddersfield T	0	0		
2011–12	Reading	0	0		
2011–12	Huddersfield T	19	1	19	1
2012–13	Reading	16	2		
2013–14	Reading	21	1		
2014–15	Reading	1	1	38	4
2014–15	Cardiff C	41	6		
2015–16	Cardiff C	30	3		
2016–17	Cardiff C	44	4		
2017–18	Cardiff C	39	7	154	20

MURPHY, Brian (G)   160 0
H: 6 0   W: 13 00   b.Waterford 7-5-83
Internationals: Republic of Ireland U16.

2000–01	Manchester C	0	0		
2001–02	Manchester C	0	0		
2002–03	Manchester C	0	0		
2002–03	Oldham Ath	0	0		
2002–03	Peterborough U	1	0	1	0
From Waterford					
2003–04	Swansea C	11	0		
2004–05	Swansea C	2	0		
2005–06	Swansea C	0	0		
2006–07	Swansea C	0	0	13	0
2007	Bohemians	29	0		
2008	Bohemians	33	0		
2009	Bohemians	35	0	97	0
2009–10	Ipswich T	16	0		
2010–11	Ipswich T	4	0		
2011–12	Ipswich T	0	0	20	0
2011–12	QPR	0	0		
2012–13	QPR	0	0		
2013–14	QPR	2	0		
2014–15	QPR	0	0	2	0
2015–16	Portsmouth	21	0		
2016–17	Portsmouth	0	0	21	0
2016–17	Cardiff C	5	0		
2017–18	Cardiff C	1	0	6	0

O'KEEFE, Stuart (M)   127 7
H: 5 8   W: 10 00   b.Eye 4-3-91

2008–09	Southend U	3	0		
2009–10	Southend U	7	0		
2010–11	Southend U	0	0	10	0
2010–11	Crystal Palace	4	0		
2011–12	Crystal Palace	13	0		
2012–13	Crystal Palace	5	0		
2013–14	Crystal Palace	12	1		
2014–15	Crystal Palace	2	0	36	1
2014–15	Blackpool	4	0	4	0
2014–15	Cardiff C	6	0		
2015–16	Cardiff C	24	2		
2016–17	Cardiff C	8	0		
2016–17	Milton Keynes D	18	4	18	4
2017–18	Cardiff C	0	0	38	2
2017–18	Portsmouth	21	0	21	0

PATERSON, Callum (D)   169 43
H: 6 0   W: 12 00   b.London 13-10-94
Internationals: Scotland U18, U19, U21, Full caps.

2012–13	Hearts	22	3		
2013–14	Hearts	37	11		
2014–15	Hearts	29	6		
2015–16	Hearts	29	5		
2016–17	Hearts	20	8	137	33
2017–18	Cardiff C	32	10	32	10

PELTIER, Lee (D)   394 5
H: 5 10   W: 12 00   b.Liverpool 11-12-86
Internationals: England U18.

2004–05	Liverpool	0	0		
2005–06	Liverpool	0	0		
2006–07	Liverpool	0	0		
2006–07	Hull C	7	0	7	0
2007–08	Liverpool	0	0		
2007–08	Yeovil T	34	0		
2008–09	Yeovil T	35	1	69	1
2009–10	Huddersfield T	42	0		
2010–11	Huddersfield T	38	1		
2011–12	Leicester C	40	2		
2012–13	Leicester C	0	0	40	2
2012–13	Leeds U	41	0		
2013–14	Leeds U	25	1	66	1
2013–14	Nottingham F	7	0	7	0
2014–15	Huddersfield T	11	0	91	1
2014–15	Cardiff C	15	0		
2015–16	Cardiff C	41	0		
2016–17	Cardiff C	28	0		
2017–18	Cardiff C	30	0	114	0

PILKINGTON, Anthony (M)   345 69
H: 5 11   W: 12 00   b.Blackburn 3-11-87
Internationals: Republic of Ireland U21, Full caps.

2006–07	Stockport Co	24	5		
2007–08	Stockport Co	29	6		
2008–09	Stockport Co	24	5	77	16
2008–09	Huddersfield T	16	2		
2009–10	Huddersfield T	43	7		
2010–11	Huddersfield T	31	10	90	19
2011–12	Norwich C	30	8		
2012–13	Norwich C	30	5		
2013–14	Norwich C	15	1	75	14
2014–15	Cardiff C	20	1		
2015–16	Cardiff C	41	9		
2016–17	Cardiff C	34	7		
2017–18	Cardiff C	8	3	103	20

RALLS, Joe (M)   201 20
H: 5 10   W: 11 00   b.Farnborough 13-10-93
Internationals: England U19.

2011–12	Cardiff C	10	1		
2012–13	Cardiff C	4	0		
2013–14	Cardiff C	0	0		
2013–14	Yeovil T	37	3	37	3
2014–15	Cardiff C	28	2		
2015–16	Cardiff C	43	1		
2016–17	Cardiff C	42	6		
2017–18	Cardiff C	37	7	164	17

RICHARDS, Ashley (M)   127 0
H: 6 1   W: 12 04   b.Swansea 12-4-91
Internationals: Wales U17, U19, U21, Full caps.

2009–10	Swansea C	15	0		
2010–11	Swansea C	6	0		
2011–12	Swansea C	8	0		
2012–13	Swansea C	0	0		
2012–13	Crystal Palace	11	0	11	0
2013–14	Swansea C	0	0		
2013–14	Huddersfield T	9	0	9	0
2014–15	Swansea C	10	0	39	0
2014–15	Fulham	14	0		
2015–16	Fulham	22	0	36	0
2016–17	Cardiff C	26	0		
2017–18	Cardiff C	6	0	32	0

TOMLIN, Lee (F)   281 60
H: 5 11   W: 11 09   b.Leicester 12-1-89
Internationals: England C.

2010–11	Peterborough U	37	8		
2011–12	Peterborough U	37	8		
2012–13	Peterborough U	42	11		
2013–14	Peterborough U	19	5	135	32
2013–14	Middlesbrough	14	4		
2014–15	Middlesbrough	42	7	56	11
2015–16	Bournemouth	6	0	6	0
2015–16	Bristol C	18	6		
2016–17	Bristol C	38	6	56	12
2017–18	Cardiff C	13	1	13	1
2017–18	Nottingham F	15	4	15	4

WARD, Danny (M)   298 47
H: 5 11   W: 12 05   b.Bradford 11-12-91

2008–09	Bolton W	0	0		
2009–10	Bolton W	2	0		
2009–10	Swindon T	28	7	28	7
2010–11	Bolton W	0	0	2	0
2010–11	Coventry C	5	0	5	0
2010–11	Huddersfield T	7	3		
2011–12	Huddersfield T	39	4		
2012–13	Huddersfield T	28	2		
2013–14	Huddersfield T	38	10		
2014–15	Huddersfield T	12	0	124	19
2014–15	Rotherham U	16	3		
2015–16	Rotherham U	34	4		
2016–17	Rotherham U	41	10	91	17
2017–18	Cardiff C	18	4	18	4

WILSON, Ben (G)   24 0
H: 6 1   W: 11 09   b.Stanley 9-8-92

2010–11	Sunderland	0	0		
2011–12	Sunderland	0	0		
2013–14	Accrington S	0	0		
2013–14	Cardiff C	0	0		
2014–15	Cardiff C	0	0		
2015–16	Cardiff C	0	0		
2015–16	AFC Wimbledon	8	0	8	0
2016–17	Cardiff C	3	0		
2016–17	Rochdale	8	0	8	0
2017–18	Cardiff C	0	0	3	0
2017–18	Oldham Ath	5	0	5	0

ZOHORE, Kenneth (F)   145 38
H: 6 4   W: 12 06   b.Copenhagen 31-1-94
Internationals: Denmark U17, U18, U19, U21.

2009–10	Copenhagen	1	0		
2010–11	Copenhagen	15	1		
2011–12	Copenhagen	0	0	16	1
2011–12	Fiorentina	0	0		
2012–13	Fiorentina	0	0		
2013–14	Fiorentina	0	0		
2013–14	Brondby	25	5	25	5
2014–15	Fiorentina	0	0		
2014–15	Gothenburg	11	2	11	2
2015–16	Odense BK	16	7	16	7
2015–16	KV Kortrijk	0	0		
2015–16	Cardiff C	12	2		
2016–17	Cardiff C	29	12		
2017–18	Cardiff C	36	9	77	23

Players retained or with offer of contract
Brown, Ciaron Maurice; Duffus, Tyrone Errol; Humphries, Lloyd; McKay, Jack; McKay, Paul; Veale, Jamie Lawrence; Waite, James Tyler.

Scholars
Bodenham, Jack Tomas; Bowen, Sam Lewis; Burwood, Warren Robert John; Davies, Connor William; Davies, Jac Tomos; Duffey, Jordan James; Jones, Trystan Rhys; Madden, Alfie William; Patten, Keenan; Proctor, Keiron; Ratcliffe, George; Reynolds, Ryan Michael; Sharif, Badedi Adam Mohamed; Smith, Henry William Leonard; Spence, Sion; Williams, Cai; Williams-Margetson, Ben; Wootton, Laurence Thomas.

Non-contract
Evans, Jacob Finlay.

CARLISLE U (22)

ADAMS, Nicky (F)   426 36
H: 5 10   W: 11 00   b.Bolton 16-10-86
Internationals: Wales U21.

2005–06	Bury	15	1		
2006–07	Bury	19	1		
2007–08	Bury	43	12		
2008–09	Leicester C	12	0		
2008–09	Rochdale	14	1		
2009–10	Leicester C	18	0	30	0
2009–10	Leyton Orient	6	0	6	0
2010–11	Brentford	7	0	7	0
2010–11	Rochdale	30	0		
2011–12	Rochdale	41	4	85	5
2012–13	Crawley T	46	8		
2013–14	Crawley T	24	1	70	9
2013–14	Rotherham U	15	1	15	1
2013–14	Bury	0	0		
2014–15	Bury	38	1	115	15
2015–16	Northampton T	39	3	39	3
2016–17	Carlisle U	42	3		
2017–18	Carlisle U	17	0	59	3

BACON, Morgan (G)   0 0
H: 6 2   W: 12 13   b. 1-6-98

2015–16	Carlisle U	0	0
2016–17	Carlisle U	0	0
2017–18	Carlisle U	0	0

BENNETT, Richie (F)   38 6
b.Oldham 3-3-91
From Ashton U, Northwich Vic, Barrow.

2017–18	Carlisle U	38	6	38	6

CAMPBELL-RYCE, Jamal (M)   479 41
H: 5 7   W: 12 03   b.Lambeth 6-4-83
Internationals: Jamaica Full caps.

2002–03	Charlton Ath	1	0		
2002–03	Leyton Orient	17	2		
2003–04	Charlton Ath	2	0		
2003–04	Wimbledon	4	0	4	0
2004–05	Charlton Ath	0	0	3	0
2004–05	Chesterfield	14	0		
2004–05	Rotherham U	24	0		
2005–06	Rotherham U	7	0	31	0
2005–06	Southend U	13	0		
2005–06	Colchester U	4	0	4	0
2006–07	Southend U	43	2		
2007–08	Southend U	2	0	58	2
2007–08	Barnsley	37	3		
2008–09	Barnsley	40	9		
2009–10	Barnsley	13	0	90	12

2009–10	Bristol C	14	0		
2010–11	Bristol C	31	2		
2011–12	Bristol C	17	0	62	2
2011–12	*Leyton Orient*	8	1	25	3
2012–13	Notts Co	37	8		
2013–14	Notts Co	36	3		
2014–15	Sheffield U	19	4		
2014–15	*Notts Co*	4	0	77	11
2015–16	Sheffield U	18	0	37	4
2015–16	*Chesterfield*	9	2	23	2
2016–17	Barnet	32	1		
2017–18	Barnet	24	4	56	5
2017–18	Carlisle U	9	0	9	0

COSGROVE, Sam (F)   8   1
b.Beverley 2-12-96

2014–15	Wigan Ath	0	0		
2015–16	Wigan Ath	0	0		
2016–17	Wigan Ath	0	0		
2017–18	Carlisle U	8	1	8	1

Transferred to Aberdeen, January 2018.

DEVITT, Jamie (F)   241   32
H: 5 10   W: 10 05   b.Dublin 6-7-90
Internationals: Republic of Ireland U21.

2007–08	Hull C	0	0		
2008–09	Hull C	0	0		
2009–10	Hull C	0	0		
2009–10	*Darlington*	6	1	6	1
2009–10	*Shrewsbury T*	9	2	9	2
2009–10	*Grimsby T*	15	5	15	5
2010–11	Hull C	16	0		
2011–12	Hull C	0	0		
2011–12	*Bradford C*	7	1	7	1
2011–12	*Accrington S*	16	2	16	2
2012–13	Hull C	0	0	16	0
2012–13	*Rotherham U*	1	0	1	0
2013–14	Chesterfield	7	0	7	0
2013–14	Morecambe	14	2		
2014–15	Morecambe	36	3		
2015–16	Morecambe	39	6	89	11
2016–17	Carlisle U	35	0		
2017–18	Carlisle U	40	10	75	10

EGAN, Jack (F)   0   0

2017–18	Carlisle U	0	0		

ELLIS, Mark (D)   271   19
H: 6 2   W: 12 04   b.Kingsbridge 30-9-88

2007–08	Bolton W	0	0		
2009–10	Torquay U	27	3		
2010–11	Torquay U	27	2		
2011–12	Torquay U	35	3	89	8
2012–13	Crewe Alex	44	5		
2013–14	Crewe Alex	37	1	81	6
2014–15	Shrewsbury T	32	2		
2015–16	Shrewsbury T	9	1	41	3
2015–16	Carlisle U	30	0		
2016–17	Carlisle U	7	0		
2017–18	Carlisle U	23	2	60	2

ETUHU, Kelvin (F)   194   11
H: 5 11   W: 11 02   b.Kano 30-5-88

2005–06	Manchester C	0	0		
2006–07	Manchester C	0	0		
2006–07	*Rochdale*	4	2	4	2
2007–08	Manchester C	6	1		
2007–08	*Leicester C*	4	0	4	0
2008–09	Manchester C	4	0		
2009–10	Manchester C	0	0		
2009–10	*Cardiff C*	16	0	16	0
2010–11	Manchester C	0	0	10	1
2011–12	Kavala				
2011–12	Portsmouth	13	1		
2012–13	Portsmouth	0	0	13	1
2012–13	Barnsley	26	0		
2013–14	Barnsley	20	0	46	0
2014–15	Bury	43	2		
2015–16	Bury	18	0		
2016–17	Bury	20	2	81	4
2017–18	Carlisle U	20	3	20	3

GRAINGER, Danny (D)   284   29
H: 5 10   W: 10 10   b.Kettering 28-7-86

2008–09	Dundee U	9	0	9	0
2009–10	St Johnstone	36	1		
2010–11	St Johnstone	33	2	69	3
2011–12	Hearts	27	0		
2012–13	Hearts	13	2	40	2
2013–14	St Mirren	13	0	13	0
2013–14	Dunfermline Ath	11	2	11	2
2014–15	Carlisle U	41	3		
2015–16	Carlisle U	36	5		
2016–17	Carlisle U	31	6		
2017–18	Carlisle U	34	8	142	22

HILL, Clint (D)   587   34
H: 6 0   W: 11 06   b.Liverpool 19-10-78

1997–98	Tranmere R	14	0		
1998–99	Tranmere R	33	4		
1999–2000	Tranmere R	29	5		
2000–01	Tranmere R	34	5		
2001–02	Tranmere R	30	2	140	16
2002–03	Oldham Ath	17	1	17	1
2003–04	Stoke C	12	0		
2004–05	Stoke C	32	1		
2005–06	Stoke C	13	0		
2006–07	Stoke C	18	2		
2007–08	Stoke C	5	0	80	3
2007–08	Crystal Palace	28	3		
2008–09	Crystal Palace	43	1		
2009–10	Crystal Palace	43	1	114	5
2010–11	QPR	44	2		
2011–12	QPR	22	0		
2011–12	*Nottingham F*	5	0	5	0
2012–13	QPR	31	0		
2013–14	QPR	40	1		
2014–15	QPR	19	1		
2015–16	QPR	13	1	169	5
2016–17	Rangers	24	3	24	3
2017–18	Carlisle U	38	1	38	1

HOLT, Jordan (M)   0   0
H: 5 9   W: 11 00   b.Carlisle 4-5-94
Internationals: Wales U19.

2016–17	Carlisle U	0	0		
2017–18	Carlisle U	0	0		

HOPE, Hallam (F)   135   22
H: 5 10   W: 12 00   b.Manchester 17-3-94
Internationals: England U16, U17, U18, U19.

2010–11	Everton	0	0		
2011–12	Everton	0	0		
2013–14	Everton	0	0		
2013–14	*Northampton T*	3	1	3	1
2014–15	Bury	8	5		
2014–15	Everton	0	0		
2014–15	*Sheffield W*	4	0	4	0
2014–15	Bury	19	0		
2015–16	Bury	6	0		
2015–16	*Carlisle U*	21	4		
2016–17	Bury	33	3	66	8
2017–18	Carlisle U	41	9	62	13

HUTCHINSON, Aidan (D)   0   0
b. 19-9-99

2017–18	Carlisle U	0	0		

JONES, Mike (M)   419   35
H: 5 11   W: 12 04   b.Birkenhead 15-8-87

2005–06	Tranmere R	1	0		
2006–07	Tranmere R	0	0		
2006–07	*Shrewsbury T*	13	1	13	1
2007–08	Tranmere R	9	1	10	1
2008–09	Bury	46	4		
2009–10	Bury	41	5		
2010–11	Bury	42	8		
2011–12	Bury	24	3	153	20
2011–12	Sheffield W	10	0		
2012–13	Sheffield W	0	0	10	0
2012–13	Crawley T	40	1		
2013–14	Crawley T	42	3	82	4
2014–15	Oldham Ath	45	6		
2015–16	Oldham Ath	35	3	80	9
2016–17	Carlisle U	28	0		
2017–18	Carlisle U	43	0	71	0

JOYCE, Luke (M)   392   13
H: 5 11   W: 12 03   b.Bolton 9-7-87

2005–06	Wigan Ath	0	0		
2006–07	Carlisle U	0	0		
2006–07	Carlisle U	16	1		
2007–08	Carlisle U	3	1		
2008–09	Carlisle U	7	0		
2009–10	*Accrington S*	41	1		
2010–11	Accrington S	27	1		
2011–12	Accrington S	43	2		
2012–13	Accrington S	44	0		
2013–14	Accrington S	46	1		
2014–15	Accrington S	45	3	246	8
2015–16	Carlisle U	37	0		
2016–17	Carlisle U	45.	1		
2017–18	Carlisle U	38	2	146	5

KENNEDY, Jason (M)   406   39
H: 6 1   W: 13 02   b.Stockton 11-9-86

2004–05	Middlesbrough	1	0		
2005–06	Middlesbrough	3	0		
2006–07	Middlesbrough	0	0		
2006–07	*Boston U*	13	1	13	1
2006–07	*Bury*	12	0	12	0
2007–08	Middlesbrough	0	0	4	0
2007–08	*Livingston*	18	2	18	2
2007–08	*Darlington*	13	2		

2008–09	Darlington	46	5	59	7
2009–10	Rochdale	42	0		
2010–11	Rochdale	45	4		
2011–12	Rochdale	44	4		
2012–13	Rochdale	46	4		
2013–14	Bradford C	8	1		
2013–14	*Rochdale*	7	0	184	12
2014–15	Bradford C	20	2	28	3
2014–15	Carlisle U	11	3		
2015–16	Carlisle U	44	2		
2016–17	Carlisle U	27	9		
2017–18	Carlisle U	6	0	88	14

LAMBE, Reggie (M)   213   25
H: 5 7   W: 10 09   b.Bermuda 4-2-91
Internationals: Bermuda Full caps.

2009–10	Ipswich T	0	0		
2010–11	Ipswich T	2	0	2	0
2010–11	*Bristol R*	7	0	7	0
2012	Toronto	27	2		
2013	Toronto	27	0	54	2
2014	Nykoping	11	1	11	1
2014–15	Mansfield T	30	5		
2015–16	Mansfield T	37	5	67	10
2016–17	Carlisle U	38	6		
2017–18	Carlisle U	34	6	72	12

LIDDLE, Gary (D)   489   27
H: 6 1   W: 12 06   b.Middlesbrough 15-6-86

2003–04	Middlesbrough	0	0		
2004–05	Middlesbrough	0	0		
2005–06	Middlesbrough	0	0		
2006–07	Hartlepool U	42	3		
2007–08	Hartlepool U	41	2		
2008–09	Hartlepool U	43	0		
2009–10	Hartlepool U	40	3		
2010–11	Hartlepool U	42	6		
2011–12	Hartlepool U	39	4	247	18
2012–13	Notts Co	46	0		
2013–14	Notts Co	32	4	78	4
2014–15	Bradford C	41	1		
2015–16	Bradford C	20	2	61	3
2015–16	Chesterfield	15	0		
2016–17	Chesterfield	26	1	41	1
2017–18	Carlisle U	21	1		
2017–18	Carlisle U	41	0	62	1

MILLER, Shaun (F)   327   74
H: 5 10   W: 11 08   b.Alsager 25-9-87

2006–07	Crewe Alex	7	3		
2007–08	Crewe Alex	15	1		
2008–09	Crewe Alex	33	4		
2009–10	Crewe Alex	33	7		
2010–11	Crewe Alex	42	18		
2011–12	Crewe Alex	33	5		
2012–13	Sheffield U	15	4		
2013–14	Sheffield U	13	0	28	4
2013–14	*Shrewsbury T*	8	3	8	3
2014–15	Coventry C	12	1	12	1
2014–15	*Crawley T*	5	0	5	0
2014–15	*York C*	6	0	6	0
2015–16	Morecambe	37	15	37	15
2016–17	Carlisle U	30	4		
2017–18	Carlisle U	23	3	53	7
2017–18	*Crewe Alex*	15	6	178	44

MILLER, Tom (D)   87   7
H: 5 11   W: 11 07   b.Ely 29-6-90
From Rangers, Dundalk, Newport Co,
Lincoln C.

2015–16	Carlisle U	29	5		
2016–17	Carlisle U	41	0		
2017–18	Carlisle U	17	2	87	7

NABI, Samir (M)   2   0
H: 5 11   W: 12 00   b.Birmingham 16-12-96

2016	Delhi Dynamos	1	0	1	0
2016–17	Carlisle U	1	0		
2017–18	Carlisle U	0	0	1	0

O'SULLIVAN, John (M)   101   7
H: 5 11   W: 13 01   b.Birmingham 18-9-93
Internationals: Republic of Ireland U19, U21.

2011–12	Blackburn R	0	0		
2012–13	Blackburn R	1	0		
2013–14	Blackburn R	0	0		
2014–15	Blackburn R	2	0		
2014–15	*Accrington S*	13	4		
2014–15	*Barnsley*	8	0	8	0
2015–16	Blackburn R	2	0		
2015–16	*Rochdale*	2	0	2	0
2015–16	*Bury*	19	0	19	0
2016–17	Blackburn R	0	0	5	0
2016–17	*Accrington S*	19	1	32	5
2016–17	Carlisle U	17	1		
2017–18	Carlisle U	18	1	35	2

PARKES, Tom (D)   239   5
H: 6 3   W: 12 05   b.Sutton-in-Ashfield 15-1-92
Internationals: England U17. England C.

2008–09	Leicester C	0	0		
2009–10	Leicester C	0	0		
2009–10	Burton Alb	22	1		
2010–11	Leicester C	0	0		
2010–11	Yeovil T	1	0	1	0
2010–11	Burton Alb	5	0		
2011–12	Leicester C	0	0		
2011–12	Burton Alb	4	0	31	1
2011–12	Bristol R	14	0		
2012–13	Leicester C	0	0		
2012–13	Bristol R	40	1		
2013–14	Bristol R	44	1		
2015–16	Bristol R	31	0	129	2
2016–17	Leyton Orient	41	1	41	1
2017–18	Carlisle U	37	1	37	1

RIGG, Steven (M)   49   6
H: 6 0   W: 12 08   b.Keswick 30-6-92

2014–15	Carlisle U	28	6		
2015–16	Carlisle U	8	0		
2016–17	Queen of the South	10	0	10	0
2017–18	Carlisle U	3	0	39	6

Transferred to Erie Commodores April 2018.

SALKELD, Cameron (M)   6   0
H: 6 0   W: 10 03   b. 1-12-98

2016–17	Carlisle U	0	0		
2017–18	Carlisle U	0	0		
2017–18	Annan Ath	6	0	6	0

STOCKTON, Cole (F)   125   26
H: 6 1   W: 11 11   b.Huyton 13-3-94

2011–12	Tranmere R	1	0		
2012–13	Tranmere R	31	3		
2013–14	Tranmere R	21	2		
2014–15	Tranmere R	22	4		
2015–16	Tranmere R	0	0		
2015–16	Morecambe	7	2		
2016–17	Tranmere R	0	0	75	9
2016–17	Morecambe	19	5	26	7
2017–18	Hearts	12	9	12	9
2017–18	Carlisle U	12	1	12	1

Players retained or with offer of contract
Brown, Max William.

Scholars
Adewusi, Samuel Adebola Ife Oluwa G O; Ashton, Lee Andrew John; Belchior, Rodrigues Pires Papa; Brockbank, Liam; Casson, Ceiran; Cowburn, Max David; Dixon, Joshua; Goldthorpe, Alexis Ewart; Hodgson, Kelly Jay Alexander; Hutchinson, Aidan John; Kerr, Keighran Ronnie David; Lloyd, Luke Martin; McCarron, Liam James; Miller, Jaic Lee; Olsen, Keiron; Taylor, Luke William; Ward, Regan; Watson, Dean Allan.

CHARLTON ATH (23)

AHEARNE-GRANT, Karlan (F)   70   6
H: 6 0   b.London 19-12-97
Internationals: England U17, U18, U19.

2014–15	Charlton Ath	5	0		
2015–16	Charlton Ath	17	1		
2015–16	Cambridge U	3	0	3	0
2016–17	Charlton Ath	8	0		
2017–18	Charlton Ath	22	1	52	2
2017–18	Crawley T	15	9	15	9

AJOSE, Nicholas (F)   250   78
H: 5 8   W: 11 00   b.Bury 7-10-91
Internationals: England U16, U17. Nigeria U20.

2009–10	Manchester U	0	0		
2010–11	Manchester U	0	0		
2010–11	Bury	28	13		
2011–12	Peterborough U	2	0		
2011–12	Scunthorpe U	7	0	7	0
2011–12	Chesterfield	12	1	12	1
2012–13	Crawley T	19	2	19	2
2012–13	Peterborough U	0	0		
2012–13	Bury	19	4		
2013–14	Peterborough U	22	7	24	7
2013–14	Swindon T	16	6		
2014–15	Leeds U	3	0		
2014–15	Crewe Alex	27	8	27	8
2015–16	Leeds U	0	0	3	0
2015–16	Swindon T	38	24		
2016–17	Charlton Ath	21	6		
2016–17	Swindon T	15	5	69	35
2017–18	Charlton Ath	12	1	33	7
2017–18	Bury	9	1	56	18

ARIBO, Joe (M)   45   5
b.Camberwell 21-7-96
From Staines T.

2015–16	Charlton Ath	0	0		
2016–17	Charlton Ath	19	0		
2017–18	Charlton Ath	26	5	45	5

BARNES, Aaron (D)   1   0
b. 14-10-96

2016–17	Charlton Ath	1	0		
2017–18	Charlton Ath	0	0	1	0

BAUER, Patrick (D)   134   10
H: 6 4   W: 13 08   b.Backnang 28-10-92
Internationals: Germany U17, U18, U20.

2010–11	Stuttgart	0	0		
2011–12	Stuttgart	0	0		
2012–13	Stuttgart	0	0		
2013–14	Maritimo	16	0		
2014–15	Maritimo	29	2	45	2
2015–16	Charlton Ath	19	1		
2016–17	Charlton Ath	36	4		
2017–18	Charlton Ath	34	3	89	8

BEST, Leon (F)   286   58
H: 6 1   W: 13 03   b.Nottingham 19-9-86
Internationals: Republic of Ireland U21, Full caps.

2004–05	Southampton	3	0		
2004–05	QPR	5	0	5	0
2005–06	Southampton	3	0		
2005–06	Sheffield W	13	2		
2006–07	Southampton	9	4	15	4
2006–07	Bournemouth	15	3	15	3
2006–07	Yeovil T	15	10	15	10
2007–08	Coventry C	34	8		
2008–09	Coventry C	31	2		
2009–10	Coventry C	27	9	92	19
2009–10	Newcastle U	13	0		
2010–11	Newcastle U	11	6		
2011–12	Newcastle U	18	4	42	10
2012–13	Blackburn R	6	0		
2013–14	Blackburn R	8	2		
2013–14	Sheffield W	15	4	28	6
2014–15	Blackburn R	0	0		
2014–15	Derby Co	5	0	15	0
2014–15	Brighton & HA	13	0	13	0
2015–16	Blackburn R	0	0	14	2
2015–16	Rotherham U	16	4		
2016–17	Rotherham U	0	0	16	4
2016–17	Ipswich T	11	0	11	0
2017–18	Charlton Ath	5	0	5	0

CARTER, Matt (M)   0   0

2016–17	West Ham U	0	0		
2017–18	Charlton Ath	0	0		

CHARLES, Regan (M)   1   0
H: 5 9   W: 10 12   b.London 1-3-97
From Arsenal.

2015–16	Charlton Ath	1	0		
2016–17	Charlton Ath	0	0		
2017–18	Charlton Ath	0	0	1	0

CLARKE, Billy (F)   325   68
H: 5 7   W: 10 01   b.Cork 13-12-87
Internationals: Republic of Ireland U17, U19, U21.

2004–05	Ipswich T	0	0		
2005–06	Ipswich T	2	0		
2005–06	Colchester U	6	0	6	0
2006–07	Ipswich T	27	3		
2007–08	Ipswich T	20	0		
2007–08	Falkirk	8	1	8	1
2008–09	Ipswich T	0	0	49	3
2008–09	Darlington	20	8	20	8
2008–09	Northampton T	5	3	5	3
2008–09	Brentford	8	6	8	6
2009–10	Blackpool	18	1		
2010–11	Blackpool	0	0		
2011–12	Blackpool	9	0	27	1
2011–12	Sheffield U	5	1	5	1
2011–12	Crawley T	17	3		
2012–13	Crawley T	36	10		
2013–14	Crawley T	29	7	82	20
2014–15	Bradford C	36	13		
2015–16	Bradford C	29	4		
2016–17	Bradford C	33	7	98	24
2017–18	Charlton Ath	17	1	17	1

CUMMINGS, Joe (D)   0   0

2016–17	Sheffield U	0	0		
2017–18	Sheffield U	0	0		
2017–18	Charlton Ath	0	0		

DIJKSTEEL, Anfernee (M)   10   0
b. 27-10-96
Internationals: Netherlands U20.

2016–17	Charlton Ath	0	0		
2017–18	Charlton Ath	10	0	10	0

DODOO, Joseph (F)   30   5
H: 6 0   W: 12 08   b.Nottingham 6-1-95
Internationals: England U18.

2013–14	Leicester C	0	0		
2014–15	Leicester C	0	0		
2015–16	Leicester C	1	0	1	0
2015–16	Bury	4	1	4	1
2016–17	Rangers	20	3		
2017–18	Rangers	0	0	20	3

On loan from Rangers.

2017–18	Charlton Ath	5	1	5	1

FORSTER-CASKEY, Jake (M)   165   16
H: 5 10   W: 10 00   b.Southend 25-4-94
Internationals: England U16, U17, U18, U20, U21.

2009–10	Brighton & HA	1	0		
2010–11	Brighton & HA	0	0		
2011–12	Brighton & HA	4	1		
2012–13	Brighton & HA	3	0		
2012–13	Oxford U	16	3	16	3
2013–14	Brighton & HA	28	3		
2014–15	Brighton & HA	29	1		
2015–16	Brighton & HA	2	0	67	5
2015–16	Milton Keynes D	20	1	20	1
2016–17	Charlton Ath	15	2		
2016–17	Rotherham U	6	0	6	0
2017–18	Charlton Ath	41	5	56	7

FOSU, Tarique (M)   78   18
H: 5 7   W: 10 08   b. 5-11-95
Internationals: England U18.

2013–14	Reading	0	0		
2014–15	Reading	1	0		
2015–16	Reading	0	0		
2015–16	Fleetwood T	6	1	6	1
2015–16	Accrington S	8	3	8	3
2016–17	Reading	0	0	1	0
2016–17	Colchester U	33	5	33	5
2017–18	Charlton Ath	30	9	30	9

HACKETT-FAIRCHILD, Recco (F)   5   0
H: 6 3   W: 11 00   b. 30-6-98
From Norwich C.

2017–18	Charlton Ath	5	0	5	0

HANLAN, Brandon (F)   27   2
H: 6 0   W: 11 07   b.Chelsea 31-5-97

2016–17	Charlton Ath	9	0		
2017–18	Colchester U	18	2	18	2
2017–18	Charlton Ath	0	0	9	0

JACKSON, Johnnie (M)   445   70
H: 6 1   W: 12 00   b.Camden 15-8-82
Internationals: England U17, U18, U20.

1999–2000	Tottenham H	0	0		
2000–01	Tottenham H	0	0		
2001–02	Tottenham H	0	0		
2002–03	Tottenham H	0	0		
2002–03	Swindon T	13	1	13	1
2002–03	Colchester U	8	0		
2003–04	Tottenham H	11	1		
2003–04	Coventry C	5	2	5	2
2004–05	Tottenham H	8	0		
2004–05	Watford	15	0	15	0
2005–06	Tottenham H	1	0	20	1
2005–06	Derby Co	6	0	6	0
2006–07	Colchester U	32	2		
2007–08	Colchester U	46	7		
2008–09	Colchester U	29	4		
2009–10	Colchester U	0	0	115	13
2009–10	Notts Co	24	2	24	2
2009–10	Charlton Ath	4	0		
2010–11	Charlton Ath	30	13		
2011–12	Charlton Ath	36	12		
2012–13	Charlton Ath	43	12		
2013–14	Charlton Ath	38	5		
2014–15	Charlton Ath	26	2		
2015–16	Charlton Ath	29	3		
2016–17	Charlton Ath	30	4		
2017–18	Charlton Ath	11	0	247	51

KASHI, Ahmed (M)   207   7
H: 5 10   W: 12 00   b.Aubervilliers 18-11-88
Internationals: Algeria Full caps.

2008–09	Chateauroux	21	2		
2009–10	Chateauroux	23	1		
2010–11	Chateauroux	17	1		
2011–12	Chateauroux	24	0	85	4
2012–13	Metz	25	0		
2013–14	Metz	33	0		
2014–15	Metz	19	1	77	1

2015–16	Charlton Ath	11	0		
2017–18	Charlton Ath	34	2	45	2

KENNEDY, Mikhail (D) 2 0
b. 18-8-96
Internationals: Northern Ireland U17, U19, U21.

2014–15	Charlton Ath	0	0		
2015–16	Charlton Ath	2	0		
2016–17	Charlton Ath	0	0		
2017–18	Charlton Ath	0	0	2	0

KONSA, Ezri (D) 71 0
H: 6 0 W: 12 02 b. 23-10-97
Internationals: England U20.

2015–16	Charlton Ath	0	0		
2016–17	Charlton Ath	32	0		
2017–18	Charlton Ath	39	0	71	0

LAPSLIE, George (M) 1 0
b. 5-9-97

2016–17	Charlton Ath	0	0		
2017–18	Charlton Ath	1	0	1	0

LENNON, Harry (M) 43 4
H: 6 3 W: 11 11 b.Barking 16-12-94

2012–13	Charlton Ath	0	0		
2013–14	Charlton Ath	2	0		
2014–15	Charlton Ath	0	0		
2014–15	*Cambridge U*	2	0	2	0
2014–15	*Gillingham*	2	0		
2015–16	Charlton Ath	19	2		
2015–16	*Gillingham*	6	2	8	2
2016–17	Charlton Ath	2	0		
2017–18	Charlton Ath	10	0	33	2

MAGENNIS, Josh (F) 282 48
H: 6 2 W: 14 07 b.Bangor 15-8-90
Internationals: Northern Ireland U17, U19, U21, Full caps.

2009–10	Cardiff C	9	0	9	0
2009–10	*Grimsby T*	2	0	2	0
2010–11	Aberdeen	29	3		
2011–12	Aberdeen	23	1		
2012–13	Aberdeen	35	5		
2013–14	Aberdeen	18	1	105	10
2013–14	*St Mirren*	13	0	13	0
2014–15	Kilmarnock	38	8		
2015–16	Kilmarnock	34	10	72	18
2016–17	Charlton Ath	39	10		
2017–18	Charlton Ath	42	10	81	20

MALONEY, Taylor (M) 1 0
H: 5 9 W: 10 02 b. 21-1-99

2017–18	Charlton Ath	1	0	1	0

MARSHALL, Mark (M) 258 21
H: 5 7 W: 10 07 b.Jamaica 9-5-86

2008–09	Swindon T	12	0		
2009–10	Swindon T	7	0	19	0
2009–10	*Hereford U*	8	0	8	0
2010–11	Barnet	46	6		
2011–12	Barnet	25	1	71	7
2013–14	Coventry C	14	0	14	0
2014–15	Port Vale	46	7	46	7
2015–16	Bradford C	31	0		
2016–17	Bradford C	42	6	73	6
2017–18	Charlton Ath	27	1	27	1

MASCOLL, Jamie (M) 0 0
From Dulwich Hamlet.

2017–18	Charlton Ath	0	0		

MAYNARD-BREWER, Ashley (G) 0 0
b. 25-6-99
Internationals: Australia U23.

2017–18	Charlton Ath	0	0		

PAGE, Lewis (D) 44 1
b.London 20-5-96

2014–15	West Ham U	0	0		
2015–16	West Ham U	0	0		
2015–16	*Cambridge U*	6	0	6	0
2016–17	West Ham U	0	0		
2016–17	*Coventry C*	22	0	22	0
2016–17	Charlton Ath	8	0		
2017–18	Charlton Ath	8	1	16	1

PEARCE, Jason (D) 399 18
H: 5 11 W: 12 00 b.Hillingdon 6-12-87

2006–07	Portsmouth	0	0		
2007–08	Bournemouth	33	1		
2008–09	Bournemouth	44	2		
2009–10	Bournemouth	39	1		
2010–11	Bournemouth	46	3	162	7
2011–12	Portsmouth	43	2	43	2
2011–12	Leeds U	0	0		
2012–13	Leeds U	33	0		
2013–14	Leeds U	45	2		
2014–15	Leeds U	21	0	99	2
2014–15	Wigan Ath	16	2		
2015–16	Wigan Ath	31	2	47	4
2016–17	Charlton Ath	23	1		
2017–18	Charlton Ath	25	2	48	3

PHILLIPS, Dillon (M) 8 0
H: 6 2 W: 11 11 b. 11-6-95

2012–13	Charlton Ath	0	0		
2013–14	Charlton Ath	0	0		
2014–15	Charlton Ath	0	0		
2015–16	Charlton Ath	0	0		
2016–17	Charlton Ath	8	0		
2017–18	Charlton Ath	0	0	8	0

REEVES, Ben (D) 159 28
H: 5 10 W: 10 07 b.Verwood 19-11-91
Internationals: Northern Ireland Full caps.

2008–09	Southampton	0	0		
2009–10	Southampton	0	0		
2010–11	Southampton	0	0		
2011–12	Southampton	2	0		
2011–12	*Dagenham & R*	5	0	5	0
2012–13	Southampton	3	0	5	0
2012–13	*Southend U*	1	0	10	1
2013–14	Milton Keynes D	28	7		
2014–15	Milton Keynes D	30	7		
2015–16	Milton Keynes D	18	3		
2016–17	Milton Keynes D	34	7	110	24
2017–18	Charlton Ath	29	3	29	3

SARR, Naby (D) 40 1
H: 6 5 W: 14 11 b.Marseille 13-8-93
Internationals: France U20, U21.

2012–13	Lyon	0	0		
2013–14	Lyon	2	0	2	0
2014–15	Sporting Lisbon	8	0	8	0
2015–16	Charlton Ath	12	1		
2017–18	Charlton Ath	18	0	30	1

SOLLY, Chris (D) 251 2
H: 5 8 W: 10 07 b.Rochester 20-1-91
Internationals: England U16, U17.

2008–09	Charlton Ath	0	0		
2009–10	Charlton Ath	9	0		
2010–11	Charlton Ath	14	1		
2011–12	Charlton Ath	44	0		
2012–13	Charlton Ath	45	1		
2013–14	Charlton Ath	12	0		
2014–15	Charlton Ath	38	0		
2015–16	Charlton Ath	34	0		
2016–17	Charlton Ath	27	0		
2017–18	Charlton Ath	27	0	251	2

UMERAH, Josh (F) 12 0
b.Catford 1-4-98

2015–16	Charlton Ath	1	0		
2016–17	*Kilmarnock*	4	0	4	0
2017–18	Charlton Ath	0	0	2	0
2017–18	*Wycombe W*	6	2	6	2

WATT, Tony (F) 158 33
H: 5 8 W: 12 00 b.Bellshill 29-3-93
Internationals: Scotland U19, U20, U21, Full caps.

2009–10	Airdrieonians	1	0		
2010–11	Airdrieonians	15	3	16	3
2011–12	Celtic	3	2		
2012–13	Celtic	20	5		
2013–14	Celtic	2	0	25	7
2013–14	*Lierse*	17	8	17	8
2014–15	Standard Liege	13	2	13	2
2014–15	Charlton Ath	22	5		
2015–16	Charlton Ath	14	2		
2015–16	*Cardiff C*	9	2	9	2
2015–16	*Blackburn R*	9	1	9	1
2016–17	Charlton Ath	16	2		
2016–17	*Hearts*	16	1	16	1
2017–18	Charlton Ath	1	0	53	9

Transferred to OH Leuven, August 2017.

YAMFAM, Louis (F) 0 0
b. 24-3-98

2014–15	Stevenage	0	0		
2015–16	Stevenage	0	0		
2017–18	Charlton Ath	0	0		

Players retained or with offer of contract
Blumberg, Ryan; Bowry, Daniel Robert; Hall-Anderson, Terrique Dominic; Vetokele, Igor; Yao, Kenneth William.

Scholars
Birch, Daniel George; Carey, Luke Anthony; Dempsey, Ben Michael; Doughty, Alfie Henry; Godding, Ryan Geoffrey; Gody, Naka James; Harvey, Edward James; Isiaka, Kareem; Keefe, Samuel James; Kirunda; Tyrone Rhakeem; Moore, Charlie John; Morgan, Albie Robert; Nwosu, Samuel Chibuike; Osaghae, Joseph Etinosa; Pollard, Harry Shaw; Powell, Johl Cameron; Sarpong, Wiredu Brendan Nana Akwasi; Vennings, James Frederick; Willis, Alexander William; Zemura, Jordan Bekithemba.

CHELSEA (24)

ABRAHAM, Tammy (F) 74 28
H: 6 3 W: 12 13 b.London 2-10-97
Internationals: England U18, U19, U21, Full caps.

2015–16	Chelsea	2	0		
2016–17	Chelsea	0	0		
2016–17	*Bristol C*	41	23	41	23
2017–18	Chelsea	0	0	2	0
2017–18	*Swansea C*	31	5	31	5

AINA, Ola (D) 47 0
H: 5 9 W: 10 03 b.London 8-10-96
Internationals: England U16, U17, U18, U19, U20. Nigeria Full caps.

2015–16	Chelsea	0	0		
2016–17	Chelsea	3	0		
2017–18	Chelsea	0	0	3	0
2017–18	*Hull C*	44	0	44	0

ALONSO, Marcus (D) 213 25
H: 6 2 W: 13 05 b.Madrid 28-12-90
Internationals: Spain U19, Full caps.

2008–09	RM Castilla	11	0		
2009–10	RM Castilla	28	3	39	3
2009–10	Real Madrid	1	0	1	0
2010–11	Bolton W	4	0		
2011–12	Bolton W	5	1		
2012–13	Bolton W	26	4	35	5
2013–14	Fiorentina	3	0		
2013–14	*Sunderland*	16	0	16	0
2014–15	Fiorentina	22	1		
2015–16	Fiorentina	31	3		
2016–17	Fiorentina	2	0	58	4
2016–17	Chelsea	31	6		
2017–18	Chelsea	33	7	64	13

AMPADU, Ethan (M) 9 0
b.Exeter 14-9-00
Internationals: England U16, Wales U17, U19, Full caps.

2016–17	Exeter C	8	0	8	0
2017–18	Chelsea	1	0	1	0

AZPILICUETA, Cesar (D) 343 6
H: 5 10 W: 10 13 b.Pamplona 28-8-89
Internationals: Spain U16, U17, U19, U20, U21, U23, Full caps.

2006–07	Osasuna	1	0		
2007–08	Osasuna	29	0		
2008–09	Osasuna	36	0		
2009–10	Osasuna	33	0	99	0
2010–11	Marseille	15	0		
2011–12	Marseille	30	1		
2012–13	Marseille	2	0	47	1
2012–13	Chelsea	27	0		
2013–14	Chelsea	29	0		
2014–15	Chelsea	29	0		
2015–16	Chelsea	37	2		
2016–17	Chelsea	38	1		
2017–18	Chelsea	37	2	197	5

BAKAYOKO, Tiemoue (M) 116 6
H: 6 1 W: 12 02 b.Paris 17-8-94
Internationals: France U16, U17, U18, U20, U21, Full caps.

2013–14	Rennes	24	1	24	1
2014–15	Monaco	12	0		
2015–16	Monaco	19	1		
2016–17	Monaco	32	2	63	3
2017–18	Chelsea	29	2	29	2

BAKER, Lewis (M) 92 19
b.Luton 25-4-95
Internationals: England U17, U19, U20, U21.

2012–13	Chelsea	0	0		
2013–14	Chelsea	0	0		
2014–15	Chelsea	0	0		
2014–15	*Sheffield W*	4	0	4	0
2014–15	*Milton Keynes D*	12	3	12	3
2015–16	Chelsea	0	0		
2015–16	*Vitesse*	31	5		
2016–17	Chelsea	0	0		
2016–17	*Vitesse*	33	10	64	15
2017–18	Chelsea	0	0		
2017–18	*Middlesbrough*	12	1	12	1

BARKLEY, Ross (M) 169 25
H: 6 2 W: 12 00 b.Liverpool 5-12-93
Internationals: England U16, U17, U19, U20, U21, Full caps.

2010–11	Everton	0	0		

2011–12	Everton	6	0		
2012–13	Everton	7	0		
2012–13	Sheffield W	13	4	**13**	**4**
2012–13	Leeds U	4	0	**4**	**0**
2013–14	Everton	34	6		
2014–15	Everton	29	2		
2015–16	Everton	38	8		
2016–17	Everton	36	5		
2017–18	Everton	0	0	**150**	**21**
2017–18	Chelsea	2	0	**2**	**0**

BATSHUAYI, Michy (F)   **201 79**
H: 5 11 W: 12 04 b.Brussels 2-10-93
Internationals: Belgium U21, Full caps.

2010–11	Standard Liege	2	0		
2011–12	Standard Liege	23	6		
2012–13	Standard Liege	34	12		
2013–14	Standard Liege	38	21	**97**	**39**
2014–15	Marseille	26	9		
2015–16	Marseille	36	17	**62**	**26**
2016–17	Chelsea	20	5		
2017–18	Chelsea	12	2	**32**	**7**
2017–18	Borussia Dortmund	10	7	**10**	**7**

BEENEY, Mitchell (G)   **5 0**
H: 6 0 W: 12 04 b.Leeds 3-10-95
Internationals: England U19.

2014–15	Chelsea	0	0		
2015–16	Chelsea	0	0		
2015–16	Newport Co	4	0	**4**	**0**
2016–17	Chelsea	0	0		
2016–17	Crawley T	1	0	**1**	**0**
2017–18	Chelsea	0	0		

BLACKMAN, Jamal (G)   **85 0**
H: 6 6 W: 14 09 b.Croydon 27-10-93
Internationals: England U16, U17, U18, U19.

2011–12	Chelsea	0	0		
2012–13	Chelsea	0	0		
2013–14	Chelsea	0	0		
2014–15	Chelsea	0	0		
2014–15	Middlesbrough	0	0		
2015–16	Chelsea	0	0		
2015–16	Ostersunds FK	12	0	**12**	**0**
2016–17	Chelsea	0	0		
2016–17	Wycombe W	42	0	**42**	**0**
2017–18	Chelsea	0	0		
2017–18	Sheffield U	31	0	**31**	**0**

BOGA, Jeremie (F)   **85 6**
H: 5 8 W: 10 10 b.Marseille 3-1-97
Internationals: France U16, U19, Ivory Coast Full caps.

2014–15	Chelsea	0	0		
2015–16	Chelsea	0	0		
2015–16	Rennes	27	2	**27**	**2**
2016–17	Chelsea	0	0		
2016–17	Granada	26	2	**26**	**2**
2017–18	Chelsea	1	0	**1**	**0**
2017–18	Birmingham C	31	2	**31**	**2**

BROWN, Isaiah (M)   **72 8**
H: 6 0 W: 10 13 b.Peterborough 7-1-97
Internationals: England U16, U17, U19, U20.

2012–13	WBA	1	0	**1**	**0**
2013–14	Chelsea	0	0		
2014–15	Chelsea	0	0		
2015–16	Chelsea	0	0		
2015–16	Vitesse	22	1	**22**	**1**
2016–17	Chelsea	0	0		
2016–17	Rotherham U	20	3	**20**	**3**
2016–17	Huddersfield T	15	4	**15**	**4**
2017–18	Chelsea	0	0	**1**	**0**
2017–18	Brighton & HA	13	0	**13**	**0**

CABALLERO, Willy (G)   **324 0**
H: 6 1 W: 12 08 b.Santa Elena 28-9-81
Internationals: Argentina U21, Full caps.

2001–04	Boca Juniors	15	0	**15**	**0**
2004–08	Elche	67	0		
2008–09	Elche	38	0		
2009–10	Elche	39	0		
2010–11	Elche	22	0	**166**	**0**
2010–11	Malaga	15	0		
2011–12	Malaga	28	0		
2012–13	Malaga	36	0		
2013–14	Malaga	38	0	**117**	**0**
2014–15	Manchester C	2	0		
2015–16	Manchester C	4	0		
2016–17	Manchester C	17	0	**23**	**0**
2017–18	Chelsea	3	0	**3**	**0**

CAHILL, Gary (D)   **390 30**
H: 6 2 W: 12 06 b.Dronfield 19-12-85
Internationals: England U20, U21, Full caps.

2003–04	Aston Villa	0	0		
2004–05	Aston Villa	0	0		
2004–05	Burnley	27	1	**27**	**1**
2005–06	Aston Villa	7	1		
2006–07	Aston Villa	20	0		
2007–08	Aston Villa	1	0	**28**	**1**
2007–08	Sheffield U	16	2	**16**	**2**
2007–08	Bolton W	13	0		
2008–09	Bolton W	33	3		
2009–10	Bolton W	29	5		
2010–11	Bolton W	36	3		
2011–12	Bolton W	19	2	**130**	**13**
2011–12	Chelsea	10	1		
2012–13	Chelsea	26	2		
2013–14	Chelsea	30	1		
2014–15	Chelsea	36	1		
2015–16	Chelsea	23	2		
2016–17	Chelsea	37	6		
2017–18	Chelsea	27	0	**189**	**13**

CHALOBAH, Trevor (D)   **0 0**
H: 6 3 b.Freetown 5-7-99
Internationals: England U16, U17, U19, U20, U21.

2017–18	Chelsea	0	0		

CHRISTENSEN, Andreas (D)   **90 5**
H: 6 2 W: 11 09 b.Allerod 10-4-96
Internationals: Denmark U16, U17, U19, U21, Full caps.

2012–13	Chelsea	0	0		
2013–14	Chelsea	0	0		
2014–15	Chelsea	1	0		
2015–16	Chelsea	0	0		
2015–16	Borussia M'gladbach	31	3		
2016–17	Chelsea	0	0		
2016–17	Borussia M'gladbach	31	2	**62**	**5**
2017–18	Chelsea	27	0	**28**	**0**

CLARKE-SALTER, Jake (D)   **24 1**
H: 6 2 W: 11 00 b.Carshalton 22-9-97
Internationals: England U18, U19, U20, U21.

2015–16	Chelsea	1	0		
2016–17	Chelsea	0	0		
2016–17	Bristol R	12	1	**12**	**1**
2017–18	Chelsea	0	0		
2017–18	Sunderland	11	0	**11**	**0**

COLLINS, Bradley (G)   **39 0**
H: 6 0 W: 10 12 b. 18-2-97

2017–18	Chelsea	0	0		
2017–18	Forest Green R	39	0	**39**	**0**

COURTOIS, Thibaut (G)   **278 0**
H: 6 6 W: 14 02 b.Bree 11-5-92
Internationals: Belgium U18, Full caps.

2008–09	Genk	1	0		
2009–10	Genk	0	0		
2010–11	Genk	40	0	**41**	**0**
2011–12	Chelsea	0	0		
2011–12	Atletico Madrid	37	0		
2012–13	Chelsea	0	0		
2012–13	Atletico Madrid	37	0		
2013–14	Chelsea	0	0		
2013–14	Atletico Madrid	37	0	**111**	**0**
2014–15	Chelsea	32	0		
2015–16	Chelsea	23	0		
2016–17	Chelsea	36	0		
2017–18	Chelsea	35	0	**126**	**0**

DASILVA, Jay (D)   **48 0**
b. 22-4-98
Internationals: England U16, U17, U18, U19, U20.

2016–17	Chelsea	0	0		
2016–17	Charlton Ath	10	0		
2017–18	Chelsea	0	0		
2017–18	Charlton Ath	38	0	**48**	**0**

DRINKWATER, Daniel (M)   **276 17**
H: 5 10 W: 11 00 b.Manchester 5-3-90
Internationals: England U18, U19, Full caps.

2008–09	Manchester U	0	0		
2009–10	Manchester U	0	0		
2009–10	Huddersfield T	33	2	**33**	**2**
2010–11	Manchester U	0	0		
2010–11	Cardiff C	9	0	**9**	**0**
2010–11	Watford	12	0	**12**	**0**
2011–12	Manchester U	0	0		
2011–12	Barnsley	17	1	**17**	**1**
2011–12	Leicester C	19	2		
2012–13	Leicester C	42	1		
2013–14	Leicester C	45	7		
2014–15	Leicester C	23	0		
2015–16	Leicester C	35	2		
2016–17	Leicester C	29	1		
2017–18	Leicester C	0	0	**193**	**13**
2017–18	Chelsea	12	1	**12**	**1**

EDUARDO, Carvalho (G)   **275 0**
H: 6 2 W: 13 03 b.Mirandela 19-9-82
Internationals: Portugal U21, Full caps.

2005–06	Braga	0	0		
2006–07	Braga	0	0		
2006–07	Beira-Mar Aveiro	15	0	**15**	**0**
2007–08	Braga	0	0		
2007–08	Victoria Setubal	30	0	**30**	**0**
2008–09	Braga	30	0		
2009–10	Braga	30	0		
2010–11	Genoa	37	0		
2011–12	Genoa	0	0		
2011–12	Benfica	1	0	**1**	**0**
2011–12	Genoa	0	0		
2012–13	Istanbul BB	33	0	**33**	**0**
2013–14	Genoa	0	0	**37**	**0**
2013–14	Braga	29	0	**89**	**0**
2014–15	Dinamo Zagreb	34	0		
2015–16	Dinamo Zagreb	32	0		
2016–17	Dinamo Zagreb	4	0	**70**	**0**
2016–17	Chelsea	0	0		
2017–18	Chelsea	0	0		

EMERSON, dos Santos (D)   **66 2**
H: 5 9 W: 9 13 b.Santos 13-3-94
Internationals: Brazil U17.

2011	Santos	0	0		
2012	Santos	1	0		
2013	Santos	14	1		
2014	Santos	3	0	**18**	**1**
2014–15	Palermo	9	0	**9**	**0**
2015–16	Roma	8	1		
2016–17	Roma	25	0		
2017–18	Roma	1	0	**34**	**1**
2017–18	Chelsea	5	0	**5**	**0**

FABREGAS, Francesc (M)   **440 78**
H: 5 11 W: 11 01 b.Arenys de Mar 4-5-87
Internationals: Spain Youth, U21, Full caps.

2003–04	Arsenal	0	0		
2004–05	Arsenal	33	2		
2005–06	Arsenal	35	3		
2006–07	Arsenal	38	2		
2007–08	Arsenal	32	7		
2008–09	Arsenal	22	3		
2009–10	Arsenal	27	15		
2010–11	Arsenal	25	3	**212**	**35**
2011–12	Barcelona	28	9		
2012–13	Barcelona	32	11		
2013–14	Barcelona	36	8	**96**	**28**
2014–15	Chelsea	34	3		
2015–16	Chelsea	37	5		
2016–17	Chelsea	29	5		
2017–18	Chelsea	32	2	**132**	**15**

GIROUD, Olivier (F)   **345 140**
H: 6 3 W: 13 11 b.Chambery 30-9-86
Internationals: France Full caps.

2005–06	Grenoble	3	0		
2006–07	Grenoble	15	2	**18**	**2**
2008–09	Tours	23	8		
2009–10	Tours	38	21	**61**	**29**
2010–11	Montpellier	37	12		
2011–12	Montpellier	36	21	**73**	**33**
2012–13	Arsenal	34	11		
2013–14	Arsenal	36	16		
2014–15	Arsenal	27	14		
2015–16	Arsenal	38	16		
2016–17	Arsenal	29	12		
2017–18	Arsenal	16	4	**180**	**73**
2017–18	Chelsea	13	3	**13**	**3**

HAZARD, Eden (M)   **354 105**
H: 5 7 W: 8 11 b.La Louviere 7-1-91
Internationals: Belgium U15, U16, U17, U19, Full caps.

2007–08	Lille	3	0		
2008–09	Lille	30	4		
2009–10	Lille	37	5		
2010–11	Lille	38	0		
2011–12	Lille	38	20	**146**	**36**
2012–13	Chelsea	34	9		
2013–14	Chelsea	35	14		
2014–15	Chelsea	38	14		
2015–16	Chelsea	31	4		
2016–17	Chelsea	36	16		
2017–18	Chelsea	34	12	**208**	**69**

HECTOR, Michael (D)   **230 13**
H: 6 4 W: 12 13 b.Newham 19-7-92
Internationals: Jamaica Full caps.

2009–10	Reading	0	0		
2010–11	Reading	0	0		
2011	Dundalk	11	2	**11**	**2**
2011–12	Reading	0	0		
2011–12	Barnet	27	2	**27**	**2**
2012–13	Reading	0	0		
2012–13	Shrewsbury T	8	0	**8**	**0**
2012–13	Aldershot T	8	1	**8**	**1**
2012–13	Cheltenham T	18	1	**18**	**1**
2013–14	Reading	9	0		
2013–14	Aberdeen	20	1	**20**	**1**

Season	Club				
2014–15	Reading	41	3		
2015–16	Chelsea	0	0		
2015–16	*Reading*	30	1	80	4
2016–17	Chelsea	0	0		
2016–17	*Eintract Frankfurt*	22	1	22	1
2017–18	Chelsea	0	0		
2017–18	*Hull C*	36	1	36	1

HOUGHTON, Jordan (M)   90   3
H: 6 2   W: 12 13   b.Chertsey 9-11-95
Internationals: England U16, U17, U20.

Season	Club				
2015–16	Chelsea	0	0		
2015–16	*Gillingham*	11	1	11	1
2015–16	*Plymouth Arg*	10	1	10	1
2016–17	Chelsea	0	0		
2016–17	*Doncaster R*	32	1		
2017–18	Chelsea	0	0		
2017–18	*Doncaster R*	37	0	69	1

HUDSON-ODOI, Callum (M)   2   0
H: 6 0   b.Wandsworth 7-11-00
Internationals: England U16, U17.

Season	Club				
2017–18	Chelsea	2	0	2	0

KALAS, Tomas (D)   153   2
H: 6 0   W: 12 00   b.Olomouc 15-5-93
Internationals: Czech Republic U17, U18, U19, U21, Full caps.

Season	Club				
2009–10	Sigma Olomouc	1	0		
2010–11	Chelsea	0	0		
2010–11	*Sigma Olomouc*	4	0	5	0
2011–12	Chelsea	0	0		
2012–13	Chelsea	0	0		
2012–13	*Vitesse*	34	1	34	1
2013–14	Chelsea	2	0		
2014–15	Chelsea	0	0		
2014–15	*Cologne*	0	0		
2014–15	*Middlesbrough*	17	0		
2015–16	Chelsea	0	0		
2015–16	*Middlesbrough*	26	0	43	0
2016–17	Chelsea	0	0		
2016–17	*Fulham*	36	1		
2017–18	Chelsea	0	0	2	0
2017–18	*Fulham*	33	0	69	1

KANE, Todd (D)   105   7
H: 5 11   W: 11 00   b.Huntingdon 17-9-93
Internationals: England U19.

Season	Club				
2011–12	Chelsea	0	0		
2012–13	Chelsea	0	0		
2012–13	*Preston NE*	3	0	3	0
2012–13	*Blackburn R*	14	0		
2013–14	Chelsea	0	0		
2013–14	*Blackburn R*	27	2	41	2
2014–15	Chelsea	0	0		
2014–15	*Bristol C*	5	0	5	0
2014–15	*Nottingham F*	8	1	8	1
2015–16	Chelsea	0	0		
2015–16	*NEC*	31	1	31	1
2016–17	Chelsea	0	0		
2017–18	Chelsea	0	0		
2017–18	*FC Groningen*	0	0		
2017–18	*Oxford U*	17	3	17	3

KANTE, Ngolo (M)   219   10
H: 5 7   W: 11 00   b.Paris 29-3-91
Internationals: France Full caps.

Season	Club				
2011–12	Boulogne	1	0		
2012–13	Boulogne	37	3	38	3
2013–14	Caen	38	2		
2014–15	Caen	37	2	75	4
2015–16	Leicester C	37	1	37	1
2016–17	Chelsea	35	1		
2017–18	Chelsea	34	1	69	2

KENEDY, Robert (F)   59   5
H: 6 0   W: 12 08   b.Santa Rita do Sapucai 8-2-96
Internationals: Brazil U17, U20, U23.

Season	Club				
2013	Fluminense	9	0		
2014	Fluminense	20	2		
2015	Fluminense	1	0	30	2
2015–16	Chelsea	14	1		
2016–17	Chelsea	1	0		
2016–17	*Watford*	1	0	1	0
2017–18	Chelsea	0	0	15	1
2017–18	*Newcastle U*	13	2	13	2

LOFTUS-CHEEK, Ruben (M)   46   3
H: 6 4   W: 11 03   b.Lewisham 23-1-96
Internationals: England U16, U17, U19, U21, Full caps.

Season	Club				
2012–13	Chelsea	0	0		
2013–14	Chelsea	0	0		
2014–15	Chelsea	3	0		
2015–16	Chelsea	13	1		
2016–17	Chelsea	6	0		
2017–18	Chelsea	0	0	22	1
2017–18	*Crystal Palace*	24	2	24	2

LUIZ, David (D)   232   13
H: 6 2   W: 13 03   b.Sao Paulo 22-4-87
Internationals: Brazil U20, Full caps.

Season	Club				
2005	Vitoria	0	0		
2006	Vitoria	26	1	26	1
2006–07	Benfica	10	0		
2007–08	Benfica	8	0		
2008–09	Benfica	19	2		
2009–10	Benfica	29	2		
2010–11	Benfica	16	0	82	4
2010–11	Chelsea	12	2		
2011–12	Chelsea	20	2		
2012–13	Chelsea	30	2		
2013–14	Chelsea	19	0		
2014–15	Paris St Germain	0	0		
2016–17	PSG	0	0		
2016–17	Chelsea	33	1		
2017–18	Chelsea	10	1	124	8

MORATA, Alvaro (F)   157   51
H: 6 2   W: 12 08   b.Madrid 23-10-92
Internationals: Spain U17, U18, U19, U21, Full caps.

Season	Club				
2010–11	Real Madrid	1	0		
2011–12	Real Madrid	1	0		
2012–13	Real Madrid	7	0		
2013–14	Real Madrid	23	8		
2014–15	Juventus	29	8		
2015–16	Juventus	34	7	63	15
2016–17	Real Madrid	26	15	63	25
2017–18	Chelsea	31	11	31	11

MOSES, Victor (M)   276   31
H: 5 10   W: 11 07   b.Lagos 12-12-90
Internationals: England U16, U17, U19, U21. Nigeria Full caps.

Season	Club				
2007–08	Crystal Palace	13	3		
2008–09	Crystal Palace	27	2		
2009–10	Crystal Palace	18	6	58	11
2009–10	Wigan Ath	14	1		
2010–11	Wigan Ath	21	1		
2011–12	Wigan Ath	38	6		
2012–13	Wigan Ath	1	0	74	8
2012–13	Chelsea	23	1		
2013–14	Chelsea	0	0		
2013–14	*Liverpool*	19	1	19	1
2014–15	Chelsea	0	0		
2014–15	*Stoke C*	19	3	19	3
2015–16	Chelsea	0	0		
2015–16	*West Ham U*	21	1	21	1
2016–17	Chelsea	34	3		
2017–18	Chelsea	28	3	85	7

MUSONDA, Charly (M)   55   2
H: 5 8   W: 10 10   b.Brussels 15-10-96
Internationals: Belgium U16, U17, U19, U21.

Season	Club				
2015–16	Chelsea	0	0		
2015–16	*Real Betis*	16	1		
2016–17	Chelsea	0	0		
2016–17	Real Betis	8	0		
2016–17	Chelsea	0	0		
2016–17	*Real Betis*	24	1	48	2
2017–18	Chelsea	3	0	3	0
2017–18	*Celtic*	4	0	4	0

PALMER, Kasey (M)   43   6
H: 5 11   W: 10 10   b.London 9-11-96
Internationals: England U17, U18, U20, U21.

Season	Club				
2015–16	Chelsea	0	0		
2016–17	Chelsea	0	0		
2016–17	*Huddersfield T*	24	4		
2017–18	Chelsea	0	0		
2017–18	*Huddersfield T*	4	0	28	4
2017–18	*Derby Co*	15	2	15	2

PEDRO, Rodriguez (F)   299   78
H: 5 7   W: 10 01   b.Santa Cruz de Tenerife 28-7-87
Internationals: Spain U21, Full caps.

Season	Club				
2007–08	Barcelona	2	0		
2008–09	Barcelona	6	0		
2009–10	Barcelona	34	12		
2010–11	Barcelona	33	13		
2011–12	Barcelona	29	5		
2012–13	Barcelona	28	7		
2013–14	Barcelona	37	15		
2014–15	Barcelona	35	6	204	58
2015–16	Chelsea	29	7		
2016–17	Chelsea	35	9		
2017–18	Chelsea	31	4	95	20

PIAZON, Lucas (M)   115   24
H: 6 0   W: 11 11   b.Curitiba 20-1-94
Internationals: Brazil U15, U17, U20, U23.

Season	Club				
2011–12	Chelsea	0	0		
2012–13	Chelsea	0	0		
2012–13	*Malaga*	11	0	11	0
2013–14	Chelsea	0	0		

Season	Club				
2013–14	*Vitesse*	29	11		
2014–15	Chelsea	0	0		
2014–15	*Vitesse*	0	0	29	11
2014–15	*Eintracht Frankfurt*	0	0		
2015–16	Chelsea	0	0		
2015–16	*Reading*	23	3	23	3
2016–17	Chelsea	0	0		
2016–17	*Fulham*	29	5		
2017–18	Chelsea	0	0	1	0
2017–18	*Fulham*	22	5	51	10

RUDIGER, Antonio (D)   149   6
H: 6 3   W: 13 05   b.Berlin 3-3-93
Internationals: Germany U18, U19, U20, U21, Full caps.

Season	Club				
2011–12	Stuttgart	1	0		
2012–13	Stuttgart	16	0		
2013–14	Stuttgart	30	2		
2014–15	Stuttgart	19	0	66	2
2015–16	Roma	30	2		
2016–17	Roma	26	0	56	2
2017–18	Chelsea	27	2	27	2

SCOTT, Kyle (M)   0   0
H: 5 8   W: 9 06   b.Bath 12-12-97
Internationals: England U16, Republic of Ireland U17, USA U18, U20.

Season	Club		
2017–18	Chelsea	0	0

STERLING, Dujon (D)   0   0
H: 5 11   b.London 3-11-99
Internationals: England U16, U17, U19.

Season	Club		
2017–18	Chelsea	0	0

TOMORI, Fikayo (D)   35   0
H: 6 0   W: 11 11   b.Calgary 19-12-97
Internationals: Canada U20. England U19, U20, U21.

Season	Club				
2015–16	Chelsea	1	0		
2016–17	Chelsea	0	0		
2016–17	*Brighton & HA*	9	0	9	0
2017–18	Chelsea	0	0	1	0
2017–18	*Hull C*	25	0	25	0

UGBO, Ike (F)   31   3
H: 6 1   W: 11 07   b.Lewisham 21-9-98
Internationals: Engalnd U17, U20.

Season	Club				
2017–18	Chelsea	0	0		
2017–18	*Barnsley*	16	1	16	1
2017–18	*Milton Keynes D*	15	2	15	2

WILLIAN, da Silva (M)   302   46
H: 5 9   W: 11 10   b.Ribeirao 9-8-88
Internationals: Brazil U20, Full caps.

Season	Club				
2006	Corinthians	5	0		
2007	Corinthians	0	0	5	0
2008–09	Shakhtar Donetsk	29	5		
2009–10	Shakhtar Donetsk	22	5		
2010–11	Shakhtar Donetsk	28	3		
2011–12	Shakhtar Donetsk	27	5		
2012–13	Shakhtar Donetsk	14	2	120	20
2012–13	Anzhi Makhachkala	7	1		
2013–14	Anzhi Makhachkala	4	0	11	1
2013–14	Chelsea	25	4		
2014–15	Chelsea	36	2		
2015–16	Chelsea	35	5		
2016–17	Chelsea	34	8		
2017–18	Chelsea	36	6	166	25

ZAPPACOSTA, Davide (D)   203   10
H: 6 1   W: 11 00   b.Sora 11-6-92
Internationals: Italy U21, Full caps.

Season	Club				
2009–10	Isola Liri				
2010–11	Isola Liri	11	1	13	1
2011–12	Avellino	27	0		
2012–13	Avellino	24	1		
2013–14	Avellino	32	2	83	3
2014–15	Atalanta	29	3	29	3
2015–16	Torino	25	1		
2016–17	Torino	29	1		
2017–18	Torino	2	0	56	2
2017–18	Chelsea	22	1	22	1

ZOUMA, Kurt (D)   142   5
H: 6 2   W: 13 04   b.Lyon 27-10-94
Internationals: France U16, U17, U19, U20, U21, Full caps.

Season	Club				
2011–12	St Etienne	20	1		
2012–13	St Etienne	18	2		
2013–14	Chelsea	0	0		
2013–14	*St Etienne*	23	0	61	3
2014–15	Chelsea	15	0		
2015–16	Chelsea	23	1		
2016–17	Chelsea	9	0		
2017–18	Chelsea	0	0	47	1
2017–18	*Stoke C*	34	1	34	1

Players retained or with offer of contract
Angban, Bekanty Victorien; Baba, Abdul Rahman; Baxter, Nathan; Brown, Charlie;

Bulka, Marcin; Colkett, Charlie; Colley, Joseph; Cumming, James Andrew; Da Silva Costa, Diego; Dabo, Sheik Mohamed Fankaty; De Souza, Nathan Allan; Familia-Castillo, Juan Carlos; Feruz, Islam; Gallagher, Conor; Grant, Joshua; Guehi, Addji Keaninkin Marc-Israel; Hazard, Kylian; James, Reece; Lamptey, Tariq; Maddox, Jacob; McCormick, Luke; McEachran, George James; Miazga, Matthew; Mount, Mason; Nartey, Richard Nicos Tettey; Omeruo, Kenneth; Pantic, Danilo; Pasalic, Mario; Quintero Quintero, Josimar Aldair; Rodriguez Gonzalez, Jhoao Leandro; Russell, Jonathan; Sammut, Ruben ; St Clair, Harvey ; Taylor-Crossdale, Martell; Thompson, Jared; Uwakwe, Tariq; Van Ginkel, Marco Wulfert Cornelius; Wakefield, Charlie Mark; Wakely, Jack.

Scholars
Gilmour, Billy Clifford; Lavinier, Marcel; Mola, Clinton; Panzo, Jonathan William; Redan, Daishawn Orpheo Marvin; Tie, Nicolas; Ziger, Karlo.

CHELTENHAM T (25)

ATANGANA, Nigel (M)   **120   2**
H: 6 2   W: 11 05   b.Corbeil-Essonnes 9-9-89

2014–15	Portsmouth	30	1	
2015–16	Portsmouth	13	0	43 1
2015–16	Leyton Orient	16	0	
2016–17	Leyton Orient	29	0	45 0
2017–18	Cheltenham T	32	1	32 1

BOWER, Matthew (D)   **3   0**
H: 6 6   W: 11 05   b. 11-12-98

2016–17	Cheltenham T	0	0	
2017–18	Cheltenham T	3	0	3 0

BOYLE, William (D)   **80   7**
H: 6 2   W: 11 00   b.Garforth 1-9-95

2014–15	Huddersfield T	1	0	
2015–16	Huddersfield T	1	0	
2015–16	York C	12	0	12 0
2016–17	Huddersfield T	0	0	0 0
2016–17	Kilmarnock	11	0	11 0
2016–17	Cheltenham T	21	2	
2017–18	Cheltenham T	34	5	55 7

CRANSTON, Jordan (D)   **69   0**
H: 5 11   W: 13 01   b.Wednesfield 11-3-93
Internationals: Wales U19.

2012–13	Wolverhampton W	0	0	
2013–14	Wolverhampton W	0	0	
2014–15	Notts Co	9	0	9 0
2015–16	Cheltenham T	0	0	
2016–17	Cheltenham T	38	0	
2017–18	Cheltenham T	22	0	60 0

DAVEY, Alex (D)   **39   0**
H: 6 3   W: 13 03   b.Luton 24-11-94
Internationals: Scotland U19.

2012–13	Chelsea	0	0	
2013–14	Chelsea	0	0	
2014–15	Chelsea	0	0	
2014–15	Scunthorpe U	13	0	13 0
2015–16	Chelsea	0	0	
2015–16	Peterborough U	7	0	7 0
2016	Stabaek	5	0	5 0
2016–17	Chelsea	0	0	
2016–17	Crawley T	14	0	
2017–18	Crawley T	0	0	14 0
2017–18	Cheltenham T			

DAWES, Will (M)   **0   0**
b.Bristol 5-9-00

2017–18	Cheltenham T	0	0	

DAWSON, Kevin (M)   **206   15**
H: 5 10   W: 12 08   b.Dublin 30-6-90
Internationals: Republic of Ireland U18.

2011	Shelbourne	26	2	
2012	Shelbourne	25	2	51 4
2012–13	Yeovil T	20	2	
2013–14	Yeovil T	35	1	
2014–15	Yeovil T	17	1	
2015–16	Yeovil T	10	0	
2016–17	Yeovil T	39	2	121 6
2016–17	Cheltenham T	3	0	
2017–18	Cheltenham T	34	5	34 5

EISA, Mohamed (F)   **45   23**
H: 6 0   W: 11 00   b. 12-7-94
From Dartford, Corinthian, Greenwich Bor.

2017–18	Cheltenham T	45	23	45 23

FLINDERS, Scott (G)   **388   1**
Internationals: England U20.

2004–05	Barnsley	11	0	
2005–06	Barnsley	3	0	14 0
2006–07	Crystal Palace	8	0	
2006–07	Gillingham	9	0	9 0
2006–07	Brighton & HA	12	0	12 0
2007–08	Crystal Palace	0	0	
2007–08	Yeovil T	9	0	9 0
2008–09	Crystal Palace	0	0	8 0
2009–10	Hartlepool U	4	0	
2010–11	Hartlepool U	26	1	
2011–12	Hartlepool U	45	0	
2012–13	Hartlepool U	46	0	
2013–14	Hartlepool U	43	0	
2014–15	Hartlepool U	46	0	252 1
2015–16	York C	43	0	43 0
From Macclesfield T.				
2017–18	Cheltenham T	41	0	41 0

FORSTER, Jordon (D)   **100   7**
b.Edinburgh 23-9-93

2010–11	Hibernian	0	0	
2011–12	Hibernian	0	0	
2011–12	Berwick R	10	2	10 2
2012–13	Hibernian	3	0	
2012–13	East Fife	12	0	12 0
2013–14	Hibernian	26	4	
2014–15	Hibernian	17	1	
2015–16	Hibernian	0	0	
2015–16	Plymouth Arg	12	0	12 0
2016–17	Hibernian	16	0	62 5
2017–18	Cheltenham T	4	0	4 0

GORDON, Jaanai (F)   **30   2**
H: 5 10   W: 10 02   b.Northampton 7-12-95

2012–13	Peterborough U	3	0	
2013–14	Peterborough U	1	0	4 0
2013–14	West Ham U	0	0	
2014–15	West Ham U	0	0	
2015–16	West Ham U	0	0	
2016	Sligo	12	1	12 1
2016–17	West Ham U	0	0	
2016–17	Newport Co	10	1	10 1
2017–18	Cheltenham T	4	0	4 0

GRAHAM, Brian (F)   **290   84**
H: 6 1   W: 11 00   b.Glasgow 23-11-87

2005–06	Greenock Morton	1	0	
2006–07	Greenock Morton	1	0	
2007–08	Greenock Morton	13	1	
2008–09	Greenock Morton	0	0	
2008–09	East Fife	33	15	33 15
2009–10	Greenock Morton	22	2	
2010–11	Greenock Morton	28	7	65 10
2011–12	Raith R	24	11	
2012–13	Raith R	34	18	58 29
2013–14	Dundee U	30	6	
2014–15	Dundee U	1	0	31 6
2014–15	St Johnstone	24	9	24 9
2015–16	Ross Co	23	6	
2016–17	Ross Co	1	0	24 6
2016–17	Hibernian	28	4	
2017–18	Hibernian	0	0	28 4
2017–18	Cheltenham T	27	5	27 5

GRIMES, Jamie (D)   **43   3**
H: 6 2   W: 12 10   b.Nottingham 22-12-90
From Swansea C, Redditch U, Bedford T, Kidderminster H, Dover Ath.

2017–18	Cheltenham T	43	3	43 3

GRIMSHAW, Ross (G)   **0   0**

2017–18	Cheltenham T	0	0	

HOLMAN, Dan (F)   **30   2**
H: 5 11   W: 11 03   b.Northampton 5-6-92

2014–15	Colchester U	4	0	
2015–16	Colchester U	0	0	4 0
2015–16	Woking	0	0	
2015–16	Cheltenham T	0	0	
2016–17	Cheltenham T	24	1	
2017–18	Cheltenham T	2	1	26 2

LLEWELYN, Lee (M)   **0   0**
b.Gloucester 14-11-99

2017–18	Cheltenham T	0	0	

LLOYD, George (M)   **7   2**
H: 5 8   W: 9 13   b. 11-2-00

2017–18	Cheltenham T	7	2	7 2

LOVETT, Rhys (G)   **1   0**
b. 15-5-97
From Rochdale.

2016–17	Cheltenham T	0	0	
2017–18	Cheltenham T	1	0	1 0

O'SHAUGHNESSY, Daniel (D)   **38   3**
H: 6 1   W: 12 00   b.Riihimaki 14-9-94
Internationals: Finland U16, U17, U18, U20, U21, Full caps.

2014–15	Brentford	0	0	
2015–16	Brentford	0	0	
2015–16	FC Midtjylland	1	0	1 0
2016–17	Cheltenham T	27	3	
2017–18	Cheltenham T	10	0	37 3
Transferred to HJK, January 2018.				

ODELUSI, Sanmi (F)   **72   6**
H: 6 0   W: 11 11   b.London 11-6-93

2012–13	Bolton W	1	0	
2013–14	Bolton W	5	0	
2013–14	Milton Keynes D	10	0	10 0
2014–15	Bolton W	0	0	6 0
2015–16	Coventry C	14	3	14 3
2015–16	Wigan Ath	3	0	
2016–17	Wigan Ath	0	0	
2016–17	Rochdale	15	0	15 0
2016–17	Blackpool	7	1	7 1
2017–18	Wigan Ath	0	0	3 0
2017–18	Colchester U	8	1	8 1
2017–18	Cheltenham T	9	1	9 1

PAGE, Adam (M)   **0   0**

2017–18	Cheltenham T	0	0	

PELL, Harry (M)   **185   21**
H: 6 4   W: 13 05   b.Tilbury 21-10-91

2010–11	Bristol R	10	0	10 0
2010–11	Hereford U	7	0	
2011–12	Hereford U	30	3	37 3
2012–13	AFC Wimbledon	17	2	
2013–14	AFC Wimbledon	33	4	
2014–15	AFC Wimbledon	9	0	59 6
2016–17	Cheltenham T	42	7	
2017–18	Cheltenham T	37	5	79 12

SELLARS, Jerell (F)   **39   2**
b. 28-4-95

2015–16	Aston Villa	0	0	
2015–16	Wycombe W	8	0	8 0
2016–17	Aston Villa	0	0	
2017–18	Cheltenham T	31	2	31 2

STORER, Kyle (M)   **44   0**
H: 5 11   W: 11 11   b.Nuneaton 30-4-87

2014–15	Cheltenham T	0	0	
2016–17	Cheltenham T	23	0	
2017–18	Cheltenham T	21	0	44 0

THOMAS, Josh (M)   **0   0**
H: 5 8   W: 9 13   b. 17-4-99

2016–17	Cheltenham T	0	0	
2017–18	Cheltenham T	0	0	

TOZER, Ben (D)   **265   10**
H: 6 1   W: 12 11   b.Plymouth 1-3-90

2007–08	Swindon T	2	0	2 0
2007–08	Newcastle U	0	0	
2008–09	Newcastle U	1	0	
2009–10	Newcastle U	0	0	
2010–11	Newcastle U	0	0	1 0
2010–11	Northampton T	31	3	
2011–12	Northampton T	45	3	
2012–13	Northampton T	46	0	
2013–14	Northampton T	29	0	
2013–14	Colchester U	1	0	1 0
2014–15	Northampton T	22	0	173 6
2015–16	Yeovil T	26	0	26 0
2016–17	Newport Co	23	1	
2017–18	Newport Co	39	3	62 4
2017–18	Cheltenham T	0	0	

WINCHESTER, Carl (D)   **184   14**
H: 5 10   W: 11 08   b.Belfast 12-4-93
Internationals: Northern Ireland U16, U17, U18, U19, U21, Full caps.

2010–11	Oldham Ath	6	1	
2011–12	Oldham Ath	12	0	
2012–13	Oldham Ath	9	0	
2013–14	Oldham Ath	12	1	
2014–15	Oldham Ath	41	4	
2015–16	Oldham Ath	31	1	
2016–17	Oldham Ath	9	1	120 8
2016–17	Cheltenham T	20	1	
2017–18	Cheltenham T	44	5	64 6

WRIGHT, Danny (F)   **74   12**
H: 6 2   W: 13 08   b.Doncaster 10-9-84
From Histon, Cambridge U, Forest Green R, Gateshead, Kidderminster H.

2016–17	Cheltenham T	41	9	
2017–18	Cheltenham T	33	3	74 12

Scholars
Brennan, Archie Noel; Briscoe, Tyreece Morgan Owen; Clayton, Lewis Scott; Clift, Finley Lewis; Davis, Ryan Alan James; Dawes, William John; Duncan, Camden Lloyd; Grimshaw, Ross Nathaniel; Hailwood, Ben Andrew; Handley, Thomas Tristan; Llewelyn, Lee Lance; Price, Oliver Stephen; Richards, Ioan; Scott, Miles Norman Daniel.

CHESTERFIELD (26)

ANYON, Joe (G) **41 0**
H: 6 4 W: 14 01 b.Blackpool 29-12-86
Internationals: England U16.

2006–07	Port Vale	0	0		
2010–11	Lincoln C	0	0		
2010–11	*Morecambe*	0	0		
2012–13	Shrewsbury T	0	0		
2013–14	Shrewsbury T	11	0		
2014–15	Shrewsbury T	0	0	**11**	**0**
2014–15	Scunthorpe U	0	0		
2015–16	Scunthorpe U	8	0		
2016–17	Scunthorpe U	8	0	**16**	**0**
2016–17	Chesterfield	0	0		
2017–18	Chesterfield	14	0	**14**	**0**

BARRY, Bradley (D) **87 1**
H: 6 0 W: 12 00 b.Hastings 13-12-95

2013–14	Brighton & HA	0	0		
2014–15	Brighton & HA	0	0		
2015–16	Swindon T	35	0		
2016–17	Swindon T	23	1	**58**	**1**
2016–17	Chesterfield	0	0		
2017–18	Chesterfield	29	0	**29**	**0**

BREWSTER, Delial (F) **2 0**
b.Southport 7-11-77

2015–16	Everton	0	0		
2016–17	Everton	0	0		
2017–18	Chesterfield	2	0	**2**	**0**

BROWNELL, Jack (M) **1 0**
b.Sheffield

2016–17	Chesterfield	1	0		
2017–18	Chesterfield	0	0	**1**	**0**

COKE, Giles (M) **288 26**
H: 6 0 W: 11 11 b.Westminster 3-6-86

2004–05	Mansfield T	9	0		
2005–06	Mansfield T	40	4		
2006–07	Mansfield T	21	1	**70**	**5**
2007–08	Northampton T	20	5		
2008–09	Northampton T	32	2	**52**	**7**
2009–10	Motherwell	32	2	**32**	**2**
2010–11	Sheffield W	27	4		
2011–12	Sheffield W	0	0		
2011–12	*Bury*	30	6	**30**	**6**
2012–13	Sheffield W	16	0		
2012–13	*Swindon T*	4	0	**4**	**0**
2013–14	Sheffield W	28	1		
2014–15	Sheffield W	13	1	**84**	**6**
2014–15	*Bolton W*	4	0	**4**	**0**
2015–16	Ipswich T	10	0	**10**	**0**
2017–18	Chesterfield	2	0	**2**	**0**

DENNIS, Kristian (F) **82 28**
H: 5 11 W: 11 00 b.Macclesfield 12-3-90

2007–08	Macclesfield T	1	0		
2008–09	Macclesfield T	3	1		
2009–10	Macclesfield T	0	0	**4**	**1**

From Woodley Sports, Mossley, Curzon Ashton, Stockport Co.

2015–16	Chesterfield	0	0		
2016–17	Chesterfield	35	8		
2017–18	Chesterfield	43	19	**78**	**27**

DIMAIO, Connor (D) **47 1**
H: 5 10 W: 11 05 b.Chesterfield 28-1-96
Internationals: Republic of Ireland U16, U17, U19, U21.

2013–14	Sheffield U	3	0		
2014–15	Sheffield U	0	0		
2015–16	Sheffield U	0	0	**3**	**0**
2015–16	Chesterfield	11	1		
2016–17	Chesterfield	23	0		
2017–18	Chesterfield	10	0	**44**	**1**

DODDS, Louis (M) **401 70**
H: 5 10 W: 12 04 b.Sheffield 8-10-86

2005–06	Leicester C	0	0		
2006–07	Leicester C	0	0		
2006–07	*Rochdale*	12	2	**12**	**2**
2007–08	Leicester C	0	0		
2007–08	*Lincoln C*	41	9	**41**	**9**
2008–09	Port Vale	44	7		
2009–10	Port Vale	44	6		
2010–11	Port Vale	33	7		
2011–12	Port Vale	35	8		
2012–13	Port Vale	30	7		
2013–14	Port Vale	29	4		
2014–15	Port Vale	37	4		
2015–16	Port Vale	37	8	**289**	**51**
2016–17	Shrewsbury T	38	8		
2017–18	Shrewsbury T	9	0	**47**	**8**
2017–18	Chesterfield	12	0	**12**	**0**

EVATT, Ian (D) **534 23**
H: 6 3 W: 13 12 b.Coventry 19-11-81

1998–99	Derby Co	0	0		
1999–2000	Derby Co	0	0		
2000–01	Derby Co	1	0		
2001–02	*Northampton T*	11	0	**11**	**0**
2001–02	Derby Co	3	0		
2002–03	Derby Co	30	0	**34**	**0**
2003–04	Chesterfield	43	5		
2004–05	Chesterfield	41	4		
2005–06	QPR	27	0		
2006–07	QPR	0	0	**27**	**0**
2006–07	Blackpool	44	0		
2007–08	Blackpool	29	0		
2008–09	Blackpool	33	1		
2009–10	Blackpool	36	4		
2010–11	Blackpool	38	1		
2011–12	Blackpool	39	3		
2012–13	Blackpool	11	0	**230**	**9**
2013–14	Chesterfield	35	1		
2014–15	Chesterfield	39	1		
2015–16	Chesterfield	23	1		
2016–17	Chesterfield	30	2		
2017–18	Chesterfield	21	0	**232**	**14**

GERMAN, Ricky (F) **9 0**
H: 6 2 W: 12 08 b.Brent 13-1-99

2016–17	Chesterfield	7	0		
2017–18	Chesterfield	2	0	**9**	**0**

HINES, Zavon (F) **131 12**
H: 5 10 W: 10 07 b.Jamaica 27-12-88
Internationals: England U21.

2007–08	West Ham U	0	0		
2007–08	*Coventry C*	7	1	**7**	**1**
2008–09	West Ham U	0	0		
2009–10	West Ham U	13	1		
2010–11	West Ham U	9	0	**22**	**1**
2011–12	Burnley	13	0	**13**	**0**
2011–12	*Bournemouth*	8	1	**8**	**1**
2012–13	Bradford C	32	2		
2013–14	Bradford C	0	0	**32**	**2**
2013–14	Dagenham & R	27	6		
2014–15	Dagenham & R	0	0		
2015–16	Dagenham & R	6	0	**33**	**6**
2016–17	Southend U	5	0	**5**	**0**

From Maidstone U.

2017–18	Chesterfield	11	1	**11**	**1**

HIRD, Samuel (D) **365 11**
H: 5 7 W: 10 12 b.Askern 7-9-87

2005–06	Leeds U	0	0		
2006–07	Leeds U	0	0		
2006–07	*Doncaster R*	5	0		
2007–08	Doncaster R	4	0		
2007–08	*Grimsby T*	17	0	**17**	**0**
2008–09	Doncaster R	37	1		
2009–10	Doncaster R	36	0		
2010–11	Doncaster R	32	0		
2011–12	Doncaster R	31	0	**145**	**1**
2012–13	Chesterfield	41	2		
2013–14	Chesterfield	35	2		
2014–15	Chesterfield	28	3		
2015–16	Chesterfield	40	2		
2016–17	Chesterfield	35	1		
2017–18	Chesterfield	24	0	**203**	**10**

HOLMES, Jack (M) **0 0**

2017–18	Chesterfield	0	0		

JONES, Brad (G) **0 0**
b. 17-11-00

2017–18	Chesterfield	0	0		

LEE, Tommy (G) **402 0**
H: 6 2 W: 12 00 b.Keighley 3-1-86

2005–06	Manchester U	0	0		
2005–06	*Macclesfield T*	11	0		
2006–07	Macclesfield T	34	0		
2007–08	Macclesfield T	18	0	**63**	**0**
2007–08	*Rochdale*	11	0	**11**	**0**
2008–09	Chesterfield	28	0		
2009–10	Chesterfield	42	0		
2010–11	Chesterfield	46	0		
2011–12	Chesterfield	35	0		
2012–13	Chesterfield	32	0		
2013–14	Chesterfield	46	0		
2014–15	Chesterfield	46	0		
2015–16	Chesterfield	46	0		
2017–18	Chesterfield	7	0	**328**	**0**

MAGUIRE, Laurence (D) **29 0**
H: 5 10 W: 11 00 b.Sheffield 8-2-97

2013–14	Chesterfield	0	0		
2014–15	Chesterfield	0	0		
2015–16	Chesterfield	0	0		
2016–17	Chesterfield	11	0		
2017–18	Chesterfield	18	0	**29**	**0**

McCOURT, Jak (M) **74 6**
H: 5 10 W: 10 10 b.Leicester 6-7-95

2013–14	Leicester C	0	0		
2013–14	*Torquay U*	11	0	**11**	**0**
2014–15	Leicester C	0	0		
2015–16	Leicester C	0	0		
2015–16	*Port Vale*	2	0	**2**	**0**
2015–16	Barnsley	1	0	**1**	**0**
2016–17	Northampton T	26	1	**26**	**1**
2017–18	Chesterfield	34	5	**34**	**5**

McGINN, Paul (D) **210 5**
H: 5 9 W: 10 05 b.Glasgow 22-10-90

2008–09	Queen's Park	1	0		
2009–10	Queen's Park	6	0		
2010–11	Queen's Park	26	1		
2011–12	Queen's Park	34	0		
2012–13	St Mirren	0	0		
2012–13	*Queen's Park*	8	1	**75**	**2**
2012–13	*Dumbarton*	14	1		
2013–14	Dumbarton	35	0	**49**	**1**
2014–15	Dundee	34	1		
2015–16	Dundee	34	0	**68**	**1**
2016–17	Chesterfield	18	1		
2017–18	Chesterfield	0	0	**18**	**1**

Transferred to Partick Thistle August 2017.

MITCHELL, Reece (M) **32 2**
b.London 19-7-95
Internationals: England U16.
From Chelsea.

2016–17	Chesterfield	28	2		
2017–18	Chesterfield	4	0	**32**	**2**

O'GRADY, Chris (F) **461 87**
H: 6 3 W: 12 04 b.Nottingham 25-1-86

2002–03	Leicester C	1	0		
2003–04	Leicester C	0	0		
2004–05	Leicester C	0	0		
2004–05	*Notts Co*	9	0	**9**	**0**
2005–06	Leicester C	13	1		
2005–06	*Rushden & D*	22	4	**22**	**4**
2006–07	Leicester C	10	0	**24**	**1**
2006–07	Rotherham U	13	4		
2007–08	Rotherham U	38	9	**51**	**13**
2008–09	Oldham Ath	13	0	**13**	**0**
2008–09	*Bury*	6	0	**6**	**0**
2008–09	*Bradford C*	2	0	**2**	**0**
2008–09	*Stockport Co*	18	2	**18**	**2**
2009–10	Rochdale	43	22		
2010–11	Rochdale	46	9		
2011–12	Rochdale	1	0	**90**	**31**
2011–12	Sheffield W	32	5		
2012–13	Sheffield W	21	4	**53**	**9**
2012–13	*Barnsley*	16	5		
2013–14	Barnsley	40	15	**56**	**20**
2014–15	Brighton & HA	28	1		
2014–15	*Sheffield U*	4	1	**4**	**1**
2015–16	Brighton & HA	3	0		
2015–16	*Nottingham F*	21	2	**21**	**2**
2016–17	Brighton & HA	0	0	**31**	**1**
2016–17	*Burton Alb*	26	1	**26**	**1**
2017–18	Chesterfield	35	2	**35**	**2**

OFOEGBU, Ify (D) **0 0**

2016–17	Chesterfield	0	0		
2017–18	Chesterfield	0	0		

PARKIN, Dylan (G) **0 0**
b. 11-11-99

2016–17	Chesterfield	0	0		
2017–18	Chesterfield	0	0		

RAWSON, Luke (F) **1 0**
b. 25-3-01

2017–18	Chesterfield	1	0	**1**	**0**

ROWLEY, Joe (M) **35 4**
H: 5 11 W: 11 00 b. 3-6-99

2016–17	Chesterfield	7	1		
2017–18	Chesterfield	28	3	**35**	**4**

SINNOTT, Jordan (M) **19 2**
H: 5 11 W: 11 12 b. 14-2-94

2012–13	Huddersfield T	1	0		
2013–14	Huddersfield T	0	0		
2013–14	*Bury*	9	1	**9**	**1**
2014–15	Huddersfield T	1	0	**2**	**0**

From Altrincham, Halifax T.

2017–18	Chesterfield	8	1	**8**	**1**

SMITH, George (D) — 55 0
H: 6 0 W: 12 02 b.Barnsley 14-8-96

Season	Club	App	Gls	App	Gls
2014–15	Barnsley	18	0		
2015–16	Barnsley	19	0	37	0
2015–16	Crawley T	4	0	4	0
2017–18	Northampton T	6	0	6	0
2017–18	Chesterfield	8	0	8	0

TALBOT, Drew (F) — 357 23
H: 5 10 W: 11 00 b.Barnsley 19-7-86

Season	Club	App	Gls	App	Gls
2003–04	Sheffield W	0	0		
2004–05	Sheffield W	21	4		
2005–06	Sheffield W	0	0		
2006–07	Sheffield W	8	0	29	4
2006–07	Scunthorpe U	3	1	3	1
2006–07	Luton T	15	3		
2007–08	Luton T	27	0		
2008–09	Luton T	7	0	49	3
2008–09	Chesterfield	17	2		
2009–10	Chesterfield	30	6		
2010–11	Chesterfield	44	3		
2011–12	Chesterfield	43	2		
2012–13	Chesterfield	42	2		
2013–14	Chesterfield	25	0		
2014–15	Chesterfield	9	0		
2014–15	Plymouth Arg	9	0	9	0
2015–16	Chesterfield	34	0		
2016–17	Portsmouth	5	0		
2017–18	Portsmouth	4	0	9	0
2017–18	Chesterfield	14	0	258	15

UGWU, Chigozie (F) — 105 10
H: 6 2 W: 12 00 b.Oxford 22-4-93

Season	Club	App	Gls	App	Gls
2011–12	Reading	0	0		
2012–13	Reading	0	0		
2012–13	Yeovil T	15	3		
2012–13	Plymouth Arg	6	0	6	0
2013–14	Reading	0	0		
2013–14	Shrewsbury T	7	1	7	1
2014–15	Dunfermline Ath	14	7	14	7
2014–15	Yeovil T	22	5	37	8
2015–16	Wycombe W	29	2	29	2
2017–18	Chesterfield	12	0	12	0

WAKEFIELD, Charlie (M) — 2 0
b.Derby 5-7-99
From Chelsea.

Season	Club	App	Gls	App	Gls
2016–17	Chesterfield	1	0		
2017–18	Chesterfield	1	0	2	0

WEIR, Robbie (M) — 275 12
H: 5 9 W: 11 07 b.Belfast 9-12-88
Internationals: Northern Ireland U18, U19, U21, B.

Season	Club	App	Gls	App	Gls
2007–08	Sunderland	0	0		
2008–09	Sunderland	0	0		
2009–10	Sunderland	0	0		
2010–11	Sunderland	0	0		
2010–11	Tranmere R	18	0		
2011–12	Tranmere R	39	3	57	3
2012–13	Burton Alb	42	5		
2013–14	Burton Alb	41	2		
2014–15	Burton Alb	41	0		
2015–16	Burton Alb	36	0	160	7
2016–17	Leyton Orient	17	0	17	0
2017–18	Chesterfield	41	2	41	2

WHITMORE, Alex (D) — 58 1
H: 5 11 W: 10 10 b.Newcastle upon Tyne 7-9-95

Season	Club	App	Gls	App	Gls
2016–17	Burnley	0	0		
2016–17	Morecambe	35	0	35	0
2017–18	Burnley	0	0		
2017–18	Bury	8	0	8	0
2017–18	Chesterfield	15	1	15	1

WILLIAMS, Jerome (D) — 78 1
H: 5 11 W: 12 02 b.Croydon 7-3-95
Internationals: England U18, U19.

Season	Club	App	Gls	App	Gls
2013–14	Crystal Palace	0	0		
2014–15	Crystal Palace	0	0		
2014–15	Southend U	21	0	21	0
2015–16	Crystal Palace	0	0		
2015–16	Burton Alb	15	1	15	1
2016–17	Leyton Orient	13	0	13	0
2016–17	Peterborough U	10	0	10	0
2017–18	Chesterfield	19	0	19	0

WILLOCK, Marshall (D) — 0 0
b.Birmingham 7-4-00
From Walsall, Solihull Moors.

Season	Club	App	Gls	App	Gls
2017–18	Chesterfield	0	0		

WISEMAN, Scott (D) — 382 7
H: 6 0 W: 11 06 b.Hull 9-10-85
Internationals: England U20. Gilbraltar Full caps.

Season	Club	App	Gls	App	Gls
2003–04	Hull C	2	0		
2004–05	Hull C	3	0		
2004–05	Boston U	2	0	2	0
2005–06	Hull C	11	0		
2006–07	Hull C	0	0	16	0
2006–07	Rotherham U	18	1	18	1
2006–07	Darlington	10	0		
2007–08	Darlington	7	0	17	0
2008–09	Rochdale	32	0		
2009–10	Rochdale	36	1		
2010–11	Rochdale	37	0		
2011–12	Barnsley	43	1		
2012–13	Barnsley	36	0		
2013–14	Barnsley	23	0	102	1
2013–14	Preston NE	15	0		
2014–15	Preston NE	22	2	37	2
2015–16	Scunthorpe U	24	0		
2016–17	Scunthorpe U	24	2	48	2
2017–18	Chesterfield	24	0	24	0
2017–18	Rochdale	13	0	118	1

Scholars
Amantchi, Hanani Levi Micael; Foster, Robbie Sylvain; Hand, Dylan Patrick; Holmes, Jack Thomas; Howard, Brandon Michael; Jones, Bradley James Roger; Ofoegbu, Ifeanyi Convenant; Rawson, Luke; Render, Alexander Kristian; Sennett-Neilson, Aaron; Sharman, Jamie Robert; Walker, Zak Neil.

COLCHESTER U (27)

BARNES, Dillon (G) — 2 0
H: 6 4 W: 11 11 b. 8-4-96
From Bedford T.

Season	Club	App	Gls	App	Gls
2015–16	Colchester U	0	0		
2016–17	Colchester U	0	0		
2017–18	Colchester U	2	0	2	0

COMLEY, Brandon (M) — 85 1
H: 5 11 W: 11 05 b.Islington 18-11-95

Season	Club	App	Gls	App	Gls
2014–15	QPR	1	0		
2015–16	QPR	0	0		
2015–16	Carlisle U	12	0	12	0
2016–17	QPR	1	0	2	0
2016–17	Grimsby T	33	0		
2017–18	Grimsby T	5	0	33	0
2017–18	Colchester U	38	1	38	1

DICKENSON, Brennan (F) — 141 18
H: 6 0 W: 12 07 b.Ferndown 26-2-93

Season	Club	App	Gls	App	Gls
2012–13	Brighton & HA	1	0		
2012–13	Chesterfield	11	1	11	1
2012–13	AFC Wimbledon	7	2	7	2
2013–14	Brighton & HA	0	0		
2013–14	Northampton T	13	1	13	1
2014–15	Gillingham	34	1		
2015–16	Gillingham	33	1	67	2
2016–17	Colchester U	36	12		
2017–18	Colchester U	7	0	43	12

EASTMAN, Tom (D) — 272 14
H: 6 3 W: 13 12 b.Clacton 21-10-91

Season	Club	App	Gls	App	Gls
2009–10	Ipswich T	1	0		
2010–11	Ipswich T	9	0	10	0
2011–12	Colchester U	25	3		
2011–12	Crawley T	6	0	6	0
2012–13	Colchester U	29	2		
2013–14	Colchester U	36	0		
2014–15	Colchester U	46	1		
2015–16	Colchester U	43	2		
2016–17	Colchester U	35	3		
2017–18	Colchester U	42	3	256	14

EDGE, Charley (F) — 1 0
b.Aberystwyth 14-5-97
Internationals: Wales U17.
From Everton.

Season	Club	App	Gls	App	Gls
2016–17	Colchester U	1	0		
2017–18	Colchester U	0	0	1	0

GILMARTIN, Rene (G) — 64 0
H: 6 5 W: 13 06 b.Dublin 31-5-87
Internationals: Republic of Ireland U19, U21.

Season	Club	App	Gls	App	Gls
2005–06	Walsall	2	0		
2006–07	Walsall	0	0		
2007–08	Walsall	0	0		
2008–09	Walsall	11	0		
2009–10	Walsall	22	0	35	0
2010–11	Watford	0	0		
2011–12	Watford	2	0		
2011–12	Yeovil T	8	0	8	0
2011–12	Crawley T	6	0	6	0
2012–13	Plymouth Arg	13	0		
2013–14	Plymouth Arg	0	0	13	0
2014–15	Watford	0	0		
2015–16	Watford	0	0		
2016–17	Watford	0	0		
2017–18	Colchester U	2	0	2	0

GONDOH, Ryan (F) — 2 0
b.6-6-97

Season	Club	App	Gls	App	Gls
2015–16	Barnet	0	0		

From Metropolitan Police, Kingstonian, Carshalton Ath, Maldon & Tiptree.

Season	Club	App	Gls	App	Gls
2017–18	Colchester U	2	0	2	0

GUTHRIE, Kurtis (F) — 58 13
H: 5 11 W: 11 00 b.Jersey 21-4-93
Internationals: England C.

Season	Club	App	Gls	App	Gls
2011–12	Accrington S	13	0		
2012–13	Accrington S	0	0	13	0
2012–13	Bath City	0	0		
2012–13	Welling	0	0		
2016–17	Colchester U	33	12		
2017–18	Colchester U	12	1	45	13

ISSA, Tariq (M) — 2 0
H: 5 7 W: 10 08 b.2-9-97

Season	Club	App	Gls	App	Gls
2016–17	Colchester U	0	0		
2017–18	Colchester U	2	0	2	0

JACKSON, Ryan (M) — 183 5
H: 5 9 W: 10 03 b.Streatham 31-7-90
Internationals: England C.

Season	Club	App	Gls	App	Gls
2011–12	AFC Wimbledon	7	0	7	0
2013–14	Newport Co	29	0		
2014–15	Newport Co	34	0	63	0
2015–16	Gillingham	37	2		
2016–17	Gillingham	34	1	71	3
2017–18	Colchester U	42	2	42	2

JAMES, Cameron (D) — 22 0
H: 6 0 W: 12 00 b.Chelmsford 11-2-98

Season	Club	App	Gls	App	Gls
2015–16	Colchester U	1	0		
2016–17	Colchester U	14	0		
2017–18	Colchester U	7	0	22	0

JOHNSTONE, Denny (F) — 62 6
H: 6 2 W: 13 01 b.Dumfries 9-1-95
Internationals: Scotland U16, U17, U18, U19.

Season	Club	App	Gls	App	Gls
2013–14	Celtic	0	0		
2014–15	Birmingham C	2	0		
2014–15	Cheltenham T	5	1	5	1
2014–15	Burton Alb	5	1	5	1
2015–16	Birmingham C	0	0	2	0
2016–17	Colchester U	28	2		
2017–18	Colchester U	2	0	30	2
2017–18	St Johnstone	20	2	20	2

KENT, Frankie (D) — 87 2
H: 6 2 W: 12 00 b.Romford 21-11-95

Season	Club	App	Gls	App	Gls
2013–14	Colchester U	1	0		
2014–15	Colchester U	10	0		
2015–16	Colchester U	26	0		
2016–17	Colchester U	13	0		
2017–18	Colchester U	37	2	87	2

KINSELLA, Lewis (D) — 25 0
H: 5 9 W: 11 05 b.Watford 2-9-94

Season	Club	App	Gls	App	Gls
2013–14	Aston Villa	0	0		
2014–15	Aston Villa	0	0		
2014–15	Luton T	3	0	3	0
2015–16	Aston Villa	0	0		
2016–17	Colchester U	13	0		
2017–18	Colchester U	9	0	22	0

KPEKAWA, Cole (D) — 34 0
H: 6 3 W: 12 08 b.Blackpool 20-5-96
Internationals: England U20.

Season	Club	App	Gls	App	Gls
2014–15	QPR	1	0		
2014–15	Colchester U	4	0		
2014–15	Portsmouth	2	0	2	0
2015–16	QPR	5	0	6	0
2015–16	Leyton Orient	9	0	9	0
2016–17	Barnsley	7	0	7	0
2017–18	Colchester U	6	0	10	0

LAPSLIE, Tom (M) — 87 2
H: 5 6 W: 10 12 b.Waltham Forest 5-5-95

Season	Club	App	Gls	App	Gls
2013–14	Colchester U	0	0		
2014–15	Colchester U	11	1		
2015–16	Colchester U	10	1		
2016–17	Colchester U	37	0		
2017–18	Colchester U	29	0	87	2

LOFT, Doug (M) — 306 25
H: 6 0 W: 12 01 b.Maidstone 25-12-86

Season	Club	App	Gls	App	Gls
2005–06	Brighton & HA	3	1		
2006–07	Brighton & HA	11	1		
2007–08	Brighton & HA	0	0		
2008–09	Brighton & HA	12	0	39	2
2008–09	Dagenham & R	11	0	11	0
2009–10	Port Vale	32	3		
2010–11	Port Vale	29	1		
2011–12	Port Vale	44	4		
2012–13	Port Vale	32	1		
2013–14	Port Vale	37	9	174	18
2014–15	Gillingham	36	1		
2015–16	Gillingham	26	4	62	5

| 2016–17 | Colchester U | 8 | 0 | | |
| 2017–18 | Colchester U | 12 | 0 | 20 | 0 |

MANDRON, Mikael (F) 69 11
H: 6 3 W: 12 13 b.Boulogne 11-10-94
Internationals: Scotland U20.

2011–12	Sunderland	0	0		
2012–13	Sunderland	2	0		
2013–14	Sunderland	0	0		
2013–14	*Fleetwood T*	11	1	11	1
2014–15	Sunderland	1	0		
2014–15	*Shrewsbury T*	3	0	3	0
2015–16	Sunderland	0	0	3	0
2015–16	*Hartlepool U*	5	0	5	0
2016–17	Wigan Ath	3	0	3	0
2017–18	Colchester U	44	10	44	10

McKEOWN, Eoin (F) 0 0
b.London

| 2017–18 | Colchester U | 0 | 0 | | |

MURRAY, Sean (M) 153 15
H: 5 9 W: 10 10 b.Abbots Langley 11-10-93
Internationals: Republic of Ireland U17, U19, U21.

2010–11	Watford	2	0		
2011–12	Watford	18	7		
2012–13	Watford	15	1		
2013–14	Watford	34	3		
2014–15	Watford	6	0		
2015–16	Watford	0	0		
2015–16	*Wigan Ath*	7	0	7	0
2016–17	Watford	0	0	75	11
2016–17	*Swindon T*	18	1	18	1
2016–17	Colchester U	16	0		
2017–18	Colchester U	37	3	53	3

O'SULLIVAN, Tommy (M) 29 1
H: 5 9 W: 11 04 b.Mountain Ash 18-1-95
Internationals: Wales U17, U19, U21.

2012–13	Cardiff C	0	0		
2013–14	Cardiff C	0	0		
2014–15	Cardiff C	0	0		
2014–15	*Port Vale*	5	0	5	0
2015–16	Cardiff C	0	0		
2015–16	*Newport Co*	20	1	20	1
2016–17	Colchester U	3	0		
2017–18	Colchester U	1	0	4	0

OGEDI-UZOKWE, Junior (F) 9 1
b. 20-3-94
From Maldon & Tiptree

| 2017–18 | Colchester U | 9 | 1 | 9 | 1 |

PROSSER, Luke (D) 202 10
H: 6 2 W: 12 04 b.Waltham Cross 28-5-88

2005–06	Port Vale	0	0		
2006–07	Port Vale	0	0		
2007–08	Port Vale	5	0		
2008–09	Port Vale	26	1		
2009–10	Port Vale	2	1	33	2
2010–11	Southend U	17	1		
2011–12	Southend U	21	1		
2012–13	Southend U	25	0		
2013–14	Southend U	25	3		
2014–15	Southend U	30	0		
2015–16	Southend U	13	2	131	7
2015–16	*Northampton T*	8	0	8	0
2016–17	Colchester U	14	0		
2017–18	Colchester U	16	1	30	1

ROONEY, Paul (D) 0 0
b.Dublin 22-3-97
From St Patricks Ath, Bohemians.

| 2016–17 | Millwall | 0 | 0 | | |
| 2017–18 | Colchester U | 0 | 0 | | |

SENIOR, Courtney (F) 19 4
b. 30-6-97

2014–15	Wycombe W	1	0	1	0
2015–16	Brentford	0	0		
2017–18	Colchester U	18	4	18	4

SIMS, Oliver (F) 0 0

| 2017–18 | Colchester U | 0 | 0 | | |

SLATER, Craig (M) 117 11
H: 5 10 W: 11 09 b.Glasgow 26-4-94
Internationals: Scotland U16, U17, U19, U21.
From St Mirren.

2012–13	Kilmarnock	2	0		
2013–14	Kilmarnock	22	1		
2014–15	Kilmarnock	26	4		
2015–16	Kilmarnock	26	2	76	7
2016–17	Colchester U	28	3		
2017–18	Colchester U	6	0	34	3
2017–18	*Dundee U*	7	1	7	1

SZMIDICS, Sammie (M) 99 21
H: 5 6 W: 10 01 b.Colchester 24-9-95

2013–14	Colchester U	7	0		
2014–15	Colchester U	31	4		
2015–16	Colchester U	5	0		
2016–17	Colchester U	19	5		
2017–18	Colchester U	37	12	99	21

VINCENT-YOUNG, Kane (D) 70 1
H: 5 11 W: 11 00 b.Camden Town 15-3-96

2014–15	Colchester U	0	0		
2015–16	Colchester U	14	0		
2016–17	Colchester U	18	0		
2017–18	Colchester U	38	1	70	1

WALKER, Sam (G) 259 0
H: 6 5 W: 14 00 b.Gravesend 2-10-91

2009–10	Chelsea	0	0		
2010–11	Chelsea	0	0		
2010–11	*Barnet*	7	0	7	0
2011–12	Chelsea	0	0		
2011–12	*Northampton T*	21	0	21	0
2011–12	*Yeovil T*	20	0	20	0
2012–13	Chelsea	0	0		
2012–13	*Bristol R*	11	0	11	0
2012–13	*Colchester U*	19	0		
2013–14	Colchester U	46	0		
2014–15	Colchester U	45	0		
2015–16	Colchester U	46	0		
2016–17	Colchester U	46	0		
2017–18	Colchester U	44	0	200	0

WRIGHT, Diaz (M) 0 0

| 2016–17 | Colchester U | 0 | 0 | | |
| 2017–18 | Colchester U | 0 | 0 | | |

WRIGHT, Drey (M) 134 8
H: 5 9 W: 10 11 b.Greenwich 30-4-94

2012–13	Colchester U	21	3		
2013–14	Colchester U	11	0		
2014–15	Colchester U	5	0		
2015–16	Colchester U	11	0		
2016–17	Colchester U	42	2		
2017–18	Colchester U	44	3	134	8

Players retained or with offer of contract
Barnes, Aaron Christopher; Brown, George Alan; Dunne, Louis Anthony; Krasniqi, Arjanit; Sheriff, De-Carrey Deavon.

Scholars
Ager, Dean Fred; Anderson, Callum George; Chilvers, Noah Christopher; Clampin, Ryan; Ferliss, Shakeem Devante; Howard, Robert William; Jones, Callum Wiliam Adam; Jopling, Kyle Oliver; Kensdale, Oliver James; Keys, George Harvey; Madley, Jack Martin; Maughn, Maxwell David Thomas; Michaels, Kieran James; Mudd, Reuben Alan; Sims, Oliver James Richard; Stone, Frankie Alfie.

COVENTRY C (28)

ADDAI, Corey (G) 0 0
b. 10-10-97

2015–16	Coventry C	0	0		
2016–17	Coventry C	0	0		
2017–18	Coventry C	0	0		

ANDREU, Tony (M) 221 57
H: 5 10 W: 11 05 b.Cagnes-Sur-Mer 22-5-88

2009–10	Nyon	29	2		
2010–11	Nyon	21	2		
2011–12	Nyon	27	6	77	10
2012–13	Livingston	33	7	33	7
2013–14	Hamilton A	35	13		
2014–15	Hamilton A	23	12	58	25
2014–15	*Norwich C*	6	0		
2015–16	Norwich C	0	0		
2015–16	*Rotherham U*	11	2	11	2
2016–17	Norwich C	0	0	6	0
2016–17	*Dundee U*	31	13	31	13
2017–18	Coventry C	5	0	5	0

BAYLISS, Tom (M) 24 5
b. 6-4-99

| 2017–18 | Coventry C | 24 | 5 | 24 | 5 |

BEAVON, Stuart (F) 298 52
H: 5 7 W: 10 10 b.Reading 5-5-84

2008–09	Wycombe W	8	0		
2009–10	Wycombe W	25	3		
2010–11	Wycombe W	37	3		
2011–12	Wycombe W	43	21		
2012–13	Wycombe W	2	1	115	28
2012–13	Preston NE	31	6		
2013–14	Preston NE	27	3	58	9
2014–15	Burton Alb	44	6		
2015–16	Burton Alb	43	7		
2016–17	Burton Alb	10	0	97	13
2016–17	Coventry C	14	2		
2017–18	Coventry C	14	0	28	2

BIAMOU, Maxime (F) 84 14
b. 13-11-90

| 2014–15 | Villemobmble Sports | 15 | 3 | 15 | 3 |
| 2015–16 | Yzeure | 30 | 6 | 30 | 6 |

From Sutton U.

| 2017–18 | Coventry C | 39 | 5 | 39 | 5 |

BILSON, Tom (G) 0 0
b.Shrewsbury

| 2017–18 | Coventry C | 0 | 0 | | |

BURGE, Lee (G) 100 0
H: 5 11 W: 11 00 b.Hereford 9-1-93

2011–12	Coventry C	0	0		
2012–13	Coventry C	0	0		
2013–14	Coventry C	0	0		
2014–15	Coventry C	18	0		
2015–16	Coventry C	9	0		
2016–17	Coventry C	33	0		
2017–18	Coventry C	40	0	100	0

CAMWELL, Chris (D) 1 0
b. 27-10-98

| 2016–17 | Coventry C | 1 | 0 | | |
| 2017–18 | Coventry C | 0 | 0 | 1 | 0 |

DAVIES, Tom (D) 65 1
H: 5 11 W: 11 00 b.Warrington 18-4-92

2014–15	Fleetwood T	0	0		
2015–16	Accrington S	32	1	32	1
2016–17	Portsmouth	12	0		
2017–18	Portsmouth	0	0	12	0
2017–18	Coventry C	21	0	21	0

DOYLE, Micky (M) 629 35
H: 5 10 W: 11 00 b.Dublin 8-7-81
Internationals: Republic of Ireland U21, Full caps.

2003–04	Coventry C	40	5		
2004–05	Coventry C	44	4		
2005–06	Coventry C	44	0		
2006–07	Coventry C	40	3		
2007–08	Coventry C	42	7		
2008–09	Coventry C	37	2		
2009–10	Coventry C	0	0		
2009–10	*Leeds U*	42	0	42	0
2010–11	Coventry C	18	1		
2010–11	Sheffield U	16	0		
2011–12	Sheffield U	43	3		
2012–13	Sheffield U	43	3		
2013–14	Sheffield U	43	2		
2014–15	Sheffield U	43	1	188	9
2015–16	Portsmouth	44	2		
2016–17	Portsmouth	46	1	90	3
2017–18	Coventry C	44	3	309	23

FINN, Kyle (M) 0 0
b. 7-12-98

| 2017–18 | Coventry C | 0 | 0 | | |

FORD, Reece (D) 0 0
b. 29-10-98

| 2017–18 | Coventry C | 0 | 0 | | |

GRIMMER, Jack (M) 123 3
H: 6 0 W: 12 06 b.Aberdeen 25-1-94
Internationals: Scotland U16, U17, U18, U19, U21.

2009–10	Aberdeen	2	0		
2010–11	Aberdeen	2	0		
2011–12	Aberdeen	0	0	4	0
2011–12	Fulham	0	0		
2012–13	Fulham	0	0		
2013–14	Fulham	0	0		
2013–14	*Port Vale*	13	1	13	1
2014–15	Fulham	13	0		
2014–15	*Shrewsbury T*	6	0		
2015–16	Fulham	0	0		
2015–16	*Shrewsbury T*	21	1		
2016–17	Fulham	0	0	13	0
2016–17	*Shrewsbury T*	24	0	51	1
2017–18	Coventry C	42	1	42	1

HAYNES, Ryan (D) 88 1
H: 5 7 W: 10 10 b.Northampton 27-9-95

2012–13	Coventry C	1	0		
2013–14	Coventry C	2	0		
2014–15	Coventry C	26	1		
2015–16	Coventry C	9	0		
2015–16	*Cambridge U*	10	0	10	0
2016–17	Coventry C	19	0		
2017–18	Coventry C	21	0	78	1

HICKMAN, Jak (F) 0 0
b. 11-9-98

| 2017–18 | Coventry C | 0 | 0 | | |

HYAM, Dominic (D) 30 0
H: 6 2 W: 11 00 b.Leuchars 20-12-95
Internationals: Scotland U19, U21.

2014–15	Reading	0	0	
2015–16	Reading	0	0	
2015–16	Dagenham & R	16	0	16 0
2016–17	Reading	0	0	
2016–17	Portsmouth	0	0	
2017–18	Coventry C	14	0	14 0

JONES, Jodi (F) 94 10
b.London 22-10-97

2014–15	Dagenham & R	8	1	
2015–16	Dagenham & R	27	3	35 4
2015–16	Coventry C	6	0	
2016–17	Coventry C	34	1	
2017–18	Coventry C	19	5	59 6

KELLY, Liam (M) 253 27
H: 6 2 W: 13 11 b.Milton Keynes 10-2-90
Internationals: Scotland U19, U21, Full caps.

2009–10	Kilmarnock	15	1	
2010–11	Kilmarnock	32	7	
2011–12	Kilmarnock	34	1	
2012–13	Kilmarnock	19	6	100 15
2012–13	Bristol C	5	0	
2013–14	Bristol C	2	0	21 0
2014–15	Oldham Ath	37	1	
2015–16	Oldham Ath	41	6	78 7
2016–17	Leyton Orient	21	4	21 4
2017–18	Coventry C	33	1	33 1

KELLY-EVANS, Devon (M) 14 1
H: 5 10 W: 12 06 b.Coventry 21-9-96

2016–17	Coventry C	0	0	
2017–18	Coventry C	14	1	14 1

KELLY-EVANS, Dion (D) 28 0
H: 5 10 W: 12 06 b.Coventry 21-9-96

2014–15	Coventry C	0	0	
2015–16	Coventry C	1	0	
2016–17	Coventry C	25	0	
2017–18	Coventry C	2	0	28 0

LEAHY, Darragh (M) 0 0
b. 15-4-98
Internationals: Republic of Ireland U17, U19.

2017–18	Coventry C	0	0	

Transferred to Bohemians, January 2018.

MAYCOCK, Callum (D) 4 0
b. 23-12-97

2016–17	Coventry C	3	0	
2017–18	Coventry C	1	0	4 0

McDONALD, Rod (D) 67 3
H: 6 3 W: 12 13 b.Crewe 11-4-92

2010–11	Oldham Ath	0	0	

From Colwyn Bay, Nantwich T, Hereford U,
AFC Telford U.

2015–16	Northampton T	23	3	
2016–17	Northampton T	7	0	30 3
2016–17	Coventry C	0	0	
2017–18	Coventry C	37	0	37 0

McNULTY, Marc (M) 229 81
H: 5 10 W: 11 00 b.Edinburgh 14-9-92

2009–10	Livingston	9	1	
2010–11	Livingston	5	1	
2011–12	Livingston	30	11	
2012–13	Livingston	26	7	
2013–14	Livingston	35	17	105 37
2014–15	Sheffield U	31	9	
2015–16	Sheffield U	5	1	
2015–16	Portsmouth	27	10	27 10
2016–17	Sheffield U	4	0	40 10
2016–17	Bradford C	15	1	15 1
2017–18	Coventry C	0	0	
2017–18	Coventry C	42	23	42 23

O'BRIEN, Liam (G) 62 0
H: 6 1 W: 12 06 b.Ruislip 30-11-91
Internationals: England U19.

2008–09	Portsmouth	0	0	
2009–10	Portsmouth	0	0	
2010–11	Barnet	8	0	
2011–12	Barnet	10	0	
2012–13	Barnet	3	0	21 0
2013–14	Brentford	0	0	
2014–15	Dagenham & R	10	0	
2015–16	Dagenham & R	24	0	34 0
2016–17	Portsmouth	0	0	
2017–18	Coventry C	7	0	7 0

PEARSON, James (D) 18 0
H: 6 1 W: 11 11 b.Sheffield 19-1-93

2013–14	Leicester C	0	0	
2013–14	Carlisle U	3	0	3 0
2014–15	Leicester C	0	0	
2014–15	Peterborough U	0	0	

2015–16	Barnet	15	0	
2016–17	Barnet	0	0	15 0
2017–18	Coventry C	0	0	

PONTICELLI, Jordan (F) 19 3
b. 10-9-98

2017–18	Coventry C	19	3	19 3

REID, Kyel (M) 306 26
H: 5 10 W: 12 05 b.Deptford 26-11-87
Internationals: England U17, U18, U19.

2004–05	West Ham U	0	0	
2005–06	West Ham U	2	0	
2006–07	West Ham U	0	0	
2006–07	Barnsley	26	2	26 2
2007–08	West Ham U	1	0	
2007–08	Crystal Palace	2	0	2 0
2008–09	West Ham U	0	0	3 0
2008–09	Blackpool	7	0	7 0
2008–09	Wolverhampton W	8	1	8 1
2009–10	Sheffield U	7	0	7 0
2009–10	Charlton Ath	17	4	
2010–11	Charlton Ath	32	1	49 5
2011–12	Bradford C	37	4	
2012–13	Bradford C	33	2	
2013–14	Bradford C	26	4	
2014–15	Preston NE	14	0	
2015–16	Preston NE	1	0	15 0
2015–16	Bradford C	34	3	130 13
2016–17	Coventry C	29	2	
2017–18	Colchester U	17	3	17 3
2017–18	Coventry C	13	0	42 2

SAYOUD, Bilal (M) 0 0
b. 5-5-97

2015–16	Coventry C	0	0	
2017–18	Coventry C	0	0	

SHIPLEY, Jordan (M) 31 4
b. 26-6-97

2016–17	Coventry C	1	0	
2017–18	Coventry C	30	4	31 4

STOKES, Chris (M) 90 3
H: 5 7 W: 10 04 b.Trowbridge 8-3-91
Internationals: England U17, C.

2009–10	Crewe Alex	2	0	2 0

From Forest Green R.

2014–15	Coventry C	16	1	
2015–16	Coventry C	36	2	
2016–17	Coventry C	7	0	
2017–18	Coventry C	29	0	88 3

THOMAS, Kwame (F) 41 3
H: 5 10 W: 12 00 b.Nottingham 28-9-95
Internationals: England U16, U17, U20.

2011–12	Derby Co	0	0	
2012–13	Derby Co	0	0	
2013–14	Derby Co	0	0	
2014–15	Derby Co	4	0	
2014–15	Notts Co	5	0	5 0
2015–16	Derby Co	0	0	4 0
2015–16	Blackpool	18	0	18 0
2016–17	Coventry C	14	3	
2017–18	Coventry C	0	0	14 3

THOMPSON, Jordan (D) 0 0

2016–17	Coventry C	0	0	
2017–18	Coventry C	0	0	

VINCENTI, Peter (F) 264 45
H: 6 2 W: 11 13 b.St Peter 7-7-86

2007–08	Millwall	1	0	
2010–11	Stevenage	1	1	5 1
2010–11	Aldershot T	23	6	
2011–12	Aldershot T	42	6	
2012–13	Aldershot T	39	2	104 14
2013–14	Rochdale	42	5	
2014–15	Rochdale	37	13	
2015–16	Rochdale	38	8	
2016–17	Rochdale	14	1	131 27
2017–18	Coventry C	24	3	24 3

WESTBROOKE, Zain (M) 1 0
b. 28-10-96
From Chelsea.

2016–17	Brentford	1	0	
2017–18	Brentford	0	0	1 0
2017–18	Coventry C	0	0	

WILLIS, Jordan (D) 141 3
H: 5 11 W: 11 00 b.Coventry 24-8-94
Internationals: England U18, U19.

2011–12	Coventry C	3	0	
2012–13	Coventry C	1	0	
2013–14	Coventry C	28	0	
2014–15	Coventry C	34	0	
2015–16	Coventry C	4	0	
2016–17	Coventry C	36	3	
2017–18	Coventry C	35	0	141 3

Players retained or with offer of contract
Bosma, Bouwe Jacob.

Scholars
Bannatyne-Billson, Thomas David;
Burroughs, Jack Stephen; Crowther, Morgan
James John Arthur; Doyle, Liam Thomas;
Eccles, Joshua Elliot; Endall, Joshua
Anthony; Fixter, Dylan George Cobb; Green,
Lewis Craig; Green, Sion Nathan; Hunt,
George Elliott; Johnson, Tyler Marc;
Lautaru, Costelus; McMahon, Ross Joseph;
Naylor, Samuel Thomas; Rowe, Luke James
Albert; Stedman, Billy Jay; White, Lewis
George; Whitmore, Aaron Jay.

CRAWLEY T (29)

BOLDEWIJN, Enzio (F) 226 32
H: 6 1 W: 12 06 b.Almere 17-11-92

2010–11	Utrecht	0	0	
2011–12	Utrecht	11	0	11 0
2012–13	Den Bosch	31	1	31 1
2013–14	Almere City	27	2	
2014–15	Almere City	31	7	
2015–16	Almere City	35	7	93 16
2015–16	Crawley T	0	0	
2016–17	Crawley T	46	5	
2017–18	Crawley T	45	10	91 15

BULMAN, Dannie (M) 481 22
H: 5 9 W: 11 12 b.Ashford 24-1-79

1998–99	Wycombe W	11	1	
1999–2000	Wycombe W	29	1	
2000–01	Wycombe W	36	4	
2001–02	Wycombe W	46	5	
2002–03	Wycombe W	42	3	
2003–04	Wycombe W	38	0	202 14

From Stevenage, Crawley T.

2010–11	Oxford U	5	0	5 0
2011–12	Crawley T	41	3	
2012–13	Crawley T	36	1	
2013–14	Crawley T	39	0	
2014–15	AFC Wimbledon	41	1	
2015–16	AFC Wimbledon	42	3	
2016–17	AFC Wimbledon	38	0	121 4
2017–18	Crawley T	37	0	153 4

CAMARA, Panutche (F) 30 2
H: 6 1 W: 9 13 b. 28-2-97
From Dulwich Hamlet.

2017–18	Crawley T	30	2	30 2

CLIFFORD, Billy (M) 74 1
H: 5 7 W: 10 03 b.Slough 18-10-92

2010–11	Chelsea	0	0	
2011–12	Chelsea	0	0	
2012–13	Chelsea	0	0	
2012–13	Colchester U	18	1	18 1
2013–14	Chelsea	0	0	
2013–14	Yeovil T	0	0	
2014–15	Walsall	13	0	13 0
2016–17	Crawley T	36	0	
2017–18	Crawley T	7	0	43 0

CONNOLLY, Mark (D) 184 10
H: 6 1 W: 12 01 b.Monaghan 16-12-91
Internationals: Republic of Ireland U17, U19,
U21.

2009–10	Bolton W	0	0	
2009–10	St Johnstone	1	0	1 0
2010–11	Bolton W	0	0	
2011–12	Bolton W	0	0	
2011–12	Macclesfield T	7	0	7 0
2012–13	Crawley T	33	2	
2013–14	Crawley T	36	1	
2014–15	Kilmarnock	26	2	26 2
2016–17	Crawley T	41	3	
2017–18	Crawley T	40	2	150 8

COX, Dean (M) 399 62
H: 5 4 W: 9 08 b.Cuckfield 12-8-87

2005–06	Brighton & HA	1	0	
2006–07	Brighton & HA	42	6	
2007–08	Brighton & HA	42	6	
2008–09	Brighton & HA	40	4	
2009–10	Brighton & HA	21	0	146 16
2010–11	Leyton Orient	45	11	
2011–12	Leyton Orient	38	7	
2012–13	Leyton Orient	44	4	
2013–14	Leyton Orient	45	12	
2014–15	Leyton Orient	37	6	
2015–16	Leyton Orient	14	3	
2016–17	Leyton Orient	4	1	227 44
2016–17	Crawley T	22	2	
2017–18	Crawley T	4	0	26 2

DJALO, Kaby (M)   89   5
H: 5 7   W: 10 03   b.Bissau 5-2-92
Internationals: Portugal U17, U18, U21.
Guinea-Bissau Full caps.
From Chelsea.

2011–12	AEL Limassol	4	0		
2012–13	AEL Limassol	0	0	4	0
2013–14	Gaz Metan Mediaz	3	0		
2014–15	Gaz Metan Mediaz	0	0	3	0
2014–15	*Pogon Siedice*	12	0	12	0
2015	PS Kemi	23	3		
2016	PS Kemi	17	1	40	4
2016–17	Crawley T	28	1		
2017–18	Crawley T	2	0	30	1

DOHERTY, Josh (M)   16   0
H: 5 10   W: 11 00   b.Newtownards 15-3-96
Internationals: Northern Ireland U17, U19, U21.

2013–14	Watford	1	0		
2014–15	Watford	0	0		
2015–16	Watford	0	0	1	0

From Leyton Orient, Ards.

2017–18	Crawley T	15	0	15	0

GARNETT, Addison (D)   2   0
H: 6 4   W: 14 02   b.London 13-9-96

2016–17	Crawley T	2	0		
2017–18	Crawley T	0	0	2	0

HARROLD, Matt (F)   404   75
H: 6 1   W: 11 10   b.Leyton 25-7-84

2003–04	Brentford	13	2		
2004–05	Brentford	19	0	32	2
2004–05	*Grimsby T*	6	2	6	2
2005–06	Yeovil T	42	9		
2006–07	Yeovil T	5	0	47	9
2006–07	Southend U	36	3		
2007–08	Southend U	16	0		
2008–09	Southend U	0	0	52	3
2008–09	Wycombe W	37	9		
2009–10	Wycombe W	36	8	73	17
2010–11	Shrewsbury T	41	8	41	8
2011–12	Bristol R	40	16		
2012–13	Bristol R	2	0		
2013–14	Bristol R	30	6	76	24
2014–15	Crawley T	20	1		
2014–15	*Cambridge U*	7	1	7	1
2015–16	Crawley T	37	8		
2016–17	Crawley T	11	0		
2017–18	Crawley T	2	0	70	9

LELAN, Josh (D)   59   0
H: 6 1   W: 11 00   b.Derby 21-12-94
Internationals: Kenya Full caps.

2012–13	Derby Co	0	0		
2013–14	Derby Co	0	0		
2014–15	Derby Co	0	0		
2014–15	*Swindon T*	5	0	5	0
2015–16	Northampton T	11	0		
2016–17	Northampton T	0	0	11	0
2016–17	Crawley T	13	0		
2017–18	Crawley T	30	0	43	0

McNERNEY, Joe (D)   61   5
H: 6 4   W: 13 03   b. 24-1-89
From Woking.

2015–16	Crawley T	11	1		
2016–17	Crawley T	34	3		
2017–18	Crawley T	16	1	61	5

MERSIN, Yusuf (G)   10   0
H: 6 5   W: 13 05   b.Greenwich 23-9-94
Internationals: Turkey U16, U17, U18.
From Liverpool, Kasimpasa.

2016–17	Crawley T	8	0		
2017–18	Crawley T	2	0	10	0

MORRIS, Glenn (G)   276   0
H: 6 0   W: 12 03   b.Woolwich 20-12-83

2001–02	Leyton Orient	2	0		
2002–03	Leyton Orient	23	0		
2003–04	Leyton Orient	27	0		
2004–05	Leyton Orient	12	0		
2005–06	Leyton Orient	4	0		
2006–07	Leyton Orient	3	0		
2007–08	Leyton Orient	16	0		
2008–09	Leyton Orient	26	0		
2009–10	Leyton Orient	11	0	124	0
2010–11	Southend U	33	0		
2011–12	Southend U	24	0		
2012–13	Southend U	0	0	57	0
2012–13	Aldershot T	2	0	2	0
2014–15	Gillingham	10	0		
2015–16	Gillingham	0	0	10	0
2016–17	Crawley T	39	0		
2017–18	Crawley T	44	0	83	0

OKOYE, Nathan (D)   0   0
b.Tel Aviv 8-11-95

2017–18	Crawley T	0	0

PAYNE, Josh (M)   152   12
H: 6 0   W: 11 09   b.Basingstoke 25-11-90
Internationals: England C.

2008–09	West Ham U	2	0		
2008–09	*Cheltenham T*	11	1	11	1
2009–10	West Ham U	0	0		
2009–10	Colchester U	3	0	3	0
2009–10	Wycombe W	3	1	3	1
2010–11	West Ham U	0	0	2	0
2010–11	Doncaster R	0	0		
2010–11	Oxford U	28	1		
2011–12	Oxford U	6	0	34	1
2011–12	Aldershot T	17	2		
2012–13	Aldershot T	15	1	32	3
2016–17	Crawley T	32	1		
2017–18	Crawley T	35	5	67	6

RANDALL, Mark (M)   165   7
H: 6 0   W: 12 12   b.Milton Keynes 28-9-89
Internationals: England U17, U18.

2006–07	Arsenal	0	0		
2007–08	Arsenal	1	0		
2007–08	*Burnley*	10	0	10	0
2008–09	Arsenal	1	0		
2009–10	Arsenal	0	0		
2009–10	*Milton Keynes D*	16	0		
2010–11	Arsenal	0	0	2	0
2010–11	*Rotherham U*	10	1	10	1
2011–12	Chesterfield	16	1		
2012–13	Chesterfield	29	1		
2013–14	Chesterfield	0	0	45	2
2013–14	Milton Keynes D	4	0		
2014–15	Milton Keynes D	9	0		
2015–16	Milton Keynes D	0	0	29	0
2015–16	Barnet	12	2	12	2
2016–17	Newport Co	25	1	25	1
2017–18	Crawley T	32	1	32	1

ROBERTS, Jordan (M)   76   11
H: 5 11   W: 12 13   b.Watford 5-1-94
Internationals: England C.

2011–12	Aldershot T	4	0		
2012–13	Aldershot T	5	0	9	0

From Havant & Waterlooville, Bishops Stortford, Aldershot T.

2015–16	*Inverness CT*	9	2	9	2
2016–17	Crawley T	23	3		
2017–18	Crawley T	35	6	58	9

SANOH, Moussa (F)   98   9
b.Nijmegen 20-7-95
Internationals: Netherlands U17, U19.

2013–14	Jong PSV	1	0		
2014–15	Jong PSV	32	2		
2015–16	Jong PSV	13	2	46	4
2015–16	RKC Waalwijk	14	0		
2016–17	RKC Waalwijk	26	5	40	5
2017–18	Crawley T	12	0	12	0

SMITH, Jimmy (M)   403   46
H: 6 0   W: 10 03   b.Newham 7-1-87
Internationals: England U16, U17, U19.

2004–05	Chelsea	0	0		
2005–06	Chelsea	1	0		
2006–07	Chelsea	0	0		
2006–07	*QPR*	29	6	29	6
2007–08	Chelsea	0	0		
2007–08	*Norwich C*	9	0	9	0
2008–09	Chelsea	0	0	1	0
2008–09	*Sheffield W*	12	0	12	0
2008–09	*Leyton Orient*	16	0		
2009–10	Leyton Orient	40	2		
2010–11	Leyton Orient	31	7		
2011–12	Leyton Orient	38	6		
2012–13	Leyton Orient	35	3		
2013–14	Leyton Orient	0	0	160	18
2013–14	Stevenage	42	3	42	3
2014–15	Crawley T	36	1		
2015–16	Crawley T	31	1		
2016–17	Crawley T	46	7		
2017–18	Crawley T	37	10	150	19

TAJBAKHSH, Aryan (M)   21   0
H: 6 1   W: 11 06   b.Istanbul 20-10-90
From Cray W.

2016–17	Crawley T	4	0		
2017–18	Crawley T	17	0	21	0

VERHEYDT, Thomas (F)   81   17
b. 24-1-92

2015–16	Maastricht	23	4		
2016–17	Maastricht	38	11	61	15
2017–18	MVV	0	0		
2017–18	Crawley T	20	2	20	2

YORWERTH, Josh (D)   84   4
H: 6 1   W: 11 09   b.Bridgend 1-1-95
Internationals: Wales U17, U19, U21.

2014–15	Cardiff C	0	0		
2015–16	Ipswich T	0	0		
2015–16	*Crawley T*	24	0		
2016–17	Crawley T	21	3		
2017–18	Crawley T	39	1	84	4

YOUNG, Lewis (M)   235   3
H: 5 10   W: 11 02   b.Stevenage 27-9-89

2008–09	Watford	1	0		
2009–10	Watford	0	0	1	0
2009–10	*Hereford U*	6	0	6	0
2010–11	Burton Alb	19	0	19	0
2011–12	Northampton T	30	0	30	0
2012–13	Yeovil T	15	0		
2013–14	Yeovil T	0	0	15	0
2013–14	Bury	4	0	4	0
2014–15	Crawley T	38	0		
2015–16	Crawley T	38	0		
2016–17	Crawley T	43	0		
2017–18	Crawley T	41	3	160	3

Players retained or with offer of contract
Pereira, Camara Panutche Amadu.

CREWE ALEX (30)

AINLEY, Callum (M)   88   6
H: 5 8   W: 10 01   b.Middlewich 2-11-97

2015–16	Crewe Alex	16	1		
2016–17	Crewe Alex	27	1		
2017–18	Crewe Alex	45	4	88	6

BAKAYOGO, Zaoumana (D)   238   6
H: 5 9   W: 10 08   b.Paris 11-8-86
Internationals: Ivory Coast U23.

2006–07	Millwall	5	0		
2007–08	Millwall	10	0	15	0

From Alfortville.

2009–10	Tranmere R	29	0		
2010–11	Tranmere R	27	1		
2011–12	Tranmere R	26	0		
2012–13	Tranmere R	46	4	128	5
2013–14	Leicester C	0	0		
2013–14	*Yeovil T*	1	0	1	0
2015–16	Crewe Alex	22	1		
2016–17	Crewe Alex	40	0		
2017–18	Crewe Alex	32	0	94	1

BOWERY, Jordan (F)   246   37
H: 6 1   W: 12 00   b.Nottingham 2-7-91

2008–09	Chesterfield	10	0		
2009–10	Chesterfield	10	0		
2010–11	Chesterfield	27	1		
2011–12	Chesterfield	40	8		
2012–13	Chesterfield	3	1	83	10
2012–13	Aston Villa	10	0		
2013–14	Aston Villa	9	0	19	0
2013–14	*Doncaster R*	3	0	3	0
2014–15	Rotherham U	33	5		
2015–16	Rotherham U	7	0	40	5
2015–16	*Bradford C*	3	0	3	0
2015–16	Oxford U	17	7	17	7
2016–17	Leyton Orient	17	1	17	1
2016–17	*Crewe Alex*	19	2		
2017–18	Crewe Alex	45	12	64	14

DAGNALL, Chris (F)   453   116
H: 5 8   W: 12 03   b.Liverpool 15-4-86

2003–04	Tranmere R	10	1		
2004–05	Tranmere R	23	6		
2005–06	Tranmere R	6	0	39	7
2005–06	Rochdale	21	3		
2006–07	Rochdale	37	17		
2007–08	Rochdale	14	7		
2008–09	Rochdale	40	7		
2009–10	Rochdale	45	20	157	54
2010–11	Scunthorpe U	37	5		
2011–12	Scunthorpe U	23	4	60	9
2011–12	Barnsley	9	0		
2011–12	*Bradford C*	7	1	7	1
2012–13	Barnsley	36	5		
2013–14	Barnsley	8	1	53	6
2013–14	*Coventry C*	6	1	6	1
2013–14	Leyton Orient	20	6		
2014–15	Leyton Orient	38	11	58	17
2015–16	Kerala Blasters	0	0		
2015–16	Hibernian	0	0		
2016–17	Crewe Alex	41	14		
2017–18	Crewe Alex	32	7	73	21

DALE, Owen (F)   4   0
H: 5 9   W: 10 03   b.Warrington 1-11-98

2016–17	Crewe Alex	0	0		
2017–18	Crewe Alex	4	0	4	0

FINNEY, Oliver (M) 2 0
b.Stoke-on-Trent 15-12-97
2015–16 Crewe Alex 0 0
2016–17 Crewe Alex 1 0
2017–18 Crewe Alex 1 0 2 0

GARRATT, Ben (G) 185 0
H: 6 1 W: 10 06 b.Market Drayton 25-4-94
Internationals: England U17, U18, U19.
2011–12 Crewe Alex 0 0
2012–13 Crewe Alex 1 0
2013–14 Crewe Alex 26 0
2014–15 Crewe Alex 30 0
2015–16 Crewe Alex 46 0
2016–17 Crewe Alex 46 0
2017–18 Crewe Alex 36 0 185 0

JAASKELAINEN, William (G) 0 0
b. 25-7-98
Internationals: Finland U17, U18, U21.
2015–16 Bolton W 0 0
2017–18 Bolton W 0 0
2017–18 Crewe Alex 0 0

JONES, James (M) 106 12
H: 5 9 W: 10 10 b.Winsford 1-2-96
Internationals: Scotland U19, U20, U21.
2014–15 Crewe Alex 24 1
2015–16 Crewe Alex 31 0
2016–17 Crewe Alex 45 10
2017–18 Crewe Alex 6 1 106 12

KIRK, Charlie (M) 61 5
H: 5 7 W: 11 00 b.Winsford 24-12-97
2015–16 Crewe Alex 14 0
2016–17 Crewe Alex 22 0
2017–18 Crewe Alex 25 5 61 5

LOWERY, Tom (M) 38 0
b.Holmes Chapel 31-12-97
2016–17 Crewe Alex 7 0
2017–18 Crewe Alex 31 0 38 0

LUNDSTRAM, Josh (M) 0 0
2017–18 Crewe Alex 0 0

NG, Perry (D) 60 4
H: 5 11 W: 12 02 b.Liverpool 24-6-94
2014–15 Crewe Alex 0 0
2015–16 Crewe Alex 6 0
2016–17 Crewe Alex 16 0
2017–18 Crewe Alex 38 4 60 4

NOLAN, Eddie (D) 251 3
H: 6 0 W: 13 05 b.Waterford 5-8-88
Internationals: Republic of Ireland U21, B, Full caps.
2005–06 Blackburn R 0 0
2006–07 Blackburn R 0 0
2006–07 Stockport Co 4 0 4 0
2007–08 Blackburn R 0 0
2007–08 Hartlepool U 11 0 11 0
2008–09 Blackburn R 0 0
2008–09 Preston NE 21 0
2009–10 Preston NE 19 0
2009–10 Sheffield W 14 1 14 1
2010–11 Preston NE 0 0 40 0
2010–11 Scunthorpe U 35 0
2011–12 Scunthorpe U 30 1
2012–13 Scunthorpe U 12 0
2013–14 Scunthorpe U 39 0
2014–15 Scunthorpe U 6 0 122 1
2015–16 York C 15 1 15 1
2016–17 Blackpool 3 0 3 0
2017–18 Crewe Alex 42 0 42 0

OFFORD, Luke (M) 0 0
b.Chichester 19-11-99
2017–18 Crewe Alex 0 0

PICKERING, Harry (M) 35 3
H: 6 1 W: 12 04 b.21-12-98
2017–18 Crewe Alex 35 3 35 3

PORTER, Chris (F) 458 133
H: 6 1 W: 12 09 b.Wigan 12-12-83
2002–03 Bury 2 0
2003–04 Bury 37 9
2004–05 Bury 32 9 71 18
2005–06 Oldham Ath 31 7
2006–07 Oldham Ath 35 21 66 28
2007–08 Motherwell 37 14
2008–09 Motherwell 22 9 59 23
2008–09 Derby Co 5 3
2009–10 Derby Co 21 4
2010–11 Derby Co 18 2 44 9
2011–12 Sheffield U 34 5
2012–13 Sheffield U 21 3
2012–13 Shrewsbury T 5 1 5 1
2013–14 Sheffield U 32 7
2013–14 *Chesterfield* 3 0 3 0
2014–15 Sheffield U 1 0 88 15
2014–15 Colchester U 21 7
2015–16 Colchester U 32 7
2016–17 Colchester U 38 16 91 30
2017–18 Colchester U 31 9 31 9

RAY, George (D) 105 3
H: 5 10 W: 11 03 b.Warrington 13-10-93
Internationals: Wales U21.
2011–12 Crewe Alex 0 0
2012–13 Crewe Alex 4 0
2013–14 Crewe Alex 9 0
2014–15 Crewe Alex 35 2
2015–16 Crewe Alex 22 0
2016–17 Crewe Alex 23 1
2017–18 Crewe Alex 12 0 105 3

RAYNES, Michael (D) 396 13
H: 6 4 W: 12 00 b.Wythenshawe 15-10-87
2004–05 Stockport Co 19 0
2005–06 Stockport Co 25 1
2006–07 Stockport Co 9 0
2007–08 Stockport Co 27 0
2008–09 Stockport Co 35 3
2009–10 Stockport Co 25 1 140 5
2009–10 Scunthorpe U 12 0
2010–11 Scunthorpe U 22 0 34 0
2011–12 Rotherham U 33 0 33 0
2012–13 Oxford U 38 1
2013–14 Oxford U 27 0
2014–15 Oxford U 4 0 69 1
2014–15 Mansfield T 10 0 10 0
2015–16 Carlisle U 40 3
2016–17 Carlisle U 41 2 81 5
2017–18 Crewe Alex 29 2 29 2

REILLY, Lewis (F) 5 0
b. 7-7-99
2017–18 Crewe Alex 5 0 5 0

RICHARDS, Dave (G) 11 0
H: 5 11 W: 11 11 b.Abergavenny 31-12-93
2013–14 Cardiff C 0 0
2014–15 Bristol C 0 0
2014–15 Bristol C 0 0
2015–16 Crewe Alex 0 0
2016–17 Crewe Alex 0 0
2017–18 Crewe Alex 11 0 11 0

SASS-DAVIES, Billy (D) 0 0
b.Manchester 17-2-00
2017–18 Crewe Alex 0 0

WALKER, Brad (M) 134 11
H: 6 1 W: 12 08 b. 25-4-95
2012–13 Hartlepool U 0 0
2013–14 Hartlepool U 36 3
2014–15 Hartlepool U 28 5
2015–16 Hartlepool U 23 1
2016–17 Hartlepool U 20 1 107 10
2017–18 Crewe Alex 27 1 27 1

WINTLE, Ryan (M) 38 3
H: 5 5 W: 10 01 b.Newcastle-under-Lyme 13-6-97
2015–16 Crewe Alex 3 0
2016–17 Crewe Alex 17 1
2017–18 Crewe Alex 18 2 38 3

Scholars
Adebisi, Rio Adesola Frederick; Appleyard, William Hugh; Barlow, Luke James; Booth, Samuel James; Fenton, Mathew Adam; Griffiths, Regan Jon; Harrison, Oliver Charlie; Heath, Connor John; Hurst, Alexander Charles; Johnson, Travis Joel Gary; Linton, Malachi Derek David; Lomas, Aaron Philip; Lynch, Joseph Steven; Manuel, Adao Luis; Odipe, Olaolu Josiah James; Offord, Luke William; Sass-Davies, William John; Thompson, Joseph Jordan Cosgrove; Walsh, Luke Albert.

CRYSTAL PALACE (31)

BENTEKE, Christian (F) 289 105
H: 6 3 W: 13 00 b.Kinshasa 3-12-90
Internationals: Belgium U17, U18, U19, U21, Full caps.
2007–08 Genk 7 0
2008–09 Genk 3 0
2008–09 Standard Liege 9 3
2009–10 KV Kortrijk 24 9 24 9
2010–11 Standard Liege 24 9
2010–11 KV Mechelen 15 5 15 5
2011–12 Standard Liege 0 0 18 3
2011–12 Genk 32 16
2012–13 Genk 5 3 47 19
2012–13 Aston Villa 34 19
2013–14 Aston Villa 26 10
2014–15 Aston Villa 29 13 89 42
2015–16 Liverpool 29 9 29 9
2016–17 Crystal Palace 36 15
2017–18 Crystal Palace 31 3 67 18

CABAYE, Yohan (M) 366 57
H: 5 9 W: 11 05 b.Tourcoing 14-1-86
Internationals: France U16, U18, U19, U20, U21, Full caps.
2004–05 Lille 6 0
2005–06 Lille 27 1
2006–07 Lille 22 3
2007–08 Lille 36 7
2008–09 Lille 32 5
2009–10 Lille 32 13
2010–11 Lille 36 2 191 31
2011–12 Newcastle U 34 4
2012–13 Newcastle U 26 6
2013–14 Newcastle U 19 7 79 17
2015–16 Crystal Palace 33 5
2016–17 Crystal Palace 32 4
2017–18 Crystal Palace 31 0 96 9

DALY, James (F) 0 0
2017–18 Crystal Palace 0 0

DANN, Scott (D) 377 29
H: 6 2 W: 12 00 b.Liverpool 14-2-87
Internationals: England U21.
2004–05 Walsall 1 0
2005–06 Walsall 0 0
2006–07 Walsall 30 4
2007–08 Walsall 38 3 59 7
2007–08 Coventry C 16 0
2008–09 Coventry C 31 3 47 3
2009–10 Birmingham C 30 0
2010–11 Birmingham C 20 2
2011–12 Birmingham C 0 0 50 2
2011–12 Blackburn R 27 1
2012–13 Blackburn R 46 4
2013–14 Blackburn R 25 0 98 5
2013–14 Crystal Palace 14 1
2014–15 Crystal Palace 34 2
2015–16 Crystal Palace 35 5
2016–17 Crystal Palace 23 3
2017–18 Crystal Palace 17 1 123 12

DELANEY, Damien (D) 575 16
H: 6 3 W: 14 00 b.Cork 20-7-81
Internationals: Republic of Ireland Full caps.
2000–01 Leicester C 5 0
2001–02 Leicester C 0 0
2001–02 Stockport Co 12 1 12 1
2001–02 Huddersfield T 2 0 2 0
2002–03 Leicester C 0 0 8 0
2002–03 Mansfield T 7 0 7 0
2002–03 Hull C 30 1
2003–04 Hull C 46 2
2004–05 Hull C 43 1
2005–06 Hull C 46 0
2006–07 Hull C 37 1
2007–08 Hull C 22 0 224 5
2007–08 QPR 17 1
2008–09 QPR 37 1
2009–10 QPR 0 0 54 2
2009–10 Ipswich T 36 0
2010–11 Ipswich T 32 2
2011–12 Ipswich T 29 0
2012–13 Ipswich T 1 0 98 2
2012–13 Crystal Palace 40 3
2013–14 Crystal Palace 37 1
2014–15 Crystal Palace 29 0
2015–16 Crystal Palace 32 2
2016–17 Crystal Palace 30 0
2017–18 Crystal Palace 2 0 170 6

HENNESSEY, Wayne (G) 268 0
H: 6 0 W: 11 06 b.Anglesey 24-1-87
Internationals: Wales U17, U19, U21, Full caps.
2004–05 Wolverhampton W 0 0
2005–06 Wolverhampton W 0 0
2006–07 Wolverhampton W 0 0
2006–07 *Bristol C* 0 0
2007–08 Stockport Co 15 0 15 0
2007–08 Wolverhampton W 46 0
2008–09 Wolverhampton W 35 0
2009–10 Wolverhampton W 13 0
2010–11 Wolverhampton W 24 0
2011–12 Wolverhampton W 34 0
2012–13 Wolverhampton W 0 0 152 0
2013–14 Wolverhampton W 0 0
2013–14 Yeovil T 12 0 12 0
2013–14 Crystal Palace 1 0
2014–15 Crystal Palace 3 0
2015–16 Crystal Palace 29 0

2016–17	Crystal Palace	29	0	
2017–18	Crystal Palace	27	0	89 0

HENRY, Dion (G)   1 0
H: 5 11   W: 10 03   b.Ipswich 12-9-97

2014–15	Peterborough U	0	0	
2015–16	Peterborough U	1	0	
2016–17	Peterborough U	0	0	1 0
2017–18	Crystal Palace	0	0	

INNISS, Ryan (D)   59 0
H: 6 5   W: 13 02   b.Kent 5-6-95
Internationals: England U16, U17.

2012–13	Crystal Palace	0	0	
2013–14	Crystal Palace	0	0	
2013–14	*Cheltenham T*	2	0	2 0
2013–14	*Gillingham*	3	0	3 0
2014–15	Crystal Palace	0	0	
2014–15	*Yeovil T*	6	0	6 0
2014–15	*Port Vale*	5	0	
2015–16	Crystal Palace	0	0	
2015–16	*Port Vale*	15	0	20 0
2016–17	Crystal Palace	0	0	
2016–17	*Southend U*	10	0	10 0
2017–18	Crystal Palace	0	0	
2017–18	*Colchester U*	18	0	18 0

JACH, Jaroslaw (D)   68 4
H: 6 3   W: 12 11   b.Bielawa 17-2-94
Internationals: Poland U21, Full caps.

2013–14	Zagkebie Lubin	2	0	
2014–15	Zagkebie Lubin	13	0	
2015–16	Zagkebie Lubin	13	2	
2016–17	Zagkebie Lubin	23	1	51 3
2017–18	Zaglebie Lubin	17	1	17 1
2017–18	Crystal Palace	0	0	

KAIKAI, Sullay (F)   91 20
H: 6 0   W: 11 07   b.London 26-8-95

2013–14	Crystal Palace	0	0	
2013–14	*Crawley T*	5	0	5 0
2014–15	Crystal Palace	0	0	
2014–15	*Cambridge U*	25	5	25 5
2015–16	Crystal Palace	1	0	
2015–16	*Shrewsbury T*	26	12	26 12
2016–17	Brentford	18	3	18 3
2016–17	Crystal Palace	0	0	
2017–18	Crystal Palace	1	0	3 0
2017–18	*Charlton Ath*	14	0	14 0

KELLY, Martin (D)   128 1
H: 6 3   W: 12 02   b.Bolton 27-4-90
Internationals: England U19, U20, U21, Full caps.

2007–08	Liverpool	0	0	
2008–09	Liverpool	0	0	
2008–09	*Huddersfield T*	7	1	7 1
2009–10	Liverpool	11	0	
2011–12	Liverpool	12	0	
2012–13	Liverpool	4	0	
2013–14	Liverpool	5	0	33 0
2014–15	Crystal Palace	31	0	
2015–16	Crystal Palace	13	0	
2016–17	Crystal Palace	29	0	
2017–18	Crystal Palace	15	0	88 0

KIRBY, Nya (M)   0 0
H: 5 9   W: 10 06   b.Islington 31-1-00
Internationals: England U16, U17, U18.
From Tottenham H.

2017–18	Crystal Palace	0	0	

LEE, Chung Yong (M)   265 28
H: 5 11   W: 10 09   b.Seoul 2-7-88
Internationals: South Korea U17, U20, U23, Full caps.

2006	FC Seoul	2	0	
2007	FC Seoul	15	3	
2008	FC Seoul	20	5	
2009	FC Seoul	14	2	51 10
2009–10	Bolton W	34	4	
2010–11	Bolton W	31	3	
2011–12	Bolton W	2	0	
2012–13	Bolton W	41	4	
2013–14	Bolton W	45	3	
2014–15	Bolton W	23	3	176 17
2014–15	Crystal Palace	3	0	
2015–16	Crystal Palace	13	1	
2016–17	Crystal Palace	15	0	
2017–18	Crystal Palace	7	0	38 1

LOKILO, Jason (M)   0 0
H: 5 9   b.Brussel 17-9-98
Internationals: DR Congo U20.

2014–15	Anderlecht	0	0	
2015–16	Crystal Palace	0	0	
2017–18	Crystal Palace	0	0	

LUMEKA, Levi (M)   1 0
H: 5 7   W: 11 03   b.Newham 5-9-98

2017–18	Crystal Palace	1	0	1 0

McARTHUR, James (M)   419 34
H: 5 6   W: 9 13   b.Glasgow 7-10-87
Internationals: Scotland U21, Full caps.

2004–05	Hamilton A	6	0	
2005–06	Hamilton A	20	1	
2006–07	Hamilton A	36	1	
2007–08	Hamilton A	34	4	
2008–09	Hamilton A	37	2	
2009–10	Hamilton A	35	1	168 9
2010–11	Wigan Ath	18	0	
2011–12	Wigan Ath	31	3	
2012–13	Wigan Ath	34	3	
2013–14	Wigan Ath	41	4	
2014–15	Wigan Ath	5	1	129 11
2014–15	Crystal Palace	32	2	
2015–16	Crystal Palace	28	2	
2016–17	Crystal Palace	29	5	
2017–18	Crystal Palace	33	5	122 14

MILIVOJEVIC, Luka (M)   221 34
H: 6 0   b.Kragujevac 7-4-91
Internationals: Serbia U21, Full caps.

2007–08	Radnicki Kraguejevac	5	1	5 1
2008–09	Rad Belgrade	1	0	
2009–10	Rad Belgrade	9	0	
2010–11	Rad Belgrade	26	0	
2011–12	Rad Belgrade	13	3	49 3
2011–12	Red Star Belgrade	11	1	
2012–13	Red Star Belgrade	25	6	36 7
2013–14	Anderlecht	16	0	
2014–15	Anderlecht	3	0	19 0
2014–15	Olympiacos	23	2	
2015–16	Olympiacos	22	3	
2016–17	Olympiacos	17	6	62 11
2016–17	Crystal Palace	14	2	
2017–18	Crystal Palace	36	10	50 12

MUTCH, Jordon (M)   180 17
H: 5 9   W: 10 03   b.Derby 2-12-91
Internationals: England U17, U19, U20, U21.

2007–08	Birmingham C	0	0	
2008–09	Birmingham C	0	0	
2009–10	Birmingham C	0	0	
2009–10	*Hereford U*	3	0	3 0
2009–10	*Doncaster R*	17	2	17 2
2010–11	Birmingham C	3	0	
2010–11	*Watford*	23	5	23 5
2011–12	Birmingham C	21	2	24 2
2012–13	Cardiff C	22	0	
2013–14	Cardiff C	35	7	57 7
2014–15	QPR	9	0	9 0
2014–15	Crystal Palace	7	0	
2015–16	Crystal Palace	20	0	
2016–17	Crystal Palace	4	0	
2016–17	*Reading*	9	1	9 1
2017–18	Crystal Palace	0	0	31 0
2017–18	*Vancouver Whitecaps*	7	0	7 0

PHILLIPS, Michael (M)   0 0

2016–17	Crystal Palace	0	0	
2017–18	Crystal Palace	0	0	

PUNCHEON, Jason (M)   411 59
H: 5 9   W: 12 05   b.Croydon 26-6-86

2003–04	Wimbledon	8	0	8 0
2004–05	Milton Keynes D	25	1	
2005–06	Milton Keynes D	1	0	
2006–07	Barnet	37	5	
2007–08	Barnet	41	10	78 15
2008–09	Plymouth Arg	6	0	
2008–09	*Milton Keynes D*	27	4	
2009–10	Plymouth Arg	0	0	6 0
2009–10	*Milton Keynes D*	24	7	77 12
2009–10	Southampton	19	3	
2010–11	Southampton	15	0	
2010–11	*Millwall*	7	5	7 5
2010–11	*Blackpool*	11	3	11 3
2011–12	Southampton	8	0	
2011–12	*QPR*	2	0	2 0
2012–13	Southampton	32	6	
2013–14	Southampton	0	0	74 9
2013–14	Crystal Palace	34	7	
2014–15	Crystal Palace	37	6	
2015–16	Crystal Palace	31	2	
2016–17	Crystal Palace	36	0	
2017–18	Crystal Palace	10	0	148 15

RAKIP, Erdal (M)   90 11
H: 5 9   W: 9 13   b.Malmo 13-2-96
Internationals: Sweden U17, U19, U21.

2013	Malmo	1	0	
2014	Malmo	15	0	
2015	Malmo	20	1	
2016	Malmo	27	2	
2017	Malmo	27	8	90 11
2017–18	Benfica	0	0	

On loan from Benfica.

2017–18	Crystal Palace	0	0	

RIEDEWALD, Jairo (D)   75 2
H: 6 0   W: 12 06   b.Amsterdam 9-9-96
Internationals: Netherlands U16, U17, U19, U21, Full caps.

2013–14	Ajax	5	2	
2014–15	Ajax	19	0	
2015–16	Ajax	23	0	
2016–17	Ajax	16	0	63 2
2017–18	Crystal Palace	12	0	12 0

SAKHO, Mamadou (D)   234 10
H: 6 2   W: 12 07   b.Paris 13-2-90
Internationals: France U16, U17, U18, U19, U21, Full caps.

2006–07	Paris St Germain	0	0	
2007–08	Paris St Germain	12	0	
2008–09	Paris St Germain	23	1	
2009–10	Paris St Germain	32	0	
2010–11	Paris St Germain	35	4	
2011–12	Paris St Germain	29	3	
2012–13	Paris St Germain	27	2	151 7
2013–14	Liverpool	18	1	
2014–15	Liverpool	16	0	
2015–16	Liverpool	22	1	
2016–17	Liverpool	0	0	
2016–17	*Crystal Palace*	8	0	
2017–18	Liverpool	0	0	56 2
2017–18	Crystal Palace	19	1	27 1

SAKO, Bakary (M)   331 64
H: 5 11   W: 11 12   b.Ivry Sur Seine 26-4-88
Internationals: France U21. Mali U17, Full caps.

2006–07	Chateauroux	17	0	
2007–08	Chateauroux	12	1	
2008–09	Chateauroux	35	9	64 10
2009–10	St Etienne	30	1	
2010–11	St Etienne	38	7	
2011–12	St Etienne	36	5	
2012–13	St Etienne	2	0	106 13
2012–13	Wolverhampton W	37	9	
2013–14	Wolverhampton W	40	12	
2014–15	Wolverhampton W	41	15	118 36
2015–16	Crystal Palace	20	2	
2016–17	Crystal Palace	7	0	
2017–18	Crystal Palace	16	3	43 5

SCHLUPP, Jeffrey (M)   174 16
H: 5 8   W: 11 00   b.Hamburg 23-12-92
Internationals: Ghana Full caps.

2010–11	Leicester C	0	0	
2010–11	*Brentford*	9	6	9 6
2011–12	Leicester C	21	2	
2012–13	Leicester C	19	3	
2013–14	Leicester C	26	1	
2014–15	Leicester C	32	3	
2015–16	Leicester C	24	1	
2016–17	Leicester C	4	0	126 10
2016–17	Crystal Palace	15	0	
2017–18	Crystal Palace	24	0	39 0

SORLOTH, Alexander (F)   93 28
H: 6 4   W: 14 02   b.Trondheim 5-12-95
Internationals: Norway U16, U17, U18, U19, U21, Full caps.

2013	Rosenborg	0	0	
2014	Rosenborg	6	0	6 0
2015	Bodo/Glimt	26	13	26 13
2015–16	Groningen	13	2	
2016–17	Groningen	25	3	38 5
2017–18	Midtjylland	19	10	19 10
2017–18	Crystal Palace	4	0	4 0

SOUARE, Pape (D)   126 3
H: 5 10   W: 10 10   b.Mbao 6-6-90
Internationals: Senegal U23, Full caps.

2010–11	Lille	4	0	
2011–12	Lille	7	0	
2012–13	Lille	0	0	
2012–13	*Reims*	23	0	23 0
2013–14	Lille	33	3	
2014–15	Lille	12	0	56 3
2014–15	Crystal Palace	9	0	
2015–16	Crystal Palace	34	0	
2016–17	Crystal Palace	3	0	
2017–18	Crystal Palace	1	0	47 0

SPERONI, Julian (G)   464 0
H: 6 0   W: 11 00   b.Buenos Aires 18-5-79
Internationals: Argentina U20, U21.

1999–2000	Platense	2	0	
2000–01	Platense	0	0	2 0
2001–02	Dundee	17	0	

2002–03	Dundee	38	0		
2003–04	Dundee	37	0	92	0
2004–05	Crystal Palace	6	0		
2005–06	Crystal Palace	4	0		
2006–07	Crystal Palace	5	0		
2007–08	Crystal Palace	46	0		
2008–09	Crystal Palace	45	0		
2009–10	Crystal Palace	45	0		
2010–11	Crystal Palace	45	0		
2011–12	Crystal Palace	42	0		
2012–13	Crystal Palace	46	0		
2013–14	Crystal Palace	37	0		
2014–15	Crystal Palace	36	0		
2015–16	Crystal Palace	2	0		
2016–17	Crystal Palace	0	0		
2017–18	Crystal Palace	11	0	370	0

TOMKINS, James (D)   267 14
H: 6 3   W: 11 10   b.Basildon 29-3-89
Internationals: England U16, U17, U18, U19, U20, U21. Great Britain.

2005–06	West Ham U	0	0		
2006–07	West Ham U	0	0		
2007–08	West Ham U	6	0		
2008–09	West Ham U	12	1		
2008–09	Derby Co	7	0	7	0
2009–10	West Ham U	23	0		
2010–11	West Ham U	19	1		
2011–12	West Ham U	44	4		
2012–13	West Ham U	26	1		
2013–14	West Ham U	31	0		
2014–15	West Ham U	22	1		
2015–16	West Ham U	25	0	208	8
2016–17	Crystal Palace	24	3		
2017–18	Crystal Palace	28	3	52	6

TOWNSEND, Andros (M)   236 23
H: 6 0   W: 12 00   b.Chingford 16-7-91
Internationals: England U16, U17, U19, U21, Full caps.

2008–09	Tottenham H	0	0		
2008–09	Yeovil T	10	1	10	1
2009–10	Tottenham H	0	0		
2009–10	Leyton Orient	22	2	22	2
2009–10	Milton Keynes D	9	2	9	2
2010–11	Tottenham H	0	0		
2010–11	Ipswich T	13	1	13	1
2010–11	Watford	3	0	3	0
2010–11	Millwall	11	2	11	2
2011–12	Tottenham H	0	0		
2011–12	Leeds U	6	1	6	1
2011–12	Birmingham C	15	0	15	0
2012–13	Tottenham H	5	0		
2012–13	QPR	12	2	12	2
2013–14	Tottenham H	25	1		
2014–15	Tottenham H	17	2		
2015–16	Tottenham H	3	0	50	3
2015–16	Newcastle U	13	4	13	4
2016–17	Crystal Palace	36	3		
2017–18	Crystal Palace	36	2	72	5

VAN AANHOLT, Patrick (D)   232 20
H: 5 9   W: 10 08   b.Den Bosch 3-7-88
Internationals: Netherlands U16, U17, U18, U19, U20, U21, Full caps.

2007–08	Chelsea	0	0		
2008–09	Chelsea	0	0		
2009–10	Chelsea	2	0		
2009–10	Coventry C	20	0	20	0
2009–10	Newcastle U	7	0	7	0
2010–11	Chelsea	0	0		
2010–11	Leicester C	12	1	12	1
2011–12	Chelsea	0	0		
2011–12	Wigan Ath	3	0	3	0
2011–12	Vitesse	9	0		
2012–13	Chelsea	0	0		
2012–13	Vitesse	31	0		
2013–14	Chelsea	0	0		
2013–14	Vitesse	27	4	67	5
2014–15	Sunderland	28	0		
2015–16	Sunderland	33	4		
2016–17	Sunderland	21	3	82	7
2016–17	Crystal Palace	11	2		
2017–18	Crystal Palace	28	5	39	7

WAN BISSAKA, Aaron (M)   7 0
b. 26-11-97
Internationals: DR Congo U20. England U20.

2016–17	Crystal Palace	0	0		
2017–18	Crystal Palace	7	0	7	0

WARD, Joel (D)   295 10
H: 6 2   W: 11 13   b.Emsworth 29-10-89

2008–09	Portsmouth	0	0		
2008–09	Bournemouth	21	1	21	1
2009–10	Portsmouth	3	0		
2010–11	Portsmouth	42	3		
2011–12	Portsmouth	44	3	89	6

2012–13	Crystal Palace	25	0		
2013–14	Crystal Palace	36	0		
2014–15	Crystal Palace	37	1		
2015–16	Crystal Palace	30	2		
2016–17	Crystal Palace	38	0		
2017–18	Crystal Palace	19	0	185	3

WILLIAMS, Jon (M)   118 3
H: 5 6   W: 10 00   b.Tunbridge Wells 9-10-93
Internationals: Wales U17, U19, U21, Full caps.

2010–11	Crystal Palace	0	0		
2011–12	Crystal Palace	14	0		
2012–13	Crystal Palace	29	0		
2013–14	Crystal Palace	9	0		
2013–14	Ipswich T	13	1		
2014–15	Crystal Palace	2	0		
2014–15	Ipswich T	7	1		
2015–16	Crystal Palace	1	0		
2015–16	Nottingham F	10	0	10	0
2015–16	Milton Keynes D	13	0	13	0
2016–17	Crystal Palace	0	0		
2016–17	Ipswich T	8	0	28	2
2017–18	Crystal Palace	0	0	55	0
2017–18	Sunderland	12	1	12	1

ZAHA, Wilfried (F)   269 35
H: 5 11   W: 10 05   b.Ivory Coast 10-11-92
Internationals: England U19, U21, Full caps. Ivory Coast Full caps.

2009–10	Crystal Palace	1	0		
2010–11	Crystal Palace	41	1		
2011–12	Crystal Palace	41	6		
2012–13	Crystal Palace	43	6		
2012–13	Manchester U	0	0		
2013–14	Manchester U	2	0	2	0
2013–14	Cardiff C	12	0	12	0
2014–15	Crystal Palace	31	4		
2015–16	Crystal Palace	34	2		
2016–17	Crystal Palace	35	7		
2017–18	Crystal Palace	29	9	255	35

Players retained or with offer of contract
Brown, Tyler; Dreher, Luke Garry; Flanagan, Kian; Jno Baptiste, Francis; McGregor, Giovanni Donald; Mitchell, Tyrick; O'Dwyer, Oliver; Tavares, Nikola; Wickham, Connor Neil Ralph; Woods, Samuel John.

Scholars
Boateng, David Nketiah; Bryon, Lewis; Daly, James Stanley; Donkin, William Rupert James; Gurung, Bivesh; Hanson, Ryan David; Hungbo, Joseph Oluwagbemiga; Malcolm, Joshua; Matthews, Drew; Onoabhagbe, Ehizojie Martins; Robertson, Sean Dominic; Trehy, Cian; Watson, Courtney Alfie Haynes; Webber, Oliver Henry.

DERBY CO (32)

ANYA, Ikechi (M)   190 12
H: 5 5   W: 11 04   b.Glasgow 3-1-88
Internationals: Scotland Full caps.

2004–05	Wycombe W	3	0		
2005–06	Wycombe W	2	0		
2006–07	Wycombe W	13	0		
2007–08	Wycombe W	0	0	18	0
2008–09	Northampton T	14	3	14	3
2010–11	Celta Vigo	0	0	1	0
From Cadiz					
2012–13	Watford	25	3		
2013–14	Watford	35	5		
2014–15	Watford	35	0		
2015–16	Watford	28	0		
2016–17	Watford	1	0	124	8
2016–17	Derby Co	26	1		
2017–18	Derby Co	7	0	33	1

BAIRD, Chris (D)   324 7
H: 5 10   W: 11 11   b.Ballymoney 25-2-82
Internationals: Northern Ireland U18, U21, Full caps.

2000–01	Southampton	0	0		
2001–02	Southampton	0	0		
2002–03	Southampton	3	0		
2003–04	Southampton	4	0		
2003–04	Walsall	10	0	10	0
2003–04	Watford	8	0	8	0
2004–05	Southampton	0	0		
2005–06	Southampton	17	0		
2006–07	Southampton	44	3	68	3
2007–08	Fulham	18	0		
2008–09	Fulham	10	0		
2009–10	Fulham	32	0		
2010–11	Fulham	29	2		
2011–12	Fulham	19	0		

2012–13	Fulham	19	2		
2013–14	Reading	9	0	9	0
2013–14	Burnley	7	0	7	0
2013–14	WBA	19	0	19	0
2015–16	Derby Co	14	0		
2015–16	Fulham	7	0	134	4
2016–17	Derby Co	33	0		
2017–18	Derby Co	22	0	69	0

BENNETT, Mason (F)   69 4
H: 5 10   W: 10 02   b.Shirebrook 15-7-96
Internationals: England U16, U17, U19.

2011–12	Derby Co	9	0		
2012–13	Derby Co	6	0		
2013–14	Derby Co	13	1		
2013–14	Chesterfield	5	0	5	0
2014–15	Derby Co	2	0		
2014–15	Bradford C	11	1	11	1
2015–16	Derby Co	0	0		
2015–16	Burton Alb	16	1	16	1
2016–17	Derby Co	2	0		
2017–18	Derby Co	3	0	35	1
2017–18	Notts Co	2	1	2	1

BENT, Darren (F)   486 180
H: 5 11   W: 12 07   b.Wandsworth 6-2-84
Internationals: England U15, U16, U17, U19, U21, Full caps.

2001–02	Ipswich T	5	1		
2002–03	Ipswich T	35	12		
2003–04	Ipswich T	37	16		
2004–05	Ipswich T	45	20	122	49
2005–06	Charlton Ath	36	18		
2006–07	Charlton Ath	32	13	68	31
2007–08	Tottenham H	27	6		
2008–09	Tottenham H	33	12		
2009–10	Tottenham H	0	0	60	18
2009–10	Sunderland	38	24		
2010–11	Sunderland	20	8	58	32
2010–11	Aston Villa	16	9		
2011–12	Aston Villa	22	9		
2012–13	Aston Villa	16	3		
2013–14	Aston Villa	0	0		
2013–14	Fulham	24	3	24	3
2014–15	Aston Villa	7	0	61	21
2014–15	Brighton & HA	5	2	5	2
2014–15	Derby Co	15	10		
2015–16	Derby Co	21	2		
2016–17	Derby Co	37	10		
2017–18	Derby Co	0	0	73	22
2017–18	Burton Alb	15	2	15	2

BIRD, Max (M)   0 0
H: 6 0   W: 10 10   b.Burton 18-9-00

2017–18	Derby Co	0	0	

BOGLE, Jayden (D)   0 0
b. 27-7-00
From Stoke C.

2017–18	Derby Co	0	0	

BRYSON, Craig (M)   458 59
H: 5 7   W: 10 00   b.Rutherglen 6-11-86
Internationals: Scotland U21, Full caps.

2003–04	Clyde	7	0		
2004–05	Clyde	28	3		
2005–06	Clyde	33	2		
2006–07	Clyde	34	3	95	8
2007–08	Kilmarnock	19	4		
2008–09	Kilmarnock	33	2		
2009–10	Kilmarnock	33	4		
2010–11	Kilmarnock	33	2	118	12
2011–12	Derby Co	44	6		
2012–13	Derby Co	37	5		
2013–14	Derby Co	45	16		
2014–15	Derby Co	38	4		
2015–16	Derby Co	21	3		
2016–17	Derby Co	34	2		
2017–18	Derby Co	4	1	223	37
2017–18	Cardiff C	22	2	22	2

BUTTERFIELD, Jacob (D)   288 26
H: 5 10   W: 11 00   b.Bradford 10-6-90
Internationals: England U21.

2007–08	Barnsley	3	0		
2008–09	Barnsley	3	0		
2009–10	Barnsley	20	1		
2010–11	Barnsley	40	2		
2011–12	Barnsley	24	5	90	8
2012–13	Norwich C	0	0		
2012–13	Bolton W	8	0	8	0
2012–13	Crystal Palace	9	0	9	0
2013–14	Norwich C	0	0		
2013–14	Middlesbrough	3	1	31	3
2014–15	Huddersfield T	45	6		
2015–16	Huddersfield T	1	1	50	7
2015–16	Derby Co	37	7		
2016–17	Derby Co	40	1		

2017–18	Derby Co	3	0	80	8
2017–18	Sheffield W	20	0	20	0

CARSON, Scott (G) 438 0
H: 6 0 W: 13 06 b.Whitehaven 3-9-85
Internationals: England U18, U21, B, Full caps.

2002–03	Leeds U	0	0		
2003–04	Leeds U	3	0		
2004–05	Leeds U	0	0	3	0
2004–05	Liverpool	4	0		
2005–06	Liverpool	0	0		
2005–06	Sheffield W	9	0	9	0
2006–07	Liverpool	0	0		
2006–07	Charlton Ath	36	0	36	0
2007–08	Liverpool	0	0	4	0
2007–08	Aston Villa	35	0	35	0
2008–09	WBA	35	0		
2009–10	WBA	43	0		
2010–11	WBA	32	0	110	0
2011–12	Bursaspor	34	0		
2012–13	Bursaspor	29	0	63	0
2013–14	Wigan Ath	16	0		
2014–15	Wigan Ath	34	0	50	0
2015–16	Derby Co	36	0		
2016–17	Derby Co	46	0		
2017–18	Derby Co	46	0	128	0

DAVIES, Curtis (D) 440 23
H: 6 2 W: 11 13 b.Waltham Forest 15-3-85
Internationals: England U21.

2003–04	Luton T	6	0		
2004–05	Luton T	44	1		
2005–06	Luton T	6	1	56	2
2005–06	WBA	33	2		
2006–07	WBA	32	0		
2007–08	WBA	0	0	65	2
2007–08	Aston Villa	12	1		
2008–09	Aston Villa	35	1		
2009–10	Aston Villa	2	1		
2010–11	Aston Villa	0	0	49	3
2010–11	Leicester C	12	0	12	0
2010–11	Birmingham C	6	0		
2011–12	Birmingham C	42	5		
2012–13	Birmingham C	41	6	89	11
2013–14	Hull C	37	2		
2014–15	Hull C	21	0		
2015–16	Hull C	39	2		
2016–17	Hull C	26	0	123	4
2017–18	Derby Co	46	1	46	1

ELSNIK, Timi (M) 22 3
H: 5 10 W: 10 03 b.Kidricevo 29-4-98
Internationals: Slovenia U16, U17, U19.

2015–16	Derby Co	0	0		
2016–17	Derby Co	0	0		
2017–18	Derby Co	0	0		
2017–18	Swindon T	22	3	22	3

FORSYTH, Craig (M) 269 19
H: 6 0 W: 12 00 b.Carnoustie 24-2-89
Internationals: Scotland Full caps.

2006–07	Dundee	1	0		
2007–08	Dundee	0	0		
2007–08	Montrose	9	0	9	0
2008–09	Dundee	1	0		
2008–09	Arbroath	26	2	26	2
2009–10	Dundee	24	2		
2010–11	Dundee	33	8	59	10
2011–12	Watford	20	3		
2012–13	Watford	2	0	22	3
2012–13	Bradford C	7	0	7	0
2012–13	Derby Co	10	0		
2013–14	Derby Co	46	2		
2014–15	Derby Co	44	1		
2015–16	Derby Co	12	0		
2016–17	Derby Co	3	1		
2017–18	Derby Co	31	0	146	4

GORDON, Kellan (M) 26 3
b.Burton 25-12-97

2017–18	Derby Co	0	0		
2017–18	Swindon T	26	3	26	3

GUY, Callum (M) 28 0
b. 25-11-96

2015–16	Derby Co	0	0		
2016–17	Derby Co	0	0		
2016–17	Port Vale	11	0	11	0
2017–18	Derby Co	0	0		
2017–18	Bradford C	17	0	17	0

HANSON, Jamie (F) 48 1
H: 6 3 W: 12 06 b.Burton-upon-Trent 10-11-95
Internationals: England U20.

2012–13	Derby Co	0	0	
2013–14	Derby Co	0	0	
2014–15	Derby Co	2	1	

2015–16	Derby Co	18	0		
2016–17	Derby Co	5	0		
2016–17	Wigan Ath	17	0	17	0
2017–18	Derby Co	6	0	31	1

HUDDLESTONE, Tom (M) 424 17
H: 6 2 W: 11 02 b.Nottingham 28-12-86
Internationals: England U16, U17, U19, U20, U21, Full caps.

2003–04	Derby Co	43	0		
2004–05	Derby Co	45	0		
2005–06	Tottenham H	4	0		
2005–06	Wolverhampton W	13	1	13	1
2006–07	Tottenham H	21	1		
2007–08	Tottenham H	28	3		
2008–09	Tottenham H	22	0		
2009–10	Tottenham H	33	2		
2010–11	Tottenham H	14	2		
2011–12	Tottenham H	2	0		
2012–13	Tottenham H	20	0		
2013–14	Tottenham H	0	0	144	8
2013–14	Hull C	36	3		
2014–15	Hull C	31	0		
2015–16	Hull C	37	2		
2016–17	Hull C	31	1	135	6
2017–18	Derby Co	44	2	132	2

JEROME, Cameron (F) 480 113
H: 6 1 W: 13 06 b.Huddersfield 14-8-86
Internationals: England U21.

2004–05	Cardiff C	29	6		
2005–06	Cardiff C	44	18	73	24
2005–06	Birmingham C	0	0		
2006–07	Birmingham C	38	7		
2007–08	Birmingham C	33	7		
2008–09	Birmingham C	43	9		
2009–10	Birmingham C	32	11		
2010–11	Birmingham C	34	3		
2011–12	Birmingham C	1	0	181	37
2011–12	Stoke C	23	4		
2012–13	Stoke C	26	3		
2013–14	Stoke C	0	0	50	7
2013–14	Crystal Palace	28	2	28	2
2014–15	Norwich C	41	18		
2015–16	Norwich C	34	3		
2016–17	Norwich C	40	16		
2017–18	Norwich C	15	1	130	38
2017–18	Derby Co	18	5	18	5

JOHNSON, Brad (M) 420 60
H: 6 0 W: 12 10 b.Hackney 28-4-87

2004–05	Cambridge U	1	0	1	0
2005–06	Northampton T	3	0		
2006–07	Northampton T	27	5		
2007–08	Northampton T	23	2	53	7
2007–08	Leeds U	21	3		
2008–09	Leeds U	15	1		
2008–09	Brighton & HA	10	4	10	4
2009–10	Leeds U	36	7		
2010–11	Leeds U	45	5	117	16
2011–12	Norwich C	28	2		
2012–13	Norwich C	37	1		
2013–14	Norwich C	32	3		
2014–15	Norwich C	41	15		
2015–16	Norwich C	4	0	142	21
2015–16	Derby Co	31	5		
2016–17	Derby Co	33	3		
2017–18	Derby Co	33	4	97	12

KEOGH, Richard (D) 495 16
H: 6 0 W: 11 02 b.Harlow 11-8-86
Internationals: Republic of Ireland U21, Full caps.

2004–05	Stoke C	0	0		
2005–06	Bristol C	9	1		
2005–06	Wycombe W	3	0	3	0
2006–07	Bristol C	31	2		
2007–08	Bristol C	0	0	40	3
2007–08	Huddersfield T	9	1	9	1
2007–08	Carlisle U	7	0		
2007–08	Cheltenham T	10	0	10	0
2008–09	Carlisle U	32	1		
2009–10	Carlisle U	41	3	80	4
2010–11	Coventry C	46	1		
2011–12	Coventry C	45	0	91	1
2012–13	Derby Co	46	4		
2013–14	Derby Co	41	1		
2014–15	Derby Co	45	0		
2015–16	Derby Co	46	1		
2016–17	Derby Co	42	0		
2017–18	Derby Co	42	1	262	7

LAWRENCE, Tom (F) 146 23
H: 5 9 W: 11 11 b.Wrexham 13-1-94
Internationals: Wales U17, U19, U21, Full caps.

2012–13	Manchester U	0	0		
2013–14	Manchester U	1	0	1	0

2013–14	Carlisle U	9	3	9	3
2013–14	Yeovil T	19	2	19	2
2014–15	Leicester C	3	0		
2014–15	Rotherham U	6	1	6	1
2015–16	Leicester C	0	0		
2015–16	Blackburn R	21	2	21	2
2015–16	Cardiff C	14	0	14	0
2016–17	Leicester C	0	0	3	0
2016–17	Ipswich T	34	9	34	9
2017–18	Derby Co	39	6	39	6

LEDLEY, Joe (M) 441 52
H: 6 0 W: 11 06 b.Cardiff 23-1-87
Internationals: Wales U17, U19, U21, Full caps.

2004–05	Cardiff C	28	3		
2005–06	Cardiff C	42	3		
2006–07	Cardiff C	46	2		
2007–08	Cardiff C	41	10		
2008–09	Cardiff C	40	4		
2009–10	Cardiff C	29	3	226	25
2010–11	Celtic	29	2		
2011–12	Celtic	32	7		
2012–13	Celtic	25	7		
2013–14	Celtic	20	4	106	20
2013–14	Crystal Palace	14	2		
2014–15	Crystal Palace	32	2		
2015–16	Crystal Palace	19	1		
2016–17	Crystal Palace	18	1	83	6
2017–18	Derby Co	26	1	26	1

LOWE, Max (D) 21 0
H: 5 9 W: 11 09 b.Birmingham 11-5-97
Internationals: England U16, U17, U18, U20.

2013–14	Derby Co	0	0		
2014–15	Derby Co	0	0		
2015–16	Derby Co	0	0		
2016–17	Derby Co	9	0		
2017–18	Derby Co	0	0	9	0
2017–18	Shrewsbury T	12	0	12	0

MARTIN, Chris (F) 386 111
H: 6 2 W: 12 06 b.Beccles 4-11-88
Internationals: England U19. Scotland Full caps.

2006–07	Norwich C	18	4		
2007–08	Norwich C	7	0		
2008–09	Norwich C	0	0		
2008–09	Luton T	40	11	40	11
2009–10	Norwich C	42	17		
2010–11	Norwich C	30	4		
2011–12	Norwich C	4	0		
2011–12	Crystal Palace	26	7	26	7
2012–13	Norwich C	1	0	102	25
2012–13	Swindon T	12	1	12	1
2012–13	Derby Co	13	2		
2013–14	Derby Co	44	20		
2014–15	Derby Co	35	18		
2015–16	Derby Co	45	15		
2016–17	Derby Co	5	0		
2016–17	Fulham	31	10	31	10
2017–18	Derby Co	23	1	165	56
2017–18	Reading	10	1	10	1

MITCHELL, Jonathan (G) 5 0
H: 5 11 W: 13 08 b.Hartlepool 24-11-94
Internationals: England U21.

2014–15	Derby Co	0	0		
2015–16	Derby Co	0	0		
2015–16	Luton T	5	0	5	0
2016–17	Derby Co	0	0		
2017–18	Derby Co	0	0		

NUGENT, Dave (F) 545 150
H: 5 11 W: 12 13 b.Liverpool 2-5-85
Internationals: England U20, U21, Full caps.

2001–02	Bury	5	0		
2002–03	Bury	31	4		
2003–04	Bury	26	3		
2004–05	Bury	26	11	88	18
2004–05	Preston NE	18	8		
2005–06	Preston NE	32	10		
2006–07	Preston NE	44	15	94	33
2007–08	Portsmouth	15	0		
2008–09	Portsmouth	16	3		
2009–10	Portsmouth	3	0		
2009–10	Burnley	30	6	30	6
2010–11	Portsmouth	44	13	78	16
2011–12	Leicester C	42	15		
2012–13	Leicester C	42	14		
2013–14	Leicester C	46	20		
2014–15	Leicester C	29	5	159	54
2015–16	Middlesbrough	38	8		
2016–17	Middlesbrough	4	0	42	8
2016–17	Derby Co	17	6		
2017–18	Derby Co	37	9	54	15

OLSSON, Marcus (M)   265 14
H: 5 11 W: 10 10 b.Gavle 17-5-88
Internationals: Sweden U21, Full caps.

2008	Halmstad	21	2		
2009	Halmstad	20	4		
2010	Halmstad	30	4		
2011	Halmstad	29	2	100	12
2011–12	Blackburn R	12	0		
2012–13	Blackburn R	23	1		
2013–14	Blackburn R	8	0		
2014–15	Blackburn R	41	0		
2015–16	Blackburn R	20	0	104	1
2015–16	Derby Co	16	1		
2016–17	Derby Co	30	0		
2017–18	Derby Co	15	0	61	1

PEARCE, Alex (D)   312 20
H: 6 0 W: 11 10 b.Wallingford 9-11-88
Internationals: Scotland U19, U21, Full caps.

2006–07	Reading	0	0		
2006–07	Northampton T	15	1	15	1
2007–08	Reading	0	0		
2007–08	Bournemouth	11	0	11	0
2007–08	Norwich C	11	0	11	0
2008–09	Reading	16	1		
2008–09	Southampton	9	2	9	2
2009–10	Reading	25	4		
2010–11	Reading	21	1		
2011–12	Reading	46	5		
2012–13	Reading	19	0		
2013–14	Reading	45	3		
2014–15	Reading	40	0	212	14
2015–16	Derby Co	0	0		
2015–16	Bristol C	7	0	7	0
2016–17	Derby Co	40	2		
2017–18	Derby Co	7	1	47	3

ROOS, Kelle (G)   49 0
H: 6 4 W: 14 02 b.Rijkevoort 31-5-92

2013–14	Derby Co	0	0		
2014–15	Derby Co	0	0		
2015–16	Derby Co	0	0		
2015–16	Rotherham U	4	0	4	0
2015–16	AFC Wimbledon	17	0	17	0
2016–17	Derby Co	0	0		
2016–17	Bristol R	16	0	16	0
2017–18	Derby Co	5	0		
2017–18	Port Vale	8	0	8	0
2017–18	Plymouth Arg	4	0	4	0

RUSSELL, Johnny (F)   284 61
H: 5 10 W: 12 03 b.Glasgow 8-4-90
Internationals: Scotland U19, U21, Full caps.

2006–07	Dundee U	1	0		
2007–08	Dundee U	2	0		
2008–09	Dundee U	0	0		
2009–10	Dundee U	0	0		
2010–11	Dundee U	30	9		
2011–12	Dundee U	37	9		
2012–13	Dundee U	32	13	102	31
2013–14	Derby Co	39	9		
2014–15	Derby Co	39	6		
2015–16	Derby Co	45	9		
2016–17	Derby Co	36	2		
2017–18	Derby Co	23	4	182	30

Transferred to Sporting Kansas City, January 2018.

SHACKELL, Jason (D)   445 13
H: 6 4 W: 13 06 b.Stevenage 27-9-83

2002–03	Norwich C	2	0		
2003–04	Norwich C	6	0		
2004–05	Norwich C	11	0		
2005–06	Norwich C	17	0		
2006–07	Norwich C	43	3		
2007–08	Norwich C	39	0		
2008–09	Norwich C	15	0	133	3
2008–09	Wolverhampton W	12	0		
2009–10	Wolverhampton W	0	0	12	0
2009–10	Doncaster R	21	1	21	1
2010–11	Barnsley	44	3		
2011–12	Barnsley	0	0	44	3
2011–12	Derby Co	46	1		
2012–13	Burnley	44	2		
2013–14	Burnley	46	2		
2014–15	Burnley	38	0	128	4
2015–16	Derby Co	46	1		
2016–17	Derby Co	8	0		
2017–18	Derby Co	0	0	100	2
2017–18	Millwall	7	0	7	0

THOMAS, Luke (F)   2 0
H: 5 7 W: 10 08 b. 19-2-99

2015–16	Derby Co	0	0		
2016–17	Derby Co	0	0		
2017–18	Derby Co	2	0	2	0

THORNE, George (M)   105 4
H: 6 2 W: 13 01 b.Chatham 4-1-93
Internationals: England U16, U17, U18, U19.

2009–10	WBA	1	0		
2010–11	WBA	1	0		
2011–12	WBA	3	0		
2011–12	Portsmouth	14	0	14	0
2012–13	WBA	5	0		
2012–13	Peterborough U	7	1	7	1
2013–14	WBA	0	0	10	0
2013–14	Watford	8	0	8	0
2013–14	Derby Co	9	1		
2014–15	Derby Co	3	0		
2015–16	Derby Co	34	2		
2017–18	Derby Co	20	0	66	3

VERNAM, Charles (F)   22 2
b. 8-10-96

2013–14	Derby Co	0	0		
2014–15	Derby Co	0	0		
2015–16	Derby Co	0	0		
2016	Vestmannaeyjar	9	1	9	1
2016–17	Derby Co	0	0		
2016–17	Coventry C	4	0	4	0
2017–18	Derby Co	0	0		
2017–18	Grimsby T	9	1	9	1

VYDRA, Matej (F)   227 72
H: 5 10 W: 11 09 b.Chotebor 1-5-92
Internationals: Czech Republic U16, U17, U18, U19, U21, Full caps.

2009–10	Banik Ostrava	13	4	13	4
2010–11	Udinese	2	0		
2011–12	Udinese	0	0		
2011–12	Club Brugge	1	0	1	0
2012–13	Udinese	0	0		
2012–13	Watford	41	20		
2013–14	Udinese	0	0		
2013–14	WBA	23	3	23	3
2014–15	Udinese	0	0	2	0
2014–15	Watford	42	16		
2015–16	Watford	0	0		
2015–16	Reading	31	3	31	3
2016–17	Watford	1	0	84	36
2017–18	Derby Co	40	21	73	26

WEIMANN, Andreas (F)   234 32
H: 5 9 W: 11 09 b.Vienna 5-8-91
Internationals: Austria U17, U19, U20, U21, Full caps.

2008–09	Aston Villa	0	0		
2009–10	Aston Villa	0	0		
2010–11	Aston Villa	1	0		
2010–11	Watford	18	4		
2011–12	Aston Villa	14	2		
2011–12	Watford	3	0	21	4
2012–13	Aston Villa	30	7		
2013–14	Aston Villa	37	5		
2014–15	Aston Villa	31	3	113	17
2015–16	Derby Co	30	4		
2016–17	Derby Co	11	0		
2016–17	Wolverhampton W	19	2	19	2
2017–18	Derby Co	40	5	81	9

WISDOM, Andre (D)   128 0
H: 6 1 W: 12 04 b.Leeds 9-5-93
Internationals: England U16, U17, U19, U21.

2009–10	Liverpool	0	0		
2010–11	Liverpool	0	0		
2011–12	Liverpool	0	0		
2012–13	Liverpool	12	0		
2013–14	Liverpool	2	0		
2013–14	Derby Co	34	0		
2014–15	Liverpool	0	0		
2014–15	WBA	24	0	24	0
2015–16	Liverpool	0	0		
2015–16	Norwich C	10	0	10	0
2016–17	Liverpool	0	0	14	0
2016–17	Red Bull Salzburg	16	0	16	0
2017–18	Derby Co	30	0	64	0

ZANZALA, Offrande (F)   8 1
b. 13-12-97

2015–16	Derby Co	0	0		
2015–16	Stevenage	2	0	2	0
2016–17	Derby Co	0	0		
2017–18	Derby Co	0	0		
2017–18	Accrington S	6	1	6	1

Players retained or with offer of contract
Babos, Alexander Jon; Barnes, Joshua Edwin; Bateman, Joseph Joshua; Blackman, Nicholas Alexander; Cresswell, Cameron Ian; Hunt, Max; MacDonald, Calum Ross; McAllister, Kyle; Mitchell-Lawson, Jayden; Rashid, Fuseine; Ravas, Henrich; Sostaric, Karic Sven; Walker, Lewis Jon; Wassall, Ethan Luca; Yates, Matthew Dean.

Scholars
Brown, Jordan Brian; Buchanan, Lee David; Davie, Adam Edward; Dixon, Connor Liam; French, Samuel Nicholas; Fryatt, Joseph Eric; Greco, Yoann; Haywood, Jack; Knight, Jason Paul; Mills, Jordan Mathew; Minkley, Callum; Thomas, Cain; Whittaker, Morgan Reece; Wise, Henry Dennis Paul.

DONCASTER R (33)

ALCOCK, Craig (D)   293 3
H: 5 8 W: 11 00 b.Cornwall 8-12-87

2006–07	Yeovil T	1	0		
2007–08	Yeovil T	8	0		
2008–09	Yeovil T	30	1		
2009–10	Yeovil T	42	1		
2010–11	Yeovil T	26	1	107	3
2011–12	Peterborough U	41	0		
2012–13	Peterborough U	27	0		
2013–14	Peterborough U	28	0	96	0
2014–15	Sheffield U	24	0		
2015–16	Sheffield U	3	0	27	0
2015–16	Doncaster R	27	0		
2016–17	Doncaster R	27	0		
2017–18	Doncaster R	9	0	63	0

AMOS, Danny (D)   3 0
H: 5 11 W: 10 10 b.Sheffield 22-12-99
Internationals: Northern Ireland U19.

2016–17	Doncaster R	0	0		
2017–18	Doncaster R	3	0	3	0

ANDREW, Danny (D)   132 4
H: 5 11 W: 11 06 b.Holbeach 23-12-90

2009–10	Peterborough U	2	0	2	0
2009–10	Cheltenham T	10	0		
2010–11	Cheltenham T	43	4		
2011–12	Cheltenham T	10	0		
2012–13	Cheltenham T	1	0	64	4

From Gloucester C, Macclesfield T.

2014–15	Fleetwood T	7	0		
2015–16	Fleetwood T	9	0	16	0
2016–17	Grimsby T	46	0	46	0
2017–18	Doncaster R	4	0	4	0

BAUDRY, Mathieu (D)   228 16
H: 6 2 W: 12 08 b.Le Havre 24-2-88

2007–08	Troyes	0	0		
2008–09	Troyes	17	0		
2009–10	Troyes	7	0	26	1
2010–11	Bournemouth	3	1		
2011–12	Bournemouth	7	0	10	1
2011–12	Dagenham & R	11	0	11	0
2012–13	Leyton Orient	24	3		
2013–14	Leyton Orient	39	2		
2014–15	Leyton Orient	31	1		
2015–16	Leyton Orient	34	2	128	8
2016–17	Doncaster R	31	5		
2017–18	Doncaster R	22	1	53	6

BEESTIN, Alfie (F)   29 2
H: 5 10 W: 11 11 b.Leeds 1-10-97

2016–17	Doncaster R	3	0		
2017–18	Doncaster R	26	2	29	2

BEN KHEMIS, Issam (F)   6 0
H: 5 9 W: 11 05 b.Paris 10-1-96
Internationals: Tunisia Full caps.

2015–16	Lorient	1	0		
2016–17	Lorient	2	0		
2017–18	Lorient	0	0	3	0
2017–18	Doncaster R	3	0	3	0

BLAIR, Matty (M)   201 17
H: 5 10 W: 11 09 b.Coventry 30-11-87
Internationals: England C.

2012–13	York C	44	6	44	6
2013–14	Fleetwood T	24	3		
2013–14	Northampton T	3	1	3	1
2014–15	Fleetwood T	8	0	32	3
2014–15	Cambridge U	2	0	2	0
2015–16	Mansfield T	3	0		
2015–16	Mansfield T	32	2	35	2
2016–17	Doncaster R	45	3		
2017–18	Doncaster R	40	2	85	5

BUTLER, Andy (D)   518 48
H: 6 0 W: 13 00 b.Doncaster 4-11-83

2003–04	Scunthorpe U	35	2		
2004–05	Scunthorpe U	37	10		
2005–06	Scunthorpe U	16	1		
2006–07	Scunthorpe U	11	1		
2006–07	Grimsby T	4	0	4	0
2007–08	Scunthorpe U	36	2	135	16
2008–09	Huddersfield T	42	4		

2009–10	Huddersfield T	11	0	53	4
2009–10	Blackpool	7	0	7	0
2010–11	Walsall	31	4		
2011–12	Walsall	42	5		
2012–13	Walsall	41	3		
2013–14	Walsall	45	2		
2014–15	Sheffield U	0	0		
2014–15	*Walsall*	7	0	166	14
2014–15	Doncaster R	33	3		
2015–16	Doncaster R	40	4		
2016–17	Doncaster R	44	3		
2017–18	Doncaster R	36	4	153	14

COPPINGER, James (F)   584 66
H:5 7   W:10 03   b.Middlesbrough 10-1-81
Internationals: England U16.

1997–98	Newcastle U	0	0		
1998–99	Newcastle U	0	0		
1999–2000	Newcastle U	0	0		
1999–2000	*Hartlepool U*	10	3		
2000–01	Newcastle U	1	0		
2001–02	Newcastle U	0	0	1	0
2001–02	*Hartlepool U*	14	2	24	5
2002–03	Exeter C	43	5	43	5
2004–05	Doncaster R	31	0		
2005–06	Doncaster R	36	5		
2006–07	Doncaster R	39	4		
2007–08	Doncaster R	39	5		
2008–09	Doncaster R	32	5		
2009–10	Doncaster R	39	4		
2010–11	Doncaster R	40	7		
2011–12	Doncaster R	38	2		
2012–13	Doncaster R	25	2		
2012–13	*Nottingham F*	6	0	6	0
2013–14	Doncaster R	41	4		
2014–15	Doncaster R	34	4		
2015–16	Doncaster R	39	3		
2016–17	Doncaster R	39	10		
2017–18	Doncaster R	38	3	510	56

EVINA, Cedric (D)   161 3
H:5 11   W:12 08   b.Cameroon 16-11-91

2009–10	Arsenal	0	0		
2010–11	Arsenal	0	0		
2010–11	Oldham Ath	27	2	27	2
2011–12	Charlton Ath	3	0		
2012–13	Charlton Ath	12	0		
2013–14	Charlton Ath	8	0	23	0
2014–15	Doncaster R	19	0		
2015–16	Doncaster R	42	1		
2016–17	Doncaster R	16	0		
2017–18	Doncaster R	0	0	77	1
2017–18	*Crawley T*	34	0	34	0

FIELDING, Reece (M)   0 0
H:6 2   W:12 00   b.Doncaster 23-10-98

| 2016–17 | Doncaster R | 0 | 0 | | |
| 2017–18 | Doncaster R | 0 | 0 | | |

FLETCHER, Jacob (F)   1 0
b.16-5-00

| 2016–17 | Doncaster R | 0 | 0 | | |
| 2017–18 | Doncaster R | 1 | 0 | 1 | 0 |

GARRETT, Tyler (D)   18 0
b.26-10-96

2015–16	Bolton W	3	0	3	0
2016–17	Doncaster R	2	0		
2017–18	Doncaster R	13	0	15	0

HORTON, Branden (D)   0 0
b.9-9-00

| 2017–18 | Doncaster R | 0 | 0 | | |

JAMES, Morgan (D)   0 0

| 2016–17 | Doncaster R | 0 | 0 | | |
| 2017–18 | Doncaster R | 0 | 0 | | |

JONES, Louis (G)   0 0

2015–16	Doncaster R	0	0		
2016–17	Doncaster R	0	0		
2017–18	Doncaster R	0	0		

KIWOMYA, Alex (M)   55 8
H:5 10   W:10 08   b.Sheffield 20-5-96
Internationals: England U16, U17, U18, U19.

2014–15	Chelsea	0	0		
2014–15	*Barnsley*	5	0	5	0
2015–16	Chelsea	0	0		
2015–16	*Fleetwood T*	4	0	4	0
2016–17	Chelsea	0	0		
2016–17	*Crewe Alex*	37	4	34	7
2017–18	Doncaster R	12	1	12	1

LAWLOR, Ian (G)   70 0
H:6 4   W:12 08   b.Dublin 27-10-94
Internationals: Republic of Ireland U17, U19, U21.

2011–12	Manchester C	0	0		
2012–13	Manchester C	0	0		
2013–14	Manchester C	0	0		
2014–15	Manchester C	0	0		
2015–16	Manchester C	0	0		
2015–16	*Barnet*	5	0	5	0
2015–16	*Bury*	12	0	12	0
2016–17	Doncaster R	19	0		
2017–18	Doncaster R	34	0	53	0

LONGBOTTOM, William (F)   4 0
H:5 9   W:9 11   b.Leeds 12-12-98

2015–16	Doncaster R	1	0		
2016–17	Doncaster R	3	0		
2017–18	Doncaster R	0	0	4	0

LUND, Mitchell (D)   50 1
H:6 1   W:11 11   b.Leeds 27-8-96

2014–15	Doncaster R	4	0		
2015–16	Doncaster R	30	1		
2016–17	Doncaster R	6	0		
2017–18	Doncaster R	0	0	40	1
2017–18	*Morecambe*	10	0	10	0

MANDEVILLE, Liam (F)   56 9
H:5 11   W:12 02   b.Lincoln 17-2-97

2014–15	Doncaster R	3	0		
2015–16	Doncaster R	8	1		
2016–17	Doncaster R	21	7		
2017–18	Doncaster R	17	1	49	9
2017–18	*Colchester U*	7	0	7	0

MAROSI, Marko (G)   42 0
H:6 3   W:12 08   b.23-10-93
Internationals: Slovakia U21.

2013–14	Wigan Ath	0	0		
2014–15	Doncaster R	3	0		
2015–16	Doncaster R	1	0		
2016–17	Doncaster R	25	0		
2017–18	Doncaster R	13	0	42	0

MARQUIS, John (F)   228 66
H:6 1   W:11 03   b.Lewisham 16-5-92

2009–10	Millwall	0	0		
2010–11	Millwall	11	4		
2011–12	Millwall	17	1		
2012–13	Millwall	10	0		
2013–14	Millwall	2	0		
2013–14	*Portsmouth*	5	1	5	1
2013–14	*Torquay U*	5	3	5	3
2013–14	*Northampton T*	14	2		
2014–15	Millwall	1	0		
2014–15	*Cheltenham T*	13	1	13	1
2014–15	*Gillingham*	21	8	21	8
2015–16	Millwall	10	0	52	5
2015–16	*Leyton Orient*	13	0	13	0
2015–16	*Northampton T*	15	6	29	8
2016–17	Doncaster R	45	26		
2017–18	Doncaster R	45	14	90	40

MASON, Niall (M)   78 3
b.10-1-97

2015–16	Aston Villa	0	0		
2016–17	Aston Villa	0	0		
2016–17	*Doncaster R*	38	0		
2017–18	Doncaster R	40	3	78	3

MAY, Alfie (F)   43 7
H:5 9   W:11 05   b.2-7-93
From Hythe T.

| 2016–17 | Doncaster R | 16 | 3 | | |
| 2017–18 | Doncaster R | 27 | 4 | 43 | 7 |

McCULLOUGH, Luke (D)   100 0
H:6 2   W:12 11   b.Portadown 15-2-94
Internationals: Northern Ireland U16, U17, U19, U20, U21, Full caps.

2012–13	Manchester U	0	0		
2012–13	*Cheltenham T*	1	0	1	0
2013–14	Doncaster R	14	0		
2014–15	Doncaster R	33	0		
2015–16	Doncaster R	32	0		
2016–17	Doncaster R	7	0		
2017–18	Doncaster R	13	0	99	0

MORRIS, James (F)   0 0

| 2017–18 | Doncaster R | 0 | 0 | | |

OGLEY, Declan (G)   0 0

| 2017–18 | Doncaster R | 0 | 0 | | |

PRIOR, Cody (D)   0 0

| 2017–18 | Doncaster R | 0 | 0 | | |

ROWE, Tommy (M)   374 57
H:5 11   W:12 11   b.Manchester 1-5-89

2006–07	Stockport Co	0	0		
2007–08	Stockport Co	24	6		
2008–09	Stockport Co	44	7	72	13
2008–09	Peterborough U	0	0		
2009–10	Peterborough U	32	2		
2010–11	Peterborough U	35	5		
2011–12	Peterborough U	43	4		
2012–13	Peterborough U	31	5		
2013–14	Peterborough U	34	7	175	23
2014–15	Wolverhampton W	14	0		
2015–16	Wolverhampton W	3	0	17	0
2015–16	*Scunthorpe U*	14	1	14	1
2015–16	Doncaster R	10	3		
2016–17	Doncaster R	46	13		
2017–18	Doncaster R	40	4	96	20

SCATTERGOOD, Lewis (F)   0 0

| 2016–17 | Doncaster R | 0 | 0 | | |
| 2017–18 | Doncaster R | 0 | 0 | | |

TOWNROW, Keegan (D)   0 0

| 2017–18 | Doncaster R | 0 | 0 | | |

WALKER, Tyler (F)   0 0

| 2016–17 | Doncaster R | 0 | 0 | | |
| 2017–18 | Doncaster R | 0 | 0 | | |

WHITEMAN, Ben (M)   73 13
b.Rochdale 17-6-96

2014–15	Sheffield U	0	0		
2015–16	Sheffield U	6	0		
2016–17	Sheffield U	2	0	8	0
2016–17	*Mansfield T*	23	7	23	7
2017–18	Doncaster R	42	6	42	6

WILLIAMS, Andy (F)   417 95
H:5 11   W:11 09   b.Hereford 14-8-86

2006–07	Hereford U	41	8		
2007–08	Bristol R	41	4		
2008–09	Bristol R	4	1		
2008–09	*Hereford U*	26	2	67	10
2009–10	Bristol R	43	3	88	8
2010–11	Yeovil T	37	6		
2011–12	Yeovil T	35	16		
2012–13	Swindon T	40	11		
2013–14	Swindon T	3	0		
2013–14	*Yeovil T*	9	0	81	22
2014–15	Swindon T	46	21	89	32
2015–16	Doncaster R	46	12		
2016–17	Doncaster R	37	11		
2017–18	Doncaster R	9	0	92	23

WRIGHT, Joe (D)   75 0
H:6 4   W:12 06   b.26-2-95
Internationals: Wales U21.

2013–14	Huddersfield T	0	0		
2014–15	Huddersfield T	0	0		
2015–16	Huddersfield T	0	0		
2015–16	*Accrington S*	20	0	20	0
2016–17	Doncaster R	22	0		
2017–18	Doncaster R	33	0	55	0

Players retained or with offer of contract
Blaney, Shane; Khemis, Issam Ben.

Scholars
Baldock-Smith, Cameron; Barnett, Cameron; Bingley, Kane Joseph; Boocock, Rieves; Fletcher, Jacob Frederick; Foulkes, Cameron; Gibbons, Myron Jordan; Greaves, A.j. Anthony Junior Nelson; Horton, Branden; James, Morgan Daniel; Leverton, James Leslie; Morris, James; Ogley, Declan; Overton, Matthew James; Prior, Cody Patrick James; Scattergood, Lewis Matthew; Townrow, Keegan Terry.

EVERTON (34)

BAINES, Leighton (D)   479 33
H:5 8   W:11 00   b.Liverpool 11-12-84
Internationals: England U21, Full caps.

2002–03	Wigan Ath	6	0		
2003–04	Wigan Ath	26	0		
2004–05	Wigan Ath	41	1		
2005–06	Wigan Ath	37	0		
2006–07	Wigan Ath	35	3		
2007–08	Wigan Ath	0	0	145	4
2007–08	Everton	22	0		
2008–09	Everton	31	1		
2009–10	Everton	37	1		
2010–11	Everton	38	5		
2011–12	Everton	33	4		
2012–13	Everton	38	5		
2013–14	Everton	32	5		
2014–15	Everton	31	2		
2015–16	Everton	18	2		
2016–17	Everton	32	2		
2017–18	Everton	22	2	334	29

BANINGIME, Beni (M)   8 0
H:5 10   W:11 00   b.Kinshasa 9-9-98

| 2017–18 | Everton | 8 | 0 | 8 | 0 |

BESIC, Muhamed (M) 102 2
H: 5 10 W: 11 11 b.Berlin 10-9-92
Internationals: Bosnia-Herzegovina U21, Full caps.

2010–11	Hamburg	3	0	
2011–12	Hamburg	0	0	
2012–13	Hamburg	0	0	3 0
2012–13	Ferencvaros	22	1	
2013–14	Ferencvaros	25	0	47 1
2014–15	Everton	23	0	
2015–16	Everton	12	0	
2016–17	Everton	0	0	
2017–18	Everton	2	0	37 0
2017–18	*Middlesbrough*	15	1	15 1

BOLASIE, Yannick (M) 278 28
H: 6 2 W: 13 02 b.DR Congo 24-5-89
Internationals: DR Congo Full caps.

2008–09	Plymouth Arg	0	0	
2008–09	Barnet	20	3	
2009–10	Plymouth Arg	16	1	
2009–10	Barnet	22	2	42 5
2010–11	Plymouth Arg	35	7	51 8
2011–12	Bristol C	23	1	
2012–13	Bristol C	0	0	23 1
2012–13	Crystal Palace	43	3	
2013–14	Crystal Palace	29	0	
2014–15	Crystal Palace	34	4	
2015–16	Crystal Palace	26	5	
2016–17	Crystal Palace	1	0	133 12
2016–17	Everton	13	1	
2017–18	Everton	16	1	29 2

BROADHEAD, Nathan (F) 0 0
H: 5 10 W: 11 07 b.Bangor 5-4-98
Internationals: Wales U17, U19, U20, U21.

2017–18	Everton	0	0

BROWNING, Tyias (D) 44 0
H: 5 11 W: 12 00 b.Liverpool 27-5-94
Internationals: England U17, U19, U20.

2011–12	Everton	0	0	
2012–13	Everton	0	0	
2013–14	Everton	0	0	
2013–14	*Wigan Ath*	2	0	2 0
2014–15	Everton	2	0	
2015–16	Everton	5	0	
2016–17	Everton	0	0	
2016–17	*Preston NE*	8	0	8 0
2017–18	Everton	0	0	7 0
2017–18	*Sunderland*	27	0	27 0

BYRNE, Sam (F) 17 1
Internationals: Republic of Ireland U16, U17, U19, U21.

2013–14	Manchester U	0	0	
2013–14	*Carlisle U*	17	1	17 1
2014–15	Everton	0	0	
2015–16	Everton	0	0	
2016–17	Everton	0	0	
2017–18	Everton	0	0	

CALVERT-LEWIN, Dominic (M) 74 10
b. 16-3-97
Internationals: England U20, U21.

2013–14	Sheffield U	0	0	
2014–15	Sheffield U	0	0	
2015–16	Sheffield U	9	0	
2015–16	*Northampton T*	20	5	20 5
2016–17	Sheffield U	0	0	11 0
2016–17	Everton	11	1	
2017–18	Everton	32	4	43 5

CHARSLEY, Harry (M) 1 0
H: 5 10 W: 10 01 b.Wirral 1-11-96
Internationals: Republic of Ireland U17, U19, U21.

2017–18	Everton	0	0	
2017–18	*Bolton W*	1	0	1 0

COLEMAN, Seamus (D) 227 19
H: 6 4 W: 10 07 b.Donegal 11-10-88
Internationals: Republic of Ireland U21, U23, Full caps.

2008–09	Everton	0	0	
2009–10	Everton	3	0	
2009–10	*Blackpool*	9	1	9 1
2010–11	Everton	34	4	
2011–12	Everton	18	0	
2012–13	Everton	26	0	
2013–14	Everton	36	6	
2014–15	Everton	35	3	
2015–16	Everton	28	1	
2016–17	Everton	26	4	
2017–18	Everton	12	0	218 18

COLLINS, Michael (D) 0 0
b. 22-9-00

2017–18	Everton	0	0

CONNOLLY, Callum (D) 55 6
b.Liverpool 23-9-97
Internationals: England U17, U18, U19, U20, U21.

2015–16	Everton	1	0	
2015–16	Barnsley	3	0	3 0
2016–17	Everton	0	0	
2016–17	*Wigan Ath*	17	2	17 2
2017–18	Everton	0	0	1 0
2017–18	*Ipswich T*	34	4	34 4

DAVIES, Tom (M) 59 4
b.Liverpool 30-6-98
Internationals: England U16, U17, U18, U19, U21.

2015–16	Everton	2	0	
2016–17	Everton	24	2	
2017–18	Everton	33	2	59 4

DENNY, Alex (M) 0 0
H: 6 1 W: 12 11 b.Chester 12-4-00
Internationals: England U17, U18.

2017–18	Everton	0	0

DOWELL, Kieran (F) 40 9
H: 5 9 W: 9 04 b.Ormskirk 10-10-97
Internationals: England U16, U17, U18, U19, U20, U21.

2014–15	Everton	0	0	
2015–16	Everton	2	0	
2017–18	Everton	0	0	2 0
2017–18	*Nottingham F*	38	9	38 9

DUKE-McKENNA, Stephen (M) 0 0
b.Liverpool 17-8-00

2017–18	Everton	0	0

FEENEY, Morgan (D) 0 0
H: 6 3 W: 12 02 b.Bootle 6-2-98
Internationals: England U17, U18, U19.

2017–18	Everton	0	0

FUNES MORI, Ramiro (D) 131 11
H: 6 3 W: 13 12 b.Mendoza 5-3-91
Internationals: Argentina Full caps.

2010–11	River Plate	0	0	
2011–12	River Plate	19	2	
2012–13	River Plate	10	0	
2013–14	River Plate	19	1	
2014	River Plate	17	2	
2015	River Plate	11	2	76 7
2015–16	Everton	28	4	
2016–17	Everton	23	0	
2017–18	Everton	4	0	55 4

GALLOWAY, Brendon (D) 37 0
H: 6 2 W: 13 10 b.Zimbabwe 17-3-96
Internationals: England U17, U18, U19, U20, U21.

2011–12	Milton Keynes D	1	0	
2012–13	Milton Keynes D	1	0	
2013–14	Milton Keynes D	8	0	10 0
2014–15	Everton	2	0	
2015–16	Everton	15	0	
2016–17	Everton	0	0	
2016–17	*WBA*	3	0	3 0
2017–18	Everton	0	0	17 0
2017–18	*Sunderland*	7	0	7 0

GANA, Idrissa (M) 235 8
H: 5 9 W: 11 05 b.Dakar 26-9-89
Internationals: Senegal Full caps.

2010–11	Lille	11	0	
2011–12	Lille	25	0	
2012–13	Lille	29	0	
2013–14	Lille	37	1	
2014–15	Lille	32	4	134 5
2015–16	Aston Villa	35	0	35 0
2016–17	Everton	33	1	
2017–18	Everton	33	2	66 3

GARBUTT, Luke (D) 91 5
H: 5 10 W: 11 07 b.Harrogate 21-5-93
Internationals: England U16, U17, U18, U19, U20, U21.

2010–11	Everton	0	0	
2011–12	Everton	0	0	
2011–12	*Cheltenham T*	34	2	34 2
2012–13	Everton	0	0	
2013–14	Everton	1	0	
2013–14	*Colchester U*	19	2	19 2
2014–15	Everton	4	0	
2015–16	Everton	0	0	
2015–16	*Fulham*	25	1	25 1
2016–17	Everton	0	0	
2016–17	*Wigan Ath*	8	0	8 0
2017–18	Everton	0	0	5 0

GORDON, Anthony (M) 0 0
b. 24-2-01

2017–18	Everton	0	0

GRANT, Conor (M) 74 4
H: 5 9 W: 12 08 b.Fazakerley 18-4-95
Internationals: England U18.

2013–14	Everton	0	0	
2014–15	Everton	0	0	
2014–15	*Motherwell*	11	1	11 1
2015–16	Everton	0	0	
2015–16	*Doncaster R*	19	2	
2016–17	Everton	0	0	
2016–17	*Ipswich T*	6	0	6 0
2016–17	*Doncaster R*	21	1	40 3
2017–18	Everton	0	0	
2017–18	*Crewe Alex*	17	0	17 0

GRAY, Louis (G) 0 0
H: 6 1 W: 11 11 b.Wrexham 11-8-95
From Wrexham.

2017–18	Everton	0	0
2017–18	*Carlisle U*	0	0

HEWELT, Mateusz (G) 0 0
b. 23-9-96

2016–17	Everton	0	0
2017–18	Everton	0	0

HOLGATE, Mason (D) 53 1
H: 5 11 W: 11 11 b.Doncaster 22-10-96
Internationals: England U20, U21.

2014–15	Barnsley	20	1	20 1
2015–16	Everton	18	0	
2016–17	Everton	0	0	
2017–18	Everton	15	0	33 0

HORNBY, Fraser (M) 0 0
b.Northampton 13-9-99
Internationals: Scotland U17, U19, U21.
From Northampton T.

2017–18	Everton	0	0

JAGIELKA, Phil (D) 569 31
H: 6 0 W: 13 01 b.Manchester 17-8-82
Internationals: England U20, U21, B, Full caps.

1999–2000	Sheffield U	1	0	
2000–01	Sheffield U	15	0	
2001–02	Sheffield U	23	3	
2002–03	Sheffield U	42	0	
2003–04	Sheffield U	43	3	
2004–05	Sheffield U	46	0	
2005–06	Sheffield U	46	8	
2006–07	Sheffield U	38	4	254 18
2007–08	Everton	34	1	
2008–09	Everton	34	0	
2009–10	Everton	12	0	
2010–11	Everton	33	1	
2011–12	Everton	30	2	
2012–13	Everton	36	2	
2013–14	Everton	26	0	
2014–15	Everton	37	4	
2015–16	Everton	21	0	
2016–17	Everton	27	3	
2017–18	Everton	25	0	315 13

KEANE, Michael (D) 173 12
H: 5 7 W: 12 13 b.Stockport 11-1-93
Internationals: Republic of Ireland U17, U19. England U19, U20, U21, Full caps.

2011–12	Manchester U	0	0	
2012–13	Manchester U	0	0	
2012–13	*Leicester C*	22	2	22 2
2013–14	Manchester U	0	0	
2013–14	*Derby Co*	7	0	7 0
2013–14	*Blackburn R*	13	3	13 3
2014–15	Manchester U	1	0	1 0
2014–15	Burnley	21	0	
2015–16	Burnley	44	5	
2016–17	Burnley	35	2	100 7
2017–18	Everton	30	0	30 0

KENNY, Jonjoe (D) 45 0
H: 5 9 W: 10 08 b.Kirkdale 15-3-97
Internationals: England U16, U17, U18, U19, U20, U21.

2014–15	Everton	0	0	
2015–16	Everton	1	0	
2015–16	*Wigan Ath*	7	0	7 0
2015–16	*Oxford U*	17	0	17 0
2016–17	Everton	1	0	
2017–18	Everton	19	0	21 0

KLAASSEN, Davy (M) 133 44
H: 6 1 W: 12 02 b.Hilversum 21-2-93
Internationals: Netherlands U16, U17, U19, U21, Full caps.

2011–12	Ajax	4	1
2012–13	Ajax	2	0
2013–14	Ajax	26	10
2014–15	Ajax	30	6
2015–16	Ajax	31	13

2016–17	Ajax	33	14	**126**	**44**
2017–18	Everton	7	0	**7**	**0**

LAVERY, Shayne (M)   **0**   **0**
b. 8-12-98
Internationals: Northern Ireland U17, U19, U21, Full caps.
From Glenavon.

2017–18	Everton	0	0		

LOOKMAN, Ademola (F)   **71**   **16**
H: 5 9   b.Wandsworth 18-7-98
Internationals: England U19, U20, U21.

2015–16	Charlton Ath	24	5		
2016–17	Charlton Ath	21	5	**45**	**10**
2016–17	Everton	8	1		
2017–18	Everton	7	0	**15**	**1**
2017–18	*RB Leipzig*	11	5	**11**	**5**

MARTINA, Cuco (D)   **219**   **5**
H: 6 1   W: 11 05   b.Rotterdam 25-9-89
Internationals: Curacao Full caps.

2008–09	Roosendaal	14	0		
2009–10	Roosendaal	23	1		
2010–11	Roosendaal	32	1	**69**	**2**
2011–12	Waalwijk	23	0		
2012–13	Waalwijk	34	1	**57**	**1**
2013–14	FC Twente	16	1		
2014–15	FC Twente	32	0	**48**	**1**
2015–16	Southampton	15	1		
2016–17	Southampton	9	0	**24**	**1**
2017–18	Everton	21	0	**21**	**0**

MATHIS, Boris (F)   **5**   **0**
b.Bron 15-8-97
From Metz.

2017–18	Everton	0	0		
2017–18	*Northampton T*	5	0	**5**	**0**

McCARTHY, James (M)   **322**   **27**
H: 5 11   W: 11 05   b.Glasgow 12-11-90
Internationals: Republic of Ireland U17, U18, U19, U21, Full caps.

2006–07	Hamilton A	23	1		
2007–08	Hamilton A	35	7		
2008–09	Hamilton A	37	6	**95**	**14**
2009–10	Wigan Ath	20	1		
2010–11	Wigan Ath	24	3		
2011–12	Wigan Ath	33	0		
2012–13	Wigan Ath	38	3		
2013–14	Wigan Ath	5	0	**120**	**7**
2013–14	Everton	34	1		
2014–15	Everton	28	2		
2015–16	Everton	29	2		
2016–17	Everton	12	1		
2017–18	Everton	4	0	**107**	**6**

MIRALLAS, Kevin (F)   **341**   **78**
H: 6 0   W: 11 10   b.Leige 5-10-87
Internationals: Belgium U16, U17, U18, U19, U21, Full caps.

2004–05	Lille	1	1		
2005–06	Lille	15	1		
2006–07	Lille	23	2		
2007–08	Lille	35	6	**74**	**10**
2008–09	St Etienne	30	3		
2009–10	St Etienne	23	0	**53**	**3**
2010–11	*Olympiacos*	26	14		
2011–12	*Olympiacos*	24	20		
2012–13	*Olympiacos*	0	0		
2012–13	Everton	27	6		
2013–14	Everton	32	8		
2014–15	Everton	29	7		
2015–16	Everton	23	4		
2016–17	Everton	35	4		
2017–18	Everton	5	0	**151**	**29**
2017–18	*Olympiacos*	13	2	**63**	**36**

NIASSE, Oumar (F)   **106**   **36**
H: 6 0   b.Ouakam 18-4-90
Internationals: Senegal U23, Full caps.

2013–14	Akhisar Belediyespor	34	12	**34**	**12**
2014–15	Lokomotiv Moscow	13	4		
2015–16	Lokomotiv Moscow	15	8	**28**	**12**
2015–16	Everton	5	0		
2016–17	Everton	0	0		
2016–17	*Hull C*	17	4	**17**	**4**
2017–18	Everton	22	8	**27**	**8**

PENNINGTON, Matthew (D)   **77**   **3**
H: 6 1   W: 12 02   b.Warrington 6-10-94
Internationals: England U19.

2013–14	Everton	0	0		
2013–14	*Tranmere R*	17	2	**17**	**2**
2014–15	Everton	0	0		
2014–15	*Coventry C*	24	0	**24**	**0**
2015–16	Everton	4	0		
2015–16	*Walsall*	5	0	**5**	**0**
2016–17	Everton	3	1		

2017–18	Everton	0	0	**7**	**1**
2017–18	*Leeds U*	24	0	**24**	**0**

PICKFORD, Jordan (G)   **156**   **0**
H: 6 1   b.Washington 7-3-94
Internationals: England U16, U17, U18, U19, U20, U21, Full caps.

2010–11	Sunderland	0	0		
2011–12	Sunderland	0	0		
2012–13	Sunderland	0	0		
2013–14	Sunderland	0	0		
2013–14	*Burton Alb*	12	0	**12**	**0**
2013–14	*Carlisle U*	18	0	**18**	**0**
2014–15	Sunderland	0	0		
2014–15	*Bradford C*	33	0	**33**	**0**
2015–16	Sunderland	2	0		
2015–16	*Preston NE*	24	0	**24**	**0**
2016–17	Sunderland	29	0	**31**	**0**
2017–18	Everton	38	0	**38**	**0**

ROBINSON, Antonee (D)   **30**   **0**
H: 6 0   W: 11 07   b.Milton Keynes 8-8-97
Internationals: USA U18, Full caps.

2015–16	Everton	0	0		
2016–17	Everton	0	0		
2017–18	Everton	0	0		
2017–18	*Bolton W*	30	0	**30**	**0**

ROBLES, Joel (G)   **66**   **0**
H: 6 5   W: 13 04   b.Leganes 17-6-90
Internationals: Spain U16, U17, U21, U23.

2009–10	Atletico Madrid	2	0		
2011–12	*Rayo Vallecano*	13	0	**13**	**0**
2012–13	Atletico Madrid	0	0	**2**	**0**
2012–13	*Wigan Ath*	9	0	**9**	**0**
2013–14	Everton	2	0		
2014–15	Everton	7	0		
2015–16	Everton	13	0		
2016–17	Everton	20	0		
2017–18	Everton	0	0	**42**	**0**

ROONEY, Wayne (F)   **491**   **208**
H: 5 10   W: 12 13   b.Liverpool 24-10-85
Internationals: England U15, U17, U19, U21, Full caps.

2002–03	Everton	33	6		
2003–04	Everton	34	9		
2004–05	Manchester U	29	11		
2005–06	Manchester U	36	16		
2006–07	Manchester U	35	14		
2007–08	Manchester U	27	12		
2008–09	Manchester U	30	12		
2009–10	Manchester U	32	26		
2010–11	Manchester U	28	11		
2011–12	Manchester U	34	27		
2012–13	Manchester U	27	12		
2013–14	Manchester U	29	17		
2014–15	Manchester U	33	12		
2015–16	Manchester U	28	8		
2016–17	Manchester U	25	5	**393**	**183**
2017–18	Everton	31	10	**98**	**25**

SANDRO, Ramirez (F)   **68**   **16**
H: 5 8   W: 11 03   b.Las Palmas 9-7-95
Internationals: Spain U16, U17, U18, U19, U21.

2014–15	Barcelona	7	2		
2015–16	Barcelona	10	0	**17**	**2**
2016–17	*Malaga*	30	14	**30**	**14**
2017–18	Everton	8	0	**8**	**0**
2017–18	*Sevilla*	13	0	**13**	**0**

SCHNEIDERLIN, Morgan (M)   **312**   **16**
H: 5 11   W: 11 11   b.Obernai 8-11-89
Internationals: France U16, U17, U18, U19, U20, U21, Full caps.

2007–08	Strasbourg	5	0	**5**	**0**
2008–09	Southampton	30	0		
2009–10	Southampton	37	1		
2010–11	Southampton	27	0		
2011–12	Southampton	42	2		
2012–13	Southampton	36	5		
2013–14	Southampton	33	2		
2014–15	Southampton	26	4	**231**	**14**
2015–16	Manchester U	29	1		
2016–17	Manchester U	3	0	**32**	**1**
2016–17	Everton	14	1		
2017–18	Everton	30	0	**44**	**1**

SIGURDSSON, Gylfi (M)   **305**   **77**
H: 6 1   W: 12 02   b.Reykjavik 9-9-89
Internationals: Iceland U17, U18, U19, U21, Full caps.

2007–08	Reading	0	0		
2008–09	Reading	0	0		
2008–09	*Shrewsbury T*	5	1	**5**	**1**
2008–09	*Crewe Alex*	15	3	**15**	**3**
2009–10	Reading	38	16		
2010–11	Reading	4	2	**42**	**18**

2010–11	Hoffenheim	28	9		
2011–12	Hoffenheim	6	0	**34**	**9**
2011–12	*Swansea C*	18	7		
2012–13	Tottenham H	33	3		
2013–14	Tottenham H	25	5	**58**	**8**
2014–15	Swansea C	32	7		
2015–16	Swansea C	36	11		
2016–17	Swansea C	38	9	**124**	**34**
2017–18	Everton	27	4	**27**	**4**

STEKELENBURG, Maarten (G)   **293**   **0**
H: 6 6   W: 14 05   b.Haarlem 22-9-82
Internationals: Netherlands U21, Full caps.

2001–02	Ajax	0	0		
2002–03	Ajax	9	0		
2003–04	Ajax	10	0		
2004–05	Ajax	11	0		
2005–06	Ajax	27	0		
2006–07	Ajax	32	0		
2007–08	Ajax	31	0		
2008–09	Ajax	12	0		
2009–10	Ajax	33	0		
2010–11	Ajax	26	0	**191**	**0**
2011–12	Roma	29	0		
2012–13	Roma	18	0	**47**	**0**
2013–14	Fulham	19	0		
2014–15	Fulham	0	0		
2014–15	Monaco	0	0		
2015–16	Fulham	0	0	**19**	**0**
2015–16	*Southampton*	17	0	**17**	**0**
2016–17	Everton	19	0		
2017–18	Everton	0	0	**19**	**0**

TOSUN, Cenk (M)   **220**   **85**
H: 6 0   W: 12 04   b.Wetzlar 7-6-91
Internationals: Germany U16, U18, U19, U21. Turkey U21, Full caps.

2009–10	Eintracht Frankfurt	1	0	**1**	**0**
2010–11	Gaziantepspor	14	10		
2011–12	Gaziantepspor	32	6		
2012–13	Gaziantepspor	32	10		
2013–14	Gaziantepspor	31	13	**109**	**39**
2014–15	Besiktas	18	5		
2015–16	Besiktas	29	8		
2016–17	Besiktas	33	20		
2017–18	Besiktas	16	8	**96**	**41**
2017–18	Everton	14	5	**14**	**5**

VLASIC, Nikola (M)   **98**   **11**
H: 5 10   W: 12 08   b.Split 4-10-97
Internationals: Croatia U16, U17, U18, U19, U21, Full caps.

2014–15	Hajduk Split	27	3		
2015–16	Hajduk Split	23	1		
2016–17	Hajduk Split	30	4		
2017–18	Hajduk Split	6	3	**86**	**11**
2017–18	Everton	12	0	**12**	**0**

WALCOTT, Theo (F)   **305**   **72**
H: 5 9   W: 11 01   b.Stanmore 16-3-89
Internationals: England U16, U17, U19, U21, Full caps.

2005–06	Southampton	21	4	**21**	**4**
2005–06	Arsenal	0	0		
2006–07	Arsenal	16	0		
2007–08	Arsenal	25	4		
2008–09	Arsenal	22	2		
2009–10	Arsenal	23	3		
2010–11	Arsenal	28	9		
2011–12	Arsenal	35	8		
2012–13	Arsenal	32	14		
2013–14	Arsenal	13	5		
2014–15	Arsenal	14	5		
2015–16	Arsenal	28	5		
2016–17	Arsenal	28	10		
2017–18	Arsenal	6	0	**270**	**65**
2017–18	Everton	14	3	**14**	**3**

WILLIAMS, Ashley (D)   **544**   **19**
H: 6 0   W: 11 02   b.Wolverhampton 23-8-84
Internationals: Wales Full caps.

2003–04	Stockport Co	10	0		
2004–05	Stockport Co	44	1		
2005–06	Stockport Co	36	1		
2006–07	Stockport Co	46	1		
2007–08	Stockport Co	26	0	**162**	**3**
2007–08	*Swansea C*	3	0		
2008–09	Swansea C	46	2		
2009–10	Swansea C	46	5		
2010–11	Swansea C	46	3		
2011–12	Swansea C	37	1		
2012–13	Swansea C	37	0		
2013–14	Swansea C	34	1		
2014–15	Swansea C	37	0		
2015–16	Swansea C	36	2	**322**	**14**
2016–17	Everton	36	1		
2017–18	Everton	24	1	**60**	**2**

WILLIAMS, Joe (M) 34 1
H: 5 10 W: 10 06 b.Liverpool 8-12-96
Internationals: England U20.

Season	Club	Apps	Gls	Tot Apps	Tot Gls
2014–15	Everton	0	0		
2015–16	Everton	0	0		
2016–17	Everton	0	0		
2017–18	Everton	0	0		
2017–18	*Barnsley*	34	1	34	1

Players retained or with offer of contract
Adeniran, Dennis Emmanuel Abiodun; Bowler, Joshua Luke; Bramall, Daniel Luke; Evans, Antony Kenneth; Foulds, Matthew Colin; Gibson, Lewis Jack; Kiersey, Jack Alexander; Markelo, Nathangelo Alexandro; Onyekuru, Henry Chukwuemeka; Renshaw, Christopher Thomas; Sambou, Bassala; Tarashaj, Shani.

Scholars
Adedoyin, Korede Yemi; Anderson, Joseph William; Collins, Michael Kieran; Denny, Alexander; Gordon, Anthony Michael; Hansen, Nicolas Defreitas; Hilton, Joseph Robert; Hornby, Fraser; Iversen, Einar Hjellestad; John, Kyle Alex; Mampala, Manasse; McKeown, Bernard Joshua; Murphy, Tomas Bernard; Ouzounidis, Con; Phillips, Kieran James; Richards, Elliot Thomas; Simms, Ellis Reco; Stanley, Kameron Mark James; Warnock, Ethan Daniel; Warren, Tom; Zuk, Pawel Andrzej.

EXETER C (35)

ARCHIBALD-HENVILLE, Troy (D)192 6
H: 6 2 W: 13 03 b.Newham 4-11-88

Season	Club	Apps	Gls	Tot Apps	Tot Gls
2007–10	Tottenham H	0	0		
2008–09	Tottenham H	0	0		
2008–09	Norwich C	0	0		
2008–09	Exeter C	19	0		
2009–10	Tottenham H	0	0		
2009–10	Exeter C	15	0		
2010–11	Exeter C	36	1		
2011–12	Exeter C	45	2		
2012–13	Swindon T	5	0		
2013–14	Carlisle U	4	0		
2013–14	Swindon T	14	0	19	0
2014–15	Carlisle U	24	1		
2015–16	Carlisle U	12	2	40	3
2016–17	Exeter C	3	0		
2017–18	Exeter C	15	0	133	3

BOATENG, Hiram (M) 89 2
H: 5 7 W: 11 00 b.Wandsworth 8-1-96

Season	Club	Apps	Gls	Tot Apps	Tot Gls
2012–13	Crystal Palace	0	0		
2013–14	Crystal Palace	0	0		
2013–14	Crawley T	1	0	1	0
2014–15	Crystal Palace	0	0		
2015–16	Crystal Palace	1	0		
2015–16	*Plymouth Arg*	24	1	24	1
2016–17	Crystal Palace	0	0	1	0
2016–17	*Bristol R*	9	0	9	0
2016–17	*Northampton T*	16	0	16	0
2017–18	Exeter C	38	1	38	1

BROWN, Troy (D) 247 15
H: 6 1 W: 12 01 b.Croydon 17-9-90
Internationals: Wales U17, U19, U21.

Season	Club	Apps	Gls	Tot Apps	Tot Gls
2009–10	Ipswich T	1	0		
2010–11	Ipswich T	12	0	13	0
2011–12	Rotherham U	6	1	6	1
2011–12	*Aldershot T*	17	2		
2012–13	Aldershot T	34	3	51	5
2013–14	Cheltenham T	39	4		
2014–15	Cheltenham T	43	1	82	5
2015–16	Exeter C	40	1		
2016–17	Exeter C	30	2		
2017–18	Exeter C	25	1	95	4

BRUNT, Ryan (F) 124 20
H: 6 1 W: 11 11 b.Birmingham 26-5-93

Season	Club	Apps	Gls	Tot Apps	Tot Gls
2011–12	Stoke C	0	0		
2011–12	*Tranmere R*	15	1	15	1
2012–13	Stoke C	0	0		
2012–13	*Leyton Orient*	18	3	18	3
2012–13	Bristol R	18	5		
2013–14	Bristol R	11	0		
2014–15	Bristol R	0	0	29	5
2014–15	*York C*	6	0	6	0
2014–15	*Stevenage*	5	0	5	0
2015–16	Plymouth Arg	16	2		
2015–16	Plymouth Arg	34	9	50	11
2017–18	Exeter C	1	0	1	0

BYRNE, Alex (M) 1 0
H: 5 9 W: 11 07 b.Barnstaple 15-6-96

Season	Club	Apps	Gls	Tot Apps	Tot Gls
2014–15	Exeter C	0	0		
2015–16	Exeter C	0	0		
2016–17	Exeter C	0	0		
2017–18	Exeter C	1	0	1	0

COLLINS, Archie (M) 0 0

Season	Club	Apps	Gls
2016–17	Exeter C	0	0
2017–18	Exeter C	0	0

CROLL, Luke (D) 32 0
H: 6 1 W: 12 08 b.Lambeth 10-1-95

Season	Club	Apps	Gls	Tot Apps	Tot Gls
2014–15	Crystal Palace	0	0		
2015–16	Crystal Palace	0	0		
2015–16	*Plymouth Arg*	3	0	3	0
2016–17	Crystal Palace	0	0		
2016–17	*Exeter C*	19	0		
2017–18	Exeter C	10	0	29	0

DEAN, Will (M) 0 0
b. 7-8-00

Season	Club	Apps	Gls
2017–18	Exeter C	0	0

DOWN, Toby (D) 0 0

Season	Club	Apps	Gls
2016–17	Exeter C	0	0
2017–18	Exeter C	0	0

HAMON, James (G) 23 0
H: 6 1 W: 11 00 b. 1-7-95

Season	Club	Apps	Gls	Tot Apps	Tot Gls
2013–14	Exeter C	0	0		
2014–15	Exeter C	21	0		
2015–16	Exeter C	1	0		
2016–17	Exeter C	1	0		
2017–18	Exeter C	0	0	23	0

HARLEY, Ryan (M) 269 41
H: 5 11 W: 11 00 b.Bristol 22-1-85

Season	Club	Apps	Gls	Tot Apps	Tot Gls
2004–05	Bristol C	2	0		
2005–06	Bristol C	0	0	2	0
2008–09	Exeter C	31	4		
2009–10	Exeter C	44	10		
2010–11	Exeter C	21	6		
2010–11	Swansea C	0	0		
2010–11	*Exeter C*	21	4		
2011–12	Swansea C	0	0		
2011–12	Brighton & HA	16	2		
2012–13	Brighton & HA	2	0	18	2
2012–13	*Milton Keynes D*	8	0	8	0
2013–14	Swindon T	21	1		
2014–15	Swindon T	0	0	21	1
2014–15	Exeter C	25	4		
2015–16	Exeter C	28	4		
2016–17	Exeter C	31	5		
2017–18	Exeter C	19	1	220	38

HARTRIDGE, Alex (D) 0 0

Season	Club	Apps	Gls
2017–18	Exeter C	0	0

HOLMES, Lee (M) 295 26
H: 5 8 W: 10 06 b.Mansfield 2-4-87
Internationals: England U16, U17, U19.

Season	Club	Apps	Gls	Tot Apps	Tot Gls
2002–03	Derby Co	2	0		
2003–04	Derby Co	23	2		
2004–05	Derby Co	3	0		
2004–05	*Swindon T*	15	1		
2005–06	Derby Co	18	0		
2006–07	Derby Co	0	0		
2006–07	*Bradford C*	16	0	16	0
2007–08	Derby Co	0	0	46	2
2007–08	*Walsall*	19	4	19	4
2008–09	Southampton	11	0		
2009–10	Southampton	5	0		
2010–11	Southampton	7	0		
2011–12	Southampton	6	1	29	1
2011–12	*Oxford U*	7	2	7	2
2011–12	*Swindon T*	10	1	25	2
2012–13	Preston NE	28	3		
2013–14	Preston NE	32	3		
2014–15	Preston NE	0	0	60	6
2014–15	*Portsmouth*	5	0	5	0
2014–15	Exeter C	8	0		
2015–16	Exeter C	37	2		
2016–17	Exeter C	16	5		
2017–18	Exeter C	27	2	88	9

JAMES, Lloyd (M) 319 14
H: 5 11 W: 11 01 b.Bristol 16-2-88
Internationals: Wales U17, U19, U21.

Season	Club	Apps	Gls	Tot Apps	Tot Gls
2005–06	Southampton	0	0		
2006–07	Southampton	0	0		
2007–08	Southampton	0	0		
2008–09	Southampton	41	0		
2009–10	Southampton	30	2	71	2
2010–11	Colchester U	28	0		
2011–12	Colchester U	23	1	51	1
2011–12	*Crawley T*	6	0	6	0
2012–13	Leyton Orient	28	0		
2013–14	Leyton Orient	42	3		
2014–15	Leyton Orient	13	1		
2015–16	Leyton Orient	25	4	108	8
2016–17	Exeter C	43	1		
2017–18	Exeter C	40	2	83	3

JAY, Matt (D) 24 1
H: 5 10 W: 10 12 b.Torbay 27-2-96

Season	Club	Apps	Gls	Tot Apps	Tot Gls
2013–14	Exeter C	2	0		
2014–15	Exeter C	3	0		
2015–16	Exeter C	0	0		
2016–17	Exeter C	2	0		
2017–18	Exeter C	17	1	24	1

KEY, Josh (M) 0 0
b. 1-11-99

Season	Club	Apps	Gls
2017–18	Exeter C	0	0

KITE, Harry (M) 0 0
b.Exeter 29-6-00

Season	Club	Apps	Gls
2017–18	Exeter C	0	0

McALINDEN, Liam (F) 117 16
H: 6 1 W: 11 10 b.Cannock 26-9-93
Internationals: Northern Ireland U21. Republic of Ireland U21.

Season	Club	Apps	Gls	Tot Apps	Tot Gls
2010–11	Wolverhampton W	0	0		
2011–12	Wolverhampton W	0	0		
2012–13	Wolverhampton W	1	0		
2013–14	Wolverhampton W	7	1		
2013–14	*Shrewsbury T*	9	3		
2014–15	Wolverhampton W	6	0		
2014–15	*Fleetwood T*	19	4	19	4
2015–16	Wolverhampton W	0	0	14	3
2015–16	*Shrewsbury T*	8	0	17	3
2015–16	*Crawley T*	6	1	6	1
2016–17	Exeter C	32	5		
2017–18	Exeter C	29	2	61	7

MOORE-TAYLOR, Jordan (D) 160 10
H: 5 10 W: 13 01 b.Exeter 21-1-94

Season	Club	Apps	Gls	Tot Apps	Tot Gls
2012–13	Exeter C	7	0		
2013–14	Exeter C	29	1		
2014–15	Exeter C	26	2		
2015–16	Exeter C	32	0		
2016–17	Exeter C	42	5		
2017–18	Exeter C	24	2	160	10

MOXEY, Dean (D) 292 11
H: 6 2 W: 11 00 b.Exeter 14-1-86
Internationals: England C.

Season	Club	Apps	Gls	Tot Apps	Tot Gls
2008–09	Exeter C	43	4		
2009–10	Derby Co	30	0		
2010–11	Derby Co	22	2	52	2
2010–11	Crystal Palace	17	1		
2011–12	Crystal Palace	24	0		
2012–13	Crystal Palace	30	0		
2013–14	Crystal Palace	20	0	91	4
2014–15	Bolton W	30	1		
2015–16	Bolton W	33	0		
2016–17	Bolton W	19	0	72	1
2017–18	Exeter C	34	3	77	7

PYM, Christy (G) 108 0
H: 6 0 W: 11 09 b.Exeter 24-4-95
Internationals: England U20.

Season	Club	Apps	Gls	Tot Apps	Tot Gls
2012–13	Exeter C	0	0		
2013–14	Exeter C	9	0		
2014–15	Exeter C	25	0		
2015–16	Exeter C	0	0		
2016–17	Exeter C	28	0		
2017–18	Exeter C	46	0	108	0

RANDALL, Joel (M) 0 0
b.Salisbury 29-10-99

Season	Club	Apps	Gls
2017–18	Exeter C	0	0

SEABORNE, Danny (D) 195 2
H: 6 0 W: 11 10 b.Barnstaple 5-3-87

Season	Club	Apps	Gls	Tot Apps	Tot Gls
2008–09	Exeter C	33	1		
2009–10	Exeter C	19	0		
2009–10	Southampton	16	0		
2010–11	Southampton	24	0		
2011–12	Southampton	4	0		
2012–13	Southampton	0	0	44	0
2012–13	*Charlton Ath*	7	0	7	0
2012–13	*Bournemouth*	13	0	13	0
2013–14	*Yeovil T*	10	0	10	0
2013–14	Coventry U	21	1	21	1
2014–15	Partick Thistle	0	0		
2015–16	Partick Thistle	32	0	32	0
2016–17	Hamilton A	11	0	11	0
2017–18	Exeter C	5	0	57	1

SIMPSON, Robbie (F) 285 31
H: 6 1 W: 11 11 b.Poole 15-3-85

Season	Club	Apps	Gls	Tot Apps	Tot Gls
2007–08	Coventry C	28	1		
2008–09	Coventry C	33	3	61	4
2009–10	Huddersfield T	13	0		
2010–11	Huddersfield T	0	0		
2010–11	*Brentford*	27	4	27	4

2011–12	Huddersfield T	0	0	13	0
2011–12	Oldham Ath	29	6		
2012–13	Oldham Ath	37	2		
2013–14	Oldham Ath	0	0	66	8
2013–14	Leyton Orient	14	0	14	0
2014–15	Cambridge U	35	8		
2015–16	Cambridge U	32	4	67	12
2016–17	Exeter C	26	1		
2017–18	Exeter C	11	2	37	3

SPARKES, Jack (M)   3 0
b.Exeter 29-9-00

| 2017–18 | Exeter C | 3 | 0 | 3 | 0 |

STOCKLEY, Jayden (F)   167 46
H: 6 2   W: 12 07   b.Poole 10-10-93

2009–10	Bournemouth	2	0		
2010–11	Bournemouth	4	0		
2011–12	Bournemouth	10	0		
2011–12	*Accrington S*	9	3	9	3
2012–13	Bournemouth	0	0		
2013–14	Bournemouth	0	0		
2013–14	*Leyton Orient*	8	1	8	1
2013–14	*Torquay U*	19	1	19	1
2014–15	Bournemouth	0	0		
2014–15	*Cambridge U*	3	2	3	2
2014–15	*Luton T*	13	3	13	3
2015–16	Bournemouth	0	0	16	0
2015–16	Portsmouth	9	2	9	2
2015–16	*Exeter C*	22	10		
2016–17	Aberdeen	27	5	27	5
2017–18	Exeter C	41	19	63	29

STOREY, Jordan (D)   13 2
H: 6 2   W: 12 00   b. 2-9-97

| 2016–17 | Exeter C | 0 | 0 | | |
| 2017–18 | Exeter C | 13 | 2 | 13 | 2 |

SWEENEY, Pierce (D)   69 8
H: 5 10   W: 12 07   b.Dublin 11-9-94
Internationals: Republic of Ireland U17, U19, U21.

2012–13	Reading	0	0		
2013–14	Reading	0	0		
2014–15	Reading	0	0		
2015–16	Reading	0	0		
2016–17	Exeter C	29	0		
2017–18	Exeter C	40	8	69	8

TAYLOR, Jake (M)   189 22
H: 5 10   W: 12 01   b.Ascot 1-12-91
Internationals: Wales U17, U19, U21, Full caps.

2010–11	Reading	1	0		
2011–12	Reading	0	0		
2011–12	*Aldershot T*	3	0	3	0
2011–12	*Exeter C*	30	3		
2012–13	Reading	0	0		
2012–13	*Cheltenham T*	8	1	8	1
2012–13	*Crawley T*	4	0	4	0
2013–14	Reading	8	0		
2014–15	Reading	22	2		
2014–15	*Leyton Orient*	3	0	3	0
2015–16	Reading	0	0	31	2
2015–16	*Motherwell*	7	0	7	0
2015–16	Exeter C	16	4		
2016–17	Exeter C	43	4		
2017–18	Exeter C	44	8	133	19

TILLSON, Jordan (D)   87 2
H: 6 0   W: 11 09   b.Bath 5-3-93

2012–13	Exeter C	0	0		
2013–14	Exeter C	1	0		
2014–15	Exeter C	3	0		
2015–16	Exeter C	26	1		
2016–17	Exeter C	20	0		
2017–18	Exeter C	37	1	87	2

WOODMAN, Craig (D)   508 7
H: 5 9   W: 10 11   b.Tiverton 22-12-82

1999–2000	Bristol C	0	0		
2000–01	Bristol C	2	0		
2001–02	Bristol C	6	0		
2002–03	Bristol C	10	0		
2003–04	Bristol C	21	0		
2004–05	Bristol C	3	0		
2004–05	*Mansfield T*	8	1	8	1
2004–05	*Torquay U*	22	1		
2005–06	Bristol C	37	1		
2005–06	*Torquay U*	2	0	24	1
2006–07	Bristol C	11	0	90	1
2007–08	Wycombe W	29	0		
2008–09	Wycombe W	46	1		
2009–10	Wycombe W	44	1	119	2
2010–11	Brentford	41	1		
2011–12	Brentford	18	0	59	1
2012–13	Exeter C	44	0		
2013–14	Exeter C	41	1		
2014–15	Exeter C	32	0		

2015–16	Exeter C	25	0		
2016–17	Exeter C	33	0		
2017–18	Exeter C	33	0	208	1

Players retained or with offer of contract
Seymour, Benjamin Mark; Smallcombe, Max Frederick.

Scholars
Belsten, Joe; Dean, William Luke; Dodd, James John; Dyer, Jordan Paul; Gardner, Harry; Hancock, Joshua Matthew; Haynes, Samuel Lee; Key, Joshua Myles Abraham; Kite, Harry; Norman, Felix; O'Loughlin, Joseph Samuel; Parsons, Brandon Jack; Randall, Joel John; Simpson, Theo Jon; Thomas, Mitchell; White, Lucas Graham.

Non-contract
Green, Daniel Robert; Oakley, Matthew; Taylor, Matthew James; Tisdale, Paul Robert.

FLEETWOOD T (36)

BAINES, Lewis (D)   0 0

| 2017–18 | Fleetwood T | 0 | 0 | | |

BIGGINS, Harrison (M)   7 0
b. 15-3-96
From Stocksbridge Park Steels.

| 2017–18 | Fleetwood T | 7 | 0 | 7 | 0 |

BOLGER, Cian (D)   180 11
H: 6 4   W: 12 05   b.Co. Kildare 12-3-92
Internationals: Republic of Ireland U19, U21.

2009–10	Leicester C	0	0		
2010–11	Leicester C	0	0		
2010–11	*Bristol R*	6	0		
2011–12	Leicester C	0	0		
2011–12	*Bristol R*	39	2		
2012–13	Leicester C	0	0		
2012–13	*Bristol R*	3	0	48	2
2012–13	Bolton W	0	0		
2013–14	Bolton W	9	0		
2013–14	*Colchester U*	4	0	4	0
2013–14	*Southend U*	1	0		
2014–15	Southend U	23	1		
2015–16	Southend U	22	0	46	1
2015–16	*Bury*	9	0	9	0
2016–17	Fleetwood T	32	5		
2017–18	Fleetwood T	41	3	73	8

BURNS, Wes (F)   131 15
H: 5 8   W: 10 10   b.Cardiff 28-12-95
Internationals: Wales U21.

2012–13	Bristol C	6	0		
2013–14	Bristol C	20	1		
2014–15	Bristol C	3	1		
2014–15	*Oxford U*	9	1	9	1
2014–15	*Cheltenham T*	14	4	14	4
2015–16	Bristol C	14	1	43	3
2015–16	*Fleetwood T*	14	5		
2016–17	Fleetwood T	10	0		
2016–17	*Aberdeen*	13	0	13	0
2017–18	Fleetwood T	28	2	52	7

CAIRNS, Alex (G)   69 0
H: 6 0   W: 11 05   b.Doncaster 4-1-93

2011–12	Leeds U	1	0		
2012–13	Leeds U	0	0		
2013–14	Leeds U	0	0		
2014–15	Leeds U	0	0	1	0
2015–16	Chesterfield	0	0		
2015–16	Rotherham U	0	0		
2016–17	Fleetwood T	30	0		
2017–18	Fleetwood T	38	0	68	0

CRELLIN, Billy (G)   0 0
Internationals: England U17, U18.

| 2017–18 | Fleetwood T | 0 | 0 | | |

DEMPSEY, Kyle (M)   151 14
b.Whitehaven 17-9-95

2013–14	Carlisle U	4	0		
2014–15	Carlisle U	43	10	47	10
2015–16	Huddersfield T	21	1		
2016–17	Huddersfield T	0	0	21	1
2016–17	*Fleetwood T*	38	2		
2017–18	Fleetwood T	45	1	83	3

DIAGOURAGA, Toumani (M)   401 16
H: 6 2   W: 11 05   b.Paris 10-6-87

2004–05	Watford	0	0		
2005–06	Watford	1	0		
2005–06	*Swindon T*	8	0	8	0
2006–07	Watford	0	0		
2006–07	*Rotherham U*	7	0	7	0
2007–08	Watford	0	0	1	0
2007–08	*Hereford U*	41	2		

2008–09	Hereford U	45	2	86	4
2009–10	Peterborough U	19	0	19	0
2009–10	*Brentford*	20	0		
2010–11	Brentford	32	1		
2011–12	Brentford	35	4		
2012–13	Brentford	39	1		
2013–14	Brentford	19	0		
2013–14	*Portsmouth*	8	0	8	0
2014–15	Brentford	38	0		
2015–16	Brentford	27	0	210	6
2015–16	*Leeds U*	17	2		
2016–17	Leeds U	1	0		
2016–17	*Ipswich T*	12	0	12	0
2017–18	Leeds U	0	0	18	2
2017–18	*Plymouth Arg*	15	3	15	3
2017–18	Fleetwood T	17	1	17	1

DONOHUE, Michael (M)   0 0
From Everton.

| 2017–18 | Fleetwood T | 0 | 0 | | |

EASTHAM, Ashley (D)   235 11
H: 6 3   W: 12 06   b.Preston 22-3-91

2009–10	Blackpool	1	0		
2009–10	*Cheltenham T*	20	0		
2010–11	Blackpool	0	0		
2010–11	*Cheltenham T*	9	0	29	0
2010–11	*Carlisle U*	0	0		
2011–12	Blackpool	0	0		
2011–12	*Bury*	25	2		
2012–13	Blackpool	0	0	1	0
2012–13	*Fleetwood T*	1	0		
2012–13	*Notts Co*	4	0	4	0
2012–13	*Bury*	19	0	44	2
2013–14	Rochdale	15	0		
2014–15	Rochdale	41	2		
2015–16	Rochdale	20	2	76	4
2016–17	Fleetwood T	35	2		
2017–18	Fleetwood T	45	3	81	5

EKPOLO, Godswill (D)   9 0
H: 5 11   W: 11 07   b.Benin City 14-5-95
Internationals: Nigeria U17.
From Barcelona.

| 2016–17 | Fleetwood T | 6 | 0 | | |
| 2017–18 | Fleetwood T | 3 | 0 | 9 | 0 |

Transferred to Merida AD, January 2018.

GLENDON, George (M)   56 0
H: 5 10   W: 11 00   b.Manchester 3-5-95
Internationals: England U16, U17.

2013–14	Manchester C	0	0		
2014–15	Manchester C	0	0		
2015–16	Manchester C	0	0		
2016–17	Fleetwood T	26	0		
2017–18	Fleetwood T	30	0	56	0

GRANT, Robert (M)   327 70
H: 5 11   W: 12 00   b.Liverpool 1-7-90

2006–07	Accrington S	1	0		
2007–08	Accrington S	7	0		
2008–09	Accrington S	15	1		
2009–10	Accrington S	42	14		
2010–11	Scunthorpe U	27	0		
2010–11	*Rochdale*	6	2		
2011–12	Scunthorpe U	29	7		
2011–12	*Accrington S*	8	3	73	18
2012–13	Scunthorpe U	3	0	59	7
2012–13	*Rochdale*	36	15	42	17
2013–14	Blackpool	6	0		
2013–14	*Fleetwood T*	1	0		
2014–15	Blackpool	0	0	6	0
2014–15	*Shrewsbury T*	33	6	33	6
2015–16	Fleetwood T	38	10		
2016–17	Fleetwood T	46	9		
2017–18	Fleetwood T	29	3	114	22

HIGHAM, Luke (M)   11 0
H: 6 1   W: 12 02   b.Blackpool 21-10-96

2014–15	Blackpool	0	0		
2015–16	Blackpool	11	0		
2016–17	Blackpool	0	0	11	0
2017–18	Fleetwood T	0	0		

HUNTER, Ashley (F)   124 23
H: 5 10   W: 10 08   b.Derby 29-9-93

2014–15	Fleetwood T	12	1		
2015–16	Fleetwood T	24	5		
2016–17	Fleetwood T	44	8		
2017–18	Fleetwood T	44	9	124	23

JONES, Gethin (D)   33 0
H: 5 10   W: 11 09   b.Perth 13-10-95
Internationals: Wales U17, U19, U21.

2014–15	Everton	0	0		
2014–15	*Plymouth Arg*	6	0	6	0
2015–16	Everton	0	0		
2016–17	Everton	0	0		
2016–17	*Barnsley*	17	0	17	0
2017–18	Fleetwood T	10	0	10	0

KERRIGAN, Dominic (D)   0 0

2017–18	Fleetwood T	0	0		

MADDEN, Patrick (F)   330 102
H: 6 0   W: 11 13   b.Dublin 4-3-90
Internationals: Republic of Ireland U19, U21, U23, Full caps.

2008	Bohemians	18	4		
2009	Bohemians	2	0		
2009	Shelbourne	13	6	13	6
2010	Bohemians	34	10	54	14
2010–11	Carlisle U	13	0		
2011–12	Carlisle U	18	1		
2012–13	Carlisle U	1	1	32	2
2012–13	Yeovil T	35	22		
2013–14	Yeovil T	9	0	44	22
2013–14	Scunthorpe U	21	5		
2014–15	Scunthorpe U	46	14		
2015–16	Scunthorpe U	46	20		
2016–17	Scunthorpe U	34	11		
2017–18	Scunthorpe U	20	2	167	52
2017–18	Fleetwood T	20	6	20	6

MAGUIRE, Joe (D)   5 0
H: 5 10   W: 11 00   b.Manchester 18-1-96

2015–16	Liverpool	0	0		
2015–16	*Leyton Orient*	0	0		
2016–17	Liverpool	0	0		
2016–17	Fleetwood T	3	0		
2017–18	Fleetwood T	2	0	5	0

McALENY, Conor (F)   85 21
H: 5 10   W: 12 05   b.Liverpool 12-8-92

2009–10	Everton	0	0		
2010–11	Everton	0	0		
2011–12	Everton	2	0		
2011–12	*Scunthorpe U*	3	0	3	0
2012–13	Everton	0	0		
2013–14	Everton	0	0		
2013–14	*Brentford*	4	0	4	0
2014–15	Everton	0	0		
2014–15	*Cardiff C*	8	2	8	2
2015–16	Everton	0	0		
2015–16	*Charlton Ath*	8	0	8	0
2015–16	*Wigan Ath*	13	4	13	4
2016–17	Everton	0	0	2	0
2016–17	*Oxford U*	18	10	18	10
2017–18	Fleetwood T	29	5	29	5

MORELLI, Joao (F)   0 0

2017–18	Levadia Tallinn	0	0
2017–18	Fleetwood T	0	0

NADESAN, Ashley (F)   16 4
H: 6 2   W: 11 11   b. 9-9-94

2015–16	Fleetwood T	0	0		
2016–17	Fleetwood T	0	0		
2017–18	Fleetwood T	1	0	1	0
2017–18	*Carlisle U*	15	4	15	4

NEAL, Chris (G)   225 0
H: 6 2   W: 12 04   b.St Albans 23-10-85

2004–05	Preston NE	1	0		
2005–06	Preston NE	0	0		
2006–07	Preston NE	0	0		
2006–07	*Shrewsbury T*	0	0		
2007–08	*Morecambe*	0	0		
2007–08	Preston NE	0	0		
2008–09	Preston NE	0	0	1	0
2009–10	Shrewsbury T	7	0		
2010–11	Shrewsbury T	22	0		
2011–12	Shrewsbury T	35	0	64	0
2012–13	Port Vale	46	0		
2013–14	Port Vale	31	0		
2014–15	Port Vale	40	0		
2015–16	Port Vale	6	0	123	0
2015–16	*Doncaster R*	2	0	2	0
2015–16	*Bury*	10	0	10	0
2016–17	Fleetwood T	17	0		
2017–18	Fleetwood T	8	0	25	0

NIRENNOLD, Victor (D)   43 2
H: 6 4   W: 12 13   b.Rennes 5-4-91
From Miami City.

2015–16	Fleetwood T	17	0		
2016–17	Fleetwood T	26	2		
2017–18	Fleetwood T	0	0	43	2

OSBORNE, Elliot (M)   11 0
b. 2-5-96

2016–17	Fleetwood T	0	0		
2017–18	Fleetwood T	0	0		
2017–18	*Morecambe*	11	0	11	0

POND, Nathan (M)   163 2
H: 6 3   W: 11 00   b.Preston 5-1-85

2012–13	Fleetwood T	12	0		
2013–14	Fleetwood T	41	1		
2014–15	Fleetwood T	27	1		
2015–16	Fleetwood T	21	0		
2016–17	Fleetwood T	32	0		
2017–18	Fleetwood T	30	0	163	2

REID, Alex (F)   0 0

2016–17	Fleetwood T	0	0
2017–18	Fleetwood T	0	0

SCHWABL, Markus (D)   200 1
H: 6 0   W: 11 09   b. 26-8-90

2008–09	Unterhaching	0	0		
2009–10	Unterhaching	17	0		
2010–11	Unterhaching	5	1		
2011–12	Unterhaching	32	0		
2012–13	Unterhaching	36	0		
2013–14	1860 Munich	4	0	4	0
2014–15	Unterhaching	28	0	118	1
2015–16	Aalen	37	0		
2016–17	Aalen	18	0	55	0
2016–17	Fleetwood T	13	0		
2017–18	Fleetwood T	10	0	23	0

SHERON, Nathan (D)   0 0
b.Whiston 4-10-97

2017–18	Fleetwood T	0	0

SOWERBY, Jack (F)   38 3
b. 23-3-95

2014–15	Fleetwood T	0	0		
2015–16	Fleetwood T	8	0		
2016–17	Fleetwood T	8	1		
2017–18	Fleetwood T	22	2	38	3

Players retained or with offer of contract
Bartosinski, Jakub Pawel; Djabi, Mamadou; Garner, Gerard; Mooney, Daniel John; Urwin, Matthew William.

Scholars
Bani, Alkeo; Bishop, Jack Matthew; Bridge, Owen James; Clayton, Graham Alexander; Collings, Liam; Dodd, Alexander Paul; Finlayson, Connor James; Holgate, Harrison James; Kerrigan, Dominic James; Mashigo, Katlego Keabetswe; McCaragher, Gregory Adam; O'Halleron, Sam James; Rydel, Ryan Steven; Turner, Henry; Unsworth, Benjamin John.

FOREST GREEN R (37)

ANDERSON, Tom (M)   0 0
b. 7-1-99

2017–18	Forest Green R	0	0

BELFORD, Cameron (G)   162 0
H: 6 1   W: 11 10   b.Nuneaton 16-10-88

2007–08	Bury	1	0		
2008–09	Bury	1	0		
2009–10	Bury	7	0		
2010–11	Bury	39	0		
2011–12	Bury	23	0		
2011–12	*Southend U*	13	0		
2012–13	Bury	7	0		
2012–13	*Southend U*	4	0	17	0
2012–13	*Accrington S*	5	0	5	0
2013–14	Bury	0	0	78	0
2014–15	*Swindon T*	1	0	1	0
From Wrexham.					
2016–17	Stranraer	36	0		
2017–18	Stranraer	22	0	58	0
On loan from Stranraer.					
2017–18	Forest Green R	3	0	3	0

BENNETT, Dale (D)   66 1
H: 5 11   W: 12 02   b.Enfield 6-1-90

2008–09	Watford	0	0		
2009–10	Watford	10	0		
2010–11	Watford	10	0		
2011–12	Watford	2	0		
2011–12	*Brentford*	5	1	5	1
2012–13	Watford	0	0	22	0
2012–13	*AFC Wimbledon*	5	0	5	0
2012–13	*Yeovil T*	1	0	1	0
2017–18	Forest Green R	33	0	33	0

BROWN, Reece (M)   54 2
H: 5 9   W: 12 04   b.Dudley 3-3-96
Internationals: England U16, U17, U18, U20.

2013–14	Birmingham C	6	0		
2014–15	Birmingham C	1	0		
2014–15	*Notts Co*	3	0	3	0
2015–16	Birmingham C	1	0		
2016–17	Birmingham C	8	0	16	0
2016–17	*Chesterfield*	2	0	2	0
2017–18	Forest Green R	33	2	33	2

BUGIEL, Omar (F)   19 3
H: 6 0   W: 12 02   b. 3-1-94
Internationals: Lebanon Full caps.
From Worthing.

2017–18	Forest Green R	19	3	19	3

COLLINS, Lee (D)   362 7
H: 6 1   W: 11 10   b.Telford 23-9-83

2006–07	Wolverhampton W	0	0		
2007–08	Wolverhampton W	0	0		
2007–08	*Hereford U*	16	0	16	0
2008–09	Wolverhampton W	0	0		
2008–09	Port Vale	39	1		
2009–10	Port Vale	45	1		
2010–11	Port Vale	42	2		
2011–12	Port Vale	16	0	142	4
2011–12	Barnsley	7	0		
2012–13	Barnsley	0	0	7	0
2012–13	*Shrewsbury T*	8	0	8	0
2012–13	Northampton T	15	0		
2013–14	Northampton T	22	1		
2014–15	Northampton T	37	0	74	1
2015–16	Mansfield T	35	0		
2016–17	Mansfield T	37	0	72	0
2017–18	Forest Green R	43	2	43	2

COOPER, Charlie (M)   25 1
b. 1-5-97
From Birmingham C.

2017–18	Forest Green R	25	1	25	1

DOIDGE, Christian (F)   88 30
H: 6 1   W: 12 02   b.Newport 25-8-92

2014–15	Dagenham & R	11	2		
2015–16	Dagenham & R	35	8	46	10
2017–18	Forest Green R	42	20	42	20

EVANS, Callum (D)   5 0
H: 5 10   W: 11 05   b.Bristol 11-10-95
From Manchester U.

2015–16	Barnsley	0	0		
2016–17	Barnsley	3	0	3	0
2017–18	Forest Green R	2	0	2	0

GRUBB, Dayle (M)   21 5
H: 6 0   W: 12 13   b. 24-7-91
From Weston-super-Mare

2017–18	Forest Green R	21	5	21	5

GUNNING, Gavin (D)   209 9
H: 5 11   W: 13 08   b.Dublin 26-1-91
Internationals: Republic of Ireland U17, U19, U21.

2007–08	Blackburn R	0	0		
2008–09	Blackburn R	0	0		
2009–10	Blackburn R	0	0		
2009–10	*Tranmere R*	6	0	6	0
2009–10	*Rotherham U*	21	0	21	0
2010–11	Blackburn R	0	0		
2010–11	*Bury*	2	0	2	0
2010–11	*Motherwell*	14	0	14	0
2011–12	Dundee U	31	2		
2012–13	Dundee U	25	3		
2013–14	Dundee U	27	3		
2014–15	Birmingham C	0	0		
2015–16	Oldham Ath	0	0		
2015–16	*Dundee U*	19	0	102	8
2016–17	*Greenock Morton*	10	0	10	0
2016–17	Grimsby T	14	0	14	0
2017–18	Port Vale	19	0	19	0
2017–18	Forest Green R	21	1	21	1

HENDY, Sam (M)   0 0

2017–18	Forest Green R	0	0

HOLLIS, Haydn (D)   137 7
H: 6 4   W: 13 01   b.Selston 14-10-92

2011–12	Notts Co	1	0		
2012–13	Notts Co	6	0		
2013–14	Notts Co	10	4		
2014–15	Notts Co	41	0		
2015–16	Notts Co	29	2		
2016–17	Notts Co	31	1		
2017–18	Notts Co	0	0	118	7
2017–18	Forest Green R	19	0	19	0

JAMES, Luke (F)   190 21
H: 6 0   W: 12 08   b.Amble 4-11-94

2011–12	Hartlepool U	19	3		
2012–13	Hartlepool U	26	3		
2013–14	Hartlepool U	42	13		
2014–15	Hartlepool U	4	0		
2014–15	*Peterborough U*	32	1		
2015–16	Peterborough U	0	0		
2015–16	*Bradford C*	9	0	9	0
2015–16	*Hartlepool U*	20	1	111	20
2016–17	Peterborough U	0	0	32	1
2016–17	*Bristol R*	24	0	24	0
2017–18	Forest Green R	14	0	14	0

LAIRD, Scott (D) — 271 24
H: 5 11 W: 11 05 b.Taunton 15-5-88
Internationals: Scotland U16. England C.

Season	Club	Apps	Gls	Tot A	Tot G
2006-07	Plymouth Arg	0	0		
2007-08	Plymouth Arg	0	0		
2010-11	Stevenage	44	4		
2011-12	Stevenage	46	8	90	12
2012-13	Preston NE	19	4		
2013-14	Preston NE	34	1		
2014-15	Preston NE	31	0	84	5
2015-16	Scunthorpe U	32	2		
2016-17	Scunthorpe U	1	0	33	2
2016-17	*Walsall*	28	3	28	3
2017-18	Forest Green R	36	2	36	2

MARSH-BROWN, Keanu (F) — 80 7
H: 5 11 W: 12 04 b.Hammersmith 10-8-92
Internationals: England U16, U17. England C.

Season	Club	Apps	Gls	Tot A	Tot G
2009-10	Fulham	0	0		
2010-11	Fulham	0	0		
2010-11	*Milton Keynes D*	17	2	17	2
2010-11	*Dundee U*	1	0		
2011-12	Fulham	0	0		
2011-12	*Oldham Ath*	11	1	11	1
2011-12	*Dundee U*	11	0	12	0
2012-13	Yeovil T	21	1	21	1
2012-13	Barnet	5	1	5	1
2017-18	Forest Green R	14	2	14	2

MONTHE, Emmanuel (D) — 13 0
H: 6 0 W: 12 08 b. 26-1-95
From Southport, Whitehawk, Hayes & Yeading, Havant & Waterford, Bath C.

Season	Club	Apps	Gls	Tot A	Tot G
2017-18	Forest Green R	13	0	13	0

MULLINGS, Shamir (F) — 7 1
H: 6 4 W: 12 08 b. 30-10-93
From Southend U, Bromley, Havant & Waterlooville, Chelmsford C.

Season	Club	Apps	Gls	Tot A	Tot G
2017-18	Forest Green R	7	1	7	1

OSBOURNE, Isaiah (M) — 222 4
H: 6 2 W: 12 06 b.Birmingham 5-11-87
Internationals: England U16.

Season	Club	Apps	Gls	Tot A	Tot G
2005-06	Aston Villa	0	0		
2006-07	Aston Villa	11	0		
2007-08	Aston Villa	8	0		
2008-09	Aston Villa	0	0		
2008-09	*Nottingham F*	8	0	8	0
2009-10	Aston Villa	0	0		
2009-10	*Middlesbrough*	9	0	9	0
2010-11	Aston Villa	0	0	19	0
2010-11	*Sheffield W*	10	0	10	0
2011-12	Hibernian	30	1	30	1
2012-13	Blackpool	28	1		
2013-14	Blackpool	21	4	52	2
2014-15	Scunthorpe U	28	0	28	0
2015-16	Walsall	0	0		
2016-17	Walsall	30	1	30	1
2017-18	Forest Green R	36	0	36	0

PICKERING, Harry (D) — 1 0
b.Chester 29-12-98

Season	Club	Apps	Gls	Tot A	Tot G
2016-17	Port Vale	0	0		
2016-17	Crewe Alex	1	0	1	0
2017-18	Forest Green R	0	0		

RAWSON, Farrend (D) — 64 3
H: 6 1 W: 11 07 b.Nottingham 11-7-96

Season	Club	Apps	Gls	Tot A	Tot G
2014-15	Derby Co	0	0		
2014-15	*Rotherham U*	4	0		
2015-16	Derby Co	0	0		
2015-16	*Rotherham U*	16	2	20	2
2016-17	Derby Co	0	0		
2016-17	*Coventry C*	14	0	14	0
2017-18	Derby Co	0	0		
2017-18	*Accrington S*	12	0	12	0
2017-18	Forest Green R	18	1	18	1

REID, Reuben (F) — 384 106
H: 6 0 W: 12 02 b.Bristol 26-7-88

Season	Club	Apps	Gls	Tot A	Tot G
2005-06	Plymouth Arg	1	0		
2006-07	Plymouth Arg	6	0		
2006-07	*Rochdale*	2	0	2	0
2006-07	*Torquay U*	7	2	7	2
2007-08	Plymouth Arg	0	0		
2007-08	*Wycombe W*	11	1	11	1
2007-08	*Brentford*	10	1	10	1
2008-09	Rotherham U	41	18	41	18
2009-10	WBA	4	0		
2009-10	*Peterborough U*	13	0	13	0
2010-11	WBA	0	0	4	0
2010-11	*Walsall*	18	3	18	3
2010-11	*Oldham Ath*	19	2		
2011-12	Oldham Ath	20	5	39	7
2012-13	Yeovil T	19	4	19	4
2012-13	*Plymouth Arg*	18	2		
2013-14	Plymouth Arg	46	17		
2014-15	Plymouth Arg	42	18		
2015-16	Plymouth Arg	29	7		
2016-17	Plymouth Arg	0	0	142	44
2016-17	Exeter C	36	13		
2017-18	Exeter C	21	7	57	20
2017-18	Forest Green R	21	6	21	6

ROBERTS, Mark (D) — 304 24
H: 6 1 W: 12 00 b.Northwich 16-10-83

Season	Club	Apps	Gls	Tot A	Tot G
2002-03	Crewe Alex	0	0		
2003-04	Crewe Alex	.0	0		
2004-05	Crewe Alex	6	0		
2005-06	Crewe Alex	0	0		
2005-06	*Chester C*	1	0	1	0
2006-07	Crewe Alex	0	0	6	0
2007-08	Accrington S	34	0	34	0

From Northwich Vic.

Season	Club	Apps	Gls	Tot A	Tot G
2010-11	Stevenage	42	6		
2011-12	Stevenage	46	6		
2012-13	Stevenage	44	2	132	14
2013-14	Fleetwood T	33	3		
2014-15	Fleetwood T	27	3	60	6
2015-16	Cambridge U	30	2		
2016-17	Cambridge U	27	2	57	4
2017-18	Forest Green R	14	0	14	0

RUSSELL, Sam (G) — 5 0
H: 6 0 W: 10 12 b.Middlesbrough 4-10-82
From Middlesbrough, Rochdale, Wrexham, Darlington.

Season	Club	Apps	Gls	Tot A	Tot G
2017-18	Forest Green R	5	0	5	0

SIMPSON, Jordan (M) — 1 0
H: 5 10 W: 11 05 b. 28-11-98

Season	Club	Apps	Gls	Tot A	Tot G
2016-17	Swindon T	0	0		
2017-18	Swindon T	0	0		
2017-18	Forest Green R	1	0	1	0

SPURRIER, Lewis (F) — 0 0

Season	Club	Apps	Gls	Tot A	Tot G
2017-18	Forest Green R	0	0		

TRAORE, Drissa (M) — 53 0
H: 5 9 W: 11 11 b. 25-3-92
Internationals: Ivory Coast U20.

Season	Club	Apps	Gls	Tot A	Tot G
2012-13	Le Havre	5	0		
2013-14	Le Havre	0	0	5	0
2014-15	Notts Co	4	0	4	0
2015-16	Swindon T	24	0		
2016-17	Swindon T	0	0	24	0
2017-18	Forest Green R	20	0	20	0

WHITTLE, Alex (D) — 80 1
H: 5 9 W: 11 11
b.Liverpool 15-3-93

Season	Club	Apps	Gls	Tot A	Tot G
2012-13	Dunfermline Ath	24	0		
2013-14	Dunfermline Ath	30	1		
2014-15	Dunfermline Ath	24	0	78	1

From Southport, AFC Fylde, York C.

Season	Club	Apps	Gls	Tot A	Tot G
2017-18	Forest Green R	2	0	2	0

WISHART, Daniel (F) — 32 0
H: 6 0 W: 12 04 b. 28-5-92
Internationals: England C.
From Hayes & Yeading U, Alfreton T, Sutton U.

Season	Club	Apps	Gls	Tot A	Tot G
2017-18	Forest Green R	32	0	32	0

Players retained or with offer of contract
Robert, Fabien.

Scholars
Hendy, Samuel Joseph; Kalnins, Rendijs; Lehmann, Declan; Malshanskyj, Jay Perry; Marsh, Taylor; Spurrier, Lewis Jon James; Youssef, Elias.

FULHAM (38)

ADEBAYO, Elijah (D) — 7 2
b.Brent 7-1-98

Season	Club	Apps	Gls	Tot A	Tot G
2017-18	Fulham	0	0		
2017-18	*Cheltenham T*	7	2	7	2

AYITE, Floyd (M) — 240 40
H: 5 9 W: 10 10 b.Bordeaux 15-12-88
Internationals: Togo Full caps.

Season	Club	Apps	Gls	Tot A	Tot G
2008-09	Bordeaux	0	0		
2008-09	*Angers*	33	3	33	3
2009-10	Bordeaux	0	0		
2009-10	*Nancy*	6	0	6	0
2010-11	Bordeaux	7	0		
2011-12	Bordeaux	0	0	7	0
2011-12	Reims	18	3		
2012-13	Reims	23	2		
2013-14	Reims	32	5	73	10
2014-15	Bastia	30	6		
2015-16	Bastia	32	8	62	14
2016-17	Fulham	31	9		
2017-18	Fulham	28	4	59	13

BETTINELLI, Marcus (G) — 121 0
H: 6 4 W: 12 13 b.Camberwell 24-5-92
Internationals: England U21.

Season	Club	Apps	Gls	Tot A	Tot G
2010-11	Fulham	0	0		
2011-12	Fulham	0	0		
2012-13	Fulham	0	0		
2013-14	Fulham	0	0		
2013-14	*Accrington S*	39	0	39	0
2014-15	Fulham	39	0		
2015-16	Fulham	11	0		
2016-17	Fulham	6	0		
2017-18	Fulham	26	0	82	0

BUTTON, David (G) — 289 0
H: 6 3 W: 13 00 b.Stevenage 27-2-89
Internationals: England U16, U17, U19, U20.

Season	Club	Apps	Gls	Tot A	Tot G
2005-06	Tottenham H	0	0		
2006-07	Tottenham H	0	0		
2007-08	*Rochdale*	0	0		
2008-09	Tottenham H	0	0		
2008-09	*Bournemouth*	4	0	4	0
2008-09	*Luton T*	0	0		
2008-09	*Dagenham & R*	3	0	3	0
2009-10	Tottenham H	0	0		
2009-10	*Crewe Alex*	10	0	10	0
2009-10	*Shrewsbury T*	26	0	26	0
2010-11	Tottenham H	0	0		
2010-11	*Plymouth Arg*	30	0	30	0
2011-12	Tottenham H	0	0		
2011-12	*Leyton Orient*	1	0	1	0
2011-12	*Doncaster R*	7	0	7	0
2011-12	*Barnsley*	9	0	9	0
2012-13	Tottenham H	0	0		
2012-13	*Charlton Ath*	5	0	5	0
2013-14	Brentford	42	0		
2014-15	Brentford	46	0		
2015-16	Brentford	46	0	134	0
2016-17	Fulham	40	0		
2017-18	Fulham	20	0	60	0

CAIRNEY, Tom (M) — 264 35
H: 6 0 W: 11 05 b.Nottingham 20-1-91
Internationals: Scotland U19, U21, Full caps.

Season	Club	Apps	Gls	Tot A	Tot G
2009-10	Hull C	11	1		
2010-11	Hull C	22	1		
2011-12	Hull C	27	0		
2012-13	Hull C	10	0		
2013-14	Hull C	0	0	70	2
2013-14	*Blackburn R*	37	5		
2014-15	Blackburn R	39	3	76	8
2015-16	Fulham	39	8		
2016-17	Fulham	45	12		
2017-18	Fulham	34	5	118	25

CHRISTIE, Cyrus (D) — 239 5
H: 6 2 W: 12 03 b.Coventry 30-9-92
Internationals: Republic of Ireland Full caps.

Season	Club	Apps	Gls	Tot A	Tot G
2011-12	Coventry C	37	0		
2012-13	Coventry C	31	2		
2013-14	Coventry C	34	0	102	2
2014-15	Derby Co	38	0		
2015-16	Derby Co	42	1		
2016-17	Derby Co	27	1		
2017-18	Derby Co	0	0	107	2
2017-18	*Middlesbrough*	25	1	25	1
2017-18	Fulham	5	0	5	0

CISSE, Ibrahima (M) — 105 2
H: 6 0 W: 12 02 b.Liege 28-2-94
Internationals: Belgium U17, U18, U19, U21.

Season	Club	Apps	Gls	Tot A	Tot G
2011-12	Standard Liege	0	0		
2012-13	Standard Liege	18	1		
2013-14	Standard Liege	16	0		
2014-15	Mechelen	33	1		
2015-16	Mechelen	15	0	48	1
2016-17	Standard Liege	17	0	51	1
2017-18	Mechelen	6	0	6	0

DE LA TORRE, Luca (M) — 5 0
H: 5 9 W: 9 13 b.San Diego 23-5-98
Internationals: USA U17, U20, Full caps.

Season	Club	Apps	Gls	Tot A	Tot G
2016-17	Fulham	0	0		
2017-18	Fulham	5	0	5	0

DJALO, Marcelo (D) — 27 2
H: 6 4 W: 13 10 b.Barcelona 8-10-93
From Badalona.

Season	Club	Apps	Gls	Tot A	Tot G
2014-15	Granada	0	0		
2015-16	Girona	0	0		
2016-17	Lugo	25	2	25	2
2017-18	Lugo	2	0	2	0

EDUN, Tayo (D) — 2 0
H: 5 9 b.London 14-5-98
Internationals: England U17, U18, U19, U20.

Season	Club	Apps	Gls	Tot A	Tot G
2016-17	Fulham	0	0		
2017-18	Fulham	2	0	2	0

FREDERICKS, Ryan (M)   **145** **1**
H: 5 8 W: 11 10 b.Potters Bar 10-10-92
Internationals: England U19.

2010–11	Tottenham H	0	0	
2011–12	Tottenham H	0	0	
2012–13	Tottenham H	0	0	
2012–13	Brentford	4	0	4 0
2013–14	Tottenham H	0	0	
2013–14	Millwall	14	1	14 1
2014–15	Tottenham H	0	0	
2014–15	Middlesbrough	17	0	17 0
2015–16	Bristol C	4	0	4 0
2015–16	Fulham	32	0	
2016–17	Fulham	30	0	
2017–18	Fulham	44	0	106 0

HUMPHRYS, Stephen (F)   **32** **4**
b.Oldham 15-9-97

2016–17	Fulham	2	0	
2016–17	Shrewsbury T	14	2	14 2
2017–18	Fulham	0	0	2 0
2017–18	Rochdale	16	2	16 2

JOHANSEN, Stefan (F)   **250** **39**
H: 6 0 W: 12 04 b.Vardo 8-1-91
Internationals: Norway U16, U17, U18, U19, U21, U23, Full caps.

2007	Bodo/Glimt	4	0	
2008	Bodo/Glimt	1	0	
2009	Bodo/Glimt	4	0	
2010	Bodo/Glimt	20	0	29 0
2011	Stromsgodset	13	1	
2012	Stromsgodset	27	3	
2013	Stromsgodset	27	4	67 8
2013–14	Celtic	16	2	
2014–15	Celtic	34	9	
2015–16	Celtic	23	1	73 12
2016–17	Fulham	36	11	
2017–18	Fulham	45	8	81 19

KAIT, Mattias (M)   **6** **0**
H: 6 0 W: 11 11 b.Tallinn 29-6-98
Internationals: Estonia U16, U17, U19, U21, U23, Full caps.
From Levadia.

2017–18	Fulham	0	0	
2017–18	Ross Co	6	0	6 0

KAMARA, Aboubakar (F)   **89** **22**
H: 5 10 W: 12 08 b.Gonesse 7-3-95

2013–14	Monaco	0	0	
2014–15	Monaco	2	0	2 0
2015–16	Kortrijk	12	0	12 0
2015–16	Amiens	16	5	
2016–17	Amiens	29	10	45 15
2017–18	Fulham	30	7	30 7

KEBANO, Neeskens (M)   **136** **28**
H: 5 11 W: 11 11 b.Montereau 10-3-92
Internationals: France U17, U18, U19, U20. DR Congo Full caps.

2010–11	Paris Saint-Germain	3	0	
2011–12	Paris Saint-Germain	0	0	
2012–13	Paris Saint-Germain	0	0	3 0
2012–13	Caen	12	1	12 1
2013–14	Charleroi	26	5	
2014–15	Charleroi	33	12	
2015–16	Charleroi	5	1	64 18
2016–17	Genk	3	0	3 0
2016–17	Fulham	28	6	
2017–18	Fulham	26	3	54 9

MADL, Michael (D)   **238** **12**
b. 21-3-88
Internationals: Austria U20, U21, Full caps.

2006–07	Austria Vienna	5	0	
2007–08	Austria Vienna	0	0	
2007–08	Wacker Innsbruck	21	2	21 2
2008–09	Austria Vienna	17	0	
2009–10	Austria Vienna	1	0	23 0
2010–11	Wiener Neustadt	23	0	
2011–12	Wiener Neustadt	31	3	54 3
2012–13	Sturm Graz	33	1	
2013–14	Sturm Graz	28	1	
2014–15	Sturm Graz	32	1	
2015–16	Sturm Graz	18	1	111 4
2015–16	Fulham	13	1	
2016–17	Fulham	16	0	
2017–18	Fulham	0	0	29 1

Transferred to Austria Vienna, January 2018.

McDONALD, Kevin (M)   **440** **36**
H: 6 2 W: 13 03 b.Carnoustie 4-11-88
Internationals: Scotland U19, U21, Full caps.

2005–06	Dundee	26	3	
2006–07	Dundee	31	2	
2007–08	Dundee	34	9	91 14
2008–09	Burnley	25	1	
2009–10	Burnley	26	1	
2010–11	Burnley	0	0	51 2
2010–11	Scunthorpe U	5	1	5 1
2010–11	Notts Co	11	0	11 0
2011–12	Sheffield U	31	3	
2012–13	Sheffield U	45	1	
2013–14	Sheffield U	1	1	77 5
2013–14	Wolverhampton W	41	5	
2014–15	Wolverhampton W	46	0	
2015–16	Wolverhampton W	33	3	120 8
2016–17	Fulham	43	3	
2017–18	Fulham	42	3	85 6

MOLLO, Yohan (M)   **229** **23**
H: 5 9 W: 11 09 b.Martigues 18-7-89
Internationals: France U21.

2008–09	Monaco	24	2	
2009–10	Monaco	18	0	
2010–11	Monaco	0	0	42 2
2010–11	Caen	35	4	35 4
2011–12	Granada	6	0	6 0
2011–12	Nancy	19	3	
2012–13	Nancy	17	3	
2013–14	Nancy	2	0	38 6
2013–14	Saint Etienne	17	1	
2014–15	Saint Etienne	23	4	
2015–16	Saint Etienne	20	0	
2015–16	Krylya Sovetov	23	0	
2016–17	Saint Etienne	0	0	60 5
2016–17	Krylya Sovetov	12	5	35 5
2016–17	Zenit St Petersburg	7	1	7 1
2017–18	Zenit St Petersburg	0	0	
2017–18	Fulham	6	0	6 0

NORMAN, Magnus (G)   **0** **0**
H: 6 3 W: 12 13 b.Kingston Upon Thames 19-1-97
Internationals: England U16, U18.

2017–18	Fulham	0	0

O'RILEY, Matt (M)   **0** **0**
H: 6 2 W: 12 02 b.Hounslow 21-11-00
Internationals: England U16, U18.

2017–18	Fulham	0	0

ODOI, Dennis (D)   **324** **11**
H: 5 10 W: 11 09 b.Leuven 27-5-88
Internationals: Belgium U20, U21, Full caps.

2006–07	Oud-Heverlee Leuven	3	0	
2007–08	Oud-Heverlee Leuven	21	0	
2008–09	Oud-Heverlee Leuven	33	3	57 3
2009–10	Sint-Truiden	26	1	
2010–11	Sint-Truiden	33	2	59 3
2011–12	Anderlecht	19	0	
2012–13	Anderlecht	14	0	33 0
2013–14	Lokeren	37	1	
2014–15	Lokeren	35	0	
2015–16	Lokeren	35	1	107 2
2016–17	Fulham	30	2	
2017–18	Fulham	38	1	68 3

RAFA SOARES, Luis (D)   **50** **4**
H: 6 0 W: 11 11 b. 9-5-95
Internationals: Portugal U16, U17, U18, U19, U20, U21.

2013–14	Porto	0	0	
2014–15	Porto	0	0	
2015–16	Porto	0	0	
2015–16	Academica	15	1	15 1
2016–17	Porto	0	0	
2016–17	Rio Ave	32	3	32 3
2017–18	Porto	0	0	

On loan from Porto.

2017–18	Fulham	3	0	3 0

REAM, Tim (D)   **380** **9**
H: 6 1 W: 11 05 b.St Louis 5-10-87
Internationals: USA Full caps.

2006	St Louis Billikens	19	0	
2007	St Louis Billikens	19	0	
2008	St Louis Billikens	22	0	
2008	Chicago Fire	12	0	
2009	Chicago Fire	7	0	19 0
2009	St Louis Billikens	22	6	82 6
2010	New York RB	30	1	
2011	New York RB	28	0	58 1
2011–12	Bolton W	13	0	
2012–13	Bolton W	15	0	
2013–14	Bolton W	42	0	
2014–15	Bolton W	44	0	114 0
2015–16	Fulham	29	0	
2016–17	Fulham	34	1	
2017–18	Fulham	44	1	107 2

RODAK, Marek (G)   **55** **0**
H: 6 2 W: 10 12 b. 13-12-96
Internationals: Slovakia U17, U19, U21.

2014–15	Fulham	0	0
2015–16	Fulham	0	0
2016–17	Fulham	0	0
2016–17	Accrington S	20	0 20 0
2017–18	Fulham	0	0
2017–18	Rotherham U	35	0 35 0

RUI FONTE, Pedro (F)   **141** **21**
H: 6 0 W: 12 13 b.Lisbon 23-3-90
Internationals: Portugal U16, U17, U18, U19, U20, U21.

2008–09	Arsenal	0	0	
2008–09	Crystal Palace	10	0	10 0
2009–10	Setubal	13	0	13 0
2010–11	Espanyol	11	0	
2011–12	Espanyol	19	1	
2012–13	Espanyol	10	0	40 1
2013–14	Benfica	0	0	
2014–15	Benfica	0	0	
2014–15	Belenenses	12	2	12 2
2015–16	Braga	15	4	
2016–17	Braga	22	10	
2017–18	Braga	2	1	39 15
2017–18	Fulham	27	3	27 3

SESSEGNON, Ryan (D)   **71** **20**
H: 5 10 W: 11 02 b.Roehampton 18-5-00
Internationals: England U16, U17, U19, U21.

2016–17	Fulham	25	5	
2017–18	Fulham	46	15	71 20

SESSEGNON, Steven (D)   **0** **0**
H: 5 8 W: 10 06 b.Roehampton 18-5-00
Internationals: England U16, U17, U18.

2017–18	Fulham	0	0

WOODROW, Cauley (F)   **101** **17**
H: 6 0 W: 12 04 b.Hemel Hempstead 2-12-94
Internationals: England U17, U20, U21.

2011–12	Fulham	0	0	
2012–13	Fulham	0	0	
2013–14	Fulham	6	1	
2013–14	Southend U	19	2	19 2
2014–15	Fulham	29	3	
2015–16	Fulham	14	4	
2015–16	Fulham	5	0	
2016–17	Burton Alb	14	5	14 5
2017–18	Fulham	0	0	54 8
2017–18	Bristol C	14	2	14 2

Players retained or with offer of contract
Andrason, Atli Hrafn; Asare, Zico Kukuu; Ashby-Hammond, Taye; Atkinson, Robert Philip; Bakumo-Abraham, Jason Timiebi; Davies, Aron Paul; Fossey, Marlon Joseph; Francois, Tyrese Jay; Garrido, Rodriguez Jose; Harris, Jayden John-Lloyd; Jenz, Moritz; Kelly, Vishna Christopher; Opoku, Jerome; Santos, Clase Nicolas; Thorsteinsson, Jon Dagur; York, Reece Cable.

Scholars
Armsworth, Scott David; Ashby-Hammond, Luca; Davis, Benjamin James; De Havilland Ryan James; Elstone, Michael Colin; Felix, Joseph Rabole; Frei, Elias; Hilton, Sonny; Martin, Daniel John; Mundle-Smith, Jaydn Josiah; Schwarzer, Julian; Spence, Diop Tehuti Djed-Hetep; Tahir, Showkat Mohamed.

GILLINGHAM (39)

ARNOLD, Steve (G)   **33** **0**
H: 6 1 W: 13 02 b.Welham Green 22-8-89
Internationals: England C.

2012–13	Stevenage	30	0	
2013–14	Stevenage	3	0	33 0

From Forest Green R, Dover sign.

2017–18	Gillingham	0	0

BINGHAM, Billy (D)   **177** **8**
H: 5 11 W: 11 02 b.Welling 15-7-90

2008–09	Dagenham & R	2	0	
2009–10	Dagenham & R	2	0	
2010–11	Dagenham & R	6	0	
2011–12	Dagenham & R	27	2	
2012–13	Dagenham & R	18	2	
2013–14	Dagenham & R	30	0	
2014–15	Dagenham & R	34	4	117 8
2015–16	Crewe Alex	21	0	
2016–17	Crewe Alex	30	0	51 0
2017–18	Gillingham	9	0	9 0

BYRNE, Mark (M)   **274** **24**
H: 5 9 W: 11 00 b.Dublin 9-11-88

2006–07	Nottingham F	0	0	
2007–08	Nottingham F	1	0	
2008–09	Nottingham F	1	0	
2009–10	Nottingham F	0	0	
2010–11	Nottingham F	0	0	2 0

2010–11	*Barnet*	28	6		
2011–12	Barnet	43	5		
2012–13	Barnet	40	3	111	14
2014–15	Newport Co	42	4		
2015–16	Newport Co	46	2	88	6
2016–17	Gillingham	31	1		
2017–18	Gillingham	42	3	73	4

CHAPMAN, Ben (M)   0 0

2016–17	Gillingham	0	0		
2017–18	Gillingham	0	0		

CUNDLE, Gregory (F)   8 0
b. 20-3-97

2015–16	Gillingham	0	0		
2016–17	Gillingham	2	0		
2017–18	Gillingham	6	0	8	0

EAVES, Tom (M)   173 37
H: 6 3   W: 13 07   b.Liverpool 14-1-92

2009–10	Oldham Ath	15	0		
2010–11	Bolton W	0	0		
2010–11	*Oldham Ath*	0	0	15	0
2011–12	Bolton W	0	0		
2012–13	Bolton W	3	0		
2012–13	*Bristol R*	16	7	16	7
2012–13	Shrewsbury T	10	6		
2013–14	Bolton W	0	0		
2013–14	*Rotherham U*	8	0	8	0
2013–14	*Shrewsbury T*	25	2	35	8
2014–15	Bolton W	1	0		
2014–15	*Yeovil T*	5	0		
2014–15	*Bury*	9	1	9	1
2015–16	Bolton W	0	0	45	4
2016–17	Yeovil T	40	4	45	4
2017–18	Gillingham	41	17	41	17

EHMER, Max (M)   223 11
H: 6 2   W: 11 00   b.Frankfurt 3-2-92

2009–10	QPR	0	0		
2010–11	QPR	0	0		
2010–11	*Yeovil T*	27	0		
2011–12	QPR	0	0		
2011–12	*Yeovil T*	24	0	51	0
2011–12	*Preston NE*	9	0	9	0
2012–13	QPR	0	0		
2012–13	*Stevenage*	6	1	6	1
2013–14	QPR	1	0		
2013–14	*Carlisle U*	12	1	12	1
2014–15	QPR	0	0	1	0
2014–15	*Gillingham*	27	1		
2015–16	Gillingham	30	0		
2016–17	Gillingham	45	6		
2017–18	Gillingham	42	2	144	8

GARMSTON, Bradley (D)   78 2
H: 5 9   W: 10 12   b.Greenwich 18-1-94
Internationals: Republic of Ireland U17, U9, U21.

2012–13	WBA	0	0		
2012–13	*Colchester U*	13	0	13	0
2013–14	WBA	0	0		
2014–15	WBA	0	0		
2014–15	*Gillingham*	8	1		
2015–16	Gillingham	33	0		
2016–17	Gillingham	5	0		
2017–18	Gillingham	19	1	65	2

HADDLER, Tom (G)   1 0
b. 30-7-96

2014–15	Gillingham	0	0		
2015–16	Gillingham	0	0		
2016–17	Gillingham	0	0		
2017–18	Gillingham	1	0	1	0

HESSENTHALER, Jake (M)   159 7
b.Gravesend 20-4-94

2012–13	Gillingham	0	0		
2013–14	Gillingham	19	1		
2014–15	Gillingham	37	1		
2015–16	Gillingham	38	4		
2016–17	Gillingham	28	1		
2017–18	Gillingham	37	0	159	7

HOLY, Tomas (G)   121 0
H: 6 9   W: 16 05   b.Rychnov nad Kneznou 10-12-91
Internationals: Czech Republic U16, U17, U18.

2010–11	Sparta Prague	0	0		
2011–12	Sparta Prague	0	0		
2012–13	Sparta Prague	0	0		
2013–14	Sparta Prague	0	0		
2013–14	*Vlasim*	9	0	9	0
2014–15	Sparta Prague	0	0		
2014–15	*Viktoria Zizkov*	14	0		
2014–15	*Viktoria Zizkov*	27	0	41	0
2015–16	Sparta Prague	0	0		
2015–16	*Zlin*	20	0	20	0

2016–17	*Fastav Zlin*	0	0		
2016–17	Gillingham	6	0		
2017–18	Gillingham	45	0	51	0

LACEY, Alex (D)   89 4
b.Milton Keynes 31-5-93

2014–15	Luton T	18	0	18	0
2015–16	Yeovil T	20	0		
2016–17	Yeovil T	40	3	60	3
2016–17	Gillingham	0	0		
2017–18	Gillingham	11	1	11	1

LIST, Elliott (M)   44 2
b.Camberwell 12-5-97
From Crystal Palace.

2015–16	Gillingham	6	0		
2016–17	Gillingham	15	0		
2017–18	Gillingham	23	2	44	2

M'BO, Noel (F)   0 0

2015–16	Gillingham	0	0		
2016–17	Gillingham	0	0		
2017–18	Gillingham	0	0		

MARTIN, Lee (M)   295 20
H: 5 10   W: 10 03   b.Taunton 9-2-87

2004–05	Manchester U	0	0		
2005–06	Manchester U	0	0		
2006–07	Manchester U	0	0		
2006–07	*Rangers*	7	0	7	0
2006–07	*Stoke C*	13	1	13	1
2007–08	Manchester U	0	0		
2007–08	*Plymouth Arg*	12	2	12	2
2007–08	*Sheffield U*	6	0	6	0
2008–09	Manchester U	1	0		
2008–09	*Nottingham F*	13	1	13	1
2009–10	Manchester U	0	0	1	0
2009–10	*Ipswich T*	16	1		
2010–11	Ipswich T	16	0		
2010–11	*Charlton Ath*	20	2	20	2
2011–12	Ipswich T	34	5		
2012–13	Ipswich T	34	0		
2013–14	Ipswich T	0	0	100	6
2013–14	Millwall	26	1		
2014–15	Millwall	27	1		
2015–16	Millwall	8	0	61	2
2015–16	*Northampton T*	10	0	10	0
2016–17	Gillingham	17	0		
2017–18	Gillingham	35	6	52	6

MOUSSA, Franck (M)   253 38
H: 5 8   W: 10 08   b.Brussels 24-7-89
Internationals: Belgium U18, U19.

2005–06	Southend U	1	0		
2006–07	Southend U	4	0		
2007–08	Southend U	16	0		
2008–09	Southend U	26	2		
2008–09	*Wycombe W*	9	0	9	0
2009–10	Southend U	43	5		
2010–11	Leicester C	8	1		
2010–11	*Doncaster R*	14	2	14	2
2011–12	Leicester C	0	0	8	1
2011–12	*Chesterfield*	10	4	10	4
2012–13	Nottingham F	0	0		
2012–13	*Coventry C*	38	6		
2013–14	Coventry C	39	12	77	18
2014–15	Charlton Ath	14	1		
2015–16	Charlton Ath	6	0	20	1
2015–16	*Southend U*	1	1	91	8
2016–17	Walsall	22	4	22	4
2017–18	Gillingham	2	0	2	0

MURPHY, Rhys (F)   139 36
H: 6 1   W: 11 13   b.Shoreham 6-11-90
Internationals: England U16, U17, U19. Republic of Ireland U21.

2007–08	Arsenal	0	0		
2008–09	Arsenal	0	0		
2009–10	Arsenal	0	0		
2009–10	*Brentford*	5	0	5	0
2010–11	Arsenal	0	0		
2011–12	Arsenal	0	0		
2011–12	*Preston NE*	5	0	5	0
2012–13	Arsenal	0	0		
2012–13	Stormvogels Telstar	26	8	26	8
2013–14	Dagenham & R	32	13		
2014–15	Dagenham & R	9	1	41	14
2014–15	Oldham Ath	11	0		
2015–16	Oldham Ath	13	3	24	3
2015–16	Crawley T	15	9		
2015–16	*AFC Wimbledon*	7	1	7	1
2016–17	Forest Green R	0	0		
2016–17	*Crawley T*	15	1	30	10
2017–18	Forest Green R	0	0		
2017–18	Gillingham	1	0	1	0

NASH, Liam (F)   12 0
H: 5 9   W: 11 03   b. 9-1-96
From Hullbridge Sports, Billericay T, Aveley, Great Wakering R, Maldon & Tiptree.

2017–18	Gillingham	12	0	12	0

NASSERI, David (M)   29 3
b. 26-7-96

2013–14	Bury	0	0		
2014–15	Birmingham C	0	0		

From Macclesfield T.

2017–18	Syrianska FC	25	2	25	2
2017–18	Gillingham	4	1	4	1

NUGENT, Ben (D)   128 3
H: 6 1   W: 13 00   b.Street 28-11-93

2012–13	Cardiff C	12	1		
2013–14	Cardiff C	0	0		
2013–14	Brentford	0	0		
2013–14	*Peterborough U*	11	0	11	0
2014–15	Cardiff C	0	0	12	1
2014–15	*Yeovil T*	23	1	23	1
2015–16	Crewe Alex	39	1		
2016–17	Crewe Alex	20	0	59	1
2017–18	Gillingham	23	0	23	0

O'MARA, Finn (D)   2 0
H: 6 0   W: 11 09   b. 2-3-99

2016–17	Gillingham	0	0		
2017–18	Gillingham	2	0	2	0

O'NEILL, Luke (D)   112 3
H: 6 0   W: 11 04   b.Slough 20-8-91
Internationals: England U17.

2009–10	Leicester C	1	0	1	0
2009–10	*Tranmere R*	4	0	4	0

From Kettering T, Mansfield T

2012–13	Burnley	0	0		
2013–14	Burnley	0	0		
2013–14	*York C*	15	1	15	1
2013–14	*Southend U*	1	0		
2014–15	Burnley	0	0	1	0
2014–15	*Scunthorpe U*	13	0	13	0
2014–15	*Leyton Orient*	8	0	8	0
2015–16	Southend U	14	0		
2016–17	Southend U	17	1	32	1
2017–18	Southend U	38	1	38	1

OLDAKER, Darren (M)   8 0
b.London 4-1-99

2015–16	Gillingham	0	0		
2016–17	Gillingham	5	0		
2017–18	Gillingham	3	0	8	0

PARKER, Josh (F)   147 27
H: 5 11   W: 12 00   b.Slough 1-12-90
Internationals: Antigua and Barbuda Full caps.

2009–10	QPR	4	0		
2010–11	QPR	1	0	5	0
2010–11	*Northampton T*	3	0	3	0
2010–11	*Wycombe W*	1	0	1	0
2011–12	Oldham Ath	13	0	13	0
2011–12	*Dagenham & R*	8	0	8	0
2012–13	Oxford U	15	0	15	0
2013–14	Domzale	25	11	25	11
2014–15	Red Star Belgrade	9	2		
2015–16	Red Star Belgrade	3	2	12	4
2015–16	*Aberdeen*	7	0	7	0
2016–17	Gillingham	16	2		
2017–18	Gillingham	42	10	58	12

SCARLETT, Miquel (D)   0 0

2017–18	Gillingham	0	0		

SIMPSON, Aaron (M)   0 0

2016–17	Gillingham	0	0		
2017–18	Gillingham	0	0		

STARKEY, Jesse (M)   2 0
b. 1-9-95
Internationals: England U18.
From Chelsea, Brighton & HA.

2016–17	Swindon T	1	0	1	0
2017–18	Gillingham	1	0	1	0

STEVENSON, Bradley (M)   0 0

2016–17	Gillingham	0	0		
2017–18	Gillingham	0	0		

TUCKER, Jack (D)   1 0
b. 13-11-99

2017–18	Gillingham	1	0	1	0

WAGSTAFF, Scott (M)   258 26
H: 5 10   W: 10 03   b.Maidstone 31-3-90

2007–08	Charlton Ath	2	0		
2008–09	Charlton Ath	2	0		
2008–09	*Bournemouth*	5	0	5	0
2009–10	Charlton Ath	30	4		
2010–11	Charlton Ath	40	8		

2011–12	Charlton Ath	34	4		
2012–13	Charlton Ath	9	1	117	17
2012–13	*Leyton Orient*	7	0	7	0
2013–14	Bristol C	37	5		
2014–15	Bristol C	26	2		
2015–16	Bristol C	9	1	72	8
2016–17	Gillingham	26	1		
2017–18	Gillingham	31	0	57	1

WILKINSON, Conor (F)   100 12
H: 6 1 W: 12 02 b.Croydon 23-1-95
Internationals: Republic of Ireland U17, U19, U21.

2012–13	Millwall	0	0		
2013–14	Bolton W	0	0		
2013–14	*Torquay U*	3	0	3	0
2014–15	Bolton W	4	0		
2014–15	*Oldham Ath*	17	3	17	3
2015–16	Bolton W	0	0		
2015–16	Barnsley	8	1	8	1
2015–16	Newport Co	12	1	12	1
2015–16	Portsmouth	1	0	1	0
2016–17	Bolton W	9	0	13	0
2016–17	*Chesterfield*	12	4	12	4
2017–18	Gillingham	34	3	34	3

ZAKUANI, Gaby (D)   417 15
H: 6 1 W: 12 13 b.DR Congo 31-5-86
Internationals: DR Congo Full caps.

2002–03	Leyton Orient	1	0		
2003–04	Leyton Orient	10	2		
2004–05	Leyton Orient	33	0		
2005–06	Leyton Orient	43	1	87	3
2006–07	Fulham	0	0		
2006–07	*Stoke C*	9	0		
2007–08	Fulham	0	0		
2007–08	*Stoke C*	19	0	28	0
2008–09	Fulham	0	0		
2008–09	Peterborough U	32	1		
2009–10	Peterborough U	29	0		
2010–11	Peterborough U	30	2		
2011–12	Peterborough U	41	1		
2012–13	Peterborough U	33	1		
2013–14	Peterborough U	15	0		
2014–15	*Kalloni*	15	1	15	1
2014–15	Peterborough U	22	1		
2015–16	Peterborough U	24	3	226	9
2016–17	Northampton T	21	2	21	2
2017–18	Gillingham	40	0	40	0

Players retained or with offer of contract
Wignal-List, Elliott Ricardo.

Scholars
Arnold, Henry George; Arthurs, Jude Robert; Bramble, Thomas-James Everton; Campbell, Roman Cameron; Catherall, Louie Sydney; Conway, Jack William James; Divine, Danny Paul; Gildea, Jaydn; Hlabi, Lenny; Huckle, Ryan Cockburn; Morrell, Jack Lawrence; Noyelle, Charles William; Scarlett, Miquel Howard Hugh; Sheminant, George; Tucker, Jack Robert; White, Theodore Stephen; Woods, Henry.

GRIMSBY T (40)

BERRETT, James (M)   320 33
H: 5 10 W: 10 13 b.Halifax 13-1-89
Internationals: Republic of Ireland U18, U19, U21.

2006–07	Huddersfield T	2	0		
2007–08	Huddersfield T	15	1		
2008–09	Huddersfield T	9	1		
2009–10	Huddersfield T	9	0	35	2
2010–11	Carlisle U	46	10		
2011–12	Carlisle U	42	9		
2012–13	Carlisle U	42	2		
2013–14	Carlisle U	40	2	170	23
2014–15	Yeovil T	28	1	28	1
2015–16	York C	36	4	36	4
2016–17	Grimsby T	19	2		
2017–18	Grimsby T	32	1	51	3

BOLARINWA, Tom (M)   37 2
H: 5 11 W: 11 11 b.Greenwich 21-1-90
From Sutton U.

2016–17	Grimsby T	34	2		
2017–18	Grimsby T	3	0	37	2

CARDWELL, Harry (F)   16 0
b. 23-10-96
Internationals: Scotland U19, U21.
From Reading.

2017–18	Grimsby T	16	0	16	0

CLARKE, Nathan (D)   510 13
H: 6 2 W: 12 00 b.Halifax 30-11-83

2001–02	Huddersfield T	36	1		
2002–03	Huddersfield T	3	0		
2003–04	Huddersfield T	26	1		
2004–05	Huddersfield T	37	0		
2005–06	Huddersfield T	46	0		
2006–07	Huddersfield T	16	0		
2007–08	Huddersfield T	44	2		
2008–09	Huddersfield T	38	3		
2009–10	Huddersfield T	17	1		
2010–11	Huddersfield T	1	0		
2010–11	*Colchester U*	18	0	18	0
2011–12	Huddersfield T	0	0	264	8
2011–12	*Oldham Ath*	16	1	16	1
2011–12	*Bury*	11	0	11	0
2012–13	Leyton Orient	34	0		
2013–14	Leyton Orient	46	2		
2014–15	Leyton Orient	33	0	113	2
2015–16	Bradford C	25	0		
2016–17	Bradford C	0	0	25	0
2016–17	Coventry C	18	0	18	0
2017–18	Grimsby T	45	2	45	2

CLEMENTS, Chris (M)   160 16
H: 5 9 W: 10 04 b.Birmingham 6-2-90

2008–09	Crewe Alex	0	0		
2009	*IBV*	15	1	15	1
2009–10	Crewe Alex	0	0		
2010–11	Crewe Alex	0	0		
2013–14	Mansfield T	23	1		
2014–15	Mansfield T	34	1		
2015–16	Mansfield T	38	5		
2016–17	Mansfield T	20	3	115	10
2016–17	Grimsby T	16	4		
2017–18	Grimsby T	0	0	16	4
2017–18	*Forest Green R*	14	1	14	1

CLIFTON, Harry (M)   10 0
H: 5 11 W: 13 12 b. 12-6-98

2016–17	Grimsby T	0	0		
2017–18	Grimsby T	10	0	10	0

COLLINS, Danny (D)   409 18
H: 6 2 W: 11 13 b.Buckley 6-8-80
Internationals: England C. Wales Full caps.

2004–05	Chester C	12	1	12	1
2004–05	Sunderland	14	0		
2005–06	Sunderland	23	1		
2006–07	Sunderland	38	0		
2007–08	Sunderland	36	1		
2008–09	Sunderland	35	1		
2009–10	Sunderland	3	0	149	3
2009–10	Stoke C	25	0		
2010–11	Stoke C	25	0		
2011–12	Stoke C	0	0	50	0
2011–12	*Ipswich T*	16	3	16	3
2011–12	*West Ham U*	11	1	11	1
2012–13	Nottingham F	40	0		
2013–14	Nottingham F	23	1		
2014–15	Nottingham F	8	1	71	2
2015–16	Rotherham U	24	2		
2016–17	Rotherham U	0	0	24	2
2016–17	Grimsby T	36	2		
2017–18	Grimsby T	40	4	76	6

DAVIES, Ben (M)   489 77
H: 5 7 W: 12 03 b.Birmingham 27-5-81

2000–01	Kidderminster H	3	0		
2001–02	Kidderminster H	9	0	12	0
2004–05	Chester C	44	2		
2005–06	Chester C	45	7	89	9
2006–07	Shrewsbury T	43	12		
2007–08	Shrewsbury T	27	6		
2008–09	Shrewsbury T	42	12	112	30
2009–10	Notts Co	45	15		
2010–11	Notts Co	22	5	67	20
2011–12	Derby Co	13	1		
2011–12	Derby Co	35	2		
2012–13	Derby Co	23	4		
2013–14	Derby Co	4	0	75	7
2013–14	*Sheffield U*	18	3		
2014–15	Sheffield U	14	4	32	7
2015–16	Portsmouth	43	1	43	1
2016–17	Grimsby T	25	1		
2017–18	Grimsby T	34	2	59	3

DAVIES, Mikey (D)   0 0
b.Cambridge 5-10-99

2017–18	Grimsby T	0	0		

DEMBELE, Siriki (M)   36 4
b. 7-9-96
From Dundee U.

2017–18	Grimsby T	36	4	36	4

DIXON, Paul (D)   384 6
H: 5 9 W: 11 01 b.Aberdeen 11-10-86
Internationals: Scotland U21, Full caps.

2005–06	Dundee	29	2		
2006–07	Dundee	33	0		
2007–08	Dundee	30	0	92	2
2008–09	Dundee U	29	1		
2009–10	Dundee U	25	0		
2010–11	Dundee U	30	0		
2011–12	Dundee U	37	3		
2012–13	Huddersfield T	37	0		
2013–14	Huddersfield T	37	0		
2014–15	Huddersfield T	11	0	85	0
2014–15	Dundee U	15	0		
2015–16	Dundee U	28	0		
2016–17	Dundee U	17	0	181	4
2017–18	Grimsby T	26	0	26	0

FOX, Andrew (D)   50 1
b. 15-1-93

2015–16	Peterborough U	18	1	18	1
2016–17	Stevenage	9	0	9	0
2017–18	AFC Eskilstuna	13	0	13	0
2017–18	Grimsby T	10	0	10	0

HALL-JOHNSON, Reece (M)   12 0
H: 5 8 W: 10 08 b.Aylesbury 9-5-95

2013–14	Norwich C	0	0		
2014–15	Norwich C	0	0		
2015–16	Norwich C	0	0		

From Maidstone U, Bishop's Stortford, Braintree T.

2017–18	Grimsby T	12	0	12	0

HOOPER, JJ (F)   95 16
H: 6 1 W: 13 01 b.Greenwich 9-10-93

2013–14	Northampton T	3	0		

From Havant & Waterlooville.

2015–16	Port Vale	28	5		
2016–17	Port Vale	23	5	51	10
2016–17	*Northampton T*	10	0	13	0
2017–18	Grimsby T	31	6	31	6

KEEBLE, Jack (D)   0 0

2017–18	Grimsby T	0	0		

KELLY, Sam (M)   57 3
b. 21-10-93

2014–15	Norwich C	0	0		
2015–16	Port Vale	28	3		
2016–17	Port Vale	21	0	49	3
2017–18	Grimsby T	8	0	8	0

KILLIP, Ben (G)   7 0
H: 6 2 W: 11 09 b. 24-11-95
From Norwich C.

2017–18	Grimsby T	7	0	7	0

McALLISTER, Sean (M)   189 5
H: 5 8 W: 10 07 b.Bolton 15-8-87

2005–06	Sheffield W	2	0		
2006–07	Sheffield W	6	1		
2007–08	Sheffield W	8	0		
2007–08	*Mansfield T*	7	0	7	0
2007–08	Bury	0	0		
2008–09	Sheffield W	40	3		
2009–10	Sheffield W	12	0	68	4
2010–11	Shrewsbury T	18	0		
2011–12	Shrewsbury T	17	1	35	1
2012–13	Port Vale	2	0	2	0
2013–14	Scunthorpe U	39	0		
2014–15	Scunthorpe U	23	0		
2015–16	Scunthorpe U	11	0	73	0
2016–17	Grimsby T	3	0		
2017–18	Grimsby T	1	0	4	0

McKEOWN, James (G)   82 0
H: 6 1 W: 14 00 b.Birmingham 24-7-89
Internationals: Republic of Ireland U19.

2005–06	Walsall	0	0		
2006–07	Walsall	0	0		
2007–08	Peterborough U	1	0		
2008–09	Peterborough U	1	0		
2009–10	Peterborough U	4	0	6	0
2016–17	Grimsby T	39	0		
2017–18	Grimsby T	37	0	76	0

McMILLAN, Alex (D)   0 0

2017–18	Grimsby T	0	0		

McSHEFFREY, Gary (F)   486 103
H: 5 8 W: 10 06 b.Coventry 13-8-82
Internationals: England U18, U20.

1998–99	Coventry C	1	0		
1999–2000	Coventry C	3	0		
2000–01	Coventry C	0	0		
2001–02	*Stockport Co*	5	1	5	1
2001–02	Coventry C	8	1		
2002–03	Coventry C	29	4		
2003–04	Coventry C	19	11		

2003–04	Luton T	18	9	
2004–05	Coventry C	37	12	
2004–05	Luton T	5	1	23 10
2005–06	Coventry C	43	15	
2006–07	Coventry C	3	1	
2006–07	Birmingham C	40	13	
2007–08	Birmingham C	32	3	
2008–09	Birmingham C	6	0	
2008–09	Nottingham F	4	0	4 0
2009–10	Birmingham C	5	0	83 16
2009–10	Leeds U	10	1	10 1
2010–11	Coventry C	33	8	
2011–12	Coventry C	39	8	
2012–13	Coventry C	32	1	
2013–14	Coventry C	0	0	247 61
2013–14	Chesterfield	9	1	9 1
2013–14	Scunthorpe U	13	0	
2014–15	Scunthorpe U	41	7	
2015–16	Scunthorpe U	26	5	80 12
2015–16	Doncaster R	7	1	
2016–17	Doncaster R	12	0	19 1

From Eastleigh.

2017–18	Grimsby T	6	0	6 0

MILLS, Zak (D) 58 0
b. 28-5-92
From Histon, Boston U.

2016–17	Grimsby T	30	0	
2017–18	Grimsby T	28	0	58 0

OSBORNE, Jamey (M) 21 1
H: 6 1   W: 12 04   b.Solihull 7-6-92
From Hednesford T, Redditch U, Solihull Moors.

2016–17	Grimsby T	19	1	
2017–18	Grimsby T	2	0	21 1

OSBORNE, Karleigh (D) 242 8
H: 6 2   W: 12 04   b.Southall 19-3-88

2004–05	Brentford	1	0	
2005–06	Brentford	1	0	
2006–07	Brentford	21	0	
2007–08	Brentford	29	1	
2008–09	Brentford	23	4	
2009–10	Brentford	19	0	
2010–11	Brentford	42	1	
2011–12	Brentford	25	0	161 6
2012–13	Millwall	13	1	
2013–14	Millwall	1	0	14 1
2013–14	Bristol C	27	1	
2014–15	Bristol C	1	0	
2014–15	Colchester U	4	0	4 0
2015–16	Bristol C	0	0	28 1
2015–16	AFC Wimbledon	23	0	23 0
2016–17	Plymouth Arg	1	0	1 0
2016–17	Kilmarnock	1	0	1 0
2017–18	Grimsby T	10	0	10 0

POWLES, Emil (D) 0 0
b. 1-10-00

2017–18	Grimsby T	0	0	

ROSE, Mitchell (M) 103 12
H: 5 9   W: 12 03   b.Doncaster 4-7-94

2012–13	Rotherham U	5	0	
2013–14	Rotherham U	0	0	
2014–15	Rotherham U	0	0	5 0
2014–15	Crawley T	1	0	1 0
2015–16	Mansfield T	34	2	
2016–17	Mansfield T	18	2	52 4
2016–17	Newport Co	12	0	12 0
2016–17	Grimsby T	0	0	
2017–18	Grimsby T	33	8	33 8

SAWYER, Tom (M) 0 0

2017–18	Grimsby T	0	0	

SUMMERFIELD, Luke (M) 333 24
H: 6 0   W: 11 00   b.Ivybridge 6-12-87

2004–05	Plymouth Arg	1	0	
2005–06	Plymouth Arg	0	0	
2006–07	Plymouth Arg	23	1	
2006–07	Bournemouth	8	1	8 1
2007–08	Plymouth Arg	7	0	
2008–09	Plymouth Arg	29	2	
2009–10	Plymouth Arg	12	0	
2009–10	Leyton Orient	14	0	14 0
2010–11	Plymouth Arg	7	1	79 4
2011–12	Cheltenham T	41	4	41 4
2012–13	Shrewsbury T	36	2	
2013–14	Shrewsbury T	28	1	64 3
2014–15	York C	31	4	
2015–16	York C	34	7	65 11
2016–17	Grimsby T	23	1	
2017–18	Grimsby T	39	0	62 1

VERNON, Scott (F) 456 93
H: 6 1   W: 11 06   b.Manchester 13-12-83

2002–03	Oldham Ath	8	1	

2003–04	Oldham Ath	45	12	
2004–05	Oldham Ath	22	7	75 20
2004–05	Blackpool	4	3	
2005–06	Blackpool	17	1	
2005–06	Colchester U	7	1	
2006–07	Blackpool	38	11	
2007–08	Blackpool	15	4	74 19
2007–08	Colchester U	17	5	
2008–09	Colchester U	33	4	
2008–09	Northampton T	6	1	6 1
2009–10	Colchester U	7	3	64 13
2009–10	Gillingham	1	0	1 0
2009–10	Southend U	17	4	17 4
2010–11	Aberdeen	33	10	
2011–12	Aberdeen	35	11	
2012–13	Aberdeen	35	3	
2013–14	Aberdeen	25	6	128 30
2014–15	Shrewsbury T	22	1	
2015–16	Shrewsbury T	13	1	35 2
2016–17	Grimsby T	28	3	
2017–18	Grimsby T	28	1	56 4

WARRINGTON, Andy (G) 372 0
H: 6 3   W: 12 13   b.Sheffield 10-6-76

1994–95	York C	0	0	
1995–96	York C	6	0	
1996–97	York C	27	0	
1997–98	York C	17	0	
1998–99	York C	11	0	61 0
2003–04	Doncaster R	46	0	
2004–05	Doncaster R	34	0	
2005–06	Doncaster R	9	0	
2006–07	Doncaster R	0	0	89 0
2006–07	Bury	20	0	20 0
2007–08	Rotherham U	46	0	
2008–09	Rotherham U	38	0	
2009–10	Rotherham U	46	0	
2010–11	Rotherham U	38	0	
2011–12	Rotherham U	7	0	
2012–13	Rotherham U	27	0	
2013–14	Rotherham U	0	0	202 0
2016–17	Grimsby T	0	0	
2017–18	Grimsby T	0	0	

WOOLFORD, Martyn (M) 320 34
H: 6 0   W: 11 09   b.Castleford 13-10-85
Internationals: England C.

2008–09	Scunthorpe U	39	4	
2009–10	Scunthorpe U	40	5	
2010–11	Scunthorpe U	24	6	103 15
2010–11	Bristol C	15	0	
2011–12	Bristol C	25	1	
2012–13	Bristol C	15	3	55 4
2012–13	Millwall	15	1	
2013–14	Millwall	40	7	
2014–15	Millwall	38	3	93 11
2015–16	Sheffield U	28	1	28 1
2016–17	Fleetwood T	10	1	10 1
2017–18	Grimsby T	31	2	31 2

Players retained or with offer of contract
Wright, Max.

Scholars
Battersby, Oliver Ben; Briggs, Corey Jack; Buckley, Brandon Adam; Burchell, Lawrence; Burrell, Rumarn Kameron-Scott; Curran, Jock Alan; Davis, Michael John; Evans, Ryan Lewis Lee; Flowerdew, Benjamen John; Goddard, Jamie Alexander; Jamieson, Thomas Andrew; Lawman, Myles Luke; McMillan, Alexander James; Paul-Jones, Ty-Rhys Jaden; Powles, Emil Kendal; Poynter, Conley Kevin; Richardson, Kyle William; Saunders, Oliver Matthew; Sesay, Bilal Abdulai; Slater, Declan Anthony.

Non-contract
Warrington, Andrew Clifford.

HUDDERSFIELD T (41)

BILLING, Phillip (M) 54 3
H: 6 4   W: 12 08   b.11-6-96
Internationals: Denmark U19, U21.

2013–14	Huddersfield T	1	0	
2014–15	Huddersfield T	0	0	
2015–16	Huddersfield T	13	1	
2016–17	Huddersfield T	24	2	
2017–18	Huddersfield T	16	0	54 3

COLEMAN, Joel (G) 48 0
H: 6 6   W: 12 13   b.Bolton 26-9-95

2013–14	Oldham Ath	0	0	
2014–15	Oldham Ath	11	0	
2015–16	Oldham Ath	32	0	43 0
2016–17	Huddersfield T	5	0	
2017–18	Huddersfield T	0	0	5 0

DEPOITRE, Laurent (F) 207 67
H: 6 3   W: 14 05   b.Tournai 7-12-88
Internationals: Belgium Full caps.

2010–11	Aalst	14	8	
2011–12	Aalst	33	8	47 16
2012–13	Oostende	34	14	
2013–14	Oostende	28	6	62 20
2014–15	Gent	29	12	
2015–16	Gent	27	12	
2016–17	Gent	2	0	58 24
2016–17	Porto	7	1	7 1
2017–18	FC Porto	0	0	
2017–18	Huddersfield T	33	6	33 6

GREEN, Rob (G) 609 0
H: 6 3   W: 14 09   b.Chertsey 18-1-80
Internationals: England U16, U18, B, Full caps.

1997–98	Norwich C	0	0	
1998–99	Norwich C	2	0	
1999–2000	Norwich C	3	0	
2000–01	Norwich C	5	0	
2001–02	Norwich C	41	0	
2002–03	Norwich C	46	0	
2003–04	Norwich C	46	0	
2004–05	Norwich C	38	0	
2005–06	Norwich C	42	0	223 0
2006–07	West Ham U	26	0	
2007–08	West Ham U	38	0	
2008–09	West Ham U	38	0	
2009–10	West Ham U	38	0	
2010–11	West Ham U	37	0	
2011–12	West Ham U	42	0	219 0
2012–13	QPR	16	0	
2013–14	QPR	45	0	
2014–15	QPR	36	0	
2015–16	QPR	24	0	121 0
2016–17	Leeds U	46	0	
2017–18	Leeds U	0	0	46 0
2017–18	Huddersfield T	0	0	

HADERGJONAJ, Florent (D) 121 2
H: 6 0   W: 11 11   b.Langnau 31-7-94
Internationals: Switzerland U20, U21, Full caps.

2013–14	Young Boys	11	1	
2014–15	Young Boys	26	0	
2015–16	Young Boys	32	0	
2016–17	Young Boys	2	0	71 1
2016–17	Ingolstadt 04	25	1	25 1
2017–18	FC Ingolstadt	2	0	2 0

On loan from FC Ingolstadt.

2017–18	Huddersfield T	23	0	23 0

HEFELE, Michael (D) 159 0
H: 6 4   W: 13 10   b.Pfaffenhofen 1-9-90

2010–11	Unterhaching	27	0	
2011–12	Unterhaching	6	1	33 1
2012–13	Greuther Furth	1	0	
2013–14	Greuther Furth	2	0	3 0
2013–14	Wacker Burghausen	15	0	15 0
2014–15	Dynamo Dresden	31	3	
2015–16	Dynamo Dresden	38	7	69 10
2016–17	Huddersfield T	37	3	
2017–18	Huddersfield T	2	0	39 3

HIWULA, Jordy (F) 138 31
H: 5 10   W: 11 12   b.Manchester 24-9-94
Internationals: England U18, U19.

2013–14	Manchester C	0	0	
2014–15	Manchester C	0	0	
2014–15	Yeovil T	8	0	8 0
2014–15	Walsall	19	9	
2015–16	Huddersfield T	0	0	
2015–16	Wigan Ath	14	2	14 2
2015–16	Walsall	13	3	32 12
2016–17	Huddersfield T	0	0	
2016–17	Bradford C	41	9	41 9
2017–18	Huddersfield T	0	0	
2017–18	Fleetwood T	43	8	43 8

HOGG, Jonathan (M) 256 2
H: 5 7   W: 10 05   b.Middlesbrough 6-12-88

2007–08	Aston Villa	0	0	
2008–09	Aston Villa	0	0	
2009–10	Aston Villa	0	0	
2009–10	Darlington	5	1	5 1
2010–11	Aston Villa	5	0	
2010–11	Portsmouth	19	0	19 0
2011–12	Aston Villa	0	0	5 0
2011–12	Watford	40	0	
2012–13	Watford	38	0	78 0
2013–14	Huddersfield T	34	0	
2014–15	Huddersfield T	26	0	
2015–16	Huddersfield T	22	0	
2016–17	Huddersfield T	37	1	
2017–18	Huddersfield T	30	0	149 1

HOLMES-DENNIS, Tareiq (M) 63 1
H: 5 9 W: 11 11 b.Farnborough 31-10-95
Internationals: England U18.

2012–13	Charlton Ath	0	0	
2013–14	Charlton Ath	0	0	
2014–15	Charlton Ath	0	0	
2014–15	*Oxford U*	14	0	14 0
2014–15	*Plymouth Arg*	17	1	17 1
2015–16	Charlton Ath	11	0	
2016–17	*Oldham Ath*	10	0	10 0
2016–17	Charlton Ath	1	0	12 0
2016–17	Huddersfield T	9	0	
2017–18	Huddersfield T	0	0	9 0
2017–18	*Portsmouth*	1	0	1 0

INCE, Tom (M) 265 73
H: 5 10 W: 10 06 b.Stockport 30-1-92
Internationals: England U17, U19, U21.

2009–10	Liverpool	0	0	
2010–11	Liverpool	0	0	
2010–11	*Notts Co*	6	2	6 2
2011–12	Blackpool	33	6	
2012–13	Blackpool	44	18	
2013–14	Blackpool	23	7	100 31
2013–14	*Crystal Palace*	8	1	8 1
2014–15	*Hull C*	7	0	7 0
2014–15	*Nottingham F*	6	0	6 0
2014–15	Derby Co	18	11	
2015–16	Derby Co	42	12	
2016–17	Derby Co	45	14	105 37
2017–18	Huddersfield T	33	2	33 2

JORGENSEN, Mathias Zanka (D) 237 12
H: 6 3 W: 12 06 b.Copenhagen 23-4-90
Internationals: Denmark U16, U17, U18, U21, Full caps.

2007–08	Copenhagen	12	1	
2008–09	Copenhagen	20	0	
2009–10	Copenhagen	24	4	
2010–11	Copenhagen	25	1	
2011–12	Copenhagen	11	0	
2012–13	PSV Eindhoven	5	2	
2013–14	PSV Eindhoven	9	0	14 2
2014–15	Copenhagen	29	1	
2015–16	Copenhagen	31	3	
2016–17	Copenhagen	33	0	185 10
2017–18	Huddersfield T	38	0	38 0

KACHUNGA, Elias (F) 170 38
H: 5 9 W: 10 01 b.Cologne 22-4-92
Internationals: Germany U19, U21, DR Congo Full caps.

2009–10	Borussia M'gladbach	0	0	
2010–11	Borussia M'gladbach	0	0	
2011–12	Borussia M'gladbach	0	0	
2011–12	*Osnabrück*	17	10	17 10
2012–13	Borussia M'gladbach	0	0	2 0
2012–13	*Hertha Berlin*	2	0	2 0
2012–13	Paderborn	13	3	
2013–14	Paderborn	33	6	
2014–15	Paderborn	32	6	78 15
2015–16	Ingolstadt	10	0	
2016–17	Ingolstadt	0	0	10 0
2016–17	*Huddersfield T*	42	12	
2017–18	Huddersfield T	19	1	61 13

KONGOLO, Terence (D) 122 1
H: 6 0 W: 11 00 b.Rotterdam 14-2-94
Internationals: Netherlands U16, U17, U18, U19, U21, Full caps.

2011–12	Feyenoord	1	0	
2012–13	Feyenoord	5	0	
2013–14	Feyenoord	17	0	
2014–15	Feyenoord	31	0	
2015–16	Feyenoord	29	0	
2016–17	Feyenoord	23	1	106 1
2017–18	Monaco	3	0	3 0

On loan from Monaco.

2017–18	Huddersfield T	13	0	13 0

LOSSL, Jonas (G) 259 0
H: 6 5 W: 14 00 b.Kolding 1-2-89
Internationals: Denmark U17, U18, U19, U20, U21, Full caps.

2009–10	Midtjylland	12	0	
2010–11	Midtjylland	30	0	
2011–12	Midtjylland	25	0	
2012–13	Midtjylland	27	0	
2013–14	Midtjylland	33	0	127 0
2014–15	Guingamp	30	0	
2015–16	Guingamp	37	0	67 0
2016–17	Mainz 05	27	0	27 0
2017–18	Mainz	0	0	

On loan from Mainz.

2017–18	Huddersfield T	38	0	38 0

LOWE, Chris (D) 254 15
H: 5 7 W: 10 10 b.Plauen 16-4-89

2008–09	Chemnitzer	17	1	
2009–10	Chemnitzer	34	4	
2010–11	Chemnitzer	33	4	84 9
2011–12	Borussia Dortmund	7	0	
2012–13	Borussia Dortmund	0	0	7 0
2012–13	Kaiserslautern	14	0	
2013–14	Kaiserslautern	29	1	
2014–15	Kaiserslautern	33	2	
2015–16	Kaiserslautern	23	1	99 4
2016–17	Huddersfield T	41	2	
2017–18	Huddersfield T	23	0	64 2

MALONE, Scott (D) 258 20
H: 5 9 W: 11 11 b.Rowley Regis 25-3-91
Internationals: England U19.

2008–09	Wolverhampton W	0	0	
2008–09	*Ujpest*	7	1	7 1
2009–10	Wolverhampton W	0	0	
2009–10	*Southend U*	17	0	17 0
2010–11	Wolverhampton W	0	0	
2010–11	*Burton Alb*	22	1	22 1
2011–12	Wolverhampton W	0	0	
2011–12	Bournemouth	32	5	32 5
2012–13	Millwall	15	1	
2013–14	Millwall	33	3	
2014–15	Millwall	20	1	68 5
2014–15	Cardiff C	13	0	
2015–16	Cardiff C	41	2	54 2
2016–17	Fulham	36	6	36 6
2017–18	Huddersfield T	22	0	22 0

MOOY, Aaron (M) 204 31
H: 5 9 W: 10 10 b.Sydney 15-9-90
Internationals: Australia U20, U23, Full caps.

2009–10	Bolton W	0	0	
2010–11	St Mirren	13	0	
2011–12	St Mirren	8	1	21 1
2012–13	Western Sydney W	23	1	
2013–14	Western Sydney W	26	3	49 4
2014–15	Melbourne C	27	7	
2015–16	Melbourne C	26	11	53 18
2016–17	Manchester C	0	0	
2016–17	*Huddersfield T*	45	4	
2017–18	Huddersfield T	36	4	81 8

MOUNIE, Steve (F) 97 32
H: 6 3 W: 12 08 b.Parakou 29-9-94
Internationals: Benin Full caps.

2014–15	Montpellier	0	0	
2015–16	Montpellier	2	0	
2015–16	*Nimes*	32	11	32 11
2016–17	Montpellier	35	14	37 14
2017–18	Huddersfield T	28	7	28 7

O'BRIEN, Lewis (M) 0 0
H: 5 8 W: 9 13 b.Colchester 14-10-98

2017–18	Huddersfield T	0	0

PAYNE, Jack (M) 146 21
H: 5 5 W: 9 06 b.Tower Hamlets 25-10-94

2013–14	Southend U	11	0	
2014–15	Southend U	34	6	
2015–16	Southend U	32	9	77 15
2016–17	Huddersfield T	23	2	
2017–18	Huddersfield T	0	0	23 2
2017–18	*Oxford U*	28	3	28 3
2017–18	*Blackburn R*	18	1	18 1

PRITCHARD, Alex (M) 143 26
H: 5 7 W: 9 11 b.Grays 3-5-93
Internationals: England U20, U21.

2011–12	Tottenham H	0	0	
2012–13	Tottenham H	0	0	
2012–13	*Peterborough U*	6	0	6 0
2013–14	Tottenham H	1	0	
2013–14	*Swindon T*	36	6	36 6
2014–15	Tottenham H	0	0	
2014–15	*Brentford*	45	12	45 12
2015–16	Tottenham H	1	0	2 0
2015–16	*WBA*	2	0	2 0
2016–17	Norwich C	30	6	
2017–18	Norwich C	8	1	38 7
2017–18	Huddersfield T	14	1	14 1

PYKE, Rekeil (F) 19 0
H: 5 10 W: 10 03 b. 1-9-97

2016–17	Huddersfield T	0	0	
2016–17	*Colchester U*	12	0	12 0
2017–18	Huddersfield T	0	0	
2017–18	*Port Vale*	7	0	7 0

QUANER, Collin (F) 149 19
H: 6 3 W: 12 11 b.Dusseldorf 18-6-91
From Fortuna Dusseldorf.

2010–11	Armenia Bielefeld	17	1	17 1
2011–12	Ingolstadt 04	15	1	
2012–13	Ingolstadt 04	1	0	
2013–14	Ingolstadt 04	11	1	27 2
2013–14	Rostock	7	0	7 0
2014–15	Aalen	27	6	27 6
2015–16	Union Berlin	15	1	
2016–17	Union Berlin	14	7	29 8
2016–17	Huddersfield T	16	2	
2017–18	Huddersfield T	26	0	42 2

SABIRI, Abdelhamid (M) 44 23
H: 6 0 W: 12 08 b.Goulmima 28-11-96

2015–16	Sportfreunde Siegen	30	18	30 18
2016–17	Nuremburg	9	5	9 5
2017–18	Nurnberg	0	0	
2017–18	Huddersfield T	5	0	5 0

SCANNELL, Sean (F) 306 20
H: 5 9 W: 11 07 b.Croydon 19-9-90
Internationals: Republic of Ireland U17, U18, U19, U21, B.

2007–08	Crystal Palace	23	2	
2008–09	Crystal Palace	25	2	
2009–10	Crystal Palace	26	2	
2010–11	Crystal Palace	19	2	
2011–12	Crystal Palace	37	4	130 12
2012–13	Huddersfield T	34	2	
2013–14	Huddersfield T	38	1	
2014–15	Huddersfield T	42	4	
2015–16	Huddersfield T	29	1	
2016–17	Huddersfield T	15	0	
2017–18	*Burton Alb*	18	0	18 0
2017–18	Huddersfield T	0	0	158 8

SCHINDLER, Christopher (D) 233 6
H: 6 2 W: 12 02 b.Munich 29-4-90
Internationals: Germany U21.

2009–10	1860 Munich	0	0	
2010–11	1860 Munich	16	1	
2011–12	1860 Munich	30	1	
2012–13	1860 Munich	18	0	
2013–14	1860 Munich	26	0	
2014–15	1860 Munich	29	1	
2015–16	1860 Munich	33	1	152 4
2016–17	Huddersfield T	44	2	
2017–18	Huddersfield T	37	0	81 2

SMITH, Tommy (D) 167 4
H: 6 1 W: 13 02 b.Warrington 14-4-92

2012–13	Huddersfield T	0	0	
2013–14	Huddersfield T	24	0	
2014–15	Huddersfield T	41	0	
2015–16	Huddersfield T	36	0	
2016–17	Huddersfield T	42	4	
2017–18	Huddersfield T	24	0	167 4

STANKOVIC, Jon (M) 25 0
H: 6 3 W: 12 04 b.Ljubijana 14-1-96
Internationals: Slovenia U16, U17, U18, U19, U21.

2012–13	Domzale	6	0	
2013–14	Domzale	12	0	
2014–15	Domzale	0	0	
2015–16	Domzale	0	0	18 0
2016–17	Huddersfield T	7	0	
2017–18	Huddersfield T	0	0	7 0

VAN LA PARRA, Rajiv (M) 242 23
H: 5 11 W: 11 05 b.Rotterdam 4-6-91
Internationals: Netherlands, U17, U19, U21.

2008–09	Caan	2	0	
2009–10	Caan	8	1	
2010–11	Caan	6	0	16 1
2011–12	Heerenveen	23	4	
2012–13	Heerenveen	31	5	
2013–14	Heerenveen	32	5	86 14
2014–15	Wolverhampton W	40	1	
2015–16	Wolverhampton W	13	0	53 1
2015–16	*Brighton & HA*	6	2	6 2
2015–16	Huddersfield T	8	0	
2016–17	Huddersfield T	40	2	
2017–18	Huddersfield T	33	3	81 5

WHITEHEAD, Dean (M) 548 26
H: 5 11 W: 12 06 b.Abingdon 12-1-82

1999–2000	Oxford U	0	0	
2000–01	Oxford U	20	0	
2001–02	Oxford U	40	1	
2002–03	Oxford U	18	1	
2003–04	Oxford U	44	7	122 9
2004–05	Sunderland	42	5	
2005–06	Sunderland	37	3	
2006–07	Sunderland	45	4	
2007–08	Sunderland	27	1	
2008–09	Sunderland	34	0	
2009–10	Sunderland	0	0	185 13
2009–10	Stoke C	36	0	
2010–11	Stoke C	37	2	
2011–12	Stoke C	33	0	
2012–13	Stoke C	26	1	132 3
2013–14	Middlesbrough	37	1	

2014–15	Middlesbrough	18	0	55 1
2015–16	Huddersfield T	34	0	
2016–17	Huddersfield T	16	0	
2017–18	Huddersfield T	4	0	54 0

WILLIAMS, Daniel (M)   213 14
H: 6 0 W: 11 12 b.Karlsruhe 8-3-89
Internationals: USA Full caps.

2009–10	SC Freiburg	5	0	
2010–11	SC Freiburg	7	0	
2011–12	SC Freiburg	1	0	13 0
2011–12	Hoffenheim	24	0	
2012–13	Hoffenheim	21	1	45 1
2013–14	Reading	30	3	
2014–15	Reading	25	1	
2015–16	Reading	39	5	
2016–17	Reading	41	4	135 13
2017–18	Huddersfield T	20	0	20 0

WILLIAMS, Jordan (D)   9 0
b. 22-10-99
Internationals: England U17, U18.

2017–18	Huddersfield T	0	0	
2017–18	Bury	9	0	9 0

Players retained or with offer of contract
Barrett, Jake George; Booty, Regan Jak; Crichlow-Noble, Romoney; Edmonds-Green, Rarmani River Miguel Joseph; High, Scott John; Hudson, Mark Alexander; Mewitt, Luke Edward; Obiero, Micah Obonyo Dulo; Schofield, Ryan James; Spratt, Harry; Tear, Darren Dominic.

Scholars
Daly, Matthew Paul; Danaher, George Charles; Davison-Hale, Harrison William Roger; Dyson, Oliver Jason Lee; Eli, Jordan James Raphael; Gibson, Samuel Joseph; Jackson, Ben Joseph; Marriott, Isaac William; Mills, Benjamin Peter; O'Malley, Mason Lewis; Raymond, Dahomey Asher; Rowe, Aaron Kevin Isaac; Taylor, Cameron Gerrard; Thompson, Oran James.

HULL C (42)

ANDREW, Charlie (G)   0 0
b.Hull 6-1-00

2017–18	Hull C	0	0

ANNAN, Will (M)   0 0
H: 5 11 W: 11 00 b.Kingston upon Hull 5-9-96
Internationals: Scotland U19.

2017–18	Hull C	0	0

BARKWORTH, Ellis (M)   0 0
H: 5 9 W: 11 09 b.Hull 15-10-97

2017–18	Hull C	0	0

BATTY, Daniel (D)   1 0
b.Featherstone 10-12-97

2016–17	Hull C	0	0	
2017–18	Hull C	1	0	1 0

BOWEN, Jarrod (F)   49 14
b.Leominster 1-1-96

2014–15	Hull C	0	0	
2015–16	Hull C	0	0	
2016–17	Hull C	7	0	
2017–18	Hull C	42	14	49 14

BURTON, Callum (G)   1 0
H: 6 2 W: 12 00 b.Newport, Shropshire 15-8-96
Internationals: England U16, U17, U18.

2013–14	Shrewsbury T	0	0	
2014–15	Shrewsbury T	0	0	
2015–16	Shrewsbury T	1	0	
2016–17	Shrewsbury T	0	0	1 0
2017–18	Hull C	0	0	

CAMPBELL, Frazier (F)   232 46
H: 5 11 W: 12 04 b.Huddersfield 13-9-87
Internationals: England U16, U17, U18, U21, Full caps.

2005–06	Manchester U	0	0	
2006–07	Manchester U	0	0	
2007–08	Manchester U	1	0	
2007–08	*Hull C*	34	15	
2008–09	Manchester U	1	0	
2008–09	*Tottenham H*	10	1	10 1
2009–10	Manchester U	0	0	2 0
2009–10	Sunderland	31	4	
2010–11	Sunderland	3	0	
2011–12	Sunderland	12	1	
2012–13	Sunderland	12	1	58 6
2012–13	Cardiff C	12	7	
2013–14	Cardiff C	37	6	49 13
2014–15	Crystal Palace	20	4	
2015–16	Crystal Palace	11	0	
2016–17	Crystal Palace	12	1	43 5
2017–18	Hull C	36	6	70 21

CLACKSTONE, Josh (D)   8 0
b. 18-9-96

2016–17	Hull C	0	0	
2016–17	Notts Co	8	0	8 0
2017–18	Hull C	0	0	

CLARK, Max (D)   63 1
H: 5 11 W: 11 07 b.Hull 19-1-96
Internationals: England U16, U17.

2015–16	Hull C	0	0	
2015–16	Cambridge U	9	0	
2016–17	Hull C	0	0	
2016–17	Cambridge U	27	1	36 1
2017–18	Hull C	27	0	27 0

DAWSON, Michael (D)   441 22
H: 6 2 W: 12 02 b.Leyburn 18-11-83
Internationals: England U21, B, Full caps.

2000–01	Nottingham F	0	0	
2001–02	Nottingham F	0	0	
2002–03	Nottingham F	38	5	
2003–04	Nottingham F	30	1	
2004–05	Nottingham F	14	1	83 7
2004–05	Tottenham H	5	0	
2005–06	Tottenham H	32	0	
2006–07	Tottenham H	37	1	
2007–08	Tottenham H	27	1	
2008–09	Tottenham H	16	1	
2009–10	Tottenham H	29	2	
2010–11	Tottenham H	24	1	
2011–12	Tottenham H	7	0	
2012–13	Tottenham H	27	1	
2013–14	Tottenham H	32	0	236 7
2014–15	Hull C	28	1	
2015–16	Hull C	32	1	
2016–17	Hull C	22	3	
2017–18	Hull C	40	3	122 8

DICKO, Nouha (M)   211 61
H: 5 8 W: 11 00 b.Paris 14-5-92
Internationals: Mali Full caps.

2009–10	Strasbourg B	18	4	
2010–11	Strasbourg B	24	8	42 12
2010–11	Strasbourg	3	0	3 0
2011–12	Wigan Ath	0	0	
2011–12	Blackpool	10	4	
2012–13	Wigan Ath	0	0	
2012–13	Blackpool	22	5	32 9
2012–13	Wolverhampton W	4	1	
2013–14	Wigan Ath	0	0	
2013–14	*Rotherham U*	5	5	5 5
2013–14	Wolverhampton W	19	12	
2014–15	Wolverhampton W	37	14	
2015–16	Wolverhampton W	5	0	
2016–17	Wolverhampton W	30	3	
2017–18	Wolverhampton W	5	1	100 31
2017–18	Hull C	29	4	29 4

DIOMANDE, Adama (F)   192 67
H: 5 11 W: 11 11 b.Oslo 14-2-90
Internationals: Norway U23, Full caps.

2008	Lyn	2	0	
2009	Lyn	1	0	3 0
2010	Skeid	12	8	12 8
2010	Hodd	10	4	
2011	Hodd	28	14	38 18
2012	Stromsgodset	21	7	
2013	Stromsgodset	25	8	46 15
2014–15	Dynamo Minsk	23	3	23 3
2015	Stabaek	21	17	21 17
2015–16	Hull C	11	3	
2016–17	Hull C	22	2	
2017–18	Hull C	16	1	49 6

Transferred to Los Angeles, May 2018.

EDWARDS, Jonathan (M)   15 1
H: 5 11 W: 10 01 b.Luton 24-11-96

2014–15	Peterborough U	3	0	
2015–16	Peterborough U	0	0	3 0
2016–17	Hull C	0	0	
2017–18	Hull C	0	0	
2017–18	Accrington S	2	0	12 1

EDWARDS, Luke (M)   0 0
b.Aberdare 24-6-99

2017–18	Hull C	0	0

EVANDRO, Goebel (M)   279 44
H: 5 10 W: 9 11 b.Blumenau 23-8-86
Internationals: Brazil U20.

2005	Atletico Paranaense	28	4	
2006	Atletico Paranaense	16	2	
2007	Atletico Paranaense	15	1	
2008	Atletico Paranaense	0	0	
2008	*Goias*	3	0	3 0
2008	Palmeiras	26	0	
2009	Atletico Paranaense	0	0	
2009	*Palmeiras*	8	2	34 2
2009	Atletico Mineiro	28	3	
2010	Atletico Paranaense	0	0	59 7
2010	*Atletico Mineiro*	2	0	30 3
2010	*Vitoria*	7	2	7 2
2010–11	Red Star Belgrade	9	5	
2011–12	Red Star Belgrade	25	8	
2012–13	Red Star Belgrade	1	0	35 13
2012–13	Estoril	25	3	
2013–14	Estoril	28	11	53 14
2014–15	Porto	21	1	
2015–16	Porto	11	1	
2016–17	Porto	7	0	39 2
2016–17	Hull C	11	0	
2017–18	Hull C	8	1	19 1

FLEMING, Brandon (D)   0 0
b.Dewsbury 3-12-99

2017–18	Hull C	0	0

GROSICKI, Kamil (M)   323 56
H: 5 11 W: 12 04 b.Szczecin 8-6-88
Internationals: Poland U19, U21, Full caps.

2005–06	Pognon Szczecin	2	0	
2006–07	Pognon Szczecin	21	2	23 2
2007–08	Legia Warsaw	11	1	
2007–08	*Sion*	8	2	8 2
2008–09	Legia Warsaw	0	0	11 1
2008–09	Jagiellonia	13	4	
2009–10	Jagiellonia	30	4	
2010–11	Jagiellonia	15	6	58 14
2010–11	Sivasspor	17	6	
2011–12	Sivasspor	40	7	
2012–13	Sivasspor	28	2	
2013–14	Sivasspor	5	0	90 15
2013–14	Rennes	13	0	
2014–15	Rennes	19	0	
2015–16	Rennes	33	9	
2016–17	Rennes	16	4	81 13
2016–17	Hull C	15	0	
2017–18	Hull C	37	9	52 9

HAMILTON, Tyler (M)   0 0
H: 5 9 W: 10 01 b.Kingston upon Hull 5-1-99

2017–18	Hull C	0	0

HENRIKSEN, Markus (M)   232 39
H: 6 2 W: 13 05 b.Trondheim 25-7-92
Internationals: Norway U16, U17, U18, U19, U21, U23, Full caps.

2009	Rosenborg	3	0	
2010	Rosenborg	28	7	
2011	Rosenborg	29	3	
2012	Rosenborg	18	1	78 11
2012–13	AZ Alkmaar	29	3	
2013–14	AZ Alkmaar	26	2	
2014–15	AZ Alkmaar	22	7	
2015–16	AZ Alkmaar	28	12	
2016–17	AZ Alkmaar	3	2	108 26
2016–17	Hull C	15	0	
2017–18	Hull C	31	2	46 2

HERNANDEZ, Abel (F)   247 79
H: 6 1 W: 11 00 b.Pando Canelones 8-8-90
Internationals: Uruguay U20, U23, Full caps.

2006–07	Central Espanol	6	0	
2007–08	Central Espanol	24	9	30 9
2008–09	Penarol	8	3	8 3
2008–09	Palermo	6	0	
2009–10	Palermo	21	7	
2010–11	Palermo	22	3	
2011–12	Palermo	20	6	
2012–13	Palermo	14	1	
2013–14	Palermo	28	14	111 31
2014–15	Hull C	25	4	
2015–16	Hull C	39	20	
2016–17	Hull C	24	4	
2017–18	Hull C	10	8	98 36

HINCHLIFFE, Ben (M)   0 0

2016–17	Hull C	0	0
2017–18	Hull C	0	0

IRVINE, Jackson (M)   171 18
H: 5 10 W: 11 00 b.Melbourne 7-3-93
Internationals: Scotland U19. Australia U20, U23, Full caps.

2012–13	Celtic	1	0	
2013–14	Celtic	0	0	
2013–14	*Kilmarnock*	27	1	27 1
2014–15	Celtic	0	0	1 0
2014–15	*Ross Co*	28	2	
2015–16	Ross Co	36	0	64 4

2016–17	Burton Alb	42	10		
2017–18	Burton Alb	3	1	45	11
2017–18	Hull C	34	2	34	2

KEANE, Will (F) 63 5
H: 6 2　W: 11 05　b.Stockport 11-1-93
Internationals: England U16, U17, U19, U20, U21.

2009–10	Manchester U	0	0		
2010–11	Manchester U	0	0		
2011–12	Manchester U	1	0		
2012–13	Manchester U	0	0		
2013–14	Manchester U	0	0		
2013–14	*Wigan Ath*	4	0	4	0
2013–14	*QPR*	10	0	10	0
2014–15	Manchester U	0	0		
2014–15	*Sheffield W*	13	3	13	3
2015–16	Manchester U	1	0		
2015–16	*Preston NE*	20	1	20	1
2016–17	Manchester U	0	0		
2016–17	Hull C	5	0		
2017–18	Hull C	9	1	14	1

KINGSLEY, Stephen (D) 140 1
H: 5 10　W: 10 09　b.Stirling 23-7-94
Internationals: Scotland U18, U19, U21, Full caps.

2010–11	Falkirk	3	0		
2011–12	Falkirk	15	0		
2012–13	Falkirk	35	0		
2013–14	Falkirk	35	1	88	1
2014–15	Swansea C	0	0		
2014–15	*Yeovil T*	12	0	12	0
2015–16	Swansea C	4	0		
2015–16	*Crewe Alex*	12	0	12	0
2016–17	Swansea C	13	0	17	0
2017–18	Hull C	11	0	11	0

LARSSON, Sebastian (M) 403 33
H: 5 11　W: 11 02　b.Eskilstuna 6-6-85
Internationals: Sweden U16, U17, U19, U21, Full caps.

2002–03	Arsenal	0	0		
2003–04	Arsenal	0	0		
2004–05	Arsenal	0	0		
2005–06	Arsenal	3	0		
2006–07	Arsenal	0	0	3	0
2006–07	Birmingham C	43	4		
2007–08	Birmingham C	35	6		
2008–09	Birmingham C	38	1		
2009–10	Birmingham C	33	4		
2010–11	Birmingham C	35	4	184	19
2011–12	Sunderland	32	7		
2012–13	Sunderland	38	1		
2013–14	Sunderland	31	1		
2014–15	Sunderland	36	3		
2015–16	Sunderland	18	0		
2016–17	Sunderland	21	0	176	12
2017–18	Hull C	40	2	40	2

LENIHAN, Brian (D) 30 0
H: 5 10　W: 12 00　b.Cork 8-6-94
Internationals: Republic of Ireland U21.

2012	Cork C	3	0		
2013	Cork C	3	0		
2014	Cork C	21	0	27	0
2014–15	Hull C	0	0		
2014–15	*Blackpool*	2	0	2	0
2015–16	Hull C	1	0		
2017–18	Hull C	0	0	1	0

LUER, Greg (F) 19 0
H: 5 11　W: 11 07　b.Brighton 6-12-94

2014–15	Hull C	0	0		
2014–15	*Port Vale*	2	0	2	0
2015–16	Hull C	2	0		
2015–16	*Scunthorpe U*	4	0	4	0
2015–16	*Stevenage*	10	0	10	0
2016–17	Hull C	0	0		
2017–18	Hull C	1	0	3	0

MACDONALD, Angus (D) 82 1
H: 6 0　W: 11 00　b.Winchester 15-10-92
Internationals: England C, U16, U19.

2011–12	Reading	0	0		
2011–12	*Torquay U*	2	0		
2012–13	Reading	0	0		
2012–13	*AFC Wimbledon*	4	0	4	0
2012–13	*Torquay U*	14	0	16	0

From Salisbury C, Torquay U.

2016–17	Barnsley	39	1		
2017–18	Barnsley	11	0	50	1
2017–18	Hull C	12	0	12	0

MANNION, Will (G) 0 0
b. 1-4-98
Internationals: England U19.
From AFC Wimbledon.

2016–17	Hull C	0	0		
2017–18	Hull C	0	0		
2017–18	*Plymouth Arg*	0	0		

MARSHALL, David (G) 411 0
H: 6 3　W: 13 04　b.Glasgow 5-3-85
Internationals: Scotland Youth, U21, B, Full caps.

2003–04	Celtic	11	0		
2004–05	Celtic	18	0		
2005–06	Celtic	4	0		
2006–07	Celtic	2	0	35	0
2006–07	Norwich C	2	0		
2007–08	Norwich C	46	0		
2008–09	Norwich C	46	0	94	0
2008–09	Cardiff C	0	0		
2009–10	Cardiff C	43	0		
2010–11	Cardiff C	11	0		
2011–12	Cardiff C	45	0		
2012–13	Cardiff C	46	0		
2013–14	Cardiff C	37	0		
2014–15	Cardiff C	38	0		
2015–16	Cardiff C	40	0		
2016–17	Cardiff C	4	0	264	0
2016–17	Hull C	16	0		
2017–18	Hull C	2	0	18	0

MAZUCH, Ondrej (D) 186 7
H: 6 2　W: 13 12　b.Hodonin 15-3-89
Internationals: Czech Republic U16, U17, U19, U20, U21, Full caps.

2006–07	Brno	24	1	24	1
2007–08	Fiorentina	0	0		
2008–09	Fiorentina	0	0		
2009–10	Fiorentina	0	0		
2009–10	Anderlecht	30	4		
2010–11	Anderlecht	35	1	65	5
2011–12	Dnipro Dnipropetrovsk	10	0		
2012–13	Dnipro Dnipropetrovsk	19	0		
2013–14	Dnipro Dnipropetrovsk	26	0		
2014–15	Dnipro Dnipropetrovsk	10	0	65	0
2015–16	Sparta Prague	4	0		
2016–17	Sparta Prague	14	1	18	1
2017–18	Hull C	14	0	14	0

McGREGOR, Allan (G) 417 0
H: 6 0　W: 11 08　b.Edinburgh 31-1-82
Internationals: Scotland U21, B, Full caps.

1998–99	Rangers	0	0		
1999–2000	Rangers	0	0		
2000–01	Rangers	0	0		
2001–02	Rangers	2	0		
2002–03	Rangers	4	0		
2004–05	Rangers	2	0		
2005–06	Rangers	0	0		
2005–06	*Dunfermline Ath*	26	0	26	0
2006–07	Rangers	31	0		
2007–08	Rangers	31	0		
2008–09	Rangers	27	0		
2009–10	Rangers	34	0		
2010–11	Rangers	37	0		
2011–12	Rangers	37	0	205	0
2012–13	Besiktas	27	0	27	0
2013–14	Hull C	26	0		
2014–15	Hull C	26	0		
2015–16	Hull C	44	0		
2016–17	*Cardiff C*	19	0	19	0
2017–18	Hull C	44	0	140	0

McKENZIE, Robbie (M) 0 0
b.Kingston upon Hull 25-9-98

2017–18	Hull C	0	0		

MEYLER, David (M) 184 16
H: 6 3　W: 11 09　b.Cork 29-5-89
Internationals: Republic of Ireland U21, Full caps.

2008	Cork C	2	0	2	0
2008–09	Sunderland	0	0		
2009–10	Sunderland	10	0		
2010–11	Sunderland	5	0		
2011–12	Sunderland	7	0		
2012–13	Sunderland	3	0	25	0
2012–13	Hull C	28	5		
2013–14	Hull C	30	2		
2014–15	Hull C	28	1		
2015–16	Hull C	26	2		
2016–17	Hull C	20	1		
2017–18	Hull C	25	5	157	16

OLLEY, Greg (M) 0 0
b. 2-2-96
From Newcastle U.

2016–17	Hull C	0	0		
2017–18	Hull C	0	0		

RITSON, Lewis (D) 0 0
b.South Shields 1-11-98

2017–18	Hull C	0	0		

STEWART, Kevin (D) 48 3
H: 5 7　W: 11 06　b.Enfield 7-9-93

2012–13	Tottenham H	0	0		
2012–13	Crewe Alex	4	0		
2013–14	Crewe Alex	0	0	4	0
2014–15	Liverpool	0	0		
2014–15	*Cheltenham T*	4	1	4	1
2014–15	*Burton Alb*	7	2	7	2
2015–16	Liverpool	7	0		
2015–16	*Swindon T*	5	0	5	0
2016–17	Liverpool	4	0	11	0
2017–18	Hull C	17	0	17	0

TORAL, Jon (M) 109 17
H: 6 0　W: 12 07　b.Reus 5-2-95

2013–14	Arsenal	0	0		
2014–15	Arsenal	0	0		
2014–15	*Brentford*	34	6	34	6
2015–16	Arsenal	0	0		
2015–16	*Birmingham C*	36	8	36	8
2016–17	Arsenal	0	0		
2016–17	*Rangers*	12	2	12	2
2017–18	Hull C	27	1	27	1

WEIR, James (M) 8 0
H: 5 10　W: 11 03　b.Preston 4-8-95
Internationals: England U18, U19.

2014–15	Manchester U	0	0		
2015–16	Manchester U	1	0		
2016–17	Manchester U	0	0	1	0
2016–17	Hull C	0	0		
2016–17	*Wigan Ath*	4	0	4	0
2017–18	Hull C	3	0	3	0

YATES, James (D) 0 0
H: 5 11　W: 10 01　b.Huyton 3-4-98
Internationals: England U16, U17, U18.
From Everton.

2017–18	Hull C	0	0		

Players retained or with offer of contract
Chadwick, William Anthony; Curry, Adam; Lewis-Potter, Keane William; Powell, Thomas David.

Scholars
Adamson, Benjamin Peter; Andrew, Charlie Alfred; Dunkerley, Charlie; Foulkes, Harrison Andrew; Greaves, Jacob John; Hawkins, Daniel Thomas; Holmes, Elliot Charles; Jacob, Matthew James; Nicholls, Matthew Jake; Rouse, Jay; Salam, Ahmed Mamdoh Abdel; Saltmer, Jonathan David; Sheaf, Max; Taylor, William Leeson; Thacker, Joshua; Wilson-Rhiney, Mason Alexander.

IPSWICH T (43)

ADEYEMI, Tom (M) 223 19
H: 6 1　W: 12 04　b.Milton Keynes 24-10-91

2008–09	Norwich C	0	0		
2009–10	Norwich C	11	0		
2010–11	Norwich C	0	0		
2010–11	*Bradford C*	34	5	34	5
2011–12	Norwich C	0	0		
2011–12	*Oldham Ath*	36	2	36	2
2012–13	Norwich C	0	0	11	0
2012–13	*Brentford*	30	2	30	2
2013–14	*Birmingham C*	35	1	35	1
2014–15	Cardiff C	20	1		
2015–16	Cardiff C	0	0		
2015–16	*Leeds U*	23	2	23	2
2016–17	Cardiff C	0	0	20	1
2016–17	*Rotherham U*	29	6	29	6
2017–18	Ipswich T	5	0	5	0

BIALKOWSKI, Bartosz (G) 255 0
H: 6 3　W: 12 10　b.Braniewo 6-7-87
Internationals: Poland U20, U21, Full caps.

2004–05	Gornik Zabrze	7	0	7	0
2005–06	Southampton	5	0		
2006–07	Southampton	8	0		
2007–08	Southampton	1	0		
2008–09	Southampton	0	0		
2009–10	Southampton	7	0		
2009–10	*Barnsley*	2	0	2	0
2010–11	Southampton	0	0		

2011–12	Southampton	1	0	**22**	**0**
2012–13	Notts Co	40	0		
2013–14	Notts Co	44	0	**84**	**0**
2014–15	Ipswich T	31	0		
2015–16	Ipswich T	20	0		
2016–17	Ipswich T	44	0		
2017–18	Ipswich T	45	0	**140**	**0**

BISHOP, Teddy (M)   **60 1**
H: 5 11 W: 10 03 b.Cambridge 15-7-96

2013–14	Ipswich T	0	0		
2014–15	Ipswich T	33	1		
2015–16	Ipswich T	4	0		
2016–17	Ipswich T	19	0		
2017–18	Ipswich T	4	0	**60**	**1**

BRU, Kevin (M)   **235 13**
H: 6 0 W: 11 05 b.Paris 12-12-88
Internationals: France U19. Mauritius Full caps.

2006–07	Rennes	2	0	**2**	**0**
2007–08	Chataeroux	10	0	**10**	**0**
2008–09	Clermont Foot Avergne	25	2	**25**	**2**
2009–10	Dijon	14	2		
2010–11	Dijon	11	0	**25**	**2**
2010–11	Bologne	9	0		
2011–12	Bologne	19	2	**28**	**2**
2012–13	Istres	31	2	**31**	**2**
2013–14	Levski Sofia	20	1	**20**	**1**
2014–15	Ipswich T	31	1		
2015–16	Ipswich T	28	2		
2016–17	Ipswich T	26	1		
2017–18	Ipswich T	9	0	**94**	**4**

CARAYOL, Mustapha (F)   **207 31**
H: 5 10 W: 11 11 b.Gambia 10-6-89
Internationals: Gambia Full caps.

2007–08	Milton Keynes D	0	0		
2009–10	Torquay U	20	6	**20**	**6**
2010–11	Lincoln C	33	3	**33**	**3**
2011–12	Bristol R	30	4		
2012–13	Bristol R	0	0	**30**	**4**
2012–13	Middlesbrough	18	3		
2013–14	Middlesbrough	32	8		
2014–15	Middlesbrough	0	0		
2014–15	*Brighton & HA*	5	0	**5**	**0**
2015–16	Middlesbrough	0	0	**50**	**11**
2015–16	*Huddersfield T*	15	3	**15**	**3**
2015–16	*Leeds U*	12	1	**12**	**1**
2016–17	Nottingham F	19	1		
2017–18	Nottingham F	15	1	**34**	**2**
2017–18	Ipswich T	8	1	**8**	**1**

CHAMBERS, Luke (D)   **592 33**
H: 6 1 W: 11 13 b.Kettering 29-8-85

2002–03	Northampton T	1	0		
2003–04	Northampton T	24	0		
2004–05	Northampton T	27	0		
2005–06	Northampton T	43	0		
2006–07	Northampton T	29	1	**124**	**1**
2006–07	Nottingham F	14	0		
2007–08	Nottingham F	42	6		
2008–09	Nottingham F	39	2		
2009–10	Nottingham F	23	3		
2010–11	Nottingham F	44	6		
2011–12	Nottingham F	43	0	**205**	**17**
2012–13	Ipswich T	44	3		
2013–14	Ipswich T	46	3		
2014–15	Ipswich T	45	1		
2015–16	Ipswich T	45	3		
2016–17	Ipswich T	46	4		
2017–18	Ipswich T	37	1	**263**	**15**

COTTER, Barry (D)   **2 0**
b. 4-12-98
From Limerick.

2017–18	Ipswich T	2	0	**2**	**0**

CROWE, Michael (G)   **0 0**
H: 6 2 W: 11 11 b.London 13-11-95
Internationals: Wales U19, U21, Full caps.

2013–14	Ipswich T	0	0		
2014–15	Ipswich T	0	0		
2014–15	Woking	0	0		
2015–16	Ipswich T	0	0		
2015–16	*Stevenage*	0	0		
2016–17	Ipswich T	0	0		
2017–18	Ipswich T	0	0		

DOWNES, Flynn (M)   **20 0**
H: 5 8 W: 11 00 b. 20-1-99
Internationals: England U19.

2016–17	Ipswich T	0	0		
2017–18	Ipswich T	10	0	**10**	**0**
2017–18	*Luton T*	10	0	**10**	**0**

DOZZELL, Andre (M)   **9 1**
b.Ipswich 2-5-99
Internationals: England U16, U17, U18, U19.

2015–16	Ipswich T	2	1		
2016–17	Ipswich T	6	0		
2017–18	Ipswich T	1	0	**9**	**1**

DRINAN, Aaron (F)   **0 0**
b.Cork 6-5-98
From Cork C, Waterford U.

2017–18	Ipswich T	0	0		

EMMANUEL, Josh (D)   **52 0**
H: 5 11 W: 11 00 b.London 18-8-97

2015–16	Ipswich T	4	0		
2015–16	*Crawley T*	2	0	**2**	**0**
2016–17	Ipswich T	15	0		
2017–18	Ipswich T	0	0	**19**	**0**
2017–18	*Rotherham U*	31	0	**31**	**0**

FOLAMI, Ben (F)   **4 0**
b.Sydney 8-6-99

2017–18	Ipswich T	4	0	**4**	**0**

FOWLER, George (D)   **0 0**

2016–17	Ipswich T	0	0		
2017–18	Ipswich T	0	0		

GARNER, Joe (F)   **363 108**
H: 5 10 W: 11 02 b.Blackburn 12-4-88
Internationals: England U16, U17, U19.

2004–05	Blackburn R	0	0		
2005–06	Blackburn R	0	0		
2006–07	Blackburn R	0	0		
2006–07	Carlisle U	18	5		
2007–08	Carlisle U	31	14		
2008–09	Nottingham F	28	7		
2009–10	Nottingham F	18	2		
2010–11	Nottingham F	0	0		
2010–11	*Huddersfield T*	16	0	**16**	**0**
2010–11	*Scunthorpe U*	18	6	**18**	**6**
2011–12	Nottingham F	2	0	**48**	**9**
2011–12	Watford	22	1		
2012–13	Watford	2	0	**24**	**1**
2012–13	*Carlisle U*	16	7	**65**	**26**
2012–13	Preston NE	14	0		
2013–14	Preston NE	35	18		
2014–15	Preston NE	37	25		
2015–16	Preston NE	41	6		
2016–17	Preston NE	2	0	**129**	**49**
2016–17	Rangers	31	7	**31**	**7**
2017–18	Ipswich T	32	10	**32**	**10**

GERKEN, Dean (G)   **255 0**
H: 6 2 W: 12 00 b.Southend 22-5-85

2003–04	Colchester U	1	0		
2004–05	Colchester U	13	0		
2005–06	Colchester U	7	0		
2006–07	Colchester U	27	0		
2007–08	Colchester U	40	0		
2008–09	Colchester U	21	0	**109**	**0**
2008–09	*Darlington*	7	0	**7**	**0**
2009–10	Bristol C	39	0		
2010–11	Bristol C	1	0		
2011–12	Bristol C	10	0		
2012–13	Bristol C	3	0	**53**	**0**
2013–14	Ipswich T	41	0		
2014–15	Ipswich T	16	0		
2015–16	Ipswich T	26	0		
2016–17	Ipswich T	2	0		
2017–18	Ipswich T	1	0	**86**	**0**

GLEESON, Stephen (M)   **349 26**
H: 6 2 W: 11 00 b.Dublin 3-8-88
Internationals: Republic of Ireland U21, Full caps.

2006–07	Wolverhampton W	3	0		
2006–07	*Stockport Co*	14	2		
2007–08	Wolverhampton W	0	0		
2007–08	*Hereford U*	4	0	**4**	**0**
2007–08	*Stockport Co*	6	0		
2008–09	Wolverhampton W	0	0	**3**	**0**
2008–09	*Stockport Co*	21	2	**41**	**4**
2008–09	*Milton Keynes D*	5	0		
2009–10	Milton Keynes D	29	0		
2010–11	Milton Keynes D	36	2		
2011–12	Milton Keynes D	5	0		
2012–13	Milton Keynes D	30	6		
2013–14	Milton Keynes D	35	3	**174**	**16**
2014–15	Birmingham C	39	0		
2015–16	Birmingham C	44	5		
2016–17	Birmingham C	29	1		
2017–18	Birmingham C	5	0	**117**	**6**
2017–18	Ipswich T	10	0	**10**	**0**

HUWS, Emyr (M)   **94 10**
H: 5 10 W: 11 07 b.Llanelli 30-9-93
Internationals: Wales U17, U19, U21, Full caps.

2010–11	Manchester C	0	0		
2011–12	Manchester C	0	0		
2012–13	Manchester C	0	0		
2012–13	*Northampton T*	10	0	**10**	**0**
2013–14	Manchester C	0	0		
2013–14	*Birmingham C*	17	2	**17**	**2**
2014–15	Wigan Ath	16	0		
2015–16	Wigan Ath	0	0	**16**	**0**
2015–16	*Huddersfield T*	30	5	**30**	**5**
2016–17	Cardiff C	3	0		
2016–17	*Ipswich T*	13	3		
2017–18	Cardiff C	0	0	**3**	**0**
2017–18	Ipswich T	5	0	**18**	**3**

HYAM, Luke (M)   **136 3**
H: 5 10 W: 11 05 b.Ipswich 24-10-91

2010–11	Ipswich T	10	0		
2011–12	Ipswich T	8	0		
2012–13	Ipswich T	30	1		
2013–14	Ipswich T	35	1		
2014–15	Ipswich T	16	1		
2015–16	Ipswich T	15	0		
2015–16	*Rotherham U*	5	0	**5**	**0**
2017–18	Ipswich T	17	0	**131**	**3**

KENLOCK, Myles (D)   **36 0**
H: 6 1 W: 10 08 b.Croydon 29-11-96

2015–16	Ipswich T	2	0		
2016–17	Ipswich T	18	0		
2017–18	Ipswich T	16	0	**36**	**0**

KNUDSEN, Jonas (D)   **225 8**
H: 6 1 W: 11 05 b.Esbjerg 16-9-92
Internationals: Denmark U18, U19, U20, U21, Full caps.

2009–10	Esbjerg	7	0		
2010–11	Esberg	5	0	**5**	**0**
2011–12	Esbjerg	0	0		
2012–13	Esbjerg	32	1		
2013–14	Esbjerg	31	1		
2014–15	Esbjerg	28	2		
2015–16	Esbjerg	2	0	**100**	**4**
2015–16	Ipswich T	42	1		
2016–17	Ipswich T	36	2		
2017–18	Ipswich T	42	1	**120**	**4**

McDONNELL, Adam (M)   **2 0**
H: 5 9 W: 11 05 b.Dublin 14-5-97
Internationals: Republic of Ireland U16, U17, U18, U19.
From Shelbourne.

2014–15	Ipswich T	0	0		
2015–16	Ipswich T	1	0		
2016–17	Ipswich T	0	0		
2017–18	Ipswich T	1	0	**2**	**0**

McGOLDRICK, David (F)   **338 85**
H: 6 1 W: 11 10 b.Nottingham 29-11-87
Internationals: Republic of Ireland Full caps.

2003–04	Notts Co	4	0		
2004–05	Notts Co	0	0		
2005–06	Southampton	1	0		
2005–06	*Notts Co*	6	0	**10**	**0**
2006–07	Southampton	9	0		
2006–07	*Bournemouth*	12	6	**12**	**6**
2007–08	Southampton	8	0		
2007–08	*Port Vale*	17	2	**17**	**2**
2008–09	Southampton	46	12	**64**	**12**
2009–10	Nottingham F	33	3		
2010–11	Nottingham F	21	5		
2011–12	Nottingham F	9	0		
2011–12	*Sheffield W*	4	1	**4**	**1**
2012–13	Nottingham F	0	0	**63**	**8**
2012–13	*Coventry C*	22	16	**22**	**16**
2012–13	*Ipswich T*	13	4		
2013–14	Ipswich T	31	14		
2014–15	Ipswich T	26	7		
2015–16	Ipswich T	24	4		
2016–17	Ipswich T	30	5		
2017–18	Ipswich T	22	6	**146**	**40**

McKENDRY, Conor (M)   **0 0**
b.Carnlough 21-10-98
Internationals: Northern Ireland U16, U17.
From Glenavon.

2017–18	Ipswich T	0	0		

McLOUGHLIN, Shane (D)   **1 0**
b.Castleisland 1-3-97
Internationals: Republic of Ireland U18, U19.

2014–15	Ipswich T	0	0		
2015–16	Ipswich T	0	0		
2016–17	Ipswich T	0	0		
2017–18	Ipswich T	1	0	**1**	**0**

MORRIS, Ben (F)   3   0
b. 6-6-99
Internationals: England U17, U18.

2016–17	Ipswich T	0	0		
2017–18	Ipswich T	3	0	3	0

NYDAM, Tristan (M)   18   0
H: 5 7   W: 9 06   b. 6-11-99
Internationals: England U18, U19.

2016–17	Ipswich T	0	0		
2017–18	Ipswich T	18	0	18	0

PATTERSON, Monty (F)   4   0
b.Auckland 12-6-96
Internationals: New Zealand U17, U20, U23, Full caps.

2017–18	Ipswich T	0	0		
2017–18	*Wellington Phoenix*	4	0	4	0

ROWE, Danny (M)   18   1
H: 6 0   b.Wythenshawe 9-3-92

2017–18	Ipswich T	4	0		
2017–18	Ipswich T	2	0	6	0
2017–18	*Lincoln C*	12	1	12	1

SEARS, Freddie (F)   327   57
H: 5 8   W: 10 01   b.Hornchurch 27-11-89
Internationals: England U19, U20, U21.

2007–08	West Ham U	7	1		
2008–09	West Ham U	17	0		
2009–10	West Ham U	1	0		
2009–10	*Crystal Palace*	18	0	18	0
2009–10	*Coventry C*	10	0	10	0
2010–11	West Ham U	11	1		
2010–11	*Scunthorpe U*	9	0	9	0
2011–12	West Ham U	10	0	46	2
2011–12	*Colchester C*	11	2		
2012–13	Colchester U	35	7		
2013–14	Colchester U	32	12		
2014–15	Colchester U	24	10	102	31
2014–15	Ipswich T	21	9		
2015–16	Ipswich T	45	6		
2016–17	Ipswich T	40	7		
2017–18	Ipswich T	36	2	142	24

SKUSE, Cole (M)   480   11
H: 6 1   W: 11 05   b.Bristol 29-3-86

2004–05	Bristol C	7	0		
2005–06	Bristol C	38	2		
2006–07	Bristol C	42	0		
2007–08	Bristol C	25	0		
2008–09	Bristol C	33	2		
2009–10	Bristol C	43	2		
2010–11	Bristol C	30	1		
2011–12	Bristol C	36	2		
2012–13	Bristol C	25	0	279	9
2013–14	Ipswich T	43	0		
2014–15	Ipswich T	40	1		
2015–16	Ipswich T	39	0		
2016–17	Ipswich T	40	0		
2017–18	Ipswich T	39	1	201	2

SMITH, Chris (D)   0   0
b.Ipswich 21-2-98

2017–18	Ipswich T	0	0

SMITH, Tommy (D)   261   21
H: 6 2   W: 12 02   b.Macclesfield 31-3-90
Internationals: England U17, U18. New Zealand Full caps.

2007–08	Ipswich T	0	0		
2008–09	Ipswich T	2	0		
2009–10	Ipswich T	14	0		
2009–10	*Brentford*	8	0	8	0
2010–11	Ipswich T	22	3		
2010–11	*Colchester U*	6	0	6	0
2011–12	Ipswich T	26	3		
2012–13	Ipswich T	38	3		
2013–14	Ipswich T	45	6		
2014–15	Ipswich T	42	4		
2015–16	Ipswich T	45	2		
2016–17	Ipswich T	10	0		
2017–18	Ipswich T	3	0	247	21

Transferred to Colorado Rapids, January 2018.

SPENCE, Jordan (D)   218   6
H: 6 2   W: 12 07   b.Woodford 24-5-90
Internationals: England U16, U17, U18, U19, U21.

2007–08	West Ham U	0	0		
2008–09	West Ham U	0	0		
2008–09	*Leyton Orient*	20	0	20	0
2009–10	West Ham U	1	0		
2009–10	*Scunthorpe U*	9	0	9	0
2010–11	West Ham U	2	0		
2010–11	*Bristol C*	11	0		
2011–12	West Ham U	0	0		
2011–12	*Bristol C*	10	0	21	0
2012–13	West Ham U	4	0		
2013–14	West Ham U	0	0	7	0
2013–14	*Sheffield W*	4	0	4	0
2013–14	*Milton Keynes D*	29	2		
2014–15	*Milton Keynes D*	38	0		
2015–16	*Milton Keynes D*	33	0		
2016–17	*Milton Keynes D*	0	0	100	2
2016–17	Ipswich T	17	0		
2017–18	Ipswich T	40	4	57	4

WAGHORN, Martyn (F)   274   76
H: 5 9   W: 13 01   b.South Shields 23-1-90
Internationals: England U19, U21.

2007–08	Sunderland	3	0		
2008–09	Sunderland	1	0		
2008–09	*Charlton Ath*	7	1	7	1
2009–10	Sunderland	0	0		
2009–10	*Leicester C*	43	12		
2010–11	Sunderland	2	0	6	0
2010–11	Leicester C	30	4		
2011–12	Leicester C	4	1		
2011–12	*Hull C*	5	1	5	1
2012–13	Leicester C	24	3		
2013–14	Leicester C	2	0	103	20
2013–14	*Millwall*	14	3	14	3
2013–14	*Wigan Ath*	15	5		
2014–15	Wigan Ath	23	3	38	8
2015–16	Rangers	25	20		
2016–17	Rangers	32	7	57	27
2017–18	Ipswich T	44	16	44	16

WARD, Grant (M)   154   11
H: 5 10   W: 11 07   b.Lewisham 5-12-94

2013–14	Tottenham H	0	0		
2014	*Chicago Fire*	23	1	23	1
2014–15	Tottenham H	0	0		
2014–15	*Coventry C*	11	0	11	0
2015–16	Tottenham H	0	0		
2015–16	*Rotherham U*	40	2	40	2
2016–17	Ipswich T	43	6		
2017–18	Ipswich T	37	2	80	8

WEBBER, Patrick (D)   0   0

2016–17	Ipswich T	0	0
2017–18	Ipswich T	0	0

WEBSTER, Adam (D)   118   6
H: 6 1   W: 11 11   b.West Wittering 4-1-95
Internationals: England U18, U19.

2011–12	Portsmouth	3	0		
2012–13	Portsmouth	18	0		
2013–14	Portsmouth	4	2		
2014–15	Portsmouth	15	1		
2015–16	Portsmouth	27	2	67	5
2016–17	Ipswich T	23	1		
2017–18	Ipswich T	28	0	51	1

WOOLFENDEN, Luke (D)   2   0
b.Ipswich 21-10-98

2017–18	Ipswich T	2	0	2	0

Players retained or with offer of contract
George-Kenlock, Myles Lewis; Wright, Harry Edward.

Scholars
Barley, Henry James Stuart; Brown, Kai Stephen; Cahill, Steven John; Clements, Bailey James; Crowe, Dylan; Dobra, Armando; Egan, Toby Joe; El, Mizouni Idris; Foudil, Lounes Mohamed; Henry, Ashton Donald; Hughes, Thomas; Lankester, Jack Richard; Marshall, Ross Steven; McGavin, Brett; Murrell, Ellis Andrew John; Ndaba, Corrie Richard; Ronan, Kian; Vega, Luca; Ware, Mitchell Vincent; Wilton, Albert.

LEEDS U (44)

ALIOSKI, Ezgjan (M)   179   30
b.Prilep 12-2-92
Internationals: Macedonia U19, U21, Full caps.

2012–13	Young Boys	0	0		
2012–13	Schaffhausen	10	0		
2013–14	Schaffhausen	26	2		
2014–15	Schaffhausen	35	2		
2015–16	Schaffhausen	16	0	87	4
2015–16	Lugano	16	3		
2016–17	Lugano	34	16	50	19
2017–18	Leeds U	42	7	42	7

ANITA, Vurnon (M)   260   7
H: 5 5   W: 10 04   b.Willemstad 4-4-89
Internationals: Netherlands U15, U17, U19, U20, U21, Full caps.

2005–06	Ajax	1	0		
2006–07	Ajax	1	0		
2008–09	Ajax	16	0		
2009–10	Ajax	26	0		
2010–11	Ajax	31	3		
2011–12	Ajax	33	2		
2012–13	Ajax	1	0	109	5
2012–13	Newcastle U	25	0		
2013–14	Newcastle U	34	1		
2014–15	Newcastle U	19	0		
2015–16	Newcastle U	28	1		
2016–17	Newcastle U	27	0	133	2
2017–18	Leeds U	18	0	18	0

ANTONSSON, Marcus (F)   159   41
H: 5 11   W: 12 08   b.Unnaryds 8-5-91

2010	Halmstad	1	0		
2011	Halmstad	6	0		
2012	Halmstad	18	1		
2013	Halmstad	20	4		
2014	Halmstad	26	6	71	11
2015	Kalmar	29	12		
2016	Kalmar	12	10	41	22
2016–17	Leeds U	16	1		
2017–18	Leeds U	0	0	16	1
2017–18	*Blackburn R*	31	7	31	7

AYLING, Luke (D)   315   6
H: 5 11   W: 10 08   b.Lambeth 25-8-91

2009–10	Arsenal	0	0		
2009–10	*Yeovil T*	4	0		
2010–11	*Yeovil T*	37	0		
2011–12	Yeovil T	44	0		
2012–13	Yeovil T	39	0		
2013–14	Yeovil T	42	2	166	2
2014–15	Bristol C	46	4		
2015–16	Bristol C	33	0		
2016–17	Bristol C	1	0	80	4
2016–17	Leeds U	42	0		
2017–18	Leeds U	27	0	69	0

BERARDI, Gaetano (D)   247   0
H: 5 10   W: 11 00   b.Sorengo 21-8-88
Internationals: Switzerland U20, U21, Full caps.

2006–07	Brescia	1	0		
2007–08	Brescia	9	0		
2008–09	Brescia	26	0		
2009–10	Brescia	29	0		
2010–11	Brescia	27	0		
2011–12	Brescia	13	0	105	0
2011–12	Sampdoria	9	0		
2012–13	Sampdoria	21	0		
2013–14	Sampdoria	5	0	35	0
2014–15	Leeds U	22	0		
2015–16	Leeds U	28	0		
2016–17	Leeds U	26	0		
2017–18	Leeds U	31	0	107	0

CIBICKI, Pawel (M)   90   21
b. 9-1-94
Internationals: Poland U19, U20. Sweden U21.

2013	Malmo	7	0		
2014	Malmo	21	3		
2015	Malmo	9	3		
2016	Malmo	0	0		
2016	*Jonkopings Sodra*	26	10	26	10
2017	Malmo	20	5	57	11
2017–18	Malmo FF	0	0		
2017–18	Leeds U	7	0	7	0

CLARKE, Jack (F)   0   0
b.York 23-11-00

2017–18	Leeds U	0	0

COOPER, Liam (D)   201   9
H: 6 2   W: 13 07   b.Hull 30-8-91
Internationals: Scotland U17, U19.

2008–09	Hull C	0	0		
2009–10	Hull C	2	0		
2010–11	Hull C	2	0		
2010–11	*Carlisle U*	6	1	6	1
2011–12	Hull C	7	0		
2011–12	*Huddersfield T*	4	0	4	0
2012–13	Hull C	0	0	11	0
2012–13	Chesterfield	29	2		
2013–14	Chesterfield	41	3		
2014–15	Chesterfield	1	0	71	5
2014–15	Leeds U	29	1		
2015–16	Leeds U	39	1		
2016–17	Leeds U	11	0		
2017–18	Leeds U	30	1	109	3

COYLE, Lewie (M)   57   0
H: 5 8   W: 10 08   b.Hull 15-10-95

2015–16	Leeds U	11	0		
2016–17	Leeds U	4	0		
2017–18	Leeds U	0	0	15	0
2017–18	*Fleetwood T*	42	0	42	0

DALLAS, Stuart (M) — 201 44
H: 6 0 W: 12 09 b.Cookstown 19-4-91
Internationals: Northern Ireland U21, U23, Full caps.

Season	Club	App	Gls		
2010–11	Crusaders	13	16		
2011–12	Crusaders	8	8	21	24
2012–13	Brentford	7	0		
2013–14	Brentford	18	2		
2013–14	*Northampton T*	12	3	12	3
2014–15	Brentford	38	6	63	8
2015–16	Leeds U	45	5		
2016–17	Leeds U	31	2		
2017–18	Leeds U	29	2	105	9

DE BOCK, Laurens (D) — 222 2
b.7-11-92
Internationals: Belgium U16, U17, U18, U19, U21.

Season	Club	App	Gls		
2009–10	Lokeren	5	0		
2010–11	Lokeren	25	0		
2011–12	Lokeren	29	1		
2012–13	Lokeren	21	0	80	1
2012–13	Club Brugge	11	0		
2013–14	Club Brugge	33	0		
2014–15	Club Brugge	36	0		
2015–16	Club Brugge	31	1		
2016–17	Club Brugge	18	0		
2017–18	Club Brugge	6	0	135	1
2017–18	Leeds U	7	0	7	0

DENTON, Tyler (D) — 15 0
H: 5 8 W: 10 06 b.Dewsbury 6-9-95
Internationals: England U17.

Season	Club	App	Gls		
2016–17	Leeds U	0	0		
2017–18	Port Vale	15	0	15	0
2017–18	Leeds U	0	0		

DIAZ, Hugo (D) — 1 0
b.9-2-97
From Deportivo La Coruna.

Season	Club	App	Gls		
2017–18	Leeds U	1	0	1	0

EDMONDSON, Ryan (F) — 1 0
b.20-5-01
From Leeds U.

Season	Club	App	Gls		
2017–18	Leeds U	1	0	1	0

EKUBAN, Caleb (F) — 140 30
b.Villafranca 23-2-94

Season	Club	App	Gls		
2012–13	Chievo Verona	0	0		
2013–14	Chievo Verona	0	0		
2013–14	*Sudtirol*	7	1	7	1
2013–14	*Lumezzane*	13	2		
2014–15	Chievo Verona	0	0		
2014–15	*Lumezzane*	35	5	48	7
2015–16	Chievo Verona	0	0		
2015–16	*Renate*	31	4	31	4
2016–17	Chievo Verona	0	0		
2016–17	*Partizani Tirana*	34	17	34	17
2017–18	Leeds U	20	1	20	1

FORSHAW, Adam (M) — 210 14
H: 6 1 W: 11 02 b.Liverpool 8-10-91

Season	Club	App	Gls		
2009–10	Everton	0	0		
2010–11	Everton	1	0		
2011–12	Everton	0	0	1	0
2011–12	*Brentford*	7	0		
2012–13	Brentford	43	3		
2013–14	Brentford	39	8	89	11
2014–15	Wigan Ath	16	1	16	1
2014–15	Middlesbrough	18	0		
2015–16	Middlesbrough	29	2		
2016–17	Middlesbrough	34	0		
2017–18	Middlesbrough	11	0	92	2
2017–18	Leeds U	12	0	12	0

GOMES, Madger (M) — 0 0
b.Alicante 1-2-97
Internationals: Spain U17, U18.
From Villareal, Liverpool.

Season	Club	App	Gls		
2017–18	Leeds U	0	0		

GROT, Jay-Roy (F) — 51 6
H: 6 4 W: 14 09 b.Arnhem 13-3-98
Internationals: Netherlands U19, U19.

Season	Club	App	Gls		
2015–16	NEC	10	0		
2016–17	NEC	20	5		
2017–18	NEC	1	0	31	5
2017–18	Leeds U	20	1	20	1

HERNANDEZ, Pablo (M) — 338 54
H: 5 8 W: 10 00 b.Castellon 11-4-85
Internationals: Spain Full caps.

Season	Club	App	Gls		
2005–06	Valencia	1	0		
2006–07	*Cadiz*	14	4	14	4
2007–08	Getafe	28	3	28	3
2008–09	Valencia	21	4		
2009–10	Valencia	33	5		
2010–11	Valencia	26	5		
2011–12	Valencia	30	3	111	17
2012–13	Swansea C	30	3		
2013–14	Swansea C	27	2	57	5
2014–15	Al Arabi	13	6		
2014–15	*Al-Nasr*	12	3	12	3
2015–16	Al Arabi	0	0	13	6
2015–16	*Rayo Vallecano*	27	3	27	3
2016–17	Leeds U	35	6		
2017–18	Leeds U	41	7	76	13

JANSSON, Pontus (D) — 199 17
H: 6 3 W: 13 08 b.Arlov 13-2-91
Internationals: Sweden U17, U19, U21, Full caps.

Season	Club	App	Gls		
2009	Malmo	2	0		
2009	*IFK Malmo*	9	4	9	4
2010	Malmo	18	1		
2011	Malmo	15	2		
2012	Malmo	30	1		
2013	Malmo	24	1		
2014	Malmo	9	1	98	6
2014–15	Torino	9	0		
2015–16	Torino	7	1	16	1

On loan from Torino.

Season	Club	App	Gls		
2016–17	Leeds U	34	3		
2017–18	Leeds U	42	3	76	6

KITCHING, Liam (D) — 0 0

Season	Club	App	Gls		
2017–18	Leeds U	0	0		

KLICH, Mateusz (M) — 166 22
H: 6 0 W: 10 10 b.Tarnow 13-6-90
Internationals: Poland U18, U19, U20, U21, Full caps.

Season	Club	App	Gls		
2008–09	Cracovia	8	0		
2009–10	Cracovia	21	1		
2010–11	Cracovia	27	4	56	5
2011–12	Wolfsburg	0	0		
2012–13	Wolfsburg	0	0		
2012–13	Zwolle	13	2		
2013–14	Zwolle	30	4	43	6
2014–15	Wolfsburg	0	0		
2014–15	Kaiserslautern	5	1		
2015–16	Kaiserslautern	16	3	21	4
2016–17	FC Twente	29	6	29	6
2017–18	Leeds U	4	0	4	0
2017–18	FC Utrecht	13	1	13	1

LASOGGA, Pierre-Michel (F) — 191 58
H: 6 2 W: 13 12 b.Gladbeck 15-12-91
Internationals: Germany U21.

Season	Club	App	Gls		
2009–10	Bayer Leverkusen	0	0		
2010–11	Hertha Berlin	25	13		
2011–12	Hertha Berlin	32	8		
2012–13	Hertha Berlin	7	1	64	22
2013–14	Hamburg	20	13		
2014–15	Hamburg	26	4		
2015–16	Hamburg	30	8		
2016–17	Hamburg	20	1		
2017–18	Hamburg	0	0	96	26

On loan from Hamburg.

Season	Club	App	Gls		
2017–18	Leeds U	31	10	31	10

LONERGAN, Andrew (G) — 346 1
H: 6 4 W: 13 02 b.Preston 19-10-83
Internationals: Republic of Ireland U16. England U20.

Season	Club	App	Gls		
2000–01	Preston NE	1	0		
2001–02	Preston NE	0	0		
2002–03	Preston NE	0	0		
2002–03	*Darlington*	2	0	2	0
2003–04	Preston NE	8	0		
2004–05	Preston NE	23	1		
2005–06	Preston NE	0	0		
2005–06	*Wycombe W*	2	0	2	0
2006–07	Preston NE	13	0		
2006–07	*Swindon T*	1	0	1	0
2007–08	Preston NE	43	0		
2008–09	Preston NE	46	0		
2009–10	Preston NE	45	0		
2010–11	Preston NE	29	0	208	1
2011–12	Leeds U	35	0		
2012–13	Bolton W	5	0		
2013–14	Bolton W	17	0		
2014–15	Bolton W	29	0	51	0
2015–16	Fulham	29	0	29	0
2016–17	Wolverhampton W	11	0		
2017–18	Wolverhampton W	0	0	11	0
2017–18	Leeds U	7	0	42	0

MURPHY, Luke (M) — 321 30
H: 6 1 W: 11 05 b.Alsager 21-10-89

Season	Club	App	Gls		
2008–09	Crewe Alex	9	1		
2009–10	Crewe Alex	32	3		
2010–11	Crewe Alex	39	3		
2011–12	Crewe Alex	42	8		
2012–13	Crewe Alex	39	6	161	21
2013–14	Leeds U	37	3		
2014–15	Leeds U	30	3		
2015–16	Leeds U	36	1		
2016–17	Leeds U	0	0		
2016–17	Burton Alb	19	1		
2017–18	Leeds U	0	0	103	7
2017–18	Burton Alb	38	1	57	2

NICELL, Callum (M) — 0 0
b.30-10-99
Internationals: Republic of Ireland U18, U19.

Season	Club	App	Gls		
2017–18	Leeds U	0	0		

O'CONNOR, Paudie (D) — 4 0
b.Limerick 14-7-97
From Limerick.

Season	Club	App	Gls		
2017–18	Leeds U	4	0	4	0

O'KANE, Eunan (M) — 276 18
H: 5 8 W: 13 04 b.Derry 10-7-90
Internationals: Northern Ireland U16, U17, U19, U20, U21. Republic of Ireland U21, Full caps.

Season	Club	App	Gls		
2007–08	Everton	0	0		
2008–09	Everton	0	0		
2009–10	Coleraine	13	4	13	4
2009–10	Torquay U	16	1		
2010–11	Torquay U	45	6		
2011–12	Torquay U	45	5		
2012–13	Torquay U	0	0	106	12
2013–14	Bournemouth	37	1		
2014–15	Bournemouth	11	0		
2015–16	Bournemouth	16	0	101	2
2016–17	Leeds U	24	0		
2017–18	Leeds U	32	0	56	0

PEACOCK-FARRELL, Bailey (G) — 12 0
H: 6 2 W: 11 07 b.Darlington 29-10-96
Internationals: Northern Ireland U21, Full caps.

Season	Club	App	Gls		
2015–16	Leeds U	1	0		
2016–17	Leeds U	0	0		
2017–18	Leeds U	11	0	12	0

PEARCE, Tom (D) — 5 1
b.Ormskirk 12-4-98
Internationals: England U21.
From Everton.

Season	Club	App	Gls		
2017–18	Leeds U	5	1	5	1

PHILIPS, Kalvin (M) — 86 9
H: 5 10 W: 11 05 b.Leeds 2-12-95

Season	Club	App	Gls		
2014–15	Leeds U	2	1		
2015–16	Leeds U	10	0		
2016–17	Leeds U	33	1		
2017–18	Leeds U	41	7	86	9

REY, Oriol (D) — 0 0
b.Barcelona 25-2-98
From Barcelona.

Season	Club	App	Gls		
2017–18	Leeds U	0	0		

ROBERTS, Tyler (F) — 45 9
H: 5 11 W: 11 11 b.Gloucester 12-1-98
Internationals: Wales U16, U17, U19, U20, U21.

Season	Club	App	Gls		
2014–15	WBA	0	0		
2015–16	WBA	1	0		
2016–17	WBA	0	0	1	0
2016–17	*Oxford U*	14	0	14	0
2016–17	*Shrewsbury T*	13	4	13	4
2017–18	Leeds U	0	0		
2017–18	Walsall	17	5	17	5

ROOFE, Kemar (M) — 151 39
H: 5 10 W: 11 03 b.Walsall 6-1-93

Season	Club	App	Gls		
2011–12	WBA	0	0		
2012–13	WBA	0	0		
2012–13	*Northampton T*	6	0	6	0
2013–14	WBA	0	0		
2013–14	*Cheltenham T*	9	1	9	1
2014–15	WBA	0	0		
2014–15	*Colchester U*	2	0	2	0
2014–15	Oxford U	16	6		
2015–16	Oxford U	40	18	56	24
2016–17	Leeds U	42	3		
2017–18	Leeds U	36	11	78	14

SACKO, Hadi (F) — 93 7
H: 6 0 W: 12 06 b.Corbeil-Essonnes 24-3-94
Internationals: France U16, U18, U19, U20. Mali Full caps.

Season	Club	App	Gls		
2012–13	Bordeaux	4	0		
2013–14	Bordeaux	5	0		
2013–14	*Le Havre*	18	4	18	4
2014–15	Bordeaux	2	0	11	0
2014–15	Sporting Lisbon	0	0		
2015–16	Sporting Lisbon	0	0		

SAMUEL, Saiz (F) — continued

2015–16	Sochaux	12	1	12	1
2016–17	Sporting Lisbon	0	0		
2016–17	Leeds U	38	2		
2017–18	Leeds U	14	0	52	2

SAMUEL, Saiz (F)   122 21
H: 5 9 W: 10 10 b.Madrid 22-1-91
Internationals: Spain U19.

2009–10	Real Madrid	0	0		
2010–11	Real Madrid	0	0		
2011–12	Melilla	16	1	16	1
2011–12	Getafe	1	0		
2012–13	Getafe	0	0	1	0
2013–14	Almeria	0	0		
2014–15	Atletico Madrid	0	0		
2015–16	Atletico Madrid	0	0		
2015–16	Huesca	29	3		
2016–17	Huesca	42	12		
2017–18	Leeds U	35	4	71	15
2017–18	Leeds U	34	5	34	5

SHAUGHNESSY, Conor Glynn (M)   9 0
H: 6 3 W: 11 09 b.30-6-96
Internationals: Republic of Ireland U16, U17, U18, U21, Full caps.

2013–14	Reading	0	0		
2017–18	Leeds U	9	0	9	0

STEVENS, Jordan (M)   9 0
b. 25-3-00

2017–18	Forest Green R	9	0	9	0
2017–18	Leeds U	0	0		

STOKES, Eoghan (F)   0 0
b. 22-11-95
Internationals: Republic of Ireland U16, U17, U19.

2013–14	Leeds U	0	0		
2014–15	Leeds U	0	0		
2015–16	Leeds U	0	0		
2016–17	Leeds U	0	0		
2017–18	Leeds U	0	0		

Transferred to Bohemians, January 2018.

STRUIJK, Pascal (D)   0 0
Internationals: Netherlands U17.
From Ajax.

2017–18	Leeds U	0	0		

VIEIRA, Romario (M)   0 0
Internationals: Guinea-Bissau Full caps.
From Tadcaster Alb.

2017–18	Leeds U	0	0		

VIEIRA, Ronaldo (M)   63 1
H: 5 11 W: 12 04 b.Bissau 10-8-98
Internationals: England U20, U21.

2015–16	Leeds U	1	0		
2016–17	Leeds U	34	1		
2017–18	Leeds U	28	0	63	1

WIEDWALD, Felix (G)   145 0
H: 6 3 W: 12 13 b.Thedinghausen 15-3-90
Internationals: Germany U20.

2009–10	Werder Bremen	0	0		
2010–11	Werder Bremen	0	0		
2011–12	Duisburg	20	0		
2012–13	Duisburg	27	0	47	0
2013–14	Eintracht Frankfurt	0	0		
2014–15	Eintracht Frankfurt	10	0	11	0
2015–16	Werder Bremen	34	0		
2016–17	Werder Bremen	25	0	59	0
2017–18	Leeds U	28	0	28	0

WILKS, Mallik (F)   25 3
b.Leeds 15-12-98

2016–17	Leeds U	0	0		
2017–18	Leeds U	0	0		
2017–18	Accrington S	19	3	19	3
2017–18	Grimsby T	6	0	6	0

Players retained or with offer of contract
Amissah, Samuel; Balboa, Balboa Adrian; Bouy, Ouasim; Dalby, Samuel George; Downing, Matthew Christopher; Gotts, Robbie; Halme, Aapo Ilmari; Hosannah, Bryce Joseph; Huffer, William Matthew Scobie; Ideguchi, Yosuke; Kamwa, Bobby-Emmanuel; Machuca, Mauricio Alejandro; McCalmont, Alfie John; Miazek, Kamil; Mihaylov, Dzhoshkun Temenuzhkov; Oduor, Clarke Sydney Omondi; Sarkic, Oliver; Shackleton, Jamie Stuart; Siddiki, El Horfi Ousama; Wollerton, Alexander.

Scholars
Abioye, Moses Falola; Casey, Oliver Joseph; Edmondson, Ryan David; Hudson, Theodore Douglas; Huggins, Niall Joseph; Keogh, Matthew Liam; Kroma, Moise; Lyons, Luke Anthony; Male, Harrison Darren; Odunston, Lucas Thomas; Rae, Joshua Hugh; Stanley, Joseph Thomas.

LEICESTER C (45)

ADRIEN SILVA, Sebastien (M)   220 36
H: 5 9 W: 11 11 b.Angouleme 15-3-89
Internationals: Portugal U16, U17, U18, U19, U21, Full caps.

2007–08	Sporting Lisbon	6	0		
2008–09	Sporting Lisbon	13	0		
2009–10	Sporting Lisbon	13	0		
2010–11	Sporting Lisbon	0	0		
2010–11	Maccabi Haifa	6	0	6	0
2010–11	Academica	6	1	6	1
2011–12	Sporting Lisbon	0	0		
2011–12	Academica	28	4	28	4
2012–13	Sporting Lisbon	19	3		
2013–14	Sporting Lisbon	28	8		
2014–15	Sporting Lisbon	30	8		
2015–16	Sporting Lisbon	29	8		
2016–17	Sporting Lisbon	27	4		
2017–18	Sporting Lisbon	3	0	168	31
2017–18	Leicester C	12	0	12	0

ALBRIGHTON, Marc (M)   213 15
H: 6 2 W: 12 06 b.Tamworth 18-11-89
Internationals: England U20, U21.

2008–09	Aston Villa	0	0		
2009–10	Aston Villa	3	0		
2010–11	Aston Villa	29	5		
2011–12	Aston Villa	26	2		
2012–13	Aston Villa	9	0		
2013–14	Aston Villa	19	0	86	7
2013–14	Wigan Ath	4	0	4	0
2014–15	Leicester C	18	2		
2015–16	Leicester C	38	2		
2016–17	Leicester C	33	2		
2017–18	Leicester C	34	2	123	8

AMARTEY, Daniel (M)   115 4
H: 6 0 W: 12 04 b.Accra 1-12-94
Internationals: Ghana U20, Full caps.

2013	Djurgardens	23	0		
2014	Djurgardens	11	0	34	0
2014–15	Copenhagen	29	3		
2015–16	Copenhagen	15	0	44	3
2015–16	Leicester C	5	0		
2016–17	Leicester C	24	1		
2017–18	Leicester C	8	0	37	1

BARNES, Harvey (M)   47 11
b. 8-12-97
Internationals: England U18, U20.

2016–17	Leicester C	0	0		
2016–17	Milton Keynes D	21	6	21	6
2017–18	Leicester C	3	0	3	0
2017–18	Barnsley	23	5	23	5

BENALOUANE, Yohan (D)   176 5
H: 6 1 W: 12 06 b.Bagnois-sur-Ceze 28-3-87
Internationals: France U21. Tunisia Full caps.

2007–08	St Etienne	6	1		
2008–09	St Etienne	29	1		
2009–10	St Etienne	29	1		
2010–11	St Etienne	1	0	65	3
2010–11	Cesena	15	0		
2011–12	Cesena	11	0		
2012–13	Cesena	0	0	26	0
2012–13	Parma	21	1		
2013–14	Parma	4	0	25	1
2013–14	Atalanta	17	0		
2014–15	Atalanta	27	1	44	1
2015–16	Leicester C	4	0		
2015–16	Fiorentina	0	0		
2016–17	Leicester C	11	0		
2017–18	Leicester C	1	0	16	0

CHILWELL, Ben (D)   44 1
H: 5 10 W: 11 03 b.Milton Keynes 21-12-96
Internationals: England U18, U19, U20, U21.

2015–16	Leicester C	0	0		
2015–16	Huddersfield T	8	0	8	0
2016–17	Leicester C	12	1		
2017–18	Leicester C	24	0	36	1

CHOUDHURY, Hamza (M)   34 0
H: 5 10 W: 10 01 b.Loughborough 1-10-97
Internationals: England U21.

2015–16	Leicester C	0	0		
2015–16	Burton Alb	13	0		
2016–17	Leicester C	0	0		
2016–17	Burton Alb	13	0	26	0
2017–18	Leicester C	8	0	8	0

DIABATE, Fousseni (M)   14 0
H: 5 9 W: 10 06 b.Aubervilliers 18-10-95
Internationals: Mali U20, U23.
From Rennes, Reims.

2016–17	Guingamp	0	0		
2017–18	Ajaccio GFCO	0	0		
2017–18	Leicester C	14	0	14	0

DRAGOVIC, Aleksander (D)   241 5
H: 6 0 W: 12 00 b.Vienna 6-3-91
Internationals: Austria U17, U19, Full caps.

2008–09	Austria Vienna	17	0		
2009–10	Austria Vienna	32	0		
2010–11	Austria Vienna	18	1	67	1
2010–11	Basel	16	0		
2011–12	Basel	28	1		
2012–13	Basel	32	3		
2013–14	Basel	1	0	77	4
2013–14	Dynamo Kiev	21	0		
2014–15	Dynamo Kiev	24	0		
2015–16	Dynamo Kiev	17	0		
2016–17	Dynamo Kiev	4	0	66	0
2016–17	Bayer Leverkusen	19	0		
2017–18	Bayer Leverkusen	1	0	20	0

On loan from Bayer Leverkusen.

2017–18	Leicester C	11	0	11	0

ELDER, Callum (D)   77 1
H: 5 11 W: 10 08 b.Sydney 27-1-95
Internationals: Australia U20.

2013–14	Leicester C	0	0		
2014–15	Leicester C	0	0		
2014–15	Mansfield T	21	0	21	0
2015–16	Leicester C	0	0		
2015–16	Peterborough U	18	1	18	1
2016–17	Leicester C	0	0		
2016–17	Brentford	6	0	6	0
2016–17	Barnsley	5	0	5	0
2017–18	Leicester C	0	0		
2017–18	Wigan Ath	27	0	27	0

FUCHS, Christian (D)   428 24
H: 6 1 W: 12 08 b.Pitten 7-4-86
Internationals: Austria U17, U19, U21, Full caps.

2002–03	Wiener Neustadt	12	0	12	0
2003–04	Mattersburg	13	0		
2004–05	Mattersburg	24	2		
2005–06	Mattersburg	35	1		
2006–07	Mattersburg	35	6		
2007–08	Mattersburg	33	3	140	12
2008–09	Bochum	22	2		
2009–10	Bochum	31	4		
2010–11	Bochum	0	0	53	6
2010–11	Mainz 05	31	0	31	0
2011–12	Schalke	29	2		
2012–13	Schalke	29	0		
2013–14	Schalke	16	0		
2014–15	Schalke	25	2	99	4
2015–16	Leicester C	32	0		
2016–17	Leicester C	36	2		
2017–18	Leicester C	25	0	93	2

GRAY, Demarai (M)   149 12
H: 5 10 W: 10 04 b.Birmingham 28-6-96
Internationals: England U18, U19, U20, U21.

2013–14	Birmingham C	7	1		
2014–15	Birmingham C	41	6		
2015–16	Birmingham C	24	1	72	8
2015–16	Leicester C	12	0		
2016–17	Leicester C	30	1		
2017–18	Leicester C	35	3	77	4

HAMER, Ben (G)   223 0
H: 5 11 W: 12 04 b.Chard 20-11-87

2006–07	Reading	0	0		
2007–08	Reading	0	0		
2007–08	Brentford	20	0		
2008–09	Reading	0	0		
2008–09	Brentford	45	0		
2009–10	Reading	0	0		
2010–11	Reading	0	0		
2010–11	Brentford	10	0	75	0
2010–11	Exeter C	18	0	18	0
2011–12	Charlton Ath	41	0		
2012–13	Charlton Ath	41	0		
2013–14	Charlton Ath	32	0	114	0
2014–15	Leicester C	8	0		
2015–16	Leicester C	0	0		
2015–16	Bristol C	4	0	4	0
2016–17	Leicester C	0	0		
2017–18	Leicester C	4	0	12	0

HUGHES, Sam (M)   0 0
b.West Kirby 15-4-97

2017–18	Leicester C	0	0		

HUTH, Robert (D) — 326 21
H: 6 3 W: 14 07 b.Berlin 18-8-84
Internationals: Germany U21, Full caps.

Season	Club	Apps	Gls	Tot	Gls
2001–02	Chelsea	1	0		
2002–03	Chelsea	2	0		
2003–04	Chelsea	16	0		
2004–05	Chelsea	10	0		
2005–06	Chelsea	13	0	42	0
2006–07	Middlesbrough	12	1		
2007–08	Middlesbrough	13	1		
2008–09	Middlesbrough	24	0		
2009–10	Middlesbrough	4	0	53	2
2009–10	Stoke C	32	3		
2010–11	Stoke C	35	6		
2011–12	Stoke C	34	3		
2012–13	Stoke C	35	1		
2013–14	Stoke C	12	0		
2014–15	Stoke C	1	0	149	13
2014–15	Leicester C	14	1		
2015–16	Leicester C	35	3		
2016–17	Leicester C	33	2		
2017–18	Leicester C	0	0	82	6

IBORRA, Vicente (F) — 297 35
H: 6 3 W: 12 00 b.Moncada 16-1-88

Season	Club	Apps	Gls	Tot	Gls
2007–08	Levante	14	1		
2008–09	Levante	31	2		
2009–10	Levante	36	1		
2010–11	Levante	16	0		
2011–12	Levante	33	0		
2012–13	Levante	35	4	165	8
2013–14	Sevilla	27	3		
2014–15	Sevilla	26	7		
2015–16	Sevilla	29	7		
2016–17	Sevilla	31	7	113	24
2017–18	Leicester C	19	3	19	3

IHEANACHO, Kelechi (M) — 67 15
H: 6 2 W: 13 08 b.Imo 3-10-96
Internationals: Nigeria U17, U20, Full caps.

Season	Club	Apps	Gls	Tot	Gls
2014–15	Manchester C	0	0		
2015–16	Manchester C	26	8		
2016–17	Manchester C	20	4	46	12
2017–18	Leicester C	21	3	21	3

JAKUPOVIC, Eldin (G) — 161 1
H: 6 3 W: 13 00 b.Kozarac 2-10-84
Internationals: Bosnia & Herzegovina U21, Switzerland U21, Full caps.

Season	Club	Apps	Gls	Tot	Gls
2004–05	Grasshoppers	8	0		
2005–06	FC Thun	23	0	23	0
2007–08	Grasshoppers	23	1		
2008–09	Grasshoppers	32	0	63	1
2010–11	Olympiacos Volou	26	0	26	0
2011–12	Aris Salonika	1	0	1	0
2012–13	Hull C	5	0		
2013–14	Hull C	1	0		
2013–14	Leyton Orient	13	0	13	0
2014–15	Hull C	3	0		
2015–16	Hull C	2	0		
2016–17	Hull C	22	0	33	0
2017–18	Leicester C	2	0	2	0

JAMES, Matthew (M) — 146 7
H: 6 0 W: 11 12 b.Bacup 22-7-91
Internationals: England U16, U17, U19, U20.

Season	Club	Apps	Gls	Tot	Gls
2007–08	Manchester U	0	0		
2008–09	Manchester U	0	0		
2009–10	Manchester U	0	0		
2009–10	Preston NE	18	2		
2010–11	Manchester U	0	0		
2010–11	Preston NE	10	0	28	2
2011–12	Manchester U	0	0		
2012–13	Leicester C	24	3		
2013–14	Leicester C	35	1		
2014–15	Leicester C	27	0		
2015–16	Leicester C	0	0		
2016–17	Leicester C	1	0		
2016–17	Barnsley	18	1	18	1
2017–18	Leicester C	13	0	100	4

KING, Andy (M) — 340 57
H: 6 0 W: 11 10 b.Barnstaple 29-10-88
Internationals: Wales U19, U21, Full caps.

Season	Club	Apps	Gls	Tot	Gls
2007–08	Leicester C	11	1		
2008–09	Leicester C	45	9		
2009–10	Leicester C	43	9		
2010–11	Leicester C	45	15		
2011–12	Leicester C	30	4		
2012–13	Leicester C	42	7		
2013–14	Leicester C	30	4		
2014–15	Leicester C	24	2		
2015–16	Leicester C	25	2		
2016–17	Leicester C	23	1		
2017–18	Leicester C	11	1	329	55
2017–18	Swansea C	11	2	11	2

KNIGHT, Josh (D) — 0 0
b.Leicester 7-9-97

Season	Club	Apps	Gls	Tot	Gls
2017–18	Leicester C	0	0		

MAGUIRE, Harry (D) — 242 14
H: 6 2 W: 12 06 b.Mosborough 5-3-93
Internationals: England U21, Full caps.

Season	Club	Apps	Gls	Tot	Gls
2010–11	Sheffield U	5	0		
2011–12	Sheffield U	44	1		
2012–13	Sheffield U	44	3		
2013–14	Sheffield U	41	5	134	9
2014–15	Hull C	3	0		
2014–15	Wigan Ath	16	1	16	1
2015–16	Hull C	22	0		
2016–17	Hull C	29	2	54	2
2017–18	Leicester C	38	2	38	2

MAHREZ, Riyad (M) — 216 48
H: 5 10 W: 9 10 b.Sarcelles 21-2-91
Internationals: Algeria Full caps.

Season	Club	Apps	Gls	Tot	Gls
2011–12	Le Havre	9	0		
2012–13	Le Havre	32	4		
2013–14	Le Havre	17	2	58	6
2013–14	Leicester C	19	3		
2014–15	Leicester C	30	4		
2015–16	Leicester C	37	17		
2016–17	Leicester C	36	6		
2017–18	Leicester C	36	12	158	42

MENDY, Nampalys (D) — 202 1
H: 5 6 W: 10 10 b.La Seyne-sur-Mer 9-6-92
Internationals: France U18, U19, U20, U21.

Season	Club	Apps	Gls	Tot	Gls
2010–11	Monaco	14	0		
2011–12	Monaco	28	0		
2012–13	Monaco	32	0	74	0
2013–14	Nice	36	0		
2014–15	Nice	36	0		
2015–16	Nice	38	1		
2016–17	Leicester C	4	0		
2017–18	Leicester C	0	0	4	0
2017–18	Nice	14	0	124	1

MOORE, Elliott (D) — 24 2
b. 16-3-97
Internationals: England U18, U20.

Season	Club	Apps	Gls	Tot	Gls
2016–17	Leicester C	0	0		
2017–18	Leicester C	0	0		
2017–18	OH Leuven	24	2	24	2

MORGAN, Wes (D) — 598 21
H: 6 2 W: 14 00 b.Nottingham 21-1-84
Internationals: Jamaica Full caps.

Season	Club	Apps	Gls	Tot	Gls
2002–03	Nottingham F	0	0		
2002–03	Kidderminster H	5	1	5	1
2003–04	Nottingham F	32	2		
2004–05	Nottingham F	43	1		
2005–06	Nottingham F	43	2		
2006–07	Nottingham F	38	0		
2007–08	Nottingham F	42	1		
2008–09	Nottingham F	42	1		
2009–10	Nottingham F	44	3		
2010–11	Nottingham F	46	1		
2011–12	Nottingham F	22	1	352	12
2011–12	Leicester C	17	0		
2012–13	Leicester C	45	1		
2013–14	Leicester C	45	2		
2014–15	Leicester C	37	2		
2015–16	Leicester C	38	2		
2016–17	Leicester C	27	1		
2017–18	Leicester C	32	0	241	8

MUSA, Ahmed (F) — 236 80
H: 5 9 W: 10 03 b.Jos 14-10-92
Internationals: Nigeria U20, U23, Full caps.

Season	Club	Apps	Gls	Tot	Gls
2008–09	GBS Football Academy	0	0		
2008–09	Josh UTH	18	4	18	4
2009–10	GBS Football Academy	0	0		
2009–10	Kano Pillars	25	18	25	18
2010–11	VVV Venlo	23	5		
2011–12	VVV Venlo	14	3	37	8
2011–12	CSKA Moscow	19	1		
2012–13	CSKA Moscow	28	11		
2013–14	CSKA Moscow	26	7		
2014–15	CSKA Moscow	30	10		
2015–16	CSKA Moscow	30	13		
2016–17	Leicester C	21	2		
2017–18	Leicester C	0	0	21	2
2017–18	CSKA Moscow	10	6	135	48

NDIDI, Onyinye (D) — 111 6
b. 16-12-96
Internationals: Nigeria U20, Full caps.

Season	Club	Apps	Gls	Tot	Gls
2014–15	Genk	6	0		
2015–16	Genk	36	4		
2016–17	Genk	19	0	61	4
2016–17	Leicester C	17	2		
2017–18	Leicester C	33	0	50	2

NDUKWU, Layton (F) — 0 0
Internationals: England U16, U17.

Season	Club	Apps	Gls	Tot	Gls
2017–18	Leicester C	0	0		

OKAZAKI, Shinji (F) — 342 93
H: 5 9 W: 11 00 b.Hyogo 16-4-86
Internationals: Japan U23, Full caps.

Season	Club	Apps	Gls	Tot	Gls
2005	Shimizu S-Pulse	1	0		
2006	Shimizu S-Pulse	7	0		
2007	Shimizu S-Pulse	21	5		
2008	Shimizu S-Pulse	27	10		
2009	Shimizu S-Pulse	34	14		
2010	Shimizu S-Pulse	31	13	121	42
2010–11	Stuttgart	12	2		
2011–12	Stuttgart	26	7		
2012–13	Stuttgart	25	1	63	10
2013–14	Mainz 05	33	15		
2014–15	Mainz 05	32	12	65	27
2015–16	Leicester C	36	5		
2016–17	Leicester C	30	3		
2017–18	Leicester C	27	6	93	14

SCHMEICHEL, Kasper (G) — 422 0
H: 6 1 W: 13 00 b.Copenhagen 5-11-86
Internationals: Denmark U19, U20, U21, Full caps.

Season	Club	Apps	Gls	Tot	Gls
2003–04	Manchester C	0	0		
2004–05	Manchester C	0	0		
2005–06	Manchester C	0	0		
2005–06	Darlington	4	0	4	0
2005–06	Bury	15	0		
2006–07	Manchester C	0	0		
2006–07	Falkirk	15	0	15	0
2006–07	Bury	14	0	29	0
2007–08	Manchester C	7	0		
2007–08	Cardiff C	14	0	14	0
2007–08	Coventry C	9	0	9	0
2008–09	Manchester C	1	0		
2009–10	Manchester C	0	0	8	0
2009–10	Notts Co	43	0	43	0
2010–11	Leeds U	37	0	37	0
2011–12	Leicester C	46	0		
2012–13	Leicester C	46	0		
2013–14	Leicester C	46	0		
2014–15	Leicester C	24	0		
2015–16	Leicester C	38	0		
2016–17	Leicester C	30	0		
2017–18	Leicester C	33	0	263	0

SIMPSON, Danny (D) — 301 1
H: 5 9 W: 11 05 b.Eccles 4-1-87

Season	Club	Apps	Gls	Tot	Gls
2005–06	Manchester U	0	0		
2006–07	Manchester U	0	0		
2006–07	Sunderland	14	0	14	0
2007–08	Manchester U	3	0		
2007–08	Ipswich T	8	0	8	0
2008–09	Manchester U	0	0		
2008–09	Blackburn R	12	0	12	0
2009–10	Manchester U	0	0	3	0
2009–10	Newcastle U	39	1		
2010–11	Newcastle U	30	0		
2011–12	Newcastle U	35	0		
2012–13	Newcastle U	19	0	123	1
2013–14	QPR	33	0		
2014–15	QPR	1	0	34	0
2014–15	Leicester C	14	0		
2015–16	Leicester C	30	0		
2016–17	Leicester C	35	0		
2017–18	Leicester C	28	0	107	0

SLIMANI, Islam (F) — 239 106
H: 6 2 W: 12 06 b.Algiers 18-6-88
Internationals: Algeria Full caps.

Season	Club	Apps	Gls	Tot	Gls
2008–09	JSM Cheraga	20	18	20	18
2009–10	CR Belouizdad	30	8		
2010–11	CR Belouizdad	27	10		
2011–12	CR Belouizdad	26	10		
2012–13	CR Belouizdad	15	6	98	32
2013–14	Sporting Lisbon	26	8		
2014–15	Sporting Lisbon	21	12		
2015–16	Sporting Lisbon	33	27		
2016–17	Sporting Lisbon	2	1	82	48
2016–17	Leicester C	23	7		
2017–18	Leicester C	12	1	35	8
2017–18	Newcastle U	4	0	4	0

THOMAS, George (M) — 47 5
H: 5 8 W: 12 00 b.Leicester 24-3-97
Internationals: Wales U17, U19, U20, U21, Full caps.

Season	Club	Apps	Gls	Tot	Gls
2013–14	Coventry C	1	0		
2014–15	Coventry C	6	0		
2015–16	Coventry C	7	0		
2015–16	Yeovil T	5	0	5	0
2016–17	Coventry C	28	5	42	5
2017–18	Leicester C	0	0		

ULLOA, Jose (F)   323 117
H: 6 1 W: 11 10 b.General Roca 26-7-86

2004–05	San Lorenzo	0	0		
2005–06	San Lorenzo	22	3		
2006–07	San Lorenzo	6	0	25	3
2007–08	Arsenal Sarandi	6	1	6	1
2007–08	Olimpo	8	1	8	1
2008–09	Castellon	33	17		
2009–10	Castellon	32	14		
2010–11	Castellon	1	0	66	31
2010–11	Almeria	34	7		
2011–12	Almeria	28	29		
2012–13	Almeria	10	3	72	39
2012–13	Brighton & HA	17	9		
2013–14	Brighton & HA	33	14		
2014–15	Leicester C	37	11		
2015–16	Leicester C	29	6		
2016–17	Leicester C	16	1		
2017–18	Leicester C	4	0	86	18
2017–18	*Brighton & HA*	10	1	60	24

VARDY, Jamie (F)   205 82
H: 5 10 W: 11 12 b.Sheffield 11-1-87
Internationals: England Full caps.

2012–13	Leicester C	26	4		
2013–14	Leicester C	37	16		
2014–15	Leicester C	34	5		
2015–16	Leicester C	36	24		
2016–17	Leicester C	25	13		
2017–18	Leicester C	37	20	205	82

Players retained or with offer of contract
Bolkiah, Faiq Jefri; Bramley, Max; Davies, Rhys Paul Richard; Dewsbury-Hall, Kiernan; Felix-Eppiah, Joshua; Gordon, Joshua Luke; Iversen, Daniel; Johnson, Darnell Tobias Jack; Kapustka, Bartosz; Makanjuola, Habib Abdulfatal; Martis, Liandro Rudwendry Felipe; Meite, Alassane; Muskwe, Admiral Dalindlela; Pascanu, Alexandru Stefan; Shade, Tyrese; Sherif, Lamine Kaba; Sowah, Kamal; Uche Rubio, Raul; Wood, Connor; Wright, Callum.

Scholars
Bollard, Dylan Jack; Edwards-John, Kairo; Elewa-Ikpakwu, Edward; Heaven, George William; Husek, Lukas; James, Leon Pitchaya; Keaveny, Jozsef Phelim; Leshabela, Thakgalo Khanya; Myring, Harrison; Stolarczyk, Jakub; Tee, Conor; Thomas, Luke Jonathan; Ughelumba, Calvin; Williams, Kian.

LINCOLN C (46)

ANDERSON, Harry (F)   56 6
H: 5 6 W: 9 11 b.9-1-97

2014–15	Peterborough U	10	0		
2015–16	Peterborough U	5	0		
2016–17	Peterborough U	1	0	16	0
2017–18	Lincoln C	40	6	40	6

ANTKOWIAK, Michael (G)   0 0

2017–18	Lincoln C	0	0

ARNOLD, Nathan (M)   82 8
H: 5 7 W: 10 03 b.Mansfield 26-7-87
Internationals: England C.

2005–06	Mansfield T	8	1		
2006–07	Mansfield T	22	3		
2007–08	Mansfield T	32	4	62	8
2014–15	Cambridge U	0	0		
2017–18	Lincoln C	20	0	20	0

BOSTWICK, Michael (D)   322 38
H: 6 4 W: 14 00 b.Eltham 17-5-88
Internationals: England C.

2006–07	Millwall	0	0		

From Rushden & D, Ebbsfleet U

2010–11	Stevenage	41	2		
2011–12	Stevenage	43	7	84	9
2012–13	Peterborough U	39	5		
2013–14	Peterborough U	42	4		
2014–15	Peterborough U	38	7		
2015–16	Peterborough U	36	4		
2016–17	Peterborough U	39	3	194	23
2017–18	Lincoln C	44	6	44	6

CHAPMAN, Ellis (M)   0 0
b.Lincoln 8-1-01
From Leicester C.

2017–18	Lincoln C	0	0

EARDLEY, Neal (M)   288 13
H: 5 11 W: 11 10 b.Llandudno 6-11-88
Internationals: Wales U17, U19, U21, Full caps.

2005–06	Oldham Ath	1	0		
2006–07	Oldham Ath	36	2		
2007–08	Oldham Ath	42	6		
2008–09	Oldham Ath	34	2		
2009–10	Oldham Ath	0	0	113	10
2009–10	Blackpool	24	0		
2010–11	Blackpool	31	1		
2011–12	Blackpool	26	1		
2012–13	Blackpool	23	0	104	2
2013–14	Birmingham C	5	0		
2014–15	Birmingham C	4	0		
2014–15	*Leyton Orient*	1	0	1	0
2015–16	Birmingham C	5	0	14	0
2016–17	Hibernian	2	0	2	0
2016–17	Northampton T	10	0	10	0
2017–18	Lincoln C	44	1	44	1

FARMAN, Paul (G)   0 0
H: 6 5 W: 14 07 b.North Shields 2-11-89
Internationals: England C.
From Blyth Spartans, Gateshead.

2017–18	Lincoln C	13	0	13	0

FRECKLINGTON, Lee (M)   400 61
H: 5 8 W: 11 00 b.Lincoln 8-9-85
Internationals: Republic of Ireland B.

2003–04	Lincoln C	1	0		
2004–05	Lincoln C	3	0		
2005–06	Lincoln C	18	2		
2006–07	Lincoln C	42	8		
2007–08	Lincoln C	34	4		
2008–09	Lincoln C	27	7		
2008–09	Peterborough U	7	0		
2009–10	Peterborough U	35	2		
2010–11	Peterborough U	9	1		
2011–12	Peterborough U	37	5		
2012–13	Peterborough U	5	0	93	8
2012–13	*Rotherham U*	31	6		
2013–14	Rotherham U	39	10		
2014–15	Rotherham U	29	2		
2015–16	Rotherham U	27	5		
2016–17	Rotherham U	22	1		
2017–18	Rotherham U	19	4	167	28
2017–18	Lincoln C	16	4	140	25

GREEN, Matt (F)   187 40
H: 6 0 W: 12 09 b.Bath 2-1-87
Internationals: England C.

2006–07	Cardiff C	6	0		
2007–08	Cardiff C	0	0	6	0
2007–08	*Darlington*	4	0	4	0

From Torquay U

2010–11	Oxford U	17	0	17	0
2010–11	*Cheltenham T*	19	0	19	0

From Mansfield T

2013–14	Birmingham C	10	1		
2014–15	Birmingham C	0	0	10	1
2015–16	Mansfield T	44	16		
2016–17	Mansfield T	42	10	86	26
2017–18	Lincoln C	45	13	45	13

HABERGHAM, Sam (D)   33 0
H: 6 0 W: 11 07 b.Rotherham 20-2-92
Internationals: England C, U17.
From Norwich C, Tamworth, Braintree T.

2017–18	Lincoln C	33	0	33	0

HORTON, Danny (M)   0 0
b.Lincoln 6-5-00

2017–18	Lincoln C	0	0

KNOTT, Billy (M)   156 11
H: 5 8 W: 11 02 b.Canvey Island 28-11-92
Internationals: England U16, U17, U20.

2010–11	Sunderland	0	0		
2011–12	Sunderland	0	0		
2011–12	*AFC Wimbledon*	20	3	20	3
2012–13	Sunderland	0	0		
2013–14	Sunderland	0	0		
2013–14	*Wycombe W*	17	1	17	1
2013–14	*Port Vale*	1	2	18	2
2014–15	Bradford C	40	3		
2015–16	Bradford C	24	0	64	3
2016–17	Gillingham	17	1	17	1
2017–18	Lincoln C	15	1	15	1
2017–18	*Rochdale*	4	0	4	0

LONG, Sean (D)   33 0
H: 5 10 W: 11 00 b.Dublin 2-5-95
Internationals: Republic of Ireland U16, U17, U18, U19, U21.

2013–14	Reading	0	0		
2014–15	Reading	0	0		
2015–16	Reading	0	0		
2015–16	*Luton T*	9	0	9	0
2016–17	Reading	0	0		
2016–17	*Cambridge U*	7	0	7	0
2017–18	Lincoln C	17	0	17	0

McCOMBE, Jamie (D)   396 27
H: 6 5 W: 12 05 b.Scunthorpe 1-1-83

2001–02	Scunthorpe U	17	0		
2002–03	Scunthorpe U	31	1		
2003–04	Scunthorpe U	15	0	63	1
2003–04	Lincoln C	8	0		
2004–05	Lincoln C	41	3		
2005–06	Lincoln C	38	4		
2006–07	Bristol C	41	4		
2007–08	Bristol C	34	3		
2008–09	Bristol C	28	1		
2009–10	Bristol C	16	1	119	9
2010–11	Huddersfield T	34	5		
2011–12	Huddersfield T	20	3		
2011–12	*Preston NE*	6	0	6	0
2012–13	Huddersfield T	0	0	54	8
2012–13	Doncaster R	33	1		
2013–14	Doncaster R	2	0		
2014–15	Doncaster R	18	1	53	2
2015–16	Stevenage	14	0	14	0
2017–18	Lincoln C	0	0	87	7

O'HARE, Declan (M)   0 0

2017–18	Lincoln C	0	0

PALMER, Oliver (F)   181 28
b.London 21-1-92

2013–14	Mansfield T	38	4		
2014–15	Mansfield T	16	1	54	5
2015–16	Leyton Orient	45	7		
2016–17	Leyton Orient	20	5	65	12
2016–17	*Luton T*	17	3	17	3
2017–18	Lincoln C	45	8	45	8

PETT, Tom (M)   150 21
H: 5 8 W: 11 00 b. 3-12-91
Internationals: England C.

2014–15	Stevenage	34	7		
2015–16	Stevenage	40	1		
2016–17	Stevenage	40	6		
2017–18	Stevenage	27	6	141	20
2017–18	Lincoln C	9	1	9	1

RHEAD, Matt (F)   113 17
b.Stoke-on-Trent 31-5-84

2013–14	Mansfield T	40	6		
2014–15	Mansfield T	32	3	72	9
2017–18	Lincoln C	41	8	41	8

STEWART, Cameron (M)   131 8
H: 5 8 W: 11 05 b.Manchester 8-4-91
Internationals: England U17, U19, U20.

2009–10	Manchester U	0	0		
2010–11	Manchester U	0	0		
2010–11	*Yeovil T*	5	0	5	0
2010–11	Hull C	14	0		
2011–12	Hull C	31	1		
2012–13	Hull C	2	0		
2012–13	*Burnley*	9	0	9	0
2012–13	*Blackburn R*	7	0	7	0
2013–14	Hull C	0	0	47	1
2013–14	*Charlton Ath*	18	3	18	3
2013–14	*Leeds U*	11	0	11	0
2014–15	Ipswich C	0	0		
2014–15	*Barnsley*	4	0	4	0
2015–16	Ipswich T	0	0		
2015–16	*Doncaster R*	26	4	26	4
2017–18	Lincoln C	4	0	4	0

VICKERS, Josh (G)   40 0
H: 6 0 W: 11 05 b.Billericay 1-12-95
From Arsenal.

2015–16	Swansea C	0	0		
2016–17	Swansea C	0	0		
2016–17	*Barnet*	23	0	23	0
2017–18	Lincoln C	17	0	17	0

WALTON, Richard (G)   0 0

2017–18	Lincoln C	0	0

WATERFALL, Luke (D)   44 3
H: 6 2 W: 13 02 b.Sheffield 30-7-90

2008–09	Tranmere R	0	0		

From Ilkeston, Gainsborough T

2013–14	Scunthorpe U	9	1		
2014–15	Scunthorpe U	0	0	9	1
2014–15	*Mansfield T*	5	0	5	0
2017–18	Lincoln C	30	2	30	2

WHITEHOUSE, Elliott (M)   57 3
H: 5 11 W: 12 08 b.Worksop 27-10-93
Internationals: England C.

2012–13	Sheffield U	3	0		
2013–14	Sheffield U	0	0	3	0
2013–14	York C	15	0	15	0

2014–15	Notts Co	7	1	7	1
2017–18	Lincoln C	32	2	32	2

WILSON, James (D)   196 5
H: 6 2 W: 11 05 b.Chepstow 26-2-89
Internationals: Wales U19, U21, Full caps.

2005–06	Bristol C	0	0		
2006–07	Bristol C	0	0		
2007–08	Bristol C	0	0		
2008–09	Bristol C	2	0		
2008–09	*Brentford*	14	0		
2009–10	Bristol C	0	0		
2009–10	*Brentford*	13	0	27	0
2010–11	Bristol C	2	0		
2011–12	Bristol C	21	0		
2012–13	Bristol C	6	0		
2013–14	Bristol C	0	0	31	0
2013–14	*Cheltenham T*	4	0	4	0
2013–14	Oldham Ath	16	1		
2014–15	Oldham Ath	41	1		
2015–16	Oldham Ath	43	0	100	2
2016–17	Sheffield U	7	1		
2017–18	Sheffield U	0	0	7	1
2017–18	*Walsall*	19	1	19	1
2017–18	Lincoln C	8	1	8	1

WOODYARD, Alex (M)   54 2
H: 5 9 W: 10 00 b.Gravesend 3-5-93
Internationals: England C.

2010–11	Southend U	3	0		
2011–12	Southend U	0	0		
2012–13	Southend U	5	0		
2013–14	Southend U	0	0	8	0
2017–18	Lincoln C	46	2	46	2

Scholars
Antkowiak, Michael Jerzy; Burdett, Ritchie George; Burns, Joshua James; Burutsa, Kudakwashe Bright; Cox, Lewis Stephen; Hart, Charlie; Horton, Daniel William; Hugo, James Thomas; Mathers, Jack; O'Hare, Deaglan Samuel; Smith, Jon Douglas; Troop, Harry John; Watkins, Kyle; West, Charlie Taylor; White, Luke Elliott.

LIVERPOOL (47)

ALEXANDER-ARNOLD, Trent (M)   26 1
b. 7-10-98
Internationals: England U16, U17, U18, U19, U21, Full caps.

2016–17	Liverpool	7	0		
2017–18	Liverpool	19	1	26	1

CAMACHO, Rafael (M)   0 0
Internationals: Portugal U16, U17, U18.
From Manchester C.

2017–18	Liverpool	0	0	

CAN, Emre (M)   148 14
H: 6 1 W: 11 09 b.Frankfurt 12-1-94
Internationals: Germany U16, U17, U19, U21, Full caps.

2011–12	Bayern Munich	0	0		
2012–13	Bayern Munich	4	1	4	1
2013–14	Bayer Leverkusen	29	3	29	3
2014–15	Liverpool	27	1		
2015–16	Liverpool	30	1		
2016–17	Liverpool	32	5		
2017–18	Liverpool	26	3	115	10

CHIRIVELLA, Pedro (M)   18 2
b. 23-5-97
Internationals: Spain U17.

2014–15	Valencia	0	0		
2015–16	Liverpool	1	0		
2016–17	Liverpool	0	0		
2016–17	*Go Ahead Eagles*	17	2	17	2
2017–18	Liverpool	0	0	1	0

CLYNE, Nathaniel (D)   289 5
H: 5 9 W: 10 07 b.Stockwell 5-4-91
Internationals: England U19, U21, Full caps.

2008–09	Crystal Palace	26	0		
2009–10	Crystal Palace	22	1		
2010–11	Crystal Palace	46	0		
2011–12	Crystal Palace	28	0	122	1
2012–13	Southampton	34	1		
2013–14	Southampton	25	0		
2014–15	Southampton	35	2	94	3
2015–16	Liverpool	33	1		
2016–17	Liverpool	37	0		
2017–18	Liverpool	3	0	73	1

COUTINHO, Phillippe (M)   202 50
H: 5 7 W: 10 09 b.Rio de Janeiro 12-6-92
Internationals: Brazil U17, U20, Full caps.

2009–10	Vasco da Gama	7	1	7	1
2010–11	Inter Milan	12	1		
2011–12	Inter Milan	5	1		
2011–12	*Espanyol*	16	5	16	5
2012–13	Inter Milan	10	1	27	3
2012–13	Liverpool	13	3		
2013–14	Liverpool	33	5		
2014–15	Liverpool	35	5		
2015–16	Liverpool	26	8		
2016–17	Liverpool	31	13		
2017–18	Liverpool	14	7	152	41

Transferred to Barcelona, January 2018.

EJARIA, Oviemuno (M)   13 1
W: 11 11 b.Southwark 18-11-97
Internationals: England U20, U21.
From Arsenal.

2016–17	Liverpool	2	0		
2017–18	Liverpool	0	0	2	0
2017–18	*Sunderland*	11	1	11	1

FIRMINO, Roberto (M)   281 82
H: 5 11 W: 12 00 b.Maceio 2-10-91
Internationals: Brazil Full caps.

2009	Figueirense	2	0		
2010	Figueirense	36	8	38	8
2010–11	Hoffenheim	11	3		
2011–12	Hoffenheim	30	7		
2012–13	Hoffenheim	33	5		
2013–14	Hoffenheim	33	16		
2014–15	Hoffenheim	33	7	140	38
2015–16	Liverpool	31	10		
2016–17	Liverpool	35	11		
2017–18	Liverpool	37	15	103	36

FLANAGAN, Jon (D)   55 1
H: 5 11 W: 12 06 b.Liverpool 1-1-93
Internationals: England U19, U20, U21, Full caps.

2010–11	Liverpool	7	0		
2011–12	Liverpool	5	0		
2012–13	Liverpool	0	0		
2013–14	Liverpool	23	1		
2014–15	Liverpool	0	0		
2015–16	Liverpool	5	0		
2016–17	Liverpool	0	0		
2016–17	*Burnley*	6	0	6	0
2017–18	Liverpool	0	0	40	1
2017–18	*Bolton W*	9	0	9	0

GEORGE, Shamal (G)   4 0
b.Wirral 6-1-98

2017–18	Liverpool	0	0		
2017–18	*Carlisle U*	4	0	4	0

GOMEZ, Joseph (D)   49 0
H: 6 2 W: 14 00 b.Catford 23-5-97
Internationals: England U16, U17, U19, U21, Full caps.

2014–15	Charlton Ath	21	0	21	0
2015–16	Liverpool	5	0		
2016–17	Liverpool	0	0		
2017–18	Liverpool	23	0	28	0

GRUJIC, Marko (M)   65 9
b. 13-4-96
Internationals: Serbia U16, U17, U19, U20, U21, Full caps.

2012–13	Red Star Belgrade	1	0		
2013–14	Red Star Belgrade	0	0		
2014–15	Red Star Belgrade	9	0		
2014–15	*Kolubara*	5	2	5	2
2015–16	Red Star Belgrade	29	6	39	6
2016–17	Liverpool	5	0		
2017–18	Liverpool	3	0	8	0
2017–18	*Cardiff C*	13	1	13	1

HENDERSON, Jordan (M)   288 26
H: 6 0 W: 10 07 b.Sunderland 17-6-90
Internationals: England U19, U20, U21, Full caps.

2008–09	Sunderland	1	0		
2008–09	*Coventry C*	10	1	10	1
2009–10	Sunderland	33	1		
2010–11	Sunderland	37	3	71	4
2011–12	Liverpool	37	2		
2012–13	Liverpool	30	5		
2013–14	Liverpool	35	4		
2014–15	Liverpool	37	6		
2015–16	Liverpool	17	2		
2016–17	Liverpool	24	1		
2017–18	Liverpool	27	1	207	21

INGS, Danny (F)   163 48
H: 5 10 W: 11 07 b.Winchester 3-6-92
Internationals: England U21, Full caps.

2009–10	Bournemouth	0	0		
2010–11	Bournemouth	26	7		
2011–12	Bournemouth	1	0	27	7
2011–12	Burnley	15	3		
2012–13	Burnley	33	3		
2013–14	Burnley	40	21		
2014–15	Burnley	35	11	122	38
2015–16	Liverpool	6	2		
2016–17	Liverpool	0	0		
2017–18	Liverpool	8	1	14	3

JONES, Curtis (M)   0 0
b. 30-1-01
Internationals: England U16, U17.

2017–18	Liverpool	0	0	

KARIUS, Loris (G)   120 0
H: 6 2 W: 11 11 b.Biberach 22-6-93
Internationals: Germany U16, U17, U18, U19, U20, U21.

2009–10	Manchester C	0	0		
2010–11	Manchester C	0	0		
2011–12	Manchester C	0	0		
2011–12	Manchester C	0	0		
2012–13	Mainz 05	1	0		
2013–14	Mainz 05	23	0		
2014–15	Mainz 05	33	0		
2015–16	Mainz 05	34	0	91	0
2016–17	Liverpool	10	0		
2017–18	Liverpool	19	0	29	0

KENT, Ryan (M)   71 4
H: 5 8 W: 10 03 b.Oldham 11-11-96
Internationals: England U18, U20.

2015–16	Liverpool	0	0		
2015–16	*Coventry C*	17	1	17	1
2016–17	Liverpool	0	0		
2016–17	*Barnsley*	44	3	44	3
2017–18	Liverpool	0	0		
2017–18	*SC Freiburg*	0	0		
2017–18	*Bristol C*	10	0	10	0

KLAVAN, Ragnar (D)   420 18
H: 6 1 W: 12 02 b.Viljandi 31-10-85
Internationals: Estonia U17, U18, U20, U21, Full caps.

2001	Elva	25	5	25	5
2002	Tulevik	18	0		
2003	Tulevik	10	2	28	2
2003	Flora	12	1		
2004	Flora	16	1		
2004	Valerenga	2	0		
2005	Flora	0	0	28	2
2005	Valerenga	0	0	2	0
2005–06	Heracles	15	0		
2006–07	Heracles	32	1		
2007–08	Heracles	29	2		
2008–09	Heracles	19	1	95	4
2008–09	AZ Alkmaar	12	0		
2009–10	AZ Alkmaar	11	0		
2010–11	AZ Alkmaar	28	0		
2011–12	AZ Alkmaar	27	0	78	0
2012–13	Augsburg	30	0		
2013–14	Augsburg	30	2		
2014–15	Augsburg	34	2		
2015–16	Augsburg	31	0	125	4
2016–17	Liverpool	20	0		
2017–18	Liverpool	19	1	39	1

LALLANA, Adam (M)   338 65
H: 5 8 W: 11 06 b.St Albans 10-5-88
Internationals: England U18, U19, U21, Full caps.

2005–06	Southampton	0	0		
2006–07	Southampton	1	0		
2007–08	Southampton	5	1		
2007–08	*Bournemouth*	3	0	3	0
2008–09	Southampton	40	1		
2009–10	Southampton	44	15		
2010–11	Southampton	36	8		
2011–12	Southampton	41	11		
2012–13	Southampton	30	3		
2013–14	Southampton	38	9	235	48
2014–15	Liverpool	27	5		
2015–16	Liverpool	30	4		
2016–17	Liverpool	31	8		
2017–18	Liverpool	12	0	100	17

LOVREN, Dejan (D)   298 10
H: 6 2 W: 13 02 b.Karlovac 5-7-89
Internationals: Croatia U17, U18, U19, U20, U21, Full caps.

2005–06	Dinamo Zagreb	1	0		
2006–07	Dinamo Zagreb	0	0		
2006–07	Inter Zapresic	21	0		
2007–08	Dinamo Zagreb	0	0		
2007–08	Inter Zapresic	29	1	50	1
2008–09	Dinamo Zagreb	22	1		
2009–10	Dinamo Zagreb	14	0	37	1
2009–10	Lyon	0	0		
2010–11	Lyon	28	0		
2011–12	Lyon	18	0		
2012–13	Lyon	18	1	72	2
2013–14	Southampton	31	2	31	2

2014–15	Liverpool	26	0		
2015–16	Liverpool	24	0		
2016–17	Liverpool	29	2		
2017–18	Liverpool	29	2	108	4

MANE, Sadio (F) 208 77
H: 5 9　W: 12 00　b.Sedhiou 10-4-92
Internationals: Senegal U23, Full caps.

2011–12	Metz	19	1		
2012–13	Metz	3	1	22	2
2012–13	Red Bull Salzburg	26	16		
2013–14	Red Bull Salzburg	33	13		
2014–15	Red Bull Salzburg	4	2	63	31
2014–15	Southampton	30	10		
2015–16	Southampton	37	11	67	21
2016–17	Liverpool	27	13		
2017–18	Liverpool	29	10	56	23

MARKOVIC, Lazar (F) 131 24
H: 5 9　W: 10 03　b.Cacak 2-3-94
Internationals: Serbia U17, U21, Full caps.

2010–11	Partizan Belgrade	1	0		
2011–12	Partizan Belgrade	26	6		
2012–13	Partizan Belgrade	19	7	46	13
2013–14	Benfica	26	5	26	5
2014–15	Liverpool	19	2		
2015–16	Liverpool	0	0		
2015–16	Fenerbahce	14	0	14	0
2016–17	Liverpool	0	0		
2016–17	Sporting Lisbon	6	1	6	1
2016–17	Hull C	12	2	12	2
2017–18	Liverpool	0	0	19	2
2017–18	Anderlecht	8	1	8	1

MASTERSON, Conor (D) 0 0
b.Dublin 8-9-98
Internationals: Republic of Ireland U16, U17, U18, U19.

2015–16	Liverpool	0	0	
2017–18	Liverpool	0	0	

MATIP, Joel (D) 248 16
H: 6 4　W: 13 01　b.Bochum 8-8-91
Internationals: Cameroon Full caps.

2009–10	Schalke 04	20	3		
2010–11	Schalke 04	26	0		
2011–12	Schalke 04	30	3		
2012–13	Schalke 04	32	0		
2013–14	Schalke 04	31	3		
2014–15	Schalke 04	21	2		
2015–16	Schalke 04	34	3	194	14
2016–17	Liverpool	29	1		
2017–18	Liverpool	25	1	54	2

MIGNOLET, Simon (G) 367 1
H: 6 4　W: 13 10　b.St Truiden 6-3-88
Internationals: Belgium U16, U17, U18, U19, U20, U21, Full caps.

2006–07	St Truiden	2	0		
2007–08	St Truiden	25	0		
2008–09	St Truiden	35	1		
2009–10	St Truiden	37	0		
2010–11	St Truiden	23	0	122	1
2010–11	Sunderland	23	0		
2011–12	Sunderland	29	0		
2012–13	Sunderland	38	0	90	0
2013–14	Liverpool	38	0		
2014–15	Liverpool	36	0		
2015–16	Liverpool	34	0		
2016–17	Liverpool	28	0		
2017–18	Liverpool	19	0	155	0

MILNER, James (M) 491 50
H: 5 9　W: 11 00　b.Leeds 4-1-86
Internationals: England U16, U17, U19, U20, U21, Full caps.

2002–03	Leeds U	18	2		
2003–04	Leeds U	30	3	48	5
2003–04	Swindon T	6	2	6	2
2004–05	Newcastle U	25	1		
2005–06	Newcastle U	3	0		
2005–06	Aston Villa	27	1		
2006–07	Newcastle U	35	3		
2007–08	Newcastle U	29	2		
2008–09	Newcastle U	2	0	94	6
2008–09	Aston Villa	36	3		
2009–10	Aston Villa	36	7		
2010–11	Aston Villa	1	1	100	12
2010–11	Manchester C	32	0		
2011–12	Manchester C	26	3		
2012–13	Manchester C	26	4		
2013–14	Manchester C	32	3		
2014–15	Manchester C	32	5	147	14
2015–16	Liverpool	28	5		
2016–17	Liverpool	36	7		
2017–18	Liverpool	32	0	96	12

MORENO, Alberto (D) 143 6
H: 5 7　W: 10 01　b.Seville 5-7-92
Internationals: Spain U21, Full caps.

2011–12	Sevilla	11	0		
2012–13	Sevilla	15	0		
2013–14	Sevilla	29	3	55	3
2014–15	Liverpool	28	2		
2015–16	Liverpool	32	1		
2016–17	Liverpool	12	0		
2017–18	Liverpool	16	0	88	3

OJO, Sheyi (M) 58 6
H: 5 10　W: 10 01　b.Hemel Hempstead 19-6-97
Internationals: England U16, U17, U18, U19, U20, U21.

2014–15	Liverpool	0	0		
2014–15	Wigan Ath	11	0	11	0
2015–16	Liverpool	8	0		
2015–16	Wolverhampton W	17	2	17	2
2016–17	Liverpool	0	0		
2017–18	Liverpool	0	0	8	0
2017–18	Fulham	22	4	22	4

ORIGI, Divock (F) 155 32
H: 6 1　W: 11 11　b.Oostende 18-4-95
Internationals: Belgium U16, U17, U19, U21, Full caps.

2012–13	Lille	10	1		
2013–14	Lille	30	5		
2014–15	Lille	33	8	73	14
2015–16	Liverpool	16	5		
2016–17	Liverpool	34	7		
2017–18	Liverpool	1	0	51	12
2017–18	Wolfsburg	31	6	31	6

OXLADE-CHAMBERLAIN, Alex (M) 200 21
H: 5 11　W: 11 00　b.Portsmouth 15-8-93
Internationals: England U18, U19, U21, Full caps.

2009–10	Southampton	2	0		
2010–11	Southampton	34	9	36	9
2011–12	Arsenal	16	2		
2012–13	Arsenal	25	1		
2013–14	Arsenal	14	2		
2014–15	Arsenal	23	1		
2015–16	Arsenal	22	1		
2016–17	Arsenal	29	2		
2017–18	Arsenal	3	0	132	9
2017–18	Liverpool	32	3	32	3

RANDALL, Connor (D) 28 0
H: 5 11　W: 12 00　b.Liverpool 21-10-95
Internationals: England U17.

2014–15	Liverpool	0	0		
2014–15	Shrewsbury T	1	0	1	0
2015–16	Liverpool	3	0		
2016–17	Liverpool	0	0		
2017–18	Liverpool	0	0	3	0
2017–18	Hearts	24	0	24	0

ROBERTSON, Andrew (D) 191 9
H: 5 10　W: 10 00　b.Glasgow 11-3-94
Internationals: Scotland U21, Full caps.

2012–13	Queen's Park	34	2	34	2
2013–14	Dundee U	36	3	36	3
2014–15	Hull C	24	0		
2015–16	Hull C	42	2		
2016–17	Hull C	33	1	99	3
2017–18	Liverpool	22	1	22	1

SALAH, Mohamed (M) 213 89
H: 5 9　W: 11 04　b.Basion 15-6-92
Internationals: Egypt U20, U23, Full caps.

2010–11	Al-Mokawloon	21	4		
2011–12	Al-Mokawloon	15	7	36	11
2012–13	Basle	29	5		
2013–14	Basle	18	4	47	9
2013–14	Chelsea	10	2		
2014–15	Chelsea	3	0		
2014–15	Fiorentina	16	6	16	6
2015–16	Chelsea	0	0	13	2
2015–16	Roma	34	14		
2016–17	Roma	31	15	65	29
2017–18	Liverpool	36	32	36	32

SOLANKE, Dominic (F) 46 8
H: 6 1　W: 11 11　b.Reading 14-9-97
Internationals: England U16, U17, U18, U19, U20, U21, Full caps.

2014–15	Chelsea	0	0		
2015–16	Chelsea	0	0		
2015–16	Vitesse	25	7	25	7
2016–17	Chelsea	0	0		
2017–18	Liverpool	21	1	21	1

STURRIDGE, Daniel (F) 200 74
H: 6 2　W: 12 00　b.Birmingham 1-9-89
Internationals: England U16, U17, U18, U19, U20, U21, Full caps. Great Britain.

2006–07	Manchester C	2	0		
2007–08	Manchester C	3	1		
2008–09	Manchester C	16	4		
2009–10	Manchester C	0	0	21	5
2009–10	Chelsea	13	1		
2010–11	Chelsea	13	0		
2010–11	Bolton W	12	8	12	8
2011–12	Chelsea	30	11		
2012–13	Chelsea	7	1	63	13
2012–13	Liverpool	14	10		
2013–14	Liverpool	29	21		
2014–15	Liverpool	12	4		
2015–16	Liverpool	14	8		
2016–17	Liverpool	20	3		
2017–18	Liverpool	9	2	98	48
2017–18	WBA	6	0	6	0

TONI GOMES, Correia (F) 9 0
H: 5 11　W: 11 05　b.Lille 4-11-98
Internationals: Portugal U17.

2017–18	Liverpool	0	0		
2017–18	Forest Green R	9	0	9	0

VAN DIJK, Virgil (D) 219 20
H: 6 4　W: 14 07　b.Breda 8-7-91
Internationals: Netherlands U19, U21, Full caps.

2010–11	Groningen	5	2		
2011–12	Groningen	23	3		
2012–13	Groningen	34	2	62	7
2013–14	Celtic	36	5		
2014–15	Celtic	35	4		
2015–16	Celtic	5	0	76	9
2015–16	Southampton	34	3		
2016–17	Southampton	21	1		
2017–18	Southampton	12	0	67	4
2017–18	Liverpool	14	0	14	0

VIRTUE, Matthew (M) 13 0
b.Epsom 2-5-97

2017–18	Liverpool	0	0		
2017–18	Notts Co	13	0	13	0

WARD, Danny (G) 71 0
H: 5 11　W: 13 12　b.Wrexham 22-6-93
Internationals: Wales U17, U19, U21, Full caps.

2011–12	Liverpool	0	0		
2012–13	Liverpool	0	0		
2013–14	Liverpool	0	0		
2014–15	Liverpool	0	0		
2014–15	Morecambe	5	0	5	0
2015–16	Liverpool	2	0		
2015–16	Aberdeen	21	0	21	0
2016–17	Liverpool	0	0		
2016–17	Huddersfield T	43	0	43	0
2017–18	Liverpool	0	0	2	0

WHELAN, Corey (D) 7 0
b. 12-12-97
Internationals: Republic of Ireland U17, U21.

2017–18	Liverpool	0	0		
2017–18	Yeovil T	7	0	7	0

WIJNALDUM, Georginio (M) 327 82
H: 5 8　W: 10 10　b.Rotterdam 11-11-90
Internationals: Netherlands U17, U19, U21, Full caps.

2006–07	Feyenoord	3	0		
2007–08	Feyenoord	10	1		
2008–09	Feyenoord	33	4		
2009–10	Feyenoord	31	4		
2010–11	Feyenoord	34	14	111	23
2011–12	PSV Eindhoven	32	9		
2012–13	PSV Eindhoven	33	14		
2013–14	PSV Eindhoven	11	4		
2014–15	PSV Eindhoven	33	14	109	41
2015–16	Newcastle U	38	11	38	11
2016–17	Liverpool	36	6		
2017–18	Liverpool	33	1	69	7

WILLIAMS, Jordan (M) 29 0
H: 6 0　W: 12 02　b.Bangor 6-11-95
Internationals: Wales U17, U21.

2014–15	Liverpool	0	0		
2014–15	Notts Co	8	0	8	0
2015–16	Liverpool	0	0		
2015–16	Swindon T	9	0		
2016–17	Liverpool	0	0		
2016–17	Swindon T	0	0	9	0
2017–18	Liverpool	0	0		
2017–18	Rochdale	12	0	12	0

WILSON, Harry (M)   20   7
H: 5 8   W: 11 00   b.Wrexham 22-3-97
Internationals: Wales U17, U19, U21, Full caps.

2015–16	Liverpool	0	0		
2015–16	*Crewe Alex*	7	0	7	0
2016–17	Liverpool	0	0		
2017–18	Liverpool	0	0		
2017–18	*Hull C*	13	7	13	7

WOODBURN, Ben (F)   6   0
H: 5 9   W: 11 05   b.Chester 16-11-99
Internationals: Wales U16, U17, U19, Full caps.

2016–17	Liverpool	5	0		
2017–18	Liverpool	1	0	6	0

Players retained or with offer of contract
Adekanye, Omobolaji Habeeb; Awoniyi, Taiwo; Bogdan, Adam; Cordoba, Anderson Arroyo; Coyle, Liam; Dixon-Bonner, Elijah Malik; Gallacher, Tony; Garcia Rey, Juan Manuel; Grabara, Kamil; Johnston, George; Kane, Herbie; Kelleher, Caoimhin; Lewis, Adam; McAuley, Glen; Millar, Liam; Phillips, Nathaniel Harry; Rodrigues De Souza, Allan.

Scholars
Atherton, Daniel; Boyes, Morgan; Brewster, Rhian; Clayton, Thomas; Glatzel, Paul; Griffiths, Daniel Lawrence; Jaros, Viteslav; Larouci, Yasser; Longstaff, Luis James; Raitanen, Patrik; Sharif, Abdulrahman Mohamoud; Tagseth, Edvard Sandvik; Turner, Alex; Williams, Ben; Williams, Neco Shay; Williams, Rhys.

LUTON T (48)

BERRY, Luke (D)   159   37
H: 5 10   W: 11 05   b.Bassingbourn 12-7-92

2014–15	Barnsley	31	1	31	1
2015–16	Cambridge U	46	12		
2016–17	Cambridge U	45	17		
2017–18	Cambridge U	3	0	94	29
2017–18	Luton T	34	7	34	7

COLLINS, James S (F)   340 116
H: 6 2   W: 13 08   b.Coventry 1-12-90
Internationals: Republic of Ireland U19, U21.

2008–09	Aston Villa	0	0		
2009–10	Aston Villa	0	0		
2009–10	*Darlington*	7	2	7	2
2010–11	Aston Villa	0	0		
2010–11	*Burton Alb*	10	4	10	4
2010–11	Shrewsbury T	24	8		
2011–12	Shrewsbury T	42	14		
2012–13	Swindon T	45	15	45	15
2013–14	Hibernian	36	6	36	6
2014–15	Shrewsbury T	45	15		
2015–16	Shrewsbury T	23	5	134	42
2015–16	*Northampton T*	21	8	21	8
2016–17	Crawley T	45	20	45	20
2017–18	Luton T	42	19	42	19

COOK, Jordan (F)   152   16
H: 5 10   W: 10 10   b.Hetton-le-Hole 20-3-90

2007–08	Sunderland	0	0		
2008–09	Sunderland	0	0		
2009–10	Sunderland	0	0		
2009–10	*Darlington*	5	0	5	0
2010–11	Sunderland	3	0		
2010–11	*Walsall*	8	1		
2011–12	Sunderland	0	0	3	0
2011–12	*Carlisle U*	14	4	14	4
2012–13	Charlton Ath	7	0		
2012–13	*Yeovil T*	1	0	1	0
2013–14	Charlton Ath	3	0	10	0
2014–15	Walsall	32	5		
2015–16	Walsall	34	3	74	9
2016–17	Luton T	35	3		
2017–18	Luton T	10	0	45	3

CORNICK, Harry (F)   90   13
H: 5 11   W: 13 03   b.Poole 6-3-95

2013–14	Bournemouth	0	0		
2014–15	Bournemouth	0	0		
2015–16	Bournemouth	0	0		
2015–16	*Yeovil T*	36	7	36	7
2016–17	Bournemouth	0	0		
2016–17	*Leyton Orient*	11	1	11	1
2016–17	*Gillingham*	6	0	6	0
2017–18	Luton T	37	5	37	5

COTTER, Kavan (M)   0   0
b.Harrow

2016–17	Luton T	0	0
2017–18	Luton T	0	0

CUTHBERT, Scott (D)   343   16
H: 6 2   W: 14 00   b.Alexandria 15-6-87
Internationals: Scotland U19, U20, U21, B.

2004–05	Celtic	0	0		
2005–06	Celtic	0	0		
2006–07	Celtic	0	0		
2006–07	*Livingston*	4	1	4	1
2007–08	Celtic	0	0		
2008–09	Celtic	0	0		
2008–09	*St Mirren*	29	0	29	0
2009–10	Swindon T	39	3		
2010–11	Swindon T	41	2	80	5
2011–12	Leyton Orient	33	1		
2012–13	Leyton Orient	18	0		
2013–14	Leyton Orient	44	4		
2014–15	Leyton Orient	38	2	133	7
2015–16	Luton T	36	0		
2016–17	Luton T	38	1		
2017–18	Luton T	23	2	97	3

D'ATH, Lawson (M)   146   15
H: 5 9   W: 12 02   b.Witney 24-12-92

2010–11	Reading	0	0		
2011–12	Reading	0	0		
2011–12	*Yeovil T*	14	1	14	1
2012–13	Reading	0	0		
2012–13	*Cheltenham T*	2	1	2	1
2012–13	*Exeter C*	8	1	8	1
2013–14	Reading	0	0		
2013–14	*Dagenham & R*	21	1	21	1
2014–15	Northampton T	41	7		
2015–16	Northampton T	39	4		
2016–17	Northampton T	1	0	81	11
2016–17	Luton T	11	0		
2017–18	Luton T	9	0	20	0

FAMEWO, Akin (D)   6   0
H: 5 11   W: 10 06   b.Lewisham 9-11-98

2016–17	Luton T	3	0		
2017–18	Luton T	3	0	6	0

GAMBIN, Luke (M)   103   12
H: 5 6   W: 11 00   b.Surrey 16-3-93
Internationals: Malta Full caps.

2011–12	Barnet	1	0		
2012–13	Barnet	10	2		
2015–16	Barnet	44	4		
2016–17	Barnet	19	4	74	10
2016–17	Luton T	16	1		
2017–18	Luton T	13	1	29	2

HYLTON, Danny (F)   342 103
H: 6 0   W: 11 13   b.Camden 25-2-89

2008–09	Aldershot T	29	5		
2009–10	Aldershot T	21	3		
2010–11	Aldershot T	33	5		
2011–12	Aldershot T	44	13		
2012–13	Aldershot T	27	4	154	30
2013–14	Rotherham U	1	0	1	0
2013–14	*Bury*	7	2	7	2
2013–14	*AFC Wimbledon*	17	3	17	3
2014–15	Oxford U	44	14		
2015–16	Oxford U	41	12	85	26
2016–17	Luton T	39	21		
2017–18	Luton T	39	21	78	42

ISTED, Harry (G)   0   0
b. 5-3-97
From Southampton, Stoke C.

2017–18	Luton T	0	0

JAMES, Jack (F)   0   0

2017–18	Luton T	0	0

JARVIS, Aaron (F)   1   0
H: 6 2   W: 12 08   b. 24-1-98
From Basinstoke T.

2017–18	Luton T	1	0	1	0

JERVIS, Jake (F)   216   48
H: 6 3   W: 12 13   b.Birmingham 17-9-91

2009–10	Birmingham C	0	0		
2009–10	*Hereford U*	7	2		
2010–11	Birmingham C	0	0		
2010–11	*Notts Co*	10	0	10	0
2010–11	*Hereford U*	4	0	11	2
2011–12	Birmingham C	0	0		
2011–12	*Swindon T*	12	3	12	3
2011–12	*Preston NE*	5	2	5	2
2012–13	Birmingham C	2	0	2	0
2012–13	*Carlisle U*	5	3	5	3
2012–13	*Tranmere R*	4	1	4	1
2012–13	*Portsmouth*	3	1		
2012–13	*Elazigspor*	4	1	4	1
2013–14	Portsmouth	15	4	18	5
2014–15	Ross Co	27	4	27	4
2015–16	Plymouth Arg	42	11		
2016–17	Plymouth Arg	42	12		

—(continued)—

2017–18	Plymouth Arg	24	4	108	27
2017–18	Luton T	10	0	10	0

JONES, Ciaren (D)   0   0

2017–18	Luton T	0	0

JONES, Lloyd (D)   52   3
H: 6 3   W: 11 11   b.Plymouth 7-10-95
Internationals: Wales U17, U19. England U19, U20.

2012–13	Liverpool	0	0		
2013–14	Liverpool	0	0		
2014–15	Liverpool	0	0		
2014–15	*Cheltenham T*	6	0	6	0
2014–15	*Accrington S*	11	1	11	1
2015–16	Liverpool	0	0		
2015–16	*Blackpool*	10	0	10	0
2016–17	Liverpool	0	0		
2016–17	*Swindon T*	24	2	24	2
2017–18	Liverpool	0	0		
2017–18	Luton T	1	0	1	0

JUSTIN, James (F)   47   3
H: 6 0   W: 11 03   b.Luton 11-7-97
Internationals: England U20.

2015–16	Luton T	1	0		
2016–17	Luton T	29	1		
2017–18	Luton T	17	2	47	3

LEE, Elliot (F)   74   16
H: 5 11   W: 11 05   b.Co. Durham 16-12-94

2011–12	West Ham U	0	0		
2012–13	West Ham U	0	0		
2013–14	West Ham U	1	0		
2013–14	*Colchester U*	4	1		
2014–15	West Ham U	1	0		
2014–15	*Southend U*	0	0		
2014–15	*Luton T*	11	3		
2015–16	West Ham U	0	0	2	0
2015–16	*Blackpool*	4	0	4	0
2015–16	*Colchester U*	15	2	19	3
2016–17	Barnsley	6	0	6	0
2017–18	Luton T	32	10	43	13

LEE, Oliver (M)   176   16
H: 5 11   W: 12 07   b.Hornchurch 11-7-91

2009–10	West Ham U	0	0		
2010–11	West Ham U	0	0		
2010–11	*Dagenham & R*	5	0		
2011–12	West Ham U	0	0		
2011–12	*Dagenham & R*	16	3	21	3
2011–12	*Gillingham*	8	0	8	0
2012–13	Barnet	11	0	11	0
2012–13	Birmingham C	0	0		
2013–14	Birmingham C	16	1		
2014–15	Birmingham C	0	0	16	1
2014–15	*Plymouth Arg*	15	2	15	2
2015–16	Luton T	34	3		
2016–17	Luton T	33	1		
2017–18	Luton T	38	6	105	10

McCORMACK, Alan (M)   410   26
H: 5 8   W: 11 00   b.Dublin 10-1-84
Internationals: Republic of Ireland U19.

2002–03	Preston NE	0	0		
2003–04	Preston NE	5	0		
2003–04	*Leyton Orient*	10	0	10	0
2004–05	Preston NE	3	0		
2004–05	*Southend U*	7	2		
2005–06	Preston NE	0	0		
2005–06	*Motherwell*	24	2	24	2
2006–07	Preston NE	3	0	11	0
2006–07	*Southend U*	22	3		
2007–08	Southend U	42	8		
2008–09	Southend U	34	2		
2009–10	Southend U	41	3	146	18
2010–11	Charlton Ath	24	1	24	1
2011–12	Swindon T	40	2		
2012–13	Swindon T	40	0	80	2
2013–14	Brentford	43	1		
2014–15	Brentford	18	1		
2015–16	Brentford	27	0		
2016–17	Brentford	11	0	99	2
2017–18	Luton T	16	1	16	1

McQUOID, Josh (F)   213   23
H: 5 9   W: 10 10   b.Southampton 15-12-89
Internationals: Northern Ireland U19, U21, B, Full caps.

2006–07	Bournemouth	2	0		
2007–08	Bournemouth	5	0		
2008–09	Bournemouth	16	0		
2009–10	Bournemouth	29	1		
2010–11	Bournemouth	17	9		
2010–11	Millwall	11	1		
2011–12	Millwall	5	0	16	1
2011–12	*Burnley*	17	1	17	1
2012–13	Bournemouth	34	3		
2013–14	Bournemouth	1	0		

2013–14	Peterborough U	14	1	14	1
2014–15	Bournemouth	0	0	104	13
2014–15	*Coventry C*	14	3	14	3
2015–16	Luton T	29	3		
2016–17	Luton T	3	0		
2016–17	*Stevenage*	16	1	16	1
2017–18	Luton T	0	0	32	3

MEAD, Joe (D)   0   0
b.Luton
| 2017–18 | Luton T | 0 | 0 | | |

MULLINS, John (D)   442   26
H: 5 11 W: 12 07 b.Hampstead 6-11-85
2004–05	Reading	0	0		
2004–05	*Kidderminster H*	21	2	21	2
2005–06	Reading	0	0		
2006–07	Mansfield T	43	2		
2007–08	Mansfield T	43	2	86	4
2008–09	Stockport Co	33	3		
2009–10	Stockport Co	36	1	69	4
2010–11	Rotherham U	35	1		
2011–12	Rotherham U	35	2		
2012–13	Rotherham U	29	4	99	7
2012–13	Oxford U	8	2		
2013–14	Oxford U	35	3		
2014–15	Oxford U	44	2		
2015–16	Oxford U	40	0	127	7
2016–17	Luton T	23	0		
2017–18	Luton T	17	2	40	2

MUSONDA, Frankie (D)   3   0
H: 6 0 W: 11 03 b.Bedford 12-12-97
2015–16	Luton T	3	0		
2016–17	Luton T	0	0		
2017–18	Luton T	0	0	3	0

NEUFVILLE, Josh (M)   0   0
b.Luton
| 2017–18 | Luton T | 0 | 0 | | |

PECK, Jake (M)   0   0
| 2017–18 | Luton T | 0 | 0 | | |

POTTS, Danny (D)   94   6
H: 5 8 W: 11 00 b.Barking 13-4-94
Internationals: USA U20. England U18, U19, U20.
2011–12	West Ham U	3	0		
2012–13	West Ham U	2	0		
2012–13	*Colchester U*	5	0	5	0
2013–14	West Ham U	0	0		
2013–14	*Portsmouth*	5	0	5	0
2014–15	West Ham U	0	0	5	0
2015–16	Luton T	14	0		
2016–17	Luton T	23	0		
2017–18	Luton T	42	6	79	6

REA, Glen (D)   109   3
H: 6 0 W: 11 07 b.Brighton 3-9-94
Internationals: Republic of Ireland U21.
2013–14	Brighton & HA	0	0		
2014–15	Brighton & HA	0	0		
2015–16	Brighton & HA	0	0		
2015–16	*Southend U*	14	0	14	0
2015–16	*Luton T*	10	0		
2016–17	Luton T	39	2		
2017–18	Luton T	46	1	95	3

RICHARDSON, Drew (M)   0   0
b.Luton 14-1-01
| 2017–18 | Luton T | 0 | 0 | | |

RUDDOCK, Pelly (M)   107   7
H: 5 9 W: 9 13 b.Hendon 17-7-93
2011–12	West Ham U	0	0		
2013–14	West Ham U	0	0		
2014–15	Luton T	16	1		
2015–16	Luton T	21	2		
2016–17	Luton T	42	2		
2017–18	Luton T	28	2	107	7

SENIOR, Jack (D)   10   0
H: 5 8 W: 9 13 b.Halifax 13-1-97
2015–16	Huddersfield T	0	0		
2016–17	*Luton T*	10	0		
2017–18	Luton T	0	0	10	0

SHAMALO, Michael (F)   0   0
| 2017–18 | Luton T | 0 | 0 | | |

SHEA, James (G)   104   0
H: 5 11 W: 12 00 b.Islington 16-6-91
2009–10	Arsenal	0	0		
2010–11	Arsenal	0	0		
2011–12	Arsenal	0	0		
2011–12	*Dagenham & R*	1	0	1	0
2012–13	Arsenal	0	0		
2013–14	Arsenal	0	0		
2014–15	AFC Wimbledon	38	0		
2015–16	AFC Wimbledon	21	0		
2016–17	AFC Wimbledon	36	0	95	0
2017–18	Luton T	8	0	8	0

SHEEHAN, Alan (D)   359   24
H: 5 11 W: 11 02 b.Athlone 14-9-86
Internationals: Republic of Ireland U21.
2004–05	Leicester C	1	0		
2005–06	Leicester C	2	0		
2006–07	Leicester C	0	0		
2006–07	*Mansfield T*	10	0	10	0
2007–08	Leicester C	20	1	23	1
2007–08	Leeds U	10	1		
2008–09	Leeds U	11	1		
2008–09	*Crewe Alex*	3	0	3	0
2009–10	Leeds U	0	0	21	2
2009–10	*Oldham Ath*	8	1	8	1
2009–10	*Swindon T*	22	1		
2010–11	Swindon T	21	1	43	2
2011–12	Notts Co	39	2		
2012–13	Notts Co	33	0		
2013–14	Notts Co	42	7		
2014–15	Bradford C	23	1		
2014–15	*Peterborough U*	2	0	2	0
2015–16	Bradford C	2	0	25	1
2015–16	*Notts Co*	14	2	128	11
2015–16	*Luton T*	20	1		
2016–17	Luton T	34	2		
2017–18	Luton T	42	3	96	6

SHINNIE, Andrew (M)   184   25
H: 5 11 W: 10 13 b.Aberdeen 17-7-89
Internationals: Scotland U19, U21, Full caps.
2005–06	Rangers	0	0		
2006–07	Rangers	2	0		
2007–08	Rangers	0	0		
2008–09	Rangers	0	0		
2009–10	Rangers	0	0		
2010–11	Rangers	0	0	2	0
2011–12	Inverness CT	19	7		
2012–13	Inverness CT	38	12	57	19
2013–14	Birmingham C	26	2		
2014–15	Birmingham C	27	2		
2015–16	Birmingham C	14	0		
2015–16	*Rotherham U*	3	0	3	0
2016–17	Birmingham C	0	0	67	4
2016–17	*Hibernian*	27	1	27	1
2017–18	Luton T	28	1	28	1

STACEY, Jack (M)   92   3
H: 6 4 W: 13 05 b.Bracknell 6-4-96
2014–15	Reading	6	0		
2015–16	Reading	0	0		
2015–16	*Barnet*	2	0	2	0
2015–16	*Carlisle U*	9	2	9	2
2016–17	Reading	0	0	6	0
2016–17	*Exeter C*	34	0	34	0
2017–18	Luton T	41	1	41	1

STECH, Marek (G)   139   0
H: 6 3 W: 14 00 b.Prague 28-1-90
Internationals: Czech Republic U17 U21, Full caps.
2008–09	West Ham U	0	0		
2008–09	*Wycombe W*	2	0	2	0
2009–10	West Ham U	0	0		
2009–10	*Bournemouth*	1	0	1	0
2010–11	West Ham U	0	0		
2011–12	West Ham U	0	0		
2011–12	*Yeovil T*	5	0		
2011–12	*Leyton Orient*	2	0	2	0
2012–13	Yeovil T	46	0		
2013–14	Yeovil T	26	0	77	0
2014–15	Sparta Prague	17	0		
2015–16	Sparta Prague	2	0		
2016–17	Sparta Prague	0	0	19	0
2017–18	Luton T	38	0	38	0

TOMLINSON, Connor (F)   0   0
b. 12-2-01
| 2016–17 | Luton T | 0 | 0 | | |
| 2017–18 | Luton T | 0 | 0 | | |

Players retained or with offer of contract
Read, Arthur James.

Scholars
Belgrove, Scott; Byron, Toby Joshua Olakunle; Gordon-Stearn, Ciaran Gabriel Cornelius; James, Jack Alexander; Jones, Ciaren Alexander; Mead, Joe Thomas; Neufville, Joshua Tyler; Panter, Corey James Rodney; Parker, Tiernan Christopher Luke; Peck, Jake David; Phelan, Kai Mackenzie; Richardson, Drew Philip; Shamalo, Michel Oladie Ndjova; Sorunke, Olaoluwakitan Jonathan; Tomlinson, Connor Alexander.

MANCHESTER C (49)

ADARABIOYO, Tosin (D)   0   0
H: 6 3 b. 24-9-97
Internationals: England U16, U17, U18, U19.
2014–15	Manchester C	0	0		
2015–16	Manchester C	0	0		
2016–17	Manchester C	0	0		
2017–18	Manchester C	0	0		

AGUERO, Sergio (F)   435   240
H: 5 8 W: 11 09 b.Buenos Aires 2-6-88
Internationals: Argentina U17, U20, U23, Full caps.
2002–03	Independiente	1	0		
2003–04	Independiente	5	0		
2004–05	Independiente	12	5		
2005–06	Independiente	36	18	54	23
2006–07	Atletico Madrid	38	6		
2007–08	Atletico Madrid	37	19		
2008–09	Atletico Madrid	37	17		
2009–10	Atletico Madrid	31	12		
2010–11	Atletico Madrid	32	20	175	74
2011–12	Manchester C	34	23		
2012–13	Manchester C	30	12		
2013–14	Manchester C	23	17		
2014–15	Manchester C	33	26		
2015–16	Manchester C	30	24		
2016–17	Manchester C	31	20		
2017–18	Manchester C	25	21	206	143

AMBROSE, Thierry (F)   31   10
H: 5 10 W: 11 00 b.Sens 28-3-97
Internationals: France U16, U17, U18, U19.
2014–15	Manchester C	0	0		
2015–16	Manchester C	0	0		
2016–17	Manchester C	0	0		
2017–18	Manchester C	0	0		
2017–18	*NAC Breda*	31	10	31	10

BARKER, Brandon (M)   53   5
H: 5 9 W: 10 10 b.Manchester 4-10-96
Internationals: England U18, U19, U20.
2014–15	Manchester C	0	0		
2015–16	Manchester C	0	0		
2015–16	*Rotherham U*	4	1	4	1
2016–17	Manchester C	0	0		
2017–18	*NAC Breda*	22	2	22	2
2017–18	Manchester C	0	0		
2017–18	*Hibernian*	27	2	27	2

BERNARDO SILVA, Mota (M)   137   30
H: 5 8 W: 9 11 b.Lisbon 10-8-94
Internationals: Portugal U19, U21, Full caps.
2013–14	Benfica	1	0	1	0
2014–15	Monaco	32	9		
2015–16	Monaco	32	7		
2016–17	Monaco	37	8	101	24
2017–18	Manchester C	35	6	35	6

BRAVO, Claudio (G)   417   2
H: 6 0 W: 11 00 b.Viluco 13-4-83
Internationals: Chile U23, Full caps.
2003	Colo Colo	25	1		
2004	Colo Colo	18	0		
2005	Colo Colo	36	0		
2006	Colo Colo	14	0	93	1
2006–07	Real Sociedad	29	0		
2007–08	Real Sociedad	0	0		
2008–09	Real Sociedad	32	0		
2009–10	Real Sociedad	25	1		
2010–11	Real Sociedad	38	0		
2011–12	Real Sociedad	37	0		
2012–13	Real Sociedad	31	0		
2013–14	Real Sociedad	37	0	229	1
2014–15	Barcelona	37	0		
2015–16	Barcelona	32	0		
2016–17	Barcelona	1	0	70	0
2016–17	Manchester C	22	0		
2017–18	Manchester C	3	0	25	0

BRYAN, Kean (M)   44   2
H: 6 1 b.Manchester 1-11-96
Internationals: England U16, U17, U19, U20.
2016–17	Manchester C	0	0		
2016–17	*Bury*	12	0	12	0
2017–18	Manchester C	0	0		
2017–18	*Oldham Ath*	32	2	32	2

BUCKLEY-RICKETT, Isaac (M)   17   0
H: 5 10 W: 10 10 b. 14-3-98
Internationals: England U18, U19, U20.
2017–18	Manchester C	0	0		
2017–18	*FC Twente*	6	0	6	0
2017–18	*Oxford U*	11	0	11	0

CELINA, Bersant (F) — 63 12
H: 5 4　W: 9 06　b.Prizren 9-9-96
Internationals: Norway U16, U17. Kosovo Full caps.

2014–15	Manchester C	0	0		
2015–16	Manchester C	1	0		
2016–17	Manchester C	0	0		
2016–17	*FC Twente*	27	5	27	5
2017–18	Manchester C	0	0	1	0
2017–18	*Ipswich T*	35	7	35	7

DANILO, da Silva (D) — 219 22
H: 6 0　W: 11 07　b.Bicas 15-7-91
Internationals: Brazil U20, U23, Full caps.

2009	America Mineiro	8	0		
2010	America Mineiro	7	0	15	0
2010	Santos	26	4		
2011	Santos	23	1	49	5
2011–12	Porto	6	0		
2012–13	Porto	28	2		
2013–14	Porto	28	3		
2014–15	Porto	29	6	91	11
2015–16	Real Madrid	24	2		
2016–17	Real Madrid	17	1		
2017–18	Real Madrid	0	0	41	3
2017–18	Manchester C	23	3	23	3

DAVENPORT, Jacob (M) — 17 1
b.Manchester 28-12-98

2017–18	Manchester C	0	0		
2017–18	*Burton Alb*	17	1	17	1

DE BRUYNE, Kevin (M) — 249 55
H: 5 11　W: 12 00　b.Ghent 28-6-91
Internationals: Belgium U18, U19, U21, Full caps.

2008–09	Genk	2	0		
2009–10	Genk	30	3		
2010–11	Genk	32	5		
2011–12	Genk	15	6	79	14
2011–12	Chelsea	0	0		
2012–13	Chelsea	0	0		
2012–13	Werder Bremen	33	10	33	10
2013–14	Chelsea	3	0	3	0
2014–15	Wolfsburg	34	10		
2015–16	Wolfsburg	2	0	36	10
2015–16	Manchester C	25	7		
2016–17	Manchester C	36	6		
2017–18	Manchester C	37	8	98	21

DELE-BASHIRU, Ayotomiwa (M) — 0 0
H: 6 0　W: 10 10　b.17-9-99
Internationals: England U16.

2017–18	Manchester C	0	0

DELPH, Fabian (D) — 207 13
H: 5 8　W: 11 00　b.Bradford 21-11-89
Internationals: England U19, U21, Full caps.

2006–07	Leeds U	1	0		
2007–08	Leeds U	1	0		
2008–09	Leeds U	42	6		
2009–10	Aston Villa	8	0		
2010–11	Aston Villa	7	0		
2011–12	Aston Villa	11	0		
2011–12	*Leeds U*	5	0	49	6
2012–13	Aston Villa	24	0		
2013–14	Aston Villa	34	3		
2014–15	Aston Villa	28	0	112	3
2015–16	Manchester C	17	2		
2016–17	Manchester C	7	1		
2017–18	Manchester C	22	1	46	4

DENAYER, Jason (D) — 92 5
H: 6 0　W: 12 13　b.Brussels 28-6-95
Internationals: Belgium U19, U21, Full caps.

2013–14	Manchester C	0	0		
2014–15	Manchester C	0	0		
2014–15	*Celtic*	29	5	29	5
2015–16	Manchester C	0	0		
2015–16	Galatasaray	17	0		
2016–17	Manchester C	0	0		
2016–17	*Sunderland*	24	0	24	0
2017–18	Manchester C	0	0		
2017–18	*Galatasaray*	22	0	39	0

DIAZ, Brahim (M) — 5 0
H: 5 7　W: 10 10　b.3-8-99
Internationals: Spain U17, U19, U21.
From Malaga.

2016–17	Manchester C	0	0		
2017–18	Manchester C	5	0	5	0

DUHANEY, Demeaco (D) — 0 0
H: 5 11　W: 11 00　b.Manchester 13-10-98
Internationals: England U18, U20.

2017–18	Manchester C	0	0

EDERSON, de Moraes (G) — 139 0
H: 6 2　W: 13 08　b.Osasco 17-8-93
Internationals: Brazil U23, Full caps.

2011–12	Ribeirao	29	0	29	0
2012–13	Rio Ave	2	0		
2013–14	Rio Ave	18	0		
2014–15	Rio Ave	17	0	37	0
2015–16	Benfica	10	0		
2016–17	Benfica	27	0	37	0
2017–18	Manchester C	36	0	36	0

FERNANDINHO, Luis (M) — 391 51
H: 5 10　W: 10 09　b.Londrina 4-5-85
Internationals: Brazil Full caps.

2003	Paranaense	29	5		
2004	Paranaense	41	9		
2005	Paranaense	2	0	72	14
2005–06	Shakhtar Donetsk	22	1		
2006–07	Shakhtar Donetsk	25	1		
2008–09	Shakhtar Donetsk	21	5		
2009–10	Shakhtar Donetsk	24	4		
2010–11	Shakhtar Donetsk	15	3		
2011–12	Shakhtar Donetsk	24	5		
2012–13	Shakhtar Donetsk	23	2	154	20
2013–14	Manchester C	33	5		
2014–15	Manchester C	33	3		
2015–16	Manchester C	33	2		
2016–17	Manchester C	32	2		
2017–18	Manchester C	34	5	165	17

FODEN, Phil (M) — 5 0
H: 5 7　W: 11 00　b.28-5-00
Internationals: England U16, U17, U18, U19.

2016–17	Manchester C	0	0		
2017–18	Manchester C	5	0	5	0

GABRIEL JESUS, Fernando (F) — 86 36
b.3-4-97
Internationals: Brazil U20, U23, Full caps.

2015	Palmeiras	20	4		
2016	Palmeiras	27	12		
2016–17	Palmeiras	0	0	47	16
2016–17	Manchester C	10	7		
2017–18	Manchester C	29	13	39	20

GARCIA, Aleix (D) — 25 1
H: 5 8　W: 9 08　b.Ulldecona 28-6-97
Internationals: Spain U16, U17, U18, U19, U21.

2014–15	Villareal	1	0	1	0
2015–16	Manchester C	0	0		
2016–17	Manchester C	4	0		
2017–18	Manchester C	0	0	4	0
2017–18	*Girona*	20	1	20	1

GUNDOGAN, Ilkay (M) — 193 23
H: 5 11　W: 11 00　b.Gelsenkirchen 24-10-90
Internationals: Germany U18, U19, U20, U21, Full caps.

2008–09	Bochum	0	0		
2008–09	Nuremburg	1	0		
2009–10	Nuremburg	22	1		
2010–11	Nuremburg	25	5	48	6
2011–12	Borussia Dortmund	28	3		
2012–13	Borussia Dortmund	28	3		
2013–14	Borussia Dortmund	1	0		
2014–15	Borussia Dortmund	23	3		
2015–16	Borussia Dortmund	25	1	105	10
2016–17	Manchester C	10	3		
2017–18	Manchester C	30	4	40	7

GUNN, Angus (G) — 46 0
H: 6 0　W: 12 02　b.Norwich 22-1-96
Internationals: England U16, U17, U18, U19, U21.

2013–14	Manchester C	0	0		
2014–15	Manchester C	0	0		
2015–16	Manchester C	0	0		
2016–17	Manchester C	0	0		
2017–18	Manchester C	0	0		
2017–18	*Norwich C*	46	0	46	0

HARRISON, Jack (M) — 59 14
b.Stoke-on-Trent 20-11-96
Internationals: England U21.

2016	New York C	21	4		
2017	New York C	34	10	55	14
2017–18	New York C	0	0		
2017–18	*Middlesbrough*	4	0	4	0
2017–18	Manchester C	0	0		

HART, Joe (G) — 420 0
H: 6 3　W: 13 03　b.Shrewsbury 19-4-87
Internationals: England U19, U21, Full caps.

2004–05	Shrewsbury T	6	0		
2005–06	Shrewsbury T	46	0	52	0
2006–07	Manchester C	1	0		
2006–07	*Tranmere R*	6	0	6	0
2006–07	*Blackpool*	5	0	5	0
2007–08	Manchester C	26	0		
2008–09	Manchester C	23	0		
2009–10	Manchester C	0	0		
2009–10	*Birmingham C*	36	0	36	0
2010–11	Manchester C	38	0		
2011–12	Manchester C	38	0		
2012–13	Manchester C	38	0		
2013–14	Manchester C	31	0		
2014–15	Manchester C	36	0		
2015–16	Manchester C	35	0		
2016–17	Manchester C	0	0		
2016–17	*Torino*	36	0	36	0
2017–18	Manchester C	0	0	266	0
2017–18	*West Ham U*	19	0	19	0

KOMPANY, Vincent (D) — 338 22
H: 6 3　W: 12 05　b.Brussels 10-4-86
Internationals: Belgium U16, U17, Full caps.

2004–05	Anderlecht	29	2		
2005–06	Anderlecht	32	2	61	4
2006–07	Hamburg	6	0		
2007–08	Hamburg	22	1		
2008–09	Hamburg	1	0	29	1
2008–09	Manchester C	34	1		
2009–10	Manchester C	25	2		
2010–11	Manchester C	37	0		
2011–12	Manchester C	31	3		
2012–13	Manchester C	26	1		
2013–14	Manchester C	28	4		
2014–15	Manchester C	25	0		
2015–16	Manchester C	14	2		
2016–17	Manchester C	11	3		
2017–18	Manchester C	17	1	248	17

KONGOLO, Rodney (M) — 35 0
H: 6 2　W: 12 04　b.9-1-98
Internationals: Netherlands U16, U17, U19, U20.
From Feyenoord.

2017–18	Manchester C	0	0		
2017–18	*Doncaster R*	35	0	35	0

LAPORTE, Aymeric (D) — 203 9
H: 6 2　W: 13 05　b.Agen 27-5-94
Internationals: France U17, U18, U19, U21.

2011–12	Basconia	33	2	33	2
2012–13	Athletic Bilbao	15	0		
2013–14	Athletic Bilbao	35	2		
2014–15	Athletic Bilbao	33	0		
2015–16	Athletic Bilbao	26	3		
2016–17	Athletic Bilbao	33	2		
2017–18	Athletic Bilbao	19	0	161	7
2017–18	Manchester C	9	0	9	0

MAFFEO, Pablo (D) — 60 1
b.12-6-97
Internationals: Spain U16, U17, U19, U21.
From Espanyol.

2015–16	Manchester C	0	0		
2015–16	Girona	13	0		
2016–17	Manchester C	0	0		
2016–17	Girona	14	1		
2017–18	Manchester C	0	0		
2017–18	*Girona*	33	0	60	1

MANGALA, Eliaquim (D) — 217 10
H: 6 2　W: 11 09　b.Colombes 13-2-91
Internationals: France U21, Full caps.

2008–09	Standard Liege	11	0		
2009–10	Standard Liege	31	1		
2010–11	Standard Liege	35	1	77	2
2011–12	Porto	7	0		
2012–13	Porto	23	4		
2013–14	Porto	21	2	51	6
2014–15	Manchester C	25	0		
2015–16	Manchester C	23	0		
2016–17	Manchester C	0	0		
2016–17	*Valencia*	30	2	30	2
2017–18	Manchester C	9	0	57	0
2017–18	*Everton*	2	0	2	0

MENDY, Benjamin (D) — 170 2
H: 5 11　W: 11 05　b.Longjumeau 17-7-94
Internationals: France U16, U17, U18, U19, U21, Full caps.

2011–12	Le Havre	29	0		
2012–13	Le Havre	28	0	57	0
2013–14	Marseille	24	1		
2014–15	Marseille	33	0		
2015–16	Marseille	24	1	81	2
2016–17	Monaco	25	0	25	0
2017–18	Manchester C	7	0	7	0

NMECHA, Lukas (F) — 2 0
H: 6 0　W: 12 08　b.Hamburg 14-12-98
Internationals: England U16, U17, U18, U19, U21.

2017–18	Manchester C	2	0	2	0

OLIVER, Charlie (D)   **1 0**
H: 6 1   W: 11 05   b. 17-11-97
| 2017–18 | Manchester C | 0 | 0 | | |
| 2017–18 | Fleetwood T | 1 | 0 | 1 | 0 |

OTAMENDI, Nicolas (D)   **251 20**
H: 5 10   W: 11 09   b.Buenos Aires 12-2-88
Internationals: Argentina Full caps.
2007–08	Velez Sarsfield	1	0		
2008–09	Velez Sarsfield	18	0		
2009–10	Velez Sarsfield	19	1		
2010–11	Velez Sarsfield	2	0	40	1
2010–11	Porto	15	5		
2011–12	Porto	20	1		
2012–13	Porto	29	1		
2013–14	Porto	13	0	77	7
2013–14	Atletico Mineiro	5	0	5	0
2014–15	Valencia	35	6	35	6
2015–16	Manchester C	30	1		
2016–17	Manchester C	30	1		
2017–18	Manchester C	34	4	94	6

ROBERTS, Patrick (M)   **75 15**
H: 5 6   W: 10 06   b.Kingston upon Thames 5-2-97
Internationals: England U16, U17, U18, U19, U20.
2013–14	Fulham	2	0		
2014–15	Fulham	17	0	19	0
2015–16	Manchester C	1	0		
2015–16	Celtic	11	6		
2016–17	Manchester C	0	0		
2016–17	Celtic	32	9		
2017–18	Manchester C	0	0	1	0
2017–18	Celtic	12	0	55	15

SANE, Leroy (M)   **105 26**
H: 5 8   W: 9 13   b.Essen 11-1-96
Internationals: Germany U19, U21, Full caps.
2013–14	Schalke 04	1	0		
2014–15	Schalke 04	13	3		
2015–16	Schalke 04	33	8	47	11
2016–17	Manchester C	26	5		
2017–18	Manchester C	32	10	58	15

SILVA, David (F)   **451 78**
H: 5 7   W: 10 07   b.Arguineguin 8-1-86
Internationals: Spain U16, U17, U19, U20, U21, Full caps.
2003–04	Mestalla	14	1	14	1
2004–05	Eibar	35	5	35	5
2005–06	Celta Vigo	34	3	34	3
2006–07	Valencia	36	5		
2007–08	Valencia	34	4		
2008–09	Valencia	19	4		
2009–10	Valencia	30	8	119	21
2010–11	Manchester C	35	4		
2011–12	Manchester C	36	6		
2012–13	Manchester C	32	4		
2013–14	Manchester C	32	12		
2014–15	Manchester C	24	2		
2015–16	Manchester C	34	4		
2016–17	Manchester C	29	9	249	48

SMITH-BROWN, Ashley (D)   **69 2**
H: 5 10   W: 10 10   b.Manchester 31-3-96
Internationals: England U16, U17, U18, U19, U20.
2016–17	Manchester C	0	0		
2016–17	NAC Breda	29	1		
2016–17	Manchester C	0	0		
2016–17	NAC Breda	29	1	58	2
2017–18	Manchester C	0	0		
2017–18	Hearts	2	0	2	0
2017–18	Oxford U	9	0	9	0

STERLING, Raheem (F)   **192 49**
H: 5 7   W: 10 00   b.Kingston 8-12-94
Internationals: England U16, U17, U19, U21, Full caps.
2011–12	Liverpool	3	0		
2012–13	Liverpool	24	2		
2013–14	Liverpool	33	9		
2014–15	Liverpool	35	7	95	18
2015–16	Manchester C	31	6		
2016–17	Manchester C	33	7		
2017–18	Manchester C	33	18	97	31

STONES, John (D)   **146 1**
H: 6 2   W: 11 00   b.Barnsley 28-5-94
Internationals: England U19, U20, U21, Full caps.
2011–12	Barnsley	2	0		
2012–13	Barnsley	22	0	24	0
2012–13	Everton	0	0		
2013–14	Everton	21	0		
2014–15	Everton	23	1		
2015–16	Everton	33	0	77	1

| 2016–17 | Manchester C | 27 | 0 | | |
| 2017–18 | Manchester C | 18 | 0 | 45 | 0 |

TASENDE, Jose (D)   **65 3**
H: 5 7   W: 10 10   b.Coristanco 4-1-97
Internationals: Spain U17.
2014–15	Manchester C	0	0		
2015	New York C	14	0	14	0
2015–16	Manchester C	0	0		
2016–17	Manchester C	0	0		
2016–17	Mallorca	17	0	17	0
2017–18	Manchester C	0	0		
2017–18	NAC Breda	34	3	34	3

TOURE, Yaya (M)   **454 80**
H: 6 3   W: 14 02   b.Sokoura Bouake 13-5-83
Internationals: Ivory Coast Full caps.
2001–02	Beveren	28	0		
2002–03	Beveren	30	3		
2003–04	Beveren	12	0	70	3
2003–04	Metalurgs Donetsk	11	1		
2004–05	Metalurgs Donetsk	22	2	33	3
2005–06	Olympiacos	20	3	20	3
2006–07	Monaco	27	5	27	5
2007–08	Barcelona	26	1		
2008–09	Barcelona	25	2		
2009–10	Barcelona	23	1	74	4
2010–11	Manchester C	35	8		
2011–12	Manchester C	32	6		
2012–13	Manchester C	32	7		
2013–14	Manchester C	35	20		
2014–15	Manchester C	29	10		
2015–16	Manchester C	32	6		
2016–17	Manchester C	25	5		
2017–18	Manchester C	10	0	230	62

WALKER, Kyle (D)   **287 5**
H: 5 10   W: 11 07   b.Sheffield 28-5-90
Internationals: England U19, U21, Full caps.
2008–09	Sheffield U	2	0		
2008–09	Northampton T	9	0	9	0
2009–10	Tottenham H	2	0		
2009–10	Sheffield U	26	0	28	0
2010–11	Tottenham H	1	0		
2010–11	QPR	20	0	20	0
2010–11	Aston Villa	15	1	15	1
2011–12	Tottenham H	37	2		
2012–13	Tottenham H	36	0		
2013–14	Tottenham H	26	1		
2014–15	Tottenham H	15	0		
2015–16	Tottenham H	33	1		
2016–17	Tottenham H	33	0	183	4
2017–18	Manchester C	32	0	32	0

ZINCHENKO, Alexander (M)   **51 2**
H: 5 9   W: 9 08   b.Radomyshl 15-12-96
Internationals: Ukraine U16, U17, U18, U19, U21, Full caps.
2014–15	Ufa	7	0		
2015–16	Ufa	24	2	31	2
2016–17	Manchester C	0	0		
2016–17	PSV	12	0		
2017–18	Manchester C	0	0	12	0
2017–18	Manchester C	8	0	8	0

Players retained or with offer of contract
Agyepong, Thomas; Agyiri, Ernest; Amankwah, Yeboah; Antuna Romero, Carlos Uriel; Bolton, Luke Phillip; Brattan, Nathan Luke; Bryan, Kean Shay; Bytyqi, Sinan; Caceres, Anthony; Corrigan, Ryan; Dilrosun, Javairo Joreno Faustino; Diskerud, Mikkel Morgenstar Palssonn; Esmoris Tasende, Jose Angel; Fernandes Cantin, Paolo; Francis, Edward Albert; Garcia Alonso, Manuel; Garre, Benjamin Antonio; Gonzalez, Lorenzo Jose; Grimshaw, Daniel James; Herrera Ravelo, Yangel Clemente; Humphreys-Grant, Cameron; Ilic, Luka; Kayode, Olarenwaju Ayobami; Kigbu, Ahogrenashinme; Latibeaudiere, Joel Owen; Mari Villar, Pablo; Matondo, Rabbi; Moreno Duran, Marlos; Muric, Arijanet Anan; Nemane, Aaron Evans; Nwakali, Chidiebere Chikioke; Poveda-Ocampo, Ian Carlo; Pozo La Rosa, Iker; Richards, Taylor Jerome; Rosler, Colin; Ross Palmer Brown, Erik; Smith, Matthew; Tanor, Collins; Wilson, Tyreke; Yeboah, Yaw.

Scholars
Anderson, Curtis Rainford; Dele-Bashiru, Oluwafisayo Faruq; Frimpong, Jeremie; Garcia Martret, Eric; Nmecha, Felix Kalu; Ogbeta, Nathanael; Ogunby, Henri William; Scott, Thomas Henry; Simmonds, Keyendrah Qwamalik Tegan; Touaizi Zoubdi, Nabil.

MANCHESTER U (50)

ANDER HERRERA, Aguera (M)   **270 22**
H: 6 0   W: 10 10   b.Bilbao 14-8-89
Internationals: Spain U20, U21, U23, Full caps.
2008–09	Real Zaragoza	17	2		
2009–10	Real Zaragoza	30	2		
2010–11	Real Zaragoza	19	1	66	5
2011–12	Athletic Bilbao	32	1		
2012–13	Athletic Bilbao	29	1	29	1
2013–14	Athletic Bilbao	33	5	65	6
2014–15	Manchester U	26	6		
2015–16	Manchester U	27	3		
2016–17	Manchester U	31	1		
2017–18	Manchester U	26	0	110	10

BAILLY, Eric (D)   **78 1**
H: 6 2   W: 12 02   b.Bingerville 12-4-94
Internationals: Ivory Coast Full caps.
2014–15	Espanyol	5	0	5	0
2014–15	Villareal	10	0		
2015–16	Villareal	25	0	35	0
2016–17	Manchester U	25	0		
2017–18	Manchester U	13	1	38	1

BLIND, Daley (M)   **209 7**
H: 5 11   W: 10 10   b.Amsterdam 9-3-90
Internationals: Netherlands U16, U17, U19, U21, Full caps.
2008–09	Ajax	5	0		
2009–10	Ajax	0	0		
2009–10	Groningen	17	0	17	0
2010–11	Ajax	10	0		
2011–12	Ajax	21	0		
2012–13	Ajax	34	2		
2013–14	Ajax	29	1		
2014–15	Ajax	3	0	102	3
2014–15	Manchester U	25	2		
2015–16	Manchester U	35	1		
2016–17	Manchester U	23	1		
2017–18	Manchester U	7	0	90	4

BORTHWICK-JACKSON, Cameron (D)   **17 0**
H: 6 3   W: 13 10   b.Manchester 2-2-97
Internationals: England U16, U17, U19, U20.
2015–16	Manchester U	10	0		
2016–17	Manchester U	0	0		
2016–17	Wolverhampton W	6	0	6	0
2017–18	Manchester U	0	0	10	0
2017–18	Leeds U	1	0	1	0

CARRICK, Michael (M)   **524 27**
H: 6 1   W: 11 10   b.Wallsend 28-7-81
Internationals: England U18, U21, B, Full caps.
1998–99	West Ham U	0	0		
1999–2000	West Ham U	8	1		
1999–2000	Swindon T	6	2	6	2
1999–2000	Birmingham C	2	0	2	0
2000–01	West Ham U	33	1		
2001–02	West Ham U	30	2		
2002–03	West Ham U	30	1		
2003–04	West Ham U	35	1		
2004–05	West Ham U	0	0	136	6
2004–05	Tottenham H	29	0		
2005–06	Tottenham H	35	2	64	2
2006–07	Manchester U	33	3		
2007–08	Manchester U	31	2		
2008–09	Manchester U	28	4		
2009–10	Manchester U	30	3		
2010–11	Manchester U	28	0		
2011–12	Manchester U	30	2		
2012–13	Manchester U	36	1		
2013–14	Manchester U	29	1		
2014–15	Manchester U	18	1		
2015–16	Manchester U	28	0		
2016–17	Manchester U	23	0		
2017–18	Manchester U	2	0	316	17

CASTRO, Joel (G)   **7 0**
H: 6 2   W: 12 13   b. 28-6-96
Internationals: Switzerland U16, U17. Portugal U17, U18, U19, U20, U21.
2015–16	Manchester U	0	0		
2015–16	Rochdale	6	0	6	0
2016–17	Belenenses	0	0		
2016–17	Manchester U	1	0		
2017–18	Manchester U	0	0	1	0

DARMIAN, Matteo (D)   **224 5**
H: 6 0   W: 11 00   b.Legnano 2-12-89
Internationals: Italy U17, U18, U19, U20, U21, Full caps.
2006–07	AC Milan	1	0		
2007–08	AC Milan	0	0		
2008–09	AC Milan	3	0		

Season	Club	Apps	Gls	Tot Apps	Tot Gls
2009–10	AC Milan	0	0	4	0
2009–10	Padova	22	1	22	1
2010–11	Palermo	11	0	11	0
2011–12	Torino	33	1		
2012–13	Torino	30	0		
2013–14	Torino	37	0		
2014–15	Torino	33	2	133	0
2015–16	Manchester U	28	1		
2016–17	Manchester U	18	0		
2017–18	Manchester U	8	0	54	1

DE GEA, David (G) 294 0
H: 6 3   W: 12 13   b.Madrid 7-11-90
Internationals: Spain U15, U17, U19, U20, U21, U23, Full caps.

Season	Club	Apps	Gls	Tot Apps	Tot Gls
2009–10	Atletico Madrid	19	0		
2010–11	Atletico Madrid	38	0	57	0
2011–12	Manchester U	29	0		
2012–13	Manchester U	28	0		
2013–14	Manchester U	37	0		
2014–15	Manchester U	37	0		
2015–16	Manchester U	34	0		
2016–17	Manchester U	35	0		
2017–18	Manchester U	37	0	237	0

FELLAINI, Marouane (M) 308 43
H: 6 4   W: 13 05   b.Brussels 22-11-87
Internationals: Belgium U18, U19, U21, Full caps.

Season	Club	Apps	Gls	Tot Apps	Tot Gls
2006–07	Standard Liege	29	0		
2007–08	Standard Liege	30	6		
2008–09	Standard Liege	3	0	62	6
2008–09	Everton	30	8		
2009–10	Everton	23	2		
2010–11	Everton	20	1		
2011–12	Everton	34	3		
2012–13	Everton	31	11		
2013–14	Everton	3	0	141	25
2013–14	Manchester U	16	0		
2014–15	Manchester U	27	6		
2015–16	Manchester U	18	1		
2016–17	Manchester U	28	1		
2017–18	Manchester U	16	4	105	12

FOSU-MENSAH, Timothy (D) 33 0
H: 5 10   W: 10 10   b.Amsterdam 3-1-98
Internationals: Netherlands U16, U17, U19, U21, Full caps.

Season	Club	Apps	Gls	Tot Apps	Tot Gls
2015–16	Manchester U	8	0		
2016–17	Manchester U	4	0		
2017–18	Manchester U	0	0	12	0
2017–18	Crystal Palace	21	0	21	0

GOMES, Angel (M) 1 0
b.Enfield 31-8-00
Internationals: England U16, U17, U18.

Season	Club	Apps	Gls	Tot Apps	Tot Gls
2016–17	Manchester U	1	0		
2017–18	Manchester U	0	0	1	0

HAMILTON, Ethan (M) 0 0
b.Edinburgh 18-10-98
Internationals: Scotland U19.

Season	Club	Apps	Gls	Tot Apps	Tot Gls
2017–18	Manchester U	0	0		

HENDERSON, Dean (G) 45 0
H: 6 3   W: 12 13   b.Whitehaven 12-3-97
Internationals: England U16, U17, U20, U21.

Season	Club	Apps	Gls	Tot Apps	Tot Gls
2015–16	Manchester U	0	0		
2016–17	Manchester U	0	0		
2016–17	Grimsby T	7	0	7	0
2017–18	Manchester U	0	0		
2017–18	Shrewsbury T	38	0	38	0

IBRAHIMOVIC, Zlatan (F) 517 319
H: 6 4   W: 13 03   b.Malmo 3-10-81
Internationals: Sweden U18, U21, Full caps.

Season	Club	Apps	Gls	Tot Apps	Tot Gls
1999	Malmo	6	1		
2000	Malmo	26	12		
2001	Malmo	8	3	40	16
2001–02	Ajax	24	6		
2002–03	Ajax	25	13		
2003–04	Ajax	22	13		
2004–05	Ajax	3	3	74	35
2004–05	Juventus	35	16		
2005–06	Juventus	35	7	70	23
2006–07	Inter Milan	27	15		
2007–08	Inter Milan	26	17		
2008–09	Inter Milan	35	25	88	57
2009–10	Barcelona	29	16		
2010–11	Barcelona	0	0	29	16
2010–11	AC Milan	29	14		
2011–12	AC Milan	32	28	61	42
2012–13	Paris Saint-Germain	34	30		
2013–14	Paris Saint-Germain	33	26		
2014–15	Paris Saint-Germain	24	19		
2015–16	Paris Saint-Germain	31	38	122	113
2016–17	Manchester U	28	17		
2017–18	Manchester U	5	0	33	17

Transferred to LA Galaxy, March 2018.

JOHNSTONE, Samuel (G) 140 0
H: 6 0   W: 12 10   b.Preston 25-3-93
Internationals: England U16, U17, U19, U20.

Season	Club	Apps	Gls	Tot Apps	Tot Gls
2009–10	Manchester U	0	0		
2010–11	Manchester U	0	0		
2011–12	Manchester U	0	0		
2011–12	Scunthorpe U	12	0	12	0
2012–13	Walsall	7	0	7	0
2013–14	Manchester U	0	0		
2013–14	Yeovil T	1	0	1	0
2013–14	Doncaster R	18	0		
2014–15	Manchester U	0	0		
2014–15	Doncaster R	10	0	28	0
2014–15	Preston NE	22	0		
2015–16	Manchester U	0	0		
2015–16	Preston NE	4	0	26	0
2016–17	Manchester U	0	0		
2016–17	Aston Villa	21	0		
2017–18	Manchester U	0	0		
2017–18	Aston Villa	45	0	66	0

JONES, Phil (D) 180 2
H: 5 11   W: 11 02   b.Preston 21-2-92
Internationals: England U19, U21, Full caps.

Season	Club	Apps	Gls	Tot Apps	Tot Gls
2009–10	Blackburn R	9	0		
2010–11	Blackburn R	26	0	35	0
2011–12	Manchester U	29	1		
2012–13	Manchester U	17	0		
2013–14	Manchester U	26	1		
2014–15	Manchester U	22	0		
2015–16	Manchester U	10	0		
2016–17	Manchester U	18	0		
2017–18	Manchester U	23	0	145	2

LINDELOF, Victor (D) 115 2
H: 6 2   W: 12 11   b.Vasteras 17-7-94
Internationals: Sweden U17, U19, U21, Full caps.

Season	Club	Apps	Gls	Tot Apps	Tot Gls
2009	Vasteras	1	0		
2010	Vasteras	9	0		
2011	Vasteras	27	0		
2012	Vasteras	13	0	50	0
2012–13	Benfica	1	0		
2013–14	Benfica	1	0		
2014–15	Benfica	0	0		
2015–16	Benfica	15	1		
2016–17	Benfica	32	1	48	2
2017–18	Manchester U	17	0	17	0

LINGARD, Jesse (M) 131 24
H: 5 3   W: 11 11   b.Warrington 15-12-92
Internationals: England U17, U21, Full caps.

Season	Club	Apps	Gls	Tot Apps	Tot Gls
2011–12	Manchester U	0	0		
2012–13	Manchester U	0	0		
2012–13	Leicester C	5	0	5	0
2013–14	Manchester U	0	0		
2013–14	Birmingham C	13	6	13	6
2013–14	Brighton & HA	15	3	15	3
2014–15	Manchester U	1	0		
2014–15	Derby Co	14	2	14	2
2015–16	Manchester U	25	4		
2016–17	Manchester U	25	1		
2017–18	Manchester U	33	8	84	13

LUKAKU, Romelu (F) 293 134
H: 6 3   W: 13 00   b.Antwerp 13-5-93
Internationals: Belgium U15, U18, U21, Full caps.

Season	Club	Apps	Gls	Tot Apps	Tot Gls
2008–09	Anderlecht	1	0		
2009–10	Anderlecht	33	15		
2010–11	Anderlecht	37	16		
2011–12	Anderlecht	2	2	73	33
2011–12	Chelsea	8	0		
2012–13	Chelsea	0	0		
2012–13	WBA	35	17	35	17
2013–14	Chelsea	2	0	10	0
2013–14	Everton	31	15		
2014–15	Everton	36	10		
2015–16	Everton	37	18		
2016–17	Everton	37	25	141	68
2017–18	Manchester U	34	16	34	16

MARTIAL, Anthony (F) 138 35
H: 5 11   W: 12 08   b.Massy 5-12-95
Internationals: France U16, U17, U18, U19, U21, Full caps.

Season	Club	Apps	Gls	Tot Apps	Tot Gls
2012–13	Lyon	3	0	3	0
2013–14	Monaco	11	2		
2014–15	Monaco	35	9		
2015–16	Monaco	3	0	49	11
2015–16	Manchester U	31	11		
2016–17	Manchester U	25	4		
2017–18	Manchester U	30	9	86	24

MATA, Juan (M) 389 91
H: 5 7   W: 11 00   b.Ocon de Villafranca 28-4-88
Internationals: Spain U16, U17, U19, U20, U21, U23, Full caps.

Season	Club	Apps	Gls	Tot Apps	Tot Gls
2006–07	Real Madrid B	39	10	39	10
2007–08	Valencia	24	5		
2008–09	Valencia	37	11		
2009–10	Valencia	35	9		
2010–11	Valencia	33	8	129	33
2011–12	Chelsea	34	6		
2012–13	Chelsea	35	12		
2013–14	Chelsea	13	0	82	18
2013–14	Manchester U	15	6		
2014–15	Manchester U	33	9		
2015–16	Manchester U	38	6		
2016–17	Manchester U	25	6		
2017–18	Manchester U	28	3	139	30

MATIC, Nemanja (M) 325 17
H: 6 4   W: 13 02   b.Sabac 1-8-88
Internationals: Serbia U21, Full caps.

Season	Club	Apps	Gls	Tot Apps	Tot Gls
2005–06	Jedinstvo	7	0		
2006–07	Jedinstvo	9	0	16	0
2006–07	Kosice	13	1		
2007–08	Kosice	25	1		
2008–09	Kosice	29	2	67	4
2009–10	Chelsea	2	0		
2010–11	Chelsea	0	0		
2010–11	Vitesse	27	2	27	2
2011–12	Benfica	16	1		
2012–13	Benfica	26	3		
2013–14	Benfica	14	2	56	6
2013–14	Chelsea	17	0		
2014–15	Chelsea	36	1		
2015–16	Chelsea	33	2		
2016–17	Chelsea	35	1	123	4
2017–18	Manchester U	36	1	36	1

McTOMINAY, Scott (M) 15 0
H: 5 10   W: 10 03   b.Lancaster 8-12-96
Internationals: Scotland Full caps.

Season	Club	Apps	Gls	Tot Apps	Tot Gls
2016–17	Manchester U	2	0		
2017–18	Manchester U	13	0	15	0

MITCHELL, Demetri (D) 10 0
H: 5 9   W: 11 11   b.Manchester 11-1-97
Internationals: England U16, U17, U18, U20.

Season	Club	Apps	Gls	Tot Apps	Tot Gls
2016–17	Manchester U	1	0		
2017–18	Manchester U	0	0	1	0
2017–18	Hearts	9	0	9	0

PEREIRA, Andreas (M) 63 6
H: 5 10   W: 10 06   b.Duffel 1-1-96
Internationals: Belgium U16, U17. Brazil U17, U20, U23.

Season	Club	Apps	Gls	Tot Apps	Tot Gls
2014–15	Manchester U	1	0		
2015–16	Manchester U	4	0		
2016–17	Granada	35	5	35	5
2017–18	Manchester U	0	0	5	0
2017–18	Valencia	23	1	23	1

POGBA, Paul (M) 184 39
H: 6 1   W: 12 08   b.Lagny-sur-Marne 15-3-93
Internationals: France U16, U17, U18, U19, U20, Full caps.

Season	Club	Apps	Gls	Tot Apps	Tot Gls
2009–10	Manchester U	0	0		
2010–11	Manchester U	0	0		
2011–12	Manchester U	3	0		
2012–13	Juventus	27	5		
2013–14	Juventus	36	7		
2014–15	Juventus	26	8		
2015–16	Juventus	35	8	124	28
2016–17	Manchester U	30	5		
2017–18	Manchester U	27	6	60	11

POOLE, Regan (D) 37 0
b.Cardiff 18-6-98
Internationals: Wales U17, U19, U20, U21.

Season	Club	Apps	Gls	Tot Apps	Tot Gls
2014–15	Newport Co	11	0		
2015–16	Newport Co	4	0	15	0
2015–16	Manchester U	0	0		
2016–17	Manchester U	0	0		
2017–18	Manchester U	0	0		
2017–18	Northampton T	22	0	22	0

RASHFORD, Marcus (F) 78 17
H: 5 11   W: 11 00   b.Manchester 31-10-97
Internationals: England U16, U18, U20, U21, Full caps.

Season	Club	Apps	Gls	Tot Apps	Tot Gls
2015–16	Manchester U	11	5		
2016–17	Manchester U	32	5		
2017–18	Manchester U	35	7	78	17

REDMOND, Devonte (M) 1 0
H: 6 1 W: 11 11 b. 19-9-96
2017–18	Manchester U	0	0	
2017–18	*Scunthorpe U*	1	0	1 0

ROJO, Marcos (D) 168 9
H: 6 2 W: 12 06 b.La Plata 20-3-90
Internationals: Argentina Full caps.
2008–09	Estudiantes	6	1	
2009–10	Estudiantes	18	0	
2010–11	Estudiantes	19	2	43 3
2011–12	Spartak Moscow	8	0	8 0
2012–13	Sporting Lisbon	24	1	
2013–14	Sporting Lisbon	25	4	49 5
2014–15	Manchester U	22	0	
2015–16	Manchester U	16	0	
2016–17	Manchester U	21	1	
2017–18	Manchester U	9	0	68 1

ROMERO, Sergio (G) 176 0
H: 6 4 W: 13 01 b.Yrigoyen 22-2-87
Internationals: Argentina U20, Full caps.
2006–07	Racing Club	5	0	5 0
2007–08	AZ Alkmaar	12	0	
2008–09	AZ Alkmaar	28	0	
2009–10	AZ Alkmaar	27	0	
2010–11	AZ Alkmaar	23	0	
2011–12	AZ Alkmaar	0	0	90 0
2011–12	Sampdoria	29	0	
2012–13	Sampdoria	32	0	
2013–14	Sampdoria	0	0	
2013–14	Monaco	3	0	3 0
2014–15	Sampdoria	10	0	71 0
2015–16	Manchester U	4	0	
2016–17	Manchester U	2	0	
2017–18	Manchester U	1	0	7 0

SANCHEZ, Alexis (F) 419 138
H: 5 6 W: 11 09 b.Tocopilla 19-12-88
Internationals: Chile U20, Full caps.
2005	Cobreloa	35	3	
2006	Cobreloa	12	6	47 9
2006–07	Colo Colo	32	5	32 5
2007–08	River Plate	23	4	23 4
2008–09	Udinese	32	3	
2009–10	Udinese	32	5	
2010–11	Udinese	31	12	95 20
2011–12	Barcelona	25	11	
2012–13	Barcelona	29	8	
2013–14	Barcelona	34	19	88 38
2014–15	Arsenal	35	16	
2015–16	Arsenal	30	13	
2016–17	Arsenal	38	24	
2017–18	Arsenal	19	7	122 60
2017–18	Manchester U	12	2	12 2

SHAW, Luke (D) 103 0
H: 6 1 W: 11 11 b.Kingston 12-7-95
Internationals: England U16, U17, U21, Full caps.
2011–12	Southampton	0	0	
2012–13	Southampton	25	0	
2013–14	Southampton	35	0	60 0
2014–15	Manchester U	16	0	
2015–16	Manchester U	5	0	
2016–17	Manchester U	11	0	
2017–18	Manchester U	11	0	43 0

SMALLING, Chris (D) 195 11
H: 6 4 W: 14 02 b.Greenwich 22-11-89
Internationals: England U18, U20, U21, Full caps.
2008–09	Fulham	1	0	
2009–10	Fulham	12	0	13 0
2010–11	Manchester U	16	0	
2011–12	Manchester U	19	1	
2012–13	Manchester U	15	0	
2013–14	Manchester U	25	1	
2014–15	Manchester U	25	4	
2015–16	Manchester U	35	0	
2016–17	Manchester U	18	1	
2017–18	Manchester U	29	4	182 11

TUANZEBE, Axel (D) 10 0
H: 6 0 W: 11 11 b.Bunia 14-11-97
Internationals: England U19, U20, U21.
2015–16	Manchester U	0	0	
2016–17	Manchester U	4	0	
2017–18	Manchester U	1	0	5 0
2017–18	*Aston Villa*	5	0	5 0

VALENCIA, Antonio (M) 408 35
H: 5 10 W: 12 04 b.Lago Agrio 5-8-85
Internationals: Ecuador U20, 21, U23, Full caps.
2002	El Nacional	1	0	
2003	El Nacional	26	2	
2004	El Nacional	42	5	

2005	El Nacional	14	4	83 11
2005–06	Villarreal	2	0	2 0
2005–06	*Recreativo*	4	0	4 0
2006–07	Wigan Ath	22	1	
2007–08	Wigan Ath	31	3	
2008–09	Wigan Ath	31	3	84 7
2009–10	Manchester U	34	5	
2010–11	Manchester U	10	1	
2011–12	Manchester U	27	4	
2012–13	Manchester U	30	1	
2013–14	Manchester U	29	2	
2014–15	Manchester U	32	0	
2015–16	Manchester U	14	0	
2016–17	Manchester U	28	1	
2017–18	Manchester U	31	3	235 17

WILSON, James (F) 52 9
H: 6 0 W: 12 04 b.Biddulph 1-12-95
Internationals: England U16, U19, U20, U21.
2013–14	Manchester U	1	2	
2014–15	Manchester U	13	1	
2015–16	Manchester U	0	0	
2015–16	*Brighton & HA*	25	5	25 5
2016–17	Manchester U	0	0	
2016–17	*Derby Co*	4	0	4 0
2017–18	Manchester U	0	0	15 3
2017–18	*Sheffield U*	8	1	8 1

YOUNG, Ashley (M) 405 62
H: 5 10 W: 10 03 b.Stevenage 9-7-85
Internationals: England U21, Full caps.
2002–03	Watford	0	0	
2003–04	Watford	5	3	
2004–05	Watford	34	0	
2005–06	Watford	39	13	
2006–07	Watford	20	3	98 19
2006–07	Aston Villa	13	2	
2007–08	Aston Villa	37	9	
2008–09	Aston Villa	36	7	
2009–10	Aston Villa	37	5	
2010–11	Aston Villa	34	7	157 30
2011–12	Manchester U	25	6	
2012–13	Manchester U	19	0	
2013–14	Manchester U	20	2	
2014–15	Manchester U	26	2	
2015–16	Manchester U	18	1	
2016–17	Manchester U	12	0	
2017–18	Manchester U	30	2	150 13

Players retained or with offer of contract

Baars, Millen; Barlow, Aidan Will; Bohui, Joshua Raymond; Boonen, Indy Zeb Pepe; Burkart, Nishan Connell; Chong, Tahith; Dearnley, Zachary Harry; Dunne, Max Edward; Ercolani, Luca; Fojticek, Alex; Gribbin, Callum Anthony; Kehinde, Tosin Samuel; Levitt, Dylan James Christopher; McIntosh-Buffonge, Darren Raekwon; O'Connor, Lee Patrick; O'Hara, Kieran Michael; Olosunde, Matthew Olawale; Puigmal Martinez, Arnau; Ramazani, Largie; Sang, Thomas Roy; Tanner, George; Traore, Aliou Badara; Warren, Tyrell Nathaniel; Whelan, Callum Tyler; Williams, Brandon Paul Brian; Williams, Ro-Shaun Oman; Willock, Matthew.

Scholars

Bernard, Di'Shon Joel; Bughail-Mellor, D'Mani Lucell; Galbraith, Ethan Stuart William; Garner, James David; Laird, Ethan Benjamin; McGhee, Dion Alex; Thompson, James George.

MANSFIELD T (51)

ANDERSON, Paul (M) 325 32
H: 5 9 W: 10 04 b.Leicester 23-7-88
Internationals: England U19.
2005–06	Hull C	0	0	
2005–06	Liverpool	0	0	
2006–07	Liverpool	0	0	
2007–08	Liverpool	0	0	
2007–08	*Swansea C*	31	7	31 7
2008–09	Liverpool	0	0	
2008–09	*Nottingham F*	26	2	
2009–10	Nottingham F	37	4	
2010–11	Nottingham F	36	3	
2011–12	Nottingham F	17	0	
2012–13	Nottingham F	0	0	116 9
2012–13	Bristol C	29	3	29 3
2013–14	Ipswich T	31	5	
2014–15	Ipswich T	35	1	66 6
2015–16	Bradford C	11	0	
2016–17	Bradford C	3	0	14 0
2016–17	Northampton T	36	6	36 6
2016–17	Mansfield T	0	0	
2017–18	Mansfield T	33	1	33 1

ANGOL, Lee (M) 78 21
H: 5 10 W: 11 04 b. 4-8-94
2012–13	Wycombe W	3	0	
2013–14	Wycombe W	0	0	3 0
2014–15	Luton T	0	0	
2015–16	Peterborough U	33	11	
2016–17	Peterborough U	13	1	46 12
2017–18	Mansfield T	29	9	29 9

ATKINSON, Will (M) 330 25
H: 5 10 W: 10 07 b.Beverley 14-10-88
2006–07	Hull C	0	0	
2007–08	Hull C	0	0	
2007–08	*Port Vale*	4	0	4 0
2007–08	*Mansfield T*	12	0	
2008–09	Hull C	0	0	
2009–10	Hull C	2	1	
2009–10	*Rochdale*	15	3	
2010–11	Hull C	4	0	
2010–11	*Rotherham U*	3	1	3 1
2010–11	*Rochdale*	21	2	36 5
2011–12	Hull C	0	0	6 1
2011–12	*Plymouth Arg*	22	4	22 4
2011–12	*Bradford C*	12	1	
2012–13	Bradford C	42	1	54 2
2013–14	Southend U	45	2	
2014–15	Southend U	36	2	
2015–16	Southend U	36	2	
2016–17	Southend U	37	4	154 10
2017–18	Mansfield T	39	2	51 2

BENNETT, Rhys (D) 180 8
H: 6 3 W: 12 00 b.Manchester 1-9-91
2011–12	Bolton W	1	0	
2011–12	*Falkirk*	19	0	19 0
2013–14	Rochdale	22	0	
2014–15	Rochdale	39	2	
2015–16	Rochdale	16	2	77 4
2016–17	Mansfield T	46	2	
2017–18	Mansfield T	38	2	84 4

BENNING, Malvind (D) 159 8
H: 5 10 W: 12 00 b.Sandwell 2-11-93
2012–13	Walsall	10	0	
2013–14	Walsall	0	0	
2014–15	Walsall	20	0	46 2
2014–15	*York C*	9	0	9 0
2015–16	Mansfield T	31	4	
2016–17	Mansfield T	45	1	
2017–18	Mansfield T	28	1	104 6

BUTCHER, Calum (D) 111 9
H: 6 1 W: 13 01 b.Rochford 26-2-91
2007–08	Tottenham H	0	0	
2008–09	Tottenham H	0	0	
2009–10	Tottenham H	0	0	
2009–10	*Barnet*	3	0	3 0
From Hayes & Yeading.				
2013–14	Dundee U	6	0	
2014–15	Dundee U	15	1	21 1
2015–16	Burton Alb	39	5	
2016–17	Burton Alb	1	0	40 5
2016–17	Millwall	30	2	
2017–18	Millwall	0	0	30 2
2017–18	Mansfield T	17	1	17 1

BYROM, Joel (M) 194 14
H: 6 0 W: 12 04 b.Accrington 14-9-86
Internationals: England C.
2004–05	Blackburn R	0	0	
2005–06	Blackburn R	0	0	
2006–07	Accrington S	1	0	1 0
From Clitheroe, Southport, Clitheroe, Northwich Vic.				
2010–11	Stevenage	7	0	
2011–12	Stevenage	32	4	39 4
2012–13	Preston NE	22	2	
2013–14	Preston NE	11	2	33 4
2013–14	*Oldham Ath*	4	0	4 0
2014–15	Northampton T	39	3	
2015–16	Northampton T	35	2	
2016–17	Northampton T	2	0	76 5
2016–17	Mansfield T	22	0	
2017–18	Mansfield T	19	1	41 1

DIAMOND, Zander (D) 407 29
H: 6 2 W: 11 07 b.Alexandria 3-12-85
Internationals: Scotland U21, B.
2003–04	Aberdeen	19	2	
2004–05	Aberdeen	29	3	
2005–06	Aberdeen	33	0	
2006–07	Aberdeen	21	0	
2007–08	Aberdeen	26	3	
2008–09	Aberdeen	28	4	
2009–10	Aberdeen	16	3	
2010–11	Aberdeen	32	1	204 16
2011–12	Oldham Ath	23	2	23 2
2012–13	Burton Alb	37	4	

2013–14	Burton Alb	10	1	47	5
2013–14	*Northampton T*	14	1		
2014–15	Northampton T	21	1		
2015–16	Northampton T	39	1		
2016–17	Northampton T	39	0	113	3
2016–17	Mansfield T	0	0		
2017–18	Mansfield T	20	3	20	3

DIGBY, Paul (M)   44   0
H: 5 9   W: 10 00   b.Sheffield 2-2-95
Internationals: England U19, U20.

2011–12	Barnsley	4	0		
2012–13	Barnsley	0	0		
2013–14	Barnsley	5	0		
2014–15	Barnsley	11	0		
2015–16	Barnsley	1	0	21	0
2015–16	*Ipswich T*	4	0		
2016–17	Ipswich T	4	0	8	0
2016–17	Mansfield T	0	0		
2017–18	Mansfield T	15	0	15	0

GRAHAM, Jordan (F)   0   0
b.Peterborough 30-12-97

2017–18	Mansfield T	0	0		

HAKEEM, Zayn (M)   1   0
b. 15-2-99
Internationals: Antigua and Barbuda U20.

2015–16	Mansfield T	1	0		
2016–17	Mansfield T	0	0		
2017–18	Mansfield T	0	0	1	0

HAMILTON, CJ (M)   62   2
H: 5 7   W: 11 09   b.Harrow 23-3-95

2015–16	Sheffield U	0	0		
2016–17	Mansfield T	29	0		
2017–18	Mansfield T	33	2	62	2

HUNT, Johnny (M)   27   1
H: 5 11   W: 10 03   b.Liverpool 23-8-90
Internationals: England C.

2014–15	Cambridge U	9	1	9	1
2017–18	Mansfield T	18	0	18	0

LOGAN, Conrad (G)   222   0
H: 6 2   W: 14 00   b.Letterkenny 18-4-86

2003–04	Leicester C	0	0		
2004–05	Leicester C	0	0		
2005–06	Leicester C	0	0		
2005–06	*Boston U*	13	0	13	0
2006–07	Leicester C	18	0		
2007–08	Leicester C	0	0		
2007–08	*Stockport Co*	34	0		
2008–09	Leicester C	0	0		
2008–09	*Luton T*	22	0	22	0
2008–09	*Stockport Co*	7	0	41	0
2009–10	Leicester C	2	0		
2010–11	Leicester C	3	0		
2010–11	*Bristol R*	16	0	16	0
2011–12	Leicester C	0	0		
2011–12	*Rotherham U*	19	0	19	0
2012–13	Leicester C	0	0		
2013–14	Leicester C	0	0		
2014–15	Leicester C	0	0	23	0
2014–15	*Rochdale*	19	0		
2016–17	Rochdale	24	0	43	0
2016–17	Mansfield T	0	0		
2017–18	Mansfield T	45	0	45	0

MACDONALD, Alex (F)   273   27
H: 5 7   W: 11 04   b.Warrington 14-4-90
Internationals: Scotland U19, U21.

2007–08	Burnley	2	0		
2008–09	Burnley	3	0		
2009–10	Burnley	0	0		
2009–10	*Falkirk*	11	1	11	1
2010–11	Burnley	0	0		
2010–11	*Inverness CT*	10	1	10	1
2011–12	Burnley	1	0		
2011–12	*Plymouth Arg*	18	4		
2012–13	Burnley	1	0	11	0
2012–13	*Plymouth Arg*	16	1	34	5
2012–13	*Burton Alb*	15	1		
2013–14	Burton Alb	35	0		
2014–15	Burton Alb	21	6	71	7
2014–15	Oxford U	15	3		
2015–16	Oxford U	40	5		
2016–17	Oxford U	22	1	77	9
2016–17	Mansfield T	18	1		
2017–18	Mansfield T	41	3	59	4

MELLIS, Jacob (M)   201   14
H: 5 11   W: 10 11   b.Nottingham 8-1-91
Internationals: England U16, U17, U19.

2009–10	Chelsea	0	0		
2009–10	*Southampton*	12	0	12	0
2010–11	Chelsea	0	0		
2011–12	*Barnsley*	15	2		
2012–13	Barnsley	36	6		

2013–14	Barnsley	30	2	81	10
2014–15	Blackpool	13	0	13	0
2014–15	*Oldham Ath*	7	0	7	0
2015–16	Bury	23	0		
2016–17	Bury	35	3	58	3
2017–18	Mansfield T	30	1	30	1

MIRFIN, David (D)   448   21
H: 6 3   W: 13 00   b.Sheffield 18-4-85

2002–03	Huddersfield T	1	0		
2003–04	Huddersfield T	21	2		
2004–05	Huddersfield T	41	4		
2005–06	Huddersfield T	31	1		
2006–07	Huddersfield T	38	1		
2007–08	Huddersfield T	29	1	161	9
2008–09	Scunthorpe U	33	0		
2009–10	Scunthorpe U	37	1		
2010–11	Scunthorpe U	23	3		
2011–12	Watford	4	0	4	0
2011–12	*Scunthorpe U*	19	1		
2012–13	Scunthorpe U	30	0		
2013–14	Scunthorpe U	45	2		
2014–15	Scunthorpe U	0	0		
2014–15	*Hartlepool U*	15	0	15	0
2015–16	Scunthorpe U	35	2		
2016–17	Scunthorpe U	34	2	256	11
2016–17	Mansfield T	0	0		
2017–18	Mansfield T	12	1	12	1

OLEJNIK, Robert (G)   329   0
H: 6 0   W: 15 06   b.Vienna 26-11-86
Internationals: Austria U21.

2004–05	Aston Villa	0	0		
2005–06	Aston Villa	0	0		
2006–07	Aston Villa	0	0		
2006–07	*Lincoln C*	0	0		
2007–08	Falkirk	13	0		
2008–09	Falkirk	15	0		
2009–10	Falkirk	38	0		
2010–11	Falkirk	36	0	102	0
2011–12	Torquay U	46	0	46	0
2012–13	Peterborough U	46	0		
2013–14	Peterborough U	42	0		
2014–15	Peterborough U	0	0	88	0
2014–15	*Scunthorpe U*	13	0	13	0
2014–15	*York C*	16	0	16	0
2015–16	Exeter C	45	0		
2016–17	Exeter C	18	0	63	0
2017–18	Mansfield T	1	0	1	0

PEARCE, Krystian (D)   287   18
H: 6 1   W: 13 05   b.Birmingham 5-1-90
Internationals: England U17, U19.

2006–07	Birmingham C	0	0		
2007–08	Birmingham C	0	0		
2007–08	*Port Vale*	12	0	12	0
2007–08	*Notts Co*	8	1		
2008–09	Birmingham C	0	0		
2008–09	*Scunthorpe U*	39	0	39	0
2009–10	Birmingham C	0	0		
2009–10	*Peterborough U*	2	0	2	0
2009–10	Huddersfield T	1	0	1	0
2010–11	Notts Co	27	1		
2011–12	Notts Co	27	3		
2012–13	Notts Co	2	1	64	6
2012–13	*Barnet*	17	1	17	1
2013–14	Torquay U	35	4	35	4
2015–16	Mansfield T	38	3		
2016–17	Mansfield T	41	3		
2017–18	Mansfield T	38	1	117	7

POTTER, Alfie (M)   233   27
H: 5 7   W: 9 06   b.Islington 9-1-89
From Kettering T.

2007–08	Peterborough U	2	0	2	0

From Kettering T.

2010–11	Oxford U	38	2		
2011–12	Oxford U	25	2		
2012–13	Oxford U	43	10		
2013–14	Oxford U	24	4		
2014–15	Oxford U	15	2	145	20
2014–15	*AFC Wimbledon*	15	1	15	1
2014–15	Northampton T	0	0		
2015–16	Northampton T	21	1		
2016–17	Northampton T	11	0	32	1
2016–17	Mansfield T	12	1		
2017–18	Mansfield T	27	4	39	5

ROSE, Danny (M)   162   42
H: 5 8   W: 9 00   b.Barnsley 10-12-93

2010–11	Barnsley	1	0		
2011–12	Barnsley	4	0		
2012–13	Barnsley	8	1		
2013–14	Barnsley	3	0		
2013–14	*Bury*	6	3		
2014–15	Barnsley	1	0	17	1
2014–15	*Bury*	35	10		
2015–16	Bury	28	5	69	18

2016–17	Mansfield T	37	9		
2017–18	Mansfield T	39	14	76	23

SPENCER, James (F)   179   35
H: 6 1   W: 13 00   b.Leeds 13-12-91

2008–09	Huddersfield T	0	0		
2009–10	Huddersfield T	0	0		
2010–11	Huddersfield T	0	0		
2010–11	*Morecambe*	32	8	32	8
2011–12	Huddersfield T	0	0		
2011–12	*Cheltenham T*	41	10	41	10
2012–13	Huddersfield T	1	0		
2012–13	*Brentford*	2	0	2	0
2013–14	Huddersfield T	0	0	1	0
2013–14	*Scunthorpe U*	13	1	13	1
2013–14	Notts Co	13	5		
2014–15	Notts Co	9	1		
2015–16	Notts Co	7	0	29	6
2015–16	Cambridge U	18	6	18	6
2016–17	Plymouth Arg	25	3	25	3
2016–17	Mansfield T	0	0		
2017–18	Mansfield T	18	1	18	1

STERLING-JAMES, Omari (M)   35   1
b.Birmingham 15-9-93
Internationals: St Kitts and Nevis Full caps.

2014–15	Cheltenham T	22	1	22	1

From Gloucester C, Solihull Moors.

2017–18	Mansfield T	13	0	13	0

TAFT, George (D)   85   3
H: 5 9   W: 11 09   b.Leicester 29-7-93
Internationals: England U18, U19.

2010–11	Leicester C	0	0		
2011–12	Leicester C	0	0		
2012–13	Leicester C	0	0		
2013–14	Leicester C	0	0		
2013–14	*York C*	3	0	3	0
2014–15	Burton Alb	30	1		
2015–16	Burton Alb	0	0	30	1
2015–16	*Cambridge U*	11	1		
2016–17	Mansfield T	13	0		
2017–18	Mansfield T	0	0	13	0
2017–18	*Cambridge U*	28	1	39	2

THOMAS, Jack (M)   53   3
H: 5 9   W: 10 10   b.Sutton-in-Ashfield 3-6-96

2013–14	Mansfield T	1	0		
2014–15	Mansfield T	12	1		
2015–16	Mansfield T	33	2		
2016–17	Mansfield T	6	0		
2017–18	Mansfield T	1	0	53	3

WHITE, Hayden (D)   99   3
H: 6 1   W: 10 10   b.Greenwich 15-4-95

2013–14	Bolton W	2	0		
2014–15	Bolton W	3	0		
2014–15	*Carlisle U*	8	0	8	0
2014–15	*Bury*	2	0	2	0
2014–15	*Notts Co*	3	0	3	0
2015–16	Bolton W	0	0	5	0
2015–16	*Blackpool*	29	1	29	1
2016–17	Peterborough U	6	0	6	0
2017–18	*Mansfield T*	18	1		
2017–18	Mansfield T	28	1	46	2

Players retained or with offer of contract
Baldwin, Kane; Bloor, Teddy John; Gibbens, Lewis Joseph; Healey, Cameron; Law, Jason; Smith, Alistair Oluwashaun; Ward, Keaton Brodie; Wilder, Henri Liam; Wilson, Samuel John.

Scholars
Bircumshaw, Harry; Blake, Nyle Hedley; Briggs, Andrew Robert; Cashmore, Kamen Austin; Cornell, Jack Michael; Darby, Kieran Thomas; Fikula, Steven Johnson; Gledhill, Thomas Henry; Marrs, Keaton Bailey; Morgan, Luke James; O'Sullivan, Riley-Cole Matthew; Purvin, Daniel James; Sarson, Rhys Malcolm; Sinclair, Tyrese; Sundby, Xavier Le Flock; Tague, James Nicholas; Walker, Aiden.

MIDDLESBROUGH (52)

ASSOMBALONGA, Britt (F)   199   83
H: 5 9   W: 11 13   b.Kinshasa 6-12-92
Internationals: DR Congo Full caps.

2010–11	Watford	0	0		
2011–12	Watford	4	0		
2012–13	Watford	0	0		
2012–13	*Southend U*	43	15	43	15
2013–14	Watford	4	0	4	0
2013–14	Peterborough U	43	23	43	23
2014–15	Nottingham F	29	15		

2015–16	Nottingham F	4	1		
2016–17	Nottingham F	32	14	65	30
2017–18	Middlesbrough	44	15	44	15

AYALA, Daniel (M)   184   20
H: 6 3   W: 13 03   b.Sevilla 7-11-90
Internationals: Spain U21.

2007–08	Liverpool	0	0		
2008–09	Liverpool	0	0		
2009–10	Liverpool	5	0		
2010–11	Liverpool	0	0	5	0
2010–11	Hull C	12	1	12	1
2010–11	Derby Co	17	0	17	0
2011–12	Norwich C	7	0		
2012–13	Norwich C	0	0		
2012–13	Nottingham F	12	1	12	1
2013–14	Norwich C	0	0	7	0
2013–14	Middlesbrough	19	3		
2014–15	Middlesbrough	30	4		
2015–16	Middlesbrough	35	3		
2016–17	Middlesbrough	14	1		
2017–18	Middlesbrough	33	7	131	18

BAMFORD, Patrick (F)   164   55
H: 6 1   W: 11 02   b.Newark 5-9-93
Internationals: Republic of Ireland U18. England U18, U19, U21.

2010–11	Nottingham F	0	0		
2011–12	Nottingham F	2	0	2	0
2011–12	Chelsea	0	0		
2012–13	Chelsea	0	0		
2012–13	Milton Keynes D	14	4		
2013–14	Chelsea	0	0		
2013–14	Milton Keynes D	23	14	37	18
2013–14	Derby Co	21	8	21	8
2014–15	Chelsea	0	0		
2014–15	Middlesbrough	38	17		
2015–16	Chelsea	0	0		
2015–16	Crystal Palace	6	0	6	0
2015–16	Norwich C	7	0	7	0
2016–17	Chelsea	0	0		
2016–17	Burnley	6	0	6	0
2016–17	Middlesbrough	8	1		
2017–18	Middlesbrough	39	11	85	29

BRAITHWAITE, Martin (F)   258   61
H: 5 11   W: 12 02   b.Esbjerg 5-6-91
Internationals: Denmark U17, U19, U21, Full caps.

2009–10	Esbjerg	10	0		
2010–11	Esbjerg	16	0		
2011–12	Esbjerg	26	5		
2012–13	Esbjerg	33	9		
2013–14	Esbjerg	4	3	89	17
2013–14	Toulouse	32	7		
2014–15	Toulouse	34	6		
2015–16	Toulouse	36	11		
2016–17	Toulouse	34	11	136	35
2017–18	Middlesbrough	19	5	19	5
2017–18	Bordeaux	14	4	14	4

CHAPMAN, Harry (M)   35   3
H: 5 10   W: 11 00   b.Hartlepool 5-11-97
Internationals: England U18, U20.

2015–16	Middlesbrough	0	0		
2015–16	Barnsley	11	1	11	1
2016–17	Middlesbrough	0	0		
2016–17	Sheffield U	12	1	12	1
2017–18	Middlesbrough	0	0		
2017–18	Blackburn R	12	1	12	1

CLAYTON, Adam (M)   323   20
H: 5 9   W: 11 11   b.Manchester 14-1-89
Internationals: England U20.

2007–08	Manchester C	0	0		
2008–09	Manchester C	0	0		
2009–10	Manchester C	0	0		
2009–10	Carlisle U	28	1	28	1
2010–11	Leeds U	4	0		
2010–11	Peterborough U	7	0	7	0
2010–11	Milton Keynes D	6	1	6	1
2011–12	Leeds U	43	6	47	6
2012–13	Huddersfield T	43	4		
2013–14	Huddersfield T	42	7	85	11
2014–15	Middlesbrough	41	0		
2015–16	Middlesbrough	43	1		
2016–17	Middlesbrough	34	0		
2017–18	Middlesbrough	32	0	150	1

COOKE, Callum (F)   48   6
H: 5 8   W: 11 05   b.Peterlee 21-2-97
Internationals: England U16, U17, U18.

2016–17	Middlesbrough	0	0		
2016–17	Crewe Alex	18	4	18	4
2017–18	Middlesbrough	0	0		
2017–18	Blackpool	30	2	30	2

CRANIE, Martin (D)   345   2
H: 6 1   W: 12 09   b.Yeovil 23-9-86
Internationals: England U17, U18, U19, U20, U21.

2003–04	Southampton	1	0		
2004–05	Southampton	3	0		
2004–05	Bournemouth	3	0	3	0
2005–06	Southampton	11	0		
2006–07	Southampton	1	0	16	0
2006–07	Yeovil T	12	0	12	0
2007–08	Portsmouth	2	0		
2007–08	QPR	6	0	6	0
2008–09	Portsmouth	0	0		
2008–09	Charlton Ath	19	0	19	0
2009–10	Portsmouth	0	0	2	0
2009–10	Coventry C	40	1		
2010–11	Coventry C	36	0		
2011–12	Coventry C	38	0	114	1
2012–13	Barnsley	36	0		
2013–14	Barnsley	35	0		
2014–15	Barnsley	39	1	110	1
2015–16	Huddersfield T	37	0		
2016–17	Huddersfield T	14	0		
2017–18	Huddersfield T	3	0	54	0
2017–18	Middlesbrough	9	0	9	0

DA SILVA, Fabio (M)   153   3
H: 5 8   W: 10 03   b.Rio de Janeiro 9-7-90
Internationals: Brazil U17, Full caps.

2008–09	Manchester U	0	0		
2009–10	Manchester U	5	0		
2010–11	Manchester U	11	1		
2011–12	Manchester U	5	0		
2012–13	Manchester U	0	0		
2012–13	QPR	21	0	21	0
2013–14	Manchester U	1	0	22	1
2013–14	Cardiff C	13	0		
2014–15	Cardiff C	28	0		
2015–16	Cardiff C	23	1	64	1
2016–17	Middlesbrough	24	0		
2017–18	Middlesbrough	22	1	46	1

DE ROON, Marten (M)   215   12
H: 6 1   W: 12 00   b. 29-3-91
Internationals: Netherlands U19, Full caps.

2009–10	Sparta Rotterdam	3	0		
2010–11	Sparta Rotterdam	27	0		
2011–12	Sparta Rotterdam	28	2	58	2
2012–13	Heerenveen	24	1		
2013–14	Heerenveen	31	3		
2014–15	Heerenveen	32	1	87	5
2015–16	Atalanta	36	1	36	1
2016–17	Middlesbrough	33	4		
2017–18	Middlesbrough	1	0	34	4

Transferred to Atalanta, August 2017.

DOWNING, Stewart (M)   500   46
H: 5 11   W: 10 04   b.Middlesbrough 22-7-84
Internationals: England U21, B, Full caps.

2001–02	Middlesbrough	3	0		
2002–03	Middlesbrough	2	0		
2003–04	Middlesbrough	20	0		
2003–04	Sunderland	7	3	7	3
2004–05	Middlesbrough	35	5		
2005–06	Middlesbrough	12	1		
2006–07	Middlesbrough	34	2		
2007–08	Middlesbrough	38	9		
2008–09	Middlesbrough	37	0		
2009–10	Aston Villa	25	2		
2010–11	Aston Villa	38	7	63	9
2011–12	Liverpool	36	0		
2012–13	Liverpool	29	3		
2013–14	Liverpool	0	0	65	3
2013–14	West Ham U	32	1		
2014–15	West Ham U	37	6	69	7
2015–16	Middlesbrough	45	3		
2016–17	Middlesbrough	30	1		
2017–18	Middlesbrough	40	3	296	24

FLETCHER, Ashley (F)   69   8
b.Keighley 12-10-95
Internationals: England U20.

2015–16	Manchester U	0	0		
2015–16	Barnsley	21	5	21	5
2016–17	West Ham U	16	0	16	0
2017–18	Middlesbrough	16	1	16	1
2017–18	Sunderland	16	2	16	2

FRIEND, George (D)   313   10
H: 6 2   W: 13 01   b.Barnstaple 19-10-87

2008–09	Exeter C	4	0		
2008–09	Wolverhampton W	6	0		
2009–10	Wolverhampton W	1	0	7	0
2009–10	Millwall	6	1	6	1
2009–10	Southend U	6	1	6	1
2009–10	Scunthorpe U	4	0	4	0
2009–10	Exeter C	13	1	17	1
2010–11	Doncaster R	32	1		

2011–12	Doncaster R	27	0		
2012–13	Doncaster R	0	0	59	1
2012–13	Middlesbrough	34	0		
2013–14	Middlesbrough	41	3		
2014–15	Middlesbrough	42	1		
2015–16	Middlesbrough	40	1		
2016–17	Middlesbrough	24	0		
2017–18	Middlesbrough	33	2	214	7

FRY, Dael (D)   30   0
H: 6 1   W: 11 05   b.Middlesbrough 30-8-97
Internationals: England U17, U18, U19, U20, U21.

2015–16	Middlesbrough	7	0		
2016–17	Middlesbrough	0	0		
2016–17	Rotherham U	10	0	10	0
2017–18	Middlesbrough	13	0	20	0

FRYER, Joe (G)   42   0
b.Chester-le-Street 14-11-95

2016–17	Middlesbrough	0	0		
2016–17	Hartlepool U	14	0	14	0
2017–18	Middlesbrough	0	0		
2017–18	Stevenage	28	0	28	0

GESTEDE, Rudy (F)   247   61
H: 6 4   W: 13 07   b.Nancy 10-10-88
Internationals: France U19. Benin Full caps.

2008–09	Metz	5	0		
2009–10	Cannes	22	4	22	4
2010–11	Metz	11	3	16	3
2010–11	Metz B	3	1	3	1
2011–12	Cardiff C	25	2		
2012–13	Cardiff C	27	5		
2013–14	Cardiff C	3	0	55	7
2013–14	Blackburn R	27	13		
2014–15	Blackburn R	39	20	66	33
2015–16	Aston Villa	32	5		
2016–17	Aston Villa	18	4	50	9
2016–17	Middlesbrough	16	1		
2017–18	Middlesbrough	19	3	35	4

GIBSON, Ben (D)   226   5
H: 6 1   W: 12 04   b.Nunthorpe 15-1-93
Internationals: England U17, U20, U21.

2010–11	Middlesbrough	1	0		
2011–12	Middlesbrough	0	0		
2011–12	Plymouth Arg	13	0	13	0
2012–13	Middlesbrough	1	0		
2012–13	Tranmere R	28	1	28	1
2013–14	Middlesbrough	31	1		
2014–15	Middlesbrough	36	0		
2015–16	Middlesbrough	33	1		
2016–17	Middlesbrough	38	1		
2017–18	Middlesbrough	45	1	185	4

HOWSON, Jonathan (M)   404   48
H: 5 11   W: 12 01   b.Morley 21-5-88
Internationals: England U21.

2006–07	Leeds U	9	1		
2007–08	Leeds U	26	3		
2008–09	Leeds U	40	4		
2009–10	Leeds U	45	4		
2010–11	Leeds U	46	10		
2011–12	Leeds U	19	1	185	23
2011–12	Norwich C	11	1		
2012–13	Norwich C	30	2		
2013–14	Norwich C	27	2		
2014–15	Norwich C	34	8		
2015–16	Norwich C	36	3		
2016–17	Norwich C	38	6	176	22
2017–18	Middlesbrough	43	3	43	3

JOHNSON, Marvin (F)   111   10
H: 5 10   W: 11 09   b.Birmingham 1-12-90
From Solihull Moors, Kidderminster H.

2014–15	Motherwell	11	0		
2015–16	Motherwell	38	5		
2016–17	Motherwell	4	0	53	6
2016–17	Oxford U	39	3		
2017–18	Oxford U	2	0	41	3
2017–18	Middlesbrough	17	1	17	1

KONSTANTOPOULOS, Dimitrios (G)   312   0
H: 6 4   W: 14 02   b.Kalamata 29-11-78
Internationals: Greece U21, Full caps.

2003–04	Hartlepool U	0	0		
2004–05	Hartlepool U	25	0		
2005–06	Hartlepool U	46	0		
2006–07	Hartlepool U	46	0	117	0
2007–08	Coventry C	21	0		
2008–09	Coventry C	0	0		
2008–09	Swansea C	4	0	4	0
2008–09	Cardiff C	6	0	6	0
2009–10	Coventry C	3	0	24	0
2010–11	Kerkyra	30	0	30	0
2011–12	AEK Athens	9	0		
2012–13	AEK Athens	24	0	33	0

2013–14	Middlesbrough	12	0		
2014–15	Middlesbrough	40	0		
2015–16	Middlesbrough	46	0		
2016–17	Middlesbrough	0	0		
2017–18	Middlesbrough	0	0	98	0

LEADBITTER, Grant (M) 442 53
H: 5 9 W: 11 06 b.Chester-le-Street 7-1-86
Internationals: England U16, U17, U19, U20, U21.

2002–03	Sunderland	0	0		
2003–04	Sunderland	0	0		
2004–05	Sunderland	0	0		
2005–06	Sunderland	12	0		
2005–06	Rotherham U	5	1	5	1
2006–07	Sunderland	44	7		
2007–08	Sunderland	31	2		
2008–09	Sunderland	23	2		
2009–10	Sunderland	1	0	111	11
2009–10	Ipswich T	38	3		
2010–11	Ipswich T	44	5		
2011–12	Ipswich T	34	5		
2012–13	Ipswich T	0	0	116	13
2012–13	Middlesbrough	42	3		
2013–14	Middlesbrough	39	6		
2014–15	Middlesbrough	43	11		
2015–16	Middlesbrough	41	4		
2016–17	Middlesbrough	13	1		
2017–18	Middlesbrough	32	3	210	28

McGINLEY, Nathan (D) 11 0
b.Middlesbrough 15-9-96

2017–18	Middlesbrough	0	0		
2017–18	Wycombe W	11	0	11	0

MEJIAS, Tomas (G) 11 0
H: 6 5 W: 13 02 b.Madrid 30-1-89
Internationals: Spain U19, U20.

2010–11	Real Madrid	1	0		
2011–12	Real Madrid	0	0		
2012–13	Real Madrid	0	0		
2013–14	Real Madrid	0	0	1	0
2013–14	*Middlesbrough*	1	0		
2014–15	Middlesbrough	7	0		
2015–16	Middlesbrough	0	0		
2016–17	Middlesbrough	0	0		
2016–17	*Rayo Vallecano*	2	0	2	0
2017–18	Middlesbrough	0	0	8	0

MILLER, George (F) 48 15
H: 5 10 W: 10 01 b.Bolton 11-8-98

2015–16	Bury	1	0		
2016–17	Bury	28	7		
2017–18	Middlesbrough	0	0		
2017–18	*Bury*	19	8	48	15

PEARS, Aynsley (G) 0 0
b. 23-4-98
Internationals: England U19, U20.

2017–18	Middlesbrough	0	0		

RANDOLPH, Darren (G) 320 0
H: 6 1 W: 12 02 b.Dublin 12-5-87
Internationals: Republic of Ireland U21, B, Full caps.

2004–05	Charlton Ath	0	0		
2005–06	Charlton Ath	0	0		
2006–07	Charlton Ath	1	0		
2006–07	*Gillingham*	3	0	3	0
2007–08	Charlton Ath	1	0		
2007–08	*Bury*	14	0	14	0
2008–09	Charlton Ath	1	0		
2008–09	*Hereford U*	13	0	13	0
2009–10	Charlton Ath	11	0	14	0
2010–11	Motherwell	37	0		
2011–12	Motherwell	38	0		
2012–13	Motherwell	36	0	111	0
2013–14	Birmingham C	46	0		
2014–15	Birmingham C	45	0	91	0
2015–16	West Ham U	6	0		
2016–17	West Ham U	22	0	28	0
2017–18	Middlesbrough	46	0	46	0

RIPLEY, Connor (G) 116 0
H: 5 11 W: 11 13 b.Middlesbrough 13-2-93
Internationals: England U19, U20.

2010–11	Middlesbrough	1	0		
2011–12	Middlesbrough	1	0		
2011–12	*Oxford U*	1	0	1	0
2012–13	Middlesbrough	0	0		
2013–14	Middlesbrough	0	0		
2013–14	*Bradford C*	0	0		
2014	*Ostersunds*	14	0	14	0
2014–15	Middlesbrough	0	0		
2015–16	Middlesbrough	0	0		
2015–16	*Motherwell*	36	0	36	0
2016–17	Middlesbrough	0	0		
2016–17	*Oldham Ath*	46	0	46	0
2017–18	Middlesbrough	0	0	2	0
2017–18	*Burton Alb*	2	0	2	0
2017–18	*Bury*	15	0	15	0

SHOTTON, Ryan (D) 228 13
H: 6 3 W: 13 05 b.Stoke 30-9-88

2006–07	Stoke C	0	0		
2007–08	Stoke C	0	0		
2008–09	Stoke C	0	0		
2008–09	*Tranmere R*	33	5	33	5
2009–10	Stoke C	0	0		
2009–10	*Barnsley*	30	0	30	0
2010–11	Stoke C	2	0		
2011–12	Stoke C	23	1		
2012–13	Stoke C	23	0		
2013–14	Stoke C	0	0	48	1
2013–14	*Wigan Ath*	9	1	9	1
2014–15	Derby Co	25	2		
2015–16	Derby Co	6	0	31	2
2015–16	Birmingham C	9	1		
2016–17	Birmingham C	43	2		
2017–18	Birmingham C	1	0	53	3
2017–18	Middlesbrough	24	1	24	1

TAVERNIER, Marcus (M) 12 1
b.Leeds 22-3-99
Internationals: England U19.

2017–18	Middlesbrough	5	1	5	1
2017–18	*Milton Keynes D*	7	0	7	0

TRAORE, Adama (F) 73 5
H: 5 10 W: 12 00 b.L'Hospitalet de
Llobregat 25-1-96
Internationals: Spain U16, U17, U19, U21.

2013–14	Barcelona	1	0		
2014–15	Barcelona	0	0	1	0
2015–16	Aston Villa	10	0		
2016–17	Aston Villa	1	0	11	0
2016–17	Middlesbrough	27	0		
2017–18	Middlesbrough	34	5	61	5

WING, Lewis (M) 20 3
b.Durham 23-5-95
From Shildon.

2017–18	Middlesbrough	0	0		
2017–18	*Yeovil T*	20	3	20	3

Players retained or with offer of contract
Armstrong, Luke Thomas; Barragan, Antonio Juan; Brynn, Solomon; Cook, James Michael; Coulson, Hayden Ross; Curry, Mitchell; De, Sart Julien Ariel; Liddle, Ben George; Mahmutovic, Enes; O'Neill, Tyrone; Pattison, Alexander Antony; Reading, Patrick James; Renton, Anthony Peter; Soisalo, Mikael; Sylla, Amadou; Walker, Stephen.

Scholars
Brahimi, Billal; Charlton, Kieran; Cooke, Liam; Dale, Nathan Alan; Dodds, Daniel; Drummond, Luke Jon; Guru, Nathan; Hemming, Zachary; Hood, Nicholas Joseph; James, Bradley David; Malley, Connor; McGill, Gabriel Edward; Robinson, Jack; Spence, Kian Alec; Storey, Keiran; Watts, Layton; Wearne, Stephen Christopher; Wilson, Jay Harry.

MILLWALL (53)

ABDOU, Nadjim (M) 461 13
H: 5 10 W: 11 02 b.Martigues 13-7-84
Internationals: Comoros Full caps.

2002–03	Martigues	26	1	26	1
2003–04	Sedan	17	0		
2004–05	Sedan	32	2		
2005–06	Sedan	14	0		
2006–07	Sedan	17	0	80	2
2007–08	Plymouth Arg	31	1	31	1
2008–09	Millwall	36	3		
2009–10	Millwall	43	1		
2010–11	Millwall	34	0		
2011–12	Millwall	40	0		
2012–13	Millwall	39	1		
2013–14	Millwall	24	0		
2014–15	Millwall	33	1		
2015–16	Millwall	29	1		
2016–17	Millwall	12	0		
2017–18	Millwall	0	0	290	7
2017–18	*AFC Wimbledon*	34	2	34	2

ARCHER, Jordan (G) 160 0
H: 6 1 W: 12 08 b.Walthamstow 12-4-93
Internationals: Scotland U19, U20, U21, Full caps.

2011–12	Tottenham H	0	0		
2012–13	Tottenham H	0	0		
2012–13	*Wycombe W*	27	0	27	0
2013–14	Tottenham H	0	0		
2014–15	Tottenham H	0	0		
2014–15	*Northampton T*	13	0	13	0
2014–15	Millwall	0	0		
2015–16	Millwall	39	0		
2016–17	Millwall	36	0		
2017–18	Millwall	45	0	120	0

BROWN, James (D) 27 0
H: 6 1 W: 12 06 b. 12-1-98

2016–17	Millwall	0	0		
2017–18	Millwall	0	0		
2017–18	*Carlisle U*	27	0	27	0

CAHILL, Tim (M) 588 148
H: 5 10 W: 10 12 b.Sydney 6-12-79
Internationals: Western Samoa Youth. Australia U23, Full caps.

1997–98	Millwall	1	0		
1998–99	Millwall	36	6		
1999–2000	Millwall	45	12		
2000–01	Millwall	41	9		
2001–02	Millwall	43	13		
2002–03	Millwall	11	3		
2003–04	Millwall	40	9		
2004–05	Everton	33	11		
2005–06	Everton	32	6		
2006–07	Everton	18	5		
2007–08	Everton	18	7		
2008–09	Everton	30	8		
2009–10	Everton	33	8		
2010–11	Everton	27	9		
2011–12	Everton	35	2	226	56
2012	New York Red Bulls	12	1		
2013	New York Red Bulls	27	1		
2014	New York Red Bulls	23	2	62	14
2015	Shanghai Greenland	28	11	28	11
2016	Hangzhou Greentown	17	4	17	4
2016–17	Melbourne City	22	11		
2017–18	Melbourne City	6	0	28	11
2017–18	Millwall	10	0	227	52

COOPER, Jake (D) 95 0
H: 6 4 W: 13 05 b.Bracknell 3-2-95
Internationals: England U18, U20.

2013–14	Reading	0	0		
2014–15	Reading	15	2		
2015–16	Reading	24	2		
2016–17	Reading	3	0	42	4
2016–17	*Millwall*	15	2		
2017–18	Millwall	38	4	53	6

ELLIOTT, Tom (F) 212 35
H: 6 3 W: 12 00 b.Hunslet 9-11-90
Internationals: England U16, U18.

2006–07	Leeds U	3	0		
2007–08	Leeds U	0	0		
2008–09	Leeds U	0	0		
2008–09	*Macclesfield T*	6	0	6	0
2009–10	Leeds U	0	0		
2009–10	*Bury*	16	1	16	1
2010–11	Leeds U	0	0	3	0
2010–11	*Rotherham U*	6	0	6	0
2011–12	*Hamilton A*	7	0	7	0
2011–12	Stockport Co	42	7	42	7
2014–15	Cambridge U	30	8	30	8
2015–16	AFC Wimbledon	39	6		
2016–17	AFC Wimbledon	39	9	78	15
2017–18	Millwall	24	4	24	4

FERGUSON, Shane (D) 155 6
H: 5 9 W: 10 01 b.Limavady 12-7-91
Internationals: Northern Ireland U17, U19, U21, B, Full caps.

2008–09	Newcastle U	0	0		
2009–10	Newcastle U	0	0		
2010–11	Newcastle U	7	0		
2011–12	Newcastle U	7	0		
2012–13	Newcastle U	9	0		
2012–13	*Birmingham C*	11	1		
2013–14	Newcastle U	0	0		
2013–14	*Birmingham C*	18	0	29	1
2014–15	Newcastle U	0	0		
2014–15	*Rangers*	0	0		
2015–16	Newcastle U	0	0	23	0
2015–16	Millwall	39	3		
2016–17	Millwall	40	2		
2017–18	Millwall	24	0	103	5

GREGORY, Lee (F) 160 54
H: 6 2 b.Sheffield 26-8-88

2014–15	Millwall	39	9		
2015–16	Millwall	41	18		
2016–17	Millwall	37	17		
2017–18	Millwall	43	10	160	54

HUTCHINSON, Shaun (D)   217   13
H: 6 1   W: 12 04   b.Newcastle upon Tyne 23-11-90

Season	Club	App	Gls	Tot	Tot
2008–09	Motherwell	1	0		
2009–10	Motherwell	5	3		
2010–11	Motherwell	19	1		
2011–12	Motherwell	30	1		
2012–13	Motherwell	31	1		
2013–14	Motherwell	35	1	121	7
2014–15	Fulham	25	2		
2015–16	Fulham	9	0	34	2
2016–17	Millwall	16	2		
2017–18	Millwall	46	2	62	4

KING, Tom (G)   29   0
H: 6 1   b.Plymouth 9-3-95
Internationals: England U17.

Season	Club	App	Gls	Tot	Tot
2011–12	Crystal Palace	0	0		
2012–13	Crystal Palace	0	0		
2014–15	Millwall	0	0		
2015–16	Millwall	0	0		
2016–17	Millwall	11	0		
2017–18	Millwall	0	0	11	0
2017–18	*Stevenage*	18	0	18	0

MARTIN, David E (G)   332   0
H: 6 1   W: 13 04   b.Romford 22-1-86
Internationals: England U16, U17, U18, U19.

Season	Club	App	Gls	Tot	Tot
2003–04	Wimbledon	2	0	2	0
2004–05	Milton Keynes D	15	0		
2005–06	Milton Keynes D	0	0		
2005–06	Liverpool	0	0		
2006–07	Liverpool	0	0		
2006–07	*Accrington S*	10	0	10	0
2007–08	Liverpool	0	0		
2008–09	Liverpool	0	0		
2008–09	*Leicester C*	25	0	25	0
2009–10	Liverpool	0	0		
2009–10	*Tranmere R*	3	0	3	0
2009–10	*Leeds U*	0	0		
2009–10	*Derby Co*	2	0	2	0
2010–11	Milton Keynes D	43	0		
2011–12	Milton Keynes D	46	0		
2012–13	Milton Keynes D	31	0		
2013–14	Milton Keynes D	40	0		
2014–15	Milton Keynes D	39	0		
2015–16	Milton Keynes D	35	0		
2016–17	Milton Keynes D	40	0	289	0
2017–18	Millwall	1	0	1	0

MBULU, Christian (D)   0   0
b. 6-8-96

Season	Club	App	Gls
2015–16	Millwall	0	0
2016–17	Millwall	0	0
2017–18	Millwall	0	0

McLAUGHLIN, Conor (D)   224   8
H: 6 0   W: 11 02   b.Belfast 26-7-91
Internationals: Northern Ireland U21, Full caps.

Season	Club	App	Gls	Tot	Tot
2009–10	Preston NE	0	0		
2010–11	Preston NE	7	0		
2011–12	Preston NE	17	0	24	0
2011–12	*Shrewsbury T*	4	0	4	0
2012–13	Fleetwood T	19	0		
2013–14	Fleetwood T	35	0		
2014–15	Fleetwood T	39	1		
2015–16	Fleetwood T	37	2		
2016–17	Fleetwood T	42	4	172	7
2017–18	Millwall	24	1	24	1

MEREDITH, James (D)   231   4
H: 6 1   W: 11 06   b.Albury, Australia 4-4-88
Internationals: Australia Full caps.

Season	Club	App	Gls	Tot	Tot
2006–07	Derby Co	0	0		
2006–07	*Chesterfield*	1	0	1	0
2007–08	Shrewsbury T	3	0	3	0

From York C

Season	Club	App	Gls	Tot	Tot
2012–13	Bradford C	32	1		
2013–14	Bradford C	26	0		
2014–15	Bradford C	40	0		
2015–16	Bradford C	42	1		
2016–17	Bradford C	41	2	181	4
2017–18	Millwall	46	0	46	0

MORISON, Steven (F)   369   92
H: 6 2   W: 13 07   b.Enfield 29-8-83
Internationals: England C. Wales Full caps.

Season	Club	App	Gls	Tot	Tot
2001–02	Northampton T	1	0		
2002–03	Northampton T	13	1		
2003–04	Northampton T	5	1		
2004–05	Northampton T	4	1	23	3

From Stevenage B.

Season	Club	App	Gls	Tot	Tot
2008–09	Millwall	0	0		
2009–10	Millwall	43	20		
2010–11	Millwall	40	15		
2011–12	Norwich C	34	9		
2012–13	Norwich C	19	1	53	10
2012–13	*Leeds U*	15	3		
2013–14	*Leeds U*	0	0		
2013–14	Millwall	41	8		
2014–15	*Leeds U*	26	2	41	5
2015–16	Millwall	46	15		
2016–17	Millwall	38	11		
2017–18	Millwall	44	5	252	74

NELSON, Sid (D)   67   1
H: 6 1   b.London 1-1-96

Season	Club	App	Gls	Tot	Tot
2013–14	Millwall	0	0		
2014–15	Millwall	14	0		
2015–16	Millwall	9	0		
2016–17	Millwall	3	0		
2016–17	*Newport Co*	14	0	14	0
2017–18	Millwall	0	0	26	0
2017–18	*Yeovil T*	12	0	12	0
2017–18	*Chesterfield*	15	1	15	1

O'BRIEN, Aiden (F)   147   29
H: 5 8   W: 10 12   b.Islington 4-10-93
Internationals: Republic of Ireland U17, U19, U21.

Season	Club	App	Gls	Tot	Tot
2010–11	Millwall	0	0		
2011–12	Millwall	0	0		
2012–13	Millwall	0	0		
2012–13	*Crawley T*	9	0	9	0
2013–14	Millwall	0	0		
2013–14	*Torquay U*	3	0	3	0
2014–15	Millwall	19	2		
2015–16	Millwall	43	10		
2016–17	Millwall	43	13		
2017–18	Millwall	30	4	135	29

ONYEDINMA, Fred (M)   144   16
H: 6 1   b.London 24-11-96

Season	Club	App	Gls	Tot	Tot
2013–14	Millwall	4	0		
2014–15	Millwall	2	0		
2014–15	*Wycombe W*	25	8	25	8
2015–16	Millwall	34	4		
2016–17	Millwall	42	3		
2017–18	Millwall	37	1	119	8

ROMEO, Mahlon (M)   78   2
H: 5 10   W: 11 05   b.Westminster 19-9-95
Internationals: Antigua and Barbuda Full caps.

Season	Club	App	Gls	Tot	Tot
2012–13	Gillingham	1	0		
2013–14	Gillingham	0	0		
2014–15	Gillingham	0	0	1	0
2015–16	Millwall	18	1		
2016–17	Millwall	32	0		
2017–18	Millwall	27	1	77	2

SAVILLE, George (M)   156   20
H: 5 9   W: 11 07   b.Camberley 1-6-93
Internationals: Northern Ireland Full caps.

Season	Club	App	Gls	Tot	Tot
2010–11	Chelsea	0	0		
2011–12	Chelsea	0	0		
2012–13	Chelsea	0	0		
2012–13	*Millwall*	3	0		
2013–14	Chelsea	0	0		
2013–14	*Brentford*	40	3	40	3
2014–15	Wolverhampton W	7	0		
2014–15	*Bristol C*	7	1	7	1
2015–16	Wolverhampton W	19	5		
2015–16	*Millwall*	12	0		
2016–17	Wolverhampton W	24	1	50	6
2017–18	Millwall	44	10	59	10

SMITH, Harry (F)   23   3
H: 6 5   b. 18-5-95
From Sittingbourne, Folkestone Invicta.

Season	Club	App	Gls	Tot	Tot
2016–17	Millwall	9	1		
2017–18	Millwall	0	0	9	1
2017–18	*Swindon T*	14	2	14	2

THOMPSON, Ben (M)   69   1
H: 5 11   W: 12 04   b. 3-10-95

Season	Club	App	Gls	Tot	Tot
2014–15	Millwall	0	0		
2015–16	Millwall	28	1		
2016–17	Millwall	38	0		
2017–18	Millwall	3	0	69	1

TOFFOLO, Harry (D)   77   2
H: 6 0   W: 11 03   b. 19-8-95
Internationals: England U18, U19, U20.

Season	Club	App	Gls	Tot	Tot
2014–15	Norwich C	0	0		
2014–15	*Swindon T*	28	1	28	1
2015–16	Norwich C	0	0		
2015–16	*Rotherham U*	7	0	7	0
2015–16	*Peterborough U*	7	0	7	0
2016–17	Norwich C	0	0		
2016–17	*Scunthorpe U*	22	2	22	2
2017–18	Norwich C	0	0		
2017–18	*Doncaster R*	13	0	13	0
2017–18	Millwall	0	0		

TUNNICLIFFE, Ryan (M)   170   5
H: 6 0   W: 14 02   b.Bury 30-12-92
Internationals: England U16, U17.

Season	Club	App	Gls	Tot	Tot
2009–10	Manchester U	0	0		
2010–11	Manchester U	0	0		
2011–12	Manchester U	0	0		
2011–12	*Peterborough U*	27	0	27	0
2012–13	Manchester U	0	0		
2012–13	*Barnsley*	2	0	2	0
2013–14	Manchester U	0	0		
2013–14	*Ipswich T*	27	0	27	0
2013–14	Fulham	3	0		
2013–14	*Wigan Ath*	5	0		
2014–15	Fulham	22	0		
2014–15	*Blackburn R*	17	1	17	1
2015–16	Fulham	27	2		
2016–17	Fulham	7	0	59	2
2016–17	*Wigan Ath*	9	1	14	1
2017–18	Millwall	24	1	24	1

TWARDEK, Kris (M)   14   0
b.Toronto 8-3-97
Internationals: Czech Republic U17, U18, U19. Canada Full caps.

Season	Club	App	Gls	Tot	Tot
2015–16	Millwall	0	0		
2016–17	Millwall	0	0		
2017–18	Millwall	2	0	2	0
2017–18	*Carlisle U*	12	0	12	0

WALLACE, Jed (M)   199   37
H: 5 10   W: 10 12   b.Reading 15-12-93
Internationals: England U19.

Season	Club	App	Gls	Tot	Tot
2011–12	Portsmouth	0	0		
2012–13	Portsmouth	22	6		
2013–14	Portsmouth	44	7		
2014–15	Portsmouth	44	14	110	27
2015–16	Wolverhampton W	9	0		
2015–16	*Millwall*	12	1		
2016–17	Wolverhampton W	9	0	18	0
2016–17	*Millwall*	16	3		
2017–18	Millwall	43	6	71	10

WEBSTER, Byron (D)   262   20
H: 6 5   W: 12 07   b.Sherburn-in-Elmet 31-3-87

Season	Club	App	Gls	Tot	Tot
2007–08	Siad Most	23	4		
2008–09	Siad Most	0	0	23	4
2009–10	Doncaster R	5	0		
2010–11	Doncaster R	7	0	12	0
2010–11	*Hereford U*	2	0	2	0
2011–12	*Northampton T*	8	0		
2011–12	Northampton T	13	0	21	0
2012–13	Yeovil T	44	5		
2013–14	Yeovil T	41	3		
2014–15	Millwall	11	0		
2014–15	*Yeovil T*	14	0	99	8
2015–16	Millwall	40	6		
2016–17	Millwall	44	2		
2017–18	Millwall	10	0	105	8

WILLIAMS, Shaun (M)   358   53
H: 5 9   W: 11 11   b.Dublin 19-10-86
Internationals: Republic of Ireland U21, U23.

Season	Club	App	Gls	Tot	Tot
2007	Drogheda U	0	0		
2007	Dundalk	19	9	19	9
2008	Drogheda U	4	0		
2008	Finn Harps	14	2	14	2
2009	Drogheda U	1	0	5	0
2009	Sporting Fingal	13	7		
2010	Sporting Fingal	32	5	45	12
2011–12	Milton Keynes D	39	8		
2012–13	Milton Keynes D	44	3		
2013–14	Milton Keynes D	25	8	108	19
2013–14	Millwall	17	1		
2014–15	Millwall	38	2		
2015–16	Millwall	33	2		
2016–17	Millwall	44	4		
2017–18	Millwall	35	2	167	11

Players retained or with offer of contract
Donovan, Harry; McNamara, Danny John; Sandford, Ryan David Luca; Strachan, Robert Alex; White, Lewis Antonio.

Scholars
Alexander, George John; Debrah, Jesse John Kodjo; Duncan, Reuben John; Hanson, Jethro Kirk; Jackson, Samuel John; Mitchell, Billy James; Neary, Matthew Kieron; Olaofe, Isaac Tanitoluwaloba; Queeley, Kristopher Reuben; Saunders-Henry, Mason Bradley; Skeffington, Samuel; Taylor, Harry Gavin; Tiensia, Junior Yoann Peniel; Topalloj, Besart; West, Lewis Callum; Wicks, Joseph Ryan; Wright, Joseph Dennis.

MILTON KEYNES D (54)

AGARD, Kieran (F) 263 67
H: 5 10 W: 10 10 b.Newham 10-10-89

2006-07	Everton	0	0		
2007-08	Everton	0	0		
2008-09	Everton	0	0		
2009-10	Everton	1	0		
2010-11	Everton	0	0	1	0
2010-11	Kilmarnock	8	1	8	1
2010-11	Peterborough U	0	0		
2011-12	Yeovil T	29	6	29	6
2012-13	Rotherham U	30	6		
2013-14	Rotherham U	46	21		
2014-15	Rotherham U	2	0	78	27
2014-15	Bristol C	39	13		
2015-16	Bristol C	25	2	64	15
2016-17	Milton Keynes D	42	12		
2017-18	Milton Keynes D	41	6	83	18

ANEKE, Chuks (M) 129 35
H: 6 3 W: 13 01 b.Newham 3-7-93
Internationals: England U16, U17, U18, U19.

2010-11	Arsenal	0	0		
2011-12	Arsenal	0	0		
2011-12	Stevenage	6	0	6	0
2011-12	Preston NE	7	1	7	1
2012-13	Arsenal	0	0		
2012-13	Crewe Alex	30	6		
2013-14	Arsenal	0	0		
2013-14	Crewe Alex	40	15	70	21
2014-15	Arsenal	0	0		
2014-15	Zulte-Waregem	0	0		
2016-17	Milton Keynes D	15	4		
2017-18	Milton Keynes D	31	9	46	13

ASONGANYI, Dylan (F) 0 0

2017-18	Milton Keynes D	0	0

BIRD, Jay (F) 0 0

2017-18	Milton Keynes D	0	0

BRITTAIN, Callum (F) 35 2
H: 5 10 W: 10 10 b.Bedford 12-3-98
Internationals: England U20.

2015-16	Milton Keynes D	0	0		
2016-17	Milton Keynes D	9	0		
2017-18	Milton Keynes D	26	2	35	2

CISSE, Ousseynou (D) 200 7
H: 6 5 W: 13 05 b.Dakar 4-6-91
Internationals: Mali Full caps.

2009-10	Amiens	9	0		
2010-11	Amiens	8	0		
2011-12	Amiens	19	0	36	0
2012-13	Dijon	24	0		
2013-14	Dijon	36	4		
2014-15	Dijon	35	1	95	5
2015-16	Rayo Vallecano	0	0		
2015-16	Waasland-Beveren	12	1	12	1
2016-17	Tours	25	1	25	1
2017-18	Milton Keynes D	32	0	32	0

GILBEY, Alex (M) 150 12
H: 6 0 W: 11 07 b.Dagenham 9-12-94

2011-12	Colchester U	0	0		
2012-13	Colchester U	3	0		
2013-14	Colchester U	36	1		
2014-15	Colchester U	34	1		
2015-16	Colchester U	37	5	110	7
2016-17	Wigan Ath	15	2		
2017-18	Wigan Ath	2	0	17	2
2017-18	Milton Keynes D	23	3	23	3

JACKSON, Oran (D) 1 0
b. 16-10-98

2015-16	Milton Keynes D	1	0		
2016-17	Milton Keynes D	0	0		
2017-18	Milton Keynes D	0	0	1	0

JONES, Alfie (G) 0 0

2017-18	Milton Keynes D	0	0

KASUMU, David (M) 1 0
b. 5-10-99

2015-16	Milton Keynes D	0	0		
2016-17	Milton Keynes D	0	0		
2017-18	Milton Keynes D	1	0	1	0

LEWINGTON, Dean (D) 602 31
H: 5 11 W: 11 07 b.Kingston 18-5-84

2002-03	Wimbledon	1	0		
2003-04	Wimbledon	28	1	29	1
2004-05	Milton Keynes D	43	2		
2005-06	Milton Keynes D	44	1		
2006-07	Milton Keynes D	45	1		
2007-08	Milton Keynes D	45	0		
2008-09	Milton Keynes D	40	2		
2009-10	Milton Keynes D	42	1		
2010-11	Milton Keynes D	42	3		
2011-12	Milton Keynes D	46	3		
2012-13	Milton Keynes D	38	1		
2013-14	Milton Keynes D	43	1		
2014-15	Milton Keynes D	41	3		
2015-16	Milton Keynes D	46	1		
2016-17	Milton Keynes D	36	1		
2017-18	Milton Keynes D	22	0	573	20

LOGAN, Hugo (F) 0 0
b. 21-9-98
Internationals: England U17.

2016-17	Milton Keynes D	0	0
2017-18	Milton Keynes D	0	0

McGRANDLES, Conor (M) 90 7
H: 6 0 W: 10 00 b.Falkirk 24-9-95

2012-13	Falkirk	26	2		
2013-14	Falkirk	36	5		
2014-15	Falkirk	3	0		
2014-15	Norwich C	1	0		
2015-16	Norwich C	0	0	1	0
2015-16	Falkirk	5	0	70	7
2017-18	Milton Keynes D	19	0	19	0

MUIRHEAD, Robbie (F) 129 14
b. 8-3-96
Internationals: Scotland U16, U17, U18, U19.

2012-13	Kilmarnock	1	0		
2013-14	Kilmarnock	21	2	22	2
2014-15	Kilmarknock	20	2	20	2
2014-15	Dundee U	13	2		
2015-16	Dundee U	0	0	13	2
2015-16	Partick Thistle	8	2	8	2
2016-17	Hearts	17	1	17	1
2016-17	Milton Keynes D	19	2		
2017-18	Milton Keynes D	30	3	49	5

NESBITT, Aidan (M) 119 3
b. 5-2-97
Internationals: Scotland U17, U19, U20, U21.

2015-16	Partick Thistle	70	0	70	0
2016-17	Celtic	0	0		
2016-17	Greenock Morton	30	1	30	1
2017-18	Celtic	0	0		
2017-18	Milton Keynes D	19	2	19	2

NICHOLLS, Lee (G) 128 0
H: 6 3 W: 13 05 b.Huyton 5-10-92
Internationals: England U19.

2009-10	Wigan Ath	0	0		
2010-11	Wigan Ath	0	0		
2010-11	Hartlepool U	0	0		
2010-11	Shrewsbury T	0	0		
2010-11	Sheffield W	0	0		
2011-12	Wigan Ath	0	0		
2011-12	Accrington S	9	0	9	0
2012-13	Wigan Ath	0	0		
2012-13	Northampton T	46	0	46	0
2013-14	Wigan Ath	6	0		
2014-15	Wigan Ath	1	0		
2015-16	Wigan Ath	2	0	9	0
2015-16	Bristol R	15	0	15	0
2016-17	Milton Keynes D	8	0		
2017-18	Milton Keynes D	41	0	49	0

NOMBE, Sam (F) 6 0
H: 5 9 W: 11 00 b. 22-10-98

2016-17	Milton Keynes D	0	0		
2017-18	Milton Keynes D	6	0	6	0

PAWLETT, Peter (M) 205 19
H: 5 10 W: 10 10 b.Hedon 3-2-91
Internationals: Scotland U19, U21.

2008-09	Aberdeen	5	0		
2009-10	Aberdeen	14	0		
2010-11	Aberdeen	13	1		
2011-12	Aberdeen	21	0		
2012-13	Aberdeen	12	0		
2012-13	St Johnstone	9	0	9	0
2013-14	Aberdeen	35	5		
2014-15	Aberdeen	36	6		
2015-16	Aberdeen	18	1		
2016-17	Aberdeen	18	3	172	16
2017-18	Milton Keynes D	24	3	24	3

RASULO, Georgio (M) 17 0
b.Banbury 23-1-97
Internationals: England U16, U17.

2012-13	Milton Keynes D	1	0		
2013-14	Milton Keynes D	7	0		
2014-15	Milton Keynes D	0	0		
2014-15	Oxford U	1	0	1	0
2015-16	Milton Keynes D	1	0		
2015-16	Oldham Ath	3	0	3	0
2016-17	Milton Keynes D	3	0		
2017-18	Milton Keynes D	1	0	13	0

SIETSMA, Wieger (G) 11 0
b. 11-7-95

2015-16	Heerenveen	0	0		
2016-17	Heerenveen	0	0		
2016-17	Emmen	6	0	6	0
2017-18	Milton Keynes D	5	0	5	0

SOW, Osman (F) 133 34
H: 6 4 b.Stockholm 22-4-90

2011-12	FC Dacia	13	1		
2012-13	FC Dacia	8	2	21	3
2013	Syrianska FC	7	2	7	2
2013-14	Crystal Palace	0	0		
2014-15	Hearts	22	11		
2015-16	Hearts	23	9	45	20
2016	Henan Jianye	30	4	30	4
2016-17	Emirates	11	3	11	3
2017-18	Milton Keynes D	19	2	19	2

THOMAS-ASANTE, Brandon (F) 21 0
H: 5 11 W: 12 08 b. 29-12-98

2016-17	Milton Keynes D	6	0		
2017-18	Milton Keynes D	15	0	21	0

UPSON, Edward (M) 285 18
H: 5 10 W: 11 07 b.Bury St Edmunds 21-11-89
Internationals: England U17, U19.

2006-07	Ipswich T	0	0		
2007-08	Ipswich T	0	0		
2008-09	Ipswich T	0	0		
2009-10	Ipswich T	0	0		
2009-10	Barnet	9	1	9	1
2010-11	Yeovil T	23	0		
2011-12	Yeovil T	41	3		
2012-13	Yeovil T	41	2		
2013-14	Yeovil T	24	4	129	9
2013-14	Millwall	10	0		
2014-15	Millwall	26	2		
2015-16	Millwall	32	0	68	2
2016-17	Milton Keynes D	42	3		
2017-18	Milton Keynes D	37	3	79	6

WALSH, Joe (D) 166 10
H: 5 11 W: 11 00 b.Cardiff 15-5-92
Internationals: Wales U17, U19, U21.

2010-11	Swansea C	0	0		
2011-12	Swansea C	0	0		
2012-13	Crawley T	30	2		
2013-14	Crawley T	39	5		
2014-15	Crawley T	28	1	97	8
2014-15	Milton Keynes D	2	0		
2015-16	Milton Keynes D	18	1		
2016-17	Milton Keynes D	39	1		
2017-18	Milton Keynes D	10	0	69	2

WILLIAMS, George B (D) 101 4
H: 5 9 W: 11 00 b.Hillingdon 14-4-93

2011-12	Milton Keynes D	2	0		
From Worcester C.					
2014-15	Barnsley	4	0		
2015-16	Barnsley	19	1	23	1
2016-17	Milton Keynes D	33	2		
2017-18	Milton Keynes D	43	1	78	3

WOOTTON, Scott (D) 145 3
H: 6 2 W: 13 00 b.Birkenhead 12-9-91
Internationals: England U17.

2009-10	Manchester U	0	0		
2010-11	Manchester U	0	0		
2010-11	Tranmere R	7	1	7	1
2011-12	Manchester U	0	0		
2011-12	Peterborough U	11	0		
2011-12	Nottingham F	13	0	13	0
2012-13	Peterborough U	2	1	13	1
2013-14	Manchester U	0	0		
2013-14	Leeds U	20	0		
2014-15	Leeds U	23	0		
2014-15	Rotherham U	7	0	7	0
2015-16	Leeds U	23	0	66	0
2016-17	Milton Keynes D	1	1		
2017-18	Milton Keynes D	38	0	39	1

Players retained or with offer of contract
Sole, Liam Anthony.

Scholars
Ackom, Delsin; Bell, Bradley Steven; Bird, Jay; Evans, Joseph William; Hope, Tommy William; Hourican-Harvey, Jack; Jones, Alfie; Martin, Recoe Reshan; Pattison, Charlie George; Pickworth, Nathan Michael; Sorinola, Matthew Alexander; Tapp, Finley; Wright, Jenson.

MORECAMBE (55)

BROUGH, Patrick (M)   60   0
H: 5 8   b.Carlisle 20-2-96

2013–14	Carlisle U	3	0		
2014–15	Carlisle U	29	0		
2015–16	Carlisle U	7	0		
2016–17	Carlisle U	1	0	40	0
2017–18	Morecambe	20	0	20	0

BROWNSWORD, Tyler (D)   0   0

2017–18	Morecambe	0	0

CAMPBELL, Adam (F)   117   11
H: 5 7   W: 11 07   b.North Shields 1-1-95
Internationals: England U16, U17, U19.

2011–12	Newcastle U	0	0		
2012–13	Newcastle U	3	0		
2013–14	Newcastle U	0	0		
2013–14	Carlisle U	1	0	1	0
2013–14	St Mirren	11	2	11	2
2014–15	Newcastle U	0	0	3	0
2014–15	Fleetwood T	2	0	2	0
2014–15	Hartlepool U	2	0	2	0
2015–16	Notts Co	44	4		
2016–17	Notts Co	29	4	73	8
2017–18	Morecambe	25	1	25	1

CONLAN, Luke (D)   67   0
H: 5 11   W: 11 05   b.Portaferry 31-10-94
Internationals: Northern Ireland U16, U17, U19, U21.

2011–12	Burnley	0	0		
2012–13	Burnley	0	0		
2013–14	Burnley	0	0		
2014–15	Burnley	0	0		
2015–16	Burnley	0	0		
2015–16	St Mirren	3	0	3	0
2015–16	Morecambe	16	0		
2016–17	Morecambe	21	0		
2017–18	Morecambe	27	0	64	0

DEAKIN, Reece (F)   0   0
From Airbus UK Broughton.

2017–18	Morecambe	0	0

ELLISON, Kevin (M)   589   121
H: 6 0   W: 12 00   b.Liverpool 23-2-79

2000–01	Leicester C	1	0		
2001–02	Leicester C	0	0	1	0
2001–02	Stockport Co	11	0		
2002–03	Stockport Co	23	1		
2003–04	Stockport Co	14	1	48	2
2003–04	Lincoln C	11	0	11	0
2004–05	Chester C	24	9		
2004–05	Hull C	16	1		
2005–06	Hull C	23	1	39	2
2006–07	Tranmere R	34	4	34	4
2007–08	Chester C	36	11		
2008–09	Chester C	39	8	99	28
2008–09	Rotherham U	0	0		
2009–10	Rotherham U	39	8		
2010–11	Rotherham U	23	3	62	11
2010–11	Bradford C	7	1	7	1
2011–12	Morecambe	34	15		
2012–13	Morecambe	40	11		
2013–14	Morecambe	42	10		
2014–15	Morecambe	43	11		
2015–16	Morecambe	44	9		
2016–17	Morecambe	45	8		
2017–18	Morecambe	40	9	288	73

FLEMING, Andy (M)   250   18
H: 6 1   W: 12 00   b.Liverpool 18-2-89
Internationals: England C.

2006–07	Wrexham	2	0		
2007–08	Wrexham	4	0	6	0
2010–11	Morecambe	30	2		
2011–12	Morecambe	17	2		
2012–13	Morecambe	32	5		
2013–14	Morecambe	35	2		
2014–15	Morecambe	35	2		
2015–16	Morecambe	33	3		
2016–17	Morecambe	30	2		
2017–18	Morecambe	32	0	244	18

HAWLEY, Kyle (F)   1   0

2016–17	Morecambe	1	0		
2017–18	Morecambe	0	0	1	0

HEDLEY, Ben (M)   1   0

2015–16	Morecambe	0	0		
2016–17	Morecambe	1	0		
2017–18	Morecambe	0	0	1	0

JORDAN, Luke (M)   7   0
H: 5 10   W: 11 07   b. 21-11-98

2016–17	Morecambe	6	0		
2017–18	Morecambe	1	0	7	0

KENYON, Alex (M)   162   6
H: 5 11   W: 11 12   b.Preston 17-7-92

2013–14	Morecambe	39	0		
2014–15	Morecambe	37	3		
2015–16	Morecambe	29	3		
2016–17	Morecambe	19	0		
2017–18	Morecambe	38	0	162	6

LAVELLE, Sam (D)   27   1
H: 6 0   W: 12 00   b. 3-10-96
Internationals: Scotland U18, U19.

2017–18	Morecambe	27	1	27	1

MAHER, Niall (G)   0   0

2015–16	Morecambe	0	0
2016–17	Morecambe	0	0
2017–18	Morecambe	0	0

McGOWAN, Aaron (D)   102   1
b.Maghull 20-9-95

2012–13	Morecambe	1	0		
2013–14	Morecambe	2	0		
2014–15	Morecambe	8	1		
2015–16	Morecambe	21	0		
2016–17	Morecambe	30	0		
2017–18	Morecambe	40	0	102	1

McGURK, Adam (F)   226   32
H: 5 9   W: 12 13   b.Larne 24-1-89
Internationals: Northern Ireland U21.

2005–06	Aston Villa	0	0		
2006–07	Aston Villa	0	0		
2007–08	Aston Villa	0	0		
2008–09	Aston Villa	0	0		
2009–10	Aston Villa	0	0		
From Hednesford T.					
2010–11	Tranmere R	21	3		
2011–12	Tranmere R	31	4		
2012–13	Tranmere R	27	3	79	0
2013–14	Burton Alb	34	9		
2014–15	Burton Alb	37	6	71	15
2015–16	Portsmouth	27	2	27	2
2016–17	Cambridge U	15	0		
2017–18	Cambridge U	0	0	15	0
2017–18	Morecambe	34	5	34	5

NIZIC, Daniel (G)   12   0
H: 6 2   W: 12 00   b.Sydney 15-3-95
Internationals: Australia U20, U23.

2015–16	Burnley	0	0		
2015–16	Crewe Alex	0	0		
2016–17	Morecambe	5	0		
2017–18	Morecambe	7	0	12	0

OLD, Steven (D)   206   15
H: 6 3   W: 13 05   b. 17-2-86
Internationals: New Zealand U17, U20, U23, Full caps.

2005–06	Young Heart Manawatu	19	1	19	1
2006–07	Newcastle Jets	9	0	9	0
2007–08	Wellington Phoenix	12	1	12	1
2008	Macarthur Rams	4	1	4	1
2008–09	Kilmarnock	0	0		
2009–10	Kilmarnock	10	0		
2010–11	Kilmarnock	0	0	10	0
2010–11	Cowdenbeath	4	0	4	0
From Basingstoke T, Sutton U.					
2013	Shijiazhuang Yongchang	28	1	28	1
2014	Ljungskile	22	4		
2015	Ljungskile	24	2	46	6
2016	GAIS	21	0		
2017	GAIS	12	1	33	1
2017–18	Morecambe	41	4	41	4

OLIVER, Vadaine (F)   154   21
H: 6 2   W: 12 04   b.Sheffield 21-10-91

2010–11	Sheffield W	0	0		
2011–12	Sheffield W	0	0		
2013–14	Crewe Alex	25	2		
2014–15	Crewe Alex	9	1	34	3
2014–15	Mansfield T	30	7	30	7
2015–16	York C	37	7	37	7
2016–17	Notts Co	19	1	19	1
2017–18	Morecambe	34	3	34	3

ROCHE, Barry (G)   539   1
H: 6 5   W: 14 08   b.Dublin 6-4-82
Internationals: Republic of Ireland U21.

1999–2000	Nottingham F	0	0		
2000–01	Nottingham F	2	0		
2001–02	Nottingham F	0	0		
2002–03	Nottingham F	1	0		
2003–04	Nottingham F	8	0		
2004–05	Nottingham F	2	0	13	0
2005–06	Chesterfield	41	0		
2006–07	Chesterfield	40	0		
2007–08	Chesterfield	45	0	126	0
2008–09	Morecambe	46	0		
2009–10	Morecambe	42	0		
2010–11	Morecambe	42	0		
2011–12	Morecambe	44	0		
2012–13	Morecambe	42	0		
2013–14	Morecambe	45	0		
2014–15	Morecambe	14	0		
2015–16	Morecambe	42	1		
2016–17	Morecambe	41	0		
2017–18	Morecambe	42	0	400	1

ROSE, Michael (D)   449   32
H: 5 11   W: 12 04   b.Salford 28-7-82
Internationals: England C.

1999–2000	Manchester U	0	0		
2000–01	Manchester U	0	0		
2001–02	Manchester U	0	0		
From Hereford U					
2004–05	Yeovil T	40	1		
2005–06	Yeovil T	1	0	41	1
2005–06	Cheltenham T	3	0	3	0
2005–06	Scunthorpe U	15	0	15	0
2006–07	Stockport Co	25	3		
2007–08	Stockport Co	28	3		
2008–09	Stockport Co	27	0		
2009–10	Stockport Co	24	2	104	8
2009–10	Norwich C	12	1	12	1
2010–11	Swindon T	35	3	35	3
2010–11	Colchester U	0	0		
2011–12	Colchester U	14	0		
2012–13	Colchester U	22	2	36	2
2012–13	Rochdale	14	2		
2013–14	Rochdale	42	4		
2014–15	Rochdale	32	1		
2015–16	Rochdale	30	1	118	8
2016–17	Morecambe	43	7		
2017–18	Morecambe	42	2	85	9

THOMPSON, Gary (M)   402   60
H: 6 0   W: 14 02   b.Kendal 24-11-80

2007–08	Morecambe	40	7		
2008–09	Scunthorpe U	24	3		
2009–10	Scunthorpe U	36	9		
2010–11	Scunthorpe U	12	1		
2011–12	Scunthorpe U	39	7	111	20
2012–13	Bradford C	41	6		
2013–14	Bradford C	44	2	85	8
2014–15	Notts Co	41	12	41	12
2015–16	Wycombe W	43	7		
2016–17	Wycombe W	42	3	85	10
2017–18	Morecambe	40	3	80	10

TURNER, Rhys (F)   67   6
b.Preston 22-7-95

2013–14	Oldham Ath	2	0		
2014–15	Oldham Ath	14	3		
2015–16	Oldham Ath	6	0	22	3
2015–16	York C	9	1	9	1
2016–17	Morecambe	30	2		
2017–18	Morecambe	6	0	36	2

WILDIG, Aaron (M)   180   12
H: 5 9   W: 11 02   b.Hereford 15-4-92
Internationals: Wales U16.

2009–10	Cardiff C	11	1		
2010–11	Cardiff C	2	0		
2010–11	Hamilton A	3	0	3	0
2011–12	Cardiff C	0	0	13	1
2011–12	Shrewsbury T	12	2		
2012–13	Shrewsbury T	21	1		
2013–14	Shrewsbury T	30	2		
2014–15	Shrewsbury T	1	0	64	5
2014–15	Morecambe	9	1		
2015–16	Morecambe	32	2		
2016–17	Morecambe	28	2		
2017–18	Morecambe	31	1	100	6

WINNARD, Dean (D)   293   5
H: 5 9   W: 10 04   b.Wigan 20-8-89

2006–07	Blackburn R	0	0		
2007–08	Blackburn R	0	0		
2008–09	Blackburn R	0	0		
2009–10	Accrington S	44	0		
2010–11	Accrington S	45	1		
2011–12	Accrington S	30	1		
2012–13	Accrington S	40	1		
2013–14	Accrington S	39	2		
2014–15	Accrington S	37	0		
2015–16	Accrington S	15	0	250	5
2016–17	Morecambe	23	0		
2017–18	Morecambe	20	0	43	0

YAWSON, Steven (M)   1   0

2016–17	Morecambe	1	0		
2017–18	Morecambe	0	0	1	0

Scholars

Armstrong, Cameron James; Coady, Harrison Jack; Davis, Leif; Dorward, Henry; Dutton-Kay, Nathan Ryan; Eme, Ezeikel Equiano; Fairclough, Luke James; Fletcher, Benjamin James; Hawley, Kyle; Herbert, Kai; Ingham, Benjamin Marc; Jones, Ellis; Jumeau, Olivier Philippe; Nelligan, Joe; Twiname, Toby; Young, Kaleb Harry Peter.

NEWCASTLE U (56)

AARONS, Rolando (M)   33   2
H: 5 9   W: 10 08   b.Kingston 16-11-95
Internationals: England U20.

2014–15	Newcastle U	4	1	
2015–16	Newcastle U	10	1	
2016–17	Newcastle U	4	0	
2017–18	Newcastle U	4	0	22 2
2017–18	*Verona*	11	0	11 0

ARMSTRONG, Adam (F)   132   36
H: 5 8   W: 10 12   b.Newcastle upon Tyne 10-2-97
Internationals: England U16, U17, U18, U19, U20, U21.

2013–14	Newcastle U	4	0		
2014–15	Newcastle U	11	0		
2015–16	Newcastle U	0	0		
2015–16	Coventry C	40	20	40	20
2016–17	Newcastle U	2	0		
2016–17	Barnsley	34	6	34	6
2017–18	Newcastle U	0	0	17	0
2017–18	Bolton W	20	1	20	1
2017–18	Blackburn R	21	9	21	9

ATSU, Christian (F)   147   21
H: 5 8   W: 10 09   b.Ada Foah 10-1-92
Internationals: Ghana Full caps.

2010–11	Porto	0	0		
2011–12	Porto	0	0		
2011–12	Rio Ave	27	6	27	6
2012–13	Porto	17	1	17	1
2013–14	Chelsea	0	0		
2013–14	Vitesse	26	5	26	5
2014–15	Chelsea	0	0		
2014–15	Everton	5	0	5	0
2015–16	Chelsea	0	0		
2015–16	Bournemouth	0	0		
2015–16	Malaga	12	2	12	2
2016–17	Chelsea	0	0		
2016–17	*Newcastle U*	32	5		
2017–18	Newcastle U	28	2	60	7

BARLASER, Daniel (M)   4   0
H: 6 0   W: 9 11   b.Gateshead 18-1-97
Internationals: Turkey U16, U17.

2015–16	Newcastle U	0	0	
2016–17	Newcastle U	0	0	
2017–18	Newcastle U	0	0	
2017–18	Crewe Alex	4	0	4 0

CAMERON, Kyle (D)   32   1
H: 6 3   W: 12 00   b.Hexham 15-1-97
Internationals: England U16. Scotland U17, U19, U21.

2015–16	Newcastle U	0	0	
2015–16	York C	18	1	18 1
2016–17	Newcastle U	0	0	
2016–17	Newport Co	6	0	6 0
2017–18	Newcastle U	0	0	
2017–18	Queen of the South	8	0	8 0

CLARK, Ciaran (D)   188   12
H: 6 2   W: 12 00   b.Harrow 26-9-89
Internationals: England U17, U18, U19, U20. Republic of Ireland Full caps.

2008–09	Aston Villa	0	0		
2009–10	Aston Villa	1	0		
2010–11	Aston Villa	19	3		
2011–12	Aston Villa	15	1		
2012–13	Aston Villa	29	1		
2013–14	Aston Villa	27	0		
2014–15	Aston Villa	25	1		
2015–16	Aston Villa	18	1	134	7
2016–17	Newcastle U	34	3		
2017–18	Newcastle U	20	2	54	5

COLBACK, Jack (M)   274   14
H: 5 9   W: 11 05   b.Killingworth 24-10-89
Internationals: England U20.

2007–08	Sunderland	0	0	
2008–09	Sunderland	0	0	
2009–10	Sunderland	1	0	
2009–10	Ipswich T	37	4	
2010–11	Sunderland	11	0	
2010–11	Ipswich T	13	0	50 4

2011–12	Sunderland	35	1	
2012–13	Sunderland	35	0	
2013–14	Sunderland	33	3	115 4
2014–15	Newcastle U	35	4	
2015–16	Newcastle U	29	1	
2016–17	Newcastle U	29	0	
2017–18	Newcastle U	0	0	93 5
2017–18	*Nottingham F*	16	1	16 1

DARLOW, Karl (G)   168   0
H: 6 1   W: 12 05   b.Northampton 8-10-90

2009–10	Nottingham F	0	0	
2010–11	Nottingham F	1	0	
2011–12	Nottingham F	0	0	
2012–13	Nottingham F	20	0	
2012–13	Walsall	9	0	9 0
2013–14	Nottingham F	43	0	
2014–15	Newcastle U	0	0	
2014–15	*Nottingham F*	42	0	106 0
2015–16	Newcastle U	9	0	
2016–17	Newcastle U	34	0	
2017–18	Newcastle U	10	0	53 0

DIAME, Mohamed (M)   351   33
H: 6 1   W: 11 02   b.Creteil 14-6-87
Internationals: Senegal U23, Full caps.

2006–07	Lens	0	0		
2007–08	Linares	31	1	31	1
2008–09	Rayo Vallecano	35	2	35	2
2009–10	Wigan Ath	34	1		
2010–11	Wigan Ath	36	1		
2011–12	Wigan Ath	26	3	96	5
2012–13	West Ham U	33	3		
2013–14	West Ham U	35	4		
2014–15	West Ham U	3	0	71	7
2015–16	Hull C	12	4		
2015–16	Hull C	38	9	50	13
2016–17	Newcastle U	37	3		
2017–18	Newcastle U	31	2	68	5

DUBRAVKA, Martin (G)   215   0
H: 6 3   W: 13 01   b.Zilina 15-1-89
Internationals: Slovakia U19, U21, Full caps.

2008–09	Zilina	1	0	
2009–10	Zilina	26	0	
2010–11	Zilina	24	0	
2011–12	Zilina	8	0	
2012–13	Zilina	26	0	
2013–14	Zilina	13	0	98 0
2013–14	Esbjerg	15	0	
2014–15	Esbjerg	33	0	
2015–16	Esbjerg	18	0	66 0
2016–17	Slovan Liberec	28	0	28 0
2017–18	Sparta Prague	11	0	11 0

On loan from Sparta Prague.

2017–18	Newcastle U	12	0	12 0

DUMMETT, Paul (D)   161   0
H: 5 10   W: 10 02   b.Newcastle upon Tyne 26-9-91
Internationals: Wales U21, Full caps.

2010–11	Newcastle U	0	0		
2011–12	Newcastle U	0	0		
2012–13	St Mirren	30	2	30	2
2013–14	Newcastle U	18	1		
2014–15	Newcastle U	25	0		
2015–16	Newcastle U	23	1		
2016–17	Newcastle U	45	0		
2017–18	Newcastle U	20	0	131	2

ELLIOT, Rob (G)   162   0
H: 6 3   W: 14 10   b.Chatham 30-4-86
Internationals: Republic of Ireland U19, Full caps.

2004–05	Charlton Ath	0	0		
2004–05	Notts Co	4	0	4	0
2005–06	Charlton Ath	0	0		
2006–07	Charlton Ath	0	0		
2006–07	Accrington S	7	0	7	0
2007–08	Charlton Ath	1	0		
2008–09	Charlton Ath	23	0		
2009–10	Charlton Ath	33	0		
2010–11	Charlton Ath	35	0		
2011–12	Charlton Ath	4	0	96	0
2011–12	Newcastle U	10	0		
2012–13	Newcastle U	2	0		
2014–15	Newcastle U	3	0		
2015–16	Newcastle U	21	0		
2016–17	Newcastle U	3	0		
2017–18	Newcastle U	16	0	55	0

GAYLE, Dwight (F)   178   64
H: 5 10   W: 11 07   b.Walthamstow 20-10-89

2011–12	Dagenham & R	0	0		
2012–13	Dagenham & R	18	7	18	7
2012–13	Peterborough U	29	13	29	13
2013–14	Crystal Palace	23	7		
2014–15	Crystal Palace	25	5		

2015–16	Crystal Palace	16	3	64	15
2016–17	Newcastle U	32	23		
2017–18	Newcastle U	35	6	67	29

GILLIEAD, Alex (F)   104   7
H: 6 0   W: 11 00   b.Shotley Bridge 11-2-96
Internationals: England U16, U17, U18, U20.

2014–15	Newcastle U	0	0		
2015–16	Newcastle U	0	0		
2015–16	Carlisle U	35	5	35	5
2016–17	Newcastle U	0	0		
2016–17	Luton T	18	1	18	1
2016–17	Bradford C	9	0		
2017–18	Newcastle U	0	0		
2017–18	Bradford C	42	1	51	1

HAIDARA, Massadio (D)   83   0
H: 5 11   W: 11 10   b.Trappes 2-12-92
Internationals: France U19, U20, U21.

2010–11	AS Nancy	8	0		
2011–12	AS Nancy	19	0		
2012–13	AS Nancy	17	0	44	0
2012–13	Newcastle U	4	0		
2013–14	Newcastle U	11	0		
2014–15	Newcastle U	15	0		
2015–16	Newcastle U	7	0		
2016–17	Newcastle U	1	0		
2017–18	Newcastle U	1	0	39	0

HAYDEN, Isaac (D)   77   4
H: 6 2   W: 12 06   b.Chelmsford 22-3-95
Internationals: England U16, U17, U18, U19, U20, U21.

2011–12	Arsenal	0	0		
2012–13	Arsenal	0	0		
2013–14	Arsenal	0	0		
2014–15	Arsenal	0	0		
2015–16	Arsenal	0	0		
2015–16	Hull C	18	1	18	1
2016–17	Newcastle U	33	2		
2017–18	Newcastle U	26	1	59	3

HEARDMAN, Tom (F)   2   0
H: 6 2   W: 12 08   b.Gosforth 12-9-95

2015–16	Newcastle U	0	0	
2016–17	Newcastle U	0	0	
2016–17	Hartlepool U	2	0	2 0
2017–18	Newcastle U	0	0	
2017–18	Bury	0	0	

JESUS GAMEZ, Duarte (D)   261   1
H: 6 0   W: 11 00   b.Malaga 10-4-85
Internationals: Spain U23.

2005–06	Malaga	15	0		
2006–07	Malaga	1	0		
2007–08	Malaga	35	1		
2008–09	Malaga	35	0		
2009–10	Malaga	32	0		
2010–11	Malaga	30	0		
2011–12	Malaga	26	0		
2012–13	Malaga	28	0		
2013–14	Malaga	28	0	230	0
2014–15	Atletico Madrid	14	0		
2015–16	Atletico Madrid	10	0	24	0
2016–17	Newcastle U	5	0		
2017–18	Newcastle U	2	0	7	0

JOSELU, Mato (F)   178   40
H: 6 3   W: 12 08   b.Stuttgart, Germany 27-3-90
Internationals: Spain U19, U20, U21.

2008–09	Celta Vigo	2	0		
2009–10	Real Madrid	0	0		
2009–10	Celta Vigo	24	4	26	4
2010–11	Real Madrid	1	1		
2011–12	Real Madrid	0	0	1	1
2012–13	Hoffenheim	25	5		
2013–14	Hoffenheim	0	0	25	5
2013–14	Eintracht Frankfurt	24	9	24	9
2014–15	Hannover 96	30	8	30	8
2015–16	Stoke C	22	4		
2016–17	Stoke C	0	0	22	4
2016–17	Deportivo La Coruna	20	5	20	5
2017–18	Newcastle U	30	4	30	4

LASCELLES, Jamaal (D)   159   12
H: 6 2   W: 13 01   b.Derby 11-11-93
Internationals: England U18, U19, U20, U21.

2010–11	Nottingham F	0	0		
2011–12	Nottingham F	1	0		
2011–12	Stevenage	7	1	7	1
2012–13	Nottingham F	29	2		
2013–14	Nottingham F	29	2		
2014–15	Newcastle U	0	0		
2014–15	Nottingham F	26	1	58	3
2015–16	Newcastle U	18	2		
2016–17	Newcastle U	43	3		
2017–18	Newcastle U	33	3	94	8

LAZAAR, Achraf (D)   124   4
H: 5 8   W: 10 08   b.Casablanca 22-1-92
Internationals: Morocco Full caps.

2011–12	Varese	0	0		
2012–13	Varese	21	0		
2013–14	Varese	17	0	38	0
2013–14	Palermo	14	0		
2014–15	Palermo	29	2		
2015–16	Palermo	30	1		
2016–17	Palermo	0	0	73	3
2016–17	Newcastle U	4	0		
2017–18	Newcastle U	0	0	4	0
2017–18	*Benevento*	9	1	9	1

LEJEUNE, Florian (D)   205   13
H: 6 2   W: 12 11   b.Paris 20-5-91
Internationals: France U20.

2008–09	Agde	3	2	3	2
2009–10	Istres	14	0		
2010–11	Istres	28	3	42	3
2011–12	Villarreal	2	0		
2012–13	Villarreal	3	0	5	0
2012–13	Brest	10	0		
2013–14	Brest	11	0	21	0
2014–15	Girona	38	4		
2015–16	Manchester C	0	0		
2015–16	Girona	38	3	76	7
2016–17	Eibar	34	1	34	1
2017–18	Newcastle U	24	0	24	0

LONGSTAFF, Sean (M)   74   14
H: 5 11   W: 10 03   b.North Shields 30-10-97

2016–17	Newcastle U	0	0		
2016–17	Kilmarnock	16	3		
2016–17	Newcastle U	0	0		
2016–17	Kilmarnock	16	3	32	6
2017–18	Newcastle U	0	0		
2017–18	*Blackpool*	42	8	42	8

MANQUILLO, Javier (D)   88   1
H: 5 11   W: 12 04   b.Madrid 5-5-94
Internationals: Spain U16, U17, U18, U19, U20, U21.

2012–13	Atletico Madrid	3	0		
2013–14	Atletico Madrid	0	0		
2014–15	Atletico Madrid	0	0		
2014–15	Liverpool	10	0	10	0
2015–16	Atletico Madrid	0	0		
2015–16	Marseille	31	0	31	0
2016–17	Atletico Madrid	0	0	6	0
2016–17	Sunderland	20	1	20	1
2017–18	Newcastle U	21	0	21	0

MBEMBA, Chancel (D)   117   7
H: 6 0   W: 12 00   b.Kinshasa 8-8-94
Internationals: DR Congo Full caps.

2011–12	Anderlecht	0	0		
2012–13	Anderlecht	0	0		
2013–14	Anderlecht	35	5		
2014–15	Anderlecht	28	1	63	6
2015–16	Newcastle U	33	0		
2016–17	Newcastle U	12	1		
2017–18	Newcastle U	9	0	54	1

MERINO, Mikel (M)   99   9
H: 6 2   W: 12 04   b.Pamplona 22-6-96
Internationals: Spain U19, U20.

2013–14	Osasuna	8	0		
2014–15	Osasuna	29	1		
2015–16	Osasuna	38	7	67	8
2016–17	Borussia Dortmund	8	0		
2017–18	Borussia Dortmund	0	0	8	0

On loan from Borussia Dortmund.

2017–18	*Newcastle U*	24	1	24	1

MITROVIC, Aleksandar (F)   204   82
H: 6 2   W: 13 10   b.Smederevo 16-9-94
Internationals: Serbia U21, Full caps.

2011–12	Teleoptik	25	7	25	7
2012–13	Partizan Belgrade	25	10		
2013–14	Partizan Belgrade	3	3	28	13
2013–14	Anderlecht	32	16		
2014–15	Anderlecht	37	20	69	36
2015–16	Newcastle U	34	9		
2016–17	Newcastle U	25	4		
2017–18	Newcastle U	6	1	65	14
2017–18	*Fulham*	17	12	17	12

MURPHY, Jacob (M)   138   26
H: 5 9   W: 11 03   b.Wembley 24-2-95
Internationals: England U18, U19, U20, U21.

2013–14	Norwich C	0	0		
2013–14	Swindon T	6	0	6	0
2013–14	Southend U	7	1	7	1
2014–15	Norwich C	0	0		
2014–15	Blackpool	9	2	9	2
2014–15	Scunthorpe U	3	0	3	0
2014–15	Colchester U	11	4	11	4
2015–16	Norwich C	0	0		
2015–16	Coventry C	40	9	40	9
2016–17	Norwich C	37	9	37	9
2017–18	Newcastle U	25	1	25	1

PEREZ, Ayoze (F)   188   47
H: 5 10   W: 10 06   b.Santa Cruz de Tenerife 23-7-93
Internationals: Spain U21.

2012–13	Tenerife	16	1		
2013–14	Tenerife	30	16	46	17
2014–15	Newcastle U	36	7		
2015–16	Newcastle U	34	6		
2016–17	Newcastle U	36	9		
2017–18	Newcastle U	36	8	142	30

RITCHIE, Matt (M)   374   86
H: 5 8   W: 11 00   b.Gosport 10-9-89
Internationals: Scotland Full caps.

2008–09	Portsmouth	0	0		
2008–09	Dagenham & R	37	11	37	11
2009–10	Portsmouth	2	0		
2009–10	Notts Co	16	3	16	3
2009–10	Swindon T	4	0		
2010–11	Portsmouth	5	0	7	0
2010–11	Swindon T	36	7		
2011–12	Swindon T	40	10		
2012–13	Swindon T	27	9	107	26
2012–13	Bournemouth	17	3		
2013–14	Bournemouth	30	9		
2014–15	Bournemouth	46	15		
2015–16	Bournemouth	37	4	130	31
2016–17	Newcastle U	42	12		
2017–18	Newcastle U	35	3	77	15

SAIVET, Henri (M)   184   22
H: 5 9   W: 10 08   b.Dakar 26-10-90
Internationals: France U16, U17, U18, U21. Senegal Full caps.

2007–08	Bordeaux	1	0		
2008–09	Bordeaux	1	0		
2009–10	Bordeaux	3	0		
2010–11	Bordeaux	6	0		
2010–11	Angers	18	3	18	3
2011–12	Bordeaux	24	1		
2012–13	Bordeaux	34	8		
2013–14	Bordeaux	33	6		
2014–15	Bordeaux	14	0		
2015–16	Bordeaux	18	2	134	17
2015–16	Newcastle U	4	0		
2016–17	Newcastle U	0	0		
2016–17	St Etienne	27	1	27	1
2017–18	Newcastle U	1	1	5	1
2017–18	*Sivasspor*	0	0		

SHELVEY, Jonjo (M)   265   31
H: 6 1   W: 11 02   b.Romford 27-2-92
Internationals: England U16, U17, U19, U21, Full caps.

2007–08	Charlton Ath	2	0		
2008–09	Charlton Ath	16	3		
2009–10	Charlton Ath	24	4	42	7
2010–11	Liverpool	15	0		
2011–12	Liverpool	13	1		
2011–12	Blackpool	10	6	10	6
2012–13	Liverpool	19	1	47	2
2013–14	Swansea C	32	6		
2014–15	Swansea C	31	3		
2015–16	Swansea C	16	1	79	10
2015–16	Newcastle U	15	0		
2016–17	Newcastle U	42	5		
2017–18	Newcastle U	30	1	87	6

STERRY, Jamie (D)   28   0
H: 5 11   W: 11 00   b.Newcastle upon Tyne 21-11-95

2014–15	Newcastle U	0	0		
2015–16	Newcastle U	1	0		
2016–17	Newcastle U	2	0		
2016–17	Coventry C	16	0	16	0
2017–18	Newcastle U	0	0	3	0
2017–18	*Crewe Alex*	9	0	9	0

TONEY, Ivan (F)   144   36
H: 5 10   W: 12 00   b.Northampton 16-3-96

2012–13	Northampton T	0	0		
2013–14	Northampton T	13	3		
2014–15	Northampton T	40	8	53	11
2015–16	Newcastle U	2	0		
2015–16	Barnsley	15	1	15	1
2016–17	Newcastle U	0	0		
2016–17	Shrewsbury T	19	6	19	6
2016–17	Scunthorpe U	15	6		
2017–18	Newcastle U	0	0	2	0
2017–18	Wigan Ath	24	4	24	4
2017–18	*Scunthorpe U*	16	8	31	14

WOODMAN, Freddie (G)   30   0
H: 6 1   W: 10 12   b.London 4-3-97
Internationals: England U16, U17, U18, U19, U20, U21.

2014–15	Newcastle U	0	0		
2014–15	Hartlepool U	0	0		
2015–16	Newcastle U	0	0		
2015–16	Crawley T	11	0	11	0
2016–17	Newcastle U	0	0		
2016–17	Kilmarnock	14	0	14	0
2017–18	Newcastle U	0	0		
2017–18	*Aberdeen*	5	0	5	0

YEDLIN, DeAndre (D)   147   3
H: 5 9   W: 11 07   b.Seattle 9-7-93
Internationals: USA U20, Full caps.

2013	Seattle Sounders	33	2		
2014	Seattle Sounders	29	0	62	2
2014–15	Tottenham H	1	0		
2015–16	Tottenham H	0	0	1	0
2015–16	Sunderland	23	0	23	0
2016–17	Newcastle U	27	1		
2017–18	Newcastle U	34	0	61	1

Players retained or with offer of contract
Bailey, Owen John Edward; Bartlett, Tyrique; Charman, Luke; Cumbreras, Jesus Nunez; Fernandez Satue, Victor; Gibson, Liam Steven; Harker, Nathan; Huuhtanen, Otto Eemeli; O'Connor, Stefan Ramone Sewell; Roberts, Callum; Sangare, Mohammed; Sels, Matz Willy E; Sorensen, Elias Fritjof Graenge; Yarney, Josef Charles.

Scholars
Allan, Thomas David; Allen, Max; Barrett, Ryan Thomas; Cass, Lewis Graham; Cole, Thomas Anthony; Joyce, Samuel Edward; Langley, Daniel David; Longstaff, Matthew Ben; Madia, Deese Kasinga; McEntee, Oisin Michael; Walters, Oliver Reece; Watts, Kelland John William James; Wilson, Adam Ayiro; Young, Jack.

NEWPORT CO (57)

AMOND, Padraig (F)   368   99
H: 5 11   W: 12 05   b.Carlow 15-4-88
Internationals: Republic of Ireland U21.

2006	Shamrock R	10	1		
2007	Shamrock R	6	1		
2007	Kildare Co	13	5	13	5
2008	Shamrock R	26	9		
2009	Shamrock R	20	4	62	15
2010	Sligo R	27	17	27	17
2010–11	Pacos	0	0	17	0
2011–12	Accrington S	42	7		
2012–13	Accrington S	36	9		
2013–14	Accrington S	45	11	78	16
2013–14	Morecambe	45	11		
2014–15	Morecambe	37	8	82	19
2016–17	Hartlepool U	46	14	46	14
2017–18	Newport Co	43	13	43	13

BARNUM-BOBB, Jazzi (D)   39   1
b.Enfield 15-9-95

2014–15	Cardiff C	0	0		
2015–16	Cardiff C	0	0		
2015–16	Newport Co	12	0		
2016–17	Newport Co	26	1		
2017–18	Newport Co	1	0	39	1

BENNETT, Scott (D)   228   20
H: 5 10   W: 12 10   b.Newquay 30-11-90

2008–09	Exeter C	0	0		
2009–10	Exeter C	0	0		
2010–11	Exeter C	1	0		
2011–12	Exeter C	15	3		
2012–13	Exeter C	43	6		
2013–14	Exeter C	45	6		
2014–15	Exeter C	28	3	132	18
2015–16	Notts Co	6	0	6	0
2015–16	Newport Co	12	0		
2015–16	York C	11	0	11	0
2016–17	Newport Co	39	0		
2017–18	Newport Co	28	2	79	2

BITTNER, James (G)   4   0
H: 6 2   W: 12 09   b.Devizes 2-2-82
Internationals: England C.

2001–02	Bournemouth	0	0		

From Exeter C.

2005–06	Torquay U	0	0		

From Woking, Salisbury C, Chippenham T, Forest Green R, Hereford U.

2013–14	Newport Co	0	0		

From Salisbury C.

2014–15	Plymouth Arg	1	0		
2015–16	Plymouth Arg	1	0	2	0
2016–17	Newport Co	2	0		
2017–18	Newport Co	0	0	2	0

BUTLER, Dan (D)   132   4
b.Cowes 26-8-94

2012–13	Portsmouth	17	0		
2013–14	Portsmouth	1	0		
2014–15	Portsmouth	30	0	48	0
2016–17	Newport Co	40	3		
2017–18	Newport Co	44	1	84	4

COLLINS, Lewis (M)   0   0
b.Newport 9-5-01

2017–18	Newport Co	0	0

DAY, Joe (G)   172   0
H: 6 1   W: 12 00   b.Brighton 13-8-90

2011–12	Peterborough U	0	0		
2012–13	Peterborough U	0	0		
2013–14	Peterborough U	4	0		
2014–15	Peterborough U	0	0	4	0
2014–15	*Newport Co*	36	0		
2015–16	Newport Co	41	0		
2016–17	Newport Co	45	0		
2017–18	Newport Co	46	0	168	0

DEMETRIOU, Mickey (D)   121   14
b.Durrington 12-3-90
Internationals: England C.

2014–15	Shrewsbury T	42	3		
2015–16	Shrewsbury T	1	0		
2015–16	*Cambridge U*	15	0	15	0
2016–17	Shrewsbury T	0	0	43	3
2016–17	Newport Co	17	4		
2017–18	Newport Co	46	7	63	11

DOLAN, Matthew (M)   171   13
b.Hartlepool 11-2-93

2010–11	Middlesbrough	0	0		
2011–12	Middlesbrough	0	0		
2012–13	Middlesbrough	0	0		
2012–13	*Yeovil T*	8	1		
2013–14	Middlesbrough	0	0		
2013–14	*Hartlepool U*	20	2		
2013–14	*Bradford C*	11	0		
2014–15	Bradford C	13	0	24	0
2014–15	*Hartlepool U*	2	0	22	2
2015–16	Yeovil T	39	3		
2016–17	Yeovil T	38	4	85	8
2017–18	Newport Co	40	3	40	3

FLYNN, Michael (M)   333   42
H: 5 10   W: 13 04   b.Newport 17-10-80

2002–03	Wigan Ath	17	1		
2003–04	Wigan Ath	8	0		
2004–05	Wigan Ath	13	1	38	2
2004–05	*Blackpool*	6	0		
2004–05	Gillingham	16	3		
2005–06	Gillingham	36	6		
2006–07	Gillingham	45	10	97	19
2007–08	Blackpool	28	3	34	3
2008–09	*Darlington*	0	0		
2008–09	Huddersfield T	25	4	25	4
2009–10	Bradford C	42	6		
2010–11	Bradford C	19	0		
2011–12	Bradford C	30	4	91	10
2013–14	Newport Co	32	4		
2014–15	Newport Co	11	0		
2016–17	Newport Co	5	0		
2017–18	Newport Co	0	0	48	4

FOULSTON, Jay (D)   0   0
b. 27-11-00

2017–18	Newport Co	0	0

HAYES, Paul (F)   532   117
H: 6 0   W: 12 12   b.Dagenham 20-9-83

2002–03	Scunthorpe U	18	8		
2003–04	Scunthorpe U	35	2		
2004–05	Scunthorpe U	46	18		
2005–06	Barnsley	45	6		
2006–07	Barnsley	30	5		
2006–07	*Huddersfield T*	4	1	4	1
2007–08	Scunthorpe U	40	8		
2008–09	Scunthorpe U	44	17		
2009–10	Scunthorpe U	45	9		
2010–11	Preston NE	23	2	23	2
2010–11	*Barnsley*	7	0	82	11
2011–12	Charlton Ath	19	3	19	3
2011–12	*Wycombe W*	6	6		
2012–13	Brentford	23	4		
2012–13	*Crawley T*	11	2	11	2
2013–14	Brentford	0	0	23	4
2013–14	*Plymouth Arg*	6	0	6	0
2013–14	Scunthorpe U	16	4	244	56
2014–15	Wycombe W	39	12		

2015–16	Wycombe W	37	4		
2016–17	Wycombe W	23	3		
2017–18	Wycombe W	2	0	107	25
2017–18	Newport Co	13	3	13	3

HILLMAN, Thomas (D)   0   0
b. 20-11-00

2017–18	Newport Co	0	0

JACKSON, Marlon (F)   83   3
H: 5 11   W: 11 12   b.Bristol 6-12-90
Internationals: England C.

2009–10	Bristol C	0	0		
2009–10	*Hereford U*	5	0	5	0
2009–10	*Aldershot T*	22	1		
2010–11	Bristol C	4	0		
2010–11	*Aldershot T*	9	0	31	1
2011–12	Bristol C	0	0	4	0
2011–12	*Northampton T*	6	1	6	1
2011–12	*Cheltenham T*	1	0	1	0
2013–14	Bury	8	1	8	1

From Lincoln C, Halifax T, Oxford C,
Tranmere R.

2016–17	Newport Co	22	0		
2017–18	Newport Co	6	0	28	0

JAHRALDO-MARTIN, Calaum (F)   26   1
b.Hemel Hempstead 27-4-93
Internationals: Antigua and Barbuda U20,
Full caps.

2013–14	Hull C	0	0		
2014–15	Hull C	0	0		
2014–15	*Tranmere R*	2	0	2	0
2015–16	Hull C	0	0	1	0
2015–16	*Leyton Orient*	15	1	15	1
2016–17	Oldham Ath	4	0	4	0
2017–18	Newport Co	4	0	4	0

LABADIE, Joss (M)   247   35
H: 5 7   W: 11 02   b.Croydon 31-8-90

2008–09	WBA	0	0		
2008–09	*Shrewsbury T*	1	0		
2009–10	WBA	0	0		
2009–10	*Shrewsbury T*	13	5	14	5
2009–10	*Cheltenham T*	11	0	11	0
2009–10	*Tranmere R*	9	3		
2010–11	Tranmere R	34	2		
2011–12	Tranmere R	27	5	70	10
2012–13	Notts Co	24	2		
2012–13	*Torquay U*	7	4		
2013–14	Notts Co	15	1	39	3
2013–14	*Torquay U*	10	1	17	5
2014–15	Dagenham & R	24	2		
2015–16	Dagenham & R	28	4	52	6
2016–17	Newport Co	19	3		
2017–18	Newport Co	25	3	44	6

NOUBLE, Frank (F)   213   28
H: 6 3   W: 12 08   b.Lewisham 24-9-91
Internationals: England U17, U19.

2009–10	West Ham U	8	0		
2009–10	*WBA*	3	0	3	0
2009–10	*Swindon T*	8	0	8	0
2010–11	West Ham U	2	0		
2010–11	*Swansea C*	6	1	6	1
2010–11	*Barnsley*	4	0		
2010–11	*Charlton Ath*	9	1	9	1
2011–12	West Ham U	3	1	13	1
2011–12	Gillingham	13	5		
2011–12	*Barnsley*	6	0	10	0
2012–13	Wolverhampton W	2	0	2	0
2012–13	*Ipswich T*	17	2		
2013–14	Ipswich T	38	2		
2014–15	Ipswich T	1	0	56	4
2014–15	*Coventry C*	31	6	31	6
2016–17	Gillingham	12	1	25	6
2016–17	*Southend U*	5	0	5	0
2017–18	Newport Co	45	9	45	9

O'BRIEN, Mark (D)   105   1
H: 5 11   W: 12 02   b.Dublin 20-11-92
Internationals: Republic of Ireland U19.

2008–09	Derby C	1	0		
2009–10	Derby C	0	0		
2010–11	Derby C	0	0		
2011–12	Derby C	20	0		
2012–13	Derby C	9	0		
2013–14	Derby C	0	0	32	0
2014–15	Motherwell	19	0	19	0
2015–16	Luton T	6	0	6	0

From Southport.

2016–17	Newport Co	20	1		
2017–18	Newport Co	28	0	48	1

OWEN-EVANS, Tom (F)   52   1
H: 5 11   W: 10 06   b.Bristol 18-3-97

2014–15	Newport Co	1	0		
2015–16	Newport Co	15	0		
2016–17	Newport Co	24	1		
2017–18	Newport Co	12	0	52	1

PIPE, David (M)   337   8
H: 5 9   W: 12 01   b.Caerphilly 5-11-83
Internationals: Wales U21, Full caps.

2002–03	Coventry C	21	1		
2003–04	Coventry C	0	0	21	1
2003–04	Notts Co	18	0		
2004–05	Notts Co	41	2		
2005–06	Notts Co	43	2		
2006–07	Notts Co	39	0	141	4
2007–08	Bristol R	40	2		
2008–09	Bristol R	39	1		
2009–10	Bristol R	7	0	86	3
2009–10	*Cheltenham T*	8	0	8	0
2013–14	Newport Co	25	0		

From Forest Green R, Eastleigh.

2016–17	Newport Co	21	0		
2017–18	Newport Co	35	0	81	0

PRESS, Evan (M)   0   0
b. 20-6-00

2017–18	Newport Co	0	0

REYNOLDS, Lamar (F)   10   0
H: 5 10   W: 11 07   b. 16-8-95
From Brentwood T.

2017–18	Newport Co	10	0	10	0

RIGG, Sean (F)   355   38
H: 5 9   W: 12 01   b.Bristol 1-10-88

2006–07	Bristol R	18	1		
2007–08	Bristol R	31	1		
2008–09	Bristol R	8	0		
2009–10	Bristol R	0	0	57	2
2009–10	*Port Vale*	26	3		
2010–11	Port Vale	25	3		
2011–12	Port Vale	42	10	93	16
2012–13	Oxford U	44	5		
2013–14	Oxford U	28	2	72	7
2014–15	AFC Wimbledon	44	5		
2015–16	AFC Wimbledon	39	2	83	7
2016–17	Newport Co	34	6		
2017–18	Newport Co	16	0	50	6

SHEEHAN, Josh (M)   59   9
H: 6 0   W: 11 11   b.Pembrey 30-3-95
Internationals: Wales U19, U21.

2013–14	Swansea C	0	0		
2014–15	Swansea C	0	0		
2014–15	*Yeovil T*	13	0		
2015–16	Swansea C	0	0		
2015–16	*Yeovil T*	13	2	26	2
2016–17	Swansea C	0	0		
2016–17	*Newport Co*	20	5		
2017–18	Newport Co	13	2	33	7

TAYLOR, Owen (M)   0   0
b. 6-3-01

2017–18	Newport Co	0	0

TOURAY, Momodou (F)   1   0
H: 5 11   W: 10 06   b. 30-7-99
Internationals: Wales U18, U19.

2016–17	Newport Co	0	0		
2017–18	Newport Co	1	0	1	0

WILLIAMS, Aaron (F)   33   5
H: 5 11   W: 12 05   b. 21-10-93
Internationals: England C.

2012–13	Walsall	6	0		
2013–14	Walsall	0	0	6	0

From Worcester C, Rushall Olympic,
Nuneaton T.

2015–16	Peterborough U	10	2		
2016–17	Peterborough U	0	0	10	2
2016–17	Newport Co	17	3		
2017–18	Newport Co	0	0	17	3

WILLMOTT, Robbie (M)   101   6
H: 5 9   W: 12 00   b.Harlow 16-5-90
Internationals: England C.

2013–14	Newport Co	46	3		
2014–15	Newport Co	16	1		
2017–18	Newport Co	39	2	101	6

Scholars
Beckett, Callum Peter; Bishop, Liam
Lawrence; Collins, Lewis Rhys; Cook,
Michael John; Edwards, Owura Nsiah;
Hillman, Thomas Patrick; Hunt, Joe Lewis;
Mayor, Matthew Ryan; Murray, Lucas Elliot;
Press, Evan Lewis; Savigar, Thomas Anthony
MacQuillan; Taylor, Owen Philip; Warman,
Liam; Williams, Jay Andrew; Williams,
Joshua Lee.

Non-contract
Flynn, Michael John Samuel.

NORTHAMPTON T (58)

ANAELE, Prudence (D)   0   0
2017–18   Northampton T   0   0

BARNETT, Leon (D)   302   15
H: 6 0   W: 12 04   b.Stevenage 30-11-85

2003–04	Luton T	0	0		
2004–05	Luton T	0	0		
2005–06	Luton T	20	0		
2006–07	Luton T	39	3	59	3
2007–08	WBA	32	3		
2008–09	WBA	11	0		
2009–10	WBA	2	0		
2009–10	Coventry C	20	0	20	0
2010–11	WBA	0	0	45	3
2010–11	Norwich C	25	1		
2011–12	Norwich C	17	1		
2012–13	Norwich C	8	0		
2012–13	*Cardiff C*	8	0	8	0
2013–14	Norwich C	0	0	50	2
2013–14	Wigan Ath	41	4		
2014–15	Wigan Ath	20	0		
2015–16	Wigan Ath	20	1	81	5
2016–17	Bury	24	1	24	1
2017–18	Northampton T	15	1	15	1

BOWDITCH, Dean (F)   400   79
H: 5 11   W: 11 05   b.Bishops Stortford 15-6-86
Internationals: England U16, U17, U19.

2002–03	Ipswich T	5	0		
2003–04	Ipswich T	16	4		
2004–05	Ipswich T	21	3		
2004–05	*Burnley*	10	1	10	1
2005–06	Ipswich T	21	0		
2005–06	*Wycombe W*	11	1	11	1
2006–07	Ipswich T	9	1		
2006–07	*Brighton & HA*	3	1		
2007–08	Ipswich T	0	0		
2007–08	*Northampton T*	10	2		
2007–08	*Brighton & HA*	5	0	8	1
2008–09	Ipswich T	1	0	73	8
2008–09	*Brentford*	9	2	9	2
2009–10	Yeovil T	30	10		
2010–11	Yeovil T	41	15	71	25
2011–12	Milton Keynes D	41	12		
2012–13	Milton Keynes D	39	8		
2013–14	Milton Keynes D	12	1		
2014–15	Milton Keynes D	35	7		
2015–16	Milton Keynes D	37	4		
2016–17	Milton Keynes D	28	5	192	37
2017–18	Northampton T	11	0	21	2
2017–18	*Stevenage*	5	2	5	2

BRIDGE, Jack (M)   11   0
H: 5 10   W: 11 07   b. 21-9-95

2013–14	Southend U	0	0		
2014–15	Southend U	0	0		
2015–16	Southend U	2	0		
2016–17	Southend U	4	0		
2017–18	Southend U	1	0	7	0
2017–18	Northampton T	4	0	4	0

BUCHANAN, David (M)   447   3
H: 5 7   W: 11 03   b.Rochdale 6-5-86
Internationals: Northern Ireland U19, U21.

2004–05	Bury	3	0		
2005–06	Bury	23	0		
2006–07	Bury	41	0		
2007–08	Bury	35	0		
2008–09	Bury	46	0		
2009–10	Bury	38	0	186	0
2010–11	Hamilton A	28	1	28	1
2011–12	Tranmere R	41	1	41	1
2012–13	Preston NE	33	0		
2013–14	Preston NE	19	0		
2014–15	Preston NE	17	0	69	0
2015–16	Northampton T	46	0		
2016–17	Northampton T	45	0		
2017–18	Northampton T	32	1	123	1

BUNNEY, Joe (F)   134   16
H: 5 11   W: 11 00   b.Manchester 26-9-93

2012–13	Rochdale	1	1		
2013–14	Rochdale	21	3		
2014–15	Rochdale	19	2		
2015–16	Rochdale	32	9		
2016–17	Rochdale	29	1		
2017–18	Rochdale	20	0	122	16
2017–18	Northampton T	12	0	12	0

CODDINGTON, Luke (G)   1   0
b.Middlesbrough 6-6-95
Internationals: England U17, U18, U19.

2013–14	Middlesbrough	0	0
2014–15	Middlesbrough	0	0
2015–16	Middlesbrough	0	0
2016–17	Huddersfield T	0	0
2017–18	Northampton T	1	0	1	0

CORNELL, David (G)   56   0
H: 5 11   W: 11 07   b.Gorseinon 28-3-91
Internationals: Wales U17, U19, U21.

2009–10	Swansea C	0	0		
2010–11	Swansea C	0	0		
2011–12	Swansea C	0	0		
2011–12	*Hereford U*	25	0	25	0
2012–13	Swansea C	0	0		
2013–14	Swansea C	0	0		
2013–14	*St Mirren*	5	0	5	0
2014–15	Swansea C	0	0		
2014–15	*Portsmouth*	0	0		
2015–16	Oldham Ath	14	0	14	0
2016–17	Northampton T	6	0		
2017–18	Northampton T	6	0	12	0

CROOKS, Matt (M)   96   13
H: 6 0   W: 11 05   b.Leeds 20-1-94

2011–12	Huddersfield T	0	0		
2012–13	Huddersfield T	0	0		
2013–14	Huddersfield T	0	0		
2014–15	Huddersfield T	1	0	1	0
2014–15	*Hartlepool U*	3	0	3	0
2014–15	Accrington S	16	0		
2015–16	Accrington S	32	6	48	6
2016–17	Rangers	2	0	2	0
2016–17	*Scunthorpe U*	12	3	12	3
2017–18	Northampton T	30	4	30	4

FACEY, Shay (D)   45   1
H: 5 10   W: 10 00   b.Manchester 7-1-95
Internationals: England U16, U17, U19, U20.

2013–14	Manchester C	0	0		
2014–15	Manchester C	0	0		
2014–15	New York City	0	0		
2015–16	Manchester C	0	0		
2015–16	*New York City*	22	0	22	0
2015–16	*Rotherham U*	5	0	5	0
2016–17	Manchester C	0	0		
2016–17	*Heerenveen*	3	0		
2017–18	Heerenveen	0	0	3	0
2017–18	Northampton T	15	1	15	1

FOLEY, Sam (M)   198   16
H: 6 0   W: 11 08   b.St Albans 17-10-86

2012–13	Yeovil T	41	5		
2013–14	Yeovil T	7	0		
2013–14	*Shrewsbury T*	9	0	9	0
2014–15	Yeovil T	40	2	88	7
2015–16	Port Vale	45	6		
2016–17	Port Vale	32	1	77	7
2016–17	Northampton T	0	0		
2017–18	Northampton T	24	2	24	2

GILLARD, James (F)   0   0
2017–18   Northampton T   0   0

GOFF, James (G)   0   0
2017–18   Northampton T   0   0

HANLEY, Raheem (D)   5   0
H: 5 8   W: 11 00   b.Blackburn 24-3-94
Internationals: England U19.

2011–12	Blackburn R	0	0		
2012–13	Blackburn R	0	0		
2013–14	Blackburn R	0	0		
2013–14	Swansea C	0	0		
2014–15	Swansea C	0	0		
2015–16	Swansea C	0	0		
2016–17	Northampton T	1	0		
2017–18	Northampton T	4	0	5	0

HOSKINS, Sam (F)   139   15
H: 5 8   W: 10 07   b.Dorchester 4-2-93

2011–12	Southampton	0	0		
2011–12	*Preston NE*	0	0		
2011–12	*Rotherham U*	8	2	8	2
2012–13	Southampton	0	0		
2012–13	*Stevenage*	14	1	14	1
2013–14	Yeovil T	19	0		
2014–15	Yeovil T	12	1	31	1
2015–16	Northampton T	34	6		
2016–17	Northampton T	25	3		
2017–18	Northampton T	27	2	86	11

IACIOFANO, Joe (F)   1   0
b.Northampton 9-9-98

2016–17	Northampton T	1	0
2017–18	Northampton T	0	0	1	0

KASIM, Yaser (M)   126   7
H: 5 11   W: 11 07   b.Baghdad 10-5-91
Internationals: Iraq U23, Full caps.

2010–11	Brighton & HA	0	0		
2011–12	Brighton & HA	0	0		
2012–13	Brighton & HA	0	0	1	0

LOBJOIT, Leon (M)   0   0
H: 6 2   W: 12 10   b.London 4-1-95

2012–13	Coventry C	0	0
2013–14	Coventry C	0	0
2014–15	Coventry C	0	0
2017–18	Northampton T	0	0

LUCKASSEN, Kevin (F)   66   9
H: 6 1   W: 12 08   b. 27-7-93

2011–12	AZ Alkmaar	0	0		
2012–13	AZ Alkmaar	0	0		
2013–14	Ross Co	14	0	14	0
2014–15	Slovan Liberec	16	2		
2015–16	Slovan Liberec	9	2	25	4
2016–17	St Polten	23	4	23	4
2017–18	Liberec	0	0		
2017–18	Northampton T	4	1	4	1

McGUGAN, Lewis (M)   286   56
H: 5 9   W: 11 06   b.Long Eaton 25-10-88
Internationals: England U17, U19.

2006–07	Nottingham F	13	2		
2007–08	Nottingham F	33	6		
2008–09	Nottingham F	33	5		
2009–10	Nottingham F	18	3		
2010–11	Nottingham F	40	13		
2011–12	Nottingham F	35	3		
2012–13	Nottingham F	30	8	202	40
2013–14	Watford	34	10		
2014–15	Watford	6	0	40	10
2014–15	*Sheffield W*	22	3		
2015–16	Sheffield W	13	3		
2016–17	Sheffield W	0	0	35	6
2017–18	Northampton T	9	0	9	0

McWILLIAMS, Cameron (M)   0   0
2017–18   Northampton T   0   0

McWILLIAMS, Shaun (M)   24   0
b.Northampton 14-8-98

2014–15	Northampton T	0	0		
2015–16	Northampton T	0	0		
2016–17	Northampton T	5	0		
2017–18	Northampton T	19	0	24	0

MOLONEY, Brendan (M)   230   4
H: 6 1   W: 11 12   b.Killarney 18-1-89
Internationals: Republic of Ireland U21.

2005–06	Nottingham F	0	0		
2006–07	Nottingham F	1	0		
2007–08	Nottingham F	2	0		
2007–08	*Chesterfield*	9	1	9	1
2008–09	Nottingham F	12	0		
2009–10	Nottingham F	0	0		
2009–10	Notts Co	18	1	18	1
2009–10	*Scunthorpe U*	3	0	3	0
2010–11	Nottingham F	6	0		
2011–12	Nottingham F	8	0		
2012–13	Nottingham F	13	0	42	0
2013–14	Bristol C	17	0		
2013–14	Bristol C	32	0	49	0
2014–15	Yeovil T	5	0	5	0
2014–15	*Northampton T*	22	1		
2015–16	Northampton T	25	1		
2016–17	Northampton T	23	0		
2017–18	Northampton T	34	0	104	2

O'DONNELL, Richard (G)   214   0
H: 6 2   W: 13 05   b.Sheffield 12-9-88

2007–08	Sheffield W	0	0		
2007–08	*Rotherham U*	0	0		
2007–08	*Oldham Ath*	4	0	4	0
2008–09	Sheffield W	0	0		
2009–10	Sheffield W	0	0		
2010–11	Sheffield W	9	0		
2011–12	Sheffield W	6	0	15	0
2011–12	*Macclesfield T*	11	0	11	0
2012–13	Chesterfield	14	0	14	0
2013–14	Walsall	46	0		
2014–15	Walsall	44	0	90	0
2015–16	Wigan Ath	10	0	10	0
2015–16	Bristol C	21	0		
2016–17	Bristol C	8	0	29	0
2016–17	Rotherham U	12	0		
2017–18	Rotherham U	10	0	22	0
2017–18	Northampton T	19	0	19	0

O'TOOLE, John (M)   341   59
H: 6 2   W: 13 07   b.Harrow 30-9-88
Internationals: Republic of Ireland U21.

2007–08	Watford	35	3		
2008–09	Watford	22	7		
2008–09	*Sheffield U*	9	1	9	1

2009–10	Watford	0	0	57	10
2009–10	Colchester U	31	2		
2010–11	Colchester U	11	0		
2011–12	Colchester U	15	0		
2012–13	Colchester U	15	0	72	2
2012–13	*Bristol R*	18	3		
2013–14	*Bristol R*	41	13	59	16
2014–15	Northampton T	35	2		
2014–15	*Southend U*	2	0	2	0
2015–16	Northampton T	38	12		
2016–17	Northampton T	40	10		
2017–18	Northampton T	29	6	142	30

PEREIRA, Hildeberto (F)   37   2
H: 5 9   W: 11 00   b.Lisbon 2-3-96
Internationals: Portugal U18, U19, U20.

2015–16	Benfica	0	0		
2016–17	Benfica	0	0		
2016–17	*Nottingham F*	22	2	22	2
2017–18	*Legia Warsaw*	3	0	3	0

On loan from Legia Warsaw.

2017–18	Northampton T	12	0	12	0

PHILLIPS, Aaron (D)   75   2
H: 5 7   W: 11 00   b.Warwick 20-11-93

2012–13	Coventry C	0	0		
2013–14	Coventry C	11	1		
2014–15	Coventry C	19	0		
2015–16	Coventry C	23	0	53	1
2016–17	Northampton T	20	1		
2017–18	Northampton T	2	0	22	1

PIERRE, Aaron (D)   148   7
H: 6 1   W: 13 12   b.Southall 17-2-93
Internationals: Grenada Full caps.

2011–12	Brentford	0	0		
2012–13	Brentford	0	0		
2013–14	Brentford	0	0		
2013–14	Wycombe W	8	1		
2014–15	Wycombe W	42	4		
2015–16	Wycombe W	40	2		
2016–17	Wycombe W	39	2	129	9
2017–18	Northampton T	19	0	19	0

POWELL, Daniel (F)   260   39
H: 5 11   W: 13 03   b.Luton 12-3-91

2008–09	Milton Keynes D	7	1		
2009–10	Milton Keynes D	2	1		
2010–11	Milton Keynes D	29	9		
2011–12	Milton Keynes D	43	6		
2012–13	Milton Keynes D	34	7		
2013–14	Milton Keynes D	32	1		
2014–15	Milton Keynes D	42	8		
2015–16	Milton Keynes D	22	2		
2016–17	Milton Keynes D	20	2	231	37
2017–18	Northampton T	29	2	29	2

ROBERTS, Morgan (F)   1   0
b. 22-12-00

2017–18	Northampton T	1	0	1	0

TAYLOR, Ash (M)   328   23
H: 6 0   W: 12 00   b.Bromborough 2-9-90
Internationals: Wales U19, U21.

2008–09	Tranmere R	1	0		
2009–10	Tranmere R	33	1		
2010–11	Tranmere R	26	0		
2011–12	Tranmere R	37	2		
2012–13	Tranmere R	44	2		
2013–14	Tranmere R	42	3	183	8
2014–15	Aberdeen	32	3		
2015–16	Aberdeen	37	4		
2016–17	Aberdeen	31	2	100	9
2017–18	Northampton T	45	6	45	6

TURNBULL, Jordan (D)   136   1
H: 6 1   W: 11 05   b.Trowbridge 30-10-94
Internationals: England U19, U20.

2014–15	Southampton	0	0		
2014–15	*Swindon T*	44	1		
2015–16	Southampton	0	0		
2015–16	*Swindon T*	42	0	86	1
2016–17	Coventry C	36	0		
2017–18	Coventry C	0	0	36	0
2017–18	*Partick Thistle*	1	0		
2017–18	Northampton T	14	0	14	0

VAN VEEN, Kevin (F)   165   56
H: 6 1   W: 11 11   b.Eindhoven 1-6-91

2013–14	JVC Cuyk	29	20	29	20
2014–15	FC Oss	20	16	20	16
2014–15	Scunthorpe U	20	2		
2015–16	Scunthorpe U	20	2		
2015–16	*Cambuur Leeuwarden*	12	1	12	1
2016–17	Scunthorpe U	33	10		
2017–18	Scunthorpe U	21	5	94	19
2017–18	Northampton T	10	0	10	0

WATERS, Billy (M)   106   16
H: 5 9   W: 11 07   b.Epsom 15-10-94

2012–13	Crewe Alex	0	0		
2013–14	Crewe Alex	9	0		
2014–15	Crewe Alex	16	2	25	2
2016–17	Cheltenham T	46	12	46	12
2017–18	Northampton T	17	0	17	0
2017–18	*Cambridge U*	18	2	18	2

WHALER, Sean (M)   0   0

2017–18	Northampton T	0	0		

Scholars
Anaele, Prudence Chukwudike; Bako, Shama; Daldy, Jack Ryland; Gillard, James William; Hughes, Ryan Annesley; Irwin, Lewis Cameron Leigh; Jarvis, Joseph; Lashley, Bradley; Marett, Vaughn Andrew Ronnie; McWilliams, Camron Ashley; Newell, Jack Michael; North, Adam Peter; Patrick, Seth; Roberts, Morgan; Slinn, Matthew; Williams, Jay; Wilson, Jarvis Zachary.

NORWICH C (59)

ADAMS, Ebou (M)   5   0
b. 15-1-96
Internationals: Gambia Full caps.
From Dartford.

2017–18	Norwich C	0	0		
2017–18	*Shrewsbury T*	5	0	5	0

CANTWELL, Todd (M)   10   2

2017–18	Norwich C	0	0		
2017–18	*Fortuna Sittard*	10	2	10	2

FRANKE, Marcel (D)   150   8
H: 6 4   W: 13 03   b.Dresden 5-4-93

2010–11	Dynamo Dresden	6	0		
2011–12	Dynamo Dresden	2	0		
2012–13	Dynamo Dresden	2	0		
2013–14	Hallescher	36	2		
2014–15	Hallescher	32	4	68	6
2015–16	Greuther Furth	22	0		
2016–17	Greuther Furth	31	2	53	2
2017–18	Norwich C	5	0	5	0
2017–18	*Dynamo Dresden*	16	0	24	0

GODFREY, Ben (M)   54   2
H: 6 0   W: 11 09   b.York 15-1-98

2014–15	York C	0	0		
2015–16	York C	12	1	12	1
2015–16	Norwich C	0	0		
2016–17	Norwich C	2	0		
2017–18	Norwich C	0	0	2	0
2017–18	*Shrewsbury T*	40	1	40	1

HANLEY, Grant (D)   225   9
H: 6 2   W: 12 00   b.Dumfries 20-11-91
Internationals: Scotland U19, U21, Full caps.

2008–09	Blackburn R	0	0		
2009–10	Blackburn R	1	0		
2010–11	Blackburn R	7	0		
2011–12	Blackburn R	23	1		
2012–13	Blackburn R	39	2		
2013–14	Blackburn R	38	1		
2014–15	Blackburn R	31	1		
2015–16	Blackburn R	44	2	183	7
2016–17	Newcastle U	10	1		
2017–18	Newcastle U	0	0	10	1
2017–18	Norwich C	32	1	32	1

HERNANDEZ, Onel (M)   91   6
b.Moron 1-2-93
Internationals: Germany U18.

2010–11	Arminia Bielefeld	10	1		
2011–12	Arminia Bielefeld	18	0	28	0
2012–13	Werder Bremen	0	0		
2013–14	Werder Bremen	0	0		
2013–14	Wolfsburg	0	0		
2014–15	Wolfsburg	0	0		
2015–16	Wolfsburg	0	0		
2016–17	Eintracht Brauschweig	34	5	34	5
2017–18	Eintracht Brauschweig	17	1	17	1
2017–18	Norwich C	12	0	12	0

HOOLAHAN, Wes (M)   526   69
H: 5 6   W: 10 03   b.Dublin 10-8-83
Internationals: Republic of Ireland U21, B, Full caps.

2001–02	Shelbourne	20	3		
2002–03	Shelbourne	23	0		
2004	Shelbourne	31	2		
2005	Shelbourne	29	4	103	9
2005–06	Livingston	16	0	16	0
2006–07	Blackpool	42	8		
2007–08	Blackpool	45	5	87	13
2008–09	Norwich C	32	2		
2009–10	Norwich C	37	11		
2010–11	Norwich C	41	10		
2011–12	Norwich C	33	4		
2012–13	Norwich C	33	3		
2013–14	Norwich C	16	1		
2014–15	Norwich C	36	4		
2015–16	Norwich C	30	4		
2016–17	Norwich C	33	7		
2017–18	Norwich C	29	1	320	47

HUSBAND, James (D)   114   4
H: 5 10   W: 10 00   b.Leeds 3-1-94

2011–12	Doncaster R	3	0		
2012–13	Doncaster R	33	3		
2013–14	Doncaster R	28	1	64	4
2014–15	Middlesbrough	3	0		
2014–15	*Fulham*	5	0		
2015–16	Middlesbrough	0	0		
2015–16	*Fulham*	12	0	17	0
2015–16	*Huddersfield T*	11	0	11	0
2016–17	Middlesbrough	1	0	4	0
2017–18	Norwich C	18	0	18	0

IVO PINTO, Daniel (D)   229   3
H: 6 0   W: 11 07   b.Lourosa 7-1-90
Internationals: Portugal U16, U17, U18, U19, U21.

2008–09	Porto	0	0		
2009–10	Porto	0	0		
2009–10	*Vicente*	1	0	1	0
2009–10	*Vitoria Setubal*	2	0	2	0
2010–11	Porto	0	0		
2010–11	*Covilha*	22	0	22	0
2011–12	Rio Ave	0	0		
2011–12	*Uniao Leiria*	25	0	25	0
2012–13	Cluj	27	0	27	0
2013–14	Dinamo Zagreb	28	0		
2014–15	Dinamo Zagreb	29	0		
2015–16	Dinamo Zagreb	13	0	70	0
2015–16	Norwich C	10	0		
2016–17	Norwich C	37	1		
2017–18	Norwich C	35	2	82	3

JAIYESIMI, Diallang (M)   30   0
b.Southwark 18-3-99
From Dulwich Hamlet.

2017–18	Norwich C·	0	0		
2017–18	*Grimsby T*	30	0	30	0

JONES, Paul (G)   281   0
H: 6 3   W: 13 00   b.Maidstone 28-6-86

2008–09	Exeter C	46	0		
2009–10	Exeter C	26	0		
2010–11	Exeter C	18	0		
2010–11	*Peterborough U*	1	0		
2011–12	Peterborough U	35	0	36	0
2012–13	Crawley T	46	0		
2013–14	Crawley T	46	0		
2014–15	Portsmouth	46	0		
2015–16	Portsmouth	9	0	55	0
2015–16	*Crawley T*	8	0	100	0
2016–17	Norwich C	0	0		
2017–18	Norwich C	0	0		
2017–18	*Exeter C*	0	0	90	0

KLOSE, Timm (D)   213   15
H: 6 5   W: 13 10   b.Frankfurt am Main 9-5-88
Internationals: Switzerland U21, U23, Full caps.

2009–10	Thun	29	2		
2010–11	Thun	30	3	59	5
2011–12	Nuremburg	13	0		
2012–13	Nuremburg	32	2	45	2
2013–14	Wolfsburg	10	0		
2014–15	Wolfsburg	12	1		
2015–16	Wolfsburg	8	1	30	2
2015–16	Norwich C	10	1		
2016–17	Norwich C	32	1		
2017–18	Norwich C	37	4	79	6

LEITNER, Moritz (M)   129   2
H: 5 9   W: 10 03   b.Munich 8-12-92
Internationals: Austria U17. Germany U19, U20, U21.

2010–11	1860 Munich	16	0	16	0
2010–11	Borussia Dortmund	0	0		
2010–11	*Augsburg*	9	0		
2011–12	Borussia Dortmund	17	0		
2012–13	Borussia Dortmund	25	0		
2013–14	Borussia Dortmund	0	0		
2013–14	*Stuttgart*	21	1		
2014–15	Borussia Dortmund	0	0		
2014–15	*Stuttgart*	19	1	40	2
2015–16	Borussia Dortmund	8	0	50	0
2016–17	*Lazio*	2	0	2	0
2017–18	*Augsburg*	0	0	9	0

On loan from Augsburg.

2017–18	Norwich C	12	0	12	0

LEWIS, Jamal (D)   22   0
b. 25-1-98
Internationals: Northern Ireland U19, U21, Full caps.

2017–18	Norwich C	22	0	22	0

MADDISON, James (M)   96   22
H: 5 10   W: 11 07   b.Coventry 23-11-96
Internationals: England U21.

2013–14	Coventry C	0	0		
2014–15	Coventry C	12	2		
2015–16	Norwich C	0	0		
2015–16	Coventry C	23	3	35	5
2016–17	Norwich C	3	1		
2016–17	Aberdeen	14	2	14	2
2017–18	Norwich C	44	14	47	15

MARTIN, Russell (M)   471   23
H: 6 0   W: 11 08   b.Brighton 4-1-86
Internationals: Scotland Full caps.

2004–05	Wycombe W	7	0		
2005–06	Wycombe W	23	3		
2006–07	Wycombe W	42	2		
2007–08	Wycombe W	44	0	116	5
2008–09	Peterborough U	46	1		
2009–10	Peterborough U	10	0	56	1
2009–10	Norwich C	26	0		
2010–11	Norwich C	46	5		
2011–12	Norwich C	33	2		
2012–13	Norwich C	31	3		
2013–14	Norwich C	31	0		
2014–15	Norwich C	45	2		
2015–16	Norwich C	30	3		
2016–17	Norwich C	37	1		
2017–18	Norwich C	5	0	284	16
2017–18	Rangers	15	1	15	1

MATTHEWS, Remi (G)   54   0
H: 6 0   W: 12 04   b.Gorleston 10-2-94

2014–15	Norwich C	0	0		
2014–15	Burton Alb	0	0		
2015–16	Norwich C	0	0		
2015–16	Burton Alb	2	0	2	0
2015–16	Doncaster R	9	0	9	0
2016–17	Norwich C	0	0		
2016–17	Hamilton A	17	0	17	0
2017–18	Norwich C	0	0		
2017–18	Plymouth Arg	26	0	26	0

McGOVERN, Michael (G)   290   0
H: 6 2   W: 13 07   b.Enniskillen 12-7-84
Internationals: Northern Ireland U19, U21, Full caps.

2004–05	Celtic	0	0		
2004–05	Stranraer	19	0	19	0
2005–06	Celtic	0	0		
2006–07	Celtic	0	0		
2006–07	St Johnstone	1	0	1	0
2007–08	Celtic	0	0		
2008–09	Dundee U	0	0		
2009–10	Ross Co	35	0		
2010–11	Ross Co	36	0	71	0
2011–12	Falkirk	35	0		
2012–13	Falkirk	35	0		
2013–14	Falkirk	34	0	104	0
2014–15	Hamilton A	38	0		
2015–16	Hamilton A	37	0	75	0
2016–17	Norwich C	20	0		
2017–18	Norwich C	0	0	20	0

MORRIS, Carlton (F)   98   14
H: 6 1   W: 13 05   b.Cambridge 16-12-95
Internationals: England U19.

2014–15	Norwich C	1	0		
2014–15	Oxford U	8	0	7	0
2014–15	York C	8	0	8	0
2015–16	Norwich C	0	0		
2015–16	Hamilton A	32	8	32	8
2016–17	Norwich C	0	0		
2016–17	Rotherham U	8	0	8	0
2017–18	Norwich C	0	0		
2017–18	Shrewsbury T	42	6	42	6

MURPHY, Josh (F)   137   17
H: 5 8   W: 10 07   b.Wembley 24-2-95
Internationals: England U18, U19, U20.

2012–13	Norwich C	0	0		
2013–14	Norwich C	9	0		
2014–15	Norwich C	13	1		
2014–15	Wigan Ath	5	0	5	0
2015–16	Norwich C	0	0		
2015–16	Milton Keynes D	42	5	42	5
2016–17	Norwich C	27	4		
2017–18	Norwich C	41	7	90	12

NAISMITH, Steven (F)   361   85
H: 5 10   W: 11 04   b.Irvine 14-9-86
Internationals: Scotland U21, B, Full caps.

2003–04	Kilmarnock	1	0		
2004–05	Kilmarnock	24	1		
2005–06	Kilmarnock	36	13		
2006–07	Kilmarnock	37	15		
2007–08	Kilmarnock	4	0	102	29
2007–08	Rangers	21	5		
2008–09	Rangers	7	0		
2009–10	Rangers	28	3		
2010–11	Rangers	31	11		
2011–12	Rangers	11	9	98	28
2012–13	Everton	31	4		
2013–14	Everton	31	5		
2014–15	Everton	31	6		
2015–16	Everton	10	3	103	18
2015–16	Norwich C	13	1		
2016–17	Norwich C	29	5		
2017–18	Norwich C	2	0	44	6
2017–18	Hearts	14	4	14	4

NELSON OLIVEIRA, Miguel (F)   208   45
H: 6 1   W: 12 13   b.Barcelos 8-8-91
Internationals: Portugal U16, U17, U19, U20, U21, Full caps.

2009–10	Benfica	0	0		
2009–10	Rio Ave	10	0	10	0
2010–11	Benfica	0	0		
2010–11	Pacos Ferreira	23	4	23	4
2011–12	Benfica	12	0		
2012–13	Benfica	0	0		
2012–13	La Coruna	30	4	30	4
2013–14	Benfica	0	0		
2013–14	Rennes	30	8	30	8
2014–15	Benfica	0	0		
2014–15	Swansea C	10	1	10	1
2015–16	Benfica	0	0	12	0
2015–16	Nottingham F	28	9	28	9
2016–17	Norwich C	28	11		
2017–18	Norwich C	37	8	65	19

PHILLIPS, Adam (M)   4   0
b.Garstang 15-1-98
Internationals: England U16, U17.

2014–15	Liverpool	0	0		
2015–16	Liverpool	0	0		
2017–18	Norwich C	0	0		
2017–18	Cambridge U	4	0	4	0

RAGGETT, Sean (D)   27   2
H: 5 11   W: 12 04   b.Gillingham 17-4-93
Internationals: England C.
From Dover Ath.

2017–18	Lincoln C	25	2	25	2
2017–18	Norwich C	2	0	2	0

SRBENY, Dennis (F)   104   39
b.Berlin 5-5-94

2013–14	Hansa Rostock	2	0		
2014–15	Hansa Rostock	18	1	20	1
2015–16	BFC Dynamo	22	10		
2016–17	BFC Dynamo	33	18	55	28
2017–18	Paderborn	15	9	15	9
2017–18	Norwich C	14	1	14	1

STIEPERMANN, Marco (M)   199   21
H: 5 11   W: 11 11   b.Dortmund 9-2-91
Internationals: Germany U16, U17, U18, U19, U20.

2008–09	Borussia Dortmund	0	0		
2009–10	Borussia Dortmund	3	1		
2010–11	Borussia Dortmund	4	0		
2011–12	Borussia Dortmund	0	0	7	1
2011–12	Aachen	21	2	21	2
2012–13	Energie Cottbus	27	2		
2013–14	Energie Cottbus	29	5	56	7
2014–15	Greuther Furth	31	4		
2015–16	Greuther Furth	30	5	61	9
2016–17	Bochum	31	1	31	1
2017–18	VfL Bochum	0	0		
2017–18	Norwich C	23	1	23	1

TETTEY, Alexander (M)   310   19
H: 5 11   W: 10 09   b.Accra 4-4-86
Internationals: Norway U18, U19, U21, Full caps.

2004–05	Rosenborg	0	0		
2005–06	Rosenborg	10	1		
2006–07	Rosenborg	21	1		
2007–08	Rosenborg	25	4		
2008–09	Rosenborg	28	6		
2009–10	Rosenborg	1	0	85	12
2009–10	Rennes	24	0		
2010–11	Rennes	17	1		
2011–12	Rennes	19	1	60	2
2012–13	Norwich C	27	0		
2013–14	Norwich C	21	1		
2014–15	Norwich C	36	2		
2015–16	Norwich C	23	2		
2016–17	Norwich C	35	0		
2017–18	Norwich C	23	0	165	5

TRYBULL, Tom (M)   96   4
H: 5 11   W: 11 05   b.Berlin 9-3-93
Internationals: Germany U17, U18, U19, U20.

2010–11	Hansa Rostock	17	0	17	0
2011–12	Werder Bremen	15	1		
2012–13	Werder Bremen	4	0		
2013–14	Werder Bremen	2	0	21	1
2013–14	St Pauli	12	0		
2014–15	St Pauli	3	0	15	0
2015–16	Greuther Furth	0	0		
2016–17	Den Haag	23	1	23	1
2017–18	Norwich C	20	2	20	2

VRANCIC, Mario (M)   194   19
H: 6 1   W: 12 02   b.Slavonski Brod 23-5-89
Internationals: Germany U17, U19, U20. Bosnia-Herzegovina Full caps.

2006–07	Mainz 05	1	0		
2007–08	Mainz 05	5	0		
2008–09	Mainz 05	3	0		
2009–10	Mainz 05	0	0	9	0
2009–10	Rot Weiss Ahlen	12	0	12	0
2010–11	Borussia Dortmund	0	0		
2011–12	Borussia Dortmund	0	0		
2012–13	Paderborn	33	5		
2013–14	Paderborn	30	5		
2014–15	Paderborn	30	2	93	12
2015–16	Darmstadt	22	2		
2016–17	Darmstadt	23	4	45	6
2017–18	Norwich C	35	1	35	1

WATKINS, Marley (M)   185   24
H: 5 10   W: 10 03   b.London 17-10-90
Internationals: Wales Full caps.

2008–09	Cheltenham T	12	0		
2009–10	Cheltenham T	13	1		
2010–11	Cheltenham T	1	0	26	1

From Bath C, Hereford U

2013–14	Inverness CT	26	1		
2014–15	Inverness CT	33	7	59	8
2015–16	Barnsley	34	5		
2016–17	Barnsley	42	10	76	15
2017–18	Norwich C	24	0	24	0

WILDSCHUT, Yanic (F)   229   28
H: 6 2   W: 13 08   b.Amsterdam 1-11-91
Internationals: Netherlands U21.

2010–11	Zwolle	33	3	33	3
2011–12	VVV	29	7		
2012–13	VVV	32	1	61	8
2013–14	Heerenveen	18	2		
2013–14	Den Haag	7	0	7	0
2014–15	Heerenveen	4	0	22	2
2014–15	Middlesbrough	11	2		
2015–16	Middlesbrough	1	0	12	2
2015–16	Wigan Ath	34	7		
2016–17	Wigan Ath	25	4	59	11
2016–17	Norwich C	9	1		
2017–18	Norwich C	16	1	25	2
2017–18	Cardiff C	10	0	10	0

ZIMMERMANN, Christoph (D)   39   1
b.Dusseldorf 12-1-93

2011–12	Borussia M'gladbach	0	0		
2012–13	Borussia M'gladbach	0	0		
2013–14	Borussia M'gladbach	0	0		
2014–15	Borussia Dortmund	0	0		
2015–16	Borussia Dortmund	0	0		
2016–17	Borussia Dortmund	0	0		
2017–18	Norwich C	39	1	39	1

Players retained or with offer of contract
Abrahams, Tristan; Aransibia, Devonte; Fonkeu, Pierre; Jarvis, Matthew Thomas; Kamal, Bilal Noradin; McCracken, Jon Douglas; McIntosh, Louis; McLean, Kenneth; Milovanovic, Saul John; Mourgos, Savvas; Odusina, Oluwarotimi Mark; Oxborough, Aston Jay; Power, Simon; Thomas, Jordan James Chatterton; Thompson, Louis Clyde William.

Scholars
Aarons, Maximillian James; Akyeampong-Ekumah, Aaron; Barkarson, Atli; Barnes, Finlay; Da, Costa Rui Giovanni; Dickerson, Ryan James; Hale-Brown, Fergal Stanley; Hutchinson, Shae Armari Akpojotor; Idah, Adam; Lomas, Louis James; Mehmeti, Anis; Parsons, Connor; Payne, Alfred Edward; Spyrou, Anthony Jeffrey John; Thompson-Brissett, Jaden Lee; Thorvaldsson, Isak.

NOTTINGHAM F (60)

ARIYIBI, Gboly (M) 121 6
H: 6 0 W: 11 05 b.West Virginia 18-1-95
Internationals: USA U20, U23.

2013–14	Leeds U	2	0	**2**	**0**
2013–14	*Tranmere R*	2	0	**2**	**0**
2014–15	Chesterfield	17	1		
2015–16	Chesterfield	38	2		
2016–17	Chesterfield	28	0	**83**	**3**
2016–17	Nottingham F	0	0		
2017–18	Nottingham F	0	0		
2017–18	*Milton Keynes D*	22	3	**22**	**3**
2017–18	*Northampton T*	12	0	**12**	**0**

BOUCHALAKIS, Andreas (M) 114 11
b.Heraklion 5-4-93
Internationals: Greece U19, U20, U21.

2011–12	Ergotelis	2	0		
2012–13	Ergotelis	39	5		
2013–14	Olympiacos	0	0		
2013–14	*Ergotelis*	30	2	**71**	**7**
2014–15	Olympiacos	9	1		
2015–16	Olympiacos	5	1		
2016–17	Olympiacos	8	0	**22**	**2**
2017–18	Nottingham F	21	2	**21**	**2**

BRERETON, Ben (F) 53 8
b.Stoke-on-Trent 18-4-99
Internationals: England U19.
From Stoke C.

2016–17	Nottingham F	18	3		
2017–18	Nottingham F	35	5	**53**	**8**

BRIDCUTT, Liam (M) 268 3
H: 5 9 W: 11 07 b.Reading 8-5-89
Internationals: Scotland Full caps.

2007–08	Chelsea	0	0		
2007–08	*Yeovil T*	9	0	**9**	**0**
2008–09	Chelsea	0	0		
2008–09	*Watford*	6	0	**6**	**0**
2009–10	Chelsea	0	0		
2009–10	*Stockport Co*	15	0	**15**	**0**
2010–11	Chelsea	0	0		
2010–11	Brighton & HA	37	2		
2011–12	Brighton & HA	43	0		
2012–13	Brighton & HA	41	0		
2013–14	Brighton & HA	11	0	**132**	**2**
2013–14	Sunderland	12	0		
2014–15	Sunderland	18	0		
2015–16	Sunderland	0	0	**30**	**0**
2015–16	*Leeds U*	24	0		
2016–17	Leeds U	25	0	**49**	**0**
2017–18	Nottingham F	27	1	**27**	**1**

CASH, Matty (M) 63 5
H: 6 2 W: 10 01 b.Slough 7-8-97

2015–16	Nottingham F	0	0		
2015–16	*Dagenham & R*	12	3	**12**	**3**
2016–17	Nottingham F	28	0		
2017–18	Nottingham F	23	2	**51**	**2**

CLOUGH, Zach (F) 95 26
H: 5 7 b.Manchester 8-3-95

2013–14	Bolton W	0	0		
2014–15	Bolton W	8	5		
2015–16	Bolton W	28	7		
2016–17	Bolton W	23	9		
2016–17	Nottingham F	14	4		
2017–18	Nottingham F	13	0	**27**	**4**
2017–18	*Bolton W*	9	1	**68**	**22**

COHEN, Chris (M) 364 21
H: 5 11 W: 10 11 b.Norwich 5-3-87

2003–04	West Ham U	7	0		
2004–05	West Ham U	11	0		
2005–06	West Ham U	0	0	**18**	**0**
2005–06	*Yeovil T*	30	1		
2006–07	Yeovil T	44	6	**74**	**7**
2007–08	Nottingham F	41	2		
2008–09	Nottingham F	41	2		
2009–10	Nottingham F	44	3		
2010–11	Nottingham F	42	2		
2011–12	Nottingham F	7	0		
2012–13	Nottingham F	38	2		
2013–14	Nottingham F	16	1		
2014–15	Nottingham F	6	0		
2015–16	Nottingham F	15	1		
2016–17	Nottingham F	20	1		
2017–18	Nottingham F	2	0	**272**	**14**

CUMMINGS, Jason (F) 143 58
H: 5 10 W: 10 10 b.Edinburgh 1-8-95
Internationals: Scotland U19, U21, Full caps.

2013–14	Hibernian	16	0		
2014–15	Hibernian	33	18		
2015–16	Hibernian	33	18		
2016–17	Hibernian	32	19	**114**	**55**

2017–18	Nottingham F	14	1	**14**	**1**
2017–18	*Rangers*	15	2	**15**	**2**

DARIKWA, Tendayi (D) 176 10
H: 6 2 W: 12 02 b.Nottingham 13-12-91
Internationals: Zimbabwe Full caps.

2010–11	Chesterfield	0	0		
2011–12	Chesterfield	2	0		
2012–13	Chesterfield	36	5		
2013–14	Chesterfield	41	3		
2014–15	Chesterfield	46	1	**125**	**9**
2015–16	Burnley	21	1		
2016–17	Burnley	0	0	**21**	**1**
2017–18	Nottingham F	30	0	**30**	**0**

DEJAGAH, Ashkan (F) 243 33
H: 5 11 W: 11 08 b.Tehran 5-7-86
Internationals: Germany U17, U18, U19, U20,
U21. Iran Full caps.

2004–05	Hertha Berlin	1	0		
2005–06	Hertha Berlin	3	0		
2006–07	Hertha Berlin	22	1	**26**	**1**
2007–08	Wolfsburg	31	8		
2008–09	Wolfsburg	27	3		
2009–10	Wolfsburg	22	1		
2010–11	Wolfsburg	21	3		
2011–12	Wolfsburg	26	3		
2012–13	Wolfsburg	1	0		
2013–14	Fulham	21	0		
2013–14	Fulham	22	5	**43**	**5**
2014–15	Al-Arabi	24	5		
2015–16	Al-Arabi	21	4		
2016–17	Al-Arabi	0	0	**45**	**9**
2016–17	Wolfsburg	0	0		
2017–18	Wolfsburg	0	0	**128**	**18**
2017–18	Nottingham F	1	0	**1**	**0**

EVTIMOV, Dimitar (G) 23 0
H: 6 3 W: 13 00 b.Plevan 7-9-93
Internationals: Bulgaria U19, U21.

2012–13	Nottingham F	0	0		
2013–14	Nottingham F	1	0		
2014–15	Nottingham F	0	0		
2014–15	*Mansfield T*	10	0	**10**	**0**
2015–16	Nottingham F	1	0		
2016–17	Nottingham F	0	0		
2016–17	*Olhanense*	10	0	**10**	**0**
2017–18	*Port Vale*	1	0	**1**	**0**
2017–18	Nottingham F	0	0	**2**	**0**

FOX, Danny (D) 393 15
H: 5 11 W: 12 06 b.Winsford 29-5-86
Internationals: England U21. Scotland Full
caps.

2004–05	Everton	0	0		
2004–05	*Stranraer*	11	1	**11**	**1**
2005–06	Walsall	33	0		
2006–07	Walsall	44	3		
2007–08	Walsall	22	3	**99**	**6**
2007–08	Coventry C	18	1		
2008–09	Coventry C	39	5		
2009–10	Coventry C	0	0	**57**	**6**
2009–10	Celtic	15	0	**15**	**0**
2009–10	Burnley	14	1		
2010–11	Burnley	35	0		
2011–12	Burnley	1	0	**50**	**1**
2011–12	Southampton	41	0		
2012–13	Southampton	20	1		
2013–14	Southampton	3	0	**64**	**1**
2013–14	Nottingham F	14	0		
2014–15	Nottingham F	27	0		
2015–16	Nottingham F	10	0		
2016–17	Nottingham F	23	0		
2017–18	Nottingham F	23	0	**97**	**0**

FUENTES, Juan (D) 199 2
H: 5 10 W: 11 05 b.Cordoba 5-1-90

2008–09	Cordoba	0	0		
2009–10	Cordoba	26	0		
2010–11	Cordoba	22	0		
2011–12	Cordoba	31	0		
2012–13	Cordoba	35	2	**114**	**2**
2013–14	Espanyol	35	0		
2014–15	Espanyol	22	0		
2015–16	Espanyol	10	0	**67**	**0**
2016–17	Osasuna	17	0		
2017–18	Osasuna	0	0	**17**	**0**
2017–18	Nottingham F	1	0	**1**	**0**

GRANT, Jorge (M) 79 21
H: 5 9 W: 11 07 b.Oxford 26-9-94

2013–14	Nottingham F	0	0		
2014–15	Nottingham F	1	0		
2015–16	Nottingham F	10	0		
2016–17	Nottingham F	6	0		
2016–17	*Notts Co*	17	6		
2017–18	Nottingham F	0	0	**17**	**0**
2017–18	*Notts Co*	45	15	**62**	**21**

GUEDIOURA, Adlene (M) 267 20
H: 6 1 W: 12 08 b.La Roche-sur-Yon
12-11-85
Internationals: Algeria Full caps.

2004–05	Sedan	0	0		
2005–06	Noisy-Le-Sec	15	1	**15**	**1**
2006–07	L'Entente	21	3	**21**	**3**
2007–08	Creteil	24	6	**24**	**6**
2008–09	Kortrijk	10	0	**10**	**0**
2008–09	Charleroi	12	0		
2009–10	Charleroi	13	1	**25**	**1**
2009–10	Wolverhampton W	14	1		
2010–11	Wolverhampton W	10	1		
2011–12	Wolverhampton W	10	0	**34**	**2**
2011–12	Nottingham F	19	1		
2012–13	Nottingham F	35	3		
2013–14	Nottingham F	5	0		
2013–14	Crystal Palace	8	0		
2014–15	Crystal Palace	7	0		
2014–15	*Watford*	17	3		
2015–16	Crystal Palace	0	0	**15**	**0**
2015–16	Watford	18	0		
2016–17	Watford	12	0	**47**	**3**
2016–17	Middlesbrough	5	0		
2017–18	Middlesbrough	1	0	**6**	**0**
2017–18	Nottingham F	11	0	**70**	**4**

HENDERSON, Stephen (G) 163 0
H: 6 3 W: 11 00 b.Dublin 2-5-88
Internationals: Republic of Ireland U16, U17,
U19, U21.

2005–06	Aston Villa	0	0		
2006–07	Aston Villa	0	0		
2007–08	Bristol C	1	0		
2008–09	Bristol C	1	0		
2009–10	Bristol C	3	0		
2009–10	*Aldershot T*	8	0	**8**	**0**
2010–11	Bristol C	0	0	**5**	**0**
2010–11	*Yeovil T*	33	0	**33**	**0**
2011–12	Portsmouth	25	0		
2011–12	West Ham U	0	0		
2012–13	West Ham U	0	0		
2012–13	*Ipswich T*	24	0	**24**	**0**
2013–14	West Ham U	0	0		
2013–14	*Bournemouth*	2	0	**2**	**0**
2014–15	Charlton Ath	31	0		
2015–16	Charlton Ath	22	0	**53**	**0**
2016–17	Nottingham F	12	0		
2017–18	Nottingham F	0	0	**12**	**0**
2017–18	*Portsmouth*	1	0	**26**	**0**

HOBBS, Jack (D) 276 4
H: 6 3 W: 13 05 b.Portsmouth 18-8-88
Internationals: England U19.

2004–05	Lincoln C	1	0	**1**	**0**
2005–06	Liverpool	0	0		
2006–07	Liverpool	0	0		
2007–08	Liverpool	2	0		
2007–08	*Scunthorpe U*	9	1	**9**	**1**
2008–09	Liverpool	0	0	**2**	**0**
2008–09	Leicester C	44	1		
2009–10	Leicester C	44	0		
2010–11	Leicester C	26	0	**114**	**1**
2010–11	*Hull C*	13	0		
2011–12	Hull C	40	1		
2012–13	Hull C	22	0	**75**	**1**
2013–14	Nottingham F	27	1		
2014–15	Nottingham F	17	0		
2015–16	Nottingham F	20	0		
2016–17	Nottingham F	9	0		
2017–18	Nottingham F	2	0	**75**	**1**

IACOVITTI, Alex (D) 24 1
b. 2-9-97
Internationals: Scotland U17, U19, U21.

2015–16	Nottingham F	0	0		
2016–17	Nottingham F	2	0		
2016–17	*Mansfield T*	8	0	**8**	**0**
2017–18	Nottingham F	0	0	**2**	**0**
2017–18	*Forest Green R*	14	1	**14**	**1**

KAPINO, Stefanos (G) 73 0
H: 6 5 W: 13 05 b.Athens 18-3-94
Internationals: Greece U17, U19, U20, U21,
Full caps.

2011–12	Panathinaikos	12	0		
2012–13	Panathinaikos	1	0		
2013–14	Panathinaikos	28	0	**41**	**0**
2014–15	Mainz 05	2	0	**2**	**0**
2015–16	Olympiacos	3	0		
2016–17	Olympiacos	18	0		
2017–18	Olympiacos	5	0	**26**	**0**
2017–18	Nottingham F	4	0	**4**	**0**

LAM, Thomas (D) — 114 9
H: 6 2 W: 11 07 b.Amsterdam 18-12-93
Internationals: Finland U17, U18, U19, U21, Full caps.

2011–12	AZ Alkmaar	0	0	
2012–13	AZ Alkmaar	6	0	
2013–14	AZ Alkmaar	0	0	6 0
2014–15	PEC Zwolle	28	2	
2015–16	PEC Zwolle	33	2	61 4
2016–17	Nottingham F	19	2	
2017–18	Nottingham F	0	0	19 2
2017–18	FC Twente	28	3	28 3

LICHAJ, Eric (D) — 236 6
H: 5 11 W: 12 07 b.Chicago 17-11-88
Internationals: USA U17, U20, Full caps.

2007–08	Aston Villa	0	0	
2008–09	Aston Villa	0	0	
2009–10	Aston Villa	0	0	
2009–10	Lincoln C	6	0	6 0
2009–10	Leyton Orient	9	1	9 1
2010–11	Aston Villa	5	0	
2010–11	Leeds U	16	0	16 0
2011–12	Aston Villa	10	1	
2012–13	Aston Villa	17	0	32 1
2013–14	Nottingham F	24	0	
2014–15	Nottingham F	42	0	
2015–16	Nottingham F	43	1	
2016–17	Nottingham F	41	2	
2017–18	Nottingham F	23	1	173 4

LOLLEY, Joe (F) — 102 12
H: 5 10 W: 11 05 b.Redditch 25-8-92
Internationals: England C.

2013–14	Huddersfield T	6	1	
2014–15	Huddersfield T	17	2	
2015–16	Huddersfield T	32	4	
2015–16	Scunthorpe U	6	0	6 0
2016–17	Huddersfield T	19	1	
2017–18	Huddersfield T	6	1	80 9
2017–18	Nottingham F	16	3	16 3

MANCIENNE, Michael (D) — 291 0
H: 6 0 W: 11 09 b.Isleworth 8-1-88
Internationals: England U16, U17, U18, U19, U21.

2005–06	Chelsea	0	0	
2006–07	Chelsea	0	0	
2006–07	QPR	28	0	
2007–08	Chelsea	0	0	
2007–08	QPR	30	0	58 0
2008–09	Chelsea	4	0	
2008–09	Wolverhampton W	10	0	
2009–10	Chelsea	0	0	
2009–10	Wolverhampton W	30	0	
2010–11	Chelsea	0	0	4 0
2010–11	Wolverhampton W	16	0	56 0
2011–12	Hamburg	16	0	
2012–13	Hamburg	21	0	
2013–14	Hamburg	12	0	49 0
2014–15	Nottingham F	36	0	
2015–16	Nottingham F	31	0	
2016–17	Nottingham F	28	0	
2017–18	Nottingham F	29	0	124 0

McKAY, Barrie (M) — 170 21
H: 5 9 W: 11 00 b.Paisley 30-12-94
Internationals: Scotland U18, U19, U21, Full caps.

2011–12	Rangers	1	0	
2012–13	Rangers	31	1	
2013–14	Rangers	2	0	
2013–14	Greenock Morton	18	3	18 3
2014–15	Rangers	0	0	
2014–15	Raith R	23	1	23 1
2015–16	Rangers	34	6	
2016–17	Rangers	35	5	103 12
2017–18	Nottingham F	26	5	26 5

MURPHY, Daryl (F) — 392 96
H: 6 2 W: 13 12 b.Waterford 15-3-83
Internationals: Republic of Ireland U21, Full caps.

2000–01	Luton T	0	0	
2001–02	Luton T	0	0	
2005–06	Sunderland	18	1	
2005–06	Sheffield W	4	0	4 0
2006–07	Sunderland	38	10	
2007–08	Sunderland	28	3	
2008–09	Sunderland	23	0	
2009–10	Sunderland	3	0	110 14
2009–10	Ipswich T	18	6	
2010–11	Celtic	18	3	
2011–12	Ipswich T	33	4	
2012–13	Celtic	1	0	19 3
2012–13	Ipswich T	39	7	
2013–14	Ipswich T	45	13	
2014–15	Ipswich T	44	27	
2015–16	Ipswich T	34	10	
2016–17	Ipswich T	4	0	217 67
2016–17	Newcastle U	15	5	15 5
2017–18	Nottingham F	27	7	27 7

OSBORN, Ben (D) — 173 14
H: 5 9 W: 11 11 b.Derby 5-8-94
Internationals: England U18, U19, U20.

2011–12	Nottingham F	0	0	
2012–13	Nottingham F	0	0	
2013–14	Nottingham F	8	0	
2014–15	Nottingham F	37	3	
2015–16	Nottingham F	36	3	
2016–17	Nottingham F	46	4	
2017–18	Nottingham F	46	4	173 14

SMITH, Jordan (G) — 44 0
b.Nottingham 8-8-94
Internationals: Costa Rica U17, U20, Full caps.

2013–14	Nottingham F	0	0	
2014–15	Nottingham F	0	0	
2015–16	Nottingham F	0	0	
2016–17	Nottingham F	15	0	
2017–18	Nottingham F	29	0	44 0

TOBIAS FIGUEIREDO, Pereira (D) — 64 4
b.Satao 2-2-94
Internationals: Portugal U17, U18, U19, U20, U21, U23.

2012–13	Sporting Lisbon	0	0	
2013–14	Sporting Lisbon	0	0	
2013–14	Reus	13	1	13 1
2014–15	Sporting Lisbon	14	2	
2015–16	Sporting Lisbon	1	0	
2016–17	Sporting Lisbon	2	0	
2016–17	Nacional	22	1	22 1
2017–18	Sporting Lisbon	0	0	17 2

On loan from Sporting Lisbon.

2017–18	Nottingham F	12	0	12 0

TRAORE, Armand (D) — 163 4
H: 6 1 W: 12 12 b.Paris 8-10-89
Internationals: France U19, U21. Senegal Full caps.

2006–07	Arsenal	0	0	
2007–08	Arsenal	3	0	
2008–09	Arsenal	0	0	
2008–09	Portsmouth	19	1	19 1
2009–10	Arsenal	9	0	
2010–11	Arsenal	0	0	
2010–11	Juventus	10	0	10 0
2011–12	Arsenal	1	0	13 0
2011–12	QPR	23	0	
2012–13	QPR	26	0	
2013–14	QPR	22	2	
2014–15	QPR	16	0	
2015–16	QPR	0	0	87 2
2016–17	Nottingham F	12	0	
2017–18	Nottingham F	18	0	30 0
2017–18	Cardiff C	4	1	4 1

VAUGHAN, David (M) — 452 27
H: 5 7 W: 11 00 b.Abergele 18-2-83
Internationals: Wales U19, U21, Full caps.

2000–01	Crewe Alex	1	0	
2001–02	Crewe Alex	13	0	
2002–03	Crewe Alex	32	3	
2003–04	Crewe Alex	31	0	
2004–05	Crewe Alex	44	6	
2005–06	Crewe Alex	34	5	
2006–07	Crewe Alex	29	4	
2007–08	Crewe Alex	1	0	185 18
2007–08	Real Sociedad	7	1	7 1
2008–09	Blackpool	33	1	
2009–10	Blackpool	41	1	
2010–11	Blackpool	35	2	109 4
2011–12	Sunderland	22	2	
2012–13	Sunderland	24	1	
2013–14	Sunderland	3	0	49 3
2013–14	Nottingham F	9	0	
2014–15	Nottingham F	13	0	
2015–16	Nottingham F	35	1	
2016–17	Nottingham F	31	0	
2017–18	Nottingham F	14	0	102 1

VELLIOS, Apostolos (F) — 86 14
H: 6 3 W: 12 06 b.Salonika 8-1-92
Internationals: Greece U17, U19, U21, Full caps.

2008–09	Iraklis	1	0	
2009–10	Iraklis	9	2	
2010–11	Iraklis	12	2	22 4
2010–11	Everton	3	0	
2011–12	Everton	13	3	
2012–13	Everton	6	0	
2013–14	Everton	0	0	
2013–14	Blackpool	2	0	2 0
2014–15	Everton	0	0	22 3

WALKER, Tyler (F) — 58 10
H: 5 10 W: 9 13 b.17-10-96
Internationals: England U20.

2013–14	Nottingham F	0	0	
2014–15	Nottingham F	7	1	
2015–16	Nottingham F	0	0	
2015–16	Burton Alb	6	1	6 1
2016–17	Nottingham F	0	0	
2016–17	Stevenage	8	3	8 3
2016–17	Port Vale	6	2	6 2
2017–18	Nottingham F	12	3	33 4
2017–18	Bolton W	5	0	5 0

WARD, Jamie (M) — 381 89
H: 5 5 W: 9 04 b.Birmingham 12-5-86
Internationals: Northern Ireland U18, U21, Full caps.

2003–04	Aston Villa	0	0	
2004–05	Aston Villa	0	0	
2005–06	Aston Villa	0	0	
2005–06	Stockport Co	9	1	9 1
2006–07	Torquay U	25	9	25 9
2006–07	Chesterfield	9	3	
2007–08	Chesterfield	35	12	
2008–09	Chesterfield	23	14	67 29
2008–09	Sheffield U	16	2	
2009–10	Sheffield U	28	7	
2010–11	Sheffield U	19	0	63 9
2010–11	Derby Co	13	5	
2011–12	Derby Co	37	4	
2012–13	Derby Co	25	12	
2013–14	Derby Co	38	7	
2014–15	Derby Co	25	6	138 34
2015–16	Nottingham F	31	2	
2016–17	Nottingham F	18	1	
2016–17	Burton Alb	18	4	18 4
2017–18	Nottingham F	8	0	57 3
2017–18	Cardiff C	4	0	4 0

WATSON, Ben (M) — 384 36
H: 5 10 W: 10 11 b.Camberwell 9-7-85
Internationals: England U21.

2002–03	Crystal Palace	5	0	
2003–04	Crystal Palace	16	1	
2004–05	Crystal Palace	21	0	
2005–06	Crystal Palace	42	4	
2006–07	Crystal Palace	25	3	
2007–08	Crystal Palace	42	5	
2008–09	Crystal Palace	18	5	169 18
2008–09	Wigan Ath	10	2	
2009–10	Wigan Ath	5	1	
2009–10	QPR	16	2	16 2
2009–10	WBA	7	1	7 1
2010–11	Wigan Ath	29	3	
2011–12	Wigan Ath	21	3	
2012–13	Wigan Ath	12	1	
2013–14	Wigan Ath	25	2	
2014–15	Wigan Ath	9	1	111 13
2014–15	Watford	20	0	
2015–16	Watford	35	2	
2016–17	Watford	4	0	
2017–18	Watford	8	0	67 2
2017–18	Nottingham F	14	0	14 0

WORRALL, Joe (D) — 66 2
H: 6 3 b.Nottingham 10-1-97
Internationals: England U20 U21.

2015–16	Nottingham F	0	0	
2015–16	Dagenham & R	14	1	14 1
2016–17	Nottingham F	21	0	
2017–18	Nottingham F	31	1	52 1

YATES, Ryan (M) — 53 5
b.Nottingham 21-11-97

2016–17	Nottingham F	0	0	
2016–17	Shrewsbury T	12	0	12 0
2017–18	Nottingham F	0	0	
2017–18	Notts Co	25	3	25 3
2017–18	Scunthorpe U	16	2	16 2

Players retained or with offer of contract
Ahmedhodzic, Anel; Appiah, Arvin Amoakoh; Asare, Keith; Bossin, Liam Cathal; Coveney, Joseph Charles; Crookes, Adam Mark; Edser, Toby George; Erlandsson, Tim Anders Junior; Gomis, Virgil Vilela; Harbottle, Riley-Jay; Hayes, Kieran; Lawrence-Gabriel, Jordan Jay; Lolley, Joseph; Sodeinde, Victor Adeoluwa; Wright, Jordan Ian.

Scholars
Barnes, Joshua William; Charlesworth, Choz Micheal; En-Neyah, Yassine; Greenwood,

Samuel; Johnson, Brennan Price; McCormick, Luke; Preston, Daniel James; Ram, Max Benjamin; Richardson, Jaydan De'Chante; Shelvey, George William; Smith, Connor David; Soloha, Rudolfs Oskars; Stewart, Ethan; Swan, William Jonathan; Taylor, Jake Jon; Willetts, Jake Anthony.

NOTTS CO (61)

ALESSANDRA, Lewis (F) — 339 52
H: 5 9 W: 11 07 b.Heywood 8-2-89

2007–08	Oldham Ath	15	2		
2008–09	Oldham Ath	32	5		
2009–10	Oldham Ath	1	0		
2010–11	Oldham Ath	19	1	67	8
2011–12	Morecambe	42	4		
2012–13	Morecambe	40	3	82	7
2013–14	Plymouth Arg	42	7		
2014–15	Plymouth Arg	44	11	86	18
2015–16	Rochdale	8	1	8	1
2015–16	York C	11	2	11	2
2016–17	Hartlepool U	46	9	46	9
2017–18	Notts Co	39	7	39	7

AMEOBI, Shola (F) — 391 66
H: 6 3 W: 11 13 b.Zaria 12-10-81
Internationals: England U21. Nigeria Full caps.

1998–99	Newcastle U	0	0		
1999–2000	Newcastle U	0	0		
2000–01	Newcastle U	20	2		
2001–02	Newcastle U	15	0		
2002–03	Newcastle U	28	5		
2003–04	Newcastle U	26	7		
2004–05	Newcastle U	31	2		
2005–06	Newcastle U	30	9		
2006–07	Newcastle U	12	3		
2007–08	Newcastle U	6	0		
2007–08	Stoke C	6	0	6	0
2008–09	Newcastle U	22	4		
2009–10	Newcastle U	18	10		
2010–11	Newcastle U	28	6		
2011–12	Newcastle U	27	2		
2012–13	Newcastle U	23	1		
2013–14	Newcastle U	26	2	312	53
2014–15	Crystal Palace	4	0	4	0
2015–16	Bolton W	8	2	8	2
2015–16	Fleetwood T	10	1		
2016–17	Fleetwood T	5	0	10	1
2016–17	Notts Co	17	4		
2017–18	Notts Co	34	6	51	10

BIRD, Pierce (D) — 1 0
H: 6 2 W: 14 00 b. 16-4-99
From Dunkirk.

2017–18	Notts Co	1	0	1	0

BRISLEY, Shaun (D) — 299 13
H: 6 2 W: 12 02 b.Macclesfield 6-5-90

2007–08	Macclesfield T	10	2		
2008–09	Macclesfield T	38	0		
2009–10	Macclesfield T	33	1		
2010–11	Macclesfield T	14	0		
2011–12	Macclesfield T	29	3	124	6
2011–12	Peterborough U	11	0		
2012–13	Peterborough U	2	0		
2013–14	Peterborough U	22	0		
2014–15	Peterborough U	15	1		
2014–15	Scunthorpe U	7	0	7	0
2015–16	Peterborough U	2	0	78	1
2015–16	Northampton T	9	1	9	1
2015–16	Leyton Orient	16	1	16	1
2016–17	Carlisle U	28	2	28	2
2017–18	Notts Co	37	2	37	2

COLLIN, Adam (G) — 280 0
H: 6 2 W: 12 00 b.Penrith 9-12-84

2003–04	Newcastle U	0	0		
2003–04	Oldham Ath	0	0		

From Workington

2009–10	Carlisle U	29	0		
2010–11	Carlisle U	46	0		
2011–12	Carlisle U	46	0		
2012–13	Carlisle U	12	0	133	0
2013–14	Rotherham U	34	0		
2014–15	Rotherham U	36	0		
2015–16	Rotherham U	1	0	71	0
2015–16	Aberdeen	3	0	3	0
2016–17	Notts Co	43	0		
2017–18	Notts Co	30	0	73	0

DICKINSON, Carl (D) — 370 8
H: 6 1 W: 12 04 b.Swadlincote 31-3-87

2004–05	Stoke C	1	0		
2005–06	Stoke C	5	0		
2006–07	Stoke C	13	0		
2006–07	Blackpool	7	0	7	0
2007–08	Stoke C	27	0		
2008–09	Stoke C	5	0		
2008–09	Leeds U	7	0	7	0
2009–10	Stoke C	0	0		
2009–10	Barnsley	28	1	28	1
2010–11	Stoke C	0	0	51	0
2010–11	Portsmouth	36	0		
2011–12	Watford	39	2		
2012–13	Watford	4	0	43	2
2012–13	Portsmouth	6	0	42	0
2012–13	Coventry C	6	0	6	0
2013–14	Port Vale	40	0		
2014–15	Port Vale	43	1		
2015–16	Port Vale	44	3	127	4
2016–17	Notts Co	34	0		
2017–18	Notts Co	25	1	59	1

DUFFY, Richard (D) — 443 12
H: 5 9 W: 10 03 b.Swansea 30-8-85
Internationals: Wales U17, U19, U21, Full caps.

2002–03	Swansea C	2	0		
2003–04	Swansea C	18	1		
2003–04	Portsmouth	0	0		
2004–05	Portsmouth	0	0		
2004–05	Burnley	7	1	7	1
2005–06	Coventry C	14	0		
2005–06	Portsmouth	32	0		
2006–07	Portsmouth	0	0		
2006–07	Coventry C	13	0		
2006–07	Swansea C	11	0	29	1
2007–08	Portsmouth	0	0		
2007–08	Coventry C	2	0	61	0
2008–09	Portsmouth	0	0	1	0
2008–09	Millwall	12	0	12	0
2009–10	Exeter C	42	1		
2010–11	Exeter C	42	2		
2011–12	Exeter C	28	0	112	3
2012–13	Port Vale	36	0		
2013–14	Port Vale	28	0		
2014–15	Port Vale	27	1		
2015–16	Port Vale	45	0	136	1
2016–17	Notts Co	42	4		
2017–18	Notts Co	43	2	85	6

FITZSIMONS, Ross (G) — 17 0
H: 6 1 W: 11 10 b.Hammersmith 28-5-94

2012–13	Crystal Palace	0	0		
2013–14	Crystal Palace	0	0		
2014–15	Bolton W	0	0		
2015–16	Bolton W	0	0		

From Bishop's Stortford, Braintree T, Chelmsford C.

2017–18	Notts Co	17	0	17	0

FORTE, Jonathan (M) — 384 75
H: 6 0 W: 12 02 b.Sheffield 25-7-86
Internationals: England U16, U17, U18. Barbados Full caps.

2003–04	Sheffield U	7	0		
2004–05	Sheffield U	22	1		
2005–06	Sheffield U	1	0		
2005–06	Doncaster R	13	4		
2005–06	Rotherham U	11	4	11	4
2006–07	Sheffield U	1	0		
2006–07	Doncaster R	41	5	54	9
2007–08	Scunthorpe U	38	4		
2008–09	Scunthorpe U	6	2		
2008–09	Notts Co	18	8		
2009–10	Scunthorpe U	28	2		
2010–11	Scunthorpe U	24	3	98	9
2010–11	Southampton	10	2		
2011–12	Southampton	1	0		
2011–12	Preston NE	3	0	3	0
2011–12	Notts Co	10	5		
2012–13	Southampton	0	0		
2012–13	Crawley T	12	3	12	3
2013–14	Sheffield U	12	1	42	2
2013–14	Southampton	0	0	11	2
2014–15	Oldham Ath	34	15		
2015–16	Oldham Ath	26	3	60	18
2016–17	Notts Co	35	8		
2017–18	Notts Co	30	7	93	28

HAWKRIDGE, Terry (M) — 92 4
H: 5 9 W: 11 00 b.Nottingham 23-2-90

2013–14	Scunthorpe U	45	1		
2014–15	Scunthorpe U	11	0		
2014–15	Mansfield T	5	0	5	0
2015–16	Scunthorpe U	0	0	56	1
2015–16	Lincoln C	0	0		
2017–18	Notts Co	31	3	31	3

HEWITT, Elliott (D) — 187 7
H: 5 11 W: 11 10 b.Rhyl 30-5-94
Internationals: Wales U17, U21.

2010–11	Macclesfield T	1	0		
2011–12	Macclesfield T	21	0	22	0
2012–13	Ipswich T	7	0		
2013–14	Ipswich T	4	0		
2013–14	Gillingham	20	0	20	0
2014–15	Ipswich T	3	0	14	0
2014–15	Colchester U	21	1	21	1
2015–16	Notts Co	38	0		
2016–17	Notts Co	29	2		
2017–18	Notts Co	43	4	110	6

HODGE, Elliot (M) — 1 0
b. 23-12-95

2017–18	Notts Co	1	0	1	0

HOWES, Alex (M) — 2 0

2016–17	Notts Co	2	0		
2017–18	Notts Co	0	0	2	0

HUNT, Nicky (D) — 353 3
H: 6 1 W: 13 07 b.Westhoughton 3-9-83
Internationals: England U21.

2000–01	Bolton W	1	0		
2001–02	Bolton W	0	0		
2002–03	Bolton W	0	0		
2003–04	Bolton W	31	1		
2004–05	Bolton W	29	0		
2005–06	Bolton W	20	0		
2006–07	Bolton W	33	0		
2007–08	Bolton W	14	0		
2008–09	Bolton W	9	0		
2008–09	Birmingham C	11	0	11	0
2009–10	Bolton W	0	0	128	1
2009–10	Derby Co	21	0	21	0
2010–11	Bristol C	7	0		
2011–12	Bristol C	0	0	7	0
2011–12	Preston NE	17	1	17	1
2011–12	Rotherham U	9	0	9	0
2012–13	Accrington S	11	0		
2013–14	Accrington S	37	0		
2014–15	Accrington S	29	0	77	0
2015–16	Mansfield T	19	0	19	0
2015–16	Leyton Orient	16	0		
2016–17	Leyton Orient	35	1	51	1
2017–18	Notts Co	13	0	13	0

HUSIN, Noor (M) — 23 2
H: 5 10 W: 10 03 b.Mazar-i-Sharif 3-3-97

2015–16	Reading	0	0		
2016–17	Crystal Palace	0	0		
2016–17	Accrington S	11	1	11	1
2017–18	Notts Co	12	1	12	1

JONES, Daniel (D) — 256 10
H: 6 2 W: 13 00 b.Rowley Regis 14-7-86

2005–06	Wolverhampton W	1	0		
2006–07	Wolverhampton W	8	0		
2007–08	Wolverhampton W	1	0		
2007–08	Northampton T	33	3	33	3
2008–09	Wolverhampton W	0	0		
2008–09	Oldham Ath	23	1	23	1
2009–10	Wolverhampton W	0	0	10	0
2009–10	Notts Co	7	0		
2009–10	Bristol R	17	0	17	0
2010–11	Sheffield W	25	0		
2011–12	Sheffield W	3	0		
2012–13	Sheffield W	9	0	37	0
2012–13	Port Vale	16	1		
2013–14	Port Vale	20	0	36	1
2014–15	Chesterfield	33	0		
2015–16	Chesterfield	19	1		
2016–17	Chesterfield	14	0	66	1
2017–18	Notts Co	27	4	34	4

MILSOM, Robert (M) — 186 4
H: 5 10 W: 11 04 b.Redhill 2-1-87

2005–06	Fulham	0	0		
2006–07	Fulham	0	0		
2007–08	Fulham	0	0		
2007–08	Brentford	6	0	6	0
2008–09	Fulham	1	0		
2008–09	Southend U	6	0	6	0
2009–10	Fulham	0	0		
2010	TPS Turku	14	0	14	0
2010–11	Fulham	0	0	1	0
2011–12	Aberdeen	18	1		
2011–12	Aberdeen	22	1		
2012–13	Aberdeen	13	0	53	2
2013–14	Rotherham U	27	1		
2014–15	Rotherham U	8	0	35	1
2014–15	Bury	2	0	2	0
2015–16	Notts Co	14	0		
2016–17	Notts Co	38	0		
2017–18	Notts Co	17	1	69	1

NOBLE, Liam (M)   227 35
H: 5 9   W: 10 05   b.Newcastle 8-5-91

2009–10	Sunderland	0	0		
2010–11	Sunderland	0	0		
2010–11	Carlisle U	21	3		
2011–12	Sunderland	0	0		
2011–12	Carlisle U	40	6		
2012–13	Carlisle U	35	6		
2013–14	Carlisle U	34	5	130	20
2014–15	Notts Co	33	5		
2015–16	Notts Co	37	8		
2017–18	Forest Green R	9	1	9	1
2017–18	Notts Co	18	1	88	14

O'CONNOR, Michael (M)   356 35
H: 6 1   W: 11 08   b.Belfast 6-10-87
Internationals: Northern Ireland U21, B, Full caps.

2005–06	Crewe Alex	2	0		
2006–07	Crewe Alex	29	0		
2007–08	Crewe Alex	23	0		
2008–09	Crewe Alex	23	3	77	3
2008–09	Lincoln C	10	1	10	1
2009–10	Scunthorpe U	32	2		
2010–11	Scunthorpe U	32	8		
2011–12	Scunthorpe U	33	1	97	11
2012–13	Rotherham U	35	6		
2013–14	Rotherham U	29	2	64	8
2014–15	Port Vale	44	6		
2015–16	Port Vale	26	4	70	10
2016–17	Notts Co	32	2		
2017–18	Notts Co	6	0	38	2

OSBORNE, Samuel (F)   3 0
From Dunkirk.

2016–17	Notts Co	3	0		
2017–18	Notts Co	0	0	3	0

PINDROCH, Branislav (G)   83 0
b. 30-10-91

2010–11	Dukla	9	0		
2011–12	Dukla	0	0	9	0
2012–13	Karvina	1	0		
2013–14	Karvina	26	0		
2014–15	Karvina	17	0		
2015–16	Karvina	28	0		
2016–17	Karvina	1	0	73	0
2017–18	Notts Co	1	0	1	0

SAUNDERS, Callum (F)   30 2
H: 5 10   W: 11 11   b.Istanbul 26-9-95
Internationals: Wales U19, U21.

2014–15	Crewe Alex	4	0		
2015–16	Crewe Alex	18	2		
2016–17	Crewe Alex	5	0	27	2
2017–18	Notts Co	3	0	3	0

SMITH, Alan (F)   471 47
H: 5 10   W: 12 04   b.Rothwell 28-10-80
Internationals: England U21, B, Full caps.

1997–98	Leeds U	0	0		
1998–99	Leeds U	22	7		
1999–2000	Leeds U	26	4		
2000–01	Leeds U	33	11		
2001–02	Leeds U	23	4		
2002–03	Leeds U	33	3		
2003–04	Leeds U	35	9	172	38
2004–05	Manchester U	31	6		
2005–06	Manchester U	21	1		
2006–07	Manchester U	9	0	61	7
2007–08	Newcastle U	33	0		
2008–09	Newcastle U	6	0		
2009–10	Newcastle U	32	0		
2010–11	Newcastle U	11	0		
2011–12	Newcastle U	2	0	84	0
2011–12	Milton Keynes D	16	1		
2012–13	Milton Keynes D	27	1		
2013–14	Milton Keynes D	24	0	67	2
2014–15	Notts Co	23	0		
2015–16	Notts Co	28	0		
2016–17	Notts Co	19	0		
2017–18	Notts Co	17	0	87	0

STEAD, Jon (F)   542 127
H: 6 3   W: 13 03   b.Huddersfield 7-4-83
Internationals: England U21.

2001–02	Huddersfield T	0	0		
2002–03	Huddersfield T	42	6		
2003–04	Huddersfield T	26	16		
2003–04	Blackburn R	13	6		
2004–05	Blackburn R	29	2	42	8
2005–06	Sunderland	30	1		
2006–07	Sunderland	5	1	35	2
2006–07	Derby Co	17	3	17	3
2006–07	Sheffield U	14	5		
2007–08	Sheffield U	24	3		
2008–09	Sheffield U	1	0	39	8
2008–09	Ipswich T	39	12		
2009–10	Ipswich T	22	6		
2009–10	Coventry C	10	2	10	2
2010–11	Ipswich T	3	1	64	19
2010–11	Bristol C	27	9		
2011–12	Bristol C	24	6		
2012–13	Bristol C	28	5	79	20
2013–14	Huddersfield T	12	1		
2013–14	*Oldham Ath*	5	0	5	0
2013–14	Bradford C	8	1		
2014–15	Huddersfield T	7	1	87	24
2014–15	Bradford C	32	6	40	7
2015–16	Notts Co	43	11		
2016–17	Notts Co	38	14		
2017–18	Notts Co	43	9	124	34

THOMPSON, Curtis (M)   90 2
H: 5 10   W: 12 06   b.Nottingham 2-9-93

2011–12	Notts Co	0	0		
2012–13	Notts Co	2	0		
2013–14	Notts Co	11	0		
2014–15	Notts Co	31	0		
2015–16	Notts Co	26	2		
2016–17	Notts Co	13	0		
2017–18	Notts Co	0	0	83	2
2017–18	*Wycombe W*	7	0	7	0

TOOTLE, Matt (D)   284 6
H: 5 9   W: 11 00   b.Widnes 11-10-90

2009–10	Crewe Alex	28	1		
2010–11	Crewe Alex	39	0		
2011–12	Crewe Alex	37	0		
2012–13	Crewe Alex	37	1		
2013–14	Crewe Alex	43	0		
2014–15	Crewe Alex	15	0	199	2
2015–16	Shrewsbury T	16	0	16	0
2016–17	Notts Co	33	2		
2017–18	Notts Co	36	2	69	4

WALKER, Liam (M)   162 42
H: 5 9   W: 11 11   b.13-4-88
Internationals: Gilbralta Full caps.

2006–07	Algeciras	0	0		
2007–08	Algeciras	0	0		
2008–09	Atletico Zabal	8	6	8	6
2009–10	Balompedica	0	0		
2009–10	Los Barrios	13	2	13	2
2010–11	Balompedica	13	1	13	1
2011–12	San Roque Lepe	0	0		
2012–13	Portsmouth	26	2	26	2
2013–14	San Roque Lepe	9	2	9	2
2013–14	Bnei Yehuda Tel-Aviv	13	1	13	1
2014–15	Lincoln Red Imps	24	12		
2015–16	Lincoln Red Imps	19	3	43	15
2016–17	Europa	26	13	26	13
2017–18	Notts Co	11	0	11	0

Scholars
Betts, Owen Adam; Brown-Hill, Dominic; Bugg, Harry Joseph; Campbell, Remaye Orvil Kelvin; Culverwell, Max Edward; Dearle, Peter James; Duncan, Coden; Dunn, Declan Nicholas; Ebanks, Ryan Jenson; Hall, Curtis James; Howes, Alex Jacob; Kennedy-Williams, Tyreece; Newell, Owen Jay; Osborne, Samuel Paul; Ramirez, Inscoe Oscar; Richards, Jordon George; Searson-Smithard, Joseph Luke; Towers, Edwin James.

OLDHAM ATH (62)

AMADI-HOLLOWAY, Aaron (D)   123 10
H: 6 2   W: 13 00   b.Newark 22-2-93
Internationals: Wales U17, U19.

2012–13	Bristol C	0	0		
2013–14	Bristol C	0	0		
2013–14	Newport Co	4	0	4	0
2014–15	Wycombe W	29	3		
2015–16	Wycombe W	23	3	52	6
2015–16	*Oldham Ath*	10	2		
2016–17	Fleetwood T	6	0	6	0
2016–17	Oldham Ath	15	0		
2017–18	Oldham Ath	36	2	61	4

ANTOINE, Francois (M)   0 0

2017–18	Oldham Ath	0	0

BANKS, Oliver (D)   142 15
H: 6 3   W: 11 11   b.Rotherham 21-9-92

2010–11	Rotherham U	1	1		
2011–12	Rotherham U	0	0	1	1
2013–14	Chesterfield	25	7		
2014–15	Chesterfield	0	0		
2014–15	*Northampton T*	3	0	3	0
2015–16	Chesterfield	32	2	81	9
2016–17	Oldham Ath	33	2		
2017–18	Oldham Ath	7	0	40	2
2017–18	*Swindon T*	17	3	17	3

BENTEKE, Jonathan (F)   43 4
b. 28-4-95
From Standard Liege.

2013–14	Vise	20	2	20	2
2014–15	Zulte-Waregem	6	2		
2015–16	Zulte-Waregem	15	0		
2016–17	Zulte-Waregem	0	0	21	2
2016–17	Crystal Palace	1	0	1	0
2017–18	Oldham Ath	1	0	1	0

BENYU, Kundai (M)   5 0
b. 12-12-97
Internationals: Zimbabwe Full caps.

2014–15	Ipswich T	0	0		
2015–16	Ipswich T	0	0		
2016–17	Ipswich T	0	0		

From Aldershot T.

2017–18	Celtic	1	0	1	0

On loan from Celtic.

2017–18	Oldham Ath	4	0	4	0

BOYLING, Joe (G)   0 0

2017–18	Oldham Ath	0	0

BYRNE, Jack (M)   73 9
H: 5 9   W: 11 07   b.Dublin 24-4-96
Internationals: Republic of Ireland U16, U17, U18, U19, U21.

2015–16	Manchester C	0	0		
2015–16	*Cambuur*	27	4	27	4
2016–17	Manchester C	0	0		
2016–17	*Blackburn R*	4	0	4	0
2016–17	Wigan Ath	2	0	2	0
2017–18	Oldham Ath	40	5	40	5

CLARKE, Peter (D)   612 45
H: 6 0   W: 12 00   b.Southport 3-1-82
Internationals: England U21.

1998–99	Everton	0	0		
1999–2000	Everton	0	0		
2000–01	Everton	1	0		
2001–02	Everton	7	0		
2002–03	Everton	0	0		
2002–03	*Blackpool*	16	3		
2002–03	*Port Vale*	13	1	13	1
2003–04	Everton	1	0		
2003–04	*Coventry C*	5	0	5	0
2004–05	Everton	0	0	9	0
2004–05	Blackpool	38	5		
2005–06	Blackpool	46	6		
2006–07	Southend U	38	2		
2007–08	Southend U	45	4		
2008–09	Southend U	4	0	126	10
2009–10	Huddersfield T	46	5		
2010–11	Huddersfield T	46	4		
2011–12	Huddersfield T	31	0		
2012–13	Huddersfield T	43	0		
2013–14	Huddersfield T	26	0	192	9
2014–15	Blackpool	39	2	139	16
2015–16	Bury	45	1		
2016–17	Oldham Ath	46	5		
2017–18	Oldham Ath	19	2	65	7
2017–18	Bury	18	1	63	2

DAVIES, Craig (F)   441 102
H: 6 2   W: 13 05   b.Burton-on-Trent 9-1-86
Internationals: Wales U17, U19, U21, Full caps.

2004–05	Oxford U	28	6		
2005–06	Oxford U	20	2	48	8
2005–06	Verona	0	0		
2006–07	Wolverhampton W	23	0	23	0
2007–08	Oldham Ath	32	10		
2008–09	Oldham Ath	12	0		
2008–09	*Stockport Co*	9	5	9	5
2008–09	Brighton & HA	16	1		
2009–10	Brighton & HA	5	0	21	1
2009–10	*Yeovil T*	19	0	19	0
2009–10	Port Vale	24	7	24	7
2010–11	Chesterfield	23	11	41	23
2011–12	Barnsley	40	11		
2012–13	Barnsley	38	8	60	19
2013–14	Bolton W	18	4		
2013–14	Bolton W	8	0		
2013–14	*Preston NE*	15	5	15	5
2014–15	Bolton W	27	6	53	10
2015–16	Wigan Ath	26	2		
2016–17	Wigan Ath	14	1	40	3
2016–17	Scunthorpe U	19	0	19	0
2017–18	Oldham Ath	40	11	84	21

DE LA PAZ, Zeus (G)   14 0
b. 11-3-95
Internationals: Curacao U20, Full caps.

2013–14	PSV Eindhoven	0	0
2014–15	PSV Eindhoven	0	0

From Nuneaton T.

2017	Cincinnati Dutch Lions	14	0	14 0
2017–18	Oldham Ath	0	0	

DUFFUS, Courtney (F)   9 0
H: 5 7 W: 12 00 b.Cheltenham 24-10-95
Internationals: Republic of Ireland U21.

2013–14	Everton	0	0	
2014–15	Everton	0	0	
2014–15	Bury	3	0	3 0
2015–16	Everton	0	0	
2016–17	Everton	0	0	
2017–18	Oldham Ath	6	0	6 0

DUMMIGAN, Cameron (D)   68 3
H: 5 11 W: 11 00 b.Lurgan 2-6-96
Internationals: Northern Ireland U17, U19, U21.

2013–14	Burnley	0	0	
2014–15	Burnley	0	0	
2015–16	Burnley	0	0	
2015–16	Oldham Ath	26	1	
2016–17	Oldham Ath	12	0	
2017–18	Oldham Ath	30	2	68 3

EDMUNDSON, Sam (D)   20 1
H: 6 1 W: 11 11 b.Timperley 15-8-97

2015–16	Oldham Ath	2	0	
2016–17	Oldham Ath	3	0	
2017–18	Oldham Ath	15	1	20 1

FANE, Ousmane (M)   80 0
H: 6 4 W: 12 08 b.Paris 13-12-93
From Kidderminster H.

2016–17	Oldham Ath	39	0	
2017–18	Oldham Ath	41	0	80 0

FAWNS, Mason (M)   4 0
b. 10-1-99

2017–18	Oldham Ath	4	0	4 0

FLYNN, Ryan (M)   266 24
H: 5 8 W: 10 00 b.Falkirk 4-9-88
Internationals: Scotland U19.

2006–07	Liverpool	0	0	
2007–08	Hereford U	0	0	
2007–08	Liverpool	0	0	
2008–09	Liverpool	0	0	
2009–10	Liverpool	0	0	
2009–10	Falkirk	36	5	
2010–11	Falkirk	33	5	69 10
2011–12	Sheffield U	26	2	
2012–13	Sheffield U	36	3	
2013–14	Sheffield U	32	5	
2014–15	Sheffield U	32	1	
2015–16	Sheffield U	27	2	153 13
2016–17	Oldham Ath	37	1	
2017–18	Oldham Ath	7	0	44 1

Transferred to St Mirren, January 2018.

GARDNER, Dan (M)   152 13
H: 6 1 W: 12 05 b.Manchester 5-4-90

2009–10	Crewe Alex	2	0	2 0

From Droylsden, FC Halifax T.

2013–14	Chesterfield	16	3	
2014–15	Chesterfield	17	1	
2014–15	*Tranmere R*	4	2	4 2
2015–16	Chesterfield	30	4	
2015–16	Bury	6	0	6 0
2016–17	Chesterfield	34	2	97 10
2017–18	Oldham Ath	43	1	43 1

GERRARD, Anthony (D)   424 19
H: 6 2 W: 13 07 b.Huyton 6-2-86
Internationals: Republic of Ireland U18.

2004–05	Everton	0	0	
2004–05	Walsall	8	0	
2005–06	Walsall	34	0	
2006–07	Walsall	35	1	
2007–08	Walsall	44	3	
2008–09	Walsall	42	3	163 7
2009–10	Cardiff C	39	2	
2010–11	Cardiff C	0	0	
2010–11	*Hull C*	41	5	41 5
2011–12	Cardiff C	20	1	
2012–13	Cardiff C	0	0	59 3
2012–13	Huddersfield T	38	1	
2013–14	Huddersfield T	40	1	
2014–15	Huddersfield T	3	0	81 2
2014–15	*Oldham Ath*	0	0	
2015–16	Shrewsbury T	11	0	11 0
2015–16	Oldham Ath	18	0	
2016–17	Oldham Ath	14	0	
2017–18	Oldham Ath	31	2	69 2

GREEN, Paul (M)   506 44
H: 5 9 W: 10 02 b.Pontefract 10-4-83
Internationals: Republic of Ireland Full caps.

2003–04	Doncaster R	43	8	
2004–05	Doncaster R	42	7	
2005–06	Doncaster R	34	3	
2006–07	Doncaster R	41	2	
2007–08	Doncaster R	38	5	198 25
2008–09	Derby Co	29	3	
2009–10	Derby Co	33	2	
2010–11	Derby Co	36	2	
2011–12	Derby Co	27	1	125 8
2012–13	Leeds U	32	4	
2013–14	Leeds U	9	0	41 4
2013–14	*Ipswich T*	14	2	14 2
2014–15	Rotherham U	37	3	
2015–16	Rotherham U	24	0	61 3
2017–18	Oldham Ath	41	1	
2017–18	Oldham Ath	6	0	47 1
2017–18	*Crewe Alex*	20	1	20 1

HAYMER, Tom (D)   7 1
b. 16-11-99

2017–18	Oldham Ath	7	1	7 1

HUNT, Robert (M)   44 0
H: 5 7 W: 10 08 b.Dagenham 7-7-95

2013–14	Brighton & HA	0	0	
2014–15	Brighton & HA	0	0	
2015–16	Brighton & HA	0	0	
2016–17	Brighton & HA	1	0	1 0
2016–17	*Oldham Ath*	10	0	
2017–18	Oldham Ath	33	0	43 0

KYEREMEH, Gyamfi (M)   2 0
b. 9-3-95

2014–15	Waasland Beveren	1	0	
2015–16	Eintracht Braunschweig	0	0	
2016–17	Eintracht Braunschweig	0	0	
2017–18	Oldham Ath	1	0	1 0

MANTACK, Kallum (D)   1 0
H: 5 8 W: 11 11 b.1-5-98

2016–17	Oldham Ath	0	0	
2017–18	Oldham Ath	1	0	1 0

MAOUCHE, Mohamed (M)   63 4
b. 22-1-93

2010–11	Saint-Etienne	0	0	
2011–12	Servette	0	0	
2012–13	Servette	0	0	
2013–14	Servette	0	0	
2014–15	Lausanne Sport	16	1	16 1
2015–16	Tours	15	0	
2016–17	Tours	31	3	
2017–18	Tours	0	0	46 3
2017–18	Oldham Ath	1	0	1 0

McELENEY, Patrick (F)   9 1
H: 5 9 W: 11 03 b.26-9-92
Internationals: Northern Ireland U16. Republic of Ireland 17, U19.

2017–18	Oldham Ath	9	1	9 1

McLAUGHLIN, Ryan (D)   65 3
H: 5 9 W: 10 12 b.Belfast 30-9-94
Internationals: Northern Ireland U16, U17, U19, U21, Full caps.

2011–12	Liverpool	0	0	
2013–14	Liverpool	0	0	
2013–14	*Barnsley*	9	0	9 0
2014–15	Liverpool	0	0	
2015–16	Liverpool	0	0	
2015–16	*Aberdeen*	4	0	4 0
2016–17	Oldham Ath	36	2	
2017–18	Oldham Ath	16	1	52 3

MENIG, Queensy (F)   96 17
H: 5 9 W: 10 12 b.Amsterdam 19-8-95
Internationals: Netherlands U17, U19, U20, U21.

2014–15	Ajax	3	0	3 0
2015–16	PEC Zwolle	35	6	
2016–17	PEC Zwolle	31	9	
2017–18	Nantes	0	0	

On loan from Nantes.

2017–18	Oldham Ath	14	1	14 1
2017–18	*PEC Zwolle*	13	1	79 16

MOIMBE, Wilfried (D)   205 1
H: 5 8 W: 10 03 b.Vichy 18-10-88

2005–06	Bordeaux	0	0	
2006–07	Bordeaux	0	0	
2007–08	Bordeaux	0	0	
2008–09	Reims	19	0	19 0
2009–10	Ajaccio	26	0	26 0
2010–11	Tours	18	0	
2011–12	Tours	20	0	
2012–13	Tours	32	0	70 0
2013–14	Brest	30	0	
2014–15	Brest	26	1	56 1
2015–16	Nantes	15	0	
2016–17	Nantes	8	0	
2017–18	Nantes	0	0	23 0
2017–18	Oldham Ath	11	0	11 0

NEPOMUCENO, Gevaro (F)   168 10
H: 5 9 W: 10 08 b.10-11-92
Internationals: Curacao Full caps.

2010–11	Den Bosch	2	0	
2011–12	Den Bosch	13	1	15 1
2012–13	Fortuna Sittard	17	2	
2013–14	Fortuna Sittard	38	5	55 7
2014–15	Petrolui Ploiesti	25	1	
2015–16	Petrolui Ploiesti	22	0	47 1
2015–16	Maritimo Funchal	7	0	
2016–17	Maritimo Funchal	5	0	12 0
2016–17	Famalicao	13	0	13 0
2017–18	Maritimo	0	0	
2017–18	Oldham Ath	26	1	26 1

OBADEYI, Temitope (F)   192 22
H: 5 10 W: 11 09 b.Birmingham 29-10-89
Internationals: England U19, U20.

2006–07	Bolton W	0	0	
2007–08	Bolton W	0	0	
2008–09	Bolton W	3	0	
2009–10	Bolton W	0	0	
2009–10	*Swindon T*	12	2	12 2
2009–10	Rochdale	11	1	
2010–11	Bolton W	0	0	
2010–11	*Shrewsbury T*	9	0	9 0
2011–12	Bolton W	0	0	3 0
2011–12	*Chesterfield*	5	0	5 0
2011–12	*Rochdale*	6	1	17 2
2012–13	Rio Ave	11	0	11 0
2013–14	Bury	7	0	7 0
2013–14	*Plymouth Arg*	14	1	14 1
2014–15	Kilmarnock	29	9	
2015–16	Kilmarnock	30	3	59 12
2016–17	Dundee U	18	2	18 2
2016–17	Oldham Ath	15	2	
2017–18	Oldham Ath	22	1	37 3

OMRANI, Abdelhakim (F)   81 6
H: 6 2 W: 13 05 b.18-2-91
Internationals: France U19.

2008–09	Lens	2	0	
2009–10	Lens	0	0	
2010–11	Lens	2	0	
2011–12	Lens	0	0	4 0
2012–13	Le Mans	13	1	13 1
2013–14	Nimes	21	3	
2014–15	Nimes	7	1	28 4
2015–16	Chamois Niortais	18	0	18 0
2016–17	Sedan	10	1	10 1
2017–18	Oldham Ath	8	0	8 0

OSEI, Darius (F)   22 1
H: 5 11 W: 10 12 b.2-6-95
From Stalybridge Celtic.

2016–17	Oldham Ath	19	0	
2017–18	Oldham Ath	3	1	22 1

PLACIDE, Johnny (G)   182 0
H: 5 11 W: 12 13 b.Montfermeil 29-1-88
Internationals: France U21. Haiti U23, Full caps.

2008–09	Le Havre	4	0	
2009–10	Le Havre	30	0	
2010–11	Le Havre	34	0	
2011–12	Le Havre	23	0	
2012–13	Le Havre	6	0	97 0
2012–13	Reims	4	0	
2013–14	Reims	4	0	
2014–15	Reims	22	0	
2015–16	Reims	19	0	49 0
2016–17	Guingamp	0	0	
2017–18	Oldham Ath	36	0	36 0

SCHOLES-BEARD, Ryan (M)   0 0

2017–18	Oldham Ath	0	0	

SHERIDAN, Jay (D)   0 0

2017–18	Oldham Ath	0	0	

STOTT, Jamie (D)   4 0
b. 22-12-97

2016–17	Oldham Ath	4	0	
2017–18	Oldham Ath	0	0	4 0

UCHE, Chinedy (M)   0 0

2017–18	Oldham Ath	0	0	

WILSON, Brian (D)   446 17
H: 5 11 W: 11 00 b.Manchester 9-5-83

2001–02	Stoke C	2	0	
2002–03	Stoke C	3	0	
2003–04	Stoke C	2	0	6 0
2003–04	Cheltenham T	14	0	
2004–05	Cheltenham T	43	3	
2005–06	Cheltenham T	43	1	
2006–07	Cheltenham T	25	2	125 14
2006–07	Bristol C	19	0	
2007–08	Bristol C	18	1	

Season	Club	App	Gls	Tot App	Tot Gls
2008–09	Bristol C	20	0		
2009–10	Bristol C	3	0	60	1
2010–11	Colchester U	26	1		
2011–12	Colchester U	46	0		
2012–13	Colchester U	41	0		
2013–14	Colchester U	38	0	151	1
2014–15	Oldham Ath	33	0		
2015–16	Oldham Ath	26	0		
2016–17	Oldham Ath	26	1		
2017–18	Oldham Ath	19	0	104	1

Scholars
Amankwaa, Samuel Osei; Antoine, Francois Bernard; Arthur, Festus; Baldwin, Declan James; Dry, Edward MacKenzie; Hamer, Thomas Philip; Lent, Tommy; Leonard, Ryan Michael Raymond; McFarlane, Ewan Glenn; Norman, Max John; Norris, Harry Robert; Robinson, Harry David; Scholes-Beard, Ryan Stewart; Sheridan, Jay Anthony; Sheriff, Kelfala; Swaby-Neavin, Javid Reece; Uche, Chinedu Oyinoluwa Praise; Whalley, Bailey Michael.

OXFORD U (63)

ASHBY, Josh (M)　　5　0
b.Oxford 3-5-96

Season	Club	App	Gls	Tot App	Tot Gls
2013–14	Oxford U	0	0		
2014–15	Oxford U	2	0		
2015–16	Oxford U	3	0		
2016–17	Oxford U	0	0		
2017–18	Oxford U	0	0	5	0

BAPTISTE, Shandon (M)　　0　0
Internationals: Grenada Full caps.

2017–18	Oxford U	0	0

BRANNAGAN, Cameron (M)　　28　0
H: 5 11　W: 11 03　b.Manchester 9-5-96
Internationals: England U18, U20.

Season	Club	App	Gls	Tot App	Tot Gls
2013–14	Liverpool	0	0		
2014–15	Liverpool	0	0		
2015–16	Liverpool	3	0		
2016–17	Liverpool	0	0		
2016–17	*Fleetwood T*	13	0	13	0
2017–18	Liverpool	0	0	3	0
2017–18	Oxford U	12	0	12	0

CARROLL, Canice (M)　　16　1
b.26-1-99
Internationals: Republic of Ireland U17.

2015–16	Oxford U	0	0		
2016–17	Oxford U	4	0		
2017–18	Oxford U	12	1	16	1

DICKIE, Rob (D)　　54　3
H: 6 0　W: 11 09　b.Wokingham 3-3-96
Internationals: England U18, U19.

Season	Club	App	Gls	Tot App	Tot Gls
2015–16	Reading	1	0		
2016–17	Reading	0	0		
2016–17	*Cheltenham T*	20	2	20	2
2017–18	Reading	0	0	1	0
2017–18	*Lincoln C*	18	0	18	0
2017–18	Oxford U	15	1	15	1

EASTWOOD, Simon (G)　　155　0
H: 6 2　W: 10 13　b.Huddersfield 26-6-89
Internationals: England U18.

Season	Club	App	Gls	Tot App	Tot Gls
2005–06	Huddersfield T	0	0		
2006–07	Huddersfield T	0	0		
2007–08	Huddersfield T	0	0		
2008–09	Huddersfield T	1	0		
2009–10	Huddersfield T	0	0	1	0
2009–10	*Bradford C*	22	0	22	0
2012–13	Portsmouth	27	0	27	0
2013–14	Blackburn R	7	0		
2014–15	Blackburn R	6	0		
2015–16	Blackburn R	0	0	13	0
2016–17	Oxford U	46	0		
2017–18	Oxford U	46	0	92	0

FERNANDEZ CODINA, Josep (M) 10　1
H: 6 0　W: 13 05　b.2-2-95
From Barcelona.

2017–18	Oxford U	10	1	10	1

Transferred to Cornella January 2018.

HALL, Robert (F)　　137　19
H: 6 2　W: 10 05　b.Aylesbury 20-10-93
Internationals: England U16, U17, U18, U19.

Season	Club	App	Gls	Tot App	Tot Gls
2010–11	West Ham U	0	0		
2011–12	West Ham U	3	0		
2011–12	*Oxford U*	13	5		
2011–12	*Milton Keynes D*	2	0		
2012–13	West Ham U	1	0	4	0
2012–13	*Birmingham C*	13	0	13	0
2012–13	*Bolton W*	1	0		
2013–14	Bolton W	22	1		
2014–15	Bolton W	9	0		
2014–15	*Milton Keynes D*	7	3		
2015–16	Bolton W	0	0	32	1
2015–16	*Milton Keynes D*	27	2	36	5
2016–17	Oxford U	26	6		
2017–18	Oxford U	13	2	52	13

HEMMINGS, Kane (F)　　141　45
b.Burton 8-4-92

Season	Club	App	Gls	Tot App	Tot Gls
2011–12	Rangers	4	0	4	0

From Cowdenbeath.

Season	Club	App	Gls	Tot App	Tot Gls
2014–15	Barnsley	23	3	23	3
2015–16	Dundee	37	21	37	21
2016–17	Oxford U	40	6		
2017–18	Oxford U	0	0	40	6
2017–18	*Mansfield T*	37	15	37	15

HENRY, James (M)　　353　55
H: 6 1　W: 11 11　b.Reading 10-6-89
Internationals: Scotland U16, U19. England U18, U19.

Season	Club	App	Gls	Tot App	Tot Gls
2006–07	Reading	0	0		
2006–07	*Nottingham F*	1	0	1	0
2007–08	Reading	0	0		
2007–08	*Bournemouth*	11	4	11	4
2007–08	*Norwich C*	3	0	3	0
2008–09	Reading	7	0		
2008–09	*Millwall*	16	3		
2009–10	Reading	3	0	10	0
2009–10	Millwall	9	5		
2010–11	Millwall	42	5		
2011–12	Millwall	39	0		
2012–13	Millwall	35	5		
2013–14	Millwall	5	0	146	18
2013–14	Wolverhampton W	32	10		
2014–15	Wolverhampton W	37	5		
2015–16	Wolverhampton W	39	7		
2016–17	Wolverhampton W	2	0	110	22
2016–17	*Bolton W*	30	1	30	1
2017–18	Oxford U	42	10	42	10

HOPKINS, Albie (M)　　0　0

2017–18	Oxford U	0	0

JAMES, Owen (F)　　1　0
b. 13-10-00

2017–18	Oxford U	1	0	1	0

LEDSON, Ryan (M)　　93　4
H: 5 9　W: 10 12　b.Liverpool 19-8-97
Internationals: England U16, U17, U18, U19, U20.

Season	Club	App	Gls	Tot App	Tot Gls
2013–14	Everton	0	0		
2014–15	Everton	0	0		
2015–16	Everton	0	0		
2015–16	*Cambridge U*	27	0	27	0
2016–17	Oxford U	22	1		
2017–18	Oxford U	44	3	66	4

LONG, Sam (D)　　18　1
H: 5 10　W: 11 11　b.Oxford 16-1-95

Season	Club	App	Gls	Tot App	Tot Gls
2012–13	Oxford U	1	0		
2013–14	Oxford U	3	0		
2014–15	Oxford U	10	1		
2015–16	Oxford U	1	0		
2016–17	Oxford U	3	0		
2017–18	Oxford U	0	0	18	1

MARTIN, Aaron (D)　　128　6
H: 6 3　W: 11 13　b.Newport (IW) 29-9-87

Season	Club	App	Gls	Tot App	Tot Gls
2009–10	Southampton	2	0		
2010–11	Southampton	8	0		
2011–12	Southampton	10	1		
2012–13	Southampton	0	0		
2012–13	*Crystal Palace*	4	0	4	0
2012–13	*Coventry C*	12	0		
2013–14	Southampton	0	0	20	1
2013–14	*Birmingham C*	8	0	8	0
2014–15	*Yeovil T*	12	3	12	3
2014–15	Coventry C	27	0		
2015–16	Coventry C	29	2	68	2
2016–17	Oxford U	4	0		
2017–18	Oxford U	12	0	16	0

MEHMETI, Agon (F)　　197　40
H: 6 0　W: 11 05　b. 20-11-89
Internationals: Sweden U19, U21. Albania Full caps.

Season	Club	App	Gls	Tot App	Tot Gls
2008	Malmo	21	3		
2009	Malmo	22	5		
2010	Malmo	24	11		
2011	Malmo	21	4		
2011–12	Palermo	3	0		
2012–13	Palermo	0	0	3	0
2012–13	Novara	22	6	22	6
2013–14	Olhanense	20	2	20	2
2014	Malmo	10	2		
2015	Malmo	15	2	113	27
2016	Stabaek	24	4	24	4
2016–17	Genclerbirligi	2	0	2	0
2017–18	Oxford U	13	1	13	1

MOUSINHO, John (M)　　401　21
H: 6 1　W: 12 07　b.Hounslow 30-4-86

Season	Club	App	Gls	Tot App	Tot Gls
2005–06	Brentford	7	0		
2006–07	Brentford	34	0		
2007–08	Brentford	23	2	64	2
2008–09	Wycombe W	34	2		
2009–10	Wycombe W	39	1	73	3
2010–11	Stevenage	38	7		
2011–12	Stevenage	19	3		
2012–13	Preston NE	24	1		
2013–14	Preston NE	2	0	26	1
2013–14	*Gillingham*	4	1	4	1
2013–14	*Stevenage*	16	1	73	11
2014–15	Burton Alb	42	2		
2015–16	Burton Alb	46	0		
2016–17	Burton Alb	32	0		
2017–18	Burton Alb	1	0	121	2
2017–18	Oxford U	40	1	40	1

NAPA, Malachi (M)　　14　0
b. 26-5-99
From Reading.

2017–18	Oxford U	14	0	14	0

NELSON, Curtis (D)　　264　11
H: 6 0　W: 11 07　b.Newcastle-under-Lyme 21-5-93
Internationals: England U18.

Season	Club	App	Gls	Tot App	Tot Gls
2010–11	Plymouth Arg	35	0		
2011–12	Plymouth Arg	17	0		
2012–13	Plymouth Arg	27	3		
2013–14	Plymouth Arg	44	1		
2014–15	Plymouth Arg	42	1		
2015–16	Plymouth Arg	46	3	211	8
2016–17	Oxford U	33	2		
2017–18	Oxford U	20	1	53	3

NOVILLO, Harry (F)　　2　1
H: 6 0　W: 12 08　b.Lyon 11-2-92

2017–18	Oxford U	2	1	2	1

OBIKA, Jonathan (F)　　251　53
H: 6 0　W: 12 00　b.Enfield 12-9-90
Internationals: England U19, U20.

Season	Club	App	Gls	Tot App	Tot Gls
2008–09	Tottenham H	0	0		
2008–09	*Yeovil T*	10	4		
2009–10	Tottenham H	0	0		
2009–10	*Yeovil T*	22	6		
2009–10	*Millwall*	12	2	12	2
2010–11	Tottenham H	0	0		
2010–11	*Crystal Palace*	7	0	7	0
2010–11	*Peterborough U*	1	1	1	1
2010–11	*Swindon T*	5	0		
2010–11	*Yeovil T*	11	3		
2011–12	Tottenham H	0	0		
2011–12	*Yeovil T*	27	4	70	17
2012–13	Tottenham H	0	0		
2012–13	*Charlton Ath*	10	3		
2013–14	Tottenham H	0	0		
2013–14	*Brighton & HA*	5	0	5	0
2013–14	*Charlton Ath*	12	0	22	3
2014–15	Tottenham H	0	0		
2014–15	Swindon T	32	8		
2015–16	Swindon T	32	11		
2016–17	Swindon T	30	6	99	25
2017–18	Oxford U	35	5	35	5

RAGLAN, Charlie (D)　　72　1
H: 6 0　W: 11 13　b.Wythenshawe 28-4-93

Season	Club	App	Gls	Tot App	Tot Gls
2011–12	Port Vale	0	0		
2012–13	Port Vale	0	0		
2013–14	Port Vale	0	0		
2014–15	Chesterfield	18	1		
2015–16	Chesterfield	27	0		
2016–17	Chesterfield	1	0	46	1
2016–17	*Oxford U*	16	0		
2017–18	Oxford U	0	0	16	0
2017–18	*Port Vale*	10	0	10	0

RIBEIRO, Christian (D)　　172　9
H: 5 11　W: 12 02　b.Neath 14-12-89
Internationals: Wales U17, U19, U21, Full caps.

Season	Club	App	Gls	Tot App	Tot Gls
2006–07	Bristol C	0	0		
2007–08	Bristol C	0	0		
2008–09	Bristol C	5	0		
2009–10	Bristol C	5	0		
2009–10	*Stockport Co*	7	0	7	0
2009–10	*Colchester U*	2	0	2	0
2010–11	Bristol C	9	0		
2011–12	Bristol C	0	0	14	0
2011–12	*Carlisle U*	5	0	5	0
2011–12	*Scunthorpe U*	10	0		
2012–13	Scunthorpe U	28	2		
2013–14	Scunthorpe U	21	0	59	2
2014–15	Exeter C	37	2		

2015–16	Exeter C	35	4	**72 6**
2016–17	Oxford U	3	0	
2017–18	Oxford U	10	1	**13 1**

RICARDINHO, Ferreira (D)   **392 20**
H: 5 6   W: 10 08   b.Curitiba 9-9-84

2003	Coritiba	2	0	
2004	Coritiba	34	2	
2005	Coritiba	37	5	
2006	Coritiba	34	3	
2007	Coritiba	13	1	
2007	*Atletico Mineiro*	4	0	**4 0**
2008	Coritiba	37	2	**157 13**
2009	Malmo	29	1	
2010	Malmo	22	0	
2011	Malmo	30	0	
2012	Malmo	28	2	
2013	Malmo	27	0	
2014	Malmo	23	0	**159 3**
2014–15	Gabala	10	0	
2015–16	Gabala	16	0	
2016–17	Gabala	10	1	
2017–18	Gabala	0	0	**36 1**
2017–18	Oxford U	36	3	**36 3**

ROBERTS, James (F)   **32 3**
b.Stoke Mandeville 21-6-96

2012–13	Oxford U	0	0	
2013–14	Oxford U	0	0	
2014–15	Oxford U	25	3	
2015–16	Oxford U	4	0	
2015–16	*Barnet*	2	0	**2 0**
2016–17	Oxford U	0	0	
2017–18	Oxford U	1	0	**30 3**

ROTHWELL, Joe (M)   **76 6**
H: 6 1   W: 12 02   b.Manchester 11-1-95
Internationals: England U16, U17, U19, U20.

2014–15	Manchester U	0	0	
2014–15	*Blackpool*	3	0	**3 0**
2015–16	Manchester U	0	0	
2015–16	*Barnsley*	4	0	**4 0**
2016–17	Oxford U	33	1	
2017–18	Oxford U	36	5	**69 6**

RUFFELS, Joshua (M)   **137 8**
H: 5 10   W: 11 11   b.Oxford 23-10-93

2011–12	Coventry C	1	0	
2012–13	Coventry C	0	0	**1 0**
2013–14	Oxford U	29	1	
2014–15	Oxford U	33	0	
2015–16	Oxford U	16	0	
2016–17	Oxford U	20	2	
2017–18	Oxford U	38	5	**136 8**

SHEARER, Scott (G)   **335 0**
H: 6 3   W: 12 00   b.Glasgow 15-2-81
Internationals: Scotland B.

2000–01	Albion R	3	0	
2001–02	Albion R	10	0	
2002–03	Albion R	36	0	**49 0**
2003–04	Coventry C	30	0	
2004–05	Coventry C	8	0	**38 0**
2004–05	*Rushden & D*	13	0	**13 0**
2005–06	Bristol R	45	0	
2006–07	Bristol R	2	0	**47 0**
2006–07	*Shrewsbury T*	20	0	**20 0**
2007–08	Wycombe W	5	0	
2008–09	Wycombe W	29	0	
2009–10	Wycombe W	29	0	
2010–11	Wycombe W	0	0	**63 0**
2011–12	Crawley T	25	0	**25 0**
2012–13	Rotherham U	19	0	
2013–14	Rotherham U	12	0	**31 0**
2014–15	Crewe Alex	2	0	**2 0**
2014–15	*Burton Alb*	1	0	**1 0**
2015–16	Mansfield T	21	0	
2016–17	Mansfield T	25	0	**46 0**
2016–17	Oxford U	0	0	
2017–18	Oxford U	0	0	

STEPHENS, Jack (G)   **0 0**
b. 2-8-97

2014–15	Oxford U	0	0	
2015–16	Oxford U	0	0	
2016–17	Oxford U	0	0	
2017–18	Oxford U	0	0	

THOMAS, Wesley (F)   **265 67**
H: 5 10   W: 11 00   b.Barking 23-1-87

2008–09	Dagenham & R	1	0	
2009–10	Dagenham & R	23	3	**28 3**
2010–11	Cheltenham T	41	18	**41 18**
2011–12	Crawley T	6	1	**6 1**
2011–12	Bournemouth	36	11	
2012–13	Bournemouth	6	0	
2012–13	*Portsmouth*	6	3	**6 3**
2012–13	*Blackpool*	9	3	**9 3**
2012–13	*Birmingham C*	11	3	

2013–14	Bournemouth	10	0	**52 11**
2013–14	*Rotherham U*	13	5	**13 5**
2014–15	Birmingham C	33	4	
2015–16	Birmingham C	0	0	**44 7**
2015–16	*Swindon T*	6	2	**6 2**
2015–16	*Bradford C*	0	1	**10 1**
2016–17	Oxford U	13	3	
2017–18	Oxford U	37	10	**50 13**

TIENDALLI, Dwight (D)   **201 5**
H: 5 9   W: 11 08   b.Surinam 21-10-85
Internationals: Netherlands U21, Full caps.

2004–05	FC Utrecht	10	1	
2005–06	FC Utrecht	29	2	
2006–07	FC Utrecht	1	0	**40 3**
2006–07	Feyenoord	13	0	
2007–08	*S Rotterdam*	13	0	**13 0**
2008–09	Feyenoord	22	0	**35 0**
2009–10	FC Twente	26	1	
2010–11	FC Twente	18	0	
2011–12	FC Twente	20	0	**71 1**
2012–13	Swansea C	14	1	
2013–14	Swansea C	10	0	
2014–15	Swansea C	3	0	
2014–15	*Middlesbrough*	2	0	**2 0**
2015–16	Swansea C	0	0	**27 1**
2017–18	Oxford U	13	0	**13 0**

VAN KESSEL, Gino (F)   **127 40**
b. 9-3-93
Internationals: Curacao Full caps.

2012–13	Ajax	0	0	
2012–13	Almere C	10	1	**10 1**
2013–14	Ajax	0	0	
2013–14	Trencin	25	10	
2014–15	Arles	14	2	**14 2**
2014–15	Trencin	14	6	
2015–16	Trencin	33	17	**72 33**
2016–17	Slavia Prague	7	2	
2016–17	*Lechia Gdansk*	3	0	**3 0**
2016–17	Slavia Prague	0	0	**7 2**

On loan from Slavia Prague.

2017–18	Oxford U	21	2	**21 2**

WILLIAMSON, Mike (D)   **352 14**
H: 6 4   W: 13 03   b.Stoke 8-11-83

2001–02	Torquay U	3	0	
2001–02	Southampton	0	0	
2002–03	Southampton	0	0	
2003–04	Southampton	0	0	
2003–04	*Torquay U*	11	0	**14 0**
2003–04	*Doncaster R*	0	0	
2004–05	Southampton	0	0	
2004–05	Wycombe W	37	2	
2005–06	Wycombe W	39	5	
2006–07	Wycombe W	33	1	
2007–08	Wycombe W	12	0	
2008–09	Wycombe W	22	3	**143 11**
2008–09	Watford	17	1	
2009–10	Watford	4	1	**21 2**
2009–10	Portsmouth	0	0	
2009–10	Newcastle U	16	0	
2010–11	Newcastle U	29	0	
2011–12	Newcastle U	22	0	
2012–13	Newcastle U	19	0	
2013–14	Newcastle U	33	0	
2014–15	Newcastle U	31	1	
2015–16	Newcastle U	0	0	**150 1**
2015–16	Wolverhampton W	5	0	
2016–17	Wolverhampton W	5	0	**10 0**
2017–18	Oxford U	14	0	**14 0**

Scholars
Baker, Nathan Luke; Berry-Hargreaves, Matthew Owen; Bryan, Graham John; Carr, Daniel Joshua; Chilcott, Ben William; Clayton, Niall Liam; Cowan, James Scott; Crooks, Ryan; Harris, Max James; Heap, Aaron John Harrison; Hopkins, Albert Oscar; Lofthouse, Kyran Aiden; Mannings, Rex Arnold; McCreadie, Aaron; McDonnell, Harry Robin; Niblett, Freddie; Noel-Williams, Dejon George Franklin.

PETERBOROUGH U (64)

ANDERSON, Jermaine (M)   **76 5**
b. 16-5-96
Internationals: England U18, U20.

2012–13	Peterborough U	1	0	
2013–14	Peterborough U	13	0	
2014–15	Peterborough U	24	1	
2015–16	Peterborough U	14	4	
2016–17	Peterborough U	4	0	
2017–18	Peterborough U	17	0	**76 5**

BALDWIN, Jack (D)   **177 8**
H: 6 1   W: 11 00   b.Barking 30-6-93

2011–12	Hartlepool U	17	0	
2012–13	Hartlepool U	32	2	
2013–14	Hartlepool U	28	2	**77 4**
2013–14	Peterborough U	11	0	
2014–15	Peterborough U	11	0	
2015–16	Peterborough U	18	1	
2016–17	Peterborough U	27	1	
2017–18	Peterborough U	33	2	**100 4**

BORG, Andrea (M)   **3 0**
b. 12-11-99
Internationals: Malta U19.

2016–17	Peterborough U	3	0	
2017–18	Peterborough U	0	0	**3 0**

BURROWS, Harrison (M)   **0 0**

2017–18	Peterborough U	0	0	

CARTWRIGHT, Samuel (D)   **0 0**

2017–18	Peterborough U	0	0	

CHETTLE, Callum (M)   **18 0**
b. 28-8-96
Internationals: England C.
From Ilkeston, Nuneaton T.

2015–16	Peterborough U	5	0	
2016–17	Peterborough U	11	0	
2017–18	Peterborough U	2	0	**18 0**

COOPER, George (M)   **135 16**
H: 5 9   W: 11 05   b.Warrington 2-11-96

2014–15	Crewe Alex	22	3	
2015–16	Crewe Alex	27	1	
2016–17	Crewe Alex	46	9	
2017–18	Crewe Alex	27	1	**122 14**
2017–18	Peterborough U	13	2	**13 2**

DA SILVA LOPES, Leonardo (M)   **87 2**
H: 5 6   W: 9 08   b.Lisbon 30-11-98
Internationals: Portugal U20.

2014–15	Peterborough U	2	0	
2015–16	Peterborough U	8	0	
2016–17	Peterborough U	38	2	
2017–18	Peterborough U	39	0	**87 2**

DOUGHTY, Michael (M)   **151 10**
H: 6 1   W: 12 10   b.Westminster 20-11-92
Internationals: Wales U19, U21.

2010–11	QPR	0	0	
2011–12	QPR	0	0	
2011–12	*Crawley T*	16	0	**16 0**
2011–12	*Aldershot T*	5	0	**5 0**
2012–13	QPR	0	0	
2012–13	*St Johnstone*	5	0	**5 0**
2013–14	QPR	0	0	
2013–14	*Stevenage*	36	2	**36 2**
2014–15	QPR	3	0	
2014–15	*Gillingham*	9	0	**9 0**
2015–16	QPR	5	0	
2015–16	Swindon T	20	5	
2016–17	QPR	4	0	**12 0**
2016–17	Swindon T	14	2	**34 7**
2017–18	Peterborough U	34	1	**34 1**

EDWARDS, Gwion (M)   **163 25**
H: 5 9   W: 12 00   b.Carmarthen 1-3-93
Internationals: Wales U19, U21.

2011–12	Swansea C	0	0	
2012–13	Swansea C	0	0	
2012–13	*St Johnstone*	6	0	
2013–14	Swansea C	0	0	
2013–14	*St Johnstone*	13	0	**19 0**
2013–14	*Crawley T*	6	2	
2014–15	Crawley T	37	4	
2015–16	Crawley T	42	8	**85 14**
2016–17	Peterborough U	33	7	
2017–18	Peterborough U	26	4	**59 11**

FORRESTER, Chris (M)   **107 6**
b.Dublin 17-12-92
Internationals: Republic of Ireland U21.
From Bohemians, St Patrick's Ath.

2015–16	Peterborough U	35	2	
2016–17	Peterborough U	43	4	
2017–18	Peterborough U	29	0	**107 6**

FREESTONE, Lewis (D)   **8 0**
b.King's Lynn 26-10-99

2016–17	Peterborough U	4	0	
2017–18	Peterborough U	4	0	**8 0**

GRANT, Anthony (M)   **435 15**
H: 5 10   W: 11 01   b.Lambeth 4-6-87
Internationals: England U16, U17, U19.

2004–05	Chelsea	0	0	
2005–06	Chelsea	0	0	
2005–06	*Oldham Ath*	2	0	**2 0**
2006–07	Chelsea	0	0	

Season	Club	A	G	A	G
2006–07	Wycombe W	40	0	40	0
2007–08	Chelsea	0	0	1	0
2007–08	Luton T	4	0	4	0
2007–08	Southend U	10	0		
2008–09	Southend U	35	1		
2009–10	Southend U	38	0		
2010–11	Southend U	43	8		
2011–12	Southend U	33	1	159	10
2012–13	Stevenage	41	0	41	0
2013–14	Crewe Alex	38	2		
2014–15	Crewe Alex	43	2	81	4
2015–16	Port Vale	38	1		
2016–17	Port Vale	20	0	58	1
2016–17	Peterborough U	11	0		
2017–18	Peterborough U	38	0	49	0

HUGHES, Andrew (D)   149   6
b.Cardiff 5-6-92
Internationals: Wales U18, U23.

Season	Club	A	G	A	G
2013–14	Newport Co	26	2		
2014–15	Newport Co	16	1		
2015–16	Newport Co	25	0	67	3
2016–17	Peterborough U	39	1		
2017–18	Peterborough U	43	2	82	3

INMAN, Bradden (M)   165   24
H: 5 9   W: 11 03   b.Adelaide 10-12-91
Internationals: Scotland U19, U21.

Season	Club	A	G	A	G
2009–10	Newcastle U	0	0		
2010–11	Newcastle U	0	0		
2011–12	Newcastle U	0	0		
2012–13	Newcastle U	0	0		
2012–13	Crewe Alex	21	5		
2013–14	Newcastle U	0	0		
2013–14	Crewe Alex	36	4		
2014–15	Crewe Alex	21	1		
2015–16	Crewe Alex	39	10	117	20
2016–17	Peterborough U	11	0		
2017–18	Peterborough U	0	0	11	0
2017–18	Rochdale	37	4	37	- 4

KANU, Idris (F)   18   0
b. 5-12-99
From Aldershot T.

Season	Club	A	G	A	G
2017–18	Peterborough U	18	0	18	0

LLOYD, Danny (F)   31   8
b.3-12-91
From Stockport Co.

Season	Club	A	G	A	G
2017–18	Peterborough U	31	8	31	8

MADDISON, Marcus (M)   150   35
H: 5 9   W: 11 03   b.Sedgefield 26-9-93
Internationals: England U20.

Season	Club	A	G	A	G
2014–15	Peterborough U	29	7		
2015–16	Peterborough U	39	11		
2016–17	Peterborough U	41	9		
2017–18	Peterborough U	41	8	150	35

MARRIOTT, Jack (F)   135   50
H: 5 8   W: 11 03   b.Beverley 9-9-94

Season	Club	A	G	A	G
2012–13	Ipswich T	1	0		
2013–14	Ipswich T	1	0		
2013–14	Gillingham	1	0	1	0
2014–15	Ipswich T	0	0	2	0
2014–15	Carlisle U	4	0	4	0
2014–15	Colchester U	5	1	5	1
2015–16	Luton T	40	14		
2016–17	Luton T	39	8	79	22
2017–18	Peterborough U	44	27	44	27

MILLER, Ricky (F)   30   2
b. 13-3-89

Season	Club	A	G	A	G
2014–15	Luton T	12	1	12	1

From Dover Ath.

Season	Club	A	G	A	G
2017–18	Peterborough U	10	0	10	0
2017–18	Mansfield T	8	1	8	1

MORIAS, Junior (F)   73   10
H: 5 8   W: 10 10   b.Kingston 4-7-95

Season	Club	A	G	A	G
2012–13	Wycombe W	19	0		
2013–14	Wycombe W	9	0		
2014–15	Wycombe W	0	0	28	0

From Boreham Wood, Whitehawk, St Albans C.

Season	Club	A	G	A	G
2016–17	Peterborough U	20	4		
2017–18	Peterborough U	25	6	45	10

O'MALLEY, Conor (G)   9   0
H: 6 3   W: 13 01   b. 1-8-94
From St Patrick's Ath.

Season	Club	A	G	A	G
2017–18	Peterborough U	9	0	9	0

PENFOLD, Morgan (F)   0   0

Season	Club	A	G	A	G
2016–17	Peterborough U	0	0		
2017–18	Peterborough U	0	0		

PENNY, Alex (D)   7   0
H: 6 1   W: 11 07   b. 16-2-97
Internationals: Wales U16.
From Bedworth U, Stourbridge, Hinckley, Nuneaton T.

Season	Club	A	G	A	G
2017–18	Peterborough U	7	0	7	0

SHEPHARD, Liam (D)   88   1
H: 5 10   W: 10 08   b.Rhondda 22-11-94
Internationals: Wales U21.

Season	Club	A	G	A	G
2013–14	Swansea C	0	0		
2014–15	Swansea C	0	0		
2014–15	Yeovil T	20	0		
2015–16	Swansea C	0	0		
2015–16	Yeovil T	6	0		
2016–17	Swansea C	0	0		
2016–17	Yeovil T	38	1	64	1
2017–18	Peterborough U	24	0	24	0

TAFAZOLLI, Ryan (D)   168   12
H: 6 5   W: 12 03   b.Sutton 28-9-91

Season	Club	A	G	A	G
2010–11	Southampton	0	0		

From Salisbury, Cambridge C, Carshalton Ath

Season	Club	A	G	A	G
2013–14	Mansfield T	24	2		
2014–15	Mansfield T	36	1		
2015–16	Mansfield T	44	5	104	8
2016–17	Peterborough U	31	3		
2017–18	Peterborough U	33	1	64	4

TAYLOR, Steven (D)   279   18
H: 6 2   W: 13 01   b.Greenwich 23-1-86
Internationals: England U16, U17, U20, U21, B.

Season	Club	A	G	A	G
2002–03	Newcastle U	0	0		
2003–04	Newcastle U	1	0		
2003–04	Wycombe W	6	0	6	0
2004–05	Newcastle U	13	0		
2005–06	Newcastle U	12	0		
2006–07	Newcastle U	27	2		
2007–08	Newcastle U	31	1		
2008–09	Newcastle U	27	4		
2009–10	Newcastle U	21	1		
2010–11	Newcastle U	14	3		
2011–12	Newcastle U	14	0		
2012–13	Newcastle U	25	0		
2013–14	Newcastle U	10	1		
2014–15	Newcastle U	10	1		
2015–16	Newcastle U	10	0	215	13
2016	Portland Timbers	11	2	11	2
2016–17	Ipswich T	3	0	3	0
2017–18	Peterborough U	44	3	44	3

TIBBETTS, Josh (G)   0   0
b. 5-7-98
From Birmingham C.

Season	Club	A	G	A	G
2017–18	Peterborough U	0	0		

TYLER, Mark (G)   488   0
H: 6 0   W: 12 09   b.Norwich 2-4-77
Internationals: England U18.

Season	Club	A	G	A	G
1994–95	Peterborough U	5	0		
1995–96	Peterborough U	0	0		
1996–97	Peterborough U	3	0		
1997–98	Peterborough U	46	0		
1998–99	Peterborough U	27	0		
1999–2000	Peterborough U	32	0		
2000–01	Peterborough U	40	0		
2001–02	Peterborough U	44	0		
2002–03	Peterborough U	29	0		
2003–04	Peterborough U	43	0		
2004–05	Peterborough U	46	0		
2005–06	Peterborough U	40	0		
2006–07	Peterborough U	41	0		
2007–08	Peterborough U	17	0		
2008–09	Peterborough U	0	0		
2008–09	Bury	11	0	11	0
2014–15	Luton T	31	0		
2015–16	Luton T	27	0	58	0
2015–16	Peterborough U	3	0		
2016–17	Peterborough U	3	0		
2017–18	Peterborough U	0	0	419	0

WARD, Joe (M)   17   0
b. 9-4-95
Internationals: England C.

Season	Club	A	G	A	G
2015–16	Brighton & HA	0	0		
2016–17	Brighton & HA	0	0		
2017–18	Peterborough U	17	0	17	0

Players retained or with offer of contract
Nabi, Adil; Stevens, Matthew.

Scholars
Barker, Kyle Lennon; Brookes, Harry; Douglas, Kasey Jamal; Douglas, Rio Davon; Elsom, Lewis John; Fieldhouse, Ewan Jack; Fosu, Mikkel; Garner, Frazer James; Gurney, Jack Ethan; Hart, Aaron Richard; Javed-Akhtar, Mohammed Hamza; Maddison, Layton Luca Robert; Shackleton, Oliver James; Strachan, Luke Robert.

Non-contract
Tyler, Mark Richard.

PLYMOUTH ARG (65)

AINSWORTH, Lionel (F)   253   35
H: 5 9   W: 9 10   b.Nottingham 1-10-87
Internationals: England U16, U17, U18, U19.

Season	Club	A	G	A	G
2005–06	Derby Co	2	0		
2006–07	Derby Co	0	0		
2006–07	Bournemouth	7	0	2	0
2006–07	Wycombe W	7	0	7	0
2007–08	Hereford U	15	4		
2007–08	Watford	8	0		
2008–09	Watford	7	0	15	0
2008–09	Hereford U	7	3	22	7
2008–09	Huddersfield T	14	0		
2009–10	Huddersfield T	11	0		
2009–10	Brentford	9	0	9	0
2010–11	Shrewsbury T	33	9		
2010–11	Huddersfield T	0	0	25	0
2011–12	Shrewsbury T	21	2	54	11
2011–12	Burton Alb	7	0	7	0
2012–13	Rotherham U	16	0		
2012–13	Aldershot T	7	0	7	0
2013–14	Rotherham U	0	0	16	0
2013–14	Motherwell	29	11		
2014–15	Motherwell	34	6	63	17
2017–18	Plymouth Arg	19	0	19	0

BATTLE, Alex (F)   1   0
b. 23-1-99

Season	Club	A	G	A	G
2017–18	Plymouth Arg	1	0	1	0

BLISSETT, Nathan (F)   24   3
H: 6 0   W: 12 04   b.West Bromwich 29-6-90
From Kidderminster H.

Season	Club	A	G	A	G
2015–16	Bristol R	2	0	2	0
2016–17	Plymouth Arg	9	2		
2017–18	Plymouth Arg	13	1	22	3

BRADLEY, Sonny (D)   247   16
H: 6 0   W: 11 05   b.Hedon 14-6-92

Season	Club	A	G	A	G
2011–12	Hull C	2	0		
2011–12	Aldershot T	14	0		
2012–13	Hull C	0	0	2	0
2012–13	Aldershot T	42	1	56	1
2013–14	Portsmouth	33	2	33	2
2014–15	Crawley T	26	1		
2015–16	Crawley T	46	1	72	2
2016–17	Plymouth Arg	44	7		
2017–18	Plymouth Arg	40	4	84	11

CAREY, Graham (M)   289   54
H: 6 0   W: 10 03   b.Dublin 20-5-89
Internationals: Republic of Ireland U21.

Season	Club	A	G	A	G
2008–09	Celtic	0	0		
2009	Bohemians	15	2	15	2
2009–10	Celtic	0	0		
2009–10	St Mirren	15	3		
2010–11	Celtic	0	0		
2010–11	Huddersfield T	19	2	19	2
2011–12	St Mirren	29	2		
2012–13	St Mirren	26	1	70	6
2013–14	Ross Co	36	3		
2014–15	Ross Co	22	2	58	5
2015–16	Plymouth Arg	39	11		
2016–17	Plymouth Arg	46	14		
2017–18	Plymouth Arg	42	14	127	39

CHILDS, Max (G)   0   0

Season	Club	A	G	A	G
2017–18	Plymouth Arg	0	0		

CHURCH, Simon (F)   248   42
H: 6 0   W: 13 04   b.Amersham 10-12-88
Internationals: Wales U21, Full caps.

Season	Club	A	G	A	G
2007–08	Reading	0	0		
2007–08	Crewe Alex	12	1	12	1
2007–08	Yeovil T	6	0	6	0
2008–09	Reading	0	0		
2008–09	Wycombe W	9	0	9	0
2008–09	Leyton Orient	13	5	13	5
2009–10	Reading	36	10		
2010–11	Reading	37	5		
2011–12	Reading	31	7		
2012–13	Reading	0	0	104	22
2012–13	Huddersfield T	7	1	7	1
2013–14	Charlton Ath	38	3		
2014–15	Charlton Ath	17	2	55	5
2015–16	Milton Keynes D	19	2	19	2
2015–16	Aberdeen	13	6	13	6
2016–17	Roda JC	4	0	4	0
2017–18	Scunthorpe U	4	0	4	0
2017–18	Plymouth Arg	2	0	2	0

CIFTCI, Nadir (F) 146 37
H: 5 11 W: 12 02 b.Karakocan 12-2-92
Internationals: Netherlands U17. Turkey U19.
2009–10	Portsmouth	0	0		
2010–11	Portsmouth	19	1	19	1
2011–12	Kayserispor	11	0	11	0
2012–13	NAC Breda	7	0	7	0
2013–14	Dundee U	32	11		
2014–15	Dundee U	36	14	68	25
2015–16	Celtic	11	4		
2015–16	Celtic	11	4		
2016–17	Celtic	1	0		
2017–18	Celtic	0	0	23	8
On loan from Celtic.
2017–18	Plymouth Arg	7	0	7	0
2017–18	*Motherwell*	11	3	11	3

COOPER, Michael (G) 1 0
b. 8-10-99
| 2017–18 | Plymouth Arg | 1 | 0 | 1 | 0 |

EDWARDS, Ryan (D) 185 4
b.Liverpool 7-10-93
2011–12	Blackburn R	0	0		
2012–13	Rochdale	26	0	26	0
2012–13	Blackburn R	0	0		
2012–13	*Fleetwood T*	9	0	9	0
2013–14	Blackburn R	0	0		
2013–14	*Chesterfield*	5	0	5	0
2013–14	*Tranmere R*	0	0		
2013–14	Morecambe	9	0		
2014–15	Morecambe	31	0		
2015–16	Morecambe	37	0		
2016–17	Morecambe	43	1	120	1
2017–18	Plymouth Arg	25	3	25	3

FLETCHER, Alex (F) 14 1
H: 5 10 W: 10 10 b. 9-2-99
| 2016–17 | Plymouth Arg | 0 | 0 | | |
| 2017–18 | Plymouth Arg | 14 | 1 | 14 | 1 |

FOX, David (M) 339 16
H: 5 9 W: 11 08 b.Leek 13-12-83
Internationals: England U16, U17, U19, U20.
2000–01	Manchester U	0	0		
2001–02	Manchester U	0	0		
2002–03	Manchester U	0	0		
2003–04	Manchester U	0	0		
2004–05	Manchester U	0	0		
2004–05	*Shrewsbury T*	4	1	4	1
2005–06	Manchester U	0	0		
2005–06	Blackpool	7	1		
2006–07	Blackpool	37	4		
2007–08	Blackpool	28	1		
2008–09	Blackpool	22	0	94	6
2009–10	Colchester U	18	3		
2010–11	Norwich C	32	1		
2011–12	Norwich C	28	0		
2012–13	Norwich C	2	0		
2013–14	Norwich C	0	0	62	1
2013–14	*Barnsley*	7	0	7	0
2014–15	Colchester U	30	2	48	5
2015–16	Crewe Alex	39	2	39	2
2016–17	Plymouth Arg	40	0		
2017–18	Plymouth Arg	45	1	85	1

GRANT, Joel (F) 308 50
H: 6 0 W: 12 01 b.Acton 26-8-87
Internationals: Jamaica U20. Full caps.
| 2005–06 | Watford | 7 | 0 | | |
| 2006–07 | Watford | 0 | 0 | 7 | 0 |
From Aldershot T.
2008–09	Crewe Alex	28	2		
2009–10	Crewe Alex	43	9		
2010–11	Crewe Alex	25	5	96	16
2011–12	Wycombe W	30	4		
2012–13	Wycombe W	41	10	71	14
2013–14	Yeovil T	34	3		
2014–15	Yeovil T	21	3	55	6
2015–16	Exeter C	26	4		
2016–17	Exeter C	20	4	46	8
2017–18	Plymouth Arg	33	6	33	6

LAMEIRAS, Ruben (M) 101 9
H: 5 9 W: 11 00 b.Lisbon 22-12-94
2014–15	Tottenham H	0	0		
2015	*Atvidabergs*	11	0	11	0
2015–16	Coventry C	29	2		
2016–17	Coventry C	27	1	56	3
2017–18	Plymouth Arg	34	6	34	6

LAW, Ryan (D) 0 0
| 2017–18 | Plymouth Arg | 0 | 0 | | |

LETHEREN, Kyle (G) 73 0
H: 6 2 W: 13 00 b.Swansea 26-12-87
Internationals: Wales U21.
| 2010–11 | Kilmarnock | 0 | 0 | | |
| 2011–12 | Kilmarnock | 2 | 0 | | |

2012–13	Kilmarnock	9	0	11	0
2013–14	Dundee	35	0		
2014–15	Dundee	15	0	50	0
2015–16	Blackpool	5	0		
2016–17	Blackpool	0	0	5	0
From York C.
2017–18	Plymouth Arg	7	0	7	0

LOLOS, Klaidi (F) 0 0
| 2017–18 | Plymouth Arg | 0 | 0 | | |

McCORMICK, Luke (G) 183 0
H: 6 0 W: 13 12 b.Coventry 15-8-83
2012–13	Oxford U	15	0	15	0
2013–14	Plymouth Arg	27	0		
2014–15	Plymouth Arg	46	0		
2015–16	Plymouth Arg	40	0		
2016–17	Plymouth Arg	46	0		
2017–18	Plymouth Arg	9	0	168	0

MILLER, Gary (D) 302 4
H: 6 1 W: 11 03 b.Glasgow 15-4-87
2005–06	Livingston	4	0		
2006–07	Livingston	13	0		
2006–07	*Ayr U*	15	1	15	1
2007–08	Livingston	20	0		
2007–08	Ross Co	20	0		
2008–09	Livingston	23	0	40	0
2009–10	Ross Co	32	0		
2010–11	Ross Co	31	0		
2011–12	Ross Co	36	1	119	1
2012–13	St Johnstone	17	0		
2013–14	St Johnstone	25	1		
2014–15	St Johnstone	19	0	61	1
2015–16	Partick Thistle	21	1	21	1
2016–17	Plymouth Arg	31	0		
2017–18	Plymouth Arg	15	0	46	0

NESS, Jamie (M) 129 7
H: 6 2 W: 10 13 b.Irvine 2-3-91
Internationals: Scotland U17, U19, U21.
2010–11	Rangers	11	0		
2011–12	Rangers	5	1	16	1
2012–13	Stoke C	0	0		
2013–14	Stoke C	0	0		
2013–14	*Leyton Orient*	13	1	13	1
2014–15	Stoke C	0	0		
2014–15	*Crewe Alex*	34	2	34	2
2015–16	Scunthorpe U	27	0		
2016–17	Scunthorpe U	12	0	39	0
2017–18	Plymouth Arg	27	3	27	3

PATON, Paul (M) 361 13
H: 5 11 W: 11 10 b.Paisley 18-4-87
Internationals: Northern Ireland Full caps.
2005–06	Queen's Park	23	0		
2006–07	Queen's Park	34	1		
2007–08	Queen's Park	34	0	91	1
2008–09	Partick Thistle	35	3		
2009–10	Partick Thistle	29	1		
2010–11	Partick Thistle	26	1		
2011–12	Partick Thistle	33	0		
2012–13	Partick Thistle	24	0	147	5
2013–14	Dundee U	37	2		
2014–15	Dundee U	24	2		
2015–16	Dundee U	14	2	75	6
2016–17	St Johnstone	28	1		
2017–18	St Johnstone	17	0	45	1
2017–18	Plymouth Arg	3	0	3	0

ROONEY, Daniel (M) 0 0
b. 30-11-98
Internationals: Northern Ireland U17, U19.
| 2017–18 | Plymouth Arg | 0 | 0 | | |

SANGSTER, Cameron (M) 2 0
H: 6 1 W: 11 11 b. 29-12-99
| 2017–18 | Plymouth Arg | 2 | 0 | 2 | 0 |

SARCEVIC, Antoni (M) 189 24
H: 5 10 W: 11 00 b.Manchester 13-3-92
Internationals: England C.
2009–10	Crewe Alex	0	0		
2010–11	Crewe Alex	6	1		
2011–12	Crewe Alex	6	0	12	1
2013–14	Fleetwood T	42	13		
2014–15	Fleetwood T	37	2		
2015–16	Fleetwood T	39	3	118	18
2016–17	*Shrewsbury T*	12	0	12	0
2016–17	Plymouth Arg	17	2		
2017–18	Plymouth Arg	30	3	47	5

SAWYER, Gary (D) 337 7
H: 6 0 W: 11 08 b.Bideford 5-7-85
2004–05	Plymouth Arg	0	0		
2005–06	Plymouth Arg	0	0		
2006–07	Plymouth Arg	22	0		
2007–08	Plymouth Arg	31	1		
2008–09	Plymouth Arg	13	3		
2009–10	Plymouth Arg	29	1		

2009–10	*Bristol C*	2	0	2	0
2010–11	Bristol R	37	0		
2011–12	Bristol R	24	0	61	0
2012–13	Leyton Orient	34	1		
2013–14	Leyton Orient	22	0		
2014–15	Leyton Orient	13	0	69	1
2015–16	Plymouth Arg	43	0		
2016–17	Plymouth Arg	21	0		
2017–18	Plymouth Arg	46	1	205	6

SOKOLIK, Jakub (D) 81 2
H: 5 6 W: 12 02 b.Ostrava 28-8-93
Internationals: Czech Republic U16, U17, U18.
2010–11	Liverpool	0	0		
2011–12	Liverpool	0	0		
2012–13	Liverpool	0	0		
2013–14	Liverpool	0	0		
2013–14	Southend U	10	0		
2014–15	Yeovil T	11	0		
2014–15	Southend U	1	0		
2015–16	Yeovil T	34	1	45	1
2016–17	Southend U	5	0	16	0
2016–17	Plymouth Arg	18	1		
2017–18	Plymouth Arg	2	0	20	1

SONGO'O, Yann (D) 114 6
H: 6 0 W: 12 00 b.Yaounde 17-11-91
Internationals: France U16. Cameroon U20.
2011–12	Sabadell	6	0	6	0
2013	Sporting Kansas C	0	0		
2013	*Orlando C*	12	1	12	1
2013–14	Blackburn R	0	0		
2013–14	*Ross Co*	17	3	17	3
2014–15	Blackburn R	0	0		
2016–17	Plymouth Arg	46	2		
2017–18	Plymouth Arg	33	0	79	2

TAYLOR, Ryan (F) 315 51
H: 6 2 W: 10 10 b.Rotherham 4-5-88
2005–06	Rotherham U	1	0		
2006–07	Rotherham U	10	0		
2007–08	Rotherham U	35	6		
2008–09	Rotherham U	33	4		
2009–10	Rotherham U	19	0		
2009–10	*Exeter C*	7	0	7	0
2010–11	Rotherham U	34	11	132	21
2011–12	Bristol C	7	1		
2012–13	Bristol C	25	1		
2013–14	Bristol C	7	0	39	2
2013–14	Portsmouth	18	6		
2014–15	Portsmouth	37	9	55	15
2015–16	Oxford U	22	3		
2016–17	Oxford U	21	1	43	4
2016–17	Plymouth Arg	18	4		
2017–18	Plymouth Arg	21	5	39	9

TAYLOR-SINCLAIR, Aaron (D) 231 11
H: 6 1 W: 11 07 b.Aberdeen 8-4-91
2008–09	Montrose	1	0		
2009–10	Montrose	30	2		
2010–11	Montrose	35	3	66	5
2011–12	Partick Thistle	30	1		
2012–13	Partick Thistle	28	1		
2013–14	Partick Thistle	36	2	94	4
2014–15	Wigan Ath	0	0		
2015–16	Doncaster R	43	2		
2016–17	Doncaster R	4	0	47	2
2017–18	Plymouth Arg	24	0	24	0

TE LOEKE, Robbert (G) 96 0
H: 6 4 W: 13 10 b.Arnhem 1-12-88
2007–08	Werder Bremen	0	0		
2008–09	Cambur	0	0		
2009–10	Cambur	0	0		
2010–11	Cambur	0	0		
2011–12	Cambur	17	0	17	0
2012–13	Veendam	0	0		
2013–14	Dordrecht	4	0		
2014–15	Dordrecht	3	0		
2015–16	Dordrecht	34	0	41	0
2016–17	Achilles '29	38	0	38	0
2017–18	Plymouth Arg	0	0		

THRELKELD, Oscar (D) 94 3
H: 6 0 W: 12 04 b.Bolton 15-12-94
2013–14	Bolton W	2	0		
2014–15	Bolton W	4	0		
2015–16	Bolton W	3	0	9	0
2015–16	Plymouth Arg	25	1		
2016–17	Plymouth Arg	36	2		
2017–18	Plymouth Arg	24	0	85	3

WYLDE, Gregg (M) 189 18
H: 5 9 W: 11 04 b.Kirkintilloch 23-3-91
Internationals: Scotland U17, U19, U21.
2009–10	Rangers	4	0		
2010–11	Rangers	30	0		
2011–12	Rangers	42	4	76	4

2012–13	Bolton W	0	0
2012–13	*Bury*	4	0	4	0
2013–14	Aberdeen	8	1	8	1
2013–14	St Mirren	17	2	17	2
2015–16	Plymouth Arg	43	7
2016–17	Millwall	5	0	5	0
2016–17	*Northampton T*	12	1	12	1
2017–18	Plymouth Arg	9	1	52	8
2017–18	*Morecambe*	15	2	15	2

Scholars
Burn, Andrew; Childs, Max Timothy; Craske, Billy Frederick; Crawford, Elliott Ian; Downing, Harry Edward; Garside, Rio Shawn Terry; Goulty, Aaron Richard; Hodges, Harry Kenneth; Jephcott, Luke Owen; Law, Ryan James; Lolos, Klaidi; Peck, Michael Dennis; Purrington, Tom; Randell, Adam Fletcher; Sangster, Cameron; Ward, Matthew Lawrence.

PORT VALE (66)

ANGUS, Dior (F)   **3**   **1**
H: 6 0   W: 12 00   b. 18-1-94
From Solihull Moors, Kidderminster H, Daventry T, Stratford T, Redditch U.

2017–18	Port Vale	3	1	3	1

BARNETT, Tyrone (F)   **279**   **59**
H: 6 3   W: 13 05   b.Stevenage 28-10-85

2010–11	Macclesfield T	45	13	45	13
2011–12	Crawley T	26	14	26	14
2011–12	Peterborough U	13	4
2012–13	Peterborough U	18	1
2012–13	*Ipswich T*	3	0	3	0
2013–14	Peterborough U	21	6
2013–14	*Bristol C*	17	1	17	1
2014–15	Peterborough U	4	0	56	11
2014–15	*Oxford U*	12	4	12	4
2014–15	Shrewsbury T	18	4
2015–16	Shrewsbury T	21	4	39	8
2015–16	*Southend U*	20	5	20	5
2016–17	AFC Wimbledon	36	2	36	2
2017–18	Port Vale	25	1	25	1

BENNS, Harry (M)   **1**   **0**
b. 13-1-00

2017–18	Port Vale	1	0	1	0

BOOT, Ryan (G)   **23**   **0**
H: 6 1   W: 11 03   b.Rocester 9-11-94

2012–13	Port Vale	0	0
2013–14	Port Vale	0	0
2014–15	Port Vale	0	0
2015–16	Port Vale	0	0
2016–17	Port Vale	1	0
2017–18	Port Vale	22	0	23	0

CALVELEY, Mike (M)   **2**   **0**
H: 5 10   W: 10 10   b. 22-6-99

2017–18	Port Vale	2	0	2	0

DAVIS, Joe (D)   **68**   **0**
H: 6 0   W: 11 07   b.Burnley 10-11-93

2010–11	Port Vale	1	0
2011–12	Port Vale	8	0
2012–13	Port Vale	7	0
2013–14	Port Vale	11	0
2014–15	Leicester C	0	0
2015–16	Leicester C	0	0
2015–16	Fleetwood T	19	0
2016–17	*Fleetwood T*	4	0	23	0
2017–18	Port Vale	18	0	45	0

DE FREITAS, Anthony (M)   **35**   **0**
b. 10-5-94
Internationals: France U20.
From Monaco.

2016–17	Port Vale	24	0
2017–18	Port Vale	11	0	35	0

FORRESTER, Anton (F)   **65**   **10**
H: 6 0   W: 12 00   b.Liverpool 11-2-94

2010–11	Everton	0	0
2011–12	Everton	0	0
2012–13	Blackburn R	0	0
2013–14	Blackburn R	0	0
2013–14	*Bury*	28	6	28	6
2014–15	Blackburn R	0	0
2015–16	Blackburn R	0	0
2015–16	*Morecambe*	3	0	3	0
2016–17	Port Vale	21	2
2017–18	Port Vale	13	2	34	4

GIBBONS, James (D)   **30**   **0**
H: 5 9   W: 9 11   b. 16-3-98

2016–17	Port Vale	0	0
2017–18	Port Vale	30	0	30	0

HANNANT, Luke (M)   **18**   **1**
b. 4-11-93
From Dereham T, Team Northumbria, Gateshead.

2017–18	Port Vale	18	1	18	1

HORNBY, Sam (G)   **11**   **0**
b. 14-2-95
From Brackley T, Kidderminster H.

2015–16	Burton Alb	0	0
2017–18	Port Vale	11	0	11	0

HOWE, Callum (D)   **3**   **0**
H: 6 0   W: 11 07   b.Doncaster 9-4-94

2012–13	Scunthorpe U	0	0
2013–14	Scunthorpe U	0	0
2014–15	Scunthorpe U	0	0
2017–18	Lincoln C	0	0
2017–18	Port Vale	3	0	3	0

KAY, Antony (D)   **568**   **47**
H: 5 11   W: 11 08   b.Barnsley 21-10-82
Internationals: England U18.

1999–2000	Barnsley	0	0
2000–01	Barnsley	7	0
2001–02	Barnsley	1	0
2002–03	Barnsley	16	0
2003–04	Barnsley	43	3
2004–05	Barnsley	39	6
2005–06	Barnsley	36	1
2006–07	Barnsley	32	1	174	11
2007–08	Tranmere R	38	6
2008–09	Tranmere R	44	11	82	17
2009–10	Huddersfield T	40	6
2010–11	Huddersfield T	27	3
2011–12	Huddersfield T	28	1
2012–13	Huddersfield T	0	0	95	10
2012–13	Milton Keynes D	33	1
2013–14	Milton Keynes D	30	2
2014–15	Milton Keynes D	45	1
2015–16	Milton Keynes D	34	2	142	6
2016–17	*Bury*	42	0	42	0
2017–18	Port Vale	33	3	33	3

KELLY, Graham (D)   **1**   **0**
b. 16-10-97
Internationals: Republic of Ireland U18, U19.

2015–16	Sheffield U	1	0
2016–17	Sheffield U	0	0	1	0
2017–18	Port Vale	0	0

LAINTON, Robert (G)   **59**   **0**
H: 6 2   W: 12 06   b.Ashton-under-Lyne 12-10-89

2009–10	Bolton W	0	0
2010–11	Bolton W	0	0
2011–12	Bolton W	0	0
2012–13	Bolton W	0	0
2013–14	Bury	4	0
2013–14	*Burton Alb*	14	0	14	0
2014–15	Bury	17	0
2015–16	Bury	10	0
2016–17	Bury	7	0	38	0
2016–17	*Cheltenham T*	1	0	1	0
2017–18	Port Vale	6	0	6	0

MIDDLETON, Harry (M)   **69**   **0**
H: 5 11   W: 11 00   b.Doncaster 12-4-95

2012–13	Doncaster R	0	0
2013–14	Doncaster R	0	0
2014–15	Doncaster R	4	0
2015–16	Doncaster R	34	0
2016–17	Doncaster R	25	0	63	0
2017–18	Port Vale	6	0	6	0

MONTANO, Cristian (F)   **160**   **20**
H: 5 11   W: 12 00   b.Cali 11-12-91

2010–11	West Ham U	0	0
2011–12	West Ham U	0	0
2011–12	*Notts Co*	15	4	15	4
2011–12	*Swindon T*	4	1	4	1
2011–12	*Dagenham & R*	10	3	10	3
2011–12	*Oxford U*	9	2	9	2
2012–13	Oldham Ath	30	1
2013–14	Oldham Ath	10	2	40	3
2015–16	Bristol R	27	2
2016–17	Bristol R	25	1	52	3
2017–18	Port Vale	30	4	30	4

POPE, Tom (F)   **399**   **107**
H: 6 3   W: 11 03   b.Stoke 27-8-85

2005–06	Crewe Alex	0	0
2006–07	Crewe Alex	4	0
2007–08	Crewe Alex	26	7
2008–09	Crewe Alex	26	10	56	17
2009–10	Rotherham U	35	3
2010–11	Rotherham U	18	1	53	4
2010–11	*Port Vale*	13	3
2011–12	Port Vale	41	5

PUGH, Danny (M)   **358**   **17**
H: 6 0   W: 12 10   b.Cheadle Hulme 19-10-82

2000–01	Manchester U	0	0
2001–02	Manchester U	0	0
2002–03	Manchester U	1	0
2003–04	*Manchester U*	0	0	1	0
2004–05	Leeds U	38	5
2005–06	Leeds U	12	0
2006–07	Preston NE	45	4
2007–08	Preston NE	7	0
2007–08	Stoke C	30	0
2008–09	Stoke C	17	0
2009–10	Stoke C	7	1
2010–11	Stoke C	10	0
2010–11	*Preston NE*	5	0	57	4
2011–12	Stoke C	3	0	67	1
2011–12	Leeds U	34	2
2012–13	Leeds U	4	0
2012–13	*Sheffield W*	16	1	16	1
2013–14	Leeds U	20	2	108	9
2014–15	Coventry C	5	0	5	0
2015–16	Bury	39	0	39	0
2016–17	Blackpool	18	0	18	0
2016–17	Port Vale	14	0
2017–18	Port Vale	33	2	47	2

REEVES, William (M)   **15**   **0**
b. 18-12-96

2015–16	Port Vale	0	0
2016–17	Port Vale	12	0
2017–18	Port Vale	3	0	15	0

REGIS, Chris (M)   **1**   **0**
b. 11-11-96
Internationals: England U17.
From Southampton.

2016–17	Colchester U	0	0
2017–18	Port Vale	1	0	1	0

SMITH, Nathan (D)   **92**   **5**
H: 6 0   W: 11 05   b.Madeley 3-4-96

2013–14	Port Vale	0	0
2014–15	Port Vale	0	0
2015–16	Port Vale	0	0
2016–17	Port Vale	46	4
2017–18	Port Vale	46	1	92	5

TONGE, Michael (M)   **477**   **34**
H: 6 0   W: 11 10   b.Manchester 7-4-83
Internationals: England U20, U21.

2000–01	Sheffield U	2	0
2001–02	Sheffield U	30	3
2002–03	Sheffield U	44	6
2003–04	Sheffield U	46	4
2004–05	Sheffield U	34	2
2005–06	Sheffield U	30	3
2006–07	Sheffield U	27	2
2007–08	Sheffield U	45	1
2008–09	*Sheffield U*	4	0	262	21
2008–09	Stoke C	10	0
2009–10	Stoke C	0	0
2009–10	*Preston NE*	7	0
2009–10	*Derby Co*	18	2	18	2
2010–11	Stoke C	2	0
2010–11	*Preston NE*	5	1	12	1
2011–12	Stoke C	0	0
2011–12	*Barnsley*	10	0	10	0
2012–13	Stoke C	0	0	12	0
2012–13	Leeds U	35	4
2013–14	Leeds U	23	0
2014–15	Leeds U	10	0	68	4
2014–15	*Millwall*	6	0	6	0
2015–16	Stevenage	29	2
2016–17	Stevenage	27	1	56	3
2017–18	Port Vale	33	3	33	3

TURNER, Dan (F)   **34**   **3**
b. 23-6-98

2015–16	Port Vale	1	0
2016–17	Port Vale	16	0
2017–18	Port Vale	17	3	34	3

WALFORD, Charlie (D)   **0**   **0**

2017–18	Port Vale	0	0

WILSON, Lawrie (D)   **226**   **16**
H: 5 11   W: 11 06   b.London 11-9-87

2006–07	Colchester U	0	0
2010–11	Stevenage	42	5
2011–12	Stevenage	46	5	88	10

2012–13	Charlton Ath	30	2		
2013–14	Charlton Ath	42	2		
2014–15	Charlton Ath	24	0	96	4
2014–15	Rotherham U	3	0	3	0
2015–16	Bolton W	12	1		
2015–16	Peterborough U	2	0	2	0
2016–17	Bolton W	18	1	30	2
2017–18	Port Vale	7	0	7	0

WORRALL, David (M) 343 27
H: 6 0 W: 11 03 b.Manchester 12-6-90

2006–07	Bury	0	0		
2007–08	Bury	0	0		
2007–08	WBA	0	0		
2008–09	Accrington S	4	0	4	0
2008–09	Shrewsbury T	9	0	9	0
2009–10	WBA	0	0		
2009–10	Bury	40	4		
2010–11	Bury	40	2		
2011–12	Bury	41	3		
2012–13	Bury	41	2	163	11
2013–14	Rotherham U	3	1	3	1
2013–14	Oldham Ath	18	1	18	1
2014–15	Southend U	38	6		
2015–16	Southend U	35	3	73	9
2016–17	Millwall	33	1	33	1
2017–18	Port Vale	40	4	40	4

YATES, Adam (D) 289 4
H: 5 10 W: 10 07 b.Stoke 28-5-83
Internationals: England C.

2000–01	Crewe Alex	0	0		
2001–02	Crewe Alex	0	0		
2002–03	Crewe Alex	0	0		
2003–04	Crewe Alex	0	0		
2004–05	Crewe Alex	0	0		
2005–06	Crewe Alex	0	0		
2006–07	Crewe Alex	0	0		
2007–08	Morecambe	44	0		
2008–09	Morecambe	32	0	76	0
2009–10	Port Vale	32	0		
2010–11	Port Vale	46	0		
2011–12	Port Vale	38	2		
2012–13	Port Vale	26	0		
2013–14	Port Vale	34	1		
2014–15	Port Vale	25	1		
2015–16	Port Vale	11	0		
2015–16	Northampton T	1	0	1	0
2016–17	Port Vale	0	0		
2017–18	Port Vale	0	0	212	4

Scholars
Beeston, Max Charlie; Benns, Harry Francis; Berks, Joseph Peter; Blight, Mawgan Anthony; Campbell-Gordon, Ryan Joseph; Crockwell, Dequan Takai Eugene; Daulby, Thomas William; Ede, Joshua Lennon; Green-Birch, Lucas Gabriel; Grimshaw, Jack Cameron; Hill, Zak Thomas; Jackson, Finley Thomas; Johnson, Kyle Dean; Ryder-Ackland, Joshua Jordan; Steele, James David; Thomas, Jake Stephen; Wakefield, Jack James; Ward, Matthew Joseph.

PORTSMOUTH (67)

BAKER, Carl (M) 357 64
H: 6 2 W: 12 06 b.Prescot 26-12-82
Internationals: England C.

2007–08	Morecambe	42	10	42	10
2008–09	Stockport Co	22	3		
2009–10	Stockport Co	20	9	42	12
2009–10	Coventry C	22	0		
2010–11	Coventry C	32	1		
2011–12	Coventry C	26	1		
2012–13	Coventry C	43	12		
2013–14	Coventry C	37	7	160	21
2014–15	Milton Keynes D	32	9		
2015–16	Milton Keynes D	34	3	66	12
2016–17	Portsmouth	45	9		
2017	ATK	0	0		
2017–18	Portsmouth	2	0	47	9

BASS, Alex (G) 1 0
H: 6 2 W: 11 00 b.Southampton 1-1-97

2014–15	Portsmouth	0	0		
2015–16	Portsmouth	0	0		
2016–17	Portsmouth	0	0		
2017–18	Portsmouth	1	0	1	0

BURGESS, Christian (D) 188 8
H: 6 5 W: 13 02 b. 7-10-91

2012–13	Middlesbrough	1	0		
2013–14	Middlesbrough	0	0	1	0
2013–14	Hartlepool U	41	0	41	0
2014–15	Peterborough U	30	2	30	2
2015–16	Portsmouth	37	2		
2016–17	Portsmouth	44	4		
2017–18	Portsmouth	35	0	116	6

CASEY, Matthew (D) 0 0

2017–18	Portsmouth	0	0	

CHAPLIN, Conor (M) 104 22
H: 5 10 W: 10 12 b.Worthing 16-2-97

2014–15	Portsmouth	9	1		
2015–16	Portsmouth	30	8		
2016–17	Portsmouth	39	8		
2017–18	Portsmouth	26	5	104	22

CLARKE, Matthew (M) 108 4
H: 5 11 W: 11 00 b.Ipswich 22-9-96

2013–14	Ipswich T	0	0		
2014–15	Ipswich T	4	0		
2015–16	Ipswich T	0	0	4	0
2015–16	*Portsmouth*	29	1		
2016–17	Portsmouth	33	1		
2017–18	Portsmouth	42	2	104	4

CLOSE, Ben (M) 53 2
H: 5 9 W: 11 11 b.Portsmouth 8-8-96

2013–14	Portsmouth	0	0		
2014–15	Portsmouth	6	0		
2015–16	Portsmouth	7	0		
2016–17	Portsmouth	0	0		
2017–18	Portsmouth	40	2	53	2

DONOHUE, Dion (M) 88 1
H: 5 11 W: 10 06 b.Bodedern 26-8-93

2015–16	Chesterfield	17	0		
2016–17	Chesterfield	37	1		
2017–18	Chesterfield	2	0	56	1
2017–18	Portsmouth	32	0	32	0

EVANS, Gary (F) 412 69
H: 6 0 W: 12 08 b.Stockport 26-4-88

2007–08	Macclesfield T	42	7		
2008–09	Macclesfield T	40	12	82	19
2009–10	Bradford C	43	11		
2010–11	Bradford C	36	3	79	14
2011–12	Rotherham U	32	7		
2012–13	Rotherham U	13	2	45	9
2012–13	Fleetwood T	16	1		
2013–14	Fleetwood T	34	6		
2014–15	Fleetwood T	43	2	93	10
2015–16	Portsmouth	40	10		
2016–17	Portsmouth	41	5		
2017–18	Portsmouth	32	2	113	17

HANCOTT, Joe (D) 0 0

2017–18	Portsmouth	0	0	

HAUNSTRUP, Brandon (D) 17 0
b. 26-10-96

2015–16	Portsmouth	1	0		
2016–17	Portsmouth	0	0		
2017–18	Portsmouth	16	0	17	0

HAWKINS, Oliver (F) 49 8
b. 8-4-92
From North Greenford U, Hillingdon Bor, Nothwood, Hemel Hemstead T.

2015–16	Dagenham & R	18	1	18	1
2017–18	Portsmouth	31	7	31	7

KABAMBA, Nicke (F) 13 0
H: 6 3 W: 11 11 b.Brent 1-2-93
From Uxbridge, Hayes, Burnham, Hampton & Richmond.

2016–17	Portsmouth	4	0		
2017–18	Portsmouth	1	0	5	0
2017–18	Colchester U	8	0	8	0

LALKOVIC, Milan (F) 137 14
H: 5 9 W: 10 01 b.Kosice 9-12-92
Internationals: Slovakia U17, U19, U21.

2010–11	Chelsea	0	0		
2011–12	Chelsea	0	0		
2011–12	Doncaster R	6	0	6	0
2011–12	Den Haag	2	0	2	0
2012–13	Chelsea	0	0		
2012–13	Vitoria Guimaraes	8	0	8	0
2013–14	Chelsea	0	0		
2013–14	Walsall	38	6		
2014–15	Mlada Boleslav	6	0	6	0
2014–15	Barnsley	17	0	17	0
2015–16	Walsall	40	7	78	13
2016–17	Portsmouth	13	1		
2016–17	Ross Co	6	0	6	0
2017–18	Portsmouth	1	0	14	1

LETHBRIDGE, Bradley (F) 0 0

2017–18	Portsmouth	0	0	

LOWE, Jamal (F) 66 10
H: 6 0 W: 12 06 b.Harrow 21-7-94
Internationals: England C.

2012–13	Barnet	8	0	8	0

From St Albans C, Hemel Hempstead T, Hampton & Richmond.

2016–17	Portsmouth	14	4		
2017–18	Portsmouth	44	6	58	10

MAIN, Curtis (F) 181 26
H: 5 9 W: 12 02 b.South Shields 20-6-92

2007–08	Darlington	1	0		
2008–09	Darlington	18	2		
2009–10	Darlington	26	3		
2010–11	Darlington	0	0	45	5
2011–12	Middlesbrough	12	2		
2012–13	Middlesbrough	13	3		
2013–14	Middlesbrough	23	1	48	6
2013–14	Shrewsbury T	5	0	5	0
2014–15	Doncaster R	38	8		
2015–16	Doncaster R	10	1	48	9
2015–16	Oldham Ath	18	4	18	4
2016–17	Portsmouth	12	2		
2017–18	Portsmouth	5	0	17	2

Transferred to Motherwell, January 2018.

MAY, Adam (M) 15 0
b. 6-12-97

2014–15	Portsmouth	1	0		
2015–16	Portsmouth	1	0		
2016–17	Portsmouth	0	0		
2017–18	Portsmouth	13	0	15	0

McGEE, Luke (G) 83 0
H: 6 2 W: 12 08 b.Edgware 9-2-95
Internationals: England U17.

2014–15	Tottenham H	0	0		
2015–16	Tottenham H	0	0		
2016–17	Tottenham H	0	0		
2016–17	*Peterborough U*	39	0	39	0
2017–18	Portsmouth	44	0	44	0

NAISMITH, Kal (F) 159 32
H: 5 7 W: 13 02 b.Glasgow 18-2-92
Internationals: Scotland U16, U17.

2013–14	Accrington S	38	10		
2014–15	Accrington S	35	4	73	14
2015–16	Portsmouth	19	3		
2015–16	Hartlepool U	4	0	4	0
2016–17	Portsmouth	37	13		
2017–18	Portsmouth	26	2	82	18

OXLADE-CHAMBERLAIN, Christian (D) 0 0
b. 24-6-98

2015–16	Portsmouth	0	0	
2016–17	Portsmouth	0	0	
2017–18	Portsmouth	0	0	

PITMAN, Brett (F) 447 153
H: 6 0 W: 11 00 b.Jersey 31-1-88

2005–06	Bournemouth	19	1		
2006–07	Bournemouth	29	5		
2007–08	Bournemouth	39	6		
2008–09	Bournemouth	39	17		
2009–10	Bournemouth	46	26		
2010–11	Bournemouth	2	3		
2010–11	Bristol C	39	13		
2011–12	Bristol C	35	7		
2012–13	Bristol C	3	0	77	20
2012–13	Bournemouth	26	19		
2013–14	Bournemouth	34	5		
2014–15	Bournemouth	34	13	268	95
2015–16	Ipswich T	42	10		
2016–17	Ipswich T	22	4	64	14
2017–18	Portsmouth	38	24	38	24

ROSE, Danny (M) 184 14
H: 5 7 W: 10 04 b.Bristol 21-2-88
Internationals: England C.

2006–07	Manchester U	0	0		
2007–08	Manchester U	0	0		

From Oxford U, Newport Co

2012–13	Fleetwood T	0	0		
2012–13	Aldershot T	34	2	34	2
2013–14	Oxford U	40	4		
2014–15	Oxford U	29	2		
2015–16	Oxford U	13	0	82	6
2015–16	Northampton T	15	1	15	1
2016–17	Portsmouth	38	5		
2017–18	Portsmouth	15	0	53	5

SMITH, Dan (M) 0 0

2017–18	Portsmouth	0	0	

THOMPSON, Nathan (D) 203 4
H: 5 7 W: 11 02 b.Chester 9-11-90

2009–10	Swindon T	0	0		
2010–11	Swindon T	3	0		

Season	Club	App	Gls	Tot App	Tot Gls
2011–12	Swindon T	5	0		
2012–13	Swindon T	26	0		
2013–14	Swindon T	41	1		
2014–15	Swindon T	35	0		
2015–16	Swindon T	23	1		
2016–17	Swindon T	34	2	167	4
2017–18	Portsmouth	36	0	36	0

WHATMOUGH, Jack (D)   60   1
b.Gosport 19-8-96
Internationals: England U18, U19.

Season	Club	App	Gls	Tot App	Tot Gls
2012–13	Portsmouth	0	0		
2013–14	Portsmouth	12	0		
2014–15	Portsmouth	22	0		
2015–16	Portsmouth	2	0		
2016–17	Portsmouth	10	1		
2017–18	Portsmouth	14	0	60	1

WIDDRINGTON, Theo (M)   0   0

Season	Club	App	Gls	Tot App	Tot Gls
2017–18	Portsmouth	0	0		

Scholars
Brooks, Jordan Antony Brian; Casey, Matthew Adam; Chandler, Jack Raymond; Collins, Jack; Dandy, Joe Mark James; Flint, Joshua Huchson; Hancott, Joe Mark; Johnston, Oscar William James; Lethbridge, Bradley Stephen; Maloney, Leon Harry; Mayes, Matthew James; Read, Frederick Edward; Smith, Daniel Lewis; Whiting, James Christopher John.

PRESTON NE (68)

BARKHUIZEN, Tom (F)   194   42
H: 5 9   W: 11 00   b.Blackpool 4-7-93

Season	Club	App	Gls	Tot App	Tot Gls
2011–12	Blackpool	0	0		
2011–12	*Hereford U*	38	11	38	11
2012–13	Blackpool	0	0		
2012–13	*Fleetwood T*	13	1	13	1
2013–14	Blackpool	14	1		
2014–15	Blackpool	7	0	21	1
2014–15	Morecambe	5	0		
2015–16	Morecambe	40	10		
2016–17	Morecambe	14	5	59	15
2016–17	Preston NE	17	6		
2017–18	Preston NE	46	8	63	14

BODIN, Billy (M)   227   50
H: 5 11   W: 11 00   b.Swindon 24-3-92
Internationals: Wales U17, U19, U21, Full caps.

Season	Club	App	Gls	Tot App	Tot Gls
2009–10	Swindon T	0	0		
2010–11	Swindon T	5	0		
2011–12	Swindon T	11	3	16	3
2011–12	*Torquay U*	17	5		
2011–12	*Crewe Alex*	8	0	8	0
2012–13	Torquay U	43	5		
2013–14	Torquay U	27	1	87	11
2014–15	Northampton T	4	0	4	0
2015–16	Bristol R	38	13		
2016–17	Bristol R	36	13		
2017–18	Bristol R	21	9	95	35
2017–18	Preston NE	17	1	17	1

BOYLE, Andrew (D)   16   1
H: 5 10   W: 12 02   b.Dublin 7-3-91
Internationals: Republic of Ireland U18, U19, Full caps.
From Dundalk.

Season	Club	App	Gls	Tot App	Tot Gls
2016–17	Preston NE	7	0		
2017–18	Preston NE	3	0	10	0
2017–18	*Doncaster R*	6	1	6	1

BROWNE, Alan (M)   139   14
H: 5 8   W: 11 03   b.Cork 15-4-95
Internationals: Republic of Ireland U19, U21, Full caps.

Season	Club	App	Gls	Tot App	Tot Gls
2013–14	Preston NE	8	1		
2014–15	Preston NE	20	3		
2015–16	Preston NE	36	3		
2016–17	Preston NE	31	0		
2017–18	Preston NE	44	7	139	14

CLARKE, Tom (D)   292   14
H: 6 0   W: 11 02   b.Sowerby Bridge 21-12-87
Internationals: England U18, U19.

Season	Club	App	Gls	Tot App	Tot Gls
2004–05	Huddersfield T	12	0		
2005–06	Huddersfield T	17	1		
2006–07	Huddersfield T	9	0		
2007–08	Huddersfield T	3	0		
2008–09	Huddersfield T	15	1		
2008–09	*Bradford C*	6	0	6	0
2009–10	Huddersfield T	21	0		
2010–11	Huddersfield T	5	1		
2011–12	Huddersfield T	14	0		
2011–12	*Leyton Orient*	10	0	10	0
2012–13	Huddersfield T	0	0	96	3
2013–14	Preston NE	42	4		
2014–15	Preston NE	43	1		
2015–16	Preston NE	35	0		
2016–17	Preston NE	42	4		
2017–18	Preston NE	18	2	180	11

CUNNINGHAM, Greg (D)   236   8
H: 6 0   W: 11 00   b.Galway 31-1-91
Internationals: Republic of Ireland U17, U21, Full caps.

Season	Club	App	Gls	Tot App	Tot Gls
2008–09	Manchester C	0	0		
2009–10	Manchester C	2	0		
2010–11	Manchester C	0	0		
2010–11	*Leicester C*	13	0	13	0
2011–12	Manchester C	0	0		
2011–12	*Nottingham F*	27	0	27	0
2012–13	Manchester C	0	0	2	0
2012–13	Bristol C	30	1		
2013–14	Bristol C	37	1		
2014–15	Bristol C	24	2	91	4
2015–16	Preston NE	43	2		
2016–17	Preston NE	40	1		
2017–18	Preston NE	20	1	103	4

DAVIES, Ben (D)   129   2
H: 6 1   W: 11 09   b.Barrow 11-8-95

Season	Club	App	Gls	Tot App	Tot Gls
2012–13	Preston NE	3	0		
2013–14	Preston NE	0	0		
2013–14	*York C*	44	0	44	0
2014–15	Preston NE	4	0		
2014–15	*Tranmere R*	3	0	3	0
2015–16	Preston NE	0	0		
2015–16	*Newport Co*	19	0	19	0
2016–17	Preston NE	0	0		
2016–17	*Fleetwood T*	22	1	22	1
2017–18	Preston NE	34	1	41	1

DOYLE, Eoin (F)   299   98
H: 6 0   W: 11 07   b.Tallaght 12-3-88

Season	Club	App	Gls	Tot App	Tot Gls
2009	Sligo	15	3		
2010	Sligo	35	6		
2011	Sligo	34	20	84	29
2011–12	Hibernian	13	1		
2012–13	Hibernian	36	10	49	11
2013–14	Chesterfield	43	11		
2014–15	Chesterfield	26	21	69	32
2014–15	Cardiff C	16	5		
2015–16	Cardiff C	0	0	16	5
2015–16	Preston NE	28	4		
2016–17	Preston NE	11	1		
2016–17	*Portsmouth*	12	2	12	2
2017–18	Preston NE	0	0	39	5
2017–18	*Oldham Ath*	30	14	30	14

EARL, Joshua (D)   19   0
b. 24-10-98

Season	Club	App	Gls	Tot App	Tot Gls
2017–18	Preston NE	19	0	19	0

FISHER, Darnell (M)   108   1
H: 5 9   W: 11 00   b.Reading 1-5-94

Season	Club	App	Gls	Tot App	Tot Gls
2012–13	Celtic	0	0		
2013–14	Celtic	12	0		
2014–15	Celtic	5	0		
2015–16	Celtic	0	0	17	0
2015–16	*St Johnstone*	23	1	23	1
2016–17	Rotherham U	34	0	34	0
2017–18	Preston NE	34	0	34	0

GALLAGHER, Paul (F)   466   78
H: 6 1   W: 11 00   b.Glasgow 9-8-84
Internationals: Scotland U21, B, Full caps.

Season	Club	App	Gls	Tot App	Tot Gls
2002–03	Blackburn R	1	0		
2003–04	Blackburn R	26	3		
2004–05	Blackburn R	16	2		
2005–06	Blackburn R	1	0		
2005–06	Stoke C	37	11		
2006–07	Blackburn R	16	1		
2007–08	Blackburn R	0	0		
2007–08	*Preston NE*	19	1		
2007–08	*Stoke C*	7	0	44	11
2008–09	Blackburn R	0	0		
2008–09	*Plymouth Arg*	40	13	40	13
2009–10	Blackburn R	1	0	61	6
2009–10	Leicester C	41	7		
2010–11	Leicester C	41	10		
2011–12	Leicester C	28	8		
2012–13	Leicester C	8	0		
2012–13	*Sheffield U*	6	1	6	1
2013–14	Leicester C	0	0		
2013–14	*Preston NE*	28	6		
2014–15	Leicester C	0	0	118	25
2014–15	Preston NE	46	7		
2015–16	Preston NE	41	5		
2016–17	Preston NE	31	1		
2017–18	Preston NE	32	2	197	22

GRIMSHAW, Liam (D)   18   0
H: 5 10   W: 11 11   b.Burnley 2-2-95
Internationals: England U18.

Season	Club	App	Gls	Tot App	Tot Gls
2013–14	Manchester U	0	0		
2013–14	*Morecambe*	0	0		
2015–16	Manchester U	0	0		
2015–16	*Motherwell*	0	0		
2015–16	Preston NE	0	0		
2016–17	Preston NE	5	0		
2016–17	*Chesterfield*	13	0	13	0
2017–18	Preston NE	0	0	5	0

Transferred to Motherwell, August 2017.

HARROP, Josh (M)   39   3
H: 5 9   W: 11 00   b.Stockport 15-12-95
Internationals: England U20.

Season	Club	App	Gls	Tot App	Tot Gls
2016–17	Manchester U	1	1	1	1
2017–18	Preston NE	38	2	38	2

HORGAN, Daryl (M)   39   3
H: 5 7   W: 10 10   b.Galway 10-8-92
Internationals: Republic of Ireland U19, U21, Full caps.
From Dundalk.

Season	Club	App	Gls	Tot App	Tot Gls
2016–17	Preston NE	19	2		
2017–18	Preston NE	20	1	39	3

HUDSON, Matthew (G)   1   0
H: 6 4   b.Southport 29-7-98

Season	Club	App	Gls	Tot App	Tot Gls
2014–15	Preston NE	0	0		
2015–16	Preston NE	1	0		
2016–17	Preston NE	0	0		
2017–18	Preston NE	0	0	1	0

HUNTINGTON, Paul (D)   342   22
H: 6 3   W: 12 08   b.Carlisle 17-9-87
Internationals: England U18.

Season	Club	App	Gls	Tot App	Tot Gls
2005–06	Newcastle U	0	0		
2006–07	Newcastle U	11	1		
2007–08	Newcastle U	0	0	11	1
2007–08	Leeds U	17	2		
2008–09	Leeds U	4	0		
2009–10	Leeds U	0	0	21	2
2009–10	*Stockport Co*	26	0	26	0
2010–11	Yeovil T	40	5		
2011–12	Yeovil T	37	2	77	7
2012–13	Preston NE	37	3		
2013–14	Preston NE	23	2		
2014–15	Preston NE	32	5		
2015–16	Preston NE	38	0		
2016–17	Preston NE	33	1		
2017–18	Preston NE	44	1	207	12

JOHNSON, Daniel (M)   158   26
H: 5 8   W: 10 07   b.Kingston, Jamaica 8-10-92

Season	Club	App	Gls	Tot App	Tot Gls
2010–11	Aston Villa	0	0		
2011–12	Aston Villa	0	0		
2012–13	Aston Villa	0	0		
2012–13	*Yeovil T*	5	0	5	0
2013–14	Aston Villa	0	0		
2014–15	Aston Villa	0	0		
2014–15	*Chesterfield*	11	0	11	0
2014–15	*Oldham Ath*	6	3	6	3
2014–15	Preston NE	20	8		
2015–16	Preston NE	43	8		
2016–17	Preston NE	40	4		
2017–18	Preston NE	33	3	136	23

MAGUIRE, Sean (F)   166   70
H: 5 9   W: 11 10   b.Luton 1-5-94
Internationals: Republic of Ireland U19, U21, Full caps.

Season	Club	App	Gls	Tot App	Tot Gls
2010–11	West Ham U	0	0		
2011	Waterford U	8	1		
2011–12	West Ham U	0	0		
2012	Waterford U	26	13	34	14
2012–13	West Ham U	0	0		
2013–14	West Ham U	0	0		
2014	*Sligo R*	18	1	18	1
2014–15	West Ham U	0	0		
2014–15	*Accrington S*	33	7	33	7
2015	Dundalk	6	0	6	0
2016	Cork C	30	18		
2017	Cork C	21	20	51	38
2017–18	Preston NE	24	10	24	10

MAXWELL, Chris (G)   178   0
H: 6 0   W: 11 07   b.Wrexham 30-7-90
Internationals: Wales U17, U19, U21, U23.

Season	Club	App	Gls	Tot App	Tot Gls
2012–13	Fleetwood T	0	0		
2013–14	Fleetwood T	18	0		
2014–15	Fleetwood T	46	0		
2015–16	Fleetwood T	46	0	110	0
2016–17	Preston NE	38	0		
2017–18	Preston NE	30	0	68	0

MAY, Stevie (F) — 167 75
H: 5 3 W: 9 07 b.Perth 3-11-92
Internationals: Scotland U20, U21, Full caps.

2008–09	St Johnstone	1	1		
2009–10	St Johnstone	0	0		
2010–11	St Johnstone	19	2		
2011–12	St Johnstone	1	0		
2011–12	*Alloa Ath*	22	19	22	19
2012–13	St Johnstone	3	0		
2012–13	*Hamilton A*	33	25	33	25
2013–14	St Johnstone	38	20	62	23
2014–15	Sheffield W	39	7		
2015–16	Sheffield W	0	0	39	7
2015–16	Preston NE	7	0		
2016–17	Preston NE	4	1		
2017–18	Preston NE	0	0	11	1

Transferred to Aberdeen, August 2017.

MOULT, Louis (F) — 123 42
H: 6 0 W: 13 05 b.Stoke 14-5-92

2009–10	Stoke C	1	0		
2010–11	Stoke C	0	0		
2010–11	*Bradford C*	11	1	11	1
2011–12	Stoke C	0	0		
2011–12	*Accrington S*	4	0	4	0
2012–13	Stoke C	0	0	1	0
2012–13	*Northampton T*	13	1	13	1

From Nuneaton T, Wrexham.

2015–16	Motherwell	38	15		
2016–17	Motherwell	31	15		
2017–18	Motherwell	15	8	84	38
2017–18	Preston NE	10	2	10	2

O'CONNOR, Kevin (D) — 12 0
b.Enniscorthy 7-5-95
Internationals: Republic of Ireland U17, U21.
From Waterford U, Cork C.

2017–18	Preston NE	8	0	8	0
2017–18	*Fleetwood T*	4	0	4	0

O'REILLY, Adam (M) — 0 0
b. 11-5-01
Internationals: Republic of Ireland U17.

2017–18	Preston NE	0	0

PEARSON, Ben (M) — 126 3
H: 5 5 W: 11 03 b.Oldham 4-1-95
Internationals: England U16, U17, U18, U19, U21, Full caps.

2013–14	Manchester U	0	0		
2014–15	Manchester U	0	0		
2014–15	*Barnsley*	22	1		
2015–16	Manchester U	0	0		
2015–16	*Barnsley*	23	1	45	2
2015–16	Preston NE	15	0		
2016–17	Preston NE	31	1		
2017–18	Preston NE	35	0	81	1

PRINGLE, Ben (M) — 220 24
H: 5 8 W: 11 10 b.Whitley Bay 25-7-88

2009–10	Derby Co	5	0		
2010–11	Derby Co	15	0	20	0
2010–11	*Torquay U*	5	0	5	0
2011–12	Rotherham U	21	4		
2012–13	Rotherham U	41	7		
2013–14	Rotherham U	45	5		
2014–15	Rotherham U	40	3	147	19
2015–16	Fulham	15	2	15	2
2015–16	*Ipswich T*	10	2	10	2
2016–17	Preston NE	10	0		
2017–18	Preston NE	0	0	10	0
2017–18	*Oldham Ath*	13	1	13	1

ROBINSON, Callum (F) — 132 23
H: 5 10 W: 11 11 b.Birmingham 2-2-95
Internationals: England U16, U17, U19, U20.

2013–14	Aston Villa	4	0		
2014–15	Aston Villa	0	0		
2014–15	*Preston NE*	25	4		
2015–16	Aston Villa	0	0	4	0
2015–16	*Bristol C*	6	0	6	0
2015–16	*Preston NE*	14	2		
2016–17	Preston NE	42	10		
2017–18	Preston NE	41	7	122	23

RUDD, Declan (G) — 135 0
H: 6 3 W: 12 06 b.Diss 16-1-91
Internationals: England U16, U17, U19, U20, U21, Full caps.

2008–09	Norwich C	0	0		
2009–10	Norwich C	0	0		
2010–11	Norwich C	1	0		
2011–12	Norwich C	2	0		
2012–13	Norwich C	0	0		
2012–13	*Preston NE*	14	0		
2013–14	Norwich C	0	0		
2013–14	*Preston NE*	46	0		
2014–15	Norwich C	0	0		
2015–16	Norwich C	11	0		
2016–17	Norwich C	0	0	21	0
2016–17	*Charlton Ath*	38	0	38	0
2017–18	Preston NE	16	0	76	0

SIMPSON, Connor (F) — 3 0
b.Guisborough 24-1-00

2016–17	Hartlepool U	2	0	2	0
2017–18	Preston NE	1	0	1	0

SPURR, Tommy (D) — 357 10
H: 6 1 W: 11 05 b.Leeds 13-9-87

2005–06	Sheffield W	2	0		
2006–07	Sheffield W	36	0		
2007–08	Sheffield W	41	2		
2008–09	Sheffield W	41	2		
2009–10	Sheffield W	46	1		
2010–11	Sheffield W	26	0	192	5
2011–12	Doncaster R	19	0		
2012–13	Doncaster R	46	1		
2013–14	Doncaster R	0	0	65	1
2013–14	Blackburn R	43	3		
2014–15	Blackburn R	12	0		
2015–16	Blackburn R	23	0	78	3
2016–17	Preston NE	17	1		
2017–18	Preston NE	5	0	22	1

VERMIJL, Marnick (D) — 93 6
H: 5 11 W: 11 12 b.Overpelt 13-1-92
Internationals: Belgium U17, U18, U19, U21.

2010–11	Manchester U	0	0		
2011–12	Manchester U	0	0		
2012–13	Manchester U	0	0		
2013–14	Manchester U	0	0		
2013–14	*NEC*	28	3	28	3
2014–15	Manchester U	0	0		
2014–15	Sheffield W	11	0		
2015–16	Preston NE	28	1		
2016–17	Sheffield W	0	0	11	0
2016–17	Preston NE	18	2		
2017–18	Preston NE	2	0	48	3
2017–18	*Scunthorpe U*	6	0	6	0

WELSH, John (M) — 342 17
H: 5 7 W: 12 02 b.Liverpool 10-1-84
Internationals: England U16, U19, U20, U21.

2000–01	Liverpool	0	0		
2001–02	Liverpool	0	0		
2002–03	Liverpool	0	0		
2003–04	Liverpool	1	0		
2004–05	Liverpool	3	0		
2005–06	Liverpool	0	0	4	0
2005–06	Hull C	32	2		
2006–07	Hull C	18	1		
2007–08	Hull C	0	0		
2007–08	*Chester C*	6	0	6	0
2008–09	Hull C	0	0	50	3
2008–09	*Carlisle U*	4	0	4	0
2008–09	*Bury*	5	0	5	0
2009–10	Tranmere R	45	4		
2010–11	Tranmere R	41	4		
2011–12	Tranmere R	44	3	130	11
2012–13	Preston NE	36	1		
2013–14	Preston NE	36	2		
2014–15	Preston NE	32	0		
2015–16	Preston NE	24	0		
2016–17	Preston NE	6	0		
2017–18	Preston NE	9	0	143	3

WOODS, Calum (D) — 266 11
H: 5 11 W: 11 07 b.Liverpool 5-2-87

2006–07	Dunfermline Ath	12	0		
2007–08	Dunfermline Ath	25	0		
2008–09	Dunfermline Ath	30	5		
2009–10	Dunfermline Ath	29	2		
2010–11	Dunfermline Ath	32	3	128	10
2011–12	Huddersfield T	26	0		
2012–13	Huddersfield T	27	0		
2013–14	Huddersfield T	19	1	72	1
2014–15	Preston NE	18	0		
2015–16	Preston NE	32	0		
2016–17	Preston NE	0	0		
2017–18	Preston NE	16	0	66	0

Scholars
Armer, Jack; Baxter, Jack Thomas; Brannigan, Darren Lee; Campbell, Kamol Shawn; Cottam, James; Fensome, Lewis George; Garstang, Harry Charles; Jolly, Jerome Thomas; Lenton, Callum; Lyons, Charlie; Mason, Myles Jacob David; Ngongo, Precieux Luz; O'Neil, Oscar Brian; O'Reilly, Adam Kieran; Pollard, Joshua Thomas; Rahman, Hafizul; Simmons, Lewis; Smart, Kian Michael Allan; Stead, Thomas; Wood, Alexander Stuart.

QPR (69)

BAPTISTE, Alex (D) — 476 24
H: 6 0 W: 11 11 b.Sutton-in-Ashfield 31-1-86

2002–03	Mansfield T	4	0		
2003–04	Mansfield T	17	0		
2004–05	Mansfield T	41	1		
2005–06	Mansfield T	41	1		
2006–07	Mansfield T	46	3		
2007–08	Mansfield T	25	0	174	5
2008–09	Blackpool	21	1		
2009–10	Blackpool	42	3		
2010–11	Blackpool	21	2		
2011–12	Blackpool	43	1		
2012–13	Blackpool	43	1	170	8
2013–14	Bolton W	39	4		
2014–15	Bolton W	0	0	39	4
2014–15	*Blackburn R*	32	3	32	3
2015–16	Middlesbrough	0	0		
2015–16	*Sheffield U*	11	1	11	1
2016–17	Middlesbrough	0	0		
2016–17	*Preston NE*	24	3	24	3
2017–18	QPR	26	0	26	0

BIDWELL, Jake (D) — 272 5
H: 6 0 W: 11 00 b.Southport 21-3-93
Internationals: England U16, U17, U18, U19.

2009–10	Everton	0	0		
2010–11	Everton	0	0		
2011–12	*Brentford*	24	0		
2012–13	Everton	0	0		
2012–13	*Brentford*	40	0		
2013–14	Brentford	38	0		
2014–15	Brentford	43	0		
2015–16	Brentford	45	3	190	3
2016–17	QPR	36	0		
2017–18	QPR	46	2	82	2

BORYSIUK, Ariel (M) — 230 7
H: 5 10 W: 11 00 b.Biala Podlaska 29-7-91
Internationals: Poland U17, U19, U20, U21, Full caps.

2007–08	Legia Warsaw	8	1		
2008–09	Legia Warsaw	18	0		
2009–10	Legia Warsaw	23	0		
2010–11	Legia Warsaw	26	2		
2011–12	Legia Warsaw	15	1		
2011–12	Kaiserslautern	12	0		
2012–13	Kaiserslautern	28	0		
2013–14	Kaiserslautern	4	0		
2013–14	*Volga*	4	0	4	0
2014–15	Kaiserslautern	0	0	44	0
2014–15	Lechia Gdansk	34	0		
2015–16	Lechia Gdansk	20	2		
2015–16	*Legia Warsaw*	13	0	103	4
2016–17	QPR	11	0		
2016–17	*Lechia Gdansk*	14	1	68	3
2017–18	QPR	0	0	11	0

Transferred to Lechia Gdansk, January 2018.

CAULKER, Steven (D) — 211 12
H: 6 3 W: 12 00 b.Feltham 29-12-91
Internationals: England U19 U21, Full caps. Great Britain.

2009–10	Tottenham H	0	0		
2009–10	*Yeovil T*	44	0	44	0
2010–11	Tottenham H	0	0		
2010–11	*Bristol C*	29	2	29	2
2011–12	Tottenham H	0	0		
2011–12	*Swansea C*	26	0	26	0
2012–13	Tottenham H	18	2	18	2
2013–14	Cardiff C	38	5	38	5
2014–15	QPR	35	1		
2015–16	QPR	0	0		
2015–16	*Southampton*	3	0	3	0
2015–16	*Liverpool*	3	0	3	0
2016–17	QPR	13	2		
2017–18	QPR	2	0	50	3

Transferred to Dundee, February 2018.

CHAIR, Ilias (M) — 6 1
b.Lierse 30-10-97

2015–16	Lierse	2	0		
2016–17	Lierse	0	0	2	0
2017–18	QPR	4	1	4	1

COUSINS, Jordan (D) — 158 7
H: 5 10 W: 11 05 b.Greenwich 6-3-94
Internationals: England U16, U17, U18, U20.

2011–12	Charlton Ath	0	0		
2012–13	Charlton Ath	0	0		
2013–14	Charlton Ath	42	2		
2014–15	Charlton Ath	0	0		
2015–16	Charlton Ath	39	2	125	7
2016–17	QPR	18	0		
2017–18	QPR	15	0	33	0

EZE, Eberechi (M)   36   7
H: 5 8   W: 10 08   b. 29-6-98
From Millwall.

Season	Club	App	Gls	App	Gls
2016–17	QPR	0	0		
2017–18	*Wycombe W*	20	5	20	5
2017–18	QPR	16	2	16	2

FREEMAN, Luke (F)   290   34
H: 6 0   W: 10 00   b.Dartford 22-3-92
Internationals: England U16, U17.

Season	Club	App	Gls	App	Gls
2007–08	Gillingham	1	0	1	0
2008–09	Arsenal	0	0		
2009–10	Arsenal	0	0		
2010–11	Arsenal	0	0		
2010–11	*Yeovil T*	13	2	13	2
2011–12	Arsenal	0	0		
2011–12	Stevenage	26	7		
2012–13	Stevenage	39	2		
2013–14	Stevenage	45	6	110	15
2014–15	Bristol C	46	7		
2015–16	Bristol C	41	1		
2016–17	Bristol C	18	2	105	10
2016–17	QPR	16	2		
2017–18	QPR	45	5	61	7

FURLONG, Darnell (D)   94   2
b. 31-10-95

Season	Club	App	Gls	App	Gls
2014–15	QPR	3	0		
2015–16	QPR	0	0		
2015–16	*Northampton T*	10	0	10	0
2015–16	*Cambridge U*	21	0	21	0
2016–17	QPR	14	0		
2016–17	*Swindon T*	24	2	24	2
2017–18	QPR	22	0	39	0

GOSS, Sean (M)   19   2
H: 5 10   W: 11 03   b.Wegberg 1-10-95

Season	Club	App	Gls	App	Gls
2015–16	Manchester U	0	0		
2016–17	Manchester U	0	0		
2016–17	QPR	6	0		
2017–18	QPR	0	0	6	0
2017–18	*Rangers*	13	2	13	2

HALL, Grant (D)   124   2
H: 5 9   W: 11 02   b.Brighton 29-10-91

Season	Club	App	Gls	App	Gls
2009–10	Brighton & HA	0	0		
2010–11	Brighton & HA	0	0		
2011–12	Brighton & HA	1	0	1	0
2012–13	Tottenham H	0	0		
2013–14	*Swindon T*	27	0	27	0
2014–15	Tottenham H	0	0		
2014–15	*Birmingham C*	7	0	7	0
2014–15	*Blackpool*	12	1	12	1
2015–16	QPR	39	1		
2016–17	QPR	34	0		
2017–18	QPR	4	0	77	1

HAMALAINEN, Niko (M)   4   0
b.Florida 3-5-97
Internationals: Finland U18, U19, U21.

Season	Club	App	Gls	App	Gls
2014–15	QPR	0	0		
2015–16	QPR	0	0		
2015–16	*Dagenham & R*	1	0	1	0
2016–17	QPR	3	0		
2017–18	QPR	0	0	3	0

INGRAM, Matt (G)   150   0
H: 6 3   W: 12 13   b.Croydon 18-12-93

Season	Club	App	Gls	App	Gls
2011–12	Wycombe W	0	0		
2012–13	Wycombe W	8	0		
2013–14	Wycombe W	46	0		
2014–15	Wycombe W	46	0		
2015–16	Wycombe W	24	0	124	0
2015–16	QPR	4	0		
2016–17	QPR	0	0		
2017–18	*Northampton T*	20	0	20	0
2017–18	QPR	2	0	6	0

KAKAY, Osman (D)   21   0
b.Westminster 25-8-97

Season	Club	App	Gls	App	Gls
2015–16	QPR	0	0		
2015–16	*Livingston*	10	0	10	0
2016–17	QPR	1	0		
2016–17	Chesterfield	8	0		
2017–18	*Chesterfield*	0	0	8	0
2017–18	QPR	2	0	3	0

LUMLEY, Joe (G)   44   0
H: 6 3   W: 11 07   b.Harlow 15-2-95

Season	Club	App	Gls	App	Gls
2013–14	QPR	0	0		
2014–15	QPR	0	0		
2014–15	*Accrington S*	5	0	5	0
2014–15	*Morecambe*	0	0		
2015–16	QPR	1	0		
2015–16	*Stevenage*	0	0		
2016–17	QPR	0	0		
2016–17	*Bristol R*	19	0	19	0
2017–18	QPR	2	0	3	0
2017–18	*Blackpool*	17	0	17	0

LUONGO, Massimo (F)   198   20
H: 5 8   W: 11 10   b.Sydney 25-9-92
Internationals: Australia U20, Full caps.

Season	Club	App	Gls	App	Gls
2010–11	Tottenham H	0	0		
2011–12	Tottenham H	0	0		
2012–13	Tottenham H	0	0		
2012–13	*Ipswich T*	9	0	9	0
2012–13	*Swindon T*	7	1		
2013–14	Swindon T	44	6		
2014–15	Swindon T	34	6	85	13
2015–16	QPR	30	0		
2016–17	QPR	35	1		
2017–18	QPR	39	6	104	7

LYNCH, Joel (D)   336   17
H: 6 1   W: 12 10   b.Eastbourne 3-10-87
Internationals: England Youth. Wales Full caps.

Season	Club	App	Gls	App	Gls
2005–06	Brighton & HA	16	1		
2006–07	Brighton & HA	39	0		
2007–08	Brighton & HA	22	1		
2008–09	Brighton & HA	2	0	79	2
2008–09	*Nottingham F*	23	0		
2009–10	Nottingham F	10	0		
2010–11	Nottingham F	12	0		
2011–12	Nottingham F	35	3	80	3
2012–13	Huddersfield T	22	1		
2013–14	Huddersfield T	29	2		
2014–15	Huddersfield T	34	3		
2015–16	Huddersfield T	37	2	122	8
2016–17	QPR	30	3		
2017–18	QPR	25	1	55	4

MACKIE, Jamie (F)   329   49
H: 5 8   W: 11 00   b.Dorking 22-9-85
Internationals: Scotland Full caps.

Season	Club	App	Gls	App	Gls
2003–04	Wimbledon	13	0	13	0
2004–05	Milton Keynes D	3	0	3	0
From Exeter C					
2007–08	Plymouth Arg	13	3		
2008–09	Plymouth Arg	43	5		
2009–10	Plymouth Arg	42	8	98	16
2010–11	QPR	25	9		
2011–12	QPR	31	7		
2012–13	QPR	29	2		
2013–14	*Nottingham F*	45	4	45	4
2014–15	*Reading*	32	5	32	5
2015–16	QPR	15	1		
2016–17	QPR	18	1		
2017–18	QPR	20	4	138	24

MANNING, Ryan (F)   37   3
H: 5 8   W: 10 06   b.Galway 14-6-96
Internationals: Republic of Ireland U17, U19, U21.
From Galway U.

Season	Club	App	Gls	App	Gls
2016–17	QPR	18	1		
2017–18	QPR	19	2	37	3

NGBAKOTO, Yeni (F)   216   47
H: 5 8   W: 11 03   b.Croix 23-1-92
Internationals: France U17, U18. DR Congo Full caps.

Season	Club	App	Gls	App	Gls
2009–10	Metz	0	0		
2010–11	Metz	22	2		
2011–12	Metz	20	0		
2012–13	Metz	38	11		
2013–14	Metz	37	14		
2014–15	Metz	30	5		
2015–16	Metz	38	12	185	44
2016–17	QPR	26	3		
2017–18	QPR	5	0	31	3

Transferred to Guingamp, January 2018.

ONUOHA, Nedum (D)   333   11
H: 6 2   W: 12 04   b.Warri 12-11-86
Internationals: England U20, U21.

Season	Club	App	Gls	App	Gls
2004–05	Manchester C	17	0		
2005–06	Manchester C	10	0		
2006–07	Manchester C	18	0		
2007–08	Manchester C	16	1		
2008–09	Manchester C	23	1		
2009–10	Manchester C	10	0		
2010–11	Manchester C	0	0		
2010–11	*Sunderland*	31	1	31	1
2011–12	Manchester C	1	0	95	3
2011–12	QPR	16	0		
2012–13	QPR	23	0		
2013–14	QPR	26	2		
2014–15	QPR	23	0		
2015–16	QPR	46	2		
2016–17	QPR	44	3		
2017–18	QPR	29	0	207	7

OTEH, Aramide (F)   6   1
b.London 10-9-98
From Tottenham H.

Season	Club	App	Gls	App	Gls
2017–18	QPR	6	1	6	1

OWENS, Charlie (M)   0   0
b. 7-12-97
Internationals: Northern Ireland U19, U21.

Season	Club	App	Gls	App	Gls
2017–18	QPR	0	0		

PERCH, James (D)   410   16
H: 5 11   W: 11 05   b.Mansfield 29-9-85

Season	Club	App	Gls	App	Gls
2002–03	Nottingham F	0	0		
2003–04	Nottingham F	0	0		
2004–05	Nottingham F	22	0		
2005–06	Nottingham F	38	3		
2006–07	Nottingham F	46	5		
2007–08	Nottingham F	30	0		
2008–09	Nottingham F	37	3		
2009–10	Nottingham F	17	1	190	12
2010–11	Newcastle U	13	0		
2011–12	Newcastle U	25	0		
2012–13	Newcastle U	27	1	65	1
2013–14	Wigan Ath	40	0		
2014–15	Wigan Ath	41	3	81	3
2015–16	QPR	35	0		
2016–17	QPR	32	0		
2017–18	QPR	7	0	74	0

PETRASSO, Michael (M)   40   5
H: 5 6   W: 10 01   b.Toronto 9-7-95
Internationals: Canada U17, U20, U23, Full caps.

Season	Club	App	Gls	App	Gls
2013–14	QPR	1	0		
2013–14	*Oldham Ath*	11	1	11	1
2013–14	*Coventry C*	7	1	7	1
2014–15	QPR	0	0		
2014–15	*Leyton Orient*	3	0	3	0
2014–15	*Notts Co*	8	3	8	3
2015–16	QPR	8	0		
2016–17	QPR	2	0		
2017–18	QPR	0	0	11	0

Transferred to Montreal Impact, January 2018.

ROBINSON, Jack (D)   117   2
H: 5 11   W: 10 08   b.Warrington 1-9-93
Internationals: England U16, U17, U18, U19, U21.

Season	Club	App	Gls	App	Gls
2009–10	Liverpool	1	0		
2010–11	Liverpool	2	0		
2011–12	Liverpool	0	0		
2012–13	Liverpool	0	0		
2012–13	*Wolverhampton W*	11	0	11	0
2013–14	Liverpool	0	0	3	0
2013–14	*Blackpool*	34	0	34	0
2014–15	QPR	0	0		
2014–15	*Huddersfield T*	30	0	30	0
2015–16	QPR	1	0		
2016–17	QPR	0	0		
2017–18	QPR	31	2	39	2

SAMUEL, Bright (F)   82   5
H: 5 9   W: 11 05   b. 1-2-97

Season	Club	App	Gls	App	Gls
2014–15	Blackpool	6	0		
2015–16	Blackpool	23	0		
2016–17	Blackpool	31	4		
2017–18	Blackpool	4	0	64	4
2017–18	QPR	18	1	18	1

SCOWEN, Josh (M)   229   14
H: 5 10   W: 11 09   b.Cheshunt 28-3-93

Season	Club	App	Gls	App	Gls
2010–11	Wycombe W	2	0		
2011–12	Wycombe W	0	0		
2012–13	Wycombe W	34	1		
2013–14	Wycombe W	37	1		
2014–15	Wycombe W	18	1	91	3
2014–15	Barnsley	21	4		
2015–16	Barnsley	34	4		
2016–17	Barnsley	41	2	96	10
2017–18	QPR	42	1	42	1

SHODIPO, Olamide (M)   23   0
b.Dublin 5-7-97
Internationals: Republic of Ireland U19, U21.

Season	Club	App	Gls	App	Gls
2016–17	QPR	11	0		
2016–17	*Port Vale*	6	0	6	0
2017–18	QPR	0	0	11	0
2017–18	*Colchester U*	6	0	6	0

SMITH, Matt (F)   234   53
H: 6 6   W: 14 00   b.Birmingham 7-6-89

Season	Club	App	Gls	App	Gls
2011–12	Oldham Ath	28	3		
2011–12	*Macclesfield T*	8	1	8	1
2012–13	Oldham Ath	34	6	62	9
2013–14	Leeds U	39	12		
2014–15	Leeds U	3	0	42	12
2014–15	Fulham	15	5		
2014–15	*Bristol C*	14	7	14	7
2015–16	Fulham	20	2		
2016–17	Fulham	16	2	51	9
2016–17	QPR	16	4		
2017–18	QPR	41	11	57	15

SMITHIES, Alex (G)   354   0
H: 6 1 W: 10 01 b.Huddersfield 25-3-90
Internationals: England U16, U17, U18, U19.

2006–07	Huddersfield T	0	0	
2007–08	Huddersfield T	2	0	
2008–09	Huddersfield T	27	0	
2009–10	Huddersfield T	46	0	
2010–11	Huddersfield T	22	0	
2011–12	Huddersfield T	13	0	
2012–13	Huddersfield T	46	0	
2013–14	Huddersfield T	46	0	
2014–15	Huddersfield T	44	0	
2015–16	Huddersfield T	1	0	247 0
2015–16	QPR	18	0	
2016–17	QPR	46	0	
2017–18	QPR	43	0	107 0

SMYTH, Paul (M)   13   2
b. 10-9-97
Internationals: Northern Ireland U19, U21, Full caps.

2017–18	Linfield	0	0	
2017–18	QPR	13	2	13 2

SYLLA, Idrissa (F)   218   61
H: 6 2 W: 11 11 b.Conakry 3-12-90
Internationals: Guinea Full caps.

2010–11	Le Mans	0	0	
2010–11	Bastia	27	7	27 7
2011–12	Le Mans	25	9	
2012–13	Le Mans	27	5	52 14
2013–14	Zulte Waregem	27	9	
2014–15	Zulte Waregem	20	5	47 14
2014–15	Anderlecht	0	0	
2015–16	Anderlecht	30	7	
2016–17	Anderlecht	4	2	34 9
2016–17	QPR	32	10	
2017–18	QPR	26	7	58 17

TILT, Chay (M)   0   0
From WBA.

2017–18	QPR	0	0

WASHINGTON, Conor (F)   194   44
H: 5 10 W: 11 09 b.Chatham 18-5-92
Internationals: Northern Ireland Full caps.

2013–14	Newport Co	24	4	24 4
2013–14	Peterborough U	17	4	
2014–15	Peterborough U	40	13	
2015–16	Peterborough U	25	10	82 27
2015–16	QPR	15	0	
2016–17	QPR	40	7	
2017–18	QPR	33	6	88 13

WHEELER, David (M)   160   34
H: 5 11 W: 12 00 b.Brighton 4-10-90
Internationals: England U18.

2013–14	Exeter C	35	3	
2014–15	Exeter C	45	7	
2015–16	Exeter C	31	6	
2016–17	Exeter C	38	17	
2017–18	Exeter C	2	0	151 33
2017–18	QPR	9	1	9 1

WILLIAMS, Jack (M)   1   0
b.London 11-9-97

2017–18	QPR	0	0	
2017–18	Wycombe W	1	0	1 0

WSZOLEK, Pawel (M)   178   15
H: 6 1 W: 12 04 b.Tczew 30-4-92
Internationals: Poland U17, U18, U19, Full caps.

2010–11	Polonia Warsaw	7	0	
2011–12	Polonia Warsaw	26	2	
2012–13	Polonia Warsaw	27	7	60 9
2013–14	Sampdoria	19	1	
2014–15	Sampdoria	6	0	
2015–16	Sampdoria	2	0	27 1
2015–16	Verona	26	0	
2016–17	Verona	0	0	26 0
2016–17	QPR	29	3	
2017–18	QPR	36	2	65 5

Players retained or with offer of contract
Alfa, Odysseus Naphtali; Brzozowski, Marcin Maurycy; Dalling, Deshane; Dieng, Seny Timothy; Phillips, Giles Ene Malachi.

Scholars
Akinola, Romoluwa Ayomide; Bansal-McNulty, Amrit Padraig Singh; Bettache, Faysal; Bowman, Myles Thomas; Brooks, Marcus Adolphus Lee; Carlyle, Nathan Trevor; Dauti, Mus; Dickinson, Tyla Dez; Disubi, Daniel; Dos, Santos Cardoso Hugo Alexandre; Drewe, Aaron Michael; Eshun, Kingsley Lewis; Fox, Charles John; Frailing, Jake Lewis John; Francis-Adeyinka, Jardel Adeolu Adesola Joshua; Genovesi, Caden Seamus; Gubbins, Joseph Matthew; Kendall, Charley George; McLeod, Kraig Nathaniel Noel; Mesias, Aiden Justino Araujo; Miller, Gilbert Scott Wallace; Orafu, Nathaniel Ikechukwu Benson; Platt, Mickel Anton; Remy, Shiloh Samuel; Ribeiro, Mateus Leandro Rivaldo; White, Harvey Batterson; Williams-Lowe, Kayden Lavon; Woollard-Innocent, Kai Hamilton.

READING (70)

ALUKO, Sone (M)   302   46
H: 5 8 W: 9 10 b.Birmingham 19-2-89
Internationals: England U16, U17, U18, U19. Nigeria U20, Full caps.

2005–06	Birmingham C	0	0	
2006–07	Birmingham C	0	0	
2007–08	Birmingham C	0	0	
2007–08	Aberdeen	20	3	
2008–09	Birmingham C	0	0	
2008–09	Blackpool	1	0	1 0
2008–09	Aberdeen	32	2	
2009–10	Aberdeen	22	3	
2010–11	Aberdeen	28	2	102 10
2011–12	Rangers	21	12	21 12
2012–13	Hull C	23	8	
2013–14	Hull C	17	1	
2014–15	Hull C	25	1	
2015–16	Hull C	25	3	90 13
2016–17	Fulham	45	8	
2017–18	Fulham	4	0	49 8
2017–18	Reading	39	3	39 3

ANDRESSON, Axel (D)   0   0
b. 27-1-98
Internationals: Iceland U17, U19, U21.

2016–17	Reading	0	0
2017–18	Reading	0	0

BACUNA, Leandro (M)   202   15
H: 6 2 W: 12 00 b.Groningen 21-8-91
Internationals: Netherlands U19, U21. Curacao Full caps.

2009–10	FC Groningen	20	2	
2012–13	FC Groningen	33	5	53 7
2013–14	Aston Villa	35	5	
2014–15	Aston Villa	19	0	
2015–16	Aston Villa	31	1	
2016–17	Aston Villa	30	1	
2017–18	Aston Villa	1	0	116 7
2017–18	Reading	33	1	33 1

BARRETT, Josh (F)   9   0
b. 21-6-98
Internationals: Republic of Ireland U17, U19, U21.

2015–16	Reading	3	0	
2016–17	Reading	0	0	
2017–18	Reading	0	0	3 0
2017–18	Coventry C	6	0	6 0

BARROW, Modou (F)   193   51
H: 5 9 W: 9 13 b.Banjul 13-10-92
Internationals: Gambia Full caps.

2010	Mjolby AI	15	6	15 6
2011	Mjolby Sodra	19	23	19 23
2012	Norrkping	7	0	7 0
2013	Varbergs	28	2	28 2
2014	Ostersunds FK	19	9	19 9
2014–15	Swansea C	11	0	
2014–15	Nottingham F	4	0	4 0
2015–16	Swansea C	22	1	
2015–16	Blackburn R	4	0	4 0
2016–17	Swansea C	18	0	51 1
2016–17	Leeds U	5	0	5 0
2017–18	Reading	41	10	41 10

BEERENS, Roy (F)   316   53
H: 5 8 W: 9 13 b.Bladel 22-12-87
Internationals: Netherlands U21, B, Full caps.

2005–06	PSV Eindhoven	2	0	
2006–07	PSV Eindhoven	7	1	9 1
2006–07	NEC	14	2	14 2
2007–08	Heerenveen	28	6	
2008–09	Heerenveen	29	9	
2009–10	Heerenveen	29	4	
2010–11	Heerenveen	28	6	114 25
2011–12	AZ Alkmaar	26	3	
2012–13	AZ Alkmaar	34	5	
2013–14	AZ Alkmaar	33	5	93 13
2014–15	Hertha Berlin	27	4	
2015–16	Hertha Berlin	2	0	29 4
2016–17	Reading	40	6	
2017–18	Reading	17	2	57 8

Transferred to Vitesse, January 2018.

BLACKETT, Tyler (D)   86   0
H: 6 1 W: 11 12 b.Manchester 2-4-94
Internationals: England U16, U17, U18, U19, U21.

2012–13	Manchester U	0	0	
2013–14	Manchester U	0	0	
2013–14	Blackpool	5	0	5 0
2013–14	Birmingham C	8	0	8 0
2014–15	Manchester U	11	0	
2015–16	Manchester U	0	0	11 0
2015–16	Celtic	3	0	3 0
2016–17	Reading	34	0	
2017–18	Reading	25	0	59 0

BODVARSSON, Jon Dadi (F)   251   45
H: 6 3 W: 13 05 b.Selfoss 25-5-92
Internationals: Iceland U19, U21, Full caps.

2008	Selfoss	0	0	
2009	Selfoss	16	1	
2010	Selfoss	21	3	
2011	Selfoss	21	7	
2012	Selfoss	22	7	80 18
2013	Viking	23	1	
2014	Viking	29	5	
2015	Viking	29	9	81 15
2015–16	Kaiserslautern	15	2	15 2
2016–17	Wolverhampton W	42	3	42 3
2017–18	Reading	33	7	33 7

BOND, Jonathan (G)   91   0
H: 6 3 W: 13 03 b.Hemel Hempstead 19-5-93
Internationals: Wales U17, U19. England U20, U21.

2010–11	Watford	0	0	
2011–12	Watford	1	0	
2011–12	Dagenham & R	5	0	5 0
2011–12	Bury	6	0	6 0
2012–13	Watford	8	0	
2013–14	Watford	10	0	
2014–15	Watford	3	0	22 0
2015–16	Reading	14	0	
2016–17	Reading	0	0	
2016–17	Gillingham	7	0	7 0
2017–18	Reading	0	0	14 0
2017–18	Peterborough U	37	0	37 0

CLEMENT, Pelle (M)   24   0
b.Amsterdam 19-5-96
Internationals: Netherlands U21.

2014–15	Ajax	0	0	
2015–16	Ajax	0	0	
2016–17	Ajax	1	0	1 0
2017–18	Reading	23	0	23 0

EAST, Ryan (M)   0   0
b. 7-8-98

2017–18	Reading	0	0

EDWARDS, Dave (M)   438   60
H: 5 11 W: 11 04 b.Shrewsbury 3-2-86
Internationals: Wales U21, Full caps.

2002–03	Shrewsbury T	1	0	
2003–04	Shrewsbury T	0	0	
2004–05	Shrewsbury T	27	5	
2005–06	Shrewsbury T	30	2	
2006–07	Shrewsbury T	45	5	103 12
2007–08	Luton T	19	4	19 4
2007–08	Wolverhampton W	10	1	
2008–09	Wolverhampton W	44	3	
2009–10	Wolverhampton W	20	1	
2010–11	Wolverhampton W	15	1	
2011–12	Wolverhampton W	26	3	
2012–13	Wolverhampton W	24	2	
2013–14	Wolverhampton W	30	9	
2014–15	Wolverhampton W	41	6	
2015–16	Wolverhampton W	29	5	
2016–17	Wolverhampton W	44	10	
2017–18	Wolverhampton W	1	0	284 41
2017–18	Reading	32	3	32 3

EVANS, George (M)   110   8
H: 6 0 W: 11 12 b.Cheadle 13-1-96
Internationals: England U17, U19, U20.

2012–13	Manchester C	0	0	
2013–14	Manchester C	0	0	
2013–14	Crewe Alex	23	1	23 1
2014–15	Manchester C	0	0	
2014–15	Scunthorpe U	16	1	16 1
2015–16	Manchester C	0	0	
2015–16	Walsall	12	3	12 3
2015–16	Reading	6	0	
2016–17	Reading	35	2	
2017–18	Reading	18	1	59 3

FROST, Tyler (M)   0   0
b. 7-7-99

2017–18	Reading	0	0

GRAVENBERCH, Danzell (D)   59   1
H: 6 1   W: 12 08   b.Amsterdam 13-2-94
Internationals: Netherlands U16, U17, U18, U19.

2013–14	Ajax	0	0		
2013–14	NEC	6	0	6	0
2014–15	Ajax	0	0		
2014–15	Universitatea Cluj	17	1	17	1
2015–16	Dordrecht	28	0	28	0
2016–17	Reading	2	0		
2017–18	Reading	0	0	2	0
2017–18	Roeselare	6	0	6	0

GUNTER, Chris (D)   412   4
H: 5 11   W: 11 02   b.Newport 21-7-89
Internationals: Wales U17, U19, U21, Full caps.

2006–07	Cardiff C	15	0		
2007–08	Cardiff C	13	0	28	0
2007–08	Tottenham H	2	0		
2008–09	Tottenham H	3	0	5	0
2008–09	Nottingham F	8	0		
2009–10	Nottingham F	44	1		
2010–11	Nottingham F	43	0		
2011–12	Nottingham F	46	1	141	2
2012–13	Reading	20	0		
2013–14	Reading	44	0		
2014–15	Reading	38	0		
2015–16	Reading	44	0		
2016–17	Reading	46	1		
2017–18	Reading	46	1	238	2

HOLMES, Thomas (D)   1   0
b. 12-3-00

2017–18	Reading	1	0	1 0

JAAKKOLA, Anssi (G)   123   0
H: 6 4   W: 13 12   b.Kemi 13-3-87
Internationals: Finland U21, Full caps.

2005	TP-47	3	0		
2006	TP-47	14	0	17	0
2006–07	Siena	0	0		
2007–08	Siena	1	0		
2008–09	Siena	0	0		
2008–09	Colligiana	7	0	7	0
2009–10	Siena	0	0	1	0
2010–11	Slavia Prague	2	0	2	0
2010–11	Kilmarnock	8	0		
2011–12	Kilmarnock	5	0		
2012–13	Kilmarnock	0	0	13	0
2013–14	Ajax Cape Town	24	0		
2014–15	Ajax Cape Town	28	0		
2015–16	Ajax Cape Town	26	0	78	0
2016–17	Reading	0	0		
2017–18	Reading	5	0	5	0

KELLY, Liam (M)   62   6
b. 22-11-95
Internationals: Republic of Ireland U19, U21.

2014–15	Reading	0	0		
2015–16	Reading	0	0		
2016–17	Reading	28	1		
2017–18	Reading	34	5	62	6

KERMORGANT, Yann (F)   434 123
H: 6 0   W: 13 03   b.Vannes 8-11-81
Internationals: Brittany Full caps.

2004–05	Chatellerault	24	14	29	14
2005–06	Grenoble	26	6		
2006–07	Grenoble	32	10	58	16
2007–08	Reims	33	4		
2008–09	Reims	34	9	67	13
2009–10	Leicester C	20	1		
2010–11	Leicester C	0	0	20	1
2010–11	Arles-Avignon	26	3	26	3
2011–12	Charlton Ath	36	12		
2012–13	Charlton Ath	32	12		
2013–14	Charlton Ath	21	5	89	29
2013–14	Bournemouth	16	9		
2014–15	Bournemouth	38	15		
2015–16	Bournemouth	7	0	61	24
2015–16	Reading	17	3		
2016–17	Reading	42	18		
2017–18	Reading	25	2	84	23

LEGG, George (G)   3   0
b. 30-4-96

2016–17	Reading	0	0		
2017–18	Reading	0	0		
2017–18	Barnet	3	0	3	0

LOADER, Danny (F)   0   0
Internationals: England U16, U17, U18.
From Wycombe W.

2017–18	Reading	0	0	

MANNONE, Vito (G)   156   0
H: 6 0   W: 11 08   b.Milan 2-3-88
Internationals: Italy U21.

2005–06	Arsenal	0	0		
2006–07	Arsenal	0	0		
2006–07	Barnsley	2	0	2	0
2007–08	Arsenal	0	0		
2008–09	Arsenal	1	0		
2009–10	Arsenal	5	0		
2010–11	Arsenal	0	0		
2010–11	Hull C	10	0		
2011–12	Arsenal	0	0		
2011–12	Hull C	21	0	31	0
2012–13	Arsenal	9	0	15	0
2013–14	Sunderland	29	0		
2014–15	Sunderland	10	0		
2015–16	Sunderland	19	0		
2016–17	Sunderland	9	0	67	0
2017–18	Reading	41	0	41	0

McCLEARY, Garath (M)   303 35
H: 5 10   W: 12 06   b.Oxford 15-5-87
Internationals: Jamaica Full caps.

2007–08	Nottingham F	8	1		
2008–09	Nottingham F	39	1		
2009–10	Nottingham F	24	0		
2010–11	Nottingham F	18	2		
2011–12	Nottingham F	22	9	111	13
2011–12	Reading	0	0		
2012–13	Reading	31	3		
2013–14	Reading	42	5		
2014–15	Reading	26	1		
2015–16	Reading	34	4		
2016–17	Reading	41	9		
2017–18	Reading	18	0	192	22

McSHANE, Paul (D)   329 14
H: 6 0   W: 11 05   b.Wicklow 6-1-86
Internationals: Republic of Ireland U21, Full caps.

2002–03	Manchester U	0	0		
2003–04	Manchester U	0	0		
2004–05	Manchester U	0	0		
2004–05	Walsall	4	1	4	1
2005–06	Manchester U	0	0		
2005–06	Brighton & HA	38	3	38	3
2006–07	WBA	32	2	32	2
2007–08	Sunderland	21	0		
2008–09	Sunderland	3	0		
2008–09	Hull C	17	1		
2009–10	Sunderland	0	0	24	0
2009–10	Hull C	27	0		
2010–11	Hull C	19	0		
2010–11	Barnsley	10	1	10	1
2011–12	Hull C	5	0		
2011–12	Crystal Palace	11	0	11	0
2012–13	Hull C	25	2		
2013–14	Hull C	10	0		
2014–15	Hull C	20	1	119	4
2015–16	Reading	35	0		
2016–17	Reading	30	3		
2017–18	Reading	26	0	91	3

MEITE, Yakou (M)   37   4
H: 6 0   W: 11 05   b.Paris 11-2-96
Internationals: Ivory Coast U17, U20, U23.

2015–16	Paris Saint-Germain	1	0	1	0
2016–17	Reading	14	1		
2017–18	Reading	0	0	14	1
2017–18	Sochaux	22	3	22	3

MENDES, Joseph (F)   137 21
H: 6 1   W: 12 08   b.Evreux 30-3-91

2010–11	Grenoble	14	1	14	1
2011–12	Epinal	22	3	22	3
2012–13	Le Mans	20	3	20	3
2013–14	Lokomotiv Plovdiv	7	0	7	0
2014–15	Le Havre	22	2		
2015–16	Le Havre	37	9	59	11
2016–17	Reading	12	3		
2017–18	Reading	3	0	15	3

MOORE, Liam (D)   182   5
H: 6 1   W: 13 08   b.Loughborough 31-1-93
Internationals: England U17, U20, U21.

2011–12	Leicester C	2	0		
2011–12	Bradford C	17	0	17	0
2012–13	Leicester C	16	0		
2012–13	Brentford	7	0		
2013–14	Leicester C	30	1		
2014–15	Leicester C	11	0		
2014–15	Brentford	3	0	10	0
2015–16	Leicester C	0	0	59	1
2015–16	Bristol C	10	0	10	0
2016–17	Reading	40	1		
2017–18	Reading	46	3	86	4

OBITA, Jordan (M)   169   7
H: 5 11   W: 11 08   b.Oxford 8-12-93
Internationals: England U18, U19, U21.

2010–11	Reading	0	0		
2011–12	Reading	0	0		
2011–12	Barnet	5	0	5	0
2011–12	Gillingham	6	3	6	3
2012–13	Reading	0	0		
2012–13	Portsmouth	8	1	8	1
2012–13	Oldham Ath	8	0	8	0
2013–14	Reading	34	1		
2014–15	Reading	43	0		
2015–16	Reading	26	0		
2016–17	Reading	37	2		
2017–18	Reading	2	0	142	3

POPA, Adrian (F)   294 40
H: 5 7   W: 11 00   b.Horezu 24-7-88
Internationals: Romania Full caps.

2006–07	Stiinta Timisoara	3	2		
2007–08	Stiinta Timisoara	25	2		
2008–09	Stiinta Timisoara	0	0	28	4
2008–09	Buftea	11	2	11	2
2008–09	Gloria Buzzau	11	0	11	0
2009–10	Universitatea Cluj	23	3	23	3
2010–11	Concordia Chiajna	27	4		
2011–12	Concordia Chiajna	30	3		
2012–13	Concordia Chiajna	4	3	61	10
2012–13	Steau Bucharest	30	1		
2013–14	Steau Bucharest	28	7		
2014–15	Steau Bucharest	28	5		
2015–16	Steau Bucharest	32	4		
2016–17	Steau Bucharest	19	3	137	20
2016–17	Reading	8	1		
2017–18	Reading	6	0	14	1
2017–18	Al-Taawoun	9	0	9	0

QUINN, Stephen (M)   356 25
H: 5 6   W: 9 08   b.Dublin 4-4-86
Internationals: Republic of Ireland U21, Full caps.

2005–06	Sheffield U	0	0		
2005–06	Milton Keynes D	15	0	15	0
2005–06	Rotherham U	16	0	16	0
2006–07	Sheffield U	15	2		
2007–08	Sheffield U	19	2		
2008–09	Sheffield U	43	7		
2009–10	Sheffield U	44	4		
2010–11	Sheffield U	37	1		
2011–12	Sheffield U	45	4		
2012–13	Sheffield U	3	0	206	20
2012–13	Hull C	42	3		
2013–14	Hull C	15	0		
2014–15	Hull C	28	1	85	4
2015–16	Reading	27	1		
2016–17	Reading	7	0		
2017–18	Reading	0	0	34	1

RICHARDS, Omar (D)   13   2
H: 6 1   W: 10 12   b. 15-2-98

2017–18	Reading	13	2	13	2

RINOMHOTA, Andy (M)   0   0
b. 21-4-97
From AFC Portchester.

2017–18	Reading	0	0	

SMITH, Sam (F)   8   1
H: 5 11   W: 11 07   b. 8-3-98

2017–18	Reading	8	1	8	1

SWIFT, John (M)   109 19
H: 6 0   W: 11 07   b.Portsmouth 23-6-95
Internationals: England U16, U17, U18, U19, U20, U21.

2013–14	Chelsea	1	0		
2014–15	Chelsea	0	0		
2014–15	Rotherham U	3	0	3	0
2014–15	Swindon T	18	2	18	2
2015–16	Chelsea	0	0	1	0
2015–16	Brentford	27	7	27	7
2016–17	Reading	36	8		
2017–18	Reading	24	2	60	10

TIAGO ILORI, Almeida (D)   55   1
H: 6 3   W: 12 07   b.London 26-2-93
Internationals: Portugal U18, U19, U20, U21, U23.

2011–12	Sporting Lisbon	1	0		
2012–13	Sporting Lisbon	11	1	12	1
2013–14	Liverpool	0	0		
2013–14	Granada	9	0	9	0
2014–15	Liverpool	0	0		
2014–15	Bordeaux	0	0		
2015–16	Aston Villa	0	0		
2016–17	Liverpool	0	0		
2016–17	Reading	5	0		
2017–18	Reading	29	0	34	0

VAN DEN BERG, Joey (M)   262 26
H: 5 10 W: 11 00 b.Nijeveen 13-2-86

2004–05	Heerenveen	1	0		
2005–06	Heerenveen	1	0		
2005–06	Almere C	19	1	19	1
2007–08	Go Ahead Eagles	11	1	11	1
2010–11	PEC Zwolle	27	5		
2011–12	PEC Zwolle	30	7		
2012–13	PEC Zwolle	16	3	73	15
2012–13	Heerenveen	13	0		
2013–14	Heerenveen	29	2		
2014–15	Heerenveen	29	2		
2015–16	Heerenveen	26	4	99	8
2016–17	Reading	27	0		
2017–18	Reading	33	1	60	1

Players retained or with offer of contract
Coleman, Ethan Jay; Driscoll, Liam Michael-Owen; Harriott, Callum Kyle; Holsgrove, Jordan William; House, Benjamin; Howe, Teddy William; McIntyre, Thomas Peter; Medford-Smith, Ramarni Nelson; Novakovich, Andrija; Osho, Gabriel Jeremiah Adedayo; Rollinson, Joel Robert Paul; Shokunbi, Ademola Oluwaseyi Abiodun; Southwood, Luke Kevin; Ward, Lewis Moore; Watson, Tennai Rosharne; Wieser, Sandro.

Scholars
Andresson, Jokull; Balogun, Jamal Clinton; Buchanan, Jack James; Burley, Andre Maurice Keith; Desbois, Adam Jack; Elva-Fountaine, Marcel Patrick Joshua; Green, Cameron Oliver; Hansen, Michenaidgelo Marjorick Nildion; Hillson, James Andrew; Lawrence, Charles James; Moore, Shamar Andrew; Nditi, Roberto Yohana; Nolan, Jack Daniel; Obamakinwa, Emmanuel Olorunfemi Joshua; Odimayo, Akinwale Joseph; Okuboyejo, Leon Sholafunmibabajide; Omolabi, Moroyin Oladimeji Opemipo; Pemberton, Jacob; Philby, Henry Thomas; Saydee, Terrance; Simmo, Khalid Zakaria; Stevens, Tommy; Wallace, Jazz Oreet; Wilson, Joseph Robert.

ROCHDALE (71)

ADSHEAD, Daniel (M)   1 0
H: 5 6 W: 10 03 b. 2-9-01

2017–18	Rochdale	1	0	1	0

ANDREW, Calvin (F)   328 33
H: 6 0 W: 12 11 b.Luton 19-12-86

2004–05	Luton T	8	0		
2005–06	Luton T	1	1		
2005–06	*Grimsby T*	8	1	8	1
2005–06	*Bristol C*	3	0	3	0
2006–07	Luton T	7	1		
2007–08	Luton T	39	2	55	4
2008–09	Crystal Palace	7	0		
2008–09	*Brighton & HA*	9	2	9	2
2009–10	Crystal Palace	27	1		
2010–11	Crystal Palace	13	0		
2010–11	*Millwall*	3	0	3	0
2010–11	*Swindon T*	10	1	10	1
2011–12	Crystal Palace	6	0	53	1
2011–12	*Leyton Orient*	10	0	10	0
2012–13	Port Vale	22	1		
2013–14	Port Vale	0	0	22	1
2013–14	Mansfield T	15	1	15	1
2013–14	York C	8	1	8	1
2014–15	Rochdale	32	5		
2015–16	Rochdale	30	6		
2016–17	Rochdale	39	7		
2017–18	Rochdale	31	3	132	21

BARRY-MURPHY, Brian (M)   458 17
H: 5 10 W: 13 01 b.Cork 27-7-78
Internationals: Republic of Ireland U21.

1995–96	Cork C	13	0		
1996–97	Cork C	25	0		
1997–98	Cork C	15	1		
1998–99	Cork C	27	1	80	2
1999–2000	Preston NE	1	0		
2000–01	Preston NE	14	0		
2001–02	Preston NE	4	0		
2001–02	*Southend U*	8	1	8	1
2002–03	Preston NE	2	0	21	0
2002–03	*Hartlepool U*	7	0	7	0
2002–03	Sheffield W	17	0		
2003–04	Sheffield W	41	0	58	0
2004–05	Bury	45	6		
2005–06	Bury	40	3		
2006–07	Bury	14	0		
2007–08	Bury	31	1		
2008–09	Bury	42	2		
2009–10	Bury	46	1	218	13
2010–11	Rochdale	32	0		
2011–12	Rochdale	22	1		
2012–13	Rochdale	8	0		
2013–14	Rochdale	3	0		
2014–15	Rochdale	0	0		
2015–16	Rochdale	1	0		
2016–17	Rochdale	0	0		
2017–18	Rochdale	0	0	66	1

BROWN, Reece (D)   94 1
H: 6 2 W: 13 02 b.Manchester 1-11-91
Internationals: England U19, U20.

2010–11	Manchester U	0	0		
2010–11	*Bradford C*	3	0	3	0
2011–12	Manchester U	0	0		
2011–12	*Doncaster R*	3	0	3	0
2011–12	*Oldham Ath*	15	0	15	0
2012–13	Manchester U	0	0		
2012–13	*Coventry C*	6	0	6	0
2012–13	*Ipswich T*	1	0	1	0
2013–14	Watford	1	0	1	0
2013–14	*Carlisle U*	12	0	12	0
2014–15	Barnsley	13	0	13	0
2015–16	Bury	28	0		
2016–17	Sheffield U	2	0	2	0
2016–17	Bury	7	1	35	1
2017–18	Rochdale	3	0	3	0

CAMPS, Callum (M)   132 16
b.Stockport 30-11-95
Internationals: Northern Ireland U18, U21.

2012–13	Rochdale	2	0		
2013–14	Rochdale	0	0		
2014–15	Rochdale	12	1		
2015–16	Rochdale	32	5		
2016–17	Rochdale	44	8		
2017–18	Rochdale	42	2	132	16

CANAVAN, Niall (D)   196 18
H: 6 3 W: 12 00 b.Guiseley 11-4-91
Internationals: Republic of Ireland U21.

2009–10	Scunthorpe U	7	1		
2010–11	Scunthorpe U	8	0		
2010–11	*Shrewsbury T*	3	0	3	0
2011–12	Scunthorpe U	12	1		
2012–13	Scunthorpe U	40	6		
2013–14	Scunthorpe U	45	4		
2014–15	Scunthorpe U	32	3		
2015–16	Scunthorpe U	10	0	154	15
2015–16	*Rochdale*	11	1		
2016–17	Rochdale	25	2		
2017–18	Rochdale	3	0	39	3

CANNON, Andy (M)   89 4
H: 5 9 W: 11 09 b.Ashton-under-Lyne 14-3-96

2014–15	Rochdale	18	0		
2015–16	Rochdale	25	0		
2016–17	Rochdale	25	2		
2017–18	Rochdale	21	2	89	4

COLLIS, Steve (G)   88 0
H: 6 3 W: 12 05 b.Harrow 18-3-81

1999–2000	Barnet	0	0		
2000–01	Nottingham F	0	0		
2001–02	Nottingham F	0	0		
2003–04	Yeovil T	11	0		
2004–05	Yeovil T	9	0		
2005–06	Yeovil T	23	0	43	0
2006–07	Southend U	1	0		
2007–08	Southend U	20	0	21	0
2008–09	Crewe Alex	18	0		
2009–10	Crewe Alex	1	0	19	0
2009–10	Bristol C	0	0		
2009–10	*Torquay U*	1	0	1	0
2010–11	Peterborough U	0	0		
2010–11	*Northampton T*	4	0	4	0
2011–12	Macclesfield T	0	0		
2012–13	Rochdale	0	0		
2013–14	Rochdale	0	0		
2014–15	Rochdale	0	0		
2015–16	Rochdale	0	0		
2017–18	Rochdale	0	0		

DAVIES, Steve (F)   324 90
H: 6 0 W: 12 00 b.Liverpool 29-12-87

2005–06	Tranmere R	22	2		
2006–07	Tranmere R	28	1		
2007–08	Tranmere R	10	2	60	5
2008–09	Derby Co	19	3		
2009–10	Derby Co	18	1		
2010–11	Derby Co	20	5		
2011–12	Derby Co	26	11		
2012–13	Derby Co	0	0	83	20
2012–13	*Bristol C*	37	13	37	13
2013–14	Blackpool	28	3		
2014–15	Blackpool	17	5	45	8

2014–15	*Sheffield U*	13	2	13	2
2015–16	Bradford C	25	5	25	5
2016–17	Rochdale	29	9		
2017–18	Rochdale	32	7	61	16

DELANEY, Ryan (D)   48 8
H: 6 0 W: 11 05 b.Wexford 6-9-96
Internationals: Republic of Ireland U21.
From Wexford.

2016–17	Burton Alb	0	0		
2017	Cork C	30	6	30	6
2017–18	Rochdale	18	2	18	2

DONE, Matt (M)   390 40
H: 5 10 W: 10 04 b.Oswestry 22-6-88

2005–06	Wrexham	6	0		
2006–07	Wrexham	34	1		
2007–08	Wrexham	26	0	66	1
2008–09	Hereford U	36	0		
2009–10	Hereford U	20	0	56	0
2010–11	Rochdale	33	5		
2011–12	Barnsley	31	4		
2012–13	Barnsley	13	0	44	4
2012–13	*Hibernian*	7	0	7	0
2013–14	Rochdale	38	0		
2014–15	Rochdale	23	10		
2014–15	Sheffield U	15	7		
2015–16	Sheffield U	31	4		
2016–17	Sheffield U	31	3	77	14
2017–18	Rochdale	46	6	140	21

GILLAM, Matthew (F)   8 1
H: 5 9 W: 11 07 b. 4-10-98

2016–17	Rochdale	0	0		
2017–18	Rochdale	8	1	8	1

HENDERSON, Ian (F)   471 109
H: 5 10 W: 11 06 b.Thetford 25-1-85
Internationals: England U18, U20.

2002–03	Norwich C	20	1		
2003–04	Norwich C	19	4		
2004–05	Norwich C	24	1		
2005–06	Norwich C	2	0	68	6
2006–07	*Rotherham U*	18	1	18	1
2007–08	Northampton T	23	0		
2008–09	Northampton T	3	0	26	0
2008–09	Luton T	19	1	19	1
2009–10	Colchester U	13	2		
2009–10	*Ankaragucu*	2	0	2	0
2010–11	Colchester U	36	10		
2011–12	Colchester U	46	9		
2012–13	Colchester U	22	3	117	24
2012–13	Rochdale	12	3		
2013–14	Rochdale	45	11		
2014–15	Rochdale	44	22		
2015–16	Rochdale	39	13		
2016–17	Rochdale	42	15		
2017–18	Rochdale	39	13	221	77

KEANE, Keith (M)   255 8
H: 5 9 W: 11 01 b.Luton 20-11-86
Internationals: Republic of Ireland U19, U21.

2003–04	Luton T	15	1		
2004–05	Luton T	17	0		
2005–06	Luton T	10	1		
2006–07	Luton T	19	1		
2007–08	Luton T	28	1		
2008–09	Luton T	40	0	129	4
2012–13	Preston NE	26	1		
2013–14	Preston NE	38	2		
2014–15	Preston NE	0	0	64	3
2014–15	*Crawley T*	12	0	12	0
2014–15	Stevenage	7	0		
2015–16	Stevenage	6	1	13	1
2016–17	Cambridge U	1	0	5	0
2016–17	*Rochdale*	29	0		
2017–18	Rochdale	3	0	32	0

KEARNEY, Keith (D)   0 0
Internationals: Northern Ireland U16, U17.

2017–18	Rochdale	0	0		

KITCHING, Mark (D)   19 2
b.Guisborough 4-9-95

2013–14	Middlesbrough	0	0		
2014–15	Middlesbrough	0	0		
2015–16	Middlesbrough	0	0		
2015–16	*York C*	1	0	1	0
2016–17	Middlesbrough	0	0		
2016–17	*Rochdale*	0	0		
2017–18	Rochdale	13	2	18	2

LILLIS, Josh (G)   272 0
H: 6 0 W: 12 08 b.Derby 24-6-87

2006–07	Scunthorpe U	1	0		
2007–08	Scunthorpe U	3	0		
2008–09	Scunthorpe U	5	0		

2008–09	*Notts Co*	5	0	**5**	**0**
2009–10	Scunthorpe U	8	0		
2009–10	*Grimsby T*	4	0	**4**	**0**
2009–10	*Rochdale*	1	0		
2010–11	Scunthorpe U	15	0		
2010–11	*Rochdale*	23	0		
2011–12	Scunthorpe U	6	0	**38**	**0**
2012–13	Rochdale	46	0		
2013–14	Rochdale	45	0		
2014–15	Rochdale	16	0		
2015–16	Rochdale	40	0		
2016–17	Rochdale	14	0		
2017–18	Rochdale	40	0	**225**	**0**

McGAHEY, Harrison (D) 108 0
b.Preston 26-9-95

2013–14	Blackpool	4	0	**4**	**0**
2014–15	Sheffield U	15	0		
2014–15	*Tranmere R*	4	0	**4**	**0**
2015–16	Sheffield U	7	0	**22**	**0**
2016–17	Rochdale	36	0		
2017–18	Rochdale	42	0	**78**	**0**

McNULTY, Jim (D) 328 6
H: 6 1 W: 12 00 b.Runcorn 13-2-85
Internationals: Scotland U17, U19.

2006–07	Macclesfield T	15	0		
2007–08	Macclesfield T	19	1	**34**	**1**
2007–08	Stockport Co	11	0		
2008–09	Stockport Co	26	1	**37**	**1**
2008–09	Brighton & HA	5	1		
2009–10	Brighton & HA	8	0		
2009–10	*Scunthorpe U*	3	0		
2010–11	Brighton & HA	0	0	**13**	**1**
2010–11	*Scunthorpe U*	6	0	**9**	**0**
2011–12	Barnsley	44	2		
2012–13	Barnsley	12	0		
2013–14	Barnsley	0	0	**56**	**2**
2013–14	*Tranmere R*	12	0	**12**	**0**
2013–14	Bury	21	0		
2014–15	Bury	25	0	**46**	**0**
2015–16	Rochdale	46	0		
2016–17	Rochdale	35	0		
2017–18	Rochdale	40	1	**121**	**1**

MOORE, Brendan (G) 6 0
b. 16-4-92
From Fleetwood T, Torquay U.

2017–18	Rochdale	6	0	**6**	**0**

MORLEY, Aaron (M) 2 0

2016–17	Rochdale	2	0		
2017–18	Rochdale	0	0	**2**	**0**

NTLHE, Kgosietsile (D) 118 4
H: 5 9 W: 10 05 b.Pretoria 21-2-94
Internationals: South Africa U20, Full caps.

2010–11	Peterborough U	0	0		
2011–12	Peterborough U	2	0		
2012–13	Peterborough U	12	1		
2013–14	Peterborough U	27	2		
2014–15	Peterborough U	28	1		
2015–16	Peterborough U	7	0		
2016–17	Peterborough U	0	0	**76**	**4**
2016–17	Stevenage	22	0	**22**	**0**
2017–18	Rochdale	20	0	**20**	**0**

RAFFERTY, Joe (D) 187 3
H: 6 0 W: 11 11 b.Liverpool 6-10-93
Internationals: Republic of Ireland U18, U19.

2012–13	Rochdale	21	0		
2013–14	Rochdale	31	0		
2014–15	Rochdale	31	1		
2015–16	Rochdale	31	1		
2016–17	Rochdale	40	0		
2017–18	Rochdale	33	1	**187**	**3**

RATHBONE, Oliver (M) 60 3
H: 5 7 W: 10 06 b.Blackburn 10-10-96
From Manchester U.

2016–17	Rochdale	27	2		
2017–18	Rochdale	33	1	**60**	**3**

SLEW, Jordan (F) 127 11
H: 6 3 W: 12 11 b.Sheffield 7-9-92
Internationals: England U19.

2010–11	Sheffield U	7	2		
2011–12	Sheffield U	4	1	**11**	**3**
2011–12	Blackburn R	1	0		
2011–12	*Stevenage*	9	0	**9**	**0**
2012–13	Blackburn R	0	0		
2012–13	*Oldham Ath*	3	0	**3**	**0**
2012–13	*Rotherham U*	7	0	**7**	**0**
2013–14	Blackburn R	0	0		
2013–14	*Ross Co*	20	1	**20**	**1**
2014–15	Blackburn R	0	0	**1**	**0**
2014–15	*Port Vale*	9	2	**9**	**2**
2014–15	Cambridge U	13	1		
2015–16	Cambridge U	10	0	**23**	**1**
2015–16	Chesterfield	7	0	**7**	**0**
2016–17	Plymouth Arg	32	4	**32**	**4**
2017–18	Rochdale	5	0	**5**	**0**

THOMPSON, Joe (M) 219 23
H: 6 0 W: 9 07 b.Rochdale 5-3-89

2005–06	Rochdale	1	0		
2006–07	Rochdale	13	0		
2007–08	Rochdale	11	1		
2008–09	Rochdale	30	5		
2009–10	Rochdale	36	6		
2010–11	Rochdale	32	2		
2011–12	Rochdale	17	1		
2012–13	Tranmere R	19	1		
2012–13	*Rochdale*	7	0		
2013–14	Tranmere R	6	2	**25**	**3**
2014–15	Bury	1	0	**1**	**0**
2015–16	Carlisle U	15	1	**15**	**1**
2016–17	Rochdale	21	3		
2017–18	Rochdale	10	1	**178**	**19**

WILLIAMS, Jordan (M) 22 0
b.Warrington 13-12-92

2017–18	Rochdale	11	0	**11**	**0**
2017–18	*Lincoln C*	11	0	**11**	**0**

Scholars
Appiah, Nathaniel Amoako; Bradley, Lewis Derek; Hamzat, Sikirulahi Adejuwon; Hopper, Harrison George; Hoti, Florent; Kearney, Keith Leeroy; Kengni, Kuemo Neil Astrio; Muralitharan, Jai Ravin; Murray, Elliott Roy; Neild, James; Renner, Joseph Edward; Tavares, Desiderio Fabio Andre; Wade, Bradley Calvin; Ward, Isaac Benjamin; White, Louis Vincent; Yonsian, Monimon de Louis-Florian.

ROTHERHAM U (72)

AJAYI, Semi (D) 70 5
H: 6 4 W: 13 00 b.Croydon 9-11-93
Internationals: Nigeria U20.

2012–13	Charlton Ath	0	0		
2013–14	Charlton Ath	0	0		
2014–15	Arsenal	0	0		
2014–15	*Cardiff C*	0	0		
2015–16	Cardiff C	0	0		
2015–16	*AFC Wimbledon*	5	0	**5**	**0**
2015–16	*Crewe Alex*	13	0	**13**	**0**
2016–17	Cardiff C	0	0		
2016–17	*Rotherham U*	17	1		
2017–18	Rotherham U	35	4	**52**	**5**

BALL, David (F) 284 63
H: 6 0 W: 11 08 b.Whitefield 14-12-89

2007–08	Manchester C	0	0		
2008–09	Manchester C	0	0		
2009–10	Manchester C	0	0		
2010–11	Manchester C	0	0		
2010–11	*Swindon T*	18	2	**18**	**2**
2010–11	Peterborough U	19	5		
2011–12	Peterborough U	22	4		
2011–12	*Rochdale*	14	3	**14**	**3**
2012–13	Peterborough U	0	0	**41**	**9**
2012–13	Fleetwood T	34	7		
2013–14	Fleetwood T	30	8		
2014–15	Fleetwood T	32	8		
2015–16	Fleetwood T	37	4		
2016–17	Fleetwood T	46	14	**179**	**41**
2017–18	Rotherham U	32	8	**32**	**8**

BALL, Dominic (D) 67 1
H: 6 0 W: 12 06 b.Welwyn Garden City 2-8-95
Internationals: Northern Ireland U16, U17, U19, U21. England U19, U20.

2013–14	Tottenham H	0	0		
2014–15	Tottenham H	0	0		
2014–15	*Cambridge U*	11	0	**11**	**0**
2015–16	Tottenham H	0	0		
2015–16	*Rangers*	21	0	**21**	**0**
2016–17	Rotherham U	13	0		
2016–17	*Peterborough U*	6	1	**6**	**1**
2017–18	Rotherham U	0	0	**13**	**0**
2017–18	*Aberdeen*	16	0	**16**	**0**

BILBOE, Laurence (G) 0 0
b. 21-2-98

2016–17	Rotherham U	0	0		
2017–18	Rotherham U	0	0		

BRAY, Alex (M) 17 1
H: 5 10 W: 10 06 b.Bath 25-7-95
Internationals: Wales U19.

2013–14	Swansea C	0	0		
2014–15	Swansea C	0	0		
2014–15	*Plymouth Arg*	1	0	**1**	**0**
2015–16	Swansea C	0	0		
2016–17	Swansea C	0	0		
2016–17	*Rotherham U*	5	0		
2017–18	Rotherham U	0	0	**5**	**0**
2017–18	*Forest Green R*	11	1	**11**	**1**

CLARKE-HARRIS, Jonson (F) 162 24
H: 6 0 W: 11 01 b.Leicester 21-7-94

2012–13	Peterborough U	0	0		
2012–13	*Southend U*	3	0	**3**	**0**
2012–13	*Bury*	12	4	**12**	**4**
2013–14	Oldham Ath	40	6		
2014–15	Oldham Ath	5	1	**45**	**7**
2014–15	Rotherham U	15	3		
2014–15	*Milton Keynes D*	5	0	**5**	**0**
2014–15	*Doncaster R*	9	1	**9**	**1**
2015–16	Rotherham U	35	6		
2016–17	Rotherham U	7	0		
2017–18	Rotherham U	14	0	**71**	**9**
2017–18	*Coventry C*	17	3	**17**	**3**

CUMMINGS, Shaun (D) 168 2
H: 6 0 W: 11 10 b.Hammersmith 25-2-89
Internationals: Jamaica Full caps.

2007–08	Chelsea	0	0		
2008–09	Chelsea	0	0		
2008–09	*Milton Keynes D*	32	0	**32**	**0**
2009–10	Chelsea	0	0		
2009–10	*WBA*	3	0	**3**	**0**
2009–10	Reading	8	0		
2010–11	Reading	10	0		
2011–12	Reading	34	0		
2012–13	Reading	9	0		
2013–14	Reading	11	0		
2014–15	Reading	5	1	**77**	**1**
2014–15	Millwall	12	0		
2015–16	Millwall	16	1		
2016–17	Millwall	16	0	**44**	**1**
2017–18	Rotherham U	12	0	**12**	**0**

FORDE, Anthony (M) 180 11
H: 5 9 W: 10 10 b.Limerick 16-11-93
Internationals: Republic of Ireland U19, U21.

2011–12	Wolverhampton W	6	0		
2012–13	Wolverhampton W	12	0		
2012–13	*Scunthorpe U*	8	0	**8**	**0**
2013–14	Wolverhampton W	3	0	**21**	**0**
2014–15	Walsall	37	3		
2015–16	Walsall	41	4	**78**	**7**
2016–17	Rotherham U	32	2		
2017–18	Rotherham U	41	2	**73**	**4**

HINDS, Akeem (D) 0 0

2017–18	Rotherham U	0	0		

IHIEKWE, Michael (D) 82 2
H: 6 1 W: 12 02 b.Liverpool 20-11-92
Internationals: England C.

2011–12	Wolverhampton W	0	0		
2012–13	Wolverhampton W	0	0		
2013–14	Wolverhampton W	0	0		
2013–14	*Cheltenham T*	13	0	**13**	**0**
2014–15	Tranmere R	38	1	**38**	**1**
2017–18	Rotherham U	31	1	**31**	**1**

KAYODE, Joshua (F) 0 0

2017–18	Rotherham U	0	0		

MATTOCK, Joe (D) 293 6
H: 5 11 W: 12 05 b.Leicester 15-5-90
Internationals: England U17, U19, U21.

2006–07	Leicester C	4	0		
2007–08	Leicester C	31	0		
2008–09	Leicester C	31	1		
2009–10	Leicester C	0	0	**66**	**1**
2009–10	WBA	29	0		
2010–11	WBA	0	0		
2010–11	*Sheffield U*	13	0	**13**	**0**
2011–12	WBA	0	0	**29**	**0**
2011–12	*Portsmouth*	7	0	**7**	**0**
2011–12	*Brighton & HA*	15	1	**15**	**1**
2012–13	Sheffield W	7	0		
2013–14	Sheffield W	23	2		
2014–15	Sheffield W	27	0	**57**	**2**
2015–16	Rotherham U	35	1		
2016–17	Rotherham U	36	0		
2017–18	Rotherham U	35	1	**106**	**2**

McGINLEY, Reece (F) 0 0
Internationals: Northern Ireland U17, U19.

2017–18	Rotherham U	0	0		

MURR, Lewis (M) 0 0

2017–18	Rotherham U	0	0		

NEWELL, Joe (M) 204 17
H: 5 11 W: 11 02 b.Tamworth 15-3-93

2010–11	Peterborough U	2	0		
2011–12	Peterborough U	14	1		
2012–13	Peterborough U	30	0		

Season	Club	Apps	Gls	Tot A	Tot G
2013–14	Peterborough U	11	0		
2014–15	Peterborough U	39	2	96	3
2015–16	Rotherham U	35	5		
2016–17	Rotherham U	34	2		
2017–18	Rotherham U	39	7	108	14

ONARIASE, Manny (D)   27   1
H: 6 1 b.29-1-95

Season	Club	Apps	Gls	Tot A	Tot G
2014–15	West Ham U	0	0		
2015–16	West Ham U	0	0		
2016–17	Brentford	0	0		
2016–17	*Cheltenham T*	22	1		
2017–18	West Ham U	0	0		
2017–18	*Cheltenham T*	5	0	27	1

PALMER, Matthew (M)   164   7
H: 5 10 W: 12 06 b.Derby 1-8-93

Season	Club	Apps	Gls	Tot A	Tot G
2012–13	Burton Alb	2	0		
2013–14	Burton Alb	40	0		
2014–15	Burton Alb	33	4		
2015–16	Burton Alb	14	0		
2015–16	*Oldham Ath*	14	1	14	1
2016–17	Burton Alb	36	1		
2017–18	Burton Alb	11	1	136	6
2017–18	Rotherham U	14	0	14	0

POTTER, Darren (M)   409   17
H: 6 0 W: 10 08 b.Liverpool 21-12-84
Internationals: Republic of Ireland Full caps.

Season	Club	Apps	Gls	Tot A	Tot G
2001–02	Liverpool	0	0		
2002–03	Liverpool	0	0		
2003–04	Liverpool	0	0		
2004–05	Liverpool	2	0		
2005–06	Liverpool	0	0		
2005–06	*Southampton*	10	0	10	0
2006–07	Liverpool	0	0	2	0
2006–07	Wolverhampton W	38	0		
2007–08	Wolverhampton W	18	0		
2008–09	Wolverhampton W	0	0	56	0
2008–09	*Sheffield W*	17	2		
2009–10	Sheffield W	46	3		
2010–11	Sheffield W	33	3	96	8
2011–12	Milton Keynes D	40	2		
2012–13	Milton Keynes D	46	4		
2013–14	Milton Keynes D	29	0		
2014–15	Milton Keynes D	40	2		
2015–16	Milton Keynes D	37	0		
2016–17	Milton Keynes D	37	1	229	9
2017–18	Rotherham U	16	0	16	0

PRICE, Lewis (G)   148   0
H: 5 10 W: 13 05 b.Bournemouth 19-7-84
Internationals: Wales U19, U21, Full caps.

Season	Club	Apps	Gls	Tot A	Tot G
2002–03	Ipswich T	0	0		
2003–04	Ipswich T	1	0		
2004–05	Ipswich T	8	0		
2004–05	*Cambridge U*	6	0	6	0
2005–06	Ipswich T	25	0		
2006–07	Ipswich T	34	0	68	0
2007–08	Derby Co	6	0		
2008–09	Derby Co	0	0		
2008–09	*Milton Keynes D*	2	0	2	0
2008–09	*Luton T*	1	0	1	0
2009–10	Derby Co	0	0	6	0
2009–10	Brentford	13	0	13	0
2010–11	Crystal Palace	1	0		
2011–12	Crystal Palace	5	0		
2012–13	Crystal Palace	0	0		
2013–14	Crystal Palace	0	0		
2013–14	*Mansfield T*	5	0	5	0
2014–15	Crystal Palace	0	0	6	0
2014–15	*Crawley T*	18	0	18	0
2015–16	*Sheffield W*	5	0	5	0
2016–17	Rotherham U	17	0		
2017–18	Rotherham U	1	0	18	0

PROCTOR, Jamie (F)   232   38
H: 6 2 W: 12 03 b.Preston 25-3-92

Season	Club	Apps	Gls	Tot A	Tot G
2009–10	Preston NE	1	0		
2010–11	Preston NE	5	1		
2010–11	*Stockport Co*	7	0	7	0
2011–12	Preston NE	31	3	37	4
2012–13	Swansea C	0	0		
2012–13	*Shrewsbury T*	2	0	2	0
2012–13	Crawley T	3	0		
2013–14	Crawley T	44	6	62	13
2014–15	Fleetwood T	41	8		
2015–16	Fleetwood T	23	4	64	12
2015–16	Bradford C	18	5	18	5
2016–17	Bolton W	21	0	21	0
2016–17	*Carlisle U*	17	4	17	4
2017–18	Rotherham U	14	0	14	0

PURRINGTON, Ben (D)   72   0
H: 5 9 W: 11 07 b.Exeter 5-5-96

Season	Club	Apps	Gls	Tot A	Tot G
2013–14	Plymouth Arg	12	0		
2014–15	Plymouth Arg	8	0		
2015–16	Plymouth Arg	13	0		
2016–17	Plymouth Arg	19	0	52	0
2016–17	Rotherham U	10	0		
2017–18	Rotherham U	10	0	20	0

SMITH, Michael (F)   202   50
H: 6 4 W: 11 02 b.Wallsend 17-10-91

Season	Club	Apps	Gls	Tot A	Tot G
2011–12	Charlton Ath	0	0		
2011–12	*Accrington S*	6	3	6	3
2012–13	Charlton Ath	0	0		
2012–13	*Colchester U*	8	1	8	1
2013–14	Charlton Ath	0	0		
2013–14	*AFC Wimbledon*	23	9	23	9
2013–14	Swindon T	20	8		
2014–15	Swindon T	40	13		
2015–16	Swindon T	5	0	65	21
2015–16	Barnsley	13	0	13	0
2015–16	Portsmouth	16	4		
2016–17	Portsmouth	18	3	34	7
2016–17	Northampton T	14	2		
2017–18	Northampton T	0	0	14	2
2017–18	Bury	19	1	19	1
2017–18	Rotherham U	20	6	20	6

TAYLOR, Jon (M)   268   44
H: 5 11 W: 12 04 b.Liverpool 23-12-89

Season	Club	Apps	Gls	Tot A	Tot G
2009–10	Shrewsbury T	2	0		
2010–11	Shrewsbury T	20	6		
2011–12	Shrewsbury T	33	0		
2012–13	Shrewsbury T	37	7		
2013–14	Shrewsbury T	41	9	133	22
2014–15	Peterborough U	24	3		
2015–16	Peterborough U	44	11	68	14
2016–17	Rotherham U	42	4		
2017–18	Rotherham U	25	4	67	8

VAULKS, Will (D)   192   16
H: 5 11 b.Birkenhead 13-9-93

Season	Club	Apps	Gls	Tot A	Tot G
2012–13	Tranmere R	6	0		
2012–13	Falkirk	6	0		
2013–14	Falkirk	33	1		
2014–15	Falkirk	34	3		
2015–16	Falkirk	35	6	108	10
2016–17	Rotherham U	40	1		
2017–18	Rotherham U	44	5	84	6

WARREN, Mason (D)   0   0
b.Doncaster 28-3-97

Season	Club	Apps	Gls	Tot A	Tot G
2015–16	Rotherham U	0	0		
2016–17	Rotherham U	0	0		
2017–18	Rotherham U	0	0		

WILES, Ben (M)   0   0

Season	Club	Apps	Gls	Tot A	Tot G
2017–18	Rotherham U	0	0		

WILLIAMS, Ryan (F)   110   12
H: 5 11 W: 12 00 b.Perth 28-10-93
Internationals: Australia U20, U23.

Season	Club	Apps	Gls	Tot A	Tot G
2011–12	Portsmouth	4	0	4	0
2011–12	Fulham	0	0		
2012–13	Fulham	0	0		
2013–14	Fulham	0	0		
2013–14	*Oxford U*	36	7	36	7
2014–15	Fulham	2	0	2	0
2014–15	*Barnsley*	5	0		
2015–16	Barnsley	5	0		
2016–17	Barnsley	16	1	26	1
2017–18	Rotherham U	42	4	42	4

WOOD, Richard (D)   414   25
H: 6 3 W: 12 13 b.Ossett 5-7-85

Season	Club	Apps	Gls	Tot A	Tot G
2002–03	Sheffield W	3	1		
2003–04	Sheffield W	12	0		
2004–05	Sheffield W	34	1		
2005–06	Sheffield W	30	1		
2006–07	Sheffield W	12	0		
2007–08	Sheffield W	27	2		
2008–09	Sheffield W	42	0		
2009–10	Sheffield W	11	2	171	7
2009–10	Coventry C	24	3		
2010–11	Coventry C	40	1		
2011–12	Coventry C	17	1		
2012–13	Coventry C	36	3	117	8
2013–14	Charlton Ath	21	0	21	0
2014–15	Rotherham U	6	0		
2014–15	*Crawley T*	10	3	10	3
2015–16	Rotherham U	13	0		
2015–16	*Fleetwood T*	6	0	6	0
2015–16	*Chesterfield*	5	0	5	0
2016–17	Rotherham U	29	3		
2017–18	Rotherham U	36	4	84	7

YATES, Jerry (M)   39   2
H: 5 9 W: 10 10 b.Doncaster 10-11-96

Season	Club	Apps	Gls	Tot A	Tot G
2014–15	Rotherham U	0	0		
2015–16	Rotherham U	0	0		
2016–17	Rotherham U	21	1		
2017–18	Rotherham U	17	1	39	2

Players retained or with offer of contract
Ogunfaolu-Kayode, Joshua Akinola.

SCUNTHORPE U (73)

ADELAKUN, Hakeeb (F)   139   16
H: 6 3 W: 11 11 b.Hackney 11-6-96

Season	Club	Apps	Gls	Tot A	Tot G
2012–13	Scunthorpe U	2	0		
2013–14	Scunthorpe U	28	2		
2014–15	Scunthorpe U	32	6		
2015–16	Scunthorpe U	21	2		
2016–17	Scunthorpe U	17	3		
2017–18	Scunthorpe U	39	4	139	16

BISHOP, Neil (M)   440   26
H: 6 1 W: 12 10 b.Stockton 7-8-81
Internationals: England C.

Season	Club	Apps	Gls	Tot A	Tot G
2007–08	Barnet	39	2		
2008–09	Barnet	44	1	83	3
2009–10	Notts Co	43	1		
2010–11	Notts Co	43	1		
2011–12	Notts Co	41	2		
2012–13	Notts Co	41	7	168	11
2013–14	Blackpool	35	1	35	1
2014–15	Scunthorpe U	35	4		
2015–16	Scunthorpe U	42	1		
2016–17	Scunthorpe U	42	5		
2017–18	Scunthorpe U	35	1	154	11

BURGESS, Cameron (D)   70   3
H: 6 4 W: 12 11 b.Aberdeen 21-10-95
Internationals: Scotland U19. Australia U20, U23.

Season	Club	Apps	Gls	Tot A	Tot G
2014–15	Fulham	4	0		
2014–15	*Ross Co*	0	0		
2015–16	Fulham	0	0		
2016–17	Fulham	0	0	4	0
2016–17	*Oldham Ath*	23	1	23	1
2016–17	*Bury*	18	0	18	0
2017–18	Scunthorpe U	25	2	25	2

BUTROID, Lewis (D)   7   0
H: 5 9 W: 10 08 b. 17-9-98

Season	Club	Apps	Gls	Tot A	Tot G
2016–17	Scunthorpe U	0	0		
2017–18	Scunthorpe U	7	0	7	0

CLARKE, Jordan (D)   232   9
H: 6 0 W: 11 02 b.Coventry 19-11-91
Internationals: England U19, U20.

Season	Club	Apps	Gls	Tot A	Tot G
2009–10	Coventry C	12	0		
2010–11	Coventry C	21	1		
2011–12	Coventry C	19	1		
2012–13	Coventry C	20	0		
2013–14	Coventry C	41	1		
2014–15	Coventry C	11	1	124	4
2014–15	*Yeovil T*	5	2	5	2
2015–16	Scunthorpe U	24	0		
2015–16	Scunthorpe U	33	2		
2016–17	Scunthorpe U	23	1		
2017–18	Scunthorpe U	23	0	103	3

CROFTS, Andrew (D)   422   36
H: 5 10 W: 12 09 b.Chatham 29-5-84
Internationals: Wales U19, U21, Full caps.

Season	Club	Apps	Gls	Tot A	Tot G
2000–01	Gillingham	1	0		
2001–02	Gillingham	0	0		
2002–03	Gillingham	8	0		
2003–04	Gillingham	8	0		
2004–05	Gillingham	27	2		
2005–06	Gillingham	45	2		
2006–07	Gillingham	43	8		
2007–08	Gillingham	41	5		
2008–09	Gillingham	9	0		
2008–09	*Peterborough U*	9	0	9	0
2009–10	Brighton & HA	44	8		
2010–11	Norwich C	44	8		
2011–12	Norwich C	24	0		
2012–13	Norwich C	0	0	68	8
2012–13	Brighton & HA	24	0		
2013–14	Brighton & HA	23	5		
2014–15	Brighton & HA	7	0		
2015–16	Brighton & HA	17	0	115	10
2015–16	*Gillingham*	6	0	180	17
2016–17	Charlton Ath	45	1		
2017–18	Charlton Ath	1	0	46	1
2017–18	Scunthorpe U	4	0	4	0

GILKS, Matthew (G)   **418**   **0**
H: 6 3   W: 13 12   b.Rochdale 4-6-82
Internationals: Scotland Full caps.

2000–01	Rochdale	3	0	
2001–02	Rochdale	19	0	
2002–03	Rochdale	20	0	
2003–04	Rochdale	12	0	
2004–05	Rochdale	30	0	
2005–06	Rochdale	46	0	
2006–07	Rochdale	46	0	**176** **0**
2007–08	Norwich C	0	0	
2008–09	Blackpool	5	0	
2008–09	*Shrewsbury T*	4	0	**4** **0**
2009–10	Blackpool	26	0	
2010–11	Blackpool	18	0	
2011–12	Blackpool	42	0	
2012–13	Blackpool	45	0	
2013–14	Blackpool	46	0	**182** **0**
2014–15	Burnley	0	0	
2015–16	Burnley	0	0	
2016–17	Rangers	0	0	
2016–17	Wigan Ath	14	0	**14** **0**
2017–18	Scunthorpe U	42	0	**42** **0**

GOODE, Charlie (D)   **43**   **2**
b. 3-8-95
Internationals: England C.

2015–16	Scunthorpe U	10	1
2016–17	Scunthorpe U	20	0
2017–18	Scunthorpe U	13	1	**43** **2**

HOLMES, Duane (M)   **110**   **11**
H: 5 8   W: 10 03   b.Wakefield 6-11-94

2012–13	Huddersfield T	0	0	
2013–14	Huddersfield T	16	0	
2013–14	*Yeovil T*	5	0	**5** **0**
2014–15	Huddersfield T	0	0	
2014–15	*Bury*	6	0	**6** **0**
2015–16	Huddersfield T	6	1	**22** **1**
2016–17	Scunthorpe U	32	3	
2017–18	Scunthorpe U	45	7	**77** **10**

HOPPER, Tom (F)   **137**   **27**
H: 6 1   W: 12 00   b.Boston 14-12-93
Internationals: England U18.

2011–12	Leicester C	0	0	
2012–13	Leicester C	0	0	
2012–13	*Bury*	22	3	**22** **3**
2013–14	Leicester C	0	0	
2014–15	Leicester C	0	0	
2015–16	*Scunthorpe U*	12	4	
2015–16	Scunthorpe U	34	8	
2016–17	Scunthorpe U	31	5	
2017–18	Scunthorpe U	38	7	**115** **24**

HORNSHAW, George (M)   **0**   **0**

2017–18	Scunthorpe U	0	0

KELSEY, Adam (G)   **0**   **0**

2016–17	Scunthorpe U	0	0
2017–18	Scunthorpe U	0	0

LEWIS, Clayton (M)   **40**   **13**
H: 5 7   W: 11 05   b. 12-2-97
Internationals: New Zealand U20, Full caps.

2013–14	Team Wellington	0	0	
2014–15	Wanderers	11	3	**11** **3**
2015–16	Auckland C	12	5	
2016–17	Auckland C	13	5	**25** **10**
2017–18	Auckland City	0	0	
2017–18	Scunthorpe U	4	0	**4** **0**

MANTOM, Sam (M)   **181**   **20**
H: 5 9   W: 11 00   b.Stourbridge 20-2-92
Internationals: England U17.

2010–11	WBA	0	0	
2010–11	Tranmere R	2	0	**2** **0**
2010–11	Oldham Ath	4	0	**4** **0**
2011–12	Walsall	13	3	
2011–12	WBA	0	0	
2012–13	Walsall	29	2	
2013–14	Walsall	43	5	
2014–15	Walsall	12	0	
2015–16	Walsall	37	8	**134** **18**
2016–17	Scunthorpe U	26	2	
2017–18	Scunthorpe U	8	0	**34** **2**
2017–18	*Southend U*	7	0	**7** **0**

McARDLE, Rory (D)   **421**   **21**
H: 6 1   W: 11 04   b.Doncaster 1-5-87
Internationals: Northern Ireland U21, Full caps.

2005–06	Sheffield W	0	0	
2005–06	*Rochdale*	19	1	
2006–07	Sheffield W	1	0	**1** **0**
2006–07	Rochdale	25	0	
2007–08	Rochdale	43	3	
2008–09	Rochdale	41	2	

2009–10	Rochdale	20	0	**148** **6**
2010–11	Aberdeen	28	2	
2011–12	Aberdeen	25	0	**53** **2**
2012–13	Bradford C	40	2	
2013–14	Bradford C	41	3	
2014–15	Bradford C	43	3	
2015–16	Bradford C	35	3	
2016–17	Bradford C	24	1	**183** **12**
2017–18	Scunthorpe U	36	1	**36** **1**

MORRIS, Josh (M)   **196**   **41**
H: 5 9   W: 10 00   b.Preston 30-9-91
Internationals: England U20.

2010–11	Blackburn R	4	0	
2011–12	Blackburn R	2	0	
2011–12	*Yeovil T*	5	0	**5** **0**
2012–13	Blackburn R	10	0	
2012–13	*Rotherham U*	5	0	**5** **0**
2013–14	Blackburn R	4	0	
2013–14	*Carlisle U*	6	0	**6** **0**
2013–14	*Fleetwood T*	14	2	
2014–15	Blackburn R	0	0	**20** **0**
2014–15	*Fleetwood T*	45	8	**59** **10**
2015–16	Bradford C	13	1	**13** **1**
2016–17	Scunthorpe U	44	19	
2017–18	Scunthorpe U	44	11	**88** **30**

NOVAK, Lee (F)   **301**   **66**
H: 6 0   W: 12 04   b.Newcastle upon Tyne 28-9-88

2008–09	Huddersfield T	0	0	
2009–10	Huddersfield T	37	12	
2010–11	Huddersfield T	31	5	
2011–12	Huddersfield T	41	13	
2012–13	Huddersfield T	35	4	**144** **34**
2013–14	Birmingham C	38	9	
2014–15	Birmingham C	21	1	
2015–16	Birmingham C	0	0	**59** **10**
2015–16	*Chesterfield*	35	14	**35** **14**
2016–17	Charlton Ath	29	2	
2017–18	Charlton Ath	2	0	**31** **2**
2017–18	Scunthorpe U	32	6	**32** **6**

OJO, Funso (M)   **184**   **3**
H: 5 10   W: 11 03   b.Antwerp 28-8-91
Internationals: Belgium U16, U17, U20, U21.

2008–09	PSV Eindhoven	1	0	
2009–10	PSV Eindhoven	3	0	
2010–11	PSV Eindhoven	2	0	
2010–11	*VVV Venlo*	8	0	**8** **0**
2011–12	PSV Eindhoven	5	0	**11** **0**
2012–13	Beerschott	24	1	**24** **1**
2013–14	Antwerp	8	0	**8** **0**
2013–14	Dordrecht	13	0	
2014–15	Dordrecht	19	0	**32** **0**
2015–16	Willem II	32	0	
2016–17	Willem II	28	0	**60** **0**
2017–18	Scunthorpe U	41	2	**41** **2**

SUTTON, Levi (M)   **24**   **0**
b. 24-3-96

2014–15	Scunthorpe U	0	0	
2015–16	Scunthorpe U	1	0	
2016–17	Scunthorpe U	8	0	
2017–18	Scunthorpe U	15	0	**24** **0**

TOWNSEND, Conor (D)   **129**   **6**
H: 5 4   W: 9 11   b.Hessle 4-3-93

2011–12	Hull C	0	0	
2012–13	Hull C	0	0	
2012–13	*Chesterfield*	20	1	**20** **1**
2013–14	Hull C	0	0	
2013–14	*Carlisle U*	12	0	**12** **0**
2014–15	Hull C	0	0	
2014–15	*Dundee U*	17	0	**17** **0**
2014–15	*Scunthorpe U*	6	0	
2015–16	Hull C	0	0	
2015–16	*Scunthorpe U*	20	1	
2016–17	Scunthorpe U	24	0	
2017–18	Scunthorpe U	30	4	**80** **5**

WALLACE, Murray (D)   **194**   **10**
H: 6 2   W: 11 07   b.Glasgow 10-1-93
Internationals: Scotland U20, U21.

2011–12	Falkirk	19	2	**19** **2**
2011–12	Huddersfield T	0	0	
2012–13	Huddersfield T	6	1	
2013–14	Huddersfield T	17	0	
2014–15	Huddersfield T	26	2	
2015–16	Huddersfield T	2	0	**51** **3**
2015–16	*Scunthorpe U*	33	2	
2016–17	Scunthorpe U	46	2	
2017–18	Scunthorpe U	45	1	**124** **5**

WATSON, Rory (G)   **4**   **0**
b. 5-2-96

2014–15	Hull C	0	0
2015–16	Hull C	0	0
2015–16	*Scunthorpe U*	0	0

2016–17	Scunthorpe U	0	0	
2017–18	Scunthorpe U	4	0	**4** **0**

WILLIAMS, Luke (F)   **99**   **11**
H: 6 1   W: 11 08   b.Middlesbrough 11-6-93
Internationals: England U17, U19, U20.

2009–10	Middlesbrough	4	0	
2010–11	Middlesbrough	6	0	
2011–12	Middlesbrough	9	0	
2012–13	Middlesbrough	11	2	
2013–14	Middlesbrough	9	0	
2013–14	*Hartlepool U*	7	2	**7** **2**
2014–15	Middlesbrough	4	0	**34** **2**
2014–15	*Scunthorpe U*	6	2	
2014–15	*Coventry C*	5	0	**5** **0**
2014–15	*Peterborough U*	2	0	**2** **0**
2015–16	Scunthorpe U	28	5	
2016–17	Scunthorpe U	0	0	
2016–17	*Northampton T*	8	0	**8** **0**
2017–18	Scunthorpe U	2	0	**43** **7**

WOOTTON, Kyle (M)   **59**   **8**
H: 6 2   W: 12 04   b. 11-10-96

2014–15	Scunthorpe U	12	1	
2015–16	Scunthorpe U	20	3	
2016–17	Scunthorpe U	2	1	
2016–17	*Cheltenham T*	16	2	**16** **2**
2017–18	Stevenage	8	1	**8** **1**
2017–18	Scunthorpe U	1	0	**35** **5**

Scholars
Ablett, Harvey; Allasan, David; Appleby,
Alexander Benn; Bartholomew, Kane Rhys;
Busby, Joe David; Colclough, Liam Thomas;
Collins, Louis Michael; Harrison, Jack;
Hornshaw, George Matthew; Kalu, James
Emmanuel; Lilley, Sam Joshua; Morfoot,
Cameron John; Okafor, Miracle
Chimeremeze; Porter, Kyle Blue; Pugh,
Thomas Edward; Riches, Samuel David;
Train, Ewan.

SHEFFIELD U (74)

BALDOCK, George (M)   **182**   **6**
H: 5 9   W: 10 07   b.Buckingham 26-1-93

2009–10	Milton Keynes D	2	0	
2010–11	Milton Keynes D	2	0	
2011–12	Milton Keynes D	0	0	
2011–12	*Northampton T*	5	0	**5** **0**
2012–13	Milton Keynes D	2	0	
2013–14	Milton Keynes D	38	2	
2014–15	Milton Keynes D	9	0	
2014–15	*Oxford U*	12	1	
2015–16	Milton Keynes D	15	0	
2015–16	*Oxford U*	27	2	**39** **3**
2016–17	Milton Keynes D	39	0	**104** **2**
2017–18	Sheffield U	34	1	**34** **1**

BASHAM, Chris (M)   **286**   **13**
H: 5 11   W: 12 00   b.Hebburn 20-7-88

2007–08	Bolton W	0	0	
2007–08	*Rochdale*	13	0	**13** **0**
2008–09	Bolton W	11	1	
2009–10	Bolton W	8	0	**19** **1**
2010–11	Blackpool	2	0	
2011–12	Blackpool	17	2	
2012–13	Blackpool	26	1	
2013–14	Blackpool	40	2	**85** **5**
2014–15	Sheffield U	37	0	
2015–16	Sheffield U	44	3	
2016–17	Sheffield U	43	2	
2017–18	Sheffield U	45	2	**169** **7**

BENNETT, Jake (F)   **0**   **0**
b.Telford 22-2-96
From Mickleover Sports.

2017–18	Sheffield U	0	0

BROOKS, David (M)   **30**   **3**
b. 8-7-98
Internationals: England U20. Wales U21, Full caps.

2015–16	Sheffield U	0	0	
2016–17	Sheffield U	0	0	
2017–18	Sheffield U	30	3	**30** **3**

CARRUTHERS, Samir (F)   **148**   **7**
H: 5 8   W: 11 00   b.Islington 4-4-93
Internationals: Republic of Ireland U19, U21.

2011–12	Aston Villa	3	0	
2012–13	Aston Villa	0	0	
2013–14	Aston Villa	0	0	**3** **0**
2013–14	*Milton Keynes D*	23	2	
2014–15	Milton Keynes D	32	1	
2015–16	Milton Keynes D	39	1	
2016–17	Milton Keynes D	23	1	**117** **6**
2017–18	Sheffield U	14	0	
2017–18	Sheffield U	14	1	**28** **1**

CLARKE, Leon (F)   417 132
H: 6 2 W: 14 02 b.Birmingham 10-2-85

2003–04	Wolverhampton W	0	0		
2003–04	Kidderminster H	4	0	4	0
2004–05	Wolverhampton W	28	7		
2005–06	Wolverhampton W	24	1		
2005–06	QPR	1	0		
2005–06	Plymouth Arg	5	0	5	0
2006–07	Wolverhampton W	22	5		
2006–07	Sheffield W	10	1		
2006–07	Oldham Ath	5	3	5	3
2007–08	Sheffield W	8	3		
2007–08	Southend U	16	8	16	8
2008–09	Sheffield W	29	8		
2009–10	Sheffield W	36	6	83	18
2010–11	QPR	13	0	14	0
2010–11	Preston NE	6	1	6	1
2011–12	Swindon T	2	0	2	0
2011–12	Chesterfield	14	9	14	9
2011–12	Charlton Ath	7	0		
2011–12	Crawley T	4	1	4	1
2012–13	Charlton Ath	0	0	7	0
2012–13	Scunthorpe U	15	11	15	11
2012–13	Coventry C	12	8		
2013–14	Coventry C	23	15	35	23
2013–14	Wolverhampton W	13	1		
2014–15	Wolverhampton W	16	2	103	16
2014–15	Wigan Ath	10	1	10	1
2015–16	Bury	32	15	32	15
2016–17	Sheffield U	23	7		
2017–18	Sheffield U	39	19	62	26

COUTTS, Paul (M)   300 10
H: 5 9 W: 11 11 b.Aberdeen 22-7-88
Internationals: Scotland U21.

2008–09	Peterborough U	37	0		
2009–10	Peterborough U	16	0	53	0
2009–10	Preston NE	13	1		
2010–11	Preston NE	23	1		
2011–12	Preston NE	41	2	77	4
2012–13	Derby Co	44	3		
2013–14	Derby Co	8	0		
2014–15	Derby Co	7	0	59	3
2014–15	Sheffield U	20	0		
2015–16	Sheffield U	32	0		
2016–17	Sheffield U	43	2		
2017–18	Sheffield U	16	1	111	3

DONALDSON, Clayton (F)   411 135
H: 6 1 W: 11 07 b.Bradford 7-2-84
Internationals: England C. Jamaica Full caps.

2002–03	Hull C	2	0		
2003–04	Hull C	0	0		
2004–05	Hull C	0	0	2	0
From York C					
2007–08	Hibernian	17	5	17	5
2008–09	Crewe Alex	37	6		
2009–10	Crewe Alex	37	13		
2010–11	Crewe Alex	43	28	117	47
2011–12	Brentford	46	11		
2012–13	Brentford	44	18		
2013–14	Brentford	46	17	136	46
2014–15	Birmingham C	46	15		
2015–16	Birmingham C	40	11		
2016–17	Birmingham C	23	6		
2017–18	Birmingham C	4	0	113	32
2017–18	Sheffield U	26	5	26	5

DUFFY, Mark (M)   331 32
H: 5 9 W: 11 05 b.Liverpool 7-10-85

2008–09	Morecambe	9	1		
2009–10	Morecambe	35	4		
2010–11	Morecambe	22	0	66	5
2010–11	Scunthorpe U	22	1		
2011–12	Scunthorpe U	37	2		
2012–13	Scunthorpe U	43	5	102	8
2013–14	Doncaster R	36	2	36	2
2014–15	Birmingham C	4	0		
2014–15	Chesterfield	3	0	3	0
2015–16	Birmingham C	0	0	4	0
2015–16	Burton Alb	45	8	45	8
2016–17	Sheffield U	39	6		
2017–18	Sheffield U	36	3	75	9

EASTWOOD, Jake (G)   5 0
b. 3-10-96

2017–18	Chesterfield	4	0	4	0
2017–18	Sheffield U	1	0	1	0

EVANS, Ched (F)   181 58
H: 6 0 W: 12 00 b.Rhyl 28-12-88
Internationals: Wales U21, Full caps.

2006–07	Manchester C	0	0		
2007–08	Manchester C	0	0		
2007–08	Norwich C	28	10	28	10
2008–09	Manchester C	16	1	16	1
2009–10	Sheffield U	33	4		
2010–11	Sheffield U	34	9		
2011–12	Sheffield U	36	29		
2016–17	Chesterfield	25	5	25	5
2017–18	Sheffield U	9	0	112	42

EVANS, Lee (M)   133 10
H: 6 1 W: 13 12 b.Newport 24-7-94
Internationals: Wales U21, Full caps.

2012–13	Wolverhampton W	0	0		
2013–14	Wolverhampton W	26	2		
2014–15	Wolverhampton W	18	1		
2015–16	Wolverhampton W	0	0		
2015–16	Bradford C	35	4	35	4
2016–17	Wolverhampton W	15	0		
2017–18	Wolverhampton W	0	0	59	3
2017–18	Wigan Ath	20	1	20	1
2017–18	Sheffield U	19	2	19	2

FLECK, John (M)   295 16
H: 5 9 W: 11 05 b.Glasgow 24-8-91
Internationals: Scotland U17, U19, U21.

2007–08	Rangers	1	0		
2008–09	Rangers	8	1		
2009–10	Rangers	15	1		
2010–11	Rangers	13	0		
2011–12	Rangers	4	0	41	2
2011–12	Blackpool	7	0	7	0
2012–13	Coventry C	35	3		
2013–14	Coventry C	43	1		
2014–15	Coventry C	44	0		
2015–16	Coventry C	40	4	162	8
2016–17	Sheffield U	44	4		
2017–18	Sheffield U	41	2	85	6

FREEMAN, Kieron (D)   179 13
H: 5 10 W: 12 05 b.Nottingham 21-3-92
Internationals: Wales U17, U19, U21.

2010–11	Nottingham F	0	0		
2011–12	Nottingham F	0	0		
2011–12	Notts Co	19	1		
2012–13	Derby Co	19	0		
2013–14	Derby Co	6	0		
2013–14	Notts Co	16	0	35	1
2014–15	Derby Co	0	0	25	0
2014–15	Mansfield T	11	0	11	0
2014–15	Sheffield U	19	1		
2015–16	Sheffield U	19	0		
2015–16	Portsmouth	7	0	7	0
2016–17	Sheffield U	41	10		
2017–18	Sheffield U	10	1	101	12

HANSON, James (F)   314 78
H: 6 4 W: 12 04 b.Bradford 9-11-87

2009–10	Bradford C	34	12		
2010–11	Bradford C	36	6		
2011–12	Bradford C	39	13		
2012–13	Bradford C	43	10		
2013–14	Bradford C	35	12		
2014–15	Bradford C	38	9		
2015–16	Bradford C	41	11		
2016–17	Bradford C	17	4	283	77
2017–18	Sheffield U	13	1		
2017–18	Sheffield U	1	0	14	1
2017–18	Bury	17	0	17	0

HENEGHAN, Ben (D)   41 1
b.Bolton 19-9-93
Internationals: England C.

2016–17	Motherwell	37	0		
2017–18	Motherwell	4	1	41	1
2017–18	Sheffield U	0	0		

HOLMES, Ricky (M)   256 50
H: 6 2 W: 11 11 b.Southend 19-6-87
Internationals: England C.

2010–11	Barnet	25	2		
2011–12	Barnet	41	8		
2012–13	Barnet	25	5	91	15
2013–14	Portsmouth	40	2		
2014–15	Portsmouth	10	0	53	2
2014–15	Northampton T	21	5		
2015–16	Northampton T	28	9	49	14
2016–17	Charlton Ath	35	13		
2017–18	Charlton Ath	23	6	58	19
2017–18	Sheffield U	5	0	5	0

HUSSEY, Chris (D)   219 5
H: 5 10 W: 10 03 b.Hammersmith 2-1-89

2009–10	Coventry C	8	0		
2010–11	Coventry C	11	0		
2010–11	Crewe Alex	1	0		
2011–12	Coventry C	29	0		
2012–13	Coventry C	10	0	58	0
2012–13	AFC Wimbledon	19	0		
2013–14	AFC Wimbledon	0	0	19	0
2013–14	Burton Alb	27	1	27	1
2014–15	Bury	11	2		
2014–15	Bury	38	0		
2015–16	Bury	41	1	90	3

LAFFERTY, Danny (D)   171 13
H: 6 0 W: 12 08 b.Derry 1-4-89
Internationals: Northern Ireland U17, U19, U21, B, Full caps.

2009–10	Celtic	0	0		
2009–10	Ayr U	14	1	14	1
2010	Derry C	12	0		
2011	Derry C	34	7	46	7
2011–12	Burnley	5	0		
2012–13	Burnley	24	0		
2013–14	Burnley	10	0		
2014–15	Burnley	1	0		
2014–15	Rotherham U	11	0	11	0
2015–16	Burnley	0	0		
2015–16	Oldham Ath	15	1	15	1
2016–17	Burnley	0	0	40	0
2016–17	Sheffield U	37	4		
2017–18	Sheffield U	8	0	45	4

LAVERY, Caolan (F)   110 22
H: 5 11 W: 11 12 b.Red Deer 22-10-92
Internationals: Canada U17. Northern Ireland U19, U21.

2012–13	Sheffield W	0	0		
2012–13	Southend U	3	0	3	0
2013–14	Sheffield W	21	4		
2013–14	Plymouth Arg	8	3	8	3
2014–15	Sheffield W	13	2		
2014–15	Chesterfield	8	3	8	3
2015–16	Sheffield W	0	0	34	6
2015–16	Portsmouth	4	3	13	4
2016–17	Sheffield U	27	4		
2017–18	Sheffield U	3	0	30	4
2017–18	Rotherham U	14	2	14	2

LEONARD, Ryan (D)   242 20
H: 6 0 W: 11 01 b.Plympton 24-5-92

2009–10	Plymouth Arg	1	0		
2010–11	Plymouth Arg	0	0	1	0
2011–12	Southend U	17	1		
2012–13	Southend U	22	2		
2013–14	Southend U	43	5		
2014–15	Southend U	41	3		
2015–16	Southend U	37	2		
2016–17	Southend U	43	3		
2017–18	Southend U	25	4	228	20
2017–18	Sheffield U	13	0	13	0

LONG, George (G)   168 0
H: 6 0 W: 12 05 b.Sheffield 5-11-93
Internationals: England U18, U20.

2010–11	Sheffield U	1	0		
2011–12	Sheffield U	2	0		
2012–13	Sheffield U	36	0		
2013–14	Sheffield U	27	0		
2014–15	Sheffield U	0	0		
2014–15	Oxford U	10	0	10	0
2014–15	Motherwell	13	0	13	0
2015–16	Sheffield U	31	0		
2016–17	Sheffield U	3	0		
2017–18	Sheffield U	0	0	100	0
2017–18	AFC Wimbledon	45	0	45	0

LUNDSTRAM, John (M)   181 9
H: 5 11 W: 11 09 b.Liverpool 18-2-94
Internationals: England U17, U18, U19, U20.

2011–12	Everton	0	0		
2012–13	Everton	0	0		
2012–13	Doncaster R	14	0	14	0
2013–14	Everton	0	0		
2013–14	Yeovil T	14	2	14	2
2013–14	Leyton Orient	7	0		
2014–15	Everton	0	0		
2014–15	Blackpool	17	0	17	0
2014–15	Leyton Orient	4	0	11	0
2015–16	Scunthorpe U	7	0	7	0
2015–16	Oxford U	37	3		
2016–17	Oxford U	45	1	82	4
2017–18	Sheffield U	36	3	36	3

MOORE, Simon (G)   153 0
H: 6 3 W: 12 02 b.Sandown 19-5-90
Internationals: Isle of Wight Full caps.

2009–10	Brentford	1	0		
2010–11	Brentford	10	0		
2011–12	Brentford	10	0		
2012–13	Brentford	43	0	64	0
2013–14	Cardiff C	0	0		
2013–14	Bristol C	11	0	11	0
2014–15	Cardiff C	10	0		
2015–16	Cardiff C	7	0	17	0
2016–17	Cardiff C	43	0		
2017–18	Sheffield U	18	0	61	0

NORRINGTON-DAVIES, Rhys (D) 0 0
b. 22-4-99
Internationals: Wales U19, U21.
2017-18 Sheffield U 0 0

O'CONNELL, Jack (D) 194 10
H: 6 3 W: 13 05 b.Liverpool 29-3-94
Internationals: England U18, U19.
2012-13	Blackburn R	0	0		
2012-13	Rotherham U	3	0	3	0
2012-13	York C	18	0	18	0
2013-14	Blackburn R	0	0		
2013-14	Rochdale	38	0		
2014-15	Blackburn R	0	0		
2014-15	Rochdale	29	5	67	5
2014-15	Brentford	0	0		
2015-16	Brentford	16	1	16	1
2016-17	Sheffield U	44	4		
2017-18	Sheffield U	46	0	90	4

REED, Louis (M) 81 4
b. 25-7-97
Internationals: England U18, U19, U20.
2013-14	Sheffield U	1	0		
2014-15	Sheffield U	19	0		
2015-16	Sheffield U	19	0		
2016-17	Sheffield U	0	0		
2017-18	Sheffield U	0	0	39	0
2017-18	Chesterfield	42	4	42	4

SHARP, Billy (F) 472 204
H: 5 9 W: 11 00 b.Sheffield 5-2-86
2004-05	Sheffield U	2	0		
2004-05	Rushden & D	16	9	16	9
2005-06	Scunthorpe U	37	23		
2006-07	Scunthorpe U	45	30	82	53
2007-08	Sheffield U	29	4		
2008-09	Sheffield U	22	4		
2009-10	Sheffield U	0	0		
2009-10	Doncaster R	33	15		
2010-11	Doncaster R	29	15		
2011-12	Doncaster R	20	10		
2011-12	Southampton	15	9		
2012-13	Southampton	2	0		
2012-13	Nottingham F	39	10	39	10
2013-14	Southampton	0	0	17	9
2013-14	Reading	10	2	10	2
2013-14	Doncaster R	16	4	98	44
2014-15	Leeds U	33	5	33	5
2015-16	Sheffield U	44	21		
2016-17	Sheffield U	46	30		
2017-18	Sheffield U	34	13	177	72

SLATER, Regan (M) 1 0
b. 11-9-99
| 2016-17 | Sheffield U | 0 | 0 | | |
| 2017-18 | Sheffield U | 1 | 0 | 1 | 0 |

STEARMAN, Richard (D) 418 14
H: 6 2 W: 10 08 b.Wolverhampton 19-8-87
Internationals: England U16, U18, U19, U21.
2004-05	Leicester C	8	1		
2005-06	Leicester C	34	3		
2006-07	Leicester C	35	1		
2007-08	Leicester C	39	2	116	7
2008-09	Wolverhampton W	37	1		
2009-10	Wolverhampton W	16	1		
2010-11	Wolverhampton W	31	0		
2011-12	Wolverhampton W	30	0		
2012-13	Wolverhampton W	12	1		
2012-13	Ipswich T	15	0	15	0
2013-14	Wolverhampton W	40	2		
2014-15	Wolverhampton W	42	0		
2015-16	Wolverhampton W	4	0		
2015-16	Fulham	29	0		
2016-17	Fulham	0	0	29	0
2016-17	Wolverhampton W	18	0	230	5
2017-18	Sheffield U	28	2	28	2

STEVENS, Enda (D) 266 4
H: 6 0 W: 12 04 b.Dublin 9-7-90
Internationals: Republic of Ireland U21, Full caps.
2008	UCD	2	0	2	0
2009	St Patrick's Ath	30	0	30	0
2010	Shamrock R	18	0		
2011	Shamrock R	27	0	45	0
2011-12	Aston Villa	0	0		
2012-13	Aston Villa	7	0		
2013-14	Aston Villa	0	0		
2013-14	Notts Co	2	0	2	0
2013-14	Doncaster R	13	0		
2014-15	Aston Villa	0	0	7	0
2014-15	Northampton T	4	1	4	1
2014-15	Doncaster R	28	1	41	1
2015-16	Portsmouth	45	0		
2016-17	Portsmouth	45	1	90	1

| 2016-17 | Sheffield U | 0 | 0 | | |
| 2017-18 | Sheffield U | 45 | 1 | 45 | 1 |

THOMAS, Nathan (F) 105 18
H: 5 10 W: 12 08 b.Barwick 27-9-94
2013-14	Plymouth Arg	10	0		
2014-15	Plymouth Arg	9	1	19	1
2014-15	Motherwell	2	0	2	0
2015-16	Mansfield T	17	1	17	1
2015-16	Hartlepool U	22	5		
2016-17	Hartlepool U	33	9	55	14
2017-18	Sheffield U	3	0		
2017-18	Shrewsbury T	11	2	11	2

WRIGHT, Jake (D) 276 0
H: 5 10 W: 11 07 b.Keighley 11-3-86
| 2005-06 | Bradford C | 1 | 0 | 1 | 0 |
From Halifax T, Crawley T
2009-10	Brighton & HA	6	0	6	0
2010-11	Oxford U	35	0		
2011-12	Oxford U	43	0		
2012-13	Oxford U	42	0		
2013-14	Oxford U	31	0		
2014-15	Oxford U	42	0		
2015-16	Oxford U	29	0	222	0
2016-17	Sheffield U	30	0		
2017-18	Sheffield U	17	0	47	0

Players retained or with offer of contract
Ferguson, Keenan Tyrone Glendon; Gilmour, Harvey James; Hallam, Jordan Paul; Hirst, Horatio Michael James; Mallon, Stephen; Oure, Ondji; Semple, Callum Charlie; Smith, Tyler Gavin Junior.

Scholars
Belchouan, Seri Jean Leroy; Broadbent, George; Cantrill, George; Dewhurst, Marcus Robert; Doherty, Jordan; Graham, Samuel; Greaves, Oliver; Mason, Livesey; McClellan, Samuel Alexander; Ompreon, Samuel; Parkhouse, David Cain; Portman, William Tendai; Potts, Reon Ben; Slater, Regan; Warhurst, Hugo John; Weaver, Thomas.

SHEFFIELD W (75)

ABDI, Almen (M) 316 57
H: 5 11 W: 12 11 b.Prizren 21-10-86
Internationals: Switzerland, U21, Full caps.
2003-04	FC Zurich	11	0		
2004-05	FC Zurich	5	0		
2005-06	FC Zurich	12	0		
2006-07	FC Zurich	28	5		
2007-08	FC Zurich	31	7		
2008-09	FC Zurich	32	19		
2009-10	FC Zurich	8	0	127	31
2009-10	Le Mans	13	0	13	0
2010-11	Udinese	19	0		
2011-12	Udinese	22	0	41	0
2012-13	Watford	38	12		
2013-14	Watford	13	2		
2014-15	Watford	32	9		
2015-16	Watford	32	2	115	25
2016-17	Sheffield W	16	1		
2017-18	Sheffield W	4	0	20	1

BAKER, Ashley (D) 1 0
b. 30-10-96
| 2017-18 | Sheffield W | 1 | 0 | 1 | 0 |

BANNAN, Barry (D) 246 7
H: 5 10 W: 10 08 b.Glasgow 1-12-89
Internationals: Scotland U21, Full caps.
2008-09	Aston Villa	0	0		
2008-09	Derby Co	10	1	10	1
2009-10	Aston Villa	0	0		
2009-10	Blackpool	20	1	20	1
2010-11	Aston Villa	12	0		
2010-11	Leeds U	7	0	7	0
2011-12	Aston Villa	28	1		
2012-13	Aston Villa	24	0		
2013-14	Aston Villa	0	0	64	1
2013-14	Crystal Palace	15	1		
2014-15	Crystal Palace	7	0		
2014-15	Bolton W	16	0	16	0
2015-16	Crystal Palace	0	0	22	1
2015-16	Sheffield W	35	2		
2016-17	Sheffield W	43	1		
2017-18	Sheffield W	29	0	107	3

BOYD, George (M) 447 85
H: 5 10 W: 11 07 b.Chatham 2-10-85
Internationals: Scotland B, Full caps.
2006-07	Peterborough U	20	6		
2007-08	Peterborough U	46	12		
2008-09	Peterborough U	46	9		
2009-10	Peterborough U	32	9		

2009-10	Nottingham F	6	1	6	1
2010-11	Peterborough U	43	15		
2011-12	Peterborough U	45	7		
2012-13	Peterborough U	31	6	263	64
2012-13	Hull C	13	4		
2013-14	Hull C	29	2		
2014-15	Hull C	1	0	43	6
2014-15	Burnley	35	5		
2015-16	Burnley	44	5		
2016-17	Burnley	36	2	115	12
2017-18	Sheffield W	20	2	20	2

CLARE, Sean (M) 38 3
H: 6 3 b.Sheffield 18-9-96
2015-16	Sheffield W	0	0		
2015-16	Bury	4	0	4	0
2016-17	Sheffield W	0	0		
2016-17	Accrington S	8	1	8	1
2017-18	Sheffield W	5	1	5	1
2017-18	Gillingham	21	1	21	1

DAWSON, Cameron (G) 10 0
H: 6 0 W: 10 12 b.Sheffield 7-7-95
Internationals: England U18, U19.
2013-14	Sheffield W	0	0		
2013-14	Plymouth Arg	0	0		
2014-15	Sheffield W	0	0		
2015-16	Sheffield W	0	0		
2016-17	Wycombe W	1	0	1	0
2016-17	Sheffield W	4	0		
2017-18	Chesterfield	2	0	2	0
2017-18	Sheffield W	3	0	7	0

FLETCHER, Steven (F) 415 110
H: 6 1 W: 12 00 b.Shrewsbury 26-3-87
Internationals: Scotland U20, U21, B, Full caps.
2003-04	Hibernian	5	0		
2004-05	Hibernian	20	5		
2005-06	Hibernian	34	8		
2006-07	Hibernian	31	6		
2007-08	Hibernian	32	13		
2008-09	Hibernian	34	11	156	43
2009-10	Burnley	35	8	35	8
2010-11	Wolverhampton W	29	10		
2011-12	Wolverhampton W	32	12	61	22
2012-13	Sunderland	28	11		
2013-14	Sunderland	20	3		
2014-15	Sunderland	30	5		
2015-16	Sunderland	16	4	94	23
2015-16	Marseille	12	2	12	2
2016-17	Sheffield W	38	10		
2017-18	Sheffield W	19	2	57	12

FORESTIERI, Fernando (F) 257 65
H: 5 8 W: 10 07 b.Rosario 16-1-90
Internationals: Italy U17, U19, U20, U21.
2006-07	Genoa	1	1	1	1
2007-08	Siena	17	1		
2008-09	Siena	2	0	19	1
2008-09	Vicenza	13	5	13	5
2009-10	Malaga	19	1	19	1
2010-11	Empoli	17	3	17	3
2011-12	Bari	27	2	27	2
2012-13	Udinese	0	0		
2012-13	Watford	28	8		
2013-14	Watford	28	7		
2014-15	Watford	24	5	80	20
2015-16	Sheffield W	36	15		
2016-17	Sheffield W	35	12		
2017-18	Sheffield W	10	5	81	32

FOX, Morgan (D) 148 3
H: 6 1 W: 12 03 b.Chelmsford 21-9-93
Internationals: Wales U21.
2012-13	Charlton Ath	0	0		
2013-14	Charlton Ath	6	0		
2013-14	Notts Co	7	1	7	1
2014-15	Charlton Ath	31	0		
2015-16	Charlton Ath	42	1		
2016-17	Charlton Ath	24	0	103	1
2016-17	Sheffield W	10	1		
2017-18	Sheffield W	28	0	38	1

FREDERICO VENANCIO, Andre (D)135 7
H: 6 1 W: 12 02 b.Setubal 4-2-93
Internationals: Portugal U20, U21.
2012-13	Vitoria Setubal	7	1		
2013-14	Vitoria Setubal	18	1		
2014-15	Vitoria Setubal	31	1		
2015-16	Vitoria Setubal	31	0		
2016-17	Vitoria Setubal	26	3		
2017-18	Vitoria Setubal	2	0	115	6
On loan from Vitoria Setubal.
2017-18	Sheffield W	20	1	20	1

HOOPER, Gary (F) 370 168
H: 5 9 W: 11 02 b.Loughton 26-1-88
2006–07	Southend U	19	0		
2006–07	*Leyton Orient*	4	2	4	2
2007–08	Southend U	13	2	32	2
2007–08	*Hereford U*	19	11	19	11
2008–09	Scunthorpe U	45	24		
2009–10	Scunthorpe U	35	19	80	43
2010–11	Celtic	26	20		
2011–12	Celtic	37	24		
2012–13	Celtic	32	19	95	63
2013–14	Norwich C	32	6		
2014–15	Norwich C	30	12		
2015–16	Norwich C	2	0	64	18
2015–16	Sheffield W	29	13		
2016–17	Sheffield W	23	6		
2017–18	Sheffield W	24	10	76	29

HUNT, Jack (D) 263 2
H: 5 9 W: 11 02 b.Rothwell 6-12-90
2009–10	Huddersfield T	0	0		
2010–11	Huddersfield T	19	1		
2010–11	*Chesterfield*	20	0	20	0
2011–12	Huddersfield T	43	1		
2012–13	Huddersfield T	40	0		
2013–14	Huddersfield T	2	0	104	2
2013–14	Crystal Palace	0	0		
2013–14	*Barnsley*	11	0	11	0
2014–15	Crystal Palace	0	0		
2014–15	*Nottingham F*	17	0	17	0
2014–15	*Rotherham U*	16	0	16	0
2015–16	Sheffield W	34	0		
2016–17	Sheffield W	32	0		
2017–18	Sheffield W	29	0	95	0

HUTCHINSON, Sam (M) 111 4
H: 6 0 W: 11 07 b.Windsor 3-8-89
Internationals: England U18, U19.
2006–07	Chelsea	1	0		
2007–08	Chelsea	0	0		
2008–09	Chelsea	0	0		
2009–10	Chelsea	2	0		
2010–11	Chelsea	0	0		
2011–12	Chelsea	2	0		
2012–13	Chelsea	0	0		
2012–13	*Nottingham F*	9	1	9	1
2013–14	Chelsea	0	0	5	0
2013–14	*Vitesse*	1	0	1	0
2013–14	*Sheffield W*	10	1		
2014–15	Sheffield W	20	0		
2015–16	Sheffield W	25	0		
2016–17	Sheffield W	33	2		
2017–18	Sheffield W	8	0	96	3

JONES, David (M) 370 27
H: 5 11 W: 10 10 b.Southport 4-11-84
Internationals: England U21.
2003–04	Manchester U	0	0		
2004–05	Manchester U	0	0		
2005–06	Manchester U	0	0		
2005–06	*Preston NE*	24	3	24	3
2005–06	*NEC Nijmegen*	17	6	17	6
2006–07	Manchester U	0	0		
2006–07	Derby Co	28	6		
2007–08	Derby Co	14	1	42	7
2008–09	Wolverhampton W	34	4		
2009–10	Wolverhampton W	20	1		
2010–11	Wolverhampton W	12	1	66	6
2011–12	Wigan Ath	16	0		
2012–13	Wigan Ath	13	0	29	0
2012–13	*Blackburn R*	12	2	12	2
2013–14	Burnley	46	1		
2014–15	Burnley	36	0		
2015–16	Burnley	41	1		
2016–17	Burnley	1	0	124	2
2016–17	Sheffield W	29	0		
2017–18	Sheffield W	27	1	56	1

KEAN, Jake (G) 114 0
H: 6 4 W: 11 13 b.Derby 4-2-91
Internationals: England U20.
2010–11	Blackburn R	0	0		
2010–11	*Hartlepool U*	19	0	19	0
2011–12	Blackburn R	1	0		
2011–12	*Rochdale*	14	0	14	0
2012–13	Blackburn R	18	0		
2013–14	Blackburn R	18	0		
2014–15	Blackburn R	0	0	37	0
2014–15	*Yeovil T*	5	0	5	0
2014–15	*Oldham Ath*	11	0	11	0
2015–16	Norwich C	0	0		
2015–16	*Colchester U*	3	0	3	0
2015–16	*Swindon T*	3	0	3	0
2016–17	Sheffield W	0	0		
2016–17	*Mansfield T*	19	0	19	0
2017–18	Sheffield W	0	0		
2017–18	*Grimsby T*	3	0	3	0

KIRBY, Connor (M) 1 0
b. 10-9-98
2017–18	Sheffield W	1	0	1	0

LEE, Kieran (D) 291 25
H: 6 1 W: 12 00 b.Stalybridge 22-6-88
2006–07	Manchester U	1	0		
2007–08	Manchester U	0	0	1	0
2007–08	*QPR*	7	0	7	0
2008–09	Oldham Ath	7	0		
2009–10	Oldham Ath	24	1		
2010–11	Oldham Ath	43	2		
2011–12	Oldham Ath	43	2	117	5
2012–13	Sheffield W	23	0		
2013–14	Sheffield W	26	1		
2014–15	Sheffield W	33	6		
2015–16	Sheffield W	43	5		
2016–17	Sheffield W	26	5		
2017–18	Sheffield W	15	3	166	20

LEES, Tom (D) 349 12
H: 6 1 W: 12 04 b.Warwick 28-11-90
Internationals: England U21.
2008–09	Leeds U	0	0		
2009–10	Leeds U	0	0		
2009–10	*Accrington S*	39	0	39	0
2010–11	Leeds U	0	0		
2010–11	*Bury*	45	4	45	4
2011–12	Leeds U	42	2		
2012–13	Leeds U	40	1		
2013–14	Leeds U	41	0	123	3
2014–15	Sheffield W	44	0		
2015–16	Sheffield W	34	3		
2016–17	Sheffield W	35	1		
2017–18	Sheffield W	29	1	142	5

LOOVENS, Glenn (D) 375 14
H: 5 10 W: 11 08 b.Doetinchem 22-10-83
Internationals: Netherlands U21, Full caps.
2001–02	Feyenoord	8	0		
2002–03	Feyenoord	12	0		
2003–04	Feyenoord	1	0		
2003–04	*Excelsior*	24	2	24	2
2004–05	Feyenoord	6	0	27	0
2004–05	*De Graafschap*	11	0	11	0
2005–06	Cardiff C	33	2		
2006–07	Cardiff C	30	1		
2007–08	Cardiff C	36	0		
2008–09	Cardiff C	1	0	100	3
2008–09	Celtic	17	3		
2009–10	Celtic	20	3		
2010–11	Celtic	13	1		
2011–12	Celtic	11	1	61	8
2012–13	*Real Zaragoza*	21	0	21	0
2013–14	Sheffield W	22	0		
2014–15	Sheffield W	26	0		
2015–16	Sheffield W	31	0		
2016–17	Sheffield W	32	1		
2017–18	Sheffield W	20	0	131	1

LUCAS JOAO, Eduardo (F) 167 36
H: 6 4 W: 12 08 b.Luanda 4-9-93
Internationals: Portugal U20, U21, U23, Full caps.
2012–13	Nacional	0	0		
2012–13	*Mirandela*	27	12	27	12
2013–14	Nacional	16	0		
2014–15	Nacional	30	6	46	6
2015–16	Sheffield W	40	6		
2016–17	Sheffield W	10	0		
2016–17	*Blackburn R*	13	3	13	3
2017–18	Sheffield W	31	9	81	15

MARCO MATIAS, Andre (F) 180 35
H: 5 10 W: 10 08 b.Barreiro 10-5-89
Internationals: Portugal U18, U19, U21.
2008–09	Sporting Lisbon	1	0		
2008–09	*Varzim*	12	0	12	0
2009–10	Sporting Lisbon	0	0		
2009–10	*Fatima*	7	2	7	2
2009–10	*Real Massama*	15	0	15	0
2010–11	Vit Guimaraes	0	0		
2010–11	Freamunde	24	5		
2011–12	Vit Guimaraes	0	0		
2011–12	Freamunde	19	2	43	7
2012–13	Vit Guimaraes	20	0		
2013–14	Vit Guimaraes	22	6	42	6
2014–15	Nacional	33	17	33	17
2015–16	Sheffield W	17	3		
2016–17	Sheffield W	2	0		
2017–18	Sheffield W	9	0	28	3

NIELSEN, Frederik (D) 3 0
b. 7-2-98
Internationals: Denmark U16, U17, U19.
From Nottingham F.
2017–18	Sheffield W	3	0	3	0

NUHIU, Atdhe (F) 303 53
H: 6 6 W: 13 05 b.Prishtina 29-7-89
Internationals: Austria U19, U20, U21.
Kosovo Full caps.
2008–09	Austria Karnten	16	2		
2009–10	Austria Karnten	3	0	19	2
2009–10	SV Ried	27	6	27	6
2010–11	Rapid Vienna	28	5		
2011–12	Rapid Vienna	31	8	59	13
2012–13	Eskisehirspor	28	2	28	2
2013–14	Sheffield W	38	8		
2014–15	Sheffield W	43	8		
2015–16	Sheffield W	41	3		
2016–17	Sheffield W	20	0		
2017–18	Sheffield W	28	11	170	30

O'GRADY, Connor (D) 0 0
b.Sheffield 5-12-97
2016–17	Sheffield W	0	0		
2017–18	Sheffield W	0	0		

PALMER, Liam (M) 201 1
H: 6 2 W: 12 10 b.Worksop 19-9-91
Internationals: Scotland U19, U21.
2010–11	Sheffield W	9	0		
2011–12	Sheffield W	14	1		
2012–13	Sheffield W	0	0		
2012–13	*Tranmere R*	43	0		
2013–14	*Tranmere R*	0	0	43	0
2013–14	Sheffield W	39	0		
2014–15	Sheffield W	35	0		
2015–16	Sheffield W	15	0		
2016–17	Sheffield W	21	0		
2017–18	Sheffield W	25	0	158	1

PELUPESSY, Joey (M) 123 3
H: 5 8 W: 9 13 b.Nijverdal 15-5-93
2012–13	FC Twente	3	0		
2013–14	FC Twente	0	0	3	0
2014–15	Heracles	17	1		
2015–16	Heracles	34	0		
2016–17	Heracles	34	1		
2017–18	Heracles	18	0	103	2
2017–18	Sheffield W	17	1	17	1

PENNEY, Matt (D) 3 0
b.Chesterfield 11-2-98
2016–17	Sheffield W	0	0		
2016–17	*Bradford C*	1	0	1	0
2017–18	Sheffield W	0	0		
2017–18	*Mansfield T*	2	0	2	0

PRESTON, Fraser (G) 0 0
b. 1-10-98
Internationals: Scotland U16, U19.
2017–18	Sheffield W	0	0		

PUDIL, Daniel (D) 323 28
H: 6 1 W: 12 11 b.Prague 27-9-85
Internationals: Czech Republic U19, U21, Full caps.
2003–04	Blsany	2	2	2	2
2005–06	Liberec	3	4		
2006–07	Liberec	3	3	6	7
2007–08	Slavia Prague	9	6	16	6
2008–09	Genk	29	4		
2009–10	Genk	27	1		
2010–11	Genk	32	0		
2011–12	Genk	18	0	106	5
2011–12	Cesena	7	1	7	1
2012–13	Watford	37	1		
2013–14	Watford	37	2		
2014–15	Watford	23	0		
2015–16	Watford	0	0	97	3
2015–16	*Sheffield W*	36	2		
2016–17	Sheffield W	26	2		
2017–18	Sheffield W	27	0	89	4

REACH, Adam (M) 223 23
H: 6 1 W: 11 07 b.Gateshead 3-2-93
Internationals: England U20.
2010–11	Middlesbrough	1	1		
2011–12	Middlesbrough	1	0		
2012–13	Middlesbrough	16	2		
2013–14	Middlesbrough	2	0		
2013–14	*Shrewsbury T*	22	3	22	3
2013–14	*Bradford C*	18	3	18	3
2014–15	Middlesbrough	39	2		
2015–16	Middlesbrough	4	1		
2015–16	*Preston NE*	35	4	35	4
2016–17	Middlesbrough	0	0	63	6
2016–17	Sheffield W	39	3		
2017–18	Sheffield W	46	4	85	7

RHODES, Jordan (F)   385 179
H: 6 1   W: 11 03   b.Oldham 5-2-90
Internationals: Scotland U21, Full caps.

Season	Club	A	G	Tot A	Tot G
2007–08	Ipswich T	8	1		
2008–09	Ipswich T	2	0	10	1
2008–09	Rochdale	5	2	5	2
2008–09	Brentford	14	7	14	7
2009–10	Huddersfield T	45	19		
2010–11	Huddersfield T	37	16		
2011–12	Huddersfield T	40	35		
2012–13	Huddersfield T	2	2	124	72
2012–13	Blackburn R	43	27		
2013–14	Blackburn R	46	25		
2014–15	Blackburn R	45	21		
2015–16	Blackburn R	25	10	159	83
2015–16	Middlesbrough	18	6		
2016–17	Middlesbrough	6	0	24	6
2016–17	Sheffield W	3	2		
2017–18	Sheffield W	31	5	49	8

STOBBS, Jack (M)   10 0
H: 5 11   W: 13 05   b.Leeds 27-2-97

Season	Club	A	G	Tot A	Tot G
2013–14	Sheffield W	1	0		
2014–15	Sheffield W	0	0		
2015–16	Sheffield W	1	0		
2016–17	Sheffield W	0	0		
2017–18	Port Vale	5	0	5	0
2017–18	Sheffield W	3	0	5	0

THORNILEY, Jordan (D)   25 0
b.Warrington 24-11-96
From Everton.

Season	Club	A	G	Tot A	Tot G
2016–17	Sheffield W	0	0		
2017–18	Sheffield W	11	0	11	0
2017–18	Accrington S	14	0	14	0

VAN AKEN, Joost (D)   98 3
H: 5 10   W: 11 11   b.Haarlem 13-5-94
Internationals: Netherlands U21.

Season	Club	A	G	Tot A	Tot G
2013–14	Heerenveen	6	2		
2014–15	Heerenveen	30	0		
2015–16	Heerenveen	20	0		
2016–17	Heerenveen	26	1		
2017–18	Heerenveen	2	0	84	3
2017–18	Sheffield W	14	0	14	0

WALLACE, Ross (M)   427 44
H: 5 6   W: 9 12   b.Dundee 23-5-85
Internationals: Scotland U18, U19, U21, B, Full caps.

Season	Club	A	G	Tot A	Tot G
2001–02	Celtic	0	0		
2002–03	Celtic	0	0		
2003–04	Celtic	8	1		
2004–05	Celtic	16	0		
2005–06	Celtic	11	0		
2006–07	Celtic	2	0	37	1
2006–07	Sunderland	32	6		
2007–08	Sunderland	21	2		
2008–09	Sunderland	0	0	53	8
2008–09	Preston NE	39	5		
2009–10	Preston NE	41	7	80	12
2010–11	Burnley	40	3		
2011–12	Burnley	44	5		
2012–13	Burnley	36	3		
2013–14	Burnley	14	0		
2014–15	Burnley	15	1	149	12
2015–16	Sheffield W	40	4		
2016–17	Sheffield W	41	5		
2017–18	Sheffield W	27	2	108	11

WESTWOOD, Keiren (G)   415 0
H: 6 1   W: 13 10   b.Manchester 23-10-84
Internationals: Republic of Ireland Full caps.

Season	Club	A	G	Tot A	Tot G
2001–02	Manchester C	0	0		
2002–03	Manchester C	0	0		
2003–04	Manchester C	0	0		
2003–04	Oldham Ath	0	0		
2004–05	Manchester C	0	0		
2005–06	Manchester C	0	0		
2005–06	Carlisle U	35	0		
2006–07	Carlisle U	46	0		
2007–08	Carlisle U	46	0	127	0
2008–09	Coventry C	46	0		
2009–10	Coventry C	44	0		
2010–11	Coventry C	41	0	131	0
2011–12	Sunderland	9	0		
2012–13	Sunderland	0	0		
2013–14	Sunderland	10	0	19	0
2014–15	Sheffield W	43	0		
2015–16	Sheffield W	34	0		
2016–17	Sheffield W	43	0		
2017–18	Sheffield W	18	0	138	0

WILDSMITH, Joe (G)   38 0
H: 6 0   W: 10 03   b.Sheffield 28-12-95
Internationals: England U20.

Season	Club	A	G	Tot A	Tot G
2013–14	Sheffield W	0	0		
2014–15	Sheffield W	0	0		
2014–15	Barnsley	2	0	2	0
2015–16	Sheffield W	9	0		
2016–17	Sheffield W	1	0		
2017–18	Sheffield W	26	0	36	0

WINNALL, Sam (F)   208 83
H: 5 9   W: 11 04   b.Wolverhampton 19-1-91

Season	Club	A	G	Tot A	Tot G
2009–10	Wolverhampton W	0	0		
2010–11	Wolverhampton W	0	0		
2010–11	Burton Alb	19	7	19	7
2011–12	Wolverhampton W	0	0		
2011–12	Hereford U	8	2	8	2
2011–12	Inverness CT	2	0	2	0
2012–13	Wolverhampton W	0	0		
2012–13	Shrewsbury T	4	0	4	0
2013–14	Scunthorpe U	45	23	45	23
2014–15	Barnsley	32	9		
2015–16	Barnsley	43	21		
2016–17	Barnsley	22	11	97	41
2016–17	Sheffield W	14	3		
2017–18	Sheffield W	2	1	16	4
2017–18	Derby Co	17	6	17	6

Players retained or with offer of contract
Brennan, Ciaran Thomas; Clarke, Warren Eliott; Hirst, George David Eric; Hughes, Ben Anthony; Hunt, Alexander John; Lee, Jack; Lonchar, Jordan Rhys; Waldock, Liam Brian; Wallis, Daniel Michael; West, Joseph William; Williams, Liam Shaun.

Scholars
Borukov, Preslav Nikolaev; Brazinskas, Arijus; Dawodu, Joshua; Gavrilov, Stefan Emilov; Grant, Conor Michael; Hamud, Iyad Omar; Hornsby, Benjamin Jack; Kaempfe, Isaac David; Marques, O'Brien Jordan; Reaney, Joshua Craig Kenneth; Render, Joshua Ben; Shaw, Liam Darren; Swaine, Layton John; Walker, Joseph Alan.

SHREWSBURY T (76)

BARNETT, Ryan (M)   0 0

Season	Club	A	G	Tot A	Tot G
2016–17	Shrewsbury T	0	0		
2017–18	Shrewsbury T	0	0		

BECKLES, Omar (D)   76 6
H: 6 2   W: 12 04   b.Kettering 25-10-91
From Aldershot T.

Season	Club	A	G	Tot A	Tot G
2016–17	Accrington S	41	2		
2017–18	Accrington S	2	1	43	3
2017–18	Shrewsbury T	33	3	33	3

BOLTON, James (D)   33 1
H: 5 11   W: 11 11   b.Stone 13-8-94
Internationals: England C.
From Macclesfield T, Halifax T, Gateshead.

Season	Club	A	G	Tot A	Tot G
2017–18	Shrewsbury T	33	1	33	1

BROWN, Junior (M)   198 21
H: 5 9   W: 10 09   b.Crewe 7-5-89

Season	Club	A	G	Tot A	Tot G
2006–07	Crewe Alex	0	0		
2007–08	Crewe Alex	1	0	1	0
2012–13	Fleetwood T	43	11		
2013–14	Fleetwood T	21	1	64	12
2013–14	Tranmere R	9	1	9	1
2014–15	Oxford U	11	0	11	0
2014–15	Mansfield T	24	2	24	2
2015–16	Shrewsbury T	31	0		
2016–17	Shrewsbury T	43	5		
2017–18	Shrewsbury T	11	1	89	6

COYNE, Danny (G)   441 0
H: 6 0   W: 13 00   b.Prestatyn 27-8-73
Internationals: Wales U21, B, Full caps.

Season	Club	A	G	Tot A	Tot G
1991–92	Tranmere R	1	0		
1992–93	Tranmere R	1	0		
1993–94	Tranmere R	5	0		
1994–95	Tranmere R	5	0		
1995–96	Tranmere R	46	0		
1996–97	Tranmere R	21	0		
1997–98	Tranmere R	16	0		
1998–99	Tranmere R	17	0		
1999–2000	Grimsby T	44	0		
2000–01	Grimsby T	46	0		
2001–02	Grimsby T	45	0		
2002–03	Grimsby T	46	0	181	0
2003–04	Leicester C	4	0	4	0
2004–05	Burnley	20	0		
2005–06	Burnley	8	0		
2006–07	Burnley	12	0	40	0
2007–08	Tranmere R	41	0		
2008–09	Tranmere R	39	0	191	0
2009–10	Middlesbrough	23	0		
2010–11	Middlesbrough	1	0		
2011–12	Middlesbrough	1	0	25	0
2012–13	Sheffield U	0	0		
2013–14	Sheffield U	0	0		
2013–14	Shrewsbury T	0	0		
2014–15	Shrewsbury T	0	0		
2017–18	Shrewsbury T	0	0		

EISA, Abobaker (M)   5 1
From Uxbridge, Wealdstone.

Season	Club	A	G	Tot A	Tot G
2017–18	Shrewsbury T	5	1	5	1

GALLAGHER, Chris (M)   0 0
Internationals: Northern Ireland U17, U19.
From Linfield.

Season	Club	A	G	Tot A	Tot G
2017–18	Shrewsbury T	0	0		

GNAHOUA, Arthur (F)   11 1
H: 6 2   W: 12 08   b.London 5-4-92
From Stalybridge Celtic, Macclesfield T, Kidderminster H.

Season	Club	A	G	Tot A	Tot G
2017–18	Shrewsbury T	11	1	11	1

GREGORY, Cameron (G)   0 0

Season	Club	A	G	Tot A	Tot G
2017–18	Shrewsbury T	0	0		

HENDRIE, Luke (M)   76 0
b. 27-8-94
Internationals: England U16, U17.

Season	Club	A	G	Tot A	Tot G
2013–14	Derby Co	0	0		
2014–15	Derby Co	0	0		
2015–16	Burnley	0	0		
2015–16	Hartlepool U	3	0	3	0
2015–16	York C	18	0	18	0
2016–17	Burnley	0	0		
2016–17	Kilmarnock	32	0	32	0
2017–18	Burnley	0	0		
2017–18	Bradford C	13	0	13	0
2017–18	Shrewsbury T	10	0	10	0

HUGHES, George (M)   0 0

Season	Club	A	G	Tot A	Tot G
2017–18	Shrewsbury T	0	0		

JOHN-LEWIS, Lemell (M)   219 22
H: 5 10   W: 11 10   b.Hammersmith 17-5-89

Season	Club	A	G	Tot A	Tot G
2006–07	Lincoln C	21	3		
2007–08	Lincoln C	27	4		
2008–09	Lincoln C	24	1	72	8
2009–10	Lincoln C	39	2		
2010–11	Bury	39	2		
2011–12	Bury	28	5		
2012–13	Bury	16	2	83	9
2015–16	Newport Co	28	3		
2016–17	Newport Co	2	0	30	3
2017–18	Shrewsbury T	34	2	34	2

JONES, Sam (M)   46 14
H: 6 2   W: 12 08   b.Doncaster 18-9-91
Internationals: Wales U19.
From Alfreton T, Gateshead.

Season	Club	A	G	Tot A	Tot G
2016–17	Grimsby T	16	7		
2017–18	Grimsby T	25	6	41	13
2017–18	Shrewsbury T	5	1	5	1

JULES, Zak (D)   18 1
b. 2-7-97
Internationals: Scotland U17, U18, U19, U20, U21.

Season	Club	A	G	Tot A	Tot G
2016–17	Reading	0	0		
2016–17	Motherwell	10	1	10	1
2017–18	Shrewsbury T	0	0		
2017–18	Chesterfield	6	0	6	0
2017–18	Port Vale	2	0	2	0

MACGILLIVRAY, Craig (G)   20 0
H: 6 2   W: 12 04   b.Harrogate 12-1-93

Season	Club	A	G	Tot A	Tot G
2014–15	Walsall	5	0		
2015–16	Walsall	5	0		
2016–17	Walsall	5	0	12	0
2017–18	Shrewsbury T	8	0	8	0

McATEE, John (F)   1 0

Season	Club	A	G	Tot A	Tot G
2016–17	Shrewsbury T	1	0		
2017–18	Shrewsbury T	0	0	1	0

MORRIS, Bryn (M)   48 0
H: 6 0   W: 11 01   b.Hartlepool 25-4-96
Internationals: England U16, U17, U18, U19, U20.

Season	Club	A	G	Tot A	Tot G
2012–13	Middlesbrough	1	0		
2013–14	Middlesbrough	0	0		
2014–15	Middlesbrough	0	0		
2014–15	Burton Alb	5	0	5	0
2015–16	Middlesbrough	0	0		
2015–16	Coventry C	6	0	6	0
2015–16	York C	3	0	3	0
2015–16	Walsall	1	0	1	0
2016–17	Middlesbrough	0	0	2	0
2016–17	Shrewsbury T	13	0		
2017–18	Shrewsbury T	18	0	31	0

MWANDWE, Lifumpa (F)   0 0
b. 29-12-00

Season	Club	A	G	Tot A	Tot G
2017–18	Shrewsbury T	0	0		

NOLAN, Jon (M) 73 10
H: 5 11 W: 11 05 b.Huyton 22-4-92
Internationals: England C.
From Everton, Stockport Co, Lindoln C, Grimsby T.

| 2016–17 | Chesterfield | 30 | 1 | 30 | 1 |
| 2017–18 | Shrewsbury T | 43 | 9 | 43 | 9 |

NSIALA, Aristote (D) 132 5
H: 6 4 W: 14 09 b.DR Congo 25-3-92
Internationals: DR Congo Full caps.

2009–10	Everton	0	0		
2010–11	Everton	0	0		
2010–11	Macclesfield T	10	0	10	0
2011–12	Everton	0	0		
2011–12	Accrington S	19	0		
2012–13	Accrington S	17	0		
2013–14	Accrington S	0	0	36	0
2016–17	Hartlepool U	21	1	21	1
2016–17	Shrewsbury T	21	1		
2017–18	Shrewsbury T	44	3	65	4

OGOGO, Abu (M) 337 22
H: 5 8 W: 10 02 b.Epsom 3-11-89

2007–08	Arsenal	0	0		
2008–09	Arsenal	0	0		
2008–09	Barnet	9	1	9	1
2009–10	Dagenham & R	30	2		
2010–11	Dagenham & R	33	1		
2011–12	Dagenham & R	40	1		
2012–13	Dagenham & R	46	1		
2013–14	Dagenham & R	44	8		
2014–15	Dagenham & R	32	4	225	17
2015–16	Shrewsbury T	42	2		
2016–17	Shrewsbury T	26	0		
2017–18	Shrewsbury T	35	2	103	4

PAYNE, Stefan (F) 88 14
H: 5 10 W: 11 07 b.Lambeth 10-8-91
Internationals: England C.

2009–10	Fulham	0	0		
2010–11	Gillingham	16	0		
2011–12	Gillingham	12	1	28	1
2011–12	Aldershot T	1	0	1	0

From Sutton U, Macclesfield T, Ebbsfleet U, AFC Hornchurch, Dover Ath.

2015–16	Barnsley	0	0		
2016–17	Barnsley	7	0		
2016–17	Shrewsbury T	12	2		
2017–18	Barnsley	2	0	9	0
2017–18	Shrewsbury T	38	11	50	13

RILEY, Joe (D) 117 4
H: 6 0 W: 11 02 b.Salford 13-10-91

2011–12	Bolton W	3	0		
2012–13	Bolton W	3	0		
2013–14	Bolton W	0	0		
2014–15	Bolton W	0	0	3	0
2014–15	Oxford U	22	0	22	0
2014–15	Bury	17	1		
2015–16	Bury	33	1	50	2
2016–17	Shrewsbury T	32	1		
2017–18	Shrewsbury T	10	1	42	2

RODMAN, Alex (F) 167 19
H: 6 2 W: 12 08 b.Sutton Coldfield 15-2-87
Internationals: England C.

2010–11	Aldershot T	14	5		
2011–12	Aldershot T	18	1		
2012–13	Aldershot T	11	1	43	7
2012–13	York C	18	1	18	1
2015–16	Newport Co	29	4	29	4
2016–17	Notts Co	16	1	16	1
2017–18	Shrewsbury T	20	1		
2017–18	Shrewsbury T	41	5	61	6

ROWLEY, Shaun (G) 0 0
b. 11-1-96

2015–16	Shrewsbury T	0	0		
2016–17	Shrewsbury T	0	0		
2017–18	Shrewsbury T	0	0		

SADLER, Matthew (D) 410 8
H: 5 11 W: 11 08 b.Birmingham 26-2-85
Internationals: England U17, U18, U19.

2001–02	Birmingham C	0	0		
2002–03	Birmingham C	2	0		
2003–04	Birmingham C	0	0		
2003–04	Northampton T	7	0	7	0
2004–05	Birmingham C	0	0		
2005–06	Birmingham C	8	0		
2006–07	Birmingham C	36	0		
2007–08	Birmingham C	5	0	51	0
2007–08	Watford	15	0		
2008–09	Watford	15	0		
2009–10	Watford	0	0		
2009–10	Stockport Co	20	0	20	0
2010–11	Watford	0	0	30	0
2010–11	Shrewsbury T	46	0		
2011–12	Walsall	46	1	46	1
2012–13	Crawley T	46	1		
2013–14	Crawley T	46	1		
2014–15	Rotherham U	0	0		
2014–15	Crawley T	10	0	102	2
2014–15	Oldham Ath	8	0	8	0
2014–15	Shrewsbury T	0	0		
2015–16	Shrewsbury T	24	2		
2016–17	Shrewsbury T	34	2		
2017–18	Shrewsbury T	42	1	146	5

SHELIS, Christos (D) 0 0
b. 2-2-00
Internationals: Cyprus U17.

| 2017–18 | Shrewsbury T | 0 | 0 | | |

WHALLEY, Shaun (M) 118 20
H: 5 9 W: 10 08 b.Whiston 7-8-87

2014–15	Luton T	18	3	18	3
2015–16	Shrewsbury T	24	6		
2016–17	Shrewsbury T	32	3		
2017–18	Shrewsbury T	44	8	100	17

Players retained or with offer of contract
Sears, Ryan Joseph.

Scholars
Agbozo, Joshua Mawugniga; Atkinson, Jack Edward; Corfield, Reiss Morgan; Davies, Rhys Andrew Melville; Esien, Cameron Eniang; Gilpin, Aaron Morgan; Gregory, Cameron Akash James; Higgs, Charley Robert; Leask, Jack Nathan; Lovett, Harri Tomas; Mwandwe, Lifumpa Yande; Ofori, Tyrone Edwine Kwaku; Taylor, Brett Andrew; Taylor, Kian George.

SOUTHAMPTON (77)

AUSTIN, Charlie (F) 264 131
H: 6 2 W: 13 03 b.Hungerford 5-7-89

2009–10	Swindon T	33	19		
2010–11	Swindon T	21	12	54	31
2010–11	Burnley	4	0		
2011–12	Burnley	41	16		
2012–13	Burnley	37	25	82	41
2013–14	QPR	31	17		
2014–15	QPR	35	18		
2015–16	QPR	16	10	82	45
2015–16	Southampton	7	1		
2016–17	Southampton	15	6		
2017–18	Southampton	24	7	46	14

BARNES, Marcus (F) 8 0
b.Reading 1-12-96

| 2017–18 | Southampton | 0 | 0 | | |
| 2017–18 | Yeovil T | 8 | 0 | 8 | 0 |

BEDNAREK, Jan (D) 53 2
H: 6 2 W: 12 02 b.Slupca 12-4-96
Internationals: Poland U16, U17, U18, U19, U20, U21, Full caps.

2013–14	Lech Poznan	2	0		
2014–15	Lech Poznan	2	0		
2015–16	Gornik Leczna	17	0	17	0
2016–17	Lech Poznan	27	1	31	1
2017–18	Southampton	5	1	5	1

BERTRAND, Ryan (D) 318 6
H: 5 10 W: 11 00 b.Southwark 5-8-89
Internationals: England U17, U18, U19, U20, U21, Full caps. Great Britain.

2006–07	Chelsea	0	0		
2006–07	Bournemouth	5	0	5	0
2007–08	Chelsea	0	0		
2007–08	Oldham Ath	21	0	21	0
2008–09	Chelsea	0	0		
2008–09	Norwich C	38	0	56	0
2009–10	Chelsea	0	0		
2009–10	Reading	44	1	44	1
2010–11	Chelsea	1	0		
2010–11	Nottingham F	19	0	19	0
2011–12	Chelsea	7	0		
2012–13	Chelsea	19	0		
2013–14	Chelsea	1	0	28	0
2013–14	Aston Villa	16	0	16	0
2014–15	Southampton	34	2		
2015–16	Southampton	32	1		
2016–17	Southampton	28	2		
2017–18	Southampton	35	0	129	5

BOUFAL, Sofiane (M) 139 21
H: 5 7 W: 11 09 b.Paris 17-9-93
Internationals: Morocco Full caps.

2012–13	Angers	2	0		
2013–14	Angers	28	0		
2014–15	Angers	16	4	46	4
2014–15	Lille	14	3		
2015–16	Lille	29	11		
2016–17	Lille	0	0	43	14
2016–17	Southampton	24	1		
2017–18	Southampton	26	2	50	3

CARRILLO, Guido (F) 192 43
H: 6 3 W: 13 08 b.La Plata 25-5-91

2010–11	Estudiantes	5	0		
2011–12	Estudiantes	21	2		
2012–13	Estudiantes	29	4		
2013–14	Estudiantes	37	13		
2014	Estudiantes	17	5		
2015	Estudiantes	11	4	120	28
2015–16	Monaco	31	4		
2016–17	Monaco	19	7		
2017–18	Monaco	15	4	65	15
2017–18	Southampton	7	0	7	0

CEDRIC SOARES, Ricardo (D) 177 2
H: 5 8 W: 10 08 b.Gelsenkirchen, Germany 31-8-91
Internationals: Portugal U16, U17, U18, U19, U20, U21, Full caps.

2010–11	Sporting Lisbon	2	0		
2011–12	Sporting Lisbon	0	0		
2011–12	Academica	24	0	24	0
2012–13	Sporting Lisbon	13	1		
2013–14	Sporting Lisbon	28	1		
2014–15	Sporting Lisbon	24	0	67	2
2015–16	Southampton	24	0		
2016–17	Southampton	30	0		
2017–18	Southampton	32	0	86	0

CLASIE, Jordy (M) 216 11
H: 5 7 W: 10 12 b.Haarlem 27-7-91
Internationals: Netherlands U17, U18, U19, U21, Full caps.

2010–11	Feyenoord	2	0		
2010–11	Excelsior	32	2	32	2
2011–12	Feyenoord	33	3		
2012–13	Feyenoord	33	2		
2013–14	Feyenoord	32	1		
2014–15	Feyenoord	31	2	129	8
2015–16	Southampton	22	0		
2016–17	Southampton	16	1		
2017–18	Southampton	0	0	38	1
2017–18	Club Brugge	17	0	17	0

DAVIS, Steven (M) 455 35
H: 5 8 W: 11 04 b.Ballymena 1-1-85
Internationals: Northern Ireland U15, U16, U17, U19, U21, U23, Full caps.

2004–05	Aston Villa	28	1		
2005–06	Aston Villa	35	4		
2006–07	Aston Villa	28	0	91	5
2007–08	Fulham	22	0	22	0
2007–08	Rangers	12	0		
2008–09	Rangers	34	6		
2009–10	Rangers	36	3		
2010–11	Rangers	37	4		
2011–12	Rangers	33	5	152	18
2012–13	Southampton	32	2		
2013–14	Southampton	34	2		
2014–15	Southampton	35	0		
2015–16	Southampton	34	5		
2016–17	Southampton	32	0		
2017–18	Southampton	23	3	190	12

FORSTER, Fraser (G) 294 0
H: 6 0 W: 12 00 b.Hexham 17-3-88
Internationals: England Full caps.

2007–08	Newcastle U	0	0		
2008–09	Newcastle U	0	0		
2008–09	Stockport Co	6	0	6	0
2009–10	Newcastle U	0	0		
2009–10	Bristol R	4	0	4	0
2009–10	Norwich C	38	0	38	0
2010–11	Newcastle U	0	0		
2010–11	Celtic	36	0		
2011–12	Newcastle U	0	0		
2011–12	Celtic	33	0		
2012–13	Celtic	34	0		
2013–14	Celtic	37	0	140	0
2014–15	Southampton	30	0		
2015–16	Southampton	18	0		
2016–17	Southampton	38	0		
2017–18	Southampton	20	0	106	0

GABBIADINI, Manolo (F) 224 52
H: 5 10 W: 11 03 b.Bergamo 26-11-91
Internationals: Italy U20, U21, Full caps.

2009–10	Atalanta	2	0		
2010–11	Atalanta	0	0		
2010–11	Cittadella	27	5	27	5
2011–12	Atalanta	23	1		
2012–13	Atalanta	0	0	25	1
2012–13	Bologna	30	6	30	6
2013–14	Sampdoria	34	8		

Season	Club	App	Gls	Tot	Tot
2014–15	Sampdoria	13	7	47	15
2014–15	Napoli	20	8		
2015–16	Napoli	23	5		
2016–17	Napoli	13	3	56	16
2016–17	Southampton	11	4		
2017–18	Southampton	28	5	39	9

GALLAGHER, Sam (F) 107 18
H: 6 4 W: 11 11 b.Crediton 15-9-95
Internationals: Scotland U19, England U19, U20.

Season	Club	App	Gls	Tot	Tot
2013–14	Southampton	18	1		
2014–15	Southampton	0	0		
2015–16	Southampton	0	0		
2015–16	*Milton Keynes D*	13	0	13	0
2016–17	Southampton	0	0		
2016–17	*Blackburn R*	43	11	43	11
2017–18	Southampton	0	0	18	1
2017–18	*Birmingham C*	33	6	33	6

HOEDT, Wesley (D) 102 4
H: 6 2 W: 12 02 b.Alkmaar 6-3-94
Internationals: Netherlands U20, U20, Full caps.

Season	Club	App	Gls	Tot	Tot
2013–14	AZ Alkmaar	2	0		
2014–15	AZ Alkmaar	24	2	26	2
2015–16	Lazio	25	0		
2016–17	Lazio	23	2		
2017–18	Lazio	0	0	48	2
2017–18	Southampton	28	0	28	0

HOJBJERG, Pierre (M) 101 2
H: 6 1 W: 12 11 b. 5-8-95
Internationals: Denmark U16, U17, U19, U21, Full caps.

Season	Club	App	Gls	Tot	Tot
2012–13	Bayern Munich	2	0		
2013–14	Bayern Munich	7	0		
2014–15	Bayern Munich	8	0		
2014–15	Augsburg	16	2	16	2
2015–16	Bayern Munich	0	0	17	0
2015–16	Schalke	23	0	23	0
2016–17	Southampton	22	0		
2017–18	Southampton	23	0	45	0

LEMINA, Mario (M) 109 6
H: 6 0 W: 12 00 b.Libreville 1-9-93
Internationals: France U20, U21. Gabon Full caps.

Season	Club	App	Gls	Tot	Tot
2012–13	Lorient	10	0		
2013–14	Lorient	4	0	14	0
2013–14	Marseille	14	0		
2014–15	Marseille	23	2		
2015–16	Marseille	4	0	41	2
2015–16	Juventus	10	2		
2016–17	Juventus	19	1	29	3
2017–18	Southampton	25	1	25	1

LONG, Shane (F) 393 87
H: 5 10 W: 11 02 b.Co. Tipperary 22-1-87
Internationals: Republic of Ireland B, U21, Full caps.

Season	Club	App	Gls	Tot	Tot
2005	Cork C	1	0	1	0
2005–06	Reading	11	3		
2006–07	Reading	21	2		
2007–08	Reading	29	3		
2008–09	Reading	37	9		
2009–10	Reading	31	6		
2010–11	Reading	44	21		
2011–12	Reading	1	0	174	44
2011–12	WBA	32	8		
2012–13	WBA	34	8		
2013–14	WBA	15	3	81	19
2013–14	Hull C	15	4	15	4
2014–15	Southampton	32	5		
2015–16	Southampton	28	10		
2016–17	Southampton	32	3		
2017–18	Southampton	30	2	122	20

McCARTHY, Alex (G) 165 0
H: 6 4 W: 11 12 b.Guildford 3-12-89
Internationals: England U21.

Season	Club	App	Gls	Tot	Tot
2008–09	Reading	0	0		
2008–09	*Aldershot T*	4	0	4	0
2009–10	Reading	0	0		
2009–10	*Yeovil T*	44	0	44	0
2010–11	Reading	13	0		
2010–11	*Brentford*	3	0	3	0
2011–12	Reading	0	0		
2011–12	*Leeds U*	6	0	6	0
2011–12	*Ipswich T*	10	0	10	0
2012–13	Reading	13	0		
2013–14	Reading	44	0	70	0
2014–15	QPR	3	0	3	0
2015–16	Crystal Palace	7	0	7	0
2016–17	Southampton	0	0		
2017–18	Southampton	18	0	18	0

McQUEEN, Sam (M) 38 2
H: 5 9 W: 11 00 b.Southampton 6-2-95
Internationals: England U21.

Season	Club	App	Gls	Tot	Tot
2011–12	Southampton	0	0		
2012–13	Southampton	0	0		
2013–14	Southampton	0	0		
2014–15	Southampton	0	0		
2015–16	Southampton	0	0		
2015–16	*Southend U*	18	2	18	2
2016–17	Southampton	13	0		
2017–18	Southampton	7	0	20	0

OBAFEMI, Michael (F) 1 0
H: 5 7 W: 11 03 b.Dublin 6-7-00
Internationals: Republic of Ireland U19.
From Leyton Orient.

Season	Club	App	Gls	Tot	Tot
2017–18	Southampton	1	0	1	0

OLOMOLA, Olufela (F) 21 7
H: 5 7 b.London 5-9-97

Season	Club	App	Gls	Tot	Tot
2015–16	Southampton	0	0		
2016–17	Southampton	0	0		
2017–18	Southampton	0	0		
2017–18	*Yeovil T*	21	7	21	7

PIED, Jeremy (F) 193 11
H: 5 8 W: 10 12 b.Grenoble 23-2-89
Internationals: France U21.

Season	Club	App	Gls	Tot	Tot
2009–10	Lyon	0	0		
2009–10	Metz	37	4	37	4
2010–11	Lyon	25	3		
2011–12	Lyon	14	1		
2012–13	Lyon	1	0	40	4
2012–13	Nice	26	0		
2013–14	Nice	21	1		
2014–15	Nice	2	0		
2014–15	Guingamp	28	2	28	2
2015–16	Nice	33	0	82	1
2016–17	Southampton	4	0		
2017–18	Southampton	2	0	6	0

REDMOND, Nathan (M) 242 26
H: 5 8 W: 11 11 b.Birmingham 6-3-94
Internationals: England U16, U17, U18, U19, U20, Full caps.

Season	Club	App	Gls	Tot	Tot
2011–12	Birmingham C	24	5		
2012–13	Birmingham C	38	2	62	7
2013–14	Norwich C	34	1		
2014–15	Norwich C	43	4		
2015–16	Norwich C	35	6	112	11
2016–17	Southampton	37	7		
2017–18	Southampton	31	1	68	8

REED, Harrison (M) 56 1
H: 5 9 W: 11 09 b.Worthing 27-1-95
Internationals: England U19, U20.

Season	Club	App	Gls	Tot	Tot
2011–12	Southampton	0	0		
2012–13	Southampton	0	0		
2013–14	Southampton	4	0		
2014–15	Southampton	9	0		
2015–16	Southampton	1	0		
2016–17	Southampton	3	0		
2017–18	Southampton	0	0	17	0
2017–18	*Norwich C*	39	1	39	1

ROMEU, Oriol (M) 210 4
H: 6 0 W: 12 06 b.Ulldecona 24-9-91
Internationals: Spain U17, U19, U20, U21, U23.

Season	Club	App	Gls	Tot	Tot
2008–09	Barcelona B	5	0		
2009–10	Barcelona B	26	0		
2010–11	Barcelona B	18	1	49	1
2010–11	Barcelona	1	0	1	0
2011–12	Chelsea	16	0		
2012–13	Chelsea	6	0		
2013–14	Chelsea	0	0		
2013–14	Valencia	13	0	13	0
2014–15	Chelsea	0	0	22	0
2014–15	Stuttgart	27	0	27	0
2015–16	Southampton	29	1		
2016–17	Southampton	35	1		
2017–18	Southampton	34	1	98	3

SEAGER, Ryan (F) 26 3
H: 5 11 W: 11 00 b.Southampton 5-2-96
Internationals: England U17.

Season	Club	App	Gls	Tot	Tot
2014–15	Southampton	1	0		
2015–16	Southampton	0	0		
2015–16	*Crewe Alex*	4	1	4	1
2016–17	Southampton	0	0		
2017–18	Southampton	0	0	1	0
2017–18	*Milton Keynes D*	14	1	14	1
2017–18	*Yeovil T*	7	1	7	1

SIMS, Josh (M) 13 0
b. 28-3-97
Internationals: England U17, U18, U20.
From Portsmouth.

Season	Club	App	Gls	Tot	Tot
2016–17	Southampton	7	0		
2017–18	Southampton	6	0	13	0

STEPHENS, Jack (D) 108 3
H: 6 1 W: 13 03 b.Torpoint 27-1-94
Internationals: England U18, U19, U20, U21.

Season	Club	App	Gls	Tot	Tot
2010–11	Plymouth Arg	5	0	5	0
2010–11	Southampton	0	0		
2011–12	Southampton	0	0		
2012–13	Southampton	0	0		
2013–14	Southampton	0	0		
2013–14	*Swindon T*	10	0		
2014–15	Southampton	0	0		
2014–15	*Swindon T*	37	1	47	1
2015–16	Southampton	0	0		
2015–16	*Middlesbrough*	1	0	1	0
2015–16	*Coventry C*	16	0	16	0
2016–17	Southampton	17	0		
2017–18	Southampton	22	2	39	2

TADIC, Dusan (M) 375 91
H: 5 11 W: 12 00 b.Backa Topola 20-11-88
Internationals: Serbia Full caps.

Season	Club	App	Gls	Tot	Tot
2006–07	Vojvodina	23	3		
2007–08	Vojvodina	28	7		
2008–09	Vojvodina	29	9		
2009–10	Vojvodina	27	10	107	29
2010–11	Groningen	34	7		
2011–12	Groningen	34	7	68	14
2012–13	FC Twente	33	12		
2013–14	FC Twente	33	16	66	28
2014–15	Southampton	31	4		
2015–16	Southampton	34	7		
2016–17	Southampton	33	3		
2017–18	Southampton	36	6	134	20

TARGETT, Matt (D) 45 1
H: 6 0 W: 12 11 b.Edinburgh 18-9-95
Internationals: Scotland U19, England U19, U20, U21.

Season	Club	App	Gls	Tot	Tot
2013–14	Southampton	0	0		
2014–15	Southampton	6	0		
2015–16	Southampton	14	0		
2016–17	Southampton	5	0		
2017–18	Southampton	2	0	27	0
2017–18	*Fulham*	18	1	18	1

TAYLOR, Stuart (G) 75 0
H: 6 5 W: 13 07 b.Romford 28-11-80
Internationals: England U16, U18, U20, U21.

Season	Club	App	Gls	Tot	Tot
1998–99	Arsenal	0	0		
1999–2000	Arsenal	0	0		
1999–2000	*Bristol R*	4	0	4	0
2000–01	Arsenal	0	0		
2000–01	*Crystal Palace*	10	0	10	0
2000–01	*Peterborough U*	6	0	6	0
2001–02	Arsenal	10	0		
2002–03	Arsenal	8	0		
2003–04	Arsenal	0	0		
2004–05	Arsenal	0	0	18	0
2004–05	*Leicester C*	10	0	10	0
2005–06	Aston Villa	2	0		
2006–07	Aston Villa	6	0		
2007–08	Aston Villa	4	0		
2008–09	Aston Villa	0	0	12	0
2008–09	*Cardiff C*	8	0	8	0
2009–10	Manchester C	0	0		
2010–11	Manchester C	0	0		
2011–12	Manchester C	0	0		
2012–13	Manchester C	0	0		
2012–13	Reading	4	0		
2013–14	Reading	0	0	4	0
2014–15	Leeds U	3	0	3	0
2016–17	Southampton	0	0		
2017–18	Southampton	0	0		

WARD-PROWSE, James (M) 167 10
H: 5 8 W: 10 06 b.Portsmouth 1-11-94
Internationals: England U17, U19, U20, U21, Full caps.

Season	Club	App	Gls	Tot	Tot
2011–12	Southampton	0	0		
2012–13	Southampton	15	0		
2013–14	Southampton	34	0		
2014–15	Southampton	25	1		
2015–16	Southampton	33	2		
2016–17	Southampton	30	4		
2017–18	Southampton	30	3	167	10

YOSHIDA, Maya (D) 183 11
H: 6 2 W: 12 03 b.Nagasaki 24-8-88
Internationals: Japan U23, Full caps.

Season	Club	App	Gls	Tot	Tot
2010–11	VVV	20	0		
2011–12	VVV	32	5		

2012–13	VVV	2	0	54	5
2012–13	Southampton	32	0		
2013–14	Southampton	8	1		
2014–15	Southampton	22	1		
2015–16	Southampton	20	1		
2016–17	Southampton	23	1		
2017–18	Southampton	24	2	129	6

Players retained or with offer of contract
Bradley Green, Jamie; Cull, Alexander;
FerryWilliam; Flannigan, Jake; Freeman,
Kieran; Hansen, Kornelius Normann;
Hesketh, Jake Alexander; Johnson, Tyreke
Martin; Klarer, Christoph; Kozak, Simon;
Latham, Kingsley Finn; Lewis, Harry Charles
John; Mdlalose, Siphesihle Thembinkosi;
O'Connor, Thomas James; O'Driscoll,
Aaron; Parkes, Adam Darren; Rose, Jack
Joseph; Rowthorn, Ben John; Slattery,
Callum; Smallbone, William Anthony Patrick;
Tella, Nathan; Valery, Yan; Vokins, Jake.

Scholars
Afolabi, Jonathan; Bartlett, Daniel Grahame;
Brennan, Sean Anthony; Davis, Harrison;
Fleary, Taymar; Hale, Harlem; Hamblin,
Harry Mark; Ledwidge, Kameron Malcolm;
Nlundulu, Dan; Norton, Christian Anthony;
Olufunwa, Oludare Samuel Araba; Ramsay,
Kayne; Robise, Enzo.

SOUTHEND U (78)

BA, Amadou (F) 5 0
H: 5 9 W: 9 13 b. 15-2-98
From Le Havre.
2017–18	Southend U	5	0	5	0

BISHOP, Nathan (G) 1 0
H: 6 1 W: 11 05 b. 15-10-99
2016–17	Southend U	1	0		
2017–18	Southend U	1	0	1	0

BWOMONO, Elvis (D) 11 0
H: 5 9 W: 9 13 b. 29-11-98
2017–18	Southend U	11	0	11	0

COKER, Ben (D) 211 4
H: 5 11 W: 11 09 b.Hatfield 17-6-89
2010–11	Colchester U	20	0		
2011–12	Colchester U	20	0		
2012–13	Colchester U	1	0	41	0
2013–14	Southend U	45	2		
2014–15	Southend U	32	1		
2015–16	Southend U	40	1		
2016–17	Southend U	31	0		
2017–18	Southend U	22	0	170	4

COTTON, Nico (M) 0 0
2015–16	Southend U	0	0		
2016–17	Southend U	0	0		
2017–18	Southend U	0	0		

COUTTS, Sonny (D) 0 0
2017–18	Southend U	0	0		

COX, Simon (F) 382 105
H: 5 10 W: 10 12 b.Reading 28-4-87
Internationals: Republic of Ireland Full caps.
2005–06	Reading	2	0		
2006–07	Reading	5	0		
2006–07	Brentford	13	0	13	0
2006–07	Northampton T	8	3	8	3
2007–08	Reading	0	0		
2007–08	Swindon T	36	15		
2008–09	Swindon T	45	29	81	44
2009–10	WBA	28	9		
2010–11	WBA	19	1		
2011–12	WBA	18	0		
2012–13	WBA	0	0	65	10
2012–13	Nottingham F	39	5		
2013–14	Nottingham F	34	8	73	13
2014–15	Reading	37	8		
2015–16	Reading	13	1	52	9
2015–16	Bristol C	4	0	4	0
2016–17	Southend U	44	16		
2017–18	Southend U	42	10	86	26

DEMETRIOU, Jason (D) 370 27
H: 5 11 W: 10 08 b.Newham 18-11-87
Internationals: Cyprus Full caps.
2005–06	Leyton Orient	3	0		
2006–07	Leyton Orient	15	2		
2007–08	Leyton Orient	43	3		
2008–09	Leyton Orient	43	4		
2009–10	Leyton Orient	39	1	143	10
2010–11	AEK Larnaca	15	0		
2011–12	AEK Larnaca	23	1		
2012–13	AEK Larnaca	19	3	57	4
2013–14	An Famagusta	19	1		
2014–15	An Famagusta	25	0	44	1
2015–16	Walsall	43	3	43	3
2016–17	Southend U	41	1		
2017–18	Southend U	42	8	83	9

FERDINAND, Anton (D) 363 7
H: 6 2 W: 11 00 b.Peckham 18-2-85
Internationals: England U18, U20, U21.
2002–03	West Ham U	0	0		
2003–04	West Ham U	20	0		
2004–05	West Ham U	29	1		
2005–06	West Ham U	33	2		
2006–07	West Ham U	31	0		
2007–08	West Ham U	25	2		
2008–09	West Ham U	0	0	138	5
2008–09	Sunderland	31	0		
2009–10	Sunderland	24	0		
2010–11	Sunderland	27	0		
2011–12	Sunderland	3	0	85	0
2011–12	QPR	31	0		
2012–13	QPR	13	0		
2012–13	Bursaspor	7	0	7	0
2013–14	QPR	0	0	44	0
2013–14	Antalyaspor	3	0	3	0
2014–15	Reading	2	0		
2015–16	Reading	19	0	21	0
2016–17	Southend U	34	2		
2017–18	Southend U	31	0	65	2

FORTUNE, Marc-Antoine (F) 545 94
H: 6 0 W: 11 13 b.Cayenne 2-7-81
2000–01	Angouleme	18	3		
2001–02	Angouleme	36	12	54	15
2002–03	Nancy	19	1		
2002–03	Lille	15	0	15	0
2003–04	Rouen	34	10	34	10
2004–05	Brest	33	10	33	10
2005–06	Utrecht	31	6		
2006–07	Utrecht	22	5	53	11
2006–07	Nancy	15	5		
2007–08	Nancy	37	6		
2008–09	Nancy	19	1	90	13
2009–10	Celtic	30	10		
2010–11	Celtic	2	0	32	10
2010–11	WBA	25	2		
2011–12	WBA	17	2		
2011–12	Doncaster R	5	1	5	1
2012–13	WBA	21	2	63	6
2013–14	Wigan Ath	36	4		
2014–15	Wigan Ath	35	1	71	5
2015–16	Coventry C	25	4		
2016–17	Coventry C	0	0	25	4
2017–18	Southend U	38	4	70	9

GARD, Lewis (M) 2 0
b. 26-8-99
2017–18	Southend U	2	0	2	0

HENDRIE, Stephen (D) 127 1
H: 5 10 W: 11 00 b.Glasgow 8-1-95
Internationals: Scotland U17, U19, U21.
2010–11	Hamilton A	8	1		
2011–12	Hamilton A	25	0		
2012–13	Hamilton A	23	0		
2013–14	Hamilton A	22	0		
2014–15	Hamilton A	30	0	100	0
2015–16	West Ham U	0	0		
2015–16	Southend U	5	1		
2016–17	West Ham U	0	0		
2016–17	Blackburn R	4	0	4	0
2017–18	Southend U	12	0	17	1
2017–18	Motherwell	6	0	6	0

KIERNAN, Rob (D) 145 3
H: 6 1 W: 11 13 b.Rickmansworth 13-1-91
Internationals: Republic of Ireland U18, U19, U21.
2008–09	Watford	0	0		
2009–10	Watford	0	0		
2009–10	Kilmarnock	4	0	4	0
2010–11	Watford	0	0		
2010–11	Yeovil T	3	0	3	0
2010–11	Bradford C	8	0	8	0
2010–11	Wycombe W	2	0	2	0
2011–12	Wigan Ath	0	0		
2011–12	Accrington S	3	0	3	0
2012–13.	Burton Alb	6	0	6	0
2012–13	Brentford	8	0	8	0
2013–14	Wigan Ath	12	1		
2013–14	Southend U	12	0		
2014–15	Wigan Ath	17	0	29	1
2014–15	Birmingham C	12	1	12	1
2015–16	Rangers	33	0		
2016–17	Rangers	24	1	57	1
2017–18	Southend U	1	0	13	0

KIGHTLY, Michael (F) 278 45
H: 5 10 W: 10 10 b.Basildon 24-1-86
Internationals: England U21.
2002–03	Southend U	1	0		
2003–04	Southend U	11	0		
2004–05	Southend U	1	0		

From Grays Ath.
2006–07	Wolverhampton W	24	8		
2007–08	Wolverhampton W	21	4		
2008–09	Wolverhampton W	38	8		
2009–10	Wolverhampton W	9	0		
2010–11	Wolverhampton W	4	0		
2011–12	Wolverhampton W	18	3		
2011–12	Watford	12	3	12	3
2012–13	Wolverhampton W	0	0	114	23
2012–13	Stoke C	22	3		
2013–14	Stoke C	0	0	22	3
2013–14	Burnley	36	5		
2014–15	Burnley	17	1		
2015–16	Burnley	18	0		
2016–17	Burnley	5	0	76	6
2016–17	Burton Alb	12	4	12	4
2017–18	Southend U	29	6	42	6

KLASS, Michael (M) 0 0
From QPR.
2017–18	Southend U	0	0		

KYPRIANOU, Harry (D) 16 1
b. 16-3-97
Internationals: Cyprus U21.
2013–14	Watford	0	0		
2014–15	Watford	0	0		
2015–16	Watford	0	0		
2015–16	Southend U	0	0		
2016–17	Southend U	3	1		
2017–18	Southend U	13	0	16	1

LADAPO, Freddie (F) 49 6
H: 6 0 W: 12 06 b.Romford 1-2-93
2011–12	Colchester U	0	0		
2012–13	Colchester U	4	0		
2013–14	Colchester U	2	0	6	0
2015–16	Crystal Palace	0	0		
2016–17	Crystal Palace	0	0		
2016–17	Oldham Ath	17	2	17	2
2016–17	Shrewsbury T	15	4	15	4
2017–18	Crystal Palace	1	0	1	0
2017–18	Southend U	10	0	10	0

MATSUZAKA, Daniel (D) 0 0
H: 6 4 W: 11 11 b.Barnet 1-8-98
Internationals: Japan U19.
2014–15	Southend U	0	0		
2015–16	Southend U	0	0		
2016–17	Southend U	0	0		
2017–18	Southend U	0	0		

McGLASHAN, Jermaine (M) 283 26
H: 5 7 W: 10 00 b.Croydon 14-4-88
2010–11	Aldershot T	38	1		
2011–12	Aldershot T	23	4	61	5
2011–12	Cheltenham T	16	2		
2012–13	Cheltenham T	45	4		
2013–14	Cheltenham T	43	6	104	12
2014–15	Gillingham	40	5		
2015–16	Gillingham	17	0	57	5
2016–17	Southend U	35	3		
2017–18	Southend U	26	1	61	4

McLAUGHLIN, Stephen (M) 186 28
H: 5 9 W: 11 12 b.Derry 14-6-90
2011	Derry C	33	3		
2012	Derry C	24	10	57	13
2012–13	Nottingham F	0	0		
2013–14	Nottingham F	3	0		
2013–14	Bristol C	5	0	5	0
2014–15	Nottingham F	6	0	9	0
2014–15	Notts Co	13	0	13	0
2014–15	Southend U	6	1		
2015–16	Southend U	17	1		
2016–17	Southend U	34	7		
2017–18	Southend U	45	6	102	15

MITCHELL-NELSON, Miles (D) 0 0
2017–18	Southend U	0	0		

OXLEY, Mark (G) 178 1
H: 5 11 W: 11 05 b.Aston 2-6-90
Internationals: England U18, U20.
2008–09	Hull C	0	0		
2009–10	Hull C	0	0		
2009–10	Grimsby T	3	0	3	0
2010–11	Hull C	0	0		
2011–12	Hull C	0	0		
2012–13	Hull C	1	0		
2012–13	Burton Alb	3	0	3	0
2013–14	Hull C	0	0		
2013–14	Oldham Ath	36	0	36	0

2014–15	Hull C	0	0	1	0
2014–15	*Hibernian*	35	1		
2015–16	Hibernian	34	0	69	1
2016–17	Southend U	20	0		
2017–18	Southend U	46	0	66	0

PHILLIPS, Harry (M)   **0   0**

2017–18	Southend U	0	0		

PITOULA-WABO, Norman (F)   **3   0**
b. 6-5-98

2017–18	Southend U	3	0	3	0

RANGER, Nile (F)   **146   24**
H: 6 2   W: 13 03   b.Wood Green 11-4-91
Internationals: England U19.

2008–09	Newcastle U	0	0		
2009–10	Newcastle U	25	2		
2010–11	Newcastle U	24	0		
2011–12	Newcastle U	0	0		
2011–12	*Barnsley*	5	0	5	0
2011–12	*Sheffield W*	8	2	8	2
2012–13	Newcastle U	2	0	51	2
2013–14	*Swindon T*	23	8	23	8
2014–15	Blackpool	14	2		
2015–16	Blackpool	0	0	14	2
2016–17	Southend U	27	8		
2017–18	Southend U	18	2	45	10

ROBINSON, Theo (F)   **342   77**
H: 5 9   W: 10 03   b.Birmingham 22-1-89
Internationals: Jamaica Full caps.

2005–06	Watford	1	0		
2006–07	Watford	1	0		
2007–08	Watford	0	0		
2007–08	*Hereford U*	43	13	43	13
2008–09	Watford	3	0	5	0
2008–09	*Southend U*	21	7		
2009–10	Huddersfield T	37	13		
2010–11	Huddersfield T	1	0		
2010–11	*Millwall*	11	3		
2010–11	*Derby Co*	13	2		
2011–12	Derby Co	39	10		
2012–13	Derby Co	28	8		
2012–13	Huddersfield T	6	0	44	13
2013–14	Millwall	0	0	11	3
2013–14	Derby Co	0	0	80	20
2013–14	*Doncaster R*	31	5		
2014–15	Doncaster R	32	4	63	9
2014–15	*Scunthorpe U*	8	3	8	3
2015–16	*Motherwell*	10	0	10	0
2015–16	*Port Vale*	14	2	14	2
2016–17	Southend U	18	2		
2017–18	Southend U	25	5	64	14

SMITH, Ted (G)   **26   0**
b.Benfleet 18-1-96
Internationals: England U18, U19, U20.

2012–13	Southend U	0	0		
2013–14	Southend U	0	0		
2014–15	Southend U	4	0		
2015–16	Southend U	3	0		
2016–17	Southend U	19	0		
2017–18	Southend U	0	0	26	0

TIMLIN, Michael (M)   **345   19**
H: 5 8   W: 11 08   b.New Cross 19-3-85
Internationals: Republic of Ireland U17, U21.

2002–03	Fulham	0	0		
2003–04	Fulham	0	0		
2004–05	Fulham	0	0		
2005–06	Fulham	0	0		
2005–06	*Scunthorpe U*	1	0	1	0
2005–06	*Doncaster R*	3	0	3	0
2006–07	Fulham	0	0		
2006–07	*Swindon T*	24	1		
2007–08	Fulham	0	0		
2007–08	*Swindon T*	10	1		
2008–09	Swindon T	41	2		
2009–10	Swindon T	21	0		
2010–11	Swindon T	22	2		
2010–11	*Southend U*	8	1		
2011–12	Swindon T	1	0	119	6
2011–12	Southend U	39	4		
2012–13	Southend U	25	0		
2013–14	Southend U	36	2		
2014–15	Southend U	32	3		
2015–16	Southend U	21	2		
2016–17	Southend U	27	1		
2017–18	Southend U	34	0	222	13

TURNER, Michael (D)   **411   28**
H: 6 4   W: 13 05   b.Lewisham 9-11-83

2001–02	Charlton Ath	0	0		
2002–03	Charlton Ath	0	0		
2002–03	*Leyton Orient*	7	1	7	1
2003–04	Charlton Ath	0	0		
2004–05	Brentford	45	1		
2005–06	Brentford	46	2	91	3

2006–07	Hull C	43	3		
2007–08	Hull C	44	5		
2008–09	Hull C	38	4		
2009–10	Hull C	4	0	129	12
2009–10	Sunderland	29	2		
2010–11	Sunderland	15	0		
2011–12	Sunderland	24	0	68	2
2012–13	Norwich C	26	3		
2013–14	Norwich C	22	0		
2014–15	Norwich C	23	1		
2014–15	*Fulham*	9	1	9	1
2015–16	Norwich C	0	0		
2015–16	*Sheffield W*	11	1	11	1
2016–17	Norwich C	0	0	71	4
2017–18	Southend U	25	4	25	4

WHITE, John (D)   **388   5**
H: 6 1   W: 12 01   b.Maldon 26-7-86

2004–05	Colchester U	20	0		
2005–06	Colchester U	35	0		
2006–07	Colchester U	16	0		
2007–08	Colchester U	21	0		
2008–09	Colchester U	26	0		
2009–10	Colchester U	39	0		
2009–10	*Southend U*	5	0		
2010–11	Colchester U	22	0		
2011–12	Colchester U	26	0		
2012–13	Colchester U	22	0	227	0
2013–14	Southend U	41	1		
2014–15	Southend U	42	0		
2015–16	Southend U	29	1		
2016–17	Southend U	13	1		
2017–18	Southend U	31	2	161	5

WORDSWORTH, Anthony (M)   **298   60**
H: 6 1   W: 12 00   b.Camden 3-1-89

2007–08	Colchester U	3	0		
2008–09	Colchester U	30	3		
2009–10	Colchester U	41	11		
2010–11	Colchester U	35	5		
2011–12	Colchester U	44	13		
2012–13	Colchester U	24	3	177	35
2012–13	*Ipswich T*	7	1		
2013–14	Ipswich T	10	1		
2014–15	Ipswich T	1	0	18	2
2014–15	*Rotherham U*	6	1	6	1
2014–15	*Crawley T*	18	4	18	4
2015–16	Southend U	21	4		
2016–17	Southend U	34	11		
2017–18	Southend U	24	3	79	18

WRIGHT, Josh (M)   **304   19**
H: 5 11   W: 11 07   b.Bethnal Green 6-11-89
Internationals: England U16, U17, U18, U19.

2007–08	Charlton Ath	0	0		
2007–08	*Barnet*	32	1	32	1
2008–09	Charlton Ath	2	0	2	0
2008–09	*Brentford*	5	0	5	0
2008–09	*Gillingham*	5	0		
2009–10	Scunthorpe U	35	0		
2010–11	Scunthorpe U	36	0	71	0
2011–12	Millwall	18	1		
2012–13	Millwall	24	0		
2013–14	Millwall	3	0		
2013–14	*Leyton Orient*	2	0		
2014–15	Millwall	1	0	46	1
2014–15	*Crawley T*	4	0	4	0
2014–15	Leyton Orient	29	2	31	2
2015–16	Gillingham	41	1		
2016–17	Gillingham	41	13		
2017–18	Gillingham	3	0	90	14
2017–18	Southend U	23	1	23	1

YEARWOOD, Dru (M)   **25   0**
H: 5 9   W: 9 13   b. 17-2-00

2017–18	Southend U	25	0	25	0

Scholars
Acquah, Emile; Benton, Jon; Clark, Alex; Clifford, Thomas; Cuthbert, Harry David George; Egbri, Terrell Evieoghene Oluwatoby; Farah, Yonis Abdirizak; Gard, Lewis Thomas; Humphreys, Daniel; Hutchings, Marley Carl; Kinali, Eren; Knock, Samuel David; MacKenzie, Joseph Peter Uduakobong; Marah, Sewa Bockarie; Mitchell-Nelson, Miles Nathaniel; Pianim, Zak Michael; Rush, Matthew Thomas; Seaden, Harry John; Stewart, O'Shane Christan; Udebhu-Osimeh, Idemudia Mohammed.

STEVENAGE (79)

BEAUTYMAN, Harry (M)   **71   8**
H: 5 10   W: 11 09   b.Newham 1-4-92
Internationals: England C.

2010–11	Leyton Orient	0	0		

From Sutton U, Welling U.

2014–15	Peterborough U	18	2		
2015–16	Peterborough U	22	3	40	5
2016–17	Northampton T	21	3	21	3
2017–18	Stevenage	10	0	10	0

CONLON, Tom (M)   **62   2**
H: 5 8   W: 9 11   b.Stoke-on-Trent 3-2-96

2013–14	Peterborough U	1	0	1	0
2014–15	Stevenage	13	0		
2015–16	Stevenage	32	2		
2016–17	Stevenage	4	0		
2017–18	Stevenage	12	0	61	2

DAY, Chris (G)   **401   0**
H: 6 2   W: 13 07   b.Whipps Cross 28-7-75
Internationals: England U18, U21.

1992–93	Tottenham H	0	0		
1993–94	Tottenham H	0	0		
1994–95	Tottenham H	0	0		
1995–96	Tottenham H	0	0		
1996–97	Crystal Palace	24	0	24	0
1997–98	Watford	0	0		
1998–99	Watford	0	0		
1999–2000	Watford	11	0		
2000–01	Watford	0	0	11	0
2000–01	*Lincoln C*	14	0	14	0
2001–02	QPR	16	0		
2002–03	QPR	12	0		
2003–04	QPR	29	0		
2004–05	QPR	30	0	87	0
2004–05	*Preston NE*	6	0	6	0
2005–06	Oldham Ath	30	0	30	0
2006–07	Millwall	5	0		
2007–08	Millwall	5	0	10	0
2010–11	Stevenage	46	0		
2011–12	Stevenage	44	0		
2012–13	Stevenage	17	0		
2013–14	Stevenage	44	0		
2014–15	Stevenage	38	0		
2015–16	Stevenage	19	0		
2016–17	Stevenage	11	0		
2017–18	Stevenage	0	0	219	0

FERRY, James (M)   **0   0**
b. 20-4-97

2015–16	Brentford	0	0		
2015–16	*Wycombe W*	0	0		
2017–18	Stevenage	0	0		

FIELD, Paul (D)   **0   0**
b.Barnet 28-11-00

2017–18	Stevenage	0	0		

FRANKS, Fraser (D)   **126   7**
H: 6 0   W: 10 12   b.Hammersmith 22-11-90
Internationals: England C.

2009–10	Brentford	0	0		
2011–12	AFC Wimbledon	4	0	4	0
2014–15	Luton T	13	0	13	0
2015–16	Stevenage	38	3		
2016–17	Stevenage	41	3		
2017–18	Stevenage	30	1	109	7

GEORGIOU, Andronicos (F)   **3   0**
b.Enfield 28-10-99

2017–18	Stevenage	3	0	3	0

GODDARD, John (M)   **66   4**
H: 5 10   W: 11 09   b.Sandhurst 2-6-93
Internationals: England C.

2011–12	Reading	0	0		
2015–16	Woking	0	0		
2015–16	*Swindon T*	0	0		
2016–17	Swindon T	42	3		
2017–18	Swindon T	13	1	55	4
2017–18	Stevenage	11	0	11	0

GODDEN, Matthew (F)   **94   30**
H: 6 1   W: 12 03   b.Canterbury 29-7-91

2009–10	Scunthorpe U	0	0		
2010–11	Scunthorpe U	5	0		
2011–12	Scunthorpe U	1	0		
2012–13	Scunthorpe U	8	0		
2013–14	Scunthorpe U	4	0		
2014–15	Scunthorpe U	0	0	18	0
2016–17	Stevenage	38	20		
2017–18	Stevenage	38	10	76	30

GORMAN, Dale (D) — 62 3
H: 5 11 W: 11 00 b.Letterkenny 28-6-96
Internationals: Northern Ireland U17, U19, U21.

2014–15	Stevenage	0	0		
2015–16	Stevenage	13	0		
2016–17	Stevenage	25	1		
2017–18	Stevenage	24	2	62	3

GRAY, Jamie (F) — 11 0
b. 13-4-98
Internationals: Republic of Ireland U17, U18.

| 2016–17 | Stevenage | 3 | 0 | | |
| 2017–18 | Stevenage | 8 | 0 | 11 | 0 |

HENRY, Ronnie (D) — 227 0
H: 5 11 W: 11 10 b.Hemel Hempstead 2-1-84
Internationals: England C.

2002–03	Tottenham H	0	0		
2002–03	*Southend U*	3	0	3	0
2004	Dublin C	12	0	12	0
2010–11	Stevenage	42	0		
2011–12	Stevenage	32	0		
2014–15	Stevenage	34	0		
2015–16	Stevenage	31	0		
2016–17	Stevenage	33	0		
2017–18	Stevenage	40	0	212	0

IONTTON, Arthur (M) — 2 0
b.Enfield 16-12-00

| 2017–18 | Stevenage | 2 | 0 | 2 | 0 |

JOHNSON, Ryan (D) — 13 0
H: 6 2 W: 13 05 b. 2-10-96
Internationals: Northern Ireland U21.

2013–14	Stevenage	1	0		
2014–15	Stevenage	4	0		
2015–16	Stevenage	7	0		
2016–17	Stevenage	0	0		
2017–18	Stevenage	1	0	13	0

KENNEDY, Ben (F) — 108 21
H: 5 10 W: 11 00 b. 12-1-97
Internationals: Northern Ireland U17, U19, U21.

2014–15	Stevenage	15	4		
2015–16	Stevenage	22	2		
2016–17	Stevenage	36	8		
2017–18	Stevenage	35	7	108	21

KING, Jack (M) — 182 11
H: 6 0 W: 11 11 b.Oxford 20-8-85

2012–13	Preston NE	36	4		
2013–14	Preston NE	24	2		
2014–15	Preston NE	18	1	78	7
2015–16	Scunthorpe U	36	1		
2016–17	Scunthorpe U	0	0	36	1
2016–17	*Stevenage*	36	3		
2017–18	Stevenage	32	0	68	3

LESLIE, Joe (F) — 0 0

| 2017–18 | Stevenage | 0 | 0 | | |

LOKKO, Kevin (D) — 2 0
b.Whitechapel 3-11-95
Internationals: England C.
From Colchester U, Welling U, Maidstone U, Stevenage.

| 2017–18 | Stevenage | 2 | 0 | 2 | 0 |

MARTIN, Joe (M) — 274 13
H: 6 0 W: 12 13 b.Dagenham 29-11-88
Internationals: England U16, U17.

2005–06	Tottenham H	0	0		
2006–07	Tottenham H	0	0		
2007–08	Tottenham H	0	0		
2007–08	*Blackpool*	1	0		
2008–09	Blackpool	15	0		
2009–10	Blackpool	6	0	22	0
2010–11	Gillingham	17	1		
2011–12	Gillingham	35	1		
2012–13	Gillingham	38	2		
2013–14	Gillingham	46	2		
2014–15	Gillingham	25	2	161	8
2015–16	Millwall	29	2		
2016–17	Millwall	23	1	52	3
2017–18	Stevenage	39	2	39	2

McKEE, Mark (F) — 26 1
b. 1-12-98
Internationals: Northern Ireland U16, U17, U19.
From Cliftonville.

| 2016–17 | Stevenage | 2 | 0 | | |
| 2017–18 | Stevenage | 24 | 1 | 26 | 1 |

NEWTON, Danny (F) — 45 14
b.Liverpool 18-3-91
From Tamworth.

| 2017–18 | Stevenage | 45 | 14 | 45 | 14 |

O'DONNELL, Dylan (D) — 2 0
b.Stevenage 4-11-99
From Norwich C.

| 2017–18 | Stevenage | 2 | 0 | 2 | 0 |

O'KEEFE, Charley (D) — 0 0
b.Luton 17-4-00

| 2017–18 | Stevenage | 0 | 0 | | |

REVELL, Alex (F) — 477 94
H: 6 3 W: 13 00 b.Cambridge 7-7-83

2000–01	Cambridge U	4	0		
2001–02	Cambridge U	24	2		
2002–03	Cambridge U	9	0		
2003–04	Cambridge U	20	3	57	5
From Braintree T.					
2006–07	Brighton & HA	38	7		
2007–08	Brighton & HA	21	6	59	13
2007–08	Southend U	8	0		
2008–09	Southend U	23	4		
2009–10	Southend U	3	0	34	4
2009–10	Swindon T	10	2	10	2
2009–10	Wycombe W	15	6	15	6
2010–11	Leyton Orient	39	13		
2011–12	Leyton Orient	5	0	44	13
2011–12	Rotherham U	40	10		
2012–13	Rotherham U	41	6		
2013–14	Rotherham U	45	8		
2014–15	Rotherham U	24	4	150	28
2014–15	Cardiff C	16	2		
2015–16	Cardiff C	10	0	26	2
2015–16	Wigan Ath	6	1	6	1
2015–16	Milton Keynes D	17	4	17	4
2016–17	Northampton T	32	8		
2017–18	Northampton T	15	2	47	10
2017–18	Stevenage	12	6	12	6

SAMUEL, Alex (F) — 66 4
H: 6 0 W: 11 11 b.Neath 20-9-95
Internationals: Wales U18.
From Aberystwyth T.

2014–15	Swansea C	0	0		
2015–16	Swansea C	0	0		
2015–16	*Greenock Morton*	26	2	26	2
2016–17	Swansea C	0	0		
2016–17	*Newport Co*	18	2	18	2
2017–18	Stevenage	22	0	22	0

SLATER, Luke (D) — 2 0
H: 5 11 W: 11 00 b. 2-3-98
Internationals: Republic of Ireland U17, U18.

| 2016–17 | Stevenage | 0 | 0 | | |
| 2017–18 | Stevenage | 2 | 0 | 2 | 0 |

SMITH, Jonathan (M) — 183 13
H: 6 3 W: 11 02 b.Preston 17-10-86

2011–12	Swindon T	38	3	38	3
2012–13	York C	12	0	12	0
2014–15	Luton T	35	2		
2015–16	Luton T	37	4		
2016–17	Luton T	25	1	97	7
2017–18	Stevenage	36	3	36	3

TURGOTT, Blair (M) — 48 3
H: 6 0 W: 10 03 b.Bromley 22-5-94
Internationals: England C, U16, U17, U18, U19.

2011–12	West Ham U	0	0		
2012–13	*Bradford C*	4	0	4	0
2013–14	West Ham U	0	0		
2013–14	*Colchester U*	4	1	4	1
2013–14	*Rotherham U*	1	0	1	0
2013–14	*Dagenham & R*	5	0	5	0
2014–15	West Ham U	0	0		
2014–15	*Coventry C*	3	1	3	1
2015–16	*Leyton Orient*	31	1	31	1
From Bromley.					
2017–18	Stevenage	0	0		

VANCOOTEN, Terence (D) — 22 0
H: 6 1 W: 12 04 b. 29-12-97
Internationals: Guyana Full caps.

| 2016–17 | Reading | 0 | 0 | | |
| 2017–18 | Stevenage | 22 | 0 | 22 | 0 |

WHELPDALE, Chris (M) — 337 52
H: 6 0 W: 12 08 b.Harold Wood 27-1-87

2007–08	Peterborough U	35	3		
2008–09	Peterborough U	39	7		
2009–10	Peterborough U	29	1		
2010–11	Peterborough U	22	1	125	12
2010–11	*Gillingham*	4	3		
2011–12	Gillingham	39	12		
2012–13	Gillingham	41	7		
2013–14	Gillingham	24	1	108	23
2014–15	Stevenage	39	7		
2015–16	Stevenage	21	8		
2016–17	AFC Wimbledon	17	1	17	1
2017–18	Stevenage	27	1	87	16

WHITE, Joe (F) — 3 0
b. 16-1-99

| 2017–18 | Stevenage | 3 | 0 | 3 | 0 |

WILKINSON, Luke (D) — 213 20
H: 6 2 W: 11 09 b.Wells 2-12-92

2009–10	Portsmouth	0	0		
2010–11	Dagenham & R	0	0		
2011–12	Dagenham & R	0	0		
2012–13	Dagenham & R	43	6		
2013–14	Dagenham & R	22	0	65	6
2014–15	Luton T	42	4		
2015–16	Luton T	20	3	62	7
2015–16	Stevenage	19	2		
2016–17	Stevenage	40	4		
2017–18	Stevenage	27	1	86	7

WILMOT, Ben (M) — 10 0
H: 6 2 W: 12 08 b. 4-11-99
Internationals: England U19.

| 2016–17 | Stevenage | 0 | 0 | | |
| 2017–18 | Stevenage | 10 | 0 | 10 | 0 |

Players retained or with offer of contract
Wildin, Luther Ash; Wilmot, Benjamin Lewis.

Scholars
Draper, Harry; Field, Paul Michael; Fraser, Macsen William George; Gouldbourne, Marcus; Iontton, Arthur John; Jellis, Jamie Ryan; Leslie, Joe Ryan; O'Donnell, Dylan James Joseph; O'Keefe, Charley Jay; Ofosu, Claudio Tsikata; Omar, Ali Mohammed; Payne, Harry George; Sackey, Theophilus Eniabasi Sowah; Schmid, Ryan Stephen.

STOKE C (80)

ADAM, Charlie (M) — 361 71
H: 6 1 W: 12 00 b.Dundee 10-12-85
Internationals: Scotland U21, B, Full caps.

2004–05	Rangers	1	0		
2004–05	*Ross Co*	10	2	10	2
2005–06	Rangers	1	0		
2005–06	*St Mirren*	29	5	29	5
2006–07	Rangers	32	11		
2007–08	Rangers	16	2		
2008–09	Rangers	9	0	59	13
2008–09	Blackpool	13	2		
2009–10	Blackpool	43	16		
2010–11	Blackpool	35	12	91	30
2011–12	Liverpool	28	2	28	2
2012–13	Stoke C	27	3		
2013–14	Stoke C	31	7		
2014–15	Stoke C	29	7		
2015–16	Stoke C	22	1		
2016–17	Stoke C	24	1		
2017–18	Stoke C	11	0	144	19

AFELLAY, Ibrahim (M) — 258 44
H: 5 11 W: 10 10 b.Utrecht 2-4-86
Internationals: Netherlands Full caps.

2003–04	PSV Eindhoven	2	0		
2004–05	PSV Eindhoven	7	2		
2005–06	PSV Eindhoven	23	2		
2006–07	PSV Eindhoven	27	6		
2007–08	PSV Eindhoven	24	2		
2008–09	PSV Eindhoven	28	13		
2009–10	PSV Eindhoven	29	4		
2010–11	PSV Eindhoven	19	6	159	35
2010–11	Barcelona	16	1		
2011–12	Barcelona	4	0		
2012–13	Barcelona	3	0		
2012–13	*Schalke 04*	10	2	10	2
2013–14	Barcelona	1	0		
2014–15	Barcelona	0	0	21	1
2014–15	*Olympiacos*	19	4	19	4
2015–16	Stoke C	31	2		
2016–17	Stoke C	12	0		
2017–18	Stoke C	6	0	49	2

ALLEN, Joe (M) — 290 19
H: 5 6 W: 9 10 b.Carmarthen 14-3-90
Internationals: Wales U17, U19, U21, Full caps. Great Britain.

2006–07	Swansea C	1	0		
2007–08	Swansea C	6	0		
2008–09	Swansea C	23	1		
2009–10	Swansea C	21	0		
2010–11	Swansea C	40	2		
2011–12	Swansea C	36	4		

2012–13	Swansea C	0	0	**127**	**7**
2012–13	Liverpool	27	0		
2013–14	Liverpool	24	1		
2014–15	Liverpool	21	1		
2015–16	Liverpool	19	2	**91**	**4**
2016–17	Stoke C	36	6		
2017–18	Stoke C	36	2	**72**	**8**

BAUER, Moritz (D)   **145**   **0**
H: 5 11 W: 11 07 b.Veltheim 25-1-92
Internationals: Switzerland U19, U21. Austria Full caps.

2011–12	Grasshopper Zurich	16	0		
2012–13	Grasshopper Zurich	13	0		
2013–14	Grasshopper Zurich	15	0		
2014–15	Grasshopper Zurich	15	0		
2015–16	Grasshopper Zurich	33	0	**93**	**0**
2016–17	Ruban Kazan	21	0	**21**	**0**
2017–18	Rubin Kazan	16	0	**16**	**0**
2017–18	Stoke C	15	0	**15**	**0**

BERAHINO, Saido (F)   **165**   **35**
H: 5 10 W: 11 13 b.Burundi 4-8-93
Internationals: England U16, U17, U18, U19, U20, U21.

2010–11	WBA	0	0		
2011–12	WBA	0	0		
2011–12	*Northampton T*	14	6	**14**	**6**
2011–12	*Brentford*	8	4	**8**	**4**
2012–13	WBA	0	0		
2012–13	*Peterborough U*	10	2	**10**	**2**
2013–14	WBA	32	5		
2014–15	WBA	38	14		
2015–16	WBA	31	4		
2016–17	WBA	4	0	**105**	**23**
2017–18	Stoke C	15	0	**28**	**0**

BOJAN, Krkic (F)   **257**   **54**
H: 5 8 W: 10 03 b.Linyola 28-8-90
Internationals: Spain U17, U21, Full caps.

2007–08	Barcelona	31	10		
2008–09	Barcelona	23	2		
2009–10	Barcelona	23	8		
2010–11	Barcelona	27	6		
2011–12	Roma	33	7		
2012–13	Roma	0	0	**33**	**7**
2012–13	*AC Milan*	19	3	**19**	**3**
2013–14	Barcelona	0	0	**104**	**26**
2013–14	*Ajax*	24	3	**24**	**3**
2014–15	Stoke C	16	4		
2015–16	Stoke C	27	7		
2016–17	Stoke C	9	3		
2016–17	*Mainz*	11	1	**11**	**1**
2017–18	Stoke C	1	0	**53**	**14**
2017–18	*Alaves*	13	0	**13**	**0**

BUTLAND, Jack (G)   **182**   **0**
H: 6 4 W: 12 00 b.Clevedon 10-3-93
Internationals: England U16, U17, U19, U20, U21, Full caps.

2009–10	Birmingham C	0	0		
2010–11	Birmingham C	0	0		
2011–12	Birmingham C	0	0		
2011–12	*Cheltenham T*	24	0	**24**	**0**
2012–13	Birmingham C	46	0	**46**	**0**
2012–13	Stoke C	0	0		
2013–14	Stoke C	3	0		
2013–14	*Barnsley*	13	0	**13**	**0**
2013–14	*Leeds U*	16	0	**16**	**0**
2014–15	Stoke C	3	0		
2014–15	*Derby Co*	6	0	**6**	**0**
2015–16	Stoke C	31	0		
2016–17	Stoke C	5	0		
2017–18	Stoke C	35	0	**77**	**0**

CAMERON, Geoff (D)   **292**   **13**
H: 6 3 W: 13 02 b.Attleboro 11-7-85
Internationals: USA Full caps.

2008	Houston D	24	1		
2009	Houston D	32	2		
2010	Houston D	16	3		
2011	Houston D	37	5		
2012	Houston D	15	0	**124**	**11**
2012–13	Stoke C	35	0		
2013–14	Stoke C	37	2		
2014–15	Stoke C	27	0		
2015–16	Stoke C	30	0		
2016–17	Stoke C	19	0		
2017–18	Stoke C	20	0	**168**	**2**

CAMPBELL, Tyrese (F)   **4**   **0**
b.Derby 16-9-97
Internationals: England U17.
From Manchester C.

2017–18	Stoke C	4	0	**4**	**0**

CHOUPO-MOTING, Eric Maxim (F) **234**   **50**
H: 6 3 W: 12 13 b.Hamburg 23-3-89
Internationals: Germany U19, U21.
Cameroon Full caps.

2007–08	Hamburg	13	0		
2008–09	Hamburg	0	0		
2009–10	Hamburg	0	0		
2009–10	*Nuremberg*	25	5	**25**	**5**
2010–11	Hamburg	10	2	**23**	**2**
2011–12	Mainz 05	34	10		
2012–13	Mainz 05	8	0		
2013–14	Mainz 05	32	10	**74**	**20**
2014–15	Schalke 04	31	9		
2015–16	Schalke 04	28	6		
2016–17	Schalke 04	23	3		
2017–18	Schalke 04	0	0	**82**	**18**
2017–18	Stoke C	30	5	**30**	**5**

CROUCH, Peter (F)   **556**   **140**
H: 6 7 W: 13 03 b.Macclesfield 30-1-81
Internationals: England U20, U21, B, Full caps.

1998–99	Tottenham H	0	0		
1999–2000	Tottenham H	0	0		
2000–01	QPR	42	10	**42**	**10**
2001–02	Portsmouth	37	18		
2001–02	Aston Villa	7	2		
2002–03	Aston Villa	14	0		
2003–04	Aston Villa	16	4	**37**	**6**
2003–04	*Norwich C*	15	4	**15**	**4**
2004–05	Southampton	27	12	**27**	**12**
2005–06	Liverpool	32	8		
2006–07	Liverpool	32	9		
2007–08	Liverpool	21	5	**85**	**22**
2008–09	Portsmouth	38	11		
2009–10	Portsmouth	0	0	**75**	**29**
2009–10	Tottenham H	38	8		
2010–11	Tottenham H	34	4		
2011–12	Tottenham H	1	0	**73**	**12**
2011–12	Stoke C	32	10		
2012–13	Stoke C	34	7		
2013–14	Stoke C	34	8		
2014–15	Stoke C	33	8		
2015–16	Stoke C	11	0		
2016–17	Stoke C	27	7		
2017–18	Stoke C	31	5	**202**	**45**

DIOUF, Mame (F)   **283**   **85**
H: 6 1 W: 12 00 b.Dakar 16-12-87
Internationals: Senegal Full caps.

2007	Molde	21	9		
2008	Molde	23	7		
2009	Molde	29	16	**73**	**32**
2009–10	Manchester U	5	1		
2010–11	Manchester U	0	0		
2010–11	*Blackburn R*	26	3	**26**	**3**
2011–12	Manchester U	0	0	**5**	**1**
2011–12	*Hannover 96*	10	6		
2012–13	*Hannover 96*	28	12		
2013–14	*Hannover 96*	19	8	**57**	**26**
2014–15	Stoke C	34	11		
2015–16	Stoke C	26	5		
2016–17	Stoke C	27	1		
2017–18	Stoke C	35	6	**122**	**23**

EDWARDS, Thomas (D)   **6**   **0**
b. 22-1-99

2016–17	Stoke C	0	0		
2017–18	Stoke C	6	0	**6**	**0**

FLETCHER, Darren (M)   **341**   **23**
H: 6 0 W: 11 09 b.Edinburgh 1-2-84
Internationals: Scotland U20, U21, B, Full caps.

2000–01	Manchester U	0	0		
2001–02	Manchester U	0	0		
2002–03	Manchester U	0	0		
2003–04	Manchester U	22	0		
2004–05	Manchester U	18	3		
2005–06	Manchester U	27	1		
2006–07	Manchester U	24	3		
2007–08	Manchester U	16	0		
2008–09	Manchester U	26	3		
2009–10	Manchester U	30	4		
2010–11	Manchester U	26	2		
2011–12	Manchester U	8	1		
2012–13	Manchester U	3	1		
2013–14	Manchester U	12	0		
2014–15	Manchester U	11	0	**223**	**18**
2014–15	WBA	15	1		
2015–16	WBA	38	1		
2016–17	WBA	38	2	**91**	**4**
2017–18	Stoke C	27	1	**27**	**1**

GRANT, Lee (G)   **468**   **0**
H: 6 3 W: 13 01 b.Hemel Hempstead 27-1-83
Internationals: England U16, U17, U18, U19, U21.

2000–01	Derby Co	0	0		
2001–02	Derby Co	0	0		
2002–03	Derby Co	29	0		
2003–04	Derby Co	36	0		
2004–05	Derby Co	2	0		
2005–06	Derby Co	0	0		
2005–06	*Burnley*	1	0		
2005–06	*Oldham Ath*	16	0	**16**	**0**
2006–07	Derby Co	7	0		
2007–08	Sheffield W	44	0		
2008–09	Sheffield W	46	0		
2009–10	Sheffield W	46	0	**136**	**0**
2010–11	Burnley	25	0		
2011–12	Burnley	43	0		
2012–13	Burnley	46	0	**115**	**0**
2013–14	Derby Co	46	0		
2014–15	Derby Co	40	0		
2015–16	Derby Co	10	0		
2016–17	Derby Co	0	0	**170**	**0**
2016–17	*Stoke C*	28	0		
2017–18	Stoke C	3	0	**31**	**0**

HAUGAARD, Jakob (G)   **57**   **0**
H: 6 6 W: 13 10 b.Sundby 1-5-92
Internationals: Denmark U18, U20.

2010–11	Akademisk BK	14	0	**14**	**0**
2011–12	Midtjylland	0	0		
2012–13	Midtjylland	6	0		
2013–14	Midtjylland	1	0		
2014–15	Midtjylland	23	0	**30**	**0**
2015–16	Stoke C	5	0		
2016–17	Stoke C	0	0		
2016–17	*Wigan Ath*	8	0		
2017–18	*Wigan Ath*	0	0	**8**	**0**
2017–18	Stoke C	0	0	**5**	**0**

IMBULA, Giannelli (M)   **221**   **10**
H: 6 0 W: 12 02 b.Vilvoorde 12-9-92
Internationals: France U20, U21.

2009–10	Guingamp	2	0		
2010–11	Guingamp	28	2		
2011–12	Guingamp	27	0		
2012–13	Guingamp	34	2	**91**	**4**
2013–14	Marseille	29	1		
2014–15	Marseille	37	2	**66**	**3**
2015–16	FC Porto	10	0	**10**	**0**
2015–16	Stoke C	14	2		
2016–17	Stoke C	12	0		
2017–18	Stoke C	0	0	**26**	**2**
2017–18	*Toulouse*	28	1	**28**	**1**

IRELAND, Stephen (F)   **246**   **19**
H: 5 8 W: 10 07 b.Cork 22-8-86
Internationals: Republic of Ireland U21, Full caps.

2005–06	Manchester C	24	0		
2006–07	Manchester C	24	1		
2007–08	Manchester C	33	4		
2008–09	Manchester C	35	9		
2009–10	Manchester C	22	2		
2010–11	Manchester C	0	0	**138**	**16**
2010–11	Aston Villa	10	0		
2010–11	*Newcastle U*	2	0	**2**	**0**
2011–12	Aston Villa	24	1		
2012–13	Aston Villa	13	0		
2013–14	Aston Villa	0	0	**47**	**1**
2013–14	Stoke C	25	2		
2014–15	Stoke C	17	0		
2015–16	Stoke C	13	0		
2017–18	Stoke C	4	0	**59**	**2**

JESE, Rodriguez (F)   **101**   **18**
H: 5 10 W: 11 07 b.Madrid 26-2-93
Internationals: Spain U16, U17, U18, U19, U20, U21.

2011–12	Real Madrid	1	0		
2012–13	Real Madrid	0	0		
2013–14	Real Madrid	18	5		
2014–15	Real Madrid	16	3		
2015–16	Real Madrid	28	5	**63**	**13**
2016–17	Paris Saint-Germain	9	1		
2016–17	*Las Palmas*	16	3	**16**	**3**
2017–18	Paris Saint-Germain	0	0	**9**	**1**

On loan from Paris Saint-Germain.

2017–18	Stoke C	13	1	**13**	**1**

JOHNSON, Glen (D)   **366**   **15**
H: 6 0 W: 13 04 b.Greenwich 23-8-84
Internationals: England U20, U21, Full caps.

2001–02	West Ham U	0	0		
2002–03	West Ham U	15	0	**15**	**0**
2002–03	*Millwall*	8	0	**8**	**0**
2003–04	Chelsea	19	3		

2004–05	Chelsea	17	0		
2005–06	Chelsea	4	0		
2006–07	Chelsea	0	0		
2006–07	*Portsmouth*	26	0		
2007–08	Chelsea	2	0	**42**	**3**
2007–08	Portsmouth	29	1		
2008–09	Portsmouth	29	3		
2009–10	Portsmouth	0	0	**84**	**4**
2009–10	Liverpool	25	3		
2010–11	Liverpool	28	2		
2011–12	Liverpool	23	1		
2012–13	Liverpool	36	1		
2013–14	Liverpool	29	0		
2014–15	Liverpool	19	1	**160**	**8**
2015–16	Stoke C	25	0		
2016–17	Stoke C	23	0		
2017–18	Stoke C	9	0	**57**	**0**

MARTINS INDI, Bruno (D) 201 8
H: 6 1 W: 11 09 b.Barreiro, Portugal 8-2-92
Internationals: Netherlands U17, U19, U21, Full caps.

2010–11	Feyenoord	15	1		
2011–12	Feyenoord	29	1		
2012–13	Feyenoord	32	1		
2013–14	Feyenoord	26	2	**102**	**5**
2014–15	Porto	24	2		
2015–16	Porto	23	0		
2016–17	Porto	0	0	**47**	**2**
2016–17	*Stoke C*	35	1		
2017–18	Stoke C	17	0	**52**	**1**

NDIAYE, Papa Badou (M) 191 48
H: 5 10 W: 10 10 b.Dakar 27-10-90
Internationals: Senegal Full caps.

2012	Bodo/Glimt	29	3		
2013	Bodo/Glimt	27	12		
2014	Bodo/Glimt	30	9		
2015	Bodo/Glimt	16	4	**102**	**28**
2015–16	Osmanlispor	33	11		
2016–17	Osmanlispor	26	6	**59**	**17**
2017–18	Galatasaray	17	1	**17**	**1**
2017–18	Stoke C	13	2	**13**	**2**

NGOY, Julien (F) 19 3
H: 6 1 W: 10 01 b.Antwerp 2-11-97
Internationals: Belgium U16, U17, U21.

2016–17	Stoke C	5	0		
2017–18	Stoke C	1	0	**6**	**0**
2017–18	*Walsall*	13	3	**13**	**3**

PIETERS, Erik (D) 313 3
H: 6 0 W: 13 00 b.Tiel 7-8-88
Internationals: Netherlands U17, U19, U21, Full caps.

2006–07	FC Utrecht	20	0		
2007–08	FC Utrecht	31	2	**51**	**2**
2008–09	PSV Eindhoven	17	0		
2009–10	PSV Eindhoven	27	0		
2010–11	PSV Eindhoven	31	0		
2011–12	PSV Eindhoven	16	0		
2012–13	PSV Eindhoven	2	0	**93**	**0**
2013–14	Stoke C	36	1		
2014–15	Stoke C	31	0		
2015–16	Stoke C	35	0		
2016–17	Stoke C	36	0		
2017–18	Stoke C	31	0	**169**	**1**

SHAQIRI, Xherdan (M) 243 45
H: 5 7 W: 11 05 b.Gnjilane 10-10-91
Internationals: Switzerland U17, U18, U19, U21, Full caps.

2009–10	Basel	32	4		
2010–11	Basel	29	5		
2011–12	Basel	31	9	**92**	**18**
2012–13	Bayern Munich	26	4		
2013–14	Bayern Munich	17	6		
2014–15	Bayern Munich	9	1	**52**	**11**
2014–15	Inter Milan	15	1	**15**	**1**
2015–16	Stoke C	27	3		
2016–17	Stoke C	21	4		
2017–18	Stoke C	36	8	**84**	**15**

SHAWCROSS, Ryan (D) 359 21
H: 6 3 W: 13 13 b.Buckley 4-10-87
Internationals: England U21, Full caps.

2006–07	Manchester U	0	0		
2007–08	Manchester U	0	0		
2007–08	Stoke C	41	7		
2008–09	Stoke C	30	3		
2009–10	Stoke C	28	2		
2010–11	Stoke C	36	1		
2011–12	Stoke C	36	2		
2012–13	Stoke C	37	1		
2013–14	Stoke C	37	1		
2014–15	Stoke C	32	2		
2015–16	Stoke C	20	0		
2016–17	Stoke C	35	1		
2017–18	Stoke C	27	1	**359**	**21**

SOBHI, Ramadan (F) 96 13
b.Cairo 27-1-97
Internationals: Egypt U17, U20, U23, Full caps.

2013–14	Al Ahly	3	1		
2014–15	Al Ahly	24	5		
2015–16	Al Ahly	28	5	**55**	**11**
2016–17	Stoke C	17	0		
2017–18	Stoke C	24	2	**41**	**2**

SORENSON, Lasse (M) 1 0
b. 21-10-99
From Esbjerg.

2017–18	Stoke C	1	0	**1**	**0**

SOUTAR, Harry (D) 15 1
H: 6 6 W: 12 08 b.Aberdeen 22-6-98
Internationals: Scotland U17, U19.

2015–16	Dundee U	2	1		
2016–17	Dundee U	0	0	**2**	**1**
2016–17	Stoke C	0	0		
2017–18	Stoke C	0	0		
2017–18	*Ross Co*	13	0	**13**	**0**

STAFYLIDIS, Konstantinos (D) 129 9
H: 5 9 W: 11 09 b.Koufalia 2-12-93
Internationals: Greece U17, U19, U20, U21, Full caps.

2011–12	PAOK Salonika	11	0		
2012–13	PAOK Salonika	18	1	**29**	**1**
2013–14	Bayer Leverkusen	1	0		
2014–15	Bayer Leverkusen	0	0	**1**	**0**
2014–15	*Fulham*	38	0	**38**	**0**
2015–16	Augsburg	27	4		
2016–17	Augsburg	27	4		
2017–18	Augsburg	2	0	**56**	**8**

On loan from Augsburg.

2017–18	Stoke C	5	0	**5**	**0**

SWEENEY, Ryan (D) 52 3
b.Kingston upon Thames 15-4-97
Internationals: Republic of Ireland U19, U21.

2014–15	AFC Wimbledon	3	0		
2015–16	AFC Wimbledon	10	0	**13**	**0**
2016–17	Stoke C	0	0		
2016–17	*Bristol R*	16	0		
2017–18	Stoke C	0	0		
2017–18	*Bristol R*	23	3	**39**	**3**

TELFORD, Dominic (F) 33 4
H: 5 9 W: 11 05 b.Burnley 5-12-96

2014–15	Blackpool	14	1		
2015–16	Blackpool	0	0	**14**	**1**
2016–17	Stoke C	0	0		
2017–18	Stoke C	0	0		
2017–18	*Bristol R*	19	3	**19**	**3**

TYMON, Josh (D) 17 0
b. 22-5-99
Internationals: England U17, U18, U19, U20.

2015–16	Hull C	0	0		
2016–17	Hull C	5	0	**5**	**0**
2017–18	Stoke C	3	0	**3**	**0**
2017–18	*Milton Keynes D*	9	0	**9**	**0**

VERLINDEN, Thibaud (M) 0 0
Internationals: Belgium U16, U17, U19.
From Club Bruges.

2016–17	Stoke C	0	0		
2017–18	Stoke C	0	0		
2017–18	*St Pauli*	0	0		

WIMMER, Kevin (D) 127 6
H: 6 2 W: 13 05 b.Wels 15-11-92
Internationals: Austria U18, U21, Full caps.

2011–12	LASK Linkz	28	4	**28**	**4**
2012–13	Cologne	9	0		
2013–14	Cologne	26	2		
2014–15	Cologne	32	0	**67**	**2**
2015–16	Tottenham H	10	0		
2016–17	Tottenham H	5	0		
2017–18	Tottenham H	0	0	**15**	**0**
2017–18	Stoke C	17	0	**17**	**0**

WOLLSCHEID, Philipp (D) 225 11
H: 6 4 W: 13 03 b.Wadern 6-3-89
Internationals: Germany U20, Full caps.

2006–07	Noswendel-Wadern	8	2	**8**	**2**
2007–08	Hasborn-Dautweiler	18	0	**18**	**0**
2007–08	Saarbrucken	7	1		
2008–09	Saarbrucken	23	2	**30**	**3**
2009–10	Nuremberg II	26	1		
2010–11	Nuremberg II	14	0	**40**	**1**
2010–11	Nuremberg	19	3		
2011–12	Nuremberg	2	0	**21**	**3**
2012–13	Bayer Leverkusen	31	2		
2013–14	Bayer Leverkusen	20	0		
2014–15	Bayer Leverkusen	0	0	**51**	**2**
2014–15	*Mainz*	5	0	**5**	**0**
2014–15	Stoke C	12	0		
2015–16	Stoke C	31	0		
2016–17	Stoke C	2	0		
2016–17	*Wolfsburg*	7	0	**7**	**0**
2017–18	Stoke C	0	0	**45**	**0**

Transferred to Metz, August 2017.

Players retained or with offer of contract
Balde, Rachid; Bursik, Josef John; Deczki, Mate; Dunwoody, Jake; El Ouariachi, Mohamed; Gyollai, Daniel; Jarvis, Daniel Adam; Karamoko, Vazoumana; McJannet, Cameron Allan; Muniesa Martinez, Marc; Niakate, Moussa; Pemberton, Tre Kingsley; Shenton, Oliver; Szereto, Krisztofer; Waddington, Mark Thomas; Wimmer, Kevin.

Scholars
Butler, James Anthony; Collins, Nathan Michael; Diallo, Mohamed; Forrester, William; Jennings, James Jordan; Murphy, Max; Mvovi, Joel Kaduba; Stanton, Ethan Bradley; Toure, Abdoulaye; Twyford, Jacob Thomas; Wara, Semi Scott.

SUNDERLAND (81)

ASORO, Joel (F) 27 3
H: 5 9 W: 11 11 b. 27-4-99
Internationals: Sweden U17, U21.

2016–17	Sunderland	1	0		
2017–18	Sunderland	26	3	**27**	**3**

BEADLING, Tom (D) 13 0
H: 6 1 W: 12 08 b.Barrow-in-Furness 16-1-96

2014–15	Sunderland	0	0		
2015–16	Sunderland	0	0		
2016–17	Sunderland	0	0		
2016–17	*Bury*	2	0	**2**	**0**
2017–18	Sunderland	0	0		
2017–18	*Dunfermline Ath*	11	0	**11**	**0**

CATTERMOLE, Lee (M) 306 7
H: 5 10 W: 11 13 b.Stockton 21-3-88
Internationals: England U16, U17, U18, U19, U21.

2005–06	Middlesbrough	14	1		
2006–07	Middlesbrough	31	1		
2007–08	Middlesbrough	24	1	**69**	**3**
2008–09	Wigan Ath	33	1		
2009–10	Wigan Ath	0	0	**33**	**1**
2009–10	Sunderland	22	0		
2010–11	Sunderland	23	0		
2011–12	Sunderland	23	0		
2012–13	Sunderland	10	0		
2013–14	Sunderland	24	1		
2014–15	Sunderland	28	1		
2015–16	Sunderland	31	0		
2016–17	Sunderland	8	0		
2017–18	Sunderland	35	1	**204**	**3**

DJILOBODJI, Papy (D) 240 12
H: 6 4 W: 12 13 b.Kaolack 1-12-88
Internationals: Senegal Full caps.

2009–10	Senart-Moissy	7	1	**7**	**1**
2009–10	Nantes	13	0		
2010–11	Nantes	27	2		
2011–12	Nantes	36	4		
2012–13	Nantes	36	0		
2013–14	Nantes	28	3		
2014–15	Nantes	31	0	**171**	**9**
2015–16	Chelsea	0	0		
2015–16	*Werder Bremen*	14	2	**14**	**2**
2016–17	Sunderland	18	0		
2017–18	Sunderland	0	0	**18**	**0**
2017–18	*Dijon*	30	0	**30**	**0**

EMBLETON, Elliot (M) 2 0
H: 5 8 W: 10 01 b. 2-4-99
Internationals: England U17, U18, U19, U20.

2016–17	Sunderland	0	0		
2017–18	Sunderland	2	0	**2**	**0**

GAMBLE, Owen (M) 0 0

2017–18	Sunderland	0	0		

GIBSON, Darron (M) 130 6
H: 6 0 W: 12 04 b.Derry 25-10-87
Internationals: Republic of Ireland U21, B, Full caps.

2005–06	Manchester U	0	0		
2006–07	Manchester U	0	0		
2007–08	Manchester U	0	0		
2007–08	*Wolverhampton W*	21	1	**21**	**1**
2008–09	Manchester U	3	1		
2009–10	Manchester U	15	2		
2010–11	Manchester U	12	0		
2011–12	Manchester U	1	0	**31**	**3**

2011–12	Everton	11	1		
2012–13	Everton	23	1		
2013–14	Everton	1	0		
2014–15	Everton	9	0		
2015–16	Everton	7	0		
2016–17	Everton	0	0	51	2
2016–17	Sunderland	12	0		
2017–18	Sunderland	15	0	27	0

GOOCH, Lynden (M) 45 1
H: 5 8 W: 10 12 b.Santa Cruz 24-12-95
Internationals: Republic of Ireland U18. USA U20, Full caps.

2015–16	Sunderland	0	0		
2015–16	*Doncaster R*	10	0	10	0
2016–17	Sunderland	11	0		
2017–18	Sunderland	24	1	35	1

HONEYMAN, George (M) 48 6
H: 5 8 W: 11 05 b.Prudhoe 8-9-94

2014–15	Sunderland	0	0		
2015–16	Sunderland	1	0		
2016–17	Sunderland	5	0		
2017–18	Sunderland	42	6	48	6

HUME, Denver (D) 1 0
b. 11-8-96

2017–18	Sunderland	1	0	1	0

JONES, Billy (M) 445 25
H: 5 11 W: 13 00 b.Shrewsbury 24-3-87
Internationals: England U16, U17, U19, U20.

2003–04	Crewe Alex	27	1		
2004–05	Crewe Alex	20	0		
2005–06	Crewe Alex	44	6		
2006–07	Crewe Alex	41	1	132	8
2007–08	Preston NE	29	0		
2008–09	Preston NE	44	3		
2009–10	Preston NE	44	4		
2010–11	Preston NE	43	6	160	13
2011–12	WBA	18	0		
2012–13	WBA	27	1		
2013–14	WBA	21	0	66	1
2014–15	Sunderland	14	0		
2015–16	Sunderland	24	1		
2016–17	Sunderland	27	1		
2017–18	Sunderland	22	1	87	3

KHAZRI, Wahbi (M) 286 57
H: 6 0 W: 12 04 b.Ajaccio 8-2-91
Internationals: France U21. Tunisia U20, Full caps.

2008–09	Bastia	13	3		
2009–10	Bastia	31	2		
2010–11	Bastia	34	4		
2011–12	Bastia	33	9		
2012–13	Bastia	29	7		
2013–14	Bastia	32	6	172	31
2014–15	Bordeaux	32	9		
2015–16	Bordeaux	20	5	52	14
2015–16	Sunderland	14	2		
2016–17	Sunderland	21	1		
2017–18	Sunderland	3	0	38	3
2017–18	*Rennes*	24	9	24	9

KONE, Lamine (D) 269 14
H: 6 2 W: 13 01 b.Paris 1-2-89
Internationals: France U17, U18, U19, U20. Ivory Coast Full caps.

2006–07	Chateauroux	5	0		
2007–08	Chateauroux	16	0		
2008–09	Chateauroux	27	1		
2009–10	Chateauroux	26	3	74	4
2010–11	Lorient	7	1		
2011–12	Lorient	21	1		
2012–13	Lorient	32	3		
2013–14	Lorient	18	1		
2014–15	Lorient	30	1		
2015–16	Lorient	18	0	126	7
2015–16	Sunderland	15	2		
2016–17	Sunderland	30	1		
2017–18	Sunderland	24	0	69	3

LOVE, Donald (D) 31 0
H: 5 10 W: 11 05 b.Rochdale 2-12-94
Internationals: Scotland U17, U19, U21.

2015–16	Manchester U	1	0		
2015–16	*Wigan Ath*	7	0	7	0
2016–17	Sunderland	12	0		
2017–18	Sunderland	11	0	23	0

LUALUA, Kazenga (F) 195 18
H: 5 11 W: 12 00 b.Kinshasa 10-12-90

2007–08	Newcastle U	2	0		
2008–09	Newcastle U	3	0		
2008–09	*Doncaster R*	4	0	4	0
2009–10	Newcastle U	1	0		
2009–10	*Brighton & HA*	11	0		
2010–11	Newcastle U	2	0		

2010–11	*Brighton & HA*	11	4		
2011–12	Newcastle U	0	0	8	0
2011–12	Brighton & HA	27	1		
2012–13	Brighton & HA	22	5		
2013–14	Brighton & HA	32	1		
2014–15	Brighton & HA	34	3		
2015–16	Brighton & HA	18	3		
2016–17	Brighton & HA	3	0		
2016–17	*QPR*	11	1		
2017–18	Brighton & HA	0	0	158	17
2017–18	*QPR*	8	0	19	1
2017–18	Sunderland	6	0	6	0

MAJA, Josh (F) 17 1
H: 5 11 W: 11 09 b. 27-12-98
From Fulham.

2016–17	Sunderland	0	0		
2017–18	Sunderland	17	1	17	1

MATTHEWS, Adam (D) 197 6
H: 5 10 W: 11 02 b.Swansea 13-1-92
Internationals: Wales U17, U19, U21, Full caps.

2008–09	Cardiff C	0	0		
2009–10	Cardiff C	32	1		
2010–11	Cardiff C	8	0	40	1
2011–12	Celtic	27	0		
2012–13	Celtic	22	2		
2013–14	Celtic	23	1		
2014–15	Celtic	29	1	101	4
2015–16	Sunderland	1	0		
2015–16	*Bristol C*	9	0		
2016–17	*Bristol C*	12	0	21	0
2017–18	Sunderland	34	1	35	1

McGEADY, Aiden (M) 371 59
H: 5 10 W: 11 03 b.Glasgow 4-4-86
Internationals: Republic of Ireland Full caps.

2003–04	Celtic	4	1		
2004–05	Celtic	27	4		
2005–06	Celtic	20	4		
2006–07	Celtic	34	5		
2007–08	Celtic	36	7		
2008–09	Celtic	29	3		
2009–10	Celtic	35	7	185	31
2010–11	Spartak Moscow	11	2		
2011–12	Spartak Moscow	31	3		
2012–13	Spartak Moscow	17	5		
2013–14	Spartak Moscow	13	1	72	11
2013–14	Everton	16	0		
2014–15	Everton	16	1		
2015–16	Everton	0	0		
2015–16	*Sheffield W*	13	1	13	1
2016–17	Everton	0	0	32	1
2016–17	*Preston NE*	34	8	34	8
2017–18	Sunderland	35	7	35	7

McMANAMAN, Callum (F) 148 13
H: 5 9 W: 11 03 b.Huyton 25-4-91
Internationals: England U20.

2008–09	Wigan Ath	1	0		
2009–10	Wigan Ath	0	0		
2010–11	Wigan Ath	3	0		
2011–12	Wigan Ath	2	0		
2011–12	*Blackpool*	14	2	14	2
2012–13	Wigan Ath	20	2		
2013–14	Wigan Ath	30	3		
2014–15	Wigan Ath	23	5	79	10
2014–15	WBA	8	0		
2015–16	WBA	12	0		
2016–17	WBA	0	0	20	0
2016–17	*Sheffield W*	11	0	11	0
2017–18	Sunderland	24	1	24	1

McNAIR, Paddy (D) 49 5
H: 5 8 W: 11 05 b.Ballyclare 27-4-95
Internationals: Northern Ireland U16, U17, U19, U21, Full caps.

2011–12	Manchester U	0	0		
2012–13	Manchester U	0	0		
2013–14	Manchester U	0	0		
2014–15	Manchester U	16	0		
2015–16	Manchester U	8	0	24	0
2016–17	Sunderland	9	0		
2017–18	Sunderland	16	5	25	5

MOLYNEUX, Luke (M) 1 0
b. 29-3-98

2017–18	Sunderland	1	0	1	0

MUMBA, Bali (F) 1 0
Internationals: England U16, U17.

2017–18	Sunderland	1	0	1	0

NDONG , Didier (M) 137 5
H: 5 10 b.Lambarene 17-6-94
Internationals: Gabon U20, Full caps.

2011–12	Sfaxien	1	0		
2012–13	Sfaxien	18	1		
2013–14	Sfaxien	16	1		
2014–15	Sfaxien	5	0	40	2
2014–15	Lorient	12	0		
2015–16	Lorient	34	2		
2016–17	Lorient	2	0	48	2
2016–17	Sunderland	31	1		
2017–18	Sunderland	18	0	49	1
2017–18	*Watford*	0	0		

NELSON, Andrew (F) 16 4
b.Stockton-on-Tees 16-9-97

2016–17	Sunderland	0	0		
2016–17	*Hartlepool U*	4	0	4	0
2017–18	Sunderland	0	0		
2017–18	*Falkirk*	12	4	12	4

O'SHEA, John (D) 492 15
H: 6 3 W: 13 07 b.Waterford 30-4-81
Internationals: Republic of Ireland U21, Full caps.

1998–99	Manchester U	0	0		
1999–2000	Manchester U	0	0		
1999–2000	*Bournemouth*	10	1	10	1
2000–01	Manchester U	0	0		
2001–02	Manchester U	9	0		
2002–03	Manchester U	32	0		
2003–04	Manchester U	33	2		
2004–05	Manchester U	23	2		
2005–06	Manchester U	34	1		
2006–07	Manchester U	32	4		
2007–08	Manchester U	28	0		
2008–09	Manchester U	30	0		
2009–10	Manchester U	15	1		
2010–11	Manchester U	20	0	256	10
2011–12	Sunderland	29	0		
2012–13	Sunderland	34	2		
2013–14	Sunderland	33	1		
2014–15	Sunderland	37	0		
2015–16	Sunderland	28	0		
2016–17	Sunderland	28	0		
2017–18	Sunderland	37	1	226	4

OVIEDO, Bryan (M) 138 6
H: 5 8 W: 10 13 b.Alajuela 18-2-90
Internationals: Costa Rica U20, Full caps.

2009–10	FC Copenhagen	3	0		
2010–11	FC Copenhagen	1	0		
2010–11	*Nordsjaelland*	14	0	14	0
2011–12	FC Copenhagen	22	2		
2012–13	FC Copenhagen	4	0	30	2
2012–13	Everton	15	0		
2013–14	Everton	9	2		
2014–15	Everton	6	0		
2015–16	Everton	14	0		
2016–17	Everton	6	0	50	2
2016–17	Sunderland	10	0		
2017–18	Sunderland	34	2	44	2

ROBSON, Ethan (M) 9 0
H: 5 8 W: 10 12 b. 25-10-96

2016–17	Sunderland	0	0		
2017–18	Sunderland	9	0	9	0

RODWELL, Jack (D) 168 11
H: 6 2 W: 12 08 b.Southport 11-3-91
Internationals: England U16, U17, U19, U21, Full caps.

2007–08	Everton	2	0		
2008–09	Everton	19	0		
2009–10	Everton	26	2		
2010–11	Everton	24	0		
2011–12	Everton	14	2	85	4
2012–13	Manchester C	11	2		
2013–14	Manchester C	5	0	16	2
2014–15	Sunderland	23	3		
2015–16	Sunderland	22	1		
2016–17	Sunderland	20	0		
2017–18	Sunderland	2	1	67	5

RUITER, Robbin (G) 232 0
H: 6 5 W: 12 04 b.Amsterdam 25-3-87

2009–10	Volendam	21	0		
2010–11	Volendam	24	0		
2011–12	Volendam	25	0	70	0
2012–13	Utrecht	37	0		
2013–14	Utrecht	30	0		
2014–15	Utrecht	31	0		
2015–16	Utrecht	29	0		
2016–17	Utrecht	14	2	142	0
2017–18	FC Utrecht	0	0		
2017–18	Sunderland	20	0	20	0

STEELE, Jason (G)   272   0
H: 6 2   W: 12 07   b.Newton Aycliffe 18-8-90
Internationals: England U16, U17, U19, U21. Great Britain.

2007–08	Middlesbrough	0	0		
2008–09	Middlesbrough	0	0		
2009–10	Middlesbrough	0	0		
2009–10	*Northampton T*	13	0	13	0
2010–11	Middlesbrough	35	0		
2011–12	Middlesbrough	34	0		
2012–13	Middlesbrough	46	0		
2013–14	Middlesbrough	16	0		
2014–15	Middlesbrough	0	0	131	0
2014–15	*Blackburn R*	31	0		
2015–16	Blackburn R	41	0		
2016–17	Blackburn R	41	0	113	0
2017–18	Sunderland	15	0	15	0

STRYJEK, Maksymilian (G)   1   0
H: 6 2   W: 12 11   b.Warsaw 18-7-96
Internationals: Poland U17, U18, U19.

2014–15	Sunderland	0	0		
2015–16	Sunderland	0	0		
2016–17	Sunderland	0	0		
2017–18	Sunderland	0	0		
2017–18	*Accrington S*	1	0	1	0

WATMORE, Duncan (F)   52   4
H: 5 9   W: 11 05   b.Cheadle Hulme 8-3-94
Internationals: England U20, U21.

2013–14	Sunderland	0	0		
2013–14	*Hibernian*	9	1	9	1
2014–15	Sunderland	0	0		
2015–16	Sunderland	23	3		
2016–17	Sunderland	14	0		
2017–18	Sunderland	6	0	43	3

WILSON, Marc (M)   238   4
H: 6 2   W: 12 07   b.Lisburn 17-8-87
Internationals: Republic of Ireland U18, U19, U21, Full caps.

2005–06	Portsmouth	0	0		
2005–06	*Yeovil T*	2	0	2	0
2006–07	Portsmouth	0	0		
2006–07	*Bournemouth*	19	3		
2007–08	Portsmouth	0	0		
2007–08	*Bournemouth*	7	0		
2007–08	*Luton T*	4	0	4	0
2008–09	Portsmouth	3	0		
2009–10	Portsmouth	28	0		
2010–11	Portsmouth	4	0	35	0
2010–11	Stoke C	28	1		
2011–12	Stoke C	35	0		
2012–13	Stoke C	19	0		
2013–14	Stoke C	33	0		
2014–15	Stoke C	27	0		
2015–16	Stoke C	4	0	146	1
2016–17	*Bournemouth*	0	0	26	3
2016–17	*WBA*	4	0	4	0
2017–18	Sunderland	21	0	21	0

Players retained or with offer of contract
Borini, Fabio; Brotherton, Sam; Connelly, Lee John; Diamond, Jack Tyler; Hackett, Jake Willis; Lens, Jeremain Marciano; Mbunga-Kimpioka, Benjamin; Shields, Connor Jon; Storey, Alexander Michael; Taylor, Brandon Lewis.

Scholars
Allan, Christopher Mark; Bale, Adam James; Best, Sonny Alexander John; Connolly, Jack; Derbali, Rayed; Devine, Harrison James; Dunne, Robert Michael; Edmundsson, Andrias; Evans, Kane; Hickey, Jordan; Howard, Tomas David; Kokolo, Williams Joseph Gabriel; Leonard, Ryan John; Lilley, Joseph Isaac; McAughtrie, Fergus David; Patterson, Anthony; Scothern, Thomas; Slack, Connor James.

SWANSEA C (82)

AYEW, Andre (F)   89   21
H: 5 9   W: 11 05   b.Seclin 17-12-89
Internationals: Ghana U20, Full caps.

2015–16	Swansea C	34	12		
2016–17	West Ham U	25	6		
2017–18	West Ham U	18	3	43	9
2017–18	Swansea C	12	0	46	12

AYEW, Jordan (F)   260   48
H: 6 0   W: 12 11   b.Marseille 11-9-91
Internationals: Ghana U20, Full caps.

2009–10	Marseille	4	1		
2010–11	Marseille	22	2		
2011–12	Marseille	34	3		
2012–13	Marseille	35	7		
2013–14	Marseille	16	1	111	14
2013–14	*Sochaux*	17	5	17	5
2014–15	*Lorient*	31	12	31	12
2015–16	Aston Villa	30	7		
2016–17	Aston Villa	21	2	51	9
2016–17	Swansea C	14	1		
2017–18	Swansea C	36	7	50	8

BAKER-RICHARDSON, Courtney (F) 0 0
H: 6 1   W: 11 07   b.Coventry 5-12-95

| 2013–14 | Coventry C | 0 | 0 | | |
| 2014–15 | Coventry C | 0 | 0 | | |

From Tamworth, Nuneaton T, Redditch U, Kettering T, Leamington.

| 2017–18 | Swansea C | 0 | 0 | | |

BARTLEY, Kyle (D)   142   10
H: 5 11   W: 11 00   b.Stockport 22-5-91
Internationals: England U16, U17.

2008–09	Arsenal	0	0		
2009–10	Arsenal	0	0		
2009–10	*Sheffield U*	14	0		
2010–11	Arsenal	0	0		
2010–11	*Sheffield U*	21	0	35	0
2010–11	*Rangers*	5	1		
2011–12	Arsenal	0	0		
2011–12	*Rangers*	19	0	24	1
2012–13	Arsenal	0	0		
2012–13	Swansea C	2	0		
2013–14	Swansea C	2	0		
2013–14	*Birmingham C*	17	3	17	3
2014–15	Swansea C	7	0		
2015–16	Swansea C	5	0		
2016–17	Swansea C	0	0		
2016–17	*Leeds U*	45	6	45	6
2017–18	Swansea C	5	0	21	0

BLAIR, Ryan (M)   14   1
b.Glasgow 23-2-96

2013–14	Falkirk	0	0		
2014–15	Falkirk	0	0		
2015–16	Falkirk	7	0		
2015–16	Swansea C	0	0		
2016–17	Swansea C	0	0		
2017–18	Swansea C	0	0		
2017–18	*Falkirk*	7	1	14	1

BONY, Wilfried (F)   238   103
H: 6 0   W: 13 11   b.Bingerville 10-12-88
Internationals: Ivory Coast Full caps.

2008–09	Sparta Prague	16	3		
2009–10	Sparta Prague	29	9		
2010–11	Sparta Prague	13	10	58	22
2010–11	Vitesse	7	3		
2011–12	Vitesse	28	12		
2012–13	Vitesse	30	31	65	46
2013–14	Swansea C	34	16		
2014–15	Swansea C	20	9		
2014–15	Manchester C	10	2		
2015–16	Manchester C	26	4		
2016–17	Manchester C	0	0	36	6
2016–17	*Stoke C*	10	2	10	2
2017–18	Swansea C	15	2	69	27

BRITTON, Leon (M)   485   11
H: 5 6   W: 10 00   b.Merton 16-9-82
Internationals: England U16.

1999–2000	West Ham U	0	0		
2000–01	West Ham U	0	0		
2001–02	West Ham U	0	0		
2002–03	West Ham U	0	0		
2002–03	*Swansea C*	25	0		
2003–04	Swansea C	42	3		
2004–05	Swansea C	30	1		
2005–06	Swansea C	38	4		
2006–07	Swansea C	41	2		
2007–08	Swansea C	40	0		
2008–09	Swansea C	43	0		
2009–10	Swansea C	36	0		
2010–11	*Sheffield U*	24	0	24	0
2010–11	Swansea C	17	1		
2011–12	Swansea C	36	0		
2012–13	Swansea C	33	0		
2013–14	Swansea C	25	0		
2014–15	Swansea C	9	0		
2015–16	Swansea C	25	0		
2016–17	Swansea C	16	0		
2017–18	Swansea C	5	0	461	11

BYERS, George (M)   1   0
H: 5 11   W: 11 07   b.Ilford 29-5-96
Internationals: Scotland U16, U17.

2014–15	Watford	1	0		
2015–16	Watford	0	0	1	0
2017–18	Swansea C	0	0		

CARROLL, Tommy (M)   144   3
H: 5 10   W: 10 00   b.Watford 28-5-92
Internationals: England U19, U21.

2010–11	Tottenham H	0	0		
2010–11	*Leyton Orient*	12	0	12	0
2011–12	Tottenham H	0	0		
2011–12	*Derby Co*	12	1	12	1
2012–13	Tottenham H	7	0		
2013–14	Tottenham H	0	0		
2013–14	*QPR*	26	0	26	0
2014–15	Tottenham H	0	0		
2014–15	*Swansea C*	13	0		
2015–16	Tottenham H	19	1		
2016–17	Tottenham H	1	0	27	1
2016–17	Swansea C	17	1		
2017–18	Swansea C	37	0	67	1

CLUCAS, Sam (M)   214   29
H: 5 10   W: 11 08   b.Lincoln 25-9-90
Internationals: England C.

2009–10	Lincoln C	0	0		
2011–12	Hereford U	17	0	17	0
2013–14	Mansfield T	38	8		
2014–15	Mansfield T	5	0	43	8
2014–15	Chesterfield	41	9	41	9
2015–16	Hull C	44	6		
2016–17	Hull C	37	3		
2017–18	Hull C	3	0	84	9
2017–18	Swansea C	29	3	29	3

DAVIES, Keston (D)   2   0
H: 6 2   W: 13 01   b. 2-10-96
Internationals: Wales U17, U19.

| 2017–18 | Swansea C | 0 | 0 | | |
| 2017–18 | *Yeovil T* | 2 | 0 | 2 | 0 |

DYER, Nathan (M)   346   28
H: 5 5   W: 9 00   b.Trowbridge 29-11-87

2005–06	Southampton	17	0		
2005–06	*Burnley*	5	2	5	2
2006–07	Southampton	18	0		
2007–08	Southampton	17	1		
2008–09	Southampton	4	0	56	1
2008–09	*Sheffield U*	7	1	7	1
2008–09	Swansea C	17	2		
2009–10	Swansea C	40	2		
2010–11	Swansea C	46	2		
2011–12	Swansea C	34	5		
2012–13	Swansea C	37	3		
2013–14	Swansea C	27	6		
2014–15	Swansea C	32	3		
2015–16	Swansea C	1	0		
2015–16	*Leicester C*	12	1	12	1
2016–17	Swansea C	8	0		
2017–18	Swansea C	24	0	266	23

FABIANSKI, Lukasz (G)   234   0
H: 6 3   W: 13 01   b.Costrzyn nad Odra 18-4-85
Internationals: Poland U21, Full caps.

2005–06	Legia	30	0		
2006–07	Legia	23	0	53	0
2007–08	Arsenal	3	0		
2008–09	Arsenal	6	0		
2009–10	Arsenal	4	0		
2010–11	Arsenal	14	0		
2011–12	Arsenal	0	0		
2012–13	Arsenal	4	0		
2013–14	Arsenal	1	0	32	0
2014–15	Swansea C	37	0		
2015–16	Swansea C	37	0		
2016–17	Swansea C	37	0		
2017–18	Swansea C	38	0	149	0

FER, Leroy (M)   297   45
H: 6 2   W: 12 05   b.Zortermeer 5-1-90
Internationals: Netherlands U16, U17, U19, U21, Full caps.

2007–08	Feyenoord	13	1		
2008–09	Feyenoord	31	6		
2009–10	Feyenoord	31	2		
2010–11	Feyenoord	23	3		
2011–12	Feyenoord	4	2	102	14
2011–12	FC Twente	26	8		
2012–13	FC Twente	26	5	52	13
2013–14	Norwich C	29	3		
2014–15	Norwich C	1	0	30	3
2014–15	QPR	29	6		
2015–16	QPR	19	2	48	8
2015–16	*Swansea C*	11	0		
2016–17	Swansea C	34	6		
2017–18	Swansea C	20	1	65	7

FERNANDEZ, Federico (D)   234   6
H: 6 3   W: 13 01   b.Tres Algarrobos 21-2-89
Internationals: Argentina U20, Full caps.

| 2008–09 | Estudiantes | 14 | 2 | | |
| 2009–10 | Estudiantes | 12 | 0 | | |

2010–11	Estudiantes	33	1	**59**	**3**
2011–12	Napoli	16	0		
2012–13	Napoli	2	0		
2012–13	*Getafe*	14	1	**14**	**1**
2013–14	Napoli	26	0	**44**	**0**
2014–15	Swansea C	28	0		
2015–16	Swansea C	32	1		
2016–17	Swansea C	27	0		
2017–18	Swansea C	30	1	**117**	**2**

FULTON, Jay (M) **35** **1**
H: 5 10 W: 10 08 b.Bolton 4-4-94
Internationals: Scotland U18, U19, U21.

2013–14	Swansea C	2	0		
2014–15	Swansea C	2	0		
2015–16	Swansea C	2	0		
2015–16	*Oldham Ath*	11	0	**11**	**0**
2016–17	Swansea C	11	0		
2017–18	Swansea C	2	0	**19**	**0**
2017–18	*Wigan Ath*	5	1	**5**	**1**

GRIMES, Matt (M) **126** **9**
H: 5 10 W: 11 00 b.Exeter 15-7-95
Internationals: England U20, U21.

2013–14	Exeter C	35	1		
2014–15	Exeter C	23	4	**58**	**5**
2014–15	Swansea C	3	0		
2015–16	Swansea C	1	0		
2015–16	*Blackburn R*	13	0	**13**	**0**
2016–17	Swansea C	0	0		
2016–17	*Leeds U*	7	0	**7**	**0**
2017–18	Swansea C	0	0	**4**	**0**
2017–18	*Northampton T*	44	4	**44**	**4**

JAMES, Daniel (M) **0** **0**
b. 10-11-97
Internationals: Wales U17, U19, U20, U21, Full caps.

2015–16	Swansea C	0	0		
2016–17	Swansea C	0	0		
2017–18	Swansea C	0	0		
2017–18	*Shrewsbury T*	0	0		

KI, Sung-Yeung (M) **232** **24**
H: 6 2 W: 11 10 b.Gwangju 24-1-89
Internationals: South Korea U17, U20, U23, Full caps.

2009–10	Celtic	10	0		
2010–11	Celtic	26	3		
2011–12	Celtic	30	6	**66**	**9**
2012–13	Swansea C	29	0		
2013–14	Swansea C	1	0		
2013–14	*Sunderland*	27	3	**27**	**3**
2014–15	Swansea C	33	8		
2015–16	Swansea C	28	2		
2016–17	Swansea C	23	0		
2017–18	Swansea C	25	2	**139**	**12**

KING, Adam (M) **40** **4**
H: 5 11 W: 11 10 b.Edinburgh 11-10-95
Internationals: Scotland U18, U19, U21.

2012–13	Hearts	0	0		
2013–14	Hearts	2	0	**2**	**0**
2013–14	Swansea C	0	0		
2014–15	Swansea C	0	0		
2015–16	Swansea C	0	0		
2015–16	*Crewe Alex*	24	4	**24**	**4**
2016–17	Swansea C	0	0		
2016–17	*Southend U*	7	0	**7**	**0**
2017–18	Swansea C	0	0		
2017–18	*Mansfield T*	7	0	**7**	**0**

MARIC, Adnan (M) **0** **0**
H: 5 11 W: 12 00 b.Gothenburg 1-10-96
Internationals: Sweden U17.

2017–18	Swansea C	0	0		

MAWSON, Alfie (D) **159** **20**
H: 5 8 W: 12 11 b.Hillingdon 19-1-94
Internationals: England U21.

2012–13	Brentford	0	0		
2013–14	Brentford	0	0		
2014–15	Brentford	0	0		
2014–15	*Wycombe W*	45	6	**45**	**6**
2015–16	Barnsley	45	6		
2016–17	Barnsley	4	2	**49**	**8**
2016–17	Swansea C	27	4		
2017–18	Swansea C	38	2	**65**	**6**

McBURNIE, Oliver (F) **56** **12**
H: 6 2 W: 10 04 b.Bradford 6-4-96
Internationals: Scotland U19, U21, Full caps.

2013–14	Bradford C	8	0		
2014–15	Bradford C	7	0	**15**	**0**
2015–16	Swansea C	0	0		
2015–16	*Newport Co*	3	3	**3**	**3**
2015–16	*Bristol R*	5	0	**5**	**0**
2016–17	Swansea C	5	0		
2017–18	Swansea C	11	0	**16**	**0**
2017–18	*Barnsley*	17	9	**17**	**9**

MONTERO, Jefferson (M) **250** **34**
H: 5 8 W: 11 00 b.Babahoyo 1-9-89
Internationals: Ecuador Full caps.

2007	Emelec	22	2		
2008	Independiente de Valle	25	8		
2008–09	*Dorados*	5	1	**5**	**1**
2009	Independiente de Valle	12	11	**37**	**19**
2010–11	Villareal	9	1		
2010–11	*Levante*	11	0	**11**	**0**
2011–12	Villareal	0	0	**9**	**1**
2011–12	*Real Betis*	32	1	**32**	**1**
2012–13	Morelia	32	4		
2013–14	Morelia	25	5	**57**	**9**
2014–15	Swansea C	30	1		
2015–16	Swansea C	23	0		
2016–17	Swansea C	13	0		
2017–18	Swansea C	0	0	**66**	**1**
2017–18	*Getafe*	4	0	**4**	**0**
2017–18	*Emelec*	7	0	**29**	**2**

MULDER, Erwin (G) **226** **0**
H: 6 4 W: 13 12 b.Zevenaar 3-3-89
Internationals: Netherlands B, U19, U20.

2007–08	Feyenoord	1	0		
2008–09	Feyenoord	0	0		
2008–09	*Excelsior*	36	0	**36**	**0**
2009–10	Feyenoord	10	0		
2010–11	Feyenoord	17	0		
2011–12	Feyenoord	34	0		
2012–13	Feyenoord	22	0		
2013–14	Feyenoord	32	0		
2014–15	Feyenoord	4	0	**120**	**0**
2015–16	Heerenveen	34	0		
2016–17	Heerenveen	36	0		
2017–18	Heerenveen	0	0	**70**	**0**
2017–18	Swansea C	0	0		

NARSINGH, Luciano (F) **208** **35**
H: 5 10 W: 10 12 b.Amsterdam 13-9-90
Internationals: Netherlands U18, U19, U20, U21, Full caps.

2008–09	Heerenveen	2	0		
2009–10	Heerenveen	2	0		
2010–11	Heerenveen	24	5		
2011–12	Heerenveen	34	8	**62**	**13**
2012–13	PSV Eindhoven	18	6		
2013–14	PSV Eindhoven	20	0		
2014–15	PSV Eindhoven	32	6		
2015–16	PSV Eindhoven	30	8	**100**	**20**
2016–17	PSV	15	1	**15**	**1**
2016–17	Swansea C	13	0		
2017–18	Swansea C	18	1	**31**	**1**

NAUGHTON, Kyle (M) **283** **7**
H: 5 11 W: 11 07 b.Sheffield 11-11-88
Internationals: England U21.

2006–07	Sheffield U	0	0		
2007–08	*Gretna*	18	0	**18**	**0**
2007–08	Sheffield U	0	0		
2008–09	Sheffield U	40	1		
2009–10	Sheffield U	0	0	**40**	**1**
2009–10	Tottenham H	1	0		
2009–10	*Middlesbrough*	15	0	**15**	**0**
2010–11	Tottenham H	0	0		
2010–11	*Leicester C*	34	5	**34**	**5**
2011–12	Tottenham H	0	0		
2011–12	*Norwich C*	32	0	**32**	**0**
2012–13	Tottenham H	14	0		
2013–14	Tottenham H	22	0		
2014–15	Tottenham H	5	0	**42**	**0**
2014–15	Swansea C	10	0		
2015–16	Swansea C	27	0		
2016–17	Swansea C	31	1		
2017–18	Swansea C	34	0	**102**	**1**

NORDFELDT, Kristoffer (G) **217** **0**
H: 6 3 W: 13 05 b.Stockholm 23-6-89
Internationals: Sweden U19, U21, Full caps.

2006	Brommapojkarna	0	0		
2007	Brommapojkarna	0	0		
2008	Brommapojkarna	29	0		
2009	Brommapojkarna	21	0		
2010	Brommapojkarna	25	0		
2011	Brommapojkarna	28	0	**103**	**0**
2011–12	Heerenveen	6	0		
2012–13	Heerenveen	33	0		
2013–14	Heerenveen	35	0		
2014–15	Heerenveen	38	0	**112**	**0**
2015–16	Swansea C	1	0		
2016–17	Swansea C	1	0		
2017–18	Swansea C	0	0	**2**	**0**

OLSSON, Martin (D) **287** **8**
H: 5 7 W: 12 12 b.Gavle 17-5-88
Internationals: Sweden U19, U21, Full caps.

2005–06	Blackburn R	0	0		
2006–07	Blackburn R	0	0		
2007–08	Blackburn R	2	0		
2008–09	Blackburn R	9	0		
2009–10	Blackburn R	21	1		
2010–11	Blackburn R	29	2		
2011–12	Blackburn R	27	0		
2012–13	Blackburn R	29	0	**117**	**3**
2013–14	Norwich C	34	0		
2014–15	Norwich C	42	1		
2015–16	Norwich C	24	1		
2016–17	Norwich C	19	1	**119**	**3**
2016–17	Swansea C	15	2		
2017–18	Swansea C	36	0	**51**	**2**

RANGEL, Angel (D) **362** **11**
H: 5 11 W: 11 09 b.Barcelona 28-10-82

2006–07	Terrassa	34	2	**34**	**2**
2007–08	Swansea C	43	2		
2008–09	Swansea C	40	1		
2009–10	Swansea C	38	0		
2010–11	Swansea C	38	2		
2011–12	Swansea C	34	0		
2012–13	Swansea C	33	3		
2013–14	Swansea C	30	0		
2014–15	Swansea C	27	0		
2015–16	Swansea C	23	0		
2016–17	Swansea C	18	1		
2017–18	Swansea C	4	0	**328**	**9**

REID, Tyler (D) **7** **0**
b. 2-9-97

2017–18	Swansea C	0	0		
2017–18	*Newport Co*	7	0	**7**	**0**

ROBERTS, Connor (D) **52** **0**
H: 5 9 W: 11 03 b.Neath 23-9-95
Internationals: Wales U19, U21, Full caps.

2014–15	Swansea C	0	0		
2015–16	Swansea C	0	0		
2015–16	*Yeovil T*	45	0	**45**	**0**
2016–17	Bristol R	2	0	**2**	**0**
2016–17	Swansea C	0	0		
2017–18	Swansea C	4	0	**4**	**0**
2017–18	*Middlesbrough*	1	0	**1**	**0**

RODON, Joe (D) **12** **0**
b.Swansea 22-10-97
Internationals: Wales U20, U21.

2015–16	Swansea C	0	0		
2016–17	Swansea C	0	0		
2017–18	Swansea C	0	0		
2017–18	*Cheltenham T*	12	0	**12**	**0**

ROQUE, Mesa (M) **173** **8**
H: 5 7 W: 10 10 b.Las Palmas 7-6-89

2011–12	Las Palmas	22	0		
2012–13	Las Palmas	0	0		
2012–13	*Atletico Baleares*	33	3	**33**	**3**
2013–14	Las Palmas	0	0		
2014–15	Las Palmas	31	3		
2015–16	Las Palmas	34	1		
2016–17	Las Palmas	35	1	**122**	**5**
2017–18	Swansea C	11	0	**11**	**0**
2017–18	*Sevilla*	7	0	**7**	**0**

ROUTLEDGE, Wayne (M) **459** **39**
H: 5 6 W: 11 02 b.Sidcup 7-1-85
Internationals: England U20, U21.

2001–02	Crystal Palace	2	0		
2002–03	Crystal Palace	26	4		
2003–04	Crystal Palace	44	6		
2004–05	Crystal Palace	38	0	**110**	**10**
2005–06	Tottenham H	3	0		
2005–06	*Portsmouth*	13	0	**13**	**0**
2006–07	Tottenham H	0	0		
2006–07	*Fulham*	24	0	**24**	**0**
2007–08	Tottenham H	2	0	**5**	**0**
2007–08	Aston Villa	1	0		
2008–09	Aston Villa	1	0	**2**	**0**
2008–09	*Cardiff C*	9	2	**9**	**2**
2008–09	QPR	19	1		
2009–10	QPR	25	2		
2009–10	Newcastle U	17	3		
2010–11	Newcastle U	17	0	**34**	**3**
2010–11	*QPR*	20	5	**64**	**8**
2011–12	Swansea C	28	1		
2012–13	Swansea C	36	5		
2013–14	Swansea C	35	2		
2014–15	Swansea C	29	3		
2015–16	Swansea C	28	2		
2016–17	Swansea C	27	3		
2017–18	Swansea C	15	0	**198**	**16**

SANCHES, Renato (M) **53** **2**
H: 5 9 W: 11 11 b.Lisbon 18-8-97
Internationals: Portugal U16, U17, U19, U21, Full caps.

2014–15	Benfica	0	0		
2015–16	Benfica	24	2	**24**	**2**

| 2016–17 | Bayern Munich | 17 | 0 | | |
| 2017–18 | Bayern Munich | 0 | 0 | 17 | 0 |

On loan from Bayern Munich.

| 2017–18 | Swansea C | 12 | 0 | 12 | 0 |

VAN DER HOORN, Mike (D) 109 11
H: 6 3 W: 12 11 b.Almere 15-10-92
Internationals: Netherlands U20, U21.

2010–11	Utrecht	1	0		
2011–12	Utrecht	12	2		
2012–13	Utrecht	31	4	44	6
2013–14	Ajax	3	0		
2014–15	Ajax	15	2		
2015–16	Ajax	15	1	33	3
2016–17	Swansea C	8	1		
2017–18	Swansea C	24	1	32	2

Players retained or with offer of contract
Amat Maas, Jordi; Benda, Steven; Bia Bi, Botti Boulenin; Cooper, Brandon James; Cullen, Liam Jamie; De Boer, Kees Cornelis Henricus; Dulca, Marco-Alexandru; Evans, Jack; Evans, Keiran; Garrick, Jordon D'Andre; Gonzalez Tomas, Borja; Gorre, Kenji Joel; Gudjohnsen, Arnor Borg; Harries, Cian William Thomas; Lewis, Aaron James; Withers, Jack; Zabret, Gregor.

Scholars
Berry, Cameron; Blake, Matthew; Cabango, Benjamin; Cooper, Oliver Joseph; Davies, Thomas Craig; Erickson, Benjamin James; Evans, Cameron James; Evans, Owen Jarrett; Jones-Thomas, Mason Jake; Lewis, Joe Cameron; Owen, Bailey Elis; Price, Thomas Owen; Reed, Scott Steven Joseph; Reid, Jayden Andrew; Shepperd, Nathan; Walsh, Marc Thomas; Williams, Daniel Patrick; Wynter-Coles, Shaquille Leighton Gaston.

SWINDON T (83)

ANDERSON, Keshi (F) 66 12
H: 5 9 W: 10 10 b.Luton 15-11-95

2014–15	Crystal Palace	0	0		
2015–16	Crystal Palace	0	0		
2015–16	Doncaster R	7	3	7	3
2016–17	Crystal Palace	0	0		
2016–17	Bolton W	8	1	8	1
2016–17	Northampton T	14	3	14	3
2017–18	Swindon T	37	5	37	5

BROPHY, James (D) 64 0
b. 25-7-94
From Harrow Bor, Woodlands U, Broadfields U.

2015–16	Swindon T	28	0		
2016–17	Swindon T	30	0		
2017–18	Swindon T	6	0	64	0

CHARLES-COOK, Reice (G) 76 0
H: 6 1 W: 12 08 b.London 8-4-94

2013–14	Bury	2	0	2	0
2014–15	Coventry C	0	0		
2015–16	Coventry C	37	0		
2016–17	Coventry C	15	0	52	0
2017–18	Swindon T	22	0	22	0

CONROY, Dion (D) 21 0
b.Redhill 11-12-95
From Chelsea.

| 2016–17 | Swindon T | 14 | 0 | | |
| 2017–18 | Swindon T | 7 | 0 | 21 | 0 |

DUNNE, James (M) 314 14
H: 5 11 W: 10 12 b.Bromley 18-9-89

2007–08	Arsenal	0	0		
2008–09	Arsenal	0	0		
2008–09	*Nottingham F*	0	0		
2009–10	Exeter C	23	3		
2010–11	Exeter C	42	1		
2011–12	Exeter C	45	2	110	6
2012–13	Stevenage	42	4		
2013–14	Stevenage	13	1	55	5
2013–14	*St Johnstone*	13	0	13	0
2014–15	Portsmouth	36	1		
2015–16	Portsmouth	0	0	36	1
2015–16	*Dagenham & R*	9	0	9	0
2015–16	Cambridge U	19	1		
2016–17	Cambridge U	33	1	52	2
2017–18	Swindon T	39	0	39	0

EDWARDS, Jordan (M) 1 0
b. 26-10-99

| 2017–18 | Swindon T | 1 | 0 | 1 | 0 |

HENRY, Will (G) 5 0
b. 6-7-98

2015–16	Swindon T	2	0		
2016–17	Swindon T	3	0		
2017–18	Swindon T	0	0	5	0

IANDOLO, Ellis (M) 34 1
b. 22-8-97
From Maidstone U.

2015–16	Swindon T	12	0		
2016–17	Swindon T	10	0		
2017–18	Swindon T	12	1	34	1

KNOYLE, Kyle (D) 28 0
H: 5 10 W: 9 13 b.Newham 24-9-96
Internationals: England U18.

2015–16	West Ham U	0	0		
2015–16	*Dundee U*	9	0	9	0
2016–17	West Ham U	0	0		
2016–17	*Wigan Ath*	1	0	1	0
2017–18	Swindon T	18	0	18	0

LANCASHIRE, Oliver (D) 243 6
H: 6 1 W: 11 10 b.Basingstoke 13-12-88

2006–07	Southampton	0	0		
2007–08	Southampton	0	0		
2008–09	Southampton	11	0		
2009–10	Southampton	2	0	13	0
2009–10	*Grimsby T*	25	1	25	1
2010–11	Walsall	29	0		
2011–12	Walsall	20	1	49	1
2012–13	Aldershot T	12	0	12	0
2013–14	Rochdale	38	0		
2014–15	Rochdale	21	0		
2015–16	Rochdale	34	2	93	2
2016–17	Shrewsbury T	16	1	16	1
2017–18	Swindon T	35	1	35	1

LINGANZI, Amine (M) 93 4
H: 6 1 W: 10 00 b.Algiers 16-11-89
Internationals: DR Congo Full caps.

2008–09	St Etienne	1	0		
2009–10	St Etienne	0	0	3	0
2009–10	Blackburn R	1	0		
2010–11	Blackburn R	1	0		
2010–11	*Preston NE*	1	0	1	0
2011–12	Blackburn R	0	0		
2012–13	Blackburn R	1	0		
2012–13	*Accrington S*	13	0	13	0
2013–14	Gillingham	20	1		
2014–15	Gillingham	7	0	27	1
2015–16	Saint-Raphael	3	0	3	0
2016–17	Portsmouth	19	1	19	1
2017–18	Swindon T	25	2	25	2

McDERMOTT, Donal (F) 134 11
H: 6 6 W: 12 00 b.Co. Meath 19-10-89
Internationals: Republic of Ireland U17, U18, U19.

2007–08	Manchester C	0	0		
2008–09	Manchester C	0	0		
2008–09	*Milton Keynes D*	1	0	1	0
2009–10	Manchester C	0	0		
2009–10	*Chesterfield*	15	5	15	5
2009–10	*Scunthorpe U*	9	0	9	0
2010–11	Manchester C	0	0		
2010–11	Bournemouth	9	1		
2011–12	*Huddersfield T*	9	0	9	0
2011–12	Bournemouth	14	1		
2012–13	Bournemouth	6	0		
2013–14	Bournemouth	0	0	29	2
2014–15	Rochdale	0	0		
2015–16	Rochdale	37	2		
2016–17	Rochdale	17	1	54	3
2017–18	Swindon T	17	1	17	1

McGIVERN, Ryan (D) 199 2
H: 5 10 W: 11 07 b.Newry 8-1-90
Internationals: Northern Ireland U16, U17, U19, U21, B, Full caps.

2007–08	Manchester C	0	0		
2008–09	Manchester C	0	0		
2008–09	*Morecambe*	5	1	5	1
2009–10	Manchester C	0	0		
2009–10	*Leicester C*	12	0	12	0
2010–11	Manchester C	1	0		
2010–11	*Walsall*	15	0	15	0
2011–12	Manchester C	0	0		
2011–12	*Crystal Palace*	5	0	5	0
2011–12	*Bristol C*	31	0	31	0
2012–13	Manchester C	0	0		
2012–13	Hibernian	27	1		
2013–14	Hibernian	33	0	60	1
2014–15	Port Vale	20	0		
2015–16	Port Vale	28	0	48	0
2016–17	Shrewsbury T	15	0	15	0
2017–18	Northampton T	1	0	1	0
2017–18	Swindon T	6	0	6	0

MOORE, Stuart (G) 22 0
H: 6 2 W: 11 05 b.Sandown 8-9-94

2013–14	Reading	0	0		
2014–15	Reading	0	0		
2015–16	Reading	0	0		
2015–16	*Peterborough U*	4	0	4	0
2016–17	Reading	0	0		
2016–17	*Luton T*	8	0	8	0
2017–18	Swindon T	10	0	10	0

MULLIN, Paul (F) 162 31
H: 5 10 W: 11 01 b. 6-11-94

2013–14	Huddersfield T	0	0		
2014–15	Morecambe	42	8		
2015–16	Morecambe	40	9		
2016–17	Morecambe	40	8	122	25
2017–18	Swindon T	40	6	40	6

NORRIS, Luke (F) 175 39
H: 6 1 W: 13 05 b.Stevenage 3-6-93

2011–12	Brentford	1	0		
2012–13	Brentford	0	0		
2013–14	Brentford	1	0	2	0
2013–14	*Northampton T*	10	4	10	4
2013–14	*Dagenham & R*	19	4	19	4
2014–15	Gillingham	37	6		
2015–16	Gillingham	33	8	70	14
2016–17	Swindon T	39	4		
2017–18	Swindon T	35	13	74	17

PRESTON, Matt (D) 62 5
b. 16-3-95

2013–14	Walsall	0	0		
2014–15	Walsall	1	0		
2015–16	Walsall	10	2		
2016–17	Walsall	30	1		
2017–18	Walsall	0	0	41	3
2017–18	Swindon T	21	2	21	2

PURKISS, Ben (D) 223 0
H: 6 2 W: 10 13 b.Sheffield 1-4-84

| 2001–02 | Sheffield U | 0 | 0 | | |
| 2002–03 | Sheffield U | 0 | 0 | | |

From Gainsborough T, York C

2010–11	Oxford U	23	0	23	0
2011–12	Hereford U	15	0	15	0
2012–13	Walsall	27	0		
2013–14	Walsall	14	0		
2014–15	Walsall	32	0	73	0
2015–16	Port Vale	39	0		
2016–17	Port Vale	32	0	71	0
2017–18	Swindon T	41	0	41	0

RICHARDS, Marc (F) 554 180
H: 6 2 W: 12 06 b.Wolverhampton 8-7-82
Internationals: England U18, U20.

1999–2000	Blackburn R	0	0		
2000–01	Blackburn R	0	0		
2001–02	Blackburn R	0	0		
2001–02	*Crewe Alex*	4	0	4	0
2001–02	*Oldham Ath*	5	0	5	0
2001–02	*Halifax T*	5	0	5	0
2002–03	Blackburn R	0	0		
2002–03	*Swansea C*	17	7	17	7
2003–04	Northampton T	41	8		
2004–05	Northampton T	12	2		
2004–05	*Rochdale*	5	2	5	2
2005–06	Northampton T	0	0		
2005–06	Barnsley	38	12		
2006–07	Barnsley	31	6	69	18
2007–08	Port Vale	29	5		
2008–09	Port Vale	30	10		
2009–10	Port Vale	46	20		
2010–11	Port Vale	40	16		
2011–12	Port Vale	36	17	181	68
2012–13	Chesterfield	34	12		
2013–14	Chesterfield	38	8	72	20
2013–14	Northampton T	0	0		
2014–15	Northampton T	31	18		
2015–16	Northampton T	31	15		
2016–17	Northampton T	42	10		
2017–18	Northampton T	19	1	176	54
2017–18	Swindon T	20	11	20	11

ROBERTSON, Chris (D) 277 12
H: 6 3 W: 11 08 b.Dundee 11-10-85

2005–06	Sheffield U	0	0		
2005–06	*Chester C*	1	0	1	0
2006–07	Sheffield U	0	0		
2006–07	Torquay U	9	1		
2009–10	Torquay U	45	2		
2010–11	Torquay U	43	2		
2011–12	Torquay U	25	1	122	6
2011–12	Preston NE	18	1		
2012–13	Preston NE	21	0	39	1
2013–14	Port Vale	37	3		
2014–15	Port Vale	24	0	61	3
2015–16	Ross Co	23	0	23	0

2016–17	AFC Wimbledon	13	1	**13 1**
2017–18	Swindon T	18	1	**18 1**

ROMANSKI, Joe (D)   **2 0**
b.Reading 3-2-00

2017–18	Swindon T	2	0	**2 0**

SMITH, Tom (M)   **10 1**
H: 5 10   W: 11 00   b. 25-1-98

2014–15	Swindon T	1	0	
2015–16	Swindon T	1	1	
2016–17	Swindon T	8	0	
2017–18	Swindon T	0	0	**10 1**

TAYLOR, Matthew (D)   **626 81**
H: 5 11   W: 12 03   b.Oxford 27-11-81
Internationals: England U21, B.

1998–99	Luton T	0	0	
1999–2000	Luton T	41	4	
2000–01	Luton T	45	1	
2001–02	Luton T	43	11	**129 16**
2002–03	Portsmouth	35	7	
2003–04	Portsmouth	30	0	
2004–05	Portsmouth	32	1	
2005–06	Portsmouth	34	6	
2006–07	Portsmouth	35	8	
2007–08	Portsmouth	13	1	**179 23**
2007–08	Bolton W	16	3	
2008–09	Bolton W	34	10	
2009–10	Bolton W	37	8	
2010–11	Bolton W	36	2	**123 23**
2011–12	West Ham U	28	1	
2012–13	West Ham U	28	1	
2013–14	West Ham U	20	0	**76 2**
2014–15	Burnley	10	0	
2015–16	Burnley	27	4	**37 4**
2016–17	Northampton T	43	7	
2017–18	Northampton T	1	0	**44 7**
2017–18	Swindon T	38	6	**38 6**

THOMAS, Conor (M)   **135 2**
H: 6 1   W: 11 05   b.Coventry 29-10-93
Internationals: England U17, U18.

2010–11	Liverpool	0	0	
2010–11	Coventry C	0	0	
2011–12	Coventry C	27	1	
2012–13	Coventry C	11	0	
2013–14	Coventry C	43	0	
2014–15	Coventry C	16	0	
2015–16	Coventry C	3	0	**100 1**
2016–17	Swindon T	33	1	
2017–18	Swindon T	2	0	**35 1**

Transferred to ATK, August 2017.

TWINE, Scott (F)   **5 0**
H: 5 9   W: 10 12   b.Swindon 14-7-99

2015–16	Swindon T	0	0	
2016–17	Swindon T	1	0	
2017–18	Swindon T	4	0	**5 0**

VIGOUROUX, Lawrence (G)   **90 0**
b.London 19-11-93

2012–13	Tottenham H	0	0	
2013–14	Tottenham H	0	0	
2015–16	Swindon T	33	0	
2016–17	Swindon T	43	0	
2017–18	Swindon T	14	0	**90 0**

WOOLERY, Kaiyne (F)   **62 6**
H: 5 10   W: 11 07   b.Hackney 11-1-95

2014–15	Bolton W	1	0	
2014–15	Notts Co	5	0	**5 0**
2015–16	Bolton W	17	2	
2016–17	Bolton W	1	0	**19 2**
2016–17	Wigan Ath	1	0	**1 0**
2017–18	Swindon T	37	4	**37 4**

YOUNG, Jordan (F)   **5 1**
b. 31-7-99

2015–16	Swindon T	3	1	
2016–17	Swindon T	2	0	
2017–18	Swindon T	0	0	**5 1**

Scholars

Atik, Teoman Edward; Blackwell, Joe
Anthony; Dugan, Elliott Lucas; Dunstan-
Digweed, Jay; Giamattei, Paolo Bruno;
Graham, Ralph Cornelius; Haines, Luke
Ryan; Matthews, Archie Cameron; McLeod,
Bancroft Jacob Elijah; Pryce, Sol Easton;
Rejek, Oliver James; Romanski, Joseph Rio;
Spalding, Louis Andre; Stanley, Harry;
White, Wilf.

TOTTENHAM H (84)

ALDERWEIRELD, Toby (D)   **247 14**
H: 6 1   W: 11 11   b.Wilrijk 2-3-89
Internationals: Belgium U26, U17, U18, U19,
U21, Full caps.

2008–09	Ajax	5	0	
2009–10	Ajax	31	2	
2010–11	Ajax	26	2	
2011–12	Ajax	29	1	
2012–13	Ajax	32	2	
2013–14	Ajax	4	0	**127 7**
2013–14	Atletico Madrid	12	1	**12 1**
2014–15	Southampton	26	1	**26 1**
2015–16	Tottenham H	38	4	
2016–17	Tottenham H	30	1	
2017–18	Tottenham H	14	0	**82 5**

ALLI, Bamidele (M)   **178 59**
H: 6 1   W: 11 12   b.Watford 11-4-96
Internationals: England U17, U18, U19, U21,
Full caps.

2012–13	Milton Keynes D	0	0	
2013–14	Milton Keynes D	33	6	
2014–15	Milton Keynes D	39	16	**72 22**
2015–16	Tottenham H	33	10	
2016–17	Tottenham H	37	18	
2017–18	Tottenham H	36	9	**106 37**

AMOS, Luke (M)   **19 2**
H: 5 10   W: 11 00   b.Hatfield 23-2-97
Internationals: England U18.

2016–17	Tottenham H	0	0	
2016–17	Southend U	3	0	**3 0**
2017–18	Tottenham H	0	0	
2017–18	Stevenage	16	2	**16 2**

AURIER, Serge (D)   **193 12**
H: 5 9   W: 11 11   b.Paris 24-12-92
Internationals: Ivory Coast Full caps.

2009–10	Lens	5	0	
2010–11	Lens	26	0	
2011–12	Lens	16	0	**47 0**
2011–12	Toulouse	10	1	
2012–13	Toulouse	28	1	
2013–14	Toulouse	34	6	
2014–15	Toulouse	0	0	**72 8**
2014–15	Paris Saint-Germain	14	0	
2015–16	Paris Saint-Germain	21	2	
2016–17	Paris Saint-Germain	22	0	**57 2**
2017–18	Paris Saint-Germain	0	0	
2017–18	Tottenham H	17	2	**17 2**

CARTER-VICKERS, Cameron (D)   **34 1**
H: 6 1   W: 13 08   b.Westcliff on Sea
31-12-97
Internationals: USA U18, U20, U23, Full
caps.

2015–16	Tottenham H	0	0	
2016–17	Tottenham H	0	0	
2017–18	Tottenham H	0	0	
2017–18	Sheffield U	17	1	**17 1**
2017–18	Ipswich T	17	0	**17 0**

DAVIES, Ben (D)   **154 6**
H: 5 7   W: 12 00   b.Neath 24-4-93
Internationals: Wales U19, Full caps.

2011–12	Swansea C	0	0	
2012–13	Swansea C	37	1	
2013–14	Swansea C	34	2	**71 3**
2014–15	Tottenham H	14	0	
2015–16	Tottenham H	17	0	
2016–17	Tottenham H	23	1	
2017–18	Tottenham H	29	2	**83 3**

DEMBELE, Mousa (F)   **404 46**
H: 5 9   W: 10 01   b.Wilrijk 17-7-87
Internationals: Belgium U16, U17, U18, U19,
Full caps.

2003–04	Beerschot	1	0	
2004–05	Beerschot	19	1	**20 1**
2005–06	Willem II	33	9	**33 9**
2006–07	AZ	33	6	
2007–08	AZ	33	4	
2008–09	AZ	23	10	
2009–10	AZ	29	4	**118 24**
2010–11	Fulham	24	3	
2011–12	Fulham	36	2	
2012–13	Fulham	2	0	**62 5**
2012–13	Tottenham H	30	1	
2013–14	Tottenham H	28	1	
2014–15	Tottenham H	26	1	
2015–16	Tottenham H	29	1	
2016–17	Tottenham H	30	1	
2017–18	Tottenham H	28	0	**171 7**

DIER, Eric (D)   **162 8**
H: 6 3   W: 13 08   b.Cheltenham 15-1-94
Internationals: England U18, U19, U20, U21,
Full caps.

2012–13	Sporting Lisbon	14	1	
2013–14	Sporting Lisbon	13	0	**27 1**
2014–15	Tottenham H	28	2	
2015–16	Tottenham H	37	3	
2016–17	Tottenham H	36	2	
2017–18	Tottenham H	34	0	**135 7**

EDWARDS, Marcus (M)   **1 0**
b.London 3-12-98
Internationals: England U16, U17, U18, U19,
U20.

2016–17	Tottenham H	0	0	
2017–18	Tottenham H	0	0	
2017–18	Norwich C	1	0	**1 0**

ERIKSEN, Christian (M)   **284 66**
H: 5 9   W: 10 02   b.Middelfart 14-2-92
Internationals: Denmark U17, U18, U19, U21,
Full caps.

2009–10	Ajax	15	0	
2010–11	Ajax	28	6	
2011–12	Ajax	33	7	
2012–13	Ajax	33	10	
2013–14	Ajax	4	2	**113 25**
2013–14	Tottenham H	25	7	
2014–15	Tottenham H	38	10	
2015–16	Tottenham H	35	6	
2016–17	Tottenham H	36	8	
2017–18	Tottenham H	37	10	**171 41**

FOYTH, Juan (D)   **7 0**
H: 5 10   W: 10 12   b.La Plata 12-1-98
Internationals: Argentina U20.

2017	Estudiantes	7	0	
2017–18	Estudiantes	0	0	**7 0**

GAZZANIGA, Paulo (G)   **74 0**
H: 6 5   W: 14 02   b.Santa Fe 2-1-92

2011–12	Gillingham	20	0	**20 0**
2012–13	Southampton	9	0	
2013–14	Southampton	8	0	
2014–15	Southampton	2	0	
2015–16	Southampton	2	0	
2016–17	Southampton	0	0	**21 0**
2016–17	Rayo Vallecano	32	0	**32 0**
2017–18	Tottenham H	1	0	**1 0**

GEORGIOU, Anthony (M)   **0 0**
H: 5 10   W: 11 07   b.Lewisham 24-2-97
Internationals: Cyprus Full caps.

2017–18	Tottenham H	0	0	

HARRISON, Shayon (F)   **27 1**
H: 6 00   W: 10 10   b.Hornsey 13-7-97

2016–17	Tottenham H	0	0	
2016–17	Yeovil T	14	1	**14 1**
2017–18	Tottenham H	0	0	
2017–18	Southend U	13	0	**13 0**

JANSSEN, Vincent (F)   **146 62**
H: 5 11   W: 12 06   b.Heesch 15-6-94
Internationals: Netherlands U16, U18, U20,
U21, Full caps.

2013–14	Almere C	35	10	
2014–15	Almere C	34	19	**69 29**
2015–16	AZ Alkmaar	34	27	**34 27**
2016–17	Tottenham H	27	2	
2017–18	Tottenham H	1	0	**28 2**
2017–18	Fenerbahce	15	4	**15 4**

KANE, Harry (F)   **206 122**
H: 6 00   W: 10 00   b.Chingford 28-7-93
Internationals: England U17, U19, U20, U21,
Full caps.

2010–11	Tottenham H	0	0	
2010–11	Leyton Orient	18	5	**18 5**
2011–12	Tottenham H	0	0	
2011–12	Millwall	22	7	**22 7**
2012–13	Tottenham H	1	0	
2012–13	Norwich C	3	0	**3 0**
2012–13	Leicester C	13	2	**13 2**
2013–14	Tottenham H	10	3	
2014–15	Tottenham H	34	21	
2015–16	Tottenham H	38	25	
2016–17	Tottenham H	30	29	
2017–18	Tottenham H	37	30	**150 108**

LAMELA, Erik (F)   **205 33**
H: 6 00   W: 10 13   b.Buenos Aires 4-3-92
Internationals: Argentina U20, Full caps.

2008–09	River Plate	1	0	
2009–10	River Plate	1	0	
2010–11	River Plate	32	4	**34 4**
2011–12	Roma	29	4	

2012–13	Roma	32	15	61	19
2013–14	Tottenham H	9	0		
2014–15	Tottenham H	33	2		
2015–16	Tottenham H	34	5		
2016–17	Tottenham H	9	1		
2017–18	Tottenham H	25	2	110	10

LLORENTE, Fernando (F)   433 140
H: 6 4 W: 13 12 b.Pamplona 26-2-85
Internationals: Spain U17, U20, U21, Full caps.

2003–04	Basconia	33	12	33	12
2004–05	Atletico Bilbao	15	3		
2005–06	Atletico Bilbao	22	2		
2006–07	Atletico Bilbao	23	2		
2007–08	Atletico Bilbao	35	11		
2008–09	Atletico Bilbao	34	14		
2009–10	Atletico Bilbao	37	14		
2010–11	Atletico Bilbao	38	18		
2011–12	Atletico Bilbao	32	17		
2012–13	Atletico Bilbao	26	4	262	85
2013–14	Juventus	34	16		
2014–15	Juventus	31	7		
2015–16	Juventus	1	0	66	23
2015–16	Sevilla	23	4	23	4
2016–17	Swansea C	33	15		
2017–18	Swansea C	0	0	33	15
2017–18	Tottenham H	16	1	16	1

LLORIS, Hugo (G)   424 0
H: 6 2 W: 12 03 b.Nice 26-12-86
Internationals: France U18, U19, U20, U21, Full caps.

2005–06	Nice	5	0		
2006–07	Nice	37	0		
2007–08	Nice	30	0	72	0
2008–09	Lyon	35	0		
2009–10	Lyon	36	0		
2010–11	Lyon	37	0		
2011–12	Lyon	36	0		
2012–13	Lyon	2	0	146	0
2012–13	Tottenham H	27	0		
2013–14	Tottenham H	37	0		
2014–15	Tottenham H	35	0		
2015–16	Tottenham H	37	0		
2016–17	Tottenham H	34	0		
2017–18	Tottenham H	36	0	206	0

LOFT, Ryan (F)   10 0
H: 6 3 W: 11 07 b.Gravesend 14-9-97

2016–17	Tottenham H	0	0		
2016–17	Stevenage	9	0	9	0
2017–18	Tottenham H	0	0		
2017–18	Exeter C	1	0	1	0

LUCAS MOURA, Rodrigues (M)   233 53
H: 5 8 W: 10 06 b.Sao Paulo 13-8-92
Internationals: Brazil U20, U23, Full caps.

2010	Sao Paulo	25	4		
2011	Sao Paulo	28	9		
2012	Sao Paulo	21	6	74	19
2012–13	Paris Saint-Germain	10	0		
2013–14	Paris Saint-Germain	36	5		
2014–15	Paris Saint-Germain	29	7		
2015–16	Paris Saint-Germain	36	9		
2016–17	Paris Saint-Germain	37	12		
2017–18	Paris Saint-Germain	5	1	153	34
2017–18	Tottenham H	6	0	6	0

NKOUDOU, Georges (M)   79 39
b. 13-2-95
Internationals: France U17, U19, U20, U21.

2013–14	Nantes	6	1		
2014–15	Nantes	28	16	34	17
2015–16	Marseilles	28	22	28	22
2016–17	Marseille	0	0		
2016–17	Tottenham H	8	0		
2017–18	Tottenham H	9	0	9	0
2017–18	Burnley	8	0	8	0

OAKLEY-BOOTHE, Tashan (M)   0 0
H: 5 10 W: 11 00 b.Lambeth 14-2-00
Internationals: England U16, U17, U18.

2017–18	Tottenham H	0	0		

OGILVIE, Connor (D)   76 2
H: 6 0 W: 12 08 b.Harlow 14-2-96
Internationals: England U16, U17.

2013–14	Tottenham H	0	0		
2014–15	Tottenham H	0	0		
2015–16	Tottenham H	0	0		
2015–16	Stevenage	21	1		
2016–17	Tottenham H	0	0		
2016–17	Stevenage	18	0	39	1
2017–18	Tottenham H	0	0		
2017–18	Gillingham	37	1	37	1

ONOMAH, Joshua (M)   46 4
H: 5 11 W: 10 01 b.Enfield 27-4-97
Internationals: England U16, U17, U18, U19, U20, U21.

2013–14	Tottenham H	0	0		
2014–15	Tottenham H	0	0		
2015–16	Tottenham H	8	0		
2016–17	Tottenham H	5	0		
2017–18	Tottenham H	0	0	13	0
2017–18	Aston Villa	33	4	33	4

ROSE, Danny (M)   169 9
H: 5 8 W: 11 11 b.Doncaster 2-6-90
Internationals: England U17, U19, U21, Full caps. Great Britain.

2007–08	Tottenham H	0	0		
2008–09	Tottenham H	0	0		
2008–09	Watford	7	0	7	0
2009–10	Tottenham H	1	1		
2009–10	Tottenham H	4	0		
2010–11	Bristol C	17	0	17	0
2011–12	Tottenham H	11	0		
2012–13	Tottenham H	0	0		
2012–13	Sunderland	27	1	27	1
2013–14	Tottenham H	22	1		
2014–15	Tottenham H	28	3		
2015–16	Tottenham H	24	1		
2016–17	Tottenham H	18	2		
2017–18	Tottenham H	10	0	118	8

SANCHEZ, Davinson (D)   81 6
H: 6 2 W: 13 01 b.Caloto 12-6-96
Internationals: Columbia U17, U20, U23, Full caps.

2013	Atletico Nacional	2	0		
2014	Atletico Nacional	1	0		
2015	Atletico Nacional	5	0		
2016	Atletico Nacional	10	0	18	0
2016–17	Ajax	32	6		
2017–18	Ajax	0	0	32	6
2017–18	Tottenham H	31	0	31	0

SISSOKO, Moussa (M)   366 32
H: 6 2 W: 13 00 b.Le Blanc Mesnil 16-8-89
Internationals: France U16, U17, U18, U19, U21, Full caps.

2007–08	Toulouse	29	1		
2008–09	Toulouse	35	4		
2009–10	Toulouse	37	7		
2010–11	Toulouse	35	5		
2011–12	Toulouse	35	2		
2012–13	Toulouse	19	1	190	20
2012–13	Newcastle U	12	3		
2013–14	Newcastle U	35	3		
2014–15	Newcastle U	34	4		
2015–16	Newcastle U	37	1	118	11
2016–17	Tottenham H	25	0		
2017–18	Tottenham H	33	1	58	1

SON, Heung-Min (M)   234 71
H: 6 0 W: 12 00 b.Chuncheon 8-7-92
Internationals: South Korea U17, U23, Full caps.

2010–11	Hamburg	13	3		
2011–12	Hamburg	27	5		
2012–13	Hamburg	33	12	73	20
2013–14	Bayer Leverkusen	31	10		
2014–15	Bayer Leverkusen	30	11		
2015–16	Bayer Leverkusen	1	0	62	21
2015–16	Tottenham H	0	0		
2016–17	Tottenham H	34	14		
2017–18	Tottenham H	37	12	99	30

STERLING, Kazaiah (F)   0 0
H: 5 9 W: 11 03 b.Enfield 9-11-98
Internationals: England U17, U18. From Leyton Orient.

2017–18	Tottenham H	0	0		

TRIPPIER, Keiran (D)   254 7
H: 5 10 W: 11 00 b.Bury 19-9-90
Internationals: England U18, U19, U20, U21, Full caps.

2007–08	Manchester C	0	0		
2008–09	Manchester C	0	0		
2009–10	Manchester C	0	0		
2009–10	Barnsley	3	0		
2010–11	Manchester C	0	0		
2010–11	Barnsley	39	2	42	2
2011–12	Manchester C	0	0		
2011–12	Burnley	46	3		
2012–13	Burnley	45	0		
2013–14	Burnley	41	1		
2014–15	Burnley	38	0	170	4
2015–16	Tottenham H	6	1		
2016–17	Tottenham H	12	0		
2017–18	Tottenham H	24	0	42	1

VERTONGHEN, Jan (D)   354 30
H: 6 2 W: 12 05 b.Sint-Niklaas 24-4-87
Internationals: Belgium U16, U17, Full caps.

2006–07	Ajax	3	0		
2006–07	RKC	12	3	12	3
2007–08	Ajax	31	2		
2008–09	Ajax	26	4		
2009–10	Ajax	32	3		
2010–11	Ajax	32	6		
2011–12	Ajax	31	8	155	23
2012–13	Tottenham H	34	4		
2013–14	Tottenham H	23	0		
2014–15	Tottenham H	32	0		
2015–16	Tottenham H	29	0		
2016–17	Tottenham H	33	0		
2017–18	Tottenham H	36	0	187	4

VORM, Michel (G)   271 0
H: 6 0 W: 13 03 b.Nieuwegein 20-10-83
Internationals: Netherlands Full caps.

2005–06	Den Bosch	35	0	35	0
2006–07	Utrecht	33	0		
2007–08	Utrecht	11	0		
2008–09	Utrecht	26	0		
2009–10	Utrecht	33	0		
2010–11	Utrecht	33	0	136	0
2011–12	Swansea C	37	0		
2012–13	Swansea C	26	0		
2013–14	Swansea C	26	0	89	0
2014–15	Tottenham H	4	0		
2015–16	Tottenham H	1	0		
2016–17	Tottenham H	5	0		
2017–18	Tottenham H	1	0	11	0

WALKER-PETERS, Kyle (F)   3 0
H: 5 8 W: 9 13 b.Edmonton 13-4-97
Internationals: England U18, U19, U20, U21.

2015–16	Tottenham H	0	0		
2016–17	Tottenham H	0	0		
2017–18	Tottenham H	3	0	3	0

WALKES, Anton (M)   33 3
b. 8-2-97

2016–17	Tottenham H	0	0		
2017	Atlanta U	21	2	21	2
2017–18	Tottenham H	0	0		
2017–18	Portsmouth	12	1	12	1

WANYAMA, Victor (M)   249 21
H: 6 2 W: 11 12 b.Nairobi 25-6-91
Internationals: Kenya Full caps.

2009–10	Beerschot	19	0		
2010–11	Beerschot	30	2	49	2
2011–12	Celtic	29	4		
2012–13	Celtic	32	6	61	10
2013–14	Southampton	23	0		
2014–15	Southampton	32	3		
2015–16	Southampton	30	1	85	4
2016–17	Tottenham H	36	4		
2017–18	Tottenham H	18	1	54	5

WHITEMAN, Alfie (G)   0 0
b. 2-10-98
Internationals: England U16, U17, U18, U19.

2016–17	Tottenham H	0	0		
2017–18	Tottenham H	0	0		

WINKS, Harry (M)   37 1
H: 5 10 W: 10 03 b.Hemel Hempstead 2-2-96
Internationals: England U17, U18, U19, U20, U21, Full caps.

2013–14	Tottenham H	0	0		
2014–15	Tottenham H	0	0		
2015–16	Tottenham H	0	0		
2016–17	Tottenham H	21	1		
2017–18	Tottenham H	16	0	37	1

Players retained or with offer of contract
Austin, Brandon Anthony; Bennetts, Keanan Chidozie; Brown, Jaden; De Bie, Jonathan; Dinzeyi, Jonathan Toko Lema; Duncan, Dylan; Eyoma, Timothy Joel; Freeman, Charlie; Glover, Thomas William; Hinds, Tariq Devontae Aaron; Marsh, George Owen; Patterson, Phoenix MacLaren; Reynolds, Jamie Joe; Roles, Jack; Shashoua, Samuel; Skipp, Oliver William; Tanganga, Japhat Manzambi; Tracey, Shilow.

Scholars
Bowden, Jamie Patrick; Clarke, Rayan Romario; Griffiths, Reo Revaldo; Lyons-Foster, Brooklyn; Maghoma, Edmond-Paris; Markanday, Dilan Kumar; Mukendi, Jeremie; Okedina, Jubril Adesope; Oluwayemi, Oluwaferanmi Joshua; Pochettino, Maurizio; Richards, Rodel; Shashoua, Armando; Statham, Maxwell Louis; Tainio, Maximus Mikael; Thorpe, Elliot Morgan.

WALSALL (85)

BAKAYOKO, Amadou (F)   93   9
H: 6 4   W: 13 05   b. 1-1-96
2013–14	Walsall	6	0	
2014–15	Walsall	7	0	
2015–16	Walsall	0	0	
2016–17	Walsall	39	4	
2017–18	Walsall	41	5	93	9

CAIRNS, Joe (F)   0   0
| 2017–18 | Walsall | 0 | 0 | |

CANDLIN, Mitchell (F)   8   0
H: 6 0   W: 11 09   b. 8-6-00
| 2016–17 | Walsall | 5 | 0 | |
| 2017–18 | Walsall | 3 | 0 | 8 | 0 |

CHAMBERS, Adam (D)   530   12
H: 5 10   W: 11 12   b.Sandwell 20-11-80
1998–99	WBA	0	0	
1999–2000	WBA	0	0	
2000–01	WBA	11	1	
2001–02	WBA	32	0	
2002–03	WBA	13	0	
2003–04	WBA	0	0	
2003–04	*Sheffield W*	11	0	11	0
2004–05	WBA	0	0	56	1
2004–05	*Kidderminster H*	2	0	2	0
2006–07	Leyton Orient	38	4	
2007–08	Leyton Orient	45	3	
2008–09	Leyton Orient	33	1	
2009–10	Leyton Orient	29	1	
2010–11	Leyton Orient	29	0	174	9
2011–12	Walsall	29	2	
2012–13	Walsall	37	0	
2013–14	Walsall	45	0	
2014–15	Walsall	45	0	
2015–16	Walsall	45	0	
2016–17	Walsall	43	0	
2017–18	Walsall	43	0	287	2

COCKERILL-MOLLETT, Callum (D) 1   0
H: 5 10   W: 11 00   b. 15-1-99
| 2016–17 | Walsall | 0 | 0 | |
| 2017–18 | Walsall | 1 | 0 | 1 | 0 |

CUVELIER, Florent (M)   104   7
H: 6 0   W: 11 05   b.Brussels 12-9-92
Internationals: Belgium U16, U17, U18, U19, U20, U21.
2009–10	Portsmouth	0	0	
2010–11	Stoke C	0	0	
2011–12	Stoke C	0	0	
2011–12	*Walsall*	18	4	
2012–13	Stoke C	0	0	
2012–13	*Walsall*	19	2	
2012–13	*Peterborough U*	1	0	1	0
2013–14	Stoke C	0	0	
2013–14	*Sheffield U*	7	0	
2013–14	*Port Vale*	1	0	1	0
2014–15	Sheffield U	3	0	
2014–15	*Burton Alb*	1	1	1	1
2015–16	Sheffield U	9	0	19	0
2016–17	Walsall	22	0	
2017–18	Walsall	23	0	82	6

DEVLIN, Nicky (D)   220   3
H: 5 10   W: 11 07   b.Glasgow 17-10-93
Internationals: Scotland U19.
2010–11	Dumbarton	23	0	
2011–12	Motherwell	0	0	
2011–12	*Stenhousemuir*	6	0	
2012–13	Motherwell	0	0	
2012–13	*Dumbarton*	16	0	39	0
2012–13	*Stenhousemuir*	8	0	
2013–14	Stenhousemuir	30	0	44	0
2014–15	Ayr U	36	2	
2015–16	Ayr U	34	1	
2016–17	Ayr U	34	0	104	3
2017–18	Walsall	33	0	33	0

DOBSON, George (M)   47   2
H: 6 1   b.Harold Wood 15-11-97
From Arsenal.
2015–16	West Ham U	0	0	
2016–17	West Ham U	0	0	
2016–17	*Walsall*	21	1	
2017–18	Sparta Rotterdam	5	0	5	0
2017–18	*Walsall*	21	1	42	2

EDWARDS, Joe (D)   238   16
H: 5 8   W: 11 07   b.Gloucester 31-10-90
2009–10	Bristol C	0	0	
2010–11	Bristol C	2	0	
2011–12	Bristol C	2	0	
2011–12	*Yeovil T*	4	1	
2012–13	Bristol C	0	0	4	0

2012–13	*Yeovil T*	35	2	
2013–14	Yeovil T	46	1	
2014–15	Yeovil T	34	0	119	4
2015–16	Colchester U	42	2	42	2
2016–17	Walsall	43	3	
2017–18	Walsall	30	7	73	10

FLANAGAN, Reece (M)   39   0
b. 19-10-94
2013–14	Walsall	0	0	
2014–15	Walsall	16	0	
2015–16	Walsall	14	0	
2017–18	Walsall	9	0	39	0

GANLEY, Brandon (G)   0   0
| 2016–17 | Walsall | 0 | 0 | |
| 2017–18 | Walsall | 0 | 0 | |

GILLESPIE, Mark (G)   184   0
H: 6 3   W: 13 07   b.Newcastle upon Tyne 27-3-92
2009–10	Carlisle U	1	0	
2010–11	Carlisle U	0	0	
2011–12	Carlisle U	0	0	
2012–13	Carlisle U	35	0	
2013–14	Carlisle U	15	0	
2014–15	Carlisle U	19	0	
2015–16	Carlisle U	45	0	
2016–17	Carlisle U	46	0	161	0
2017–18	Walsall	23	0	23	0

GUTHRIE, Jon (D)   168   2
H: 5 10   W: 11 00   b.Devizes 1-2-93
2011–12	Crewe Alex	0	0	
2012–13	Crewe Alex	2	0	
2013–14	Crewe Alex	23	0	
2014–15	Crewe Alex	25	0	
2015–16	Crewe Alex	39	1	
2016–17	Crewe Alex	33	0	122	1
2017–18	Walsall	46	1	46	1

HAYLES-DOCHERTY, Tobias (F) 1   0
| 2016–17 | Walsall | 1 | 0 | |
| 2017–18 | Walsall | 0 | 0 | 1 | 0 |

JACKSON, Simeon (M)   319   72
H: 5 10   W: 10 12   b.Kingston, Jamaica 28-3-87
Internationals: Canada U20, Full caps.
2004–05	Rushden & D	1	0	
2005–06	Rushden & D	14	5	
2006–07	Rushden & D	0	0	
2007–08	Rushden & D	0	0	17	5
2007–08	Gillingham	18	4	
2008–09	Gillingham	41	17	
2009–10	Gillingham	42	14	101	35
2010–11	Norwich C	38	13	
2011–12	Norwich C	22	3	
2012–13	Norwich C	13	1	73	17
2013–14	E Braunschweig	9	0	9	0
2013–14	Millwall	14	2	14	2
2014–15	Coventry C	28	3	28	3
2015–16	Barnsley	9	0	9	0
2015–16	Blackburn R	17	2	17	2
2016–17	Walsall	38	7	
2017–18	Walsall	8	0	46	7
2017–18	*Grimsby T*	5	1	5	1

KINSELLA, Liam (M)   38   1
b.Colchester 23-2-96
Internationals: Republic of Ireland U19.
2013–14	Walsall	0	0	
2014–15	Walsall	4	0	
2015–16	Walsall	7	1	
2016–17	Walsall	8	0	
2017–18	Walsall	19	0	38	1

LEAHY, Luke (M)   173   13
H: 5 10   W: 11 07   b.Coventry 19-11-92
2012–13	Falkirk	8	1	
2013–14	Falkirk	19	1	
2014–15	Falkirk	33	3	
2015–16	Falkirk	36	3	
2016–17	Falkirk	31	3	127	11
2017–18	Walsall	46	2	46	2

MASON, Stefan (M)   0   0
| 2017–18 | Walsall | 0 | 0 | |

MORRIS, Kieron (M)   126   13
H: 5 10   W: 11 01   b.Hereford 3-6-94
2012–13	Walsall	0	0	
2013–14	Walsall	2	0	
2014–15	Walsall	14	2	

2015–16	Walsall	33	3	
2016–17	Walsall	35	5	
2017–18	Walsall	42	3	126	13

O'SULLIVAN, Daniel (M)   0   0
| 2017–18 | Walsall | 0 | 0 | |

OLIVER, Rory (M)   0   0
| 2017–18 | Walsall | 0 | 0 | |

OZTUMER, Erhun (M)   136   37
b.Greenwich 29-5-91
2014–15	Peterborough U	20	1	
2015–16	Peterborough U	30	6	50	7
2016–17	Walsall	41	15	
2017–18	Walsall	45	15	86	30

ROBERTS, Kory (D)   25   0
H: 6 0   W: 11 07   b.Birmingham 17-12-97
| 2016–17 | Walsall | 4 | 0 | |
| 2017–18 | Walsall | 21 | 0 | 25 | 0 |

ROBERTS, Liam (G)   25   0
H: 6 0   W: 12 13   b.Walsall 24-11-94
2012–13	Walsall	0	0	
2013–14	Walsall	0	0	
2014–15	Walsall	0	0	
2015–16	Walsall	1	0	
2017–18	Walsall	24	0	25	0

SANGHA, Jordan (M)   0   0
b. 4-1-98
2015–16	Walsall	0	0	
2016–17	Walsall	0	0	
2017–18	Walsall	0	0	

SHORROCK, Will (M)   1   0
H: 5 6   W: 11 00   b. 30-1-99
| 2016–17 | Walsall | 0 | 0 | |
| 2017–18 | Walsall | 1 | 0 | 1 | 0 |

VANN, Daniel (D)   0   0
| 2016–17 | Walsall | 0 | 0 | |
| 2017–18 | Walsall | 0 | 0 | |

Scholars
Bates, Alfie; Brown, Joseph Grant; Cairns, Joseph Lawrence; Dawe, Ethan Bradley; Fisher, Cody Lee; Flanagan, Kian Jay; Freemantle, Ethan James; Friel, Benjamin Michael; Ganley, Brandon Rooney; Kendrick, Ben; Leak, Thomas John; Leivesley, Samuel James; Little, Luke Thomas; Mason, Stefan Richard; Massamba, Debert; Nolan, Owen Henry; O'Sullivan, Daniel Joseph; Ruddock, Tyreece.

WATFORD (86)

AMRABAT, Nordin (F)   331   50
H: 5 10   W: 12 02   b.Naarden 31-3-87
Internationals: Netherlands U21. Morocco Full caps.
2006–07	Omniworld	36	14	36	14
2007–08	VVV-Venlo	33	10	33	10
2008–09	PSV Eindhoven	25	5	
2009–10	PSV Eindhoven	25	3	
2010–11	PSV Eindhoven	6	1	56	9
2010–11	Kayserispor	14	1	
2011–12	Kayserispor	25	5	39	6
2012–13	Galatasaray	30	1	
2013–14	Galatasaray	4	0	
2013–14	*Malaga*	15	2	
2014–15	Galatasaray	0	0	34	1
2014–15	*Malaga*	31	6	
2015–16	Malaga	13	0	59	8
2015–16	Watford	12	0	
2016–17	Watford	29	0	
2017–18	Watford	3	0	44	0
2017–18	*Leganes*	30	2	30	2

BACHMANN, Daniel (G)   9   0
H: 6 3   W: 12 11   b.Vienna 9-7-94
Internationals: Austria U16, U17, U18, U19, U21.
2011–12	Stoke C	0	0	
2012–13	Stoke C	0	0	
2013–14	Stoke C	0	0	
2014–15	Stoke C	0	0	
2015–16	Stoke C	0	0	
2015–16	*Ross Co*	1	0	1	0
2015–16	*Bury*	8	0	8	0
2016–17	Stoke C	0	0	
2017–18	Watford	0	0	

BRITOS, Miguel (D)   273   13
H: 6 2   W: 12 13   b.Montevideo 17-7-85
2005–06	Fenix	12	0	12	0
2006–07	Juventud	33	3	33	3
2007–08	Montevideo W	26	1	26	1

2008–09	Bologna	14	1		
2009–10	Bologna	23	0		
2010–11	Bologna	34	3	71	4
2011–12	Napoli	11	1		
2012–13	Napoli	22	0		
2013–14	Napoli	16	1		
2014–15	Napoli	19	1	68	3
2015–16	Watford	24	0		
2016–17	Watford	27	1		
2017–18	Watford	12	1	63	2

CAPOUE, Etienne (M) 291 22
H: 6 2　W: 11 10　b.Niort 11-7-88
Internationals: France U18, U19, U21, Full caps.

2006–07	Toulouse	0	0		
2007–08	Toulouse	5	0		
2008–09	Toulouse	32	1		
2009–10	Toulouse	33	0		
2010–11	Toulouse	37	2		
2011–12	Toulouse	33	3		
2012–13	Toulouse	34	7	174	13
2013–14	Tottenham H	12	1		
2014–15	Tottenham H	12	0	24	1
2015–16	Watford	33	0		
2016–17	Watford	37	7		
2017–18	Watford	23	1	93	8

CARRILLO, Andre (F) 178 17
H: 5 11　W: 10 12　b.Lima 14-6-91
Internationals: Peru Full caps.

2009	Alianza Lima	1	0		
2010	Alianza Lima	10	0		
2011	Alianza Lima	9	3	20	3
2011–12	Sporting Lisbon	24	2		
2012–13	Sporting Lisbon	23	1		
2013–14	Sporting Lisbon	27	2		
2014–15	Sporting Lisbon	32	5		
2015–16	Sporting Lisbon	4	1	110	11
2016–17	Benfica	20	2		
2017–18	Benfica	0	0	20	2

On loan from Benfica.

2017–18	Watford	28	1	28	1

CATHCART, Craig (D) 254 10
H: 6 2　W: 11 06　b.Belfast 6-2-89
Internationals: Northern Ireland U16, U17, U20, U21, Full caps.

2005–06	Manchester U	0	0		
2006–07	Manchester U	0	0		
2007–08	Manchester U	0	0		
2007–08	Antwerp	13	2	13	2
2008–09	Manchester U	0	0		
2008–09	Plymouth Arg	31	1	31	1
2009–10	Manchester U	0	0		
2009–10	Watford	12	0		
2010–11	Blackpool	30	1		
2011–12	Blackpool	27	0		
2012–13	Blackpool	25	1		
2013–14	Blackpool	30	1	112	3
2014–15	Watford	29	3		
2015–16	Watford	35	1		
2016–17	Watford	15	0		
2017–18	Watford	7	0	98	4

CHALOBAH, Nathaniel (D) 109 9
H: 6 1　W: 11 11　b.Sierra Leone 12-12-94
Internationals: England U16, U17, U18, U19, U20, U21.

2010–11	Chelsea	0	0		
2011–12	Chelsea	0	0		
2012–13	Chelsea	0	0		
2012–13	Watford	38	5		
2013–14	Chelsea	0	0		
2013–14	Nottingham F	12	2	12	2
2013–14	Middlesbrough	19	1	19	1
2014–15	Chelsea	0	0		
2014–15	Burnley	4	0	4	0
2014–15	Reading	15	1	15	1
2015–16	Chelsea	0	0		
2015–16	Napoli	5	0	5	0
2016–17	Chelsea	10	0	10	0
2017–18	Watford	6	0	44	5

CLEVERLEY, Tom (M) 231 25
H: 5 9　W: 10 07　b.Basingstoke 12-8-89
Internationals: England U20, U21, Full caps. Great Britain.

2007–08	Manchester U	0	0		
2008–09	Manchester U	0	0		
2008–09	Leicester C	15	2	15	2
2009–10	Manchester U	0	0		
2009–10	Watford	33	11		
2010–11	Manchester U	0	0		
2010–11	Wigan Ath	25	3	25	3
2011–12	Manchester U	10	0		
2012–13	Manchester U	22	2		

2013–14	Manchester U	22	1		
2014–15	Manchester U	1	0	55	3
2014–15	Aston Villa	31	3	31	3
2015–16	Everton	22	2		
2016–17	Everton	10	0	32	2
2016–17	Watford	17	0		
2017–18	Watford	23	1	73	12

DEENEY, Troy (F) 432 133
H: 5 11　W: 12 00　b.Solihull 29-6-88

2006–07	Walsall	1	0		
2007–08	Walsall	35	1		
2008–09	Walsall	45	12		
2009–10	Walsall	42	14	123	27
2010–11	Watford	36	3		
2011–12	Watford	43	11		
2012–13	Watford	40	19		
2013–14	Watford	44	24		
2014–15	Watford	42	21		
2015–16	Watford	38	13		
2016–17	Watford	37	10		
2017–18	Watford	29	5	309	106

DEULOFEU, Gerard (F) 98 11
H: 5 10　W: 11 01　b.Riudarenes 13-3-94
Internationals: Spain U16, U17, U19, U20, U21, Full caps.

2010–11	Barcelona	0	0		
2011–12	Barcelona	1	0		
2012–13	Barcelona	1	0		
2013–14	Barcelona	0	0		
2013–14	Everton	25	3		
2014–15	Everton	26	2		
2016–17	Everton	11	0	62	5
2016–17	AC Milan	17	4	17	4
2017–18	Barcelona	10	1	12	1

On loan from Barcelona.

2017–18	Watford	7	1	7	1

DJA DJEDJE, Brice (D) 166 5
H: 5 9　W: 11 00　b.Abidjan 23-12-90
Internationals: Ivory Coast Full caps.
From Paris Saint-Germain.

2010–11	Evian	18	1		
2011–12	Evian	34	2		
2012–13	Evian	27	1		
2013–14	Evian	14	1	93	5
2013–14	Marseilles	11	0		
2014–15	Marseilles	33	0		
2015–16	Marseilles	19	0	63	0
2016–17	Watford	0	0		
2017–18	Watford	0	0		
2017–18	Lens	10	0	10	0

DOUCOURE, Abdoulaye (M) 147 20
b.Meulan-en-Yvelines 1-1-93
Internationals: France U17, U18, U19, U20, U21.

2012–13	Rennes	4	1		
2013–14	Rennes	20	6		
2014–15	Rennes	35	3		
2015–16	Rennes	16	2	75	12
2015–16	Watford	0	0		
2015–16	Granada	10	0	15	0
2016–17	Watford	20	1		
2017–18	Watford	37	7	57	8

FEMENIA, Kiko (M) 180 10
H: 5 9　W: 9 11　b.Sanet i Negrals 2-2-91
Internationals: Spain U18, U19, U20.

2007–08	Hercules	1	0		
2008–09	Hercules	1	0		
2009–10	Hercules	35	3		
2010–11	Hercules	34	1	71	4
2011–12	Barcelona	0	0		
2012–13	Barcelona	0	0		
2013–14	Real Madrid	0	0		
2014–15	Alcorcon	17	0	17	0
2015–16	Alaves	38	5		
2016–17	Alaves	31	0	69	5
2017–18	Watford	23	1	23	1

FOLIVI, Michael (F) 2 0
H: 5 11　W: 12 06　b.Brent 25-2-98

2016–17	Watford	1	0		
2016–17	Coventry C	1	0	1	0
2017–18	Watford	0	0	1	0

GOMES, Heurelho (G) 435 0
H: 6 3　W: 12 13　b.Minas Gerais 15-2-81
Internationals: Brazil U23, Full caps.

2001	Cruzeiro	0	0		
2002	Cruzeiro	14	0		
2003	Cruzeiro	40	0		
2004	Cruzeiro	5	0	59	0
2004–05	PSV Eindhoven	30	0		
2005–06	PSV Eindhoven	32	0		
2006–07	PSV Eindhoven	32	0		

2007–08	PSV Eindhoven	34	0	128	0
2008–09	Tottenham H	34	0		
2009–10	Tottenham H	31	0		
2010–11	Tottenham H	30	0		
2011–12	Tottenham H	0	0		
2012–13	Tottenham H	0	0		
2012–13	Hoffenheim	9	0	9	0
2013–14	Tottenham H	0	0	95	0
2014–15	Watford	44	0		
2015–16	Watford	38	0		
2016–17	Watford	38	0		
2017–18	Watford	24	0	144	0

GRAY, Andre (F) 155 55
H: 5 10　W: 12 06　b.Shrewsbury 26-6-91
Internationals: England C.

2009–10	Shrewsbury T	4	0	4	0

From Hinckley U, Luton T.

2014–15	Brentford	45	16		
2015–16	Brentford	2	2	47	18
2015–16	Burnley	41	23		
2016–17	Burnley	32	9	73	32
2017–18	Watford	31	5	31	5

HOLEBAS, Jose (M) 297 34
H: 6 0　W: 12 06　b.Aschaffenburg 27-6-84
Internationals: Greece Full caps.

2005–06	Viktoria Kahl	33	15	33	15
2006–07	1860 Munich	0	0		
2007–08	1860 Munich	19	2		
2008–09	1860 Munich	24	1		
2009–10	1860 Munich	31	4	74	7
2010–11	Olympiacos	24	1		
2011–12	Olympiacos	23	2		
2012–13	Olympiacos	28	4		
2013–14	Olympiacos	19	2	94	9
2014–15	Roma	24	1	24	1
2015–16	Watford	11	0		
2016–17	Watford	33	2		
2017–18	Watford	28	0	72	2

HUGHES, Will (M) 180 11
H: 6 1　W: 11 08　b.Weybridge 7-4-95
Internationals: England U17, U21.

2011–12	Derby Co	3	0		
2012–13	Derby Co	35	2		
2013–14	Derby Co	41	3		
2014–15	Derby Co	42	2		
2015–16	Derby Co	6	0		
2016–17	Derby Co	38	2	165	9
2017–18	Watford	15	2	15	2

JANMAAT, Daryl (D) 292 20
H: 6 1　W: 12 13　b.Leidschendam 22-7-89
Internationals: Netherlands U20, U21, Full caps.

2007–08	Den Haag	25	2	25	2
2008–09	Heerenveen	10	0		
2009–10	Heerenveen	28	0		
2010–11	Heerenveen	24	3		
2011–12	Heerenveen	22	2	84	5
2012–13	Feyenoord	32	3		
2013–14	Feyenoord	30	2	62	5
2014–15	Newcastle U	37	1		
2015–16	Newcastle U	32	2		
2016–17	Newcastle U	2	0	71	3
2016–17	Watford	27	2		
2017–18	Watford	23	3	50	5

KABASELE, Christian (D) 194 20
b.Lubumbashi 24-2-91
Internationals: Belgium U19, U20, Full caps.

2008–09	Eupen	3	0		
2009–10	Eupen	3	0		
2010–11	Eupen	3	0		
2010–11	Mechelen	4	1	4	1
2011–12	Ludogorets	11	3	11	3
2012–13	Eupen	26	4		
2013–14	Eupen	26	2	59	6
2014–15	Genk	34	2		
2015–16	Genk	42	4	76	6
2016–17	Watford	16	2		
2017–18	Watford	28	2	44	4

KABOUL, Younes (D) 249 15
H: 6 2　W: 13 07　b.Annemasse 4-1-86
Internationals: France U21, Full caps.

2004–05	Auxerre	12	1		
2005–06	Auxerre	9	0		
2006–07	Auxerre	31	2	52	3
2007–08	Tottenham H	21	3		
2008–09	Portsmouth	20	1		
2009–10	Portsmouth	19	3	39	4
2009–10	Tottenham H	10	0		
2010–11	Tottenham H	21	1		
2011–12	Tottenham H	33	1		
2012–13	Tottenham H	13	1		
2013–14	Tottenham H	13	1		
2014–15	Tottenham H	11	0	110	6

2015–16	Sunderland	23	0		
2016–17	Sunderland	1	0	24	0
2016–17	Watford	22	2		
2017–18	Watford	2	0	24	2

KARNEZIS, Orestis (G)   182   0
H: 6 2   W: 12 06   b.Athens 11-7-85
Internationals: Greece U21, Full caps.

2007–08	Panathinaikos	1	0		
2008–09	Panathinaikos	0	0		
2009–10	Panathinaikos	1	0		
2010–11	Panathinaikos	0	0		
2011–12	Panathinaikos	22	0		
2012–13	Panathinaikos	29	0	53	0
2013–14	Granada	6	0	6	0
2014–15	Udinese	37	0		
2015–16	Udinese	38	0		
2016–17	Udinese	33	0		
2017–18	Udinese	0	0	108	0

On loan from Udinese.

2017–18	Watford	15	0	15	0

LEWIS, Dennon (M)   10   0
b. 9-5-97

2015–16	Watford	0	0		
2016–17	Watford	0	0		
2017–18	Watford	0	0		
2017–18	*Crawley T*	10	0	10	0

LUKEBAKIO, Dodi (M)   61   7
H: 6 2   W: 12 02   b.Asse 24-9-97
Internationals: Belgium U21. DR Congo Full caps.

2015–16	Anderlecht	17	1		
2016–17	Anderlecht	0	0		
2016–17	*Toulouse*	5	0	5	0
2016–17	*Charleroi*	19	3		
2017–18	Anderlecht	0	0	17	1
2017–18	*Charleroi*	19	3	38	6
2017–18	Watford	1	0	1	0

MARIAPPA, Adrian (D)   319   6
H: 5 10   W: 11 12   b.Harrow 3-10-86
Internationals: Jamaica Full caps.

2005–06	Watford	3	0		
2006–07	Watford	19	0		
2007–08	Watford	25	0		
2008–09	Watford	39	1		
2009–10	Watford	46	1		
2010–11	Watford	45	1		
2011–12	Watford	39	1		
2012–13	Reading	29	1		
2013–14	Reading	0	0	29	1
2013–14	Crystal Palace	24	1		
2014–15	Crystal Palace	12	0		
2015–16	Crystal Palace	3	0	39	1
2016–17	Watford	7	0		
2017–18	Watford	28	0	251	4

MASON, Brandon (M)   3   0
H: 5 9   W: 11 00   b.Westminster 30-9-97

2016–17	Watford	2	0		
2017–18	Watford	0	0	2	0
2017–18	*Dundee U*	1	0	1	0

MUKENA, Joy (D)   0   0
b.Enfield 3-7-99
From Tottenham H.

2017–18	Watford	0	0	

OKAKA, Stefano (F)   274   53
H: 6 2   W: 12 04   b.Castiglion del Lago 9-8-89
Internationals: Italy U19, U20, U21, Full caps.

2005–06	Roma	9	0		
2006–07	Roma	6	1		
2007–08	Roma	0	0		
2007–08	*Modena*	33	7	33	7
2008–09	Roma	8	0		
2008–09	*Brescia*	17	2	17	2
2009–10	Roma	6	0		
2009–10	*Fulham*	11	2	11	2
2010–11	Roma	4	0	33	1
2010–11	*Bari*	10	2	10	2
2011–12	Parma	14	3		
2012–13	Parma	0	0		
2012–13	*Spezia*	38	7	38	7
2013–14	Parma	2	0	16	3
2013–14	Sampdoria	13	5		
2014–15	Sampdoria	32	4	45	9
2015–16	Anderlecht	37	15	37	15
2016–17	Watford	0	0		
2017–18	Watford	15	1	34	5

PANTILIMON, Costel (G)   175   0
H: 6 5   W: 15 02   b.Bacau 1-2-87
Internationals: Romania U17, U19, U21, Full caps.

2005–06	Aerostar Bacau	9	0	9	0
2006–07	Poli Timisoara	8	0		
2007–08	Poli Timisoara	5	0	13	0
2008–09	Timisoara	31	0		
2009–10	Timisoara	21	0		
2010–11	Timisoara	28	0	80	0
2011–12	Manchester C	0	0		
2012–13	Manchester C	0	0		
2013–14	Manchester C	7	0	7	0
2014–15	Sunderland	28	0		
2015–16	Sunderland	17	0	45	0
2015–16	Watford	0	0		
2016–17	Watford	2	0		
2017–18	Watford	0	0	2	0
2017–18	*Deportivo La Coruna*	6	0	6	0
2017–18	*Nottingham F*	13	0	13	0

PEREYRA, Roberto (M)   220   19
H: 6 2   W: 11 11   b.Argentina 17-1-91
Internationals: Argentina U20, Full caps.

2008–09	River Plate	1	0		
2009–10	River Plate	15	0		
2010–11	River Plate	27	0	43	0
2011–12	Udinese	11	1		
2012–13	Udinese	37	5		
2013–14	Udinese	36	2		
2014–15	Udinese	0	0	84	8
2014–15	*Juventus*	35	4		
2015–16	Juventus	13	0	48	4
2016–17	Watford	13	2		
2017–18	Watford	32	5	45	7

PRODL, Sebastien (D)   267   17
H: 6 4   W: 13 05   b.Graz 21-6-87
Internationals: Austria U19, U20, Full caps.

2006–07	Sturm Graz	16	1		
2007–08	Sturm Graz	27	3	43	4
2008–09	Werder Bremen	20	0		
2009–10	Werder Bremen	9	1		
2010–11	Werder Bremen	25	1		
2011–12	Werder Bremen	16	2		
2012–13	Werder Bremen	28	1		
2013–14	Werder Bremen	27	2		
2014–15	Werder Bremen	22	3	149	10
2015–16	Watford	21	2		
2016–17	Watford	33	1		
2017–18	Watford	21	0	75	3

RICHARLISON, de Andrade (F)   104   23
H: 5 10   W: 11 03   b.Nova Venecia 10-5-97
Internationals: Brazil U20.

2015	America Mineiro	24	9	24	9
2016	Fluminense	28	4		
2017	Fluminense	14	5		
2017–18	Fluminense	0	0	42	9
2017–18	Watford	38	5	38	5

ROWAN, Charlie (D)   0   0

2016–17	Watford	0	0	
2017–18	Watford	0	0	
2017–18	*Accrington S*	0	0	

SINCLAIR, Jerome (F)   17   0
H: 5 8   W: 12 06   b.Birmingham 20-9-96
Internationals: England U16, U17.

2012–13	Liverpool	0	0		
2013–14	Liverpool	0	0		
2014–15	Liverpool	2	0		
2014–15	*Wigan Ath*	1	0	1	0
2015–16	Liverpool	0	0	2	0
2016–17	Watford	5	0		
2016–17	*Birmingham C*	5	0	5	0
2017–18	Watford	4	0	9	0

STEWART, Carl (M)   0   0

2016–17	Watford	0	0	
2017–18	Watford	0	0	

SUCCESS, Isaac (F)   77   8
H: 6 1   W: 11 03   b. 7-1-96
Internationals: Nigeria U17, U20, Full caps.

2014–15	Granada	19	1		
2015–16	Granada	30	6	49	7
2016–17	Watford	19	1		
2017–18	Watford	0	0	19	1
2017–18	*Malaga*	9	0	9	0

WAGUE, Molla (D)   93   7
H: 6 4   W: 13 10   b.Verdon 21-2-91
Internationals: France U19. Mali Full caps.

2011–12	Caen	5	1		
2012–13	Caen	20	2		
2013–14	Caen	24	1	49	4
2014–15	Granada	0	0		
2014–15	*Udinese*	10	2		
2015–16	Granada	0	0		
2015–16	Udinese	21	0		
2016–17	Grananda	0	0		
2016–17	Udinese	6	0		
2016–17	Leicester C	0	0		
2017–18	Udinese	1	0	38	2

On loan from Udinese.

2017–18	Watford	6	1	6	1

WILLIAMS, Randell (F)   6   1
H: 6 3   b.London 30-12-96
From Tower Hamlets.

2016–17	Crystal Palace	0	0		
2017–18	Watford	0	0		
2017–18	*Wycombe W*	6	1	6	1

ZARATE, Mauro (F)   328   92
H: 5 8   W: 10 10   b.Haedo 18-3-87
Internationals: Argentina U20.

2003–04	Velez Sarsfield	4	1		
2004–05	Velez Sarsfield	14	2		
2005–06	Velez Sarsfield	33	3		
2006–07	Velez Sarsfield	32	16		
2007–08	Al-Sadd	6	0	6	0
2007–08	*Birmingham C*	14	4	14	4
2008–09	Al-Saad	0	0		
2008–09	*Lazio*	36	13		
2009–10	Lazio	32	3		
2010–11	Lazio	35	9		
2011–12	Lazio	0	0		
2011–12	*Inter Milan*	22	2	22	2
2012–13	Lazio	1	0	104	25
2013–14	Velez Sarsfield	29	19		
2014–15	West Ham U	7	2		
2014–15	*QPR*	4	0	4	0
2014–15	West Ham U	15	3	22	5
2015–16	Fiorentina	13	3		
2016–17	Fiorentina	7	2	20	5
2016–17	Watford	3	0		
2017–18	Watford	0	0	3	0
2017–18	*Al-Nasr*	8	3	8	3
2018	*Velez Sarsfield*	13	7	125	48

ZEEGELAAR, Marvin (F)   136   4
H: 6 1   W: 13 02   b.Amsterdam 12-8-90

2008–09	Ajax	0	0		
2009–10	Ajax	2	0		
2010–11	Ajax	2	0	4	0
2010–11	*Excelsior*	16	0	16	0
2012–13	Elazigspor	19	0		
2013–14	Elazigspor	15	0	34	0
2013–14	*Blackpool*	2	0	2	0
2014–15	Rio Ave	25	1		
2015–16	Rio Ave	12	3	37	4
2015–16	Sporting Lisbon	11	0		
2016–17	Sporting Lisbon	20	0	31	0
2017–18	Watford	12	0	12	0

Players retained or with offer of contract
Alvarado Hoyos, Jamie Alberto; Barrozo Rodrigues, Matheus Aias; Becerra Maya, Juan Camillo; Bradbury, Harvey Lee; Charles, Ashley James; Cholevas, Chose Loint; Dahlberg, Pontus; Eleftheriou, Andrew; Estupinan Tenorio, Pervis Josue; Fobi, Kingsley; Foulquier, Dimitri; Gordon, Lewis; Hernandez Suarez, Juan Camilo; Hoban, Thomas Michael; Howes, Samuel Scott; Huerta Jerez, Valbur Robert; Jakubiak, Alexander Louis; Marreh, Sulayman; McLean Cassidy, Ryan Michael; Montenegro Zuniga, Eduardo Antonio; Oulare, Mamadou Obbi; Penaranda Maestre, Adalberto; Pereira, Dion Enrico; Santana Ferreira, Matheus Henrique; Segura Portocarrero, Jorge Andres; Suarez Charris, Luis Javier; Velasquez Reyes, Williams Daniel.

Scholars
Adebiyi, Emmanuel; Bennetts, Jayden; Forster, Harry James; Hoskins, James Michael; Hudson, Harry Jonathan; Leighton, Tom Craig; Miller, Reece; Mullings, Michael Koray; Phillips, Daniel Shaquille Jabari; Sanders, Kai Sidney; Sesay, Samuel Santigie; Suckling, Ryan George; Tricker, Ben.

WBA (87)

BARRY, Gareth (M)   653   53
H: 5 11   W: 12 06   b.Hastings 23-2-81
Internationals: England B, U21, Full caps.

1997–98	Aston Villa	1	0	
1998–99	Aston Villa	32	2	
1999–2000	Aston Villa	30	1	
2000–01	Aston Villa	30	0	
2001–02	Aston Villa	20	0	

Season	Club	Apps	Gls	Tot A	Tot G
2002–03	Aston Villa	35	3		
2003–04	Aston Villa	36	3		
2004–05	Aston Villa	34	7		
2005–06	Aston Villa	36	3		
2006–07	Aston Villa	35	8		
2007–08	Aston Villa	37	9		
2008–09	Aston Villa	38	5	365	41
2009–10	Manchester C	34	2		
2010–11	Manchester C	33	2		
2011–12	Manchester C	34	1		
2012–13	Manchester C	31	1		
2013–14	Manchester C	0	0	132	6
2013–14	*Everton*	32	3		
2014–15	Everton	33	0		
2015–16	Everton	33	0		
2016–17	Everton	33	2	131	5
2017–18	WBA	25	1	25	1

BRUNT, Chris (M) 483 65
H: 6 1 W: 13 04 b.Belfast 14-12-84
Internationals: Northern Ireland U19, U21, U23, Full caps.

Season	Club	Apps	Gls	Tot A	Tot G
2002–03	Middlesbrough	0	0		
2003–04	Middlesbrough	0	0		
2003–04	Sheffield W	9	2		
2004–05	Sheffield W	42	4		
2005–06	Sheffield W	44	7		
2006–07	Sheffield W	44	11		
2007–08	Sheffield W	1	0	140	24
2007–08	WBA	34	4		
2008–09	WBA	34	8		
2009–10	WBA	40	13		
2010–11	WBA	34	4		
2011–12	WBA	29	2		
2012–13	WBA	31	2		
2013–14	WBA	28	3		
2014–15	WBA	34	2		
2015–16	WBA	22	0		
2016–17	WBA	31	3		
2017–18	WBA	26	0	343	41

BURKE, Oliver (M) 67 7
H: 5 9 W: 11 11 b.Melton Mowbray 7-4-97
Internationals: Scotland U19, U20, Full caps.

Season	Club	Apps	Gls	Tot A	Tot G
2014–15	Nottingham F	2	0		
2014–15	*Bradford C*	2	0	2	0
2015–16	Nottingham F	18	2		
2016–17	Nottingham F	5	4	25	6
2016–17	RB Leipzig	25	1	25	1
2017–18	WBA	15	0	15	0

CAMPBELL, Tahvon (F) 61 4
b. 10-1-97

Season	Club	Apps	Gls	Tot A	Tot G
2015–16	WBA	0	0		
2015–16	Yeovil T	17	1		
2016–17	WBA	0	0		
2016–17	*Yeovil T*	19	1	36	2
2016–17	Notts Co	11	0	11	0
2017–18	WBA	0	0		
2017–18	Forest Green R	14	2	14	2

CHADLI, Nacer (M) 300 74
H: 6 2 W: 12 07 b.Liege 3-6-88
Internationals: Morocco Full caps. Belgium Full caps.

Season	Club	Apps	Gls	Tot A	Tot G
2007–08	AGOVV	19	2		
2008–09	AGOVV	34	9		
2009–10	AGOVV	39	17	92	28
2010–11	FC Twente	33	7		
2011–12	FC Twente	25	6		
2012–13	FC Twente	26	12	84	25
2013–14	Tottenham H	24	1		
2014–15	Tottenham H	35	11		
2015–16	Tottenham H	29	3	88	15
2016–17	WBA	31	5		
2017–18	WBA	5	1	36	6

DAWSON, Craig (D) 256 35
H: 6 0 W: 12 04 b.Rochdale 6-5-90
Internationals: England U21. Great Britain.

Season	Club	Apps	Gls	Tot A	Tot G
2008–09	Rochdale	1	0		
2009–10	Rochdale	42	9		
2010–11	WBA	0	0		
2010–11	*Rochdale*	45	10	87	19
2011–12	WBA	8	0		
2012–13	WBA	1	0		
2012–13	Bolton W	16	4	16	4
2013–14	WBA	12	0		
2014–15	WBA	29	2		
2015–16	WBA	38	4		
2016–17	WBA	37	4		
2017–18	WBA	28	2	153	12

EDWARDS, Kyle (M) 23 0
H: 5 8 W: 10 01 b.Dudley 17-2-98
Internationals: England U16, U17.

Season	Club	Apps	Gls	Tot A	Tot G
2015–16	WBA	0	0		
2017–18	WBA	0	0		
2017–18	Exeter C	23	0	23	0

EVANS, Jonny (D) 267 12
H: 6 2 W: 12 02 b.Belfast 3-1-88
Internationals: Northern Ireland U16, U17, U21, Full caps.

Season	Club	Apps	Gls	Tot A	Tot G
2004–05	Manchester U	0	0		
2005–06	Manchester U	0	0		
2006–07	Manchester U	0	0		
2006–07	Antwerp	14	2	14	2
2006–07	Sunderland	18	1		
2007–08	Manchester U	0	0		
2007–08	Sunderland	15	0	33	1
2008–09	Manchester U	17	0		
2009–10	Manchester U	18	0		
2010–11	Manchester U	13	0		
2011–12	Manchester U	29	1		
2012–13	Manchester U	23	3		
2013–14	Manchester U	17	0		
2014–15	Manchester U	14	0		
2015–16	Manchester U	0	0	131	4
2015–16	WBA	30	1		
2016–17	WBA	31	2		
2017–18	WBA	28	2	89	5

FERGUSON, Nathan (D) 0 0
b. 6-10-00
Internationals: England U18.

Season	Club	Apps	Gls	Tot A	Tot G
2017–18	WBA	0	0		

FIELD, Sam (M) 19 1
b. 8-5-98
Internationals: England U18, U19, U20.

Season	Club	Apps	Gls	Tot A	Tot G
2015–16	WBA	1	0		
2016–17	WBA	8	0		
2017–18	WBA	10	1	19	1

FITZWATER, Jack (D) 30 4
H: 6 2 W: 11 00 b.Solihull 23-9-97

Season	Club	Apps	Gls	Tot A	Tot G
2015–16	WBA	0	0		
2015–16	*Chesterfield*	1	0	1	0
2016–17	WBA	0	0		
2017–18	WBA	0	0		
2017–18	*Forest Green R*	14	1	14	1
2017–18	Walsall	15	3	15	3

FOSTER, Ben (G) 351 0
H: 6 2 W: 12 08 b.Leamington Spa 3-4-83
Internationals: England Full caps.

Season	Club	Apps	Gls	Tot A	Tot G
2000–01	Stoke C	0	0		
2001–02	Stoke C	0	0		
2002–03	Stoke C	0	0		
2003–04	Stoke C	0	0		
2004–05	Stoke C	0	0		
2004–05	*Kidderminster H*	2	0	2	0
2004–05	Wrexham	17	0	17	0
2005–06	Manchester U	0	0		
2005–06	Watford	44	0		
2006–07	*Watford*	29	0	73	0
2007–08	Manchester U	1	0		
2008–09	Manchester U	2	0		
2009–10	Manchester U	9	0	12	0
2010–11	Birmingham C	38	0		
2011–12	Birmingham C	0	0	38	0
2011–12	*WBA*	37	0		
2012–13	WBA	30	0		
2013–14	WBA	24	0		
2014–15	WBA	28	0		
2015–16	WBA	15	0		
2016–17	WBA	38	0		
2017–18	WBA	37	0	209	0

GABR, Ali (D) 129 4
H: 6 4 W: 11 09 b.Ismailia 1-1-89
Internationals: Egypt Full caps.

Season	Club	Apps	Gls	Tot A	Tot G
2009–10	Ismaily	2	0		
2010–11	Ismaily	1	0		
2011–12	Ismaily	0	0	3	0
2012–13	Ittihad Alexandria	13	0		
2013–14	Ittihad Alexandria	14	0	27	0
2014–15	Zamalek	33	1		
2015–16	Zamalek	26	1		
2016–17	Zamalek	25	2		
2017–18	Zamalek	15	0	99	4

On loan from Zamalek.

Season	Club	Apps	Gls	Tot A	Tot G
2017–18	WBA	0	0		

GARDNER, Craig (M) 306 35
H: 5 10 W: 11 13 b.Solihull 25-11-86
Internationals: England U21.

Season	Club	Apps	Gls	Tot A	Tot G
2004–05	Aston Villa	0	0		
2005–06	Aston Villa	8	0		
2006–07	Aston Villa	13	2		
2007–08	Aston Villa	23	3		
2008–09	Aston Villa	14	0		
2009–10	Aston Villa	1	0	59	5
2009–10	Birmingham C	13	1		
2010–11	Birmingham C	29	8		
2011–12	Sunderland	30	3		

Season	Club	Apps	Gls	Tot A	Tot G
2012–13	Sunderland	33	6		
2013–14	Sunderland	18	2	81	11
2014–15	WBA	35	3		
2015–16	WBA	34	3		
2016–17	WBA	9	0	78	6
2016–17	*Birmingham C*	20	2		
2017–18	Birmingham C	26	2	88	13

GIBBS, Kieran (M) 177 2
H: 5 10 W: 10 02 b.Lambeth 26-9-89
Internationals: England U19, U20, U21, Full caps.

Season	Club	Apps	Gls	Tot A	Tot G
2007–08	Arsenal	0	0		
2007–08	*Norwich C*	7	0	7	0
2008–09	Arsenal	8	0		
2009–10	Arsenal	3	0		
2010–11	Arsenal	7	0		
2011–12	Arsenal	16	1		
2012–13	Arsenal	27	0		
2013–14	Arsenal	28	0		
2014–15	Arsenal	22	0		
2015–16	Arsenal	15	1		
2016–17	Arsenal	11	0		
2017–18	Arsenal	0	0	137	2
2017–18	WBA	33	0	33	0

HARPER, Rekeem (M) 5 0
H: 6 0 W: 10 01 b. 8-3-00

Season	Club	Apps	Gls	Tot A	Tot G
2016–17	WBA	0	0		
2017–18	WBA	1	0	1	0
2017–18	*Blackburn R*	4	0	4	0

HEGAZI, Ahmed (D) 119 2
H: 6 5 W: 11 03 b.Ismalia 25-1-91
Internationals: Egypt U20, U23, Full caps.

Season	Club	Apps	Gls	Tot A	Tot G
2009–10	Ismaily	12	0		
2010–11	Ismaily	7	0		
2011–12	Ismaily	9	0	28	0
2012–13	Fiorentina	2	0		
2013–14	Fiorentina	1	0		
2014–15	Fiorentina	0	0	3	0
2014–15	Perugia	10	0	10	0
2015–16	Al Ahly	29	0		
2016–17	Al Ahly	11	0	40	0
2017–18	WBA	38	2	38	2

HOWKINS, Kyle (D) 27 0
H: 6 5 W: 12 11 b.Walsall 4-5-96

Season	Club	Apps	Gls	Tot A	Tot G
2015–16	WBA	0	0		
2016–17	WBA	0	0		
2016–17	*Mansfield T*	15	0	15	0
2017–18	WBA	0	0		
2017–18	*Cambridge U*	2	0	2	0
2017–18	Port Vale	10	0	10	0

JAMESON, Kyle (D) 0 0
b.Urmston 11-9-98
From Chelsea.

Season	Club	Apps	Gls	Tot A	Tot G
2017–18	WBA	0	0		

KRYCHOWIAK, Grzegorz (M) 243 14
H: 6 1 W: 13 01 b.Gryfice 29-1-90
Internationals: Poland U20, U21, Full caps.

Season	Club	Apps	Gls	Tot A	Tot G
2009–10	Bordeaux	0	0		
2009–10	Reims	19	2		
2010–11	Bordeaux	0	0		
2010–11	Reims	35	2		
2011–12	Bordeaux	2	0	2	0
2011–12	Nantes	21	0	21	0
2012–13	Reims	35	4		
2013–14	Reims	35	4	124	12
2014–15	Sevilla	32	2		
2015–16	Sevilla	26	0	58	2
2016–17	Paris Saint-Germain	11	0		
2016–17	Paris Saint-Germain	0	0	11	0

On loan from Paris Saint-Germain.

Season	Club	Apps	Gls	Tot A	Tot G
2017–18	WBA	27	0	27	0

LEKO, Jonathan (M) 25 0
H: 6 0 W: 11 11 b.Kinshasa 24-4-99
Internationals: England U16, U17, U18, U19.

Season	Club	Apps	Gls	Tot A	Tot G
2015–16	WBA	5	0		
2016–17	WBA	9	0		
2017–18	*Bristol C*	11	0	11	0
2017–18	WBA	0	0	14	0

LIVERMORE, Jake (M) 259 13
H: 5 9 W: 12 08 b.Enfield 14-11-89
Internationals: England Full caps.

Season	Club	Apps	Gls	Tot A	Tot G
2006–07	Tottenham H	0	0		
2007–08	Tottenham H	0	0		
2007–08	Milton Keynes D	5	0	5	0
2008–09	Tottenham H	0	0		
2008–09	Crewe Alex	0	0		
2009–10	Tottenham H	1	0		
2009–10	Derby Co	16	1	16	1
2009–10	Peterborough U	9	1	9	1
2010–11	Tottenham H	0	0		
2010–11	Ipswich T	12	0	12	0

Season	Club	Apps	Gls		
2010–11	Leeds U	5	0	5	0
2011–12	Tottenham H	24	0		
2012–13	Tottenham H	11	0		
2013–14	Tottenham H	0	0	36	0
2013–14	Hull C	36	3		
2014–15	Hull C	35	1		
2015–16	Hull C	34	4		
2016–17	Hull C	21	1	126	9
2016–17	WBA	16	0		
2017–18	WBA	34	2	50	2

McAULEY, Gareth (D)   464   35
H: 6 3 W: 13 00 b.Larne 5-12-79
Internationals: Northern Ireland B, Full caps.

Season	Club	Apps	Gls		
2004–05	Lincoln C	37	3		
2005–06	Lincoln C	35	5	72	8
2006–07	Leicester C	30	3		
2007–08	Leicester C	44	2	74	5
2008–09	Ipswich T	35	0		
2009–10	Ipswich T	41	5		
2010–11	Ipswich T	39	2	115	7
2011–12	WBA	32	2		
2012–13	WBA	36	3		
2013–14	WBA	32	2		
2014–15	WBA	24	1		
2015–16	WBA	34	1		
2016–17	WBA	36	6		
2017–18	WBA	9	0	203	15

McCLEAN, James (M)   304   38
H: 5 11 W: 11 00 b.Derry 22-4-89
Internationals: Northern Ireland U21. Republic of Ireland Full caps.

Season	Club	Apps	Gls		
2009	Derry C	27	1		
2010	Derry C	30	10		
2011	Derry C	16	7	73	18
2011–12	Sunderland	23	5		
2012–13	Sunderland	36	2		
2013–14	Sunderland	0	0	59	7
2013–14	Wigan Ath	37	3		
2014–15	Wigan Ath	36	6	73	9
2015–16	WBA	35	2		
2016–17	WBA	34	1		
2017–18	WBA	30	1	99	4

MELBOURNE, Max (D)   3   0
b.Solihull 24-10-98

Season	Club	Apps	Gls		
2017–18	WBA	0	0		
2017–18	Ross Co	3	0	3	0

MORRISON, James (M)   357   37
H: 5 10 W: 10 06 b.Darlington 25-5-86
Internationals: England U17, U18, U19, U20. Scotland Full caps.

Season	Club	Apps	Gls		
2003–04	Middlesbrough	1	0		
2004–05	Middlesbrough	14	0		
2005–06	Middlesbrough	24	1		
2006–07	Middlesbrough	28	2	67	3
2007–08	WBA	35	4		
2008–09	WBA	30	3		
2009–10	WBA	11	1		
2010–11	WBA	31	4		
2011–12	WBA	30	5		
2012–13	WBA	35	5		
2013–14	WBA	32	1		
2014–15	WBA	33	2		
2015–16	WBA	18	3		
2016–17	WBA	31	5		
2017–18	WBA	4	1	290	34

MYHILL, Boaz (G)   381   0
H: 6 3 W: 14 06 b.California 9-11-82
Internationals: England U20. Wales Full caps.

Season	Club	Apps	Gls		
2000–01	Aston Villa	0	0		
2001–02	Aston Villa	0	0		
2001–02	Stoke C	0	0		
2002–03	Aston Villa	0	0		
2002–03	Bristol C	0	0		
2002–03	Bradford C	2	0	2	0
2003–04	Aston Villa	0	0		
2003–04	Macclesfield T	15	0	15	0
2003–04	Stockport Co	2	0	2	0
2003–04	Hull C	23	0		
2004–05	Hull C	45	0		
2005–06	Hull C	45	0		
2006–07	Hull C	46	0		
2007–08	Hull C	43	0		
2008–09	Hull C	28	0		
2009–10	Hull C	27	0	257	0
2010–11	WBA	6	0		
2011–12	WBA	0	0		
2011–12	Birmingham C	42	0	42	0
2012–13	WBA	8	0		
2013–14	WBA	14	0		
2014–15	WBA	11	0		
2015–16	WBA	23	0		
2016–17	WBA	0	0		
2017–18	WBA	1	0	63	0

NYOM, Allan (D)   308   2
H: 5 7 W: 12 11 b.Neuilly-sur-Seine 10-5-88
Internationals: Cameroon Full caps.

Season	Club	Apps	Gls		
2008–09	Arles-Avignon	37	0	37	0
2009–10	Udinese	0	0		
2010–11	Udinese	0	0		
2010–11	Granada	43	1		
2011–12	Udinese	0	0		
2011–12	Granada	32	0		
2012–13	Udinese	0	0		
2012–13	Granada	35	0		
2013–14	Udinese	0	0		
2013–14	Granada	34	0		
2014–15	Udinese	0	0		
2014–15	Granada	34	1	178	2
2015–16	Watford	32	0		
2016–17	Watford	0	0	32	0
2016–17	WBA	32	0		
2017–18	WBA	29	0	61	0

PALMER, Alex (G)   0   0
b. 10-8-96
Internationals: England U16.

Season	Club	Apps	Gls		
2014–15	WBA	0	0		
2015–16	WBA	0	0		
2016–17	WBA	0	0		
2017–18	WBA	0	0		

PHILLIPS, Matthew (M)   325   45
H: 6 0 W: 12 10 b.Aylesbury 13-3-91
Internationals: England U19, U20. Scotland Full caps.

Season	Club	Apps	Gls		
2007–08	Wycombe W	2	0		
2008–09	Wycombe W	37	3		
2009–10	Wycombe W	36	5		
2010–11	Wycombe W	3	0	78	8
2010–11	Blackpool	27	1		
2011–12	Blackpool	33	7		
2011–12	Sheffield U	6	5	6	5
2012–13	Blackpool	34	4		
2013–14	Blackpool	0	0	94	12
2013–14	QPR	21	3		
2014–15	QPR	25	3		
2015–16	QPR	44	8	90	14
2016–17	WBA	27	4		
2017–18	WBA	30	2	57	6

ROBSON-KANU, Hal (F)   290   38
H: 5 7 W: 11 08 b.Acton 21-5-89
Internationals: England U19, U20. Wales U21, Full caps.

Season	Club	Apps	Gls		
2007–08	Reading	0	0		
2007–08	Southend U	8	3		
2008–09	Reading	0	0		
2008–09	Southend U	14	2	22	5
2008–09	Swindon T	20	4	20	4
2009–10	Reading	17	0		
2010–11	Reading	27	5		
2011–12	Reading	36	4		
2012–13	Reading	25	7		
2013–14	Reading	36	4		
2014–15	Reading	29	1		
2015–16	Reading	28	3		
2016–17	Reading	0	0	198	24
2016–17	WBA	29	3		
2017–18	WBA	21	2	50	5

RODRIGUEZ, Jay (F)   263   68
H: 6 0 W: 12 00 b.Burnley 29-7-89
Internationals: England U21, Full caps.

Season	Club	Apps	Gls		
2007–08	Burnley	0	0		
2007–08	Stirling Alb	11	3	11	3
2008–09	Burnley	25	2		
2009–10	Burnley	0	0		
2009–10	Barnsley	6	1	6	1
2010–11	Burnley	42	14		
2011–12	Burnley	37	15	105	31
2012–13	Southampton	35	6		
2013–14	Southampton	33	15		
2014–15	Southampton	0	0		
2015–16	Southampton	12	0		
2016–17	Southampton	24	5	104	26
2017–18	WBA	37	7	37	7

RONDON, Jose Salomon (F)   343   109
H: 6 1 W: 13 08 b.Caracas 16-9-89
Internationals: Venezuela U20, Full caps.

Season	Club	Apps	Gls		
2006–07	Aragua	21	7		
2007–08	Aragua	28	8	49	15
2008–09	Las Palmas	10	0		
2009–10	Las Palmas	36	12	46	12
2010–11	Malaga	30	14		
2011–12	Malaga	37	11	67	25
2012–13	Rubin Kazan	25	7		
2013–14	Rubin Kazan	6	6	36	13
2013–14	Zenit St Petersburg	10	7		
2014–15	Zenit St Petersburg	26	13		
2015–16	Zenit St Petersburg	1	0	37	20
2015–16	WBA	34	9		
2016–17	WBA	38	8		
2017–18	WBA	36	7	108	24

TULLOCH, Rayhaan (F)   0   0
b.Birmingham 20-1-01
Internationals: England U16, U17.

Season	Club	Apps	Gls		
2017–18	WBA	0	0		

WILSON, Kane (D)   19   1
H: 5 10 W: 11 03 b. 11-3-00
Internationals: England U16, U17.

Season	Club	Apps	Gls		
2016–17	WBA	0	0		
2017–18	WBA	0	0		
2017–18	Exeter C	19	1	19	1

YACOB, Claudio (M)   285   5
H: 5 11 W: 11 06 b.Carcarana 18-7-87
Internationals: Argentina U20, Full caps.

Season	Club	Apps	Gls		
2006–07	Racing Club	12	0		
2007–08	Racing Club	24	0		
2008–09	Racing Club	25	1		
2009–10	Racing Club	26	0		
2010–11	Racing Club	21	2		
2011–12	Racing Club	17	1	125	4
2012–13	WBA	30	0		
2013–14	WBA	27	1		
2014–15	WBA	20	0		
2015–16	WBA	34	0		
2016–17	WBA	33	0		
2017–18	WBA	16	0	160	1

Players retained or with offer of contract
Bradley, Alex; House, Bradley Roy; Keranovic, Jasmin; Morton, Callum Damian Peter; O'Shea, Dara; Pierce, Benjamin Alan; Soule, Jamie; Zhang, Yuning.

Scholars
Ashton, Eoin Thomas; Asomugha, Stanley; Azaz, Finn; Brown, Zak; Cann, Ted Barnaby; Chambers, Maurice Jack; Clayton-Phillips, Nicholas; Dyce, Tyrese; Harmon, George; Healy, Kevin; Martinez, Pablo Jacob; Meredith, Daniel William; Ojebode, Yusuff Akinola Olatunji; Przybek, Adam; Sharpe, Thomas; Taylor, Peter James; White, Aksum; Wilding, Samuel.

WEST HAM U (88)

ADRIAN (G)   157   0
H: 6 2 W: 12 00 b.Seville 3-1-87

Season	Club	Apps	Gls		
2008–09	Real Betis	0	0		
2009–10	Real Betis	0	0		
2010–11	Real Betis	0	0		
2011–12	Real Betis	0	0		
2012–13	Real Betis	32	0	32	0
2013–14	West Ham U	20	0		
2014–15	West Ham U	38	0		
2015–16	West Ham U	32	0		
2016–17	West Ham U	16	0		
2017–18	West Ham U	19	0	125	0

ANTONIO, Michael (M)   284   61
H: 6 0 W: 11 11 b.Wandsworth 28-3-90

Season	Club	Apps	Gls		
2008–09	Reading	0	0		
2008–09	Cheltenham T	9	0	9	0
2009–10	Reading	1	0		
2009–10	Southampton	28	3	28	3
2010–11	Reading	21	1		
2011–12	Reading	6	0		
2011–12	Colchester U	15	4	15	4
2011–12	Sheffield W	14	5		
2012–13	Reading	0	0	28	1
2012–13	Sheffield W	37	8		
2013–14	Sheffield W	27	4	78	17
2014–15	Nottingham F	46	14		
2015–16	Nottingham F	4	2	50	16
2015–16	West Ham U	26	8		
2016–17	West Ham U	29	9		
2017–18	West Ham U	21	3	76	20

ARNAUTOVIC, Marko (F)   275   59
H: 6 4 W: 13 00 b.Floridsdorf 19-4-89
Internationals: Austria U18, U19, U21, Full caps.

Season	Club	Apps	Gls		
2006–07	FC Twente	2	0		
2007–08	FC Twente	14	0		
2008–09	FC Twente	28	12		
2009–10	FC Twente	0	0	44	12
2009–10	Inter Milan	3	0	3	0
2010–11	Werder Bremen	25	3		
2011–12	Werder Bremen	19	6		
2012–13	Werder Bremen	26	5		
2013–14	Werder Bremen	2	0	72	14
2013–14	Stoke C	30	4		

2014–15	Stoke C	29	1		
2015–16	Stoke C	34	11		
2016–17	Stoke C	32	6	125	22
2017–18	West Ham U	31	11	31	11

BROWNE, Marcus (M) 0 0
b. 18-12-97

2015–16	West Ham U	0	0		
2016–17	West Ham U	0	0		
2016–17	Wigan Ath	0	0		
2017–18	West Ham U	0	0		

BURKE, Reece (D) 74 4
H: 6 2 W: 12 11 b.London 2-9-96
Internationals: England U18, U19, U20.

2013–14	West Ham U	0	0		
2014–15	West Ham U	5	0		
2015–16	West Ham U	0	0		
2015–16	*Bradford C*	34	2	34	2
2016–17	West Ham U	0	0		
2016–17	*Wigan Ath*	10	1	10	1
2017–18	West Ham U	0	0	5	0
2017–18	*Bolton W*	25	1	25	1

BYRAM, Samuel (M) 157 9
H: 5 11 W: 11 04 b.Thurrock 16-9-93

2012–13	Leeds U	44	3		
2013–14	Leeds U	25	0		
2014–15	Leeds U	39	3		
2015–16	Leeds U	22	3	130	9
2015–16	West Ham U	4	0		
2016–17	West Ham U	18	0		
2017–18	West Ham U	5	0	27	0

CARROLL, Andy (F) 249 71
H: 6 4 W: 11 00 b.Gateshead 6-1-89
Internationals: England U19, U21, Full caps.

2006–07	Newcastle U	4	0		
2007–08	Newcastle U	4	0		
2007–08	*Preston NE*	11	1	11	1
2008–09	Newcastle U	14	3		
2009–10	Newcastle U	39	17		
2010–11	Newcastle U	19	11	80	31
2010–11	Liverpool	7	2		
2011–12	Liverpool	35	4		
2012–13	Liverpool	2	0	44	6
2012–13	*West Ham U*	24	7		
2013–14	West Ham U	15	2		
2014–15	West Ham U	14	5		
2015–16	West Ham U	27	9		
2016–17	West Ham U	18	7		
2017–18	West Ham U	16	3	114	33

COLLINS, James M (D) 345 14
H: 6 2 W: 14 05 b.Newport 23-8-83
Internationals: Wales U19, U20, U21, Full caps.

2000–01	Cardiff C	3	0		
2001–02	Cardiff C	7	1		
2002–03	Cardiff C	2	0		
2003–04	Cardiff C	20	1		
2004–05	Cardiff C	34	1	66	3
2005–06	West Ham U	14	2		
2006–07	West Ham U	16	0		
2007–08	West Ham U	3	0		
2008–09	West Ham U	18	0		
2009–10	West Ham U	30	0		
2009–10	Aston Villa	27	1		
2010–11	Aston Villa	32	3		
2011–12	Aston Villa	32	1	91	5
2012–13	West Ham U	29	0		
2013–14	West Ham U	24	1		
2014–15	West Ham U	27	0		
2015–16	West Ham U	19	0		
2016–17	West Ham U	22	2		
2017–18	West Ham U	13	1	188	6

CRESSWELL, Aaron (D) 339 16
H: 5 7 W: 10 05 b.Liverpool 15-12-89
Internationals: England Full caps.

2008–09	Tranmere R	13	1		
2009–10	Tranmere R	14	0		
2010–11	Tranmere R	43	4	70	5
2011–12	Ipswich T	44	1		
2012–13	Ipswich T	46	3		
2013–14	Ipswich T	42	2	132	6
2014–15	West Ham U	38	2		
2015–16	West Ham U	37	2		
2016–17	West Ham U	26	0		
2017–18	West Ham U	36	1	137	5

CULLEN, Josh (M) 70 1
H: 5 8 W: 11 00 b.Southend-on-Sea 4-7-96
Internationals: England U16. Republic of Ireland U19, U21.

2014–15	West Ham U	0	0		
2015–16	West Ham U	1	0		
2015–16	*Bradford C*	15	0		
2016–17	West Ham U	0	0		
2016–17	*Bradford C*	40	1	55	1
2017–18	West Ham U	2	0	3	0
2017–18	*Bolton W*	12	0	12	0

DIANGANA, Grady (M) 0 0

2016–17	West Ham U	0	0		
2017–18	West Ham U	0	0		

EVRA, Patrice (D) 532 16
H: 5 8 W: 11 10 b.Dakar 15-5-81
Internationals: France U21, Full caps.

1998–99	Marsala	24	3	24	3
1999–2000	Monza	3	0	3	0
2000–01	Nice	5	0		
2001–02	Nice	34	1	39	1
2002–03	Monaco	36	1		
2003–04	Monaco	33	0		
2004–05	Monaco	36	0		
2005–06	Monaco	15	0	120	1
2005–06	Manchester U	11	0		
2006–07	Manchester U	24	1		
2007–08	Manchester U	33	0		
2008–09	Manchester U	28	0		
2009–10	Manchester U	38	0		
2010–11	Manchester U	35	1		
2011–12	Manchester U	37	0		
2012–13	Manchester U	34	4		
2013–14	Manchester U	33	1	273	7
2014–15	Juventus	21	1		
2015–16	Juventus	26	2		
2016–17	Juventus	6	0	53	3
2017–18	Marseille	11	1		
2017–18	Marseille	4	0	15	1
2017–18	West Ham U	5	0	5	0

FERNANDES, Edimilson (M) 73 1
b. 15-4-96
Internationals: Switzerland U21, Full caps.

2014–15	Sion	26	1		
2015–16	Sion	5	0	31	1
2016–17	West Ham U	28	0		
2017–18	West Ham U	14	0	42	0

FONTE, Jose (D) 446 24
H: 6 2 W: 12 08 b.Penafiel 22-12-83
Internationals: Portugal U21, B, Full caps.

2004–05	Felgueiros	28	1	28	1
2005–06	Setubal	15	0	15	0
2005–06	Benfica	1	0	1	0
2005–06	Pacos	11	1	11	1
2006–07	Amadora	25	1	25	1
2007–08	Crystal Palace	22	1		
2008–09	Crystal Palace	38	4		
2009–10	Crystal Palace	22	1	82	6
2009–10	Southampton	21	0		
2010–11	Southampton	43	7		
2011–12	Southampton	42	1		
2012–13	Southampton	27	2		
2013–14	Southampton	36	3		
2014–15	Southampton	37	0		
2015–16	Southampton	37	2		
2016–17	Southampton	17	0	260	15
2016–17	West Ham U	16	0		
2017–18	West Ham U	8	0	24	0

Transferred to Dalian Yifang, February 2018.

HAKSABANOVIC, Sead (M) 68 12
H: 5 9 W: 10 12 b.Hyltebruk 4-5-99
Internationals: Sweden U17, U19. Montenegro Full caps.

2015	Halmstads	20	0		
2016	Halmstads	30	8		
2017	Halmstads	18	4	68	12
2017–18	Halmstad	0	0		
2017–18	West Ham U	0	0		

HERNANDEZ, Javier (F) 315 117
H: 5 8 W: 9 11 b.Guadalajara 1-6-88
Internationals: Mexico U20, Full caps.

2005–06	Tapatio	10	0		
2006–07	Tapatio	12	3		
2006–07	Guadalajara	7	1		
2007–08	Guadalajara	5	0		
2007–08	Tapatio	15	6		
2008–09	Tapatio	7	2	45	11
2008–09	Guadalajara	22	4		
2009–10	Guadalajara	28	21	62	26
2010–11	Manchester U	27	13		
2011–12	Manchester U	28	10		
2012–13	Manchester U	22	10		
2013–14	Manchester U	24	4		
2014–15	Manchester U	1	0		
2014–15	*Real Madrid*	23	7	23	7
2015–16	Manchester U	1	0	103	37
2015–16	Bayer Leverkusen	28	17		
2016–17	Bayer Leverkusen	26	11	54	28
2017–18	West Ham U	28	8	28	8

HOLLAND, Nathan (M) 0 0
b. 19-6-98
Internationals: England U16, U17, U18, U19.

2016–17	West Ham U	0	0		
2017–18	West Ham U	0	0		

HUGILL, Jordan (F) 140 32
H: 6 0 W: 10 01 b.Middlesbrough 4-6-92

2013–14	Port Vale	20	4	20	4
2014–15	Preston NE	3	0		
2014–15	*Tranmere R*	6	1	6	1
2014–15	*Hartlepool U*	8	4	8	4
2015–16	Preston NE	29	3		
2016–17	Preston NE	44	12		
2017–18	Preston NE	27	8	103	23
2017–18	West Ham U	3	0	3	0

JOAO MARIO, Eduardo (M) 137 25
H: 5 10 W: 11 11 b.Porto 19-1-93
Internationals: Portugal U16, U17, U18, U19, U20, U21, Full caps.

2011–12	Sporting Lisbon	0	0		
2012–13	Sporting Lisbon	1	0		
2013–14	Sporting Lisbon	0	0		
2013–14	*Vitoria Setubal*	15	9	15	9
2014–15	Sporting Lisbon	30	5		
2015–16	Sporting Lisbon	33	6		
2015–16	Sporting Lisbon	1	0	65	11
2016–17	Inter Milan	30	3		
2017–18	Inter Milan	14	0	44	3

On loan from Inter Milan.

2017–18	West Ham U	13	2	13	2

JOHNSON, Ben (M) 0 0
b. 21-1-00

2017–18	West Ham U	0	0		

KOUYATE, Cheikhou (M) 318 19
H: 6 3 W: 11 11 b.Dakar 21-12-89
Internationals: Senegal U20, Full caps.

2007–08	Brussels	10	0		
2008–09	Brussels	0	0	10	0
2008–09	Kortrijk	26	3	26	3
2009–10	Anderlecht	21	1		
2010–11	Anderlecht	23	1		
2011–12	Anderlecht	38	0		
2012–13	Anderlecht	33	1		
2013–14	Anderlecht	38	1	153	4
2014–15	West Ham U	31	4		
2015–16	West Ham U	34	5		
2016–17	West Ham U	31	1		
2017–18	West Ham U	33	2	129	12

LANZINI, Manuel (M) 224 42
H: 5 7 W: 11 00 b.Ituzaingo 15-2-93
Internationals: Argentina U20, Full caps.

2010–11	River Plate	22	0		
2010–11	Fluminense	22	2		
2011–12	River Plate	0	0		
2011–12	Fluminense	6	1	28	3
2012–13	River Plate	26	8	26	8
2013–14	River Plate	36	4	58	4
2014–15	Al-Jazira	24	8		
2015–16	Al-Jazira	0	0	24	8
2015–16	*West Ham U*	26	6		
2016–17	West Ham U	35	8		
2017–18	West Ham U	27	5	88	19

MAKASI, Moses (M) 7 1
H: 5 11 W: 11 05 b. 22-9-95

2016–17	West Ham U	0	0		
2017–18	West Ham U	0	0		
2017–18	*Plymouth Arg*	7	1	7	1

MARTINEZ, Antonio (F) 26 2
b.Barrio del Progreso 30-6-97
Internationals: Spain U17, U18, U19.

2015–16	Valencia	0	0		
2016–17	West Ham U	0	0		
2016–17	*Oxford U*	15	1	15	1
2017–18	West Ham U	0	0		
2017–18	*Valladolid*	11	1	11	1

MASUAKU, Arthur (D) 118 2
b. 7-11-93
Internationals: France U18, U19.

2012–13	Valenciennes	0	0		
2013–14	Valenciennes	27	1	27	1
2014–15	Olympiacos	27	0		
2015–16	Olympiacos	24	1	51	1
2016–17	West Ham U	13	0		
2017–18	West Ham U	27	0	40	0

NEUFVILLE, Vashon (D) 0 0
H: 5 8 W: 10 08 b. 18-7-99
Internationals: England U16, U17.

2017–18	West Ham U	0	0		

NOBLE, Mark (M)   394 46
H: 5 11   W: 12 00   b.West Ham 8-5-87
Internationals: England U16, U17, U18, U19, U21.

2004–05	West Ham U	13	0	
2005–06	West Ham U	5	0	
2005–06	*Hull C*	5	0	5 0
2006–07	West Ham U	10	2	
2006–07	*Ipswich T*	13	1	13 1
2007–08	West Ham U	31	3	
2008–09	West Ham U	29	3	
2009–10	West Ham U	27	2	
2010–11	West Ham U	26	4	
2011–12	West Ham U	45	8	
2012–13	West Ham U	28	4	
2013–14	West Ham U	38	3	
2014–15	West Ham U	28	2	
2015–16	West Ham U	37	7	
2016–17	West Ham U	30	3	
2017–18	West Ham U	29	4	376 45

OBIANG, Pedro (M)   199 7
H: 6 1   W: 12 13   b.Alcala de Henares 13-5-90
Internationals: Spain U17, U19, U20, U21.

2008–09	Sampdoria	0	0	
2009–10	Sampdoria	0	0	
2010–11	Sampdoria	4	0	
2011–12	Sampdoria	33	0	
2012–13	Sampdoria	34	1	
2013–14	Sampdoria	27	0	
2014–15	Sampdoria	34	3	132 4
2015–16	West Ham U	24	0	
2016–17	West Ham U	22	1	
2017–18	West Ham U	21	2	67 3

OGBONNA, Angelo (D)   290 2
H: 6 2   W: 13 08   b.Cassino 23-5-88
Internationals: Italy U21, Full caps.

2006–07	Torino	4	0	
2007–08	Torino	0	0	
2007–08	*Crotone*	22	0	22 0
2008–09	Torino	19	0	
2009–10	Torino	28	1	
2010–11	Torino	35	0	
2011–12	Torino	39	0	
2012–13	Torino	22	0	147 1
2013–14	Juventus	16	0	
2014–15	Juventus	25	0	41 0
2015–16	West Ham U	28	0	
2016–17	West Ham U	20	0	
2017–18	West Ham U	32	1	80 1

OXFORD, Reece (D)   20 0
H: 6 3   W: 13 08   b.Edmonton 16-12-98
Internationals: England U16, U17, U18, U19, U20.

2014–15	West Ham U	0	0	
2015–16	West Ham U	7	0	
2016–17	West Ham U	0	0	
2016–17	*Reading*	5	0	5 0
2017–18	West Ham U	1	0	8 0
2017–18	*Borussia M'gladbach*	7	0	7 0

PASK, Josh (D)   15 0
b. 1-11-97

2014–15	West Ham U	0	0	
2015–16	*Dagenham & R*	5	0	5 0
2016–17	West Ham U	0	0	
2016–17	*Gillingham*	10	0	10 0
2017–18	West Ham U	0	0	

QUINA, Domingos (F)   0 0
b. 18-11-99
Internationals: Portugal U17, U18, U19.

2016–17	West Ham U	0	0
2017–18	West Ham U	0	0

REID, Winston (D)   277 11
H: 6 3   W: 13 10   b.North Shore 3-7-88
Internationals: Denmark U19, U20, U21. New Zealand Full caps.

2005–06	Midtjylland	9	0	
2006–07	Midtjylland	11	0	
2007–08	Midtjylland	9	0	
2008–09	Midtjylland	25	2	
2009–10	Midtjylland	29	0	83 2
2010–11	West Ham U	7	0	
2011–12	West Ham U	28	3	
2012–13	West Ham U	36	1	
2013–14	West Ham U	22	1	
2014–15	West Ham U	30	1	
2015–16	West Ham U	34	1	
2016–17	West Ham U	30	2	
2017–18	West Ham U	17	0	194 9

RICE, Declan (M)   27 0
b. 14-1-99
Internationals: Republic of Ireland U16, U17, U19, U21, Full caps.

2016–17	West Ham U	1	0	
2017–18	West Ham U	26	0	27 0

SAKHO, Diafra (F)   183 62
H: 6 0   W: 12 06   b.Guediawaye 24-12-89
Internationals: Senegal Full caps.

2009–10	Metz	5	0	
2010–11	Metz	30	5	
2011–12	Metz	9	0	
2011–12	*Boulogne*	7	0	7 0
2012–13	Metz	33	19	
2013–14	Metz	37	20	114 44
2014–15	West Ham U	23	10	
2015–16	West Ham U	21	5	
2016–17	West Ham U	4	1	
2017–18	West Ham U	14	2	62 18

Transferred to Rennes, January 2018.

SAMUELSEN, Martin (F)   40 2
H: 6 2   W: 11 05   b.Haugesund 17-4-97
Internationals: Norway U16, U17, U18, U21, Full caps.

2015–16	West Ham U	0	0	
2015–16	*Peterborough U*	17	1	
2016–17	West Ham U	0	0	
2016–17	*Blackburn R*	3	0	3 0
2016–17	*Peterborough U*	11	1	
2017–18	*Peterborough U*	0	0	28 2
2017–18	West Ham U	0	0	
2017–18	*Burton Alb*	9	0	9 0

SNODGRASS, Robert (M)   426 85
H: 6 0   W: 12 02   b.Glasgow 7-9-87
Internationals: Scotland U20, U21, Full caps.

2003–04	Livingston	0	0	
2004–05	Livingston	17	2	
2005–06	Livingston	27	4	
2006–07	Livingston	6	0	
2006–07	*Stirling Alb*	12	5	12 5
2007–08	Livingston	31	9	81 15
2008–09	Leeds U	42	9	
2009–10	Leeds U	44	7	
2010–11	Leeds U	37	6	
2011–12	Leeds U	43	13	166 35
2012–13	Norwich C	37	6	
2013–14	Norwich C	30	6	67 12
2014–15	Hull C	1	0	
2015–16	Hull C	24	4	
2016–17	Hull C	20	7	45 11
2016–17	West Ham U	15	0	
2017–18	West Ham U	0	0	15 0
2017–18	*Aston Villa*	40	7	40 7

TROTT, Nathan (G)   0 0
H: 6 0   W: 11 00   b. 21-11-98
Internationals: Bermuda U17. England U18, U20.

2017–18	West Ham U	0	0

ZABALETA, Pablo (D)   413 20
H: 5 8   W: 10 12   b.Buenos Aires 16-1-85
Internationals: Argentina U20, U23, Full caps.

2002–03	San Lorenzo	11	0	
2003–04	San Lorenzo	27	3	
2004–05	San Lorenzo	28	5	66 8
2005–06	Espanyol	27	2	
2006–07	Espanyol	21	0	
2007–08	Espanyol	32	1	80 3
2008–09	Manchester C	29	1	
2009–10	Manchester C	27	0	
2010–11	Manchester C	26	2	
2011–12	Manchester C	21	1	
2012–13	Manchester C	30	2	
2013–14	Manchester C	35	1	
2014–15	Manchester C	29	1	
2015–16	Manchester C	13	0	
2016–17	Manchester C	20	1	230 9
2017–18	West Ham U	37	0	37 0

Players retained or with offer of contract
Afolayan, Oladapo Joshua; Akinola, Olatunji Oluwasehun; Costa Da Rosa, Bernardo; Coventry, Conor; Hector-Ingram, Jahmal Justin; Kemp, Daniel; Lewis, Alfie; Powell, Joe; Scully, Anthony Richard; Sylvestre, Noha.

Scholars
Adarkwa, Sean Jordan; Alese, Ajibola; Anang, Joseph Tetteh; Barrett, Mason; Belic, Kristijan; Dalipi, Kevin; El Mhassani, Anouar; Hannam, Reece Phillip Peter; Longelo Mbule, Emmanuel; Matrevic, sRihards; Mingi, Jade Jay; Ngakia, Jeremy; Spyridis, Odysseas; Watson, Louie Shaun; Wells, Ben.

WIGAN ATH (89)

BANINGIME, Divin (F)   0 0
b. 13-10-00

2017–18	Wigan Ath	0	0

BARRIGAN, James (F)   0 0
b. 25-1-98

2016–17	Wigan Ath	0	0
2017–18	Wigan Ath	0	0

BERRY, James (F)   0 0
b.Wigan 10-2-00

2017–18	Wigan Ath	0	0

BRUCE, Alex (D)   280 6
H: 6 0   W: 11 06   b.Norwich 28-9-84
Internationals: Republic of Ireland B, U21, Full caps. Northern Ireland Full caps.

2002–03	Blackburn R	0	0	
2003–04	Blackburn R	0	0	
2004–05	Blackburn R	0	0	
2004–05	*Oldham Ath*	12	0	12 0
2004–05	Birmingham C	0	0	
2004–05	*Sheffield W*	6	0	6 0
2005–06	Birmingham C	6	0	6 0
2005–06	*Tranmere R*	11	0	11 0
2006–07	Ipswich T	41	0	
2007–08	Ipswich T	36	0	
2008–09	Ipswich T	25	1	
2009–10	Ipswich T	13	1	
2009–10	*Leicester C*	3	0	3 0
2010–11	Ipswich T	0	0	115 2
2010–11	Leeds U	21	1	
2011–12	Leeds U	8	0	29 1
2011–12	*Huddersfield T*	3	0	3 0
2012–13	Hull C	32	0	
2013–14	Hull C	20	0	
2014–15	Hull C	22	0	
2015–16	Hull C	11	1	
2016–17	*Wigan Ath*	0	0	85 1
2017–18	Bury	2	1	2 1
2017–18	Wigan Ath	6	1	8 1

BURGESS, Luke (M)   0 0
b. 3-3-99

2017–18	Wigan Ath	0	0

BURKE, Luke (D)   5 0
b. 22-9-97

2015–16	Wigan Ath	0	0	
2016–17	Wigan Ath	5	0	
2017–18	Wigan Ath	0	0	5 0

BURN, Dan (D)   210 9
H: 6 6   W: 13 00   b.Blyth 1-5-92

2009–10	Darlington	4	0	4 0
2010–11	Fulham	0	0	
2011–12	Fulham	0	0	
2012–13	Fulham	0	0	
2012–13	*Yeovil T*	34	2	34 2
2013–14	Fulham	9	0	
2013–14	*Birmingham C*	24	0	24 0
2014–15	Fulham	20	1	
2015–16	Fulham	32	0	61 1
2016–17	Wigan Ath	42	1	
2017–18	Wigan Ath	45	5	87 6

BYRNE, Nathan (D)   221 14
H: 5 10   W: 10 10   b.St Albans 5-6-92

2010–11	Tottenham H	0	0	
2010–11	*Brentford*	11	0	11 0
2011–12	Tottenham H	0	0	
2011–12	*Bournemouth*	9	0	9 0
2012–13	Tottenham H	0	0	
2012–13	*Crawley T*	12	1	12 1
2012–13	*Swindon T*	7	0	
2013–14	Swindon T	36	4	
2014–15	Swindon T	42	3	
2015–16	Swindon T	5	3	90 10
2015–16	Wolverhampton W	24	2	
2016–17	Wolverhampton W	0	0	24 2
2016–17	Wigan Ath	14	0	
2016–17	*Charlton Ath*	17	1	17 1
2017–18	Wigan Ath	44	0	58 0

COLCLOUGH, Ryan (F)   124 23
H: 5 9   W: 13 01   b.Budapest 27-12-94

2012–13	Crewe Alex	18	1	
2013–14	Crewe Alex	8	2	
2014–15	Crewe Alex	7	2	
2015–16	Crewe Alex	27	7	60 12
2015–16	Wigan Ath	10	2	
2016–17	*Milton Keynes D*	18	5	18 5
2016–17	Wigan Ath	10	0	
2017–18	Wigan Ath	26	4	46 6

COLE, Devante (F)   136 30
H: 6 1 W: 11 06 b.Alderley Edge 10-5-95
Internationals: England U16,U17,U18, U19.

2013–14	Manchester C	0	0	
2014–15	Manchester C	0	0	
2014–15	*Barnsley*	19	5	19 5
2014–15	*Milton Keynes D*	15	3	15 3
2015–16	Bradford C	19	5	19 5
2015–16	Fleetwood T	14	2	
2016–17	Fleetwood T	35	5	
2017–18	Fleetwood T	28	10	77 17
2017–18	Wigan Ath	6	0	6 0

CULSHAW, Mitchell (M)   0 0
b.Liverpool 15-9-01

2017–18	Wigan Ath	0	0

DANIELS, Donervorn (D)   103 6
H: 6 1 W: 14 05 b.Montserrat 24-11-93
Internationals: England U20.

2011–12	WBA	0	0	
2012–13	WBA	0	0	
2012–13	*Tranmere R*	13	1	13 1
2013–14	WBA	0	0	
2013–14	*Gillingham*	3	1	3 1
2014–15	WBA	0	0	
2014–15	*Blackpool*	19	1	19 1
2014–15	*Aberdeen*	9	0	9 0
2015–16	Wigan Ath	42	3	
2016–17	Wigan Ath	1	0	
2017–18	*Rochdale*	15	0	15 0
2017–18	Wigan Ath	1	0	44 3

DOWNEY, Joe (M)   0 0
b. 9-9-99

2017–18	Wigan Ath	0	0

DUNKLEY, Cheyenne (D)   121 14
H: 6 2 W: 13 05 b.Wolverhampton 13-2-92
Internationals: England C.
From Kidderminster H.

2014–15	Oxford U	9	0	
2015–16	Oxford U	29	4	
2016–17	Oxford U	40	3	78 7
2017–18	Wigan Ath	43	7	43 7

EVANS, Owen (G)   0 0
Internationals: Wales U19, U21.
From Hereford U.

2016–17	Wigan Ath	0	0
2017–18	Wigan Ath	0	0

FLORES, Jordan (F)   38 5
H: 5 9 W: 10 08 b.Wigan 4-10-95

2014–15	Wigan Ath	1	0	
2015–16	Wigan Ath	3	1	
2016–17	Wigan Ath	2	0	
2016–17	*Blackpool*	19	3	19 3
2017–18	Wigan Ath	0	0	6 1
2017–18	*Chesterfield*	13	1	13 1

GOLDEN, Tylor (D)   0 0
b.Ipswich 8-11-99

2017–18	Wigan Ath	0	0

GREGORY, Joshua (M)   0 0
b.Wigan 5-6-98

2016–17	Wigan Ath	0	0
2017–18	Wigan Ath	0	0

GRIGG, Will (M)   293 101
H: 5 11 W: 11 00 b.Solihull 3-7-91
Internationals: Northern Ireland U19, U21,
Full caps.

2008–09	Walsall	1	0	
2009–10	Walsall	0	0	
2010–11	Walsall	28	4	
2011–12	Walsall	29	4	
2012–13	Walsall	41	19	99 27
2013–14	Brentford	34	5	
2014–15	Brentford	0	0	34 5
2014–15	*Milton Keynes D*	44	20	44 20
2015–16	Wigan Ath	40	25	
2016–17	Wigan Ath	33	5	
2017–18	Wigan Ath	43	19	116 49

HILTON, Tom (D)   0 0
b.Manchester 30-9-99

2017–18	Wigan Ath	0	0

HUNT, Noel (F)   368 72
H: 5 8 W: 11 05 b.Waterford 26-12-82
Internationals: Republic of Ireland U21, B,
Full caps.

2002–03	Dunfermline Ath	12	1	
2003–04	Dunfermline Ath	13	2	
2004–05	Dunfermline Ath	23	1	
2005–06	Dunfermline Ath	32	4	80 8
2006–07	Dundee U	28	10	
2007–08	Dundee U	36	13	64 23

2008–09	Reading	37	11	
2009–10	Reading	10	2	
2010–11	Reading	33	10	
2011–12	Reading	41	8	
2012–13	Reading	24	2	145 33
2013–14	Leeds U	19	0	
2014–15	Leeds U	1	0	20 0
2014–15	*Ipswich T*	11	3	11 3
2015–16	Southend U	21	4	21 4
2016–17	Portsmouth	20	1	20 1
2017–18	Wigan Ath	7	0	7 0

JACOBS, Michael (M)   297 47
H: 5 9 W: 11 08 b.Rothwell 23-3-92

2009–10	Northampton T	0	0	
2010–11	Northampton T	41	5	
2011–12	Northampton T	46	6	87 11
2012–13	Derby Co	38	2	
2013–14	Derby Co	3	0	41 2
2013–14	Wolverhampton W	30	8	
2014–15	Wolverhampton W	12	0	42 8
2014–15	*Blackpool*	5	1	5 1
2015–16	Wigan Ath	35	10	
2016–17	Wigan Ath	43	3	
2017–18	Wigan Ath	44	12	122 25

JAMES, Reece (D)   62 2
H: 5 6 W: 11 03 b.Bacup 7-11-93

2012–13	Manchester U	0	0	
2013–14	Manchester U	0	0	
2013–14	*Carlisle U*	1	0	1 0
2014–15	Manchester U	0	0	
2014–15	*Rotherham U*	7	0	7 0
2014–15	*Huddersfield T*	6	1	6 1
2015–16	Wigan Ath	26	1	
2016–17	Wigan Ath	0	0	
2017–18	Wigan Ath	22	0	48 1

JONES, Jamie (G)   270 0
H: 6 2 W: 14 05 b.Kirkby 18-2-89

2007–08	Everton	0	0	
2008–09	Leyton Orient	20	0	
2009–10	Leyton Orient	36	0	
2010–11	Leyton Orient	35	0	
2011–12	Leyton Orient	6	0	
2012–13	Leyton Orient	26	0	
2013–14	Leyton Orient	28	0	151 0
2014–15	Preston NE	17	0	
2014–15	*Coventry C*	4	0	4 0
2014–15	*Rochdale*	13	0	13 0
2015–16	Preston NE	0	0	17 0
2015–16	*Colchester U*	17	0	17 0
2015–16	Stevenage	17	0	
2016–17	Stevenage	36	0	53 0
2017–18	Wigan Ath	15	0	15 0

KELLETT, Andy (D)   66 7
H: 5 8 W: 12 06 b.Bolton 10-11-93

2012–13	Bolton W	0	0	
2013–14	Bolton W	3	0	
2014–15	Bolton W	1	0	
2014–15	*Plymouth Arg*	12	1	12 1
2014–15	*Manchester U*	0	0	
2015–16	Bolton W	0	0	4 0
2016–17	Wigan Ath	9	2	
2016–17	Wigan Ath	5	0	
2017–18	Wigan Ath	0	0	14 2
2017–18	*Chesterfield*	36	4	36 4

LANG, Callum (F)   30 10
H: 5 11 W: 11 00 b. 8-9-98

2016–17	Wigan Ath	0	0	
2017–18	Wigan Ath	0	0	
2017–18	*Morecambe*	30	10	30 10

LAURENT, Josh (M)   54 2
H: 6 0 W: 11 00 b.Leytonstone 6-5-95

2013–14	QPR	0	0	
2014–15	QPR	0	0	
2015–16	Brentford	0	0	
2015–16	*Newport Co*	3	0	3 0
2015–16	Hartlepool U	3	0	
2016–17	Hartlepool U	25	1	28 1
2016–17	Wigan Ath	1	0	
2017–18	Wigan Ath	0	0	1 0
2017–18	*Bury*	22	1	22 1

LAVERCOMBE, Dan (G)   0 0
H: 6 3 W: 11 03 b.Torquay 16-5-96

2013–14	Torquay U	0	0

From Torquay U.

2015–16	Wigan Ath	0	0
2016–17	Wigan Ath	0	0
2017–18	Wigan Ath	0	0

LONG, Adam (D)   0 0
b. 11-00-00

2017–18	Wigan Ath	0	0

MACDONALD, Shaun (M)   208 11
H: 6 1 W: 11 04 b.Swansea 17-6-88
Internationals: Wales U19, U21, Full caps.

2005–06	Swansea C	7	0	
2006–07	Swansea C	8	0	
2007–08	Swansea C	1	0	
2008–09	Swansea C	5	0	
2008–09	*Yeovil T*	4	2	
2009–10	Swansea C	3	0	
2009–10	*Yeovil T*	31	3	
2010–11	Swansea C	0	0	
2010–11	*Yeovil T*	26	4	61 9
2011–12	Swansea C	0	0	24 0
2011–12	Bournemouth	25	1	
2012–13	Bournemouth	28	0	
2013–14	Bournemouth	23	0	
2014–15	Bournemouth	5	0	
2015–16	Bournemouth	3	0	84 1
2016–17	Wigan Ath	39	1	
2017–18	Wigan Ath	0	0	39 1

MAFFEO, Victor (D)   0 0
b.Barcelona 18-9-00

2017–18	Wigan Ath	0	0

MALUMO, Mwiya (F)   0 0
b. 26-10-99
From Oldham Ath.

2017–18	Wigan Ath	0	0

MASSEY, Gavin (F)   267 37
H: 5 11 W: 11 06 b.Watford 14-10-92

2009–10	Watford	3	0	
2010–11	Watford	3	0	
2011–12	Watford	3	0	
2011–12	*Yeovil T*	16	3	16 3
2011–12	*Colchester U*	8	0	
2012–13	Watford	0	0	7 0
2012–13	Colchester U	40	6	
2013–14	Colchester U	30	3	
2014–15	Colchester U	46	7	
2015–16	Colchester U	42	4	166 20
2016–17	Leyton Orient	36	8	36 8
2017–18	Wigan Ath	42	6	42 6

McGUFFIE, Will (D)   0 0
b.Birkenhead 27-10-00
From Wolverhampton W.

2017–18	Wigan Ath	0	0

MERRIE, Christopher (M)   0 0
b.Liverpool 2-11-98
From Everton.

2017–18	Wigan Ath	0	0

MORSY, Sam (M)   256 15
H: 5 9 W: 12 06 b.Wolverhampton 10-9-91
Internationals: Egypt Full caps.

2009–10	Port Vale	1	0	
2010–11	Port Vale	16	1	
2011–12	Port Vale	26	1	
2012–13	Port Vale	28	2	71 4
2013–14	Chesterfield	34	1	
2014–15	Chesterfield	39	2	
2015–16	Chesterfield	26	4	99 7
2015–16	Wigan Ath	16	1	
2016–17	*Barnsley*	14	0	14 0
2016–17	Wigan Ath	15	1	
2017–18	Wigan Ath	41	2	72 4

PERKINS, David (M)   413 15
H: 5 6 W: 11 06 b.Heysham 21-6-82
Internationals: England C.

2006–07	Rochdale	18	0	
2007–08	Rochdale	40	4	58 4
2008–09	Colchester U	38	5	
2009–10	Colchester U	5	1	
2009–10	*Chesterfield*	13	1	13 1
2009–10	*Stockport Co*	22	0	22 0
2010–11	Colchester U	36	1	79 7
2011–12	Barnsley	33	1	
2012–13	Barnsley	35	1	
2013–14	Barnsley	23	0	91 2
2013–14	Blackpool	20	0	
2014–15	Blackpool	45	0	65 0
2015–16	Wigan Ath	45	0	
2016–17	Wigan Ath	27	0	
2017–18	Wigan Ath	13	1	85 1

PERRIN, Jordan (G)   0 0
b. 18-9-99
From Arsenal.

2017–18	Wigan Ath	0	0

PLANT, Anthony (D)   0 0
b.St Helens 26-10-99

2017–18	Wigan Ath	0	0

POWELL, Nick (F) 155 43
H: 6 0　W: 10 05　b.Crewe 23-3-94
Internationals: England U16, U17, U18, U19, U21.

2010–11	Crewe Alex	17	0		
2011–12	Crewe Alex	38	14	55	14
2012–13	Manchester U	2	1		
2013–14	Manchester U	0	0		
2013–14	Wigan Ath	31	7		
2014–15	Manchester U	0	0		
2014–15	Leicester C	3	0	3	0
2015–16	Manchester U	1	0	3	1
2015–16	Hull C	3	0	3	0
2016–17	Wigan Ath	21	6		
2017–18	Wigan Ath	39	15	91	28

POWER, Max (M) 235 23
H: 5 11　W: 11 13　b.Bebington 27-7-93

2010–11	Tranmere R	0	0		
2011–12	Tranmere R	4	0		
2012–13	Tranmere R	27	3		
2013–14	Tranmere R	33	2		
2014–15	Tranmere R	45	7	109	12
2015–16	Wigan Ath	44	6		
2016–17	Wigan Ath	40	5		
2017–18	Wigan Ath	40	5	126	11

ROBERTS, Gary (F) 448 81
H: 5 10　W: 11 09　b.Chester 18-3-84
Internationals: England C.

2006–07	Accrington S	14	8	14	8
2006–07	Ipswich T	33	2		
2007–08	Ipswich T	21	1	54	3
2007–08	Crewe Alex	4	0	4	0
2008–09	Huddersfield T	43	9		
2009–10	Huddersfield T	43	7		
2010–11	Huddersfield T	37	9		
2011–12	Huddersfield T	39	6	162	31
2012–13	Swindon T	39	4	39	4
2013–14	Chesterfield	40	11		
2014–15	Chesterfield	34	6	74	17
2015–16	Portsmouth	33	7		
2016–17	Portsmouth	41	10		
2017–18	Portsmouth	0	0	74	17
2017–18	Wigan Ath	27	1	27	1

ROBERTS, Theo (G) 0 0
b. 10-9-98

| 2016–17 | Wigan Ath | 0 | 0 | | |
| 2017–18 | Wigan Ath | 0 | 0 | | |

STUBBS, Sam (D) 5 0
b. 20-11-98

2016–17	Wigan Ath	0	0		
2017–18	Wigan Ath	0	0		
2017–18	Crewe Alex	5	0	5	0

THOMAS, Terell (D) 3 0
H: 6 0　b. 13-10-97

2014–15	Charlton Ath	0	0		
2015–16	Charlton Ath	0	0		
2016–17	Charlton Ath	0	0		
2017–18	Wigan Ath	3	0	3	0

VAUGHAN, James (F) 264 76
H: 5 11　W: 13 00　b.Birmingham 14-7-88
Internationals: England U17, U19, U21.

2004–05	Everton	2	1		
2005–06	Everton	1	0		
2006–07	Everton	14	4		
2007–08	Everton	8	1		
2008–09	Everton	13	0		
2009–10	Everton	8	1		
2009–10	Derby Co	2	0	2	0
2010–11	Everton	1	0	47	7
2010–11	Crystal Palace	30	9	30	9
2011–12	Norwich C	5	0		
2012–13	Norwich C	0	0	5	0
2012–13	Huddersfield T	33	14		
2013–14	Huddersfield T	23	10		
2014–15	Huddersfield T	26	7		
2015–16	Huddersfield T	4	0	86	31
2015–16	Birmingham C	15	0	15	0
2016–17	Bury	37	24	37	24
2017–18	Sunderland	23	2	23	2
2017–18	Wigan Ath	19	3	19	3

WALKER, Jamie (M) 187 40
H: 5 9　W: 11 00　b.Edinburgh 25-6-93
Internationals: Scotland U16, U17, U19, U21.

2011–12	Hearts	0	0		
2011–12	Raith R	23	3	23	3
2012–13	Hearts	24	2		
2013–14	Hearts	26	3		
2014–15	Hearts	33	11		
2015–16	Hearts	23	7		
2016–17	Hearts	34	12		
2017–18	Hearts	16	2	156	37
2017–18	Wigan Ath	8	0	8	0

WEIR, Jensen (M) 0 0
b.Warrington 31-1-02

| 2017–18 | Wigan Ath | 0 | 0 | | |

WHITEHEAD, Danny (M) 8 0
H: 5 10　W: 10 11　b.Trafford 23-10-93

2013–14	West Ham U	0	0		
2014–15	West Ham U	0	0		
2014–15	Accrington S	2	0	2	0
From Macclesfield T.					
2015–16	Wigan Ath	0	0		
2016–17	Wigan Ath	0	0		
2016–17	Cheltenham T	6	0	6	0
2017–18	Wigan Ath	0	0		

Players retained or with offer of contract
Morgan, Craig.

Scholars
Baningime, Divin; Berry-McNally, James Jon; Cotter, James; Culshaw, Mitchell Scott; Downey, Joseph Paul; Golden, Tylor Reed; Hilton, Thomas Andrew Fred; Jolley, Charlie Patrick; Long, Adam David; Maffeo, Becerra Victor Alfonso; Malumo, Mwiya; McGaughey, Kain Alex; McGuffie, Will Jared; Monaghan, Neil Stephen; Perrin, Jordan-John Richard; Plant, Anthony; Roberts, Bradley Ian; Roberts, Theo Paul; Smith, Scott.

WOLVERHAMPTON W (90)

ARMSTRONG, Daniel (M) 6 0
b. 11-10-97

| 2017–18 | Wolverhampton W | 0 | 0 | | |
| 2017–18 | Dunfermline Ath | 6 | 0 | 6 | 0 |

BATTH, Danny (D) 267 17
H: 6 3　W: 13 05　b.Brierley Hill 21-9-90

2009–10	Wolverhampton W	0	0		
2009–10	Colchester U	17	1	17	1
2010–11	Wolverhampton W	0	0		
2010–11	Sheffield U	1	0	1	0
2010–11	Sheffield W	10	0		
2011–12	Wolverhampton W	0	0		
2011–12	Sheffield W	44	2	54	2
2012–13	Wolverhampton W	12	1		
2013–14	Wolverhampton W	46	2		
2014–15	Wolverhampton W	44	4		
2015–16	Wolverhampton W	38	2		
2016–17	Wolverhampton W	39	4		
2017–18	Wolverhampton W	16	1	195	14

BENNETT, Ryan (M) 321 15
H: 6 2　W: 11 00　b.Thurrock 6-3-90
Internationals: England U18, U21.

2006–07	Grimsby T	5	0		
2007–08	Grimsby T	40	1		
2008–09	Grimsby T	45	5		
2009–10	Grimsby T	13	0	103	6
2009–10	Peterborough U	22	1		
2010–11	Peterborough U	34	4		
2011–12	Peterborough U	32	1	88	6
2011–12	Norwich C	8	0		
2012–13	Norwich C	15	1		
2013–14	Norwich C	16	1		
2014–15	Norwich C	7	0		
2015–16	Norwich C	22	0		
2016–17	Norwich C	33	0	101	2
2017–18	Wolverhampton W	29	1	29	1

BOLY, Willy (D) 162 8
H: 6 1　W: 12 11　b. 3-2-91
Internationals: France U16, U17, U19.

2010–11	Auxerre	8	1		
2011–12	Auxerre	33	1		
2012–13	Auxerre	25	1		
2013–14	Auxerre	30	0		
2014–15	Auxerre	1	0	97	3
2014–15	Braga	0	0		
2015–16	Braga	22	2		
2016–17	Braga	3	0	25	2
2016–17	Porto	4	0	4	0
2017–18	FC Porto	0	0		
On loan from FC Porto.					
2017–18	Wolverhampton W	36	3	36	3

BURGOYNE, Harry (G) 9 0
H: 6 4　W: 13 05　b.Ludlow 28-12-96

2015–16	Wolverhampton W	0	0		
2016–17	Barnet	2	0	2	0
2016–17	Wolverhampton W	6	0		
2017–18	Wolverhampton W	1	0	7	0

BUUR, Oskar (D) 11 1
b.Skanderborg 31-3-98
Internationals: Denmark U16, U17, U18, U19.

2014–15	AGF	8	0		
2015–16	AGF	1	0		
2016–17	AGF	1	0	10	0
2017–18	Wolverhampton W	1	1	1	1

COADY, Conor (D) 207 9
H: 6 1　W: 11 05　b.Liverpool 25-2-93
Internationals: England U16, U17, U18, U19, U20.

2010–11	Liverpool	0	0		
2011–12	Liverpool	0	0		
2012–13	Liverpool	1	0		
2013–14	Liverpool	0	0	1	0
2013–14	Sheffield U	39	5	39	5
2014–15	Huddersfield T	45	3	45	3
2015–16	Wolverhampton W	37	0		
2016–17	Wolverhampton W	40	0		
2017–18	Wolverhampton W	45	1	122	1

COLLINS, Aaron (F) 48 4
b. 27-5-97
Internationals: Wales U19.

2014–15	Newport Co	2	0		
2015–16	Newport Co	18	2		
2015–16	Wolverhampton W	0	0		
2016–17	Wolverhampton W	0	0		
2016–17	Notts Co	18	2	18	2
2017–18	Wolverhampton W	0	0		
2017–18	Newport Co	10	0	30	2

DESLANDES, Sylvain (D) 6 0
H: 6 1　W: 11 11　b.Kouoptamo 25-4-97
Internationals: France U16, U17, U18, U19, U20.

2014–15	Caen	0	0		
2015–16	Wolverhampton W	3	0		
2016–17	Wolverhampton W	0	0		
2016–17	Bury	0	0		
2017–18	Wolverhampton W	1	0	4	0
2017–18	Portsmouth	2	0	2	0

DOHERTY, Matthew (M) 216 15
H: 6 0　W: 12 08　b.Dublin 17-1-92
Internationals: Republic of Ireland U19, U21, Full caps.

2010–11	Wolverhampton W	0	0		
2011–12	Wolverhampton W	1	0		
2011–12	Hibernian	13	2	13	2
2012–13	Wolverhampton W	13	1		
2012–13	Bury	17	1	17	1
2013–14	Wolverhampton W	18	1		
2014–15	Wolverhampton W	33	0		
2015–16	Wolverhampton W	34	2		
2016–17	Wolverhampton W	42	4		
2017–18	Wolverhampton W	45	4	186	12

DOUGLAS, Barry (D) 257 22
H: 5 9　W: 10 00　b.Glasgow 4-9-89
Internationals: Scotland Full caps.

2008–09	Queen's Park	30	2		
2009–10	Queen's Park	35	8	65	10
2010–11	Dundee U	23	2		
2011–12	Dundee U	10	1		
2012–13	Dundee U	28	1	61	4
2013–14	Lech Poznan	18	0		
2014–15	Lech Poznan	27	3		
2015–16	Lech Poznan	13	0	58	3
2015–16	Konyaspor	12	0		
2016–17	Konyaspor	22	0	34	0
2017–18	Wolverhampton W	39	5	39	5

EBANKS-LANDELL, Ethan (M) 129 12
H: 5 6　W: 11 02　b.Oldbury 16-12-92

2009–10	Wolverhampton W	0	0		
2010–11	Wolverhampton W	0	0		
2011–12	Wolverhampton W	0	0		
2012–13	Wolverhampton W	0	0		
2012–13	Bury	24	0	24	0
2013–14	Wolverhampton W	7	2		
2014–15	Wolverhampton W	14	2		
2015–16	Wolverhampton W	21	1		
2016–17	Wolverhampton W	0	0		
2016–17	Sheffield U	34	5	34	5
2017–18	Wolverhampton W	0	0	42	5
2017–18	Milton Keynes D	29	2	29	2

ENNIS, Niall (F) 1 0
H: 5 10　W: 12 00　b.Wolverhampton 20-5-99
Internationals: England U17, U18.

| 2017–18 | Wolverhampton W | 0 | 0 | | |
| 2017–18 | Shrewsbury T | 1 | 0 | 1 | 0 |

ENOBAKHARE, Bright (F) 41 1
H: 6 0　W: 12 06　b. 8-2-98

| 2015–16 | Wolverhampton W | 7 | 0 | | |

2016–17	Wolverhampton W	13	0		
2017–18	Wolverhampton W	21	1	41	1

FLATT, Jonathan (G)   4 0
H: 6 1   W: 13 12   b.Wolverhampton 12-9-94

2013–14	Wolverhampton W	0	0		
2014–15	Wolverhampton W	0	0		
2014–15	*Chesterfield*	0	0		
2015–16	Wolverhampton W	0	0		
2015–16	*Cheltenham T*	0	0		
2016–17	Wolverhampton W	0	0		
2017–18	Wolverhampton W	0	0		
2017–18	*Cheltenham T*	4	0	4	0

GRAHAM, Jordan (M)   25 1
H: 6 0   W: 10 10   b.Coventry 5-3-95
Internationals: England U16, U17.

2011–12	Aston Villa	0	0		
2012–13	Aston Villa	0	0		
2013–14	Aston Villa	0	0		
2013–14	*Ipswich T*	2	0	2	0
2013–14	*Bradford C*	1	0	1	0
2014–15	Wolverhampton W	0	0		
2015–16	Wolverhampton W	11	1		
2015–16	*Oxford U*	5	0	5	0
2016–17	Wolverhampton W	2	0		
2017–18	Wolverhampton W	1	0	14	1
2017–18	*Fulham*	3	0	3	0

HAUSE, Kortney (D)   104 5
H: 6 2   W: 13 03   b.Goodmayes 16-7-95
Internationals: England U20, U21.

2012–13	Wycombe W	9	1		
2013–14	Wycombe W	14	1	23	2
2013–14	Wolverhampton W	0	0		
2014–15	Wolverhampton W	17	0		
2014–15	*Gillingham*	14	1	14	1
2015–16	Wolverhampton W	25	0		
2016–17	Wolverhampton W	24	2		
2017–18	Wolverhampton W	1	0	67	2

HELDER COSTA, Wander (M)   102 18
H: 5 10   W: 11 07   b.Luanda 12-1-94
Internationals: Portugal U16, U17, U18, U19, U20, U21, U23.

2013–14	Benfica	0	0		
2014–15	Benfica	0	0		
2014–15	*Deportivo La Coruna*	6	0	6	0
2015–16	Benfica	0	0		
2015–16	*Monaco*	25	3	25	3
2016–17	Benfica	0	0		
2016–17	*Wolverhampton W*	35	10		
2017–18	Wolverhampton W	36	5	71	15

IORFA, Dominic (D)   114 1
H: 6 2   W: 12 04   b.Southend-on-Sea 24-6-95
Internationals: England U18, U20, U21.

2013–14	Wolverhampton W	0	0		
2013–14	*Shrewsbury T*	7	0	7	0
2014–15	Wolverhampton W	20	0		
2015–16	Wolverhampton W	42	0		
2016–17	Wolverhampton W	22	0		
2017–18	Wolverhampton W	0	0	84	0
2017–18	*Ipswich T*	23	1	23	1

IVAN CAVALEIRO, Ricardo (M)   127 18
H: 5 9   W: 11 07   b.Vialonga 18-10-93
Internationals: Portugal U17, U18, U19, U20, U21, Full caps.

2012–13	Benfica	0	0		
2013–14	Benfica	8	0		
2014–15	Benfica	0	0	8	0
2014–15	*Deportivo La Coruna*	34	3	34	3
2015–16	*Monaco*	12	1	12	1
2016–17	Wolverhampton W	31	5		
2017–18	Wolverhampton W	42	9	73	14

JOHNSON, Connor (D)   0 0
b.Kettering 10-3-98

2016–17	Wolverhampton W	0	0
2017–18	Wolverhampton W	0	0

JOTA, Diogo (F)   112 39
H: 5 10   W: 11 00   b.Massarelos 4-12-96
Internationals: Portugal U19, U21, U23.

2014–15	Pacos Ferreira	10	2		
2015–16	Pacos Ferreira	31	12	41	14
2016–17	Atletico Madrid	0	0		
2016–17	*Porto*	27	8	27	8
2017–18	Atletico Madrid	0	0		

On loan from Atletico Madrid.

2017–18	Wolverhampton W	44	17	44	17

LEO BONATINI, Lohner (F)   122 45
b. 28-3-94
Internationals: Brazil U17.

2013	Cruzeiro	0	0
2013	Goias	5	0
2014	Cruzeiro	0	0

2014	Goias	1	0	6	0
2014–15	Estoril	15	4		
2015	Cruzeiro	0	0		
2015–16	Estoril	33	17	48	21
2016–17	Al Hilal	25	12		
2017–18	Al Hilal	0	0	25	12

On loan from Al Hilal.

2017–18	Wolverhampton W	43	12	43	12

MARSHALL, Ben (F)   316 38
H: 5 11   W: 11 13   b.Salford 29-3-91
Internationals: England U21.

2009–10	Stoke C	0	0		
2009–10	*Northampton T*	15	2	15	2
2009–10	*Cheltenham T*	6	2	6	2
2009–10	*Carlisle U*	20	3		
2010–11	Stoke C	0	0		
2010–11	*Carlisle U*	33	3	53	6
2011–12	Stoke C	0	0		
2011–12	*Sheffield W*	5	2	22	5
2011–12	Leicester C	16	3		
2012–13	Leicester C	40	4		
2013–14	Leicester C	0	0	56	7
2013–14	Blackburn R	18	2		
2014–15	Blackburn R	42	6		
2015–16	Blackburn R	44	2		
2016–17	Blackburn R	22	1	126	11
2016–17	Wolverhampton W	16	2		
2017–18	Wolverhampton W	6	0	22	2
2017–18	*Millwall*	16	3	16	3

MASON, Joe (F)   230 52
H: 5 9   W: 11 11   b.Plymouth 13-5-91
Internationals: Republic of Ireland U18, U19, U21.

2009–10	Plymouth Arg	19	3		
2010–11	Plymouth Arg	34	7	53	10
2011–12	Cardiff C	39	9		
2012–13	Cardiff C	28	6		
2013–14	Cardiff C	0	0		
2013–14	*Bolton W*	16	6		
2014–15	Cardiff C	7	1		
2014–15	*Bolton W*	12	4	28	10
2015–16	Cardiff C	23	6	97	22
2015–16	Wolverhampton W	16	3		
2016–17	Wolverhampton W	19	3		
2017–18	Wolverhampton W	0	0	35	6
2017–18	*Burton Alb*	6	1	6	1
2018	*Colorado Rapids*	11	3	11	3

Transferred to Colorado Rapids, February 2018.

MIR, Rafa (F)   4 0
H: 6 1   W: 11 11   b.Murcia 18-6-97

2014–15	Valencia	0	0		
2015–16	Valencia	0	0		
2016–17	Valencia	2	0		
2017–18	Valencia	0	0	2	0
2017–18	Wolverhampton W	2	0	2	0

N'DIAYE, Alfred (M)   210 11
H: 6 2   W: 13 08   b.Paris 6-3-90
Internationals: France U17, U19, U20, U21. Senegal Full caps.

2008–09	AS Nancy	24	0		
2009–10	AS Nancy	23	0		
2010–11	AS Nancy	13	0	60	0
2011–12	Bursaspor	32	3		
2012–13	Bursaspor	13	1	45	4
2012–13	Sunderland	16	0		
2013–14	Sunderland	0	0	16	0
2013–14	*Eskisehirspor*	16	3	16	3
2013–14	*Real Betis*	16	0	16	0
2016–17	Villarreal	7	0		
2016–17	*Hull C*	15	1	15	1
2017–18	Villarreal	2	0	9	0

On loan from Villarreal.

2017–18	Wolverhampton W	33	3	33	3

NAZON, Duckens (F)   37 12
b.Paris 7-4-94
Internationals: Haiti U20, Full caps.
From Kerala Blasters.

2017–18	Wolverhampton W	0	0		
2017–18	*Coventry C*	21	6	21	6
2017–18	*Oldham Ath*	16	6	16	6

NEVES, Ruben (M)   101 9
H: 5 11   W: 12 08   b. 13-3-97
Internationals: Portugal U16, U17, U18, U21, U23, Full caps.

2014–15	Porto	24	1		
2015–16	Porto	22	1		
2016–17	Porto	13	1	59	3
2017–18	Wolverhampton W	42	6	42	6

NORRIS, Will (G)   70 0
H: 6 5   W: 11 09   b.Royston 12-7-93

2014–15	Cambridge U	3	0

2015–16	Cambridge U	21	0		
2016–17	Cambridge U	45	0	69	0
2017–18	Wolverhampton W	1	0	1	0

POTE, Pedro Goncalves (M)   0 0
Internationals: Portugal U18, U20.
From Braga, Valencia.

2017–18	Wolverhampton W	0	0

PRICE, Jack (M)   108 2
H: 6 3   W: 13 10   b.Shrewsbury 19-12-92

2011–12	Wolverhampton W	0	0		
2012–13	Wolverhampton W	0	0		
2013–14	Wolverhampton W	26	0		
2014–15	Wolverhampton W	23	1		
2014–15	*Yeovil T*	6	0	6	0
2014–15	*Leyton Orient*	5	0	5	0
2015–16	Wolverhampton W	24	1		
2016–17	Wolverhampton W	19	0		
2017–18	Wolverhampton W	5	0	97	2

Transferred to Colorado Rapids, January 2018.

RANDALL, Will (M)   18 0
H: 5 11   W: 10 03   b.Swindon 2-5-97

2013–14	Swindon T	1	0		
2014–15	Swindon T	4	0		
2015–16	Swindon T	4	0	9	0
2015–16	Wolverhampton W	0	0		
2016–17	Wolverhampton W	0	0		
2016–17	*Walsall*	2	0	2	0
2017–18	Wolverhampton W	0	0		
2017–18	*Forest Green R*	7	0	7	0

RODERICK MIRANDA, Jefferson (D)1234
H: 6 3   W: 12 08   b.Odivelas 30-3-91
Internationals: Portugal U17, U18, U19, U20.

2009–10	Benfica	0	0		
2010–11	Benfica	5	0		
2011–12	Benfica	0	0		
2011–12	*Servette*	24	0	24	0
2012–13	Benfica	2	0	7	0
2012–13	*Deportivo La Coruna*	3	0	3	0
2013–14	Rio Ave	18	0		
2014–15	Rio Ave	3	0		
2015–16	Rio Ave	18	1		
2016–17	Rio Ave	33	3	72	4
2017–18	Wolverhampton W	17	0	17	0

RONAN, Connor (M)   23 0
H: 5 8   W: 11 00   b.Rochdale 6-3-98
Internationals: England U17. Republic of Ireland U17, U19, U21.

2015–16	Wolverhampton W	0	0		
2016–17	Wolverhampton W	4	0		
2017–18	Wolverhampton W	3	0	7	0
2017–18	*Portsmouth*	16	0	16	0

RUBEN VINAGRE, Goncalo (D)   9 1
b. 9-4-99
Internationals: Portugal U16, U17, U18, U19.

2016–17	Monaco	0	0		
2017–18	Monaco	0	0		

On loan from Monaco.

2017–18	Wolverhampton W	9	1	9	1

RUDDY, Jack (G)   17 0
H: 6 1   W: 13 01   b.Glasgow 18-5-97
Internationals: Scotland U21.

2014–15	Bury	0	0		
2015–16	Bury	1	0		
2016–17	Bury	0	0	1	0
2016–17	Wolverhampton W	0	0		
2017–18	Wolverhampton W	0	0		
2017–18	*Oldham Ath*	5	0	5	0
2017–18	*Ayr U*	11	0	11	0

RUDDY, John (G)   414 0
H: 6 3   W: 12 07   b.St Ives 24-10-86
Internationals: England Full caps.

2003–04	Cambridge U	0	0		
2004–05	Cambridge U	38	0	39	0
2005–06	Everton	0	0		
2005–06	*Walsall*	5	0	5	0
2005–06	*Rushden & D*	3	0	3	0
2005–06	*Chester C*	4	0	4	0
2006–07	Everton	0	0		
2006–07	*Stockport Co*	11	0		
2006–07	*Wrexham*	5	0	5	0
2006–07	*Bristol C*	1	0	1	0
2007–08	Everton	0	0		
2007–08	*Stockport Co*	12	0	23	0
2008–09	Everton	0	0		
2008–09	*Crewe Alex*	19	0	19	0
2009–10	Everton	0	0	1	0
2009–10	*Motherwell*	34	0	34	0
2010–11	Norwich C	45	0		
2011–12	Norwich C	37	0		
2012–13	Norwich C	15	0		

2013–14	Norwich C	38	0		
2014–15	Norwich C	46	0		
2015–16	Norwich C	27	0		
2016–17	Norwich C	27	0	235	0
2017–18	Wolverhampton W	45	0	45	0

SAISS, Romain (M) 223 14
H: 6 3 W: 12 00 b.Bourg-de-Peage 26-3-90
Internationals: Morocco Full caps.

2010–11	Valence	13	4	13	4
2011–12	Clermont	17	1		
2012–13	Clermont	31	0	48	1
2013–14	Le Havre	27	1		
2014–15	Le Havre	34	2	61	3
2015–16	Angers	35	2	35	2
2016–17	Wolverhampton W	24	0		
2017–18	Wolverhampton W	42	4	66	4

STEVENSON, Ben (M) 46 4
H: 6 0 W: 10 08 b.Leicester 23-3-97

2015–16	Coventry C	0	0		
2016–17	Coventry C	28	2		
2017–18	Coventry C	5	0	33	2
2017–18	Wolverhampton W	0	0		
2017–18	Colchester U	13	2	13	2

WHITE, Morgan (M) 20 0
b. 27-1-00
Internationals: England U16, U17.

2016–17	Wolverhampton W	7	0		
2017–18	Wolverhampton W	13	0	20	0

WILSON, Donovan (F) 9 1
b.Yate 14-3-97

2014–15	Wolverhampton W	0	0		
2015–16	Wolverhampton W	0	0		
2016–17	Wolverhampton W	1	0		
2017–18	Wolverhampton W	0	0	1	0
2017–18	Port Vale	8	1	8	1

ZYRO, Michal (M) 116 19
b.Warsaw 20-9-92
Internationals: Poland U19, U21, Full caps.

2009–10	Legia Warsaw	1	0		
2010–11	Legia Warsaw	6	0		
2011–12	Legia Warsaw	25	1		
2012–13	Legia Warsaw	9	2		
2013–14	Legia Warsaw	23	4		
2014–15	Legia Warsaw	27	5		
2015–16	Legia Warsaw	5	1	96	13
2015–16	Wolverhampton W	7	3		
2016–17	Wolverhampton W	0	0		
2017–18	Wolverhampton W	0	0	7	3
2017–18	Charlton Ath	13	3	13	3

Players retained or with offer of contract
Ashley-Seal, Bernard Patrick; Beasley, Harry Alexander; Csoka, Daniel; Gladon, Paul; Goodliffe, Ben David; Harris-Sealy, Andrew Jay; Hayden, Aaron Edward-George; Herc, Christian; Heredia, Fontana Carlos; Ikeme, Carl; John, Cameron Bradley; Leak, Ryan David; McKenna, Daniel; Neto, Hanne Boubacar Rafael; Ofosu-Ayeh, Phil; Oniangue, Prince Alban; Otasowie, Ebeguowen; Rasmussen, Oskar Buur; Samuels, Austin Jordan; Sauvage, Enzo Claude; Seedorf, Sherwin; Simpson, Aaron; Sondergaard, Andreas; Watt, Elliot William; Yang, Ming-Yang.

Scholars
Berkoe, Kevin; Bexton, Thomas; Brown, Rory Francis; Carr, Bradley Paul; Crabtree, Aaron; Feeney, Kieran Jack; Giles, Ryan John; Hesson, Joshua Scott; Lattie, Diego Omar; Moan, Dominic; O'Sullivan, Ray; Perry, Taylor; Sanderson, Dion Dannie Leonard; Taylor, Terence; Thompson, Callum Niall; Townsend, Taylor; Whittingham, Joel Cameron.

WYCOMBE W (91)

AINSWORTH, Gareth (M) 539 105
H: 5 10 W: 12 05 b.Blackburn 10-5-73

1991–92	Preston NE	5	0		
1992–93	Cambridge U	4	1	4	1
1992–93	Preston NE	26	0		
1993–94	Preston NE	38	11		
1994–95	Preston NE	16	1		
1995–96	Preston NE	2	0		
1995–96	Lincoln C	31	12		
1996–97	Lincoln C	46	22		
1997–98	Lincoln C	6	3	83	37
1997–98	Port Vale	40	5		
1998–99	Port Vale	15	5	55	10
1998–99	Wimbledon	8	0		
1999–2000	Wimbledon	2	2		
2000–01	Wimbledon	12	2		
2001–02	Wimbledon	5	0		
2001–02	Preston NE	5	1	92	13
2002–03	Wimbledon	12	2	36	6
2002–03	Walsall	5	1	5	1
2002–03	Cardiff C	9	0	9	0
2003–04	QPR	29	6		
2004–05	QPR	22	2		
2005–06	QPR	43	9		
2006–07	QPR	22	1		
2007–08	QPR	24	3		
2008–09	QPR	0	0		
2009–10	QPR	1	0	141	21
2009–10	Wycombe W	14	2		
2010–11	Wycombe W	43	10		
2011–12	Wycombe W	32	2		
2012–13	Wycombe W	25	2		
2013–14	Wycombe W	0	0		
2014–15	Wycombe W	0	0		
2015–16	Wycombe W	0	0		
2016–17	Wycombe W	0	0		
2017–18	Wycombe W	0	0	114	16

AKINFENWA, Adebayo (F) 552 177
H: 5 11 W: 13 07 b.Nigeria 10-5-82

2001	Atlantas	19	4		
2002	Atlantas	4	1	23	5
From Barry T					
2003–04	Boston U	3	0	3	0
2003–04	Leyton Orient	1	0	1	0
2003–04	Rushden & D	0	0		
2003–04	Doncaster R	9	4	9	4
2004–05	Torquay U	37	14	37	14
2005–06	Swansea C	34	9		
2006–07	Swansea C	25	5		
2007–08	Swansea C	0	0	59	14
2007–08	Millwall	7	0	7	0
2007–08	Northampton T	15	7		
2008–09	Northampton T	33	13		
2009–10	Northampton T	40	17		
2010–11	Gillingham	44	11		
2011–12	Northampton T	39	18		
2012–13	Northampton T	41	16	168	71
2013–14	Gillingham	34	10	78	21
2014–15	AFC Wimbledon	45	13		
2015–16	AFC Wimbledon	38	6	83	19
2016–17	Wycombe W	42	12		
2017–18	Wycombe W	42	17	84	29

BEAN, Marcus (M) 435 27
H: 5 11 W: 11 06 b.Hammersmith 2-11-84
Internationals: Jamaica Full caps.

2002–03	QPR	7	0		
2003–04	QPR	31	1		
2004–05	QPR	20	1		
2004–05	Swansea C	8	0		
2005–06	QPR	9	0	67	2
2005–06	Swansea C	9	1	17	1
2005–06	Blackpool	17	1		
2006–07	Blackpool	6	0		
2007–08	Blackpool	0	0	23	1
2007–08	Rotherham U	12	1	12	1
2008–09	Brentford	44	9		
2009–10	Brentford	31	0		
2010–11	Brentford	37	3		
2011–12	Brentford	32	2	144	14
2012–13	Colchester U	19	0		
2013–14	Colchester U	35	5		
2014–15	Colchester U	3	0	69	5
2014–15	Portsmouth	6	1	6	1
2014–15	Wycombe W	17	0		
2015–16	Wycombe W	30	0		
2016–17	Wycombe W	19	0		
2017–18	Wycombe W	31	2	97	2

BLOOMFIELD, Matt (M) 416 34
H: 5 9 W: 11 00 b.Felixstowe 8-2-84
Internationals: England U19.

2001–02	Ipswich T	0	0		
2002–03	Ipswich T	0	0		
2003–04	Ipswich T	0	0		
2003–04	Wycombe W	12	1		
2004–05	Wycombe W	26	2		
2005–06	Wycombe W	39	5		
2006–07	Wycombe W	41	4		
2007–08	Wycombe W	35	4		
2008–09	Wycombe W	20	0		
2009–10	Wycombe W	14	2		
2010–11	Wycombe W	34	3		
2011–12	Wycombe W	31	2		
2012–13	Wycombe W	2	1		
2013–14	Wycombe W	32	0		
2014–15	Wycombe W	33	1		
2015–16	Wycombe W	27	1		
2016–17	Wycombe W	33	5		
2017–18	Wycombe W	37	3	416	34

BROWN, Scott (G) 360 0
H: 6 2 W: 13 01 b.Wolverhampton 26-4-85
From Welshpool T

2003–04	Bristol C	0	0		
2004–05	Cheltenham T	0	0		
2005–06	Cheltenham T	1	0		
2006–07	Cheltenham T	11	0		
2007–08	Cheltenham T	0	0		
2008–09	Cheltenham T	35	0		
2009–10	Cheltenham T	46	0		
2010–11	Cheltenham T	46	0		
2011–12	Cheltenham T	22	0		
2012–13	Cheltenham T	46	0		
2013–14	Cheltenham T	45	0		
2014–15	Aberdeen	25	0		
2015–16	Aberdeen	13	0	38	0
2016–17	Wycombe W	3	0		
2016–17	*Cheltenham T*	21	0	273	0
2017–18	Wycombe W	46	0	49	0

COWAN-HALL, Paris (F) 167 26
H: 5 8 W: 11 08 b.Portsmouth 5-10-90

2008–09	Portsmouth	0	0		
2009–10	Portsmouth	0	0		
2009–10	*Grimsby T*	3	0	3	0
2010–11	Portsmouth	0	0		
2010–11	Scunthorpe U	1	0	1	0
2012–13	Plymouth Arg	40	3	40	3
2013–14	Wycombe W	25	4		
2014–15	Wycombe W	20	6		
2014–15	Millwall	5	0		
2015–16	Millwall	3	0	8	0
2015–16	*Bristol R*	3	0	3	0
2015–16	*Wycombe W*	5	1		
2016–17	Wycombe W	28	4		
2017–18	Wycombe W	34	8	112	23

DE HAVILLAND, Will (D) 19 0
H: 6 0 W: 11 00 b.Huntingdon 8-11-94

2013–14	Millwall	0	0		
2014–15	Sheffield W	0	0		
2015–16	Sheffield W	0	0		
2016–17	Wycombe W	16	0		
2017–18	Wycombe W	3	0	19	0

EL-ABD, Adam (D) 425 9
H: 5 10 W: 13 05 b.Brighton 11-9-84
Internationals: Egypt Full caps.

2003–04	Brighton & HA	11	0		
2004–05	Brighton & HA	16	0		
2005–06	Brighton & HA	29	0		
2006–07	Brighton & HA	42	1		
2007–08	Brighton & HA	35	1		
2008–09	Brighton & HA	31	0		
2009–10	Brighton & HA	35	1		
2010–11	Brighton & HA	37	1		
2011–12	Brighton & HA	23	0		
2012–13	Brighton & HA	32	1		
2013–14	Brighton & HA	9	0	300	5
2013–14	Bristol C	14	0		
2014–15	Bristol C	2	0		
2014–15	*Bury*	24	1	24	1
2015–16	Bristol C	0	0	16	0
2015–16	*Swindon T*	13	0	13	0
2015–16	*Gillingham*	8	0	8	0
2016–17	Shrewsbury T	28	2	28	2
2017–18	Wycombe W	36	1	36	1

FREEMAN, Nick (M) 41 3
b. 7-11-95
From Histon, Hemel Hempstead T, Biggleswade T.

2016–17	Wycombe W	14	0		
2017–18	Wycombe W	27	3	41	3

GAPE, Dominic (M) 68 2
H: 5 11 W: 10 13 b.Southampton 9-9-94

2012–13	Southampton	0	0		
2013–14	Southampton	0	0		
2014–15	Southampton	1	0		
2015–16	Southampton	0	0		
2016–17	Wycombe W	0	0	1	0
2016–17	Wycombe W	32	1		
2017–18	Wycombe W	35	1	67	2

HARRIMAN, Michael (D) 192 10
H: 5 6 W: 11 10 b.Chichester 23-10-92
Internationals: Republic of Ireland U18, U19, U21.

2010–11	QPR	0	0		
2011–12	QPR	1	0		
2012–13	QPR	1	0		
2012–13	*Wycombe W*	20	0		
2013–14	QPR	0	0		
2013–14	*Gillingham*	34	1	34	1
2014–15	QPR	0	0	2	0
2014–15	*Luton T*	35	1	35	1
2015–16	Wycombe W	45	7		

2016–17	Wycombe W	38	0		
2017–18	Wycombe W	18	1	121	8

JACOBSON, Joe (D)   393 24
H: 5 11 W: 12 06 b.Cardiff 17-11-86
Internationals: Wales U21.

2005–06	Cardiff C	1	0		
2006–07	Cardiff C	0	0	1	0
2006–07	*Accrington S*	6	1		
2006–07	*Bristol R*	11	0		
2007–08	Bristol R	40	1		
2008–09	Bristol R	22	0	73	1
2009–10	Oldham Ath	15	0		
2010–11	Oldham Ath	1	0	16	0
2010–11	Accrington S	26	2	32	3
2011–12	Shrewsbury T	30	1		
2012–13	Shrewsbury T	30	2		
2013–14	Shrewsbury T	41	4	110	7
2014–15	Wycombe W	42	3		
2015–16	Wycombe W	34	1		
2016–17	Wycombe W	39	3		
2017–18	Wycombe W	46	6	161	13

JOMBATI, Sido (D)   230 8
H: 6 0 W: 11 11 b.Lisbon 8-8-87

2011–12	Cheltenham T	36	2		
2012–13	Cheltenham T	37	1		
2013–14	Cheltenham T	43	1	116	4
2014–15	Wycombe W	35	0		
2015–16	Wycombe W	34	1		
2016–17	Wycombe W	25	2		
2017–18	Wycombe W	20	1	114	4

KASHKET, Scott (M)   46 12
H: 5 9 W: 10 06 b.London 6-7-95

2014–15	Leyton Orient	1	0		
2015–16	Leyton Orient	15	1		
2016–17	Leyton Orient	0	0	16	1
2017–18	Wycombe W	21	10		
2017–18	Wycombe W	9	1	30	11

MACKAIL-SMITH, Craig (F)   391 118
H: 6 3 W: 12 04 b.Watford 25-2-84
Internationals: England C. Scotland Full caps.

2006–07	Peterborough U	15	8		
2007–08	Peterborough U	36	12		
2008–09	Peterborough U	46	23		
2009–10	Peterborough U	43	10		
2010–11	Peterborough U	45	27		
2011–12	Brighton & HA	45	9		
2012–13	Brighton & HA	29	11		
2013–14	Brighton & HA	5	0		
2014–15	Brighton & HA	30	1	109	21
2014–15	*Peterborough U*	3	0		
2015–16	Luton T	33	4		
2016–17	Luton T	2	0	35	4
2016–17	*Peterborough U*	18	5	206	85
2017–18	Wycombe W	41	8	41	8

MAKABU-MAKALAMBY, Yves (G) 64 0
b.Brussels 31-1-86
Internationals: Belgium U23, DR Congo Full caps.

2005–06	Chelsea	0	0		
2005–06	*Watford*	0	0		
2006–07	Chelsea	0	0		
2007–08	Hibernian	29	0		
2008–09	Hibernian	21	0		
2009–10	Hibernian	7	0	57	0
2010–11	Swansea C	0	0		
2011–12	Mechelen	1	0	1	0
2013–14	Royal Antwerp	3	0		
2014–15	Royal Antwerp	0	0	3	0
2014–15	Otelul Galati	2	0		
2017–18	Otelul Galati	0	0	2	0
2017–18	Wycombe W	1	0	1	0

MULLER, Max (D)   49 1
b. 16-5-94

2013–14	SV Sandhausen	0	0		
2014–15	SV Sandhausen	0	0		
2015–16	Austria Salzburg	20	1	20	1
2016–17	Wycombe W	9	0		
2017–18	Wycombe W	0	0	9	0
2017–18	*Morecambe*	20	0	20	0

O'NIEN, Luke (M)   102 15
b. 21-11-94

2013–14	Watford	1	0		
2014–15	Watford	0	0	1	0
2015–16	Wycombe W	35	5		
2016–17	Wycombe W	31	3		
2017–18	Wycombe W	35	7	101	15

RICHARDSON, Barry (G)   308 0
H: 6 1 W: 12 01 b.Willington Quay 5-8-69

1987–88	Sunderland	0	0		
1988–89	Scunthorpe U	0	0		
1989–90	Scarborough	24	0		
1990–91	Scarborough	6	0	30	0
1991–92	Northampton T	27	0		
1992–93	Northampton T	42	0		
1993–94	Northampton T	27	0	96	0
1994–95	Preston NE	17	0		
1995–96	Preston NE	3	0	20	0
1995–96	Lincoln C	34	0		
1996–97	Lincoln C	36	0		
1997–98	Lincoln C	26	0		
1998–99	Lincoln C	13	0		
1999–2000	Lincoln C	22	0		
1999–2000	Mansfield T	6	0	6	0
1999–2000	Sheffield W	0	0		
2000–01	Lincoln C	0	0	131	0

From Doncaster R.

2001–02	Halifax T	24	0	24	0

From Gainsborough T.

2003–04	Doncaster R	0	0		
2004–05	Nottingham F	0	0		

From Cheltenham T, Peterborough U.

2015–16	Wycombe W	1	0		
2016–17	Wycombe W	0	0		
2017–18	Wycombe W	0	0	1	0

ROWE, Daniel (D)   47 1
H: 6 2 W: 12 08 b.Middlesbrough 24-10-95

2012–13	Rotherham U	0	0		
2013–14	Rotherham U	0	0		
2013–14	*Wycombe W*	7	0		
2014–15	Rotherham U	0	0		
2014–15	*Wycombe W*	16	0		
2015–16	Wycombe W	12	1		
2016–17	Wycombe W	12	0		
2017–18	Wycombe W	0	0	47	1

SAUNDERS, Sam (M)   282 44
H: 5 6 W: 11 04 b.Erith 29-8-83

2007–08	Dagenham & R	22	0		
2008–09	Dagenham & R	40	14	62	14
2009–10	Brentford	26	1		
2010–11	Brentford	21	2		
2011–12	Brentford	37	10		
2012–13	Brentford	31	3		
2013–14	Brentford	17	5		
2014–15	Brentford	5	2		
2015–16	*Wycombe W*	11	2		
2015–16	Brentford	25	3		
2016–17	Brentford	8	0	170	26
2016–17	Wycombe W	17	1		
2017–18	Wycombe W	22	1	50	4

SOUTHWELL, Dayle (F)   25 1
H: 5 11 W: 12 08 b.Grimsby 20-10-93
Internationals: England C.
From Grimsby T, Boston U.

2016–17	Wycombe W	13	1		
2017–18	Wycombe W	12	0	25	1

STEWART, Anthony (D)   141 7
H: 5 10 W: 12 03 b.Brixton 18-9-92

2011–12	Wycombe W	4	0		
2012–13	Wycombe W	19	1		
2013–14	Wycombe W	33	3		
2014–15	Crewe Alex	10	0	10	0
2015–16	Wycombe W	27	1		
2016–17	Wycombe W	31	1		
2017–18	Wycombe W	17	1	131	7

TYSON, Nathan (F)   502 110
H: 5 10 W: 10 02 b.Reading 4-5-82
Internationals: England U20.

1999–2000	Reading	1	0		
2000–01	Reading	0	0		
2001–02	Reading	1	0		
2001–02	*Swansea C*	11	1	11	1
2001–02	*Cheltenham T*	8	1	8	1
2002–03	Reading	23	1		
2003–04	Reading	8	0	33	1
2003–04	Wycombe W	21	9		
2004–05	Wycombe W	42	22		
2005–06	Wycombe W	15	11		
2005–06	Nottingham F	28	10		
2006–07	Nottingham F	24	7		
2007–08	Nottingham F	34	9		
2008–09	Nottingham F	35	5		
2009–10	Nottingham F	33	2		
2010–11	Nottingham F	30	2	184	35
2011–12	Derby Co	23	0		
2012–13	Derby Co	16	4	39	4
2012–13	*Millwall*	4	0	4	0
2013–14	*Blackpool*	10	0	10	0
2013–14	*Fleetwood T*	4	0	4	0
2013–14	Notts Co	10	0	10	0
2014–15	Doncaster R	39	12		
2015–16	Doncaster R	32	6	71	18
2016–17	Kilmarnock	17	0	17	0
2017–18	Wycombe W	33	8	111	50

YEOVIL T (92)

ALFEI, Daniel (D)   59 0
H: 5 11 W: 12 02 b.Swansea 23-2-92
Internationals: Wales U17, U19, U21.

2010–11	Swansea C	1	0		
2011–12	Swansea C	0	0		
2012–13	Swansea C	0	0		
2013–14	Swansea C	0	0		
2013–14	*Portsmouth*	15	0	15	0
2014–15	Swansea C	0	0		
2014–15	*Northampton T*	11	0	11	0
2015–16	Swansea C	0	0	1	0
2015–16	*Mansfield T*	12	0	12	0
2016–17	Aberystwyth T	18	0	18	0
2017–18	Yeovil T	2	0	2	0

BAILEY, James (M)   233 5
H: 6 0 W: 12 05 b.Bollington 18-9-88

2006–07	Crewe Alex	0	0		
2007–08	Crewe Alex	1	0		
2008–09	Crewe Alex	24	0		
2009–10	Crewe Alex	21	0	46	0
2010–11	Derby Co	36	1		
2011–12	Derby Co	22	0		
2012–13	Derby Co	0	0		
2012–13	*Coventry C*	30	2	30	2
2013–14	Derby Co	1	0	59	1
2014–15	Barnsley	25	0	25	0
2015	Pune C	8	1	8	1
2016	Ottawa Fury	29	0	29	0
2016–17	Carlisle U	12	0	12	0
2017–18	Yeovil T	24	1	24	1

BROWNE, Rhys (M)   40 4
H: 5 10 W: 12 08 b.Romford 16-11-95
Internationals: Antigua and Barbuda Full caps.
From Norwich C, Charlton Ath, Aldershot T.

2016–17	Grimsby T	5	0	5	0
2017–18	Yeovil T	35	4	35	4

DICKSON, Ryan (M)   324 10
H: 5 10 W: 11 05 b.Saltash 14-12-86

2004–05	Plymouth Arg	3	0		
2005–06	Plymouth Arg	0	0		
2006–07	Plymouth Arg	0	0		
2006–07	*Torquay U*	9	1	9	1
2007–08	Plymouth Arg	0	0	5	0
2007–08	Brentford	31	0		
2008–09	Brentford	39	1		
2009–10	Brentford	27	2	97	3
2010–11	Southampton	23	1		
2011–12	Southampton	0	0		
2011–12	*Yeovil T*	5	1		
2011–12	*Leyton Orient*	9	0	9	0
2012–13	Southampton	0	0	23	1
2012–13	*Bradford C*	5	1	5	1
2013–14	Colchester U	32	0	32	0
2014–15	Crawley T	32	1	32	1
2015–16	Yeovil T	37	2		
2016–17	Yeovil T	34	0		
2017–18	Yeovil T	36	0	112	3

DONNELLAN, Shaun (D)   21 0
b. 22-5-97
Internationals: Republic of Ireland U19, U21.

2015–16	WBA	0	0		
2016–17	WBA	0	0		
2016–17	*Stevenage*	0	0		
2017–18	WBA	0	0		
2017–18	*Walsall*	10	0	10	0
2017–18	Yeovil T	11	0	11	0

FISHER, Alex (F)   148 38
H: 6 2 W: 12 00 b. 30-6-90

2006–07	Oxford U	1	0		
2007–08	Oxford U	10	1		
2008–09	Oxford U	3	1	13	2
2009–10	Jerez Industrial	0	0		
2010–11	Jerez Industrial	21	11	21	11
2011–12	Tienen	7	1	7	1
2012–13	Racing Mechelen	27	7	27	7
2013–14	Heist	2	0	2	0
2013–14	Monza	14	2	14	2
2014–15	Mansfield T	14	1	14	1
2015–16	Inverness CT	0	0		
2016–17	Inverness CT	21	8	22	8
2017–18	Motherwell	11	0	11	0
2017–18	Yeovil T	17	6	17	6

GOBERN, Oscar (M)   122 4
H: 6 3 W: 10 10 b.Birmingham 26-1-91
Internationals: England U19.

2008–09	Southampton	6	0		
2009–10	Southampton	4	0		
2009–10	*Milton Keynes D*	2	0	2	0

2010–11	Southampton	11	1	21	1
2011–12	Huddersfield T	21	2		
2012–13	Huddersfield T	15	0		
2013–14	Huddersfield T	23	0		
2014–15	Huddersfield T	12	1	71	3
2014–15	*Chesterfield*	3	0	3	0
2015–16	QPR	0	0		
2015–16	*Doncaster R*	5	0	5	0
2016–17	Mansfield T	9	0	9	0
2016–17	Ross Co	0	0		
2017–18	Yeovil T	11	0	11	0

GOLUBICKAS, Paulius (F)   0   0
b. 19-8-99
Internationals: Lithuania U17, U19.

2017–18	Yeovil T	0	0		

GRAY, Jake (F)   78   9
H: 5 11   W: 11 00   b.Aylesbury 25-12-95

2014–15	Crystal Palace	0	0		
2014–15	*Cheltenham T*	4	0	4	0
2015–16	Crystal Palace	0	0		
2015–16	*Hartlepool U*	29	5	29	5
2016–17	Luton T	19	1	19	1
2017–18	Yeovil T	26	3	26	3

GREEN, Jordan (F)   47   2
H: 5 6   W: 10 03   b.London 22-2-95

2015–16	Bournemouth	0	0		
2016–17	Bournemouth	0	0		
2016–17	*Newport Co*	10	0	10	0
2017–18	Yeovil T	37	2	37	2

JAMES, Tom (D)   41   0
H: 5 11   W: 11 00   b.Leamington Spa 19-11-88
Internationals: Wales U19.

2013–14	Cardiff C	1	0		
2014–15	Cardiff C	0	0		
2015–16	Cardiff C	0	0		
2016–17	Cardiff C	0	0	1	0
2016–17	Yeovil T	2	0		
2017–18	Yeovil T	38	0	40	0

KHAN, Otis (M)   72   12
H: 5 9   W: 11 03   b.Ashton-under-Lyme 5-9-95

2013–14	Sheffield U	2	0		
2014–15	Sheffield U	0	0		
2015–16	Sheffield U	0	0	2	0
2015–16	*Barnsley*	3	0	3	0
2016–17	Yeovil T	29	6		
2017–18	Yeovil T	38	6	67	12

KRYSIAK, Artur (G)   299   0
H: 6 1   W: 12 00   b.Lodz 11-8-89
Internationals: Poland U19.

2006–07	Birmingham C	0	0		
2007–08	*Gretna*	4	0	4	0
2007–08	Birmingham C	0	0		
2008–09	Birmingham C	0	0		
2008–09	*Motherwell*	1	0	1	0
2008–09	*Swansea C*	2	0	2	0
2009–10	Birmingham C	0	0		
2009–10	*Burton Alb*	38	0	38	0
2010–11	Exeter C	10	0		
2011–12	Exeter C	38	0		
2012–13	Exeter C	42	0		
2013–14	Exeter C	37	0	127	0
2014–15	Yeovil T	15	0		
2015–16	Yeovil T	38	0		
2016–17	Yeovil T	41	0		
2017–18	Yeovil T	33	0	127	0

MADDISON, Johnny (G)   15   0
H: 6 0   W: 11 12   b.Chester le Street 4-9-94

2012–13	Crawley T	0	0		
2013–14	Crawley T	0	0		
2014–15	Crawley T	0	0		
2015–16	Leicester C	0	0		
2016–17	Yeovil T	5	0		
2017–18	Yeovil T	10	0	15	0

MUGABI, Bevis (D)   53   3
H: 6 2   W: 11 11   b.Harrow 1-5-95
Internationals: Uganda Full caps.
From Southampton.

2016–17	Yeovil T	31	1		
2017–18	Yeovil T	22	2	53	3

NELSON, Stuart (G)   425   0
H: 6 1   W: 12 12   b.Stroud 17-9-81

2003–04	Brentford	9	0		
2004–05	Brentford	43	0		
2005–06	Brentford	45	0		
2006–07	Brentford	19	0	116	0
2007–08	Leyton Orient	30	0	30	0
2008–09	Norwich C	0	0		
2010–11	Notts Co	33	0		
2011–12	Notts Co	46	0	79	0
2012–13	Gillingham	45	0		
2013–14	Gillingham	46	0		
2014–15	Gillingham	24	0		
2015–16	Gillingham	46	0		
2016–17	Gillingham	34	0		
2017–18	Gillingham	0	0	195	0
2017–18	Yeovil T	5	0	5	0

PHILLIPS, Steve (G)   510   0
H: 6 1   W: 11 10   b.Bath 6-5-78

1996–97	Bristol C	0	0		
1997–98	Bristol C	0	0		
1998–99	Bristol C	15	0		
1999–2000	Bristol C	21	0		
2000–01	Bristol C	42	0		
2001–02	Bristol C	22	0		
2002–03	Bristol C	46	0		
2003–04	Bristol C	46	0		
2004–05	Bristol C	46	0		
2005–06	Bristol C	19	0	257	0
2006–07	Bristol R	44	0		
2007–08	Bristol R	46	0		
2008–09	Bristol R	46	0		
2009–10	Bristol R	0	0	136	0
2009–10	*Shrewsbury T*	11	0	11	0
2009–10	*Crewe Alex*	28	0		
2010–11	Crewe Alex	3	0		
2011–12	Crewe Alex	46	0		
2012–13	Crewe Alex	20	0		
2013–14	Crewe Alex	9	0		
2014–15	Crewe Alex	0	0	106	0
2017–18	Yeovil T	0	0		

SANTOS, Alefe (M)   41   1
H: 5 10   W: 10 06   b.Sao Paulo 28-1-95

2012–13	Bristol R	1	0		
2013	Ponte Preta	0	0		
2013–14	Bristol R	23	1	24	1
2014–15	Derby Co	0	0		
2014–15	*Notts Co*	3	0	3	0
2015–16	Derby Co	0	0		
2016–17	Derby Co	0	0		
2017–18	Yeovil T	14	0	14	0

SCOTT, Tommy (G)   0   0
b. 13-9-99

2017–18	Yeovil T	0	0		

SMITH, Connor (M)   76   1
H: 5 11   W: 11 06   b.London 18-2-93
Internationals: Republic of Ireland U17, U19, U21.

2012–13	Watford	7	0		
2013–14	Watford	1	0		
2013–14	*Gillingham*	10	0	10	0
2014–15	Watford	0	0		
2015–16	Watford	0	0	8	0
2015–16	*Stevenage*	4	0	4	0
2015–16	AFC Wimbledon	10	0	10	0
2016–17	Plymouth Arg	25	1	25	1
2017–18	Yeovil T	19	0	19	0

SMITH, Nathan (D)   327   5
H: 5 11   W: 12 00   b.Enfield 11-1-87
Internationals: Jamaica Full caps.

2007–08	Yeovil T	7	0		
2008–09	Yeovil T	33	1		
2009–10	Yeovil T	34	0		
2010–11	Yeovil T	40	0		
2011–12	Chesterfield	25	0		
2012–13	Chesterfield	29	0		
2013–14	Chesterfield	13	0	67	0
2014–15	Yeovil T	41	0		
2015–16	Yeovil T	40	1		
2016–17	Yeovil T	34	2		
2017–18	Yeovil T	31	1	260	5

SOWUNMI, Omar (D)   52   3
H: 6 6   W: 14 09   b.Colchester 7-11-95

2015–16	Yeovil T	5	1		
2016–17	Yeovil T	11	0		
2017–18	Yeovil T	36	2	52	3

ZOKO, Francois (F)   512   100
H: 6 0   W: 11 05   b.Daloa 13-9-83
Internationals: Ivory Coast U20, U23.

2001–02	Nancy	24	3		
2002–03	Nancy	28	2		
2003–04	Nancy	19	3	71	8
2004–05	Laval	27	7		
2005–06	Laval	33	2	60	9
2006–07	Mons	23	4		
2007–08	Mons	32	8	55	12
2008–09	Hacettepe	27	1	27	1
2009–10	Ostend	11	4	11	4
2010–11	Carlisle U	44	6		
2011–12	Carlisle U	45	13		
2012–13	Carlisle U	0	0	89	19
2012–13	Notts Co	38	7		
2013–14	Notts Co	1	0	39	7
2013–14	*Stevenage*	33	10	33	10
2014–15	Blackpool	14	1	14	1
2014–15	*Bradford C*	16	1	16	1
2016–17	Yeovil T	25	7		
2017–18	Yeovil T	37	13	97	28

Scholars
Cherrett, Bradley Frederick; Dix, Lewis; Fripp, Charlie John; Golubickas, Paulius; Gyebi, Jeremiah Boateng; Haughton, Harry Robert; Hayes, Thomas; Hilton-Jones, Jack Alexander; John, Alex Ryan; Nzembela, Neville Nchang Kabamba; Ojo, Taiwo Daniel; Rice-Lethaby, Jack Renauld; Rogers, Gabriel Eric; Scott, Tommy; Shako, Nestor Kasende; Tomlinson, Joseph William George; Wan, Nathaniel Shio Hong.

ENGLISH LEAGUE PLAYERS – INDEX

NATIONAL LIST OF REFEREES FOR SEASON 2018–19

Adcock, James
Atkinson, Martin
Attwell, Stuart
Backhouse, Anthony
Bankes, Peter
Bond, Darren
Boyeson, Carl
Bramall, Tom
Breakspear, Charles
Brooks, John
Brown, Mark
Busby, John
Clark, Richard
Coggins, Antony
Collins, Lee
Coote, David
Coy, Martin
Davies, Andy
Dean, Mike
Donohue, Matthew
Drysdale, Darren
Duncan, Scott
East, Roger
Eltringham, Geoff
England, Darren
Friend, Kevin

Haines, Andy
Hair, Neil
Handley, Darren
Harrington, Tony
Heywood, Mark
Hicks, Craig
Hooper, Simon
Horwood, Graham
Huxtable, Brett
Ilderton, Eddie
Johnson, Kevin
Jones, Rob
Joyce, Ross
Kavanagh, Chris
Kettle, Trevor
Kinseley, Nick
Langford, Oliver
Lewis, Rob
Linington, James
Madley, Andy
Madley, Bobby
Marriner, Andre
Marsden, Paul
Martin, Stephen
Mason, Lee
Moss, Jonathan

Nield, Tom
Oldham, Scott
Oliver, Michael
Pawson, Craig
Probert, Lee
Robinson, Tim
Salisbury, Graham
Salisbury, Michael
Sarginson, Chris
Scott, Graham
Simpson, Jeremy
Stockbridge, Seb
Stroud, Keith
Swabey, Lee
Taylor, Anthony
Tierney, Paul
Toner, Ben
Ward, Gavin
Webb, David
Whitestone, Dean
Woolmer, Andy
Wright, Peter
Yates, Ollie
Young, Alan

ASSISTANT REFEREES

Amey, Justin
Amphlett, Marvyn
Aspinall, Natalie
Atkin, Rob
Avent, David
Aylott, Andrew
Barnard, Nik
Bartlett, Richard
Beck, Simon
Bennett, Simon
Benton, David
Beswick, Gary
Betts, Lee
Bickle, Oliver
Blunden, Darren
Bristow, Matthew
Brown, Stephen
Burt, Stuart
Butler, Stuart
Byrne, George
Byrne, Helen
Cann, Darren
Cheosiaua, Ravel

Child, Stephen
Clark, Joe
Clayton, Alan
Clayton, Simon
Cobb, Ben
Cook, Dan
Cook, Daniel
Cooper, Ian
Cooper, Nick
Cropp, Barry
Crowhurst, Leigh
Crysell, Adam
Cunliffe, Mark
Da Costa, Anthony
Dabbs, Robert
Davies, Neil
Denton, Michael
Dermott, Philip
Dudley, Ian
Duncan, Mark
Dwyer, Mark
Eaton, Derek
Farrell, Conor

Finch, Stephen
Fitch-Jackson, Carl
Flynn, John
Foley, Matt
Ford, Declan
Fox, Andrew
Freeman, Lee
Fyvie, Graeme
Ganfield, Ronald
Garratt, Andrew
George, Michael
Gill, Bhupinder
Gooch, Peter
Gordon, Barry
Graham, Paul
Gratton, Danny
Greenhalgh, Nick
Griffiths, Mark
Grunnill, Wayne
Halliday, Andrew
Hanley, Michael
Harty, Thomas
Hatzidakis, Constantine

Haycock, Ken
Hendley, Andrew
Hilton, Gary
Hobday, Paul
Hodskinson, Paul
Holmes, Adrian
Hopton, Nick
Howick, Kevin
Howson, Akil
Hudson, Shaun
Hunt, Jonathan
Husband, Christopher
Hussin, Ian
Hyde, Robert
Isherwood, Chris
Jones, Mark
Jones, Matthew
Kane, Graham
Karaivanov, Hristo
Kelly, Paul
Kendall, Richard
Khan, Abbas
Khatib, Billy
Kidd, Christopher
Kirkup, Peter
Laver, Andrew
Leach, Daniel
Ledger, Scott
Lee, Matthew
Lennard, Harry
Lewis, Samuel
Liddle, Geoffrey
Lister, Paul
Long, Simon
Lugg, Nigel

Mainwaring, James
Maskell, Garry
Massey-Ellis, Sian
Matthews, Adam
McDonough, Mick
McGrath, Matthew
Mellor, Gareth
Merchant, Robert
Meredith, Steven
Moore, Anthony
Morris, Kevin
Mulraine, Kevin
Newhouse, Paul
Nunn, Adam
Ogles, Samuel
Parry, Matthew
Pashley, Alix
Peart, Tony
Perry, Marc
Plane, Steven
Plowright, David
Pottage, Mark
Powell, Christopher
Ramsey, Thomas
Rashid, Lisa
Rathbone, Ian
Read, Gregory
Rees, Paul
Robathan, Daniel
Rushton, Steven
Russell, Geoffrey
Russell, Mark
Scholes, Mark
Searle, Isaac
Sharp, Neil

Shaw, Simon
Siddall, Iain
Simpson, Joe
Smallwood, Billy
Smart, Edward
Smedley, Ian
Smith, Matthew
Smith, Rob
Smith, Wade
Street, Duncan
Taylor, Craig
Taylor, Grant
Tranter, Adrian
Treleaven, Dean
Venamore, Lee
Viccars, Gareth
Wade, Christopher
Wade, Stephen
Walchester, Callum
Ward, Christopher
Warren, George
Waters, Adrian
Webb, Michael
West, Richard
Wigglesworth, Richard
Wild, Richard
Wilding, Darren
Wilkes, Matthew
Williams, Andrew
Williams, Ollie
Wilson, James
Wilson, Marc
Wood, Timothy
Woodward, Richard
Yates, Paul

MANAGERS – IN AND OUT 2017–18

AUGUST 2017
31   Justin Edinburgh sacked as manager of Northampton T. Assistant manager David Kerslake takes temporary charge.

SEPTEMBER 2017
4   Jimmy Floyd Hasselbaink appointed manager of Northampton T.
11   Frank de Boer sacked as manager of Crystal Palace after 77 days and 5 games in charge.
12   Roy Hodgson appointed manager of Crystal Palace.
16   Harry Redknapp sacked as manager of Birmingham C. Development squad manager Lee Carsley takes temporary charge.
Gary Caldwell sacked as manager of Chesterfield. Director of recruitment and development Guy Branston takes temporary charge.
Michael Brown sacked as manager of Port Vale. Assistant managers David Kelly and Chris Morgan take temporary charge.
25   Ady Pennock leaves as manager of Gillingham by mutual consent. Director of Football Peter Taylor takes temporary charge.
John Sheridan leaves as manager of Oldham Ath by mutual consent. First-team coach Richie Wellens takes temporary charge.
29   Steve Cotterill appointed manager of Birmingham C.
Jack Lester appointed manager of Chesterfield.

OCTOBER 2017
4   Neil Aspin appointed manager of Port Vale.
17   Craig Shakespeare sacked as manager of Leicester C. Assistant manager Michael Appleton takes temporary charge.
18   Richie Wellens appointed manager of Oldham Ath after being in temporary charge.
23   Ronald Koeman sacked as manager of Everton. Under 23s manager David Unsworth takes temporary charge.
25   Claude Puel appointed manager of Leicester C.
26   Pedro Caixinha sacked as manager of Rangers. Graeme Murty takes temporary charge.
30   Lee Clark sacked as manager of Bury.
31   Simon Grayson sacked as manager of Sunderland. Robbie Stockdale and Billy McKinlay take temporary charge.

NOVEMBER 2017
6   Slavin Bilic sacked as manager of West Ham U.
7   David Moyes appointed manager of West Ham U.
13   Rossi Eames sacked as manager of Barnet. Mark McGhee appointed new manager.
16   Steve Lovell appointed manager of Gillingham.
19   Chris Coleman appointed manager of Sunderland.
20   Tony Pulis sacked as manager of WBA. Assistant manager Gary Megson takes temporary charge.
22   Chris Lucketti appointed manager of Bury.
29   Alan Pardew appointed manager of WBA.
30   Sam Allardyce appointed manager of Everton.

DECEMBER 2017
3   Leonid Slutsky leaves as manager of Hull C by mutual consent.
7   Nigel Adkins appointed manager of Hull C.
20   Paul Clement sacked as manager of Swansea C. Midfielder Leon Britton takes temporary charge.
22   Graeme Murty appointed manager of Rangers for the remainder of the season.
23   Gary Monk sacked as manager of Middlesbrough. Academy manager Craig Liddle takes temporary charge.
24   Carlos Carvalhal sacked as manager of Sheffield W. Coach Lee Bullen takes temporary charge.
26   Tony Pulis appointed manager of Middlesbrough.
28   Carlos Carvalhal appointed manager of Swansea C.
31   Mark Warburton sacked as manager of Nottingham F. Academy manager Gary Brazil takes temporary charge.

JANUARY 2018
5   Jos Luhukay appointed manager of Sheffield W.
6   Mark Hughes sacked as manager of Stoke C.
8   Aitor Karanka appointed manager of Nottingham F.
15   Paul Lambert appointed manager of Stoke C.
Chris Lucketti sacked as manager of Bury. Ryan Lowe and Ryan Kidd take temporary charge.
Graham Westley appointed manager of Barnet. Previous manager Mark McGhee appointed head of technical.
17   Phil Brown sacked by Southend U. Academy manager Ricky Duncan and Under 23s manager Kevin Maher take temporary charge.
20   Robbie Neilson sacked by Milton Keynes D.
21   Marco Silva sacked as manager of Watford. Javi Gracia appointed new manager.
22   Pep Clotet sacked as manager of Oxford U. Derek Fazackerley takes temporary charge.
23   Dan Micciche appointed manager of Milton Keynes D.
Chris Powell appointed manager of Southend U.

FEBRUARY 2018
4   Thomas Christiansen sacked as manager of Leeds U.
5   Stuart McCall sacked as manager of Bradford C.
6   Paul Heckingbottom leaves Barnsley to become manager of Leeds U.
9   Shaun Derry sacked as manager of Cambridge U. Joe Dunne takes temporary charge.

11 Simon Grayson appointed manager of Bradford C.
  Russell Slade sacked as manager of Grimsby T.
16 Jose Morais appointed manager of Barnsley.
17 Uwe Rosler sacked as manager of Fleetwood T.
22 John Sheridan appointed manager of Fleetwood T.
27 Steve Evans leaves Mansfield Town to become manager of Peterborough U.

MARCH 2018
1 David Flitcroft leaves Swindon T to become manager of Mansfield T.
2 Michael Jolley appointed manager of Grimsby T.
3 Steve Cotterill sacked as manager of Birmingham C.
4 Garry Monk appointed manager of Birmingham C.
12 Mauricio Pellegrino sacked as manager of Southampton.
  Jon Whitney sacked as manager of Walsall.
  Phil Brown appointed manager of Swindon T.
14 Mark Hughes appointed manager of Southampton.
16 Dean Keates leaves Wrexham and is appointed new manager of Walsall.
18 Darren Sarll sacked as manager of Stevenage.
19· Graham Westley sacked as manager of Barnet. Martin Allen appointed manager.
20 Dino Maamria appointed manager of Stevenage.
21 Jaap Stam sacked as manager of Reading.
22 Karl Robinson leaves as manager of Charlton Ath by mutual consent and is appointed manager of Oxford U. Lee
  Bowyer takes temporary charge at Charlton Ath.
23 Paul Clement appointed manager of Reading.
24 Graham Alexander sacked as manager of Scunthorpe U. First-team coach Nick Daws takes temporary charge.

APRIL 2018
2 Alan Pardew leaves WBA by mutual consent. First-team coach Darren Moore takes temporary charge.
  Jimmy Floyd Hasselbaink sacked as manager of Northampton T. Assistant manager Dean Austin takes temporary
  charge.
10 Mick McCarthy leaves as manager of Ipswich T. Head of coaching and player development, Bryan Klug takes
  temporary charge.
18 Fleetwood T announce that Joey Barton will be new manager from 2 June.
20 Arsene Wenger announces that he will leave Arsenal at the end of the current season.
22 Dan Micciche sacked as manager of Milton Keynes D. Assistant manager Keith Millen takes temporary charge.
23 Jack Lester leaves as manager of Chesterfield. Club captain Ian Evatt takes temporary charge.
26 Keith Curle to leave Carlisle U at the end of the season.
29 Chris Coleman sacked as manager of Sunderland. First-team coach Robbie Stockdale takes temporary charge.

MAY 2018
1 Graeme Murty sacked as manager of Rangers.
2 Joe Dunne appointed manager of Cambridge U after being in temporary charge.
4 Steven Gerrard appointed manager of Rangers.
6 Jose Morais sacked as manager of Barnsley.
8 Simon Grayson leaves Bradford C.
10 Martin Allen leaves as manager of Barnet.
  Ian Holloway sacked as manager of QPR.
  Ryan Lowe appointed manager of Bury after being in temporary charge.
12 Dean Austin appointed manager of Northampton T.
15 Martin Allen appointed manager of Chesterfield.
16 Sam Allardyce sacked as manager of Everton.
  David Moyes sacked as manager of West Ham U.
18 Carlos Carvalhal leaves as manager of Swansea C.
  Paul Lambert leaves as manager of Stoke C.
  Steve McClaren appointed manager of QPR.
  Darren Moore appointed manager of WBA.
22 Manuel Pellegrini appointed manager of West Ham U.
  Gary Rowett leaves Derby Co to become manager of Stoke C.
23 Unai Emery appointed manager of Arsenal.
25 Jack Ross appointed manager of Sunderland.
  Nick Daws appointed manager of Scunthorpe U.
30 Paul Hurst leaves Shrewsbury T to become manager of Ipswich T.
31 Marco Silva appointed manager of Everton.
  Frank Lampard appointed manager of Derby Co.

JUNE 2018
1 Paul Heckingbotom sacked as manager of Leeds U.
  John Askew leaves Macclesfield T to become manager of Shrewsbury T.
  Paul Tisdale leaves as manager of Exeter C. Matt Taylor appointed manager.
4 Darren Ferguson resigns as manager of Doncaster R.
5 John Sheridan appointed manager of Carlisle U.
6 Daniel Stendel appointed manager of Barnsley.
  Paul Tisdale appointed manager of Milton Keynes D.
8 Richie Wellens sacked as manager of Oldham Ath.
13 Frankie Bunn appointed manager of Oldham Ath.
15 Marcelo Bielsa appointed manager of Leeds U.
18 Michael Collins appointed manager of Bradford C.
27 Grant McCann appointed manager of Doncaster R.

TRANSFERS 2017–18

JUNE 2017	From	To	Fee in £
30 Adeyemi, Tom	Cardiff C	Ipswich T	Free
30 Ake, Nathan	Chelsea	Bournemouth	Undisclosed
26 Anderton, Nick	Barrow	Blackpool	Undisclosed
1 Andrew, Danny	Grimsby T	Doncaster R	Free
13 Baldock, George	Milton Keynes D	Sheffield U	Undisclosed
22 Ball, David	Fleetwood T	Rotherham U	Free
15 Beautyman, Harry	Northampton T	Stevenage	Free
29 Benyu, Kundai	Ipswich T	Celtic	Compensation
27 Biamou, Maxime	Sutton U	Coventry C	Undisclosed
2 Bigirimana, Gael	Coventry C	Motherwell	Free
15 Binnom-Williams, Jerome	Peterborough U	Chesterfield	Free
23 Bowditch, Dean	Milton Keynes D	Northampton T	Free
20 Boyce, Liam	Ross Co	Burton Alb	Undisclosed
15 Brewster, Delial	Everton	Chesterfield	Free
29 Brough, Patrick	Carlisle U	Morecambe	Free
1 Brown, Reece	Birmingham C	Forest Green R	Free
16 Browne, Rhys	Grimsby T	Yeovil T	Undisclosed
30 Buckley, Will	Sunderland	Bolton W	Free
6 Burgess, Cameron	Fulham	Scunthorpe U	Undisclosed
28 Buxton, Jake	Wigan Ath	Burton Alb	Free
8 Camara, Panutche	Dulwich Hamlet	Crawley T	Undisclosed
16 Camp, Lee	Rotherham U	Cardiff C	Free
21 Campbell, Adam	Notts Co	Morecambe	Free
19 Chicksen, Adam	Charlton Ath	Bradford C	Free
8 Clarke, Billy	Bradford C	Charlton Ath	Undisclosed
23 Clarke, Nathan	Coventry C	Grimsby T	Free
22 Clayton, Max	Bolton W	Blackpool	Free
29 Collins, James	Crawley T	Luton T	Free
15 Cooper, Charlie	Birmingham C	Forest Green R	Free
26 Croll, Luke	Crystal Palace	Exeter C	Free
17 Cummings, Jason	Hibernian	Nottingham F	Undisclosed
27 Dack, Bradley	Gillingham	Blackburn R	£750,000
22 Davies, Craig	Scunthorpe U	Oldham Ath	Free
7 Davies, Curtis	Hull C	Derby Co	Undisclosed
21 Davis, Joe	Fleetwood T	Port Vale	Free
1 Deegan, Gary	Shrewsbury T	Cambridge U	Free
29 Defoe, Jermain	Sunderland	Bournemouth	Free
26 Devlin, Nicky	Ayr U	Walsall	Free
7 Dolan, Matt	Yeovil T	Newport Co	Free
29 Doughty, Michael	QPR	Peterborough U	Undisclosed
5 Dunkley, Chey	Oxford U	Wigan Ath	Free
22 Eaves, Tom	Yeovil T	Gillingham	Free
30 Edwards, Liam	Swansea C	Hull C	Free
13 Edwards, Ryan	Morecambe	Plymouth Arg	Undisclosed
9 Elliott, Tom	AFC Wimbledon	Millwall	Free
29 Etuhu, Kelvin	Bury	Carlisle U	Free
28 Fischer, Viktor	Middlesbrough	Mainz	Undisclosed
1 Fletcher, Darren	WBA	Stoke C	Free
19 Fosu, Tariqe	Reading	Charlton Ath	Undisclosed
2 Gardner, Dan	Chesterfield	Oldham Ath	Free
16 Garner, Joe	Rangers	Ipswich T	Undisclosed
16 Gilks, Matt	Wigan Ath	Scunthorpe U	Free
23 Gillespie, Mark	Carlisle U	Walsall	Free
28 Gladwin, Ben	QPR	Blackburn R	Undisclosed
30 Gogia, Akaki	Brentford	Dynamo Dresden	Undisclosed
28 Gomis, Bafetimbi	Swansea C	Galatasaray	Undisclosed
23 Grant, Joel	Exeter C	Plymouth Arg	Free
26 Gray, Jake	Luton T	Yeovil T	Undisclosed
26 Green, Matt	Mansfield T	Lincoln C	Free
21 Griffiths, Russell	Everton	Motherwell	Free
22 Guthrie, Jon	Crewe Alex	Walsall	Free
23 Harrop, Josh	Manchester U	Preston NE	Undisclosed
16 Hartley, Peter	Bristol R	Blackpool	Free
29 Hendrie, Stephen	West Ham U	Southend U	Free
13 Hofmann, Philipp	Brentford	Greuter Furth	Undisclosed
29 Hope, Hallam	Bury	Carlisle U	Free
21 Hornby, Sam	Burton Alb	Port Vale	Free
24 Hughes, Will	Derby Co	Watford	£8m
30 Humphrey, Chris	Hibernian	Bury	Free
28 Huws, Emyr	Cardiff C	Ipswich T	Undisclosed
30 Jackson, Ryan	Gillingham	Colchester U	Free
26 Jules, Zak	Reading	Shrewsbury T	Undisclosed
28 Kay, Antony	Bury	Port Vale	Free
19 Kelleher, Fiacre	Celtic	Oxford U	Undisclosed
22 Kelly, Graham	Sheffield U	Port Vale	Free
11 Kelly, Sean	AFC Wimbledon	Ross Co	Free
16 Kiwomya, Alex	Chelsea	Doncaster R	Free
27 Knott, Billy	Gillingham	Lincoln C	Free
28 Lafferty, Kyle	Norwich C	Hearts	Free
20 Lainton, Rob	Bury	Port Vale	Free
20 Laird, Scott	Scunthorpe U	Forest Green R	Free

8 Lameiras, Ruben	Coventry C	Plymouth Arg	Free
28 Lancashire, Olly	Shrewsbury T	Swindon T	Free
6 Le Fondre, Adam	Cardiff C	Bolton W	Free
14 Leahy, Luke	Falkirk	Walsall	Free
22 Lindsay, Liam	Partick Thistle	Barnsley	Undisclosed
29 Linganzi, Amine	Portsmouth	Swindon T	Free
16 Little, Mark	Bristol C	Bolton W	Free
15 Maguire, Harry	Hull C	Leicester C	£17m
3 Maguire, Sean	Cork C	Preston NE	Undisclosed
28 Marriott, Jack	Luton T	Peterborough U	Undisclosed
16 Marshall, Mark	Bradford C	Charlton Ath	Free
27 Martin, Joe	Millwall	Stevenage	Free
23 McAleny, Conor	Everton	Fleetwood T	Free
21 McArdle, Rory	Bradford C	Scunthorpe U	Free
29 McCartan, Shay	Accrington S	Bradford C	Free
13 McCarthy, Jason	Southampton	Barnsley	Undisclosed
5 McClean, Kyle	Nottingham F	St Johnstone	Free
1 McCormack, Alan	Brentford	Luton T	Free
22 McDonald, Cody	Gillingham	AFC Wimbledon	Free
23 McGeehan, Cameron	Luton T	Barnsley	Undisclosed
5 Mitov, Dimitar	Charlton Ath	Cambridge U	Free
20 Montano, Cristian	Bristol R	Port Vale	Free
15 Moore, Brendan	Torquay U	Rochdale	Free
30 Mooy, Aaron	Manchester C	Huddersfield T	£8m
27 Moxey, Dean	Bolton W	Exeter C	Free
27 Mullin, Paul	Morecambe	Swindon T	Undisclosed
22 Ness, Jamie	Scunthorpe U	Plymouth Arg	Free
19 Newton, Danny	Tamworth	Stevenage	Undisclosed
2 Nolan, Jon	Chesterfield	Shrewsbury T	Undisclosed
20 Nordtveit, Havard	West Ham U	Hoffenheim	Undisclosed
8 O'Connell, Eoghan	Celtic	Bury	Undisclosed
30 O'Connor, Kevin	Cork C	Preston NE	Undisclosed
29 O'Grady, Chris	Brighton & HA	Chesterfield	Free
8 Olejnik, Bobby	Exeter C	Mansfield T	Free
30 Oliver, Vadaine	York C	Morecambe	Free
6 O'Neill, Luke	Southend U	Gillingham	Free
9 O'Shea, Jay	Chesterfield	Bury	Free
8 Oshilaja, Deji	Cardiff C	AFC Wimbledon	Free
26 Palmer, Ollie	Leyton Orient	Lincoln C	Free
7 Paterson, Callum	Hearts	Cardiff C	Free
15 Pickford, Jordan	Sunderland	Everton	£25m rising to £30m
30 Pinnock, Ethan	Forest Green R	Barnsley	Undisclosed
28 Poleon, Dominic	AFC Wimbledon	Bradford C	Undisclosed
14 Potter, Darren	Milton Keynes D	Rotherham U	Free
23 Power, Alan	Lincoln C	Kilmarnock	Free
28 Purkiss, Ben	Port Vale	Swindon T	Free
7 Raglan, Charlie	Chesterfield	Oxford U	Free
30 Randall, Mark	Newport Co	Crawley T	Free
27 Reynolds, Lamar	Brentwood	Newport Co	Free
22 Robertson, Chris	AFC Wimbledon	Swindon T	Free
16 Rodgers, Harvey	Hull C	Fleetwood T	Free
13 Rose, Andy	Coventry C	Motherwell	Free
20 Rudd, Declan	Norwich C	Preston NE	Undisclosed
16 Ryan, Mathew	Valencia	Brighton & HA	Undisclosed
26 Saville, George	Wolverhampton W	Millwall	Undisclosed
17 Scougall, Stefan	Sheffield U	St Johnstone	Free
15 Sinnott, Jordan	FC Halifax T	Chesterfield	Free
1 Skarz, Joe	Oxford U	Bury	Free
20 Smallwood, Richie	Rotherham U	Blackburn R	Free
21 Smith, Connor	Plymouth Arg	Yeovil T	Free
3 Smith, Michael	Peterborough U	Hearts	Undisclosed
27 Sousa, Erico	Tranmere R	Accrington S	Free
26 Stacey, Jack	Reading	Luton T	Undisclosed
27 Sterling-James, Omari	Solihull Moors	Mansfield T	Free
13 Stockdale, David	Brighton & HA	Birmingham C	Free
5 Tanner, Craig	Reading	Motherwell	Free
28 Tanser, Scott	Port Vale	St Johnstone	Free
23 Taylor, Paul	Peterborough U	Bradford C	Free
28 Taylor-Sinclair, Aaron	Doncaster R	Plymouth Arg	Free
16 Thomas, Terell	Charlton Ath	Wigan Ath	Free
1 Thompson, Adam	Southend U	Bury	Free
28 Thompson, Garry	Wycombe W	Morecambe	Free
22 Thompson, Nathan	Swindon T	Portsmouth	Free
15 Tilt, Curtis	Wrexham	Blackpool	Free
26 Traore, Bertrand	Chelsea	Lyon	£8.8m
27 Turgott, Blair	Bromley	Stevenage	Free
20 Turton, Ollie	Crewe Alex	Blackpool	Free
29 Vickers, Josh	Swansea C	Lincoln C	Free
21 Vincenti, Peter	Rochdale	Coventry C	Free
26 Wallace, Jed	Wolverhampton W	Millwall	Undisclosed
23 Ward, Danny	Rotherham U	Cardiff C	Undisclosed
26 Warnock, Stephen	Wigan Ath	Burton Alb	Free
8 Waters, Billy	Cheltenham T	Northampton T	Undisclosed
1 Watkins, Marley	Barnsley	Norwich C	Free
13 Whittingham, Peter	Cardiff C	Blackburn R	Free
29 Wilkinson, Conor	Bolton W	Gillingham	Undisclosed
7 Williams, Jordan	Barrow	Rochdale	£100,000

20 Williams, Ryan	Barnsley	Rotherham U	Free
30 Willock, Chris	Arsenal	Benfica	Undisclosed
28 Wylde, Gregg	Millwall	Plymouth Arg	Free
7 Zakuani, Gabriel	Northampton T	Gillingham	Free
28 Zubar, Stephane	Weymouth	Yeovil T	Free

JULY 2017

31 Abrahams, Tristan	Leyton Orient	Norwich C	Undisclosed
18 Akpan, Hope	Blackburn R	Burton Alb	Free
6 Aldred, Tom	Blackpool	Bury	Free
28 Alfei, Daniel	Aberystwyth	Yeovil T	Free
17 Al-Habsi, Ali	Reading	Al-Hilal	Undisclosed
-17 Ali, Mukhtar	Chelsea	Vitesse Arnhem	Undisclosed
14 Ameobi, Sammy	Newcastle U	Bolton W	Free
1 Ampadu, Ethan	Exeter C	Chelsea	Undisclosed
20 Anderson, Harry	Peterborough U	Lincoln C	Undisclosed
6 Anita, Vurnon	Newcastle U	Leeds U	Free
22 Arnautovic, Marko	Stoke C	West Ham U	£20m rising to £25m
17 Assombalonga, Britt	Nottingham F	Middlesbrough	£15m
6 Azeez, Ade	Partick Thistle	Cambridge U	Undisclosed
1 Bachmann, Daniel	Stoke C	Watford	Free
4 Bailey, James	Carlisle U	Yeovil T	Free
28 Baker, Nathan	Aston Villa	Bristol C	Undisclosed
25 Bardsley, Phil	Stoke C	Burnley	Undisclosed
6 Barnett, Tyrone	AFC Wimbledon	Port Vale	Undisclosed
25 Bennett, Richard	Barrow	Carlisle U	Undisclosed
31 Berghuis, Steven	Watford	Feyenoord	Undisclosed
18 Bingham, Billy	Crewe Alex	Gillingham	Free
31 Bird, Pierce	Dunkirk	Notts Co	Free
14 Bodvarsson, Jon Dadi	Wolverhampton W	Reading	Undisclosed
20 Bolton, James	Gateshead	Shrewsbury T	Undisclosed
20 Bostwick, Michael	Peterborough U	Lincoln C	Undisclosed
3 Boyd, George	Burnley	Sheffield W	Free
8 Bradbury, Harvey	Portsmouth	Watford	Free
10 Brindley, Richard	Colchester U	Barnet	Free
24 Brisley, Shaun	Carlisle U	Notts Co	Free
4 Broadfoot, Kirk	Rotherham U	Kilmarnock	Free
26 Burton, Callum	Shrewsbury T	Hull C	Undisclosed
1 Caballero, Willy	Manchester C	Chelsea	Free
20 Caddis, Paul	Birmingham C	Blackburn R	Free
18 Campbell, Fraizer	Crystal Palace	Hull C	Free
17 Cardwell, Harry	Reading	Grimsby T	Free
13 Chalobah, Nathaniel	Chelsea	Watford	Undisclosed
18 Christiansen, Lasse Vigen	Fulham	Brondby	Undisclosed
7 Christie, Cyrus	Derby Co	Middlesbrough	Undisclosed
28 Cooper, Jake	Reading	Millwall	Undisclosed
11 Cork, Jack	Swansea C	Burnley	£10m
26 Coulthirst, Shaquile	Peterborough U	Barnet	Free
7 Coveney, Joe	Manchester C	Nottingham F	Free
18 Crooks, Matt	Rangers	Northampton T	Undisclosed
17 Crowley, Dan	Arsenal	Willem II	Undisclosed
7 Darby, Stephen	Bradford C	Bolton W	Free
26 Darikwa, Tendayi	Burnley	Nottingham F	Undisclosed
14 Deulofeu, Gerard	Everton	Barcelona	£10.6m
29 Dixon, Paul	Dundee U	Grimsby T	Free
16 Dobson, George	West Ham U	Sparta Rotterdam	Undisclosed
6 Dorrans, Graham	Norwich C	Rangers	Undisclosed
17 Duffus, Courtney	Everton	Oldham Ath	Undisclosed
7 Eisa, Mohamed	Greenwich Bor	Cheltenham T	Free
3 El-Abd, Adam	Shrewsbury T	Wycombe W	Free
19 Elmohamady, Ahmed	Hull C	Aston Villa	£1m
28 Erwin, Lee	Leeds U	Kilmarnock	Free
15 Fazio, Federico	Tottenham H	Roma	Undisclosed
26 Fisher, Darnell	Rotherham U	Preston NE	Undisclosed
28 Fletcher, Ashley	West Ham U	Middlesbrough	£6.5m
20 Forde, David	Millwall	Cambridge U	Free
3 Forster, Jordon	Hibernian	Cheltenham T	Undisclosed
20 Frei, Kerim	Birmingham C	Istanbul Basaksehir	Undisclosed
1 Fryers, Zeki	Crystal Palace	Barnsley	Free
18 Fulton, Ryan	Liverpool	Hamilton A	Free
7 Gilmartin, Rene	Watford	Colchester U	Free
17 Gouffran, Yoan	Newcastle U	Goztepe	Free
31 Greer, Gordon	Blackburn R	Kilmarnock	Free
6 Grimmer, Jack	Fulham	Coventry C	Free
28 Gunning, Gavin	Grimsby T	Port Vale	Free
6 Hendry, Jack	Wigan Ath	Dundee	Free
12 Henry, James	Wolverhampton W	Oxford U	Free
9 Hinds, Kaylen	Arsenal	Wolfsburg	Undisclosed
8 Howes, Sam	West Ham U	Watford	Free
7 Howson, Jonny	Norwich C	Middlesbrough	Undisclosed
15 Huddlestone, Tom	Hull C	Derby Co	£2m
13 Hunt, Rob	Brighton & HA	Oldham Ath	Undisclosed
11 Husband, James	Middlesbrough	Norwich C	Undisclosed
4 Ince, Tom	Derby Co	Huddersfield T	Undisclosed
2 Isgrove, Lloyd	Southampton	Barnsley	Free
21 Jackson, Kayden	Barnsley	Accrington S	Undisclosed
19 Jakupovic, Eldin	Hull C	Leicester C	Undisclosed

13	James, Luke	Peterborough U	Forest Green R	Free
12	Januzaj, Adnan	Manchester U	Real Sociedad	£9.8m
3	Jones, Dan	Chesterfield	Notts Co	Free
4	Jozabed	Fulham	Celta Vigo	Undisclosed
13	Kamara, Glen	Arsenal	Dundee	Free
4	Kasim, Yaser	Swindon T	Northampton T	Free
3	Keane, Michael	Burnley	Everton	£30m
1	Keown, Niall	Reading	Partick Thistle	Undisclosed
7	Kightly, Michael	Burnley	Southend U	Free
15	Killip, Ben	Norwich C	Grimsby T	Free
6	Kipre, Cedric	Leicester C	Motherwell	Free
22	Kolarov, Aleksandar	Manchester C	Roma	£4.5m
17	Kpekawa, Cole	Barnsley	Colchester U	Undisclosed
4	Lee, Elliot	Barnsley	Luton T	Free
18	Leiva, Lucas	Liverpool	Lazio	£5m
10	Lukaku, Romelu	Everton	Manchester U	£75m
25	Lundstram, John	Oxford U	Sheffield U	Undisclosed
6	MacGillivray, Craig	Walsall	Shrewsbury T	Free
20	Maguire, Chris	Oxford U	Bury	Free
4	Mahoney, Connor	Blackburn R	Bournemouth	Undisclosed
11	Mandanda, Steve	Crystal Palace	Marseille	Undisclosed
21	Mandron, Mikael	Wigan Ath	Colchester U	Undisclosed
19	Mannone, Vito	Sunderland	Reading	£2m
21	Manu, Elvis	Brighton & HA	Genclerbirligi	Free
17	Martina, Cuco	Southampton	Everton	Free
6	Massey, Gavin	Leyton Orient	Wigan Ath	Free
31	Matic, Nemanja	Chelsea	Manchester U	£40m
7	Maynard, Nicky	Milton Keynes D	Aberdeen	Free
8	McCourt, Jak	Northampton T	Chesterfield	
13	McDermott, Donal	Rochdale	Swindon T	Free
13	McGeady, Aiden	Everton	Sunderland	Undisclosed
12	McGee, Luke	Tottenham H	Portsmouth	Undisclosed
6	McKay, Barrie	Rangers	Nottingham F	Undisclosed
25	Mckay, Billy	Wigan Ath	Ross Co	Undisclosed
6	McLaughlin, Conor	Fleetwood T	Millwall	Free
14	Miller, George	Bury	Middlesbrough	Undisclosed
21	Murphy, Daryl	Newcastle U	Nottingham F	Undisclosed
19	Murphy, Jacob	Norwich C	Newcastle U	£12m
21	Nash, Liam	Maldon & Tiptree	Gillingham	Free
25	Newell, George	Bolton W	Motherwell	Free
17	Nichols, Tom	Peterborough U	Bristol R	Undisclosed
3	Nolan, Eddie	Blackpool	Crewe Alex	Free
16	Nolito	Manchester C	Sevilla	£7.9m
11	Norris, Will	Cambridge U	Wolverhampton W	Undisclosed
12	Ntcham, Olivier	Manchester C	Celtic	£4.5m
27	Ntlhe, Kgosi	Stevenage	Rochdale	Free
6	Obika, Jonathan	Swindon T	Oxford U	Free
20	O'Brien, Jim	Shrewsbury T	Ross Co	Free
6	O'Connor, Stefan	Arsenal	Newcastle U	Free
4	O'Donnell, Stephen	Luton T	Kilmarnock	Free
27	Osborne, Karleigh	Kilmarnock	Grimsby T	Free
20	Parish, Elliot	Accrington S	Dundee	Free
4	Parkes, Tom	Leyton Orient	Carlisle U	Free
19	Penny, Alex	Nuneaton T	Peterborough U	Undisclosed
28	Phillips, Adam	Liverpool	Norwich C	Free
22	Pickering, Harry	Port Vale	Forest Green R	Free
21	Pierre, Aaron	Wycombe W	Northampton T	Free
14	Pitman, Brett	Ipswich T	Portsmouth	Undisclosed
3	Proctor, Jamie	Bolton W	Rotherham U	Undisclosed
22	Randolph, Darren	West Ham U	Middlesbrough	£5m
4	Reeves, Jake	AFC Wimbledon	Bradford C	Undisclosed
1	Roberts, Marc	Barnsley	Birmingham C	Undisclosed
21	Robertson, Andrew	Hull C	Liverpool	£8m rising to £10m
2	Rodriguez, Jay	Southampton	WBA	£12m
9	Rooney, Wayne	Manchester U	Everton	Free
1	Ross, Craig	Macclesfield T	Barnet	Free
10	Ruddy, John	Norwich C	Wolverhampton W	Free
6	Ryan, Jimmy	Fleetwood T	Blackpool	Free
21	Saadi, Idriss	Cardiff C	Strasbourg	Undisclosed
19	Samuel, Dominic	Reading	Blackburn R	Undisclosed
31	Sang, Chris	Wigan Ath	Bury	Free
25	Santos, Alefe	Derby Co	Yeovil T	Free
31	Saunders, Callum	Crewe Alex	Notts Co	Free
1	Scowen, Josh	Barnsley	QPR	Free
7	Sellars, Jerell	Aston Villa	Cheltenham T	Free
3	Shea, James	AFC Wimbledon	Luton T	Free
10	Shephard, Liam	Swansea C	Peterborough U	Free
19	Simpson, Jordan	Swindon T	Forest Green R	Free
6	Slocombe, Sam	Blackpool	Bristol R	Free
6	Smith, Adam	Northampton T	Bristol R	Free
11	Solanke, Dominic	Chelsea	Liverpool	Undisclosed
6	Stearman, Richard	Fulham	Sheffield U	Undisclosed
26	Steele, Jason	Blackburn R	Sunderland	Undisclosed
21	Stewart, Kevin	Liverpool	Hull C	£8m
11	Suarez, Mario	Watford	Guizhou Hengfeng Zhicheng	Undisclosed
19	Szczesny, Wojciech	Arsenal	Juventus	£10m
6	Taylor, Ash	Aberdeen	Northampton T	Free

6 Taylor, Charlie	Leeds U	Burnley	Tribunal
25 Taylor, Steven	Ipswich T	Peterborough U	Free
3 Terry, John	Chelsea	Aston Villa	Free
13 Tomlin, Lee	Bristol C	Cardiff C	£2.9m
21 Trotter, Liam	Bolton W	AFC Wimbledon	Free
29 Tunnicliffe, Ryan	Fulham	Millwall	Undisclosed
11 Turner, Michael	Norwich C	Southend U	Free
6 Tymon, Josh	Hull C	Stoke C	Undisclosed
25 Tyson, Nathan	Kilmarnock	Wycombe W	Free
13 Valencia, Enner	West Ham U	Tigres	Undisclosed
18 Vancooten, Terence	Reading	Stevenage	Free
13 Vaughan, James	Bury	Sunderland	£900,000
25 Veretout, Jordan	Aston Villa	Fiorentina	Undisclosed
4 Walker, Brad	Hartlepool U	Crewe Alex	Undisclosed
14 Walker, Kyle	Tottenham H	Manchester C	£45m
7 Walters, Jon	Stoke C	Burnley	£3m
18 Watkins, Ollie	Exeter C	Brentford	Undisclosed
20 Whelan, Glenn	Stoke C	Aston Villa	£1m
28 Whelpdale, Chris	AFC Wimbledon	Stevenage	Free
15 Whittaker, Steven	Norwich C	Hibernian	Free
3 Williams, Ben	Bury	Blackpool	Free
26 Williamson, Mike	Wolverhampton W	Oxford U	Free
3 Wisdom, Andre	Liverpool	Derby Co	Undisclosed
6 Yarney, Josef	Everton	Newcastle U	Free
11 Zieler, Ron-Robert	Leicester C	Stuttgart	Undisclosed

AUGUST 2017

31 Allen, Jamie	Rochdale	Burton Alb	Undisclosed
29 Aluko, Sone	Fulham	Reading	£7.5m
10 Andreu, Tony	Norwich C	Coventry C	Free
17 Arnold, Steve	Dover Ath	Gillingham	Free
13 Bacuna, Leandro	Aston Villa	Reading	Undisclosed
31 Bakinson, Tyreeq	Luton T	Bristol C	Undisclosed
7 Baptiste, Alex	Middlesbrough	QPR	Free
3 Barrow, Modou	Swansea C	Reading	£1.5m
15 Barry, Gareth	Everton	WBA	Undisclosed
22 Beckles, Omar	Accrington S	Shrewsbury T	Undisclosed
21 Bennacer, Ismael	Arsenal	Empoli	Undisclosed
25 Berry, Luke	Cambridge U	Luton T	Undisclosed
31 Birighitti, Mark	Swansea C	NAC Breda	Free
26 Blackman, Andre	Crawley T	Barnet	Free
31 Boateng, Hiram	Crystal Palace	Exeter C	Free
17 Bogle, Omar	Wigan Ath	Cardiff C	Undisclosed
31 Bony, Wilfried	Manchester C	Swansea C	£12m
31 Brayford, John	Sheffield U	Burton Alb	Free
22 Bridcutt, Liam	Leeds U	Nottingham F	Undisclosed
2 Brown, Jevani	St Neots T	Cambridge U	Free
13 Bruce, Alex	Hull C	Bury	Free
31 Bruce, Alex	Bury	Wigan Ath	Free
1 Brunt, Ryan	Plymouth Arg	Exeter C	Free
4 Bunn, Harry	Huddersfield T	Bury	Undisclosed
31 Butcher, Calum	Millwall	Mansfield T	Free
31 Callachan, Ross	Raith R	Hearts	Undisclosed
31 Charles-Cook, Reice	Coventry C	Swindon T	Undisclosed
23 Clucas, Sam	Hull C	Swansea C	Undisclosed
17 Coddington, Luke	Huddersfield T	Northampton T	Free
31 Colin, Maxime	Brentford	Birmingham C	Undisclosed
8 Cornick, Harry	Bournemouth	Luton T	Undisclosed
1 Cosgrove, Sam	Wigan Ath	Carlisle U	Free
9 Cummings, Shaun	Millwall	Rotherham U	Free
31 Davies, Tom	Portsmouth	Coventry C	Undisclosed
28 de Jong, Siem	Newcastle U	Ajax	£4m
10 De Roon, Marten	Middlesbrough	Atalanta	Undisclosed
30 Dean, Harlee	Brentford	Birmingham C	Undisclosed
29 Dicko, Nouha	Wolverhampton W	Hull C	Undisclosed
31 Donaldson, Clayton	Birmingham C	Sheffield U	Undisclosed
3 Done, Matt	Sheffield U	Rochdale	Free
18 Donohue, Dion	Chesterfield	Portsmouth	Undisclosed
3 Eardley, Neal	Northampton	Lincoln C	Free
26 Edwards, Dave	Wolverhampton W	Reading	Undisclosed
14 Feghouli, Sofiane	West Ham U	Galatasaray	£3.87m
4 Fernando	Manchester C	Galatasaray	Undisclosed
31 Flinders, Scott	Macclesfield T	Cheltenham T	Free
23 Gazzaniga, Paulo	Southampton	Tottenham H	Undisclosed
30 Gibbs, Kieran	Arsenal	WBA	£7m
31 Gilbey, Alex	Wigan Ath	Milton Keynes D	Undisclosed
10 Graham, Brian	Hibernian	Cheltenham T	Free
9 Gray, Andre	Burnley	Watford	Undisclosed
16 Green, Jordan	Bournemouth	Yeovil T	Free
28 Green, Robert	Leeds U	Huddersfield T	Free
31 Grimshaw, Liam	Preston NE	Motherwell	Free
30 Hanley, Grant	Newcastle U	Norwich C	Undisclosed
31 Hart, Sam	Liverpool	Blackburn R	Undisclosed
31 Hawkins, Oliver	Dagenham & R	Portsmouth	Undisclosed
31 Heneghan, Ben	Motherwell	Sheffield U	Undisclosed
1 Hodge, Elliot	Lincoln C	Notts Co	Undisclosed
31 Holden, Rory	Derry C	Bristol C	Undisclosed

8	Hooper, JJ	Port Vale	Grimsby T	Free
1	Hunt, Nicky	Leyton Orient	Notts Co	Undisclosed
3	Hunt, Noel	Portsmouth	Wigan Ath	Free
3	Iheanacho, Kelechi	Manchester C	Leicester C	£25m
30	Irvine, Jackson	Burton Alb	Hull C	Undisclosed
15	Jaaskelainen, Will	Bolton W	Crewe Alex	Free
31	Jameson, Kyle	Chelsea	WBA	Undisclosed
31	Jarvis, Aaron	Basingstoke	Luton T	Undisclosed
31	Johnson, Marvin	Oxford U	Middlesbrough	Undisclosed
7	Jones, Jamie	Stevenage	Wigan Ath	Free
16	Joselu	Stoke C	Newcastle U	£5m
31	Jota	Brentford	Birmingham C	Undisclosed
1	Kanu, Idris	Aldershot T	Peterborough U	Undisclosed
3	Kiernan, Rob	Rangers	Southend U	Undisclosed
23	Kingsley, Stephen	Swansea C	Hull C	Undisclosed
2	Knoyle, Kyle	West Ham U	Swindon T	Free
9	Larsson, Seb	Sunderland	Hull C	Free
1	Lavelle, Sam	Bolton W	Morecambe	Free
15	Lawrence, Tom	Leicester C	Derby Co	Undisclosed
2	Leutwiler, Jayson	Shrewsbury T	Blackburn R	Undisclosed
31	Llorente, Fernando	Swansea C	Tottenham H	£15m
2	Lokko, Kevin	Maidstone U	Stevenage	Undisclosed
28	Lonergan, Andy	Wolverhampton W	Leeds U	Free
31	Lowe, Jason	Blackburn R	Birmingham C	Free
17	Mackail-Smith, Craig	Luton T	Wycombe W	Free
31	Malen, Donyell	Arsenal	PSV Eindhoven	Undisclosed
31	Mars, Malakai	Chelsea	Barnet	Undisclosed
10	May, Stevie	Preston NE	Aberdeen	Undisclosed
31	McGinn, Paul	Chesterfield	Partick Thistle	Free
31	McGurk, Adam	Cambridge U	Morecambe	Free
25	McLaughlin, Jon	Burton Alb	Hearts	Free
31	McManaman, Callum	WBA	Sunderland	Undisclosed
31	Middleton, Harry	Doncaster R	Port Vale	Free
31	Miller, Will	Tottenham H	Burton Alb	Undisclosed
22	Mourgos, Savvas	Arsenal	Norwich C	Undisclosed
31	Mousinho, John	Burton Alb	Oxford U	Free
21	Nasri, Samir	Manchester C	Antalyaspor	£3.2m
1	Navas, Jesus	Manchester C	Sevilla	Free
31	Nesbitt, Aidan	Celtic	Milton Keynes D	Undisclosed
31	Noone, Craig	Cardiff C	Bolton W	Undisclosed
31	Novak, Lee	Charlton Ath	Scunthorpe U	Free
15	Nugent, Ben	Crewe Alex	Gillingham	Free
31	Odelusi, Sanmi	Wigan Ath	Colchester U	Free
31	Onariase, Manny	Brentford	Rotherham U	Undisclosed
31	Oxlade-Chamberlain, Alex	Arsenal	Liverpool	£35m
18	Paulista, Gabriel	Arsenal	Valencia	Undisclosed
18	Payne, Stefan	Barnsley	Shrewsbury T	Undisclosed
4	Pearson, James	Barnet	Coventry C	Free
4	Pearson, Matty	Accrington S	Barnsley	Undisclosed
2	Plummer, Ellis	Manchester C	Motherwell	Free
3	Potts, Brad	Blackpool	Barnsley	Undisclosed
16	Quigley, Scott	The New Saints	Blackpool	£35,000
18	Raggett, Sean	Lincoln T	Norwich C	Undisclosed fee
4	Ramirez, Gaston	Middlesbrough	Sampdoria	Undisclosed
3	Reeves, Ben	Milton Keynes D	Charlton Ath	Free
25	Riviere, Emmanuel	Newcastle U	Metz	Undisclosed
29	Roberts, Gary	Portsmouth	Wigan Ath	Free
24	Roberts, Mark	Cambridge U	Forest Green R	Free
31	Sancho, Jadon	Manchester C	Borussia Dortmund	£10m
30	Shotton, Ryan	Birmingham C	Middlesbrough	Undisclosed
16	Sigurdsson, Gylfi	Swansea C	Everton	£45m
7	Smith, Jonathan	Luton T	Stevenage	Free
31	Smith, Michael	Portsmouth	Bury	Free
6	Stiepermann, Marco	Bochum	Norwich C	Undisclosed
31	Stockley, Jayden	Aberdeen	Exeter C	Undisclosed
2	Stokes, Anthony	Blackburn R	Hibernian	Free
22	Taylor, Matt	Northampton T	Swindon T	Free
8	Thomas, George	Coventry C	Leicester C	Undisclosed
4	Tonge, Michael	Stevenage	Port Vale	Free
24	Toral, Jon	Arsenal	Hull C	Undisclosed
14	Vassell, Isaac	Luton T	Birmingham C	Undisclosed
7	Waghorn, Martyn	Rangers	Ipswich T	Undisclosed
14	Watt, Tony	Charlton Ath	Oud-Heverlee Leuven	Undisclosed
31	Wells, Nahki	Huddersfield T	Burnley	£5m
31	Wheeler, David	Exeter C	QPR	Undisclosed
3	Wilbraham, Aaron	Bristol C	Bolton W	Undisclosed
31	Wilson, Marc	Bournemouth	Sunderland	Undisclosed
29	Wimmer, Kevin	Tottenham H	Stoke C	£18m
30	Wollscheid, Philipp	Stoke C	Metz	Free
21	Wood, Chris	Leeds U	Burnley	£15m
7	Woolery, Kaiyne	Wigan Ath	Swindon T	£350,000
31	Woolford, Martyn	Fleetwood T	Grimsby T	Free
24	Worrall, David	Millwall	Port Vale	Free

SEPTEMBER 2017

1	Briggs, Matthew	Colchester U	Chesterfield T	Free
5	Doherty, Josh	Ards	Crawley T	Undisclosed

1 Drinkwater, Danny	Leicester C	Chelsea	£35m
1 Gordon, Jaanai	West Ham U	Cheltenham T	Undisclosed
20 Krul, Tim	Newcastle U	Brighton & HA	Free
1 Martin, David	Milton Keynes D	Millwall	Free
29 McCormack, Ross	Aston Villa	Melbourne C	Undisclosed
1 Osayi-Samuel, Bright	Blackpool	QPR	Undisclosed
1 Remy, Loic	Chelsea	Las Palmas	Free
16 Roos, Kelle	Derby Co	Port Vale	Emergency loan
1 Sakho, Mamadou	Liverpool	Crystal Palace	£26m
1 Tarpey, Dave	Maidenhead	Barnet	Undisclosed

OCTOBER 2017

20 Matthews, Remi	Norwich C	Plymouth Arg	Emergency loan

NOVEMBER 2017

28 Mannion, Will	Hull C	Plymouth Arg	Emergency loan

DECEMBER 2017

8 Roos, Kelle	Derby Co	Plymouth Arg	Emergency loan

JANUARY 2018

31 Afolayan, Oladapo	Solihull	West Ham U	Undisclosed
16 Anderson, Keshi	Crystal Palace	Swindon T	Undisclosed
1 Angus, Dior	Redditch	Port Vale	Undisclosed
31 Ayew, Andre	West Ham U	Swansea	£18m
5 Barkley, Ross	Everton	Chelsea	£15m
31 Barnes, Aaron	Charlton Ath	Colchester U	Undisclosed
9 Bauer, Moritz	Rubin Kazan	Stoke C	Undisclosed
31 Beerens, Roy	Reading	Vitesse Arnhem	Undisclosed
26 Belford, Cameron	Stranraer	Forest Green R	Free
19 Bell, Amari'i	Fleetwood T	Blackburn R	Undisclosed
31 Bennett, Kyle	Portsmouth	Bristol R	Free
16 Blaney, Shane	Finn Harps	Doncaster R	Undisclosed
3 Bodin, Billy	Bristol R	Preston NE	Undisclosed
11 Brannagan, Cameron	Liverpool	Oxford U	Undisclosed
5 Bridge, Jack	Southend U	Northampton T	Undisclosed
16 Bunney, Joe	Rochdale	Northampton T	Undisclosed
15 Byrne, Jack	Wigan Ath	Oldham Ath	Undisclosed
31 Campbell-Ryce, Jamal	Barnet	Carlisle U	Undisclosed
31 Carayol, Mustapha	Nottingham F	Ipswich T	Free
31 Christie, Cyrus	Middlesbrough	Fulham	Undisclosed
19 Church, Simon	Scunthorpe U	Plymouth Arg	Free
31 Cole, Devante	Fleetwood T	Wigan Ath	Undisclosed
17 Comley, Brandon	QPR	Colchester U	Undisclosed
18 Cooper, George	Crewe Alex	Peterborough U	Undisclosed
11 Coquelin, Francis	Arsenal	Valencia	£12m
31 Cosgrove, Sam	Carlisle U	Aberdeen	Free
1 Costa, Diego	Chelsea	Atletico Madrid	Undisclosed
31 Cotter, Barry	Limerick	Ipswich T	Undisclosed
8 Coutinho, Philippe	Liverpool	Barcelona	£142m
31 Craig, Tony	Millwall	Bristol R	Free
31 Cranie, Martin	Huddersfield T	Middlesbrough	Undisclosed
31 Debuchy, Mathieu	Arsenal	Saint-Etienne	Free
9 Delaney, Ryan	Burton Alb	Rochdale	Undisclosed
7 Diagouraga, Toumani	Plymouth Arg	Fleetwood T	Free
4 Dickie, Rob	Reading	Oxford U	Undisclosed
5 Dodds, Louis	Shrewsbury T	Chesterfield	Free
27 Donnellan, Shaun	WBA	Yeovil T	Free
8 Downing, Paul	Milton Keynes D	Blackburn R	Undisclosed
4 Drinan, Aaron	Waterford	Ipswich T	Undisclosed
31 Eisa, Abo	Wealdstone	Shrewsbury T	Undisclosed
10 Evans, Lee	Wolverhampton W	Sheffield U	£750,000
5 Facey, Shay	Manchester C	Northampton T	Undisclosed
26 Fisher, Alex	Motherwell	Yeovil T	Free
18 Forshaw, Adam	Middlesbrough	Leeds U	£4.5m
11 Francis, Akeel	Rotherham U	Accrington S	Free
11 Frecklington, Lee	Rotherham U	Lincoln C	Undisclosed
25 Gallagher, Tony	Falkirk	Liverpool	£200,000
31 Giroud, Olivier	Arsenal	Chelsea	£18m
19 Gleeson, Stephen	Birmingham C	Ipswich T	Free
31 Goddard, John	Swindon T	Stevenage	Undisclosed
3 Gondoh, Ryan	Maldon & Tiptree	Colchester U	Undisclosed
1 Grubb, Dayle	Weston-super-Mare	Forest Green R	Undisclosed
31 Guedioura, Adlene	Middlesbrough	Nottingham F	Undisclosed
4 Gunning, Gavin	Port Vale	Forest Green R	Free
18 Hannant, Luke	Gateshead	Port Vale	Undisclosed
30 Harrison, Jack	New York City	Manchester C	Undisclosed
24 Hartley, Peter	Blackpool	Motherwell	Undisclosed
9 Hendrie, Luke	Burnley	Shrewsbury T	Undisclosed
9 Hollis, Haydn	Notts Co	Forest Green R	Free
15 Holmes, Ricky	Charlton Ath	Sheffield U	Undisclosed
31 Howe, Callum	Lincoln C	Port Vale	Undisclosed
31 Hugill, Jordan	Preston NE	West Ham U	Undisclosed
12 Husin, Noor	Crystal Palace	Notts Co	Undisclosed
16 Jerome, Cameron	Norwich C	Derby Co	Undisclosed
31 Jervis, Jake	Plymouth Arg	Luton T	Undisclosed
1 John, Declan	Cardiff C	Rangers	Undisclosed
5 Johnson, Callum	Middlesbrough	Accrington S	Undisclosed
5 Jones, Gethin	Everton	Fleetwood T	Undisclosed

31 Jones, Lloyd	Liverpool	Luton T	Undisclosed
31 Jones, Sam	Grimsby T	Shrewsbury T	Undisclosed
31 Ladapo, Freddie	Crystal Palace	Southend U	Undisclosed
23 Lennon, Aaron	Everton	Burnley	Undisclosed
9 Leonard, Ryan	Southend U	Sheffield U	Undisclosed
8 Livesey, Jack	Partick Thistle	Burton Alb	Undisclosed
31 Lolley, Joe	Huddersfield T	Nottingham F	Undisclosed
25 LuaLua, Kazenga	Brighton & HA	Sunderland	Free
31 MacDonald, Angus	Barnsley	Hull C	Undisclosed
2 Madden, Paddy	Scunthorpe U	Fleetwood T	Undisclosed
31 Madine, Gary	Bolton W	Cardiff C	About £6m
16 Madl, Michael	Fulham	Austria Vienna	Undisclosed
3 Main, Curtis	Portsmouth	Motherwell	Undisclosed
19 Maxted, Jonny	Guiseley	Accrington S	Undisclosed
1 McEleney, Patrick	Dundalk	Oldham Ath	Undisclosed
12 McGinley, Nathan	Middlesbrough	Wycombe W	Undisclosed
30 McGuane, Marcus	Arsenal	Barcelona	Undisclosed
22 McLean, Kenny	Aberdeen	Norwich C	Undisclosed
11 Mensah, Bernard	Aldershot T	Bristol R	Undisclosed
31 Middleton, Glenn	Norwich C	Rangers	Undisclosed
31 Mills, Matt	Nottingham F	Barnsley	Free
22 Mkhitaryan, Henrikh	Manchester U	Arsenal	Swap for Alexis Sanchez
8 Moore, Kieffer	Ipswich T	Barnsley	Undisclosed
27 Moore, Stuart	Barrow	Swindon T	Free
1 Moult, Louis	Motherwell	Preston NE	£500,000
31 Murphy, Rhys	Forest Green R	Gillingham	Free
3 Ngbakoto, Yeni	QPR	Guingamp	Undisclosed
31 Nicholson, Jordan	Peterborough U	Barnet	Undisclosed
1 Noble, Liam	Forest Green R	Notts Co	Free
8 Nsue, Emilio	Birmingham C	Apoel	Undisclosed
5 Odelusi, Sanmi	Colchester U	Cheltenham T	Free
8 O'Donnell, Richard	Rotherham U	Northampton T	Undisclosed
30 Ogbene, Chiedozie	Limerick	Brentford	Undisclosed
3 Ogedi-Uzokwe, Junior	Maldon & Tiptree	Colchester U	Undisclosed
3 O'Shaughnessy, Daniel	Cheltenham T	HJK Helsinki	Free
25 Palmer, Matty	Burton Alb	Rotherham U	Undisclosed
31 Pett, Tom	Stevenage	Lincoln C	Undisclosed
5 Pigott, Joe	Maidstone	AFC Wimbledon	Undisclosed
8 Price, Jack	Wolverhampton W	Colorado Rapids	Undisclosed
12 Pritchard, Alex	Norwich C	Huddersfield T	Undisclosed
4 Rawson, Farrend	Derby Co	Forest Green R	Undisclosed
5 Reid, Reuben	Exeter C	Forest Green R	Undisclosed
30 Revell, Alex	Northampton T	Stevenage	Free
15 Richards, Marc	Northampton T	Swindon T	Free
31 Roberts, Tyler	WBA	Leeds U	£2.5m
31 Rodgers, Harvey	Fleetwood T	Accrington S	Undisclosed
24 Rooney, Paul	Millwall	Colchester U	Undisclosed
31 Russell, Johnny	Derby Co	Sporting Kansas City	Undisclosed
29 Sakho, Diafra	West Ham U	Rennes	Undisclosed
22 Sanchez, Alexis	Arsenal	Manchester U	Swap for Henrikh Mkhitaryan
18 Sigurdsson, Ragnar	Fulham	FC Rostov	Undisclosed
11 Simpson, Connor	Hartlepool U	Preston NE	Undisclosed
31 Smith, George	Northampton T	Chesterfield	Undisclosed
11 Smith, Michael	Bury	Rotherham U	Undisclosed
22 Smith, Tommy	Ipswich T	Colorado Rapids	Undisclosed
31 Stevens, Jordan	Forest Green R	Leeds U	Undisclosed
31 Stevenson, Ben	Coventry C	Wolverhampton W	Undisclosed
26 Stockton, Cole	Hearts	Carlisle U	Free
29 Toffolo, Harry	Norwich C	Millwall	Undisclosed
11 Turnbull, Jordan	Coventry C	Northampton T	Free
1 van Dijk, Virgil	Southampton	Liverpool	£75m
30 van Veen, Kevin	Scunthorpe U	Northampton	Undisclosed
12 Vaughan, James	Sunderland	Wigan Ath	Undisclosed
17 Walcott, Theo	Arsenal	Everton	£20m
8 Walker, Jamie	Hearts	Wigan Ath	Undisclosed
5 Walsh, Liam	Everton	Bristol C	Undisclosed
10 Ward, Joe	Woking	Peterborough U	Undisclosed
31 White, Joe	Dagenham & R	Stevenage	Undisclosed
11 Whiteman, Ben	Sheffield U	Doncaster R	Undisclosed
18 Whitmore, Alex	Burnley	Chesterfield	Free
1 Whittle, Alex	York C	Forest Green R	Free
12 Williams, Danny	Dundee	Accrington S	Free
31 Withers, Jack	Boston U	Swansea C	Undisclosed

FEBRUARY 2018

10 Vibe, Lasse	Brentford	Changchun Yatai	Undisclosed
5 Watson, Ben	Watford	Nottingham Forest	Free

MARCH 2018

13 Ledger, Michael	Sunderland	Notodden FK	Undisclosed

MAY 2018

17 Anderson, Tom	Burnley	Doncaster R	Free
25 Andrade, Bruno	Boreham Wood	Lincoln C	Free
14 Arfield, Scott	Burnley	Rangers	Free
9 Ball, James	Stockport Co	Stevenage	Undisclosed
15 Barratt, Sam	Maidenhead U	Southend U	Undisclosed
30 Baxter, Jose	Everton	Oldham Ath	Free

	From	To	Fee
16 Bennett, Rhys	Mansfield T	Peterborough U	Free
18 Bennetts, Keanan	Tottenham H	Borussia Moenchengladbach	Undisclosed
18 Broom, Ryan	Bristol R	Cheltenham T	Free
14 Brown, Scott	Wycombe W	Port Vale	Free
29 Campbell-Ryce, Jamal	Carlisle U	Stevenage	Free
15 Chapman, Aaron	Accrington S	Peterborough U	Free
30 Charles-Cook, Regan	Charlton Ath	Gillingham	Free
25 Chesmain, Noah	Millwall	Colchester U	Free
23 Clarke, Eddie	Tranmere R	Fleetwood T	Free
22 Cook, Andy	Tranmere R	Walsall	Free
30 Crawford, Tom	Chester FC	Notts Co	Undisclosed
30 Cuthbert, Scott	Luton T	Stevenage	Free
24 Daniel, Colin	Blackpool	Peterborough U	Free
17 Daniels, Brendon	Alfreton T	Port Vale	Free
30 Dawson, Michael	Hull C	Nottingham F	Free
31 Dennis, Kristian	Chesterfield	Notts Co	Undisclosed
23 Dennis, Louis	Bromley	Portsmouth	Free
31 Dooley, Stephen	Coleraine	Rochdale	Free
29 Evans, Will	Aldershot T	Chesterfield	Free
23 Finnerty, James	Aston Villa	Rochdale	Free
10 Green, Paul	Oldham Ath	Crewe Alex	Free
29 Hussey, Chris	Sheffield U	Cheltenham T	Free
22 Jalal, Shwan	Macclesfield T	Chesterfield	Free
21 John, Louis	Sutton U	Cambridge U	Free
17 Joyce, Luke	Carlisle U	Port Vale	Free
22 Kellermann, James	Aldershot T	St Mirren	Free
31 Kellett, Andy	Wigan Ath	Notts Co	Free
17 Ledson, Ryan	Oxford U	Preston NE	Undisclosed
16 Lee, Olly	Luton T	Hearts	Free
23 Legge, Leon	Cambridge U	Port Vale	Free
14 Maffeo, Pablo	Manchester C	Stuttgart	Undisclosed
16 McGregor, Allan	Hull C	Rangers	Free
17 Miller, Shaun	Carlisle U	Crewe Alex	Free
23 Montgomery, James	Gateshead	Forest Green R	Free
16 Mullins, Johnny	Luton T	Cheltenham T	Free
18 Murphy, Jamie	Brighton & HA	Rangers	Undisclosed
30 Naismith, Kal	Portsmouth	Wigan Ath	Free
18 Norman, Cameron	King's Lynn	Oxford U	Free
21 Nottingham, Michael	Salford	Blackpool	Free
25 O'Hara, Mark	Dundee	Peterborough U	Undisclosed
21 Olomola, Olufela	Southampton	Scunthorpe U	Free
30 Parrett, Dean	AFC Wimbledon	Gillingham	Free
10 Pell, Harry	Cheltenham T	Colchester U	Undisclosed
24 Perkins, David	Wigan Ath	Rochdale	Free
29 Preston, Matt	Swindon T	Mansfield T	Undisclosed
27 Pritchard, Harry	Maidenhead U	Blackpool	Free
23 Rawlinson, Connell	The New Saints	Port Vale	Free
25 Riley, Joe	Manchester U	Bradford C	Undisclosed
30 Taft, George	Mansfield T	Cambridge U	Free
24 Tozer, Ben	Newport Co	Cheltenham T	Free
22 Upson, Ed	Milton Keynes D	Bristol R	Free
25 Vose, Bailey	Brighton & HA	Colchester U	Undisclosed
22 Watters, Max	Ashford U	Doncaster R	Undisclosed
22 Wedgbury, Sam	Wrexham	Chesterfield	Free
10 Westbrooke, Zain	Brentford	Coventry C	Free
24 Weston, Curtis	Barnet	Chesterfield	Free
30 Whitmore, Alex	Chesterfield	Grimsby T	Undisclosed
16 Wildin, Luther	Nuneaton Bor	Stevenage	Undisclosed
21 Williams, Andy	Doncaster R	Northampton T	Free
25 Wilmot, Ben	Stevenage	Watford	Undisclosed
31 Winchester, Carl	Cheltenham T	Forest Green R	Free
31 Wood, Will	Southampton	Accrington S	Free
30 Woodyard, Alex	Lincoln C	Peterborough U	Undisclosed
9 Wright, Drey	Colchester U	St Johnstone	Free
31 Wright, Josh	Southend U	Bradford C	Free

THE NEW FOREIGN LEGION 2017–18

JUNE 2017	From	To	Fee in £
29 Cissé, Ousseynou	Tours	Milton Keynes D	Free
28 Clement, Pelle	Ajax	Reading	Undisclosed
23 Depoitre, Laurent	Porto	Huddersfield T	Undisclosed
28 Diedhiou, Famara	Angers	Bristol C	£5.3m
15 Klaassen, Davy	Ajax	Everton	£23.6m
23 Klich, Mateusz	FC Twente	Leeds U	Undisclosed
6 Kolasinac, Sead	Schalke	Arsenal	Free
14 Lindelof, Victor	Benfica	Manchester U	£31m
27 Loeke, Robbert te	Achilles '29	Plymouth Arg	Free
30 Lossl, Jonas	Mainz	Huddersfield T	Loan
13 Miranda, Roderick	Rio Ave	Wolverhampton W	Undisclosed
8 Moraes, Ederson	Benfica	Manchester C	£35m
20 Ofosu-Ayeh, Phil	Eintracht Braunschweig	Wolverhampton W	Free
30 Onyekuru, Henry	Eupen	Everton	£7m
27 Pisano, Eros	Hellas Verona	Bristol C	Free

2	Sacko, Hadi	Sporting Lisbon	Leeds U	Undisclosed
22	Salah, Mohamed	Roma	Liverpool	£34m
5	Sanoh, Moussa	RKC Waalwijk	Crawley T	Free
14	Stech, Marek	Sparta Prague	Luton T	Undisclosed
8	Vrancic, Mario	Darmstadt	Norwich C	Undisclosed
30	Wiedwald, Felix	Werder Bremen	Leeds U	Undisclosed
15	Zimmermann, Christoph	Borussia Dortmund	Norwich C	Free

JULY 2017

13	Alioski, Ezgjan	FC Lugano	Leeds U	Undisclosed
15	Bakayoko, Tiemoue	Monaco	Chelsea	Undisclosed
1	Bednarek, Jan	Lech Poznan	Southampton	Undisclosed
8	Boly, Willy	FC Porto	Wolverhampton W	Loan
27	Bouchalakis, Andreas	Olympiakos	Nottingham F	Free
13	Braithwaite, Martin	Toulouse	Middlesbrough	Undisclosed
7	Cisse, Ibrahima	Standard Liege	Fulham	Undisclosed
6	Damour, Loic	Bourg-Peronnas	Cardiff C	Free
23	Danilo	Real Madrid	Manchester C	£26.5m
3	Djalo, Marcelo	CD Lugo	Fulham	Undisclosed
1	Douglas, Barry	Konyaspor	Wolverhampton W	Undisclosed
11	Ekuban, Caleb	Chievo Verona	Leeds U	Undisclosed
1	Femenia, Kiko	Alaves	Watford	Free
14	Franke, Marcel	Greuther Furth	Norwich C	Undisclosed
17	Hegazi, Ahmed	Al Ahly	WBA	Loan
24	Hernandez, Javier	Bayer Leverkusen	West Ham U	£16m
1	Iborra, Vincent	Sevilla	Leicester C	£10.5m
7	Jorgensen, Mathias	FC Copenhagen	Huddersfield T	Undisclosed
25	Jota, Diogo	Atletico Madrid	Wolverhampton W	Loan
31	Kamara, Aboubakar	SC Amiens	Fulham	Undisclosed
6	Lacazette, Alexandre	Lyon	Arsenal	£46.5m rising to £52.6m
4	Lejeune, Florian	Eibar	Newcastle U	£8.7m
15	Luiz, Douglas	Vasco Da Gama	Manchester C	Undisclosed
20	Mafoumbi, Christoffer	Free State Stars	Blackpool	Free
21	Manquillo, Javier	Atletico Madrid	Newcastle U	Undisclosed
14	Maupay, Neal	Saint-Etienne	Brentford	Undisclosed
26	Mazuch, Ondrej	Sparta Prague	Hull C	Undisclosed
24	Mendy, Benjamin	Monaco	Manchester C	£52m
28	Merino, Mikel	Borussia Dortmund	Newcastle U	Loan
6	Mesa, Roque	Las Palmas	Swansea C	£11m
4	Mikkelsen, Thomas	Odense	Ross Co	Free
7	Mokotjo, Kamo	FC Twente	Brentford	Undisclosed
21	Morata, Alvaro	Real Madrid	Chelsea	£60m
6	Mounie, Steve	Montpellier	Huddersfield T	£11.44m
14	N'Doye, Cheikh	Angers	Birmingham C	Free
8	Neves, Ruben	FC Porto	Wolverhampton W	£15.8m
18	Ojo, Funso	Willem II	Scunthorpe U	Free
27	Old, Steve	GAIS	Morecambe	Undisclosed
3	Ramirez, Sandro	Malaga	Everton	£5.2m
24	Riedewald, Jairo	Ajax	Crystal Palace	Undisclosed
9	Rudiger, Antonio	Roma	Chelsea	Undisclosed
13	Saiz, Samuel	SD Huesca	Leeds U	Undisclosed
7	Sietsma, Wieger	Heerenveen	Milton Keynes D	Free
31	Suttner, Markus	Ingolstadt	Brighton & HA	Undisclosed
6	Verheydt, Thomas	MVV Maastricht	Crawley T	Undisclosed
20	Vinagre, Ruben	Monaco	Wolverhampton W	Loan
25	Walker, Liam	Europa FC	Notts Co	Free
18	Xemi	Barcelona	Oxford U	Free
3	Yuning, Zhang	Vitesse	WBA	Undisclosed

AUGUST 2017

10	Ahannach, Soufyan	Almere C	Brighton & HA	Undisclosed
31	Aurier, Serge	Paris Saint-Germain	Tottenham H	£23m
3	Ben Khemis, Issam	Lorient	Doncaster R	Free
1	Bonatini, Leo	Al Hilal	Wolverhampton W	Loan
2	Buoy, Ouasim	Juventus	Leeds U	Free
25	Burke, Oliver	RB Leipzig	WBA	Undisclosed
17	Cavare, Dimitri	Stade Rennais	Barnsley	Undisclosed
7	Choupo-Moting, Eric Maxim	Schalke	Stoke C	Free
31	Cibicki, Pawel	Malmo	Leeds U	Undisclosed
31	Dragovic, Aleksandar	Bayer Leverkusen	Leicester C	Loan
8	Eliasson, Niclas	IFK Norrkoping	Bristol C	£1.8m
10	Fasan, Leonardo	Udinese	Bury	Free
1	Fonte, Rui	Braga	Fulham	Undisclosed
30	Foyth, Juan	Estudiantes	Tottenham H	£8m
24	Grot, Jay-Roy	NEC Nijmegen	Leeds U	Undisclosed
24	Hadergjonaj, Florent	Ingolstadt	Huddersfield T	Loan
7	Haksabanovic, Sead	Halmstad	West Ham U	£2.7m
20	Izquierdo, Jose	Club Brugge	Brighton & HA	£13.5m
4	Jorgensen, Simon Bloch	Bronshoj	Accrington S	Free
31	Karnezis, Orestis	Udinese	Watford	Loan
18	Kayode, Olarenwaju	Austria Vienna	Manchester C	Undisclosed
30	Krychowiak, Grzegorz	Paris Saint-Germain	WBA	Loan
31	Lasogga, Pierre-Michel	Hamburg	Leeds U	Loan
8	Lemina, Mario	Juventus	Southampton	£15.4m rising to £18.1m
11	Martins Indi, Bruno	Porto	Stoke C	£7m
31	Mollo, Yohan	Zenit St Petersburg	Fulham	Free
31	N'Diaye, Alfred	Villarreal	Wolverhampton W	Loan
8	Pekalski, Ivo	Halmstad	Oxford U	Undisclosed

7 Propper, Davy	PSV Eindhoven	Brighton & HA	£6m
31 Raeder, Lukas	Vitoria Setubal	Bradford C	Free
3 Ricardinho	Qabala	Oxford U	Free
8 Richarlison	Fluminense	Watford	£11m
16 Rodriguez, Jese	Paris Saint-Germain	Stoke C	Loan
2 Ruiter, Robbin	Utrecht	Sunderland	Free
23 Sabiri, Abdelhamid	Nuremberg	Huddersfield T	Undisclosed
31 Sanches, Renato	Bayern Munich	Swansea C	Loan
23 Sanchez, Davinson	Ajax	Tottenham H	Undisclosed
31 Schelotto, Ezequiel	Sporting Lisbon	Brighton & HA	£2.75m
22 Soares, Rafa	Porto	Fulham	Loan
14 Sow, Osman	Henan Jianye	Milton Keynes D	Undisclosed
31 Steele, Luke	Panathinaikos	Bristol C	Free
12 Thiam, Mamadou	Dijon	Barnsley	Undisclosed
4 Trybull, Tom	ADO Den Haag	Norwich C	Free
30 van Aken, Joost	Heerenveen	Sheffield W	Undisclosed
16 Venancio, Frederico	Vitoria Setubal	Sheffield W	Loan
31 Vlasic, Nikola	Hajduk Split	Everton	£10m
31 Wague, Molla	Udinese	Watford	Loan
31 Zappacosta, Davide	Torino	Chelsea	Undisclosed
31 Zeegelaar, Marvin	Sporting Lisbon	Watford	£2.75m

SEPTEMBER 2017

6 Gyokeres, Viktor	IF Brommapojkarna	Brighton & HA	Undisclosed
7 Mehmeti, Agon	Genclerbirligi	Oxford U	Free
6 Menig, Queensy	Nantes	Oldham Ath	Loan
6 Omrani, Abdelhakim	Sedan	Oldham Ath	Undisclosed

DECEMBER 2017

18 Hegazi, Ahmed	Al Ahly	WBA	Undisclosed

JANUARY 2018

1 Gyokeres, Viktor	IF Brommapojkarna	Brighton & HA	Undisclosed
1 Ideguchi, Yosuke	Gamba Osaka	Leeds U	£500,000
1 Marcondes, Emiliano	Nordsjaelland	Brentford	Undisclosed
1 Silva, Adrien	Sporting Lisbon	Leicester C	£22m
3 Kongolo, Terence	Monaco	Huddersfield T	Loan
3 Dobson, George	Sparta Rotterdam	Walsall	Undisclosed
3 Halme, Aapo	HJK Helsinki	Leeds U	Undisclosed
3 Mir, Rafael	Valencia	Wolverhampton W	Undisclosed
3 Pereira, Hildeberto	Legia Warsaw	Northampton T	Loan
4 Mavropanos, Konstantinos	PAS Giannina	Arsenal	Undisclosed
5 Tosun, Cenk	Besiktas	Everton	£27m
8 Paz, Zeus de la	Cincinnati Dutch Lions	Oldham Ath	Free
9 Ideguchi, Yosuke	Gamba Osaka	Leeds U	Undisclosed
11 Bock, Laurens de	Club Brugge	Leeds U	Undisclosed
13 Diabate, Fousseni	Gazelec Ajaccio	Leicester C	Undisclosed
18 Pelupessy, Joey	Heracles Almelo	Sheffield W	Undisclosed
18 Stafylidis, Kostas	Augsburg	Stoke C	Loan
19 Locadia, Jurgen	PSV Eindhoven	Brighton & HA	£14m
19 Pinillos, Dani	Cordoba	Barnsley	Undisclosed
23 Jach, Jaroslaw	Zaglebie Lubin	Crystal Palace	Undisclosed
25 Bruenker, Kai	SC Freiburg	Bradford C	Undisclosed
25 Carrillo, Guido	Monaco	Southampton	Undisclosed
25 Diony, Lois	Saint-Etienne	Bristol C	Loan
25 Hernandez, Onel	Eintracht Braunschweig	Norwich C	Undisclosed
25 Leitner, Moritz	FC Augsburg	Norwich C	Loan
25 Mario, Joao	Inter Milan	West Ham U	Loan
25 Srbeny, Dennis	Paderborn	Norwich C	Undisclosed
26 McGowan, Ryan	Al-Sharjah	Bradford C	Free
29 Deulofeu, Gerard	Barcelona	Watford	Loan
29 Gabr, Ali	Zamalek	WBA	Loan
30 Figueiredo, Tobias	Sporting Lisbon	Nottingham F	Loan
30 Jota, Diogo	Atletico Madrid	Wolverhampton W	Undisclosed
30 Laporte, Aymeric	Athletic Bilbao	Manchester C	£57m
30 Lukebakio, Dodi	Anderlecht	Watford	Undisclosed
30 Palmieri, Emerson	Roma	Chelsea	£17.6m
31 Aubameyang, Pierre-Emerick	Borussia Dortmund	Arsenal	£56m
31 Knasmullner, Christoph	Admira Wacker	Barnsley	Undisclosed
31 Moimbe, Wilfried	Nantes	Oldham Ath	Free
31 Moura, Lucas	Paris Saint-Germain	Tottenham H	£23m
31 Ndiaye, Badou	Galatasaray	Stoke C	£14m
31 Sorloth, Alexander	Midtjylland	Crystal Palace	Undisclosed

MARCH 2018

9 Baker, Carl	ATK	Coventry C	Free
9 Fox, Andrew	AFC Eskilstuna	Grimsby T	Free

MAY 2018

25 Andone, Florin	Deportivo La Coruna	Brighton & HA	Undisclosed
22 Balogun, Leon	Mainz	Brighton & HA	Free
30 Dubravka, Martin	Sparta Prague	Newcastle U	Undisclosed
28 Fabinho	Monaco	Liverpool	£39m
25 Thomas, Conor	ATK	Cheltenham T	Free
17 Yiadom, Andy	Barnsley	Reading	Free

ENGLISH LEAGUE HONOURS 1888–2018

Won or placed on goal average (ratio), goal difference or most goals scored. ‡Not promoted after play-offs. No official competition during 1915–19 and 1939–46, regional leagues operated.

FOOTBALL LEAGUE (1888–89 to 1891–92) – TIER 1

MAXIMUM POINTS: *a* 44; *b* 60.

1	1888–89*a*	Preston NE	40	Aston Villa	29	Wolverhampton W	28
1	1889–90*a*	Preston NE	33	Everton	31	Blackburn R	27
1	1890–91*a*	Everton	29	Preston NE	27	Notts Co	26
1	1891–92*b*	Sunderland	42	Preston NE	37	Bolton W	36

DIVISION 1 (1892–93 to 1991–92)

MAXIMUM POINTS: *a* 44; *b* 52; *c* 60; *d* 68; *e* 76; *f* 84; *g* 126; *h* 120; *k* 114.

1	1892–93*c*	Sunderland	48	Preston NE	37	Everton	36
1	1893–94*c*	Aston Villa	44	Sunderland	38	Derby Co	36
1	1894–95*c*	Sunderland	47	Everton	42	Aston Villa	39
1	1895–96*c*	Aston Villa	45	Derby Co	41	Everton	39
1	1896–97*c*	Aston Villa	47	Sheffield U*	36	Derby Co	36
1	1897–98*c*	Sheffield U	42	Sunderland	37	Wolverhampton W*	35
1	1898–99*d*	Aston Villa	45	Liverpool	43	Burnley	39
1	1899–1900*d*	Aston Villa	50	Sheffield U	48	Sunderland	41
1	1900–01*d*	Liverpool	45	Sunderland	43	Notts Co	40
1	1901–02*d*	Sunderland	44	Everton	41	Newcastle U	37
1	1902–03*d*	The Wednesday	42	Aston Villa*	41	Sunderland	41
1	1903–04*d*	The Wednesday	47	Manchester C	44	Everton	43
1	1904–05*d*	Newcastle U	48	Everton	47	Manchester C	46
1	1905–06*e*	Liverpool	51	Preston NE	47	The Wednesday	44
1	1906–07*e*	Newcastle U	51	Bristol C	48	Everton*	45
1	1907–08*e*	Manchester U	52	Aston Villa*	43	Manchester C	43
1	1908–09*e*	Newcastle U	53	Everton	46	Sunderland	44
1	1909–10*e*	Aston Villa	53	Liverpool	48	Blackburn R*	45
1	1910–11*e*	Manchester U	52	Aston Villa	51	Sunderland*	45
1	1911–12*e*	Blackburn R	49	Everton	46	Newcastle U	44
1	1912–13*e*	Sunderland	54	Aston Villa	50	Sheffield W	49
1	1913–14*e*	Blackburn R	51	Aston Villa	44	Middlesbrough*	43
1	1914–15*e*	Everton	46	Oldham Ath	45	Blackburn R*	43
1	1919–20*f*	WBA	60	Burnley	51	Chelsea	49
1	1920–21*f*	Burnley	59	Manchester C	54	Bolton W	52
1	1921–22*f*	Liverpool	57	Tottenham H	51	Burnley	49
1	1922–23*f*	Liverpool	60	Sunderland	54	Huddersfield T	53
1	1923–24*f*	Huddersfield T*	57	Cardiff C	57	Sunderland	53
1	1924–25*f*	Huddersfield T	58	WBA	56	Bolton W	55
1	1925–26*f*	Huddersfield T	57	Arsenal	52	Sunderland	48
1	1926–27*f*	Newcastle U	56	Huddersfield T	51	Sunderland	49
1	1927–28*f*	Everton	53	Huddersfield T	51	Leicester C	48
1	1928–29*f*	Sheffield W	52	Leicester C	51	Aston Villa	50
1	1929–30*f*	Sheffield W	60	Derby Co	50	Manchester C*	47
1	1930–31*f*	Arsenal	66	Aston Villa	59	Sheffield W	52
1	1931–32*f*	Everton	56	Arsenal	54	Sheffield W	50
1	1932–33*f*	Arsenal	58	Aston Villa	54	Sheffield W	51
1	1933–34*f*	Arsenal	59	Huddersfield T	56	Tottenham H	49
1	1934–35*f*	Arsenal	58	Sunderland	54	Sheffield W	49
1	1935–36*f*	Sunderland	56	Derby Co*	48	Huddersfield T	48
1	1936–37*f*	Manchester C	57	Charlton Ath	54	Arsenal	52
1	1937–38*f*	Arsenal	52	Wolverhampton W	51	Preston NE	49
1	1938–39*f*	Everton	59	Wolverhampton W	55	Charlton Ath	50
1	1946–47*f*	Liverpool	57	Manchester U*	56	Wolverhampton W	56
1	1947–48*f*	Arsenal	59	Manchester U*	52	Burnley	52
1	1948–49*f*	Portsmouth	58	Manchester U*	53	Derby Co	53
1	1949–50*f*	Portsmouth*	53	Wolverhampton W	53	Sunderland	52
1	1950–51*f*	Tottenham H	60	Manchester U	56	Blackpool	50
1	1951–52*f*	Manchester U	57	Tottenham H*	53	Arsenal	53
1	1952–53*f*	Arsenal*	54	Preston NE	54	Wolverhampton W	51
1	1953–54*f*	Wolverhampton W	57	WBA	53	Huddersfield T	51
1	1954–55*f*	Chelsea	52	Wolverhampton W*	48	Portsmouth*	48
1	1955–56*f*	Manchester U	60	Blackpool*	49	Wolverhampton W	49
1	1956–57*f*	Manchester U	64	Tottenham H*	56	Preston NE	56
1	1957–58*f*	Wolverhampton W	64	Preston NE	59	Tottenham H	51
1	1958–59*f*	Wolverhampton W	61	Manchester U	55	Arsenal*	50
1	1959–60*f*	Burnley	55	Wolverhampton W	54	Tottenham H	53
1	1960–61*f*	Tottenham H	66	Sheffield W	58	Wolverhampton W	57
1	1961–62*f*	Ipswich T	56	Burnley	53	Tottenham H	52
1	1962–63*f*	Everton	61	Tottenham H	55	Burnley	54
1	1963–64*f*	Liverpool	57	Manchester U	53	Everton	52
1	1964–65*f*	Manchester U*	61	Leeds U	61	Chelsea	56

	Season		Pts		Pts		Pts
1	1965–66f	Liverpool	61	Leeds U*	55	Burnley	55
1	1966–67f	Manchester U	60	Nottingham F*	56	Tottenham H	56
1	1967–68f	Manchester C	58	Manchester U	56	Liverpool	55
1	1968–69f	Leeds U	67	Liverpool	61	Everton	57
1	1969–70f	Everton	66	Leeds U	57	Chelsea	55
1	1970–71f	Arsenal	65	Leeds U	64	Tottenham H*	52
1	1971–72f	Derby Co	58	Leeds U*	57	Liverpool*	57
1	1972–73f	Liverpool	60	Arsenal	57	Leeds U	53
1	1973–74f	Leeds U	62	Liverpool	57	Derby Co	48
1	1974–75f	Derby Co	53	Liverpool*	51	Ipswich T	51
1	1975–76f	Liverpool	60	QPR	59	Manchester U	56
1	1976–77f	Liverpool	57	Manchester C	56	Ipswich T	52
1	1977–78f	Nottingham F	64	Liverpool	57	Everton	55
1	1978–79f	Liverpool	68	Nottingham F	60	WBA	59
1	1979–80f	Liverpool	60	Manchester U	58	Ipswich T	53
1	1980–81f	Aston Villa	60	Ipswich T	56	Arsenal	53
1	1981–82g	Liverpool	87	Ipswich T	83	Manchester U	78
1	1982–83g	Liverpool	82	Watford	71	Manchester U	70
1	1983–84g	Liverpool	80	Southampton	77	Nottingham F*	74
1	1984–85g	Everton	90	Liverpool*	77	Tottenham H	77
1	1985–86g	Liverpool	88	Everton	86	West Ham U	84
1	1986–87g	Everton	86	Liverpool	77	Tottenham H	71
1	1987–88h	Liverpool	90	Manchester U	81	Nottingham F	73
1	1988–89k	Arsenal*	76	Liverpool	76	Nottingham F	64
1	1989–90k	Liverpool	79	Aston Villa	70	Tottenham H	63
1	1990–91k	Arsenal[1]	83	Liverpool	76	Crystal Palace	69
1	1991–92g	Leeds U	82	Manchester U	78	Sheffield W	75

[1] Arsenal deducted 2pts due to player misconduct in match on 20/10/1990 v Manchester U at Old Trafford.

FA PREMIER LEAGUE (1992–93 to 2017–18)

MAXIMUM POINTS: a 126; b 114.

	Season		Pts		Pts		Pts
1	1992–93a	Manchester U	84	Aston Villa	74	Norwich C	72
1	1993–94a	Manchester U	92	Blackburn R	84	Newcastle U	77
1	1994–95a	Blackburn R	89	Manchester U	88	Nottingham F	77
1	1995–96b	Manchester U	82	Newcastle U	78	Liverpool	71
1	1996–97b	Manchester U	75	Newcastle U*	68	Arsenal*	68
1	1997–98b	Arsenal	78	Manchester U	77	Liverpool	65
1	1998–99b	Manchester U	79	Arsenal	78	Chelsea	75
1	1999–2000b	Manchester U	91	Arsenal	73	Leeds U	69
1	2000–01b	Manchester U	80	Arsenal	70	Liverpool	69
1	2001–02b	Arsenal	87	Liverpool	80	Manchester U	77
1	2002–03b	Manchester U	83	Arsenal	78	Newcastle U	69
1	2003–04b	Arsenal	90	Chelsea	79	Manchester U	75
1	2004–05b	Chelsea	95	Arsenal	83	Manchester U	77
1	2005–06b	Chelsea	91	Manchester U	83	Liverpool	82
1	2006–07b	Manchester U	89	Chelsea	83	Liverpool*	68
1	2007–08b	Manchester U	87	Chelsea	85	Arsenal	83
1	2008–09b	Manchester U	90	Liverpool	86	Chelsea	83
1	2009–10b	Chelsea	86	Manchester U	85	Arsenal	75
1	2010–11b	Manchester U	80	Chelsea*	71	Manchester C	71
1	2011–12b	Manchester C*	89	Manchester U	89	Arsenal	70
1	2012–13b	Manchester U	89	Manchester C	78	Chelsea	75
1	2013–14b	Manchester C	86	Liverpool	84	Chelsea	82
1	2014–15b	Chelsea	87	Manchester C	79	Arsenal	75
1	2015–16b	Leicester C	81	Arsenal	71	Tottenham H	70
1	2016–17b	Chelsea	93	Tottenham H	86	Manchester C	78
1	2017–18b	Manchester C	100	Manchester U	81	Tottenham H	77

DIVISION 2 (1892–93 to 1991–92) – TIER 2

MAXIMUM POINTS: a 44; b 56; c 60; d 68; e 76; f 84; g 126; h 132; k 138.

	Season		Pts		Pts		Pts
2	1892–93a	Small Heath	36	Sheffield U	35	Darwen	30
2	1893–94b	Liverpool	50	Small Heath	42	Notts Co	39
2	1894–95c	Bury	48	Notts Co	39	Newton Heath*	38
2	1895–96c	Liverpool*	46	Manchester C	46	Grimsby T*	42
2	1896–97c	Notts Co	42	Newton Heath	39	Grimsby T	38
2	1897–98c	Burnley	48	Newcastle U	45	Manchester C	39
2	1898–99d	Manchester C	52	Glossop NE	46	Leicester Fosse	45
2	1899–1900d	The Wednesday	54	Bolton W	52	Small Heath	46
2	1900–01d	Grimsby T	49	Small Heath	48	Burnley	44
2	1901–02d	WBA	55	Middlesbrough	51	Preston NE*	42
2	1902–03d	Manchester C	54	Small Heath	51	Woolwich A	48
2	1903–04d	Preston NE	50	Woolwich A	49	Manchester U	48
2	1904–05d	Liverpool	58	Bolton W	56	Manchester U	53
2	1905–06e	Bristol C	66	Manchester U	62	Chelsea	53
2	1906–07e	Nottingham F	60	Chelsea	57	Leicester Fosse	48
2	1907–08e	Bradford C	54	Leicester Fosse	52	Oldham Ath	50
2	1908–09e	Bolton W	52	Tottenham H*	51	WBA	51
2	1909–10e	Manchester C	54	Oldham Ath*	53	Hull C*	53
2	1910–11e	WBA	53	Bolton W	51	Chelsea	49

	Season		Pts		Pts		Pts
2	1911–12e	Derby Co*	54	Chelsea	54	Burnley	52
2	1912–13e	Preston NE	53	Burnley	50	Birmingham	46
2	1913–14e	Notts Co	53	Bradford PA*	49	Woolwich A	49
2	1914–15e	Derby Co	53	Preston NE	50	Barnsley	47
2	1919–20f	Tottenham H	70	Huddersfield T	64	Birmingham	56
2	1920–21f	Birmingham*	58	Cardiff C	58	Bristol C	51
2	1921–22f	Nottingham F	56	Stoke C*	52	Barnsley	52
2	1922–23f	Notts Co	53	West Ham U*	51	Leicester C	51
2	1923–24f	Leeds U	54	Bury*	51	Derby Co	51
2	1924–25f	Leicester C	59	Manchester U	57	Derby Co	55
2	1925–26f	Sheffield W	60	Derby Co	57	Chelsea	52
2	1926–27f	Middlesbrough	62	Portsmouth*	54	Manchester C	54
2	1927–28f	Manchester C	59	Leeds U	57	Chelsea	54
2	1928–29f	Middlesbrough	55	Grimsby T	53	Bradford PA*	48
2	1929–30f	Blackpool	58	Chelsea	55	Oldham Ath	53
2	1930–31f	Everton	61	WBA	54	Tottenham H	51
2	1931–32f	Wolverhampton W	56	Leeds U	54	Stoke C	52
2	1932–33f	Stoke C	56	Tottenham H	55	Fulham	50
2	1933–34f	Grimsby T	59	Preston NE	52	Bolton W*	51
2	1934–35f	Brentford	61	Bolton W*	56	West Ham U	56
2	1935–36f	Manchester U	56	Charlton Ath	55	Sheffield U*	52
2	1936–37f	Leicester C	56	Blackpool	55	Bury	52
2	1937–38f	Aston Villa	57	Manchester U*	53	Sheffield U	53
2	1938–39f	Blackburn R	55	Sheffield U	54	Sheffield W	53
2	1946–47f	Manchester C	62	Burnley	58	Birmingham C	55
2	1947–48f	Birmingham C	59	Newcastle U	56	Southampton	52
2	1948–49f	Fulham	57	WBA	56	Southampton	55
2	1949–50f	Tottenham H	61	Sheffield W*	52	Sheffield U*	52
2	1950–51f	Preston NE	57	Manchester C	52	Cardiff C	50
2	1951–52f	Sheffield W	53	Cardiff C*	51	Birmingham C	51
2	1952–53f	Sheffield U	60	Huddersfield T	58	Luton T	52
2	1953–54f	Leicester C*	56	Everton	56	Blackburn R	55
2	1954–55f	Birmingham C*	54	Luton T*	54	Rotherham U	54
2	1955–56f	Sheffield W	55	Leeds U	52	Liverpool*	48
2	1956–57f	Leicester C	61	Nottingham F	54	Liverpool	53
2	1957–58f	West Ham U	57	Blackburn R	56	Charlton Ath	55
2	1958–59f	Sheffield W	62	Fulham	60	Sheffield U*	53
2	1959–60f	Aston Villa	59	Cardiff C	58	Liverpool*	50
2	1960–61f	Ipswich T	59	Sheffield U	58	Liverpool	52
2	1961–62f	Liverpool	62	Leyton Orient	54	Sunderland	53
2	1962–63f	Stoke C	53	Chelsea*	52	Sunderland	52
2	1963–64f	Leeds U	63	Sunderland	61	Preston NE	56
2	1964–65f	Newcastle U	57	Northampton T	56	Bolton W	50
2	1965–66f	Manchester C	59	Southampton	54	Coventry C	53
2	1966–67f	Coventry C	59	Wolverhampton W	58	Carlisle U	52
2	1967–68f	Ipswich T	59	QPR*	58	Blackpool	58
2	1968–69f	Derby Co	63	Crystal Palace	56	Charlton Ath	50
2	1969–70f	Huddersfield T	60	Blackpool	53	Leicester C	51
2	1970–71f	Leicester C	59	Sheffield U	56	Cardiff C*	53
2	1971–72f	Norwich C	57	Birmingham C	56	Millwall	55
2	1972–73f	Burnley	62	QPR	61	Aston Villa	50
2	1973–74f	Middlesbrough	65	Luton T	50	Carlisle U	49
2	1974–75f	Manchester U	61	Aston Villa	58	Norwich C	53
2	1975–76f	Sunderland	56	Bristol C*	53	WBA	53
2	1976–77f	Wolverhampton W	57	Chelsea	55	Nottingham F	52
2	1977–78f	Bolton W	58	Southampton	57	Tottenham H*	56
2	1978–79f	Crystal Palace	57	Brighton & HA*	56	Stoke C	56
2	1979–80f	Leicester C	55	Sunderland	54	Birmingham C*	53
2	1980–81f	West Ham U	66	Notts Co	53	Swansea C*	50
2	1981–82g	Luton T	88	Watford	80	Norwich C	71
2	1982–83g	QPR	85	Wolverhampton W	75	Leicester C	70
2	1983–84g	Chelsea*	88	Sheffield W	88	Newcastle U	80
2	1984–85g	Oxford U	84	Birmingham C	82	Manchester C*	74
2	1985–86g	Norwich C	84	Charlton Ath	77	Wimbledon	76
2	1986–87g	Derby Co	84	Portsmouth	78	Oldham Ath‡	75
2	1987–88h	Millwall	82	Aston Villa*	78	Middlesbrough	78
2	1988–89k	Chelsea	99	Manchester C	82	Crystal Palace	81
2	1989–90k	Leeds U*	85	Sheffield U	85	Newcastle U‡	80
2	1990–91k	Oldham Ath	88	West Ham U	87	Sheffield W	82
2	1991–92k	Ipswich T	84	Middlesbrough	80	Derby Co	78

FIRST DIVISION (1992–93 to 2003–04)

MAXIMUM POINTS: 138

	Season		Pts		Pts		Pts
2	1992–93	Newcastle U	96	West Ham U*	88	Portsmouth‡	88
2	1993–94	Crystal Palace	90	Nottingham F	83	Millwall‡	74
2	1994–95	Middlesbrough	82	Reading‡	79	Bolton W	77
2	1995–96	Sunderland	83	Derby Co	79	Crystal Palace‡	75
2	1996–97	Bolton W	98	Barnsley	80	Wolverhampton W‡	76
2	1997–98	Nottingham F	94	Middlesbrough	91	Sunderland‡	90

2	1998–99	Sunderland	105	Bradford C	87	Ipswich T‡	86
2	1999–2000	Charlton Ath	91	Manchester C	89	Ipswich T	87
2	2000–01	Fulham	101	Blackburn R	91	Bolton W	87
2	2001–02	Manchester C	99	WBA	89	Wolverhampton W‡	86
2	2002–03	Portsmouth	98	Leicester C	92	Sheffield U‡	80
2	2003–04	Norwich C	94	WBA	86	Sunderland‡	79

FOOTBALL LEAGUE CHAMPIONSHIP (2004–05 to 2017–18)

MAXIMUM POINTS: 138

2	2004–05	Sunderland	94	Wigan Ath	87	Ipswich T‡	85
2	2005–06	Reading	106	Sheffield U	90	Watford	81
2	2006–07	Sunderland	88	Birmingham C	86	Derby Co	84
2	2007–08	WBA	81	Stoke C	79	Hull C	75
2	2008–09	Wolverhampton W	90	Birmingham C	83	Sheffield U‡	80
2	2009–10	Newcastle U	102	WBA	91	Nottingham F‡	79
2	2010–11	QPR	88	Norwich C	84	Swansea C*	80
2	2011–12	Reading	89	Southampton	88	West Ham U	86
2	2012–13	Cardiff C	87	Hull C	79	Watford‡	77
2	2013–14	Leicester C	102	Burnley	93	Derby Co‡	85
2	2014–15	Bournemouth	90	Watford	89	Norwich C	86
2	2015–16	Burnley	93	Middlesbrough*	89	Brighton & HA‡	89
2	2016–17	Newcastle U	94	Brighton & HA	93	Reading‡	85
2	2017–18	Wolverhampton W	99	Cardiff C	90	Fulham	88

DIVISION 3 (1920–1921) – TIER 3

MAXIMUM POINTS: *a* 84.

3	1920–21*a*	Crystal Palace	59	Southampton	54	QPR	53

DIVISION 3—SOUTH (1921–22 to 1957–58)

MAXIMUM POINTS: *a* 84; *b* 92.

3	1921–22*a*	Southampton*	61	Plymouth Arg	61	Portsmouth	53
3	1922–23*a*	Bristol C	59	Plymouth Arg*	53	Swansea T	53
3	1923–24*a*	Portsmouth	59	Plymouth Arg	55	Millwall	54
3	1924–25*a*	Swansea T	57	Plymouth Arg	56	Bristol C	53
3	1925–26*a*	Reading	57	Plymouth Arg	56	Millwall	53
3	1926–27*a*	Bristol C	62	Plymouth Arg	60	Millwall	56
3	1927–28*a*	Millwall	65	Northampton T	55	Plymouth Arg	53
3	1928–29*a*	Charlton Ath*	54	Crystal Palace	54	Northampton T*	52
3	1929–30*a*	Plymouth Arg	68	Brentford	61	QPR	51
3	1930–31*a*	Notts Co	59	Crystal Palace	51	Brentford	50
3	1931–32*a*	Fulham	57	Reading	55	Southend U	53
3	1932–33*a*	Brentford	62	Exeter C	58	Norwich C	57
3	1933–34*a*	Norwich C	61	Coventry C*	54	Reading*	54
3	1934–35*a*	Charlton Ath	61	Reading	53	Coventry C	51
3	1935–36*a*	Coventry C	57	Luton T	56	Reading	54
3	1936–37*a*	Luton T	58	Notts Co	56	Brighton & HA	53
3	1937–38*a*	Millwall	56	Bristol C	55	QPR*	53
3	1938–39*a*	Newport Co	55	Crystal Palace	52	Brighton & HA	49
3	1946–47*a*	Cardiff C	66	QPR	57	Bristol C	51
3	1947–48*a*	QPR	61	Bournemouth	57	Walsall	51
3	1948–49*a*	Swansea T	62	Reading	55	Bournemouth	52
3	1949–50*a*	Notts Co	58	Northampton T*	51	Southend U	51
3	1950–51*b*	Nottingham F	70	Norwich C	64	Reading*	57
3	1951–52*b*	Plymouth Arg	66	Reading*	61	Norwich C	61
3	1952–53*b*	Bristol R	64	Millwall*	62	Northampton T	62
3	1953–54*b*	Ipswich T	64	Brighton & HA	61	Bristol C	56
3	1954–55*b*	Bristol C	70	Leyton Orient	61	Southampton	59
3	1955–56*b*	Leyton Orient	66	Brighton & HA	65	Ipswich T	64
3	1956–57*b*	Ipswich T*	59	Torquay U	59	Colchester U	58
3	1957–58*b*	Brighton & HA	60	Brentford*	58	Plymouth Arg	58

DIVISION 3—NORTH (1921–22 to 1957–58)

MAXIMUM POINTS: *a* 76; *b* 84; *c* 80; *d* 92.

3	1921–22*a*	Stockport Co	56	Darlington*	50	Grimsby T	50
3	1922–23*a*	Nelson	51	Bradford PA	47	Walsall	46
3	1923–24*b*	Wolverhampton W	63	Rochdale	62	Chesterfield	54
3	1924–25*b*	Darlington	58	Nelson*	53	New Brighton	53
3	1925–26*b*	Grimsby T	61	Bradford PA	60	Rochdale	59
3	1926–27*b*	Stoke C	63	Rochdale	58	Bradford PA	55
3	1927–28*b*	Bradford PA	63	Lincoln C	55	Stockport Co	54
3	1928–29*b*	Bradford C	63	Stockport Co	62	Wrexham	52
3	1929–30*b*	Port Vale	67	Stockport Co	63	Darlington*	50
3	1930–31*b*	Chesterfield	58	Lincoln C	57	Wrexham*	54
3	1931–32*c*	Lincoln C*	57	Gateshead	57	Chester	50
3	1932–33*b*	Hull C	59	Wrexham	57	Stockport Co	54
3	1933–34*b*	Barnsley	62	Chesterfield	61	Stockport Co	59

3	1934–35b	Doncaster R	57	Halifax T	55	Chester	54
3	1935–36b	Chesterfield	60	Chester*	55	Tranmere R	55
3	1936–37b	Stockport Co	60	Lincoln C	57	Chester	53
3	1937–38b	Tranmere R	56	Doncaster R	54	Hull C	53
3	1938–39b	Barnsley	67	Doncaster R	56	Bradford C	52
3	1946–47b	Doncaster R	72	Rotherham U	64	Chester	56
3	1947–48b	Lincoln C	60	Rotherham U	59	Wrexham	50
3	1948–49b	Hull C	65	Rotherham U	62	Doncaster R	50
3	1949–50b	Doncaster R	55	Gateshead	53	Rochdale*	51
3	1950–51d	Rotherham U	71	Mansfield T	64	Carlisle U	62
3	1951–52d	Lincoln C	69	Grimsby T	66	Stockport Co	59
3	1952–53d	Oldham Ath	59	Port Vale	58	Wrexham	56
3	1953–54d	Port Vale	69	Barnsley	58	Scunthorpe U	57
3	1954–55d	Barnsley	65	Accrington S	61	Scunthorpe U*	58
3	1955–56d	Grimsby T	68	Derby Co	63	Accrington S	59
3	1956–57d	Derby Co	63	Hartlepools U	59	Accrington S*	58
3	1957–58d	Scunthorpe U	66	Accrington S	59	Bradford C	57

DIVISION 3 (1958–59 to 1991–92)

MAXIMUM POINTS: 92; 138 FROM 1981–82.

3	1958–59	Plymouth Arg	62	Hull C	61	Brentford*	57
3	1959–60	Southampton	61	Norwich C	59	Shrewsbury T*	52
3	1960–61	Bury	68	Walsall	62	QPR	60
3	1961–62	Portsmouth	65	Grimsby T	62	Bournemouth*	59
3	1962–63	Northampton T	62	Swindon T	58	Port Vale	54
3	1963–64	Coventry C*	60	Crystal Palace	60	Watford	58
3	1964–65	Carlisle U	60	Bristol C*	59	Mansfield T	59
3	1965–66	Hull C	69	Millwall	65	QPR	57
3	1966–67	QPR	67	Middlesbrough	55	Watford	54
3	1967–68	Oxford U	57	Bury	56	Shrewsbury T	55
3	1968–69	Watford*	64	Swindon T	64	Luton T	61
3	1969–70	Orient	62	Luton T	60	Bristol R	56
3	1970–71	Preston NE	61	Fulham	60	Halifax T	56
3	1971–72	Aston Villa	70	Brighton & HA	65	Bournemouth*	62
3	1972–73	Bolton W	61	Notts Co	57	Blackburn R	55
3	1973–74	Oldham Ath	62	Bristol R*	61	York C	61
3	1974–75	Blackburn R	60	Plymouth Arg	59	Charlton Ath	55
3	1975–76	Hereford U	63	Cardiff C	57	Millwall	56
3	1976–77	Mansfield T	64	Brighton & HA	61	Crystal Palace*	59
3	1977–78	Wrexham	61	Cambridge U	58	Preston NE*	56
3	1978–79	Shrewsbury T	61	Watford*	60	Swansea C	60
3	1979–80	Grimsby T	62	Blackburn R	59	Sheffield W	58
3	1980–81	Rotherham U	61	Barnsley*	59	Charlton Ath	59
3	1981–82	Burnley*	80	Carlisle U	80	Fulham	78
3	1982–83	Portsmouth	91	Cardiff C	86	Huddersfield T	82
3	1983–84	Oxford U	95	Wimbledon	87	Sheffield U*	83
3	1984–85	Bradford C	94	Millwall	90	Hull C	87
3	1985–86	Reading	94	Plymouth Arg	87	Derby Co	84
3	1986–87	Bournemouth	97	Middlesbrough	94	Swindon T	87
3	1987–88	Sunderland	93	Brighton & HA	84	Walsall	82
3	1988–89	Wolverhampton W	92	Sheffield U*	84	Port Vale	84
3	1989–90	Bristol R	93	Bristol C	91	Notts Co	87
3	1990–91	Cambridge U	86	Southend U	85	Grimsby T*	83
3	1991–92	Brentford	82	Birmingham C	81	Huddersfield T‡	78

SECOND DIVISION (1992–93 to 2003–04)

MAXIMUM POINTS: 138

3	1992–93	Stoke C	93	Bolton W	90	Port Vale‡	89
3	1993–94	Reading	89	Port Vale	88	Plymouth Arg*‡	85
3	1994–95	Birmingham C	89	Brentford‡	85	Crewe Alex‡	83
3	1995–96	Swindon T	92	Oxford U	83	Blackpool‡	82
3	1996–97	Bury	84	Stockport Co	82	Luton T‡	78
3	1997–98	Watford	88	Bristol C	85	Grimsby T	72
3	1998–99	Fulham	101	Walsall	87	Manchester C	82
3	1999–2000	Preston NE	95	Burnley	88	Gillingham	85
3	2000–01	Millwall	93	Rotherham U	91	Reading‡	86
3	2001–02	Brighton & HA	90	Reading	84	Brentford*‡	83
3	2002–03	Wigan Ath	100	Crewe Alex	86	Bristol C*‡	83
3	2003–04	Plymouth Arg	90	QPR	83	Bristol C‡	82

FOOTBALL LEAGUE ONE (2004–05 to 2017–18)

MAXIMUM POINTS: 138

3	2004–05	Luton T	98	Hull C	86	Tranmere R‡	79
3	2005–06	Southend U	82	Colchester U	79	Brentford‡	76
3	2006–07	Scunthorpe U	91	Bristol C	85	Blackpool	83
3	2007–08	Swansea C	92	Nottingham F	82	Doncaster R*	80
3	2008–09	Leicester C	96	Peterborough U	89	Milton Keynes D‡	87
3	2009–10	Norwich C	95	Leeds U	86	Millwall	85
3	2010–11	Brighton & HA	95	Southampton	92	Huddersfield T‡	87

3	2011–12	Charlton Ath	101	Sheffield W	93	Sheffield U‡	90
3	2012–13	Doncaster R	84	Bournemouth	83	Brentford‡	79
3	2013–14	Wolverhampton W	103	Brentford	94	Leyton Orient‡	86
3	2014–15	Bristol C	99	Milton Keynes D	91	Preston NE	89
3	2015–16	Wigan Ath	87	Burton Alb	85	Walsall‡	84
3	2016–17	Sheffield U	100	Bolton W	86	Scunthorpe U*‡	82
3	2017–18	Wigan Ath	98	Blackburn R	96	Shrewsbury T‡	87

DIVISION 4 (1958–59 to 1991–92) – TIER 4

MAXIMUM POINTS: 92; 138 FROM 1981–82.

4	1958–59	Port Vale	64	Coventry C*	60	York C	60	Shrewsbury T	58
4	1959–60	Walsall	65	Notts Co*	60	Torquay U	60	Watford	57
4	1960–61	Peterborough U	66	Crystal Palace	64	Northampton T*	60	Bradford PA	60
4	1961–62²	Millwall	56	Colchester U	55	Wrexham	53	Carlisle U	52
4	1962–63	Brentford	62	Oldham Ath*	59	Crewe Alex	59	Mansfield T*	57
4	1963–64	Gillingham*	60	Carlisle U	60	Workington	59	Exeter C	58
4	1964–65	Brighton & HA	63	Millwall*	62	York C	62	Oxford U	61
4	1965–66	Doncaster R*	59	Darlington	59	Torquay U	58	Colchester U*	56
4	1966–67	Stockport Co	64	Southport*	59	Barrow	59	Tranmere R	58
4	1967–68	Luton T	66	Barnsley	61	Hartlepools U	60	Crewe Alex	58
4	1968–69	Doncaster R	59	Halifax T	57	Rochdale*	56	Bradford C	56
4	1969–70	Chesterfield	64	Wrexham	61	Swansea C	60	Port Vale	59
4	1970–71	Notts Co	69	Bournemouth	60	Oldham Ath	59	York C	56
4	1971–72	Grimsby T	63	Southend U	60	Brentford	59	Scunthorpe U	57
4	1972–73	Southport	62	Hereford U	58	Cambridge U	57	Aldershot*	56
4	1973–74	Peterborough U	65	Gillingham	62	Colchester U	60	Bury	59
4	1974–75	Mansfield T	68	Shrewsbury T	62	Rotherham U	59	Chester*	57
4	1975–76	Lincoln C	74	Northampton T	68	Reading	60	Tranmere R	58
4	1976–77	Cambridge U	65	Exeter C	62	Colchester U*	59	Bradford C	59
4	1977–78	Watford	71	Southend U	60	Swansea C*	56	Brentford	56
4	1978–79	Reading	65	Grimsby T*	61	Wimbledon*	61	Barnsley	61
4	1979–80	Huddersfield T	66	Walsall	64	Newport Co	61	Portsmouth*	60
4	1980–81	Southend U	67	Lincoln C	65	Doncaster R	56	Wimbledon	55
4	1981–82	Sheffield U	96	Bradford C*	91	Wigan Ath	91	Bournemouth	88
4	1982–83	Wimbledon	98	Hull C	90	Port Vale	88	Scunthorpe U	83
4	1983–84	York C	101	Doncaster R	85	Reading*	82	Bristol C	82
4	1984–85	Chesterfield	91	Blackpool	86	Darlington	85	Bury	84
4	1985–86	Swindon T	102	Chester C	84	Mansfield T	81	Port Vale	79
4	1986–87	Northampton T	99	Preston NE	90	Southend U	80	Wolverhampton W‡	79
4	1987–88	Wolverhampton W	90	Cardiff C	85	Bolton W	78	Scunthorpe U*‡	77
4	1988–89	Rotherham U	82	Tranmere R	80	Crewe Alex	78	Scunthorpe U*‡	77
4	1989–90	Exeter C	89	Grimsby T	79	Southend U	75	Stockport Co‡	74
4	1990–91	Darlington	83	Stockport Co*	82	Hartlepool U	82	Peterborough U	80
4	1991–92³	Burnley	83	Rotherham U*	77	Mansfield T	77	Blackpool	76

²*Maximum points:* 88 owing to Accrington Stanley's resignation.
³*Maximum points:* 126 owing to Aldershot being expelled (and only 23 teams started the competition).

THIRD DIVISION (1992–93 to 2003–04)

MAXIMUM POINTS: a 126; b 138.

4	1992–93a	Cardiff C	83	Wrexham	80	Barnet	79	York C	75
4	1993–94a	Shrewsbury T	79	Chester C	74	Crewe Alex	73	Wycombe W	70
4	1994–95a	Carlisle U	91	Walsall	83	Chesterfield	81	Bury‡	80
4	1995–96b	Preston NE	86	Gillingham	83	Bury	79	Plymouth Arg*	78
4	1996–97b	Wigan Ath*	87	Fulham	87	Carlisle U	84	Northampton T	72
4	1997–98b	Notts Co	99	Macclesfield T	82	Lincoln C	72	Colchester U*	74
4	1998–99b	Brentford	85	Cambridge U	81	Cardiff C	80	Scunthorpe U	74
4	1999–2000b	Swansea C	85	Rotherham U	84	Northampton T	82	Darlington‡	79
4	2000–01b	Brighton & HA	92	Cardiff C	82	Chesterfield⁴	80	Hartlepool U‡	77
4	2001–02b	Plymouth Arg	102	Luton T	97	Mansfield T	79	Cheltenham T	78
4	2002–03b	Rushden & D	87	Hartlepool U	85	Wrexham	84	Bournemouth	74
4	2003–04b	Doncaster R	92	Hull C	88	Torquay U*	81	Huddersfield T	81

⁴*Chesterfield deducted 9pts for irregularities.*

FOOTBALL LEAGUE TWO (2004–05 to 2017–18)

MAXIMUM POINTS: 138

4	2004–05	Yeovil T	83	Scunthorpe U*	80	Swansea C	80	Southend U	80
4	2005–06	Carlisle U	86	Northampton T	83	Leyton Orient	81	Grimsby T‡	78
4	2006–07	Walsall	89	Hartlepool U	88	Swindon T	85	Milton Keynes D‡	84
4	2007–08	Milton Keynes D	97	Peterborough U	92	Hereford U	88	Stockport Co	82
4	2008–09	Brentford	85	Exeter C	79	Wycombe W*	78	Bury‡	78
4	2009–10	Notts Co	93	Bournemouth	83	Rochdale	82	Morecambe*‡	73
4	2010–11	Chesterfield	86	Bury	81	Wycombe W	80	Shrewsbury T‡	79
4	2011–12	Swindon T	93	Shrewsbury T	88	Crawley T	84	Southend U‡	83
4	2012–13	Gillingham	83	Rotherham U	79	Port Vale	78	Burton Alb	76
4	2013–14	Chesterfield	84	Scunthorpe U*	81	Rochdale	81	Fleetwood T	76
4	2014–15	Burton Alb	94	Shrewsbury T	89	Bury	85	Wycombe W*‡	84
4	2015–16	Northampton T	99	Oxford U	86	Bristol R*	85	Accrington S‡	85
4	2016–17	Portsmouth*	87	Plymouth Arg	87	Doncaster R	85	Luton T‡	77
4	2017–18	Accrington S	93	Luton T	88	Wycombe W	84	Exeter C‡	80

LEAGUE TITLE WINS

DIVISION 1 (1888–89 to 1991–92) – TIER 1
Liverpool 18, Arsenal 10, Everton 9, Aston Villa 7, Manchester U 7, Sunderland 6, Newcastle U 4, Sheffield W 4 (2 as The Wednesday), Huddersfield T 3, Leeds U 3, Wolverhampton W 3, Blackburn R 2, Burnley 2, Derby Co 2, Manchester C 2, Portsmouth 2, Preston NE 2, Tottenham H 2, Chelsea 1, Ipswich T 1, Nottingham F 1, Sheffield U 1, WBA 1.

FA PREMIER LEAGUE (1992–93 to 2017–18) – TIER 1
Manchester U 13, Chelsea 5, Arsenal 3, Manchester C 3, Blackburn R 1, Leicester C 1.

DIVISION 2 (1892–93 TO 1991–92) – TIER 2
Leicester C 6, Manchester C 6, Sheffield W 5 (1 as The Wednesday), Birmingham C 5 (1 as Small Heath), Derby Co 4, Liverpool 4, Ipswich T 3, Leeds U 3, Middlesbrough 3, Notts Co 3, Preston NE 3, Aston Villa 2, Bolton W 2, Burnley 2, Chelsea 2, Grimsby T 2, Manchester U 2, Norwich C 2, Nottingham F 2, Stoke C 2, Tottenham H 2, WBA 2, West Ham U 2, Wolverhampton W 2, Blackburn R 1, Blackpool 1, Bradford C 1, Brentford 1, Bristol C 1, Bury 1, Coventry C 1, Crystal Palace 1, Everton 1, Fulham 1, Huddersfield T 1, Luton T 1, Millwall 1, Newcastle U 1, Oldham Ath 1, Oxford U 1, QPR 1, Sheffield U 1, Sunderland 1.

FIRST DIVISION (1992–93 to 2003–04) – TIER 2
Sunderland 1, Bolton W 1, Charlton Ath 1, Crystal Palace 1, Fulham 1, Manchester C 1, Middlesbrough 1, Newcastle U 1, Norwich C 1, Nottingham F 1, Portsmouth 1.

FOOTBALL LEAGUE CHAMPIONSHIP (2004–05 to 2017–18) – TIER 2
Newcastle U 2, Reading 2, Sunderland 2, Wolverhampton W 2, Bournemouth 1, Burnley 1, Cardiff C 1, Leicester C 1, QPR 1, WBA 1,

DIVISION 3—SOUTH (1920–21 to 1957–58) – TIER 3
Bristol C 3, Charlton Ath 2, Ipswich T 2, Millwall 2, Notts Co 2, Plymouth Arg 2, Swansea T 2, Brentford 1, Brighton & HA 1, Bristol R 1, Cardiff C 1, Coventry C 1, Crystal Palace 1, Fulham 1, Leyton Orient 1, Luton T 1, Newport Co 1, Norwich C 1, Nottingham F 1, Portsmouth 1, QPR 1, Reading 1, Southampton 1.

DIVISION 3—NORTH (1921–22 to 1957–58) – TIER 3
Barnsley 3, Doncaster R 3, Lincoln C 3, Chesterfield 2, Grimsby T 2, Hull C 2, Port Vale 2, Stockport Co 2, Bradford C 1, Bradford PA 1, Darlington 1, Derby Co 1, Nelson 1, Oldham Ath 1, Rotherham U 1, Scunthorpe U 1, Stoke C 1, Tranmere R 1, Wolverhampton W 1.

DIVISION 3 (1958–59 to 1991–92) – TIER 3
Oxford U 2, Portsmouth 2, Aston Villa 1, Blackburn R 1, Bolton W 1, Bournemouth 1, Bradford C 1, Brentford 1, Bristol R 1, Burnley 1, Bury 1, Cambridge U 1, Carlisle U 1, Coventry C 1, Grimsby T 1, Hereford U 1, Hull C 1, Mansfield T 1, Northampton T 1, Oldham Ath 1, Orient 1, Plymouth Arg 1, Preston NE 1, QPR 1, Reading 1, Rotherham U 1, Shrewsbury T 1, Southampton 1, Sunderland 1, Watford 1, Wolverhampton W 1, Wrexham 1.

SECOND DIVISION (1992–93 to 2003–04) – TIER 3
Birmingham C 1, Brighton & HA 1, Bury 1, Fulham 1, Millwall 1, Plymouth Arg 1, Preston NE 1, Reading 1, Stoke C 1, Swindon T 1, Watford 1, Wigan Ath 1.

FOOTBALL LEAGUE ONE (2004–05 to 2017–18) – TIER 3
Wigan Ath 2, Brighton & HA 1, Bristol C 1, Charlton Ath 1, Doncaster R 1, Leicester C 1, Luton T 1, Norwich C 1, Scunthorpe U 1, Sheffield U 1, Southend U 1, Swansea C 1, Wolverhampton W 1.

DIVISION 4 (1958–59 to 1991–92) – TIER 4
Chesterfield 2, Doncaster R 2, Peterborough U 2, Brentford 1, Brighton & HA 1, Burnley 1, Cambridge U 1, Darlington 1, Exeter C 1, Gillingham 1, Grimsby T 1, Huddersfield T 1, Lincoln C 1, Luton T 1, Mansfield T 1, Millwall 1, Northampton T 1, Notts Co 1, Port Vale 1, Reading 1, Rotherham U 1, Sheffield U 1, Southend U 1, Southport 1, Stockport Co 1, Swindon T 1, Walsall 1, Watford 1, Wimbledon 1, Wolverhampton W 1, York C 1.

THIRD DIVISION (1992–93 to 2003–04) – TIER 4
Brentford 1, Brighton & HA 1, Cardiff C 1, Carlisle U 1, Doncaster R 1, Notts Co 1, Plymouth Arg 1, Preston NE 1, Rushden & D 1, Shrewsbury T 1, Swansea C 1, Wigan Ath 1.

FOOTBALL LEAGUE TWO (2004–05 to 2017–18) – TIER 4
Chesterfield 2, Accrington S 1, Brentford 1, Burton Alb 1, Carlisle U 1, Gillingham 1, Milton Keynes D 1, Northampton T 1, Notts Co 1, Portsmouth 1, Swindon T 1, Walsall 1, Yeovil T 1.

PROMOTED AFTER PLAY-OFFS

1986–87	Charlton Ath to Division 1; Swindon T to Division 2; Aldershot to Division 3
1987–88	Middlesbrough to Division 1; Walsall to Division 2; Swansea C to Division 3
1988–89	Crystal Palace to Division 1; Port Vale to Division 2; Leyton Orient to Division 3
1989–90	Sunderland to Division 1; Notts Co to Division 2; Cambridge U to Division 3
1990–91	Notts Co to Division 1; Tranmere R to Division 2; Torquay U to Division 3
1991–92	Blackburn R to Premier League; Peterborough U to Division 2; Blackpool to Second Division
1992–93	Swindon T to Premier League; WBA to First Division; York C to Second Division
1993–94	Leicester C to Premier League; Burnley to First Division; Wycombe W to Second Division
1994–95	Bolton W to Premier League; Huddersfield T to First Division; Wycome Wanderers to Second Division
1995–96	Leicester C to Premier League; Bradford C to First Division; Plymouth Arg to Second Division
1996–97	Crystal Palace to Premier League; Crewe Alex to First Division; Northampton T to Second Division
1997–98	Charlton Ath to Premier League; Grimsby T to First Division; Colchester U to Second Division
1998–99	Watford to Premier League; Manchester C to First Division; Scunthorpe U to Second Division
1999–2000	Ipswich to Premier League; Gillingham to First Division; Peterborough U to Second Division
2000–01	Bolton W to Premier league; Walsall to First Division; Blackpool to Second Division
2001–02	Birmingham C to Premier League; Stoke C to First Division; Cheltenham T to Second Division
2002–03	Wolverhampton W to Premier League; Cardiff C to First Division; Bournemouth to Second Division
2003–04	Crystal Palace to Premier League; Brighton & HA to First Division; Huddersfield T to Second Division
2004–05	West Ham U to Premier League; Sheffield W to Championship; Southend U to Football League One
2005–06	Watford to Premier League; Barnsley to Championship; Cheltenham T to Football League One
2006–07	Derby Co to Premier League; Blackpool to Championship; Bristol R to Football League One
2007–08	Hull C to Premier League; Doncaster R to Championship; Stockport Co to Football League One
2008–09	Burnley to Premier League; Scunthorpe U to Championship; Gillingham to Football League One
2009–10	Blackpool to Premier League; Millwall to Championship; Dagenham & R to Football League One
2010–11	Swansea C to Premier League; Peterborough U to Championship; Stevenage to Football League One
2011–12	West Ham U to Premier League; Huddersfield T to Championship; Crewe Alex to Football League One
2012–13	Crystal Palace to Premier League; Yeovil T to Championship; Bradford C to Football League One
2013–14	QPR to Premier League; Rotherham U to Championship; Fleetwood T to Football League One
2014–15	Norwich C to Premier League; Preston NE to Championship; Southend U to Football League One
2015–16	Hull C to Premier League; Barnsley to Championship; AFC Wimbledon to Football League One
2016–17	Huddersfield T to Premier League; Millwall to Championship; Blackpool to Football League One
2017–18	Fulham to Premier League; Rotherham U to Championship; Coventry C to Football League One

RELEGATED CLUBS

1891–92 League extended. Newton Heath, Sheffield W and Nottingham F admitted. *Second Division formed* including Darwen.
1892–93 In Test matches, Sheffield U and Darwen won promotion in place of Notts Co and Accrington S.
1893–94 In Tests, Liverpool and Small Heath won promotion. Newton Heath and Darwen relegated.
1894–95 After Tests, Bury promoted, Liverpool relegated.
1895–96 After Tests, Liverpool promoted, Small Heath relegated.
1896–97 After Tests, Notts Co promoted, Burnley relegated.
1897–98 Test system abolished after success of Stoke C and Burnley. League extended. Blackburn R and Newcastle U elected to First Division. *Automatic promotion and relegation introduced.*

DIVISION 1 TO DIVISION 2 (1898–99 to 1991–92)

1898–99 Bolton W and Sheffield W
1899–1900 Burnley and Glossop
1900–01 Preston NE and WBA
1901–02 Small Heath and Manchester C
1902–03 Grimsby T and Bolton W
1903–04 Liverpool and WBA
1904–05 League extended. Bury and Notts Co, two bottom clubs in First Division, re-elected.
1905–06 Nottingham F and Wolverhampton W
1906–07 Derby Co and Stoke C
1907–08 Bolton W and Birmingham C
1908–09 Manchester C and Leicester Fosse
1909–10 Bolton W and Chelsea
1910–11 Bristol C and Nottingham F
1911–12 Preston NE and Bury
1912–13 Notts Co and Woolwich Arsenal
1913–14 Preston NE and Derby Co
1914–15 Tottenham H and Chelsea*
1919–20 Notts Co and Sheffield W
1920–21 Derby Co and Bradford PA
1921–22 Bradford C and Manchester U
1922–23 Stoke C and Oldham Ath
1923–24 Chelsea and Middlesbrough
1924–25 Preston NE and Nottingham F
1925–26 Manchester C and Notts Co
1926–27 Leeds U and WBA
1927–28 Tottenham H and Middlesbrough
1928–29 Bury and Cardiff C
1929–30 Burnley and Everton
1930–31 Leeds U and Manchester U
1931–32 Grimsby T and West Ham U
1932–33 Bolton W and Blackpool
1933–34 Newcastle U and Sheffield U
1934–35 Leicester C and Tottenham H
1935–36 Aston Villa and Blackburn R
1936–37 Manchester U and Sheffield W
1937–38 Manchester C and West Bromwich Albion
1938–39 Birmingham C and Leicester C
1946–47 Brentford and Leeds U
1947–48 Blackburn R and Grimsby T
1948–49 Preston NE and Sheffield U
1949–50 Manchester C and Birmingham C
1950–51 Sheffield W and Everton
1951–52 Huddersfield T and Fulham

1952–53 Stoke C and Derby Co
1953–54 Middlesbrough and Liverpool
1954–55 Leicester C and Sheffield W
1955–56 Huddersfield T and Sheffield U
1956–57 Charlton Ath and Cardiff C
1957–58 Sheffield W and Sunderland
1958–59 Portsmouth and Aston Villa
1959–60 Luton T and Leeds U
1960–61 Preston NE and Newcastle U
1961–62 Chelsea and Cardiff C
1962–63 Manchester C and Leyton Orient
1963–64 Bolton W and Ipswich T
1964–65 Wolverhampton W and Birmingham C
1965–66 Northampton T and Blackburn R
1966–67 Aston Villa and Blackpool
1967–68 Fulham and Sheffield U
1968–69 Leicester C and QPR
1969–70 Sunderland and Sheffield W
1970–71 Burnley and Blackpool
1971–72 Huddersfield T and Nottingham F
1972–73 Crystal Palace and WBA
1973–74 Southampton, Manchester U, Norwich C
1974–75 Luton T, Chelsea, Carlisle U
1975–76 Wolverhampton W, Burnley, Sheffield U
1976–77 Sunderland, Stoke C, Tottenham H
1977–78 West Ham U, Newcastle U, Leicester C
1978–79 QPR, Birmingham C, Chelsea
1979–80 Bristol C, Derby Co, Bolton W
1980–81 Norwich C, Leicester C, Crystal Palace
1981–82 Leeds U, Wolverhampton W, Middlesbrough
1982–83 Manchester C, Swansea C, Brighton & HA
1983–84 Birmingham C, Notts Co, Wolverhampton W
1984–85 Norwich C, Sunderland, Stoke C
1985–86 Ipswich T, Birmingham C, WBA
1986–87 Leicester C, Manchester C, Aston Villa
1987–88 Chelsea**, Portsmouth, Watford, Oxford U
1988–89 Middlesbrough, West Ham U, Newcastle U
1989–90 Sheffield W, Charlton Ath, Millwall
1990–91 Sunderland and Derby Co
1991–92 Luton T, Notts Co, West Ham U
***Relegated after play-offs.**
***Subsequently re-elected to Division 1 when League was extended after the War.*

FA PREMIER LEAGUE TO DIVISION 1 (1992–93 to 2003–04)

1992–93 Crystal Palace, Middlesbrough, Nottingham F
1993–94 Sheffield U, Oldham Ath, Swindon T
1994–95 Crystal Palace, Norwich C, Leicester C, Ipswich T
1995–96 Manchester C, QPR, Bolton W
1996–97 Sunderland, Middlesbrough, Nottingham F
1997–98 Bolton W, Barnsley, Crystal Palace

1998–99 Charlton Ath, Blackburn R, Nottingham F
1999–2000 Wimbledon, Sheffield W, Watford
2000–01 Manchester C, Coventry C, Bradford C
2001–02 Ipswich T, Derby Co, Leicester C
2002–03 West Ham U, WBA, Sunderland
2003–04 Leicester C, Leeds U, Wolverhampton W

FA PREMIER LEAGUE TO CHAMPIONSHIP (2004–05 to 2017–18)

2004–05 Crystal Palace, Norwich C, Southampton
2005–06 Birmingham C, WBA, Sunderland
2006–07 Sheffield U, Charlton Ath, Watford
2007–08 Reading, Birmingham C, Derby Co
2008–09 Newcastle U, Middlesbrough, WBA
2009–10 Burnley, Hull C, Portsmouth
2010–11 Birmingham C, Blackpool, West Ham U

2011–12 Bolton W, Blackburn R, Wolverhampton W
2012–13 Wigan Ath, Reading, QPR
2013–14 Norwich C, Fulham, Cardiff C
2014–15 Hull C, Burnley, QPR
2015–16 Newcastle U, Norwich C, Aston Villa
2016–17 Hull C, Middlesbrough, Sunderland
2017–18 Swansea C, Stoke C, WBA

DIVISION 2 TO DIVISION 3 (1920–21 to 1991–92)

1920–21 Stockport Co
1921–22 Bradford PA and Bristol C
1922–23 Rotherham Co and Wolverhampton W

1923–24 Nelson and Bristol C
1924–25 Crystal Palace and Coventry C
1925–26 Stoke C and Stockport Co

1926–27 Darlington and Bradford C
1927–28 Fulham and South Shields
1928–29 Port Vale and Clapton Orient
1929–30 Hull C and Notts Co
1930–31 Reading and Cardiff C
1931–32 Barnsley and Bristol C
1932–33 Chesterfield and Charlton Ath
1933–34 Millwall and Lincoln C
1934–35 Oldham Ath and Notts Co
1935–36 Port Vale and Hull C
1936–37 Doncaster R and Bradford C
1937–38 Barnsley and Stockport Co
1938–39 Norwich C and Tranmere R
1946–47 Swansea T and Newport Co
1947–48 Doncaster R and Millwall
1948–49 Nottingham F and Lincoln C
1949–50 Plymouth Arg and Bradford PA
1950–51 Grimsby T and Chesterfield
1951–52 Coventry C and QPR
1952–53 Southampton and Barnsley
1953–54 Brentford and Oldham Ath
1954–55 Ipswich T and Derby Co
1955–56 Plymouth Arg and Hull C
1956–57 Port Vale and Bury
1957–58 Doncaster R and Notts Co
1958–59 Barnsley and Grimsby T
1959–60 Bristol C and Hull C
1960–61 Lincoln C and Portsmouth
1961–62 Brighton & HA and Bristol R
1962–63 Walsall and Luton T

1963–64 Grimsby T and Scunthorpe U
1964–65 Swindon T and Swansea T
1965–66 Middlesbrough and Leyton Orient
1966–67 Northampton T and Bury
1967–68 Plymouth Arg and Rotherham U
1968–69 Fulham and Bury
1969–70 Preston NE and Aston Villa
1970–71 Blackburn R and Bolton W
1971–72 Charlton Ath and Watford
1972–73 Huddersfield T and Brighton & HA
1973–74 Crystal Palace, Preston NE, Swindon T
1974–75 Millwall, Cardiff C, Sheffield W
1975–76 Oxford U, York C, Portsmouth
1976–77 Carlisle U, Plymouth Arg, Hereford U
1977–78 Blackpool, Mansfield T, Hull C
1978–79 Sheffield U, Millwall, Blackburn R
1979–80 Fulham, Burnley, Charlton Ath
1980–81 Preston NE, Bristol C, Bristol R
1981–82 Cardiff C, Wrexham, Orient
1982–83 Rotherham U, Burnley, Bolton W
1983–84 Derby Co, Swansea C, Cambridge U
1984–85 Notts Co, Cardiff C, Wolverhampton W
1985–86 Carlisle U, Middlesbrough, Fulham
1986–87 Sunderland**, Grimsby T, Brighton & HA
1987–88 Huddersfield T, Reading, Sheffield U**
1988–89 Shrewsbury T, Birmingham C, Walsall
1989–90 Bournemouth, Bradford C, Stoke C
1990–91 WBA and Hull C
1991–92 Plymouth Arg, Brighton & HA, Port Vale

FIRST DIVISION TO SECOND DIVISION (1992–93 to 2003–04)

1992–93 Brentford, Cambridge U, Bristol R
1993–94 Birmingham C, Oxford U, Peterborough U
1994–95 Swindon T, Burnley, Bristol C, Notts Co
1995–96 Millwall, Watford, Luton T
1996–97 Grimsby T, Oldham Ath, Southend U
1997–98 Manchester C, Stoke C, Reading

1998–99 Bury, Oxford U, Bristol C
1999–2000 Walsall, Port Vale, Swindon T
2000–01 Huddersfield T, QPR, Tranmere R
2001–02 Crewe Alex, Barnsley, Stockport Co
2002–03 Sheffield W, Brighton & HA, Grimsby T
2003–04 Walsall, Bradford C, Wimbledon

FOOTBALL LEAGUE CHAMPIONSHIP TO FOOTBALL LEAGUE ONE (2004–05 to 2017–18)

2004–05 Gillingham, Nottingham F, Rotherham U
2005–06 Crewe Alex, Millwall, Brighton & HA
2006–07 Southend U, Luton T, Leeds U
2007–08 Leicester C, Scunthorpe U, Colchester U
2008–09 Norwich C, Southampton, Charlton Ath
2009–10 Sheffield W, Plymouth Arg, Peterborough U
2010–11 Preston NE, Sheffield U, Scunthorpe U

2011–12 Portsmouth, Coventry C, Doncaster R
2012–13 Peterborough U, Wolverhampton W, Bristol C
2013–14 Doncaster R, Barnsley, Yeovil T
2014–15 Millwall, Wigan Ath, Blackpool
2015–16 Charlton Ath, Milton Keynes D, Bolton W
2016–17 Blackburn R, Wigan Ath, Rotherham U
2017–18 Barnsley, Burton Alb, Sunderland

DIVISION 3 TO DIVISION 4 (1958–59 to 1991–92)

1958–59 Stockport Co, Doncaster R, Notts Co, Rochdale
1959–60 York C, Mansfield T, Wrexham, Accrington S
1960–61 Tranmere R, Bradford C, Colchester U, Chesterfield
1961–62 Torquay U, Lincoln C, Brentford, Newport Co
1962–63 Bradford PA, Brighton & HA, Carlisle U, Halifax T
1963–64 Millwall, Crewe Alex, Wrexham, Notts Co
1964–65 Luton T, Port Vale, Colchester U, Barnsley
1965–66 Southend U, Exeter C, Brentford, York C
1966–67 Swansea T, Darlington, Doncaster R, Workington
1967–68 Grimsby T, Colchester U, Scunthorpe U, Peterborough U (demoted)
1968–69 Northampton T, Hartlepool, Crewe Alex, Oldham Ath
1969–70 Bournemouth, Southport, Barrow, Stockport Co
1970–71 Reading, Bury, Doncaster R, Gillingham
1971–72 Mansfield T, Barnsley, Torquay U, Bradford C
1972–73 Rotherham U, Brentford, Swansea C, Scunthorpe U
1973–74 Cambridge U, Shrewsbury T, Southport, Rochdale

1974–75 Bournemouth, Tranmere R, Watford, Huddersfield T
1975–76 Aldershot, Colchester U, Southend U, Halifax T
1976–77 Reading, Northampton T, Grimsby T, York C
1977–78 Port Vale, Bradford C, Hereford U, Portsmouth
1978–79 Peterborough U, Walsall, Tranmere R, Lincoln C
1979–80 Bury, Southend U, Mansfield T, Wimbledon
1980–81 Sheffield U, Colchester U, Blackpool, Hull C
1981–82 Wimbledon, Swindon T, Bristol C, Chester
1982–83 Reading, Wrexham, Doncaster R, Chesterfield
1983–84 Scunthorpe U, Southend U, Port Vale, Exeter C
1984–85 Burnley, Orient, Preston NE, Cambridge U
1985–86 Lincoln C, Cardiff C, Wolverhampton W, Swansea C
1986–87 Bolton W**, Carlisle U, Darlington, Newport Co
1987–88 Rotherham U**, Grimsby T, York C, Doncaster R
1988–89 Southend U, Chesterfield, Gillingham, Aldershot
1989–90 Cardiff C, Northampton T, Blackpool, Walsall
1990–91 Crewe Alex, Rotherham U, Mansfield T
1991–92 Bury, Shrewsbury T, Torquay U, Darlington

*** Relegated after play-offs.*

SECOND DIVISION TO THIRD DIVISION (1992–93 to 2003–04)

1992–93 Preston NE, Mansfield T, Wigan Ath, Chester C
1993–94 Fulham, Exeter C, Hartlepool U, Barnet
1994–95 Cambridge U, Plymouth Arg, Cardiff C, Chester C, Leyton Orient
1995–96 Carlisle U, Swansea C, Brighton & HA, Hull C

1996–97 Peterborough U, Shrewsbury T, Rotherham U, Notts Co
1997–98 Brentford, Plymouth Arg, Carlisle U, Southend U
1998–99 York C, Northampton T, Lincoln C, Macclesfield T

1999–2000 Cardiff C, Blackpool, Scunthorpe U, Chesterfield
2000–01 Bristol R, Luton T, Swansea C, Oxford U
2001–02 Bournemouth, Bury, Wrexham, Cambridge U

2002–03 Cheltenham T, Huddersfield T, Mansfield T Northampton T
2003–04 Grimsby T, Rushden & D, Notts Co, Wycombe W

FOOTBALL LEAGUE 1 TO FOOTBALL LEAGUE TWO (2004–05 to 2017–18)

2004–05 Torquay U, Wrexham, Peterborough U, Stockport Co
2005–06 Hartlepool U, Milton Keynes D, Swindon T, Walsall
2006–07 Chesterfield, Bradford C, Rotherham U, Brentford
2007–08 Bournemouth, Gillingham, Port Vale, Luton T
2008–09 Northampton T, Crewe Alex, Cheltenham T, Hereford U
2009–10 Gillingham, Wycombe W, Southend U, Stockport Co
2010–11 Dagenham & R, Bristol R, Plymouth Arg, Swindon T

2011–12 Wycombe W, Chesterfield, Exeter C, Rochdale
2012–13 Scunthorpe U, Bury, Hartlepool U, Portsmouth
2013–14 Tranmere R, Carlisle U, Shrewsbury T, Stevenage
2014–15 Notts Co, Crawley T, Leyton Orient, Yeovil T
2015–16 Doncaster R, Blackpool, Colchester U, Crewe Alex
2016–17 Port Vale, Swindon T, Coventry C, Chesterfield
2017–18 Oldham Ath, Northampton T, Milton Keynes D, Bury

LEAGUE STATUS FROM 1986–87

RELEGATED FROM LEAGUE

1986–87 Lincoln C	1987–88 Newport Co
1988–89 Darlington	1989–90 Colchester U
1990–91 —	1991–92 —
1992–93 Halifax T	1993–94 —
1994–95 —	1995–96 —
1996–97 Hereford U	1997–98 Doncaster R
1998–99 Scarborough	1999–2000 Chester C
2000–01 Barnet	2001–02 Halifax T
2002–03 Shrewsbury T, Exeter C	
2003–04 Carlisle U, York C	
2004–05 Kidderminster H, Cambridge U	
2005–06 Oxford U, Rushden & D	
2006–07 Boston U, Torquay U	
2007–08 Mansfield T, Wrexham	
2008–09 Chester C, Luton T	
2009–10 Grimsby T, Darlington	
2010–11 Lincoln C, Stockport Co	
2011–12 Hereford U, Macclesfield T	
2012–13 Barnet, Aldershot T	
2013–14 Bristol R, Torquay U	
2014–15 Cheltenham T, Tranmere R	
2015–16 Dagenham & R, York C	
2016–17 Hartlepool U, Leyton Orient	
2017–18 Barnet, Chesterfield	

PROMOTED TO LEAGUE

1986–87 Scarborough	1987–88 Lincoln C
1988–89 Maidstone U	1989–90 Darlington
1990–91 Barnet	1991–92 Colchester U
1992–93 Wycombe W	1993–94 —
1994–95 —	1995–96 —
1996–97 Macclesfield T	1997–98 Halifax T
1998–99 Cheltenham T	1999–2000 Kidderminster H
2000–01 Rushden & D	2001–02 Boston U
2002–03 Yeovil T, Doncaster R	
2003–04 Chester C, Shrewsbury T	
2004–05 Barnet, Carlisle U	
2005–06 Accrington S, Hereford U	
2006–07 Dagenham & R, Morecambe	
2007–08 Aldershot T, Exeter C	
2008–09 Burton Alb, Torquay U	
2009–10 Stevenage B, Oxford U	
2010–11 Crawley T, AFC Wimbledon	
2011–12 Fleetwood T, York C	
2012–13 Mansfield T, Newport Co	
2013–14 Luton T, Cambridge U	
2014–15 Barnet, Bristol R	
2015–16 Cheltenham T, Grimsby T	
2016–17 Lincoln C, Forest Green R	
2017–18 Macclesfield T, Tranmere R	

APPLICATIONS FOR RE-ELECTION

FOURTH DIVISION

Eleven: Hartlepool U.
Seven: Crewe Alex.
Six: Barrow (lost League place to Hereford U 1972), Halifax T, Rochdale, Southport (lost League place to Wigan Ath 1978), York C.
Five: Chester C, Darlington, Lincoln C, Stockport Co, Workington (lost League place to Wimbledon 1977).
Four: Bradford PA (lost League place to Cambridge U 1970), Newport Co, Northampton T.
Three: Doncaster R, Hereford U.
Two: Bradford C, Exeter C, Oldham Ath, Scunthorpe U, Torquay U.
One: Aldershot, Colchester U, Gateshead (lost League place to Peterborough U 1960), Grimsby T, Swansea C, Tranmere R, Wrexham, Blackpool, Cambridge U, Preston NE.
Accrington S resigned and Oxford U were elected 1962.
Port Vale were forced to re-apply following expulsion in 1968.
Aldershot expelled March 1992. Maidstone U resigned August 1992.

THIRD DIVISIONS NORTH & SOUTH

Seven: Walsall.
Six: Exeter C, Halifax T, Newport Co.
Five: Accrington S, Barrow, Gillingham, New Brighton, Southport.
Four: Rochdale, Norwich C.
Three: Crystal Palace, Crewe Alex, Darlington, Hartlepool U, Merthyr T, Swindon T.
Two: Aberdare Ath, Aldershot, Ashington, Bournemouth, Brentford, Chester, Colchester U, Durham C, Millwall, Nelson, QPR, Rotherham U, Southend U, Tranmere R, Watford, Workington.
One: Bradford C, Bradford PA, Brighton & HA, Bristol R, Cardiff C, Carlisle U, Charlton Ath, Gateshead, Grimsby T, Mansfield T, Shrewsbury T, Torquay U, York C.

LEAGUE ATTENDANCES SINCE 1946–47

Season	Matches	Total	Div. 1	Div. 2	Div. 3 (S)	Div. 3 (N)
1946–47	1848	35,604,606	15,005,316	11,071,572	5,664,004	3,863,714
1947–48	1848	40,259,130	16,732,341	12,286,350	6,653,610	4,586,829
1948–49	1848	41,271,414	17,914,667	11,353,237	6,998,429	5,005,081
1949–50	1848	40,517,865	17,278,625	11,694,158	7,104,155	4,440,927
1950–51	2028	39,584,967	16,679,454	10,780,580	7,367,884	4,757,109
1951–52	2028	39,015,866	16,110,322	11,066,189	6,958,927	4,880,428
1952–53	2028	37,149,966	16,050,278	9,686,654	6,704,299	4,708,735
1953–54	2028	36,174,590	16,154,915	9,510,053	6,311,508	4,198,114
1954–55	2028	34,133,103	15,087,221	8,988,794	5,996,017	4,051,071
1955–56	2028	33,150,809	14,108,961	9,080,002	5,692,479	4,269,367
1956–57	2028	32,744,405	13,803,037	8,718,162	5,622,189	4,601,017
1957–58	2028	33,562,208	14,468,652	8,663,712	6,097,183	4,332,661

Season	Matches	Total	Div. 1	Div. 2	Div. 3	Div. 4
1958–59	2028	33,610,985	14,727,691	8,641,997	5,946,600	4,276,697
1959–60	2028	32,538,611	14,391,227	8,399,627	5,739,707	4,008,050
1960–61	2028	28,619,754	12,926,948	7,033,936	4,784,256	3,874,614
1961–62	2015	27,979,902	12,061,194	7,453,089	5,199,106	3,266,513
1962–63	2028	28,885,852	12,490,239	7,792,770	5,341,362	3,261,481
1963–64	2028	28,535,022	12,486,626	7,594,158	5,419,157	3,035,081
1964–65	2028	27,641,168	12,708,752	6,984,104	4,436,245	3,512,067
1965–66	2028	27,206,980	12,480,644	6,914,757	4,779,150	3,032,429
1966–67	2028	28,902,596	14,242,957	7,253,819	4,421,172	2,984,648
1967–68	2028	30,107,298	15,289,410	7,450,410	4,013,087	3,354,391
1968–69	2028	29,382,172	14,584,851	7,382,390	4,339,656	3,075,275
1969–70	2028	29,600,972	14,868,754	7,581,728	4,223,761	2,926,729
1970–71	2028	28,194,146	13,954,337	7,098,265	4,377,213	2,764,331
1971–72	2028	28,700,729	14,484,603	6,769,308	4,697,392	2,749,426
1972–73	2028	25,448,642	13,998,154	5,631,730	3,737,252	2,081,506
1973–74	2027	24,982,203	13,070,991	6,326,108	3,421,624	2,163,480
1974–75	2028	25,577,977	12,613,178	6,955,970	4,086,145	1,992,684
1975–76	2028	24,896,053	13,089,861	5,798,405	3,948,449	2,059,338
1976–77	2028	26,182,800	13,647,585	6,250,597	4,152,218	2,132,400
1977–78	2028	25,392,872	13,255,677	6,474,763	3,332,042	2,330,390
1978–79	2028	24,540,627	12,704,549	6,153,223	3,374,558	2,308,297
1979–80	2028	24,623,975	12,163,002	6,112,025	3,999,328	2,349,620
1980–81	2028	21,907,569	11,392,894	5,175,442	3,637,854	1,701,379
1981–82	2028	20,006,961	10,420,793	4,750,463	2,836,915	1,998,790
1982–83	2028	18,766,158	9,295,613	4,974,937	2,943,568	1,552,040
1983–84	2028	18,358,631	8,711,448	5,359,757	2,729,942	1,557,484
1984–85	2028	17,849,835	9,761,404	4,030,823	2,667,008	1,390,600
1985–86	2028	16,488,577	9,037,854	3,551,968	2,490,481	1,408,274
1986–87	2028	17,379,218	9,144,676	4,168,131	2,350,970	1,715,441
1987–88	2030	17,959,732	8,094,571	5,341,599	2,751,275	1,772,287
1988–89	2036	18,464,192	7,809,993	5,887,805	3,035,327	1,791,067
1989–90	2036	19,445,442	7,883,039	6,867,674	2,803,551	1,891,178
1990–91	2036	19,508,202	8,618,709	6,285,068	2,835,759	1,768,666
1991–92	2064*	20,487,273	9,989,160	5,809,787	2,993,352	1,694,974

Season	Matches	Total	FA Premier	Div. 1	Div. 2	Div. 3
1992–93	2028	20,657,327	9,759,809	5,874,017	3,483,073	1,540,428
1993–94	2028	21,683,381	10,644,551	6,487,104	2,972,702	1,579,024
1994–95	2028	21,856,020	11,213,168	6,044,293	3,037,752	1,560,807
1995–96	2036	21,844,416	10,469,107	6,566,349	2,843,652	1,965,308
1996–97	2036	22,783,163	10,804,762	6,931,539	3,195,223	1,851,639
1997–98	2036	24,692,608	11,092,106	8,330,018	3,503,264	1,767,220
1998–99	2036	25,435,542	11,620,326	7,543,369	4,169,697	2,102,150
1999–2000	2036	25,341,090	11,668,497	7,810,208	3,700,433	2,161,952
2000–01	2036	26,030,167	12,472,094	7,909,512	3,488,166	2,160,395
2001–02	2036	27,756,977	13,043,118	8,352,128	3,963,153	2,398,578
2002–03	2036	28,343,386	13,468,965	8,521,017	3,892,469	2,460,935
2003–04	2036	29,197,510	13,303,136	8,772,780	4,146,495	2,975,099

Season	Matches	Total	FA Premier	Championship	League One	League Two
2004–05	2036	29,245,870	12,878,791	9,612,761	4,270,674	2,483,644
2005–06	2036	29,089,084	12,871,643	9,719,204	4,183,011	2,315,226
2006–07	2036	29,541,949	13,058,115	10,057,813	4,135,599	2,290,422
2007–08	2036	29,914,212	13,708,875	9,397,036	4,412,023	2,396,278
2008–09	2036	29,881,966	13,527,815	9,877,552	4,171,834	2,304,765
2009–10	2036	30,057,892	12,977,251	9,909,882	5,043,099	2,127,660
2010–11	2036	29,459,105	13,406,990	9,595,236	4,150,547	2,306,332
2011–12	2036	29,454,401	13,148,465	9,784,100	4,091,897	2,429,939
2012–13	2036	29,225,443	13,653,958	9,662,232	3,485,290	2,423,963
2013–14	2036	29,629,309	13,930,810	9,168,922	4,126,701	2,402,876
2014–15	2036	30,052,575	13,746,753	9,838,940	3,884,414	2,582,468
2015–16	2036	30,207,923	13,852,291	9,705,865	3,955,385	2,694,382
2016–17	2036	31,727,248	13,612,316	11,106,918	4,385,178	2,622,836
2017–18	2036	32,656,695	14,560,349	11,313,826	4,303,525	2,478,995

*Figures include matches played by Aldershot.

Football League official total for their three divisions in 2001–02 was 14,716,162.

ENGLISH LEAGUE ATTENDANCES 2017–18

PREMIER LEAGUE ATTENDANCES

| | Average Gate | | | Season 2017–18 | |
	2016–17	2017–18	+/–%	Highest	Lowest
Arsenal	59,957	59,323	–1.06	59,547	58,420
Bournemouth	11,182	10,641	–4.84	10,998	10,242
Brighton & HA	27,996	30,403	+8.60	30,634	29,676
Burnley	20,558	20,688	+0.63	21,841	18,862
Chelsea	41,508	41,282	–0.54	41,616	38,910
Crystal Palace	25,161	25,063	–0.39	25,840	23,477
Everton	39,310	38,797	–1.31	39,221	37,580
Huddersfield T	20,343	24,032	+18.13	24,169	23,548
Leicester C	31,893	31,636	–0.81	32,202	30,203
Liverpool	53,016	53,049	+0.06	53,287	50,752
Manchester C	54,019	54,070	+0.10	54,452	53,241
Manchester U	75,290	74,976	–0.42	75,118	74,726
Newcastle U	51,106	51,992	+1.73	52,311	50,174
Southampton	30,936	30,794	–0.46	31,930	27,714
Stoke City	27,433	29,280	+6.73	30,022	27,458
Swansea C	20,619	20,623	+0.02	20,933	19,580
Tottenham H	31,639	68,052	+115.09	83,222	50,034
Watford	20,571	20,231	–1.65	20,552	20,002
WBA	23,876	24,520	+2.70	26,223	22,704
West Ham U	56,972	56,885	–0.15	56,988	56,197

TOTAL ATTENDANCES: 14,560,349 (380 games)
Average 38,317 (+6.96%)
HIGHEST: 83,222 Tottenham H v Arsenal
LOWEST: 10,242 Bournemouth v WBA
HIGHEST AVERAGE: 74,976 Manchester U
LOWEST AVERAGE: 10,641 Bournemouth

SKY BET ENGLISH FOOTBALL LEAGUE CHAMPIONSHIP ATTENDANCES

| | Average Gate | | | Season 2017–18 | |
	2016–17	2017–18	+/–%	Highest	Lowest
Aston Villa	32,107	32,097	–0.03	41,745	26,631
Barnsley	13,857	13,704	–1.11	17,163	10,920
Birmingham C	18,717	21,042	+12.42	27,608	18,301
Bolton W	15,194	15,887	+4.56	21,097	13,113
Brentford	10,467	10,234	–2.23	12,367	7,957
Bristol C	19,256	20,953	+8.81	25,540	17,203
Burton Alb	5,228	4,645	–11.14	6,535	2,750
Cardiff C	16,564	20,164	+21.73	32,478	15,951
Derby Co	29,085	27,175	–6.57	31,196	23,296
Fulham	19,199	19,896	+3.63	24,547	15,792
Hull C	20,761	15,622	–24.75	18,026	13,524
Ipswich T	16,981	16,272	–4.17	24,928	13,031
Leeds U	27,698	31,525	+13.82	35,377	26,434
Middlesbrough	30,449	25,544	–16.11	29,443	22,848
Millwall	9,340	13,368	+43.13	17,614	9,817
Norwich C	26,354	25,959	–1.50	27,100	24,841
Nottingham F	20,333	24,680	+21.38	29,106	20,596
Preston NE	12,607	13,774	+9.25	18,570	10,796
QPR	14,616	13,928	–4.71	16,934	11,488
Reading	17,505	16,656	–4.85	21,771	6,769
Sheffield U	21,892	26,854	+22.67	31,120	24,409
Sheffield W	27,129	25,995	–4.18	32,839	22,733
Sunderland	41,287	27,635	–33.07	31,237	24,894
Wolverhampton W	21,570	28,298	+31.19	30,239	23,045

TOTAL ATTENDANCES: 11,313,826 (552 games)
Average 20,496 (+1.86%)
HIGHEST: 41,745 Aston Villa v Derby Co
LOWEST: 2,750 Burton Alb v Reading
HIGHEST AVERAGE: 32,097 Aston Villa
LOWEST AVERAGE: 4,645 Burton Alb

Premier League and Football League attendance averages and highest crowd figures for 2017–18 are unofficial.

SKY BET ENGLISH FOOTBALL LEAGUE ONE ATTENDANCES

	Average Gate			Season 2017–18	
	2016–17	*2017–18*	*+/–%*	*Highest*	*Lowest*
AFC Wimbledon	4,477	4,325	–3.39	4,850	3,819
Blackburn R	12,688	12,832	+1.14	27,600	10,011
Blackpool	3,456	4,178	+20.87	7,371	2,650
Bradford C	18,167	19,787	+8.92	21,403	18,799
Bristol R	9,302	8,933	–3.97	10,029	7,531
Bury	3,845	3,931	+2.25	7,159	2,784
Charlton Ath	11,162	11,846	+6.13	17,581	8,801
Doncaster R	6,021	8,213	+36.40	12,481	7,013
Fleetwood T	3,245	3,140	–3.23	5,035	2,088
Gillingham	6,129	5,370	–12.39	8,163	4,002
Milton Keynes D	10,307	9,202	–10.71	14,762	7,258
Northampton T	6,245	5,830	–6.63	7,231	4,788
Oldham Ath	4,514	4,442	–1.58	7,784	2,975
Oxford U	8,297	7,376	–11.10	9,510	6,337
Peterborough U	5,581	5,669	+1.57	8,619	2,531
Plymouth Arg	9,652	10,413	+7.88	14,634	7,411
Portsmouth	16,823	17,917	+6.50	19,210	17,118
Rochdale	3,556	3,471	–2.39	6,524	2,138
Rotherham U	9,783	8,514	–12.97	11,725	7,330
Scunthorpe U	4,536	4,364	–3.79	6,359	3,120
Shrewsbury T	5,507	6,249	+13.47	8,202	4,666
Southend U	7,406	7,195	–2.85	9,588	5,608
Walsall	5,072	4,760	–6.16	8,919	3,225
Wigan Ath	11,722	9,152	–21.93	12,554	7,777

TOTAL ATTENDANCES: 4,303,525 (552 games)
Average 7,796 (–1.86%)
HIGHEST: 27,600 Blackburn R v Oxford U
LOWEST: 2,088 Fleetwood T v Gillingham
HIGHEST AVERAGE: 19,787 Bradford C
LOWEST AVERAGE: 3,140 Fleetwood T

SKY BET ENGLISH FOOTBALL LEAGUE TWO ATTENDANCES

	Average Gate			Season 2017–18	
	2016–17	*2017–18*	*+/–%*	*Highest*	*Lowest*
Accrington S	1,699	1,979	+16.45	4,753	1,119
Barnet	2,260	2,113	–6.49	5,539	1,123
Cambridge U	4,737	4,523	–4.52	6,722	3,524
Carlisle U	5,114	4,609	–9.88	6,036	3,562
Cheltenham T	3,323	3,172	–4.56	5,050	2,266
Chesterfield	5,929	5,354	–9.68	7,967	3,955
Colchester U	3,973	3,321	–16.43	5,461	2,552
Coventry C	9,118	9,255	+1.50	28,343	6,151
Crawley T	2,492	2,268	–8.98	5,008	1,455
Crewe Alex	3,882	3,876	–0.16	6,680	3,042
Exeter C	4,166	4,005	–3.87	4,760	3,382
Forest Green R	1,753	2,772	+58.11	3,880	1,825
Grimsby T	5,259	4,658	–11.45	7,669	3,023
Lincoln C	5,162	8,782	+70.12	10,004	7,320
Luton T	8,043	8,676	+7.87	10,063	7,046
Mansfield T	3,774	4,309	+14.18	7,525	2,866
Morecambe	1,703	1,492	–12.38	3,319	893
Newport Co	2,854	3,489	+22.28	5,741	2,275
Notts Co	5,970	7,911	+32.51	17,274	3,738
Port Vale	4,813	4,583	–4.79	7,127	3,129
Stevenage	2,899	2,611	–9.95	4,365	1,788
Swindon T	7,026	6,380	–9.19	8,526	5,439
Wycombe W	3,917	4,705	+20.12	8,802	3,295
Yeovil T	3,567	2,941	–17.54	4,834	2,205

TOTAL ATTENDANCES: 2,478,995 (552 games)
Average 4,491 (–5.49%)
HIGHEST: 28,343 Coventry C v Accrington S
LOWEST: 893 Morecambe v Colchester U
HIGHEST AVERAGE: 9,255 Coventry C
LOWEST AVERAGE: 1,492 Morecambe

LEAGUE CUP FINALS 1961–2018

*Played as a two-leg final until 1966. All subsequent finals played at Wembley except between 2001 and 2007 (inclusive) which were played at Millennium Stadium, Cardiff. *After extra time.*

FOOTBALL LEAGUE CUP

1961	Rotherham U v Aston Villa	2-0
	Aston Villa v Rotherham U	3-0*
	Aston Villa won 3-2 on aggregate.	
1962	Rochdale v Norwich C	0-3
	Norwich C v Rochdale	1-0
	Norwich C won 4-0 on aggregate.	
1963	Birmingham C v Aston Villa	3-1
	Aston Villa v Birmingham C	0-0
	Birmingham C won 3-1 on aggregate.	
1964	Stoke C v Leicester C	1-1
	Leicester C v Stoke C	3-2
	Leicester C won 4-3 on aggregate.	
1965	Chelsea v Leicester C	3-2
	Leicester C v Chelsea	0-0
	Chelsea won 3-2 on aggregate.	
1966	West Ham U v WBA	2-1
	WBA v West Ham U	4-1
	WBA won 5-3 on aggregate.	
1967	QPR v WBA	3-2
1968	Leeds U v Arsenal	1-0
1969	Swindon T v Arsenal	3-1*
1970	Manchester C v WBA	2-1*
1971	Tottenham H v Aston Villa	2-0
1972	Stoke C v Chelsea	2-1
1973	Tottenham H v Norwich C	1-0
1974	Wolverhampton W v Manchester C	2-1
1975	Aston Villa v Norwich C	1-0
1976	Manchester C v Newcastle U	2-1
1977	Aston Villa v Everton	0-0
Replay	Aston Villa v Everton	1-1*
	(at Hillsborough)	
Replay	Aston Villa v Everton	3-2*
	(at Old Trafford)	
1978	Nottingham F v Liverpool	0-0*
Replay	Nottingham F v Liverpool	1-0
	(at Old Trafford)	
1979	Nottingham F v Southampton	3-2
1980	Wolverhampton W v Nottingham F	1-0
1981	Liverpool v West Ham U	1-1*
Replay	Liverpool v West Ham U	2-1
	(at Villa Park)	

MILK CUP

1982	Liverpool v Tottenham H	3-1*
1983	Liverpool v Manchester U	2-1*
1984	Liverpool v Everton	0-0*
Replay	Liverpool v Everton	1-0
	(at Maine Road)	
1985	Norwich C v Sunderland	1-0
1986	Oxford U v QPR	3-0

LITTLEWOODS CUP

1987	Arsenal v Liverpool	2-1
1988	Luton T v Arsenal	3-2
1989	Nottingham F v Luton T	3-1
1990	Nottingham F v Oldham Ath	1-0

RUMBELOWS LEAGUE CUP

1991	Sheffield W v Manchester U	1-0
1992	Manchester U v Nottingham F	1-0

COCA-COLA CUP

1993	Arsenal v Sheffield W	2-1
1994	Aston Villa v Manchester U	3-1
1995	Liverpool v Bolton W	2-1
1996	Aston Villa v Leeds U	3-0
1997	Leicester C v Middlesbrough	1-1*
Replay	Leicester C v Middlesbrough	1-0*
	(at Hillsborough)	
1998	Chelsea v Middlesbrough	2-0*

WORTHINGTON CUP

1999	Tottenham H v Leicester C	1-0
2000	Leicester C v Tranmere R	2-1
2001	Liverpool v Birmingham C	1-1*
	Liverpool won 5-4 on penalties.	
2002	Blackburn R v Tottenham H	2-1
2003	Liverpool v Manchester U	2-0

CARLING CUP

2004	Middlesbrough v Bolton W	2-1
2005	Chelsea v Liverpool	3-2*
2006	Manchester U v Wigan Ath	4-0
2007	Chelsea v Arsenal	2-1
2008	Tottenham H v Chelsea	2-1*
2009	Manchester U v Tottenham H	0-0*
	Manchester U won 4-1 on penalties.	
2010	Manchester U v Aston Villa	2-1
2011	Birmingham C v Arsenal	2-1
2012	Liverpool v Cardiff C	2-2*
	Liverpool won 3-2 on penalties.	

CAPITAL ONE CUP

2013	Swansea C v Bradford C	5-0
2014	Manchester C v Sunderland	3-1
2015	Chelsea v Tottenham H	2-0
2016	Manchester C v Liverpool	1-1*
	Manchester C won 3-1 on penalties.	

EFL CUP

2017	Manchester U v Southampton	3-2

CARABAO CUP

2018	Manchester C v Arsenal	3-0

LEAGUE CUP WINS

Liverpool 8, Aston Villa 5, Chelsea 5, Manchester C 5, Manchester U 5, Nottingham F 4, Tottenham H 4, Leicester C 3, Arsenal 2, Birmingham C 2, Norwich C 2, Wolverhampton W 2, Blackburn R 1, Leeds U 1, Luton T 1, Middlesbrough 1, Oxford U 1, QPR 1, Sheffield W 1, Stoke C 1, Swansea C 1, Swindon T 1, WBA 1.

APPEARANCES IN FINALS

Liverpool 12, Manchester U 9, Arsenal 8, Aston Villa 8, Tottenham H 8, Chelsea 7, Manchester C 6, Nottingham F 6, Leicester C 5, Norwich C 4, Birmingham C 3, Middlesbrough 3, WBA 3, Bolton W 2, Everton 2, Leeds U 2, Luton T 2, QPR 2, Sheffield W 2, Southampton 2, Stoke C 2, Sunderland 2, West Ham U 2, Wolverhampton W 2, Blackburn R 1, Bradford C 1, Cardiff C 1, Newcastle U 1, Oldham Ath 1, Oxford U 1, Rochdale 1, Rotherham U 1, Swansea C 1, Swindon T 1, Tranmere R 1, Wigan Ath 1.

APPEARANCES IN SEMI-FINALS

Liverpool 17, Arsenal 15, Aston Villa 14, Manchester U 14, Tottenham H 14, Chelsea 13, Manchester C 10, West Ham U 9, Blackburn R 6, Nottingham F 6, Birmingham C 5, Everton 5, Leeds U 5, Leicester C 5, Middlesbrough 5, Norwich C 5, Bolton W 4, Burnley 4, Crystal Palace 4, Ipswich T 4, Sheffield W 4, Sunderland 4, WBA 4, Bristol C 3, QPR 3, Southampton 3, Swindon T 3, Wolverhampton W 3, Cardiff C 2, Coventry C 2, Derby Co 2, Luton T 2, Oxford U 2, Plymouth Arg 2, Sheffield U 2, Tranmere R 2, Watford 2, Wimbledon 2, Blackpool 1, Bradford C 1, Bury 1, Carlisle U 1, Chester C 1, Huddersfield T 1, Hull C 1, Newcastle U 1, Oldham Ath 1, Peterborough U 1, Rochdale 1, Rotherham U 1, Shrewsbury T 1, Stockport Co 1, Swansea C 1, Walsall 1, Wigan Ath 1, Wycombe W 1.

CARABAO CUP 2017–18

■ *Denotes player sent off.*

FIRST ROUND

Tuesday, 8 August 2017

Accrington S (1) 3 *(Richards-Everton 20, Clark 86, Kee 90)*
Preston NE (0) 2 *(Hugill 70, 90)* 2879

Accrington S: (442) Bloch Jorgensen; Hornby-Forbes, Hughes, Richards-Everton, Dallison; Clark, Brown (Conneely 81), Nolan, McConville; Edwards (Kee 46), Jackson.
Preston NE: (442) Maxwell; Vermijl, Boyle, Davies, O'Connor; Horgan, Grimshaw (Maguire 65), Gallagher, Robinson (Browne 80); Mavididi (Johnson 53), Hugill.
Referee: Eddie Ilderton.

AFC Wimbledon (1) 1 *(Robinson 25)*
Brentford (0) 3 *(Sawyers 69, Watkins 105, Shaibu 119)* 3229

AFC Wimbledon: (442) Long; Fuller, Nightingale, Robinson, Kennedy (Oshilaja 71); Hartigan, Francomb (Egan 82), Parrett, Barcham (Kaja 91); Taylor, McDonald (Appiah 67).
Brentford: (4231) Daniels; Colin, Dean, Barbet, Chatzitheodoridis (Dalsgaard 97); Sawyers, Mokotjo (McEachran 67); Clarke (Jozefzoon 56), Maupay (Shaibu 99), Yennaris; Watkins.
aet. Referee: Dean Whitestone.

Barnsley (2) 4 *(Bradshaw 2, 46, Lund 22 (og), Hedges 90)*
Morecambe (1) 3 *(Lavelle 45, Rose 49 (pen), Oliver 82)* 4062

Barnsley: (442) Davies; Pearson, MacDonald, Pinnock, Yiadom; Potts (Hedges 89), Moncur, Williams J (Mowatt 89), Hammill; Ugbo (Payne 77), Bradshaw.
Morecambe: (3412) Nizic; Lund (Ellison 50), Lavelle, Kenyon; Brough, Rose, Fleming, McGowan; Campbell (Thompson 69); Oliver, Turner (Deakin 74).
Referee: Darren Bond.

Birmingham C (3) 5 *(Adams 27, 42, 66, Davis 38, Tesche 49)*
Crawley T (0) 1 *(Camara 86)* 7814

Birmingham C: (451) Kuszczak; Nsue (Harding 58), Grounds, Roberts, Robinson; Gleeson, Maghoma (Cotterill, Davis (Tesche 46), Kieftenbeld; Adams (Gardner 69).
Crawley T: (442) Morris; Payne, McNerney, Blackman, Yorwerth; Djalo (Boldewijn 54), Cox, Tajbakhsh (Clifford 65), Lewis; Harrold, Sanoh (Camara 71).
Referee: Michael Salisbury.

Bradford C (1) 2 *(Poleon 35, Jones 84)*
Doncaster R (1) 3 *(May 8, Kongolo 71, Whiteman 88)* 3175

Bradford C: (41212) Doyle; McMahon, Knight-Percival, Vincelot■, Field (Taylor 76); Dieng; Gilliead (Kilgallon 64), Reeves; Pybus; Patrick (Jones 78), Poleon.
Doncaster R: (352) Lawlor; Wright, Butler, Garrett (Beestin 67); Mason, Kongolo (Alcock 79), Rowe, Whiteman, Andrew; Marquis, May.
Referee: Darren Drysdale.

Bristol C (4) 5 *(Hegeler 2, Baker 14, Smith 19, Hinds 39, Paterson 80)*
Plymouth Arg (0) 0 9838

Bristol C: (442) Fielding; Vyner, Hegeler (Kelly 70), Baker, Magnusson; Brownhill, Smith (Morrell 59), O'Dowda; Reid (Paterson 46), Hinds.
Plymouth Arg: (433) te Loeke; Miller, Bradley, Sokolik, Taylor-Sinclair; Songo'o, Lameiras, Carey; Ainsworth (Threlkeld 46 (Edwards 67)), Blissett, Wylde (Sarcevic 46).
Referee: Oliver Langford.

Bristol R (2) 4 *(Bodin 13, 42, Harrison 61, Sercombe 70)*
Cambridge U (0) 1 *(Ikpeazu 66)* 4114

Bristol R: (433) Smith; Leadbitter (Partington 52), Lockyer, Sweeney, Brown; Sinclair, Sercombe, Lines (Moore 67); Bodin, Nichols, Harrison (Gaffney 67).
Cambridge U: (343) Mitov; Taylor, Legge, Darling; Amoo (Brown 70), Osadebe, Lewis (Deegan 69), Dunk; Azeez, Ikpeazu, Elito (Carroll 69).
Referee: Kevin Johnson.

Cardiff C (0) 2 *(Mendez-Laing 48, Halford 113)*
Portsmouth (1) 1 *(Morrison 32 (og))* 6592

Cardiff C: (442) Murphy; Richards, Morrison, Ecuele Manga, Halford; Kennedy (Hoilett 87), O'Keefe, Damour (Ralls 102), Pilkington (Mendez-Laing 46); Tomlin (Meite 97), Ward D.
Portsmouth: (442) McGee; Talbot, Whatmough, Burgess, Haunstrup (Close 106); Evans, May, Rose, Bennett (Baker 98); Naismith (Kabamba 65), Pitman (Chaplin 114).
aet. Referee: Stephan Martin.

Coventry C (1) 1 *(Nazon 22)*
Blackburn R (2) 3 *(Evans 16, Smallwood 33, Samuel 56)* 5372

Coventry C: (4231) O'Brien; Grimmer, Hyam, McDonald, Camwell; Stevenson, Shipley; Devon Kelly-Evans (Beavon 62), Nazon, Jones (Finn 75); Biamou (Ponticelli 63).
Blackburn R: (343) Raya; Nyambe, Ward, Mulgrew (Doyle 76); Caddis, Smallwood, Evans (Chapman 71), Williams; Bennett, Samuel, Feeney (Gladwin 66).
Referee: Darren England.

Exeter C (0) 1 *(Holmes 54)*
Charlton Ath (0) 2 *(Clarke 72, Charles-Cook 79)* 2699

Exeter C: (442) Pym; Sweeney, Archibald-Henville (Jay 81), Brown, Croll; Holmes (Byrne 73), James, Tillson, Taylor; Reid (Brunt 81), McAlinden.
Charlton Ath: (4231) Phillips; Dijksteel, Konsa, Sarr, Jackson; Crofts■, Aribo; Charles-Cook, Reeves (Clarke 59), Ahearne-Grant; Watt (Hackett-Fairchild 67).
Referee: Tim Robinson.

Fleetwood T (0) 1 *(Hiwula 69)*
Carlisle U (1) 2 *(Miller S 22, Miller T 101)* 1711

Fleetwood T: (343) Cairns; Rodgers■, Bolger, Eastham; Coyle (Ekpolo 76), Schwabl (Dempsey 61), O'Neill, Maguire; Hunter (McAleny 61), Hiwula (Burns 91), Cole.
Carlisle U: (442) Bonham; Liddle, Parkes, Ellis, Grainger; Lambe, Joyce, Jones (Adams 112), Devitt (Cosgrove 90); Bennett (Hope 70), Miller S (Miller T 65).
aet. Referee: Graham Salisbury.

Forest Green R (0) 0
Milton Keynes D (0) 1 *(Ariyibi 110)* 1608

Forest Green R: (532) Russell; Bennett, Fitzwater, Collins L, Monthe (Laird 103), Wishart (Traore 73); Noble, Brown (Marsh-Brown 58), Cooper; James, Doidge (Mullings 73).
Milton Keynes D: (433) Nicholls; Brittain (Lewington 105), Ebanks-Landell, Downing, Williams GB; Tshibola, Cisse, Upson; Ariyibi, Seager (Nombe 80), Muirhead (Agard 63).
aet. Referee: Lee Swabey.

Luton T (0) 0
Ipswich T (1) 2 *(McGoldrick 34, 90)* 4610

Luton T: (442) Stech; Stacey, Cuthbert, Rea, Sheehan; Ruddock, Lee O, Shinnie, Lee E (Gambin 74); Cook (Mullins 86), Collins.
Ipswich T: (442) Gerken; Iorfa, Chambers, Webster (Woolfenden 46), Knudsen; Downes, Skuse (McDonnell 73), Nydam (Waghorn 63), Kenlock; Celina, McGoldrick.
Referee: Andy Haines.

Mansfield T (0) 0
Rochdale (1) 1 *(Camps 17)* 1457

Mansfield T: (442) Olejnik; Bennett, Pearce, Mirfin, Benning; Atkinson, Digby, Byrom (Hamilton 70), Anderson (Potter 80); Spencer (Rose 78), Sterling-James.
Rochdale: (442) Lillis; Rafferty, McNulty, Canavan, Ntlhe (Andrew 90); Jordan LR Williams (Davies 65), Camps, Brown, Rathbone, Done (Inman 80), Henderson.
Referee: Andrew Madley.

Millwall (0) 2 *(Elliott 54, 67)*
Stevenage (0) 0 3096
Millwall: (442) King; Romeo, Webster, Cooper (Gregory 35 (Butcher 71)), Craig; Worrall, Thompson, Saville (Williams 74), Ferguson; Elliott, Onyedinma.
Stevenage: (442) Fryer; Henry, Franks, Wilkinson, Martin; Pett (Turgott 73), Whelpdale (Smith 59), Gorman, McKee; Godden (Newton 48), Samuel.
Referee: Simon Hooper.

Norwich C (3) 3 *(Jerome 27, Hoolahan 39, Maddison 42)*
Swindon T (1) 2 *(Lancashire 25, Mullin 62)* 13,166
Norwich C: (433) Gunn; Ivo Pinto (Martin 78), Zimmermann, Franke, Husband; Reed (Tettey 79), Hoolahan (Watkins 88), Maddison; Vrancic, Jerome, Murphy.
Swindon T: (4231) Vigouroux; Purkiss, Lancashire, Robertson, Hussey; Dunne, Thomas; Mullin, Smith T (Iandolo 50), Brophy; Smith H.
Referee: Geoff Eltringham.

Nottingham F (1) 2 *(Carayol 29 (pen), Cummings 75)*
Shrewsbury T (0) 1 *(Whalley 79 (pen))* 7546
Nottingham F: (442) Evtimov; Lichaj, Mills, Hobbs, Fox (Darikwa 63); Dowell (Osborn 63), Bouchalakis, Cohen, Carayol; Vellios (Walker 74), Cummings.
Shrewsbury T: (451) Henderson; Brown, Bolton, Nsiala, Sadler; Rodman, Nolan, Ogogo, Adams (Dodds 83), Gnahoua (Whalley 66); Ennis (John-Lewis 83).
Referee: John Busby.

Oxford U (3) 3 *(Johnson 21, Obika 31, Fernandez Codina 42)*
Cheltenham T (1) 4 *(Eisa 9, 99, Wright 66, 90)* 3179
Oxford U: (4411) Eastwood; Ribeiro, Nelson, Martin, Johnson (Carroll 67); Hall, Ledson, Ruffels, Rothwell (Henry 97); Fernandez Codina (Payne 71); Obika (Thomas 78).
Cheltenham T: (442) Flatt; Forster, Boyle, Grimes, Cranston; Winchester (Pell 54), Storer (O'Shaughnessy 79), Atangana (Page 99), Sellars; Holman (Wright 46), Eisa.
aet. Referee: Graham Horwood.

Peterborough U (1) 1 *(Edwards 30)*
Barnet (2) 3 *(Akpa Akpro 22, Vilhete 39, Coulthirst 58)* 2725
Peterborough U: (3412) Bond; Tafazolli, Baldwin, Penny (Da Silva Lopes 68); Lloyd (Hughes 46), Doughty (Kanu 74), Forrester, Edwards; Maddison; Marriott, Morias.
Barnet: (532) Stephens; Taylor H, Santos, Nelson, Tutonda, Johnson; Fonguck (Clough 88), Campbell-Ryce (Ruben Bover 55), Vilhete; Coulthirst (Amaluzor 68), Akpa Akpro.
Referee: Tony Harrington.

QPR (1) 1 *(Ngbakoto 36)*
Northampton T (0) 0 4317
QPR: (41212) Ingram; Furlong, Onuoha, Caulker, Robinson; Borysiuk; Ngbakoto, Freeman (Chair 63); Manning, Sylla (Petrasso 74), Smith (Washington 57).
Northampton T: (541) Cornell; Buchanan (Smith 81), Barnett■, Taylor A, Pierre, Phillips; Long (Lobjoit 70), Crooks, Kasim, Waters; Revell (Richards 69).
Referee: Charles Breakspear.

Reading (0) 2 *(Kelly 71, 86)*
Gillingham (0) 0 5936
Reading: (442) Jaakkola; Gunter, Moore, Evans, Richards (Andresson 63); Kelly, Barrett (Quinn 58), Clement, Rinomhota; Smith, Mendes (Barrow 46).
Gillingham: (3412) Holy; O'Neill, Ehmer, Ogilvie; Wagstaff, Hessenthaler (Chapman 78), Wright, Oldaker; Parker; Eaves (Nash 74), Cundle (Wilkinson 69).
Referee: Brett Huxtable.

Rotherham U (1) 2 *(Proctor 39, Forde 78)*
Lincoln C (0) 1 *(Knott 64)* 5489
Rotherham U: (442) O'Donnell; Emmanuel, Ajayi, Ihiekwe, Mattock; Williams (Forde 63), Frecklington (Vaulks 90), Potter, Newell; Proctor (Clarke-Harris 87); Moore.
Lincoln C: (4411) Vickers; Long, Dickie, Raggett, Eardley; Maguire-Drew (Arnold 68), Bostwick, Woodyard, Anderson; Knott (Rhead 82); Green (Palmer 63).
Referee: Sebastian Stockbridge.

Scunthorpe U (0) 3 *(Madden 69 (pen), 105, Holmes 86)*
Notts Co (1) 3 *(Grant 22, Brisley 90, Yates 117)* 1874
Scunthorpe U: (352) Gilks; Wallace, McArdle, Goode (Adelakun 46); Clarke (Burgess 112), Morris (Holmes 52), Mantom (Redmond 89), Ojo, Townsend; van Veen, Madden.
Notts Co: (442) Fitzsimons; Hunt (Tootle 72), Brisley, Hollis, Dickinson; Hawkridge (Hodge 88), Milsom, Yates, Grant (Thompson 94); Stead (Smith 77), Forte.
aet; Scunthorpe U won 6-5 on penalties.
Referee: David Webb.

Sheffield W (2) 4 *(Hooper 43, Fletcher 45, Bannan 75, Hutchinson 83)*
Chesterfield (1) 1 *(Dennis 38 (pen))* 11,682
Sheffield W: (442) Wildsmith; Hunt (Hutchinson 59), Lees, Pudil, Reach; Wallace, Bannan, Abdi (Nuhiu 69), Jones; Fletcher (Marco Matias 76), Hooper.
Chesterfield: (532) Anyon; Hird, Maguire, Wiseman, O'Grady (Mitchell 90), Barry; McCourt, Reed, Ugwu (German 80); Dennis (Brewster 69), Donohue.
Referee: Ross Joyce.

Southend U (0) 0
Newport Co (0) 2 *(McCoulsky 52, 58)* 2998
Southend U: (442) Smith; Demetriou, White, Kiernan, Hendrie; McGlashan (Ba 66), Leonard, Yearwood, McLaughlin; Cox (Fortune 65), Robinson (Timlin 81).
Newport Co: (352) Day; White, Bennett (Labadie 46), Demetriou; Pipe, Willmott, Dolan, Owen-Evans, Butler; McCoulsky (Foulston 90), Reynolds (Nouble 67).
Referee: James Linnington.

Wigan Ath (2) 2 *(Laurent 17, Flores 45)*
Blackpool (0) 1 *(Gnanduillet 59)* 3391
Wigan Ath: (442) Evans; Burke, Thomas (Stubbs 65), Daniels, James; Gilbey, Flores, Merrie (Lang 65), Laurent; Colclough, Grigg (Burgess 73).
Blackpool: (442) Williams; Taylor, Aimson, Hartley, Anderton; Solomon-Otabor (Richards 87), Longstaff, Samuel (Matt 70), Delfouneso; Gnanduillet, Clayton (Philliskirk 64).
Referee: Christopher Sarginson.

Wolverhampton W (0) 1 *(Dicko 76)*
Yeovil T (0) 0 9478
Wolverhampton W: (343) Norris; Boly, Batth, Bennett; Graham, Price, Edwards (Enobakhare 69), Ruben Vinagre; Dicko, Leo Bonatini (Jota 69), Ronan (Saiss 81).
Yeovil T: (343) Krysiak; James, Sowunmi, Smith N; Alfei, Bailey, Smith C (Gray 81), Dickson; Browne, Zoko (Surridge 55), Khan (Olomola 66).
Referee: Robert Lewis.

Wycombe W (0) 0
Fulham (0) 2 *(Piazon 67, Odoi 81)* 3639
Wycombe W: (433) Brown; Harriman, Muller, El-Abd, Jacobson; Rowe, Bean, Bloomfield; Cowan-Hall (Tyson 46), Hayes (Akinfenwa 72), Williams J (Freeman 74).
Fulham: (433) Rodak; Sessegnon S, Djalo, Madl, Odoi; O'Riley (Sessegnon R 81), Cisse, Edun; Piazon, Woodrow, Kamara.
Referee: Gavin Ward.

Wednesday, 9 August 2017

Colchester U (1) 1 *(Kent 39)*
Aston Villa (2) 2 *(Hogan 7, Kent 19 (og))* 6603
Colchester U: (343) Walker; James, Kent, Kpekawa; Jackson, Lapslie (Slater 65), Murray, Reid (Kinsella 69); Drey Wright (Johnstone 82), Mandron, Szmodics.
Aston Villa: (442) Steer; Bree, Chester, Samba, Bjarnason; Adomah (Hepburn-Murphy 69), Hourihane, Onomah, Green (de Laet 85); O'Hare, Hogan (Davis 73).
Referee: John Brooks.

Crewe Alex (1) 1 *(Porter 42)*
Bolton W (0) 2 *(Armstrong 70, Osede 81)* 3167
Crewe Alex: (433) Garratt; Nolan, Raynes, Walker (Bowery 87), Ng; Porter, Wintle, Lowery; Cooper, Ainley (Pickering 84), Dagnall.

Bolton W: (532) Alnwick; Robinson, Osede, Pratley (Karacan 67), Darby, Little (Morais 66); Earing, Buckley, Burke; Armstrong, Wilbraham (Madine 66).
Referee: Mark Heywood.

Leeds U (1) 4 *(Samuel 12, 60, 62, Ekuban 83)*
Port Vale (1) 1 *(Tonge 36)*   15,431
Leeds U: (4231) Wiedwald; Ayling (Gomes 70), Shaughnessy, Borthwick-Jackson, Anita; Klich (Bridcutt 58), Vieira; Dallas, Samuel, Sacko (Alioski 57); Ekuban.
Port Vale: (4411) Lainton (Hornby 46); Kay, Davis, Smith, Gunning■; Reeves, Tonge, Pugh (Harness 80), Turner; Pyke; Forrester (Pope 62).
Referee: Peter Bankes.

Oldham Ath (0) 2 *(Green 55, Davies 67 (pen))*
Burton Alb (0) 3 *(Varney 47, Lund 69, Akins 86 (pen))*
                                                       2176
Oldham Ath: (532) Ben Wilson; Dummigan (Obadeyi 75), Brian Wilson, Clarke, Gerrard, Hunt; Fane (Fawns 90), Green, McLaughlin; Duffus (Davies 55), Holloway.
Burton Alb: (433) Ripley; Mousinho (Irvine 88), Naylor, McFadzean, McCrory; Sbarra, Palmer, Akpan (Lund 60); Varney (Sordell 84), Akins, Fox.
Referee: Scott Duncan.

Sheffield U (0) 3 *(Roberts 74 (og), Thomas 79, Lafferty 82)*
Walsall (1) 2 *(Bakayoko 13, Oztumer 90 (pen))*   5210
Sheffield U: (352) Eastwood; Brayford, Wright, Lafferty; Bennett (Basham 58), Lundstram, Duffy, Brooks, Thomas; Lavery (Fleck 86), Hanson (Evans C 52).
Walsall: (442) Gillespie; Edwards, Guthrie, Devlin, Leahy; Chambers, Kinsella (Kouhyar 84), Bakayoko (Jackson 76), Morris; Roberts K, Oztumer.
Referee: Andy Davies.

Thursday, 10 August 2017

Bury (0) 0
Sunderland (0) 1 *(Honeyman 69)*   3470
Bury: (532) Murphy; Jones, Thompson (Ismail 59), Aldred, Whitmore, Leigh; Dawson (Tutte 16), Dai (Beckford 72), Reilly; Ajose, Bunn.
Sunderland: (4411) Steele; Matthews, Browning, O'Shea, Galloway; Honeyman, Ndong, Gibson, McGeady (Asoro 59); Khazri (Gooch 77); Grabban (Vaughan 46).
Referee: Robert Jones.

Tuesday, 22 August 2017

Grimsby T (0) 0
Derby Co (0) 1 *(Vydra 53 (pen))*   3033
Grimsby T: (4411) McKeown; Davies■, Clarke, Collins, Dixon; Bolarinwa, Berrett, Rose, Kelly (Mills 64); Dembele (Jaiyesimi 80); Hooper (Cardwell 64).
Derby Co: (442) Mitchell; Forsyth, Pearce, Shackell, Baird; Bennett (Gordon 75), Butterfield, Bryson, Lawrence (Elsnik 81); Vydra (Anya 67), Martin.
Referee: Trevor Kettle.

SECOND ROUND
Tuesday, 22 August 2017

Accrington S (0) 1 *(Dallison 88)*
WBA (2) 3 *(Rondon 11, Phillips 31, Rodriguez 64)* 2699
Accrington S: (442) Chapman; Donacien, Richards-Everton, Hughes, Dallison; Clark, Nolan, Brown (Conneely 67), McConville; Edwards (Kee 53), Jackson (Leacock-McLeod 67).
WBA: (4231) Myhill; Nyom, Hegazi, Dawson, McClean; Morrison (Harper 77), Barry (Livermore 66); Phillips, Rodriguez (Leko 66), Chadli; Rondon.
Referee: Jeremy Simpson.

Aston Villa (3) 4 *(Hogan 19, 44, Adomah 36, Bjarnason 74)*
Wigan Ath (1) 1 *(Colclough 43)*   18,108
Aston Villa: (4411) Steer; de Laet, Elphick, Clark, Bjarnason; Bree, Doyle-Hayes (Lyden 78), Gardner, Adomah; O'Hare (McCormack 73); Hogan (Suliman 81).
Wigan Ath: (4231) Jones; Burke, Thomas, Daniels, Elder; Perkins, Power; Gilbey (Burgess 62), Laurent, Colclough (Hunt 80); Grigg (Lang 66).
Referee: Darren Drysdale.

Birmingham C (1) 1 *(Kieftenbeld 11)*
Bournemouth (0) 2 *(Fraser 46, Pugh 68)*   8245
Birmingham C: (352) Kuszczak; Shotton, Roberts, Grounds; Nsue (Harding 23), Davis, Gleeson, Kieftenbeld, Bramall (Robinson 78); Maghoma, Vassell (Jutkiewicz 46).
Bournemouth: (442) Boruc; Smith A, Mings, Cook S, Smith B; Fraser (Ibe 82), Gosling, Cook L, Pugh; Defoe, Mousset (Afobe 77).
Referee: Geoff Eltringham.

Bolton W (1) 3 *(Dervite 42, Armstrong 57 (pen), Karacan 64)*
Sheffield W (0) 2 *(Rhodes 76, 83)*   6385
Bolton W: (532) Alnwick; Robinson, Dervite, Beevers, Darby, Little; Buckley (Morais 65), Osede, Karacan (Pratley 69); Armstrong (Le Fondre 73), Wilbraham.
Sheffield W: (4411) Wildsmith; Reach, Pudil, Lees, Palmer; Forestieri (Marco Matias 70), Bannan, Abdi, Wallace (Lucas Joao 74); Rhodes, Winnall (Nuhiu 69).
Referee: David Webb.

Brighton & HA (0) 1 *(Tilley 54)*
Barnet (0) 0   11,414
Brighton & HA: (4411) Maenpaa; Rosenior, Hunemeier, Goldson, Bong (Mateju 46); Skalak, Ince, Molumby, Knockaert (Tilley 46); Towell; Hemed (Connolly 76).
Barnet: (343) Ross; Santos, Clough, Tutonda; Taylor H, Taylor J, Fonguck, Vilhete; Campbell-Ryce (Akinola 65), Coulthirst (Amaluzor 71); Akpa Akpro (Ruben Bover 76).
Referee: Stephen Martin.

Cardiff C (0) 1 *(Pilkington 76)*
Burton Alb (1) 2 *(Naylor 26, Fox 70)*   5820
Cardiff C: (532) Murphy; Richards, Ecuele Manga, Halford (Damour 81), Connolly, Coxe; O'Keefe, Kennedy (Mendez-Laing 77), Tomlin; Ward D, Bogle (Pilkington 74).
Burton Alb: (442) Ripley; Flanagan, Turner, Naylor, McCrory; Scannell (Sordell 62), Fox (McFadzean 76), Irvine, Palmer; Akins, Sbarra (Murphy 90).
Referee: John Busby.

Carlisle U (0) 1 *(Grainger 60)*
Sunderland (1) 2 *(Love 25, Gooch 80)*   8187
Carlisle U: (4411) Bonham; Liddle, Ellis, Parkes, Grainger; Lambe, Jones, Joyce (Hope 85), Adams (Kennedy 88); Devitt (Miller S 85); Bennett.
Sunderland: (433) Ruiter; Matthews, O'Shea, Djilobodji, Oviedo (McGeady 72); Love (Kone 65), Ndong, Gibson; Gooch, Asoro (Vaughan 66), Khazri.
Referee: Darren Bond.

Crystal Palace (0) 2 *(McArthur 76, 84)*
Ipswich T (0) 1 *(Celina 90)*   9837
Crystal Palace: (343) Speroni; Kelly, Dann (Fosu-Mensah 46), Ward; Schlupp, McArthur, Puncheon, Van Aanholt (Townsend 57); Cabaye, KaiKai (Lee 75), Lokilo.
Ipswich T: (442) Gerken; Woolfenden, Webber, Fowler, Nydam (Smith 81); Rowe, McDonnell, Downes, Celina; McLoughlin (Patterson 81); Folami (Morris 62).
Referee: Andy Davies.

Doncaster R (0) 2 *(May 48, Rowe 54)*
Hull C (0) 0   7139
Doncaster R: (352) Marosi; Alcock, Wright, Andrew; Blair, Whiteman, Kongolo (Mason 83), Ben Khemis, Rowe (Garrett 74); Marquis (Williams 60), May.
Hull C: (4411) Mannion; Lenihan, Clackstone, McKenzie, Fleming (Barkworth 68); Annan, Weir, Batty, Hamilton (Hinchcliffe 77); Olley; Luer.
Referee: Graham Salisbury.

Fulham (0) 0
Bristol R (1) 1 *(Harrison 13)*   6243
Fulham: (433) Bettinelli; Sessegnon S, Madl, Djalo, Edun (Sessegnon R 82); Cisse, Norwood, O'Riley; Kebano, Kamara, Ojo.
Bristol R: (433) Slocombe; Bola, Lockyer, Sweeney, Brown; Sercombe, Lines, Sinclair; Bodin (Nichols 61), Harrison (Gaffney 68), Moore (Broom 82).
Referee: Dean Whitestone.

Leeds U (1) 5 *(Roofe 44, 49, 65, Samuel 78, Vieira 89)*
Newport Co (1) 1 *(Labadie 33)*   17,098
Leeds U: (4231) Green; Ayling, Shaughnessy, Borthwick-Jackson, Anita (Cooper 60); Klich, Vieira; Roofe (Alioski 75), Gomes, Dallas; Stokes (Samuel 66).
Newport Co: (352) Day; O'Brien, White, Demetriou; Pipe, Dolan, Labadie, Rigg (Tozer 71), Willmott; McCoulsky (Nouble 54), Reynolds (Quigley 66).
Referee: Ross Joyce.

Middlesbrough (2) 3 *(Da Silva 17, Baker 30, Fletcher 55)*
Scunthorpe U (0) 0   12,679
Middlesbrough: (4231) Konstantopoulos; Roberts, Fry, Ayala, Da Silva; Forshaw, Leadbitter (Wing 80); Traore, Baker, Tavernier (Downing 64); Fletcher (Gestede 81).
Scunthorpe U: (451) Gilks; Sutton, Wallace, McArdle, Townsend; Adelakun, Mantom, Bishop (Redmond 70), Holmes, Morris; Madden (Hopper 62).
Referee: Andrew Madley.

Milton Keynes D (1) 1 *(Seager 17)*
Swansea C (1) 4 *(Fer 19, 59, Abraham 71, Ayew J 86)*   5162
Milton Keynes D: (4411) Sietsma; Brittain, Downing, Walsh (Tshibola 75), Lewington; Ariyibi (Thomas-Asante 67), Upson, McGrandles, Muirhead; Rasulo; Seager (Nombe 54).
Swansea C: (4231) Nordfeldt; Rangel, van der Hoorn, Bartley (Mawson 82), Olsson; Fulton (Narsingh 75), Roque; Ayew J, Fer, Carroll (King 87); Abraham.
Referee: Rob Jones.

Norwich C (1) 4 *(Murphy 21, 52, Watkins 74, Trybull 89)*
Charlton Ath (1) 1 *(Novak 5)*   12,521
Norwich C: (4141) McGovern; Ivo Pinto, Martin, Franke (Zimmermann 61), Stiepermann; Tettey; Hoolahan (Trybull 77), Naismith, Maddison (Wildschut 79), Murphy; Watkins.
Charlton Ath: (4231) Phillips; Charles-Cook (Dasilva 67), Sarr, Konsa, Jackson; Aribo, Dijksteel; Fosu (Pearce 57), Clarke (Magennis 58), Ahearne-Grant; Novak.
Referee: Andy Haines.

QPR (1) 1 *(Furlong 43)*
Brentford (3) 4 *(Borysiuk 10 (og), Egan 19, Maupay 32, Clarke 83)*   9719
QPR: (41212) Ingram; Furlong, Manning (Freeman 51), Caulker (Smith 75), Baptiste; Borysiuk; Ngbakoto, Wszolek (Mackie 69); Robinson; Chair, Sylla.
Brentford: (442) Daniels; Colin, Bjelland, Jozefzoon, Yennaris; Mokotjo (Woods 69), Egan, Sawyers, Clarke; Maupay (Shaibu 69), Chatzitheodoridis (Dalsgaard 77).
Referee: Christopher Sarginson.

Reading (1) 3 *(Bacuna 34, Evans 105, Smith 116)*
Millwall (1) 1 *(Ferguson 37)*   7148
Reading: (4231) Jaakkola; Gunter, Tiago Ilori, Evans, Andresson (Blackett 90); Quinn (Barrow 71), Bacuna (Loader 95); Rinomhota, McCleary (Clement 46), Popa; Smith.
Millwall: (442) King; Romeo, Webster, Cooper, Craig; Butcher (O'Brien 85), Tunnicliffe (Williams 78), Thompson, Ferguson (Wallace 96); Elliott (Morison 66), Onyedinma.
aet. Referee: Charles Breakspear.

Sheffield U (0) 1 *(Lavery 83)*
Leicester C (0) 4 *(Gray 52, Slimani 63, 67, Musa 90)*   11,280
Sheffield U: (352) Eastwood; Freeman, Wright (Basham 68), O'Connell; Baldock (Coutts 68), Brooks, Lundstram, Carruthers, Lafferty; Evans C (Sharp 62), Lavery.
Leicester C: (442) Hamer; Amartey, Maguire (Knight 81), Fuchs, Chilwell; Musa, Ndidi (Mendy 77), King, Gray; Ulloa, Slimani.
Referee: Tony Harrington.

Watford (0) 2 *(Capoue 47, Mariappa 90)*
Bristol C (0) 3 *(Hinds 60, Reid 67, Eliasson 90)*   9003
Watford: (4231) Gomes; Holebas▪, Kabasele, Prodl, Mariappa; Watson, Capoue (Cleverley 79); Richarlison, Hughes (Gray 71), Amrabat (Success 46); Deeney.

Bristol C: (442) Fielding; Kelly, Flint, Magnusson, Vyner; O'Dowda, O'Neil, Hegeler (Smith 60), Eliasson; Hinds (Taylor 77), Diedhiou (Reid 46).
Referee: Tim Robinson.

Wednesday, 23 August 2017

Blackburn R (0) 0
Burnley (2) 2 *(Cork 27, Brady 45)*   16,313
Blackburn R: (433) Raya; Williams, Ward, Mulgrew, Caddis; Feeney (Conway 46), Smallwood, Whittingham (Samuel 46); Chapman, Antonsson, Gladwin (Bennett 46).
Burnley: (442) Pope; Taylor, Long, Tarkowski, Bardsley; Brady (Gudmundsson 78), Cork, Westwood, Arfield; Walters (Wood 43), Barnes.
Referee: Simon Hooper.

Cheltenham T (0) 0
West Ham U (2) 2 *(Sakho 40, Ayew 43)*   6259
Cheltenham T: (442) Flatt; Forster, Grimes, Boyle (Dawson 46), Cranston; Pell, Storer, Atangana, Winchester; Wright (Graham 64), Eisa (Holman 71).
West Ham U: (433) Adrian; Byram, Collins, Ogbonna, Masuaku; Obiang, Rice, Noble (Kouyate 73); Fernandes (Quina 88), Sakho (Hernandez 64), Ayew.
Referee: Oliver Langford.

Huddersfield T (0) 2 *(Billing 52 (pen), Lolley 54)*
Rotherham U (1) 1 *(Ajayi 1)*   8290
Huddersfield T: (4231) Coleman; Williams J, Hefele, Schindler (Billing 46), Malone; Williams D, Whitehead; Lolley (Ince 82), Palmer (Kachunga 74), Quaner; Depoitre.
Rotherham U: (442) O'Donnell; Cummings, Ajayi, Wood, Purrington; Taylor, Vaulks, Dominic Ball (Bray 81), Forde; David Ball (Clarke-Harris 64), Proctor (Moore 46).
Referee: Peter Bankes.

Newcastle U (2) 2 *(Mitrovic 3, Aarons 45)*
Nottingham F (2) 3 *(Cummings 29, 31, Walker 97)*   27,709
Newcastle U: (4411) Darlow; Sterry (Lazaar 58), Hanley, Mbemba, Jesus Gamez; Murphy, Saivet, Barlaser (Hayden 70), Aarons (Ritchie 77); Diame; Mitrovic (Joselu 106).
Nottingham F: (433) Smith; Lichaj, Mancienne, Worrall, Fox; Osborn, Clough, Bouchalakis (McKay 46); Brereton (Walker 77), Cummings (Murphy 97), Dowell (Hobbs 62).
aet. Referee: Darren England.

Southampton (0) 0
Wolverhampton W (0) 2 *(Batth 67, Wilson 87)*   17,931
Southampton: (4231) Forster; Pied, Yoshida, Bednarek (Redmond 73), McQueen; Romeu, Stephens; Ward-Prowse, Tadic, Boufal (Gabbiadini 76); Austin (Long 76).
Wolverhampton W: (3421) Norris; Bennett, Batth, Deslandes; Graham, Price, Edwards, Ruben Vinagre; Ivan Cavaleiro (Wilson 86), Marshall (Ronan 46); Dicko (Zyro 74).
Referee: James Linington.

Stoke C (3) 4 *(Allen 16, 42, Crouch 29, Sobhi 80)*
Rochdale (0) 0   9930
Stoke C: (3421) Grant; Zouma (Soutar 60), Wollscheid, Martins Indi; Pieters (Verlinden 70), Allen (Fletcher 46), Adam, Tymon; Sobhi, Krkic; Crouch.
Rochdale: (442) Moore; Rafferty, Canavan, McGahey, Ntlhe; Cannon, Keane (Davies 46), Kitching, Inman (Jordan LR Williams 53); Done (Gillam 81), Henderson.
Referee: Scott Duncan.

Tuesday, 12 September 2017

Barnsley (1) 3 *(Jackson 18, Bradshaw 73, Hammill 88)*
Derby Co (2) 2 *(Russell 6, Bennett 39)*   7163
Barnsley: (433) Davies; McCarthy, Jackson, Pinnock, Pearson; Potts (McGeehan 88), Williams J, Moncur (Thiam 68); Hedges (Hammill 61), Bradshaw, Barnes.
Derby Co: (4231) Mitchell; Wisdom, Pearce, Shackell, Forsyth; Thorne, Bird (Guy 81); Anya, Russell, Bennett (Lawrence 81); Martin.
Referee: Eddie Ilderton.

THIRD ROUND

Tuesday, 19 September 2017

Aston Villa (0) 0

Middlesbrough (0) 2 *(Bamford 58 (pen), 67)*   11,197

Aston Villa: (4231) Steer; Hutton, Elphick■, Samba, de Laet; Lansbury (McCormack 41), Doyle-Hayes; Onomah (Taylor 81), O'Hare, Bjarnason; Hogan (Lyden 63).
Middlesbrough: (4231) Konstantopoulos; Roberts, Ayala, Gibson (Fry 46), Friend; Howson, Forshaw; Bamford, Wing (Downing 63), Tavernier; Fletcher (Miller 82).
Referee: Stephen Martin.

Bournemouth (0) 1 *(King 99)*

Brighton & HA (0) 0   10,372

Bournemouth: (4411) Boruc; Fraser (Hyndman 117), Francis, Cook S, Smith B; Ibe (Smith A 103), Cook L, Gosling, Stanislas (Pugh 63); Mousset (King 79); Afobe.
Brighton & HA: (343) Krul; Rosenior (Mateju 110), Goldson, Hunemeier, Schelotto (Propper 106), Molumby, Hutchinson, Bong; Skalak (March 104), Murphy, Izquierdo (Knockaert 104).
aet. Referee: Kevin Friend.

Brentford (0) 1 *(Clarke 90)*

Norwich C (1) 3 *(Vrancic 10 (pen), 51, Murphy 68)*   4863

Brentford: (4231) Daniels; Clarke, Barbet, Mepham, Chatzitheodoridis; Mokotjo, Yennaris; Jozefzoon (Dalsgaard 70), McEachran, Archibald (Watkins 53); Maupay (Shaibu 54).
Norwich C: (442) Gunn; Ivo Pinto, Klose (Franke 82), Zimmermann, Husband; Vrancic, Hoolahan, Reed, Trybull (Stiepermann 73); Watkins, Murphy (Wildschut 76).
Referee: James Linnington.

Bristol C (0) 2 *(Diedhiou 50, Taylor 61)*

Stoke C (0) 0   13,826

Bristol C: (442) Steele; Vyner, Flint, Hegeler, Magnusson; Eliasson (Bryan 80), Pack, Brownhill, O'Dowda; Diedhiou (Reid 83), Taylor (Smith 88).
Stoke C: (3421) Grant; Wimmer, Zouma, Martins Indi; Johnson, Adam (Shaqiri 74), Fletcher, Tymon (Berahino 46); Sobhi, Choupo-Moting; Crouch (Diouf 81).
Referee: Geoff Eltringham.

Burnley (0) 2 *(Wood 89 (pen), Brady 90)*

Leeds U (0) 2 *(Sacko 80, Hernandez 90 (pen))*   11,799

Burnley: (442) Pope; Bardsley, Tarkowski, Long, Taylor; Gudmundsson, Westwood (Defour 120), Hendrick (Cork 91), Arfield (Brady 72); Vokes (Wood 72), Barnes.
Leeds U: (4231) Lonergan; Ayling, Shaughnessy, Berardi, Borthwick-Jackson (Sacko 60); Klich, Vieira; Roofe (Alioski 104), Grot (Lasogga 85), Dallas; Cibicki (Hernandez 79).
aet; Leeds U won 5-3 on penalties.
Referee: Darren Bond.

Crystal Palace (1) 1 *(Sako 13)*

Huddersfield T (0) 0   6607

Crystal Palace: (4231) Speroni; Kelly, Tomkins, Sakho (Delaney 70), Van Aanholt; Milivojevic, Riedewald (Cabaye 80); Townsend, Lee, Schlupp (Souare 46); Sako.
Huddersfield T: (4231) Coleman; Hadergjonaj, Hefele, Cranie, Malone; Hogg (Whitehead 71), Billing; Ince (Mooy 70), Lolley (Sabiri 46), van La Parra; Kachunga.
Referee: Lee Probert.

Leicester C (0) 2 *(Okazaki 65, Slimani 78)*

Liverpool (0) 0   31,609

Leicester C: (442) Hamer; Amartey, Morgan, Dragovic, Chilwell; Albrighton, Ndidi (Choudhury 84), Iborra, Gray; Ulloa (Okazaki 53), Slimani.
Liverpool: (433) Ward; Flanagan, Gomez, Klavan, Robertson; Wijnaldum (Ings 73), Henderson, Grujic; Oxlade-Chamberlain, Solanke, Coutinho (Woodburn 46).
Referee: Stuart Attwell.

Reading (0) 0

Swansea C (0) 2 *(Mawson 52, Ayew J 83)*   8729

Reading: (433) Jaakkola; Gunter, Tiago Ilori, Moore, Obita (Blackett 62); Swift (Kelly 54), Evans, Bacuna; Beerens, Clement, Popa (Bodvarsson 74).
Swansea C: (433) Nordfeldt; Rangel, van der Hoorn, Mawson, Olsson; Sanches, Roque, Fer; Narsingh (Fernandez 70), Bony (Abraham 81), Routledge (Ayew J 62).
Referee: Andy Davies.

Tottenham H (0) 1 *(Alli 65)*

Barnsley (0) 0   23,926

Tottenham H: (4231) Vorm; Walker-Peters, Foyth, Vertonghen, Trippier; Winks, Dembele (Dier 79); Son, Alli (Oakley-Boothe 90), Sissoko; Llorente (Nkoudou 67).
Barnsley: (433) Davies; McCarthy, MacDonald, Lindsay, Fryers; Potts (Moncur 71), Bird, Williams J (Bradshaw 79); Barnes (Hammill 71), Ugbo, Hedges.
Referee: Tim Robinson.

West Ham U (2) 3 *(Ogbonna 4, Sakho 31, Masuaku 90)*

Bolton W (0) 0   35,806

West Ham U: (4231) Adrian; Byram, Rice, Ogbonna, Masuaku; Noble (Quina 77), Kouyate; Ayew, Haksabanovic (Holland 61), Arnautovic; Sakho (Hernandez 70).
Bolton W: (352) Howard; Robinson, Beevers, Pratley; Wheater, Noone (Earing 70), Morais, King (Armstrong 80), Taylor; Le Fondre, Wilbraham.
Referee: Simon Hooper.

Wolverhampton W (0) 1 *(Enobakhare 98)*

Bristol R (0) 0   12,740

Wolverhampton W: (343) Norris; Roderick Miranda, Coady, Batth; Buur (Wilson 91), N'Diaye, Price, Deslandes (Douglas 60); Marshall (Ronan 68), Enobakhare, Zyro (Ivan Cavaleiro 68).
Bristol R: (433) Slocombe; Leadbitter (Partington 97), Lockyer■, Broadbent (Moore 106), Bola; Sercombe, Clarke O, Lines; Bodin, Harrison (Gaffney 90), Nichols (Telford 86).
aet. Referee: Tony Harrington.

Wednesday, 20 September 2017

Arsenal (1) 1 *(Walcott 25)*

Doncaster R (0) 0   44,064

Arsenal: (3421) Ospina; Chambers (Da Silva 46), Mertesacker, Holding; Nelson (Willock 84), Elneny, Wilshere, Maitland-Niles; Walcott (Iwobi 76), Sanchez; Giroud.
Doncaster R: (541) Lawlor; Blair, Wright, Butler, Mason, Rowe; Coppinger (Mandeville 62), Houghton (Alcock 62), Whiteman, Kongolo; May (Marquis 76).
Referee: Scott Duncan.

Chelsea (3) 5 *(Kenedy 13, Batshuayi 19, 53, 86, Musonda 40)*

Nottingham F (0) 1 *(Darikwa 90)*   40,621

Chelsea: (343) Caballero; Rudiger, Christensen (Clarke-Salter 71), Cahill; Zappacosta (Sterling 76), Fabregas (Ampadu 56), Bakayoko, Kenedy; Musonda, Batshuayi, Hazard E.
Nottingham F: (352) Henderson; Worrall, Hobbs, Mancienne; Lichaj, Bouchalakis, Osborn, Dowell (Clough 74), Fox (Darikwa 59); Cummings, Walker (Brereton 65).
Referee: Christopher Kavanagh.

Everton (1) 3 *(Calvert-Lewin 39, 52, Niasse 83)*

Sunderland (0) 0   23,000

Everton: (433) Stekelenburg; Kenny, Keane, Williams, Holgate; Davies, Besic, Klaassen; Calvert-Lewin (Niasse 66), Sandro (Lookman 73), Vlasic (Lennon 82).
Sunderland: (4411) Steele; Love, Jones, Kone, Matthews; Honeyman (Williams 63), Gibson, Ndong, Gooch; Rodwell (McManaman 55); Vaughan (Robson 86).
Referee: Oliver Langford.

Manchester U (3) 4 *(Rashford 5, 17, Lingard 36,*
Martial 60)
Burton Alb (0) 1 *(Dyer 90)*   54,256
Manchester U: (4231) Romero (Joel Pereira 78);
Darmian, Lindelof, Smalling, Blind; Ander Herrera,
Carrick; Lingard, Mata (Shaw 46), Martial; Rashford
(McTominay 64).
Burton Alb: (532) Ripley; Lund, Flanagan, Naylor,
Turner (Warnock 46), Dyer; Allen (Murphy 46), Akpan
(Akins 78), Palmer; Mason, Varney.
Referee: Graham Scott.

WBA (0) 1 *(Yacob 72)*
Manchester C (1) 2 *(Sane 3, 77)*   14,953
WBA: (352) Foster; Dawson, McAuley (Phillips 62),
Evans; Nyom, Krychowiak, Yacob (McClean 80),
Morrison, Gibbs; Rodriguez (Rondon 67), Robson-Kanu.
Manchester C: (433) Bravo; Danilo, Stones, Mangala,
Delph; Bernardo Silva, Toure, Gundogan (Walker 59);
Sterling, Gabriel Jesus, Sane (Fernandinho 79).
Referee: Michael Jones.

FOURTH ROUND
Tuesday, 24 October 2017
Arsenal (0) 2 *(Nketiah 85, 96)*
Norwich C (1) 1 *(Murphy 34)*   58,444
Arsenal: (3421) Macey; Debuchy, Elneny, Holding;
Nelson (Nketiah 85), Coquelin, Wilshere (Willock 114),
Maitland-Niles (Akpom 70); Walcott, Iwobi (Da Silva
105); Giroud.
Norwich C: (4231) Gunn; Ivo Pinto, Zimmermann, Klose,
Husband; Trybull, Reed (Jerome 101); Vrancic
(Wildschut 90), Maddison (Hoolahan 90), Murphy
(Stiepermann 73); Oliveira.
aet. Referee: Andrew Madley.

Bournemouth (0) 3 *(Simpson 49, Wilson C 75 (pen),*
Afobe 83)
Middlesbrough (0) 1 *(Tavernier 56)*   10,254
Bournemouth: (442) Boruc; Smith A (Ake 84), Simpson,
Cook S, Daniels; Fraser (Afobe 77), Gosling, Arter,
Pugh; Wilson C, Mousset (Ibe 70).
Middlesbrough: (4231) Konstantopoulos; Roberts, Fry,
Ayala, Friend; Clayton, Forshaw; Traore, Baker
(Fletcher 83), Tavernier (Downing 76); Bamford.
Referee: Simon Hooper.

Bristol C (2) 4 *(Taylor 32, Djuric 39, Bryan 60,*
O'Dowda 66)
Crystal Palace (1) 1 *(Sako 21)*   21,901
Bristol C: (442) Steele; Pisano (Paterson 65), Flint,
Wright, Magnusson; O'Dowda, Brownhill, Pack, Bryan;
Diedhiou (Djuric 31 (Bakinson 80)), Taylor.
Crystal Palace: (442) Hennessey; Fosu-Mensah,
Tomkins, Kelly, Van Aanholt (Lumeka 83); Puncheon,
Riedewald; Lee (Ladapo 57), Loftus-Cheek, KaiKai
(Souare 64); Sako.
Referee: Tim Robinson.

Leicester C (1) 3 *(Iheanacho 30, Slimani 71, Mahrez 88)*
Leeds U (1) 1 *(Hernandez 26)*   31,516
Leicester C: (442) Hamer; Iborra, Dragovic, Maguire,
Chilwell; Albrighton (Mahrez 65), Amartey, King, Gray;
Iheanacho (Vardy 81), Slimani.
Leeds U: (4231) Wiedwald; Anita, Jansson, Shaughnessy,
Borthwick-Jackson (Ayling 46); Phillips (Vieira 71),
Klich; Roofe, Grot, Hernandez (Cibicki (Sacko 65).
Referee: Lee Probert.

Manchester C (0) 0
Wolverhampton W (0) 0   50,755
Manchester C: (343) Bravo; Danilo (Walker 103),
Adarabioyo (Stones 91), Mangala; Zinchenko, Toure,
Gundogan, Sterling; Bernardo Silva (Sane 95), Gabriel
Jesus (De Bruyne 82), Aguero.
Wolverhampton W: (343) Norris; Batth, Coady, Hause;
Bennett, N'Diaye, Price, Ruben Vinagre; Marshall
(Ronan 73), Enobakhare (Leo Bonatini 91), Helder
Costa (Ivan Cavaleiro 79).
aet; Manchester C won 4-1 on penalties.
Referee: Kevin Friend.

Swansea C (0) 0
Manchester U (1) 2 *(Lingard 21, 59)*   20,083
Swansea C: (4231) Nordfeldt; Rangel, van der Hoorn,
Mawson, Olsson (Naughton 39); Ki, Roque (Fer 67);
Routledge, Clucas, Ayew J; McBurnie (Abraham 72).
Manchester U: (3412) Romero; Lindelof, Smalling,
Tuanzebe; Darmian, Ander Herrera (Matic 67),
McTominay, Blind; Lingard; Rashford (Lukaku 67),
Martial (Shaw 87).
Referee: Robert Madley.

Wednesday, 25 October 2017
Chelsea (1) 2 *(Rudiger 26, Willian 90)*
Everton (0) 1 *(Calvert-Lewin 90)*   40,655
Chelsea: (343) Caballero; Rudiger, Christensen, Cahill;
Zappacosta, Ampadu, Drinkwater (Fabregas 62),
Kenedy; Willian, Batshuayi (Morata 85), Musonda
(Pedro 70).
Everton: (451) Pickford; Kenny, Jagielka, Williams,
Baines; Lennon (Lookman 73), McCarthy (Calvert-
Lewin 64), Baningime, Davies, Mirallas; Rooney (Niasse
81).
Referee: Neil Swarbrick.

Tottenham H (2) 2 *(Sissoko 6, Alli 37)*
West Ham U (0) 3 *(Ayew 55, 60, Ogbonna 70)*   36,168
Tottenham H: (352) Vorm; Foyth, Alderweireld, Davies;
Trippier, Sissoko, Dier, Alli, Rose (Eriksen 81); Llorente
(Dembele 72), Son (Nkoudou 83).
West Ham U: (3412) Adrian; Kouyate, Rice, Ogbonna;
Byram, Fernandes (Obiang 77), Noble, Cresswell;
Lanzini (Arnautovic 88); Carroll, Ayew.
Referee: Mike Dean.

QUARTER-FINALS
Tuesday, 19 December 2017
Arsenal (1) 1 *(Welbeck 42)*
West Ham U (0) 0   44,741
Arsenal: (433) Ospina; Debuchy, Chambers, Holding,
Kolasinac; Coquelin (Da Silva 90), Elneny, Willock
(Sheaf 84); Walcott, Giroud (Nelson 78), Welbeck.
West Ham U: (532) Hart; Cresswell (Carroll 65), Reid,
Collins, Ogbonna, Masuaku; Rice, Obiang, Quina
(Arnautovic 83); Hernandez (Sakho 65), Ayew.
Referee: Kevin Friend.

Leicester C (0) 1 *(Vardy 90 (pen))*
Manchester C (1) 1 *(Bernardo Silva 26)*   31,562
Leicester C: (4411) Hamer; Amartey, Dragovic
(Benalouane 111), Maguire, Fuchs; Albrighton (Mahrez
57), King, Iborra, Chilwell (Gray 71); Okazaki;
Iheanacho (Vardy 57).
Manchester C: (433) Bravo; Danilo, Adarabioyo,
Mangala (Walker 81), Zinchenko; Gundogan, Toure,
Foden (Dele-Bashiru 90); Bernardo Silva, Gabriel Jesus,
Diaz (Nmecha 88).
aet; Manchester C won 4-3 on penalties.
Referee: Robert Madley.

Wednesday, 20 December 2017
Bristol C (0) 2 *(Bryan 51, Smith 90)*
Manchester U (0) 1 *(Ibrahimovic 58)*   26,088
Bristol C: (4411) Steele; Wright, Flint, Baker, Magnusson
(Taylor 69); Brownhill (Eliasson 74), Pack, Smith, Bryan;
Paterson; Reid.
Manchester U: (433) Romero; Darmian (Smalling 90),
Lindelof, Rojo, Shaw; McTominay, Blind (Lukaku 61),
Pogba; Rashford, Ibrahimovic (Mkhitaryan 69); Martial.
Referee: Mike Dean.

Chelsea (1) 2 *(Willian 13, Morata 90)*
Bournemouth (0) 1 *(Gosling 90)*   41,168
Chelsea: (343) Caballero; Rudiger, Ampadu, Cahill;
Zappacosta, Drinkwater, Fabregas, Kenedy; Willian
(Hazard E 61), Batshuayi (Morata 73), Pedro (Bakayoko
61).
Bournemouth: (532) Boruc; Smith A, Francis, Cook S,
Simpson, Fraser; Arter (Cook L 74), Surman, Gosling;
Defoe (Ibe 17), Mousset (Wilson C 71).
Referee: Lee Mason.

SEMI-FINALS FIRST LEG

Tuesday, 9 January 2018

Manchester C (0) 2 *(De Bruyne 55, Aguero 90)*

Bristol C (1) 1 *(Reid 44 (pen))*　　　　　　43,426

Manchester C: (433) Bravo; Danilo, Stones, Mangala, Zinchenko (Walker 79); De Bruyne, Toure (Aguero 70), Gundogan; Bernardo Silva, Sterling, Sane.
Bristol C: (4411) Fielding; Wright, Flint, Baker, Magnusson (Walsh 72); Brownhill, Pack, Smith, Bryan; Paterson; Reid.
Referee: Anthony Taylor.

Wednesday, 10 January 2018

Chelsea (0) 0

Arsenal (0) 0　　　　　　　　　　40,097

Chelsea: (3511) Courtois; Azpilicueta, Christensen, Rudiger; Moses, Drinkwater (Willian 68), Kante, Fabregas, Alonso; Hazard E (Bakayoko 84); Morata (Batshuayi 87).
Arsenal: (3421) Ospina; Chambers, Mustafi, Holding; Bellerin, Xhaka, Wilshere (Elneny 57), Maitland-Niles; Iwobi, Welbeck; Lacazette (Sanchez 66).
Referee: Martin Atkinson.

SEMI-FINALS SECOND LEG

Tuesday, 23 January 2018

Bristol C (0) 2 *(Pack 64, Flint 90)*

Manchester C (1) 3 *(Sane 43, Aguero 49, De Bruyne 90)*
　　　　　　　　　　　　　　　　26,003

Bristol C: (451) Steele; Smith, Flint, Wright, Magnusson (Baker 46); Paterson (Kent 73), Walsh (Diedhiou 46), Brownhill, Pack, Bryan; Reid.
Manchester C: (433) Bravo; Walker (Danilo 85), Stones, Otamendi, Zinchenko; De Bruyne, Fernandinho, Silva; Bernardo Silva, Aguero (Gundogan 82), Sane.
Manchester C won 5-3 on aggregate.
Referee: Graham Scott.

Wednesday, 24 January 2018

Arsenal (1) 2 *(Rudiger 12 (og), Xhaka 60)*

Chelsea (1) 1 *(Hazard 7)*　　　　　　58,964

Arsenal: (433) Ospina; Bellerin, Koscielny, Mustafi, Monreal; Wilshere, Elneny, Xhaka; Ozil, Lacazette (Kolasinac 84), Iwobi (Ramsey 84).
Chelsea: (3421) Caballero; Azpilicueta, Christensen, Rudiger; Moses (Zappacosta 72), Kante, Bakayoko, Alonso; Willian (Barkley 30), Pedro (Batshuayi 65); Hazard E.
Arsenal won 2-1 on aggregate.
Referee: Michael Oliver.

CARABAO CUP FINAL 2018

Sunday, 25 February 2018

(at Wembley Stadium, attendance 85,671)

Arsenal (0) 0　　　Manchester C (1) 3

Arsenal: (3421) Ospina; Chambers (Welbeck 65), Mustafi, Koscielny; Bellerin, Ramsey (Iwobi 73), Xhaka, Monreal (Kolasinac 26); Ozil, Wilshere; Aubameyang.

Manchester C: (4231) Bravo; Walker, Kompany, Otamendi, Danilo; Fernandinho (Bernardo Silva 52), Gundogan; De Bruyne, Silva, Sane (Gabriel Jesus 77); Aguero (Foden 89).
Scorers: Aguero 18, Kompany 58, Silva 65.

Referee: Craig Pawson.

Man of the Match Vincent Kompany celebrates his goal in Manchester City's 3-0 defeat of Arsenal at the EFL Cup Final at Wembley on 25 February. (NurPhoto/SIPA USA/PA Images)

LEAGUE CUP ATTENDANCES 1960–2018

Season	Attendances	Games	Average
1960–61	1,204,580	112	10,755
1961–62	1,030,534	104	9,909
1962–63	1,029,893	102	10,097
1963–64	945,265	104	9,089
1964–65	962,802	98	9,825
1965–66	1,205,876	106	11,376
1966–67	1,394,553	118	11,818
1967–68	1,671,326	110	15,194
1968–69	2,064,647	118	17,497
1969–70	2,299,819	122	18,851
1970–71	2,035,315	116	17,546
1971–72	2,397,154	123	19,489
1972–73	1,935,474	120	16,129
1973–74	1,722,629	132	13,050
1974–75	1,901,094	127	14,969
1975–76	1,841,735	140	13,155
1976–77	2,236,636	147	15,215
1977–78	2,038,295	148	13,772
1978–79	1,825,643	139	13,134
1979–80	2,322,866	169	13,745
1980–81	2,051,576	161	12,743
1981–82	1,880,682	161	11,681
1982–83	1,679,756	160	10,498
1983–84	1,900,491	168	11,312
1984–85	1,876,429	167	11,236
1985–86	1,579,916	163	9,693
1986–87	1,531,498	157	9,755
1987–88	1,539,253	158	9,742
1988–89	1,552,780	162	9,585
1989–90	1,836,916	168	10,934
1990–91	1,675,496	159	10,538
1991–92	1,622,337	164	9,892
1992–93	1,558,031	161	9,677
1993–94	1,744,120	163	10,700
1994–95	1,530,478	157	9,748
1995–96	1,776,060	162	10,963
1996–97	1,529,321	163	9,382
1997–98	1,484,297	153	9,701
1998–99	1,555,856	153	10,169
1999–2000	1,354,233	153	8,851
2000–01	1,501,304	154	9,749
2001–02	1,076,390	93	11,574
2002–03	1,242,478	92	13,505
2003–04	1,267,729	93	13,631
2004–05	1,313,693	93	14,216
2005–06	1,072,362	93	11,531
2006–07	1,098,403	93	11,811
2007–08	1,332,841	94	14,179
2008–09	1,329,753	93	14,298
2009–10	1,376,405	93	14,800
2010–11	1,197,917	93	12,881
2011–12	1,209,684	93	13,007
2012–13	1,210,031	93	13,011
2013–14	1,362,360	93	14,649
2014–15	1,274,413	93	13,690
2015–16	1,430,554	93	15,382
2016–17	1,462,722	93	15,728
2017–18	1,454,912	93	15,644

CARABAO CUP 2017–18

Round	Aggregate	Games	Average
One	176,766	35	5,050
Two	262,282	25	10,491
Three	348,368	16	21,773
Four	269,776	8	33,722
Quarter-finals	143,559	4	35,890
Semi-finals	168,490	4	42,123
Final	85,671	1	85,671
Total	1,454,912	93	15,644

FOOTBALL LEAGUE TROPHY
FINALS 1984–2018

The 1984 final was played at Boothferry Park, Hull. All subsequent finals played at Wembley except between 2001 and 2007 (inclusive) which were played at Millennium Stadium, Cardiff.

ASSOCIATE MEMBERS' CUP
1984	Bournemouth v Hull C	2-1

FREIGHT ROVER TROPHY
1985	Wigan Ath v Brentford	3-1
1986	Bristol C v Bolton W	3-0
1987	Mansfield T v Bristol C	1-1*
	Mansfield T won 5-4 on penalties	

SHERPA VANS TROPHY
1988	Wolverhampton W v Burnley	2-0
1989	Bolton W v Torquay U	4-1

LEYLAND DAF CUP
1990	Tranmere R v Bristol R	2-1
1991	Birmingham C v Tranmere R	3-2

AUTOGLASS TROPHY
1992	Stoke C v Stockport Co	1-0
1993	Port Vale v Stockport Co	2-1
1994	Swansea C v Huddersfield T	1-1*
	Swansea C won 3-1 on penalties	

AUTO WINDSCREENS SHIELD
1995	Birmingham C v Carlisle U	1-0*
1996	Rotherham U v Shrewsbury T	2-1
1997	Carlisle U v Colchester U	0-0*
	Carlisle U won 4-3 on penalties	
1998	Grimsby T v Bournemouth	2-1
1999	Wigan Ath v Millwall	1-0
2000	Stoke C v Bristol C	2-1

LDV VANS TROPHY
2001	Port Vale v Brentford	2-1
2002	Blackpool v Cambridge U	4-1
2003	Bristol C v Carlisle U	2-0
2004	Blackpool v Southend U	2-0
2005	Wrexham v Southend U	2-0*

FOOTBALL LEAGUE TROPHY
2006	Swansea C v Carlisle U	2-1

JOHNSTONE'S PAINT TROPHY
2007	Doncaster R v Bristol R	3-2*
2008	Milton Keynes D v Grimsby T	2-0
2009	Luton T v Scunthorpe U	3-2*
2010	Southampton v Carlisle U	4-1
2011	Carlisle U v Brentford	1-0
2012	Chesterfield v Swindon T	2-0
2013	Crewe Alex v Southend U	2-0
2014	Peterborough U v Chesterfield	3-1
2015	Bristol C v Walsall	2-0
2016	Barnsley v Oxford U	3-2

EFL CHECKATRADE TROPHY
2017	Coventry v Oxford U	2-1
2018	Lincoln C v Shrewsbury T	1-0

*After extra time.

FOOTBALL LEAGUE TROPHY WINS

Bristol C 3, Birmingham C 2, Blackpool 2, Carlisle U 2, Port Vale 2, Stoke C 2, Swansea C 2, Wigan Ath 2, Barnsley 1, Bolton W 1, Bournemouth 1, Chesterfield 1, Coventry C 1, Crewe Alex 1, Doncaster R 1, Grimsby T 1, Lincoln C 1, Luton T 1, Mansfield T 1, Milton Keynes D 1, Peterborough U 1, Rotherham U 1, Southampton 1, Tranmere R 1, Wolverhampton W 1, Wrexham 1.

APPEARANCES IN FINALS

Carlisle U 6, Bristol C 5, Brentford 3, Southend U 3, Birmingham C 2, Blackpool 2, Bolton W 2, Bournemouth 2, Bristol R 2, Chesterfield 2, Grimsby T 2, Oxford U 2, Port Vale 2, Shrewsbury T 2, Stockport Co 2, Stoke C 2, Swansea C 2, Tranmere R 2, Wigan Ath 2, Barnsley 1, Burnley 1, Cambridge U 1, Colchester U 1, Coventry C 1, Crewe Alex 1, Doncaster R 1, Huddersfield T 1, Hull C 1, Lincoln C 1, Luton T 1, Mansfield T 1, Millwall 1, Milton Keynes D 1, Peterborough U 1, Rotherham U 1, Scunthorpe U 1, Southampton 1, Swindon T 1, Torquay U 1, Walsall 1, Wolverhampton W 1, Wrexham 1.

EFL TROPHY ATTENDANCES 2017–18

Round	Aggregate	Games	Average
One	132,065	96	1,376
Two	19,207	16	1,200
Three	15,333	8	1,917
Quarter-finals	12,604	4	3,151
Semi-finals	13,562	2	6,781
Final	41,261	1	41,261
Total	234,032	127	1,843

EFL CHECKATRADE TROPHY 2017–18

■ *Denotes player sent off.*
In the group stages an additional point was awarded to the team that won on penalties when a match was drawn after 90 minutes.

NORTHERN SECTION GROUP A
Tuesday, 29 August 2017
Fleetwood T (1) 3 *(Ekpolo 27, Cargill 61, Burns 85)*
Leicester C U21 (0) 0   517
Fleetwood T: (343) Neal; Eastham, Pond, Cargill; Ekpolo, Schwabl, Glendon, Bell (Maguire 46); Hunter (Grant 84), Hiwula (Sowerby 77), Burns.
Leicester C U21: (433) Bramley; Debayo, Hughes, Knight, Wood; Watts, Choudhury, Sheriff (Thandi 46); Martis (Felix-Eppiah 63), Gordon, Ndukwu (Muskwe 46).
Referee: Martin Coy.

Morecambe (0) 0
Carlisle U (2) 2 *(Hope 1, Kennedy 44)*   1228
Morecambe: (352) Nizic; Winnard (Deakin 60), Lavelle, Muller; McGowan, Fleming, Wildig, Osborne, Conlan (Lund 83); Campbell, Ellison (Thompson 71).
Carlisle U: (442) George; Brown, Ellis, Parkes, Grainger; Kennedy (Adams 64), Joyce, Jones, Devitt; Hope (Bennett 69), Miller S (Nabi 69).
Referee: Sebastian Stockbridge.

Tuesday, 3 October 2017
Carlisle U (0) 0
Leicester C U21 (1) 1 *(Ndukwu 20)*   1009
Carlisle U: (442) George; Miller T, Liddle, Parkes, Grainger; Lambe, Jones (Adams 76), Nabi (Joyce 65), Devitt; Bennett, Cosgrove (Miller S 64).
Leicester C U21: (442) Bramley; Knight, Hughes, Dewsbury-Hall, Wood; Felix-Eppiah (Ughelumba 72), Choudhury, Sheriff, Ndukwu (Leshabela 68); Gordon, Muskwe (Shade 90).
Referee: Ben Toner.

Fleetwood T (1) 2 *(Burns 25, McGowan 72 (og))*
Morecambe (0) 1 *(Ekpolo 51 (og))*   768
Fleetwood T: (352) Neal; Rodgers, Bolger (Pond 46), Cargill; Ekpolo, Sowerby, Schwabl, O'Neill (Nadesan 69), Maguire; Burns, Hunter (Hiwula 83).
Morecambe: (4231) Nizic; McGowan, Muller (Winnard 59 (Lund 82)), Lavelle, Conlan; Kenyon, Rose; Campbell, Fleming, Deakin (Ellison 75); Turner.
Referee: Eddie Ilderton.

Tuesday, 7 November 2017
Morecambe (1) 2 *(Thompson 8, Osborne 90)*
Leicester C U21 (1) 2 *(Ndukwu 25, Knight 85)*   432
Morecambe: (4231) Nizic; Lund, Lavelle, Old, Conlan (McGowan 83); Osborne, Rose; Thompson (Turner 68), Fleming (Yawson 77), Campbell; Oliver.
Leicester C U21: (433) Bramley; Wood, Knight, Hughes, Johnson; Choudhury, Dewsbury-Hall, Sheriff (Rubio 75); Felix-Eppiah (Ughelumba 88), Gordon, Ndukwu (Shade 62).
Morecambe won 4-2 on penalties.
Referee: Robert Jones.

Wednesday, 8 November 2017
Carlisle U (0) 1 *(Miller S 86)*
Fleetwood T (2) 2 *(Sowerby 10, Burns 44)*   909
Carlisle U: (352) George; Miller T, Parkes, Grainger; Brown, Jones (Joyce 66), Devitt, Etuhu (O'Sullivan 66), Lambe (Rigg 77); Cosgrove, Miller S.
Fleetwood T: (352) Neal; Rodgers, Sheron, Cargill (Higham 46); Ekpolo (Nirennold 69), Schwabl, Sowerby, Biggins, Maguire; Burns, Nadesan (Donohue 74).
Referee: Martin Coy.

Northern Group A	P	W	D	L	F	A	GD	Pts
Fleetwood T	3	3	0	0	7	2	5	9
Leicester C U21	3	1	1	1	3	5	–2	4
Carlisle U	3	1	0	2	3	3	0	3
Morecambe	3	0	1	2	3	6	–3	2

NORTHERN SECTION GROUP B
Tuesday, 29 August 2017
Blackpool (0) 1 *(Sinclair-Smith 87)*
Wigan Ath (0) 1 *(Gilbey 63)*   1532
Blackpool: (442) Williams; Mellor, Taylor, Hartley (Gnanduillet 46), Anderton; Philliskirk, Turenne Des Pres, D'Almeida (Sinclair-Smith 71), Delfouneso; Clayton, Quigley (Roache 70).
Wigan Ath: (442) Jones; Daniels, Perkins, Thomas, Burke; Laurent, Merrie (Barrigan 77), Power, Burgess (Hunt 68); Gilbey, Lang (Maffeo 68).
Wigan Ath won 5-4 on penalties.
Referee: Jeremy Simpson.

Tuesday, 19 September 2017
Accrington S (0) 3 *(Brown 54, Wilks 69, Nolan 90)*
Middlesbrough U21 (1) 2 *(Gibson 31, Armstrong 65)*   587
Accrington S: (442) Chapman; Hornby-Forbes, Sykes, Dallison, Ogle (Donacien 82); Sousa, Brown, Johnson (Nolan 82), Leacock-McLeod (Watson 86); Edwards, Wilks.
Middlesbrough U21: (442) Hemming; Dale, Brewitt, McGinley, Coulson (Storey 75); Gibson, Malley, Liddle, Soisalo (Sinior 87); Curry (O'Neill 59), Armstrong.
Referee: Graham Salisbury.

Tuesday, 3 October 2017
Accrington S (1) 1 *(Sousa 38)*
Blackpool (1) 2 *(Philliskirk 33, Clayton 88)*   975
Accrington S: (442) Chapman; Ogle, Sykes, Richards-Everton, Dallison (Donacien 86); Hornby-Forbes, Johnson, Brown, Sousa (Edwards 80); Leacock-McLeod, Wilks.
Blackpool: (3412) Mafoumbi; Tilt (Roache 46), Aimson, Anderton; Mellor, Cooke, Delfouneso, Taylor; Philliskirk; Quigley (Sinclair-Smith 71), Clayton.
Referee: Stuart Attwell.

Tuesday, 24 October 2017
Wigan Ath (2) 4 *(Evans 33 (pen), Maffeo 41, Hunt 72, Colclough 74)*
Middlesbrough U21 (0) 1 *(Armstrong 53)*   876
Wigan Ath: (4231) Sarkic; James, Thomas, Long (Bruce 74), Golden; Perkins, Evans; Maffeo (Malumo 70), Burgess, Colclough (Baningime 79); Hunt.
Middlesbrough U21: (541) Hemming; Hegarty (Wilson 73), Gibson, Cook, McGinley, Brewitt; Johnson (Sylla 68), Soisalo (Armstrong 46), Malley, Liddle; Miller.
Referee: Mark Heywood.

Wednesday, 1 November 2017
Blackpool (2) 4 *(Philliskirk 24, 89, Longstaff 43, D'Almeida 56)*
Middlesbrough U21 (0) 1 *(Armstrong 54)*   691
Blackpool: (433) Williams; Richards, Mellor (Taylor 61), Tilt, Anderton; Longstaff (Spearing 76), Philliskirk, D'Almeida; Solomon-Otabor, Quigley (Gnanduillet 76), Clayton.
Middlesbrough U21: (541) Mejias; Hegarty, Shotton, Coulson (O'Neill 77), McGinley, Brewitt; Armstrong, Wing, Sylla (Malley 46), Liddle; Miller.
Referee: Martin Coy.

Tuesday, 7 November 2017
Wigan Ath (0) 0
Accrington S (2) 4 *(Edwards 12, Sousa 30, 56, Leacock-McLeod 89)*   1473
Wigan Ath: (4231) Roberts; Plant, Thomas, Long, Golden; Merrie, McGuffie (Weir 69); Barrigan, Burgess, Baningime (Maffeo 57); Malumo (Culshaw 84).
Accrington S: (442) Stryjek; Hornby-Forbes, Richards-Everton, Rawson, Kee (Ogle 4); Sousa (Clark 87), Brown, Nolan, Leacock-McLeod; Edwards, Wilks.
Referee: Jeremy Simpson.

Northern Group B	P	W	D	L	F	A	GD	Pts
Blackpool	3	2	1	0	7	3	4	7
Accrington S	3	2	0	1	8	4	4	6
Wigan Ath	3	1	1	1	5	6	–1	4
Middlesbrough U21	3	0	0	3	4	11	–7	0

NORTHERN SECTION GROUP C

Tuesday, 29 August 2017

Blackburn R (0) 1 *(Nuttall 77)*

Stoke C U21 (0) 0 1501

Blackburn R: (4231) Fisher; Travis, Nyambe (Smallwood 46); Williams (Platt 38), Doyle; Tomlinson, Whittingham; Feeney, Chapman, Gladwin (Nuttall 64); Graham.
Stoke C U21: (4231) Haugaard (Gyollai 85); Wara, Soutar, Banks, McJannaett; Waddington, Adam; Pemberton, Shenton, Jarvis; Campbell.
Referee: Darren Handley.

Tuesday, 19 September 2017

Bury (0) 0

Rochdale (3) 4 *(Bunney 12, Inman 18, 34, Henderson 51)*
1451

Bury: (4411) Fasan; Williams (Leigh 46), Whitmore (Reilly 46), Shotton, Skarz; Cooney, Styles (Bunn 46), Dai, Alexandru Dobre; Danns; Lowe.
Rochdale: (442) Lillis; Rafferty, McGahey, Jordan M Williams (Rathbone 73), Ntlhe; Adshead, Camps, Inman (Cannon 69), Jodan LR Williams; Henderson (Slew 55), Bunney.
Referee: Mark Heywood.

Tuesday, 3 October 2017

Blackburn R (0) 0

Bury (0) 1 *(Bunn 77)* 2025

Blackburn R: (442) Fisher; Travis, Nyambe, Platt, Hart; Chapman (Rankin-Costello 57), Harper, Whittingham, Conway (Mols 64); Graham (Nuttall 57), Gladwin.
Bury: (352) Fasan; Edwards, O'Connell (Shotton 70), Skarz; Williams (Humphrey 79), Ince, Maguire, Reilly (Tutte 81), Leigh; Bunn, Smith.
Referee: Scott Oldham.

Rochdale (0) 0

Stoke C U21 (0) 0 731

Rochdale: (433) Moore; Rafferty, M Jordan Williams, Ntlhe, Bunney (Jordan LR Williams 76); Rathbone, Adshead, Kitching; Done, Slew, Inman (Andrew 76).
Stoke C U21: (532) Haugaard; Edwards■, Banks, Soutar, Wara, McJannaett; Waddington, Adam (Pemberton 75), Afellay (Jarvis 63); Campbell, Ngoy (Shenton 63).
Stoke C U21 won 5-4 on penalties. Referee: Martin Coy.

Tuesday, 7 November 2017

Rochdale (0) 1 *(Slew 72)*

Blackburn R (1) 1 *(Nuttall 42)* 1080

Rochdale: (433) Lillis; Rafferty, McGahey, Canavan (Gillam 71), Ntlhe; Rathbone (Inman 53), Camps, Adshead; Jordan LR Williams (Done 52), Slew, Bunney.
Blackburn R: (442) Fisher; Nyambe, Ward, Wharton■, Hart; Bennett, Harper, Smallwood, Gladwin; Samuel (Platt 31), Nuttall.
Rochdale won 5-3 on penalties.
Referee: Anthony Backhouse.

Wednesday, 8 November 2017

Bury (3) 3 *(Ajose 5, Leigh 18, Reilly 19)*

Stoke C U21 (0) 1 *(Afellay 75)* 686

Bury: (532) Fasan; Williams, Whitmore, O'Connell, Aldred, Leigh; Danns (Hill 82), Ince, Reilly; Ajose (Maguire 80), Sang (Harker 75).
Stoke C U21: (343) Bursik; Wara, Soutar, Martins Indi; Pemberton, Shenton, Adam, Banks; Afellay, Berahino, Jarvis (Campbell 76).
Referee: Graham Salisbury.

Northern Group C	P	W	D	L	F	A	GD	Pts
Rochdale	3	1	2	0	5	1	4	6
Bury	3	2	0	1	4	5	-1	6
Blackburn R	3	1	1	1	2	2	0	4
Stoke C U21	3	0	1	2	1	4	-3	2

NORTHERN SECTION GROUP D

Tuesday, 29 August 2017

Crewe Alex (0) 1 *(Bowery 88)*

Newcastle U U21 (1) 2 *(Smith L 4, Nolan 68 (og))* 1351

Crewe Alex: (3421) Garratt; Sass-Davies, Nolan, Bakayogo; Ainley, Lowery (Wintle 70), Walker,

Pickering; Cooper (Reilly 89), Kirk (Dale 69); Bowery.
Newcastle U U21: (4411) Woolston; Sterry (O'Connor 72), Good, Cameron, Gillesphey; Roberts (Sangare 67), Hunter, Barlaser, Fernandez (Smith C 46); Smith L; Charman.
Referee: Robert Jones.

Oldham Ath (0) 0

Port Vale (0) 0 1429

Oldham Ath: (442) Ben Wilson; Brian Wilson, Gerrard, Clarke, Hunt; Gardner, Banks, Fawns, Byrne; Holloway, Osei (Mantack 65).
Port Vale: (442) Boot; Wilson L, Smith, Davis, Gunning; Montano (Denton 74), Worrall (Pope 73), Tonge, de Freitas; Turner, Pyke (Harness 39).
Port Vale won 4-2 on penalties.
Referee: Michael Salisbury.

Tuesday, 3 October 2017

Crewe Alex (0) 0

Oldham Ath (1) 1 *(Byrne 42)* 976

Crewe Alex: (442) Richards; Ng, Raynes, Stubbs, Bakayogo; Kirk (Ainley 61), Walker (Dale 82), Lowery, Cooper; Porter (Dagnall 77), Bowery.
Oldham Ath: (442) Placide; Brian Wilson, Gerrard, Bryan, Hunt; Omrani (Banks 82), Byrne, Fane, Gardner; Doyle, Menig (Obadeyi 70).
Referee: Sebastian Stockbridge.

Port Vale (1) 1 *(Barnett 21)*

Newcastle U U21 (0) 0 824

Port Vale: (352) Roos; Davis, Smith, Gunning; Gibbons, Whitfield (Reeves 79), Pugh (Denton 87), Harness (Stobbs 79), Yates; Barnett, Turner.
Newcastle U U21: (4231) Harker; Sterry, Yarney, Cameron, Gillesphey; O'Connor, Barlaser; Sangare (McNall 80), Smith C, Fernandez (Gallacher 72); Charman.
Referee: David Coote.

Tuesday, 7 November 2017

Oldham Ath (1) 4 *(Byrne 13, 63, Doyle 61, 69)*

Newcastle U U21 (0) 1 *(Aarons 78)* 1107

Oldham Ath: (442) Placide; Brian Wilson, Gerrard, Bryan, Nepomuceno; Flynn (Maouche 72), Omrani, Byrne, Gardner (Obadeyi 65); Doyle (Duffus 72), Holloway.
Newcastle U U21: (4231) Harker; Sterry, Good, Gillesphey, Cameron; Barlaser, Ward; Roberts, Fernandez (Kitchen 71), Aarons; McNall (Bailey 64).
Referee: Carl Boyeson.

Port Vale (2) 4 *(Regis 3, Forrester 8, Reeves 65, Montano 90)*

Crewe Alex (1) 2 *(Reilly 31, 70)* 1322

Port Vale: (442) Boot; Gibbons, Smith, Gunning, Yates; Stobbs, Calveley (Reeves 46), Tonge, Montano; Regis (Turner 62), Forrester (de Freitas 90).
Crewe Alex: (442) Garratt; Nolan, Raynes, Stubbs, Bakayogo; Cooper (Ainley 61), Lowery, Walker, Kirk; Reilly, Porter.
Referee: John Brooks.

Northern Group D	P	W	D	L	F	A	GD	Pts
Port Vale	3	2	1	0	5	2	3	8
Oldham Ath	3	2	1	0	5	1	4	7
Newcastle U U21	3	1	0	2	3	6	-3	3
Crewe Alex	3	0	0	3	3	7	-4	0

NORTHERN SECTION GROUP E

Tuesday, 29 August 2017

Coventry C (0) 2 *(Andreu 51, McNulty 63 (pen))*

Shrewsbury T (2) 3 *(Payne 30, Gnahoua 33, Riley 90)* 1968

Coventry C: (4231) Burge; Grimmer, Hyam, Pearson, Dion Kelly-Evans (Maycock 46); Stevenson (Shipley 40), Doyle (Beavon 52); Jones, Andreu, Vincenti; McNulty.
Shrewsbury T: (442) MacGillivray; Bolton■, Nsiala, Beckles, Brown; Whalley (Adams 74), Godfrey, Nolan, Gnahoua (Riley 73); John-Lewis, Payne.
Referee: Tom Nield.

Tuesday, 19 September 2017

Walsall (0) 3 *(Flanagan 55, Ismail 73, Leahy 80)*

WBA U21 (1) 1 *(Tulloch 45)*   1055

Walsall: (442) Roberts L; Kinsella, Roberts K, Guthrie, Leahy; Ismail (Shorrock 83), Morris (Sangha 90), Flanagan, Kouhyar; Agyei (Candlin 75), Bakayoko.
WBA U21: (4231) Palmer; Soleman, Ferguson, Jameson (McCourt 85), Melbourne; Field (Azaz 46), Chambers; Bradley, Tulloch, Clayton-Phillips (Rogers 67); Morton.
Referee: Darren Handley.

Tuesday, 3 October 2017

Shrewsbury T (1) 3 *(John-Lewis 24, Morris C 49, Dodds 75)*

WBA U21 (0) 0   1404

Shrewsbury T: (442) MacGillivray; Riley, Sadler, Beckles, Shelis; Dodds, Adams (Hughes 76), Morris B, Gnahoua; Morris C (Mwandwe 89), John-Lewis (Barnett 67).
WBA U21: (451) Palmer; White (Clayton-Phillips 67), Melbourne, Jameson, McCourt; Soleman, Brown (Azaz 74), Bradley, Chambers, Burke (Pierce 62); Morton.
Referee: Michael Salisbury.

Walsall (1) 2 *(Ismail 32 (pen), Agyei 90)*

Coventry C (0) 2 *(McNulty 54 (pen), Ponticelli 59)*   1517

Walsall: (442) Roberts L; Devlin, Roberts K, Guthrie, Leahy; Ismail (Oztumer 68), Flanagan, Kouhyar (Edwards 63), Morris; Bakayoko, Agyei.
Coventry C: (4231) O'Brien; Dion Kelly-Evans, Hyam, Grimmer, Camwell; Maycock (Sayoud 74), Stevenson, Vincenti, McNulty, Shipley; Beavon (Ponticelli 46).
Coventry C won 4-3 on penalties.
Referee: Robert Lewis.

Tuesday, 7 November 2017

Coventry C (0) 2 *(Stevenson 58, Biamou 62)*

WBA U21 (0) 1 *(Burke 72)*   1429

Coventry C: (4231) O'Brien; Dion Kelly-Evans (Bayliss 75), Willis (Thompson 59), Hyam, Stokes; Stevenson, Maycock; Vincenti (Biamou 46), Devon Kelly-Evans, Thomas; Beavon.
WBA U21: (433) Palmer; Soleman, Jameson, Ferguson, Melbourne; Bradley (Hall 81), Brown, Azaz (Soule 78); Burke, Morton, Clayton-Phillips (Wilding 65).
Referee: John Busby.

Shrewsbury T (0) 0

Walsall (0) 1 *(Bakayoko 90)*   1701

Shrewsbury T: (352) MacGillivray; Godfrey■, Beckles, Sadler; Riley, Ogogo, Gnahoua (Shelis 82), Morris B, Rodman (Whalley 68); Payne, John-Lewis (Morris C 68).
Walsall: (451) Roberts L; Kinsella, Wilson, Guthrie, Leahy (Devlin 82); Ismail, Chambers, Morris, Edwards (Oztumer 85), Kouhyar (Flanagan 74); Bakayoko.
Referee: Trevor Kettle.

Northern Group E	P	W	D	L	F	A	GD	Pts
Walsall	3	2	1	0	6	3	3	7
Shrewsbury T	3	2	0	1	6	3	3	6
Coventry C	3	1	1	1	6	6	0	5
WBA U21	3	0	0	3	2	8	–6	0

NORTHERN SECTION GROUP F

Tuesday, 15 August 2017

Rotherham U (0) 1 *(David Ball 64)*

Manchester C U21 (0) 1 *(Garre 90)*   2562

Rotherham U: (433) O'Donnell; Cummings, Dominic Ball, Wood, Purrington; Forde, Vaulks, Taylor; David Ball (Kayode 85), Clarke-Harris, Yates (Bray 57).
Manchester C U21: (433) Muric; Duhaney (Matondo 75), Oliver, Latibeaudiere, Francis; Smith, Davenport, Dele-Bashiru (Richards 69); Dilrosun, Nmecha, Gonzalez (Garre 62).
Manchester C U21 won 4-2 on penalties
Referee: Anthony Backhouse.

Tuesday, 29 August 2017

Chesterfield (1) 2 *(Dennis 24, Sinnott 79)*

Bradford C (1) 4 *(Patrick 45, Jones 57, 62, Hanson 80)* 1099

Chesterfield: (442) Anyon; Flores, Evatt, Maguire, Wiseman; Reed, McCourt, Dimaio (Wakefield 12 (O'Grady 66)), Sinnott; Ugwu, Dennis (Kellett 66).

Bradford C: (4312) Sattelmaier (Doyle 38); Hendrie, Barr, Vincelot, Hanson; Gilliead (Law 46), Devine, Pybus (Gibson 86); Taylor; Patrick, Jones.
Referee: Carl Boyeson.

Tuesday, 3 October 2017

Rotherham U (0) 1 *(Vaulks 71)*

Chesterfield (1) 2 *(De Girolamo 9, McCourt 89)*   2043

Rotherham U: (442) O'Donnell; Emmanuel, Ajayi, Onariase, Hinds; Forde, Vaulks, Towell (Wiles 46), Bray (Newell 64); Yates, Clarke-Harris (David Ball 65).
Chesterfield: (442) Anyon; Barry, Wiseman, Evatt, Kellett; De Girolamo (Dennis 70), Weir, McCourt, Flores; Rowley (Sinnott 57), O'Grady.
Referee: Darren Handley.

Tuesday, 24 October 2017

Bradford C (2) 2 *(Thompson 18, Jones 35)*

Manchester C U21 (0) 1 *(Matondo 57)*   1260

Bradford C: (442) Raeder; Hendrie (Hudson 46), Thompson, Knight-Percival, Hanson (Laird 77); Gibson (Patrick 84), Devine, Pybus, Robinson; McCartan, Jones.
Manchester C U21: (4231) Muric; Duhaney, Oliver, Francis, Wilson; Smith, Dele-Bashiru; Matondo, Richards, Garre; Gonzalez (Pozo 77).
Referee: Eddie Ilderton.

Tuesday, 7 November 2017

Bradford C (0) 0

Rotherham U (3) 3 *(Yates 17, Clarke-Harris 31 (pen), Towell 45)*   931

Bradford C: (442) Sattelmaier; Devine, Thompson, Laird, Robinson; Gibson, Pybus, Dieng (Maltby 82), Patrick (Hudson 64); McCartan, Poleon (Staunton 74).
Rotherham U: (442) Price; Emmanuel, Onariase, Mattock, Hinds; Taylor (Bray 62), Towell, Wiles, Forde (McGinley 81); Clarke-Harris (Kayode 74), Yates.
Referee: Rob Lewis.

Wednesday, 29 November 2017

Chesterfield (0) 2 *(Rowley 73, O'Grady 90)*

Manchester C U21 (0) 2 *(Francis 88, Nmecha 90)*   1266

Chesterfield: (442) Anyon; Barry, Hird, Maguire, Binnom-Williams; Reed, Dimaio (Wakefield 86), McCourt (Weir 57), Kellett; O'Grady, De Girolamo (Rowley 73).
Manchester C U21: (433) Muric; Duhaney, Oliver■, Francis, Wilson; Dele-Bashiru, Davenport, Smith (Richards 69); Dilrosun (Diallo 80), Nmecha, Garre (Gonzalez 63).
Chesterfield won 4-3 on penalties.
Referee: Darren Drysdale.

Northern Group F	P	W	D	L	F	A	GD	Pts
Bradford C	3	2	0	1	6	6	0	6
Chesterfield	3	1	1	1	6	7	–1	5
Rotherham U	3	1	1	1	5	3	2	4
Manchester C U21	3	0	2	1	4	5	–1	3

NORTHERN SECTION GROUP G

Tuesday, 15 August 2017

Notts Co (2) 2 *(Forte 30, Hollis 36)*

Everton U21 (0) 1 *(Donkor 55)*   1409

Notts Co: (442) Pindroch; Hunt, Hewitt, Hollis, Dickinson; Grant (Hodge 68), Walker, Milsom, Alessandra (Thompson 76); Forte (Saunders 70), Smith.
Everton U21: (4411) Gray; Jones, Feeney (Gibson 56), Connolly, Foulds; Bowler (Evans 46), Charsley, Baningime, Garbutt (Donkor 46); Grant; Sambou.
Referee: Scott Oldham.

Tuesday, 29 August 2017

Mansfield T (1) 1 *(Potter 6)*

Lincoln C (1) 3 *(Whitehouse 40, Palmer 79, Green 90)* 2495

Mansfield T: (442) Olejnik; White, Pearce, Taft, Hunt; MacDonald (Hamilton 82), Digby, Thomas (Atkinson 72), Potter; Spencer (Rose 82), Sterling-James.
Lincoln C: (451) Farman; Long, Waterfall, Dickie, Habergham (Eardley 65); Anderson, Woodyard (Bostwick 65), Whitehouse, Knott, Maguire-Drew (Green 77); Palmer.
Referee: David Webb.

Tuesday, 24 October 2017

Lincoln C (2) 2 *(Maguire-Drew 3, 23)*

Everton U21 (0) 1 *(Adeniran 81)* 3713

Lincoln C: (4411) Farman; Long, Waterfall, Dickie, Habergham; Maguire-Drew, Bostwick (Chapman 70), Whitehouse, Ginnelly (Stewart 46); Knott; Palmer (Green 70).
Everton U21: (433) Hewelt; Markelo, Foulds, Feeney, Garbutt; Charsley, Adeniran, Baxter; Broadhead (Donkor 83), Evans (Bowler 63), Sambou (Lavery 76).
Referee: Graham Salisbury.

Notts Co (1) 1 *(Smith 34)*

Mansfield T (1) 2 *(Angol 1, Hamilton 73)* 2290

Notts Co: (442) Pindroch; Hunt, Hollis, Brisley, Jones (Dickinson 62); Saunders, Hodge, Milsom (Grant 81), Thompson; Walker, Smith (Alessandra 80).
Mansfield T: (442) Olejnik; Anderson, Digby, Bennett, Benning; Sterling-James (Potter 90), Mellis, Byrom (Thomas 57), Hamilton; Angol (Hemmings 90), Spencer.
Referee: Graham Horwood.

Tuesday, 31 October 2017

Mansfield T (0) 1 *(Diamond 81)*

Everton U21 (0) 0 964

Mansfield T: (442) Olejnik; White, Digby, Diamond, Hunt; Potter (Anderson 90), Atkinson, Butcher, Sterling-James (Hamilton 80); Angol (Thomas 90), Spencer.
Everton U21: (442) Gray; Markelo, Foulds, Ouzounidis, Garbutt; Bowler (Hornby 28), Charsley, Adeniran, Evans; Sambou (Lavery 76), Broadhead (Donkor 82).
Referee: Michael Salisbury.

Tuesday, 7 November 2017

Lincoln C (1) 2 *(Bird 37 (og), Ginnelly 86)*

Notts Co (1) 1 *(Forte 27)* 3026

Lincoln C: (4231) Vickers; Long, Waterfall, Raggett, Eardley; Whitehouse, Bostwick (Woodyard 46); Stewart (Anderson 59), Knott (Chapman 86), Ginnelly; Palmer.
Notts Co: (442) Pindroch; Hunt, Hollis, Bird, Jones; Thompson (Grant 64), Smith, Walker, Milsom (Stead 85); Alessandra, Forte (Saunders 73).
Referee: Tom Nield.

Northern Group G	P	W	D	L	F	A	GD	Pts
Lincoln C	3	3	0	0	7	3	4	9
Mansfield T	3	2	0	1	4	4	0	6
Notts Co	3	1	0	2	4	5	–1	3
Everton U21	3	0	0	3	2	5	–3	0

NORTHERN SECTION GROUP H

Tuesday, 29 August 2017

Grimsby T (1) 1 *(Cardwell 29)*

Doncaster R (1) 1 *(Williams 38)* 862

Grimsby T: (4231) Killip; Mills, Osborne K (Clarke 70), Collins, Davies B; Clifton (Bolarinwa 79), Summerfield; Jaiyesimi (Hooper 63), Jones, Kelly; Cardwell.
Doncaster R: (41212) Marosi; Alcock, Butler (Longbottom 46), Wright (Mason 46), Garrett; Middleton; Kongolo, Ben Khemis; Beestin; Williams, Mandeville.
Doncaster R won 4-3 on penalties.
Referee: Mike Jones.

Scunthorpe U (2) 3 *(van Veen 3, Holmes 45, Morris 90)*

Sunderland U21 (0) 1 *(Greenwood 65)* 1127

Scunthorpe U: (442) Watson; Clarke, Goode, Burgess, Butroid; Adelakun (Morris 84), Mantom, Redmond, Holmes; van Veen, Hopper (Madden 84).
Sunderland U21: (433) Talbot; Love, Matthews, Beadling, Hume; Robson (Gamble 21), Rodwell, Bale (Diamond 83); Greenwood, Gooch, Molyneux.
Referee: Darren Drysdale.

Tuesday, 3 October 2017

Doncaster R (0) 1 *(Ben Khemis 69)*

Sunderland U21 (0) 0 1520

Doncaster R: (352) Marosi; Alcock, Fielding, Garrett; Walker, Fletcher, Ben Khemis, Mason (Prior 62); Toffolo (James 63); Williams (Morris 46), Mandeville.

Sunderland U21: (442) Mika; Love, Beadling, Rodwell, Galloway; Molyneux, Gamble (Diamond 78), Robson, Hume (Bale 46); Nelson, Greenwood.
Referee: Ross Joyce.

Scunthorpe U (1) 2 *(Hopper 43, 80)*

Grimsby T (1) 1 *(Jaiyesimi 32)* 1987

Scunthorpe U: (442) Watson; Sutton, Burgess, Wallace, Butroid; Adelakun, Mantom, Redmond, van Veen; Madden, Hopper.
Grimsby T: (352) Killip; Mills (Woolford 71), Osborne K, Collins; Bolarinwa, Rose, Jaiyesimi (Dembele 78), Clifton, Kelly; Cardwell, Hooper (Vernon 82).
Referee: Tom Nield.

Tuesday, 31 October 2017

Doncaster R (1) 1 *(Mandeville 37)*

Scunthorpe U (0) 1 *(Lewis 55)* 1717

Doncaster R: (41212) Marosi; Alcock (Prior 72), Baudry (Fletcher 72), Amos, Garrett; Mason; James, Beestin; Ben Khemis; Williams (Scattergood 44), Mandeville.
Scunthorpe U: (433) Watson; Clarke, Goode, Burgess, Butroid; Lewis, Ojo (Holmes 75), Redmond; Madden, Church (Adelakun 46), van Veen.
Doncaster R won 3-2 on penalties.
Referee: Ben Toner.

Wednesday, 8 November 2017

Grimsby T (0) 1 *(Hooper 78 (pen))*

Sunderland U21 (0) 1 *(Love 79)* 248

Grimsby T: (433) Killip; Mills, Osborne K, Osborne J (McAllister 69), Kelly; Clifton (Powles 88), Rose, Jaiyesimi; Cardwell, Matt, Hooper.
Sunderland U21: (451) Talbot; Love, Galloway, Beadling, Bale; Molyneux, Gamble (Hackett 82), Rodwell, Robson, McManaman; Diamond (Greenwood 76).
Sunderland U21 won 7-6 on penalties.
Referee: Scott Oldham.

Northern Group H	P	W	D	L	F	A	GD	Pts
Scunthorpe U	3	2	1	0	6	3	3	7
Doncaster R	3	1	2	0	3	2	1	7
Grimsby T	3	0	2	1	3	4	–1	2
Sunderland U21	3	0	1	2	2	5	–3	2

SOUTHERN SECTION GROUP A

Wednesday, 16 August 2017

Portsmouth (0) 3 *(Lowe 54, 67, Naismith 57)*

Fulham U21 (1) 3 *(Humphrys 21, George C Williams 62 (pen), Adebayo 82)* 1520

Portsmouth: (433) Bass; Evans, Davies, Whatmough, Hancott; Baker (Bennett 60), Close (Talbot 76), May; Lowe, Main (Chaplin 68), Naismith.
Fulham U21: (4411) Norman; Sessegnon S, Opoku (Harris 76), Davies, Kavanagh; Humphrys, O'Riley, Kait (Kwietniewski 79), Thorsteinsson; George C Williams; Adebayo.
Fulham U21 won 4-2 on penalties.
Referee: Antony Coggins.

Tuesday, 29 August 2017

Crawley T (0) 0

Charlton Ath (1) 2 *(Reeves 37, Lapslie 70)* 1666

Crawley T: (442) Mersin; Young (Tajbakhsh 14), McNerney, Yorwerth, Djalo; Lewis, Bulman (Clifford 33), Payne, Meite; Verheijdt (Sanoh 55), Camara.
Charlton Ath: (442) Phillips; Konsa, Dijksteel, Sarr, Barnes (Jackson 68); Charles-Cook, Crofts (Maloney 89), Aribo, Reeves (Lapslie 54); Ahearne-Grant, Hackett-Fairchild.
Referee: Nicholas Kinsley.

Tuesday, 3 October 2017

Portsmouth (2) 3 *(Clarke 30, Hawkins 35, O'Keefe 71)*

Crawley T (0) 1 *(Sanoh 65)* 1527

Portsmouth: (433) McGee; Evans, Hawkins, Clarke, Donohue; May (Haunstrup 62), Rose (Lowe 62), O'Keefe (Close 88); Bennett, Main, Naismith.
Crawley T: (4231) Mersin; Tajbakhsh (Lewis 76), Yorwerth, McNerney, Djalo (Smith 87); Bulman, Payne; Camara (Boldewijn 76), Clifford, Sanoh; Meite.
Referee: Tim Robinson.

Wednesday, 1 November 2017

Charlton Ath (1) 3 *(Reeves 30, Dodoo 89, Aribo 90)*

Fulham U21 (1) 2 *(Thorsteinsson 4, Thompson 63)*   741

Charlton Ath: (4231) Phillips; Barnes, Cummings, Jackson (Maloney 75), Mascoll; Aribo, Dijksteel; Marshall (Hackett-Fairchild 69), Reeves (Lapslie 69), Dodoo; Ahearne-Grant.
Fulham U21: (4231) Norman; Jenz, Davies, Atkinson, Spence; Harris, O'Riley; Kwietniewski (Thompson 46), Kait, Thorsteinsson; Adebayo (Elstone 79).
Referee: Craig Hicks.

Tuesday, 7 November 2017

Charlton Ath (0) 0

Portsmouth (1) 1 *(Main 19)*   1307

Charlton Ath: (4231) Phillips; Dijksteel, Bauer, Sarr, Mascoll; Kashi, Aribo; Fosu (Reeves 9), Clarke, Ahearne-Grant (Holmes 69); Dodoo (Hackett-Fairchild 59).
Portsmouth: (4231) McGee; Evans, Thompson, Hawkins, Donohue; May, Rose; Lalkovic (Kennedy 58), Chaplin (O'Keefe 86), Naismith; Main (Lowe 57).
Referee: Nicholas Kinseley.

Wednesday, 29 November 2017

Crawley T (0) 1 *(Meite 74)*

Fulham U21 (2) 3 *(Adebayo 31, Graham 45, 85)*   435

Crawley T: (442) Mersin; Lelan, McNerney, Yorwerth (Tajbakhsh 16), Doherty; Lewis, Randall (Clifford 46), Payne (Sanoh 46), Djalo; Camara, Meite.
Fulham U21: (442) Ashby-Hammond; Jenz, Davies, Madl, Rafa Soares; Cisse (Thorsteinsson 69), Kait, O'Riley, Mollo (Kwietniewski 75); Graham, Adebayo.
Referee: John Busby.

Southern Group A	P	W	D	L	F	A	GD	Pts
Portsmouth	3	2	1	0	7	4	3	7
Charlton Ath	3	2	0	1	5	3	2	6
Fulham U21	3	1	1	1	8	7	1	5
Crawley T	3	0	0	3	2	8	–6	0

SOUTHERN SECTION GROUP B

Tuesday, 29 August 2017

Colchester U (1) 2 *(Szmodics 5, Mckeown 87)*

Reading U21 (2) 2 *(Barrett 19, House 42)*   572

Colchester U: (4231) Gilmartin; Vincent-Young (Jackson 46), Eastman, James, Kinsella; Diaz Wright, Murray; Drey Wright, Szmodics (O'Sullivan 46), Issa (Mckeown 78); Mandron.
Reading U21: (442) Legg; Andresson, Medford-Smith, Osho, Holmes; East, Frost, Holsgrove, Smith; Barrett, House (Rollinson 88).
Colchester U won 6-5 on penalties.
Referee: Gavin Ward.

Gillingham (1) 2 *(Parker 8, Ferdinand 57 (og))*

Southend U (1) 1 *(McLaughlin 31)*   1549

Gillingham: (442) Arnold; O'Neill, Ehmer, Nugent, Ogilvie (Simpson 79); Parker, Hessenthaler, Oldaker, Wagstaff (Byrne 90); Wilkinson, Cundle (List 70).
Southend U: (442) Oxley; Bwomono, White (Kyprianou 85), Ferdinand, Timlin; McGlashan, Yearwood (Klass 62), Leonard, McLaughlin; Robinson, Ba (Cox 70).
Referee: Andy Haines.

Tuesday, 3 October 2017

Colchester U (0) 0

Gillingham (0) 1 *(Ehmer 90)*   684

Colchester U: (343) Walker; James, Kent, Kpekawa; Vincent-Young, Comley, Murray, Kinsella; Guthrie (Kabamba 46), Mandron (Senior 60), Odelusi (Slater 78).
Gillingham: (352) Arnold; O'Mara, Ehmer, Nugent; Parker (Nash 82), Clare (Chapman 73), Hessenthaler, Oldaker, Simpson; List (Bingham 46), Eaves.
Referee: John Brooks.

Southend U (1) 1 *(Robinson 31)*

Reading U21 (0) 0   1148

Southend U: (442) Oxley; Bwomono, White, Kyprianou, Hendrie; McGlashan (McLaughlin 90), Yearwood, Klass, Bridge (Cotton 73); Fortune, Robinson (Ba 67).

Reading U21: (442) Legg; Medford-Smith, Osho, Sheppard, Holmes; East, Rinomhota (Frost 56), Burley, Smith; House (Barrett 67), Clement.
Referee: Andy Haines.

Tuesday, 7 November 2017

Gillingham (4) 7 *(Cundle 1, Wilkinson 12, Wagstaff 29, O'Neill 39, M'Bo 80, Oldaker 82, 90)*

Reading U21 (1) 5 *(Rollinson 38, Popa 49, 83, Medford-Smith 57, Sheppard 68)*   1039

Gillingham: (442) Nelson; O'Neill, O'Mara, Ehmer (Tucker 46), Simpson; Wagstaff, Oldaker, Chapman, List (M'Bo 46); Wilkinson (Stevenson 55), Cundle.
Reading U21: (442) Legg; Medford-Smith, Osho, Sheppard, Holmes; East, Frost, Burley, Rollinson; Popa, Barrett.
Referee: Craig Hicks.

Southend U (1) 2 *(Wright 37, Robinson 49)*

Colchester U (0) 0   2781

Southend U: (442) Oxley; Bwomono, White, Turner (Ferdinand 70), Timlin; McGlashan, Wright, Leonard, McLaughlin; Robinson (Ba 73), Ranger (Cox 79).
Colchester U: (3412) Gilmartin; Eastman, Kent, James (Szmodics 62); Vincent-Young, Lapslie, Slater (Hanlan 81), Kinsella; O'Sullivan (Mandron 73); Odelusi, Kabamba.
Referee: Stuart Attwell.

Southern Group B	P	W	D	L	F	A	GD	Pts
Gillingham	3	3	0	0	10	6	4	9
Southend U	3	2	0	1	4	2	2	6
Colchester U	3	0	1	2	2	5	–3	2
Reading U21	3	0	1	2	7	10	–3	1

SOUTHERN SECTION GROUP C

Tuesday, 15 August 2017

Swindon T (0) 2 *(Norris 47 (pen), Mullin 74)*

West Ham U U21 (1) 3 *(Samuelsen 6, Makasi 68, Kemp 86)*   2082

Swindon T: (442) Henry; Purkiss, Lancashire, Conroy, Hussey; Iandolo, Linganzi, Dunne, McDermott (Brophy 66); Norris (Smith H 62), Woolery (Mullin 62).
West Ham U U21: (4231) Trott; Neufville■, Akinola, Pask, Pike; Quina (Diangana 62), Makasi; Holland (Coventry 87), Samuelsen, Haksabanovic (Kemp 72); Martinez.
Referee: John Busby.

Tuesday, 29 August 2017

Wycombe W (1) 1 *(Southwell 5)*

Bristol R (2) 5 *(Telford 9, 42, Broom 54, 85, Sercombe 63)*   1132

Wycombe W: (433) Brown; Harriman, El-Abd (Stewart 62), Jombati, Williams; Bean, Gape, O'Nien; Southwell (Cowan-Hall 71), Freeman, Umerah.
Bristol R: (442) Slocombe; Partington, Broadbent, Burn (Menayese 79), Bola; Broom, Sercombe (Hargreaves 83), Clarke O, Moore (Russe 71); Telford, Gaffney.
Referee: James Linington.

Tuesday, 31 October 2017

Bristol R (1) 1 *(Nichols 1)*

West Ham U U21 (1) 3 *(Martinez 43 (pen), 76, Samuelsen 50)*   1508

Bristol R: (442) Slocombe; Leadbitter, Burn, Sweeney, Bola; Broom (Hargreaves 66), Russe, Sinclair, Moore; Telford, Nichols (Dunnwald 66).
West Ham U U21: (433) Trott; Pike, Rice, Pask, Johnson; Quina, Samuelsen (Diangana 73), Coventry; Haksabanovic (Kemp 73), Martinez (Hector-Ingram 90), Holland.
Referee: Robert Jones.

Swindon T (0) 1 *(Preston 88)*

Wycombe W (0) 0   1236

Swindon T: (4231) Charles-Cook; Knoyle, Robertson, Preston, Iandolo; Dunne, Elsnik (McDermott 77); Mullin (Smith H 59), Woolery, Gordon (Goddard 68); Anderson.
Wycombe W: (433) Makabu-Makalamby; Gape, De Havilland, El-Abd (Bean 70), Jacobson; O'Nien, Eze, Bloomfield; Cowan-Hall, Southwell, Freeman (Saunders 80).
Referee: Kevin Johnson.

Wednesday, 8 November 2017

Bristol R (1) 2 *(Sweeney 26, Sercombe 73)*

Swindon T (2) 4 *(Goddard 17 (pen), Mullin 37,
Gordon 58, Woolery 87)*   1657

Bristol R: (433) Smith; Partington, Sweeney, Burn
(Leadbitter 75), Bola; Sercombe, Lines, Clarke O;
Harrison, Telford (Gaffney 56), Moore (Nichols 57).
Swindon T: (433) Charles-Cook; Knoyle, Robertson,
Lancashire (Preston 46); Iandolo; Gordon, Elsnik
(Dunne 57), Goddard; Mullin, Anderson (McDermott
62), Woolery.
Referee: Andre Marriner.

Tuesday, 28 November 2017

Wycombe W (1) 2 *(De Havilland 31, Jombati 55)*

West Ham U U21 (0) 0   699

Wycombe W: (343) Makabu-Makalamby; De Havilland,
El-Abd, Scarr (Stewart 63); Jombati, Saunders
(Bloomfield 82), O'Nien, Williams J; Eze, Southwell,
Freeman.
West Ham U U21: (4231) Trott; Johnson, Collins
(Diangana 24), Akinola, Neufville (Powell 47); Coventry,
Makasi; Haksabanovic (Browne 70), Quina, Samuelsen;
Hector-Ingram.
Referee: Charles Breakspear.

Southern Group C	P	W	D	L	F	A	GD	Pts
Swindon T	3	2	0	1	7	5	2	6
West Ham U U21	3	2	0	1	6	5	1	6
Bristol R	3	1	0	2	8	8	0	3
Wycombe W	3	1	0	2	3	6	–3	3

SOUTHERN SECTION GROUP D

Tuesday, 15 August 2017

Plymouth Arg (0) 2 *(Fletcher 88, 90)*

Chelsea U21 (0) 2 *(Hudson-Odoi 62, 74)*   3962

Plymouth Arg: (433) te Loeke; Miller, Songo'o, Sokolik,
Taylor-Sinclair; Sarcevic (Fox 46), Lameiras (Blissett 90),
Ness (Carey 61); Ainsworth, Fletcher, Wylde.
Chelsea U21: (4231) Cumming; James, Colley, Ampadu,
DaSilva (Familio-Castillo 74); Sammut, McCormick;
Sterling, Hudson-Odoi (Muheim 90), Christie-Davies;
Taylor-Crossdale (Maddox 59).
Plymouth Arg won 5-4 on penalties.
Referee: Brett Huxtable.

Tuesday, 29 August 2017

Exeter C (0) 1 *(Sparkes 80)*

Yeovil T (0) 3 *(Surridge 46, Browne 75, Khan 78)*   1509

Exeter C: (442) Hamon; Taylor, Moore-Taylor (James
59), Brown, Croll (Kite 9); Sparkes, Byrne, Archibald-
Henville, Holmes; Reid (McAlinden 64), Jay.
Yeovil T: (442) Krysiak; Alfei (Sid Nelson 86), Mugabi,
Smith N, James; Green, Bailey (Santos 46), Gray, Khan;
Olomola (Browne 39), Surridge.
Referee: Oliver Langford.

Tuesday, 3 October 2017

Plymouth Arg (1) 2 *(Edwards 19, Blissett 75)*

Exeter C (1) 2 *(McAlinden 13, Edwards 70)*   3800

Plymouth Arg: (4231) Letheren; Sokolik, Edwards,
Songo'o, Sawyer; Sarcevic, Ness; Jervis, Carey (Lameiras
67), Wylde; Blissett (Ciftci 90).
Exeter C: (442) Hamon; Wilson, Archibald-Henville
(Sweeney 82), Croll, Moxey (Woodman 67); Sparkes,
James, Boateng (Taylor 76), Edwards; Jay, McAlinden.
Plymouth Arg won 5-3 on penalties.
Referee: Christopher Sarginson.

Wednesday, 25 October 2017

Yeovil T (1) 1 *(Browne 22)*

Chelsea U21 (1) 1 *(McCormick 34)*   1896

Yeovil T: (433) Krysiak; Mugabi, Smith N (Davies 67),
Sid Nelson, James; Worthington, Gray (Zoko 83), Santos;
Khan, Surridge, Browne (Olomola 64).
Chelsea U21: (3511) Cumming; Colley, Nartey (DaSilva
77), Chalobah; James (Muheim 90), McCormick,
Sammut, Maddox, Grant; Hazard K (St Clair 62); Taylor-
Crossdale.
Yeovil T won 5-3 on penalties.
Referee: Kevin Johnson.

Tuesday, 28 November 2017

Exeter C (1) 1 *(Reid 7)*

Chelsea U21 (1) 3 *(Hudson-Odoi 29, James 68, Grant 83)*
                                                      1294

Exeter C: (352) Hamon; Storey, Collins, Woodman;
Wilson (Dean 63), Edwards, Harley (Hartridge 46),
Byrne, Sparkes (Randall 62); Reid, Jay.
Chelsea U21: (3421) Bulka; James, Nartey, Chalobah;
Sterling, Sammut, Maddox, Grant; Hazard K (St Clair 75),
Christie-Davies (Taylor-Crossdale 62); Hudson-Odoi.
Referee: Kevin Johnson.

Yeovil T (0) 2 *(James 61, Surridge 88)*

Plymouth Arg (1) 1 *(Taylor 16)*   1110

Yeovil T: (433) Krysiak; Mugabi (James 46), Sowunmi,
Davies, Dickson; Gray (Khan 46), Smith C, Santos;
Green, Olomola, Zoko (Surridge 83).
Plymouth Arg: (41212) Mannion; Miller (Wylde 80),
Bradley, Edwards, Taylor-Sinclair; Songo'o; Sarcevic,
Threlkeld; Carey; Taylor (Ainsworth 72), Fletcher (Jervis
62).
Referee: Brett Huxtable.

Southern Group D	P	W	D	L	F	A	GD	Pts
Yeovil T	3	2	1	0	6	3	3	8
Chelsea U21	3	1	2	0	6	4	2	5
Plymouth Arg	3	0	2	1	5	6	–1	4
Exeter C	3	0	1	2	4	8	–4	1

SOUTHERN SECTION GROUP E

Tuesday, 15 August 2017

Cheltenham T (0) 1 *(Storer 48)*

Swansea C U21 (0) 2 *(Gorre 73, Lewis 83)*   801

Cheltenham T: (442) Lovett; Thomas, Grimes (Boyle 61),
Bower, O'Shaughnessy; Lloyd, Pell (Storer 46),
Winchester (Cranston 46), Page; Holman, Graham.
Swansea C U21: (451) Zabret; Reid, Harries, Rodon,
Lewis; Garrick (Gorre 61), Byers, Evans, Maric, Adam
King; Bia Bi (Baker-Richardson 53).
Referee: Kevin Johnson.

Tuesday, 29 August 2017

Forest Green R (1) 2 *(Wishart 20, James 84)*

Newport Co (0) 0   1090

Forest Green R: (451) Russell; Bennett, Iacovitti,
Roberts, Laird; Wishart, Cooper (Brown 78), Noble,
Traore (Monthe 68); James; Doidge (Mullings 78).
Newport Co: (442) Bittner; Pipe (Barnum-Bobb 46),
Bennett, White, Butler; Rigg, Tozer (Amond 71), Owen-
Evans, Jahraldo-Martin; Willmott (Cole 46), Quigley.
Referee: Brett Huxtable.

Tuesday, 3 October 2017

Cheltenham T (0) 1 *(Hinds 50)*

Forest Green R (0) 2 *(Brown 79, Stevens 80)*   1576

Cheltenham T: (352) Flatt; Davey, Boyle, Bower; Moore,
Sellars (Grimes 73), Storer (Winchester 57), Atangana,
Cranston; Hinds (Eisa 64), Wright■.
Forest Green R: (442) Russell; Bennett, Roberts,
Fitzwater, Wishart (Iacovitti 90); Cooper (Stevens 76),
Traore, Brown, Osbourne; James, Doidge (Bugiel 73).
Referee: Trevor Kettle.

Tuesday, 10 October 2017

Newport Co (0) 1 *(McCoulsky 76)*

Swansea C U21 (0) 2 *(Gorre 70, Foulston 83 (og))*   750

Newport Co: (442) Day; Barnum-Bobb, Foulston, Butler,
White; Owen-Evans, Rigg (Amond 85), Bennett,
Jahraldo-Martin (Dolan 54); Reynolds, McCoulsky.
Swansea C U21: (451) Zabret; Reid, Harries, Rodon,
Lewis; Gorre (Garrick 81), Fulton, Evans (James 65),
Byers, Adam King; Baker-Richardson.
Referee: Brett Huxtable.

Tuesday, 31 October 2017

Forest Green R (0) 0

Swansea C U21 (0) 2 *(Adam King 75, 79)*   590

Forest Green R: (3421) Collins B; Iacovitti (Stevens 19),
Roberts, Fitzwater; Randall, Monthe, Traore (Brown 61),
Laird; Correia Gomes, James; Bugiel (Marsh-Brown 69).

Swansea C U21: (41212) Zabret; Reid, Harries, Rodon, Lewis; Blair; Adam King, Maric; Byers; Gorre, Baker-Richardson (Cullen 55).
Referee: Graham Horwood.

Tuesday, 7 November 2017
Newport Co (0) 1 *(Reynolds 48)*
Cheltenham T (2) 2 *(Graham 3, Pell 11)*   540
Newport Co: (433) Bittner; Hillman, Bennett, Foulston, Butler; Rigg, Press, Collins; Jackson (Taylor 70), Quigley (Amond 81), Reynolds.
Cheltenham T: (442) Flinders; Moore, Boyle, Grimes, O'Shaughnessy; Winchester, Pell, Dawson, Sellars; Graham (Eisa 46), Hinds (Storer 67).
Referee: Simon Hooper.

Southern Group E	P	W	D	L	F	A	GD	Pts
Swansea C U21	3	3	0	0	6	2	4	9
Forest Green R	3	2	0	1	4	3	1	6
Cheltenham T	3	1	0	2	4	5	–1	3
Newport Co	3	0	0	3	2	6	–4	0

SOUTHERN SECTION GROUP F

Tuesday, 15 August 2017
Luton T (1) 2 *(Gambin 19, McQuoid 51)*
Tottenham H U21 (1) 2 *(Shea 21 (og), Loft 47)*   2699
Luton T: (41212) Shea; Justin (James 46), Famewo, Mullins, Senior; Bakinson; Cook, Gambin; Cornick (Down 77); Hylton (McQuoid 46), Lee E.
Tottenham H U21: (4231) Austin; Dinzeyi (Eyoma 52), Maghoma, Tanganga, Bennetts; Skipp; Pritchard; Tracey (Shashoua 81), Duncan, Miller; Loft (Sterling 77).
Luton T won 4-2 on penalties.
Referee: Craig Hicks.

Tuesday, 29 August 2017
Barnet (2) 3 *(Ruben Bover 13, Coulthirst 25, Blackman 89)*
AFC Wimbledon (2) 4 *(Hartigan 5, Kaja 16, McDonald 48, Clough 56 (og))*   696
Barnet: (352) Ross; Smith, Clough, Tutonda; Vilhete, Taylor J, Ruben Bover (Akpa Akpro 74), Fonguck (Taylor H 62), Blackman; Akinola, Coulthirst (Amaluzor 82).
AFC Wimbledon: (442) McDonnell; Sibbick, Kennedy (Kalambayi 66), Nightingale, Oshilaja; Forrester (Francomb 66), Egan, Hartigan, McDonald; Kaja (Bellikli 74); Appiah.
Referee: Dean Whitestone.

Tuesday, 3 October 2017
AFC Wimbledon (2) 4 *(Sibbick 19, 60, Kaja 38, Parrett 90)*
Tottenham H U21 (2) 3 *(Tracey 16, Shashoua 34, Sterling 59)*   608
AFC Wimbledon: (433) McDonnell; Sibbick, Kennedy, Robinson, Charles; Egan, Hartigan, Soares (Trotter 46); Kaja, McDonald (Taylor 56), Forrester (Parrett 64).
Tottenham H U21: (433) Austin; Marsh, Maghoma, Skipp, Bennetts; Tracey (Loft 71); Pritchard, Dinzeyi (Lyons-Foster 71); Shashoua (Griffiths 90), Amos, Sterling.
Referee: Antony Coggins.

Luton T (0) 1 *(Lee E 64)*
Barnet (1) 2 *(Taylor J 63 (pen))*   1530
Luton T: (4231) Shea; Justin, Famewo, Mullins, Senior; Ruddock, D'Ath (Musonda 46); Berry, Lee E, Cook; Jarvis.
Barnet: (4231) Ross; Pascal, Clough, Santos, Tutonda; Taylor J, Fonguck; Mason-Clark, Ruben Bover (Shomotun 73), Blackman (Kyei 69); Hinckson-Mars (Aghadiuno 61).
Luton T won 4-3 on penalties.
Referee: John Busby.

Tuesday, 31 October 2017
AFC Wimbledon (1) 1 *(Taylor 14)*
Luton T (1) 2 *(Shinnie 12, 75)*   581
AFC Wimbledon: (433) McDonnell; Sibbick, Robinson, Oshilaja, Meades (Egan 73); Hartigan, Abdou, Kennedy; Forrester (Barcham 62), Taylor (Kaja 41), McDonald.

Luton T: (4411) Shea; Justin, Famewo, Musonda, Senior; Gambin, Rea, Ruddock, D'Ath; Shinnie (Berry 79); Lee E (Jarvis 83).
Referee: Gavin Ward.

Tuesday, 28 November 2017
Barnet (0) 2 *(Maghoma 48 (og), Nicholls 57)*
Tottenham H U21 (1) 1 *(Harrison 16)*   445
Barnet: (433) Ross; Taylor H, Santos, Nelson, Blackman; Watson, Vilhete, Fonguck (Coker 82); Nicholls, Coulthirst (Amaluzor 73), Kyei (Tutonda 73).
Tottenham H U21: (4132) Whiteman; Marsh, Eyoma, Tanganga, Bennetts; Maghoma; Harrison, Edwards (Sterling 82), Roles; Amos (Shashoua 72), Loft (Tracey 63).
Referee: Lee Collins.

Southern Group F	P	W	D	L	F	A	GD	Pts
Luton T	3	1	2	0	5	4	1	7
AFC Wimbledon	3	2	0	1	9	8	1	6
Barnet	3	1	1	1	6	6	0	4
Tottenham H U21	3	0	1	2	6	8	–2	1

SOUTHERN SECTION GROUP G

Tuesday, 29 August 2017
Milton Keynes D (1) 2 *(Ariyibi 32, Tshibola 66 (pen))*
Brighton & HA U21 (0) 0   1541
Milton Keynes D: (442) Sietsma; Williams GB, Downing, Cisse, Lewington; Ariyibi (Logan 73), McGrandles, Tshibola (Rasulo 78), Nombe; Thomas-Asante, Muirhead (Seager 53).
Brighton & HA U21: (442) Sanchez; Moore, Hutchinson, Kerr, Cox; Tilley, Sanders, Mandroiu, Collar; Connolly (Ajiboye 67), O'Sullivan (Cashman 80).
Referee: Craig Hicks.

Stevenage (1) 2 *(Beautyman 19, Samuel 82)*
Oxford U (2) 6 *(Henry 30, Hall 43, 52, Obika 50, Rothwell 55, Payne 64)*   799
Stevenage: (442) Day; Vancooten, King J (Wilkinson 46), Toner, Martin; Beautyman, Conlon, Smith (Ferry 46), Pett; Godden (Gray 65), Samuel.
Oxford U: (4411) Eastwood; Tiendalli, Ribeiro, Martin, Carroll; Henry, Rothwell, Fernandez Codina (Ruffels 85); Hall; Payne (Baptiste 71); Obika (Roberts 79).
Referee: Charles Breakspear.

Tuesday, 3 October 2017
Milton Keynes D (0) 0
Stevenage (0) 0   2031
Milton Keynes D: (4231) Sietsma; Kasumu, Williams GB, Walsh, Lewington; McGrandles, Tshibola (Logan 77); Muirhead (Nombe 84), Aneke (Thomas-Asante 46), Nesbitt; Seager.
Stevenage: (451) Day; Wade-Slater, Wilmot, Wilkinson, Toner; Whelpdale, Ferry, Conlon, Gorman (Pett 77); Beautyman (Georgiou 62); Wootton (Newton 46).
Milton Keynes D won 5-4 on penalties.
Referee: Nicholas Kinseley.

Oxford U (2) 2 *(Van Kessel 22, 28)*
Brighton & HA U21 (1) 2 *(Tilley 36, Mandroiu 67)*   1074
Oxford U: (352) Shearer; Williamson, Martin, Nelson; Henry, Ledson (Rothwell 71), Mowatt (Ashby 80), Fernandez Codina, Ruffels; Mehmeti (Roberts 8), Van Kessel.
Brighton & HA U21: (442) Sanchez; Morrison, Moore, Kerr, Cox; Sanders, Collar, Tilley, Mandroiu; Ahannach, Alzate.
Brighton & HA U21 won 5-4 on penalties.
Referee: Dean Whitestone.

Tuesday, 7 November 2017
Oxford U (2) 3 *(Payne 33, 39 (pen), Hall 64)*
Milton Keynes D (3) 4 *(Thomas-Asante 10, Ariyibi 40, 45, Seager 66)*   1182
Oxford U: (4411) Eastwood; Ribeiro (Carroll 60), Nelson, Mousinho, Tiendalli; Hall, Fernandez Codina, Ruffels, Rothwell; Payne (Henry 68); Obika.
Milton Keynes D: (4132) Sietsma; B Williams, Wootton (Logan 79), Ebanks-Landell, Lewington; Upson; Ariyibi, Thomas-Asante, Nesbitt (Pawlett 60); Seager (Agard 67); Muirhead.
Referee: Christopher Sarginson.

Stevenage (2) 3 *(Samuel 19, 82, Wootton 45 (pen))*

Brighton & HA U21 (0) 1 *(Murphy 90)*   389

Stevenage: (442) Fryer; Wilmot, Toner, Wilkinson (Whelpdale 82), Vancooten; Wade-Slater, Beautyman (Ferry 70), Conlon, McKee; Wootton (Georgiou 59), Samuel.
Brighton & HA U21: (442) Krul; Schelotto, Hutchinson (Cox 59), Hunemeier, Rosenior; Molumby, Collar, Tilley (Ahannach 46), Brown; Murphy, Connolly (Alzate 90).
Referee: Charles Breakspear.

Southern Group G	P	W	D	L	F	A	GD	Pts
Milton Keynes D	3	2	1	0	6	3	3	8
Oxford U	3	1	1	1	11	8	3	4
Stevenage	3	1	1	1	5	7	-2	4
Brighton & HA U21	3	0	1	2	3	7	-4	2

SOUTHERN SECTION GROUP H

Tuesday, 29 August 2017

Northampton T (1) 1 *(Revell 29)*

Cambridge U (1) 1 *(Mingoia 27)*   1453

Northampton T: (442) Coddington; Moloney, Taylor A, Barnett, Buchanan; Waters, McWilliams, Grimes, Powell; Revell, Long (Iaciofano 81).
Cambridge U: (41212) Mitov; Davies (Taylor 90), Legge, Darling, Carroll; O'Neil; Mingoia, Lewis (Elito 66); Osadebe; Brown, Ibehre (Azeez 61).
Northampton T won 5-4 on penalties.
Referee: John Brooks.

Peterborough U (2) 2 *(Morias 2, Maddison 21 (pen))*

Southampton U21 (0) 0   2282

Peterborough U: (3412) O'Malley; Hughes, Baldwin, Tafazolli; Edwards, Forrester, Doughty (Anderson 62), Da Silva Lopes (Shephard 76); Maddison; Morias (Marriott 62), Kanu.
Southampton U21: (4231) McCarthy; Bakary, Cook, O'Driscoll, Wood; Jones, Little; Barnes (Obafemi 62), Slattery, Johnson (Tella 76); Afolabi (Smallbone 90).
Referee: Trevor Kettle.

Tuesday, 3 October 2017

Cambridge U (0) 0

Southampton U21 (1) 1 *(Jones 36)*   480

Cambridge U: (4411) Mitov; Davies, Taylor, Howkins, Carroll; Mingoia (Dunk 57), Deegan (Osadebe 57), O'Neil, Elito (Amoo 57); Brown; Foy.
Southampton U21: (4231) McCarthy; Bakary (Valery 46), Cook, O'Driscoll, Wood; Jones, Rowthorn (Hamblin 80); Hale, Slattery (Smallbone 88), Johnson; Barnes.
Referee: Charles Breakspear.

Peterborough U (1) 1 *(Lloyd 43)*

Northampton T (0) 1 *(Baldwin 79 (og))*   2745

Peterborough U: (442) O'Malley; Shephard, Baldwin, Tafazolli, Hughes; Da Silva Lopes, Grant, Doughty, Lloyd; Miller (Marriott 66), Kanu.
Northampton T: (442) Cornell; Moloney (Revell 89), Taylor A, Smith, Pierre; Powell, Kasim, McGugan (Bowditch 69), Foley (Grimes 75); Richards, Waters.
Northampton T won 4-2 on penalties.
Referee: Gavin Ward.

Tuesday, 7 November 2017

Cambridge U (0) 0

Peterborough U (0) 2 *(Taylor S 50, Marriott 81)*   3138

Cambridge U: (4411) Mitov; Halliday, Taylor, Legge, Carroll; Elito, Lewis, O'Neil, Maris (Dunk 60); Brown (Ibehre 60); Ikpeazu (Worman 83).
Peterborough U: (3412) O'Malley; Tafazolli, Baldwin, Taylor S; Da Silva Lopes (Hughes 70), Doughty, Grant, Edwards (Kanu 83); Maddison (Anderson 83); Marriott, Lloyd.
Referee: Gavin Ward.

Northampton T (0) 3 *(Foley 72, McGugan 83, Taylor A 90)*

Southampton U21 (1) 3 *(Hesketh 6, 51, Johnson 59)*   1118

Northampton T: (442) Cornell; Moloney, Taylor A, McGivern, Smith; Kasim (McGugan 69), Foley, Crooks (Grimes 63), Bowditch; Hanley (Long 64), Richards.

Southampton U21: (433) McCarthy; Valery, Cook, O'Driscoll, Wood; Hesketh (Little 75), Jones, Slattery; Tella (Obafemi 62), Afolabi, Johnson.
Northampton T won 4-2 on penalties.
Referee: Brett Huxtable.

Southern Group H	P	W	D	L	F	A	GD	Pts
Peterborough U	3	2	1	0	5	1	4	7
Northampton T	3	0	3	0	5	5	0	6
Southampton U21	3	1	1	1	4	5	-1	4
Cambridge U	3	0	1	2	1	4	-3	1

NORTHERN SECTION SECOND ROUND

Tuesday, 28 November 2017

Rochdale (1) 1 *(Gillam 33 (pen))*

Doncaster R (0) 1 *(Mandeville 72)*   786

Rochdale: (532) Lillis; Cannon, McGahey, McNulty, Ntlhe (Kitching 42), Bunney; Adshead, Camps, Rathbone (Inman 80); Andrew, Gillam (Jordan LR Williams 57).
Doncaster R: (343) Marosi; Alcock, Baudry, Garrett; Blair, Mason, Whiteman (Rowe 90), Toffolo (Butler 70); Beestin, Mandeville, Ben Khemis.
Rochdale won 5-4 on penalties.
Referee: Darren Handley.

Saturday, 2 December 2017

Walsall (1) 1 *(Oztumer 45)*

Bury (1) 2 *(Ajose 7, 65)*   1065

Walsall: (442) Roberts L; Kinsella, Guthrie, Roberts K, Leahy; Kouhyar (Bakayoko 69), Chambers, Morris, Flanagan (Agyei 72); Oztumer, Roberts T.
Bury: (442) Fasan; Edwards, O'Connell, Cameron, Leigh (Williams 46); O'Shea, Tutte, Ince, Reilly; Ajose (Humphrey 90), Smith.
Referee: Michael Salisbury.

Tuesday, 5 December 2017

Bradford C (0) 0

Oldham Ath (1) 1 *(Obadeyi 3)*   1036

Bradford C: (442) Raeder; Hanson, Thompson, Knight-Percival, Hendrie; Gilliead (Poleon 46), Devine, Pybus (Law 68), Gibson; McCartan, Patrick (Taylor 75).
Oldham Ath: (4231) Placide; Dummigan, Gerrard, Bryan, Brian Wilson; Green, Gardner (Omrani 80); Obadeyi, Flynn (Fane 69), Nepomuceno (McLaughlin 77); Doyle.
Referee: David Webb.

Fleetwood T (1) 2 *(Sowerby 17, Reid 88)*

Chesterfield (0) 0   372

Fleetwood T: (352) Neal; Rodgers, Sheron, Cargill; Ekpolo, Sowerby (Nirennold 58), Schwabl, O'Neill (Biggins 46), Maguire; Hiwula (Reid 64), Hunter.
Chesterfield: (4231) Anyon; Barry, Wiseman, Maguire, Briggs; Dimaio (Dennis 79), Weir; Mitchell (Kellett 46), De Girolamo (Reed 46), Rowley; O'Grady.
Referee: Ross Joyce.

Lincoln C (2) 3 *(Palmer 37, Green 45, Raggett 61)*

Accrington S (2) 2 *(Wilks 7, Farman 42 (og))*   3026

Lincoln C: (442) Farman; Long, Waterfall, Raggett, Habergham; Anderson, Woodyard, Whitehouse, Ginnelly (Arnold 86); Palmer (Rhead 90), Green (Dickie 81).
Accrington S: (442) Stryjek; Donacien, Richards-Everton, Hughes, Thorniley (Rawson 65); Clark (Jackson 65), Brown, Nolan, McConville; Kee, Wilks (Sykes 86).
Referee: Christopher Sarginson.

Port Vale (1) 1 *(Montano 1)*

Shrewsbury T (0) 2 *(Dodds 68, Whalley 81)*   965

Port Vale: (4411) Boot; Gibbons, Anderson, Smith, Gunning; Montano, Pugh (Turner 75), Reeves, Denton; Harness (Whitfield 62); Barnett.
Shrewsbury T: (4411) MacGillivray; Riley, Nsiala, Beckles, Sadler; Whalley, Morris B, Ogogo, Rodman (John-Lewis 46); Dodds; Morris C (Gnahoua 80).
Referee: Graham Salisbury.

Scunthorpe U (1) 1 *(van Veen 45)*

Leicester C U21 (2) 2 *(Thomas 3, Hughes 12)*	824

Scunthorpe U: (442) Watson; Sutton, Goode, Wallace (Burgess 46), Butroid; Lewis, Redmond, Hornshaw, Townsend; Madden (Church 65), van Veen.
Leicester C U21: (442) Hamer; Benalouane, Hughes, Dragovic, Wood; Thomas (Knight 90), Choudhury, Amartey, Ndukwu (Felix-Eppiah 70); Ulloa, Iheanacho (Muskwe 82).
Referee: Trevor Kettle.

Wednesday, 6 December 2017

Blackpool (1) 1 *(Mellor 38)*

Mansfield T (0) 1 *(Butcher 88)*	587

Blackpool: (433) Mafoumbi; Mellor, Taylor, Robertson (Aimson 46), D'Almeida; Clayton (Delfouneso 68), Cooke, Anderton; Philliskirk, Gnanduillet, Quigley.
Mansfield T: (3412) Olejnik; Digby, Pearce, Mirfin (Hakeem 82); Potter, Atkinson (Thomas 70), Mellis, Benning; Butcher; Spencer, Angol (Sterling-James 66).
Blackpool won 5-4 on penalties.
Referee: Sebastian Stockbridge.

SOUTHERN SECTION SECOND ROUND

Saturday, 2 December 2017

Portsmouth (1) 2 *(Evans 41, O'Keefe 58)*

Northampton T (0) 0	1780

Portsmouth: (4231) McGee; Thompson, Burgess, Clarke, Haunstrup (Talbot 69); Rose, O'Keefe; Evans, Chaplin, Lowe (Kennedy 89); Main.
Northampton T: (442) Cornell; Moloney, Taylor, Barnett, Buchanan; Hoskins (Bowditch 64), Poole (Waters 79), McGugan, Crooks; Richards, Long (Foley 46).
Referee: Tom Nield.

Tuesday, 5 December 2017

Gillingham (1) 1 *(Byrne 9 (pen))*

Oxford U (1) 2 *(Payne 31, Mowatt 90)*	1224

Gillingham: (41212) Nelson; Clare (Oldaker 77), Lacey, Nugent, Ogilvie; Ehmer; Wagstaff, Byrne; Martin (Cundle 61); Wilkinson (Eaves 46), Parker.
Oxford U: (4231) Eastwood; Carroll, Martin, Mousinho, Ricardinho; Ledson, Ruffels; Henry (Napa 65), Payne, Mowatt (Baptiste 90); Obika.
Referee: Charles Breakspear.

Luton T (1) 4 *(D'Ath 28, Jarvis 56, Cotter 86, Cook 90)*

West Ham U U21 (0) 0	1670

Luton T: (4132) Shea; Justin, Musonda, Famewo, Senior; Ruddock; D'Ath (Down 88), Cook, Gambin; Jarvis, Cotter.
West Ham U U21: (433) Trott; Johnson, Akinola (Hector-Ingram 70), Pike, Powell; Makasi, Coventry (Diangana 53), Quina; Haksabanovic, Martinez, Samuelsen.
Referee: Darren Drysdale.

Swansea C U21 (2) 2 *(Gorre 9, Garrick 41)*

Charlton Ath (2) 3 *(Hackett-Fairchild 15, 52, Ahearne-Grant 32)*	410

Swansea C U21: (4231) Zabret; Reid, Rodon, Harries, Lewis; Adam King, Blair (Evans 58); Garrick, Byers, Gorre; Cullen (Baker-Richardson 69).
Charlton Ath: (4231) Phillips; Barnes, Charles-Cook, Pearce (Lennon 46), Mascoll; Jackson, Dijksteel; Ahearne-Grant, Aribo (Lapslie 69), Hackett-Fairchild; Best (Carter 88).
Referee: Lee Swabey.

Swindon T (0) 0

Forest Green R (0) 1 *(Doidge 79)*	1320

Swindon T: (532) Vigouroux; Knoyle, Lancashire, Robertson, Preston, Iandolo; Mullin (Gordon 69), Linganzi (Dunne 65), Taylor; Norris (Woolery 52), Anderson**.
Forest Green R: (352) Collins B; Iacovitti (Cooper 46), Monthe, Fitzwater; Bennett**, Collins L, Brown, Laird (Stevens 62), Wishart; Doidge, James (Correia Gomes 66).
Referee: Robert Lewis.

Yeovil T (0) 2 *(Davies 49, Gray 87)*

AFC Wimbledon (0) 0	886

Yeovil T: (442) Krysiak; Mugabi, Davies, Sowunmi, James; Green (Gray 82), Smith C, Gobern (Worthington 75), Khan; Surridge (Zoko 70), Olomola.
AFC Wimbledon: (3421) McDonnell; Sibbick, Robinson, Kalambayi; Nightingale, Kennedy (Ashley 80), Francomb, Abdou; Forrester (Nelson-Roberts 61), Kaja; McDonald (Evans 61).
Referee: Graham Horwood.

Wednesday, 6 December 2017

Milton Keynes D (0) 0

Chelsea U21 (3) 4 *(Batshuayi 22, 42, Hudson-Odoi 45, Musonda 56)*	1549

Milton Keynes D: (4132) Sietsma; Williams GB, Wootton, Walsh, Golbourne; McGrandles (Upson 64); Nesbitt, Thomas-Asante, Ariyibi (Pawlett 64); Seager (Nombe 53), Muirhead.
Chelsea U21: (4231) Eduardo; Sterling, Clarke-Salter, Chalobah (Sammut 72), Kenedy; Ampadu, James; Hudson-Odoi (Hazard K 72), Scott (Christie-Davies 82), Musonda; Batshuayi.
Referee: Gavin Ward.

Peterborough U (1) 2 *(Edwards 16, Maddison 62)*

Southend U (0) 0	1707

Peterborough U: (4231) Bond; Anderson, Baldwin, Tafazolli, Hughes; Forrester, Penny; Maddison (Lloyd 78), Da Silva Lopes, Edwards (Kanu 73); Marriott (Miller 73).
Southend U: (442) Oxley; Demetriou, Ferdinand, White, Hendrie; McGlashan (Cox 75), Wordsworth (McLaughlin 65), Wright, Timlin; Ranger, Ba (Robinson 61).
Referee: John Busby.

THIRD ROUND

Tuesday, 9 January 2018

Bury (1) 2 *(Bunn 45, Dai 55)*

Fleetwood T (2) 3 *(Hiwula 14, 50, Grant 17 (pen))*	698

Bury: (442) Ripley; Edwards, O'Connell (Bunn 44), Skarz, Leigh; Maguire, Reilly, Ince (Lowe 86), Cooney; Ajose, Hanson (Dai 46).
Fleetwood T: (352) Cairns; Rodgers, Sheron, Cargill; Nirennold, Biggins, Sowerby (Hunter 80), Grant (Schwabl 61), Maguire; Hiwula, McAleny (Nadesan 67).
Referee: Sebastian Stockbridge.

Charlton Ath (1) 1 *(Ahearne-Grant 7)*

Oxford U (0) 1 *(Thomas 54)*	1146

Charlton Ath: (3412) Phillips; Dijksteel, Konsa, Jackson; Marshall, Kashi (Lapslie 59), Aribo, Dasilva; Reeves; Magennis (Mavididi 64), Ahearne-Grant (Hackett-Fairchild 34).
Oxford U: (442) Shearer; Carroll, Williamson, Martin, Ricardinho (Tiendalli 46); Payne, Ledson, Mowatt, Van Kessel (Napa 57); Obika, Thomas (Mehmeti 74).
Oxford U won 3-0 on penalties.
Referee: Andy Haines.

Luton T (0) 0

Peterborough U (0) 0	2253

Luton T: (442) Shea; Stacey, Musonda, Sheehan, Senior; D'Ath (Lee O 82), Ruddock, Famewo, Gambin (McQuoid 25); Cornick (Shinnie 64), Cook.
Peterborough U: (4231) Bond; Shephard, Tafazolli, Baldwin, Hughes; Da Silva Lopes (Doughty 33), Grant; Lloyd (Kanu 57), Morias (Anderson 68), Maddison; Marriott.
Peterborough U won 7-6 on penalties.
Referee: Antony Coggins.

Portsmouth (0) 1 *(Pitman 90)*

Chelsea U21 (0) 2 *(Musonda 58, 90)*	3116

Portsmouth: (4231) McGee; Thompson (Pitman 53), Burgess, Clarke, Donohue; Close, May; Lowe, Ronan (Chaplin 76), Kennedy; Hawkins (Naismith 53).
Chelsea U21: (4231) Bulka; Sterling, Ampadu, Chalobah, Grant (Colley 83); Scott (McCormick 87), Sammut; Musonda, Maddox (Redan 28), Hudson-Odoi; St Clair.
Referee: Gavin Ward.

Rochdale (0) 0

Lincoln C (0) 1 *(Palmer 88)* 1171

Rochdale: (352) Lillis; McGahey, McNulty, Ntlhe; Rafferty (Henderson 81), Cannon, Adshead (Camps 71), Kitching, Bunney; Inman, Andrew (Jordan LR Williams 71).
Lincoln C: (442) Farman; Eardley, Waterfall, Bostwick, Habergham; Anderson, Whitehouse, Woodyard, Rowe (Arnold 56); Rhead (Palmer 62), Green (Knott 70).
Referee: Ben Toner.

Yeovil T (2) 2 *(Smith N 3, Smith C 26)*

Forest Green R (0) 0 1395

Yeovil T: (442) Krysiak; Whelan, Sowunmi, Smith N, James; Gray (Zoko 70), Smith C, Santos (Bird 66), Khan; Green, Surridge.
Forest Green R: (352) Collins B; Roberts (Spurrier 71), Monthe, Laird (Traore 46); James, Simpson, Cooper, Brown, Whittle (Wishart 69); Marsh-Brown, Grubb.
Referee: John Busby.

Wednesday, 10 January 2018

Shrewsbury T (0) 0

Blackpool (0) 0 1362

Shrewsbury T: (41212) Henderson; Riley, Bolton, Nsiala, Lowe; Ogogo, Morris B, Gnahoua (Rodman 74); Dodds; John-Lewis, Payne.
Blackpool: (433) Lumley; Turton, Aimson, Tilt, Anderton; Ryan, D'Almeida (McAlister 59), Cooke; Philliskirk, Correia (Roache 74), Quigley (Delfouneso 74).
Shrewsbury T won 4-2 on penalties.
Referee: Christopher Sarginson.

Wednesday, 17 January 2018

Oldham Ath (0) 4 *(Davies 50, 56, Gerrard 76, Obadeyi 86)*

Leicester C U21 (1) 2 *(Knight 43, Musa 68)* 4192

Oldham Ath: (4231) Placide; Haymer (Maouche 69), Gerrard, Edmundson, Brian Wilson; Fane (Omrani 82), Benyu (Holloway 46); Obadeyi, Pringle, Nepomuceno; Davies.
Leicester C U21: (433) Hamer; Knight, Huth, Hughes, Wood; Dewsbury-Hall (Felix-Eppiah 82), Choudhury, Barnes; Thomas, Musa, Diabate (Gordon 69).
Referee: Darren Handley.

QUARTER-FINALS

Tuesday, 23 January 2018

Chelsea U21 (2) 3 *(St Clair 10, Redan 16, Fanilia-Castilo 65)*

Oxford U (0) 0 2643

Chelsea U21: (343) Bulka; James (Grant 72), Ampadu, Chalobah; Sterling, Sammut, Scott, Fanilia-Castilo; St Clair (Christie-Davies 82), Redan (Maddox 66), Hudson-Odoi.
Oxford U: (442) Eastwood; Tiendalli, Martin, Ledson, Ruffels; Obika (Mehmeti 77), Ricardinho, Raglan, Mousinho; Buckley-Rickett, Van Kessel (Napa 66).
Referee: John Brooks.

Lincoln C (1) 4 *(Rowe 43, Rhead 55, Anderson 90, Green 90)*

Peterborough U (1) 2 *(Eardley 14 (og), Lloyd 50)* 6663

Lincoln C: (442) Farman; Habergham, Bostwick, Waterfall, Eardley; Anderson, Whitehouse, Frecklington (Long 64), Rowe (Stewart 69); Green, Rhead (Palmer 65).
Peterborough U: (442) Bond; Hughes, Tafazolli, Baldwin, Shephard; Forrester, Grant, Maddison, Ward (Da Silva Lopes 69); Lloyd, Morias (Kanu 69).
Referee: Michael Salisbury.

Shrewsbury T (1) 2 *(Payne 1, Rodman 88)*

Oldham Ath (0) 1 *(Holloway 67)* 1984

Shrewsbury T: (442) Henderson; Bolton, Sadler, Nsiala, Beckles; Whalley, Morris B, Nolan, Lowe (Rodman 72); Gnahoua (Dodds 63), Payne (John-Lewis 89).
Oldham Ath: (442) Placide; Haymer (Dummigan 57), Brian Wilson, Bryan, Edmundson; Maouche (McLaughlin 46), Gardner, Byrne, Pringle; Holloway (Duffus 83), Davies.
Referee: Darren Handley.

Tuesday, 6 February 2018

Yeovil T (1) 3 *(Bolger 23 (og), Whelan 56, Zoko 90)*

Fleetwood T (1) 2 *(Bolger 17, Hiwula 80)* 1314

Yeovil T: (442) Krysiak; Whelan, Sowunmi, Smith N, James; Browne (Santos 84), Bird (Smith C 90), Gray, Green; Surridge (Zoko 61), Fisher.
Fleetwood T: (433) Cairns; Coyle, Eastham, Bolger, O'Connor; Sowerby, Schwabl (Biggins 58), Grant (Dempsey 71); Burns (Hunter 72), Hiwula, McAleny.
Referee: Gavin Ward.

SEMI-FINALS

Tuesday, 6 February 2018

Lincoln C (0) 1 *(Waterfall 72)*

Chelsea U21 (0) 1 *(Redan 78)* 9444

Lincoln C: (442) Allsop; Eardley, Waterfall, Bostwick, Habergham; Rowe (Frecklington 90), Whitehouse, Woodyard, Anderson (Stewart 90); Rhead (Palmer 67), Green.
Chelsea U21: (3421) Bulka; James, Ampadu, Nartey; Sterling (Maddox 60), Chalobah, Sammut (Hazard K 90), Fanilia-Castilo; Hudson-Odoi, St Clair; Redan.
Lincoln C won 4-2 on penalties
Referee: David Webb.

Tuesday, 6 March 2018

Shrewsbury T (0) 1 *(Morris C 63)*

Yeovil T (0) 0 4118

Shrewsbury T: (451) Henderson; Godfrey, Nsiala, Sadler, Beckles; Whalley, Ogogo, Morris B, Nolan (John-Lewis 90), Rodman (Thomas 69); Morris C (Payne 81).
Yeovil T: (433) Maddison; Whelan, Sowunmi, James, Dickson; Gobern (Surridge 46), Smith C, Bird (Santos 72); Green (Browne 49), Zoko, Khan.
Referee: Darren Drysdale.

EFL CHECKATRADE TROPHY FINAL 2018

Sunday, 8 April 2018

(at Wembley Stadium, attendance 41,261)

Lincoln C (1) 1   Shrewsbury T (0) 0

Lincoln C: (433) Allsop; Eardley, Bostwick, Waterfall, Habergham; Whitehouse, Woodyard, Frecklington; Rowe (Anderson 64), Rhead (Palmer 63), Green (Long 90).

Scorer: Whitehouse 16.

Shrewsbury T: (4141) Henderson; Bolton, Nsiala, Sadler, Beckles; Morris B (Rodman 67); Whalley (Gnahoua 86), Nolan, Godfrey, Thomas (Payne 75); Morris C.

Referee: Gavin Ward.

FA CUP FINALS 1872–2018

VENUES

1872 and 1874–92	Kennington Oval	1895–1914	Crystal Palace
1873	Lillie Bridge	1915	Old Trafford, Manchester
1893	Fallowfield, Manchester	1920–22	Stamford Bridge
1894	Everton	2001–06	Millennium Stadium, Cardiff
1923–2000	Wembley Stadium (old)	2007 to date	Wembley Stadium (new)

THE FA CUP

1872	Wanderers v Royal Engineers	1-0
1873	Wanderers v Oxford University	2-0
1874	Oxford University v Royal Engineers	2-0
1875	Royal Engineers v Old Etonians	1-1*
Replay	Royal Engineers v Old Etonians	2-0
1876	Wanderers v Old Etonians	1-1*
Replay	Wanderers v Old Etonians	3-0
1877	Wanderers v Oxford University	2-1*
1878	Wanderers v Royal Engineers	3-1

Wanderers won the cup outright, but it was restored to the Football Association.

1879	Old Etonians v Clapham R	1-0
1880	Clapham R v Oxford University	1-0
1881	Old Carthusians v Old Etonians	3-0
1882	Old Etonians v Blackburn R	1-0
1883	Blackburn Olympic v Old Etonians	2-1*
1884	Blackburn R v Queen's Park, Glasgow	2-1
1885	Blackburn R v Queen's Park, Glasgow	2-0
1886	Blackburn R v WBA	0-0
Replay	Blackburn R v WBA	2-0
	(at Racecourse Ground, Derby Co)	

A special trophy was awarded to Blackburn R for third consecutive win.

1887	Aston Villa v WBA	2-0
1888	WBA v Preston NE	2-1
1889	Preston NE v Wolverhampton W	3-0
1890	Blackburn R v The Wednesday	6-1
1891	Blackburn R v Notts Co	3-1
1892	WBA v Aston Villa	3-0
1893	Wolverhampton W v Everton	1-0
1894	Notts Co v Bolton W	4-1
1895	Aston Villa v WBA	1-0

FA Cup was stolen from a shop window in Birmingham and never found.

1896	The Wednesday v Wolverhampton W	2-1
1897	Aston Villa v Everton	3-2
1898	Nottingham F v Derby Co	3-1
1899	Sheffield U v Derby Co	4-1
1900	Bury v Southampton	4-0
1901	Tottenham H v Sheffield U	2-2
Replay	Tottenham H v Sheffield U	3-1
	(at Burnden Park, Bolton W)	
1902	Sheffield U v Southampton	1-1
Replay	Sheffield U v Southampton	2-1
1903	Bury v Derby Co	6-0
1904	Manchester C v Bolton W	1-0
1905	Aston Villa v Newcastle U	2-0
1906	Everton v Newcastle U	1-0
1907	The Wednesday v Everton	2-1
1908	Wolverhampton W v Newcastle U	3-1
1909	Manchester U v Bristol C	1-0
1910	Newcastle U v Barnsley	1-1
Replay	Newcastle U v Barnsley	2-0
	(at Goodison Park, Everton)	
1911	Bradford C v Newcastle U	0-0
Replay	Bradford C v Newcastle U	1-0
	(at Old Trafford, Manchester U)	

Trophy was given to Lord Kinnaird – he made nine FA Cup Final appearances – for services to football.

1912	Barnsley v WBA	0-0
Replay	Barnsley v WBA	1-0
	(at Bramall Lane, Sheffield U)	

1913	Aston Villa v Sunderland	1-0
1914	Burnley v Liverpool	1-0
1915	Sheffield U v Chelsea	3-0
1920	Aston Villa v Huddersfield T	1-0*
1921	Tottenham H v Wolverhampton W	1-0
1922	Huddersfield T v Preston NE	1-0
1923	Bolton W v West Ham U	2-0
1924	Newcastle U v Aston Villa	2-0
1925	Sheffield U v Cardiff C	1-0
1926	Bolton W v Manchester C	1-0
1927	Cardiff C v Arsenal	1-0
1928	Blackburn R v Huddersfield T	3-1
1929	Bolton W v Portsmouth	2-0
1930	Arsenal v Huddersfield T	2-0
1931	WBA v Birmingham	2-1
1932	Newcastle U v Arsenal	2-1
1933	Everton v Manchester C	3-0
1934	Manchester C v Portsmouth	2-1
1935	Sheffield W v WBA	4-2
1936	Arsenal v Sheffield U	1-0
1937	Sunderland v Preston NE	3-1
1938	Preston NE v Huddersfield T	1-0*
1939	Portsmouth v Wolverhampton W	4-1
1946	Derby Co v Charlton Ath	4-1*
1947	Charlton Ath v Burnley	1-0*
1948	Manchester U v Blackpool	4-2
1949	Wolverhampton W v Leicester C	3-1
1950	Arsenal v Liverpool	2-0
1951	Newcastle U v Blackpool	2-0
1952	Newcastle U v Arsenal	1-0
1953	Blackpool v Bolton W	4-3
1954	WBA v Preston NE	3-2
1955	Newcastle U v Manchester C	3-1
1956	Manchester C v Birmingham C	3-1
1957	Aston Villa v Manchester U	2-1
1958	Bolton W v Manchester U	2-0
1959	Nottingham F v Luton T	2-1
1960	Wolverhampton W v Blackburn R	3-0
1961	Tottenham H v Leicester C	2-0
1962	Tottenham H v Burnley	3-1
1963	Manchester U v Leicester C	3-1
1964	West Ham U v Preston NE	3-2
1965	Liverpool v Leeds U	2-1*
1966	Everton v Sheffield W	3-2
1967	Tottenham H v Chelsea	2-1
1968	WBA v Everton	1-0*
1969	Manchester C v Leicester C	1-0
1970	Chelsea v Leeds U	2-2*
Replay	Chelsea v Leeds U	2-1
	(at Old Trafford, Manchester U)	
1971	Arsenal v Liverpool	2-1*
1972	Leeds U v Arsenal	1-0
1973	Sunderland v Leeds U	1-0
1974	Liverpool v Newcastle U	3-0
1975	West Ham U v Fulham	2-0
1976	Southampton v Manchester U	1-0
1977	Manchester U v Liverpool	2-1
1978	Ipswich T v Arsenal	1-0
1979	Arsenal v Manchester U	3-2
1980	West Ham U v Arsenal	1-0
1981	Tottenham H v Manchester C	1-1*
Replay	Tottenham H v Manchester C	3-2

1982	Tottenham H v QPR	1-1*
Replay	Tottenham H v QPR	1-0
1983	Manchester U v Brighton & HA	2-2*
Replay	Manchester U v Brighton & HA	4-0
1984	Everton v Watford	2-0
1985	Manchester U v Everton	1-0*
1986	Liverpool v Everton	3-1
1987	Coventry C v Tottenham H	3-2*
1988	Wimbledon v Liverpool	1-0
1989	Liverpool v Everton	3-2*
1990	Manchester U v Crystal Palace	3-3*
Replay	Manchester U v Crystal Palace	1-0
1991	Tottenham H v Nottingham F	2-1*
1992	Liverpool v Sunderland	2-0
1993	Arsenal v Sheffield W	1-1*
Replay	Arsenal v Sheffield W	2-1*
1994	Manchester U v Chelsea	4-0

THE FA CUP SPONSORED BY LITTLEWOODS POOLS

1995	Everton v Manchester U	1-0
1996	Manchester U v Liverpool	1-0
1997	Chelsea v Middlesbrough	2-0
1998	Arsenal v Newcastle U	2-0

THE AXA-SPONSORED FA CUP

1999	Manchester U v Newcastle U	2-0
2000	Chelsea v Aston Villa	1-0
2001	Liverpool v Arsenal	2-1
2002	Arsenal v Chelsea	2-0

THE FA CUP

2003	Arsenal v Southampton	1-0
2004	Manchester U v Millwall	3-0
2005	Arsenal v Manchester U	0-0*
	Arsenal won 5-4 on penalties.	
2006	Liverpool v West Ham U	3-3*
	Liverpool won 3-1 on penalties.	

THE FA CUP SPONSORED BY E.ON

2007	Chelsea v Manchester U	1-0*
2008	Portsmouth v Cardiff C	1-0
2009	Chelsea v Everton	2-1
2010	Chelsea v Portsmouth	1-0
2011	Manchester C v Stoke C	1-0

THE FA CUP WITH BUDWEISER

2012	Chelsea v Liverpool	2-1
2013	Wigan Ath v Manchester C	1-0
2014	Arsenal v Hull C	3-2*

THE FA CUP

2015	Arsenal v Aston Villa	4-0

THE EMIRATES FA CUP

2016	Manchester U v Crystal Palace	2-1*
2017	Arsenal v Chelsea	2-1
2018	Chelsea v Manchester U	1-0

After extra time.

FA CUP WINS

Arsenal 13, Manchester U 13, Chelsea 8, Tottenham H 8, Aston Villa 7, Liverpool 7, Blackburn R 6, Newcastle U 6, Everton 5, Manchester C 5, The Wanderers 5, WBA 5, Bolton W 4, Sheffield U 4, Wolverhampton W 4, Sheffield W 3, West Ham U 3, Bury 2, Nottingham F 2, Old Etonians 2, Portsmouth 2, Preston NE 2, Sunderland 2, Barnsley 1, Blackburn Olympic 1, Blackpool 1, Bradford C 1, Burnley 1, Cardiff C 1, Charlton Ath 1, Clapham R 1, Coventry C 1, Derby Co 1, Huddersfield T 1, Ipswich T 1, Leeds U 1, Notts Co 1, Old Carthusians 1, Oxford University 1, Royal Engineers 1, Southampton 1, Wigan Ath 1, Wimbledon 1.

APPEARANCES IN FINALS

Arsenal 20, Manchester U 20, Liverpool 14, Chelsea 13, Everton 13, Newcastle U 13, Aston Villa 11, Manchester C 10, WBA 10, Tottenham H 9, Blackburn R 8, Wolverhampton W 8, Bolton W 7, Preston NE 7, Old Etonians 6, Sheffield U 6, Sheffield W 6, Huddersfield T 5, Portsmouth 5, *The Wanderers 5, West Ham U 5, Derby Co 4, Leeds U 4, Leicester C 4, Oxford University 4, Royal Engineers 4, Southampton 4, Sunderland 4, Blackpool 3, Burnley 3, Cardiff C 3, Nottingham F 3, Barnsley 2, Birmingham C 2, *Bury 2, Charlton Ath 2, Clapham R 2, Crystal Palace 2, Notts Co 2, Queen's Park (Glasgow) 2, *Blackburn Olympic 1, *Bradford C 1, Brighton & HA 1, Bristol C 1, *Coventry C 1, Fulham 1, Hull C 1, *Ipswich T 1, Luton T 1, Middlesbrough 1, Millwall 1, *Old Carthusians 1, QPR 1, Stoke C 1, Watford 1, *Wigan Ath 1, *Wimbledon 1.
* *Denotes undefeated in final.*

APPEARANCES IN SEMI-FINALS

Arsenal 29, Manchester U 29, Everton 26, Liverpool 24, Chelsea 23, Aston Villa 21, Tottenham H 21, WBA 20, Blackburn R 18, Newcastle U 17, Sheffield W 16, Bolton W 14, Sheffield U 14, Wolverhampton W 14, Derby Co 13, Manchester C 13, Nottingham F 12, Southampton 12, Sunderland 12, Preston NE 10, Birmingham C 9, Burnley 8, Leeds U 8, Huddersfield T 7, Leicester C 7, Portsmouth 7, West Ham U 7, Old Etonians 6, Fulham 6, Oxford University 6, Watford 6, Millwall 5, Notts Co 5, The Wanderers 5, Cardiff C 4, Crystal Palace (professional club) 4, Luton T 4, Queen's Park (Glasgow) 4, Royal Engineers 4, Stoke C 4, Barnsley 3, Blackpool 3, Ipswich T 3, Middlesbrough 3, Norwich C 3, Old Carthusians 3, Oldham Ath 3, The Swifts 3, Blackburn Olympic 2, Bristol C 2, Bury 2, Charlton Ath 2, Grimsby T 2, Hull C 2, Reading 2, Swansea T 2, Swindon T 2, Wigan Ath 2, Wimbledon 2, Bradford C 1, Brighton & HA 1, Cambridge University 1, Chesterfield 1, Coventry C 1, Crewe Alex 1, Crystal Palace (amateur club) 1, Darwen 1, Derby Junction 1, Glasgow R 1, Marlow 1, Old Harrovians 1, Orient 1, Plymouth Arg 1, Port Vale 1, QPR 1, Shropshire W 1, Wycombe W 1, York C 1.

FA CUP ATTENDANCES 1969–2018

	1st Round	2nd Round	3rd Round	4th Round	5th Round	6th Round	Semi-finals & Final	Total	No. of matches	Average per match
1969–70	345,229	195,102	925,930	651,374	319,893	198,537	390,700	3,026,765	170	17,805
1970–71	329,687	230,942	956,683	757,852	360,687	304,937	279,644	3,220,432	162	19,879
1971–72	277,726	236,127	986,094	711,399	486,378	230,292	248,546	3,158,562	160	19,741
1972–73	259,432	169,114	938,741	735,825	357,386	241,934	226,543	2,928,975	160	18,306
1973–74	214,236	125,295	840,142	747,909	346,012	233,307	273,051	2,779,952	167	16,646
1974–75	283,956	170,466	914,994	646,434	393,323	268,361	291,369	2,968,903	172	17,261
1975–76	255,533	178,099	867,880	573,843	471,925	206,851	205,810	2,759,941	161	17,142
1976–77	379,230	192,159	942,523	631,265	373,330	205,379	258,216	2,982,102	174	17,139
1977–78	258,248	178,930	881,406	540,164	400,751	137,059	198,020	2,594,578	160	16,216
1978–79	243,773	185,343	880,345	537,748	243,683	263,213	249,897	2,604,002	166	15,687
1979–80	267,121	204,759	804,701	507,725	364,039	157,530	355,541	2,661,416	163	16,328
1980–81	246,824	194,502	832,578	534,402	320,530	288,714	339,250	2,756,800	169	16,312
1981–82	236,220	127,300	513,185	356,987	203,334	124,308	279,621	1,840,955	160	11,506
1982–83	191,312	150,046	670,503	452,688	260,069	193,845	291,162	2,209,625	154	14,348
1983–84	192,276	151,647	625,965	417,298	181,832	185,382	187,000	1,941,400	166	11,695
1984–85	174,604	137,078	616,229	320,772	269,232	148,690	242,754	1,909,359	157	12,162
1985–86	171,142	130,034	486,838	495,526	311,833	184,262	192,316	1,971,951	168	11,738
1986–87	209,290	146,761	593,520	349,342	263,550	119,396	195,533	1,877,400	165	11,378
1987–88	204,411	104,561	720,121	443,133	281,461	119,313	177,585	2,050,585	155	13,229
1988–89	212,775	121,326	690,199	421,255	206,781	176,629	167,353	1,966,318	164	12,173
1989–90	209,542	133,483	683,047	412,483	351,423	123,065	277,420	2,190,463	170	12,885
1990–91	194,195	121,450	594,592	530,279	276,112	124,826	196,434	2,038,518	162	12,583
1991–92	231,940	117,078	586,014	372,576	270,537	155,603	201,592	1,935,340	160	12,095
1992–93	241,968	174,702	612,494	377,211	198,379	149,675	293,241	2,047,670	161	12,718
1993–94	190,683	118,031	691,064	430,234	172,196	134,705	228,233	1,965,146	159	12,359
1994–95	219,511	125,629	640,017	438,596	257,650	159,787	174,059	2,015,249	161	12,517
1995–96	185,538	115,669	748,997	391,218	274,055	174,142	156,500	2,046,199	167	12,252
1996–97	209,521	122,324	651,139	402,293	199,873	67,035	191,813	1,843,998	151	12,211
1997–98	204,803	130,261	629,127	455,557	341,290	192,651	172,007	2,125,696	165	12,883
1998–99	191,954	132,341	609,486	431,613	359,398	181,005	202,150	2,107,947	155	13,599
1999–2000	181,485	127,728	514,030	374,795	182,511	105,443	214,921	1,700,913	158	10,765
2000–01	171,689	122,061	577,204	398,241	256,899	100,663	177,778	1,804,535	151	11,951
2001–02	198,369	119,781	566,284	330,434	249,190	173,757	171,278	1,809,093	148	12,224
2002–03	189,905	104,103	577,494	404,599	242,483	156,244	175,498	1,850,326	150	12,336
2003–04	162,738	117,967	624,732	347,964	292,521	156,780	167,401	1,870,103	149	12,551
2004–05	161,197	98,702	602,152	477,472	339,082	127,914	193,233	1,999,752	146	13,697
2005–06	188,876	107,456	654,570	388,339	286,225	163,449	177,723	1,966,638	160	12,291
2006–07	168,884	113,924	708,628	478,924	340,612	230,064	177,810	2,218,846	158	14,043
2007–08	175,195	99,528	704,300	356,404	276,903	142,780	256,210	2,011,320	152	13,232
2008–09	161,526	96,923	631,070	529,585	297,364	149,566	264,635	2,131,669	163	13,078
2009–10	147,078	100,476	613,113	335,426	288,604	144,918	254,806	1,884,421	151	12,480
2010–11	169,259	101,291	637,202	390,524	284,311	164,092	250,256	1,996,935	150	13,313
2011–12	155,858	92,267	640,700	391,214	250,666	194,971	262,064	1,987,740	151	13,164
2012–13	135,642	115,965	645,676	373,892	288,509	221,216	234,210	2,015,110	156	12,917
2013–14	144,709	75,903	668,242	346,706	254,084	156,630	243,350	1,889,624	149	12,682
2014–15	156,621	111,434	609,368	515,229	208,908	233,341	258,780	2,093,681	153	13,684
2015–16	134,914	94,855	755,187	397,217	235,433	227,262	253,793	2,098,661	149	14,085
2016–17	147,448	97,784	685,467	409,084	212,842	163,620	261,552	1,977,797	156	12,678
2017–18	125,978	87,075	712,036	371,650	210,328	140,641	245,730	1,893,438	149	12,708

THE EMIRATES FA CUP 2017–18
PRELIMINARY AND QUALIFYING ROUNDS

After extra time.

EXTRA PRELIMINARY ROUND

Penrith v West Auckland T	2-1
Billingham v Pickering T	0-3
Barnoldswick T v Jarrow Roofing Boldon CA	3-1
Sunderland RCA v Garforth T	3-1
Shildon v Morpeth T	2-0
Consett v Bishop Auckland	3-3, 5-2
Washington v Dunston UTS	0-3
Bridlington T v Billingham Synthonia	2-0
Newton Aycliffe v Chester-le-Street T	1-0
Seaham Red Star v Whitley Bay	1-1, 1-4
Thackley v Harrogate Railway Ath	3-4
Guisborough T v Stockton T	4-2
Ashington v Sunderland Ryhope CW	1-0
Newcastle Benfield v West Allotment Celtic	1-0
Albion Sports v Nelson	2-0
Team Northumbria v Heaton Stannington	0-1
Marske U v North Shields	4-4, 1-0
Litherland Remyca v AFC Liverpool	2-0
AFC Emley v Burscough	0-3
Squires Gate v Ashton Ath	0-4
Cammell Laird 1907 v Maltby Main	4-1
Padiham v City of Liverpool	1-2
Pontefract Collieries v Alsager T	1-0
Hallam v Bootle	3-0
Runcorn T v AFC Darwen	3-2
Northwich Vic v 1874 Northwich	2-2, 0-2
Widnes v Handsworth Parramore	0-5
Congleton T v New Mills	4-2
Irlam v Abbey Hey	1-2
Armthorpe Welfare v Liversedge	1-1, 3-5
Parkgate v Barnton	4-2
Athersley Recreation v West Didsbury & Chorlton	0-5
Charnock Richard v Penistone Church	3-4
Maine Road v Winsford U	3-2
Runcorn Linnets v Hemsworth MW	2-0
Hanley T v Atherstone T	4-1
Coventry U v Rugby T	1-2
Sporting Khalsa v Stourport Swifts	2-2, 3-2*
(1-1 at the end of normal time)	
AFC Wulfrunians v Shawbury U	3-0
Wolverhampton SC v Haughmond	2-3
Tividale v Highgate U	1-1, 3-2
Walsall Wood v Whitchurch Alport	3-1
Coventry Sphinx v Boldmere St Michaels	0-2
Daventry T v Worcester C	0-1
Wolverhampton Casuals v Malvern T	7-0
Westfields v Bewdley T	3-1
Coleshill T v Wellington	6-2
Bromsgrove Sporting v Rocester	2-2, 3-0
Brocton v Cadbury Ath	3-0
Kimberley MW v Blaby & Whetstone Ath	2-4
Tie awarded to Kimberley MW as Blaby & Whetstone	
Ath fielded ineligible player	
Oadby T v St Andrews	1-1, 2-2*
Oadby T won 3-1 on penalties	
Birstall U v South Normanton Ath	3-0
Bottesford T v Long Eaton U	6-0
Leicester Road v Sleaford T	2-1
Dunkirk v Leicester Nirvana	2-1
Kirby Muxloe v Barton T	4-2
AFC Mansfield v Hall Road Rangers	2-1
Staveley MW v Loughborough University	2-1
Retford U v Quorn	1-1, 0-3
Clipstone v West Bridgford	3-1
Heanor T v Aylestone Park	0-1
Worksop T v Hinckley	1-2
Boston T v Radford	2-2, 2-2*
Boston T won 4-3 on penalties	
Rainworth MW v Shepshed Dynamo	0-1
Harrowby U v Grimsby Bor	0-3
Biggleswade v Wisbech T	1-4
Swaffham T v Rothwell Corinthians	3-1
Raunds T v Yaxley	1-1, 2-4*
(2-2 at the end of normal time)	
Peterborough Northern Star v Deeping Rangers	2-3
Cogenhoe U v Godmanchester R	3-0

Ely C v Holbeach U	0-2
Huntingdon T v Newport Pagnell T	1-4
Eynesbury R v Thetford T	3-2
Northampton Sileby Rangers v Harborough T	0-5
Wellingborough Whitworths v Desborough T	0-4
Fakenham T v Wellingborough T	0-2
Histon v Northampton ON Chenecks	0-1
Potton U v Biggleswade U	0-0, 2-1
Hoddesdon T v Haverhill R	1-2
Sawbridgeworth T v West Essex	0-3
Enfield 1893 v Haverhill Bor	1-2
Redbridge v Stansted	3-1
Takeley v Wivenhoe T	3-1
Kirkley & Pakefield v Saffron Walden T	1-2
Southend Manor v Wroxham	1-0
Framlingham T v Wadham Lodge	0-0, 3-1
FC Broxbourne Bor v Tower Hamlets	1-1, 0-1
Barkingside v Stowmarket T	0-4
Ilford v Woodbridge T	1-0
FC Clacton v Clapton	0-1
Hadleigh U v Sporting Bengal U	3-2
FC Romania v Waltham Forest	2-2, 2-1
Hackney Wick v Long Melford	0-1
Felixstowe & Walton U v Brantham Ath	2-7
Stanway R v Gorleston	2-4
Hullbridge Sports v Ipswich W	5-1
St Margaretsbury v Burnham Ramblers	3-2
Great Yarmouth T v Diss T	5-0
Newmarket T v Great Wakering R	5-1
Walsham Le Willows v Basildon U	2-2, 0-3
Welwyn Garden C v North Greenford U	2-4
Cockfosters v Risborough Rangers	1-1, 2-2*
Cockfosters won 4-2 on penalties	
Holmer Green v AFC Hayes	4-0
Lydney T v Wantage T	1-3
Langford v Hadley	1-9
Highworth T v London Colney	1-1, 4-2
Stotfold v Berkhamsted	1-12
Woodley U v Tuffley R	1-2
Southall v Harpenden T	5-1
Flackwell Heath v Burnham	5-0
Highmoor Ibis v Buckingham T	3-1
Fairford T v Longlevens	1-1, 1-5
Edgware T v Leverstock Green	1-1, A-A, 3-5
First replay abandoned due to serious injury to a player,	
Leverstock Green leading 3-2	
Chipping Sodbury T v Brackley T Saints	3-1
Leighton T v Oxhey Jets	4-0
Windsor v Wembley	1-4
Brimscombe & Thrupp v Sun Sports	4-0
Royal Wootton Bassett T v Crawley Green	1-2
Colney Heath v Tring Ath	1-0
Ardley U v Baldock T	1-3
Corinthian v Deal T	2-2, 1-4
Hassocks v Hollands & Blair	2-3
Sheppey U v AFC Croydon Ath	3-2
Crowborough Ath v Lingfield	2-0
Sutton Common R v Canterbury C	2-0
Newhaven v Peacehaven & Telscombe	0-0, 2-0
Colliers Wood U v AFC Uckfield T	2-2, 2-0
Chessington & Hook U v Lancing	2-2, 3-1
East Preston v Saltdean U	2-1
Epsom & Ewell v Banstead Ath	1-2
Hailsham T v Redhill	1-8
Loxwood v Holmesdale	3-1
Tunbridge Wells v Beckenham T	1-0
Walton & Hersham v Mile Oak	7-0
Sevenoaks T v Broadbridge Heath	3-1
Hanworth Villa v Bedfont & Feltham	5-0
Glebe v Lordswood	1-0
Whitstable T v Croydon	2-3
Worthing U v Steyning T	2-4
Arundel v Pagham	0-4
Horley T v Raynes Park Vale	5-1
Abbey Rangers v Cray Valley (PM)	1-3
Eastbourne T v Bearsted	2-1
Spelthorne Sports v Chertsey T	1-3
Rochester U v Erith T	1-1, 0-5
Erith & Belvedere v Wick	4-0

AC London v Crawley Down Gatwick	3-2
Chatham T v Littlehampton T	1-1, 1-2
Little Common v Eastbourne U	1-2
Rushtall v CB Hounslow U	0-0, 1-2
Haywards Heath T v Bedfont Sports	A-A, 5-2
First match abandoned after 45 mins due to waterlogged pitch, 1-1	
Horsham YMCA v Three Bridges	0-2
Bracknell T v Cowes Sports	3-0
Thatcham T v Petersfield T	5-0
Christchurch v AFC Portchester	1-5
Farnham T v Fawley	3-2
Bashley v Fareham T	2-4
Hamworthy U v Bemerton Heath Harlequins	4-1
Team Solent v Brockenhurst	2-5
Badshot Lea v Verwood T	1-1, 3-3*
Badshot Lea won 3-1 on penalties	
Amesbury T v Eversley & California	4-0
Camberley T v Blackfield & Langley	0-0, 2-1*
(1-1 at the end of normal time)	
Whitchurch U v Laverstock & Ford	0-3
Ringwood T v Ascot U	0-6
Binfield v Chichester C	4-3
Horndean v Melksham T	2-1
Knaphill v Bournemouth	0-0, 2-0
Newport (IW) v Guildford C	2-2, 0-3
Godalming T v Westfield	2-1
Sholing v Alresford T	1-2
Lymington T v Andover T	0-2
Clevedon T v Bitton	2-2, 1-0
Cadbury Heath v Longwell Green Sports	4-1
Plymouth Parkway v Portland U	0-1
AFC St Austell v Bridport	1-1, 0-1
Wells C v Cribbs	2-1
Shaftesbury T v Exmouth T	0-0, 2-1*
(1-1 at the end of normal time)	
Shepton Mallet v Tavistock	1-4
Buckland Ath v Bodmin T	2-3
Cheddar v Willand R	0-2
Wellington v Hengrove Ath	1-3
Street v Hallen	1-1, 4-1
Brislington v Sherborne T	6-1
Bridgwater T v Keynsham T	5-2
Bradford T v Odd Down	3-4

PRELIMINARY ROUND

Albion Sports v Newton Aycliffe	2-1
South Shields v Bridlington T	3-1
Pickering T v Clitheroe	1-2
Sunderland RCA v Ashington	4-0
Guisborough T v Shildon	1-5
Goole v Newcastle Benfield	1-2
Barnoldswick T v Dunston UTS	2-1
Tadcaster Alb v Colne	0-1
Harrogate Railway Ath v Kendal T	1-1, 1-4
Scarborough Ath v Marske U	1-1, 2-1*
(1-1 at the end of normal time)	
Consett v Heaton Stannington	4-0
Penrith v Whitley Bay	1-1, 1-3
Abbey Hey v Maine Road	2-2, A-A, 2-1
First replay abandoned after 105 minutes due to serious injury to a player, 1-1	
Sheffield v Ossett T	0-2
Penistone Church v Litherland Remyca	2-0
Bamber Bridge v Brighouse T	3-2
Hallam v Atherton Colleries	1-4
Frickley Ath v Runcorn T	2-1
Ramsbottom U v Liversedge	2-3
Pontefract Collieries v Skelmersdale U	1-2
Ashton Ath v Runcorn Linnets	4-2
Parkgate v Handsworth Parramore	2-4
Trafford v Kidsgrove Ath	2-2, 0-2
Prescot Cables v City of Liverpool	2-2, 2-8
1874 Northwich v West Didsbury & Chorlton	3-3, 3-1
Glossop North End v Mossley	0-2
Hyde U v Congleton T	4-2
Ossett Alb v Droylsden	3-4
Colwyn Bay v Stocksbridge Park Steels	3-0
Radcliffe Bor v Burscough	1-1, 3-0
Leek T v Cammell Laird 1907	2-0
Sporting Khalsa v Market Drayton T	1-1, 1-1*
Market Drayton T won 4-1 on penalties	
Alvechurch v Hanley T	2-0
Walsall Wood v Tividale	0-1
Bedworth U v Haughmond	0-2

Rugby T v Romulus	2-3
Bromsgrove Sporting v Coleshill T	3-4
Wolverhampton Casuals v Boldmere St Michaels	2-2, 0-5
Worcester C v Chasetown	1-1, 0-2
Brocton v Gresley	2-0
Newcastle T v Evesham U	1-1, 3-2*
(2-2 at the end of normal time)	
AFC Wulfrunians v Westfields	1-1, 0-1
Birstall U v Cleethorpes T	0-3
Shepshed Dynamo v Kimberley MW	3-0
Kirby Muxloe v Dunkirk	0-2
Grimsby Bor v Leicester Road	4-1
Oadby T v Loughborough Dynamo	1-3
Hinckley v Aylestone Park	4-1
Quorn v AFC Mansfield	1-3
Staveley MW v Basford U	0-1
Boston T v Carlton T	3-2
Lincoln U v Belper T	0-0, 4-1
Bottesford T v Clipstone	4-1
Wisbech T v Spalding U	2-2, 2-0
Dereham T v Corby T	3-0
Cambridge C v Stamford	1-0
Barton R v Deeping Rangers	1-2
Yaxley v Harborough T	5-3
Holbeach U v Northampton ON Chenecks	6-1
Potton U v AFC Dunstable	2-0
Newport Pagnell T v Kempston R	3-3, 1-4
Arlesey T v Desborough T	3-1
Soham T Rangers v Cogenhoe U	3-2
Eynesbury R v Peterborough Sports	1-1, 0-2
Wellingborough T v AFC Rushden & Diamonds	0-4
Bedford T v Swaffham T	3-1
St Margaretsbury v Hullbridge Sports	2-2, 1-1*
St Margaretsbury won 5-4 on penalties	
Bury T v Tilbury	1-2
Southend Manor v Gorleston	2-3
Bowers & Pitsea v Haringey Bor	0-2
Maldon & Tiptree v Waltham Abbey	5-1
AFC Hornchurch v Brentwood T	2-0
Canvey Island v Witham T	0-2
Clapton v Norwich U	2-0
Framlingham T v Mildenhall T	0-1
Haverhill R v Heybridge Swifts	1-1, 1-6
Newmarket T v Ware	1-2
Tower Hamlets v Takeley	0-4
Brantham Ath v Cheshunt	3-6
Stowmarket T v Romford	1-1, 1-3
AFC Sudbury v Aveley	4-0
Ilford v Haverhill Bor	1-1, 2-5
Hertford T v Hadleigh U	4-1
Great Yarmouth T v Basildon U	1-0
Grays Ath v Redbridge	2-0
Long Melford v FC Romania	1-2
Barking v Saffron Walden T	0-0, 4-3
Potters Bar T v West Essex	4-1
Slimbridge v Cinderford T	1-2
Flackwell Heath v Didcot T	1-2
Baldock T v North Greenford U	3-1
Chalfont St Peter v Beaconsfield T	2-2, 1-3
Ashford T (Middlesex) v Wembley	3-0
Colney Heath v Shortwood U	2-0
Kidlington v Wantage T	1-0
Swindon Supermarine v Northwood	1-0
Hayes & Yeading U v Brimscombe & Thrupp	1-0
Leighton T v Tuffley R	2-3
Crawley Green v Berkhamsted	2-3
Chipping Sodbury T v Bishop's Cleeve	1-3
Leverstock Green v Aylesbury U	1-1, 1-4
Southall v Hadley	2-4
Aylesbury v Cirencester T	2-1
Uxbridge v Thame U	0-4
Highworth T v Marlow	2-3
Hanwell T v Longlevens	1-0
Highmoor Ibis v North Leigh	1-3
Cockfosters v Holmer Green	3-0
Pagham v Sittingbourne	1-1, 1-0
Hollands & Blair v Crowborough Ath	1-4
Erith & Belvedere v Cray Valley (PM)	1-4
Whyteleafe v Erith T	1-1, 3-3*
Erith T won 4-1 on penalties	
Carshalton Ath v Walton & Hersham	1-1, 1-1*
Carshalton Ath won 5-4 on penalties	
Haywards Heath T v South Park	2-0
Colliers Wood U v Shoreham	1-1, 1-3*
(1-1 at the end of normal time)	
Sutton Common R v Eastbourne T	1-2

Corinthian Casuals v Hythe T	1-1, 3-1
Greenwich Bor v Three Bridges	4-1
Deal T v Glebe	2-2, 0-3
Walton Casuals v Molesey	3-1
Redhill v Ashford U	1-3
Ramsgate v Hanworth Villa	3-1
East Grinstead T v VCD Ath	3-2
Cray W v Sevenoaks T	2-3
Banstead Ath v Loxwood	6-3
East Preston v Thamesmead T	0-8
Littlehampton T v Eastbourne U	1-3
Chipstead v Horley T	2-0
Tunbridge Wells v CB Hounslow U	3-1
Steyning T v Phoenix Sports	0-5
Chertsey T v Horsham	1-3
Herne Bay v Chessington & Hook U	2-1
Lewes v Newhaven	3-3, 4-1
Sheppey U v Hastings U	0-2
Croydon v Faversham T	0-0, 1-2
AC London v Egham T	1-5
Bracknell T v Winchester C	0-4
Fleet T v AFC Totton	1-1, 0-5
Andover T v Wimborne T	3-3, 2-1
Godalming T v Farnham T	3-0
AFC Portchester v Amesbury T	3-1
Hamworthy U v Ascot U	4-1
Binfield v Horndean	1-1, 0-3
Brockenhurst v Hartley Wintney	1-5
Guildford C v Camberley T	4-0
Salisbury v Fareham T	3-2
Badshot Lea v Moneyfields	0-3
Laverstock & Ford v Knaphill	2-4
Alresford T v Thatcham T	0-2
Portland U v Paulton R	0-3
Barnstaple T v Clevedon T	1-0
Tavistock v Shaftesbury T	2-1
Bideford v Wells C	6-0
Cadbury Heath v Yate T	1-0
Bridgwater T v Brislington	1-0
Hengrove Ath v Bodmin T	1-4
Willand R v Bristol Manor Farm	2-1
Odd Down v Mangotsfield U	1-0
Taunton T v Larkhall Ath	3-0
Bridport v Street	3-1

FIRST QUALIFYING ROUND

Penistone Church v Whitby T	3-2
Albion Sports v Barnoldswick T	3-2
City of Liverpool v Nantwich T	1-2
Warrington T v Grimsby Bor	1-0
Ashton Ath v Bamber Bridge	2-1
Kidsgrove Ath v Clitheroe	3-2
Stalybridge Celtic v Farsley Celtic	2-1
Marine v Ashton U	1-3
Shaw Lane v Radcliffe Bor	3-1
Scarborough Ath v Workington	1-0
Bottesford T v Shildon	0-1
Cleethorpes T v Atherton Colleries	1-2
Colne v Lancaster C	0-1
Ossett T v Consett	2-1
Hyde U v Kendal T	1-0
Droylsden v Colwyn Bay	4-3
Abbey Hey v Altrincham	3-3, 1-2
Skelmersdale U v Handsworth Parramore	1-2
Buxton v Frickley Ath	3-2
Whitley Bay v Newcastle Benfield	0-2
Sunderland RCA v Liversedge	0-0, 4-0
Mossley v 1874 Northwich	2-2, 0-2
Witton Alb v South Shields	0-2
Halesowen T v Basford U	0-3
Boston T v Hednesford T	2-0
Kempston R v Wisbech T	2-1
Loughborough Dynamo v Stourbridge	1-3
Market Drayton T v Alvechurch	1-5
AFC Mansfield v Dunkirk	3-2
Soham T Rangers v Westfields	0-0, 0-1
Peterborough Sports v Stafford Rangers	3-4
Rushall Olympic v Potton U	1-0
Sutton Coldfield T v Barwell	0-2
St Ives T v Coalville T	2-1
Grantham T v Holbeach U	2-1
Haughmond v Matlock T	3-2
Tividale v AFC Rushden & Diamonds	2-3
Lincoln U v Redditch U	0-1
Shepshed Dynamo v Leek T	6-1

Romulus v Kettering T	0-3
Stratford T v Newcastle T	4-0
King's Lynn T v Coleshill T	4-1
Mickleover Sports v Hinckley	2-1
Boldmere St Michaels v Chasetown	0-3
Yaxley v Dereham T	0-1
Brocton v Deeping Rangers	2-4
Cambridge C v St Neots T	3-1
Maldon & Tiptree v Hayes & Yeading U	3-3, 3-4*
(3-3 at the end of normal time)	
Tilbury v Aylesbury U	0-1
North Leigh v Biggleswade T	2-2, 2-3
Romford v AFC Hornchurch	0-1
Baldock T v Thame U	4-3
Hendon v Wingate & Finchley	1-1, 2-4*
(2-2 at the end of normal time)	
Beaconsfield T v Marlow	0-2
Colney Heath v Cockfosters	3-0
Berkhamsted v Slough T	1-3
Clapton v Needham Market	0-3
Royston v Dunstable T	2-0
Billericay T v Didcot T	5-0
Bedford T v Lowestoft T	0-2
Ware v Witham T	2-1
Thurrock v Harlow T	1-1, 1-2
Hadley v FC Romania	2-3
Great Yarmouth T v Chesham U	0-2
Hertford T v Grays Ath	1-1, 3-2*
(2-2 at the end of normal time)	
Haringey Bor v Hitchin T	1-1, 1-1*
Haringey Bor won 3-2 on penalties	
Potters Bar T v Bishop's Stortford	1-0
Gorleston v Barking	0-4
Arlesey T v Heybridge Swifts	0-7
AFC Sudbury v Mildenhall T	1-1, 4-2
Aylesbury v Leiston	1-3
Hanwell T v Brightlingsea Regent	4-1
St Margaretsbury v Kidlington	1-6
Cheshunt v Takeley	2-0
Haverhill Bor v Kings Langley	0-8
Enfield T v Harrow Bor	2-1
Littlehampton T v Chipstead	2-2, 0-4
Ashford T (Middlesex) v Corinthian Casuals	2-0
Phoenix Sports v Eastbourne T	2-0
Ramsgate v Egham T	3-3, 4-2
Margate v East Grinstead T	3-1
Faversham T v Tonbridge Angels	3-1
Crowborough Ath v Sevenoaks T	2-0
Dulwich Hamlet v Hastings U	3-1
Tooting & Mitcham U v Merstham	2-0
Thamesmead T v Lewes	3-0
Herne Bay v Walton Casuals	3-1
Metropolitan Police v Staines T	3-2
Folkestone Invicta v Greenwich Bor	3-2
Dorking W v Worthing	3-2
Horsham v Ashford U	6-0
Haywards Heath T v Tunbridge Wells	2-2, 0-3*
(0-0 at the end of normal time)	
Banstead Ath v Glebe	0-4
Carshalton Ath v Pagham	5-3
Kingstonian v Shoreham	3-2
Leatherhead v Cray Valley (PM)	6-0
Erith T v Burgess Hill T	0-3
Hereford v Godalming T	8-0
Banbury U v Tiverton T	4-2
Bridport v Barnstaple T	1-0
Gosport Bor v Bridgwater T	1-0
Frome T v AFC Totton	2-1
AFC Portchester v Dorchester T	1-0
Farnborough v Salisbury	2-3
Odd Down v Weymouth	0-5
Tavistock v Taunton T	2-2, 2-1
Merthyr T v Willand R	6-1
Tuffley R v Swindon Supermarine	0-5
Horndean v Bodmin T	0-2
Paulton R v Winchester C	1-0
Guildford C v Knaphill	1-3
Basingstoke T v Hartley Wintney	2-2, 0-1
Bideford v Bishop's Cleeve	5-1
Hamworthy U v Thatcham T	1-5
Cinderford T v Moneyfields	2-1
Andover T v Cadbury Heath	1-2

SECOND QUALIFYING ROUND

Salford C v York C	1-2

Darlington 1883 v South Shields	0-3
Southport v Bradford (Park Avenue)	0-3
Ossett T v Atherton Collieries	1-0
Newcastle Benfield v Ashton U	2-1
Warrington T v Hyde U	1-1, 0-2
Harrogate T v Penistone Church	3-0
Spennymoor T v Gainsborough Trinity	1-2
Handsworth Parramore v	
FC United of Manchester	1-1 2-6
Albion Sports v Ashton Ath	0-4
Shildon v Altrincham	1-0
Scarborough Ath v Sunderland RCA	2-0
Blyth Spartans v Shaw Lane	1-2
1874 Northwich v North Ferriby U	1-0
Stockport Co v Curzon Ashton	1-0
Stalybridge Celtic v Chorley	1-3
Lancaster C v Droylsden	4-0
Stafford Rangers v Tamworth	1-0
Boston U v Haughmond	1-1, 5-0
Shepshed Dynamo v Nantwich T	0-1
Deeping Rangers v Kidderminster H	2-4
AFC Mansfield v Rushall Olympic	0-0, 2-1
Kempston R v Hereford	0-4
Stratford T v Redditch U	4-1
AFC Telford U v Barwell	2-0
Nuneaton T v King's Lynn T	3-1
Kettering T v Kidsgrove Ath	2-0
Basford U v Mickleover Sports	1-0
Alfreton T v AFC Rushden & Diamonds	2-2, 3-1
Westfields v Leamington	0-2
Grantham T v Alvechurch	3-4
Buxton v Chasetown	4-1
Stourbridge v St Ives T	2-0
Dereham T v Boston T	1-2
Leiston v Crowborough Ath	4-2
Concord Rangers v Tunbridge Wells	4-0
Braintree T v Royston T	2-2, 2-1
AFC Sudbury v Chipstead	3-0
Biggleswade T v East Thurrock U	0-1
St Albans C v Cambridge C	3-3, 2-0
Horsham v Herne Bay	2-5
Hemel Hempstead T v Wingate & Finchley	0-0, 2-1*
(1-1 at the end of normal time)	
Lowestoft T v Harlow T	0-1
Metropolitan Police v Heybridge Swifts	2-2, 1-1*
Heybridge Swifts won 4-3 on penalties	
Chelmsford C v Ramsgate	7-0
Ware v Leatherhead	2-5
Kings Langley v Margate	0-1
Thamesmead T v Billericay T	1-1, 0-5
Baldock T v Aylesbury U	1-2
Hertford T v AFC Hornchurch	1-2
Glebe v Phoenix Sports	2-2, 1-1*
Phoenix Sports won 5-4 on penalties	
FC Romania v Hayes & Yeading U	2-2, 0-2*
(0-0 at the end of normal time)	
Kingstonian v Brackley T	0-3
Eastbourne Bor v Carshalton Ath	4-3
Folkestone Invicta v Tooting & Mitcham U	3-1
Cheshunt v Dorking W	1-3
Wealdstone v Faversham T	4-0
Colney Heath v Burgess Hill T	3-3, 0-3
Welling U v Haringey Bor	1-2
Dartford v Barking	3-1
Hampton & Richmond Bor v Potters Bar T	1-1, 3-0
Whitehawk v Oxford C	1-3
Marlow v Ashford T (Middlesex)	0-2
Needham Market v Chesham U	2-0
Slough T v Dulwich Hamlet	3-2
Hanwell T v Enfield T	0-0, 0-5
Havant & Waterlooville v Merthyr T	2-1
Bodmin T v Bideford	1-1, 0-1
Bridport v Cadbury Heath	2-2, 3-2*
(2-2 at the end of normal time)	
Gosport Bor v Swindon Supermarine	1-2
Bognor Regis T v Weston Super Mare	2-1
Cinderford T v Hartley Wintney	1-0
Tavistock v Frome T	1-2
Weymouth v Chippenham T	2-0
Banbury U v Thatcham T	2-0
Bath C v Knaphill	6-0
Truro C v AFC Portchester	2-0
Salisbury v Poole T	0-2
Paulton R v Kidlington	3-2
Gloucester C v Hungerford T	0-3

THIRD QUALIFYING ROUND

1874 Northwich v Ossett T	2-2, 0-0*
Ossett T won 5-4 on penalties	
AFC Mansfield v Boston U	0-2
Stafford Rangers v AFC Telford U	1-1, 1-4
Newcastle Benfield v Kidderminster H	0-1
Nantwich T v Nuneaton T	3-1
Boston T v Hyde U	2-3
Banbury U v Shildon	2-3
Scarborough Ath v Stratford T	2-2, 4-1*
(1-1 at the end of normal time)	
Basford U v Kettering T	2-3
Shaw Lane v Lancaster C	2-1
Buxton v Alvechurch	2-1
Stockport Co v FC United of Manchester	3-3, 0-1
Ashton Ath v Chorley	0-1
Leamington v Gainsborough Trinity	0-0, 0-2
Stourbridge v Alfreton T	3-1
South Shields v York C	3-2
Harrogate T v Bradford (Park Avenue)	0-0, 2-0
Swindon Supermarine v Paulton R	2-3
Enfield T v Phoenix Sports	3-0
Hayes & Yeading U v Havant & Waterlooville	0-4
Hereford v AFC Hornchurch	2-0
Slough T v Poole T	2-1
Brackley T v Braintree T	4-1
Concord Rangers v Dorking W	3-0
East Thurrock U v Harlow T	2-2, 2-1
Chelmsford C v Weymouth	2-1
Cinderford T v Hampton & Richmond Bor	2-3
Oxford C v Leiston	4-2
Margate v Herne Bay	2-0
St Albans C v Bridport	2-1
Heybridge Swifts v Frome T	2-1
Truro C v AFC Sudbury	4-1
Eastbourne Bor v Bognor Regis T	0-2
Bath C v Hemel Hempstead T	3-0
Needham Market v Dartford	1-6
Haringey Bor v Bideford	4-1
Folkestone Invicta v Aylesbury U	2-1
Hungerford T v Billericay T	1-1, 1-6
Burgess Hill T v Wealdstone	1-0
Ashford T (Middlesex) v Leatherhead	1-2

FOURTH QUALIFYING ROUND

FC Halifax T v Tranmere R	1-3
Solihull Moors v Ossett T	1-1, 2-1
South Shields v Hartlepool U	1-2
Shaw Lane v Barrow	2-1
Chorley v Boston U	0-0, 4-3*
(3-3 at the end of normal time)	
AFC Telford U v FC United of Manchester	3-1
Harrogate T v Gainsborough Trinity	1-2
Nantwich T v Kettering T	1-1, 1-0
Buxton v Gateshead	1-2
Guiseley v Shildon	6-0
AFC Fylde v Wrexham	1-0
Kidderminster H v Chester FC	2-0
Scarborough Ath v Hyde U	0-2
Stourbridge v Macclesfield T	0-5
Brackley T v Billericay T	3-3, 1-2
Dagenham & Redbridge v Leyton Orient	0-0, 0-1
Eastleigh v Hereford	1-2
Aldershot T v Torquay U	1-0
Bath C v Chelmsford C	0-0, 0-1
Oxford C v Bognor Regis T	1-0
Maidenhead U v Havant & Waterlooville	2-1
Haringey Bor v Heybridge Swifts	2-4
Woking v Concord Rangers	1-1, 2-1*
(1-1 at the end of normal time)	
Hampton & Richmond Bor v Truro C	0-2
Dover Ath v Bromley	0-0, 0-3
Slough T v Folkestone Invicta	1-0
Burgess Hill T v Dartford	0-1
St Albans C v Boreham Wood	1-3
Maidstone U v Enfield T	2-2, 3-1*
(1-1 at the end of normal time)	
Margate v Leatherhead	1-2
Paulton R v Sutton U	2-3
East Thurrock U v Ebbsfleet U	0-0, 0-3

THE EMIRATES FA CUP 2017–18
COMPETITION PROPER

■ *Denotes player sent off.*

FIRST ROUND

Friday, 3 November 2017

Hyde U (0) 0
Milton Keynes D (2) 4 *(Nesbitt 14, Aneke 45,*
Ebanks-Landell 67, Upson 73) 3123
Hyde U: (442) Crookes; Harrison, Coates, Miller, Burke;
Pratt, Lipka, Stockdill, Porrritt (Boyle 82); Beadle (Jones
77), Khamsuk (Gay 65).
Milton Keynes D: (4231) Nicholls; Brittain, Ebanks-Landell,
Walsh, Williams GB; Gilbey (Nombe 77), Upson; Seager
(Pawlett 69), Aneke (McGrandles 77), Nesbitt; Agard.
Referee: David Webb.

Notts Co (2) 4 *(Yates 30, 31, Stead 58, Grant 90)*
Bristol R (2) 2 *(Sercombe 8, Sinclair 12)* 4228
Notts Co: (442) Fitzsimons; Tootle, Duffy, Brisley,
Dickinson (Jones 90); Hawkridge, Yates, Hewitt, Grant;
Stead (Smith 87), Ameobi (Forte 87).
Bristol R: (41212) Smith; Partington (Leadbitter 69),
Lockyer, Broadbent, Brown; Sinclair (Harrison 60);
Sercombe, Lines; Clarke O; Nichols (Telford 82), Gaffney.
Referee: Graham Salisbury.

Port Vale (1) 2 *(Gunning 16, Pope 53)*
Oxford U (0) 0 3443
Port Vale: (4231) Boot; Gibbons, Anderson, Smith,
Gunning; Pugh, Kay; Worrall (Forrester 78), Harness
(Turner 84), Denton; Pope (Stobbs 90).
Oxford U: (4411) Eastwood; Ribeiro, Williamson (Martin
46), Mousinho, Tiendalli; Henry, Ledson, Ruffels
(Rothwell 63), Mowatt (Hall 55); Payne; Thomas.
Referee: Mark Heywood.

Saturday, 4 November 2017

AFC Fylde (1) 4 *(Rowe 14, 48, Smith 54, Finley 64)*
Kidderminster H (0) 2 *(Taylor 74, Brown 90)* 1482
AFC Fylde: (442) Lynch; Francis-Angol, Tunnicliffe,
Bond, Finley (Montrose 80); Smith (Grand 84), Burke
(Ezewele 86), Taylor, Edmundson; Rowe, Muldoon.
Kidderminster H: (442) Hall; Pearson, Taylor, Croasdale,
Horsfall; O'Connor, Sonupe (Weeks 70); McQuilkin,
Ironside; Ngwatala, Wright (Brown 61).
Referee: Daniel Middleton.

AFC Wimbledon (1) 1 *(Taylor 7)*
Lincoln C (0) 0 3394
AFC Wimbledon: (433) Long; Fuller, Oshilaja, Charles,
Kennedy; Forrester, Abdou (Robinson 85), Soares;
McDonald, Taylor (Meades 29), Barcham.
Lincoln C: (433) Vickers; Long, Dickie, Waterfall,
Eardley; Bostwick, Knott (Ginnelly 85), Woodyard;
Green, Palmer (Rhead 68), Arnold (Whitehouse 83).
Referee: Andy Woolmer.

Blackburn R (0) 3 *(Nuttall 63, Graham 70, Antonsson 81)*
Barnet (1) 1 *(Akinola 31)* 3710
Blackburn R: (433) Leutwiler; Caddis, Downing,
Mulgrew, Williams; Harper, Evans, Hart (Nuttall 46);
Gladwin (Antonsson 70), Graham, Dack (Bennett 74).
Barnet: (433) Ross; Watson, Clough, Santos, Tutonda;
Taylor J, Fonguck (Aghadiuno 82), Vilhete; Akinola
(Ruben Bover 71), Nicholls, Akpa Akpro.
Referee: Carl Boyeson.

Boreham Wood (0) 2 *(Turgott 68, Holman 88)*
Blackpool (0) 1 *(Philliskirk 62)* 1041
Boreham Wood: (352) Smith G; Champion, Stephens,
Wells; Smith K, Ricketts, Murtagh, Balanta (Turgott 65),
Woodards; Jeffers (Holman 66), Andrade.
Blackpool: (352) Allsop; Mellor, Aimson, Anderton
(Gnanduillet 88); Turton, Ryan (Longstaff 77), Spearing,
Cooke, Taylor; Philliskirk (Solomon-Otabor 77),
Delfouneso.
Referee: Christopher Sarginson.

Bradford C (2) 2 *(Gilliead 4, Jones 44)*
Chesterfield (0) 0 4747
Bradford C: (442) Doyle; Hendrie, Kilgallon, Thompson,
Knight-Percival; Gilliead (Robinson 87), Vincelot, Dieng
(Devine 78), Taylor; Wyke, Jones (Law 71).
Chesterfield: (4411) Anyon; Barry, Evatt, Hird, Wiseman;
Kellett, McCourt, Reed (O'Grady 71), Dimaio (Sinnott
78); Rowley (Mitchell 84); Dennis.
Referee: Anthony Backhouse.

Carlisle U (2) 3 *(Bennett 22, 60, Hope 36)*
Oldham Ath (0) 2 *(Clarke 64, Holloway 72)* 3965
Carlisle U: (352) Bonham; Liddle, Parkes, Hill; Brown,
Lambe (Devitt 78), Joyce, Jones, Grainger; Bennett
(Miller S 86), Hope (Etuhu 69).
Oldham Ath: (442) Placide; Dummigan, Clarke, Gardner,
Hunt (Nepomuceno 70); Fane, Menig (Holloway 63),
Green (Flynn 66), Bryan; Davies, Doyle.
Referee: Gary Hilton.

Cheltenham T (0) 2 *(Dawson 52, Finney 62 (og))*
Maidstone U (3) 4 *(Sam-Yorke 20, 53, Pigott 21,*
Hines 43) 2799
Cheltenham T: (442) Flinders; Winchester, Grimes,
Moore (Boyle 31); Cranston; Dawson■, Pell, Storer
(Wright 32), Morrell (Sellars 62); Eisa, Graham.
Maidstone U: (433) Worgan; Nana Ofori-Twumasi
(Okuonghae 56), Wynter, Finney, Anderson; Lewis,
Prestedge, Reason (Wraight 81); Hines, Pigott (Loza 84),
Sam-Yorke■.
Referee: Kevin Johnson.

Colchester U (0) 0
Oxford C (0) 1 *(Paterson 46)* 1775
Colchester U: (3412) Walker; Eastman, Inniss, Kent
(Kinsella 59); Jackson, Loft (Slater 57), Comley
(O'Sullivan 80), Doey Wright; Reid; Mandron, Hanlan.
Oxford C: (451) Stevens; Welch-Hayes, Oastler,
Henderson, Grant; Sinclair, Pearce, Poku, Fofana,
McEachran (Hirst 80); Paterson (Forde 90).
Referee: Alan Young.

Crewe Alex (0) 2 *(Walker 47, Ainley 89)*
Rotherham U (1) 1 *(Vaulks 21)* 2597
Crewe Alex: (442) Richards; Ng, Raynes, Walker,
Pickering; Ainley, Lowery, Grant, Cooper; Bowery
(Porter 75), Dagnall.
Rotherham U: (442) O'Donnell; Cummings, Ajayi, Wood
(Ihiekwe 83), Emmanuel; Williams (Taylor 62), Vaulks,
Potter, Newell; David Ball (Towell 68), Moore.
Referee: Scott Oldham.

Ebbsfleet U (2) 2 *(Kedwell 35 (pen), Coulson 37)*
Doncaster R (2) 6 *(Rowe 45, 85, Marquis 45,*
Coppinger 52, 83 (pen), Houghton 78) 2069
Ebbsfleet U: (442) Ashmore; Magri, Clark, Mambo
(Brandy 58), Bush■; Cook (Shields 76), Powell, Rance,
Coulson; Weston, Kedwell (McCoy 84).
Doncaster R: (3421) Lawlor; Alcock (Mason 46), Baudry,
Butler; Toffolo, Houghton, Kongolo, Blair; Rowe
(Beestin 86), Coppinger (Ben Khemis 84); Marquis.
Referee: Lee Collins.

Forest Green R (1) 1 *(Doidge 42)*
Macclesfield T (0) 0 1387
Forest Green R: (3421) Collins B; Fitzwater, Collins L,
Monthe; Bennett, Traore (Stevens 90), Osbourne, Laird;
Marsh-Brown (Bugiel 70), Brown; Doidge.
Macclesfield T: (433) Jalal; Hodgkiss, Lowe, Kennedy
(Pilkington 45), Fitzpatrick; Baba (Whitaker 75),
Whitehead, Lloyd; Durrell, Marsh, Arthur (Wilson 80).
Referee: Trevor Kettle.

Gainsborough Trinity (0) 0
Slough T (1) 6 *(Lench 35, 46, 84, Flood 52, Williams 71, Fraser 75)* 1630
Gainsborough Trinity: (442) Ravas; Lacey (Wafula 60), Jacklin, Stainfield, Taylor (Simmons 46); King, Richards, Clarke (Wells 61), Davie; Jarman, Worsfold.
Slough T: (442) Turner; Smart, Nisbet, Hollis, Wells; Dobson (Webb 82), Togwell, Lench, Harris (Fraser 70); Williams (James 79), Flood.
Referee: Peter Wright.

Gateshead (2) 2 *(Burrow 30, Johnson 34)*
Chelmsford C (0) 0 732
Gateshead: (442) Montgomery; Williams (Vassell 66), Kerr, Byrne, Barrow; York (Preston 62), Penn, McLaughlin, Hannant (Maxwell 75); Johnson, Burrow.
Chelmsford C: (442) Beasant; Omozusi, Porter, Spillane, Braham-Barrett; Green, Stevenson (West 46), Smith, Johnson; Barnard (Hitchcock 65), Dickson (Batt 56).
Referee: Peter Gibbons.

Gillingham (1) 2 *(Parker 20, Eaves 75)*
Leyton Orient (0) 1 *(Dayton 79)* 3659
Gillingham: (352) Holy; Ehmer, Zakuani, Ogilvie (O'Neill 80); Clare, Hessenthaler, Martin, Byrne, Parker; Eaves (Wilkinson 76), List (Wagstaff 57).
Leyton Orient: (352) Grainger; Clark (Lawless 46), Sendles-White, Widdowson■; Caprice, Boco (Harrold 69), Westbrooke (Sotiriou 87), Dayton, Judd; Bonne, Mooney.
Referee: John Brooks.

Hereford (0) 1 *(Mills 68)*
AFC Telford U (0) 0 4712
Hereford: (442) Horsell; O'Shea, Green, Deaman, Oates; Reffell, Purdie, Dinsley (Haysham 17), Preen (Page 78); Mills (Smith 84), Symons.
AFC Telford U: (4231) Singh; Simpson (Barnes-Homer 83), Sutton, Johnson, Harris; Royle■, Cowans; Murphy, Dwyer (Lussey 62), Newby; Dinanga.
Referee: Thomas Bramall.

Luton T (1) 1 *(Collins 45)*
Portsmouth (0) 0 5333
Luton T: (4312) Stech; Stacey, Cuthbert, Sheehan, Potts; Lee O, Ruddock, Berry; Shinnie (Cornick 83); Collins, Hylton.
Portsmouth: (4231) McGee; Thompson■, Burgess, Clarke, Haunstrup; Close, O'Keefe; Lowe, Hawkins, Kennedy (Bennett 63); Pitman (Chaplin 63).
Referee: Sebastian Stockbridge.

Morecambe (1) 3 *(Ellison 4, Fleming 67, Loach 85 (og))*
Hartlepool U (0) 0 2004
Morecambe: (4231) Roche; McGowan, Muller, Old, Brough; Kenyon, Fleming; Thompson (Rose 87), Wildig (Campbell 70), Ellison; McGurk (Oliver 65).
Hartlepool U: (4141) Loach; Richardson, Donnelly, Laing, Adams; Featherstone; Oates, George (Munns 75), Woods (Rodney 60), Deverdics; Franks.
Referee: Tom Nield.

Newport Co (1) 2 *(Nouble 18, McCoulsky 46)*
Walsall (0) 1 *(Bakayoko 77)* 2701
Newport Co: (532) Day; Pipe, White, O'Brien (Bennett 69), Demetriou, Butler; Tozer, Dolan, Willmott; McCoulsky (Amond 81), Nouble.
Walsall: (442) Gillespie; Kinsella, Donnellan, Guthrie, Leahy; Chambers, Edwards, Morris (Bakayoko 62), Ismail; Roberts T, Oztumer (Kouhyar 74).
Referee: Gavin Ward.

Northampton T (0) 0
Scunthorpe U (0) 0 2820
Northampton T: (433) Cornell; McWilliams, Taylor A, Pierre, Buchanan; Poole, McGugan, Powell; O'Toole (Richards 51), Long (Bowditch 85), Hoskins (Waters 70).
Scunthorpe U: (442) Gilks; Clarke, Burgess, McArdle, Wallace; Adelakun (Holmes 65), Crofts, Ojo, Morris; Hopper, Novak (van Veen 77).
Referee: Robert Jones.

Peterborough U (0) 1 *(Marriott 52)*
Tranmere R (0) 1 *(Cook 72)* 3750
Peterborough U: (4231) O'Malley; Baldwin, Taylor S, Tafazolli, Hughes; Doughty (Anderson 79), Grant; Maddison, Da Silva Lopes (Miller 86), Edwards (Kanu 71); Marriott.
Tranmere R: (433) Davies; McEveley, McNulty, Sutton, Ridehalgh; Norburn, Mottley-Henry, Hughes; Norwood, Jennings (Cole 69), McDonagh (Cook 68).
Referee: Charles Breakspear.

Plymouth Arg (1) 1 *(Carey 9)*
Grimsby T (0) 0 5137
Plymouth Arg: (4141) Matthews; Sawyer, Edwards, Bradley, Taylor-Sinclair; Songo'o; Carey, Fox, Diagouraga, Grant (Ainsworth 90); Jervis.
Grimsby T: (442) McKeown; Davies B, Collins, Clarke, Dixon; Dembele (Cardwell 81), Berrett, Summerfield, Woolford (Jaiyesimi 68); Vernon (Matt 68), Jones.
Referee: John Busby.

Rochdale (2) 4 *(Inman 10, 53, Henderson 31 (pen), 84)*
Bromley (0) 0 2241
Rochdale: (433) Lillis; Rafferty, McGahey, McNulty, Ntlhe; Rathbone (Kitching 84), Camps, Henderson; Inman, Done (Slew 81), Andrew.
Bromley: (442) Gregory; Dunne (Francis-Adeyinka 70), Johnson R (Sutherland 19), Holland, Johnson D; Wanadio (Mekki 58), Raymond, Higgs, Rees; Dennis, Williams■.
Referee: Andrew Miller.

Shaw Lane (1) 1 *(Bennett 41)*
Mansfield T (1) 3 *(Pearce 34, Rose 73, 78)* 1700
Shaw Lane: (4231) Stewart; Austin, Lugsden, Qualter, Serrant (Whitehouse 43); Norris, Harris; Byrne, Bennett (Reeves 72), Walker (Adabaki 86); Clayton.
Mansfield T: (442) Logan; Anderson, Diamond, Pearce, Benning; MacDonald, Mellis (Digby 90), Byrom, Hamilton; Rose (Spencer 82), Hemmings (Atkinson 90).
Referee: Ben Toner.

Shrewsbury T (2) 5 *(Rodman 20, Whalley 24 (pen), Payne 62, Gnahoua 66, Morris C 68)*
Aldershot T (0) 0 3859
Shrewsbury T: (4141) MacGillivray; Riley, Sadler, Nsiala, Beckles; Godfrey, Whalley, Morris B, Nolan (Gnahoua 44), Rodman (Morris C 67); Payne (Dodds 82).
Aldershot T: (4231) Smith; Alexander, Reynolds (Fowler 69), Evans, McDonnell, Oyeleke (Gallagher 69), Kellermann; Fenelon (Rowe 69), Robert, Mensah; Rendell.
Referee: Ross Joyce.

Stevenage (1) 5 *(Godden 16, 76, 89, Smith 68, 73)*
Nantwich T (0) 0 1436
Stevenage: (433) Fryer; Henry, Wilkinson, King J (Wilmot 84), Martin; Beautyman, Smith, Whelpdale (Gorman 64); Newton (Wootton 75), Godden, Pett.
Nantwich T: (4411) Jaaskelainen; Bourne (Webster 83), Stair, Mullarkey, Wildin; Morgan (Jones 65), Bichakhchyan, Hughes, Cotterell (Forbes 75); Cooke; Clayton.
Referee: Michael Salisbury.

Wigan Ath (1) 2 *(Toney 29, Evans 71)*
Crawley T (1) 1 *(Roberts 20)* 3288
Wigan Ath: (4231) Sarkic; Byrne, Burn, Bruce, James; Morsy, Evans; Roberts G (Colclough 81), Powell, Massey (Perkins 73); Toney (Grigg 74).
Crawley T: (4231) Morris; Young, McNerney, Connolly, Doherty (Clifford 80); Bulman (Tajbakhsh 74), Lelan; Boldewijn, Smith, Roberts (Verheijdt 60); Camara.
Referee: Martin Coy.

Yeovil T (1) 1 *(Khan 29 (pen))*
Southend U (0) 0 2079
Yeovil T: (433) Krysiak; Mugabi, Sowunmi, Smith N, James; Gray (Santos 83), Bailey, Worthington; Browne, Surridge, Khan.

Southend U: (442) Oxley; Demetriou, White, Ferdinand, Timlin; Wright (McGlashan 77), Leonard, Wordsworth (McLaughlin 55), Kightly; Fortune (Ranger 51), Cox.
Referee: Craig Hicks.

Sunday, 5 November 2017

Cambridge U (1) 1 *(Ibehre 45)*

Sutton U (0) 0 3070

Cambridge U: (442) Forde; Halliday, Legge, Taylor, Carroll (Taft 90); Mingoia (Lewis 82), O'Neil, Brown (Dunk 89), Maris■; Ikpeazu, Ibehre.
Sutton U: (442) Butler; John, Beckwith, Collins, Thomas A (Coombes 83); Cadogan, Davis, Bailey (Lafayette 27), Dundas; Wright (Jeffrey 62), Taylor.
Referee: Darren Handley.

Charlton Ath (1) 3 *(Reeves 10, 70, Marshall 53)*

Truro C (0) 1 *(Harvey 59)* 4494

Charlton Ath: (4231) Amos; Solly, Konsa, Sarr, Dasilva; Jackson, Forster-Caskey; Holmes, Reeves (Clarke 81), Marshall (Fosu 64); Dodoo (Ahearne-Grant 71).
Truro C: (442) McHale; Palfrey, Gerring, Richards, Riley-Lowe; Lamont (Yetton 84), Keats, Palmer, Harvey; Cooke (Allen 71), Harding (Neal 71).
Referee: Dean Whitestone.

Coventry C (2) 2 *(Ponticelli 33, 44)*

Maidenhead U (0) 0 3370

Coventry C: (4231) Burge; Grimmer, Davies, McDonald, Haynes; Doyle, Shipley (Maycock 74); Jones, McNulty, Vincenti (Biamou 46); Ponticelli (Nazon 74).
Maidenhead U: (442) Pentney; Clerima, Goodman, Massey, Steer; Barratt (Hyde 46), Comley, Upward, Pritchard (Peters 82); Clifton, Smith (Mulley 59).
Referee: Scott Duncan.

Dartford (3) 5 *(Sho-Silva 83)*

Swindon T (3) 5 *(Elsnik 12, 26, Smith H 23, Linganzi 47, Mullin 50)* 2705

Dartford: (451) Ibrahim; Harris, Sho-Silva, Bonner, Onyemah; Hayes (Mfula 67), Brown (Wood 66), Noble, Bradbrook, Della Verde (Murphy 54); Pavey.
Swindon T: (433) Charles-Cook; Purkiss, Lancashire, Preston, Taylor; Linganzi, Dunne, Elsnik (Goddard 38); McDermott (Gordon 74), Mullin (Woolery 54), Smith H.
Referee: Darren Drysdale.

Exeter C (0) 3 *(Stockley 59, 63, McAlinden 86)*

Heybridge Swifts (0) 1 *(Bantrick 70)* 3004

Exeter C: (442) Pym; Sweeney, Brown, Moore-Taylor, Woodman (Holmes 61); Taylor, James (Edwards 71), Boateng, Moxey; Reid (McAlinden 75), Stockley.
Heybridge Swifts: (442) Sambridge; Ramon, Henshaw, Cawley, Sampayo; Bantrick (Brown 87), Chatting, Griffiths (Godbold 64), Luque; Dark, Callander (Gardner 68).
Referee: Neil Hair.

Guiseley (0) 0

Accrington S (0) 0 1611

Guiseley: (442) Maxted; Brown, Palmer, M'Boungou, Holden; Hurst (Haworth 86), Lawlor, Lenighan, Molyneux (Rooney 80); Odejayi, Fondop-Talom.
Accrington S: (442) Chapman; Donacien, Hughes, Richards-Everton, Thorniley; Clark, Brown (Johnson 61), Conneely, McConville; Kee, Jackson.
Referee: Antony Coggins.

Leatherhead (1) 1 *(Midson 21)*

Billericay (0) 1 *(Bricknell 67 (pen))* 1797

Leatherhead: (442) Oualah; Clohessy, Ambroisine, Minshull, Richards; Blackman (Theobalds 81), Nnamani, Moore, Gallagher; McManus (Davies 82), Midson.
Billericay: (442) Julian; Evans, Chambers (Pennant 46), Swaine, Konchesky, Modeste, Deering, Waldren (Paine 62), Robinson; Theophanous (Bricknell 46), Cunnington.
Referee: Alan Dale.

Solihull Moors (0) 0

Wycombe W (2) 2 *(Freeman 16, Mackail-Smith 28)* 1544

Solihull Moors: (532) Bannister; Green K, Green P, St. Ledger, Daly, Asante; Carter, Sammons (Camwell 56), Murombedzi; Hylton, Afolayan (Carline 85).
Wycombe W: (4231) Brown; Freeman (Cowan-Hall 68), Stewart (El-Abd 74), Scarr, Jacobson; Gape, Bean; Saunders, Bloomfield, Mackail-Smith (Southwell 90); Akinfenwa.
Referee: Brett Huxtable.

Woking (1) 1 *(Philpot 25)*

Bury (1) 1 *(Smith 1)* 1858

Woking: (4231) Baxter; Young, Orlu, Wynter, Ralph; Jones, Isaac; Philpot, Charles-Cook (Appau 79), Ward; Effiong.
Bury: (3412) Fasan; Williams, Edwards, Aldred; Humphrey (Ince 58), Tutte, O'Shea, Leigh; Mayor (Alexandru Dobre 76); Maguire, Smith.
Referee: Darren England.

Monday, 6 November 2017

Chorley (0) 1 *(Carver 58)*

Fleetwood T (0) 2 *(Cole 77, Sowerby 90)* 3526

Chorley: (352) Byrne; Leather, Teague, Jordan; Challoner, O'Keefe, Wilson, Cottrell, Blakeman; Carver (Darr 90), Walker.
Fleetwood T: (352) Cairns; Bolger, Pond (Hiwula 61), Eastham; Coyle■, Dempsey, Glendon, O'Neill (Burns 64); Bell; Hunter (Sowerby 82), Cole.
Referee: Eddie Ilderton.

FIRST ROUND REPLAYS

Tuesday, 14 November 2017

Accrington S (0) 1 *(McConville 47)*

Guiseley (0) 1 *(Rooney 79 (pen))* 1166

Accrington S: (442) Chapman; Donacien, Richards-Everton, Hughes, Thorniley; Sousa (Leacock-McLeod 10 (Wilks 91)), Nolan, Johnson (Brown 80), McConville; Jackson, Kee.
Guiseley: (442) Maxted; Brown, M'Boungou■, Koue Niate, Holden; Hurst (McFadzean 107), Lawlor, Lenighan, Molyneux (Haworth 88); Fondop-Talom, Odejayi (Rooney 46).
aet; Guiseley won 4-3 on penalties.
Referee: Thomas Harty.

Bury (0) 0

Woking (1) 3 *(Charles-Cook 30, Effiong 71, Philpot 86)* 1513

Bury: (3412) Fasan; Aldred, O'Connell, Cameron (Maguire 74); Edwards, Danns (Reilly 69), Ince (Tutte 46), Leigh; O'Shea; Ajose, Smith.
Woking: (4231) Baxter; Young, Wynter, Orlu, Ralph; Jones, Isaac (Appau 90); Charles-Cook (Philpot 77), Ferdinand, Ward (Saraiva 84); Effiong.
Referee: Ross Joyce.

Scunthorpe U (1) 1 *(Adelakun 32)*

Northampton T (0) 0 1880

Scunthorpe U: (442) Gilks; Clarke, Goode, Wallace, Townsend; Adelakun (McArdle 86), Ojo, Burgess, Holmes (van Veen 76); Hopper, Novak (Madden 65).
Northampton T: (4411) Cornell; McWilliams, Taylor A, Pierre, McGivern; Bowditch (Waters 73), Kasim (O'Toole 83), Foley, Smith (McGugan 84); Crooks; Richards.
Referee: Robert Lewis.

Wednesday, 15 November 2017

Tranmere R (0) 0

Peterborough U (2) 5 *(Lloyd 16, 22, 73, Baldwin 67, Maddison 75 (pen))* 4199

Tranmere R: (3412) Davies; Sutton, McNulty, McEveley (Buxton 46); Mottley-Henry, Harris■, Norburn (Cole 73), Ridehalgh; Jennings; McDonagh (Cook 67), Norwood.
Peterborough U: (4312) O'Malley; Baldwin, Taylor S, Tafazolli (Forrester 77), Hughes; Da Silva Lopes, Grant, Doughty (Anderson 68); Maddison; Marriott (Kanu 69), Lloyd.
Referee: Michael Salisbury.

Thursday, 16 November 2017

Billericay (0) 1 *(Cunnington 61)*

Leatherhead (0) 3 *(Midson 68, 82 (pen), Moore 90)*   3400

Billericay: (343) Julian; Chambers (Modeste 46), Swaine■, Foley; Pennant (Waldren 46), Deering (Bricknell 66), Konchesky, Evans; Robinson, Cunnington, Theophanous.
Leatherhead: (343) Oualah; Ambroisine, Nnamani, Minshull; Clohessy, Moore, Blackman, Richards; McManus (Wood 88), Midson, Theobalds.
Referee: Dean Whitestone.

SECOND ROUND

Friday, 1 December 2017

AFC Fylde (0) 1 *(Rowe 70 (pen))*

Wigan Ath (1) 1 *(Grigg 44)*   3351

AFC Fylde: (4141) Lynch; Richards (Grand 89), Edmundson, Tunnicliffe, Francis-Angol; Montrose; Ezewele (Blinkhorn 62), Finley (Taylor 90), Bond, Smith; Rowe.
Wigan Ath: (4231) Jones; Byrne, Dunkley, Burn, James; Evans, Morsy; Massey (Powell 73), Power, Jacobs (Roberts G 90); Grigg (Toney 88).
Referee: Darren Drysdale.

Saturday, 2 December 2017

Bradford C (1) 3 *(Vincelot 38, Knight-Percival 50, Wyke 64)*

Plymouth Arg (0) 1 *(Carey 63)*   4957

Bradford C: (4411) Sattelmaier; McMahon, Knight-Percival, Kilgallon, Robinson; Gilliead, Reeves (Hendrie 66), Vincelot, Law; Taylor (Poleon 78); Wyke.
Plymouth Arg: (433) McCormick; Sawyer (Ainsworth 78), Edwards, Bradley, Taylor-Sinclair; Diagouraga, Songo'o (Taylor 66), Fox; Carey, Jervis, Grant (Sarcevic 80).
Referee: Tony Harrington.

Fleetwood T (1) 1 *(Cole 29)*

Hereford (1) 1 *(Dinsley 23)*   2567

Fleetwood T: (343) Neal; Eastham, Pond (Bolger 90), Cargill; Coyle, Glendon (O'Neill 73), Dempsey, Bell (Hiwula 64); Burns, Cole, Hunter.
Hereford: (451) Horsell; O'Shea, Deaman, Green, Oates; Smith (Symons 75), Murphy, Reffell, Dinsley (Haysham 87), Preen; Mills.
Referee: Sebastian Stockbridge.

Forest Green R (1) 3 *(Doidge 26, 90, Laird 88)*

Exeter C (0) 3 *(Moore-Taylor 58, Stockley 64, 90)*   2250

Forest Green R: (352) Collins B; Bennett, Roberts, Iacovitti, James, Brown (Stevens 82), Collins L, Laird, Wishart; Doidge, Bugiel (Correia Gomes 65).
Exeter C: (352) Pym; Sweeney, Archibald-Henville (Harley 55), Moore-Taylor; Wilson (Tillson 65), James, Taylor, Boateng, Moxey; Stockley, McAlinden (Reid 79).
Referee: Gavin Ward.

Gillingham (1) 1 *(O'Neill 5)*

Carlisle U (1) 1 *(Grainger 18 (pen))*   3178

Gillingham: (442) Holy; O'Neill, Ehmer, Zakuani, Ogilvie; Clare (Martin 46), Hessenthaler, Byrne, Wagstaff; Eaves (Parker 75), Wilkinson.
Carlisle U: (451) Bonham; Brown, Liddle, Hill, Grainger (Miller T 71); Lambe (Hope 88), Joyce, Parkes, Jones, Etuhu; Bennett (O'Sullivan 81).
Referee: Andy Woolmer.

Milton Keynes D (0) 4 *(Nesbitt 54, Agard 64, 70, Pawlett 89)*

Maidstone U (1) 1 *(Okuonghae 25)*   4804

Milton Keynes D: (4231) Nicholls; Williams GB, Wootton, Ebanks-Landell (Walsh 71), Golbourne; McGrandles, Upson; Nesbitt (Pawlett 80), Aneke, Ariyibi; Seager (Agard 63).
Maidstone U: (343) Worgan; Finney, Okuonghae, Wynter; Hare, Lewis, Reason (Paxman 83), Anderson; Hines (Loza 77), Sam-Yorke (Collins 68), Pigott.
Referee: Martin Coy.

Notts Co (1) 3 *(Duffy 31, Stead 56 (pen), Grant 90)*

Oxford C (0) 2 *(Sinclair 53, Paterson 73)*   5092

Notts Co: (442) Fitzsimons; Tootle, Duffy, Brisley, Dickinson; Hawkridge, Yates, Hewitt, Grant; Stead, Alessandra (Forte 66).
Oxford C: (4231) Stevens; Oxlade-Chamberlain, Oastler, Navarro, Grant (Fleet 72); Fofana, Poku; Pearce (Jones 85), Sinclair, McEachran; Paterson.
Referee: John Brooks.

Port Vale (0) 1 *(Pope 63)*

Yeovil T (0) 1 *(Green 89)*   3316

Port Vale: (4321) Boot; Gibbons, Anderson, Smith, Gunning; Worrall (Harness 71), Tonge, Montano (Forrester 46); Kay, Pugh (Denton 46); Pope.
Yeovil T: (442) Krysiak; James, Smith N, Sowunmi, Dickson; Olomola, Santos (Smith C 82), Bailey (Gobern 69), Khan (Green 68); Zoko, Surridge.
Referee: Scott Oldham.

Shrewsbury T (2) 2 *(Rodman 32, Whalley 37 (pen))*

Morecambe (0) 0   3184

Shrewsbury T: (4141) MacGillivray; Bolton, Beckles, Nsiala, Sadler; Morris B; Whalley (Morris C 80), Nolan, Godfrey (Dodds 59), Rodman (Gnahoua 70); Payne.
Morecambe: (4231) Roche; Lund, Muller, Old, Brough (McGowan 46); Kenyon (Oliver 46), Fleming; Thompson, Wildig, Campbell (Lang 78); McGurk.
Referee: Craig Hicks.

Stevenage (3) 5 *(Samuel 18, Godden 23, Pett 45, Newton 72, 77)*

Swindon T (2) 2 *(Linganzi 33, Taylor 42)*   1883

Stevenage: (442) Fryer; Henry, King J, Wilkinson, Martin; Whelpdale, Smith, McKee, Pett; Godden (Conlon 84), Samuel (Newton 54).
Swindon T: (4231) Vigouroux; Purkiss, Preston, Lancashire, Taylor; Dunne, Linganzi, Mullin, Goddard (Brophy 82), Woolery (Norris 46); Gordon (Smith H 64).
Referee: Nicholas Kinseley.

Sunday, 3 December 2017

AFC Wimbledon (1) 3 *(McDonald 10, Taylor 70, 81 (pen))*

Charlton Ath (1) 1 *(Ahearne-Grant 22)*   3270

AFC Wimbledon: (4231) Long; Fuller, Oshilaja, Charles, Meades; Trotter, Soares; Barcham (Kennedy 89), Forrester (Francomb 75), Taylor; McDonald (Abdou 82).
Charlton Ath: (4231) Amos; Dijksteel, Konsa, Sarr, Dasilva; Forster-Caskey, Aribo (Lennon 88); Marshall (Hackett-Fairchild 76), Ahearne-Grant (Best 74), Holmes; Magennis.
Referee: James Linington.

Blackburn R (3) 3 *(Samuel 11, 20, Graham 15)*

Crewe Alex (1) 3 *(Porter 35 (pen), 66, Nolan 63)*   4472

Blackburn R: (343) Leutwiler; Nyambe, Ward (Downing 46), Wharton; Caddis, Harper■, Evans, Bennett■; Samuel, Graham (Smallwood 46), Antonsson (Travis 57).
Crewe Alex: (3412) Richards; Walker (Nolan 46), Stubbs, Lowery; Ng, Bowery, Ainley (Reilly 87), Pickering; Cooper; Porter, Dagnall.
Referee: David Webb.

Coventry C (2) 3 *(Nazon 27, McNulty 40, Shipley 48)*

Boreham Wood (0) 0   2985

Coventry C: (4231) Burge; Grimmer, Willis, Davies, Haynes; Stevenson, Doyle (Bayliss 84); Nazon (Vincenti 65), Shipley (Devon Kelly-Evans 71), McNulty; Biamou.
Boreham Wood: (3412) Smith G; Champion, Stephens, Wells; Smith K, Ricketts (Turley 86), Murtagh, Shakes; Turgott (Balanta 60); Holman (Jeffers 60), Andrade.
Referee: Darren Handley.

Doncaster R (1) 3 *(Rowe 16, 67, Mandeville 90)*

Scunthorpe U (0) 0   5251

Doncaster R: (4411) Lawlor; Mason, Butler, Wright, Garrett (Toffolo 53); Blair (Kongolo 46), Whiteman, Rowe, Beestin (Mandeville 72); Coppinger; Marquis.
Scunthorpe U: (442) Gilks; Holmes, McArdle, Burgess, Wallace; Adelakun (van Veen 75), Bishop, Crofts (Goode 75), Morris; Madden, Hopper (Church 75).
Referee: Mark Heywood.

Gateshead (0) 0
Luton T (1) 5 *(Lee O 40, Potts 62, Lee E 67, Hylton 90,*
Berry 90) 1339
Gateshead: (433) Hanford; Tinkler, Byrne, Kerr, Barrow
(Fyfield 45); Hannant, Maxwell (Preston 54),
McLaughlin; Johnson, Burrow, O'Donnell (Peniket 55).
Luton T: (41212) Stech; Stacey, Mullins, Sheehan, Potts;
Rea (Ruddock 74); Lee O (Gambin 69), Berry; Shinnie;
Hylton, Lee E (Cook 69).
Referee: Ben Toner.

Mansfield T (1) 3 *(Spencer 31, 52, 65 (pen))*
Guiseley (0) 0 4081
Mansfield T: (442) Logan; White, Bennett, Diamond,
Hunt; Anderson (Potter 69), Atkinson, MacDonald
(Butcher 73), Hamilton; Spencer (Sterling-James 88),
Rose.
Guiseley: (442) Maxted; Brown, Palmer, M'Boungou■,
Holden■; Hughes (Hurst 46), Lenighan, Lawlor,
Molyneux (Purver 55); Fondop-Talom, Odejayi (Lowe
43).
Referee: Carl Boyeson.

Newport Co (1) 2 *(Labadie 2, 82)*
Cambridge U (0) 0 2748
Newport Co: (352) Day; White, O'Brien, Demetriou;
Pipe, Labadie (Rigg 84), Dolan (Willmott 77), Tozer,
Butler; McCoulsky (Amond 64), Nouble.
Cambridge U: (442) Forde; Halliday, Taylor, Legge,
Carroll; Brown, O'Neil, Elito, Dunk (Amoo 65); Ibehre
(Azeez 63), Ikpeazu.
Referee: Kevin Johnson.

Woking (0) 1 *(Ward 84)*
Peterborough U (1) 1 *(Tafazolli 24)* 3072
Woking: (343) Baxter; Ramsey (Young 63), Ralph, Jones;
Carter (Philpot 74), Ward, Ferdinand, Wynter; Isaac,
Effiong, Charles-Cook.
Peterborough U: (352) Bond; Hughes, Tafazolli, Penny;
Edwards (Baldwin 85), Forrester, Da Silva Lopes,
Taylor S, Grant; Maddison, Marriott.
Referee: Christopher Sarginson.

Wycombe W (1) 3 *(Saunders 29, Mackail-Smith 76,*
Akinfenwa 90)
Leatherhead (1) 1 *(Midson 8 (pen))* 3835
Wycombe W: (433) Brown; Jombati, Stewart, El-Abd,
Jacobson; Saunders (Scarr 84), O'Nien, Bloomfield;
Southwell (Freeman 62), Akinfenwa, Mackail-Smith.
Leatherhead: (541) Oualah; Clohessy, Ambroisine,
Nnamani, Minshull, Richards; McManus (Omofe 85),
Moore■, Blackman, Theobalds (Gallagher 70); Midson.
Referee: Tim Robinson.

Monday, 4 December 2017

Slough T (0) 0
Rochdale (1) 4 *(Andrew 13, Camps 68, Henderson 89,*
Done 90) 1950
Slough T: (4231) Turner; Smart (Fraser 80), Hollis,
Nisbet, Wells; Togwell, Dunn; Harris (Williams 59),
Lench, Dobson (Webb 75); Flood.
Rochdale: (433) Lillis; Rafferty, McGahey, Daniels,
Bunney; Rathbone, Camps, Henderson; Gillam (Done
64), Andrew, Inman (Cannon 70).
Referee: Robert Jones.

SECOND ROUND REPLAYS
Tuesday, 12 December 2017

Exeter C (0) 2 *(Sweeney 73 (pen), Stockley 115)*
Forest Green R (1) 1 *(Doidge 30 (pen))* 2923
Exeter C: (442) Pym; Sweeney, Moore-Taylor, Seaborne
(Harley 71), Woodman; Taylor, James, Tillson■, Moxey
(Boateng 53); Stockley, McAlinden (Edwards 71).
Forest Green R: (532) Collins B; Marsh-Brown (James
74), Monthe■, Collins L, Laird, Wishart; Stevens (Bugiel
58), Cooper, Brown; Doidge, Correia Gomes (Roberts
101).
aet.
Referee: Andy Davies.

Peterborough U (2) 5 *(Doughty 29, Marriott 45, 69,*
Maddison 78 (pen), Edwards 90)
Woking (1) 2 *(Effiong 19, Young 68)* 3022
Peterborough U: (4231) Bond; Penny, Tafazolli, Taylor S,
Hughes; Grant, Doughty (Forrester 84); Edwards, Da
Silva Lopes (Lloyd 61), Maddison; Marriott.
Woking: (4231) Baxter; Ramsey (Young 46), Orlu,
Wynter, Ralph; Ferdinand, Jones; Ward, Carter (Philpot
70), Saraiva (Banton 57); Effiong.
Referee: Antony Coggins.

Wigan Ath (1) 3 *(Toney 31, Grigg 80, 84)*
AFC Fylde (1) 2 *(Grand 40, Rowe 65)* 3124
Wigan Ath: (4231) Sarkic; Byrne, Burn, Bruce, Elder;
Perkins, Power; Roberts G (Dunkley 87), Massey (Hunt
73), Colclough (Grigg 61); Toney.
AFC Fylde: (433) Lynch; Richards, Tunnicliffe, Grand,
Francis-Angol; Finley, Montrose, Bond (Blinkhorn 85);
Ezewele (Muldoon 54), Rowe, Smith.
Referee: Darren England.

Yeovil T (1) 3 *(Khan 45 (pen), 95, Zoko 109)*
Port Vale (0) 2 *(Harness 83, Kay 108)* 1588
Yeovil T: (442) Krysiak; James, Sowunmi, Smith N,
Dickson; Gray (Green 77), Smith C (Worthington 27),
Bailey, Khan (Santos 115); Surridge (Olomola 69), Zoko.
Port Vale: (4141) Boot; Gibbons■, Smith, Anderson,
Gunning; Kay; Worrall (Harness 69), Whitfield (Denton
61), Tonge (Reeves 93), Montano■; Pope (Barnett 61).
aet.
Referee: Gavin Ward.

Wednesday, 13 December 2017

Crewe Alex (0) 0
Blackburn R (1) 1 *(Graham 24)* 2241
Crewe Alex: (442) Garratt; Ng, Raynes, Nolan,
Bakayogo; Ainley (Kirk 42), Lowery, Pickering, Cooper;
Porter (Reilly 79), Dagnall (Bowery 70).
Blackburn R: (442) Leutwiler; Caddis, Ward, Mulgrew,
Williams; Tomlinson, Harper (Travis 46), Smallwood,
Conway (Hart 56); Graham (Dack 63), Nuttall.
Referee: Anthony Backhouse.

Thursday, 14 December 2017

Hereford (0) 0
Fleetwood T (1) 2 *(Bolger 10, 58)* 4235
Hereford: (4411) Horsell; O'Shea, Deaman, Green,
Oates; Preen (Smith 69), Murphy, Dinsley, Symons;
Reffell; Mills.
Fleetwood T: (352) Cairns; Eastham, Bolger, Cargill;
Burns (Coyle 66), Sowerby, Glendon (Schwabl 83),
O'Neill, Bell; Hiwula (Hunter 72), Cole.
Referee: David Coote.

Tuesday, 19 December 2017

Carlisle U (2) 3 *(Hope 7, 37, Miller S 90)*
Gillingham (0) 1 *(Wagstaff 47)* 2357
Carlisle U: (352) Bonham; Liddle, Hill, Parkes; Brown
(Miller S 61), Lambe, Jones, Devitt (O'Sullivan 90),
Grainger (Miller T 90); Hope, Bennett.
Gillingham: (442) Holy; O'Neill, Lacey (Garmston 64),
Ehmer, Nugent; Wagstaff, Clare (List 81), Byrne
(Wilkinson 85), Martin; Eaves, Parker.
Referee: Mark Heywood.

THIRD ROUND
Friday, 5 January 2018

Liverpool (1) 2 *(Milner 35 (pen), van Dijk 84)*
Everton (0) 1 *(Sigurdsson 67)* 52,513
Liverpool: (4231) Karius; Gomez (Solanke 77), Matip,
van Dijk, Robertson; Can, Milner (Alexander-Arnold
77); Oxlade-Chamberlain, Lallana (Wijnaldum 70),
Mane; Firmino.
Everton: (4231) Pickford; Kenny, Holgate, Jagielka,
Martina; McCarthy (Davies 86), Schneiderlin; Bolasie,
Rooney (Lookman 52), Sigurdsson; Calvert-Lewin
(Niasse 82).
Referee: Robert Madley.

Manchester U (0) 2 *(Lingard 84, Lukaku 90)*
Derby Co (0) 0   73,899
Manchester U: (4141) Romero; Lindelof, Smalling, Blind, Shaw; Ander Herrera; Mata (Martial 67), Mkhitaryan (Lukaku 46), Pogba, Lingard; Rashford (Fellaini 80).
Derby Co: (4231) Carson; Wisdom, Keogh, Pearce, Olsson; Huddlestone, Thorne; Russell (Hanson 78), Lawrence (Bennett 81), Weimann; Winnall (Vydra 67).
Referee: Kevin Friend.

Saturday, 6 January 2018
Aston Villa (1) 1 *(Davis 8)*
Peterborough U (0) 3 *(Marriott 75, 90, Tafazolli 83)* 21,677
Aston Villa: (442) Steer; de Laet, Bree, Terry, Taylor; Onomah, Hourihane, Bjarnason (Hepburn-Murphy 80), Green (Lansbury 46); Davis, O'Hare (Grealish 80).
Peterborough U: (4231) Bond; Shephard, Tafazolli, Taylor S, Hughes; Forrester, Grant; Maddison, Da Silva Lopes (Morias 72), Lloyd; Marriott.
Referee: Robert Jones.

Birmingham C (0) 1 *(Gallagher 56)*
Burton Alb (0) 0   7623
Birmingham C: (4231) Stockdale; Colin, Roberts, Dean, Grounds; Gardner, Kieftenbeld; Maghoma (N'Doye 88), Davis, Boga (Dacres-Cogley 80); Gallagher.
Burton Alb: (343) Bywater; Turner, Buxton, McFadzean; Brayford (Sordell 74), Murphy (Akpan 86), Naylor, Flanagan; Miller (Sbarra 46), Akins, Dyer.
Referee: Jeremy Simpson.

Blackburn R (0) 0
Hull C (0) 1 *(Aina 58)*   6777
Blackburn R: (442) Leutwiler; Caddis, Nyambe, Mulgrew, Williams; Bennett, Tomlinson (Dack 61), Evans (Travis 43), Conway; Nuttall (Graham 61), Samuel.
Hull C: (4231) Marshall; Aina, Hector, Tomori, Clark; Henriksen, Stewart (Meyler 80); Bowen, Evandro (Irvine 61), Toral; Diomande (Campbell 76).
Referee: Oliver Langford.

Bolton W (0) 1 *(Osede 64)*
Huddersfield T (0) 2 *(van La Parra 51, Williams D 52)* 11,574
Bolton W: (532) Howard; Little (Hall 85), Beevers, Osede, Wheater, Robinson; Ameobi (Noone 76), Vela (King 85), Morais; Le Fondre, Wilbraham.
Huddersfield T: (442) Coleman; Smith, Kongolo, Hefele (Whitehead 85), Malone; Lolley (Billing 76), Hogg, Williams D, Sabiri; Depoitre, Quaner (van La Parra 39).
Referee: Roger East.

Bournemouth (0) 2 *(Mousset 55, Cook S 90)*
Wigan Ath (2) 2 *(Grigg 4, Hyndman 29 (og))*   9894
Bournemouth: (442) Boruc; Smith A, Cook S, Ake, Smith B (Pugh 46); Mahoney (Ibe 46), Hyndman, Surman, Fraser; Afobe (Wilson C 71), Mousset.
Wigan Ath: (4231) Walton; Byrne, Dunkley, Burn, James; Morsy, Power; Jacobs, Powell (Perkins 57), Massey (Roberts G 83); Grigg (Toney 65).
Referee: Andrew Madley.

Brentford (0) 0
Notts Co (0) 1 *(Stead 65)*   6935
Brentford: (451) Daniels; Clarke, Mepham, Barbet, Chatzitheodoridis (Canos 77); Jozefzoon, Mokotjo (Watkins 63), Macleod (Judge 70), McEachran, Marcondes; Maupay.
Notts Co: (442) Fitzsimons; Tootle, Brisley, Duffy, Jones; Grant (Walker 90), Yates, Hewitt, Hawkridge (Noble 74); Stead (Smith 81), Alessandra.
Referee: Tim Robinson.

Cardiff C (0) 0
Mansfield T (0) 0   6378
Cardiff C: (433) Murphy; Richards, Morrison (Damour 75), Ecuele Manga, Bennett; Paterson, Halford, Tomlin; Mendez-Laing, Zohore (Pilkington 80), Healey (Hoilett 77).

Mansfield T: (442) Logan; Anderson, Pearce, Bennett, Benning; Potter, Mellis (Atkinson 90), MacDonald, Hamilton; Hemmings (Spencer 45), Angol (Sterling-James 75).
Referee: Lee Probert.

Carlisle U (0) 0
Sheffield W (0) 0   7793
Carlisle U: (352) Bonham; Liddle, Hill, Parkes; Brown, Lambe (O'Sullivan 86), Jones, Devitt, Grainger; Cosgrove (Bennett 78), Hope (Miller S 78).
Sheffield W: (442) Wildsmith; Palmer, Frederico Venancio, Loovens, Fox; Jones, Wallace, Boyd (Rhodes 68), Reach; Nuhiu (Marco Matias 79), Lucas Joao.
Referee: David Webb.

Coventry C (1) 2 *(Willis 24, Grimmer 68)*
Stoke C (0) 1 *(Adam 54 (pen))*   14,199
Coventry C: (442) O'Brien; Grimmer, Willis, Davies, Stokes; Maguire-Drew (Stevenson 63), Bayliss, Doyle, Shipley (Haynes 90); Biamou, McNulty.
Stoke C: (352) Butland; Zouma, Cameron (Crouch 52), Wimmer; Edwards, Allen, Ireland (Choupo-Moting 72), Adam (Shaqiri 75), Sobhi; Berahino, Diouf.
Referee: Martin Atkinson.

Doncaster R (0) 0
Rochdale (1) 1 *(Andrew 18)*   4513
Doncaster R: (41212) Lawlor; Blair, Butler, Baudry, Mason (Garrett 79); Houghton; Kongolo, Rowe; Beestin (Coppinger 64); Marquis, May (Mandeville 88).
Rochdale: (352) Lillis; Daniels, McNulty, Ntlhe; Cannon (McGahey 90), Adshead (Keane 64), Henderson, Kitching, Bunney (Jordan LR Williams 69); Andrew, Done.
Referee: Andy Woolmer.

Exeter C (0) 0
WBA (2) 2 *(Rondon 2, Rodriguez 25)*   5638
Exeter C: (442) Pym; Sweeney, Archibald-Henville, Seaborne, Moxey; Taylor, Boateng (James 63), Tillson, Harley (Jay 87); McAlinden (Holmes 55), Stockley.
WBA: (442) Foster; Nyom, McAuley, Hegazi, Gibbs (Robson-Kanu 12); Brunt, Krychowiak (Livermore 85), Barry, McClean; Rodriguez (Field 69), Rondon.
Referee: Lee Mason.

Fleetwood T (0) 0
Leicester C (0) 0   5001
Fleetwood T: (433) Neal; Coyle, Bolger, Eastham (Pond 15); Bell; Glendon, Schwabl, Dempsey; Burns (McAleny 69), Cole, Hunter.
Leicester C: (433) Jakupovic; Amartey, Dragovic, Benalouane, Chilwell; Adrien Silva (Okazaki 57), King, James; Gray, Slimani (Iheanacho 80), Barnes (Albrighton 57).
Referee: Simon Hooper.

Fulham (0) 0
Southampton (1) 1 *(Ward-Prowse 29)*   17,327
Fulham: (433) Button; Fredericks, Kalas (Ojo 66), Ream, Odoi; Norwood, McDonald (Kebano 56), Johansen; Piazon, Rui Fonte (Kamara 76), Sessegnon R.
Southampton: (4231) McCarthy; Bednarek, Stephens, Yoshida, Bertrand; Romeu, Hojbjerg (Lemina 80); Ward-Prowse, Davis, Boufal (Redmond 70); Long (Gabbiadini 86).
Referee: Michael Oliver.

Ipswich T (0) 0
Sheffield U (1) 1 *(Thomas 25)*   12,057
Ipswich T: (4231) Bialkowski; Iorfa, Chambers, Knudsen, Kenlock; Connolly, Hyam (Waghorn 61); Sears, Bru, Celina; McGoldrick.
Sheffield U: (352) Blackman; Carter-Vickers, Stearman, Wright; Baldock, Carruthers, Thomas (Slater 46), Basham, Lafferty; Sharp (Fleck 88), Lavery (Donaldson 72).
Referee: Mike Jones.

Manchester C (0) 4 *(Aguero 56, 58, Sane 71,*
Bernardo Silva 82)
Burnley (1) 1 *(Barnes 25)* 53,285
Manchester C: (433) Bravo; Danilo, Stones, Otamendi,
Zinchenko (Walker 72); Gundogan (De Bruyne 76),
Fernandinho, Silva; Sterling, Aguero (Bernardo Silva 79),
Sane.
Burnley: (4411) Pope; Lowton, Long, Mee, Taylor;
Gudmundsson (Walters 75), Cork (Wells 69), Westwood,
Barnes; Hendrick; Vokes.
Referee: Graham Scott.

Middlesbrough (2) 2 *(Gestede 10, Braithwaite 42)*
Sunderland (0) 0 26,399
Middlesbrough: (4231) Randolph; Shotton, Ayala,
Gibson, Friend (Christie 90); Leadbitter, Howson; Traore
(Johnson 81), Braithwaite (Clayton 65), Downing;
Gestede.
Sunderland: (541) Steele; Jones, Browning, O'Shea,
Wilson, Oviedo; Honeyman, Love, Robson (Embleton
81), McManaman (Asoro 53); Maja (Vaughan 74).
Referee: Chris Kavanagh.

Millwall (1) 4 *(O'Brien 35, 56, Thompson 47,*
Onyedinma 61)
Barnsley (1) 1 *(Potts 11)* 5319
Millwall: (442) Martin; McLaughlin, Hutchinson, Cooper,
Craig; Wallace (Twardek 75), Thompson, Williams J,
Onyedinma (Romeo 85); Morison (Gregory 72),
O'Brien.
Barnsley: (433) Davies; Cavare, Pinnock, Lindsay,
McCarthy; Gardner, Williams■, Potts (Mallan 73);
Isgrove (Moncur 64), Bradshaw, Hammill (Thiam 64).
Referee: Darren Bond.

Newcastle U (3) 3 *(Perez 30, 36, Shelvey 39)*
Luton T (0) 1 *(Hylton 49)* 47,069
Newcastle U: (4231) Woodman; Manquillo, Lascelles
(Hayden 30), Clark, Dummett; Shelvey (Diame 71),
Merino (Saivet 81); Murphy, Perez, Ritchie; Gayle.
Luton T: (4312) Stech; Justin, Mullins, Rea, Potts; Lee O,
Ruddock (Cornick 46), Berry; Shinnie (Gambin 82);
Collins (Lee E 68), Hylton.
Referee: Neil Swarbrick.

Norwich C (0) 0
Chelsea (0) 0 23,598
Norwich C: (343) Gunn; Hanley, Zimmermann, Klose;
Ivo Pinto, Tettey, Trybull, Lewis; Pritchard (Wildschut
87), Maddison, Murphy (Oliveira 83).
Chelsea: (343) Caballero; Rudiger, Luiz, Cahill;
Zappacosta, Drinkwater, Bakayoko, Kenedy (Musonda
78); Willian, Batshuayi (Morata 74), Pedro (Sterling 89).
Referee: Stuart Attwell.

QPR (0) 0
Milton Keynes D (0) 1 *(Cisse 60)* 6314
QPR: (352) Smithies; Baptiste (Hall 11), Onuoha,
Robinson; Cousins (Wszolek 46), Chair (Eze 61),
Scowen, Freeman, Bidwell; Smyth, Smith.
Milton Keynes D: (442) Nicholls; Williams GB, Walsh,
Cisse, Wootton; Brittain (Ebanks-Landell 80),
McGrandles, Upson, Muirhead (Agard 77); Aneke, Ugbo
(Thomas-Asante 90).
Referee: James Linington.

Stevenage (0) 0
Reading (0) 0 3877
Stevenage: (442) King T; Henry, King J, Wilmot (Franks
89); Martin; Pett, Smith, McKee, Kennedy (Samuel 73);
Godden, Newton.
Reading: (442) Jaakkola; Bacuna (Gunter 90), Richards,
McShane, Tiago Ilori; van den Berg, Evans, Edwards
(Swift 81), Kelly; McCleary (Kermorgant 65), Barrow.
Referee: Ben Toner.

Watford (1) 3 *(Carrillo 37, Deeney 57, Capoue 85)*
Bristol C (0) 0 13,269
Watford: (451) Gomes; Janmaat, Wague, Kabasele,
Zeegelaar; Pereyra (Holebas 70), Capoue, Cleverley,
Doucoure (Watson 81), Carrillo (Richarlison 69);
Deeney.
Bristol C: (442) Steele; Vyner, Magnusson, Flint, Kelly;
Eliasson, Smith (Pack 46), Edwards, Lemonheigh-Evans;
Woodrow (Hinds 77), Taylor (Engvall 63).
Referee: Craig Pawson.

Wolverhampton W (0) 0
Swansea C (0) 0 22,976
Wolverhampton W: (343) Norris; Bennett, Coady, Hause;
Doherty, Gibbs-White (Douglas 45), N'Diaye, Ruben
Vinagre■; Helder Costa, Leo Bonatini (Mir 77),
Enobakhare (Ivan Cavaleiro 65).
Swansea C: (352) Nordfeldt; Roberts, Fernandez (Ayew J
56), van der Hoorn; Bartley, Dyer, Fer■, Sanches (Carroll
34), Olsson; Routledge, Bony (Roque 74).
Referee: Anthony Taylor.

Wycombe W (1) 1 *(O'Nien 45)*
Preston NE (2) 5 *(Harrop 2, 85, Browne 38, 78 (pen),*
Horgan 50) 4928
Wycombe W: (433) Brown; Bean, Scarr, El-Abd,
Jacobson (Cowan-Hall 79); Saunders (De Havilland 46),
O'Nien, Bloomfield (Kashket 71); Freeman, Akinfenwa,
Tyson.
Preston NE: (433) Rudd; Woods (Boyle 79), Clarke,
Huntington, Cunningham; Browne, Welsh, Harrop;
Horgan, Robinson (Gallagher 84), Bodin (Johnson 79).
Referee: Peter Bankes.

Yeovil T (0) 2 *(Barnes 61, Green 76)*
Bradford C (0) 0 3040
Yeovil T: (442) Krysiak; James, Mugabi, Smith N,
Dickson; Gray, Green, Bird (Wing 78), Khan (Santos 90);
Zoko, Barnes (Whelan 85).
Bradford C: (442) Raeder; Hanson, Kilgallon (Thompson
46), Vincelot, Robinson; Gilliead, Law, Dieng (Devine
70), McCartan (Poleon 75); Wyke, Taylor.
Referee: John Brooks.

Sunday, 7 January 2018
Newport Co (0) 2 *(Shaughnessy 76 (og), McCoulsky 89)*
Leeds U (1) 1 *(Berardi 9)* 6887
Newport Co: (451) Day; Pipe, White, Demetriou, Butler;
Willmott (O'Brien 90), Bennett, Labadie, Dolan
(McCoulsky 69), Nouble; Amond (Hayes 86).
Leeds U: (442) Lonergan; Anita, Shaughnessy, Berardi,
Borthwick-Jackson (Cooper 60); Sacko, Phillips, Klich,
Cibicki; Grot (Samuel■ 75), Lasogga.
Referee: Mike Dean.

Nottingham F (2) 4 *(Lichaj 20, 44, Brereton 64 (pen),*
Dowell 85 (pen))
Arsenal (1) 2 *(Mertesacker 23, Welbeck 79)* 27,182
Nottingham F: (4231) Smith; Lichaj, Worrall■,
Mancienne, Traore; Vaughan, Osborn; Cash (McKay 87),
Dowell (Mills 90), Clough (Walker 56); Brereton.
Arsenal: (4231) Ospina; Debuchy (Akpom 87),
Mertesacker, Holding, Maitland-Niles; Elneny, Willock
(Nketiah 65); Walcott, Iwobi, Nelson; Welbeck.
Referee: Jon Moss.

Shrewsbury T (0) 0
West Ham U (0) 0 9535
Shrewsbury T: (4141) Henderson; Bolton, Nsiala, Sadler,
Beckles; Godfrey; Whalley (Gnahoua 88), Nolan, Ogogo,
Rodman (Lowe 76); Morris C (Payne 82).
West Ham U: (352) Hart; Reid (Quina 86), Ogbonna,
Rice; Burke, Cullen, Obiang, Kouyate, Masuaku;
Hernandez (Martinez 71), Ayew.
Referee: Paul Tierney.

Tottenham H (0) 3 *(Kane 63, 65, Vertonghen 71)*

AFC Wimbledon (0) 0   47,527

Tottenham H: (442) Vorm; Trippier, Foyth, Vertonghen, Walker-Peters; Sissoko (Alli 65), Wanyama, Dembele, Lamela; Kane (Nkoudou 79), Llorente (Son 59).
AFC Wimbledon: (451) Long; Fuller, Oshilaja, Charles, Meades; Francomb, Soares (Hartigan 79), Trotter, Abdou (McDonald 70), Barcham (Forrester 69); Taylor.
Referee: David Coote.

Monday, 8 January 2018

Brighton & HA (1) 2 *(Stephens 25, Murray 87)*

Crystal Palace (0) 1 *(Sako 69)*   14,507

Brighton & HA: (442) Krul; Schelotto, Goldson, Hunemeier, Bong; March, Stephens (Propper 61), Kayal, Izquierdo; Brown (Baldock 6), Hemed (Murray 81).
Crystal Palace: (4231) Hennessey; Fosu-Mensah, Kelly, Delaney, Schlupp (Souare 13); Cabaye, Riedewald; Townsend (KaiKai 46), McArthur, Van Aanholt; Sako.
Referee: Andre Marriner.

THIRD ROUND REPLAYS

Tuesday, 16 January 2018

Leicester C (1) 2 *(Iheanacho 43, 77)*

Fleetwood T (0) 0   17,237

Leicester C: (4411) Jakupovic; Amartey, Dragovic, Benalouane, Fuchs; Mahrez (Vardy 81), Adrien Silva, Iborra, Gray; Iheanacho (Okazaki 81); Slimani (Albrighton 56).
Fleetwood T: (451) Neal; Jones, Pond, Bolger, Bell; Hunter, Glendon, Schwabl (Grant 72), Dempsey, McAleny (Burns 65); Hiwula (Cole 65).
Referee: Jonathan Moss.

Mansfield T (1) 1 *(Rose 35)*

Cardiff C (1) 4 *(Ecuele Manga 34, Hoilett 66, 89, Pilkington 71)*   5746

Mansfield T: (4411) Logan; White, Bennett, Pearce, Benning; Anderson (Potter 79), Mellis, Byrom (Angol 74), Hamilton; MacDonald; Rose.
Cardiff C: (4231) Etheridge; Richards, Ecuele Manga, Morrison, Bennett; Paterson, Ralls (Halford 74); Pilkington, Damour, Hoilett (Healey 90); Zohore (Bogle 85).
Referee: Geoff Eltringham.

Reading (2) 3 *(Bodvarsson 32, 44, 64)*

Stevenage (0) 0   4986

Reading: (4231) Jaakkola; Bacuna (Richards 80), Tiago Ilori, Blackett, Gunter; Edwards, Kelly; Aluko, Clement, Beerens; Bodvarsson.
Stevenage: (442) King T; Henry, King J, Wilmot, Martin; Pett, Smith, McKee (Conlon 71), Kennedy (Samuel 71); Newton (Georgiou 85), Godden.
Referee: Tim Robinson.

Sheffield W (1) 2 *(Marco Matias 28, Nuhiu 66)*

Carlisle U (0) 0   12,003

Sheffield W: (532) Dawson; Hunt, O'Grady, Frederico Venancio, Nielsen, Fox; Jones (Reach 79), Butterfield, Boyd; Nuhiu, Marco Matias.
Carlisle U: (541) Bonham; Brown (O'Sullivan 64), Liddle, Ellis (Miller S 67), Parkes, Grainger; Lambe, Joyce, Jones, Devitt; Bennett (Hope 58).
Referee: Michael Salisbury.

West Ham U (0) 1 *(Burke 112)*

Shrewsbury T (0) 0   39,867

West Ham U: (352) Hart; Byram (Zabaleta 90), Burke, Ogbonna; Oxford (Noble 69), Masuaku, Cullen, Obiang, Lanzini; Ayew (Arnautovic 69), Martinez.
Shrewsbury T: (4141) Henderson; Beckles, Sadler, Nsiala, Lowe (Bolton 101); Godfrey; Riley (Dodds 74), Nolan, Ogogo, Whalley (Rodman 78); Payne (Morris C 84).
aet.
Referee: Jeremy Simpson.

Wednesday, 17 January 2018

Chelsea (0) 1 *(Batshuayi 55)*

Norwich C (0) 1 *(Lewis 90)*   39,684

Chelsea: (343) Caballero; Ampadu (Christensen 81), Luiz, Azpilicueta; Zappacosta, Drinkwater (Hazard E 100), Bakayoko, Kenedy (Kante 86); Willian, Batshuayi (Morata■ 81), Pedro■.
Norwich C: (3412) Gunn; Hanley (Cantwell 86 (Stiepermann 120)), Zimmermann, Klose; Ivo Pinto (Tettey 116), Reed (Hoolahan 82), Vrancic, Lewis; Maddison; Oliveira, Murphy.
aet; Chelsea won 5-3 on penalties.
Referee: Graham Scott.

Swansea C (1) 2 *(Ayew J 11, Bony 69)*

Wolverhampton W (0) 1 *(Jota 66)*   8294

Swansea C: (4231) Nordfeldt; Roberts, Mawson, Fernandez, Naughton; Carroll, Roque (Ki 73); Narsingh (Dyer 73), Fer, Ayew J; Bony (Clucas 79).
Wolverhampton W: (343) Norris; Roderick Miranda, Batth, Hause; Doherty, Gibbs-White, N'Diaye, Douglas; Helder Costa (Saiss 73), Mir (Leo Bonatini 64), Enobakhare (Jota 64).
Referee: Chris Kavanagh.

Wigan Ath (1) 3 *(Morsy 9, Burn 73, Elder 76)*

Bournemouth (0) 0   4709

Wigan Ath: (4231) Jones; Power, Dunkley, Bruce, Elder; Perkins, Morsy; Colclough (Burn 71), Roberts G (Jacobs 86), Massey; Grigg (Hunt 51).
Bournemouth: (4411) Boruc; Fraser (Hyndman 78), Cook S, Simpson, Daniels; Mahoney (Ibe 64), Surman (Taylor 87), Arter, Pugh; Mousset; Afobe.
Referee: Stuart Attwell.

FOURTH ROUND

Friday, 26 January 2018

Sheffield W (1) 3 *(Nuhiu 29, 53, Boyd 61)*

Reading (0) 1 *(Dawson 87 (og))*   14,848

Sheffield W: (532) Dawson; Hunt, Frederico Venancio, Loovens, Pudil (Palmer 63), Fox; Boyd, Pelupessy, Reach (Jones 71); Marco Matias (Rhodes 89), Nuhiu.
Reading: (442) Jaakkola; Gunter, Moore, Tiago Ilori, Bacuna (Evans 79); Beerens, Clement, Edwards, McCleary (Barrow 66); Kermorgant (Smith 79), Bodvarsson.
Referee: John Brooks.

Yeovil T (0) 0

Manchester U (1) 4 *(Rashford 41, Ander Herrera 61, Lingard 89, Lukaku 90)*   9195

Yeovil T: (442) Krysiak; James, Sowunmi, Smith N, Dickson; Gray, Wing (Smith C 83), Bird (Browne 56), Green (Fisher 69); Surridge, Zoko.
Manchester U: (433) Romero; Darmian, Lindelof, Rojo, Shaw; Ander Herrera, Carrick, McTominay; Mata (Lukaku 65), Rashford (Gomes 88), Sanchez (Lingard 72).
Referee: Paul Tierney.

Saturday, 27 January 2018

Huddersfield T (1) 1 *(Mounie 21)*

Birmingham C (0) 1 *(Jutkiewicz 54)*   13,047

Huddersfield T: (4231) Coleman; Hadergjonaj, Hefele, Kongolo, Lowe (Malone 82); Hogg, Williams D (Billing 36); Quaner, Sabiri, van La Parra (Lolley 57); Mounie.
Birmingham C: (3511) Stockdale; Dean (Grounds 46), Roberts, Jenkinson; Lowe (Gardner 88), Morrison, N'Doye, Adams (Boga 76), Bramall; Jota; Jutkiewicz.
Referee: Neil Swarbrick.

Hull C (2) 2 *(Bowen 18, Dicko 40)*

Nottingham F (0) 1 *(Vellios 88)*   13,450

Hull C: (4231) Marshall; Aina, Mazuch, Hector, Clark; Stewart, Henriksen; Bowen, Irvine (Batty 87), Diomande (Grosicki 71); Dicko (Keane 63).
Nottingham F: (4231) Smith; Lichaj, Worrall, Mancienne, Fox; Carayol (Clough 46), Bouchalakis (Vaughan 46); Cash, Osborn, Dowell; Brereton (Vellios 81).
Referee: Stuart Attwell.

Liverpool (1) 2 *(Firmino 5, Salah 78)*
WBA (3) 3 *(Rodriguez 7, 11, Matip 45 (og))*　53,342
Liverpool: (433) Mignolet; Alexander-Arnold, Matip, van Dijk, Moreno; Oxlade-Chamberlain (Ings 65), Can (Milner 65), Wijnaldum; Salah, Firmino, Mane (Henderson 65).
WBA: (442) Foster; Nyom, Dawson, Evans, Gibbs (Hegazi 37); Livermore, Barry (Yacob 71), Krychowiak, Brunt; Robson-Kanu (Phillips 39), Rodriguez.
Referee: Craig Pawson.

Middlesbrough (0) 0
Brighton & HA (0) 1 *(Murray 90)*　20,475
Middlesbrough: (4231) Randolph; Shotton, Ayala (Fry 65), Gibson, Friend; Howson, Clayton; Traore, Braithwaite (Downing 56), Bamford; Fletcher (Assombalonga 56).
Brighton & HA: (442) Krul; Rosenior, Goldson, Hunemeier, Suttner; Knockaert, Stephens (Propper 46), Kayal, Skalak (Izquierdo 61); Baldock, Hemed (Murray 72).
Referee: Anthony Taylor.

Millwall (1) 2 *(Wallace 17 (pen), Thompson 90)*
Rochdale (1) 2 *(Henderson 32, Done 53)*　8346
Millwall: (442) Martin; Romeo, Cooper, Shackell (Morison 59), Craig; Wallace, Thompson, Tunnicliffe (Williams 84), Ferguson; Onyedinma (Gregory 85), Elliott.
Rochdale: (352) Lillis; Daniels, McNulty, Delaney; Rafferty, Cannon (Rathbone 80), Camps (Adshead 51), Kitching, Done; Henderson, Andrew.
Referee: Andrew Madley.

Milton Keynes D (0) 0
Coventry C (0) 1 *(Biamou 64)*　14,925
Milton Keynes D: (4231) Nicholls; Williams GB, Wootton, Cisse, Lewington (Ebanks-Landell 56); Upson (McGrandles 75), Gilbey; Tavernier, Agard (Nesbitt 66), Ugbo; Sow.
Coventry C: (433) Burge; Grimmer, Willis, McDonald, Stokes; Bayliss (Dion Kelly-Evans 82), Kelly (Stevenson 76), Doyle; McNulty, Biamou, Barrett (Shipley 59).
Referee: Peter Banks.

Newport Co (1) 1 *(Amond 38)*
Tottenham H (0) 1 *(Kane 82)*　9836
Newport Co: (451) Day; Pipe, White, Demetriou, Butler; Willmott, Tozer, Labadie (Dolan 84), Bennett, Nouble; Amond (McCoulsky 74).
Tottenham H: (3142) Vorm; Foyth, Dier, Vertonghen; Wanyama; Trippier, Sissoko, Dembele (Davies 81), Walker-Peters (Son 46); Llorente (Alli 66), Kane.
Referee: Roger East.

Notts Co (0) 1 *(Stead 62)*
Swansea C (1) 1 *(Narsingh 45)*　9802
Notts Co: (442) Collin; Hunt, Duffy, Brisley, Dickinson; Grant, Husin (Smith 90), Hewitt, Hawkridge; Ameobi (Alessandra 84), Stead.
Swansea C: (343) Nordfeldt; van der Hoorn, Bartley, Mawson; Roberts, Fer (Clucas 63), Sanches (Ki 32), Carroll; Narsingh, Bony, Abraham (Ayew J 70).
Referee: Michael Jones.

Peterborough U (0) 1 *(Hughes 58)*
Leicester C (3) 5 *(Diabate 9, 87, Iheanacho 12, 29, Ndidi 90)*　13,193
Peterborough U: (4231) Bond; Shephard, Taylor S, Tafazolli, Hughes; Forrester, Grant; Maddison (Borg 89), Da Silva Lopes (Morias 61), Lloyd (Kanu 80); Marriott.
Leicester C: (4231) Hamer; Simpson, Benalouane, Maguire, Fuchs; Adrien Silva, Iborra (Albrighton 65); Diabate, Barnes (Ndidi 64), Gray; Iheanacho (Chilwell 80).
Referee: Michael Oliver.

Sheffield U (0) 1 *(Sharp 80 (pen))*
Preston NE (0) 0　15,680
Sheffield U: (352) Moore; Lundstram, Wright, Stearman; Baldock, Fleck, Duffy, Heneghan (Basham 59), Lafferty; Sharp (Stevens 90), Donaldson (Evans C 59).
Preston NE: (4231) Rudd; Clarke, Fisher (Woods 68), Huntington, Earl; Horgan (Barkhuizen 59), Browne; Welsh (Hugill 68), Johnson, Bodin; Moult.
Referee: Graham Scott.

Southampton (1) 1 *(Stephens 4)*
Watford (0) 0　25,195
Southampton: (4231) McCarthy; Cedric, Stephens, Hoedt, Bertrand (Pied 40); Romeu, Davis; Hojbjerg, Boufal (Yoshida 67), Tadic (Carrillo 83); Long.
Watford: (4231) Karnezis; Janmaat (Sinclair 74), Mariappa, Kabasele, Holebas; Watson, Capoue (Okaka 46); Richarlison, Carrillo (Pereyra 57), Doucoure; Gray.
Referee: Robert Madley.

Wigan Ath (1) 2 *(Grigg 7, 62 (pen))*
West Ham U (0) 0　14,194
Wigan Ath: (4231) Walton; Byrne, Dunkley, Burn, Elder (James 86); Power, Morsy; Massey (Colclough 76), Powell, Jacobs; Grigg (Roberts G 88).
West Ham U: (442) Hart; Zabaleta (Joao Mario 46), Burke, Ogbonna, Cresswell; Byram, Cullen, Obiang (Oxford 36), Masuaku■; Martinez (Haksabanovic 81), Hernandez.
Referee: Chris Kavanagh.

Sunday, 28 January 2018
Cardiff C (0) 0
Manchester C (2) 2 *(De Bruyne 8, Sterling 37)*　32,339
Cardiff C: (4231) Etheridge; Richards, Morrison, Ecuele Manga, Bennett■; Grujic, Ralls (Damour 88); Mendez-Laing (Feeney 78), Paterson, Hoilett; Zohore (Pilkington 67).
Manchester C: (433) Bravo; Walker, Kompany, Otamendi, Danilo; De Bruyne, Fernandinho, Gundogan; Bernardo Silva (Diaz 89), Sterling, Sane (Aguero 46).
Referee: Lee Mason.

Chelsea (2) 3 *(Batshuayi 31, 44, Alonso 72)*
Newcastle U (0) 0　41,049
Chelsea: (3421) Caballero; Rudiger, Christensen, Cahill; Zappacosta, Drinkwater, Kante (Ampadu 78), Alonso; Pedro (Hudson-Odoi 81), Hazard E (Barkley 73); Batshuayi.
Newcastle U: (532) Darlow; Manquillo (Murphy 77), Mbemba, Lascelles, Clark, Haidara; Hayden (Atsu 83), Saivet, Shelvey; Ritchie, Gayle (Joselu 64).
Referee: Kevin Friend.

FOURTH ROUND REPLAYS
Tuesday, 6 February 2018
Birmingham C (0) 1 *(Adams 52)*
Huddersfield T (0) 4 *(Roberts 60 (og), Mounie 94, van La Parra 97, Ince 106)*　13,175
Birmingham C: (352) Stockdale; Dean, Roberts, Morrison; Jenkinson (Dacres-Cogley 71), Lowe (Lakin 101), Gardner, N'Doye (Jota 46), Bramall; Jutkiewicz (Boga 86), Adams.
Huddersfield T: (442) Lossl; Smith (Hadergjonaj 46), Kongolo, Jorgensen, Malone (Lowe 95); Sabiri (van La Parra 56), Billing, Mooy, Ince; Quaner (Scannell 99), Mounie.
aet.
Referee: Chris Kavanagh.

Rochdale (0) 1 *(Henderson 53)*
Millwall (0) 0　2790
Rochdale: (352) Lillis; McGahey, McNulty, Delaney; Rafferty, Cannon, Camps, Kitching, Done; Henderson, Andrew.
Millwall: (442) Martin; McLaughlin, Hutchinson, Shackell, Meredith; Tunnicliffe (Gregory 63), Williams, Thompson, Ferguson (Morison 63); Elliott, Onyedinma (Wallace 77).
Referee: Tim Robinson.

Swansea C (4) 8 *(Abraham 18, 45, Dyer 20, 30,*
Naughton 53, Routledge 57, Carroll 65, James 82)
Notts Co (1) 1 *(Husin 35)*   7822

Swansea C: (4411) Nordfeldt; Naughton, van der Hoorn (Maric 78), Bartley, Roberts; Narsingh, Carroll, Clucas (Ki 46); Routledge; Dyer (James 62); Abraham.
Notts Co: (4411) Collin; Hunt, Duffy, Brisley, Dickinson; Grant, Virtue, Husin (Milsom 62), Hawkridge; Alessandra (Forte 62); Stead (Smith 64).
Referee: Martin Atkinson.

Wednesday, 7 February 2018

Tottenham H (2) 2 *(Butler 26 (og), Lamela 34)*
Newport Co (0) 0   38,947

Tottenham H: (4231) Vorm; Aurier, Foyth, Alderweireld, Rose (Walker-Peters 86); Wanyama (Alli 78), Winks; Sissoko, Lamela, Son (Eriksen 61); Llorente.
Newport Co: (451) Day; Pipe (McCoulsky 67), White (O'Brien 77), Demetriou, Butler; Willmott, Tozer (Dolan 59), Labadie, Bennett, Nouble; Amond.
Referee: Stuart Attwell.

FIFTH ROUND

Friday, 16 February 2018

Chelsea (4) 4 *(Willian 2, 32, Pedro 27, Giroud 42)*
Hull C (0) 0   39,591

Chelsea: (343) Caballero; Rudiger, Ampadu, Cahill; Zappacosta, Drinkwater, Fabregas (Scott 62), Emerson; Willian, Giroud (Morata 70), Pedro (Hudson-Odoi 46).
Hull C: (4141) Marshall; Meyler, Dawson, MacDonald, Clark; Stewart; Wilson (Toral 55), Evandro, Irvine (Batty 88), Diomande; Dicko (Campbell 72).
Referee: Andre Marriner.

Leicester C (0) 1 *(Vardy 66)*
Sheffield U (0) 0   28,336

Leicester C: (4411) Schmeichel; Simpson, Morgan, Maguire, Chilwell; Gray, Iborra, Ndidi, Mahrez (James 90); Iheanacho; Vardy (Albrighton 84).
Sheffield U: (352) Blackman; Basham, Wright (Evans C 76), O'Connell; Baldock, Carruthers (Duffy 76), Lundstram, Lafferty, Stevens; Donaldson, Wilson (Brooks 46).
Referee: Lee Mason.

Saturday, 17 February 2018

Brighton & HA (2) 3 *(Locadia 15, Goldson 34, Ulloa 61)*
Coventry C (0) 1 *(Clarke-Harris 77)*   26,966

Brighton & HA: (442) Krul (Maenpaa 46); Saltor, Goldson, Hunemeier, Suttner; Knockaert, Kayal, Stephens (Propper 46), March; Locadia (Baldock 77), Ulloa.
Coventry C: (442) Burge; Grimmer (McDonald 57), Willis, Hyam, Haynes; Bayliss, Kelly, Shipley, Barrett (Biamou 79); McNulty (Ponticelli 74), Clarke-Harris.
Referee: Craig Pawson.

Huddersfield T (0) 0
Manchester U (1) 2 *(Lukaku 3, 55)*   17,861

Huddersfield T: (4231) Lossl; Hadergjonaj (Smith 70), Jorgensen, Schindler, Kongolo (Malone 70); Williams D, Billing; Quaner, Ince, van La Parra (Sabiri 84); Mounie.
Manchester U: (433) Romero; Young, Smalling, Lindelof, Shaw; McTominay, Carrick, Matic; Mata (Lingard 81), Lukaku (Bailly 90), Sanchez (Martial 75).
Referee: Kevin Friend.

Sheffield W (0) 0
Swansea C (0) 0   19,427

Sheffield W: (352) Dawson; Frederico Venancio, Pudil, Fox; Hunt, Butterfield (Pelupessy 70), Jones, Reach, Boyd; Wallace (Lucas Joao 80), Nuhiu.
Swansea C: (343) Nordfeldt; Naughton, Bartley, van der Hoorn; Roberts, Ki, Carroll, Olsson (Clucas 79); Narsingh (Dyer 64), Abraham (Ayew J 67), Routledge.
Referee: Paul Tierney.

WBA (0) 1 *(Rondon 58)*
Southampton (1) 2 *(Hoedt 11, Tadic 56)*   17,600

WBA: (442) Foster; Dawson, McAuley, Hegazi, Evans; Phillips (Burke 89), Krychowiak (Field 82), Barry (Brunt 72), McClean; Rondon, Rodriguez.
Southampton: (4231) McCarthy; Cedric, Stephens, Hoedt, Bertrand; Hojbjerg (Romeu 78), Lemina; Ward-Prowse, Tadic, Redmond (Gabbiadini 72); Carrillo (Sims 85).
Referee: Chris Kavanagh.

Sunday, 18 February 2018

Rochdale (1) 2 *(Henderson 45, Davies 90)*
Tottenham H (0) 2 *(Lucas Moura 59, Kane 88 (pen))*   8480

Rochdale: (352) Lillis; McGahey, McNulty (Inman 89), Delaney; Rafferty (Rathbone 81), Cannon, Camps, Kitching, Done; Humphrys (Davies 75), Henderson.
Tottenham H: (4231) Vorm; Trippier, Foyth, Alderweireld, Rose; Wanyama; Lucas Moura (Alli 71), Sissoko, Winks (Lamela 62); Son; Llorente (Kane 76).
Referee: Robert Madley.

Monday, 19 February 2018

Wigan Ath (0) 1 *(Grigg 79)*
Manchester C (0) 0   19,242

Wigan Ath: (4321) Walton; Byrne, Dunkley, Burn, Elder; Massey (Colclough 77), Power, Perkins; Powell (Fulton 27), Roberts G (Jacobs 55); Grigg.
Manchester C: (433) Bravo; Danilo, Stones, Laporte, Delph*****; Gundogan, Fernandinho, Silva (De Bruyne 65); Bernardo Silva, Aguero, Sane (Walker 46).
Referee: Anthony Taylor.

FIFTH ROUND REPLAYS

Tuesday, 27 February 2018

Swansea C (0) 2 *(Ayew J 55, Dyer 80)*
Sheffield W (0) 0   8198

Swansea C: (343) Nordfeldt; van der Hoorn, Fernandez, Bartley; Roberts, Ki (Olsson 46), Carroll, Clucas; Dyer (Britton 83), Abraham, Routledge (Ayew J 46).
Sheffield W: (352) Dawson; Frederico Venancio, Loovens, Pudil; Hunt (Palmer 38), Butterfield (Nuhiu 68), Jones, Reach, Boyd; Rhodes (Abdi 81), Lucas Joao.
Referee: Stuart Attwell.

Wednesday, 28 February 2018

Tottenham H (1) 6 *(Son 23, 65, Llorente 47, 53, 59,*
Walker-Peters 90)
Rochdale (1) 1 *(Humphrys 31)*   24,627

Tottenham H: (4231) Vorm; Trippier, Foyth, Dier, Rose; Sissoko, Winks (Dembele 62); Lucas Moura (Walker-Peters 82), Lamela, Son (Alli 67); Llorente.
Rochdale: (532) Lillis; Rafferty, McGahey, McNulty, Delaney, Done; Cannon (Adshead 76), Camps, Kitching (Thompson 64); Humphrys (Davies 58), Henderson.
Referee: Paul Tierney.

SIXTH ROUND

Saturday, 17 March 2018

Manchester U (1) 2 *(Lukaku 37, Matic 83)*
Brighton & HA (0) 0   74,241

Manchester U: (4231) Romero; Valencia, Bailly, Smalling, Shaw (Young 46); McTominay, Matic, Mata (Rashford 75), Lingard (Fellaini 89), Martial; Lukaku.
Brighton & HA: (433) Krul; Schelotto, Duffy, Dunk, Suttner; Gross, Propper, Kayal; March (Izquierdo 68), Ulloa (Murray 76), Locadia.
Referee: Andre Marriner.

Swansea C (0) 0
Tottenham H (2) 3 *(Eriksen 11, 62, Lamela 45)*   17,498

Swansea C: (541) Nordfeldt; Naughton (Narsingh 46), van der Hoorn (Roberts 81), Bartley, Mawson, Olsson; Dyer (Routledge 86), Ki, Carroll, Clucas; Abraham.
Tottenham H: (4231) Vorm; Trippier, Sanchez, Vertonghen, Davies; Dier, Sissoko; Lucas Moura (Llorente 73), Lamela (Alli 81), Eriksen; Son.
Referee: Kevin Friend.

Sunday, 18 March 2018

Leicester C (0) 1 *(Vardy 76)*

Chelsea (1) 2 *(Morata 42, Pedro 105)*   31,792

Leicester C: (4411) Schmeichel; Simpson (Diabate 106), Morgan, Maguire, Chilwell; Mahrez, Iborra (Adrien Silva 106), Ndidi, Albrighton (Gray 115); Iheanacho (Okazaki 68); Vardy.

Chelsea: (3421) Caballero; Azpilicueta, Christensen (Cahill 101), Rudiger; Moses, Kante, Bakayoko (Fabregas 46), Alonso; Willian (Pedro 92), Hazard E; Morata (Giroud 105).

aet.

Referee: Craig Pawson.

Wigan Ath (0) 0

Southampton (0) 2 *(Hojbjerg 62, Cedric 90)*   17,110

Wigan Ath: (4231) Walton; Byrne (Hunt 80), Dunkley, Burn, Elder; Power, Morsy; Massey (Powell 66), Roberts G (Colclough 66), Jacobs; Grigg.

Southampton: (442) McCarthy; Cedric, Stephens, Hoedt, Bertrand; Tadic, Hojbjerg, Lemina, Boufal (Redmond 65); Carrillo (Long 81), Gabbiadini (Romeu 87).

Referee: Michael Oliver.

Saturday, 21 April 2018

Manchester U (1) 2 *(Sanchez 24, Ander Herrera 62)*

Tottenham H (1) 1 *(Alli 11)*   84,667

Manchester U: (433) de Gea; Valencia (Darmian 80), Smalling, Jones, Young; Ander Herrera, Matic, Pogba; Lingard (Rashford 83), Lukaku, Sanchez (Fellaini 90).

Tottenham H: (4231) Vorm; Trippier, Sanchez, Vertonghen, Davies (Lucas Moura 68); Dier, Dembele (Wanyama 78); Eriksen, Alli, Son (Lamela 86); Kane.

Referee: Anthony Taylor.

Sunday, 22 April 2018

Chelsea (0) 2 *(Giroud 46, Morata 82)*

Southampton (0) 0   73,416

Chelsea: (3421) Caballero; Azpilicueta, Cahill, Rudiger; Moses, Fabregas (Pedro 76), Kante, Emerson; Willian (Bakayoko 64), Hazard E; Giroud (Morata 80).

Southampton: (352) McCarthy; Bednarek (Gabbiadini 78), Yoshida, Hoedt; Cedric, Lemina, Romeu, Hojbjerg (Tadic 63), Bertrand; Long (Redmond 63), Austin.

Referee: Martin Atkinson.

THE FA CUP FINAL 2018

Saturday, 19 May 2018

(at Wembley Stadium, attendance 87,647)

Chelsea (1) 1   **Manchester U (0) 0**

Chelsea: (3511) Courtois; Azpilicueta, Cahill, Rudiger; Moses, Fabregas, Kante, Bakayoko, Alonso; Hazard E (Willian 90); Giroud (Morata 89).
Scorer: Hazard E 22 (pen).

Manchester U: (41212) de Gea; Valencia, Smalling, Jones (Mata 87), Young; Ander Herrera; Matic, Pogba; Lingard (Martial 73); Rashford (Lukaku 73), Sanchez.

Referee: Michael Oliver.

Chelsea's Eden Hazard strokes home the penalty kick which won the FA Cup Final against Manchester United at Wembley on 19 May. (Reuters/Lee Smith)

NATIONAL LEAGUE 2017–18

(P) *Promoted into division at end of 2016–17 season.*   (R) *Relegated into division at end of 2016–17 season.*

			Home				Away					Total						
		P	W	D	L	F	A	W	D	L	F	A	W	D	L	F	A	GD	Pts
1	Macclesfield T	46	13	7	3	31	19	14	4	5	36	27	27	11	8	67	46	21	92
2	Tranmere R¶	46	15	2	6	48	23	9	8	6	30	23	24	10	12	78	46	32	82
3	Sutton U	46	12	6	5	36	28	11	4	8	31	25	23	10	13	67	53	14	79
4	Boreham Wood	46	12	5	6	33	25	8	10	5	31	22	20	15	11	64	47	17	75
5	Aldershot T	46	11	7	5	35	23	9	8	6	29	29	20	15	11	64	52	12	75
6	Ebbsfleet U (P)	46	11	7	5	35	23	8	10	5	29	27	19	17	10	64	50	14	74
7	AFC Fylde (P)	46	11	9	3	51	27	9	4	10	31	29	20	13	13	82	56	26	73
8	Dover Ath	46	12	5	6	32	17	8	8	7	30	27	20	13	13	62	44	18	73
9	Bromley	46	10	8	5	38	23	9	5	9	37	35	19	13	14	75	58	17	70
10	Wrexham	46	10	10	3	31	17	7	9	7	18	22	17	19	10	49	39	10	70
11	Dagenham & R	46	13	3	7	40	32	6	8	9	29	30	19	11	16	69	62	7	68
12	Maidenhead U (P)	46	11	6	6	36	26	6	7	10	29	40	17	13	16	65	66	–1	64
13	Leyton Orient (R)	46	8	6	9	33	26	8	6	9	25	30	16	12	18	58	56	2	60
14	Eastleigh	46	6	11	6	33	34	7	6	10	32	38	13	17	16	65	72	–7	56
15	Hartlepool U (R)	46	7	6	10	24	26	7	8	8	29	37	14	14	18	53	63	–10	56
16	FC Halifax T (P)	46	9	6	8	31	30	4	9	17	28	31	13	16	17	48	58	–10	55
17	Gateshead	46	8	8	7	34	27	4	10	9	28	31	12	18	16	62	58	4	54
18	Solihull Moors	46	8	7	8	28	30	6	5	12	21	30	14	12	20	49	60	–11	54
19	Maidstone U	46	6	9	8	25	31	7	6	10	27	33	13	15	18	52	64	–12	54
20	Barrow	46	4	10	9	23	29	7	6	10	28	34	11	16	19	51	63	–12	49
21	Woking	46	9	5	9	32	32	4	4	15	23	44	13	9	24	55	76	–21	48
22	Torquay U	46	5	6	12	26	36	5	6	12	19	37	10	12	24	45	73	–28	42
23	Chester FC	46	5	5	13	20	37	3	8	12	22	42	8	13	25	42	79	–37	37
24	Guiseley	46	3	8	11	21	33	4	3	16	23	56	7	12	27	44	89	–45	33

¶*Tranmere R promoted via play-offs.*

NATIONAL LEAGUE PLAY-OFFS 2017–18

■ *Denotes player sent off.*

NATIONAL LEAGUE ELIMINATORS
Wednesday 2 May 2018
Aldershot T (0) 1 *(Kabamba 106)*
Ebbsfleet U (0) 1 *(Winfield 119)*   3319
Aldershot T: Ward; Alexander, Evans, Oyeleke, Rendell, McClure (Robert 65), Kabamba, Gallagher (Kellerman 57 (Rowe 76), McDonnell, Kinsella, Reynolds, Ward.
Ebbsfleet U: Ashmore; Connors, Rance, Winfield, Clark, Powell, Drury (Wabo 107), Kedwell, Coulson (Weston 90), Wilson, Whitely (McCoy 105).
aet; Ebbsfleet U won 5-4 on penalties.
Referee: Allan Young.

Thursday 3 May 2018
Boreham Wood (2) 2 *(Turley 6, Andrade 17)*
AFC Fylde (1) 1 *(Grand 30)*   1244
Boreham Wood: Smith G; Smith K (Shakes 45), Woodards, Ricketts, Stephens, Champion, Murtagh, Andrade, Turley, Balanta, Folivi (Quigley 87).
AFC Fylde: Lynch; Montrose (Jones 77), Francis-Angol, Tunnicliffe, Bond, Finley, Rowe, Muldoon, Grand (Hardy 63), Smith (Blinkhorn 81), Lawlor.
Referee: Joe Johnson.

SEMI-FINALS
Saturday 5 May 2018
Tranmere R (1) 4 *(Norwood 33, 101, Ginnelly 56, Cole 106)*
Ebbsfleet U (1) 2 *(Coulson 16 Weston 51)*   8898
Tranmere R: Davies; Ginnelly (Harris 95), Cole, McNulty, Norburn, Ridehalgh, Sutton, Buxton (Monthe 82), Cook, Norwood, Hughes.

Ebbsfleet U: Ashmore; Connors (Wabo 104), Rance, Winfield■, Clark, Powell (McCoy 69), Drury, Kedwell, Coulson (Weston 34), Wilson, Whitely.
aet.
Referee: Peter Wright.

Sunday 6 May 2018
Sutton U (0) 2 *(Bolarinwa 82, Lafayette 90)*
Boreham Wood (1) 3 *(Balanta 42, Lafayette 53 (og), Folivi 88)*   2730
Sutton U: Butler; Thomas T (Lafayette 46), John, Collins, Eastmond, Bailey, Thomas A, Wright (Harrison 58), Taylor, Butler, Bolarinwa, Beautyman (Cadogan 46).
Boreham Wood: Smith G; Woodards, Ricketts, Stephens, Shakes, Champion, Murtagh, Andrade (Thomas 90), Balanta (Davey 87), Folivi (Quigley 90), Doe.
Referee: Matt Donohue.

FINAL
Wembley, Saturday 12 May 2018
Tranmere R (1) 2 *(Cook 6, Norwood 80)*
Boreham Wood (1) 1 *(Andrade 45)*   16,306
Tranmere R: Davies; Monthe, McNulty, Hughes, Ridehalgh■, Sutton (Harris 45), Cole (Clarke 9), Norburn, Ginnelly (Jennings 34), Cook, Norwood.
Boreham Wood: Smith G; Champion, Woodards (Thomas 83), Doe, Shakes, Folivi (Quigley 70), Andrade, Murtagh, Ricketts, Balanta, Stephens.
Referee: Neil Hair.
Tranmere R promoted to EFL League Two.

NATIONAL LEAGUE PROMOTED TEAMS ROLL CALL 2017–18

MACCLESFIELD TOWN

Player	H	W	DOB
Arthur, Koby (M)	5 6	10 10	31/01/1996
Baba, Noe (M)	6 0	11 09	08/08/1996
Blissett, Nathan (F)	6 0	12 04	29/06/1990
Burgess, Scott (M)	5 10	11 00	27/06/1996
Durrell, Elliott (M)	5 10	11 11	31/07/1989
Evans, Callum (D)	5 10	11 05	11/10/1995
Fitzpatrick, David (D)	5 10	11 07	22/02/1990
Hancox, Mitch (M)	5 10	11 03	09/11/1993
Hodgkiss, Jared (D)	5 7	11 05	15/11/1986
Jalal, Shwan (G)	6 2	14 00	14/08/1983
Kennedy, Kieran (D)	5 10	11 00	23/09/1993
Lloyd, Ryan (M)	5 10	10 03	01/02/1994
Lowe, Keith (D)	6 2	13 10	13/09/1985
Marsh, Tyrone (F)	5 11	12 08	24/12/1993
Pilkington, George (D)	6 0	12 05	07/11/1981
Ramsbottom, Sam (G)	6 1	11 00	03/04/1996
Richards, Courtney (M)	5 11	12 08	22/11/1993
Whitaker, Danny (M)	5 10	11 00	14/11/1980
Wilson, Scott (F)			11/01/1993

TRANMERE ROVERS

Player	H	W	DOB
Buxton, Adam (D)	6 1	12 11	12/05/1992
Clarke, Eddie (D)			29/12/1998
Cole, Larnell (M)	5 4	12 04	09/03/1993
Cook, Andy (F)	6 0	11 03	18/10/1990
Davies, Scott (G)	6 0	11 00	27/02/1987
Drysdale, Declan (D)			14/11/1999
Duggan, Mitch (M)	5 9	11 00	20/03/1997
Dunn, Jack (F)	5 8	10 08	19/11/1994
Ginnelly, Josh (M)	5 6	10 03	24/03/1997
Green, Devarn (F)	5 6	10 02	26/08/1996
Gumbs, Evan (D)	5 10	12 00	21/07/1997
Harris, Jay (M)	5 7	11 07	15/04/1987
Hughes, Jeff (M)	6 0	11 02	29/05/1985
Jennings, Connor (F)	6 0	11 05	29/10/1991
Kirby, Jake (M)	5 11	12 04	09/05/1994
Mangan, Andy (F)	6 0	11 09	30/08/1986
McNulty, Steve (D)	6 1	13 12	26/09/1983
Monthe, Emmanuel (D)	6 0	12 08	26/01/1995
Norburn, Ollie (M)	6 1	12 13	26/10/1992
Norwood, James (F)	6 0	12 13	05/09/1990
Pilling, Luke (G)	5 11	10 12	25/07/1997
Ridehalgh, Liam (D)	5 10	11 05	20/04/1991
Rokka, Elliot (M)			16/03/1996
Solomon-Davies, Josh (D)			21/11/1999
Spellman, Carl (M)			
Sutton, Ritchie (D)	6 0	11 05	29/04/1986
Taylor, Rhys (G)	6 1	13 01	07/04/1990
Tollitt, Ben (M)	6 0	12 00	30/11/1994
Traore, Drissa (M)	5 9	11 11	25/03/1992
Walker-Rice, Danny (F)			
Wallace, James (M)	5 11	13 02	19/12/1991

NATIONAL LEAGUE ATTENDANCES BY CLUB 2017–18

	Aggregate 2017–18	Average 2017–18	Highest Attendance 2017–18
Tranmere R	117,645	5,115	7,385 v Macclesfield T
Wrexham	106,917	4,649	8,471 v Tranmere R
Leyton Orient	99,921	4,344	5,728 v Aldershot T
Hartlepool U	77,052	3,350	6,833 v Wrexham
Aldershot T	55,873	2,429	4,358 v Macclesfield T
Maidstone U	55,478	2,412	3,225 v Leyton Orient
Sutton U	50,910	2,213	3,541 v Aldershot T
Woking	46,563	2,024	3,790 v Aldershot T
Eastleigh	45,077	1,960	3,312 v AFC Fylde
Macclesfield T	42,296	1,839	4,201 v Dagenham & R
Chester	42,005	1,826	4,079 v Wrexham
AFC Fylde	41,498	1,804	3,065 v Tranmere R
Torquay U	39,830	1,732	3,162 v Tranmere R
FC Halifax T	39,691	1,726	3,113 v Tranmere R
Ebbsfleet U	35,955	1,563	2,852 v Sutton U
Maidenhead U	33,924	1,475	2,544 v Leyton Orient
Dagenham & R	33,671	1,464	3,144 v Leyton Orient
Bromley	33,245	1,445	3,346 v Leyton Orient
Dover Ath	31,420	1,366	2,860 v AFC Fylde
Barrow	27,140	1,180	1,796 v Leyton Orient
Solihull Moors	20,223	879	2,658 v Hartlepool U
Guiseley	20,096	874	1,723 v Hartlepool U
Gateshead	19,117	831	3,538 v Hartlepool U
Boreham Wood	15,061	655	1,920 v Leyton Orient

NATIONAL LEAGUE LEADING GOALSCORERS 2017–18

Player	Club	League	FA Cup	FA Trophy	Play-Offs	Total
Daniel Rowe	AFC Fylde	24	5	1	0	30
Andy Cook	Tranmere R	26	1	0	1	28
Bruno Andrade	Boreham Wood	20	2	2	2	26
Macauley Bonne	Leyton Orient	22	1	2	0	25
James Norwood	Tranmere R	20	1	0	3	24
Louis Dennis	Bromley	13	1	7	0	21
Daniel Kedwell	Ebbsfleet U	18	1	1	0	20
Joshua Rees	Bromley	16	1	3	0	20
Ryan Bird	Dover Ath	16	0	2	0	18
Morgan Ferrier	Boreham Wood	15	0	0	0	15
(Includes 8 League goals for Dagenham & R)						
Harry Pritchard	Maidenhead U	13	0	2	0	15
Scott Wilson	Macclesfield T	14	0	0	0	14

NATIONAL LEAGUE NORTH 2017–18

(P) *Promoted into division at end of 2016–17 season.*   (R) *Relegated into division at end of 2016–17 season.*

			Home					Away					Total					
		P	W	D	L	F	A	W	D	L	F	A	W	D	L	F	A	GD	Pts
1	Salford C	42	15	2	4	44	24	13	5	3	36	21	28	7	7	80	45	35	91
2	Harrogate T¶	42	15	4	2	60	18	11	3	7	40	31	26	7	9	100	49	51	85
3	Brackley T	42	13	5	3	39	16	10	6	5	33	21	23	11	8	72	37	35	80
4	Kidderminster H	42	13	5	3	50	25	7	7	7	26	25	20	12	10	76	50	26	72
5	Stockport Co	42	12	5	4	41	19	8	4	9	34	38	20	9	13	75	57	18	69
6	Chorley	42	10	8	3	28	14	8	6	7	24	25	18	14	10	52	39	13	68
7	Bradford Park Avenue	42	9	4	8	38	30	9	5	7	28	26	18	9	15	66	56	10	63
8	Spennymoor T (P)	42	9	6	6	31	28	9	3	9	40	39	18	9	15	71	67	4	63
9	Boston U	42	11	5	5	40	30	6	4	11	27	36	17	9	16	67	66	1	60
10	Blyth Spartans (P)	42	11	1	9	39	24	8	1	12	37	45	19	2	21	76	69	7	59
11	York C (R)	42	9	7	5	31	27	7	3	11	34	35	16	10	16	65	62	3	58
12	Darlington 1883	42	9	5	7	37	26	5	8	8	21	32	14	13	15	58	58	0	55
13	Nuneaton T	42	8	7	6	28	23	6	6	9	22	34	14	13	15	50	57	–7	55
14	AFC Telford U	42	8	3	10	32	41	8	2	11	23	28	16	5	21	55	69	–14	53
15	Southport (R)	42	8	4	9	34	32	6	4	11	26	40	14	8	20	60	72	–12	50
16	FC United of Manchester	42	12	2	7	35	26	2	6	13	23	46	14	8	20	58	72	–14	50
17	Alfreton T	42	7	3	11	31	33	7	4	10	36	38	14	7	21	67	71	–4	49
18	Curzon Ashton	42	9	7	5	29	23	3	6	12	23	43	12	13	17	52	66	–14	49
19	Leamington (P)	42	8	4	9	30	30	5	6	10	21	35	13	10	19	51	65	–14	49
20	Gainsborough Trinity	42	11	1	9	33	30	3	3	15	14	43	14	4	24	47	73	–26	46
21	Tamworth	42	7	6	8	35	34	4	3	14	20	43	11	9	22	55	77	–22	42
22	North Ferriby U (R)	42	1	5	15	11	49	3	4	14	14	52	4	9	29	25	101	–76	21

¶*Harrogate T promoted via play-offs.*

NATIONAL LEAGUE NORTH PLAY-OFFS 2017–18

■ *Denotes player sent off.*

NATIONAL LEAGUE NORTH ELIMINATORS

Wednesday 2 May 2018

Kidderminster H (0) 0

Bradford Park Avenue (1) 2 *(Boyes 10, Johnson 78)* 2291

Kidderminster H: Hall; Vaughan, Taylor, Croasdale, Horsfall, O'Connor, Weeks (Waring 79), McQuilkin (Sonupe 61), Ironside, Bradley, N'Gwatala.
Bradford Park Avenue: Drench; Ross, Atkinson, Wroe, Killock, Havern, Brooksby, Spencer, Boyes, Johnson, Mulhern (Vidal 84).
Referee: Declan Bourne.

Wednesday 2 May 2018

Stockport Co (0) 0

Chorley (0) 1 *(Walker 68))* 6230

Stockport Co: Hincliffe; Cowan, Miniham, Winter, Smalley, O'Halloran (Stephenson 80), Thomas, Turnbull (Turner 73), Oswell, Warburton, Ball.
Chorley: Urwin; Challoner, Molyneux■, Teague, Leather, Anson, Newby (Whitham 90), O'Keefe, Carver, Walker (Wilson 78), Cottrell.
Referee: Gareth Rhodes.

SEMI-FINALS

Sunday 6 May

Brackley T (0) 1 *(Williams A 111)*

Bradford Park Avenue (0) 0 923

Brackley T: Lewis; Lowe (Myles-Tebbutt 98), Franklin, Byrne, Gudger, Dean, Walker G (Murombedzi 90), Armson, Williams, Ndlovu (Brown 91), Walker A.
Bradford Park Avenue: Drench; Ross, Atkinson, Wroe, Killock, Havern, Brooksby (Boshell 61), Spencer (Toulson 109), Boyes, Johnson (Vidal 98), Mulhern.
aet.
Referee: Martin Woods.

Sunday 6 May 2018

Harrogate T (0) 2 *(Knowles 61 (pen), 90)*

Chorley (1) 1 *(O'Keefe 36)* 2307

Harrogate T: Belshaw; Fallowfield, Parker, Falkingham, Burrell, McCombe, Thomson, Emmett, Beck, Knowles, Leesley (Wright 80).
Chorley: Urwin; Challoner, Molyneux■, Teague, Leather, Anson (Wilson 67), Newby, O'Keefe, Carver, Walker (Whitham 57), Cottrell.
Referee: Rebecca Welsh.

PROMOTION FINAL

Harrogate, Sunday 13 May 2018

Harrogate T (2) 3 *(Knowles 26 (pen), 40, Leesley 71)*

Brackley T (0) 0 3000

Harrogate T: Belshaw; Fallowfield, Parker, Falkingham, Burrell, McCombe, Thomson, Emmett (Agnew 90), Beck (Wright 12 (Kerry 45)), Knowles, Leesley.
Brackley T: Lewis; Franklin, Dean, Gudger (Miles-Tebbutt 84), Armson, Walker A (Lowe 58), Walker G, Byrne, Murombedzi, Williams, Ndlovu (Brown 66).
Referee: Leigh Doughty.
Harrogate T promoted to National League.

NATIONAL LEAGUE SOUTH 2017–18

(P) *Promoted into division at end of 2016–17 season.*   (R) *Relegated into division at end of 2016–17 season.*

				Home				Away					Total					
		P	W	D	L	F	A	W	D	L	F	A	W	D	L	F	A	GD	Pts
1	Havant & Waterlooville (P)	42	11	7	3	40	20	14	4	3	30	10	25	11	6	70	30	40	86
2	Dartford	42	15	3	3	51	20	11	5	5	30	24	26	8	8	81	44	37	86
3	Chelmsford C	42	10	6	5	37	24	11	5	5	31	21	21	11	10	68	45	23	74
4	Hampton & Richmond Bor	42	9	11	1	30	16	9	7	5	28	21	18	18	6	58	37	21	72
5	Hemel Hempstead T	42	12	5	4	37	20	7	8	6	34	31	19	13	10	71	51	20	70
6	Braintree T* (R)¶	42	11	6	4	40	23	8	7	6	33	32	19	13	10	73	55	18	69
7	Truro C	42	10	4	7	39	29	10	5	6	32	26	20	9	13	71	55	16	69
8	St Albans C	42	11	4	6	40	28	8	4	9	31	30	19	8	15	71	58	13	65
9	Bath C	42	8	7	6	31	20	9	5	7	33	28	17	12	13	64	48	16	63
10	Welling U	42	8	4	9	36	31	9	6	6	32	28	17	10	15	68	59	9	61
11	Wealdstone	42	11	3	7	36	29	5	8	8	28	33	16	11	15	64	62	2	59
12	Weston-super-Mare	42	11	2	8	38	30	5	5	11	28	43	16	7	19	66	73	−7	55
13	Chippenham T (P)	42	10	7	4	38	25	5	2	14	26	45	15	9	18	64	70	−6	54
14	Gloucester C†	42	8	3	10	27	31	7	5	9	29	39	15	8	19	56	70	−14	53
15	East Thurrock U	42	5	6	10	32	32	8	5	8	36	52	13	11	18	68	84	−16	50
16	Oxford C	42	7	6	8	34	30	6	4	11	26	39	13	10	19	60	69	−9	49
17	Concord Rangers	42	9	5	7	26	26	3	5	13	20	36	12	10	20	46	62	−16	46
18	Eastbourne Bor	42	5	4	12	29	40	8	3	10	28	40	13	7	22	57	80	−23	46
19	Hungerford T	42	6	4	11	26	29	6	3	12	19	39	12	7	23	45	68	−23	43
20	Poole T	42	4	4	13	21	41	7	5	9	26	32	11	9	22	47	73	−26	42
21	Whitehawk	42	4	7	10	24	40	4	3	14	27	49	8	10	24	51	89	−38	34
22	Bognor Regis T (P)	42	4	4	13	25	39	1	8	12	16	39	5	12	25	41	78	−37	27

Braintree T deducted 1 point for fielding an ineligible player. †Gloucester C transferred from National League South. ¶Braintree T promoted via play-offs.

NATIONAL LEAGUE SOUTH PLAY-OFFS 2017–18

NATIONAL LEAGUE SOUTH ELIMINATORS

Wednesday 2 May 2018

Hampton & Richmond Bor (1) 3 *(Cook 34, Hudson-Odoi 99, 118)*

Truro C (1) 1 *(Neal 8)*   922

Hampton & Richmond Bor: Dieng; Wynter, Casey, Cook, Wassmer, McAuley, Kretzschmar (Mulley 80), Jeffers, Kiernan (Charles 105), Roberts (Hudson-Odoi 85).
Truro C: Wollacott; Thompson, Riley-Lowe (Allen 106), Palmer, Gerring, Hartridge, Lamont (Harvey 106), Owen-Evans, Neal, Cooke, Harding (Yetton 119).
aet. Referee: Paul Howard.

Wednesday 2 May 2018

Hemel Hempstead T (0) 0

Braintree T (0) 0   1165

Hemel Hempstead T: Walker; Howe, Connolly, Parkes, Ward, Kaloczi (Oliyide 71), Moyo, Watt, Yakubu (Doyley 90), Saunders (Shulton 60), McCall.
Braintree T: McDonald; Muleba, Gabriel, Hill, Okoye, Wright, Allen, Crook (Wyatt 70), Grant (Michael-Percil 75), Thompson, Barrington.
aet; Braintree T won 3-2 on penalties.
Referee: Will Finnie.

SEMI-FINALS

Sunday 6 May

Chelmsford C (0) 0

Hampton & Richmond Bor (0) 1 *(Kretzschmar 54 (pen))*
                                                               1651

Chelmsford C: Jessup; Barnum-Bobb!, Barrett, Porter, Spillane, Omozusi, Oyenuga (West 71), Church, Fenwick, Dickson (Roberts 78), Giles (Graham 65).
Hampton & Richmond Bor: Dieng; Wynter, Casey, Cook, Wassmer, McAuley (Mulley 76), Kretzschmar, Baptiste, Jeffers, Kiernan (Charles 86), Hudson-Odoi (Roberts 71).
Referee: Joshua Smith.

Sunday 6 May 2018

Dartford (0) 0

Braintree T (0) 1 *(Crook 72)*   1704

Dartford: Schotterl; Collier, Onyemah, Bonner, Vint, Brown (Pugh 79), Noble, Bradbrook, Pavey (Murphy 79), Ofori-Acheampong (Hayes 61), Mills.
Braintree T: McDonald; Muleba, Gabriel, Hill, Okoye, Wright, Allen (Frimpong 90), Crook, Grant (Michael-Percil 59), Thompson, Barrington (Wyatt 84).
Referee: Lloyd Wood.

PROMOTION FINAL

Hampton, Sunday 13 May 2018

Hampton & Richmond Bor (1) 1 *(Kretzschmar 8)*

Braintree T (1) 1 *(Grant 45)*   3127

Hampton & Richmond Bor: Dieng; Wynter, Casey, Cook, Wassmer, McAuley (Mulley 64), Kretzschmar (Charles 79), Baptiste, Jeffers, Kiernan, Roberts (Hudson-Odoi 56).
Braintree T: McDonald; Muleba, Gabriel, Hill, Okoye, Wright, Allen (Michael-Percil 62), Crook, Grant (Wyatt 104), Thompson, Barrington.
aet; Braintree T won 4-3 on penalties.
Referee: Tom Reeves.
Braintree T promoted to National League.

AFC FYLDE

Ground: Mill Farm Sports Village, Coronation Way, Wesham PR4 3JZ.
Tel: (01772) 682 593.   *Website:* afcfylde.co.uk   *Email:* info@afcfylde.co.uk   *Year Formed:* 1988.
Record Attendance: 3,858 v Chorley, National League North, 26 December 2016.   *Nickname:* 'The Coasters'.
Manager: Dave Challinor.   *Colours:* White shirts with blue trim, white shorts with blue trim, white socks.

AFC FYLDE – NATIONAL LEAGUE 2017–18 LEAGUE RECORD

Match No.	Date	Venue	Opponents	Result	H/T Score	Lg Pos.	Goalscorers	Attendance
1	Aug 5	H	Boreham Wood	D 2-2	1-1	7	Woodards (og) [17], Smith [74]	1641
2	8	A	Chester FC	D 1-1	1-1	14	Muldoon [43]	2223
3	12	A	Ebbsfleet U	D 3-3	3-2	15	Jones [8], Rowe [15], Finley [34]	1270
4	15	H	Maidenhead U	L 1-4	1-2	18	Montrose [45]	1657
5	19	H	Dagenham & R	D 2-2	1-1	20	Jones [14], Grand [85]	1590
6	26	A	Hartlepool U	W 2-0	1-0	17	Jones [40], Rowe [84]	2954
7	28	H	Barrow	W 1-0	0-0	12	Hardy [56]	2234
8	Sept 2	A	FC Halifax T	L 1-2	0-0	17	Rowe [56]	1775
9	9	H	Bromley	D 2-2	0-1	18	Tasdemir [67], Rowe [69]	1514
10	12	A	Macclesfield T	L 1-2	0-1	20	Muldoon [49]	1065
11	16	A	Eastleigh	D 2-2	1-1	20	Jones [45], Tunnicliffe [60]	3312
12	23	H	Woking	L 1-2	1-0	20	Tunnicliffe [18]	1532
13	30	A	Leyton Orient	W 2-1	1-0	19	Rowe 2 [15, 48]	4357
14	Oct 3	H	Gateshead	D 0-0	0-0	19		1494
15	7	A	Sutton U	L 1-2	0-2	19	Grand [85]	2127
16	24	H	Wrexham	W 2-0	1-0	18	Smith [8], Muldoon [77]	1816
17	28	A	Solihull Moors	W 4-0	2-0	16	Smith [44], Rowe [45], Finley [76], Muldoon [87]	668
18	Nov 11	A	Aldershot T	L 1-2	0-1	18	Rowe [56]	2011
19	18	H	Torquay U	W 2-0	1-0	16	Rowe 2 [34, 69]	1552
20	25	A	Dover Ath	W 1-0	0-0	16	Rowe [78]	2860
21	Dec 9	A	Boreham Wood	L 0-1	0-1	17		401
22	23	H	Ebbsfleet U	D 1-1	0-0	17	Rowe [89]	1512
23	26	A	Tranmere R	L 1-4	0-2	19	Smith [58]	6669
24	30	A	Maidenhead U	W 2-1	0-1	15	Montrose [71], Muldoon [83]	1315
25	Jan 1	H	Tranmere R	W 5-2	3-0	13	Rowe [21], Muldoon [28], Francis-Angol [36], Tunnicliffe [55], Tasdemir [90]	3065
26	6	A	Bromley	W 1-0	1-0	11	Muldoon [28]	1239
27	9	H	Chester FC	D 1-1	0-0	11	Rowe [55]	1531
28	13	H	Guiseley	W 2-1	1-1	11	Smith [18], Rowe [88]	1535
29	20	H	Macclesfield T	W 6-0	4-0	9	Montrose [6], Muldoon [23], Finley 2 [34, 57], Smith [46], Bond [81]	1982
30	23	H	Maidstone U	W 3-0	2-0	6	Bond [13], Rowe [42], Tunnicliffe [84]	1408
31	27	A	Woking	L 0-1	0-0	9		1856
32	Feb 3	A	Eastleigh	D 2-2	0-1	9	Francis-Angol [64], Jones [85]	1626
33	10	A	Gateshead	W 2-1	2-0	7	Rowe 2 [16, 37]	752
34	17	H	Leyton Orient	L 0-1	0-1	7		2206
35	20	A	Guiseley	L 0-1	0-0	9		613
36	24	H	Dover Ath	W 3-1	0-0	7	Rowe [69], Tasdemir [77], Hardy [90]	1622
37	Mar 10	H	Aldershot T	W 7-1	5-1	8	Rowe 3 [2, 18, 19], Finley 2 [10, 62], Grand [46], Muldoon [65]	2081
38	17	H	Hartlepool U	D 3-3	0-1	8	Bond 2 [46, 55], Hardy [77]	1753
39	24	A	Dagenham & R	L 0-2	0-2	8		1168
40	30	H	FC Halifax T	W 2-0	0-0	8	Smith [47], Hardy [54]	2313
41	Apr 3	A	Barrow	W 3-1	1-1	7	Smith [24], Rowe [54], Tasdemir [90]	901
42	7	H	Sutton U	W 2-1	0-1	7	Smith [77], Rowe [80]	1789
43	10	A	Torquay U	W 3-1	2-1	4	Muldoon [24], Tunnicliffe 2 [28, 78]	1416
44	14	A	Maidstone U	L 0-1	0-0	5		2254
45	21	H	Solihull Moors	D 1-1	0-1	5	Bond [50]	2045
46	28	A	Wrexham	D 0-0	0-0	7		3931

Final League Position: 7

GOALSCORERS

League (82): Rowe 24, Muldoon 10, Smith 9, Finley 6, Tunnicliffe 6, Bond 5, Jones 5, Hardy 4, Tasdemir 4, Grand 3, Montrose 3, Francis-Angol 2, own goal 1.
FA Cup (8): Rowe 5 (1 pen), Finley 1, Grand 1, Smith 1.
FA Trophy (2): Rowe 1, Tasdemir 1.
National League Play-Offs (1): Montrose 1.

Taylor R 10	Ezewele 2 + 3	Francis-Angol 43	Langley 4	Tunnicliffe 46	Montrose 42 + 2	Bond 41 + 3	Hardy 18 + 6	Finley 33	Rowe 46	Muldoon 35 + 9	Jones 14 + 9	Smith 30 + 14	Blinkhorn 1 + 20	Grand 30 + 5	McCready 3 + 6	Burke 29 + 3	Richards 7 + 3	Tasdemir 6 + 20	Lynch 36	Taylor J 5 + 12	Edmundson 10	Mangan 3 + 1	Chettle 4 + 5	Stubbs 6 + 1	Flores 1	Lawlor 1 + 5	Match No.
1	2[1]	3	4	5	6	7	8[2]	9	10	11	12	13															1
1	2	3	4	5	6	12	7	10[1]	11	9	8																2
1	12	3	4	5	2	6	7	11	10[1]	9[2]	8[1]	13	14														3
1	13	2	3[4]	4	9	5	14	6[2]	11[3]	10	8[1]	7	12														4
1	2	3	8	5	6[1]	7	11	10	9[2]	12	13	4															5
1	2	3	5	6	7[2]	8	10	11	9[1]	12	4	13															6
1	12	2[2]	3	5	7	8[1]	9	10	11	6[3]	13	14	4														7
1	10[3]	3	2	4[1]	5[2]	6	7	8	13	14	9	11	12														8
1	3	4	8	6[1]	7	10	11[3]	9[2]	13	2	14	5	12														9
1	3	4	8[1]	7	6	11	10	13	9[2]	2	5	12															10
	3	2	6	7	11	10[1]	9[2]	8[1]	14	5	13	4	12						1								11
	2	3	7	6[2]	10	11[3]	9	12	13	4	14	5	8[1]						1								12
	3	4	2[8]	5	6[3]	7	13	14	10[2]	9	8[1]	11	12						1								13
	4	5	6[2]	7[3]	11	12	13	10[1]	14	2	8	3	9						1								14
	3	4[2]	2[8]	5	6[3]	7	8	13	14	10	9[1]	11							1	12							15
	3	4	6	7[2]	10	11[3]	13	9[1]	14	5	12								1	8	2						16
	2	4	13	5	6[1]	10	11	8[2]	3	12									1	7	9						17
	2	3	13	6	7	10	11[4]	8[1]	4	12									1	9[2]	5						18
	2	3[2]	8	6	11	9[1]	7[2]	14	4	13									1	12	5	10					19
	5	3	2	7	6[2]	10[2]	12	13	4	9[1]									1	14	8	11					20
	5	4	6	7[1]	8	9	11[3]	13	14	3	12								1	2	10[2]						21
	3	4	9	5[2]	8[4]	10	11[1]	12	14	7	6[3]								1	2	13						22
	5	6	4	13	11	12	9[1]	2	14	8	10[1]								1	7[2]	3						23
	3	4	2	14	5[4]	6[2]	12	10[3]	9[1]	7	8								1	13	11						24
	3	4	2	5	6[2]	7[3]	10[1]	14	8	9	13								1	12	11						25
	3	4	2	5	6[3]	7	10[1]	14	8	13	9	12							1	11[2]	12						26
	3	4	2	13	5	6	7[3]	10[2]	14	8	9	12							1	11[1]							27
	3	4	2	5	6[2]	7	13	9[1]	8	10[3]									1	14	12	11					28
	3	4	2	5	6[2]	7	8[1]	9[2]	10	12									1	14	13	11					29
	3	4	2	5	6	7[1]	8[2]	9	14	10	12								1	13	11						30
	4	5	8	7[3]	9	10	11[1]	6[2]	14	3	12								1	13	2						31
	2	3	6	7	13	11	10	12	8[1]	4	14								1	9[3]	5[2]						32
	3	4	2	5	14	6[3]	7[1]	8	11[2]	13	9	10							1	12							33
	3	4	2	5[2]	12	6	7	8[1]	11	13	14	10							1								34
	2	3	7[1]	8[2]	9	11	12	14	10[3]	13	4	5							1	6							35
	2	3	9	5	12	7	10	11	6[2]	4	13								1	8[1]							36
	3	4	6	5	7[1]	8[4]	10[3]	11	14	2	12	9[2]							1	13							37
	3	4	2	5	6[1]	7	8	13	9	12	10[2]								1	14	11[3]						38
	2	5	6	7	9	10[1]	13	8[2]	12	3	4	14							1	11[2]							39
	4[3]	5	6	7	8[1]	11[2]	10	14	9	3	2	13							1	12							40
	2	5	7	8[2]	9	10	11[1]	6[3]	3	4	12								1	13	14						41
	3	4	9	6	7[2]	8	11	13	10[3]	5	2	12							1	14							42
	2	3	7	5	9	6	10[3]	11[2]	8[1]	14	4	13							1	12							43
	2	3	8	6	7[1]	10[2]	11	9	13	4[3]	5	14							1	12							44
	3	4	2	5	6	7	10	8	12	9									1	11[1]							45
	4	5[3]	9	7	8[1]	10	11[2]	13	6	3	2[8]								1	14	12						46

FA Cup

Fourth Qualifying	Wrexham	(h)	1-0
First Round	Kidderminster H	(h)	4-2
Second Round	Wigan Ath	(h)	1-1
Replay	Wigan Ath	(a)	2-3

FA Trophy

First Round	Chester FC	(a)	2-2

(aet; Chester FC won 5-4 on penalties)

National League Play-Offs

Eliminator	Boreham Wood	(a)	1-2

ALDERSHOT TOWN

Ground: The EBB Stadium at the Recreation Ground, High Street, Aldershot, Hampshire GU11 1TW.
Tel: (01252) 320211.   *Website:* www.theshots.co.uk   *Email:* admin@theshots.co.uk   *Year Formed:* 1926.
Record Attendance: 19,138 v Carlisle U, FA Cup 4th rd (replay), 28 January 1970.   *Nickname:* 'The Shots'.
Manager: Gary Waddock.   *Colours:* Red shirts with blue trim, blue shorts with red trim, red socks with white trim.

ALDERSHOT TOWN – NATIONAL LEAGUE 2017–18 LEAGUE RECORD

Match No.	Date	Venue	Opponents	Result	H/T Score	Lg Pos.	Goalscorers	Attendance
1	Aug 5	A	FC Halifax T	W 2-0	0-0	1	Fenelon [59], Rowe (pen) [90]	2108
2	8	H	Torquay U	W 3-2	1-1	1	Fenelon [5], Taylor [48], Okojie [85]	2662
3	12	H	Guiseley	W 6-0	4-0	1	McClure 2 [20, 74], Reynolds [37], Kellermann [43], Fenelon [45], Rowe [53]	1938
4	15	H	Maidstone U	D 1-1	0-0	1	Gallagher [76]	2524
5	19	A	Boreham Wood	L 1-2	0-2	3	Alexander [51]	809
6	26	H	Chester FC	L 1-2	1-0	5	McClure [34]	2056
7	28	A	Eastleigh	D 0-0	0-0	5		2525
8	Sept 2	H	Solihull Moors	W 1-0	1-0	5	Fenelon [9]	1803
9	9	H	Dover Ath	L 0-2	0-1	7		1862
10	12	A	Ebbsfleet U	W 2-0	1-0	3	Rowe [14], Rendell [67]	1402
11	16	A	Gateshead	W 1-0	0-0	1	Robert [83]	654
12	23	H	Leyton Orient	D 2-2	2-1	2	Alexander [9], McClure [20]	3060
13	30	A	Macclesfield T	L 0-2	0-1	8		1350
14	Oct 3	H	Dagenham & R	D 1-1	1-0	7	McDonnell [23]	1903
15	7	A	Maidenhead U	D 3-3	2-1	8	Kellermann 2 [16, 90], McDonnell [42]	2425
16	21	H	Tranmere R	W 2-1	0-1	7	Robert [80], Rendell [90]	2714
17	24	H	Sutton U	D 2-2	2-2	6	Mensah [14], Rendell (pen) [43]	2259
18	28	A	Barrow	L 1-3	0-2	9	McDonnell [46]	1128
19	Nov 11	A	AFC Fylde	W 2-1	1-0	7	Fenelon [20], Evans [86]	2011
20	18	A	Hartlepool U	W 2-0	1-0	5	Mensah [44], Kellermann [87]	3732
21	25	H	Wrexham	W 2-0	2-0	6	Mensah [15], Fenelon [33]	2377
22	28	A	Bromley	W 2-0	1-0	1	Mensah [28], Rendell [68]	1171
23	Dec 2	H	Torquay U	D 0-0	0-0	4		1851
24	9	H	FC Halifax T	L 0-1	0-1	6		1912
25	23	A	Guiseley	D 1-1	0-1	5	Fenelon [90]	820
26	26	H	Woking	W 3-1	2-1	3	Fenelon 2 [12, 27], Oyeleke [64]	4181
27	30	H	Maidstone U	D 1-1	0-0	2	Kellermann [90]	2287
28	Jan 1	A	Woking	W 2-1	1-0	2	Rendell 2 [28, 90]	3790
29	6	A	Dover Ath	W 2-1	1-1	2	Kellermann [45], Kabamba [67]	1237
30	20	H	Ebbsfleet U	D 0-0	0-0	2		2457
31	27	A	Leyton Orient	W 3-2	1-2	2	Fenelon [44], Evans [48], McDonnell [76]	5728
32	Feb 10	A	Dagenham & R	W 2-0	1-0	2	Kellermann [4], Rendell [49]	1509
33	17	H	Macclesfield T	L 1-2	0-1	3	Rendell (pen) [62]	4358
34	20	H	Bromley	D 1-1	0-1	3	Oyeleke [90]	1909
35	24	A	Wrexham	D 2-2	1-1	4	Fenelon [42], Reynolds [75]	4662
36	Mar 6	H	Hartlepool U	W 2-1	1-1	3	Rendell [13], Oyeleke [60]	1665
37	10	A	AFC Fylde	L 1-7	1-5	4	McQuoid [5]	2081
38	17	A	Chester FC	D 0-0	0-0	6		1612
39	24	H	Boreham Wood	W 2-0	1-0	5	Gallagher [11], McClure [75]	2448
40	30	A	Solihull Moors	D 0-0	0-0	4		1734
41	Apr 2	H	Eastleigh	L 0-2	0-1	5		2853
42	7	H	Maidenhead U	W 1-0	0-0	3	Kabamba [89]	2318
43	14	A	Tranmere R	L 0-2	0-0	6		5444
44	17	H	Gateshead	W 1-0	0-0	3	Rendell [45]	1893
45	21	H	Barrow	D 1-1	0-0	4	Rendell [90]	2947
46	28	A	Sutton U	L 1-2	0-0	5	Rendell (pen) [57]	3541

Final League Position: 5

GOALSCORERS

League (64): Rendell 12 (3 pens), Fenelon 11, Kellermann 7, McClure 5, McDonnell 4, Mensah 4, Oyeleke 3, Rowe 3 (1 pen), Alexander 2, Evans 2, Gallagher 2, Kabamba 2, Reynolds 2, Robert 2, McQuoid 1, Okojie 1, Taylor 1.
FA Cup (1): Rendell 1.
FA Trophy (0).
National League Play-Offs (1): Kabamba 1.

Cole 21	De Havilland 7 + 1	Alexander 43	Arnold 5 + 2	Oyeleke 34 + 6	Gallagher 23 + 12	Rowe 30 + 10	Taylor 17 + 8	Rendell 25 + 13	Fenelon 31 + 4	Kellermann 32 + 6	Okojie 1 + 8	McClure 19 + 15	Arthur 10 + 3	Lyons-Foster 1 + 5	Fowler 24	McDonnell 28 + 2	Wrightman — + 2	Bozier — + 3	Robert 12 + 11	Evans 32 + 1	Mensah 14	Pring — + 1	Smith 1	Ward 24	Blanchfield — + 1	Kinsella 18	Kababa 3 + 7	McQuoid 13 + 3	Match No.
1	2	3	4	5	6	7	8	9¹	10²	11	12	13																	1
1	2	3	5	4	6	7²	8	9¹	14	10	12	13	11³																2
1	3	4	2³	12	5	13	7²	9	14	10¹	6		11		8														3
1	4	5	3	2	6	13	8	9²	10	7²	12	11¹	14																4
1	5	4	3	2	6	7	8	9¹	10	12	13	11²	14																5
1	2	3	4	14	5		7	9	13	12	6³	11¹	10	8²															6
1		3	4	2¹	5²		8	9	11	10	7	13	12	6⁴															7
1		3	2		13	6	10		9²	5	11¹	8	4	7	12²	14													8
1		3	2		5³	7		10		6	11	9¹	4²	8	14	13	12												9
1		2	4		5	7		11		6¹	9		3	8	12														10
1	4	2	14	7	9		11		6¹	10²	5²	13	3	8	12														11
1	11	2	3²	5	7		12		6	4¹	9	10	8	13															12
1	5²	3	4	6		8¹	10	12	7	11	2³	9	14	13															13
1	2	3		5	6⁴	14	11²	13	12	10³	8	7	9¹	4															14
1	13	2	3	5	12	11	10¹	6	14	8³	7²	9	4																15
1	5	2		4	12	9	10¹	6	13	7	11	3	8⁴																16
1	2	3	5	6³	7	11	10²	14	8	12	4	9¹	13																17
	4	2	5	12	7²	10	6	13	9¹	3	11	1																	18
	3	2	12⁸	13	7²	14	9	8³	5¹	6	10	4	11	1															19
	4	2	13	7	12	9⁶	6	14	5	8	11²	3	10¹	1															20
	4	2¹	12	7	13	10³	6	14	5	8	11³	3	9	1															21
	2	5	7¹	13	10²	6	14	12	3	8⁴	9³	4	11	1															22
	4	2	13	6²	8	12	7	10	3	11¹	5	9	1																23
	3	2²	12	13	7	9	10¹	6	14	4³	8	5	11	1															24
	3	2	13	7	8¹	11	9	6²	12	5	4	10	1																25
	10	2	5	8	11	6	4³	12	9	13	3	7²	1																26
	2	5	8³	13	11	6	4³	9	14	12	10	3¹	7	1															27
	2	4	7	9²¹	11	5	8	13	10	3	6¹	1	12																28
	2	6	7	12	11²	10¹	8	14	4	3	9	1	5³	13															29
	2	5	7	12	11	13	4¹	8	10	3	1	9	6²	7²															30
	2	5	14	8³	6	4¹	13	11	9	3	1	10	12	7²															31
	2	6²	14	8	11³	7¹	5	9	12	3	1	4	13	10															32
	10	12	6	11¹	3	5²	9	7	14	2⁸	1	8	13	4³															33
	5	2	6	7	14	13	12	4	8	9²	1	3	10³	11¹															34
1	3		5²	7³	6	12	10	9	14		13	4	2	11³															35
1	14	2	6	7	12	10	9²	13	5	8¹	3	4	11³																36
1	2	7	13	8²	12	10	14	4	6³	11¹	5	3	9																37
1	5²	2	6	7³	14	9¹	12	10²	8	3	4	13	11																38
	5	2	7	6¹	12	14	13	9⁴	10³	8	3	1	4	11															39
	4	2	5	6¹	14	9¹	12	10	7³	13	3	1	8	11															40
	10	2	5	14	12	13	4	8²	6	11³	3	1	9	7¹															41
	4	2	6¹	9	10	7²	14	8	11³	3	1	5	13	12															42
	10	2	4	11²	12	7¹	13	8	3	1	9	5	6																43
	4	2	6	7²14	10	9¹	8	11³	13	3	1	5	12																44
	4	2	6	7³13	9	11	8¹	10²	14	5	1	3	12																45
	11	2¹	5	14	9	6	4³	8	12	3	1	10	13	7³															46

FA Cup

Fourth Qualifying	Torquay U	(h)	1-0
First Round	Shrewsbury T	(a)	0-5

FA Trophy

First Round	East Thurrock U	(a)	0-4

National League Play-Offs

Eliminator	Ebbsfleet U	(h)	1-1

aet; AFC Fylde won 5-4 on penalties.

BARROW

Ground: Furness Building Society Stadium, Wilkie Road, Barrow-in-Furness, Cumbria LA14 5UW.
Tel: (01229) 666010.   *Website:* www.barrowafc.com   *Email:* office@barrowafc.com   *Year Formed:* 1901.
Record Attendance: 16,854 v Swansea T, FA Cup 3rd rd, 9 January 1954.   *Nickname:* 'The Bluebirds'.
Manager: Ian Evatt.   *Colours:* White shirts with blue trim, blue shorts, white socks with blue trim.

BARROW – NATIONAL LEAGUE 2017–18 LEAGUE RECORD

Match No.	Date		Venue	Opponents	Result	H/T Score	Lg Pos.	Goalscorers	Atten- dance
1	Aug	5	A	Dagenham & R	L	1-2	0-2	19	Jones [86]	1362
2		8	H	FC Halifax T	D	0-0	0-0	20		1410
3		12	H	Woking	W	3-0	1-0	12	Yussuf [20], White 2 [47, 83]	1075
4		15	A	Solihull Moors	D	3-3	2-0	13	Nieskens [20], Jones [31], Panayiotou (pen) [90]	558
5		19	A	Dover Ath	D	1-1	0-0	12	White [53]	927
6		26	H	Maidenhead U	D	1-1	0-1	16	Diarra [56]	1154
7		28	A	AFC Fylde	L	0-1	0-0	19		2234
8	Sept	2	H	Boreham Wood	W	2-1	2-1	16	Gomis [3], Barthram [37]	1159
9		9	A	Tranmere R	L	0-1	0-0	20		4269
10		12	H	Guiseley	D	0-0	0-0	18		1072
11		16	H	Torquay U	D	1-1	0-1	18	Harrison [90]	1190
12		23	A	Sutton U	L	2-3	1-1	19	Harrison 2 [39, 62]	1909
13		30	H	Maidstone U	L	0-1	0-0	20		1097
14	Oct	3	A	Hartlepool U	L	0-1	0-0	20		3082
15		7	H	Leyton Orient	D	2-2	2-2	20	Gomis [23], White [41]	1796
16		21	A	Ebbsfleet U	L	2-3	0-1	20	Gomis 2 [71, 90]	1402
17		24	A	Chester FC	L	2-3	2-2	22	Yussuf [45], Harrison [45]	1548
18		28	H	Aldershot T	W	3-1	2-0	21	Yussuf 3 [5, 39, 65]	1128
19	Nov	11	H	Macclesfield T	L	0-2	0-1	21		1644
20		18	A	Eastleigh	W	2-0	1-0	20	Harrison [32], Dunne [55]	1708
21		21	A	Gateshead	W	2-1	1-1	19	Harrison [33], Panayiotou [58]	663
22		25	H	Bromley	L	0-3	0-1	19		941
23	Dec	2	A	FC Halifax T	W	1-0	0-0	18	White [69]	1618
24		9	H	Dagenham & R	L	0-1	0-0	19		917
25		23	A	Woking	W	2-1	2-1	19	Diarra [2], Dunne [28]	1816
26		26	H	Wrexham	D	1-1	1-1	20	Diarra [2]	1648
27		30	H	Solihull Moors	L	1-2	0-0	20	Hall [55]	1315
28	Jan	1	A	Wrexham	D	3-3	2-2	20	White [31], Jones [37], MacDonald [90]	4390
29		6	H	Tranmere R	D	1-1	1-0	20	Harrison (pen) [5]	1470
30	Feb	3	A	Torquay U	L	1-3	0-0	20	Harrison (pen) [74]	1553
31		13	H	Sutton U	D	1-1	1-0	20	Gomis [10]	643
32		17	A	Maidstone U	W	1-0	1-0	19	James, L [31]	2338
33		20	H	Gateshead	D	1-1	1-0	20	James, L (pen) [18]	860
34	Mar	10	A	Macclesfield T	L	1-3	1-1	20	James, L [11]	1748
35		17	A	Maidenhead U	W	1-0	0-0	19	James, L [49]	1030
36		21	A	Hartlepool U	L	1-2	1-1	20	James, L [19]	1018
37		24	H	Dover Ath	D	0-0	0-0	20		908
38		30	A	Boreham Wood	D	0-0	0-0	20		623
39	Apr	3	H	AFC Fylde	L	1-3	1-1	20	Waterston [29]	901
40		7	A	Leyton Orient	L	1-4	1-1	21	James, L [7]	3979
41		10	H	Eastleigh	W	3-2	1-0	21	Hall [15], Makoma [62], Walters [79]	817
42		14	H	Ebbsfleet U	L	0-1	0-1	21		1189
43		17	A	Guiseley	W	1-0	0-0	20	Hall [48]	611
44		21	A	Aldershot T	D	1-1	0-0	20	James, L [72]	2947
45		24	A	Bromley	D	0-0	0-0	20		1331
46		28	H	Chester FC	L	1-2	0-1	20	White [54]	1788

Final League Position: 20

GOALSCORERS

League (51): Harrison 8 (2 pens), James, L 7 (1 pen), White 7, Gomis 5, Yussuf 5, Diarra 3, Hall 3, Jones 3, Dunne 2, Panayiotou 2 (1 pen), Barthram 1, MacDonald 1, Makoma 1, Nieskens 1, Walters 1, Waterston 1.
FA Cup (1): Harrison 1 (1 pen).
FA Trophy (1): Harrison 1.

Moore 18	Diarra 38	Audel 5 + 2	Jones 31 + 2	Barthram 28 + 2	Dunne 21	Hall 37	Gomis 38 + 5	Harvey 13	White 22 + 22	Yussuf 16 + 5	Panayiotou 10 + 21	Cockerline 1 + 4	Nieskens 8	Hughes 7 + 2	Bauress 17 + 14	Makoma 11 + 5	Harrison 21 + 5	Thompson 7 + 1	Bignot 11 + 1	Dixon 11	Fitzpatrick 1 + 3	Diagne 12 + 5	Clements 7	Holt 15 + 8	MacDonald 21	Walters 11 + 4	Arnold 17	Cook 13	Humphrey 1 + 1	James L 17	James K 13 + 1	Waterston 7 + 2	Match No.
1	2	3	4	5	6	7¹	8	9	10²	11	12	13																					1
1	5		3	2	4	9	8	7³	10²	11			12	6	13	14																	2
1	5		3	2	4	8	9²	7	10	11¹	14	12	6				13																3
1	4	12	2	5³	3⁶	8	9	7²	10		13		11¹	6		14																	4
1	3	2	5			8	7	9		10¹	12	4	6	11																			5
1	4	2³	3	12		9	8	11¹	13	10²		5	7	6		14																	6
1	5		4	3		7	8	10¹	11	14		6	12	2⁵	9²	13																	7
1	5		3	2	4	8	9	7⁴	13	10¹	12	6				11²																	8
1	5	12	3	2	4	8	9		14	10¹	13	6⁵		7²	11																		9
1	6		3	2	5	8	9		12	10²	13		7	11¹																			10
1	5		3	2⁴	4	8	9¹		14	10³	12		6	11	7	13																	11
			3		5	7	8	10	12		6¹		11	4	2	1	9²	13															12
			3	2	4	8¹		7	10		12		11	5		1	6	9															13
			3	2	4		9	7	10			8	11	5		1	6																14
			2	3		8¹	7	10			6	12	11	4		1	5	9															15
			2		8	13	7³	10²	12	14		3¹	11	4	5	1	6	9															16
			2		4	8		10²	12	7¹	3	11	13	5	1	6	9																17
1			2		7	8²	12	10¹	13	6	3	11	4	5		9																	18
1	4		2³		7	8	13	10²	6	3	11	5	12	9¹	14																		19
1	6		5	7	8	12	9³	11¹	2	14	10³	3	4	13																			20
1	5		4	7	8	12	9³	6	11²	14	10¹	2	3	13																			21
1			4	7	12	10	9	6¹	11²	5	3	8	13																				22
1	6	13	4	7	8	12	9²	11	5¹	10	2	3																					23
1	5		4	7	8	9³	14	11¹	6	10²	2	13	3	12																			24
4		2¹	6	3	7	8	13	12		14	10	1	9³	5	11²																		25
5	11	6	4	8	14	12	7	10³	2	1	13	9³	3																				26
5	11²	2	4	7	8	6	12	13	10¹	1	9	3																					27
5	2	3	4	8	12	11¹	10	9²	7²	13	1	14	6																				28
5	4	11²	2	7³	8	13	6	12	10	1	14	9¹	3																				29
4	3	2	7	8	13	11²	12	14	9¹	1	5	6¹	10																				30
4	6⁵	2	7	8	11²	14	12	13	9¹	3	1	5	10																				31
5	4³	2	7	8	9²	14	11	3	1	6	12	10¹	13																				32
4	6¹	2	8	9³	12	13	14	10²	3	1	5	11	7																				33
4	2	8	6	9¹	5⁵	13	7⁴	12	1	11	10	3	14																				34
3		5	6⁵	13	12	8	4	11²	1	2	10	7	9¹																				35
3	13	7	14	5	8³	12	4	11²	1	2	10	6	9¹																				36
3	5	7	13	12	6	9²	4	11¹	1	2	10	8																					37
4	13	6³	7	12	14	2	9³	5	11¹	1	3	10	8																				38
3	5	13	14	6	8²	2	10³	1	4	9	7	11¹																					39
4	6⁶	2	8³	11¹	13	12	5	14	1	3	9	7	10²																				40
4	6	8¹	13	5	2	12	2	11²	1	3	10	7	9																				41
4	6	8¹	13	12	2	5	11	1	3	9	7	10²																					42
4	8	3	9	12	13	2⁴	14	10⁴	5	6	1	11³	7¹																				43
3	5	7	14	10	12	13⁶	2²	8¹	4	9¹	1	11	6																				44
5	3	6	8	10	12	4	2¹	13	1	11	7	9²																					45
3	7³	4	8	10	12	14	2	6¹	5²	9	1	11	13																				46

FA Cup

Fourth Qualifying	Shaw Lane		(a)	1-2

FA Trophy

First Round	Nuneaton T		(a)	1-0
Second Round	Brackley T		(a)	0-0
Replay	Brackley T		(h)	0-2

BOREHAM WOOD

Ground: Meadow Park, Broughinge Road, Borehamwood, Hertfordshire WD6 5AL.   *Tel:* (02089) 535097.
Website: borehamwoodfootballclub.co.uk   *Email:* see website.   *Year Formed:* 1948.
Record Attendance: 4,030 v Arsenal, Friendly, 13 July 2001.   *Nickname:* 'The Wood'   *Manager:* Luke Garrard.
Colours: White shirts with black trim, black shorts with white trim, white socks.

BOREHAM WOOD – NATIONAL LEAGUE 2017–18 LEAGUE RECORD

Match No.	Date		Venue	Opponents	Result	H/T Score	Lg Pos.	Goalscorers	Attendance
1	Aug	5	A	AFC Fylde	D 2-2	1-1	8	Shakes [45], Smith, K [56]	1641
2		8	H	Dagenham & R	L 1-2	1-2	16	Andrade (pen) [7]	635
3		12	H	Solihull Moors	W 4-1	3-1	11	Turley [34], Andrade [40], Benson [44], Balanta [59]	319
4		15	A	Torquay U	W 4-2	0-0	6	Balanta [50], Andrade [57], Jeffers [73], Sach [90]	1864
5		19	H	Aldershot T	W 2-1	2-0	4	Andrade [27], Jeffers [40]	809
6		26	A	Tranmere R	D 2-2	2-0	3	Andrade (pen) [53], Balanta [68]	4295
7		28	H	Wrexham	L 0-1	0-0	7		765
8	Sept	2	A	Barrow	L 1-2	1-2	10	Andrade [38]	1159
9		9	H	Leyton Orient	W 2-0	1-0	8	Woodards [35], Murtagh [50]	1920
10		12	A	Dover Ath	W 1-0	1-0	4	Turgott [44]	1012
11		16	A	Maidenhead U	L 1-2	0-1	11	Ricketts [90]	1351
12		23	H	Ebbsfleet U	L 0-1	0-0	12		622
13		30	A	Gateshead	D 1-1	0-1	11	Shakes [87]	606
14	Oct	3	H	Eastleigh	W 1-0	0-0	10	Andrade [77]	404
15		7	H	FC Halifax T	D 1-1	1-0	11	Andrade [7]	562
16		21	A	Chester FC	W 2-1	2-0	8	Jeffers [31], Andrade [38]	1501
17		24	A	Guiseley	D 0-0	0-0	9		706
18		28	H	Bromley	D 2-2	2-2	10	Holman [25], Turley [40]	1128
19	Nov	11	H	Hartlepool U	D 0-0	0-0	10		773
20		18	A	Macclesfield T	D 0-0	0-0	10		1324
21		21	A	Maidstone U	W 4-0	2-0	9	Smith, K [13], Holman 2 [40, 53], Turgott (pen) [77]	1945
22		25	H	Woking	W 2-1	1-0	7	Champion [22], Andrade [82]	543
23	Dec	9	H	AFC Fylde	W 1-0	1-0	7	Balanta [6]	401
24		23	A	Solihull Moors	D 0-0	0-0	7		419
25		26	H	Sutton U	L 0-4	0-2	8		455
26		30	H	Torquay U	W 2-0	1-0	7	Balanta [11], Andrade (pen) [81]	627
27	Jan	1	A	Sutton U	D 1-1	0-0	8	Balanta [90]	2007
28		6	A	Leyton Orient	D 0-0	0-0	8		4094
29		9	A	Dagenham & R	W 3-2	1-0	5	Andrade 2 (1 pen) [12, 48 (p)], Balanta [59]	1117
30		20	H	Dover Ath	L 2-3	0-0	8	Stephens [70], Davey [87]	527
31		27	A	Ebbsfleet U	W 3-0	1-0	8	Balanta [34], Turley [47], Quigley [66]	1366
32	Feb	10	A	Eastleigh	W 2-0	0-0	6	Ferrier [58], Andrade (pen) [67]	1751
33		17	H	Gateshead	W 2-1	1-0	6	Andrade 2 [35, 75]	464
34		20	H	Maidstone U	W 1-0	1-0	4	Balanta [36]	428
35		24	A	Woking	D 0-0	0-0	5		1744
36	Mar	10	A	Hartlepool U	D 0-0	0-0	5		2538
37		13	H	Maidenhead U	D 1-1	1-1	6	Ferrier [4]	401
38		17	H	Tranmere R	W 2-1	1-0	3	Balanta [45], Andrade [79]	801
39		24	A	Aldershot T	L 0-2	0-1	6		2448
40		30	H	Barrow	D 0-0	0-0	6		623
41	Apr	2	A	Wrexham	W 1-0	1-0	3	Andrade (pen) [10]	4746
42		7	A	FC Halifax T	L 1-2	0-1	5	Ferrier [53]	1460
43		10	H	Macclesfield T	L 0-2	0-1	6		602
44		14	H	Chester FC	W 4-2	2-0	6	Folivi [6], Andrade (pen) [44], Ferrier [58], Shakes [90]	551
45		21	A	Bromley	L 2-3	2-1	6	Ferrier 2 [3, 25]	1282
46		28	H	Guiseley	W 3-1	2-1	4	Andrade [3], Ferrier [16], Smith, K [69]	701

Final League Position: 4

GOALSCORERS
League (64): Andrade 20 (7 pens), Balanta 10, Ferrier 7, Holman 3, Jeffers 3, Shakes 3, Smith, K 3, Turley 3, Turgott 2 (1 pen), Benson 1, Champion 1, Davey 1, Folivi 1, Murtagh 1, Quigley 1, Ricketts 1, Sach 1, Stephens 1, Woodards 1.
FA Cup (5): Andrade 2 (1 pen), Jeffers 1, Holman 1, Turgott 1.
FA Trophy (7): Andrade 2 (1 pen), Jeffers 1, Murtagh 1, Quigley 1, Shakes 1, Smith K 1.
National League Play-Offs (6): Andrade 2, Balanta 1, Turley 1, Folivi 1, own goal 1.

Smith G 46	Smith K 43	Woodards 25 + 7	Stephens 41	Turley 30 + 1	Ricketts 42	Shakes 36 + 6	Champion 42	Murtagh 44	Benson 4 + 10	Balanta 26 + 6	Andrade 44 + 1	Johnson 2	Jeffers 14 + 12	Sach — + 7	Keita — + 1	Wells 16	Turgott 10 + 3	Thomas — + 3	Holman 9 + 3	Chesmain 2 + 1	Jarvis 1 + 3	Davey 8 + 4	Quigley 5 + 4	Folivi 1 + 12	Ferrier 14 + 1	Harfield — + 1	Doe 1 + 1	Match No.
1	2	3^5	4	5	6	7	8	9	10	11	12																	1
1	2			4	5	6	7	8^2	10^1	11		9	3	12	13													2
1	2		3	9	4	5	6	7^2	11^3	10^1	8		12	14	13													3
1	4	13	2	5	6	7	8	12	11	9^2	3^1	10^3	14															4
1	2	13	3	4^1	9	5	6	7	12	11	8^2		10															5
1	2	3	4	5	6	7	8	12	11	9			10^1															6
1	2		4	5	6	7	8^2	10^1	11	9			12	13		3												7
1	2	12	4	3^1	5	6^1	7	8	14	11	9		10^3	13														8
1	2	3	5		6	7	8	12		9			11^1			4	10											9
1	5	4	2		7	6	8			11			10			3	9											10
1	2^5	5	3		6	7	8	12		9			10^3	13		4	11^{12}	14										11
1	2	5	14	3^2	6	7	8	12		9			13			4	10^1		11^3									12
1	2	5	9	3	6	7	8			12						4	10^2	13	11^1									13
1	2	3	6		4	7	8	9		10			12			5			11^1									14
1	2	3	5		6	7	8	9	12	10						4			11^1									15
1	2	3	5		8	13	6	7		11^1	9		10^2			4			12									16
1	2	5	11	3	6	7	8	9		10						4												17
1	2		4	5	6	7	8	10^2	11	9			12			3	13		11^1									18
1	2		4	5		6	7	8		9			12			3	10		11^1									19
1	2	3	6		4	7	8	9		10			11^1			5			12									20
1	2	3	5		6	7	8	13	12	9^2						4	10^1		11									21
1	2	5	3		6	7	8	14	12	9^1			13			4	10^3		11^2									22
1	3		2		5	6	7	8		11	9		10^1			4			12									23
1	2	3	8		4	5	6	13	7				12				9^1	10^3	11									24
1	4	3	2		5	6	7	8^4	11^2	9^1			10^3				13		14	12								25
1	2	4	8		3	12	5	6	9^1	7			14				13	10^3	11^2									26
1	2	3^1	5	10	4	13	6	7	12	8			9^2				11^3		14									27
1	2	3^5	4		6	7	8	9		11			10						12	5								28
1	2	12	9		3	4	5	6		10			7^2			13				11	8^1							29
1	2	13	5			6	7	8		11			9							4	10^2	12						30
1	5	8	3	4		6		2	7				9	11							10^1	12						31
1	2	3	5	10	4		6	7		11			8^2									9^1	13	12				32
1	2^1	3	5	8	4	12		6		9^2	7											10	13	11				33
1		5	3	4	8^1	6		7		10	9^3											2	14	12	11^2	13		34
1		2	4	5	6	7		8^2	10	9												3	13	12	11^1			35
1	5	6^1	4	3	2	12	7	8		10	9														11			36
1	2	5	4	8		6	7			11^1	9					3							12	10				37
1	2	3^1	5	9	4	12	6	7		10^3	8														11	13		38
1	2	3		4	6^2	7	8	9^1			10^3							14					13	12	11		5	39
1	2	12	4	10	3	5	6	7			8^2											9^1	13	11				40
1	2	4	5	3	8	6	7	9			10^2												13	12	11^1			41
1	4	5^1	3	2	6^3	7	8	9	13		10											12	14		11			42
1	2	3^1	4		10	9	6	7		12	8^1											5		13	11			43
1	2	3	5		4	6	7	8			9^2					12							13	10^1	11			44
1	2	3	5		4	6	7	8			10		9												11			45
1	2	13	4	9	3	5	6	7^2		10^1	8												14	12	11^2			46

FA Cup

Fourth Qualifying	St Albans C		(a)	3-1
First Round	Blackpool		(a)	2-1
Second Round	Coventry C		(a)	0-3

National League Play-Offs

Eliminator	AFC Fylde		(h)	2-1
Semi-Finals	Sutton U		(a)	3-2
Final	Tranmere R		Wembley	1-2

FA Trophy

First Round	Dartford		(a)	1-1
Replay	Dartford		(h)	2-2
(aet; Boreham Wood won 3-1 on penalties)				
Second Round	Gateshead		(a)	3-3
Replay	Gateshead		(h)	1-2

BROMLEY

Ground: The Stadium, Hayes Lane, Bromley BR2 9EF. *Tel:* (02084) 605291. *Website:* bromleyfc.tv
Email: info@bromleyfc.co.uk *Year Formed:* 1892. *Record Attendance:* 10,798 v Nigeria, Friendly, 24 September 1949.
Nickname: 'The Ravens', 'The Lillywhites'. *Manager:* Neil Smith. *Colours:* White shirts with black trim,
black shorts with white trim, white socks.

BROMLEY – NATIONAL LEAGUE 2017–18 LEAGUE RECORD

Match No.	Date		Venue	Opponents	Result	H/T Score	Lg Pos.	Goalscorers	Attendance
1	Aug	5	H	Eastleigh	D 0-0	0-0	13		1228
2		8	A	Dover Ath	W 2-1	1-0	5	Rees 36, Dennis 71	1145
3		12	A	Macclesfield T	D 0-0	0-0	9		1281
4		15	H	Leyton Orient	W 6-1	2-0	4	Porter 11, Holland 2 39, 75, Rees 55, Mekki 62, Williams 88	3346
5		19	H	Hartlepool U	W 2-0	1-0	2	Rees 36, Wanadio 58	1709
6		26	A	Dagenham & R	L 1-5	1-3	4	Wanadio 26	1415
7		28	H	Sutton U	L 0-1	0-1	8		2239
8	Sept	2	A	Wrexham	L 0-2	0-0	13		4032
9		9	A	AFC Fylde	D 2-2	1-0	13	Sutherland 8, Rees 50	1514
10		12	H	Torquay U	W 3-1	1-1	12	Williams 3 20, 58, 88	1029
11		16	H	Solihull Moors	W 1-0	0-0	6	Porter 88	1003
12		23	A	FC Halifax T	L 1-2	0-0	10	Porter 62	1760
13		30	H	Tranmere R	L 0-1	0-0	13		2056
14	Oct	3	A	Maidstone U	W 2-0	1-0	12	Okuonghae (og) 38, Dennis 90	2541
15		7	A	Gateshead	W 2-1	0-0	7	Dennis 84, Williams 90	853
16		21	H	Woking	W 2-0	2-0	6	Holland 42, Rees 45	1577
17		24	H	Maidenhead U	L 2-3	2-3	8	Wanadio 10, Rees 23	1056
18		28	A	Boreham Wood	D 2-2	2-2	7	Rees 32, Wanadio 38	1128
19	Nov	11	A	Guiseley	W 1-0	0-0	6	Allen 90	1074
20		18	H	Chester FC	D 1-1	1-1	7	Dennis 15	1129
21		25	A	Barrow	W 3-0	1-0	8	Raymond 24, Wanadio 58, Vose 81	941
22		28	H	Aldershot T	L 0-2	0-1	8		1171
23	Dec	2	A	Dover Ath	D 2-2	2-0	7	Dennis 33, Holland 42	1201
24		9	A	Eastleigh	D 4-4	2-2	8	Rees 26, Williams 37, Dennis 2 50, 87	1751
25		23	H	Macclesfield T	D 1-1	0-1	8	Dennis 70	1445
26		26	A	Ebbsfleet U	L 1-2	1-2	10	Dennis 19	1567
27		30	A	Leyton Orient	W 1-0	0-0	9	Dennis 22	5227
28	Jan	1	H	Ebbsfleet U	W 4-2	3-1	6	Holland 17, Porter 28, Wanadio 36, Dennis 85	1302
29		6	H	AFC Fylde	L 0-1	0-1	9		1239
30		20	A	Torquay U	W 4-0	1-0	7	Dennis 41, Mekki 65, Wanadio 73, Rees 80	1547
31		27	H	FC Halifax T	W 3-0	0-0	7	Dennis 50, Rees 2 54, 58	1524
32	Feb	10	H	Maidstone U	D 2-2	2-1	8	Rees 5, Porter 45	2027
33		17	A	Tranmere R	L 0-1	0-1	8		5536
34		20	A	Aldershot T	D 1-1	1-0	8	Woolfenden 23	1909
35	Mar	10	H	Guiseley	W 2-1	0-0	8	Rees 73, Bugiel 90	906
36		20	A	Solihull Moors	L 0-2	0-1	10		624
37		27	A	Hartlepool U	L 1-2	1-1	10	Rees 45	3041
38		30	H	Wrexham	D 1-1	0-0	10	Hanlan (pen) 66	1403
39	Apr	2	A	Sutton U	W 3-0	2-0	10	Hanlan 6, Mekki (pen) 45, Rees 80	2233
40		7	H	Gateshead	D 0-0	0-0	10		1035
41		10	A	Chester FC	L 2-3	0-1	10	Rees 66, Bugiel 80	754
42		14	A	Woking	W 2-0	1-0	10	Higgs 32, Johnson, R 68	2027
43		17	H	Dagenham & R	W 3-1	0-0	10	Holland 2 57, 71, Raymond 90	1007
44		21	H	Boreham Wood	W 3-2	1-0	10	Higgs 35, Hanlan (pen) 56, Bugiel 90	1282
45		24	H	Barrow	D 0-0	0-0	8		1331
46		28	A	Maidenhead U	L 2-5	1-3	9	Porter 22, Bugiel 68	1418

Final League Position: 9

GOALSCORERS

League (75): Rees 16, Dennis 13, Holland 7, Wanadio 7, Porter 6, Williams 6, Bugiel 4, Hanlan 3 (2 pens), Mekki 3
(1 pen), Higgs 2, Raymond 2, Allen 1, Johnson, R 1, Sutherland 1, Vose 1, Woolfenden 1, own goal 1.
FA Cup (3): Dennis 1, Mekki 1, Rees 1.
FA Trophy (21): Dennis 7, Rees 3, Porter 2, Hanlan 2 (1 pen), Holland 2, Bugiel 1, Higgs 1, Raymond 1, Wanadio 1,
own goal 1.

Gregory 46	Chorley 17 + 6	Wynter 12 + 2	Sterling 43 + 1	Wanadio 38 + 2	Mekki 29 + 8	Holland 45	Raymond 32 + 5	Rees 38 + 5	Williams 11 + 15	Dennis 30 + 12	Allen 3 + 9	Sutherland 26 + 7	Porter 28 + 10	Dunne 14 + 3	Higgs 21 + 10	Johnson D 17 + 6	Johnson R 17 + 1	Campbell 1 + 1	Francis-Adeyinka 1 + 1	Vose 1 + 5	Woolfenden 17 + 3	Bugiel 7 + 9	Hanlan 11 + 4	McLoughlin 1 + 1	Match No.
1	2	3	4	5^1	6	7	8	9	10	11	12														1
1	4	2	5	3^2	6^1	7		9	11	10^2	12	8	13	14											2
1	3	4	5	6^2	12		2	10^2	11		8^1	9	13		14										3
1	3^1	2	5	4	9	6	14	10^3	12	11		8	7^2			13									4
1	3	7	8	9	6	4	13	2	12	5^1		11	10^2												5
1	2	3	4^1	5^1	7	6		10	12	11		9	8^2	13	14										6
1		7		10^1	13	4	5	3	6^1	12		11			8	9	2								7
1	4		5	10	8	3	6^2	7	13	9	12		11^1		2										8
1	2	12	5	3			6	8^2	10	11^1	14	7	9	4^3	13										9
1	5^1	4^3	2	3	8	7		9	11	10^2		6		14	13	12									10
1		2	5	3^1	6^2	8	9	11	10^3	12	14	7	13			4									11
1		2	5	3^1	7^1	8	6^2	10	11	13	14	9	12			4									12
1			3	4	8^2	9		10	13	11	12	7	6^1	2				5							13
1	12		10	4^2	14	7		2	13	6	3^3		11^1	5	8	9									14
1	14		4	5^1	13	6		11	12	10	8^2		9^3	2	7	3									15
1			3^1	4	8^2	6	7	11	10^3	12		14	2	9	13				5						16
1	14	10	11	7	4	5^1	3	6				12	13^4	2^2	8^3	9									17
1	2		4	6^2	7	8	9	10	11^1	5		12	13			3		13							18
1			5	6^2	9^1	3	8	7				10	13		2						11	12			19
1			4	5	8^2	6	7	10^3				11	12	9^1	2	3					13	14			20
1			4	5^1	6	8	9^3	11		10^2		12	13		7	3	2				14				21
1			3	4^1	7^2	6		5^3	10	14		11	9		12	8^4	2					13			22
1	2		4	5^1		7		8	10	12		11	13		3	6						9^2			23
1	14		4	13	7^3	5	6^2	10	12	11		9	8		2^1	3									24
1		2	3	5	13		10	11^2	12			9	8		6	4					7^1				25
1	14	7	8^1	13	3	4^2	12	5					9			6	10				11				26
1	3	7	8^2	6^3	14	2	13	5				10	9^1			12					11				27
1			4	5^2	7^3	6	14	10	13	11		9	8^1		12	3					2				28
1		7	8	6^3	3	4	2	13	5				9^2			14	10				11	12			29
1	3	5	4^1	8	6	7^3	10	12	9			13								14	2	11^1			30
1	2	3	4	6^1	7	8^3		10	11			12	13			14					5	9^2			31
1	3	8	9^3	4	5	2	7	10				12									11^1	13	6		32
1	2^1	3	4^2	6	7^3	9		11		14		8				13					5	12	10		33
1	14		4			5	6	11^1		10		12	8^3	7		2					3	9^2			34
1			3^1	2^2	12	9	8^3	13		11		6	7			4					5	14	10		35
1	2		6^1	4	7^2			11		13		9^3			8	5		14			3	10	12		36
1	14		3^2	6	9			11		13	12		8^1	2		4		3^4			7	10	5^4		37
1			4		8	6	7^1	13				5	10^2		9	14	3^4				2	12	11^3		38
1	4		2	9^1	5	7	12		14			8	10^3		6^2						3	13	11		39
1	2		3	9^1	5	6^2	13		12			10	8^3	7			2				4	14	11		40
1		3	12		5	6^2	9		11^1			8	7			2					4	13	10		41
1	6	7		3	4		14					10	8^3	2^1	5			9			12	11^1	13		42
1		3	4^3			6	7	14				10	9	2^1	8			5			13	11^1	12		43
1		6	7^3	13	3	4		14				10^1	8	2^2	5			9			11	12			44
1		3^2		13	5	6		12				9	8^1	2^3	7			4			14	10	11		45
1	14		4	7^2	5	6	10			13		9	2^2	8		3^1					11	12			46

FA Cup

Fourth Qualifying	Dover Ath	(a)	0-0	
Replay	Dover Ath	(h)	3-0	
First Round	Rochdale	(a)	0-4	

FA Trophy

First Round	Hartley Wintney	(a)	2-0	
Second Round	Blyth Spartans	(a)	4-1	
Third Round	Workington	(a)	1-1	
Replay	Workington	(h)	7-1	
Fourth Round	Spennymoor T	(h)	0-0	
Replay	Spennymoor T	(a)	2-1	
Semi-Final 1st leg	Gateshead	(h)	3-2	
Semi-Final 2nd leg	Gateshead	(a)	1-1	
(Bromley won 4-3 on aggregate)				
Final	Brackley T	Wembley	1-1	
(Brackley T won 5-4 on penalties)				

CHESTER FC

Ground: Swansway Chester Stadium, Bumpers Lane, Chester CH1 4LT.   *Tel:* (01244) 371376.
Website: www.chesterfc.com   *Email:* info@chesterfc.com   *Year Formed:* 1885, renamed Chester City 1983, reformed
as Chester FC 2010.   *Record Attendance:* 20,500 v Chelsea, FA Cup 3rd rd (replay), 16 January 1952 (at Sealand
Road).   *Nickname:* 'The Blues'.   *Joint Managers:* Anthony Johnson and Bernard Morley.   *Colours:* Blue and white
striped shirts, white shorts with blue trim, white socks with blue trim.

CHESTER FC – NATIONAL LEAGUE 2017–18 LEAGUE RECORD

Match No.	Date		Venue	Opponents	Result		H/T Score	Lg Pos.	Goalscorers	Attendance
1	Aug	8	H	AFC Fylde	D	1-1	1-1	15	Dawson [45]	2223
2		12	H	FC Halifax T	D	0-0	0-0	18		2082
3		15	A	Hartlepool U	D	1-1	1-0	17	Akintunde [1]	3071
4		19	H	Sutton U	L	2-3	1-2	21	Mahon [45], Dawson [63]	1670
5		26	A	Aldershot T	W	2-1	0-1	18	Dawson (pen) [48], James [82]	2056
6		28	H	Macclesfield T	L	0-2	0-1	20		2363
7	Sept	2	A	Torquay U	D	1-1	0-1	21	Hannah [90]	1455
8		5	A	Solihull Moors	L	0-2	0-1	21		651
9		9	H	Ebbsfleet U	D	1-1	0-0	21	Akintunde [82]	1591
10		12	A	Gateshead	L	2-3	0-1	21	Hannah [73], Waters [90]	657
11		16	A	Dover Ath	L	0-4	0-1	21		1102
12		23	H	Maidenhead U	W	2-0	1-0	21	Astles [6], Hannah (pen) [73]	1839
13	Oct	3	H	Woking	L	0-2	0-1	21		1658
14		7	A	Tranmere R	D	0-0	0-0	21		7172
15		21	A	Boreham Wood	L	1-2	0-2	22	Bell [77]	1501
16		24	H	Barrow	W	3-2	2-2	20	Archer [11], Hall-Johnson [25], Dawson [90]	1548
17		28	A	Maidstone U	L	0-1	0-0	22		2351
18	Nov	4	A	Eastleigh	D	2-2	0-1	22	Akintunde [60], Astles [88]	1868
19		8	H	Wrexham	L	0-1	0-1	22		4079
20		18	A	Bromley	D	1-1	1-1	21	Hannah [14]	1129
21		21	A	Leyton Orient	D	2-2	2-1	21	Akintunde [15], Hannah [40]	3352
22		25	H	Dagenham & R	L	0-4	0-0	21		1638
23	Dec	9	H	Solihull Moors	W	1-0	0-0	21	Hannah [77]	1430
24		23	A	FC Halifax T	L	0-4	0-4	21		2040
25		26	H	Guiseley	L	0-2	0-2	22		1634
26	Jan	1	A	Guiseley	D	1-1	0-0	22	James [61]	855
27		6	A	Ebbsfleet U	W	1-0	1-0	21	White [20]	1389
28		9	A	AFC Fylde	D	1-1	0-0	21	White [68]	1531
29		20	H	Gateshead	L	1-3	0-2	22	White [70]	1580
30		23	H	Hartlepool U	D	1-1	0-0	22	White [77]	1421
31		27	A	Maidenhead U	L	0-3	0-3	22		1510
32	Feb	10	A	Woking	L	0-1	0-1	23		1367
33		17	H	Eastleigh	W	3-1	2-1	22	Hannah 2 [19, 43], Akintunde [90]	1604
34		20	H	Leyton Orient	L	0-1	0-0	22		1935
35		24	A	Dagenham & R	L	2-3	1-1	22	Archer [31], Waters [62]	1254
36	Mar	6	A	Dover Ath	L	0-2	0-0	22		1182
37		11	A	Wrexham	L	0-2	0-0	22		6511
38		17	H	Aldershot T	D	0-0	0-0	23		1612
39		24	A	Sutton U	L	2-3	0-2	23	Akintunde [60], White [87]	2195
40		30	H	Torquay U	L	0-2	0-1	23		1830
41	Apr	2	A	Macclesfield T	L	0-1	0-0	23		2996
42		7	H	Tranmere R	L	0-2	0-1	23		3103
43		10	H	Bromley	W	3-2	1-0	23	Vose [45], Archer [77], Brown [90]	754
44		14	A	Boreham Wood	L	2-4	0-2	23	Akintunde 2 [73, 90]	551
45		21	H	Maidstone U	L	1-3	0-2	23	Noble [58]	1728
46		28	A	Barrow	W	2-1	1-0	23	Archer [20], Crawford [76]	1788

Final League Position: 23

GOALSCORERS

League (42): Akintunde 8, Hannah 8 (1 pen), White 5, Archer 4, Dawson 4 (1 pen), Astles 2, James 2, Waters 2, Bell 1,
Brown 1, Crawford 1, Hall-Johnson 1, Mahon 1, Noble 1, Vose 1.
FA Cup (0).
FA Trophy (2): Dawson 1, Hannah 1.

Mitchell 8	Halls 39	McCombe 22 + 1	Astles 40 + 1	Rowe-Turner 26 + 3	Dawson 31 + 4	Turnbull 17 + 4	James 32	Mahon 23 + 9	Akintunde 33 + 7	White 20 + 10	Hannah 21 + 9	Bell 5 + 8	Downes — + 1	Chapell 3 + 6	Thomson 2	Joyce 6 + 5	Davies 1 + 1	Noble 1	Lynch 14	Crawford 15 + 2	Shaw 9 + 4	Sheron 3	Waters 3 + 4	Hall-Johnson 11	Zanzala 1 + 3	Hellawell — + 1	Gough 15 + 1	Archer 12 + 8	Rainey 2	Anderson 13 + 1	Slew — + 1	Hornby 13	Jones 14	Udoh 2 + 1	Murombedzi 2	Brown 1 + 5	Hobson 13	Roberts 12	Vose 10 + 1	Firth 11	Cunningham — + 2	Match No.
1	2	3	4	5	6	7	8	9^2	10^1	11^{13}	12	13		14																												1
1	2	3	4	5	6	7	8	9^2	12	10^1	11	13																														2
1	2	5	6	3	10	8	4	7^1	11^3	12	9^2	13		14																												3
1	2	3	4	5	6	7	8	9	11					10^1		12																										4
1	2	3	4	5	6	7	8	9	11^1					12	13	10^2																										5
	2	3	4	5	11	6^1	7	9				10		8			1	12																								6
	2	3^2	4	5	6		8	9^1	11^3		14	10	13	7			1			12																						7
	2	4^2		3	9^1	6	5	12				10	7	8			1			13	11																					8
1	2	4		3	13	7	6	12	9			10^1	11							8^2			5																			9
	4	3		5	12	7^1	8	9	11^2	13	10			6^3					2	14																						10
	2	3	4	5	9		8	6^1	13	10^3	11	12		7^2		1				14																						11
	2	3	5	6	8	12	4	9^2	10^3		11	14		13		1			7^1																							12
	2	3^4	4	5	8	13	6	9^3	10		11	14			12	1			7^1																							13
	2	5	3	4	8	7	6		9		11			12		1			10^1																							14
		3	4	2	7^3	14	5			11^2	12	13		6^1		1			8				9	10																		15
		3	4		7	8	6			13	10^3	14		1		9^2				2	12	5	11^1																			16
	2	4	5	14	8	6^2	3			13	7^3			1		9	12	11	10^1																							17
1	2		4	3	7		6		8^2			10^1	12	13		1			9			5	11																			18
	2		5	3	7	12	4^1		8^2	13	6			1		9^2	14	11	10																							19
	2	4		3	8	7	6		9	11^3	10	12		1		5																										20
	2	3		4^1	7		5		9		10	11		1		8				6	12																					21
	2	5	12	3	8		4	9		6	7^2			1		10				11^1		13																				22
5^1		3	6	8		9	10	13						12		7			4			1	2	11^2																		23
	3	4		7		6^2	13	8	12			9		10^1		2			1	5	11																					24
	3	5^4	7		6	14	12	10^3	11^2			8^1		9		4	13		1	2																						25
3	4	5		7^1	6	10	13	8^1	11^2			14		9		2			1			12																				26
2	3			9	5	7		10^1	11	12		8		6		4			1																							27
	2		6	4^1	3		8	5	12			9		10		11			1	7																						28
2	4		7^2	5	3	13	9	6		12				11		1	8		10^1																							29
4		2	5	8^1	6	7		9^2	10			10		12		1	3																									30
2	12	4	5	8^1	6	7		9^2	11^3			10		13		1	3^8	14																								31
	3	4	13		8^1	5^2	9	10	12			11		6		2	7																									32
2	4	13			6^1	12		11				7^2		14		10	5	1		3	8	9^3																				33
2	4				6^3	14	12	10				8		13		11^1	5^2	1		3	7	9																				34
2	4				12		10					8		6		11	5^1	1		3	7	9																				35
2^2	3				13		11	12				8		7		10	4^1			5	9	6	1																			36
2	4	8		14	10^3	13	12	7				9^2		11^1		5				3		6	1																			37
2	3	14		12	13	10^3	8					8^2		11		6^2		5		4	9	7^1	1																			38
6	4	12		14	9	10		8^2				13		5^1		3				2	7	11^3	1																			39
3		6	5	8^8	10^2	7	11^3					13		4						2	9^1	12	1	14																		40
2	3				4	8	5					9				11			7			6	10	1																		41
2	4				9	10	11^2					8				12	5					13	3^7	6^1	1																	42
3	5				6^1	8	11^3					9		12	13	4^2						14	2	10^7	1																	43
	4				9	10	11^1	14				7				5^3						12	2	6^8	8	1	13															44
2^2	5				9	7^1				4	8	10				3^{12}	13					6		11		1																45
2	3				4^1	6	13		10			7				9^{82}	11					5		12		1																46

FA Cup
Fourth Qualifying   Kidderminster H   (a)   0-2

FA Trophy
First Round   AFC Fylde   (h)   2-2
(aet; Chester FC won 5-4 on penalties)
Second Round   East Thurrock U   (a)   0-1

DAGENHAM & REDBRIDGE

Ground: Chigwell Construction Stadium, Victoria Road, Dagenham, Essex RM10 7XL.
Tel: (020) 8592 1549.   *Website:* www.daggers.co.uk   *Email:* info@daggers.co.uk   *Year Formed:* 1992.
Record Attendance: 5,949 v Ipswich T, FA Cup 3rd rd, 5 January 2002.   *Nickname:* 'The Daggers'.
Joint Managers: Peter Taylor and Terry Harris.   *Colours:* Red and blue halved shirts, blue shorts, red socks.

DAGENHAM & REDBRIDGE – NATIONAL LEAGUE 2017–18 LEAGUE RECORD

Match No.	Date	Venue	Opponents	Result	H/T Score	Lg Pos.	Goalscorers	Attendance
1	Aug 5	H	Barrow	W 2-1	2-0	3	Whitely (pen) [18], Cheek [21]	1362
2	8	A	Boreham Wood	W 2-1	2-1	2	Okenabirhie [2], Whitely [18]	635
3	12	A	Eastleigh	D 2-2	1-2	2	Whitely 2 (1 pen) [13, 74 (p)]	1614
4	15	H	Ebbsfleet U	D 3-3	2-0	5	Whitely [22], Lokko [45], Ferrier [64]	1686
5	19	A	AFC Fylde	D 2-2	1-1	7	Ferrier [45], Ling [90]	1590
6	26	H	Bromley	W 5-1	3-1	1	Cheek 2 [15, 29], Lokko [44], Ferrier [74], Whitely [81]	1415
7	28	A	Maidstone U	D 0-0	0-0	2		2544
8	Sept 2	H	Gateshead	W 3-1	1-1	1	White [13], Ferrier [80], Romain [87]	1358
9	9	A	Hartlepool U	L 0-1	0-0	2		3366
10	12	H	Sutton U	L 1-2	1-1	8	Whitely [22]	1261
11	16	H	FC Halifax T	W 3-1	3-0	3	Robson [17], Whitely [22], Garner (og) [45]	1282
12	23	A	Solihull Moors	D 2-2	1-2	7	Enigbokan-Bloomfield [6], Howell [90]	625
13	30	H	Torquay U	W 1-0	0-0	2	Okenabirhie (pen) [90]	1421
14	Oct 3	A	Aldershot T	D 1-1	0-1	4	Ling [86]	1903
15	7	A	Woking	L 0-1	0-0	6		2509
16	21	H	Wrexham	L 0-1	0-0	9		1492
17	24	H	Macclesfield T	W 1-0	0-0	7	Ferrier [50]	1185
18	28	H	Maidenhead U	D 1-1	0-1	6	Cheek [55]	1384
19	Nov 11	A	Tranmere R	L 0-2	0-2	9		5227
20	18	H	Guiseley	W 3-2	2-2	8	Ferrier [29], Doe [45], Howell [80]	1116
21	21	H	Dover Ath	W 1-0	1-0	5	Ferrier [23]	1263
22	25	A	Chester FC	W 4-0	0-0	4	Ling [56], Howell [75], Cheek 2 [79, 90]	1638
23	Dec 9	A	Barrow	W 1-0	0-0	5	Ferrier [56]	917
24	23	H	Eastleigh	L 1-2	1-1	6	Cheek [17]	1263
25	26	A	Leyton Orient	L 0-2	0-0	7		5125
26	30	A	Ebbsfleet U	D 1-1	0-1	8	Enigbokan-Bloomfield [86]	1684
27	Jan 1	H	Leyton Orient	D 0-0	0-0	8		3144
28	6	H	Hartlepool U	W 4-2	1-0	6	Sparkes 2 [39, 81], Cheek [66], Okenabirhie [79]	1290
29	9	H	Boreham Wood	L 2-3	0-1	7	Cheek [55], Sparkes [90]	1117
30	20	A	Sutton U	L 1-2	0-0	10	Okenabirhie [84]	2077
31	27	H	Solihull Moors	L 1-3	1-2	10	Okenabirhie [40]	2217
32	Feb 10	A	Aldershot T	L 0-2	0-1	11		1509
33	17	A	Torquay U	W 3-0	0-0	11	Okenabirhie 2 [50, 90], Robson [76]	1931
34	20	A	Dover Ath	L 0-1	0-1	11		677
35	24	H	Chester FC	W 3-2	1-1	11	Okenabirhie 2 [11, 85], Halls (og) [88]	1254
36	Mar 10	H	Tranmere R	L 0-4	0-0	11		1411
37	13	A	FC Halifax T	L 1-2	1-0	11	Adams [40]	1315
38	24	H	AFC Fylde	W 2-0	2-0	11	Kandi [33], Enigbokan-Bloomfield [42]	1168
39	30	A	Gateshead	D 0-0	0-0	11		764
40	Apr 2	H	Maidstone U	W 2-1	1-0	11	Okenabirhie [25], Robson [64]	1633
41	7	H	Woking	D 1-1	1-0	11	Sparkes [9]	1391
42	14	A	Wrexham	W 2-1	0-1	11	Okenabirhie [50], Raven (og) [75]	4193
43	17	A	Bromley	L 1-3	0-0	11	Howell [54]	1007
44	19	A	Guiseley	W 5-3	4-3	11	Cheek 3 [16, 36, 67], Gordon [26], Okenabirhie (pen) [44]	311
45	21	H	Maidenhead U	W 1-0	1-0	11	Cheek [11]	1433
46	28	A	Macclesfield T	L 0-2	0-0	11		4201

Final League Position: 11

GOALSCORERS

League (69): Cheek 13, Okenabirhie 12 (2 pens), Ferrier 8, Whitely 8 (2 pens), Howell 4, Sparkes 4, Enigbokan-Bloomfield 3, Ling 3, Robson 3, Lokko 2, Adams 1, Doe 1, Gordon 1, Kandi 1, Romain 1, White 1, own goals 3.
FA Cup (0).
FA Trophy (2): Cheek 1, own goal 1.

Cousins 46	N'Gala 9	Ling 28 + 1	Lokko 23 + 2	Pennell 22	Robson 45	Whitely 23 + 4	Boucaud 40 + 1	Ferrier 27 + 3	Okenabirhie 34 + 4	Cheek 27 + 7	Hawkins 2 + 5	Howells 35 + 6	Robinson 24 + 9	Doe 15 + 2	Romain 1 + 9	White 1 + 2	Howell 26 + 7	Nunn 24 + 1	Wheeler — + 1	Adams 16 + 5	Kandi 5 + 13	Enigbokan-Bloomfield 10 + 16	Sparkes 21 + 4	Bonds 1 + 4	Gordon 1 + 1	Mongoy — + 1	Match No.
1	2	3	4	5	6	7	8	9²	10¹	11	12	13															1
1	4	6	5	2	3	8	7	9²	10¹	11³	12	14	13														2
1	6	5	12	2	3	7	8		10	11³	14	9¹		4²	13												3
1	4	6	5	2	3	8	7		10⁵	11	9²	12			13												4
1	7³	9	2	3	11	8	5	6¹	10²	12	13		4		14												5
1	5	4	2	3	8	7	11²		10			9¹	12	6	13												6
1	9⁴	7	2	3	11²	8	5	6¹	10	12				4	13												7
1	9	3	4		8	6	7²		11			5		12	10¹		2	13									8
1	3	8	2¹	4	10³	9	6	7²	11	5	14			13			12										9
1	3	8		4	10	9	6¹	7²	13	5		11³		2			14	12									10
1	3	9		4	10	8	7		11	5				2				6¹	12								11
1	3	8		4	10²	9	6	12		5³		13		7	2		14		11¹								12
1	3			4	8	9	10	12		5¹	7	6	13		2				11²								13
1	3	2		6	9²	8	11	10		7¹	5	12		13	4												14
1	2³			6		9	11	10²		3	13	5	12	7	4		8¹		14								15
1	8	7⁸		3	10	6	5		9¹	11		2		4					12								16
1	8	3		10²	7	6	12	9¹		11		2		4			5³		13								17
1	8	3		10²	7	6	12	9¹		11		2		4			5		13								18
1	14	4		9³	8			10¹	11	2		3	12	6	5²		7			13							19
1	2	4		6	7	9¹	11		10	3		5		8			12										20
1	8	7		3	10	6	5²		9¹	11		2		4					12	13							21
1	8	7		3	10²	6	5¹		9	11		2		4			5		13	12							22
1	4	6		5	9¹	8	10³		11²	3		2		7			14	13	12								23
1	4	3¹		6		9	10		11³	5	13	2		7²					12	14	8						24
1	5	12		4	9	7	10		11²	2	6¹	3							13	8							25
1	5	3		2	12	8	14	10	11¹	4	7			6³						13	9²						26
1	5	4		3	13	7	14	10	12	2	6			8²						11¹	9³						27
1	4	3		2		9	12	11	10	5	6	13		7²							8¹						28
1	5	4		3	12	7	9	10³	11	2	6¹	13		8²							14						29
1	6³	5		4		7	9	10	11²	2	14	3		12					13	8¹							30
1	3		5		4	11	8	9	10¹	13		2		12			7²				6						31
1			3	4	13	9		11	10⁵	5	6			7	2¹				12	14	8²						32
1			3	4					10¹	5	6			7	2		8	12	11	9²	13						33
1			4	3					11	12		5	6	8	2		7	13	10²	9¹							34
1	4			3				11²	10	5	6			8¹	2		7	12	13	9							35
1			3	4				8	10²	11	5	6¹		2	7		12	13	9								36
1			3	5	13			10¹	11²	4	6³			7	2		8	12	14	9							37
1			3	4		6		11		5		12		2	7		9¹	10	8								38
1			4	3		6		11		5		12		2	7		9¹	10	8								39
1			3	4		6		11	10	5	13			12	2		7	9¹	8²								40
1			4	3		6¹		11	13	5	14			12	2		7	9³	10²	8							41
1			5	3		6¹		11³	12	4	13			8	2		7		10²	9	14						42
1			4	3		6³		11	12	5	13			8¹	2		7		10²	9	14						43
1	4		3					11³	10¹	12	6			7	2		8²		13		9	5	14				44
1	4			3		7		11	10	5	6			8¹	2				12	9							45
1			3	4		9³		11	10	5	6¹			7²	2				13	8	12	14					46

DOVER ATHLETIC

Ground: Crabbie Athletic Ground, Lewisham Road, River, Dover, Kent CT17 0JB.   *Tel:* (01304) 822373.
Website: doverathletic.com   *Email:* enquiries@doverathletic.com   *Year Formed:* 1894 as Dover FC, reformed as
Dover Ath 1983.   *Record Attendance:* 7,000 v Folkestone, 13 October 1951 (Dover FC); 5,645 v Crystal Palace,
FA Cup 3rd rd, 4 January 2015 (Dover Ath).   *Nickname:* 'The Whites'.   *Manager:* Chris Kinnear.
Colours: White shirts with grey trim, black shorts, black socks.

DOVER ATHLETIC – NATIONAL LEAGUE 2017–18 LEAGUE RECORD

Match No.	Date		Venue	Opponents	Result		H/T Score	Lg Pos.	Goalscorers	Atten- dance
1	Aug	5	A	Hartlepool U	W	1-0	1-0	5	Allen 29	3954
2		8	H	Bromley	L	1-2	0-1	10	Gregory (og) 75	1145
3		12	H	Wrexham	W	1-0	1-0	6	Bird 18	1012
4		15	A	FC Halifax T	W	2-1	0-0	3	Brundle 87, Sho-Silva 90	1486
5		19	H	Barrow	D	1-1	0-0	5	Bird 72	927
6		25	H	Macclesfield T	L	0-1	0-0	5		1270
7		28	H	Ebbsfleet U	D	1-1	1-0	9	Bird 17	1625
8	Sept	2	A	Tranmere R	W	1-0	0-0	6	Bird 79	4101
9		9	A	Aldershot T	W	2-0	1-0	1	Gallifuoco 35, Daniel 65	1862
10		12	H	Boreham Wood	L	0-1	0-1	5		1012
11		16	H	Chester FC	W	4-0	1-0	2	Gallifuoco 22, Pinnock 62, Nortey 70, Brundle 83	1102
12		23	A	Guiseley	D	1-1	1-1	3	Nortey 40	805
13		30	H	Solihull Moors	W	1-0	0-0	1	Bird 80	2795
14	Oct	3	A	Sutton U	D	2-2	1-0	2	Gallifuoco 36, Parry 90	2206
15		7	A	Torquay U	W	2-0	1-0	2	Lewis 5, Bird 63	1915
16		21	H	Maidenhead U	D	1-1	0-0	2	Bird 76	837
17		24	H	Woking	W	3-1	2-0	1	Bird 2 5, 21, Parry 56	1017
18		28	A	Gateshead	D	0-0	0-0	1		816
19	Nov	11	H	Eastleigh	W	2-0	1-0	1	Alabi 32, Essam 57	1273
20		18	A	Leyton Orient	D	1-1	1-0	1	Nortey 23	4548
21		21	A	Dagenham & R	L	0-1	0-1	2		1263
22		25	H	AFC Fylde	L	0-1	0-0	5		2860
23	Dec	2	A	Bromley	D	2-2	0-2	5	Brundle 55, Richards 90	1201
24		9	H	Hartlepool U	W	4-0	2-0	4	Pinnock 2 3, 25, Bird 2 79, 90	1083
25		23	A	Wrexham	D	0-0	0-0	3		4980
26		26	H	Maidstone U	D	2-2	0-2	5	Nortey 58, Bird 80	2369
27		30	H	FC Halifax T	D	0-0	0-0	4		1127
28	Jan	1	A	Maidstone U	D	2-2	1-0	4	Ilesanmi 27, Nortey 76	2502
29		6	H	Aldershot T	L	1-2	1-1	5	Parry 45	1237
30		20	A	Boreham Wood	W	3-0	0-0	6	Parry 52, Daniel 72, Ilesanmi 85	527
31		27	A	Guiseley	W	2-1	1-0	6	Brundle 5, Pinnock 88	2327
32	Feb	10	H	Sutton U	L	0-1	0-1	9		1027
33		17	A	Solihull Moors	L	2-3	1-1	9	Bird 22, Pinnock 60	679
34		20	H	Dagenham & R	W	1-0	1-0	7	Pinnock 29	677
35		24	A	AFC Fylde	L	1-3	0-0	9	Pinnock 57	1622
36	Mar	3	H	Leyton Orient	W	1-0	0-0	7	Pinnock 82	1348
37		6	A	Chester FC	W	2-0	0-0	6	Lokko 64, Astles (og) 71	1182
38		17	H	Macclesfield T	W	2-0	2-0	7	Marsh-Brown 2 2, 36	837
39		24	A	Barrow	D	0-0	0-0	7		908
40		27	A	Eastleigh	L	1-2	1-0	7	Bird 22	1450
41	Apr	2	A	Ebbsfleet U	L	1-2	0-0	7	Marsh-Brown (pen) 90	1735
42		7	H	Torquay U	W	1-0	0-0	8	Bird (pen) 57	1128
43		14	A	Maidenhead U	L	2-3	0-0	8	Jeffrey 49, Parry 54	1155
44		17	A	Tranmere R	L	0-1	0-1	9		1231
45		21	H	Gateshead	W	3-2	1-1	7	Gallifuoco 36, Bird (pen) 68, Azeez 89	1424
46		28	A	Woking	W	2-1	1-1	8	Gallifuoco 26, Marsh-Brown 90	2593

Final League Position: 8

GOALSCORERS
League (62): Bird 16 (2 pens), Pinnock 8, Gallifuoco 5, Nortey 5, Parry 5, Brundle 4, Marsh-Brown 4 (1 pen), Daniel 2, Ilesanmi 2, Alabi 1, Allen 1, Azeez 1, Essam 1, Jeffrey 1, Lewis 1, Lokko 1, Richards 1, Sho-Silva 1, own goals 2.
FA Cup (0).
FA Trophy (10): Pinnock 5, Bird 2, Alabi 1, Brundle 1, Parry 1.

Match No.	Walker 46	Passley 31+3	Brundle 46	Ilesanmi 45	Nortey 32+1	Parry 45+1	Essam 46	Gallifuoco 45	Richards 8+6	Allen 10+2	Bird 43+3	Sho-Silva 2+12	Pinnock 39+3	Daniel 5+34	Fazakerley 6+5	Essuman —+1	Deen-Conteh —+4	Lewis 5+1	Alabi 7+4	Jeffrey 13+8	Okosieme 2+7	Bellamy 9+7	Azeez 8+4	Lokko 11+1	Marsh-Brown 2+4
1	1	2	3	4	5²	6	7	8	9³	10¹	11	12	13	14											
2	1	2	6²	5	8	3¹	4	7	11	9	10	12	13												
3	1	2	4	3	5	7	6	8	11¹	9	10²	12		13											
4	1	2	5	4	3	7	8	6	9¹	10	11²	12		13											
5	1		7	6	8	4	5	3³	9²	10¹	11	13		14	2	12									
6	1	2	9	5	4¹	3³	8	7	6²		11	10	14	12			13								
7	1	6	5	7¹	2	3	4	8			11	10	9³	13			12								
8	1	2	6	3	7²	4	5	9				10³	11¹	12	8	14	13								
9	1	2	7	4	3	5	6	8				10³	11²	13	9¹	12	14								
10	1	2	7	5¹	8²	3	4	6	14			9³	10	12	11	13									
11	1	2	7	5³	6	3	4	8	13			11¹	12	9	10²			14							
12	1	2	3	4	7¹	5	6	10				13	11²	14	9	8³		12							
13	1	2	7	5		3	4	6				12	10	13	11³	9¹	14		8²						
14	1	2	5	6		3	4	7	14			11²	10¹	13	8¹²				9						
15	1	2	7	3		5	6	4				8	10		9¹	12			11						
16	1	2	7	6		4	3		13			10			9²	12	5		8	11¹					
17	1	2	7	5		3	4	6				10			9	12		8	11¹						
18	1		4	5		6	3	2	8			10		7	12	9			11¹						
19	1	2	6	5	7	3	4	8			11	9			12				10¹						
20	1	2²	7	6	8	5	3	4				10¹			9	13	12		11						
21	1		6	2	10¹	4	5	3				9		7	13	8			11²	12					
22	1		7	5	8²	3	4	6			11	10		12	2²		14		9¹	13					
23	1		6	2	3¹	4	5	8	14		11		7		10³				9²	12	13				
24	1		5	7	6	3	4				11	10			9	12			8¹	2					
25	1	3¹	7	4	2	5	6²	8	14		11				9	13			12	10²					
26	1	2	7	6	8	4	3	5				10			9	12			11¹						
27	1	2	7	5	8²	3	4	6				10	11²	12					13	9¹	14				
28	1	2	7	3	10	5	6	4				9¹		8	11²				13			12			
29	1	2	4	7	5²	3	6	8	10³			11¹		9					13			14			
30	1	2	8	3	4²	5	7	6			11	9		12						10¹	13				
31	1	2	7	3	10¹	5	6	4				9		8²						11³	14	12			
32	1	2	7	5	8²	3	4	6	9¹			10			11	12		13							
33	1	7	2	3²	5	6	9				11		8	13						10¹	4	12			
34	1	2¹	6	3	14	4	5	7			11		8²							9²	13	10			
35	1	2³	6	5	4²	3	7	10			9		14							12	8	11¹	13		
36	1	2²	7	5	8¹	14	4	6			10³		11							12	13	9	3		
37	1	14	6	2	3	4	7				10¹		8²	13						12	9¹	11	5		
38	1		8	6	3	4	2		14		9²		13							12	7	10³	5		11¹
39	1		6	3		4	5	8	12		7³		14							13	9	11²	2		10¹
40	1		5	2		3	4	8			10¹		7							12		9	11	6	
41	1	12	6	2	4²	5	3	8³			7¹									13		10	11	9	14
42	1	2	6	3		5	7	8			9		11							10¹		12	4		
43	1		6	3		4	5	8			11	7³								12	9¹	14	10²	13	2
44	1		2	6		3	5	7	14			8³	13							9¹	10	11²	4		12
45	1	12	7	5	8	3	2²	6			10¹		11³							9	13		4		14
46	1		2	5	3²	6¹	7	8			11³		10							9	12	13	4		14

FA Cup
Fourth Qualifying Bromley (h) 0-0
Replay Bromley (a) 0-3

FA Trophy
First Round Eastbourne Bor (h) 3-0
Second Round Marine (h) 4-3
Third Round Leyton Orient (h) 3-4

EASTLEIGH

Ground: The Silverlake Stadium, Ten Acres, Stoneham Lane, Eastleigh, Hampshire SO50 9HT.   *Tel:* (02380) 613361.
Website: eastleighfc.com   *Email:* admin@eastleighfc.com   *Year Formed:* 1946.
Record Attendance: 5,250 v Bolton W, FA Cup 3rd rd, 9 January 2016.   *Nickname:* 'Spitfires'.
Manager: Andy Hessenthaler.   *Colours:* Blue shirts with white trim, white shorts, blue socks.

EASTLEIGH – NATIONAL LEAGUE 2017–18 LEAGUE RECORD

Match No.	Date	Venue	Opponents	Result	H/T Score	Lg Pos.	Goalscorers	Attendance
1	Aug 5	A	Bromley	D	0-0	0-0	14		1228
2	8	H	Sutton U	W	1-0	0-0	7	Williamson [59]	1744
3	12	H	Dagenham & R	D	2-2	2-1	8	Williamson 2 (1 pen) [44, 45 (p)]	1614
4	15	A	Woking	L	1-2	0-1	15	Obileye (pen) [67]	1796
5	19	H	Tranmere R	W	2-0	0-0	10	Williamson [64], McAllister [79]	1906
6	26	A	Leyton Orient	D	1-1	1-0	10	Obileye [45]	4373
7	28	H	Aldershot T	D	0-0	0-0	11		2525
8	Sept 2	A	Ebbsfleet U	D	2-2	1-1	12	Constable [19], McAllister [80]	1423
9	9	A	Guiseley	D	0-0	0-0	12		735
10	12	H	Maidstone U	L	0-1	0-0	15		1820
11	16	H	AFC Fylde	D	2-2	1-1	16	Johnson [26], McSheffrey [54]	3312
12	23	A	Hartlepool U	W	2-1	0-0	15	Howe [48], Yeates [52]	3374
13	Oct 3	A	Boreham Wood	L	0-1	0-0	17		404
14	7	A	Wrexham	L	1-2	1-0	18	Williamson [43]	3907
15	21	H	Gateshead	W	3-2	1-0	16	Williamson [4], Constable [62], Strevens [90]	1597
16	24	H	Solihull Moors	L	1-2	0-1	17	Williamson [59]	2577
17	28	A	Macclesfield T	W	2-1	1-0	18	Yeates 2 [45, 50]	1352
18	Nov 4	H	Chester FC	D	2-2	1-0	16	Williamson [2], McSheffrey [53]	1868
19	11	A	Dover Ath	L	0-2	0-1	17		1273
20	18	H	Barrow	L	0-2	0-1	18		1708
21	21	H	Maidenhead U	D	2-2	0-1	18	Obileye (pen) [84], Williamson [90]	1525
22	25	A	FC Halifax T	D	3-3	2-1	18	Matthews [16], Zebroski [22], Heslop [63]	1407
23	Dec 2	A	Sutton U	L	0-1	0-1	19		1967
24	9	H	Bromley	D	4-4	2-2	18	McCallum 3 [10, 19, 58], Matthews [88]	1751
25	23	A	Dagenham & R	W	2-1	1-1	18	Zebroski [32], McCallum [60]	1263
26	26	H	Torquay U	D	1-1	0-0	17	Miley [72]	2092
27	30	H	Woking	D	2-2	0-0	18	Zebroski [64], Howe [90]	2067
28	Jan 6	H	Guiseley	W	4-2	2-1	15	Miley [2], Zebroski [36], Yeates [58], Howe [65]	2001
29	13	A	Torquay U	W	2-1	1-1	14	Matthews [9], Hoyte [70]	1486
30	20	A	Maidstone U	W	3-2	1-2	12	Obileye 2 [10, 86], Broom [79]	2133
31	27	A	Hartlepool U	W	4-3	2-2	12	Obileye [23], Zebroski 3 [45, 65, 75]	2153
32	Feb 3	A	AFC Fylde	D	2-2	1-0	11	Broom 2 [24, 67]	1626
33	10	H	Boreham Wood	L	0-2	0-0	12		1751
34	17	A	Chester FC	L	1-3	1-2	13	Yeates [20]	1604
35	20	A	Maidenhead U	L	1-3	1-1	14	Obileye (pen) [45]	1055
36	24	H	FC Halifax T	D	0-0	0-0	13		1852
37	Mar 17	H	Leyton Orient	D	0-0	0-0	14		2013
38	24	A	Tranmere R	L	1-3	0-1	16	Zebroski [88]	4619
39	27	A	Dover Ath	W	2-1	0-1	12	McCallum 2 [84, 90]	1450
40	Apr 2	A	Aldershot T	W	2-0	1-0	12	Zebroski [43], McCallum [63]	2853
41	7	H	Wrexham	D	1-1	0-1	13	Cresswell [90]	1765
42	10	A	Barrow	L	2-3	0-1	13	Zebroski [60], Williamson [90]	817
43	14	A	Gateshead	L	0-2	0-1	16		612
44	17	H	Ebbsfleet U	L	0-1	0-0	16		1614
45	21	H	Macclesfield T	L	0-2	0-1	16		2372
46	28	A	Solihull Moors	W	4-1	1-0	14	Matthews 3 [34, 51, 53], McCallum [68]	1014

Final League Position: 14

GOALSCORERS

League (65): Williamson 10 (1 pen), Zebroski 10, McCallum 8, Obileye 7 (3 pens), Matthews 6, Yeates 5, Broom 3, Howe 3, Constable 2, McAllister 2, McSheffrey 2, Miley 2, Cresswell 1, Heslop 1, Hoyte 1, Johnson 1, Strevens 1.
FA Cup (1): Howe 1.
FA Trophy (1): Miley 1.

Stack 27	Hoyte 31	Green 11+6	Johnson 11+2	Boyce 38	Togwell 19+2	Wood 34+1	Yeates 37+8	Hollands 29+4	McCallum 23+3	Williamson 24+12	Zebroski 29+10	McAllister 2+22	Stearn 1+4	Constable 13+12	Obiley 23+11	Matthews 25+14	Flitney 18+2	Howe 26	Miley 34+3	McSheffrey 11	Strevens 1+6	Cresswell 12+1	Shaw 5+1	Heslop 5	Hudson-Odoi 5+1	Broom 10+3	Read 1	Childs 1	Dennett —+1	Match No.
1	2	3	4	5	6	7	8^3	9	10^1	11^2	12	13	14																	1
1	2	3	5	4	7	6^1	8	9	10^2	11^3	12	13		14																2
1	2	3		5	6	7	8^2	9	10^3	11^1	12			13	4	14														3
	4	5		3	6	7^1	8	9^3	10	11^2	13				14	12	1	2												4
				9	4	5	6	8	10^1	7^2	12		3^3	14	2	13	1	11												5
1			12	3	5	6^1	7	8		11^2	10^3	13		9	2	14	4													6
		5	12	3	7^3	8	9	14		11^1	13	10			4^2	6	1	2												7
1		2	9	3	5^1	8			6^2	13	14			4	7^3	12		11	10											8
1		2	8	3^2	5	7				12	14			4^1	6	13			10	9	11^3									9
1		5	3		6^1	7				12	13	14	11^3	4^2	9				2	8	10									10
1		2	3	4^2	12	6	7			14	10	13				9^3			5	8	11^1									11
1				4	6	7^2	8^2			11^1	13			10	2	14			3	5	9	12								12
				4	5	6	7			13	10^3	14		9^1	2		1		3	8	11^2	12								13
	2			3	5	9	8			10	13	7^1	14				1		4	12	11^3	6^2								14
	2				7	13	6	8^3	10^2		12			9	4				1	5	11^1	14	3							15
	2				12	7				9^3	10	14	13	8	3				1	4	6^1	11^2	5							16
		2^2	4		6	7				9		13		11	12				1	5	8	10^1	14	3^3						17
	2		4		6	7				9^2		13		10	3^1	14			1	5	8	11^3	12							18
	2		6		7	4^1				9			14	10^2	12				1	5	8	11^3	13		3					19
1	5		4		6					12	9	10^3		11^2	14	13			3	8^1			2	7						20
1	2		7^3		4^1					3^2	8		14	6	9				10	12			11	5	13					21
	2		6		4					3^3	8^1	12	13	14	9^2	1^1	10	7					11	5						22
1	2		5							6	14	10^2		11	13				12	9^3			4	8^1	3	7				23
1	2		3		5^1	12		8	10^3	11	14					13			4	9					6	7^2				24
1	2		4		5	13	7^3	11	10					14	12	9^1			3	8					6^2					25
1	2		8		3	12	7	4		5^2	14			13					10^1	11	9				6^3					26
1^1	2		8		3	5	7^3	4^2		6	13			14					10	12	11	9								27
	4		2^1		5	6	8				11			12	10		1		3	9					7					28
	2		12	3	4^1	8^2					13	5		14	6	10	1		11	9					7^3					29
	4		2	5	6	7^2					11	10^1		13	3	9^3	1		8			14			12					30
	2			8	3^3	4	5^1	10^2	6		12	7		11			1		9						13					31
1	2				5	6	7				10			11	4^1	9			12			3			8					32
1	2			8^2	3	5	12				10	6^1		13	14	11			9^3			4			7					33
1	2			10	3	5	6	9^3	13	11^1	7			14	12							4			8^3					34
1	2				5	6^3	7^2			11^1	13	10		14	4	9			8				3	12						35
1	5			2	4	6^1	8	13		10	12	11^2			3	9			7											36
1	2			4	9	3	5	7		6	11			8	12				10^1											37
1	5				4	6	7	8^2		11^1	14	12		3^3	10				9				2		13					38
1					4	13	5	6		11	12	10		3^2	9^1				8				2		7					39
1			14	9	2	4	6^1	13	5^3	12	7			11	10								3		8^2					40
1			14	13	3	4^2	5^1	6		10	12	11^3			9				8				2		7					41
1^1	2		12		3^3	5	6			11	14	10			9		13		8				4^2		7					42
	3	4	5				6	8	14	10	11^1			12	13	1			9						7^3	2^2				43
	2	13	3				4^2	5	7	10^3	12	11		14	9	1			8^1						6					44
	2	12	3				4^1	5^3	7	11	13	10		14	9	1			8^2						6					45
	2	3		8				13	7	4^1	10	5		6	11^2				9									1	12	46

FA Cup
Fourth Qualifying Hereford (h) 1-2

FA Trophy
First Round Ebbsfleet U (a) 1-2

EBBSFLEET UNITED

Ground: The Kuflink Stadium, Stonebridge Road, Northfleet, Kent DA11 9GN.
Tel: (01474) 533 796. *Website:* ebbsfleetunited.co.uk *Email:* info@eufc.co.uk *Year Formed:* 1946 (as Gravesend and Northfleet), 2007 (renamed Ebbsfleet United).
Record Attendance: 12,032 v Sunderland, FA Cup 4th rd, 12 February 1963. *Nickname:* 'The Fleet'.
Manager: Daryl McMahon. *Colours:* Red shirts with white trim, white shorts, red socks.

EBBSFLEET UNITED – NATIONAL LEAGUE 2017–18 LEAGUE RECORD

Match No.	Date		Venue	Opponents	Result	H/T Score	Lg Pos.	Goalscorers	Attendance
1	Aug	5	A	Guiseley	D 2-2	0-1	9	Weston [63], McQueen [66]	848
2		8	H	Maidstone U	W 2-0	0-0	3	Coulson [65], Kedwell [76]	2519
3		12	H	AFC Fylde	D 3-3	2-3	7	Clark [18], Kedwell [28], Drury [89]	1270
4		15	A	Dagenham & R	D 3-3	0-2	8	Powell [59], Coulson [67], Kedwell [80]	1686
5		19	A	Maidenhead U	D 1-1	0-1	11	Coulson [50]	1628
6		26	H	Gateshead	D 0-0	0-0	12		1446
7		28	A	Dover Ath	D 1-1	0-1	13	McQueen [76]	1625
8	Sept	2	H	Eastleigh	D 2-2	1-1	15	Powell [45], Kedwell [68]	1423
9		9	A	Chester FC	D 1-1	0-1	17	Powell [58]	1591
10		12	H	Aldershot T	L 0-2	0-1	19		1402
11		16	H	Tranmere R	D 0-0	0-0	19		1525
12		23	A	Boreham Wood	W 1-0	0-0	16	Kedwell (pen) [78]	622
13		30	H	FC Halifax T	W 2-0	0-0	12	Shields 2 [47, 71]	1643
14	Oct	3	A	Solihull Moors	W 3-1	2-0	11	Weston [27], Kedwell [31], Mills [83]	579
15		7	A	Macclesfield T	L 0-1	0-1	14		1635
16		21	H	Barrow	W 3-2	1-0	10	McLean [24], Drury [76], Powell [80]	1402
17		24	H	Torquay U	L 0-1	0-0	12		1525
18		28	A	Sutton U	D 0-0	0-0	13		2197
19	Nov	11	H	Leyton Orient	W 2-1	2-0	11	Drury [6], Kedwell [40]	2021
20		18	A	Wrexham	L 0-2	0-1	12		4150
21		21	A	Woking	L 0-1	0-1	15		1580
22		25	H	Hartlepool U	W 3-0	1-0	12	Weston [22], Kedwell [67], Coulson [81]	1416
23	Dec	9	A	Guiseley	W 4-0	2-0	10	Powell [21], Kedwell (pen) [43], Bush [77], Weston [79]	1127
24		23	A	AFC Fylde	D 1-1	0-0	10	Kedwell [53]	1512
25		26	H	Bromley	W 2-1	2-1	9	Powell [15], Kedwell [30]	1567
26		30	H	Dagenham & R	D 1-1	1-0	10	Powell [33]	1684
27	Jan	1	A	Bromley	L 2-4	1-3	10	Drury [39], Shields [54]	1302
28		6	H	Chester FC	L 0-1	0-1	10		1389
29		9	A	Maidstone U	W 2-1	0-0	10	Powell 2 [46, 61]	2396
30		20	A	Aldershot T	D 0-0	0-0	11		2457
31		27	H	Boreham Wood	L 0-3	0-1	11		1366
32	Feb	3	A	Tranmere R	L 0-3	0-2	12		5138
33		10	H	Solihull Moors	W 1-0	0-0	10	Coulson [72]	1117
34		17	A	FC Halifax T	W 2-1	0-1	10	Whitely [55], Coulson [60]	1762
35		20	H	Woking	W 2-1	1-0	10	Kedwell 2 (1 pen) [41 (p), 49]	1146
36		24	A	Hartlepool U	W 1-0	1-0	8	Rance [17]	2895
37	Mar	10	A	Leyton Orient	D 1-1	1-1	9	Whitely [15]	4127
38		24	H	Maidenhead U	D 1-1	1-0	9	Coulson [4]	1503
39	Apr	2	A	Dover Ath	W 2-1	0-0	9	Shields [55], Drury [90]	1735
40		7	A	Macclesfield T	D 2-2	0-1	9	Kedwell (pen) [70], Rance [78]	1501
41		10	H	Wrexham	W 3-0	0-0	9	Whitely [50], Kedwell [83], Coulson [90]	1376
42		14	A	Barrow	W 1-0	1-0	9	Rance [32]	1189
43		17	A	Eastleigh	W 1-0	0-0	7	Clark [82]	1614
44		21	A	Sutton U	L 0-1	0-0	8		2852
45		24	A	Gateshead	W 5-2	1-1	5	Kedwell 3 (1 pen) [33 (p), 61, 71], Coulson [74], Powell [83]	411
46		28	A	Torquay U	D 1-1	0-0	6	Connors [69]	1728

Final League Position: 6

GOALSCORERS

League (64): Kedwell 18 (5 pens), Powell 10, Coulson 9, Drury 5, Shields 4, Weston 4, Rance 3, Whitely 3, Clark 2, McQueen 2, Bush 1, Connors 1, McLean 1, Mills 1.
FA Cup (5): Drury 1, Coulson 1, Kedwell 1 (1 pen), McLean 1, Weston 1.
FA Trophy (3): Kedwell 1, Shields 1, Weston 1.
National League Play-Offs (3): Coulson 1, Weston 1, Winfield 1.

Ashmore 46	Coulson 40 + 6	Weston 23 + 17	Winfield 25 + 1	Magri 32 + 1	Clark 37 + 1	Drury 37 + 3	Payne 21 + 2	Powell 33 + 8	Kedwell 43 + 2	McQueen 9 + 4	McLean 2 + 8	McCoy 15 + 4	Shields 17 + 16	Connors 22 + 2	Mills 3 + 7	Mambo 9	Bush 29 + 5	Graham 4 + 1	Cook 5 + 4	Rance 30 + 4	Brandy — + 1	Bubb — + 7	Wilson 12 + 1	Whitely 12 + 1	Pitouia-Wabo — + 6	Match No.
1	2	3	4	5	6	7	8	9	10	11¹	12															1
1	2	6¹	5²	4	3	9	8	7	10	11²	13	12	14													2
1	6	10²		4	3	9	8	7³	11	12				2	13	5¹	14									3
1	3	8²		4		7³	9	12	11	10¹	14	2	13	6		5										4
1	3	8²		4		13	9¹	7	10	12	11³	5		6	14	2										5
1	2	12		4		7	8	9¹	11	10		13		3	5	6²										6
1	2²	7³				8	9	11¹	10		3	13	12	4	5	6	14									7
1	6³					7	8	11²	10¹	14	2	9	13	3	4	5	12									8
1	13		3	12	14	7	9³	10	11		6²			2¹	4	5	8									9
1	2	13		3	4		8	6	11	10			12		9		7¹	5²								10
1	9	10		2¹	3	6	8	7	13	12			5	11²	4											11
1	10³	6		9	3	5	7¹	4	13	14			2	8²	11		12									12
1	13	5		2	3	8²		6	11	10¹		12	9	4		7										13
1	4²	9³		3		8	11	2	10¹	6	12		5	14	13	7										14
1	5¹	9		6		8		13	2	10	3²	11	7	12	4											15
1	13	12		2	3	7		6	11		10¹	9²	5	4	8											16
1	13	7	14	3	10	9	11		12	2¹	6¹	5²	4	8												17
1	6²	12		2	3	8	7³	11		13		4	5¹	10	9	14										18
1	2¹	10²		3	4	8	13	11		12	6	5	7	9												19
1	11	7	10	4	5	6		14	2	9¹	12	8²	3	13³												20
1	4²		3	2	9	8	11	12	6	13	5	10¹	7													21
1	8¹	10		2	3	7	12	11³	14	6	5	4	13	9²												22
1	9¹	8	12	2	3	6		7	11	13	10	5²	4													23
1	4	10¹	2	5	3²	9	8	11		13	6	12	7													24
1	10	7³	4	2	3	8	9²	11		12	13	5¹	14	6												25
1	2¹	7	5	6	4	8		10²	11	3	12		9	13												26
1	10²	12	4	2	3	7	9²	11		14	6	5¹	8	13												27
1	2²	9	5	3¹	4	7	13	8	11	10		6		12												28
1	11	12	3	5	4	6	7	8¹	10		9²				13		2									29
1	9	12	3	8		5	7	4³	6¹	2			10		14		13	11²								30
1	10¹	14	3	5		7	8	9³	11		2²	12			4		13	6								31
1	4¹	8	2	3		9		11		6					5		7	12	10							32
1	12	10	4	5	3	13	8	9²	11			2¹			6		7									33
1	5	11¹	3	2	4	6	8	14	10		13				7³		9²	12								34
1	10¹		4	2	3	9	7²	12	11		13	5			8		6									35
1	2²	13	5	3	4	10	8		11		12	6			9		7¹									36
1	10¹		4	2²	3	9	7	13	11			5			12		8	6								37
1	2	5		4	10	13	8¹	11			12	6			9¹		3	7²	14							38
1	9²	12	4		3	7		13	11		2	10			5		6	8¹								39
1	8¹	13	4		3	9		11			2²	10			5		7	6	12							40
1	4	13	5		3	9	8¹	11			2	10³			6		14	7¹	12							41
1	8²	12	3		4	5		6			7	14			9¹		2	10	11³	13						42
1	2¹	12	5		3	8	13	11			6²				4		9	10	7							43
1	13	12	4		3	9²	8	11			10¹				5		7	2²	6	14						44
1	6	12	3		4	7	8¹	11			2				9		5	10¹	13							45
1	2	12	4		3	8	7²	11			13				5¹		6	9	10							46

FA Cup

Fourth Qualifying	East Thurrock U	(a)	0-0	
Replay	East Thurrock U	(h)	3-0	
First Round	Doncaster R	(h)	2-6	

FA Trophy

First Round	Eastleigh	(h)	2-1	
Second Round	Warrington T	(h)	1-1	
Replay	Warrington T	(a)	0-3	

National League Play-Offs

Eliminator	Aldershot T	(a)	1-1
(aet; AFC Fylde won 5-4 on penalties.)			
Semi-Finals	Tranmere R	(a)	2-4
(aet)			

FC HALIFAX TOWN

Ground: The MBi Shay Stadium, Halifax HX1 2YT.
Tel: (01422) 341 222. *Website:* fchalifaxtown.com *Email:* mikesharman@fchalifaxtown.com *Year Formed:* 1911.
Record Attendance: 36,855 v Tottenham H, FA Cup 5th rd, 15 February 1953. *Nickname:* 'The Shaymen'.
Manager: Jamie Fullarton. *Colours:* Blue shirts with white trim, blue shorts with white trim, blue socks with white trim.

FC HALIFAX TOWN – NATIONAL LEAGUE 2017–18 LEAGUE RECORD

Match No.	Date		Venue	Opponents	Result		H/T Score	Lg Pos.	Goalscorers	Attendance
1	Aug	5	H	Aldershot T	L	0-2	0-0	23		2108
2		8	A	Barrow	D	0-0	0-0	23		1410
3		12	A	Chester FC	D	0-0	0-0	19		2082
4		15	H	Dover Ath	L	1-2	0-0	20	Denton [90]	1486
5		19	A	Solihull Moors	W	1-0	1-0	16	Morgan [28]	684
6		26	H	Guiseley	W	2-0	1-0	13	Kosylo [26], Brown [78]	1777
7		28	A	Gateshead	D	0-0	0-0	16		1118
8	Sept	2	H	AFC Fylde	W	2-1	0-0	8	Denton 2 [58, 77]	1775
9		9	H	Maidenhead U	W	3-2	1-0	6	Morgan [29], Kosylo 2 [55, 67]	1727
10		12	A	Leyton Orient	W	3-0	2-0	2	Morgan [5], Denton [29], Kosylo (pen) [74]	3600
11		16	A	Dagenham & R	L	1-3	0-3	8	Brown [70]	1282
12		23	H	Bromley	W	2-1	0-0	4	Kosylo [55], Denton [70]	1760
13		30	A	Ebbsfleet U	L	0-2	0-0	10		1643
14	Oct	3	H	Wrexham	D	0-0	0-0	9		2136
15		7	A	Boreham Wood	D	1-1	0-1	10	Morgan [81]	562
16		21	H	Torquay U	D	1-1	0-0	11	Waring [68]	1764
17		24	H	Maidstone U	L	0-2	0-1	13		1410
18		28	A	Tranmere R	L	2-4	0-2	15	Brown [51], Batty [65]	4826
19	Nov	11	H	Woking	D	0-0	0-0	16		1710
20		18	A	Sutton U	L	2-3	0-1	17	Denton [64], Garner [85]	1968
21		21	A	Hartlepool U	L	0-4	0-3	17		2755
22		25	H	Eastleigh	D	3-3	1-2	17	McManus (pen) [39], Denton [74], Batty [90]	1407
23	Dec	2	A	Barrow	L	0-1	0-0	17		1618
24		9	A	Aldershot T	W	1-0	1-0	16	McManus [39]	1912
25		23	H	Chester FC	W	4-0	4-0	14	Denton [6], McManus [28], Clarke [33], MacDonald [38]	2040
26		26	A	Macclesfield T	L	1-2	1-1	14	Denton [11]	2313
27		30	A	Dover Ath	D	0-0	0-0	14		1127
28	Jan	1	H	Macclesfield T	L	1-4	0-1	16	Waring [70]	1962
29		6	A	Maidenhead U	D	0-0	0-0	16		1229
30		27	A	Bromley	L	0-3	0-0	18		1524
31		30	H	Leyton Orient	L	1-2	1-2	19	Denton [32]	1352
32	Feb	10	A	Wrexham	D	1-1	1-1	18	Garner [45]	4998
33		17	H	Ebbsfleet U	L	1-2	1-0	20	Kosylo (pen) [37]	1762
34		20	H	Hartlepool U	W	2-0	0-0	18	Hotte [74], Tomlinson [77]	1584
35		24	A	Eastleigh	D	0-0	0-0	17		1852
36	Mar	3	A	Woking	W	3-1	1-0	17	Kosylo 2 (1 pen) [33 (p), 66], Thomson [80]	1619
37		13	H	Dagenham & R	W	2-1	0-1	15	Howell (og) [68], Fondop-Talom [69]	1315
38		17	A	Guiseley	D	1-1	0-1	15	Tomlinson [68]	1106
39		24	H	Solihull Moors	D	0-0	0-0	15		1849
40		30	H	AFC Fylde	L	0-2	0-0	17		2313
41	Apr	7	H	Boreham Wood	W	2-1	1-0	15	Brown [20], Fondop-Talom [64]	1460
42		10	H	Sutton U	W	2-1	1-0	14	Fondop-Talom [18], Tomlinson [89]	1274
43		12	H	Gateshead	D	2-2	0-2	12	Fondop-Talom [46], Kosylo [90]	1302
44		14	A	Torquay U	L	0-1	0-0	15		1567
45		21	H	Tranmere R	L	0-2	0-2	15		3113
46		28	A	Maidstone U	D	0-0	0-0	16		2832

Final League Position: 16

GOALSCORERS

League (48): Denton 10, Kosylo 9 (3 pens), Brown 4, Fondop-Talom 4, Morgan 4, McManus 3 (1 pen), Tomlinson 3, Batty 2, Garner 2, Waring 2, Clarke 1, Hotte 1, MacDonald 1, Thomson 1, own goal 1.
FA Cup (1): Own goal 1.
FA Trophy (2): Kosylo 2.

Johnson 44	Duckworth 16+2	Wilde 32+2	Garner 30	Brown 39	Hotte 30+2	Oliver 25+6	MacDonald 25+4	Kosylo 30+3	Tomlinson 19+14	Denton 28+3	Charles 5+6	Clarke 9+8	Riley 2+1	Dixon 3+1	McManus 32+5	Morgan 12+8	Moyo 19+3	Lynch 6+7	King —+2	Waring 5+5	Nicholson 2+1	Batty 4+1	Middleton 3+2	Clackstone 5	Hibbs 17+8	Collins 22	Khan —+1	Tuton 4+3	Fondop-Talom 10+2	Maher 9	Hanley 4+3	Thomson 8+3	Hanson 1+1	Graham 6+1	Match No.
1	2	3	4	5	6	7	8^2	9	10^1	11	12	13																							1
1	2	3	6	5	7	8	13	12^2	11	10				4^1	9																				2
1	2^2	3	5	4	6	7	13	11^3		10	9				8^1	12	14																		3
1		3	5	4		7	12	10		11	9^1				6^2	13	2	8																	4
1		3	5		6		8^3	9	10	13				4^1	14	12	11^2	2	7																5
1	2^1	12	3	4	7	8	6	9^2	14	10					5	11^3	13																		6
1		4	6	5	7	8	12	10^4		13	11				3	9^2	2^1																		7
1	2	4	3	5^2	7			9^3		13	6	11	14		8	10^1	12																		8
1	2	5	4	6	7	8		9^1	12	10					3	11^2	13																		9
1	2	4	3	6		8	10^2	5^1	12	7	14				9	11^3	13																		10
1	2	4	3	6^1		8	10^2	5		7	12				9	11	13																		11
1		3	5^4	4	6	7	8	9^3	14	10					12	11^1	2^3	13																	12
1		3	4		8		5^2	7^2	9	10	13	12			14	11	2^1	6																	13
1		3	4	8	6		5^1	9	12	10					2	11	13	7^2																	14
1		3	4	6	7		9	11^2	10^4	14					5	12	2	8^3	13																15
1		3	5	4	7	8^1	6	10^2		9	12				2	13	11																		16
1	2	4	3	6^1	7^3	8^2	9	12		5	10	13	14		11						1														17
1		3	7	6		8^1	12	10		11		13			5	2^5	9				4														18
1	2^4	4	3	5		8	12	6	7	13					11	1	9	10																	19
1	3	2	7	13	8		10^3	11		12	6	14			5^2	9^1	4																		20
1		3	4		5	10^3	7		6	12					9	14	13																		21
1^1		3		7	6^3		11	10		9					5	4^1		14	12	13		2^2	8												22
		3	5	4			14	6^1		11^2	10				8					13					9^3	1		12	2^2	7					23
1		3	5	4			10^1			12	7^3				6		2			11			13		8	9									24
1		3	6	4			13	9^3		12	11^2				7^1		2			14					8	10									25
1		3	5	4			7			12	11	8^1			6^2		2			13					9	10									26
1	4	5	3				7			12	10	9^4			11^1		2								8	6									27
1		3	4				5	7		10^2	11^3	6^1			13		2			12					8	9	14								28
1		3	5	4			6	13	10^1	12		7					2			11^2					8	9									29
1	5	2	4	3	12			13		7					14										8^1	9^3			10						30
1	3	5	4				8	6		7					9^1		2								12	10			11						31
1	12	4	3		7^2	9^1	5		6			14			8^3		2								10	11		13							32
1	13	4	3		6	7^2	10	14	11						5		2^3								9^1	8		12							33
1		5	4	8	13			9	11						3										6^2	7			10^1	12					34
1	4		5^1	2	6			10	11			13			3										7	8			9^2	12					35
1	5		2	6	14			9^1	10						3										7^3	8		11^2	4	12	13				36
1	3		2	7				10	11						4										12	8		9^2	6	5^1	13				37
1	6		5	7^1				11	10	13					3										12	8		2^2	4	9	6^1				38
1		3	5	7				11	10						4										13	8		9	6^1	2^2	12				39
1	10		2	4				3^1	6						5										12	9		13	11^2	7	8				40
1	4	3	2	12	9			11							13	7^2									10	5			8^1	6					41
1	12	6^1	8					10							2	5									7			11	3	9	4			42
1	3	2^1		7				12	9						8^2	6									11	4	13	10					5		43
1	5		6^1					10	11^1						2										13	7		9	4	12	8^2	3			44
1	2		6^3	14				8							5										12	7		10	4^1	11	9^1	13	3	45
1	2			7				10	9						4										8^1	6		11	3	5	12			46

FA Cup
Fourth Qualifying   Tranmere R   (h)   1-3

FA Trophy
First Round   Macclesfield T   (h)   1-0
Second Round   Maidenhead U   (h)   1-4

GATESHEAD

Ground: Gateshead International Stadium, Neilson Road, Gateshead, Tyne and Wear NE10 0EF.
Tel: (0191) 4783883.   *Website:* www.gateshead-fc.com   *Email:* info@gateshead-fc.com
Year Formed: 1889 (Reformed 1977).   *Record Attendance:* 20,752 v Lincoln C, Division 3N (at Redheugh Park),
25 September 1937.   *Nickname:* 'The Tynesiders', 'The Heed'.   *Manager:* Steve Watson.
Colours: White shirts with black trim, black shorts, white socks with black trim.

GATESHEAD – NATIONAL LEAGUE 2017–18 LEAGUE RECORD

Match No.	Date	Venue	Opponents	Result	H/T Score	Lg Pos.	Goalscorers	Attendance
1	Aug 5	A	Woking	L	1-2	1-2	20	Johnson [26]	1705
2	8	H	Guiseley	W	1-0	0-0	11	Byrne [53]	629
3	12	H	Torquay U	W	3-0	1-0	3	Higgins (og) [19], Peniket [78], Anderson (og) [82]	756
4	15	A	Wrexham	L	0-1	0-0	9		4097
5	19	H	Macclesfield T	W	3-0	2-0	6	Kerr [5], Burrow [45], Preston [72]	633
6	26	A	Ebbsfleet U	D	0-0	0-0	6		1446
7	28	H	FC Halifax T	D	0-0	0-0	6		1118
8	Sept 2	A	Dagenham & R	L	1-3	1-1	11	Lokko (og) [24]	1358
9	9	A	Sutton U	D	1-1	1-1	11	Johnson (pen) [15]	1805
10	12	H	Chester FC	W	3-2	1-0	11	Halls (og) [41], Peniket [46], Mitchell (og) [90]	657
11	16	H	Aldershot T	L	0-1	0-0	14		654
12	23	A	Maidstone U	D	2-2	0-1	14	Peniket [69], Johnson [80]	2530
13	30	H	Boreham Wood	D	1-1	1-0	14	York [30]	606
14	Oct 3	A	AFC Fylde	D	0-0	0-0	15		1494
15	7	H	Bromley	L	1-2	0-1	16	Johnson [68]	853
16	21	A	Eastleigh	L	2-3	0-1	17	Preston [74], Vassell [87]	1597
17	24	A	Leyton Orient	W	2-0	1-0	15	Burrow 2 [9, 80]	3468
18	28	H	Dover Ath	D	0-0	0-0	17		816
19	Nov 11	A	Maidenhead U	W	3-0	2-0	15	Hannant 2 [5, 50], Johnson [8]	1377
20	18	H	Tranmere R	W	1-0	0-0	11	Sutton (og) [90]	1140
21	21	H	Barrow	L	1-2	1-1	13	York [43]	663
22	25	A	Solihull Moors	D	1-1	1-0	15	Burrow [12]	534
23	Dec 12	A	Torquay U	D	1-1	1-0	16	Preston [28]	1405
24	26	H	Hartlepool U	D	2-2	1-1	16	Barrow 2 [45, 51]	3538
25	Jan 1	A	Hartlepool U	D	2-2	1-1	17	Peniket [41], York [79]	3241
26	6	H	Sutton U	L	0-2	0-0	18		493
27	20	A	Chester FC	W	3-1	2-0	15	McLaughlin [45], Burrow [45], Preston [52]	1580
28	23	H	Woking	D	1-1	0-0	15	Fox [80]	470
29	27	H	Maidstone U	W	2-1	1-1	14	McNall [3], Fox [87]	771
30	30	H	Wrexham	D	0-0	0-0	14		658
31	Feb 10	H	AFC Fylde	L	1-2	0-2	15	Peniket [90]	752
32	13	A	Guiseley	W	1-0	1-0	13	York [6]	541
33	17	A	Boreham Wood	L	1-2	0-1	14	York [55]	464
34	20	A	Barrow	D	1-1	0-1	13	Preston [80]	860
35	Mar 10	H	Maidenhead U	W	7-1	2-1	12	Peniket [22], Fyfield [27], Johnson 3 [59, 76, 79], McLaughlin [81], Burrow [90]	581
36	13	H	Solihull Moors	D	2-2	0-1	12	McLaughlin [68], Daly (og) [90]	486
37	27	A	Macclesfield T	L	0-1	0-0	14		1537
38	30	H	Dagenham & R	D	0-0	0-0	13		764
39	Apr 7	A	Bromley	D	0-0	0-0	14		1035
40	10	A	Tranmere R	L	2-4	2-1	16	York [39], Barrow [43]	4328
41	12	A	FC Halifax T	D	2-2	1-0	16	Burrow 2 [37, 90]	1302
42	14	H	Eastleigh	W	2-0	1-0	13	Johnson [45], Burrow [52]	612
43	17	A	Aldershot T	L	0-1	0-1	13		1893
44	21	A	Dover Ath	L	2-3	1-1	14	Vassell [20], Johnson (pen) [84]	1424
45	24	H	Ebbsfleet U	L	2-5	1-1	14	Johnson 2 [45, 66]	411
46	28	H	Leyton Orient	L	1-3	0-1	17	Johnson (pen) [90]	1056

Final League Position: 17

GOALSCORERS

League (62): Johnson 13 (3 pens), Burrow 9, Peniket 6, York 6, Preston 5, Barrow 3, McLaughlin 3, Fox 2, Hannant 2, Vassell 2, Byrne 1, Fyfield 1, Kerr 1, McNall 1, own goals 9.
FA Cup (4): Burrow 2 (1 pen), Johnson 1, McLaughlin 1.
FA Trophy (21): Johnson 6 (1 pen), Peniket 5, Burrow 3 (1 pen), McLaughlin 2, Barrow 1, Byrne 1, Hannant 1, McNall 1, Vassell 1.

Montgomery 25 + 1	Vassell 29 + 5	Barrow 34	Kerr 24 + 3	Byrne 39	Fyfield 32 + 2	Penn 36 + 4	McLaughlin 42 + 4	Preston 24 + 17	Johnson 26 + 9	Burrow 34 + 10	Tinkler 11 + 4	Peniket 30 + 10	Williams 18 + 2	Mellish 9 + 1	York 18 + 12	Hanford 21 + 1	Hannant 18 + 1	O'Donnell 6 + 5	Langstaff 1 + 4	Maxwell 6 + 2	Green 5 + 3	Fox 11 + 1	McNall 3 + 4	Greenwood 4 + 4	Match No.
1	2	3	4^2	5	6	7^1	8	9	10	11	12	13													1
1	4		3	2^1	6	8	11	9^2	10	7	13	5	12												2
1	3	6^1	12^1	4	5	8	9	13	10^1	11	7	14	2												3
1	3		4^3	5	6	8^2	7	14	13	11	2	10	9^1		12										4
1	8		3	4^1	2	7	6	11	13	10		9^2	5		12										5
1	2		4	3	7	8	9^1	14	10^1	13	11	5	6^2		12										6
1^1	3		4	5	7	8	9^3	10	11	2	6^2	14	12		13										7
	2	3	4^2	9	7	6	13	12	5	11		10^1				1	8								8
	2	3	4	5	9	8	12	7	13	6^1		11^2				1	10								9
	3		4	5	8	9	10^3	13	11	2		14	1		7^1	6^2	12								10
	3		4	5	8^1	9	14	10^2	13	11^1	2		1		7	6	12								11
1	2^*		4	5		6	12	10^1	14	11	3	9^2			8	13			7^3						12
1	5		3	4	14	8	13	10^3	12	11^1	2	6			9				7^2						13
1	4	3	2	5		8		11	10			6			9	1	7								14
2	6		3	5	7	9		10	11			12	4^1		1	8									15
3	5	4			6^2	8	9	12			10	2			11^1	1	7	13							16
	5	3	4		7^1	8	10		11			2			1	6	9	12							17
	5	4	3		7	10^1		11		12	2				1	8	9	6							18
	2^1	4	3		7^2	13	12	11	10	5	14				1	8	9^3	6							19
	2		3	4	7	6	9^1	10	11	5	12				1	8^2				13					20
	5^2		3	4	12	8		9	11	2	13				10^1	1	7	14		6^2					21
	2	3	5^1	13	8^4	12	10^1		9	4	11^2				14	1		6	7						22
5		3	4		6	12	8^2	10	11	2	9^1	13				1	7^3	14							23
12	5	4^2	3		11^3	13	14	6	10	2	9				7^1	1	8								24
3	5		4		6^2	8	10^1	12	11	2	9				13	1	7								25
	6	3	5			8	12	13	10^2	2	9				11	1	7			4^1					26
2	5	12	3	4	6	8	10		11						9^1						7				27
4^1	2	12	5	3	6	8^2		11							9	1					7	13			28
13		6	3	4	5	9^2	8	14	12	11					2^3	1^1					7	10^1			29
1		5	2	3	4	7	8		11^1	10					9						6	12			30
1	12	6		2^1	3	5^2	8	14		10^1		11	4		9						7	13			31
1	2	4			3	7	9	8		10			11	12	5^1						6				32
1	2	3			4	10	9	8^2	13	7^3		6^1			5							11	14	12	33
1	2	3			5^4	12	6	10	14	13		11^1	4									7^1	8^3	9^2	34
1	14	3	4	2^2	5		8	12	11	13		10			6^3							7		9^1	35
1		5	4	3^2	2	12	6	8^1	10	14		11			13					12		7^3		9^4	36
1		2	3	4	5	7	6	11^3	9^1	10		8			13					12					37
1	5	2		4	3	7	6	12	9	10		11^2			13					8^1					38
1	2	3		4	14		8	12		10		11	5^1								7	6	10^2	13	39
1	2	5		3	4	8	9	13		10		11			6^2						7^1	12^3		14	40
1	12	2	3	4^2	5	7	8	13	9	10		11^1			6^3						14				41
1	2	4	3			6	7	9	11	10		12			5^1			13				8^2			42
1	2	3	4			7^2	6	10	9	13		5^1	8	14							12			11^3	43
	2	6	3	4		7	8	12	9	10^4		13	5^1	14	1				11^3						44
1	2	5	3			6	7	8	11	12		10^2			4	9^1						13			45
12	5	2	3	4^3	6^2	7	8	9	10	11^1					1						13			14	46

FA Cup

Fourth Qualifying	Buxton	(a)	2-1
First Round	Chelmsford C	(h)	2-0
Second Round	Luton T	(h)	0-5

FA Trophy

First Round *(aet)*	Guiseley	(h)	2-1
Second Round	Boreham Wood	(h)	3-3
Replay	Boreham Wood	(a)	2-1
Third Round	Maidstone U	(a)	2-2
Replay	Maidstone U	(h)	3-0
Fourth Round	Leyton Orient	(a)	3-3
Replay	Leyton Orient	(h)	3-2
Semi-Final 1st leg	Bromley	(a)	2-3
Semi-Final 2nd leg	Bromley	(h)	1-1

(Bromley won 4-3 on aggregate)

GUISELEY

Ground: Nethermoor Park, Otley Road, Guiseley, Leeds LS20 8BT. *Tel:* (01943) 873223. *Website:* guiseleyafc.co.uk
Email: see website. *Year Formed:* 1909. *Record Attendance:* 6,548 v Carlisle U, FA Cup 1st rd, 13 November 1994
(at Valley Parade); 3,000 v Leeds U, Friendly, 8 July 2017 (at Nethermoor Park). *Nickname:* 'The Lions'.
Joint Managers: Marcus Bignot and Russ O'Neill *Colours:* White shirts with blue trim, blue shorts with white trim,
blue socks with white trim.

GUISELEY – NATIONAL LEAGUE 2017–18 LEAGUE RECORD

Match No.	Date	Venue	Opponents	Result	H/T Score	Lg Pos.	Goalscorers	Attendance
1	Aug 5	H	Ebbsfleet U	D	2-2	1-0	10	Rooney [16], Thompson [77]	848
2	8	A	Gateshead	L	0-1	0-0	17		629
3	12	A	Aldershot T	L	0-6	0-4	23		1938
4	15	H	Tranmere R	D	0-0	0-0	22		1231
5	19	H	Torquay U	W	3-2	1-2	19	Lawlor [13], Hurst [86], Mulhern [90]	791
6	26	A	FC Halifax T	L	0-2	0-1	21		1777
7	28	H	Hartlepool U	L	0-1	0-0	22		1723
8	Sept 2	A	Leyton Orient	L	1-4	1-2	22	Odejayi [36]	4323
9	9	H	Eastleigh	D	0-0	0-0	23		735
10	12	A	Barrow	D	0-0	0-0	23		1072
11	16	A	Wrexham	D	1-1	1-0	22	Correia [27]	3916
12	23	H	Dover Ath	D	1-1	1-1	22	Rooney [29]	805
13	30	A	Maidenhead U	L	0-3	0-3	22		1224
14	Oct 3	H	Macclesfield T	L	1-2	1-1	22	Fondop-Talom [42]	812
15	7	A	Maidstone U	D	1-1	0-1	22	Mulhern (pen) [90]	2552
16	21	H	Solihull Moors	W	4-2	1-1	21	Molyneux [23], Liburd [65], Lawlor [68], Rooney [86]	735
17	24	H	Boreham Wood	D	0-0	0-0	21		706
18	28	H	Woking	W	3-2	1-1	20	Liburd 2 [34, 49], Fondop-Talom [74]	1783
19	Nov 11	H	Bromley	L	0-1	0-0	20		1074
20	18	A	Dagenham & R	L	2-3	2-2	22	Molyneux [18], Fondop-Talom [23]	1116
21	25	H	Sutton U	L	0-2	0-2	23		929
22	Dec 9	A	Ebbsfleet U	L	0-4	0-2	23		1127
23	23	H	Aldershot T	D	1-1	1-0	23	Purver [9]	820
24	26	A	Chester FC	W	2-0	2-0	21	McFadzean [4], Roberts [15]	1634
25	30	A	Tranmere R	L	0-4	0-0	22		5271
26	Jan 1	H	Chester FC	D	1-1	0-0	23	Palmer [90]	855
27	6	A	Eastleigh	L	2-4	1-2	23	Liburd [18], Roberts [79]	2001
28	13	A	AFC Fylde	L	1-2	1-1	23	Roberts [30]	1535
29	27	A	Dover Ath	L	1-2	0-1	23	Southwell [63]	2327
30	Feb 3	H	Wrexham	L	0-2	0-1	24		1338
31	10	A	Macclesfield T	L	1-2	1-0	24	Liburd [10]	1464
32	13	H	Gateshead	L	0-1	0-1	24		541
33	17	H	Maidenhead U	L	1-3	1-2	24	Southwell [19]	777
34	20	H	AFC Fylde	W	1-0	0-0	24	Rooney [86]	613
35	24	A	Sutton U	L	0-4	0-1	24		1915
36	Mar 10	A	Bromley	L	1-2	0-0	24	Rooney [88]	906
37	17	H	FC Halifax T	D	1-1	1-0	24	Odejayi [13]	1106
38	30	H	Leyton Orient	L	1-3	0-0	24	Widdowson (og) [76]	1216
39	Apr 2	A	Hartlepool U	W	1-0	0-0	24	Southwell [90]	2634
40	7	H	Maidstone U	D	0-0	0-0	24		957
41	14	A	Solihull Moors	L	1-3	0-2	24	Southwell [49]	915
42	17	H	Barrow	L	0-1	0-0	24		611
43	19	A	Dagenham & R	L	3-5	3-4	24	Purver [27], Hudson [33], Lenighan [38]	311
44	21	H	Woking	L	1-2	0-1	24	Southwell [61]	562
45	24	A	Torquay U	W	4-3	2-1	24	Southwell [5], Hatfield [37], Liburd 2 [60, 80]	1007
46	28	A	Boreham Wood	L	1-3	1-2	24	Southwell [21]	701

Final League Position: 24

GOALSCORERS

League (44): Liburd 7, Southwell 7, Rooney 5, Fondop-Talom 3, Roberts 3, Lawlor 2, Molyneux 2, Mulhern 2 (1 pen),
Odejayi 2, Purver 2, Correia 1, Hatfield 1, Hudson 1, Hurst 1, Lenighan 1, McFadzean 1, Palmer 1, Thompson 1, own
goal 1.
FA Cup (7): Fondop-Talam 2, Hatfield 2, Rooney 2 (1 pen), Haworth 1.
FA Trophy (1): Liburd 1.

Maxted 17	Brown 20	Frempah 3	Lowe 14	Lawlor 20 + 1	Williams 8	Hurst 14 + 8	Wesolowski 2 + 5	Rooney 24 + 7	Molyneux 18 + 3	Hudson 2	Thompson 6 + 6	Green E 2	Correia 6 + 5	Mulhern 2 + 9	Purver 24 + 4	Hatfield 27 + 3	McFadzean 16 + 8	East 4 + 1	Atkinson 11	Morrison 3	Odejayi 27 + 9	Green J 18 + 1	Palmer 36 + 1	Lenighan 17 + 3	Freestone 2	Fondop-Talom 8 + 11	Haworth 1 + 6	Holden 16 + 2	M'Boungou 4 + 1	Lihurd 19 + 9	Harvey 19	Koue Niate 3 + 3	Crookes 13 + 2	Roberts 10 + 8	Hughes 4 + 1	Sheppard 5	Southwell 18	Coddington 11	St. Ledger 6 + 1	Flowers 13	Nirennold 13 + 1	Match No.
1	2	3	4	5	6[2]	7[1]		8	9		10	11[3]	12	13	14																											1
1	3	5	6	2		7[2]		9[3]	4		11	13	12	10[1]	8	14																										2
1	2	3		5			8		10[1]		4[3]	13		11[2]		9	14		6	7	12																					3
	4	5	6	2				8	10[1]					12		9	7				3	11	1																			4
	2	5	6[2]	4			14	8	12		11[2]		13			9	7[1]				3	10	1																			5
	2	4	7[3]	5	6			8	13		10[1]		12			9	14				3	11[2]	1																			6
		2	4			14		6	12			7		10	9	5	8[9]	11[2]			13	1	3																			7
		2		5	7			9[1]	4		13			12	10	8		6			11[2]	1	3																			8
	2	3	7			13		8	6[2]		10	12			9				5	11	1	4																				9
	4	5	7			13		9	3[2]	12	10[1]					8			2	11	1	4																				10
	2	3	5[3]			13		7	8[2]	14	9[1]				6			12	11	10	1	4																				11
	2	9				13		8	4[2]	12	10[1]				7			5	6	11	1	3																				12
	4	5[2]	7			13		9	3[1]	11			14		8			2	10[3]	1	6	12																				13
1	2							6	9[1]	13				7				3	10[2]	4	8	5	11	12																		14
1	5		12					9[2]	4			13		7				3[1]	10[3]	6	8	2	11	14																		15
1	2		4		5			14	7					6[3]				8[2]	3	9		10[1]		11	12	13																16
1	2		7			8[1]		13	4								12		3	9		10[2]	6	5	11																	17
1	5		7			8		13	4[2]										10[3]	6		12	2	3	11[1]	9	14															18
1	2		4			5[2]			6[1]								7[3]		3[1]	13	14		9	8	10	11	12															19
1			6			7		13	2[2]		14						10[3]		5	8		11[1]	3		12	9	4															20
1			5			6		14	3[2]		13		7				11[3]		2	8[1]		10	12	4			9															21
1	2	3						5	6[1]							14			12	4	7	13	8[2]			10[1]	11	9														22
1	5		4										7		9				3	8	12		10[1]	6		2	11															23
1	3		5					13			8		6				12		4	9		10[2]		7		2	11[1]															24
1								13			14		3				2		14	12		5		6[1]	7	4	9	10[1]	8[2]	11												25
1	2	5[1]							7				6			13			4	7[1]		10		9	12	3	11															26
1									6				5[2]			13			4	7[1]		10		11	8		2	12	9	3												27
									4				12			14		1	2		13		5	6[2]	7		9	10[3]	8[1]	11	3											28
									3							4[1]			5		12		13	7		8	9[2]		11	2	1	6	10									29
									3							4[2]			5	12	13		14	7		8	9[3]			2[1]	1	6	10	11								30
								7					6[2]						8	14		11	9		2	12	13		10[3]	1	4	3	5[1]									31
													14	5		13			2	6[1]	12		11	7		3		8[2]		10[3]	1		4	9								32
							14							6	7	10[2]			2	8[1]		12		13		3				5[3]	11	1		4	9							33
							14	7				13	6[2]	8[1]				5					4	10	9[3]		2	12		11	1	3										34
							14	7				13	6	8[3]				2					4	10	9[1]		3	12		11	1	5[2]										35
							12	6				7[1]	5			11[1]			2				4	13			14	10[2]		9	1			3	8[1]							36
							6[1]					7	5	12		9[2]			4				2[1]	10	8	13		11	1			3	7									37
	3[3]		4	9[2]				7	6					11	12	5						13	10[1]			14		8	1[1]			2										38
				12			7[2]					5	3	13		6[1]	2					8	14			9[3]		4			10	11										39
				3[2]								7	4	6[1]		8	2					9	13			12		5			10	11										40
	2[3]		13	14								6[1]	8	12		10[2]	3					4	11			9					5	7										41
			4[1]	2[3]	6							12	5[2]	13		14	3					8	9			7					10	11										42
	2[1]			14	8[3]		3					6[2]	5			11	12	7			9			10					1	4		13	12									43
				4								6[1]	3		7[2]		1	2			12	8	9			13		5		10	11										44
				9								7	8	5	6[2]	10[1]	1	4					13	12				11		3[1]	2											45
				4					6[2]			8	3	7	9[1]		1	2					10				13		5	12	11											46

FA Cup

Fourth Qualifying	Shildon	(h)	6-0
First Round	Accrington S	(h)	0-0
Replay	Accrington S	(h)	1-1
(aet; Guiseley won 4-3 on penalties)			
Second Round	Mansfield T	(a)	0-3

FA Trophy

First Round	Gateshead	(a)	1-2
(aet)			

HARTLEPOOL UNITED

Ground: Victoria Park, Clarence Road, Hartlepool TS24 8BZ. *Tel:* (01429) 272 584.
Website: www.hartlepoolunited.co.uk *Email:* enquires@hartlepoolunited.co.uk
Year Formed: 1908. *Record Attendance:* 17,426 v Manchester U, FA Cup 3rd rd, 5 January 1957.
Nickname: 'The Pool', 'Monkey Hangers'. *Manager:* Matthew Bates. *Colours:* Blue shirts with white stripes, blue shorts with white trim, white socks with blue trim.

HARTLEPOOL UNITED – NATIONAL LEAGUE 2017–18 LEAGUE RECORD

Match No.	Date	Venue	Opponents	Result	H/T Score	Lg Pos.	Goalscorers	Attendance
1	Aug 5	H	Dover Ath	L	0-1	0-1	21		3954
2	8	A	Macclesfield T	D	1-1	0-1	21	Cassidy [58]	1519
3	12	A	Maidenhead U	L	1-2	0-1	20	Amond (pen) [87]	1491
4	15	H	Chester FC	D	1-1	0-1	19	Cassidy [71]	3071
5	19	A	Bromley	L	0-2	0-1	22		1709
6	26	H	AFC Fylde	L	0-2	0-1	23		2954
7	28	A	Guiseley	W	1-0	0-0	21	Franks [49]	1723
8	Sept 2	H	Maidstone U	W	3-1	1-0	20	Watson [19], Franks [57], Simpson [68]	4137
9	9	H	Dagenham & R	W	1-0	0-0	19	Franks [75]	3366
10	12	A	Wrexham	D	0-0	0-0	17		4144
11	16	H	Leyton Orient	W	2-1	1-1	15	Franks [45], Oates [47]	3867
12	23	H	Eastleigh	L	1-2	0-0	17	Munns [90]	3374
13	30	A	Woking	D	1-1	1-1	18	Donaldson [26]	2479
14	Oct 3	A	Barrow	W	1-0	0-0	14	Woods [90]	3082
15	7	A	Solihull Moors	W	2-1	0-0	13	Oates [47], Franks [90]	2658
16	21	H	Sutton U	D	1-1	1-0	14	Oates [39]	4526
17	24	H	Tranmere R	D	1-1	0-0	14	Deverdics [50]	3371
18	28	A	Torquay U	W	2-0	0-0	12	Oates [54], Franks [68]	1987
19	Nov 11	A	Boreham Wood	D	0-0	0-0	12		773
20	18	H	Aldershot T	L	0-2	0-1	14		3732
21	21	H	FC Halifax T	W	4-0	3-0	11	Deverdics [4], Donnelly (pen) [7], Oates [31], Newton [89]	2755
22	25	A	Ebbsfleet U	L	0-3	0-1	13		1416
23	Dec 2	H	Macclesfield T	L	1-2	1-0	13	Woods [39]	3082
24	9	A	Dover Ath	L	0-4	0-2	14		1083
25	23	H	Maidenhead U	L	1-2	1-0	15	Cassidy [28]	2756
26	26	A	Gateshead	D	2-2	1-1	15	Donnelly (pen) [17], Woods [72]	3538
27	Jan 1	H	Gateshead	D	2-2	1-1	15	Watson 2 [7, 64]	3241
28	6	A	Dagenham & R	L	2-4	0-1	17	Woods 2 [59, 84]	1290
29	20	H	Wrexham	L	0-2	0-0	18		6833
30	23	A	Chester FC	D	1-1	0-0	18	Woods [62]	1421
31	27	A	Eastleigh	L	3-4	2-2	17	Woods 2 [9, 29], Newton [88]	2153
32	Feb 17	H	Woking	W	3-2	3-0	18	Rodney [19], Cassidy [34], Oates [43]	3018
33	20	A	FC Halifax T	L	0-2	0-0	19		1584
34	24	H	Ebbsfleet U	L	0-1	0-1	19		2895
35	Mar 6	A	Aldershot T	L	1-2	1-1	19	Adams [45]	1665
36	10	H	Boreham Wood	D	0-0	0-0	19		2538
37	17	A	AFC Fylde	D	3-3	1-0	20	Tunnicliffe (og) [39], Cassidy [88], Rodney [90]	1753
38	21	A	Barrow	W	2-1	1-1	19	Newton [45], Magnay [50]	1018
39	27	A	Bromley	W	2-1	1-1	18	Hawkes [10], Woods [64]	3041
40	30	H	Maidstone U	W	2-1	1-0	16	Woods 2 (1 pen) [26, 89 (p)]	2559
41	Apr 2	H	Guiseley	L	0-1	0-0	16		2634
42	7	H	Solihull Moors	L	0-1	0-0	17		2782
43	14	A	Sutton U	D	1-1	1-1	19	Hawkes [26]	2272
44	17	H	Leyton Orient	W	1-0	1-0	17	Laing [38]	2656
45	21	H	Torquay U	D	1-1	1-0	17	Donaldson [14]	3254
46	28	A	Tranmere R	W	2-1	1-0	15	Donnelly (pen) [45], Oates [74]	5499

Final League Position: 15

GOALSCORERS

League (53): Woods 11 (1 pen), Oates 7, Franks 6, Cassidy 5, Donnelly 3 (3 pens), Newton 3, Watson 3, Deverdics 2, Donaldson 2, Hawkes 2, Rodney 2, Adams 1, Amond 1 (1 pen), Laing 1, Magnay 1, Munns 1, Simpson 1, own goal 1.
FA Cup (2): Deverdics 1, Rodney 1.
FA Trophy (0).

Loach 46	Magnay 35	Laing 35 + 4	Harrison 22 + 5	Donnelly 25 + 2	Newton 26 + 1	Woods 37 + 2	Hawkins 31 + 4	Munns 5 + 12	Donaldson 14 + 6	Amond 4	Cassidy 33 + 2	Oates 25 + 11	Deverdics 27 + 2	Adams 27 + 6	Rodney 21 + 20	Featherstone 36	Franks 19 + 1	Watson 8 + 1	Richardson 3 + 3	Ledger 9 + 2	Simpson 2 + 5	Thorne 2	George 6 + 1	Adeloye 1 + 8	Hawkes 7 + 5	Owen — + 1	Cunningham — + 1	Match No.
1	2	3	4	5	6	7^1	8^1	9^2	10	11	12	13	14															1
1	2	5	3	4	6		9	8^1	7	11	10		12															2
1	2	6	5	4^3	7	12	8^2	9^1		11	10			14	3	13												3
1	2	3	4	12	8		13	6		11	10			9^2	5^3	14	7^1											4
1	2	3^1	4	6	9			7			11	10^2	5	13	8	12												5
1		4^2	2	8		14	9^1	7^3		11	5	13	6	10	3	12												6
1		4	2^1			9	5		12	11		7		10^2	8	6	3	13										7
1	2					8	7		12		13	5		9^1	6	11	4				3	10^2						8
1	2	14				8	7		13		12	5^3		9^1	6	11	3				4	10^2						9
1	2	13			7	8		12			11^1	5	9^2	6	10	3	4											10
1	2	13	6			8	9				10^1	5	12	7	11	3^2	4											11
1	2	3	4			9	8^3	14	10^1	11^2	5	13	7	6							12							12
1	2	5	4			7	8	9^2			13	3	12	6	10													13
1	2	3	4			7	8	13	9^2		12	5	10^1	6	11													14
1	3	2	4		6		9^2	13			12	8	14	10^1	7	5							11^3					15
1	2	3	5			8^3	7				10^1	6	12	11^2	9		4	13			14							16
1	2^1	3	4			7^2	8				10	5	14	11^2	6	9		12	13									17
1	3	13	2			8^3		14			11	9	5		6	10		12	4^2				7					18
1		4	3						12		9^2	8^1	5	11	6	10		2					7	13				19
1		3	4	14			13		10	12	9	5^2	11^1	7	6		2						8^3					20
1	4	3	2	8	7		13		10^3	11	5^2	9^1	6							14			12					21
1	5	4	2	8	7		13		10	9	3	11^2	6^1										12					22
1	2	4	3	6^2	8	7	12	9^3		10	11	5	13										14					23
1	2	4		6	5	8		9			10	11	7^4	13					3^2				12					24
1	3	12	4	7	6				10^2	11	8	5	13		9				2^3	14								25
1		11		10		7	9				3	5	8	2^4	4^1		6						12					26
1		2		6	7	12			10^3	9^2	5		11^1		8	4		3	14				13					27
1	2	13		4		8	10^1			11		9	3^2	12		7	5	6										28
1	2	3		4		8	7				10		9	5	11	6^1							12					29
1	2	4	3			7	9			11		10	5			6^1							12					30
1	2^4	3	4			7	8				10		9	5	12	6							11^1					31
1	4	2	3			8	12				10	11^2		5	9	6							7^1		13			32
1	3	5	4	2		8					10	11		6	9	7												33
1	2	4	3			12	8	13			10	11	5	9^2		6							7^1					34
1	2	5	3	4^1	7	8					10	11^2	12	13	9								6^1		14			35
1	2	12	5^1	4	3^1	9	8^2				10	11^3		6	13	7									14			36
1	2	3	4			7^2	9^1	8	12		10	11		5	13	6												37
1	2	4	3^2	6		9	8^1				10	11^3		5	12	7									13	14		38
1	3	4	2			9	8	13			10	11^2		5	12	6							7^1					39
1	4	3		5		9	8				11	10^1	2	12		6							7					40
1	4	3				8	9	2			10	12		5	11^1	6							7^2					41
1	4	3				7^2	9	2			10	11^1		5	12	6							8					42
1	3	2	14	5			9^2	7			10^1	11		12		4	13	6					8^3					43
1	4	3	14			8	9^4	2			11^3	10		12	5	13^6	6						7^1					44
1	3	4		8^2		2	12	9			11	10^1		5		6							7			13	13^4	45
1	6	2	14	4	5		7				8^3	11	12	3	10^1	9^2									13			46

FA Cup

Fourth Qualifying	South Shields	(a)	2-1
First Round	Morecambe	(a)	0-3

FA Trophy

First Round	Workington	(a)	0-1

LEYTON ORIENT

Ground: Matchroom Stadium, Brisbane Road, Leyton, London E10 5NF.
Tel: (0871) 310 1881.   *Website:* www.leytonorient.com   *Email:* info@leytonorient.net   *Year Formed:* 1881.
Record Attendance: 34,345 v West Ham U, FA Cup 4th rd, 25 January 1964.   *Nickname:* 'The O's'.
Manager: Justin Edinburgh.   *Colours:* Red shirts with white trim, red shorts with white trim, red socks.

LEYTON ORIENT – NATIONAL LEAGUE 2017–18 LEAGUE RECORD

Match No.	Date	Venue	Opponents	Result	H/T Score	Lg Pos.	Goalscorers	Attendance
1	Aug 5	A	Sutton U	L	0-2	0-2	24		3198
2	8	H	Solihull Moors	W	3-1	1-0	9	Lee [21], Mooney [47], Elokobi [78]	4411
3	12	H	Maidstone U	W	2-0	0-0	4	Mooney [60], Boco [90]	5085
4	15	A	Bromley	L	1-6	0-2	11	Bonne [67]	3346
5	19	A	Woking	W	2-0	0-0	8	Bonne 2 [50, 86]	2885
6	26	H	Eastleigh	D	1-1	0-1	8	Clay [90]	4373
7	28	A	Maidenhead U	W	1-0	1-0	3	Bonne [6]	2544
8	Sept 2	H	Guiseley	W	4-1	2-1	2	Bonne 3 (2 pens) [43 (p), 45 (p), 82], Harrold [66]	4323
9	9	A	Boreham Wood	L	0-2	0-1	4		1920
10	12	H	FC Halifax T	L	0-3	0-2	9		3600
11	16	A	Hartlepool U	L	1-2	1-1	13	McAnuff [19]	3867
12	23	A	Aldershot T	D	2-2	1-2	13	Clay [39], Boco [82]	3060
13	30	H	AFC Fylde	L	1-2	0-1	15	McAnuff [72]	4357
14	Oct 4	A	Tranmere R	L	1-2	1-1	17	Harrold [22]	4145
15	7	A	Barrow	D	2-2	2-2	17	Mooney [19], Clay [27]	1796
16	21	H	Macclesfield T	L	0-1	0-1	18		4562
17	24	H	Gateshead	L	0-2	0-1	19		3468
18	28	A	Wrexham	D	2-2	1-1	19	Bonne [22], Ellis [85]	4432
19	Nov 11	A	Ebbsfleet U	L	1-2	0-2	19	Dayton [87]	2021
20	18	H	Dover Ath	D	1-1	0-1	19	Clay [78]	4548
21	21	H	Chester FC	D	2-2	1-2	20	Bonne [6], McAnuff [60]	3352
22	25	A	Torquay U	L	0-3	0-2	20		1913
23	Dec 2	A	Solihull Moors	L	0-1	0-0	20		1118
24	9	H	Sutton U	W	4-1	1-0	20	Bonne 2 (1 pen) [7 (p), 81], Harrold [54], Dayton [86]	4180
25	23	A	Maidstone U	W	2-0	1-0	20	N'Gala [38], Bonne [52]	3225
26	26	H	Dagenham & R	W	2-0	0-0	18	Coulson [49], Bonne [59]	5125
27	30	H	Bromley	L	0-1	0-1	19		5227
28	Jan 1	A	Dagenham & R	D	0-0	0-0	19		3144
29	6	H	Boreham Wood	D	0-0	0-0	19		4094
30	27	H	Aldershot T	L	2-3	1-1	19	Bonne [1], Elokobi [52]	5728
31	30	A	FC Halifax T	W	2-1	2-1	17	Bonne [18], Koroma [38]	1352
32	Feb 10	H	Tranmere R	D	1-1	0-1	17	Davies (og) [52]	4631
33	17	A	AFC Fylde	W	1-0	1-0	16	Bonne (pen) [42]	2206
34	20	A	Chester FC	W	1-0	0-0	15	Brophy [68]	1935
35	Mar 3	A	Dover Ath	L	0-1	0-0	16		1348
36	10	H	Ebbsfleet U	D	1-1	1-1	15	Clark (og) [32]	4127
37	13	H	Torquay U	L	0-1	0-1	16		2900
38	17	A	Eastleigh	D	0-0	0-0	17		2013
39	24	H	Woking	W	3-0	2-0	14	Bonne 2 (1 pen) [10, 17 (p)], Brophy [80]	5673
40	30	A	Guiseley	W	3-1	0-0	12	McAnuff 2 [48, 75], Mooney [90]	1216
41	Apr 7	H	Barrow	W	4-1	1-1	12	Jones (og) [28], Koroma [72], Bonne 2 [90, 90]	3979
42	14	A	Macclesfield T	D	1-1	1-1	14	Koroma [42]	3110
43	17	A	Hartlepool U	L	0-1	0-1	14		2656
44	21	H	Wrexham	W	1-0	1-0	13	Bonne [29]	5166
45	24	H	Maidenhead U	L	0-1	0-1	13		3145
46	28	A	Gateshead	W	3-1	1-0	13	Bonne [17], McAnuff [53], Koroma [60]	1056

Final League Position: 13

GOALSCORERS

League (58): Bonne 22 (5 pens), McAnuff 6, Clay 4, Koroma 4, Mooney 4, Harrold 3, Boco 2, Brophy 2, Dayton 2, Elokobi 2, Coulson 1, Ellis 1, Lee 1, N'Gala 1, own goals 3.
FA Cup (2): Bonne 1, Dayton 1.
FA Trophy (13): Bonne 2, Coulson 2, Harrold 2, Koroma 2, Mooney 2, Adams 1, Brophy 1, Elokobi.

Grainger 20	Caprice 35	Coulson 27	Elokobi 21	Widdowson 35 + 1	Lawless 23 + 3	Lee 6 + 2	Dayton 25 + 3	McAnuff 34 + 3	Mooney 22 + 13	Bonne 43 + 1	Koroma 16 + 15	Clay 38 + 5	Boco 5 + 12	Ochieng 3 + 2	Harrold 9 + 15	Sendles-White 8 + 5	Clark 1	Happe 21 + 5	Dalby — + 2	Brophy 22 + 2	Ellis 7	Judd 7 + 3	Westbrooke 3 + 2	Sotiriou — + 3	Sargeant 2 + 1	N'Gala 5	Brill 24	Reynolds 2 + 7	Holman 9 + 1	Adams 16	Ling 12 + 1	Ekpiteta 5 + 2	Clayden — + 1	Match No.
1	2	3	4	5	6	7^3	8^2	9^1	10	11	12	13	14																					1
1	2	3	4	5	6	7^2	8^3	9^1	10	11	14	12	13																					2
1	2	3	4	5	6	7	8^2	9^1	10^3	11	13	12	14																					3
1	2	3	4	5	6	7	12	13	10	11	9^2				8^1																			4
1	2	5	4	3	6	8^3	9^2	7^1	11	10	13	12	14																					5
1	2	5	4	3	6		9	7^1	11^2	10	13	8	12																					6
1	2	3	4	5	6		8^2	13	12	11	10^1	7	9^3	14																				7
1	2	3	4	5			6	9	10^3	11^1	14	8			7^2	12	13																	8
1	2	3^1	4	5			8^3	9	10	11	14	7			6^2	12	13																	9
1	2			5	6			9	12	11	13	7	8^1			10^2	3	4																10
1	2			5	7			9	10^3	11	6^1	8^2	14	13			3		4	12														11
1	2	8^1		3	4		11^2	6		7		9	12			5		13	10															12
1	2				3^1		10	4	6^2	5		7	13			12		8		9	11													13
1	2^1				3		10^3	4	14	5		6	13			7^2	12	8		9	11													14
1	2^1			3	6		14	7^2	10	11		8				5^3	13			9	4	12												15
1	2			5			8		10^3	11		7	9^1				4		12	3	6^2	13	14											16
1	2			5^2			12	7^1	10^2	11		8	14				4		9	3	6		13											17
1	2^2						9^3		10^1	11		13	8		12	4		5		6	3	14	7											18
1	2^1				7^3		9	13	10				12		11	4		5^2		6	3	14	8											19
	2			5	7^1		8	9		10		6			12	3		4		11						1								20
	2			5	6^3		8^2	9	14	11		7^1			12	3^4		4		10		13	1											21
1^3	2^4			5			8	9		10^2	7	12			11	4				6^1	14	13	3											22
				5			9	8	12	11		7		6^1	10^2			4	13		2					3	1							23
				5	6		9	8	12	11	13^1	7			10^2			4			2					3	1							24
	2	4		5	6		9^2	8	10^1	11		7			12	13										3	1							25
	2	3		5	6		9^2	8	10^1	11		7			12	13		4									1							26
	2	4		5	6		9	8^1	10^2	11		7			13			12								3^4	1							27
	2	3		5	7		9		10^1	11	6	8			12			4									1							28
	2	3		5	8		9	6	13	11		7			10^2			4									1	12						29
	2	7	4^3		3^1		10^2	5		6	12	8			13			9									1	14	11					30
	2	3	5					8		11	9	7						4									1		10	6				31
	2	3	4^3	5	14				11	8	7				12			9^2									1	13	10	6^1				32
	2	3	4	5	12				11	8^2	7				13			9									1		10^1	6				33
	2	3		5	12				11	6^3	8				13			4		9							1		10^2	7^1	14			34
2^1	3	4							11	6	8				14					12							1	9^1	10	7	5^2	13		35
	2	3	4					12	10	8^2	6							9									1	13	11^1	7	5			36
	5^1	4	3	13				11	10	14	7	7^3			12			6									1	9^2		8	2			37
	3	4	5					6^1		13	12	8			10			9									1		11^2	7	2			38
		4	3	2				6^1	14	10^3	13	7			11^2			8									1		12	9	5			39
		5	3	2				6	12	11	13	7						8									1		10^2	9^1	4			40
		3^2	4	5				6	10^3	11	13	8^1						9									1	14		7	2	12		41
		4	5					6	12	11	10^1	8						9									1			7	2	3		42
		3^3	2					4	14	5	6	8^1						12		9^2							1	13		10^1	11	7		43
				13				2	12	3	5	7						8		9^1	4						1			10^2	11	6		44
				12				6		11	10	8^1						4		9^2	5						1	13		7	2	3		45
					7			8	10	11^1	9							4			2						1			6	5	3	12	46

FA Cup

Fourth Qualifying	Dagenham & R	(a)	0-0
Replay	Dagenham & R	(h)	1-0
First Round	Gillingham	(a)	1-2

FA Trophy

First Round	Haringey Bor	(a)	2-1
Second Round	Bognor Regis T	(a)	2-1
(aet)			
Third Round	Dover Ath	(a)	4-3
Fourth Round	Gateshead	(h)	3-3
Replay	Gateshead	(a)	2-3

MACCLESFIELD TOWN

Ground: Moss Rose Stadium, London Road, Macclesfield, Cheshire SK11 7SP.   *Tel:* (01625) 264 686.
Website: www.mtfc.co.uk   *Email:* reception@mtfc.co.uk   *Year Formed:* 1874.
Record Attendance: 9,008 v Winsford U, Cheshire Senior Cup 2nd rd, 4 February 1948.
Nickname: 'The Silkmen'.   *Manager:* John Askey.   *Colours:* Blue shirts with white trim, white shorts, blue socks with white trim.

MACCLESFIELD TOWN – NATIONAL LEAGUE 2017–18 LEAGUE RECORD

Match No.	Date		Venue	Opponents	Result		H/T Score	Lg Pos.	Goalscorers	Attendance
1	Aug	5	A	Wrexham	W	1-0	1-0	6	Baba [12]	6118
2		8	H	Hartlepool U	D	1-1	1-0	6	Whitaker [38]	1519
3		12	H	Bromley	D	0-0	0-0	10		1281
4		15	A	Sutton U	L	1-2	1-0	16	Wilson [2]	1986
5		19	A	Gateshead	L	0-3	0-2	18		633
6		25	H	Dover Ath	W	1-0	0-0	11	Marsh [49]	1270
7		28	A	Chester FC	W	2-0	1-0	10	Hancox [7], Kennedy [62]	2363
8	Sept	2	H	Woking	L	1-3	1-2	14	Durrell [18]	1289
9		9	A	Solihull Moors	W	1-0	0-0	9	Wilson [62]	808
10		12	H	AFC Fylde	W	2-1	1-0	7	Wilson 2 [14, 90]	1065
11		16	H	Maidstone U	L	1-4	0-2	12	Arthur [80]	1347
12		23	A	Torquay U	W	1-0	0-0	8	Wilson [49]	1835
13		30	H	Aldershot T	W	2-0	1-0	4	Lloyd [1], Durrell [58]	1350
14	Oct	3	A	Guiseley	W	2-1	1-1	1	Whitaker [16], Durrell [86]	812
15		7	H	Ebbsfleet U	W	1-0	1-0	1	Hancox [42]	1635
16		21	A	Leyton Orient	W	1-0	1-0	1	Wilson [45]	4562
17		24	A	Dagenham & R	L	0-1	0-0	2		1185
18		28	H	Eastleigh	L	1-2	0-1	2	Whitehead [90]	1352
19	Nov	11	A	Barrow	W	2-0	1-0	2	Hodgkiss [27], Durrell [61]	1644
20		18	H	Boreham Wood	D	0-0	0-0	4		1324
21		21	H	Tranmere R	D	2-2	1-2	3	Wilson [40], Marsh [90]	1709
22		25	A	Maidenhead U	D	1-1	0-0	3	Lloyd [54]	1165
23	Dec	2	A	Hartlepool U	W	2-1	0-1	3	Lloyd [85], Lowe [90]	3082
24		9	H	Wrexham	W	4-1	1-0	1	Wilson 3 [6, 78, 82], Fitzpatrick [90]	2402
25		23	A	Bromley	D	1-1	1-0	1	Lloyd [39]	1445
26		26	H	FC Halifax T	W	2-1	1-1	1	Whitehead [45], Marsh [78]	2313
27		30	H	Sutton U	W	1-0	1-0	1	Whitaker (pen) [10]	2246
28	Jan	1	A	FC Halifax T	W	4-1	1-0	1	Hancox 3 (1 pen) [45, 48, 72 (p)], Wilson [60]	1962
29		6	A	Solihull Moors	D	0-0	0-0	1		1771
30		20	A	AFC Fylde	L	0-6	0-4	1		1982
31		27	H	Torquay U	D	1-1	0-0	1	Whitehead [72]	1699
32	Feb	10	H	Guiseley	W	2-1	0-1	1	Blissett [61], Marsh [72]	1464
33		17	A	Aldershot T	W	2-1	1-0	1	Whitaker (pen) [3], Blissett [48]	4358
34		20	A	Tranmere R	W	4-1	1-0	1	Whitaker 2 (1 pen) [45, 62 (p)], Durrell 2 [55, 66]	7385
35		24	H	Maidenhead U	W	1-0	0-0	1	Wilson [90]	1668
36	Mar	10	H	Barrow	W	3-1	1-1	1	Hancox [35], Whitaker [70], Durrell [77]	1748
37		17	A	Dover Ath	L	0-2	0-2	1		837
38		21	A	Maidstone U	D	2-2	0-1	1	Whitaker [52], Durrell [75]	1994
39		27	H	Gateshead	W	1-0	0-0	1	Blissett [89]	1537
40		30	A	Woking	W	3-2	1-1	1	Blissett [35], Marsh [54], Whitehead [90]	2158
41	Apr	2	H	Chester FC	W	1-0	0-0	1	Whitehead [53]	2996
42		7	A	Ebbsfleet U	D	2-2	1-0	1	Blissett [29], Marsh [59]	1501
43		10	A	Boreham Wood	W	2-0	1-0	1	Marsh 2 [20, 58]	602
44		14	H	Leyton Orient	D	1-1	1-1	1	Whitaker [17]	3110
45		21	A	Eastleigh	W	2-0	1-0	1	Marsh [3], Hancox [60]	2372
46		28	H	Dagenham & R	W	2-0	0-0	1	Wilson 2 [79, 82]	4201

Final League Position: 1

GOALSCORERS
League (67): Wilson 14, Marsh 9, Whitaker 9 (3 pens), Durrell 8, Hancox 7 (1 pen), Blissett 5, Whitehead 5, Lloyd 4, Arthur 1, Baba 1, Fitzpatrick 1, Hodgkiss 1, Kennedy 1, Lowe 1.
FA Cup (5): Arthur 1, Burgess 1, Durrell 1, Marsh 1, Whitehead 1.
FA Trophy (0).

Jalal 40 + 1	Yates 7	Baba 9 + 3	Fitzpatrick 46	Lowe 46	Pilkington 30 + 3	Durrell 31 + 4	Lloyd 25 + 2	Burgess 20 + 11	Whitaker 43 + 1	Marsh 28 + 13	Richards 2 + 4	Wilson 23 + 12	Kennedy 21 + 11	Arthur 3 + 10	Toure 8 + 3	O'Brien 2 + 1	Hancox 31 + 8	Whitehead 34 + 1	Hodgkiss 29 + 1	Ramsbottom 4 + 2	Blissett 15 + 2	Evans 9 + 5	Match No.
1	2	3	4	5	6	7^1	8	9	10	11^2	12	13											1
1	5	6	2	3	4^2	7^1	8	9^3	10	11		13	12	14									2
1^3	6	4	2	3		7^2		9	10	14	5	8^1	11	12	13								3
		6	3	4			12	8	14	13	5^1	11^3	2	9^2	10	1	7						4
	5	7^1	2	3				6^2	8	9	12	10	4	13	11	1							5
1		3	13	5	2	6^2	9	7	8	11^1	4	10	12										6
1		3	14	4	5	6^3	8	9	10^2	13	12	2	11^1	7									7
1	5		2	3		6		8^1	9	10	12	4	13	11^2	7								8
1		7	2	3		4^2		13	11		6^1	5	8	12	10	9							9
1		6	2	3		7	12	9^3	5	14		11^2	4	13	10^1	8							10
1		7	3^1	4		5	6^2	9^1	10	11	2	14	12	8	13								11
1			5	3	4	9^3	11	13	7^2	12		10^1	14				8	6	2				12
1			3	4	5	6^3	7	12	10^1	13		11^2	14				8	9	2				13
1			5	3	4	7^1	9		8	13		10^2	14	12			11^3	6	2				14
1			3	4	5	6^1	7	13	10	12		11^2					8	9	2				15
1^2			3	4	5	6	7		10	13		11^2	2				8	9			12		16
			2	3	4	5	7		11	12		6^2	8	10^1	13			9				1	17
1			3	4	5	6	7		10^1	12		11	13				8^2	9	2				18
1			5	3	4	9^2	11	6	7	13		10^1					12	8	2				19
1			3	4	5	6	8	10^2	11			7^1			13		12	9	2				20
1			3	4	5	6	8	10^2	11^1	13		7		12				9	2				21
1			3	4	5	6	7	10		11							8	9	2				22
1			3	4	5	12	7	10^2	11	6^3		13	14				8^1	9	2				23
1			3	4			7	10	11	5		6	8					9	2				24
1			4	5		12	6	9^1	7	10		11^2	3				13	8	2				25
1			3	4		12	6	8^2	9	11		10^1	5				13	7	2				26
1*			3	4	12	5^2	8		11	6		7^3	9				14	10	2^1	13			27
	10		2	3	4	13	6^2	9		12		11^1	5	14			7	8^3		1			28
	13		2	3	5	6	7		10	11		14	4^1				8^2	9	12^3	1			29
13			2	3	4	5	7	10^2	11	6^3		12	8					9			11	14	30
1			4	5	13	6^1	7		9	11^3		10	3				14	8			12	2^3	31
1			3	4	5	6^1		13	11	7^2			12				9	10	2		8		32
1			3	4	5	6^1		11		7^2			13				9	10	2		8	12	33
1			3	4	5	6^1		13	9	10^2			7				8	2			11	12	34
1			3	4	5	6		11		7^2		12					9^1	10	2		8	13	35
1			3	4	5	6^2	12	11	13	7							9^1	10	2		8		36
1		5	3	4	6		14	8	12	10^3		9^2	7				9^2	7	2^1		11	13	37
1			3	4		7		10					6				8	9	2		11	5	38
1		5	4	3	6^1		9	10²	13			7					7	8	2		11	12	39
1			3	4	5			9	10			6					8	2			11	7	40
1		5	3	4		12	8	10^1		13							9	7^2	2		11	6	41
1		3	6	4		8^2	7	9^1	12	13							11		5	10^*	2		42
1			3	4	5			9	10	12							7	8^1	2		11	6	43
1		5	4	3		12	7	10	13			9					6^2	2			11	8^1	44
1			3	4	5		9	11	13			5	7				8	2			10	6	45
1			3	4	14	12	8	10	13	5		7	9^2				2	11^2	6^1				46

FA Cup

Fourth Qualifying   Stourbridge   (a) 5-0
First Round   Forest Green R   (a) 0-1

FA Trophy

First Round   FC Halifax T   (a) 0-1

MAIDENHEAD UNITED

Ground: York Road, Maidenhead, Berkshire SL6 1SF.   *Tel:* (01628) 636 314.
Website: pitchero.com/clubs/maidenheadunited   *Email:* social@maidenheadunitedfc.org   *Year Formed:* 1870.
Record Attendance: 7,920 v Southall, FA Amateur Cup quarter-final, 7 March 1936.   *Nickname:* 'The Magpies'.
Manager: Alan Devonshire.   *Colours:* Black and white striped shirts, black shorts, white socks.

MAIDENHEAD UNITED – NATIONAL LEAGUE 2017–18 LEAGUE RECORD

Match No.	Date	Venue	Opponents	Result	H/T Score	Lg Pos.	Goalscorers	Attendance
1	Aug 5	A	Maidstone U	D	1-1	0-0	11	Barratt [88]	2298
2	8	H	Wrexham	L	1-2	1-1	18	Tarpey [42]	1631
3	12	H	Hartlepool U	W	2-1	1-0	14	Tarpey 2 [34, 58]	1491
4	15	A	AFC Fylde	W	4-1	2-1	7	Tarpey 4 (2 pens) [26 (p), 37 (p), 58, 78]	1657
5	19	H	Ebbsfleet U	D	1-1	1-0	9	Pritchard [26]	1628
6	26	A	Barrow	D	1-1	1-0	9	Clifton [28]	1154
7	28	H	Leyton Orient	L	0-1	0-1	14		2544
8	Sept 2	A	Sutton U	W	2-0	0-0	7	Upward [73], Odametey [90]	2158
9	9	A	FC Halifax T	L	2-3	0-1	10	Goodman [79], Marks [90]	1727
10	12	H	Tranmere R	W	1-0	0-0	10	Pritchard [88]	1483
11	16	H	Boreham Wood	W	2-1	1-0	5	Clifton [43], Upward [61]	1351
12	23	A	Chester FC	L	0-2	0-1	11		1839
13	30	H	Guiseley	W	3-0	3-0	9	Upward [3], Pritchard [5], Comley [35]	1224
14	Oct 3	A	Torquay U	L	0-4	0-4	13		1567
15	7	H	Aldershot T	D	3-3	1-2	12	Clifton [18], Inman [63], Pritchard (pen) [86]	2425
16	21	A	Dover Ath	D	1-1	0-0	12	Hyde [90]	837
17	24	A	Bromley	W	3-2	3-2	11	Clifton 3 (1 pen) [17, 21 (p), 35]	1056
18	28	H	Dagenham & R	D	1-1	1-0	11	Clerima [39]	1384
19	Nov 11	H	Gateshead	L	0-3	0-2	14		1377
20	18	A	Woking	D	1-1	1-1	13	Clifton [10]	1878
21	21	A	Eastleigh	D	2-2	1-0	12	Odametey [41], Pritchard (pen) [51]	1525
22	25	H	Macclesfield T	D	1-1	0-0	14	Hyde [88]	1165
23	Dec 2	A	Wrexham	L	0-2	0-1	14		3968
24	9	H	Maidstone U	D	0-0	0-0	13		1313
25	23	A	Hartlepool U	W	2-1	0-1	11	Marks 2 [52, 78]	2756
26	26	H	Solihull Moors	W	1-0	0-0	11	Smith [60]	1261
27	30	H	AFC Fylde	L	1-2	1-0	11	Pritchard (pen) [42]	1315
28	Jan 1	A	Solihull Moors	L	1-3	0-0	11	Emmanuel [53]	602
29	6	H	FC Halifax T	D	0-0	0-0	12		1229
30	20	A	Tranmere R	L	2-3	0-1	13	Barratt [55], Clerima [84]	4980
31	27	H	Chester FC	W	3-0	3-0	13	Pritchard 2 (1 pen) [12 (p), 14], Barratt [35]	1510
32	Feb 10	H	Torquay U	L	1-2	0-1	14	Upward [69]	1433
33	17	A	Guiseley	W	3-1	2-1	12	Hyde [30], Pritchard 2 [43, 48]	777
34	20	A	Eastleigh	W	3-1	1-1	12	Emmanuel [21], Marks [56], Pritchard [64]	1055
35	24	A	Macclesfield T	L	0-1	0-0	12		1668
36	Mar 10	A	Gateshead	L	1-7	1-2	13	Hyde [25]	581
37	13	A	Boreham Wood	D	1-1	1-1	13	Emmanuel [29]	401
38	17	H	Barrow	L	0-1	0-0	13		1030
39	24	A	Ebbsfleet U	D	1-1	0-1	12	Pritchard [81]	1503
40	Apr 7	A	Aldershot T	L	0-1	0-0	16		2318
41	10	H	Woking	W	2-1	0-0	15	Clifton [81], Marks [88]	1301
42	14	H	Dover Ath	W	3-2	0-0	12	Hyde [52], Upward [60], Kilman [90]	1155
43	17	H	Sutton U	W	2-1	2-0	12	Pritchard [25], Goodman [32]	2201
44	21	A	Dagenham & R	L	0-1	0-1	12		1433
45	24	A	Leyton Orient	W	1-0	1-0	12	Upward [5]	3145
46	28	H	Bromley	W	5-2	3-1	12	Barratt 2 [3, 49], Smith [5], Owusu [32], Marks [61]	1418

Final League Position: 12

GOALSCORERS

League (65): Pritchard 13 (4 pens), Clifton 8 (1 pen), Tarpey 7 (2 pens), Marks 6, Upward 6, Barratt 5, Hyde 5, Emmanuel 3, Clerima 2, Goodman 2, Odametey 2, Smith 2, Comley 1, Inman 1, Kilman 1, Owusu 1.
FA Cup (2): Barratt 1, Upward 1.
FA Trophy (9): Emmanuel 3, Hyde 2, Pritchard 2 (1 pen), Barratt 1, Upward 1.

Pentney 46	Clerima 33	Odametey 44+1	Massey 44	Inman 7+5	Tarpey 6	Comley 29+3	Marks 23+12	Pritchard 41+2	Upward 33+6	Kilman 27+6	Clifton 20+17	Barratt 19+13	Goodman 34+4	Hyde 16+16	Mulley 5+10	Peters 11+3	Smith 17+14	McKenzie -+2	Steer 31+1	Emmanuel 17+4	Owusu 2+8	Osho 2+1	Match No.
1	2	3	4	5¹	6	7	8	9³	10²	11	12	13	14										1
1	2	3¹	4	5	6	7	8³	9²	10	11	14	13					12						2
1	2	6	3	14		7	8	11¹	9²	10²	4	12					5		13				3
1	2	7	3		6³	8	12	9¹	10²	4		13	5	11	14								4
1	10		5	13	6²	7	11³	8	9	4	14		3¹	12		2							5
1	8	5					12		13	3	7³	6¹	2	11²	10	4	9	14					6
1	2	6	4	5¹	7	8	11	9	10²		13	14	12							3³			7
1	2	6³	3			7	11²	9	10	4	14	8¹	5		12		13						8
1	2	6	5			7²	11	9		4¹	12	8	3		13		10						9
1	2	10	4	14		6		8¹		9¹	7⁴	5	12	11³		13	3						10
1	2¹	4	5	6		7		9	11		10²	8¹	13		12	14	3						11
1	2	4³	5	6		7		9	11	14	10	13	8¹		12		3¹						12
1	3	6	5	14		7²		9¹	11³	13	10	8	2				12		4				13
1	3	4				5	7²	9³		8¹	6	11	13			10	12	14	2				14
1	4	6	5	12		7		8	10	3	9¹	13	2²	11³			14						15
1		7²	3	6				8	14	12	13	4	10		5¹	11			2	9¹			16
1	2	13	3	4			7	9	10³	8	6¹		14		11		12	5²					17
1	2	4¹	5			12		9	14		8¹	10	7	13		11		3	6²				18
1		6	2			7²		8	10¹	9		4	13	14	3	12	5	11³					19
1	2	4	5			12	7	9	8		10²	6¹	11³	14	13		3						20
1	2	3	4			6¹	8	14	9		7³	10	12	13⁸		11			5²				21
1	2	6	4			14	8	12	9	7³		13		5	10¹		3	11²					22
1	2	6	3			12	7³	9⁸	13	8¹		11²		4	10		5	14					23
1	2	4	5			13	7		9²	8³		10	6¹		11		3	12	14				24
1	2	4	5			7³	8		9	12		10	14	13		11		3¹	6²				25
1		6	2			12	7	13	3	8		5	11²	10¹	4	9³			14				26
1	2	4	5			7	8		9²	14		10¹		13	12	11		3	6³				27
1	2	4	5			7	13	8		9⁸			11²	10	12¹		3	6¹	14				28
1	2	9	4			6	10	7	8		5						3	11¹	12				29
1	2	7	4			13	11	8	9²	5¹		12	6				3	10⁵	14				30
1	2	10	4			6¹	11²	8	9		13	7³	5	14		12	3						31
1		5				6	11	8	9	2		7¹	4	12		3²	10		13				32
1	2	5				6	13	8	10	12	9²	7¹	4	11			3						33
1	2	6¹	3			7	11³	8	9	4	14		5	12					10²	13			34
1	2		4			14	6¹	8	9	7²	12	10	5			11		3³		13			35
1	5	6	2				8	10³	3	9	7⁴	4¹	11				14				13	12	36
1	2	6	4			7	11	8	9				12				3	10¹				5	37
1		6⁵	2			7³	11	8	13		12	4	14			9²	5	10				3	38
1	2	6	3			11	8	9²		13	7¹	4	12				5	10					39
1	2	6	4			14	10	7	8¹	5²		13	12	11²		9	3						40
1		6	3			7	10	8	9	4¹	14	13	5	12			2	11³					41
1		6	2			7	12	13	10	3	9¹	8	4	11²			5						42
1		7	4			6²	11	8¹	10	5	9	13	2			12	3						43
1		6	3			7³	14	8¹	9	5	13	12	4	11			2	10²					44
1		8	5			7	11²	10⁸	3	12	9	4³				14	2	13	6¹				45
1	2²	7	4			8	11¹	13		6	14	10	12			9	3	5³					46

FA Cup

Fourth Qualifying	Havant & Waterlooville	(h)	2-1
First Round	Coventry C	(a)	0-2

FA Trophy

First Round	Woking	(a)	2-0
Second Round	FC Halifax T	(a)	4-1
Third Round	Stockport Co	(h)	1-1
Replay	Stockport Co	(a)	2-3
(aet)			

MAIDSTONE UNITED

Ground: Gallagher Stadium, James Whatman Way, Maidstone ME14 1LQ. *Tel:* (01622) 753817.
Website: www.maidstoneunited.co.uk *Email:* See website. *Year Formed:* 1897. Reformed 1992.
Record Attendance: 4,101 v Crystal Palace, Friendly, 15 July 2017 (Gallagher Stadium).
Nickname: 'The Stones'. *Manager:* Jay Saunders. *Colours:* Amber shirts with black trim, black shorts, black socks.

MAIDSTONE UNITED – NATIONAL LEAGUE 2017–18 LEAGUE RECORD

Match No.	Date		Venue	Opponents	Result	H/T Score	Lg Pos.	Goalscorers	Attendance
1	Aug	5	H	Maidenhead U	D 1-1	0-0	12	Pigott [51]	2298
2		8	A	Ebbsfleet U	L 0-2	0-0	22		2519
3		12	A	Leyton Orient	L 0-2	0-0	22		5085
4		15	H	Aldershot T	D 1-1	0-0	21	Hare [90]	2524
5		19	H	Wrexham	W 2-1	2-1	17	Wynter [15], Richards, J [33]	2192
6		26	A	Sutton U	W 3-1	0-1	14	Okuonghae [68], Paxman [74], Pigott [82]	2312
7		28	H	Dagenham & R	D 0-0	0-0	17		2544
8	Sept	2	A	Hartlepool U	L 1-3	0-1	19	Ter Horst [90]	4137
9		9	H	Woking	W 3-1	1-0	15	Hines [34], Sam-Yorke [67], Pigott [77]	2527
10		12	A	Eastleigh	W 1-0	0-0	13	Hines [69]	1820
11		16	A	Macclesfield T	W 4-1	2-0	7	Hines 2 [11, 65], Wynter [24], Pigott [74]	1347
12		23	H	Gateshead	D 2-2	1-0	9	Hines (pen) [11], Wynter [67]	2530
13		30	A	Barrow	W 1-0	0-0	5	Pigott (pen) [52]	1097
14	Oct	3	H	Bromley	L 0-2	0-1	8		2541
15		7	H	Guiseley	D 1-1	1-0	9	Hines [12]	2552
16		24	A	FC Halifax T	W 2-0	1-0	10	Pigott [15], Reason (pen) [61]	1410
17		28	H	Chester FC	W 1-0	0-0	5	Finney [90]	2351
18	Nov	11	A	Torquay U	W 1-0	1-0	5	Pigott [30]	1799
19		18	A	Solihull Moors	D 1-1	1-0	6	Pigott [1]	2463
20		21	H	Boreham Wood	L 0-4	0-2	7		1945
21		25	A	Tranmere R	L 0-4	0-2	10		4126
22	Dec	9	A	Maidenhead U	D 0-0	0-0	11		1313
23		23	H	Leyton Orient	L 0-2	0-1	12		3225
24		26	A	Dover Ath	D 2-2	2-0	12	Pigott 2 [36, 41]	2369
25		30	A	Aldershot T	D 1-1	0-0	12	Collins [48]	2287
26	Jan	1	H	Dover Ath	D 2-2	0-1	12	Wraight [69], Anderson [90]	2502
27		6	A	Woking	D 4-4	3-2	13	Lewis 2 [25, 53], Reason (pen) [41], Pigott [42]	1874
28		9	H	Ebbsfleet U	L 1-2	0-0	13	Anderson [54]	2396
29		20	H	Eastleigh	L 2-3	2-1	14	Ter Horst [1], Lewis [34]	2133
30		23	A	AFC Fylde	L 0-3	0-2	14		1408
31		27	A	Gateshead	L 1-2	1-1	16	Reason (pen) [19]	771
32	Feb	10	A	Bromley	D 2-2	1-2	16	Loza [35], Turgott [77]	2027
33		17	H	Barrow	L 0-1	0-1	17		2338
34		20	A	Boreham Wood	L 0-1	0-1	17		428
35		24	H	Tranmere R	L 2-3	2-1	18	Finney [27], Lafayette (pen) [41]	2502
36	Mar	10	H	Torquay U	W 1-0	0-0	18	Hare [88]	2211
37		17	H	Sutton U	W 1-0	0-0	16	Lewis [75]	2065
38		21	H	Macclesfield T	D 2-2	1-0	16	Wynter [19], Lafayette [83]	1994
39		24	A	Wrexham	L 0-1	0-0	17		4443
40		30	H	Hartlepool U	L 1-2	0-1	18	Lafayette [90]	2559
41	Apr	2	A	Dagenham & R	L 1-2	0-1	18	Wynter [82]	1633
42		7	A	Guiseley	D 0-0	0-0	18		957
43		10	A	Solihull Moors	L 0-1	0-1	19		665
44		14	H	AFC Fylde	W 1-0	1-0	18	Turgott [23]	2254
45		21	A	Chester FC	W 3-1	2-0	18	Turgott (pen) [19], Phillips [32], Hare [74]	1728
46		28	H	FC Halifax T	D 0-0	0-0	19		2832

Final League Position: 19

GOALSCORERS

League (52): Pigott 11 (1 pen), Hines 6 (1 pen), Wynter 5, Lewis 4, Hare 3, Lafayette 3 (1 pen), Reason 3 (3 pens), Turgott 3 (1 pen), Anderson 2, Finney 2, Ter Horst 2, Collins 1, Loza 1, Okuonghae 1, Paxman 1, Phillips 1, Richards, J 1, Sam-Yorke 1, Wraight 1.
FA Cup (10): Hines 2, Pigott 2, Sam-Yorke 2, Finney 1, Okuonghae 1, Reason 1, Wynter 1.
FA Trophy (8): Loza 2, Okuonghae 1, Osei 1, Pigott 1, Prestedge 1, Reason 1, Wraight 1.

Worgan 46	Hare 26 + 2	Finney 24 + 2	Prestedge 24 + 9	Lewis 41	Sam-Yorke 26 + 6	Paxman 10 + 13	Anderson 41 + 1	Nana Ofori-Twumasi 32 + 1	Willard 1 + 2	Pigott 28	Wraight 10 + 11	Phipps 1 + 1	Reason 37 + 5	Wynter 40 + 1	Richards J 3 + 10	Okuonghae 21 + 2	Hines 16 + 4	Ter Horst 9 + 9	Muldoon 2 + 3	Loza 16 + 12	Bartlett —+1	Collins 3 + 1	Osei 3 + 3	Richards C —+1	Coker 4 + 2	Beckwith 4	Lafayette 9 + 1	Turgott 12 + 2	De Havilland 9 + 1	Phillips 6 + 2	Luer 2 + 4	Match No.
1	2	3	4	5	6	7^2	8	9	10^1	11	12	13																				1
1	3	5^1	6	7^4	11	12	2	4	13	10	8^2		9^3	14																		2
1	2	3^1		5	6	8	10	12	11		7^2		9	4	13																	3
1	2		6	10	7	5		11		8^1			9	3	12	4																4
1	2		6	10^1	13	5		11		8			7	4	9^2	3	12															5
1	2	6^1	7	10	13	5		11		9^2			8	4		3	12															6
1	2		8	10	7	5		11^1		6			4			3	9	12														7
1	2		8	10^1	7	5		11	14	6^2			4	12	3	9^3	13															8
1	2	6	7	10	13	5		11^3		12			4	14	3	8^1	9^2															9
1	2^1	6	7	10^2		5	13	11		8			4			3	9	12														10
1	14	2	5		13	6^2	8	11		7^3		3	12	4	10	9^1																11
1		6	7		12	5	2	11		8^1		4	13	3	9	10^2																12
1		6	7		5	2		11	12	8			4	9^2	3		10^1	13														13
1		2^1	5	14	6	8		11	13	7^3		3	12	4	10^2	9																14
1	12	6	7		3	2		11	13	8		5	9^3	4	10^2	14																15
1	5	4	12	7	9^1		2			11	6^3		8	3			10^2	14		13												16
1	2	3	13	5	6		9			11^3	7^1		8	4			10^2	14		12												17
1	13	4	6	7		5	2			11			9	3			10^1		8^2	12												18
1		2	8	6		5	3			11			7	4^2		12	13	10^1		9												19
1		4	6^3	7		5	2	11		8				12	3	10^1	13		9^2	14												20
1		4	7^1	6	9	5	2	11	13				8	3	10^2				12													21
1		3	13	6	10	5	2	11		7			4			9^2			12			8^1										22
1		3	7^2	6	9^1	5	2	11		8			4			12			10	13												23
1		3^3	13	6		5	2	11		7			4	12	9^1			10^2	8													24
1	14		13	5		6	8	10	12	7		2	9^1			4^2		11^3														25
1	5^2		6	7	12	14	13	2		11	8^3		4		3	10^1		9														26
1		12	5	6		8	10	11		7^1			9	2	3			13	4^2													27
1	5		7^1	8	13	14	6	2		11			9	4	3^3			10^2				12										28
1	3		6	11	8	5	2			7			4			9				10^1	12											29
1	2^3	5	6	7^2	8	9				14	3	13	4		11^1	12		10														30
1	6^3	7	10		3	2				8^2	4		5	14	13	9		11^1		12												31
1		7	14	12	5	2				6^1	4					9				8^3	10^2					9	3^4	11	13			32
1	2		7	12	8	5^1				6^2	4		3			9											11	10	13			33
1	2	5	9^4	10^1	12		6			8^2	3^3					13				14		4	11			7						34
1	5	4		10	7		8			6						12						3	11			9	2					35
1	5	4	13		9^1	6				8	7					12						3	11	10^2			2					36
1	5	4	13	7	11		8			12	6		3			9^1								10^2			2					37
1	6	5		8	11^1	3				7^2	4^3					10						13	9			2	12	14			38
1	3	4		7	12	6				5						11^1						10	9			2	8^2	13			39
1	6	4		7	12	14	5			8	3					13						11	9^2	2^1				10^3			40
1		4		8	10^2	5	2			7^1	3					12		14				14	11	9^3			6	13				41
1		4	6^3	7	10	5	2			13	14					11							9^2				8^1				42
1		3^1	7^2	8	10		2	6		9^3	4					13						14	5	12	11							43
1	5	4		7			6			13	12^3					11^1						8^3		10	2		9^2	14				44
1	2	3	12	7			5	6		13	14		4^4			11^3						8^1	10	9^2								45
1	3	4		7	12	5	2			10	6		14			13						9^2	11^3	8^1								46

FA Cup

Fourth Qualifying	Enfield	(h)	2-2
Replay (aet)	Enfield	(a)	3-1
First Round	Cheltenham T	(a)	4-2
Second Round	Milton Keynes D	(a)	1-4

FA Trophy

First Round	Torquay U	(a)	4-0
Second Round	Heybridge Swifts	(h)	2-1
Third Round	Gateshead	(a)	2-2
Replay	Gateshead	(h)	0-3

SOLIHULL MOORS

Ground: The Automated Technology Group Stadium, Damson Parkway, Solihull, West Midlands B91 2PP.
Tel: (0121) 205 6770.   *Website:* www.solihullmoorsfc.co.uk   *Email:* info@solihullmoorsfc.co.uk   *Year Formed:* 2007.
Record Attendance: 2,658 v Hartlepool U, National League, 7 October 2017.   *Nickname:* 'Moors'.
Manager: Tim Flowers.   *Colours:* Blue shirts with yellow trim, blue shorts, blue socks with yellow trim.

SOLIHULL MOORS – NATIONAL LEAGUE 2017–18 LEAGUE RECORD

Match No.	Date	Venue	Opponents	Result	H/T Score	Lg Pos.	Goalscorers	Attendance
1	Aug 8	A	Leyton Orient	L	1-3	0-1	24	Afolayan [76]	4411
2	12	A	Boreham Wood	L	1-4	1-3	24	Kelleher [32]	319
3	15	H	Barrow	D	3-3	0-2	23	Kettle [61], Afolayan [70], Carter [73]	558
4	19	H	FC Halifax T	L	0-1	0-1	23		684
5	26	A	Torquay U	W	2-1	0-0	22	Campbell [47], Vaughan [74]	1862
6	28	H	Tranmere R	L	0-2	0-1	23		1312
7	Sept 2	A	Aldershot T	L	0-1	0-1	23		1803
8	5	H	Chester FC	W	2-0	1-0	22	Afolayan 2 [16, 77]	651
9	9	H	Macclesfield T	L	0-1	0-0	22		808
10	12	A	Woking	L	1-2	0-1	22	Carter [74]	1402
11	16	A	Bromley	L	0-1	0-0	23		1003
12	23	H	Dagenham & R	D	2-2	2-1	23	Carter [11], Afolayan [40]	625
13	30	A	Dover Ath	L	0-1	0-0	23		2795
14	Oct 3	H	Ebbsfleet U	L	1-3	0-2	23	Carter [57]	579
15	7	H	Hartlepool U	L	1-2	0-0	23	Carter (pen) [86]	2658
16	21	A	Guiseley	L	2-4	1-1	24	Afolayan 2 [43, 67]	735
17	24	A	Eastleigh	W	2-1	1-0	24	Hylton [4], Afolayan [56]	2577
18	28	H	AFC Fylde	L	0-4	0-2	24		668
19	Nov 11	H	Sutton U	L	0-2	0-1	24		729
20	18	A	Maidstone U	D	1-1	0-1	23	Thomas, Kwame [64]	2463
21	21	A	Wrexham	L	0-1	0-1	24		3896
22	25	H	Gateshead	D	1-1	0-1	24	Atkinson [65]	534
23	Dec 2	H	Leyton Orient	W	1-0	0-0	24	Daly [58]	1118
24	9	A	Chester FC	L	0-1	0-0	24		1430
25	23	H	Boreham Wood	D	0-0	0-0	24		419
26	26	A	Maidenhead U	L	0-1	0-0	24		1261
27	30	A	Barrow	W	2-1	0-0	24	Carter [57], Reckord (pen) [84]	1315
28	Jan 1	H	Maidenhead U	W	3-1	0-0	21	Afolayan 2 [63, 72], Carter [64]	602
29	6	A	Macclesfield T	D	0-0	0-0	22		1771
30	20	H	Woking	W	3-0	1-0	21	Thomas, Kwame [6], Hylton 2 [57, 72]	638
31	27	A	Dagenham & R	W	3-1	2-1	21	Yussuf 2 [11, 12], Afolayan [71]	2217
32	Feb 10	A	Ebbsfleet U	L	0-1	0-0	21		1117
33	17	H	Dover Ath	W	3-2	1-1	21	Storer, K [29], Thomas, Kwame [75], Reid [84]	679
34	20	H	Wrexham	D	0-0	0-0	21		1228
35	Mar 10	A	Sutton U	L	0-1	0-1	21		1990
36	13	A	Gateshead	D	2-2	1-0	21	Reid [32], Lait [87]	486
37	17	H	Torquay U	D	1-1	0-1	21	Yussuf [82]	781
38	20	H	Bromley	W	2-0	1-0	21	Thomas, Kwame [13], Reid [90]	624
39	24	A	FC Halifax T	D	0-0	0-0	21		1849
40	30	H	Aldershot T	D	0-0	0-0	21		1734
41	Apr 7	A	Hartlepool U	W	1-0	0-0	20	Yussuf [88]	2782
42	10	H	Maidstone U	W	1-0	0-0	18	Williams [25]	665
43	14	A	Guiseley	W	3-1	2-0	17	Frempah (og) [6], Osborne [19], Kelleher [60]	915
44	21	A	AFC Fylde	D	1-1	1-0	19	Sterling-James [5]	2045
45	24	A	Tranmere R	W	2-1	1-0	15	Osborne [31], Reid [64]	3496
46	28	H	Eastleigh	L	1-4	0-1	18	Yussuf [75]	1014

Final League Position: 18

GOALSCORERS
League (49): Afolayan 11, Carter 7 (1 pen), Yussuf 5, Reid 4, Thomas, Kwame 4, Hylton 3, Kelleher 2, Osborne 2, Atkinson 1, Campbell 1, Daly 1, Kettle 1, Lait 1, Reckord 1 (1 pen), Sterling-James 1, Storer, K 1, Vaughan 1, Williams 1, own goal 1.
FA Cup (3): Carter 1 (1 pen), Kettle 1, Murombedzi 1.
FA Trophy (2): Hylton 1 (1 pen), Osborne 1.

Trueman 4	Thomas Kalern 3+3	Carter 44+1	Murombedzi 25+2	Benbow 2+2	Storer J 1+1	Cullinane-Liburd 11+1	Afolayan 22+8	Edwards J 3+3	Green P 15+8	Carline 21+12	Kelleher 37+1	Dunkley 3+8	Tonks 2+1	Kettle 13+3	Martinez 2	Cleary 2+1	Storer K 16	Campbell 8+5	Edwards O —+4	Vaughan 12	Green K 31	Daly 38	Westbrooke 1+1	Frempah —+1	Fox 2+3	Richards 10	Yussuf 12+1	McDonald 3+2	Payne 3	Reid 3+12	Brodie 3+2	Maye 1+2	Williams 14	Bowen 9+1	Asante 7+3	Hylton 23+4	Townsend 5	Camwell —+1	Lait 1+5	Sammons 1	Higgs —+1	Sterling-James 4+4	Martin —+2	Thomas Kwame 24+1	O'Leary 23	Atkinson 3	Coyle 1	Osborne 21+1	Match No.
		2¹	3	4		5²	6	7	8	9	10	11	12	13																																			1
1		5	6	10³		7	11	12	2	9¹	3	13	8³	4	14																																		2
1	14	7	6	13		3	12	8³	10	5	9¹	2	4	11²																																		3
		6	7¹	12³		4	10	14	13	9	5	8²	3				11	1	2																														4
	14	7	6			8	10³	13	5²	9	3	12	4			11¹	1	2																														5
		3	5			6	13	7		10	11	8²	9¹	4			12	1	2																														6
	3	7²	8			10		9	6	13		5¹	11	1	2	4	12																															7
	6	7		4	10²		12	8		13		5		11¹	1	2	3	9⁴																														8
	3¹	4	6			7	8			12		5	10	1	2	9	11																															9
1	12	6	5			4	9	7¹	14	13	3	10²	2	8	11³																																	10
		7	6			5³	11²			8¹	14	4	12	1	2	3	13	9	10																													11
		6	8			10¹			3	14	1	2	4	12	7	9²	5	11³	13																													12
		7	6²			10¹			8		3	14	1	2	4	9³	13	5	11	12																											13
		6				10			8¹		3		13	1	2	4	14	9	12	5	11²	7³																									14
		5	7	13	11²			8	3			9	1	4	2	6	10¹	12																													15
		4	6	7³	12	14		9		5		1	2²	8	11							3¹	10	13																							16
		6	8			10		4			14		2	3	7¹		12			5	11³	9²	1	13																							17
		6	7			10		2³			12	4	3					5	11¹	9	1	8²	13	14																							18
		7	8			12		3³	9	5		2	4					6	11¹	10	1		13																								19
		7	8			11¹			9	6		2	5			10		3	12		1																	4									20
		6	7²			13		8³	4		14	2	5			9		3	10	12	1																11¹										21
		7	13			12		3	5			4				6¹		2	10²	9																	11	1	8								22
		3	13			6²	7		9			8						2	12	5																	11	1	4	10¹							23
13		3⁴				6¹		7¹	14	9									8																	2²	12	5						11	1	4	10		24
5		3	4	8⁴		12		6	13	9						2	7																										11¹	1	10		25
4		9	8	13		11¹		5²	12	2						3	6														10														1	7		26
5		3	4¹			6		7	9							2	8												12												11	1	10		27
7		3	4			6¹		12	13	9	1					2	8																	5										11²	1	10⁴		28
3		7	8			4	12	6								2	5																	10¹								11	1			29
7³		3				6¹	14					4²	12	2	8	13					5													5							11	1	10		30
7		3				12	14		9			4	13	2	8						5¹													6³							11	1	10²		31
8		3³				14			10			4²	13	2	9						5¹	12												6							7	1	11		32
4		7							3			8	13	2	9					9¹	12	2	10¹																	11	1	6		33
3		8							5			7		4						11¹	12	2	10																	9	1	6		34
8		2²						13	10			4		9					5¹	12	3	6¹																		7	1	11		35
3		7						12	5			8		4						10²	2	9	13																11¹	1	6		36
4		2²						13	14	6			3²		5				11	10¹	8	9																	12	1	7		37
4		6						12	14	2			7		5				9³	13	3	10¹																	11	1	8³		38
5		9						6	8	4			3						10⁴	13	2	12														7			11¹	1	8		39
4		12							7			5		6					9¹	13	2	10²	14													3²			11	1	8		40
8		2					14	10				4		9⁴			2		5	13	2	6²														12			7¹	1	11³		41
5		5					7	4				6		2			2		9¹	12	3	10¹														13			11	1	8		42
3		3					7	5				6		2					9⁴	13	4	10¹	14												12			11	1	8²		43
5		5					7³	3				9		2	6					12	4	10¹	14												8⁴			11	1	13		44
3		3					13	10				6		2	9					12	4	7¹	14												5¹			8²	1	11		45
							8³	10			1	4		2	9					12	6	13													5¹			14		7¹	11	46

FA Cup

Fourth Qualifying	Ossett T	(h)	1-1
Replay	Ossett T	(a)	2-1
First Round	Wycombe W	(h)	0-2

FA Trophy

First Round	Tranmere R	(h)	2-0
Second Round	Spennymoor T	(a)	0-2

SUTTON UNITED

Ground: Borough Sports Ground, Gander Green Lane, Sutton, Surrey SM1 2EY.   *Tel:* (0208) 644 4440.
Website: www.suttonunited.net   *Email:* info@suttonunited.net   *Year Formed:* 1898.
Record Attendance: 14,000 v Leeds U, FA Cup 4th rd, 24 January 1970.   *Nickname:* 'The U's'.
Manager: Paul Doswell.   *Colours:* Amber shirts with chocolate trim, amber shorts with chocolate trim, amber socks
with chocolate trim.

SUTTON UNITED – NATIONAL LEAGUE 2017–18 LEAGUE RECORD

Match No.	Date	Venue	Opponents	Result	H/T Score	Lg Pos.	Goalscorers	Attendance
1	Aug 5	H	Leyton Orient	W 2-0	2-0	2	Collins (pen) [15], Beckwith [34]	3198
2	8	A	Eastleigh	L 0-1	0-0	8		1744
3	12	A	Tranmere R	W 1-0	1-0	5	Dundas [32]	5050
4	15	H	Macclesfield T	W 2-1	0-1	2	Emmanuel [85], Wright [86]	1986
5	19	A	Chester FC	W 3-2	2-1	1	John [5], Wright [44], Cadogan [90]	1670
6	26	H	Maidstone U	L 1-3	1-0	2	Wright [35]	2312
7	28	A	Bromley	W 1-0	1-0	1	Eastmond [24]	2239
8	Sept 2	H	Maidenhead U	L 0-2	0-0	4		2158
9	9	H	Gateshead	D 1-1	1-1	5	Walton (pen) [28]	1805
10	12	A	Dagenham & R	W 2-1	1-1	1	Dundas [45], Davis [90]	1261
11	16	A	Woking	L 0-2	0-0	4		2193
12	23	H	Barrow	W 3-2	1-1	1	Thomas, A [26], Taylor [49], Emmanuel [52]	1909
13	30	A	Wrexham	D 1-1	0-1	3	Lafayette [90]	4815
14	Oct 3	H	Dover Ath	D 2-2	0-1	5	Wright [70], Cadogan [80]	2206
15	7	H	AFC Fylde	W 2-1	2-0	4	Dundas [41], Grand (og) [42]	2127
16	21	A	Hartlepool U	D 1-1	0-1	5	Wright [90]	4526
17	24	A	Aldershot T	D 2-2	2-2	4	John [4], Dundas [31]	2259
18	28	H	Ebbsfleet U	D 0-0	0-0	4		2197
19	Nov 11	A	Solihull Moors	W 2-0	1-0	4	Lafayette [29], Dundas [86]	729
20	18	H	FC Halifax T	W 3-2	1-0	3	Lafayette 2 [45, 73], Dundas [58]	1968
21	21	A	Torquay U	L 0-1	0-1	4		1970
22	25	A	Guiseley	W 2-0	2-0	1	Dundas [12], Bolarinwa [36]	929
23	Dec 2	H	Eastleigh	W 2-0	1-0	1	Bolarinwa [13], Wright [82]	1967
24	9	A	Leyton Orient	L 1-4	0-1	2	Wright [83]	4180
25	23	H	Tranmere R	L 1-3	1-2	4	Davis [25]	2237
26	26	A	Boreham Wood	W 4-0	2-0	1	Collins [32], Bailey [45], Eastmond 2 [68, 73]	455
27	30	H	Macclesfield T	L 0-1	0-1	3		2246
28	Jan 1	H	Boreham Wood	D 1-1	0-0	3	Collins (pen) [57]	2007
29	6	A	Gateshead	W 2-0	0-0	3	Wright 2 [74, 81]	493
30	20	H	Dagenham & R	W 2-1	0-0	3	Wright [57], Bolarinwa [61]	2077
31	Feb 10	A	Dover Ath	W 1-0	1-0	5	Cadogan [26]	1027
32	13	A	Barrow	D 1-1	0-1	4	Wright [73]	643
33	17	H	Wrexham	D 1-1	0-1	5	Walton [47]	2621
34	20	A	Torquay U	W 3-2	2-2	2	Harrison [6], Walton [45], Collins (pen) [90]	1302
35	24	A	Guiseley	W 4-0	1-0	2	Thomas, T [34], Harrison [50], Eastmond [56], Coddington (og) [75]	1915
36	Mar 6	H	Woking	W 2-0	1-0	2	Harrison [33], Bolarinwa [54]	2019
37	10	H	Solihull Moors	W 1-0	1-0	2	Bolarinwa [37]	1990
38	17	H	Maidstone U	L 0-1	0-0	2		2065
39	24	A	Chester FC	W 3-2	2-0	1	Beautyman [13], Harrison [45], Stearn [79]	2195
40	Apr 2	H	Bromley	L 0-3	0-2	2		2233
41	7	A	AFC Fylde	L 1-2	1-0	2	Wright [20]	1789
42	10	A	FC Halifax T	L 1-2	0-1	3	Lafayette [82]	1274
43	14	H	Hartlepool U	D 1-1	1-1	3	Lafayette [9]	2272
44	17	H	Maidenhead U	L 1-2	0-2	4	Eastmond [88]	2201
45	21	A	Ebbsfleet U	W 1-0	0-0	3	Bolarinwa [77]	2852
46	28	H	Aldershot T	W 2-1	0-0	3	Wright [49], Lafayette [79]	3541

Final League Position: 3

GOALSCORERS

League (67): Wright 13, Dundas 7, Lafayette 7, Bolarinwa 6, Eastmond 5, Collins 4 (3 pens), Harrison 4, Cadogan 3,
Walton 3 (1 pen), Davis 2, Emmanuel 2, John 2, Bailey 1, Beautyman 1, Beckwith 1, Stearn 1, Taylor 1, Thomas, A 1,
Thomas, T 1, own goals 2.
FA Cup (3): Cadogan 2, John 1.
FA Trophy (5): Wright 2, Dundas 1, Cadogan 1, Coombes 1.
National League Play-Offs (2): Bolarinwa 1, Lafayette 1.

Butler 44	Thomas A 34+3	Beckwith 12	Collins 40	Davis 38+2	Cadogan 29+10	Eastmond 35+1	Bailey 27+3	Spence 11+4	Lafayette 22+5	Dundas 25+12	Wright 26+14	Emmanuel 5+5	Monakana —+1	Taylor 18+11	Amankwaah 2	John 33+2	Walton 24+4	Jeffrey 2+8	Thomas K 2+1	Downer 12+4	Coombes 2+11	Bolariwwa 22+1	Egan —+4	Stearn —+10	Thomas T 19	Evans 2	Beautyman 10+4	Hudson-Odoi —+2	Harrison 10+3	Match No.
1	2	3	4	5	6	7	8[1]	9	10	11	12																			1
1	2	3	4	5[1]	6	7	8	9[3]	11	13	10[2]	12	14																	2
1	3		4	5	6	12	7	8	13	9[1]	10[2]	11			2															3
1	3	4[3]	5	7[1]		6	8	2	9	10[2]	11	14		13		12														4
1	2		4	5[2]	13	8	9	10	6	7[3]	11[1]	14		12		3														5
1	3		5	6[3]	13	7	8			11	10[2]	14		9[1]	2	4	12													6
1	2		4		5	6	7		12		11[1]			8		3	10	9												7
1	2		4	12	14	5	6		9	10[3]	11[2]			8		3	7[1]	13												8
1	2		4	5[1]	7	8[2]	13		6[3]	12				10		3	9	14	11											9
1	2		4	13	6		7		5	8[2]				14		3	9	12	11[3]	10[1]										10
1	2		4	5[3]	7		8		6	9[1]	12			11[2]		3	10	13		14										11
1	2		4	6[2]	7	8		5	11	12			10[1]	9		3	13													12
1	2		4			6		11		9[1]	10[2]			8		3	7	12	13	5										13
1	2		4		6	7	13	5[3]	11	12	14			9		3	8[2]	10[1]												14
1	2		4		6[3]	8	9		5[1]	7	12	14		11[2]		3	10	13												15
1	2		4	5[1]	6	7	8		11[2]	13	12			10		3	9[1]					14								16
1		2	4	5	6		7		10	9[2]	11[1]			8		3		13		12										17
1	12	2	4	5	7		8		11[3]	9	10[1]			6[2]		3		13		14										18
1	2	3	5	6	9[1]				10	11				8[2]	4			13		7	12									19
1	2	3	5	6	7		12		11	10[3]	13			8[2]	4					9[1]	14									20
1	2[3]		4	6	7		12		10	10[2]				8[1]	3				5	9	14	13								21
1		2	5[1]	6		7	3	10	11					8				4		9[2]	12	13								22
1		2	8[3]	5[1]	12	6	4	10	11	13				14	7				3	9[2]										23
1		2		4[1]	6[2]	7	8	3	5[3]	12		13		9				10		11	14									24
1			3	5	13	7[3]	8		9[1]	11	10			2	6				4[2]	14	12									25
1	3		4	5[1]		6[1]	7	13		10	11[2]			14		8			2	12	9									26
1	2[1]		3	4	6[2]	7	8		5		12			14		10[3]				13	11			9						27
1	2		3	4	14	7	8[2]	12	13	6	10[3]			11					5[1]					9						28
	2		4	6		7			14	11[1]	13			12	3				10[3]	8[2]		5	1	9						29
		3	4	5	6					13	8[2]			12	2		9		10[1]			7	1	11						30
1	13		3	4	5[3]		6[1]		12		8			2		9		14	10[2]			7		11■						31
1			3	5[1]	6		7[1]		11[3]	10				2		8		12	13	9		4			14					32
1			3	12	9[2]	6[2]			10[1]					2		7	5	13	8		4				14	11				33
1	2		4	6	7[1]	8[2]				12				3		9			14	10[3]	13	5				11				34
1	2		4	6	7[2]	8				12				3		9			13	10		5		12		11[1]				35
1	2		4	6	12	7			14	11[2]				3		13				8[1]		5		9[3]	10					36
1	2		4	5[2]	6	13				8[1]	12			14		9						11[3]		10						37
1	2		4	5	12	6				14	8[2]			3		9[1]					13	7		10[3]	11					38
1	13	2	4[1]	5	6					14	8[2]			3							9	12	7	10[3]	11					39
1		2	5[1]	6	7					14	12			4		8[3]					9	13	3	10[2]	11[1]					40
1	2			6	7	8			12	11[3]				3		10			5[2]		9[1]	14	4		13					41
1	4			6	7[2]	8		13	10	11[3]				5		9[1]			3			2		12	14					42
1	2	3		5[2]	12	7	8		9		10[3]			14									13	4	6	11[1]				43
1	2		3	5		6	7		9	10[2]	12			14									13	4	8[1]	11[3]				44
1	2		4		6[2]	7	8		12		11[1]			9	3								10		5	13				45
1	2	3	5	6[1]	7[3]	8		13		9[2]				10	4							11			12	14				46

FA Cup

Fourth Qualifying	Paulton R	(a)	3-2	
First Round	Cambridge U	(a)	0-1	

FA Trophy

First Round	Truro C	(h)	1-0
Second Round	Hendon	(h)	3-0
Third Round	Brackley T	(a)	1-3

National League Play-Offs

Semi-Final	Boreham Wood	(h)	2-3

TORQUAY UNITED

Ground: The Launa Windows Stadium, Plainmoor, Marnham Road, Torquay, Devon TQ1 3PS.
Tel: (01803) 328666.   *Website:* www.torquayunited.com   *Email:* reception@torquayunited.com
Year Formed: 1899.   *Record Attendance:* 21,908 v Huddersfield T, FA Cup 4th rd, 29 January 1955.
Nickname: 'The Gulls'.   *Manager:* Gary Owers.   *Colours:* Yellow shirts with blue trim, blue shorts with yellow trim, white socks.

TORQUAY UNITED – NATIONAL LEAGUE 2017–18 LEAGUE RECORD

Match No.	Date	Venue	Opponents	Result	H/T Score	Lg Pos.	Goalscorers	Attendance
1	Aug 5	H	Tranmere R	D	0-0	0-0	15		3162
2	8	A	Aldershot T	L	2-3	1-1	19	Young [9], Pittman [90]	2662
3	12	A	Gateshead	L	0-3	0-1	21		756
4	15	H	Boreham Wood	L	2-4	0-0	24	Keating 2 [58, 72]	1864
5	19	A	Guiseley	L	2-3	2-1	24	McGinty [36], Keating [40]	791
6	26	H	Solihull Moors	L	1-2	0-0	24	Pittman [75]	1862
7	28	A	Woking	L	1-4	1-2	24	Gray [45]	1936
8	Sept 2	H	Chester FC	D	1-1	1-0	24	Dowling [12]	1455
9	9	H	Wrexham	D	0-0	0-0	24		1841
10	12	A	Bromley	L	1-3	1-1	24	Pittman [24]	1029
11	16	A	Barrow	D	1-1	1-0	24	Gray [6]	1190
12	23	H	Macclesfield T	L	0-1	0-0	24		1835
13	30	A	Dagenham & R	L	0-1	0-0	24		1421
14	Oct 3	A	Maidenhead U	W	4-0	4-0	24	McQuoid [4], Young [12], Murphy [21], Reid [44]	1567
15	7	H	Dover Ath	L	0-2	0-1	24		1915
16	21	A	FC Halifax T	D	1-1	0-0	23	Reid [76]	1764
17	24	A	Ebbsfleet U	W	1-0	0-0	23	Reid [62]	1525
18	28	H	Hartlepool U	L	0-2	0-0	23		1987
19	Nov 11	H	Maidstone U	L	0-1	0-1	23		1799
20	18	A	AFC Fylde	L	0-2	0-1	24		1552
21	21	A	Sutton U	W	1-0	1-0	23	Keating [10]	1970
22	25	H	Leyton Orient	W	3-0	2-0	22	McQuoid [15], Young [29], Reid [47]	1913
23	Dec 2	H	Aldershot T	D	0-0	0-0	21		1851
24	9	A	Tranmere R	L	0-3	0-1	22		4569
25	12	H	Gateshead	D	1-1	1-0	22	McGinty [90]	1405
26	26	A	Eastleigh	D	1-1	0-0	23	Reid (pen) [47]	2092
27	30	A	Boreham Wood	L	0-2	0-1	23		627
28	Jan 6	A	Wrexham	L	0-4	0-3	24		4242
29	13	H	Eastleigh	L	1-2	1-1	24	Young [34]	1486
30	20	H	Bromley	L	0-4	0-1	24		1547
31	27	A	Macclesfield T	D	1-1	0-0	24	Romain [79]	1699
32	Feb 3	H	Barrow	W	3-1	0-0	23	McGinty [52], Dowling [55], Young [66]	1553
33	10	A	Maidenhead U	W	2-1	1-0	22	Barnes [35], Romain [85]	1433
34	17	H	Dagenham & R	L	0-3	0-0	23		1931
35	20	H	Sutton U	L	2-3	2-2	23	McGinty [12], Williams [45]	1302
36	Mar 10	A	Maidstone U	L	0-1	0-0	23		2211
37	13	A	Leyton Orient	W	1-0	1-0	22	Romain [37]	2900
38	17	A	Solihull Moors	D	1-1	1-0	22	Williams (pen) [41]	781
39	30	A	Chester FC	W	2-0	1-0	22	Healey [3], Romain [66]	1830
40	Apr 2	H	Woking	W	2-1	1-0	22	Williams (pen) [14], Lemonheigh-Evans [68]	1837
41	7	A	Dover Ath	L	0-1	0-0	22		1128
42	10	H	AFC Fylde	L	1-3	1-2	22	Williams (pen) [5]	1416
43	14	H	FC Halifax T	W	1-0	0-0	22	Reid [58]	1567
44	21	A	Hartlepool U	D	1-1	0-1	22	Healey [82]	3254
45	24	H	Guiseley	L	3-4	1-2	22	Healey 3 [16, 72, 86]	1007
46	28	H	Ebbsfleet U	D	1-1	0-0	22	Healey (pen) [71]	1728

Final League Position: 22

GOALSCORERS

League (45): Healey 6 (1 pen), Reid 6 (1 pen), Young 5, Keating 4, McGinty 4, Romain 4, Williams 4 (3 pens), Pittman 3, Dowling 2, Gray 2, McQuoid 2, Barnes 1, Lemonheigh-Evans 1, Murphy 1.
FA Cup (0).
FA Trophy (0).

Clarke 10	McGinty 46	Gowling 24 + 1	Higgins 16 + 1	Lathrope 16 + 3	Chaney 6	Young 46	Gosling 9 + 5	Klukowski 7 + 1	Pitman 8 + 11	Keating 16 + 23	Reid 33 + 8	Lee 1 + 1	Lemonheigh-Evans 11 + 4	Gray 7 + 6	Sokolik 5	Anderson 7 + 2	Fallon 1 + 4	Healey 7 + 1	Haworth 3 + 3	Lavercombe 2	Dorel 34 + 1	Dowling 15 + 6	Cole 3	Efete 24 + 2	Evans 10	Myrie-Williams 3 + 7	Murphy 6 + 2	McCuoid 13 + 1	Davis 33	Barnum-Bobb 7	Davey 7	Gnabouyou — + 5	Andresson 4 + 1	O'Sullivan 5 + 2	Fletcher 2 + 1	Balatoni 16	Mitchell — + 2	Romain 13	Barnes 16	Williams 14 + 2	Match No.
1	2	3	4	5²	6	7	8¹	9	10³	11	12	13	14																												1
1	5	4		6³	7	13	8	12	10¹	11	2²	9	3	14																											2
1	3		11	2⁴	4	5	7	9	6³	13	10¹		14	8			12																								3
1	2	4		5¹	6³	7	8	9	10²	11	12		13	3	14																										4
1	2		3	6	4	5	7	8	11	9²	10¹		12				13																								5
	3		2	4³	5¹	6	7	8	10	9	11²	13	12	14		1																									6
	4		3			5	9¹	6	7	8	12	11	2	10²	13	1																									7
	2		9			3			12	4	7		6	5	8¹		1	10	11																						8
	4	5	2			6			12	10¹	11		7		8		1	9	3																						9
	5		3			6			9²	12	11		10		13	7¹	1	8	2	4																				10
	3	4				7			11²	12	10		9	6		1	8¹		2	5	13																			11
	3	4				5			13	9	8¹	7		1	2	6	10	11¹	12																					12
	4	5	3	8		6			12	10			1	2		7	11¹	9	7																					13
	4	3	2¹	7⁷		8			12	6	14		1	9	13	11¹	10³	5																						14
	4	3	2¹	7³		8			13	14	6		1	9	12	11²	10	5																						15
	4	5	10			6			12	9			1	2		7	11¹	8	3																					16
	3	4	6			8			12	10²			1	13	2	5	14	11¹	9³	7																				17
	3	6	5²	13		7²			8	10		14	1	12	2	4¹	11	9																						18
	6	4	13			9			14	11		1	8¹	3	5²	12	10³	7	2																					19
	5	6	14			7			13	10		1	4²	2¹	9³	12	11	8	3																					20
	3	12	7			8			13	9	11²	1	2		10¹	6	4	5																						21
	3		7			8			9¹	11		1	5		12	10²	6	4	2	13																				22
	4		8			7			11	10		1	3		9¹	6	2	5	12																					23
	5		4			6		14	7¹	10		1	2²		8³	3	9	11	13	12																				24
	5		7			8		14	9¹	11		1		13	10³	6	2	3	12	4²																				25
	5		4			6	12	13	7²	8¹		1	10⁸	2		3		9	11																					26
	5		4			6	8³	12	7¹	9		1		2	13	3		10	14	11²																				27
	5		4²			6	13		12	8		1	9	2		3			10	7	11¹																			28
1	4					5	6²		13	8			9	2		3			7	11¹	10	12																		29
1	4					5	6		14	8³			10	2		3			7²	12	11	13	9¹																	30
1¹	2	3				8			11³	12		10¹	6			7				14	4		9	5	13															31
	3	4				8			13	12		1	9¹	2		6					5	7²	11	10																32
	2	3¹				8				12		1	10	6		7					5	9	4	11																33
	3					8	14		12	10²	13		4	1	9	2					6¹			5³	11															34
	3					8			13		12		4	1	10	2¹					6		9	5	11²															35
	3	12				8			4	14	13		10¹	5³		1	8				2			9	7²	6	11													36
	2	3²				8			14	13	10		5³			1	2				7		12	4	9³	6	11													37
	3					4		14		10		5	13	1			2				6³	9		8¹	7	11²														38
	3	2				7			13	12	10			9²			1				6			5	8	4	11¹													39
	4	3				6			12	10				9			1				7			2	8	5	11¹													40
1	2	3				6			13	10			9⁸					12			5²			8⁸	4¹	11														41
1	4	5				6			12	9	10		13			2					8			7¹	3²	11														42
	3	4				6			13	8³	10			9¹		1	12				2			5	2	11														43
	3	4				5		14	6	6	10			9		1	12	13			2			8³	7²	11¹														44
	3	4				5		14	6³	10⁸				9		1	12				2			8¹	11	7	13													45
	3	4				7			12	10				9		1		2			6			8	5	11¹														46

FA Cup
Fourth Qualifying   Aldershot T   (a)   0-1

FA Trophy
First Round   Maidstone U   (h)   0-4

TRANMERE ROVERS

Ground: Prenton Park, Prenton Road West, Prenton, Wirral CH42 9PY. *Tel:* (03330) 144452.
Website: www.tranmererovers.co.uk *Email:* customerservice@tranmererovers.co.uk *Year Formed:* 1884.
Record Attendance: 24,424 v Stoke C, FA Cup 4th rd, 5 February 1972. *Nickname:* 'Rovers' *Manager:* Micky Mellon.
Colours: White shirts with blue trim, white shorts with blue trim, white socks with blue trim.

TRANMERE ROVERS – NATIONAL LEAGUE 2017–18 LEAGUE RECORD

Match No.	Date	Venue	Opponents	Result	H/T Score	Lg Pos.	Goalscorers	Attendance
1	Aug 5	A	Torquay U	D 0-0	0-0	16		3162
2	8	H	Woking	W 3-1	2-1	4	Cook [18], Norburn [31], McEveley [60]	4698
3	12	H	Sutton U	L 0-1	0-1	13		5050
4	15	A	Guiseley	D 0-0	0-0	14		1231
5	19	A	Eastleigh	L 0-2	0-0	15		1906
6	26	H	Boreham Wood	D 2-2	0-0	19	Cook [82], Mangan [90]	4295
7	28	A	Solihull Moors	W 2-0	1-0	15	Norburn [19], Cook [82]	1312
8	Sept 2	H	Dover Ath	L 0-1	0-0	18		4101
9	9	H	Barrow	W 1-0	0-0	14	Norwood [90]	4269
10	12	A	Maidenhead U	L 0-1	0-0	16		1483
11	16	A	Ebbsfleet U	D 0-0	0-0	17		1525
12	23	H	Wrexham	L 0-1	0-0	18		6802
13	30	A	Bromley	W 1-0	0-0	17	Norwood [90]	2056
14	Oct 4	H	Leyton Orient	W 2-1	1-1	14	Cook [25], Norwood [70]	4145
15	7	H	Chester FC	D 0-0	0-0	15		7172
16	21	A	Aldershot T	L 1-2	1-0	15	McNulty [17]	2714
17	24	A	Hartlepool U	D 1-1	0-0	16	McEveley [57]	3371
18	28	H	FC Halifax T	W 4-2	2-0	14	Norwood 2 [5, 14], Cole [52], Mottley-Henry [57]	4826
19	Nov 11	H	Dagenham & R	W 2-0	2-0	13	Norwood [4], Norburn [41]	5227
20	18	A	Gateshead	L 0-1	0-0	15		1140
21	21	A	Macclesfield T	D 2-2	2-1	14	Cole [19], Cook [42]	1709
22	25	H	Maidstone U	W 4-0	2-0	11	Norwood 2 [7, 83], Cook [16], Norburn [77]	4126
23	Dec 9	H	Torquay U	W 3-0	1-0	9	Jennings [35], Cook 2 [79, 82]	4569
24	23	A	Sutton U	W 3-1	2-1	9	Buxton [10], Jennings [44], Cook [90]	2237
25	26	H	AFC Fylde	W 4-1	2-0	6	Sutton 2 [37, 43], Jennings 2 [52, 68]	6669
26	30	H	Guiseley	W 4-0	0-0	6	Norwood [65], Jennings 2 [70, 78], Cook [86]	5271
27	Jan 1	A	AFC Fylde	L 2-5	0-3	7	Banks [58], Jennings (pen) [90]	3065
28	6	A	Barrow	D 1-1	0-1	7	Norwood [90]	1470
29	13	A	Woking	W 1-0	1-0	5	Cook [28]	2115
30	20	H	Maidenhead U	W 3-2	1-0	5	Norwood [4], Ginnelly [49], Hughes [78]	4980
31	27	A	Wrexham	D 2-2	2-2	5	Sutton [10], Cook [45]	8471
32	Feb 3	H	Ebbsfleet U	W 3-0	2-0	4	Cook [16], Norwood 2 [35, 63]	5138
33	10	A	Leyton Orient	D 1-1	1-0	4	Sutton [43]	4631
34	17	H	Bromley	W 1-0	1-0	2	Jennings [35]	5536
35	20	H	Macclesfield T	L 1-4	0-1	6	Cook [49]	7385
36	24	A	Maidstone U	W 3-2	1-2	3	Finney (og) [85], Cook [39], Buxton (pen) [88]	2502
37	Mar 10	A	Dagenham & R	W 4-0	0-0	3	Cook 2 [47, 69], Norwood 2 [68, 90]	1411
38	17	A	Boreham Wood	L 1-2	0-1	4	Norwood [66]	801
39	24	H	Eastleigh	W 3-1	1-0	3	Sutton [9], Cook 2 [78, 90]	4619
40	Apr 7	A	Chester FC	W 2-0	1-0	4	Cook [45], Norwood [64]	3103
41	10	H	Gateshead	W 4-2	1-2	2	Cook 4 [45, 53, 60, 69]	4328
42	14	H	Aldershot T	W 2-0	0-0	2	Norwood 2 [70, 80]	5444
43	17	A	Dover Ath	W 1-0	1-0	2	Cook [39]	1231
44	21	A	FC Halifax T	W 2-0	2-0	2	Cook [4], Norwood [23]	3113
45	24	H	Solihull Moors	L 1-2	0-1	2	Green [67]	3496
46	28	H	Hartlepool U	L 1-2	0-1	2	Hughes [76]	5499

Final League Position: 2

GOALSCORERS
League (78): Cook 26, Norwood 20, Jennings 8 (1 pen), Sutton 5, Norburn 4, Buxton 2 (1 pen), Cole 2, Hughes 2, McEveley 2, Banks 1, Ginnelly 1, Green 1, Mangan 1, McNulty 1, Mottley-Henry 1, own goal 1.
FA Cup (4): Cook 1, Jennings 1, Norwood 1, Ridehalgh 1.
FA Trophy (0).
National League Play-Offs (6): Norwood 3, Cole 1, Cook 1, Ginnelly 1.

Davies 40	Buxton 35+2	Ridehalgh 35+2	McNulty 41	McEveley 9+2	Harris 26+12	Hughes 24+7	Norburn 42	Jennings 39+4	Norwood 40+2	Alabi 4+5	Sutton 41+2	Cook 37+4	Dunn 6+3	Mangan 3+11	Duggan 9+2	Waring —+3	Gumbs 2+2	Tollitt 6+6	Mottley-Henry 11+1	McDonagh 1+7	Clarke 12+2	Cole 9+4	Banks 8	Green 1+2	Kay —+2	Kirby 1+2	Pilling —+1	Taylor 6	Ginnelly 9+1	Monthe 4	Traore 2+1	Wallace —+2	Rokka 1	Drysdale 1	Solomon-Davies 1	Spellman —+1	Walker-Rice —+1	Match No.
1	2	3	4¹	5	6	7	8¹	9	10⁸	11²	12	13																										1
1	2	5			3	6	7	8	9		12	4	11²	10¹	13																							2
1	5	2			3	6²	8	7	10		12	4	9	11¹	13																							3
1	3	4	5	2	6¹	7	9	8		12		10	11																									4
1	2	5	3			7¹	6	8	9²	11	13	4	10	12																								5
1		2	4	5	14	7²	6	10¹	9	11³	3	12		13	8																							6
1	14	2	4	3	7	9	8¹	13	12		5	10		11³	6²																							7
1	14	2	4	5	6	9	7¹	13	12		3	10		11²	8³																							8
1	5	6	2	3¹	8³	7	9	14	10		4	11²	13				12																					9
1	5	3	2		13	8	7	11¹	9	14	6	10³	12						4³																			10
1	3	6	2	5¹	7	8	9¹	10	11		4				12																							11
1	4	8	2		9		3	6	10	7¹	11	12	5²			13																						12
1	2	5	3			8	7	9	11	10	4						6																					13
1	2	3	5		13	11	10²	9	8		4	7							6¹	12																		14
1	2	3	5		13	7	6¹	8	9		4	11²								10	12																	15
1		5	12	6	10	7	8	11¹	4				2						9²	13	3																	16
1	4	3¹	12	5		7	8	10		2	9			6					11																			17
1	2	4		5	11		7	6¹	3	13				9			6²		8	10		12⁴																18
1	2	4	12	7¹	5	10		9		3	8¹			6²					11	14	13																	19
1	4	3²	2			7		11		5	9			13					10¹		8	6	12															20
1	2	4				7	12	6³		3	5¹								8	13	10	9²	11	14														21
1	3				6¹	8	10			5	11					4			9²	2		7	12	13														22
1	2		4		12	8	7	6¹		3	5								9	13	10	11²																23
1	2		4			6	9	10		3	8¹								11	12	5	7																24
1	3		5		12	6	8	10		4	9¹					13			11²	14	2	7³																25
1	2		4		12	14	8²	7	6		3	5							10	9¹	11		13															26
1¹	3	7	8		14		6²	5	4		11	9							13	2¹	10		12															27
2³	14	4			5¹	12	9	8	7		3	6							11	10²			13	1														28
	5	12	2²		4	13	11	9	3		7	6⁴							10	8¹			1															29
	2	3	5		6	13	7	11	10		4				12										8¹	1	9²											30
	2	3	5		6		7	10	9		4	11								12						1	8¹											31
	3	5			6	13	7²10	10¹		4	9	14							12	2						1	8³											32
	4	2			6		7	11	10		5	9							12			3				1	8¹											33
1	2	3	5		6	13	7¹	11	10		4	9							12								8²											34
1	2	3	5			7		8	11	10		4	9						6																			35
1	2				4	10¹	8	7	6²		3	5	9	14	12³				13													11						36
1	2	5	3			7¹		9	11		12	10							13										6²	4³	8	14						37
1	2	5	3			7		9	11			10							12										6¹	4	8							38
1	2	5	3			8	7	9	11		4	10		12					6¹													13						39
1	2	3	5		14	7	8¹	10	9²		4	11		12					6³													13						40
1	2	3	5		7		8	11	10³		4	9²		13					6¹		12										14							41
1	2	3	5		13	11	10	9	8²		4	7³		14					6¹		12											8¹						42
1	2	3	5		12	7	6	10	9		4	11							8¹																			43
1	3¹	8	2		12	9	4	6	5		7	11²		14					10³										13									44
									2	4	5								10			9²			1	3	11						6¹	7	8	12	13	45
1		2	4		5	8	6		10		3	11			12					9¹							7											46

FA Cup
Fourth Qualifying   FC Halifax T   (a)   3-1
First Round   Peterborough U   (a)   1-1
Replay   Peterborough U   (h)   0-5

FA Trophy
First Round   Solihull Moors   (a)   0-2

National League Play-Offs
Semi-Finals   Ebbsfleet U   (h)   4-2
(aet)
Final   Boreham Wood   Wembley   2-1

WOKING

Ground: The Laithwaite Community Stadium, Kingfield, Woking, Surrey GU22 9AA.   *Tel:* (01483) 722 470.
Website: wokingfc.co.uk   *Email:* admin@wokingfc.co.uk   *Year Formed:* 1889.   *Record Attendance:* 6,064 v Coventry C,
FA Cup 3rd rd, 4 February 1997.   *Nickname:* 'The Cardinals'.   *Manager:* Alan Dowson.   *Colours:* Red and white
halved shirts, black shorts with red trim, white socks with red trim.

WOKING – NATIONAL LEAGUE 2017–18 LEAGUE RECORD

Match No.	Date	Venue	Opponents	Result		H/T Score	Lg Pos.	Goalscorers	Attendance
1	Aug 5	H	Gateshead	W	2-1	2-1	4	Effiong [18], Ward [44]	1705
2	8	A	Tranmere R	L	1-3	1-2	13	Carter [43]	4698
3	12	A	Barrow	L	0-3	0-1	17		1075
4	15	H	Eastleigh	W	2-1	1-0	12	Effiong [43], Hoyte (og) [54]	1796
5	19	H	Leyton Orient	L	0-2	0-0	14		2885
6	26	A	Wrexham	L	0-1	0-1	20		3875
7	28	H	Torquay U	W	4-1	2-1	18	Ward [23], Ferdinand [33], Carter [51], Bawling [58]	1936
8	Sept 2	A	Macclesfield T	W	3-1	2-1	9	Banton [27], Ward [41], Effiong [89]	1289
9	9	A	Maidstone U	L	1-3	0-1	16	Ward [72]	2527
10	12	H	Solihull Moors	W	2-1	1-0	14	Banton [30], Carter [82]	1402
11	16	H	Sutton U	W	2-0	0-0	10	Charles-Cook 2 [49, 90]	2193
12	23	A	AFC Fylde	W	2-1	0-1	6	Ward [53], Philpot [54]	1532
13	30	H	Hartlepool U	D	1-1	1-1	7	Philpot [45]	2479
14	Oct 3	A	Chester FC	W	2-0	1-0	3	Ferdinand [10], Philpot [71]	1658
15	7	H	Dagenham & R	W	1-0	0-0	3	Charles-Cook [78]	2509
16	21	A	Bromley	L	0-2	0-2	4		1577
17	24	A	Dover Ath	L	1-3	0-2	5	Ward [54]	1017
18	28	H	Guiseley	L	2-3	1-1	8	Appau [14], Charles-Cook [65]	1783
19	Nov 11	A	FC Halifax T	D	0-0	0-0	8		1710
20	18	H	Maidenhead U	D	1-1	1-1	9	Carter [39]	1878
21	21	H	Ebbsfleet U	W	1-0	1-0	8	Effiong [30]	1580
22	25	A	Boreham Wood	L	1-2	0-1	9	Effiong [90]	543
23	Dec 23	H	Barrow	L	1-2	1-2	13	Carter [21]	1816
24	26	A	Aldershot T	L	1-3	1-2	13	Effiong [14]	4181
25	30	A	Eastleigh	D	2-2	0-0	13	Carter [70], Effiong (pen) [83]	2067
26	Jan 1	H	Aldershot T	L	1-2	0-1	14	Ferdinand [47]	3790
27	6	H	Maidstone U	D	4-4	2-3	14	Ferdinand [21], Effiong [34], Carter [50], Banton [60]	1874
28	13	H	Tranmere R	L	0-1	0-1	15		2115
29	20	A	Solihull Moors	L	0-3	0-1	16		638
30	23	A	Gateshead	D	1-1	0-0	16	Grego-Cox [51]	470
31	27	H	AFC Fylde	W	1-0	0-0	15	Stojsavljevic [49]	1856
32	Feb 10	H	Chester FC	W	1-0	1-0	13	Hobson (og) [23]	1367
33	17	A	Hartlepool U	L	2-3	0-3	15	Grego-Cox [85], Edwards [90]	3018
34	20	A	Ebbsfleet U	L	1-2	0-1	16	Carter [61]	1146
35	24	H	Boreham Wood	D	0-0	0-0	15		1744
36	Mar 6	A	Sutton U	L	0-2	0-1	15		2019
37	10	H	FC Halifax T	L	1-3	0-1	16	Carter [50]	1619
38	17	H	Wrexham	D	2-2	1-1	18	Staunton [12], Jones [80]	1458
39	24	A	Leyton Orient	L	0-3	0-2	18		5673
40	30	H	Macclesfield T	L	2-3	1-1	19	Carter [20], Grego-Cox [84]	2158
41	Apr 2	A	Torquay U	L	1-2	0-1	19	Grego-Cox [65]	1837
42	7	A	Dagenham & R	D	1-1	0-1	19	Staunton [47]	1391
43	10	A	Maidenhead U	L	1-2	0-0	20	Edwards [76]	1301
44	14	H	Bromley	L	0-2	0-1	20		2027
45	21	A	Guiseley	W	2-1	1-0	21	Carter [26], Orlu [85]	562
46	28	H	Dover Ath	L	1-2	1-1	21	Carter [38]	2593

Final League Position: 21

GOALSCORERS

League (55): Carter 12, Effiong 8 (1 pen), Ward 6, Charles-Cook 4, Ferdinand 4, Grego-Cox 4, Banton 3, Philpot 3, Edwards 2, Staunton 2, Appau 1, Bawling 1, Jones 1, Orlu 1, Stojsavljevic 1, own goals 2.
FA Cup (10): Charles-Cook 2, Effiong 2, Philpot 2, Carter 1, Smith 1, Ward 1, Young 1.
FA Trophy (0).

Baxter 42	Ramsey 23+5	Ralph 32	Staunton 40	Orlu 22+4	Jones 25+6	Isaac 33+5	Bawling 8+4	Ward 25+2	Saraiva 7+11	Effiong 19+9	Carter 32+9	Philpot 14+12	Ferdinand 41+3	Wynter 24+1	Young 31+3	Banton 17+8	Appau 3+7	Charles-Cook 19+4	Stojsavljevic 2+4	Mason 3	Wollacott 1	Edwards 3+11	Cook 14+3	Grego-Cox 16+2	Lathrope 3+1	Theophanous 7+4	Match No.
1	2	3	4	5	6	7	8^1	9^3	10^2	11	12	13	14														1
1	2	3	5	6	4	8^1	7	11		9	10^2	13	12														2
1	2	3	5	6	4	13	7^2	10		11	8^1	12	14	9^1													3
1	4^2	5	3	2	6	7		9		10	12	11^1	8		13												4
1	2	3	4	5		7	6^1	9		10	12	11	8^2		13												5
1	2	3	4	5		7^1	6^2	10		11	8^1	12	9		13	14											6
1	13	3^1	4	5		6	12	10		11	8^3	14	7		2	9^2											7
1	12	2	3	4^3		6		10		11	8	14	9		5^2	7^1	13										8
1	2	3					4^3	13	11		5	7^1	14	10	8	9	6^2	12									9
1	2	3	4			6		9^2		11	12	13	7		5	10		8^1									10
1	2^0	3	4			6		9		13	12	11^1	7		5	14	10^2	8									11
1	11		4			5		10		11	13	7^1	9^2	6	3	2	12	14	8^3								12
1		3	4			6		13		9	12	10^1	11^2		7	5	2	8									13
1		3				6				9^1	12	5^3	14	8	11^2	7	4	2				10	13				14
1		3	13			6		10		9	12	11^2			7	5	2	8^1	4								15
1	2^2	4	3^1			6		10		12	11	9^8	8	5	7^3	13		14									16
1	4	2	6^1	5		11		9		10	7	3	12	8													17
1		3	5^2	12	2	7^1		9		13	11	6	4					8^3	10	14							18
1	5	3	6	12		13		10		11^1	7	4	2					8^2	9								19
																		14	9	1							20
	3							4	12	6	10^3	14	11	8^1	11^2	7	5	2		9^2	1						21
	13	3		4		6		7^1		9^2	14	11	12	10	8	5		2^3		1							22
	14	3		4		5^3				9	12	11	8	13	7	6		2^2	10^1		1						23
1	2	3	4	14	5			11		12	6	8^1	13	10	9^3			7^2									24
1	5		4	3	6	7^*		9^1	11^3	12	13	10^2	8		2	14											25
1	3^2		4	5	6			8		13	11	10	12^7		2	9^1											26
1	3		4	5	6			8		13	11	10^2			7			2	9^1			12					27
1	3		5	4				9^1	11	7			6		2		8^2					13	10	12			28
1	2		5	4	7^1			3^2		8		6			12	13						10	11	9			29
1	3^2		5	4	6^1					7		8		2	14	13		12				10	9	11^3			30
1	3^2		4	12	6^3					8		7		2	10^1		5					14	9	11	13		31
1		3	4	5	12	13				8		7		2^*	10^2			9					11	6¹			32
1		3	4	5	12	14				8		7^1		2	9^3			13				10	11	6^2			33
1		3	4	5	6	8^1		14		13		7		2	9^2			10					11^2			12	34
1	5	3		4	13					8		7		2				12				9	11^1	6^2	10		35
1	2	4	5	3				14		7		8		6	13			12				9^3	10^1	11^2			36
1		3	4	5	6^2			14	12	7		2	8^1	10				13				9^3	11				37
1	13	3	5	4				12		7		6		2^1	9^2	8							10	11			38
1		2	5	4^1				9^2		8	10	12	3^3	6		7		14	13					11			39
1	3^1		4		5	6^2				8		7	2	13				9					10	11		12	40
1	2^1		4		3	5^2				7		9	8		13			6					10	11		12	41
1	2		3			5				7		9	8	4				6^2				12	13	11	10^1		42
1	3		4	14		8^3				6		9	5	2				7^1				12	13	10		11^2	43
1	2	3	4			5^2		12		7		10	8					6^1				13	11	9			44
1	2	3	4	14	6	7^2				9		8	5					13					10^1	12		11^3	45
1	3	4	5		2^3	7^2	13			9		8	6					12					10^1	11		14	46

FA Cup

Fourth Qualifying	Concord Rangers	(h)	1-1	
Replay *(aet)*	Concord Rangers	(a)	2-1	
First Round	Bury	(h)	1-1	
Replay	Bury	(a)	3-0	
Second Round	Peterborough U	(h)	1-1	
Replay	Peterborough U	(a)	2-5	

FA Trophy

First Round	Maidenhead U	(h)	0-2

WREXHAM

Ground: Racecourse Ground, Mold Road, Wrexham, Wales LL11 2AH. *Tel:* (01978) 891 864.
Website: wrexhamafc.co.uk *Email:* info@wrexhamfc.tv *Year Formed:* 1872.
Record Attendance: 34,445 v Manchester U, FA Cup 4th rd, 26 January 1957. *Nickname:* 'Red Dragons'.
Manager: Sam Ricketts. *Colours:* Red shirts with white trim, white shorts with red trim, white socks.

WREXHAM – NATIONAL LEAGUE 2017–18 LEAGUE RECORD

Match No.	Date		Venue	Opponents	Result		H/T Score	Lg Pos.	Goalscorers	Atten- dance
1	Aug	5	H	Macclesfield T	L	0-1	0-1	22		6118
2		8	A	Maidenhead U	W	2-1	1-1	12	Smith, M [40], Massanka [77]	1631
3		12	A	Dover Ath	L	0-1	0-1	16		1012
4		15	H	Gateshead	W	1-0	0-0	10	Reid [70]	4097
5		19	A	Maidstone U	L	1-2	1-2	13	Reid [10]	2192
6		26	H	Woking	W	1-0	1-0	11	Jennings [43]	3875
7		28	A	Boreham Wood	W	1-0	0-0	4	Reid [61]	765
8	Sept	2	H	Bromley	W	2-0	0-0	3	Massanka 2 [46, 70]	4032
9		9	A	Torquay U	D	0-0	0-0	3		1841
10		12	H	Hartlepool U	D	0-0	0-0	6		4144
11		16	H	Guiseley	D	1-1	0-1	9	Wedgbury [90]	3916
12		23	A	Tranmere R	W	1-0	0-0	5	Holroyd [58]	6802
13		30	H	Sutton U	D	1-1	1-0	6	Kelly [16]	4815
14	Oct	3	A	FC Halifax T	D	0-0	0-0	6		2136
15		7	H	Eastleigh	W	2-1	0-1	5	Pearson [73], Holroyd [78]	3907
16		21	A	Dagenham & R	W	1-0	0-0	3	Robson (og) [90]	1492
17		24	A	AFC Fylde	L	0-2	0-1	3		1816
18		28	H	Leyton Orient	D	2-2	1-1	3	Holroyd 2 [1, 71]	4432
19	Nov	8	A	Chester FC	W	1-0	1-0	2	Pearson [43]	4079
20		18	H	Ebbsfleet U	W	2-0	1-0	2	Holroyd 2 (1 pen) [28, 74 (p)]	4150
21		21	H	Solihull Moors	W	1-0	1-0	1	Rutherford [39]	3896
22		25	A	Aldershot T	L	0-2	0-2	2		2377
23	Dec	2	H	Maidenhead U	W	2-0	1-0	2	Holroyd [19], Jennings [75]	3968
24		9	A	Macclesfield T	L	1-4	0-1	3	Boden [74]	2402
25		23	H	Dover Ath	D	0-0	0-0	2		4980
26		26	A	Barrow	D	1-1	1-1	4	Pearson [25]	1648
27	Jan	1	H	Barrow	D	3-3	2-2	5	Holroyd [19], Jennings [45], Boden [76]	4390
28		6	H	Torquay U	W	4-0	3-0	4	Holroyd 3 [9, 37, 89], Smith, M [30]	4242
29		20	A	Hartlepool U	W	2-0	0-0	4	Quigley 2 [54, 72]	6833
30		27	H	Tranmere R	D	2-2	2-2	3	Quigley [12], Holroyd (pen) [16]	8471
31		30	A	Gateshead	D	0-0	0-0	3		658
32	Feb	3	H	Guiseley	W	2-0	1-0	1	Holroyd [16], Pearson [71]	1338
33		10	H	FC Halifax T	D	1-1	1-1	3	Boden [19]	4998
34		17	A	Sutton U	D	1-1	1-0	4	Quigley [20]	2621
35		20	A	Solihull Moors	D	0-0	0-0	5		1228
36		24	H	Aldershot T	D	2-2	1-1	6	Quigley 2 [21, 57]	4662
37	Mar	11	A	Chester FC	W	2-0	0-0	4	Quigley [61], Deverdics [69]	6511
38		17	A	Woking	D	2-2	1-1	5	Staunton (og) [33], Kelly [60]	1458
39		24	H	Maidstone U	W	1-0	0-0	4	Pearson [75]	4443
40		30	A	Bromley	D	1-1	0-0	3	Jennings [52]	1403
41	Apr	2	H	Boreham Wood	L	0-1	0-1	4		4746
42		7	A	Eastleigh	D	1-1	1-0	6	Quigley [20]	1765
43		10	A	Ebbsfleet U	L	0-3	0-0	7		1376
44		14	H	Dagenham & R	L	1-2	1-0	7	Rutherford [23]	4193
45		21	A	Leyton Orient	L	0-1	0-1	10		5166
46		28	H	AFC Fylde	D	0-0	0-0	10		3931

Final League Position: 10

GOALSCORERS

League (49): Holroyd 13 (2 pens), Quigley 8, Pearson 5, Jennings 4, Boden 3, Massanka 3, Reid 3, Kelly 2, Rutherford 2, Smith, M 2, Deverdics 1, Wedgbury 1, own goals 2.
FA Cup (0).
FA Trophy (0).

Dunn 35	Jennings 40	Smith M 44	Pearson 45	Wedgbury 41	Holroyd 33 + 1	Carrington 17 + 9	Rutherford 40 + 3	Kelly 42 + 1	Roberts 38 + 1	Boden 23 + 11	Massanka 8 + 15	Mackreth 7 + 25	Wright 19 + 11	Hurst 6 + 11	Reid 14 + 4	Dibble 5	Smith L 4 + 3	Preston 1	Coddington 5	Marx 1	Miller 4 + 1	Quigley 16 + 1	Raven 5 + 2	Deverdics 10 + 2	Franks 2 + 5	Ainge 1 + 9	Match No.
1	2	3	4	5	6¹	7³	8²	9	10	11	12	13	14														1
1	2	3	4	6		7	8²	9	5	11³	10¹	12	13	14													2
1	2	3	5	7			8³	12	9²	4	11¹	13	6	10	14												3
1	3	4	5	7			8	13	9	2	10³	11²	6¹		14	12											4
5	4	3	7			6	9¹	8²	2	10³	12		13	14	11	1											5
	3	4	5	7			12	8²		14	10¹	6³	9	2	11	1	13										6
	3	4	5	7			8			12	10¹		9	2	11	1	6										7
	3	4	5	6				9	10²	13	7¹		11	2	8	1	12										8
	3	4²	5	6		14	7			12	13	11³	8	2¹	10	1	9										9
	2	3	4	12	6	7		8	9¹	14	13	10			5²		11³	1									10
	2	3	4	5	6²	7	8	9	10	11³	14	13			12				1								11
	2		4	5	6²	12	8	9	10				13	11	7		3		1								12
	2	3	4		10	6	7¹	8	5			13	14	9³	12	11²			1								13
	5	4	2	9	10²	7	6¹	8	3	14	12	13			11³				1								14
	5	3	4	8	11	7³	6	9	2	10²			12		14	13			1								15
1	2	3	4		5³	7²	8	9	10	14	13	12	11		6¹												16
1	5	3		8	10	12	6	9¹	2³		13	14	7		11²				4								17
1	3¹	4	5		11²	12	7	8			10³	6	9	2	13		14										18
1	2³	3	4	5	7	12	8	9¹	10	13	6²	14	11														19
1		2	3	4	5	7	8	9²	10		12	13	11		6¹												20
1		2	3	5	11	6	7	8¹	4		12		9	13	10²												21
1		2	3	6	11	5	7	8³	4	14	13	12	9¹		10²												22
1	2	4	5	7¹	10²	12	8	9	3	11	14	6³		13													23
1	3	4	5		6	7	8¹	9²	10	11		13	2									12					24
1	2	4	5	6	10		7	8	3	11	12											9¹					25
1	2	3	4²	5	6	8	9	10³	11		13	12		14								7¹					26
1	3	4	5	6	11		7²	8¹	2	9		12	13									10					27
1	5³	3	4	8	11	12	6²	7	2¹	10		13		14								9					28
1	3	4	5	6	11		7	8	2	9¹		12	13									10²					29
1	2¹	4	5	6	10		7³	8	3	9		13	14									11²	12				30
1	2	3	4	5	7		8	9¹	10	11		13	12									6²					31
1	2	3	4	5	6¹		8	9	10	11		12														7	32
1	2	3	4	5	6		8⁸	9	10	11²												12		7¹	13		33
1	2	3	4	6	11		8²	5	9¹	14	13											10³		7	12		34
1	2	3	4	6	11		8²	14	5	13	9											10²		7	12		35
1	2	3	4	6	11¹			9	5													10		7	8	12	36
1		2³	3	5	7	12	9³	10	11			13										6	4	8²		14	37
1		2	4	6	8	9	10³	11	12		14											5²	3	7¹	13		38
1	2	3	4	6	11		8	9	5													10²		7¹	12	13	39
1	3	4	5	6	10		8³	9	2	13												11¹		7²	12	14	40
1	2	4	5	6	10			8	3⁸	9¹		14										11³	12		7²	13	41
1	2	3	4	6	10³	14	7	8²				9										11¹	5	13		12	42
1	5	3	4		6²	8			13		12	7¹										11	2	9		10	43
1	2	3	4	7			8¹	9		10		6										11	5			12	44
1	2	3	4	6			8	9	10	11²		5¹	12									7				13	45
1	5	3	4	7			6	9	2	11	12²	8										10¹		13			46

FA Cup
Fourth Qualifying   AFC Fylde   (a)   0-1

FA Trophy
First Round   Harrogate T   (h)   0-2

SCOTTISH LEAGUE TABLES 2017–18

(P) *Promoted into division at end of 2016–17 season.*   (R) *Relegated into division at end of 2016–17 season.*

SPFL LADBROKES PREMIERSHIP 2017–18

		Home					Away					Total						
		P	W	D	L	F	A	W	D	L	F	A	W	D	L	F	A	GD	Pts
1	Celtic	38	11	7	1	38	9	13	3	3	35	16	24	10	4	73	25	48	82
2	Aberdeen	38	11	4	4	30	16	11	3	5	26	21	22	7	9	56	37	19	73
3	Rangers	38	10	2	7	32	20	11	5	3	44	30	21	7	10	76	50	26	70
4	Hibernian (P)	38	11	4	4	39	27	7	9	3	23	19	18	13	7	62	46	16	67
5	Kilmarnock	38	9	3	7	27	26	7	8	4	22	21	16	11	11	49	47	2	59
6	Hearts	38	8	7	3	23	13	4	6	10	16	26	12	13	13	39	39	0	49
7	Motherwell	38	8	5	7	26	22	5	4	9	17	27	13	9	16	43	49	–6	48
8	St Johnstone	38	5	7	7	17	27	7	3	9	25	26	12	10	16	42	53	–11	46
9	Dundee	38	6	3	10	18	27	5	3	11	18	30	11	6	21	36	57	–21	39
10	Hamilton A	38	5	3	11	26	35	4	3	12	21	33	9	6	23	47	68	–21	33
11	Partick Thistle®	38	6	4	9	20	24	2	5	12	11	37	8	9	21	31	61	–30	33
12	Ross Co	38	3	7	9	23	29	3	4	12	17	33	6	11	21	40	62	–22	29

Top 6 teams split after 33 games, teams in the bottom six cannot pass teams in the top six after the split.
®Partick Thistle relegated after play-offs.

SPFL LADBROKES CHAMPIONSHIP 2017–18

		Home					Away					Total						
		P	W	D	L	F	A	W	D	L	F	A	W	D	L	F	A	GD	Pts
1	St Mirren	36	14	2	2	37	12	9	3	6	26	24	23	5	8	63	36	27	74
2	Livingston (P)¶	36	8	7	3	26	16	9	4	5	30	21	17	11	8	56	37	19	62
3	Dundee U	36	12	3	3	30	16	6	4	8	22	26	18	7	11	52	42	10	61
4	Dunfermline Ath	36	11	4	3	38	18	5	7	6	22	17	16	11	9	60	35	25	59
5	Inverness CT (R)	36	9	5	4	31	17	7	4	7	22	20	16	9	11	53	37	16	57
6	Queen of the South	36	5	7	6	26	26	9	3	6	33	27	14	10	12	59	53	6	52
7	Greenock Morton	36	7	3	8	23	22	6	8	4	24	18	13	11	12	47	40	7	50
8	Falkirk	36	7	6	5	27	22	5	5	8	18	27	12	11	13	45	49	–4	47
9	Dumbarton®	36	4	3	11	13	32	3	6	9	14	31	7	9	20	27	63	–36	30
10	Brechin C (P)	36	0	4	14	10	40	0	0	18	10	50	0	4	32	20	90	–70	4

¶Livingston promoted after play-offs. ®Dumbarton relegated after play-offs.

SPFL LADBROKES LEAGUE ONE 2017–18

		Home					Away					Total						
		P	W	D	L	F	A	W	D	L	F	A	W	D	L	F	A	GD	Pts
1	Ayr U (R)	36	11	2	5	43	20	13	2	3	49	22	24	4	8	92	42	50	76
2	Raith R (R)	36	15	3	0	36	9	7	6	5	32	23	22	9	5	68	32	36	75
3	Alloa Ath¶	36	10	4	4	32	24	7	5	6	24	19	17	9	10	56	43	13	60
4	Arbroath (P)	36	7	5	6	30	25	10	3	5	40	26	17	8	11	70	51	19	59
5	Stranraer	36	9	1	8	32	35	7	4	7	26	31	16	5	15	58	66	–8	53
6	East Fife	36	8	1	9	33	37	5	2	11	16	30	13	3	20	49	67	–18	42
7	Airdrieonians	36	8	6	4	28	19	2	5	11	18	41	10	11	15	46	60	–14	41
8	Forfar Ath (P)	36	6	3	9	20	30	5	2	11	20	35	11	5	20	40	65	–25	38
9	Queen's Park®	36	2	7	9	22	41	5	3	10	20	31	7	10	19	42	72	–30	31
10	Albion R	36	3	3	12	22	40	5	3	10	35	40	8	6	22	57	80	–23	30

¶Alloa Ath promoted after play-offs. ®Queen's Park relegated after play-offs.

SPFL LADBROKES LEAGUE TWO 2017–18

		Home					Away					Total						
		P	W	D	L	F	A	W	D	L	F	A	W	D	L	F	A	GD	Pts
1	Montrose	36	11	4	3	31	22	12	4	2	29	13	23	8	5	60	35	25	77
2	Peterhead (R)	36	11	2	5	37	21	13	2	3	42	18	24	4	8	79	39	40	76
3	Stirling Alb	36	8	4	6	30	24	8	3	7	31	28	16	7	13	61	52	9	55
4	Stenhousemuir (R)¶	36	9	1	8	32	26	6	8	4	24	21	15	9	12	56	47	9	54
5	Clyde	36	7	6	5	23	23	7	3	8	29	27	14	9	13	52	50	2	51
6	Elgin C	36	10	4	4	31	16	4	3	11	23	45	14	7	15	54	61	–7	49
7	Annan Ath	36	6	8	4	24	17	6	3	9	25	24	12	11	13	49	41	8	47
8	Berwick Rangers	36	5	6	7	21	27	4	4	10	10	32	9	10	17	31	59	–28	37
9	Edinburgh C	36	4	4	10	19	31	3	5	10	18	31	7	9	20	37	62	–25	30
10	Cowdenbeath	36	3	3	12	12	35	1	7	10	11	21	4	10	22	23	56	–33	22

¶Stenhousemuir promoted after play-offs. Cowdenbeath not relegated after play-offs.

SCOTTISH LEAGUE ATTENDANCES 2017–18

SPFL LADBROKES PREMIERSHIP ATTENDANCES

	Average Gate			Season 2017–18	
	2016–17	2017–18	+/–%	Highest	Lowest
Aberdeen	12,641	15,775	+24.80	20,528	13,531
Celtic	54,624	57,528	+5.31	59,259	53,883
Dundee	6,432	5,947	–7.53	9,193	4,863
Hamilton A	2,531	3,095	+22.31	5,406	1,272
Hearts	16,326	18,429	+12.88	32,852	15,357
Hibernian	15,394	18,124	+17.73	20,193	15,459
Kilmarnock	4,964	5,391	+8.60	11,490	3,337
Motherwell	4,486	5,448	+21.46	9,974	3,196
Partick Thistle	4,282	4,580	+6.94	8,264	2,452
Rangers	48,893	49,174	+0.57	50,215	47,272
Ross Co	4,103	4,624	+12.70	6,590	3,509
St Johnstone	4,392	3,809	–13.28	6,887	2,037

SPFL LADBROKES CHAMPIONSHIP ATTENDANCES

	Average Gate			Season 2017–18	
	2016–17	2017–18	+/–%	Highest	Lowest
Brechin C	429	923	+115.41	2,627	445
Dumbarton	1,130	832	–26.38	1,652	392
Dundee U	6,584	5,505	–16.39	6,936	3,620
Dunfermline Ath	4,438	5,243	+18.15	7,585	2,249
Falkirk	5,032	4,676	–7.07	6,094	3864
Greenock Morton	2,362	1,986	–15.93	4,661	1,134
Inverness CT	3,946	2,395	–39.31	3,415	1,801
Livingston	797	1,350	+69.41	2,708	732
Queen of the South	1,857	1,457	–21.50	2,019	1,062
St Mirren	3,599	4,448	+23.60	6,422	3,023

SPFL LADBROKES LEAGUE ONE ATTENDANCES

	Average Gate			Season 2017–18	
	2016–17	2017–18	+/–%	Highest	Lowest
Airdrieonians	830	768	–7.45	1,129	450
Albion R	450	457	+1.57	1,032	167
Alloa Ath	531	643	+21.04	1,749	363
Arbroath	727	772	+6.32	1,110	600
Ayr U	1,866	1,589	–14.87	2,441	1,139
East Fife	626	683	+9.12	1,850	390
Forfar Ath	654	619	–5.48	990	428
Queen's Park	645	688	+6.64	1,233	428
Raith R	2,631	1,886	–28.31	4,496	1,260
Stranraer	409	443	+8.12	1,143	201

SPFL LADBROKES LEAGUE TWO ATTENDANCES

	Average Gate			Season 2017–18	
	2016–17	2017–18	+/–%	Highest	Lowest
Annan Ath	386	346	–10.34	507	248
Berwick R	427	434	+1.67	596	295
Clyde	526	515	–2.06	804	402
Cowdenbeath	345	320	–7.48	406	216
Edinburgh C	401	325	–18.83	464	223
Elgin C	687	607	–11.58	883	393
Montrose	606	682	+12.68	2,380	353
Peterhead	505	641	+27.06	1,049	394
Stenhousemuir	429	444	+3.47	976	220
Stirling Alb	639	658	+2.88	1,012	395

ABERDEEN

Year Formed: 1903. *Ground & Address:* Pittodrie Stadium, Pittodrie St, Aberdeen AB24 5QH. *Telephone:* 01224 650400. *Fax:* 01224 644173. *E-mail:* feedback@afc.co.uk *Website:* www.afc.co.uk
Ground Capacity: 20,866 (all seated). *Size of Pitch:* 105m × 66m.
Chairman: Stewart Milne. *Chief Executive:* Duncan Fraser.
Manager: Derek McInnes. *Assistant Manager:* Tony Docherty. *U-20 Coach:* Paul Sheerin.
Club Nicknames: 'The Dons', 'The Reds', 'The Dandies'.
Previous Grounds: None.
Record Attendance: 45,061 v Hearts, Scottish Cup 4th rd, 13 March 1954.
Record Transfer Fee received: £1,750,000 for Eoin Jess to Coventry C (February 1996).
Record Transfer Fee paid: £1,000,000 for Paul Bernard from Oldham Ath (September 1995).
Record Victory: 13-0 v Peterhead, Scottish Cup 3rd rd, 10 February 1923.
Record Defeat: 0-9 v Celtic, Premier League, 6 November 2010.
Most Capped Player: Alex McLeish, 77 (Scotland).
Most League Appearances: 556: Willie Miller, 1973-90.
Most League Goals in Season (Individual): 38: Benny Yorston, Division I, 1929-30.
Most Goals Overall (Individual): 199: Joe Harper, 1969-72; 1976-81.

ABERDEEN – SPFL LADBROKES PREMIERSHIP 2017–18 LEAGUE RECORD

Match No.	Date	Venue	Opponents	Result	H/T Score	Lg Pos.	Goalscorers	Atten- dance
1	Aug 6	H	Hamilton A	W 2-0	1-0	3	O'Connor [26], Storey [90]	15,165
2	12	A	Ross Co	W 2-1	1-1	4	Reynolds [23], Logan [71]	5965
3	19	H	Dundee	W 2-1	1-0	3	May 2 [11, 79]	15,646
4	26	A	Partick Thistle	W 4-3	2-2	1	Christie [5], McLean (pen) [42], Wright [52], Rooney [84]	4768
5	Sept 9	A	Hearts	D 0-0	0-0	2		24,248
6	16	H	Kilmarnock	D 1-1	1-0	2	May [10]	15,037
7	24	A	Motherwell	W 1-0	0-0	2	Considine [57]	4535
8	30	H	St Johnstone	W 3-0	2-0	2	Rooney 3 (1 pen) [7, 18, 81 (p)]	14,879
9	Oct 14	A	Hibernian	W 1-0	1-0	2	Mackay-Steven [38]	19,038
10	25	H	Celtic	L 0-3	0-2	2		20,528
11	28	H	Ross Co	W 2-1	1-1	2	Christie [12], McLean (pen) [52]	13,918
12	Nov 4	A	Hamilton A	D 2-2	1-1	2	Stewart [27], Arnason [74]	3099
13	18	H	Motherwell	L 0-2	0-1	2		14,013
14	26	A	Kilmarnock	W 3-1	2-0	2	McLean [1], Broadfoot (og) [12], May [74]	4198
15	29	A	Rangers	L 0-3	0-2	2		48,647
16	Dec 3	H	Rangers	L 1-2	0-1	3	Ross, F [85]	18,983
17	8	A	Dundee	W 1-0	0-0	2	McKenna [48]	6451
18	13	A	St Johnstone	W 3-0	2-0	3	Rooney [20], Arnason [33], Christie [60]	2911
19	16	H	Hibernian	W 4-1	3-0	2	Shinnie [11], Mackay-Steven 3 [36, 45, 62]	14,923
20	23	A	Celtic	L 0-3	0-1	2		58,975
21	27	H	Partick Thistle	W 1-0	0-0	2	Rooney [61]	14,830
22	30	H	Hearts	D 0-0	0-0	2		18,371
23	Jan 24	A	Rangers	L 0-2	0-1	3		49,707
24	27	H	Kilmarnock	W 3-1	0-1	2	Rooney [49], McKenna [52], McGinn [72]	13,723
25	31	A	Ross Co	W 4-2	3-0	2	McLean 2 [28, 64], Rooney 2 (1 pen) [32 (p), 34]	4318
26	Feb 3	H	Hamilton A	W 3-0	1-0	2	Considine 2 [24, 87], McGinn [80]	13,531
27	17	A	Hibernian	L 0-2	0-0	2		19,551
28	25	H	Celtic	L 0-2	0-1	3		17,206
29	Mar 10	A	Partick Thistle	D 0-0	0-0	3		3931
30	17	H	Dundee	W 1-0	1-0	3	Shinnie [35]	15,208
31	31	H	St Johnstone	W 4-1	2-0	3	Christie [34], May [41], Stewart 2 [51, 82]	14,161
32	Apr 3	A	Motherwell	W 2-0	0-0	2	Arnason [65], McLean [68]	4127
33	7	A	Hearts	L 0-2	0-2	3		18,056
34	21	A	Kilmarnock	W 2-0	1-0	2	McLean [37], Logan [59]	5067
35	27	H	Hearts	W 2-0	2-0	2	O'Connor [21], Mackay-Steven [37]	14,045
36	May 5	H	Hibernian	D 0-0	0-0	2		17,822
37	8	H	Rangers	D 1-1	1-0	2	McLean (pen) [14]	17,745
38	13	A	Celtic	W 1-0	0-0	2	Considine [47]	58,388

Final League Position: 2

Honours

League Champions: Division I 1954-55; Premier Division 1979-80, 1983-84, 1984-85.
Runners-up: Premiership 2014-15, 2015-16, 2016-17, 2017-18; Division I 1910-11, 1936-37, 1955-56, 1970-71, 1971-72; Premier Division 1977-78, 1980-81, 1981-82, 1988-89, 1989-90, 1990-91, 1992-93, 1993-94.
Scottish Cup Winners: 1947, 1970, 1982, 1983, 1984, 1986, 1990; *Runners-up:* 1937, 1953, 1954, 1959, 1967, 1978, 1993, 2000, 2017.
League Cup Winners: 1955-56, 1976-77, 1985-86, 1989-90, 1995-96, 2013-14; *Runners-up:* 1946-47, 1978-79, 1979-80, 1987-88, 1988-89, 1992-93, 1999-2000, 2016-17.
Drybrough Cup Winners: 1971, 1980.

European: *European Cup:* 12 matches (1980-81, 1984-85, 1985-86); *Cup Winners' Cup:* 39 matches (1967-68, 1970-71, 1978-79, 1982-83 winners, 1983-84 semi-finals, 1986-87, 1990-91, 1993-94); *UEFA Cup:* 56 matches (*Fairs Cup:* 1968-69. *UEFA Cup:* 1971-72, 1972-73, 1973-74, 1977-78, 1979-80, 1981-82, 1987-88, 1988-89, 1989-90, 1991-92, 1994-95, 1996-97, 2000-01, 2002-03, 2007-08). *Europa League:* 24 matches (2009-10, 2014-15, 2015-16, 2016-17, 2017-18).

Club colours: All: Red with white trim.

Goalscorers: *League (56):* Rooney 9 (2 pens), McLean 8 (3 pens), Mackay-Steven 5, May 5, Christie 4, Considine 4, Arnason 3, Stewart 3, Logan 2, McGinn 2, McKenna 2, O'Connor 2, Shinnie 2, Reynolds 1, Ross F 1, Storey 1, Wright 1, own goal 1.
William Hill Scottish FA Cup (10): Mackay-Steven 3, Christie 2, McLean 2 (1 pen), Rooney 2 (1 pen), Shinnie 1.
Betfred Scottish League Cup (1): McLean 1.
UEFA Europa League (5): Christie 2, Mackay-Steven 1, Shinnie 1, Stewart 1.

Lewis J 31	Considine A 30 + 2	O'Connor A 37 + 1	Arnason K 16 + 5	Logan S 37	Tansey G 8 + 1	Shinnie G 35	McLean K 37	Wright S 6 + 10	Christie R 28 + 4	Maynard N 2 + 17	Reynolds M 6 + 7	Stewart G 17 + 13	Storey M — + 1	Mackay-Steven G 22 + 9	May S 25 + 4	Rooney A 17 + 19	Ball D 9 + 7	McKenna S 30	Ross F 1 + 3	Harvie D — + 2	McGinn N 10 + 1	Rogers D 2 + 1	Nwakali C 3 + 2	Woodman F 5	Cosgrove S 4 + 1	Campbell D — + 1	Match No.
1	2	3	4^3	5	6	7	8	9	10^2	11^1	12	13	14														1
1	5	4		2	7	6	9	13	12	14		3		8^2	10^1	11^1											2
1	5	3		2	6^2	8	7		10	13		4	12		9^1	11^3	14										3
1	4	3		2	6	5	7	9	8	13	14	10^1				11^3	12										4
1	5	3		2		7	8	9	6	13	14		12	11	10^2	4^1											5
1	5	4	3	2		8	7	9	12	11^1		6^2		13	10	14											6
1	6	3	4	2	9^2	8	10	7^1		12		11^3	14	13	5												7
1		6	3	2		7	5	12	9^1	13		8		11^2	10			4	14								8
1		6	3	2		5	9		8^1	14	13	7^1	10^2	11	12			4									9
1	5	6	3	2	13	8	9	12		14		7^2	10^5	11^1				4									10
1		6	3	2		5	7	10^2	9	12		8^2	13	11^1	14			4									11
1		6	3	2		5	8		9	13		7		10^1	11^2	12		4									12
1	5	7	3	2	6^2		8	13	10		14			9^1	12	11^3		4									13
1	5	3		2	7	6	9		8^1	14	12	10^1		11^2		13		4									14
1	5	7	3^1	2	6^2		8	11	9		13		12^3	10	14			4									15
1	5^2	3		2	7	6	10^1	13		8		9^3		11				4	12	14							16
1	5	3	12	2	7	8	11	6	10									4			9^1						17
1	12	3	6	2	5	7	10	14	8^1	13				9^3	11^2			4									18
1	5	3		2	7	6	13	8	14	12		10^1		9^3	11^2			4									19
1	5	3	4		9	8		12	6	7^3		11^2	2	13	14												20
1	5^5	3		2	6	7	12	9	13	8^2		10	11	14				4									21
1	5^1	7	3^2	2		8	6	14	10	13	12	9^2	11					4									22
1	5	3		2	7	6	9		8^1	10	11	13						4	12	14							23
1	5	3	12	2	6	9	14		10	11	7^2							4			8^3	1	13				24
1	5	14	3	2	7	6	12	9^5		13	10	11						4			8^2	1					25
1	5	3		2	7^1	6	9	13		10^3	11^2	14						4			8	12	1				26
1	5	3	13	2		6	9	14		10^2	12	11^1						4			8		7^3	1			27
1	5	6	3^2	2		9		14		10	11^3	13						4			8	7^1	1		12		28
1	5	3		2	7	9	8		14	13	11^3	12						4			6^1				10^2		29
1	5	3		2	7	9	10		12	13	11^3	14						4			8^1			1	6^2		30
1	5	3		2	7	6	9	12	8	10^1	11^2	14	13					4^1									31
1	5	6	3^3	2	7	9	14	10^2		8^1	11	13	12					4									32
1	5	3	12	2	6	9	8^1		10^2	13	11	14						4					7^3				33
1		3	14	2	7	9	10^1		5	8^2	13	11^3	12	6				4									34
1	14	6		2	5	7	13		8	9^3	12	3	4	10^2							11^3						35
1		3		2	7		13	5	12	8^2	9^1	14	6	4	10^2						11						36
1	5	3		2	10	6	9		12	8^1	13	14	7^2	4							11^3						37
1	5	3		2^8	7	9		4	8^1	10^6	14	13	6								11^3	12					38

AIRDRIEONIANS

Year Formed: 2002. *Ground & Address:* The Penny Cars Stadium, New Broomfield, Craigneuk Avenue, Airdrie ML6 8QZ. *Telephone:* (Stadium) 01236 622000. *Fax:* 0141 221 1497. *Postal Address:* 60 St Enoch Square, Glasgow G1 4AG.
E-mail: enquiries@airdriefc.com *Website:* www.airdriefc.com
Ground Capacity: 10,101 (all seated). *Size of Pitch:* 105m × 67m.
Chairman: Bobby Watson. *Vice-Chairman:* Martin Ferguson.
Manager: Stevie Findlay. *First-Team Coach:* David Proctor.
Club Nickname: 'The Diamonds'.
Record Attendance: 9,044 v Rangers, League 1, 23 August 2013.
Record Victory: 11-0 v Gala Fairydean, Scottish Cup 3rd rd, 19 November 2011.
Record Defeat: 0-7 v Partick Thistle, First Division, 20 October 2012.
Most League Appearances: 222: Paul Lovering, 2004-12.
Most League Goals in Season (Individual): 23: Andy Ryan, 2016-17.
Most Goals Overall (Individual): 43: Bryan Prunty, 2005-08, 2015-16.

AIRDRIEONIANS – SPFL LADBROKES LEAGUE ONE 2017–18 LEAGUE RECORD

Match No.	Date	Venue	Opponents	Result	H/T Score	Lg Pos.	Goalscorers	Atten- dance
1	Aug 5	A	Forfar Ath	L	1-2	0-1	7	Loudon [58]	674
2	12	H	Arbroath	D	1-1	0-1	8	Ryan [50]	740
3	19	A	Albion R	W	2-1	2-1	5	Tierney 2 [3, 17]	863
4	26	H	Alloa Ath	W	2-0	1-0	4	Conroy (pen) [16], Hastie [88]	771
5	Sept 9	A	Stranraer	L	1-3	0-1	4	Furtado [56]	431
6	16	H	East Fife	L	0-1	0-1	8		783
7	23	A	Raith R	L	0-2	0-0	8		1726
8	30	H	Queen's Park	W	4-2	1-1	7	Stewart 2 [7, 67], Cairns [50], Furtado [71]	747
9	Oct 14	A	Ayr U	D	2-2	1-0	7	McGregor [29], Furtado [65]	1513
10	21	A	Arbroath	L	1-7	1-4	8	Conroy (pen) [12]	740
11	28	H	Albion R	D	2-2	2-1	8	Brownlie [24], Stewart [45]	960
12	Nov 4	A	Alloa Ath	L	0-1	0-1	8		631
13	11	H	Stranraer	W	2-0	0-0	8	Conroy 2 [61, 68]	641
14	25	H	East Fife	L	1-6	1-3	8	Stewart [1]	619
15	Dec 2	H	Forfar Ath	W	2-1	0-0	7	Furtado [68], Hastie [79]	507
16	10	H	Raith R	D	2-2	2-1	7	Hastie [23], Russell [38]	450
17	16	A	Queen's Park	D	1-1	1-1	7	Watt [10]	593
18	23	A	Ayr U	W	2-0	2-0	6	Russell [4], Brownlie [26]	1113
19	Jan 2	A	Albion R	D	2-2	0-0	6	Furtado [70], Cairns [75]	1032
20	6	H	East Fife	D	0-0	0-0	6		734
21	13	A	Stranraer	L	2-3	1-1	7	Carrick [2], Furtado [64]	406
22	27	H	Arbroath	D	0-0	0-0	7		850
23	Feb 3	A	Forfar Ath	W	1-0	1-0	7	Carrick [40]	551
24	10	A	Raith R	L	1-2	1-0	7	Carrick [44]	1685
25	17	H	Queen's Park	W	2-1	2-0	6	Brownlie [3], Duffy (pen) [25]	908
26	24	A	Ayr U	L	0-3	0-0	7		1456
27	Mar 10	A	East Fife	L	1-2	1-1	7	Higgins, D [32]	473
28	13	H	Stranraer	W	2-1	1-1	7	Conroy (pen) [11], Duffy [71]	512
29	17	A	Alloa Ath	D	2-2	1-2	7	Carrick [29], Duffy [58]	526
30	20	H	Alloa Ath	D	2-2	2-1	7	Duffy [18], Higgins, D [45]	516
31	24	H	Raith R	L	1-2	0-2	7	Stewart [46]	915
32	31	A	Queen's Park	D	0-0	0-0	7		702
33	Apr 7	H	Ayr U	L	1-2	1-1	7	Carrick [10]	1129
34	14	A	Albion R	W	2-0	1-0	7	Brown, A [32], Fry [88]	826
35	21	A	Arbroath	L	0-2	0-1	7		732
36	28	H	Forfar Ath	L	1-2	0-1	7	Conroy (pen) [77]	730

Final League Position: 7

Honours
League Champions: Second Division 2003-04.
Runners-up: Second Division 2007-08.
League Challenge Cup Winners: 2008-09; *Runners-up:* 2003-04.

Club colours: Shirt: White with red diamond. Shorts: White with red trim. Socks: White with red trim.

Goalscorers: *League (46):* Conroy 6 (4 pens), Furtado 6, Carrick 5, Stewart 5, Duffy 4 (1 pen), Brownlie 3, Hastie 3, Cairns 2, Higgins D 2, Russell 2, Tierney 2, Brown A 1, Fry 1, Loudon 1, McGregor 1, Ryan 1, Watt 1.
William Hill Scottish FA Cup (2): Hastie 1, McGregor 1.
Betfred Scottish League Cup (4): Russell 2, Cairns 1, Ryan 1 (1 pen).
Irn-Bru Scottish League Challenge Cup (0).

Ferguson R 26	Stewart S 33	Cairns D 22 + 5	Brownlie D 27	MacDonald K 36	Higgins J 1 + 1	Fry T 20 + 10	Conroy R 22 + 1	Brown A 8 + 9	Ryan A 2	Loudon M 1 + 1	Russell C 14 + 11	Leighton R 1 + 4	Thomson S — + 5	McIntosh S 15 + 6	McGregor J 25 + 2	Balaton C 2	Watt L 22 + 4	Hastie J 21 + 10	Tierney R 4 + 1	Furtado W 18	Allan J 2 + 7	Gourlay K 3	Mason K 1	Edwards J 12	Carrick D 16	Duffy D 9 + 1	O'Neil C 10	Brown R 8 + 1	Higgins D 6 + 2	Muir W 6	Kilday L 3	Match No.
1	2	3	4	5	6¹	7	8	9²	10	11³	12	13	14																			1
1	6	3	4	5		7	8	9		11	12	10²	13		2¹																	2
1	2			5		9²	7	10						12	13	3	4	6	8	11¹												3
1	2			5		9¹	6							13	12	4	3	7	8	11	10²											4
1	2	4		5		11	8							13	6²	3		7	10¹	9	12											5
1	2	3		5		9¹	8³							13	14		6	7¹	11²	10	12											6
1	7	6	3	5			8					10¹					2	4	9		11	12										7
1	10²	8	3	5		7						12					2	4	9	11¹		6	13									8
1	6	11	3	5		9	8										2	4²	7¹	12		10	13									9
1	6	7		5	12	9	8								14		3	4	2¹	13	11³	10³										10
	6	7¹	4	5		11	8										2	3	9	10	12	1										11
	6		3	5		9	8					13					2	4	7²	10³	14	11³	12	1								12
	6	13	4	5		11²	8										2	3	7	12		9	10¹	1								13
	6	4		5		10¹	8	13				12					2	3	7	9²		11			1							14
1	6	2		5		12	8¹	7				10	13				3²	4	14	11				9³								15
1	5	9	2	4		13						10²		12	3		7	8		11				6¹								16
1	5	6	2	4		12		13				10¹			3		7	9		11				8²								17
1	5	7	2	4		12		13				11¹			3		6	8²		10				9								18
1	8	7	2	5		12		13				10²			3		4	9¹		11				6								19
1	5		3	4		10		12				13	14			6	2¹	7	9²	11				8³								20
1	5	12	3	4		14						13				6	2	7²	9¹	10				8³	11							21
1	6	13	5	9				12				14				7	3⁴	2¹	8					4³	11	10²						22
1	6	3	5	9		8						12					13	14						4¹	11²	10	2	7³				23
1	6	8	4	3		9²						14						13						5¹	10	11³	2	7				24
1	6	7	3	5		9²												13							11	10¹	2	8²	13			25
1	6	7	4	5		9²												13							11	10¹	2	8				26
	6	4		5				13	9²			10					3			12				7³	11	14		8¹	2	1		27
	6²	7	3	5		9	8¹										14			13	12				11³	10	2		4	1		28
	6	7	4	5		8															9				10	11	2		3	1		29
	6	7	4	5		8³						12						13		9					11	10¹	2	14	3	1		30
	6		4	5		9	13					10¹					7⁴	12							11		2	8²	3	1		31
1	8	7²		5			6	13				9¹		12	4		10								11	2⁴					3	32
1	8¹			5		12	6	13				9			2	4	7⁴	10²							11						3	33
1		3	4		12	7¹	8					11	2					9						5	10		6					34
1	13	3	4		12	7	6²					11³						9							10		2	8¹	14		5	35
	12		3⁴		13	8	6²					11¹			4		7	9						5	10			2	1			36

ALBION ROVERS

Year Formed: 1882. *Ground & Address:* Cliftonhill Stadium, Main St, Coatbridge ML5 3RB. *Telephone/Fax:* 01236 606334.
E-mail: general@albionroversfc.co.uk *Website:* albionroversfc.co.uk
Ground capacity: 1,572 (seated: 489). *Size of Pitch:* 101m × 66m.
Chairman Ronnie Boyd.
Manager: John Brogan. *Assistant Manager:* Colin Mitchell.
Club Nickname: 'The Wee Rovers'.
Previous Grounds: Cowheath Park, Meadow Park, Whifflet.
Record Attendance: 27,381 v Rangers, Scottish Cup 2nd rd, 8 February 1936.
Record Transfer Fee received: £40,000 from Motherwell for Bruce Cleland (1979).
Record Transfer Fee paid: £7000 for Gerry McTeague to Stirling Alb, September 1989.
Record Victory: 12-0 v Airdriehill, Scottish Cup 1st rd, 3 September 1887.
Record Defeat: 1-11 v Partick Thistle, League Cup 2nd rd, 11 August 1993.
Most Capped Player: Jock White, 1 (2), Scotland.
Most League Appearances: 399: Murdy Walls, 1921-36.
Most League Goals in Season (Individual): 41: Jim Renwick, Division II, 1932-33.
Most Goals Overall (Individual): 105: Bunty Weir, 1928-31.

ALBION ROVERS – SPFL LADBROKES LEAGUE ONE 2017–18 LEAGUE RECORD

Match No.	Date	Venue	Opponents	Result	H/T Score	Lg Pos.	Goalscorers	Attendance
1	Aug 5	H	Ayr U	L	1-5	0-3	10	Shields [87]	806
2	12	A	Queen's Park	W	5-2	2-1	5	Marr [40], Trouten 2 (1 pen) [43 (p), 76], Shields 2 [47, 63]	645
3	19	H	Airdrieonians	L	1-2	1-2	7	Vitoria [10]	863
4	26	A	Forfar Ath	W	2-0	1-0	5	Trouten [34], Shields [86]	537
5	Sept 9	A	Arbroath	W	4-1	2-0	3	Trouten [43], Fisher [44], Perry [63], Shields [75]	669
6	16	H	Stranraer	L	0-4	0-3	5		353
7	23	A	Alloa Ath	W	5-2	2-0	4	Shields [5], Trouten 2 [28, 73], Higgins [51], Vitoria [80]	488
8	30	H	Raith R	W	2-1	1-0	3	Trouten [38], Shields [83]	616
9	Oct 14	A	East Fife	L	4-5	1-2	3	Marr [8], Reid [54], Vitoria [68], Trouten [78]	502
10	21	A	Queen's Park	L	0-1	0-0	4		425
11	28	A	Airdrieonians	D	2-2	1-2	5	Trouten [37], Fisher [65]	960
12	Nov 4	H	Forfar Ath	L	3-4	1-1	7	Trouten (pen) [4], Shields [56], Higgins [90]	367
13	11	H	Alloa Ath	L	0-2	0-1	7		393
14	Dec 2	A	Ayr U	L	2-3	1-1	8	Higgins [25], Trouten [75]	1426
15	19	A	Stranraer	D	2-2	1-1	8	Trouten 2 (1 pen) [7, 52 (p)]	303
16	23	H	East Fife	W	3-2	2-2	8	Shields [23], Trouten [25], McLaughlin [72]	248
17	30	A	Queen's Park	D	2-2	0-2	8	Trouten [88], Vitoria [90]	609
18	Jan 2	A	Airdrieonians	D	2-2	0-0	8	Trouten [57], McLaughlin [90]	1032
19	6	A	Alloa Ath	L	1-3	1-2	8	Vitoria [14]	458
20	13	A	Forfar Ath	L	2-4	1-2	8	Fisher [18], Marr [60]	505
21	27	H	Stranraer	L	1-3	0-1	8	Reid [52]	388
22	Feb 3	A	Arbroath	L	0-1	0-1	8		600
23	6	A	Raith R	L	1-3	0-1	8	Hopkins [54]	1294
24	17	H	Raith R	D	2-2	1-1	9	Trouten 2 (1 pen) [11, 90 (p)]	519
25	24	A	East Fife	L	0-2	0-2	9		390
26	Mar 10	A	Stranraer	W	3-2	0-2	8	Fisher [51], Hester [82], McLeish [86]	281
27	13	H	Queen's Park	D	1-1	1-0	9	Davidson [23]	296
28	17	H	Arbroath	L	1-2	1-1	9	Trouten [17]	274
29	20	H	Ayr U	L	2-3	1-2	9	Hester [39], Trouten [66]	652
30	24	H	Alloa Ath	L	1-3	0-2	9	Vitoria [77]	289
31	27	A	Arbroath	L	1-2	1-1	9	Higgins [23]	167
32	31	A	Raith R	L	0-2	0-0	9		1456
33	Apr 7	H	Forfar Ath	L	0-1	0-0	9		269
34	14	A	Airdrieonians	L	0-2	0-1	9		826
35	21	H	East Fife	W	1-0	1-0	9	Higgins [1]	262
36	28	A	Ayr U	L	0-2	0-1	10		2441

Final League Position: 10

Honours
League Champions: Division II 1933-34; Second Division 1988-89; League Two 2014-15.
Runners-up: Division II 1913-14, 1937-38, 1947-48; Third Division 2010-11.
Promoted via play-offs: 2010-11 (to Second Division).
Scottish Cup Runners-up: 1920.

Club colours: Shirt: Yellow with red trim. Shorts: Red. Socks: Red.

Goalscorers: *League (57):* Trouten 20 (4 pens), Shields 9, Vitoria 6, Higgins 5, Fisher 4, Marr 3, Hester 2, McLaughlin 2, Reid 2, Davidson 1, Hopkins 1, McLeish 1, Perry 1.
William Hill Scottish FA Cup (4): Fisher 1, Trouten 1, Vitoria 1, own goal 1.
Betfred Scottish League Cup (12): Trouten 7 (2 pens), Shields 3, Davidson 1, Fisher 1.
Irn-Bru Scottish League Challenge Cup (0).

Bowman G 13	Reid A 28+1	Marr J 16+2	Perry R 28+1	McLaughlin S 35	Holmes G 29	Fisher G 29	Davidson R 29+2	Trouten A 33	Higgins S 21+8	Vitoria J 17+16	Shields C 19+2	Gallagher J —+4	McManus R —+2	Hopkins M 2+6	Lightbody D 13+3	McMullin M 12+11	Trialist A —+1	McLeish C 12+5	Potts D 11	Watters R 3+7	Wright K 12	Baur D 10+2	MacDonald C 1	Mbayo H 7	Queen P —+2	Hester K 5+2	Guthrie J —+1	Scullion C 4+5	McLean S 7	Match No.
1	2	3	4	5	6¹	7	8	9	10	11²	12	13																		1
1	2	4	3	5	7³	8	6¹	11	9²	10		14	12	13																2
1	2	3¹	4	5	7	8	6³	11	9¹	10		13			12	14														3
1	2		4	5	7²	8	6	11	13		10				3	9¹	12													4
1	5	13	3	2	4	9	8	7	12	14	10²				6³	11¹														5
1	2	13⁴	3	5	4	9	8²	7	12	14	10				6³	11¹														6
1	2		4	5	7²	6	8	11	10³	13	9¹				3	14		12												7
1	2		4	5	6¹	7	8	11	10²	13	9³				3	12		14												8
1	2	3	4	5	7	6	8	11	9¹	12	10¹				13															9
1	2	4²	13	5	7	6	8	9	11	10¹	12				3⁴															10
1	2	3¹	4	5¹	6	7³	14	9	10¹	12	11				13			8⁸												11
1	2	3¹		7	6	12	9	13	11	10					4	5		8⁸												12
1	3			2	6	7	8	9	12	11	10¹				4	5														13
	2	3¹	4	5	7	6	8	9	11²	12	10				13				1											14
	3		4	5	6	7	8	9		13	11²				10¹	2	12		1											15
	3		4	5	6	7	8	10²	12	11¹	9				2				1	13										16
	3		4	5	7	8	6	11		9¹	13	10			2²	12			1											17
	3		4	5	7	8		9		11	10				12	2	6¹		1											18
	3		4²	5	7	8	6	9	13	11	10¹				2	12			1											19
	3	4		2		8	6	9⁴	10	11²	7		12⁴	13	5				1											20
	2			5	8¹	7	9		11²	13	10				12	6				1	3	4								21
			2		7³		8²	9	10	11¹		12			5	6		13	1	3		4	14							22
			2				7	9	11²	12		6¹			5	8		13	1	3		4		10						23
	3		2		6²	7	8	11	10						12	5			1			4	13	9¹						24
	3		2		6	7³	8	9	11	10⁴	12				14	5¹			1			4	13							25
		3	2	6²	7¹	8	9		10							13		11³	1	5		4		12	14					26
		3	2	6	7	8	10		11¹							13		12	1	5		4³		9²		14				27
13	2	3	5		7		11		12						6¹	8		10	1		4							9¹		28
	2²	3	4	8		7		10	14	12			13		6³	1		5								11		9¹		29
	2	3	4	6		7		8	10	12						1		5								11¹			9	30
	2²	3	4	5				8	9	10	11¹				6	1		12										13	7	31
	2	3	4	5	7			8	10	9	11¹					1												12	6	32
	2	3	4	5	7				10²	11		13			8³	1	12	14								9¹			6	33
	2		3	5		9¹	8	11		10²		13			6¹	12	1	4								14	7			34
		3	2	7²		8	11³	10	12						5	13	14	1	4							9¹	6			35
	2		3	5	7		8	10²	12						9			11¹	1	4							13	6		36

ALLOA ATHLETIC

Year Formed: 1878. *Ground & Address:* Indodrill Stadium, Recreation Park, Clackmannan Rd, Alloa FK10 1RY.
Telephone: 01259 722695. *Fax:* 01259 210886. *E-mail:* fcadmin@alloaatheltic.co.uk *Website:* www.alloaathletic.co.uk
Ground Capacity: 3,100 (seated: 919). *Size of Pitch:* 102m × 69m.
Chairman: Mike Mulraney. *Secretary:* Ewen Cameron.
Player/Manager: Jim Goodwin. *Assistant Manager:* Paddy Connolly.
Club Nicknames: 'The Wasps', 'The Hornets'.
Previous Grounds: West End Public Park, Gabberston Park, Bellevue Park.
Record Attendance: 13,000 v Dunfermline Ath, Scottish Cup 3rd rd replay, 26 February 1939.
Record Transfer Fee received: £100,000 for Martin Cameron to Bristol R (July 2000).
Record Transfer Fee paid: £26,000 for Ross Hamilton from Stenhousemuir (July 2000).
Record Victory: 9-0 v Selkirk, Scottish Cup 1st rd, 28 November 2005.
Record Defeat: 0-10 v Dundee, Division II, 8 March 1947; v Third Lanark, League Cup, 8 August 1953.
Most Capped Player: Jock Hepburn, 1, Scotland.
Most League Appearances: 239: Peter Smith 1960-69.
Most League Goals in Season (Individual): 49: 'Wee' Willie Crilley, Division II, 1921-22.
Most Goals Overall (Individual): 91: Willie Irvine, 1996-2001.

ALLOA ATHLETIC – SPFL LADBROKES LEAGUE ONE 2017–18 LEAGUE RECORD

Match No.	Date		Venue	Opponents	Result		H/T Score	Lg Pos.	Goalscorers	Attendance
1	Aug	5	H	Raith R	D	1-1	1-0	5	Cawley [16]	1114
2		12	A	East Fife	L	0-1	0-0	9		589
3		19	H	Queen's Park	W	1-0	0-0	6	Martin [85]	508
4		26	A	Airdrieonians	L	0-2	0-1	7		771
5	Sept	9	H	Forfar Ath	W	2-1	0-0	7	Cawley [88], Renton [90]	511
6		16	A	Ayr U	D	3-3	1-1	7	McKeown [36], Cawley [61], Taggart (pen) [84]	1306
7		23	H	Albion R	L	2-5	0-2	7	Renton [57], Taggart [64]	488
8		30	A	Arbroath	D	1-1	1-0	8	Gold (og) [35]	640
9	Oct	14	A	Stranraer	L	0-2	0-0	8		409
10		21	H	East Fife	W	4-1	2-1	7	Crossan [25], Hetherington [45], Graham [60], Flannigan [74]	556
11		28	A	Queen's Park	W	4-0	1-0	6	Crossan [26], Malcolm [60], Graham [70], Meggatt [86]	556
12	Nov	4	H	Airdrieonians	W	1-0	1-0	3	Malcolm [41]	631
13		11	A	Albion R	W	2-0	1-0	3	Flannigan [5], Renton [90]	393
14		25	H	Ayr U	L	1-2	0-1	4	Taggart [76]	854
15	Dec	2	A	Raith R	L	1-2	0-0	4	Cawley [88]	1400
16		9	A	Forfar Ath	W	2-0	0-0	3	Renton 2 [67, 87]	428
17		23	H	Stranraer	W	1-0	0-0	3	Stewart [57]	449
18	Jan	2	H	Queen's Park	D	2-2	1-1	3	Stewart [4], Renton [85]	476
19		6	H	Albion R	W	3-1	2-1	3	Stewart [19], Crossan [43], Flannigan [88]	458
20		13	A	East Fife	L	1-2	0-1	4	Martin [68]	492
21		27	H	Raith R	D	0-0	0-0	5		904
22	Feb	3	A	Ayr U	W	2-1	2-1	4	McCart [14], Stewart [17]	1139
23		10	A	Forfar Ath	W	1-0	1-0	3	Graham [27]	508
24		17	A	Arbroath	D	0-0	0-0	3		652
25		24	A	Stranraer	L	0-1	0-1	4		282
26	Mar	6	H	Arbroath	W	5-3	4-1	4	Fleming (pen) [6], Stewart 3 [9, 15, 42], Flannigan [79]	363
27		10	A	Queen's Park	W	2-1	0-0	4	Crane [61], Kirkpatrick [75]	428
28		13	H	East Fife	L	1-2	0-0	4	Fleming (pen) [58]	402
29		17	H	Airdrieonians	D	2-2	2-1	4	Flannigan [22], Cawley [40]	526
30		20	A	Airdrieonians	D	2-2	1-2	4	Fleming (pen) [45], Kirkpatrick [67]	516
31		24	A	Albion R	W	3-1	2-0	3	Hetherington 2 [36, 87], Kirkpatrick [42]	289
32		31	H	Arbroath	W	3-2	2-2	3	Smith [26], Kirkpatrick 2 [41, 77]	604
33	Apr	7	H	Stranraer	L	0-1	0-0	4		472
34		14	A	Forfar Ath	W	1-0	1-0	4	Crane [15]	533
35		22	H	Ayr U	W	2-1	0-0	4	Flannigan [21], Crane [33]	1749
36		28	A	Raith R	D	0-0	0-0	3		4496

Final League Position: 3

Honours
League Champions: Division II 1921-22; Third Division 1997-98, 2011-12.
Runners-up: Division II 1938-39; Second Division 1976-77, 1981-82, 1984-85, 1988-89, 1999-2000, 2001-02, 2009-10, 2012-13; League One 2016-17.
Promoted via play-offs: 2012-13 (to First Division); 2017-18 (to Championship).
League Challenge Cup Winners: 1999-2000; *Runners-up:* 2001-02, 2014-15.

Club colours: Shirt: Gold and black hoops. Shorts: Black. Socks: Black with gold hoops.

Goalscorers: *League (56):* Stewart 7, Flannigan 6, Renton 6, Cawley 5, Kirkpatrick 5, Crane 3, Crossan 3, Fleming 3 (3 pens), Graham 3, Hetherington 3, Taggart 3 (1 pen), Malcolm 2, Martin 2, McCart 1, McKeown 1, Meggatt 1, Smith 1, own goal 1.
William Hill Scottish FA Cup (2): Malcolm 2.
Betfred Scottish League Cup (2): Flannigan 1, McKeown 1.
Irn-Bru Scottish League Challenge Cup (5): Malcolm 2, Cawley 1, Crane 1, Flannigan 1.
Play-Offs (6): Stewart 3, Kirkpatrick 2, Flannigan 1.

Parry N 36	Taggart S 35	Graham A 33	Meggatt D 9+2	Crane C 32+1	Robertson J 29+6	Flannigan J 33+1	Cawley K 26+7	Fleming G 27+1	Cook A 5+4	Malcolm C 11+9	Renton K 16+15	Hetherington S 29+3	Martin A —+16	Crossan P 17+11	McKeown F 4	Goodwin J 2+1	Hoggan R —+1	Stewart R 17+2	McCart J 13	Kirkpatrick J 16	Smith C 6+7	Monaghan D —+1	Match No.
1	2	3	4	5	6	7	8	9[1]	10[3]	11[12]	12	13	14										1
1	2	3	4	5	6	8	7	9	10[1]	11	12												2
1	2	3	4	5	7	8	6		9[1]	10	11[12]	12	13										3
1	2	3	4	5	7	9	6	11[1]		10[3]	13	8[2]	14	12									4
1	2	4[5]		5	6	8	7		10[2]	12	11	9[13]			3	14							5
1	2		5	14	7[2]	9	6	11[13]		13	10[1]	8	12		3	4							6
1	2		5		6	10	7[1]	9[3]		13	11	8	14	12	3	4[2]							7
1	2	4	5	7	6	9		13	12	10[1]	8		11[3]	3									8
1	2	3	4	5[1]	7	8	6[2]	14	9[3]	12	10	13	11										9
1	3	4	5	2	9	6[1]	7	13	10[3]	12	8	14	11[2]										10
1	4	3	14	5	2	9	6	7[1]	10[2]	12	8	13	11[3]										11
1	4	3		5	2	9	6	7	11[2]	12	8	13	10[5]										12
1	3	4		5	2	9	8	7	12	10[1]	13	6	11[2]										13
1	4	3		5	2	9	6	7[1]	13	10	12	8	11[2]										14
1	3	4		5	2	9	6	7[1]		10[1]	12	8	13	11[2]									15
1	3	4		5	2		6[2]	7		10[1]	11	8	13	9				12					16
1	2	3		5	4	9		7		12	11[2]	8	13	10[1]				6					17
1	4	3		5	2	9		6[2]		12	11	7[1]	13	10				8					18
1	4	3		5	2	10	12	6[1]		13	11[3]	7	14	9[2]				8					19
1	2	4	3[1]	5	10	9	6[2]			13	11	8	12					7					20
1	2	3		5	13	10	12	6		11[2]	7							8	4	9[1]			21
1	2[3]	3		5	12	9	6[2]	7		8		13						11	4	10[1]	14		22
1	2	3		5	14	10	7[1]	6[3]		8		12						11	4	9[2]	13		23
1	4	3		5	2	9		7		10		8							11	6[4]			24
1	2	3		5	6[1]	9	13			11	7	8[2]						12	4	10			25
1	2	3	9	13	12	5	6[3]			14	7	8[1]						10[2]	4	11			26
1	2	3		5	7	8	13			10[3]	14	11[2]						12	4	6	9[1]		27
1	2	3		5		10[1]	8[3]	6[4]		14	7[2]	12						11	4	9	13		28
1	2	3		5	13	9[2]	6	7[3]		8	14							11	4	10[1]	12		29
1	2	3		5	14	9[4]	6[1]	7[3]		8	13	12						10	4	11	12		30
1	2	3		5	7	9[1]	13			14	8	12						10[2]	4	11[1]	6		31
1	2	3		5	7	9[1]	13			8	12							10	4	11	6[1]		32
1	5	3		2	7	12				13	8	9[1]						11	4	10	6[2]		33
1		3		5	2	9	6[2]	7[1]		14	8	12						10[1]	4[1]	11	13		34
1	4	3		5	2	9[2]	6[1]	7		14	8	12						11[3]		10	13		35
1	4	3	12	5	2		9	8[2]		11[1]								10		7	6	13	36

ANNAN ATHLETIC

Year Formed: 1942. *Ground & Address:* Galabank, North Street, Annan DG12 5DQ. *Telephone:* 01461 204108.
E-mail: annanathletic.enquiries@btconnect.com *Website:* www.annanathleticfc.com
Ground capacity: 2,517 (seated: 500). *Size of Pitch:* 100m × 62m.
Chairman: Philip Jones. *Vice-Chairman:* Gordon Hyslop.
Secretary: Alan Irving.
Player/Manager: Peter Murphy.
Assistant Manager: John Joyce.
Club Nicknames: 'Galabankies', 'Black and Golds'.
Previous Ground: Mafeking Park.
Record attendance: 2,517, v Rangers, Third Division, 15 September 2012.
Record Victory: 6-0 v Elgin C, Third Division, 7 March 2009.
Record Defeat: 1-8 v Inverness CT, Scottish Cup 3rd rd, 24 January 1998.
Most League Appearances: 285: Peter Watson, 2008-18.
Most League Goals in Season (Individual): 22: Peter Weatherson, 2014-15.
Most Goals Overall (Individual): 56: Peter Weatherson, 2013-17.

ANNAN ATHLETIC – SPFL LADBROKES LEAGUE TWO 2017–18 LEAGUE RECORD

Match No.	Date	Venue	Opponents	Result	H/T Score	Lg Pos.	Goalscorers	Atten-dance
1	Aug 5	H	Peterhead	L	1-2	1-0	8	Watson [28]	331
2	12	A	Clyde	L	1-2	0-1	9	Omar [76]	412
3	19	A	Berwick R	W	5-1	3-1	7	Swinglehurst [20], Sinnamon [27], Murphy [44], Smith (pen) [75], Henderson [78]	494
4	26	H	Montrose	L	0-1	0-1	9		412
5	Sept 9	A	Elgin C	W	1-0	1-0	7	Smith (pen) [24]	546
6	16	H	Stenhousemuir	D	1-1	0-1	6	Smith (pen) [68]	373
7	23	A	Stirling Alb	L	2-3	1-2	8	Moxon [8], Smith [61]	617
8	30	H	Cowdenbeath	W	1-0	1-0	7	Smith [37]	363
9	Oct 21	A	Edinburgh C	W	1-0	0-0	6	Smith (pen) [72]	249
10	28	H	Peterhead	L	0-1	0-1	7		512
11	Nov 4	H	Berwick R	D	0-0	0-0	7		442
12	11	A	Montrose	D	1-1	0-1	7	Swinglehurst [61]	353
13	18	A	Cowdenbeath	D	1-1	1-0	7	Smith [43]	249
14	25	H	Clyde	D	0-0	0-0	6		375
15	Dec 2	H	Elgin C	W	2-0	1-0	6	Smith [5], Watson [57]	322
16	9	A	Stenhousemuir	W	3-1	0-0	5	Henderson 3 [70, 80, 90]	242
17	16	H	Stirling Alb	D	1-1	0-1	5	Luke [87]	316
18	23	H	Edinburgh C	W	2-1	1-1	5	Fergusson [13], Brannan [61]	304
19	Jan 2	A	Clyde	D	0-0	0-0	4		477
20	6	H	Montrose	L	0-1	0-1	5		339
21	13	A	Berwick R	W	2-0	0-0	4	Henderson [68], Smith [88]	388
22	27	A	Edinburgh C	L	2-3	0-2	5	Smith (pen) [71], Henderson [88]	259
23	Feb 3	H	Cowdenbeath	D	1-1	0-0	6	Omar [71]	299
24	10	A	Elgin C	L	1-2	1-1	6	Swinglehurst [7]	573
25	17	A	Stirling Alb	L	0-3	0-0	6		648
26	20	H	Peterhead	D	3-3	0-2	6	Henderson 2 [64, 74], Watson [84]	267
27	24	H	Stenhousemuir	W	2-0	0-0	6	Roberts [84], O'Keefe [90]	307
28	Mar 10	H	Edinburgh C	L	2-3	0-0	6	O'Keefe [86], Henderson (pen) [89]	248
29	13	A	Montrose	L	1-2	0-1	6	Roberts [48]	355
30	17	H	Clyde	D	1-1	0-0	6	Henderson [69]	371
31	24	A	Peterhead	L	0-1	0-0	7		708
32	31	H	Berwick R	D	0-0	0-0	7		378
33	Apr 7	H	Elgin C	W	4-1	1-0	7	Roberts [26], Smith [50], O'Keefe [79], Henderson [86]	282
34	14	A	Stenhousemuir	L	2-3	1-1	7	Swinglehurst [19], Smith [62]	378
35	21	H	Stirling Alb	W	3-1	1-1	7	Henderson 3 [20, 48, 62]	507
36	28	A	Cowdenbeath	W	2-0	2-0	7	Henderson 2 [2, 4]	233

Final League Position: 7

Honours
League Two Runners-up: 2013-14.
League Challenge Cup: Semi-finals: 2009-10, 2011-12.

Club colours: Shirt: Gold with black trim. Shorts: Black. Socks: Gold with black and white rings.

Goalscorers: *League (49):* Henderson 16 (1 pen), Smith 12 (5 pens), Swinglehurst 4, O'Keefe 3, Roberts 3, Watson 3, Omar 2, Brannan 1, Fergusson 1, Luke 1, Moxon 1, Murphy 1, Sinnamon 1.
William Hill Scottish FA Cup (0).
Betfred Scottish League Cup (2): Sinnamon 1, Swinglehurst 1.
Irn-Bru Scottish League Challenge Cup (3): Smith 3 (1 pen).

Atkinson J 14	Hooper S 27+5	Watson P 26+3	Swinglehurst S 30	Brannan J 25+2	Sinnamon R 29	Murphy P 5+1	Moxon O 27+5	Orsi D 20+1	Stevenson R 3	Smith A 36	McWaters A —+1	Sonkur A 7+4	Omar R 27+1	Luke B 5+9	Trialist A —+1	Trialist B —+2	Creaney J 17+1	Henderson B 25+8	Roberts S 16+5	Cunningham J —+3	Pearson E —+1	Fergusson R 3+3	Mitchell A 22	Rutkiewicz K —+2	Hogg R —+2	Henry J 10	O'Keefe C 5+6	Armour B 3+12	Home E 14+2	Salkeld C —+6	Hannay Z —+2	Match No.
1	2	3	4	5	6	7^1	8	9	10	11	12																					1
1	2	4	5	11^3	3^1	8			6	10^2		7	9	12	13	14																2
1	2	3	4		7	8^1	14	12	6^3	10			11^2	9			5	13														3
1	2	3	4		7^1	8	12	6		10			11^2	9			5	13														4
1	2	3	4^3	5	8	13	7	6^2		10			11	9^1	12		14															5
1	2	3	4	5	7	8	6^1			10^2			11	9^3			13	12	14													6
1	2	4	3	5	8	7^1	6^2			10			11				12	9^3	13	14												7
1	2	3	4^3	5	7	8	6^1			10		13	11	14			12	9^2														8
1	2	3	4	5	7	8	6^1			10			11	12			13	9^2														9
1	2	3	4	5	8	7	6^2			10			11	13			12	9^1														10
1	2	3	4	5	8	7	6^1			10^2			9				11	13	12													11
1	2	3	4^4	5	8	7	6^2			10		12	13				11	9^1														12
1	2		5	8	4	7	6			10		3	12				11	9^1														13
1	2	3	4	5	8	7	6^1			11			9	13				10^2														14
	3	4	5		8	7^1	6^3			10			9	13			2	11^2	12				1		14							15
	12	4	3^3	2	7	8	6^2			10		14	9^1				5	11					1		13							16
	12	3	4	2	7^2		6^1			9		8	13				5	11					1		10							17
	3	13	4	2		8	6^2			9			7	12			5	11					1		10^1							18
	12	3	4	2^4		8	6^1			9			7				5	10					1		11							19
	2	3	4			8^2	6			10			7	9^1			5	11					1		12	13						20
	2	3	4				6^1			11			7^1				5	10					1		14	8	9^2	12	13			21
	4	3	2				6^1			10			12	7			5	11					1				9	8				22
	2	3	4	13						9			7				8^2	10					1				5	11^1	6	12		23
	3	14	4	2	13					10							5^2	9^3					1				7	6^1	11	8	12	24
	2	3	4	5	7^2		14			10							11	9^1					1				8	12	13			25
	3	4			7^1		8^2			10			6				5	11^3	12				1				9	14	2	13		26
	3	4			7^1		8^2			10^3			6				5	11	12				1				9	14	13	2		27
	3	4			8		7^1			10^2			9				5	11	12				1				6^3	14	13	2		28
	3	14	4		7		8^3			10^1			6				5^2	11	9				1					13	12	2		29
	3		4	14	8^1		7			10			9				5^2	11	6^3				1					12	13	2		30
	2	3^1	4		8		7			11			6^2				10^1	9					1					12	5	13		31
		4	2		9^2		8			10		3					11	7					1				6^1	12	5		13	32
	3		2		8		6			10		4					11^2	9^3					1				7^1	12	14	5	13	33
		4	2		8		9^2			11		3					10^1	6^3					1				7	12	13	5	14	34
	14	4	2		9^2		12			10		3					11	6					1				8^1	7^3	13	5		35
	12	3^3	2	4	5^1					10			6				13	11	9^2				1				7^1		8		14	36

ARBROATH

Year Formed: 1878. *Ground & Address:* Gayfield Park, Arbroath DD11 1QB. *Telephone:* 01241 872157. *Fax:* 01241 431125. *E-mail:* afc@gayfield.fsnet.co.uk *Website:* www.arbroathfc.co.uk
Ground Capacity: 6,600 (seated: 861). *Size of Pitch:* 105m × 65m.
Chairman: Mike Caird. *Secretary:* Dr Gary Callon.
Manager: Dick Campbell. *Assistant Manager:* Ian Campbell.
Club Nickname: 'The Red Lichties'.
Previous Grounds: Lesser Gayfield.
Record Attendance: 13,510 v Rangers, Scottish Cup 3rd rd, 23 February 1952.
Record Transfer Fee received: £120,000 for Paul Tosh to Dundee (August 1993).
Record Transfer Fee paid: £20,000 for Douglas Robb from Montrose (1981).
Record Victory: 36-0 v Bon Accord, Scottish Cup 1st rd, 12 September 1885.
Record Defeat: 0-8 v Kilmarnock, Division II, 3 January 1949; 1-9 v Celtic, League Cup 3rd rd, 25 August 1993.
Most Capped Player: Ned Doig, 2 (5), Scotland.
Most League Appearances: 445: Tom Cargill, 1966-81.
Most League Goals in Season (Individual): 45: Dave Easson, Division II, 1958-59.
Most Goals Overall (Individual): 120: Jimmy Jack, 1966-71.

ARBROATH – SPFL LADBROKES LEAGUE ONE 2017–18 LEAGUE RECORD

Match No.	Date		Venue	Opponents	Result		H/T Score	Lg Pos.	Goalscorers	Atten- dance
1	Aug	5	H	Queen's Park	W	2-0	1-0	2	Denholm [37], Yule [62]	769
2		12	A	Airdrieonians	D	1-1	1-0	3	Kader [33]	740
3		19	H	East Fife	L	2-3	1-3	4	Doris [16], Denholm [68]	808
4		26	A	Ayr U	W	2-1	1-1	3	Kader [45], Whatley [59]	1569
5	Sept	9	H	Albion R	L	1-4	0-2	6	Hester [66]	669
6		16	H	Forfar Ath	W	5-0	1-0	3	McCord 2 (1 pen) [42 (p), 67], O'Brien [52], Hester [80], Linn (pen) [90]	968
7		23	A	Stranraer	W	6-2	4-1	2	O'Brien [16], Denholm 2 [18, 42], McCord 3 (1 pen) [33, 49, 68 (p)]	360
8		30	H	Alloa Ath	D	1-1	0-1	4	McCord (pen) [56]	640
9	Oct	14	A	Raith R	L	0-2	0-2	5		1827
10		21	H	Airdrieonians	W	7-1	4-1	3	Swankie [18], McCord 2 (1 pen) [27 (p), 89], Denholm 2 [34, 60], Linn [36], Hester [82]	740
11		28	A	East Fife	L	1-3	1-0	4	Linn [16]	565
12	Nov	4	H	Ayr U	L	1-4	0-1	5	Swankie [86]	922
13		11	A	Queen's Park	W	2-0	1-0	4	Swankie [19], Hamilton [55]	764
14		25	H	Forfar Ath	W	2-1	1-1	3	McIntosh [32], Linn [90]	924
15	Dec	2	H	Stranraer	L	1-2	1-0	3	McCord [15]	642
16		23	H	Raith R	L	1-2	0-2	5	Matthews (og) [55]	1035
17		30	H	East Fife	D	1-1	0-0	5	McIntosh [73]	649
18	Jan	2	A	Forfar Ath	W	1-0	1-0	4	McIntosh [43]	990
19		6	A	Ayr U	W	2-1	0-1	4	Wallace [68], McIntosh [88]	1436
20		13	H	Queen's Park	W	2-1	1-1	3	Swankie [43], Gold [60]	751
21		27	A	Airdrieonians	D	0-0	0-0	3		850
22	Feb	3	H	Albion R	W	1-0	1-0	3	Kader [28]	600
23		17	A	Alloa Ath	D	0-0	0-0	4		652
24		20	A	Stranraer	W	4-1	1-1	3	Wallace 2 (2 pens) [39, 63], McKenna [47], Denholm [83]	201
25		24	A	Raith R	D	2-2	0-1	3	Wallace (pen) [64], McIntosh [90]	1707
26	Mar	6	A	Alloa Ath	L	3-5	1-4	3	McKenna [39], Linn [55], Denholm [67]	363
27		10	H	Forfar Ath	W	2-0	1-0	3	O'Brien [45], McIntosh [89]	882
28		14	H	Ayr U	D	1-1	1-0	3	Denholm [45]	653
29		17	A	Albion R	W	2-1	1-1	3	Kader [37], Wallace (pen) [54]	274
30		24	H	Stranraer	L	2-3	2-0	4	Kader [2], Swankie [13]	726
31		27	A	Albion R	W	2-1	1-1	3	Wallace [38], Hamilton [89]	167
32		31	A	Alloa Ath	L	2-3	2-2	4	McKenna [21], Wallace [22]	604
33	Apr	7	H	Raith R	D	1-1	0-1	3	McIntosh [74]	1110
34		14	A	East Fife	W	5-0	2-0	3	McKenna [33], Wallace [39], McIntosh [55], Hamilton [60], Linn [78]	554
35		21	H	Airdrieonians	W	2-0	1-0	3	Denholm [28], Hamilton [58]	732
36		28	A	Queen's Park	L	0-3	0-1	4		892

Final League Position: 4

Honours
League Champions: Third Division 2010-11; League Two 2016-17.
Runners-up: Division II 1934-35, 1958-59, 1967-68, 1971-72; Second Division 2000-01; Third Division 1997-98, 2006-07.
Promoted via play-offs: 2007-08 (to Second Division).
Scottish Cup: Quarter-finals 1993.

Club colours: Shirt: Maroon with white trim. Shorts: Maroon. Socks: Maroon.

Goalscorers: *League (70):* Denholm 10, McCord 9 (4 pens), McIntosh 8, Wallace 8 (4 pens), Linn 6 (1 pen), Kader 5, Swankie 5, Hamilton 4, McKenna 4, Hester 3, O'Brien 3, Doris 1, Gold 1, Whatley 1, Yule 1, own goal 1.
William Hill Scottish FA Cup (4): McIntosh 2, Hamilton 1, McCord 1.
Betfred Scottish League Cup (6): Denholm 2, Doris 2, Gold 1, Yule 1.
Irn-Bru Scottish League Challenge Cup (0).
Play-Offs (2): Linn 1, Swankie 1.

Hutton D 31+1	Gold D 22+10	Little R 33+2	O'Brien T 32+1	Hamilton C 34	Kader O 16+13	Yule B 30+4	Whatley M 34+1	Denholm D 26+7	Doris S 5	Linn B 24+6	Skelly J —+8	McCord R 12+7	Prunty B —+8	Swankie G 26+4	Hester K —+13	Henry J 4+3	Fraser G —+3	Martin S 20+2	Douglas R 1	McIntosh L 10+11	Wallace R 18	McKenna M 14	Gomes R 4	Match No.
1	2	3	4	5	6	7	8¹	9	10²	11³	12	13	14											1
1	2²	3	4	5	6	7	8	9	10³	11¹		12		13	14									2
1		3²	4	5	12	7	2	9	10	6¹		8		14	11¹³	13								3
1	2²		4	3	5	6³	7	8	9	10	12	14		11¹		13								4
1	5	4	3	2	9²	7	8³	6		11¹	12	13		10	14									5
1	5	14	4	3	6¹	8	7³	10		11		9²		13		2	12							6
1	5		4	3	6²	8	7	10		11¹		9⁴		12	14	2	13							7
1	5	13	3	4	6¹	7	8	11		9²		10		12		2¹	14							8
1	2	4	3	5		7	8	10		9²	13	11¹		6				12						9
1	2	3	4¹	5		8	7	11		9	13³	10	14	6²				12						10
1	2	3	4	5	13	8	7	11		6		10³		9¹				12						11
1	2	3	4	5	13	8²	7¹	11		6²		10		9	12		14							12
13		3	4	5	6³	2¹	7	10		9²			14	11	12			8	1					13
1	12	2	3	4		6	7	8²		10		11	14		13			5¹		9³				14
1	5	2	3			7	12	9		10³	14	8²	13	6		11¹								15
1	9¹	3	4	5	13	8	2	6		11³		12	14					7		10²				16
1	12	2	3	4	14	6³	5	9		10²		8¹		11				7		13				17
1	12	2	3	4		7	5	8		9²		13		14				6		10³	11¹			18
1	13	2	3ˢ	4	12	7	8	9³		5²			14					6		11¹	10			19
1	8	3		4	6¹	2	7	12		9								5		10	11			20
1	5¹	2	3	4	9	14	6	12		8²		11						7		13	10³			21
1	5	2	3	4	9³	12	8			14		11¹						7		13	10²	6		22
1	5¹	2	3	4	9	14	8	13		12		6²						7		11	10			23
1	14	2	3	4		8	13	5		9		6²						7		12	11¹	10³		24
1	12	2	3	4	13	6		9¹		5¹		8						7		14	11²	10		25
1	13	2	3	4	5	7³	6	14		9		8²						12		10¹	11			26
13		3	4	14		7	6	9		5³				8²				12		10¹	11²		1	27
12³	2	3	4	14		7²	6	9¹		5				11				8		13	10		1	28
	2	7	5	6		4	9²			14	12			11³				3		13	10	8¹	1	29
12		2	3	4	5¹		6	9		13	14			11				7			10²	8	13	30
1	6²	2	7	5	13	3	4	12		9²				11				14			10	8³		31
1	8	2		4		5	3	12		14				9²	13			6		11	10³	7¹		32
1	2³	3	4	5	14	7²	8			13	12			9				10		11¹		6		33
1	9	2	3	4¹	12	14	7²			13				8				6			11	10	5³	34
1	2		4	12		6	7	9³		5	14			10²				3			13	11	8¹	35
1	4	3		14		8¹	2	6³		11²	13			9				5			12	10	7	36

AYR UNITED

Year Formed: 1910. *Ground & Address:* Somerset Park, Tryfield Place, Ayr KA8 9NB. *Telephone:* 01292 263435.
Fax: 01292 281314. *E-mail:* info@ayrunitedfc.co.uk *Website:* ayrunitedfc.co.uk
Ground Capacity: 10,185 (seated: 1,597). *Size of Pitch:* 101m × 66m.
Chairman: Lachlan Cameron.
Managing Director: Lewis Grant.
Manager: Ian McCall. *Assistant Manager:* Neil Scally.
Club Nickname: 'The Honest Men'.
Previous Grounds: None.
Record Attendance: 25,225 v Rangers, Division I, 13 September 1969.
Record Transfer Fee received: £300,000 for Steve Nicol to Liverpool (October 1981).
Record Transfer Fee paid: £90,000 for Mark Campbell from Stranraer (March 1999).
Record Victory: 11-1 v Dumbarton, League Cup, 13 August 1952.
Record Defeat: 0-9 in Division I v Rangers (1929); v Hearts (1931); B Division v Third Lanark (1954).
Most Capped Player: Jim Nisbet, 3, Scotland.
Most League Appearances: 459: John Murphy, 1963-78.
Most League League and Cup Goals in Season (Individual): 66: Jimmy Smith, 1927-28.
Most League and Cup Goals Overall (Individual): 213: Peter Price, 1955-61.

AYR UNITED – SPFL LADBROKES LEAGUE ONE 2017–18 LEAGUE RECORD

Match No.	Date	Venue	Opponents	Result	H/T Score	Lg Pos.	Goalscorers	Attendance
1	Aug 5	A	Albion R	W 5-1	3-0	1	McDaid [2], Moffat [34], Moore 3 (1 pen) [39, 70 (p), 79]	806
2	12	H	Forfar Ath	W 3-0	2-0	1	Moore [34], McDaid [37], Crawford [81]	1399
3	19	A	Stranraer	W 4-3	1-1	1	McDaid [42], Moore [49], Moffat [59], Boyle [85]	1070
4	26	H	Arbroath	L 1-2	1-1	2	Higgins [42]	1569
5	Sept 9	A	Raith R	L 1-2	1-0	2	Shankland [45]	2286
6	16	H	Alloa Ath	D 3-3	1-1	2	Shankland 2 [4, 90], Adams [80]	1306
7	23	A	Queen's Park	W 2-0	1-0	3	Adams [23], Shankland [68]	1051
8	30	H	East Fife	W 3-0	1-0	2	Shankland [7], Geggan [50], Higgins [73]	1382
9	Oct 14	H	Airdrieonians	D 2-2	0-1	2	Geggan 2 [55, 57]	1513
10	21	A	Forfar Ath	W 5-0	1-0	2	Moffat 3 [15, 64, 81], Shankland [52], Moore [85]	664
11	28	H	Stranraer	W 2-0	0-0	2	Moffat [66], Shankland [80]	1473
12	Nov 4	A	Arbroath	W 4-1	1-0	1	Shankland 2 [36, 57], Gold (og) [53], Moore [58]	922
13	14	H	Raith R	W 3-0	2-0	1	Shankland [16], Crawford [22], Moore [90]	2040
14	25	A	Alloa Ath	W 2-1	1-0	1	Moffat [4], Moore [90]	854
15	Dec 2	H	Albion R	W 3-2	1-1	1	Moore [16], Shankland [73], Higgins [77]	1426
16	9	H	Queen's Park	W 3-2	1-1	1	Moore (pen) [24], McDaid [79], Forrest [88]	1320
17	16	A	East Fife	W 4-1	0-1	1	Rose 2 [57, 72], Moore [75], Shankland [88]	637
18	23	A	Airdrieonians	L 0-2	0-2	1		1113
19	30	H	Forfar Ath	L 2-3	1-0	1	Moffat [45], Shankland [67]	1477
20	Jan 2	A	Stranraer	W 5-1	2-0	1	Shankland 2 [8, 53], Moffat [39], Forrest 2 [49, 63]	1143
21	6	H	Arbroath	L 1-2	1-0	2	Forrest [4]	1436
22	13	A	Raith R	D 1-1	1-0	2	Shankland [34]	3064
23	27	A	Queen's Park	W 4-1	2-0	1	Moore [5], Forrest [43], McGuffie 2 [80, 87]	1233
24	Feb 3	H	Alloa Ath	L 1-2	1-2	2	Shankland [10]	1139
25	17	H	East Fife	W 3-0	1-0	2	McDaid [32], Shankland [53], Forrest (pen) [60]	1170
26	24	H	Airdrieonians	W 3-0	0-0	2	Geggan [50], Shankland 2 (1 pen) [81 (p), 84]	1456
27	Mar 10	H	Raith R	W 3-0	2-0	2	Shankland [34], Adams [43], Moffat [53]	2126
28	14	A	Arbroath	D 1-1	0-1	1	McGuffie [86]	653
29	17	A	Forfar Ath	W 2-0	1-0	1	Moffat [10], Moore (pen) [81]	629
30	20	A	Albion R	W 3-2	2-1	1	Moore [28], Adams [36], Shankland [75]	652
31	24	H	Queen's Park	W 4-0	3-0	1	Shankland 3 [10, 29, 34], Moore (pen) [76]	1600
32	31	A	East Fife	W 3-2	1-1	1	Forrest [4], Bell [72], Moore (pen) [88]	759
33	Apr 7	A	Airdrieonians	W 2-1	1-1	1	Crawford [37], Shankland [70]	1129
34	14	H	Stranraer	L 1-2	1-1	1	Adams [16]	2323
35	22	A	Alloa Ath	L 1-2	0-2	2	Moore [50]	1749
36	28	H	Albion R	W 2-0	1-0	1	Moore [34], McDaid [86]	2441

Final League Position: 1

Honours
League Champions: Division II 1911-12, 1912-13, 1927-28, 1936-37, 1958-59, 1965-66; Second Division 1987-88, 1996-97; League One 2017-18.
Runners-up: Division II 1910-11, 1955-56, 1968-69; Second Division 2008-09; League One 2015-16.
Promoted via play-offs: 2008-09 (to First Division); 2010-11 (to First Division); 2015-16 (to Championship).
Scottish Cup: Semi-finals 2002.
League Cup: Runners-up: 2001-02.
League Challenge Cup Runners-up: 1990-91, 1991-92.

Club colours: Shirt: White with black trim. Shorts: Black. Socks: White.

Goalscorers: *League (92):* Shankland 26 (1 pen), Moore 19 (5 pens), Moffat 11, Forrest 7 (1 pen), McDaid 6, Adams 5, Geggan 4, Crawford 3, Higgins 3, McGuffie 3, Rose 2, Bell 1, Boyle 1, own goal 1.
William Hill Scottish FA Cup (11): McDaid 4, Moore 3, Shankland 3, Forrest 1.
Betfred Scottish League Cup (15): McDaid 3, Moore 3, Crawford 2, Geggan 2, Moffat 2, Docherty 1, McGuffie 1, own goal 1.
Irn-Bru Scottish League Challenge Cup (6): Moore 2, Forrest 1, Gilmour 1, McCowan 1, Murphy 1.

Hart J 25	Geggan A 25+1	Higgins C 19	Reid C 19+4	Boyle P 26+1	Crawford R 21+1	McDaid D 28+6	Adams J 21+4	Docherty R 14+2	Moffat M 30+5	Moore C 15+16	Rose M 33+1	McGuffie C 6+23	Forrest A 16+13	Gilmour B 7+7	Ferguson D 21+3	Shankland L 30	Murphy L —+5	McCowan L —+1	Faulds S —+3	Hilton J —+1	Bell S 15	Ruddy J 11	Kerr M 14	Match No.
1	2	3	4	5	6³	7	8²	9	10¹	11	12	13	14											1
1	2	3	12	5	8	6³		7	10¹	11	4	9¹	13	14										2
1	2	4	9	5	7	6¹		8	10¹	11²	3	12	13	14										3
1	2	4	12	5	7¹	6		8²	10	11	3	13	9³	14										4
1	7	4*	2		8	6			10		3		9¹		12	5	11²	13							5
1	2	4			6	8	7²		10		3		9¹		13	5	11	12						6
1	2	3	5		6¹	7	8			11²	4	12			9¹	10	14	13						7
1	7	3	2¹	5	6³		8²		10		4	13	9		12	11	14							8
1	8	3	5²	6	12		7		10	14	4	9¹		13	2	11²								9
1	8³	3	5	6	12		7		10	14	4	13	9²		2	11¹								10
1	8²	3	5	9	6³	13	7		10¹	12	4		14		2	11								11
1	8		5	9	6³	3	7		10¹	12	4	14	13		2	11²								12
1	6	3	5	9		8	7		10¹	12	4		13		2	11²								13
1	6¹	5	3	8⁰	11²		7		9	13	4	12	14		2	10								14
1		3	2		12	8	7¹		9	11³	4	13	14	6²	5	10								15
1		3	2³	13		14	7		8	10²	4	9¹	12	6	5	11								16
1	7	3		5		9²	8³		10	13	4	14	6¹	12	2	11								17
1	7¹	4		5²	12			11	9	3	13	6³	8		2	10	14							18
1	7³	3		5		6¹	12		10	13	4	14	9	8	2	11²								19
1		3	7	5		6	8		11³	12	4²		9¹		2	10				13	14			20
1		3³	4	5		6¹	7		10	13			9		2	11			12		8			21
		3	5			6	7¹		10	12	4		9		2	11				8	1			22
	12	3	5			6	7¹		13	10¹	4	14	9²		2	11				1	8			23
		4	5			6	12		10	13	3	14	9¹		2³	11				8	1	7²		24
	2	14	5			6	8		10³	13	4		9¹	12		11				3	1	7²		25
	2		5	13	6		8	14	12	10¹	4		9²			11				3	1	7³		26
	2	12	5²	9¹	6		8	14	11		4			13	10					3	1	7³		27
	2	5		9²	6¹	8			10³	12	4	14	13			11				3	1	7		28
	2		5	7	9²				11³	12	3	13	6		10					4	1	8		29
	2		5	9		7			13	10²	3	12	6¹		11					4	1	8		30
		2	5	7	6				10	12	3	13	9¹		11¹		14			4	1	8²		31
		2	5	7²	9¹	14			13	10³	3	12	6		11					4	1	8		32
	2²	3	5³	9	6¹	7			10			13	14		12	11				4		8		33
1		5²		6	13	7			14	11	4	12³	9¹		2	10⁴				3		8		34
1	2¹			9	6²	8			10	11	4	13	12		5					3		7		35
1				8	6	3			10	11	2	12	9¹		5					4		7		36

BERWICK RANGERS

Year Formed: 1881. *Ground & Address:* Shielfield Park, Tweedmouth, Berwick-upon-Tweed TD15 2EF. *Telephone:* 01289 307424. *Fax:* 01289 309424. *Email:* club@berwickrangers.com *Website:* berwickrangers.com
Ground Capacity: 4,131 (seated: 1,366). *Size of Pitch:* 101m × 64m.
Chairman: Len Eyre. *Vice-Chairman:* John Bell. *Football Secretary:* Dennis McCleary.
Manager: Robbie Horn. *Assistant Manager:* David Burrell. *First-Team Coach:* Jim McQueen.
Club Nicknames: 'The Borderers', 'Black and Gold', 'The Wee Gers'.
Previous Grounds: Bull Stob Close, Pier Field, Meadow Field, Union Park, Old Shielfield.
Record Transfer Fee received: £80,000 for John Hughes to Swansea C (November 1989).
Record Transfer Fee paid: £27,000 for Sandy Ross from Cowdenbeath (March 1991).
Record Attendance: 13,283 v Rangers, Scottish Cup 1st rd, 28 January 1967.
Record Victory: 8-1 v Forfar Ath, Division II, 25 December 1965; v Vale of Leithen, Scottish Cup, December 1966.
Record Defeat: 1-9 v Hamilton A, First Division, 9 August 1980.
Most League Appearances: 439: Eric Tait, 1970-87.
Most League Goals in Season (Individual): 33: Ken Bowron, Division II, 1963-64.
Most Goals Overall (Individual): 114: Eric Tait, 1970-87.

BERWICK RANGERS – SPFL LADBROKES LEAGUE TWO 2017–18 LEAGUE RECORD

Match No.	Date	Venue	Opponents	Result	H/T Score	Lg Pos.	Goalscorers	Attendance
1	Aug 5	H	Clyde	W 3-1	1-1	1	Irving 2 45, 89, Murrell 83	547
2	12	A	Stirling Alb	L 0-4	0-2	6		618
3	19	H	Annan Ath	L 1-5	1-3	9	McKenna 5	494
4	26	A	Cowdenbeath	W 1-0	1-0	5	Murrell 18	380
5	Sept 9	A	Edinburgh C	L 0-1	0-1	8		308
6	16	H	Elgin C	W 3-2	0-1	5	Murrell 2 73, 83, McKenna 87	492
7	23	A	Stenhousemuir	L 0-3	0-2	6		348
8	30	A	Peterhead	W 2-0	0-0	5	Fleming 74, McKenna 83	507
9	Oct 21	H	Montrose	L 0-1	0-1	7		508
10	28	H	Cowdenbeath	W 1-0	0-0	6	McKenna (pen) 80	487
11	Nov 4	A	Annan Ath	D 0-0	0-0	6		442
12	11	H	Edinburgh C	D 1-1	0-0	6	McKenna 57	467
13	25	A	Elgin C	L 1-5	0-1	7	Phillips 58	508
14	Dec 2	H	Stirling Alb	W 1-0	1-0	7	McKenna 7	442
15	9	A	Montrose	L 0-3	0-3	7		430
16	23	A	Clyde	D 0-0	0-0	7		503
17	Jan 2	A	Edinburgh C	L 0-3	0-1	7		446
18	6	A	Stirling Alb	L 0-2	0-1	7		597
19	13	H	Annan Ath	L 0-2	0-0	7		388
20	27	A	Cowdenbeath	W 3-1	1-1	7	Hamilton 19, Thomson 54, See 82	332
21	30	H	Peterhead	L 2-3	1-2	7	Hamilton 43, See 52	330
22	Feb 3	A	Stenhousemuir	L 0-4	0-2	7		323
23	10	H	Clyde	L 0-1	0-0	8		474
24	17	A	Peterhead	D 1-1	1-0	8	Thomson 33	604
25	24	H	Montrose	D 2-2	1-2	8	See 23, Willis 63	417
26	Mar 10	A	Elgin C	L 0-3	0-2	8		531
27	13	H	Stirling Alb	L 0-1	0-1	9		302
28	24	H	Edinburgh C	D 1-1	0-0	9	Hamilton 55	516
29	27	H	Elgin C	D 2-2	0-1	9	Hamilton 69, Murrell 87	323
30	31	A	Annan Ath	D 0-0	0-0	9		378
31	Apr 7	H	Peterhead	L 1-3	0-2	9	Hamilton 78	403
32	14	A	Montrose	L 0-1	0-1	9		805
33	17	H	Stenhousemuir	D 0-0	0-0	9		326
34	21	H	Cowdenbeath	W 1-0	1-0	8	Todd 12	596
35	24	H	Stenhousemuir	D 2-2	2-2	8	Hamilton 28, Willis 33	295
36	28	A	Clyde	W 2-1	1-0	8	Hamilton 2 7, 62	804

Final League Position: 8

Honours
League Champions: Second Division 1978-79; Third Division 2006-07.
Runners-up: Second Division 1993-94; Third Division 1999-2000, 2005-06.
Scottish Cup: Quarter-finals 1953-54, 1979-80.
League Cup: Semi-finals 1963-64.
League Challenge Cup: Quarter-finals 2004-05.

Club colours: Shirt: Black and gold vertical stripes. Shorts: Black. Socks: Black with gold tops.

Goalscorers: *League (31):* Hamilton 8, McKenna 6 (1 pen), Murrell 5, See 3, Irving 2, Thomson 2, Willis 2, Fleming 1, Phillips 1, Todd 1.
William Hill Scottish FA Cup (0).
Betfred Scottish League Cup (4): Murrell 1, Rutherford 1, Scullion 1, Thomson 1.
Irn-Bru Scottish League Challenge Cup (2): McKenna 1, Thomson 1.

McCrorie R 33	Donaldson C 4+1	Fleming O 18+3	Waugh K 2+1	McDonald C 11+5	Stewart K 29+3	McKenna M 19	Lavery D 25+7	Irving A 12+6	Rutherford G 3+4	Murrell A 14+16	Watt D — +1	Orru J 10+5	Notman S 27+1	Fairbairn J 11+2	McKinlay K 15	Phillips G 27+5	Thomson S 16+17	Scullion P 10+1	Godinho M 13	Wilson R 20	O'Kane D 14+1	See O 10+3	Simpson P 1+4	Petkov A 5+1	Hamilton J 14+2	Cook J 4+3	Willis P 12+1	Todd J 14+1	Brennan S 3	Match No.
1	2	3	4	5	6	7	8	9	10[2]	11[1]	12	13																		1
1	2[1]	3	4[2]	5	7	6	8	9	11[1]	10			14	12	13															2
1		3		5	8[2]	6	7	12	14	11[3]			2[1]			4	9	10	13											3
1	2[2]	3		5	12	10	7[3]	13	14	11[1]						4	9	6	8											4
1				5[2]	7	9[3]	11	13	12	10[1]			6			4	8	14	3	2										5
1				6[2]	9		8	10[1]	12				7	3	5	11	13	4	2											6
1	2[2]			7[1]	6	12	9	13	11[3]				8	3	5	10	14	4												7
1	2			5		8	10[3]	13		11[1]			7	12	4[2]	9	14	3	6											8
1	2			7[3]	13	11	6	14		10[3]			8		4[1]	9	12	3	5											9
1	3	14	12	6[1]	9	10[2]	8		13				7[3]		5	11	4	2												10
1	2			13	14	11	8[3]	6[2]	12				7	3		9	10[1]	4	5											11
1	4			12	7	9[1]	10	6[2]	13				2			8	11	3	5											12
1	5			2[2]	6	11	13	12	10[2]				7[1]		4	9	14	3	8											13
1				13	8	11[2]	12	6[1]	10[3]				7	3	4	9	14	5	2											14
1	13			12	8	11	7[3]	6[2]	10				3	4	9	14		5[1]	2											15
1				9	6	11[2]	10[3]	8[1]	13				7	3	4	12	14	5	2											16
1				9	8	10	11[2]	7	12				6	4[1]	2	13		5	3											17
1				9[3]	8[1]	10	11[2]	6	12				7	3	4	14	13	5	2											18
1	2[2]			5	10	14	12		6				4	8	9[1]			3	7	11[3]	13									19
1	3			2	10[3]		12	14	4				5	8[2]		7	11		6	9[1]	13									20
1	3			2	12		6[2]	4					5	7		8[1]	10	13	9	11										21
1	2	9[4]	12		14		4[4]	8[2]					7	10[1]		6[3]	5	3	11	13										22
1			9		12	5	7		10				3	6		11[1]	2	8	4											23
1	14		2	9[2]		12	6		5	10[1]			3[3]	7	11			8	4											24
1			2	9		6			5	10[1]			3	7	11		12	8	4											25
1			2		7		5	11[2]		4			6	10	14	8[1]	12	13	9[3]	3										26
1			2	13		5[2]	6		10	12			3	11		7[1]	8	9	4											27
1			2	12	13	5	6		10				3	7	11[1]		8[2]	9	4											28
1			2	9	14		5[1]	6		10[3]	13		3	7[1]	12		11	8	4											29
1			2	9		5	6		12	10[2]			3	7	13	11[1]		8	4											30
1	13		2	9		5	6		14	10[3]			3	7[1]	12		11	8[2]	4											31
1	2		6	7		12	5	8		9[1]	13		3	10[3]	14		11		4[2]											32
	2		6	7		11[1]	9	5[2]		8	12		3	13			10		4										1	33
	2		5[2]	6		10[1]	9		8	13			3	7		11[3]	12	14	4										1	34
1	14		6		12		5	13	8[1]				3	7		11[3]	10[2]	2	9	4										35
	2		12		10[1]	9	6[4]		8	13			3			11[2]	5	7	4										1	36

BRECHIN CITY

Year Formed: 1906. *Ground & Address:* Glebe Park, Trinity Rd, Brechin, Angus DD9 6BJ. *Telephone:* 01356 622856.
Fax: 01382 206331. *E-mail:* secretary@brechincityfc.com *Website:* www.brechincity.com
Ground Capacity: 4,123 (seated: 1,528). *Size of Pitch:* 101m × 61m.
Chairman: Ken Ferguson. *Vice-Chairman:* Martin Smith. *Secretary:* Grant Hood.
Manager: Darren Dods. *Assistant Manager:* Lee Bailey.
Club Nicknames: 'The City', 'The Hedgemen'.
Previous Grounds: Nursery Park.
Record Attendance: 8,122 v Aberdeen, Scottish Cup 3rd rd, 3 February 1973.
Record Transfer Fee received: £100,000 for Scott Thomson to Aberdeen (1991) and Chris Templeman to Morton (2004).
Record Transfer Fee paid: £16,000 for Sandy Ross from Berwick R (1991).
Record Victory: 12-1 v Thornhill, Scottish Cup 1st rd, 28 January 1926.
Record Defeat: 0-10 v Airdrieonians, Albion R and Cowdenbeath, all in Division II, 1937-38.
Most League Appearances: 459: David Watt, 1975-89.
Most League Goals in Season (Individual): 26: Ronald McIntosh, Division II, 1959-60.
Most Goals Overall (Individual): 131: Ian Campbell, 1977-85.

BRECHIN CITY – SPFL LADBROKES CHAMPIONSHIP 2017–18 LEAGUE RECORD

Match No.	Date	Venue	Opponents	Result		H/T Score	Lg Pos.	Goalscorers	Attendance
1	Aug 5	A	Queen of the South	L	1-4	0-2	10	O'Neil, C [75]	1209
2	12	H	Livingston	D	2-2	0-2	9	Orsi [54], Graham [61]	579
3	19	A	Dundee U	L	0-1	0-0	8		6060
4	26	H	Inverness CT	L	0-4	0-2	10		703
5	Sept 9	H	Falkirk	D	1-1	0-1	10	Graham [72]	748
6	16	A	Dumbarton	L	1-2	1-0	10	Sinclair [2]	589
7	23	H	Dunfermline Ath	L	0-3	0-1	10		1214
8	30	A	St Mirren	L	1-2	1-1	10	Orsi [38]	3928
9	Oct 14	H	Greenock Morton	L	0-1	0-0	10		624
10	21	H	Queen of the South	L	0-1	0-0	10		562
11	28	A	Livingston	L	2-3	1-1	10	Sinclair [8], Orsi (pen) [85]	926
12	Nov 4	H	Dumbarton	L	0-1	0-0	10		538
13	25	H	Dundee U	D	1-1	0-1	10	Crighton [47]	2627
14	28	A	Inverness CT	L	0-4	0-2	10		1801
15	Dec 2	A	Greenock Morton	L	1-4	1-2	10	Layne [41]	1388
16	9	H	St Mirren	L	1-2	1-1	10	Layne [27]	812
17	23	A	Dunfermline Ath	L	1-2	0-1	10	McLennan [59]	4595
18	30	H	Inverness CT	L	2-3	2-1	10	Sinclair 2 (1 pen) [18 (p), 39]	571
19	Jan 2	A	Dundee U	L	1-4	0-2	10	Sinclair (pen) [64]	5532
20	6	H	Greenock Morton	D	1-1	1-1	10	McLennan [7]	694
21	13	H	Livingston	L	0-2	0-1	10		551
22	27	A	Queen of the South	L	1-3	0-2	10	Orsi [85]	1211
23	Feb 6	A	Falkirk	L	1-3	0-2	10	Mackin [67]	4214
24	17	H	Falkirk	L	0-1	0-0	10		805
25	24	A	St Mirren	L	0-1	0-1	10		4358
26	Mar 13	A	Dumbarton	L	0-1	0-1	10		403
27	17	H	Dumbarton	L	1-3	1-3	10	Storie [38]	445
28	20	H	Dunfermline Ath	L	0-3	0-2	10		611
29	24	A	Greenock Morton	L	0-2	0-0	10		1831
30	31	A	Falkirk	L	0-3	0-2	10		4422
31	Apr 3	A	Inverness CT	L	0-4	0-2	10		1963
32	7	H	St Mirren	L	0-1	0-1	10		2447
33	14	A	Dunfermline Ath	L	0-4	0-2	10		4898
34	17	H	Dundee U	L	0-5	0-0	10		1427
35	21	A	Livingston	L	0-3	0-0	10		943
36	28	H	Queen of the South	L	1-5	0-2	10	Layne [78]	661

Final League Position: 10

Honours
League Champions: Second Division 1982-83, 1989-90, 2004-05; Third Division 2001-02; C Division 1953-54.
Runners-up: Second Division 1992-93, 2002-03; Third Division 1995-96.
Promoted via play-offs: 2016-17 (to Championship).
League Challenge Cup Runners-up: 2002-03.

Club colours: Shirt: Red with black trim. Shorts: Black with red trim. Socks: Black with red trim.

Goalscorers: *League (20):* Sinclair 5 (2 pens), Orsi 4 (1 pen), Layne 3, Graham 2, McLennan 2, Crighton 1, Mackin 1, O'Neil C 1, Storie 1.
William Hill Scottish FA Cup (3): Layne 2, Sinclair 1.
Betfred Scottish League Cup (1): Layne 1.
Irn-Bru Scottish League Challenge Cup (1): McLean 1.

Smith G 31	McLean P 26 + 1	Spark E 24 + 4	Crighton S 33 + 1	Dyer W 28 + 1	Love A 1 + 4	Fusco G 16 + 2	Graham F 24 + 10	O'Neil C 2 + 2	Jackson A 5 + 5	Layne I 20 + 14	Orsi K 24 + 9	Sinclair J 23 + 6	Ford E — + 1	Lynas A 17 + 10	Dale J 30 + 2	Watt L 16 + 13	McGeever R 5	McLennan C 12 + 3	Smith E 19 + 3	Tapping C 17	Morrison C 7 + 5	Mackin D 8 + 3	O'Neil P 5 + 1	Gatzhalov K 2	Storie C 1 + 1	Match No.
1	2	3	4	5	6	7^1	8	9^2	10	11^3	12	13	14													1
1	2		4	9		3	8			11	12	10^1	6	5	7											2
1		4	10^2	3	5		9	14	11^1	13	8	7		2^3	6	12										3
1	2	9^3	3	4	13		6^1	14		10	11	5^2		8	7	12										4
1	4^3	13	2	9			6			14	11^1	8^2		5	7	12	3	10								5
1	4	13	2	9			6			14	11^2	8^1		5^3	7	12	3	10^3								6
1	4	13	2	9	12		6^3	5^1		10	8			7	14		3	11^2								7
1	4	5	2	9	12		6			14	11^3	8^1		7	13		3	10^2								8
1	2		4	9	13		7			14	10	8^2		5	6	12	3^1	11^3								9
1		3	2	9	13^4	4				14	10^1	12		8^3	5	7	6	11^2								10
1	4	3	6	5			13			10	12	9^2		2	7	8^3		11^1	14							11
1	4	2^2	3	6	5		12			11^1	10	9^3		14	8	7		13								12
1	2	5	4	9			7^2			11	10^1	13			6	8		12	3							13
1	2	5	4	9^1			7			11	14	13		12	6	8^1		10^2	3							14
1	3	5	2				7^2		13	10	11^1	12		9	6	8			4							15
1	2	5	3	9^2		4		13		14	11	10^1		7	12	8^3		6								16
1	2^2	5	3		4			14		10	11^1	9^3		8	12	6		13	7							17
1		9	3		4			8	13	11		6^1		5	7	12		10^2	2							18
1		9	3		4			8^1	12	11^2	14	6^3		5	7	13		10	2							19
1	3	5^4	4		12		6			11^1	14	9^2		2	7	13		10		8						20
1	3	5	4		6			10^2	12	13		9^1		2	7			11^3	14	8						21
1	3	5	4		6			14		11^2	12	9^1		2	8^1					13	7	10				22
1		5	2		4	3		14		11^2				13	7^3	12		8			6	9^1	10			23
	5	3	8		4		13	14		12^4		6^1		10	2	7		9^2			11^3		1			24
	5	3	8^1					13		12		6^1		10	2	7		9^2		11			1	4	14	25
	9	3			12			14	13	11^3		7^2		8	2	6		5		10			1	4^1		26
	2	3	5		4		9	13		8		10			7			12		11^1	1				6^2	27
1	14	2^1	12	5		4^2				10		8		13	7			9^3		3	6	11				28
1^3	4		3	9				8		11^1	13	7^2		5	2	6		10			12	14				29
2^4		3^4	9			7		10^1		11^2		6^1		13	12	5		4			8	14				30
3	12	5	4			7		11		10	14			13	8^3	9^1		2			6^2					31
	2	5			4^3	7^1				11	10	9^2		12	6			3		8	14	13				32
	2		4		5	7^3				11	10^2	9^1		13	6			3		8	14	12				33
1	4		2		3		5	12		10		9^3		6^1	14	7^2		8			13	11				34
1	4		3		5		12			11		7		2	6^2			13		8	10	9^1				35
	4		2		9	7	13			12	11	5^3		8^1	14			3^2		6		10	1			36

CELTIC

Year Formed: 1888. *Ground & Address:* Celtic Park, Glasgow G40 3RE. *Telephone:* 0871 226 1888. *Fax:* 0141 551 8106.
E-mail: customerservices@celticfc.co.uk *Website:* www.celticfc.net
Ground Capacity: 60,832 (all seated). *Size of Pitch:* 105m × 68m.
Chairman: Ian Bankier. *Chief Executive:* Peter Lawwell.
Manager: Brendan Rodgers. *Assistant Manager:* Chris Davies. *First-Team Coach:* John Kennedy.
Club Nicknames: 'The Bhoys', 'The Hoops', 'The Celts'. *Previous Grounds:* None.
Record Attendance: 92,000 v Rangers, Division I, 1 January 1938.
Record Transfer Fee received: £12,500,000 for Victor Wanyama to Southampton (July 2013).
Record Transfer Fee paid: £9,000,000 for Odsonne Édouard from Paris Saint-Germain (June 2018).
Record Victory: 11-0 Dundee, Division I, 26 October 1895. *Record Defeat:* 0-8 v Motherwell, Division I, 30 April 1937.
Most Capped Player: Pat Bonner, 80, Republic of Ireland. *Most League Appearances:* 486: Billy McNeill, 1957-75.
Most League Goals in Season (Individual): 50: James McGrory, Division I, 1935-36.
Most Goals Overall (Individual): 397: James McGrory, 1922-39.

Honours
League Champions: (49 times) Division I 1892-93, 1893-94, 1895-96, 1897-98, 1904-05, 1905-06, 1906-07, 1907-08, 1908-09,
1909-10, 1913-14, 1914-15, 1915-16, 1916-17, 1918-19, 1921-22, 1925-26, 1935-36, 1937-38, 1953-54, 1965-66, 1966-67,
1967-68, 1968-69, 1969-70, 1970-71, 1971-72, 1972-73, 1973-74; Premier Division 1976-77, 1978-79, 1980-81, 1981-82,
1985-86, 1987-88, 1997-98, 2000-01, 2001-02, 2003-04, 2005-06, 2006-07, 2007-08, 2011-12, 2012-13; Premiership 2013-14,
2014-15, 2015-16, 2016-17, 2017-18. *Runners-up:* 31 times.
Scottish Cup Winners: (38 times) 1892, 1899, 1900, 1904, 1907, 1908, 1911, 1912, 1914, 1923, 1925, 1927, 1931, 1933, 1937,
1951, 1954, 1965, 1967, 1969, 1971, 1972, 1974, 1975, 1977, 1980, 1985, 1988, 1989, 1995, 2001, 2004, 2005, 2007, 2011, 2013,
2017, 2018. *Runners-up:* 18 times.
League Cup Winners: (17 times) 1956-57, 1957-58, 1965-66, 1966-67, 1967-68, 1968-69, 1969-70, 1974-75, 1982-83,
1997-98, 1999-2000, 2000-01, 2005-06, 2008-09, 2014-15, 2016-17, 2017-18. *Runners-up:* 15 times.

CELTIC – SPFL LADBROKES PREMIERSHIP 2017–18 LEAGUE RECORD

Match No.	Date	Venue	Opponents	Result	H/T Score	Lg Pos.	Goalscorers	Atten- dance
1	Aug 5	H	Hearts	W 4-1	1-0	1	Griffiths 2 [29, 63], Sinclair [51], McGregor [73]	58,843
2	11	A	Partick Thistle	W 1-0	1-0	1	Ntcham [25]	8041
3	19	A	Kilmarnock	W 2-0	1-0	1	Forrest [40], McGregor [88]	10,069
4	26	H	St Johnstone	D 1-1	0-1	2	McGregor [79]	58,446
5	Sept 8	A	Hamilton A	W 4-1	3-0	1	Armstrong [17], Sinclair 2 [29, 42], Edouard [65]	5208
6	16	H	Ross Co	W 4-0	2-0	1	Rogic [13], Dembele [42], Forrest 2 [52, 74]	58,624
7	23	A	Rangers	W 2-0	0-0	1	Rogic [50], Griffiths [65]	50,116
8	30	H	Hibernian	D 2-2	1-0	1	McGregor 2 [15, 80]	59,259
9	Oct 14	H	Dundee	W 1-0	0-0	1	Ntcham [61]	57,610
10	25	A	Aberdeen	W 3-0	2-0	1	Tierney [13], Dembele 2 [39, 63]	20,528
11	28	H	Kilmarnock	D 1-1	1-0	1	Griffiths [43]	58,060
12	Nov 4	A	St Johnstone	W 4-0	1-0	1	Sinclair [28], Dembele [72], Anderson (og) [75], Ntcham [89]	6800
13	18	A	Ross Co	W 1-0	0-0	1	Griffiths [78]	6590
14	29	A	Motherwell	D 1-1	0-0	1	Sinclair (pen) [88]	9164
15	Dec 2	H	Motherwell	W 5-1	2-0	1	Edouard 3 [16, 33, 85], Forrest 2 [76, 88]	57,817
16	10	A	Hibernian	D 2-2	0-0	1	Sinclair 2 [59, 64]	20,193
17	13	H	Hamilton A	W 3-1	3-1	1	Ntcham [12], Forrest [40], Sinclair [41]	53,883
18	17	A	Hearts	L 0-4	0-2	1		18,555
19	20	H	Partick Thistle	W 2-0	1-0	1	Armstrong [35], Tierney [67]	54,187
20	23	H	Aberdeen	W 3-0	1-0	1	Lustig [40], Hayes [69], Ntcham [76]	58,975
21	26	A	Dundee	W 2-0	2-0	1	Forrest [8], Griffiths [43]	9193
22	30	H	Rangers	D 0-0	0-0	1		59,004
23	Jan 23	A	Partick Thistle	W 2-1	0-1	1	Sinclair (pen) [55], Griffiths [70]	6920
24	27	H	Hibernian	W 1-0	1-0	1	Griffiths [27]	58,998
25	30	H	Hearts	W 3-1	3-0	1	Edouard [3], Boyata [25], Dembele [36]	56,296
26	Feb 3	A	Kilmarnock	L 0-1	0-0	1		10,702
27	18	H	St Johnstone	D 0-0	0-0	1		56,867
28	25	A	Aberdeen	W 2-0	1-0	1	Dembele [37], Tierney [83]	17,206
29	Mar 11	A	Rangers	W 3-2	2-2	1	Rogic [11], Dembele [45], Edouard [69]	50,215
30	18	A	Motherwell	D 0-0	0-0	1		8717
31	31	H	Ross Co	W 3-0	1-0	1	Dembele (pen) [25], Armstrong [48], Rogic [60]	58,765
32	Apr 4	H	Dundee	D 0-0	0-0	1		55,768
33	8	A	Hamilton A	W 2-1	1-1	1	McGregor [3], Griffiths [46]	4851
34	21	A	Hibernian	L 1-2	0-1	1	Edouard [87]	19,886
35	29	A	Rangers	W 5-0	3-0	1	Edouard 2 [14, 41], Forrest [45], Rogic [47], McGregor [53]	58,320
36	May 6	A	Hearts	W 3-1	1-1	1	Boyata [21], Dembele [51], Sinclair [90]	19,031
37	9	H	Kilmarnock	D 0-0	0-0	1		54,916
38	13	H	Aberdeen	L 0-1	0-0	1		58,388

Final League Position: 1

Scottish League Clubs – Celtic

European: *European Cup/Champions League:* 200 matches (1966-67 winners, 1967-68, 1968-69, 1969-70 runners-up, 1970-71, 1971-72, 1972-73, 1973-74 semi-finals, 1974-75, 1977-78, 1979-80, 1981-82, 1982-83, 1986-87, 1988-89, 1998-99, 2001-02, 2002-03, 2003-04, 2004-05, 2005-06, 2006-07, 2007-08, 2008-09, 2009-10, 2010-11, 2012-13, 2013-14, 2014-15, 2015-16, 2016-17, 2017-18). *Cup Winners' Cup:* 38 matches (1963-64 semi-finals, 1965-66 semi-finals, 1975-76, 1980-81, 1984-85, 1985-86, 1989-90, 1995-96). *UEFA Cup:* 75 matches (*Fairs Cup:* 1962-63, 1964-65). *UEFA Cup:* 1976-77, 1983-84, 1987-88, 1991-92, 1992-93, 1993-94, 1996-97, 1997-98, 1998-99, 1999-2000, 2000-01, 2001-02, 2002-03 runners-up, 2003-04 quarter-finals). *Europa League:* 32 matches (2009-10, 2010-11, 2011-12, 2014-15, 2015-16, 2017-18).

Club colours: Shirt: Green and white hoops. Shorts: White. Socks: Green with white hoops.

Goalscorers: *League (73):* Sinclair 10 (2 pens), Dembele 9 (1 pen), Edouard 9, Griffiths 9, Forrest 8, McGregor 7, Ntcham 5, Rogic 5, Armstrong 3, Tierney 3, Boyata 2, Hayes 1, Lustig 1, own goal 1.
William Hill Scottish FA Cup (17): Forrest 4, Dembele 3 (2 pens), Ntcham 3 (1 pen), Edouard 2, McGregor 2, Boyata 1, Rogic 1, Sinclair 1.
Betfred Scottish League Cup (15): Dembele 3 (1 pen), Forrest 3, Griffiths 2 (1 pen), Lustig 2, Armstrong 1, McGregor 1, Ralston 1, Sinclair 1 (1 pen), Tierney 1.
UEFA Champions League (20): Sinclair 7, Forrest 2, Griffiths 2, Rogic 2, Armstrong 1, Dembele 1, McGregor 1, Ntcham 1, Roberts 1, own goals 2.
UEFA Europa League (1): McGregor 1.

Gordon C 26	Lustig M 25+1	Simunovic J 13+2	Bitton N 10+4	Tierney K 30+2	Ntcham J 24+5	Brown S 34	Forrest J 31+4	McGregor C 29+7	Sinclair S 23+12	Griffiths L 11+14	Hayes J 6+8	Rogic T 18+5	Armstrong S 15+12	Ralston A 3	Ajer K 23+1	Miller C 3	Benyu K 1	Edouard O 12+10	Roberts P 7+5	Dembele M 17+8	Boyata D 28	De Vries D 5+1	Gamboa C 2	Eboue K 5+1	Henderson L —+1	Johnston M 1+2	Musonda C 2+2	Hendry J 7+4	Bain S 7	Henderson E —+1	Match No.
1	2	3	4	5	6[2]	7	8	9[1]	10	11[1]	12	13	14																		1
1	2	4	3	5	7[2]	6	11	9[1]	10	12	8[3]	13	14																		2
1	14		12	4[3]		6	11[1]	8		13		9	7	2	3	5		10[2]													3
1	3		4	5	7[2]	6	8[3]	14	10	11	13	9	12	2[1]																	4
1	2	3[1]	14	4	12	6	9	5	8		13		7[1]					10	11[2]												5
1		4	3			7	5	13	14	11[1]	9	6	8[3]	2				12		10[2]											6
1	2		4	5	6		13	12	10	11[1]			9[2]	7						8[1]	14	3									7
1	2		4		6		5[1]	8	12	13	9	7						10[3]	14	11[1]	3										8
		3	5	6				9	10	11[2]			14					8	13	4	1			2[3]		7[1]	12				9
1	2	3	4	5	6		8[2]		10	12	14	13	9[1]		7					11[3]											10
1	2		3	5	6[3]				12	11	9	13			4			8[2]	14							7		10[1]			11
1	2		3	5	13	6	8[1]	9[2]	10			14	12		7[3]					11	4										12
1	2		3	5	13	6	8[2]	9	10	12			14		7					11	4										13
1	2[3]	3		5		7	10	9	13	11		12	6[1]		4			14	8[2]												14
1	2			5	7[2]	6	12	13	10[3]			8[1]	9	14	3			11			4										15
1	2	3		5	6[2]	7	8[1]	9	10			13			14			11[3]		12	4										16
		13	4			6	7	5[2]	9	11	12	14	2		10[3]				8	3[1]									1		17
1	2	3		5[2]	6[1]	7	8	9[3]	10	11		12	13					14			4										18
1		3		5		6	8[3]	9	10[1]	14	12		7		2			11[2]			4						13				19
1	2			5	7	6	12	13	10[1]			8[2]	4		9			14		11[3]	3										20
1	2			5	7[2]	6	8	9		11[1]	10[3]	13			4					14	3						12				21
1	2			5	13	6	8		7	10[2]	12		14							9	4			11[3]		3					22
1	2[2]	13	14	5	7	6	8	9	10[3]	12				3				11[1]			4										23
1[2]				4		7	6	8[3]	9	10	11[1]				2					12	3	13		14							24
	3			9	6	5[3]	14	13	7						2			11[2]	10[1]	4			1	8			12				25
	3		12	10	8	6	7					13			4[1]			14	11				1	5[2]				9	2		26
		14			12	7	10		9[2]						4		5[3]	11[1]	13				1	2	6			8	3		27
	2[3]	3		5	7	8	6[2]	12		9[1]					10[2]			14	11		4						13		1		28
		3[1]		5	7	6	8	4	10						9[2]	14		13		11[1]	2						12		1		29
						7[3]	6	5[1]	8	13	9				4			11[2]	14	10	3						12	2	1		30
	2	3				6	8[1]	5	10	14		9	7					13	11[2]	4[3]							12		1		31
1	2					13	6	8	5	10[1]	12	9[2]	7					14	11[3]	4								3			32
				8	7	6		9	10	12					3			13	5[3]	11[2]	4						14	2[1]	1		33
1				5	7[2]	9	6	8[3]	10	12	11[1]				3			13	14		4							2			34
1	2[3]			5	6	7	8	9	10	12	14				4			11[1]			3						13				35
	2	3				7	6	8	5	12					9[1]	13		4		10[3]	14	11[1]							1		36
		3		13		6	8	7	11			12	9[3]		4	5[1]		10[2]										2	1	14	37
	2					5[3]	7[1]	6	8	10	13	12	4		9	14				11[2]	3								1		38

CLYDE

Year Formed: 1877. *Ground & Address:* Broadwood Stadium, Cumbernauld, G68 9NE. *Telephone:* 01236 451511.
Fax: 01236 733490. *E-mail:* info@clydefc.co.uk *Website:* www.clydefc.co.uk
Ground Capacity: 8,006 (all seated). *Size of Pitch:* 100m × 68m.
Chairman: Norrie Innes. *Vice Chairman:* John Taylor.
Manager: Danny Lennon. *Assistant Manager:* Allan Moore.
Club Nickname: 'The Bully Wee'.
Previous Grounds: Barrowfield Park 1877-98, Shawfield Stadium 1898-1986, Firhill Stadium 1986-91, Douglas Park 1991-94.
Record Attendance: 52,000 v Rangers, Division I, 21 November 1908.
Record Transfer Fee received: £200,000 from Blackburn R for Gordon Greer (May 2001).
Record Transfer Fee paid: £14,000 for Harry Hood from Sunderland (1966).
Record Victory: 11-1 v Cowdenbeath, Division II, 6 October 1951.
Record Defeat: 0-11 v Dumbarton, Scottish Cup 4th rd, 22 November, 1879; v Rangers, Scottish Cup 4th rd, 13 November 1880.
Most Capped Player: Tommy Ring, 12, Scotland.
Most League Appearances: 420: Brian Ahern, 1971-81; 1987-88.
Most League Goals in Season (Individual): 32: Bill Boyd, 1932-33.
Most Goals Overall (Individual): 124: Tommy Ring, 1950-60.

CLYDE – SPFL LADBROKES LEAGUE TWO 2017–18 LEAGUE RECORD

Match No.	Date	Venue	Opponents	Result	H/T Score	Lg Pos.	Goalscorers	Attendance
1	Aug 5	A	Berwick R	L 1-3	1-1	9	Goodwillie [23]	547
2	12	H	Annan Ath	W 2-1	1-0	5	Cuddihy [33], Osadolor [61]	412
3	19	A	Elgin C	L 2-3	2-1	8	Goodwillie [21], Stewart [31]	559
4	26	H	Stenhousemuir	D 1-1	0-1	8	Nicoll [77]	440
5	Sept 9	A	Stirling Alb	W 3-2	1-1	6	Goodwillie [41], Burbidge [47], Cuddihy [79]	865
6	16	H	Edinburgh C	L 2-3	1-1	8	Wright [11], Goodwillie [87]	466
7	23	H	Cowdenbeath	D 1-1	0-0	7	Osadolor [75]	418
8	30	A	Montrose	L 2-3	1-3	8	Osadolor [3], Goodwillie [74]	463
9	Oct 21	H	Peterhead	L 1-4	1-1	8	Ramsay [11]	403
10	28	H	Elgin C	L 2-4	1-1	8	Goodwillie [6], Osadolor [81]	402
11	Nov 4	A	Stenhousemuir	D 1-1	0-1	8	Goodwillie [50]	596
12	11	H	Stirling Alb	D 1-1	0-0	8	Goodwillie (pen) [88]	770
13	25	A	Annan Ath	D 0-0	0-0	8		375
14	Dec 2	H	Montrose	D 0-0	0-0	8		409
15	23	H	Berwick R	D 0-0	0-0	8		503
16	Jan 2	H	Annan Ath	D 0-0	0-0	8		477
17	6	A	Elgin C	L 1-2	0-1	9	Goodwillie [68]	566
18	13	H	Stenhousemuir	L 0-3	0-1	9		581
19	20	A	Montrose	W 3-1	1-0	8	Love [24], Goodwillie [50], Lamont [62]	543
20	27	A	Peterhead	W 1-0	0-0	8	Goodwillie [85]	449
21	Feb 3	H	Edinburgh C	W 3-2	2-1	8	Goodwillie 2 [14, 89], Cuddihy [34]	421
22	10	A	Berwick R	W 1-0	0-0	7	Goodwillie (pen) [90]	474
23	17	H	Cowdenbeath	W 2-0	0-0	7	Goodwillie 2 (1 pen) [47, 69 (p)]	613
24	24	A	Stirling Alb	L 1-2	1-1	7	Nicoll [38]	1012
25	27	H	Peterhead	L 1-2	0-2	7	Goodwillie [64]	394
26	Mar 10	A	Stenhousemuir	W 3-2	2-0	7	McStay [8], Goodwillie 2 [29, 51]	488
27	13	H	Elgin C	W 1-0	0-0	7	Goodwillie [60]	423
28	17	A	Annan Ath	D 1-1	0-0	7	Nicoll [64]	371
29	20	A	Edinburgh C	W 3-0	2-0	6	Nicoll [21], Boyle [26], Goodwillie [50]	310
30	24	H	Montrose	W 3-0	3-0	6	Lamont [31], McNiff [41], Goodwillie [45]	571
31	27	A	Cowdenbeath	W 3-0	1-0	4	McStay 2 [12, 82], Goodwillie [61]	374
32	31	A	Peterhead	L 0-3	0-1	6		724
33	Apr 7	A	Cowdenbeath	L 0-1	0-0	6		406
34	14	H	Stirling Alb	W 2-1	0-0	5	Boyle 2 [51, 58]	715
35	21	A	Edinburgh C	W 3-1	1-0	5	Goodwillie 2 (1 pen) [34 (p), 46], Cogill [65]	408
36	28	H	Berwick R	L 1-2	0-1	5	Boyle [57]	804

Final League Position: 5

Honours
League Champions: Division II 1904-05, 1951-52, 1956-57, 1961-62, 1972-73; Second Division 1977-78, 1981-82, 1992-93, 1999-2000.
Runners-up: Division II 1903-04, 1905-06, 1925-26, 1963-64; First Division 2002-03, 2003-04.
Scottish Cup Winners: 1939, 1955, 1958; *Runners-up:* 1910, 1912, 1949.
League Challenge Cup Runners-up: 2006-07.

Club colours: Shirt: White with red trim. Shorts: Black. Socks: Red.

Goalscorers: *League (52):* Goodwillie 25 (4 pens), Boyle 4, Nicoll 4, Osadolor 4, Cuddihy 3, McStay 3, Lamont 2, Burbidge 1, Cogill 1, Love 1, McNiff 1, Ramsay 1, Stewart 1, Wright 1.
William Hill Scottish FA Cup (0).
Betfred Scottish League Cup (7): Goodwillie 2, Breslin 1, Miller 1, Nicoll 1, Ramsay 1, Wright 1.
Irn-Bru Scottish League Challenge Cup (2): McNiff 1, Osadolor 1.

Currie B 32	Home C 20+1	Breslin J 7+3	Nicoll K 24+2	McNiff M 36	Stewart J 28	Cuddihy B 32+2	Miller D 4+1	Flynn M 3	Goodwillie D 36	Osadolor S 9+12	Wright M 10+6	Burbidge M 4+4	Millar A 5+4	Ramsay D 15+1	Belkacem I —+1	Crawford D 1	Bradley K 1	Munro A 10	Lamont M 18+9	Duffie K 20+3	Ferguson S —+8	Lowdon J 7+7	Gormley D 2+3	Lang T 10	Love A 7+6	Martin A 2+7	Grant R 10+6	Boyle J 10+6	Cogill D 15+1	McStay C 15	Gourlay K 3	Kipre S —+3	Match No.
1	2¹	3	4	5	6	7³	8	9	10	11²	12	13	14																				1
1	2	4		3	5	7	6	8	10¹	11	12	13	14	9¹																			2
1⁸	2	4		3	5	8	6	7²	10	11¹	12	13		9³	14																		3
	5	3	2	9	6	7¹			10	11	13	12	8			1	4²																4
1	2	9¹	3	5	6	13			10	8	7²	11						4	12														5
1	2	6	4	5	8				11	12	9²	7²						3⁸	10¹	13	14												6
1	2⁸	6	4	5	9				11	13	8¹	7²	10²						3	12	14												7
1	12		3	4	5	7			11	10	8³	6²	9¹					14	2	13													8
1	3		7¹	4	5²	8			11	10	6²	9						14	2	12	13												9
1			4	5	7				10	11	6¹	8³						3	14	2	12	9²											10
1	4	13		2	9	8			11	12	5²		7					3				6	10¹										11
1	2		7	4		8			11	10²	12		6¹					3	13	5		9											12
1	2	14		4	5	8¹			10	11²			7					3	6	13	9²	12											13
1	2			3	5	6²			11	13	10¹		8²					4		7		9	12										14
1	2	13	7		4	5			11	14	6²		8²					3	12			9	10¹										15
1	3		6⁸	2					11	14	8¹		9²					4	12	5	13				7²	10							16
1	3	7²		2		8			11	9³				14				4		13	5	12	6	10¹									17
1	3		6	4	5¹				11	13			10²	8					14	2		12			7³	9							18
1	4		7	3	9	6			11										5	12					2	8¹							19
1	3		7	4	5	6			10	13			11¹					8							2	9²	12						20
1	3		7	4	5¹	6			10				11²					8							2	9³	12	13	14				21
1	3		8	4		7			11				10³					9	12						2¹		14	13	5	6²			22
1	3		6	4		8			11	13								9³							2		12	14	10⁸	5	7¹		23
1	3		8³	5		6			11	14								7²							2		13	12	10	4¹	9		24
	4		6³	3		8²			11	13								12							2		14	9	10	5	7¹	1	25
1			3	5	6				11	12			14					8²	2						10³	9	13	4	7¹			26
1			3	5	6				11									8	2						10²	9¹	12	4	7			27
1		7	4	5	6				10									9	2	13					11¹	3²	8					28
1		7³	3	5	6				10									9³	2	14					12	11	4	8²	13			29
1			4	5	6				11²									9³	2	14	12				7	10¹	3	8	13			30
12			4	5	9²				11									8¹	2	13	14				7	10³	3	6			1	31
		7³	3	5²	6¹				11									9	2	13	14				12	10	4¹			1		32
1			4	5	8				11									10²	2						9³	13	7	12	3	6¹	14	33
1		9	3	5	12				11									10	2						13		8	6¹	4	7²		34
1		7	4	5	13				11									10¹	2						12		6	9²	3	8		35
1			4	5¹	8²				11	13	14							9³	2						12		6	10	3	7		36

COWDENBEATH

Year Formed: 1882. *Ground & Address:* Central Park, Cowdenbeath KY4 9QQ. *Telephone:* 01383 610166. *Fax:* 01383 512132.
E-mail: office@cowdenbeathfc.com *Website:* www.cowdenbeathfc.com
Ground Capacity: 4,370 (seated: 1,431). *Size of Pitch:* 95m × 60m.
Chairman: Donald Findlay QC. *Finance Director and Secretary:* David Allan.
Club Nicknames: 'The Blue Brazil', 'Cowden', 'The Miners'.
Manager: Gary Bollan. *Assistant Manager:* Mark Fotheringham. *First-Team Coach:* Ian Flaherty.
Previous Grounds: North End Park.
Record Attendance: 25,586 v Rangers, League Cup quarter-final, 21 September 1949.
Record Transfer Fee received: £30,000 for Nicky Henderson to Falkirk (March 1994).
Record Victory: 12-0 v Johnstone, Scottish Cup 1st rd, 21 January 1928.
Record Defeat: 1-11 v Clyde, Division II, 6 October 1951; 0-10 v Hearts, Championship, 28 February 2015.
Most Capped Player: Jim Paterson, 3, Scotland.
Most League and Cup Appearances: 491, Ray Allan 1972-75, 1979-89.
Most League Goals in Season (Individual): 54, Rab Walls, Division II, 1938-39.
Most Goals Overall (Individual): 127, Willie Devlin, 1922-26, 1929-30.

COWDENBEATH – SPFL LADBROKES LEAGUE TWO 2017–18 LEAGUE RECORD

Match No.	Date		Venue	Opponents	Result		H/T Score	Lg Pos.	Goalscorers	Attendance
1	Aug	5	A	Elgin C	D	1-1	1-1	5	Syme [11]	584
2		12	H	Edinburgh C	W	1-0	1-0	4	Stirling [30]	341
3		19	A	Montrose	L	0-1	0-1	5		456
4		26	H	Berwick R	L	0-1	0-1	7		380
5	Sept	9	A	Stenhousemuir	L	0-1	0-1	9		409
6		16	H	Peterhead	L	0-4	0-3	10		301
7		23	A	Clyde	D	1-1	0-0	10	Swan (pen) [90]	418
8		30	A	Annan Ath	L	0-1	0-1	10		363
9	Oct	21	H	Stirling Alb	L	0-3	0-2	10		371
10		28	A	Berwick R	L	0-1	0-0	10		487
11	Nov	4	H	Montrose	L	1-3	0-2	10	Buchanan [52]	349
12		11	H	Elgin C	L	1-3	0-2	10	Muirhead [85]	326
13		18	H	Annan Ath	D	1-1	0-1	10	Miller [70]	249
14		25	A	Edinburgh C	D	0-0	0-0	10		346
15	Dec	19	A	Stenhousemuir	D	1-1	1-0	10	Buchanan [27]	245
16		23	A	Peterhead	L	2-3	1-0	10	Muirhead [33], Buchanan [54]	593
17	Jan	2	A	Montrose	D	1-1	0-0	10	Buchanan [80]	543
18		6	H	Edinburgh C	L	0-2	0-2	10		365
19		13	A	Elgin C	L	0-1	0-0	10		609
20		27	H	Berwick R	L	1-3	1-1	10	Swan (pen) [45]	332
21		31	A	Stirling Alb	L	0-1	0-1	10		395
22	Feb	3	A	Annan Ath	D	1-1	1-0	10	Smith, B [29]	299
23		10	H	Stirling Alb	L	1-2	0-0	10	Swan (pen) [81]	366
24		17	A	Clyde	L	0-2	0-0	10		613
25		24	H	Peterhead	L	0-2	0-1	10		216
26	Mar	13	A	Edinburgh C	D	1-1	0-0	10	Cox [87]	256
27		17	H	Elgin C	W	3-1	2-0	10	Buchanan [39], Sheerin [41], Cox [86]	242
28		20	A	Stenhousemuir	W	2-1	2-0	10	Malcolm [22], Buchanan [29]	312
29		24	A	Stirling Alb	D	2-2	0-1	10	Buchanan [54], Malcolm [71]	748
30		27	H	Clyde	L	0-3	0-1	10		374
31		31	H	Stenhousemuir	D	1-1	1-1	10	Sheerin [39]	277
32	Apr	7	H	Clyde	W	1-0	0-0	10	Smith, B [68]	406
33		10	H	Montrose	L	0-3	0-1	10		378
34		14	A	Peterhead	L	0-1	0-0	10		785
35		21	A	Berwick R	L	0-1	0-1	10		596
36		28	H	Annan Ath	L	0-2	0-2	10		233

Final League Position: 10

Honours

League Champions: Division II 1913-14, 1914-15, 1938-39; Second Division 2011-12; Third Division 2005-06.
Runners-up: Division II 1921-22, 1923-24, 1969-70; Second Division 1991-92; Third Division 2000-01, 2008-09.
Promoted via play-offs: 2009-10 (to First Division).
Scottish Cup: Quarter-finals 1931.
League Cup: Semi-finals 1959-60, 1970-71.

Club colours: Shirt: Royal blue with white trim. Shorts: White. Socks: Black with red tops.

Goalscorers: *League (23):* Buchanan 7, Swan 3 (3 pens), Cox 2, Malcolm 2, Muirhead 2, Sheerin 2, Smith B 2, Miller 1, Stirling 1, Syme 1.
William Hill Scottish FA Cup (0).
Betfred Scottish League Cup (5): Muirhead 2, Syme 2, Connelly 1.
Irn-Bru Scottish League Challenge Cup (0).
Play-Offs (3): Swan 2, Smith B 1.

McGovern J 8	Pyper J 28	Runsby S 26 + 5	Syme D 15 + 2	Smith A 9	Swan H 27 + 3	Stirling B 5 + 2	Mullen F 32 + 1	Buchanan R 25 + 4	Connelly R 4 + 6	Muirhead C 14 + 11	Morris J 5 + 3	Miller K 29 + 3	Rutherford S 9	Smith B 30 + 4	McNally M 16 + 4	Denton C — + 3	Whittaker J 3 + 6	Garden J 4 + 7	McGurn D 27	Malcolm B 19	Scullion C 2	Henderson C — + 1	Fotheringham M 1 + 1	Reilly B 6 + 9	Malone A 3	Cox D 16	Luke B 4 + 2	Gilfillan B 11 + 1	Hornby J 5	Sheerin J 12	Penman B 1	McManus S — + 1	Match No.
1	2	3	4	5	6	7	8	9²	10¹	11	12	13																					1
1	2	4	3		7²	6	9	13	12	11		10	5	8¹																			2
1	2	4	3		6	9³	7¹	8²	14	13	10			12	5	11																	3
1	2	4	8	10	13	3¹	7	6		12		11		5	9²																		4
1		4	8	11	9³	3	6²		7	12	10¹	5	13	2	14																		5
1		4	3	6¹	14	8	9	10³	11	7		2	13	5²	12																		6
1		4	3	6	5	2	9⁶	8³	13	10¹	7	11		14	12																		7
1		3	4	6	5	14	2	9	8²	13	10¹	7		11		12																	8
		3	4		9¹	7	8	10		12	13	5	6²	2	14	11³	1																9
		3	4		9		8	10	12	7¹		5²	6	2	13	11¹	1																10
		3	4	2		7	6	9¹	12	10	8	5²	13	14	11³	1																	11
	2	3	4⁴	13		7⁸	8	12³	14	10	6	5	11¹		9²	1																	12
	3	4		5		13		11¹	9	10	2	6	12	1	7	8²																	13
	3	4		5	12		10²	8	11	2	6	13	1	7	9¹																		14
	3	4		5	6	9	12	11¹	7	10	2		1	8																			15
	3	4		5	6	9⁴		10¹	7	11	2	12	1	8																			16
	3	4		5	6	9		10¹	7	11	2	13	1	8		12²																	17
	3	4	14	5		7	13	11²	8	10	2	6²	12	1			9¹																18
	2	4	3	5	7			8⁴		10	13	12	14	1	9²			6¹	11³														19
	2	4	3	10	6				8	12		1	5				7¹	11²	9	13													20
	3	4		5	6	9		8		11¹	2		1	7			12	10															21
	3⁴	4		5	6	10		8		9²	2		1	7			13	11¹	12														22
	3	13	5		6			7		9²	2		1	8			12	11¹	10	10													23
8	4		5		6		13		7	11	2	12	1	9			10¹			3²													24
	3	4			2			7	9			1	8	6¹		10	12		5	11													25
	3			12	2	6	13	7	9			1	8¹			10		4	5²	11													26
	3	12		5²	2	8		7	9¹			1	6	13		11		4	10														27
	3	12		5³	2	11		8	9	14		1	7			13	6²	4¹	10														28
	3	12		5	2	9		8				1	7			13	6¹	11	4²	10													29
	3	4		5	2	11		6	8¹			1	7			12	9		10														30
	3	12		5	2	11		6	14			1	7³			13	9	8¹	4²	10													31
	3			5	2	9	12	7	10	13		1				8²	6¹	4	11														32
	3			5	6	11	12	8	2			1	7			9¹	4	10															33
	3				2	9	12	7	10			1	8			6¹	4	5	11														34
	3	13			2	14	8³	7²	11			1				12	6	9	4¹	5	10												35
	3	4	7			11²	13	6	2³			12	9¹	8			5	10	1	14													36

DUMBARTON

Year Formed: 1872. *Ground:* C&G Systems Stadium, Castle Road, Dumbarton G82 1JJ. *Telephone/Fax:* 01389 762569.
E-mail: enquiries@dumbartonfc.com *Website:* www.dumbartonfootballclub.com
Ground Capacity: total: 2,025 (all seated). *Size of Pitch:* 98m × 67m.
Chairman: John Steele. *Vice-Chairman:* Colin Hosie.
Manager: Stephen Aitken. *Assistant Manager:* Ian Durrant.
Club Nickname: 'The Sons', 'Sons of the Rock'.
Previous Grounds: Broadmeadow, Ropework Lane, Townend Ground, Boghead Park, Cliftonhill Stadium.
Record Attendance: 18,000 v Raith R, Scottish Cup, 2 March 1957.
Record Transfer Fee received: £300,000 for Neill Collins to Sunderland (July 2004).
Record Transfer Fee paid: £50,000 for Charlie Gibson from Stirling Alb (1989).
Record Victory: 13-1 v Kirkintilloch Central, Scottish Cup 1st rd, 1 September 1888.
Record Defeat: 1-11 v Albion R, Division II, 30 January 1926: v Ayr U, League Cup, 13 August 1952.
Most Capped Player: James McAulay, 9, Scotland.
Most League Appearances: 298: Andy Jardine, 1957-67.
Most Goals in Season (Individual): 38: Kenny Wilson, Division II, 1971-72. *(League and Cup):* 46 Hughie Gallacher, 1955-56.
Most Goals Overall (Individual): 202: Hughie Gallacher, 1954-62

DUMBARTON – SPFL LADBROKES CHAMPIONSHIP 2017–18 LEAGUE RECORD

Match No.	Date	Venue	Opponents	Result	H/T Score	Lg Pos.	Goalscorers	Atten- dance
1	Aug 5	H	Greenock Morton	D	0-0	0-0	6		1161
2	12	A	Falkirk	D	1-1	1-1	7	Roy [13]	3864
3	19	A	Queen of the South	L	0-1	0-1	6		1442
4	26	A	Dunfermline Ath	L	0-4	0-2	8		1028
5	Sept 9	A	Dundee U	D	1-1	1-0	8	Smith [4]	5331
6	16	H	Brechin C	W	2-1	0-1	7	Stewart [82], Froxylias [86]	589
7	23	H	Inverness CT	W	2-1	0-1	7	Froxylias [47], Wardrop [63]	594
8	30	A	Livingston	L	1-2	0-1	7	Walsh [76]	938
9	Oct 14	H	St Mirren	L	0-2	0-1	7		1178
10	21	A	Greenock Morton	D	1-1	1-0	7	Stewart [5]	1428
11	28	H	Dundee U	L	0-2	0-2	8		968
12	Nov 4	A	Brechin C	W	1-0	0-0	8	Dyer (og) [90]	538
13	25	A	Dunfermline Ath	D	2-2	0-0	7	Walsh [51], Froxylias [68]	4505
14	28	H	Queen of the South	D	2-2	1-0	8	Fordyce (og) [11], Morrison [81]	474
15	Dec 2	A	St Mirren	W	1-0	0-0	7	Walsh [80]	3591
16	16	H	Inverness CT	L	0-1	0-1	8		2103
17	23	H	Falkirk	D	0-0	0-0	8		874
18	26	H	Livingston	L	1-4	1-2	8	Roy [25]	495
19	Jan 2	A	Queen of the South	D	0-0	0-0	8		1269
20	6	H	Dunfermline Ath	L	0-1	0-1	8		1086
21	13	A	St Mirren	L	0-2	0-0	8		1652
22	27	A	Livingston	L	0-2	0-2	9		732
23	Feb 20	H	Greenock Morton	L	0-1	0-0	9		836
24	24	A	Falkirk	D	0-0	0-0	9		6094
25	Mar 10	H	Queen of the South	L	0-1	0-0	9		642
26	13	H	Brechin C	W	1-0	1-0	9	Froxylias [37]	403
27	17	A	Brechin C	W	3-1	3-1	9	Gallagher, C [11], Crighton (og) [24], Handling [43]	445
28	27	A	St Mirren	L	0-5	0-2	9		3964
29	31	H	Livingston	L	0-3	0-3	9		670
30	Apr 3	A	Dundee U	L	0-2	0-2	9		3620
31	7	H	Dundee U	W	3-2	1-0	9	Gallagher, C [11], Barr 2 [59, 79]	994
32	10	A	Greenock Morton	L	2-3	0-0	9	Handling [55], O'Ware (og) [87]	1134
33	14	A	Inverness CT	L	1-5	1-2	9	Gallagher, G [13]	2355
34	18	H	Inverness CT	L	0-1	0-0	9		392
35	21	H	Falkirk	L	2-5	1-1	9	Gallagher, C [37], Burt [87]	942
36	28	A	Dunfermline Ath	L	0-4	0-3	9		5506

Final League Position: 9

Honours
League Champions: Division I 1890-91 (shared with Rangers), 1891-92; Division II 1910-11, 1971-72; Second Division 1991-92; Third Division 2008-09.
Runners-up: First Division 1983-84; Division II 1907-08; Second Division 1994-95; Third Division 2001-02.
Scottish Cup Winners: 1883; *Runners-up:* 1881, 1882, 1887, 1891, 1897.
League Challenge Cup: Runners-up: 2017-18.

Club colours: Shirt: White with yellow and black horizontal stripe. Shorts: White. Socks: White.

Goalscorers: *League (27):* Froxylias 4, Gallagher C 3, Walsh 3, Barr 2, Handling 2, Roy 2, Stewart 2, Burt 1, Gallagher G 1, Morrison 1, Smith 1, Wardrop 1, own goals 4.
William Hill Scottish FA Cup (4): Gallagher C 2, Carswell 1, Russell 1.
Betfred Scottish League Cup (2): Barr 1, Nade 1.
Irn-Bru Scottish League Challenge Cup (10): Froxylias 2, Stewart 2, Barr 1, Gallagher C 1 (1 pen), Handling 1, McLaughlin 1, Roy 1, Wilson D 1.
Play-Offs (4): Barr 1, Carswell 1, Gallagher C 1, Hill 1.

Gallacher S 34	Hill D 18 + 2	Barr C 32	Dowie A 31	Wardrop S 22	Roy A 7 + 9	Wilson D 15 + 7	Walsh T 27 + 1	McLaughlin C 23	Nade C 8 + 12	Stewart M 15 + 9	Gallagher C 17 + 11	Smith D 12 + 5	Johnston C 1 + 6	Carswell S 25 + 1	Hutton K 28 + 3	Handling D 11 + 5	Morrison G 6 + 8	Froxylias D 17 + 6	Dick L 13	Russell I 4 + 3	Nisbet K 6 + 3	Wilson A 3	Burt L 4 + 9	Stirling A 12	Gallagher G 3 + 5	Ewings J 2 + 1	Match No.
1	2	3	4	5	6	7^1	8^2	9	10	11	12	13															1
1	4	7	3	2	9^2	8	6^3	5	11	10^1			14	12	13												2
1	4		3	2	13	9^2	8^3	5	12	11	14	6^1			10	7											3
1		4	3^4	2^4	8	14	10^2	5	11		13	12			7	6	9^1										4
1	4	3		8	14	6	11	5	12		13	2^2		7			9^1	10^3									5
1	4	3			8	9	5	13	12		6^3			7^2	14		11^1	10									6
1	3	7	4	2		13	10^3	5	11^1	9^2	14			6	12	8											7
1	4^3	8	3	2	14	13	9	5	10^1	11^2				7	12	6											8
1	4	3	2	13	7	9^2	5	11^3	10^1			14		8	12	6											9
1	4	7	3	2	14	9	10^2	5	11^3	13				8	12	7											10
1	4	6^3	3	2	13	9^1	10^2	5	11^3	14				8	12	7											11
1	4		3	2	10^1	13	9	5	11^3	8^2	14			6	7	12											12
1		3	4	2		9^2	5	13	10	6^1	14	8	7		11^3	12											13
1		3	4	2	14	10	5	13	11^2	6^1		8	7		12	9^1											14
1	4	3	2	12		9	5	14	8^2	10^1		7	6		11^2	13											15
1	4	3	2	11^1	12	6	5	13	7^3		9	8			10^2	14											16
1	3	4	2	9^1	10	5^1	11	13	12	14	8	7			6^2												17
1	4	3	2	11^3		10	12	6^2	5	9^1	8	7^4	14		13												18
1	8	4	3	9^3	11	14	10^1	2	7		13	12	6^2	5													19
1	4	7	3^1	9	10	12	8^3	2	14	6		13	11^2	5													20
1	4	3	13	10	11	8^2	2	6	7	9^1			5	12													21
1	4^1	2	3	14	9^3	13	8	7	6			12	5	10^2	11												22
1				11^3		2	6	7	13	8^3	5	14	12	4	9^1	10											23
1		4	3	2	14	12	8^3	6	7	9^2		5	11^1	13	10												24
1	4		3	2	13	10^1	7	8	9^2	14	5	6^1	11	12													25
1	4	3	2	14	8	7	11^1	6^2	5	10^3	12	13	9														26
1	13	4	3	2^2	5^3	6	12	7	8	10	11^1	14	9														27
1		3	4	14	13	12	2	6	7	9^1	5	10^3	11^1	8													28
1	4	3		10^1		12	11^3	7	8	6^2	5	13	2^4	9	14												29
1	4	3		8^1	5	13	11^2	7^3	10	6	2		14	9	12												30
1		3	4	8	6	5^2	14	11^3	7	10	2		13	9	12												31
1		3	4	7	6^3	5	14	11	8	10^1	2^2		13	9	12												32
1	14	3	4	7^1	5	13	11^3	8	10	6	12	9	2^2														33
1^1	3	7	4	9	5^4	10^3	12	8	14	6	11	2	13														34
	4	3		8^1	9	11^2	5	7	12	10^3	14	13	6	2	1												35
	4	3^4		13	2	6	7	14	9^1	11^1	5	8^2	10	12	1												36

DUNDEE

Year Formed: 1893. *Ground & Address:* Dens Park Stadium, Sandeman St, Dundee DD3 7JY. *Telephone:* 01382 889966.
Fax: 01382 832284. *E-mail:* reception@dundeefc.co.uk *Website:* www.dundeefc.co.uk
Ground Capacity: 11,850 (all seated). *Size of Pitch:* 101m × 66m.
Chairman: Tim Keyes. *Managing Director:* John Nelms.
Manager: Neil McCann. *Assistant Manager:* Graham Gartland. *Youth Development:* Jimmy Boyle.
Club Nicknames: 'The Dark Blues' or 'The Dee'.
Previous Grounds: Carolina Port 1893-98.
Record Attendance: 43,024 v Rangers, Scottish Cup 2nd rd, 7 February 1953.
Record Transfer Fee received: £1,500,000 for Robert Douglas to Celtic (October 2000).
Record Transfer Fee paid: £600,000 for Fabian Caballero from Sol de América (Paraguay) (July 2000).
Record Victory: 10-0 Division II v Alloa Ath, 9 March 1947 and v Dunfermline Ath, 22 March 1947.
Record Defeat: 0-11 v Celtic, Division I, 26 October 1895.
Most Capped Player: Alex Hamilton, 24, Scotland.
Most League Appearances: 400: Barry Smith, 1995-2006.
Most League Goals in Season (Individual): 52: Alan Gilzean, 1960-64.
Most Goals Overall (Individual): 113: Alan Gilzean 1960-64.

DUNDEE – SPFL LADBROKES PREMIERSHIP 2017–18 LEAGUE RECORD

Match No.	Date	Venue	Opponents	Result	H/T Score	Lg Pos.	Goalscorers	Attendance
1	Aug 5	H	Ross Co	L	1-2	0-1	9	Hendry [86]	5032
2	12	A	Hamilton A	L	0-3	0-2	12		1694
3	19	A	Aberdeen	L	1-2	0-1	12	Deacon [53]	15,646
4	27	H	Hibernian	D	1-1	1-1	11	Holt (pen) [9]	6004
5	Sept 9	A	Rangers	L	1-4	0-1	12	El Bakhtaoui [90]	49,164
6	16	H	St Johnstone	W	3-2	1-0	9	Leitch-Smith 2 [9, 65], Moussa (pen) [78]	6001
7	23	A	Kilmarnock	D	1-1	1-0	9	El Bakhtaoui [4]	3452
8	30	H	Hearts	W	2-1	1-0	8	Waddell 2 [44, 90]	7028
9	Oct 14	A	Celtic	L	0-1	0-0	8		57,610
10	21	A	Partick Thistle	L	1-2	1-0	9	Leitch-Smith [8]	3358
11	25	H	Motherwell	L	0-1	0-1	10		5254
12	28	H	Hamilton A	L	1-3	0-1	12	Leitch-Smith (pen) [67]	4863
13	Nov 4	A	Hibernian	L	1-2	1-1	12	Haber [21]	16,936
14	18	H	Kilmarnock	D	0-0	0-0	12		5853
15	24	H	Rangers	W	2-1	0-0	11	O'Hara 2 [66, 80]	8548
16	Dec 2	A	Ross Co	W	2-0	1-0	9	O'Hara [18], El Bakhtaoui [89]	3896
17	8	H	Aberdeen	L	0-1	0-0	10		6451
18	12	A	Hearts	L	0-2	0-1	11		15,566
19	16	H	Partick Thistle	W	3-0	2-0	10	Moussa 2 (2 pens) [19, 65], O'Hara [35]	5101
20	23	A	Motherwell	D	1-1	0-0	10	McGowan [47]	4173
21	26	H	Celtic	L	0-2	0-2	10		9193
22	30	A	St Johnstone	W	2-0	1-0	10	Haber [3], Leitch-Smith [90]	4769
23	Jan 24	H	Hibernian	L	0-1	0-0	10		5323
24	27	A	Hamilton A	W	2-1	0-1	9	Henvey [77], Leitch-Smith [90]	1776
25	Feb 3	H	Ross Co	L	1-4	0-0	9	Waddell [67]	4971
26	13	A	Kilmarnock	L	2-3	1-1	9	Moussa (pen) [31], Caulker [56]	3768
27	17	A	Partick Thistle	W	2-1	0-1	8	Murray 2 [84, 90]	4267
28	24	H	Motherwell	L	0-1	0-1	9		5003
29	Mar 10	H	St Johnstone	L	0-4	0-2	10		5336
30	17	A	Aberdeen	L	0-1	0-1	10		15,208
31	Apr 1	H	Hearts	D	1-1	1-1	10	Moussa [28]	5496
32	4	A	Celtic	D	0-0	0-0	10		55,768
33	7	A	Rangers	L	0-4	0-1	10		49,142
34	21	H	St Johnstone	W	2-1	1-0	9	Moussa 2 [1, 88]	5592
35	28	A	Motherwell	L	1-2	1-1	10	Kusunga [23]	4064
36	May 5	H	Hamilton A	W	1-0	1-0	9	Holt [18]	5195
37	8	A	Ross Co	W	1-0	0-0	9	Murray [51]	3976
38	12	H	Partick Thistle	L	0-1	0-0	9		6756

Final League Position: 9

Honours
League Champions: Division I 1961-62; First Division 1978-79, 1991-92, 1997-98; Championship 2013-14; Division II 1946-47.
Runners-up: Division I 1902-03, 1906-07, 1908-09, 1948-49; First Division 1980-81, 2007-08, 2009-10, 2011-12.
Scottish Cup Winners: 1910; *Runners-up:* 1925, 1952, 1964, 2003.
League Cup Winners: 1951-52, 1952-53, 1973-74; *Runners-up:* 1967-68, 1980-81, 1995-96.
League Challenge Cup Winners: 1990-91, 2009-10.

European: *European Cup:* 8 matches (1962-63 semi-finals). *Cup Winners' Cup:* 2 matches: (1964-65).
UEFA Cup: 22 matches: (*Fairs Cup:* 1967-68 semi-finals. *UEFA Cup:* 1971-72, 1973-74, 1974-75, 2003-04).

Club colours: All: Navy blue.

Goalscorers: *League (36):* Moussa 7 (4 pens), Leitch-Smith 6 (1 pen), O'Hara 4, El Bakhtaoui 3, Murray 3, Waddell 3, Haber 2, Holt 2 (1 pen), Caulker 1, Deacon 1, Hendry 1, Henvey 1, Kusunga 1, McGowan 1.
William Hill Scottish FA Cup (3): Allan 1, Moussa 1, O'Hara 1.
Betfred Scottish League Cup (10): Moussa 5, El Bakhtaoui 2, Hendry 1, McGowan 1, O'Hara 1.

Bain S 12	Kerr C 27+5	Waddell K 10+6	O'Dea D 14+2	Holt K 22+2	Kamara G 37	Allan S 8+8	Deacon R 25+3	Wolters R 4+5	O'Hara M 26+6	Moussa S 21+5	Hendry J 23+1	El Bakhtaoui F 16+12	McGowan P 30+4	Haber M 9+2	Williams D —+2	Vincent J 2+1	Spence L 14+4	Leitch-Smith A 14+14	Meekings J 21+1	Curran J 5+3	Aurtenetxe J 14+2	Parish E 25	Lambert J —+1	Henvey M —+4	Etxabeguren Leanizbarrutia J —+1	Murray S 13+1	Caulker S 12	Kusunga G 7+2	Piggott J —+1	Wighton C 5+2	Ferie C 1+1	Scott C —+3	Jefferies D 1+1	Match No.
1	2	3³	4	5	6	7	8	9¹	10	11²	12	13	14																					1
1	2	13	4³	5	8	7	6²	14	3	10	9¹	11	12																					2
1	2	4	5	6¹	7	8	14	3	10³	12	11²	13	9																					3
1	2	4	5	7¹	9	6	12	13	3	11	10	8²																						4
1	2	4	5	8¹	9	6²	13	11	3	10	14	7	12																					5
1	2	13	4⁵	5	7	6¹	12	10²	3	11	8	9																						6
1	2	4	5	8³	9²	6¹	14	12	3	10	13	7	11																					7
1	12	4	3²	9	7	5¹	8	11³	2	14	10	6	13																					8
1		4	9	7	10	5	12	3¹	14	8²	6	11³	2	13																				9
1		4	9	6	12		13	10²	2	14	7³		8	11¹	3	5																		10
1	12	4²	8	6	11¹		9²	2	13	10	7	14	3	5																				11
1	12	4	6	8¹	14	2	9	10	7	11	3²	5³	13																					12
	2²		5	6	8³	12	3	10	9¹	11	7	14	4	13	1																			13
	2	4⁵		6	13	5²	8	3	11¹	7³	10	12	14	9	1																			14
	2			6	13	5¹	8	12	3	10	7	11²	4	9	1																			15
	2	14		6	12	8³	7	11¹	3	10	9²	13	4	5	1																			16
	2	14		7	12	6²	9	11	3	10	8¹	13	4³	5	1																			17
12	2		7	11	9²	5	10	4³	13	6¹	14	3	8	1																				18
	2		7	12	5¹	10²	3	11³	6	13	9	4	14	8	1																			19
	2		7	12	6	11	3	9¹	8	10	4	5	1																					20
	2	12	8	6	10	3	9²	7	11³	4¹	5	1	13	14																				21
	3³		7	9¹	6	4	13	8	10	11²	5	1	14	12																				22
		13	7	12	6	3	10³	8	11	4	5²	9¹	1	14																				23
2	12		5	7	13	6	11	3	9²	8¹	10	4³	1	14																				24
2	3	4	5²	8³	13	6	14	7	10¹	12	9	1	11																					25
12	4		7	5¹	6²	10	13	8	14	9	1	11	2	3³																				26
2			9¹	6	10²	8	13	12	3	5	1	11	4																					27
5¹		7	8	6	10²	14	9³	12	3	13	1	11	4	2																				28
2²			6	7	13	14	9¹	11	4	8	5	1	10³	3	12																			29
13	4	9	7	8	6	11²	10	5	3¹	1	12	2																						30
		4¹	13	7	9	6	11³	8	14	2	5²	1	10	3	12																			31
		9	6	10²	5	12	7³	8	13	4	1	11¹	2	3	14																			32
		8	7	9	5	10²	6¹	13	3	13	1	11	4	2	12	14																		33
2		5	7		6	10	8	12	1	11¹	4	3	9																					34
2		13	5	7		6	11²	8	12	1	10	4	3³	9¹	14																			35
2		3	5	7	10³	6²		11	12	1	9	4	8¹	14	13																			36
2		4	5	6	12	8³	13	7	9¹	1	10	3	14	11²																				37
2			5	7	6³	12	14	8¹	1	10	4	11²	1	13	3																			38

DUNDEE UNITED

Year Formed: 1909 (1923). *Ground & Address:* Tannadice Park, Tannadice St, Dundee DD3 7JW. *Telephone:* 01382 833166. *Fax:* 01382 889398. *E-mail:* admin@dundeeunited.co.uk *Website:* www.dundeeunitedfc.co.uk
Ground Capacity: 14,223 (all seated). *Size of Pitch:* 100m × 66m.
Chairman: Stephen Thompson, OBE.
Manager: Csaba László. *Assistant Manager:* Laurie Ellis.
Club Nicknames: 'The Terrors', 'The Arabs'.
Previous Grounds: None.
Record Attendance: 28,000 v Barcelona, Fairs Cup, 16 November 1966.
Record Transfer Fee received: £4,000,000 for Duncan Ferguson from Rangers (July 1993).
Record Transfer Fee paid: £750,000 for Steven Pressley from Coventry C (July 1995).
Record Victory: 14-0 v Nithsdale Wanderers, Scottish Cup 1st rd, 17 January 1931.
Record Defeat: 1-12 v Motherwell, Division II, 23 January 1954.
Most Capped Player: Maurice Malpas, 55, Scotland.
Most League Appearances: 618: Maurice Malpas, 1980-2000.
Most Appearances in European Matches: 76: Dave Narey (record for Scottish player).
Most League Goals in Season (Individual): 40: John Coyle, Division II, 1955-56.
Most Goals Overall (Individual): 199: Peter McKay, 1947-54.

DUNDEE UNITED – SPFL LADBROKES CHAMPIONSHIP 2017–18 LEAGUE RECORD

Match No.	Date		Venue	Opponents	Result		H/T Score	Lg Pos.	Goalscorers	Atten- dance
1	Aug	5	A	Inverness CT	W	1-0	1-0	3	McMullan (pen) [13]	3415
2		12	H	Queen of the South	W	2-1	1-1	1	McDonald [18], Fraser [68]	5842
3		19	H	Brechin C	W	1-0	0-0	1	McDonald [80]	6060
4		26	A	St Mirren	L	0-3	0-1	4		4768
5	Sept	9	H	Dumbarton	D	1-1	0-1	4	Keatings [87]	5331
6		16	A	Falkirk	D	0-0	0-0	4		4874
7		23	H	Greenock Morton	W	2-1	0-0	2	Keatings [65], McDonald [83]	5569
8		30	A	Dunfermline Ath	W	3-1	2-0	2	Fyvie 2 [35, 59], McDonald [43]	7585
9	Oct	14	A	Livingston	L	0-2	0-1	4		2282
10		21	H	Inverness CT	L	0-2	0-2	4		5560
11		28	A	Dumbarton	W	2-0	2-0	4	Stanton 2 [2, 15]	968
12	Nov	4	H	St Mirren	W	2-1	1-0	2	Durnan [11], Stanton [79]	6936
13		19	H	Falkirk	W	3-0	3-0	1	McDonald [21], Robson [41], Flood [45]	5915
14		25	A	Brechin C	D	1-1	1-0	1	McDonald [29]	2627
15	Dec	2	H	Dunfermline Ath	W	2-1	2-0	1	Fraser 2 [15, 42]	5790
16		9	A	Greenock Morton	W	2-0	0-0	1	King 2 [61, 90]	2021
17		23	H	Livingston	W	3-0	2-0	1	McMullan 2 [22, 88], McDonald [37]	6221
18		29	A	St Mirren	L	0-2	0-0	2		6214
19	Jan	2	H	Brechin C	W	4-1	2-0	2	McDonald 2 [1, 49], Stanton [7], Keatings (pen) [52]	5532
20		6	A	Falkirk	L	1-6	1-2	2	King [6]	5326
21		13	A	Dunfermline Ath	D	0-0	0-0	2		7139
22		27	H	Greenock Morton	L	0-3	0-1	2		5730
23	Feb	23	A	Livingston	L	1-2	0-1	3	Smith, M [74]	1604
24	Mar	13	A	Queen of the South	W	3-1	1-1	3	Mikkelsen [24], Smith, M 2 [48, 57]	1480
25		17	H	Inverness CT	D	1-1	0-1	3	Mikkelsen [64]	4772
26		20	H	Queen of the South	L	2-3	0-2	3	Durnan [57], McDonald [68]	4088
27		24	A	Dunfermline Ath	D	1-1	0-0	4	McDonald [55]	5830
28		27	A	Inverness CT	L	0-1	0-1	4		2328
29		31	A	Greenock Morton	D	1-1	0-0	5	Mohsni [59]	2319
30	Apr	3	H	Dumbarton	W	2-0	2-0	4	McMullan [30], Mohsni [45]	3620
31		7	A	Dumbarton	L	2-3	0-1	4	Ralston [51], McDonald [70]	994
32		10	H	St Mirren	W	1-0	1-0	4	King [3]	5905
33		14	H	Falkirk	W	1-0	1-0	4	Mikkelsen [7]	5170
34		17	A	Brechin C	W	5-0	0-0	3	McDonald 2 [51, 79], King [56], Fraser [81], Mohsni [88]	1427
35		21	A	Queen of the South	L	0-3	0-2	3		1531
36		28	H	Livingston	W	2-0	0-0	3	Slater [54], McDonald [85]	5226

Final League Position: 3

Honours: *League Champions:* Premier Division 1982-83;. Division II 1924-25, 1928-29.
Runners-up: Division II 1930-31, 1959-60; First Division 1995-96.
Scottish Cup Winners: 1994, 2010; *Runners-up:* 1974, 1981, 1985, 1987, 1988, 1991, 2005, 2014.
League Cup Winners: 1979-80, 1980-81; *Runners-up:* 1981-82, 1984-85, 1997-98, 2007-08, 2014-15.
League Challenge Cup Winners, 2016-17; *Runners-up:* 1995-96.

European: *European Cup:* 8 matches (1983-84, semi-finals). *Cup Winners' Cup:* 10 matches (1974-75, 1988-89, 1994-95).
UEFA Cup: 86 matches (*Fairs Cup:* 1966-67, 1969-70, 1970-71. *UEFA Cup:* 1975-76, 1977-78, 1978-79, 1979-80, 1980-81, 1981-82, 1982-83, 1984-85, 1985-86, 1986-87 runners-up, 1987-88, 1989-90, 1990-91, 1993-94, 1997-98, 2005-06). *Europa League:* 6 matches (2010-2011, 2011-12, 2012-13).

Club colours: Shirt: Tangerine with black trim. Shorts: Tangerine. Socks: Tangerine.

Goalscorers: *League (52):* McDonald 15, King 5, Fraser 4, McMullan 4 (1 pen), Stanton 4, Keatings 3 (1 pen), Mikkelsen 3, Mohsni 3, Smith M 3, Durnan 2, Fyvie 2, Flood 1, Ralston 1, Robson 1, Slater 1.
William Hill Scottish FA Cup (4): Durnan 1, Lyng 1, McMullan 1, Stanton 1.
Betfred Scottish League Cup (11): King 3, McMullan 3, Durnan 1, Fraser 1 (1 pen), Keatings 1 (1 pen), Smith M 1, Stanton 1.
Irn-Bru Scottish League Challenge Cup (7): Nkoyi 3 (1 pen), Chalmers 1, Flood 1, Fyvie 1, McMullan 1.
Play-Offs (5): Fraser 1, McDonald 1, Mikkelsen 1, Ralston 1, Stanton 1.

Lewis H 30	Toshney L 4	Scobbie T 18+1	Edjenguele W 9+4	Robson J 30	Allardice S 1+3	Briels J 6+4	Stanton S 32+3	Fraser S 14+9	McMullan P 22+8	King B 32+3	Keatings J 8+8	Flood W 26+4	Murdoch S 25+2	Durnan M 26+1	Fyvie F 14+1	McDonald S 31+3	Quinn P 12+4	Nkoyi P —+8	Smith M 8+9	Glass D —+2	Chalmers L —+2	Ballantyne C —+1	Mason B 1	Slater C 3+4	Lyng E 3+3	Mikkelsen T 9+4	Kadded I —+1	Martin L —+1	Gillespie G 5+1	Mehmet D 6	Ralston A 11	Mohsni B 10	Match No.
1	2	3	4	5	6^1	7	8	9^2	10	11	12	13																					1
1		3		5		13	8	12	6^8	9	11^3	14	2	4	7^2	10^1																	2
1				5			8	6^1		11		9		7	2	3	6^1	10	4	12													3
1				5			8		11	9		7	2	3	6^1	10	4	12															4
1		4	5			9^5	6^2	7	8	13	14		2		10	11	3	12															5
1	4	12	9		10	8		5		7^1	13		2	11	6	3^2																	6
1	2^3		4	5			8^1	14		6	9	11^2		12	3	7	10	13															7
1		4	5			7	12			9	6	11^1	2		3	8	10^2		13														8
1		3	5			8^2	12			6	9	10	2		4	7	11		13														9
1	2	4	5			9^3	14	6^2	12	11	7	13	3		8^1	10																	10
1	4		5			8	10^3	13	6^1	12	7	2	3						9^2	14													11
1	4		5			7	10			9	13	8	2	3	12	11^1			6^2														12
1	4		5			6	10^3	12	9		7^1	2	3	8	11^2	14	13																13
1	4^8		5			6^1	10	13	9^6	12	7	2	3	8	11																		14
1		13	5			8^5	9^2	14	10	12	6^1	2	3	7	11	4																	15
1	4	13	5			7	10^1	6^3	9			2	3	8	11^2	12	14																16
1	2		5	13		6	9^2	8^3	10			3	7^1	11	4		12		14														17
1	2		5	14		7	9^3	8^1	10	13	6^2	3		11	4		12																18
1	2		5	13		7		6^8	9	10^2	8^1	3^3		11	4		14			12													19
1	4	2				9			10	8^2	6		11	3	14		13		5	7^1	12												20
1	4	5				6^1		10	8	2		9	12								7	11											21
1		5				7		10^2		6	2	4	9^1	3							13	8	11^3	12	14								22
1	4	5				9	14	8		6	2	3	11^3		13						10^1	12			7^2								23
1	4	9				8	13	7^1		6^2	5	2	3	11							14	10^1			11^3								24
1	4	5				9	14	13	10		7	2	3	12	6^1	8^2						11^3											25
	5	4				7	12	8^3	10^2	14	6	3		9							13				11					1	2^1		26
1	4^3		5			6	10^1	14		7	9	12	11				8^2				13									2	3		27
1		2	9			8^3	7^1		14	6	3		10			12					13	11^2						5	4				28
1						7^2	13	9	8		6^3	3	4	11^1	12	10							14				5	2					29
1						7^1	12	10	9		8	5	4	11^2		6^2					13	14					2	3					30
1	4					6		11	10	7	5		9			8^1						12					2	3					31
						12	7		8^1	10^2		6	5	4			13				11				9	1	2	3					32
	13		5^2				14	8^3	10^1	7	3		9			12					11				6^1	1	2	4					33
		5		13	9	14	10^3	8		7^1	3		12								11				6^2	1	2	4					34
	5	14				7	13	10^2	8^1	6	4		11								12	9^3				1	2	3					35
		5				14	7	9^2	10			4			11		13				8^1	12			6^3	1	2	3					36

DUNFERMLINE ATHLETIC

Year Formed: 1885. *Ground & Address:* East End Park, Halbeath Road, Dunfermline KY12 7RB.
Telephone: 01383 724295. *Fax:* 01383 745 959. *E-mail:* enquiries@dafc.co.uk
Website: www.dafc.co.uk
Ground Capacity: 11,380 (all seated). *Size of Pitch:* 105m × 65m.
Chairman: Ross McArthur. *Vice-Chairman:* Billy Braisby.
Manager: Allan Johnston. *Assistant Manager:* Sandy Clark. *Head Coach:* John Potter.
Club Nickname: 'The Pars'.
Previous Grounds: None.
Record Attendance: 27,816 v Celtic, Division I, 30 April 1968.
Record Transfer Fee received: £650,000 for Jackie McNamara to Celtic (October 1995).
Record Transfer Fee paid: £540,000 for Istvan Kozma from Bordeaux (September 1989).
Record Victory: 11-2 v Stenhousemuir, Division II, 27 September 1930.
Record Defeat: 1-13 v St. Bernard's, Scottish Cup, 1st rd; 15 September 1883.
Most Capped Player: Colin Miller 16 (61), Canada.
Most League Appearances: 497: Norrie McCathie, 1981-96.
Most League Goals in Season (Individual): 53: Bobby Skinner, Division II, 1925-26.
Most Goals Overall (Individual): 212: Charles Dickson, 1954-64.

DUNFERMLINE ATHLETIC – SPFL LADBROKES CHAMPIONSHIP 2017–18 LEAGUE RECORD

Match No.	Date		Venue	Opponents	Result	H/T Score	Lg Pos.	Goalscorers	Atten- dance
1	Aug	5	A	Livingston	D 1-1	0-1	4	Higginbotham (pen) [63]	2301
2		12	H	Inverness CT	W 5-1	3-1	2	Smith [2], Ashcroft [14], Cardle 2 [41, 90], Hopkirk [67]	4391
3		19	A	Falkirk	W 3-1	2-0	2	McManus [5], Cardle 2 [11, 90]	5751
4		26	A	Dumbarton	W 4-0	2-0	1	Cardle [5], Higginbotham [28], Clark [87], Ryan [90]	1028
5	Sept	9	A	Greenock Morton	L 2-3	2-0	2	Cardle [9], Higginbotham (pen) [33]	1918
6		16	H	St Mirren	W 3-0	1-0	1	McManus [20], Hopkirk [45], Morris [56]	6628
7		23	A	Brechin C	W 3-0	1-0	1	Ashcroft [28], McManus [55], Clark [70]	1214
8		30	H	Dundee U	L 1-3	0-2	3	Smith [77]	7585
9	Oct	14	A	Queen of the South	D 0-0	0-0	3		1834
10		21	H	Livingston	W 3-1	3-0	2	Higginbotham 2 [2, 38], Aird [30]	5059
11		28	A	Inverness CT	L 0-1	0-1	3		2948
12	Nov	4	A	Falkirk	D 1-1	1-0	4	Higginbotham (pen) [28]	5465
13		21	H	Greenock Morton	D 1-1	1-1	3	Ryan [21]	4816
14		25	H	Dumbarton	D 2-2	0-0	4	Morris [55], Clark [88]	4505
15	Dec	2	A	Dundee U	L 1-2	0-2	4	McManus (pen) [75]	5790
16		9	H	Queen of the South	L 2-5	0-2	4	Clark [47], McManus [85]	4694
17		16	A	St Mirren	L 0-1	0-1	3		3665
18		23	H	Brechin C	W 2-1	1-0	4	McManus [22], Paton [49]	4595
19	Jan	2	H	Falkirk	W 2-0	1-0	3	Clark [16], McManus [51]	7140
20		6	A	Dumbarton	W 1-0	1-0	3	Cardle [24]	1086
21		13	H	Dundee U	D 0-0	0-0	3		7139
22		26	H	St Mirren	L 1-2	0-1	5	Clark [49]	5479
23	Feb	3	A	Greenock Morton	L 1-2	1-1	4	Beadling [23]	1588
24		10	A	Livingston	D 0-0	0-0	5		1579
25		24	A	Queen of the South	D 0-0	0-0	6		1429
26	Mar	10	A	St Mirren	L 0-2	0-0	5		4240
27		13	H	Inverness CT	W 1-0	1-0	5	Craigen [6]	2249
28		17	H	Greenock Morton	D 0-0	0-0	5		4613
29		20	A	Brechin C	W 3-0	2-0	5	Clark 3 [8, 9, 54]	611
30		24	A	Dundee U	D 1-1	0-0	4	Clark [52]	5830
31		31	H	Queen of the South	W 3-1	2-0	3	Clark 3 [33, 38, 90]	4762
32	Apr	3	A	Livingston	W 1-0	1-0	3	Ashcroft [11]	4572
33		7	A	Falkirk	W 2-1	1-0	3	Higginbotham [24], Aird [48]	5784
34		14	H	Brechin C	W 4-0	2-0	4	Ashcroft [2], Aird [25], Ryan [72], Higginbotham (pen) [87]	4898
35		21	A	Inverness CT	D 2-2	1-1	4	Ryan [13], Clark [90]	3316
36		28	H	Dumbarton	W 4-0	3-0	4	Higginbotham 2 [18, 25], Aird [45], Williamson [65]	5506

Final League Position: 4

Honours
League Champions: First Division 1988-89, 1995-96, 2010-11; Division II 1925-26; Second Division 1985-86; League One 2015-16.
Runners-up: First Division 1986-87, 1993-94, 1994-95, 1999-2000; Division II 1912-13, 1933-34, 1954-55, 1957-58, 1972-73; Second Division 1978-79; League One 2013-14.
Scottish Cup Winners: 1961, 1968; *Runners-up:* 1965, 2004, 2007.
League Cup Runners-up: 1949-50, 1991-92, 2005-06.
League Challenge Cup Runners-up: 2007-08.

European: *Cup Winners' Cup:* 14 matches (1961-62, 1968-69 semi-finals). *UEFA Cup:* 32 matches (*Fairs Cup:* 1962-63, 1964-65, 1965-66, 1966-67, 1969-70. *UEFA Cup:* 2004-05, 2007-08).

Club colours: Shirt: Black and white stripes. Shorts: Black. Socks: White with black trim.

Goalscorers: *League (60):* Clark 14, Higginbotham 10 (4 pens), Cardle 7, McManus 7 (1 pen), Aird 4, Ashcroft 4, Ryan 4, Hopkirk 2, Morris 2, Smith 2, Beadling 1, Craigen 1, Paton 1, Williamson 1.
William Hill Scottish FA Cup (5): McManus 2, Clark 1, Ryan 1, Talbot 1.
Betfred Scottish League Cup (13): Clark 4, Cardle 3, McManus 3, Paton 1, Smith 1, own goal 1.
Irn-Bru Scottish League Challenge Cup (5): Ryan 3, Clark 2.
Play-Offs (1): McManus 1.

Murdoch S 18	Williamson R 36	Mvoto J 11 + 2	Ashcroft L 33	Martin L 13 + 3	Higginbotham K 26 + 6	Wedderburn N 23 + 4	Paton M 8 + 3	Smith C 8 + 5	Aird F 11 + 10	Hopkirk D 3 + 5	Shiels D 16 + 3	Morris C 28 + 2	Talbot J 25 + 1	Lochhead S — +1	Splaine A 3 + 4	McManus D 28 + 4	Ryan A 5 + 14	Clark N 31 + 1	Robinson L 18	Craigen J 14 + 1	Beadling T 11	Vincent J 10	Armstrong D 1 + 5		Match No.
1	2	3	4	5	6	7	8	9	10²	11¹	12	13													1
1	2		4	12	6	8²		9	11		10¹	7	3	5²	13	14									2
1	2		4		6³	8		9	11²	14	12	7	3	5			10¹	13							3
1	2		4		6	8		9¹	11²		12	7	3	5			10³	13	14						4
1	2		4	12	6	8		9	13		14	7	3	5²			10¹		11²						5
1	2		4		6²	8		9¹			12	7	3	5		13	10		11						6
1	2		4		6	8			12			9¹	7³	3	5		13	10³	14	11					7
1	2		4		6	8			12			9¹	7³	3	5		13	10²	14	11					8
1	2		4		6	8			10				3	5		7	9¹	12	11						9
1	2		3		6	8		12	11²	9¹			4	5		7		13	10						10
1	2		3		6	8		12	11³	9¹		14	4	5		7³	13		10						11
1	2	12	4		6⁸	8			9²		13		7	3	5		10⁸		11¹						12
1	2		4			8	12	9¹	13	6		7	3	5			11	10²							13
1	2		4		6³	8	12	13	11	9¹		7³	3	5		14		10							14
1	2		4	7	8¹	6	10	9			12		3	5		11									15
1	2		4	7²	13	8¹	6	9		14		12	3	5³			10		11						16
1	2		4		7¹	6	12	9²		13		8	3	5			10		11						17
1	2		4		12	8	6	9¹		13		7³	3	5			10²	14	11						18
	2	3	4		12	8	6	9¹				7		5			10²	13	11	1					19
	2	3	4		14	8	6	9	12			7¹		5			10³	13	11²	1					20
	2	4			13	8	6¹	9³		12		7	3	5			10	14	11²	1					21
	2	3			6²	8	9¹			13		7²	4	5			10	14	11	1	12				22
	2	3				8		9				4	5			10		11	1	6	7				23
	2	3	4										5			10	8¹	11	1	6	7	9	12		24
	2	3	4		12			13				5				11	10²	9	1	6¹	7	8			25
	2	3	4	13			12				14	5⁸				10¹		11	1	9²	7	8	6³		26
	2		4	5	6							3				10		11	1	9	7	8			27
	2		4	5	6			13				3				10		11²	1	9¹	7	8	12		28
	2		4	5	6			14				3				10³	13	11²	1	9	7	8¹	12		29
	2		4	5	6	12						3				10		11	1	9¹	7	8			30
	2		4	5	6¹	13			9²			3				10		11	1	8	7		12		31
	2		4	5	6	12			9²			3				10¹	13	11	1	8	7			32
	2	13	4	5	6²	12		14	9¹			3				10		11	1	8	7³				33
	2	3	4	5	6			14	9							10³	12	11²	1	8		7¹	13		34
	2	4	3	5	6³			12	9¹		14					13	11	10	1	8²	7				35
	2		4¹	5	6²			13	9			3	12			14	11	10³	1	8	7				36

EAST FIFE

Year Formed: 1903. *Ground & Address:* Bayview Stadium, Harbour View, Methil, Fife KY8 3RW. *Telephone:* 01333 426323. *Fax:* 01333 426376. *E-mail:* office@eastfifefc.info. *Website:* www.eastfifefc.info
Ground Capacity: 1,992. *Size of Pitch:* 105m × 65m.
Chairman: Jim Stevenson. *Vice-Chairman:* David Marshall.
Manager: Darren Young. *Assistant Manager:* Tony McMinn.
Club Nickname: 'The Fifers'.
Previous Ground: Bayview Park.
Record Attendance: 22,515 v Raith Rovers, Division I, 2 January 1950 (Bayview Park); 4,700 v Rangers, League One, 26 October 2013 (Bayview Stadium).
Record Transfer Fee received: £150,000 for Paul Hunter from Hull C (March 1990).
Record Transfer Fee paid: £70,000 for John Sludden from Kilmarnock (July 1991).
Record Victory: 13-2 v Edinburgh C, Division II, 11 December 1937.
Record Defeat: 0-9 v Hearts, Division I, 5 October 1957.
Most Capped Player: George Aitken, 5 (8), Scotland.
Most League Appearances: 517: David Clarke, 1968-86.
Most League Goals in Season (Individual): 41: Jock Wood, Division II; 1926-27 and Henry Morris, Division II, 1947-48.
Most Goals Overall (Individual): 225: Phil Weir, 1922-35.

EAST FIFE – SPFL LADBROKES LEAGUE ONE 2017–18 LEAGUE RECORD

Match No.	Date	Venue	Opponents	Result		H/T Score	Lg Pos.	Goalscorers	Attendance
1	Aug 5	A	Stranraer	L	0-1	0-0	8		409
2	12	H	Alloa Ath	W	1-0	0-0	4	Hurst, G 56	589
3	19	A	Arbroath	W	3-2	3-1	3	O'Brien (og) 3, Flanagan 26, Duggan 39	808
4	26	H	Raith R	L	0-5	0-3	6		1850
5	Sept 9	H	Queen's Park	L	0-1	0-0	8		496
6	16	A	Airdrieonians	W	1-0	0-0	6	Docherty (pen) 45	783
7	23	H	Forfar Ath	W	3-0	2-0	5	Duggan 4, Docherty 2 (2 pens) 21, 62	519
8	30	A	Ayr U	L	0-3	0-1	5		1382
9	Oct 14	H	Albion R	W	5-4	2-1	4	Duggan 4, Docherty (pen) 42, Hurst, G 2 80, 90, Linton 90	502
10	21	A	Alloa Ath	L	1-4	1-2	5	Wilkie 8	556
11	28	H	Arbroath	W	3-1	0-1	3	Duggan 2 59, 67, Lamont 67	565
12	Nov 4	A	Raith R	L	0-1	0-1	4		2656
13	11	A	Forfar Ath	L	0-2	0-0	5		647
14	25	H	Airdrieonians	W	6-1	3-1	5	Wilkie 2 25, 51, Duggan 29, Lamont 39, Kane 58, Hurst, G 79	619
15	Dec 2	A	Queen's Park	L	1-2	1-1	5	Duggan 16	506
16	9	H	Stranraer	D	1-1	1-0	5	Duggan 23	521
17	16	H	Ayr U	L	1-4	1-0	6	Duggan 36	637
18	23	A	Albion R	L	2-3	2-2	7	Dunsmore 6, Hurst, G 27	248
19	30	A	Arbroath	D	1-1	0-0	6	Docherty (pen) 90	649
20	Jan 2	H	Raith R	L	2-3	1-2	7	Wilkie 20, Linton 56	1795
21	6	A	Airdrieonians	D	0-0	0-0	7		734
22	13	H	Alloa Ath	W	2-1	1-0	6	Lamont 42, Docherty 75	492
23	27	H	Forfar Ath	L	1-2	1-1	6	Docherty (pen) 45	556
24	Feb 3	A	Stranraer	W	2-0	0-0	6	Linton (pen) 58, Lamont 61	383
25	10	H	Queen's Park	L	0-2	0-1	6		558
26	17	A	Ayr U	L	0-3	0-1	7		1170
27	24	H	Albion R	W	2-0	2-0	6	Dunsmore 13, Duggan 23	390
28	Mar 10	A	Airdrieonians	W	2-1	1-1	6	Duggan 13, Wilkie 90	473
29	13	A	Alloa Ath	W	2-1	0-0	5	Smith 54, Duggan 62	402
30	24	A	Forfar Ath	L	0-2	0-1	6		607
31	27	A	Raith R	L	0-2	0-1	6		1485
32	31	H	Ayr U	L	2-3	1-1	6	Duggan 2 22, 53	759
33	Apr 7	A	Queen's Park	W	3-2	2-1	6	McManus 8, Dunsmore 16, Slattery 75	458
34	14	H	Arbroath	L	0-5	0-2	6		554
35	21	A	Albion R	L	0-1	0-1	6		262
36	28	H	Stranraer	L	2-3	0-1	6	Watson 58, Page 79	426

Final League Position: 6

Honours
League Champions: Division II 1947-48; Third Division 2007-08; League Two 2015-16.
Runners-up: Division II 1929-30, 1970-71;. Second Division 1983-84, 1995-96; Third Division 2002-03.
Scottish Cup Winners: 1938; *Runners-up:* 1927, 1950.
League Cup Winners: 1947-48, 1949-50, 1953-54.

Club colours: Shirt: Gold and black stripes. Shorts: White. Socks: Black.

Goalscorers: *League (49):* Duggan 14, Docherty 7 (6 pens), Hurst G 5, Wilkie 5, Lamont 4, Dunsmore 3, Linton 3 (1 pen), Flanagan 1, Kane 1, McManus 1, Page 1, Slattery 1, Smith 1, Watson 1, own goal 1.
William Hill Scottish FA Cup (2): Page 1, Smith 1.
Betfred Scottish League Cup (3): Docherty 1 (1 pen), Duggan 1, Willis 1.
Irn-Bru Scottish League Challenge Cup (0).

Goodfellow R 14	Dunsmore A 32 + 1	Watson C 19 + 3	Gordon B 5	Docherty M 23	Wilson K 2 + 6	Millar K 33	Slattery P 17 + 7	Flanagan N 12 + 5	Willis P 8 + 2	Duggan C 36	Hurst G 12 + 6	Wilkie K 16 + 9	Linton S 20 + 6	Lamont M 17 + 4	Hurst M 14	Page J 28 + 1	Reilly B 2 + 5	Kane C 13 + 6	Mutch R — + 8	Smith K 9 + 12	Piggott J 10	Thomson C 8	McManus C 11	Livingstone A 9	Jones R 2 + 8	Knox M 5 + 5	Allardice S 11	MacKenzie B 8	Match No.
1	2	3	4	5	6^1	7	8^2	9	10	11	12	13																	1
1	2	3	4	5	13	6	7	8^3	10	11^1	9^2	12	14																2
1	2	3	4	5	14	7	12	8^1	6	10^3	11^2	9	13																3
1	2	3	4	5		7	12	8^2	6^3	10^1	11	9	13	14															4
	2	3^1	4	5	13			9	10^2	11^3	8	6	7	12	1	14													5
	2		4			9	7	12	10^2	11^3	8	6^1	5		1	3	13	14											6
	2	3				9^1	12	7	8	6	11	10^2	5^3		1	4	13	14											7
	2	3				9^1	13	8	10	6	11^3	12	5^2		1	4^1		14	7										8
	2	3^2				8	6	7	9	10^1	11	12	5		1	4			13										9
	2					4	12	8	5	6^1	7	11^2	9^3	10	1	14	13	3											10
	2					5	8	9	10^3	11^2	7^1	6^1			1	4	13	14	12	3									11
	2					9	7	5	14	10^1	11	6^1			1	4		8^2	13	12	3								12
	2					5^2	7	6	8^1	13	11	10			1	4		9^3	14	12	3								13
	2	14				7^3	6	12	11	13	9^2	8			1	4	3	10^1	5										14
	2	10				8^3	14	11	13	7	12	6^1			1	4	3^2	9	5										15
	2					7	6	12	11	13	9^3	5	8^1		1	4		14	10^2	3									16
	2					5	6	11	12	9	7	8			1	3		10^1	4										17
	2^3					5	7	10	8	11^1	6	9^2			1	3	13	12	14	4									18
1						5	7	13	10	11^1	12	9	6^2			4	3	14	8^3	2									19
1	2					7^2	6	14	11	9^3	10	5	8^1			4	3	13	12										20
1	2					6	7	12	9	11	10^1	5	8^2			4	3	13											21
1	2					7	6		10	11	9^1	5	8			4	3				12								22
1	2					6		7^1		11	9	5	10			4	3				12	8							23
1	2	13					8	14	11^2		5	6^1				4	3						10^3	7	9	12			24
1	2	14						7^2	10		5	6^3				4	3						11	8	9^1	12	13		25
1	2	3					9	6		11^3	12	5				4^2							13	8	10^1	14	7		26
6^1	2						9	7		11^2	12	5				4							13	10	14	8^3	3	1	27
6	2						8^3	9^2		10	14	5	12			4							13	7	11^1		3	1	28
13	2^2						7	14		10		6^1				4						11^3	5	8	9	12	3	1	29
	2						7^3			11	12	5	9			4						10^1	6^2	8	13	14	3	1	30
	2						8	5^2		11	13	12				4						6^1	7	10	14	9^1	3	1	31
6	2^1						8			11	10^2	5				4						7	9	13	12	3	1	32
6	2						8	12		11		9^1				4^2			14			13	10	7	5^1	3	1	33
	2						8	9		11		12				4^1						6^1	10	7^2	5	13	3	1	34
1	2						5	8		9		10				3							7^1	6	11	12	4		35
1	6	2					7	8		10	13					4			12				9	5^1	11^2		3		36

EDINBURGH CITY

Year formed: 1928 (disbanded 1955, reformed from Postal United in 1986).
Ground & Address: Ainslie Park Stadium, 94 Pilton Drive, Edinburgh EH5 2HF (for 3 seasons from 2017-18 whilst Meadowbank Stadium is redeveloped). *Telephone:* 0845 463 1932.
E-mail: admin@edinburghcityfc.com *Website:* edinburghcityfc.com
Ground Capacity: 3,127 (seated 504). *Size of Pitch:* 96m × 66m
Chairman: Jim Brown. *Secretary:* Gavin Kennedy.
Manager: James McDonaugh. *Coach:* Colin Jack.
Previous names: Postal United.
Club Nickname: 'The Citizens'.
Previous Grounds: City Park 1928-55; Fernieside 1986-95; Meadowbank Stadium 1996-2017.
Record victory: 5-0 v King's Park, Division II (1935-36); 6-1 and 7-2 v Brechin City, Division II (1937-38).
Record defeat: 1-11 v Rangers, Scottish Cup, 19 January 1929.
Most League Appearances: 58: Marc Laird, 2016-18.
Most League Goals in Season (Individual): 9: Dougie Gair, League Two, 2016-17.
Most Goals Overall (Individual): 9: Dougie Gair, 2016-17.

EDINBURGH CITY – SPFL LADBROKES LEAGUE TWO 2017–18 LEAGUE RECORD

Match No.	Date	Venue	Opponents	Result	H/T Score	Lg Pos.	Goalscorers	Attendance
1	Aug 5	H	Montrose	L 1-3	0-2	10	Allan [83]	341
2	12	A	Cowdenbeath	L 0-1	0-1	10		341
3	19	A	Stirling Alb	L 0-2	0-2	10		610
4	26	H	Elgin C	L 0-3	0-2	10		350
5	Sept 9	H	Berwick R	W 1-0	1-0	10	Grimes [2]	308
6	16	A	Clyde	W 3-2	1-1	9	Belmokhtar 2 [22, 64], Beattie [90]	466
7	23	H	Peterhead	L 0-3	0-1	9		356
8	30	A	Stenhousemuir	L 0-3	0-0	9		412
9	Oct 21	H	Annan Ath	L 0-1	0-0	9		249
10	28	A	Montrose	L 0-1	0-0	9		446
11	Nov 4	H	Stirling Alb	L 1-2	1-1	9	Shepherd [18]	421
12	11	A	Berwick R	D 1-1	0-0	9	Garcia Tena [47]	467
13	25	H	Cowdenbeath	D 0-0	0-0	9		346
14	Dec 2	A	Peterhead	L 0-3	0-0	9		539
15	9	A	Elgin C	D 1-1	0-0	9	El Alagui [51]	565
16	16	H	Stenhousemuir	L 1-2	1-2	9	Laird [35]	271
17	23	A	Annan Ath	L 1-2	1-1	9	El Alagui [29]	304
18	Jan 2	H	Berwick R	W 3-0	1-0	9	Grimes [30], Shepherd 2 [76, 80]	446
19	6	A	Cowdenbeath	W 2-0	0-0	8	Shepherd [38], Scullion [42]	365
20	13	H	Montrose	L 0-2	0-2	8		464
21	27	H	Annan Ath	W 3-2	2-0	9	Grimes 2 [14, 33], Shepherd [51]	259
22	Feb 3	A	Clyde	L 2-3	1-2	9	Shepherd [42], Walker (pen) [51]	421
23	10	H	Peterhead	D 0-0	0-0	9		301
24	17	A	Stenhousemuir	L 0-1	0-1	9		385
25	24	H	Elgin C	W 4-0	2-0	9	Beattie [16], Walker [41], Rodger [48], El Alagui [51]	223
26	Mar 10	A	Annan Ath	W 3-2	0-0	9	Shepherd [57], Garcia Tena [63], Beattie [65]	248
27	13	H	Cowdenbeath	D 1-1	0-0	8	Taylor [71]	256
28	17	H	Stirling Alb	D 2-2	1-1	8	Shepherd [24], Rodger [78]	312
29	20	A	Clyde	L 0-3	0-2	8		310
30	24	A	Berwick R	D 1-1	0-0	8	Grimes [65]	516
31	27	A	Stirling Alb	D 2-2	1-1	8	Taylor [11], El Alagui [70]	433
32	31	A	Montrose	L 0-3	0-2	8		583
33	Apr 7	H	Stenhousemuir	L 1-4	0-2	8	Blues [71]	233
34	14	A	Elgin C	D 1-1	0-1	8	Rodger [49]	699
35	21	H	Clyde	L 1-3	0-1	9	Beattie (pen) [71]	408
36	28	A	Peterhead	L 1-2	0-1	9	Rodger [82]	1049

Final League Position: 9

Honours
League Champions: Scottish Lowland League Champions: 2014-15.
Promoted via play-offs: 2015-16 (to League Two).

Club colours: Shirt: White. Shorts: Black. Socks: White.

Goalscorers: *League (37):* Shepherd 8, Grimes 5, Beattie 4 (1 pen), El Alagui 4, Rodger 4, Belmokhtar 2, Garcia Tena 2, Taylor 2, Walker 2 (1 pen), Allan 1, Blues 1, Laird 1, Scullion 1.
William Hill Scottish FA Cup (0).
Betfred Scottish League Cup (3): Grimes 3.
Irn-Bru Scottish League Challenge Cup (0).

Antell C 35	Hall C 8+7	Veriaque D 1	Harrison S 6+3	Mackie S 4+2	Walker J 26+1	Laird M 34	Thomson C 30+2	Allan L 3+8	Grimes A 24+5	Malin G 4+8	Smith I 3+5	Olanrewaju M —+5	Bloch Jorgensen S —+1	Caddow J 10+3	Rodger G 19+1	Morrison S 20+1	Beattie C 20+4	Dunn J 18+3	Morton F 1	Blake A 6+1	Belmokhtar A 3+2	Garcia Tena J 21	McKee C 8+3	El Alagui F 19+4	Shepherd S 19+1	Henderson L 8	Scullion P 15+2	Watson K —+5	Donnelly-Kay N —+2	Blues C 14+2	Taylor G 10+4	Paton F —+1	McLean L 4+3	Shiels M 3	Kennedy L —+1	Barfoot M —+1	Smith J —+1	Match No.
1	2^2	3	$4^\bullet$	5	6	7	8	9	10^1	11^1	12	13	14																									1
1					5	7^2	8	6	13	11	12	9		2^1	3	4	10																					2
1				6^2	7	5	14	11		8^1	12	13		9	2^3	4	3	10																				3
1			13	10		7	$6^\bullet$	14	9^2		11^3	12		5^1	4	2	3	8																				4
	14				12		7		11^2	8^3	9^1	13		2	4	3	10	5	1	6																		5
1					5		8	9	10^2	13	14			2	4	3	12	7			6^3	11^1																6
1						7	8	13	11	14	12			2	5	4	6^2					9^3	10^1	3														7
1	2^2				5		9	6^2	7	13	10			12		3		8^1				14	11	4														8
1	8^1					7	10	6	13	9	14					4	2	11^3					5^2	3	12													9
1		14				6	9	7	12	10^2						2	4	11^1				8	13	3^3	5													10
1		3	13			7^3	6^1	8			12					4^2	2					5	14		9	10	11											11
1	2					7	8	5		12	6^1						3						4		9	10	11											12
1	2^1					8	7	6		12						5	3						4	11	10	9												13
1						8	7	6	5^3	13	12				2		3						$4^\bullet$	10	11^1	9												14
1			13			7	6^2	5	9^1	12					2		4	3					10	11	8													15
1						6	7	5	12	9	13		14		2		4						3^2	10^1	11^3	8												16
1			14			7	8	2	6^3	9^2	12				3		4	13					10	11^1	5													17
1				5^3	12	6	7			9^2							3					2	8	10	11^1			4	13	14								18
1				5^2	12	6	7					14					3^1					2	11	10	8			4		13								19
1				5^1	2^3	6	8	14		7^2												4		$10^\bullet$	11	9	3			13	12							20
1					2	7^2	6	5		10^3						13								4^1	11	9	3	14		8	12							21
1						7	6	9		10^1						2	5							4	12	11	3			8								22
1			13			7^2	6	5		10^1		14					2^1					3		4						8	11^3							23
1						7	8	12								2^1	3	9							5	11	10			4	6							24
1						7	6	5								4	2	9^1								12	11	3	14		$8^\bullet$		10^3	13				25
1						7		2^2								5	4	6				3	13		11	10			12	8	9^1							26
1						7^2	6	5								2	3	9				4	10^1		11		13			8	12							27
1			9^1			7^2	6	5								4	13	12				3	14	11^3	2					8	10							28
1						7^3	6	5			14					4	3	9^1				2		11	10^2		13			8	12							29
1						7	2	10						12		4^2	9							11	5			3		8	6^1		13					30
1			12			7		9^3								4	5					2	8^1		11		3	14		6	10^2		13					31
1						6		5		8						4	13					2		11^2	12		3			7	9		10					32
1				4		6		12								11	9^1					8		14	2^3		3			7	13		10^2	5				33
1			12			7		5	8^2							2	3	14							11^3		4			6	10^1		13	9				34
1			12			6		5		7^2						4	2	3				8			13		11				10^1		14					35
1	5^2					6										8	2	7				4^1			11		3			9	10^3				12	13	14	36

ELGIN CITY

Year Formed: 1893. *Ground and Address:* Borough Briggs, Borough Briggs Road, Elgin IV30 1AP.
Telephone: 01343 551114. *Fax:* 01343 547921. *E-mail:* office@elgincity.com *Website:* www.elgincity.net
Ground Capacity: 3,927 (seated: 478). *Size of pitch:* 102m × 68m.
Chairman: Graham Tatters. *Secretary:* Kate Taylor.
Manager: Gavin Price. *Assistant Manager:* Keith Gibson.
Previous names: 1900-03 Elgin City United.
Club Nicknames: 'City', 'The Black & Whites'.
Previous Grounds: Association Park 1893-95; Milnfield Park 1895-1909; Station Park 1909-19; Cooper Park 1919-21.
Record Attendance: 12,608 v Arbroath, Scottish Cup, 17 February 1968.
Record Transfer Fee received: £32,000 for Michael Teasdale to Dundee (January 1994).
Record Transfer Fee paid: £10,000 for Russell McBride from Fraserburgh (July 2001).
Record Victory: 18-1 v Brora Rangers, North of Scotland Cup, 6 February 1960.
Record Defeat: 1-14 v Hearts, Scottish Cup, 4 February 1939.
Most League Appearances: 306: Mark Nicholson, 2007-17.
Most League Goals in Season (Individual): 21: Craig Gunn, 2015-16.
Most Goals Overall (Individual): 128: Craig Gunn, 2009-17.

ELGIN CITY – SPFL LADBROKES LEAGUE TWO 2017–18 LEAGUE RECORD

Match No.	Date		Venue	Opponents	Result	H/T Score	Lg Pos.	Goalscorers	Attendance
1	Aug	5	H	Cowdenbeath	D 1-1	1-1	6	Cooper [26]	584
2		12	A	Peterhead	L 0-3	0-2	8		691
3		19	H	Clyde	W 3-2	1-2	6	Reid [39], McLeish [67], Cameron (pen) [90]	559
4		26	A	Edinburgh C	W 3-0	2-0	3	Strapp [20], Cameron [36], Allan [82]	350
5	Sept	9	H	Annan Ath	L 0-1	0-1	5		546
6		16	A	Berwick R	L 2-3	1-0	7	Anderson 2 [4, 49]	492
7		23	H	Montrose	W 3-0	1-0	5	Anderson [19], Cameron (pen) [50], Reid [86]	549
8		30	A	Stirling Alb	D 2-2	0-2	6	McLeish [68], Allan [74]	691
9	Oct	21	H	Stenhousemuir	W 2-0	0-0	5	Cameron (pen) [56], Reilly [75]	654
10		28	A	Clyde	W 4-2	1-1	5	Anderson [36], McLeish [58], McHardy [73], Allan [89]	402
11	Nov	4	A	Peterhead	L 0-2	0-1	5		883
12		11	A	Cowdenbeath	W 3-1	2-0	5	Cameron 2 (1 pen) [8 (pl. 41)], Reilly [66]	326
13		25	H	Berwick R	W 5-1	1-0	3	Anderson 2 [35, 66], McHardy [48], Cameron [64], Byrne [88]	508
14	Dec	2	A	Annan Ath	L 0-2	0-1	4		322
15		9	H	Edinburgh C	D 1-1	0-0	4	Allan [89]	565
16		16	A	Montrose	L 0-3	0-1	6		559
17		23	A	Stenhousemuir	L 1-4	0-2	6	Bronsky [81]	373
18	Jan	2	A	Peterhead	L 0-7	0-1	6		779
19		6	H	Clyde	W 2-1	1-0	6	Cameron [18], Dodd [87]	566
20		13	A	Cowdenbeath	W 1-0	0-0	6	Eadie [85]	609
21		27	H	Stenhousemuir	W 2-0	1-0	4	McLeish [33], Reilly (pen) [90]	553
22	Feb	3	A	Stirling Alb	L 1-3	0-2	5	Allan [83]	544
23		10	A	Annan Ath	W 2-1	1-1	5	Reilly [11], McDonald [73]	573
24		17	H	Montrose	D 2-2	1-1	5	Cameron [9], McLeish [57]	700
25		24	A	Edinburgh C	L 0-4	0-2	5		223
26	Mar	10	H	Berwick R	W 3-0	2-0	5	Reilly [20], Bronsky [30], McHardy [78]	531
27		13	A	Clyde	L 0-1	0-0	5		423
28		17	A	Cowdenbeath	L 1-3	0-2	5	Sutherland, S [61]	242
29		20	H	Stirling Alb	L 0-2	0-0	5		393
30		24	A	Stenhousemuir	W 2-0	1-0	5	McLeish [24], McHardy [56]	422
31		27	A	Berwick R	D 2-2	1-0	6	Bronsky [40], McHardy [75]	323
32		31	H	Stirling Alb	W 3-0	3-0	6	Flanagan [7], Cameron [18], Sutherland, S [24]	676
33	Apr	7	A	Annan Ath	L 1-4	0-1	5	Sutherland, S [68]	282
34		14	H	Edinburgh C	D 1-1	1-0	6	Sutherland, S [3]	699
35		21	H	Peterhead	L 0-1	0-0	6		786
36		28	A	Montrose	D 1-1	1-0	6	Sutherland, S [45]	2380

Final League Position: 6

Honours
League Runners-up: League Two 2015-16.
Scottish Cup: Quarter-finals 1968.
Highland League Champions: winners 15 times.

Club colours: Shirt: Black and white stripes. Shorts: Black. Socks: White.

Goalscorers: *League (54):* Cameron 10 (4 pens), Anderson 6, McLeish 6, Allan 5, McHardy 5, Reilly 5 (1 pen), Sutherland S 5, Bronsky 3, Reid 2, Byrne 1, Cooper 1, Dodd 1, Eadie 1, Flanagan 1, McDonald 1, Strapp 1.
William Hill Scottish FA Cup (0).
Betfred Scottish League Cup (2): Reilly 2.
Irn-Bru Scottish League Challenge Cup (4): Allan 1, Bronsky 1, Dodd 1, McLeish 1.

Waters M 20 + 2	Cooper M 20	Eadie C 29	Bronsky S 25 + 1	McHardy D 28 + 6	Dodd C 11 + 10	Cameron B 35	McGovern J 36	Reid J 5 + 6	Reilly T 33	Allan J 25 + 9	McLeish C 31 + 4	Sutherland A 10 + 10	Ferguson C 1 + 9	McKinnon R 1	Trialist A — + 1	Smith S 15 + 10	Strapp L 11 + 2	Anderson B 13 + 1	Dingwall T 3	Byrne D 2 + 19	Ross I 2	Elbouzedi Z 2 + 1	McDonald A 14 + 2	Long B 14	McLear L — + 1	Trialist B — + 1	Sutherland S 7 + 2	Whitehead A — + 1	Flanagan N 3	Match No.
1	2	3	4	5	6	7	8	9¹	10³	11¹	12	13	14																	1
1		2	4	3	9	7	6	8¹	11	10¹	12			5²	13	14														2
1		2	3	4	9³	10	7	6¹	8	13	11²	12	14				5													3
1		2	3	4	6²	11	7	9¹	8	13	10³	12				14	5													4
1		2	3	4	9²	10	7	6²	8	12	11¹		14			5	13													5
1	2		3	4	9³	6	7	12	8	13	10²		14			5	11³													6
1	9²	4	2	3	12	8	7¹	14	6	13	10					5	11³													7
1	2³	3	4	6	14	5	7²	13	8	12	10					9		11¹												8
1	2	3	4	12	6	7	14	8	13	10²	11¹					5		9³												9
1	2	3	4		6	7	13	8³	12	10²	11¹		14			5		9												10
1		3		4	2	6	7	13	8¹	12	10²	11³	14			5		9												11
1		3	4		2	6²	7		8		10	13	14		12	5¹		9³		11										12
1		2	3	4	12	6	7		8	5	10³						9¹	11¹	14											13
1		2	3	4	12	6	7¹		8	5	10³					14	9¹	11	13											14
1		2	3	4	11²	6	7		8	5	10¹	12						9		13										15
1		2	3	4	12	6	7		8²	5	10¹					14	11³	9		13										16
1	2	4	3			9	8		6	5	12	11³				7¹	14	10²		13										17
13	2		4		3		10	7		8	5	11³	14			9		6¹				1²	12							18
1	2		4			14	13	6	7		5	12	11¹			8							10²		9¹		3			19
1	2	3			12	14	10	7		6	5²		11¹			8							13		9		4			20
	2	3			14	12	8	6	9	5	11¹	10³				7²							13		4		1			21
	2	4			14	9	10	8¹	7	5	11²	12				6³							13		3		1			22
	2	3			14	12³	10	8	7	5	11²	9				6¹							13		4		1			23
	2		3	13		10	8	7		5	11²	9¹	14			6³							12		4		1			24
	2	4¹	13			11	7	8³	5	10	9²	12				6							3	1		14				25
	2		4	9		10	7²	8	5	11³		12				6¹							3	1		13				26
	2	3	9			10	7	8	5	11¹		6²				13							12		4	1				27
12	6		3	4		11	5	8	9	10		7²									2	11			13					28
1	5		3	4		6	7		9	10²	12					8¹			13				2			11				29
	5	6	2	4		10	7²	9	11³		8¹					13							3	1		12	14			30
		2	4	3		6	8	7	5	10		9				12								1		11¹				31
		2¹	3	4		6	7	8	9	10²		13				14		12	1					11			5³			32
		4	3			8	7	6	5²	10¹		13				12							2	1		11		9		33
		2¹	3	4		7	8	6		10		12				5	1									11		9		34
		2²	3	4		6	8	7	5	10	13	9¹				12				1						11				35
		2	4	3¹		6	8	7¹	5	11	14	9¹				13	1	12						10						36

FALKIRK

Year Formed: 1876. *Ground & Address:* The Falkirk Stadium, 4 Stadium Way, Falkirk FK2 9EE. *Telephone:* 01324 624121. *Fax:* 01324 612418. *Email:* post@falkirkfc.co.uk *Website:* www.falkirkfc.co.uk
Ground Capacity: 8,750 (all seated). *Size of Pitch:* 105m × 68m.
Chair: Margaret Lang. *Chief Executive:* Craig Campbell.
Manager: Paul Hartley. *Assistant Manager:* Gordon Young.
Club Nickname: 'The Bairns'.
Previous Grounds: Randyford 1876-81; Blinkbonny Grounds 1881-83; Brockville Park 1883-2003.
Record Attendance: 23,100 v Celtic, Scottish Cup 3rd rd, 21 February 1953.
Record Transfer Fee received: £945,000 for Conor McGrandles to Norwich C (August 2014).
Record Transfer Fee paid: £225,000 to Chelsea for Kevin McAllister (August 1991).
Record Victory: 11-1 v Tillicoultry, Scottish Cup 1st rd, 7 Sep 1889.
Record Defeat: 1-11 v Airdrieonians, Division I, 28 April 1951.
Most Capped Player: Alex Parker, 14 (15), Scotland.
Most League Appearances: 451: Tom Ferguson, 1919-32.
Most League Goals in Season (Individual): 43: Evelyn Morrison, Division I, 1928-29.
Most Goals Overall (Individual): 154: Kenneth Dawson, 1934-51.

FALKIRK – SPFL LADBROKES CHAMPIONSHIP 2017–18 LEAGUE RECORD

Match No.	Date	Venue	Opponents	Result	H/T Score	Lg Pos.	Goalscorers	Attendance
1	Aug 5	A	St Mirren	L 1-3	1-1	9	Austin [2]	4639
2	12	H	Dumbarton	D 1-1	1-1	8	Hippolyte (pen) [24]	3864
3	19	A	Dunfermline Ath	L 1-3	0-2	9	Taiwo [83]	5751
4	26	H	Queen of the South	L 1-4	0-2	9	Gasparotto [89]	4108
5	Sept 9	A	Brechin C	D 1-1	1-0	9	Harris [15]	748
6	16	H	Dundee U	D 0-0	0-0	9		4874
7	23	H	Livingston	L 0-2	0-0	9		4091
8	30	A	Greenock Morton	W 1-0	0-0	9	McKee [62]	1992
9	Oct 14	H	Inverness CT	D 0-0	0-0	9		4107
10	21	H	St Mirren	D 0-0	0-0	9		5080
11	28	A	Queen of the South	L 2-4	0-2	9	McKee [86], McGhee [89]	1716
12	Nov 4	H	Dunfermline Ath	D 1-1	0-1	9	McGhee [64]	5465
13	19	A	Dundee U	L 0-3	0-3	9		5915
14	25	H	Greenock Morton	L 0-3	0-2	9		4361
15	Dec 19	A	Livingston	D 0-0	0-0	9		1287
16	23	A	Dumbarton	D 0-0	0-0	9		874
17	30	H	Queen of the South	W 3-2	3-1	9	Grant [20], Hippolyte [42], Longridge [44]	4285
18	Jan 2	A	Dunfermline Ath	L 0-2	0-1	9		7140
19	6	H	Dundee U	W 6-1	2-1	9	Grant [21], Tumility [41], Longridge 2 [57, 73], Robson [65], Kidd [90]	5326
20	9	A	Inverness CT	L 1-4	0-3	9	Longridge [86]	2014
21	13	A	Greenock Morton	W 1-0	1-0	9	Sibbald [20]	2084
22	27	H	Inverness CT	W 3-1	0-0	8	Muirhead 2 (2 pens) [48, 66], Nelson [87]	4251
23	Feb 3	H	Livingston	L 1-3	0-1	8	Jakubiak [72]	4123
24	6	A	Brechin C	W 3-1	2-0	8	Jakubiak [13], Loy [28], Longridge [71]	4214
25	17	A	Brechin C	W 1-0	0-0	8	Jakubiak [90]	805
26	24	H	Dumbarton	D 0-0	0-0	8		6094
27	Mar 10	H	Greenock Morton	W 3-1	3-0	7	Muirhead (pen) [4], Nelson [18], Jakubiak [30]	4218
28	17	A	Livingston	D 0-0	0-0	7		1319
29	31	H	Brechin C	W 3-0	2-0	7	Muirhead [17], Sibbald [29], Nelson [60]	4422
30	Apr 3	A	Queen of the South	D 2-2	1-0	8	Nelson [5], Longridge [87]	1062
31	7	H	Dunfermline Ath	L 1-2	0-1	8	Muirhead (pen) [79]	5784
32	10	A	Inverness CT	L 0-1	0-0	8		2053
33	14	A	Dundee U	L 0-1	0-1	8		5170
34	17	A	St Mirren	W 2-1	0-0	8	McKee [83], Sibbald [90]	3761
35	21	A	Dumbarton	W 5-2	1-1	8	Jakubiak [19], Longridge [47], Robson [59], Sibbald [70], McKee [86]	942
36	28	H	St Mirren	W 1-0	0-0	8	Blair [85]	5508

Final League Position: 8

Honours
League Champions: Division II 1935-36, 1969-70, 1974-75; First Division 1990-91, 1993-94, 2002-03, 2004-05; Second Division 1979-80;
Runners-up: Division I 1907-08, 1909-10; First Division 1985-86, 1988-89, 1997-98, 1998-99; Division II 1904-05, 1951-52, 1960-61; Championship: 2015-16, 2016-17.
Scottish Cup Winners: 1913, 1957; *Runners-up:* 1997, 2009, 2015.
League Cup Runners-up: 1947-48.
League Challenge Cup Winners: 1993-94, 1997-98, 2004-05, 2011-12.

European: *Europa League:* 2 matches (2009-10).

Club colours: All: Navy blue with white trim.

Goalscorers: *League (45):* Longridge 7, Jakubiak 5, Muirhead 5 (4 pens), McKee 4, Nelson 4, Sibbald 4, Grant 2, Hippolyte 2 (1 pen), McGhee 2, Robson 2, Austin 1, Blair 1, Gasparotto 1, Harris 1, Kidd 1, Loy 1, Taiwo 1, Tumility 1.
William Hill Scottish FA Cup (5): Jakubiak 2, Muirhead 1, Sibbald 1, Tumility 1.
Betfred Scottish League Cup (14): Austin 3, Hippolyte 3, McKee 3, Harris 2, Craigen 1, Miller 1, Muirhead 1 (1 pen).
Irn-Bru Scottish League Challenge Cup (4): Austin 1, Balatoni 1, Craigen 1, Hippolyte 1.

Thomson R 20	Muirhead A 33	Grant P 24 + 3	Watson P 14 + 4	Gallacher T 11	Harris A 10 + 11	Kerr M 15	McKee J 16 + 5	Hippolyte M 8 + 2	Austin N 8 + 6	Loy R 9 + 9	Miller L 3 + 10	Shepherd S — + 2	Gasparotto L 3 + 2	Taiwo T 21 + 1	O'Hara K 5 + 13	Sibbald C 25 + 5	Craigen J 5 + 5	Blues C 2 + 4	McGhee J 32	Balatoni C 8	Mitchell D 1	Dunne C 3 + 2	Longridge L 24 + 1	Tumility R 17	Mutch R 5	Kidd L 10 + 6	Welsh S 7 + 4	Robson T 18	Nelson A 12	Jakubiak A 13 + 2	Hazard C 10 + 1	Blair R 4 + 3	Match No.
1	2ᵃ	3	4	5	6¹	7	8	9	10³	11²	12	13	14																				1
1		3	4	5	12	7²	8	11	10²	9¹	13			2	6	14																	2
1	2³	13	3	5	14	8	7	11²			12ᵃ				4	6	10¹	9ᵃ															3
1	2		4	5	7		9		12	10¹				3	6	11			8²	13													4
1	2			5	6	8			10²	11³	13			9	14	12	7¹	3	4														5
1	5			11	6	3	7¹			9	12			4	13	10²	8	2															6
1	2			5	6³	7		14	11²	12		13		9	10	8		4¹	3														7
	2	4			9	8	6		11²		12	14		7¹	10³		13	5	3	1													8
1	5	3			6³	8	7	11	14					9¹	10²		13	12	2	4													9
1	2	4			6³	7	8	10	11²		13	14			9¹		5	3	12														10
1	2		4	14	8	7	11²	10¹	13	12					9³		5	3	6														11
1	2	3			7	9³	11	14	12	10					13		6	4²	8	5													12
1	2	3		5²	6	7	8⁹		13		11¹					12	9	4	14	10													13
1	2	4		13	8³		6¹	11		12					7	14	3		9²	10	5												14
	2	3		8		7		12	13	11³				6¹	9²	14		4		10	5	1											15
	3	4		8²	14	7		12	13	11¹				6³	9			2		10	5	1											16
	7	4	3	12			10¹							6	8		9			11	5	1	2										17
	2	3¹		12					13					6²	7		4			10	5	1	8	9	11								18
1	2	3	13				14							6³	7		4¹			11	5		8	12	9	10²							19
1	2	3	12				14							13	7		4³			11	5		8	6¹	9	10²							20
1	2	3	12						13					6	7		4			11	5²		8		9	11¹							21
1	2	3												6¹	13	7		4			11	5		8		9	10²	12					22
1	2	3					14		13					8²	7		4			10	5		6¹		9	11³	12						23
	2	4				6³			11					13	14	7¹		3			9	5			8			10²	1	12			24
	2	3²				12			10¹					6	13	7		4			9	5			8			11	1				25
	3					7			12					6¹	8		4			9	2			5	11	10	1						26
	2	3				13								6¹			4			9²	5		12	14	8	11	10	1	7³				27
	2	3	14							12				6			4			8	5³		13		9¹	11²	10	1	7				28
	4	3¹		13	14									7		5²				6			2	12	8	11	10	1	9³				29
	3	4		13										6		5				12			2³	9	7	11	10	1	8¹				30
	2	3¹	4	12										14	6	5				11			13	9²	7	8³	10	1					31
	3	12	4											7²	14	6				8			11	2¹		13	9	5¹	10	1			32
1	2	12	3					14						8		7				4			10	5²		13	6³	9¹		11			33
1²	2³	3	4		6¹		8							7	13	9				5			10			14				11	12		34
	4	3			8									7¹	14	9³				2			11			6²	12	5		10	1	13	35
	4	3	12		6³									13	9			2		11			1		8¹	7²	5		10			14	36

FORFAR ATHLETIC

Year Formed: 1885. *Ground & Address:* Station Park, Carseview Road, Forfar DD8 3BT. *Telephone:* 01307 463576.
Fax: 01307 466956. *E-mail:* info@forfarathletic.co.uk *Website:* www.forfarathletic.co.uk
Ground Capacity: 6,777 (seated: 739). *Size of Pitch:* 103m × 64m.
Chairman: Ross Graham. *Secretary:* David McGregor.
Manager: Jim Weir. *Assistant Manager:* John Baird.
Club Nicknames: 'The Loons', 'The Sky Blues'.
Previous Grounds: None.
Record Attendance: 10,780 v Rangers, Scottish Cup 2nd rd, 2 February 1970.
Record Transfer Fee received: £65,000 for David Bingham to Dunfermline Ath (September 1995).
Record Transfer Fee paid: £50,000 for Ian McPhee from Airdrieonians (1991).
Record Victory: 14-1 v Lindertis, Scottish Cup 1st rd, 1 September 1888.
Record Defeat: 2-12 v King's Park, Division II, 2 January 1930.
Most League Appearances: 463: Ian McPhee, 1978-88 and 1991-98.
Most League Goals in Season (Individual): 46: Dave Kilgour, Division II, 1929-30.
Most Goals Overall: 125: John Clark, 1978-91.

FORFAR ATHLETIC – SPFL LADBROKES LEAGUE ONE 2017–18 LEAGUE RECORD

Match No.	Date	Venue	Opponents	Result		H/T Score	Lg Pos.	Goalscorers	Attendance
1	Aug 5	H	Airdrieonians	W	2-1	1-0	3	Cox [45], Millar [63]	674
2	12	A	Ayr U	L	0-3	0-2	6		1399
3	19	A	Raith R	L	1-3	1-1	9	Millar [18]	1589
4	26	H	Albion R	L	0-2	0-1	9		537
5	Sept 9	A	Alloa Ath	L	1-2	0-0	10	See [52]	511
6	16	H	Arbroath	L	0-5	0-1	10		968
7	23	A	East Fife	L	0-3	0-2	10		519
8	30	H	Stranraer	D	1-1	1-0	10	Peters [4]	474
9	Oct 14	A	Queen's Park	D	1-1	0-0	10	Millar (pen) [66]	517
10	21	H	Ayr U	L	0-5	0-1	10		664
11	28	H	Raith R	D	1-1	0-0	10	Millar (pen) [73]	865
12	Nov 4	A	Albion R	W	4-3	1-1	9	Reid (og) [10], Cox 2 [60, 77], Peters [89]	367
13	11	H	East Fife	W	2-0	0-0	9	Malone [59], Travis [67]	647
14	25	A	Arbroath	L	1-2	1-1	9	Cox [9]	924
15	Dec 2	A	Airdrieonians	L	1-2	0-0	9	Easton [53]	507
16	9	H	Alloa Ath	L	0-2	0-0	9		428
17	16	A	Stranraer	L	0-3	0-0	9		276
18	23	H	Queen's Park	L	0-3	0-2	10		544
19	30	A	Ayr U	W	3-2	0-1	10	Hornby [75], Aitken 2 [83, 88]	1477
20	Jan 2	H	Arbroath	L	0-1	0-1	10		990
21	6	A	Raith R	L	1-2	1-2	10	Peters [21]	1575
22	13	H	Albion R	W	4-2	2-1	10	Millar (pen) [8], Travis 2 [22, 89], Munro [56]	505
23	27	A	East Fife	W	2-1	1-1	9	Easton (pen) [18], Aitken [77]	556
24	Feb 3	H	Airdrieonians	L	0-1	0-1	9		551
25	10	A	Alloa Ath	L	0-1	0-1	10		508
26	17	H	Stranraer	W	5-1	4-0	8	Aitken 2 [2, 6], Dingwall [24], Hurst [29], Easton [72]	428
27	24	A	Queen's Park	D	2-2	1-1	8	Hilson [4], Easton [75]	570
28	Mar 10	A	Arbroath	L	0-2	0-1	9		882
29	13	H	Raith R	W	2-1	0-0	8	Aitken 2 [68, 76]	509
30	17	H	Ayr U	L	0-2	0-1	8		629
31	24	H	East Fife	W	2-0	1-0	8	Easton [9], Hilson [69]	607
32	31	A	Stranraer	L	0-2	0-2	8		290
33	Apr 7	A	Albion R	W	1-0	0-0	8	Peters [90]	269
34	14	H	Alloa Ath	L	0-1	0-1	8		533
35	21	H	Queen's Park	D	1-1	1-0	8	Maciver [13]	580
36	28	A	Airdrieonians	W	2-1	1-0	8	Hurst [11], Millar [80]	730

Final League Position: 8

Honours
League Champions: Second Division 1983-84; Third Division 1994-95; C Division 1948-49.
Runners-up: Third Division 1996-97, 2009-10; League Two 2016-17.
Promoted via play-offs: 2009-10 (to Second Division); 2016-17 (to League One).
Scottish Cup: Semi-finals 1982.
League Cup: Semi-finals 1977-78.
League Challenge Cup: Semi-finals 2004-05.

Club colours: Shirt: Sky blue. Shorts: White. Socks: Sky blue.

Goalscorers: *League (40):* Aitken 7, Millar 6 (3 pens), Easton 5 (1 pen), Cox 4, Peters 4, Travis 3, Hilson 2, Hurst 2, Dingwall 1, Hornby 1, Maciver 1, Malone 1, Munro 1, See 1, own goal 1.
William Hill Scottish FA Cup (0).
Betfred Scottish League Cup (3): Millar 1 (1 pen), Scott 1, own goal 1.
Irn-Bru Scottish League Challenge Cup (1): Millar 1.

McCallum M 36	Bain J 34	Travis M 31 + 3	Mensing S 7	Quigley C 10 + 1	Cox D 16 + 1	Millar M 24 + 3	Malone E 21 + 2	Scott M 8 + 1	Lister J 6 + 2	See O 8 + 11	Easton D 27 + 5	Aitken M 20 + 9	McBride S 4 + 5	Kennedy M 7 + 1	Manitelemio R 3	Cregg P 12 + 2	Peters J 11 + 20	Whyte D 25	MacKintosh M 17	Duthie C 6 + 4	Lochhead S 4 + 3	Milne L 2 + 1	McNaughton K 9 + 2	Starkey B — + 5	Hornby J 3	Hilson D 11 + 1	Munro A 9 + 2	Dingwall R 14	Maciver R 4 + 6	Hurst G 7 + 6	Brotherston D — + 2	Allan J — + 1	Match No.
1	2	3	4	5	6¹	7	8	9	10	11²	12	13																					1
1	2	3	4	5	6¹	8	7³	9		10²	12	11	14	13																			2
1	5¹	12	3		9¹	7	8			10³	14	11²			6	2	4	13															3
1		2	3			7	8	12	11	14	10¹	13▪			5	4	6²	9³															4
1	2	4			6	8		9	12	10¹	13				5	3	7	11²															5
1	2	3	4	5	6	8	14	9¹	11³	10¹	13					7	12																6
1	2	12	3¹	14	11	7	6	9	13			5▪			8³	10²	4																7
1	2	3		5	6	7	9²		11¹	12		13	8			10		4															8
1	2	4		5	6³	7		8		12	10²	13	9			14	11¹	3															9
1	2	4		5	11	7		6³		10²	12	9	13			8¹	14	3															10
1	2	4			11	7		6³		13	9²	14	5			12	3	8	10¹														11
1	2	4			10³	7				6²	11	13	5			14	3	8	9¹	12													12
1	2	4			11²	7				12	10¹	6	5			13	3	8	9														13
1	2	4		5	6³	7				10²	9¹	11				8	14	3		12	13												14
1	2	3		5	6¹	8▪				10³	9²	11				7	14	4		12	13												15
1	2	4			14					13	10	6				8	11¹	3		12	9³		7²										16
1	2	4		5						12	10¹	6				8	14	3				11	7²	13									17
1	2	4				7	3			11¹	10	12				8	14			9	6²		5³	13									18
1		4				8	9			12		10				7	13			2	6¹	11²	3	5									19
1	5	4				14	13	7		10²	12	6				8	11			2			3³	9¹									20
1	2	4				8	6	7		13		9				11²	3³		10			14		5¹	12								21
1	3	6				10	8	4³		9¹	12	14				11²	2		13			7				5							22
1	5	4								7¹	8	13				11³			2	12		6	14				3	9	10²				23
1	5	4				13	12			7²	8					14	2					6³					3	9	10¹	11			24
1	5	4				11	8¹			12	10					13	2³	7									3	6	14	9²			25
1	2					7	3			10³	9	14				13	4	5								11¹		8	12	6²			26
1	2	14				7³	3▪			10¹	9					13	4	5								11	12	8		6²			27
1	5	3								9²	6³					14	2	8				13				10	4	7	12	11¹			28
1	5	4					8			11¹	9						2	6								10	3	7		12			29
1	5	4²					8³			9¹	10					13	2	6				14				11	3²	7		12			30
1	2	3				7	4			11³	9¹						5	6								10²		8	13	12	14		31
1	2	3					4			9	10▪					14	5	6				8²				11		7¹	13	12			32
1	2	3				4	7³			11³	9▪					14	5	6								10	12	8		13			33
1	5	4					8			10¹						11²	2	6								9	3	7	14	13	12³		34
1	2	4					9¹			12	5	7														10	3▪	8	6	11¹²		13	35
1	2	3				7				9¹	12	4	5			13										10	8	6	11¹				36

GREENOCK MORTON

Year Formed: 1874. *Ground & Address:* Cappielow Park, Sinclair St, Greenock PA15 2TU. *Telephone:* 01475 723571.
Fax: 01475 781084. *E-mail:* admin@gmfc.net *Website:* www.gmfc.net
Ground Capacity: 11,612 (seated: 6,062). *Size of Pitch:* 100m × 65m.
Chairman: Crawford Rae. *Chief Executive:* Warren Hawke.
Manager: Ray McKinnon. *First-Team Coach:* Darren Taylor.
Club Nickname: 'The Ton'.
Previous Grounds: Grant Street 1874, Garvel Park 1875, Cappielow Park 1879, Ladyburn Park 1882, Cappielow Park 1883.
Record Attendance: 23,500 v Celtic, 29 April 1922.
Record Transfer Fee received: £500,000 for Derek Lilley to Leeds U (March 1997).
Record Transfer Fee paid: £250,000 for Janne Lindberg and Marko Rajamäki from MyPa, Finland (November 1994).
Record Victory: 11-0 v Carfin Shamrock, Scottish Cup 4th rd, 13 November 1886.
Record Defeat: 1-10 v Port Glasgow Ath, Division II, 5 May, 1894 and v St Bernards, Division II, 14 October 1933.
Most Capped Player: Jimmy Cowan, 25, Scotland.
Most League Appearances: 534: Derek Collins, 1987-98, 2001-05.
Most League Goals in Season (Individual): 58: Allan McGraw, Division II, 1963-64.
Most Goals Overall (Individual): 136: Andy Ritchie, 1976-83.

GREENOCK MORTON – SPFL LADBROKES CHAMPIONSHIP 2017–18 LEAGUE RECORD

Match No.	Date		Venue	Opponents	Result	H/T Score	Lg Pos.	Goalscorers	Attendance
1	Aug	5	A	Dumbarton	D 0-0	0-0	7		1161
2		12	H	St Mirren	W 4-1	1-1	3	Tidser 2 (2 pens) [26, 50], McHugh [72], Murdoch [77]	4661
3		19	A	Inverness CT	D 1-1	0-1	5	Thomson [51]	2202
4		26	H	Livingston	L 0-1	0-0	5		1599
5	Sept	9	H	Dunfermline Ath	W 3-2	0-2	5	Thomson [47], Harkins [73], Quitongo [90]	1918
6		16	A	Queen of the South	W 2-1	2-1	3	Forbes [16], Quitongo [20]	1725
7		23	A	Dundee U	L 1-2	0-0	5	McHugh [75]	5569
8		30	H	Falkirk	L 0-1	0-0	6		1992
9	Oct	14	A	Brechin C	W 1-0	0-0	5	Murdoch [81]	624
10		21	H	Dumbarton	D 1-1	0-1	6	McHugh [50]	1428
11		28	A	St Mirren	D 2-2	0-0	6	Murdoch [68], Harkins (pen) [79]	5496
12	Nov	4	H	Queen of the South	L 1-2	1-1	6	Harkins (pen) [7]	1677
13		21	A	Dunfermline Ath	D 1-1	1-1	6	Oliver [34]	4816
14		25	A	Falkirk	W 3-0	2-0	6	Harkins [9], Thomson 2 [43, 61]	4361
15	Dec	2	H	Brechin C	W 4-1	2-1	5	Oliver [4], Tiffoney [44], Harkins (pen) [72], Quitongo [83]	1388
16		9	H	Dundee U	L 0-2	0-0	6		2021
17		23	H	Inverness CT	W 1-0	1-0	4	Harkins (pen) [22]	1547
18	Jan	2	H	St Mirren	D 1-1	0-1	5	O'Ware [80]	4126
19		6	A	Brechin C	D 1-1	1-1	6	McHugh [12]	694
20		13	H	Falkirk	L 0-1	0-1	7		2084
21		27	A	Dundee U	W 3-0	1-0	6	O'Ware [35], Tiffoney [47], Iredale [80]	5730
22	Feb	3	H	Dunfermline Ath	W 2-1	1-1	4	Tidser [37], Oliver [90]	1588
23		17	A	Queen of the South	D 1-1	0-1	4	Oliver [55]	1489
24		20	A	Dumbarton	W 1-0	0-0	4	O'Ware [74]	836
25		24	A	Inverness CT	W 2-0	1-0	3	Tiffoney [28], Harkins (pen) [70]	2359
26		27	H	Livingston	L 0-1	0-0	3		1373
27	Mar	10	A	Falkirk	L 1-3	0-3	3	Harkins [90]	4218
28		13	A	Livingston	D 1-1	0-0	4	Oliver [88]	862
29		17	A	Dunfermline Ath	D 0-0	0-0	4		4613
30		24	H	Brechin C	W 2-0	0-0	3	Baird 2 [50, 72]	1831
31		31	H	Dundee U	D 1-1	0-0	3	Ross [90]	2319
32	Apr	7	A	Livingston	L 2-3	1-1	5	O'Ware [18], Lamie [69]	1028
33		10	A	Dumbarton	W 3-2	0-0	5	Fraser [62], Baird [69], Iredale [90]	1134
34		14	H	Queen of the South	L 0-1	0-0	5		1514
35		21	A	St Mirren	L 1-2	1-1	6	Doyle [30]	6422
36		28	H	Inverness CT	L 0-3	0-2	7		1539

Final League Position: 7

Honours
League Champions: First Division 1977-78, 1983-84, 1986-87; Division II 1949-50, 1963-64, 1966-67; Second Division 1994-95, 2006-07; League One 2014–15; Third Division 2002-03.
Runners-up: Division 1 1916-17; First Division 2012-13; Second Division 2005-06;. Division II 1899-1900, 1928-29, 1936-37.
Scottish Cup Winners: 1922; *Runners-up:* 1948.
League Cup Runners-up: 1963-64.
League Challenge Cup Runners-up: 1992-93.

European: *UEFA Cup:* 2 matches (*Fairs Cup*: 1968-69).

Club colours: Shirt: Blue and white hoops. Shorts: White with blue trim. Socks: White with blue tops.

Goalscorers: *League (47):* Harkins 8 (5 pens), Oliver 5, McHugh 4, O'Ware 4, Thomson 4, Baird 3, Murdoch 3, Quitongo 3, Tidser 3 (2 pens), Tiffoney 3, Iredale 2, Doyle 1, Forbes 1, Fraser 1, Lamie 1, Ross 1.
William Hill Scottish FA Cup (5): Iredale 1, McHugh 1, Oliver 1, Quitongo 1, Ross 1.
Betfred Scottish League Cup (8): McHugh 3, Thomson 2, Barr 1, Quitongo 1, own goal 1.
Irn-Bru Scottish League Challenge Cup (0).

Gaston D 32	Doyle M 35	McManus C 3+2	Lamie R 32+1	Russell M 27+2	Murdoch A 33+1	Forbes R 15+1	Tidser M 24+4	Quitongo J 13+2	McHugh B 19+13	Thomson R 17+8	Tiffoney S 17+14	O'Ware T 33	Harkins G 27+7	Oliver G 25+7	Armour B —+7	Barr D 1+1	Langan R —+3	Gasparotto L 10+1	Iredale J 9	Ross F 9+6	Strapp L 1+2	Brennan C 4+1	Purdue J —+1	Baird J 6+2	Fraser G 3+4	Hynes D 1	Eardley B —+1	Match No.
1	2	3	4	5	6	7	8	9^1	10	11	12																	1
1	2^3	12	4	5	7	6^2	8	10^1	11	9		3	13	14														2
1	2		4	5	7	6^3	8	10^2	11^1	9	13	3	14	12														3
1	2		4	5	6	7^3	8^1	10	11^2	9	14	3	12	13														4
1	2	14	4	5	6	7^3	8	12	10^2	9		3	13	11^1														5
1	2	7	4	5	6^2		8	10^3	13	12	14	3	9^1	11														6
1	2		4	5	8	6^1	7	11^2	12	9		3	14	10^3	13													7
1	2	8^2	4	5	7	6		10^3	12	14		3	9	11^1	13													8
1	2		4	5	8	6^1	7	10^1	11^3	9	12	3	13	14														9
1	2		4	5	7	12		9	11^2	10^1	13	3	8	6														10
1	2		4	5	7	9		10^2	12	13	6^1	3	8^3	11	14													11
1	2		4	5	6^1		11	12	9^2			8^3	10	13	3		14											12
1	5		4	9	6	8		11^1	12	13		3	7^2	10				2										13
1	2		4	5	7	6^2		10	11^1	9		3	8^3	13	12	14												14
1	2		5		7^1	6	12	13		11		9^3	4	8^2	10			14	3									15
1	2		5		7^3	6^1	12	11	14		9^{13}	4	8	10				3										16
1	2		5		6^2		8	11^1	13	9	12	4	7	10^3	14			3										17
1	2		4	5	6		8	11^1	13	9	12	3	7^2	10														18
1	2	3	5	6			13	10^1	11	9	7	8^3	12	14				4^2										19
1	2		4	5^2	13		8		11	9	6	3	7^1	10			12											20
1	5		12	6	7			13		9^1	2	8	10^3					3	4	11^2	14							21
1	2			7		6^1		12		10	4	8	11					3	5	9								22
1	2	14	9	7		13		11^2	12	3	8	10						4	5^3	6^1								23
	2		5	9	7		8	11^2		13	4	12	10					3^1	6		1							24
1	2	3	5	7		9		12		10^2	4	8	11							6^1		13						25
1	2		4	9^1	7		6^2	10			3	8	13							12	5			11				26
1	2		4	5	8		6	11		9	3	7												10				27
1			4	9	2^1		8			10	3	7	11							5	6^2				13	12		28
1	9		4		2		8			11	3	7	10							5	6^1					12		29
1	2		4	7^2		6	13			9	3		10							5^1	12	14		11^3	8			30
1	2		4	5	7		6	14	13	9^2	3	8	11^1							12				10^3				31
1	2		5	14	7		6	13	11	9^1	3	8^3	10^2					4		12								32
1^3	2		4			7^2		14	11^1	13	3	8								5	9	12		10	6			33
	2^2		4	9^3	7			11	12	6	3	8								5	13	1		10^1	14			34
	2^3		4		7	6		14	11	3	8	8^1	10							5	9^2	1		12	13			35
	3		4	5	6^3			11^2	8	10		12	13					12		13				7^1	2	14		36

HAMILTON ACADEMICAL

Year Formed: 1874. *Ground:* New Douglas Park, Cadzow Avenue, Hamilton ML3 0FT. *Telephone:* 01698 368652.
Fax: 01698 285422. *E-mail:* office@acciesfc.co.uk *Website:* www.hamiltonacciesfc.co.uk
Ground Capacity: 6,078 (all seated). *Size of Pitch:* 105m × 68m.
Chairman: Ronnie MacDonald. *Vice-Chairman:* Les Gray.
Manager: Martin Canning. *First-Team Coach:* Guillaume Beuzelin.
Club Nickname: 'The Accies'.
Previous Grounds: Bent Farm, South Avenue, South Haugh, Douglas Park, Cliftonhill Stadium, Firhill Stadium.
Record Attendance: 28,690 v Hearts, Scottish Cup 3rd rd, 3 March 1937 (at Douglas Park); 5,895 v Rangers, 28 February 2009 (at New Douglas Park).
Record Transfer Fee received: £1,200,000 (rising to £3,200,000) for James McCarthy to Wigan Ath (July 2009).
Record Transfer Fee paid: £180,000 for Tomas Cerny from Sigma Olomouc (July 2009).
Record Victory: 10-2 v Greenock Morton, Scottish Championship, 3 May 2014.
Record Defeat: 1-11 v Hibernian, Division I, 6 November 1965.
Most Capped Player: Colin Miller, 29 (61), Canada, 1988-94.
Most League Appearances: 452: Rikki Ferguson, 1974-88.
Most League Goals in Season (Individual): 35: David Wilson, Division I; 1936-37.
Most Goals Overall (Individual): 246: David Wilson, 1928-39.

HAMILTON ACADEMICAL – SPFL LADBROKES PREMIERSHIP 2017–18 LEAGUE RECORD

Match No.	Date		Venue	Opponents		Result	H/T Score	Lg Pos.	Goalscorers	Atten- dance
1	Aug	6	A	Aberdeen	L	0-2	0-1	11		15,165
2		12	H	Dundee	W	3-0	2-0	5	MacKinnon [24], Boyd [36], Imrie (pen) [85]	1694
3		19	A	Hibernian	W	3-1	0-0	4	Bingham 2 (1 pen) [52 lpl, 88], Longridge [69]	16,633
4		26	A	Kilmarnock	D	2-2	0-1	4	Skondras [72], Crawford (pen) [88]	3706
5	Sept	8	H	Celtic	L	1-4	0-3	6	Gogic [86]	5208
6		16	H	Hearts	L	1-2	1-2	8	Bingham [33]	3326
7		23	A	St Johnstone	L	1-2	1-0	8	Docherty [24]	2880
8		29	H	Rangers	L	1-4	1-3	8	Redmond [1]	5400
9	Oct	14	H	Motherwell	L	1-2	1-1	9	Skondras [15]	3869
10		21	A	Ross Co	L	1-2	0-0	10	Docherty [52]	3509
11		24	H	Partick Thistle	D	0-0	0-0	9		2236
12		28	A	Dundee	W	3-1	1-0	8	Skondras [39], Templeton [64], Rojano [86]	4863
13	Nov	4	H	Aberdeen	D	2-2	1-1	9	Imrie [19], Templeton [76]	3099
14		18	A	Rangers	W	2-0	0-0	7	Templeton [47], Lyon [81]	48,892
15		25	H	Hibernian	D	1-1	0-1	8	Rojano [72]	2945
16	Dec	2	A	Hearts	D	1-1	0-0	8	Tomas [69]	15,357
17		9	H	St Johnstone	L	0-1	0-0	9		1451
18		13	A	Celtic	L	1-3	1-3	9	Redmond [29]	53,883
19		16	H	Ross Co	W	3-2	1-0	9	Imrie (pen) [30], Sarris [75], Lindsay (og) [89]	1272
20		23	A	Partick Thistle	L	0-1	0-1	9		2912
21		30	A	Motherwell	W	3-1	1-1	9	Imrie (pen) [41], Bingham [53], Docherty [76]	4890
22	Jan	24	H	Hearts	L	0-3	0-0	9		2077
23		27	H	Dundee	L	1-2	1-0	10	O'Hara (og) [2]	1776
24	Feb	3	A	Aberdeen	L	0-3	0-1	11		13,531
25		18	A	Rangers	L	3-5	2-4	11	Lyon [5], Templeton [22], Imrie (pen) [88]	5406
26		24	H	Partick Thistle	W	2-1	1-1	10	Rojano [11], Templeton [90]	2243
27	Mar	10	H	Motherwell	W	2-0	1-0	9	Ogboe [11], Templeton [69]	3182
28		17	A	Ross Co	D	2-2	0-1	9	Imrie (pen) [49], Ogboe [62]	3586
29		28	A	St Johnstone	L	0-1	0-1	9		2037
30		31	A	Kilmarnock	L	0-2	0-2	9		4672
31	Apr	3	A	Hibernian	L	1-3	1-1	9	Ogboe [9]	15,818
32		8	H	Celtic	L	1-2	1-1	9	Bingham [18]	4851
33		14	H	Kilmarnock	L	1-2	0-0	9	Fasan (og) [73]	4348
34		21	A	Partick Thistle	L	1-2	1-0	10	Templeton [43]	3839
35		28	H	Ross Co	W	2-0	0-0	9	Imrie (pen) [56], Templeton [67]	2057
36	May	5	A	Dundee	L	0-1	0-1	10		5195
37		8	H	St Johnstone	L	1-2	0-0	10	Imrie [82]	2367
38		12	A	Motherwell	L	0-3	0-1	10		4699

Final League Position: 10

Honours
League Champions: Division II 1903-04; First Division 1985-86, 1987-88, 2007-08; Third Division 2000-01.
Runners-up: Division II 1952-53, 1964-65; Second Division 1996-97, 2003-04; Championship 2013-14.
Promoted via play-offs: 2013-14 (to Premiership).
Scottish Cup Runners-up: 1911, 1935. *League Cup:* Semi-finalists three times.
League Challenge Cup Winners: 1991-92, 1992-93; *Runners-up:* 2005-06, 2011-12.

Club colours: Shirt: Red and white hoops. Shorts: White. Socks: White.

Goalscorers: *League (47):* Imrie 8 (6 pens), Templeton 8, Bingham 5 (1 pen), Docherty 3, Ogboe 3, Rojano 3, Skondras 3, Lyon 2, Redmond 2, Boyd 1, Crawford 1 (1 pen), Gogic 1, Longridge 1, MacKinnon 1, Sarris 1, Tomas 1, own goals 3.
William Hill Scottish FA Cup (0).
Betfred Scottish League Cup (11): Boyd 2, Crawford 2, Want 2, Bingham 1 (1 pen), Donati 1, Longridge 1, MacKinnon 1, Templeton 1.

Woods G 32	McMann S 30+4	Tomas X 36	Sarris G 19+2	Skondras G 20+1	Imrie D 33+2	Crawford A 11+3	Docherty G 21	MacKinnon D 31	Bingham R 18+14	Boyd S 7+6	Templeton D 20+7	Donati M 6+4	Longridge L 3+6	Redmond D 11+14	Gillespie G 1+2	Gogic A 15+3	Cunningham R —+6	Jamieson D 1+1	Bia Bi B 3+2	Fulton R 5+1	Rojano A 14+12	Lyon D 21+6	Ferguson L 12+1	Ogboe M 12+4	Want S 13	Hughes R 2+1	van der Weg K 10+1	Jenkins R 9+2	Miller M 1+5	Scott C 1+1	Match No.
1	2	3⁴	4	5²	6	7	8	9	10¹	11³	12	13	14																		1
1	5		3	2	6	9²	7	8	10³	11¹	13	4	12	14																	2
1	5	3	4	2	7	9¹	8	6	11¹	10²		12	13	14																	3
1	5	3	9	2	7¹	4	8	6	10³	12	11²					13	14														4
1	5	4	3	2	6²	7	9	8	11³	10¹	14	12				13															5
1	5	4	3	2	10¹	9	6	7	11³	12	8²					14	13														6
1¹		3		2	8	9	6	7¹	11	14	4³	10²		5		12	13														7
	4	2	5	9	7³	6		10	14	12	11²	8¹				13		1													8
	4	3	6³	9	8	5	11	13	7¹	12		2				10²	1			14											9
	4	3	9		6	7	11²	8³	14	13		2				10¹	1		12	5											10
1	4	3³	5	8	6	7	13	9	12	14		2				11²			10												11
1	4	3		9	7	10¹	13⁴	11²	6⁴			2				12	14														12
1	5	3		2	8		9	7	13	14	10²					12	4				11³	6¹									13
1	4	3		5	9	7²	6	13		10³		12	14	2⁴							11¹	8									14
1	4	3¹	2	5	9		6	7	13		10	14	12								11²	8³									15
1	4	3	2	5	8		9²	6	12		10			13							11	7									16
1	4	3	2	5	9¹		8³	7	12		10			13			14				11	6²									17
1	4	3	12	9	8	6	11¹	7						10³	5²	2	14					13									18
1		3	4	5⁴	9	13	6	7	10²			11³		8¹		2					12	14									19
1	4	3	2		8	13	5	7	12		11			6¹		14					10²	9³									20
1	4	3		9	11²	5	8	10			6³	7¹		13		2	14				12										21
1	4	3		9		7		10			8¹	2				12	5	6	11												22
1		3	14	5	9		7		11■			8²	2			10³	12	6¹	13	4											23
1	9	3	7	5¹							8³			2	12	13	6	10	11²	4	14										24
1	9	3	2	5	13			12			10²					14	6	8	11¹			4³	7								25
1	12	4	3¹	9				8						2⁴		10	7	6	11	5³		14	13								26
1	9	3			12			5²			13					10³	6	8	11²	2		4	7	14							27
1	9	3		12				14			5³			13		10¹	6	8	11²	2		4	7								28
1	5	3	4³	6				7	10²	9						12	8	11¹	2			13	14								29
1	8³	3	4	9	6											11	14	10	12	2	5²		7¹	13							30
1	12	3	2	9⁴	14		7	13			5³					10²	6	8	11¹	4											31
	9	3	12		10³		6	11			8²					1	14	5⁴	13		2	4	7								32
1	4	3	2²	10	8⁴		7	11¹	12							13		6	14	5	9										33
1	14	3		9				10³	8²		12							5	6	11	2	4¹	7	13							34
1		3	9		7	14		10			12							5	8²	11³	2	4	6¹		13						35
1¹	14	4	9		6			11³	8²		12					13	5	10	3	2	7										36
	4	3	9		6	14		10³	8¹	1	12					5		11²	2		7	13									37
	4	3	9		7	14				1	11¹	5				12³		10	2		6	8⁴									38

HEART OF MIDLOTHIAN

Year Formed: 1874. *Ground & Address:* Tynecastle Stadium, McLeod Street, Edinburgh EH11 2NL. *Telephone:* 0333 043 1874. *Fax:* 0131 200 7222. *E-mail:* supporterservices@homplc.co.uk *Website:* www.heartsfc.co.uk
Ground Capacity: 17,529. *Size of Pitch:* 100m × 64m.
Chief Executive and Chairwoman: Ann Budge.
Director of Football and Manager: Craig Levein. *Assistant Head Coach:* Austin MacPhee.
Club Nicknames: 'Hearts', 'Jambos', 'Jam Tarts'.
Previous Grounds: The Meadows 1874, Powderhall 1878, Old Tynecastle 1881 Tynecastle Park, 1886.
Record Attendance: 53,396 v Rangers, Scottish Cup 3rd rd, 13 February 1932 (57,857 v Barcelona, 28 July 2007 at Murrayfield).
Record Transfer Fee received: £9,000,000 for Craig Gordon to Sunderland (August 2008).
Record Transfer Fee paid: £850,000 for Mirsad Beslija from Genk (January 2006).
Record Victory: 15-0 v King's Park, Scottish Cup 2nd rd, 13 February 1937 (21-0 v Anchor, EFA Cup, 30 October 1880).
Record Defeat: 1-8 v Vale of Leven, Scottish Cup 3rd rd, 1883; 0-7 v Celtic, Scottish Cup 4th rd, 1 December 2013.
Most Capped Player: Steven Pressley, 32, Scotland.
Most League Appearances: 515: Gary Mackay, 1980-97.
Most League Goals in Season (Individual): 44: Barney Battles, 1930-31.
Most Goals Overall (Individual): 214: John Robertson, 1983-98.

HEART OF MIDLOTHIAN – SPFL LADBROKES PREMIERSHIP 2017–18 LEAGUE RECORD

Match No.	Date	Venue	Opponents	Result	H/T Score	Lg Pos.	Goalscorers	Attendance
1	Aug 5	A	Celtic	L	1-4	0-1	12	Goncalves [84]	58,843
2	12	A	Kilmarnock	W	1-0	1-0	8	Goncalves [6]	5076
3	19	A	Rangers	D	0-0	0-0	7		49,677
4	26	A	Motherwell	L	1-2	1-2	8	Lafferty [30]	6568
5	Sept 9	H	Aberdeen	D	0-0	0-0	8		24,248
6	16	A	Hamilton A	W	2-1	2-1	7	Callachan [3], Lafferty (pen) [23]	3326
7	23	A	Partick Thistle	D	1-1	0-1	7	Callachan [80]	4671
8	30	A	Dundee	L	1-2	0-1	7	Lafferty [71]	7028
9	Oct 14	A	Ross Co	W	2-1	1-1	7	Goncalves [34], Walker [59]	4819
10	21	H	St Johnstone	W	1-0	0-0	5	Lafferty [74]	18,534
11	24	A	Hibernian	L	0-1	0-1	7		20,165
12	28	A	Rangers	L	1-3	1-1	7	Lafferty [24]	32,852
13	Nov 5	H	Kilmarnock	L	1-2	-	6	Goncalves [76]	16,347
14	19	H	Partick Thistle	D	1-1	0-0	7	Goncalves [54]	16,999
15	25	H	Ross Co	D	0-0	0-0	7		15,601
16	Dec 2	H	Hamilton A	D	1-1	0-0	6	Walker [47]	15,357
17	9	H	Motherwell	W	1-0	1-0	6	Lafferty [39]	15,984
18	12	H	Dundee	W	2-0	1-0	5	Goncalves [30], Berra [77]	15,566
19	17	H	Celtic	W	4-0	2-0	5	Cochrane [26], Lafferty [35], Milinkovic 2 (1 pen) [48, 76 (p)]	18,555
20	23	A	St Johnstone	D	0-0	0-0	5		4975
21	27	H	Hibernian	D	0-0	0-0	5		19,316
22	30	A	Aberdeen	D	0-0	0-0	5		18,371
23	Jan 24	A	Hamilton A	W	3-0	0-0	5	Callachan [67], Milinkovic [73], Zanatta [87]	2077
24	27	H	Motherwell	D	1-1	0-0	5	Milinkovic [80]	16,717
25	30	A	Celtic	L	1-3	0-3	5	Lafferty [67]	56,296
26	Feb 3	H	St Johnstone	W	1-0	0-0	5	Milinkovic [46]	16,197
27	17	A	Ross Co	D	1-1	0-0	5	Lafferty [53]	4936
28	24	A	Rangers	L	0-2	0-1	5		49,927
29	27	H	Kilmarnock	D	1-1	1-1	5	Naismith [27]	15,862
30	Mar 9	A	Hibernian	L	0-2	0-0	6		20,166
31	17	H	Partick Thistle	W	3-0	3-0	6	Lafferty [17], Naismith [21], Souttar [44]	17,179
32	Apr 1	A	Dundee	D	1-1	1-1	6	Callachan [2]	5496
33	7	H	Aberdeen	W	2-0	2-0	6	Naismith [18], Milinkovic [20]	18,056
34	22	A	Rangers	L	1-2	0-0	6	Berra [71]	47,272
35	27	A	Aberdeen	L	0-2	0-2	6		14,045
36	May 6	H	Celtic	L	1-3	1-1	6	Lafferty [18]	19,031
37	9	H	Hibernian	W	2-1	1-0	6	Lafferty [26], Naismith [57]	19,324
38	13	A	Kilmarnock	L	0-1	0-1	6		6273

Final League Position: 6

Honours
League Champions: Division I 1894-95, 1896-97, 1957-58, 1959-60; First Division 1979-80; Championship 2014-15.
Runners-up: Division I 1893-94, 1898-99, 1903-04, 1905-06, 1914-15, 1937-38, 1953-54, 1956-57, 1958-59, 1964-65; Premier Division 1985-86, 1987-88, 1991-92, 2005-06; First Division 1977-78, 1982-83.
Scottish Cup Winners: 1891, 1896, 1901, 1906, 1956, 1998, 2006, 2012; *Runners-up:* 1903, 1907, 1968, 1976, 1986, 1996.
League Cup Winners: 1954-55, 1958-59, 1959-60, 1962-63; *Runners-up:* 1961-62, 1996-97, 2012-13.

European: *European Cup:* 8 matches (1958-59, 1960-61, 2006-07). *Cup Winners' Cup:* 10 matches (1976-77, 1996-97, 1998-99). *UEFA Cup:* 46 matches (*Fairs Cup:* 1961-62, 1963-64, 1965-66. *UEFA Cup:* 1984-85, 1986-87, 1988-89, 1990-91, 1992-93, 1993-94, 2000-01, 2003-04, 2004-05, 2006-07). *Europa League:* 12 matches (2010-11, 2011-12, 2012-13, 2016-17).

Club colours: Shirt: Maroon. Shorts: White with maroon trim. Socks: Maroon.

Goalscorers: *League (39):* Lafferty 12 (1 pen), Goncalves 6, Milinkovic 6 (1 pen), Callachan 4, Naismith 4, Berra 2, Walker 2, Cochrane 1, Souttar 1, Zanatta 1.
William Hill Scottish FA Cup (5): Lafferty 3 (1 pen), Cowie 1, Mitchell 1.
Betfred Scottish League Cup (7): Lafferty 4 (1 pen), Berra 1, Cowie 1, Goncalves 1.

The following is the players' appearance and scoring grid. Column headers (with total appearances + substitute appearances) read left to right; goals scored in a match are shown as a superscript on the shirt number. The final column is the match number.

Hamilton J 5	Brandon J 11+1	Hughes A 17+2	Berra C 37	Grzelak R 9+4	Smith M 29+2	Busbeu P 9+8	Cowie D 25+3	Djoum A 15+1	Moore L 10+5	Lafferty K 30+5	Randall C 22+2	Goncalves E 16+4	Sammon C —+1	Souttar J 31	Nowak K —+3	Stockton C 4+8	Smith C —+1	Martin M —+1	Makovora L —+1	Walker J 14+2	McLaughlin J 33	Callachan R 18+5	Milinkovic M 15+9	Smith-Brown A 1+1	Currie R —+1	Cochrane H 14+8	Henderson E 3+9	Baur D 1+1	Keena A —+1	McDonald A 5+8	Mitchell D 9	Irving A 2+2	Naismith S 12+2	Zanatta D —+1	Amankwaa D 5+6	Adao J 9+1	Godinho M 5	Logan C 1	Hamilton C 1	Match No.
1	2	3	4	5^1	6	7^2	8	9	10	11^3	12	13	14																											1
1	2^2		4	9	5	6^3	7		11^1	8	10^4			3	12	13	14																							2
1	2^2		4	14	5	13	7	8		11	9^1	10		3	12						6^3																			3
1			4	5	2	14	8	6	13	10	7^1	12		3		11^2					6^3																			4
	3	4	9		6	10		12	5	11^2				3						8^1	1	7	13																	5
	4	9	2	12	13	8^1		10		11^3				3						7^2	1	6	14	5																6
	3	4	9^3	5^2		8^1			6	11				2						10	1	7	13	12	14															7
	3^4	4	5	12			10	9	11					2						6	1	7	13				8^1													8
13	3	14	5	7	6^1		11	2^4	10^2					4						9	1		8^1	12																9
2		4	5	8^1			10		11^2					3	14		6	1	7	9^3		12	13																	10
5^1		4	10^2	2			11	6	13					3	14		7	1	8			12	9^1																	11
	4	5	2			7^3	10		11					3	13	14	9^2	1	8	12		6^1																		12
	4	2	6				9^2	10^1	7^3	11				3	13		1	8	14			12	5																	13
5	3	4		2		6^1	7		10^3	11^2				13	12	1	8	9			14																			14
2	3^1	4		5	12	13	8		14	11^2				10	6	1	9			7^1																				15
2^8	13	4		5	7		8	12	14		9^1			3	10	6^3	1	11^2																						16
	4		5	6	7	9^1	10	11	2					3	14	8^2	1	13	12^3																					17
	4	5		8		7^3	9^2	14	2	11^1				3	10		1	13			12		6																	18
2		4	14	3	6^2	8		11^3	5					13			1	9^1	10		7			12																19
	4	14	5^1	6	7		11^3	2	13					3			1	10			9^4		8^2																	20
5	12	4			7	6		11	2^1	10				3		9	1	13	8^2																					21
2	6	4		5^2		7		13^4		10				3			1		11	9		12	8^1																	22
		3				6^2	12	11^3		2				4			1	9	13		8^1					5	7	10	14											23
	3	4	5			6			14					2			1	7^3	12				9^1	8	10^2	11			13											24
	4		12	6	9			11^1	2					3			1	7^3	10	8^2					5	14	13													25
	4	12	13					11	2^1					3			1		10				14	5	9	7^3	6^2													26
	4	2		7^2	9^1		11							3			1	8	10^3		13		14	5	12		6													27
	4	5		2	12		11							3			1	7		9^1	10^1	13	6		14		8^2													28
	3	4	13		6^1		11	2						3			1	14	9^2	7			5^3	10	12	8														29
	4		5^3				10^2	11	2					3			1		9^1	14		12	7	13	8	6														30
	5	4	7		6^2	14	11							3			1		12	13			10	9^3	8^1	2														31
	5	4	6		12	10								3			1	8^1	14	13			11	9^2	7^3	2														32
	3	4	7		6	11	5							2			1	10^2	13			9	12	8																33
	3^4	4	6		7	13	11	5						2			1	14				9	10^2	12	8^1															34
	3	4	6		7^2	8	11	5^1						2			1	12	10^3	14	13	9																		35
	4	2	9		11^3	10^1								3			1	8	13	14		5	6	12	7^2															36
	3	4	2	12		10								1			13	11^3	8^1			14	5	6	9^2	7														37
1	3		6		5	10								12	13		8	11	7^1	14		9^1																2^3	4	38

HIBERNIAN

Year Formed: 1875. *Ground & Address:* Easter Road Stadium, 12 Albion Place, Edinburgh EH7 5QG. *Telephone:* 0131 661 2159. *Fax:* 0131 659 6488. *E-mail:* club@hibernianfc.co.uk *Website:* www.hibernianfc.co.uk
Ground Capacity: 20,421 (all seated). *Size of Pitch:* 105m × 68m.
Chairman: Rod Petrie. *Chief Executive:* Leean Dempster.
Head Coach: Neil Lennon. *Assistant Head Coach:* Garry Parker.
Club Nickname: 'Hibs', 'Hibees'.
Previous Grounds: Meadows 1875-78, Powderhall 1878-79, Mayfield 1879-80, First Easter Road 1880-92, Second Easter Road 1892-.
Record Attendance: 65,860 v Hearts, Division I, 2 January 1950.
Record Transfer Fee received: £4,400,000 for Scott Brown from Celtic (2007).
Record Transfer Fee paid: £700,000 for Ulises de la Cruz to LDU Quito (2001).
Record Victory: 15-1 v Pebbles Rovers, Scottish Cup 2nd rd, 11 February 1961.
Record Defeat: 0-10 v Rangers, Division I, 24 December 1898.
Most Capped Player: Lawrie Reilly, 38, Scotland.
Most League Appearances: 446: Arthur Duncan, 1969-84.
Most League Goals in Season (Individual): 42: Joe Baker, 1959-60.
Most Goals Overall (Individual): 233: Lawrie Reilly, 1945-58.

HIBERNIAN – SPFL LADBROKES PREMIERSHIP 2017–18 LEAGUE RECORD

Match No.	Date	Venue	Opponents	Result	H/T Score	Lg Pos.	Goalscorers	Attendance
1	Aug 5	H	Partick Thistle	W 3-1	2-1	2	Boyle [14], Whittaker [33], Murray, S (pen) [52]	17,634
2	12	A	Rangers	W 3-2	2-1	3	Murray, S [21], Tavernier (og) [39], Slivka [65]	49,636
3	19	H	Hamilton A	L 1-3	0-0	5	Stokes [90]	16,633
4	27	A	Dundee	D 1-1	1-1	6	Stokes [39]	6004
5	Sept 9	A	St Johnstone	D 1-1	0-0	6	Paton (og) [61]	5591
6	16	H	Motherwell	D 2-2	1-0	6	Stokes 2 (1 pen) [21 (p), 57]	17,335
7	23	A	Ross Co	W 1-0	1-0	4	Hanlon [13]	4181
8	30	A	Celtic	D 2-2	0-1	6	McGinn 2 [53, 77]	59,259
9	Oct 14	A	Aberdeen	L 0-1	0-1	6		19,038
10	24	H	Hearts	W 1-0	1-0	5	Murray, S [3]	20,165
11	28	A	Motherwell	W 1-0	1-0	5	Boyle [27]	6043
12	31	A	Kilmarnock	W 3-0	1-0	3	McGinn [10], Murray, S [61], Boyle [90]	5005
13	Nov 4	H	Dundee	W 2-1	1-1	3	Boyle [1], Murray, S [63]	16,936
14	18	H	St Johnstone	L 1-2	0-0	3	Stokes (pen) [90]	17,044
15	25	A	Hamilton A	D 1-1	1-0	3	Murray, S [29]	2945
16	Dec 2	A	Partick Thistle	W 1-0	0-0	3	Barton (og) [48]	4997
17	10	H	Celtic	D 2-2	0-0	4	Ambrose [76], Shaw [79]	20,193
18	13	H	Rangers	L 1-2	1-2	4	Stevenson [9]	20,057
19	16	A	Aberdeen	L 1-4	0-3	4	Stokes [89]	14,923
20	23	H	Ross Co	W 2-1	1-1	4	Stokes [21], Shaw [75]	16,228
21	27	A	Hearts	D 0-0	0-0	4		19,316
22	30	H	Kilmarnock	D 1-1	1-1	4	Shaw [23]	17,666
23	Jan 24	A	Dundee	W 1-0	0-0	4	McGinn [52]	5323
24	27	A	Celtic	L 0-1	0-1	4		58,998
25	31	H	Motherwell	W 2-1	1-0	4	Kamberi [28], Barker [47]	15,459
26	Feb 3	A	Rangers	W 2-1	1-0	4	McGinn [41], Maclaren (pen) [75]	49,986
27	17	H	Aberdeen	W 2-0	0-0	4	Boyle [46], Kamberi [60]	19,551
28	24	A	Kilmarnock	D 2-2	2-0	4	Kamberi [1], Porteous [9]	5348
29	Mar 9	H	Hearts	W 2-0	0-0	4	Allan, S [59], Maclaren [80]	20,166
30	16	A	St Johnstone	D 1-1	1-0	4	Ambrose [2]	3652
31	31	H	Partick Thistle	W 2-0	0-0	4	Maclaren [71], Hanlon [76]	17,497
32	Apr 3	H	Hamilton A	W 3-1	1-1	4	Kamberi 3 [17, 63, 85]	15,818
33	7	A	Ross Co	D 1-1	0-1	4	Shaw [90]	5389
34	21	H	Celtic	W 2-1	1-0	4	Maclaren [24], Slivka [80]	19,886
35	28	H	Kilmarnock	W 5-3	1-1	4	Allan, S [29], Whittaker [54], Maclaren [64], Kamberi [76], Barker [90]	17,470
36	May 5	A	Aberdeen	D 0-0	0-0	4		17,822
37	9	A	Hearts	L 1-2	0-1	4	Kamberi (pen) [48]	19,324
38	13	H	Rangers	D 5-5	3-3	4	Kamberi (pen) [10], Allan, S [19], Maclaren 3 [22, 70, 90]	19,579

Final League Position: 4

Honours
League Champions: Division I 1902-03, 1947-48, 1950-51, 1951-52; First Division 1980-81, 1998-99; Championship 2016-17; Division II 1893-94, 1894-95, 1932-33.
Runners-up: Division I 1896-97, 1946-47, 1949-50, 1952-53, 1973-74, 1974-75; Championship 2014-15.
Scottish Cup Winners: 1887, 1902, 2016; *Runners-up:* 1896, 1914, 1923, 1924, 1947, 1958, 1972, 1979, 2001, 2012, 2013.
League Cup Winners: 1972-73, 1991-92, 2006-07; *Runners-up:* 1950-51, 1968-69, 1974-75, 1985-86, 1993-94, 2003-04, 2015-16.
Drybrough Cup Winners: 1972-73, 1973-74.

European: *European Cup:* 6 matches (1955-56 semi-finals). *Cup Winners' Cup:* 6 matches (1972-73). *UEFA Cup:* 64 matches (*Fairs Cup:* 1960-61 semi-finals, 1961-62, 1962-63, 1965-66, 1967-68, 1968-69, 1970-71. *UEFA Cup:* 1973-74, 1974-75, 1975-76, 1976-77, 1978-79, 1989-90, 1992-93, 2001-02, 2005-06. *Europa League:* 4 matches 2010-11, 2013-14).

Club colours: Shirt: Green with white sleeves. Shorts: White. Socks: Green.

Goalscorers: *League (62):* Kamberi 9 (2 pens), Maclaren 8 (1 pen), Stokes 7 (2 pens), Murray S 6 (1 pen), Boyle 5, McGinn 5, Shaw 4, Allan S 3, Ambrose 2, Barker 2, Hanlon 2, Slivka 2, Whittaker 2, Porteous 1, Stevenson 1, own goals 3.
William Hill Scottish FA Cup (0).
Betfred Scottish League Cup (23): Murray S 8, Stokes 4 (2 pens), Murray F 2, Porteous 2, Ambrose 1, Boyle 1, Graham 1 (1 pen), Matulevicius 1, McGinn 1, Shaw 1, Swanson 1.

Marciano O 34	Whittaker S 19 + 7	Ambrose E 37 + 1	Hanlon P 36	Stevenson L 35	McGeouch D 30 + 5	Bartley M 20 + 6	McGinn J 35	Swanson D 4 + 13	Boyle M 34	Murray S 17 + 5	Stokes A 15 + 3	Slivka V 9 + 13	Murray F — + 2	McGregor D 22 + 2	Gray D 6 + 1	Barker B 17 + 10	Matulevicius D — + 12	Laidlaw R 3	Shaw O 5 + 11	Porteous R 2 + 4	Maclaren J 11 + 4	Kamberi F 14	Rheras F — + 1	Allan S 12	Bell C 1 + 1	Match No.
1	2	3	4	5	6	7³	8	9¹	10	11²	12	13	14													1
1	5	3	4	9	6		7	12		11¹	10	8¹		2	13											2
1	5	3	4	8	6³		7	9²		10	11	13		2¹	12	14										3
1	5	12	4		14	7	6			9	10²	11		3¹	2	8¹										4
1	5	4	3		7	8	12	9	10	11²				2	6¹	13										5
1	5	3	4		14	7³	8	9²	10¹	11	13			2	6	12										6
	2	3	4	5	6²	7	8	9	10¹	11	12	13				1										7
	2	4	3	5	10	7²	6	8	13	11	9¹			12		1										8
	2	3	4	5	10	7¹	9	13	8	14	11³	6²		12		1										9
1	2	3	4	5	7	8	9		6²	11¹		13		10	12											10
1	2	3	4	5	6	8	7		11³	10²		13		9¹	14	12										11
1		3	4	5	6	7	8¹		9	10³		13		2	11²	14										12
1		3	4	5	7³	8	9		6	11	12	14		2²	10¹		13									13
1		3	4	5	13	7²	8		6	11	10			2²	9¹	14		12								14
1	2	3	4	5	6³	7	8		10	11²		12		9¹	14	13										15
1		2	4	9	6	7			5¹	11³	10²	8		3	13	14	12									16
1	2²	3	4	5	7	8³	9		6		11	13	14	10¹		12										17
1	13	3	4	8	6		7		5	9¹	11			2	12		10²									18
1	12	3	4	9	6	7²	10		5	11	13			2³	8		14									19
1		2	4	5	7	12	8		6	10				3	9¹		11									20
1		2	4	9	6	7	8		5¹	12	10			3	13³	14	11²									21
1		2	4	5	7		6	8³	9	12	11²	13		3		14	10¹									22
1		2	4	5	7		6	12	11²	10¹	8			3	9³		14			13						23
1		2	3	5	7		9	13	6³	12		8		4	11¹	14										24
1		2	4	5	8	12	9		6		7²			3⁴	10¹				14		11	13				25
1	4		5	9	2	8	14	6								10²		13	3	12³	11			7¹		26
1		2	4	5	7	12	8¹	13	6					3						11	10			9²		27
1	14		2	8	6	13	7		5³					3					12	4	10²	11		9¹		28
1	13	2	4	9	6¹²	8	14		5					3							11²	10		7²		29
1⁸	13	2	4	9		7	8		5					3							11²	10	6¹	12		30
	12	2	4	9	6	8¹	14		5					3				13			10²	11	7¹		1	31
1	6³	2	4	9	8²	12	14		5					3				13			10¹	11	7			32
1	12	2	4	8	6		7	13	5					3				14			11²	10	9³			33
1	2	3	4	5	7			8	9¹	6					13		12				10²	11				34
1	6	2	4	9		7	13		5					3			12				10¹	11	8²			35
1	6	2	4	8	13		7		5					3			12				11¹	10	9²			36
1	7	2	4³	9	12		8		5¹			14		3		10					13	11	6²			37
1	2	3¹	4	5²	7			8	14					6		13	12				10	11	9¹			38

INVERNESS CALEDONIAN THISTLE

Year Formed: 1994. *Ground & Address:* Tulloch Caledonian Stadium, Stadium Road, Inverness IV1 1FF. *Telephone:*
01463 222880. *Fax:* 01463 227479. *E-mail:* info@ictfc.co.uk *Website:* ictfc.co.uk
Ground Capacity: 7,780 (all seated). *Size of Pitch:* 105m × 68m.
Chairman: Graham Rae. *Chief Executive:* Yvonne Crook.
Manager: John Robertson. *Assistant Manager:* Brian Rice.
Club Nicknames: 'Caley Thistle', 'Caley Jags', 'ICT'.
Record Attendance: 7,753 v Rangers, SPL, 20 January 2008.
Record Transfer Fee received: £400,000 for Marius Niculae to Dinamo Bucharest (July 2008).
Record Transfer Fee paid: £65,000 for John Rankin from Ross Co (July 2006).
Record Victory: 8-1 v Annan Ath, Scottish Cup 3rd rd, 24 January 1998; 7-0 v Ayr U, First Division, 24 April 2010; 7-0 v
Arbroath, League Cup Northern Section Group C, 30 July 2016.
Record Defeats: 0-6 v Airdrieonians, First Division, 21 Sep 2000; 0-6 v Celtic, League Cup 3rd rd, 22 Sep 2010; 0-6 v
Celtic, Scottish Premiership, 27 April 2014; 0-6 v Celtic, Scottish Cup 5th rd, 11 February 2017.
Most Capped Player: Richard Hastings, 38 (59), Canada.
Most League Appearances: 490: Ross Tokely, 1995-2012.
Most League Goals in Season: 27: Iain Stewart, 1996-97; Denis Wyness, 2002-03.
Most Goals Overall (Individual): 118: Denis Wyness, 2000-03, 2005-08.

INVERNESS CALEDONIAN THISTLE –
SPFL LADBROKES CHAMPIONSHIP 2017–18 LEAGUE RECORD

Match No.	Date	Venue	Opponents	Result	H/T Score	Lg Pos.	Goalscorers	Atten- dance
1	Aug 5	H	Dundee U	L	0-1	0-1	8		3415
2	12	A	Dunfermline Ath	L	1-5	1-3	10	Vigurs [18]	4391
3	19	H	Greenock Morton	D	1-1	1-0	10	Warren [19]	2202
4	26	A	Brechin C	W	4-0	2-0	7	Vigurs 2 [27, 73], McKay [32], Cooper [62]	703
5	Sept 9	A	St Mirren	L	2-4	0-1	7	Baird [61], Polworth [69]	3610
6	16	H	Livingston	L	1-3	1-1	8	Bell [27]	2007
7	23	A	Dumbarton	L	1-2	1-0	8	Bell [8]	594
8	30	H	Queen of the South	D	0-0	0-0	9		2082
9	Oct 14	A	Falkirk	D	0-0	0-0	9		4107
10	21	A	Dundee U	W	2-0	2-0	8	Vigurs [28], Bell [36]	5560
11	28	H	Dunfermline Ath	W	1-0	1-0	7	Bell [23]	2948
12	Nov 4	A	Livingston	D	0-0	0-0	7		1262
13	25	H	St Mirren	L	0-2	0-0	8		2687
14	28	H	Brechin C	W	4-0	2-0	7	McKay [7], Baird [9], Bell [52], Oakley [87]	1801
15	Dec 2	A	Queen of the South	D	0-0	0-0	8		1293
16	16	H	Dumbarton	W	1-0	1-0	7	Tremarco [34]	2103
17	23	A	Greenock Morton	L	0-1	0-1	7		1547
18	30	A	Brechin C	W	3-2	1-2	7	McLennan (og) [4], Oakley 2 [65, 78]	571
19	Jan 2	H	Livingston	D	1-1	1-0	7	Doran [6]	2239
20	6	A	St Mirren	L	0-1	0-1	7		4448
21	9	H	Falkirk	W	4-1	3-0	7	Oakley [10], Bell [28], Mulraney [30], Baird [88]	2014
22	13	H	Queen of the South	W	3-1	2-0	6	Vigurs [3], Chalmers [29], Doran [58]	2209
23	27	A	Falkirk	L	1-3	0-0	7	Mackay [84]	4251
24	Feb 24	H	Greenock Morton	L	0-2	0-1	7		2359
25	Mar 13	A	Dunfermline Ath	L	0-1	0-1	8		2249
26	17	A	Dundee U	D	1-1	1-0	8	Vigurs [30]	4772
27	27	H	Dundee U	W	1-0	1-0	7	Doran [44]	2328
28	31	H	St Mirren	D	2-2	0-1	8	Warren [78], Polworth [81]	3025
29	Apr 3	H	Brechin C	W	4-0	2-0	7	Chalmers 2 [12, 58], Donaldson [22], Oakley [66]	1963
30	7	A	Queen of the South	W	2-0	2-0	7	Austin [9], Oakley [30]	1140
31	10	H	Falkirk	W	1-0	0-0	6	Mulraney [81]	2053
32	14	H	Dumbarton	W	5-1	2-1	6	Doran [17], Austin 3 [41, 50, 66], Vigurs [63]	2355
33	18	A	Dumbarton	W	1-0	0-0	5	Vigurs [56]	392
34	21	H	Dunfermline Ath	D	2-2	1-1	5	Chalmers [16], Austin [48]	3316
35	24	A	Livingston	W	1-0	0-0	5	Polworth [46]	740
36	28	A	Greenock Morton	W	3-0	2-0	5	Oakley 2 [20, 37], Austin [55]	1539

Final League Position: 5

Honours
League Champions: First Division 2003-04, 2009-10; Third Division 1996-97.
Runners-up: Second Division 1998-99.
Scottish Cup Winners: 2015; Semi-finals 2003, 2004; Quarter-finals 1996.
League Cup Runners-up: 2013-14.
League Challenge Cup Winners: 2003-04, 2017-18; *Runners-up:* 1999-2000, 2009-10.

European: *Europa League:* 4 matches (2015-16).

Club colours: Shirt: Blue with vertical red stripes. Shorts: Blue. Socks: Blue with red stripes.

Goalscorers: *League (53):* Oakley 8, Vigurs 8, Austin 6, Bell 6, Chalmers 4, Doran 4, Baird 3, Polworth 3, McKay 2, Mulraney 2, Warren 2, Cooper 1, Donaldson 1, Mackay 1, Tremarco 1, own goal 1.
William Hill Scottish FA Cup (2): Doran 1, Oakley 1.
Betfred Scottish League Cup (5): Oakley 2, Warren 2, Baird 1.
Irn-Bru Scottish League Challenge Cup (12): Calder 2, Polworth 2, Tremarco 2, Bell 1, Chalmers 1, Mackay 1, Mulraney 1, Oakley 1, Raven 1.

Ridgers M 34	Raven D 15+3	McKay B 34+1	Elsdon M 3	Chalmers J 33+1	Polworth L 35	Draper R 1	Vigurs I 30	Calder R 10+13	Oakley G 22+11	Baird J 18+4	Mulraney J 15+11	Bell C 20+8	Zschusschen F —+2	Seedorf C 12+2	Cooper A 3+3	Warren G 19+3	Trafford C 21+5	Donaldson C 25+1	Tremarco C 23+2	Fon Williams O 2	Mackay D —+7	Doran A 11+7	Austin N 9+4	Brown J —+1	Harper C 1	Elbouzedi Z —+4	Match No.
1	2	3	4	5	6	7	8	9[1]	10[3]	11[2]	12	13	14														1
1	14	3	4	5	7		8[1]	9	11[3]	10	6[2]	13		2	12												2
1	14	4		9	6		8	5[2]	11[1]	10[3]	13	12			2[4]	3	7										3
1	2	4	3[1]	5	6		8	13	10	14	11[3]					9[2]	7	12									4
1	2	4		5	9		8	11[1]	10			12				6	3	7									5
1	2	3		5[1]	8		7	12	11[3]	13	9					10[2]	4	6	14								6
	8	2		9	7			6[2]	13	12	10					3[1]	11	4	5[1]	1							7
	2	3		6	7			12	10[2]	9[1]	13	11					8	4	5	1							8
1	2	3		8	6		9		10	7[1]	11						4	5			12						9
1	2	3		9	7		8[1]	14	10	6[3]	11[2]	12	13					4	5								10
1	2	3		9	7		8	12	13	11[4]	6[3]	10[1]	14					4	5								11
1	2	3		9	7		8	13	12	11[2]	6	10						4	5[1]								12
1	2	9[2]			7		8[4]	12	13	10[3]	6[1]	11				3	14	4	5								13
1	2	3		9	7			13	10[1]	6[3]	11[2]	14				8		4	5			12					14
1	2	3		8[4]	6		7	14	12	10[1]	9	11[3]	13					4	5								15
1	2	3		9	8			14	12	11[3]	6[2]	10[1]				7		4	5			13					16
1	2[4]	3		9	7		8	13	11[1]	6[2]	10[3]	12		14				4	5								17
1		3		9	7		8	14	12	10[3]	6	11[2]		2[1]	13			4	5[5]								18
1	13	2		5[1]	6		7[4]	12	10	9[2]						3	8	4				11[3]	14				19
1	2	4		9	6			12	10[3]	13	14					3	7		5			8[1]	11[2]				20
1	2			9	7		8	12	10	14	6[2]	11[3]				3		4	5[1]			13					21
1	2			9	8		7[1]	5	11	12	10[2]					3	13	4				6					22
1	2			8	5			10[2]	12	9[4]	11[3]					7	3					13	14				23
1		3		9	7		8	5	11					2		4	6[1]				13	10	12[2]				24
1	12	7		6	8			10	9[3]	13				2		3		4				11[1]				5[2] 14	25
1	4	9		8	7			10[2]	12	11[3]				2		3	6[1]		5			13	14				26
1	2	13		6	7			10						3			8[2]	4	5			12	11			9[1]	27
1	2			7	8			13	10							3	9	4	5			12	6[1]			11[1]	28
1		4		6	8		7[3]	5	11	10				2		14	9[2]	3[1]				12	13				29
1	2	6[2]		7	8			10								4	9	3	5			12	13			11[1]	30
1	2	6		8	7			10	13							3	9[1]	4	5			12				11[2]	31
1		4		9	8		7[1]		10	14	13			2		3	6[1]		5			11[2]				12	32
1	2			9	8		7	5	10	14	12				4[1]	3	13					6[1]				11[3]	33
1		3		5	7			13	10						2	9	4	8				12	6[1]			11[2]	34
1		3		8	6			10	12	11[2]				2		7		4	5				9[1]			13	35
1		3		9	6		8	13	12					2		7[1]	4[2]		5				11[3]			14	36

KILMARNOCK

Year Formed: 1869. *Ground & Address:* Rugby Park, Kilmarnock KA1 2DP. *Telephone:* 01563 545300. *Fax:* 01563 522181. *Email:* info@kilmarnockfc.co.uk *Website:* www.kilmarnockfc.co.uk
Ground Capacity: 18,128 (all seated). *Size of Pitch:* 102m × 67m.
Chief Executive: Kirsten Robertson. *Director:* Billy Bowie.
Manager: Steve Clarke. *Assistant Manager:* Alex Dyer.
Club Nickname: 'Killie'.
Previous Grounds: Rugby Park (Dundonald Road); The Grange; Holm Quarry; Rugby Park 1899.
Record Attendance: 35,995 v Rangers, Scottish Cup Quarter-final, 10 March 1962.
Record Transfer Fee received: £1,900,000 for Steven Naismith to Rangers (2007).
Record Transfer Fee paid: £340,000 for Paul Wright from St Johnstone (1995).
Record Victory: 11-1 v Paisley Academical, Scottish Cup 1st rd, 18 January 1930.
Record Defeat: 1-9 v Celtic, Division I, 13 August 1938.
Most Capped Player: Joe Nibloe, 11, Scotland.
Most League Appearances: 481: Alan Robertson, 1972-88.
Most League Goals in Season (Individual): 34: Harry 'Peerie' Cunningham 1927-28; Andy Kerr 1960-61.
Most Goals Overall (Individual): 148: Willy Culley, 1912-23.

KILMARNOCK – SPFL LADBROKES PREMIERSHIP 2017–18 LEAGUE RECORD

Match No.	Date	Venue	Opponents	Result	H/T Score	Lg Pos.	Goalscorers	Atten- dance
1	Aug 5	H	St Johnstone	L	1-2	0-1	10	Boyd, K [59]	3935
2	12	H	Hearts	L	0-1	0-1	9		5076
3	19	H	Celtic	L	0-2	0-1	10		10,069
4	26	H	Hamilton A	D	2-2	1-0	10	Longridge (og) [3], Erwin [58]	3706
5	Sept 9	A	Motherwell	L	0-2	0-0	11		4621
6	16	A	Aberdeen	D	1-1	0-1	12	Jones [48]	15,037
7	23	A	Dundee	D	1-1	0-1	12	Greer [64]	3452
8	30	H	Ross Co	L	0-2	0-2	12		3337
9	Oct 14	A	Partick Thistle	W	2-0	1-0	11	Boyd, K [39], Frizzell [63]	3662
10	25	A	Rangers	D	1-1	0-1	11	Burke [90]	47,981
11	28	A	Celtic	D	1-1	0-1	11	Jones [60]	58,060
12	31	H	Hibernian	L	0-3	0-1	11		5005
13	Nov 5	A	Hearts	W	2-1	-	10	Boyd, K [31], Frizzell [86]	16,347
14	18	A	Dundee	D	0-0	0-0	10		5853
15	26	H	Aberdeen	L	1-3	0-2	10	Jones [66]	4198
16	Dec 2	A	St Johnstone	W	2-1	1-1	10	Findlay [10], Brophy [66]	2950
17	9	H	Partick Thistle	W	5-1	2-1	8	Boyd, K 2 (1 pen) [12, 79 (p)], Brophy 2 [20, 65], Keown (og) [60]	4339
18	12	A	Ross Co	D	2-2	0-2	8	Brophy [61], Boyd, K [86]	3021
19	16	H	Motherwell	W	1-0	1-0	8	Boyd, S [42]	4179
20	23	H	Rangers	W	2-1	0-1	6	Boyd, K 2 [77, 80]	11,490
21	30	A	Hibernian	D	1-1	1-1	6	Boyd, K [1]	17,666
22	Jan 27	A	Aberdeen	L	1-3	1-0	7	Boyd, K [28]	13,723
23	Feb 3	H	Celtic	W	1-0	0-0	6	Mulumbu [70]	10,702
24	13	H	Dundee	W	3-2	1-1	7	Brophy [5], Boyd, K [74], Wilson [87]	3768
25	17	A	Motherwell	W	1-0	1-0	6	O'Donnell [34]	5322
26	24	H	Hibernian	D	2-2	0-2	6	Jones [58], Boyd, K [61]	5348
27	27	A	Hearts	D	1-1	1-1	6	Brophy [3]	15,862
28	Mar 7	H	St Johnstone	W	2-0	1-0	5	Boyd, K (pen) [30], Erwin [58]	3807
29	10	H	Ross Co	W	3-2	1-0	5	Erwin [16], Boyd, K [46], Brophy [74]	4001
30	17	A	Rangers	W	1-0	0-0	5	Boyd, K [54]	49,396
31	31	H	Hamilton A	W	2-0	2-0	5	Erwin [5], O'Donnell [45]	4672
32	Apr 7	A	Partick Thistle	W	1-0	1-0	5	Findlay [35]	4227
33	14	A	Hamilton A	W	2-1	0-0	5	Broadfoot [63], Boyd, K [79]	4348
34	21	A	Aberdeen	L	0-2	0-1	5		5067
35	28	H	Hibernian	L	3-5	1-1	5	Boyd, K 2 [33, 80], Findlay [61]	17,470
36	May 5	A	Rangers	L	0-1	0-0	5		49,703
37	9	A	Celtic	D	0-0	0-0	5		54,916
38	13	H	Hearts	W	1-0	1-0	5	Erwin [10]	6273

Final League Position: 5

Honours
League Champions: Division I 1964-65;. Division II 1897-98, 1898-99.
Runners-up: Division I 1959-60, 1960-61, 1962-63, 1963-64; First Division 1975-76, 1978-79, 1981-82, 1992-93; Division II 1953-54, 1973-74; Second Division 1989-90.
Scottish Cup Winners: 1920, 1929, 1997; *Runners-up:* 1898, 1932, 1938, 1957, 1960.
League Cup Winners: 2011-12; *Runners-up:* 1952-53, 1960-61, 1962-63, 2000-01, 2006-07.

European: *European Cup:* 4 matches (1965-66). *Cup Winners' Cup:* 4 matches (1997-98). *UEFA Cup:* 32 matches (*Fairs Cup:* 1964-65, 1966-67 semi-finals, 1969-70, 1970-71. *UEFA Cup:* 1998-99, 1999-2000, 2001-02).

Club colours: Shirt: Blue with white stripes. Shorts: White. Socks: Blue.

Goalscorers: *League (49):* Boyd K 18 (2 pens), Brophy 7, Erwin 5, Jones 4, Findlay 3, Frizzell 2, O'Donnell 2, Boyd S 1, Broadfoot 1, Burke 1, Greer 1, Mulumbu 1, Wilson 1, own goals 2.
William Hill Scottish FA Cup (7): Boyd K 2 (1 pen), O'Donnell 2, Brophy 1, Erwin 1 (1 pen), Tshibola 1.
Betfred Scottish League Cup (9): Boyd K 3, McKenzie 2, Thomas 2, Burke 1, Erwin 1.

MacDonald J 35	Wilson 17 + 6	Greer G 20	Broadfoot K 29 + 1	Taylor G 36 + 2	Thomas D 7 + 2	Burke C 9 + 11	Frizzell A 10 + 5	Jones J 28 + 4	McKenzie R 21 + 4	Boyd K 30 + 4	Erwin L 14 + 20	Power A 21 + 3	O'Donnell S 35 + 1	Samizadeh A — +1	Smith S 3	Brophy E 15 + 13	Findlay S 29 + 3	Waters C 3 + 2	Hawkshaw D 2 + 3	Dicker G 20 + 1	Mulumbu Y 16 + 2	Boyd S 10 + 1	Kiltie G 5 + 4	Tshibola A 9 + 3	Simpson A 1 + 3	Fasan L 3	Cameron I — + 3	Match No.
1	2	3	4	5	6¹	7²	8	9	10	11	12	13																1
1	2³	3	4⁸	5²	9	6¹	8	12	7	10	11		13	14														2
1	4	3		5	6²	13	8	10	7	11		2			9¹	12												3
1	6	3		5	7¹		8	10	13	11²	12		2		9	4												4
1	7	3¹	12	5	6	9²	14	13			11		2		8	10³	4											5
1	7¹	3		5		13	8	9²	10		11		2			4	6	12										6
1		3		5			9¹	10	8	12	11		2			4	6	7										7
1		3	5	8			9	10		12	11¹		2		13	4	6²	7										8
1	2	3	9²	14		11	8	6³	10¹	12	7	5				4	13											9
1		4	3	8		12	9²	10	6	11¹	13	7	2			5												10
1		4	3	8¹	13	9²		10	6	11¹		7	2			12	5	14										11
1		4	3	8		9	12	10	6²	11	13	7	2			5												12
1		3	4	8		9¹	13	10	6¹	11²	12	7	2			5		14										13
1		3	4	7		9²		10	6	11¹	12	8	2			13	5											14
1		3	4	9		8²	10⁸	6¹	12	11³	7	2				14	5		13									15
1		4	3	9	6²	12			11¹	13	7	2			10³	5	14	8										16
1		4	3	14		12		9		11²	13	6	2			10³	5		7	8¹								17
1	4¹	3	13		14		6³		11		7	2			10	5²		8	9	12								18
1		4	5	9¹		12		11	14	6¹	2				10²		7	8	3	13								19
1		4	5	14			9¹	13	6	2				10³	12	7	8	3										20
1		4	5	9¹	14	11¹	12	10²	13	8	2				6	7	3											21
1		4	5		11	9³	10¹	12	8¹	2		13			6	7	3	14										22
1	4	3	5		9¹	6	11²	13	2		10³	14			7	8		12										23
1	13		3	9		6	11¹	12	2		10¹	5	8⁸		4²		7	14										24
1	13		3	8	14		9⁴	6	11²	12	2		10¹	5	7	4												25
1		3	5		11	9	10²		6¹	2		12	4		7	8		13										26
1	14	4³	3	5		9	6		13	7	2		10²	12	8		11¹											27
1		3	5¹		13	9³		11²	10	8	2		12	4	7		6	14										28
1		3	5²			6	10²	11		14	4	7	13		9¹	8	12											29
1		3	5		10	13	11²	14	12	2		9⁴	4	6	7¹		8²											30
1	14		5		12	6	10²	11	8¹	2		9³	4	7		3	13											31
1		3	5		11	12	10¹	9²	8	2		13	4	7	6²		14											32
		3	5		10	8¹	11¹		12		13	4	6	7	9²		14				2	1	14					33
		3	8	14		10	12	6		2		9²	5	7		4³	11¹						1	13				34
		3	5		6		10	11¹	7	2		13	4	8	12		9²			1								35
1	14		3	5		11		10³	12	2		9²	4	7	6¹		13	8										36
1	14		5	13		12	10		2		9²	4	7	6¹	3	11²	8											37
1	7³		5	13		10¹		12		2		9²	4		8	3	9²	6						14				38

LIVINGSTON

Year Formed: 1974. *Ground:* Tony Macaroni Arena, Almondvale Stadium, Alderstone Road, Livingston EH54 7DN.
Telephone: 01506 417000. *Fax:* 01506 429948.
Email: lfcreception@livingstonfc.co.uk *Website:* livingstonfc.co.uk
Ground Capacity: 9,865 (all seated). *Size of Pitch:* 98m × 69m.
Chairman: Robert Wilson. *Secretary:* Brian Ewing.
Player/Manager: Kenny Miller. *Coach:* David Martindale.
Club Nickname: 'Livi Lions'.
Previous Grounds: Meadowbank Stadium (as Meadowbank Thistle).
Record Attendance: 10,024 v Celtic, Premier League, 18 August 2001.
Record Transfer Fee received: £1,000,000 for David Fernandez to Celtic (June 2002).
Record Transfer Fee paid: £120,000 for Wes Hoolahan from Shelbourne (December 2005).
Record Victory: 8-0 v Stranraer, League Cup, 1st rd, 31 July 2012.
Record Defeat: 0-8 v Hamilton A. Division II, 14 December 1974.
Most League Appearances: 446: Walter Boyd, 1979-89.
Most League Goals in Season (Individual): 22: Leigh Griffiths, 2008-09; Iain Russell, 2010-11; Liam Buchanan, 2016-17.
Most Goals Overall (Individual): 64: David Roseburgh, 1986-93.

LIVINGSTON – SPFL LADBROKES CHAMPIONSHIP 2017–18 LEAGUE RECORD

Match No.	Date	Venue	Opponents	Result	H/T Score	Lg Pos.	Goalscorers	Atten-dance
1	Aug 5	H	Dunfermline Ath	D 1-1	1-0	5	Pitman [30]	2301
2	12	A	Brechin C	D 2-2	2-0	6	Mackin [25], Pitman [44]	579
3	19	H	St Mirren	L 1-3	1-1	7	Halkett [15]	1609
4	26	A	Greenock Morton	W 1-0	0-0	6	Mullen [60]	1599
5	Sept 9	H	Queen of the South	D 2-2	1-0	6	Mullin (pen) [40], Mackin [81]	1113
6	16	A	Inverness CT	W 3-1	1-1	6	Todorov [24], Robinson [52], Halkett [72]	2007
7	23	A	Falkirk	W 2-0	0-0	4	Mullen [47], Mullin [53]	4091
8	30	H	Dumbarton	W 2-1	1-0	4	Lithgow [19], Halkett [85]	938
9	Oct 14	H	Dundee U	W 2-0	1-0	2	Mullen [7], Todorov [76]	2282
10	21	A	Dunfermline Ath	L 1-3	0-3	3	Mullen [87]	5059
11	28	H	Brechin C	W 3-2	1-1	3	McMillan [3], Halkett [60], Mackin [69]	926
12	Nov 4	H	Inverness CT	D 0-0	0-0	3		1262
13	25	A	Queen of the South	W 3-0	1-0	3	Penrice [32], Mullin [68], Byrne [81]	1328
14	28	A	St Mirren	L 1-3	1-0	3	Carrick [30]	3177
15	Dec 19	H	Falkirk	D 0-0	0-0	4		1287
16	23	A	Dundee U	L 0-3	0-2	6		6221
17	26	A	Dumbarton	W 4-1	2-1	3	Halkett [27], Pitman [43], Mackin [58], Robinson [80]	495
18	Jan 2	A	Inverness CT	D 1-1	0-1	3	Lithgow [82]	2239
19	6	H	Queen of the South	L 0-1	0-1	5		1067
20	13	A	Brechin C	W 2-0	1-0	4	Halkett (pen) [12], Robinson [69]	551
21	27	H	Dumbarton	W 2-0	2-0	3	Lithgow [23], Hardie [28]	732
22	Feb 3	A	Falkirk	W 3-1	1-0	3	Lithgow [39], Hardie [59], De Vita [62]	4123
23	10	H	Dunfermline Ath	D 0-0	0-0	2		1579
24	17	H	St Mirren	W 4-1	3-1	2	Hardie 2 [9, 15], Miller [22], Robinson [90]	2708
25	23	H	Dundee U	W 2-1	1-0	2	Robinson [22], Hardie [90]	1604
26	27	A	Greenock Morton	W 1-0	0-0	2	Cadden [47]	1373
27	Mar 13	A	Greenock Morton	D 1-1	0-0	2	Longridge [90]	862
28	17	H	Falkirk	D 0-0	0-0	2		1319
29	24	A	Queen of the South	D 3-3	1-2	2	De Vita [41], Halkett [52], Hardie [60]	1153
30	31	A	Dumbarton	W 3-0	3-0	2	Miller [34], Hardie [36], De Vita [45]	670
31	Apr 3	A	Dunfermline Ath	L 0-1	0-1	2		4572
32	7	H	Greenock Morton	W 3-2	1-1	2	Longridge [35], Lithgow 2 [53, 86]	1028
33	14	A	St Mirren	D 0-0	0-0	2		6172
34	21	H	Brechin C	W 3-0	0-0	2	Pitman [67], Longridge [73], Hardie [86]	943
35	24	H	Inverness CT	L 0-1	0-0	2		740
36	28	A	Dundee U	L 0-2	0-0	2		5226

Final League Position: 2

Honours
League Champions: First Division 2000-01; Second Division 1986-87, 1998-99, 2010-11; League One 2016-17; Third Division 1995-96, 2009-10.
Runners-up: Second Division 1982-83; First Division 1987-88; Championship 2017-18.
Promoted via play-offs: 2017-18 (to Premiership).
Scottish Cup: Semi-finals 2001, 2004.
League Cup Winners: 2003-04. Semi-finals 1984-85.
League Challenge Cup Winners: 2014-15; *Runners-up:* 2000-01.

European: *UEFA Cup:* 4 matches (2002-03).

Club colours: All: Black with yellow trim.

Goalscorers: *League (56):* Hardie 8, Halkett 7 (1 pen), Lithgow 6, Robinson 5, Mackin 4, Mullen 4, Pitman 4, De Vita 3, Longridge 3, Mullin 3 (1 pen), Miller 2, Todorov 2, Byrne 1, Cadden 1, Carrick 1, McMillan 1, Penrice 1.
William Hill Scottish FA Cup (2): Mackin 2.
Betfred Scottish League Cup (12): Carrick 2, De Vita 2, Robinson 2, Halkett 1, Jacobs 1, Lithgow 1, Mackin 1, Todorov 1, own goal 1.
Irn-Bru Scottish League Challenge Cup (3): Mackin 1, Mullen 1, Todorov 1.
Play-Offs (7): Jacobs 2, Pitman 2, De Vita 1, Lithgow 1, Mullin 1.

Alexander N 34	Gallagher D 30 + 1	Halkett C 34 + 1	Lithgow A 33	Mullin J 20 + 8	Byrne S 32 + 1	Pitman S 35	Jacobs K 13 + 7	Longridge J 23 + 8	Carrick D 4 + 5	Mullen D 11	De Vita R 21 + 9	Cadden N 15 + 11	Todorov N 10 + 8	Mackin N 7 + 7	Robinson S 9 + 8	Thomson J 1 + 1	Penrice J 11 + 2	McMillan J 3 + 10	Knox M — + 2	Boyd S 4 + 6	Maley G 2	Thompson J 7 + 4	Buchanan G 7 + 1	Miller L 13 + 3	Hardie R 15 + 1	Frizzell A 2 + 3	Match No.
1	2	3	4	5^2	6	7	8	9	10^1	11^3	12	13	14														1
1	2	3	4	5^2	6	7		9	13	11^3	8^1	14		10	12												2
1	2	3		5	8^3	6		4	10^2	11		9^1	12	14	13		7										3
1	2	3	4	5	8^2	6	7	12		11	14		10^3		13	9^1											4
1	2	3	4	5	7	6	8^2	9	13	11^1	14		10^2	12													5
1		3	4	6	8	7		5		11^2	12	10	9^1	2^3		14	13										6
1	2^1	3	4	5	7	6	14	9		10^1		13	11^3		8^2	12											7
1		3	4	5^2	7	6	13	9^1		11		10^3	2	12		8	14										8
1		3	4	5	7	6		9^2	12^3	11	14	10^1	2		8	13											9
1	12	3	2	5^2	7	6		9^3	11^1	10	14		4		8	13											10
1	2	3	4	5	7	6	13		11^2		10^1	12		8	9^3	14											11
1	2	3	4	5^2	7	10	6	9		11^1		12	14	13		8^2											12
1	2	3	4	5	7	6	8	14	13		10^1		12	11^2		9^3											13
1	2	3	4	5^2	8	7	6	9	11^1		13	10^3	12	14													14
1	2	3	4	5	7	6		9^3	14	12	11^2	13		8^1		10											15
	4	2	3	5^2	6	7	13	8^2		14		10^1		12	9		11	1									16
1	4	3	2		8	7	6^1	9		11^3	5^2		10	12	13		14										17
1	4	3	2	7^3	6	11		5	12		9	8^1	14	10^1	13												18
1		3	2	14	7	6		4^3		9		10	11^1	5^2	8		13	12									19
1	2	5	4		7	8	6^3	9		12		14	13	10^1			11^2		3								20
1	7	3	4	14		6			5	9^3		12					13		8^1	2^3	10	11					21
1	2	4	3	13	6	7			5	9^2		12					8	14	10^1	11^3							22
1	2	3	4		6^2	7			5	9		14		13		12	6^1		10^1	11^3							23
1	2	3	4		7	6	12		5^1	9^2		8		13	14				10	11^3							24
1	2	3	4	12	7	6		13	5^1	9^2		8							10	11							25
1	2	3	4		6	7	12	14	5^3	9		8^2		13					10	11							26
1	2	3	4	5^1	7^5	6	13	12		9^2				14			8		10^1	11							27
1	7	3	4	5^1		6	8	9^3		12				14		10^2			2	13	11						28
1	6	3	4		12	7	8	11		5	14		9^2							2^3	10^1	13					29
1	3			12	8	7		4		6^2	9^1					5	14		13	2	11	10^3					30
1	2	3	4		6	7^1	5	9		8^1		10^2								14		13	11	12			31
1		3	4		7	6	12	9		5^2	13								8^3	2	11	10^1	14				32
1	2	3	4	14	7	6		9		5^2	12						13			11	11^2	10	8^1				33
1	2	3	4	12	7	6	8	13		5^3	9^2		14									10^1	11				34
	4	14		6^2			5			9	12		11			2^1			1	8	3	13	10	7^3			35
1	2	3	4	14	7^3	6	8	13		9^2									5^1		11	10	12				36

MONTROSE

Year Formed: 1879. *Ground & Address:* Links Park, Wellington St, Montrose DD10 8QD. *Telephone:* 01674 673200.
Fax: 01674 677311. *E-mail:* office@montrosefc.co.uk *Website:* www.montrosefc.co.uk
Ground Capacity: total: 4,936, (seated: 1,338). *Size of Pitch:* 100m × 64m.
Chairman: John Crawford. *Secretary:* Brian Petrie.
Manager: Stewart Petrie. *Assistant Manager:* Ross Campbell.
Club Nickname: 'The Gable Endies'.
Previous Grounds: None.
Record Attendance: 8,983 v Dundee, Scottish Cup 3rd rd, 17 March 1973.
Record Transfer Fee received: £50,000 for Gary Murray to Hibernian (December 1980).
Record Transfer Fee paid: £17,500 for Jim Smith from Airdrieonians (February 1992).
Record Victory: 12-0 v Vale of Leithen, Scottish Cup 2nd rd, 4 January 1975.
Record Defeat: 0-13 v Aberdeen, 17 March 1951.
Most Capped Player: Alexander Keillor, 2 (6), Scotland.
Most League Appearances: 432: David Larter, 1987-98.
Most League Goals in Season (Individual): 28: Brian Third, Division II, 1972-73.
Most Goals Overall (Individual): 126: Bobby Livingstone, 1967-79.

MONTROSE – SPFL LADBROKES LEAGUE TWO 2017–18 LEAGUE RECORD

Match No.	Date	Venue	Opponents	Result	H/T Score	Lg Pos.	Goalscorers	Attendance
1	Aug 5	A	Edinburgh C	W 3-1	2-0	2	Templeman [28], McLaren [30], Campbell, I [46]	341
2	12	H	Stenhousemuir	D 1-1	0-0	3	Webster [78]	455
3	19	H	Cowdenbeath	W 1-0	1-0	2	Dillon [19]	456
4	26	A	Annan Ath	W 1-0	1-0	2	Watson [43]	412
5	Sept 9	A	Peterhead	D 1-1	0-0	2	Templeman [90]	614
6	16	H	Stirling Alb	L 1-3	0-1	2	Ferguson [90]	568
7	23	A	Elgin C	L 0-3	0-1	4		549
8	30	H	Clyde	W 3-2	3-1	3	Campbell, I (pen) [10], Templeman [20], Webster [26]	463
9	Oct 21	A	Berwick R	W 1-0	1-0	2	Johnston [30]	508
10	28	H	Edinburgh C	W 1-0	0-0	2	Johnston [60]	446
11	Nov 4	A	Cowdenbeath	W 3-1	2-0	2	Masson 2 [10, 21], Johnston [59]	349
12	11	H	Annan Ath	D 1-1	1-0	2	Templeman [8]	353
13	25	A	Stenhousemuir	W 1-0	1-0	1	Masson [15]	418
14	Dec 2	A	Clyde	D 0-0	0-0	1		409
15	9	H	Berwick R	W 3-0	3-0	1	Fraser 2 [2, 28], Templeman [19]	430
16	16	H	Elgin C	W 3-0	1-0	1	Masson [6], Steeves [54], Redman [73]	559
17	23	A	Stirling Alb	W 1-0	0-0	1	Fraser [58]	710
18	30	H	Peterhead	L 2-6	1-2	1	Dillon [41], Hay [75]	932
19	Jan 2	H	Cowdenbeath	D 1-1	0-0	1	Fraser [68]	543
20	6	A	Annan Ath	W 1-0	1-0	1	Milne [39]	339
21	13	A	Edinburgh C	W 2-0	2-0	1	Bolochoweckyj [36], Milne [39]	464
22	20	H	Clyde	L 1-3	0-1	1	Fraser (pen) [67]	543
23	27	H	Stirling Alb	W 2-1	0-1	1	Johnston [75], Allan [81]	531
24	Feb 3	A	Peterhead	W 1-0	0-0	1	Templeman [73]	762
25	10	H	Stenhousemuir	W 1-0	0-0	1	Redman [80]	1182
26	17	A	Elgin C	D 2-2	1-1	1	Fraser [41], Rennie [75]	700
27	24	A	Berwick R	D 2-2	2-1	1	Wilson (og) [8], Fraser [43]	417
28	Mar 13	A	Annan Ath	W 2-1	1-0	2	Templeman 2 [40, 64]	355
29	17	H	Peterhead	W 3-2	0-1	1	Masson [61], Templeman [71], Milne [82]	699
30	24	A	Clyde	L 0-3	0-3	2		571
31	31	H	Edinburgh C	W 3-0	2-0	2	Milne 2 (1 pen) [4, 19 (p)], Rennie [90]	583
32	Apr 7	A	Stirling Alb	W 5-0	1-0	2	Rennie [27], Milne 3 [63, 78, 90], Ballantyne [75]	692
33	10	A	Cowdenbeath	W 3-0	1-0	1	Milne 2 [26, 60], Rennie [47]	378
34	14	H	Berwick R	W 1-0	1-0	1	Templeman [10]	805
35	21	A	Stenhousemuir	W 2-0	2-0	1	Templeman [2], Milne [8]	976
36	28	H	Elgin C	D 1-1	0-1	1	Redman [50]	2380

Final League Position: 1

Honours
League Champions: Second Division 1984-85; League Two 2017-18.
Runners-up: Second Division 1990-91; Third Division 1994-95.
Scottish Cup: Quarter-finals 1973, 1976.
League Cup: Semi-finals 1975-76.
League Challenge Cup: Semi-finals 1992-93, 1996-97.

Club colours: Shirt: Blue. Shorts: Blue. Socks: White.

Goalscorers: *League (60):* Milne 11 (1 pen), Templeman 11, Fraser 7 (1 pen), Masson 5, Johnston 4, Rennie 4, Redman 3, Campbell I 2 (1 pen), Dillon 2, Webster 2, Allan 1, Ballantyne 1, Bolochoweckyj 1, Ferguson 1, Hay 1, McLaren 1, Steeves 1, Watson 1, own goal 1.
William Hill Scottish FA Cup (1): Webster 1.
Betfred Scottish League Cup (2): Hay 1, Watson 1.
Irn-Bru Scottish League Challenge Cup (5): Ballantyne 2, Campbell I 1, Masson 1, Steeves 1.

Fleming A 35	Allan M 29+1	Dillon S 36	Campbell I 20	Steeves A 36	Thomson K 1	Fotheringham M 12+7	Callaghan L 19+8	McLaren C 8+11	Templeman C 31+4	Johnston C 14+12	Campbell R —+4	Hunt R —+1	Webster G 13+12	Ballantyne C 24+1	Hay K 3+6	Redman J 25+5	Watson P 18+10	Ferguson R —+4	Masson T 24+3	Fraser G 15+8	Milne L 13+3	Bolochoweckyj M 15	Millar J 1	Rennie M 4+7	Match No.
1	2	3	4	5	6	7	8	9	10[1]	11[2]	12	13													1
1	2[2]	3	4	5		7[3]	8	11	10	9[1]			6	12	13	14									2
1		3	4	5		7[3]	8	11	10	12				9[2]	2	14	6	13							3
1	8	3	4	2				9	11[2]	10[1]	14	13	12	5		6	7[3]								4
1	2	3	4[3]	9		13	8[1]	12	11				10	5		6	7[2]	14							5
1	2	3	4	8			12	13	11[2]				9[3]	5	10	6	7[1]	14							6
1	4[1]	3	2	5		7[3]	6	12	11				13	9	10[2]	8	14								7
1	14	3	4	5		7[3]	8	9[2]	11	10[5]			6	2		13	12								8
1	2	3	4	5		9[2]	14	12	11				13	6		7			8[1]	10[1]					9
1	4	3	2	5		6[3]	11[2]	10	12				9	13		7[1]			8	14					10
1	2[3]	3	4	5		9[3]	13	11	10[5]	12			6	8		7	14								11
1	6	3	9	4		13	12	10	11[3]	14			2	5[1]	8	7[2]									12
1	2	3	4	9		8	10[2]	11	13	5[3]			12	7[1]		6	14								13
1	9	4	7	5		12	14	13	8	11[3]	3		6	2[2]		10[1]									14
1	2	3	4	9		7[2]		14	11[3]				5	13	8	12	6[1]		10						15
1	2	3	4	9		7[1]		11[2]	12				14	5		6	13		8[3]	10					16
1	4	3	5	9		8[2]		10	12				14	2		7	13		6[1]	11[3]					17
1	2	3	4	9		12	14	11[1]	6				5	13		7[3]			8	10[2]					18
1	2	3	4	5		6[3]	11[1]	12	14				9[2]			7			8	10	13				19
1	2			5		12		11	13				9[1]			8	7[2]		14	10[2]	6	4			20
1	4	2		9		12	5[1]	11[2]	10				6			8[3]			13	14	7	3			21
	2	3	4	5		14	9[1]	13	11[2]				12	6[5]	7				10	8			1		22
1	2	3		9		14	6	11	12				5	7[2]					8	10[1]		4[3]		13	23
1	2	3		5		8[3]	11[1]	10	13				6[2]			9	14		7		12	4		13	24
1	2	4		5		8[2]		10	11[3]				6			12	14		7	9[1]	3			13	25
1		3		5		9	14	11[2]	12				6[1]			8	7		2	10[3]		4		13	26
1		3		9		8[2]	14	10[1]					5[3]			7	4		6	11	12	2		13	27
1		3		5		7[1]	12		11[2]	13	14			6		8	2		10	9[3]		4			28
1		3		5		13	12		11		14		5	6		4	7[1]		10	8[2]	2[3]				29
1		3		5		6[1]		10[2]	12				7	13	8[3]	4	2		11	9				14	30
1	2	3		5		6[3]		11[2]					5		7	14	13	12	8[1]	4				10	31
1	8	4		5		14		10[2]					2		6[2]	12	7	13	9	3[1]				11	32
1	8	4		5				10[2]	12				14	2		6	7[3]	13	9	3				11[1]	33
1	2	3		9				11					13	5	14	7		6[2]	12	8[3]	4			10[1]	34
1	2	3		5		13	11[1]	10[3]					6		9	14		8	7[2]	4				12	35
1	2	3		9		13	7[3]	10[1]					5		8	14		6	11[2]	4				12	36

MOTHERWELL

Year Formed: 1886. *Ground & Address:* Fir Park Stadium, Motherwell ML1 2QN. *Telephone:* 01698 333333. *Fax:* 01698 338001.
E-mail: mfcenquiries@motherwellfc.co.uk *Website:* www.motherwellfc.co.uk
Ground Capacity: 13,742 (all seated). *Size of Pitch:* 105m × 65m.
Chairman: James McMahon. *Chief Executive:* Alan Burrows.
Manager: Steve Robinson. *Assistant Manager:* Keith Lasley.
Club Nicknames: 'The Well', 'The Steelmen'.
Previous Grounds: The Meadows, Dalziel Park.
Record Attendance: 35,632 v Rangers, Scottish Cup 4th rd replay, 12 March 1952.
Record Transfer Fee received: £1,750,000 for Phil O'Donnell to Celtic (September 1994).
Record Transfer Fee paid: £500,000 for John Spencer from Everton (January 1999).
Record Victory: 12-1 v Dundee U, Division II, 23 January 1954.
Record Defeat: 0-8 v Aberdeen, Premier Division, 26 March 1979.
Most Capped Player: Stephen Craigan, 54, Northern Ireland.
Most League Appearances: 626: Bobby Ferrier, 1918-37.
Most League Goals in Season (Individual): 52: Willie McFadyen, Division I, 1931-32.
Most Goals Overall (Individual): 283: Hugh Ferguson, 1916-25.

MOTHERWELL – SPFL LADBROKES PREMIERSHIP 2017–18 LEAGUE RECORD

Match No.	Date		Venue	Opponents	Result	H/T Score	Lg Pos.	Goalscorers	Atten- dance
1	Aug	6	H	Rangers	L	1-2	1-1	9	Heneghan [40]	9974
2		12	A	St Johnstone	L	1-4	1-2	11	Rose [28]	3451
3		19	H	Ross Co	W	2-0	0-0	8	Tait [53], Moult (pen) [74]	3911
4		26	H	Hearts	W	2-1	2-1	6	Bowman [37], Moult [41]	6568
5	Sept	9	A	Kilmarnock	W	2-0	0-0	5	Bowman [65], Moult (pen) [88]	4621
6		16	A	Hibernian	D	2-2	0-1	5	Moult 2 [64, 74]	17,335
7		24	H	Aberdeen	L	0-1	0-0	6		4535
8		30	H	Partick Thistle	W	3-0	1-0	5	Hartley [7], Tanner [56], Bowman [82]	4692
9	Oct	14	A	Hamilton A	W	2-1	1-1	4	Rose [32], Hartley [51]	3869
10		25	A	Dundee	W	1-0	1-0	3	Tanner [5]	5254
11		28	H	Hibernian	L	0-1	0-1	4		6043
12	Nov	4	A	Ross Co	L	2-3	0-3	5	Bowman [48], Moult [79]	4014
13		18	A	Aberdeen	W	2-0	1-0	5	Moult 2 [42, 54]	14,013
14		29	H	Celtic	D	1-1	0-0	5	Lustig (og) [78]	9164
15	Dec	2	A	Celtic	L	1-5	0-2	5	Frear [65]	57,817
16		9	A	Hearts	L	0-1	0-1	5		15,984
17		13	A	Partick Thistle	L	2-3	0-3	6	Bowman [56], Tanner [79]	2452
18		16	A	Kilmarnock	L	0-1	0-1	7		4179
19		23	H	Dundee	D	1-1	0-0	8	Tanner (pen) [61]	4173
20		27	A	Rangers	L	0-2	0-0	8		49,273
21		30	H	Hamilton A	L	1-3	1-1	8	Tanner [3]	4890
22	Jan	24	A	Ross Co	W	2-0	1-0	6	Soutar (og) [45], Main [47]	3196
23		27	A	Hearts	D	1-1	0-0	6	Main [90]	16,717
24		31	A	Hibernian	L	1-2	0-1	6	Main [78]	15,459
25	Feb	3	H	Partick Thistle	D	1-1	0-0	7	Ciftci [79]	4607
26		6	H	St Johnstone	W	2-0	0-0	6	Campbell [64], Main [70]	3227
27		17	H	Kilmarnock	L	0-1	0-1	7		5322
28		24	A	Dundee	W	1-0	1-0	7	Tanner [33]	5003
29	Mar	10	A	Hamilton A	L	0-2	0-1	7		3182
30		18	H	Celtic	D	0-0	0-0	7		8717
31		31	H	Rangers	D	2-2	2-0	7	Main (pen) [9], Campbell [16]	8915
32	Apr	3	H	Aberdeen	L	0-2	0-0	7		4127
33		7	A	St Johnstone	D	0-0	0-0	7		2409
34		21	A	Ross Co	D	0-0	0-0	7		3879
35		28	H	Dundee	W	2-1	1-1	7	Bowman [28], Kipre [52]	4064
36	May	5	H	St Johnstone	L	1-5	0-3	7	Bigirimana [78]	3524
37		8	A	Partick Thistle	W	1-0	0-0	7	Bowman [60]	3320
38		12	H	Hamilton A	W	3-0	1-0	7	Ciftci 2 [31, 70], Aldred [73]	4699

Final League Position: 7

Honours
League Champions: Division I 1931-32;. First Division 1981-82, 1984-85; Division II 1953-54, 1968-69.
Runners-up: Premier Division 1994-95, 2012-13; Premiership 2013-14; Division I 1926-27, 1929-30, 1932-33, 1933-34;Division II 1894-95, 1902-03.
Scottish Cup: 1952, 1991; *Runners-up:* 1931, 1933, 1939, 1951, 2011, 2018.
League Cup Winners: 1950-51; *Runners-up:* 1954-55, 2004-05, 2017-18.

European: *Champions League:* 2 matches (2012-13). *Cup Winners' Cup:* 2 matches (1991-92). *UEFA Cup:* 8 matches (1994-95, 1995-96, 2008-09). *Europa League:* 18 matches (2009-10, 2010-11, 2012-13, 2013-14, 2014-15).

Club colours: Shirt: Amber with maroon band. Shorts: Maroon. Socks: Amber and maroon bands.

Goalscorers: *League (43):* Moult 8 (2 pens), Bowman 7, Tanner 6 (1 pen), Main 5 (1 pen), Ciftci 3, Campbell 2, Hartley 2, Rose 2, Aldred 1, Bigirimana 1, Frear 1, Heneghan 1, Kipre 1, Tait 1, own goals 2.
William Hill Scottish FA Cup (9): Main 3, Tanner 2 (1 pen), Bowman 1, McHugh 1, own goals 2.
Betfred Scottish League Cup (20): Moult 5, Cadden 4, Bowman 2, Frear 2, Bigirimana 1, Dunne 1, Hartley 1, MacLean 1, Tait 1, Tanner 1, own goal 1.

Carson T 33	Tait R 33+1	Heneghan B 4	Kipre C 35+1	Dunne C 34	Cadden C 30+3	Rose A 22+6	McHugh C 33+2	Frear E 14+9	Tanner C 16+10	Moult L 13+2	Bowman R 23+9	Fisher A 6+5	Newell G 1+7	Bigirimana G 11+16	Griffiths R 5+1	Campbell A 25+4	MacLean R 1+7	Hartley P 14	Hammell S 2+2	Grimshaw L 11+6	Petravicius D 2+11	Aldred D 17	Ciftci N 8+3	Main C 16	Hendrie S 4+2	Maguire B 3	Scott J —+2	Turnbull D 2	Brown L —+1	Match No.
1	2	3	4	5	6	7³	8	9²	10	11¹	12	13	14																	1
1▪	2²	3	4	5▪	6	9	7▪		14	12	10³	11		8¹	13															2
	2	4	3	5	6		8		9³	10	12	11²		7¹	1	13	14													3
1	2	3	4	5	6¹	8	7	9²	11	10	13			12																4
1	8	2	4³	5	7¹	6			10	11				13		9		3²	12	14										5
1	9	2	4	5	7³	6²			12	10	11¹			13		8		3	14											6
1	9²	2	4	5	7¹	13	14		11	10³	12			6		8		3												7
1	8	2	4	5	12	6³	13	9¹	11	10	7			13		14		3												8
1	6	3	5	2²	7³	8	12	14	11¹	10	13			9		4														9
1	9	2	4	12	7	5	6¹	13	10²	11	8					3³		14												10
1		2	4	5	6¹	7²	9³	12	11	10	13			8		3		14												11
1	9	8	4³	5	6²	7	13	10¹	11	12				2		3		14												12
1	5	2	4	9	6	7	12		11³	10²	14			13		3		8¹												13
1	5	2	4	9	12	7³	8¹	13	10	14				6		3		11²												14
1	2		3	5	6³	8	12	13	9²	10¹	11			7		4		14												15
	5		2	4	6¹	8³	3	9	13		11	10²		12		7	14													16
	5		2	4		8³	3	9	12		10			13	1	7	14			6⁴	11¹									17
	5		2	3		12	8		9		10	11¹	13	7²	1		14		4	6³										18
1	9		2	4	5³	14	7	13	10		11²			12		8		3	6¹											19
1	5		2	4		9¹	7³	11	13		10²	14		6		12		3	8											20
1	2		3		9³	6	10	13	11²		7			8¹	14	4▪	5													21
			2	4	6	9	5	8²						7	13	14			12				3	10¹	11³					22
1	9²		2	4	6	5	7	12						13	8¹				5³				3	10³	11					23
1	9		2	4	12	6¹	7²	10						13	8			5³				3	14	11						24
1	12		2	4	5²		6	13	9¹					7				14				3	11	8³						25
1	6	3	5	2	9	8			12					14	7¹			13				4	11³	10²						26
1	5		4		6³	7¹	3	8	9		12			13				14				2	11²	10						27
1	8	2	4	5	13	7		9²	12	14				6								3	10³	11¹						28
1	5²	2	4	9	10³	7		8						14	13	6¹						3	12							29
1	5	2⁴	4	6		7	9¹		11					8								3	10	12						30
1	5	2	4	6		7	9²		11¹					8				13				3	10	12						31
1	2	3		6		7³	9¹	11						14	12	8¹	13					4	10	5						32
1	6	3		12	14	5	9³		10					13	7							8	4	11⁴	2¹					33
1	9	2	4	6	8²	12			11					13	7							5³	3	10¹		14				34
1	9	2	4	5	7				11¹					13	8²	14						6	3	10²		12				35
1			4	6	5³	9²			12					13	8							7¹	14	3	11	10	2			36
1		2	4	5		7	13		11					12	8							3	14	10³	9¹			6²		37
	5		13			9³								6	1		8¹				7	12	3	11	4²	2		10	14	38

PARTICK THISTLE

Year Formed: 1876. *Ground & Address:* Firhill Stadium, 80 Firhill Rd, Glasgow G20 7AL. *Telephone:* 0141 579 1971.
Fax: 0141 945 1525. *E-mail:* mail@ptfc.co.uk *Website:* ptfc.co.uk
Ground Capacity: 10,102 (all seated). *Size of Pitch:* 105m × 68m.
Chairman: David Beattie. *Interim Chief Executive:* Gerry Britton.
Manager: Alan Archibald. *Assistant Manager:* Scott Paterson.
Club Nickname: 'The Jags'.
Previous Grounds: Overnewton Park; Jordanvale Park; Muirpark; Inchview; Meadowside Park.
Record Attendance: 49,838 v Rangers, Division I, 18 February 1922. *Ground Record:* 54,728, Scotland v Ireland, 25 February 1928.
Record Transfer Fee received: £200,000 for Mo Johnston to Watford (July 1981).
Record Transfer Fee paid: £85,000 for Andy Murdoch from Celtic (February 1991).
Record Victory: 16-0 v Royal Albert, Scottish Cup 1st rd, 17 January 1931.
Record Defeat: 0-10 v Queen's Park, Scottish Cup 5th rd, 3 December 1881.
Most Capped Player: Alan Rough, 51 (53), Scotland.
Most League Appearances: 410: Alan Rough, 1969-82.
Most League Goals in Season (Individual): 41: Alex Hair, Division I, 1926-27.
Most Goals Overall (Individual): 229: Willie Sharp, 1939-57.

PARTICK THISTLE – SPFL LADBROKES PREMIERSHIP 2017–18 LEAGUE RECORD

Match No.	Date		Venue	Opponents	Result		H/T Score	Lg Pos.	Goalscorers	Attendance
1	Aug	5	A	Hibernian	L	1-3	1-2	11	Erskine [7]	17,634
2		11	H	Celtic	L	0-1	0-1	12		8041
3		19	A	St Johnstone	L	0-1	0-1	11		3470
4		26	H	Aberdeen	L	3-4	2-2	11	Erskine [8], Doolan [13], Keown [54]	4768
5	Sept	9	A	Ross Co	D	1-1	1-0	10	Spittal [22]	3660
6		15	H	Rangers	D	2-2	0-1	10	Spittal [50], Erskine [60]	8264
7		23	H	Hearts	D	1-1	1-0	11	Spittal [18]	4671
8		30	A	Motherwell	L	0-3	0-1	11		4692
9	Oct	14	H	Kilmarnock	L	0-2	0-1	12		3662
10		21	H	Dundee	W	2-1	0-1	12	Edwards [75], Storey [90]	3358
11		24	A	Hamilton A	D	0-0	0-0	11		2236
12		28	H	St Johnstone	W	1-0	1-0	10	Storey [14]	2870
13	Nov	4	A	Rangers	L	0-3	0-2	10		49,502
14		19	A	Hearts	D	1-1	0-0	11	Doolan [85]	16,999
15	Dec	2	H	Hibernian	L	0-1	0-0	12		4997
16		9	A	Kilmarnock	L	1-5	1-2	12	Erskine [16]	4339
17		13	H	Motherwell	W	3-2	3-0	12	Spittal [16], Edwards [22], Sammon [28]	2452
18		16	A	Dundee	L	0-3	0-2	12		5101
19		20	A	Celtic	L	0-2	0-1	12		54,187
20		23	H	Hamilton A	W	1-0	1-0	11	Keown [26]	2912
21		27	A	Aberdeen	L	0-1	0-0	12		14,830
22		30	H	Ross Co	W	2-0	1-0	11	Doolan [35], Sammon [86]	2870
23	Jan	23	H	Celtic	L	1-2	1-0	11	Sammon (pen) [34]	6920
24		27	A	St Johnstone	W	3-1	1-0	11	Lawless [13], Sammon [64], Edwards [90]	2848
25	Feb	3	A	Motherwell	D	1-1	0-0	10	Doolan [53]	4607
26		6	H	Rangers	L	0-2	0-1	10		7332
27		17	H	Dundee	L	1-2	1-0	10	Sammon [42]	4267
28		24	A	Hamilton A	L	1-2	1-1	11	Sammon (pen) [9]	2243
29	Mar	10	H	Aberdeen	D	0-0	0-0	11		3931
30		17	A	Hearts	L	0-3	0-3	11		17,179
31		31	A	Hibernian	L	0-2	0-0	11		17,497
32	Apr	3	A	Ross Co	L	0-4	0-2	12		3944
33		7	H	Kilmarnock	L	0-1	0-1	12		4227
34		21	H	Hamilton A	W	2-1	0-1	11	Doolan [64], Edwards [72]	3839
35		28	A	St Johnstone	D	1-1	0-1	11	Sammon (pen) [89]	2925
36	May	4	H	Ross Co	D	1-1	1-1	11	Erskine [21]	4312
37		8	H	Motherwell	L	0-1	0-0	11		3320
38		12	A	Dundee	W	1-0	0-0	11	Doolan [63]	6756

Final League Position: 11

Honours
League Champions: First Division 1975-76, 2001-02, 2012-13; Division II 1896-97, 1899-1900, 1970-71; Second Division 2000-01.
Runners-up: First Division 1991-92, 2008-09; Division II 1901-02.
Promoted via play-offs: 2005-06 (to First Division).
Scottish Cup Winners: 1921; *Runners-up:* 1930.
League Cup Winners: 1971-72; *Runners-up:* 1953-54, 1956-57, 1958-59.
League Challenge Cup Runners-up: 2012-13.

European: *Fairs Cup:* 4 matches (1963-64). *UEFA Cup:* 2 matches (1972-73). *Intertoto Cup:* 4 matches (1995-96).

Club colours: Shirt: Yellow with red stripes. Shorts: Red with yellow trim. Socks: Red with yellow tops.

Goalscorers: *League (31):* Sammon 7 (3 pens), Doolan 6, Erskine 5, Edwards 4, Spittal 4, Keown 2, Storey 2, Lawless 1.
William Hill Scottish FA Cup (4): Sammon 3, Doolan 1.
Betfred Scottish League Cup (13): Doolan 3, Lawless 3 (1 pen), Spittal 3, Erskine 2, Edwards 1, Elliot 1.
Play-Offs (1): Doolan 1.

Cerny T 34	Elliot C 17	Keown N 30	Devine D 26	Booth C 11+1	Barton A 27+6	Osman A 12+1	Bannigan S 4+2	Lawless S 21+6	Doolan K 18+15	Erskine C 19+9	Nisbet K —+6	Nitriansky M 4+3	Turnbull J 19	Edwards R 30+6	Sammon C 21+10	Storey M 24+10	McCarthy A 10+5	Spittal B 24+9	Scully R 4+2	McGinn P 25+1	Woods M 16+2	Fraser G —+5	Dumbuya M 4+1	Cargill B 16	Penrice J 2	Match No.
1	2	3	4	5	6	7	8	9^2	10^1	11	12	13														1
1	2	3		5	6		7^1	8^3	11^2	13			4	9	10	12	14									2
1	2	3	5^9	7	6		8^3	14	10		12		4	9^2	13	11										3
1	5	3^8		7			6^1	13	11	9^3		14	2	4	12	10		8^2								4
1^3	2		5	6			7^2		11^1	14			4	3	9	8	13	10	12							5
	5	3	4	6		13		10^4		7	9	12	11^1		8^3	1	2									6
8^1	2	3		6		13		11^2		14	12	4	7		10^9		9	1	5							7
1		2	3^1	6		14	10^3	13		5	4	7	12	11		9^2	8									8
1		4	3	7^2		11	9		2		6	12	10^1	13	8		5									9
1		3	4	6		10	14	9^4		5	7	11^2	12	8^1	13		2									10
1		2	3	7		9	11		4	8		10		6			5									11
1		3	2	7		8	12		4	6	10^1	11		9^2		5	13									12
1		2	3	8		9^2	12		14	4	6	10^1	11^3	7		5		13								13
1		4	5	7		9^2	12	10^1	14	3	8		11^1	6		2		13								14
1		3	4	7		10^1	12	9^3		5	6	13	11^2	8		2		14								15
1		3	4	6^1		8^2	11^3	9		5	7	14	13	10		2	12									16
1		2	3	7		13	14		4	6	11	10^1	9^1		5	8^2	12									17
1		2	4	7		13	14	12		3	6	10^1	11^2	9		5	8^2									18
1		3	4	9		5	13	12		2	7		11^1	8^2	10^3	6		14								19
1		2	4	3		8	10^2	11^1		6	14	12	13	9		5	7^3									20
1		3	4	9		5^1		13		2	7	11	12	8^2	10	6										21
1		2		3		9	8		4	6	12	11^2	13	10		5	7^1									22
1		3	12	6		13	14		7	11^2	10^1	9	8^3			2	4	5								23
1		3	5	13	6	9^2		8^1		12	11	10		2	7		4									24
1		3		8	7	11^1		9	10	12		5	6		2	4										25
1		3		6		13	12	9	11^1	10		8^3		2	7		14	4	5^2							26
1		3	5	6		13	8^2	9	11	10^1		12		7		2	4									27
1		3	9	5		8	14	11^3	13	7	10^1	12		6^2		2	4									28
1	2	3	5			9^1		6^2	12	11	10	7	13	8		4										29
1	2	3	5	12	7^3	9^1	10	6^2		14	11	13	8		4											30
1^1	9	2^8		3	6	13		8	10	11^2	7^3	14	12	5		4										31
	5	2	14	3	6	13		7^1	10	11^2		12	1	9^2	8		4									32
	2	4	5	14	6^2	10	12	9		11^3	13	7	8^1	1		3										33
1	2	4	5	14		10^1	11	9	13	12		7^1	8^3			3										34
1	2	3	5^2			10^1	11	9	13	12		7^3	8	14	6	4										35
1	5	3	12			10^1	9	7^3	11	14	8	13		2	6	4^2										36
1	5	3	7^1			12	10^3	6^2	9	11	13	14		2	8	4										37
1	5	3	8	14		9	13	6^1	10^3	11^2	12		2	7		4										38

PETERHEAD

Year Formed: 1891. *Ground and Address:* Balmoor Stadium, Balmoor Terrace, Peterhead AB42 1EU.
Telephone: 01779 478256. *Fax:* 01779 490682. *E-mail:* office@peterheadfc.co.uk *Website:* www.peterheadfc.com
Ground Capacity: 3,150 (seated: 1,000). *Size of Pitch:* 101m × 64m.
Chairman: Rodger Morrison. *Vice-Chairman:* Ian Grant.
Manager: Jim McInally. *Assistant Coach:* David Nicholls.
Club Nickname: 'Blue Toon'.
Previous Ground: Recreation Park.
Record Attendance: 8,643 v Raith R, Scottish Cup 4th rd replay, 25 February 1987 (Recreation Park); 4,855 v Rangers, Third Division, 19 January 2013 (at Balmoor).
Record Victory: 9-0 v Colville Park, Scottish Cup 2nd rd, 14 October 2017.
Record Defeat: 0-13 v Aberdeen, Scottish Cup 3rd rd, 10 February 1923.
Most League Appearances: 275: Martin Bavidge, 2003-13.
Most League Goals in Season (Individual): 32: Rory McAllister, 2013-14.
Most Goals Overall (Individual): 119: Rory McAllister, 2011-16.

PETERHEAD – SPFL LADBROKES LEAGUE TWO 2017–18 LEAGUE RECORD

Match No.	Date	Venue	Opponents	Result	H/T Score	Lg Pos.	Goalscorers	Atten- dance
1	Aug 5	A	Annan Ath	W 2-1	0-1	4	McCracken [86], Stevenson [90]	331
2	12	H	Elgin C	W 3-0	2-0	2	McAllister 2 (1 pen) [23, 45 (p)], Smith [57]	691
3	19	A	Stenhousemuir	L 1-3	1-1	3	Robertson [30]	220
4	26	H	Stirling Alb	L 2-4	1-4	4	Cairney [5], McAllister (pen) [53]	632
5	Sept 9	H	Montrose	D 1-1	0-0	4	Leitch [71]	614
6	16	A	Cowdenbeath	W 4-0	3-0	3	Smith 2 [4, 19], Gibson [22], Brown, S [76]	301
7	23	A	Edinburgh C	W 3-0	1-0	2	Brown, Jason [21], McLean [82], Brown, S [84]	356
8	30	H	Berwick R	L 0-2	0-0	4		507
9	Oct 21	A	Clyde	W 4-1	1-1	3	Smith [28], Leitch [65], McLean [66], McAllister [74]	403
10	28	H	Annan Ath	W 1-0	1-0	3	McAllister [45]	512
11	Nov 4	H	Elgin C	W 2-0	1-0	3	McAllister 2 [24, 71]	883
12	11	H	Stenhousemuir	L 2-3	0-1	3	Leitch [57], Brown, Jason [78]	525
13	Dec 2	H	Edinburgh C	W 3-0	0-0	3	McAllister 2 (1 pen) [47 (p), 72], Brown, Jordon [73]	539
14	5	A	Stirling Alb	W 1-0	1-0	1	McAllister [42]	456
15	23	H	Cowdenbeath	W 3-2	0-1	2	McAllister [48], Brown, Jason [52], Brown, Jordon [90]	593
16	30	A	Montrose	W 6-2	2-1	2	Brown, Jason 2 [5, 17], Smith [46], Robertson [51], Gibson [58], McAllister [69]	932
17	Jan 2	H	Elgin C	W 7-0	1-0	2	McAllister [27], Brown, Jordon [54], Riley [65], Stevenson 2 [71, 78], Robertson [84], McLean [87]	779
18	6	A	Stenhousemuir	W 4-1	1-1	2	McAllister 2 (1 pen) [45 (p), 46], Robertson [72], McLean [80]	449
19	13	H	Stirling Alb	W 4-3	2-2	2	Gibson [1], McAllister (pen) [23], McLean 2 [68, 72]	649
20	27	A	Clyde	L 0-1	0-0	2		449
21	30	A	Berwick R	W 3-2	2-1	2	McCracken [15], McAllister (pen) [41], Leitch [71]	330
22	Feb 3	H	Montrose	L 0-1	0-0	2		762
23	10	A	Edinburgh C	D 0-0	0-0	2		301
24	17	H	Berwick R	D 1-1	0-1	2	McAllister (pen) [76]	604
25	20	A	Annan Ath	D 3-3	2-0	2	McLean 3 (1 pen) [30, 35, 72 (p)]	267
26	24	A	Cowdenbeath	W 2-0	1-0	2	McLean [18], Belmokhtar [90]	216
27	27	H	Clyde	W 2-1	2-0	1	McLean [37], Leitch [41]	394
28	Mar 10	A	Stirling Alb	W 1-0	0-0	1	Stevenson [61]	541
29	13	H	Stenhousemuir	L 1-2	0-2	1	McAllister [80]	471
30	17	A	Montrose	L 2-3	1-0	2	Brown, Jordon [37], Smith [63]	699
31	24	A	Annan Ath	W 1-0	0-0	1	Stevenson [83]	708
32	31	A	Clyde	W 3-0	1-0	1	McLean 2 (1 pen) [4, 68 (p)], McAllister [79]	724
33	Apr 7	A	Berwick R	W 3-1	2-0	1	McLean 2 [32, 65], Brown, Jason [43]	403
34	14	H	Cowdenbeath	W 1-0	0-0	2	Brown, Jordon [80]	785
35	21	A	Elgin C	W 1-0	0-0	2	Brown, Jason [74]	786
36	28	H	Edinburgh C	W 2-1	1-0	2	Scullion (og) [4], Brown, S [90]	1049

Final League Position: 2

Honours
League Champions: League Two 2013-14.
Runners up: Third Division 2004-05, 2012-13; League Two 2017-18.
Scottish Cup: Quarter-finals 2001.
League Challenge Cup: Runners up: 2015-16.

Club colours: Shirt: Royal blue with light blue sleeves. Shorts: Royal blue with white trim. Socks: Light blue.

Goalscorers: *League (79):* McAllister 20 (7 pens), McLean 15 (2 pens), Jason Brown 7, Smith 6, Jordon Brown 5, Leitch 5, Stevenson 5, Robertson 4, Brown S 3, Gibson 3, McCracken 2, Belmokhtar 1, Cairney 1, Riley 1, own goal 1.
William Hill Scottish FA Cup (5): McAllister 2, Jason Brown 1, Jordon Brown 1, Robertson 1.
Betfred Scottish League Cup (7): McAllister 3 (2 pens), Cairney 1, Jason Brown 1, McCracken 1, Stevenson 1.
Irn-Bru Scottish League Challenge Cup (4): Adams 1, Lawrence 1, McAllister 1, McLean 1 (1 pen).
Play-Offs (5): Robertson 2, Jason Brown 1, McAllister 1, McLean 1.

Fleming G 36	Ross S 3 + 1	McCracken D 28 + 1	Robertson M 26 + 1	Brown Jason 35	Brown Jordon 11 + 19	Brown S 23 + 9	Stevenson J 30 + 1	Gibson W 35	Cairney P 3 + 2	Smith A 21 + 6	McLean R 17 + 14	Leitch J 31 + 2	Riley N 1 + 15	Ferry S 25 + 2	McAllister R 29 + 2	Dikobo M 1 + 3	Adams S — + 6	Gabriel S — + 1	McIlduff A 30	Lawrence M 2	Norris A 2 + 8	Johnston C 6 + 4	Belmokhtar A 1 + 9	Match No.
1	2	3	4	5	6^1	7^2	8	9	10^3	11	12	13	14											1
1	2^3	3^2	4	5		12	9	8	14	10^1		6	13^4	7	11									2
1	13	3	4^1	2			7	5	6	9	10^3	11^2	8			12	14							3
1	4^4	3		6	2^1	9	8	14		10	13		7	11		5^2		12^3						4
1		4	3	13	2		8			11^2	10^1	6	12	7	9^3		14		5					5
1		3	4	12	5		9			6	10^2	13		8	11^3		14		5				6^2	6
1		4	3	8	2	9				11^3	12	7^1	14	10	13				5				6^2	7
1		4^2	3	13	2	6	9			11^1	12	8^3		7	10		14		5					8
1		4	3	13	6	2^3	8			9^2	11^1	7	12		10	14			5					9
1	3^1	4	2	12	6		11			13	10	8	14	7	9^3				5					10
1		4	3	13	2		6			11^2	9^1	8	12	7	10^3		14		5					11
1		3	4	2	13	6^1	12	9		11	8	14	7^1	10					5^2					12
1		3	4	2	12		6^1	9		14	11	8	13	7^2	10^3				5					13
1		3	4	2	13		9^2	7		14	10^3	6^1	12	8	11				5					14
1		3	4	2	13		6^1	9	14	11^2	8^3	12	7	10					5					15
1		3	4	2	8^2	12	6	7		11	13	9^3			10^1				5		14			16
1		3	4	2	10^2	13	6	8		14	9^1	12	7	11^3					5					17
1		3	4	2	8^1	13	6^2	9		11^3	12	7	14	10					5					18
1		3	4	2	10^3	13	6	8		12	9^1	14	7	11^1					5					19
1		4	3^3	2	11^2	13	6	7		9^1	8	12		10					5		14			20
1		3		4	12	6	2^1	8		13	9	10^2	7	11^3					5		14			21
1		4		3	8^2	2	7			12	11^{11}	9		6	10				5			13		22
1		3		4	13	7	2^1	6		9^2	12	8		14	10				5				11^3	23
1		3	4	2	7^1	6				10^2	12			8	11		14		5			13	9^3	24
1		4		2	14	7	6	9			12	8			10^1				5^1		3^2	11^3	13	25
1		3	4	2	14	7	6	9		11^2	10^3	8							5^1			13	12	26
1		3	4	2	14	13	5	6		11	9^1			7							8^2	10^1	12	27
1		3		2	14	7	6	11		13	8^3			9					5		12	4^1	10^2	28
1	4^2	3		2	14	6	8^1	9			10^3			7	11				5			13	12	29
1		4	3	7^2	12	2	9			8^1	10			11					5		13	6^1	14	30
1		4	3	9^3		2	6			11	12	8		7	10^1				5^2			14	13	31
1		4	3	8^1	12	2	9			10	11^3	6		7^2	13				5			14		32
1		4		14	8	2	10			9^1	11^3	6		7^4	12				5				13	33
1		4	3	13	6	2	9			8^1	12	10^2		7	11				5^3				14	34
1		4	13	3		7	2	9		6^1	11	12		8^3	10				5				14	35
1		4	3	2	12	7	5	9		8^1	10^3	6		11^2								14	13	36

QUEEN OF THE SOUTH

Year Formed: 1919. *Ground & Address:* Palmerston Park, Dumfries DG2 9BA. *Telephone:* 01387 254853.
Fax: 01387 240470. *E-mail:* admin@qosfc.com *Website:* www.qosfc.com
Ground Capacity: 8,690 (seated: 3,377) *Size of Pitch:* 102m × 66m.
Chairman: Billy Hewitson. *Vice-Chairman:* Craig Paterson.
Player/Manager: Gary Naysmith. *Assistant Manager:* Dougie Anderson. *Coach:* Eddie Warwick.
Club Nickname: 'The Doonhamers'.
Previous Grounds: None.
Record Attendance: 26,552 v Hearts, Scottish Cup 3rd rd, 23 February 1952.
Record Transfer Fee received: £250,000 for Andy Thomson to Southend U (July 1994).
Record Transfer Fee paid: £30,000 for Jim Butter from Alloa Ath (1995).
Record Victory: 11-1 v Stranraer, Scottish Cup 1st rd, 16 January 1932.
Record Defeat: 2-10 v Dundee, Division I, 1 December 1962.
Most Capped Player: Billy Houliston, 3, Scotland.
Most League Appearances: 731: Allan Ball, 1963-82.
Most League Goals in Season (Individual): 37: Jimmy Gray, Division II, 1927-28.
Most Goals in Season: 41: Jimmy Rutherford, 1931-32; Nicky Clark, 2012-13.
Most Goals Overall (Individual): 251: Jim Patterson, 1949-63.

QUEEN OF THE SOUTH – SPFL LADBROKES CHAMPIONSHIP 2017–18 LEAGUE RECORD

Match No.	Date	Venue	Opponents	Result	H/T Score	Lg Pos.	Goalscorers	Atten- dance
1	Aug 5	H	Brechin C	W 4-1	2-0	1	Lyle 2 [28, 42], Rankin [59], Dykes [78]	1209
2	12	A	Dundee U	L 1-2	1-1	4	Fordyce [25]	5842
3	19	H	Dumbarton	W 1-0	1-0	3	Fordyce [44]	1442
4	26	A	Falkirk	W 4-1	2-0	2	Kerr [2], Dobbie 3 (1 pen) [41, 46, 49 (p)]	4108
5	Sept 9	A	Livingston	D 2-2	0-1	3	Stirling [71], Lyle [77]	1113
6	16	H	Greenock Morton	L 1-2	1-2	5	Lyle [21]	1725
7	24	A	St Mirren	L 1-3	0-2	6	Kerr [64]	3023
8	30	A	Inverness CT	D 0-0	0-0	5		2082
9	Oct 14	H	Dunfermline Ath	D 0-0	0-0	6		1834
10	21	H	Brechin C	W 1-0	0-0	5	Kerr [60]	562
11	28	H	Falkirk	W 4-2	2-0	5	Dobbie [16], Dykes [19], Brownlie [75], Lyle [90]	1716
12	Nov 4	A	Greenock Morton	W 2-1	1-1	5	Dobbie [43], Fordyce [47]	1677
13	25	H	Livingston	L 0-3	0-1	5		1328
14	28	A	Dumbarton	D 2-2	0-1	5	Dobbie (pen) [70], Carswell (og) [84]	474
15	Dec 2	A	Inverness CT	D 0-0	0-0	6		1293
16	9	A	Dunfermline Ath	W 5-2	2-0	3	Kane 2 [8, 27], Dobbie 3 (1 pen) [74, 80 (p), 90]	4694
17	23	H	St Mirren	L 2-3	2-2	5	Dobbie [1], Kane [6]	2019
18	30	A	Falkirk	L 2-3	1-3	6	Dobbie [45], Kerr [90]	4285
19	Jan 2	H	Dumbarton	D 0-0	0-0	6		1269
20	6	A	Livingston	W 1-0	1-0	4	Kane [39]	1067
21	13	A	Inverness CT	L 1-3	0-2	5	Bell [85]	2209
22	27	H	Brechin C	W 3-1	2-0	5	Dobbie 3 [7, 13, 73]	1211
23	Feb 3	A	St Mirren	L 0-2	0-2	6		4585
24	17	H	Greenock Morton	D 1-1	1-0	6	Dobbie [33]	1489
25	24	H	Dunfermline Ath	D 0-0	0-0	6		1429
26	Mar 10	A	Dumbarton	W 1-0	0-0	5	Thomas [48]	642
27	13	H	Dundee U	L 1-3	1-1	6	Thomas [21]	1480
28	17	H	St Mirren	L 1-3	1-1	6	Marshall [21]	1902
29	20	A	Dundee U	W 3-2	2-0	6	Thomson 2 [21, 75], Jacobs (pen) [41]	4088
30	24	H	Livingston	D 3-3	2-1	6	Thomson [28], Dykes [30], Todorov [90]	1153
31	31	A	Dunfermline Ath	L 1-3	0-2	6	Marshall [69]	4762
32	Apr 3	H	Falkirk	D 2-2	0-1	6	Thomson [51], Brownlie [73]	1062
33	7	H	Inverness CT	L 0-2	0-2	6		1140
34	14	A	Greenock Morton	W 1-0	0-0	7	Dykes [69]	1514
35	21	A	Dundee U	W 3-0	2-0	7	Dykes [9], Thomson [31], Murray [77]	1531
36	28	A	Brechin C	W 5-1	2-0	6	Dobbie 3 [45, 60, 74], Dykes 2 [45, 65]	661

Final League Position: 6

Honours
League Champions: Division II 1950-51; Second Division 2001-02, 2012-13.
Runners-up: Division II 1932-33, 1961-62, 1974-75; Second Division 1980-81, 1985-86.
Scottish Cup Runners-up: 2007-08.
League Cup: semi-finals 1950-51, 1960-61.
League Challenge Cup Winners: 2002-03, 2012-13; *Runners-up:* 1997-98, 2010-11.

European: *UEFA Cup:* 2 matches (2008-09).

Club colours: All: Royal blue with white trim.

Goalscorers: *League (59):* Dobbie 18 (3 pens), Dykes 7, Lyle 5, Thomson 5, Kane 4, Kerr 4, Fordyce 3, Brownlie 2, Marshall 2, Thomas 2, Bell 1, Jacobs 1 (1 pen), Murray 1, Rankin 1, Stirling 1, Todorov 1, own goal 1.
William Hill Scottish FA Cup (3): Dobbie 1, Fergusson 1, Lyle 1.
Betfred Scottish League Cup (6): Dobbie 4, Brownlie 1, Rooney 1.
Irn-Bru Scottish League Challenge Cup (12): Dobbie 4, Lyle 2, Rooney 2, Brownlie 1, Dykes 1, Kane 1, Kerr 1.

Martin A 22	Rooney S 14+10	Fordyce C 28+1	Brownlie D 32+1	Marshall J 29	Murray C 10+10	Rankin J 31+3	Jacobs K 29	Carmichael D 3+4	Lyle D 9+17	Dykes L 30+4	Leighfield J 14+2	Stirling A 5+8	Akubuine J —+1	Tapping C 7+7	Dobbie S 31	Kane C 12+4	Kerr J 18	Fergusson R 4+4	McFadden J 6+5	Mercer S 18+2	Thomson J 16+1	Bell O —+4	Beerman M 1+2	Cameron K 7+1	Thomas D 12+2	Todorov N —+8	Todd J 8	Match No.
1^3	2	3	4	5	6	7	8^1	9^2	10	11	12	13	14															1
1	2	4	3	5		7	6	12	10^1	9^3			14		8^1	11	13											2
1	2	3	4	5	13	8	7	6^2	10^1	14		12			11	9^2												3
1		2	3	5	12	6	7		13	9^2					8^1	11	10^1	4	14									4
	2	3		5		7^2	8		13	9^1	1	12			6	10	11^3	4	14									5
1		2	3	5		7^1	8		10	14	12				6^3	9	11^2	4	13									6
1	6	2	3^3	5		7	8		11^2	9^1					13	10	12	4	14									7
1	2^1	3	14	5		7	9		12					6^3	8	10	11^2	4	13									8
1		2	4	5	6^3	8^2	7		12	11		13			14	10		3	9^1									9
1		2	4	5^1	6^2	8	7		12	11					14	10		3	9^3	13								10
1	12	2	3		6^3	8	7		13	11					14	10		4	9^1	5^2								11
1	14	2	3	5^3	6^1	8	7		13	11					12	10		4	9^2									12
1	13	2	4	5		8^3	7^4		10^1	6					14	11^2	12	3	9									13
1	12	2^3	3	5	9	8			11			14			7^3	10	13	4	6^1									14
1	14		4	5		8	7		13	6		9^1			11^3	10^4		3	12	2								15
1	12		3	5		8	7			6		9^1			11	10		4		2								16
1	13		4	5^3		8	7^1		14	9		6^2			12	11	10	3		2								17
1	2		3		13	8			14	9		6^2			4^2	10	11	5		7^1	12							18
1	2		3		6^1	8			12	9		13			11^2	10		4		5	7							19
1	2		3		6	8				9					11^1	10		4		5	7	12						20
	2		4		6^1	8				9^3	1				10	11^2	3	13	5	7	14	12						21
1		2	3		14	8^3			13	6					11			10^2		9	7	12	5^1	4				22
1^2	2	3	4		7				10						9			11^3	5^1	6					8	12	14	23
		3	4	5	12	8^2	7								10			11^1		2					6	13		24
	2^3	3	4	5	11^2	8^1	7		9						10			12				14			6	13		25
		3	4	5	13	7			11^1	9^3	1				10^2					2	9			14	6^2	12		26
		3	4	5	13	8^3	7		14	11^1	1				10^2				12	2	9				6			27
		3		5		8	7		11	13	1				10^2					2	9^1			4	6	12		28
	2^1	12	3	5	14		8	7	13	11	1							9^2						4	10^3		6	29
	2	3		5		8	13		12	10^2					11					7				4	9^3	14	6^1	30
	14	3	4	5		7^1	6		12	11^3	1									2^3				9	8	13	10	31
	13	2	3	5		8	7		12	11^2	1									6				4^1	9^3	14	10	32
	2	3		5	8^1	7^2			6^3	14	1	12			11					10				4	13	9		33
1		3	4	5	12	13	7		11						10^2				14	2	8				6^1	9^3		34
	14	3	4	5	12		7		13	11	1				10^2					2	8				6^2	9^1		35
	3	4		5	13	12	8^1		11		1				10					2^3	7	14			6^2	9		36

QUEEN'S PARK

Year Formed: 1867. *Ground & Address:* Hampden Park, Mount Florida, Glasgow G42 9BA. *Telephone:* 0141 632 1275.
Fax: 0141 636 1612. *E-mail:* secretary@queensparkfc.co.uk *Website:* queensparkfc.co.uk
Ground Capacity: 51,866 (all seated). *Size of Pitch:* 105m × 68m.
President: Gerry Crawley. *Treasurer:* David Gordon.
Head Coach: Gus MacPherson. *Assistant Head Coach:* Chris Hillcoat.
Club Nickname: 'The Spiders'.
Previous Grounds: 1st Hampden (Recreation Ground); (Titwood Park was used as an interim measure between 1st &
2nd Hampdens); 2nd Hampden (Cathkin); 3rd Hampden.
Record Attendance: 95,772 v Rangers, Scottish Cup 1st rd, 18 January 1930.
Record for Ground: 149,547 Scotland v England, 1937.
Record Transfer Fees: Not applicable due to amateur status.
Record Victory: 16-0 v St. Peter's, Scottish Cup 1st rd, 12 Sep 1885.
Record Defeat: 0-9 v Motherwell, Division I, 26 April 1930.
Most Capped Player: Walter Arnott, 14, Scotland.
Most League Appearances: 532: Ross Caven, 1982-2002.
Most League Goals in Season (Individual): 30: William Martin, Division I, 1937-38.
Most Goals Overall (Individual): 163: James B. McAlpine, 1919-33.

QUEEN'S PARK – SPFL LADBROKES LEAGUE ONE 2017–18 LEAGUE RECORD

Match No.	Date		Venue	Opponents	Result		H/T Score	Lg Pos.	Goalscorers	Attendance
1	Aug	5	A	Arbroath	L	0-2	0-1	9		769
2		12	H	Albion R	L	2-5	1-2	10	Burns [11], Orr [81]	645
3		19	A	Alloa Ath	L	0-1	0-0	10		508
4		26	H	Stranraer	D	2-2	1-2	10	Brady [38], Neill (og) [90]	595
5	Sept	9	A	East Fife	W	1-0	0-0	9	Millen (pen) [56]	496
6		16	H	Raith R	L	0-5	0-2	9		873
7		23	H	Ayr U	L	0-2	0-1	9		1051
8		30	A	Airdrieonians	L	2-4	1-1	9	Docherty, D 2 [11, 80]	747
9	Oct	14	H	Forfar Ath	D	1-1	0-0	9	Donnelly [89]	517
10		21	A	Albion R	W	1-0	0-0	9	Orr [48]	425
11		28	H	Alloa Ath	L	0-4	0-1	9		556
12	Nov	4	A	Stranraer	L	0-3	0-2	10		495
13		11	H	Arbroath	L	0-2	0-1	10		764
14		25	A	Raith R	L	0-2	0-0	10		1260
15	Dec	2	H	East Fife	W	2-1	1-1	10	Donnelly 2 [18, 51]	506
16		9	A	Ayr U	L	2-3	1-1	10	McVey [42], Reid (og) [48]	1320
17		16	H	Airdrieonians	D	1-1	1-1	10	Cummins [38]	593
18		23	A	Forfar Ath	W	3-0	2-0	9	Cummins [2], Leitch [43], Docherty, D [90]	544
19		30	H	Albion R	D	2-2	2-0	9	Iredale [3], Cummins (pen) [11]	609
20	Jan	2	A	Alloa Ath	D	2-2	1-1	9	Donnelly [39], Cummins (pen) [54]	476
21		6	H	Stranraer	D	2-2	0-0	9	Donnelly [80], Cummins (pen) [90]	607
22		13	A	Arbroath	L	1-2	1-1	9	McGhee [12]	751
23		27	H	Ayr U	L	1-4	0-2	10	Cummins [89]	1233
24	Feb	3	A	Raith R	L	1-3	1-3	10	Keena [41]	777
25		10	A	East Fife	W	2-0	1-0	9	Keena 2 [25, 85]	558
26		17	A	Airdrieonians	L	1-2	0-2	10	Cummins [86]	908
27		24	H	Forfar Ath	D	2-2	1-1	10	Cummins [34], Keena [52]	570
28	Mar	10	H	Alloa Ath	L	1-2	0-0	10	Keena [47]	428
29		13	A	Albion R	D	1-1	0-1	10	Burns [51]	296
30		17	A	Stranraer	W	3-2	2-0	10	Keena 2 [17, 30], Burns [73]	255
31		24	A	Ayr U	L	0-4	0-3	10		1600
32		31	A	Airdrieonians	D	0-0	0-0	10		702
33	Apr	7	H	East Fife	L	2-3	1-2	10	Keena [41], Galt [62]	458
34		14	A	Raith R	L	0-2	0-2	10		1391
35		21	A	Forfar Ath	D	1-1	0-1	10	Donnelly [68]	580
36		28	H	Arbroath	W	3-0	1-0	9	Leitch [1], Donnelly 2 [46, 70]	892

Final League Position: 9

Honours
League Champions: Division II 1922-23; B Division 1955-56; Second Division 1980-81; Third Division 1999-2000.
Runners-up: Third Division 2011-12; League Two 2014-15.
Promoted via play-offs: 2006-07 (to Second Division); 2015-16 (to League One).
Scottish Cup Winners: 1874, 1875, 1876, 1880, 1881, 1882, 1884, 1886, 1890, 1893; *Runners-up:* 1892, 1900.
FA Cup Runners-up: 1884, 1885.
FA Charity Shield: 1899 (shared with Aston Villa).

Club colours: Shirt: Black and white thin hoops. Shorts: White. Socks: Black.

Goalscorers: *League (42):* Cummins 8 (3 pens), Donnelly 8, Keena 8, Burns 3, Docherty D 3, Leitch 2, Orr 2, Brady 1, Galt 1, Iredale 1, McGhee 1, McVey 1, Millen 1 (1 pen), own goals 2.
William Hill Scottish FA Cup (1): own goal 1.
Betfred Scottish League Cup (9): Brady 2, Cummins 1, Docherty D 1, Galt 1, Millen 1 (1 pen), Orr 1, Wharton 1, own goal 1.
Irn-Bru Scottish League Challenge Cup (1): Cummins 1.
Play-Offs (2): Leitch 1, McLauchlan 1.

Muir W 12	Millen R 25	Wharton B 4	Cummins A 31	Galt D 30 + 2	Docherty D 19 + 9	Green K 7 + 2	McVey C 21 + 3	Burns S 31 + 3	Orr T 7 + 15	Brady A 26 + 6	Duff C 3 + 10	Green D 3 + 2	MacPherson E 1 + 3	Bailey M 5 + 2	Mortimer W 9 + 5	Fotheringham G 29	Iredale J 14	Donnelly L 21 + 5	Summers C 16 + 4	Gibson S 14 + 2	MacLennan J 1 + 7	White M 24	McGhee L 8 + 3	Leitch R 14 + 6	Gullan J 1 + 6	Keena A 13 + 1	Nimmo D 4	McLauchlan G 2	Miller A — + 1	Ruth M 1 + 2	Match No.
1	2	3	4¹	5	6	7	8²	9	10³	11	12	13	14																		1
1	2		4³	5	7¹	3	9	13	8	11	6	10²	12	14																	2
1	2	3	4	6			11	9	10¹	8		12	5				7														3
1	2	3	4	11		7²	9	10³	8	14	12	13				5		6¹													4
1	2	3	5	14		13	9	12	11	7³	6	8²				4		10¹													5
1	2	3	8	6¹			10³	12	9	13		14			7		4	11²	5												6
1	2	3	11	6			14	12	8	13					9³		7¹	4	10²	5											7
1	2	3	11	10			12	13	8						6¹		7	4²	9	5³	14										8
1	2		8¹	7¹	3		10	11²	9	12					6		4	14	5	13											9
1	5		4	13	7		10¹	9		2					8		6	11²	3		12										10
1	5		3	13	7	2²		12	10¹	8¹	14				6		4	11	9												11
1	6		4		8²		9	10	14	12	13				7		5	11¹	3³	2											12
	5		2		7¹		8	14	11	9					6	3³	10²			4	13	1	12								13
		4	9			10	2		13	6²		12		7¹	14		5	11³	1	3		8									14
			9	13		7	2		12	10²		8	4	11³		5		14	1	3	6¹										15
			10	8¹		2	9	12	7	13		11²		4		5			1	3	6										16
		3	10	14	12	6	2		7	13		11¹		4²	9³	5		1		8											17
		3	10	12		6	2		7			11¹		4	9³	5		13	1	8											18
		3	10	12		6	2		7			11²		4	9³	5		13	1	8											19
		4	10		3	6	2		13	12		11²		7	9³	5			1	8											20
		4		13	3³	6	2	14	10			11²		7	9	5¹			1	12	8										21
		4	8	13		2²			7¹			11	6		10	5	12	14	1	3	9³										22
		4	10		3²	6	2		11³			7		9¹	12	5			1	8	13	14									23
2		4	10	9²		7¹	5		13	6⁴		14			3			1	3	8³	12	11									24
2		3	10	8¹		9	5		7²						6			1	12	13	11	4									25
		3	6	7²		2	14	9¹							8	11³		5	1	12	13	10	4								26
5		2	10	6²			9		8³						13	4¹			1	12	14	11	3								27
2		3	10	9		6³	5							14	7	13			1	12	8¹		11	4²							28
2		3	11¹	8²			7	9	13	12					6			5	1		8					10	4				29
2		3	8¹	9¹		6²	10		12						7			5	1	4	14	13	11								30
2		3	7²			10		9	8						14	12		5	1	4³	6¹	11			13						31
2		3	8			12	5	14	6¹						7	9³		4	1		10	11²			13						32
		6		12		8³	5	11	13						7	9		4	1		10¹		3²	14							33
5		3	6			10³	7	14	4²						8	13		9	1	2¹	12	11									34
2		3	10¹	12			5	14	9³						6	8		4	1		13	11			7²						35
2		3	10	12		14	5		7²						13	6		9³	4	1		8	11¹								36

RAITH ROVERS

Year Formed: 1883. *Ground & Address:* Stark's Park, Pratt St, Kirkcaldy KY1 1SA. *Telephone:* 01592 263514. *Fax:* 01592 642833. *E-mail:* info@raithrovers.net *Website:* www.raithrovers.net
Ground Capacity: 8,473 (all seated). *Size of Pitch:* 103m × 64m.
Chairman: Bill Clark. *Deputy Chairman:* David Sinton.
Manager: Barry Smith. *Coach:* Kevin Cuthbert.
Club Nickname: 'Rovers'.
Previous Grounds: Robbie's Park.
Record Attendance: 31,306 v Hearts, Scottish Cup 2nd rd, 7 February 1953.
Record Transfer Fee received: £900,000 for Steve McAnespie to Bolton W (September 1995).
Record Transfer Fee paid: £225,000 for Paul Harvey from Airdrieonians (July 1996).
Record Victory: 10-1 v Coldstream, Scottish Cup 2nd rd, 13 February 1954.
Record Defeat: 2-11 v Morton, Division II, 18 March 1936.
Most Capped Player: David Morris, 6, Scotland.
Most League Appearances: 430: Willie McNaught, 1946-51.
Most League Goals in Season (Individual): 38: Norman Haywood, Division II, 1937-38.
Most Goals Overall (Individual): 154: Gordon Dalziel (League), 1987-94.

RAITH ROVERS – SPFL LADBROKES LEAGUE ONE 2017–18 LEAGUE RECORD

Match No.	Date	Venue	Opponents	Result	H/T Score	Lg Pos.	Goalscorers	Atten- dance
1	Aug 5	A	Alloa Ath	D 1-1	0-1	6	Vaughan [90]	1114
2	12	H	Stranraer	W 3-0	1-0	2	Vaughan 2 [43, 64], Spence [61]	1625
3	19	H	Forfar Ath	W 3-1	1-1	2	Vaughan [31], Buchanan [85], Spence [88]	1589
4	26	A	East Fife	W 5-0	3-0	1	Barr [5], Vaughan 2 [20, 80], Spence [39], Buchanan [69]	1850
5	Sept 9	H	Ayr U	W 2-1	0-1	1	Vaughan [50], Thomson [59]	2286
6	16	A	Queen's Park	W 5-0	2-0	1	Buchanan [3], Vaughan [7], Zanatta [56], Barr [80], Thomson [90]	873
7	23	H	Airdrieonians	W 2-0	0-0	1	Thomson [74], Zanatta [89]	1726
8	30	A	Albion R	L 1-2	0-1	1	Spence [87]	616
9	Oct 14	H	Arbroath	W 2-0	2-0	1	Vaughan [33], Thomson [38]	1827
10	28	A	Forfar Ath	D 1-1	0-1	1	Herron [59]	865
11	Nov 4	H	East Fife	W 1-0	1-0	2	Vaughan [29]	2656
12	14	A	Ayr U	L 0-3	0-2	2		2040
13	25	H	Queen's Park	W 2-0	0-0	2	Zanatta [64], Spence [66]	1260
14	Dec 2	A	Alloa Ath	W 2-1	0-0	2	Spence [55], Buchanan [68]	1400
15	10	A	Airdrieonians	D 2-2	1-2	2	Spence [22], Court [90]	450
16	23	H	Arbroath	W 2-1	2-0	2	Spence [19], Zanatta [32]	1035
17	30	H	Stranraer	W 3-0	2-0	2	Spence [13], Buchanan [27], Vaughan [69]	1432
18	Jan 2	A	East Fife	W 3-2	2-1	2	Robertson [8], Buchanan [25], Zanatta [78]	1795
19	6	H	Forfar Ath	W 2-1	2-1	1	Spence [13], Hornby (og) [26]	1575
20	13	H	Ayr U	D 1-1	0-1	1	Spence [47]	3064
21	20	A	Stranraer	L 0-1	0-1	1		449
22	27	A	Alloa Ath	D 0-0	0-0	2		904
23	Feb 3	A	Queen's Park	W 3-1	3-1	1	Murray [15], Furtado [18], Buchanan [30]	777
24	6	H	Albion R	W 3-1	1-0	1	Herron 2 [7, 63], Thomson [76]	1294
25	10	H	Airdrieonians	W 2-1	0-1	1	Furtado [64], Vaughan [77]	1685
26	17	A	Albion R	D 2-2	1-1	1	Murray [40], Marr (og) [82]	519
27	24	A	Arbroath	D 2-2	1-0	1	Thomson [43], Furtado [74]	1707
28	Mar 10	A	Ayr U	L 0-3	0-2	1		2126
29	13	A	Forfar Ath	L 1-2	0-0	1	Vaughan [78]	509
30	24	A	Airdrieonians	W 2-1	2-0	2	Vaughan [8], Thomson [20]	915
31	27	H	East Fife	W 2-0	1-0	2	Barr [39], Davidson [85]	1485
32	31	H	Albion R	W 2-0	0-0	2	Barr [86], Zanatta [89]	1456
33	Apr 7	A	Arbroath	D 1-1	1-0	2	Buchanan (pen) [39]	1110
34	14	H	Queen's Park	W 2-0	2-0	2	Barr [10], Zanatta [39]	1391
35	21	A	Stranraer	W 3-0	2-0	1	Murray [5], Buchanan [44], Vaughan [78]	524
36	28	A	Alloa Ath	D 0-0	0-0	2		4496

Final League Position: 2

Honours
League Champions: First Division 1992-93, 1994-95; Second Division 2002-03, 2008-09; Division II 1907-08, 1909-10 (shared with Leith Ath), 1937-38, 1948-49.
Runners-up: Division II 1908-09, 1926-27, 1966-67;. Second Division 1975-76, 1977-78, 1986-87; League One 2017-18.
Scottish Cup Runners-up: 1913.
League Cup Winners: 1994-95; *Runners-up:* 1948-49.
League Challenge Cup Winners: 2013-14.

European: *UEFA Cup:* 6 matches (1995-96).

Club colours: Shirt: Navy with white trim. Shorts: White with navy trim. Socks: Navy.

Goalscorers: *League (68):* Vaughan 15, Spence 11, Buchanan 9 (1 pen), Thomson 7, Zanatta 7, Barr 5, Furtado 3, Herron 3, Murray 3, Court 1, Davidson 1, Robertson 1, own goals 2.
William Hill Scottish FA Cup (0).
Betfred Scottish League Cup (9): Vaughan 4 (1 pen), Buchanan 3, Matthews 1, Spence 1.
Irn-Bru Scottish League Challenge Cup (10): Vaughan 4, Barr 2, Buchanan 1, Callachan 1, Osei-Opoku 1, Spence 1.
Play-Offs (1): Murray 1.

Lennox A 14	Thomson J 36	McKay D 13+4	Benedictus K 14	Murray E 34	Vaughan L 35	Matthews R 25+9	Robertson S 28+2	Callachan R 4	Buchanan L 30+3	Spence G 22+10	Barr B 26+6	McHattie K 11+1	Court J —+14	Berry J —+4	Osei-Opoku Y —+5	Brian R 1	Davidson I 28+1	Smith Graeme 21+1	Herron J 14+5	Zanatta D 17+8	Smith J —+1	Watson J 4	Furtado W 11+5	Hendry R 8+3	Match No.
1	2	3¹	4	5	6	7²	8³	9	10	11	12	13	14												1
1	2		4	3	6¹	12	8²	7	10³	11	9	5		13	14										2
	5	3			9	13	7²	8	10¹	11	6	2	12				1	4							3
	5	3			9³	12	7	8	10¹	11²	6	2	14		13		4	1							4
	2	4¹	5	9	7	8		11²	10³	6			14				3	1	12	13					5
	2	13		5	10	8	4		11³	6¹	9		14				3²	1	7	12					6
	2			5	11	8	3		10²	9¹	6		13				7	1	4	12					7
	2	4		5	11	7¹			10	12	9						3	1	6	8²	13				8
	5	13		4	11	6	7		12	10²	9						3	1	8			2¹			9
	2			3	11	12	7		9²	10¹	8	5					4¹	1	6	13					10
	2			4	9	8	3		11	10¹	6	5					1	7	12						11
	2	13		4	9	7¹	3³		10	14	6	5	12				1	8	11²						12
	5	3		4	9	6	8		11²	10¹			13	14			1	7³	12	2					13
	5	3		4	8	6¹	7		10²	9	12						13	1	11	2					14
	5	3		4	8	6¹	7		11	10²	12	13					1	9	2						15
	2	4		5	8	6	7		11¹	10	12						3	1	9						16
	2	5		4	9	7	6		10²	11¹			12		13		3	1	8						17
	2	5		3	7	8	6		11¹	10			12				4	1	9						18
	2	3		5	7	6	8		11¹	10			12				4	1	9						19
	2	4		5	9	6	8		11	10	12						3	1	7¹						20
	2	4		5	7	6	8¹		11²	10	9		13				3	1				12			21
1	2	12		4	8	7			11²	10¹	6	5¹	14				3		13			9			22
1	2	3		5	8				11¹	12	6						4		7	9²			10	13	23
1	2	4		5	9	14	12		10²	13	6¹						3		7	8			11³		24
1	2		4	5	8	13	12		10¹		6²						3		7	9			11		25
1	2		4	3	8	12			11³	13	9						7		5¹	10²			6	14	26
1	2		4	5	11	8	7¹		12	13	6						3			9²			10		27
1	2	3		4	9	7			13		10	5	12							6²			11	8¹	28
1	2	4		5	6	8³			11²	10¹	12		14				3		13				9	7	29
1	2	4		5	10	9	7¹			6							3		12				11	8	30
1	2	4		5	11	6	7²			12	9						3		13				10¹	8	31
1	2	4		5	10	6²	7¹			11³	9						3		13	14			12	8	32
1¹	2		4	5		6²	7		11	13	9³		14				3	12					10	8	33
	2			4	11³	12	7		10²		6	5					3	1	8¹	9			14	13	34
	2			4	11¹	13	7		10³	12	6	5					3	1		9²			14	8	35
	2			4	11		7		10²	13	9¹	5	14				3	1		6²			12	8	36

RANGERS

Year Formed: 1873. *Ground & Address:* Ibrox Stadium, 150 Edmiston Drive, Glasgow G51 2XD.
Telephone: 0871 702 1972. *Fax:* 0870 600 1978. *Website:* rangers.co.uk
Ground Capacity: 51,082 (all seated). *Size of Pitch:* 105m × 68m.
Chairman: Dave King. *Deputy Chairman:* Douglas Park.
Manager: Steven Gerrard. *Assistant Manager:* Gary McAllister.
Club Nickname: 'The Gers', 'The Teddy Bears'.
Previous Grounds: Flesher's Haugh, Burnbank, Kinning Park, Old Ibrox.
Record Attendance: 118,567 v Celtic, Division I, 2 January 1939.
Record Transfer Fee received: £9,000,000 for Alan Hutton to Tottenham H (January 2008).
Record Transfer Fee paid: £12,000,000 for Tore Andre Flo from Chelsea (November 2000).
Record Victory: 14-2 v Blairgowrie, Scottish Cup 1st rd, 20 January, 1934.
Record Defeat: 1-7 v Celtic, League Cup Final, 19 October 1957.
Most Capped Player: Ally McCoist, 60, Scotland. *Most League Appearances:* 496: John Greig, 1962-78.
Most League Goals in Season (Individual): 44: Sam English, Division I, 1931-32.
Most Goals Overall (Individual): 355: Ally McCoist; 1985-98.

Honours
League Champions: (54 times) Division I 1890-91 (shared with Dumbarton), 1898-99, 1899-1900, 1900-01, 1901-02, 1910-11,
1911-12, 1912-13, 1917-18, 1919-20, 1920-21, 1922-23, 1923-24, 1924-25, 1926-27, 1927-28, 1928-29, 1929-30, 1930-31, 1932-33,
1933-34, 1934-35, 1936-37, 1938-39, 1946-47, 1948-49, 1949-50, 1952-53, 1955-56, 1956-57, 1958-59, 1960-61, 1962-63, 1963-64,
1974-75. Premier Division: 1975-76, 1977-78, 1986-87, 1988-89, 1989-90, 1990-91, 1991-92, 1992-93, 1993-94, 1994-95, 1995-96,
1996-97, 1998-99, 1999-2000, 2002-03, 2004-05, 2008-09, 2009-10, 2010-11. *Runners-up, tier 1:* 30 times. Championship
2015-16. League One 2013-14. Third Division 2012-13.
Scottish Cup Winners: (33 times) 1894, 1897, 1898, 1903, 1928, 1930, 1932, 1934, 1935, 1936, 1948, 1949, 1950, 1953, 1960, 1962,
1963, 1964, 1966, 1973, 1976, 1978, 1979, 1981, 1992, 1993, 1996, 1999, 2000, 2002, 2003, 2008, 2009; *Runners-up:* 18 times.

RANGERS – SPFL LADBROKES PREMIERSHIP 2017–18 LEAGUE RECORD

Match No.	Date	Venue	Opponents	Result		H/T Score	Lg Pos.	Goalscorers	Attendance
1	Aug 6	A	Motherwell	W	2-1	1-1	4	Dorrans 2 (1 pen) [4, 58 (p)]	9974
2	12	H	Hibernian	L	2-3	1-2	6	Morelos [3], Tavernier [81]	49,636
3	19	H	Hearts	D	0-0	0-0	6		49,677
4	27	A	Ross Co	W	3-1	2-0	5	Morelos 2 [31, 41], Herrera [89]	6400
5	Sept 9	H	Dundee	W	4-1	1-0	4	Morelos 2 [41, 86], Windass [66], Pena [83]	49,164
6	15	A	Partick Thistle	D	2-2	1-0	3	Morelos [19], Dorrans [77]	8264
7	23	H	Celtic	L	0-2	0-0	5		50,116
8	29	A	Hamilton A	W	4-1	3-1	3	John 2 [21, 25], Candeias [27], Dorrans (pen) [59]	5400
9	Oct 13	A	St Johnstone	W	3-0	1-0	3	Pena 2 [27, 78], Dorrans [86]	6887
10	25	A	Kilmarnock	D	1-1	1-0	4	Holt [44]	47,981
11	28	A	Hearts	W	3-1	1-1	3	Miller 2 [43, 65], Windass [72]	32,852
12	Nov 4	H	Partick Thistle	W	3-0	2-0	4	McCrorie [30], Candeias [39], Windass [47]	49,502
13	18	H	Hamilton A	L	0-2	0-0	4		48,892
14	24	A	Dundee	L	1-2	0-0	4	Windass [70]	8548
15	29	H	Aberdeen	W	3-0	2-0	3	Tavernier 2 (1 pen) [7 (p), 70], Pena [27]	48,647
16	Dec 3	A	Aberdeen	W	2-1	1-0	2	Wilson, D [14], Windass [63]	18,983
17	9	A	Ross Co	W	2-1	0-1	2	Morelos [59], Wilson, D [83]	48,139
18	13	A	Hibernian	W	2-1	2-1	2	Windass [42], Morelos [45]	20,057
19	16	H	St Johnstone	L	1-3	1-1	3	Morelos [5]	47,923
20	23	A	Kilmarnock	L	1-2	1-0	3	John [39]	11,490
21	27	H	Motherwell	W	2-0	0-0	3	Wilson, D [56], Morelos [76]	49,273
22	30	A	Celtic	D	0-0	0-0	3		59,004
23	Jan 24	H	Aberdeen	W	2-0	1-0	2	Morelos [32], Tavernier (pen) [80]	49,707
24	28	A	Ross Co	W	2-1	1-0	2	Candeias [21], Cummings [82]	6541
25	Feb 3	H	Hibernian	L	1-2	0-1	3	Goss [73]	49,986
26	6	A	Partick Thistle	W	2-0	1-0	3	Windass [39], Tavernier [58]	7332
27	18	A	Hamilton A	W	5-3	4-2	2	Murphy [10], Windass 3 [19, 34, 72], Morelos [27]	5406
28	24	H	Hearts	W	2-0	1-0	2	Murphy [41], Martin [88]	49,927
29	27	A	St Johnstone	W	4-1	3-0	2	Tavernier (pen) [12], Windass [25], Goss [40], Morelos [56]	5737
30	Mar 11	H	Celtic	L	2-3	2-2	2	Windass [3], Candeias [26]	50,215
31	17	H	Kilmarnock	L	0-1	0-0	2		49,396
32	31	A	Motherwell	D	2-2	0-2	2	Tavernier (pen) [51], Murphy [53]	8915
33	Apr 7	H	Dundee	W	4-0	1-0	2	Miller [39], Morelos [68], Murphy [79], Candeias [90]	49,142
34	22	H	Hearts	W	2-1	0-0	2	Cummings [47], Candeias [64]	47,272
35	29	A	Celtic	L	0-5	0-3	3		58,320
36	May 5	H	Kilmarnock	W	1-0	0-0	3	Bates [85]	49,703
37	8	A	Aberdeen	D	1-1	0-1	3	McCrorie [63]	17,745
38	13	A	Hibernian	D	5-5	3-3	3	Tavernier [25], Rossiter [27], Bruno Alves [40], Holt [54], Windass [68]	19,579

Final League Position: 3

League Cup Winners: (27 times) 1946-47, 1948-49, 1960-61, 1961-62, 1963-64, 1964-65, 1970-71, 1975-76, 1977-78, 1978-79, 1981-82, 1983-84, 1984-85, 1986-87, 1987-88, 1988-89, 1990-91, 1992-93, 1993-94, 1996-97, 1998-99, 2001-02, 2002-03, 2004-05, 2007-08, 2009-10, 2010-11; *Runners-up:* 7 times.
League Challenge Cup Winners: 2015-16; *Runners-up:* 2013-14.

European: *European Cup:* 161 matches (1956-57, 1957-58, 1959-60 semi-finals, 1961-62, 1963-64, 1964-65, 1975-76, 1976-77, 1978-79, 1987-88, 1989-90, 1990-91, 1991-92, 1992-93 final pool, 1993-94, 1994-95, 1995-96; 1996-97, 1997-98, 1999-2000, 2000-01, 2001-02, 2003-04, 2004-05, 2005-06, 2007-08, 2008-09, 2009-10, 2010-11, 2011-12).
Cup Winners' Cup: 54 matches (1960-61 runners-up, 1962-63, 1966-67 runners-up, 1969-70, 1971-72 winners, 1973-74, 1977-78, 1979-80, 1981-82, 1983-84).
UEFA Cup: 88 matches (*Fairs Cup:* 1967-68, 1968-69 semi-finals, 1970-71. *UEFA Cup:* 1982-83, 1984-85, 1985-86, 1986-87, 1988-89, 1997-98, 1998-99, 1999-2000, 2000-01, 2002-03, 2004-05, 2006-07, 2007-08 runners-up). *Europa League:* 8 matches (2010-11, 2011-12, 2017-18).

Club colours: Shirt: Royal blue with white trim. Shorts: White with blue trim. Socks: Black with red tops.

Goalscorers: *League (76):* Morelos 14, Windass 13, Tavernier 8 (4 pens), Candeias 6, Dorrans 5 (2 pens), Murphy 4, Pena 4, John 3, Miller 3, Wilson D 3, Cummings 2, Goss 2, Holt 2, McCrorie 2, Bates 1, Bruno Alves 1, Herrera 1, Martin 1, Rossiter 1.
William Hill Scottish FA Cup (13): Windass 5 (1 pen), Cummings 4, Morelos 2, Murphy 1, own goal 1.
Betfred Scottish League Cup (9): Candeias 2, Morelos 2, Bruno Alves 1, Herrera 1, Miller 1, Pena 1, Tavernier 1.
UEFA Europa League (1): Miller 1.

Foderingham W 33	Hodson L 5 + 1	Fabio Cardoso S 9 + 3	Bruno Alves E 17 + 3	Wallace L 5	Candeias D 34 + 3	Jack R 17	Dorrans G 16	Windass J 31 + 2	Miller K 15 + 3	Herrera E 2 + 17	Tavernier J 37 + 1	Wilson D 12 + 2	Morelos A 29 + 6	Pena C 6 + 6	Kranjcar N 4 + 3	Hardie R — + 7	Rossiter J 1 + 1	Nenane A — + 5	John D 25 + 1	McCrorie R 19 + 2	Holt J 23 + 3	Dalcio G — + 1	Barjonas J 1 + 4	Bates D 13 + 2	Martin R 15	Goss S 10 + 3	Murphy J 16	Cummings J 6 + 9	Halliday A 5 + 6	Docherty G 7 + 4	Alnwick J 5	O'Halloran M — + 1	Match No.
1	2²	3	4	5	6	7	8	9	10³	11¹	12	13	14																				1
1	5³	3	4		6²	7¹	8	9	10	13	2	12	11¹	14																			2
1		3	4	5	6	7	8¹	9¹	11		2		10	12	13																		3
1		3	4	5	6	7	8	10²	12		2	11³	13	9¹					14														4
1		3	4	5	6²	7	8	12	11¹		2	10	13	9³					14														5
1		3	4	5³	6	7	8	9	10¹	13	2		11	14						12													6
1	5	3			9³	7	8	11³	12	13	2		10	6¹					14		4												7
1		3			6³	7¹	8	9		13	2		11²	10¹					5	4	12	14											8
1		3	4		6		8	9¹		14	2		11¹	10²					13	5	12	7											9
1			4		6	7¹	10¹	9²		12	2		11³						13	5	3	8	14										10
1					9	7		11²	6³	13	2	4	10¹			14			5	3	8	12											11
1					6	7		9¹	10		2	4	11²	12	13				5	3	8												12
1	5				6	7		9³	10¹	13	2	4	11³			12			14	3	8												13
1					6²	7		9	10	12	2	4	11¹			13			5	3	8												14
1		3			12	7		11¹	10²	13	2	4		9¹		14			5	6	8												15
1	12				13	6⁴		11¹	9	14	5	2²	10³						8	4	7		3										16
1		3			7			11	10²	14	2	4	12	9³					5	6¹	8	13											17
1		3			12			9	11¹	14	2	4	10²						5	6	7	8³	13										18
1		3			7²	8		10		13	2	4¹	11	12					5	6	9												19
1	5¹				6			11		12	2	4	10						9	7	8		3										20
1		3				7²			11	2	4	10¹	13	9³	14				5	6	8		12										21
1		4²	6			10		14	2	3	11³	13	9¹						5	8	7		12										22
1	14				8³			9²		2			11¹						5		6				4	3	7	10	12	13			23
1					8³			9		2			11¹						5		7				4	3	6²	10	13	14	12		24
1					8²			9		2			11¹						5	6¹					4	3	7	10	12		13		25
1					8²			9		2			13						5¹	6					4	3	7	10	11¹	12	14		26
1					10			9²	12	2			11¹						5						4	3	8³	6	13	14	7		27
1					8			9		2			11²						5	13					4	3	7	10	12	6¹			28
1		13			8²			9		2			11						5						4	3	7	10¹	12	5	6		29
1	12	4			8			9		2			11						5					3²			7¹	10	13	6			30
1		4			8²			9¹	14	2			13						5	12					3		7³	10	11	6			31
1		4	6		8	10¹			2			11							5						3		9	12	7				32
1	13				8	7		9³		2			11						5	3¹					4	14	10		12	6²			33
					8¹	7		9²		2			11						5	3	6				4		10	11³	12		1	14	34
					8	7¹		9²		2			12							3	6				4		10	11	5	13	1		35
					8	6			2			11						12	7²					3	4	13	10	9¹	5		1		36
					7	9²			2			11						6	8¹					3	4	12	10	13	5		1		37
14	12		8		13			2									7³			6⁴				3	4	9⁴	10	11⁵	5		1		38

ROSS COUNTY

Year Formed: 1929. *Ground & Address:* The Global Energy Stadium, Victoria Park, Dingwall IV15 9QZ. *Telephone:* 01349 860860. *Fax:* 01349 866277. *E-mail:* info@rosscountyfootballclub.co.uk
Website: www.rosscountyfootballclub.co.uk
Ground Capacity: 6,700 (all seated). *Size of Ground:* 105 × 68m.
Chairman: Roy MacGregor. *Club Secretary:* Fiona MacBean.
Co-managers: Steven Ferguson and Stuart Kettlewell.
Club Nickname: 'The Staggies'.
Record Attendance: 6,110 v Celtic, Premier League, 18 August 2012.
Record Transfer Fee received: £500,000 for Liam Boyce to Burton Albion (June 2017).
Record Transfer Fee paid: £50,000 for Derek Holmes from Hearts (October 1999).
Record Victory: 11-0 v St Cuthbert Wanderers, Scottish Cup 1st rd, 11 December 1993.
Record Defeat: 0-7 v Kilmarnock, Scottish Cup 3rd rd, 17 February 1962.
Most League Appearances: 230: Mark McCulloch, 2002-09.
Most League Goals in Season: 24: Andrew Barrowman, 2007-08.
Most League Goals (Overall): 48: Liam Boyce, 2014-17.

ROSS COUNTY – SPFL LADBROKES PREMIERSHIP 2017–18 LEAGUE RECORD

Match No.	Date	Venue	Opponents	Result	H/T Score	Lg Pos.	Goalscorers	Attendance
1	Aug 5	A	Dundee	W 2-1	1-0	3	Lindsay [35], Routis [61]	5032
2	12	H	Aberdeen	L 1-2	1-1	7	Curran [2]	5965
3	19	A	Motherwell	L 0-2	0-0	9		3911
4	27	H	Rangers	L 1-3	0-2	9	Mikkelsen [59]	6400
5	Sept 9	H	Partick Thistle	D 1-1	0-1	9	Schalk (pen) [86]	3660
6	16	A	Celtic	L 0-4	0-2	10		58,624
7	23	H	Hibernian	L 0-1	0-1	10		4181
8	30	A	Kilmarnock	W 2-0	2-0	10	Curran [34], van der Weg [44]	3337
9	Oct 14	A	Hearts	L 1-2	1-1	10	Keillor-Dunn [36]	4819
10	21	H	Hamilton A	W 2-1	0-0	8	Schalk [70], Mikkelsen [86]	3509
11	24	A	St Johnstone	D 0-0	0-0	8		2267
12	28	A	Aberdeen	L 1-2	1-1	9	Gardyne [8]	13,918
13	Nov 4	H	Motherwell	W 3-2	3-0	8	Gardyne 2 [13, 42], Keillor-Dunn [26]	4014
14	18	H	Celtic	L 0-1	0-0	9		6590
15	25	A	Hearts	D 0-0	0-0	9		15,601
16	Dec 2	H	Dundee	L 0-2	0-1	11		3896
17	9	A	Rangers	L 1-2	1-0	11	Curran [10]	48,139
18	12	H	Kilmarnock	D 2-2	2-0	10	Routis [31], Naismith [41]	3021
19	16	H	Hamilton A	L 2-3	0-1	11	Curran [73], van der Weg [84]	1272
20	23	A	Hibernian	L 1-2	1-1	12	Curran [14]	16,228
21	27	H	St Johnstone	D 1-1	0-1	11	Schalk (pen) [54]	3636
22	30	A	Partick Thistle	L 0-2	0-1	12		2870
23	Jan 24	A	Motherwell	L 0-2	0-1	12		3196
24	28	H	Rangers	L 1-2	0-1	12	Ngog (pen) [90]	6541
25	31	A	Aberdeen	L 2-4	0-3	12	Schalk 2 [77, 82]	4318
26	Feb 3	A	Dundee	W 4-1	0-0	12	Keillor-Dunn [49], Schalk 2 [61, 64], Chow [90]	4971
27	17	H	Hearts	D 1-1	0-0	12	Naismith [76]	4936
28	24	A	St Johnstone	L 0-2	0-2	12		2533
29	Mar 10	H	Kilmarnock	L 2-3	0-1	12	McKay [86], Schalk [90]	4001
30	17	H	Hamilton A	D 2-2	1-0	12	Lindsay [23], Davies [76]	3586
31	31	A	Celtic	L 0-3	0-1	12		58,765
32	Apr 3	H	Partick Thistle	W 4-0	2-0	11	Schalk 3 [35, 56, 72], Draper [41]	3944
33	7	A	Hibernian	D 1-1	1-0	11	McKay [28]	5389
34	21	H	Motherwell	D 0-0	0-0	12		3879
35	28	A	Hamilton A	L 0-2	0-0	12		2057
36	May 4	A	Partick Thistle	D 1-1	1-1	12	McKay [42]	4312
37	8	H	Dundee	L 0-1	0-0	12		3976
38	12	A	St Johnstone	D 1-1	1-0	12	Curran [3]	3279

Final League Position: 12

Honours
League Champions: First Division 2011-12; Second Division 2007-08; Third Division 1998-99.
Scottish Cup Runners-up: 2010.
League Cup Winners: 2015-16.
League Challenge Cup Winners: 2006-07, 2010-11; *Runners-up:* 2004-05, 2008-09.

Club colours: Shirt: Navy blue with white and red trim. Shorts: Navy blue with white trim. Socks: Navy blue.

Goalscorers: *League (40):* Schalk 11 (2 pens), Curran 6, Gardyne 3, Keillor-Dunn 3, McKay 3, Lindsay 2, Mikkelsen 2, Naismith 2, Routis 2, van der Weg 2, Chow 1, Davies 1, Draper 1, Ngog 1 (1 pen).
William Hill Scottish FA Cup (0).
Betfred Scottish League Cup (10): Curran 4 (2 pens), Mikkelsen 2, Schalk 2, Fraser 1, own goal 1.

Fox S 26+1	Fraser M 38	Kelly S 11+2	Davies A 25	Naismith J 34+1	Gardyne M 28+5	Routis C 23+3	Lindsay J 21+5	Chow T 10+4	Dow R 4+14	Schalk A 19+11	van der Weg K 16+3	Mikkelsen T 2+7	Tumilty R 1+1	Draper R 25+3	Curran C 20+15	O'Brien J 22+3	Keillor-Dunn D 18+11	McKay N 14+9	McCarey A 12+2	Eagles C 7+1	Effiong I 2	Souter H 11+2	Ngog D 4+6	Fontaine L 14	Kait M 3+3	Tansey G 2+1	Melbourne M 6	Match No.
1	2	3		4	5	6²	7¹	8	9	10	11¹	12	13	14														1
1	3		4	2	6	8²	9		10¹	5	13			7³	11	12	14											2
1	2	14	4²	6	9	12	3	7		10³	5¹			11	8¹		13											3
1	4	5	3	2	8			6³	9¹	10²		12		14	11	7	13											4
	4	5	3³	2	6	8				12	14	11²		7	10¹		9	13	1									5
	3	9²	4	2	6			13	14	11	5			7³	12	10	8¹		1									6
1	4		3	2	6		14			13	5		9²	7³	11¹	8	12	10										7
1	3	14	4	2	6		7	12	13		5			8²	11	9¹	10¹											8
1	4		3	2	6²		9			13	5	12		7³	11¹	8	10	14										9
1	4		3	2	6		8²			13	5	12		14	11¹	7	9	10³										10
1¹	3		4	2	13			7	6³		5	11²		8	12	9	10		14									11
	3	4		2	6	14	9		12	13	5¹			8	11	7	10²		1									12
	3	5	4	2	6	9	13		12				14	7	10¹	8²	11³		1									13
	3	5	4	2	6				14	12		13		7	10³	8²	11¹		1									14
	3	5	4²	2	6	8	12		13	11¹				7	14	9	10		1									15
	3	2		4	6³	7	9			11²	5¹			8	12		14	13	1	10								16
1	3	5³	4	2	7¹	9	6		13		14			11	8	12		10²										17
1	3		4	2			8	9		12			14	11²	7	10³	13		6¹									18
1	3			2	7⁴	4	6	9²		12	5			11	8	13	14		10³									19
1	4		3	2			7	12	6²		5			8³	11	14	13	10		9¹								20
1	3		4²	2	6	7	12	8		10	5			11¹		13	14		9²									21
1	2	9²	3	5	6¹	4	10	8		7				12		13	11³		14									22
	7		3³	2	9²	4				5				6		8	14	11	1			10¹	12	13				23
	3			2	7	6¹		12		14	5			8	11²	9	10³		1			4	13					24
1	5			2	13			7	12	14				8¹	10		9			6²	11³	4		3				25
1	5			2		8		12		11³				13	7¹	9	14			3	10²	4	6					26
1	5			2		7				14	11			13	8¹	9				4	10¹	3	6²	12				27
1	5			2		8				14	7			13⁴	9¹	10				4	11²	3	12	6¹				28
	3		2³	6	12			10	14					7		8	9¹	13	1			11²	4			5		29
	2¹	3	5	13	9	6	8²		11					7	12		10	1				11¹	4					30
12	6	5⁴	2	14	8			13	9²					10	7		11³			3		4						31
1	2			6¹	7	9		13	10³					8	12		11²			4	14	3		5				32
1	5			2		9²	7		14	10¹				6	13		11³			3		4	12	8				33
1	9			12	8¹	2⁸	7		10					5	13		11³			3	14	4		6				34
1	5¹	3		13			6		10					7	14		11²			2	12	4		8¹	9			35
1	2		5	9		7³			10					6	14		12	11¹		3		4	13	8²				36
1²	5	3	2	6		8			10²					7	13		9	11¹	12			14	4					37
1	5	3¹	2	6		8			13					7	11	14	10³			12		4	9²					38

ST JOHNSTONE

Year Formed: 1884. *Ground & Address:* McDiarmid Park, Crieff Road, Perth PH1 2SJ. *Telephone:* 01738 459090. *Fax:* 01738 625 771. *Email:* enquiries@perthstsaints.co.uk *Website:* perthstjohnstonefc.co.uk
Ground Capacity: 10,673 (all seated). *Size of Pitch:* 105m × 68m.
Chairman: Steve Brown. *Vice-Chairman:* Charlie Fraser.
Manager: Tommy Wright. *Assistant Manager:* Callum Davidson.
Club Nickname: 'Saints'.
Previous Grounds: Recreation Grounds, Muirton Park.
Record Attendance: 29,972 v Dundee, Scottish Cup 2nd rd, 10 February 1951 (Muirton Park): 10,545 v Dundee, Premier Division, 23 May 1999 (McDiarmid Park).
Record Transfer Fee received: £1,750,000 for Callum Davidson to Blackburn R (March 1998).
Record Transfer Fee paid: £400,000 for Billy Dodds from Dundee (January 1994).
Record Victory: 9-0 v Albion R, League Cup, 9 March 1946.
Record Defeat: 1-10 v Third Lanark, Scottish Cup 1st rd, 24 January 1903.
Most Capped Player: Nick Dasovic, 26, Canada.
Most League Appearances: 359: Steven Anderson, 2004-18.
Most League Goals in Season (Individual): 36: Jimmy Benson, Division II, 1931-32.
Most Goals Overall (Individual): 140: John Brogan, 1977-83.

ST JOHNSTONE – SPFL LADBROKES PREMIERSHIP 2017–18 LEAGUE RECORD

Match No.	Date	Venue	Opponents	Result		H/T Score	Lg Pos.	Goalscorers	Attendance
1	Aug 5	A	Kilmarnock	W	2-1	1-0	4	Wotherspoon [10], O'Halloran [89]	3935
2	12	H	Motherwell	W	4-1	2-1	1	MacLean [8], O'Halloran 2 [18, 74], Davidson [90]	3451
3	19	H	Partick Thistle	W	1-0	1-0	2	O'Halloran [33]	3470
4	26	A	Celtic	D	1-1	1-0	3	MacLean [39]	58,446
5	Sept 9	H	Hibernian	D	1-1	0-0	3	O'Halloran [48]	5591
6	16	A	Dundee	L	2-3	0-1	4	Craig 2 (2 pens) [75, 84]	6001
7	23	H	Hamilton A	W	2-1	0-1	2	MacLean [49], Davidson [84]	2880
8	30	A	Aberdeen	L	0-3	0-2	4		14,879
9	Oct 13	H	Rangers	L	0-3	0-1	4		6887
10	21	A	Hearts	L	0-1	0-0	6		18,534
11	24	H	Ross Co	D	0-0	0-0	6		2267
12	28	A	Partick Thistle	L	0-1	0-1	6		2870
13	Nov 4	H	Celtic	L	0-4	0-1	7		6800
14	18	A	Hibernian	W	2-1	0-0	6	Davidson [74], MacLean [90]	17,044
15	Dec 2	H	Kilmarnock	L	1-2	1-1	7	MacLean [43]	2950
16	9	A	Hamilton A	W	1-0	0-0	7	Scougall [66]	1451
17	13	H	Aberdeen	L	0-3	0-2	7		2911
18	16	A	Rangers	W	3-1	1-1	6	Alston [10], Johnstone [61], Cummins [71]	47,923
19	23	H	Hearts	D	0-0	0-0	7		4975
20	27	A	Ross Co	D	1-1	1-0	6	Johnstone [2]	3636
21	30	H	Dundee	L	0-2	0-1	7		4769
22	Jan 27	H	Partick Thistle	L	1-3	0-1	8	Craig (pen) [74]	2848
23	Feb 3	A	Hearts	L	0-1	0-0	8		16,197
24	6	A	Motherwell	L	0-2	0-0	8		3227
25	18	A	Celtic	D	0-0	0-0	9		56,867
26	24	H	Ross Co	W	2-0	0-0	8	Davidson 2 [29, 40]	2533
27	27	H	Rangers	L	1-4	0-3	8	Kerr [82]	5737
28	Mar 7	A	Kilmarnock	L	0-2	0-1	8		3807
29	10	A	Dundee	W	4-0	2-0	8	Piggott (og) [24], Kane 2 [37, 66], Alston [64]	5336
30	16	H	Hibernian	D	1-1	0-1	8	Kane [83]	3652
31	28	H	Hamilton A	W	1-0	1-0	7	McMann (og) [5]	2037
32	31	A	Aberdeen	L	1-4	0-2	8	Willock [68]	14,161
33	Apr 7	H	Motherwell	D	0-0	0-0	8		2409
34	21	A	Dundee	L	1-2	0-1	8	MacLean [85]	5592
35	28	H	Partick Thistle	D	1-1	1-0	8	Shaughnessy [39]	2925
36	May 5	A	Motherwell	W	5-1	3-0	8	MacLean 3 [31, 40, 56], Anderson [36], McMillan [81]	3524
37	8	A	Hamilton A	W	2-1	0-0	8	McMillan (pen) [65], Wotherspoon [80]	2367
38	12	H	Ross Co	D	1-1	0-1	8	Wotherspoon [90]	3279

Final League Position: 8

Honours
League Champions: First Division 1982-83, 1989-90, 1996-97, 2008-09; Division II 1923-24, 1959-60, 1962-63.
Runners-up: Division II 1931-32; First Division 2005-06, 2006-07; Second Division 1987-88.
Scottish Cup Winners: 2014.
League Cup Runners-up: 1969-70, 1998-99.
League Challenge Cup Winners: 2007-08; *Runners-up:* 1996-97.

European: *UEFA Cup:* 10 matches (1971-72, 1999-2000). *Europa League:* 14 matches (2012-13, 2013-14, 2014-15, 2015-16, 2017-18).

Club colours: Shirt: Blue with white sleeves. Shorts: White with blue trim. Socks: Blue.

Goalscorers: *League (42):* MacLean 9, Davidson 5, O'Halloran 5, Craig 3 (3 pens), Kane 3, Wotherspoon 3, Alston 2, Johnstone 2, McMillan 2 (1 pen), Anderson 1, Cummins 1, Kerr 1, Scougall 1, Shaughnessy 1, Willock 1, own goals 2.
William Hill Scottish FA Cup (4): Kane 3, McClean 1.
Betfred Scottish League Cup (0).
UEFA Europa League (1): Shaughnessy 1.

Mannus A 22	Foster R 22 + 2	Shaughnessy J 38	Anderson S 34	Easton B 12 + 1	Aiston B 17 + 7	Davidson M 29	Paton P 16 + 1	Wotherspoon D 25 + 10	Scougall S 18 + 6	Cummins G 6 + 9	O'Halloran M 12 + 4	Kane C 10 + 2	Craig L 17 + 10	MacLean S 26 + 4	Hendry C 1 + 4	Thomson Craig — + 4	Comrie A 12	Tanser S 24 + 5	Johnstone D 8 + 12	Millar C 13 + 3	Gordon L 5 + 2	Clark Z 16	McClean K — + 5	Watson K 1 + 1	McMillan D 2 + 2	Kerr J 15	Willock M 6 + 5	Williams G 10 + 1	Robertson J — + 2	McCann A 1 + 2	Match No.
1	2	3	4	5	6	7	8	9²	10³	11¹	12	13	14																		1
1	2	3	4	5	13	7	8	6²	9³	12	10			11¹	14																2
1	2	3	4	5		7	8	6	9³	13	11¹		14	10²			12														3
1	2	3	4	5		8¹	6	7³			10²		12	11				9	13	14											4
1	2	3	4	5		7¹	8	6³	9²		10		12	11					14	13											5
1	2	4	3	5			6	9¹	13	12	8³		7	11	14		10²														6
1	2²	3	4	5		7	8	13	6³	10		9¹	11				12		14												7
1		3	4	5		7	8²	12	6	11			10³				2	9¹	14	13											8
1		3	4¹	5			8	12	6	9	11¹			10²		13	2	14		7³											9
1		3		5	13		6⁵	8	12	11			9	10³			2	14		7¹	4										10
		3	4	5	6²	7	8	12	9	13	11³		14	10¹			2									1					11
	4	3	5⁵			9	6	10	7¹	11	12		8²	14			2	13								1					12
6²	3	4			8		7	10³	9¹		12			13	11		2	5								1	14				13
12	4	3			6¹	7	8			13	11		9	10			2²	5								1					14
	2	4			6¹	7	8	12	13	10²			9³	11	14			5		3						1					15
2	3	4			6		8		7	10¹		9		13	11²			5	12							1					16
2	3	4			14	7²	8	9	10³	12	6		11		13			5								1					17
2	3	4			7		6	13	8³	12		10²						5	11¹	9						1	14				18
2	3	4			6		8	12	10¹		13		9³		14			5	11	7²						1					19
2	3	4			13		6¹			12		8	9	10				5	11²	7						1					20
2⁴	3	4	13	6²	7		8	10			9		14					5³	11¹						12	1					21
	3	4		14			6	9		12	8	11⁴					5		10¹	7						1		2	13³		22
1	5	2	3²		12	6		8¹		11	13	14		9	10³												4	7¹			23
1	2²	3	4		9	8		7³		11		10¹					6	13					14				5	12			24
1	9²	3	4		5	7		8		14		11		12			6³										2	13	10¹		25
1		2	4		6		8		9¹			10²		13	11			5	12	7³					14			3			26
1		3	2		7		9⁴			12		11¹	10					5		13							4	8	6		27
1			4		6		8	9				11²					2	5	13	7⁹	12		14				3⁴		10¹		28
1		3	4		6²		8			12		11	9	10				5		7¹					13			2			29
1		2	4		6¹		8			13		11	9	10				5	14	7³	3²								12		30
1		2	4		6		7					10	8	11				5									3	12	9¹		31
1	14	2	4		12³		8²		10			11	9					5	6	7¹							3	13			32
1	6	3	4		7		8					11¹		10				5	13								2	12	9²		33
	6	2	3				12	13					9	11				5		7¹						1	4	8³	10⁵	14	34
	6	2	4					8				10						5								1	3	7	11¹	12	35
	6	2	4		8			9	13			10¹						5	12							1	3	7³	11²	14	36
	6	2			8			9	14							13		5					12	4		1	11²	3	7¹	10³	37
1		2			7			9	12							14	6¹	5				13	4				11	3	10³	8²	38

ST MIRREN

Year Formed: 1877. *Ground & Address:* The Paisley 2021 Stadium, St Mirren Park, Greenhill Road, Paisley PA3 1RU.
Telephone: 0141 889 2558. *Fax:* 0141 848 6444. *E-mail:* info@stmirren.com *Website:* www.stmirren.com
Ground Capacity: 8,023 (all seated). *Size of Pitch:* 105m × 68m.
Chairman: Gordon Scott. *Chief Executive:* Tony Fitzpatrick.
Manager: Alan Stubbs. *Assistant Manager:* Brian Rice.
Club Nickname: 'The Buddies'.
Previous Grounds: Shortroods 1877-79, Thistle Park Greenhill 1879-83, Westmarch 1883-94, Love Street 1894-2009.
Record Attendance: 47,438 v Celtic, League Cup, 20 August 1949.
Record Transfer Fee received: £850,000 for Ian Ferguson to Rangers (February 1988).
Record Transfer Fee paid: £400,000 for Thomas Stickroth from Bayer Uerdingen (March 1990).
Record Victory: 15-0 v Glasgow University, Scottish Cup 1st rd, 30 January 1960.
Record Defeat: 0-9 v Rangers, Division I, 4 December 1897.
Most Capped Player: Godmundur Torfason, 29, Iceland.
Most League Appearances: 399: Hugh Murray, 1997-2012.
Most League Goals in Season (Individual): 45: Dunky Walker, Division I, 1921-22.
Most Goals Overall (Individual): 221: David McCrae, 1923-34.

ST MIRREN – SPFL LADBROKES CHAMPIONSHIP 2017–18 LEAGUE RECORD

Match No.	Date	Venue	Opponents	Result	H/T Score	Lg Pos.	Goalscorers	Attendance
1	Aug 5	H	Falkirk	W 3-1	1-1	2	Demetriou [33], Smith, C [46], Reilly [69]	4639
2	12	A	Greenock Morton	L 1-4	1-1	5	Smith, C [41]	4661
3	19	A	Livingston	W 3-1	1-1	4	Halkett (og) [9], Reilly 2 [51, 60]	1609
4	26	H	Dundee U	W 3-0	1-0	3	Morgan 2 [26, 48], McShane [78]	4768
5	Sept 9	H	Inverness CT	W 4-2	1-0	1	Morgan [31], Buchanan [63], Smith, C [73], McShane [74]	3610
6	16	A	Dunfermline Ath	L 0-3	0-2	2		6628
7	24	A	Queen of the South	W 3-1	2-0	2	Smith, C [24], Morgan 2 [27, 54]	3023
8	30	H	Brechin C	W 2-1	1-1	1	Smith, C [14], Hilson [78]	3928
9	Oct 14	A	Dumbarton	W 2-0	1-0	1	Reilly [36], Sutton [70]	1178
10	21	A	Falkirk	D 0-0	0-0	1		5080
11	28	H	Greenock Morton	D 2-2	0-0	1	McShane (pen) [66], Reilly [72]	5496
12	Nov 4	A	Dundee U	L 1-2	0-1	1	Eckersley [90]	6936
13	25	A	Inverness CT	W 2-0	0-0	2	McShane (pen) [52], Reilly [90]	2687
14	28	H	Livingston	W 3-1	0-1	1	Morgan [51], Alexander (og) [66], McShane (pen) [78]	3177
15	Dec 2	H	Dumbarton	L 0-1	0-0	2		3591
16	9	A	Brechin C	W 2-1	1-1	2	Reilly [20], Smith, C (pen) [64]	812
17	16	H	Dunfermline Ath	W 1-0	1-0	2	Smith, C [38]	3665
18	23	A	Queen of the South	W 3-2	2-2	1	Reilly 2 [19, 35], MacKenzie [68]	2019
19	29	H	Dundee U	W 2-0	0-0	1	Morgan 2 [59, 78]	6214
20	Jan 2	A	Greenock Morton	D 1-1	1-0	1	Morgan [25]	4126
21	6	H	Inverness CT	W 1-0	1-0	1	Reilly [26]	4448
22	13	A	Dumbarton	W 2-0	0-0	1	Smith, C [47], McGinn [58]	1652
23	26	A	Dunfermline Ath	W 2-1	1-0	1	Smith, C [13], Baird [64]	5479
24	Feb 3	A	Queen of the South	W 2-0	2-0	1	Smith, L [4], Davis (pen) [32]	4585
25	17	A	Livingston	L 1-4	1-3	1	Flynn [2]	2708
26	24	H	Brechin C	W 1-0	1-0	1	O'Neil, P (og) [15]	4358
27	Mar 10	H	Dunfermline Ath	W 2-0	0-0	1	Davis (pen) [69], Smith, L [72]	4240
28	17	A	Queen of the South	W 3-1	1-1	1	Mullen [17], Morgan [52], Magennis [63]	1902
29	27	H	Dumbarton	W 5-0	2-0	1	Morgan 2 [13, 85], Smith, C [32], Mullen [49], Reilly [70]	3964
30	31	A	Inverness CT	D 2-2	1-0	1	Davis (pen) [4], Morgan [70]	3025
31	Apr 7	A	Brechin C	W 1-0	1-0	1	Magennis [7]	2447
32	10	A	Dundee U	L 0-1	0-1	1		5905
33	14	H	Livingston	D 0-0	0-0	1		6172
34	17	H	Falkirk	L 1-2	0-0	1	Hippolyte (pen) [55]	3761
35	21	H	Greenock Morton	W 2-1	1-1	1	Mullen [10], Morgan [72]	6422
36	28	A	Falkirk	L 0-1	0-0	1		5508

Final League Position: 1

Honours
League Champions: First Division 1976-77, 1999-2000, 2005-06; Division II 1967-68; Championship 2017-18.
Runners-up: First Division 2004-05; Division II 1935-36.
Scottish Cup Winners: 1926, 1959, 1987; *Runners-up:* 1908, 1934, 1962.
League Cup Winners: 2012-13; *Runners-up:* 1955-56, 2009-10.
League Challenge Cup Winners: 2005-06; *Runners-up:* 2016-17.
B&Q Cup Runners-up: 1993-94. *Anglo-Scottish Cup:* 1979-80.

European: *Cup Winners' Cup:* 4 matches (1987-88). *UEFA Cup:* 10 matches (1980-81, 1983-84, 1985-86).

Club colours: Shirt: Black and white stripes. Shorts: Black. Socks: Black with white hooped tops.

Goalscorers: *League (63):* Morgan 14, Reilly 11, Smith C 10 (1 pen), McShane 5 (3 pens), Davis 3 (3 pens), Mullen 3, Magennis 2, Smith L 2, Baird 1, Buchanan 1, Demetriou 1, Eckersley 1, Flynn 1, Hilson 1, Hippolyte 1 (1 pen), MacKenzie 1, McGinn 1, Sutton 1, own goals 3.
William Hill Scottish FA Cup (8): Reilly 5, Baird 1, Morgan 1, Smith C 1.
Betfred Scottish League Cup (9): Reilly 3, Morgan 2, Buchanan 1, Ross C Stewart 1, Smith C 1, own goal 1.
Irn-Bru Scottish League Challenge Cup (6): Reilly 3, Morgan 1, Ross C Stewart 1, Sutton 1.

Samson C 36	Irvine G 5+2	Baird J 27+4	MacKenzie G 12+2	Demetriou G 17+6	Smith C 33+1	McGinn S 35	McShane I 26+5	Morgan L 34+1	Sutton J 2+14	Reilly G 27+8	Stewart Ross C 1+8	Kirkpatrick J 1+7	O'Keefe C —+2	Buchanan G 7+3	Eckersley A 24	Smith L 32	Whyte D —+1	Todd J 1+2	Duffy D —+2	McCart J 3	Hilson D —+2	Magennis K 25+2	MacPherson C —+4	Davis H 20	Mullen D 11+8	Flynn R 11+2	Hill M 2+1	Hippolyte M 2+6	Donati M 1	Erhahon E 1	Match No.
1	2	3	4	5	6^1	7	8	9	10^2	11^3	12	13	14																		1
1	2	3^4	4	5	6	7	8	9	10^2	11^1	13					12															2
1	2^a			8	10^1	6	7	9	12	11^2		13			3	4	5														3
1		2		8	10	6	7	9^1		11^2	14	12			3	4	5^3	13													4
1	5	2		8^1	9^3	6	7	10^2		11		12			3	4						13	14								5
1		2		8^2	9^3	7	6	10	12	11	13				3^4	4^1	5			14											6
1	14	3			9	6	7	10		11^2	12	13			2			8^1		4											7
1		3		5^1	9	6	7	10	14	11^3	12	8^1				2		4	13												8
1		3	14		9	6	7	10^2	12	11^3	8^1			4	5	2						13									9
1		3			10	6^1	7	9	12	11^2		13		4	5	2						8^2	14								10
1		3		5	9	6	7	10		11	12			4		2						8^1									11
1	4				9	6	7	10	12	11^1					5	2				3	13	8^1									12
1	3	12		9^2	7	6	10		11^1					5	2	13						8		4							13
1	3	13		9^3	6	7	10	14	11^1					12	5	2						8^2		4							14
1	3	8^4			7	6^1	10	12	11^2	11^2	13			5	2							9		4							15
1	3			9^3	7	6^1	10^2	12	11		14			13	5	2						8		4							16
1	3			9^2	6	7	10		11^1					5	2							8	13	4	12						17
1	3	4	12	10^1	6	7	9		11^2					5^3	2						8	14	13								18
1	3			5	9^2	6	7	10^3	12				13		2						8	14	4	11^2							19
1	3			5	9^2	6	7	10	13	12					2						8	4	11^1								20
1	13	3		5	9^1	7	6^2	10		11					2						8	4	12								21
1	3			5	9^1	7	6	10	13	11^2					2						8	4	12								22
1	3	14			9^2	7	6^1	10		11^3				5	2						8	4	13	12							23
1	3			9^1	6	13	10		11^3						2						7	4	12	8^2	14						24
1	3	12		9^2	7		10		11^1					5	2						6	4	13	8^3		14					25
1	14	3		9^2	7	6^3	10		11^1					5	2						8	4		12		13					26
1	12	3		9	6	14			11^1					5	2						7^2	4	10^3	8		13					27
1		4	3	12	9^2	6	14	10		13				5^1	2						7		11^3	8							28
1		3	12	9	6	14	10		13					5^2	2						7^3	4	11^1	8							29
1		13	3		9^1	7		8		12				5	2						6	4	11^2	10							30
1		3			9^2	6	13	8		12				5	2						7	4	11^1	10							31
1		3			9^3	6^1		10	13	12				5	2						7	4	11^2	8	14						32
1		3			9^2	6		10		12				5	2						7	4	11^1	8	13						33
1	2	3		5	14	7		6^1	13	10^3											12		9^2	8	11	4					34
1	12	3^3	5	9	7		10^1	13							2						6	4	11	8^2	14						35
1		4		5		6	10	13	11^2					12							8	3	9	7	7^1						36

STENHOUSEMUIR

Year Formed: 1884. *Ground & Address:* Ochilview Park, Gladstone Rd, Stenhousemuir FK5 4QL. *Telephone:* 01324 562992. *Fax:* 01324 562980. *E-mail:* info@stenhousemuirfc.com *Website:* www.stenhousemuirfc.com
Ground Capacity: 3,776 (seated: 626). *Size of Pitch:* 101m × 66m.
Chairman: Gordon Thompson. *Vice-Chairman:* David Reid. *Secretary/General Manager:* Margaret Kilpatrick.
Manager: Brown Ferguson. *Assistant Manager:* Jim Paterson.
Club Nickname: 'The Warriors'.
Previous Grounds: Tryst Ground 1884-86, Goschen Park 1886-90.
Record Attendance: 12,500 v East Fife, Scottish Cup Quarter-final, 11 March 1950.
Record Transfer Fee received: £70,000 for Euan Donaldson to St Johnstone (May 1995).
Record Transfer Fee paid: £20,000 to Livingston for Ian Little (June 1995); £20,000 to East Fife for Paul Hunter (September 1995).
Record Victory: 9-2 v Dundee U, Division II, 16 April 1937.
Record Defeat: 2-11 v Dunfermline Ath, Division II, 27 September 1930.
Most League Appearances: 434: Jimmy Richardson, 1957-73.
Most League Goals in Season (Individual): 32: Robert Taylor, Division II, 1925-26.

STENHOUSEMUIR – SPFL LADBROKES LEAGUE TWO 2017–18 LEAGUE RECORD

Match No.	Date	Venue	Opponents	Result	H/T Score	Lg Pos.	Goalscorers	Attendance
1	Aug 5	H	Stirling Alb	L	2-3	2-1	7	Paton [21], McGuigan [39]	606
2	12	A	Montrose	D	1-1	0-0	7	McGuigan [70]	455
3	19	H	Peterhead	W	3-1	1-1	4	McGuigan [7], Blockley [52], Longworth [81]	220
4	26	A	Clyde	D	1-1	1-0	6	McGuigan [31]	440
5	Sept 9	H	Cowdenbeath	W	1-0	1-0	3	Blockley [42]	409
6	16	A	Annan Ath	D	1-1	1-0	4	McGuigan [5]	373
7	23	H	Berwick R	W	3-0	2-0	3	McGuigan 2 [5, 87], Scullion (og) [14]	348
8	30	H	Edinburgh C	W	3-0	0-0	2	McMenamin [65], McGuigan 2 (1 pen) [79 (p), 87]	412
9	Oct 21	A	Elgin C	L	0-2	0-0	4		654
10	28	A	Stirling Alb	W	2-1	1-0	4	McGuigan (pen) [26], Longworth [48]	768
11	Nov 4	H	Clyde	D	1-1	1-0	4	McGuigan (pen) [20]	596
12	11	A	Peterhead	W	3-2	1-0	4	McGuigan 2 (1 pen) [13, 81 (p)], Dunlop, M [71]	525
13	25	H	Montrose	L	0-1	0-1	5		418
14	Dec 9	H	Annan Ath	L	1-3	0-0	6	McMenamin [69]	242
15	16	A	Edinburgh C	W	2-1	2-1	4	Paton [25], McGuigan [41]	271
16	19	A	Cowdenbeath	D	1-1	0-1	4	McGuigan [60]	245
17	23	H	Elgin C	W	4-1	2-0	3	Cook [33], Paton [39], McGuigan [87], Murray [90]	373
18	Jan 2	H	Stirling Alb	W	2-1	0-0	3	Scott [47], Meechan [52]	626
19	6	H	Peterhead	L	1-4	1-1	3	McGuigan (pen) [28]	449
20	13	A	Clyde	W	3-0	1-0	4	Meechan [11], Longworth [72], Murray [83]	581
21	27	A	Elgin C	L	0-2	0-1	3		553
22	Feb 3	H	Berwick R	W	4-0	2-0	3	Scott 2 [12, 71], Paton [35], Cook [68]	323
23	10	A	Montrose	L	0-1	0-0	4		1182
24	17	H	Edinburgh C	W	1-0	1-0	4	McGuigan [13]	385
25	24	A	Annan Ath	L	0-2	0-0	4		307
26	Mar 10	H	Clyde	L	2-3	0-2	4	Ferns [56], Paton [76]	488
27	13	A	Peterhead	W	2-2	2-0	4	McGuigan [17], McMenamin [31]	471
28	20	H	Cowdenbeath	L	1-2	0-2	4	Longworth [73]	312
29	24	H	Elgin C	L	0-2	0-1	4		422
30	31	A	Cowdenbeath	D	1-1	1-1	5	McGuigan [38]	277
31	Apr 7	A	Edinburgh C	W	4-1	2-0	4	Paton [7], McMenamin [17], Dallas 2 [58, 79]	233
32	14	A	Annan Ath	W	3-2	1-1	4	Paton 2 (1 pen) [24, 53 (p)], Ferry [90]	378
33	17	A	Berwick R	D	0-0	0-0	4		326
34	21	H	Montrose	L	0-2	0-2	4		976
35	24	A	Berwick R	D	2-2	2-2	4	Dallas [39], McMenamin [43]	295
36	28	A	Stirling Alb	D	1-1	1-0	4	McMenamin [38]	894

Final League Position: 4

Honours
League Runners-up: Third Division 1998-99.
Promoted via play-offs: 2008-09 (to Second Division); 2017-18 (to League One).
Scottish Cup: Semi-finals 1902-03. Quarter-finals 1948-49, 1949-50, 1994-95.
League Cup: Quarter-finals 1947-48, 1960-61, 1975-76.
League Challenge Cup Winners: 1995-96.

Club colours: Shirt: Maroon with white trim. Shorts: White. Socks: Maroon.

Goalscorers: *League (56):* McGuigan 20 (5 pens), Paton 8 (1 pen), McMenamin 6, Longworth 4, Dallas 3, Scott 3, Blockley 2, Cook 2, Meechan 2, Murray 2, Dunlop M 1, Ferns 1, Ferry 1, own goal 1.
William Hill Scottish FA Cup (1): Paterson 1.
Betfred Scottish League Cup (3): Longworth 1, McGuigan 1 (1 pen), McMenamin 1.
Irn-Bru Scottish League Challenge Cup (0).
Play-Offs (5): Dunlop M 2, McGuigan 2, Scott 1.

Smith C 30	Marsh D 12+8	Dunlop R 36	Dunlop M 36	Meechan R 35	McGuigan M 30+1	Blockley N 6	Ferry M 35	Donaldson R 36	Longworth J 15+15	Paton H 31	McMenamin C 12+19	Gilmour R —+3	Ferns E 15+17	Scott M 13+11	Paterson N 15+3	Murray 16+13	Allen P —+3	Cook A 20+3	Halleran T 1+3	McMinn L 6	Cunningham A —+2	Dallas A 6	Match No.
1	2¹	3	4	5⁴	6	7	8	9	10	11³	12	13	14										1
1	2²	3	4	5	6	7¹	8	9	10³	11	14	13	12										2
1		4	3	2	10³	8¹	6	5	11	7		13	9²	12	14								3
1		4	3	2	10	7²	6	5	11	8		13	9¹	12									4
1		4	3	2	10	7¹	8	5	11²	6	12	14	13	9³									5
1	3	4	2	10	7¹	8	5	11²	6		14	12	9³	13									6
1	3	4	2	10	7	5	12	8¹	11²	13	9³	6	14										7
1	3	4	2	10	8	5	13	7	11¹	12	6²	9³	14										8
1	3	4	2³	11	7	5	12	8²	10¹	9	14	6	13										9
1	13	4	3	2	10¹	8	9	11²	7	14	6⁵	5	12										10
1	14	3	4	5	10¹	6	2	11	7	9³	13	8¹	12										11
1	13	2	3	5	10¹	6	4	11	7³	14	9	12	8²										12
1		2	3	5	10	6	4	11²	8	13	9	12	7¹	14									13
1	12	2	3	5	10	7	4²	11	14	8	6¹	13	9										14
1	8	3	4	2	9²	7	5	14	6¹	12	10³	13	11										15
1	7	3	2	5	10	6	4	12	11²	13	8¹	9											16
1	7	2	3	5	10	6	4	8³	14	11²	12	13	9¹										17
1	6	3	4	2	11	7	5	14	8²	10³	13	12	9¹										18
1	6²	4	3	2	10³	7	5	12	8	13	11	14	9¹										19
1	6	3	4	2	11	7	5	12	13	9	10²	8¹	14										20
1	8³	4	2	11	7		5	13	12	14	9²	10	6¹										21
1	3	4	2	11²	6		5	14	7	13	12	10¹	8²	9									22
1		4	3	2	11¹	8	5	14	7	13	12	10	6²	9									23
1	14	2	3	5	10	7	4	11¹	6	13	12	8³	9²								1		24
1	3	4	2	11	9	5	13	8	12	6	7¹	10									1		25
1	8²	2	3	5	10	7	4	11³	6	14	13	9¹	12								1		26
1	13	3	4	2	11	7	5	14	8¹	10²	6	9³							1			12	27
1		2	3	5⁴	10	7	4	13	6	11³	12	8¹	9						1			14	28
1	6	2	3	10	5	4	11¹	12	9	7	13	8²							1				29
1		2	3	5	10	6	4	11²	8	12	9	7¹	13										30
1	14	2	3³	5	6	4	8²	10	9¹	7	13	12										11	31
1	14	2	3	5	6	4	13	7	10²	9¹	8³											11	32
1		2	3	5	8	4	10²	7	6¹	13	12	9										11	33
1		2	3	5⁴	7	4	13	8	10	14	12	6¹	9									11³	34
1	3¹	8	4	2	5	7	10	6²	12	9	13											11	35
1		4	3	2	13	7	5	8	10¹	6	12	9²	14									11³	36

STIRLING ALBION

Year Formed: 1945. *Ground & Address:* Forthbank Stadium, Springkerse, Stirling FK7 7UJ. *Telephone:* 01786 450399.
Fax: 01786 448592. *Email:* office@stirlingalbionfc.co.uk *Website:* www.stirlingalbionfc.co.uk
Ground Capacity: 3,808 (seated: 2,508). *Size of Pitch:* 101m × 68m.
Chairman: Stuart Brown. *General Manager:* Andy Kennedy.
Manager: Dave Mackay. *Assistant Manager:* Frazer Wright.
Club Nickname: 'The Binos'.
Previous Grounds: Annfield 1945-92.
Record Attendance: 26,400 v Celtic, Scottish Cup 4th rd, 14 March 1959 (Annfield); 3,808 v Aberdeen, Scottish Cup 4th rd, 15 February 1996 (Forthbank).
Record Transfer Fee received: £90,000 for Stephen Nicholas to Motherwell (March 1999).
Record Transfer Fee paid: £25,000 for Craig Taggart from Falkirk (August 1994).
Record Victory: 20-0 v Selkirk, Scottish Cup 1st rd, 8 December 1984.
Record Defeat: 0-9 v Dundee U, Division I, 30 December 1967; 0-9 v Ross Co, Scottish Cup 5th rd, 6 February 2010.
Most League Appearances: 504: Matt McPhee, 1967-81.
Most League Goals in Season (Individual): 27: Joe Hughes, Division II, 1969-70.
Most Goals Overall (Individual): 129: Billy Steele, 1971-83.

STIRLING ALBION – SPFL LADBROKES LEAGUE TWO 2017–18 LEAGUE RECORD

Match No.	Date		Venue	Opponents	Result	H/T Score	Lg Pos.	Goalscorers	Atten- dance
1	Aug	5	A	Stenhousemuir	W 3-2	1-2	3	Smith, D [33], Morrison [54], Kavanagh [82]	606
2		12	H	Berwick R	W 4-0	2-0	1	Smith, D 2 [23, 35], Kavanagh [54], Smith, R [79]	618
3		19	H	Edinburgh C	W 2-0	2-0	1	Smith, D [31], Kavanagh [44]	610
4		26	A	Peterhead	W 4-2	4-1	1	Morrison [18], Smith, D 2 [21, 36], Kavanagh [25]	632
5	Sept	9	H	Clyde	L 2-3	1-1	1	MacDonald [11], Morrison [60]	865
6		16	A	Montrose	W 3-1	1-0	1	Morrison 2 [13, 90], Dickson [46]	568
7		23	H	Annan Ath	W 3-2	2-1	1	Smith, D [11], Morrison 2 [30, 74]	617
8		30	H	Elgin C	D 2-2	2-0	1	Smith, D 2 [6, 23]	691
9	Oct	21	A	Cowdenbeath	W 3-0	2-0	1	Smith, D [28], MacDonald [33], McLaughlin [67]	371
10		28	H	Stenhousemuir	L 1-2	0-1	1	Smith, D [73]	768
11	Nov	4	A	Edinburgh C	W 2-1	1-1	1	Kavanagh [37], Morrison [53]	421
12		11	A	Clyde	D 1-1	0-0	1	Smith, D [78]	770
13	Dec	2	A	Berwick R	L 0-1	0-1	2		442
14		5	H	Peterhead	L 0-1	0-1	3		456
15		16	A	Annan Ath	D 1-1	1-0	3	Caddis [9]	316
16		23	H	Montrose	L 0-1	0-0	4		710
17	Jan	2	A	Stenhousemuir	L 1-2	0-0	5	Smith, D [90]	626
18		6	H	Berwick R	W 2-0	1-0	4	Smith, D 2 [24, 58]	597
19		13	A	Peterhead	L 3-4	2-2	5	Robertson [6], Smith, D 2 [32, 90]	649
20		27	A	Montrose	L 1-2	1-0	6	Smith, D [14]	531
21		31	H	Cowdenbeath	W 1-0	1-0	4	Pyper (og) [35]	395
22	Feb	3	H	Elgin C	W 3-1	2-0	4	Smith, D 2 [9, 31], MacDonald [71]	544
23		10	A	Cowdenbeath	W 2-1	0-0	3	MacDonald 2 (1 pen) [71 (p), 85]	366
24		17	H	Annan Ath	W 3-0	0-0	3	McGeachie [56], MacDonald 2 [70, 78]	648
25		24	H	Clyde	W 2-1	1-1	3	Smith, D [4], MacDonald [58]	1012
26	Mar	10	H	Peterhead	L 0-1	0-0	3		541
27		13	A	Berwick R	W 1-0	1-0	3	Little [41]	302
28		17	A	Edinburgh C	D 2-2	1-1	3	Jardine [32], McLaughlin [90]	312
29		20	A	Elgin C	W 2-0	0-0	3	Hamilton [53], Robertson [63]	393
30		24	H	Cowdenbeath	D 2-2	1-0	3	Jardine [39], McLaughlin (pen) [64]	748
31		27	H	Edinburgh C	D 2-2	1-1	3	Smith, D [24], Smith, R [56]	433
32		31	A	Elgin C	L 0-3	0-3	3		676
33	Apr	7	H	Montrose	L 0-5	0-1	3		692
34		14	A	Clyde	L 1-2	0-0	3	Jardine [53]	715
35		21	A	Annan Ath	L 1-3	1-1	3	McLaughlin [7]	507
36		28	H	Stenhousemuir	D 1-1	0-1	3	MacDonald [74]	894

Final League Position: 3

Honours
League Champions: Division II 1952-53, 1957-58, 1960-61, 1964-65; Second Division 1976-77, 1990-91, 1995-96, 2009-10.
Runners-up: Division II 1948-49, 1950-51; Second Division 2006-07; Third Division 2003-04.
Promoted via play-offs: 2006-07 (to First Division); 2013-14 (to League One).
League Cup: Semi-finals 1961-62.
League Challenge Cup: Semi-finals 1995-96, 1999-2000.

Club colours: Shirt: Red with white sleeves. Shorts: Red with white trim. Socks: Red.

Goalscorers: *League (61):* Smith D 22, MacDonald 9 (1 pen), Morrison 8, Kavanagh 5, McLaughlin 4 (1 pen), Jardine 3, Robertson 2, Smith R 2, Caddis 1, Dickson 1, Hamilton 1, Little 1, McGeachie 1, own goal 1.
Betfred Scottish League Cup (6): Morrison 2, Caddis 1 (1 pen), Kavanagh 1, MacDonald 1 (1 pen), Smith D 1.
Irn-Bru Scottish League Challenge Cup (1): Smith D 1.
Play-Offs (0).

Binnie C 29	McNeil E 35	McGeachie R 36	Smith R 16+5	Noble S 7+3	Morrison C 16	Caddis L 14+9	Black A 20+4	Dickson S 12+10	MacDonald P 27+6	Smith D 30+1	Kavanagh R 20+16	Hamilton L 31+1	McMullan C —+3	Robertson W 20+4	Cameron R —+1	McLaughlin N 13+17	Foden M 2	Banner K 7+1	Stanger G 5+6	Thomson C 3	Moon K 16	Jardine D 16	Barr D 12	Little A 4+4	Wight C 5	Match No.
1	2¹	3	4	5	6³	7	8	9	10	11²	12	13	14													1
1	2	3	4	5	6	7	8		10¹	9²				12	13											2
1	2	3	4		6¹	7	8²		10	11	9	5		12		13										3
1	2	3	4		6	7	8		10¹	11	9	5		12												4
1	4	2	3	14	7	8	6¹		9	10	11³	5²		13		12										5
1	3	2	4		6	9¹	7	12	10¹	11²	13	5		8		14										6
	2	3	4		6	7		9	10²	11	13	5	14	8²		12	1									7
	2	3	4	9	6	7	8²		10	11¹	12	5				13	1									8
1	2	3	4		8²	9	6		11¹	10	13	5		7		12										9
1	2	3	4		6	7⁴	9¹	12	11	13	5	14		8³		10										10
1	4	3	5	9		7	6	8	11¹	10		2				12										11
1	5	4						8	6	9	10	11				3	12	2	7¹							12
1	2	3			6	7	8	13	12	9	11²	5				10¹				4						13
1	2²	3		13	6	8	7*	9	10	11¹	12	4								5						14
1	5¹	3	12			9	7	10	11	13	4	6²							2	8						15
1	2	3	4		6	14		9	10	13	12	5¹		8¹		11²					7					16
1	2		4	5	6¹	7²	8³	9	10	11	12	14		13		3										17
1	2	4	3		5³	12	6¹	13	10	11²	9	8				7			14							18
1	2	4	3		6²				10	11	9	5		7		12		8¹	13							19
1	3	2				12	7³		10	11	9	5		6		13		4¹	14			8²				20
1	4	2	3			13			10²	11	12	5		7		9¹		14				8³	6			21
1	2	3				12			11	9	8¹	5		6³		13		14			7²	10	4			22
1	3	2				14			11	10	9¹	5		7²		13		12			8³	6	4			23
1	2	3				13			10	11	6¹	5		9		12					7²	8	4			24
1	5¹	2				13	14		10²	11	9	4		6				8²			7	3	12			25
	5	2				14			11²	10	9	4		13				6¹	8³		7	3	12			26
1	2	5				13	14		11³	9	4	6		12							8	7	3²	10¹		27
1	5	2				13		9	11²	12	4⁴	6		10							7¹	8	3	14		28
	5	2				13	14		12	9	4	6²		11		7¹					8	3	10³		1	29
	2	5				13	14		12	11	7	3³		9¹		6					8²	10	4		1	30
	2	4	5					8	12	9	13	10¹		3		6					7			11²	1	31
	5	2	3¹				12	7²	11	9	13	4				10						8		11	1	32
	2	3	5³						10¹	11²	13	4		8*		9		14			7	6		12	1	33
1	5	4					14		8³	13	12	9				11			2		7	6¹	3	10⁴		34
1	3	2					14		12	10²	9	13		5		8³		11			7¹	6	4			35
1	9	5					13		7	14	12	11²		2³		10					3	6¹	8	4		36

STRANRAER

Year Formed: 1870. *Ground & Address:* Stair Park, London Rd, Stranraer DG9 8BS. *Telephone and Fax:* 01776 703271.
E-mail: secretary@stranraerfc.org *Website:* www.stranraerfc.org
Ground Capacity: 4,178 (seated: 1,830). *Size of Pitch:* 103m × 64m.
Chairman: Alex Connor. *Vice-Chairman:* David Broadfoot.
Manager: Stephen Farrell. *Assistant Manager:* Chris Aitken.
Club Nicknames: 'The Blues', 'The Clayholers'.
Previous Grounds: None.
Record Attendance: 6,500 v Rangers, Scottish Cup 1st rd, 24 January 1948.
Record Transfer Fee received: £90,000 for Mark Campbell to Ayr U (1999).
Record Transfer Fee paid: £35,000 for Michael Moore from St Johnstone (March 2005).
Record Victory: 9-0 v St Cuthbert Wanderers, Scottish Cup 2nd rd, 23 October 2010; 9-0 v Wigtown & Bladnoch, Scottish Cup 2nd rd, 22 October 2011.
Record Defeat: 1-11 v Queen of the South, Scottish Cup 1st rd, 16 January 1932.
Most League Appearances: 301: Keith Knox, 1986-90; 1999-2001.
Most League Goals in Season (Individual): 27: Derek Frye, 1977-78.
Most Goals Overall (Individual): 136: Jim Campbell, 1965-75.

STRANRAER – SPFL LADBROKES LEAGUE ONE 2017–18 LEAGUE RECORD

Match No.	Date		Venue	Opponents	Result		H/T Score	Lg Pos.	Goalscorers	Atten- dance
1	Aug	5	H	East Fife	W	1-0	0-0	4	Hamill [65]	409
2		12	A	Raith R	L	0-3	0-1	7		1625
3		19	H	Ayr U	L	3-4	1-1	8	Wallace, R [16], Thomson 2 [79, 81]	1070
4		26	A	Queen's Park	D	2-2	2-1	8	Wallace, R [1], Anderson [9]	595
5	Sept	9	H	Airdrieonians	W	3-1	1-0	5	Anderson 2 [10, 68], Agnew (pen) [66]	431
6		16	A	Albion R	W	4-0	3-0	4	Agnew 3 (2 pens) [11, 23 (p), 83 (p)], Woods [31]	353
7		23	H	Arbroath	L	2-6	1-4	6	Thomson [21], Agnew [65]	360
8		30	A	Forfar Ath	D	1-1	0-1	6	Stoney [90]	474
9	Oct	14	H	Alloa Ath	W	2-0	0-0	6	Wallace, R [58], Hamill [81]	409
10		28	A	Ayr U	L	0-2	0-0	7		1473
11	Nov	4	H	Queen's Park	W	3-0	2-0	6	Anderson [12], Bell [44], Wallace, R [87]	495
12		11	A	Airdrieonians	L	0-2	0-0	6		641
13	Dec	2	A	Arbroath	W	2-1	0-1	6	Turner [53], Beith [78]	642
14		9	A	East Fife	D	1-1	0-1	6	Wallace, R [70]	521
15		16	H	Forfar Ath	W	3-0	0-0	3	Wallace, R (pen) [56], Beith 2 [84, 90]	276
16		19	H	Albion R	D	2-2	1-1	3	Wallace, R 2 (2 pens) [37, 88]	303
17		23	A	Alloa Ath	L	0-1	0-0	4		449
18		30	A	Raith R	L	0-3	0-2	4		1432
19	Jan	2	H	Ayr U	L	1-5	0-2	5	Turner [80]	1143
20		6	A	Queen's Park	D	2-2	0-0	5	Beith [78], Turner [90]	607
21		13	H	Airdrieonians	W	3-2	1-1	5	Okoh 2 [36, 61], Beith [75]	406
22		20	H	Raith R	W	1-0	1-0	4	Beith [9]	449
23		27	A	Albion R	W	3-1	1-0	3	Beith 2 [8, 89], Robertson [74]	388
24	Feb	3	H	East Fife	L	0-2	0-0	5		383
25		17	A	Forfar Ath	L	1-5	0-4	5	Woods [89]	428
26		20	H	Arbroath	L	1-4	1-1	5	MacPherson [9]	201
27		24	A	Alloa Ath	W	1-0	1-0	5	Lyon [45]	282
28	Mar	10	H	Albion R	L	2-3	2-0	5	Turner 2 [34, 35]	281
29		13	A	Airdrieonians	L	1-2	1-1	6	Turner (pen) [4]	512
30		17	H	Queen's Park	L	2-3	0-2	6	Robertson [67], Agnew (pen) [90]	255
31		24	A	Arbroath	W	3-2	0-2	5	Okoh [68], Anderson [73], Agnew (pen) [86]	726
32		31	H	Forfar Ath	W	2-0	2-0	5	Agnew [6], Lyon [32]	290
33	Apr	7	A	Alloa Ath	W	1-0	0-0	5	Neill [54]	472
34		14	A	Ayr U	W	2-1	1-1	5	Anderson [3], Agnew (pen) [85]	2323
35		21	H	Raith R	L	0-3	0-2	5		524
36		28	A	East Fife	W	3-2	1-0	5	Agnew [36], Anderson 2 [48, 53]	426

Final League Position: 5

Honours
League Champions: Second Division 1993-94, 1997-98; Third Division 2003-04.
Runners-up: Second Division 2004-05; Third Division 2007-08; League One 2014-15.
Promoted via play-offs: 2011-12 (to Second Division).
Scottish Cup: Quarter-finals 2003
League Challenge Cup Winners: 1996-97. Semi-finals: 2000-01, 2014-15.

Club colours: Shirt: Blue with white trim. Shorts: White with blue trim. Socks: Blue.

Goalscorers: *League (58):* Agnew 10 (6 pens), Anderson 8, Beith 8, Wallace R 8 (3 pens), Turner 6 (1 pen), Okoh 3, Thomson 3, Hamill 2, Lyon 2, Robertson 2, Woods 2, Bell 1, MacPherson 1, Neill 1, Stoney 1.
William Hill Scottish FA Cup (0).
Betfred Scottish League Cup (4): Agnew 2 (1 pen), Neill 1, Robertson 1.
Irn-Bru Scottish League Challenge Cup (6): Wallace R 2, Agnew 1 (1 pen), Okoh 1, Stoney 1, own goal 1.

Belford C 22	Robertson S 30+1	Barron D 13	Neill M 31+4	Dick L 14+1	Hamill J 36	Bell S 18+1	Anderson G 31+4	Turner K 26+8	Thomson R 27	Wallace R 17	Woods P 18+12	Agnew S 18+8	Okoh C 16+15	Lang T 2+1	Wallace T —+1	Stoney D 2+9	Elliott C 2+8	Gray D —+5	Beith A 14	McGowan C 17+2	Lyon R 6+7	Dykes D 8+6	Currie M 14	Hawkshaw D 6+6	MacPherson C 8+1	Scott G —+4	Baxter J —+1	Match No.
1	2	3	4	5	6	7	8	9^2	10^3	11^1	12	13	14															1
1	2	3	4	5	6^1	7	8^2	9	10^1	11	12	13	14															2
1	2^3	14	5	6	4	8	12	7	10	13	9^2	11^1		3														3
1	2		4	5	6	3	8^3	7^2	9	11	10^1		13			12			14									4
1	2^4	3	4	5	8	12	9^3	13	7	11^2	6	10^1							14									5
1	3	4	5	2	6	8^1	13	7	11	9^2	10^3	12							14									6
1	3	4	5	2	7	10^1	12	6	11^3	9^2	8	13							14									7
1	3		4	5	7	10	12	6	11^3	9^2	8	14			2^1				13									8
1	2	3	9	5	4	8^2	6	7	11^3	10^1	12					13	14											9
1	3^2		4^2	5	2^1	9	8^1	7	11	10	6^3		14			13	12											10
1	2	12	4	5	3	8^3	13	6	10	9^2	7	14	11^1															11
1	4	3	5	2	7	12	9	10	6^1	8^2	13	11^3				14												12
1	3	4	2	5	7	8^2	9	10	11^2	12						13			6									13
1	14	3	4	5^1	2	7	8^2	9^1	10	11	12					13				6^1								14
1	2^2	3	4	5^3	8	9^1	10	6	11	12					14						7	13						15
1	5	3^3	4^1	13	2	8^2	9	10	6	11	12										7	14						16
1	3	4	5	2	7	9^3	13	10^1	11	6^2	12					14				8								17
1	4	5	3	2	7	6^1	8^2	9^3	11	12	13					14				10								18
1	3^3		4^2	2	7	6	8	9	11^1	12						13			14	10	5							19
1	3		4	2	8		9	6			12		11^1							10^2	7	5	13					20
1	3		4	2			8^2	9	7		10^1	14	11^3							6	5	13	12					21
1	3		4	2			12	9	6		10^2	14	11^1							7	5	13	8^3					22
	2	5	4	2			12	6			9^2	10	11^3					14		7	3	8^1	1					23
	3	4	2				12	9			10^3	6^2	11						14	7	5	13	1	8^1				24
	3	5^1	4	2			10	7	6		13	11^2	8							12			1	14	9^3			25
	3	4^2	12	2			6^1	11			10^3	8	13							7	5	14	1		9			26
	3	14	4	12			9	7			13	11^1								8	6^2	5	1	10^3	2			27
	3		4	2			10	9	7		12	13	11^2						14	5	8^3		1	6^1				28
	3		4	2			10	9	7^3		12	13	11^2						14	5	13	6^2	1	8^1				29
	3		4	2			8	9			12	10	11^1							5	7^2	13	1		6			30
	3		4	2		6		10	9		12		14							5	7^2	11^3	1	13	8			31
	3		4	2		8^1		10			11^2	13								5	6^2	14	1	7				32
	3		4	2		6		9			10	11^3								5	7^2	14	1	8^1	13	12		33
	2	4	3	10	7		8				11^2	13					13			5	6^1		1	14	9^3	12		34
	2	4	3	10	7		8				11^3	9^1					12			5	14	1	6^2				13	35
	2	3	5		9	10^3	8				11^1	12				4				14	1	7^2	6	13				36

SCOTTISH LEAGUE HONOURS 1890–2018

=Until 1921–22 season teams were equal if level on points, unless a play-off took place. §Not promoted after play-offs.
*Won or placed on goal average (ratio), goal difference or most goals scored (goal average from 1921–22 until 1971–72
when it was replaced by goal difference). No official competition during 1939–46; regional leagues operated.

DIVISION 1 (1890–91 to 1974–75) – TIER 1

Tier	Season	Max Pts	First	Pts	Second	Pts	Third	Pts
1	1890–91	36	Dumbarton=	29	Rangers=	29	Celtic	21

Dumbarton and Rangers held title jointly after indecisive play-off ended 2-2. Celtic deducted 4 points for fielding an ineligible player.

Tier	Season	Max Pts	First	Pts	Second	Pts	Third	Pts
1	1891–92	44	Dumbarton	37	Celtic	35	Hearts	34
1	1892–93	36	Celtic	29	Rangers	28	St Mirren	20
1	1893–94	36	Celtic	29	Hearts	26	St Bernard's	23
1	1894–95	36	Hearts	31	Celtic	26	Rangers	22
1	1895–96	36	Celtic	30	Rangers	26	Hibernian	24
1	1896–97	36	Hearts	28	Hibernian	26	Rangers	25
1	1897–98	36	Celtic	33	Rangers	29	Hibernian	22
1	1898–99	36	Rangers	36	Hearts	26	Celtic	24
1	1899–1900	36	Rangers	32	Celtic	25	Hibernian	24
1	1900–01	40	Rangers	35	Celtic	29	Hibernian	25
1	1901–02	36	Rangers	28	Celtic	26	Hearts	22
1	1902–03	44	Hibernian	37	Dundee	31	Rangers	29
1	1903–04	52	Third Lanark	43	Hearts	39	Celtic / Rangers=	38
1	1904–05	52	Celtic=	41	Rangers=	41	Third Lanark	35

Celtic won title after beating Rangers 2-1 in play-off.

Tier	Season	Max Pts	First	Pts	Second	Pts	Third	Pts
1	1905–06	60	Celtic	49	Hearts	43	Airdrieonians	38
1	1906–07	68	Celtic	55	Dundee	48	Rangers	45
1	1907–08	68	Celtic	55	Falkirk	51	Rangers	50
1	1908–09	68	Celtic	51	Dundee	50	Clyde	48
1	1909–10	68	Celtic	54	Falkirk	52	Rangers	46
1	1910–11	68	Rangers	52	Aberdeen	48	Falkirk	44
1	1911–12	68	Rangers	51	Celtic	45	Clyde	42
1	1912–13	68	Rangers	53	Celtic	49	Hearts / Airdrieonians=	41
1	1913–14	76	Celtic	65	Rangers	59	Hearts / Morton=	54
1	1914–15	76	Celtic	65	Hearts	61	Rangers	50
1	1915–16	76	Celtic	67	Rangers	56	Morton	51
1	1916–17	76	Celtic	64	Morton	54	Rangers	53
1	1917–18	68	Rangers	56	Celtic	55	Kilmarnock / Morton=	43
1	1918–19	68	Celtic	58	Rangers	57	Morton	47
1	1919–20	84	Rangers	71	Celtic	68	Motherwell	57
1	1920–21	84	Rangers	76	Celtic	66	Hearts	50
1	1921–22	84	Celtic	67	Rangers	66	Raith R	51
1	1922–23	76	Rangers	55	Airdrieonians	50	Celtic	46
1	1923–24	76	Rangers	59	Airdrieonians	50	Celtic	46
1	1924–25	76	Rangers	60	Airdrieonians	57	Hibernian	52
1	1925–26	76	Celtic	58	Airdrieonians*	50	Hearts	50
1	1926–27	76	Rangers	56	Motherwell	51	Celtic	49
1	1927–28	76	Rangers	60	Celtic*	55	Motherwell	55
1	1928–29	76	Rangers	67	Celtic	51	Motherwell	50
1	1929–30	76	Rangers	60	Motherwell	55	Aberdeen	53
1	1930–31	76	Rangers	60	Celtic	58	Motherwell	56
1	1931–32	76	Motherwell	66	Rangers	61	Celtic	48
1	1932–33	76	Rangers	62	Motherwell	59	Hearts	50
1	1933–34	76	Rangers	66	Motherwell	62	Celtic	47
1	1934–35	76	Rangers	55	Celtic	52	Hearts	50
1	1935–36	76	Celtic	66	Rangers*	61	Aberdeen	61
1	1936–37	76	Rangers	61	Aberdeen	54	Celtic	52
1	1937–38	76	Celtic	61	Hearts	58	Rangers	49
1	1938–39	76	Rangers	59	Celtic	48	Aberdeen	46
1	1946–47	60	Rangers	46	Hibernian	44	Aberdeen	39
1	1947–48	60	Hibernian	48	Rangers	46	Partick Thistle	36
1	1948–49	60	Rangers	46	Dundee	45	Hibernian	39
1	1949–50	60	Rangers	50	Hibernian	49	Hearts	43
1	1950–51	60	Hibernian	48	Rangers*	38	Dundee	38
1	1951–52	60	Hibernian	45	Rangers	41	East Fife	37
1	1952–53	60	Rangers*	43	Hibernian	43	East Fife	39
1	1953–54	60	Celtic	43	Hearts	38	Partick Thistle	35
1	1954–55	60	Aberdeen	49	Celtic	46	Rangers	41
1	1955–56	68	Rangers	52	Aberdeen	46	Hearts*	45
1	1956–57	68	Rangers	55	Hearts	53	Kilmarnock	42
1	1957–58	68	Hearts	62	Rangers	49	Celtic	46
1	1958–59	68	Rangers	50	Hearts	48	Motherwell	44
1	1959–60	68	Hearts	54	Kilmarnock	50	Rangers*	42
1	1960–61	68	Rangers	51	Kilmarnock	50	Third Lanark	42
1	1961–62	68	Dundee	54	Rangers	51	Celtic	46
1	1962–63	68	Rangers	57	Kilmarnock	48	Partick Thistle	46
1	1963–64	68	Rangers	55	Kilmarnock	49	Celtic*	47
1	1964–65	68	Kilmarnock*	50	Hearts	50	Dunfermline Ath	49
1	1965–66	68	Celtic	57	Rangers	55	Kilmarnock	45

1	1966–67	68	Celtic	58	Rangers	55	Clyde	46
1	1967–68	68	Celtic	63	Rangers	61	Hibernian	45
1	1968–69	68	Celtic	54	Rangers	49	Dunfermline Ath	45
1	1969–70	68	Celtic	57	Rangers	45	Hibernian	44
1	1970–71	68	Celtic	56	Aberdeen	54	St Johnstone	44
1	1971–72	68	Celtic	60	Aberdeen	50	Rangers	44
1	1972–73	68	Celtic	57	Rangers	56	Hibernian	45
1	1973–74	68	Celtic	53	Hibernian	49	Rangers	48
1	1974–75	68	Rangers	56	Hibernian	49	Celtic*	45

PREMIER DIVISION (1975–76 to 1997–98)

1	1975–76	72	Rangers	54	Celtic	48	Hibernian	43
1	1976–77	72	Celtic	55	Rangers	46	Aberdeen	43
1	1977–78	72	Rangers	55	Aberdeen	53	Dundee U	40
1	1978–79	72	Celtic	48	Rangers	45	Dundee U	44
1	1979–80	72	Aberdeen	48	Celtic	47	St Mirren	42
1	1980–81	72	Celtic	56	Aberdeen	49	Rangers*	44
1	1981–82	72	Celtic	55	Aberdeen	53	Rangers	43
1	1982–83	72	Dundee U	56	Celtic*	55	Aberdeen	55
1	1983–84	72	Aberdeen	57	Celtic	50	Dundee U	47
1	1984–85	72	Aberdeen	59	Celtic	52	Dundee U	47
1	1985–86	72	Celtic*	50	Hearts	50	Dundee U	47
1	1986–87	88	Rangers	69	Celtic	63	Dundee U	60
1	1987–88	88	Celtic	72	Hearts	62	Rangers	60
1	1988–89	72	Rangers	56	Aberdeen	50	Celtic	46
1	1989–90	72	Rangers	51	Aberdeen*	44	Hearts	44
1	1990–91	72	Rangers	55	Aberdeen	53	Celtic*	41
1	1991–92	88	Rangers	72	Hearts	63	Celtic	62
1	1992–93	88	Rangers	73	Aberdeen	64	Celtic	60
1	1993–94	88	Rangers	58	Aberdeen	55	Motherwell	54
1	1994–95	108	Rangers	69	Motherwell	54	Hibernian	53
1	1995–96	108	Rangers	87	Celtic	83	Aberdeen*	55
1	1996–97	108	Rangers	80	Celtic	75	Dundee U	60
1	1997–98	108	Celtic	74	Rangers	72	Hearts	67

PREMIER LEAGUE (1998–99 to 2012–13)

1	1998–99	108	Rangers	77	Celtic	71	St Johnstone	57
1	1999–2000	108	Rangers	90	Celtic	69	Hearts	54
1	2000–01	114	Celtic	97	Rangers	82	Hibernian	66
1	2001–02	114	Celtic	103	Rangers	85	Livingston	58
1	2002–03	114	Rangers*	97	Celtic	97	Hearts	63
1	2003–04	114	Celtic	98	Rangers	81	Hearts	68
1	2004–05	114	Rangers	93	Celtic	92	Hibernian*	61
1	2005–06	114	Celtic	91	Hearts	74	Rangers	73
1	2006–07	114	Celtic	84	Rangers	72	Aberdeen	65
1	2007–08	114	Celtic	89	Rangers	86	Motherwell	60
1	2008–09	114	Rangers	86	Celtic	82	Hearts	59
1	2009–10	114	Rangers	87	Celtic	81	Dundee U	63
1	2010–11	114	Rangers	93	Celtic	92	Hearts	63
1	2011–12	114	Celtic	93	Rangers	73	Motherwell	62

Rangers deducted 10 points for entering administration.

| 1 | 2012–13 | 114 | Celtic | 79 | Motherwell | 63 | St Johnstone | 56 |

SPFL SCOTTISH PREMIERSHIP (2013–14 to 2017–18)

1	2013–14	114	Celtic	99	Motherwell	70	Aberdeen	68
1	2014–15	114	Celtic	92	Aberdeen	75	Inverness CT	65
1	2015–16	114	Celtic	86	Aberdeen	71	Hearts	65
1	2016–17	114	Celtic	106	Aberdeen	76	Rangers	67
1	2017–18	114	Celtic	82	Aberdeen	73	Rangers	70

DIVISION 2 (1893–93 to 1974–75) – TIER 2

Tier	Season	Max Pts	First	Pts	Second	Pts	Third	Pts
2	1893–94	36	Hibernian	29	Cowlairs	27	Clyde	24
2	1894–95	36	Hibernian	30	Motherwell	22	Port Glasgow Ath	20
2	1895–96	36	Abercorn	27	Leith Ath	23	Renton / Kilmarnock=	21
2	1896–97	36	Partick Thistle	31	Leith Ath	27	Airdrieonians / Kilmarnock=	21
2	1897–98	36	Kilmarnock	29	Port Glasgow Ath	25	Morton	22
2	1898–99	36	Kilmarnock	32	Leith Ath	27	Port Glasgow Ath	25
2	1899–1900	36	Partick Thistle	29	Morton	28	Port Glasgow Ath	20
2	1900–01	36	St Bernard's	26	Airdrieonians	23	Abercorn	21
2	1901–02	44	Port Glasgow Ath	32	Partick Thistle	30	Motherwell	26
2	1902–03	44	Airdrieonians	35	Motherwell	28	Ayr U / Leith Ath=	27
2	1903–04	44	Hamilton A	37	Clyde	29	Ayr U	28
2	1904–05	44	Clyde	32	Falkirk	28	Hamilton A	27
2	1905–06	44	Leith Ath	34	Clyde	31	Albion R	27
2	1906–07	44	St Bernard's	32	Vale of Leven=	27	Arthurlie=	27
2	1907–08	44	Raith R	30	Dumbarton=	27	Ayr U=	27

Dumbarton deducted 2 points for registration irregularities.

2	1908–09	44	Abercorn	31	Raith R=	28	Vale of Leven=	28
2	1909–10	44	Leith Ath=	33	Raith R=	33	St Bernard's	27

Leith Ath and Raith R held title jointly, no play-off game played.

2	1910–11	44	Dumbarton	31	Ayr U	27	Albion R	25
2	1911–12	44	Ayr U	35	Abercorn	30	Dumbarton	27
2	1912–13	52	Ayr U	34	Dunfermline Ath	33	East Stirling	32
2	1913–14	44	Cowdenbeath	31	Albion R	27	Dunfermline Ath / Dundee U=	26
2	1914–15	52	Cowdenbeath=	37	St Bernard's=	37	Leith Ath=	37

Cowdenbeath won title after a round robin tournament between the three tied clubs.

2	1921–22	76	Alloa Ath	60	Cowdenbeath	47	Armadale	45
2	1922–23	76	Queen's Park	57	Clydebank	50	St Johnstone	48

Clydebank and St Johnstone both deducted 2 points for fielding an ineligible player.

2	1923–24	76	St Johnstone	56	Cowdenbeath	55	Bathgate	44
2	1924–25	76	Dundee U	50	Clydebank	48	Clyde	47
2	1925–26	76	Dunfermline Ath	59	Clyde	53	Ayr U	52
2	1926–27	76	Bo'ness	56	Raith R	49	Clydebank	45
2	1927–28	76	Ayr U	54	Third Lanark	45	King's Park	44
2	1928–29	72	Dundee U	51	Morton	50	Arbroath	47
2	1929–30	76	Leith Ath*	57	East Fife	57	Albion R	54
2	1930–31	76	Third Lanark	61	Dundee U	50	Dunfermline Ath	47
2	1931–32	76	East Stirling*	55	St Johnstone	55	Raith R*	46
2	1932–33	68	Hibernian	54	Queen of the South	49	Dunfermline Ath	47

Armadale and Bo'ness were expelled for failing to meet match guarantees. Their records were expunged.

2	1933–34	68	Albion R	45	Dunfermline Ath*	44	Arbroath	44
2	1934–35	68	Third Lanark	52	Arbroath	50	St Bernard's	47
2	1935–36	68	Falkirk	59	St Mirren	52	Morton	48
2	1936–37	68	Ayr U	54	Morton	51	St Bernard's	48
2	1937–38	68	Raith R	59	Albion R	48	Airdrieonians	47
2	1938–39	68	Cowdenbeath	60	Alloa Ath*	48	East Fife	48
2	1946–47	52	Dundee	45	Airdrieonians	42	East Fife	31
2	1947–48	60	East Fife	53	Albion R	42	Hamilton A	40
2	1948–49	60	Raith R*	42	Stirling Alb	42	Airdrieonians*	41
2	1949–50	60	Morton	47	Airdrieonians	44	Dunfermline Ath*	36
2	1950–51	60	Queen of the South*	45	Stirling Alb	45	Ayr U*	36
2	1951–52	60	Clyde	44	Falkirk	43	Ayr U	39
2	1952–53	60	Stirling Alb	44	Hamilton A	43	Queen's Park	37
2	1953–54	60	Motherwell	45	Kilmarnock	42	Third Lanark*	36
2	1954–55	60	Airdrieonians	46	Dunfermline Ath	42	Hamilton A	39
2	1955–56	72	Queen's Park	54	Ayr U	51	St Johnstone	49
2	1956–57	72	Clyde	64	Third Lanark	51	Cowdenbeath	45
2	1957–58	72	Stirling Alb	55	Dunfermline Ath	53	Arbroath	47
2	1958–59	72	Ayr U	60	Arbroath	51	Stenhousemuir	46
2	1959–60	72	St Johnstone	53	Dundee U	50	Queen of the South	49
2	1960–61	72	Stirling Alb	55	Falkirk	54	Stenhousemuir	50
2	1961–62	72	Clyde	54	Queen of the South	53	Morton	44
2	1962–63	72	St Johnstone	55	East Stirling	49	Morton	48
2	1963–64	72	Morton	67	Clyde	53	Arbroath	46
2	1964–65	72	Stirling Alb	59	Hamilton A	50	Queen of the South	45
2	1965–66	72	Ayr U	53	Airdrieonians	50	Queen of the South	47
2	1966–67	76	Morton	69	Raith R	58	Arbroath	57
2	1967–68	72	St Mirren	62	Arbroath	53	East Fife	49
2	1968–69	72	Motherwell	64	Ayr U	53	East Fife*	48
2	1969–70	72	Falkirk	56	Cowdenbeath	55	Queen of the South	50
2	1970–71	72	Partick Thistle	56	East Fife	51	Arbroath	46
2	1971–72	72	Dumbarton*	52	Arbroath	52	Stirling Alb*	50
2	1972–73	72	Clyde	56	Dumfermline Ath	52	Raith R*	47
2	1973–74	72	Airdrieonians	60	Kilmarnock	58	Hamilton A	55
2	1974–75	76	Falkirk	54	Queen of the South*	53	Montrose	53

Elected to First Division: 1894 Clyde; 1895 Hibernian; 1896 Abercorn; 1897 Partick Thistle; 1899 Kilmarnock; 1900 Morton and Partick Thistle; 1902 Port Glasgow; 1903 Airdrieonians and Motherwell; 1905 Falkirk and Aberdeen; 1906 Clyde and Hamilton A; 1910 Raith R; 1913 Ayr U and Dumbarton.

FIRST DIVISION (1975–76 to 2012–13)

2	1975–76	52	Partick Thistle	41	Kilmarnock	35	Montrose	30
2	1976–77	78	St Mirren	62	Clydebank	58	Dundee	51
2	1977–78	78	Morton*	58	Hearts	58	Dundee	57
2	1978–79	78	Dundee	55	Kilmarnock*	54	Clydebank	54
2	1979–80	78	Hearts	53	Airdrieonians	51	Ayr U*	44
2	1980–81	78	Hibernian	57	Dundee	52	St Johnstone	51
2	1981–82	78	Motherwell	61	Kilmarnock	51	Hearts	50
2	1982–83	78	St Johnstone	55	Hearts	54	Clydebank	50
2	1983–84	78	Morton	54	Dumbarton	51	Partick Thistle	46
2	1984–85	78	Motherwell	50	Clydebank	48	Falkirk	45
2	1985–86	78	Hamilton A	56	Falkirk	45	Kilmarnock*	44
2	1986–87	88	Morton	57	Dunfermline Ath	56	Dumbarton	53
2	1987–88	88	Hamilton A	56	Meadowbank Thistle	52	Clydebank	49
2	1988–89	78	Dunfermline Ath	54	Falkirk	52	Clydebank	48
2	1989–90	78	St Johnstone	58	Airdrieonians	54	Clydebank	44
2	1990–91	78	Falkirk	54	Airdrieonians	53	Dundee	52
2	1991–92	88	Dundee	58	Partick Thistle*	57	Hamilton A	57
2	1992–93	88	Raith R	65	Kilmarnock	54	Dunfermline Ath	52

Tier	Season	Max Pts	First	Pts	Second	Pts	Third	Pts
2	1993–94	88	Falkirk	66	Dunfermline Ath	65	Airdrieonians	54
2	1994–95	108	Raith R	69	Dunfermline Ath*	68	Dundee	68
2	1995–96	108	Dunfermline Ath	71	Dundee U*	67	Greenock Morton	67
2	1996–97	108	St Johnstone	80	Airdrieonians	60	Dundee*	58
2	1997–98	108	Dundee	70	Falkirk	65	Raith R*	60
2	1998–99	108	Hibernian	89	Falkirk	66	Ayr U	62
2	1999–2000	108	St Mirren	76	Dunfermline Ath	71	Falkirk	68
2	2000–01	108	Livingston	76	Ayr U	69	Falkirk	56
2	2001–02	108	Partick Thistle	66	Airdrieonians	56	Ayr U*	52
2	2002–03	108	Falkirk	81	Clyde	72	St Johnstone	67
2	2003–04	108	Inverness CT	70	Clyde	69	St Johnstone	57
2	2004–05	108	Falkirk	75	St Mirren*	60	Clyde	60
2	2005–06	108	St Mirren	76	St Johnstone	66	Hamilton A	59
2	2006–07	108	Gretna	66	St Johnstone	65	Dundee*	53
2	2007–08	108	Hamilton A	76	Dundee	69	St Johnstone	58
2	2008–09	108	St Johnstone	65	Partick Thistle	55	Dunfermline Ath	51
2	2009–10	108	Inverness CT	73	Dundee	61	Dunfermline Ath	58
2	2010–11	108	Dunfermline Ath	70	Raith R	60	Falkirk	58
2	2011–12	108	Ross Co	79	Dundee	55	Falkirk	52
2	2012–13	108	Partick Thistle	78	Greenock Morton	67	Falkirk	53

SPFL SCOTTISH CHAMPIONSHIP (2013–14 to 2017–18)

Tier	Season	Max Pts	First	Pts	Second	Pts	Third	Pts
2	2013–14	108	Dundee	69	Hamilton A	67	Falkirk§	66
2	2014–15	108	Hearts	91	Hibernian§	70	Rangers§	67
2	2015–16	108	Rangers	81	Falkirk*§	70	Hibernian§	70
2	2016–17	108	Hibernian	71	Falkirk§	60	Dundee U§	57
2	2017–18	108	St Mirren	74	Livingston	62	Dundee U§	61

SECOND DIVISION (1975–76 to 2012–13) – TIER 3

Tier	Season	Max Pts	First	Pts	Second	Pts	Third	Pts
3	1975–76	52	Clydebank*	40	Raith R	40	Alloa Ath	35
3	1976–77	78	Stirling Alb	55	Alloa Ath	51	Dunfermline Ath	50
3	1977–78	78	Clyde*	53	Raith R	53	Dunfermline Ath*	48
3	1978–79	78	Berwick R	54	Dunfermline Ath	52	Falkirk	50
3	1979–80	78	Falkirk	50	East Stirling	49	Forfar Ath	46
3	1980–81	78	Queen's Park	50	Queen of the South	46	Cowdenbeath	45
3	1981–82	78	Clyde	59	Alloa Ath*	50	Arbroath	50
3	1982–83	78	Brechin C	55	Meadowbank Thistle	54	Arbroath	49
3	1983–84	78	Forfar Ath	63	East Fife	47	Berwick R	43
3	1984–85	78	Montrose	53	Alloa Ath	50	Dunfermline Ath	49
3	1985–86	78	Dunfermline Ath	57	Queen of the South	55	Meadowbank Thistle	49
3	1986–87	78	Meadowbank Thistle	55	Raith R*	52	Stirling Alb*	52
3	1987–88	78	Ayr U	61	St Johnstone	59	Queen's Park	51
3	1988–89	78	Albion R	50	Alloa Ath	45	Brechin C	43
3	1989–90	78	Brechin C	49	Kilmarnock	48	Stirling Alb	47
3	1990–91	78	Stirling Alb	54	Montrose	46	Cowdenbeath	45
3	1991–92	78	Dumbarton	52	Cowdenbeath	51	Alloa Ath	50
3	1992–93	78	Clyde	54	Brechin C*	53	Stranraer	53
3	1993–94	78	Stranraer	56	Berwick R	48	Stenhousemuir*	47
3	1994–95	108	Greenock Morton	64	Dumbarton	60	Stirling Alb	58
3	1995–96	108	Stirling Alb	81	East Fife	67	Berwick R	60
3	1996–97	108	Ayr U	77	Hamilton A	74	Livingston	64
3	1997–98	108	Stranraer	61	Clydebank	60	Livingston	59
3	1998–99	108	Livingston	77	Inverness CT	72	Clyde	53
3	1999–2000	108	Clyde	65	Alloa Ath	64	Ross Co	62
3	2000–01	108	Partick Thistle	75	Arbroath	58	Berwick R*	54
3	2001–02	108	Queen of the South	67	Alloa Ath	59	Forfar Ath	53
3	2002–03	108	Raith R	59	Brechin C	55	Airdrie U	54
3	2003–04	108	Airdrie U	70	Hamilton A	62	Dumbarton	60
3	2004–05	108	Brechin C	72	Stranraer	63	Greenock Morton	62
3	2005–06	108	Gretna	88	Greenock Morton§	70	Peterhead*§	57
3	2006–07	108	Greenock Morton	77	Stirling Alb	69	Raith R§	62
3	2007–08	108	Ross Co	73	Airdrie U	66	Raith R§	60
3	2008–09	108	Raith R	76	Ayr U	74	Brechin C§	62
3	2009–10	108	Stirling Alb*	65	Alloa Ath§	65	Cowdenbeath	59
3	2010–11	108	Livingston	82	Ayr U*	59	Forfar Ath§	59
3	2011–12	108	Cowdenbeath	71	Arbroath§	63	Dumbarton	58
3	2012–13	108	Queen of the South	92	Alloa Ath	67	Brechin C	61

SPFL SCOTTISH LEAGUE ONE (2013–14 to 2017–18)

Tier	Season	Max Pts	First	Pts	Second	Pts	Third	Pts
3	2013–14	108	Rangers	102	Dunfermline Ath§	63	Stranraer§	51
3	2014–15	108	Greenock Morton	69	Stranraer§	67	Forfar Ath	66
3	2015–16	108	Dunfermline Ath	79	Ayr U	61	Peterhead§	59
3	2016–17	108	Livingston	81	Alloa Ath§	62	Airdrieonians§	52
3	2017–18	108	Ayr U	76	Raith R§	75	Alloa Ath	60

THIRD DIVISION (1994–95 to 2012–13) – TIER 4

Tier	Season	Max Pts	First	Pts	Second	Pts	Third	Pts
4	1994–95	108	Forfar Ath	80	Montrose	67	Ross Co	60
4	1995–96	108	Livingston	72	Brechin C	63	Inverness CT	57

4	1996–97	108	Inverness CT	76	Forfar Ath*	67	Ross Co	67
4	1997–98	108	Alloa Ath	76	Arbroath	68	Ross Co	67
4	1998–99	108	Ross Co	77	Stenhousemuir	64	Brechin C	59
4	1999–2000	108	Queen's Park	69	Berwick R	66	Forfar Ath	61
4	2000–01	108	Hamilton A*	76	Cowdenbeath	76	Brechin C	72
4	2001–02	108	Brechin C	73	Dumbarton	61	Albion R	59
4	2002–03	108	Greenock Morton	72	East Fife	71	Albion R	70
4	2003–04	108	Stranraer	79	Stirling Alb	77	Gretna	68
4	2004–05	108	Gretna	98	Peterhead	78	Cowdenbeath	51
4	2005–06	108	Cowdenbeath*	76	Berwick R§	76	Stenhousemuir§	73
4	2006–07	108	Berwick R	75	Arbroath§	70	Queen's Park	68
4	2007–08	108	East Fife	88	Stranraer	65	Montrose§	59
4	2008–09	108	Dumbarton	67	Cowdenbeath	63	East Stirling§	61
4	2009–10	108	Livingston	78	Forfar Ath	63	East Stirling§	61
4	2010–11	108	Arbroath	66	Albion R	61	Queen's Park*§	59
4	2011–12	108	Alloa Ath	77	Queen's Park§	63	Stranraer	58
4	2012–13	108	Rangers	83	Peterhead§	59	Queen's Park§	56

SPFL SCOTTISH LEAGUE TWO (2013–14 to 2017–18)

4	2013–14	108	Peterhead	76	Annan Ath§	63	Stirling Alb	57
4	2014–15	108	Albion R	71	Queen's Park§	61	Arbroath§	56
4	2015–16	108	East Fife	62	Elgin C§	59	Clyde§	56
4	2016–17	108	Abroath	66	Forfar Ath	64	Annan Ath§	58
4	2017–18	108	Montrose	77	Peterhead§	76	Stirling Alb§	55

RELEGATED CLUBS

RELEGATED FROM DIVISION I (1921–22 to 1973–74)

1921–22 *Dumbarton, Queen's Park, Clydebank
1922–23 Albion R, Alloa Ath
1923–24 Clyde, Clydebank
1924–25 Ayr U, Third Lanark
1925–26 Raith R, Clydebank
1926–27 Morton, Dundee U
1927–28 Bo'ness, Dunfermline Ath
1928–29 Third Lanark, Raith R
1929–30 Dundee U, St Johnstone
1930–31 Hibernian, East Fife
1931–32 Dundee U, Leith Ath
1932–33 Morton, East Stirling
1933–34 Third Lanark, Cowdenbeath
1934–35 St Mirren, Falkirk
1935–36 Airdrieonians, Ayr U
1936–37 Dunfermline Ath, Albion R
1937–38 Dundee, Morton
1938–39 Queen's Park, Raith R
1946–47 Kilmarnock, Hamilton A
1947–48 Airdrieonians, Queen's Park
1948–49 Morton, Albion R
1949–50 Queen of the South, Stirling Alb
1950–51 Clyde, Falkirk

1951–52 Morton, Stirling Alb
1952–53 Motherwell, Third Lanark
1953–54 Airdrieonians, Hamilton A
1954–55 *No clubs relegated as league extended to 18 teams*
1955–56 Clyde, Stirling Alb
1956–57 Dunfermline Ath, Ayr U
1957–58 East Fife, Queen's Park
1958–59 Falkirk, Queen of the South
1959–60 Stirling Alb, Arbroath
1960–61 Clyde, Ayr U
1961–62 St Johnstone, Stirling Alb
1962–63 Clyde, Raith R
1963–64 Queen of the South, East Stirling
1964–65 Airdrieonians, Third Lanark
1965–66 Morton, Hamilton A
1966–67 St Mirren, Ayr U
1967–68 Motherwell, Stirling Alb
1968–69 Falkirk, Arbroath
1969–70 Raith R, Partick Thistle
1970–71 St Mirren, Cowdenbeath
1971–72 Clyde, Dunfermline Ath
1972–73 Kilmarnock, Airdrieonians
1973–74 East Fife, Falkirk

Season 1921–22 – only 1 club promoted, 3 clubs relegated.

RELEGATED FROM PREMIER DIVISION (1974–75 to 1997–98)

1974–75 *No relegation due to League reorganisation*
1975–76 Dundee, St Johnstone
1976–77 Hearts, Kilmarnock
1977–78 Ayr U, Clydebank
1978–79 Hearts, Motherwell
1979–80 Dundee, Hibernian
1980–81 Kilmarnock, Hearts
1981–82 Partick Thistle, Airdrieonians
1982–83 Morton, Kilmarnock
1983–84 St Johnstone, Motherwell
1984–85 Dumbarton, Morton
1985–86 *No relegation due to League reorganisation*

1986–87 Clydebank, Hamilton A
1987–88 Falkirk, Dunfermline Ath, Morton
1988–89 Hamilton A
1989–90 Dundee
1990–91 *No clubs relegated*
1991–92 St Mirren, Dunfermline Ath
1992–93 Falkirk, Airdrieonians
1993–94 St Johnstone, Raith R, Dundee
1994–95 Dundee U
1995–96 Partick Thistle, Falkirk
1996–97 Raith R
1997–98 Hibernian

RELEGATED FROM PREMIER LEAGUE (1998–99 to 2012–13)

1998–99 Dunfermline Ath
1999–2000 *No relegation due to League reorganisation*
2000–01 St Mirren
2001–02 St Johnstone
2002–03 *No clubs relegated*
2003–04 Partick Thistle
2005–06 Livingston
2006–07 Dunfermline Ath

2007–08 Gretna
2008–09 Inverness CT
2009–10 Falkirk
2010–11 Hamilton A
2011–12 Dunfermline Ath, Rangers (demoted to Third Division)
2012–13 Dundee

RELEGATED FROM SPFL SCOTTISH PREMIERSHIP (2013–14 to 2017–18)

2013–14 Hibernian, Hearts
2014–15 St Mirren
2015–16 Dundee U

2016–17 Inverness CT
2017–18 Ross Co, Partick Thistle

RELEGATED FROM FIRST DIVISION (1975–76 to 2012–13)

1975–76	Dunfermline Ath, Clyde	1994–95	Ayr U, Stranraer
1976–77	Raith R, Falkirk	1995–96	Hamilton A, Dumbarton
1977–78	Alloa Ath, East Fife	1996–97	Clydebank, East Fife
1978–79	Montrose, Queen of the South	1997–98	Partick Thistle, Stirling Alb
1979–80	Arbroath, Clyde	1998–99	Hamilton A, Stranraer
1980–81	Stirling Alb, Berwick R	1999–2000	Clydebank
1981–82	East Stirling, Queen of the South	2000–01	Greenock Morton, Alloa Ath
1982–83	Dunfermline Ath, Queen's Park	2001–02	Raith R
1983–84	Raith R, Alloa Ath	2002–03	Alloa Ath, Arbroath
1984–85	Meadowbank Thistle, St Johnstone	2003–04	Ayr U, Brechin C
1985–86	Ayr U, Alloa Ath	2004–05	Partick Thistle, Raith R
1986–87	Brechin C, Montrose	2005–06	Stranraer, Brechin C
1987–88	East Fife, Dumbarton	2006–07	Airdrie U, Ross Co
1988–89	Kilmarnock, Queen of the South	2007–08	Stirling Alb
1989–90	Albion R, Alloa Ath	2008–09	Livingstone *(for breaching rules)*, Clyde
1990–91	Clyde, Brechin C	2009–10	Airdrie U, Ayr U
1991–92	Montrose, Forfar Ath	2010–11	Cowdenbeath, Stirling Alb
1992–93	Meadowbank Thistle, Cowdenbeath	2011–12	Ayr U, Queen of the South
1993–94	Dumbarton, Stirling Alb, Clyde, Morton, Brechin C	2012–13	Dunfermline Ath, Airdrie U

RELEGATED FROM SPFL SCOTTISH CHAMPIONSHIP (2013–14 to 2017–18)

2013–14	Greenock Morton	2016–17	Raith R, Ayr U
2014–15	Cowdenbeath	2017–18	Brechin C, Dumbarton
2015–16	Livingston, Alloa Ath		

RELEGATED FROM SECOND DIVISION (1993–94 to 2012–13)

1993–94	Alloa Ath, Forfar Ath, East Stirlingshire, Montrose, Queen's Park, Arbroath, Albion R, Cowdenbeath		
1994–95	Meadowbank Thistle, Brechin C	2004–05	Arbroath, Berwick R
1995–96	Forfar Ath, Montrose	2005–06	Dumbarton
1996–97	Dumbarton, Berwick R	2006–07	Stranraer, Forfar Ath
1997–98	Stenhousemuir, Brechin C	2007–08	Cowdenbeath, Berwick R
1998–99	East Fife, Forfar Ath	2008–09	Queen's Park, Stranraer
1999–2000	Hamilton A *(after being deducted 15 points)*	2009–10	Arbroath, Clyde
2000–01	Queen's Park, Stirling Alb	2010–11	Alloa Ath, Peterhead
2001–02	Greenock Morton	2011–12	Stirling Alb
2002–03	Stranraer, Cowdenbeath	2012–13	Albion R
2003–04	East Fife, Stenhousemuir		

RELEGATED FROM SPFL SCOTTISH LEAGUE ONE (2013–14 to 2017–18)

2013–14	East Fife, Arbroath	2016–17	Peterhead, Stenhousemuir
2014–15	Stirling Alb	2017–18	Albion R, Queen's Park
2015–16	Cowdenbeath, Forfar Ath		

RELEGATED FROM SPFL SCOTTISH LEAGUE TWO (2015–16 to 2017–18)

2015–16	East Stirlingshire	2017–18	None
2016–17	None		

SCOTTISH LEAGUE CHAMPIONSHIP WINS

Rangers 54, Celtic 49, Aberdeen 4, Hearts 4, Hibernian 4, Dumbarton 2, Dundee 1, Dundee U 1, Kilmarnock 1, Motherwell 1, Third Lanark 1.

The totals for Rangers and Dumbarton each include the shared championship of 1890–91.

Since the formation of the Scottish Football League in 1890, there have been periodic reorganisations of the leagues to allow for expansion, improve competition and commercial aspects of the game. The table below lists the league names by tier and chronology. This table can be used to assist when studying the records.

Tier	Division		Tier	Division	
1	Scottish League Division I	1890–1939	3	Scottish League Division III	1923–1926
	Scottish League Division A	1946–1956		Scottish League Division C	1946–1949
	Scottish League Division I	1956–1975		Second Division	1975–2013
	Premier Division	1975–1998		SPFL League One	2013–
	Scottish Premier League	1998–2013			
	SPFL Premiership	2013–	4	Third Division	1994–2013
				SPFL League Two	2013–
2	Scottish League Division II	1893–1939			
	Scottish League Division B	1946–1956			
	Scottish League Division II	1956–1975			
	First Division	1975–2013			
	SPFL Championship	2013–			

In 2013–14 the SPFL introduced play-offs to determine a second promotion/relegation place for the Premiership, Championship and League One.

The team finishing second bottom of the Premiership plays two legs against the team from the Championship that won the eliminator games played between the teams finishing second, third and fourth.

For both the Championship and League One, the team finishing second bottom joins the teams from second, third and fourth places of the lower league in a play-off series of two-legged semi-finals and finals.

In 2014–15 a play-off was introduced for promotion/relegation from League Two. The team finishing bottom of League Two plays two legs against the victors of the eliminator games between the winners of the Highland and Lowland leagues.

SCOTTISH LEAGUE PLAY-OFFS 2017–18

■ *Denotes player sent off.*

PREMIERSHIP QUARTER-FINAL FIRST LEG
Tuesday, 1 May 2018
Dunfermline Ath (0) 0
Dundee U (0) 0   6474
Dunfermline Ath: (442) Robinson; Williamson
(Wedderburn 88), Morris, Ashcroft■, Martin;
Higginbotham (Talbot 63), Vincent, Craigen, Aird; Ryan
(McManus 25), Clark.
Dundee U: (442) Mehmet; Ralston, Murdoch, Mohsni,
Robson; Fraser, Flood, Gillespie (Stanton 68), King;
McDonald, Mikkelsen (Lyng 75).
Referee: Bobby Madden.

PREMIERSHIP QUARTER-FINAL SECOND LEG
Friday, 4 May 2018
Dundee U (0) 2 *(McDonald 57, Stanton 70)*
Dunfermline Ath (1) 1 *(McManus 14)*   7994
Dundee U: (4231) Mehmet (Lewis 64); Ralston,
Murdoch, Mohsni, Robson; Flood, Stanton; King
(Durnan 90), Fraser, McMullan (Mikkelsen 46);
McDonald.
Dunfermline Ath: (442) Robinson; Williamson, Morris,
Ashcroft, Martin; Higginbotham (Mvoto 74), Vincent,
Craigen (Cardle 84), Aird; McManus, Clark.
Dundee U won 2-1 on aggregate.
Referee: William Collum.

PREMIERSHIP SEMI-FINAL FIRST LEG
Monday, 7 May 2018
Dundee U (2) 2 *(Mikkelsen 3, Ralston 28)*
Livingston (1) 3 *(De Vita 2, Mullin 77, Pitman 80)*   5610
Dundee U: (451) Lewis; Ralston, Murdoch, Mohsni
(Durnan 90), Robson; Fraser, Flood■, McDonald,
Stanton, King (Lyng 76); Mikkelsen.
Livingston: (3421) Alexander; Lithgow, Halkett,
Gallagher; Jacobs, Pitman, Byrne, Longridge (Thompson
90); De Vita (Cadden 70), Robinson (Jacobs 79); Miller.
Referee: Nick Walsh.

PREMIERSHIP SEMI-FINAL SECOND LEG
Friday, 11 May 2018
Livingston (1) 1 *(Lithgow 6)*
Dundee U (1) 1 *(Fraser 21)*   4508
Livingston: (352) Alexander; Gallagher, Halkett,
Lithgow; Mullin (Cadden 68), Pitman, Byrne, Jacobs,
Longridge; Miller (Robinson 87), De Vita (Thompson
19).
Dundee U: (442) Lewis; Ralston, Durnan, Mohsni,
Murdoch; King, Gillespie (McMullan 83), Stanton,
Fraser; McDonald, Mikkelsen (Smith M 76).
Livingston won 4-3 on aggregate.
Referee: Don Robertson.

PREMIERSHIP FINAL FIRST LEG
Thursday, 17 May 2018
Livingston (1) 2 *(Jacobs 13, Pitman 74)*
Partick Thistle (1) 1 *(Doolan 10)*   5469
Livingston: (352) Alexander; Gallagher, Halkett,
Lithgow; Jacobs, Thompson (Mullin 60), Byrne, Pitman,
Longridge; Miller (Buchanan 87), Robinson (Cadden 78).
Partick Thistle: (4231) Cerny; McGinn, Devine, Cargill,
Booth; Woods, Barton; Lawless (Spittal 67), Doolan,
Edwards; Sammon (Storey 85).
Referee: Craig Thomson.

PREMIERSHIP FINAL SECOND LEG
Sunday, 20 May 2018
Partick Thistle (0) 0
Livingston (0) 1 *(Jacobs 46)*   7122
Partick Thistle: (4231) Cerny; McGinn, Barton, Cargill,
Elliot; Woods (Edwards 70), McCarthy (Sammon 55);
Spittal, Erskine (Booth 75), Lawless; Doolan.

Livingston: (352) Alexander; Gallagher, Halkett,
Lithgow; Jacobs, Pitman, Byrne, Thompson (Cadden 59),
Longridge; Miller (McMillan 68), Robinson (Buchanan
79).
Livingston won 3-1 on aggregate.
Referee: John Beaton.

CHAMPIONSHIP SEMI-FINALS FIRST LEG
Wednesday, 2 May 2018
Alloa Ath (1) 2 *(Stewart 23, Flannigan 58)*
Raith R (0) 0   1133
Alloa Ath: (4231) Parry; Taggart, Graham, McCart,
Crane; Hetherington (Robertson 38), Fleming (Smith
67); Cawley (Renton 83), Kirkpatrick, Flannigan;
Stewart.
Raith R: (442) Smith; Thomson, Davidson■, Murray,
McHattie; Matthews (Zanatta 60), Robertson, Hendry,
Barr (Furtado 72); Vaughan, Buchanan (Spence 54).
Referee: Don Robertson.

Arbroath (0) 1 *(Linn 64)*
Dumbarton (0) 2 *(Gallagher C 55, Barr 90)*   892
Arbroath: (3142) Hutton; Little, O'Brien, Hamilton;
Martin; Linn, Swankie, Yule, Denholm (Gold 71);
Wallace (Hester 80), McKenna (McIntosh 79).
Dumbarton: (4231) Gallacher; Smith, Dowie, Barr, Dick;
Carswell, Hutton; Stirling, Walsh (Burt 80), Gallagher C
(Russell 72); Handling.
Referee: Nick Walsh.

CHAMPIONSHIP SEMI-FINALS SECOND LEG
Saturday, 5 May 2018
Dumbarton (1) 1 *(Hill 9)*
Arbroath (1) 1 *(Swankie 27)*   872
Dumbarton: (4231) Gallacher; Smith, Dowie, Hill, Dick;
Carswell, Hutton (Gallagher G 46); Stirling, Handling,
Walsh (Burt 75); Russell (Nisbet 57).
Arbroath: (4411) Hutton; Little, O'Brien, Martin,
Hamilton; McKenna (McIntosh 74), Yule (McCord 80),
Whatley, Linn (Denholm 70); Swankie; Wallace.
Dumbarton won 3-2 on aggregate.
Referee: Craig Charleston.

Raith R (0) 1 *(Murray 53)*
Alloa Ath (1) 2 *(Kirkpatrick 40, Stewart 81)*   1831
Raith R: (433) Smith; Thomson, Benedictus, Murray,
McHattie; Robertson (Barr 50), Herron (Spence 75),
Hendry; Vaughan, Court, Furtado.
Alloa Ath: (442) Parry; Taggart, Graham, McCart, Crane;
Cawley (Renton 84), Fleming (Smith 76), Robertson,
Flannigan; Stewart (Meggatt 88), Kirkpatrick.
Alloa Ath won 4-1 on aggregate.
Referee: Stephen Finnie.

CHAMPIONSHIP FINAL FIRST LEG
Wednesday, 9 May 2018
Alloa Ath (0) 0
Dumbarton (1) 1 *(Carswell 6)*   811
Alloa Ath: (433) Parry; Taggart, Graham, McCart, Crane;
Robertson, Kirkpatrick (Smith 37), Fleming (Renton 73);
Cawley, Stewart, Flannigan.
Dumbarton: (442) Gallacher; Smith, Dowie, Carswell,
Dick; Stirling (Stewart 86), Handling (Burt 53), Hutton,
Walsh (Russell 76); Nisbet, Barr.
Referee: John McKendrick.

CHAMPIONSHIP FINAL SECOND LEG
Sunday, 13 May 2018
Dumbarton (0) 0
Alloa Ath (0) 2 *(Stewart 90, Kirkpatrick 95)*   1115
Dumbarton: (4231) Gallacher; Smith, Dowie, Hill, Dick;
Carswell, Hutton; Nisbet, Walsh (Gallagher G 83),
Stirling (Burt 70); Gallagher C (Stewart 59).

Alloa Ath: (442) Parry; Taggart, Graham, McCart, Crane; Cawley, Fleming (Renton 59), Robertson (Smith 24), Flannigan; Kirkpatrick, Stewart.
aet; Alloa Ath won 2-1 on aggregate..
Referee: John Beaton.

LEAGUE ONE SEMI-FINALS FIRST LEG
Tuesday, 1 May 2018
Stenhousemuir (1) 1 *(Scott 27)*
Queen's Park (0) 1 *(Leitch 47)* 657
Stenhousemuir: (442) Smith; Meechan, Dunlop R, Dunlop M, Donaldson; Ferns, Ferry, Paton (Longworth 88), Scott (Dallas 78); McGuigan (Cook 64), McMenamin.
Queen's Park: (4231) White; Millen, Cummins■, Gibson, Burns; Fotheringham, Brady (McVey 83); Leitch, Donnelly (McLauchlan 80), Galt (Mortimer 46); Keena.
Referee: Alan Newlands.

Wednesday, 2 May 2018
Stirling Alb (0) 0
Peterhead (1) 1 *(Robertson 29)* 729
Stirling Alb: (442) Binnie; McGeachie, Hamilton, Barr, McNeil; McLaughlin (Smith D 67), Moon (Robertson 46), Caddis, Jardine; MacDonald, Kavanagh.
Peterhead: (442) Fleming; Jason Brown, Robertson, McCracken (Smith 50), Stevenson; Brown S, Gibson (Jordon Brown 80), Ferry, Leitch; McAllister (Johnston 83), McLean.
Referee: Colin Steven.

LEAGUE ONE SEMI-FINALS SECOND LEG
Saturday, 5 May 2018
Peterhead (1) 3 *(Robertson 38, McAllister 57, Jason Brown 65)*
Stirling Alb (0) 0 861
Peterhead: (4312) Fleming; Stevenson, Jason Brown, Robertson, McIlduff; Brown S, Ferry, Leitch (Smith 59); Gibson; McAllister (Belmokhtar 72), McLean (Jordon Brown 66).
Stirling Alb: (433) Binnie; McGeachie, Stanger, Barr, McNeil (McLaughlin 61); Caddis, Black (Dickson 68), Jardine; Smith D (Noble 78), MacDonald, Kavanagh.
Peterhead won 4-0 on aggregate.
Referee: Barry Cook.

Queen's Park (1) 1 *(McLauchlan 41)*
Stenhousemuir (1) 2 *(McGuigan 17, 81)* 948
Queen's Park: (4231) White; Millen (Docherty D 76), McLauchlan, Gibson, Burns; Fotheringham, McVey (Mortimer 80); Leitch, Donnelly, Gullan (Galt 62); Keena.
Stenhousemuir: (442) Smith; Meechan, Dunlop R, Dunlop M, Donaldson; Ferns (Murray 62), Ferry, Paton, Scott (Longworth 90); McGuigan (Dallas 90), Cook.
Stenhousemuir won 3-2 on aggregate.
Referee: Euan Anderson.

LEAGUE ONE FINAL FIRST LEG
Wednesday, 9 May 2018
Stenhousemuir (0) 2 *(Dunlop M 61, 76)*
Peterhead (0) 0 796
Stenhousemuir: (442) Smith; Meechan, Dunlop R, Dunlop M, Donaldson; Ferns (Murray 75), Paton, Ferry, Cook (Marsh 86); Scott (Dallas 72), McGuigan.
Peterhead: (442) Fleming; Jason Brown (Belmokhtar 43), McCracken, McIlduff, Stevenson; Gibson, Brown S, Leitch, Smith (Jordon Brown 82); McAllister (Johnston 72), McLean.
Referee: Gavin Duncan.

LEAGUE ONE FINAL SECOND LEG
Saturday, 12 May 2018
Peterhead (0) 1 *(McLean 54)*
Stenhousemuir (0) 0 880
Peterhead: (4231) Fleming; Stevenson, McLean, McCracken■, McIlduff (Johnston 62); Brown S, Ferry; Smith (Belmokhtar 80), Jordon Brown (Norris 69), Leitch■; Gibson.
Stenhousemuir: (442) Smith; Meechan, Dunlop R, Dunlop M (Marsh 73), Donaldson; Ferns (Murray 80), Paton, Ferry, Cook; Scott, McGuigan.
Stenhousemuir won 2-1 on aggregate.
Referee: Greg Aitken.

LEAGUE TWO SEMI-FINAL FIRST LEG
Saturday, 28 April 2018
Cove R (1) 4 *(Megginson 42, McManus 48 (pen), 68, Watson 52)*
Spartans (0) 0 850
Cove R: (433) McKenzie; Redford, Watson, Kelly, Milne; Scully, Ross, McManus (Stott 81); Smith (Park 55), Megginson, Masson (Robertson 89).
Spartans: (442) Carswell; Herd, Tolmie, Corbett, McFarland; Brown, Thomson (Stevenson 62), Greenhill (Allum 62), Stevens (Lamarca); Bremner, Maxwell.
Referee: David Munro.

LEAGUE TWO SEMI-FINAL SECOND LEG
Tuesday, 1 May 2018
Spartans (0) 2 *(Dishington 79, Atkinson 86)*
Cove R (0) 1 *(McManus 67)* 655
Spartans: (442) Carswell; Herd, Cennerazzo, Tolmie, Corbett; Brown, Atkinson, Stevenson (Greenhill 76), Lamarca (Stevens 76); Dishington, Bremner (Maxwell 60).
Cove R: (433) McKenzie; Redford, Watson, Kelly, Milne; Scully, Ross, McManus (Stott 70); Park (Robertson 76), Megginson, Masson.
Cove R won 5-2 on aggregate.
Referee: Steven Reid.

LEAGUE TWO FINAL FIRST LEG
Saturday, 5 May 2018
Cove R (0) 0
Cowdenbeath (0) 0 650
Cove R: (433) McKenzie; Redford, Watson, Kelly, Milne; Scully, Ross, McManus (Robertson 81); Park, Megginson, Masson (Stott 78).
Cowdenbeath: (433) McGurn; Malcolm, Gilfillan (Rumsby 67), Pyper, Swan; Buchanan, Miller, Luke (Reilly 74); Smith B, Sheerin, Cox.
Referee: John McKendrick.

LEAGUE TWO FINAL SECOND LEG
Saturday, 12 May 2018
Cowdenbeath (1) 3 *(Swan 7, 50, Smith B 70)*
Cove R (2) 2 *(Megginson 9, 22)* 1762
Cowdenbeath: (433) McGurn; Mullen, Gilfillan (Luke 90), Pyper, Swan; Malcolm, Smith B, Miller (Rumsby 89); Cox (Reilly 69), Sheerin, Buchanan.
Cove R: (433) McKenzie; Redford (Lawrie 75), Ross■, Watson■, Milne; Scully, McManus■, Kelly; Stott, Megginson, Masson (Smith 61).
Cowdenbeath won 3-2 on aggregate.
Referee: Steven Kirkland.

SCOTTISH LEAGUE CUP FINALS 1946–2018

SCOTTISH LEAGUE CUP

1946–47	Rangers v Aberdeen	4-0
1947–48	East Fife v Falkirk	0-0*
Replay	East Fife v Falkirk	4-1
1948–49	Rangers v Raith R	2-0
1949–50	East Fife v Dunfermline Ath	3-0
1950–51	Motherwell v Hibernian	3-0
1951–52	Dundee v Rangers	3-2
1952–53	Dundee v Kilmarnock	2-0
1953–54	East Fife v Partick Thistle	3-2
1954–55	Hearts v Motherwell	4-2
1955–56	Aberdeen v St Mirren	2-1
1956–57	Celtic v Partick Thistle	0-0*
Replay	Celtic v Partick Thistle	3-0
1957–58	Celtic v Rangers	7-1
1958–59	Hearts v Partick Thistle	5-1
1959–60	Hearts v Third Lanark	2-1
1960–61	Rangers v Kilmarnock	2-0
1961–62	Rangers v Hearts	1-1*
Replay	Rangers v Hearts	3-1
1962–63	Hearts v Kilmarnock	1-0
1963–64	Rangers v Morton	5-0
1964–65	Rangers v Celtic	2-1
1965–66	Celtic v Rangers	2-1
1966–67	Celtic v Rangers	1-0
1967–68	Celtic v Dundee	5-3
1968–69	Celtic v Hibernian	6-2
1969–70	Celtic v St Johnstone	1-0
1970–71	Rangers v Celtic	1-0
1971–72	Partick Thistle v Celtic	4-1
1972–73	Hibernian v Celtic	2-1
1973–74	Dundee v Celtic	1-0
1974–75	Celtic v Hibernian	6-3
1975–76	Rangers v Celtic	1-0
1976–77	Aberdeen v Celtic	2-1*
1977–78	Rangers v Celtic	2-1*
1978–79	Rangers v Aberdeen	2-1

BELL'S LEAGUE CUP

1979–80	Dundee U v Aberdeen	0-0*
Replay	Dundee U v Aberdeen	3-0
1980–81	Dundee U v Dundee	3-0

SCOTTISH LEAGUE CUP

1981–82	Rangers v Dundee U	2-1
1982–83	Celtic v Rangers	2-1
1983–84	Rangers v Celtic	3-2*

SKOL CUP

1984–85	Rangers v Dundee U	1-0
1985–86	Aberdeen v Hibernian	3-0
1986–87	Rangers v Celtic	2-1
1987–88	Rangers v Aberdeen	3-3*
	Rangers won 5-3 on penalties.	
1988–89	Rangers v Aberdeen	3-2
1989–90	Aberdeen v Rangers	2-1*
1990–91	Rangers v Celtic	2-1*
1991–92	Hibernian v Dunfermline Ath	2-0
1992–93	Rangers v Aberdeen	2-1*

SCOTTISH LEAGUE CUP

1993–94	Rangers v Hibernian	2-1

COCA-COLA CUP

1994–95	Raith R v Celtic	2-2*
	Raith R won 6-5 on penalties.	
1995–96	Aberdeen v Dundee	2-0
1996–97	Rangers v Hearts	4-3
1997–98	Celtic v Dundee U	3-0

SCOTTISH LEAGUE CUP

1998–99	Rangers v St Johnstone	2-1

CIS INSURANCE CUP

1999–2000	Celtic v Aberdeen	2-0
2000–01	Celtic v Kilmarnock	3-0
2001–02	Rangers v Ayr U	4-0
2002–03	Rangers v Celtic	2-1
2003–04	Livingston v Hibernian	2-0
2004–05	Rangers v Motherwell	5-1
2005–06	Celtic v Dunfermline Ath	3-0
2006–07	Hibernian v Kilmarnock	5-1
2007–08	Rangers v Dundee U	2-2*
	Rangers won 3-2 on penalties.	

CO-OPERATIVE INSURANCE CUP

2008–09	Celtic v Rangers	2-0*
2009–10	Rangers v St Mirren	1-0
2010–11	Rangers v Celtic	2-1*

SCOTTISH COMMUNITIES LEAGUE CUP

2011–12	Kilmarnock v Celtic	1-0
2012–13	St Mirren v Hearts	3-2
2013–14	Aberdeen v Inverness CT	0-0*
	Aberdeen won 4-2 on penalties.	

SCOTTISH LEAGUE CUP PRESENTED BY QTS

2014–15	Celtic v Dundee U	2-0
2015–16	Ross Co v Hibernian	2-1

BETFRED SCOTTISH LEAGUE CUP

2016–17	Celtic v Aberdeen	3-0
2017–18	Celtic v Motherwell	2-0

*After extra time.

SCOTTISH LEAGUE CUP WINS

Rangers 27, Celtic 17, Aberdeen 6, Hearts 4, Dundee 3, East Fife 3, Hibernian 3, Dundee U 2, Kilmarnock 1, Livingston 1, Motherwell 1, Partick Thistle 1, Raith R 1, Ross Co 1, St Mirren 1.

APPEARANCES IN FINALS

Rangers 34, Celtic 32, Aberdeen 14, Hibernian 10, Dundee U 7, Hearts 7, Dundee 6, Kilmarnock 6, Motherwell 4, Partick Thistle 4, Dunfermline Ath 3, East Fife 3, St Mirren 3, Raith R 2, St Johnstone 2, Ayr U 1, Falkirk 1, Inverness CT 1, Livingston 1, Morton 1, Ross Co 1, Third Lanark 1.

BETFRED SCOTTISH LEAGUE CUP 2017–18

■ *Denotes player sent off.*
PW = won on penalties (2pts). PL = lost on penalties (1pt).

FIRST ROUND
NORTH SECTION – GROUP A
Saturday, 15 July 2017
Falkirk (3) 4 *(Austin 24, McKee 26, Harris 39, Muirhead 57 (pen))*
Stirling Alb (0) 1 *(Smith D 87)*   2044

Inverness CT (2) 3 *(Warren 21, 34, Oakley 57)*
Brechin C (0) 0   1419

Tuesday, 18 July 2017
Brechin C (0) 1 *(Layne 68)*
Forfar Ath (0) 1 *(Millar 90 (pen))*   526
Brechin C won 4-3 on penalties.

Stirling Alb (0) 0
Inverness CT (0) 0   591
Inverness CT won 2-0 on penalties.

Saturday, 22 July 2017
Forfar Ath (0) 1 *(Caddis 90 (og))*
Stirling Alb (2) 3 *(Morrison 7, 44, Kavanagh 76)*   441

Inverness CT (0) 0
Falkirk (2) 2 *(McKee 21, Austin 43)*   1859

Tuesday, 25 July 2017
Falkirk (3) 4 *(Hippolyte 8, 38, 50, Austin 29)*
Forfar Ath (0) 0   2187

Stirling Alb (1) 2 *(MacDonald 40 (pen), Caddis 90 (pen))*
Brechin C (0) 0   430

Saturday, 29 July 2017
Brechin C (0) 0
Falkirk (1) 3 *(Miller 20, McKee 52, Harris 72)* 712

Forfar Ath (0) 1 *(Scott 49)*
Inverness CT (0) 2 *(Oakley 54, Baird 55)*   517

Group A Table	P	W	PW	PL	L	F	A	GD	Pts
Falkirk	4	4	0	0	0	13	1	12	12
Inverness CT	4	2	1	0	1	5	3	2	8
Stirling Alb	4	2	0	1	1	6	5	1	7
Brechin C	4	0	1	0	3	1	9	–8	2
Forfar Ath	4	0	0	1	3	3	10	–7	1

NORTH SECTION – GROUP B
Saturday, 15 July 2017
Dunfermline Ath (4) 6 *(Clark 10, 20, 35, 47, Paton 33, Smith 90)*
Elgin C (0) 0   1757

Peterhead (1) 1 *(McAllister 10)*
East Fife (0) 0   454

Tuesday, 18 July 2017
East Fife (0) 0
Dunfermline Ath (0) 0   1094
Dunfermline Ath won 9-8 on penalties.

Elgin C (0) 0
Hearts (0) 1 *(Lafferty 60)*   1303

Saturday, 22 July 2017
Dunfermline Ath (3) 5 *(McManus 7, 47, Cardle 12, 22, Ross 72 (og))*
Peterhead (0) 1 *(McAllister 63 (pen))*   1878

Hearts (1) 3 *(Lafferty 22, 86 (pen), Berra 70)*
East Fife (0) 0   6265

Tuesday, 25 July 2017
East Fife (0) 3 *(Duggan 57, Docherty 66 (pen), Willis 82)*
Elgin C (0) 2 *(Reilly 49, 79)*   331

Peterhead (1) 2 *(Jason Brown 6, McAllister 90 (pen))*
Hearts (1) 1 *(Lafferty 17)*   1602

Saturday, 29 July 2017
Elgin C (0) 0
Peterhead (2) 3 *(Cairney 4, McCracken 36, Stevenson 54)*
                                                      673

Hearts (1) 2 *(Cowie 20, Goncalves 86)*
Dunfermline Ath (1) 2 *(Cardle 28, McManus 52)*   8404
Dunfermline Ath won 3-1 on penalties.

Group B Table	P	W	PW	PL	L	F	A	GD	Pts
Dunfermline Ath	4	2	2	0	0	13	3	10	10
Peterhead	4	3	0	0	1	7	6	1	9
Hearts	4	2	0	1	1	7	4	3	7
East Fife	4	1	0	1	2	3	6	–3	4
Elgin C	4	0	0	0	4	2	13	–11	0

NORTH SECTION – GROUP C
Saturday, 15 July 2017
Cowdenbeath (2) 4 *(Syme 25, 62, Muirhead 44, Connelly 89)*
Buckie Thistle (1) 2 *(Dorrat 5, Copeland 51)*   308

Dundee U (0) 2 *(McMullan 59, Keatings 72 (pen))*
Raith R (0) 0   3753

Tuesday, 18 July 2017
Raith R (0) 1 *(Vaughan 90)*
Dundee (0) 2 *(Moussa 83, Hendry 90)*   2962

Wednesday, 19 July 2017
Buckie Thistle (0) 0
Dundee U (3) 3 *(McMullan 17, King 21, Durnan 34)* 1200

Saturday, 22 July 2017
Dundee (1) 2 *(El Bakhtaoui 22, Moussa 84)*
Buckie Thistle (0) 0   2774

Sunday, 23 July 2017
Dundee U (1) 4 *(Stanton 30, King 46, Fraser 67 (pen), Smith M 80)*
Cowdenbeath (0) 1 *(Muirhead 76)*   3253

Tuesday, 25 July 2017
Buckie Thistle (1) 1 *(Mcloud 27)*
Raith R (3) 6 *(Vaughan 14 (pen), 45, Spence 40, Buchanan 65, 69, Matthews 86)*   620

Wednesday, 26 July 2017
Cowdenbeath (0) 0
Dundee (3) 3 *(Moussa 17, 23, 38)*   1321

Saturday, 29 July 2017
Raith R (2) 2 *(Vaughan 9, Buchanan 32)*
Cowdenbeath (0) 0   1480

Sunday, 30 July 2017
Dundee (0) 1 *(O'Hara 60)*
Dundee U (1) 1 *(McMullan 45)*   10,460
Dundee U won 4-3 on penalties.

Group C Table	P	W	PW	PL	L	F	A	GD	Pts
Dundee U	4	3	1	0	0	10	2	8	11
Dundee	4	3	0	1	0	8	2	6	10
Raith R	4	2	0	0	2	9	5	4	6
Cowdenbeath	4	1	0	0	3	5	11	–6	3
Buckie Thistle	4	0	0	0	4	3	15	–12	0

NORTH SECTION – GROUP D

Saturday, 15 July 2017

Hibernian (2) 4 *(Murray S 12, 53, Murray F 22, Graham 88 (pen))*
Montrose (0) 0   5226

Ross Co (1) 2 *(Fraser 40, Curran 69)*
Alloa Ath (0) 0   1108

Tuesday, 18 July 2017

Alloa Ath (0) 1 *(McKeown 89)*
Arbroath (1) 1 *(Yule 16)*   311
Arbroath won 6-5 on penalties.

Montrose (0) 0
Ross Co (4) 6 *(Mikkelsen 15, 54, Curran 27 (pen), 45, Dillon 31 (og), Schalk 58)*   421

Friday, 21 July 2017

Ross Co (0) 0
Hibernian (0) 0   2065
Ross Co won 4-3 on penalties.

Saturday, 22 July 2017

Arbroath (1) 4 *(Gold 31, Denholm 69, 74, Doris 90)*
Montrose (0) 0   817

Tuesday, 25 July 2017

Hibernian (2) 6 *(Murray S 18, 51, 90, Porteous 45, 88, McGinn 53)*
Arbroath (1) 1 *(Doris 38)*   4856

Montrose (1) 2 *(Hay 21, Watson 50)*
Alloa Ath (0) 1 *(Flannigan 82)*   257

Saturday, 29 July 2017

Alloa Ath (0) 0
Hibernian (1) 3 *(Murray F 15, Murray S 63, 80)*   1758

Arbroath (0) 0
Ross Co (0) 0   702
Ross Co won 5-4 on penalties.

Group D Table	P	W	PW	PL	L	F	A	GD	Pts
Hibernian	4	3	0	1	0	13	1	12	10
Ross Co	4	2	2	0	0	8	0	8	10
Arbroath	4	1	1	1	1	6	7	–1	6
Montrose	4	1	0	0	3	2	15	–13	3
Alloa Ath	4	0	0	1	3	2	8	–6	1

SOUTH SECTION – GROUP E

Friday, 14 July 2017

Ayr U (1) 1 *(Geggan 39)*
Kilmarnock (0) 0   6417

Saturday, 15 July 2017

Clyde (0) 2 *(Breslin 57, Goodwillie 89)*
Annan Ath (0) 1 *(Swinglehurst 90)*   415

Tuesday, 18 July 2017

Dumbarton (1) 1 *(Nade 45)*
Ayr U (1) 3 *(Dowie 36 (og), McDaid 71, Crawford 88)*   615

Kilmarnock (1) 4 *(McKenzie 7, 68, Thomas 53, 59)*
Clyde (2) 2 *(Ramsay 10, Nicoll 11)*   1871

Saturday, 22 July 2017

Annan Ath (0) 0
Kilmarnock (1) 2 *(Boyd K 7, 62)*   743

Clyde (0) 2 *(Miller 57, Wright 67)*
Dumbarton (1) 1 *(Barr 33)*   416

Tuesday, 25 July 2017

Ayr U (2) 5 *(Crawford 20, Moore 30, 64, Moffat 53, McDaid 75)*
Clyde (1) 1 *(Goodwillie 12)*   1501

Dumbarton (0) 0
Annan Ath (0) 0   366
Annan Ath won 4-3 on penalties.

Saturday, 29 July 2017

Annan Ath (0) 1 *(Sinnamon 85)*
Ayr U (4) 6 *(Docherty 1, McGuffie 3, Moffat 25, Moore 45, Geggan 67, McDaid 81)*   659

Kilmarnock (0) 3 *(Burke 53, Boyd K 72, Erwin 76)*
Dumbarton (0) 0   2444

Group E Table	P	W	PW	PL	L	F	A	GD	Pts
Ayr U	4	4	0	0	0	15	3	12	12
Kilmarnock	4	3	0	0	1	9	3	6	9
Clyde	4	2	0	0	2	7	11	–4	6
Annan Ath	4	0	1	0	3	2	10	–8	2
Dumbarton	4	0	0	1	3	2	8	–6	1

SOUTH SECTION – GROUP F

Saturday, 15 July 2017

Berwick R (0) 0
Greenock Morton (1) 1 *(Fleming 33 (og))*   701

Queen's Park (1) 1 *(Cummins 23)*
Motherwell (1) 5 *(Cadden 10, Tanner 53, Bowman 74, 77, Moult 85)*   1590

Tuesday, 18 July 2017

Edinburgh C (2) 2 *(Grimes 23, 31)*
Berwick R (1) 2 *(Murrell 30, Scullion 84)*   247
Edinburgh C won 4-2 on penalties.

Greenock Morton (0) 2 *(McHugh 85, Barr 90)*
Queen's Park (0) 2 *(Wharton 70, Orr 81)*   1220
Greenock Morton won 4-2 on penalties.

Saturday, 22 July 2017

Motherwell (2) 4 *(Dunne 3, Cadden 25, Tait 67, Moult 72)*
Greenock Morton (0) 0   3113

Queen's Park (1) 3 *(Docherty D 20, McKee 55 (og), Brady 62)*
Edinburgh C (0) 0   404

Tuesday, 25 July 2017

Berwick R (1) 2 *(Rutherford 1, Thomson 83)*
Queen's Park (3) 3 *(Millen 9 (pen), Brady 33, Galt 39)*   305

Edinburgh C (0) 1 *(Grimes 69)*
Motherwell (0) 2 *(Cadden 74, Frear 89)*   970

Saturday, 29 July 2017

Greenock Morton (1) 5 *(McHugh 14, 90, Quitongo 53, Thomson 73, 79)*
Edinburgh C (0) 0   1065

Motherwell (0) 1 *(Frear 82)*
Berwick R (0) 0   2524

Group F Table	P	W	PW	PL	L	F	A	GD	Pts
Motherwell	4	4	0	0	0	12	2	10	12
Greenock Morton	4	2	1	0	1	8	6	2	8
Queen's Park	4	2	0	1	1	9	9	0	7
Edinburgh C	4	0	1	0	3	3	12	–9	2
Berwick Rangers	4	0	0	1	3	4	7	–3	1

SOUTH SECTION – GROUP G

Saturday, 15 July 2017
East Kilbride (0) 1 *(Winter 69 (pen))*
Hamilton A (1) 3 *(MacKinnon 39, Longridge 81,*
Crawford 90) 531

Stenhousemuir (1) 1 *(McGuigan 16 (pen))*
Queen of the South (0) 3 *(Dobbie 69, 85, Rooney 83)* 384

Tuesday, 18 July 2017
Albion R (0) 1 *(Trouten 59 (pen))*
Stenhousemuir (1) 1 *(McMenamin 15)* 244
Stenhousemuir won 3-2 on penalties.

Queen of the South (0) 0
East Kilbride (0) 0 1055
East Kilbride won 4-1 on penalties.

Saturday, 22 July 2017
East Kilbride (0) 2 *(Winter 67, McMullin 68 (og))*
Albion R (2) 5 *(Trouten 2, Fisher 5, Shields 47, 54, 72)* 261

Hamilton A (0) 1 *(Boyd 88)*
Queen of the South (0) 1 *(Dobbie 89)* 1047
Hamilton A won 6-5 on penalties.

Tuesday, 25 July 2017
Albion R (1) 4 *(Trouten 9, 53, 64, Davidson 90)*
Hamilton A (2) 4 *(Donati 38, Want 45, 57,*
Bingham 74 (pen)) 497
Albion R won 4-2 on penalties.

Stenhousemuir (0) 1 *(Longworth 50)*
East Kilbride (0) 2 *(Winter 47, 63)* 201

Saturday, 29 July 2017
Hamilton A (1) 3 *(Crawford 15, Templeton 56, Boyd 74)*
Stenhousemuir (0) 0 657

Queen of the South (0) 2 *(Dobbie 64, Brownlie 85)*
Albion R (1) 2 *(Trouten 38, 82 (pen))* 1002
Queen of the South won 4-2 on penalties.

Group G Table	P	W	PW	PL	L	F	A	GD	Pts
Hamilton A	4	2	1	1	0	10	6	4	9
Albion R	4	1	1	2	0	12	9	3	7
Queen of the South	4	1	1	2	0	6	4	2	7
East Kilbride	4	1	1	0	2	5	9	-4	5
Stenhousemuir	4	0	1	0	3	3	9	-6	2

SOUTH SECTION – GROUP H

Saturday, 15 July 2017
Livingston (0) 1 *(Jacobs 46)*
Partick Thistle (1) 1 *(Erskine 14)* 1119
Livingston won 3-1 on penalties.

Stranraer (1) 1 *(Agnew 11)*
St Mirren (3) 4 *(Reilly 27, Ross C Stewart 31, Morgan 40,*
Buchanan 56) 849

Tuesday, 18 July 2017
Airdrieonians (1) 3 *(Russell 29, 67, Ryan 63 (pen))*
Stranraer (0) 1 *(Robertson 81)* 490

St Mirren (0) 0
Livingston (1) 1 *(Carrick 2)* 2104

Saturday, 22 July 2017
Livingston (1) 2 *(Mackin 21, Halkett 53)*
Airdrieonians (0) 0 617

Partick Thistle (4) 5 *(Doolan 12, Lawless 23, 33,*
Spittal 38, 59)
St Mirren (0) 0 2727

Tuesday, 25 July 2017
Airdrieonians (0) 1 *(Cairns 55)*
Partick Thistle (2) 2 *(Doolan 10, Spittal 40)* 1255

Stranraer (2) 2 *(Neill 5, Agnew 33 (pen))*
Livingston (2) 4 *(Robertson 10 (og), Carrick 32,*
Todorov 61, Robinson 80) 341

Saturday, 29 July 2017
Partick Thistle (0) 1 *(Elliot 87)*
Stranraer (0) 0 2185

St Mirren (2) 5 *(MacDonald 9 (og), Reilly 31, 69,*
Morgan 82, Smith C 88)
Airdrieonians (0) 0 1557

Group H Table	P	W	PW	PL	L	F	A	GD	Pts
Livingston	4	3	1	0	0	8	3	5	11
Partick Thistle	4	3	0	1	0	9	2	7	10
St Mirren	4	2	0	0	2	9	7	2	6
Airdrieonians	4	1	0	0	3	4	10	-6	3
Stranraer	4	0	0	0	4	4	12	-8	0

Ross Co, Partick Thistle, Dundee and Kilmarnock qualified for Round Two as best runners-up.

ROUND TWO

Tuesday, 8 August 2017
Celtic (3) 5 *(Griffiths 14 (pen), 29, Ralston 21, Tierney 65,*
Armstrong 71)
Kilmarnock (0) 0 27,407
Celtic: (4231) Gordon; Ralston, Ajer, Tierney, Miller;
Eboue (Ntcham 40), Armstrong; Hayes, Rogic, Benyu
(McGregor 70); Griffiths (Forrest 64).
Kilmarnock: (451) MacDonald; Wilson (O'Donnell 59),
Greer, Broadfoot, Taylor; Burke, McKenzie, Power,
Frizzell, Jones (Graham 46); Erwin.
Referee: Alan Muir.

Falkirk (1) 1 *(Craigen 40)*
Livingston (1) 2 *(Robinson 32, De Vita 101)* 2677
Falkirk: (442) Thomson; Gasparotto, Watson, Grant,
Gallacher; Craigen (Shepherd 102), Taiwo, Kerr, Harris
(Miller 57); Hippolyte (McKee 69), Austin (Loy 90).
Livingston: (3511) Alexander; Gallagher, Halkett,
Lithgow; Mullin, Byrne, Jacobs, Robinson (Carrick 63
(Mackin 113)), Cadden (Longridge 62); Pitman; Mullen
(De Vita 73).
aet.
Referee: Andrew Dallas.

Hibernian (2) 5 *(Stokes 20, 59, Murray S 31, Ambrose 69,*
Matulevicius 85)
Ayr U (0) 0 8135
Hibernian: (343) Marciano; Porteous, McGregor,
Ambrose; Gray, McGeouch (Matulevicius 76), McGinn,
Stevenson; Murray S (Boyle 64), Stokes, Swanson (Slivka
64).
Ayr U: (442) Hart; Higgins, Rose, Boyle, Reid; McGuffie
(Murphy 64), Docherty, Geggan, McDaid (Forrest 46);
Moffat, Moore (Ferguson 46).
Referee: Kevin Clancy.

St Johnstone (0) 0
Partick Thistle (0) 3 *(Lawless 50 (pen), Edwards 62,*
Erskine 90) 2619
St Johnstone: (4411) Mannus; Foster, Shaughnessy,
Anderson, Easton; Wotherspoon, Alston (Cummins 64),
Davidson, Craig (Scougall 58); O'Halloran; MacLean
(Kane 79).
Partick Thistle: (4231) Cerny; Elliot, Turnbull, Devine
(Keown 30); Booth; Osman, Barton; Lawless (Bannigan
77), Edwards, Erskine; Nisbet.
Referee: Euan Anderson.

Wednesday, 9 August 2017

Dundee (1) 2 *(El Bakhtaoui 30, McGowan 64)*

Dundee U (1) 1 *(King 40)* 10,472

Dundee: (4231) Bain; Kerr, Hendry, Waddell, Holt; Kamara, McGowan; Deacon (Wolters 76), Allan (Vincent 85), El Bakhtaoui; Haber.
Dundee U: (4231) Lewis; Toshney, Edjenguele, Durnan, Scobbie (Robson 18); Briels (Keatings 73), Fyvie (Murdoch 85); McMullan, Stanton, King; McDonald.
Referee: Steven McLean.

Hamilton A (0) 0

Aberdeen (1) 1 *(McLean 43)* 2768

Hamilton A: (4411) Woods; Gillespie, Sarris, Tomas (Donati 71), McMann; Docherty, MacKinnon (Redmond 68), Crawford, Imrie; Boyd; Bingham (Longridge 62).
Aberdeen: (4231) Lewis; Logan, O'Connor, Reynolds, Considine; Tansey, Shinnie; Christie (Stewart 69), McLean, Wright (Mackay-Steven 68); Maynard (Storey 72).
Referee: Nick Walsh.

Rangers (4) 6 *(Miller 5, Bruno Alves 9, Morelos 23, 75, Tavernier 27, Candeias 57)*

Dunfermline Ath (0) 0 35,262

Rangers: (442) Alnwick; Tavernier, Fabio Cardoso, Bruno Alves (Wilson 56), Hodson; Candeias, Rossiter, Dorrans (Holt 68), Windass; Morelos, Miller (Kranjcar 59).
Dunfermline Ath: (4411) Murdoch; Williamson, Morris, Ashcroft, Martin; Hopkirk (Mvoto 29), Paton, Wedderburn, Cardle (Lochhead 68); Higginbotham (Shiels 62); McManus.
Referee: Don Robertson.

Ross Co (0) 2 *(Schalk 65, Curran 104 (pen))*

Motherwell (0) 3 *(Bigirimana 50, Cadden 92, MacLean 112)* 1612

Ross Co: (4141) Fox; Fraser, Davies, Naismith, Kelly; Lindsay; Gardyne, Chow (O'Brien 13), Routis (Keillor-Dunn 99), Dow (Curran 71); Schalk (Mikkelsen 101).
Motherwell: (4411) Carson; Tait, Heneghan, Kipre, Dunne[*]; Cadden, McHugh, Rose (Plummer 105), Bigirimana (MacLean 85); Tanner (Fisher 56); Moult (Bowman 85).
aet.
Referee: Stephen Finnie.

QUARTER-FINALS

Tuesday, 19 September 2017

Hibernian (2) 3 *(Swanson 18, Boyle 32, Stokes 83 (pen))*

Livingston (2) 2 *(Lithgow 10, De Vita 28)* 8535

Hibernian: (442) Laidlaw; Gray (Whittaker 13), Ambrose, Hanlon, Stevenson; Boyle, Slivka (McGeouch 66), Bartley, McGinn; Swanson (Barker 88), Stokes.
Livingston: (352) Alexander; Todorov, Halkett, Lithgow; De Vita (Longridge 43), Jacobs (Mullen 62), Byrne, Pitman, Cadden; Carrick, Knox (Mullin 56).
Referee: Bobby Madden.

Partick Thistle (0) 1 *(Doolan 90)*

Rangers (0) 3 *(Pena 55, Candeias 94, Herrera 99)* 7394

Partick Thistle: (3421) Scully; Keown, Devine, Turnbull (Doolan 57); McGinn, Barton, Edwards, Elliot; Spittal (Nisbet 83), Lawless (Bannigan 105); Sammon.
Rangers: (4411) Alnwick; Tavernier, Fabio Cardoso, Bruno Alves (McCrorie 76), John (Hodson 79); Candeias, Jack, Dorrans, Windass; Pena (Holt 71); Morelos (Herrera 91).
aet.
Referee: Steven McLean.

Wednesday, 20 September 2017

Dundee (0) 0

Celtic (2) 4 *(Sinclair 25 (pen), Forrest 42, 90, McGregor 88)* 6917

Dundee: (4231) Bain; Kerr, Hendry, O'Dea, Holt; Kamara, Spence (McGowan 73); Wolters (Deacon 64), O'Hara, El Bakhtaoui; Leitch-Smith.
Celtic: (4231) Gordon; Lustig, Boyata (Ralston 67), Bitton, Tierney; Brown, Ntcham; Forrest, Sinclair, Roberts (McGregor 73); Griffiths (Edouard 85).
Referee: John Beaton.

Thursday, 21 September 2017

Motherwell (2) 3 *(Lewis 13 (og), Hartley 19, Moult 85)*

Aberdeen (0) 0 6430

Motherwell: (4411) Carson; Tait, Kipre, Hartley, Hammell; Cadden, McHugh, Campbell, Rose (Grimshaw 70); Bowman (Fisher 87); Moult (Tanner 90).
Aberdeen: (4141) Lewis; Logan, O'Connor, Reynolds (Arnason 52), Considine; Ball (Tansey 67); Christie, McLean, Shinnie, Mackay-Steven (Rooney 37); May.
Referee: Kevin Clancy.

SEMI-FINALS

Saturday, 21 October 2017

Hibernian (0) 2 *(Stokes 59 (pen), Shaw 70)*

Celtic (2) 4 *(Lustig 15, 42, Dembele 66, 88)* 39,813

Hibernian: (4231) Laidlaw; Gray (Whittaker 46), Ambrose, Hanlon, Stevenson; Slivka (Shaw 70), Bartley (Boyle 46); Barker, McGinn, McGeouch; Stokes.
Celtic: (4231) Gordon; Lustig, Boyata, Bitton, Tierney; Brown, Armstrong (Rogic 73); Roberts (Forrest 61), McGregor, Sinclair; Griffiths (Dembele 61).
Referee: Kevin Clancy.

Sunday, 22 October 2017

Rangers (0) 0

Motherwell (0) 2 *(Moult 52, 74)* 44,506

Rangers: (4411) Alnwick; Tavernier, Fabio Cardoso (McCrorie 67), Bruno Alves, John; Candeias, Jack, Dorrans, Windass (Herrera 75); Pena (Nemane 60); Morelos.
Motherwell: (352) Carson; Kipre, Hartley, Dunne; Cadden, Campbell (Bigirimana 72), McHugh, Rose, Tait; Bowman (Fisher 90), Moult.
Referee: Steven McLean.

BETFRED SCOTTISH LEAGUE CUP FINAL 2017–18

Sunday, 26 November 2017

(at Hampden Park, 49,483)

Motherwell (0) 0   Celtic (0) 2

Motherwell: (532) Carson; Cadden, Kipre[*], Hartley, Dunne, Tait; Grimshaw (Tanner 51), McHugh, Rose (Frear 70); Bowman (Campbell 64), Moult.
Celtic: (4231) Gordon; Lustig, Boyata, Simunovic, Tierney; Armstrong, Brown; Forrest (Roberts 78), McGregor (Rogic 89), Sinclair; Dembele (Griffiths 64).
Scorers: Forrest 49, Dembele 60 (pen)).
Referee: Craig Thomson.

IRN-BRU SCOTTISH
LEAGUE CHALLENGE CUP 2017–18

■ *Denotes player sent off.*

FIRST ROUND – NORTH

Tuesday, 15 August 2017
Aberdeen U20 **(1) 1** *(Ross F 42)*
St Johnstone U20 **(0) 0**   155

Buckie Thistle **(0) 2** *(Fraser 56, 82)*
Brechin C **(1) 1** *(McLean 14)*   453

Dundee U **(0) 2** *(Nkoyi 61, 67)*
Cowdenbeath **(0) 0**   1655

Dunfermline Ath **(2) 2** *(Ryan 24, 40)*
Arbroath **(0) 0**   1462

East Fife **(0) 0**
Peterhead **(1) 2** *(Lawrence 2, Adams 64)*   333

Formartine United **(2) 2** *(MacPhee 17, Berton 35)*
Hearts U20 **(0) 3** *(Zanatta 50, 90, Paton 119)*   200
aet.

Hibernian U20 **(0) 1** *(Murray 48)*
Elgin C **(1) 2** *(McLeish 19, Bronsky 89)*   387

Raith R **(1) 3** *(Callachan 16, Vaughan 65, Osei-Opoku 84)*
Brora **(0) 0**   971

Ross County U20 **(2) 2** *(McKay 25, Maciver 27)*
Forfar Ath **(0) 1** *(Millar 89)*   234

Stenhousemuir **(0) 0**
Cove Rangers **(2) 2** *(Dunlop R 19 (og),
Megginson 36 (pen))*   169

Stirling Alb **(0) 1** *(Smith D 90)*
Montrose **(1) 3** *(Steeves 45, Ballantyne 56, 85)*   413

Wednesday, 16 August 2017
Dundee U20 **(1) 2** *(Henvey 40, 79)*
Alloa Ath **(3) 4** *(Malcolm 13, 90, Crane 21, Flannigan 33)*
                                                            110

FIRST ROUND – SOUTH

Tuesday, 15 August 2017
Albion R **(0) 0**
Spartans **(0) 0**   155
aet; Albion R won 5-4 on penalties.
Albion R removed for fielding ineligible player.

Annan Ath **(2) 3** *(Smith 17, 23 (pen), 84)*
Celtic U20 **(1) 1** *(Hendry 30)*   278

Clyde **(1) 2** *(McNiff 2, Osadolor 48)*
Stranraer **(0) 3** *(Agnew 66 (pen), Stewart 70 (og),
Wallace R 103)*   319
aet.

Greenock Morton **(0) 0**
Livingston **(1) 2** *(Todorov 25, Mullen 70)*   1036

Hamilton A U20 **(1) 1** *(Tierney 4 (pen))*
Edinburgh City **(0) 0**   153

Kilmarnock U20 **(0) 0**
Berwick R **(2) 2** *(Thomson 19, McKenna 39)*   255

Partick Thistle U20 **(1) 6** *(McLaughlin 15, 57, 79, Lamont
52, Nisbet 60, Fitzpatrick 67)*
Stirling University **(0) 1** *(Lyons 75)*   190

Queen of the South **(3) 4** *(Lyle 14, Kerr 25, Brownlie 44,
Rooney 88)*
Airdrieonians **(0) 0**   1012

St Mirren **(0) 2** *(Ross C Stewart 87, Morgan 90)*
East Kilbride **(0) 1** *(McLaren 81)*   1357

Wednesday, 16 August 2017
Dumbarton **(1) 2** *(Gallagher C 2 (pen), Stewart 49)*
Rangers U20 **(0) 1** *(Hardie 72)*   389

East Stirling **(1) 1** *(Ure 40)*
Ayr U **(2) 5** *(Murphy 26, Gilmour 38, Moore 54,
Forrest 58, McCowan 88)*   318

Motherwell U20 **(0) 2** *(Plummer 62, Livingstone 69)*
Queen's Park **(1) 1** *(Cummins 29)*   168

James Forrest (far left) curls in Celtic's first goal in their 2-0 defeat of Motherwell in the Scottish League Cup Final at Hampden Park on 26 November. (Reuters/Lee Smith)

SECOND ROUND

Tuesday, 29 August 2017
Ayr U (1) 1 *(Moore 28)*
Montrose (1) 1 *(Campbell I 2)*   906
aet; Montrose won 6-5 on penalties.

Friday, 1 September 2017
Stranraer (1) 2 *(Wallace R 33, Stoney 90)*
Partick Thistle U20 (0) 0   228

Saturday, 2 September 2017
Aberdeen U20 (0) 2 *(Ross S 51, Anderson 89)*
Inverness CT (3) 4 *(Calder 4, Polworth 25, Raven 40, Tremarco 82)*   175

Berwick R (0) 0
Queen of the South (0) 5 *(Rooney 53, Dobbie 58, 63, Lyle 60, Kane 87)*   621

Buckie Thistle (0) 0
Dunfermline Ath (3) 3 *(Clark 7, 35, Ryan 39)*   606

Crusaders (1) 3 *(Lowry 28, Burns 84, 90)*
Motherwell U20 (0) 2 *(Turnbull 51, Newell 67)*   494

Dumbarton (0) 2 *(Wilson 81, Froxylias 120)*
Connah's Quay Nomads (1) 1 *(Morris 26 (pen))*   491
aet.

Dundee U (0) 3 *(Nkoyi 72 (pen), McMullan 90, Flood 90)*
Alloa Ath (0) 1 *(Cawley 78)*   1763

Elgin C (0) 2 *(Dodd 46, Allan 90)*
Bray (0) 0   611

Hamilton A U20 (0) 1 *(Breen 54)*
Cove Rangers (3) 3 *(Masson 14, Megginson 27 (pen), 30)*   297

Peterhead (0) 2 *(McLean 59 (pen), McAllister 78)*
Annan Ath (0) 0   529

Raith R (4) 4 *(Vaughan 7, 21, Barr 10, Buchanan 27)*
Ross County U20 (0) 0   1035

Sligo R (1) 1 *(Sharkey 18)*
Falkirk (2) 2 *(Austin 9, Craigen 28)*   520

Spartans (0) 1 *(Atkinson 74)*
Linfield (1) 2 *(Rooney 39 (pen), Lowry 49)*   902

St Mirren (1) 3 *(Reilly 8, 48, Sutton 83)*
Hearts U20 (0) 1 *(Currie 81)*   1130

Sunday, 3 September 2017
The New Saints (1) 1 *(Edwards 20)*
Livingston (0) 1 *(Mackin 64)*   403
aet; The New Saints won 6-5 on penalties.

THIRD ROUND

Friday, 6 October 2017
Dumbarton (1) 2 *(Barr 12, Stewart 65)*
Stranraer (0) 1 *(Okoh 90)*   492
Dumbarton: (4231) Gallacher (Ewings 32); Wardrop, Dowie, Barr, McLaughlin; Hutton, Wilson D; Froxylias, Stewart (Roy 79), Walsh; Gallagher C (Nade 58).
Stranraer: (451) Currie; Hamill, Robertson, Neill, Dick; Agnew (Okoh 73), Turner (Stoney 75), Bell, Thomson, Anderson; Woods (Elliott 83).
Referee: Greg Aitken.

Saturday, 7 October 2017
Cove Rangers (0) 0
Crusaders (1) 3 *(Carvill 45, Glackin 60, Caddell 90)*   268
Cove Rangers: (4231) McKenzie; Ross∎, Watson, Kelly, Milne; Strachan (Scully 70), Campbell; Park (Redford 56), Burnett, Masson (Stott 76); Megginson.

Crusaders: (4411) Dougherty; Burns, McChrystal, Beverland, Brown (McClean 47); Forsyth, Caddell, Snoddy, Carvill (Whyte 87); Glackin (Owens 77); Cushley.
Referee: Paul McLaughlin.

Dundee U (0) 1 *(Chalmers 90)*
Linfield (0) 0   1967
Dundee U: (442) Mehmet; Taylor, Allardice, Murdoch, Hornby (Dailly 81); Stanton, Thomas, Ritchie, Smith M; Nkoyi, Piggott (Chalmers 66).
Linfield: (451) Deane; Stafford, Haughey, Robinson, Clarke M; Mulgrew, Garrett, Millar, Mitchell (Clarke R 80); Burns; Waterworth (Stewart J 76).
Referee: Iwan Griffith.

Falkirk (1) 2 *(Balatoni 19, Hippolyte 59)*
Dunfermline Ath (0) 0   4082
Falkirk: (451) Mitchell (Thomson 70); Muirhead, Grant, Balatoni, McGhee; Harris, McKee, Kerr, Taiwo, Hippolyte (Craigen 75); O'Hara (Austin 83).
Dunfermline Ath: (442) Murdoch; Martin, Ashcroft, Wedderburn (Mvoto 79), Talbot; Higginbotham, Shiels∎, Splaine (Ryan 74); McManus; Smith, Clark.
Referee: Steven McLean.

Inverness CT (1) 3 *(Polworth 2, Calder 51, Mackay 90)*
Peterhead (0) 0   930
Inverness CT: (442) Fon Williams; Raven, McKay, Donaldson, Tremarco; Calder (Mackay 90), Polworth (Cooper 87), Vigurs, Chalmers; Bell (Oakley 76), Baird.
Peterhead: (442) Fleming; Stevenson, Jason Brown, McCracken, McIlduff; Gibson, Ferry, Brown S (Lawrence 87), Leitch; McAllister (Adams 76), McLean (Smith 56).
Referee: Alan Muir.

Montrose (1) 1 *(Masson 23)*
Queen of the South (0) 3 *(Dobbie 87, 120, Dykes 113)* 534
Montrose: (4411) Fleming; Ballantyne, Dillon, Campbell I, Steeves; Allan, Masson (Redman 70), Watson (Hay 114), McLaren (Webster 73); Callaghan; Templeman (Campbell R 109).
Queen of the South: (442) Martin; Rooney (Mercer 109), Fordyce, Brownlie, Marshall; Stirling (Murray 69), Rankin, Tapping (McFadden 61), Jacobs; Dobbie, Kane (Dykes 46).
aet.
Referee: Kevin Graham.

St Mirren (0) 1 *(Reilly 63)*
Raith R (0) 3 *(Vaughan 64, Spence 73, Barr 81)*   1970
St Mirren: (3412) Ross Stewart; Baird, Buchanan (Duffy 76), Eckersley; Irvine (MacPherson 56), McShane, Erhahon, Demetriou; Hilson; Ross C Stewart, Reilly (Smith C 76).
Raith R: (442) Smith; Watson, McKay, Murray, Thomson; Matthews, Berry, Herron, Barr; Spence (Court 90), Vaughan.
Referee: Euan Anderson.

The New Saints (3) 4 *(Draper 17, 61, Edwards 39, Mullan 44)*
Elgin C (0) 0   404
The New Saints: (541) Harrison; Spender (Cieslewicz 56), Rawlinson, Hudson, Leak, Mullan; Seargeant, Holland, Edwards, Brobbel (Darlington 62); Draper (Roberts 67).
Elgin C: (442) Waters; Cooper, Eadie, Bronsky, McHardy; Reid, McGovern (Sutherland A 75), Reilly, Dodd (Smith 53); Cameron, McLeish (Allan 62).
Referee: Andrew Davey.

QUARTER-FINALS

Saturday, 11 November 2017
Dumbarton (1) 2 *(McLaughlin 20, Roy 49)*
Raith R (0) 0   888
Dumbarton: (442) Gallacher; Wardrop, Barr, Dowie, McLaughlin; Gallagher C (Johnston 79), Hutton, Carswell, Walsh; Stewart (Prior 89), Roy (Wilson D 66).

Raith R: (442) Smith; Watson, Davidson (Buchanan 50), Murray, Thomson; Matthews, Berry (Robertson 50), Herron, Vaughan; Osei-Opoku (McKay 61), Spence■.
Referee: Gavin Duncan.

Dundee U (0) 1 *(Fyvie 55)*
Crusaders (0) 2 *(Cushley 67, Whyte 90)*   2048
Dundee U: (442) Mehmet; Ritchie, Quinn, Edjenguele, Hornby; McMullan, Fyvie, Allardice (King 46), Taylor; Keatings (Smith M 89), Nkoyi.
Crusaders: (442) Jensen; Ward, Beverland, McChrystal, McClean; Forsyth, Caddell (Burns 87), Snoddy (Whyte 61), Brown; Glackin (Owens 80), Cushley.
Referee: Robert Hennessey.

Inverness CT (0) 1 *(Bell 57)*
Falkirk (0) 0   1078
Inverness CT: (442) Ridgers; Raven, McKay, Donaldson, Tremarco; Cooper (Doran 72), Polworth, Vigurs, Chalmers; Baird (Oakley 79), Bell (Calder 86).
Falkirk: (4411) Thomson; Muirhead, Watson, Balatoni, McGhee; Harris, Longridge, McKee (Loy 63), Hippolyte; Craigen (Blues 85); Austin (Dunne 72).
Referee: Euan Anderson.

Sunday, 12 November 2017
The New Saints (0) 0
Queen of the South (0) 0   808
The New Saints: (4411) Harrison; Spender, Leak, Rawlinson, Marriott; Mullan, Holland (Seargeant 107), Routledge, Brobbel; Edwards (Darlington 116); Draper (Fletcher 72).

Queen of the South: (442) Martin; Rooney (Mercer 77), Brownlie, Fordyce, Marshall; Murray (Stirling 85), Jacobs, Tapping (Lyle 97), McFadden; Dobbie, Dykes (Kane 114).
aet; The New Saints won 4-3 on penalties.
Referee: Raymond Crangle.

SEMI-FINALS
Saturday, 17 February 2018
The New Saints (0) 1 *(Ebbe 52)*
Dumbarton (0) 2 *(Handling 74, Froxylias 84)*   825
The New Saints: (4231) Harrison; Spender, Hudson, Rawlinson, Marriott; Routledge, Holland; Brobbel, Edwards (Kauber 87), Ebbe; Draper.
Dumbarton: (442) Gallacher; Smith, Dowie, Barr, Hill; Gallagher C (Stewart 65), Handling (Froxylias 80), Hutton, Carswell; Russell (Burt 65), Nade.
Referee: Neil Doyle.

Sunday, 18 February 2018
Inverness CT (3) 3 *(Oakley 1, Chalmers 13, Mulraney 44)*
Crusaders (0) 2 *(Heatley 57, 79)*   1044
Inverness CT: (442) Ridgers; McKay■, Warren, Donaldson, Calder; Mulraney (Elbouzedi 79), Polworth, Vigurs, Chalmers; Oakley, Bell (Seedorf 65).
Crusaders: (4231) Jensen; Burns, Beverland, Coates, McClean; Forsyth (Owens 46), Caddell■; Glackin (Whyte 46), Snoddy (Lowry 77), Heatley; Murray.
Referee: Bryn Markham-Jones.

IRN-BRU SCOTTISH LEAGUE CHALLENGE CUP FINAL 2017–18

Saturday, 24 March 2018

(at McDiarmid Park, attendance 4602)

Dumbarton (0) 0   Inverness CT (0) 1

Dumbarton: (442) Gallacher; Smith, Dowie, Barr, McLaughlin; Gallagher C (Stewart 74), Carswell, Hutton, Walsh (Burt 81); Handling, Russell (Froxylias 68).

Inverness CT: (442) Ridgers; Seedorf, Warren, Donaldson, Tremarco; Mulraney (Doran 70), Polworth, Vigurs, Chalmers; Oakley, Bell (Mackay 78).

Scorer: Tremarco 90.

Referee: Andrew Dallas.

LEAGUE CHALLENGE FINALS 1990–2018

B&Q CENTENARY CUP

1990–91	Dundee v Ayr U	3-2*

B&Q CUP

1991–92	Hamilton A v Ayr U	1-0
1992–93	Hamilton A v Morton	3-2
1993–94	Falkirk v St Mirren	3-0
1994–95	Airdrieonians v Dundee	3-2*

SCOTTISH LEAGUE CHALLENGE CUP

1995–96	Stenhousemuir v Dundee U	0-0*
	Stenhousemuir won 5-4 on penalties.	
1996–97	Stranraer v St Johnstone	1-0
1997–98	Falkirk v Queen of the South	1-0
1998–99	*No competition.*	
	Suspended due to lack of sponsorship.	

BELL'S CHALLENGE CUP

1999–2000	Alloa Ath v Inverness CT	4-4*
	Alloa Ath won 5-4 on penalties.	
2000–01	Airdrieonians v Livingston	2-2*
	Airdrieonians won 3-2 on penalties.	
2001–02	Airdrieonians v Alloa Ath	2-1

BELL'S CUP

2002–03	Queen of the South v Brechin C	2-0
2003–04	Inverness CT v Airdrie U	2-0
2004–05	Falkirk v Ross Co	2-1
2005–06	St Mirren v Hamilton A	2-1

SCOTTISH LEAGUE CHALLENGE CUP

2006–07	Ross Co v Clyde	1-1*
	Ross Co won 5-4 on penalties.	
2007–08	St Johnstone v Dunfermline Ath	3-2

ALBA CHALLENGE CUP

2008–09	Airdrie U v Ross Co	2-2*
	Airdrie U won 3-2 on penalties.	
2009–10	Dundee v Inverness CT	3-2
2010–11	Ross Co v Queen of the South	2-0

RAMSDENS CUP

2011–12	Falkirk v Hamilton A	1-0
2012–13	Queen of the South v Partick Thistle	1-1*
	Queen of the South won 6-5 on penalties.	
2013–14	Raith R v Rangers	1-0*

PETROFAC TRAINING SCOTTISH LEAGUE CHALLENGE CUP

2014–15	Livingston v Alloa Athletic	4-0
2015–16	Rangers v Peterhead	4-0

IRN-BRU SCOTTISH LEAGUE CHALLENGE CUP

2016–17	Dundee U v St Mirren	2-1
2017–18	Inverness CT v Dumbarton	1-0

After extra time.

SCOTTISH CUP FINALS 1874–2018

SCOTTISH FA CUP

Year	Match	Score
1874	Queen's Park v Clydesdale	2-0
1875	Queen's Park v Renton	3-0
1876	Queen's Park v Third Lanark	1-1
Replay	Queen's Park v Third Lanark	2-0
1877	Vale of Leven v Rangers	1-1
Replay	Vale of Leven v Rangers	1-1
2nd Replay	Vale of Leven v Rangers	3-2
1878	Vale of Leven v Third Lanark	1-0
1879	Vale of Leven v Rangers	1-1
	Vale of Leven awarded cup, Rangers failing to appear for replay.	
1880	Queen's Park v Thornliebank	3-0
1881	Queen's Park v Dumbarton	2-1
Replay	Queen's Park v Dumbarton	3-1
	After Dumbarton protested the first game.	
1882	Queen's Park v Dumbarton	2-2
Replay	Queen's Park v Dumbarton	4-1
1883	Dumbarton v Vale of Leven	2-2
Replay	Dumbarton v Vale of Leven	2-1
1884	Queen's Park v Vale of Leven	
	Queen's Park awarded cup, Vale of Leven failing to appear.	
1885	Renton v Vale of Leven	0-0
Replay	Renton v Vale of Leven	3-1
1886	Queen's Park v Renton	3-1
1887	Hibernian v Dumbarton	2-1
1888	Renton v Cambuslang	6-1
1889	Third Lanark v Celtic	3-0
Replay	Third Lanark v Celtic	2-1
	Replay by order of Scottish FA because of playing conditions in first match.	
1890	Queen's Park v Vale of Leven	1-1
Replay	Queen's Park v Vale of Leven	2-1
1891	Hearts v Dumbarton	1-0
1892	Celtic v Queen's Park	1-0
Replay	Celtic v Queen's Park	5-1
	After mutually protested first match.	
1893	Queen's Park v Celtic	0-1
Replay	Queen's Park v Celtic	2-1
	Replay by order of Scottish FA because of playing conditions in first match.	
1894	Rangers v Celtic	3-1
1895	St Bernard's v Renton	2-1
1896	Hearts v Hibernian	3-1
1897	Rangers v Dumbarton	5-1
1898	Rangers v Kilmarnock	2-0
1899	Celtic v Rangers	2-0
1900	Celtic v Queen's Park	4-3
1901	Hearts v Celtic	4-3
1902	Hibernian v Celtic	1-0
1903	Rangers v Hearts	1-1
Replay	Rangers v Hearts	0-0
2nd Replay	Rangers v Hearts	2-0
1904	Celtic v Rangers	3-2
1905	Third Lanark v Rangers	0-0
Replay	Third Lanark v Rangers	3-1
1906	Hearts v Third Lanark	1-0
1907	Celtic v Hearts	3-0
1908	Celtic v St Mirren	5-1
1909	Celtic v Rangers	2-2
Replay	Celtic v Rangers	1-1
	Owing to riot, the cup was withheld.	
1910	Dundee v Clyde	2-2
Replay	Dundee v Clyde	0-0*
2nd Replay	Dundee v Clyde	2-1
1911	Celtic v Hamilton A	0-0
Replay	Celtic v Hamilton A	2-0
1912	Celtic v Clyde	2-0
1913	Falkirk v Raith R	2-0
1914	Celtic v Hibernian	0-0
Replay	Celtic v Hibernian	4-1
1920	Kilmarnock v Albion R	3-2
1921	Partick Thistle v Rangers	1-0
1922	Morton v Rangers	1-0
1923	Celtic v Hibernian	1-0
1924	Airdrieonians v Hibernian	2-0
1925	Celtic v Dundee	2-1
1926	St Mirren v Celtic	2-0
1927	Celtic v East Fife	3-1
1928	Rangers v Celtic	4-0
1929	Kilmarnock v Rangers	2-0
1930	Rangers v Partick Thistle	0-0
Replay	Rangers v Partick Thistle	2-1
1931	Celtic v Motherwell	2-2
Replay	Celtic v Motherwell	4-2
1932	Rangers v Kilmarnock	1-1
Replay	Rangers v Kilmarnock	3-0
1933	Celtic v Motherwell	1-0
1934	Rangers v St Mirren	5-0
1935	Rangers v Hamilton A	2-1
1936	Rangers v Third Lanark	1-0
1937	Celtic v Aberdeen	2-1
1938	East Fife v Kilmarnock	1-1
Replay	East Fife v Kilmarnock	4-2*
1939	Clyde v Motherwell	4-0
1947	Aberdeen v Hibernian	2-1
1948	Rangers v Morton	1-1*
Replay	Rangers v Morton	1-0*
1949	Rangers v Clyde	4-1
1950	Rangers v East Fife	3-0
1951	Celtic v Motherwell	1-0
1952	Motherwell v Dundee	4-0
1953	Rangers v Aberdeen	1-1
Replay	Rangers v Aberdeen	1-0
1954	Celtic v Aberdeen	2-1
1955	Clyde v Celtic	1-1
Replay	Clyde v Celtic	1-0
1956	Hearts v Celtic	3-1
1957	Falkirk v Kilmarnock	1-1
Replay	Falkirk v Kilmarnock	2-1*
1958	Clyde v Hibernian	1-0
1959	St Mirren v Aberdeen	3-1
1960	Rangers v Kilmarnock	2-0
1961	Dunfermline Ath v Celtic	0-0
Replay	Dunfermline Ath v Celtic	2-0
1962	Rangers v St Mirren	2-0
1963	Rangers v Celtic	1-1
Replay	Rangers v Celtic	3-0
1964	Rangers v Dundee	3-1
1965	Celtic v Dunfermline Ath	3-2
1966	Rangers v Celtic	0-0
Replay	Rangers v Celtic	1-0
1967	Celtic v Aberdeen	2-0
1968	Dunfermline Ath v Hearts	3-1
1969	Celtic v Rangers	4-0
1970	Aberdeen v Celtic	3-1
1971	Celtic v Rangers	1-1
Replay	Celtic v Rangers	2-1
1972	Celtic v Hibernian	6-1
1973	Rangers v Celtic	3-2
1974	Celtic v Dundee U	3-0
1975	Celtic v Airdrieonians	3-1
1976	Rangers v Hearts	3-1
1977	Celtic v Rangers	1-0
1978	Rangers v Aberdeen	2-1
1979	Rangers v Hibernian	0-0
Replay	Rangers v Hibernian	0-0*
2nd Replay	Rangers v Hibernian	3-2*
1980	Celtic v Rangers	1-0*
1981	Rangers v Dundee U	0-0*
Replay	Rangers v Dundee U	4-1
1982	Aberdeen v Rangers	4-1*
1983	Aberdeen v Rangers	1-0*
1984	Aberdeen v Celtic	2-1*
1985	Celtic v Dundee U	2-1
1986	Aberdeen v Hearts	3-0
1987	St Mirren v Dundee U	1-0*
1988	Celtic v Dundee U	2-1
1989	Celtic v Rangers	1-0

TENNENTS SCOTTISH CUP

1990	Aberdeen v Celtic	0-0*
	Aberdeen won 9-8 on penalties.	
1991	Motherwell v Dundee U	4-3*
1992	Rangers v Airdrieonians	2-1
1993	Rangers v Aberdeen	2-1
1994	Dundee U v Rangers	1-0
1995	Celtic v Airdrieonians	1-0
1996	Rangers v Hearts	5-1
1997	Kilmarnock v Falkirk	1-0
1998	Hearts v Rangers	2-1
1999	Rangers v Celtic	1-0
2000	Rangers v Aberdeen	4-0
2001	Celtic v Hibernian	3-0
2002	Rangers v Celtic	3-2
2003	Rangers v Dundee	1-0
2004	Celtic v Dunfermline Ath	3-1
2005	Celtic v Dundee U	1-0
2006	Hearts v Gretna	1-1*
	Hearts won 4-2 on penalties.	
2007	Celtic v Dunfermline Ath	1-0

SCOTTISH FA CUP

2008	Rangers v Queen of the South	3-2

HOMECOMING SCOTTISH CUP

2009	Rangers v Falkirk	1-0

ACTIVE NATION SCOTTISH CUP

2010	Dundee U v Ross Co	3-0

SCOTTISH FA CUP

2011	Celtic v Motherwell	3-0

WILLIAM HILL SCOTTISH CUP

2012	Hearts v Hibernian	5-1
2013	Celtic v Hibernian	3-0
2014	St Johnstone v Dundee U	2-0
2015	Inverness CT v Falkirk	2-1
2016	Hibernian v Rangers	3-2
2017	Celtic v Aberdeen	2-1
2018	Celtic v Motherwell	2-0

After extra time.

SCOTTISH CUP WINS

Celtic 38, Rangers 33, Queen's Park 10, Hearts 8, Aberdeen 7, Clyde 3, Hibernian 3, Kilmarnock 3, St Mirren 3, Vale of Leven 3, Dundee U 2, Dunfermline Ath 2, Falkirk 2, Motherwell 2, Renton 2, Third Lanark 2, Airdrieonians 1, Dumbarton 1, Dundee 1, East Fife 1, Inverness CT 1, Morton 1, Partick Thistle 1, St Bernard's 1, St Johnstone 1.

APPEARANCES IN FINAL

Celtic 56, Rangers 51, Aberdeen 16, Hearts 14, Hibernian 14, Queen's Park 12, Dundee U 10, Kilmarnock 8, Motherwell 8, Vale of Leven 7, Clyde 6, Dumbarton 6, St Mirren 6, Third Lanark 6, Dundee 5, Dunfermline Ath 5, Falkirk 5, Renton 5, Airdrieonians 4, East Fife 3, Hamilton A 2, Morton 2, Partick Thistle 2, Albion R 1, Cambuslang 1, Clydesdale 1, Gretna 1, Inverness CT 1, Queen of the South 1, Raith R 1, Ross Co 1, St Bernard's 1, St Johnstone 1, Thornliebank 1.

WILLIAM HILL SCOTTISH FA CUP 2017–18

■ *Denotes player sent off.*

FIRST PRELIMINARY ROUND

Burntisland Shipyard v Colville Park	0-7
Glenafton Ath v Newton Stewart	6-0
Kelty Hearts v Lothian Thistle	0-1

SECOND PRELIMINARY ROUND

Banks O'Dee v Linlithgow Rose	2-1
Colville Park v Preston Ath	5-0
Glasgow University v Threave R	1-1
Glenafton Ath v Golspie Sutherland	6-1
Lothian Thistle v Coldstream	4-0
St Cuthbert W v Girvan	3-5

SECOND PRELIMINARY ROUND REPLAY

Threave R v Glasgow University	2-1

FIRST ROUND

Spartans v Vale Of Leithen	3-0
Banks O'Dee v Huntly	4-0
Brora Rangers v Girvan	5-0
Civil Service Strollers v Strathspey Thistle	2-1
Clachnacuddin v Fort William	8-0
Colville Park v Cumbernauld Colts	2-1
Deveronvale v Hawick Royal Albert	3-1
Edinburgh University v Lossiemouth	2-1
Edusport Academy v Rothes	1-1
Formartine U v Turriff U	2-1
Fraserburgh v Forres Mechanics	2-1
Gala Fairydean v Keith	0-2
Glenafton Ath v Threave R	4-0
Lothian Thistle v Inverurie Loco Works	3-2
Nairn Co v Whitehill Welfare	1-0
Selkirk v Gretna 2008	4-0
Wick Academy v Stirling University	2-2
BSC Glasgow v Dalbeattie Star	1-0

FIRST ROUND REPLAYS

Rothes v Edusport Academy	1-3
Stirling University v Wick Academy	1-0

SECOND ROUND

Edinburgh C v Stenhousemuir	0-1
Banks O'Dee v Selkirk	2-0
Berwick R v Annan Ath	1-0
Buckie Thistle v BSC Glasgow	6-2
Civil Service Strollers v Brora Rangers	0-5
Cowdenbeath v East Kilbride	0-1
Deveronvale v Glenafton Ath	0-2
Edinburgh University v Fraserburgh	0-2
Elgin C v Edusport Academy	3-1
Formartine U v East Stirling	4-0
Keith v Clyde	0-3
Montrose v Stirling University	4-1
Nairn Co v Cove Rangers	1-2
Peterhead v Colville Park	9-0
Spartans v Clachnacuddin	5-0
Stirling Alb v Lothian Thistle	3-5

THIRD ROUND

Saturday, 18 November 2017

Airdrieonians (1) 2 *(McGregor 33, Hastie 49)*
Cove Rangers (1) 3 *(Milne 36, 89, Ross 86)*   439
Airdrieonians: (442) Mason; McIntosh, McGregor, Cairns (Brown A 78), MacDonald; Stewart, Fry, Conroy, Hastie; Russell (Allan 82), Furtado.
Cove Rangers: (4411) McKenzie; Redford, Ross, Watson, Milne; Burnett (Smith 82), Strachan, Campbell, Scully (Stott 73); Masson; Megginson.
Referee: Steven Reid.

Arbroath (2) 3 *(Hamilton 16, McIntosh 36, 70)*
Berwick R (0) 0   536
Arbroath: (343) Hutton; Little, O'Brien (McIntosh 34), Hamilton; Martin, Yule, Whatley, Kader (Gold 69); Denholm, Linn, McCord (Prunty 75).
Berwick R: (343) McCrorie; Fleming, Fairbairn (McKinlay 81), Scullion; Donaldson, McDonald, Stewart, Phillips; Thomson (Murrell 60), Lavery (Irving 71), McKenna.
Referee: Stephen Finnie.

Banks O'Dee (2) 2 *(Watt 9 (pen), 26 (pen))*
Ayr U (4) 6 *(Shankland 1, 37, McDaid 43, 45,*   *Moore 63, 66)*   469
Banks O'Dee: (4141) Shearer; Allan, McCall, Robertson, Whyte (Taylor 45); Henderson, Phillipson, Smith, Hall (Murray 67); Watt.
Ayr U: (433) Hart; Ferguson, Reid, Rose, Boyle (McDaid 36); Geggan (McGuffie 65), Docherty (McCowan 75), Crawford; Moffat, Moore, Shankland.
Referee: Craig Napier.

Buckie Thistle (2) 2 *(Mcloud 3, 43)*
Brechin C (1) 3 *(Sinclair 22, Layne 59, 86)*   295
Buckie Thistle: (442) Bell; Skinner (Milne 88), Anderson, MacKinnon, Carroll; Murray, McLean, Cheyne (Munro 68), Taylor; Mcloud, Ross S (Dorrat 76).
Brechin C: (352) Smith G; Crighton, Fusco, Smith E; McLean, Watt, Graham, Dale, Dyer; Orsi, Sinclair (Layne 54).
Referee: Grant Irvine.

Clyde (0) 0
East Fife (1) 2 *(Smith 32, Page 67)*   527
Clyde: (442) Currie; Home, Breslin (Wright 68), McNiff■, Stewart; Duffie, Nicoll (Ramsay 75), Cuddihy, Lowdon; Gormley (Osadolor 67), Goodwillie.
East Fife: (4231) Goodfellow; Dunsmore, Kane, Page, Wilson; Wilkie (Reilly 82), Docherty; Lamont (Watson 68), Millar, Smith (Mutch 75); Duggan.
Referee: David Munro.

Dumbarton (1) 1 *(Carswell 24)*
Elgin C (0) 0   491
Dumbarton: (442) Gallacher; Wardrop, Barr, Dowie, Hill; Gallagher C (Morrison 66), Hutton, Carswell, Walsh; Stewart (Nade 88), Roy (Wilson D 75).
Elgin C: (442) Waters; Dodd (Ferguson 65), McHardy, Eadie, Allan; McGovern, Bronsky, Reilly, Cameron; Sutherland (Reid 80), McLeish.
Referee: Colin Steven.

East Kilbride (1) 3 *(McNeil 6, 63, Howie 90)*
Albion R (1) 4 *(Howie 23 (og), Fisher 47, Vitoria 54,*   *Trouten 61)*   300
East Kilbride: (4231) Kean (McGinley 52); Stevenson, Howie, Proctor, Russell; Gibbons, McBride (Graham 65); Winter, Andersen (Wallace 64), Strachan; McNeil.
Albion R: (433) Bowman; McLaughlin, Reid, Perry, McLeish; Fisher, Holmes, Davidson; Trouten (Shields 76), Vitoria (Watters 90), Higgins (McMullin 79).
Referee: David Dickinson.

Formartine United (1) 1 *(Crawford 15)*
Forfar Ath (0) 0 244

Formartine United: (433) Sim; Crawford, Anderson S, Henry, MacPhee; Rodger, Lawson, Mackintosh; Burnett (Dingwall 90), Wood, Barbour.
Forfar Ath: (4411) McCallum; Bain, Whyte, Travis, Kennedy (Cregg 72); Aitken, Malone, Easton, Lochhead (Peters 58); Milne (See 76); Cox.
Referee: Mike Roncone.

Livingston (1) 2 *(Mackin 20, 61)*
Glenafton Ath (0) 0 735

Livingston: (352) Maley; Gallagher, Halkett, Lithgow; Mullin (Knox 75), Pitman, Byrne, Jacobs, Longridge (Cadden 61); Mackin (Henderson 86), Carrick.
Glenafton Ath: (433) McGarrity; McAusland, Menzies, McChesney, Cairns; Park (Moore 30), McKernon, Gray (Lynass 74); Dallas, Andrew, McCann (Borris 68).
Referee: Alan Newlands.

Lothian Thistle (0) 1 *(Wringe 47)*
St Mirren (7) 7 *(Morgan 4, Reilly 8, 32, 36, 42, Baird 17, Smith C 24)* 1322

Lothian Thistle: (3412) Swain; Sherlock, Munro, Crawford; Moore (Hare 57), Muir, Brown, O'Donnell (Hutchinson 70); Swanson (Nhamburo 73); Wringe, Devlin.
St Mirren: (4231) Samson; MacPherson, Baird, Davis, Demetriou; McGinn, McShane (Hilson 57); Morgan (Sutton 71), Smith C, Magennis; Reilly (Ross C Stewart 67).
Referee: David Lowe.

Montrose (0) 0
Queen of the South (0) 0 512

Montrose: (3142) Fleming; Allan, Campbell I, Dillon; Fotheringham (Watson 69); Ballantyne, Redman, Callaghan, Steeves; McLaren (Templeman 68), Johnston (Hay 90).
Queen of the South: (442) Martin; Rooney, Brownlie, Fordyce, Marshall; Stirling (Dykes 58), Jacobs, Rankin, McFadden (Murray 68); Lyle (Fergusson 86), Dobbie.
Referee: John McKendrick.

Peterhead (0) 3 *(Jordon Brown 55, McAllister 57, 85)*
Raith R (0) 0 671

Peterhead: (442) Fleming; Jason Brown, McCracken, Robertson, McIlduff; Leitch, Gibson, Ferry (Jordon Brown 31), Stevenson (Smith 82); McAllister (Cairney 88), McLean.
Raith R: (433) Smith; Watson, Murray, McKay, Thomson; Robertson, Matthews, Herron; Spence (Osei-Opoku 70), Court, Buchanan.
Referee: Mat Northcroft.

Queen's Park (0) 1 *(Ashcroft 65 (og))*
Dunfermline Ath (0) 4 *(Clark 48, Talbot 59, Ryan 78, McManus 89)* 1179

Queen's Park: (4231) White; Millen, Cummins, McGhee, Gibson; McVey, Fotheringham; Duff, Docherty D (Leitch 67), Galt; MacLennan (Mortimer 67).
Dunfermline Ath: (442) Murdoch; Williamson, Ashcroft, Morris, Talbot; Higginbotham, Wedderburn (Splaine 65), Shiels (Martin 77); Cardle; McManus, Clark (Ryan 71).
Referee: Steven McLean.

Spartans (1) 1 *(Dishington 17)*
Fraserburgh (0) 2 *(Campbell 47 (pen), Hay 89)* 335

Spartans: (4231) Stobie; Nixon, Tolmie, Thomson, Stevenson; Herd, McFarland; Dishington, Greenhill (Atkinson 76), Brown; Allum.
Fraserburgh: (4132) Tait; Davidson, Christie, Hay, Cowie R; Cowie D; Rae (Combe 46), Young, Beagrie, West (Buchan 84), Campbell.
Referee: Lloyd Wilson.

Stenhousemuir (1) 1 *(Paterson 27)*
Alloa Ath (0) 2 *(Malcolm 50, 67)* 400

Stenhousemuir: (442) Smith; Meechan (Marsh 84), Dunlop M, Dunlop R, Donaldson; Ferns, Ferry, Paton, Paterson (Scott 75); Longworth (McMenamin 84), McGuigan.
Alloa Ath: (442) Parry; Robertson, Graham, Taggart, Crane; Cawley, Fleming (Cook 74), Hetherington, Flannigan; Malcolm, Crossan (Renton 74).
Referee: Kevin Clancy.

Stranraer (0) 0
Brora Rangers (0) 1 *(Mackay 90)* 440

Stranraer: (442) Belford; Hamill, Barron, Neill, Dick; Woods (Turner 65), Robertson, Bell, Anderson (Okoh 81); Wallace R, Thomson.
Brora Rangers: (442) Malin; Ross, Duff, Williamson, Macdonald; Graham (John Pickles 79), Maclean, Morrison (Brindle 69), Nicolson; Sutherland (MacLeod 77), Mackay.
Referee: Barry Cook.

THIRD ROUND REPLAY
Tuesday, 21 November 2017
Queen of the South (1) 2 *(Dobbie 24, Lyle 67)*
Montrose (1) 1 *(Webster 43)* 794

Queen of the South: (442) Martin; Rooney, Fordyce, Brownlie, Marshall; Murray (McFadden 65), Jacobs, Rankin, Dykes; Lyle (Tapping 79), Dobbie.
Montrose: (442) Fleming; Ballantyne, Campbell I, Dillon, Fotheringham (Callaghan 55); Webster, Allan, Masson, Steeves; Fraser (Templeman 73), Hay (Johnston 66).
Referee: John McKendrick.

FOURTH ROUND
Saturday, 20 January 2018
Aberdeen (3) 4 *(Rooney 8 (pen), Christie 18, 33, Mackay-Steven 47)*
St Mirren (1) 1 *(Reilly 25)* 9848

Aberdeen: (4231) Lewis; Logan, O'Connor, Reynolds (Harvie 84), Considine; Shinnie, McLean; Stewart (May 79), Christie, Mackay-Steven (McGinn 66); Rooney.
St Mirren: (4231) Samson; Smith L, Baird, Davis, Demetriou; McGinn, McShane (Flynn 56); Magennis, Smith C (Hill 76), Morgan; Reilly (Mullen 65).
Referee: Don Robertson.

Alloa Ath (0) 0
Dundee U (1) 2 *(Durnan 44, Lyng 62)* 1615

Alloa Ath: (4231) Parry; Taggart, Graham, McCart, Crane; Fleming (Robertson 68), Hetherington; Cawley, Kirkpatrick, Flannigan; Renton (Malcolm 71).
Dundee U: (4231) Lewis; Flood, Quinn, Durnan, Robson; Slater (Murdoch 83), Stanton; Lyng, McDonald, King (Mason 86); Mikkelsen (Kadded 79).
Referee: Craig Charleston.

Ayr U (1) 4 *(McDaid 9, 83, Shankland 58, Moore 90)*
Arbroath (0) 1 *(McCord 79)* 1151

Ayr U: (442) Ruddy; Ferguson, Reid, Rose, Boyle; McDaid, Adams, Moffat, Forrest (McGuffie 90); Shankland, Moore (Murphy 90).
Arbroath: (352) Hutton; Little, O'Brien, Hamilton; Linn (McCord 65), Yule (Gold 65), Martin, Whatley, Denholm; Swankie, McIntosh (Kader 65).
Referee: Mike Roncone.

Celtic (2) 5 *(Forrest 2, Sinclair 11, Ntcham 49, Boyata 56, Edouard 86)*
Brechin C (0) 0 24,879

Celtic: (4231) Gordon; Lustig, Ajer, Boyata (Bitton 61), Tierney; Brown (Eboue 61), Ntcham; Forrest, McGregor, Sinclair (Johnston 69); Edouard.
Brechin C: (451) Smith G; Lynas, McLean, Crighton, Spark; Orsi (Fusco 80), Smith E, Dale, Sinclair (Watt 67), Graham; Jackson (Layne 61).
Referee: Steven McLean.

Dundee (0) 2 *(Moussa 47, O'Hara 64)*
Inverness CT (1) 2 *(Doran 16, Oakley 87)*　　3507
Dundee: (4231) Parish; Kerr, Meekings, O'Dea, Aurtenetxe; McGowan (Wolters 85), Kamara; O'Hara, Leitch-Smith, Allan (El Bakhtaoui 61); Moussa.
Inverness CT: (442) Ridgers; McKay, Warren, Donaldson, Calder; Doran, Vigurs, Trafford (Polworth 58), Chalmers; Oakley, Bell (Baird 81).
Referee: Stephen Finnie.

Dunfermline Ath (0) 1 *(McManus 57)*
Greenock Morton (1) 2 *(Oliver 24, Quitongo 85)*　　2573
Dunfermline Ath: (442) Robinson; Williamson, Morris, Mvoto, Talbot; Paton, Shiels (Higginbotham 67), Wedderburn, Cardle (Craigen 67); McManus, Clark.
Greenock Morton: (352) Gaston; O'Ware, Gasparotto, Iredale; Doyle, Murdoch, Tidser, Harkins, Tiffoney (Russell 90); Oliver (McHugh 90), Ross (Quitongo 66).
Referee: Alan Muir.

East Fife (0) 0
Brora Rangers (1) 1 *(Williamson 12)*　　685
East Fife: (4231) Goodfellow; Dunsmore, Kane, Page, Linton; Millar (Thomson 46), Slattery; Lamont (Wilson 81), Wilkie, Smith; Duggan.
Brora Rangers: (442) Malin; John Pickles, Duff, Williamson (Ross 82), Macdonald; Graham, Maclean, Morrison, Nicolson; Mackay (James Pickles 76), Sutherland (Brindle 83).
Referee: David Munro.

Kilmarnock (0) 1 *(Erwin 88 (pen))*
Ross Co (0) 0　　3595
Kilmarnock: (433) MacDonald; O'Donnell, Boyd S (Findlay 46), Broadfoot, Taylor; Power, Dicker, McKenzie; Brophy (Erwin 72), Boyd K (Kiltie 73), Jones.
Ross Co: (433) McCarey; Naismith, Davies, Routis, van der Weg; Draper, O'Brien, Lindsay (Chow■ 9); Gardyne (Eagles 76), Effiong (Schalk 86), McKay.
Referee: Bobby Madden.

Motherwell (2) 2 *(McMann 4 (og), Tanner 35 (pen))*
Hamilton A (0) 0　　4725
Motherwell: (532) Carson; Tait, Kipre, Aldred (Hammell 37), Dunne, Rose; Tanner, McHugh, Campbell; Ciftci (Bigirimana 66), Main (Fisher 78).
Hamilton A: (3142) Woods; Gogic, Tomas, McMann; Donati (Redmond 46); Lyon, Ferguson (Cunningham 77), MacKinnon, Imrie; Bingham (Hughes 80), Templeton.
Referee: Craig Thomson.

Queen of the South (0) 1 *(Fergusson 55)*
Partick Thistle (1) 2 *(Sammon 42, 81)*　　2338
Queen of the South: (442) Martin; Rooney, Fordyce (Cameron 61), Brownlie, Mercer; Dykes, Thomson, Rankin, Beerman (Murray 69); Fergusson (Stirling 82), Dobbie.
Partick Thistle: (4231) Cerny; McGinn, Keown, Osman, Booth; Barton, Erskine (McCarthy 84); Edwards, Spittal, Lawless (Doolan 72); Sammon.
Referee: William Collum.

Sunday, 21 January 2018

Hearts (0) 1 *(Cowie 87)*
Hibernian (0) 0　　18,709
Hearts: (343) McLaughlin; Souttar, Hughes, Berra; Randall, Djoum, Cochrane (Smith 90), Mitchell; Naismith, Goncalves (Moore 88), Milinkovic (Cowie 56).
Hibernian: (4141) Marciano; Ambrose, McGregor, Hanlon, Stevenson; Bartley (Murray S 77); Slivka (Barker 59), McGeouch, McGinn, Boyle; Shaw.
Referee: Kevin Clancy.

Tuesday, 23 January 2018

Livingston (0) 0
Falkirk (0) 1 *(Tumility 90)*　　1237
Livingston: (352) Alexander; Halkett, Buchanan, Lithgow; McMillan (Mullin 61), Pitman, Gallagher, Byrne, Longridge; Boyd (Miller 66), Robinson (Hardie 75).

Falkirk: (352) Thomson; Muirhead, Grant, McGhee; Tumility, Taiwo (McKee 81), Sibbald, Kidd (Blair 74), Robson; Longridge, Nelson (Jakubiak 64).
Referee: Alan Newlands.

Peterhead (1) 2 *(Jason Brown 31, Robertson 83)*
Dumbarton (1) 3 *(Gallagher C 12, 53, Russell 56)*　　691
Peterhead: (4231) Fleming; Jason Brown, McCracken, Robertson, McIlduff; Ferry, Brown S (Riley 57); Stevenson, Gibson, Leitch (Jordon Brown 66); McLean (McAllister 57).
Dumbarton: (4411) Gallacher; Smith, Dowie, Barr, Hill (Froxylias 73); Gallagher C, Carswell, Hutton, Wilson D; Walsh; Russell.
Referee: Gavin Ross.

Monday, 29 January 2018

Albion R (0) 0
St Johnstone (1) 4 *(Kane 3, 57, 70, McClean 51)*　　1130
Albion R: (532) Wright; Fisher, Lightbody, McLaughlin, McMullin, McLeish; Holmes (Gallagher 83), Davidson, Shields; Higgins (Watters 74), Vitoria (Guthrie 74).
St Johnstone: (442) Mannus; Shaughnessy, Kerr, Gordon, Craig; Alston (Comrie 69), Davidson (McCann 71), Paton, McClean; Johnstone, Kane (Wotherspoon 83).
Referee: Mat Northcroft.

Tuesday, 30 January 2018

Formartine United (0) 0
Cove Rangers (1) 2 *(Stott 32, Megginson 68)*　　776
Formartine United: (433) MacDonald; Crawford, McKeown, Anderson J (Michie 79), MacPhee; Rodger, Lawson (Gethins 74), Mackintosh; Burnett (Dingwall 69), Wood, Barbour.
Cove Rangers: (4231) McKenzie; Ross, Kelly, Watson, Redford; Campbell, Milne; Masson (McManus 74), Strachan, Stott (Scully 89); Megginson (Gray 86).
Referee: Gavin Duncan.

Wednesday, 31 January 2018

Fraserburgh (0) 0
Rangers (1) 3 *(Windass 15 (pen), 55, 67)*　　1865
Fraserburgh: (4141) Tait; Dickson, Hay, Cowie D, Cowie R; Christie (Campbell 68); Davidson, Young, Beagrie, West (Rae 69); Harris (Johnston■ 83).
Rangers: (41212) Alnwick; Hodson, Bates, Fabio Cardoso, John; Holt; Kranjcar, Halliday; Candeias (Murphy 78); Cummings (Dodoo 71), Windass (Herrera 71).
Referee: Greg Aitken.

FOURTH ROUND REPLAY

Tuesday, 30 January 2018

Inverness CT (0) 0
Dundee (0) 1 *(Allan 47)*　　1746
Inverness CT: (442) Ridgers; McKay, Warren, Donaldson, Calder (Mackay 83); Doran (Baird 67), Polworth, Vigurs, Chalmers; Oakley, Bell (Mulraney 67).
Dundee: (442) Parish; Kerr, Waddell, Hendry, Holt; Allan, O'Hara, Kamara, El Bakhtaoui (Spence 46); Leitch-Smith, Moussa (Deacon 84).
Referee: Stephen Finnie.

FIFTH ROUND

Saturday, 10 February 2018

Celtic (2) 3 *(Forrest 3, 10, 54)*
Partick Thistle (1) 2 *(Doolan 20, Sammon 84)*　　24,191
Celtic: (4231) De Vries; Lustig, Ajer, Simunovic, Tierney; Brown, Ntcham; Forrest (Eboue 87), Musonda (McGregor 65), Sinclair (Edouard 79); Dembele.
Partick Thistle: (4231) Cerny; McGinn, Devine, Cargill, Booth; Woods (McCarthy 79), Barton (Osman 57); Spittal, Edwards, Erskine; Doolan (Sammon 60).
Referee: Steven McLean.

Cove Rangers (1) 1 *(Megginson 3)*
Falkirk (1) 3 *(Jakubiak 2, 48, Sibbald 46)*　　1687
Cove Rangers: (4231) McKenzie; Ross, Watson, Kelly, Redford (Scully 75); Strachan, Milne; Masson, Campbell, Stott (Park 81); Megginson.

Falkirk: (3412) Hazard; Muirhead, Watson, McGhee; Tumility, Kidd, Robson (Taiwo 63), Sibbald (McKee 76); Longridge (Nelson 81); Jakubiak, Loy.
Referee: Alan Muir.

Dundee (0) 0
Motherwell (1) 2 *(Tanner 30, Holt 56 (og))*   4663
Dundee: (352) Parish; Kusunga, Aurtenetxe, O'Dea; Kerr, McGowan (Lambert 80), Kamara, O'Hara, Holt (Deacon 66); Moussa, Leitch-Smith.
Motherwell: (352) Carson; Kipre, Aldred, Dunne; Cadden, McHugh (Turnbull 90), Tait, Tanner (Bigirimana 70), Rose; Ciftci (Petravicius 82), Main.
Referee: Bobby Madden.

Greenock Morton (1) 3 *(Ross 12, Iredale 49, McHugh 80)*
Dumbarton (0) 0   1746
Greenock Morton: (4411) Gaston; Doyle, Gasparotto, O'Ware, Iredale; Tidser, Murdoch, Harkins (McHugh 70), Ross (Langan 87); Tiffoney (Russell 84); Oliver.
Dumbarton: (3412) Gallacher; Barr, Dowie, Wilson A; Smith, Carswell, Hutton, Walsh; Froxylias (Nade 65); Nisbet, Russell (Handling 71).
Referee: Craig Thomson.

Hearts (1) 3 *(Lafferty 7, 58, Mitchell 54)*
St Johnstone (0) 0   12,393
Hearts: (352) McLaughlin; Souttar, Hughes, Berra; Smith, Djoum, Adao (Buaben 60), Callachan, Mitchell (Randall 77); McDonald, Lafferty (Henderson 84).
St Johnstone: (541) Mannus; Foster, Shaughnessy, Anderson, Kerr, Tanser; Davidson, Millar (Johnstone 26), Willock (Alston 61); Wotherspoon; Kane.
Referee: Kevin Clancy.

Kilmarnock (1) 4 *(Tshibola 42, Boyd K 58, Brophy 76, O'Donnell 82)*
Brora Rangers (0) 0   4278
Kilmarnock: (442) Fasan; O'Donnell, Broadfoot, Boyd S, Findlay; Tshibola, Dicker, Mulumbu (Brophy 65), Jones; Kiltie (Frizzell 78), Boyd K (Erwin 75).
Brora Rangers: (4411) Malin; John Pickles, Duff, Williamson, Macdonald; Maclean, Morrison, Nicolson (Brindle 69), Mackay (James Pickles 69); Graham; Sutherland (MacLeod 78).
Referee: Euan Anderson.

Sunday, 11 February 2018

Aberdeen (3) 4 *(Rooney 20, Mackay-Steven 27, 55, McLean 35)*
Dundee U (1) 2 *(Stanton 34, McMullan 70)*   11,611
Aberdeen: (4231) Woodman; Logan, O'Connor, McKenna, Considine; Shinnie, McLean; McGinn, Christie, Mackay-Steven (Ball 82); Rooney (Maynard 90).
Dundee U: (4231) Lewis; Slater (McMullan 46), Murdoch, Durnan, Robson; Flood, Gillespie; King, Stanton, Lyng (McDonald 71); Smith (Mikkelsen 76).
Referee: William Collum.

Ayr U (1) 1 *(Forrest 11)*
Rangers (1) 6 *(Morelos 31, 72, Cummings 66, Windass 69, 81, Murphy 88)*   9346
Ayr U: (442) Ruddy; Geggan (Faulds 83), Rose, Reid, Boyle; McDaid, Moffat, Adams, Forrest (McGuffie 75); Moore (Ferguson 70), Shankland.
Rangers: (442) Foderingham; Tavernier, Martin, Bates, John; Murphy, Docherty, Goss, Windass (Halliday 84); Cummings (Herrera 76), Morelos (Miller 76).
Referee: Nick Walsh.

QUARTER-FINALS
Saturday, 3 March 2018
Aberdeen (1) 1 *(Shinnie 9)*
Kilmarnock (0) 1 *(Boyd K 68 (pen))*   8739
Aberdeen: (4231) Woodman; Logan, Arnason, McKenna, Shinnie; O'Connor, McLean; McGinn, May (Mackay-Steven 79), Christie (Nwakali 87); Rooney.

Kilmarnock: (4411) MacDonald; O'Donnell, Broadfoot, Findlay, Taylor; McKenzie (Burke 64), Dicker, Power, Jones; Brophy (Erwin 56); Boyd K (Kiltie 83).
Referee: Steven McLean.

Celtic (0) 3 *(Dembele 62, 71 (pen), Edouard 90)*
Greenock Morton (0) 0   18,255
Celtic: (4231) De Vries; Ajer, Compper (McGregor 83), Simunovic, Tierney; Brown, Ntcham; Forrest, Rogic (Musonda 68), Sinclair (Edouard 46); Dembele.
Greenock Morton: (451) Gaston; Doyle, O'Ware, Lamie, Russell; Ross (Iredale 87), Harkins, Murdoch, Tidser (McHugh 78), Tiffoney; Oliver.
Referee: John Beaton.

Sunday, 4 March 2018
Motherwell (1) 2 *(Main 7, McHugh 86)*
Hearts (0) 1 *(Lafferty 51 (pen))*   7564
Motherwell: (352) Carson; Kipre, Aldred, Dunne; Cadden, Campbell, McHugh, Tanner (Rose 90), Tait (Frear 78); Ciftci (Bowman 55), Main.
Hearts: (3511) McLaughlin; Souttar, Hughes (Amankwaa 88), Berra; Randall (Smith 90), Callachan (Milinkovic 46), Adao, Cochrane, Godinho; Naismith; Lafferty.
Referee: Andrew Dallas.

Rangers (3) 4 *(Cummings 16, 21, 75, Muirhead 44 (og))*
Falkirk (1) 1 *(Muirhead 20)*   33,968
Rangers: (4231) Alnwick; Tavernier, Bates, Bruno Alves, Halliday; Docherty, Goss (Holt 68); Candeias (Miller 80), Cummings, Windass (Dodoo 80); Morelos.
Falkirk: (352) Thomson; Muirhead, Grant (Harris 71), McGhee; Tumility, Longridge, Taiwo (McKee 58), Sibbald, Robson; Jakubiak, Nelson.
Referee: Craig Thomson.

QUARTER-FINAL REPLAY
Tuesday, 13 March 2018
Kilmarnock (0) 1 *(O'Donnell 96)*
Aberdeen (0) 1 *(McLean 103 (pen))*   8998
Kilmarnock: (4231) MacDonald; O'Donnell, Broadfoot, Findlay, Taylor; Dicker, Power (Tshibola 106); McKenzie (Brophy 70), Mulumbu (Kiltie 118); Jones; Boyd K (Erwin 91).
Aberdeen: (4231) Woodman; Logan, O'Connor, McKenna, Considine; McLean, Shinnie; McGinn, Christie (Nwakali 88), Mackay-Steven (May 65); Rooney (Stewart 77).
aet; Aberdeen won 3-2 on penalties.
Referee: Steven McLean.

SEMI-FINALS (at Hampden Park)
Saturday, 14 April 2018
Motherwell (2) 3 *(Main 20, 66, Bowman 22)*
Aberdeen (0) 0   18,470
Motherwell: (3142) Carson; Kipre, Aldred, Dunne; Rose; Tait, Cadden, Grimshaw (MacLean 88), Campbell; Main (Newell 87), Bowman (Ciftci 79).
Aberdeen: (4231) Lewis; Ball (McGinn 62), Arnason, McKenna, Considine; O'Connor, Nwakali (Mackay-Steven 44); Stewart, Christie, May; Rooney (Cosgrove 79).
Referee: Kevin Clancy.

Sunday, 15 April 2018
Celtic (2) 4 *(Rogic 22, McGregor 38, Dembele 52 (pen), Ntcham 78 (pen))*
Rangers (0) 0   49,729
Celtic: (4231) Gordon; Lustig, Ajer, Boyata, Tierney; Brown, Ntcham; Forrest (Roberts 73), Rogic (Sinclair 60), McGregor; Dembele (Griffiths 79).
Rangers: (4231) Foderingham; Tavernier, McCrorie■, Martin, John; Docherty, Halliday (Windass 41); Candeias (Bruno Alves 53), Dorrans (Holt 73), Murphy; Morelos.
Referee: Bobby Madden.

WILLIAM HILL SCOTTISH CUP FINAL 2018

Saturday, 19 May 2018

(at Hampden Park, attendance 49,967)

Celtic (2) 2   Motherwell (0) 0

Celtic: (4231) Gordon; Lustig, Boyata, Ajer (Simunovic 76), Tierney; Ntcham, Brown; Forrest (Sinclair 90), Rogic (Armstrong 72), McGregor; Dembele.
Scorers: McGregor 11, Ntcham 25.

Motherwell: (352) Carson; Kipre, Aldred, Dunne; Cadden, Campbell (Frear 78), McHugh (Bigirimana 56), Grimshaw, Tait; Main, Bowman.

Referee: Kevin Clancy.

Motherwell again suffered at the hands of Celtic in the Scottish FA Cup Final on 19 May. Here, Olivier Ntcham scores Celtic's second goal in another 2-0 victory. (Reuters/Jason Cairnduff)

SCOTTISH FOOTBALL PYRAMID 2017–18

PRESS & JOURNAL HIGHLAND LEAGUE

		P	W	D	L	F	A	GD	Pts
1	Cove Rangers	34	29	3	2	127	22	105	90
2	Formartine U	34	26	1	7	124	41	83	79
3	Inverurie Loco Works	34	25	3	6	104	37	67	78
4	Fraserburgh	34	23	4	7	101	38	63	73
5	Forres Mechanics	34	23	4	7	88	45	43	73
6	Brora Rangers	34	20	3	11	87	39	48	63
7	Buckie Thistle	34	15	6	13	80	56	24	51
8	Deveronvale	34	16	3	15	73	76	–3	51
9	Nairn Co	34	16	3	15	61	71	–10	51
10	Rothes	34	15	4	15	77	70	7	49
11	Huntly	34	15	4	15	66	81	–15	49
12	Wick Academy	34	12	10	12	67	54	13	46
13	Clachnacuddin	34	11	8	15	54	69	–15	41
14	Turriff U	34	11	4	19	54	70	–16	37
15	Keith	34	4	4	26	45	104	–59	16
16	Lossiemouth	34	4	3	27	41	125	–84	15
17	Strathspey Thistle	34	4	2	28	26	124	–98	14
18	Fort William	34	0	5	29	31	184	–153	5

FERRARI PACKAGING LOWLAND LEAGUE

		P	W	D	L	F	A	GD	Pts
1	Spartans	30	23	4	3	64	17	47	73
2	East Kilbride	30	22	5	3	76	23	53	71
3	BSC Glasgow	30	20	5	5	71	27	44	65
4	East Stirlingshire	30	19	7	4	67	31	36	64
5	Selkirk	30	15	3	12	63	50	13	48
6	Cumbernauld Colts	30	11	8	11	50	51	–1	41
7	Civil Service Strollers	30	11	7	12	47	44	3	40
8	Gretna 2008	30	12	4	14	50	56	–6	40
9	Stirling University	30	11	5	14	45	49	–4	38
10	Edusport Academy	30	9	7	14	46	49	–3	34
11	Edinburgh University	30	9	7	14	40	45	–5	34
12	Whitehill Welfare	30	11	1	18	50	66	–16	34
13	Gala Fairydean R	30	8	7	15	43	63	–20	31
14	Dalbeattie Star	30	7	8	15	46	65	–19	29
15	Vale of Leithen	30	8	5	17	44	76	–32	29
16	Hawick Royal Albert	30	1	3	26	11	108	–97	6

CENTRAL TAXIS EAST OF SCOTLAND LEAGUE

		P	W	D	L	F	A	GD	Pts
1	Kelty Hearts	24	23	0	1	143	12	131	69
2	Lothian Thistle Hutchison Vale	24	22	1	1	97	20	77	67
3	Preston Ath	24	16	3	5	74	36	38	51
4	Leith Ath	24	15	4	5	80	41	39	49
5	Tynecastle	24	13	0	11	79	48	31	39
6	Heriot-Watt University	24	11	6	7	59	53	6	39
7	Peebles R	24	12	2	10	59	73	–14	38
8	Burntisland Shipyard	24	8	1	15	52	69	–17	25
9	Stirling University Res	24	6	6	12	48	73	–25	24
10	Coldstream	24	5	3	16	52	79	–27	18
11	Eyemouth U	24	6	0	18	44	114	–70	18
12	Ormiston	24	3	3	18	17	68	–51	12
13	Tweedmouth Rangers	24	1	1	22	21	139	–118	4

SOUTH OF SCOTLAND FOOTBALL LEAGUE

		P	W	D	L	F	A	GD	Pts
1	Threave R	28	24	1	3	94	21	73	73
2	Mid-Annandale	28	21	3	4	107	42	65	66
3	Lochar Thistle	28	20	3	5	89	40	49	63
4	St Cuthbert W	28	17	3	8	87	57	30	54
5	Abbey Vale	28	15	4	9	78	50	28	49
6	Bonnyton Thistle	28	14	4	10	89	41	48	46
7	Heston R	28	15	1	12	75	71	4	46
8	Stranraer Res	28	12	6	10	90	77	13	42
9	Newton Stewart	28	12	2	14	65	64	1	38
10	Upper Annandale	28	11	4	13	66	74	–8	37
11	Nithsdale W	28	11	3	14	77	81	–4	36
12	Lochmaben	28	10	3	15	61	75	–14	33
13	Annan Ath Res	28	3	1	24	41	139	–98	10
14	Creetown	28	3	2	23	32	97	–65	11
15	Dumfries YMCA	28	2	0	26	26	148	–122	6

Wigtown & Bladnoch – withdrawn.

NORTH CALEDONIAN FOOTBALL LEAGUE

		P	W	D	L	F	A	GD	Pts
1	Orkney	16	13	0	3	82	16	66	39
2	Invergordon	16	12	2	2	48	21	27	38
3	Golspie Sutherland	16	11	2	3	51	23	28	35
4	Thurso	16	9	2	5	38	23	15	29
5	Alness U	16	8	1	7	31	55	–24	25
6	St Duthus	16	4	2	10	28	28	0	14
7	Inverness Ath	16	4	1	11	31	56	–25	13
8	Halkirk U	16	4	1	11	23	54	–31	13
9	Bunillidh Thistle	16	1	1	14	17	73	–56	4

WELSH FOOTBALL 2017–18

THE WELSH PREMIER LEAGUE 2017–18

			Home					Away					Total						
		P	W	D	L	F	A	W	D	L	F	A	W	D	L	F	A	GD	Pts
1	The New Saints	32	13	1	2	49	15	10	4	2	34	17	23	5	4	83	32	51	74
2	Bangor C*	32	11	0	5	28	13	8	3	5	21	19	19	3	10	49	32	17	60
3	Connah's Quay Nomads	32	10	4	2	30	12	7	2	7	16	17	17	6	9	46	29	17	57
4	Bala T	32	8	2	6	18	20	7	2	7	19	28	15	4	13	37	48	–11	49
5	Cefn Druids	32	6	5	5	20	18	6	3	7	18	23	12	8	12	38	41	–3	44
6	Cardiff Met University	32	7	5	4	26	17	5	2	9	20	24	12	7	13	46	41	5	43
7	Barry T	32	9	3	4	26	12	7	2	7	13	19	16	5	11	39	31	8	53
8	Newtown	32	8	1	7	33	22	4	3	9	19	33	12	4	16	52	55	–3	40
9	Aberystwyth	32	6	3	7	30	24	4	4	8	17	32	10	7	15	47	56	–9	37
10	Llandudno	32	6	5	5	24	21	3	4	9	15	23	9	9	14	39	44	–5	36
11	Carmarthen	32	4	3	9	15	27	4	2	10	20	35	8	5	19	35	62	–27	29
12	Prestatyn T	32	3	0	10	12	26	1	4	11	15	41	4	7	21	27	67	–40	19

*Top 6 teams split after 22 games. *Bangor C relegated after failing to receive licence. Carmarthen reprieved.*

PREVIOUS WELSH LEAGUE WINNERS

1993	Cwmbran Town	2000	TNS	2007	TNS	2014	The New Saints
1994	Bangor City	2001	Barry Town	2008	Llanelli	2015	The New Saints
1995	Bangor City	2002	Barry Town	2009	Rhyl	2016	The New Saints
1996	Barry Town	2003	Barry Town	2010	The New Saints	2017	The New Saints
1997	Barry Town	2004	Rhyl	2011	Bangor C	2018	The New Saints
1998	Barry Town	2005	TNS	2012	The New Saints		
1999	Barry Town	2006	TNS	2013	The New Saints		

NATHANIEL CAR SALES WELSH LEAGUE 2017–18

			Home					Away					Total						
		P	W	D	L	F	A	W	D	L	F	A	W	D	L	F	A	GD	Pts
1	Llanelli T	30	11	2	2	41	18	13	1	1	46	15	24	3	3	87	33	54	75
2	Haverfordwest Co	30	9	3	3	33	16	10	0	5	32	21	19	3	8	65	37	28	60
3	Penybont*	30	10	3	2	40	18	8	3	4	24	19	18	6	6	64	37	27	57
4	Cambrian & Clydach	30	10	1	4	34	15	6	2	6	24	24	16	3	10	58	39	19	54
5	Afan Lido	30	9	1	5	38	26	6	3	6	23	22	15	4	11	61	48	13	49
6	Goytre	30	10	1	4	30	27	5	2	8	21	35	15	3	12	51	62	–11	48
7	Goytre U	30	7	1	7	27	34	6	7	2	26	18	13	8	9	53	52	1	47
8	Cwmbran Celtic	30	7	2	6	26	23	7	2	6	41	28	14	4	12	67	51	16	46
9	Undy Ath	30	7	3	5	30	22	6	2	7	32	38	13	5	12	62	60	2	44
10	Taffs Well	30	6	4	5	24	16	5	1	9	28	32	11	5	14	52	48	4	38
11	Briton Ferry Llansawel	30	6	3	6	33	35	4	4	7	25	29	10	7	13	58	64	–6	37
12	CwmammanU	30	4	2	9	18	33	4	4	7	20	26	8	6	16	38	59	–21	30
13	Port Talbot T†	30	3	6	6	25	29	6	5	4	33	24	9	11	10	58	53	5	29
14	Monmouth T	30	5	3	7	27	33	2	1	12	17	40	7	4	19	44	73	–29	25
15	Caerau (Ely)	30	2	1	12	12	39	3	2	10	20	39	5	3	22	32	78	–46	18
16	Ton Pentre	30	0	5	10	14	40	1	2	12	12	42	1	7	22	26	82	–56	10

Penybont deducted 3 pts. †Port Talbot T deducted 9 pts.

HUWS GRAY CYMRU ALLIANCE LEAGUE 2017–18

			Home					Away					Total						
		P	W	D	L	F	A	W	D	L	F	A	W	D	L	F	A	GD	Pts
1	Caernarfon T	28	12	1	1	57	12	7	7	0	41	19	19	8	1	98	31	67	65
2	Denbigh T	28	9	1	4	33	20	10	2	2	36	23	19	3	6	69	43	26	60
3	Airbus UK Broughton	28	11	2	1	36	13	6	1	7	31	29	17	3	8	67	42	25	54
4	Guilsfield	28	7	6	1	26	19	8	2	4	28	19	15	8	5	54	38	16	53
5	Holywell T	28	6	5	3	43	20	8	3	3	32	17	14	8	6	75	37	38	50
6	Rhyl	28	8	3	3	41	25	5	5	4	21	22	13	8	7	62	45	17	47
7	Porthmadog	28	8	3	3	40	17	4	2	7	30	29	12	5	10	70	46	24	44
8	Gresford Ath*	28	8	3	3	30	22	4	3	7	27	35	12	6	10	57	57	0	39
9	Penrhyncoch	28	6	4	4	22	20	4	5	5	23	26	10	9	9	45	46	–1	39
10	Ruthin T	28	6	4	4	34	27	4	1	9	17	22	10	5	13	51	49	2	35
11	Flint Town U†	28	6	2	6	24	20	4	4	6	25	22	10	6	12	49	42	7	30
12	Holyhead Hotspur	28	6	2	6	22	22	3	1	10	18	35	9	3	16	40	57	–17	30
13	Caersws	28	3	1	10	17	34	2	2	10	22	38	5	3	20	39	72	–33	18
14	FC Queens Park	28	2	1	11	18	54	0	2	12	8	56	2	3	23	26	110	–84	9
15	Llandudno Junction	28	0	3	11	12	50	1	1	12	16	65	1	4	23	28	115	–87	7

Gresford Ath deducted 3 pts. †Flint Town U deducted 6 pts.

JD WELSH FA CUP 2017–18

After extra time.

QUALIFYING ROUND 1 – CENTRAL

Abermule v Tywyn Bryncrug	1-0
Borth United v Trewern	5-3
Churchstoke v Welshpool Town	2-3
Kerry v Hay St Marys	2-1
Llansantffraid v Montgomery Town	6-0
Machynlleth v Llandrindod Wells	0-5

QUALIFYING ROUND 1 – NORTH

Barmouth & Dyffryn v Llanfairpwll	1-0
Blaenau Ffestiniog v Llandyrnog United	3-12
Brymbo Victoria v Acton	3-6*
Cemaes Bay v CPD Llannefydd	0-5
CPD Waunfawr v Llanrwst United	4-6*
Dyffryn Nantlle v CPD Llanystumdwy	5-1
FC Penley v Mostyn Dragons	4-4*
FC Penley won 4-3 on penalties.	
Holyhead Town v Gaerwen	2-4
Lex Glyndwr v Greenfield	2-1
Llanberis v Llandudno Albion	2-3
Llanrug United v Pentraeth	4-2*
Mynydd Isa Spartans v Rhosllanerchrugog	1-3
New Brighton Villa v Brymbo	0-2
Penyffordd Lions v Cefn Albion	3-2
Penrhyndeudraeth v Bodedern Athletic	2-3
Penycae v Castell Alun Colts	5-3
Pwllheli v Llangefni Town	3-1
Rhos Aelwyd v Coedpoeth United	1-2
Rhostyllen v Llangollen Town	4-2
Rhydymwyn v Cefn Mawr Rangers	3-2
St Asaph City v Llay Welfare	1-2
Trearddur Bay v CPD Aberffraw	1-3

QUALIFYING ROUND 1 – SOUTH

Aber Valley v Cardiff Corinthians	3-4
Abertillery Bluebirds v Chepstow Town	5-4
AFC Butetown v Aberfan FC	3-2
AFC Rumney Juniors v Ferndale & Dist	4-2
Blaenrhondda v Brecon Corries	3-4
Cardiff Draconians v Canton Liberal	8-1
Carmarthen Stars v CRC Rangers	4-3
Clwb Cymric v Penrhiwfer	0-1
Cwmbran Town v Caerleon	3-1
FC Tredegar v Tredegar Town	3-3*
Tredegar Town won 7-6 on penalties.	
Llangynnwyd Rangers v Porthcawl Town	2-3
Llantwit Fardre v Grange All Stars	1-0
Merthyr Saints v Tiger Bay	6-4
Newcastle Emlyn v Pencoed Athletic	0-2
Newport YMCA v Machen	1-4
Panteg v Newport City	2-0
Penlan FC v Caerau	1-4
Penydarren BGC v Penrhiwceiber Rangers	5-3
Pontlottyn v Bridgend Street	2-6
Pontyclun v Garw SGBC	2-0
Swansea University v Cefn Cribbwr	2-2*
Cefn Cribbwr won 4-1 on penalties.	
Trebanog v Caerphilly Athletic	0-2
Trefelin BGC v Ynysygerwn	1-1*
Ynysygerwn won 3-1 on penalties.	
Treforest v Brecon Northcote	1-3*
Treharris Ath Western v Llanrumney United	7-0
Treharris removed for fielding ineligible player;	
Llanrumney reinstated.	
Trethomas Bluebirds v Ely Rangers	3-4
Villa Dino Christchurch v Neuadd Wen	4-1

QUALIFYING ROUND 2 – CENTRAL

Abermule v Borth United	3-2
Carno v Llandrindod Wells	2-1
Knighton Town v Bow Street	0-2
Llanidloes Town v Barmouth & Dyffryn	3-0
Llanrhaeadr Ym Mochnant v Kerry	3-1
Llansantffraid v Berriew	0-7
Rhayader Town v Brecon Northcote	3-2
Welshpool Town v Aberaeron	3-4

QUALIFYING ROUND 2 – NORTH

Bodedern Athletic v Aberffraw	2-0
Conwy Borough v Amlwch Town	4-1

Corwen v FC Nomads	3-1
FC Penley v Brymbo	3-2
Gaerwen v Pwllheli	6-5
Lex Glyndwr v Hawarden Rangers	1-0
Llandudno Albion v Llanefydd	1-1*
Llandudno won 5-4 on penalties.	
Llanrug United v Llandyrnog United	5-1
Llanuwchllyn v Chirk AAA	0-1
Meliden v Dyffryn Nantlle	3-3*
Meliden won 4-3 on penalties.	
Mochdre Sports v Mynydd Llandegai	3-0
Mold Alex v Acton	5-0
Penmaenmawr Phoenix v Llanrwst United	1-4
Penycae v Llay Welfare	1-3
Rhosllanerchrugog v Penyffordd Lions	2-3
Rhostyllen v Brickfield Rangers	2-7
Rhydymwyn v Buckley Town	0-2
Saltney Town v Coedpoeth United	3-0

QUALIFYING ROUND 2 – SOUTH

Aberdare Town v Dinas Powys	2-1
Abergavenny Town v AFC Porth	7-0
Abertillery Bluebirds v Cardiff Corinthians	1-2
AFC Butetown v STM Sports	3-5
AFC Llwydcoed v Panteg	3-4*
AFC Rumney Juniors v Caerphilly Athletic	1-4
Ammanford v Merthyr Saints	5-2
Brecon Corries v Penydarren BGC	1-3
Bridgend Street v Llanrumney United	7-0
Caerau v Pontyclun	2-6
Cardiff Draconians v Tredegar Town	5-1
Carmarthen Stars v Porthcawl Town	5-4
Cwmbran Town v Aberbargoed Buds	1-7
Llantwit Major v Cefn Cribbwr	2-1
Machen v Ely Rangers	4-0
Pencoed Athletic v Llantwit Fardre	2-0
Penrhiwfer v Pontypridd Town	1-3
Pontardawe Town v Garden Village	3-4
Risca United v Croesyceiliog	1-2*
Villa Dino Christchurch v Caldicot Town	2-5
West End v Ynysygerwn	1-1*
Ynysygerwn won 3-1 on penalties.	

FIRST ROUND

Aberaeron v Llanelli Town	1-6
Aberbargoed Buds v Port Talbot Town	2-0
Aberdare Town v Ammanford	0-0*
Ammanford Town won 3-2 on penalties.	
Abergavenny Town v Panteg	1-3
Abermule v Berriew	0-4
Airbus UK Broughton v Bow Street	3-0
Brickfield Rangers v Chirk AAA	1-0
Bridgend Street v Machen	4-3
Briton Ferry Llansawel v Goytre United	3-1
Buckley Town v Llanidloes Town	2-1
Caerau Ely v Cwmbran Celtic	0-1
Caernarfon Town v Lex Glyndwr	5-1
Caerphilly Athletic v Carmarthen Stars	4-1*
Caersws (walkover) v Prestatyn Town	
Caldicot Town v Goytre	2-3
Cardiff Corinthians v Penydarren BGC	0-3
Cardiff Draconians v Ton Pentre	1-2
Carno v Gresford Athletic	0-4
Conwy Borough v Bodedern Athletic	5-1
Cwmamman United v Rhayader Town	3-1
Denbigh Town v Holyhead Hotspur	4-3*
Flint Town United v Llanfair United	3-0
Gaerwen v Llandudno Junction	1-3
Garden Village v Penrhyncoch	3-4
Guilsfield v Mold Alex	4-0
Haverfordwest County v Croesyceiliog	2-1
Holywell Town v Corwen	3-0
Llandudno Albion v Rhyl	3-2
Llanrhaeadr Ym Mochnant v FC Queens Park	3-0
Llantwit Major v Taffs Well	3-2
Llay Welfare v Llanrug United	1-0
Meliden v Ruthin Town	0-4
Mochdre Sports v FC Penley	1-1*
FC Penley won 5-3 on penalties.	
Monmouth Town v Ynysygerwn	4-1
Penybont v Undy Athletic	1-0*
Pontyclun v Pencoed Athletic	0-0*
Pencoed won 8-7 on penalties.	

Pontypridd Town v Cambrian & Clydach	2-1
Porthmadog v Penyffordd Lions	3-0
Saltney Town v Llanrwst United	6-0
STM Sports v Afan Lido	5-2

SECOND ROUND

Airbus UK Broughton v Saltney Town	4-0
Ammanford v Llantwit Major	1-1*
Ammanford won 3-2 on penalties.	
Brickfield Rangers v Ruthin Town	2-4*
Buckley Town v Llandudno Albion	2-1
Caernarfon Town v Berriew	4-1
Caerphilly Athletic v Penrhyncoch	2-4
Caersws v Llanrhaeadr Ym Mochnant	1-2
Cwmamman United v Bridgend Street	3-0
Cwmbran Celtic v Llanelli Town	2-1
FC Penley v Porthmadog	0-10
Goytre v Briton Ferry Llansawel	2-1
Gresford Athletic v Conwy Borough	5-1
Haverfordwest County v Aberbargoed Buds	2-0
Holywell Town v Guilsfield	2-3
Llandudno Junction v Denbigh Town	3-2*
Llay Welfare v Flint Town United	1-3
Pencoed Athletic v Pontypridd Town	1-3
Penybont v Monmouth Town	2-1
Penydarren BGC v STM Sports	2-1
Ton Pentre v Panteg	1-2

THIRD ROUND

Aberystwyth Town v Bala Town	4-0
Airbus UK Broughton v Goytre	3-2*
Ammanford v Carmarthen Town	2-3
Bangor City v Cwmamman United	4-3
Buckley Town v Flint Town United	0-1
Caernarfon Town v Barry Town United	2-0
Connahs Quay Nomads v Cwmbran Celtic	3-0
Llandudno v Gresford Athletic	4-0
Llandudno Junction v Penydarren BGC	0-4
Llanrhaeadr Ym Mochnant v Cefn Druids	3-2
Newtown v Guilsfield	2-0
Penybont v Cardiff Metropolitan	1-3
Pontypridd Town v Haverfordwest County	3-1
Porthmadog v Panteg	7-2
Prestatyn Town v Ruthin Town	0-3
The New Saints v Penrhyncoch	6-0

FOURTH ROUND

Airbus UK Broughton v Carmarthen Town	1-4
Caernarfon Town v The New Saints	1-3
Cardiff Metropolitan v Aberystwyth Town	0-1
Connahs Quay Nomads v Porthmadog	3-1
Flint Town United v Newtown	2-2*
Newtown won 4-3 on penalties.	
Llandudno v Ruthin Town	4-3*
Llanrhaeadr Ym Mochnant v Bangor City	2-3
Pontypridd Town v Penydarren BGC	1-2

QUARTER-FINALS

Bangor City v Penydarren BGC	7-0
Carmarthen Town v Aberystwyth Town	1-3
Connahs Quay Nomads v The New Saints	2-1
Llandudno v Newtown	0-2

SEMI-FINALS

| Connahs Quay Nomads v Bangor City | 6-1 |
| Newtown v Aberystwyth Town | 1-2 |

JD WELSH FA CUP FINAL 2018

Latham Park, Newtown, Sunday 6 May 2018

Connah's Quay Nomads (3) 4 *(Bakare 23, Wilde 26, 41, Owens 90)*

Aberystwyth (1) 1 *(Wade 45)*　　　　　1455

Connah's Quay Nomads: Danby; Horan, Pearson, Edwards, Smith , Harrison, Owen J, Bakare, Wignall (Woolfe 78), Poole (Hughes 90), Wilde (Owens 73).
Aberystwyth: Mullock; Walker, Wollacott, Allen, Melvin, Young, Owens (Hobson 57), Phillips (Kellaway 78), Jones, Owen, Wade (Sherlock 70).
Referee: Iwan Griffith.

PREVIOUS WELSH CUP WINNERS

1878	Wrexham	1911	Wrexham	1954	Flint Town United	1987	Merthyr Tydfil
1879	Newtown White Star	1912	Cardiff City	1955	Barry Town	1988	Cardiff City
1880	Druids	1913	Swansea Town	1956	Cardiff City	1989	Swansea City
1881	Druids	1914	Wrexham	1957	Wrexham	1990	Hereford United
1882	Druids	1915	Wrexham	1958	Wrexham	1991	Swansea City
1883	Wrexham	1920	Cardiff City	1959	Cardiff City	1992	Cardiff City
1884	Oswestry White Stars	1921	Wrexham	1960	Wrexham	1993	Cardiff City
1885	Druids	1922	Cardiff City	1961	Swansea Town	1994	Barry Town
1886	Druids	1923	Cardiff City	1962	Bangor City	1995	Wrexham
1887	Chirk	1924	Wrexham	1963	Borough United	1996	TNS
1888	Chirk	1925	Wrexham	1964	Cardiff City	1997	Barry Town
1889	Bangor	1926	Ebbw Vale	1965	Cardiff City	1998	Bangor City
1890	Chirk	1927	Cardiff City	1966	Swansea Town	1999	Inter Cable-Tel
1891	Shrewsbury Town	1928	Cardiff City	1967	Cardiff City	2000	Bangor City
1892	Chirk	1929	Connah's Quay	1968	Cardiff City	2001	Barry Town
1893	Wrexham	1930	Cardiff City	1969	Cardiff City	2002	Barry Town
1894	Chirk	1931	Wrexham	1970	Cardiff City	2003	Barry Town
1895	Newtown	1932	Swansea Town	1971	Cardiff City	2004	Rhyl
1896	Bangor	1933	Chester	1972	Wrexham	2005	TNS
1897	Wrexham	1934	Bristol City	1973	Cardiff City	2006	Rhyl
1898	Druids	1935	Tranmere Rovers	1974	Cardiff City	2007	Carmarthen Town
1899	Druids	1936	Crewe Alexandra	1975	Wrexham	2008	Bangor City
1900	Aberystwyth Town	1937	Crewe Alexandra	1976	Cardiff City	2009	Bangor City
1901	Oswestry United	1938	Shrewsbury Town	1977	Shrewsbury Town	2010	Bangor City
1902	Wellington Town	1939	South Liverpool	1978	Wrexham	2011	Llanelli
1903	Wrexham	1940	Wellington Town	1979	Shrewsbury Town	2012	The New Saints
1904	Druids	1947	Chester	1980	Newport County	2013	Prestatyn Town
1905	Wrexham	1948	Lovell's Athletic	1981	Swansea City	2014	The New Saints
1906	Wellington Town	1949	Merthyr Tydfil	1982	Swansea City	2015	The New Saints
1907	Oswestry United	1950	Swansea Town	1983	Swansea City	2016	The New Saints
1908	Chester	1951	Merthyr Tydfil	1984	Shrewsbury Town	2017	Bala Town
1909	Wrexham	1952	Rhyl	1985	Shrewsbury Town	2018	Connah's Quay N
1910	Wrexham	1953	Rhyl	1986	Wrexham		

NATHANIEL MG WELSH LEAGUE CUP 2017–18

*After extra time.

FIRST ROUND

Holywell T v Prestatyn T	5-4*
Afan Lido v Penybont	2-1
Airbus UK Broughton v Cefn Druids	3-2
Bala T v Newtown	0-1
Bangor C v Denbigh T	5-2
Caersws v Aberystwyth T	0-2
Goytre v Cardiff Met	1-2
Haverfordwest Co v Goytre U	2-1
Llandudno v Caernarfon T	0-1
Pontypridd T v Taffs Well	3-0
Porthmadog v Holyhead Hotspur	3-5
Rhyl v Flint Town U	0-1

The semi-finalists from 2016–17, The New Saints, Barry Town U, Connah's Quay Nomads and Carmarthen T received a bye to the second round.

SECOND ROUND

Aberystwyth T v Airbus UK Broughton	1-2
Barry Town U v Afan Lido	4-2
Cardiff Met v Pontypridd T	2-1*
Connah's Quay Nomads v Bangor C	2-0
Flint T U v The New Saints	1-5
Haverfordwest Co v Carmarthen T	0-1*
Holyhead Hotspur v Caernarfon T	0-3
Newtown v Holywell T	2-0

QUARTER-FINALS

Airbus UK Broughton v Connah's Quay Nomads	0-2
Barry Town U v Cardiff Met	0-2
Carmarthen T v Newtown	0-2
The New Saints v Caernarfon	2-0

SEMI-FINALS

Cardiff Met v Newtown	1-0
Connah's Quay Nomads v The New Saints	0-1

2018 FINAL NATHANIEL MG WELSH LEAGUE CUP

Aberystwyth, Saturday 20 January 2018

The New Saints (0) 1 (Mullan 63)

Cardiff Met (0) 0   906

The New Saints: Harrison; Spender, Marriott, Rawlinson, Hudson, Holland, Routledge, Edwards, Mullan, Ruscoe, Evans.
Cardiff Met: Fuller; Rees, McCarthy, Woolridge, Evans, Baker, Lam (Hope 27), Spencer (Howell 75), Edwards J, Barnett (Thomas 66), Edwards C.
Referee: Iwan Griffith.

THE FAW TROPHY 2017–18

*After extra time.

ROUND 3

Abertillery Bluebirds v South Gower	5-1
Buckley Town v Saltney Town	6-0
Cefn Albion v Penmaenmawr Phoenix	8-3
Chirk AAA v Penrhyndeudraeth	5-2
Coedpoeth United v Conwy Borough	2-7
Corwen v Llanefydd	3-0
Cwmcarn Athletic v Hakin United	1-8
Fairfield United v Ynysddu Welfare	0-1
FC Nomads v Prestatyn Sports	3-1
Gaerwen v Greenfield	1-5
Garden Village v Pontlottyn	5-1
Goodwick United v Penlan Social	3-2
Grange Albion v Merlins Bridge	2-1
Knighton Town v Llanrhaeadr	3-1
Lex Glyndwr v Llanrug United	0-3
Llanfair United v Bow Street	2-1
Llangefni Town v Hawarden Rangers	3-1
Llanidloes Town v Llansantffraid	4-1
Llanuwchllyn v Brymbo	2-2*
Brymbo won 4-3 on penalties.	
Meliden v Llanystumdwy	4-5
Mold Alex v Dyffryn Nantlle	2-1
Mynydd Isa Spartans v Pentraeth	6-0
New Brighton Villa v Pwllheli	3-2
Newport City v Caerphilly Athletic	2-3
Penydarren BGC v Ynysygerwn	4-0
Radnor Valley v Berriew	0-2
Ragged School v FC Cwmaman	3-1
Rhos Aelwyd v Llanberis	2-1
Sully Sports v Carmarthen Stars	2-2*
Carmarthen Stars won 4-2 on penalties.	
Treowen Stars v Ton & Gelli BC	2-1
Trewern v Mochdre Sports	1-5
Villa Dino Christchurch v Cadoxton Barry FC	4-3

ROUND 4

Abertillery Bluebirds v Ragged School	2-0
Berriew v Brymbo	0-1*
Buckley Town v FC Nomads	2-1*
Caerphilly Athletic v Hakin United	2-3
Carmarthen Stars v Penydarren BGC	0-5
Chirk AAA v New Brighton Villa	4-0
Conwy Borough v Cefn Albion	2-1
Garden Village v Villa Dino Christchurch	8-0
Grange Albion v Treowen Stars	2-1
Llanfair United v Corwen	3-2*
Llangefni Town v Llanystumdwy	4-0
Llanidloes Town v Llanrug United	2-5*

ROUND 5

Mold Alex v Greenfield	2-5
Mynydd Isa Spartans v Knighton Town	4-1
Rhos Aelwyd v Mochdre Sports	2-0
Ynysddu Welfare v Goodwick United	0-1

ROUND 5

Abertillery Bluebirds v Rhos Aelwyd	1-3
Brymbo v Greenfield	2-4
Buckley Town v Garden Village	2-1
Conwy Borough v Llanfair United	5-4*
Goodwick United v Penydarren BGC	1-1*
Penydarren won 4-3 on penalties.	
Llangefni Town v Hakin United	3-1
Llanrug United v Chirk AAA	2-2*
Llanrug won 4-2 on penalties.	
Mynydd Isa Spartans v Grange Albion	1-3

QUARTER-FINALS

Conwy Borough v Grange Albion	7-1
Llanrug United v Greenfield	2-5
Penydarren BGC v Llangefni Town	2-0
Rhos Aelwyd v Buckley Town	1-0

SEMI-FINALS

Conwy Borough v Penydarren BGC	3-0
Greenfield v Rhos Aelwyd	2-3

FAW TROPHY FINAL 2018

Broughton, Saturday 7 April 2018

Rhos Aelwyd (1) 1 *(Haynes 33)*

Conwy Borough (1) 4 *(Craven 44, Hogan 51, McGonigle 57, Creamer 67)*

NORTHERN IRISH FOOTBALL 2017–18

NIFL DANSKE BANK PREMIERSHIP 2017–18

		Home					Away					Total						
		P	W	D	L	F	A	W	D	L	F	A	W	D	L	F	A	GD	Pts
1	Crusaders	38	13	5	2	47	15	15	2	1	59	23	28	7	3	106	38	68	91
2	Coleraine	38	13	5	0	38	17	13	6	1	38	14	26	11	1	76	31	45	89
3	Glenavon	38	6	9	4	36	28	13	3	3	49	24	19	12	7	85	52	33	69
4	Linfield	38	10	4	5	31	21	10	3	6	41	24	20	7	11	72	45	27	67
5	Cliftonville	38	11	2	5	38	19	9	3	8	30	26	20	5	13	68	45	23	65
6	Glentoran	38	7	3	9	25	27	7	6	6	27	25	14	9	15	52	52	0	51
7	Ballymena U	38	9	2	8	34	38	5	4	10	19	27	14	6	18	53	65	-12	48
8	Dungannon Swifts	38	9	2	8	25	30	4	4	11	17	32	13	6	19	42	62	-20	45
9	Ards	38	6	1	13	20	43	6	3	9	22	31	12	4	22	42	74	-32	40
10	Warrenpoint T	38	5	2	12	28	42	3	4	12	24	44	8	6	24	52	86	-34	30
11	Carrick Rangers	38	3	3	12	14	27	3	2	15	17	51	6	5	27	31	78	-47	23
12	Ballinamallard U	38	4	5	11	25	49	1	3	14	13	40	5	8	25	38	89	-51	23

Top 6 teams split after 33 games. Crusaders qualify for Champions League first qualifying round.
Coleraine and Glenavon qualify for Europa League first qualifying round.
Europa League play-off: Cliftonville 3 Glentoran 2. Relegation/promotion play-off: Carrick Rangers 3 Newry C 6 (agg). Carrick R relegated to NIFL Championship.

LEADING GOALSCORERS (League goals only)

25	Joe Gormley	Cliftonville
22	Gavin Whyte	Crusaders
21	Curtis Allen	Glentoran
19	Paul Heatley	Crusaders
19	Jay Donnelly	Cliftonville
18	Andrew Mitchell	Glenavon
18	Jordan Owens	Crusaders
17	Darren McCauley	Coleraine
16	Jamie McGonigle	Coleraine
14	Ryan Curran	Ballinamallard U
13	Darren Murray	Warrenpoint T, Crusaders
13	Andrew Waterworth	Linfield
12	Sammy Clingan	Glenavon
12	Rory Donnelly	Cliftonville
11	Cathair Friel	Ballymena U
11	Daniel Hughes	Dungannon Swifts, Cliftonville
11	Robbie McDaid	Glentoran
9	Josh Carson	Coleraine
9	Marc Griffin	Glenavon
9	Michael McLellan	Ards
9	Mark Sykes	Glenavon
8	Jordan Forsythe	Crusaders

IRISH LEAGUE CHAMPIONSHIP WINNERS

1891	Linfield	1914	Linfield	1949	Linfield	1973	Crusaders	1997	Crusaders
1892	Linfield	1915	Belfast Celtic	1950	Linfield	1974	Coleraine	1998	Cliftonville
1893	Linfield	1920	Belfast Celtic	1951	Glentoran	1975	Linfield	1999	Glentoran
1894	Glentoran	1921	Glentoran	1952	Glenavon	1976	Crusaders	2000	Linfield
1895	Linfield	1922	Linfield	1953	Glentoran	1977	Glentoran	2001	Linfield
1896	Distillery	1923	Linfield	1954	Linfield	1978	Linfield	2002	Portadown
1897	Glentoran	1924	Queen's Island	1955	Linfield	1979	Linfield	2003	Glentoran
1898	Linfield	1925	Glentoran	1956	Linfield	1980	Linfield	2004	Linfield
1899	Distillery	1926	Belfast Celtic	1957	Glentoran	1981	Glentoran	2005	Glentoran
1900	Belfast Celtic	1927	Belfast Celtic	1958	Ards	1982	Linfield	2006	Linfield
1901	Distillery	1928	Belfast Celtic	1959	Linfield	1983	Linfield	2007	Linfield
1902	Linfield	1929	Belfast Celtic	1960	Glenavon	1984	Linfield	2008	Linfield
1903	Distillery	1930	Linfield	1961	Linfield	1985	Linfield	2009	Glentoran
1904	Linfield	1931	Glentoran	1962	Linfield	1986	Linfield	2010	Linfield
1905	Glentoran	1932	Linfield	1963	Distillery	1987	Linfield	2011	Linfield
1906	Cliftonville/	1933	Belfast Celtic	1964	Glentoran	1988	Glentoran	2012	Linfield
	Distillery (shared)	1934	Linfield	1965	Derry City	1989	Linfield	2013	Cliftonville
1907	Linfield	1935	Linfield	1966	Linfield	1990	Portadown	2014	Cliftonville
1908	Linfield	1936	Belfast Celtic	1967	Glentoran	1991	Portadown	2015	Crusaders
1909	Linfield	1937	Belfast Celtic	1968	Glentoran	1992	Glentoran	2016	Crusaders
1910	Cliftonville	1938	Belfast Celtic	1969	Linfield	1993	Linfield	2017	Linfield
1911	Linfield	1939	Belfast Celtic	1970	Glentoran	1994	Linfield	2018	Crusaders
1912	Glentoran	1940	Belfast Celtic	1971	Linfield	1995	Crusaders		
1913	Glentoran	1948	Belfast Celtic	1972	Glentoran	1996	Portadown		

NIFL BLUEFIN SPORT CHAMPIONSHIP 2017–18

			Home				Away				Total					
		P	W	D	L	F	A	W	D	L	F	A	W	D	L	F	A	GD	Pts

		P	W	D	L	F	A	W	D	L	F	A	W	D	L	F	A	GD	Pts
1	Institute	32	11	3	2	27	10	10	2	4	28	26	21	5	6	55	36	19	68
2	Newry C	32	9	3	4	28	18	8	5	3	30	13	17	8	7	58	31	27	59
3	H&W Welders	32	11	1	4	31	21	5	7	4	23	21	16	8	8	54	42	12	56
4	Portadown	32	8	4	4	33	15	6	5	5	28	21	14	9	9	61	36	25	51
5	Ballyclare Comrades	32	9	1	6	29	26	6	2	8	27	26	15	3	14	56	52	4	48
6	Larne	32	8	6	2	33	18	4	5	7	26	29	12	11	9	59	47	12	47
7	PSNI	32	7	5	4	37	24	4	3	9	18	26	11	8	13	55	50	5	41
8	Loughgall	32	8	1	7	27	30	4	1	11	18	29	12	2	18	45	59	–14	38
9	Limavady U	32	8	5	3	31	20	2	2	12	21	38	10	7	15	52	58	–6	37
10	Knockbreda	32	5	3	8	32	27	4	6	6	18	27	9	9	14	50	54	–4	36
11	Dergview	32	6	6	4	31	24	3	3	10	18	35	9	9	14	49	59	–10	36
12	Lurgan Celtic	32	2	5	9	19	35	1	2	13	13	67	3	7	22	32	102	–70	16

Top 6 teams split after 22 games. Promotion play off: Carrick Rangers 3 Newry C 6 (agg). Newry C promoted to NIFL Premiership. NIFL Championship relegation/promotion play-off: Dergview 4 Queens University 1 (agg). Dergview not relegated.

NIFL CHAMPIONSHIP WINNERS

1996	Coleraine	2004	Loughgall	2012	Ballinamallard U
1997	Ballymena United	2005	Armagh City	2013	Ards
1998	Newry Town	2006	Crusaders	2014	Institute
1999	Distillery	2007	Institute	2015	Carrick Rangers
2000	Omagh Town	2008	Loughgall	2016	Ards
2001	Ards	2009	Portadown	2017	Warrenpoint T
2002	Lisburn Distillery	2010	Loughgall	2018	Institute
2003	Dungannon Swifts	2011	Carrick Rangers		

NIFL BLUEFIN SPORT PREMIER INTERMEDIATE LEAGUE 2017–18

		P	W	D	L	F	A	GD	Pts
1	Dundela	27	18	6	3	78	33	45	60
2	Queen's University	27	17	2	8	62	39	23	53
3	Banbridge T	27	14	8	5	55	36	19	50
4	Lisburn Distillery	27	15	3	9	46	35	11	48
5	Moyola Park	27	10	5	12	46	41	5	35
6	Tobermore U	27	8	7	12	47	60	–13	31
7	Portstewart	27	10	4	13	36	51	–15	34
8	Sports & Leisure Swifts	27	9	5	13	44	62	–18	32
9	Armagh C	27	9	4	14	39	44	–5	31
10	Annagh U	27	10	1	16	41	63	–22	31
11	Newington YC	27	7	7	13	40	56	–16	28
12	Donegal Celtic	27	7	4	16	38	52	–14	25

Top 6 teams split after 22 games. Championship relegation/promotion play-off: Dergview 4 Queen's University 1 (agg). Queen's University not promoted.

IFA DEVELOPMENT LEAGUES 2017–18

Premiership Development League

	P	W	D	L	F	A	GD	Pts
Linfield Swifts	33	28	0	5	116	31	85	84
Cliftonville Olympic	33	26	2	5	109	34	75	80
Ards II	33	20	3	10	94	62	32	63
Glentoran II	33	15	9	9	77	64	13	54
Crusaders	32	15	6	11	69	61	8	51
Glenavon	33	13	3	17	75	94	–19	42
Dungannon Swifts	33	12	2	19	70	88	–18	38
Ballymena United	33	10	7	16	61	81	–20	37
Coleraine	32	9	8	15	62	76	–14	35
Ballinamallard U	33	10	5	18	67	91	–24	35
Carrick Rangers	33	9	5	19	57	89	–32	32
Warrenpoint T	33	3	5	25	39	123	–84	14

Development League North

	P	W	D	L	F	A	GD	Pts
Institute	22	18	2	2	82	30	52	56
Dundela	22	16	2	4	65	21	44	50
H&W Welders	22	12	1	9	61	36	25	37
Ballyclare Comrades	22	10	2	10	59	50	9	32
Newington	24	10	4	10	58	71	–13	34
PSNI Olympic	24	10	2	12	55	57	–2	32
Knockbreda	24	7	3	14	43	55	–12	24
Moyola Park	24	8	0	16	36	97	–61	24
Larne Olympic	24	4	2	18	32	74	–42	14

Development League South

	P	W	D	L	F	A	GD	Pts
Portadown	16	11	2	3	55	16	39	35
Loughgall	16	10	1	5	42	18	24	31
Banbridge T	16	9	3	4	39	28	11	30
Newry C	18	7	3	8	40	41	–1	24
Lisburn Distillery	18	7	1	10	29	38	–9	22
Armagh C	18	6	2	10	27	54	–27	20
Annagh U	18	3	2	13	26	63	–37	11

TENNENT'S IRISH FA CUP 2017–18

After extra time.

FIRST ROUND

Lower Maze v St Patrick's	1-2
18th Newtownabbey OB v Comber Rec	3-2
Abbey Villa v Immaculata	0-3
Ardstraw v Richhill	10-2
Ballymacash Rangers v Shankill U	3-3*
Shankhill U won 4-2 on penalties	
Ballynahinch U v Rosario YC (walkover)	
Bangor Amateurs v Newtowne	0-3
Barn U v Rathfriland Rangers	3-8
Bloomfield v Craigavon C	1-3
Bryansburn Rangers v St Mary's YC	3-1
Coagh U v Ballymoney U	6-1
Crumlin Star v Shorts	9-1
Derriaghy CC v Bourneview Mill	3-1
Dunloy v Banbridge Rangers	3-1
Dunmurry Rec v Dromore Amateurs	4-0
Fivemiletown U v Islandmagee	1-4
Glebe Rangers v Bangor	2-0
Hanover v Chimney Corner	8-2
Killyleagh YC v Newbuildings U	5-1
Laurelvale v Broomhedge Maghaberry	6-1
1st Bangor v Tullyvallen Rangers	2-3
Lurgan T v Groomsport	3-1
Magherafelt Sky Blues v Colin Valley (walkover)	
Malachians v Downshire YM (walkover)	
Markethill Swifts (walkover) v Grove U	
Moneyslane v Sirocco Works	1-4
Orangefield OB v Dunmurry YM	3-0
Oxford U Stars v Trojans	4-3
Portaferry R v Ballynahinch Olympic	3-1
Rathfern Rangers v Lisburn Rangers	4-5
Rosemount Rec v St Luke's	3-1
Royal British Legion v Dromara Village	1-2
Saintfield U v Tandragee R	2-4
Seagoe v Larne Tech OB	1-12
Seapatrick v Ballynure OB	1-4
Suffolk v Dungiven	2-3
Valley Rangers v Oxford Sunnyside	5-0
Windmill Stars v St James' Swifts	2-1
Crumlin U v AFC Silverwood	3-2
Dollingstown v Maiden C	1-3
Crewe U v Drumaness Mills	2-3
Ards Rangers v Iveagh U	9-0

SECOND ROUND

Newcastle v Strabane Ath	3-1
Annagh U v Markethill Swifts	4-2
Ardstraw v Dundela	2-6
Killyleagh YC v Sirocco Works	2-0
Ballywalter Rec v Ballynure OB	6-3
Bryansburn Rangers v Albert Foundry	3-4
Colin Valley v Valley Rangers	1-4
Cookstown Youth v Craigavon C	6-7
Crumlin Star v Oxford U Stars	5-0
Crumlin U v Donegal Celtic	2-0
Derriaghy CC v Shankill U	1-2
Downshire YM v Moyola Park	1-10
Dromara Village v Banbridge T	0-1
Drumaness Mills v Hanover	0-2
Dunloy v Portstewart	1-2
18th Newtownabbey OB v UUJ	1-2
Glebe Rangers v Rosemount Rec	3-0
Immaculata v Larne Tech OB	2-1
Islandmagee v Ards Rangers	1-2
Laurelvale v Tullyvallen Rangers	5-2
Maiden C v Lurgan T	7-1
Tandragee R v Lisburn Rangers	3-2
Newtowne v Desertmartin	4-2
Portaferry R v Mossley	2-0
Queen's University v Dungiven	7-2
Rathfriland Rangers v Orangefield OB	4-1
Rosario YC v Brantwood	4-0
Rosario YC removed from competition; Brantwood reinstated.	
Sport & Leisure Swifts v Windmill Stars	2-0
St Patrick's v Wellington Rec	3-2
Dunmurry Rec v Tobermore U	0-7
Newington v Lisburn Distillery	0-3
Armagh C v Coagh U	2-0

THIRD ROUND

Killyleagh YC v Tobermore U	3-1
Armagh C v Crumlin Star	1-2
Banbridge T v Queen's University	1-2
Craigavon C v Albert Foundry	1-4
Crumlin U v Valley Rangers	2-0
Glebe Rangers (walkover) v UUJ	
Hanover v Shankill U	2-3
Immaculata v Brantwood	3-1*
Ballywalter Rec v Ards Rangers	3-2
Laurelvale v Moyola Park	0-5
Newcastle v Rathfriland Rangers	3-0
Newtowne v Lisburn Distillery	0-2
Portstewart v Portaferry R	2-1
Sport & Leisure Swifts v Dundela	0-2
St Patrick's v Annagh U	2-5
Tandragee R v Maiden C	1-2*

FOURTH ROUND

Crumlin U v Immaculata	2-4
Dundela v Newcastle	5-0
Glebe Rangers v Annagh U	2-1
Lisburn Distillery v Albert Foundry	3-1
Moyola Park v Ballywalter Rec	2-0
Portstewart v Maiden C	1-1*
Maiden C won 3-1 on penalties	
Queen's University v Killyleagh YC	3-1
Shankill U v Crumlin Star	0-4

FIFTH ROUND

Knockbreda v Institute	0-2
Queen's University v Dundela	0-1
Lurgan Celtic v Glentoran	1-2
Larne v Dergview	3-0
Carrick Rangers v Glenavon	1-3*
Coleraine v Lisburn Distillery	7-0
Crusaders v Maiden C	2-0
Dungannon Swifts v Limavady U	4-0
Ballinamallard U v Immaculata	4-2
Cliftonville v Warrenpoint T	4-3*
Linfield v Glebe Rangers	5-0
Loughgall v PSNI	4-1
Ballymena U v Moyola Park	4-0
Newry C v H&W Welders	2-0
Portadown v Ballyclare Comrades	1-2*
Ards v Crumlin Star	4-1

SIXTH ROUND

Ballyclare Comrades v Glentoran	0-4
Ballymena U v Ballinamallard U	2-2*
Ballymena U won 4-3 on penalties	
Cliftonville v Crusaders	4-1
Glenavon v Dungannon Swifts	3-0
Coleraine v Institute	4-0
Larne v Dundela	6-1
Linfield v Newry C	1-0
Loughgall v Ards	2-1

QUARTER-FINALS

Glenavon v Loughgall	1-2
Ballymena U v Larne	1-2
Coleraine v Glentoran	1-0
Linfield v Cliftonville	0-1

SEMI-FINALS

Cliftonville v Loughgall	4-1
Coleraine v Larne	3-1

TENNENT'S IRISH CUP FINAL 2018

Windsor Park, Belfast, Saturday 5 May 2018

Coleraine (0) 3 *(McCauley 50, Burns 78, Bradley 90)*

Cliftonville (0) 1 *(Donnelly R 53)*

Coleraine: Johns; Traynor, McConaghie, Mullan, O'Donnell, Dooley (Parkhill 32), McCauley (Smith 87), Lyons, Harkin, Bradley, McGonigle (Burns 78).
Cliftonville: Neeson; Breen (Harkin 85), Bagnall, Harney, Ives, Curran (Garrett 73), McDonald, Cosgrove, Donnelly R, Gormley, Donnelly J.
Referee: Arnold Hunter.

IRISH CUP FINALS (from 1946–47)

1946–47 Belfast Celtic 1, Glentoran 0	1984–85 Glentoran 1:1, Linfield 1:0
1947–48 Linfield 3, Coleraine 0	1985–86 Glentoran 2, Coleraine 1
1948–49 Derry City 3, Glentoran 1	1986–87 Glentoran 1, Larne 0
1949–50 Linfield 2, Distillery 1	1987–88 Glentoran 1, Glenavon 0
1950–51 Glentoran 3, Ballymena U 1	1988–89 Ballymena U 1, Larne 0
1951–52 Ards 1, Glentoran 0	1989–90 Glentoran 3, Portadown 0
1952–53 Linfield 5, Coleraine 0	1990–91 Portadown 2, Glenavon 1
1953–54 Derry City 1, Glentoran 0	1991–92 Glenavon 2, Linfield 1
1954–55 Dundela 3, Glenavon 0	1992–93 Bangor 1:1:1, Ards 1:1:0
1955–56 Distillery 1, Glentoran 0	1993–94 Linfield 2, Bangor 0
1956–57 Glenavon 2, Derry City 0	1994–95 Linfield 3, Carrick Rangers 1
1957–58 Ballymena U 2, Linfield 0	1995–96 Glentoran 1, Glenavon 0
1958–59 Glenavon 2, Ballymena U 0	1996–97 Glenavon 1, Cliftonville 0
1959–60 Linfield 5, Ards 1	1997–98 Glentoran 1, Glenavon 0
1960–61 Glenavon 5, Linfield 1	1998–99 *Portadown awarded trophy after Cliftonville*
1961–62 Linfield 4, Portadown 0	*were eliminated for using an ineligible player in*
1962–63 Linfield 2, Distillery 1	*semi-final.*
1963–64 Derry City 2, Glentoran 0	1999–2000 Glentoran 1, Portadown 0
1964–65 Coleraine 2, Glenavon 1	2000–01 Glentoran 1, Linfield 0
1965–66 Glentoran 2, Linfield 0	2001–02 Linfield 2, Portadown 1
1966–67 Crusaders 3, Glentoran 1	2002–03 Coleraine 1, Glentoran 0
1967–68 Crusaders 2, Linfield 0	2003–04 Glentoran 1, Coleraine 0
1968–69 Ards 4, Distillery 2	2004–05 Portadown 5, Larne 1
1969–70 Linfield 2, Ballymena U 1	2005–06 Linfield 2, Glentoran 1
1970–71 Distillery 3, Derry City	2006–07 Linfield 2, Dungannon Swifts 2
1971–72 Coleraine 2, Portadown 1	*(aet; Linfield won 3-2 on penalties).*
1972–73 Glentoran 3, Linfield 2	2007–08 Linfield 2, Coleraine 1
1973–74 Ards 2, Ballymena U 1	2008–09 Crusaders 1, Cliftonville 0
1974–75 Coleraine 1:0:1, Linfield 1:0:0	2009–10 Linfield 2, Portadown 1
1975–76 Carrick Rangers 2, Linfield 1	2010–11 Linfield 2, Crusaders 1
1976–77 Coleraine 4, Linfield 1	2011–12 Linfield 4, Crusaders 1
1977–78 Linfield 3, Ballymena U 1	2012–13 Glentoran 3, Cliftonville 1
1978–79 Cliftonville 3, Portadown 2	2013–14 Glenavon 2, Ballymena U 1
1979–80 Linfield 2, Crusaders 0	2014–15 Glentoran 1, Portadown 0
1980–81 Ballymena U 1, Glenavon 0	2015–16 Glenavon 2, Linfield 0
1981–82 Linfield 2, Coleraine 1	2016–17 Linfield 3, Coleraine 0
1982–83 Glentoran 1:2, Linfield 1:1	2017–18 Coleraine 3, Cliftonville 1
1983–84 Ballymena U 4, Carrick Rangers 1	

BETMcLEAN LEAGUE CUP 2017–18

After extra time.

FIRST ROUND

H&W Welders v Armagh C	3-0
Portstewart v Limavady U	2-3
Sport & Leisure Swifts v Lurgan Celtic	0-1
Dergview v Annagh U	4-0

SECOND ROUND

Ballinamallard U v Tobermore U	0-0*
Ballinamallard U won 8-7 on penalties	
Ards v Queen's University	5-0
Ballyclare Comrades v Newington YC	2-0
Ballymena U v Knockbreda	3-0
Carrick Rangers v Dergview	3-0
Cliftonville v Banbridge T	4-0
Coleraine v Larne	4-1
Crusaders v Dundela	2-1
Glenavon v Donegal Celtic	5-1
Limavady U v PSNI	0-1
Linfield v Lisburn Distillery	6-0
Loughgall v Glentoran	0-1*
Moyola Park v Institute	1-1*
Institute won 8-7 on penalties	
Newry C v Dungannon Swifts	0-4
Portadown v H&W Welders	3-2
Warrenpoint T v Lurgan Celtic	4-1

THIRD ROUND

Ards v Glenavon	4-0
Crusaders v Coleraine	3-2
Ballymena U v Portadown	2-0
Glentoran v Carrick Rangers	0-1
Warrenpoint T v Dungannon Swifts	0-1
Ballinamallard U v Linfield	0-3
Ballyclare Comrades v Institute	1-0
Cliftonville v PSNI	7-0

QUARTER-FINALS

Ballymena U v Ards	3-2*
Carrick Rangers v Cliftonville	0-1
Crusaders v Linfield	2-0
Dungannon Swifts v Ballyclare Comrades	2-1

SEMI-FINALS

Dungannon Swifts v Crusaders	2-1
Ballymena U v Cliftonville	3-1

BETMcLEAN LEAGUE CUP FINAL 2018

Windsor Park, Belfast, Sunday 17 February 2018

Dungannon Swifts (2) 3 *(Mayse 11, 37, Burke 55)*

Ballymena U (1) 1 *(Owens 17)*

Dungannon Swifts: Addis, Hegarty, Armstrong, Mayse (Teggart 75), McElroy, Harpur, O'Rourke, Lowe, Clucas (Wilson 46), Burke, Hutchinson.
Ballymena U: Glendinning, Kane, Owens, Friel, McCloskey, Burns (Weir 65), Balmer (83), Ervin, Millar, Faulkner (Shevlin 65), McMurray.
Referee: Tim Marshall.

ROLL OF HONOUR SEASON 2017–18

Competition	Winner	Runner-up
NIFL Danske Bank Premiership	Crusaders	Coleraine
Tennent's Irish FA Cup	Coleraine	Cliftonville
NIFL Championship	Institute	Newry C
NIFL Premier Intermediate	Dundela	Queen's University
BetMcLean Northern Ireland League Cup	Dungannon Swifts	Ballymena U
County Antrim Shield	Crusaders	Ballymena U
Steel & Sons Cup	Newington YC	Linfield Swifts
Co Antrim Junior Shield	Harryville Homers	Willowbank
Irish Junior Cup	Enniskillen Rangers	Greenisland
Mid Ulster Cup (Senior)	Glenavon	Newry C
Harry Cavan Youth Cup	Linfield Rangers	Cliftonville
George Wilson Memorial Cup	H&W Welders	Knockbreda
North West Senior Cup	Institute	Coleraine
The Fermanagh Mulhern Cup	Tummery Ath	Enniskillen Town U
Intermediate Cup	Queen's University	Dundela

NORTHERN IRELAND FOOTBALL WRITERS ASSOCIATION AWARDS 2017–18

BETMCLEAN MANAGER OF THE YEAR
Oran Kearney (Coleraine)

DANSKE BANK UK PLAYER OF THE YEAR
Gavin Whyte (Crusaders)

DREAM SPANISH HOMES
YOUNG PLAYER OF THE YEAR
Gavin Whyte (Crusaders)

SODEXO CHAMPIONSHIP PLAYER OF THE YEAR
Michael McCrudden (Institute)

PREMIER INTERMEDIATE PLAYER OF THE YEAR
Jordan Hughes (Dundela)

INTERNATIONAL PERSONALITY OF THE YEAR
Jonny Evans (West Bromwich Albion and Northern Ireland)

THE JIMMY DUBOIS NON-SENIOR
TEAM OF THE YEAR
Dundela

MERIT AWARD
Jackie Fullerton

JORDAN'S GIFT GOAL OF THE SEASON 2017–18
Billy Joe Burns of Crusaders v Linfield

WOMEN'S PERSONALITY OF THE YEAR
Lauren Perry, Linfield Ladies and Northern Ireland

DR MALCOLM BRODIE HALL OF FAME
Jimmy Nicholl

UHLSPORT PREMIERSHIP TEAM OF THE YEAR
Chris Johns (Coleraine)
Billy Joe Burns (Crusaders)
Stephen O'Donnell (Coleraine)
Gareth McConaghie (Coleraine)
Aaron Traynor (Coleraine)
Gavin Whyte (Crusaders)
Ciaron Harkin (Coleraine)
Mark Sykes (Glenavon)
Paul Heatley (Crusaders)
James McGonigle (Coleraine)
Joe Gormley (Cliftonville)

@BET_McLEAN NIFWA PREMIERSHIP PLAYER OF THE MONTH 2017–18

Month	Player	Team
August	Mark Haughey	Linfield
September	Darren McCauley	Coleraine
October	Rory Donnelly	Cliftonville
November	Gavin Whyte	Crusaders
December	Gavin Whyte	Crusaders
January	Gareth McConaghie	Coleraine
February	Curtis Allen	Glentoran
March	Joe Gormley	Cliftonville
April	Chris Johns	Coleraine

@BET_McLEAN NIFWA MANAGER OF THE MONTH 2017–18

Month	Player	Team
August	Oran Kearney	Coleraine
September	Oran Kearney	Coleraine
October	Oran Kearney	Coleraine
November	Stephen Baxter	Crusaders
December	Stephen Baxter	Crusaders
January	Stephen Baxter	Crusaders
February	Gary Hamilton	Glenavon
March	Oran Kearney	Coleraine
April	Stephen Baxter	Crusaders

NIFWA CHAMPIONSHIP PLAYER OF THE MONTH 2017–18

Month	Player	Team
August	Samuel McIlveen	Ballycare
September	Karl Hamill	Knockbreda
October	Declan Carville	Newry C
November	Michael McCrudden	Institute
December	Darren Stuart	Larne
January	Marty Gallagher	Institute
February	John Boyle	Newry C
March	Chris Lavery	Portadown
April	Michael McCrudden	Institute

EUROPEAN CUP FINALS

EUROPEAN CUP FINALS 1956–1992

Year	Winners v Runners-up		Venue	Attendance	Referee
1956	Real Madrid v Reims	4-3	Paris	38,239	A. Ellis (England)
1957	Real Madrid v Fiorentina	2-0	Madrid	124,000	L. Horn (Netherlands)
1958	Real Madrid v AC Milan	3-2*	Brussels	67,000	A. Alsteen (Belgium)
1959	Real Madrid v Reims	2-0	Stuttgart	72,000	A. Dutsch (West Germany)
1960	Real Madrid v Eintracht Frankfurt	7-3	Glasgow	127,621	J. Mowat (Scotland)
1961	Benfica v Barcelona	3-2	Berne	26,732	G. Dienst (Switzerland)
1962	Benfica v Real Madrid	5-3	Amsterdam	61,257	L. Horn (Netherlands)
1963	AC Milan v Benfica	2-1	Wembley	45,715	A. Holland (England)
1964	Internazionale v Real Madrid	3-1	Vienna	71,333	J. Stoll (Austria)
1965	Internazionale v Benfica	1-0	Milan	89,000	G. Dienst (Switzerland)
1966	Real Madrid v Partizan Belgrade	2-1	Brussels	46,745	R. Kreitlein (West Germany)
1967	Celtic v Internazionale	2-1	Lisbon	45,000	K. Tschenscher (West Germany)
1968	Manchester U v Benfica	4-1*	Wembley	92,225	C. Lo Bello (Italy)
1969	AC Milan v Ajax	4-1	Madrid	31,782	J. Ortiz de Mendibil (Spain)
1970	Feyenoord v Celtic	2-1*	Milan	53,187	C. Lo Bello (Italy)
1971	Ajax v Panathinaikos	2-0	Wembley	90,000	J. Taylor (England)
1972	Ajax v Internazionale	2-0	Rotterdam	61,354	R. Helies (France)
1973	Ajax v Juventus	1-0	Belgrade	89,484	M. Guglovic (Yugoslavia)
1974	Bayern Munich v Atletico Madrid	1-1	Brussels	48,722	V. Loraux (Belgium)
Replay	Bayern Munich v Atletico Madrid	4-0	Brussels	23,325	A. Delcourt (Belgium)
1975	Bayern Munich v Leeds U	2-0	Paris	48,374	M. Kitabdjian (France)
1976	Bayern Munich v Saint-Etienne	1-0	Glasgow	54,864	K. Palotai (Hungary)
1977	Liverpool v Moenchengladbach	3-1	Rome	52,078	R. Wurtz (France)
1978	Liverpool v Club Brugge	1-0	Wembley	92,500	C. Corver (Netherlands)
1979	Nottingham F v Malmo	1-0	Munich	57,500	E. Linemayr (Austria)
1980	Nottingham F v Hamburger SV	1-0	Madrid	51,000	A. Garrido (Portugal)
1981	Liverpool v Real Madrid	1-0	Paris	48,360	K. Palotai (Hungary)
1982	Aston Villa v Bayern Munich	1-0	Rotterdam	46,000	G. Konrath (France)
1983	Hamburg v Juventus	1-0	Athens	73,500	N. Rainea (Romania)
1984	Liverpool v Roma	1-1*	Rome	69,693	E. Fredriksson (Sweden)
	(Liverpool won 4-2 on penalties)				
1985	Juventus v Liverpool	1-0	Brussels	58,000	A. Daina (Switzerland)
1986	Steaua Bucharest v Barcelona	0-0*	Seville	70,000	M. Vautrot (France)
	(Steaua won 2-0 on penalties)				
1987	FC Porto v Bayern Munich	2-1	Vienna	57,500	A. Ponnet (Belgium)
1988	PSV Eindhoven v Benfica	0-0*	Stuttgart	68,000	L. Agnolin (Italy)
	(PSV won 6-5 on penalties)				
1989	AC Milan v Steaua Bucharest	4-0	Barcelona	97,000	K.-H. Tritschler (West Germany)
1990	AC Milan v Benfica	1-0	Vienna	57,500	H. Kohl (Austria)
1991	Crvena Zvezda v Olympique Marseille	0-0*	Bari	56,000	T. Lanese (Italy)
	(Crvena Zvezda won 5-3 on penalties)				
1992	Barcelona v Sampdoria	1-0*	Wembley	70,827	A. Schmidhuber (Germany)

UEFA CHAMPIONS LEAGUE FINALS 1993–2018

1993	Marseille† v AC Milan	1-0	Munich	64,400	K. Rothlisberger (Switzerland)
1994	AC Milan v Barcelona	4-0	Athens	70,000	P. Don (England)
1995	Ajax v AC Milan	1-0	Vienna	49,730	I. Craciunescu (Romania)
1996	Juventus v Ajax	1-1*	Rome	70,000	M. D. Vega (Spain)
	(Juventus won 4-2 on penalties)				
1997	Borussia Dortmund v Juventus	3-1	Munich	59,000	S. Puhl (Hungary)
1998	Real Madrid v Juventus	1-0	Amsterdam	48,500	H. Krug (Germany)
1999	Manchester U v Bayern Munich	2-1	Barcelona	90,245	P. Collina (Italy)
2000	Real Madrid v Valencia	3-0	Paris	80,000	S. Braschi (Italy)
2001	Bayern Munich v Valencia	1-1*	Milan	79,000	D. Jol (Netherlands)
	(Bayern Munich won 5-4 on penalties)				
2002	Real Madrid v Leverkusen	2-1	Glasgow	50,499	U. Meier (Switzerland)
2003	AC Milan v Juventus	0-0*	Manchester	62,315	M. Merk (Germany)
	(AC Milan won 3-2 on penalties)				
2004	FC Porto v Monaco	3-0	Gelsenkirchen	53,053	K. M. Nielsen (Denmark)
2005	Liverpool v AC Milan	3-3*	Istanbul	65,000	M. M. González (Spain)
	(Liverpool won 3-2 on penalties)				
2006	Barcelona v Arsenal	2-1	Paris	79,610	T. Hauge (Norway)
2007	AC Milan v Liverpool	2-1	Athens	74,000	H. Fandel (Germany)
2008	Manchester U v Chelsea	1-1*	Moscow	67,310	L. Michel (Slovakia)
	(Manchester U won 6-5 on penalties)				
2009	Barcelona v Manchester U	2-0	Rome	62,467	M. Busacca (Switzerland)
2010	Internazionale v Bayern Munich	2-0	Madrid	73,490	H. Webb (England)
2011	Barcelona v Manchester U	3-1	Wembley	87,695	V. Kassai (Hungary)
2012	Chelsea v Bayern Munich	1-1*	Munich	62,500	P. Proença (Portugal)
	(Chelsea won 4-3 on penalties)				
2013	Bayern Munich v Borussia Dortmund	2-1	Wembley	86,298	N. Rizzoli (Italy)
2014	Real Madrid v Atletico Madrid	4-1*	Lisbon	60,000	B. Kuipers (Netherlands)
2015	Barcelona v Juventus	3-1	Berlin	70,442	C. Cakir (Turkey)
2016	Real Madrid v Atletico Madrid	1-1*	Milan	71,942	M. Clattenburg (England)
	(Real Madrid won 5-3 on penalties)				
2017	Real Madrid v Juventus	4-1	Cardiff	65,842	F. Brych (Germany)
2018	Real Madrid v Liverpool	3-1	Kiev	61,561	M. Mazic (Serbia)

†*Subsequently stripped of title.* *After extra time.

UEFA CHAMPIONS LEAGUE 2017–18

■ *Denotes player sent off.*

FIRST QUALIFYING ROUND FIRST LEG
Tuesday, 27 June 2017
Alashkert (1) 1 *(Nenadovic 39)*
FC Santa Coloma (0) 0   3300
Alashkert: (3511) Beglaryan; Voskanyan, Stojkovic, Arakelyan; Minasyan (Grigoryan 54 (Zeljkovic 65)), Dashyan, Veranyan, Yedigaryan, Daghbashyan; Edigaryan (Badoyan 76); Nenadovic.
FC Santa Coloma: (4231) Casals; Ramos R, Lima, Ramos A, Capdevila; Rebes (Lempereur 67), Escolano; Lain (Rodriguez 60), Conde, Sosa Sebastian (Mercade 75); Gago.

Hibernians (0) 2 *(Jorginho 63, Kristensen 73)*
FCI Tallinn (0) 0   1068
Hibernians: (433) Hogg; Dias, Agius, Soares, Da Garcia; Lima (Vella 90), Kristensen, Failla; Bezzina, Jorginho (Degabriele 90), Sahanek (Mbong 78).
FCI Tallinn: (4231) Igonen; Volodin, Nesterovski (Kalimulin 38), Avilov, Kruglov; Domov, Dmitrijev; Kulinits, Nesterov (Voskoboinikov 79), Harin (Tumasyan 84); Prosa.

The New Saints (1) 1 *(Quigley 44)*
Europa (1) 2 *(Quillo 8, Gomez 78)*   1148
The New Saints: (4231) Harrison; Spender, Saunders, Rawlinson, Pryce; Edwards, Routledge; Mullan (Fletcher 90), Brobbel, Cieslewicz (Darlington 68); Quigley (Draper 73).
Europa: (41212) Munoz; Toscano, Merino, Belfortti, Toni Garcia; Moya; Quillo (Carreno 79), Walker; Yahaya; Gomez, Roldan (Joselinho 84).

Vikingur (1) 2 *(Vatnhamar G 17, Lawal 73)*
Trepca'89 (1) 1 *(Hajdari 39)*   841
Vikingur: (4411) Rasmussen; Hansen G, Gregersen, Jacobsen E, Jacobsen H; Vatnhamar G (Olsen J 90), Benjaminsen, Anghel S (Hansen H 83), Djordjevic; Vatnhamar S; Lawal.
Trepca'89: (442) Manxholli; Lladrovci (Maloku 38), Hasani, Potoku, Islami; Idrizi (Lushtaku 74), Mustafa, Izmaku, Broja; Hajdari, Oto John (Henry Chibuze 60).

Wednesday, 28 June 2017
Linfield (0) 1 *(Stewart J 89)*
La Fiorita (0) 0   2839
Linfield: (442) Carroll; Casement, Haughey, Clarke M, Stafford; Quinn (Stewart J 60), Mulgrew, Lowry, Burns (Stewart C 75); Waterworth, Smyth.
La Fiorita: (442) Vivan; Olivi, Martini, Di Maio, Gasperoni; Tommasi, Miglietta (Lunadei 90), Brighi, Rinaldi; Hirsch (Zafferani 80), Olcese (Guidi 90).

FIRST QUALIFYING ROUND SECOND LEG
Tuesday, 4 July 2017
Europa (0) 1 *(Walker 53 (pen))*
The New Saints (2) 3 *(Fletcher 37, Quigley 41, 104)*   261
Europa: (4132) Munoz; Ayew, Moya, Quillo■, Gomez■; Walker; Toscano, Roldan (Toni Garcia 73), Yahaya; Belfortti, Merino (Carreno 106).
The New Saints: (442) Harrison; Brobbel, Edwards, Fletcher (Cieslewicz 69), Mullan; Pryce (Darlington 100), Quigley, Rawlinson, Routledge; Saunders (Draper 79), Spender.
aet.

FCI Tallinn (0) 0
Hibernians (0) 1 *(Jorginho 88)*   995
FCI Tallinn: (4231) Igonen; Kulinits, Kalimulin, Avilov, Kruglov; Dmitrijev, Domov (Golovljov 80); Nesterov (Rattel 71), Tumasyan (Voskoboinikov 65), Harin; Prosa.
Hibernians: (4231) Hogg (Briffa 15); Dias, Soares, Da Garcia, Kreuzriegler; Lima, Kristensen; Sahanek (Mbong 71), Bezzina, Failla; Jorginho (Degabriele 89).

La Fiorita (0) 0
Linfield (0) 0   911
La Fiorita: (352) Vivan; Martini, Brighi (Ricchiuti 59), Di Maio; Olivi, Miglietta, Olcese, Rinaldi (Mottola 81), Tommasi; Gasperoni, Zafferani (Hirsch 69).
Linfield: (442) Carroll; Stafford, Stewart C (Burns 69), Haughey, Waterworth; Lowry, Clarke M, Casement, Mulgrew; Quinn, Smyth (Mitchell 67).

FC Santa Coloma (0) 1 *(Lima 63)*
Alashkert (1) 1 *(Nenadovic 28)*   850
FC Santa Coloma: (433) Casals; Ramos R (Martinez 88), Ramos A, Lima, Capdevila; Galan, Rebes, Conde (Lain 59); Lempereur (Santos 75), Cubas, Sosa Sebastian.
Alashkert: (352) Beglaryan; Voskanyan, Stojkovic, Arakelyan; Khovbosha, Dashyan (Minasyan 89), Veranyan, Yedigaryan, Daghbashyan; Nenadovic (Peltier 76), Manasyan (Edigaryan 69).

Trepca'89 (0) 1 *(Hasani 65)*
Vikingur (2) 4 *(Anghel S 37, Islami 40 (og),*
Vatnhamar S 52, 59)   12,000
Trepca'89: (4231) Manxholli; Islami (Oto John 57), Mustafa, Izmaku, Potoku; Broja, Maloku; Hasani, Lushtaku (Idrizi 71), Hajdari (Henry Chibuze 57); Kurtishaj■.
Vikingur: (4231) Rasmussen; Hansen G, Gregersen, Jacobsen E, Jacobsen H; Djurhuus (Hansen H 55), Anghel S (Lervig 56); Vatnhamar S, Vatnhamar G, Djordjevic; Lawal (Olsen A 82).

SECOND QUALIFYING ROUND FIRST LEG
Tuesday, 11 July 2017
Hibernians (0) 0
Red Bull Salzburg (2) 3 *(Berisha V 32, Hwang 35,*
Minamino 54)   1452
Hibernians: (442) Agius; Bezzina, Da Garcia, Dias (Mbong 76), Failla (Sahanek 65); Hogg, Jorginho, Kreuzriegler, Kristensen (Degabriele 84); Lima, Soares.
Red Bull Salzburg: (442) Walke; Berisha V, Hwang (Gulbrandsen 70), Minamino (Wolf 63), Berisha M; Caleta-Car, Lazaro, Paulo Miranda, Samassekou; Ulmer, Yabo.

Partizan Belgrade (0) 2 *(Djurdjevic 53 (pen), Leonardo 63)*
Buducnost Podgorica (0) 0   20,530
Partizan Belgrade: (442) Kljajic; Djurdjevic, Cirkovic, Jankovic (Djurickovic 80), Kosovic; Everton Bilher, Mihajlovic (Leonardo 46), Nemanja G Miletic, Ostojic; Tawamba (Ilic 85), Vulicevic.
Buducnost Podgorica: (442) Marcelja; Hocko, Mirkovic, Mitrovic, Nikac; Pejakovic (Camaj 67), Raspopovic, Simovic, Terzic (Ristovic 64 (Melunovic 78)); Tucevic, Vlaisavljevic.

Qarabag (3) 5 *(Ismayilov 10 (pen), Ndlovu 37, 45 (pen),*
Guerrier 83, Michel 90)
Samtredia (0) 0   21,500
Qarabag: (442) Sehic; Ismayilov (Guerrier 76), Ndlovu, Michel, Agolli; Diniyev (Almeida 65), Garayev, Huseynov B, Madatov; Medvedev, Sadygov (Rzezniczak 31).
Samtredia: (442) Balde; Datunaishvili, Kasradze, Manjgaladze, Markozashvili; Migineishvili, Mitchedlishvili, Razhamashvili (Beriashvili 69), Sabanadze; Samushia (Jikia 64), Sandokhadze.

Rijeka (1) 2 *(Misic 4, Matei 69)*
The New Saints (0) 0   5883
Rijeka: (4231) Sluga; Ristovski, Zuparic, Elez, Zuta (Matei 63); Bradaric, Misic, Vesovic, Gorgon (Males 78), Heber; Gavranovic (Crnic 87).
The New Saints: (433) Harrison; Routledge, Saunders, Rawlinson, Edwards; Brobbel, Spender, Pryce; Mullan, Quigley, Fletcher (Cieslewicz 70).

Wednesday, 12 July 2017

APOEL (0) 1 *(Bertoglio 72)*

F91 Dudelange (0) 0   9600

APOEL: (4231) Waterman; Roberto Lago, Artymatas, Ebecilio, de Camargo (Pote 74); Bertoglio, Oar (Vander 60); Vinicius, Milanov, Morais; Merkis.
F91 Dudelange: (442) Joubert; Malget (Jordanov 46), Lauriente, Prempeh, Schnell; Stolz, Cruz (Pokar 84), Garos, Turpel (Sinani 83); Ibrahimovic, Barbosa.

BATE Borisov (1) 1 *(Rios 43)*

Alashkert (0) 1 *(Rios 78 (og))*   11,192

BATE Borisov: (442) Scherbitski; Palyakow, Milunovic, Rios, Zhavnerchik; Stasevich, Dragun, Kendysh, Ivanic (Berezkin 74); Gordeichuk (Volodjko A 71), Signevich (Tuominem 64).
Alashkert: (442) Beglaryan; Daghbashyan, Khovbosha, Yedigaryan (Badoyan 73), Jablan; Voskanyan, Stojkovic, Veranyan, Edigaryan (Zeljkovic 86); Dashyan, Manasyan (Nenadovic 90).

Dundalk (1) 1 *(McMillan 18)*

Rosenborg (1) 1 *(Reginiussen 44)*   3050

Dundalk: (4411) Rogers; Gartland, Massey, Vemmelund (Barrett 64), Gannon; Shields, Mountney, McEleney, Benson; Duffy (Connolly 72); McMillan (Kilduff 81).
Rosenborg: (433) Hansen; Hedenstadt, Reginiussen, Bjordal, Jensen; Konradsen A, Vilhjalmsson, Skjelvik; Midtsjoe (de Lanlay 81), Helland (Jevtovic 42), Bendtner.

Spartaks Jurmala (0) 0

Astana (0) 1 *(Twumasi 73)*   1987

Spartaks Jurmala: (433) Nerugals; Stuglis E, Slampe, Simunovic, Pushnyakov; Kazacoks (Stuglis I 76), Vardanjans, Gabelok; Gauracs (Kozlovs 79), Ibragimov (Platonov 59), Kozlov.
Astana: (433) Mokin; Shitov, Anicic, Logvinenko, Shomko; Grahovac, Kleinheisler (Murtazayev 75), Maevskiy; Muzhikov (Beysebekov 88), Kabananga (Despotovic 90), Twumasi.

Hafnarfjordur (0) 1 *(Palsson 49)*

Vikingur (0) 1 *(Lawal 73 (pen))*   1523

Hafnarfjordur: (442) Nielsen; Vidarsson P (Bjornsson A 90), Doumbia, Olafsson, Bodvarsson; Vidarsson D, Bjornsson H (Gudmundsson 76), Palsson, Lennon; Vidarsson B (Gudnason 76), Finnbogason.
Vikingur: (442) Rasmussen; Hansen G (Olsen A 63), Gregersen, Djurhuus, Jacobsen E; Jacobsen H, Vatnhamar G, Benjaminsen, Vatnhamar S; Anghel S (Hansen H 84), Lawal.

Hapoel Be'er Sheva (1) 2 *(Vitor 35, Einbinder 52)*

Budapest Honved (0) 1 *(Lanzafame 63)*   15,603

Hapoel Be'er Sheva: (433) Haimov; Bitton, Korhut, Vitor, Tzedek; Radi (Ghadir 65), Einbinder, Melikson (Ohana 81); Ogu, Sahar (Barda 71), Nwakaeme.
Budapest Honved: (433) Grof; Ikenne, Lovric, Laczko (Bobal 73), Barath; Gazdag, Poloskei (de Oliveira 70), Kamber; Nagy, Lanzafame, Eppel.

IFK Mariehamn (0) 0

Legia Warsaw (3) 3 *(Guilherme 7 (pen), Nagy 40, Hamalainen 44)*   1637

IFK Mariehamn: (4411) Vaikla; Kojola, Lyyski, Maenpaa (Granlund 72), Friberg da Cruz; Span, Sellin (Wirtanen 87), Petrovic (Sid 79), Ekhalie; Dafaa; Kangaskolkka.
Legia Warsaw: (4321) Malarz; Dabrowski, Broz, Jedrzejczyk, Guilherme (Szymanski 64); Hlousek, Kopczynski (Szwoch 57), Nagy (Moneta 63); Hamalainen, Maczynski; Moulin.

Malmo (0) 1 *(Brorsson 75)*

Vardar (0) 1 *(Nikolov 63)*   20,058

Malmo: (442) Wiland; Konate (Eikrem 65), Tinnerholm, Yotun, Nielsen; Brorsson, Rakip (Svanberg 65), Lewicki, Christiansen; Cibicki (Bergqvist 85), Berget.
Vardar: (442) Gacevski; Grncarov, Hambardzumyan, Novak, Demiri; Spirovski (Kojasevic 78), Nikolov, Iseni (Gligorov 46), Felipe; Barseghyan (Blazevski 72), Balotelli.

MSK Zilina (1) 1 *(Spalek 39)*

FC Copenhagen (0) 3 *(Pavlovic 68, 73, 82)*   10,023

MSK Zilina: (442) Mandous; Mazan, Kralik, Vavro, Skvarka; Otubanjo (Sheidaev 58), Diaz, Kacer; Jankauskas (Polievka 72); Spalek (Chvatal 86), Pavlovic.
FC Copenhagen: (442) Olsen; Bengtsson (Kusk 66), Hogli, Johansson, Boilesen; Kvist, Gregus, Toutouh (Luftner 46), Verbic; Sotiriou (Santander 76), Pavlovic.

Sheriff (0) 1 *(Badibanga 79 (pen))*

Kukesi (0) 0   5772

Sheriff: (442) Mikulic; Jardan (Badibanga 69), Racu, Bayala, Cristiano; Posmac, Susic, de Nooijer (Bordian 90), Anton; Brezovec, Mugosa (Damascan 82).
Kukesi: (442) Kolici; Shameti, Serran, Cale (Carioca 89), Zeqiri (Nasr 66); Hallaci, Lena, Rrumbullaku, Musolli; Guri (Emini 83), Pejic.

Zalgiris (0) 2 *(Nyuiadzi 78, Kuklys 78)*

Ludogorets Razgrad (1) 1 *(Andrianantenaina 18)*   4911

Zalgiris: (442) Vitkauskas; Klimavicius, Vaitkunas, Mbodj, Slijngard; Kuklys, Antal (Nyuiadzi 60), Blagojevic, Ljujic (Atajic 73); Sernas; Elivelto (Luksa 88).
Ludogorets Razgrad: (442) Renan; Moti, Terziev, Campanharo, Sasha; Andrianantenaina, Wanderson (Plastun 85), Natanael, Marcelinho; Lukoki (Keseru 79), Cafu.

Zrinjski Mostar (0) 1 *(Todorovic 89)*

Maribor (1) 2 *(Zahovic 43, Tavares 90 (pen))*   7000

Zrinjski Mostar: (442) Piric; Baric, Stojkic, Jakovljevic, Katanec; Kajkut, Jovic, Pezer (Perisic 61), Cavar (Mulahusejnovic 78); Filipovic (Todorovic 61), Bilbja.
Maribor: (442) Handanovic; Suler, Rajcevic, Palcic, Vrhovec; Ahmedi, Kabha, Hotic (Tavares 71), Viler; Zahovic (Pihler 71), Bajde (Mesanovic 84).

Friday, 14 July 2017

Linfield (0) 0

Celtic (2) 2 *(Sinclair 18, Rogic 23)*   6359

Linfield: (352) Carroll; Stafford, Haughey, Clarke M (Stewart J 54); Casement, Garrett, Mulgrew, Lowry, Quinn; Smyth, Waterworth.
Celtic: (4411) Gordon; Lustig, Simunovic, Sviatchenko, Tierney; Forrest (Hayes 71), Armstrong, Brown, Sinclair; Rogic; Griffiths (Dembele 70).

SECOND QUALIFYING ROUND SECOND LEG

Tuesday, 18 July 2017

Alashkert (1) 1 *(Nenadovic 18)*

BATE Borisov (2) 3 *(Gordeichuk 23, 35, Volodjko M 78)*
                                  10,000

Alashkert: (451) Beglaryan; Khovbosha (Peltier 72), Voskanyan, Stojkovic, Jablan (Minasyan 66); Daghbashyan, Dashyan, Veranyan, Grigoryan (Manasyan 46), Yedigaryan; Nenadovic.
BATE Borisov: (4231) Scherbitski; Yablonskiy, Rios (Volodjko M 33), Milunovic (Gajduchik 43), Polyakov; Volodjko A, Dragun (Kendysh 82); Gordeichuk, Ivanic, Stasevich; Signevich.

Astana (0) 1 *(Twumasi 59)*

Spartaks Jurmala (0) 1 *(Vardanjans 72)*   20,500

Astana: (433) Mokin; Shitov, Anicic, Logvinenko, Shomko; Grahovac (Beysebekov 72), Kleinheisler (Murtazayev 76), Maevskiy; Twumasi, Kabananga, Muzhikov (Postnikov 87).
Spartaks Jurmala: (442) Nerugals; Slampe, Mihadjuks, Stuglis E, Pushnyakov; Gabelok, Vardanjans, Stuglis I (Kozlovs 83), Gauracs (Platonov 65); Ibragimov, Kozlov.

Buducnost Podgorica (0) 0

Partizan Belgrade (0) 0   9153

Buducnost Podgorica: (433) Mijatovic; Camaj (Melunovic 64), Mirkovic (Markovic 83), Nikac, Tucevic; Simovic, Mitrovic, Raspopovic; Hocko, Terzic (Pejakovic 69), Vlaisavljevic.
Partizan Belgrade: (4231) Kljajic; Vulicevic, Cirkovic, Jankovic (Mihajlovic 82), Djurickovic (Ilic 90); Ostojic, Everton Bilher; Nemanja G Miletic, Kosovic, Djurdjevic; Leonardo (Pantic 88).

Samtredia (0) 0
Qarabag (1) 1 *(Guerrier 23)* 1835
Samtredia: (4231) Migineishvili; Mtchedlishvili, Sandokhadze, Kasradze, Balde; Datunaishvili, Manjgaladze; Markozashvili (Samushia 57), Razhamashvili, Gui (Ninua 84); Sabanadze (Jikia 77).
Qarabag: (433) Kanibolotskiy; Medvedev, Huseynov B, Rzezniczak, Agolli; Michel, Garayev, Almeida (Amirguliyev 62); Madatov, Ndlovu (Ramazanov 70), Guerrier (Ismayilov 62).

The New Saints (0) 1 *(Cieslewicz 69)*
Rijeka (1) 5 *(Matei 41, Gavranovic 54, 79, Gorgon 61, Ristovski 64)* 1150
The New Saints: (442) Harrison; Pryce, Spender, Saunders, Rawlinson; Edwards (Holland 65), Routledge, Brobbel, Fletcher (Cieslewicz 56); Mullan, Quigley (Draper 62).
Rijeka: (361) Sluga; Elez, Ristovski, Zuta; Matei, Zuparic, Gorgon (Crnic 68), Misic, Bradaric, Vesovic (Gavranovic 52); Heber.

Vardar (0) 3 *(Grncarov 56, Barseghyan 61, Nikolov 90)*
Malmo (1) 1 *(Rosenberg 16 (pen))* 2800
Vardar: (442) Gacevski; Grncarov, Spirovski, Barseghyan (Brdarovski 73), Gligorov (Blazevski 46); Hambardzumyan, Nikolov, Novak, Demiri; Felipe, Balotelli (Musliu 85).
Malmo: (442) Wiland; Konate (Rakip 63), Tinnerholm, Lewicki (Svanberg 83), Christiansen; Rosenberg, Eikrem, Yotun, Berget; Nielsen, Brorsson (Bengtsson 46).

Vìkingur (0) 0
Hafnarfjordur (0) 2 *(Lennon 79 (pen), Valdimarsson 90)* 3043
Vìkingur: (4231) Rasmussen; Gregersen, Jacobsen E, Jacobsen H, Djurhuus (Olsen A[■] 26); Vatnhamar G, Anghel V; Djordjevic (Lervig 87), Benjaminsen (Hansen H 88), Anghel S; Lawal.
Hafnarfjordur: (433) Nielsen; Olafsson, Vidarsson P, Doumbia, Bodvarsson; Palsson (Crawford 61), Vidarsson D, Valdimarsson; Lennon, Finnbogason, Gudnason.

Wednesday, 19 July 2017
Budapest Honved (1) 2 *(Lanzafame 45 (pen), Barath 73)*
Hapoel Be'er Sheva (2) 3 *(Ogu 12, Nwakaeme 16, 84)* 200
Budapest Honved: (442) Grof; Barath, Bobal, Kamber, Laczko (Tomosvari 74); Poloskei (Kabangu 34), Nagy, Lovric, Gazdag; Lanzafame, Eppel.
Hapoel Be'er Sheva: (433) Haimov; Korhut (Ohayon 56), Tzedek, Vitor, Bitton; Ohana, Ogu, Einbinder; Nwakaeme, Sahar (Barda 36 (Ghadir 63)), Melikson.

Celtic (1) 4 *(Sinclair 5, 54, Rogic 48, Armstrong 90)*
Linfield (0) 0 58,075
Celtic: (4231) Gordon; Lustig, Ntcham (Armstrong 70), Simunovic, Tierney; McGregor (Benyu 76), Brown; Forrest (Hayes 70), Rogic, Sinclair; Dembele.
Linfield: (352) Carroll; Casement, Haughey, Stafford; Mitchell, Quinn, Lowry, Mulgrew, Garrett (Millar 66); Smyth (Stewart J 66), Waterworth (Stewart C 77).

F91 Dudelange (0) 0
APOEL (1) 1 *(de Camargo 39 (pen))* 1458
F91 Dudelange: (442) Joubert; Jordanov, Schnell (Pokar 46), Prempeh, Lauriente; Stolz, Garos, Stelvio Cruz, Barbosa (Sinani 73); Er Rafik (Dobros 58), Turpel.
APOEL: (442) Waterman; Milanov (Artymatas 61), Merkis, Rueda, Roberto Lago; Bertoglio, Vinicius, Morais, Ebecilio; de Camargo (Pote 80), Oar (Vander 72).

FC Copenhagen (0) 1 *(Verbic 48 (pen))*
MSK Zilina (1) 2 *(Otubanjo 19, Kasa 57)* 9140
FC Copenhagen: (442) Olsen; Boilesen, Luftner, Johansson, Bengtsson; Verbic, Gregus, Matic (Kvist 65), Toutouh; Sotiriou (Pavlovic 67), Santander.
MSK Zilina: (433) Mandous; Vallo (Kralik 75), Kasa, Vavro, Mazan; Cociuc (Sheidaev 66), Diaz, Skvarka; Spalek, Otubanjo, Polievka (Mraz 61).

Kukesi (2) 2 *(Emini 35, Pejic 45)*
Sheriff (0) 1 *(Bayala 56)* 1417
Kukesi: (442) Kolici; Rrumbullaku, Hallaci, Shameti, Serran; Musolli (Zeqiri 72), Lena, Cale (Nasr 46), Emini; Guri (Carioca 62), Pejic.
Sheriff: (352) Mikulic; Posmac, Racu, Susic; Badibanga (Bordian 82), Brezovec, de Nooijer[■], Anton, Cristiano; Mugosa (Oliveira 88), Bayala (Jardan 90).
Sheriff won on away goals.

Legia Warsaw (3) 6 *(Guilherme 6, Kojola 37 (og), Kucharczyk 40, 54 (pen), Szymanski 80, Michalak 81)*
IFK Mariehamn (0) 0 15,843
Legia Warsaw: (4231) Cierzniak; Jedrzejczyk, Dabrowski, Pazdan (Kopczynski 57); Hlousek; Maczynski, Makowski; Szymanski, Guilherme (Michalak 46), Moneta; Kucharczyk (Hamalainen 65).
IFK Mariehamn: (4411) Nordqvist; Friberg da Cruz, Kojola (Granlund 67), Lyyski, Maenpaa; Span, Ekhalie, Petrovic, Sellin (Mattsson 75); Sid; Kangaskolkka (Amani 86).

Ludogorets Razgrad (1) 4 *(Natanael 41, Wanderson 55, Keseru 56, 74)*
Zalgiris (1) 1 *(Nyuiadzi 15)* 4739
Ludogorets Razgrad: (433) Broun; Sasha, Moti, Plastun, Natanael; Abel, Marcelinho, Dyakov; Wanderson (Joao Paulo 86), Keseru (Lukoki 88), Cafu (Misidjan 81).
Zalgiris: (433) Vitkauskas; Vaitkunas, Mbodj, Klimavicius, Slijngard; Traore (Atajic 46), Blagojevic, Kuklys; Nyuiadzi (Luksa 67), Ljujic (Oyarzun 76), Elivelto.

Maribor (1) 1 *(Viler 27)*
Zrinjski Mostar (1) 1 *(Todorovic 7)* 9266
Maribor: (4231) Handanovic; Palcic, Rajcevic, Suler, Viler; Pihler, Kabha; Hotic (Mesanovic 65), Ahmedi, Bajde; Zahovic (Tavares 65).
Zrinjski Mostar: (4231) Piric; Galic, Jakovljevic, Katanec, Stojkic; Pezer (Mulahusejnovic 86), Perisic (Cavar 70); Filipovic (Kukoc 81), Bilbja, Todorovic; Jovic.

Red Bull Salzburg (2) 3 *(Rzatkowski 11, Gulbrandsen 20, Haidara 85)*
Hibernians (0) 0 5511
Red Bull Salzburg: (4312) Stankovic; Lazaro (Farkas 69), Paulo Miranda, Caleta-Car, Ulmer; Leitgeb, Samassekou, Rzatkowski (Haidara 64); Wolf; Gulbrandsen (Hwang 56), Dabbur.
Hibernians: (352) Hogg; Soares, Da Garcia, Kreuzriegler; Dias (Mbong 46), Lima, Agius, Kristensen, Failla (Degabriele 80); Bezzina (Sahanek 65), Jorginho.

Rosenborg (1) 2 *(de Lanlay 43, Vilhjalmsson 98)*
Dundalk (1) 1 *(Gartland 12)* 14,817
Rosenborg: (433) Hansen; Hedenstadt, Reginiussen, Skjelvik, Meling; Jensen, Konradsen A, Midtsjoe; Jevtovic (Rashani 106), Bendtner (Lundemo 114), de Lanlay (Vilhjalmsson 72).
Dundalk: (433) Rogers; Gannon, Vemmelund, Gartland, Massey; Mountney, Shields, Benson; McEleney (McGrath 84), McMillan (Kilduff 94), Duffy (O'Donnell 59).
aet.

THIRD QUALIFYING ROUND FIRST LEG
Tuesday, 25 July 2017
AEK Athens (0) 0
CSKA Moscow (1) 2 *(Dzagoev 45, Wernbloom 56)* 25,083
AEK Athens: (433) Anestis; Bakakis, Vranjes, Ajdarevic, Christodoulopoulos (Rodriguez 71); Andre Simoes (Klonaridis 60), Livaja (Almeida 60), Rodrigo Galo; Johansson, Chygrynskiy, Mantalos.
CSKA Moscow: (3142) Akinfeev; Fernandes, Wernbloom, Vasin; Berezutski A; Dzagoev (Natcho 75), Vitinho, Golovin (Milanov 83), Berezutski V; Schennikov, Chalov (Makarov 87).

Partizan Belgrade (1) 1 *(Tawamba 10)*
Olympiacos (1) 3 *(Nabouhane 6, 56, Emenike 90)* 24,658
Partizan Belgrade: (442) Kljajic; Ostojic, Vulicevic, Nemanja G Miletic, Cirkovic (Nemanja R Miletic 72); Jankovic (Pantic 82), Everton Bilher, Kosovic, Leonardo; Tawamba, Djurdjevic.
Olympiacos: (433) Kapino; Koutris, Diogo Figueiras, Retsos, Romao; Carcela-Gonzalez (Pardo 80), Fortounis, Odjidja-Ofoe; Marin (Zdjelar 80), Siopis, Nabouhane (Emenike 88).

Qarabag (0) 0
Sheriff (0) 0 26,000
Qarabag: (433) Sehic; Medvedev, Huseynov B, Rzezniczak (Yunuszadze 24), Garayev; Agolli, Michel, Guerrier (Ramazanov 88); Almeida, Ismayilov (Madatov 62), Ndlovu.
Sheriff: (433) Mikulic; Susic, Posmac, Racu, Oliveira; Brezovec (Bordian 77), Anton, Cristiano; Bayala (Damascan 90), Mugosa (Balima 71), Badibanga.

Slavia Prague (1) 1 *(Skoda 20 (pen))*
BATE Borisov (0) 0 18,147
Slavia Prague: (4141) Lastuvka; Frydrych, Jugas, Deli, Boril; Ngadeu Ngadjui; van Buren, Rotan (Mesanovic 66), Husbauer, Danny (Mingazov 76); Skoda.
BATE Borisov: (4231) Scherbitski; Baha, Gajduchik, Yablonskiy**, Volodjko M; Kendysh, Dragun (Berezkin 90); Stasevich (Tuominem 78), Volodjko A, Ivanic (Buljat 24); Signevich.

Steaua Bucharest (1) 2 *(Budescu 37, Teixeria 61)*
Viktoria Plzen (1) 2 *(Krmencik 23, Kopic 53)* 33,795
Steaua Bucharest: (4231) Nita; Enache, Larie, Balasa, Momcilovic; Pintilii, Junior Morais; Teixeria, Budescu (Achim 66), Tanase (William 46); Alibec (Gnohere 57).
Viktoria Plzen: (4231) Bolek; Limbersky, Reznik, Hajek, Suchan; Zivulic, Hrosovsky; Petrzela (Zeman 69), Kolar (Reznicek 84), Kopic; Krmencik (Bakos 67).

Vardar (0) 1 *(Balotelli 65)*
FC Copenhagen (0) 0 12,000
Vardar: (4231) Gacevski; Hambardzumyan, Grncarov, Novak, Demiri; Spirovski, Nikolov (Gligorov 88); Barseghyan (Brdarovski 76), Felipe, Blazevski (Kojasevic 60); Balotelli.
FC Copenhagen: (442) Olsen; Boilesen, Luftner, Johansson, Bengtsson; Verbic, Gregus, Kvist, Toutouh (Thomsen 65); Pavlovic (Sotiriou 73), Santander.

Wednesday, 26 July 2017

Astana (2) 3 *(Kabananga 36, Maevskiy 45, Twumasi 90)*
Legia Warsaw (0) 1 *(Sadiku 79)* 26,100
Astana: (442) Mokin; Shitov, Logvinenko, Anicic, Shomko; Twumasi, Maevskiy, Kleinheisler (Grahovac 80), Muzhikov; Kabananga, Despotovic (Murtazayev 20 (Postnikov 89)).
Legia Warsaw: (4231) Malarz; Jedrzejczyk, Dabrowski, Pazdan, Hlousek; Moulin, Maczynski; Guilherme, Hamalainen (Sadiku 70), Nagy (Pasquato 62); Kucharczyk (Michalak 83).

Celtic (0) 0
Rosenborg (0) 0 49,172
Celtic: (4321) Gordon; Lustig, Simunovic, Ajer, Tierney; Ntcham (Hayes 63), Brown, Forrest (Benyu 81); Sinclair, Rogic; Armstrong.
Rosenborg: (433) Hansen; Hedenstadt, Reginiussen (Bjordal 65), Skjelvik, Meling; Midtsjoe, Konradsen A, Jensen; Jevtovic (Rashani 79), Bendtner, de Lanlay (Vilhjalmsson 80).

Club Brugge (2) 3 *(Bonaventure 6, Denswil 16, 79)*
Istanbul Basaksehir (0) 3 *(Mossoro 59, 74, Elia 64)* 26,788
Club Brugge: (343) Horvath; Mechele, Engels, Denswil; Palacios, Vormer, Nakamba, De Bock (Touba 59); Rafaelov (Vanaken 75), Perbet, Bonaventure (Izquierdo 62).
Istanbul Basaksehir: (4231) Babacan; Junior Caicara, Attamah, Epureanu, Clichy; Emre (Inler 76), Tekdemir; Visca (Torun 82), Mossoro, Elia (Napoleoni 89); Adebayor.

Dynamo Kyiv (2) 3 *(Yarmolenko 15, Mbokani 34, Harmash 90)*
Young Boys (0) 1 *(Fassnacht 90)* 36,341
Dynamo Kyiv: (4411) Koval; Morozyuk, Khacheridi, Vida, Kadar; Yarmolenko, Sydorchuk (Korzun 65), Shepelev, Gonzalez (Tsygankov 81); Harmash (Buyalsky 90); Mbokani.
Young Boys: (442) von Ballmoos; Mbabu, von Bergen, Nuhu, Benito (Lotomba 76); Ravet, Aebischer (Bertone 62), Sanogo (Assale 52), Fassnacht; Hoarau, Sow.

Hapoel Be'er Sheva (1) 2 *(Nwakaeme 20, Ohana 79)*
Ludogorets Razgrad (0) 0 15,183
Hapoel Be'er Sheva: (433) Haimov; Bitton, Vitor, Tzedek, Korhut; Radi (Brown 90), Ogu, Einbinder; Melikson (Ohana 71), Ghadir (Elo 86), Nwakaeme.
Ludogorets Razgrad: (433) Broun; Sasha, Plastun, Moti, Natanael; Abel, Dyakov, Wanderson; Marcelinho, Cafu, Keseru (Misidjan 76).

Maribor (0) 1 *(Tavares 54)*
Hafnarfjordur (0) 0 8166
Maribor: (4231) Handanovic; Palcic, Rajcevic, Suler, Viler; Kabha, Vrhovec (Pihler 89); Ahmedi (Bohar 75), Tavares, Bajde; Mesanovic (Zahovic 79).
Hafnarfjordur: (442) Nielsen; Olafsson, Vidarsson P, Doumbia, Bodvarsson; Valdimarsson (Crawford 79), Palsson, Vidarsson D, Gudnason; Lennon (Bjornsson A 90), Finnbogason.

Nice (1) 1 *(Balotelli 32)*
Ajax (0) 1 *(van de Beek 49)* 31,342
Nice: (442) Cardinale; Souquet, Dante, Le Marchand, Sarr; Eysseric, Koziello, Seri, Lees-Melou (Dalbert 87); Srarfi (Marcel 77), Balotelli (Plea 70).
Ajax: (433) Onana; Veltman, Sanchez, de Ligt, Viergever; van de Beek, Schone (De Jong 73), Ziyech; Kluivert (Neres 68), Dolberg, Younes.

Red Bull Salzburg (0) 1 *(Hwang 49)*
Rijeka (1) 1 *(Gavranovic 30)* 12,714
Red Bull Salzburg: (442) Walke; Lainer, Paulo Miranda, Caleta-Car, Ulmer; Yabo (Rzatkowski 77), Samassekou, Minamino, Berisha V; Hwang (Gulbrandsen 73), Dabbur (Wolf 90).
Rijeka: (442) Sluga; Ristovski, Zuparic, Elez, Kvrzic (Zuta 73); Heber (Males 58), Bradaric, Misic, Vesovic; Gavranovic (Jelic 88), Gorgon.

Viitorul (0) 1 *(Ganea 75)*
APOEL (0) 0 3873
Viitorul: (433) Rimniceanu; Boli, Tiru, Constantin (Vina 46), Ganea; Cicaldau, Benzar, Nedelcu; Chitu (Coman 66), Tucudean**, Herea (Lopez 46).
APOEL: (4411) Waterman; Milanov, Merkis, Rueda, Lago; Bertoglio, Vinicius (Artymatas 86), Morais, Ebecilio (Vander 73); Oar; de Camargo.

THIRD QUALIFYING ROUND SECOND LEG

Tuesday, 1 August 2017

Sheriff (0) 1 *(Badibanga 90 (pen))*
Qarabag (1) 2 *(Ndlovu 45, Michel 87)* 7742
Sheriff: (433) Mikulic; Susic, Posmac, Oliveira, Cristiano; Brezovec (Balima 85), Racu, de Nooijer (Mugosa 61); Bayala, Damascan, Badibanga.
Qarabag: (433) Sehic; Medvedev (Rzezniczak 31), Huseynov B, Sadygov, Agolli; Michel, Garayev, Almeida, Guerrier, Ndlovu (Ramazanov 90), Madatov (Ismayilov 60).

Wednesday, 2 August 2017

Ajax (1) 2 *(van de Beek 26, Sanchez 57)*
Nice (1) 2 *(Souquet 3, Marcel 79)* 51,845
Ajax: (433) Onana; Veltman, Sanchez, de Ligt (Neres 86), Viergever; van de Beek, Schone (Huntelaar 82), Ziyech; Kluivert (De Jong 78), Dolberg, Younes.
Nice: (451) Cardinale; Souquet, Dante, Le Marchand, Sarr (Marcel 69); Lees-Melou, Koziello, Seri, Eysseric, Srarfi (Dalbert 46); Plea.
Nice won on away goals.

APOEL (0) 4 *(Carlao 54, Merkis 93, de Camargo 94, Efrem 105)*

Viitorul (0) 0   13,647

APOEL: (442) Waterman; Milanov, Rueda, Carlao (Merkis 81), Lago; Bertoglio, Morais, Vinicius, Aloneftis (Ebecilio 54); Vander (Efrem 88), de Camargo.
Viitorul: (433) Rimniceanu; Boli, Tiru, Constantin, Ganea; Benzar, Nedelcu (Mladen 82), Lopez; Chitu, Coman (Eric 96), Cicaldau (Herea 82).
aet.

BATE Borisov (1) 2 *(Signevich 6, Stasevich 46)*

Slavia Prague (1) 1 *(Skoda 44)*   12,436

BATE Borisov: (451) Scherbitski; Baha, Milunovic, Buljat, Polyakov (Volodjko M 46); Stasevich, Volodjko A (Gvilia 76), Ivanic, Dragun, Gordeichuk (Tuominen 88); Signevich.
Slavia Prague: (451) Lastuvka; Frydrych, Jugas, Deli, Boril; van Buren (Zmrhal 61), Rotan, Husbauer (Soucek 86), Ngadeu Ngadjui, Danny (Svento 70); Skoda.
Slavia Prague won on away goals.

CSKA Moscow (0) 1 *(Natcho 74)*

AEK Athens (0) 0   12,000

CSKA Moscow: (532) Akinfeev; Fernandes, Vasin, Berezutski V, Berezutski A, Schennikov; Wernbloom, Dzagoev (Natcho 73), Golovin (Milanov 81); Vitinho, Chalov (Olanare 69).
AEK Athens: (532) Anestis; Bakakis, Vranjes, Chygrynskiy, Cosic, Helder Lopes; Johansson, Mantalos, Andre Simoes (Galanopoulos 77); Klonaridis (Giakoumakis 77), Livaja (Christodoulopoulos 71).

FC Copenhagen (2) 4 *(Gregus 2, Barseghyan 26 (og), Santander 75, Sotiriou 88 (pen))*

Vardar (1) 1 *(Nikolov 19)*   15,224

FC Copenhagen: (442) Olsen; Luftner, Bengtsson, Johansson, Kvist; Thomsen, Gregus■, Toutouh (Amankwaa 82), Verbic; Santander (Matic 78), Pavlovic (Sotiriou 83).
Vardar: (442) Gacevski; Novak, Demiri, Hambardzumyan (Blazevski 76), Grncarov; Spirovski (Jigauri 82), Nikolov, Felipe, Balotelli; Kojasevic (Brdarovski 46), Barseghyan.

Hafnarfjordur (0) 0

Maribor (0) 1 *(Tavares 90)*   2563

Hafnarfjordur: (442) Nielsen; Doumbia, Bodvarsson, Vidarsson P, Olafsson (Gudmundsson 89); Lennon, Palsson, Valdimarsson, Vidarsson D; Gudnason, Finnbogason.
Maribor: (442) Handanovic; Rajcevic, Palcic, Suler, Vrhovec (Pihler 90); Ahmedi (Hotic 83), Kabha, Viler, Bohar (Bajde 77); Tavares, Zahovic.

Istanbul Basaksehir (2) 2 *(Adebayor 7, Visca 34)*

Club Brugge (0) 0   9168

Istanbul Basaksehir: (442) Babacan; Epureanu, Junior Caicara, Clichy, Attamah; Emre, Tekdemir, Visca (Napoleoni 88), Mossoro (Inler 71); Adebayor, Elia (Frei 78).
Club Brugge: (442) Horvath; Touba (Izquierdo 71), Mechele, Engels, Palacios; Denswil, Vormer, Rafaelov (Vanaken 46), Nakamba; Bonaventure (Diaby 56), Vossen.

Legia Warsaw (0) 1 *(Czerwinski 76)*

Astana (0) 0   24,937

Legia Warsaw: (433) Malarz; Jedrzejczyk, Czerwinski, Pazdan, Hlousek (Szymanski 69); Moulin, Guilherme, Kopczynski (Maczynski 65); Kucharczyk, Sadiku (Hamalainen 58), Nagy.
Astana: (4231) Mokin; Shitov, Logvinenko, Anicic (Postnikov 63), Shomko; Maevskiy, Kleinheisler; Twumasi, Muzhikov (Grahovac 84), Murtazayev (Beysebekov 57); Kabananga.

Ludogorets Razgrad (2) 3 *(Wanderson 9, 33, Marcelinho 56)*

Hapoel Be'er Sheva (0) 1 *(Ghadir 61)*   5398

Ludogorets Razgrad: (361) Broun; Moti, Plastun, Natanael; Sasha, Abel (Misidjan 71), Dyakov, Cafu (Joao Paulo 78), Keseru, Marcelinho; Wanderson.
Hapoel Be'er Sheva: (433) Haimov; Korhut, Bitton, Vitor, Tzedek; Radi, Einbinder (Ohana■ 58), Melikson (Taha 67); Ogu, Ghadir (Brown 89), Nwakaeme.
Hapoel Be'er Sheva won on away goals.

Olympiacos (1) 2 *(Carcela-Gonzalez 22, Fortounis 51)*

Partizan Belgrade (1) 2 *(Everton Bilher 33, Djurdjevic 85)*   23,854

Olympiacos: (4231) Kapino; Diogo Figueiras, Vukovic (Zdjelar 72), Retsos, Koutris; Ödjidja-Ofoe, Romao; Carcela-Gonzalez, Fortounis (Seba 70), Marin (Siopis 87); Nabouhane.
Partizan Belgrade: (442) Kljajic; Vulicevic, Ostojic, Cirkovic, Nemanja G Miletic; Soumah (Pantic 64), Jevtovic (Kosovic 79), Everton Bilher, Jankovic; Tawamba, Djurdjevic.

Rijeka (0) 0

Red Bull Salzburg (0) 0   8118

Rijeka: (4231) Sluga; Ristovski, Zuparic, Elez, Vesovic; Bradaric, Males; Kvrzic (Heber 87), Misic, Gorgon; Gavranovic (Jelic 74).
Red Bull Salzburg: (442) Walke; Lainer, Paulo Miranda, Caleta-Car, Ulmer; Yabo (Haidara 68), Samassekou, Minamino (Wolf 81), Berisha V; Hwang, Dabbur (Gulbrandsen 74).
Rijeka won on away goals.

Rosenborg (0) 0

Celtic (0) 1 *(Forrest 69)*   20,974

Rosenborg: (433) Hansen; Hedenstadt, Bjordal, Skjelvik, Meling; Jensen, Konradsen A, Midtsjoe; Jevtovic (Helland 72), Bendtner, de Lanlay (Vilhjalmsson 73).
Celtic: (433) Gordon; Lustig, Šimunovic, Sviatchenko (Bitton 24), Tierney; McGregor, Brown, Armstrong (Rogic 70); Forrest, Hayes (Griffiths 57), Sinclair.

Viktoria Plzen (0) 1 *(Krmencik 64)*

Steaua Bucharest (1) 4 *(Balasa 27, Teixeria 71, Tanase 76, Alibec 79 (pen))*   10,802

Viktoria Plzen: (442) Bolek; Hajek, Hejda, Kopic, Petrzela (Zeman 54); Hrosovsky, Havel, Kolar (Bakos 77), Zivulic (Horava 63); Krmencik■, Reznicek.
Steaua Bucharest: (442) Nita; Junior Morais, Momcilovic, Balasa, Pintilii; Tanase (Gnohere 83), Popescu (Achim 73), Enache, Teixeria; Man (Larie 46), Alibec.

Young Boys (1) 2 *(Hoarau 13 (pen), Benito 90)*

Dynamo Kyiv (0) 0   13,303

Young Boys: (442) Wolfli; von Bergen, Benito, Nuhu, Mbabu; Sow (Lotomba 85), Fassnacht (Sulejmani 73), Sanogo, Hoarau; Ravet, Assale (Nsame 73).
Dynamo Kyiv: (4231) Koval; Kadar, Khacheridi, Vida, Shepelev (Korzun 69); Morozyuk, Sydorchuk; Harmash (Buyalsky 84), Gonzalez (Kravets 90), Mbokani; Yarmolenko.
Young Boys won on away goals.

PLAY-OFF ROUND FIRST LEG
Tuesday, 15 August 2017

APOEL (2) 2 *(de Camargo 2, Aloneftis 10)*

Slavia Prague (0) 0   13,073

APOEL: (4411) Waterman; Milanov, Rueda, Carlao, Lago; Ebecilio (Bertoglio 83), Morais, Vinicius, Aloneftis (Farias 68); Oar (Efrem 52); de Camargo.
Slavia Prague: (4141) Lastuvka; Frydrych, Jugas, Ngadeu Ngadjui, Boril; Soucek; van Buren (Zmrhal 46), Rotan (Mesanovic 72), Husbauer, Stoch (Sykora 79); Skoda.

Qarabag (1) 1 *(Madatov 25)*

FC Copenhagen (0) 0   31,250

Qarabag: (433) Sehic; Medvedev, Huseynov B, Rzezniczak, Agolli; Michel, Almeida, Garayev; Madatov, Ndlovu (Ismayilov 90), Guerrier.
FC Copenhagen: (442) Olsen; Ankersen, Luftner, Boilesen, Bengtsson; Matic, Kvist, Verbic (Thomsen 86), Toutouh (Amankwaa 68); Pavlovic (Sotiriou 74), Santander.

Sporting Lisbon (0) 0

Steaua Bucharest (0) 0   46,678

Sporting Lisbon: (4411) Rui Patricio; Piccini, Coates, Mathieu, Fabio Coentrao (Iuri Medeiros 86); Acuna, Battaglia, Adrien Silva (Bruno Fernandes 67); Gelson Martins; Daniel Podence (Doumbia 60); Dost.
Steaua Bucharest: (4411) Nita; Enache, Larie, Momcilovic, Junior Morais; Teixeria, Pintilii■, Popescu, Golofca (William 57); Tanase (Achim 83); Alibec (Gnohere 90). ·

TSG Hoffenheim (0) 1 *(Uth 87)*
Liverpool (1) 2 *(Alexander-Arnold 35, Nordtveit 77 (og))*
25,568
TSG Hoffenheim: (433) Baumann; Kaderabek, Bicakcic (Nordtveit 52), Vogt, Hubner; Zuber, Rupp (Amiri 53), Demirbay; Kramaric, Gnabry (Uth 70), Wagner.
Liverpool: (433) Mignolet; Alexander-Arnold, Matip, Lovren, Moreno; Can, Henderson (Milner 63), Wijnaldum; Salah, Firmino (Solanke 84), Mane (Grujic 89).

Young Boys (0) 0
CSKA Moscow (0) 1 *(Nuhu 90 (og))*
20,003
Young Boys: (442) von Ballmoos; Benito, Nuhu, von Bergen, Mbabu; Ravet (Fassnacht 73), Bertone, Sanogo, Sulejmani; Assale (Nsame 85), Hoarau.
CSKA Moscow: (352) Akinfeev; Berezutski V, Vasin, Ignashevich; Fernandes, Golovin, Wernbloom, Dzagoev (Milanov 72), Schennikov; Vitinho, Chalov (Olanare 55 (Natcho 90)).

Wednesday, 16 August 2017

Celtic (2) 5 *(Postnikov 32 (og), Sinclair 42, 60, Forrest 79, Shitov 88 (og))*
Astana (0) 0
54,016
Celtic: (4411) Gordon; Lustig, Bitton, Simunovic, Tierney; Forrest (Armstrong 82), Ntcham, Brown, Sinclair; Rogic (McGregor 63); Griffiths.
Astana: (442) Mokin; Shitov, Postnikov, Logvinenko (Beysebekov 66), Shomko; Twumasi, Maevskiy, Kleinheisler, Tomasov (Murtazayev 77); Kabananga, Muzhikov (Grahovac 81).

Hapoel Be'er Sheva (2) 2 *(Nwakaeme 12, Tzedek 45 (pen))*
Maribor (1) 1 *(Tavares 10)*
15,265
Hapoel Be'er Sheva: (433) Haimov; Bitton, Taha, Tzedek, Korhut; Radi (Cuenca 84), Ogu, Einbinder; Melikson, Ghadir (Pekhart 65), Nwakaeme.
Maribor: (4411) Handanovic; Milec, Rajcevic, Suler, Viler; Hotic (Zahovic 71), Kabha, Vrhovec (Pihler 88), Bohar; Ahmedi; Tavares (Mesanovic 74).

Istanbul Basaksehir (0) 1 *(Elia 64)*
Sevilla (1) 2 *(Escudero 16, Ben Yedder 84)*
12,894
Istanbul Basaksehir: (4411) Babacan; Junior Caicara, Attamah, Epureanu, Clichy; Visca (Frei 64), Tekdemir, Emre, Elia; Mossoro (Napoleoni 82); Adebayor.
Sevilla: (433) Sergio Rico; Mercado, Pareja, Lenglet, Escudero; Nzonzi, Pizarro, Banega; Montoya (Nolito 63), Ben Yedder (Krohn-Dehli 86), Correa (Jesus Navas 83).

Napoli (1) 2 *(Mertens 13, Jorginho 69 (pen))*
Nice (0) 0
49,324
Napoli: (451) Reina; Hysaj, Albiol, Koulibaly, Ghoulam; Callejon, Allan (Rog 85), Jorginho, Hamsik (Zielinski 59), Insigne; Mertens (Milik 75).
Nice: (433) Cardinale; Souquet, Le Marchand, Dante, Sarr (Boscagli 60); Koziello■, Seri, Jallet (Burner 90); Lees-Melou, Saint-Maximin (Walter 82), Plea■.

Olympiacos (0) 2 *(Odjidja-Ofoe 66, Romao 90)*
Rijeka (1) 1 *(Heber 42)*
21,352
Olympiacos: (4231) Kapino; Elabdellaoui, Romao, Retsos, Koutris; Odjidja-Ofoe (Androutsos 79), Gillet; Carcela-Gonzalez, Marin (Pardo 75), Seba (Fortounis 65); Nabouhane.
Rijeka: (4231) Sluga; Vesovic, Zuparic, Elez, Zuta■; Bradaric, Males; Heber (Martic 88), Misic, Gorgon (Crnic 78); Gavranovic (Jelic 72).

PLAY-OFF ROUND SECOND LEG

Tuesday, 22 August 2017

Astana (1) 4 *(Ajer 26 (og), Muzhikov 48, Twumasi 49, 69)*
Celtic (1) 3 *(Sinclair 33, Ntcham 80, Griffiths 90)* 19,075
Astana: (442) Eric; Shitov, Postnikov, Anicic, Shomko; Twumasi, Maevskiy, Kleinheisler (Grahovac 13), Tomasov (Beysebekov 46 (Tagybergen 81)); Kabananga, Muzhikov.
Celtic: (451) Gordon; Lustig, Bitton, Ajer, Tierney; Forrest (Ralston 56), Ntcham, Brown, McGregor (Rogic 57), Sinclair (Armstrong 65); Griffiths.

Maribor (1) 1 *(Viler 15)*
Hapoel Be'er Sheva (0) 0
12,066
Maribor: (442) Handanovic; Suler, Rajcevic, Milec, Viler; Bohar (Billong 90), Vrhovec, Ahmedi (Pihler 83), Kabha; Tavares, Bajde (Hotic 72).
Hapoel Be'er Sheva: (442) Haimov; Korhut, Elhamed (Ohana 46), Bitton, Tzedek; Taha, Melikson, Ogu, Radi (Barda 79); Ghadir (Pekhart 56), Nwakaeme.
Maribor won on away goals.

Nice (0) 0
Napoli (0) 2 *(Callejon 48, Insigne 89)*
32,103
Nice: (4312) Cardinale; Souquet, Le Marchand, Dante, Jallet; Tameze (Lees-Melou 66), Seri, Walter (Marcel 79); Sneijder; Balotelli (Ganago 77), Saint-Maximin.
Napoli: (433) Reina; Hysaj, Albiol, Koulibaly, Ghoulam; Allan (Rog 71), Jorginho (Diawara 85), Hamsik (Zielinski 63); Callejon, Mertens, Insigne.

Rijeka (0) 0
Olympiacos (1) 1 *(Marin 25)*
8105
Rijeka: (4231) Sluga (Prskalo 51); Martic, Zuparic, Elez, Vesovic; Bradaric (Matei 77), Males; Gorgon (Kvrzic 61), Misic, Heber; Gavranovic.
Olympiacos: (4231) Kapino; Elabdellaoui, Retsos, Vukovic, Koutris (Diogo Figueiras 61); Gillet, Romao (Fortounis 80); Carcela-Gonzalez, Odjidja-Ofoe, Marin (Seba 66); Nabouhane.

Sevilla (2) 2 *(Escudero 52, Ben Yedder 75)*
Istanbul Basaksehir (1) 2 *(Elia 17, Visca 83)*
34,278
Sevilla: (433) Sergio Rico; Mercado, Pareja, Lenglet, Escudero; Nzonzi, Pizarro, Banega (Sarabia 90); Jesus Navas (Montoya 85), Ben Yedder, Correa (Nolito 72).
Istanbul Basaksehir: (4231) Babacan; Junior Caicara, Attamah, Epureanu, Clichy; Tekdemir (Inler 83), Emre; Visca, Mossoro (Napoleoni 72), Elia (Frei 83); Adebayor.

Wednesday, 23 August 2017

CSKA Moscow (1) 2 *(Schennikov 45, Dzagoev 65)*
Young Boys (0) 0
15,560
CSKA Moscow: (442) Akinfeev; Vasin, Berezutski V, Berezutski A, Fernandes; Schennikov, Wernbloom, Golovin, Dzagoev (Natcho 68); Vitinho (Ignashevich 90), Chalov (Zhamaletdinov 74).
Young Boys: (442) Ballmoos; Mbabu, Nuhu, Benito (Lotomba 74), von Bergen; Sulejmani, Nsame, Bertone, Sanogo; Ravet (Fassnacht 73), Assale.

FC Copenhagen (1) 2 *(Santander 45, Pavlovic 66)*
Qarabag (0) 1 *(Ndlovu 63)*
21,222
FC Copenhagen: (442) Olsen; Luftner, Ankersen, Boilesen, Bengtsson; Kvist (Toutouh 80), Gregus, Kusk (Amankwaa 67), Verbic; Santander (Sotiriou 70), Pavlovic.
Qarabag: (433) Sehic; Huseynov B, Rzezniczak, Guerrier (Ismayilov 11 (Sadygov 80)), Medvedev; Garayev, Michel, Almeida (Yunuszadze 90); Agolli, Ndlovu, Madatov.
Qarabag won on away goals.

Liverpool (3) 4 *(Can 10, 21, Salah 19, Firmino 63)*
TSG Hoffenheim (1) 2 *(Uth 28, Wagner 79)* 51,808
Liverpool: (433) Mignolet; Alexander-Arnold (Gomez 64), Matip, Lovren, Moreno; Can (Milner 69), Henderson, Wijnaldum; Salah, Firmino, Mane (Klavan 87).
TSG Hoffenheim: (523) Baumann; Kaderabek (Toljan 64), Nordtveit (Uth 24), Vogt, Hubner; Zuber, Geiger, Demirbay; Kramaric, Wagner, Gnabry (Szalai 56).

Slavia Prague (0) 0
APOEL (0) 0
18,844
Slavia Prague: (451) Lastuvka; Frydrych, Boril, Jugas, Danny (Sykora 71); Husbauer, Ngadeu Ngadjui, Soucek, Rotan (Mesanovic 60), van Buren; Stoch (Zmrhal 46).
APOEL: (442) Waterman; Milanov, Morais, Lago, Carlao; Rueda, Ebecilio (Merkis 82), Vinicius, Aloneftis (Farias 75); Efrem (Bertoglio 46), de Camargo.

Steaua Bucharest (1) 1 *(Junior Morais 20)*
Sporting Lisbon (1) 5 *(Doumbia 13, Acuna 60,*
Gelson Martins 64, Dost 75, Battaglia 88) 49,220
Steaua Bucharest: (442) Nita; Junior Morais, Filip,
Momcilovic, Larie; Teixeria, Popescu, Enache, Golofca
(Gnohere 62); Budescu (Tanase 46), Alibec (Man 81).

Sporting Lisbon: (451) Rui Patricio; Mathieu, Coates,
Fabio Coentrao, Bruno Fernandes; Acuna, Battaglia,
Adrien Silva (Petrovic 72), Gelson Martins (Bruno Cesar
80), Doumbia (Dost 59); Piccini.

GROUP STAGE

GROUP A

Tuesday, 12 September 2017

Benfica (0) 1 *(Seferovic 50)*
CSKA Moscow (0) 2 *(Vitinho 64 (pen),*
Zhamaletdinov 71) 38,323
Benfica: (4132) Bruno Varela; Andre Almeida, Luisao,
Lopez (Rafa Silva 88), Grimaldo (Gabriel Barbosa 77);
Filipe Augusto; Salvio, Pizzi, Zivkovic, Jonas (Jimenez
69), Seferovic.
CSKA Moscow: (352) Akinfeev; Vasin, Berezutski V,
Berezutski A; Fernandes, Golovin (Kuchaev 87),
Wernbloom, Dzagoev (Natcho 76), Schennikov; Vitinho,
Olanare (Zhamaletdinov 67).

Manchester U (1) 3 *(Fellaini 35, Lukaku 53, Rashford 84)*
FC Basel (0) 0 73,854
Manchester U: (4231) de Gea; Young, Lindelof, Smalling,
Blind; Pogba (Fellaini 19), Matic; Mata (Rashford 77),
Mkhitaryan, Martial (Lingard 69); Lukaku.
FC Basel: (343) Vaclik; Akanji, Suchy, Balanta; Lang,
Xhaka, Zuffi, Riveros (Oberlin 77); Steffen, van
Wolfswinkel (Bua 65), Elyounoussi.

Wednesday, 27 September 2017

CSKA Moscow (0) 1 *(Kuchaev 90)*
Manchester U (3) 4 *(Lukaku 4, 26, Martial 19 (pen),*
Mkhitaryan 57) 29,073
CSKA Moscow: (352) Akinfeev; Vasin, Berezutski V,
Ignashevich; Fernandes, Dzagoev (Milanov 72),
Wernbloom, Golovin, Schennikov; Chalov
(Zhamaletdinov 67), Vitinho (Kuchaev 84).
Manchester U: (343) de Gea; Smalling, Bailly, Lindelof;
Young (Darmian 67), Ander Herrera, Matic, Blind;
Mkhitaryan (Lingard 60), Lukaku, Martial (Rashford
71).

FC Basel (2) 5 *(Lang 2, Oberlin 20, 69,*
van Wolfswinkel 59 (pen), Riveros 76)
Benfica (0) 0 34,111
FC Basel: (343) Vaclik; Suchy, Akanji, Balanta (Die 79);
Xhaka, Zuffi, Lang, Petretta (Riveros 67); Steffen, van
Wolfswinkel, Oberlin (Elyounoussi 74).
Benfica: (442) Julio Cesar; Andre Almeida■, Luisao,
Jardel, Grimaldo; Zivkovic (Samaris 74), Pizzi, Fejsa,
Cervi (Salvio 46); Jonas (Rafa Silva 46), Jimenez.

Wednesday, 18 October 2017

Benfica (0) 0
Manchester U (0) 1 *(Rashford 65)* 57,684
Benfica: (433) Svilar; Douglas, Luisao■, Dias, Grimaldo;
Pizzi (Zivkovic 59), Fejsa, Filipe Augusto; Salvio (Cervi
83), Jimenez, Goncalves (Jonas 69).
Manchester U: (442) de Gea; Valencia, Lindelof,
Smalling, Blind; Mata (Lingard 82), Ander Herrera,
Matic, Rashford (Martial 76); Mkhitaryan (McTominay
90), Lukaku.

CSKA Moscow (0) 0
FC Basel (1) 2 *(Xhaka 29, Oberlin 90)* 27,996
CSKA Moscow: (343) Akinfeev; Berezutski A,
Ignashevich (Natcho 46), Vasin; Schennikov,
Wernbloom, Fernandes, Milanov (Kuchaev 70); Golovin,
Vitinho, Zhamaletdinov (Chalov 77).
FC Basel: (343) Vaclik; Akanji, Suchy, Balanta; Lang,
Xhaka, Zuffi, Petretta; Steffen (Bua 86), Elyounoussi
(Fransson 90), Ajeti (Oberlin 61).

Tuesday, 31 October 2017

FC Basel (1) 1 *(Zuffi 32)*
CSKA Moscow (0) 2 *(Dzagoev 65, Wernbloom 79)* 33,303
FC Basel: (343) Vaclik; Akanji, Suchy, Balanta; Lang,
Xhaka (Die 73), Zuffi, Petretta (Itten 85); Steffen,
Oberlin (Ajeti 71), Elyounoussi.
CSKA Moscow: (352) Akinfeev; Vasin, Berezutski V,
Berezutski A; Fernandes, Natcho (Zhamaletdinov 89),
Wernbloom, Golovin, Schennikov; Kuchaev (Milanov
90), Vitinho (Dzagoev 46).

Manchester U (1) 2 *(Svilar 45 (og), Blind 78 (pen))*
Benfica (0) 0 74,437
Manchester U: (4231) de Gea; Darmian, Bailly, Smalling,
Blind; McTominay, Matic, Mata (Ander Herrera 67),
Lingard (Mkhitaryan 46), Martial (Rashford 75);
Lukaku.
Benfica: (433) Svilar; Douglas, Jardel, Dias, Grimaldo
(Eliseu 64); Pizzi (Jonas 79), Fejsa, Samaris; Salvio,
Jimenez (Seferovic 74), Goncalves.

Wednesday, 22 November 2017

CSKA Moscow (1) 2 *(Schennikov 13, Jardel 57 (og))*
Benfica (0) 0 27,709
CSKA Moscow: (523) Akinfeev; Fernandes, Berezutski
V, Vasin, Ignashevich, Schennikov (Nababkin 49);
Natcho, Golovin; Vitinho (Kuchaev 77), Wernbloom,
Dzagoev (Gordyushenko 84).
Benfica: (433) Bruno Varela; Andre Almeida, Jardel,
Luisao, Eliseu (Zivkovic 83); Pizzi, Fejsa, Filipe Augusto
(Jimenez 58); Salvio, Jonas, Goncalves (Cervi 46).

FC Basel (0) 1 *(Lang 89)*
Manchester U (0) 0 36,000
FC Basel: (343) Vaclik; Akanji, Suchy, Balanta; Lang,
Die (Fransson 80), Zuffi, Petretta; Steffen, Oberlin,
Elyounoussi.
Manchester U: (4411) Romero; Darmian, Smalling, Blind,
Rojo; Lingard (Rashford 64), Fellaini, Ander Herrera,
Martial (Ibrahimovic 74); Pogba (Matic 65); Lukaku.

Tuesday, 5 December 2017

Benfica (0) 0
FC Basel (1) 2 *(Elyounoussi 6, Oberlin 66)* 22,470
Benfica: (433) Svilar; Douglas, Lopez, Jardel, Eliseu;
Joao Carvalho, Samaris (Andre Almeida 75), Pizzi
(Gabriel Barbosa 74); Zivkovic, Seferovic, Goncalves
(Jonas 62).
FC Basel: (343) Vaclik; Suchy, Akanji, Balanta; Lang,
Xhaka, Zuffi, Petretta (Riveros 82); Steffen (Fransson
90), Oberlin (Bua 88), Elyounoussi.

Manchester U (0) 2 *(Lukaku 65, Rashford 66)*
CSKA Moscow (1) 1 *(Vitinho 45)* 74,669
Manchester U: (343) Romero; Lindelof, Smalling, Blind;
Valencia (Tuanzebe 72), Shaw, Pogba, Ander Herrera
(McTominay 67); Mata, Lukaku (Martial 74), Rashford.
CSKA Moscow: (343) Akinfeev; Berezutski V, Vasin,
Ignashevich; Fernandes, Golovin, Kuchaev, Nababkin
(Khosonov 70); Vitinho (Zhamaletdinov 83), Chalov
(Gordyushenko 68), Dzagoev.

Group A Table	P	W	D	L	F	A	GD	Pts
Manchester U	6	5	0	1	12	3	9	15
FC Basel	6	4	0	2	11	5	6	12
CSKA Moscow	6	3	0	3	8	10	–2	9
Benfica	6	0	0	6	1	14	–13	0

GROUP B

Tuesday, 12 September 2017

Bayern Munich (1) 3 *(Lewandowski 12 (pen), Thiago 65, Kimmich 90)*

Anderlecht (0) 0 70,000

Bayern Munich: (4231) Neuer; Kimmich, Javi Martinez (Boateng 77), Sule, Rafinha; Tolisso, Thiago; Robben, Rodriguez (Coman 85), Ribery (Muller 77); Lewandowski.
Anderlecht: (541) Sels; Chipciu, Spajic, Kums■, Deschacht, Najar (Appiah 26); Stanciu (Onyekuru 58), Dendoncker, Trebel, Hanni; Teodorczyk (Harbaoui 84).

Celtic (0) 0

Paris Saint-Germain (3) 5 *(Neymar 19, Mbappe-Lottin 34, Cavani 40 (pen), 85, Lustig 83 (og))* 57,562

Celtic: (4231) Gordon; Simunovic, Ralston, Lustig, Tierney; Brown, Ntcham; Armstrong (Rogic 46), Roberts (Forrest 78), Sinclair; Griffiths (Edouard 69).
Paris Saint-Germain: (433) Areola; Dani Alves, Thiago Silva, Marquinhos, Kurzawa; Verratti, Thiago Motta, Rabiot (Draxler 61); Cavani, Neymar, Mbappe-Lottin (Lo Celso 84).

Wednesday, 27 September 2017

Anderlecht (0) 0

Celtic (1) 3 *(Griffiths 38, Roberts 50, Sinclair 90)* 19,896

Anderlecht: (541) Boeckx; Chipciu, Spajic (Mbodji 44), Dendoncker, Deschacht (Stanciu 58), Appiah; Hanni (Bruno 70), Gerkens, Trebel, Onyekuru; Teodorczyk.
Celtic: (451) Gordon; Lustig, Simunovic, Boyata, Tierney; Roberts (Forrest 77), Ntcham, Brown (Bitton 71), Rogic (McGregor 65), Sinclair; Griffiths.

Paris Saint-Germain (2) 3 *(Dani Alves 2, Cavani 31, Neymar 63)*

Bayern Munich (0) 0 46,252

Paris Saint-Germain: (433) Areola; Dani Alves, Marquinhos, Thiago Silva, Kurzawa; Verratti (Draxler 89), Thiago Motta (Lo Celso 86), Rabiot; Mbappe-Lottin (Di Maria 79), Cavani, Neymar.
Bayern Munich: (433) Ulreich; Kimmich, Sule, Javi Martinez, Alaba; Tolisso (Rudy 46), Thiago, Vidal; Muller (Robben 69), Lewandowski, Rodriguez (Coman 46).

Wednesday, 18 October 2017

Anderlecht (0) 0

Paris Saint-Germain (2) 4 *(Mbappe-Lottin 3, Cavani 44, Neymar 65, Di Maria 88)* 19,108

Anderlecht: (343) Sels; Appiah, Mbodji, Deschacht (Obradovic 89); Dendoncker, Kums (Josue Sa 57), Trebel, Onyekuru; Gerkens (Bruno 82), Teodorczyk, Hanni.
Paris Saint-Germain: (433) Areola; Dani Alves, Marquinhos, Kimpembe, Kurzawa; Verratti (Lo Celso 75), Thiago Motta (Draxler 71), Rabiot; Mbappe-Lottin, Cavani (Di Maria 74), Neymar.

Bayern Munich (2) 3 *(Muller 17, Kimmich 29, Hummels 51)*

Celtic (0) 0 70,000

Bayern Munich: (4231) Ulreich; Kimmich (Rafinha 79), Hummels, Boateng, Alaba; Robben, Rudy; Thiago (Vidal 67), Coman (Rodriguez 77), Muller; Lewandowski.
Celtic: (4411) Gordon; Gamboa, Lustig, Boyata, Tierney; Roberts (Forrest 78), Ntcham, Brown, Sinclair; Armstrong (Rogic 64); Griffiths (Dembele 64).

Tuesday, 31 October 2017

Celtic (0) 1 *(McGregor 74)*

Bayern Munich (1) 2 *(Coman 22, Javi Martinez 77)* 58,269

Celtic: (4231) Gordon; Lustig, Bitton, Boyata, Tierney; Brown, Armstrong (Griffiths 90); Forrest, McGregor, Sinclair (Rogic 64); Dembele.
Bayern Munich: (4231) Ulreich; Rafinha, Sule, Boateng, Alaba; Tolisso (Kimmich 83), Javi Martinez; Robben (Thiago 90), Vidal (Rudy 59), Coman; Rodriguez.

Paris Saint-Germain (2) 5 *(Verratti 30, Neymar 45, Kurzawa 53, 72, 78)*

Anderlecht (0) 0 46,403

Paris Saint-Germain: (433) Areola; Dani Alves, Marquinhos, Thiago Silva, Kurzawa; Verratti (Lo Celso 64), Rabiot (Pastore 76), Draxler; Mbappe-Lottin (Di Maria 64), Cavani, Neymar.
Anderlecht: (433) Boeckx; Appiah, Mbodji, Spajic (Josue Sa 45), Obradovic; Kums, Dendoncker, Trebel; Gerkens, Onyekuru (Stanciu 80), Hanni (Teodorczyk 60).

Wednesday, 22 November 2017

Anderlecht (0) 1 *(Hanni 63)*

Bayern Munich (0) 2 *(Lewandowski 51, Tolisso 77)* 19,753

Anderlecht: (433) Sels; Appiah, Spajic, Mbodji, Deschacht; Kums, Trebel, Dendoncker; Gerkens (Onyekuru 65), Teodorczyk (Harbaoui 82), Hanni (Bruno 71).
Bayern Munich: (433) Ulreich; Kimmich, Boateng, Sule, Friedl; Tolisso, Rudy, Vidal (Hummels 87); Robben (Javi Martinez 48), Lewandowski, Thiago (Rodriguez 43).

Paris Saint-Germain (4) 7 *(Neymar 9, 22, Cavani 28, 79, Mbappe-Lottin 35, Verratti 75, Dani Alves 80)*

Celtic (1) 1 *(Dembele 2)* 46,288

Paris Saint-Germain: (433) Areola; Dani Alves, Marquinhos, Thiago Silva, Kurzawa; Verratti (Lo Celso 76), Rabiot, Draxler (Pastore 66); Mbappe-Lottin (Di Maria 76), Cavani, Neymar.
Celtic: (4141) Gordon; Lustig (Bitton 13), Boyata, Simunovic, Tierney; Brown; Forrest, McGregor, Rogic, Ntcham (Eboue 69); Dembele (Griffiths 76).

Tuesday, 5 December 2017

Bayern Munich (2) 3 *(Lewandowski 8, Tolisso 37, 69)*

Paris Saint-Germain (0) 1 *(Mbappe-Lottin 50)* 70,000

Bayern Munich: (4411) Ulreich; Kimmich, Sule, Hummels, Alaba (Rafinha 85); Coman, Tolisso, Rudy, Ribery (Muller 66); Rodriguez (Vidal 83); Lewandowski.
Paris Saint-Germain: (433) Areola; Dani Alves, Marquinhos, Thiago Silva (Kimpembe 72), Kurzawa; Verratti, Rabiot, Draxler (Lo Celso 90); Mbappe-Lottin, Cavani, Neymar.

Celtic (0) 0

Anderlecht (0) 1 *(Simunovic 62 (og))* 57,931

Celtic: (4411) Gordon; Lustig, Boyata, Simunovic, Tierney; Forrest, Brown, Armstrong (Ntcham 45), Sinclair (Rogic 45); McGregor; Dembele (Edouard 74).
Anderlecht: (442) Boeckx; Appiah (Bruno 90), Mbodji (Josue Sa 75), Spajic, Obradovic; Gerkens (Teodorczyk 78), Dendoncker, Kums, Trebel; Onyekuru, Hanni.

Group B Table	P	W	D	L	F	A	GD	Pts
Paris Saint-Germain	6	5	0	1	25	4	21	15
Bayern Munich	6	5	0	1	13	6	7	15
Celtic	6	1	0	5	5	18	–13	3
Anderlecht	6	1	0	5	2	17	–15	3

GROUP C

Tuesday, 12 September 2017

Chelsea (2) 6 *(Pedro 5, Zappacosta 30, Azpilicueta 55, Bakayoko 71, Batshuayi 76, Medvedev 82 (og))*

Qarabag (0) 0 41,150

Chelsea: (343) Courtois; Azpilicueta (Rudiger 74), Christensen, Cahill; Zappacosta, Kante (Bakayoko 63), Fabregas, Alonso; Willian, Batshuayi, Pedro (Hazard 58).
Qarabag: (4141) Sehic; Medvedev, Huseynov B, Sadygov (Madatov 70), Rzezniczak; Garayev (Diniyev 70); Pedro Henrique (Elyounoussi 77), Michel, Almeida, Guerrier; Ndlovu.

Roma (0) 0

Atletico Madrid (0) 0 36,064

Roma: (433) Alisson; Bruno Peres, Manolas, Juan Jesus, Kolarov; Nainggolan (Pellegrini 79), De Rossi, Strootman; Defrel (Fazio 68), Dzeko (El Shaarawy 89), Perotti.
Atletico Madrid: (442) Oblak; Juanfran, Savic, Godin, Filipe Luis; Koke, Thomas, Gabi (Carrasco 62), Saul; Griezmann (Gaitan 79), Vietto (Correa 58).

Wednesday, 27 September 2017
Atletico Madrid (1) 1 *(Griezmann 40 (pen))*
Chelsea (0) 2 *(Morata 60, Batshuayi 90)* 60,643
Atletico Madrid: (442) Oblak; Juanfran, Godin, Lucas, Filipe Luis; Koke, Thomas (Gimenez 77), Saul, Carrasco (Torres 69); Griezmann, Correa (Gaitan 70).
Chelsea: (3421) Courtois; Azpilicueta, Luiz, Cahill; Moses, Kante, Bakayoko, Alonso; Fabregas (Christensen 85), Hazard (Willian 82); Morata (Batshuayi 81).

Qarabag (1) 1 *(Pedro Henrique 28)*
Roma (2) 2 *(Manolas 7, Dzeko 15)* 67,200
Qarabag: (4231) Sehic; Medvedev, Huseynov B, Sadygov, Agolli; Almeida, Garayev; Pedro Henrique (Elyounoussi 75), Michel (Quintana 88), Madatov (Guerrier 82); Ndlovu.
Roma: (433) Alisson; Bruno Peres, Manolas, Juan Jesus, Kolarov; Pellegrini (Strootman 82), Gonalons (De Rossi 67), Nainggolan; Defrel (Florenzi 57), Dzeko, El Shaarawy.

Wednesday, 18 October 2017
Chelsea (2) 3 *(Luiz 11, Hazard 37, 75)*
Roma (1) 3 *(Kolarov 40, Dzeko 64, 70)* 41,105
Chelsea: (352) Courtois; Azpilicueta, Christensen, Cahill; Zappacosta (Rudiger 77), Fabregas, Luiz (Pedro 57), Bakayoko, Alonso; Morata, Hazard (Willian 80).
Roma: (433) Alisson; Bruno Peres, Fazio, Juan Jesus, Kolarov; Nainggolan, Gonalons, Strootman (Florenzi 83); Gerson (Pellegrini 73), Dzeko, Perotti (El Shaarawy 88).

Qarabag (0) 0
Atletico Madrid (0) 0 47,923
Qarabag: (4411) Sehic; Medvedev (Rrezniczak 71), Huseynov B, Sadygov, Agolli; Pedro Henrique (Guerrier 69), Almeida, Garayev, Madatov; Michel (Elyounoussi 85); Ndlovu■.
Atletico Madrid: (442) Oblak; Vrsaljko, Godin, Gimenez, Filipe Luis; Gaitan (Thomas 64), Saul, Gabi, Carrasco (Correa 72); Gameiro (Torres 72), Griezmann.

Tuesday, 31 October 2017
Atletico Madrid (0) 1 *(Thomas 56)*
Qarabag (1) 1 *(Michel 40)* 55,893
Atletico Madrid: (442) Oblak; Juanfran, Savic■, Godin, Filipe Luis; Correa, Thomas (Gaitan 61), Gabi, Saul; Gameiro (Torres 70), Griezmann.
Qarabag: (4411) Sehic; Medvedev, Rrezniczak, Sadygov, Agolli; Pedro Henrique■, Almeida, Garayev, Guerrier (Yunuszadze 63); Michel (Ismayilov 90); Sheydaev (Quintana 72).

Roma (2) 3 *(El Shaarawy 1, 36, Perotti 63)*
Chelsea (0) 0 55,036
Roma: (433) Alisson; Florenzi (Manolas 75), Fazio, Juan Jesus, Kolarov; Nainggolan, De Rossi, Strootman; El Shaarawy (Gerson 74), Dzeko, Perotti (Pellegrini 86).
Chelsea: (343) Courtois; Rudiger, Luiz, Cahill (Willian 55); Azpilicueta, Fabregas (Drinkwater 71), Bakayoko, Alonso; Pedro, Morata (Batshuayi 75), Hazard.

Wednesday, 22 November 2017
Atletico Madrid (0) 2 *(Griezmann 69, Gameiro 85)*
Roma (0) 0 56,253
Atletico Madrid: (442) Oblak; Filipe Luis, Thomas, Koke (Gabi 63), Griezmann; Saul, Torres, Carrasco (Gameiro 67), Fernandez (Correa 57); Lucas, Gimenez.
Roma: (451) Alisson; Nainggolan, Pellegrini (Strootman 61), Perotti, Dzeko; Kolarov, Fazio, Gonalons (El Shaarawy 78), Bruno Peres■, Gerson (Defrel 71); Manolas.

Qarabag (0) 0
Chelsea (2) 4 *(Hazard 21 (pen), Willian 36, 85, Fabregas 72 (pen))* 67,100
Qarabag: (4411) Sehic; Medvedev, Sadygov■, Rrezniczak, Agolli; Guerrier (Yunuszadze 81), Almeida, Garayev, Madatov (Diniyev 46); Michel; Ndlovu (Quintana 85).
Chelsea: (352) Courtois; Azpilicueta, Luiz, Rudiger; Zappacosta, Fabregas, Kante (Drinkwater 75), Willian, Alonso (Cahill 58); Pedro, Hazard (Morata 65).

Tuesday, 5 December 2017
Chelsea (0) 1 *(Savic 75 (og))*
Atletico Madrid (0) 1 *(Saul 56)* 40,875
Chelsea: (3511) Courtois; Azpilicueta, Christensen, Cahill; Zappacosta (Willian 73), Fabregas, Kante, Bakayoko (Pedro 64), Moses; Hazard; Morata (Batshuayi 81).
Atletico Madrid: (442) Oblak; Gimenez (Vietto 79), Savic, Lucas, Filipe Luis; Koke, Thomas, Gabi (Correa 78), Saul; Torres (Carrasco 57), Griezmann.

Roma (0) 1 *(Perotti 54)*
Qarabag (0) 0 34,258
Roma: (433) Alisson; Florenzi, Manolas, Fazio, Kolarov; Nainggolan, De Rossi, Strootman; El Shaarawy (Gerson 72), Dzeko, Perotti (Pellegrini 80).
Qarabag: (451) Sehic; Medvedev, Rrezniczak, Yunuszadze, Abdullayev; Ismayilov (Quintana 76), Michel, Garayev, Almeida, Madatov (Ramazanov 85); Ndlovu (Sheydaev 85).

Group C Table	P	W	D	L	F	A	GD	Pts
Roma	6	3	2	1	9	6	3	11
Chelsea	6	3	2	1	16	8	8	11
Atletico Madrid	6	1	4	1	5	4	1	7
Qarabag	6	0	2	4	2	14	–12	2

GROUP D

Tuesday, 12 September 2017
Barcelona (1) 3 *(Messi 45, 69, Rakitic 56)*
Juventus (0) 0 78,658
Barcelona: (433) ter Stegen; Nelson Semedo, Pique, Umtiti, Jordi Alba; Rakitic (Paulinho 78), Busquets, Iniesta (Andre Gomes 84); Messi, Suarez L, Dembele (Sergi Roberto 71).
Juventus: (4231) Buffon; De Sciglio (Sturaro 41), Barzagli, Benatia, Alex Sandro; Pjanic, Matuidi; Bentancur (Bernardeschi 64), Dybala, Douglas Costa; Higuain (Caligara 88).

Olympiacos (0) 2 *(Pardo 89, 90)*
Sporting Lisbon (3) 3 *(Doumbia 2, Gelson Martins 13, Bruno Fernandes 43)* 30,168
Olympiacos: (4231) Kapino; Elabdellaoui, Engels, Romao, Diogo Figueiras; Carcela-Gonzalez (Pardo 78), Odjidja-Ofoe; Gillet, Marin, Fortounis (Zdjelar 46); Djurdjevic (Emenike 62).
Sporting Lisbon: (451) Rui Patricio; Piccini, Mathieu, Coates, Silva; Bruno Fernandes (Ristovski 87), William Carvalho, Battaglia, Acuna; Gelson Martins (Bruno Cesar 72); Doumbia (Dost 63).

Wednesday, 27 September 2017
Juventus (0) 2 *(Higuain 69, Mandzukic 80)*
Olympiacos (0) 0 33,460
Juventus: (4231) Buffon; Sturaro (Benatia 81), Barzagli, Chiellini, Alex Sandro; Bentancur, Matuidi; Cuadrado (Higuain 60), Dybala, Douglas Costa (Bernardeschi 84); Mandzukic.
Olympiacos: (4321) Proto; Diogo Figueiras, Engels, Nikolaou, Koutris; Romao, Zdjelar (Fortounis 77), Odjidja-Ofoe; Pardo (Nabouhane 71), Seba; Emenike (Marin 88).

Sporting Lisbon (0) 0
Barcelona (0) 1 *(Coates 49 (og))* 48,575
Sporting Lisbon: (4411) Rui Patricio; Piccini, Coates, Mathieu, Fabio Coentrao (Silva 73); Gelson Martins, William Carvalho, Battaglia, Acuna (Bruno Cesar 73); Bruno Fernandes; Doumbia (Dost 44).
Barcelona: (433) ter Stegen; Nelson Semedo, Pique, Umtiti, Jordi Alba; Rakitic, Busquets, Sergi Roberto (Andre Gomes 87); Messi, Suarez L (Aleix Vidal 89), Iniesta (Paulinho 79).

Wednesday, 18 October 2017
Barcelona (1) 3 *(Nikolaou 18 (og), Messi 61, Digne 64)*
Olympiacos (0) 1 *(Nikolaou 90)* 55,026
Barcelona: (433) ter Stegen; Sergi Roberto, Pique■, Umtiti, Digne; Paulinho, Busquets (Andre Gomes 80), Iniesta (Rakitic 67); Messi, Suarez L, Deulofeu (Mascherano 46).

Olympiacos: (433) Proto; Elabdellaoui, Botia, Nikolaou, Koutris; Gillet (Djurdjevic 54), Romao, Zdjelar; Carcela-Gonzalez (Pardo 65), Odjidja-Ofoe (Fortounis 72), Androutsos.

Juventus (1) 2 *(Pjanic 29, Mandzukic 84)*

Sporting Lisbon (1) 1 *(Alex Sandro 12 (og))*   36,288

Juventus: (4231) Buffon; Sturaro (Douglas Costa 84), Benatia (Barzagli 46), Chiellini, Alex Sandro; Pjanic, Khedira (Matuidi 61); Cuadrado, Dybala, Mandzukic; Higuain.
Sporting Lisbon: (4231) Rui Patricio; Piccini, Coates, Mathieu, Fabio Coentrao (Silva 77); William Carvalho, Battaglia (Doumbia 87); Gelson Martins (Joao Palhinha 76), Bruno Fernandes, Acuna; Dost.

Tuesday, 31 October 2017

Olympiacos (0) 0

Barcelona (0) 0   31,600

Olympiacos: (451) Proto; Elabdellaoui, Botia, Engels, Koutris; Diogo Figueiras, Romao, Tachtsidis, Odjidja-Ofoe (Gillet 75), Carcela-Gonzalez (Pardo 78); Fortounis (Djurdjevic 83).
Barcelona: (433) ter Stegen; Nelson Semedo, Mascherano, Umtiti, Jordi Alba; Sergi Roberto (Deulofeu 45), Busquets, Paulinho (Rakitic 62); Messi, Suarez L, Suarez D (Andre Gomes 76).

Sporting Lisbon (1) 1 *(Bruno Cesar 21)*

Juventus (0) 1 *(Higuain 79)*   48,442

Sporting Lisbon: (4411) Rui Patricio; Andre Pinto, Coates, Ristovski (Petrovic 90), Silva; Bruno Cesar (Joao Palhinha 63), Battaglia, Gelson Martins, Bruno Fernandes; Acuna; Dost (Doumbia 81).
Juventus: (4411) Buffon; De Sciglio (Douglas Costa 65), Barzagli, Chiellini, Alex Sandro; Cuadrado, Pjanic, Khedira (Matuidi 70); Mandzukic; Dybala (Bernardeschi 82); Higuain.

Wednesday, 22 November 2017

Juventus (0) 0

Barcelona (0) 0   40,876

Juventus: (343) Buffon; Barzagli, Benatia, Rugani; Pjanic (Bentancur 66), Cuadrado (Marchisio 70), Khedira, Alex Sandro; Dybala, Douglas Costa (Matuidi 85), Higuain.
Barcelona: (433) ter Stegen; Nelson Semedo, Pique, Umtiti, Digne; Rakitic, Busquets, Iniesta (Jordi Alba 81); Deulofeu (Messi 55), Suarez L, Paulinho.

Sporting Lisbon (2) 3 *(Dost 40, 66, Bruno Cesar 44)*

Olympiacos (0) 1 *(Odjidja-Ofoe 86)*   42,528

Sporting Lisbon: (4231) Rui Patricio; Piccini (Ristovski 85), Andre Pinto, Mathieu (Tobias Figueiredo 77), Fabio Coentrao; Battaglia, William Carvalho; Gelson Martins, Bruno Fernandes, Bruno Cesar (Mattheus Oliveira 90); Dost.
Olympiacos: (433) Proto; Diogo Figueiras, Botia, Engels, Koutris; Gillet, Romao, Tachtsidis (Odjidja-Ofoe 65); Carcela-Gonzalez (Seba 46), Fortounis (Djurdjevic 57), Pardo.

Tuesday, 5 December 2017

Barcelona (0) 2 *(Alcacer 59, Mathieu 90 (og))*

Sporting Lisbon (0) 0   48,336

Barcelona: (433) Cillessen; Nelson Semedo, Pique (Busquets 64), Vermaelen, Digne; Rakitic, Andre Gomes, Suarez D; Aleix Vidal (Messi 60), Suarez L (Paulinho 74), Alcacer.
Sporting Lisbon: (442) Rui Patricio; Piccini, Coates, Mathieu, Bruno Cesar (Fabio Coentrao 64); Battaglia, William Carvalho, Ristovski (Gelson Martins 46), Bruno Fernandes; Acuna, Ruiz (Dost 46).

Olympiacos (0) 0

Juventus (1) 2 *(Cuadrado 15, Bernardeschi 90)*   29,567

Olympiacos: (4231) Proto; Elabdellaoui, Engels, Nikolaou, Koutris; Romao, Tachtsidis; Pardo, Odjidja-Ofoe (Fortounis 61), Seba (Marin 46); Djurdjevic (Nabouhane 70).
Juventus: (4231) Szczesny; De Sciglio, Benatia, Barzagli (Rugani 70), Alex Sandro; Khedira, Matuidi; Cuadrado (Bernardeschi 84), Dybala (Pjanic 62), Douglas Costa; Higuain.

Group D Table

	P	W	D	L	F	A	GD	Pts
Barcelona	6	4	2	0	9	1	8	14
Juventus	6	3	2	1	7	5	2	11
Sporting Lisbon	6	2	1	3	8	9	–1	7
Olympiacos	6	0	1	5	4	13	–9	1

GROUP E

Wednesday, 13 September 2017

Liverpool (2) 2 *(Firmino 21, Salah 37)*

Sevilla (1) 2 *(Ben Yedder 5, Correa 72)*   52,332

Liverpool: (433) Karius; Gomez■, Matip, Lovren, Moreno; Can (Coutinho 75), Henderson, Wijnaldum; Salah (Oxlade-Chamberlain 88), Firmino, Mane (Sturridge 83).
Sevilla: (433) Sergio Rico; Mercado, Pareja, Kjaer, Escudero; Nzonzi, Banega, Pizarro (Sarabia 45); Jesus Navas (Corchia 83), Ben Yedder (Muriel 69), Correa.

Maribor (0) 1 *(Bohar 85)*

Spartak Moscow (0) 1 *(Samedov 60)*   12,566

Maribor: (4411) Handanovic; Milec, Rajcevic, Suler, Viler; Bajde (Kramaric 69), Kabha, Vrhovec (Pihler 79), Bohar; Ahmedi (Mesanovic 69); Tavares.
Spartak Moscow: (352) Rebrov; Bocchetti, Kutepov, Dzhikija; Eshchenko, Pasalic, Fernando, Glushakov (Samedov 29), Kombarov (Melgarejo 90); Luiz Adriano, Promes (Popov 87).

Tuesday, 26 September 2017

Sevilla (2) 3 *(Ben Yedder 27, 38, 83 (pen))*

Maribor (0) 0   34,705

Sevilla: (433) Sergio Rico; Corchia, Pareja, Lenglet, Escudero; Banega (Pizarro 86), Nzonzi, Vazquez (Sarabia 78); Correa, Ben Yedder, Nolito (Jesus Navas 67).
Maribor: (4231) Handanovic; Milec, Rajcevic, Billong, Viler; Kabha (Hotic 74), Vrhovec; Pihler, Ahmedi, Bohar (Kramaric 71); Tavares (Mesanovic 88).

Spartak Moscow (0) 1 *(Fernando 23)*

Liverpool (1) 1 *(Coutinho 31)*   43,376

Spartak Moscow: (541) Rebrov (Selikhov 66); Eshchenko, Tasci, Kutepov, Bocchetti, Dzhikija; Samedov (Pedro Rocha 90), Fernando, Pasalic, Popov (Melgarejo 84); Luiz Adriano.
Liverpool: (433) Karius; Alexander-Arnold, Matip, Lovren, Moreno; Can (Wijnaldum 72), Henderson, Coutinho; Salah, Firmino, Mane (Sturridge 70).

Tuesday, 17 October 2017

Maribor (0) 0

Liverpool (4) 7 *(Firmino 4, 54, Coutinho 13, Salah 19, 39, Oxlade-Chamberlain 86, Alexander-Arnold 90)*   12,508

Maribor: (4411) Handanovic; Milec, Rajcevic, Suler, Viler; Kramaric (Hotic 58), Kabha, Vrhovec, Bohar (Mesanovic 81); Ahmedi (Pihler 58); Tavares.
Liverpool: (433) Karius; Alexander-Arnold, Matip, Lovren, Moreno; Can, Wijnaldum (Solanke 76), Milner; Salah (Oxlade-Chamberlain 57), Firmino (Sturridge 68), Coutinho.

Spartak Moscow (1) 5 *(Promes 18, 90, Melgarejo 58, Glushakov 67, Luiz Adriano 74)*

Sevilla (1) 1 *(Kjaer 30)*   44,307

Spartak Moscow: (4411) Selikhov; Eshchenko, Tasci, Dzhikija, Kombarov; Samedov (Melgarejo 25), Fernando, Glushakov, Promes; Popov (Pasalic 56); Luiz Adriano.
Sevilla: (433) Sergio Rico; Mercado, Kjaer, Lenglet, Escudero; Banega, Pizarro, Krohn-Dehli (Vazquez 69); Nolito (Jesus Navas 76), Ben Yedder, Sarabia.

Wednesday, 1 November 2017

Liverpool (0) 3 *(Salah 49, Can 64, Sturridge 90)*

Maribor (0) 0   47,957

Liverpool: (433) Karius; Alexander-Arnold, Matip, Klavan, Moreno; Milner, Can, Wijnaldum (Henderson 17); Oxlade-Chamberlain, Firmino (Grujic 85), Salah (Sturridge 74).
Maribor: (343) Handanovic; Billong, Rajcevic, Suler; Milec, Pihler, Kabha, Viler; Hotic (Ahmedi 81), Mesanovic (Tavares 58), Bohar (Bajde 69).

Sevilla (1) 2 *(Lenglet 30, Banega 59)*
Spartak Moscow (0) 1 *(Ze Luis 78)* 38,002
Sevilla: (433) Sergio Rico; Mercado (Corchia 83), Kjaer, Lenglet, Escudero; Nzonzi, Banega (Krohn-Dehli 77), Pizarro; Sarabia (Jesus Navas 74), Ben Yedder, Nolito.
Spartak Moscow: (4411) Selikhov; Eshchenko (Petkovic 81), Tasci, Dzhikija, Kombarov; Promes, Fernando, Pasalic (Popov 57), Melgarejo (Ze Luis 72); Glushakov; Luiz Adriano.

Tuesday, 21 November 2017
Sevilla (0) 3 *(Ben Yedder 51, 61 (pen), Pizarro 90)*
Liverpool (3) 3 *(Firmino 2, 30, Mane 22)* 39,495
Sevilla: (433) Sergio Rico; Mercado, Geis, Lenglet, Escudero; Nzonzi (Vazquez 46), Banega, Pizarro; Sarabia, Ben Yedder (Correa 81), Nolito (Muriel 72).
Liverpool: (433) Karius; Gomez, Lovren, Klavan, Moreno (Milner 63); Wijnaldum, Henderson, Coutinho (Can 63); Salah (Oxlade-Chamberlain 86), Firmino, Mane.

Spartak Moscow (0) 1 *(Ze Luis 82)*
Maribor (0) 1 *(Mesanovic 90)* 42,920
Spartak Moscow: (4141) Selikhov; Petkovic (Zobnin 73), Tasci, Kutepov, Kombarov; Fernando; Luiz Adriano, Popov (Melgarejo 63), Pasalic (Glushakov 53), Promes; Ze Luis.
Maribor: (451) Handanovic; Milec, Suler, Billong, Viler; Bajde (Hotic 68), Pihler, Vrhovec (Vrsic 46), Kabha, Bohar (Mesanovic 83); Tavares.

Wednesday, 6 December 2017
Liverpool (3) 7 *(Coutinho 4 (pen), 15, 50, Firmino 18, Mane 47, 76, Salah 85)*
Spartak Moscow (0) 0 48,779
Liverpool: (433) Karius; Gomez, Lovren (Alexander-Arnold 60), Klavan, Moreno (Milner 45); Coutinho, Can, Wijnaldum; Salah, Firmino (Sturridge 71), Mane.
Spartak Moscow: (4411) Selikhov; Eshchenko, Tasci, Bocchetti, Dzhikija (Pasalic 59); Zobnin, Glushakov, Fernando, Promes (Samedov 75); Luiz Adriano; Ze Luis (Melgarejo 51).

Maribor (1) 1 *(Tavares 10)*
Sevilla (0) 1 *(Ganso 75)* 11,976
Maribor: (433) Handanovic; Milec, Suler, Billong, Viler; Pihler (Vrsic 79), Vrhovec, Kabha; Bajde, Tavares, Bohar (Hotic 90).
Sevilla: (433) Sergio Rico; Mercado (Jesus Navas 69), Kjaer, Lenglet, Escudero; Krohn-Dehli (Ganso 59), Pizarro, Banega; Sarabia, Ben Yedder (Muriel 76), Correa.

Group E Table	P	W	D	L	F	A	GD	Pts
Liverpool	6	3	3	0	23	6	17	12
Sevilla	6	2	3	1	12	12	0	9
Spartak Moscow	6	1	3	2	9	13	–4	6
Maribor	6	0	3	3	3	16	–13	3

GROUP F
Wednesday, 13 September 2017
Feyenoord (0) 0
Manchester C (3) 4 *(Stones 2, 63, Aguero 10, Gabriel Jesus 25)* 43,500
Feyenoord: (433) Jones; St Juste, Botteghin, Van Der Heijden, Nelom; Amrabat (Larsson 78), El Ahmadi, Vilhena; Berghuis (Toornstra 46), Kramer (Vente 72), Boetius.
Manchester C: (352) Ederson; Stones, Fernandinho (Sane 71), Otamendi; Walker, Bernardo Silva, Silva (Delph 66), De Bruyne, Mendy; Gabriel Jesus, Aguero (Sterling 59).

Shakhtar Donetsk (1) 2 *(Taison 15, Ferreyra 58)*
Napoli (0) 1 *(Milik 72 (pen))* 32,679
Shakhtar Donetsk: (4411) Pyatov; Srna, Ordets (Khocholava 90), Rakitskiy, Ismaily; Marlos (Kovalenko 77), Fred, Stepanenko, Bernard; Taison; Ferreyra (Dentinho 87).
Napoli: (433) Reina; Hysaj, Albiol, Koulibaly, Ghoulam; Zielinski (Allan 67), Diawara, Hamsik (Mertens 60); Callejon, Milik, Insigne.

Tuesday, 26 September 2017
Manchester C (0) 2 *(De Bruyne 48, Sterling 90)*
Shakhtar Donetsk (0) 0 45,310
Manchester C: (433) Ederson; Walker, Stones, Otamendi, Delph; De Bruyne, Fernandinho, Silva (Gundogan 81); Gabriel Jesus (Sterling 54), Aguero (Bernardo Silva 84), Sane.
Shakhtar Donetsk: (4411) Pyatov; Butko, Ordets, Rakitskiy, Ismaily; Marlos (Dentinho 78), Fred (Kovalenko 90), Stepanenko, Bernard (Petryak 89); Taison; Ferreyra.

Napoli (1) 3 *(Insigne 7, Mertens 49, Callejon 69)*
Feyenoord (0) 1 *(Amrabat 90)* 22,577
Napoli: (433) Reina; Hysaj, Maksimovic, Koulibaly, Ghoulam; Allan, Jorginho (Diawara 79), Hamsik (Zielinski 70); Callejon (Rog 73), Mertens, Insigne.
Feyenoord: (433) Jones; Diks, St Juste, Tapia (van Beek 77), Haps; Amrabat, El Ahmadi, Vilhena; Berghuis (Larsson 86), Toornstra (Basacikoglu 69), Boetius.

Tuesday, 17 October 2017
Feyenoord (1) 1 *(Berghuis 8)*
Shakhtar Donetsk (1) 2 *(Bernard 24, 54)* 43,500
Feyenoord: (433) Jones; Nieuwkoop (Toornstra 61), van Beek (Kramer 77), St Juste, Haps; Amrabat, El Ahmadi, Vilhena; Berghuis, Jorgensen (Larsson 66), Boetius.
Shakhtar Donetsk: (4411) Pyatov; Butko, Ordets, Rakitskiy*, Ismaily; Marlos (Zubkov 90), Fred, Stepanenko, Bernard (Kovalenko 70); Taison; Ferreyra (Khocholava 77).

Manchester C (2) 2 *(Sterling 9, Gabriel Jesus 13)*
Napoli (0) 1 *(Diawara 73 (pen))* 48,520
Manchester C: (433) Ederson; Walker, Stones, Otamendi, Delph; De Bruyne, Fernandinho, Silva (Gundogan 76); Sterling (Bernardo Silva 69), Gabriel Jesus (Danilo 86), Sane.
Napoli: (433) Reina; Hysaj (Maggio 70), Albiol, Koulibaly, Ghoulam; Zielinski, Diawara, Hamsik (Ounas 78); Callejon, Mertens, Insigne (Allan 57).

Wednesday, 1 November 2017
Napoli (1) 2 *(Insigne 21, Jorginho 62 (pen))*
Manchester C (1) 4 *(Otamendi 34, Stones 48, Aguero 69, Sterling 90)* 44,483
Napoli: (433) Reina; Hysaj, Albiol, Koulibaly, Ghoulam (Maggio 30); Allan (Rog 75), Jorginho (Ounas 82), Hamsik; Callejon, Mertens, Insigne.
Manchester C: (4411) Ederson; Danilo, Otamendi, Stones, Delph; Sterling, Fernandinho, Gundogan (Silva 70), Sane (Gabriel Jesus 89); De Bruyne; Aguero (Bernardo Silva 75).

Shakhtar Donetsk (2) 3 *(Ferreyra 15, Marlos 17, 68)*
Feyenoord (1) 1 *(Jorgensen 13)* 24,570
Shakhtar Donetsk: (4411) Pyatov; Butko, Ordets, Khocholava, Ismaily; Marlos, Fred, Stepanenko, Bernard (Alan Patrick 72); Taison; Ferreyra (Dentinho 88).
Feyenoord: (433) Jones; Nieuwkoop, St Juste, Tapia (Diks 72), Haps; Amrabat, El Ahmadi, Vilhena; Berghuis, Jorgensen (Larsson 80), Boetius.

Tuesday, 21 November 2017
Manchester C (0) 1 *(Sterling 88)*
Feyenoord (0) 0 43,548
Manchester C: (334) Ederson; Walker, Otamendi, Mangala; Danilo, Gundogan, Toure (Foden 75); De Bruyne (Gabriel Jesus 64), Bernardo Silva, Aguero, Sterling (Diaz 90).
Feyenoord: (433) Jones; Diks (Nieuwkoop 72), Tapia, van Beek, Haps; Amrabat, Toornstra, Vilhena; Berghuis (Basacikoglu 82), Boetius (Jorgensen 70), Larsson.

Napoli (0) 3 *(Insigne 56, Zielinski 81, Mertens 84)*
Shakhtar Donetsk (0) 0 10,573
Napoli: (433) Reina; Maggio, Albiol, Chiriches, Hysaj; Zielinski (Rui 86), Diawara, Hamsik (Rog 77); Callejon, Mertens, Insigne (Allan 65).
Shakhtar Donetsk: (4231) Pyatov; Butko, Ordets, Rakitskiy, Ismaily; Fred, Stepanenko (Alan Patrick 70); Marlos (Dentinho 79), Taison, Bernard; Ferreyra.

Wednesday, 6 December 2017
Feyenoord (1) 2 *(Jorgensen 33, St Juste 90)*
Napoli (1) 1 *(Zielinski 2)*   36,500
Feyenoord: (433) Vermeer; Nieuwkoop (St Juste 76), van Beek, Tapia, Malacia; Amrabat, Toornstra, Vilhena■; Berghuis (Larsson 72), Jorgensen, Boetius.
Napoli: (433) Reina; Maggio (Rui 64), Albiol, Koulibaly, Hysaj; Allan (Rog 60), Diawara, Hamsik; Callejon (Ounas 74), Mertens, Zielinski.

Shakhtar Donetsk (2) 2 *(Bernard 26, Ismaily 32)*
Manchester C (0) 1 *(Aguero 90 (pen))*   33,154
Shakhtar Donetsk: (4231) Pyatov; Butko, Ordets, Rakitskiy, Ismaily (Azevedo 63); Fred, Stepanenko; Marlos (Kovalenko 81), Taison, Bernard; Ferreyra (Khocholava 89).
Manchester C: (433) Ederson; Danilo, Adarabioyo, Mangala, Foden; Gundogan, Fernandinho (Aguero 69), Toure; Bernardo Silva, Gabriel Jesus, Sane (Diaz 61).

Group F Table	P	W	D	L	F	A	GD	Pts
Manchester C	6	5	0	1	14	5	9	15
Shakhtar Donetsk	6	4	0	2	9	9	0	12
Napoli	6	2	0	4	11	11	0	6
Feyenoord	6	1	0	5	5	14	-9	3

GROUP G

Wednesday, 13 September 2017
Porto (1) 1 *(Tosic 21 (og))*
Besiktas (2) 3 *(Anderson Talisca 14, Tosun 28, Babel 86)*   42,429
Porto: (442) Casillas; Ricardo Pereira, Felipe, Marcano, Alex Telles; Corona (Andre Andre 46), Torres (Otavio 46), Danilo Pereira (Hernani 82), Brahimi; Marega, Tiquinho Soares.
Besiktas: (4411) Fabri; Adriano (Uysal 87), Pepe, Tosic, Erkin; Quaresma (Negredo 72), Hutchinson, Ozyakup (Medel 65), Babel; Anderson Talisca; Tosun.

RB Leipzig (1) 1 *(Forsberg 33)*
Monaco (1) 1 *(Tielemans 34)*   40,068
RB Leipzig: (442) Gulacsi; Klostermann, Orban, Upamecano, Halstenberg; Sabitzer, Demme, Ilsanker, Forsberg (Kampl 63); Poulsen (Augustin 80), Werner.
Monaco: (4411) Benaglio; Toure, Glik, Jemerson, Jorge; Sidibe (Ghezzal 84), Fabinho, Joao Moutinho, Diakhaby (Balde 73); Tielemans; Falcao (Carrillo 89).

Tuesday, 26 September 2017
Besiktas (2) 2 *(Babel 11, Anderson Talisca 43)*
RB Leipzig (0) 0   36,641
Besiktas: (4231) Fabri; Medel (Uysal 60), Pepe, Tosic, Erkin; Ozyakup, Hutchinson; Quaresma, Anderson Talisca (Arslan 70), Babel; Tosun (Negredo 80).
RB Leipzig: (442) Gulacsi; Ilsanker, Orban (Kampl 46), Upamecano, Halstenberg; Sabitzer, Keita (Bruma 59), Demme, Forsberg; Augustin, Werner (Klostermann 32).

Monaco (0) 0
Porto (1) 3 *(Aboubakar 32, 69, Layun 90)*   11,703
Monaco: (451) Benaglio; Sidibe, Glik, Jemerson, Jorge; Ghezzal (Balde 74), Joao Moutinho, Fabinho, Lemar (Lopes 63), Diakhaby (Carrillo 46); Falcao.
Porto: (442) Casillas; Ricardo Pereira, Felipe, Marcano, Alex Telles; Sergio Oliveira (Reyes 86), Danilo Pereira, Herrera, Brahimi (Corona 71); Marega, Aboubakar (Layun 71).

Tuesday, 17 October 2017
Monaco (1) 1 *(Falcao 30)*
Besiktas (1) 2 *(Tosun 34, 55)*   7403
Monaco: (442) Subasic; Sidibe (Boschilia 79), Glik, Jemerson, Toure; Tielemans (Lopes 57), Joao Moutinho, Fabinho, Lemar; Balde, Falcao.
Besiktas: (4231) Fabri; Adriano, Pepe, Tosic, Erkin; Arslan (Medel 74), Hutchinson; Quaresma, Anderson Talisca (Ozyakup 74), Babel; Tosun (Negredo 89).

RB Leipzig (3) 3 *(Orban 8, Forsberg 37, Augustin 40)*
Porto (2) 2 *(Aboubakar 18, Marcano 44)*   41,496
RB Leipzig: (433) Gulacsi; Klostermann, Orban, Upamecano, Halstenberg; Keita, Sabitzer, Kampl; Bruma (Werner 75), Augustin (Poulsen 78), Forsberg (Bernardo 90).
Porto: (442) Jose Sa; Layun, Felipe, Marcano, Alex Telles; Marega, Herrera (Hernani 81), Danilo Pereira, Sergio Oliveira (Torres 58); Aboubakar, Brahimi (Corona 76).

Wednesday, 1 November 2017
Besiktas (0) 1 *(Tosun 54 (pen))*
Monaco (1) 1 *(Lopes 45)*   39,346
Besiktas: (4231) Fabri; Gonul, Pepe, Tosic (Medel 69), Adriano; Hutchinson (Anderson Talisca 83), Arslan (Mitrovic 74); Quaresma, Ozyakup, Babel; Tosun.
Monaco: (433) Subasic; Raggi, Jemerson, Glik, Jorge; Joao Moutinho, Fabinho, Tielemans (Carrillo 73); Lemar (Jovetic 26), Balde, Lopes (Diakhaby 85).

Porto (1) 3 *(Herrera 13, Danilo Pereira 61, Maxi Pereira 90)*
RB Leipzig (0) 1 *(Werner 48)*   41,616
Porto: (442) Jose Sa; Ricardo Pereira, Felipe, Marcano, Alex Telles; Corona (Maxi Pereira 72), Herrera, Danilo Pereira, Brahimi (Reyes 89); Marega (Andre Andre 12), Aboubakar.
RB Leipzig: (442) Gulacsi; Bernardo, Orban, Upamecano, Halstenberg (Klostermann 46); Forsberg, Kampl, Keita, Bruma (Werner 46); Sabitzer, Augustin (Poulsen 75).

Tuesday, 21 November 2017
Besiktas (1) 1 *(Anderson Talisca 41)*
Porto (1) 1 *(Felipe 29)*   36,919
Besiktas: (433) Fabri; Gonul, Pepe, Tosic (Medel 46), Adriano; Arslan, Hutchinson, Anderson Talisca (Ozyakup 87); Quaresma (Negredo 90), Tosun, Babel.
Porto: (4231) Jose Sa; Maxi Pereira, Felipe, Marcano, Alex Telles; Danilo Pereira, Herrera (Reyes 90); Ricardo Pereira (Corona 80), Sergio Oliveira, Brahimi; Aboubakar.

Monaco (1) 1 *(Falcao 43)*
RB Leipzig (4) 4 *(Jemerson 6 (og), Werner 9, 31 (pen), Keita 45)*   9029
Monaco: (442) Subasic; Raggi, Glik, Jemerson, Jorge; Tielemans, Fabinho, Joao Moutinho (Carrillo 83), Lopes (Ghezzal 66); Balde (Diakhaby 60), Falcao.
RB Leipzig: (442) Gulacsi; Klostermann, Orban, Upamecano, Halstenberg; Sabitzer (Demme 35), Keita, Kampl, Forsberg (Laimer 79); Poulsen, Werner (Bruma 58).

Wednesday, 6 December 2017
Porto (3) 5 *(Aboubakar 9, 33, Brahimi 45, Alex Telles 65, Tiquinho Soares 88)*
Monaco (0) 2 *(Glik 61 (pen), Falcao 78)*   42,509
Porto: (433) Jose Sa; Ricardo Pereira, Felipe■, Marcano, Alex Telles; Danilo Pereira, Herrera, Andre Andre (Reyes 42); Marega (Corona 67), Aboubakar (Tiquinho Soares 74), Brahimi.
Monaco: (4411) Benaglio; Toure, Glik, Jemerson, Kongolo; Lopes, Meite (Joao Moutinho 67), N'Doram, Ghezzal■; Carrillo (Falcao 67); Diakhaby (Balde 72).

RB Leipzig (0) 1 *(Keita 87)*
Besiktas (1) 2 *(Negredo 10 (pen), Anderson Talisca 90)*   42,558
RB Leipzig: (433) Gulacsi; Klostermann, Orban (Compper 71), Ilsanker■, Halstenberg (Bernardo 66); Kampl (Kaiser 74), Keita, Demme; Bruma, Augustin, Werner.
Besiktas: (4231) Zengin; Uysal (Adriano 50), Mitrovic, Tosic, Erkin; Medel, Ozyakup; Lens, Anderson Talisca, Pektemek (Cinar 68); Negredo (Tosun 80).

Group G Table	P	W	D	L	F	A	GD	Pts
Besiktas	6	4	2	0	11	5	6	14
Porto	6	3	1	2	15	10	5	10
RB Leipzig	6	2	1	3	10	11	-1	7
Monaco	6	0	2	4	6	16	-10	2

GROUP H

Wednesday, 13 September 2017

Real Madrid (1) 3 *(Ronaldo 12, 51 (pen), Sergio Ramos 61)*

APOEL (0) 0   71,060

Real Madrid: (433) Navas; Carvajal, Nacho, Sergio Ramos, Marcelo, Modric, Casemiro, Kovacic (Kroos 25); Isco (Ceballos 72), Ronaldo, Bale (Borja Mayoral 81).
APOEL: (442) Waterman; Vouros, Rueda, Carlao, Lago; Sallai (Farias 60), Morais, Vinicius, Aloneftis; de Camargo (Pote 82), Ebecilio (Zahid 72).

Tottenham H (2) 3 *(Son 4, Kane 15, 60)*

Borussia Dortmund (1) 1 *(Yarmolenko 11)*   67,343

Tottenham H: (541) Lloris; Aurier, Alderweireld, Sanchez, Vertonghen■, Davies; Son (Sissoko 83), Dembele, Dier, Eriksen; Kane (Llorente 87).
Borussia Dortmund: (433) Burki; Piszczek, Papastathopoulos, Toprak (Zagadou 80), Toljan; Dahoud (Castro 72), Sahin, Kagawa (Gotze 66); Yarmolenko, Aubameyang, Pulisic.

Tuesday, 26 September 2017

APOEL (0) 0

Tottenham H (1) 3 *(Kane 39, 62, 67)*   16,324

APOEL: (4231) Waterman; Vouros, Rueda, Carlao, Lago; Vinicius, Morais (Alexandrou 83); Zahid, Sallai (Makris 62), Aloneftis (Farias 75); de Camargo.
Tottenham H: (4231) Lloris; Trippier, Alderweireld, Sanchez, Davies; Winks, Dier; Aurier (Llorente 57), Sissoko (Georgiou 84), Son; Kane (Nkoudou 74).

Borussia Dortmund (0) 1 *(Aubameyang 54)*

Real Madrid (1) 3 *(Bale 18, Ronaldo 49, 79)* 65,849

Borussia Dortmund: (433) Burki; Piszczek, Papastathopoulos, Toprak, Toljan (Dahoud 60); Castro, Sahin (Weigl 60), Gotze (Pulisic 76); Yarmolenko, Aubameyang, Philipp.
Real Madrid: (451) Navas; Carvajal, Sergio Ramos, Varane, Nacho; Bale (Lucas 85), Kroos, Casemiro, Modric (Ceballos 90), Isco (Asensio 75); Ronaldo.

Tuesday, 17 October 2017

APOEL (0) 1 *(Pote 62)*

Borussia Dortmund (0) 1 *(Papastathopoulos 68)* 15,604

APOEL: (4231) Waterman (Gudino 43); Vouros, Merkis, Rueda, Lago; Vinicius, Morais; Zahid, Ebecilio (Sallai 72), Aloneftis; de Camargo (Pote 30).
Borussia Dortmund: (433) Burki; Schmelzer (Philipp 73), Papastathopoulos, Toprak (Toljan 59), Bartra; Gotze, Kagawa, Weigl; Yarmolenko (Isak 82), Pulisic, Aubameyang.

Real Madrid (0) 1 *(Ronaldo 43 (pen))*

Tottenham H (1) 1 *(Varane 28 (og))*   76,589

Real Madrid: (433) Navas; Hakimi, Sergio Ramos, Varane, Marcelo; Kroos, Casemiro, Modric; Isco (Lucas 87), Benzema (Asensio 76), Ronaldo.
Tottenham H: (4231) Lloris; Aurier, Alderweireld, Vertonghen, Sanchez; Dier, Winks; Sissoko (Son 89), Llorente (Rose 80), Eriksen; Kane.

Wednesday, 1 November 2017

Borussia Dortmund (1) 1 *(Guerreiro 29)*

APOEL (0) 1 *(Pote 51)*   64,500

Borussia Dortmund: (451) Burki; Bartra, Papastathopoulos, Toprak (Schurrle 87), Guerreiro (Schmelzer 72); Pulisic, Gotze, Weigl, Kagawa, Philipp (Yarmolenko 65); Aubameyang.

APOEL: (532) Perez; Vouros, Rueda, Merkis, Carlao, Alexandrou (Sallai 46); Morais, Zahid, Vinicius; Pote (de Camargo 74), Aloneftis (Farias 81).

Tottenham H (1) 3 *(Alli 27, 56, Eriksen 65)*

Real Madrid (0) 1 *(Ronaldo 80)*   83,782

Tottenham H: (352) Lloris; Alderweireld (Sissoko 24), Sanchez, Vertonghen; Trippier, Eriksen, Winks (Dembele 66), Dier, Davies; Kane (Llorente 78), Alli.
Real Madrid: (433) Casilla; Hakimi, Sergio Ramos, Nacho, Marcelo; Kroos, Casemiro, Modric (Hernandez 81); Isco (Borja Mayoral 73), Benzema (Asensio 74), Ronaldo.

Tuesday, 21 November 2017

APOEL (0) 0

Real Madrid (4) 6 *(Modric 23, Benzema 39, 45, Nacho 41, Ronaldo 49, 54)*   19,705

APOEL: (3421) Perez; Carlao, Rueda, Vouros; Sallai (Efrem 60), Morais (Ebecilio 66), Vinicius (Farias 59), Lago; Zahid, Aloneftis; Pote.
Real Madrid: (433) Casilla; Carvajal, Nacho, Varane, Marcelo (Hernandez 58); Modric, Kroos (Ceballos 59), Asensio; Lucas, Benzema (Borja Mayoral 64), Ronaldo.

Borussia Dortmund (1) 1 *(Aubameyang 31)*

Tottenham H (0) 2 *(Kane 49, Son 76)*   65,849

Borussia Dortmund: (433) Burki (Weidenfeller 90); Toljan, Bartra, Zagadou (Toprak 78), Schmelzer; Kagawa (Castro 66), Weigl, Gotze; Yarmolenko, Aubameyang, Guerreiro.
Tottenham H: (4231) Lloris; Aurier, Dier, Vertonghen, Rose; Winks, Sanchez; Alli (Dembele 81), Eriksen (Sissoko 85), Son; Kane (Llorente 86).

Wednesday, 6 December 2017

Real Madrid (2) 3 *(Borja Mayoral 8, Ronaldo 12, Lucas 81)*

Borussia Dortmund (1) 2 *(Aubameyang 44, 49)* 73,323

Real Madrid: (433) Navas; Sergio Ramos, Varane (Asensio 38), Nacho, Hernandez; Casemiro, Lucas, Isco (Llorente 69); Kovacic (Ceballos 57), Ronaldo, Borja Mayoral.
Borussia Dortmund: (343) Burki; Papastathopoulos, Subotic, Schmelzer; Guerreiro, Bartra (Toprak 80), Sahin (Weigl 65), Dahoud; Pulisic, Kagawa (Yarmolenko 90), Aubameyang.

Tottenham H (2) 3 *(Llorente 20, Son 37, Nkoudou 80)*

APOEL (0) 0   42,679

Tottenham H: (4231) Vorm; Aurier, Foyth, Sanchez, Rose (Walker-Peters 70); Sissoko, Winks; Nkoudou, Alli (Sterling 88), Son (Dembele 64); Llorente.
APOEL: (4231) Perez; Vouros, Rueda, Carlao, Lago; Zahid, Vinicius (Sallai 46); Morais, Aloneftis (de Camargo 75), Ebecilio; Pote (Antoniou 81).

Group H Table	P	W	D	L	F	A	GD	Pts
Tottenham H	6	5	1	0	15	4	11	16
Real Madrid	6	4	1	1	17	7	10	13
Borussia Dortmund	6	0	2	4	7	13	–6	2
APOEL	6	0	2	4	2	17	–15	2

KNOCK-OUT STAGE

ROUND OF 16 FIRST LEG

Tuesday, 13 February 2018

FC Basel (0) 0

Manchester C (3) 4 *(Gundogan 14, 53, Bernardo Silva 18, Aguero 23)*   36,000

FC Basel: (541) Vaclik; Lang, Xhaka, Lacroix, Suchy, Riveros; Elyounoussi (Bua 85), Frei, Die, Stocker (Ajeti 71); Oberlin.
Manchester C: (433) Ederson; Walker, Kompany, Otamendi, Delph; De Bruyne (Silva 63), Fernandinho, Gundogan; Bernardo Silva, Aguero (Danilo 85), Sterling (Sane 57).

Juventus (2) 2 *(Higuain 2, 9 (pen))*

Tottenham H (1) 2 *(Kane 35, Eriksen 71)*   41,232

Juventus: (433) Buffon; De Sciglio, Benatia, Chiellini, Alex Sandro; Khedira (Bentancur 66), Pjanic, Bernardeschi; Douglas Costa (Asamoah 90), Higuain, Mandzukic (Sturaro 76).
Tottenham H: (433) Lloris; Aurier, Sanchez, Vertonghen, Davies; Eriksen (Wanyama 90), Dier, Dembele; Lamela (Lucas Moura 88), Kane, Alli (Son 83).

Wednesday, 14 February 2018
Porto (0) 0
Liverpool (2) 5 *(Mane 25, 53, 85, Salah 30, Firmino 70)*
                                    47,718

Porto: (4231) Jose Sa; Ricardo Pereira, Reyes, Marcano, Alex Telles; Sergio Oliveira, Herrera; Marega, Otavio (Corona 46), Brahimi (Waris 62); Tiquinho Soares (Paciencia 74).
Liverpool: (433) Karius; Alexander-Arnold (Gomez 79), Lovren, van Dijk, Robertson; Milner, Henderson (Matip 74), Wijnaldum; Salah, Firmino (Ings 79), Mane.

Real Madrid (1) 3 *(Ronaldo 45 (pen), 83, Marcelo 86)*
Paris Saint-Germain (1) 1 *(Rabiot 33)*   78,158
Real Madrid: (433) Navas; Nacho, Varane, Sergio Ramos, Marcelo; Modric, Kroos, Casemiro (Lucas 79); Isco (Asensio 79), Benzema (Bale 68), Ronaldo.
Paris Saint-Germain: (433) Areola; Dani Alves, Marquinhos, Kimpembe, Yuri; Verratti, Lo Celso (Draxler 85), Rabiot; Mbappe-Lottin, Cavani (Meunier 66), Neymar.

Tuesday, 20 February 2018
Bayern Munich (1) 5 *(Muller 43, 66, Coman 52, Lewandowski 79, 88)*
Besiktas (0) 0   70,000
Bayern Munich: (451) Ulreich; Kimmich, Boateng, Hummels, Alaba; Muller, Vidal (Tolisso 83), Javi Martinez, Rodriguez (Robben 44), Coman (Ribery 81); Lewandowski.
Besiktas: (4231) Fabri; Adriano, Pepe, Vida■, Erkin (Gonul 69); Hutchinson, Medel (Arslan 85); Quaresma, Anderson Talisca, Babel; Vagner Love (Tosic 57).

Chelsea (0) 1 *(Willian 62)*
Barcelona (0) 1 *(Messi 75)*   37,741
Chelsea: (343) Courtois; Azpilicueta, Christensen, Rudiger; Moses, Fabregas (Drinkwater 84), Kante, Alonso; Willian, Hazard, Pedro (Morata 83).
Barcelona: (433) ter Stegen; Sergi Roberto, Pique, Umtiti, Jordi Alba; Rakitic, Busquets, Paulinho (Aleix Vidal 64); Messi, Suarez L, Iniesta (Andre Gomes 90).

Wednesday, 21 February 2018
Sevilla (0) 0
Manchester U (0) 0   39,725
Sevilla: (4231) Sergio Rico; Jesus Navas, Mercado, Lenglet, Escudero; Sarabia, Nzonzi; Banega (Pizarro 89), Correa, Vazquez; Muriel (Sandro 84).
Manchester U: (4231) de Gea; Valencia, Smalling, Lindelof, Young; Ander Herrera (Pogba 17), McTominay; Matic, Sanchez (Rashford 75), Mata (Martial 79); Lukaku.

Shakhtar Donetsk (0) 2 *(Ferreyra 52, Fred 71)*
Roma (1) 1 *(Under 41)*   35,124
Shakhtar Donetsk: (4411) Pyatov; Butko, Kryvtsov (Ordets 45), Rakitskiy, Ismaily; Marlos, Stepanenko, Fred, Bernard (Kovalenko 90); Taison; Ferreyra.
Roma: (4411) Alisson; Florenzi (Bruno Peres 72), Manolas, Fazio, Kolarov; Under (Gerson 72), De Rossi, Strootman, Perotti; Nainggolan (Defrel 83); Dzeko.

ROUND OF 16 SECOND LEG
Tuesday, 6 March 2018
Liverpool (0) 0
Porto (0) 0   48,768
Liverpool: (433) Karius; Gomez, Matip, Lovren, Moreno; Can (Klavan 80), Henderson, Milner; Mane (Salah 73), Firmino (Ings 61), Lallana.
Porto: (442) Casillas; Maxi Pereira, Felipe, Reyes, Dalot; Costa, Torres, Andre Andre (Sergio Oliveira 62), Corona; Aboubakar (Paciencia 80), Waris (Ricardo Pereira 66).

Paris Saint-Germain (0) 1 *(Cavani 71)*
Real Madrid (0) 2 *(Ronaldo 51, Casemiro 80)*   46,585
Paris Saint-Germain: (433) Areola; Dani Alves, Thiago Silva, Marquinhos, Yuri; Verratti■, Thiago Motta (Pastore 59), Rabiot; Di Maria (Draxler 76), Cavani, Mbappe-Lottin (Diarra 85).

Real Madrid: (442) Navas; Carvajal, Sergio Ramos, Varane, Marcelo; Lucas, Casemiro, Kovacic (Kroos 71), Asensio (Isco 82); Benzema (Bale 76), Ronaldo.

Wednesday, 7 March 2018
Manchester C (1) 1 *(Gabriel Jesus 8)*
FC Basel (1) 2 *(Elyounoussi 17, Lang 71)*   49,411
Manchester C: (433) Bravo; Danilo, Stones, Laporte, Zinchenko; Gundogan (Diaz 66), Toure, Foden (Adarabioyo 89); Bernardo Silva, Gabriel Jesus, Sane.
FC Basel: (343) Vaclik; Suchy, Frei, Lacroix; Lang, Die, Zuffi, Riveros; Bua (Stocker 68), Oberlin (van Wolfswinkel 73), Elyounoussi.

Tottenham H (1) 1 *(Son 39)*
Juventus (0) 2 *(Higuain 64, Dybala 67)*   84,010
Tottenham H: (433) Lloris; Trippier, Sanchez, Vertonghen, Davies; Dembele, Dier (Lamela 74), Eriksen; Alli (Llorente 85), Kane, Son.
Juventus: (433) Buffon; Barzagli, Benatia (Lichtsteiner 61), Chiellini, Alex Sandro; Khedira, Pjanic, Matuidi (Asamoah 60); Dybala, Higuain (Sturaro 83), Douglas Costa.

Tuesday, 13 March 2018
Manchester U (0) 1 *(Lukaku 84)*
Sevilla (0) 2 *(Ben Yedder 74, 78)*   74,909
Manchester U: (4231) de Gea; Valencia (Mata 77), Smalling, Bailly, Young; Fellaini (Pogba 59), Matic; Lingard (Martial 76), Sanchez, Rashford; Lukaku.
Sevilla: (4231) Sergio Rico; Mercado, Kjaer, Lenglet, Escudero; Nzonzi, Banega; Sarabia, Vazquez (Pizarro 87), Correa (Geis 89); Muriel (Ben Yedder 72).

Roma (0) 1 *(Dzeko 52)*
Shakhtar Donetsk (0) 0   47,693
Roma: (433) Alisson; Florenzi, Manolas, Fazio, Kolarov; Nainggolan, De Rossi, Strootman; Under (Gerson 65), Dzeko (El Shaarawy 89), Perotti.
Shakhtar Donetsk: (4411) Pyatov; Butko, Ordets■, Rakitskiy, Ismaily; Marlos (Dentinho 82), Fred, Stepanenko (Alan Patrick 74), Bernard; Taison; Ferreyra.
Roma won on away goals.

Wednesday, 14 March 2018
Barcelona (2) 3 *(Messi 3, 63, Dembele 20)*
Chelsea (0) 0   97,183
Barcelona: (442) ter Stegen; Sergi Roberto, Pique, Umtiti, Jordi Alba; Dembele (Aleix Vidal 66), Rakitic, Busquets (Andre Gomes 61), Iniesta (Paulinho 56); Messi, Suarez L.
Chelsea: (343) Courtois; Azpilicueta, Christensen, Rudiger; Moses (Zappacosta 67), Fabregas, Kante, Alonso; Willian, Giroud (Morata 67), Hazard (Pedro 82).

Besiktas (0) 1 *(Vagner Love 58)*
Bayern Munich (1) 3 *(Thiago 18, Gonul 46 (og), Wagner 84)*   36,885
Besiktas: (442) Zengin; Gonul, Medel, Uysal, Erkin; Ozyakup, Arslan (Hutchinson 60), Quaresma, Vagner Love (Babel 75); Pektemek, Lens (Anderson Talisca 60).
Bayern Munich: (433) Ulreich; Rafinha, Boateng, Hummels (Sule 46), Alaba; Vidal, Javi Martinez, Thiago (Rodriguez 35); Muller, Lewandowski (Wagner 68), Ribery.

QUARTER-FINALS FIRST LEG
Tuesday, 3 April 2018
Juventus (0) 0
Real Madrid (1) 3 *(Ronaldo 3, 64, Marcelo 72)*   40,849
Juventus: (4411) Buffon; De Sciglio, Barzagli, Chiellini, Asamoah (Mandzukic 68); Douglas Costa (Matuidi 69), Khedira (Cuadrado 76), Bentancur, Alex Sandro; Dybala■; Higuain.
Real Madrid: (442) Navas; Carvajal, Sergio Ramos, Varane, Marcelo; Modric (Kovacic 82), Kroos, Casemiro, Isco (Asensio 76); Benzema (Lucas 59), Ronaldo.

Sevilla (1) 1 *(Sarabia 32)*
Bayern Munich (1) 2 *(Jesus Navas 38 (og), Thiago 68)*
                                         40,635
Sevilla: (4231) Soria; Jesus Navas, Kjaer, Lenglet, Escudero; Nzonzi, Pizarro; Sarabia, Vazquez, Correa (Sandro 78); Ben Yedder (Muriel 80).
Bayern Munich: (451) Ulreich; Kimmich, Boateng, Hummels, Bernat (Rafinha 46); Muller, Vidal (Rodriguez 36), Javi Martinez, Thiago, Ribery (Robben 79); Lewandowski.

Wednesday, 4 April 2018
Barcelona (1) 4 *(De Rossi 39 (og), Manolas 57 (og), Pique 59, Suarez L 87)*
Roma (0) 1 *(Dzeko 80)*   90,106
Barcelona: (442) ter Stegen; Nelson Semedo, Pique, Umtiti, Jordi Alba; Sergi Roberto (Andre Gomes 83), Rakitic, Busquets (Paulinho 66), Iniesta (Suarez D 85); Messi, Suarez L.
Roma: (433) Alisson; Bruno Peres, Fazio, Manolas, Kolarov; Pellegrini (Gonalons 60), De Rossi (Defrel 77), Strootman; Florenzi (El Shaarawy 72), Dzeko, Perotti.

Liverpool (3) 3 *(Salah 12, Oxlade-Chamberlain 20, Mane 31)*
Manchester C (0) 0   50,685
Liverpool: (433) Karius; Alexander-Arnold, van Dijk, Lovren, Robertson; Milner, Henderson, Oxlade-Chamberlain (Moreno 85); Salah (Wijnaldum 52), Firmino (Solanke 70), Mane.
Manchester C: (433) Ederson; Walker, Otamendi, Kompany, Laporte; Gundogan (Sterling 57), Fernandinho, Silva; De Bruyne, Gabriel Jesus, Sane.

QUARTER-FINALS SECOND LEG
Tuesday, 10 April 2018
Manchester C (1) 1 *(Gabriel Jesus 2)*
Liverpool (0) 2 *(Salah 56, Firmino 77)*   53,461
Manchester C: (343) Ederson; Walker, Otamendi, Laporte; Bernardo Silva (Gundogan 74), Fernandinho, De Bruyne, Silva (Aguero 66); Sterling, Gabriel Jesus, Sane.
Liverpool: (433) Karius; Alexander-Arnold (Clyne 82), Lovren, van Dijk, Robertson; Oxlade-Chamberlain, Wijnaldum, Milner; Salah (Ings 89), Firmino (Klavan 81), Mane.

Roma (1) 3 *(Dzeko 6, De Rossi 58 (pen), Manolas 82)*
Barcelona (0) 0   56,580
Roma: (352) Alisson; Manolas, Fazio, Juan Jesus; Florenzi, Nainggolan (El Shaarawy 76), De Rossi, Strootman, Kolarov; Dzeko, Schick (Under 72).
Barcelona: (442) ter Stegen; Nelson Semedo (Dembele 85), Pique, Umtiti, Jordi Alba; Sergi Roberto, Rakitic, Busquets (Alcacer 85), Iniesta (Andre Gomes 81); Messi, Suarez L.
Roma won on away goals.

Wednesday, 11 April 2018
Bayern Munich (0) 0
Sevilla (0) 0   70,000
Bayern Munich: (4411) Ulreich; Kimmich, Boateng, Hummels, Rafinha (Sule 86); Robben, Javi Martinez, Rodriguez, Ribery (Thiago 70); Muller; Lewandowski.
Sevilla: (4231) Soria; Jesus Navas, Mercado, Lenglet, Escudero; Banega, Nzonzi, Correa (Nolito 80), Sarabia (Sandro 70); Ben Yedder (Muriel 65).

Real Madrid (0) 1 *(Ronaldo 90 (pen))*
Juventus (2) 3 *(Mandzukic 2, 37, Matuidi 61)*   75,796
Real Madrid: (442) Navas; Carvajal, Varane, Vallejo, Marcelo; Casemiro (Lucas 46), Modric (Kovacic 75), Kroos, Isco; Ronaldo, Bale (Asensio 46).
Juventus: (433) Buffon[a]; De Sciglio (Lichtsteiner 17), Benatia, Chiellini, Alex Sandro; Khedira, Pjanic, Matuidi; Douglas Costa, Higuain (Szczesny 90), Mandzukic.

SEMI-FINALS FIRST LEG
Tuesday, 24 April 2018
Liverpool (2) 5 *(Salah 36, 45, Mane 56, Firmino 61, 69)*
Roma (0) 2 *(Dzeko 81, Perotti 85 (pen))* 51,236
Liverpool: (433) Karius; Alexander-Arnold, Lovren, van Dijk, Robertson; Oxlade-Chamberlain (Wijnaldum 18), Henderson, Milner; Salah (Ings 74), Firmino (Klavan 90), Mane.
Roma: (3421) Alisson; Fazio, Manolas, Juan Jesus (Perotti 66); Florenzi, De Rossi (Gonalons 66), Strootman, Kolarov; Under (Schick 46), Nainggolan; Dzeko.
Referee: Felix Brych.

Gareth Bale's acrobatic overhead kick gives the lead back to Real Madrid in their pulsating 3-1 defeat of Liverpool in the UEFA Champions League Final in Kiev on 26 May. (Reuters/Kai Pfaffenbach)

Wednesday, 25 April 2018
Bayern Munich (1) 1 *(Kimmich 28)*
Real Madrid (1) 2 *(Marcelo 44, Asensio 57)*   70,000
Bayern Munich: (4141) Ulreich; Kimmich, Boateng (Sule 34), Hummels, Rafinha; Javi Martinez (Tolisso 75); Robben (Thiago 8), Muller, Rodriguez, Ribery; Lewandowski.
Real Madrid: (433) Navas; Carvajal (Benzema 66), Sergio Ramos, Varane, Marcelo; Modric, Casemiro (Kovacic 83), Kroos; Lucas, Ronaldo, Isco (Asensio 46).
Referee: Bjorn Kuipers.

SEMI-FINALS SECOND LEG
Tuesday, 1 May 2018
Real Madrid (1) 2 *(Benzema 11, 46)*
Bayern Munich (1) 2 *(Kimmich 3, Rodriguez 63)*   77,459
Real Madrid: (442) Navas; Lucas, Varane, Sergio Ramos, Marcelo; Asensio (Nacho 87), Kovacic (Casemiro 72), Modric, Kroos; Benzema (Bale 72), Ronaldo.
Bayern Munich: (4231) Ulreich; Kimmich, Hummels, Sule, Alaba; Tolisso (Wagner 75), Thiago; Muller, Rodriguez (Javi Martinez 83), Ribery; Lewandowski.
Referee: Cuneyt Cakir.

Wednesday, 2 May 2018
Roma (1) 4 *(Milner 16 (og), Dzeko 52, Nainggolan 87, 90 (pen))*
Liverpool (2) 2 *(Mane 9, Wijnaldum 26)*   61,889
Roma: (433) Alisson; Florenzi, Manolas, Fazio, Kolarov; Pellegrini (Under 53), De Rossi (Gonalons 69), Nainggolan; Schick, Dzeko, El Shaarawy (Antonucci 75).
Liverpool: (433) Karius; Alexander-Arnold (Clyne 90), van Dijk, Lovren, Robertson; Wijnaldum, Henderson, Milner; Salah, Firmino (Solanke 87), Mane (Klavan 83).
Referee: Damir Skomina.

CHAMPIONS LEAGUE FINAL 2018
Saturday, 26 May 2018
(in Kiev, 61,561)

Real Madrid (0) 3 *(Benzema 51, Bale 64, 83)*   **Liverpool (0) 1** *(Mane 55)*

Real Madrid: (4312) Navas; Carvajal (Nacho 37), Varane, Sergio Ramos, Marcelo; Modric, Casemiro, Kroos; Isco (Bale 61); Benzema (Asensio 89), Ronaldo.

Liverpool: (433) Karius; Alexander-Arnold, Lovren, van Dijk, Robertson; Milner (Can 83), Henderson, Wijnaldum; Salah (Lallana 30), Firmino, Mane.

Referee: Milorad Mazic.

UEFA CHAMPIONS LEAGUE 2018–19

PARTICIPATING CLUBS
The list below is provisional and is subject to pending legal proceedings and final confirmation from UEFA.

GROUP STAGE
Atletico Madrid (ESP)
Barcelona (ESP)
Bayern Munich (GER)
Borussia Dortmund (GER)
Club Brugge (BEL)
CSKA Moscow (RUS)
Galatasaray (TUR)
Internazionale (ITA)
Juventus (ITA)
Liverpool (ENG)
Lokomotiv Moscow (RUS)
Lyon (FRA)
Manchester C (ENG)
Manchester U (ENG)
Monaco (FRA)
Napoli (ITA)
Paris Saint-Germain (FRA)
Porto (POR)
Real Madrid (ESP)
Roma (ITA)
Schalke (GER)
Shakhtar Donetsk (UKR)
Tottenham H (ENG)
TSG Hoffenheim (GER)
Valencia (ESP)
Viktoria Plzen (CZE)
Plus six play-off winners.

PLAY-OFF – CHAMPIONS ROUTE
PSV Eindhoven (NED)
Young Boys (SUI)
Plus six third qualifying round winners (champions path).

PLAY-OFF – LEAGUE ROUTE
Four third qualifying round winners (league path).

THIRD QUALIFYING ROUND – CHAMPIONS ROUTE
AEK Athens (GRE)
Salzburg (AUT)
Plus ten second qualifying round winners (champions path).

THIRD QUALIFYING ROUND – LEAGUE ROUTE
Benfica (POR)
Dynamo Kyiv (UKR)
Fenerbahce (TUR)
Slavia Prague (CZE)
Spartak Moscow (RUS)
Standard Liege (BEL)
Plus two second qualifying round winners (league path).

SECOND QUALIFYING ROUND – CHAMPIONS ROUTE
BATE Borisov (BLR)
CFR Cluj (ROU)
Dinamo Zagreb (CRO)
Midtjylland (DEN)
Plus 16 first qualifying round winners.

SECOND QUALIFYING ROUND – LEAGUE ROUTE
Ajax (NED)
FC Basel (SUI)
PAOK Salonika (GRE)
Sturm Graz (AUT)

FIRST QUALIFYING ROUND
Alashkert (ARM)
APOEL (CYP)

Astana (KAZ)
Celtic (SCO)
Cork C (IRL)
Crusaders (NIR)
Crvena Zvezda (SRB)
Dudelange (LUX)
Flora Tallinn (EST)
Hapoel Be'er Sheva (ISR)
HJK Helsinki (FIN)
Kukes (ALB)
Legia Warsaw (POL)
Ludogorets Razgrad (BUL)
Malmo (SWE)
Olimpija Ljubljana (SVN)
Qarabag (AZE)
Rosenborg (NOR)
Sheriff Tiraspol (MDA)
Shkendija (MKD)
Spartak Trnava (SVK)
Spartaks Jurmala (LVA)
Suduva Marijampole (LTU)
Sutjeska Niksic (MNE)
The New Saints (WAL)
Torpedo Kutaisi (GEO)
Valletta (MLT)
Valur (ISL)
Videoton (HUN)
Víkingur Gota (FRO)
Zrinjski (BIH)
Plus the preliminary round winner.

PRELIMINARY ROUND
Drita (KOS)
FC Santa Coloma (AND)
La Fiorita (SMR)
Lincoln Red Imps (GIB)

EUROPEAN CUP-WINNERS' CUP
FINALS 1961–99

Year	Winners v Runners-up		Venue	Attendance	Referee
1961	1st Leg Fiorentina v Rangers	2-0	Glasgow	80,000	C. E. Steiner (Austria)
	2nd Leg Fiorentina v Rangers	2-1	Florence	50,000	V. Hernadi (Hungary)
1962	Atletico Madrid v Fiorentina	1-1	Glasgow	27,389	T. Wharton (Scotland)
Replay	Atletico Madrid v Fiorentina	3-0	Stuttgart	38,000	K. Tschenscher (West Germany)
1963	Tottenham Hotspur v Atletico Madrid	5-1	Rotterdam	49,000	A. van Leuwen (Netherlands)
1964	Sporting Lisbon v MTK Budapest	3-3*	Brussels	3,208	L. van Nuffel (Belgium)
Replay	Sporting Lisbon v MTK Budapest	1-0	Antwerp	13,924	G. Versyp (Belgium)
1965	West Ham U v Munich 1860	2-0	Wembley	7,974	I. Zsolt (Hungary)
1966	Borussia Dortmund v Liverpool	2-1*	Glasgow	41,657	P. Schwinte (France)
1967	Bayern Munich v Rangers	1-0*	Nuremberg	69,480	C. Lo Bello (Italy)
1968	AC Milan v Hamburg	2-0	Rotterdam	53,000	J. Ortiz de Mendibil (Spain)
1969	Slovan Bratislava v Barcelona	3-2	Basle	19,000	L. van Ravens (Netherlands)
1970	Manchester C v Gornik Zabrze	2-1	Vienna	7,968	P. Schiller (Austria)
1971	Chelsea v Real Madrid	1-1*	Athens	45,000	R. Scheurer (Switzerland)
Replay	Chelsea v Real Madrid	2-1*	Athens	19,917	R. Scheurer (Switzerland)
1972	Rangers v Dynamo Moscow	3-2	Barcelona	24,701	J. Ortiz de Mendibil (Spain)
1973	AC Milan v Leeds U	1-0	Salonika	40,154	C. Mihas (Greece)
1974	Magdeburg v AC Milan	2-0	Rotterdam	4,641	A. van Gemert (Netherlands)
1975	Dynamo Kyiv v Ferencvaros	3-0	Basle	13,000	R. Davidson (Scotland)
1976	Anderlecht v West Ham U	4-2	Brussels	51,296	R. Wurtz (France)
1977	Hamburger SV v Anderlecht	2-0	Amsterdam	66,000	P. Partridge (England)
1978	Anderlecht v Austria/WAC	4-0	Paris	48,679	H. Adlinger (West Germany)
1979	Barcelona v Fortuna Dusseldorf	4-3*	Basel	58,000	K. Palotai (Hungary)
1980	Valencia v Arsenal	0-0*	Brussels	40,000	V. Christov (Czechoslovakia)
	(Valencia won 5-4 on penalties)				
1981	Dinamo Tbilisi v Carl Zeiss Jena	2-1	Dusseldorf	4,750	R. Lattanzi (Italy)
1982	Barcelona v Standard Liege	2-1	Barcelona	80,000	W. Eschweiler (West Germany)
1983	Aberdeen v Real Madrid	2-1*	Gothenburg	17,804	G. Menegali (Italy)
1984	Juventus v Porto	2-1	Basel	55,000	A. Prokop (Egypt)
1985	Everton v Rapid Vienna	3-1	Rotterdam	38,500	P. Casarin (Italy)
1986	Dynamo Kyiv v Atletico Madrid	3-0	Lyon	50,000	F. Wohrer (Austria)
1987	Ajax v Lokomotiv Leipzig	1-0	Athens	35,107	L. Agnolin (Italy)
1988	Mechelen v Ajax	1-0	Strasbourg	39,446	D. Pauly (West Germany)
1989	Barcelona v Sampdoria	2-0	Berne	42,707	G. Courtney (England)
1990	Sampdoria v Anderlecht	2-0*	Gothenburg	20,103	B. Galler (Switzerland)
1991	Manchester U v Barcelona	2-1	Rotterdam	43,500	B. Karlsson (Sweden)
1992	Werder Bremen v Monaco	2-0	Lisbon	16,000	P. D'Elia (Italy)
1993	Parma v Antwerp	3-1	Wembley	37,393	K.-J. Assenmacher (Germany)
1994	Arsenal v Parma	1-0	Copenhagen	33,765	V. Krondl (Czech Republic)
1995	Real Zaragoza v Arsenal	2-1	Paris	42,424	P. Ceccarini (Italy)
1996	Paris Saint-Germain v Rapid Vienna	1-0	Brussels	37,000	P. Pairetto (Italy)
1997	Barcelona v Paris Saint-Germain	1-0	Rotterdam	52,000	M. Merk (Germany)
1998	Chelsea v VfB Stuttgart	1-0	Stockholm	30,216	S. Braschi (Italy)
1999	Lazio v Mallorca	2-1	Villa Park	33,021	G. Benko (Austria)

INTER-CITIES FAIRS CUP FINALS 1958–71

Year	1st Leg		Attendance	2nd Leg	Attendance		Agg	Winner
1958	London XI v Barcelona	2-2	45,466	0-6	70,000		2-8	Barcelona
1960	Birmingham C v Barcelona	0-0	40,524	1-4	70,000		1-4	Barcelona
1961	Birmingham C v Roma	2-2	21,005	0-2	60,000		2-4	Roma
1962	Valencia v Barcelona	6-2	65,000	1-1	60,000		7-3	Valencia
1963	Dinamo Zagreb v Valencia	1-2	40,000	0-2	55,000		1-4	Valencia
1964	Real Zaragoza v Valencia	2-1	50,000	(in Barcelona, one match only)				Real Zaragoza
1965	Ferencvaros v Juventus	1-0	25,000	(in Turin, one match only)				Ferencvaros
1966	Barcelona v Real Zaragoza	0-1	70,000	4-2*	70,000		4-3	Barcelona
1967	Dinamo Zagreb v Leeds U	2-0	40,000	0-0	35,604		2-0	Dynamo Zagreb
1968	Leeds U v Ferencvaros	1-0	25,368	0-0	70,000		1-0	Leeds U
1969	Newcastle U v Ujpest Dozsa	3-0	60,000	3-2	37,000		6-2	Newcastle U
1970	Anderlecht v Arsenal	3-1	37,000	0-3	51,612		3-4	Arsenal
1971	Juventus v Leeds U	0-0	(abandoned 51 minutes)		42,000			
	Juventus v Leeds U	2-2	42,000	1-1	42,483		3-3	Leeds U
	Leeds U won on away goals rule.							

Trophy Play-Off – *between first and last winners to decide who would have possession of the original trophy*
1971 Barcelona v Leeds U   2-1   50,000   (in Barcelona, one match only)

*After extra time.

UEFA CUP FINALS 1972–97

Year	1st Leg		Attendance	2nd Leg	Attendance	Agg	Winner
1972	Wolverhampton W v Tottenham H	1-2	38,562	1-1	54,303	2-3	Tottenham H
1973	Liverpool v Moenchengladbach	0-0	*(abandoned after 27 minutes)*		44,967		
	Liverpool v Moenchengladbach	3-0	41,169	0-2	35,000	3-2	Liverpool
1974	Tottenham H v Feyenoord	2-2	46,281	0-2	59,317	2-4	Feyenoord
1975	Moenchengladbach v FC Twente	0-0	42,368	5-1	21,767	5-1	Moenchengladbach
1976	Liverpool v Club Brugge	3-2	49,981	1-1	29,423	4-3	Liverpool
1977	Juventus v Athletic Bilbao	1-0	66,000	1-2	39,700	2-2	Juventus
	Juventus won on away goals rule.						
1978	Bastia v PSV Eindhoven	0-0	8,006	0-3	28,000	0-3	PSV Eindhoven
1979	RS Belgrade v Moenchengladbach	1-1	65,000	0-1	45,000	1-2	Moenchengladbach
1980	Moenchengladbach v E. Frankfurt	3-2	25,000	0-1	59,000	3-3	E. Frankfurt
	Eintracht Frankfurt won on away goals rule.						
1981	Ipswich T v AZ 67 Alkmaar	3-0	27,532	2-4	22,291	5-4	Ipswich T
1982	IFK Gothenburg v Hamburger SV	1-0	42,548	3-0	57,312	4-0	IFK Gothenburg
1983	Anderlecht v Benfica	1-0	55,000	1-1	70,000	2-1	Anderlecht
1984	Anderlecht v Tottenham H	1-1	33,000	1-1*	46,258	2-2	Tottenham H
	Tottenham H won 4-3 on penalties.						
1985	Videoton v Real Madrid	0-3	30,000	1-0	80,000	1-3	Real Madrid
1986	Real Madrid v Cologne	5-1	60,000	0-2	22,000	5-3	Real Madrid
1987	IFK Gothenburg v Dundee U	1-0	48,614	1-1	20,900	2-1	IFK Gothenburg
1988	Espanol v Bayer Leverkusen	3-0	31,180	0-3*	21,600	3-3	Bayer Leverkusen
	Bayer Leverkusen won 3-2 on penalties.						
1989	Napoli v VfB Stuttgart	2-1	81,093	3-3	64,000	5-4	Napoli
1990	Juventus v Fiorentina	3-1	47,519	0-0	30,999	3-1	Juventus
1991	Internazionale v Roma	2-0	68,887	0-1	70,901	2-1	Internazionale
1992	Torino v Ajax	2-2	65,377	0-0	40,000	2-2	Ajax
	Ajax won on away goals rule.						
1993	Borussia Dortmund v Juventus	1-3	37,000	0-3	62,781	1-6	Juventus
1994	Salzburg v Internazionale	0-1	43,000	0-1	80,345	0-2	Internazionale
1995	Parma v Juventus	1-0	22,057	1-1	80,000	2-1	Parma
1996	Bayern Munich v Bordeaux	2-0	63,000	3-1	30,000	5-1	Bayern Munich
1997	Schalke 04 v Internazionale	1-0	57,000	0-1*	81,675	1-1	Schalke 04
	Schalke 04 won 4-1 on penalties.						

UEFA CUP FINALS 1998–2009

Year	Winners v Runners-up		Venue	Attendance	Referee
1998	Internazionale v Lazio	3-0	Paris	44,412	A. L. Nieto (Spain)
1999	Parma v Olympique Marseille	3-0	Moscow	61,000	H. Dallas (Scotland)
2000	Galatasaray v Arsenal	0-0*	Copenhagen	38,919	A. L. Nieto (Spain)
	Galatasaray won 4-1 on penalties.				
2001	Liverpool v Alaves	5-4*	Dortmund	48,050	G. Veissiere (France)
	Liverpool won on sudden death 'golden goal'.				
2002	Feyenoord v Borussia Dortmund	3-2	Rotterdam	45,611	V. M. M. Pereira (Portugal)
2003	FC Porto v Celtic	3-2*	Seville	52,140	L. Michel (Slovakia)
2004	Valencia v Olympique Marseille	2-0	Gothenburg	39,000	P. Collina (Italy)
2005	CSKA Moscow v Sporting Lisbon	3-1	Lisbon	47,085	G. Poll (England)
2006	Sevilla v Middlesbrough	4-0	Eindhoven	32,100	H. Fandel (Germany)
2007	Sevilla v Espanyol	2-2*	Glasgow	47,602	M. Busacca (Switzerland)
	Sevilla won 3-1 on penalties.				
2008	Zenit St Petersburg v Rangers	2-0	Manchester	43,878	P. Fröjdfeldt (Sweden)
2009	Shakhtar Donetsk v Werder Bremen	2-1*	Istanbul	37,357	L. M. Chantalejo (Spain)

UEFA EUROPA LEAGUE FINALS 2010–18

Year	Winners v Runners-up		Venue	Attendance	Referee
2010	Atletico Madrid v Fulham	2-1*	Hamburg	49,000	N. Rizzoli (Italy)
2011	FC Porto v Braga	1-0	Dublin	45,391	V. Carballo (Spain)
2012	Atletico Madrid v Athletic Bilbao	3-0	Bucharest	52,347	W. Stark (Germany)
2013	Chelsea v Benfica	2-1	Amsterdam	46,163	B. Kuipers (Netherlands)
2014	Sevilla v Benfica	0-0*	Turin	33,120	F. Brych (Germany)
	Sevilla won 4-2 on penalties.				
2015	Sevilla v Dnipro Dnipropetrovsk	3-2	Warsaw	45,000	M. Atkinson (England)
2016	Sevilla v Liverpool	3-1	Basel	34,429	J. Eriksson (Sweden)
2017	Manchester U v Ajax	2-0	Stockholm	46,961	D. Skomina (Slovenia)
2018	Atletico Madrid v Marseille	3-0	Lyon	55,768	B. Kuipers (Netherlands)

After extra time.

UEFA EUROPA LEAGUE 2017–18

■ Denotes player sent off.

FIRST QUALIFYING ROUND FIRST LEG

AEK Larnaca v Lincoln	5-0
Bala Town v Vaduz	1-2
Beitar Jerusalem v Vasas	4-3
Chikhura Sachkhere v Rheindorf Altach	0-1
Crvena Zvezda v Floriana	3-0
Connah's Quay Nomads v HJK Helsinki	1-0
Crusaders v FK Liepaja	3-1
Dinamo Batumi v Jagiellonia Bialystock	0-1
Dinamo Minsk v NSI Runavik	2-1
Domzale v Flora Tallinn	2-0
Ferencvaros v Jelgava	2-0
Fola Esch v Milsami	2-1
Haugesund v Coleraine	7-0
IFK Norrkoping v Pristina	5-0
Irtysh v Dunav Ruse	1-0
Kairat v Atlantas	6-0
KI Klaksvik v AIK	0-0
KR Reykjavik v Seinajoki	0-0
Lech Poznan v Pelister	4-0
Levadia Tallinn v Cork C	0-2
Levski Sofia v Sutjeska	3-1
Lyngby v Bangor C	1-0
Maccabi Tel Aviv v KF Tirana	2-0
Midtjylland v Derry C	6-1
Mladost Lucani v Inter Baku	0-3
Mladost Podgorica v Gandzasar Kapan	1-0
Nomme Kalju v B36 Torshavn	2-1
Odd v Ballymena	3-0
Partizani v Botev Plovdiv	1-3
Pyunik v Slovan Bratislava	1-4
Rangers v Progres Niederkorn	1-0
Shakhtyor Soligorsk v Suduva Marijampole	0-0
Shirak v Gorica	0-2
Siroki Brijeg v Ordabasy	2-0
Skenderbeu v Sant Julia	1-0
Skendija Tetovo v Dacia	3-0
St Johnstone v Trakai	1-2
St Joseph's v AEL Limassol	0-4
Stjarnan v Shamrock R	0-1
Tre Penne v Rabotnicki Kometal	0-1
Trencin v Torpedo Kutaisi	5-1
UE Santa Coloma v Osijek	0-2
Vaasa v Olimpija Ljubljana	1-0
Valletta v Folgore Falciano	2-0
Ventspils v Valur Reykjavik	0-0
Videoton v Balzan	2-0
Vojvodina v Ruzomberok	2-1
Zaria Balti v Sarajevo	2-1
Zeljeznicar Sarajevo v Zeta	1-0
Zira v Differdange 03	2-0

FIRST QUALIFYING ROUND FIRST LEG

Thursday, 29 June 2017

Bala Town (0) 1 *(Venables 61)*

Vaduz (2) 2 *(Zarate 21, Brunner 29)* 803

Bala Town: (451) Morris; Owens, Stuart W. Jones, Stuart
J. Jones, Thompson; Sheridan, Stephens, Burke, Smith,
Venables; Davies (Hayes 86).
Vaduz: (442) Jehle; von Niederhausern, Buhler (Konrad
46), Pulijic, Borgmann; Zarate (Kamber 73), Muntwiler,
Ciccone, Brunner (Burgmeier 90); Mathys, Turkes.

Connah's Quay Nomads (1) 1 *(Woolfe 40)*

HJK Helsinki (0) 0 472

Connah's Quay Nomads: (451) Danby; Edwards,
Pearson, Horan, Harrison; Morris, Wilde, Woolfe, Poole
(Wignall 77), Smith; Owen J.
HJK Helsinki: (4231) Uusitalo; Patronen, Yaghoubi,
Rafinha, Savage; Jalasto, Onovo; Annan (Lappalainen
83), Pelvas, Obilor; Mensah (Jallow 61).

Crusaders (2) 3 *(Lowry 28, Carvill 35, Owens 55)*

FK Liepaja (0) 1 *(Karasausks 65)* 1375

Crusaders: (442) Jensen; Burns, Coates, Lowry (Glackin
73), Brown; Heatley (Whyte 82), Snoddy, Ward, Carvill
(Beverland 85); Forsyth, Owens.

FK Liepaja: (442) Dorosevs; Ivanovs, Klava, Strumia,
Hmizs; Jurkovskis, Afanasjevs (Kurtiss 59), Torres,
Karasausks; Grebis, Tomic (Kigurs 71).

Haugesund (3) 7 *(Tronstad 8, Abdi 33, Hajradinovic 42,
Ideki 49, Ibrahim 52, Huseklepp 61, Buduson 71)*

Coleraine (0) 0 2523

Haugesund: (4411) Sandvik; Knudsen, Skjerve, Kiss,
Tronstad; Haraldseid, Stolas (Bjorkkjaer 46), Ideki,
Abdi; Ibrahim (Huseklepp 54); Hajradinovic (Buduson
62).
Coleraine: (433) Doherty; Mullan, McConaghie,
O'Donnell, Harkin (Kirk 82); McCauley, Bradley,
Traynor; McGonigle (McLaughlin 72), Carson (Parkhill
82), Lyons.

Levadia Tallinn (0) 0

Cork C (1) 2 *(Buckley 43, Beattie 83)* 1500

Levadia Tallinn: (442) Lepmets; Dudarev, Manga■,
Podholjuzin, Gando; Krznaric, Roosnupp (Artjunin 45),
Marin (Andreev 72), Kobzar (Teever 88); Morelli, Hunt.
Cork C: (442) McNulty; Delaney, O'Connor, Bolger,
Keohane; McCormack, Dooley (Griffin 80), Morrissey,
Buckley (Campion 74); Sheppard (Beattie 67), Maguire.

Lyngby (1) 1 *(Blume 13)*

Bangor C (0) 0 2574

Lyngby: (433) Andersen; Christensen, Lumb, Jonasson■,
Ornskov; Christjansen (Boysen 46), Brandrup, Blume;
Rygaard (Hebo 46), Larsen, Ojo (Kjaer 68).
Bangor C: (433) Roberts C; Kennedy, Wilson, Connolly,
Roberts G; Allen, Gossett, Shaw; Hewitt, Taylor-
Fletcher, Nardiello (Rittenberg 60).

Midtjylland (3) 6 *(Dal Hende 4, Riis 15, Poulsen 44 (pen),
Kroon 59, 62, Kraev 84)*

Derry C (0) 1 *(Curtis 66)* 5122

Midtjylland: (442) Hansen J; Sparv, Korcsmar, Dal
Hende, Poulsen; Drachmann (Wikheim 46), Kroon, Riis,
Romer; Onuachu (Sorloth 57), Hassan (Kraev 72).
Derry C: (442) Doherty G; Jarvis, McEneff, Low,
Monaghan (Schubert 62); Curtis, Patterson (Daniels 74),
Holden, Boyle (Timlin 84); Doherty B, Barry.

Odd (1) 3 *(Mladenovic 1, Broberg 53, Haugen 90)*

Ballymena (0) 0 2969

Odd: (433) Myhra; Ruud, Semb Berge, Bergan, Nilsen;
Samuelsen (Nordkvelle 62), Jensen, Broberg; Diouf
(Zehninki 46), Occean, Mladenovic (Haugen 77).
Ballymena: (442) Glendinning; Kane (Faulkner 79),
Ervin, Owens (Friars 58), Flynn; Gault, McCloskey,
Millar, Braniff; McKinney, Friel (McMurray 72).

Rangers (1) 1 *(Miller 37)*

Progres Niederkorn (0) 0 48,861

Rangers: (442) Foderingham; Tavernier, Bates, Fabio
Cardoso, Wallace; Kranjcar (Rossiter 68), Holt
(Candeias 58), Jack, Dalcio; Miller, Waghorn (Morelos
76).
Progres Niederkorn: (442) Flauss; Matias Marques,
Ferino, Karayer, Schneider (Fiorani 90); Lafon, Thill S,
Watzka, Thill O (Vogel 81); Francoise, Karapetyan
(Sully 85).

St Johnstone (1) 1 *(Shaughnessy 32)*

Trakai (2) 2 *(Maksimov 13, Silenas 36)* 5636

St Johnstone: (4312) Clark; Foster, Shaughnessy,
Gilchrist, Easton; Wotherspoon (Scougall 62), Paton
(Millar 62), Alston; Craig (Kane 83); Cummins,
MacLean.
Trakai: (532) Plukas; Borovskis, Klimavicius,
Janusevskis, Silenas■, Wakili (Cyzas 81); Bychanok,
Shyshka, Vorobjovas; Dorley (Kruk 90), Maksimov
(Cesnauskis 90).

Stjarnan (0) 0
Shamrock R (1) 1 *(Shaw 38)* 1020
Stjarnan: (451) Bjornsson; Gudjonsson, Laxdal J (Aegisson 87), Laxdal D, Josefsson; Hauksson, Halldorsson, Hedinsson, Sigurdsson, Baldvinsson; Fridjonsson (Finsen 82).
Shamrock R: (4231) Chencinski; Lopes, Webster, Madden, Byrne; Clarke, Connolly (Bone 74); Finn, Miele, Shaw (O'Connor 87); Burke (McAlister 82).

FIRST QUALIFYING ROUND SECOND LEG

Balzan v Videoton	3-3
Progres Niederkorn v Rangers	2-0
AEL Limassol v St Joseph's	6-0
AIK Solna v KI Klaksvik	5-0
Atlantas v Kairat	1-2
B36 Torshavn v Nomme Kalju	1-2
Ballymena v Odd	0-2
Bangor C v Lyngby	0-3
Botev Plovdiv v Partizani	1-0
Coleraine v Haugesund	0-0
Cork C v Levadia Tallinn	4-2
Dacia v Skendija Tetovo	0-4
Derry C v Midtjylland	1-4
Differdange 03 v Zira	1-2
Dunav Ruse v Irtysh	0-2
FK Liepaja v Crusaders	2-0
(FK Liepaja won on away goals.)	
Flora Tallinn v Domzale	2-3
Floriana v Crvena Zvezda	3-3
Folgore Falciano v Valletta	0-1
Gandzasar Kapan v Mladost Podgorica	0-3
Gorica v Shirak	2-2
HJK Helsinki v Connah's Quay Nomads	3-0
Inter Baku v Mladost Lucani	2-0
Jagiellonia Bialystock v Dinamo Batumi	4-0
Jelgava v Ferencvaros	0-1
KF Tirana v Maccabi Tel Aviv	0-3
Lincoln v AEK Larnaca	1-1
Milsami v Fola Esch	1-1
NSI Runavik v Dinamo Minsk	0-2
Olimpija Ljubljana v Vaasa	0-1
Ordabasy v Siroki Brijeg	0-0
Osijek v UE Santa Coloma	4-0
Pelister v Lech Poznan	0-3
Pristina v IFK Norrkoping	0-1
Rabotnicki Kometal v Tre Penne	6-0
Rheindorf Altach v Chikhura Sachkhere	1-1
Ruzomberok v Vojvodina	2-0
Sant Julia v Skenderbeu	0-5
Sarajevo v Zaria Balti	2-1
(aet. Zaria Balti won 6-5 on penalties.)	
Seinajoki v KR Reykjavik	0-2
Shamrock R v Stjarnan	1-0
Slovan Bratislava v Pyunik	5-0
Suduva Marijampole v Shakhtyor Soligorsk	2-1
Sutjeska v Levski Sofia	0-0
Torpedo Kutaisi v Trencin	0-3
Trakai v St Johnstone	1-0
Vaduz v Bala Town	3-0
Valur Reykjavik v Ventspils	1-0
Vasas v Beitar Jerusalem	0-3
Zeta v Zeljeznicar Sarajevo	2-2

FIRST QUALIFYING ROUND SECOND LEG
Tuesday, 4 July 2017

Progres Niederkorn (0) 2 *(Francoise 66, Thill S 75)*
Rangers (0) 0 5534
Progres Niederkorn: (4321) Flauss (Schinker 32); Matias Marques, Ferino, Karayer, Lafon; Francoise, Thill S, Watzka; Thill O (Vogel 78), Schneider; Karapetyan (Fiorani 84).
Rangers: (4231) Foderingham; Tavernier, Bates, Fabio Cardoso, Wallace; Rossiter (Herrera 77), Jack; Candeias (Windass 59), Kranjcar, Miller; Morelos (Dalcio 46).

Thursday, 6 July 2017

Ballymena (0) 0
Odd (0) 2 *(Millar 79 (og), Haugen 88)* 1792
Ballymena: (442) Glendinning (Allen 89); Kane, Burns, Friars, Flynn; Gault, Millar, McCloskey (Lowry 85), Friel (McMurray 72); Braniff, McKinney.
Odd: (433) Rossbach; Ruud, Kitolano, Semb Berge, Hagen; Broberg (Haugen 77), Jensen, Nordkvelle; Samuelsen, Occean (Agdestein 81), Diouf (Riski 62).

Bangor C (0) 0
Lyngby (3) 3 *(Larsen 3, 44, Kjaer 37)* 1089
Bangor C: (433) Roberts C; Miley, Connolly (Wall 25), Kennedy, Wilson; Gossett, Hewitt, Allen; Rittenberg (Henry 73), Taylor-Fletcher, Shaw (Edwards 73).
Lyngby: (4411) Andersen; Brandrup, Christensen, Sorensen, Lumb (Hojer 46); Fosgaard, Ornskov (Hebo 43), Christjansen, Larsen (Boysen 46); Rygaard; Kjaer.

Coleraine (0) 0
Haugesund (0) 0 944
Coleraine: (442) Johns; Mullan, Douglas, O'Donnell, Traynor (Kirk 83); Carson, Harkin, Lyons, McCauley; McGonigle (Parkhill 80), Bradley (McLaughlin 80).
Haugesund: (442) Sandvik; Bjorkkjaer, Skjerve, Andreassen, Stolas (Bruno Leite 76); Buduson (Ibrahim 76), Kiss (Tronstad 76), Ideki, Abdi; Huseklepp, Gytkjaer.

Cork C (1) 4 *(Dooley 28, Maguire 46, 86, 90)*
Levadia Tallinn (2) 2 *(Kobzar 15, Andreev 33)* 6314
Cork C: (433) McNulty; Keohane, McCormack, Delaney, O'Connor; Bolger, Buckley, Morrissey; Sheppard (Beattie 69), Maguire, Dooley (Griffin 78).
Levadia Tallinn: (4231) Lepmets; Dudarev, Podholjuzin, Artjunin, Gando; Krznaric, Roosnupp; Hunt, Morelli, Kobzar (Marin 60); Andreev (Teever 87).

Derry C (1) 1 *(McEneff 41)*
Midtjylland (2) 4 *(Onuachu 7, 38, 69, Wikheim 59)* 467
Derry C: (433) Doherty G; Monaghan, Whiteside (Todd 72), Jarvis, Doherty B; McEneff, Low (Patterson 63), Holden (Timlin 76); Schubert, Boyle, Curtis.
Midtjylland: (433) Hansen J; Romer (Nissen 70), Korcsmar, Riis (Hansen K 46), Dal Hende; Drachmann, Sparv, Poulsen; Hassan, Onuachu, Kroon (Wikheim 58).

FK Liepaja (1) 2 *(Eristavi 33 (pen), Karasauks 90)*
Crusaders (0) 0 2310
FK Liepaja: (352) Ralkevics; Gueye, Strumia, Hmizs (Afanasjevs 60); Lebamba, Kurtiss (Kigurs 67), Karasausks, Torres, Keita; Eristavi, Tomic (Grebis 70).
Crusaders: (4321) Jensen; Burns, Beverland, Coates, Ward; Brown, Caddell (Forsyth 59), Snoddy; Carvill (Whyte 46), Owens; Heatley.
FK Liepaja won on away goals.

HJK Helsinki (2) 3 *(Yaghoubi 11, Pelvas 32, 55)*
Connah's Quay Nomads (0) 0 6103
HJK Helsinki: (433) Dahne; Rafinha, Halme, Patronen, Pirinen; Annan, Dahlstrom (Onovo 81), Yaghoubi; Pelvas (Lingman 90), Jallow (Mensah 86), Savage.
Connah's Quay Nomads: (451) Danby; Edwards, Horan, Pearson, Smith; Poole (Wignall 60), Morris (Williams 83), Harrison, Owen J (Phillips 71), Woolfe; Wilde.

Shamrock R (1) 1 *(Burke 20)*
Stjarnan (0) 0 3352
Shamrock R: (4321) Chencinski; Madden, Lopes, Byrne, Webster; Finn, Connolly (Bolger 87), Miele; Clarke, Burke (McAlister 78); Shaw (O'Connor 69).
Stjarnan: (4231) Bjornsson; Laxdal J, Gudjonsson, Laxdal D, Josefsson; Hauksson (Finsen 49), Hedinsson; Fridjonsson (Hilmarsson 90), Sigurdsson (Aegisson 78), Halldorsson; Baldvinsson.

Trakai (0) 1 *(Maksimov 88)*
St Johnstone (0) 0 2000
Trakai: (433) Plukas; Borovskis (Cyzas 81), Janusevskis, Klimavicius•, Wakili; Bychanok, Shyshka, Vorobjovas; Cesnauskis (Kruk 60), Maksimov (Traore 90), Dorley.
St Johnstone: (442) Clark; Foster, Shaughnessy, Gilchrist, Tanser; Alston (Cummins 76), Millar (MacLean 63), Davidson, Craig; Scougall (Wotherspoon 74), Kane.

Vaduz (3) 3 *(Turkes 23, 39, Mathys 43)*
Bala Town (0) 0 621
Vaduz: (4132) Jehle; von Niederhausern, Puljic, Konrad, Borgmann; Muntwiler (Goppel 67); Ciccone, Mathys, Kamber; Brunner (Felfel 60), Turkes (Burgmeier 46).
Bala Town: (433) Morris; Thompson, Stuart W. Jones, Stuart J. Jones (Bell 43), Stephens; Burke, Venables, Owens; Smith, Davies (Wade 60), Sheridan (Hayes 76).

SECOND QUALIFYING ROUND FIRST LEG

Aberdeen v Siroki Brijeg	1-1
Apollon Limassol v Zaria Balti	3-0
Astra Giurgiu v Zira	3-1
Beitar Jerusalem v Botev Plovdiv	1-1
Brondby v Vaasa	2-0
Cork C v AEK Larnaca	0-1
Ferencvaros v Midtjylland	2-4
FK Liepaja v Suduva Marijampole	0-2
Gabala v Jagiellonia Bialystock	1-1
Hajduk Split v Levski Sofia	1-0
Haugesund v Lech Poznan	3-2
IFK Norrkoping v Trakai	2-1
Irtysh v Crvena Zvezda	1-1
Kairat v Skenderbeu	1-1
Kesla v Fola Esch	1-0
Maccabi Tel Aviv v KR Reykjavik	3-1
Nomme Kalju v Videoton	0-3
Osijek v Lucerne	2-0
Ostersunds FK v Galatasaray	2-0
Panionios v Gorica	2-0
Progres Niederkorn v AEL Limassol	0-1
Rabotnicki Kometal v Dinamo Minsk	1-1
Rheindorf Altach v Dinamo Brest	1-1
Ruzomberok v Brann	0-1
Shamrock R v Mlada Boleslav	2-3
Skendija Tetovo v HJK Helsinki	3-1
Slovan Bratislava v Lyngby	0-1
Sturm Graz v Mladost Podgorica	0-1
Trencin v Bnei Yehuda	1-1
Vaduz v Odd	0-1
Valletta v Utrecht	0-0
Valur Reykjavik v Domzale	1-2
Zeljeznicar Sarajevo v AIK Solna	0-0

SECOND QUALIFYING ROUND FIRST LEG

Thursday, 13 July 2017

Aberdeen (1) 1 *(Christie 17)*

Siroki Brijeg (0) 1 *(Markovic 69)*   17,067

Aberdeen: (442) Lewis; Logan, O'Connor, Reynolds, Considine; Shinnie, McLean (Stewart 73), Tansey, Mackay-Steven (Maynard 63); Rooney (Storey 89), Christie.
Siroki Brijeg: (433) Bilobrk; Coric D, Bralic, Barisic, Markovic; Begonja, Matic, Loncar (Coric J 74 (Corluka 83)); Menalo (Kozul 90), Krstanovic, Cabraja.

Cork C (0) 0

AEK Larnaca (0) 1 *(Truyols 70)*   6441

Cork C: (442) McNulty; O'Connor, Delaney, Dooley (Sadlier 62), Bolger (Campion 75); McCormack, Morrissey, Beattie, Buckley; Sheppard (Griffin 79), Maguire.
AEK Larnaca: (442) Colinas Ferreras; Antoniades, Catala, Mojsov, Truyols; Laban, Trickovski (Boljevic 85), Jorge (Roushias 90), Tomas (Tete 76); Hevel, Taulemesse.

Shamrock R (0) 2 *(Burke 48, 90)*

Mlada Boleslav (1) 3 *(Mebrahtu 35, 63, Chramostra 88)*   3160

Shamrock R: (442) Chencinski; Madden, Webster, Lopes, Byrne; Finn, Connolly, Miele (McAlister 83), Clarke; Shaw, Burke.
Mlada Boleslav: (442) Divis; Mares (Fabian 73), Fleisman, Cmovs, Pauschek; Stronati, Matejovsky (Magera 90), Rada, Prikryl; Chramostra, Mebrahtu (Janos 90).

SECOND QUALIFYING ROUND SECOND LEG

AEK Larnaca v Cork C	1-0
AEL Limassol v Progres Niederkorn	2-1
AIK Solna v Zeljeznicar Sarajevo	2-0
Bnei Yehuda v Trencin	2-0
Botev Plovdiv v Beitar Jerusalem	4-0
Brann v Ruzomberok	0-2
Crvena Zvezda v Irtysh	2-0
Dinamo Brest v Rheindorf Altach	0-3
Dinamo Minsk v Rabotnicki Kometal	3-0
Domzale v Valur Reykjavik	3-2
Fola Esch v Kesla	4-1
Galatasaray v Ostersunds	1-1

Gorica v Panionios	2-3
HJK Helsinki v Skendija Tetovo	1-1
Jagiellonia Bialystock v Gabala	0-2
KR Reykjavik v Maccabi Tel Aviv	0-2
Lech Poznan v Haugesund	2-0
Levski Sofia v Hajduk Split	1-2
Lucerne v Osijek	2-1
Lyngby v Slovan Bratislava	2-1
Midtjylland v Ferencvaros	3-1
Mlada Boleslav v Shamrock R	2-0
Mladost Podgorica v Sturm Graz	0-3
Odd v Vaduz	1-0
Siroki Brijeg v Aberdeen	0-2
Skenderbeu v Kairat	2-0
Suduva Marijampole v FK Liepaja	0-1
(FK Suduva won on away goals.)	
Trakai v IFK Norrkoping	2-1
(aet; Trakai won 5-3 on penalties.)	
Utrecht v Valletta	3-1
Vaasa v Brondby	2-1
Videoton v Nomme Kalju	1-1
Zaria Balti v Apollon Limassol	1-2
Zira v Astra Giurgiu	0-0

SECOND QUALIFYING ROUND SECOND LEG

Thursday, 20 July 2017

AEK Larnaca (1) 1 *(Taulemesse 34)*

Cork C (0) 0   3771

AEK Larnaca: (4231) Colinas Ferreras; Antoniades, Truyols, Mojsov, Catala; Jorge, Tomas (Tete 72); Trickovski (Boljevic 88), Hevel, Laban; Taulemesse (Mitidis 80).
Cork C: (442) McNulty; Delaney, Bolger, Keohane (Sheppard 67), McCormack; Beattie, Dooley (Sadlier 61), O'Connor, Morrissey; Maguire, Buckley (Campion 61).

Mlada Boleslav (2) 2 *(Chramostra 9, Mebrahtu 31)*

Shamrock R (0) 0   4727

Mlada Boleslav: (442) Divis; Fleisman, Silva, Matejovsky (Magera 83), Prikryl; Mares (Janos 77), Chramostra (Fabian 64), Pauschek, Cmovs; Rada, Mebrahtu.
Shamrock R: (4411) Chencinski; Byrne (Bone 67), Webster, Lopes, Finn; Miele, Shaw, McAlister (Connolly 75), Madden; Clarke; Burke.

Siroki Brijeg (0) 0

Aberdeen (0) 2 *(Stewart 71, Mackay-Steven 77)*   4800

Siroki Brijeg: (433) Bilobrk; Coric D, Matic, Barisic, Markovic (Grubisic 78); Coric J (Loncar 51), Begonja, Bralic; Cabraja (Corluka 67), Krstanovic, Menalo.
Aberdeen: (433) Lewis; Logan, O'Connor, Reynolds, Considine; Christie, Shinnie, McLean; Stewart (Tansey 74), Stockley (Maynard 67), Mackay-Steven (Rooney 79).

THIRD QUALIFYING ROUND FIRST LEG

AA Gent v Rheindorf Altach	1-1
Aberdeen v Apollon Limassol	2-1
AEK Larnaca v Dinamo Minsk	2-0
AIK Solna v Braga	1-1
Arka Gdynia v Midtjylland	3-2
Astra Giurgiu v Oleksandriya	0-0
Austria Vienna v AEL Limassol	0-0
Bnei Yehuda v Zenit St Petersburg	0-2
Bordeaux v Videoton	2-1
Botev Plovdiv v Maritimo	0-0
Brondby v Hajduk Split	0-0
Crvena Zvezda v Sparta Prague	2-0
CSU Craiova v AC Milan	0-1
Dinamo Bucharest v Athletic Bilbao	1-1
Dinamo Zagreb v Odds	2-1
Everton v Ruzomberok	1-0
Krasnodar v Lyngby	2-1
Maccabi Tel Aviv v Panionios	1-0
Marseille v Oostende	4-2
Mlada Boleslav v Skenderbeu	2-1
Olimpik v PAOK Salonika	1-1
Ostersunds v Fola Esch	1-0
Panathinaikos v Gabala	1-0
PSV Eindhoven v Osijek	0-1
SC Freiburg v Domzale	1-0

Sturm Graz v Fenerbahce	1-2
Suduva Marijampole v Sion	3-0
Trakai v Skendija Tetovo	2-1
Utrecht v Lech Poznan	0-0

THIRD QUALIFYING ROUND FIRST LEG

Thursday, 27 July 2017

Aberdeen (1) 2 *(Christie 4, Shinnie 78)*

Apollon Limassol (0) 1 *(Jander 59)*   20,085

Aberdeen: (433) Lewis; Logan, O'Connor, Reynolds (Wright 75), Considine; McLean, Shinnie, Stewart; Christie, Maynard (Stockley 60), Mackay-Steven (Arnason 61).
Apollon Limassol: (4231) Bruno Vale; Sardinero (Vasiliou 82), Yuste, Roberge, Jander; Sachetti*, Alex (Jakolis 46); Pedro Silva, Kyriakou, Maglica; Schembri (Alef 69).

Everton (0) 1 *(Baines 65)*

Ruzomberok (0) 0   32,124

Everton: (433) Stekelenburg; Martina, Keane, Williams, Baines; Klaassen (Davies 85), Gueye, Schneiderlin; Calvert-Lewin (Sandro 62), Rooney, Mirallas (Lookman 81).
Ruzomberok: (433) Macik; Maslo P, Maslo J, Kruzliak, Kupec; Takac (Kostadinov 72), Qose, Kochan; Daniel, Haskic (Lacny 83), Gal-Andrezly (Gerec 88).

THIRD QUALIFYING ROUND SECOND LEG

AEL Limassol v Austria Vienna	1-2
Sion v Suduva Marijampole	1-1
AC Milan v CSU Craiova	2-0
Apollon Limassol v Aberdeen	2-0
Athletic Bilbao v Dinamo Bucharest	3-0
Braga v AIK Solna	2-1
(aet.)	
Dinamo Minsk v AEK Larnaca	1-1
Domzale v SC Freiburg	2-0
Fenerbahce v Sturm Graz	1-1
Fola Esch v Ostersunds	1-2
Gabala v Panathinaikos	1-2
Hajduk Split v Brondby	2-0
Lech Poznan v Utrecht	2-2
(Utrecht won on away goals.)	
Lyngby v Krasnodar	1-3
Maritimo v Botev Plovdiv	2-0
Midtjylland v Arka Gdynia	2-1
(Midtjylland won on away goals.)	
Odds v Dinamo Zagreb	0-0
Oleksandriya v Astra Giurgiu	1-0
Oostende v Marseille	0-0
Osijek v PSV Eindhoven	1-0
Panionios v Maccabi Tel Aviv	0-1
PAOK Salonika v Olimpik	2-0
Rheindorf Altach v AA Gent	3-1
Ruzomberok v Everton	0-1
Skenderbeu v Mlada Boleslav	2-1
(Skenderbeu won 4-2 on penalties.)	
Skendija Tetovo v Trakai	3-0
Sparta Prague v Crvena Zvezda	0-1
Videoton v Bordeaux	1-0
(Videoton won on away goals.)	
Zenit St Petersburg v Bnei Yehuda	0-1

THIRD QUALIFYING ROUND SECOND LEG

Thursday, 3 August 2017

Apollon Limassol (1) 2 *(Schembri 17, Zelaya 88)*

Aberdeen (0) 0   6250

Apollon Limassol: (4231) Bruno Vale; Joao Pedro, Yuste, Roberge, Jander; Alex (Zelaya 85), Kyriakou; Alef, Jakolis (Stylianou 73), Schembri (Sardinero 65); Maglica.
Aberdeen: (433) Lewis; Logan, Reynolds (Wright 78), O'Connor, Considine; Christie, Shinnie, McLean; Stewart (Tansey 64), Stockley (Maynard 54), Mackay-Steven.

Ruzomberok (0) 0

Everton (0) 1 *(Calvert-Lewin 80)*   4752

Ruzomberok: (433) Macik; Kruzliak, Maslo J, Maslo P, Menich (Lacny 46); Qose, Gal-Andrezly, Takac (Sapara 71); Kochan, Haskic (Gerec 80), Daniel.

Everton: (3412) Pickford; Schneiderlin (Barry 81), Baines, Keane; Williams, Jagielka, Gueye, Klaassen; Davies; Sandro (Calvert-Lewin 69), Rooney (Mirallas 85).

PLAY-OFF ROUND FIRST LEG

AC Milan v Skendija Tetovo	6-0
Ajax v Rosenborg	0-1
Apollon Limassol v Midtjylland	3-2
BATE Borisov v Oleksandriya	1-1
Club Brugge v AEK Athens	0-0
Dinamo Zagreb v Skenderbeu	1-1
Domzale v Marseille	1-1
Everton v Hajduk Split	2-0
Hafnarfjordur v Braga	1-2
Krasnodar v Crvena Zvezda	3-2
Legia Warsaw v Sheriff	1-1
Ludogorets Razgrad v FK Suduva	2-0
Maritimo v Dynamo Kyiv	0-0
Osijek v Austria Vienna	1-2
Panathinaikos v Athletic Bilbao	2-3
PAOK Salonika v Ostersund	3-1
Partizan Belgrade v Videoton	0-0
Rheindorf Altach v Maccabi Tel Aviv	0-1
Utrecht v Zenit St Petersburg	1-0
Vardar v Fenerbahce	2-0
Viitorul v Red Bull Salzburg	1-3
Viktoria Plzen v AEK Larnaca	3-1

PLAY-OFF ROUND FIRST LEG

Thursday, 17 August 2017

Everton (2) 2 *(Keane 30, Gueye 45)*

Hajduk Split (0) 0   34,977

Everton: (451) Pickford; Martina, Keane, Williams, Baines; Lookman, Klaassen (Calvert-Lewin 62), Gueye, Schneiderlin (Davies 46), Mirallas (Besic 76); Rooney.
Hajduk Split: (433) Stipica; Juranovic, Nizic, Rosa, Memolla; Gentzoglou (Basic 85), Radosevic, Kozulj (Erceg 66); Vlasic, Ohandza (Said 66), Barry.

PLAY-OFF ROUND SECOND LEG

AEK Athens v Club Brugge	3-0
AEK Larnaca v Viktoria Plzen	0-0
Athletic Bilbao v Panathinaikos	1-0
Austria Vienna v Osijek	0-1
(Austria Vienna won on away goals.)	
Braga v Hafnarfjordur	3-2
Crvena Zvezda v Krasnodar	2-1
(Crvena Zvezda won on away goals.)	
Dynamo Kyiv v Maritimo	3-1
Fenerbahce v Vardar	1-2
FK Suduva v Ludogorets Razgrad	0-0
Hajduk Split v Everton	1-1
Maccabi Tel Aviv v Rheindorf Altach	2-2
Marseille v Domzale	3-0
Midtjylland v Apollon Limassol	1-1
Oleksandriya v BATE Borisov	1-2
Ostersund v PAOK Salonika	2-0
(Ostersund won on away goals.)	
Red Bull Salzburg v Viitorul	4-0
Rosenborg v Ajax	3-2
Sheriff v Legia Warsaw	0-0
(Sherrif won on away goals.)	
Skenderbeu v Dinamo Zagreb	0-0
(Skenderbeu won on away goals.)	
Skendija Tetovo v AC Milan	0-1
Videoton v Partizan Belgrade	0-4
Zenit St Petersburg v Utrecht	2-0
(aet.)	

PLAY-OFF ROUND SECOND LEG

Thursday, 24 August 2017

Hajduk Split (1) 1 *(Radosevic 43)*

Everton (0) 1 *(Sigurdsson 46)*   31,645

Hajduk Split: (433) Stipica; Juranovic, Nizic, Lopez, Memolla; Gentzoglou, Radosevic, Barry (Kovacevic 85); Vlasic (Kozulj 85), Said (Tudor 74), Erceg.
Everton: (442) Pickford; Williams, Keane, Martina, Baines; Schneiderlin, Besic, Lookman (Lennon 46), Rooney; Sigurdsson, Calvert-Lewin (Davies 72).

GROUP STAGE

GROUP A

Thursday, 14 September 2017
Slavia Prague (1) 1 *(Necid 12)*
Maccabi Tel Aviv (0) 0   13,035
Slavia Prague: (4231) Kovar; Frydrych, Jugas, Deli, Sobol; Soucek, Hromada (Ngadeu Ngadjui 80); Sykora (Husbauer 63), Stoch, Zmrhal (van Buren 66); Necid.
Maccabi Tel Aviv: (433) Rajkovic; Yeini, Ben Haim I, Babin (Rikan 72), Davidadze; Susic, Filipenko (Blackman 66), Battocchio; Atar, Kjartansson, Micha (Atzily 80).

Villarreal (1) 3 *(Sansone 16, Bakambu 75, Cheryshev 77)*
Astana (0) 1 *(Logvinenko 68)*   14,670
Villarreal: (442) Barbosa; Mario, Bonera, Semedo, Jaume; Castillejo (Suarez 87), Rodri, Trigueros, Fornals (Cheryshev 74); Unal, Sansone (Bakambu 69).
Astana: (4411) Eric; Postnikov, Logvinenko, Anicic, Shomko; Beysebekov (Tagybergen 87), Maevskiy, Grahovac, Muzhikov (Shitov 83); Twumasi; Murtazayev (Tomasov 67).

Thursday, 28 September 2017
Astana (1) 1 *(Tomasov 43)*
Slavia Prague (1) 1 *(Ngadeu Ngadjui 18)* 17,215
Astana: (541) Eric; Beysebekov, Shitov, Postnikov, Logvinenko, Shomko; Tomasov (Murtazayev 81), Maevskiy, Muzhikov (Tagybergen 87), Twumasi; Kabananga.
Slavia Prague: (4231) Kovar; Boril, Jugas, Deli, Sobol; Ngadeu Ngadjui, Rotan; Sykora (van Buren 87), Stoch, Zmrhal (Hromada 62); Necid (Skoda 72).

Maccabi Tel Aviv (0) 0
Villarreal (0) 0   11,865
Maccabi Tel Aviv: (442) Rajkovic; Spungin, Babin, Ben Haim I, Davidadze; Susic (Peretz 63), Battocchio, Yeini, Blackman; Kjartansson (Itzhaki 87), Atar (Atzily 66).
Villarreal: (442) Barbosa; Mario, Bonera, Victor Ruiz, Jaume; Fornals, Trigueros (Rodri 82), Guerra, Soriano (Castillejo 69); Bakambu, Bacca (Unal 76).

Thursday, 19 October 2017
Astana (2) 4 *(Twumasi 34 (pen), 42, Kabananga 47, 52)*
Maccabi Tel Aviv (0) 0   10,350
Astana: (4411) Eric; Shitov, Logvinenko, Anicic, Shomko; Murtazayev (Tomasov 75), Beysebekov (Tagybergen 85), Maevskiy, Twumasi; Muzhikov (Grahovac 68); Kabananga.
Maccabi Tel Aviv: (433) Rajkovic; Spungin, Ben Haim I, Babin, Davidadze; Peretz (Rikan 46), Battocchio, Yeini; Susic (Atar 46), Kjartansson (Tibi 75), Blackman.

Villarreal (2) 2 *(Trigueros 41, Bacca 44)*
Slavia Prague (2) 2 *(Necid 18, Danny 30)* 15,634
Villarreal: (4312) Barbosa; Rukavina, Bonera, Victor Ruiz, Jaume; Guerra, Trigueros, Fornals (Castillejo 77); Soriano (Cheryshev 46); Bacca, Unal (Bakambu 60).
Slavia Prague: (4231) Lastuvka; Frydrych, Deli (Boril 46), Jugas, Sobol; Soucek, Hromada; Sykora (Stoch 83), Danny, Zmrhal (van Buren 69); Necid.

Thursday, 2 November 2017
Maccabi Tel Aviv (0) 0
Astana (0) 1 *(Twumasi 57)*   7934
Maccabi Tel Aviv: (442) Rajkovic; Yeini, Babin, Tibi, Davidadze (Micha 65); Dasa O, Battocchio, Rikan, Blackman (Atzily 78); Kjartansson, Atar (Schoenfeld 65).
Astana: (4141) Eric; Shitov (Anicic 88), Maliy, Postnikov, Shomko; Maevskiy; Twumasi, Beysebekov, Tagybergen (Muzhikov 72), Tomasov (Murtazayev 74); Kabananga.

Slavia Prague (0) 0
Villarreal (1) 2 *(Bacca 17, Deli 89 (og))* 18,403
Slavia Prague: (433) Lastuvka; Boril, Jugas, Deli, Sobol; Hromada (Ngadeu Ngadjui 46), Danny (van Buren 46), Soucek; Sykora (Skoda 81), Necid, Stoch.
Villarreal: (433) Barbosa; Mario, Alvaro, Victor Ruiz, Marin; Soriano (Sansone 84), Rodri, Trigueros; Bakambu, Fornals (Cheryshev 67), Bacca (Chuca 74).

Thursday, 23 November 2017
Astana (1) 2 *(Kabananga 23, Twumasi 88)*
Villarreal (1) 3 *(Raba 40, Bakambu 65, 83)* 29,800
Astana: (4141) Eric; Shitov, Postnikov, Anicic, Shomko; Logvinenko (Despotovic 83); Twumasi, Beysebekov (Grahovac 69), Maevskiy, Muzhikov (Tomasov 72); Kabananga.
Villarreal: (41212) Barbosa; Rukavina, Bonera, Victor Ruiz, Marin; Rodri; Raba (Guerra 78), Trigueros; Fornals (Bakambu 60); Sansone, Bacca (Soriano 68).

Maccabi Tel Aviv (0) 0
Slavia Prague (1) 2 *(Husbauer 45, 54)*   6874
Maccabi Tel Aviv: (442) Rajkovic; Yeini, Tibi, Ben Haim I, Davidadze; Battocchio (Susic 75), Peretz, Rikan (Golasa 60), Micha; Schoenfeld (Atar 60), Kjartansson.
Slavia Prague: (4231) Lastuvka; Frydrych, Deli, Jugas, Sobol; Ngadeu Ngadjui, Soucek; Stoch (van Buren 79), Husbauer (Danny 88), Zmrhal; Necid (Skoda 69).

Thursday, 7 December 2017
Slavia Prague (0) 0
Astana (1) 1 *(Anicic 39)*   14,198
Slavia Prague: (4231) Lastuvka; Frydrych, Ngadeu Ngadjui, Jugas, Sobol; Soucek, Rotan (van Buren 69); Stoch, Danny, Zmrhal (Sykora 77); Skoda (Necid 17).
Astana: (4411) Eric; Shitov, Logvinenko, Anicic, Shomko; Twumasi (Despotovic 90), Maevskiy, Grahovac, Tomasov (Murtazayev 68); Muzhikov (Maliy 84); Kabananga.

Villarreal (0) 0
Maccabi Tel Aviv (0) 1 *(Blackman 60)*   12,613
Villarreal: (4312) Barbosa; Rukavina, Montolio, Torres, Marin; Guerra (Raba 82), Soriano (Martinez 63), Chuca; Morlanes (Lozano 77); Gonzalez, Poveda.
Maccabi Tel Aviv: (433) Rajkovic; Spungin, Babin, Tibi, Davidadze; Peretz, Golasa, Rikan (Battocchio 83); Micha (Dasa E 73), Blackman (Atar 89), Schoenfeld.

Group A Table	P	W	D	L	F	A	GD	Pts
Villarreal	6	3	2	1	10	6	4	11
Astana	6	3	1	2	10	7	3	10
Slavia Prague	6	2	2	2	6	6	0	8
Maccabi Tel Aviv	6	1	1	4	1	8	-7	4

GROUP B

Thursday, 14 September 2017
Dynamo Kyiv (0) 3 *(Sydorchuk 47, Junior Moraes 50, Mbokani 65 (pen))*
Skenderbeu (1) 1 *(Muzaka 39)*   24,893
Dynamo Kyiv: (4231) Koval; Vida, Khacheridi, Kadar, Pivaric; Sydorchuk, Buyalsky; Tsygankov (Morozyuk 70), Harmash (Junior Moraes 46), Gonzalez (Husyev 82); Mbokani.
Skenderbeu: (4141) Shehi; Vangjeli, Radas, Jashanica (Aliti 68), Mici; Osmani (Gavazaj 60); Muzaka, Dita, Lilaj, Adeniyi (Sahiti 76); Sowe.

Young Boys (1) 1 *(Fassnacht 14)*
Partizan Belgrade (1) 1 *(Jankovic 13)*   13,004
Young Boys: (442) von Ballmoos; Mbabu, von Bergen, Nuhu, Lotomba; Fassnacht, Sanogo, Sow, Sulejmani (Schick 85); Nsame, Assale (Ngamaleu 68).
Partizan Belgrade: (442) Stojkovic; Vulicevic, Ostojic, Nemanja R. Miletic, Nemanja G. Miletic; Tosic (Pantic 88), Everton Bilher, Jevtovic, Jankovic; Ozegovic (Solomon 65), Tawamba.

Thursday, 28 September 2017
Partizan Belgrade (2) 2 *(Ozegovic 34, Tawamba 42)*
Dynamo Kyiv (0) 3 *(Junior Moraes 54 (pen), 84, Buyalsky 67)*   Behind closed doors
Partizan Belgrade: (442) Stojkovic; Vulicevic, Ostojic, Nemanja R. Miletic, Nemanja G. Miletic; Jankovic, Radin, Everton Bilher, Soumah (Pantic 75); Ozegovic (Jovanovic 78), Tawamba.
Dynamo Kyiv: (4231) Koval; Kedziora, Vida, Kadar, Pivaric; Sydorchuk, Buyalsky; Tsygankov (Junior Moraes 46), Harmash, Gonzalez (Morozyuk 90); Kravets (Besyedin 46).

Skenderbeu (0) 1 *(Sowe 65)*

Young Boys (0) 1 *(Assale 72)* 3300

Skenderbeu: (433) Shehi; Vangjeli, Jashanica, Aliti, Mici; Muzaka (Dita 76), Lilaj, Adeniyi; Gavazaj (Taku 20), Sowe, Sahiti (Nimaga 67).

Young Boys: (442) von Ballmoos; Burki, von Bergen, Wuthrich, Joss (Mbabu 76); Aebischer, Sanogo, Sulejmani (Nsame 70), Schick (Fassnacht 70); Assale, Ngamaleu.

Thursday, 19 October 2017

Dynamo Kyiv (1) 2 *(Mbokani 35, Morozyuk 47)*

Young Boys (2) 2 *(Assale 17, 39)* 21,789

Dynamo Kyiv: (442) Koval; Kedziora, Vida (Pantic 80), Kadar, Pivaric; Morozyuk, Buyalsky, Sydorchuk (Garmash 62), Gonzalez; Junior Moraes, Mbokani (Besyedin 90).

Young Boys: (442) Ballmoos; Mbabu, von Bergen, Nuhu, Lotomba; Fassnacht, Sanogo*, Sow (Aebischer 76), Sulejmani; Ngamaleu (Schick 85), Assale (Nsame 89).

Skenderbeu (0) 0

Partizan Belgrade (0) 0 6300

Skenderbeu: (433) Shehi; Vangjeli, Radas (Aliti 32), Jashanica, Mici; Muzaka (Osmani 90), Lilaj, Dita (Shkodra 80); Taku, Sowe, Adeniyi.

Partizan Belgrade: (442) Stojkovic; Vulicevic, Mitrovic, Nemanja R. Miletic, Nemanja G. Miletic; Jankovic (Ilic 87), Everton Bilher, Jevtovic, Tosic; Soumah, Tawamba (Ozegovic 65).

Thursday, 2 November 2017

Partizan Belgrade (1) 2 *(Tosic 39, Tawamba 66)*

Skenderbeu (0) 0 12,659

Partizan Belgrade: (442) Stojkovic; Vulicevic, Nemanja R. Miletic, Mitrovic, Nemanja G. Miletic; Jankovic, Everton Bilher, Jevtovic, Tosic (Pantic 82); Ozegovic (Radin 73), Tawamba (Jovanovic 87).

Skenderbeu: (442) Shehi; Vangjeli, Radas, Jashanica, Mici (Aliti 66); Muzaka, Lilaj, Taku (Sahiti 89); Gavazaj (Nespor 68), Sowe, Adeniyi.

Young Boys (0) 0

Dynamo Kyiv (0) 1 *(Buyalsky 70)* 10,077

Young Boys: (442) von Ballmoos; Mbabu, Nuhu, von Bergen, Lotomba; Sulejmani, Aebischer, Sow, Fassnacht (Schick 80); Assale, Nsame (Ngamaleu 73).

Dynamo Kyiv: (4141) Bushchan; Kedziora (Kravets 46), Khacheridi, Vida, Pivaric; Korzun; Morozyuk, Garmash, Buyalsky (Shepelev 87), Gonzalez; Junior Moraes.

Thursday, 23 November 2017

Partizan Belgrade (1) 2 *(Tawamba 12, Ozegovic 53)*

Young Boys (1) 1 *(Ngamaleu 25)* 21,000

Partizan Belgrade: (442) Stojkovic; Vulicevic, Nemanja R. Miletic, Mitrovic, Nemanja G. Miletic; Jankovic, Everton Bilher, Jevtovic, Pantic (Ilic 81); Tawamba (Ostojic 88), Ozegovic (Radin 79).

Young Boys: (442) von Ballmoos; Mbabu, Nuhu, Wuthrich (Fassnacht 83), Benito; Ngamaleu, Sow, Aebischer, Sulejmani; Assale, Nsame (Hoarau 66).

Skenderbeu (1) 3 *(Lilaj 18, Adeniyi 53, Sowe 56)*

Dynamo Kyiv (1) 2 *(Tsygankov 16, Rusyn 90)* 100

Skenderbeu: (433) Shehi; Vangjeli, Radas, Aliti, Mici; Muzaka, Osmani (Nimaga 70), Lilaj; Gavazaj (Taku 71), Adeniyi, Sowe (Dita 89).

Dynamo Kyiv: (442) Bushchan; Kedziora (Rusyn 71), Khacheridi, Kadar, Pivaric; Tsygankov, Korzun (Shaparenko 60), Shepelev, Morozyuk; Junior Moraes, Besyedin.

Behind closed doors.

Thursday, 7 December 2017

Dynamo Kyiv (3) 4 *(Morozyuk 6, Junior Moraes 28, 31, 78 (pen))*

Partizan Belgrade (1) 1 *(Jevtovic 45 (pen))* 14,678

Dynamo Kyiv: (4231) Bushchan; Kedziora, Khacheridi, Kadar, Pivaric; Shepelev, Buyalsky (Garmash 66); Morozyuk, Shaparenko (Besyedin 77), Tsygankov (Gonzalez 83); Junior Moraes.

Partizan Belgrade: (442) Stojkovic; Vulicevic, Nemanja R. Miletic, Mitrovic, Nemanja G. Miletic; Pantic, Everton Bilher (Djurickovic 77), Jevtovic, Soumah; Solomon (Ozegovic 66), Tawamba.

Young Boys (0) 2 *(Hoarau 55, Assale 90)*

Skenderbeu (0) 1 *(Gavazaj 51)* 8023

Young Boys: (433) Wolfli; Mbabu, Wuthrich, Burki, Joss; Schick, Aebischer (Bertone 71), Ngamaleu; Nsame, Teixeira, Hoarau (Assale 81).

Skenderbeu: (442) Shehi; Vangjeli, Jashanica, Aliti, Mici; Muzaka, Lilaj, Nimaga, Gavazaj; Beneyam (Taku 75), Sahiti (Osmani 68).

Group B Table	P	W	D	L	F	A	GD	Pts
Dynamo Kyiv	6	4	1	1	15	9	6	13
Partizan Belgrade	6	2	2	2	8	9	–1	8
Young Boys	6	1	3	2	7	8	–1	6
Skenderbeu	6	1	2	3	6	10	–4	5

GROUP C

Thursday, 14 September 2017

Istanbul Basaksehir (0) 0

Ludogorets Razgrad (0) 0 6804

Istanbul Basaksehir: (4231) Babacan; Junior Caicara, Attamah, Epureanu, Clichy; Inler, Emre; Visca, Mossoro (Napoleoni 81), Elia (Frei 73); Adebayor (Erdinc 65).

Ludogorets Razgrad: (433) Broun; Cicinho, Moti, Plastun, Natanael; Goralski (Sasha 77), Abel, Dyakov; Lukoki (Campanharo 86), Joao Paulo (Keseru 59), Wanderson.

TSG Hoffenheim (1) 1 *(Wagner 24)*

Braga (1) 2 *(Teixeira 45, Dyego Sousa 50)* 15,714

TSG Hoffenheim: (352) Baumann; Bicakcic (Hubner 46), Vogt, Nordtveit (Ochs 69); Rupp, Grillitsch (Polanski 56), Kaderabek, Schulz, Demirbay; Wagner, Kramaric.

Braga: (433) Matheus Magalhaes; Marcelo Goiano, Rosic, Raul Silva, Nuno Sequeira; Teixeira (Andre Horta 78), Danilo Barbosa, Vukcevic; Ricardo Esgaio, Paulinho (Hassan 83), Dyego Sousa (Fransergio 60).

Thursday, 28 September 2017

Braga (1) 2 *(Hassan 26, Fransergio 90)*

Istanbul Basaksehir (1) 1 *(Emre 28)* 10,376

Braga: (433) Matheus Magalhaes; Marcelo Goiano, Ricardo Ferreira, Raul Silva, Nuno Sequeira (Xadas 20); Ricardo Esgaio, Vukcevic, Danilo Barbosa (Fransergio 70); Teixeira (Ricardo Horta 78), Hassan, Paulinho.

Istanbul Basaksehir: (4231) Babacan; Junior Caicara, da Costa (Attamah 46), Epureanu, Clichy; Inler, Emre; Visca, Mossoro (Tekdemir 81), Elia; Erdinc (Batdal 74).

Ludogorets Razgrad (0) 2 *(Dyakov 46, Lukoki 72)*

TSG Hoffenheim (1) 1 *(Kaderabek 2)* 6155

Ludogorets Razgrad: (433) Broun; Cicinho, Plastun, Moti, Natanael; Campanharo (Goralski 79), Dyakov, Abel; Marcelinho (Sasha 90), Lukoki, Wanderson (Keseru 87).

TSG Hoffenheim: (352) Baumann; Posch, Nordtveit, Kaderabek (Ochs 56); Zuber (Geiger 55), Rupp, Vogt, Polanski; Schulz; Kramaric, Uth (Passlack 74).

Thursday, 19 October 2017

Braga (0) 0

Ludogorets Razgrad (1) 2 *(Moti 26, Raul Silva 57 (og))* 8613

Braga: (433) Matheus Magalhaes; Marcelo Goiano (Xadas 59), Ricardo Ferreira, Raul Silva, Jefferson; Vukcevic, Fransergio (Andre Horta 73), Teixeira (Fabio Martins 58); Ricardo Esgaio, Paulinho, Hassan.

Ludogorets Razgrad: (4411) Renan; Cicinho, Moti, Plastun, Natanael (Sasha 85); Forster, Abel, Goralski, Wanderson; Marcelinho (Dyakov 73); Lukoki (Keseru 83).

TSG Hoffenheim (0) 3 *(Hubner 52, Amiri 59, Schulz 75)*

Istanbul Basaksehir (0) 1 *(Napoleoni 90)* 20,000

TSG Hoffenheim: (433) Baumann; Kaderabek, Hubner, Posch (Zuber 69), Schulz; Geiger (Polanski 71), Vogt, Demirbay (Ochs 63); Amiri, Wagner, Uth.

Istanbul Basaksehir: (442) Gunok; Junior Caicara, Attamah, Epureanu, Clichy (Erdem 81); Torun, Inler, Kahveci (Tekdemir 63), Frei; Erdinc (Napoleoni 63), Batdal.

Thursday, 2 November 2017

Istanbul Basaksehir (0) 1 *(Visca 90)*
TSG Hoffenheim (0) 1 *(Grillitsch 47)*   4500

Istanbul Basaksehir: (4231) Gunok; Junior Caicara, Erdem, Epureanu, Clichy; Inler, Kahveci (Mossoro 82); Torun (Visca 62), Napoleoni (Elia 82), Frei; Erdinc.
TSG Hoffenheim: (352) Baumann; Hoogma, Nordtveit, Zuber; Grillitsch, Demirbay (Geiger 74), Vogt (Posch 25), Amiri (Ochs 60), Schulz; Kramaric, Wagner.

Ludogorets Razgrad (0) 1 *(Marcelinho 69)*
Braga (0) 1 *(Fransergio 84)*   7544

Ludogorets Razgrad: (4411) Broun; Cicinho, Plastun, Moti, Natanael; Misidjan (Campanharo 89), Abel, Goralski, Wanderson (Terziev 85); Marcelinho (Dyakov 72); Lukoki.
Braga: (433) Matheus Magalhaes; Marcelo Goiano, Ricardo Ferreira, Raul Silva, Jefferson; Ricardo Esgaio, Danilo Barbosa (Hassan 78), Vukcevic; Xadas (Ricardo Horta 57), Paulinho, Dyego Sousa (Fransergio 65).

Thursday, 23 November 2017

Braga (1) 3 *(Marcelo Goiano 1, Fransergio 81, 90)*
TSG Hoffenheim (0) 1 *(Uth 75)*   10,054

Braga: (433) Matheus Magalhaes; Marcelo Goiano, Ricardo Ferreira, Raul Silva, Jefferson; Fransergio, Danilo Barbosa, Vukcevic; Ricardo Esgaio, Paulinho (Dyego Sousa 71), Teixeira (Fabio Martins 77).
TSG Hoffenheim: (352) Baumann; Posch, Vogt, Nordtveit (Gnabry 46); Zuber (Szalai■ 66), Demirbay, Grillitsch, Geiger (Uth 52), Schulz; Amiri, Kramaric.

Ludogorets Razgrad (0) 1 *(Marcelinho 65)*
Istanbul Basaksehir (2) 2 *(Visca 20, Frei 28)*   7520

Ludogorets Razgrad: (4231) Renan; Cicinho, Plastun, Moti, Natanael; Abel, Goralski (Campanharo 83); Wanderson, Marcelinho, Lukoki (Keseru 46); Misidjan.
Istanbul Basaksehir: (4231) Gunok; Junior Caicara, Attamah, Epureanu, Erdem; Inler, Kahveci; Visca (da Costa 90), Napoleoni (Mossoro 67), Frei; Erdinc (Elia 88).

Thursday, 7 December 2017

Istanbul Basaksehir (1) 2 *(Visca 11, Emre 77 (pen))*
Braga (0) 1 *(Raul Silva 55)*   5241

Istanbul Basaksehir: (4231) Gunok; Junior Caicara, Attamah, Epureanu, Clichy; Inler, Kahveci (Emre 60); Visca (Napoleoni 85), Mossoro, Frei; Erdinc (Batdal 60).
Braga: (433) Matheus Magalhaes; Ricardo Esgaio, Bruno Viana, Raul Silva, Jefferson; Andre Horta (Teixeira 73), Danilo Barbosa, Vukcevic; Xadas (Hassan 85), Dyego Sousa, Fabio Martins (Ricardo Horta 73).

TSG Hoffenheim (1) 1 *(Ochs 26)*
Ludogorets Razgrad (0) 1 *(Wanderson 62)*   7814

TSG Hoffenheim: (442) Kobel; Lorenz, Bicakcic, Nordtveit, Rossipal; Passlack, Polanski, Hoogma, Hack (Otto 76); Zulj (Buhler 69), Ochs (Skenderovic 55).
Ludogorets Razgrad: (3421) Renan; Natanael, Plastun, Moti; Cicinho, Dyakov, Abel, Goralski (Keseru■ 46); Marcelinho (Sasha 88), Wanderson (Terziev 86); Misidjan.

Group C Table	P	W	D	L	F	A	GD	Pts
Braga	6	3	1	2	9	8	1	10
Ludogorets Razgrad	6	2	3	1	7	5	2	9
Istanbul Basaksehir	6	2	2	2	7	8	–1	8
TSG Hoffenheim	6	1	2	3	8	10	–2	5

GROUP D

Thursday, 14 September 2017

Austria Vienna (0) 1 *(Borkovic 48)*
AC Milan (3) 5 *(Calhanoglu 7, Andre Silva 10, 20, 56, Suso 63)*   31,409

Austria Vienna: (433) Hadzikic; Klein, Mohammed, Westermann (Borkovic 42 (Gluhakovic 86)), Martschinko; Holzhauser, Serbest, Prokop; Pires, Monschein, Lee (De Paula 74).

AC Milan: (352) Donnarumma G; Zapata, Bonucci, Romagnoli (Musacchio 74); Abate, Kessie (Bonaventura 62), Biglia, Calhanoglu, Antonelli; Andre Silva, Kalinic (Suso 62).

Rijeka (1) 1 *(Elez 30)*
AEK Athens (1) 2 *(Mantalos 16, Christodoulopoulos 62)*   5932

Rijeka: (4231) Prskalo; Vesovic, Zuparic, Elez, Zuta; Bradaric, Misic (Matei 80); Heber, Gavranovic (Males 58), Kvrzic (Acosty 72); Gorgon.
AEK Athens: (4312) Anestis; Cosic, Helder Lopes, Vranjes, Bakakis; Andre Simoes, Johansson, Christodoulopoulos (Ajdarevic 77); Mantalos; Klonaridis (Bakasetas 59), Livaja (Araujo 85).

Thursday, 28 September 2017

AC Milan (1) 3 *(Andre Silva 14, Musacchio 53, Cutrone 90)*
Rijeka (0) 2 *(Acosty 84, Elez 90 (pen))*   23,917

AC Milan: (352) Donnarumma G; Musacchio, Bonucci, Romagnoli; Abate, Locatelli, Calhanoglu (Bonaventura 46), Kessie (Mauri 70), Borini; Andre Silva (Suso 82), Cutrone.
Rijeka: (442) Sluga; Vesovic, Elez, Zuparic, Zuta; Kvrzic (Acosty 58), Misic, Bradaric, Heber; Puljic (Crnic 79), Pavicic (Males 71).

AEK Athens (1) 2 *(Livaja 29, 90)*
Austria Vienna (1) 2 *(Monschein 44, Tajouri 49)* 16,954

AEK Athens: (433) Anestis; Bakakis, Vranjes, Cosic (Tzanetopoulos 23 (Bakasetas 81)), Rodrigo Galo; Mantalos, Ajdarevic (Galanopoulos 54), Johansson; Christodoulopoulos, Livaja, Araujo.
Austria Vienna: (4141) Pentz; Klein, Mohammed, Serbest, Martschinko; Holzhauser; Pires, De Paula (Lee 90), Tajouri, Alhassan (Prokop 60); Monschein (Friesenbichler 70).

Thursday, 19 October 2017

AC Milan (0) 0
AEK Athens (0) 0   20,812

AC Milan: (352) Donnarumma G; Musacchio, Bonucci, Rodriguez; Calabria, Bonaventura (Kessie 72), Calhanoglu, Suso (Borini 82), Locatelli; Andre Silva (Kalinic 62), Cutrone.
AEK Athens: (343) Anestis; Vranjes, Tzanetopoulos, Bakakis; Helder Lopes, Andre Simoes, Johansson, Rodrigo Galo; Livaja (Bakasetas 75), Mantalos (Galanopoulos 90), Christodoulopoulos (Araujo 63).

Austria Vienna (0) 1 *(Friesenbichler 90)*
Rijeka (2) 3 *(Gavranovic 21, 30, Kvrzic 90)*   20,690

Austria Vienna: (442) Pentz; Klein, Westermann, Mohammed, Salamon; De Paula (Tajouri 58), Holzhauser, Serbest (Prokop 77), Pires; Friesenbichler, Monschein.
Rijeka: (4231) Sluga; Vesovic, Elez (Puncec 70), Zuparic, Zuta; Bradaric, Males; Acosty (Kvrzic 79), Misic (Pavicic 78), Gorgon; Gavranovic.

Thursday, 2 November 2017

AEK Athens (0) 0
AC Milan (0) 0   40,538

AEK Athens: (3412) Anestis; Vranjes, Cosic, Bakakis; Rodrigo Galo, Johansson, Andre Simoes, Helder Lopes; Bakasetas (Galanopoulos 66); Christodoulopoulos (Livaja 60), Araujo (Giakoumakis 79).
AC Milan: (3412) Donnarumma G; Musacchio, Bonucci, Romagnoli; Borini, Locatelli (Kessie 67), Montolivo, Rodriguez; Calhanoglu; Cutrone (Suso 46), Andre Silva (Kalinic 81).

Rijeka (0) 1 *(Pavicic 61)*
Austria Vienna (1) 4 *(Prokop 41, 62, Serbest 73, Monschein 83)*   7912

Rijeka: (4411) Prskalo; Vesovic, Puncec, Zuparic, Zuta; Acosty (Kvrzic 55), Bradaric, Misic■, Heber (Matei 53); Pavicic; Gorgon (Puljic 84).
Austria Vienna: (4231) Pentz; Gluhakovic, Mohammed, Westermann, Salamon; Holzhauser, Serbest; Tajouri (Sarkaria 86), Prokop (Alhassan 90), Pires; Friesenbichler (Monschein 71).

Thursday, 23 November 2017

AC Milan (3) 5 *(Rodriguez 27, Andre Silva 36, 70, Cutrone 43, 90)*

Austria Vienna (1) 1 *(Monschein 21)* 17,932

AC Milan: (352) Donnarumma G; Musacchio, Bonucci (Gomez 80), Zapata; Borini (Locatelli 74), Biglia, Calhanoglu, Kessie, Rodriguez (Antonelli 64); Andre Silva, Cutrone.
Austria Vienna: (4231) Pentz; De Paula, Borkovic, Mohammed, Salamon (Gluhakovic 69); Serbest, Holzhauser (Lee 86); Prokop, Alhassan, Pires (Tajouri 78); Monschein.

AEK Athens (1) 2 *(Araujo 45, Christodoulopoulos 55)*

Rijeka (2) 2 *(Gorgon 8, 26)* 17,100

AEK Athens: (433) Anestis; Rodrigo Galo (Livaja 30), Vranjes, Chygrynskiy, Helder Lopes; Galanopoulos (Kone 68), Andre Simoes, Bakakis; Christodoulopoulos (Rodriguez 85), Araujo, Bakasetas.
Rijeka: (433) Prskalo; Vesovic, Zuparic, Elez, Zuta; Bradaric, Males, Pavicic (Crnic 90); Acosty (Kvrzic 70), Gavranovic (Puljic 81), Gorgon.

Thursday, 7 December 2017

Austria Vienna (0) 0

AEK Athens (0) 0 23,133

Austria Vienna: (4141) Pentz; Blauensteiner, Mohammed, Serbest, Salamon (Sarkaria 89); Holzhauser, Tajouri (Venuto 72), Prokop, Alhassan, Pires; Friesenbichler (Monschein 77).
AEK Athens: (4321) Tsintotas; Bakakis, Vranjes, Chygrynskiy, Helder Lopes; Rodrigo Galo, Andre Simoes, Galanopoulos; Christodoulopoulos (Bakasetas 64), Livaja (Kone 90); Araujo (Klonaridis 73).

Rijeka (1) 2 *(Puljic 6, Gavranovic 46)*

AC Milan (0) 0 8021

Rijeka: (451) Sluga; Vesovic, Zuparic, Elez, Zuta; Males, Pavicic, Acosty (Puncec 75), Gavranovic (Crnic 80), Kvrzic (Mavrias 85); Puljic.
AC Milan: (532) Storari; Zapata, Paletta, Romagnoli, Calabria, Zanellato (Abate 74); Biglia, Locatelli, Antonelli (Forte 79); Cutrone, Andre Silva.

Group D Table	P	W	D	L	F	A	GD	Pts
AC Milan	6	3	2	1	13	6	7	11
AEK Athens	6	1	5	0	6	5	1	8
Rijeka	6	2	1	3	11	12	−1	7
Austria Vienna	6	1	2	3	9	16	−7	5

GROUP E

Thursday, 14 September 2017

Apollon Limassol (0) 1 *(Sardinero 90)*

Lyon (0) 1 *(Depay 53 (pen))* 5134

Apollon Limassol: (433) Bruno Vale; Joao Pedro, Yuste, Roberge, Jander; Alef, Sachetti, Alex (Martinez 76); Jakolis (Sardinero 54), Maglica (Schembri (Zelaya 85).
Lyon: (433) Lopes; Da Silva, Marcelo, Morel, Marcal; Tousart, Ferri (Alvaro 78), Fekir; Cornet, Mariano (Traore 77), Depay.

Atalanta (3) 3 *(Masiello 27, Gomez 41, Cristante 44)*

Everton (0) 0 14,490

Atalanta: (352) Berisha; Toloi, Palomino, Masiello (Caldara 76); Hateboer, Cristante (Kurtic 82), Freuler, de Roon, Castagne; Petagna (Cornelius 79), Gomez.
Everton: (4231) Stekelenburg; Holgate, Jagielka, Keane, Baines; Besic, Schneiderlin (Sandro 67); Rooney (Klaassen 66), Vlasic, Sigurdsson; Calvert-Lewin (Mirallas 76).

Thursday, 28 September 2017

Everton (1) 2 *(Rooney 21, Vlasic 66)*

Apollon Limassol (1) 1 *(Sardinero 13, Yuste 88)* 27,034

Everton: (4312) Pickford; Kenny, Holgate, Williams, Baines; Gueye (Vlasic 46), Schneiderlin, Davies (Klaassen 67); Sigurdsson, Sandro (Calvert-Lewin 67), Rooney.
Apollon Limassol: (433) Bruno Vale; Joao Pedro, Yuste, Roberge, Vasiliou (Zelaya 83); Allan, Sachetti (Jander 77), Alef; Jakolis (Schembri 61), Maglica, Sardinero.

Lyon (1) 1 *(Traore 45)*

Atalanta (0) 1 *(Gomez 57)* 27,715

Lyon: (4231) Lopes; Tete, Marcelo, Morel, Mendy; Tousart, Alvaro; Traore (Cornet 85), Fekir, Aouar (Depay 69); Mariano (Maolida 70).
Atalanta: (352) Berisha; Masiello, Caldara, Palomino; Hateboer, Cristante (Castagne 46), de Roon, Freuler, Spinazzola; Petagna (Ilicic 61), Gomez.

Thursday, 19 October 2017

Atalanta (1) 3 *(Ilicic 12, Petagna 64, Freuler 66)*

Apollon Limassol (0) 1 *(Schembri 59)* 13,803

Atalanta: (343) Berisha; Masiello, Caldara, Palomino; Hateboer, Cristante (de Roon 70), Freuler, Spinazzola; Ilicic (Cornelius 85), Petagna, Gomez (Kurtic 79).
Apollon Limassol: (433) Bruno Vale; Joao Pedro, Yuste, Pitian, Jander; Alef, Sachetti, Allan (Alex 56); Jakolis, Maglica (Zelaya 56), Schembri (Sardinero 80).

Everton (0) 1 *(Williams 69)*

Lyon (1) 2 *(Fekir 6 (pen), Traore 76)* 27,159

Everton: (4231) Pickford; Holgate, Keane, Williams, Martina; Schneiderlin (Sigurdsson 57), Davies; Vlasic, Klaassen (Lookman 46), Calvert-Lewin; Mirallas (Ramirez 68).
Lyon: (4231) Lopes; Tete, Marcelo, Diakhaby, Marcal; Tousart, Aouar; Traore, Fekir (Ferri 60), Depay (Alvaro 89); Maolida (Cornet 71).

Thursday, 2 November 2017

Apollon Limassol (0) 1 *(Zelaya 90)*

Atalanta (1) 1 *(Ilicic 35 (pen))* 5658

Apollon Limassol: (433) Bruno Vale; Joao Pedro, Yuste, Alef, Vasiliou; Sachetti, Alex (Maglica 76), Allan; Sardinero (Schembri 64), Zelaya, Papoulis (Jakolis 58).
Atalanta: (343) Berisha; Masiello, Caldara, Palomino; Cristante (de Roon 81), Freuler, Hateboer, Ilicic (Orsolini 54); Kurtic (Gosens 69), Spinazzola, Petagna.

Lyon (0) 3 *(Traore 68, Aouar 76, Depay 88)*

Everton (0) 0 48,103

Lyon: (4231) Lopes; Da Silva, Marcelo, Diakhaby, Mendy; Tousart, Alvaro (Ferri 77); Cornet, Fekir (Aouar 62), Depay; Traore (Mariano 69).
Everton: (4411) Pickford; Kenny, Williams, Holgate, Martina (Besic 43); Lookman, Schneiderlin, Gueye (Calvert-Lewin 61), Lennon (Vlasic 71); Baningime; Sigurdsson.

Thursday, 23 November 2017

Everton (0) 1 *(Sandro 71)*

Atalanta (1) 5 *(Cristante 13, 64, Gosens 86, Cornelius 88, 90)* 17,431

Everton: (4411) Robles; Kenny (Feeney 69), Williams, Keane, Martina; Klaassen (Vlasic 62), Baningime, Davies, Mirallas (Calvert-Lewin 79); Rooney; Sandro.
Atalanta: (352) Berisha; Toloi, Palomino, Masiello (Caldara 61); Hateboer (Gosens 70), Cristante (Cornelius 82), de Roon, Freuler, Castagne; Petagna, Gomez.

Lyon (2) 4 *(Diakhaby 29, Fekir 31, Mariano 67, Maolida 90)*

Apollon Limassol (0) 0 26,972

Lyon: (4231) Lopes; Da Silva, Marcelo, Morel (Tousart 46), Marcal; Alvaro, Diakhaby; Traore (Aouar 16), Fekir, Depay (Maolida 74); Mariano.
Apollon Limassol: (4231) Bruno Vale; Joao Pedro, Yuste, Roberge, Jander; Alef, Sachetti; Jakolis, Schembri (Martinez 73), Sardinero (Alex 73); Maglica (Zelaya 17).

Thursday, 7 December 2017

Apollon Limassol (0) 0

Everton (2) 3 *(Lookman 21, 28, Vlasic 87)* 4237

Apollon Limassol: (433) Kissas; Joao Pedro, Pitian, Roberge, Jander; Allan, Sachetti, Martinez (Pittas 75); Sardinero (Jakolis 62), Schembri (Zelaya 61), Papoulis.
Everton: (442) Robles; Baningime, Feeney, Besic, Charsley (Denny 90); Klaassen, Schneiderlin, Vlasic, Mirallas (Gordon 89); Lookman, Hornby (Broadhead 82).

Atalanta (1) 1 *(Petagna 10)*

Lyon (0) 0   14,500

Atalanta: (343) Berisha; Toloi, Caldara, Masiello; Hateboer, Cristante (de Roon 87), Freuler, Spinazzola; Ilicic (Palomino 83), Petagna (Kurtic 75), Gomez.
Lyon: (4231) Lopes; Da Silva, Marcelo, Diakhaby, Mendy; Ferri, Alvaro; Cornet (Geubbels 45), Fekir, Depay (Aouar 68); Mariano (Gouiri 74).

Group E Table	P	W	D	L	F	A	GD	Pts
Atalanta	6	4	2	0	14	4	10	14
Lyon	6	3	2	1	11	4	7	11
Everton	6	1	1	4	7	15	–8	4
Apollon Limassol	6	0	3	3	5	14	–9	3

GROUP F

Thursday, 14 September 2017

Fastav Zlin (0) 0

Sheriff (0) 0   4499

Fastav Zlin: (442) Dostal; Matejov, Baco, Gajic, Holzer; Ekpai (Bartosak 68), Traore, Jiracek, Vukadinovic; Zeleznik (Diop 61), Mehanovic (Dzafic 82).
Sheriff: (352) Mikulic; Racu, Posmac, Kulusic; Susic, Brezovec (Kendysh 72), Anton, de Nooijer, Cristiano; Mugosa (Damascan 80), Jairo (Tripic 87).

FC Copenhagen (0) 0

Lokomotiv Moscow (0) 0   18,000

FC Copenhagen: (442) Olsen; Ankersen, Vavro, Luftner, Boilesen; Kusk (Jensen 62), Gregus, Zeca (Kvist 86), Verbic; Sotiriou, Pavlovic (Pusic 81).
Lokomotiv Moscow: (451) Guilherme; Mykhalyk, Pejcinovic, Kvirkvelia, Rybus; Ignatiev, Denisov I, Tarasov, Fernandes, Aleksey Miranchuk (Anton Miranchuk 82); Farfan (Eder 70).

Thursday, 28 September 2017

Lokomotiv Moscow (3) 3 *(Fernandes 3 (pen), 6, 17)*

Fastav Zlin (0) 0   10,065

Lokomotiv Moscow: (442) Guilherme; Ignatiev (Rotenberg 88), Kvirkvelia, Pejcinovic, Lysov; Farfan (Anton Miranchuk 46), Tarasov, Denisov I, Fernandes; Aleksey Miranchuk (Kolomeytsev 78), Eder.
Fastav Zlin: (442) Dostal; Matejov (Kopecny 65), Baco, Gajic, Holzer; Ekpai, Traore, Jiracek, Vukadinovic; Zeleznik (Mehanovic 46), Diop (Beauguel 79).

Sheriff (0) 0

FC Copenhagen (0) 0   5070

Sheriff: (352) Mikulic; Racu, Posmac, Kulusic; Susic, Brezovec (Badibanga 81), Anton (de Nooijer 63), Kendysh, Cristiano; Anton (de Nooijer 63), Kendysh, Cristiano; Jairo, Mugosa (Damascan 70).
FC Copenhagen: (442) Olsen; Ankersen, Vavro, Bengtsson; Kusk (Boilesen 69), Zeca, Kvist, Verbic (Matic 82); Sotiriou, Pusic (Jensen 45).

Thursday, 19 October 2017

Fastav Zlin (1) 1 *(Diop 11)*

FC Copenhagen (1) 1 *(Ankersen 19)*   6245

Fastav Zlin: (442) Zlamal; Kopecny, Baco, Gajic, Holzer; Ekpai, Janicek, Traore (Zeleznik 86), Jiracek; Diop (Vukadinovic 67), Mehanovic (Dzafic 77).
FC Copenhagen: (442) Andersen; Ankersen, Vavro, Luftner, Bengtsson; Toutouh, Gregus, Kvist, Matic (Amankwaa 83); Holse (Jensen 69), Pavlovic (Sotiriou 68).

Sheriff (1) 1 *(Badibanga 32)*

Lokomotiv Moscow (1) 1 *(Anton Miranchuk 17)*   10,500

Sheriff: (433) Mikulic; Susic, Posmac, Kulusic, Cristiano; Brezovec (Balima 68), Anton, Kendysh; Jairo (Racu 81), Mugosa (Damascan 86), Badibanga.
Lokomotiv Moscow: (451) Guilherme; Ignatiev, Kvirkvelia, Pejcinovic, Rybus; Farfan, Anton Miranchuk, Tarasov, Denisov I, Fernandes; Eder (Kolomeytsev 61).

Thursday, 2 November 2017

FC Copenhagen (1) 3 *(Luftner 42, Verbic 49, 90)*

Fastav Zlin (0) 0   16,189

FC Copenhagen: (442) Olsen; Ankersen, Vavro, Luftner, Bengtsson; Kusk (Jensen 64), Zeca, Matic, Toutouh (Amankwaa 72); Sotiriou (Pavlovic 64), Verbic.
Fastav Zlin: (442) Dostal; Kopecny, Baco, Gajic, Holzer; Ekpai (Zeleznik 75), Traore, Janicek (Hnanicek 54), Jiracek; Diop (Mehanovic 65), Vukadinovic.

Lokomotiv Moscow (1) 1 *(Farfan 26)*

Sheriff (1) 2 *(Badibanga 41, Brezovec 58)*   10,118

Lokomotiv Moscow: (451) Guilherme (Medvedev 33); Ignatiev, Kvirkvelia, Pejcinovic, Lysov; Anton Miranchuk (Eder 73), Aleksey Miranchuk, Denisov I, Tarasov (Barinov 55), Fernandes; Farfan.
Sheriff: (352) Mikulic; Racu, Posmac, Kulusic; Susic, Brezovec (Balima 66), Anton, Kendysh, Cristiano (Oliveira 87); Badibanga, Jairo (de Nooijer 78).

Thursday, 23 November 2017

Lokomotiv Moscow (1) 2 *(Farfan 17, 51)*

FC Copenhagen (1) 1 *(Verbic 31)*   10,696

Lokomotiv Moscow: (442) Kochenkov; Ignatiev, Kvirkvelia, Mykhalyk (Pejcinovic 80), Denisov V; Farfan, Denisov I, Fernandes, Kolomeytsev; Aleksey Miranchuk (Barinov 90), Anton Miranchuk (Tarasov 73).
FC Copenhagen: (442) Olsen; Ankersen, Vavro, Luftner, Boilesen; Holse (Pusic 70), Kvist, Matic (Kusk 78), Verbic; Sotiriou, Zeca.

Sheriff (1) 1 *(Jairo 11)*

Fastav Zlin (0) 0   5485

Sheriff: (352) Mikulic; Racu, Posmac, Kulusic; Susic, Brezovec (de Nooijer 69), Anton, Kendysh, Cristiano; Badibanga (Damascan 90), Jairo (Balima 83).
Fastav Zlin: (442) Zlamal; Matejov, Baco, Gajic, Bartosak (Bartolomeu 80); Ekpai (Holzer 53), Hnanicek (Traore 83), Jiracek, Dzafic; Zeleznik, Mehanovic.

Thursday, 7 December 2017

Fastav Zlin (0) 0

Lokomotiv Moscow (0) 2 *(Aleksey Miranchuk 70, Farfan 74)*   4682

Fastav Zlin: (442) Zlamal; Kopecny, Hnanicek, Gajic■, Matejov (Dzafic 78); Vukadinovic, Hronek (Janicek 64), Jiracek, Holzer; Traore, Diop (Ekpai 72).
Lokomotiv Moscow: (442) Kochenkov; Ignatiev, Pejcinovic, Kvirkvelia, Lysov; Farfan (Rotenberg 81), Kolomeytsev (Tarasov 45), Denisov I, Fernandes; Anton Miranchuk (Eder 59), Aleksey Miranchuk.

FC Copenhagen (0) 2 *(Sotiriou 56, Luftner 59)*

Sheriff (0) 0   14,246

FC Copenhagen: (442) Olsen; Ankersen, Vavro, Luftner, Boilesen; Jensen (Thomsen 81), Zeca, Kvist, Verbic (Matic 88); Santander (Pavlovic 82), Sotiriou.
Sheriff: (352) Mikulic; Racu (Damascan 62), Posmac, Kulusic; Susic, Brezovec (de Nooijer 54), Anton (Mugosa 85), Kendysh, Cristiano; Badibanga, Jairo■.

Group F Table	P	W	D	L	F	A	GD	Pts
Lokomotiv Moscow	6	3	2	1	9	4	5	11
FC Copenhagen	6	2	3	1	7	3	4	9
Sheriff	6	2	3	1	4	4	0	9
Fastav Zlin	6	0	2	4	1	10	–9	2

GROUP G

Thursday, 14 September 2017

Hapoel Be'er Sheva (1) 2 *(Einbinder 3, Tzedek 60 (pen))*

Lugano (0) 1 *(Tzedek 67 (og))*   14,752

Hapoel Be'er Sheva: (433) Haimov; Elo (Elhamed 69), Taha, Tzedek, Korhut; Radi, Ogu, Einbinder (Brown 84); Melikson, Pekhart (Zrihen 67), Nwakaeme.
Lugano: (352) Da Costa; Rouiller (Yao 46), Sulmoni, Golemic; Crnigoj (Bottani 46), Sabbatini, Piccinocchi, Mariani (Milosavljevic 71), Mihajlovic; Bnou-Marzouk, Gerndt.

Steaua Bucharest (2) 3 *(Budescu 22 (pen), 44, Alibec 72)*
Viktoria Plzen (0) 0 27,000
Steaua Bucharest: (4231) Nita; Benzar R, Planic, Balasa, Junior Morais; Pintilii, Nedelcu; Golofca, Budescu (Man 83), Coman (Popescu 57); Alibec (Gnohere 75).
Viktoria Plzen: (4231) Hruska; Reznik, Hejda, Hajek, Limbersky; Zivulic (Bakos 61), Hrosovsky; Petrzela, Kolar, Kopic; Reznicek (Horava 61).

Thursday, 28 September 2017
Lugano (1) 1 *(Bottani 14)*
Steaua Bucharest (0) 2 *(Budescu 57, Junior Morais 64)*
2680
Lugano: (433) Da Costa; Mihajlovic, Sulmoni, Golemic, Daprela; Sabbatini, Ledesma, Mariani (Culina 75); Crnigoj (Bnou-Marzouk 75), Gerndt, Bottani (Milosavljevic 71).
Steaua Bucharest: (4231) Nita; Benzar R, Planic, Balasa, Junior Morais; Popescu (Man 46), Pintilii; Teixeria, Budescu (Filip 82), Tanase F; Gnohere (Coman 65).

Viktoria Plzen (1) 3 *(Petrzela 30, Kopic 75, Bakos 90)*
Hapoel Be'er Sheva (0) 1 *(Nwakaeme 70)* 10,314
Viktoria Plzen: (4231) Hruska; Reznik, Hejda, Hajek, Havel; Horava, Hrosovsky; Petrzela (Zeman 61), Kolar (Ivanschitz 73), Kopic; Krmencik (Bakos 84).
Hapoel Be'er Sheva: (352) Goresh; Brown (Ohana 80), Taha, Elhamed; Elo, Radi, Ogu, Melikson (Cuenca 80), Korhut; Sahar (Nwakaeme 62), Pekhart.

Thursday, 19 October 2017
Hapoel Be'er Sheva (0) 1 *(Cuenca 88)*
Steaua Bucharest (0) 2 *(Gnohere 70, 75)* 15,117
Hapoel Be'er Sheva: (433) Goresh; Bitton (Cuenca 74), Taha, Elhamed, Korhut; Brown, Ogu (Radi 30), Einbinder; Melikson, Sahar (Pekhart 67), Nwakaeme.
Steaua Bucharest: (4231) Nita; Benzar R (Enache 24), Planic, Balasa, Momcilovic; Nedelcu, Popescu; Man (Coman 57), Budescu, Teixeria; Tanase F (Gnohere 69).

Lugano (0) 3 *(Bottani 64, Carlinhos 70, Gerndt 88)*
Viktoria Plzen (0) 2 *(Krmencik 76, Bakos 90)* 2000
Lugano: (433) Da Costa; Mihajlovic, Rouiller, Golemic, Daprela; Piccinocchi, Ledesma, Mariani; Crnigoj (Padalino 85), Carlinhos (Sabbatini 73), Bottani (Gerndt 71).
Viktoria Plzen: (4231) Hruska; Reznik, Hubnik, Hajek, Havel; Cermak, Hrosovsky; Petrzela (Kopic 56), Kolar (Krmencik 56), Pilar (Zeman 75); Bakos.

Thursday, 2 November 2017
Steaua Bucharest (1) 1 *(Coman 31)*
Hapoel Be'er Sheva (1) 1 *(Sahar 37)* 27,174
Steaua Bucharest: (4231) Nita; Enache, Larie, Balasa, Junior Morais; Pintilii, Filip; Man (Teixeria 46), Budescu, Coman (Tanase F 65); Alibec (Gnohere 70).
Hapoel Be'er Sheva: (433) Goresh; Elo, Vitor (Ohana 71), Taha, Korhut; Radi, Elhamed, Einbinder; Cuenca (Melikson 76), Sahar (Barda 82), Nwakaeme.

Viktoria Plzen (3) 4 *(Krmencik 4, 19, Horava 45, Cermak 57)*
Lugano (1) 1 *(Mariani 15)* 9483
Viktoria Plzen: (4231) Hruska; Reznik, Hejda, Hajek, Limbersky; Horava (Zivulic 86), Hrosovsky; Petrzela, Cermak, Kopic (Pilar 74); Krmencik (Reznicek 64).
Lugano: (433) Da Costa; Mihajlovic, Sulmoni, Golemic, Daprela; Sabbatini, Ledesma (Milosavljevic 83), Mariani; Bottani, Gerndt (Bnou-Marzouk 76), Carlinhos (Vecsei 62).

Thursday, 23 November 2017
Lugano (0) 1 *(Carlinhos 50)*
Hapoel Be'er Sheva (0) 0 3000
Lugano: (433) Kiassumbua; Rouiller, Sulmoni, Golemic, Mihajlovic; Sabbatini, Piccinocchi (Culina 90), Vecsei; Carlinhos (Gerndt 55), Bottani (Ledesma 76), Mariani.
Hapoel Be'er Sheva: (433) Goresh; Bitton, Elhamed, Vitor, Korhut; Radi, Ogu (Pekhart 46), Einbinder (Ohana 57); Cuenca (Melikson 73), Sahar, Nwakaeme.

Viktoria Plzen (0) 2 *(Petrzela 49, Kopic 76)*
Steaua Bucharest (0) 0 10,197
Viktoria Plzen: (4231) Hruska; Reznik, Hejda, Hubnik, Limbersky; Horava, Hrosovsky; Petrzela (Zivulic 88), Kolar (Cermak 83), Kopic; Reznicek (Bakos 66).
Steaua Bucharest: (4231) Vlad D; Enache, Planic, Balasa, Junior Morais; Popescu, Filip (Nedelcu 46); Golofca (Tanase F 46), Man, Coman (Budescu 64); Alibec.

Thursday, 7 December 2017
Hapoel Be'er Sheva (0) 0
Viktoria Plzen (1) 2 *(Hejda 29, Horava 83)* 16,000
Hapoel Be'er Sheva: (4321) Haimov; Elo, Elhamed, Korhut, Taha; Radi, Brown, Einbinder (Melikson 58); Ohana, Cuenca (Zrihen 67); Pekhart.
Viktoria Plzen: (4231) Hruska; Reznik, Hejda, Hubnik, Limbersky; Horava, Hrosovsky; Petrzela (Pilar 58), Kolar (Cermak 77), Kopic; Krmencik (Bakos 89).

Steaua Bucharest (0) 1 *(Gnohere 61)*
Lugano (2) 2 *(Daprela 3, Vecsei 32)* 13,231
Steaua Bucharest: (442) Vlad D; Enache, Larie, Balasa, Junior Morais; Popescu, Nedelcu, Golofca (Man 46); Tanase F (Momcilovic 61); William (Gnohere 41), Coman.
Lugano: (433) Da Costa; Yao (Bnou-Marzouk 87), Kovacic, Golemic, Daprela; Milosavljevic, Piccinocchi (Sabbatini 41), Vecsei; Culina (Mihajlovic 73), Bottani, Mariani.

Group G Table	P	W	D	L	F	A	GD	Pts
Viktoria Plzen	6	4	0	2	13	8	5	12
Steau Bucharest	6	3	1	2	9	7	2	10
Lugano	6	3	0	3	9	11	−2	9
Hapoel Be'er Sheva	6	1	1	4	5	10	−5	4

GROUP H
Thursday, 14 September 2017
Arsenal (0) 3 *(Kolasinac 49, Sanchez 67, Bellerin 82)*
Cologne (1) 1 *(Cordoba 9)* 59,359
Arsenal: (343) Ospina; Holding (Kolasinac 46), Mertesacker, Monreal; Bellerin, Iwobi (Wilshere 68), Elneny, Maitland-Niles; Walcott (Nelson 83), Giroud, Sanchez.
Cologne: (4141) Horn T; Klunter (Osako 76), Mere, Heintz, Rausch; Hector (Jojic 35); Bittencourt, Hoger, Lehmann, Zoller (Risse 64); Cordoba.

Crvena Zvezda (0) 1 *(Radonjic 54)*
BATE Borisov (0) 1 *(Signevich 72)* 40,284
Crvena Zvezda: (4231) Borjan; Stojkovic, Le Tallec, Savic, Rodic; Donald, Krsticic (Milijas 89); Srnic (Pesic 77), Kanga, Radonjic (Ricardinho 71); Boakye.
BATE Borisov: (4231) Scherbitski; Palyakow, Milunovic, Gajduchik, Rios; Volodjko A (Signevich 62), Dragun; Gordeichuk, Ivanic, Stasevich (Volodjko M 82); Rodionov (Baha 75).

Thursday, 28 September 2017
BATE Borisov (1) 2 *(Ivanic 28, Gordeichuk 67)*
Arsenal (3) 4 *(Walcott 9, 22, Holding 25, Giroud 49 (pen))*
13,100
BATE Borisov: (4231) Scherbitski; Rios, Gajduchik, Milunovic, Polyakov (Volodjko M 24); Volodjko A (Baha 84), Dragun; Gordeichuk, Ivanic, Stasevich; Rodionov (Signevich 55).
Arsenal: (532) Ospina; Nelson (McGuane 79), Mustafi, Mertesacker, Holding, Maitland-Niles; Willock (Nketiah 88), Elneny, Wilshere; Walcott, Giroud.

Cologne (0) 0
Crvena Zvezda (1) 1 *(Boakye 30)* 46,195
Cologne: (352) Horn T; Mere (Bittencourt 46), Sorensen, Heintz; Olkowski (Clemens 76), Ozcan, Lehmann, Jojic, Rausch; Cordoba, Guirassy (Osako 46).
Crvena Zvezda: (4411) Borjan; Stojkovic, Babic, Le Tallec, Gobeljic; Srnic, Donald, Krsticic (Racic 77), Radonjic (Milic 72); Kanga; Boakye (Pesic 63).

Thursday, 19 October 2017

BATE Borisov (0) 1 *(Rios 55)*

Cologne (0) 0　　　　　　　　　　　　　11,783

BATE Borisov: (4231) Scherbitski; Rios, Gajduchik, Milunovic, Palyakow; Volodjko A (Baha 73), Dragun; Stasevich, Ivanic (Gordeichuk 68), Volodjko M; Signevich (Rodionov 85).
Cologne: (442) Horn T; Olkowski, Maroh, Heintz, Rausch; Clemens (Guirassy 61), Hoger, Ozcan, Jojic (Bittencourt 70); Zoller, Osako.

Crvena Zvezda (0) 0

Arsenal (0) 1 *(Giroud 85)*　　　　　　　50,327

Crvena Zvezda: (4231) Borjan; Stojkovic, Le Tallec, Savic (Babic 65), Rodic•; Krsticic, Donald; Srnic (Gobeljic 83), Kanga, Radonjic; Boakye (Pesic 80).
Arsenal: (343) Cech; Debuchy, Elneny, Holding; Nelson, Coquelin (Sheaf 89), Willock (McGuane 89), Maitland-Niles; Wilshere, Walcott, Giroud.

Thursday, 2 November 2017

Arsenal (0) 0

Crvena Zvezda (0) 0　　　　　　　　　58,285

Arsenal: (523) Macey; Nelson, Debuchy, Elneny, Holding, Maitland-Niles; Coquelin, Willock (Nketiah 68); Walcott, Giroud, Wilshere.
Crvena Zvezda: (4231) Borjan; Stojkovic, Le Tallec, Savic, Gobeljic; Krsticic, Donald; Srnic (Racic 86), Kanga (Milic 70), Radonjic (Pesic 89); Boakye.

Cologne (1) 5 *(Zoller 16, Osako 54, 82, Guirassy 63, Jojic 90)*

BATE Borisov (2) 2 *(Milunovic 31, Signevich 33)*　45,200

Cologne: (442) Horn T; Sorensen, Maroh, Heintz, Rausch; Clemens (Osako 46), Lehmann, Ozcan, Bittencourt; Zoller (Olkowski 83), Guirassy (Jojic 68).
BATE Borisov: (4231) Scherbitski; Rios, Gajduchik (Tuominem 81), Milunovic, Polyakov; Volodjko A (Rodionov 70), Dragun; Gordeichuk (Volodjko M 60), Ivanic, Stasevich; Signevich.

Thursday, 23 November 2017

BATE Borisov (0) 0

Crvena Zvezda (0) 0　　　　　　　　　12,000

BATE Borisov: (4231) Scherbitski; Rios, Buljat, Milunovic, Palyakow; Dragun, Volodjko A (Baha 55); Gordeichuk (Volodjko M 79), Ivanic, Stasevich; Rodionov (Signevich 61).
Crvena Zvezda: (4231) Borjan; Stojkovic, Le Tallec, Savic, Rodic; Donald, Krsticic; Srnic (Racic 89), Kanga, Milic (Pesic 64); Boakye (Gobeljic 90).

Cologne (0) 1 *(Guirassy 62 (pen))*

Arsenal (0) 0　　　　　　　　　　　　45,300

Cologne: (343) Horn T; Sorensen, Maroh (Rausch 38), Mere; Klunter, Ozcan, Jojic, Horn J; Cordoba (Olkowski 56), Osako (Lehmann 73), Guirassy.
Arsenal: (3421) Ospina; Debuchy (Nketiah 84), Mertesacker, Holding; Chambers (Nelson 67), Coquelin, Elneny, Maitland-Niles; Welbeck (Iwobi 46), Wilshere; Giroud.

Thursday, 7 December 2017

Arsenal (3) 6 *(Debuchy 11, Walcott 37, Wilshere 43, Polyakov 52 (og), Giroud 64 (pen), Elneny 74)*

BATE Borisov (0) 0　　　　　　　　　25,909

Arsenal: (433) Ospina; Debuchy, Holding, Chambers, Maitland-Niles; Coquelin, Elneny (Willock 76), Wilshere; Walcott (Nelson 70), Giroud, Welbeck (Nketiah 77).
BATE Borisov: (4231) Scherbitski; Rios, Polyakov, Milunovic, Volodjko M; Berezkin, Dragun; Gordeichuk, Ivanic (Yablonskiy 76), Stasevich (Tuominem 68); Rodionov (Signevich 56).

Crvena Zvezda (1) 1 *(Srnic 22)*

Cologne (0) 0　　　　　　　　　　　　51,364

Crvena Zvezda: (4231) Borjan; Stojkovic, Le Tallec, Savic, Rodic; Jovicic (Pesic 63), Donald; Srnic (Gobeljic 80), Kanga (Racic 88), Krsticic; Boakye.
Cologne: (433) Horn T; Olkowski (Klunter 66), Sorensen, Horn J, Rausch; Jojic, Lehmann, Ozcan; Clemens (Ouahim 70), Osako, Guirassy.

Group H Table	P	W	D	L	F	A	GD	Pts
Arsenal	6	4	1	1	14	4	10	13
Crvena Zvezda	6	2	3	1	3	2	1	9
Cologne	6	2	0	4	7	8	–1	6
BATE Borisov	6	1	2	3	6	16	–10	5

GROUP I

Thursday, 14 September 2017

Marseille (0) 1 *(Rami 48)*

Konyaspor (0) 0　　　　　　　　　　　8649

Marseille: (433) Pele; Sakai, Rami, Rolando, Amavi; Kamara, Gustavo, Sanson; Thauvin (Ocampos 74), Germain (Sarr 81), Payet (Zambo 89).
Konyaspor: (4231) Kirintili; Skubic, Turan, Moke, Oztorun; Findikli (Jonsson 61), Bourabia; Fofana, Araz (Milosevic 46), Sahiner (Ezekiel 72); Evouna.

Vitoria (1) 1 *(Pedro Henrique 25)*

Red Bull Salzburg (1) 1 *(Berisha 45)*　13,972

Vitoria: (433) Douglas; Garcia, Jubal Junior, Konan, Pedro Henrique; Celis, Wakaso (Rafael Miranda 77), Hurtado (Kiko 57); Rincon (Heldon 66), Texeira, Raphinha.
Red Bull Salzburg: (442) Walke; Lainer, Paulo Miranda, Caleta-Car, Ulmer; Haidara (Schlager 86), Samassekou, Wolf (Leitgeb 84), Berisha V; Dabbur, Gulbrandsen (Daka 64).

Thursday, 28 September 2017

Konyaspor (1) 2 *(Araz 24, Milosevic 48)*

Vitoria de Guimaraes (0) 1 *(Hurtado 74)*　21,116

Konyaspor: (4231) Kirintili; Skubic, Turan, Filipovic, Sahiner; Bourabia, Jonsson; Fofana, Araz (Bora 75), Milosevic (Findikli 90); Eze (Evouna 80).
Vitoria de Guimaraes: (433) Silva; Joao Aurelio, Jubal Junior, Pedro Henrique (Moreno 46), Konan; Celis, Wakaso (Ramos 46); Hurtado; Heldon, Estupinan (Ferreira 71), Raphinha.

Red Bull Salzburg (0) 1 *(Dabbur 74)*

Marseille (0) 0　　　　　　　　　　　11,832

Red Bull Salzburg: (442) Walke; Lainer, Paulo Miranda, Caleta-Car, Ulmer; Haidara, Samassekou, Schlager (Atanga 60), Berisha V; Wolf, Dabbur.
Marseille: (433) Pele; Evra, Rolando, Rami, Kamara; Sanson, Gustavo (Zambo 76), Lopez (Mitroglou 79); Thauvin (N'Jie 75), Germain, Sarr.

Thursday, 19 October 2017

Konyaspor (0) 0

Red Bull Salzburg (1) 2 *(Gulbrandsen 6, Dabbur 80)*　23,354

Konyaspor: (4231) Kirintili; Skubic, Turan, Filipovic, Oztorun; Bourabia, Jonsson (Camdali 71); Sahiner, Milosevic, Fofana (Ezekiel 76); Eze (Araz 62).
Red Bull Salzburg: (442) Walke; Lainer, Paulo Miranda, Caleta-Car, Ulmer; Haidara (Minamino 78), Wolf (Schlager 71), Samassekou, Berisha V; Gulbrandsen (Rzatkowski 88), Dabbur.

Marseille (1) 2 *(Ocampos 28, Lopez 76)*

Vitoria de Guimaraes (1) 1 *(Rafael Martins 16)*　13,359

Marseille: (442) Mandanda; Sarr, Rami, Abdennour, Evra (Amavi 58); Lopez, Kamara, Gustavo, Sanson (Zambo 81); Germain (N'Jie 88), Ocampos.
Vitoria de Guimaraes: (4231) Silva; Joao Aurelio, Jubal Junior, Marcos Valente, Konan; Wakaso, Rafael Miranda (Celis 79); Raphinha, Ramos (Ferreira 65), Heldon; Rafael Martins (Texeira 72).

Thursday, 2 November 2017

Red Bull Salzburg (0) 0

Konyaspor (0) 0　　　　　　　　　　　9000

Red Bull Salzburg: (442) Stankovic; Lainer, Paulo Miranda, Caleta-Car, Ulmer; Haidara (Yabo 74), Wolf (Minamino 69), Samassekou, Berisha V; Gulbrandsen (Schlager 87), Dabbur.
Konyaspor: (4231) Kirintili; Skubic, Ay, Moke, Oztorun; Jonsson (Camdali 46), Bourabia; Sahiner, Araz (Fofana 63), Milosevic (Findikli 89); Evouna.

Vitoria de Guimaraes (0) 1 *(Hurtado 80)*
Marseille (0) 0   14,181
Vitoria de Guimaraes: (433) Silva; Joao Aurelio (Garcia 82), Jubal Junior, Marcos Valente, Konan; Ramos, Wakaso, Hurtado (Moreno 90); Raphinha (Ferreira 70), Rafael Martins, Heldon.
Marseille: (4231) Mandanda; Sarr, Rami, Abdennour, Amavi; Kamara■, Gustavo (Mitroglou 82); Lopez (Sakai 76), Sanson, N'Jie (Thauvin 67); Germain.

Thursday, 23 November 2017
Konyaspor (0) 1 *(Skubic 81 (pen))*
Marseille (0) 1 *(Moke 90 (og))*   18,000
Konyaspor: (4231) Kirintili; Skubic, Filipovic, Moke, Oztorun; Bourabia, Findikli (Camdali 57); Araz, Milosevic, Fofana (Ezekiel 79); Evouna (Sahiner 68).
Marseille: (4231) Mandanda; Sakai, Rami, Rolando, Amavi■; Zambo (Sarr 83), Gustavo; Thauvin (N'Jie 68), Ocampos (Payet 64), Sanson; Germain.

Red Bull Salzburg (2) 3 *(Dabbur 26, Ulmer 45, Hwang 67)*
Vitoria de Guimaraes (0) 0   6474
Red Bull Salzburg: (442) Walke; Lainer, Pongracic, Caleta-Car, Ulmer; Haidara, Minamino (Rzatkowski 71), Schlager, Berisha V; Gulbrandsen (Hwang 61), Dabbur (Tetteh 86).
Vitoria de Guimaraes: (433) Douglas; Garcia, Wakaso, Pedro Henrique (Heldon 58), Konan; Ramos, Hurtado (Jubal Junior 59), Celis; Fabio Sturgeon, Rafael Martins, Raphinha (Ferreira 72).

Thursday, 7 December 2017
Marseille (0) 0
Red Bull Salzburg (0) 0   23,865
Marseille: (4231) Mandanda; Sarr, Rami, Rolando, Sakai; Zambo, Gustavo; Ocampos, Lopez, Sanson (Payet 68); N'Jie (Germain 76).
Red Bull Salzburg: (442) Walke; Lainer, Paulo Miranda, Caleta-Car, Ulmer; Haidara (Leitgeb 76), Samassekou (Yabo 61), Berisha V, Schlager; Dabbur, Gulbrandsen (Hwang 59).

Vitoria de Guimaraes (0) 1 *(Turan 79 (og))*
Konyaspor (1) 1 *(Bourabia 15)*   9040
Vitoria de Guimaraes: (433) Douglas; Garcia, Jubal Junior, Pedro Henrique, Joao Vigario (Joao Aurelio 46); Ramos (Ferreira 76), Celis, Hurtado; Raphinha, Rafael Martins (Estupinan 74), Heldon.
Konyaspor: (4231) Kirintili; Sahiner, Turan, Ay, Oztorun (Skubic 46); Camdali (Fofana 63), Moke; Bora (Milosevic 81), Bourabia, Araz; Evouna.

Group I Table	P	W	D	L	F	A	GD	Pts
Red Bull Salzburg	6	3	3	0	7	1	6	12
Marseille	6	2	2	2	4	4	0	8
Konyaspor	6	1	3	2	4	6	-2	6
Vitoria de Guimaraes	6	1	2	3	5	9	-4	5

GROUP J

Thursday, 14 September 2017
Hertha Berlin (0) 0
Athletic Bilbao (0) 0   28,832
Hertha Berlin: (4231) Kraft; Pekarik, Langkamp, Rekik, Plattenhardt, Lustenberger, Darida; Weiser, Duda, Kalou (Haraguchi 85); Ibisevic (Leckie 76).
Athletic Bilbao: (4231) Herrerin; Lekue, Etxeita, Laporte, Balenziaga; San Jose, Vesga; Williams (Susaeta 85), Muniain (Aketxe 90), Cordoba (Raul Garcia 70); Aduriz.

Zorya Luhansk (0) 0
Ostersund (0) 2 *(Ghoddos 50, Gero 90)*   5097
Zorya Luhansk: (4141) Lunin; Karavaev, Checher, Svatok, Sukhotsky; Grechyshkin (Kharatin 52); Gromov, Gordienko, Andriyevskiy (Ljubenovic 73), Lunov (Kabayev 84); Iury.
Ostersund: (442) Keita; Edwards, Papagiannopoulos, Pettersson, Mukiibi (Somi 67); Aiesh, Nouri (Gero 80); Bachirou, Sema; Hopcutt (Mensah 57); Ghoddos.

Thursday, 28 September 2017
Athletic Bilbao (0) 0
Zorya Luhansk (1) 1 *(Kharatin 28)*   32,462
Athletic Bilbao: (4231) Herrerin; Boveda, Etxeita (Iturraspe 55), Laporte, Saborit (Cordoba 65); San Jose, Benat (Aketxe 77); Williams, Raul Garcia, Muniain; Aduriz.
Zorya Luhansk: (4141) Lunin; Opanasenko, Svatok, Grechyshkin, Sukhotsky; Kharatin; Karavaev, da Silva (Gordienko 53), Andriyevskiy, Lunov (Checher 83); Gromov (Kochergin 64).

Ostersund (1) 1 *(Nouri 22 (pen))*
Hertha Berlin (0) 0   8009
Ostersund: (442) Keita; Mukiibi (Mensah 76), Papagiannopoulos, Pettersson, Somi (Widgren 56); Edwards, Nouri (Fritzson 88) Bachirou, Sema; Ghoddos, Gero.
Hertha Berlin: (442) Kraft; Pekarik, Langkamp (Darida 61), Stark, Torunarigha; Weiser, Lustenberger, Skjelbred, Lazaro (Stocker 78); Ibisevic, Esswein (Duda 65).

Thursday, 19 October 2017
Ostersund (0) 2 *(Gero 51, Edwards 64)*
Athletic Bilbao (1) 2 *(Aduriz 14, Williams 89)*   7870
Ostersund: (343) Keita; Mukiibi, Papagiannopoulos, Pettersson; Edwards, Nouri (Mensah 88), Bachirou, Widgren; Ghoddos, Gero, Sema.
Athletic Bilbao: (4231) Herrerin; Lekue, Etxeita, Laporte, Balenziaga (Boveda 46); Iturraspe, Vesga (Benat 77); Susaeta, Raul Garcia, Cordoba (Williams 66); Aduriz.

Zorya Luhansk (1) 2 *(da Silva 43, Svatok 79)*
Hertha Berlin (0) 1 *(Selke 56)*   9521
Zorya Luhansk: (4231) Lunin; Opanasenko, Pryyma (Svatok 23), Grechyshkin, Sukhotsky; Kharatin (Andriyevskiy 63), da Silva; Karavaev, Gordienko, Lunov (Gromov 80); Iury.
Hertha Berlin: (442) Jarstein; Pekarik, Stark, Rekik, Plattenhardt; Weiser, Lustenberger, Maier, Esswein (Kalou 59); Lazaro, Selke (Ibisevic 58).

Thursday, 2 November 2017
Athletic Bilbao (0) 1 *(Aduriz 70)*
Ostersund (0) 0   32,354
Athletic Bilbao: (4231) Herrerin; Lekue, Nunez■, Laporte, Balenziaga; San Jose (Susaeta 62), Iturraspe; Williams (Mikel Rico 72), Raul Garcia (Aketxe 87), Cordoba; Aduriz.
Ostersund: (433) Keita; Mukiibi, Papagiannopoulos, Pettersson, Widgren (Somi 80); Bachirou, Nouri (Aiesh 79); Edwards; Sema, Ghoddos, Gero (Hopcutt 74).

Hertha Berlin (1) 2 *(Selke 16, 73)*
Zorya Luhansk (0) 0   20,358
Hertha Berlin: (4231) Kraft; Pekarik, Stark, Torunarigha, Mittelstadt; Maier, Stocker; Esswein (Dardai 80), Duda (Skjelbred 75), Kalou (Haraguchi 58); Selke.
Zorya Luhansk: (4231) Lunin; Opanasenko, Svatok, Grechyshkin, Sukhotsky; Kharatin, Andriyevskiy; Karavaev, da Silva (Gordienko 56), Lunov (Gromov 60); Iury.

Thursday, 23 November 2017
Athletic Bilbao (1) 3 *(Aduriz 34 (pen), 66 (pen), Williams 83)*
Hertha Berlin (2) 2 *(Leckie 26, Selke 35)*   38,928
Athletic Bilbao: (4231) Herrerin; Lekue, Etxeita, Laporte, Balenziaga; San Jose (Iturraspe 46), Mikel Rico; Williams, Aketxe (Susaeta 46), Cordoba (Raul Garcia 80); Aduriz.
Hertha Berlin: (4231) Kraft; Weiser, Langkamp, Rekik, Plattenhardt; Lustenberger, Maier; Leckie (Esswein 73), Lazaro (Ibisevic 80), Mittelstadt; Selke.

Ostersund (1) 2 *(Grechyshkin 40 (og), Ghoddos 77)*
Zorya Luhansk (0) 0   7754
Ostersund: (433) Keita; Mukiibi, Papagiannopoulos, Pettersson, Somi (Widgren 90); Edwards, Nouri, Bachirou; Sema, Ghoddos, Gero (Mensah 85).

Zorya Luhansk: (4321) Lunin; Opanasenko, Svatok, Grechyshkin, Sukhotsky; Kharatin, Andriyevskiy (Babenko 61), Karavaev; Gordienko, Gromov (Lunov 47); Iury (da Silva 72).

Thursday, 7 December 2017
Hertha Berlin (0) 1 *(Pekarik 61)*
Ostersund (0) 1 *(Papagiannopoulos 58)*   14,686
Hertha Berlin: (4141) Klinsmann; Pekarik, Stark (Skjelbred 64), Torunarigha, Mittelstadt; Lustenberger; Dardai (Kade 76), Duda, Lazaro, Haraguchi (Weiser 80); Esswein.
Ostersund: (442) Keita; Mukiibi (Andersson 90), Papagiannopoulos, Pettersson, Somi (Hopcutt 77); Edwards, Nouri, Bachirou, Sema; Ghoddos, Gero (Widgren 46).

Zorya Luhansk (0) 0
Athletic Bilbao (0) 2 *(Aduriz 70, Raul Garcia 87)*   8428
Zorya Luhansk: (4231) Lunin; Gordienko, Kharatin, Svatok, Sukhotsky; Babenko (Kochergin 75), Andriyevskiy; Karavaev, Iury (da Silva 61), Lunov (Kabayev 46); Gromov.
Athletic Bilbao: (4231) Herrerin; Lekue, Nunez, Laporte, Balenziaga; San Jose, Mikel Rico; Williams (Cordoba 79), Raul Garcia (Aketxe 90), Susaeta; Aduriz (Merino 89).

Group J Table	P	W	D	L	F	A	GD	Pts
Athletic Bilbao	6	3	2	1	8	5	3	11
Ostersund	6	3	2	1	8	4	4	11
Zorya Luhansk	6	2	0	4	3	9	−6	6
Hertha Berlin	6	1	2	3	6	7	−1	5

GROUP K
Thursday, 14 September 2017
Vitesse (1) 2 *(Matavz 33, Linssen 58)*
Lazio (0) 3 *(Parolo 51, Immobile 67, Murgia 75)*   19,867
Vitesse: (433) Pasveer; Dabo (Colkett 83), Kashia, Miazga, Buttner; Bruns (Mount 88), Van der Werff, Foor; Rashica, Matavz (Castaignos 79), Linssen.
Lazio: (352) Strakosha; Bastos, de Vrij, Felipe (Immobile 46); Marusic, Di Gennaro (Milinkovic-Savic 62), Murgia, Parolo, Lukaku (Lulic 65); Luis Alberto, Caicedo.

Zulte Waregem (0) 1 *(Iseka 46)*
Nice (3) 5 *(Plea 16, 20, Dante 29, Saint-Maximin 69, Balotelli 74)*   9072
Zulte Waregem: (433) Leali; De Fauw, Derijck, Heylen, Hamalainen; de Sart, Kaya (Coopman 75), Doumbia; De Pauw (Kastanos 75), Iseka (Saponjic 84), Olayinka.
Nice: (433) Cardinale; Souquet, Le Marchand, Dante, Jallet; Lees-Melou, Seri (Tameze 77), Mendy (Srarfi 83); Saint-Maximin, Balotelli, Plea (Ganago 77).

Thursday, 28 September 2017
Lazio (1) 2 *(Caicedo 18, Immobile 90)*
Zulte Waregem (0) 0   300
Lazio: (352) Strakosha; Patric Gil, Felipe, Radu; Marusic, Parolo, Di Gennaro (Immobile 54), Murgia, Lukaku (Lulic 79); Luis Alberto, Milinkovic-Savic 54), Caicedo.
Zulte Waregem: (433) Leali; De Fauw, Baudry (Saponjic 85), Heylen, Hamalainen; Derijck, De Pauw (Olayinka 46), Doumbia; Coopman, Iseka, Kastanos (Kaya 46).

Nice (2) 3 *(Plea 16, 83, Saint-Maximin 45)*
Vitesse (0) 0   15,006
Nice: (433) Cardinale; Souquet, Le Marchand, Dante, Jallet; Koziello, Seri (Tameze 73), Lees-Melou; Saint-Maximin (Srarfi 80), Balotelli (Ganago 74), Plea.
Vitesse: (433) Pasveer; Dabo, Kashia, Miazga, Buttner (Faye 46); Bruns, Serero (Ali 79), Foor; Rashica, Matavz, Linssen (Mount 86).

Thursday, 19 October 2017
Nice (1) 1 *(Balotelli 4)*
Lazio (1) 3 *(Caicedo 5, Milinkovic-Savic 65, 89)*   21,386
Nice: (4231) Cardinale; Marlon, Dante, Le Marchand, Jallet (Srarfi 88); Mendy, Walter; Lees-Melou (Plea 71); Sneijder, Burner; Balotelli.

Lazio: (352) Strakosha; Bastos, Felipe, Radu; Patric Gil, Murgia, Di Gennaro (Luis Alberto 60), Milinkovic-Savic, Lulic; Caicedo (Lucas 75), Nani (Immobile 60).

Zulte Waregem (1) 1 *(Kashia 23 (og))*
Vitesse (1) 1 *(Bruns 27)*   9488
Zulte Waregem: (433) Bostyn; Walsh (De Fauw 68), Derijck, Heylen, Hamalainen; De Mets, Kaya (Saponjic 88), de Sart; Coopman, Iseka (De Pauw 54), Olayinka.
Vitesse: (433) Pasveer; Dabo, Kashia, Miazga, Buttner (Faye 82); Bruns (Colkett 77), Serero, Mount; Rashica, Castaignos, Linssen.

Thursday, 2 November 2017
Lazio (0) 1 *(Le Marchand 90 (og))*
Nice (0) 0   21,327
Lazio: (352) Strakosha; Patric Gil, de Vrij, Felipe; Marusic, Murgia (Lulic 60), Lucas, Luis Alberto, Lukaku (Parolo 74); Nani (Milinkovic-Savic 59), Caicedo.
Nice: (451) Benitez; Souquet, Dante, Le Marchand, Jallet; Walter, Mendy, Sneijder (Lusamba 66), Koziello (Tameze 86), Lees-Melou (Balotelli 80); Plea.

Vitesse (0) 0
Zulte Waregem (1) 2 *(Baudry 4, Kaya 70)*   17,986
Vitesse: (433) Pasveer; Dabo, Kashia (Foor 67), Miazga, Buttner[■]; Serero (Faye 58), Mount, Bruns; Rashica, Castaignos (Matavz 35), Linssen.
Zulte Waregem: (433) Bostyn; De Fauw (Heylen 87), Walsh, Baudry, Madu[■]; De Mets, De Pauw (Hamalainen 27), de Sart; Coopman, Olayinka, Kaya (Doumbia 77).

Thursday, 23 November 2017
Lazio (1) 1 *(Luis Alberto 42)*
Vitesse (1) 1 *(Linssen 13)*   8226
Lazio: (3511) Vargic; Patric Gil, Felipe, Bastos; Basta (Miceli 86), Murgia, Luis Alberto (Marusic 68), Crecco, Lukaku; Nani (Lulic 53); Palombi.
Vitesse: (433) Pasveer; Lelieveld (Dabo 81), Kashia, Miazga, Faye; Serero, Mount, Foor; Rashica (van Bergen 68), Matavz (Castaignos 62), Linssen.

Nice (2) 3 *(Balotelli 6 (pen), 31, Tameze 85)*
Zulte Waregem (0) 1 *(Hamalainen 81)*   20,274
Nice: (532) Benitez; Souquet, Burner (Lusamba 77), Dante, Le Marchand, Jallet; Koziello, Seri (Tameze 73), Lees-Melou; Balotelli (Marlon 84), Plea.
Zulte Waregem: (343) Bostyn; Baudry, De Fauw, Heylen; Walsh, Doumbia (Saponjic 78), Coopman, Hamalainen; De Pauw, Iseka, Kastanos (de Sart 46).

Thursday, 7 December 2017
Vitesse (0) 1 *(Castaignos 84)*
Nice (0) 0   17,564
Vitesse: (532) Pasveer; Lelieveld, Miazga, Kashia, Kotte, Faye; Bruns, Mount, Colkett (Foor 46); Matavz (Rashica 68), Castaignos.
Nice: (433) Cardinale; Coly, Sarr, Dante, Burner; Lusamba (Perraud 88), Koziello, Makengo; Cyprien, Srarfi (Walter 78), Plea (Diaby 65).

Zulte Waregem (1) 3 *(De Pauw 6, Heylen 60, Iseka 83)*
Lazio (0) 2 *(Caicedo 67, Lucas 76)*   8845
Zulte Waregem: (3412) Bostyn; Heylen, De Fauw, Baudry; Walsh (Saponjic 87), Doumbia (de Sart 46), Kaya, Madu (Hamalainen 46); Coopman; De Pauw, Iseka.
Lazio: (352) Vargic; Patric Gil, Felipe (Wallace Santos 65), Bastos; Basta, Murgia, Miceli (Lucas 55), Crecco (Felipe Anderson 55), Lukaku; Palombi, Caicedo.

Group K Table	P	W	D	L	F	A	GD	Pts
Lazio	6	4	1	1	12	7	5	13
Nice	6	3	0	3	12	7	5	9
Zulte Waregem	6	2	1	3	8	13	−5	7
Vitesse	6	1	2	3	5	10	−5	5

GROUP L

Thursday, 14 September 2017

Real Sociedad (3) 4 *(Llorente 10, 78, Zurutuza 10, Skjelvik 42 (og))*

Rosenborg (0) 0 21,479

Real Sociedad: (433) Rulli; Odriozola, Elustondo, Llorente, De la Bella; Prieto (Juanmi 58), Illarramendi, Zurutuza (Zubeldia 77); Vela, Willian Jose (Bautista 68), Canales.
Rosenborg: (433) Hansen; Hedenstadt, Reginiussen, Skjelvik, Meling; Jensen, Trondsen, Konradsen A (Lundemo 62); Adegbenro (Jevtovic 83), Bendtner, de Lanlay (Helland 74).

Vardar (0) 0

Zenit St Petersburg (3) 5 *(Kokorin 5, 21, Dzjuba 39, Ivanovic 66, Rigoni 89)* 11,118

Vardar: (4231) Gacevski; Hambardzumyan, Grncarov, Velkovski, Brdarovski (Glisic 44); Gligorov (Musliu 64); Nikolov; Jigauri, Felipe, Blazevski (Ytalo 70); Barseghyan.
Zenit St Petersburg: (433) Lunev; Criscito, Ivanovic (Terentjev 78), Mevlja (Zhirkov 82), Mammana; Kuzyaev, Kranevitter, Noboa; Kokorin (Rigoni 64), Dzjuba, Poloz.

Thursday, 28 September 2017

Rosenborg (1) 3 *(Bendtner 25 (pen), Konradsen A 55, Hedenstadt 68)*

Vardar (0) 1 *(Felipe 90)* 16,038

Rosenborg: (433) Hansen; Hedenstadt, Reginiussen, Skjelvik, Meling; Jensen, Lundemo (Rasmussen 85), Konradsen A (Trondsen 77); de Lanlay (Jevtovic 77), Bendtner, Adegbenro.
Vardar: (4231) Gacevski; Hambardzumyan (Markovic 84), Grncarov, Musliu, Demiri; Gligorov, Nikolov (Iseni 75); Jigauri, Felipe, Blazevski; Barseghyan (Stojchevski 75).

Zenit St Petersburg (2) 3 *(Rigoni 5, Kokorin 24, 60)*

Real Sociedad (1) 1 *(Llorente 41)* 50,487

Zenit St Petersburg: (433) Lunev; Criscito, Ivanovic, Mevlja, Mammana; Kranevitter, Kuzyaev, Paredes (Dzjuba 88); Rigoni (Erokhin 74), Driussi (Poloz 80), Kokorin.
Real Sociedad: (433) Rulli; Odriozola, Elustondo, Llorente, De la Bella; Prieto (Juanmi 64), Pardo (Illarramendi 74), Zurutuza; Canales, Bautista (Willian Jose 62), Januzaj.

Thursday, 19 October 2017

Vardar (0) 0

Real Sociedad (3) 6 *(Oyarzabal 12, Willian Jose 34, 42, 54, 58, De la Bella 90)* 20,368

Vardar: (4312) Gacevski; Hambardzumyan, Grncarov, Novak, Glisic (Demiri 72); Gligorov, Nikolov (Blazevski 46), Jigauri; Felipe; Barseghyan, Ytalo (Markovic 63).
Real Sociedad: (433) Rulli; Gorosabel, Elustondo, Llorente, De la Bella; Prieto, Zubeldia, Illarramendi (Pardo 63); Canales, Willian Jose (Bautista 60), Oyarzabal (Januzaj 56).

Zenit St Petersburg (1) 3 *(Rigoni 2, 69, 75)*

Rosenborg (0) 1 *(Meling 88)* 46,211

Zenit St Petersburg: (433) Lunev; Ivanovic, Mammana, Criscito, Mevlja; Kuzyaev, Kranevitter, Paredes (Noboa 84); Driussi (Erokhin 62), Rigoni, Kokorin (Poloz 86).
Rosenborg: (433) Hansen; Hedenstadt (Gersbach 82), Reginiussen, Bjordal, Rasmussen; Jensen, Trondsen (Lundemo 80), Konradsen A; Adegbenro (Helland 80), Bendtner, Meling.

Thursday, 2 November 2017

Real Sociedad (1) 3 *(Juanmi 31, De la Bella 69, Bautista 82)*

Vardar (0) 0 17,242

Real Sociedad: (433) Rulli; Gorosabel, Raul Navas, Martinez, De la Bella; Zurutuza (Illarramendi 46), Zubeldia, Canales; Juanmi, Willian Jose (Bautista 62), Oyarzabal (Januzaj 71).
Vardar: (433) Gacevski; Hambardzumyan, Novak, Grncarov, Glisic (Velkovski 63); Markovic (Musliu 63), Felipe, Nikolov; Jigauri, Ytalo, Barseghyan (Blazevski 75).

Rosenborg (0) 1 *(Bendtner 56 (pen))*

Zenit St Petersburg (0) 1 *(Kokorin 90)* 18,597

Rosenborg: (433) Hansen; Konradsen M (Gersbach 87), Reginiussen, Skjelvik, Meling; Jensen, Rasmussen, Trondsen; Helland (Jevtovic 72), Bendtner, Adegbenro (Bjordal 88).
Zenit St Petersburg: (433) Lunev; Mammana, Smolnikov, Mevlja, Criscito; Shatov (Driussi 75), Noboa (Dzjuba 88), Paredes; Erokhin (Kranevitter 83), Rigoni, Kokorin.

Thursday, 23 November 2017

Rosenborg (0) 0

Real Sociedad (0) 1 *(Oyarzabal 90)* 18,307

Rosenborg: (433) Hansen; Hedenstadt, Bjordal (Gersbach 87), Reginiussen, Meling; Jensen, Rasmussen (Skjelvik 78), Trondsen; Levi (Jevtovic 64), Bendtner, Adegbenro.
Real Sociedad: (433) Rulli; Odriozola, Raul Navas, Martinez, De la Bella; Prieto, Illarramendi, Canales (Zubeldia 84); Juanmi (Vela 61), Willian Jose (Bautista 74), Oyarzabal.

Zenit St Petersburg (2) 2 *(Poloz 16, Rigoni 43)*

Vardar (0) 1 *(Blazevski 90)* 38,196

Zenit St Petersburg: (433) Lodygin; Terentjev, Mevlja, Mammana (Karpov 87), Zhirkov; Noboa, Shatov (Driussi 46), Erokhin; Poloz, Dzjuba (Kranevitter 73), Rigoni.
Vardar: (4231) Gacevski; Hambardzumyan, Grncarov, Novak, Demiri; Markovic, Nikolov; Barseghyan (Stojchevski 85), Felipe, Jigauri (Petkovski 90); Ytalo (Blazevski 79).

Thursday, 7 December 2017

Real Sociedad (0) 1 *(Willian Jose 58)*

Zenit St Petersburg (1) 3 *(Erokhin 36, Ivanovic 65, Paredes 85)* 20,609

Real Sociedad: (433) Rulli; Odriozola, Llorente, Martinez, Rodrigues (De la Bella 61); Prieto, Illarramendi, Zurutuza (Canales 68); Januzaj, Willian Jose, Oyarzabal (Juanmi 59).
Zenit St Petersburg: (433) Lodygin; Mevlja, Smolnikov (Zhirkov 64), Criscito, Erokhin; Ivanovic, Poloz (Paredes 76), Kranevitter; Kokorin, Rigoni, Noboa (Kuzyaev 64).

Vardar (1) 1 *(Ytalo 10)*

Rosenborg (0) 1 *(Bendtner 45 (pen))* 7839

Vardar: (4231) Gacevski; Musliu, Grncarov, Novak, Demiri; Gligorov, Nikolov (Markovic 80); Barseghyan, Felipe, Blazevski (Jigauri 84); Ytalo.
Rosenborg: (433) Hansen; Hedenstadt, Reginiussen, Skjelvik, Gersbach (Levi 90); Konradsen M (de Lanlay 71), Rasmussen, Trondsen; Adegbenro (Botheim 90), Bendtner, Meling.

Group L Table	P	W	D	L	F	A	GD	Pts
Zenit St Petersburg	6	5	1	0	17	5	12	16
Real Sociedad	6	4	0	2	16	6	10	12
Rosenborg	6	1	2	3	6	11	–5	5
Vardar	6	0	1	5	3	20	–17	1

KNOCK-OUT STAGE

ROUND OF 32 FIRST LEG
Tuesday, 13 February 2018
Crvena Zvezda (0) 0
CSKA Moscow (0) 0 35,642
Crvena Zvezda: (4231) Borjan; Stojkovic, Savic, Le Tallec, Rodic; Donald, Jovicic; Nabouhane, Krsticic, Radonjic (Srnic 78); Pesic (Racic 85).
CSKA Moscow: (532) Akinfeev; Fernandes, Vasin, Berezutski V, Wernbloom, Kuchaev; Dzagoev, Natcho, Golovin; Vitinho (Chalov 84), Musa.

Thursday, 15 February 2018
AEK Athens (0) 1 *(Ajdarevic 80)*
Dynamo Kyiv (1) 1 *(Tsygankov 20)* 30,518
AEK Athens: (4411) Barkas; Rodrigo Galo, Vranjes, Lampropoulos, Bakakis; Bakasetas, Andre Simoes, Galanopoulos (Ajdarevic 80), Klonaridis (Christodoulopoulos 51); Livaja; Giakoumakis (Araujo 58).
Dynamo Kyiv: (4231) Boyko; Kedziora, Khacheridi, Kadar, Morozyuk; Shepelev, Buyalsky; Tsygankov, Garmash (Besyedin 78), Gonzalez; Junior Moraes (Shaparenko 90).

Astana (1) 1 *(Tomasov 7)*
Sporting Lisbon (0) 3 *(Bruno Fernandes 48 (pen), Gelson Martins 50, Doumbia 56)* 29,737
Astana: (4141) Eric; Shitov, Logvinenko■, Anicic, Shomko; Beysebekov; Twumasi, Maevskiy, Kleinheisler (Stanojevic 57), Tomasov (Murtazayev 86); Despotovic (Maliy 65).
Sporting Lisbon: (4231) Rui Patricio; Piccini, Coates, Andre Pinto, Fabio Coentrao (Battaglia 57); Acuna, William Carvalho; Ruiz, Bruno Fernandes, Gelson Martins (Ruben Ribeiro 84); Doumbia (Montero 61).

Borussia Dortmund (1) 3 *(Schurrle 30, Batshuayi 65, 90)*
Atalanta (0) 2 *(Ilicic 51, 56)* 62,500
Borussia Dortmund: (4231) Burki; Piszczek, Toprak, Papastathopoulos, Toljan; Castro, Weigl (Dahoud 80); Pulisic (Isak 85), Reus (Gotze 62), Schurrle; Batshuayi.
Atalanta: (352) Berisha; Toloi, Caldara (Palomino 85), Masiello; Hateboer, Cristante, de Roon, Freuler, Spinazzola; Ilicic (Petagna 88), Gomez (Gosens 76).

Celtic (0) 1 *(McGregor 78)*
Zenit St Petersburg (0) 0 56,743
Celtic: (4231) De Vries; Lustig, Ajer, Simunovic, Tierney; Brown, Ntcham; Forrest, McGregor, Eboue (Musonda 73); Dembele (Edouard 84).
Zenit St Petersburg: (433) Lunev; Mevlja, Criscito, Mammana, Smolnikov; Erokhin, Kuzyaev (Kranevitter 62); Paredes; Rigoni (Driussi 62), Kokorin, Zabolotny.

FC Copenhagen (1) 1 *(Fischer 15)*
Atletico Madrid (2) 4 *(Saul 21, Gameiro 37, Griezmann 71, Vitolo 77)* 34,912
FC Copenhagen: (442) Olsen; Ankersen, Vavro, Luftner, Boilesen; Skov (Bengtsson 73), Gregus, Kvist, Jensen (Santander 61); Fischer (Pavlovic 72), Sotiriou.
Atletico Madrid: (442) Moya; Juanfran, Godin, Gimenez, Lucas; Correa (Carrasco 59), Thomas, Saul, Koke (Gabi 80); Gameiro (Vitolo 69), Griezmann.

Ludogorets Razgrad (0) 0
AC Milan (1) 3 *(Cutrone 45, Rodriguez 64 (pen), Borini 90)* 7887
Ludogorets Razgrad: (4231) Renan; Cicinho, Moti, Plastun, Sasha; Abel, Dyakov; Misidjan, Marcelinho (Campanharo 78), Lukoki (Kovachev 81); Swierczok (Wanderson 46).
AC Milan: (433) Donnarumma G; Abate (Rodriguez 60), Bonucci, Romagnoli, Calabria; Kessie, Biglia, Bonaventura; Suso, Cutrone (Andre Silva 65), Calhanoglu (Borini 75).

Lyon (0) 3 *(Ndombele 46, Fekir 50, Depay 82)*
Villarreal (0) 1 *(Fornals 63)* 46,846
Lyon: (4231) Lopes; Da Silva (Mendy 84), Marcelo, Morel, Marcal; Ndombele, Tousart; Traore (Cornet 77), Fekir, Aouar (Depay 73); Mariano.
Villarreal: (4312) Sergio Asenjo; Mario, Alvaro, Victor Ruiz, Jaume; Castillejo (Unal 54), Rodri, Trigueros; Fornals (Raba 89); Bacca, Cheryshev (Soriano 74).

Marseille (1) 3 *(Germain 4, 69, Thauvin 74)*
Braga (0) 0 21,731
Marseille: (433) Pele; Sarr, Rami, Rolando, Amavi (Sakai 58); Lopez, Gustavo, Payet (Zambo 78); N'Jie, Germain (Thauvin 70), Ocampos.
Braga: (433) Matheus Magalhaes; Diogo Figueiras, Bruno Viana, Rosic, Nuno Sequeira; Ricardo Esgaio, Danilo Barbosa, Vukcevic; Dyego Sousa (Hassan 75), Paulinho (Wilson Eduardo 61), Teixeira (Andre Horta 73).

Napoli (0) 1 *(Ounas 54)*
RB Leipzig (0) 3 *(Werner 61, 90, Bruma 74)* 14,554
Napoli: (433) Reina; Maggio, Tonelli, Koulibaly, Hysaj (Rui 54); Rog, Diawara, Hamsik (Insigne 54); Ounas (Allan 60), Callejon, Zielinski.
RB Leipzig: (442) Gulacsi; Laimer, Orban, Upamecano, Klostermann; Sabitzer, Kampl, Keita (Demme 86), Bruma (Forsberg 79); Poulsen (Augustin 82), Werner.

Nice (2) 2 *(Balotelli 4, 28 (pen))*
Lokomotiv Moscow (1) 3 *(Fernandes 45 (pen), 69, 79)* 16,918
Nice: (442) Benitez; Sarr, Marlon (Burner 45), Dante, Coly■; Cyprien (Mendy 82), Seri, Lees-Melou, Saint-Maximin; Plea (Tameze 71), Balotelli.
Lokomotiv Moscow: (442) Guilherme; Ignatiev, Kvirkvelia, Pejcinovic, Denisov V (Rybus 46); Anton Miranchuk, Denisov I, Kolomeytsev (Farfan 46), Fernandes; Ari (Eder 71), Aleksey Miranchuk.

Ostersund (0) 0
Arsenal (2) 3 *(Monreal 14, Papagiannopoulos 24 (og), Ozil 58)* 7665
Ostersund: (433) Keita; Mukiibi, Papagiannopoulos, Pettersson, Widgren (Bergqvist 73); Edwards, Nouri (Tekie 46), Mensah; Sema, Ghoddos, Gero (Hopcutt 46).
Arsenal: (4411) Ospina; Bellerin, Chambers, Mustafi, Monreal (Kolasinac 73); Iwobi, Elneny, Maitland-Niles, Mkhitaryan (Nelson 84); Ozil; Welbeck (Nketiah 82).

Partizan Belgrade (0) 1 *(Tawamba 58)*
Viktoria Plzen (0) 1 *(Reznik 81)* 17,165
Partizan Belgrade: (442) Stojkovic; Vulicevic, Nemanja R. Miletic, Mitrovic■, Urosevic; Jankovic, Pantic, Jevtovic, Tosic; Soumah (Ivanovic 71), Tawamba (Markovic 90).
Viktoria Plzen: (4231) Hruska; Reznik, Hejda, Hubnik, Limbersky; Horava, Hrosovsky; Petrzela (Zeman 60), Kolar (Cermak 78), Kopic; Krmencik (Chory 90).

Real Sociedad (0) 2 *(Odriozola 57, Januzaj 80)*
Red Bull Salzburg (1) 2 *(Oyarzabal 28 (og), Minamino 90)* 19,790
Real Sociedad: (442) Rulli; Odriozola, Llorente, Moreno (Elustondo 76), Rodrigues; Prieto, Illarramendi, Zubeldia, Oyarzabal; Juanmi (Januzaj 46), Bautista (Agirretxe 68).
Red Bull Salzburg: (442) Walke; Lainer, Ramalho (Pongracic 71), Caleta-Car, Ulmer; Yabo (Minamino 76), Schlager, Samassekou, Haidara; Hwang (Gulbrandsen 46), Dabbur.

Spartak Moscow (0) 1 *(Luiz Adriano 60)*
Athletic Bilbao (3) 3 *(Aduriz 22, 39, Kutepov 45 (og))*
43,145
Spartak Moscow: (4231) Rebrov; Eshchenko, Tasci, Kutepov, Kombarov; Fernando, Glushakov (Hanni 75); Zobnin, Melgarejo (Ze Luis 59), Promes; Luiz Adriano.
Athletic Bilbao: (4231) Herrerin; De Marcos, Yeray, Etxeita, Lekue; Iturraspe, Mikel Rico; Susaeta (San Jose 72), Raul Garcia, Williams (Merino 83); Aduriz.

Steaua Bucharest (1) 1 *(Gnohere 28)*
Lazio (0) 0
33,455
Steaua Bucharest: (4231) Vlad D; Benzar R, Gaman, Planic, Junior Morais; Pintilii (Teixeira 46), Nedelcu; Man, Budescu, Tanase F (Coman 58); Gnohere (Tanase C 81).
Lazio: (352) Strakosha; Bastos, Felipe, Caceres; Basta, Milinkovic-Savic, Lucas, Murgia, Lukaku (Lulic 75); Nani (Felipe Anderson 56), Caicedo (Immobile 56).

ROUND OF 32 SECOND LEG
Wednesday, 21 February 2018
CSKA Moscow (1) 1 *(Dzagoev 45)*
Crvena Zvezda (0) 0
18,753
CSKA Moscow: (352) Akinfeev; Berezutski V, Ignashevich, Vasin (Nababkin 26); Fernandes, Dzagoev, Natcho, Vitinho (Milanov 77), Kuchaev; Musa, Wernbloom.
Crvena Zvezda: (4231) Borjan; Stojkovic, Le Tallec, Savic, Rodic; Jovicic (Racic 88), Donald (Srnic 78); Nabouhane, Krsticic, Radonjic (Hadzic 88); Pesic.

Thursday, 22 February 2018
AC Milan (1) 1 *(Borini 20)*
Ludogorets Razgrad (0) 0
17,453
AC Milan: (433) Donnarumma A; Abate, Zapata, Romagnoli (Bonucci 74), Rodriguez; Locatelli, Montolivo, Kessie (Mauri 56); Borini, Cutrone (Kalinic 56), Andre Silva.
Ludogorets Razgrad: (4411) Broun; Natanael, Moti, Terziev, Cicinho; Wanderson, Goralski, Abel (Dyakov 82), Misidjan (Lukoki 71); Marcelinho (Campanharo 63); Swierczok.

Arsenal (0) 1 *(Kolasinac 47)*
Ostersund (2) 2 *(Aiesh 22, Sema 24)*
58,405
Arsenal: (4411) Ospina; Bellerin, Chambers, Holding, Kolasinac; Mkhitaryan, Elneny, Maitland-Niles (Xhaka 46), Iwobi (Nelson 90); Wilshere (Willock 76); Welbeck.
Ostersund: (442) Keita; Mukiibi (Islamovic 72), Papagiannopoulos, Pettersson, Widgren; Aiesh (Tekie 52), Edwards, Nouri, Sema; Hopcutt (Arhin 81), Ghoddos.

Atalanta (1) 1 *(Toloi 11)*
Borussia Dortmund (0) 1 *(Schmelzer 83)*
17,492
Atalanta: (352) Berisha; Toloi (Cornelius 88), Caldara, Masiello; Hateboer, Cristante, de Roon (Petagna 87), Freuler, Spinazzola; Ilicic, Gomez.
Borussia Dortmund: (4411) Burki; Toljan (Schmelzer 46), Toprak, Papastathopoulos, Piszczek; Pulisic (Reus 59), Dahoud (Isak 82), Sahin, Schurrle; Gotze; Batshuayi.

Athletic Bilbao (0) 1 *(Etxeita 57)*
Spartak Moscow (1) 2 *(Luiz Adriano 44, Melgarejo 86)*
36,873
Athletic Bilbao: (4231) Herrerin; Lekue, Yeray, Etxeita, Saborit; Iturraspe, Mikel Rico (San Jose 54); De Marcos, Raul Garcia (Aduriz 83), Susaeta; Williams (Cordoba 90).
Spartak Moscow: (4231) Selikhov; Eshchenko, Tasci (Kutepov 10), Bocchetti, Kombarov; Pasalic (Melgarejo 74), Glushakov; Zobnin, Hanni (Ze Luis 60), Promes; Luiz Adriano.

Atletico Madrid (1) 1 *(Gameiro 7)*
FC Copenhagen (0) 0
44,035
Atletico Madrid: (442) Oblak; Godin, Koke (Saul 46), Torres, Correa (Gaitan 60); Gabi, Juanfran, Gameiro (Thomas 68), Vitolo; Gimenez, Sergi.

FC Copenhagen: (442) Andersen; Ankersen, Vavro, Luftner, Bengtsson; Thomsen, Gregus, Kvist (Skov 46); Fischer (Jensen 46); Sotiriou (Wind 80), Pavlovic.

Braga (1) 1 *(Ricardo Horta 31)*
Marseille (0) 0
9016
Braga: (433) Matheus Magalhaes; Marcelo Goiano (Fabio Martins 73), Bruno Viana, Raul Silva, Jefferson; Ricardo Esgaio, Andre Horta, Vukcevic; Wilson Eduardo, Hassan (Paulinho 54), Ricardo Horta (Xadas 73).
Marseille: (433) Pele; Sarr, Rami, Rolando, Sakai; Lopez, Gustavo, Sanson (Payet 83); N'Jie (Zambo 46), Germain (Thauvin 72), Ocampos.

Dynamo Kyiv (0) 0
AEK Athens (0) 0
27,024
Dynamo Kyiv: (4231) Boyko; Kedziora, Khacheridi, Kadar, Morozyuk; Buyalsky, Shepelev (Besyedin 76); Gonzalez, Garmash, Tsygankov; Junior Moraes (Shaparenko 90).
AEK Athens: (4231) Barkas; Bakakis, Lampropoulos, Chygrynskiy, Rodrigo Galo; Galanopoulos (Ajdarevic 81), Andre Simoes; Christodoulopoulos (Giakoumakis 74), Shojaei, Bakasetas (Klonaridis 70); Araujo.
Dynamo Kiev won on away goals.

Lazio (3) 5 *(Immobile 8, 43, 71, Bastos 36, Felipe Anderson 51)*
Steaua Bucharest (0) 1 *(Gnohere 82)*
27,597
Lazio: (352) Strakosha; Patric Gil, de Vrij, Caceres (Bastos 26); Basta, Parolo, Lucas, Luis Alberto (Murgia 68), Lulic; Felipe Anderson (Caicedo 75), Immobile.
Steaua Bucharest: (4231) Vlad D; Benzar R, Gaman (Balasa 61), Planic, Junior Morais; Nedelcu (Filip 46), Teixeira; Man, Budescu, Tanase F (Coman 46); Gnohere.

Lokomotiv Moscow (1) 1 *(Denisov I 30)*
Nice (0) 0
18,104
Lokomotiv Moscow: (433) Guilherme; Ignatiev, Kvirkvelia, Pejcinovic, Rybus; Anton Miranchuk, Denisov I, Fernandes; Farfan (Kolomeytsev 24), Ari (Eder 64), Aleksey Miranchuk (Tarasov 84).
Nice: (433) Benitez; Burner, Sarr, Dante, Perraud; Cyprien, Seri (Sacko 84), Lees-Melou; Saint-Maximin (Tameze 78), Balotelli, Plea (Makengo 78).

RB Leipzig (0) 0
Napoli (0) 2 *(Zielinski 33, Insigne 86)*
36,163
RB Leipzig: (442) Gulacsi; Laimer, Konate, Upamecano, Bernardo; Sabitzer, Demme, Kampl, Bruma (Forsberg 73); Poulsen (Ilsanker 90), Werner (Augustin 85).
Napoli: (433) Reina; Maggio, Albiol, Tonelli, Rui (Hysaj 68); Allan, Diawara (Jorginho 82), Hamsik (Callejon 65); Zielinski, Mertens, Insigne.
RB Leipzig won on away goals.

Red Bull Salzburg (1) 2 *(Dabbur 11, Berisha V 74 (pen))*
Real Sociedad (1) 1 *(Raul Navas 28)*
13,912
Red Bull Salzburg: (442) Walke; Lainer, Ramalho, Onguene, Ulmer; Yabo (Berisha V 62), Schlager, Samassekou, Haidara; Hwang (Gulbrandsen 90), Dabbur.
Real Sociedad: (4231) Rulli (Ramirez 76); Odriozola, Elustondo, Raul Navas■, De la Bella (Llorente 46); Illarramendi, Zurutuza; Januzaj, Canales, Oyarzabal; Agirretxe (Bautista 70).

Sporting Lisbon (1) 3 *(Dost 3, Bruno Fernandes 54, 63)*
Astana (1) 3 *(Tomasov 38, Twumasi 80, Shomko 90)*
30,456
Sporting Lisbon: (4141) Rui Patricio; Ristovski, Andre Pinto, Mathieu, Fabio Coentrao; Ruiz (William Carvalho 60); Battaglia, Joao Palhinha (Leao 74), Bruno Fernandes, Ruben Ribeiro (Acuna 46); Dost.
Astana: (4141) Eric; Shitov, Postnikov, Anicic, Shomko; Beysebekov; Twumasi (Murtazayev 87), Maevskiy, Kleinheisler (Stanojevic 60), Tomasov; Despotovic (Shchetkin 66).

Viktoria Plzen (0) 2 *(Krmencik 67, Cermak 90)*
Partizan Belgrade (0) 0   10,180
Viktoria Plzen: (4231) Hruska; Reznik, Hejda, Hubnik, Limbersky; Horava, Hrosovsky; Kopic, Kolar (Cermak 86), Zeman (Petrzela 71); Krmencik (Chory 83).
Partizan Belgrade: (4231) Stojkovic; Vulicevic, Nemanja R. Miletic, Ostojic, Urosevic; Jevtovic (Ozegovic 65), Zdjelar; Jankovic (Soumah 78), Pantic, Tosic; Tawamba.

Villarreal (0) 0
Lyon (0) 1 *(Traore 85)*   17,028
Villarreal: (41212) Sergio Asenjo; Mario, Alvaro, Bonera, Jaume■; Javi Fuego (Raba 74); Rodri, Trigueros (Cheryshev 57); Fornals (Castillejo 46); Bacca, Unal.
Lyon: (433) Lopes; Da Silva, Marcelo, Morel, Mendy; Tousart, Ndombele (Aouar 77), Fekir (Maolida 87); Traore, Mariano (Ferri 82), Depay.

Zenit St Petersburg (2) 3 *(Ivanovic 8, Kuzyaev 27, Kokorin 61)*
Celtic (0) 0   50,492
Zenit St Petersburg: (433) Lunev; Ivanovic (Smolnikov 87), Mammana, Criscito, Mevlja; Kranevitter, Rigoni (Driussi 84), Paredes; Kuzyaev, Kokorin, Zabolotny (Erokhin 75).
Celtic: (4411) De Vries; Tierney, Ajer, Simunovic, Lustig; Ntcham, Brown, Eboue (Rogic 46); McGregor (Sinclair 62); Forrest (Musonda 71); Dembele.

ROUND OF 16 FIRST LEG
Thursday, 8 March 2018

AC Milan (0) 0
Arsenal (2) 2 *(Mkhitaryan 15, Ramsey 45)*   72,821
AC Milan: (433) Donnarumma G; Calabria (Borini 79), Bonucci, Romagnoli, Rodriguez; Kessie, Biglia, Bonaventura; Suso, Cutrone (Andre Silva 68), Calhanoglu (Kalinic 62).
Arsenal: (4321) Ospina; Chambers (Elneny 85), Mustafi, Koscielny, Kolasinac (Maitland-Niles 62); Ramsey, Xhaka, Wilshere; Mkhitaryan, Ozil (Holding 79); Welbeck.

Atletico Madrid (1) 3 *(Saul 22, Costa 47, Koke 90)*
Lokomotiv Moscow (0) 0   40,767
Atletico Madrid: (442) Werner; Juanfran, Gimenez, Lucas, Filipe Luis; Correa (Torres 74), Thomas, Saul, Koke; Costa (Gameiro 74), Griezmann (Vitolo 67).
Lokomotiv Moscow: (442) Guilherme; Ignatiev (Lysov 53), Kvirkvelia, Corluka, Rybus; Anton Miranchuk (Kolomeytsev 71), Denisov I, Pejcinovic, Fernandes; Aleksey Miranchuk, Eder.

Borussia Dortmund (0) 1 *(Schurrle 62)*
Red Bull Salzburg (0) 2 *(Berisha V 49 (pen), 56)*   53,700
Borussia Dortmund: (4411) Burki; Castro, Papastathopoulos, Toprak, Schmelzer; Reus, Dahoud, Weigl, Schurrle; Gotze (Pulisic 61); Batshuayi (Philipp 61).
Red Bull Salzburg: (442) Walke; Lainer, Ramalho, Caleta-Car, Ulmer; Haidara (Yabo 90), Samassekou, Schlager (Minamino 73); Berisha V; Hwang (Gulbrandsen 68), Dabbur.

CSKA Moscow (0) 0
Lyon (0) 1 *(Marcelo 67)*   13,990
CSKA Moscow: (352) Akinfeev; Berezutski A, Wernbloom, Ignashevich; Nababkin, Natcho, Dzagoev (Bistrovic 82), Golovin, Kuchaev; Musa (Chalov 87), Milanov (Vitinho 73).
Lyon: (433) Lopes; Tete, Marcelo, Morel, Marcal; Ndombele, Tousart, Aouar; Traore (Cornet 76), Mariano (Mendy 89), Depay (Maolida 85).

Lazio (0) 2 *(Immobile 54, Felipe Anderson 62)*
Dynamo Kyiv (0) 2 *(Tsygankov 52, Junior Moraes 79)*   21,562
Lazio: (352) Strakosha; Wallace Santos (Nani 85), de Vrij, Radu; Basta (Patric Gil 74), Murgia (Parolo 74), Lucas, Milinkovic-Savic, Lukaku; Felipe Anderson, Immobile.

Dynamo Kyiv: (4231) Boyko; Kediziora, Burda, Kadar, Pivaric; Shaparenko (Junior Moraes 67), Buyalsky; Tsygankov, Garmash■, Morozyuk; Besyedin.

Marseille (2) 3 *(Ocampos 1, 58, Payet 14)*
Athletic Bilbao (1) 1 *(Aduriz 45 (pen))*   37,657
Marseille: (442) Mandanda; Sakai, Rami, Rolando, Amavi; Thauvin (N'Jie 62), Lopez (Sarr 86), Gustavo, Payet; Germain (Zambo 71), Ocampos.
Athletic Bilbao: (4231) Herrerin; De Marcos, Yeray, Etxeita, Balenziaga (Lekue 68); San Jose, Benat; Williams, Raul Garcia (Vesga 78), Susaeta (Cordoba 61); Aduriz.

RB Leipzig (0) 2 *(Bruma 56, Werner 77)*
Zenit St Petersburg (0) 1 *(Criscito 86)*   19,877
RB Leipzig: (442) Gulacsi; Laimer (Bernardo 46), Orban, Upamecano, Klostermann; Forsberg, Demme, Keita, Bruma (Sabitzer 74); Augustin (Poulsen 79), Werner.
Zenit St Petersburg: (433) Lunev; Ivanovic, Mammana, Criscito, Mevlja; Erokhin, Kuzyaev, Kranevitter; Zabolotny (Driussi 57), Rigoni (Poloz 80), Kokorin.

Sporting Lisbon (1) 2 *(Montero 45, 49)*
Viktoria Plzen (0) 0   26,090
Sporting Lisbon: (4411) Rui Patricio; Ristovski, Coates, Mathieu, Fabio Coentrao (Ruben Ribeiro 85); Gelson Martins, William Carvalho, Bruno Fernandes, Acuna (Battaglia 57); Ruiz (Bruno Cesar 79); Montero.
Viktoria Plzen: (4231) Hruska; Reznik, Hejda, Hubnik, Limbersky; Horava, Hrosovsky; Petrzela (Chory 62), Kolar (Kovarik 75), Zeman (Cermak 82); Krmencik.

ROUND OF 16 SECOND LEG
Thursday, 15 March 2018

Arsenal (1) 3 *(Welbeck 39 (pen), 87, Xhaka 71)*
AC Milan (1) 1 *(Calhanoglu 35)*   58,973
Arsenal: (4411) Ospina; Bellerin, Mustafi, Koscielny (Chambers 11), Monreal; Ozil, Ramsey, Xhaka, Mkhitaryan (Elneny 69); Wilshere; Welbeck.
AC Milan: (433) Donnarumma G; Borini, Bonucci, Romagnoli, Rodriguez; Kessie (Locatelli 79), Calhanoglu (Bonaventura 70), Montolivo; Suso, Cutrone (Kalinic 67), Andre Silva.

Athletic Bilbao (0) 1 *(Williams 74)*
Marseille (1) 2 *(Payet 38 (pen), Ocampos 52)*   40,586
Athletic Bilbao: (4231) Herrerin; De Marcos, Yeray (Nunez 44), Etxeita, Lekue; Iturraspe, Benat (Vesga 80); Williams, Mikel Rico (Susaeta 23), Cordoba; Aduriz■.
Marseille: (442) Mandanda; Sakai, Rami, Rolando, Amavi; Thauvin (Sarr 66), Lopez (Sanson 77), Gustavo (Zambo 55), Ocampos; Payet, Mitroglou.

Dynamo Kyiv (0) 0
Lazio (1) 2 *(Lucas 23, de Vrij 83)*   52,639
Dynamo Kyiv: (4231) Boyko; Kediziora, Burda, Kadar (Shabanov 45), Pivaric; Shepelev, Buyalsky; Morozyuk (Gonzalez 57), Junior Moraes, Tsygankov; Besyedin (Mbokani 70).
Lazio: (352) Strakosha; Felipe, de Vrij, Radu; Patric Gil (Marusic 72), Parolo, Lucas, Luis Alberto, Lulic (Lukaku 68); Felipe Anderson, Immobile (Caicedo 82).

Lokomotiv Moscow (1) 1 *(Rybus 20)*
Atletico Madrid (1) 5 *(Correa 16, Saul 47, Torres 65 (pen), 70, Griezmann 85)*   22,041
Lokomotiv Moscow: (451) Kochenkov; Rybus, Kvirkvelia, Corluka (Pejcinovic 75), Lysov; Fernandes, Anton Miranchuk, Denisov I, Kolomeytsev (Tarasov 63), Aleksey Miranchuk; Farfan (Eder 46).
Atletico Madrid: (442) Werner; Juanfran (Vrsaljko 46), Godin, Gimenez, Filipe Luis (Lucas 62); Saul (Griezmann 61), Thomas, Gabi, Koke; Torres, Correa.

Lyon (0) 2 *(Cornet 58, Mariano 71)*
CSKA Moscow (1) 3 *(Golovin 39, Musa 61,*
Wernbloom 65) 38,622
Lyon: (433) Lopes; Tete, Marcelo, Diakhaby, Marcal
(Mendy 70); Ferri (Maolida 68), Tousart, Ndombele;
Cornet, Mariano, Depay (Traore 66).
CSKA Moscow: (532) Akinfeev; Nababkin, Berezutski
A, Berezutski V (Schennikov 46), Ignashevich, Kuchaev;
Dzagoev (Gordyushenko 90), Natcho, Golovin; Musa
(Vitinho 72), Wernbloom.
CSKA Moscow won on away goals.

Red Bull Salzburg (0) 0
Borussia Dortmund (0) 0 29,520
Red Bull Salzburg: (442) Walke; Lainer, Ramalho,
Caleta-Car, Ulmer; Haidara (Yabo 82), Schlager (Wolf
79), Samassekou, Berisha V; Hwang (Gulbrandsen 66),
Dabbur.
Borussia Dortmund: (4231) Burki; Piszczek, Zagadou,
Papastathopoulos, Schmelzer; Dahoud, Castro
(Guerreiro 62); Schurrle, Reus (Isak 46), Gotze (Philipp
46); Batshuayi.

Viktoria Plzen (1) 2 *(Bakos 7, 65)*
Sporting Lisbon (0) 1 *(Battaglia 105)* 9370
Viktoria Plzen: (4231) Hruska; Havel, Reznik, Hajek,
Kovarik; Horava, Hrosovsky; Zeman (Petrzela 100),
Kolar, Kopic; Bakos (Krmencik 83).
Sporting Lisbon: (4411) Rui Patricio; Petrovic (Piccini
67), Andre Pinto, Mathieu, Fabio Coentrao; Gelson
Martins, Battaglia, Bruno Fernandes, Acuna (Montero
76); Ruiz (Ruben Ribeiro 99); Dost.
aet.

Zenit St Petersburg (1) 1 *(Driussi 45)*
RB Leipzig (1) 1 *(Augustin 22)* 44,062
Zenit St Petersburg: (433) Lunev; Ivanovic, Smolnikov
(Poloz 85), Mevlja, Criscito; Kranevitter, Paredes,
Zhirkov; Rigoni (Erokhin 90), Kokorin (Zabolotny 8),
Driussi.
RB Leipzig: (442) Gulacsi; Klostermann, Orban (Konate
46), Upamecano, Bernardo; Forsberg, Demme (Ilsanker
71), Keita, Bruma; Werner, Augustin (Poulsen 90).

QUARTER-FINALS FIRST LEG
Thursday, 5 April 2018
Arsenal (4) 4 *(Ramsey 9, 28, Lacazette 23 (pen), 35)*
CSKA Moscow (1) 1 *(Golovin 15)* 58,285
Arsenal: (4411) Cech; Bellerin, Mustafi, Koscielny,
Monreal; Mkhitaryan (Iwobi 61), Ramsey, Xhaka,
Wilshere (Elneny 75); Ozil; Lacazette (Welbeck 74).
CSKA Moscow: (352) Akinfeev; Berezutski A,
Ignashevich, Berezutski V; Kuchaev, Golovin, Natcho
(Milanov 74), Dzagoev (Vitinho 81), Schennikov; Musa
(Khosonov 83), Wernbloom.

Atletico Madrid (2) 2 *(Koke 1, Griezmann 40)*
Sporting Lisbon (0) 0 53,301
Atletico Madrid: (442) Oblak; Juanfran, Savic, Godin,
Lucas; Correa (Gameiro 53), Saul, Gabi, Koke;
Griezmann (Vitolo 89), Costa (Thomas 87).
Sporting Lisbon: (4411) Rui Patricio; Piccini, Mathieu,
Coates, Fabio Coentrao (Ruben Ribeiro 80); Ruiz,
Battaglia, William Carvalho (Acuna 45), Gelson Martins;
Bruno Fernandes (Montero 87); Dost.

Lazio (1) 4 *(Lulic 8, Parolo 49, Felipe Anderson 74,*
Immobile 76)
Red Bull Salzburg (1) 2 *(Berisha V 30 (pen), Minamino*
71)
42,538
Lazio: (352) Strakosha; Felipe, de Vrij, Radu; Basta
(Patric Gil 65), Parolo, Lucas, Milinkovic-Savic, Lulic;
Immobile (Caicedo 85), Luis Alberto (Felipe Anderson
65).
Red Bull Salzburg: (442) Walke; Lainer, Ramalho,
Caleta-Car, Ulmer; Haidara (Wolf 81), Samassekou,
Schlager, Berisha V; Gulbrandsen (Minamino 70),
Dabbur.

RB Leipzig (1) 1 *(Werner 45)*
Marseille (0) 0 34,043
RB Leipzig: (442) Gulacsi; Laimer (Bernardo 73),
Konate, Upamecano, Klostermann; Forsberg (Sabitzer
83), Demme, Keita, Bruma; Augustin (Kampl 69),
Werner.
Marseille: (442) Pele; Sakai, Kamara, Gustavo, Amavi;
Sarr, Sanson, Zambo, Ocampos; Mitroglou (Germain
80), Payet (Lopez 86).

QUARTER-FINALS SECOND LEG
Thursday, 12 April 2018
CSKA Moscow (1) 2 *(Chalov 39, Nababkin 50)*
Arsenal (0) 2 *(Welbeck 75, Ramsey 90)* 29,284
CSKA Moscow: (352) Akinfeev; Berezutski V,
Berezutski A, Ignashevich; Nababkin, Golovin, Bistrovic
(Natcho 72), Dzagoev (Vitinho 37), Kuchaev; Chalov
(Milanov 79), Musa.
Arsenal: (4321) Cech; Bellerin, Mustafi, Koscielny,
Monreal; Ramsey, Elneny, Wilshere (Chambers 68);
Welbeck, Ozil; Lacazette (Iwobi 76).
Referee: Felix Zwayer.

Marseille (3) 5 *(Ilsanker 6 (og), Sarr 10, Thauvin 38,*
Payet 60, Sakai 90)
RB Leipzig (1) 2 *(Bruma 2, Augustin 55)* 61,883
Marseille: (4231) Pele; Sakai, Kamara, Gustavo, Amavi;
Lopez, Sanson; Sarr (Rami 28), Thauvin (Ocampos 62),
Payet (Zambo 82); Mitroglou.
RB Leipzig: (442) Gulacsi; Ilsanker, Konate, Upamecano
(Bernardo 66), Klostermann; Kampl, Demme (Forsberg
54), Keita, Bruma; Augustin, Sabitzer (Poulsen 61).
Referee: Bjorn Kuipers.

Red Bull Salzburg (0) 4 *(Dabbur 56, Haidara 72,*
Hwang 74, Lainer 76)
Lazio (0) 1 *(Immobile 55)* 29,520
Red Bull Salzburg: (41212) Walke; Lainer, Ramalho,
Caleta-Car, Ulmer; Schlager; Haidara, Berisha V; Yabo
(Minamino 84); Dabbur, Hwang (Gulbrandsen 79).
Lazio: (352) Strakosha; Felipe, de Vrij, Radu; Basta
(Lukaku 60), Parolo, Lucas (Nani 78), Milinkovic-Savic
(Felipe Anderson 69), Lulic; Immobile, Luis Alberto.
Referee: Damir Skomina.

Sporting Lisbon (1) 1 *(Montero 28)*
Atletico Madrid (0) 0 28,437
Sporting Lisbon: (4231) Rui Patricio; Andre Pinto,
Coates, Mathieu (Petrovic 26), Ristovski (Doumbia 79);
Bruno Fernandes, Battaglia; Gelson Martins, Ruiz
(Ruben Ribeiro 70), Acuna; Montero.
Atletico Madrid: (442) Oblak; Juanfran, Savic, Godin,
Lucas (Vrsaljko 46); Vitolo (Correa 59) Saul, Gabi,
Koke; Griezmann, Costa (Torres 52).
Referee: Milorad Mazic.

SEMI-FINALS FIRST LEG
Thursday, 26 April 2018
Arsenal (0) 1 *(Lacazette 61)*
Atletico Madrid (0) 1 *(Griezmann 82)* 59,066
Arsenal: (4321) Ospina; Bellerin, Mustafi, Koscielny,
Monreal; Ramsey, Xhaka, Wilshere; Welbeck, Ozil;
Lacazette.
Atletico Madrid: (442) Oblak; Vrsaljko■, Gimenez,
Godin, Lucas; Correa (Savic 75), Saul, Thomas, Koke;
Gameiro (Gabi 65), Griezmann (Torres 85).
Referee: Clement Turpin.

Marseille (1) 2 *(Thauvin 15, N'Jie 63)*
Red Bull Salzburg (0) 0 62,312
Marseille: (4231) Pele; Sarr, Rami, Gustavo, Amavi;
Lopez (N'Jie 59), Sanson; Thauvin (Germain 80), Payet,
Ocampos (Zambo 52); Mitroglou.
Red Bull Salzburg: (442) Walke; Lainer, Ramalho,
Caleta-Car, Ulmer; Haidara (Yabo 81), Samassekou,
Wolf (Schlager 68), Berisha V; Hwang (Gulbrandsen 60),
Dabbur.
Referee: William Collum.

SEMI-FINALS SECOND LEG
Thursday, 3 May 2018
Atletico Madrid (1) 1 *(Costa 45)*
Arsenal (0) 0   65,000
Atletico Madrid: (442) Oblak; Thomas (Savic 90), Gimenez, Godin, Lucas; Saul, Gabi, Koke, Vitolo (Correa 74); Costa (Torres 83), Griezmann.
Arsenal: (4321) Ospina; Bellerin, Mustafi, Koscielny (Chambers 12), Monreal; Ramsey, Xhaka, Wilshere (Mkhitaryan 68); Welbeck, Ozil; Lacazette.
Referee: Gianluca Rocchi.

Red Bull Salzburg (0) 2 *(Haidara 53, Sarr 65 (og))*
Marseille (0) 1 *(Rolando 116)*   29,540
Red Bull Salzburg: (4312) Walke; Lainer, Ramalho, Caleta-Car, Ulmer (Pongracic 96); Haidara■, Samassekou, Berisha V; Schlager (Minamino 84); Dabbur, Gulbrandsen (Hwang 68).
Marseille: (4231) Pele; Sarr, Rami, Gustavo, Amavi; Lopez (Zambo 67), Sanson (Rolando 101); Thauvin, Payet, Ocampos; Germain (N'Jie 84).
aet.
Referee: Sergei Karasev.

EUROPA LEAGUE FINAL 2018
Wednesday, 16 May 2018
(in Lyon, attendance 55,768)

Marseille (0) 0   Atletico Madrid (1) 3

Marseille: (4231) Mandanda; Sarr, Rami, Gustavo, Amavi; Zambo, Sanson; Thauvin, Payet (Lopez 32), Ocampos (N'Jie 55); Germain (Mitroglou 74).
Atletico Madrid: (442) Oblak; Vrsaljko (Juanfran 46), Gimenez, Godin, Lucas; Correa (Thomas 88), Gabi, Saul, Koke; Griezmann (Torres 90), Costa.
Scorers: Griezmann 21, 49, Gabi 89.

Referee: Bjorn Kuipers.

Atletico Madrid's Antoine Griezmann scores his side's second goal of the game as they beat Marseille 3-0 in the UEFA Europa League Final in Lyon on 16 May. (Nick Potts/PA Wire/PA Images)

UEFA EUROPA LEAGUE 2018–19

PARTICIPATING CLUBS
The list below is provisional and is subject to pending legal proceedings and final confirmation from UEFA.

GROUP STAGE
AC Milan (ITA)
Akhisar Belediyespor (TUR)
Anderlecht (BEL)
Arsenal (ENG)
Bayer Leverkusen (GER)
Chelsea (ENG)
Eintracht Frankfurt (GER)
Jablonec (CZE)
Krasnodar (RUS)
Lazio (ITA)
Marseille (FRA)
Real Betis (ESP)
Rennes (FRA)
Sporting Lisbon (POR)
Villarreal (ESP)
Vorskla (UKR)
Zurich (SUI)
Plus four losing teams from the UEFA Champions League play-offs (champions path).
Plus two losing teams from the UEFA Champions League play-offs (league route).
Plus four losing teams from the UEFA Champions League third qualifying round (league route).
Plus eight winning teams from the UEFA Europa League play-offs (champions route).
Plus 13 winning teams from the UEFA Europa League play-offs (main route).

PLAY-OFF ROUND – CHAMPIONS ROUTE
Ten winning teams from UEFA Europa League third qualifying round (champions route).
Six losing teams from UEFA Champions League third qualifying round (champions path).

PLAY-OFF ROUND – MAIN ROUTE
26 winning teams from UEFA Europa League third qualifying round (main route).

THIRD QUALIFYING ROUND – CHAMPIONS ROUTE
Ten teams eliminated from UEFA Champions League second qualifying round (champions path).
Nine winning teams from UEFA Europa League second qualifying round (champions route).
One team given a bye from UEFA Europa League second qualifying round (champions route).

THIRD QUALIFYING ROUND – MAIN ROUTE
Braga (POR)
Brondby (DEN)
Universataten Craiova (ROU)
Feyenoord (NED)
Gent (BEL)
Istanbul Basaksehir (TUR)
Luzern (SUI)
Olympiacos (GRE)
Rapid Vienna (AUT)
Rijeka (CRO)
Sigma Olomouc (CZE)
Zenit St Petersburg (RUS)
Zorya Luhansk (UKR)
Plus two losing teams from UEFA Champions League second qualifying round (league route).

Plus 37 winning teams from the UEFA Europa League second qualifying round (main route).

SECOND QUALIFYING ROUND – CHAMPIONS ROUTE
16 teams eliminated from UEFA Champions League first qualifying round.
Three losing teams from UEFA Champions League preliminary round.
*one team to be given a bye to the third qualifying round by means of an additional draw following the first qualifying round draw

SECOND QUALIFYING ROUND – MAIN ROUTE
Aberdeen (SCO)
Admira Wacker Modling (AUT)
AEK Larnaca (CYP)
Asteras Tripolis (GRE)
Atalanta (ITA)
Atromitos (GRE)
AZ Alkmaar (NED)
Besiktas (TUR)
Bordeaux (FRA)
Burnley (ENG)
Dinamo Brest (BLR)
Djurgarden (SWE)
FCSB (ROU)
Genk (BEL)
Hajduk Split (CRO)
Hapoel Haifa (ISR)
Jagiellonia Bialystok (POL)
LASK Linz (AUT)
Lillestrom (NOR)
Mariupol (UKR)
RB Leipzig (GER)
Rio Ave (POR)
Sevilla (ESP)
Sparta Prague (CZE)
St Gallen (SUI)
Ufa (RUS)
Vitesse (NED)
Plus 47 winning teams from the UEFA Europa League first qualifying round.

FIRST QUALIFYING ROUND – MAIN ROUTE
AIK Solna (SWE)
Anorthosis Famagusta (CYP)
Apollon Limassol (CYP)
Balzan (MLT)
Banants (ARM)
Beitar Jerusalem (ISR)
Budapest Honved (HUN)
Buducnost Podgorica (MNE)
Chikhura Sachkhere (GEO)
Cliftonville (NIR)
Coleraine (NIR)
Connah's Quay Nomads (WAL)
Copenhagen (DEN)
CSKA Sofia (BUL)
Derry C (IRL)
Dinamo Minsk (BLR)
Dinamo Tbilisi (GEO)
Domzale (SVN)
Dunajska Streda (SVK)
Dundalk (IRL)
Ferencvaros (HUN)
FH Hafnarfjordur (ISL)
Fola Esch (LUX)
Gandzasar-Kapan (ARM)
Glenavon (NIR)
Gornik Zabrze (POL)
Hacken (SWE)
Hibernian (SCO)
IBV Vestmannaeyjar (ISL)
Ilves (FIN)
Irtysh (KAZ)
Kairat (KAZ)

Keshla (AZE)
KuPS Kuopio (FIN)
Laci (ALB)
Lahti (FIN)
Lech Poznan (POL)
Levadia Tallinn (EST)
Levski Sofia (BUL)
Liepaja (LVA)
Luftetari Gjirokaster(ALB)
Maccabi Tel-Aviv (ISR)
Maribor (SVN)
Milsami Orhei (MDA)
Molde (NOR)
Narva Trans (EST)
Neftchi (AZE)
Nomme Kalju (EST)
Nordsjaelland (DEN)
NSI Runavik (FRO)
OFK Titograd (MNE)
Osijek (CRO)
Partizan Belgrade (SRB)
Partizani (ALB)
Petrocub (MDA)
Progres Niederkorn (LUX)
Pyunik (ARM)
Qabala (AZE)
Rabotnicki (MKD)
Racing Union (LUX)
Radnicki Nis (SRB)
Rangers (SCO)
Riga (LVA)
Rudar Pljevlja (MNE)
Rudar Velenje (SVN)
Samtredia (GEO)
Sarajevo (BIH)
Sarpsborg (NOR)
Shakhtyor Soligorsk (BLR)
Shamrock R (IRL)
Shkupi (MKD)
Siroki Brijeg (BIH)
Slavia Sofia (BUL)
Slovan Bratislava (SVK)
Spartak Subotica (SRB)
Stjarnan (ISL)
Stumbras (LTU)
Tobol (KAZ)
Trencin (SVK)
Ujpest (HUN)
Vaduz (LIE)
Vardar (MKD)
Ventspils (LVA)
Viitorul (ROU)
Zalgiris Vilnius (LTU)
Zaria Balti (MDA)
Zeljeznicar (BIH)
Plus seven winning teams from the UEFA Europa League preliminary round.

PRELIMINARY ROUND
B36 Torshavn (FRO)
Bala T (WAL)
Birkirkara (MLT)
Cefn Druids (WAL)
Europa (GIB)
Folgore Falciano (SMR)
Gzira U (MLT)
KI Klaksvik (FRO)
Prishtina (KOS)
Tre Fiori (SMR)
St Joseph's (GIB)
Trakai (LTU)
Engordany (AND)
Sant Julia (AND)

BRITISH AND IRISH CLUBS IN EUROPE
SUMMARY OF APPEARANCES

EUROPEAN CUP AND CHAMPIONS LEAGUE (1955–2018)
(Winners in brackets) (SE = seasons entered).

ENGLAND	SE	P	W	D	L	F	A
Manchester U (3)	27	269	150	65	54	496	253
Liverpool (5)	22	196	109	45	42	369	172
Arsenal	21	201	101	43	57	332	218
Chelsea (1)	15	160	80	46	34	274	142
Manchester C	8	62	27	13	22	108	84
Leeds U	4	40	22	6	12	76	41
Tottenham H	4	34	16	7	11	70	46
Nottingham F (2)	3	20	12	4	4	32	14
Newcastle U	3	24	11	3	10	33	33
Everton	3	10	2	5	3	14	10
Aston Villa (1)	2	15	9	3	3	24	10
Derby Co	2	12	6	2	4	18	12
Wolverhampton W	2	8	2	2	4	12	16
Blackburn R	1	6	1	1	4	5	8
Ipswich T	1	4	3	0	1	16	5
Burnley	1	4	2	0	2	8	8
Leicester C	1	10	5	2	3	11	10

SCOTLAND							
Celtic (1)	32	200	93	33	74	297	239
Rangers	30	161	62	40	59	232	218
Aberdeen	3	12	5	4	3	14	12
Hearts	3	8	2	1	5	8	16
Dundee U	1	8	5	1	2	14	5
Dundee	1	8	5	0	3	20	14
Hibernian	1	6	3	1	2	9	5
Kilmarnock	1	4	1	2	1	4	7
Motherwell	1	2	0	0	2	0	5

WALES							
The New Saints	11	30	7	4	19	29	53
Barry T	6	14	4	1	9	11	38

	SE	P	W	D	L	F	A
Rhyl	2	4	0	0	4	1	19
Cwmbran T	1	2	1	0	1	4	4
Llanelli	1	2	1	0	1	1	4
Bangor C	1	2	0	0	2	0	13

NORTHERN IRELAND							
Linfield	28	67	7	23	37	56	118
Glentoran	12	28	3	7	18	20	59
Crusaders	5	12	1	2	9	7	43
Portadown	3	6	0	1	5	3	24
Cliftonville	3	6	0	1	5	1	20
Glenavon	1	2	0	1	1	0	3
Lisburn Distillery	1	2	0	1	1	3	8
Ards	1	2	0	0	2	3	10
Coleraine	1	2	0	0	2	1	11

REPUBLIC OF IRELAND							
Dundalk	10	28	4	9	15	23	53
Shamrock R	9	20	1	6	13	9	33
Shelbourne	6	20	4	8	8	21	31
Bohemians	6	18	4	4	10	13	29
Waterford U	6	14	3	0	11	15	47
Derry C	4	9	1	1	7	9	26
St Patrick's Ath	4	8	0	3	5	2	23
Dublin C	3	6	1	0	5	3	25
Cork C	2	8	2	1	5	7	12
Athlone T	2	4	0	2	2	7	14
Sligo R	2	4	0	0	4	0	9
Limerick	2	4	0	0	4	4	16
Drogheda U	1	4	2	1	1	6	5
Cork Hibernians	1	2	0	0	2	1	7
Cork Celtic	1	2	0	0	2	1	7

UEFA CUP AND EUROPA LEAGUE 1971–2018

ENGLAND	SE	P	W	D	L	F	A
Tottenham H (2)	15	140	78	36	26	278	121
Liverpool (3)	14	124	66	34	24	186	94
Aston Villa	13	56	24	14	18	77	60
Ipswich T (1)	10	52	30	10	12	98	53
Manchester U (1)	9	43	18	14	11	57	37
Newcastle U	8	72	42	17	13	123	60
Manchester C	8	52	28	13	11	84	51
Leeds U	8	46	20	10	16	66	48
Everton	9	52	27	8	17	87	64
Arsenal	7	39	20	7	12	75	44
Southampton	7	22	6	9	7	23	20
Blackburn R	6	22	7	8	7	27	26
Chelsea (1)	4	17	10	2	5	28	20
Wolverhampton W	4	20	13	3	4	41	23
West Ham U	4	16	6	3	7	19	16
Fulham	3	39	21	10	8	64	31
Nottingham F	3	20	10	5	5	18	16
Stoke C	3	16	8	4	4	21	16
WBA	3	12	5	2	5	15	13
Middlesbrough	2	25	13	4	8	36	24
Bolton W	2	18	6	10	2	18	14
QPR	2	12	8	1	3	39	18
Derby Co	2	10	5	2	3	32	17
Leicester C	2	4	0	1	3	3	8
Birmingham C	1	8	4	2	2	11	8
Norwich C	1	6	2	2	2	6	4
Portsmouth	1	6	2	2	2	11	10
Watford	1	6	2	1	3	10	12
Wigan Ath	1	6	1	2	3	6	7
Sheffield W	1	4	2	1	1	13	7
Millwall	1	2	0	1	1	2	4
Hull C	1	4	2	1	1	4	3

SCOTLAND							
Celtic	20	101	41	25	35	156	115
Aberdeen	20	76	24	25	27	96	97
Dundee U	19	82	33	25	24	134	89
Rangers	17	78	32	23	23	100	79
Hearts	14	50	21	10	19	61	62
Hibernian	12	34	12	9	13	41	52

	SE	P	W	D	L	F	A
Motherwell	8	26	8	2	16	33	34
St Johnstone	7	24	7	7	10	25	30
Dundee	4	14	6	0	8	24	24
Kilmarnock	3	12	4	2	6	7	14
St Mirren	3	10	2	3	5	9	12
Dunfermline Ath	2	4	0	2	2	4	6
Raith R	1	6	2	1	3	10	8
Livingston	1	4	1	2	1	7	9
Falkirk	1	2	1	0	1	1	2
Gretna	1	2	0	1	1	3	7
Queen of the South	1	2	0	0	2	2	4
Partick Thistle	1	2	0	0	2	0	4
Inverness CT	1	2	0	1	1	0	1

WALES							
Bangor C	10	22	2	2	18	10	61
The New Saints	8	18	1	2	15	12	49
Llanelli	5	12	3	3	6	12	24
Bala T	4	8	2	0	6	6	16
Rhyl	3	8	2	1	5	9	12
UWIC Inter Cardiff	3	6	1	0	5	1	18
Cwmbran T	3	6	0	0	6	0	21
Newtown	3	8	2	1	5	6	21
Air UK Broughton	3	6	0	4	2	6	9
Barry T	2	8	2	2	4	10	16
Connah's Quay Nomads	2	6	2	1	3	3	6
Carmarthen T	2	6	1	0	5	8	21
Prestatyn T	1	4	1	0	3	3	11
Afan Lido	1	2	0	1	1	1	2
Cefn Druids	1	2	0	1	1	0	5
Port Talbot T	1	2	0	0	2	1	7
Neath	1	2	0	0	2	1	6
Haverfordwest Co	1	2	0	0	2	1	4
Swansea C	1	12	4	4	4	17	10
Aberystwith T	1	2	0	0	2	0	9
Llandudno T	1	2	0	0	2	0	6

NORTHERN IRELAND							
Glentoran	18	40	3	8	29	22	97
Linfield	12	34	9	8	17	37	63
Portadown	11	28	3	7	18	16	62
Crusaders	9	20	4	3	13	19	48

	SE	P	W	D	L	F	A
Glenavon	8	18	1	2	15	7	43
Coleraine	8	16	1	4	11	8	43
Cliftonville	5	14	3	3	8	9	28
Ballymena U	2	4	1	0	3	2	9
Ards	1	2	1	0	1	4	8
Dungannon Swifts	1	2	1	0	1	1	4
Lisburn Distillery	1	2	0	0	2	1	11
Bangor	1	2	0	0	2	0	6

REPUBLIC OF IRELAND

	SE	P	W	D	L	F	A
Bohemians	14	30	3	9	18	16	56
St Patrick's Ath	10	38	10	7	21	34	57
Cork C	9	28	6	7	15	21	38
Shamrock R	8	30	7	4	19	26	55
Derry C	8	24	6	5	13	28	42
Shelbourne	6	12	0	2	10	8	28
Dundalk	6	16	4	2	10	12	35
Drogheda U	4	12	3	4	5	10	24
Sligo R	4	10	2	4	4	11	13
Longford T	3	6	1	1	4	6	12
Finn Harps	3	6	0	0	6	3	33
Athlone T	1	4	1	2	1	4	5
Limerick	1	2	0	1	1	1	4
Sporting Fingal	1	2	0	0	2	4	6
Galway U	1	2	0	0	2	2	8
Bray W	1	2	0	0	2	0	8
University College Dublin	1	4	1	0	3	3	8

EUROPEAN CUP WINNERS' CUP 1960–1999

ENGLAND

	SE	P	W	D	L	F	A
Tottenham H (1)	6	33	20	5	8	65	34
Chelsea (2)	5	39	23	10	6	81	28
Liverpool	5	29	16	5	8	57	29
Manchester U (1)	5	31	16	9	6	55	35
West Ham U (1)	4	30	15	6	9	58	42
Arsenal (1)	3	27	15	10	2	48	20
Everton (1)	3	17	11	4	2	25	9
Manchester C (1)	2	18	11	2	5	32	13
Ipswich T	1	6	3	2	1	6	3
Leeds U	1	9	5	3	1	13	3
Leicester C	1	4	2	1	1	8	5
Newcastle U	1	2	1	0	1	2	2
Southampton	1	6	4	0	2	16	8
Sunderland	1	4	3	0	1	5	3
WBA	1	6	2	2	2	8	5
Wolverhampton W	1	4	1	1	2	6	5

SCOTLAND

	SE	P	W	D	L	F	A
Rangers (1)	10	54	27	11	16	100	62
Aberdeen (1)	8	39	22	5	12	79	37
Celtic	8	38	21	4	13	75	37
Dundee U	3	10	3	3	4	9	10
Hearts	3	10	3	3	4	16	14
Dunfermline Ath	2	14	7	2	5	34	14
Airdrieonians	1	2	0	0	2	1	3
Dundee	1	2	0	1	1	3	4
Hibernian	1	6	3	1	2	19	10
Kilmarnock	1	4	1	2	1	5	6
Motherwell	1	2	1	0	1	3	3
St Mirren	1	4	1	2	1	1	2

WALES

	SE	P	W	D	L	F	A
Cardiff C	14	49	16	14	19	67	61
Wrexham	8	28	10	8	10	34	35
Swansea C	7	18	3	4	11	32	37
Bangor C	3	9	1	2	6	5	12
Barry T	1	2	0	0	2	0	7
Borough U	1	4	1	1	2	2	4
Cwmbran T	1	2	0	0	2	2	12
Merthyr Tydfil	1	2	1	0	1	2	3
Newport Co	1	6	2	3	1	12	3
The New Saints (Llansantfraid)	1	2	0	1	1	1	6

NORTHERN IRELAND

	SE	P	W	D	L	F	A
Glentoran	9	22	3	7	12	18	46
Glenavon	5	10	1	3	6	11	25
Ballymena U	4	8	0	0	8	1	25
Coleraine	4	8	0	1	7	7	34
Crusaders	3	6	0	2	4	5	18
Derry C	3	6	1	1	4	1	11
Linfield	3	6	2	0	4	6	11
Ards	2	4	0	1	3	2	17
Bangor	2	4	0	1	3	2	8
Carrick Rangers	1	4	1	0	3	7	12
Cliftonville	1	2	0	0	2	0	8
Distillery	1	2	0	0	2	1	7
Portadown	1	2	1	0	1	4	7

REPUBLIC OF IRELAND

	SE	P	W	D	L	F	A
Shamrock R	6	16	5	2	9	19	27
Shelbourne	4	10	1	1	8	9	20
Bohemians	3	8	2	2	4	6	13
Dundalk	3	8	2	1	5	7	14
Limerick U	3	6	0	1	5	2	11
Waterford U	3	8	1	1	6	6	14
Cork C	2	4	1	0	3	2	9
Cork Hibernians	2	6	2	1	3	7	8
Galway U	2	4	0	0	4	2	11
Sligo R	2	6	1	0	4	5	11
Bray W	1	2	0	1	1	1	3
Cork Celtic	1	2	0	1	1	1	3
Finn Harps	1	2	0	1	1	2	4
Home Farm	1	2	0	1	1	1	7
St Patrick's Ath	1	2	0	0	2	1	8
University College Dublin	1	2	0	1	1	0	1

INTER-CITIES FAIRS CUP 1955–1970

ENGLAND

	SE	P	W	D	L	F	A
Leeds U (2)	5	53	28	17	8	92	40
Birmingham C	4	25	14	6	5	51	38
Liverpool	4	22	12	4	6	46	15
Arsenal (1)	3	24	12	5	7	46	19
Chelsea	3	20	10	5	5	33	24
Everton	3	12	7	2	3	22	15
Newcastle U (1)	3	24	13	6	5	37	21
Nottingham F	2	6	3	0	3	8	9
Sheffield W	2	10	5	0	5	25	18
Burnley	1	8	4	3	1	16	5
Coventry C	1	4	3	0	1	9	8
London XI	1	8	4	1	3	14	13
Manchester U	1	11	6	3	2	29	10
Southampton	1	6	2	3	1	11	6
WBA	1	4	1	1	2	7	9

SCOTLAND

	SE	P	W	D	L	F	A
Hibernian	7	36	18	5	13	66	60
Dunfermline Ath	5	28	16	3	9	49	31
Kilmarnock	4	20	8	3	9	34	32
Dundee U	3	10	5	1	4	11	12
Hearts	3	12	4	4	4	20	20
Rangers	3	18	8	4	6	27	17
Celtic	2	6	1	3	2	9	10
Aberdeen	1	4	2	1	1	4	4
Dundee	1	8	5	1	2	14	6
Morton	1	2	0	0	2	3	9
Partick Thistle	1	4	3	0	1	10	7

NORTHERN IRELAND

	SE	P	W	D	L	F	A
Glentoran	4	8	1	1	6	7	22
Coleraine	2	8	2	1	5	15	23
Linfield	2	4	1	0	3	3	11

REPUBLIC OF IRELAND

	SE	P	W	D	L	F	A
Drumcondra	2	6	2	0	4	8	19
Dundalk	2	6	1	1	4	4	25
Shamrock R	2	4	0	2	2	4	6
Cork Hibernians	1	2	0	0	2	1	6
Shelbourne	1	5	1	2	2	3	4
St Patrick's Ath	1	2	0	0	2	4	9

FIFA CLUB WORLD CUP 2017

Formerly known as the FIFA Club World Championship, this tournament is played annually between the champion clubs from all 6 continental confederations, although since 2007 the champions of Oceania must play a qualifying play-off against the champion club of the host country.

(Finals in United Arab Emirates)

Denotes player sent off.

PLAY-OFF FOR QUARTER-FINALS

Wednesday 6 December 2017

Al-Jazira (1) 1 *(Romarinho 38)*
Auckland City (0) 0   4246

Al-Jazira: Ali Khaseif; Mohamad Al Attas, Mohamed Ayed (Saif Khalfan 90), Musallem Fayez, Salim Rashid, Fares Juma, Eissa Mohamed (Yaqoub Al Hosani 80), Khalfan Alrezzi (Ahmed Rabia 58), Romarinho, Boussoufa, Ali Mabkhout.
Auckland City: Zubikarai; White, Berlanga, Kim, Iwata (Lea'Alafa 84), Tavano, Riera, Howieson, Tade, De Vries, McCowatt (Morgan 60).
Referee: Malang Diedhiou (Senegal).

QUARTER-FINALS

Saturday 9 December 2017

Pachuca (0) 1 *(Guzman 112)*
Wydad Casablanca (0) 0   12,488

Pachuca: Perez; Herrera, Martinez (Raul Lopez 105), Murillo, Garcia, Guzman (Gonzalez 118), Hernandez, Aguirre (Sanchez 79), Honda, Urretaviscaya, Sagal (Jara 58).
Wydad Casablanca: Laaroubi; Noussir, Hachimi, Atouchi, El Comara, Nakach*, Saidi, El Karti, Khadrouf (Hajhouj 90), Bencharki, Aoulad Youssef (El Haddad 62).
aet.
Referee: Ravshan Irmatov (Uzbekistan).

Al-Jazira (0) 1 *(Mabkhout 52)*
Urawa Red Diamonds (0) 0   15,593

Al-Jazira: Ali Khaseif; Musallem Fayez, Mohamed Ayed (Khalfan Alrezzi 90), Fares Juma, Salim Rashid, Salem Abdulla, Mohamad Al Attas (Eissa Mohamed 89), Yaqoub Al Housani (Ahmed Rabia 84), Romarinho, Ali Mabkhout, Boussoufa.
Urawa Red Diamonds: Nishikawa; Ugajin, Abe, Endo (Ryota 72), Makino, Aoki, Rafael Silva, Yajima (Zlatan 76), Kashiwagi, Muto (Takagi 67), Koroki.
Referee: Cesar Arturo Ramos (Mexico).

MATCH FOR FIFTH PLACE

Tuesday 12 December 2017

Wydad Casablanca (1) 2 *(Haddad 21, Hajhouj 90 (pen))*
Urawa Red Diamonds (2) 3 *(Mauricio 18, 60,*
Kashiwagi 26))   4281

Wydad Casablanca: Benachour; Khadrouf (Saidi 74), Ouattara, Rabeh, Nahiri, Hajhouj, Ait Ben Idir, El Karti,

El Haddad (Daho 87), Aoulad Youssef (Tighazoui 75), Gaddarine.
Urawa Red Diamonds: Nishikawa; Moriwaki, Abe, Makino, Mauricio Antonio, Aoki, Muto, Kashiwagi, Nagasawa, Rafael Silva (Umesaki 58 (Zlatan 77)), Koroki (Kikuchi 90).
Referee: Matt Conger (New Zealand).

SEMI-FINALS

Tuesday 12 December 2017

Gremio (0) 1 *(Everton 95)*
Pachuca (0) 0   6428

Gremio: Marcelo Grohe; Edilson (Moura 90), Pedro Geromel, Kannemann, Bruno Cortez, Michel (Everton 72), Jailson, Ramiro, Luan, Fernandinho (Thyere 117), Barrios (Jael 55).
Pachuca: Perez; Herrera, Gonzalez, Murillo, Garcia (Sagal 101), Hernandez, Honda, Guzman*, Aguirre (Sanchez 67), Urretaviscaya (Cano 105), Jara (Herrera 90).
aet.
Referee: Felix Brych (Germany).

Wednesday 13 December 2017

Al-Jazira (1) 1 *(Romarinho 41)*
Real Madrid (0) 2 *(Ronaldo 53, Bale 81)*   36,650

Al-Jazira: Ali Khaseif (Khaled Al Senaani 51); Musallem Fayez, Mohamed Ayed, Fares Juma, Salim Rashid, Yaqoub Al Housani (Ahmed Rabia 72), Mohamad Al Attas, Khalifa Mubarak (Eissa Mohamed 60), Romarinho, Ali Mabkhout, Boussoufa.
Real Madrid: Navas; Hakimi, Nacho, Varane, Marcelo, Modric, Casemiro, Kovacic (Vazquez 68), Isco (Asensio 68), Ronaldo, Benzema (Bale 81).
Referee: Sandro Ricci (Brazil).

MATCH FOR THIRD PLACE

Saturday 16 December 2017

Al-Jazira (0) 1 *(Mubarak 57)*
Pachuca (1) 4 *(Urretaviscaya 37, Jara 60, De la Rosa 79,*
Sagal 84 (pen))   11,785

Al-Jazira: Khaled Al Senaani; Musallem Fayez, Saif Khalfan, Fares Juma, Salim Rashid, Yaqoub Al Housani (Abdalla Ramadan 67), Mohamad Al Attas (Salim Ali 46), Khalfan Alrezzi (Ahmed Rabia 78), Romarinho, Ali Mabkhout, Boussoufa.
Pachuca: Blanco; Lopez, Gonzalez, Murillo, Garcia, Hernandez (Lopez 85), Urretaviscaya (Figueroa 86), Sanchez, Aguirre, Jara (De La Rosa 78), Sagal.
Referee: Malang Diedhiou (Senegal).

FIFA CLUB WORLD CUP FINAL 2017

Abu Dhabi, Saturday 16 December 2017 (attendance 41,094)

Real Madrid (0) 1 *(Ronaldo 53)*   **Gremio (0) 0**

Real Madrid: Navas; Carvajal, Varane, Ramos, Marcelo, Modric, Casemiro, Kroos, Isco (Vazquez 73), Ronaldo, Benzema (Bale 79).

Gremio: Marcelo Grohe; Edilson, Pedro Geromel, Kannemann, Bruno Cortez, Michel (Maicon 84), Jailson, Ramiro (Everton 71), Luan, Fernandinho, Barrios (Jael 63).

Referee: Cesar Arturo Ramos (Mexico).

PREVIOUS FINALS

2000 Corinthians beat Vasco da Gama 4-3 on penalties after 0-0 draw	2010 Internazionale beat TP Mazembe Englebert 3-0
2001-04 Not contested	2011 Barcelona beat Santos 4-0
2005 Sao Paulo beat Liverpool 1-0	2012 Corinthians beat Chelsea 1-0
2006 Internacional beat Barcelona 1-0	2013 Bayern Munich beat Raja Casablanca 2-0
2007 AC Milan beat Boca Juniors 4-2	2014 Real Madrid beat San Lorenzo 2-0
2008 Manchester U beat Liga De Quito 1-0	2015 Barcelona beat River Plate 3-0
2009 Barcelona beat Estudiantes 2-1	2016 Real Madrid beat Kashima Antlers 4-2 (*aet.*)
	2017 Real Madrid beat Gremio 1-0

WORLD CLUB CHAMPIONSHIP

Played annually up to 1974 and intermittently since then between the winners of the European Cup and the winners of the South American Champions Cup — known as the Copa Libertadores. In 1980 the winners were decided by one match arranged in Tokyo in February 1981 which remained the venue until 2004, when the match was superseded by the FIFA Club World Championship. AC Milan replaced Marseille who had been stripped of their European Cup title in 1993.

1960 Real Madrid beat Penarol 0-0, 5-1
1961 Penarol beat Benfica 0-1, 5-0, 2-1
1962 Santos beat Benfica 3-2, 5-2
1963 Santos beat AC Milan 2-4, 4-2, 1-0
1964 Inter-Milan beat Independiente 0-1, 2-0, 1-0
1965 Inter-Milan beat Independiente 3-0, 0-0
1966 Penarol beat Real Madrid 2-0, 2-0
1967 Racing Club beat Celtic 0-1, 2-1, 1-0
1968 Estudiantes beat Manchester United 1-0, 1-1
1969 AC Milan beat Estudiantes 3-0, 1-2
1970 Feyenoord beat Estudiantes 2-2, 1-0
1971 Nacional beat Panathinaikos* 1-1, 2-1
1972 Ajax beat Independiente 1-1, 3-0
1973 Independiente beat Juventus* 1-0
1974 Atlético Madrid* beat Independiente 0-1, 2-0
1975 Independiente and Bayern Munich could not agree dates; no matches.
1976 Bayern Munich beat Cruzeiro 2-0, 0-0
1977 Boca Juniors beat Borussia Moenchengladbach* 2-2, 3-0
1978 Not contested
1979 Olimpia beat Malmö* 1-0, 2-1
1980 Nacional beat Nottingham Forest 1-0
1981 Flamengo beat Liverpool 3-0
1982 Penarol beat Aston Villa 2-0
1983 Gremio Porto Alegre beat SV Hamburg 2-1
1984 Independiente beat Liverpool 1-0

1985 Juventus beat Argentinos Juniors 4-2 on penalties after 2-2 draw
1986 River Plate beat Steaua Bucharest 1-0
1987 FC Porto beat Penarol 2-1 after extra time
1988 Nacional (Uru) beat PSV Eindhoven 7-6 on penalties after 1-1 draw
1989 AC Milan beat Atletico Nacional (Col) 1-0 after extra time
1990 AC Milan beat Olimpia 3-0
1991 Crvena Zvezda beat Colo Colo 3-0
1992 Sao Paulo beat Barcelona 2-1
1993 Sao Paulo beat AC Milan 3-2
1994 Velez Sarsfield beat AC Milan 2-0
1995 Ajax beat Gremio Porto Alegre 4-3 on penalties after 0-0 draw
1996 Juventus beat River Plate 1-0
1997 Borussia Dortmund beat Cruzeiro 2-0
1998 Real Madrid beat Vasco da Gama 2-1
1999 Manchester U beat Palmeiras 1-0
2000 Boca Juniors beat Real Madrid 2-1
2001 Bayern Munich beat Boca Juniors 1-0 after extra time
2002 Real Madrid beat Olimpia 2-0
2003 Boca Juniors beat AC Milan 3-1 on penalties after 1-1 draw
2004 Porto beat Once Caldas 8-7 on penalties after 0-0 draw

*European Cup runners-up; winners declined to take part.

EUROPEAN SUPER CUP 2017

Played annually between the winners of the European Champions' Cup and the European Cup-Winners' Cup (UEFA Cup from 2000; UEFA Europa League from 2010). AC Milan replaced Marseille in 1993–94.

Skopje, Tuesday 8 August 2017 , attendance 30,421

Real Madrid (1) 2 *(Casemiro 24, Isco 52)*

Manchester U (0) 1 *(Lukaku 62)*

Real Madrid: Navas; Carvajal, Varane, Ramos, Marcelo, Casemiro, Modric, Kroos, Isco (Vazquez 74), Bale (Asensio 74), Benzema (Ronaldo 83).

Manchester U: de Gea; Lindelof, Smalling, Darmian, Valencia, Herrera (Fellaini 56), Matic, Pogba, Lingard (Rashford 46), Mkhitaryan, Lukaku.

Referee: Gianluca Rocchi (Italy).

PREVIOUS MATCHES

1972 Ajax beat Rangers 3-1, 3-2
1973 Ajax beat AC Milan 0-1, 6-0
1974 Not contested
1975 Dynamo Kyiv beat Bayern Munich 1-0, 2-0
1976 Anderlecht beat Bayern Munich 4-1, 1-2
1977 Liverpool beat Hamburg 1-1, 6-0
1978 Anderlecht beat Liverpool 3-1, 1-2
1979 Nottingham F beat Barcelona 1-0, 1-1
1980 Valencia beat Nottingham F 1-0, 1-2
1981 Not contested
1982 Aston Villa beat Barcelona 0-1, 3-0
1983 Aberdeen beat Hamburg 0-0, 2-0
1984 Juventus beat Liverpool 2-0
1985 Juventus v Everton not contested due to UEFA ban on English clubs
1986 Steaua Bucharest beat Dynamo Kyiv 1-0
1987 FC Porto beat Ajax 1-0, 1-0
1988 KV Mechelen beat PSV Eindhoven 3-0, 0-1
1989 AC Milan beat Barcelona 1-1, 1-0
1990 AC Milan beat Sampdoria 1-1, 2-0
1991 Manchester U beat Crvena Zvezda 1-0
1992 Barcelona beat Werder Bremen 1-1, 2-1
1993 Parma beat AC Milan 0-1, 2-0
1994 AC Milan beat Arsenal 0-0, 2-0

1995 Ajax beat Zaragoza 1-1, 4-0
1996 Juventus beat Paris Saint-Germain 6-1, 3-1
1997 Barcelona beat Borussia Dortmund 2-0, 1-1
1998 Chelsea beat Real Madrid 1-0
1999 Lazio beat Manchester U 1-0
2000 Galatasaray beat Real Madrid 2-1
2001 Liverpool beat Bayern Munich 3-2
2002 Real Madrid beat Feyenoord 3-1
2003 AC Milan beat Porto 1-0
2004 Valencia beat Porto 2-1
2005 Liverpool beat CSKA Moscow 3-1
2006 Sevilla beat Barcelona 3-0
2007 AC Milan beat Sevilla 3-1
2008 Zenit beat Manchester U 2-1
2009 Barcelona beat Shakhtar Donetsk 1-0
2010 Atletico Madrid beat Internazionale 2-0
2011 Barcelona beat Porto 2-0
2012 Atletico Madrid beat Chelsea 4-1
2013 Bayern Munch beat Chelsea 5-4 on penalties after 2-2 draw
2014 Real Madrid beat Sevilla 2-0
2015 Barcelona beat Sevilla 5-4
2016 Real Madrid beat Sevilla 3-2
2017 Real Madrid beat Manchester U 2-1

INTERNATIONAL DIRECTORY

The latest available information has been given regarding numbers of clubs and players registered with FIFA, the world governing body. Where known, official colours are listed. With European countries, League tables show a number of signs: * team relegated, *+ team relegated after play-offs, + team not relegated after play-offs.

There are 211 member associations in the six FIFA Confederations, indicated in brackets after the regional heading. The four home countries, England, Scotland, Northern Ireland and Wales, are dealt with elsewhere in the Yearbook; but basic details appear in this directory. Gibraltar was admitted to full UEFA membership in 2013; Northern Cyprus is not a member of FIFA or UEFA and is the subject of an international territorial dispute. From March 2014 FIFA permitted Kosovo to play friendlies against full member nations; Kosovo was granted full membership of both FIFA and UEFA in May 2016 and entered World Cup 2018 qualification in September 2016. (Gibraltar and Kosovo play home UEFA- and FIFA-regulated competition qualifiers at neutral venues.) Gozo is included here for its close links with Maltese football. *N.B. In this edition international results for 2017–18 include matches played from 3 July 2017 to 15 July 2018.*

There are 12 associate members and others who have affiliation to their confederations; the most recent admission to full membership was South Sudan in 2011. The current associate members are as follows: AFC: Northern Mariana Islands; CAF: Reunion, Zanzibar; CONCACAF: Bonaire, French Guiana, Guadeloupe, Martinique, Saint-Martin, Sint Maarten; OFC: Kiribati, Niue, Tuvalu. Matches between full members and associate members are indicated with †.

EUROPE (UEFA)

ALBANIA

Football Association of Albania, Rruga e Elbasanit, 1000 Tirana.
Founded: 1930. *FIFA:* 1932; *UEFA:* 1954. *National Colours:* Red shirts with white trim, black shorts, red socks.

International matches 2017–18
Liechtenstein (h) 2-0, FYR Macedonia (a) 1-1, Spain (a) 0-3, Italy (h) 0-1, Turkey (a) 3-2, Norway (h) 0-1, Kosovo (n) 0-3, Ukraine (n) 1-4.

League Championship wins (1930–37; 1945–2018)
KF Tirana 24 (formerly SK Tirana; includes 17 Nentori 8); Dinamo Tirana 18; Partizani Tirana 15; Vllaznia Shkoder 9; Skenderbeu Korce 8; Elbasani 2 (incl. Labinoti 1); Flamurtari 1; Teuta Durres 1; Kukesi 1.

Cup wins (1948–2018)
KF Tirana 16 (formerly SK Tirana; includes 17 Nentori 8); Partizani Tirana 15; Dinamo Tirana 13; Vllaznia 6; Flamurtari Vlore 4; Teuta Durres 3; Elbasani 2 (incl. Labinoti 1); Besa 2; Laci 2; Apolonia Fier 1; Kukesi 1; Skenderbeu Korce 1.

Albanian Superliga 2017–18

	P	W	D	L	F	A	GD	Pts
Skenderbeu	36	22	6	8	68	41	27	72
Kukesi	36	18	9	9	61	41	20	63
Luftetari Gjirokaster	36	16	11	9	47	37	10	59
Laci	36	16	8	12	45	39	6	56
Partizani Tirana	36	15	8	13	41	36	5	53
Flamurtari	36	11	13	12	37	37	0	46
Kamza	36	12	10	14	37	41	–4	46
Teuta	36	12	10	14	55	58	–3	46
Vllaznia*	36	12	8	16	38	42	–4	44
Lushnja*	36	2	5	29	29	86	–57	11

Top scorer: Sowe (Skenderbeu) 21.
Cup Final: Skenderbeu 1, Laci 0.

ANDORRA

Federacio Andorrana de Futbol, Avda Carlemany 67, 3er Pis, Apartado postal 65, Escaldes-Engordany.
Founded: 1994. *FIFA:* 1996; *UEFA:* 1996. *National Colours:* All red.

International matches 2017–18
Qatar (n) 0-1, Switzerland (a) 0-3, Faroe Islands (a) 0-1, Portugal (h) 0-2, Latvia (a) 0-4, Liechtenstein (n) 1-0, Cape Verde Islands (n) 0-0 (2-4p).

League Championship wins (1996–2018)
FC Santa Coloma 12; Principat 3; Encamp 2; Sant Julia 2; Ranger's 2; Lusitanos 2; Constel-lacio Esportiva 1.

Cup wins (1991, 1994–2018)
FC Santa Coloma 10*; Principat 6*; Sant Julia 5; UE Santa Coloma 3; Constel-lacio Esportiva 1; Lusitanos 1.
* *Includes one unofficial title.*

Andorran Primera Divisio Qualifying Table 2017–18

	P	W	D	L	F	A	GD	Pts
FC Santa Coloma	21	15	3	3	55	16	39	48
Engordany	21	14	5	2	45	11	34	47
Sant Julia	21	12	6	3	58	15	43	42
Lusitanos	21	10	4	7	49	26	23	34
UE Santa Coloma	21	8	5	8	35	25	10	29
Inter Club d'Escaldes	21	7	4	10	33	29	4	25
Encamp	21	3	1	17	26	76	–50	10
Penya Encarnada	21	0	2	19	10	113	–103	2

Championship Round 2017–18

	P	W	D	L	F	A	GD	Pts
FC Santa Coloma	27	18	4	5	62	20	42	58
Engordany	27	16	7	4	50	17	33	55
Sant Julia	27	14	6	7	64	24	40	48
Lusitanos	27	13	5	9	59	35	24	44

Relegation Round 2017–18

	P	W	D	L	F	A	GD	Pts
UE Santa Coloma	27	12	5	10	53	29	24	41
Inter Club d'Escaldes	27	10	5	12	45	43	2	35
Encamp+	27	4	2	21	34	88	–54	14
Penya Encarnada*	27	3	2	22	15	126	–111	11

Top scorer: Sosa (FC Santa Coloma) 14.
Cup Final: FC Santa Coloma 2, Sant Julia 1.

ARMENIA

Football Federation of Armenia, Khanjyan Street 27, 0010 Yerevan.
Founded: 1992. *FIFA:* 1992; *UEFA:* 1993. *National Colours:* Red shirts with white trim, red shorts, red socks.

International matches 2017–18
Romania (a) 0-1, Denmark (h) 1-4, Poland (h) 1-6, Kazakhstan (a) 1-1, Belarus (h) 4-1, Cyprus (h) 3-2, Estonia (h) 0-0, Lithuania (h) 0-1, Malta (n) 1-1, Moldova (n) 0-0.

League Championship wins (1992–2018)
Pyunik 14 (incl. Homenetmen 1); Shirak 5*; Ararat Yerevan 2*; Araks 2 (incl. Tsement 1); Alashkert 3; FK Yerevan 1; Ulisses 1; Banants 1.
* *Includes one unofficial shared title.*

Cup wins (1992–2018)
Pyunik (incl. Homenetmen 1) 8; Mika 6; Ararat Yerevan 5; Banants 3; Tsement 2; Shirak 2; Gandzasar 1.
See also Russia section for Armenian club honours in Soviet era 1936–91.

Armenian Premier League 2017–18

	P	W	D	L	F	A	GD	Pts
Alashkert	30	14	8	8	44	31	13	50
Banants	30	11	11	8	42	34	8	44
Gandzasar	30	11	10	9	43	34	9	43
Shirak (–12)	30	14	8	8	37	31	6	38
Pyunik	30	9	9	12	37	41	–4	36
Ararat Yerevan	30	5	6	19	33	65	–32	21

Top scorers (joint): Harutyunyan (Gandzasar), Artak Yedigaryan (Alashkert) 12.
Cup Final: Gandzasar 1, Alashkert 1.
aet; Gandzasar won 4-3 on penalties.

AUSTRIA

Oesterreichischer Fussball-Bund, Ernst-Happel Stadion, Sektor A/F, Meiereistrasse 7, Wien 1021.
Founded: 1904. *FIFA:* 1905; *UEFA:* 1954. *National Colours:* Red shirts, white shorts, red socks.

International matches 2017–18

Wales (a) 0-1, Georgia (h) 1-1, Serbia (h) 3-2, Moldova (a) 1-0, Uruguay (h) 2-1, Slovenia (h) 3-0, Luxembourg (a) 4-0, Russia (h) 1-0, Germany (h) 2-1, Brazil (h) 0-3.

League Championship wins (1912–2018)

Rapid Vienna 32; Austria Vienna (formerly Amateure) 24; Red Bull Salzburg 12 (incl. Austria Salzburg 3); Wacker Innsbruck 10 (incl. Swarovski Tirol 2, Tirol Innsbruck 3); Admira Vienna (now Admira Wacker Modling) 9 (incl. Wacker Vienna 1); First Vienna 6; Wiener Sportklub 3; Sturm Graz 3; WAF 1; WAC 1; Floridsdorfer 1; Hakoah 1; LASK Linz 1; Voest Linz 1; GAK Graz 1.

Cup wins (1919–2018)

Austria Vienna (formerly Amateure) 27; Rapid Vienna 14; Wacker Innsbruck 7 (incl. Swarovski Tirol 1); Admira Vienna (now Admira Wacker Modling) 6 (incl. Wacker Vienna 1); Sturm Graz 5; Red Bull Salzburg 5; GAK Graz 4; First Vienna 3; WAC 2; Ried 2; WAF 1; Wiener Sportklub 1; Linz ASK 1; Kremser 1; Stockerau 1; Karnten 1; Horn 1; Pasching 1.

Austrian Bundesliga 2017–18

	P	W	D	L	F	A	GD	Pts
Red Bull Salzburg	36	25	8	3	81	29	52	83
Sturm Graz	36	22	4	10	68	45	23	70
Rapid Vienna	36	17	11	8	68	43	25	62
LASK Linz	36	17	6	13	49	41	8	57
Admira Wacker Modling	36	15	6	15	59	66	–7	51
Mattersburg	36	12	10	14	50	56	–6	46
Austria Vienna	36	12	7	17	51	55	–4	43
Rheindorf Altach	36	10	8	18	35	51	–16	38
Wolfsberger	36	8	9	19	31	57	–26	33
St Polten+	36	5	5	26	28	77	–49	20

Top scorer: Dabour (Red Bull Salzburg) 22.
Cup Final: Sturm Graz 1, Red Bull Salzburg 0 *aet.*

AZERBAIJAN

Association of Football Federations of Azerbaijan, 2208 Nobel prospekti, 1025 Baku.
Founded: 1992. *FIFA:* 1994; *UEFA:* 1994. *National Colours:* All red.

International matches 2017–18

Norway (a) 0-2, San Marino (h) 5-1, Czech Republic (h) 1-2, Germany (a) 1-5, Moldova (n) 0-0, Belarus (h) 0-1, FYR Macedonia (n) 1-1, Kyrgyzstan (h) 3-0, Kazakhstan (a) 0-3, Latvia (a) 3-1.

League Championship wins (1992–2018)

Neftchi 8; Qarabag 6; Kapaz 3; Shamkir 3*; FK Baku 2; Inter Baku (now Keshla) 2; Turan 1; Khazar Lankaran 1.
* *Includes one unofficial title.*

Cup wins (1992–2018)

Neftchi 7*; Qarabag 6; Kapaz 4; FK Baku 3; Khazar Lankaran 3; Inshatchi 1; Shafa 1; Keshla (formerly Inter Baku) 1.
* *Includes one title awarded by forfeit.*

Azerbaijani Premyer Liqa 2017–18

	P	W	D	L	F	A	GD	Pts
Qarabag	28	20	5	3	37	13	24	65
Qabala	28	14	7	7	43	26	17	49
Neftchi	28	14	4	10	39	28	11	46
Zira	28	12	8	8	36	30	6	44
Sumqayit	28	11	7	10	34	33	1	40
Keshla†	28	8	7	13	29	39	–10	31
Sabail	28	6	5	17	19	39	–20	23
Kapaz*	28	3	5	20	18	47	–29	14

† *Inter Baku changed its name to Keshla during season.*
Top scorer: Dabo (Qabala) 13.
Cup Final: Keshla 1, Qabala 0.

BELARUS

Belarus Football Federation, Prospekt Pobeditelei 20/3, 220020 Minsk.
Founded: 1989. *FIFA:* 1992; *UEFA:* 1993. *National Colours:* All red with white trim.

International matches 2017–18

Burkina Faso (n) 0-0 (3-0p), Thailand (a) 0-0 (4-5p), Luxembourg (a) 0-1, Sweden (h) 0-4, Netherlands (h) 1-3, France (a) 1-2, Armenia (h) 1-4, Georgia (a) 2-2, Azerbaijan (a) 1-0, Slovenia (a) 2-0, Hungary (h) 1-1, Finland (a) 0-2.

League Championship wins (1992–2017)

BATE Borisov 14; Dinamo Minsk 7; Slavia Mozyr (incl. MPKC 1) 2; Dnepr Mogilev 1; Belshina Bobruisk 1; Gomel 1; Shakhtyor Soligorsk 1.

Cup wins (1992–2018)

Dinamo Minsk 3; Belshina Bobruisk 3; BATE Borisov 3; Dynamo Brest 3; Slavia Mozyr (incl. MPKC 1) 2; Gomel 2; Shakhtyor Soligorsk 2; MTZ-RIPA 2; Naftan Novopolotsk 2; Neman Grodno 1; Dinamo 93 Minsk 1; Lokomotiv 96 1; FC Minsk 1; Torpedo-BelAZ Zhodino 1.
See also Russia section for Belarusian club honours in Soviet era 1936–91.

Belarusian Premier League 2017

	P	W	D	L	F	A	GD	Pts
BATE Borisov	30	21	5	4	61	19	42	68
Dinamo Minsk	30	22	2	6	46	15	31	68
Shakhtyor Soligorsk	30	20	5	5	52	22	30	65
Dynamo Brest	30	14	9	7	47	26	21	51
Torpedo-BelAZ Zhodino	30	14	9	7	43	27	16	51
Neman Grodno	30	14	7	9	42	32	10	49
Slutsk	30	12	8	10	30	34	–4	44
Vitebsk	30	12	7	11	35	38	–3	43
Gorodeya	30	8	14	8	37	35	2	38
Gomel	30	9	8	13	24	25	–1	35
Isloch Minsk Raion	30	10	4	16	27	46	–19	27
Dnepr Mogilev	30	6	8	16	27	48	–21	26
Krumkachy*†	30	5	10	15	26	47	–21	25
Minsk	30	3	14	13	19	39	–20	23
Slavia Mozyr*	30	4	8	18	26	50	–24	20
Naftan Novopolotsk*	30	4	6	20	18	57	–39	13

† *Krumkachy demoted for breach of league licensing rule.*
Top scorer: Gordeichuk (BATE Borisov) 18.
Cup Final: Dynamo Brest 3, BATE Borisov 2.

BELGIUM

Union Royale Belge des Societes de Football-Association, 145 Avenue Houba de Strooper, B-1020 Bruxelles.
Founded: 1895. *FIFA:* 1904; *UEFA:* 1954. *National Colours:* All red.

International matches 2017–18

Gibraltar (h) 9-0, Greece (a) 2-1, Bosnia-Herzegovina (a) 4-3, Cyprus (h) 4-0, Mexico (h) 3-3, Japan (h) 1-0, Saudi Arabia (h) 4-0, Portugal (h) 0-0, Egypt (h) 3-0, Costa Rica (h) 4-1, Panama (n) 3-0, Tunisia (n) 5-2, England (n) 1-0, Japan (n) 3-2, Brazil (n) 2-1, France (n) 0-1, England (n) 2-0.

League Championship wins (1896–2018)

Anderlecht 34; Club Brugge 15; Union St Gilloise 11; Standard Liege 10; Beerschot VAC (became Germinal) 7; RC Brussels 6; RFC Liege 5; Daring Brussels 5; Antwerp 4; Mechelen 4; Cercle Brugge 3; Genk 3; Beveren 2; RWD Molenbeek 1; Gent 1.

Cup wins (1912–14; 1927; 1935; 1954–2018)

Club Brugge 11; Anderlecht 9; Standard Liege 8; Genk 4; Gent 3; Union Saint- Gilloise 2; Waterschei (became Racing Genk) 2; Beveren 2; Cercle Brugge 2; Antwerp 2; Lierse 2; Beerschot VAC (became Germinal) 2; Beerschot Antwerpen Club (incl. Germinal Ekeren) 2; Lokeren 2; Zulte Waregem 2; Racing 1; Daring 1; Tournai 1; Mechelen 1; FC Liege 1; Westerlo 1; La Louviere 1.

Belgian First Division A Qualifying Table 2017–18

	P	W	D	L	F	A	GD	Pts
Club Brugge	30	20	7	3	68	33	35	67
Anderlecht	30	16	7	7	49	42	7	55
Sporting Charleroi	30	13	12	5	46	30	16	51
Gent	30	14	8	8	45	27	18	50
Genk	30	11	11	8	44	36	8	44
Standard Liege	30	11	11	8	43	41	2	44
Kortrijk	30	12	6	12	42	39	3	42
Antwerp	30	10	11	9	38	40	–2	41
Zulte Waregem	30	11	4	15	47	52	–5	37
Sint-Truiden	30	9	10	11	29	41	–12	37
KV Oostende	30	10	6	14	42	41	1	36
Waasland-Beveren	30	9	8	13	50	51	–1	35
Lokeren	30	8	7	15	33	49	–16	31
Royal Excel Mouscron	30	8	6	16	40	59	–19	30
Eupen	30	8	5	17	40	57	–17	29
Mechelen*	30	6	9	15	31	49	–18	27

NB: Points earned in Qualifying phase are halved and rounded up at start of Championship Play-off phase.

Championship Play-offs 2017–18

	P	W	D	L	F	A	GD	Pts
Club Brugge	10	3	3	4	17	12	5	46
Standard Liege	10	6	3	1	20	9	11	43
Anderlecht	10	4	0	6	12	15	–3	40
Gent	10	4	2	4	8	8	0	39
Genk*	10	4	4	2	13	13	0	38
Sporting Charleroi	10	2	2	6	9	22	–13	34

* *Qualified for Europa League play-off final.*

Europa League Play-offs 2017–18

Group A

	P	W	D	L	F	A	GD	Pts
Zulte Waregem	10	9	1	0	35	8	27	28
Kortrijk	10	6	1	3	18	12	6	19
Royal Excel Mouscron	10	4	2	4	18	16	2	14
OH Leuven†	10	2	3	5	12	18	–6	9
Waasland-Beveren	10	2	2	6	12	23	–11	8
Lierse†	10	2	1	7	7	25	–18	7

Group B

	P	W	D	L	F	A	GD	Pts
Lokeren	10	6	3	1	21	11	10	21
Sint-Truiden	10	5	2	3	22	15	7	17
Antwerp	10	4	2	4	13	16	–3	14
KV Oostende	10	3	5	2	21	18	3	14
Eupen	10	2	2	6	11	21	–10	8
Beerschot Wilrijk†	10	1	4	5	14	21	–7	7

† *Qualified for play-offs from First Division B. Lierse folded, forfeiting final two games as 0-5 defeats.*

Semi-final
Zulte Waregem 2, Lokeren 2
aet; Zulte Waregem won 4-3 on penalties.

Final
Genk 2, Zulte Waregem 0
Top scorer: Harbaoui (Zulte Waregem) 22.
Cup Final: Standard Liege 1, Genk 0 *aet.*

BOSNIA-HERZEGOVINA

Football Federation of Bosnia & Herzegovina, Ferhadija 30, 71000 Sarajevo.
Founded: 1992. *FIFA:* 1996; *UEFA:* 1998. *National Colours:* Blue shirts, blue shorts, blue socks with white tops.

International matches 2017–18

Cyprus (a) 2-3, Gibraltar (a) 4-0*, Belgium (h) 3-4, Estonia (a) 2-1, USA (a) 0-0, Mexico (n) 0-1, Bulgaria (a) 1-0, Senegal (n) 0-0, Montenegro (h) 0-0, Korea Republic (a) 3-1.
* *Match played in Portugal.*

League Championship wins (1998–2018)

Zeljeznicar 6; Zrinjski 6; FK Sarajevo 3; Siroki Brijeg 2; Brotnjo 1; Leotar 1; Modrica 1; Borac Banja Luka 1.

Cup wins (1998; 2000–18)

Zeljeznicar 6; FK Sarajevo 4; Siroki Brijeg 3; Modrica 1; Orasje 1; Zrinjski 1; Slavija 1; Borac Banja Luka 1; Olimpic Sarajevo 1; Radnik Bijeljina 1.
See also Serbia section for Bosnian-Herzogovinian club honours in Yugoslav Republic era 1947–91.

Bosnian-Herzegovinian Premijer Liga 2017–18

	P	W	D	L	F	A	GD	Pts
Zrinjski	22	16	2	4	40	18	22	50
Zeljeznicar	22	16	2	4	37	16	21	50
Siroki Brijeg	22	13	3	6	37	17	20	42
FK Sarajevo	22	12	4	6	44	19	25	40
Krupa na Vrbasu	22	9	8	5	29	23	6	35
Radnik Bijeljina	22	9	5	8	21	24	–3	32
Mladost Doboj Kakanj	22	7	8	7	29	28	1	29
Borac Banja Luka	22	7	5	10	14	22	–8	26
GOSK Gabela	22	7	3	12	22	30	–8	24
Sloboda Tuzla	22	5	6	11	18	25	–7	21
Celik Zenica	22	4	1	17	17	54	–37	13
Vitez	22	1	5	16	9	41	–32	8

Championship Round 2017–18

	P	W	D	L	F	A	GD	Pts
Zrinjski	32	21	6	5	58	30	28	69
Zeljeznicar	32	19	6	7	49	30	19	63
FK Sarajevo	32	17	5	10	58	28	30	56
Siroki Brijeg	32	16	8	8	52	28	24	56
Radnik Bijeljina	32	12	9	11	35	38	–3	45
Krupa na Vrbasu	32	10	10	12	35	42	–7	40

Relegation Round 2017–18

	P	W	D	L	F	A	GD	Pts
GOSK Gabela	32	13	6	13	32	36	–4	45
Mladost Doboj Kakanj	32	11	9	12	42	44	–2	42
Borac Banja Luka†	32	10	8	14	22	31	–9	38
Sloboda Tuzla	32	11	6	15	31	34	–3	36
Celik Zenica	32	8	4	10	30	61	–31	28
Vitez†	32	3	6	23	15	57	–42	15

† *Borac Banja Luka failed to obtain a new licence and were demoted.*
Top scorer: Filipovic (Zrinjski) 16.
Cup Final: Zeljeznicar 2, 4, Krupa na Vrbasu 0, 0 (agg. 6-0).

BULGARIA

Bulgarian Football Union, 26 Tzar Ivan Assen II Str., 1124 Sofia.
Founded: 1923. *FIFA:* 1992; *UEFA:* 1954. *National Colours:* White shirts, green shorts, red socks.

International matches 2017–18

Sweden (h) 3-2, Netherlands (a) 1-3, France (h) 0-1, Luxembourg (a) 1-1, Saudi Arabia (n) 1-0, Bosnia-Herzegovina (h) 0-1, Kazakhstan (n) 2-1.

League Championship wins (1925–2018)

CSKA Sofia 31; Levski Sofia 26; Slavia Sofia 7; Ludogorets Razgrad 7; Lokomotiv Sofia 4; Litex Lovech 4; Vladislav Varna (now Cherno More Varna) 3; Botev Plovdiv (includes Trakija) 2; Athletic Slava 1923 1; Sokol Varna (now Spartak Varna) 1; Sportklub Sofia (now Septemvri Sofia) 1; Ticha Varna (now Cherno More Varna) 1; Spartak Plovdiv 1; Beroe Stara Zagora 1; FC Etar 1; Lokomotiv Plovdiv 1.

Cup wins (1946–2018)

Levski Sofia (incl. Vitosha 1) 24; CSKA Sofia (incl. Sredets 3) 20; Slavia Sofia 8; Lokomotiv Sofia 4; Litex Lovech 4; Botev Plovdiv (includes Trakija) 3; Beroe Stara Zagora 2; Ludogorets Razgrad 2; Spartak Plovdiv 1; Septemvri Sofia 1; Spartak Sofia 1; Marek Dupnitsa 1; Sliven 1; Cherno More Varna 1.

Bulgarian First League 2017–18

	P	W	D	L	F	A	GD	Pts
Ludogorets Razgrad	26	21	3	2	63	13	50	66
CSKA Sofia	26	19	6	1	59	14	45	63
Levski Sofia	26	14	8	4	37	14	23	50
Beroe	26	12	9	5	33	24	9	45
Botev Plovdiv	26	11	9	6	44	29	15	42
Vereya	26	10	5	11	24	34	–10	35
Slavia Sofia	26	8	8	10	34	37	–3	32
Septemvri Sofia	26	9	4	13	25	42	–17	31
Lokomotiv Plovdiv	26	8	7	11	22	37	–15	31
Cherno More	26	7	6	13	24	32	–8	27
Pirin Blagoevgrad	26	6	8	12	20	28	–8	26
Dunav Ruse 2010	26	5	6	15	17	38	–21	21
Etar	26	4	9	13	24	45	–21	21
Vitosha Bistritsa	26	0	8	18	12	51	–39	8

Championship Round 2017–18

	P	W	D	L	F	A	GD	Pts
Ludogorets Razgrad	36	27	7	2	91	22	69	88
CSKA Sofia	36	24	9	3	80	26	54	81
Levski Sofia*	36	18	10	8	55	27	28	64
Beroe	36	16	11	9	45	43	2	59
Botev Plovdiv	36	15	11	10	62	49	13	56
Vereya	36	10	6	20	27	61	–34	36

* *Qualified for Europa League play-off final.*

Relegation Round 2017–18

Group A

	P	W	D	L	F	A	GD	Pts
Slavia Sofia	32	11	10	11	44	44	0	43
Cherno More	32	11	7	14	33	35	–2	40
Pirin Blagoevgrad *+	32	7	9	16	29	42	–13	30
Vitosha Bistritsa+	32	1	10	21	17	60	–43	13

Group B

	P	W	D	L	F	A	GD	Pts
Septemvri Sofia	32	12	5	15	32	48	–16	41
Lokomotiv Plovdiv	32	9	10	13	26	43	–17	37
Dunav 2010+	32	8	7	17	24	44	–20	31
Etar+	32	6	10	16	31	52	–21	28

Europa League Play-offs

Quarter-finals
Cherno More 2, 2, Septemvri Sofia 1, 1 (agg. 4-2)
Lokomotiv Plovdiv 3, 3, Slavia Sofia 1, 0 (agg. 6-1)

Semi-finals
Cherno More 2, 2, Lokomotiv Plovdiv 1, 2 (agg. 4-3)
Final
Levski Sofia 4, Cherno More 1
Top scorer: Keseru (Ludogorets Razgrad) 26.
Cup Final: Slavia Sofia 0, Levski Sofia 0.
aet; Slavia Sofia won 4-2 on penalties.

CHANNEL ISLANDS

Guernsey

League Championship wins (1894–2018)
Northerners 32; Guernsey Rangers 17; Vale Recreation 15; St Martin's 13; Sylvans 10; Belgrave Wanderers 8; 2nd Bn Manchesters 3; Guernsey Rovers 2; 2nd Bn Royal Irish Regt 2; 2nd Bn Wiltshires 2; 10th Comp W Div Royal Artillery 1; 2nd Bn Leicesters 1; 2nd Bn PA Somerset Light Infantry 1; 2nd Middlesex Regt 1; Athletics 1; Band Comp 2nd Bn Royal Fusiliers 1; G&H Comp Royal Fusiliers 1; Grange 1; Yorkshire Regt (Green Howards).

Guernsey Priaulx League 2017–18

	P	W	D	L	F	A	GD	Pts
Guernsey Rovers	24	18	3	3	69	21	48	57
St Martin's	24	17	3	4	69	30	39	54
Northerners	24	15	1	8	70	35	35	46
Vale Recreation	24	8	8	8	48	41	7	32
Manzur	24	9	5	10	49	63	–14	32
Guernsey Rangers	24	9	4	11	52	49	3	31
Alderney	24	8	4	12	32	52	–20	28
Sylvans	24	7	2	15	46	60	–14	23
Belgrave Wanderers	24	1	2	21	28	112	–84	5

Top scorer: Fazakerley (Guernsey Rovers) 8.

Jersey

League Championship wins (1904–2018)
Jersey Wanderers 20; First Tower United 19; St Paul's 19; Jersey Scottish 11; Beeches Old Boys 5; Magpies 4; 2nd Bn King's Own Regt 3; Oaklands 3; St Peter 3; 1st Batt Devon Regt 2; 1st Bn East Surrey Regt 2; Georgetown 2; Mechanics 2; YMCA 2; 2nd Bn East Surrey Regt 1; 20th Comp Royal Garrison Artillery 1; National Rovers 1; Sporting Academics 1; Trinity 1.

Jersey Football Combination 2017–18

	P	W	D	L	F	A	GD	Pts
St Paul's	18	14	2	2	59	20	39	44
St Peter	18	10	5	3	55	22	33	35
Jersey Wanderers	18	9	2	7	56	28	28	29
St Clement	18	9	2	7	41	38	3	29
St Ouen	18	9	1	8	34	31	3	28
Rozel Rovers	18	4	3	11	21	44	–23	15
Grouville*	18	0	1	17	9	92	–83	1

Jersey Scottish withdrew.
Top scorer: Rawlings (St Clement) 26.

Upton Park Trophy 2018 (For Guernsey & Jersey League Champions)
St Paul's 2, Guernsey Rovers 0.

Upton Park Trophy wins (1907–2018)
Northerners 17 (incl. 1 shared); First Tower United 12; Jersey Wanderers 11 (incl. 1 shared); St Martin's 11; St Paul's 11; Jersey Scottish 6; Guernsey Rangers 5; Vale Recreation 4; Belgrave Wanderers 4; Beeches Old Boys 3; Old St Paul's 3; Magpies 3; Sylvans 3; St Peter 2; Jersey Mechanics 1; Jersey YMCA 1; National Rovers 1; Sporting Academics 1; Trinity 1.

CROATIA

Croatian Football Federation, Vukovarska 269A, 10000 Zagreb.
Founded: 1912. *FIFA:* 1992; *UEFA:* 1993. *National Colours:* Red and white check shirts, white shorts, blue socks.

International matches 2017–18
Kosovo (h) 1-0, Turkey (h) 0-1, Finland (h) 1-1, Ukraine (a) 2-0, Greece (h) 4-1, Greece (a) 0-0, Peru (n) 0-2, Mexico (n) 1-0, Brazil (n) 0-2, Senegal (h) 2-1, Nigeria (n) 2-0, Argentina (n) 3-0, Iceland (n) 2-1, Denmark (n) 1-1 (3-2p), Russia (a) 2-2 (4-3p), England (n) 2-1, France (n) 2-4.

League Championship wins (1992–2018)
Dinamo Zagreb (incl. Croatia Zagreb 3) 19; Hajduk Split 6; NK Zagreb 1; Rijeka 1.

Cup wins (1992–2018)
Dinamo Zagreb (incl. Croatia Zagreb 4) 15; Hajduk Split 6; Rijeka 4; Inter Zapresic 1; Osijek 1.
See also Serbia section for Croatian club honours in Yugoslav Republic era 1947–92.

Croatian Prva HNL 2017–18

	P	W	D	L	F	A	GD	Pts
Dinamo Zagreb	36	22	7	7	68	34	34	73
Rijeka	36	22	4	10	75	32	43	70
Hajduk Split	36	19	9	8	70	38	32	66
Osijek	36	14	14	8	53	38	15	56
Lokomotiva Zagreb	36	14	9	13	47	48	–1	51
Inter Zapresic	36	11	10	15	43	64	–21	43
Slaven Koprivnica	36	11	10	15	35	45	–10	43
Rudes	36	10	10	16	41	62	–21	40
Istra 1961+	36	6	9	21	28	60	–32	27
Cibalia*	36	6	8	22	36	75	–39	26

Top scorer: Soudani (Dinamo Zagreb) 17.
Cup Final: Dinamo Zagreb 1, Hajduk Split 0.

CYPRUS

Cyprus Football Association, 10 Achaion Street, 2413 Engomi, PO Box 25071, 1306 Nicosia.
Founded: 1934. *FIFA:* 1948; *UEFA:* 1962. *National Colours:* All blue with white trim.

International matches 2017–18
Bosnia-Herzegovina (h) 3-2, Estonia (a) 0-1, Greece (h) 1-2, Belgium (a) 0-4, Georgia (a) 0-1, Armenia (a) 2-3, Montenegro (h) 0-0, Jordan (a) 0-3.

League Championship wins (1935–2018)
APOEL 27; Omonia 20; Anorthosis 13; AEL Limassol 6; EPA Larnaca 3; Olympiakos Nicosia 3; Apollon Limassol 3; Pezoporikos Larnaca 2; Trust 1; Cetinkaya 1.

Cup wins (1935–2018)
APOEL 21; Omonia 14; Anorthosis 10; Apollon Limassol 9; AEL Limassol 6; EPA Larnaca 5; Trust 3; Cetinkaya 2; AEK Larnaca 2; Pezoporikos Larnaca 1; Olympiakos Nicosia 1; Nea Salamis Famagusta 1; APOP Kinyras 1.

Cypriot First Division 2017–18

	P	W	D	L	F	A	GD	Pts
APOEL	26	20	3	3	72	25	47	63
Apollon Limassol	26	18	7	1	67	15	52	61
Anorthosis Famagusta	26	16	8	2	41	17	24	56
AEK Larnaca	26	16	5	5	57	24	33	53
AEL Limassol	26	14	6	6	35	17	18	48
Omonia	26	13	5	8	51	38	13	44
Doxa Katokopia	26	10	4	12	35	40	–5	34
Ermis Aradippou	26	9	3	14	35	49	–14	30
Paphos	26	8	12	23	38	–15	26	
Nea Salamis Famagusta	26	6	6	14	28	46	–18	24
Alki Oroklini	26	6	5	15	30	57	–27	23
Olympiakos Nicosia	26	4	8	14	22	55	–33	20
Aris	26	3	7	16	19	49	–30	16
Ethnikos Achna	26	1	5	20	19	64	–45	8

Championship Round 2017–18

	P	W	D	L	F	A	GD	Pts
APOEL	36	27	5	4	92	35	57	86
Apollon Limassol	36	25	7	4	90	26	64	82
Anorthosis Famagusta	36	19	12	5	53	29	24	69
AEK Larnaca	36	20	8	8	74	39	35	68
AEL Limassol	36	17	7	12	47	38	9	58
Omonia	36	14	5	17	58	60	–2	47

Relegation Round 2017–18

	P	W	D	L	F	A	GD	Pts
Nea Salamis Famagusta	36	14	6	16	53	55	–2	48
Ermis Aradippou	36	14	4	18	50	64	–14	46
Doxa Katokopia	36	14	4	18	54	63	–9	46
Paphos	36	11	9	16	36	51	–15	42
Alki Oroklini*	36	11	6	19	48	73	–25	39
Olympiakos Nicosia*	36	5	9	22	34	81	–47	24

Top scorer: Derbyshire (Omonia) 23.
Cup Final: AEK Larnaca 2, Apollon Limassol 1.

CZECH REPUBLIC

Fotbalova Asociace Ceske Republiky, Diskarska 2431/4, PO Box 11, Praha 6 16017.
Founded: 1901. *FIFA:* 1907; *UEFA:* 1954. *National Colours:* All red.

International matches 2017–18
Germany (h) 1-2, Northern Ireland (a) 0-2, Azerbaijan (a) 2-1, San Marino (h) 5-0, Iceland (n) 2-1, Qatar (a) 1-0, Uruguay (n) 0-2, China PR (a) 4-1, Australia (n) 0-4, Nigeria (n) 1-0.

League Championship wins – Czechoslovakia (1925–93)
Sparta Prague 21; Slavia Prague 13; Dukla Prague (prev. UDA, now Marila Pribram) 11; Slovan Bratislava (formerly NV Bratislava) 8; Spartak Trnava 5; Banik Ostrava 3; Viktoria Zizkov 1; Inter Bratislava 1; Spartak Hradec Kralove 1; Zbrojovka Brno 1; Bohemians 1; Vitkovice 1.

Cup wins – Czechoslovakia (1961–93)
Dukla Prague 8; Sparta Prague 8; Slovan Bratislava 5; Spartak Trnava 4; Banik Ostrava 3; Lokomotiva Kosice 2; TJ Gottwaldov 1; DAC 1904 Dunajska Streda 1; 1.FC Kosice 1.

League Championship wins – Czech Republic (1994–2018)
Sparta Prague 12; Viktoria Plzen 5; Slavia Prague 4; Slovan Liberec 3; Banik Ostrava 1.

Cup wins – Czech Republic (1994–2018)
Sparta Prague 6; Slavia Prague 4; Viktoria Zizkov 2; Jablonec 2; Slovan Liberec 2; Teplice 2; Mlada Boleslav 2; Hradec Kralove (formerly Spartak) 1; Banik Ostrava 1; Viktoria Plzen 1; Sigma Olomouc 1; Fastav Zlin 1.

Czech First League 2017–18

	P	W	D	L	F	A	GD	Pts
Viktoria Plzen	30	20	6	4	55	23	32	66
Slavia Prague	30	17	8	5	50	19	31	59
Jablonec	30	16	8	6	49	27	22	56
Sigma Olomouc	30	15	10	5	41	22	19	55
Sparta Prague	30	14	11	5	43	25	18	53
Slovan Liberec	30	13	7	10	37	35	2	46
Bohemians 1905	30	9	11	10	30	29	1	38
Mlada Boleslav	30	9	7	14	31	43	–12	34
Teplice	30	8	10	12	32	40	–8	34
Fastav Zlin	30	8	9	13	31	48	–17	33
Dukla Prague	30	9	5	16	32	55	–23	32
Slovacko	30	6	13	11	23	32	–9	31
Banik Ostrava	30	7	10	13	36	43	–7	31
Karvina	30	7	9	14	32	40	–8	30
Vysocina Jihlava*	30	8	6	16	30	48	–18	30
Zbrojovka Brno*	30	6	6	18	20	43	–23	24

Top scorer: Krmencik (Viktoria Plzen) 16.
Cup Final: Slavia Prague 3, Jablonec 1.

DENMARK

Dansk Boldspil-Union, Idraettens Hus, DBU Alle 1, DK-2605, Brondby.
Founded: 1889. *FIFA:* 1904; *UEFA:* 1954. *National Colours:* Red shirts, white shorts, red socks.

International matches 2017–18
Poland (h) 4-0, Armenia (a) 4-1, Montenegro (a) 1-0, Romania (h) 1-1, Republic of Ireland (h) 0-0, Republic of Ireland (a) 5-1, Sweden (n) 0-1, Jordan (n) 2-3, Panama (h) 1-0, Chile (h) 0-0, Sweden (a) 0-0, Mexico (n) 2-0, Peru (n) 1-0, Australia (n) 1-1, France (n) 0-0, Croatia (n) 1-1 (2-3p).

League Championship wins (1913–2018)
KB Copenhagen 15; FC Copenhagen 12; Brondby 10; B 93 Copenhagen 9; AB (Akademisk) 9; B 1903 Copenhagen 7; Frem 6; AGF Aarhus 5; Vejle 5; Esbjerg 5; AaB Aalborg 4; Hvidovre 3; OB Odense 3; Koge 2; B 1909 Odense 2; Lyngby 2; Midtjylland 2; Silkeborg 1; Herfolge 1; Nordsjaelland 1.

Cup wins (1955–2018)
AGF Aarhus 9; FC Copenhagen 8; Vejle 6; Brondby 7; OB Odense 5; Esbjerg 3; AaB Aalborg 3; Randers Freja 3; Lyngby 3; Frem 2; B 1909 Odense 2; B 1903 Copenhagen 2; Nordsjaelland 2; B 1913 Odense 1; KB Copenhagen 1; Vanlose 1; Hvidovre 1; B 93 Copenhagen 1; AB (Akademisk) 1; Viborg 1; Silkeborg 1; Randers 1.

Danish Superliga 2017–18

	P	W	D	L	F	A	GD	Pts
Brondby	26	18	6	2	58	24	34	60
Midtjylland	26	19	3	4	60	29	31	60
Nordsjaelland	26	15	5	6	62	41	21	50
FC Copenhagen	26	13	5	8	50	33	17	44
AaB Aalborg	26	8	12	6	28	27	1	36
Horsens	26	7	14	5	32	34	–2	35
Hobro	26	8	8	10	33	33	0	32
SonderjyskE	26	8	7	11	36	34	2	31
OB Odense	26	8	7	11	32	31	1	31
AGF Aarhus	26	7	8	11	23	36	–13	29
Silkeborg	26	8	4	14	32	49	–17	28
Lyngby	26	4	9	13	31	53	–22	21

Championship Round 2017–18

	P	W	D	L	F	A	GD	Pts
Midtjylland	36	27	4	5	80	39	41	85
Brondby	36	24	9	3	82	37	45	81
Nordsjaelland	36	17	8	11	76	58	18	59
FC Copenhagen*	36	17	7	12	65	47	18	58
AaB Aalborg	36	10	15	11	38	44	–6	45
Horsens	36	8	16	12	43	57	–14	40

* *Qualified for Europa League play-off final.*

Relegation Round 2017–18
Group 1

	P	W	D	L	F	A	GD	Pts
Hobro	32	12	8	12	41	39	2	44
AGF Aarhus	32	11	8	13	35	43	–8	41
Silkeborg*+	32	9	5	18	39	60	–21	32
FC Helsingor*+	32	8	3	21	28	61	–33	27

Group 2

	P	W	D	L	F	A	GD	Pts
OB Odense	32	11	9	12	43	37	6	42
SonderjyskE	32	11	8	13	42	40	2	41
Randers+	32	7	9	16	32	52	–20	30
Lyngby*+	32	4	11	17	35	65	–30	23

Europa League Play-offs
Semi-finals
AGF Aarhus 3, OB Odense 2, 2 (agg. 6-4)
SonderjyskE 1, 2, Hobro 0, 3 (agg. 3-3; SonderjyskE won on away goals)
Final
AGF Aarhus 2, 2, SonderjyskE 2, 0 (agg. 4-2)
Europa League Play-off
FC Copenhagen 4, AGF Aarhus 1
Top scorer: Kirkevold (Hobro) 22.
Cup Final: Brondby 3, Silkeborg 1.

ENGLAND

The Football Association, Wembley Stadium, PO Box 1966, London SW1P 9EQ.
Founded: 1863. *FIFA:* 1905; *UEFA:* 1954. *National Colours:* White shirts with light blue trim, white shorts, red socks.

ESTONIA

Eesti Jalgpalli Liit, A. Le Coq Arena, Asula 4c, 11312 Tallinn.
Founded: 1921. *FIFA:* 1923; *UEFA:* 1992. *National Colours:* Blue shirts, black shorts, white socks.

International matches 2017–18
Greece (a) 0-0, Cyprus (h) 1-0, Gibraltar (a) 6-0*, Bosnia-Herzegovina (h) 1-2, Finland (a) 0-3, Malta (a) 3-0, Fiji (a) 2-0, Vanuatu (a) 1-0, New Caledonia (a) 1-1, Sweden (n) 1-1, Armenia (a) 0-0, Georgia (a) 0-2, Lithuania (h) 2-0, Latvia (a) 0-1, Morocco (a) 1-3.
* *Match played in Portugal.*

League Championship wins (1921–40; 1992–2017)
Flora 11; Sport 9; FCI Levadia (formerly Levadia Maardu) 9; Estonia 5; Tallinna JK 2; Norma 2; Lantana (formerly Nikol) 2; Sillamae Kalev 2; Olimpia Tartu 1; TVMK Tallinn 1; Nomme Kalju 1; FCI Tallinn 1.

Cup wins (1993–2018)
FCI Levadia (incl. Levadia Maardu 2) 9; Flora 7; Tallinna Sadam 2; TVMK Tallinn 2; Lantana (formerly Nikol) 1; Norma 1; Narva Trans 1; Levadia Tallinn (pre-2004) 1; Nomme Kalju 1; FCI Tallinn 1.

Estonian Meistriliiga 2017

	P	W	D	L	F	A	GD	Pts
UE Santa Coloma	21	8	5	8	35	25	10	29
Flora	36	28	6	2	100	28	72	90
Levadia Tallinn	36	25	9	2	106	20	86	84
Nomme Kalju	36	24	6	6	101	32	69	78
FCI Tallinn	36	20	5	11	103	47	56	65
Narva Trans	36	13	6	17	46	63	–17	45
Paide Linnameeskond	36	10	8	18	47	88	–41	38
Tammeka Tartu	36	9	10	17	40	63	–23	37
Sillamae Kalev*	36	10	6	20	52	76	–24	36
Viljandi Tulevik	36	8	4	24	34	95	–61	28
Parnu Vaprus	36	2	2	32	29	146	–117	8

* *Sillamae Kalev demoted for financial reasons.*
N.B. FCI Tallinn and Levadia Tallinn merged for 2018 season, as FCI Levadia.
Top scorers (joint): Prosa (FCI Tallinn), Sappinen (Flora) 27.
Cup Final: FCI Levadia 1, Flora 0.

FAROE ISLANDS

Fotboltssamband Foroya, Gundadalur, PO Box 3028, 110 Torshavn.
Founded: 1979. *FIFA:* 1988; *UEFA:* 1990. *National Colours:* White shirts with blue trim, white shorts, white socks.

International matches 2017–18
Portugal (a) 1-5, Andorra (h) 1-0, Latvia (h) 0-0, Hungary (a) 0-1, Latvia (n) 1-1, Liechtenstein (n) 3-0.

League Championship wins (1942–2017)
HB Torshavn 22; KI Klaksvik 17; B36 Torshavn 11; TB Tvoroyri 7; GI Gota 6; B68 Toftir 3; EB/Streymur 2; Vikingur 2; SI Sorvagur 1; IF Fuglafjordur 1; B71 Sandur 1; VB Vagur 1; NSI Runavik 1.

Cup wins (1955–2017)
HB Torshavn 26; KI Klaksvik 6; GI Gota 6; TB Tvoroyri 5; B36 Torshavn 5; Vikingur 5; EB/Streymur 4; NSI Runavik 3; VB Vagur 1; B71 Sandur 1.

Faroese Premier League 2017

	P	W	D	L	F	A	GD	Pts
Vikingur	27	15	7	5	62	33	29	52
KI Klaksvik	27	14	10	3	50	26	24	52
B36 Torshavn	27	13	9	5	62	39	23	48
NSI Runavik	27	13	7	7	57	35	22	46
HB Torshavn	27	10	9	8	43	31	12	39
Skala	27	8	9	10	31	40	–9	33
EB / Streymur	27	9	5	13	34	49	–15	32
TB Tvoroyri	27	8	5	14	31	45	–14	29
07 Vestur	27	8	4	15	37	59	–22	28
IF Fuglafjordur*	27	3	3	21	23	73	–50	12

Top scorer: Lawal (Vikingur) 17.
Cup Final: NSI Runavik 1, B36 Torshavn 0.

FINLAND

Suomen Palloliitto Finlands Bollfoerbund, Urheilukatu 5, PO Box 191, 00251 Helsinki.
Founded: 1907. *FIFA:* 1908; *UEFA:* 1954. *National Colours:* White shirts with blue trim, white shorts, white socks.

International matches 2017–18
Iceland (h) 1-0, Kosovo (a) 1-0*, Croatia (a) 1-1, Turkey (h) 2-2, Estonia (h) 3-0, Jordan (n) 2-1, FYR Macedonia (n) 0-0, Malta (n) 5-0, Romania (a) 0-2, Belarus (h) 2-0.
* *Match played in Albania.*

League Championship wins (1908–2017)
HJK Helsinki 28; HPS Helsinki 9; Haka Valkeakoski 9; TPS Turku 8; HIFK Helsinki 7; KuPS Kuopio 5; Kuusysi Lahti 5; KIF Helsinki 4; AIFK Turku 3; VIFK Vaasa 3; Reipas Lahti 3; Tampere United 3; VPS Vaasa 2; KTP Kotka 2; OPS Oulu 2; Jazz Pori 2; Unitas Helsinki 1; PUS Helsinki 1; Sudet Viipuri 1; HT Helsinki 1; Ilves-Kissat 1; Pyrkiva Turku 1; KPV Kokkola 1; Ilves Tampere 1; TPV Tampere 1; MyPa Anjalankoski (renamed MYPA-47) 1; Inter Turku 1; SJK Seinajoki 1; IFK Mariehamn 1.

Cup wins (1955–2018)
HJK Helsinki 13; Haka Valkeakoski 12; Reipas Lahti 7; KTP Kotka 4; TPS Turku 3; MyPa Anjalankoski (renamed MYPA-47) 3; KuPS Kuopio 2; Mikkeli 2; Ilves Tampere 2; Kuusysi Lahti 2; RoPS Rovaniemi 2; Inter Turku 2; Pallo-Pojat 1; Drott (renamed Jaro) 1; HPS Helsinki 1; AIFK Turku 1; Jokerit (formerly PK-35) 1; Atlantis 1; Tampere United 1; FC FC Honka 1; IFK Mariehamn 1; SJK Seinajoki 1.

Finnish Veikkausliiga 2017

	P	W	D	L	F	A	GD	Pts
HJK Helsinki	33	23	7	3	78	16	62	76
KuPS Kuopio	33	16	8	9	51	36	15	56
Ilves	33	15	11	7	39	35	4	56
Lahti	33	12	13	8	46	31	15	49
IFK Mariehamn	33	13	10	10	44	42	2	49
SJK Seinajoki	33	13	8	12	42	47	–5	47
RoPS Rovaniemi	33	12	6	15	43	51	–8	42
VPS Vaasa	33	9	12	12	38	51	–13	39
Inter Turku	33	10	8	15	54	57	–3	38
PS Kemi	33	8	8	17	38	59	–21	32
HIFK Helsinki*+	33	6	11	16	37	54	–17	29
JJK Jyvaskyla*	33	6	8	19	32	63	–31	26

Top scorer: Kangaskolkka (HIFK Mariehamn) 16.
2016–17 Cup Final: HJK Helsinki 1, SJK Seinajoki 0 (omitted from last edition).
2017–18 Cup Final: Inter Turku 1, HJK Helsinki 0.

FRANCE

Federation Francaise de Football, 87 Boulevard de Grenelle, 75738 Paris Cedex 15.
Founded: 1919. *FIFA:* 1904; *UEFA:* 1954. *National Colours:* Blue shirts, white shorts, red socks.

International matches 2017–18
Netherlands (h) 4-0, Luxembourg (h) 0-0, Bulgaria (a) 1-0, Belarus (h) 2-1, Wales (h) 2-0, Germany (a) 2-2, Colombia (h) 2-3, Russia (a) 3-1, Republic of Ireland (h) 2-0, Italy (h) 3-1, USA (h) 1-1, Australia (n) 2-1, Peru (n) 1-0, Denmark (n) 0-0, Argentina (n) 4-3, Uruguay (n) 2-0, Belgium (n) 1-0, Croatia (n) 4-2.

League Championship wins (1933–2018)
Saint-Etienne 10; Olympique Marseille 9; AS Monaco 8; Nantes 8; Paris Saint-Germain 7; Olympique Lyonnais 7; Stade de Reims 6; Bordeaux 6; Lille OSC (includes Olympique Lillois) 4; OGC Nice 4; FC Sete 2; Sochaux 2; Racing Club Paris 1; Roubaix-Tourcoing 1; Strasbourg 1; Auxerre 1; Lens 1; Montpellier 1.

Cup wins (1918–2018)
Paris Saint-Germain 12; Olympique Marseille 10; Lille OSC 6; Saint-Etienne 6; Red Star 5; Racing Club Paris 5; AS Monaco 5; Olympique Lyonnais 5; Bordeaux 4; Auxerre 4; Strasbourg 3; OGC Nice 3; Nantes 3; CAS Genereaux 2; Montpellier 2; FC Sete 2; Sochaux 2; Stade de Reims 2; Sedan 2; Stade Rennais 2; Metz 2; Guingamp 2; Olympique de Pantin 1; CA Paris 1; Club Français 1; AS Cannes 1; Excelsior Roubaix 1; EF Nancy-Lorraine 1; Toulouse 1; Le Havre 1; AS Nancy 1; Bastia 1; Lorient 1.

French Ligue 1 2017–18

	P	W	D	L	F	A	GD	Pts
Paris Saint-Germain	38	29	6	3	108	29	79	93
AS Monaco	38	24	8	6	85	45	40	80
Olympique Lyonnais	38	23	9	6	87	43	44	78
Olympique Marseille	38	22	11	5	80	47	33	77
Rennes	38	16	10	12	50	44	6	58
Bordeaux	38	16	7	15	53	48	5	55
Saint-Etienne	38	15	10	13	47	50	–3	55
Nice	38	15	9	14	53	52	1	54
Nantes	38	14	10	14	36	41	–5	52
Montpellier	38	11	18	9	36	33	3	51
Dijon	38	13	9	16	55	73	–18	48
Guingamp	38	12	11	15	48	59	–11	47
Amiens	38	12	9	17	37	42	–5	45
Angers	38	9	14	15	42	52	–10	41
Strasbourg	38	9	11	18	44	67	–23	38
Caen	38	10	8	20	27	52	–25	38
Lille OSC	38	10	8	20	41	67	–26	38
Toulouse+	38	9	10	19	38	54	–16	37
Troyes+	38	9	6	23	32	59	–27	33
Metz*	38	6	8	24	34	76	–42	26

Top scorer: Cavani (Paris Saint-Germain) 28.
Cup Final: Paris Saint-Germain 2, Les Herbiers 0.

FYR MACEDONIA

Football Federation of the Former Yugoslav Republic of Macedonia, 8-ma Udarna Brigada 31-A, PO Box 84, 1000 Skopje.
Founded: 1948. *FIFA:* 1994; *UEFA:* 1994. *National Colours:* All red.

International matches 2017–18
Israel (a) 1-0, Albania (a) 1-1, Italy (a) 1-1, Liechtenstein (h) 4-0, Norway (h) 2-0, Finland (n) 0-0, Azerbaijan (n) 1-1.

League Championship wins (1992–2018)
Vardar 10*; Rabotnicki 4; Sileks 3; Sloga Jugomagnat 3; Pobeda 2; Shkendija 2; Makedonija GjP 1; Renova 1.
* *Vardar also won 1 League Championship (1986–87) in Yugoslav Republic era, later controversially annulled.*

Cup wins (1992–2018)
Vardar 5*; Rabotnicki 4; Sloga Jugomagnat 3; Sileks 2; Pelister 2; Shkendija 2; Pobeda 1; Cementarnica 55 1; Bashkimi 1; Makedonija GjP 1; Metalurg 1; Renova 1.
* *Vardar also won 1 Cup (1961) in Yugoslav Republic era.*

Macedonian Prva Liga Table 2017–18

	P	W	D	L	F	A	GD	Pts
Shkendija	36	29	4	3	101	27	74	91
Vardar	36	16	8	12	53	41	12	56
Rabotnicki	36	14	10	12	50	43	7	52
Shkupi	36	13	12	11	51	46	5	51
Sileks	36	13	11	12	30	37	–7	50
Akademija Pandev	36	10	12	14	43	47	–4	42

Renova	36	10	11	15	36	53	–17	41
Pobeda+	36	10	8	18	36	56	–20	38
Skopje*	36	7	14	15	24	43	–19	35
Pelister*	36	8	10	18	37	68	–31	34

Top scorer: Ibraimi (Shkendija) 23.
Cup Final: Shkendija 3, Pelister 0.

GEORGIA

Georgian Football Federation, 76A Chavchavadze Avenue, 0179 Tbilisi.
Founded: 1990. *FIFA:* 1992; *UEFA:* 1992. *National Colours:* All white with red trim.

International matches 2017–18

Republic of Ireland (h) 1-1, Austria (a) 1-1, Wales (h) 0-1, Serbia (a) 0-1, Cyprus (h) 1-0, Belarus (h) 2-2, Lithuania (n) 4-0, Estonia (h) 2-0, Malta (n) 1-0, Luxembourg (a) 0-1.

League Championship wins (1990–2017)

Dinamo Tbilisi 16; Torpedo Kutaisi 4; WIT Georgia 2; Metalurgi Rustavi (formerly Olimpi) 2; Zestafoni 2; Sioni Bolnisi 1; Dila Gori 1; Samtredia 1.

Cup wins (1990–2017)

Dinamo Tbilisi 13; Torpedo Kutaisi 3; Lokomotivi Tbilisi 3; Ameri Tbilisi 2; Guria Lanchkhuti 1; Dinamo Batumi 1; Zestafoni 1; WIT Georgia 1; Gagra 1; Dila Gori 1; Chikhura Sachkhere 1.
See also Russia section for Georgian club honours in Soviet era 1936–91.

Georgian Erovnuli Liga 2017

	P	W	D	L	F	A	GD	Pts
Torpedo Kutaisi	36	23	7	6	59	27	32	76
Dinamo Tbilisi	36	23	6	7	79	29	50	75
Samtredia	36	20	8	8	62	39	23	68
Saburtalo	36	18	6	12	61	42	19	60
Chikhura Sachkhere	36	17	4	15	47	54	–7	55
Lokomotivi Tbilisi	36	16	5	15	63	53	10	53
Dila Gori	36	11	8	17	41	51	–10	41
Dinamo Batumi*	36	10	3	23	28	60	–32	33
Kolkheti Poti+	36	6	8	22	31	73	–42	26
Shukura Kobuleti*	36	4	9	23	35	78	–43	21

Top scorer: Sikharulidze (Lokomotivi Tbilisi) 25.
Cup Final: Chikhura Sachkhere 0, Torpedo Kutaisi 0.
aet; Chikhura Sachkhere won 4-3 on penalties.

GERMANY

Deutscher Fussball-Bund, Hermann-Neuberger-Haus, Otto-Fleck-Schneise 6, 60528 Frankfurt Am Main.
Founded: 1900. *FIFA:* 1904; *UEFA:* 1954. *National Colours:* White shirts with red and black trim, white shorts, white socks with red tops.

International matches 2017–18

Czech Republic (a) 2-1, Norway (h) 6-0, Northern Ireland (a) 3-1, Azerbaijan (h) 5-1, England (h) 0-0, France (h) 2-2, Spain (h) 1-1, Brazil (a) 0-1, Austria (a) 1-2, Saudi Arabia (h) 2-1, Mexico (n) 0-1, Sweden (n) 2-1, Korea Republic (n) 0-2.

League Championship wins (1903–2018)

Bayern Munich 28; 1.FC Nuremberg 9; Borussia Dortmund 8; Schalke 04 7; Hamburger SV 6; VfB Stuttgart 5; Borussia Moenchengladbach 5; 1.FC Kaiserslautern 4; Werder Bremen 4; 1.FC Lokomotive Leipzig 3; SpVgg Greuther Furth 3; 1.FC Cologne 3; Viktoria Berlin 2; Hertha Berlin 2; Hannover 96 2; Dresden SC 2; Union Berlin 1; Freiburger FC 1; Phoenix Karlsruhe 1; Karlsruher FV 1; Holstein Kiel 1; Fortuna Dusseldorf 1; Rapid Vienna 1; VfR Mannheim 1; Rot-Weiss Essen 1; Eintracht Frankfurt 1; Munich 1860 1; Eintracht Braunschweig 1; VfL Wolfsburg 1.

Cup wins (1935–2018)

Bayern Munich 18; Werder Bremen 6; Schalke 04 5; Eintracht Frankfurt 5; 1.FC Nuremberg 4; Borussia Dortmund 4; 1.FC Cologne 4; VfB Stuttgart 3; Borussia Moenchengladbach 3; Hamburger SV 3; Dresden SC 2; Munich 1860 2; Karlsruhe SC 2; Fortuna Dusseldorf 2; 1.FC Kaiserslautern 2; 1.FC Lokomotive Leipzig 1; Rapid Vienna 1; First Vienna 1; Rot-Weiss Essen 1; SW Essen 1; Kickers Offenbach 1; Bayer Uerdingen 1; Hannover 96 1; Bayer Leverkusen 1; VfLWolfsburg 1.

German Bundesliga 2017–18

	P	W	D	L	F	A	GD	Pts
Bayern Munich	34	27	3	4	92	28	64	84
Schalke 04	34	18	9	7	53	37	16	63
TSG Hoffenheim	34	15	10	9	66	48	18	55
Borussia Dortmund	34	15	10	9	64	47	17	55
Bayer Leverkusen	34	15	10	9	58	44	14	55
RB Leipzig	34	15	8	11	57	53	4	53
Stuttgart	34	15	6	13	36	36	0	51
Eintracht Frankfurt	34	14	7	13	45	45	0	49
Borussia M'gladbach	34	13	8	13	47	52	–5	47
Hertha Berlin	34	10	13	11	43	46	–3	43
Werder Bremen	34	10	12	12	37	40	–3	42
Augsburg	34	10	11	13	43	46	–3	41
Hannover 96	34	10	9	15	44	54	–10	39
Mainz 05	34	9	9	16	38	52	–14	36
Freiburg	34	8	12	14	32	56	–24	36
Wolfsburg+	34	6	15	13	36	48	–12	33
Hamburger SV*	34	8	7	19	29	53	–24	31
1.FC Cologne*	34	5	7	22	35	70	–35	22

Top scorer: Lewandowski (Bayern Munich) 29.
Cup Final: Eintracht Frankfurt 3, Bayern Munich 1.

GIBRALTAR

Gibraltar Football Association, Bayside Sports Complex, PO Box 513, Gibraltar GX11 1AA.
Founded: 1895. *UEFA:* 2013. *National Colours:* Red shirts with white trim, red shorts, red socks.

International matches 2017–18

Belgium (a) 0-9, Bosnia-Herzegovina (h) 0-4*, Estonia (h) 0-6*, Greece (a) 0-4, Latvia (h) 1-0.
* Match played in Portugal.

League Championship wins (1896–2018)

Lincoln Red Imps 23 (incl. Newcastle United 5; 1 title shared); Prince of Wales 19; Glacis United 17 (incl. 1 shared); Britannia (now Britannia XI) 14; Gibraltar United 11; Europa 7; Manchester United (now Manchester 62) 7; St Theresa's 3; Chief Construction 2; Jubilee 2; Exiles 2; South United 2; Gibraltar FC 2; Albion 1; Athletic 1; Royal Sovereign 1; Commander of the Yard 1; St Joseph's 1.

Cup wins (1895–2018)

Lincoln Red Imps (incl. Newcastle United 4) 17; St Joseph's 9; Europa 7; Glacis United 5; Britannia (now Britannia XI) 3; Gibraltar United 3; Manchester United (now Manchester 62) 3; Gibraltar FC 1; HMS Hood 1; 2nd Bn The King's Regt 1; AARA 1; RAF New Camp 1; 4th Bn Royal Scots 1; Prince of Wales 1; Manchester United Reserves 1; 2nd Bn Royal Green Jackets 1; RAF Gibraltar 1; St Theresa's 1.

Gibraltarian Premier Division 2017–18

	P	W	D	L	F	A	GD	Pts
Lincoln Red Imps	27	21	2	4	71	19	52	65
Europa	27	19	3	5	67	20	47	60
St Joseph's	27	17	3	7	53	30	23	54
Gibraltar United	27	16	5	6	45	27	18	53
Mons Calpe	27	14	2	11	48	35	13	44
Gibraltar Phoenix	27	8	6	13	34	47	–13	30
Glacis United	27	7	5	15	34	44	–10	26
Lions Gibraltar	27	6	5	16	27	63	–36	23
Lynx+	27	6	4	17	22	48	–26	22
Manchester 62*	27	0	7	20	20	88	–68	7

Top scorer: Carreno (Europa) 19.
Cup Final: Europa 2, Mons Calpe 1.

GOZO

Gozo Football Association, GFA Headquarters, Mgarr Road, Xewkija, XWK 9014, Malta. (Not a member of FIFA or UEFA.)
Founded: 1936.

League Championship wins (1938–2018)

Victoria Hotspurs 12; Nadur Youngsters 11; Sannat Lions 10; Xewkija Tigers 8; Ghajnsielem 7; Xaghra United 6 (incl. Xaghra Blue Stars 1; Xaghra Young Stars 1); Salesian Youths (renamed Oratory Youths) 6; Victoria Athletics 4; Victoria Stars 1; Victoria City 1; Calypcians 1; Victoria United (renamed Victoria Wanderers) 1; Kercem Ajax 1; Zebbug Rovers 1.

Cup wins (1972–2018)

Xewkija Tigers 11; Sannat Lions 9; Nadur Youngsters 8; Ghajnsielem 6; Xaghra United 4; Kercem Ajax 2; Calypsians 1; Calypsians Bosco Youths 1; Victoria Hotspurs 1; Qala St Joseph 1; Victoria Wanderers 1.

Gozitan First Division 2017–18

	P	W	D	L	F	A	GD	Pts
Victoria Hotspurs	21	19	1	1	63	15	48	58
Nadur Youngsters	21	13	1	7	55	39	16	40

Xewkija Tigers	21	10	2	9	45	37	8	32
Ghajnsielem	21	7	6	8	30	41	–11	27
Kercem Ajax	21	7	5	9	34	50	–16	26
Gharb Rangers	21	6	4	11	28	41	–13	22
Victoria Wanderers+	21	5	4	12	35	47	–12	19
Oratory Youths*	21	3	5	13	28	48	–20	14

Top scorer: Da Silva (Victoria Hotspurs) 19.
Cup Final: Xewkija Tigers 2, Ghajnsielem 1.

GREECE

Hellenic Football Federation, Parko Goudi, PO Box 14161, 11510 Athens.
Founded: 1926. *FIFA:* 1927; *UEFA:* 1954. *National Colours:* All white.

International matches 2017–18

Estonia (h) 0-0, Belgium (h) 1-2, Cyprus (a) 2-1, Gibraltar (h) 4-0, Croatia (a) 1-4, Croatia (h) 0-0, Switzerland (h) 0-1, Egypt (n) 1-0, Saudi Arabia (n) 0-2.

League Championship wins (1927–2018)

Olympiacos 44; Panathinaikos 20; AEK Athens 12; Aris Salonika 3; PAOK 2; Larissa 1.

Cup wins (1932–2018)

Olympiacos 27; Panathinaikos 18; AEK Athens 15; PAOK 6; Panionios 2; Larissa 2; Ethnikos 1; Aris Salonika 1; Iraklis 1; Kastoria 1; OFI Crete 1.

Greek Super League 2017–18

	P	W	D	L	F	A	GD	Pts
AEK Athens	30	21	7	2	50	12	38	70
PAOK (–3)	30	21	4	5	59	19	40	64
Olympiacos (–3)	30	18	6	6	63	28	35	57
Atromitos	30	15	11	4	43	21	22	56
Asteras Tripolis	30	12	9	9	39	24	15	45
Xanthi	30	12	9	9	31	30	1	45
Panionios	30	10	10	10	32	31	1	40
Panaitolikos	30	9	8	13	31	40	–9	35
PAS Giannina	30	7	13	10	31	34	–3	34
Levadiakos	30	8	10	12	23	34	–11	34
Panathinaikos (–8)	30	10	10	10	30	30	0	32
Larissa	30	7	10	13	22	41	–19	31
Lamia	30	6	12	12	20	34	–14	30
Apollon Smirnis	30	6	11	13	23	36	–13	29
Kerkyra*	30	4	10	16	19	51	–32	22
Platanias*	30	2	4	24	14	65	–51	10

Top scorer: Prijovic (PAOK) 19.
Cup Final: PAOK 2, AEK Athens 0.

HUNGARY

Magyar Labdarugo Szovetseg, Kanai ut 2. D, 1112 Budapest.
Founded: 1901. *FIFA:* 1907; *UEFA:* 1954. *National Colours:* Red shirts, white shorts, green socks.

International matches 2017–18

Latvia (h) 3-1, Portugal (h) 0-1, Switzerland (a) 2-5, Faroe Islands (h) 1-0, Luxembourg (a) 1-2, Costa Rica (h) 1-0, Kazakhstan (h) 2-3, Scotland (h) 0-1, Belarus (a) 1-1, Australia (h) 1-2.

League Championship wins (1901–2018)

Ferencvaros 29; MTK Budapest 23; Ujpest 20; Budapest Honved 14 (incl. Kispest Honved); Debrecen 7; Vasas 6; Csepel 4; Gyor 4; Videoton 3; Budapesti TC 2; Nagyvarad 1; Vac 1; Dunaferr (renamed Dunaujvaros) 1; Zalaegerszeg 1.

Cup wins (1910–2018)

Ferencvaros 23; MTK Budapest 12; Ujpest 10; Budapest Honved 7 (inc. Kispest Honved); Debrecen 6; Vasas 4; Gyor 4; Diosgyor 2; Bocskai 1; III Keruleti TUE 1; Soroksar 1; Szolnoki MAV 1; Siofoki Banyasz 1; Bekescsaba 1; Pecsi 1; Sopron 1; Fehervar (renamed Videoton) 1; Kecskemet 1.
Cup not regularly held until 1964.

Hungarian Nemzeti Bajnoksag I 2017–18

	P	W	D	L	F	A	GD	Pts
Videoton	33	20	8	5	65	28	37	68
Ferencvaros	33	18	12	3	69	31	38	66
Ujpest	33	13	10	8	41	38	3	49
Budapest Honved	33	13	8	12	50	53	–3	47
Debrecen	33	12	8	13	53	47	6	44
Puskas Akademia	33	11	10	12	41	46	–5	43
Paksi SE	33	11	9	13	43	48	–5	42
Szombathelyi Haladas	33	11	5	17	35	50	–15	38
Mezokovesd-Zsory	33	9	10	14	35	52	–17	37
Diosgyor	33	10	6	17	44	53	–9	36

Balmazujvaros*	33	8	12	13	39	46	–7	36
Vasas Budapest*	33	9	7	17	38	61	–23	34

Top scorer: Lanzafame (Budapest Honved) 18.
Cup Final: Ujpest 2, Puskas Akademia 2.
aet; Ujpest won 5-4 on penalties.

ICELAND

Knattspyrnusamband Islands, Laugardal, 104 Reykjavik.
Founded: 1947. *FIFA:* 1947; *UEFA:* 1954. *National Colours:* All blue.

International matches 2017–18

Finland (a) 0-1, Ukraine (h) 2-0, Turkey (a) 3-0, Kosovo (h) 2-0, Czech Republic (n) 1-2, Qatar (a) 1-1, Indonesia (a) 6-0, Indonesia (a) 4-1, Mexico (n) 0-3, Peru (n) 1-3, Norway (h) 2-3, Ghana (h) 2-2, Argentina (n) 1-1, Nigeria (n) 0-2, Croatia (n) 1-2.

League Championship wins (1912–2017)

KR Reykjavik 26; Valur 21; Fram 18; IA Akranes 18; FH Hafnarfjordur 8; Vikingur 5; IBK Keflavik 4; IBV Vestmannaeyjar 3; KA Akureyri 1; Breidablik 1 ; Stjarnan 1.

Cup wins (1960–2017)

KR Reykjavik 14; Valur 11; IA Akranes 9; Fram 8; IBV Vestmannaeyjar 5; IBK Keflavik 4; Fylkir 2; FH Hafnarfjordur 2; IBA Akureyri 1; Vikingur 1; Breidablik 1.

Icelandic Urvalsdeild 2017

	P	W	D	L	F	A	GD	Pts
Valur	22	15	5	2	43	20	23	50
Stjarnan	22	10	8	4	46	25	21	38
FH Hafnarfjordur	22	9	8	5	33	25	8	35
KR Reykjavik	22	8	7	7	31	29	2	31
Grindavik	22	9	4	9	31	39	–8	31
Breidablik	22	9	3	10	34	35	–1	30
KA	22	7	8	7	37	31	6	29
Vikingur Reykjavik	22	7	6	9	32	36	–4	27
IBV Vestmannaeyjar	22	7	4	11	32	38	–6	25
Fjolnir	22	6	7	9	32	40	–8	25
Vikingur Olafsvik*	22	6	6	12	24	44	–20	22
IA Akranes*	22	3	8	11	28	41	–13	17

Top scorer: Bjarnason (Grindavik) 19.
Cup Final: IBV Vestmannaeyjar 1, FH Hafnarfjordur 0.

ISRAEL

Israel Football Association, Ramat Gan Stadium, 299 Aba Hilell Street, PO Box 3591, Ramat Gan 52134.
Founded: 1928. *FIFA:* 1929; *UEFA:* 1994. *National Colours:* Blue shirts with white trim, blue shorts, blue socks.

International matches 2017–18

FYR Macedonia (h) 0-1, Italy (a) 0-1, Liechtenstein (h) 1-0, Spain (h) 0-1, Romania (h) 1-2.

League Championship wins (1932–2018)

Maccabi Tel Aviv 21; Hapoel Tel Aviv 14 (incl. 1 shared); Maccabi Haifa 12; Hapoel Petah Tikva 6; Beitar Jerusalem 6; Maccabi Netanya 5; Hapoel Be'er Sheva 5; Hakoah Ramat Gan 2; British Police 1; Beitar Tel Aviv 1 (shared); Hapoel Ramat Gan 1; Hapoel Kfar Saba 1; Bnei Yehuda 1; Hapoel Haifa 1; Ironi Kiryat Shmona 1.

Cup wins (1928–2018)

Maccabi Tel Aviv 23; Hapoel Tel Aviv 15; Beitar Jerusalem 7; Maccabi Haifa 6; Hapoel Haifa 4; Bnei Yehuda 3; Hapoel Kfar Saba 3; Maccabi Petah Tikva 2; Beitar Tel Aviv 2; Hapoel Petah Tikva 2; Hakoah Amidar Ramat Gan 2; Hapoel Ramat Gan 2; Maccabi Hashmonai Jerusalem 1; British Police 1; Hapoel Jerusalem 1; Maccabi Netanya 1; Hapoel Yehud 1; Hapoel Lod 1; Hapoel Be'er Sheba 1; Bnei Sakhnin 1; Ironi Kiryat Shmona 1.

Israeli Premier League Qualifying Table 2017–18

	P	W	D	L	F	A	GD	Pts
Hapoel Be'er Sheva	26	17	6	3	43	18	25	57
Beitar Jerusalem	26	17	5	4	60	30	30	56
Maccabi Tel Aviv	26	16	7	3	44	20	24	55
Hapoel Haifa	26	15	7	4	36	21	15	52
Maccabi Netanya	26	12	9	5	43	29	14	45
Bnei Yehuda	26	11	7	8	32	26	6	40
Maccabi Petah Tikva	26	9	6	11	30	35	–5	33
Ironi Kiryat Shmona	26	9	5	12	28	30	–2	32
Bnei Sakhnin	26	8	6	12	24	35	–11	30
Maccabi Haifa	26	6	7	13	26	33	–7	25
Hapoel Ra'anana	26	6	6	14	23	40	–17	24

	P	W	D	L	F	A	GD	Pts
Ashdod	26	4	9	13	22	39	–17	21
Hapoel Ashkelon	26	3	8	15	19	39	–20	17
Hapoel Acre (–2)	26	4	2	20	19	54	–35	12

Championship Round 2017–18

	P	W	D	L	F	A	GD	Pts
Hapoel Be'er Sheva	36	24	8	4	70	27	43	80
Maccabi Tel Aviv	36	21	8	7	60	33	27	71
Beitar Jerusalem	36	20	8	8	75	51	24	68
Hapoel Haifa	36	17	11	8	48	39	9	62
Maccabi Netanya	36	16	10	10	59	54	5	58
Bnei Yehuda	36	13	10	13	47	41	6	49

Relegation Round 2017–18

	P	W	D	L	F	A	GD	Pts
Ironi Kiryat Shmona	33	13	6	14	39	36	3	45
Maccabi Petah Tikva	33	12	7	14	40	44	–4	43
Hapoel Ra'anana	33	11	7	15	36	45	–9	40
Maccabi Haifa	33	10	8	15	38	39	–1	38
Bnei Sakhnin	33	10	8	15	32	47	–15	38
Ashdod	33	6	10	17	29	48	–19	28
Hapoel Ashkelon*	33	4	9	20	23	51	–28	21
Hapoel Acre* (–2)	33	6	4	23	26	67	–41	20

Top scorer: Saba (Maccabi Netanya) 24.
Cup Final: Hapoel Haifa 3, Beitar Jerusalem 1 *aet*.

ITALY

Federazione Italiana Giuoco Calcio, Via Gregorio Allegri 14, 00198 Roma.
Founded: 1898. *FIFA:* 1905; *UEFA:* 1954. *National Colours:* Blue shirts, white shorts, blue socks with white tops.

International matches 2017–18

Spain (a) 0-3, Israel (h) 1-0, FYR Macedonia (h) 1-1, Albania (a) 1-0, Sweden (a) 0-1, Sweden (h) 0-0, Argentina (n) 0-2, England (a) 1-1, Saudi Arabia (n) 2-1, France (a) 1-3, Netherlands (h) 1-1.

League Championship wins (1898–2018)

Juventus 34 (excludes two titles revoked); AC Milan 18; Internazionale 18 (includes one title awarded); Genoa 9; Pro Vercelli 7; Bologna 7; Torino 7 (excludes one title revoked); Roma 3; Fiorentina 2; Lazio 2; Napoli 2; Casale 1; Novese 1; Cagliari 1; Hellas Verona 1; Sampdoria 1.

Cup wins (1928–2018)

Juventus 13; Roma 9; Internazionale 7; Fiorentina 6; Lazio 6; Torino 5; Napoli 5; AC Milan 5; Sampdoria 4; Parma 3; Bologna 2; Vado 1; Genoa 1; Venezia 1; Atalanta 1; Vicenza 1.

Italian Serie A 2017–18

	P	W	D	L	F	A	GD	Pts
Juventus	38	30	5	3	86	24	62	95
Napoli	38	28	7	3	77	29	48	91
Roma	38	23	8	7	61	28	33	77
Internazionale	38	20	12	6	66	30	36	72
Lazio	38	21	9	8	89	49	40	72
AC Milan	38	18	10	10	56	42	14	64
Atalanta	38	16	12	10	57	39	18	60
Fiorentina	38	16	9	13	54	46	8	57
Torino	38	13	15	10	54	46	8	54
Sampdoria	38	16	6	16	56	60	–4	54
Sassuolo	38	11	10	17	29	59	–30	43
Genoa	38	11	8	19	33	43	–10	41
Chievo	38	10	10	18	36	59	–23	40
Udinese	38	12	4	22	48	63	–15	40
Bologna	38	11	6	21	40	52	–12	39
Cagliari	38	11	6	21	33	61	–28	39
SPAL 2013	38	8	14	16	39	59	–20	38
Crotone*	38	9	8	21	40	66	–26	35
Hellas Verona*	38	7	4	27	30	78	–48	25
Benevento*	38	6	3	29	33	84	–51	21

Top scorers (joint): Icardi (Internazionale), Immobile (Lazio) 29.
Cup Final: Juventus 4, AC Milan 0.

KAZAKHSTAN

Football Federation of Kazakhstan, 29 Syganak Street, 9th floor, 010000 Astana.
Founded: 1914. *FIFA:* 1994; *UEFA:* 2002. *National Colours:* All yellow.

International matches 2017–18

Montenegro (h) 0-3, Poland (a) 0-3, Romania (a) 1-3, Armenia (h) 1-1, Hungary (a) 3-2, Bulgaria (n) 1-2, Azerbaijan (h) 3-0.

League Championship wins (1992–2017)

Irtysh (includes Ansat) 5; Aktobe 5; Astana 4; Yelimay (renamed Spartak Semey) 3; FC Astana-64 (includes Zhenis) 3; Kairat 2; Shakhter Karagandy 2; Taraz 1; Tobol 1.

Cup wins (1992–2017)

Kairat 8; FC Astana-64 (incl. Zhenis) 3; Astana (incl. Lokomotiv) 3; Dostyk 1; Vostok 1; Yelimay (renamed Spartak Semey) 1; Irtysh 1; Kaisar 1; Taraz 1; Almaty 1; Tobol 1; Aktobe 1; Atirau 1; Ordabasy 1; Shakhter Karagandy 1.

Kazakh Premier League 2017

	P	W	D	L	F	A	GD	Pts
Astana	33	25	4	4	74	21	53	79
Kairat	33	23	9	1	75	28	47	78
Ordabasy	33	18	4	11	44	37	7	58
Irtysh	33	12	12	9	35	32	3	48
Tobol	33	12	11	10	36	26	10	47
Kaisar	33	11	9	13	30	36	–6	42
Shakhter Karagandy	33	12	4	17	36	50	–14	40
Atyrau (–3)	33	10	8	15	34	54	–20	35
Aktobe	33	8	9	16	38	46	–8	33
Akzhayik+	33	7	9	17	29	47	–18	30
Taraz* (–6)	33	8	8	17	29	50	–21	26
Okzhetpes*	33	7	3	23	28	61	–33	24

Top scorer: Gohou (Kairat) 24.
Cup Final: Kairat 1, Atyrau 0.

KOSOVO

Football Federation of Kosovo, Rruga Agim Ramadani 45, Prishtina, Kosovo 10000. *Founded:* 1946. *FIFA:* 2016; *UEFA:* 2016. *National Colours:* All blue.

International matches 2017–18

Croatia (a) 0-1, Finland (h) 0-1*, Ukraine (h) 0-2*, Iceland (a) 0-2, Latvia (h) 4-3, Madagascar (n) 1-0, Burkina Faso (n) 2-0, Albania (n) 3-0.
* *Match played in Albania.*

League Championship wins (1945–2018)

Prishtina 14; Vellaznimi 9; KF Trepca 7; Liria 5; Buduqnosti 4; Rudari 3; Red Star 3; Besa Peje 3; Jedinstvo 2; Kosova Prishtina 2; Slloga 2; Obiliqi 2; Fushe-Kosova 2; Drita 2; Feronikeli 2; Proletari 1; KXEK Kosova 1; Rudniku 1; KNI Ramiz Sadiku 1; Dukagjini 1; Besiana 1; Hysi 1; Kosova Vushtrri 1; Trepca'89 1.

Cup wins (1992–2018)

Prishtina 5; Liria 3; Besa Peje 3; Flamurtari 2; Feronikeli 2; KF Trepca 1; KF 2 Korriku 1; Gjilani 1; Drita 1; Besiana 1; KEK-u 1; Kosova Prishtina 1; Vellaznimi 1; Hysi 1; Trepca'89 1.

Kosovar Superliga 2017

	P	W	D	L	F	A	GD	Pts
Drita	33	18	13	2	53	21	32	67
Prishtina	33	18	10	5	39	18	21	64
Llapi	33	16	6	11	51	41	10	54
Trepca'89	33	14	11	8	41	25	16	53
Feronikeli	33	10	8	5	32	18	14	48
Drenica Skenderaj	33	13	9	11	34	27	7	48
Liria Prizren	33	13	9	11	34	30	4	48
Gjilani	33	10	16	7	29	21	8	46
Vellaznimi*+	33	10	14	9	29	28	1	44
Flamurtari+	33	6	7	20	28	53	–25	25
Besa Peje*	33	6	4	23	28	64	–36	22
Vllaznia*	33	3	5	25	16	68	–52	14

Top scorers (joint): Daku (Llapi), John (Trepca'89) 17.
Cup Final: Vellaznimi 1, Prishtina 1.
aet; Prishtina won 5-4 on penalties.

LATVIA

Latvijas Futbola Federacija, Olympic Sports Centre, Grostonas Street 6B, 1013 Riga.
Founded: 1921. *FIFA:* 1922; *UEFA:* 1992. *National Colours:* All carmine red.

International matches 2017–18

Hungary (a) 1-3, Switzerland (h) 0-3, Faroe Islands (a) 0-0, Andorra (h) 4-0, Saudi Arabia (n) 0-2, Kosovo (n) 3-4, Korea Republic (a) 0-1, Faroe Islands (n) 1-1, Gibraltar (n) 1-0, Estonia (h) 1-0, Lithuania (a) 1-1, Azerbaijan (h) 1-3.

League Championship wins (1922–2017)

Skonto Riga 15; ASK Riga (incl. AVN 2) 11; Sarkanais Metalurgs Liepaja 9; RFK Riga 8; Olympija Liepaya 7; VEF Riga 6; Ventspils 6; Energija Riga (incl. ESR Riga

2) 4; Elektrons Riga (incl. Alfa 1) 4; Torpedo Riga 3; Keisermezhs Riga 2; Khimikis Daugavpils 2; RAF Yelgava 2; Daugava Liepaja 2; Liepajas Metalurgs 2; Spartaks Jurmala 2; Dinamo Riga 1; Zhmilyeva Team 1; Darba Rezervi 1; RER Riga 1; Starts Brotseni 1; Venta Ventspils 1; Jumieks Riga 1; Gauja Valmiera 1; Daugava Daugavpils 1; FK Liepaja 1.

Cup wins (1937–2017)

Skonto Riga 8; ASK Riga 7 (includes AVN 3); Elektrons Riga 7; Ventspils 7; Sarkanais Metalurgs Liepaja 4; Jelgava 4; VEF Riga 3; Tseltnieks Riga 3; RAF Yelgava 3; RFK Riga 2; Daugava Liepaja 2; Starts Brotseni 2; Selmash Liepaya 2; Yurnieks Riga 2; Khimikis Daugavpils 2; Rigas Vilki 1; Dinamo Liepaya 1; Dinamo Riga 1; RER Riga 1; Voulkan Kouldiga 1; Baltika Liepaja 1; Venta Ventspils 1; Pilots Riga 1; Lielupe Yurmala 1; Energija Riga (formerly ESR Riga) 1; Torpedo Riga 1; Daugava SKIF Riga 1; Tseltnieks Daugavpils 1; Olympija Riga 1; FK Riga 1; Liepajas Metalurgs 1; Daugava Daugavpils 1; FK Liepaja 1.

Virsliga 2017

	P	W	D	L	F	A	GD	Pts
Spartaks Jurmala	24	14	4	6	36	26	10	46
FK Liepaja	24	11	4	9	32	25	7	37
Riga FC	24	10	7	7	28	20	8	37
Ventspils	24	9	8	7	32	22	10	35
Rigas FS	24	11	2	11	29	31	–2	35
Jelgava	24	8	5	11	22	30	–8	29
Metta/LU	24	3	6	15	21	46	–25	15
Babite*	0	0	0	0	0	0	0	0

* *Babite demoted pre-season following investigation of illegal betting.*
Top scorers (joint): Karasausks (FK Liepaja), Kozlov (Spartaks Jurmala) 17.
Cup Final: FK Liepaja 2, Riga 0.

LIECHTENSTEIN

Liechtensteiner Fussballverband, Landstrasse 149, 9494 Schaan.
Founded: 1934. *FIFA:* 1974; *UEFA:* 1974. *National Colours:* Blue shirts, red shorts, blue socks.

International matches 2017–18

Albania (a) 0-2, Spain (h) 0-8, Israel (h) 0-1, FYR Macedonia (a) 0-4, Qatar (a) 2-1, Andorra (n) 0-1, Faroe Islands (n) 0-3.
Liechtenstein has no national league. Teams compete in Swiss regional leagues.

Cup wins (1937–2018)

Vaduz 46; FC Balzers 11; FC Triesen 8; USV Eschen/Mauren 5; FC Schaan 3.
Cup Final: Vaduz 3, FC Balzers 0.

LITHUANIA

Lietuvos Futbolo Federacija, Stadiono g. 2, 02106 Vilnius.
Founded: 1922. *FIFA:* 1923; *UEFA:* 1992. *National Colours:* Yellow shirts, green shorts, yellow socks.

International matches 2017–18

Scotland (h) 0-3, Slovenia (a) 0-4, Malta (a) 1-1, England (h) 0-1, Georgia (a) 0-4, Armenia (a) 1-0, Estonia (a) 0-2, Latvia (h) 1-1, Iran (n) 0-1, Poland (a) 0-2.

League Championship wins (1990–2017)

FBK Kaunas 8 (incl. Zalgiris Kaunas 1); Zalgiris Vilnius 7; Ekranas 5; Inkaras Kaunas 2; Kareda 2; Sirijus Klaipeda 1; Mazeikiai 1; Suduva 1.

Cup wins (1990–2017)

Zalgiris Vilnius 11; Ekranas 4; FBK Kaunas 2; Kareda 2; Atlantas 2; Suduva 2; Sirijus Klaipeda 1; Lietuvos Makabi Vilnius (renamed Neris Vilnius) 1; Inkaras Kaunas 1; Stumbras 1.

Lithuanian A Lyga Qualifying Table 2017

	P	W	D	L	F	A	GD	Pts
Suduva	28	17	8	3	65	28	37	59
Zalgiris Vilnius	28	17	7	4	51	22	29	58
Trakai	28	15	9	4	45	22	23	54
Atlantas	28	8	9	11	33	33	0	33
Utenis Utena	28	8	8	12	24	41	–17	32
Jonava	28	8	7	13	29	45	–16	31
Stumbras+	28	4	10	14	23	42	–19	22
Kauno Zalgiris*	28	3	6	19	19	56	–37	15

Championship Round 2017

	P	W	D	L	F	A	GD	Pts
Suduva	33	21	8	4	73	31	42	71
Zalgiris Vilnius	33	20	7	6	62	31	31	67
Trakai	33	18	10	5	53	27	26	64
Jonava	33	10	8	15	40	53	–13	38
Atlantas	33	8	12	13	39	43	–4	36
Utenis Utena	33	9	8	16	30	56	–26	33

Top scorer: Sernas (Zalgiris Vilnius) 18.
Cup Final: Stumbras 1, Zalgiris Vilnius 0.

LUXEMBOURG

Federation Luxembourgeoise de Football, BP 5 Rue de Limpach, 3932 Mondercange.
Founded: 1908. *FIFA:* 1910; *UEFA:* 1954. *National Colours:* White shirts with blue trim, white shorts, white socks.

International matches 2017–18

Belarus (h) 1-0, France (a) 0-0, Sweden (a) 0-8, Bulgaria (h) 1-1, Hungary (h) 2-1, Malta (a) 1-0, Austria (h) 0-4, Senegal (h) 0-0, Georgia (h) 1-0.

League Championship wins (1910–2018)

Jeunesse Esch 28; F91 Dudelange 14; Spora Luxembourg 11; Stade Dudelange 10; Fola Esch 7; Red Boys Differdange 6; Union Luxembourg 6; Avenir Beggen 6; US Hollerich-Bonnevoie 5; Progres NiederKorn 3; Aris Bonnevoie 3; Sporting Club 2; Racing Club 1; National Schifflange 1; Grevenmacher 1.

Cup wins (1922–2018)

Red Boys Differdange 15; Jeunesse Esch 13; Union Luxembourg 10; Spora Luxembourg 8; Avenir Beggen 7; F91 Dudelange 7; Progres NiederKorn 4; Stade Dudelange 4; Grevenmacher 4; Differdange 03 4; Fola Esch 3; Alliance Dudelange 2; US Rumelange 2; Racing Club 1; US Dudelange 1; SC Tetange 1; National Schifflange 1; Aris Bonnevoie 1; Jeunesse Hautcharage 1; Swift Hesperange 1; Etzella Ettelbruck 1; CS Petange 1; Racing 1.

Luxembourger National Division 2017–18

	P	W	D	L	F	A	GD	Pts
F91 Dudelange	26	22	2	2	81	26	55	68
Progres Niederkorn	26	20	3	3	72	28	44	63
Fola Esch	26	14	5	7	72	41	31	47
Jeunesse Esch	26	13	5	8	52	35	17	44
Differdange 03	26	11	5	10	48	38	10	38
Mondorf-les-Bains	26	10	8	8	40	36	4	38
Racing	26	9	8	9	41	40	1	35
Hostert	26	9	7	10	37	46	–9	34
UT Petange	26	9	4	13	43	51	–8	31
RM Hamm Benfica	26	8	6	12	30	45	–15	30
UNA Strassen	26	8	5	13	38	60	–22	29
Victoria Rosport+	26	7	5	14	37	59	–22	26
Rodange 91*	26	4	10	12	27	55	–28	22
Jeunesse Esch*	26	1	1	24	15	73	–58	4

Top scorer: Turpel (F91 Dudelange) 33.
Cup Final: Hostert 0, Racing 0.
aet; Racing won 4-3 on penalties.

MALTA

Malta Football Association, Millennium Stand, Floor 2, National Stadium, Ta'Qali ATD4000.
Founded: 1900. *FIFA:* 1959; *UEFA:* 1960. *National Colours:* Red shirts, white shorts, red socks.

International matches 2017–18

England (h) 4-0, Scotland (a) 0-2, Lithuania (h) 1-1, Slovakia (a) 0-3, Estonia (h) 0-3, Luxembourg (h) 0-1, Finland (n) 0-5, Armenia (n) 1-1, Georgia (n) 0-1.

League Championship wins (1910–2018)

Sliema Wanderers 26; Floriana 25; Valletta 24; Hibernians 12; Hamrun Spartans 7; Birkirkara 4; Rabat Ajax 2; St George's 1; KOMR 1; Marsalxokk 1.

Cup wins (1935–2018)

Sliema Wanderers 21; Floriana 20; Valletta 14; Hibernians 10; Hamrun Spartans 6; Birkirkara 5; Melita 1; Gzira United 1; Zurrieq 1; Rabat Ajax 1.

Maltese Premier League 2017–18

	P	W	D	L	F	A	GD	Pts
Valletta	26	17	7	2	40	11	29	58
Balzan	26	16	7	3	42	19	23	55
Gzira United	26	15	6	5	52	33	19	51
Birkirkara	26	15	2	9	44	28	16	47
Hibernians	26	13	7	6	43	16	27	46

Floriana	26	12	10	4	48	18	30	46
Sliema Wanderers	26	11	7	8	35	26	9	40
Hamrun Spartans	26	10	5	11	39	33	6	35
Senglea Athletic	26	7	5	14	29	47	–18	26
Mosta	26	7	5	14	28	52	–24	26
St Andrews	26	6	6	14	21	41	–20	24
Tarxien Rainbows+	26	6	5	15	34	56	–22	23
Naxxar Lions*	26	5	7	14	27	41	–14	22
Lija Athletic*	26	1	3	22	23	84	–61	6

Top scorer: Samb (Gzira United) 21.
Cup Final: Valletta 2, Birkirkara 1.

MOLDOVA

Federatia Moldoveneasca de Fotbal, Str. Tricolorului 39, 2012 Chisinau.
Founded: 1990. *FIFA:* 1994; *UEFA:* 1993. *National Colours:* All blue.

International matches 2017–18
Serbia (a) 0-3, Wales (h) 0-2, Republic of Ireland (a) 0-2, Austria (h) 0-1, Korea Republic (n) 0-1, Azerbaijan (n) 0-0, Saudi Arabia (a) 0-3, Ivory Coast (n) 1-2, Armenia (n) 0-0.

League Championship wins (1992–2017)
Sheriff 16; Zimbru Chisinau 8; Constructorul 1; Dacia Chisinau 1; Milsami Orhei 1.

Cup wins (1992–2018)
Sheriff 9; Zimbru Chisinau 6; Tiligul-Tiras 3; Tiraspol 3 (incl. Constructorul 2); Comrat 1; Nistru Otaci 1; Iskra-Stal 1; Milsami Orhei 1; Zaria Balti 1.

Moldovan National Division 2017

	P	W	D	L	F	A	GD	Pts
Sheriff	18	14	3	1	50	14	36	45
Milsami Orhei	18	13	1	4	26	12	14	40
Petrocub	18	7	5	6	25	16	9	26
Dacia Chisinau	18	7	5	6	23	26	–3	26
Zaria Balti	18	7	3	8	28	20	8	24
Speranta Nisporeni	18	5	6	7	18	21	–3	21
Sfintul Gheorghe	18	5	5	8	15	27	–12	20
Zimbru Chisinau	18	5	4	9	17	21	–4	19
Dinamo-Auto	18	4	3	11	14	38	–24	15
Spicul Chiscareni*	18	3	5	10	14	35	–21	14

* Spicul Chiscareni withdrew before 2018 season.
Top scorer: Damascan (Sheriff) 13.
Cup Final: Milsami Orhei 2, Zaria Balti 0 *aet*.

MONTENEGRO

Fudbalski Savez Crne Gore, Ulica 19. Decembar 13, PO Box 275, 81000 Podgorica.
Founded: 1931 *FIFA:* 2007; *UEFA:* 2007. *National Colours:* All red with gold trim.

International matches 2017–18
Kazakhstan (a) 3-0, Romania (h) 1-0, Denmark (h) 0-1, Poland (a) 2-4, Cyprus (a) 0-0, Turkey (h) 2-2, Bosnia-Herzegovina (a) 0-0, Slovenia (h) 0-2.

League Championship wins (2006–18)
Buducnost Podgorica 3; Sutjeska 3; Mogren 2; Rudar Pljevlja 2; Zeta 1; Mladost Podgorica 1 (now OFK Titograd).

Cup wins (2006–18)
Rudar Pljevlja 4; Mladost Podgorica (now OFK Titograd) 2; Mogren 1; Petrovac 1; Celik 1; Buducnost Podgorica 1; Lovcen 1: Sutjeska 1.

Montenegrin First League 2017–18

	P	W	D	L	F	A	GD	Pts
Sutjeska	36	24	7	5	55	23	32	79
Buducnost Podgorica	36	14	15	7	44	30	14	57
Mladost Podgorica	36	12	15	9	42	33	9	51
Grbalj	36	12	14	10	39	39	0	50
Zeta	36	12	13	11	40	35	5	49
Rudar Pljevlja	36	13	10	13	32	28	4	49
Iskra	36	12	9	15	33	34	–1	45
Kom Podgorica*+	36	11	10	15	36	45	–9	43
Petrovac+	36	9	11	16	25	40	–15	38
Decic*	36	3	12	21	25	64	–39	21

Top scorer: Ivanovic (Sutjeska) 14.
Cup Final: Mladost Podgorica 2, Igalo 0.

NETHERLANDS

Koninklijke Nederlandse Voetbalbond, Woudenbergseweg 56–58, Postbus 515, 3700 AM Zeist.
Founded: 1889. *FIFA:* 1904; *UEFA:* 1954. *National Colours:* Orange shirts, white shorts, orange socks.

International matches 2017–18
France (a) 0-4, Bulgaria (h) 3-1, Belarus (a) 3-1, Sweden (h) 2-0, Scotland (a) 1-0, Romania (a) 3-0, England (h) 0-1, Portugal (n) 3-0, Slovakia (a) 1-1, Italy (a) 1-1.

League Championship wins (1889–2018)
Ajax 33; PSV Eindhoven 24; Feyenoord 15; HVV The Hague 10; Sparta Rotterdam 6; RAP Amsterdam 5; Go Ahead Eagles Deventer 4; HFC Haarlem 3; HBS Craeyenhout 3; Willem II Tilburg 3; RCH Heemstede 2; Heracles 2; ADO Den Haag 2; AZ 67 Alkmaar 2; VV Concordia 1; Quick Den Haag 1; Be Quick Groningen 1; NAC Breda 1; SC Enschede 1; Volewijckers Amsterdam 1; Haarlem 1; BVV Den Bosch 1; Schiedam 1; Limburgia 1; EVV Eindhoven 1; SVV Rapid JC Den Heerlen 1; DOS Utrecht 1; DWS Amsterdam 1; FC Twente 1.

Cup wins (1899–2018)
Ajax 18; Feyenoord 13; PSV Eindhoven 9; Quick The Hague 4; AZ 67 Alkmaar 4; HFC Haarlem 3; Sparta Rotterdam 3; FC Twente 3; Utrecht 3; Haarlem 2; VOC 2; HBS Craeyenhout 2; DFC 2; RCH Haarlem 2; Wageningen 2; Willem II Tilburg 2; Fortuna 54 2; FC Den Haag (includes ADO) 2; Roda JC 2; RAP Amsterdam 1; Velocitas Breda 1; HVV Den Haag 1; Concordia Delft 1; CVV 1; Schoten 1; ZFC Zaandam 1; Longa 1; VUC 1; Velocitas Groningen 1; Roermond 1; FC Eindhoven 1; VSV 1; Quick 1888 Nijmegen 1; VVV Groningen 1; NAC Breda 1; Heerenveen 1; PEC Zwolle 1; FC Groningen 1; Vitesse 1.

Dutch Eredivisie 2017–18

	P	W	D	L	F	A	GD	Pts
PSV Eindhoven	34	26	5	3	87	39	48	83
Ajax	34	25	4	5	89	33	56	79
AZ Alkmaar	34	22	5	7	72	38	34	71
Feyenoord	34	20	6	8	76	39	37	66
Utrecht	34	14	12	8	58	53	5	54
Vitesse	34	13	10	11	63	47	16	49
ADO Den Haag	34	13	8	13	45	53	–8	47
Heerenveen	34	12	10	12	48	53	–5	46
PEC Zwolle	34	12	8	14	42	54	–12	44
Heracles Almelo	34	11	9	14	50	64	–14	42
SBV Excelsior	34	11	7	16	41	56	–15	40
FC Groningen	34	8	14	12	50	50	0	38
Willem II Tilburg	34	10	7	17	50	63	–13	37
NAC Breda	34	9	7	18	41	57	–16	34
VVV Venlo	34	7	13	14	35	54	–19	34
Roda JC*	34	8	6	20	42	69	–27	30
Sparta Rotterdam*	34	7	6	21	34	75	–41	27
FC Twente*	34	5	9	20	37	63	–26	24

Top scorer: Jahanbaksh (Feyenoord) 21.
Cup Final: Feyenoord 3, AZ Alkmaar 0.

NORTHERN CYPRUS

Cyprus Turkish Football Federation, 7 Memduh Asaf Street, 107 Koskluciftlik, Lefkosa. (Not a member of FIFA or UEFA.)
Founded: 1955; *National Colours:* Red shirts with white trim, red shorts, red socks.

League Championship wins (1956–63; 1969–74; 1976–2018)
Cetinkaya 14; Yenicami Agdelen 9; Gonyeli 9; Magusa Turk Gucu 8; Dogan Turk Birligi7; Baf Ulku 4; Kucuk Kaymakli 4; Akincilar 1; Binatli 1.

Cup wins (1956–2018)
Cetinkaya 17; Gonyeli 8; Yenicami Agdelen 7; Kucuk Kaymakli 7; Magusa Turk Gucu 5; Turk Ocagi 5; Lefke 2; Dogan Turk Birligi 2; Genclik Gucu 1; Yalova 1; Binatli 1; Cihangir 1.

Northern Cyprus Super Lig 2017–18

	P	W	D	L	F	A	GD	Pts
Yenicami Agdelen	30	18	7	5	63	33	30	61
Dogan Turk Birligi	30	17	6	7	61	42	19	57
Cetinkaya	30	16	7	7	57	42	15	55
Binatli	30	14	8	8	58	43	15	50
Alsancak Yesilova	30	12	12	6	46	35	11	48
Ulku Yurdu	30	12	9	9	63	43	20	45
Lefke	30	13	5	12	64	48	16	44
Cihangir	30	12	7	11	53	49	4	43
Kucuk Kaymakli	30	13	3	14	61	62	–1	42
Magusa Turk Gucu	30	11	8	11	54	47	7	41
Turk Ocagi	30	13	2	15	47	45	2	41
Gencler Birligi	30	10	7	13	52	60	–8	37
Genclik Gucu	30	10	4	16	40	65	–25	34
Yalova*+	30	6	7	17	45	68	–23	25

| Yeni Bogazici* | 30 | 5 | 9 | 16 | 24 | 59 | –35 | 24 |
| Ozankoy* | 30 | 4 | 7 | 19 | 29 | 76 | –47 | 19 |

Top scorer: Gok (Kucuk Kaymakli) 36.
Cup Final: Cihangir 3, Magusa Turk Gucu 1.

NORTHERN IRELAND

Irish Football Association, 20 Windsor Avenue, Belfast BT9 6EG.
Founded: 1880. *FIFA:* 1911; *UEFA:* 1954. *National Colours:* Green shirts, white shorts, green socks.

NORWAY

Norges Fotballforbund, Ullevaal Stadion, Serviceboks 1, 0840 Oslo.
Founded: 1902. *FIFA:* 1908; *UEFA:* 1954. *National Colours:* Red shirts, white shorts, red socks.

International matches 2017–18
Azerbaijan (h) 2-0, Germany (a) 0-6, San Marino (a) 8-0, Northern Ireland (h) 1-0, FYR Macedonia (a) 0-2, Slovakia (a) 0-1, Australia (h) 4-1, Albania (a) 1-0, Iceland (a) 3-2, Panama (h) 1-0.

League Championship wins (1938–2017)
Rosenborg 25; Fredrikstad 9; Viking Stavanger 8; Lillestrom 5; Valerenga 5; Larvik Turn 3; Brann 3; Molde 3; Lyn Oslo 2; Stromsgodset 2; IK Start 2; Freidig 1; Fram 1; Skeid 1; Moss 1; Stabaek 1.

Cup wins (1902–2017)
Odd Grenland 12; Fredrikstad 11; Rosenborg 11; Lyn Oslo 8; Skeid 8; Sarpsborg 6; Brann 6; Lillestrom 6; Viking Stavanger 5; Stromsgodset 5; Orn-Horten 4; Valerenga 4; Molde 4; Frigg 3; Mjondalen 3; Mercantile 2; Bodo/Glimt 2; Tromso 2; Aalesund 2; Grane Nordstrand 1; Kvik Halden 1; Sparta 1; Gjovik/Lyn 1; Moss 1; Bryne 1; Stabaek 1; Hodd 1.
(*Known as the Norwegian Championship for HM The King's Trophy.*)

Norwegian Eliteserien 2017

	P	W	D	L	F	A	GD	Pts
Rosenborg	30	18	7	5	57	20	37	61
Molde	30	16	6	8	50	35	15	54
Sarpsborg 08	30	13	12	5	50	36	14	51
Stromsgodset	30	14	8	8	45	37	8	50
Brann	30	13	8	9	51	36	15	47
Odd	30	12	6	12	27	39	–12	42
Kristiansund	30	10	10	10	44	46	–2	40
Valerenga	30	11	6	13	48	46	2	39
Stabaek	30	10	9	11	46	50	–4	39
Haugesund	30	11	6	13	35	39	–4	39
Tromso	30	10	8	12	42	49	–7	38
Lillestrom	30	10	7	13	40	43	–3	37
Sandefjord	30	11	3	16	38	51	–13	36
Sogndal*+	30	8	8	14	38	48	–10	32
Aalesund*	30	8	8	14	38	50	–12	32
Viking*	30	6	6	18	33	57	–24	24

Top scorer: Bendtner (Rosenborg) 19.
Cup Final: Lillestrom 3, Sarpsborg 08 2.

POLAND

Polski Zwiazek Pilki Noznej, ul. Bitwy Warszawskiej 1920r. 7, 02-366 Warszawa.
Founded: 1919. *FIFA:* 1923; *UEFA:* 1954. *National Colours:* White shirts with red vertical band, red shorts, white socks.

International matches 2017–18
Denmark (a) 0-4, Kazakhstan (h) 3-0, Armenia (a) 6-1, Montenegro (a) 4-2, Uruguay (h) 0-0, Mexico (h) 0-1, Nigeria (h) 0-1, Korea Republic (h) 3-2, Chile (h) 2-2, Lithuania (h) 4-0, Senegal (n) 1-2, Colombia (n) 0-3, Japan (n) 1-0.

League Championship wins (1921–2018)
Ruch Chorzow 14; Gornik Zabrze 14; Wisla Krakow 13; Legia Warsaw 13; Lech Poznan 7; Cracovia 5; Pogon Lwow 4; Widzew Lodz 4; Warta Poznan 2; Polonia Warsaw 2; Polonia Bytom 2; LKS Lodz 2; Stal Mielec 2; Slask Wroclaw 2; Zaglebie Lubin 2; Garbarnia Krakow 1; Szombierki Bytom 1.

Cup wins (1926; 1951–2018)
Legia Warsaw 19; Gornik Zabrze 6; Lech Poznan 5; Wisla Krakow 4; Zaglebie Sosnowiec 4; Ruch Chorzow 3; GKS Katowice 3; Amica Wronki 3; Polonia Warsaw 2; Slask Wroclaw 2; Arka Gdynia 2; Dyskobolia Grodzisk 2; Gwardia Warsaw 1; LKS Lodz 1; Stal Rzeszow 1; Lechia Gdansk 1; Widzew Lodz 1; Miedz Legnica 1; Wisla Plock 1; Jagiellonia Bialystok 1; Zawisza Bydgoszcz 1.

Polish Ekstraklasa Qualifying Table 2017–18

	P	W	D	L	F	A	GD	Pts
Lech Poznan	30	15	10	5	49	23	26	55
Jagiellonia Bialystok	30	16	6	8	45	36	9	54
Legia Warsaw	30	17	3	10	43	31	12	54
Wisla Plock	30	15	4	11	42	35	7	49
Gornik Zabrze	30	12	11	7	56	46	10	47
Korona Kielce	30	11	12	7	44	37	7	45
Wisla Krakow	30	12	8	10	41	36	5	44
Zaglebie Lubin	30	10	13	7	39	33	6	43
Arka Gdynia	30	10	10	10	38	32	6	40
Cracovia Krakow	30	10	9	11	40	40	0	39
Slask Wroclaw	30	7	10	13	35	48	–13	31
Pogon Szczecin	30	8	7	15	34	48	–14	31
Piast Gliwice	30	6	12	12	28	38	–10	30
Lechia Gdansk (–1)	30	7	10	13	39	51	–12	30
Nieciecza	30	7	8	15	32	52	–20	29
Sandecja Nowy Sacz	30	4	13	13	27	46	–19	25

Championship Round 2017–18

	P	W	D	L	F	A	GD	Pts
Legia Warsaw	37	22	4	11	55	35	20	70
Jagiellonia Bialystok	37	20	7	10	55	41	14	67
Lech Poznan	37	16	12	9	53	34	19	60
Gornik Zabrze	37	16	12	9	68	54	14	60
Wisla Plock	37	17	6	14	53	45	8	57
Wisla Krakow	37	15	10	12	51	42	9	55
Zaglebie Lubin	37	13	13	11	45	42	3	52
Korona Kielce	37	12	13	12	49	54	–5	49

Relegation Round 2017–18

	P	W	D	L	F	A	GD	Pts
Cracovia Krakow	37	13	11	13	51	52	–1	50
Slask Wroclaw	37	13	11	13	50	54	–4	50
Pogon Szczecin	37	12	9	16	46	54	–8	45
Arka Gdynia	37	11	10	16	46	48	–2	43
Lechia Gdansk (–1)	37	9	13	15	46	58	–12	39
Piast Gliwice	37	8	13	16	40	48	–8	37
Nieciecza*	37	9	9	19	39	66	–27	36
Sandecja Nowy Sacz*	37	6	15	14	34	54	–20	33

Top scorer: Carlitos (Wisla Krakow) 24.
Cup Final: Legia Warsaw 2, Arka Gdynia 1.

PORTUGAL

Federacao Portuguesa de Futebol, Rua Alexandre Herculano No. 58, Apartado postal 24013, Lisboa 1250-012.
Founded: 1914. *FIFA:* 1923; *UEFA:* 1954. *National Colours:* Carmine shirts with , red shorts, red and green socks.

International matches 2017–18
Faroe Islands (h) 5-1, Hungary (a) 1-0, Andorra (a) 2-0, Switzerland (h) 2-0, Saudi Arabia (h) 3-0, USA (h) 1-1, Egypt (n) 2-1, Netherlands (n) 0-3, Tunisia (n) 2-2, Belgium (n) 0-0, Algeria (h) 3-0, Spain (n) 3-3, Morocco (n) 1-0, Iran (n) 1-1, Uruguay (n) 1-2.

League Championship wins (1935–2018)
Benfica 36; Porto 28; Sporting Lisbon 18; Belenenses 1; Boavista 1.

Cup wins (1939–2018)
Benfica 26; Sporting Lisbon 16; Porto 16; Boavista 5; Belenenses 3; Vitoria de Setubal 3; Academica de Coimbra 2; Braga 2; Leixoes 1; Estrela da Amadora 1; Beira-Mar 1; Vitoria de Guimaraes 1; Desportivo das Aves 1.

Portuguese Primeira Liga 2017–18

	P	W	D	L	F	A	GD	Pts
Porto	34	28	4	2	82	18	64	88
Benfica	34	25	6	3	80	22	58	81
Sporting Lisbon	34	24	6	4	63	24	39	78
Braga	34	24	3	7	74	29	45	75
Rio Ave	34	15	6	13	40	42	–2	51
Chaves	34	13	8	13	47	55	–8	47
Maritimo	34	13	8	13	36	49	–13	47
Boavista	34	13	6	15	35	44	–9	45
Vitoria Guimaraes	34	13	4	17	45	56	–11	43
Portimonense	34	10	8	16	52	60	–8	38
Tondela	34	10	8	16	41	50	–9	38
Belenenses	34	9	10	15	33	46	–13	37
Desportivo Aves	34	9	7	18	36	51	–15	34
Vitoria Setubal	34	7	11	16	39	62	–23	32
Moreirense	34	8	8	18	29	50	–21	32
Feirense	34	9	4	21	32	48	–16	31

	P	W	D	L	F	A	GD	Pts
Pacos de Ferreira*	34	7	9	18	33	59	–26	30
Estoril*	34	8	6	20	29	61	–32	30

Top scorer: Jonas (Benfica) 34.
Cup Final: Desportivo das Aves 2, Sporting Lisbon 1.

REPUBLIC OF IRELAND

Football Association of Ireland (Cumann Peile na hEireann), National Sports Campus, Abbotstown, Dublin 15.
Founded: 1921. *FIFA:* 1923; *UEFA:* 1954. *National Colours:* Green shirts, green shorts, green socks with white tops.

League Championship wins (1922–2017)
Shamrock Rovers 17; Shelbourne 13; Dundalk 12; Bohemians 11; St Patrick's Athletic 8; Waterford United 6; Cork United 5; Drumcondra 5; Sligo Rovers 3; Cork City 3; St James's Gate 2; Cork Athletic 2; Limerick 2; Athlone Town 2; Derry City 2; Dolphin 1; Cork Hibernians 1; Cork Celtic 1; Drogheda United 1.

Cup wins (1922–2017)
Shamrock Rovers 24; Dundalk 10; Bohemians 7; Shelbourne 7; Drumcondra 5; Sligo Rovers 5; Derry City 5; Cork City 4; St Patrick's Athletic 3; St James's Gate 2; Cork (incl. Fordsons 1) 2; Waterford United 2; Cork United 2; Cork Athletic 2; Limerick 2; Cork Hibernians 2; Bray Wanderers 2; Longford Town 2; Alton United 1; Athlone Town 1; Transport 1; Finn Harps 1; Home Farm 1; UC Dublin 1; Galway United 1; Drogheda United 1; Sporting Fingal 1.

Irish Premier Division 2017

	P	W	D	L	F	A	GD	Pts
Cork City	33	24	4	5	67	23	44	76
Dundalk	33	22	3	8	72	24	48	69
Shamrock Rovers	33	17	3	13	49	41	8	54
Derry City	33	14	9	10	49	40	9	51
Bohemians	33	14	5	14	36	40	–4	47
Bray Wanderers	33	13	7	13	55	52	3	46
Limerick	33	10	10	13	41	51	–10	40
St Patrick's Athletic	33	9	12	12	45	52	–7	39
Sligo Rovers	33	8	15	10	33	44	–11	39
Galway United*	33	7	14	12	45	50	–5	35
Finn Harps*	33	9	3	21	35	67	–32	30
Drogheda United*	33	5	7	21	22	65	–43	22

Top scorer: Maguire (Cork City) 20.
Cup Final: Dundalk 1, Cork City 1.
aet; Cork City won 5-3 on penalties.

ROMANIA

Federatia Romana de Fotbal, House of Football, Str. Sergent Serbanica Vasile 12, 22186 Bucuresti.
Founded: 1909. *FIFA:* 1923; *UEFA:* 1954. *National Colours:* All yellow.

International matches 2017–18
Armenia (h) 1-0, Montenegro (a) 0-1, Kazakhstan (h) 3-1, Denmark (a) 1-1, Turkey (h) 2-0, Netherlands (h) 0-3, Israel (a) 2-1, Sweden (h) 1-0, Chile (n) 3-2, Finland (h) 2-0.

League Championship wins (1910–2018)
Steaua Bucharest (renamed FCSB) 26; Dinamo Bucharest 18; Venus Bucharest 8; Chinezul Timisoara 6; UTA Arad 6; Petrolul Ploiesti 4; Ripensia Timisoara 4; Universitatea Craiova 4; CFR Cluj 4; Rapid Bucharest 3; Olimpia Bucharest 2; United Ploiesti 2 (incl. Prahova Ploiesti 1); Colentina Bucharest 2; Arges Pitesti 2; Romano-Americana Bucharest 1; Coltea Brasov 1; Metalochimia Resita 1; Unirea Tricolor 1; CA Oradea 1; Unirea Urziceni 1; Otelul Galati 1; Astra Giurgiu 1; Viitorul Constanta 1.

Cup wins (1934–2018)
Steaua Bucharest (renamed FCSB) 23; Rapid Bucharest 13; Dinamo Bucharest 13; Universitatea Craiova 6; CFR Cluj 4; Petrolul Ploiesti 3; Ripensia Timisoara 2; UTA Arad 2; Politehnica Timisoara 2; CFR Turnu Severin 1; Metalochimia Resita 1; Universitatea Cluj (includes Stiinta) 1; Progresul Oradea (formerly ICO) 1; Progresul Bucharest 1; Ariesul Turda 1; Chimia Ramnicu Vilcea 1; Jiul Petrosani 1; FCU Craiova 1948 1; Gloria Bistrita 1; Astra Giurgiu 1; Voluntari 1.

Romanian Liga 1 Qualifying Table 2017–18

	P	W	D	L	F	A	GD	Pts
CFR Cluj	26	18	5	3	42	13	29	59
FCSB	26	16	7	3	52	18	34	55
Universitatea Craiova	26	14	9	3	41	26	15	51
Astra Giurgiu	26	12	8	6	38	27	11	44
Viitorul	26	13	5	8	34	21	13	44
CSMS Iasi	26	11	6	9	34	31	3	39
Botosani	26	11	6	9	28	26	2	39
Dinamo Bucharest	26	11	6	9	39	31	8	39
Concordia Chiajna	26	8	4	14	36	37	–1	28
Voluntari	26	7	7	12	25	35	–10	28
ACS Poli Timisoara	26	6	9	11	22	37	–15	27
Sepsi	26	5	4	17	15	44	–29	19
Gaz Metan Medis	26	2	10	14	14	39	–25	16
Juventus Bucharest	26	1	8	17	12	47	–35	11

NB: Points earned in Qualifying phase are halved and rounded up at start of Championship and Relegation Play-off phase.

Championship Round 2017–18

	P	W	D	L	F	A	GD	Pts
CFR Cluj	10	5	5	0	12	6	6	50
FCSB	10	6	3	1	14	6	8	49
Universitatea Craiova	10	3	4	3	10	10	0	38
Viitorul	10	3	4	3	13	11	2	35
Astra Giurgiu	10	3	2	5	9	11	–2	33
CSMS Iasi	10	1	1	8	5	19	–14	24

Relegation Round 2017–18

	P	W	D	L	F	A	GD	Pts
Dinamo Bucharest	14	11	1	2	29	10	19	54
Botosani	14	5	5	4	12	9	3	40
Sepsi	14	6	6	2	21	14	7	34
Gaz Metan Medias	14	6	4	4	18	15	3	30
Concordia Chiajna	14	4	4	6	13	17	–4	30
Voluntari+	14	3	4	7	16	22	–6	27
ACS Poli Timisoara*	14	3	4	7	10	16	–6	27
Juventus Bucharest*	14	3	2	9	9	25	–16	17

Top scorers (joint): Gnohere (FCSB) 15, Tucudean (Viitorul) 15 (incl. 4 for CFR Cluj).
Cup Final: Universitatea Craiova 2, Hermannstadt 0.

RUSSIA

Russian Football Union, Ulitsa Narodnaya 7, 115 172 Moscow.
Founded: 1912. *FIFA:* 1912; *UEFA:* 1954. *National Colours:* All brick red.

International matches 2017–18
Korea Republic (h) 4-2, Iran (h) 1-1, Argentina (h) 0-1, Spain (h) 3-3, Brazil (a) 0-3, France (h) 1-3, Austria (a) 0-1, Turkey (h) 1-1, Saudi Arabia (h) 5-0, Egypt (h) 3-1, Uruguay (h) 0-3, Spain (h) 1-1 (4-3p), Croatia (h) 2-2 (3-4p).

USSR League Championship wins (1936–91)
Dynamo Kyiv 13; Spartak Moscow 12; Dynamo Moscow 11; CSKA Moscow 7; Torpedo Moscow 3; Dinamo Tbilisi 2; Dnepr Dnepropetrovsk 2; Zorya Voroshilovgrad 1; Ararat Yerevan 1; Dynamo Minsk 1; Zenit Leningrad 1.

Russian League Championship wins (1992–2018)
Spartak Moscow 10; CSKA Moscow 6; Zenit St Petersburg 4; Lokomotiv Moscow 3; Rubin Kazan 2; Spartak Vladikavkaz (formerly Alania) 1.

USSR Cup wins (1936–91)
Spartak Moscow 10; Dynamo Kyiv 9; Dynamo Moscow 6; Torpedo Moscow 6; CSKA Moscow 5; Shakhtar Donetsk 4; Lokomotiv Moscow 2; Ararat Yerevan 2; Dinamo Tbilisi 2; Zenit Leningrad 1; Karpaty Lvov 1; SKA Rostov-on-Don 1; Metalist Kharkov 1; Dnepr Dnepropetrovsk 1.

Russian Cup wins (1992–2018)
CSKA Moscow 7; Lokomotiv Moscow 7; Spartak Moscow 3; Zenit St Petersburg 3; Torpedo Moscow 1; Dynamo Moscow 1; Terek Grozny (renamed Akhmat Grozny) 1; Rubin Kazan 1; Rostov 1; Tosno 1.

Russian Premier League 2017–18

	P	W	D	L	F	A	GD	Pts
Lokomotiv Moscow	30	18	6	6	41	21	20	60
CSKA Moscow	30	17	7	6	49	23	26	58
Spartak Moscow	30	16	8	6	51	32	19	56
Krasnodar	30	16	6	8	46	30	16	54
Zenit St Petersburg	30	14	11	5	46	21	25	53
Ufa	30	11	10	9	34	30	4	43
Arsenal Tula	30	12	6	12	35	41	–6	42
Dinamo Moscow	30	10	10	10	29	30	–1	40
Akhmat Grozny	30	10	9	11	30	34	–4	39
Rubin Kazan	30	9	11	10	32	30	2	38
Rostov	30	9	10	11	27	28	–1	37
Ural Sverdlovsk Oblast	30	8	13	9	31	32	–1	37

Amkar Perm*	30	9	8	13	20	30	–10	35
Anzhi+	30	6	6	18	31	55	–24	24
Tosno†	30	6	6	18	23	54	–31	24
SKA Khabarovsk*	30	2	7	21	16	55	–39	13

† *Tosno failed to obtain a licence for 2018–19 and the club was dissolved.*
Top scorer: Promes (Spartak Moscow) 15.
Cup Final: Tosno 2, Avangard Kursk 1.

SAN MARINO

Federazione Sammarinese Giuoco Calcio, Strada di Montecchio 17, 47890 San Marino.
Founded: 1931. *FIFA:* 1988; *UEFA:* 1988. *National Colours:* Cobalt blue shirts with white trim, white shorts, cobalt blue socks.

International matches 2017–18
Northern Ireland (h) 0-3, Azerbaijan (a) 1-5, Norway (h) 0-8, Czech Republic (a) 0-5.

League Championship wins (1986–2018)
Tre Fiori 7; La Fiorita 5; Domagnano 4; Folgore/Falciano 4; Faetano 3; Murata 3; Tre Penne 3; Montevito 1; Libertas 1; Cosmos 1; Pennarossa 1.

Cup wins (1937–2018)
Libertas 11; Domagnano 8; Tre Fiori 6; Tre Penne 6; Juvenes 5; La Fiorita 5; Cosmos 4; Faetano 3; Murata 3; Dogana 2; Pennarossa 2; Juvenes/Dogana 2; Folgore Falciano 1.

Campionato Sammarinese Qualifying Table 2017–18

Group A
	P	W	D	L	F	A	GD	Pts
La Fiorita	21	16	2	3	60	16	44	50
Tre Penne	21	16	2	3	52	13	39	50
Domagnano	21	11	4	6	40	35	5	37
Juvenes/Dogana	21	9	4	8	38	34	4	31
Cosmos	21	7	7	7	42	30	12	28
Pennarossa	21	6	7	8	21	36	–15	25
Faetano	21	5	4	12	36	47	–11	19
San Giovanni	21	4	1	16	18	61	–43	13

Group B
	P	W	D	L	F	A	GD	Pts
Folgore Falciano†	20	13	5	2	35	11	24	44
Libertas	20	14	2	4	42	15	27	44
Tre Fiori	20	11	5	4	45	24	21	38
Cailungo	20	6	4	10	21	29	–8	22
Virtus	20	5	4	11	25	41	–16	19
Fiorentino	20	4	2	14	13	39	–26	14
Murata	20	0	1	19	11	68	–57	1

† *Folgore Falciano placed above Libertas on superior head-to-head record.*

Play-offs
(Top three in each group qualify for Play-offs; double-elimination format (eliminated teams shown in italics); group winners receive byes in first two rounds.)
Rnd 1: Libertas 3, Domagnano 0; Tre Penne 2, Tre Fiori 2 (aet; 3-5p)
Rnd 2: Tre Fiori 1, Libertas 1 (aet; 5-4p); Tre Penne 6, *Domagnano* 4 (aet)
Rnd 3: La Fiorita 3, Folgore Falciano 1; Tre Penne 2, *Libertas* 1
Rnd 4: La Fiorita 1, Tre Fiore 0; *Tre Penne* 0, Folgore Falciano 0 (aet; 2-4p)
Semi-final: Folgore Falciano 3, *Tre Fiori* 1
Final: La Fiorita 1, Folgore Falciano 0
Top scorer: Badalassi (Tre Fiori) 26.
Cup Final: La Fiorita 3, Tre Penne 2 (aet).

SCOTLAND
Scottish Football Association, Hampden Park, Glasgow G42 9AY.
Founded: 1873. *FIFA:* 1910; *UEFA:* 1954. *National Colours:* Dark blue shirts, dark blue shorts, red socks.

SERBIA
Football Association of Serbia, Terazije 35, PO Box 263, 11000 Beograd.
Founded: 1919. *FIFA:* 1921; *UEFA:* 1954. *National Colours:* Red shirts, blue shorts, white socks.

International matches 2017–18
Moldova (h) 3-0, Republic of Ireland (a) 1-0, Austria (a) 2-3, Georgia (h) 1-0, China PR (a) 2-0, Korea Republic (a) 1-1, Morocco (n) 1-2, Nigeria (n) 2-0, Chile (n) 0-1, Bolivia (n) 5-1, Costa Rica (n) 1-0, Switzerland (n) 1-2, Brazil (n) 0-2.

Yugoslav League Championship wins (1923–41; 1947–91)
Crvena Zvezda (Red Star Belgrade) 19; Partizan Belgrade 11*; Hajduk Split 9; Gradjanski Zagreb 5; BSK Belgrade (renamed OFK) 5; Dinamo Zagreb 4; Jugoslavija Belgrade 2; Concordia Zagreb 2; Vojvodina Novi Sad 2; FC Sarajevo 2; HASK Zagreb 1; Zeljeznicar 1.
* *Total includes 1 League Championship (1986–87) originally awarded to Macedonian club Vardar.*

Serbian League Championship wins (1992–2018)
Partizan Belgrade 16; Crvena Zvezda (Red Star Belgrade) 9; Obilic 1.

Yugoslav Cup wins (1923–41; 1947–91)
Crvena Zvezda (Red Star Belgrade) 12; Hajduk Split 9; Dinamo Zagreb 7; Partizan Belgrade 5; OFK Belgrade (incl. BSK 3) 5; Rijeka 2; Velez Mostar 2; HASK Zagreb 1; Jugoslavija Belgrade 1; Vardar Skopje 1; Borac Banjaluka 1.

Serbian and Serbia-Montenegro Cup wins (1992–2018)
Crvena Zvezda (Red Star Belgrade) 12; Partizan Belgrade 9; Rijeka 2; Sartid 1; Zeleznik 1; Jagodina 1; Vojvodina 1; Cukaricki 1.

Serbian SuperLiga Qualifying Table 2017–18
	P	W	D	L	F	A	GD	Pts
Crvena Zvezda	30	25	4	1	75	15	60	77
Partizan Belgrade	30	20	7	3	59	23	36	65
Cukaricki	30	14	9	7	43	26	17	51
Radnicki Nis	30	14	8	8	46	40	6	50
Spartak Subotica	30	14	7	9	55	39	16	49
Vozdovac	30	13	8	9	41	29	12	47
Napredak	30	13	7	10	49	42	7	46
Vojvodina	30	12	8	10	33	29	4	44
Radnik Surdulica	30	10	6	14	33	52	–19	36
Mladost Lucani	30	9	8	13	36	44	–8	35
Zemun	30	9	8	13	30	38	–8	35
Macva Sabac	30	9	4	17	31	47	–16	31
Backa Palanka	30	8	6	16	30	53	–23	30
Javor Ivanjica	30	7	4	19	25	48	–23	25
Borac Cacak	30	6	5	19	25	57	–32	23
Rad	30	6	3	21	29	58	–29	21

NB: *Points earned in Qualifying phase are halved and rounded up at start of Championship and Relegation Play-off phase.*

Championship Round 2017–18
	P	W	D	L	F	A	GD	Pts
Crvena Zvezda	37	32	4	1	96	19	77	60
Partizan Belgrade	37	23	8	6	71	33	38	43
Radnicki Nis	37	18	8	11	63	51	12	37
Spartak Subotica	37	18	7	12	62	49	13	37
Vozdovac	37	16	8	13	48	42	6	33
Cukaricki	37	16	9	12	54	44	10	32
Napredak	37	15	8	14	57	55	2	30
Vojvodina	37	14	8	15	43	43	0	28

Relegation Round 2017–18
	P	W	D	L	F	A	GD	Pts
Radnik Surdulica	37	13	7	17	42	60	–18	28
Mladost Lucani	37	11	11	15	44	52	–8	27
Zemun	37	11	10	16	39	46	–7	26
Macva Sabac	37	11	8	18	38	52	–14	26
Rad	37	10	6	21	40	64	–24	26
Backa Palanka	37	11	7	19	41	64	–23	25
Javor Ivanjica*	37	10	6	21	33	57	–24	24
Borac Cacak*	37	7	5	25	31	71	–40	15

Top scorer: Pesic (Crvena Zvezda) 25.
Cup Final: Partizan Belgrade 2, Mladost Lucani 1.

SLOVAKIA
Slovensky Futbalovy Zvaz, Trnavska cesta 100, 821 01 Bratislava.
Founded: 1938. *FIFA:* 1994; *UEFA:* 1993. *National Colours:* White shirts with blue trim, white shorts, white socks.

International matches 2017–18
Slovenia (h) 1-0, England (a) 1-2, Scotland (a) 0-1, Malta (h) 3-0, Ukraine (a) 1-2, Norway (h) 1-0, UAE (n) 2-1, Thailand (a) 3-2, Netherlands (h) 1-1, Morocco (n) 1-2.

League Championship wins (1939–44; 1994–2018)
Slovan Bratislava (incl. 4 as SK Bratislava) 12; Zilina 7; Kosice 2; Inter Bratislava 2; Artmedia Petrzalka 2;

Trencin 2; Sparta Povazska Bystrica 1; OAP Bratislava 1; Ruzomberok 1; Spartak Trnava 1.
See also Czech Republic section for Slovak club honours in Czechoslovak era 1925–93.

Cup wins (1993–2018)
Slovan Bratislava 8; Inter Bratislava 3; Artmedia Petrzalka 2; Kosice 2; Trencin 2; Humenne 1; Spartak Trnava 1; Koba Senec 1; Matador Puchov 1; Dukla Banska Bystrica 1; Ruzomberok 1; ViOn Zlate Moravce 1; Zilina 1.

Slovak Super Liga 2017–18
	P	W	D	L	F	A	GD	Pts
Spartak Trnava	22	16	2	4	34	16	18	50
Slovan Bratislava	22	11	8	3	45	26	19	41
DAC Dunajska Streda	22	10	9	3	29	20	9	39
Zilina	22	12	1	9	42	35	7	37
Trencin	22	10	6	6	54	32	22	36
Ruzomberok	22	8	9	5	31	21	10	33
Nitra	22	7	9	6	19	14	5	30
ViOn Zlate Moravce	22	7	4	11	28	37	–9	25
Zemplin Michalovce	22	6	6	10	18	25	–7	24
Sport Podbrezova	22	6	2	14	19	37	–18	20
Senica	22	3	5	14	17	42	–25	14
Tatran Presov	22	3	5	14	13	44	–31	14

Championship Round 2017–18
	P	W	D	L	F	A	GD	Pts
Spartak Trnava	32	20	4	8	41	28	13	64
Slovan Bratislava	32	17	8	7	58	37	21	59
DAC Dunajska Streda	32	16	9	7	46	32	14	57
Zilina	32	17	2	13	63	51	12	53
Trencin	32	15	6	11	75	47	28	51
Ruzomberok	32	10	10	12	36	39	–3	40

Relegation Round 2017–18
	P	W	D	L	F	A	GD	Pts
Nitra	32	11	12	9	33	29	4	45
Zemplin Michalovce	32	11	8	13	35	34	1	41
Sport Podbrezova	32	11	5	16	29	43	–14	38
ViOn Zlate Moravce	32	8	7	17	39	52	–13	31
Senica+	32	6	8	18	29	58	–29	26
Tatran Presov*	32	5	11	16	22	56	–34	26

Top scorer: Mraz (Zilina) 21.
Cup Final: Slovan Bratislava 3, Ruzomberok 1.

SLOVENIA

Nogometna Zveza Slovenije, Brnciceva 41g, PP 3986, 1001 Ljubljana.
Founded: 1920. *FIFA:* 1992; *UEFA:* 1992. *National Colours:* White shirts with blue trim, white shorts, white socks.

International matches 2017–18
Slovakia (a) 0-1, Lithuania (h) 4-0, England (a) 0-1, Scotland (h) 2-2, Austria (a) 0-3, Belarus (h) 0-2, Montenegro (a) 2-0.

League Championship wins (1991–2018)
Maribor 14; Olimpija (pre-2005) 4; Gorica 4; Domzale 2; Olimpija Ljubljana 2; Koper 1.

Cup wins (1991–2018)
Maribor 9; Olimpija (pre-2005) 4; Gorica 3; Koper 3; Interblock 2; Domzale 2, Mura (pre-2004) 1; Rudar Velenje 1; Celje 1; Olimpija Ljubljana 1.

Slovenian PrvaLiga 2017–18
	P	W	D	L	F	A	GD	Pts
Olimpija Ljubljana	36	23	11	2	61	17	44	80
Maribor	36	24	8	4	76	28	48	80
Domzale	36	22	7	7	79	31	48	73
Rudar Velenje	36	15	5	16	50	49	1	50
Celje	36	14	8	14	56	51	5	50
Gorica	36	14	5	17	40	48	–8	47
Krsko	36	9	7	20	36	61	–25	34
Aluminij	36	8	9	19	40	63	–23	33
Triglav+	36	7	7	22	29	68	–39	28
Ankaran Hrvatini*	36	5	11	20	33	84	–51	26

Top scorer: Zahovic (Maribor) 18.
Cup Final: Olimpija Ljubljana 6, Aluminij 1.

SPAIN

Real Federacion Espanola de Futbol, Calle Ramon y Cajal s/n, Apartado postale 385, 28230 Las Rozas, Madrid.
Founded: 1913. *FIFA:* 1913; *UEFA:* 1954. *National Colours:* All red with yellow trim.

International matches 2017–18
Italy (h) 3-0, Liechtenstein (a) 8-0, Albania (h) 3-0, Israel (a) 1-0, Costa Rica (h) 5-0, Russia (a) 3-3, Germany (a) 1-1, Argentina (h) 6-1, Switzerland (h) 1-1, Tunisia (n) 1-0, Portugal (n) 3-3, Iran (n) 1-0, Morocco (n) 2-2, Russia (a) 1-1 (3-4p).

League Championship wins (1929–36; 1940–2018)
Real Madrid 33; Barcelona 25; Atletico Madrid 10; Athletic Bilbao 8; Valencia 6; Real Sociedad 2; Real Betis 1; Sevilla 1; Deportivo La Coruna 1.

Cup wins (1903–2018)
Barcelona 30; Athletic Bilbao (includes Vizcaya Bilbao 1) 23; Real Madrid 19; Atletico Madrid 10; Valencia 7; Real Zaragoza 6; Sevilla 5; Espanyol 4; Real Union de Irun 3; Real Sociedad (includes Ciclista) 2; Real Betis 2; Deportivo La Coruna 2; Racing de Irun 1; Arenas 1; Mallorca 1.

Spanish La Liga 2017–18
	P	W	D	L	F	A	GD	Pts
Barcelona	38	28	9	1	99	29	70	93
Atletico Madrid	38	23	10	5	58	22	36	79
Real Madrid	38	22	10	6	94	44	50	76
Valencia	38	22	7	9	65	38	27	73
Villarreal	38	18	7	13	57	50	7	61
Real Betis	38	18	6	14	60	61	–1	60
Sevilla	38	17	7	14	49	58	–9	58
Getafe	38	15	10	13	42	33	9	55
Eibar	38	14	9	15	44	50	–6	51
Girona	38	14	9	15	50	59	–9	51
Espanyol	38	12	13	13	36	42	–6	49
Real Sociedad	38	14	7	17	66	59	7	49
Celta Vigo	38	13	10	15	59	60	–1	49
Alaves	38	15	2	21	40	50	–10	47
Levante	38	11	13	14	44	58	–14	46
Athletic Bilbao	38	10	13	15	41	49	–8	43
Leganes	38	12	7	19	34	51	–17	43
Deportivo La Coruna*	38	6	11	21	38	76	–38	29
Las Palmas*	38	5	7	26	24	74	–50	22
Malaga*	38	5	5	28	24	61	–37	20

Top scorer: Messi (Barcelona) 34.
Cup Final: Barcelona 5, Sevilla 0.

SWEDEN

Svenska Fotbollfoerbundet, Evenemangsgatan 31, PO Box 1216, SE-171 23 Solna.
Founded: 1904. *FIFA:* 1904; *UEFA:* 1954. *National Colours:* Yellow shirts with blue trim, blue shorts, yellow socks.

International matches 2017–18
Bulgaria (a) 2-3, Belarus (a) 4-0, Luxembourg (h) 8-0, Netherlands (a) 0-2, Italy (h) 1-0, Italy (a) 0-0, Estonia (n) 1-1, Denmark (n) 1-0, Chile (h) 1-2, Romania (a) 0-1, Denmark (n) 0-0, Peru (h) 0-0, Korea Republic (n) 1-0, Germany (n) 1-2, Mexico (n) 3-0, Switzerland (n) 1-0, England (n) 0-2.

League Championship wins (1896–2017)
Malmo 20; IFK Gothenburg 18; IFK Norrkoping 13; Orgryte 12; AIK Stockholm 11; Djurgaarden 11; IF Elfsborg 6; Helsingborg 5; GAIS Gothenburg 4; Oster Vaxjo 4; Halmstad 4; Atvidaberg 2; Gothenburg IF 1; IFK Eskilstuna 1; Fassbergs 1; IF Gavic Brynas 1; IK Sleipner 1; Hammarby 1; Kalmar 1.
(Played in cup format from 1896–1925.)

Cup wins (1941–2018)
Malmo 14; AIK Stockholm 8; IFK Gothenburg 7; IFK Norrkoping 6; Helsingborg 5; Djurgaarden 5; Kalmar 3; IF Elfsborg 3; Atvidaberg 2; GAIS Gothenburg 1; IF Raa 1; Landskrona 1; Oster Vaxjo 1; Degerfors 1; Halmstad 1; Orgryte 1; Hacken 1; Ostersund 1.

Allsvenskan 2017
	P	W	D	L	F	A	GD	Pts
Malmo	30	19	7	4	63	27	36	64
AIK Solna	30	16	9	5	47	22	25	57
Djurgaarden	30	15	8	7	54	30	24	53
Hacken	30	14	10	6	42	28	14	52
Ostersund	30	13	11	6	48	32	16	50
IFK Norrkoping	30	14	6	10	45	40	5	48
Sirius	30	11	7	12	46	51	–5	40
Elfsborg	30	10	9	11	53	59	–6	39
Hammarby	30	9	11	10	42	43	–1	38
IFK Gothenburg	30	9	10	11	42	40	2	37
Orebro	30	10	6	14	38	54	–16	36

Kalmar	30	9	5	16	30	49	−19	32
GIF Sundsvall	30	7	10	13	29	46	−17	31
Jonkopings Sodra*+	30	6	12	12	31	46	−15	30
Halmstad*	30	5	9	16	29	45	−16	24
Eskilstuna*	30	4	8	18	28	55	−27	20

Top scorers (joint): Eriksson (Djurgaarden), Holmberg (IFK Norrkoping) 14.
Cup Final: Djurgaarden 3, Malmo 0.

SWITZERLAND

Schweizerisher Fussballverband, Worbstrasse 48, Postfach 3000, Bern 15.
Founded: 1895. *FIFA:* 1904; *UEFA:* 1954. *National Colours:* Red shirts, white shorts, red socks.

International matches 2017–18

Andorra (h) 3-0, Latvia (a) 3-0, Hungary (h) 5-2, Portugal (a) 0-2, Northern Ireland (a) 1-0, Northern Ireland (h) 0-0, Greece (a) 1-0, Panama (h) 6-0, Spain (a) 1-1, Japan (h) 2-0, Brazil (n) 1-1, Serbia (n) 2-1, Costa Rica (n) 2-2, Sweden (n) 0-1.

League Championship wins (1897–2018)

Grasshoppers 27; FC Basel 20; Servette 17; Young Boys 12; FC Zurich 12; Lausanne-Sport 7; Winterthur 3; Aarau 3; Lugano 3; La Chaux-de-Fonds 3; St Gallen 2; Neuchatel Xamax 2; Sion 2; Anglo-American Club 1; Brühl 1; Cantonal-Neuchatel 1; Etoile La Chaux-de-Fonds 1; Biel-Bienne 1; Bellinzona 1; Luzern 1.

Cup wins (1926–2018)

Grasshoppers 19; Sion 13; FC Basel 12; FC Zurich 10; Lausanne-Sport 9; Servette 7; Young Boys 6; La Chaux-de-Fonds 6; Lugano 3; Luzern 2; Urania Geneva 1; Young Fellows Zurich 1; FC Grenchen 1; St Gallen 1; Aarau 1; Wil 1.

Swiss Super League 2017–18

	P	W	D	L	F	A	GD	Pts
Young Boys	36	26	6	4	84	41	43	84
FC Basel	36	20	9	7	72	36	36	69
Luzern	36	15	9	12	51	51	0	54
Zurich	36	12	13	11	50	44	6	49
St Gallen	36	14	3	19	52	72	−20	45
Sion	36	11	9	16	53	56	−3	42
Thun	36	12	6	18	53	68	−15	42
Lugano	36	12	6	18	38	55	−17	42
Grasshopper	36	10	9	17	43	52	−9	39
Lausanne Sport*	36	9	8	19	46	67	−21	35

Top scorer: Ajeti (FC Basel) 17 (incl. 3 for St Gallen).
Cup Final: FC Zurich 2, Young Boys 1.

TURKEY

Turkiye Futbol Federasyonu, Hasan Dogan Milli Takimlar, Kamp ve Egitim Tesisleri, Riva, Beykoz, Istanbul.
Founded: 1923. *FIFA:* 1923; *UEFA:* 1962. *National Colours:* All red.

International matches 2017–18

Ukraine (a) 0-2, Croatia (h) 1-0, Iceland (h) 0-3, Finland (a) 2-2, Romania (a) 0-2, Albania (h) 2-3, Republic of Ireland (h) 1-0, Montenegro (a) 2-2, Iran (h) 2-1, Tunisia (n) 2-2, Russia (a) 1-1.

League Championship wins (1959–2018)

Galatasaray 21; Fenerbahce 19; Besiktas 13; Trabzonspor 6; Bursaspor 1.

Cup wins (1963–2018)

Galatasaray 17; Besiktas 9; Trabzonspor 8; Fenerbahce 6; Altay Izmir 2; Goztepe Izmir 2; Ankaragucu 2; Genclerbirligi 2; Kocaelispor 2; Eskisehirspor 1; Bursaspor 1; Sakaryaspor 1; Kayseri 1; Konyaspor 1; Akhisar Belediyespor 1.

Turkish Super Lig 2017–18

	P	W	D	L	F	A	GD	Pts
Galatasaray	34	24	3	7	75	33	42	75
Fenerbahce	34	21	9	4	78	36	42	72
Istanbul Basaksehir	34	22	6	6	62	34	28	72
Besiktas	34	21	8	5	69	30	39	71
Trabzonspor	34	15	10	9	63	51	12	55
Goztepe	34	13	10	11	49	50	−1	49
Sivasspor	34	14	7	13	45	53	−8	49
Kasimpasa	34	13	7	14	57	58	−1	46
Kayserispor	34	13	5	16	44	55	−11	44
Yeni Yeni Malatyaspor	34	11	10	13	38	45	−7	43
Akhisar Belediyespor	34	11	9	14	44	53	−9	42

Alanyaspor	34	11	7	16	55	59	−4	40
Bursaspor	34	11	6	17	43	48	−5	39
Antalyaspor	34	10	8	16	40	59	−19	38
Konyaspor	34	9	9	16	38	42	−4	36
Osmanlispor*	34	8	9	17	49	60	−11	33
Genclerbirligi*	34	8	9	17	37	54	−17	33
Karabukspor*	34	3	3	28	20	86	−66	12

Top scorer: Gomis (Galatasaray) 29.
Cup Final: Akhisar Belediyespor 3, Fenerbahce 2.

UKRAINE

Football Federation of Ukraine, Provulok Laboratornyi 7-A, PO Box 55, 01133 Kyiv.
Founded: 1991. *FIFA:* 1992; *UEFA:* 1992. *National Colours:* All yellow with blue trim.

International matches 2017–18

Turkey (h) 2-0, Iceland (a) 0-2, Kosovo (a) 2-0*, Croatia (h) 0-2, Slovakia (h) 2-1, Saudi Arabia (n) 1-1, Japan (n) 2-1, Morocco (n) 0-0, Albania (n) 4-1.
* *Match played in Albania.*

League Championship wins (1992–2018)

Dynamo Kyiv 15; Shakhtar Donetsk 11; Tavriya Simferopol 1.

Cup wins (1992–2018)

Shakhtar Donetsk 12; Dynamo Kyiv 11; Chornomorets Odessa 2; Vorskla Poltava 1; Tavriya Simferopol 1.
See also Russia section for Ukrainian club honours in Soviet era 1936–91.

Ukrainian Premier League 2017–18

	P	W	D	L	F	A	GD	Pts
Shakhtar Donetsk	22	16	3	3	51	18	33	51
Dynamo Kyiv	22	13	6	3	42	20	22	45
Vorskla Poltava	22	11	4	7	28	22	6	37
Zorya Luhansk	22	8	9	5	38	28	10	33
Veres	22	7	11	4	26	17	9	32
Mariupol	22	9	5	8	30	27	3	32
Olimpik Donetsk	22	7	7	8	24	26	−2	28
Oleksandria	22	4	11	7	19	23	−4	23
Zirka	22	4	7	11	13	31	−18	19
Karpaty Lviv	22	3	10	9	13	35	−22	19
Chornomorets Odessa	22	3	9	10	16	36	−20	18
Stal Kamianske	22	3	6	13	15	32	−17	15

Championship Round 2017–18

	P	W	D	L	F	A	GD	Pts
Shakhtar Donetsk	32	24	3	5	71	24	47	75
Dynamo Kyiv	32	22	7	3	64	25	39	73
Vorskla	32	14	7	11	37	35	2	49
Vorskla Poltava	32	11	10	11	44	44	0	43
Mariupol	32	10	9	13	38	41	−3	39
Veres	32	7	14	11	28	30	−2	35

Relegation Round 2017–18

	P	W	D	L	F	A	GD	Pts
Oleksandria	32	10	15	7	32	27	5	45
Karpaty Lviv	32	8	13	11	28	45	−17	37
Olimpik Donetsk	32	9	9	14	29	38	−9	36
Zirka*+	32	9	7	16	18	46	−18	31
Chornomorets Odessa*+	32	6	11	15	26	49	−23	29
Stal Kamianske*	32	6	8	18	23	44	−21	26

Top scorer: Ferreyra (Shakhtar Donetsk) 21.
Cup Final: Shakhtar Donetsk 2, Dynamo Kyiv 0.

WALES

Football Association of Wales, 11/12 Neptune Court, Vanguard Way, Cardiff CF24 5PJ.
Founded: 1876. *FIFA:* 1910; *UEFA:* 1954. *National Colours:* All red with green trim.

SOUTH AMERICA (CONMEBOL)

ARGENTINA

Asociacion del Futbol Argentino, Viamonte 1366/76, Buenos Aires 1053.
Founded: 1893. *FIFA:* 1912; *CONMEBOL:* 1916. *National Colours:* Light blue and white striped shirts, white shorts, white socks.
International matches 2017–18
Uruguay (a) 0-0, Venezuela (a) 1-1, Peru (h) 0-0, Ecuador (a) 3-1, Russia (a) 1-0, Nigeria (n) 2-4, Italy (n) 2-0, Spain (a) 1-6, Haiti (h) 4-0, Iceland (n) 1-1, Croatia (n) 0-3, Nigeria (n) 2-1, France (n) 3-4.
League champions 2017–18: Boca Juniors. *Cup winners 2017:* River Plate.

BOLIVIA

Federacion Boliviana de Futbol, Avenida Libertador Bolivar 1168, Casilla 484, Cochabamba.
Founded: 1925. *FIFA:* 1926; *CONMEBOL:* 1926. *National Colours:* Green shirts, white shorts, white socks.
International matches 2017–18
Peru (a) 1-2, Chile (h) 1-0, Brazil (h) 0-0, Uruguay (a) 2-4, Curacao (a) 1-1, Curacao (a) 0-1, USA (a) 0-3, Korea Republic (n) 0-0, Serbia (n) 1-5.
League champions 2017–18: Bolivar (Apertura 2017); Bolivar (Clausura 2017); Wilstermann (Apertura 2018).
Cup winners: No competition.

BRAZIL

Confederacao Brasileira de Futebol, Avenida Luis Carlos Prestes 130, Barra da Tijuca, Rio de Janeiro 22775-055.
Founded: 1914. *FIFA:* 1923; *CONMEBOL:* 1916. *National Colours:* Yellow shirts with green collar and cuffs, blue shorts, white socks.
International matches 2017–18
Ecuador (h) 2-0, Colombia (a) 1-1, Bolivia (a) 0-0, Chile (h) 3-0, Japan (n) 3-1, England (a) 0-0, Russia (a) 3-0, Germany (a) 1-0, Croatia (n) 2-0, Austria (a) 3-0, Switzerland (n) 1-1, Costa Rica (n) 2-0, Serbia (n) 2-0, Mexico (n) 2-0, Belgium (n) 1-2.
League champions 2017: Corinthians. *Cup winners 2017:* Cruzeiro.

CHILE

Federacion de Futbol de Chile, Avenida Quilin 5635, Comuna Penalolen, Casilla 3733, Santiago de Chile.
Founded: 1895. *FIFA:* 1913; *CONMEBOL:* 1916. *National Colours:* Red shirts with blue collars, blue shorts, white socks.
International matches 2017–18
Paraguay (h) 0-3, Bolivia (a) 0-1, Ecuador (h) 2-1, Brazil (a) 0-3, Sweden (a) 2-1, Denmark (a) 0-0, Romania (n) 2-3, Serbia (n) 1-0, Poland (a) 2-2.
League champions 2017: Colo-Colo. *Cup winners 2017:* Santiago Wanderers.

COLOMBIA

Federacion Colombiana de Futbol, Avenida 32 No. 16–22, Bogota.
Founded: 1924. *FIFA:* 1936; *CONMEBOL:* 1936. *National Colours:* Yellow shirts with blue trim, white shorts, white socks.
International matches 2017–18
Venezuela (a) 0-0, Brazil (h) 1-1, Paraguay (h) 1-2, Peru (h) 1-1, Korea Republic (a) 1-2, China PR (a) 4-0, France (a) 3-2, Australia (n) 0-0, Egypt (n) 0-0, Japan (n) 1-2, Poland (n) 3-0, Senegal (n) 1-0, England (n) 1-1 (3-4p).
League champions 2017: Atletico Nacional (Apertura); Millonarios (Finalizacion). *2018:* Deportes Tolima (Apertura). *Cup winners 2017:* Junior.

ECUADOR

Federacion Ecuatoriana del Futbol, Avenida Las Aguas y Calle Alianza, PO Box 09-01-7447, Guayaquil 593.
Founded: 1925. *FIFA:* 1927; *CONMEBOL:* 1927. *National Colours:* Yellow shirts, blue shorts, red socks.
International matches 2017–18
Trinidad & Tobago (a) 3-1, Brazil (a) 0-2, Peru (h) 1-2, Chile (a) 1-2, Argentina (h) 1-3.
League champions 2017: Emelec. *Cup winners:* No competition.

PARAGUAY

Asociacion Paraguaya de Futbol, Calle Mayor Martinez 1393, Asuncion.
Founded: 1906. *FIFA:* 1925; *CONMEBOL:* 1921. *National Colours:* Red and white striped shirts, blue shorts, blue socks.
International matches 2017–18
Chile (a) 3-0, Uruguay (h) 1-2, Colombia (a) 2-1, Venezuela (h) 0-1, USA (a) 0-1, Japan (n) 2-4.
League champions 2017: Libertad (Apertura); Cerro Porteno (Clausura). *2018:* Olimpia (Apertura). *Cup winners 2018:* Inaugural competition still being played.

PERU

Federacion Peruana de Futbol, Avenida Aviacion 2085, San Luis, Lima 30.
Founded: 1922. *FIFA:* 1924; *CONMEBOL:* 1925. *National Colours:* White shirts with red sash, white shorts, white socks.
International matches 2017–18
Bolivia (h) 2-1, Ecuador (a) 2-1, Argentina (a) 0-0,

Colombia (h) 1-1, New Zealand (a) 0-0, New Zealand (h) 2-0, Croatia (n) 2-0, Iceland (n) 3-1, Scotland (h) 2-0, Saudi Arabia (n) 3-0, Sweden (a) 0-0, Denmark (n) 0-1, France (n) 0-1, Australia (n) 2-0.
League champions 2017: Alianza Lima. *Cup winners 2017:* Deportivo Binacional.

URUGUAY

Asociacion Uruguaya de Futbol, Guayabo 1531, Montevideo 11200.
Founded: 1900. *FIFA:* 1923; *CONMEBOL:* 1916. *National Colours:* Sky blue shirts, black shorts, black socks with sky blue tops.
International matches 2017–18
Argentina (h) 0-0, Paraguay (a) 2-1, Venezuela (a) 0-0, Bolivia (h) 4-2, Poland (a) 0-0, Austria (a) 1-2, Czech Republic (n) 2-0, Wales (n) 1-0, Uzbekistan (h) 3-0, Egypt (n) 1-0, Saudi Arabia (n) 1-0, Russia (a) 3-0, Portugal (n) 2-1, France (n) 0-2.
League champions 2017: Penarol. *Cup winners:* No competition.

VENEZUELA

Federacion Venezolana de Futbol, Avenida Santos Erminy 1ra Calle las Delicias, Torre Mega II, P.H.B. Sabana Grande, 1050 Caracas.
Founded: 1926. *FIFA:* 1952; *CONMEBOL:* 1952. *National Colours:* All burgundy.
International matches 2017–18
Colombia (h) 0-0, Argentina (a) 1-1, Uruguay (h) 0-0, Paraguay (a) 1-0, Iran (n) 0-1*.
* *Behind closed doors.*
League champions 2017: Monagas. *Cup winners 2017:* Mineros de Guayana.

ASIA (AFC)

AFGHANISTAN

Afghanistan Football Federation, PO Box 128, Kabul.
Founded: 1933. *FIFA:* 1948; *AFC:* 1954. *National Colours:* All red.
International matches 2017–18
Oman (a) 0-2, Jordan (a) 1-4, Jordan (n) 3-3, Vietnam (a) 0-0, Cambodia (n) 2-1.
League champions 2017: Shaheen Asmayee. *Cup winners:* No competition.

AUSTRALIA

Football Federation Australia Ltd, Locked Bag A4071, Sydney South, NSW 1235.
Founded: 1961. *FIFA:* 1963; *AFC:* 2006. *National Colours:* Gold shirts, green shorts, white socks.
International matches 2017–18
UAE (h) 2-0*. Japan (a) 0-2, Thailand (h) 2-1, Syria (n) 1-1, Syria (h) 2-1, Honduras (a) 0-0, Honduras (h) 3-1, Norway (a) 1-4, Colombia (n) 0-0, Czech Republic (h) 4-0, Hungary (a) 2-1, France (n) 1-2, Denmark (n) 1-1, Peru (n) 0-2.
* *Match played 28.03.2017; result incorrect in last edition.*
League champions 2017–18: Sydney. *Grand Final winners 2018:* Melbourne Victory. *Cup winners 2017:* Sydney.

BAHRAIN

Bahrain Football Association, PO Box 5464, Building 315, Road 2407, Block 934, East Riffa.
Founded: 1957. *FIFA:* 1968; *AFC:* 1969. *National Colours:* All red.
International matches 2017–18
Jordan (h) 0-0, Chinese Taipei (h) 5-0, Chinese Taipei (a) 1-2, Hong Kong (a) 2-0, Singapore (a) 3-0, Kuwait (h) 0-0, Iraq (n) 1-1, Yemen (n) 1-0, Qatar (n) 1-1, Oman (n) 0-1, Palestine (h) 0-0, Turkmenistan (h) 4-0.
League champions 2017–18: Al-Muharraq. *Cup winners 2017–18:* Al-Najma.

BANGLADESH

Bangladesh Football Federation, BFF House, Motijheel Commercial Area, Dhaka 1000.
Founded: 1972. *FIFA:* 1976; *AFC:* 1974. *National Colours:* Green shirts, white shorts, green socks.
International matches 2017–18
Laos (a) 2-2.
League champions 2017–18: Dhaka Abahani. *Cup winners 2017:* Dhaka Abahani.

BHUTAN

Bhutan Football Federation, PO Box 365, Changiiji, Thimphu 11001.
Founded: 1983. *FIFA:* 2000; *AFC:* 2000. *National Colours:* Yellow and orange shirts, white shorts, orange socks.

International matches 2017–18
Palestine (h) 0-2, Palestine (a) 0-10, Oman (n) 2-4, Maldives (h) 0-7, Malaysia (h) 0-7.
League champions 2017: Transport United. *Cup winners:* No competition.

BRUNEI

National Football Association of Brunei Darussalam, NFABD House, Jalan Pusat Persidangan, Bandar Seri Begawan BB4313.
Founded: 1959. *FIFA:* 1972; *AFC:* 1969. *National Colours:* Yellow and black shirts, white shorts, yellow socks.
International matches 2017–18
Kyrgyzstan (n) 4-0.
League champions 2017–18: MS ABDB. *Cup winners 2017–18:* Indera.

CAMBODIA

Football Federation of Cambodia, National Football Centre, Road Kabsrov Sangkat Samrongkrom, Khan Dangkor, Phnom Penh 2327 PPT3.
Founded: 1933. *FIFA:* 1954; *AFC:* 1954. *National Colours:* Red and blue shirts, blue shorts, red socks.
International matches 2017–18
Vietnam (h) 1-2, Vietnam (a) 0-5, Myanmar (h) 1-2, Jordan (h) 0-1, Laos (a) 1-0, Afghanistan (n) 1-2.
League champions 2017: Boeung Ket. *Cup winners 2017:* Preah Khan Reach Svay Rieng.

CHINA PR

Football Association of the People's Republic of China, Building A, Dongjiudasha Mansion, Xizhaosi Street, Dongcheng, Beijing 100061.
Founded: 1924. *FIFA:* 1931, rejoined 1980; *AFC:* 1974. *National Colours:* All red.
International matches 2017–18
Uzbekistan (h) 1-0, Qatar (a) 2-1, Serbia (h) 0-2, Colombia (h) 0-4, Korea Republic (n) 2-2, Japan (a) 1-2, Korea DPR (n) 1-1, Wales (h) 0-6, Czech Republic (n) 1-4, Myanmar (h) 1-0, Thailand (a) 2-0.
League champions 2017: Guangzhou Evergrande. *Cup winners 2017:* Shanghai Shenhua.

CHINESE TAIPEI

Chinese Taipei Football Association, Room 210, 2F, 55 Chang Chi Street, Tatung, Taipei 10363.
Founded: 1936. *FIFA:* 1954; *AFC:* 1954. *National Colours:* All blue with white trim.
International matches 2017–18
Bahrain (a) 0-5, Mongolia (h) 4-2, Bahrain (h) 2-1, Turkmenistan (a) 1-2, Philippines (h) 3-0, Timor-Leste (h) 3-1, Laos (h) 2-0, Singapore (a) 1-0, India (a) 0-5, New Zealand (n) 0-1, Kenya (n) 0-4.
League champions 2017: Tatung. *Cup winners:* No competition.

GUAM

Guam Football Association, PO Box 20008, Barrigada, Guam 96921.
Founded: 1975. *FIFA:* 1996; *AFC:* 1996. *National Colours:* Blue shirts with white sleeves, blue shorts, blue socks.
International matches 2017–18
None played.
League champions 2017–18: Rovers. *Cup winners 2018:* BOG Strykers.

HONG KONG

Hong Kong Football Association Ltd, 55 Fat Kwong Street, Ho Man Tin, Kowloon, Hong Kong.
Founded: 1914. *FIFA:* 1954; *AFC:* 1954. *National Colours:* All red with white trim.
International matches 2017–18
Singapore (a) 1-1, Macao (h) 4-0, Malaysia (a) 1-1, Laos (h) 4-0, Malaysia (h) 2-0, Bahrain (h) 0-2, Lebanon (a) 0-1, Korea DPR (a) 0-2.
League champions 2017–18: Kitchee. *Cup winners 2017–18:* Kitchee.

INDIA

All India Football Federation, Football House, Sector 19, Phase 1 Dwarka, New Delhi 110075.
Founded: 1937. *FIFA:* 1948; *AFC:* 1954. *National Colours:* Sky blue and navy shirts, navy shorts, sky blue and navy socks.
International matches 2017–18
Mauritius (h) 2-1, St Kitts & Nevis (a) 1-1, Macao (a) 2-0, Macao (h) 4-1, Myanmar (h) 2-2, Kyrgyzstan (a) 1-2, Chinese Taipei (h) 5-0, Kenya (h) 3-0, New Zealand (h) 1-2, Kenya (h) 2-0.

League champions 2017–18: Minerva Punjab. *Cup winners 2018:* Bengaluru.

INDONESIA

Football Association of Indonesia, Gelora Bung Karno Pintu X–XI, PO Box 2305, Senayan, Jakarta 10023.
Founded: 1930. *FIFA:* 1952; *AFC:* 1954. *National Colours:* Red shirts with green trim, red shorts, red socks.
International matches 2017–18
Cambodia (a) 2-0*, Puerto Rico (h) 0-0, Fiji (h) 0-0, Guyana (h) 2-1, Iceland (h) 0-6, Iceland (h) 1-4.
* *Match played 8.06.2017; result incorrect in last edition.*
League champions 2017: Bhayangkara. *Cup winners 2018:* Competition still being played.

IRAN

Football Federation IR Iran, No. 4 Third St., Seoul Avenue, Tehran 19958-73591.
Founded: 1920. *FIFA:* 1948; AFC: 1954. *National Colours:* All white.
International matches 2017–18
Korea Republic (a) 0-0, Syria (h) 2-2, Togo (h) 2-0, Russia (a) 1-1, Panama (n) 2-1, Venezuela (n) 1-0, Sierra Leone (h) 4-0, Tunisia (a) 0-1, Algeria (n) 2-1, Uzbekistan (h) 1-0, Turkey (a) 1-2, Lithuania (n) 1-0, Morocco (n) 1-0, Spain (n) 0-1, Portugal (n) 1-1.
League champions 2017–18: Persepolis. *Cup winners 2017–18:* Esteghlal.

IRAQ

Iraq Football Association, Al-Shaab Stadium, PO Box 484, Baghdad.
Founded: 1948. *FIFA:* 1950; *AFC:* 1970. *National Colours:* All white.
International matches 2017–18
Thailand (a) 2-1, UAE (h) 1-0*, Kenya (h) 2-1, Syria (h) 1-1, Bahrain (n) 1-1, Qatar (n) 2-1, Yemen (a) 3-0, UAE (a) 0-0 (2-4p), Saudi Arabia (h) 4-1, Qatar (h) 2-3, Syria (h) 1-1, Palestine (h) 0-0.
* *Match played in Jordan.*
League champions 2016–17: Al-Quwa Al-Jawaya. *Cup winners 2016–17:* Al-Zawra'a.

JAPAN

Japan Football Association, JFA House, Football Ave., Bunkyo-ku, Tokyo 113-8311.
Founded: 1921. *FIFA:* 1929, rejoined 1950; *AFC:* 1954. *National Colours:* Blue shirts, white shorts, blue socks.
International matches 2017–18
Australia (h) 2-0, Saudi Arabia (a) 0-1, New Zealand (h) 2-1, Haiti (h) 3-3, Brazil (n) 1-3, Belgium (a) 0-1, Korea DPR (h) 1-0, China PR (h) 2-1, Korea Republic (h) 1-4, Mali (n) 1-1, Ukraine (n) 1-2, Ghana (n) 0-2, Switzerland (a) 0-2, Paraguay (n) 4-2, Colombia (n) 2-1, Senegal (n) 2-2, Poland (n) 0-1, Belgium (n) 2-3.
League champions 2017: Kawasaki Frontale. *Cup winners 2017:* Cerezo Osaka.

JORDAN

Jordan Football Association, PO Box 962024, Al-Hussein Youth City, Amman 11196.
Founded: 1949. *FIFA:* 1956; *AFC:* 1970. *National Colours:* All white with red trim.
International matches 2017–18
Bahrain (a) 0-0, Afghanistan (h) 4-1, Oman (n) 1-1, Afghanistan (n) 3-3, Cambodia (a) 1-0, Libya (n) 1-1, Finland (n) 1-2, Denmark (n) 3-2, Kuwait (h) 1-0, Vietnam (h) 1-1, Cyprus (h) 3-0.
League champions 2017–18: Al-Wehdat. *Cup winners 2017–18:* Al-Jazeera.

KOREA DPR

DPR Korea Football Association, Kumsongdong, Kwangbok Street, Mangyongdae, PO Box 818, Pyongyang.
Founded: 1945. *FIFA:* 1958; *AFC:* 1974. *National Colours:* All red.
International matches 2017–18
Thailand (a) 0-3, Burkina Faso (n) 3-3 (3-4p), Lebanon (n) 2-2, Lebanon (a) 0-5, Malaysia (n) 4-1, Malaysia (n) 4-1, Japan (a) 0-1, Korea Republic (n) 0-1, China PR (n) 1-1, Hong Kong (h) 2-0.
League champions 2017–18: Inaugural competition still being played. *Cup winners:* No competition.

KOREA REPUBLIC

Korea Football Association, KFA House 21, Gyeonghuigung-gil 46, Jongno-Gu, Seoul 110-062.
Founded: 1933, 1948. *FIFA:* 1948; *AFC:* 1954. *National Colours:* Red shirts, blue shorts, red socks.

International matches 2017–18
Iran (h) 0-0, Uzbekistan (a) 0-0, Russia (a) 2-4, Morocco (n) 1-3, Colombia (h) 2-1, Serbia (h) 1-1, China PR (n) 2-2, Korea DPR (n) 1-0, Japan (a) 4-1, Moldova (n) 1-0, Jamaica (n) 2-2, Latvia (n) 1-0, Northern Ireland (a) 1-2, Poland (a) 2-3, Honduras (h) 2-0, Bosnia-Herzegovina (h) 1-3, Bolivia (n) 0-0, Senegal (n) 0-2, Sweden (n) 0-1, Mexico (n) 1-2, Germany (n) 2-0.
League champions 2017: Jeonbuk Hyundai Motors. *Cup winners 2017:* Ulsan Hyundai.

KUWAIT

Kuwait Football Association, Block 5, Street 101, Building 141A, Jabriya, PO Box Hawalli 4020, Kuwait 32071.
Founded: 1952. *FIFA:* 1964; *AFC:* 1964. *National Colours:* All blue with white trim.
International matches 2017–18
Bahrain (a) 0-0, Saudi Arabia (h) 1-2, Oman (h) 0-1, UAE (h) 0-0, Jordan (a) 0-1, Cameroon (h) 1-3, Palestine (h) 2-0, Egypt (a) 1-1.
League champions 2017–18: Al-Kuwait. *Cup winners 2017–18:* Al-Kuwait.

KYRGYZSTAN

Football Federation of Kyrgyz Republic, Mederova Street 1 'B', PO Box 1484, Bishkek 720082.
Founded: 1992. *FIFA:* 1994; *AFC:* 1994. *National Colours:* Red shirts, red shorts, red socks with yellow tops.
International matches 2017–18
Uzbekistan (a) 0-5, Myanmar (a) 2-2, Macao (a) 4-3, Mongolia (n) 3-0, Brunei (n) 0-4, Myanmar (h) 5-1, India (h) 2-1, Azerbaijan (a) 0-3.
League champions 2017: Alay Osh. *Cup winners 2017:* Alay Osh.

LAOS

Lao Football Federation, FIFA Training Centre, Ban Houayhong, Chanthabuly, PO Box 1800, Vientiane 856-21.
Founded: 1951. *FIFA:* 1952; *AFC:* 1968. *National Colours:* All red with white trim.
International matches 2017–18
Macao (a) 1-3, Hong Kong (a) 0-4, Philippines (n) 1-3, Timor-Leste (n) 2-1, Chinese Taipei (a) 0-2, Cambodia (h) 0-1, Bangladesh (h) 2-2.
League champions 2017: Lao Toyota. *Cup winners:* No competition.

LEBANON

Association Libanaise de Football, Verdun Street, Bristol Radwan Centre, PO Box 4732, Beirut.
Founded: 1933. *FIFA:* 1936; *AFC:* 1964. *National Colours:* All red.
International matches 2017–18
Korea DPR (a) 2-2, Korea DPR (h) 5-0, Singapore (a) 1-0, Hong Kong (a) 1-0, Malaysia (h) 2-1.
League champions 2017–18: Al-Ahed. *Cup winners 2017–18:* Al-Ahed.

MACAO

Associacao de Futebol de Macao, Avenida Wai Leong, Taipa University of Science and Technology, Football Field Block 1, Taipa.
Founded: 1939. *FIFA:* 1978; *AFC:* 1978. *National Colours:* White shirts, black shorts, green socks.
International matches 2017–18
Hong Kong (a) 0-4, India (h) 0-2, Laos (h) 3-1, India (a) 1-4, Kyrgyzstan (h) 3-4, Mauritius (h) 0-1, Myanmar (a) 0-1.
League champions 2018: Benfica de Macao. *Cup winners 2017:* Benfica de Macao.

MALAYSIA

Football Association of Malaysia, 3rd Floor, Wisma FAM, Jalan SS5A/9, Kelana Jaya, Petaling Jaya 47301, Selangor Darul Ehsan.
Founded: 1933. *FIFA:* 1954; *AFC:* 1954. *National Colours:* Yellow and black shirts, black shorts, black socks.
International matches 2017–18
Syria (h) 1-2, Myanmar (a) 0-1, Hong Kong (h) 1-1, Hong Kong (a) 0-2, Korea DPR (n) 1-4, Korea DPR (h) 1-4, Mongolia (h) 2-2, Lebanon (a) 1-2, Bhutan (h) 7-0, Fiji (h) 1-0.
League champions 2017: Johor Darul Ta'zim. *Cup winners 2018:* Pahang.

MALDIVES

Football Association of Maldives, FAM House, Ujaalahingun, Male 20388.
Founded: 1982. *FIFA:* 1986; *AFC:* 1984. *National Colours:* Red and white shirts, white shorts, red socks.

International matches 2017–18
Oman (a) 0-5, Oman (h) 1-3, Palestine (a) 1-8, Singapore (a) 2-3, Bhutan (h) 7-0.
League champions 2017: New Radiant. *Cup winners:* No competition.

MONGOLIA

Mongolian Football Federation, PO Box 259, 15th Khoroo, Khan-Uul, Ulaanbaatar 210646.
Founded: 1959. *FIFA:* 1998; *AFC:* 1998. *National Colours:* Red shirts, blue shorts, red socks.
International matches 2017–18
Chinese Taipei (a) 2-4, Kyrgyzstan (n) 0-3, Malaysia (a) 2-2, Mauritius (h) 0-2.
League champions 2017: Erchim. *Cup winners 2017:* Ulaanbaatar City.

MYANMAR

Myanmar Football Federation, National Football Training Centre, Waizayanta Road, Thuwunna, Thingankyun Township, Yangon 11070.
Founded: 1947. *FIFA:* 1948; *AFC:* 1954. *National Colours:* All red.
International matches 2017–18
Malaysia (h) 1-0, Thailand (h) 1-3, Kyrgyzstan (h) 2-2, Cambodia (a) 2-1, India (a) 2-2, Kyrgyzstan (a) 1-5, Macao (h) 1-0, China PR (a) 0-1.
League champions 2017: Shan United. *Cup winners 2017:* Shan United.

NEPAL

All Nepal Football Association, ANFA House, Satdobato, Lalitpur-17, PO Box 12582, Kathmandu.
Founded: 1951. *FIFA:* 1972; *AFC:* 1954. *National Colours:* All red with white trim.
International matches 2017–18
Tajikistan (h) 1-2, Tajikistan (a) 0-3, Philippines (h) 0-0, Yemen (a) 1-2*.
* *Match played in Qatar.*
League champions: Competition to resume in 2018–19. *Cup winners 2017:* Manang Marshyangdi Club; *2018:* Nepal Police Club.

OMAN

Oman Football Association, Seeb Sports Stadium, PO Box 3462, 112 Ruwi, Muscat.
Founded: 1978. *FIFA:* 1980; *AFC:* 1980. *National Colours:* All red.
International matches 2017–18
Afghanistan (h) 2-0, Maldives (h) 5-0, Jordan (n) 1-1, Maldives (a) 3-1, Bhutan (a) 4-2, UAE (n) 0-1, Kuwait (a) 1-0, Saudi Arabia (n) 2-0, Bahrain (n) 1-0, UAE (n) 0-0 (5-4p), Palestine (h) 1-0.
League champions 2017–18: Al-Suwaiq. *Cup winners 2017–18:* Al-Nasr.

PAKISTAN

Pakistan Football Federation, PFF Football House, Ferozepur Road, Lahore 54600, Punjab.
Founded: 1947. *FIFA:* 1948; *AFC:* 1954. *National Colours:* All green and white.
International matches 2017–18
None played.
League champions: No competition since 2014–15. *Cup winners 2018:* WAPDA.

PALESTINE

Palestinian Football Association, Nr. Faisal Al-Husseini Stadium, PO Box 4373, Jerusalem-al-Ram.
Founded: 1928. *FIFA:* 1998; *AFC:* 1998. *National Colours:* All red with white trim.
International matches 2017–18
Bhutan (a) 2-0, Bhutan (h) 10-0, Maldives (h) 8-1, Bahrain (a) 0-0, Oman (a) 0-1, Iraq (a) 0-0, Kuwait (a) 0-2.
League champions 2017–18: Hilal Al-Quds. *Cup winners 2017–18:* Hilal Al-Quds.

PHILIPPINES

Philippine Football Federation, 27 Danny Floro–corner Capt. Henry Javier Streets, Oranbo, Pasig City 1600.
Founded: 1907. *FIFA:* 1930; *AFC:* 1954. *National Colours:* All blue with white trim.
International matches 2017–18
Yemen (h) 2-2, Yemen (n) 1-1, Nepal (a) 0-0, Laos (n) 3-1, Chinese Taipei (a) 0-3, Timor-Leste (n) 0-1, Fiji (h) 3-2, Tajikistan (h) 2-1.
League champions 2017: Ceres Negros. *Cup winners:* New competition beginning in 2018.

QATAR

Qatar Football Association, 28th Floor, Al Bidda Tower, Corniche Street, West Bay, PO Box 5333, Doha.
Founded: 1960. *FIFA:* 1972; *AFC:* 1974. *National Colours:* All burgundy.
International matches 2017–18
Andorra (n) 1-0, Turkmenistan (h) 2-1, Syria (a) 1-3*, China PR (h) 1-2, Singapore (h) 3-1, Curacao (h) 1-2, Czech Republic (h) 0-1, Iceland (h) 1-1, Liechtenstein (h) 1-2, Yemen (n) 4-0, Iraq (n) 1-2, Bahrain (n) 1-1, Iraq (a) 3-2, Syria (n) 2-2.
* *Match played in Malaysia.*
League champions 2017–18: Al-Duhail (formerly Lekhwiya). *Cup winners 2018:* Al-Duhail.

SAUDI ARABIA

Saudi Arabian Football Federation, Al Mather Quarter, Prince Faisal Bin Fahad Street, PO Box 5844, Riyadh 11432.
Founded: 1956. *FIFA:* 1956; *AFC:* 1972. *National Colours:* White shirts with green trim, white shorts, white socks.
International matches 2017–18
UAE (a) 1-2, Japan (h) 1-0, Latvia (n) 2-0, Portugal (a) 0-3, Bulgaria (n) 0-1, Kuwait (a) 2-1, UAE (n) 0-0, Oman (n) 0-2, Moldova (h) 3-0, Iraq (a) 1-4, Ukraine (n) 1-1, Belgium (a) 0-4, Algeria (n) 2-0, Greece (n) 2-0, Italy (n) 1-2, Germany (a) 1-2, Russia (a) 0-5, Uruguay (n) 0-1, Egypt (n) 2-1.
League champions 2017–18: Al-Hilal. *Cup winners 2018:* Al-Ittihad.

SINGAPORE

Football Association of Singapore, Jalan Besar Stadium, 100 Tyrwhitt Road, Singapore 207542.
Founded: 1892. *FIFA:* 1956; *AFC:* 1954. *National Colours:* All red.
International matches 2017–18
Hong Kong (h) 1-1, Turkmenistan (h) 1-1, Qatar (a) 1-3, Turkmenistan (a) 1-2, Lebanon (h) 0-1, Bahrain (h) 0-3, Maldives (h) 3-2, Chinese Taipei (a) 0-1.
League champions 2017: Albirex Niigata Singapore. *Cup winners 2017:* Home United.

SRI LANKA

Football Federation of Sri Lanka, 100/9 Independence Avenue, Colombo 07.
Founded: 1939. *FIFA:* 1952; *AFC:* 1954. *National Colours:* All red with white trim.
International matches 2017–18
None played.
League champions 2017–18: Colombo. *Cup winners 2016–17:* Army.

SYRIA

Syrian Arab Federation for Football, Al Faihaa Sports Complex, PO Box 421, Damascus.
Founded: 1936. *FIFA:* 1937; *AFC:* 1970. *National Colours:* All red.
International matches 2017–18
Malaysia (a) 2-1, Qatar (h) 3-1*, Iran (a) 2-2, Australia (h) 1-1*, Australia (a) 1-2, Iraq (a) 1-1, Qatar (n) 2-2, Iraq (a) 1-1.
* *Match played in Malaysia.*
League champions 2016–17: Al-Jaish. *2017–18:* Al-Jaish. *Cup winners 2017:* Al-Wahda.

TAJIKISTAN

Tajikistan Football Federation, 14/3 Ayni Street, Dushanbe 734 025.
Founded: 1936. *FIFA:* 1994; *AFC:* 1994. *National Colours:* Red, white and green shirts, white and red shorts, red and green socks.
International matches 2017–18
Nepal (a) 2-1, Nepal (h) 3-0, Yemen (h) 0-0, Philippines (a) 1-2.
League champions 2017: Istiklol. *Cup winners 2017:* Khujand.

THAILAND

Football Association of Thailand, National Stadium, Gate 3, Rama 1 Road, Patumwan, Bangkok 10330.
Founded: 1916. *FIFA:* 1925; *AFC:* 1954. *National Colours:* All red.
International matches 2017–18
Korea DPR (h) 3-0, Belarus (h) 0-0 (5-4p), Iraq (h) 1-2, Australia (a) 1-2, Myanmar (a) 3-1, Kenya (h) 1-0, Gabon (a) 0-0 (4-2p), Slovakia (h) 2-3, China PR (h) 0-2.
League champions 2017: Buriram United. *Cup winners 2017:* Chiangrai United.

TIMOR-LESTE

Federacao Futebol de Timor-Leste, Campo Democracia, Avenida Bairo Formosa, Dili.
Founded: 2002. *FIFA:* 2005; *AFC:* 2005. *National Colours:* Red shirts with black trim, red shorts, red socks.
International matches 2017–18
Laos (n) 1-2, Chinese Taipei (a) 1-3, Philippines (n) 1-0.
League champions 2017: Karketu Dili. *Cup winners 2017:* Atletico Ultramar.

TURKMENISTAN

Football Federation of Turkmenistan, Stadium Kopetdag, 245 A. Niyazov Street, Ashgabat 744 001.
Founded: 1992. *FIFA:* 1994; AFC: 1994. *National Colours:* All white.
International matches 2017–18
Qatar (a) 1-2, Singapore (a) 1-1, Singapore (h) 2-1, Chinese Taipei (h) 2-1, Bahrain (a) 0-4.
League champions 2017: Altyn Asyr. *Cup winners 2017:* Ahal.

UNITED ARAB EMIRATES (UAE)

United Arab Emirates Football Association, Zayed Sports City, PO Box 916, Abu Dhabi.
Founded: 1971. *FIFA:* 1974; *AFC:* 1974. *National Colours:* All white with red trim.
International matches
Saudi Arabia (h) 2-1, Iraq (a) 0-1*, Haiti (h) 0-1, Uzbekistan (h) 1-0, Oman (n) 1-0, Saudi Arabia (n) 0-0, Kuwait (a) 0-0, Iraq (n) 0-0 (4-2p), Oman (n) 0-0 (4-5p), Slovakia (n) 1-2, Gabon (n) 0-1.
* *Match played in Jordan.*
League champions 2017–18: Al-Ain. *Cup winners 2017–18:* Al-Ain.

UZBEKISTAN

Uzbekistan Football Federation, Massiv Almazar Furkat Street 15/1, Tashkent 700 003.
Founded: 1946. *FIFA:* 1994; *AFC:* 1994. *National Colours:* All white with blue trim.
International matches 2017–18
Kyrgyzstan (h) 5-0, China PR (a) 0-1, Korea Republic (h) 0-0, UAE (a) 0-1, Senegal (n) 1-1, Morocco (a) 0-2, Iran (a) 0-1, Uruguay (a) 0-3.
League champions 2017: Lokomotiv Tashkent. *Cup winners 2017:* Lokomotiv Tashkent.

VIETNAM

Vietnam Football Federation, Le Quang Dao Street, Phu Do Ward, Nam Tu Liem District, Hanoi 844.
Founded: 1960 (NV). *FIFA:* 1952 (SV), 1964 (NV); *AFC:* 1954 (SV), 1978 (SRV). *National Colours:* All red.
International matches 2017–18
Cambodia (a) 2-1, Cambodia (h) 5-0, Afghanistan (h) 0-0, Jordan (a) 1-1.
League champions 2017: Quang Nam. *Cup winners 2017:* Song Lam Nghe An.

YEMEN

Yemen Football Association, Quarter of Sport Al Jeraf (Ali Mohsen Al-Muraisi Stadium), PO Box 908, Al-Thawra City, Sana'a.
Founded: 1940 (SY), 1962 (NY). *FIFA:* 1967 (SY), 1980 (NY); *AFC:* 1972 (SY), 1980 (NY). *National Colours:* Red shirts, white shorts, black socks.
International matches 2017–18
Philippines (a) 2-2, Philippines (h) 1-1*, Tajikistan (a) 0-0, Qatar (n) 0-4, Bahrain (n) 0-1, Iraq (n) 0-3, Nepal (h) 2-1*.
* *Match played in Qatar.*
No club competitions since January 2015 due to civil war.

NORTH AND CENTRAL AMERICA AND CARIBBEAN (CONCACAF)

ANGUILLA

Anguilla Football Association, 2 Queen Elizabeth Avenue, PO Box 1318, The Valley, AI-2640.
Founded: 1990. *FIFA:* 1996; *CONCACAF:* 1996. *National Colours:* Turquoise and white shirts, orange and blue and shorts, turquoise and orange socks.
International matches 2017–18
None played.
League champions 2016–17: Roaring Lions; *2017–18:* Kicks United. *Cup winners:* No competition.

ANTIGUA & BARBUDA

Antigua & Barbuda Football Association, Ground Floor, Sydney Walling Stand, Antigua Recreation Ground, PO Box 773, St John's.
Founded: 1928. *FIFA:* 1970; *CONCACAF:* 1972. *National Colours:* Yellow shirts with black, red and blue stripe, yellow shorts, yellow socks.
International matches 2017–18
Bermuda (h) 3-2, Jamaica (a) 1-1, Dominica (h) 0-0, Jamaica (h) 0-2.
League champions 2017–18: Hoppers. *Cup winners:* No competition.

ARUBA

Arubaanse Voetbal Bond, Technical Centre Angel Botta, Shaba 24, PO Box 376, Noord.
Founded: 1932. *FIFA:* 1988; *CONCACAF:* 1986. *National Colours:* Yellow shirts with sky blue sleeves, yellow shorts, yellow socks.
International matches 2017–18
None played.
League champions 2017–18: Dakota. *Cup winners 2018:* Estrella.

BAHAMAS

Bahamas Football Association, Rosetta Street, PO Box N-8434, Nassau, NP.
Founded: 1967. *FIFA:* 1968; *CONCACAF:* 1981. *National Colours:* Yellow shirts, black shorts, yellow socks.
International matches 2017–18
None played.
League champions 2017–18: UB Mingoes. *Cup winners:* No competition since 2016.

BARBADOS

Barbados Football Association, Bottom Floor, ABC Marble Complex, PO Box 1362, Fontabelle, St Michael.
Founded: 1910. *FIFA:* 1968; *CONCACAF:* 1967. *National Colours:* Gold shirts with royal blue sleeves, gold shorts, white socks with gold tops.
International matches 2017–18
Bermuda (a) 3-2, Bermuda (h) 0-0, Belize (h) 0-0.
League champions 2018: Weymouth Wales. *Cup winners 2017:* Weymouth Wales.

BELIZE

Football Federation of Belize, 26 Hummingbird Highway, Belmopan, PO Box 1742, Belize City.
Founded: 1980. *FIFA:* 1986; *CONCACAF:* 1986. *National Colours:* Blue shirts with white trim, red shorts, blue socks with white tops.
International matches 2017–18
Barbados (a) 0-0.
League champions 2017–18: Verdes (Opening); Belmopan Bandits (Closing). *Cup winners:* No competition.

BERMUDA

Bermuda Football Association, 48 Cedar Avenue, PO Box HM 745, Hamilton HM11.
Founded: 1928. *FIFA:* 1962; *CONCACAF:* 1967. *National Colours:* All red.
International matches 2017–18
Barbados (h) 2-3, Antigua & Barbuda (a) 2-3, Barbados (a) 0-0.
League champions 2017–18: PHC Zebras. *Cup winners 2017–18:* Robin Hood.

BRITISH VIRGIN ISLANDS

British Virgin Islands Football Association, Botanic Station, PO Box 4269, Road Town, Tortola VG 1110.
Founded: 1974. *FIFA:* 1996; *CONCACAF:* 1996. *National Colours:* Green shirts with gold trim, gold shorts, green socks.
International matches 2017–18
None played.
League champions 2018: Islanders. *Cup winners:* No competition.

CANADA

Canadian Soccer Association, Place Soccer Canada, 237 Metcalfe Street, Ottawa, Ontario K2P 1R2.
Founded: 1912. *FIFA:* 1912; *CONCACAF:* 1961. *National Colours:* All red.
International matches 2017–18
French Guiana† (n) 4-2, Costa Rica (n) 1-1, Honduras (n) 0-0, Jamaica (n) 1-2, Jamaica (h) 2-0, El Salvador (n) 0-1, New Zealand (n) 1-0*.
* *Behind closed doors.*
Canadian teams compete in MLS and NASL. Canadian Premier League commences in April 2019. Cup winners 2017: Toronto FC.

CAYMAN ISLANDS

Cayman Islands Football Association, PO Box 178, Poindexter Road, Prospect, George Town, Grand Cayman KY1-1104.
Founded: 1966. *FIFA:* 1992; *CONCACAF:* 1990. *National Colours:* Red and white shirts, red shorts, red socks with white tops.
International matches 2017–18
None played.
League champions 2017–18: Scholars International. *Cup winners 2017–18:* Academy.

COSTA RICA

Federacion Costarricense de Futbol, 600 mts sur del Cruce de la Panasonic, San Rafael de Alajuela, Radial a Santa Ana, San Jose 670-1000.
Founded: 1921. *FIFA:* 1927; *CONCACAF:* 1961. *National Colours:* Red shirts, blue shorts, white socks.
International matches 2017–18
Honduras (n) 1-0, Canada (a) 1-1, French Guiana† (n) 3-0, Panama (n) 1-0, USA (a) 0-2, USA (a) 2-0, Mexico (h) 1-1, Honduras (a) 1-1, Panama (a) 1-2, Spain (a) 0-5, Hungary (a) 0-1, Scotland (h) 1-0, Tunisia (n) 0-1, Northern Ireland (h) 3-0, England (a) 0-2, Belgium (a) 1-4, Serbia (n) 0-1, Brazil (n) 0-2, Switzerland (n) 2-2.
League champions 2017–18: Perez Zeledion (Apertura); Deportivo Saprissa (Clausura). *Cup winners:* No competition.

CUBA

Asociacion de Futbol de Cuba, Estadio Pedro Marrero Escuela Nacional de
Futbol – Mario Lopez, Avenida 41 no. 44 y 46, La Habana.
Founded: 1924. *FIFA:* 1932; CONCACAF: 1961. *National Colours:* All red.
International matches 2017–18
Nicaragua (a) 1-3, Nicaragua (a) 3-3.
League champions 2017: Santiago de Cuba. *2018:* Santiago de Cuba. *Cup winners:* No competition.

CURACAO

Curacao Football Federation, Bonamweg 49, PO Box 341, Willemstad.
Founded: 1921 (Netherlands Antilles), 2010. *FIFA:* 1932, 2010; *CONCACAF:* 1961, 2010. *National Colours:* All blue.
International matches 2017–18
Jamaica (n) 0-2, El Salvador (n) 0-2, Mexico (n) 0-2, Qatar (a) 2-1, Bolivia (h) 1-1, Bolivia (h) 1-0.
League champions 2017: Centro Dominguito. *Cup winners:* No competition.

DOMINICA

Dominica Football Association, Patrick John Football House, Bath Estate, PO Box 1080, Roseau.
Founded: 1970. *FIFA:* 1994; *CONCACAF:* 1994. *National Colours:* Emerald green shirts with black sleeves, black shorts, emerald green socks.
International matches 2017–18
Antigua & Barbuda (a) 0-0.
League champions 2017–18: Promex Harlem United. *Cup winners:* No competition.

DOMINICAN REPUBLIC

Federacion Dominicana de Futbol, Centro Olimpico Juan Pablo Duarte, Apartado Postal 1953, Santo Domingo.
Founded: 1953. *FIFA:* 1958; *CONCACAF:* 1964. *National Colours:* All navy blue.
International matches 2017–18
Nicaragua (a) 3-0, Nicaragua (h) 1-0, Turks & Caicos Islands (h) 4-0, St Kitts & Nevis (h) 2-1.
League champions 2017: Atlantico. *Cup winners:* No competition.

EL SALVADOR

Federacion Salvadorena de Futbol, Avenida Jose Matias Delgado, Frente al Centro Espanol Colonia Escalon, Zona 10, San Salvador 1029.
Founded: 1935. *FIFA:* 1938; *CONCACAF:* 1961. *National Colours:* All blue.
International matches 2017–18
Mexico (n) 1-3, Curacao (n) 2-0, Jamaica (n) 1-1, USA (a) 0-2, Canada (n) 1-0, Honduras (n) 1-0.
League champions 2017–18: Alianza (Apertura); Alianza (Clausura). *Cup winner:* No competition.

GRENADA

Grenada Football Association, National Stadium, PO Box 326, St George's.

Founded: 1924. *FIFA:* 1978; *CONCACAF:* 1969. *National Colours:* Yellow shirts, yellow shorts, green socks. *International matches 2017–18* Guyana (h) 1-0, Panama (h) 0-5, Trinidad & Tobago (a) 2-2, St Kitts & Nevis (a) 0-1. *League champions 2017:* Hurricanes. *Cup winners:* No competition.

GUATEMALA

Federacion Nacional de Futbol de Guatemala, 2a Calle 15-57, Zona 15, Boulevard Vista Hermosa, Guatemala City 01015. *Founded:* 1919. *FIFA:* 1946; *CONCACAF:* 1961. *National Colours:* Blue shirts with white sash, blue shorts, blue socks. *International matches 2017–18* None played. *League champions 2017–18:* Antigua GFC (Apertura); Guastatoya (Clausura). *Cup winners:* No competition.

GUYANA

Guyana Football Federation, Lot 17, Dadanawa Street Section 'K', Campbellville, PO Box 10727, Georgetown. *Founded:* 1902. *FIFA:* 1970; *CONCACAF:* 1961. *National Colours:* Green shirts with white trim, green shorts, green socks. *International matches 2017–18* Grenada (a) 0-1, Trinidad & Tobago (a) 1-1, Indonesia (a) 1-2. *League champions 2017–18:* Western Tigers. *Cup winners:* No competition since 2015.

HAITI

Federation Haitienne de Football, Stade Sylvio Cator, Rue Oswald Durand, Port-au-Prince. *Founded:* 1904. *FIFA:* 1933; *CONCACAF:* 1961. *National Colours:* Blue shirts, red shorts, blue socks. *International matches 2017–18* Japan (a) 3-3, UAE (a) 1-0, Argentina (a) 0-4. *League champions 2017:* Real Hope FA (Ouverture); AS Capoise (Cloture). *Cup winners:* No competition.

HONDURAS

Federacion Nacional Autonoma de Futbol de Honduras, Colonia Florencia Norte, Edificio Plaza America Ave. Roble, 1 y 2 Nivle, PO Box 827, Tegucigalpa 504. *Founded:* 1935. *FIFA:* 1946; CONCACAF: 1961. *National Colours:* All white. *International matches 2017–18* Costa Rica (n) 0-1, French Guiana† (n) 3-0*, Canada (n) 0-0, Mexico (n) 0-1, Trinidad & Tobago (a) 2-1, USA (h) 1-1, Costa Rica (a) 1-1, Mexico (h) 3-2, Australia (h) 0-0, Australia (a) 1-3, Korea Republic (a) 0-2, El Salvador (n) 0-1. * *Match awarded 3-0 due to breach of FIFA rule.* *League champions 2017–18:* Real Espana (Apertura); Marathon (Clausura). *Cup winners 2017:* Marathon.

JAMAICA

Jamaica Football Federation Ltd, 20 St Lucia Crescent, Kingston 5. *Founded:* 1910. *FIFA:* 1962; *CONCACAF:* 1963. *National Colours:* Gold shirts, black shorts, gold socks with green tops. *International matches 2017–18* Curacao (n) 2-0, Mexico (n) 0-0, El Salvador (n) 1-1, Canada (n) 2-1, Mexico (n) 1-0, USA (a) 1-2, Trinidad & Tobago (a) 2-1, Canada (a) 0-2, Korea Republic (n) 2-2, Antigua & Barbuda (n) 1-1, St Kitts & Nevis (a) 3-1, Antigua & Barbuda (a) 2-0. *League champions 2017–18:* Portmore United. *Cup winners:* No competition.

MEXICO

Federacion Mexicana de Futbol Asociacion, A.C., Colima No. 373, Colonia Roma, Delegacion Cuauhtemoc, Mexico DF 06700. *Founded:* 1927. *FIFA:* 1929; *CONCACAF:* 1961. *National Colours:* All black with green trim. *International matches 2017–18* El Salvador (n) 3-1, Jamaica (n) 0-0, Curacao (n) 2-0, Honduras (n) 1-0, Jamaica (n) 0-1, Panama (h) 1-0, Costa Rica (a) 1-1, Trinidad & Tobago (h) 3-1, Honduras (a) 2-3, Belgium (a) 3-3, Poland (a) 1-0, Bosnia-Herzegovina (n) 1-0, Iceland (n) 3-0, Croatia (n) 0-1, Wales (n) 0-0, Scotland (h) 1-0, Denmark (a) 0-2, Germany (n) 1-0, Korea Republic (n) 2-1, Sweden (n) 0-3, Brazil (n) 0-2. *League champions 2017–18:* Tigres UANL (Apertura); Santos Laguna (Clausura). *Cup winners 2017–18:* Monterrey (Apertura); Necaxa (Clausura).

MONTSERRAT

Montserrat Football Association Inc., PO Box 505, Blakes, Montserrat. *Founded:* 1994. *FIFA:* 1996; *CONCACAF:* 1996. *National Colours:* Black shirts with red stripes, black shorts, black socks. *International matches 2017–18* None played. *No senior club competitions since 2004.*

NICARAGUA

Federacion Nicaraguense de Futbol, Porton Principal del Hospital Bautista 1 Cuadra Abajo, 1 Cuadra al Sur y 1/2 Cuadra Abajo, Apartado Postal 976, Managua. *Founded:* 1931. *FIFA:* 1950; CONCACAF: 1961. *National Colours:* All blue. *International matches 2017–18* Curacao (a) 0-0*, Martinique† (n) 0-2, Panama (n) 1-2, USA (a) 0-3, Dominican Republic (h) 0-3, Dominican Republic (a) 0-1, Cuba (h) 3-1, Cuba (h) 3-3. * *Played 18.06.2017; result incorrect in last edition.* *League champions 2017–18:* Walter Ferretti (Apertura); Diriangen (Clausura). *Cup winners:* No competition.

PANAMA

Federacion Panamena de Futbol, Ciudad Deportiva Irving Saladino, Corregimiento de Juan Diaz, Apartado Postal 0827-00391, Zona 8, Panama City. *Founded:* 1937. *FIFA:* 1938; CONCACAF: 1961. *National Colours:* All red. *International matches 2017–18* USA (a) 1-1, Nicaragua (n) 2-1, Martinique† (n) 3-0, Costa Rica (n) 0-1, Mexico (a) 0-1, Trinidad & Tobago (h) 3-0, USA (a) 0-4, Costa Rica (h) 2-1, Grenada (a) 5-0, Iran (n) 1-2, Wales (a) 1-1, Denmark (a) 0-1, Switzerland (a) 0-6, Trinidad & Tobago (a) 1-0, Northern Ireland (h) 0-0, Norway (a) 0-1, Belgium (n) 0-3, England (n) 1-6, Tunisia (n) 1-2. *League champions 2017–18:* Chorrillo (Apertura); Independiente (Clausura). *Cup winners:* No competition.

PUERTO RICO

Federacion Puertorriquena de Futbol, PO Box 367567, San Juan 00936. *Founded:* 1940. *FIFA:* 1960; *CONCACAF:* 1961. *National Colours:* Red and white striped shirts, blue shorts, blue socks. *International matches 2017–18* None played. *League champions 2016:* Metropolitan FA; *2017:* GPS Puerto Rico. *Cup winners:* No competition.

ST KITTS & NEVIS

St Kitts & Nevis Football Association, PO Box 465, Lozack Road, Basseterre. *Founded:* 1932. *FIFA:* 1992; *CONCACAF:* 1992. *National Colours:* Green and red shirts, red shorts, green socks. *International matches 2017–18* Mauritius (n) 1-1, India (a) 1-1, Grenada (h) 1-0, Dominican Republic (h) 1-2, Jamaica (h) 1-3. *League champions 2017–18:* Village Superstars. *Cup winners 2016–17:* Garden Hotspurs; *2017–18:* Cayon Rockets.

ST LUCIA

St Lucia National Football Association, Barnard Hill, PO Box 255, Castries. *Founded:* 1979. *FIFA:* 1988; *CONCACAF:* 1986. *National Colours:* Sky blue shirts with yellow sleeves, sky blue shorts, white socks. *International matches 2017–18* None played. *League champions 2017:* Northern United; *2018:* Platinum. *Cup winners:* No competition since 2013.

ST VINCENT & THE GRENADINES

St Vincent & the Grenadines Football Federation, PO Box 1278, Nichols Building (2nd Floor), Bentinck Square, Victoria Park, Kingstown. *Founded:* 1979. *FIFA:* 1988; *CONCACAF:* 1986. *National Colours:* Yellow shirts, blue shorts, blue socks. *International matches 2017–18* None played. *League champions 2016:* Hope International; *2017:* Avenues United. *Cup winners:* No competition.

SURINAME

Surinaamse Voetbal Bond, Letitia Vriesdelaan 7, PO Box 1223, Paramaribo.
Founded: 1920. *FIFA:* 1929; *CONCACAF:* 1961. *National Colours:* White shirts with green cuffs, white shorts, white socks.
International matches 2017–18
None played.
League champions 2017–18: Robinhood. *Cup winners 2017:* Inter Moengotapoe; *2018:* Robinhood.

TRINIDAD & TOBAGO

Trinidad & Tobago Football Association, 24–26 Dundonald Street, PO Box 400, Port of Spain.
Founded: 1908. *FIFA:* 1964; *CONCACAF:* 1962. *National Colours:* Red shirts with black trim, black shorts with red trim, red socks.
International matches 2017–18
Ecuador (a) 1-3, Jamaica (h) 1-2, Honduras (h) 1-2, Panama (a) 0-3, Mexico (a) 1-3, USA (h) 2-1, Grenada (h) 2-2, Guyana (h) 1-1, Guadeloupe† (a) 1-1, Martinique† (a) 0-0, Panama (h) 0-1.
League champions 2017–18: North East Stars. *Cup winners 2017:* W Connection.

TURKS & CAICOS ISLANDS

Turks & Caicos Islands Football Association, TCIFA National Academy, Venetian Road, PO Box 626, Providenciales.
Founded: 1996. *FIFA:* 1998; CONCACAF: 1996. *National Colours:* All white.
International matches 2017–18
Dominican Republic (a) 0-4.
League champions 2017: Beaches. *Cup winners:* No competition.

UNITED STATES OF AMERICA (USA)

US Soccer Federation, US Soccer House, 1801 S. Prairie Avenue, Chicago, IL 60616.
Founded: 1913. *FIFA:* 1914; CONCACAF: 1961. *National Colours:* All white.
International matches 2017–18
Panama (h) 1-1, Martinique† (h) 3-2, Nicaragua (h) 3-0, El Salvador (h) 2-0, Costa Rica (h) 2-0, Jamaica (h) 2-1, Costa Rica (h) 0-2, Honduras (a) 1-1, Panama (h) 4-0, Trinidad & Tobago (a) 1-2, Portugal (h) 1-1, Bosnia-Herzegovina (h) 0-0, Paraguay (h) 1-0, Bolivia (h) 3-0, Republic of Ireland (a) 1-2, France (a) 1-1.
League champions 2017: Toronto FC. (N.B. Teams from USA and Canada compete in MLS.) *Cup winners 2017:* Sporting Kansas City.

US VIRGIN ISLANDS

USVI Soccer Federation Inc., 498D Strawberry, PO Box 2346, Christiansted, St Croix 00851.
Founded: 1987. *FIFA:* 1998; *CONCACAF:* 1987. *National Colours:* Gold shirts with royal blue trim, gold shorts, gold socks.
International matches 2017–18
None played.
League champions 2016–17: Raymix. *Cup winners:* No competition.

OCEANIA (OFC)

AMERICAN SAMOA

Football Federation American Samoa, PO Box 982 413, Pago Pago AS 96799.
Founded: 1984. *FIFA:* 1998; *OFC:* 1998. *National Colours:* Navy blue shirts, red shorts, white socks.
International matches 2017–18
None played.
League champions 2017: Pago Youth. *Cup winners:* No competition since 2014.

COOK ISLANDS

Cook Islands Football Association, Matavera Main Road, PO Box 29, Avarua, Rarotonga.
Founded: 1971. *FIFA:* 1994; *OFC:* 1994. *National Colours:* Green shirts with white trim, green shorts, white socks.
International matches 2017–18
None played.
League champions 2017: Tupapa Maraerenga. *Cup winners 2017:* Puaikura.

FIJI

Fiji Football Association, PO Box 2514, Government Buildings, Suva.
Founded: 1938. *FIFA:* 1964; *OFC:* 1966. *National Colours:* White shirts, black shorts, white socks.

International matches 2017–18
Indonesia (a) 0-0, Estonia (h) 0-2, Solomon Islands (n) 0-0, Vanuatu (a) 1-1, Tonga (n) 4-0, New Caledonia (n) 4-1, Philippines (a) 2-3, Malaysia (a) 0-1.
League champions 2017: Lautoka. *Cup winners 2018:* Rewa.

NEW CALEDONIA

Federation Caledonienne de Football, 7 bis, Rue Suffren Quartien latin, BP 560, Noumea 99845.
Founded: 1928. *FIFA:* 2004; *OFC:* 2004. *National Colours:* Grey shirts, red shorts, grey socks.
International matches 2017–18
Estonia (h) 1-1, Vanuatu (a) 1-2, Tonga (n) 4-2, Solomon Islands (n) 0-1, Fiji (n) 1-4, Tahiti (a) 3-4.
League champions 2017: Hienghene Sport. *Cup winners 2017:* AS Lossi.

NEW ZEALAND

New Zealand Football, PO Box 301-043, Albany, Auckland.
Founded: 1891. *FIFA:* 1948; *OFC:* 1966. *National Colours:* All white.
International matches 2017–18
Solomon Islands (h) 6-1, Solomon Islands (a) 2-2, Japan (a) 1-2, Peru (h) 0-0, Peru (a) 0-2, Canada (n) 0-1*, Kenya (n) 1-2, Chinese Taipei (n) 1-0, India (a) 2-1.
* *Behind closed doors.*
League champions 2016–17: Team Wellington; *2017–18:* Auckland City. *Cup winners 2017:* Onehunga Sports.

PAPUA NEW GUINEA

Papua New Guinea Football Association, PO Box 957, Lae 411, Morobe Province.
Founded: 1962. *FIFA:* 1966; *OFC:* 1966. *National Colours:* Red shirts with black trim, red shorts, yellow socks.
International matches 2017–18
None played.
League champions 2017: Lae City Dwellers; *2018* Toti City (formerly Lae City Dwellers). *Cup winners:* No competition.

SAMOA

Football Federation Samoa, PO Box 1682, Tuanimato, Apia.
Founded: 1968. *FIFA:* 1986; *OFC:* 1986. *National Colours:* Blue, white and red shirts, blue and white shorts, red and blue socks.
International matches 2017–18
None played.
League champions 2017: Lupe o le Soaga. *Cup winners:* No competition since 2014.

SOLOMON ISLANDS

Solomon Islands Football Federation, Allan Boso Complex, Panatina Academy, PO Box 584, Honiara.
Founded: 1978. *FIFA:* 1988; *OFC:* 1988. *National Colours:* Green, gold and blue shirts, blue and white shorts, white and blue socks.
International matches 2017–18
New Zealand (a) 1-6, New Zealand (h) 2-2, Tonga (n) 8-0, Fiji (n) 0-0, New Caledonia (n) 1-0, Vanuatu (a) 2-3.
League champions 2017–18: Solomon Warriors. *Cup winners:* No competition.

TAHITI

Federation Tahitienne de Football, Rue Gerald Coppenrath, Complexe de Fautaua, PO Box 50358, Pirae 98716.
Founded: 1989. *FIFA:* 1990; *OFC:* 1990. *National Colours:* White shirts with red trim, white shorts, white socks.
International matches 2017–18
New Caledonia (h) 4-3.
League champions 2016–17: Dragon; *2017–18:* Central Sport. *Cup winners 2016:* Dragon; *2017:* Tefana.

TONGA

Tonga Football Association, Loto-Tonga Soka Centre, Valungafulu Road, Atele, PO Box 852, Nuku'alofa.
Founded: 1965. *FIFA:* 1994; OFC: 1994. *National Colours:* All red.
International matches 2017–18
Solomon Islands (n) 0-8, Vanuatu (a) 0-5, New Caledonia (n) 2-4, Fiji (n) 0-4.
League champions 2017: Veitongo. *Cup winners:* No competition since 2003.

VANUATU

Vanuatu Football Federation, VFF House, Lini Highway, PO Box 266, Port Vila.

Founded: 1934. *FIFA:* 1988; *OFC:* 1988. *National Colours:* Gold and white shirts with green sleeves, green shorts, black socks with white tops.
International matches 2017–18
Estonia (h) 0-1, New Caledonia (h) 2-1, Tonga (h) 5-0, Fiji (h) 1-1, Solomon Islands (h) 3-2.
League champions 2017–18: Erakor Golden Star. *Cup winners:* No competition.

AFRICA (CAF)
ALGERIA
Federation Algerienne De Football, Chemin Ahmed Ouaked, BP 39, Dely-Ibrahim, Algiers 16000.
Founded: 1962. *FIFA:* 1963; *CAF:* 1964. *National Colours:* All white.
International matches 2017–18
Libya (h) 1-2, Libya (a) 1-1*, Zambia (a) 1-3, Zambia (h) 0-1, Cameroon (a) 0-2, Nigeria (h) 1-1, Central African Republic (h) 3-0, Tanzania (h) 4-1, Iran (n) 1-2, Saudi Arabia (n) 0-2, Cape Verde Islands (h) 2-3, Portugal (a) 0-3.
* *Match played in Tunisia.*
League champions 2017–18: CS Constantine. *Cup winners 2017–18:* USM Bel Abbes.

ANGOLA
Federacao Angolana de Futetbol, Senado de Compl. da Cidadela Desportiva, BP 3449, Luanda.
Founded: 1979. *FIFA:* 1980; *CAF:* 1980. *National Colours:* Red shirts with yellow trim, black shorts, red socks.
International matches 2017–18
Mauritius (a) 1-0, Mauritius (h) 3-2, Madagascar (a) 0-0, Madagascar (h) 1-0, Burkina Faso (n) 0-0, Cameroon (n) 1-0, Congo (n) 0-0, Nigeria (n) 1-2, South Africa (n) 1-1 (3-5p), Zimbabwe (n) 2-2 (4-2p), Botswana (n) 1-2, Mauritius (a) 1-0, Malawi (n) 0-0.
League champions 2017: Primeiro de Agosto. *Cup winners 2017:* Petro Atletico; *2018:* Not played.

BENIN
Federation Beninoise de Football, Rue du boulevard Djassain, BP 112, 3-eme Arrondissement de Porto-Novo 01.
Founded: 1962. *FIFA:* 1962; *CAF:* 1962. *National Colours:* All yellow.
International matches 2017–18
Togo (a) 1-1, Togo (h) 1-0 (8-7p), Nigeria (n) 1-0, Nigeria (a) 0-2, Equatorial Guinea (a) 2-1, Gabon (n) 1-0, Congo (a) 1-1, Tanzania (h) 1-1.
League champions 2017: Buffles. *Cup winners:* No competition since 2014.

BOTSWANA
Botswana Football Association, PO Box 1396, Gaborone.
Founded: 1970. *FIFA:* 1978; *CAF:* 1976. *National Colours:* Blue, white and black shirts, blue shorts, blue socks.
International matches 2017–18
South Africa (a) 0-2, South Africa (h) 0-2, South Africa (a) 0-1, Ethiopia (h) 2-0, Gabon (a) 0-0, Lesotho (h) 1-0, Zimbabwe (a) 1-0, Angola (n) 2-1, Malawi (n) 1-1, Mauritius (n) 6-0, Zimbabwe (n) 1-1 (1-3p), Swaziland (n) 2-0, South Africa (a) 0-3.
League champions 2017–18: Township Rollers. *Cup winners:* No competition since 2012.

BURKINA FASO
Federation Burkinabe de Foot-Ball, Centre Technique National Ouaga 2000, BP 57, Ouagadougou 01.
Founded: 1960. *FIFA:* 1964; *CAF:* 1964. *National Colours:* Green shirts with red sleeves, green shorts, green socks.
International matches 2017–18
Belarus (n) 0-0 (0-3p), Korea DPR (n) 3-3 (4-3p), Ghana (h) 2-2, Ghana (a) 2-1, Senegal (a) 0-0, Senegal (h) 2-2, South Africa (a) 1-3, Cape Verde Islands (h) 4-0, Angola (n) 0-0, Congo (n) 0-2, Cameroon (n) 1-1, Kosovo (n) 0-2, Cameroon (n) 1-0.
League champions 2017–18: AS Fonctionnaires. *Cup winners 2017:* Etoile Filante; *2018:* Salitas.

BURUNDI
Federation de Football du Burundi, Avenue Muyinga, BP 3426, Bujumbura.
Founded: 1948. *FIFA:* 1972; *CAF:* 1972. *National Colours:* All red with white trim.
International matches 2017–18
Sudan (h) 0-0, Sudan (a) 0-1, Uganda (n) 0-0, Ethiopia (n) 4-1, South Sudan (n) 0-0, Kenya (n) 0-2, Uganda (n) 1-2.
League champions 2017–18: Le Messager Ngozi. *Cup winners 2017:* Olympic Star; *2018:* Vital'o.

CAMEROON
Federation Camerounaise de Football, Avenue du 27 aout 1940, Tsinga-Yaounde, BP 1116, Yaounde.
Founded: 1959. *FIFA:* 1962; *CAF:* 1963. *National Colours:* Green shirts, red shorts, yellow socks.
International matches 2017–18
Sao Tome & Principe (a) 2-0, Sao Tome & Principe (h) 2-0, Nigeria (a) 0-4, Nigeria (h) 1-1, Algeria (h) 2-0, Zambia (a) 2-2, Congo (n) 0-1, Angola (n) 0-1, Burkina Faso (n) 1-1, Kuwait (a) 3-1, Burkina Faso (n) 0-1.
League champions 2017: Eding Sport. *Cup winners 2017:* New Star.

CAPE VERDE ISLANDS
Federacao Caboverdiana de Futebol, Praia Cabo Verde, FCF CX, PO Box 234, Praia.
Founded: 1982. *FIFA:* 1986; *CAF:* 2000. *National Colours:* All blue with white trim.
International matches 2017–18
South Africa (h) 2-1, South Africa (a) 2-1, Senegal (h) 0-2, Burkina Faso (a) 0-4, Algeria (a) 3-2, Andorra (n) 0-0 (4-2p).
League champions 2017: Sporting Clube de Praia; *2018:* Academica de Praia. *Cup winners 2013–17:* No competition. *2018:* Sporting Clube de Praia.

CENTRAL AFRICAN REPUBLIC
Federation Centrafricaine de Football, Avenue des Martyrs, BP 344, Bangui.
Founded: 1961. *FIFA:* 1964; *CAF:* 1965. *National Colours:* All white with blue trim.
International matches 2017–18
Algeria (a) 0-3, Gambia (a) 1-1, Kenya (n) 3-2, Niger (a) 3-3, Uganda (n) 1-0.
League champions 2016–17: Olympique Real de Bangui. *Cup winners 2016:* ASDR Fatima; *2017:* ASDR Fatima.

CHAD
Federation Tchadienne de Football, BP 886, N'Djamena.
Founded: 1962. *FIFA:* 1964; *CAF:* 1964. *National Colours:* Blue shirts, yellow shorts, red socks.
International matches 2017–18
None played.
League champions 2016: Gazelle (final phase not played). *Cup winners:* No competition since 2015.

COMOROS
Federation Comorienne de Football, Route d'Itsandra, BP 798, Moroni.
Founded: 1979. *FIFA:* 2005; *CAF:* 2003. *National Colours:* All green.
International matches 2017–18
Lesotho (h) 2-0, Lesotho (a) 0-1, Namibia (h) 2-1, Namibia (a) 0-2, Mauritania (n) 1-0, Madagascar (n) 1-1, Kenya (n) 2-2, Seychelles (n) 1-1, Mozambique (n) 0-3, Madagascar (n) 0-1.
League champions 2017: Ngaya Club de Mdé. *Cup winners 2017:* Ngazi.

CONGO
Federation Congolaise de Football, 80 Rue Eugene Etienne, Centre Ville, BP Box 11, Brazzaville 00 242.
Founded: 1962. *FIFA:* 1964; *CAF:* 1965. *National Colours:* Green shirts, yellow shorts, red socks.
International matches 2017–18
DR Congo (h) 0-0, DR Congo (a) 1-1, Ghana (a) 1-1, Ghana (h) 1-5, Egypt (a) 1-2, Benin (h) 1-1, Uganda (h) 1-1, Cameroon (n) 1-0, Burkina Faso (n) 2-0, Angola (n) 0-0, Libya (n) 1-1 (3-5p).
League champions 2017: AC Leopards de Dolisie. *Cup winners 2017:* AC Leopards de Dolisie.

DR CONGO
Federation Congolaise de Football-Association, 31 Avenue de la Justice Kinshasa-Gombe, BP 1284, Kinshasa 1.
Founded: 1919. *FIFA:* 1964; *CAF:* 1964. *National Colours:* Blue shirts with red sleeves, blue shorts, blue socks.
International matches 2017–18
Congo (a) 0-0, Congo (h) 1-1, Tunisia (a) 1-2, Tunisia (h) 2-2, Libya (a) 2-1*, Guinea (h) 3-1, Tanzania (a) 0-2, Nigeria (a) 1-1.
* *Match played in Tunisia.*
League champions 2016–17: TP Mazembe. *Cup winners 2017:* AS Maniema Union.

DJIBOUTI
Federation Djiboutienne de Football, Centre Technique National, BP 2694, Ville de Djibouti.

Founded: 1979. *FIFA:* 1994; *CAF:* 1994. *National Colours:* Green shirts, white shorts, blue socks.
International matches 2017–18
Ethiopia (h) 1-5, Ethiopia (a) 0-3*.
* *Walkover; match awarded 3-0 to Ethiopia.*
League champions 2017–18: AS Ali Sabieh Djibouti Telecom. *Cup winners 2017:* Gendarmerie Nationale.

EGYPT

Egyptian Football Association, 5 Gabalaya Street, Gezira El Borg Post Office, Cairo.
Founded: 1921. *FIFA:* 1923; *CAF:* 1957. *National Colours:* Red shirts with white trim, white shorts, black socks.
International matches 2017–18
Morocco (h) 1-1, Morocco (a) 1-3, Uganda (a) 0-1, Uganda (h) 1-0, Congo (h) 2-1, Ghana (a) 1-1, Portugal (n) 1-2, Greece (n) 0-1, Kuwait (a) 1-1, Colombia (n) 0-0, Belgium (a) 0-3, Uruguay (n) 0-1, Russia (a) 1-3, Saudi Arabia (n) 1-2.
League champions 2017–18: Al-Ahly. *Cup winners 2016–17:* Al-Ahly; *2017–18:* Zamalek.

EQUATORIAL GUINEA

Federacion Ecuatoguineana de Futbol, Avenida de Hassan II, Apartado de correo 1017, Malabo.
Founded: 1957. *FIFA:* 1986; CAF: 1986. *National Colours:* All red.
International matches 2017–18
Benin (h) 1-2, Mauritius (h) 3-1, Libya (n) 0-3, Rwanda (n) 0-1, Nigeria (n) 1-3, Kenya (a) 0-1.
League champions 2017: Leones Vegetarianos. *Cup winners 2017:* Deportivo Niefang.

ERITREA

Eritrean National Football Federation, Sematat Avenue 29–31, PO Box 3665, Asmara.
Founded: 1996. *FIFA:* 1998; *CAF:* 1998. *National Colours:* Blue shirts, red shirts, green socks.
International matches 2017–18
None played.
No senior club competitions since 2014.

ETHIOPIA

Ethiopia Football Federation, Addis Ababa Stadium, PO Box 1080, Addis Ababa.
Founded: 1943. *FIFA:* 1952; *CAF:* 1957. *National Colours:* Green shirts, yellow shorts, red socks.
International matches 2017–18
Djibouti (a) 5-1, Djibouti (h) 3-0*, Zambia (a) 0-0, Sudan (h) 1-1, Sudan (a) 0-1, Botswana (a) 0-2, Rwanda (h) 2-3, Rwanda (a) 0-0, South Sudan (n) 3-0, Burundi (n) 1-4, Uganda (n) 1-1.
* *Walkover; match awarded 3-0 to Ethiopia.*
League champions 2016–17: Saint George. *Cup winners 2017:* Welayta Dicha.

GABON

Federation Gabonaise de Football, BP 181, Libreville.
Founded: 1962. *FIFA:* 1966; *CAF:* 1967. *National Colours:* Yellow shirts, blue shorts with yellow trim, blue socks with yellow tops.
International matches 2017–18
Ivory Coast (h) 0-3, Ivory Coast (a) 2-1, Morocco (a) 0-3, Benin (n) 0-1, Mali (h) 0-0, Botswana (h) 0-0, Thailand (a) 0-0 (2-4p), UAE (n) 1-0.
League champions 2016–17: CF Mounana; *2017–18:* AS Mangasport. *Cup winners:* No competition since 2016.

GAMBIA

Gambia Football Association, Kafining Layout, Bakau, PO Box 523, Banjul.
Founded: 1952. *FIFA:* 1968; *CAF:* 1966. *National Colours:* Red shirts, blue shorts, green socks.
International matches 2017–18
Guinea-Bissau (h) 1-0, Mali (h) 0-0, Mali (a) 0-4, Central African Republic (h) 1-1.
League champions 2017–18: GAMTEL. *Cup winners 2018:* Armed Forces.

GHANA

Ghana Football Association, General Secretariat, South East Ridge, PO Box AN 19338, Accra.
Founded: 1957. *FIFA:* 1958; *CAF:* 1958. *National Colours:* All white.
International matches 2017–18
DR Congo (n) 2-1*, Burkina Faso (a) 2-2, Burkina Faso (h) 1-2, Congo (h) 1-1, Congo (a) 5-1, Uganda (a) 0-0, Egypt (h) 1-1, Japan (a) 2-0, Iceland (a) 2-2.
* *Played 29.01.2017; result incorrect in last edition.*

League champions 2017: Aduana Stars. *Cup winners 2017:* Asante Kotoko.

GUINEA

Federation Guineenne de Football, Annexe 1 du Palais du Peuple, PO Box 3645, Conakry.
Founded: 1960. *FIFA:* 1962; *CAF:* 1963. *National Colours:* Red shirts, yellow shorts, green socks.
International matches 2017–18
Guinea-Bissau (a) 3-1, Guinea-Bissau (h) 7-0, Senegal (a) 1-3, Senegal (h) 5-0, Libya (h) 3-2, Libya (a) 0-1*, Tunisia (h) 1-4, DR Congo (a) 1-3, Sudan (n) 1-2, Morocco (a) 1-3, Mauritania (n) 1-0, Mauritania (a) 0-2.
* *Match played in Tunisia.*
League champions 2016–17: Horoya; *2017–18:* Horoya. *Cup winners 2017:* Hafia.

GUINEA-BISSAU

Federacao de Futebol da Guine-Bissau, Alto Bandim (Nova Sede), BP 375, Bissau 1035.
Founded: 1974. *FIFA:* 1986; *CAF:* 1986. *National Colours:* Red shirts with green and yellow trim, red shorts, red socks.
International matches 2017–18
Gambia (a) 0-1, Guinea (h) 1-3, Guinea (a) 0-7.
League champions 2017–18: Sport Bissau e Benfica. *Cup winners 2017:* FC Canchungo; *2018:* Sport Bissau e Benfica.

IVORY COAST

Federation Ivoirienne de Football, Treichville Avenue 1, 01, BP 1202, Abidjan 01.
Founded: 1960. *FIFA:* 1964; *CAF:* 1960. *National Colours:* All orange.
International matches 2017–18
Niger (a) 1-2, Niger (h) 1-0, Gabon (a) 3-0, Gabon (h) 1-2, Mali (a) 0-0, Morocco (h) 0-2, Namibia (n) 0-1, Zambia (n) 0-2, Uganda (n) 0-0, Togo (n) 2-2, Moldova (n) 2-1.
League champions 2017–18: ASEC Mimosas. *Cup winners 2017:* Africa Sports d'Abidjan.

KENYA

Football Kenya Federation, Nyayo Sports Complex, Kasarani, PO Box 12705, 00400 Nairobi.
Founded: 1960 (KFF); 2011 (FKF). *FIFA:* 1960 (2012); *CAF:* 1968 (2012). *National Colours:* All red.
International matches 2017–18
Mozambique (a) 1-1, Iraq (a) 1-2, Thailand (a) 0-1, Rwanda (h) 2-0, Libya (h) 0-0, Zanzibar† (n) 0-0, Tanzania (h) 1-0, Burundi (h) 1-0, Zanzibar† (n) 2-2 (3-2p), Comoros (n) 2-2, Central African Republic (n) 2-3, Swaziland (h) 0-1, Equatorial Guinea (h) 1-0, New Zealand (h) 2-1, India (a) 0-3, Chinese Taipei (n) 4-0, India (a) 0-2.
League champions 2017: Gor Mahia. *Cup winners 2016:* Tusker; *2017:* AFC Leopards.

LESOTHO

Lesotho Football Association, Bambatha Tsita Sports Arena, Old Polo Ground, PO Box 1879, Maseru 100.
Founded: 1932. *FIFA:* 1964; *CAF:* 1964. *National Colours:* Blue shirts, green shorts, white socks.
International matches 2017–18
Zimbabwe (n) 3-4, Tanzania (n) 0-0 (2-4p), Comoros (n) 0-2, Comoros (h) 1-0, Zimbabwe (h) 1-0, Malawi (a) 1-1, Botswana (a) 0-1, Namibia (a) 1-2, Swaziland (n) 1-0, Zimbabwe (n) 0-0 (1-3p), Madagascar (n) 1-0.
League champions 2017–18: Bantu. *Cup winners 2017:* Bantu.

LIBERIA

Liberia Football Association, Professional Building, Benson Street, PO Box 10-1066, Monrovia 1000.
Founded: 1936. *FIFA:* 1964; *CAF:* 1960. *National Colours:* Red and white shirts with black trim, red shorts, red socks with blue.
International matches 2017–18
Mauritania (h) 0-2, Mauritania (a) 1-0.
League champions 2016–17: LISCR. *Cup winners 2017:* LISCR.

LIBYA

Libyan Football Federation, General Sports Federation Building, Sports City, Goriji, PO Box 5137, Tripoli.
Founded: 1962. *FIFA:* 1964; *CAF:* 1965. *National Colours:* Red shirts, black shorts, black socks.
International matches 2017–18
Algeria (a) 2-1, Algeria (h) 1-1*, Guinea (a) 2-3, Guinea (h) 1-0*, DR Congo (h) 1-2*, Tunisia (a) 0-0, Tanzania (n)

0-0, Kenya (a) 0-0, Rwanda (n) 0-0, Zanzibar† (n) 1-0, Jordan (n) 1-1, Equatorial Guinea (n) 3-0, Nigeria (n) 0-1, Rwanda (n) 1-0, Congo (n) 1-1 (5-3p), Morocco (a) 1-3, Sudan (n) 1-1 (2-4p).
* *Match played in Tunisia.*
League champions 2017–18: Al-Nasr. *Cup winners:* No competition since 2016.

MADAGASCAR

Federation Malagasy de Football, 29 Rue de Russie Isoraka, PO Box 4409, Antananarivo 101.
Founded: 1961. *FIFA:* 1964; *CAF:* 1963. *National Colours:* All green and white.
International matches 2017–18
Mozambique (h) 2-2, Mozambique (a) 2-0, Angola (h) 0-0, Angola (a) 0-1, Comoros (n) 1-1, Togo (n) 0-0, Kosovo (n) 0-1, Mozambique (n) 2-1, Seychelles (n) 1-1, Comoros (n) 1-0, South Africa (a) 0-0 (4-3p), Zambia (n) 0-1, Lesotho (h) 0-1.
League champions 2017: CNaPS Sport. *Cup winners 2017:* Fosa Juniors.

MALAWI

Football Association of Malawi, Chiwembe Technical Centre, Off Chiwembe Road, PO Box 51657, Limbe.
Founded: 1966. *FIFA:* 1968; *CAF:* 1968. *National Colours:* All red.
International matches 2017–18
Togo (n) 1-0, Tanzania (a) 1-1, Lesotho (h) 1-1, Uganda (a) 0-0, Mauritius (n) 0-1, Botswana (n) 1-1, Angola (n) 0-0.
League champions 2017: Be Forward Wanderers. *Cup winners:* No competition since 2015.

MALI

Federation Malienne de Football, Avenue du Mali, Hamdallaye ACI 2000, BP 1020, Bamako 0000.
Founded: 1960. *FIFA:* 1964; *CAF:* 1963. *National Colours:* All yellow.
International matches 2017–18
Gambia (a) 0-0, Gambia (h) 4-0, Mauritania (a) 2-2, Mauritania (n) 0-1, Morocco (a) 0-6, Morocco (h) 0-0, Ivory Coast (h) 0-0, Gabon (a) 0-0, Japan (n) 1-1.
League champions 2016–17: Competition abandoned mid-season. *Cup winners:* 2017 final cancelled.

MAURITANIA

Federation de Foot-Ball de la Rep. Islamique de Mauritanie, Route de l'Espoire, BP 566, Nouakchott.
Founded: 1961. *FIFA:* 1970; *CAF:* 1968. *National Colours:* All green with yellow trim.
International matches 2017–18
Liberia (a) 2-0, Liberia (h) 0-1, Mali (h) 2-2, Mali (a) 1-0, Niger (n) 0-2, Comoros (n) 0-1, Morocco (a) 0-4, Sudan (n) 0-1, Guinea (n) 0-1, Guinea (n) 0-2.
League champions 2017–18: FC Nouadhibou. *Cup winners 2016:* FC Tevragh-Zeine; *2017:* FC Nouadhibou.

MAURITIUS

Mauritius Football Association, Sepp Blatter House, Trianon.
Founded: 1952. *FIFA:* 1964; *CAF:* 1963. *National Colours:* All white with red trim.
International matches 2017–18
Angola (h) 0-1, Angola (a) 2-3, India (a) 1-2, St Kitts & Nevis (n) 1-1, Equatorial Guinea (a) 1-3, Togo (a) 0-6, Macao (a) 1-0, Mongolia (a) 2-0, Malawi (n) 1-0, Angola (n) 0-1, Botswana (n) 0-6.
League champions 2017–18: Pamplemousses. *Cup winners 2017:* AS Port-Louis 2000. *2018:* Pamplemousses.

MOROCCO

Federation Royale Marocaine de Football, 51 bis, Avenue Ibn Sina, Agdal BP 51, Rabat 10 000.
Founded: 1955. *FIFA:* 1960; *CAF:* 1959. *National Colours:* Red shirts with green trim, white shorts, red socks with green trim.
International matches 2017–18
Egypt (a) 1-1, Egypt (h) 3-1, Mali (h) 6-0, Mali (a) 0-0, Gabon (h) 3-0, Korea Republic (n) 3-1, Ivory Coast (a) 2-0, Mauritania (h) 4-0, Guinea (h) 3-1, Sudan (h) 0-0, Namibia (h) 2-0, Libya (h) 3-1, Nigeria (h) 4-0, Serbia (n) 2-1, Uzbekistan (h) 2-0, Ukraine (n) 0-0, Slovakia (n) 2-1, Estonia (a) 3-1, Iran (n) 0-1, Portugal (n) 0-1, Spain (n) 2-2.
League champions 2017–18: IR Tanger. *Cup winners 2017:* Raja Casablanca.

MOZAMBIQUE

Federacao Mocambicana de Futebol, Avenida Samora Machel 11, Caixa Postal 1467, Maputo.
Founded: 1976. *FIFA:* 1980; *CAF:* 1980. *National Colours:* Red shirts, black shorts, black socks with red tops.
International matches 2017–18
Madagascar (a) 2-2, Madagascar (h) 0-2, Kenya (h) 1-1, Madagascar (n) 1-2, Comoros (n) 3-0, Seychelles (n) 2-1.
League champions 2017: UD Songo. *Cup winners 2017:* Costa do Sol.

NAMIBIA

Namibia Football Association, Richard Kamuhuka Str., Soccer House, Katutura, PO Box 1345, Windhoek 9000.
Founded: 1990. *FIFA:* 1992; *CAF:* 1992. *National Colours:* All red.
International matches 2017–18
Swaziland 1-0 (n), South Africa (a) 0-1, Zimbabwe (h) 1-0, Zimbabwe (a) 0-1 (5-4p), Comoros (a) 1-2, Comoros (h) 2-0, Zimbabwe (h) 3-1, Ivory Coast (n) 1-0, Uganda (n) 1-0, Zambia (n) 1-1, Morocco (a) 0-2, Lesotho (h) 2-1, Zambia (n) 0-0 (3-4p), South Africa (a) 1-4.
League champions 2016–17: No competition; *2017–18:* African Stars. *Cup winners 2016:* No competition; *2017:* Young African; *2018:* African Stars.

NIGER

Federation Nigerienne de Football, Avenue Francois Mitterand, BP 10299, Niamey.
Founded: 1961. *FIFA:* 1964; *CAF:* 1964. *National Colours:* White shirts, white shorts, orange socks.
International matches 2017–18
Ivory Coast (h) 2-1, Ivory Coast (a) 0-1, Togo (n) 0-2, Mauritania (n) 2-0, Central African Republic (h) 3-3, Uganda (h) 2-1.
League champions 2017–18: AS SONIDEP. *Cup winners 2017:* Sahel.

NIGERIA

Nigeria Football Federation, Plot 2033, Olusegun Obasanjo Way, Zone 7, Wuse Abuja, PO Box 5101 Garki, Abuja.
Founded: 1945. *FIFA:* 1960; *CAF:* 1960. *National Colours:* All green with white trim.
International matches 2017–18
Benin (n) 0-1, Benin (h) 2-0, Cameroon (h) 4-0, Cameroon (a) 1-1, Zambia (h) 1-0, Algeria (h) 1-1, Argentina (n) 4-2, Rwanda (n) 0-0, Libya (n) 1-0, Equatorial Guinea (n) 3-1, Angola (n) 2-1, Sudan (n) 1-0, Morocco (a) 0-4, Poland (n) 1-0, Serbia (n) 0-2, DR Congo (h) 1-1, England (a) 1-2, Czech Republic (n) 0-1, Croatia (n) 0-2, Iceland (n) 2-0, Argentina (n) 1-2.
League champions 2017: Plateau United. *Cup winners:* No competition since 2016.

RWANDA

Federation Rwandaise de Football Association, BP 2000, Kigali.
Founded: 1972. *FIFA:* 1978; *CAF:* 1976. *National Colours:* Green and yellow hooped shirts, blue shorts, green socks.
International matches 2017–18
Central African Republic (a) 1-2*, Tanzania (a) 1-1, Tanzania (h) 0-0, Sudan (h) 2-1, Uganda (a) 0-3, Uganda (h) 2-0, Ethiopia (a) 3-2, Ethiopia (h) 0-0, Kenya (a) 0-2, Zanzibar† (n) 1-3, Libya (n) 0-0, Tanzania (n) 2-1, Nigeria (n) 0-0, Equatorial Guinea (n) 1-0, Libya (n) 0-1.
* *Played 11.06.2017; result incorrect in last edition.*
League champions 2017–18: APR. *Cup winners 2016:* Rayon Sports; *2017:* APR.

SAO TOME & PRINCIPE

Federacao Santomense de Futebol, Rua Ex-Joao de Deus No. QXXIII-426/26, BP 440, Sao Tome.
Founded: 1975. *FIFA:* 1986; *CAF:* 1986. *National Colours:* Green and red shirts, black shorts, green socks.
International matches 2017–18
Cameroon (h) 0-2, Cameroon (a) 0-2, Uganda (a) 1-3.
League champions 2017: UDRA. *Cup winners 2017:* UDRA.

SENEGAL

Federation Senegalaise de Football, VDN Ouest-Foire en face du Cicesi, BP 13021, Dakar.
Founded: 1960. *FIFA:* 1964; *CAF:* 1964. *National Colours:* All white with yellow trim.
International matches 2017–18
Sierra Leone (a) 1-1, Sierra Leone (h) 3-1, Guinea (h) 3-1, Guinea (a) 0-5, Burkina Faso (h) 0-0, Burkina Faso (a)

2-2, Cape Verde Islands (a) 2-0, South Africa (a) 2-0, South Africa (h) 2-1, Uzbekistan (n) 1-1, Bosnia-Herzegovina (n) 0-0, Luxembourg (a) 0-0, Croatia (a) 1-2, Korea Republic (n) 2-0, Poland (n) 2-1, Japan (n) 2-2, Colombia (n) 0-1.
League champions 2017–18: ASC Jaraaf. *Cup winners 2017:* Mbour Petite Cote *2016:* Generation Foot.

SEYCHELLES
Seychelles Football Federation, Maison Football, Roche Caiman, PO Box 843, Mahe.
Founded: 1979. *FIFA:* 1986; *CAF:* 1986. *National Colours:* Red shirts, blue shorts, blue socks.
International matches 2017–18
Swaziland (h) 0-0, Comoros (n) 1-1, Madagascar (n) 1-1, Mozambique (n) 1-2.
League champions 2017: Saint Louis Suns United. *Cup winners 2017:* Saint Louis Suns United.

SIERRA LEONE
Sierra Leone Football Association, 21 Battery Street, Kingtom, PO Box 672, Freetown.
Founded: 1960. *FIFA:* 1960; *CAF:* 1960. *National Colours:* Green shirts, white shorts, blue socks.
International matches 2017–18
Senegal (h) 1-1, Senegal (a) 1-3, Iran (a) 0-4.
No senior club football since 2014.

SOMALIA
Somali Football Federation, Mogadishu BN 03040 (DHL only).
Founded: 1951. *FIFA:* 1962; *CAF:* 1968. *National Colours:* All blue with white trim.
International matches 2017–18
None played.
League champions 2016–17: Dekedda; *2018:* Dekedda. *Cup winners 2017:* Elman.

SOUTH AFRICA
South African Football Association, 76 Nasrec Road, Nasrec, Johannesburg 2000.
Founded: 1991. *FIFA:* 1992; *CAF:* 1992. *National Colours:* Yellow shirts with green trim, green shorts with yellow trim, yellow socks with green tops.
International matches 2017–18
Botswana (h) 2-0, Namibia (h) 1-0, Botswana (a) 2-0, Botswana (h) 1-0, Zambia (h) 2-2, Zambia (a) 0-2, Cape Verde Islands (a) 1-2, Cape Verde Islands (h) 1-2, Burkina Faso (h) 3-1, Senegal (h) 0-2, Senegal (a) 1-2, Angola (h) 1-1 (5-3p), Zambia (a) 2-0, Madagascar (h) 0-0 (3-4p), Namibia (h) 4-1, Botswana (h) 3-0.
League champions 2017–18: Mamelodi Sundowns. *Cup winners 2017–18:* Free State Stars.

SOUTH SUDAN
South Sudan Football Association, Juba National Stadium, Hai Himra, Talata, Juba.
Founded: 2011. *FIFA:* 2012; *CAF:* 2012. *National Colours:* All blue.
International matches 2017–18
Uganda (h) 0-0, Uganda (a) 1-5, Ethiopia (n) 0-3, Uganda (n) 1-5, Burundi (n) 0-0.
League champions 2016: No competition; *2017:* Al-Salam. *Cup winners 2017:* Al-Salam.

SUDAN
Sudan Football Association, Baladia Street, PO Box 437, 11111 Khartoum.
Founded: 1936. *FIFA:* 1948; *CAF:* 1957. *National Colours:* All red.
International matches 2017–18
Burundi (a) 0-0, Burundi (h) 1-0, Rwanda (a) 1-2, Ethiopia (a) 1-1, Ethiopia (h) 1-0, Guinea (n) 2-1, Mauritania (n) 1-0, Morocco (a) 0-0, Zambia (n) 1-0, Nigeria (n) 0-1, Libya (n) 1-1 (4-2p).
League champions 2017: Al-Hilal Omdurman. *Cup winners 2017:* Al-Ahly Shendi.

SWAZILAND
National Football Association of Swaziland, Sigwaca House, Plot 582, Sheffield Road, PO Box 641, Mbabane H100.
Founded: 1968. *FIFA:* 1978; *CAF:* 1976. *National Colours:* Blue and red shirts, blue shorts, blue socks.
International matches 2017–18
Namibia (n) 0-1, Zambia (h) 0-4, Zambia (a) 0-3, Seychelles (a) 0-0, Kenya (a) 1-0, Lesotho (n) 0-1, Botswana (h) 0-2.

League champions 2017–18: Mbabane Swallows. *Cup winners 2018:* Young Buffaloes.

TANZANIA
Tanzania Football Federation, Karume Memorial Stadium, Uhuru/Shauri Moyo Road, PO Box 1574, Ilala/Dar Es Salaam.
Founded: 1930. *FIFA:* 1964; *CAF:* 1964. *National Colours:* Blue shirts, black shorts, blue socks.
International matches 2017–18
Zambia (n) 2-4, Lesotho (n) 0-0 (4-2p), Rwanda (h) 1-1, Rwanda (a) 0-0, Malawi (h) 1-1, Benin (a) 1-1, Libya (n) 0-0, Zanzibar† (n) 1-2, Rwanda (n) 1-2, Kenya (a) 0-1, Algeria (a) 1-4, DR Congo (h) 2-0.
League champions 2017–18: Simba. *Cup winners 2017–18:* Mtibwa Sugar.

TOGO
Federation Togolaise de Football, Route de Kegoue, BP 05, Lome.
Founded: 1960. *FIFA:* 1964; *CAF:* 1964. *National Colours:* Yellow shirts, green shorts, yellow socks.
International matches 2017–18
Benin (h) 1-1, Benin (a) 1-1 (7-8p), Niger (n) 2-0, Malawi (n) 0-1, Iran (a) 0-2, Mauritius (h) 6-0, Madagascar (n) 0-0, Ivory Coast (n) 2-2.
League champions 2017–18: US Koroki Metete. *Cup winners 2018:* Gomido.

TUNISIA
Federation Tunisienne de Football, Stade Annexe d'El Menzah, Cite Olympique, El Menzah 1003.
Founded: 1957. *FIFA:* 1960; *CAF:* 1960. *National Colours:* All white with red trim.
International matches 2017–18
DR Congo (n) 2-1, DR Congo (a) 2-2, Guinea (a) 4-1, Libya (h) 0-0, Iran (h) 1-0, Costa Rica (n) 1-0, Portugal (a) 2-2, Turkey (n) 2-2, Spain (n) 0-1, England (n) 1-2, Belgium (n) 2-5, Panama (n) 2-1.
League champions 2017–18: Esperance de Tunis. *Cup winners 2017–18:* Club Africain.

UGANDA
Federation of Uganda Football Associations, FUFA House, Plot No. 879, Wakaliga Road, Mengo, PO Box 22518, Kampala.
Founded: 1924. *FIFA:* 1960; *CAF:* 1960. *National Colours:* Yellow shirts, black shorts, yellow socks.
International matches 2017–18
South Sudan (n) 0-0, South Sudan (h) 5-1, Rwanda (h) 3-0, Rwanda (a) 0-2, Egypt (h) 1-0, Egypt (a) 0-1, Ghana (h) 0-0, Congo (a) 1-1, Burundi (n) 0-0, South Sudan (n) 5-1, Ethiopia (n) 1-1, Zanzibar† (n) 1-2, Burundi (n) 2-1, Zambia (n) 1-3, Namibia (n) 0-1, Ivory Coast (n) 0-0, Sao Tome & Principe (h) 3-1, Malawi (h) 0-0, Central African Republic (n) 0-1, Niger (n) 1-2.
League champions 2017–18: Vipers. *Cup winners 2018:* KCCA.

ZAMBIA
Football Association of Zambia, Football House, Alick Nkhata Road, Long Acres, PO Box 34751, Lusaka.
Founded: 1929. *FIFA:* 1964; *CAF:* 1964. *National Colours:* Green shirts, green shorts, green and orange socks.
International matches 2017–18
Tanzania (n) 4-2, Zimbabwe (n) 1-3, Swaziland (a) 4-0, Swaziland (h) 3-0, Ethiopia (h) 0-0, South Africa (a) 2-2, South Africa (h) 2-0, Algeria (h) 3-1, Algeria (a) 1-0, Nigeria (a) 0-1, Cameroon (h) 2-2, Uganda (n) 3-1, Ivory Coast (n) 2-0, Namibia (n) 1-1, Sudan (n) 0-1, Zimbabwe (h) 2-2 (5-4p), South Africa (h) 0-2, Namibia (n) 0-0 (4-3p), Madagascar (n) 1-0, Zimbabwe (n) 2-4.
League champions 2017: ZESCO United. *Cup winners:* No competition.

ZIMBABWE
Zimbabwe Football Association, ZIFA House, 53 Livingston Avenue, PO Box CY 114, Causeway, Harare.
Founded: 1965. *FIFA:* 1965; *CAF:* 1980. *National Colours:* Gold shirts, gold shorts, green socks.
International matches 2017–18
Lesotho (n) 4-3, Zambia (n) 3-1, Namibia (h) 0-1, Namibia (h) 1-0 (4-5p), Lesotho (a) 0-1, Namibia (a) 1-3, Zambia (a) 2-2 (4-5p), Angola (n) 2-2 (2-4p), Botswana (h) 0-1, Botswana (n) 1-1 (3-1p), Lesotho (h) 0-0 (3-1p), Zambia (n) 4-2.
League champions 2017: FC Platinum. *Cup winners 2017:* Harare City.

FIFA WORLD CUP 2018
QUALIFYING COMPETITION – EUROPE

■ *Denotes player sent off.*

GROUP A

Tuesday, 6 September 2016

Belarus (0) 0

France (0) 0   12,920

Belarus: (451) Gorbunov; Palyakow, Sivakov, Bordachev, Politevich; Korzun, Stasevich (Krivets 69), Gordeichuk (Volodko 85), Maewski, Kalachev; Signevich (Kornilenko 80).
France: (433) Mandanda; Sidibe, Varane, Koscielny, Kurzawa; Sissoko (Dembele 70), Kante, Pogba; Griezmann, Giroud (Gameiro 82), Martial (Payet 57).

Bulgaria (1) 4 *(Rangelov 16, Marcelinho 66, Popov I 80, Tonev 90)*

Luxembourg (0) 3 *(Joachim 60, 63, Bohnert 90)*   1000

Bulgaria: (4231) Stoyanov; Popov S, Ivanov, Chorbadzhiyski, Nedyalkov; Dyakov, Marcelinho; Milanov G (Tonev 65), Popov I (Bozhilov 85), Aleksandrov M (Chochev 55); Rangelov.
Luxembourg: (442) Joubert; Jans, Martins Pereira, Chanot, Malget; Mutsch, Gerson, Philipps (Deville 84), Da Mota Alves (Bohnert 68); Joachim, Thill V (Turpel 58).

Sweden (1) 1 *(Berg 43)*

Netherlands (0) 1 *(Sneijder 67)*   36,128

Sweden: (4231) Olsen; Wendt, Lustig, Lindelof, Granqvist; Rohden (Kujovic 76), Forsberg; Hiljemark, Fransson, Guidetti (Nyman 64); Berg (Durmaz 88).
Netherlands: (433) Zoet; Janmaat, Bruma, van Dijk, Blind; Klaassen, Strootman, Wijnaldum (Dost 66); Promes (Berghuis 78), Janssen, Sneijder.

Friday, 7 October 2016

France (3) 4 *(Gameiro 23, 59, Payet 26, Griezmann 38)*

Bulgaria (1) 1 *(Aleksandrov M 6 (pen))*   65,475

France: (4231) Lloris; Sagna (Sidibe 27), Varane, Koscielny, Kurzawa; Pogba, Matuidi; Sissoko, Griezmann (Fekir 83), Payet; Gameiro (Gignac 72).
Bulgaria: (442) Stoyanov; Popov S, Aleksandrov A, Pirgov, Milanov Z; Milanov G, Dyakov, Kostadinov, Aleksandrov M (Nedelev 76); Marcelinho (Rangelov 62), Popov I (Tonev 67).

Netherlands (2) 4 *(Promes 15, 32, Klaassen 55, Janssen 64)*

Belarus (0) 1 *(Rios 48)*   41,200

Netherlands: (4411) Stekelenburg; Karsdorp, van Dijk, Bruma, Blind; Promes, Strootman (Clasie 79), Wijnaldum, Sneijder (Propper 46); Klaassen; Janssen (Dost 83).
Belarus: (4411) Gorbunov; Palyakow, Sivakov, Politevich, Bordachev; Gordeichuk (Valadzko 74); Maewski (Hleb 46); Korzun, Rios; Krivets (Kislyak 68); Kornilenko.

Luxembourg (0) 0

Sweden (0) 1 *(Lustig 58)*   2500

Luxembourg: (433) Moris; Jans, Philipps, Malget■, Carlson; Thill V (Turpel 67), Martins Pereira, Bohnert; Deville (Da Mota Alves 67), Mutsch, Joachim.
Sweden: (442) Olsen; Lustig, Lindelof, Granqvist, Olsson; Durmaz (Nyman 89), Hiljemark, Ekdal (Fransson 80), Forsberg; Guidetti (Toivonen 71), Berg.

Monday, 10 October 2016

Belarus (0) 1 *(Savitskiy 80)*

Luxembourg (0) 1 *(Joachim 85)*   9011

Belarus: (451) Gorbunov; Palyakow, Martynovich, Filipenko, Bordachev (Valadzko 79); Kalachev, Maewski (Savitskiy 91), Korzun, Hleb, Gordeichuk; Signevich (Kornilenko 60).
Luxembourg: (451) Moris; Delgado, Philipps, Martins Pereira (Veiga 34), Carlson■; Jans, Thill V (Janisch 45), Mutsch, Da Mota Alves, Bohnert (Turpel 72); Joachim.

Netherlands (0) 0

France (1) 1 *(Pogba 30)*   50,220

Netherlands: (4231) Stekelenburg; Karsdorp, Bruma, van Dijk, Blind; Strootman, Wijnaldum (Dost 62); Promes (Depay 16), Propper (Willems 84), Klaassen; Janssen.
France: (4231) Lloris; Sidibe, Varane, Koscielny, Kurzawa; Pogba, Matuidi; Sissoko, Griezmann (Kante 90), Payet (Martial 67); Gameiro (Gignac 79).

Sweden (2) 3 *(Toivonen 39, Hiljemark 45, Lindelof 58)*

Bulgaria (0) 0   21,777

Sweden: (442) Olsen; Krafth, Lindelof, Granqvist, Olsson (Augustinsson 63); Durmaz, Hiljemark, Ekdal, Forsberg (Wendt 74); Berg (Guidetti 85), Toivonen.
Bulgaria: (4411) Stoyanov; Popov S, Aleksandrov A, Bozhikov, Nedyalkov; Kostadinov (Aleksandrov M 54), Slavchev (Raynov 89), Chochev (Marcelinho 72), Milanov G; Dyakov; Popov I.

Friday, 11 November 2016

France (0) 2 *(Pogba 58, Payet 65)*

Sweden (0) 1 *(Forsberg 55)*   80,000

France: (4411) Lloris; Sidibe, Varane, Koscielny, Evra; Sissoko, Pogba, Matuidi, Payet; Griezmann (Kante 88); Giroud.
Sweden: (442) Olsen; Krafth, Lindelof, Granqvist, Augustinsson; Durmaz (Jansson 87), Johansson, Ekdal (Hiljemark 66), Forsberg; Guidetti (Thelin 73), Toivonen.

Sunday, 13 November 2016

Bulgaria (1) 1 *(Popov I 10)*

Belarus (0) 0   1994

Bulgaria: (442) Stoyanov; Popov S, Aleksandrov A, Bozhikov, Zanev; Milanov G (Chochev 53), Dyakov, Slavchev, Tonev (Kirilov 66); Delev, Popov I (Yordanov 75).
Belarus: (451) Gorbunov; Politevich, Martynovich (Shitov 35), Filipenko, Palyakow; Gordeichuk, Hleb■, Kendysh, Maewski (Kornilenko 74), Nekhaychik (Savitskiy 61); Laptsew.

Luxembourg (1) 1 *(Chanot 44 (pen))*

Netherlands (1) 3 *(Robben 36, Depay 58, 84)*   8000

Luxembourg: (541) Schon; Jans (Janisch 26), Malget, Chanot, Mahmutovic, Da Mota Alves (Kerger 75); Bohnert, Bensi (Thill V 82), Philipps, Mutsch; Turpel.
Netherlands: (433) Stekelenburg; Brenet, Bruma, van Dijk, Blind; Klaassen, Wijnaldum, Ramselaar (de Roon 88); Robben (Berghuis 45), Dost, Sneijder (Depay 45).

Saturday, 25 March 2017

Bulgaria (2) 2 *(Delev 5, 20)*

Netherlands (0) 0   10,900

Bulgaria: (4141) Mihailov; Popov S, Chorbadzhiyski, Bozhikov, Zanev (Nedyalkov 86); Manolev; Kostadinov, Slavchev, Popov I (Kraev 68), Tonev; Delev (Bodurov 88).
Netherlands: (4411) Zoet; Karsdorp, Martins Indi, de Ligt (Hoedt 46), Blind; Strootman, Klaassen, Robben, Promes (de Jong 69); Wijnaldum (Sneijder 46); Dost.

Luxembourg (1) 1 *(Joachim 34 (pen))*

France (2) 3 *(Giroud 28, 77, Griezmann 38 (pen))*   8000

Luxembourg: (4141) Moris (Schon 20); Jans, Martins Pereira, Chanot, Malget; Philipps; Bensi, Gerson, Mutsch, Da Mota Alves (Rodrigues 82); Joachim.
France: (4411) Lloris; Sidibe (Jallet 62), Koscielny, Umtiti, Mendy; Dembele, Kante, Matuidi (Rabiot 83), Payet (Mbappe 79); Griezmann; Giroud.

Sweden (1) 4 *(Forsberg 19 (pen), 49, Berg 57, Thelin 78)*
Belarus (0) 0   31,243
Sweden: (442) Olsen; Lustig, Jansson, Granqvist,
Augustinsson; Durmaz (Claesson 85), Hiljemark, Ekdal
(Johansson 68), Forsberg; Berg, Toivonen (Thelin 73).
Belarus: (442) Gorbunov; Shitov, Martynovich,
Politevich, Filipenko; Bordachev (Valadzko 69), Bressan,
Maewski (Dragun 65), Rios; Signevich (Rodionov 70),
Gordeichuk.

Friday, 9 June 2017
Belarus (1) 2 *(Sivakov 34 (pen), Savitskiy 80)*
Bulgaria (0) 1 *(Kostadinov 90)*   6150
Belarus: (352) Chernik; Politevich, Filipenko, Sivakov;
Aliseiko, Maewski (Gordeichuk 88), Dragun,
Balanovich, Matsveychyk; Laptev (Bykov 73), Savitskiy
(Skavysh 82).
Bulgaria: (433) Mihailov; Popov S, Chorbadzhiyski,
Bozhikov, Zanev; Dyakov, Popov I (Chochev 64),
Kostadinov; Manolev (Milanov G 81), Delev (Galabinov
54), Tonev.

Netherlands (2) 5 *(Robben 21, Sneijder 34, Wijnaldum 62,*
Promes 70, Janssen 83 (pen))
Luxembourg (0) 0   41,300
Netherlands: (433) Cillessen; Veltman, de Vrij, Hoedt,
Blind; Wijnaldum, Sneijder (Ake 82), Strootman;
Robben (Lens 72), Janssen, Depay (Promes 66).
Luxembourg: (451) Schon; Jans, Chanot (Delgado 25),
Mahmutovic, Malget; Bensi, Rodrigues (Bohnert 85),
Martins Pereira, Thill V (Gerson 54), Thill S; Turpel.

Sweden (1) 2 *(Durmaz 43, Toivonen 90)*
France (1) 1 *(Giroud 37)*   48,783
Sweden: (442) Olsen; Lustig, Lindelof, Granqvist,
Augustinsson; Durmaz (Claesson 76), Johansson, Ekdal
(Larsson 77), Forsberg; Berg (Guidetti 88), Toivonen.
France: (4231) Lloris; Sidibe, Varane, Koscielny, Mendy;
Pogba, Matuidi; Sissoko, Griezmann (Mbappe 76), Payet
(Lemar 76); Giroud.

Thursday, 31 August 2017
Bulgaria (2) 3 *(Manolev 12, Kostadinov 33, Chochev 79)*
Sweden (2) 2 *(Lustig 29, Berg 44)*   12,121
Bulgaria: (4411) Iliev; Popov S, Chorbadzhiyski,
Bozhikov, Zanev; Manolev (Kraev 75), Slavchev,
Kostadinov, Chochev; Milanov G (Nedelev 61); Popov I
(Dimitrov 83).
Sweden: (442) Olsen; Lustig, Lindelof, Granqvist,
Augustinsson; Durmaz (Claesson 82), Johansson
(Armenteros 85), Ekdal (Larsson 69), Forsberg; Berg,
Toivonen.

France (1) 4 *(Griezmann 14, Lemar 73, 88, Mbappe 90)*
Netherlands (0) 0   79,551
France: (4231) Lloris; Sidibe, Koscielny, Umtiti,
Kurzawa; Kante, Pogba; Coman (Lacazette 80),
Griezmann (Fekir 89), Lemar; Giroud (Mbappe 75).
Netherlands: (4231) Cillessen; Fosu-Mensah, de Vrij,
Hoedt, Blind; Wijnaldum, Strootman*; Robben, Sneijder
(Vilhena 45), Promes; Janssen (van Persie 64).

Luxembourg (0) 1 *(Da Mota Alves 60)*
Belarus (0) 0   2752
Luxembourg: (442) Joubert; Martins (Ostrowski 78),
Jans, Philipps, Janisch; Rodrigues (Turpel 55),
Skenderovic, Holter (Thill V 67), Thill O; Joachim, Da
Mota Alves.
Belarus: (352) Chernik; Politevich (Savitskiy 45),
Sivakov, Filipenko; Aliseiko, Dragun, Maewski (Saroka
77), Balanovich, Matsveychyk; Gordeichuk (Palyakow
61), Laptev.

Sunday, 3 September 2017
Belarus (0) 0
Sweden (3) 4 *(Forsberg 18, Nyman 24, Berg 37,*
Granqvist 85 (pen))   6431
Belarus: (352) Chernik; Filipenko, Sivakov, Sachivko;
Burko, Korzun, Nekhaychik (Dragun 46), Balanovich
(Savitskiy 62), Rios; Saroka, Signevich (Bykov 79).
Sweden: (442) Olsen; Lustig, Lindelof, Granqvist,
Augustinsson; Durmaz (Claesson 67), Larsson, Johansson
(Svensson 69), Forsberg; Nyman, Berg (Thelin 86).

France (0) 0
Luxembourg (0) 0   31,177
France: (442) Lloris; Sidibe, Koscielny, Umtiti,
Mbappe (Lacazette 59), Pogba, Kante, Lemar; Giroud
(Coman 60), Griezmann (Fekir 80).
Luxembourg: (451) Joubert; Jans, Malget, Philipps,
Janisch; Thill O, Martins Pereira, Skenderovic, Thill V
(Rodrigues 58), Da Mota Alves (Sinani 59); Turpel
(Holter 87).

Netherlands (1) 3 *(Propper 7, 80, Robben 67)*
Bulgaria (0) 1 *(Kostadinov 69)*   47,079
Netherlands: (4231) Cillessen; Tete, de Vrij, Hoedt,
Blind; Wijnaldum, Vilhena; Robben, Propper (van
Ginkel 86), Promes; Janssen.
Bulgaria: (4411) Iliev; Popov S, Bozhikov, Terziev,
Zanev; Zehirov (Milanov 45), Chochev, Tsvetkov
(Slavchev 24), Manolev (Galabinov 60); Kostadinov;
Popov I.

Saturday, 7 October 2017
Belarus (0) 1 *(Valadzko 55)*
Netherlands (1) 3 *(Propper 24, Robben 84 (pen), Depay 90)*
                      6850
Belarus: (4231) Chernik; Rios, Yanushkevich, Politevich,
Valadzko; Dragun, Maewski; Balanovich (Burko 76),
Karnitskiy, Stasevich; Signevich (Saroka 87).
Netherlands: (4231) Cillessen; Janmaat, van Dijk, Rekik,
Blind; Wijnaldum, Vilhena (Dost 56); Robben, Propper
(Klaassen 83), Babel; Janssen (Depay 68).

Bulgaria (0) 0
France (1) 1 *(Matuidi 3)*   12,921
Bulgaria: (442) Iliev; Popov S, Bodurov, Bozhikov,
Zanev; Manolev (Dimitrov 88), Slavchev, Kostadinov,
Nedelev; Galabinov (Kraev 48), Delev.
France: (433) Lloris; Sidibe, Varane, Umtiti, Digne;
Tolisso, Kante (Rabiot 33), Matuidi; Griezmann,
Lacazette (Payet 76), Mbappe (Giroud 84).

Sweden (3) 8 *(Granqvist 10 (pen), 67 (pen),*
Berg 18, 37, 54, 71, Lustig 60, Toivonen 76)
Luxembourg (0) 0   50,022
Sweden: (442) Olsen; Lustig (Krafth 61), Granqvist
(Helander 80), Lindelof, Augustinsson; Claesson,
Larsson, Johansson, Forsberg; Toivonen, Berg (Thelin
73).
Luxembourg: (442) Joubert; Holter, Philipps, Malget,
Janisch; Martins Pereira (Skenderovic 72), Mutsch, Thill
O (Rodrigues 45), Thill V (Turpel 45); Joachim, Da Mota
Alves.

Tuesday, 10 October 2017
France (2) 2 *(Griezmann 29, Giroud 34)*
Belarus (1) 1 *(Saroka 45)*   74,037
France: (442) Lloris; Sidibe, Varane, Umtiti, Digne;
Coman (Mbappe 62), Tolisso, Matuidi, Lemar (Payet 84);
Giroud, Griezmann (Sissoko 78).
Belarus: (433) Chernik; Matsveychyk, Yanushkevich
(Sachywka 47), Politevich, Valadzko; Dragun, Karnitskiy,
Korzun (Bykov 79); Kovalev (Skavysh 66), Saroka,
Stasevich.

Luxembourg (1) 1 *(Thill O 3)*
Bulgaria (0) 1 *(Chochev 68)*   2936
Luxembourg: (442) Joubert; Jans (Martins 81), Martins
Pereira, Malget, Janisch; Thill O, Philipps, Skenderovic,
Turpel; Joachim (Sinani 84), Rodrigues (Da Mota Alves
59).

Bulgaria: (433) Iliev; Popov S, Bodurov, Bozhikov, Zanev (Nedyalkov 14); Kraev (Galabinov 49), Slavchev (Raynov 62), Chochev; Nedelev, Popov I, Delev.

Netherlands (2) 2 *(Robben 16 (pen), 40)*
Sweden (0) 0 41,244
Netherlands: (433) Cillessen; Tete (Janmaat 71), van Dijk, Rekik, Ake; Vilhena, Wijnaldum (Klaassen 70), Blind; Robben, Janssen (Dost 46), Babel.
Sweden: (442) Olsen; Lustig, Lindelof, Granqvist, Augustinsson; Claesson (Svensson 67), Larsson (Olsson 81), Johansson, Forsberg; Toivonen (Thelin 75), Berg.

Group A Table	P	W	D	L	F	A	GD	Pts
France	10	7	2	1	18	6	12	23
Sweden	10	6	1	3	26	9	17	19
Netherlands	10	6	1	3	21	12	9	19
Bulgaria	10	4	1	5	14	19	–5	13
Luxembourg	10	1	3	6	8	26	–18	6
Belarus	10	1	2	7	6	21	–15	5

GROUP B

Tuesday, 6 September 2016
Andorra (0) 0
Latvia (0) 1 *(Sabala 48)* 1000
Andorra: (451) Pol; Jordi Rubio, Llovera, Lima, Garcia M; Clemente (Pujol 78), Alaez, Vales, Vieira, Martinez C (Moreira 85); Riera (Rebes 30).
Latvia: (451) Vanins; Maksimenko, Gabovs, Gorkss, Jagodinskis; Ikaunieks D (Torres.. 63), Ikaunieks J, Lazdins (Laizans 45), Zjuzins (Karasausks 74); Visnakovs A; Sabala.

Faroe Islands (0) 0
Hungary (0) 0 4066
Faroe Islands: (433) Nielsen; Hansen, Gregersen, Nattestad, Davidsen V; Vatnhamar, Benjaminsen, Joensen; Henriksen Olsen, Edmundsson, Hansson (Vatnsdal 90).
Hungary: (433) Gulacsi; Fiola, Guzmics, Lang, Kadar; Nemeth (Nikolic 70), Nagy A, Dzsudzsak; Kleinheisler (Stieber 80), Priskin (Szalai 27), Elek.

Switzerland (2) 2 *(Embolo 24, Mehmedi 30)*
Portugal (0) 0 36,000
Switzerland: (4231) Sommer; Lichtsteiner (Widmer 69), Schar, Djourou, Rodriguez; Behrami, Xhaka■; Embolo, Dzemaili (Fernandes G 88), Mehmedi; Seferovic (Derdiyok 78).
Portugal: (433) Rui Patricio; Cedric, Pepe, Fonte, Guerreiro; Joao Moutinho (Quaresma 68), William Carvalho (Joao Mario 45); Adrien Silva; Nani, Eder (Andre Silva 45), Bernardo Silva.

Friday, 7 October 2016
Hungary (0) 2 *(Szalai 54, 71)*
Switzerland (0) 3 *(Seferovic 51, Rodriguez 67, Stocker 89)* 21,668
Hungary: (4231) Gulacsi; Fiola, Guzmics, Lang, Kadar; Nagy A, Gera; Dzsudzsak, Kleinheisler (Nemeth 76), Stieber; Szalai (Nikolic 87).
Switzerland: (4231) Sommer; Lichtsteiner, Schar, Elvedi, Rodriguez; Behrami, Dzemaili; Embolo, Shaqiri (Fernandes G 81), Mehmedi (Stocker 88); Seferovic (Derdiyok 73).

Latvia (0) 0
Faroe Islands (1) 2 *(Nattestad 19, Edmundsson 70)* 4823
Latvia: (442) Vanins; Gabovs, Jagodinskis, Gorkss, Maksimenko; Visnakovs A, Kluskins (Zjuzins 72), Laizans, Lukjanovs (Ikaunieks J 76); Gutkovskis (Karlsons 64), Sabala.
Faroe Islands: (451) Nielsen; Davidsen V, Nattestad, Gregersen, Naes; Vatnhamar, Henriksen Olsen (Justinussen P 87), Benjaminsen, Hansson (Sorensen 72); Edmundsson (Klettskard 90).

Portugal (3) 6 *(Ronaldo 2, 4, 47, 68, Joao Cancelo 44, Andre Silva 86)*
Andorra (0) 0 25,120
Portugal: (442) Rui Patricio; Joao Cancelo, Fonte, Pepe (Gelson Martins 72), Guerreiro (Antunes 52); Quaresma, Andre Gomes (Joao Mario 66), Joao Moutinho, Bernardo Silva; Ronaldo, Andre Silva.
Andorra: (541) Gomes; Jordi Rubio■, Lima, Vales, Llovera, Garcia M (San Nicolas 49); Rodriguez, Vieira, Rebes■, Martinez C (Moreira 76); Alaez (Pujol 73).

Monday, 10 October 2016
Andorra (0) 1 *(Martinez A 90)*
Switzerland (1) 2 *(Schar 19 (pen), Mehmedi 76)* 2014
Andorra: (532) Gomes; Jesus Rubio, Garcia E, Lima, Llovera, San Nicolas; Rodriguez, Vales, Clemente (Martinez A 72); Vieira (Martinez C 79), Pujol (Riera 83).
Switzerland: (4411) Burki; Lang, Schar, Klose (Elvedi 45), Rodriguez; Shaqiri (Stocker 79), Fernandes G (Zakaria 65), Xhaka, Mehmedi; Embolo; Seferovic.

Faroe Islands (0) 0
Portugal (3) 6 *(Andre Silva 12, 22, 37, Ronaldo 65, Joao Cancelo 90, Joao Moutinho 90)* 4780
Faroe Islands: (4411) Nielsen; Hansen, Gregersen (Davidsen J 73), Nattestad, Davidsen V; Vatnhamar, Benjaminsen, Hansson, Sorensen (Joensen 66); Henriksen Olsen (Bartalsstovu 79); Edmundsson.
Portugal: (442) Rui Patricio; Joao Cancelo, Fonte, Pepe, Antunes; Quaresma (Gelson Martins 67), Andre Gomes, William Carvalho, Joao Mario (Joao Moutinho 81); Ronaldo, Andre Silva (Eder 79).

Latvia (0) 0
Hungary (1) 2 *(Gyurcso 9, Szalai 77)* 4715
Latvia: (4141) Vanins; Gabovs, Jagodinskis, Gorkss, Maksimenko; Tarasovs; Visnakovs A (Zjuzins 57), Kluskins (Ikaunieks J 69), Laizans (Karasausks 79), Ikaunieks D; Sabala.
Hungary: (442) Gulacsi; Bese, Guzmics, Kadar, Korhut; Gyurcso, Gera (Vida 84), Nagy A, Dzsudzsak; Szalai, Nikolic (Kleinheisler 45).

Sunday, 13 November 2016
Hungary (2) 4 *(Gera 33, Lang 43, Gyurcso 73, Szalai 88)*
Andorra (0) 0 20,479
Hungary: (4411) Gulacsi; Bese, Lang, Guzmics, Korhut; Gyurcso (Nemeth 81), Nagy A, Gera (Bode 84), Dzsudzsak; Kleinheisler (Stieber 73); Szalai.
Andorra: (532) Gomes; Jesus Rubio, Garcia E, Vales, Llovera, San Nicolas; Rodriguez (Moreira 82), Vieira, Martinez C (Martinez A 67); Pujol (Sanchez Soto 87), Alaez.

Portugal (1) 4 *(Ronaldo 28 (pen), 85, William Carvalho 69, Bruno Alves 90)*
Latvia (0) 1 *(Zjuzins 68)* 20,744
Portugal: (4141) Rui Patricio; Joao Cancelo, Fonte, Bruno Alves, Guerreiro; William Carvalho; Nani (Quaresma 65), Joao Mario (Gelson Martins 71), Andre Gomes (Sanches 87), Ronaldo; Andre Silva.
Latvia: (442) Vanins; Freimanis, Jagodinskis, Gorkss, Maksimenko; Gabovs, Tarasovs, Laizans, Kluskins (Visnakovs A 79); Rudnevs (Gutkovskis 87), Ikaunieks D (Zjuzins 59).

Switzerland (1) 2 *(Derdiyok 27, Lichtsteiner 83)*
Faroe Islands (0) 0 14,800
Switzerland: (433) Sommer; Lichtsteiner, Schar, Djourou, Rodriguez; Behrami, Dzemaili (Steffen 80), Xhaka; Mehmedi, Derdiyok (Seferovic 87), Stocker (Fernandes E 69).
Faroe Islands: (433) Nielsen; Naes, Nattestad, Gregersen, Hansen; Henriksen Olsen, Benjaminsen (Faero 89), Hansson; Vatnhamar (Olsen A 81), Rolantsson (Joensen 78), Edmundsson.

Saturday, 25 March 2017
Andorra (0) 0
Faroe Islands (0) 0   1755
Andorra: (4411) Gomes; Jesus Rubio (Garcia M 45), Llovera, Lima, San Nicolas; Jordi Rubio (Clemente 77), Pujol (Martinez A 54), Vales, Martinez C; Vieira; Alaez.
Faroe Islands: (433) Nielsen; Naes, Davidsen V, Gregersen, Klettskard; Davidsen J, Bartalsstovu (Hansen 70), Hansson; Edmundsson■, Vatnhamar, Sorensen (Justinussen P 82).

Portugal (2) 3 *(Andre Silva 32, Ronaldo 36, 64)*
Hungary (0) 0   57,816
Portugal: (4132) Rui Patricio; Cedric, Pepe, Fonte, Guerreiro; William Carvalho, Joao Mario (Joao Moutinho 83), Andre Gomes (Pizzi 86), Quaresma; Andre Silva (Bernardo Silva 67), Ronaldo.
Hungary: (4141) Gulacsi; Lang (Lovrencsics 46), Vinicius, Kadar, Korhut; Nagy A; Bese, Gyurcso (Kalmar 69), Gera (Pinter 85), Dzsudzsak; Szalai.

Switzerland (0) 1 *(Drmic 66)*
Latvia (0) 0   25,000
Switzerland: (4231) Sommer; Lichtsteiner, Schar, Djourou, Moubandje; Fernandes G (Drmic 64), Xhaka; Shaqiri (Zuber 78), Dzemaili, Mehmedi; Seferovic (Freuler 83).
Latvia: (442) Vanins; Freimanis, Jagodinskis, Gorkss, Solovjovs; Visnakovs A (Gabovs 55), Lazdins (Gutkovskis 77), Laizans, Kluskins; Sabala, Ikaunieks D (Rakels 69).

Friday, 9 June 2017
Andorra (1) 1 *(Rebes 26)*
Hungary (0) 0   2407
Andorra: (4411) Gomes; Jesus Rubio, Llovera, Lima, San Nicolas; Clemente (Riera 82), Vales, Rebes, Martinez A; Pujol (Ayala 88); Alaez (Maneiro 67).
Hungary: (4411) Gulacsi; Bese, Lang (Balogh 56), Toth, Vinicius; Gyurcso (Sallai 71), Nagy A, Stieber (Nagy D 21), Dzsudzsak; Kleinheisler; Eppel.

Faroe Islands (0) 0
Switzerland (1) 2 *(Xhaka 36, Shaqiri 59)*   4594
Faroe Islands: (442) Nielsen; Naes, Davidsen V, Gregersen, Davidsen J (Faero 70); Hansson (Lokin 66), Benjaminsen, Olsen K (Joensen 60), Sorensen; Vatnhamar, Justinussen F.
Switzerland: (442) Sommer; Lichtsteiner, Moubandje, Seferovic (Derdiyok 78), Xhaka; Behrami, Akanji, Dzemaili (Freuler 85), Mehmedi (Zuber 61); Djourou, Shaqiri.

Latvia (0) 0
Portugal (1) 3 *(Ronaldo 42, 63, Andre Silva 67)*   8087
Latvia: (4411) Vanins; Jagodinskis, Kolesovs, Gorkss, Maksimenko; Kluskins (Indrans 62), Kazacoks (Vardanjans 72), Laizans, Solovjovs; Sabala; Ikaunieks D (Rakels 68).
Portugal: (433) Rui Patricio; Bruno Alves, Cedric (Nelson Semedo 74), Fonte, Guerreiro; Joao Moutinho, William Carvalho, Andre Gomes; Gelson Martins (Quaresma 58), Andre Silva (Nani 80), Ronaldo.

Thursday, 31 August 2017
Hungary (2) 3 *(Kadar 6, Szalai 27, Solovjovs 68 (og))*
Latvia (1) 1 *(Freimanis 40)*   16,500
Hungary: (4231) Gulacsi; Bese, Guzmics, Kadar, Korhut; Patkai, Nagy A, Varga (Lovrencsics 86), Stieber (Elek 73), Dzsudzsak; Szalai (Bode 65).
Latvia: (352) Vanins; Kolesovs, Gorkss, Maksimenko; Freimanis, Vardanjans, Solovjovs, Indrans, Kazacoks (Visnakovs A 72); Ikaunieks D (Rakels 72), Sabala (Gutkovskis 88).

Portugal (2) 5 *(Ronaldo 3, 29 (pen), 64, William Carvalho 58, Oliveira 84)*
Faroe Islands (1) 1 *(Baldvinsson 38)*   26,514
Portugal: (442) Rui Patricio; Cedric, Pepe, Fonte, Eliseu; Joao Mario (Quaresma 59), Joao Moutinho (Andre Gomes 72), William Carvalho, Bernardo Silva; Ronaldo, Andre Silva (Oliveira 80).
Faroe Islands: (4411) Nielsen; Naes, Davidsen V, Gregersen, Faero; Sorensen, Jakobsen, Baldvinsson, Vatnhamar (Bartalsstovu 66); Edmundsson (Johannesen 74); Joensen (Lokin 81).

Switzerland (1) 3 *(Seferovic 42, 63, Lichtsteiner 67)*
Andorra (0) 0   13,600
Switzerland: (442) Sommer; Lichtsteiner, Schar, Akanji, Rodriguez; Shaqiri, Freuler, Xhaka (Zakaria 66), Zuber (Derdiyok 46); Mehmedi (Fernandes E 74), Seferovic.
Andorra: (442) Gomes; Jordi Rubio, Lima, Llovera, Garcia M; Clemente (Garcia E 83), Rebes, Vieira, Martinez A (Sanchez 76); Pujol (Moreno 90), Alaez.

Sunday, 3 September 2017
Faroe Islands (1) 1 *(Sorensen 31)*
Andorra (0) 0   4357
Faroe Islands: (343) Nielsen; Faero, Gregersen, Baldvinsson; Naes, Benjaminsen, Joensen (Jakobsen 54), Davidsen V; Vatnhamar, Edmundsson (Olsen K 85), Sorensen (Bartalsstovu 90).
Andorra: (442) Gomes; Jordi Rubio (Sanchez 69), Lima, Llovera, Jesus Rubio; Garcia E (Gomez 76), Rebes, Vieira, San Nicolas; Pujol, Martinez (Riera 88).

Hungary (0) 0
Portugal (0) 1 *(Andre Silva 48)*   21,800
Hungary: (442) Gulacsi; Fiola, Guzmics, Kadar, Korhut; Lovrencsics (Varga 77), Patkai, Elek (Pinter 67), Dzsudzsak; Priskin■, Eppel (Bode 61).
Portugal: (442) Rui Patricio; Cedric, Bruno Alves, Pepe, Fabio Coentrao (Eliseu 27); Gelson Martins (Bernardo Silva 63), Danilo Pereira, Joao Mario, Joao Moutinho; Ronaldo, Andre Silva (Quaresma 85).

Latvia (0) 0
Switzerland (1) 3 *(Seferovic 10, Dzemaili 54, Rodriguez 58 (pen))*   7587
Latvia: (532) Vanins; Solovjovs, Kolesovs, Gorkss, Dubra, Maksimenko; Vardanjans (Kazacoks 78), Laizans, Indrans (Kluskins 61); Sabala, Rakels (Ikaunieks D 68).
Switzerland: (433) Sommer; Lichtsteiner (Lang 80), Schar, Djourou, Rodriguez; Behrami, Dzemaili, Xhaka (Zakaria 76); Shaqiri, Seferovic (Derdiyok 75), Mehmedi.

Saturday, 7 October 2017
Andorra (0) 0
Portugal (0) 2 *(Ronaldo 63, Andre Silva 86)*   3193
Andorra: (442) Gomes; Jesus Rubio, Lima, Llovera, San Nicolas; Rodriguez (Sanchez Soto 87), Rebes, Vales, Clemente (Martinez A 78); Vieira (Moreno 90), Alaez.
Portugal: (442) Rui Patricio; Nelson Semedo, Pepe, Luis Neto, Eliseu; Gelson Martins (Ronaldo 46), Danilo Pereira, Joao Mario, Quaresma (William Carvalho 79); Andre Silva (Goncalo Guedes 90), Bernardo Silva.

Faroe Islands (0) 0
Latvia (0) 0   4203
Faroe Islands: (4231) Nielsen; Naes, Nattestad, Gregersen, Davidsen V; Benjaminsen, Hansson (Joensen 65); Vatnhamar (Bartalsstovu 87), Jakobsen (Johannesen 77), Sorensen; Edmundsson.
Latvia: (532) Vanins; Freimanis, Tarasovs, Gorkss, Kolesovs, Maksimenko; Kazacoks (Visnakovs A 66), Laizans, Kluskins; Sabala (Visnakovs E 83), Ikaunieks D (Uldrikis 74).

Switzerland (3) 5 *(Xhaka 18, Frei 20, Zuber 43, 49, Lichtsteiner 83)*
Hungary (0) 2 *(Guzmics 58, Ugrai 88)*   32,018
Switzerland: (4411) Sommer; Lichtsteiner, Schar, Djourou, Moubandje; Shaqiri, Freuler (Derdiyok 85), Xhaka, Zuber; Frei (Zakaria 73); Seferovic (Embolo 63).
Hungary: (4411) Gulacsi; Bese (Lang 32), Guzmics, Kadar, Korhut; Varga (Sallai 69), Nagy A, Elek (Markvart 56), Lovrencsics; Patkai; Ugrai.

Tuesday, 10 October 2017
Hungary (0) 1 *(Bode 81)*
Faroe Islands (0) 0   21,400
Hungary: (442) Gulacsi; Fiola, Guzmics, Kadar, Szabo; Stieber (Nagy D 65), Patkai, Nagy A, Dzsudzsak; Ugrai (Sallai 89), Eppel (Bode 46).

Faroe Islands: (442) Nielsen; Jonsson, Baldvinsson, Gregersen, Naes; Vatnhamar, Sorensen (Bartalsstovu 72), Benjaminsen (Hansson 65), Edmundsson; Joensen, Faero (Olsen K 88).

Latvia (2) 4 *(Ikaunieks D 11, Sabala 19, 59, Tarasovs 63)*
Andorra (0) 0 4153

Latvia: (334) Vanins; Kolesovs, Dubra, Tarasovs; Gabovs (Visnakovs A 65), Indrans, Solovjovs; Kluskins (Ulimbasevs 81), Torres, Ikaunieks D (Uldrikis 71), Sabala.
Andorra: (442) Gomes; Jesus Rubio, Lima, Llovera, Garcia M; Clemente (Martinez A 64), Rebes, Garcia E, Vieira (Riera 87); Pujol, Alaez (Sanchez Soto 82).

Portugal (1) 2 *(Djourou 42 (og), Andre Silva 57)*
Switzerland (0) 0 61,566

Portugal: (442) Rui Patricio; Cedric, Pepe, Fonte, Eliseu (Antunes 68); Joao Mario (Danilo Pereira 90), Joao Moutinho, William Carvalho, Bernardo Silva; Andre Silva (Andre Gomes 75), Ronaldo.
Switzerland: (433) Sommer; Lichtsteiner, Schar, Djourou, Rodriguez; Shaqiri, Freuler (Zakaria 45), Dzemaili (Zuber 67); Xhaka, Mehmedi (Embolo 67), Seferovic.

Group B Table	P	W	D	L	F	A	GD	Pts
Portugal	10	9	0	1	32	4	28	27
Switzerland	10	9	0	1	23	7	16	27
Hungary	10	4	1	5	14	14	0	13
Faroe Islands	10	2	3	5	4	16	–12	9
Latvia	10	2	1	7	7	18	–11	7
Andorra	10	1	1	8	2	23	–21	4

GROUP C

Sunday, 4 September 2016
Czech Republic (0) 0
Northern Ireland (0) 0 10,731

Czech Republic: (442) Vaclik; Kaderabek, Suchy, Kadlec M, Novak; Skalak (Kopic 77), Pavelka, Darida, Krejci; Skoda (Necid 68), Kadlec V (Vydra 83).
Northern Ireland: (433) McGovern; McLaughlin C, Evans J, McAuley, Ferguson; Norwood (Hodson 66), Davis, Dallas; Ward (McGinn 74), Lafferty K (Magennis 59), McNair.

Norway (0) 0
Germany (2) 3 *(Muller 16, 60, Kimmich 45)* 26,793

Norway: (442) Jarstein; Svensson, Hovland, Nordtveit, Aleesami; Diomande, Johansen (Jenssen 67), Tettey, Berisha; King (Sorloth 72), Henriksen (Selnaes 61).
Germany: (343) Neuer; Kimmich, Howedes, Hummels; Muller, Khedira (Weigl 84), Kroos, Hector; Ozil, Gotze (Brandt 73), Draxler (Meyer 84).

San Marino (0) 0
Azerbaijan (1) 1 *(Gurbanov 45)* 886

San Marino: (541) Simoncini A; Cesarini, Brolli■, Simoncini D, Vitaioli M (Valentini 85), Hirsch J; Palazzi, Tosi, Berardi M, Berardi F (Rinaldi 73); Chiaruzzi (Gasperoni L 53).
Azerbaijan: (4141) Agayev K; Garayev, Mirzabekov, Medvedev, Gurbanov (Alasgarov 69); Nazarov (Makhmudov 78); Rashad Sadygov, Ramazanov (Sheydayev 89), Amirguliev, Dashdemirov; Ismayilov.

Saturday, 8 October 2016
Azerbaijan (1) 1 *(Medvedev 11)*
Norway (0) 0 35,000

Azerbaijan: (433) Agayev K; Mirzabekov, Medvedev, Rashad Sadygov, Dashdemirov; Eddy (Alasgarov 65), Garayev, Amirguliev; Gurbanov (Sheydayev 80), Ramazanov (Guseynov 90), Nazarov.
Norway: (442) Jarstein; Svensson, Strandberg, Hovland, Aleesami; Helland (Berget 71), Skjelbred (Johansen 84), Selnaes, Diomande; King (Sorloth 61), Henriksen.

Germany (1) 3 *(Muller 13, 65, Kroos 49)*
Czech Republic (0) 0 53,000

Germany: (4231) Neuer; Kimmich, Boateng, Hummels, Hector (Howedes 67); Khedira, Kroos (Gundogan 75); Muller, Ozil, Draxler (Brandt 80); Gotze.

Northern Ireland (1) 4 *(Davis 26 (pen), Lafferty K 79, 90, Ward 85)*
San Marino (0) 0 18,234

Northern Ireland: (4411) McGovern; McLaughlin C (McNair 77), Evans J, McAuley, Ferguson; McGinn, Davis, Norwood, Dallas (Washington 65); Ward; Magennis (Lafferty K 72).
San Marino: (541) Simoncini A; Berardi M, Vitaioli F, Simoncini D, Della Valle, Palazzi■; Hirsch A (Cesarini 55), Tosi, Coppini (Golinucci E 70), Vitaioli M; Stefanelli (Zafferani 87).

Tuesday, 11 October 2016
Czech Republic (0) 0
Azerbaijan (0) 0 12,148

Czech Republic: (442) Vaclik; Gebre Selassie, Brabec, Sivok, Sykora; Skalak (Zmrhal 74), Droppa, Dockal, Krejci (Petrzela 63); Schick (Skoda 66), Kadlec V.
Azerbaijan: (4141) Agayev K; Mirzabekov, Medvedev, Guseynov, Dashdemirov; Garayev; Alasgarov (Ramazanov 70), Amirguliev, Nazarov, Gurbanov (Abdullayev 87); Sheydayev (Eddy 90).

Germany (2) 2 *(Draxler 13, Khedira 17)*
Northern Ireland (0) 0 42,132

Germany: (4231) Neuer; Kimmich, Boateng (Mustafi 69), Hummels, Hector (Volland 80); Khedira, Kroos, Muller, Ozil (Gundogan 45), Draxler; Gotze.
Northern Ireland: (532) McGovern; Hodson, Hughes, McAuley, Evans J, Ferguson; Evans C, Davis, Norwood (McNair 72); Ward (McGinn 60), Magennis (Lafferty K 76).

Norway (1) 4 *(Simoncini D 11 (og), Diomande 77, Samuelsen 81, King 83)*
San Marino (0) 1 *(Stefanelli 54)* 8298

Norway: (442) Jarstein; Svensson, Strandberg, Hovland, Aleesami; Skjelbred, Selnaes, Tettey (Samuelsen 67), Berget (Sorloth 73); Henriksen (Diomande 45); King.
San Marino: (532) Simoncini A; Brolli, Vitaioli F, Simoncini D, Della Valle, Rinaldi (Berardi M 45); Valentini (Hirsch J 67), Tosi, Mazza; Zafferani, Stefanelli (Selva 82).

Friday, 11 November 2016
Czech Republic (1) 2 *(Krmencik 11, Zmrhal 47)*
Norway (0) 1 *(King 87)* 16,411

Czech Republic: (4141) Vaclik; Kaderabek, Sivok, Brabec, Novak; Droppa (Pavelka 81); Krejci (Skalak 86), Dockal, Horava, Zmrhal; Krmencik (Schick 81).
Norway: (442) Jarstein; Elabdellaoui, Hovland, Forren, Aleesami; Skjelbred (Daehli 50), Tettey, Johansen, Berget (Elyounoussi T 71); Henriksen (Diomande 60), King.

Northern Ireland (2) 4 *(Lafferty K 27, McAuley 40, McLaughlin C 67, Brunt 83)*
Azerbaijan (0) 0 18,404

Northern Ireland: (442) McGovern; McLaughlin C, McAuley, Evans J, Brunt; Evans C (McNair 81), Norwood, Davis, Ferguson (McGinn 73); Lafferty K (Grigg 61), Magennis.
Azerbaijan: (451) Agayev K; Mirzabekov, Medvedev, Guseynov, Dashdemirov; Ismayilov, Makhmudov (Nazarov 70), Garayev, Amirguliev, Qurbanov (Ramazanov 75); Sheydayev (Yilmaz 45).

San Marino (0) 0
Germany (3) 8 *(Khedira 7, Gnabry 9, 58, 76, Hector 32, 65, Stefanelli 82 (og), Volland 85)* 3851

San Marino: (541) Simoncini A; Palazzi, Cesarini, Simoncini D, Vitaioli F, Berardi M; Zafferani (Brolli 83), Gasperoni A, Tosi (Domeniconi 59), Vitaioli M (Hirsch A 90); Stefanelli.
Germany: (4231) ter Stegen; Henrichs, Kimmich, Hummels, Hector; Khedira (Goretzka 77), Gundogan; Muller, Gnabry, Gotze (Meyer 71); Gomez (Volland 71).

Sunday, 26 March 2017

Azerbaijan (1) 1 *(Nazarov 31)*

Germany (3) 4 *(Schurrle 19, 80, Muller 36, Gomez 45)*
               30,000

Azerbaijan: (4231) Agayev K; Pashaev, Guseynov, Rashad Sadygov, Mirzabekov; Garayev, Amirguliev (Eddy 87); Ismayilov (Qurbanov 82), Huseynov, Nazarov; Sheydayev (Yilmaz 67).
Germany: (4231) Leno; Kimmich, Hummels, Howedes, Hector; Khedira, Kroos (Rudy 89); Schurrle, Muller, Draxler (Sane 85); Gomez (Ozil 61).

Northern Ireland (2) 2 *(Ward 2, Washington 32)*

Norway (0) 0   18,161

Northern Ireland: (4231) McGovern; McLaughlin C, Evans J, McAuley, Cathcart; Davis, Norwood; Ward (McGinn 80), Brunt, Dallas (Lund 88); Washington (Lafferty K 85).
Norway: (4231) Jarstein; Skjelvik, Elabdellaoui, Valsvik, Hovland; Johansen (Berge 74), Nordtveit; Elyounoussi M, King, Elyounoussi T (Daehli 53); Soderlund (Diomande 63).

San Marino (0) 0

Czech Republic (5) 6 *(Barak 17, 24, Darida 19, 77 (pen), Gebre Selassie 25, Krmencik 43)*   1000

San Marino: (541) Simoncini A; Palazzi, Cesarini, Simoncini D, Vitaioli F, Rinaldi (Tommassini 61); Vitaioli M, Domeniconi, Zafferani, Cervellini (Battistini 90); Stefanelli (Mazza 84).
Czech Republic: (4231) Vaclik; Gebre Selassie, Sivok, Brabec, Novak; Darida, Dockal; Jankto (Zmrhal 67), Krejci, Barak (Horava 75); Krmencik (Skoda 67).

Saturday, 10 June 2017

Azerbaijan (0) 0

Northern Ireland (0) 1 *(Dallas 90)*   27,978

Azerbaijan: (433) Agayev K; Medvedev, Guseynov, Rashad Sadygov, Pashaev; Huseynov, Garayev, Almeida; Ismayilov (Amirguliev 84), Sheydayev (Abdullayev 90), Nazarov (Aleskerov 76).
Northern Ireland: (532) McGovern; McLaughlin C, Hughes, McAuley (McGinn 25 (Hodson 86)), Evans J, Dallas; Brunt, Norwood, Davis; Boyce (Lafferty K 77), Magennis.

Germany (4) 7 *(Draxler 11, Wagner 16, 29, 85, Younes 39, Mustafi 47, Brandt 72)*

San Marino (0) 0   32,467

Germany: (3142) ter Stegen; Kimmich, Mustafi, Hector (Plattenhardt 55); Can; Brandt, Goretzka, Draxler (Demme 75), Younes; Wagner, Stindl (Werner 55).
San Marino: (4141) Benedettini; Bonini, Della Valle, Biordi, Cesarini (Brolli 87); Cervellini; Golinucci A, Mazza (Bernardi 69), Zafferani, Palazzi; Rinaldi (Hirsch A 78).

Norway (0) 1 *(Soderlund 56 (pen))*

Czech Republic (1) 1 *(Gebre Selassie 36)* 12,179

Norway: (442) Jarstein; Svensson, Nordtveit, Reginiussen (Valsvik 33), Aleesami; Elyounoussi M, Berge, Johansen, Berget (Daehli 61); Elyounoussi T, Soderlund (Johnsen 71).
Czech Republic: (4411) Vaclik; Kaderabek, Sivok, Brabec, Gebre Selassie; Krejci, Darida (Horava 80), Soucek, Zmrhal (Jankto 43); Dockal; Krmencik (Schick 63).

Friday, 1 September 2017

Czech Republic (0) 1 *(Darida 78)*

Germany (1) 2 *(Werner 4, Hummels 88)* 18,093

Czech Republic: (541) Vaclik; Gebre Selassie, Kalas, Suchy, Novak, Boril; Kopic (Krejci 53), Soucek, Darida, Krmencik (Kliment 76); Jankto (Zmrhal 89).
Germany: (4231) ter Stegen; Kimmich, Hummels, Ginter, Hector; Kroos, Stindl (Draxler 67); Muller, Ozil, Brandt (Rudiger 60); Werner (Can 79).

Norway (1) 2 *(King 33 (pen), Sadygov 61 (og))*

Azerbaijan (0) 0   8599

Norway: (442) Jarstein; Svensson (Elabdellaoui 90), Nordtveit, Skjelvik, Aleesami; Elyounoussi M, Berge, Johansen, Daehli (Berget 82); King, Sorloth (Elyounoussi T 74).

Azerbaijan: (451) Agayev K; Medvedev, Rashad Sadygov, Guseynov, Pashaev; Aleskerov, Huseynov■, Garayev (Amirguliev 81), Almeida, Nazarov (Ismailov 66); Madatov (Sheydayev 64).

San Marino (0) 0

Northern Ireland (0) 3 *(Magennis 70, 75, Davis 79 (pen))*
               2544

San Marino: (541) Simoncini A; Bonini, Biordi (Vitaioli F 66), Simoncini D (Gasperoni A 76), Palazzi, Grandoni; Cervellini, Battistini, Berardi F (Golinucci A 80), Rinaldi; Bernardi.
Northern Ireland: (442) McGovern; McLaughlin C, Hughes, Evans J, Brunt; Norwood, Davis, Magennis, Dallas (McGinn 78); Washington (Evans C 78), Lafferty K (Ferguson 61).

Monday, 4 September 2017

Azerbaijan (2) 5 *(Ismailov 20, 56, Abdullayev 24, Cevoli (og), Sadygov 80)*

San Marino (0) 1 *(Palazzi 73)*   8000

Azerbaijan: (433) Agayev S; Mirzabekov, Rashad Sadygov, Guliyev, Khalilzadze; Huseynov (Garayev 68), Amirguliev, Almeida; Ismailov (Ramazanov 61), Sheydayev, Abdullayev (Dadashov 71).
San Marino: (532) Simoncini A; Cesarini, Della Valle, Cevoli, Palazzi, Grandoni; Gasperoni A (Hirsch A 76), Cervellini (Tosi 27), Golinucci A; Tommassini, Rinaldi (Stefanelli 85).

Germany (4) 6 *(Ozil 10, Draxler 17, Werner 21, 40, Goretzka 50, Gomez 79)*

Norway (0) 0   53,814

Germany: (451) ter Stegen; Kimmich, Rudiger, Hummels, Hector; Rudy (Khedira 60), Muller (Goretzka 45), Kroos, Ozil, Draxler; Werner (Gomez 65).
Norway: (442) Jarstein; Elabdellaoui, Nordtveit, Skjelvik, Aleesami; Elyounoussi M (Svensson 57), Berge (Valsvik 46), Selnaes (Linnes 75), Daehli; King, Berget.

Northern Ireland (2) 2 *(Evans J 28, Brunt 41)*

Czech Republic (0) 0   18,167

Northern Ireland: (433) McGovern; McLaughlin C, Hughes, Evans J, Brunt; Magennis (Ferguson 83), Evans C, Dallas (Lafferty K 74); Davis, Washington (Hodson 58), Norwood.
Czech Republic: (343) Vaclik; Suchy, Kalas, Novak (Dockal 66); Gebre Selassie, Darida, Soucek, Boril; Jankto (Husbauer 55), Krmencik, Krejci (Kliment 55).

Thursday, 5 October 2017

Azerbaijan (0) 1 *(Ismailov 55 (pen))*

Czech Republic (1) 2 *(Kopic 35, Barak 66)* 16,200

Azerbaijan: (451) Agayev K; Mirzabekov, Guseynov, Rashad Sadygov, Pashaev; Ismailov, Huseynov (Madatov 79), Amirguliev, Almeida, Nazarov (Garayev 67); Gurbanov (Sheydayev 62).
Czech Republic: (4231) Pavlenka; Kaderabek, Brabec, Suchy, Boril; Darida (Soucek 77), Husbauer; Kopic, Barak, Jankto; Krmencik (Kliment 88).

Northern Ireland (0) 1 *(Magennis 90)*

Germany (2) 3 *(Rudy 2, Wagner 21, Kimmich 86)* 18,104

Northern Ireland: (532) McGovern; Evans J, McLaughlin C, McAuley, Hodson (Dallas 46), Brunt; Norwood, Davis, Evans C (Saville 80); Lafferty K (Washington 69), Magennis.
Germany: (4231) ter Stegen; Kimmich, Boateng, Hummels, Plattenhardt; Rudy, Kroos; Goretzka (Can 66), Muller (Stindl 83), Draxler (Sane 72); Wagner.

San Marino (0) 0

Norway (4) 8 *(Henriksen 8, King 14 (pen), 17, Elyounoussi M 40, 47, 68, Selnaes 58, Linnes 86)* 1922

San Marino: (541) Simoncini A; Brolli, Simoncini D, Cevoli, Grandoni; Berardi F (Bonini 69), Gasperoni A, Cervellini (Rinaldi 79), Battistini, Palazzi; Berardi F (Tomassini 89).
Norway: (442) Jarstein; Svensson, Nordtveit, Valsvik, Meling; Elyounoussi M (Elyounoussi T 70), Berge (Selnaes 45), Henriksen, King (Soderlund 61); Sorloth, Linnes.

Sunday, 8 October 2017
Czech Republic (3) 5 *(Krmencik 8, 23, Kopic 27, Novak 71, Kadlec V 83)*
San Marino (0) 0 5625
Czech Republic: (4411) Koubek; Kaderabek, Kalas, Luftner, Novak; Kopic (Sykora 62), Dockal, Darida, Jankto; Barak (Kadlec V 70); Krmencik (Kliment 63).
San Marino: (532) Simoncini A; Brolli, Vitaioli F (Berardi M 81), Della Valle, Palazzi, Grandoni; Battistini, Tosi, Rinaldi; Berardi F (Berretti 76), Bernardi (Bonini 64).

Germany (1) 5 *(Goretzka 8, 67, Wagner 54, Rudiger 64, Can 81)*
Azerbaijan (1) 1 *(Sheydayev 34)* 34,613
Germany: (334) Leno; Kimmich, Mustafi (Ginter 36), Sule (Rudiger 22); Brandt, Can, Sane; Goretzka, Muller (Younes 69), Stindl, Wagner.
Azerbaijan: (4141) Agayev K; Mirzabekov, Guseynov, Abishov, Khalilzadze; Garayev; Ismailov (Gurbanov 77), Amirguliev, Almeida, Huseynov (Nazarov 69); Sheydayev (Aleskerov 87).

Norway (0) 1 *(Brunt 71 (og))*
Northern Ireland (0) 0 10,244
Norway: (442) Nyland; Svensson, Reginiussen, Nordtveit, Meling; Elyounoussi M (Elyounoussi T 72), Henriksen (Selnaes 83), Berge, Johansen (Linnes 87); Soderlund, Sorloth.
Northern Ireland: (433) McGovern; McLaughlin C, McAuley, Evans J, Brunt; Davis, Evans C (Ferguson 79), Norwood (Saville 46); Magennis, Washington (Lafferty K 69), Dallas.

Group C Table	P	W	D	L	F	A	GD	Pts
Germany	10	10	0	0	43	4	39	30
Northern Ireland	10	6	1	3	17	6	11	19
Czech Republic	10	4	3	3	17	10	7	15
Norway	10	4	1	5	17	16	1	13
Azerbaijan	10	3	1	6	10	19	–9	10
San Marino	10	0	0	10	2	51	–49	0

GROUP D

Monday, 5 September 2016
Georgia (0) 1 *(Ananidze 78)*
Austria (2) 2 *(Hinteregger 16, Janko 42)* 28,500
Georgia: (4312) Loria; Lobjanidze (Chanturia 84), Kvirkvelia, Amisulashvili (Okriashvili 76), Navalovski; Kashia, Daushvili, Jigauri; Ananidze; Qazaishvili, Dvalishvili (Skhirtladze 63).
Austria: (4411) Almer; Klein, Dragovic, Hinteregger, Suttner; Harnik (Sabitzer 71), Baumgartlinger, Alaba, Arnautovic; Junuzovic (Schopf 67); Janko (Gregoritsch 76).

Serbia (0) 2 *(Kostic 62, Tadic 69 (pen))*
Republic of Ireland (1) 2 *(Hendrick 3, Murphy 81)* 7896
Serbia: (343) Rajkovic; Ivanovic, Nastasic, Vukovic; Rukavina, Milivojevic, Gudelj, Mladenovic (Tosic D 76); Tadic, Mitrovic A (Pavlovic 59), Kostic (Katai 82).
Republic of Ireland: (433) Randolph; Coleman, O'Shea, Keogh, Ward (Quinn 71); Hendrick (Murphy 75), Whelan, Brady; Walters, Long S (Clark 90), McClean.

Wales (2) 4 *(Vokes 38, Allen 44, Bale 51, 90 (pen))*
Moldova (0) 0 31,731
Wales: (532) Hennessey; Gunter, Chester, Williams A (Collins 82), Davies, Taylor; Ledley (Huws 67), Allen, King; Vokes (Robson-Kanu 75), Bale.
Moldova: (532) Cebanu; Cojocari, Cascaval, Epureanu, Armas, Jardan; Gatcan, Cebotaru (Sidorenco 75), Ionita; Ginsari (Bugaev 75), Dedov (Mihaliov 84).

Thursday, 6 October 2016
Austria (1) 2 *(Arnautovic 28, 48)*
Wales (2) 2 *(Allen 22, Wimmer 45 (og))* 44,200
Austria: (4411) Almer (Ozcan 58); Klein, Dragovic, Hinteregger, Wimmer; Sabitzer, Baumgartlinger, Alaba, Arnautovic (Schaub 87); Junuzovic (Schopf 79); Janko.
Wales: (532) Hennessey; Gunter, Chester, Davies, Williams A, Taylor (Huws 90); Ledley, Allen (Edwards 56), King; Bale, Vokes (Robson-Kanu 77).

Moldova (0) 0
Serbia (2) 3 *(Kostic 20, Ivanovic 38, Tadic 59)* 8500
Moldova: (4231) Cebanu; Racu, Carp, Epureanu, Bolohan; Cojocari, Gatcan; Andronic (Mihaliov 68), Cebotaru (Ginsari 77), Dedov (Sidorenco 63); Bugaev.
Serbia: (3421) Stojkovic; Nastasic, Ivanovic, Vukovic (Mitrovic S 70); Rukavina, Gudelj, Milivojevic, Kolarov; Kostic (Tosic Z 71), Tadic; Pavlovic (Katai 45).

Republic of Ireland (0) 1 *(Coleman 56)*
Georgia (0) 0 39,793
Republic of Ireland: (433) Randolph; Coleman, Duffy, Clark, Ward; McCarthy, Hendrick, Brady (Whelan 81); Walters, Long S (O'Shea 90), McClean.
Georgia: (433) Loria; Kakabadze, Kvirkvelia, Kashia, Navalovski (Kobakhidze 89); Daushvili (Kacharava 90), Qazaishvili, Gvilia; Okriashvili, Mchedlidze, Ananidze (Skhirtladze 74).

Sunday, 9 October 2016
Moldova (1) 1 *(Bugaev 45)*
Republic of Ireland (1) 3 *(Long S 2, McClean 69, 76)* 6089
Moldova: (4231) Calancea; Bordiyan, Posmac, Armas (Golovatenco 36), Bolohan; Gatcan, Cojocari; Andronic (Sidorenco 83), Zasavitchi (Cebotaru 61), Dedov; Bugaev.
Republic of Ireland: (4231) Randolph; Coleman, Duffy, Clark, Ward; Whelan, McCarthy (Meyler 80); Walters, Hoolahan (O'Kane 86), McClean; Long S (O'Dowda 62).

Serbia (2) 3 *(Mitrovic A 5, 23, Tadic 74)*
Austria (1) 2 *(Sabitzer 15, Janko 62)* 29,000
Serbia: (3412) Stojkovic; Ivanovic, Mitrovic S, Nastasic; Rukavina (Maksimovic 90), Milivojevic, Fejsa, Kolarov; Tadic; Mitrovic A (Gudelj 77), Kostic (Katai 65).
Austria: (4231) Ozcan; Klein, Dragovic (Prodl 71), Hinteregger, Wimmer; Baumgartlinger (Ilsanker 58), Alaba; Sabitzer, Junuzovic (Schopf 64), Arnautovic; Janko.

Wales (1) 1 *(Bale 10)*
Georgia (0) 1 *(Okriashvili 57)* 32,652
Wales: (532) Hennessey; Gunter, Chester, Williams A, Davies, Taylor (Cotterill 69); Edwards, Ledley (Huws 73), King (Robson-Kanu 61); Vokes, Bale.
Georgia: (4411) Loria; Kakabadze, Kvirkvelia, Kashia, Navalovski; Ananidze (Kacharava 90), Daushvili, Gvilia, Okriashvili (Jigauri 90); Qazaishvili; Mchedlidze (Dvalishvili 75).

Saturday, 12 November 2016
Austria (0) 0
Republic of Ireland (0) 1 *(McClean 48)* 48,500
Austria: (4231) Ozcan; Klein, Dragovic, Hinteregger, Wimmer (Ilsanker 78); Sabitzer (Harnik 73), Baumgartlinger; Alaba, Schopf (Schaub 57), Arnautovic; Janko.
Republic of Ireland: (4231) Randolph; Coleman, Duffy, Clark, Brady; Whelan (Meyler 24), Arter; Hendrick, Hoolahan (McGoldrick 78), McClean (McGeady 85); Walters.

Georgia (1) 1 *(Qazaishvili 16)*
Moldova (0) 1 *(Gatcan 78)* 40,642
Georgia: (4231) Loria; Kakabadze, Kvirkvelia, Kashia, Navalovski; Gvilia (Dvalishvili 71), Daushvili; Chanturia, Qazaishvili (Skhirtladze 80), Okriashvili; Kvilitaia (Kankava 64).
Moldova: (4231) Cebanu; Racu (Golovatenco 42), Posmac, Epureanu, Bolohan; Bordiyan, Gatcan; Jardan, Mihaliov (Andronic 77), Sidorenco (Antoniuc 70); Bugaev.

Wales (1) 1 *(Bale 30)*
Serbia (0) 1 *(Mitrovic A 86)* 32,879
Wales: (442) Hennessey; Gunter, Chester, Williams A, Taylor; Allen, Ledley (Edwards 83), Bale, Ramsey; Vokes, Robson-Kanu (Lawrence 68).
Serbia: (541) Stojkovic; Rukavina, Ivanovic, Maksimovic, Nastasic, Obradovic; Kostic (Katai 70), Matic, Milivojevic, Tadic; Mitrovic A (Gudelj 88).

Friday, 24 March 2017
Austria (0) 2 *(Sabitzer 75, Harnik 90)*
Moldova (0) 0   21,000
Austria: (3421) Lindner; Dragovic, Prodl, Hinteregger; Lazaro (Janko 69), Junuzovic, Ilsanker, Alaba; Arnautovic (Suttner 90), Sabitzer; Burgstaller (Harnik 82).
Moldova: (442) Namasco; Golovatenco, Posmac, Epureanu, Bolohan (Mihaliov 90); Dedov, Cebotaru, Gatcan, Antoniuc (Ionita 62); Ginsari (Racu 81), Bugaev.

Georgia (1) 1 *(Kacharava 5)*
Serbia (1) 3 *(Tadic 45 (pen), Mitrovic A 64, Gacinovic 86)*
                                    31,328
Georgia: (451) Loria; Kakabadze (Arabidze 70), Kashia, Kvirkvelia, Navalovski; Qazaishvili (Kvilitaia 83), Gvilia (Jigauri 90), Kvekveskiri, Kankava, Ananidze; Kacharava.
Serbia: (343) Stojkovic; Ivanovic, Maksimovic, Kolarov; Rukavina, Milivojevic, Matic, Obradovic (Vukovic 45); Kostic (Gacinovic 81), Tadic, Mitrovic A (Gudelj 71).

Republic of Ireland (0) 0
Wales (0) 0   49,989
Republic of Ireland: (4141) Randolph; Coleman (Christie 72), Keogh, O'Shea, Ward; Walters; Whelan, Hendrick, McClean, Long S; Meyler (McGeady 80).
Wales: (532) Hennessey; Gunter, Chester, Williams A; Davies, Taylor■; Ledley (Richards 72), Ramsey, Allen; Bale, Robson-Kanu (Vokes 45).

Sunday, 11 June 2017
Moldova (2) 2 *(Ginsari 15, Dedov 36)*
Georgia (0) 2 *(Merebashvili 65, Kazaishvili 70)*   4803
Moldova: (4231) Namasco; Tigirlas (Racu 77), Posmac, Epureanu, Bordian; Cebotaru, Carp (Cojocari 72); Antoniuc, Cociuc (Bugaev 73), Dedov; Ginsari.
Georgia: (343) Makaridze; Kvirkvelia, Kashia, Tabidze; Lobjanidze (Kvekveskiri 35), Kankava, Daushvili (Kazaishvili 45), Navalovski; Arabidze, Kacharava, Dvalishvili (Merebashvili 64).

Republic of Ireland (0) 1 *(Walters 85)*
Austria (1) 1 *(Hinteregger 31)*   50,000
Republic of Ireland: (4231) Randolph; Christie, Duffy, Long K, Ward (Murphy 55); Arter (Hoolahan 71), Whelan (McGeady 77); Brady, Hendrick, McClean; Walters.
Austria: (4321) Lindner; Lainer, Dragovic, Prodl, Hinteregger; Baumgartlinger, Junuzovic (Grillitsch 79), Alaba; Lazaro, Kainz (Gregoritsch 90); Burgstaller (Harnik 75).

Serbia (0) 1 *(Mitrovic A 73)*
Wales (1) 1 *(Ramsey 35 (pen))*   42,100
Serbia: (343) Stojkovic; Ivanovic, Nastasic, Vukovic; Rukavina, Milivojevic (Gudelj 63), Matic, Kolarov; Kostic (Prijovic 67), Mitrovic A, Tadic.
Wales: (352) Hennessey; Gunter, Chester, Williams A; Davies, Richards, Allen, Edwards (Huws 73), Ledley; Ramsey, Vokes (Lawrence 85).

Saturday, 2 September 2017
Georgia (1) 1 *(Qazaishvili 34)*
Republic of Ireland (1) 1 *(Duffy 4)*   19,669
Georgia: (442) Makaridze; Kashia, Kakabadze, Navalovski, Kvekveskiri; Ananidze, Kvirkvelia, Qazaishvili (Khocholava 90), Gvilia; Jigauri (Chanturia 75), Kvilitaia (Merebashvili 85).
Republic of Ireland: (442) Randolph; Ward, Clark, Duffy, Christie; Whelan (Murphy 79), Brady, McClean, Arter (McGeady 61); Walters, Long S.

Serbia (2) 3 *(Gacinovic 21, Kolarov 29, Mitrovic A 80)*
Moldova (0) 0   9974
Serbia: (4231) Rajkovic; Kolarov, Maksimovic, Ivanovic, Nastasic; Gudelj, Gacinovic, Kostic, Tadic (Ljajic 65), Matic (Radoja 76); Mitrovic A (Prijovic 81).
Moldova: (442) Gaman; Armas, Posmac, Epureanu, Ionita; Cociuc (Antoniuc 59), Cebotaru, Dedov, Cojocari (Carp 75); Anton, Ginsari.

Wales (0) 1 *(Woodburn 74)*
Austria (0) 0   32,633
Wales: (3421) Hennessey; Gunter, Williams A, Chester; Richards (King 45), Ramsey, Edwards, Davies; Lawrence (Robson-Kanu 69), Bale; Vokes (Woodburn 70).
Austria: (4411) Lindner; Lainer, Dragovic, Prodl (Danso 27), Hinteregger; Arnautovic, Baumgartlinger, Alaba, Ilsanker; Sabitzer; Harnik (Janko 81).

Tuesday, 5 September 2017
Austria (1) 1 *(Schaub 43)*
Georgia (1) 1 *(Gvilia 8)*   13,400
Austria: (442) Lindner; Dragovic, Hinteregger, Arnautovic, Alaba (Schaub 38); Harnik (Janko 68), Bauer, Baumgartlinger, Grillitsch (Ilsanker 80); Kainz, Danso.
Georgia: (451) Makaridze; Kashia, Kvirkvelia, Kankava, Qazaishvili (Khocholava 90); Ananidze, Kvilitaia (Dvalishvili 88), Gvilia (Merebashvili 68), Kvekveskiri, Kakabadze; Navalovski.

Moldova (0) 0
Wales (0) 2 *(Robson-Kanu 80, Ramsey 90)*   10,272
Moldova: (4411) Cebanu; Bordian, Posmac, Epureanu, Rozgoniuc; Graur (Ambros 85), Ionita (Bugaev 84), Anton, Dedov; Pascenco (Cojocari 70); Ginsari.
Wales: (442) Hennessey; Gunter, Chester, Williams A, Davies; Allen, Ramsey, King (Vokes 67), Lawrence (Woodburn 60); Bale, Robson-Kanu (Edwards 88).

Republic of Ireland (0) 0
Serbia (0) 1 *(Kolarov 55)*   50,153
Republic of Ireland: (433) Randolph; Christie, Duffy, Clark, Ward (O'Dowda 72); Hoolahan (Murphy 62), Meyler (Hourihane 80), Brady; Walters, Long S, McClean.
Serbia: (343) Stojkovic; Vukovic, Maksimovic■, Ivanovic; Rukavina, Milivojevic, Matic, Kolarov; Kostic (Mitrovic S 72), Mitrovic A (Prijovic 79), Tadic (Gudelj 81).

Friday, 6 October 2017
Austria (1) 3 *(Burgstaller 25, Arnautovic 76, Schaub 90)*
Serbia (1) 2 *(Milivojevic 12, Matic 84)*   42,400
Austria: (4411) Lindner; Bauer, Dragovic, Danso, Wober; Grillitsch (Lazaro 77), Baumgartlinger, Ilsanker, Arnautovic; Kainz (Schaub 61); Burgstaller (Gregoritsch 82).
Serbia: (343) Stojkovic; Ivanovic, Mitrovic S, Nastasic; Rukavina (Ljajic 68), Milivojevic, Matic, Kolarov; Gacinovic (Prijovic 87), Mitrovic A, Tadic.

Georgia (0) 0
Wales (0) 1 *(Lawrence 49)*   22,290
Georgia: (4321) Loria; Kakabadze, Kvirkvelia, Kashia, Navalovski; Merebashvili, Kvekveskiri (Jigauri 76), Qazaishvili; Kankava, Gvilia (Khocholava 89); Kvilitaia (Skhirtladze 77).
Wales: (442) Hennessey; Gunter, Williams A, Chester, Davies; King, Allen, Ledley (Edwards 81), Ramsey; Lawrence (Woodburn 90), Vokes (Robson-Kanu 73).

Republic of Ireland (2) 2 *(Murphy 2, 19)*
Moldova (0) 0   50,560
Republic of Ireland: (433) Randolph; Christie, Duffy, Clark, Ward; Hoolahan (McGeady 78), Meyler, Hendrick; O'Dowda, Long S (Maguire 82), Murphy (Arter 78).
Moldova: (451) Cebanu; Bordian, Racu, Epureanu, Rozgoniuc; Platica (Ambros 79), Gatcan■, Anton, Ionita, Dedov (Cociuc 55); Ginsari.

Monday, 9 October 2017
Moldova (0) 0
Austria (0) 1 *(Schaub 70)*   5542
Moldova: (4321) Rozgoniuc; Cebanu, Epureanu, Bolohan (Paireli 86), Bordian; Anton, Ionita■, Ivanov (Cojocari 72); Cociuc, Platica (Ambros 80); Ginsari.
Austria: (4321) Lindner; Bauer, Lienhart, Danso, Wober; Grillitsch, Baumgartlinger, Schaub; Kainz (Lazaro 59), Arnautovic (Schobesberger 81); Burgstaller (Janko 46).

Serbia (0) 1 *(Prijovic 74)*
Georgia (0) 0   42,000
Serbia: (343) Stojkovic; Ivanovic, Maksimovic, Tosic D; Rukavina, Matic, Gudelj, Kolarov; Ljajic (Prijovic 61), Mitrovic A (Milivojevic 76), Tadic (Kostic 88).
Georgia: (451) Makaridze; Kakabadze, Kashia, Khocholava, Navalovski; Qazaishvili, Gvilia, Kankava, Aburjania (Dvalishvili 82), Jigauri (Hufnagel 86); Kvilitaia (Merebashvili 78).

Wales (0) 0
Republic of Ireland (0) 1 *(McClean 57)*   32,711
Wales: (4141) Hennessey; Gunter, Williams A, Chester, Davies; Allen (Williams J 37); King (Woodburn 65), Ramsey, Lawrence, Ledley; Robson-Kanu (Vokes 71).
Republic of Ireland: (442) Randolph; Christie, Duffy, Clark, Ward; Arter (Whelan 78), Brady, Meyler, Hendrick; McClean, Murphy (Long K 90).

Group D Table	P	W	D	L	F	A	GD	Pts
Serbia	10	6	3	1	20	10	10	21
Republic of Ireland	10	5	4	1	12	6	6	19
Wales	10	4	5	1	13	6	7	17
Austria	10	4	3	3	14	12	2	15
Georgia	10	0	5	5	8	14	–6	5
Moldova	10	0	2	8	4	23	–19	2

GROUP E

Sunday, 4 September 2016
Denmark (1) 1 *(Eriksen 17)*
Armenia (0) 0   21,000
Denmark: (343) Ronnow; Kjaer, Christensen, Vestergaard; Ankersen, Kvist, Hojbjerg (Delaney 81), Durmisi; Fischer, Eriksen, Jorgensen N (Poulsen 66).
Armenia: (523) Beglaryan; Hambartsumyan, Haroyan, Mkoyan, Andonian, Hovhannisyan G; Yedigaryan, Malakyan G (Manoyan 77); Ozbiliz (Ghazaryan 41), Arshakiyan (Pizzelli 70), Kadimyan.

Kazakhstan (0) 2 *(Khizhnichenko 51, 58)*
Poland (2) 2 *(Kapustka 9, Lewandowski 35 (pen))* 19,905
Kazakhstan: (532) Pokatilov; Beisebekov, Akhmetov (Abdulin 61), Maliy, Kislitsyn, Shomko; Muzhikov, Baizhanov (Nurgaliev 69), Kuat; Islamkhan (Tagybergen 79), Khizhnichenko.
Poland: (442) Fabianski; Piszczek, Glik, Salamon, Rybus; Blaszczykowski, Krychowiak, Zielinski, Kapustka (Linetty 82); Lewandowski, Milik.

Romania (0) 1 *(Popa 85)*
Montenegro (0) 1 *(Jovetic 87)*   25,468
Romania: (4231) Pantilimon; Benzar, Moti, Grigore, Filip; Hoban, Sapunaru; Bicfalvi (Popa 76), Stancu (Keseru 90), Stanciu; Andone (Torje 70).
Montenegro: (4411) Bozovic; Tomasevic, Savic, Simic, Vukcevic; Marusic, Vesovic (Kojasevic 80), Scekic, Bakic (Mugosa 68); Jovetic; Beciraj (Nikolic 90).

Saturday, 8 October 2016
Armenia (0) 0
Romania (4) 5 *(Stancu 5 (pen), Popa 10, Marin 12, Stanciu 29, Chipciu 59)*   5500
Armenia: (4231) Beglaryan; Mkoyan, Haroyan, Andonian (Voskanyan 38), Hayrapetyan; Grigoryan, Malakyan G**[*]**; Ozbiliz (Hovhannisyan B 64), Pizzelli, Manoyan; Pogosyan (Muradyan 33).
Romania: (4231) Tatarusanu; Benzar, Sapunaru, Grigore, Latovlevici; Marin, Hoban; Popa, Stanciu (Bicfalvi 81), Chipciu (Rotariu 67); Stancu (Keseru 57).

Montenegro (1) 5 *(Tomasevic 24, Vukcevic 59, Jovetic 64, Beciraj 73, Savic 78)*
Kazakhstan (0) 0   8517
Montenegro: (442) Bozovic; Marusic, Savic, Simic, Tomasevic; Vesovic, Scekic (Bakic 83), Vukcevic (Nikolic 67), Kojasevic; Beciraj (Raicevic 75), Jovetic.
Kazakhstan: (4132) Pokatilov; Beisebekov, Kislitsyn, Logvinenko, Shomko; Maliy; Kuat (Tagybergen 76), Mukhutdinov, Nurgaliev; Khizhnichenko (Murtazaev 85), Islamkhan (Muzhikov 63).

Poland (2) 3 *(Lewandowski 20, 36 (pen), 47)*
Denmark (0) 2 *(Glik 49 (og), Poulsen 69)*   56,800
Poland: (442) Fabianski; Piszczek, Glik, Cionek, Jedrzejczyk; Blaszczykowski (Peszko 88), Krychowiak, Zielinski, Grosicki (Rybus 73); Milik (Linetty 45), Lewandowski.
Denmark: (3412) Schmeichel; Kjaer, Christensen, Vestergaard (Delaney 81); Ankersen, Kvist, Hojbjerg, Durmisi; Eriksen; Fischer (Sisto 74), Jorgensen N (Poulsen 45).

Tuesday, 11 October 2016
Denmark (0) 0
Montenegro (1) 1 *(Beciraj 32)*   24,962
Denmark: (3412) Schmeichel; Kjaer, Jorgensen M (Jorgensen N 83), Christensen; Ankersen, Hojbjerg (Sisto 63), Delaney, Durmisi; Eriksen; Fischer (Cornelius 70), Poulsen.
Montenegro: (442) Bozovic; Marusic, Simic (Sofranac 70), Savic, Tomasevic; Vesovic (Mijuskovic 90), Vukcevic, Scekic, Kojasevic (Jovovic 63); Jovetic, Beciraj.

Kazakhstan (0) 0
Romania (0) 0   12,346
Kazakhstan: (541) Pokatilov; Beisebekov, Akhmetov, Maliy, Logvinenko, Shomko; Smakov, Muzhikov, Kuat (Tagybergen 86), Baizhanov (Nurgaliev 66); Khizhnichenko (Murtazaev 82).
Romania: (4411) Tatarusanu; Benzar, Sapunaru, Grigore (Moti 26), Tosca; Hoban, Marin, Popa (Andone 84), Stanciu; Chipciu (Enache 45); Stancu.

Poland (0) 2 *(Mkoyan 47 (og), Lewandowski 90)*
Armenia (0) 1 *(Pizzelli 50)*   44,786
Poland: (442) Fabianski; Blaszczykowski, Glik, Cionek, Jedrzejczyk (Wszolek 33); Grosicki (Kapustka 70), Krychowiak, Zielinski, Rybus; Lewandowski, Teodorczyk (Wilczek 85).
Armenia: (541) Beglaryan; Minasian, Haroyan, Mkoyan, Andonian**[*]**, Hayrapetyan; Hovhannisyan K (Ozbiliz 60), Muradyan (Voskanyan 34), Grigoryan, Manoyan; Pizzelli (Hakobyan 84).

Friday, 11 November 2016
Armenia (0) 3 *(Grigoryan 50, Haroyan 74, Ghazaryan 90)*
Montenegro (2) 2 *(Kojasevic 36, Jovetic 38)*   3500
Armenia: (451) Beglaryan; Voskanyan, Haroyan, Mkoyan, Hayrapetyan; Ghazaryan, Grigoryan, Pizzelli (Hovhannisyan K 81), Malakyan G, Mkhitaryan; Koryan (Sarkisov 59).
Montenegro: (4411) Bozovic; Marusic, Savic, Basa, Stojkovic; Vesovic (Mugosa 86), Scekic, Vukcevic (Zverotic 63), Kojasevic (Jovovic 76); Jovetic; Beciraj.

Denmark (2) 4 *(Cornelius 15, Eriksen 36 (pen), 90, Ankersen 78)*
Kazakhstan (1) 1 *(Suyumbayev 17)*   18,418
Denmark: (433) Ronnow; Ankersen, Kjaer, Bjelland, Durmisi; Kvist, Delaney, Eriksen; Poulsen, Jorgensen N, Cornelius (Dolberg 81).
Kazakhstan: (532) Pokatilov; Suyumbayev, Akhmetov, Logvinenko, Shomko, Maliy; Baizhanov, Mukhutdinov, Muzhikov (Tunggyshbayev 80); Khizhnichenko (Moldakaraev 59), Islamkhan (Murtazaev 70).

Romania (0) 0
Poland (1) 3 *(Grosicki 11, Lewandowski 82, 90 (pen))*
                                                        48,531
Romania: (4231) Tatarusanu; Benzar, Chiriches, Grigore, Tosca; Hoban (Prepelita 45), Marin; Popa (Andone 45), Stanciu (Keseru 82), Chipciu; Stancu.
Poland: (4321) Fabianski; Piszczek, Glik, Pazdan, Jedrzejczyk; Krychowiak, Blaszczykowski, Grosicki (Peszko 89); Zielinski (Teodorczyk 80), Linetty (Maczynski 69); Lewandowski.

Sunday, 26 March 2017
Armenia (0) 2 *(Mkhitaryan 73, Ozbiliz 75)*
Kazakhstan (0) 0   11,500
Armenia: (433) Beglaryan; Voskanyan, Haroyan, Andonian, Hayrapetyan; Mkhitaryan, Malakyan G, Pizzelli (Manucharyan 65); Hovhannisyan K, Sarkisov (Ozbiliz 70), Ghazaryan (Barseghyan 5).

Kazakhstan: (352) Loria; Beisebekov, Maliy■, Shomko; Tunggyshbayev (Muzhikov 78), Kuat (Dmitrenko 81), Tagybergen, Islamkhan (Baizhanov 87), Suyumbayev; Nuserbaev, Nurgaliev.

Montenegro (0) 1 *(Mugosa 63)*

Poland (1) 2 *(Lewandowski 40, Piszczek 82)*   10,439

Montenegro: (442) Bozovic; Marusic (Vucinic 90), Savic, Sofranac, Stojkovic; Vesovic, Vukcevic, Scekic (Djordjevic 86), Kojasevic (Ivanic 76); Mugosa, Beciraj.
Poland: (451) Fabianski; Piszczek, Glik, Pazdan, Jedrzejczyk; Blaszczykowski, Linetty (Teodorczyk 79), Zielinski, Maczynski (Cionek 90), Grosicki (Peszko 90); Lewandowski.

Romania (0) 0

Denmark (0) 0   26,892

Romania: (3412) Tatarusanu; Sapunaru, Chiriches, Tosca; Benzar, Marin, Pintilii, Latovlevici (Rotariu 76); Stanciu; Chipciu (Ivan 86), Keseru (Alibec 63).
Denmark: (352) Schmeichel; Kjaer (Jorgensen M 46), Christensen, Vestergaard; Ankersen, Kvist, Schone (Braithwaite 69), Delaney, Durmisi; Eriksen, Cornelius.

Saturday, 10 June 2017

Kazakhstan (0) 1 *(Kuat 76)*

Denmark (1) 3 *(Jorgensen N 27, Eriksen 51 (pen), Dolberg 81)*   19,065

Kazakhstan: (451) Loria; Suyumbayev, Akhmetov, Logvinenko, Shomko (Vorogovskiy 67); Muzhikov, Zhukov, Kuat, Islamkhan■, Nurgaliev (Beisebekov 56); Nuserbaev (Tunggyshbayev 74).
Denmark: (433) Ronnow; Larsen (Dalsgaard 82), Kjaer, Vestergaard, Durmisi; Kvist (Schone 46), Eriksen, Delaney; Poulsen (Dolberg 68), Jorgensen N, Braithwaite.

Montenegro (2) 4 *(Beciraj 2, Jovetic 28, 54, 82)*

Armenia (0) 1 *(Koryan 89)*   6861

Montenegro: (4231) Petkovic; Marusic, Savic, Simic, Tomasevic (Klimenta 74); Vukcevic (Scekic 71), Kosovic; Jankovic, Jovetic, Jovovic (Haksabanovic 84); Beciraj.
Armenia: (4231) Beglaryan; Mkoyan, Voskanyan, Andonian, Daghbashyan; Mkhitaryan, Grigoryan; Hovhannisyan K, Pizzelli (Barseghyan 73); Ozbiliz (Manucharyan 60); Koryan.

Poland (1) 3 *(Lewandowski 29 (pen), 57, 62 (pen))*

Romania (0) 1 *(Stancu 77)*   57,128

Poland: (4411) Szczesny; Jedrzejczyk, Pazdan, Cionek, Piszczek; Grosicki, Linetty (Milik 73), Maczynski (Krychowiak 44), Blaszczykowski; Zielinski (Teodorczyk 81); Lewandowski.
Romania: (541) Tatarusanu; Latovlevici (Grozav 60), Tosca, Sapunaru, Chiriches, Benzar; Stancu, Pintilii, Marin (Hanca 79), Chipciu (Stanciu 60); Andone.

Friday, 1 September 2017

Denmark (2) 4 *(Delaney 16, Cornelius 42, Jorgensen N 59, Eriksen 79)*

Poland (0) 0   34,505

Denmark: (4321) Schmeichel; Dalsgaard, Kjaer, Bjelland, Larsen; Kvist, Delaney (Jensen 86), Cornelius (Bendtner 74); Eriksen, Sisto; Jorgensen N (Lerager 82).
Poland: (442) Fabianski; Piszczek (Cionek 34), Glik, Pazdan, Jedrzejczyk; Blaszczykowski (Milik 63), Maczynski, Linetty (Makuszewski 67), Grosicki; Zielinski, Lewandowski.

Kazakhstan (0) 0

Montenegro (1) 3 *(Vesovic 31, Beciraj 54, Simic 63)*   16,511

Kazakhstan: (4411) Loria; Beysebekov, Logvinenko, Akhmetov, Shomko; Zhukov (Baizhanov 17), Kuat, Nurgaliev (Turysbek 61), Suyumbayev (Tagybergen 84); Muzhikov; Murtazaev.
Montenegro: (4231) Petkovic; Marusic, Savic, Simic, Tomasevic; Vukcevic, Kosovic (Ivanic 54); Jankovic, Jovetic (Zverotic 71), Vesovic; Beciraj (Mugosa 83).

Romania (0) 1 *(Maxim 90)*

Armenia (0) 0   27,178

Romania: (4231) Tatarusanu; Benzar, Chiriches, Tosca, Ganea; Stanciu, Pintilii; Chipciu (Popa 68), Baluta (Ivan 74), Stancu (Maxim 81); Andone.

Armenia: (4231) Meliksetyan; Hambardzumyan, Haroyan, Voskanyan■, Daghbashyan; Malakyan G (Yedigaryan 45), Hovhannisyan K; Mkhitaryan, Pizzelli (Adamyan 74), Manoyan (Koryan 58); Barseghyan.

Monday, 4 September 2017

Armenia (1) 1 *(Koryan 6)*

Denmark (2) 4 *(Delaney 17, 81, 90, Eriksen 29)*   6800

Armenia: (352) Meliksetyan; Hambardzumyan, Haroyan, Andonian; Hovhannisyan K, Grigoryan, Mkhitaryan, Yedigaryan, Hayrapetyan (Daghbashyan 38); Adamyan (Barseghyan 59), Koryan (Ozbiliz 75).
Denmark: (433) Schmeichel; Dalsgaard, Kjaer, Bjelland, Larsen; Eriksen, Kvist, Delaney; Cornelius (Schone 78), Jorgensen N, Sisto (Fischer 67).

Montenegro (0) 1 *(Jovetic 75)*

Romania (0) 0   9452

Montenegro: (4411) Petkovic; Marusic, Savic, Tomasevic, Stojkovic; Jankovic (Jovovic 84), Ivanic (Mugosa 70), Vukcevic, Vesovic; Jovetic; Beciraj (Zverotic 90).
Romania: (4411) Tatarusanu; Benzar, Chiriches, Moti, Tosca; Chipciu, Gaman (Hanca 81), Marin (Stanciu 64), Maxim; Stancu; Andone (Baluta 64).

Poland (1) 3 *(Milik 11, Glik 74, Lewandowski 86 (pen))*

Kazakhstan (0) 0   56,963

Poland: (442) Fabianski; Piszczek, Glik, Pazdan, Rybus; Makuszewski (Blaszczykowski 65), Maczynski (Bednarek 88), Zielinski, Grosicki (Teodorczyk 90); Milik, Lewandowski.
Kazakhstan: (532) Loria; Suyumbayev, Logvinenko, Akhmetov, Dmitrenko, Shomko; Darabayev, Kuat, Beysebekov (Tagybergen 90); Khizhnichenko (Schetkin 68), Murtazaev.

Thursday, 5 October 2017

Armenia (1) 1 *(Hambardzumyan 39)*

Poland (3) 6 *(Grosicki 2, Lewandowski 18, 25, 64, Blaszczykowski 58, Wolski 89)*   5478

Armenia: (4141) Meliksetyan; Hovhannisyan K, Hambardzumyan, Voskanyan, Edigaryan; Malakyan G; Kadymyan (Malakyan E 62), Koryan (Manucharyan 66), Mkhitaryan, Adamyan (Manoyan 73); Barseghyan.
Poland: (4411) Szczesny; Piszczek, Glik, Pazdan (Cionek 85), Bereszynski; Blaszczykowski, Krychowiak, Linetty (Maczynski 59), Grosicki (Wolski 71); Zielinski; Lewandowski.

Montenegro (0) 0

Denmark (1) 1 *(Eriksen 16)*   10,779

Montenegro: (4231) Petkovic; Marusic, Savic, Simic, Tomasevic; Vukcevic, Ivanic; Jovetic (Djordjevic 20), Jankovic (Jovovic 85), Vesovic; Mugosa (Kojasevic 76).
Denmark: (433) Schmeichel; Kjaer, Dalsgaard, Kvist, Bjelland; Larsen (Durmisi 43), Eriksen, Delaney; Poulsen, Cornelius (Bendtner 63), Sisto.

Romania (2) 3 *(Budescu 33, 38 (pen), Keseru 73)*

Kazakhstan (0) 1 *(Turysbek 82)*   10,123

Romania: (4231) Tatarusanu; Benzar, Chiriches, Grigore, Ganea; Pintilii (Hoban 70); Marin; Chipciu, Budescu (Ionita 79), Grozav; Andone (Keseru 66).
Kazakhstan: (541) Pokatilov; Beysebekov, Maliy, Akhmetov, Dmitrenko, Suyumbayev; Tagybergen (Turysbek 66), Kuat, Darabayev, Nurgaliev (Khizhnichenko 45); Murtazaev (Schetkin 58).

Sunday, 8 October 2017

Denmark (0) 1 *(Eriksen 60 (pen))*

Romania (0) 1 *(Deac 88)*   36,084

Denmark: (4231) Schmeichel; Dalsgaard, Kjaer, Christensen, Durmisi; Kvist, Delaney; Poulsen (Schone 83), Eriksen, Sisto; Bendtner (Dolberg 69).
Romania: (4231) Tatarusanu; Balasa, Chiriches, Grigore, Ganea■; Hoban, Stanciu; Baluta (Tucudean 83), Budescu (Bancu 66), Deac; Andone (Keseru 71).

Kazakhstan (0) 1 *(Turysbek 61)*
Armenia (1) 1 *(Mkhitaryan 26)*   12,158
Kazakhstan: (343) Loria; Logvinenko, Dmitrenko, Akhmetov; Tunggyshbayev (Khizhnichenko 45), Miroshnichenko, Nurgaliev, Tagybergen; Baizhanov (Darabayev 75), Turysbek, Murtazaev.
Armenia: (4141) Beglaryan; Hambardzumyan, Mikaelyan (Andonian 67), Haroyan, Daghbashyan; Grigoryan; Simonyan, Mkhitaryan, Pizzelli (Koryan 70), Malakyan E (Hovhannisyan K 59); Adamyan.

Poland (2) 4 *(Maczynski 6, Grosicki 16, Lewandowski 86, Stojkovic 88 (og))*
Montenegro (0) 2 *(Mugosa 79, Tomasevic 85)*   57,538
Poland: (442) Szczesny; Pazdan, Glik, Bereszynski, Piszczek (Rybus 45); Maczynski (Wolski 90), Krychowiak, Grosicki (Makuszewski 90), Zielinski; Blaszczykowski, Lewandowski.
Montenegro: (442) Petkovic; Klimenta, Mijuskovic, Stojkovic, Tomasevic; Jankovic, Scekic, Vukcevic, Jovovic (Mugosa 77); Ivanic (Haksabanovic 67), Beciraj.

Group E Table	P	W	D	L	F	A	GD	Pts
Poland	10	8	1	1	28	14	14	25
Denmark	10	6	2	2	20	8	12	20
Montenegro	10	5	1	4	20	12	8	16
Romania	10	3	4	3	12	10	2	13
Armenia	10	2	1	7	10	26	–16	7
Kazakhstan	10	0	3	7	6	26	–20	3

GROUP F

Sunday, 4 September 2016
Lithuania (2) 2 *(Cernych 32, Slivka 34)*
Slovenia (0) 2 *(Krhin 77, Cesar 90)*   4114
Lithuania: (433) Setkus; Vaitkunas, Freidgeimas, Girdvainis, Slavickas; Cernych (Grigaravicius 70), Zulpa, Kuklys; Novikovas, Slivka (Chvedukas 78), Valskis (Matulevicius 84).
Slovenia: (442) Oblak; Skubic, Samardzic, Cesar, Jokic; Verbic (Novakovic 56), Krhin, Kampl, Birsa; Beric (Ilicic 46), Bezjak.

Malta (1) 1 *(Effiong 14)*
Scotland (1) 5 *(Snodgrass 10, 61 (pen), 85, Martin C 53, Fletcher S 78)*   15,069
Malta: (532) Hogg; Agius, Caruana■, Borg S, Zerafa, Scicluna (Camilleri 79); Fenech P, Sciberras, Gambin■; Schembri (Briffa 66), Effiong (Mifsud 89).
Scotland: (442) Marshall; Martin R, Robertson, Paterson, Hanley; Fletcher D, Bannan, Ritchie (Anya 86), Snodgrass; Martin C (Fletcher S 68), Burke (Forrest 66).

Slovakia (0) 0
England (0) 1 *(Lallana 90)*   18,111
Slovakia: (451) Kozacik; Pekarik, Skrtel■, Durica, Hubocan; Mak (Kubik 71), Gregus, Pecovsky (Gyomber 56), Hamsik, Svento (Kiss 78); Duris.
England: (4231) Hart; Walker, Cahill, Stones, Rose; Henderson (Alli 64), Dier; Sterling (Walcott 70), Rooney, Lallana; Kane (Sturridge 82).

Saturday, 8 October 2016
England (2) 2 *(Sturridge 29, Alli 38)*
Malta (0) 0   81,787
England: (451) Hart; Walker, Cahill, Stones, Bertrand (Rose 19); Walcott (Rashford 68), Rooney, Henderson, Alli, Lingard; Sturridge (Vardy 73).
Malta: (532) Hogg; Borg S, Muscat Z, Agius, Camilleri, Muscat A; Kristensen, Sciberras, Fenech P; Schembri (Muscat R 87), Effiong (Mifsud 76).

Scotland (0) 1 *(McArthur 89)*
Lithuania (0) 1 *(Cernych 58)*   35,966
Scotland: (442) Marshall; Paterson, Martin R, Hanley, Robertson; Snodgrass, Bannan, Fletcher D (McArthur 46), Ritchie (Griffiths 71); Burke (Forrest 57), Martin C.
Lithuania: (442) Setkus; Vaitkunas, Freidgeimas, Girdvainis, Slavickas (Andriuskevicius 63); Cernych, Zulpa (Chvedukas 65), Kuklys, Novikovas; Valskis (Grigaravicius 85), Slivka.

Slovenia (0) 1 *(Kronaveter 74)*
Slovakia (0) 0   10,492
Slovenia: (4132) Oblak; Struna, Samardzic, Cesar, Jokic; Krhin; Kurtic (Kronaveter 72), Birsa (Novakovic 68), Verbic; Ilicic, Bezjak (Mevlja 90).
Slovakia: (532) Kozacik; Pauschek (Sabo 79), Salata, Hubocan, Durica, Svento (Holubek 79); Kucka, Hrosovsky (Duris 79), Gregus; Mak, Hamsik.

Tuesday, 11 October 2016
Lithuania (0) 2 *(Cernych 75, Novikovas 84 (pen))*
Malta (0) 0   5067
Lithuania: (451) Setkus; Vaitkunas, Mikuckis, Freidgeimas, Andriuskevicius; Cernych, Zulpa, Slivka, Kuklys (Chvedukas 79), Novikovas (Grigaravicius 87); Valskis (Matulevicius 61).
Malta: (532) Hogg; Borg, Muscat Z, Agius, Caruana■, Zerafa; Kristensen (Effiong 80), Sciberras, Fenech P (Pisani 85); Mifsud, Schembri (Muscat R 83).

Slovakia (1) 3 *(Mak 18, 56, Nemec 68)*
Scotland (0) 0   11,098
Slovakia: (4231) Kozacik; Sabo, Skrtel, Durica, Holubek; Kucka, Skriniar; Duris, Hamsik (Kiss 87), Mak (Svento 80); Nemec (Bakos 69).
Scotland: (451) Marshall; Paterson, Martin R, Hanley, Tierney; Snodgrass, Bannan, Fletcher D (Griffiths 64), McArthur, Ritchie (Anya 64); Fletcher S (McGinn 76).

Slovenia (0) 0
England (0) 0   13,274
Slovenia: (442) Oblak; Struna, Samardzic, Cesar (Mevlja 68), Jokic; Kurtic, Krhin (Omladic 84), Birsa (Kronaveter 59), Verbic; Ilicic, Bezjak.
England: (433) Hart; Walker, Cahill, Stones, Rose; Henderson, Dier, Alli (Rooney 73); Walcott (Townsend 62), Sturridge (Rashford 81), Lingard.

Friday, 11 November 2016
England (1) 3 *(Sturridge 25, Lallana 51, Cahill 61)*
Scotland (0) 0   87,258
England: (4231) Hart; Rose, Stones, Cahill, Walker; Dier, Henderson; Lallana, Rooney, Sterling; Sturridge (Vardy 75).
Scotland: (4411) Gordon; Anya (Paterson 79), Wallace, Hanley, Berra; Morrison (McArthur 66), Brown, Fletcher D, Forrest; Snodgrass (Ritchie 82); Griffiths.

Malta (0) 0
Slovenia (0) 1 *(Verbic 47)*   4207
Malta: (532) Hogg; Muscat Z, Magri, Agius, Camilleri (Borg S 68), Zerafa; Muscat R, Sciberras, Gambin; Schembri, Mifsud (Farrugia 78).
Slovenia: (4312) Oblak; Skubic, Samardzic, Cesar, Trajkovski (Jovic 63); Kurtic, Krhin, Verbic; Birsa (Omladic 71); Ilicic, Novakovic (Sporar 83).

Slovakia (3) 4 *(Nemec 12, Kucka 15, Skrtel 36, Hamsik 86)*
Lithuania (0) 0   9653
Slovakia: (451) Kozacik; Pekarik, Skrtel, Durica, Hubocan; Weiss (Bero 89), Kucka, Skriniar, Hamsik, Mak (Svento 83); Nemec (Duris 77).
Lithuania: (4411) Setkus; Vaitkunas, Girdvainis, Freidgeimas, Andriuskevicius; Novikovas, Zulpa (Chvedukas 33), Kuklys, Cernych; Slivka (Ruzgis 87).

Sunday, 26 March 2017
England (1) 2 *(Defoe 22, Vardy 66)*
Lithuania (0) 0   77,690
England: (4141) Hart; Walker, Keane, Stones, Bertrand; Dier; Oxlade-Chamberlain, Lallana, Alli, Sterling (Rashford 60); Defoe (Vardy 59).
Lithuania: (4231) Setkus; Vaitkunas, Kijanskas, Klimavicius, Slavickas; Kuklys, Zulpa; Novikovas (Grigaravicius 54), Slivka (Paulius 87), Cernych; Valskis (Matulevicius 73).

Malta (1) 1 *(Farrugia 14)*

Slovakia (2) 3 *(Weiss 2, Gregus 41, Nemec 84)*   4980

Malta: (532) Hogg; Attard, Muscat Z, Magri, Camilleri (Baldacchino 80), Zerafa; Gambin (Kristensen 73), Sciberras, Fenech P; Farrugia■, Schembri (Montebello 90).
Slovakia: (4141) Kozacik; Pekarik, Skrtel, Skriniar, Hubocan; Hrosovsky; Mak (Hamsik 50), Kucka (Duris 74), Gregus, Weiss (Rusnak 86); Nemec■.

Scotland (0) 1 *(Martin C 88)*

Slovenia (0) 0   20,435

Scotland: (442) Gordon; Robertson, Martin R, Mulgrew, Tierney; Morrison (Martin C 82), Brown, Armstrong, Forrest, Snodgrass (Anya 75), Griffiths (Naismith 49).
Slovenia: (433) Oblak; Struna, Samardzic, Cesar, Jokic; Kurtic, Krhin, Kampl (Omladic 87); Ilicic, Birsa (Beric 69), Bezjak (Verbic 58).

Saturday, 10 June 2017

Lithuania (0) 1 *(Sernas 90)*

Slovakia (1) 2 *(Weiss 32, Hamsik 58)*   4083

Lithuania: (442) Zubas; Borovskij, Kijanskas, Klimavicius, Slavickas; Cernych, Slivka (Dapkus 75), Kuklys, Sernas; Valskis (Matulevicius 72), Novikovas.
Slovakia: (442) Dubravka; Pekarik, Skrtel, Durica, Hubocan (Gyomber 59); Mak (Rusnak 77), Gregus, Skriniar, Weiss; Hamsik, Duda (Benes 89).

Scotland (0) 2 *(Griffiths 87, 89)*

England (0) 2 *(Oxlade-Chamberlain 70, Kane 90)*   48,520

Scotland: (4231) Gordon; Berra, Mulgrew, Robertson, Tierney; Brown, Armstrong; Anya (Martin C 81), Snodgrass (Fraser 66); Griffiths; Morrison (McArthur 45).
England: (451) Hart; Walker, Cahill, Smalling, Bertrand; Rashford (Oxlade-Chamberlain 65), Lallana, Dier, Alli (Sterling 84), Livermore (Defoe 90); Kane.

Slovenia (1) 2 *(Ilicic 45, Novakovic 84)*

Malta (0) 0   7900

Slovenia: (4411) Oblak; Skubic (Palcic 88), Mlinar, Mevlja, Jokic; Bezjak (Omladic 59), Kurtic, Krhin, Verbic; Ilicic; Beric (Novakovic 64).
Malta: (532) Hogg; Muscat A, Muscat Z, Agius, Borg S (Magri 89), Failla; Pisani, Kristensen (Gambin 46), Fenech R; Effiong, Schembri (Mifsud 62).

Friday, 1 September 2017

Lithuania (0) 0

Scotland (2) 3 *(Armstrong 25, Robertson 31, McArthur 72)*   5067

Lithuania: (4231) Setkus; Vaitkunas, Kijanskas, Freidgeimas, Borovskij; Zulpa (Spalvis 68), Kuklys; Cernych, Slivka (Verbickas 79), Novikovas; Sernas (Matulevicius 82).
Scotland: (4231) Gordon; Berra, Mulgrew, Robertson, Tierney; Brown, Armstrong (McGinn 85); Forrest (Ritchie 66), Phillips, McArthur; Griffiths (Martin C 79).

Malta (0) 0

England (0) 4 *(Kane 53, 90, Bertrand 85, Welbeck 90)*   16,994

Malta: (532) Hogg; Borg S, Muscat Z, Agius, Magri, Zerafa (Camilleri 75); Pisani, Kristensen, Fenech R (Fenech P 83); Farrugia, Schembri (Mifsud 86).
England: (442) Hart; Jones, Bertrand, Walker, Cahill; Sterling (Rashford 45), Livermore, Alli (Vardy 69), Henderson; Kane, Oxlade-Chamberlain (Welbeck 76).

Slovakia (0) 1 *(Nemec 81)*

Slovenia (0) 0   16,896

Slovakia: (451) Dubravka; Pekarik, Gyomber, Skriniar, Hubocan; Mak, Kucka (Gregus 65), Lobotka, Hamsik (Duda 87), Weiss (Rusnak 54); Nemec.
Slovenia: (4231) Oblak; Skubic, Mevlja, Cesar, Jokic (Viler 9); Krhin (Rotman 80), Kurtic; Ilicic, Birsa (Verbic 60), Vetrih; Matavz.

Monday, 4 September 2017

England (1) 2 *(Dier 37, Rashford 59)*

Slovakia (1) 1 *(Lobotka 3)*   67,823

England: (4231) Hart; Walker, Cahill, Jones, Bertrand; Henderson, Dier; Oxlade-Chamberlain (Sterling 82), Alli (Livermore 90), Rashford (Welbeck 83); Kane.
Slovakia: (4231) Dubravka; Pekarik, Skrtel, Durica, Hubocan; Skriniar, Lobotka; Weiss (Rusnak 68), Hamsik (Duda 78), Mak; Nemec (Duris 68).

Scotland (1) 2 *(Berra 10, Griffiths 49)*

Malta (0) 0   26,371

Scotland: (433) Gordon; Berra, Mulgrew (Hanley 56), Robertson, Tierney; Brown, Phillips, Armstrong; Forrest, Griffiths (Martin C 70), McArthur (Morrison 46).
Malta: (352) Hogg; Magri, Agius, Muscat Z; Borg S (Muscat A 86), Zerafa, Kristensen (Fenech P 84), Fenech R, Pisani; Schembri (Gambin 71), Effiong.

Slovenia (1) 4 *(Ilicic 25 (pen), 61 (pen), Verbic 82, Birsa 90)*

Lithuania (0) 0   6230

Slovenia: (41212) Oblak; Skubic, Mevlja, Cesar, Viler; Rotman; Kurtic, Mevlja; Repas (Vetrih 86); Ilicic (Matavz 85), Sporar (Birsa 63).
Lithuania: (451) Setkus; Vaitkunas, Klimavicius, Kijanskas (Girdvainis 79), Borovskij; Valskis (Spalvis 65), Slivka, Kuklys, Sernas (Verbickas 81), Novikovas; Cernych.

Thursday, 5 October 2017

England (0) 1 *(Kane 90)*

Slovenia (0) 0   61,598

England: (4231) Hart; Walker, Stones, Cahill, Bertrand; Henderson, Dier; Oxlade-Chamberlain (Lingard 63), Sterling (Keane 85), Kane; Rashford.
Slovenia: (433) Oblak; Struna, Mevlja, Cesar, Jokic; Rotman (Matavz 79), Ilicic, Krhin; Bezjak (Repas 72), Sporar (Birsa 55), Verbic.

Malta (1) 1 *(Agius 23)*

Lithuania (0) 1 *(Slivka 53)*   3431

Malta: (442) Hogg; Camilleri, Borg S, Muscat Z, Zerafa; Fenech P (Attard 90), Agius, Pisani, Schembri (Failla 45); Effiong, Gambin (Borg C 85).
Lithuania: (433) Zubas; Girdvainis, Mikuckis, Vaitkunas, Andriuskevicius; Kuklys, Matulevicius (Spalvis 79), Slivka; Cernych, Valskis (Papsys 45), Novikovas.

Scotland (0) 1 *(Skrtel 89 (og))*

Slovakia (0) 0   46,773

Scotland: (433) Gordon; Berra, Mulgrew, Robertson, Tierney (Anya 82); Morrison, Fletcher D (McArthur 79), Bannan; Forrest (Martin C 60), Griffiths, Phillips.
Slovakia: (4411) Dubravka; Pekarik, Skrtel, Durica, Hubocan; Kucka (Gyomber 80), Gregus, Lobotka, Mak■; Hamsik (Duda 79); Nemec (Weiss 79).

Sunday, 8 October 2017

Lithuania (0) 0

England (1) 1 *(Kane 27 (pen))*   5067

Lithuania: (541) Setkus; Andriuskevicius, Girdvainis, Zulpa, Klimavicius, Borovskij; Slivka (Chvedukas 90), Verbickas, Novikovas, Sernas (Matulevicius 76); Cernych.
England: (343) Butland; Keane, Stones, Maguire; Trippier, Winks, Henderson, Cresswell; Alli (Lingard 80), Kane, Rashford (Sturridge 72).

Slovakia (1) 3 *(Nemec 33, 62, Duda 69)*

Malta (0) 0   17,774

Slovakia: (451) Dubravka; Pekarik, Skrtel, Skriniar, Hubocan (Mazan 86); Rusnak (Mihalik 87), Duda, Lobotka, Hamsik, Weiss; Nemec.
Malta: (442) Hogg; Borg S, Agius, Camilleri, Zerafa; Pisani, Fenech R, Fenech P (Borg C 88), Gambin (Failla 75); Effiong, Schembri.

Slovenia (0) 2 *(Bezjak 52, 72)*
Scotland (1) 2 *(Griffiths 32, Snodgrass 87)* 11,123

Slovenia: (433) Oblak; Struna (Skubic 45), Mevlja, Cesar■, Jokic; Kurtic, Rotman, Ilicic; Repas (Bezjak 45), Matavz (Vetrih 89), Verbic.
Scotland: (433) Gordon; Berra, Mulgrew, Robertson, Tierney (Fletcher S 80); McArthur (Snodgrass 78), Fletcher D, Bannan; Martin C (Anya 53), Griffiths, Phillips.

Group F Table	P	W	D	L	F	A	GD	Pts
England	10	8	2	0	18	3	15	26
Slovakia	10	6	0	4	17	7	10	18
Scotland	10	5	3	2	17	12	5	18
Slovenia	10	4	3	3	12	7	5	15
Lithuania	10	1	3	6	7	20	-13	6
Malta	10	0	1	9	3	25	-22	1

GROUP G

Monday, 5 September 2016

Israel (1) 1 *(Ben Haim II 35)*
Italy (2) 3 *(Pelle 14, Candreva 31 (pen), Immobile 83)*
29,300

Israel: (433) Goresh; Bitton B, Tibi (Gershon 50), Tzedek, Davidadze; Kayal, Bitton N (Atzily 57), Yeini; Ben Haim II (Kahat 62), Hemed, Zahavi.
Italy: (532) Buffon; Candreva (Florenzi 67), Barzagli, Bonucci, Chiellini■, Antonelli; Parolo, Verratti, Bonaventura (Ogbonna 62); Eder (Immobile 70), Pelle.

Spain (1) 8 *(Costa 11, 67, Roberto 55, Silva 59, 90, Vitolo 60, Morata 82, 83)*
Liechtenstein (0) 0 12,139

Spain: (4231) de Gea; Roberto, Pique, Sergio Ramos, Jordi Alba; Busquets, Koke; Vitolo (Asensio 79), Thiago (Nolito 46), Silva; Costa (Morata 68).
Liechtenstein: (451) Jehle; Rechsteiner (Yildiz 71), Polverino, Kaufmann, Goppel; Salanovic (Wolfinger 77), Martin Buchel, Wieser, Marcel Buchel, Burgmeier; Hasler.

Tuesday, 6 September 2016

Albania (1) 2 *(Sadiku 9, Balaj 89)*
FYR Macedonia (0) 1 *(Alioski 51)* 14,667

Albania: (433) Berisha; Hysaj, Djimsiti, Mavraj, Agolli; Abrashi (Balaj 59), Kukeli, Xhaka; Gashi (Memushaj 60), Sadiku, Hyka (Roshi 66).
FYR Macedonia: (4231) Zahov; Ristevski, Sikov, Mojsov, Zuta; Ristovski, Alioski, Stjepanovic (Petrovic 61), Spirovski, Hasani (Gjorgjev 74); Pandev.

Thursday, 6 October 2016

FYR Macedonia (0) 1 *(Nestoroski 63)*
Israel (2) 2 *(Hemed 25, Ben Haim II 43)* 6500

FYR Macedonia: (532) Bogatinov; Ristovski, Mojsov, Sikov (Ibraimi 51), Ristevski, Zuta; Hasani, Petrovic (Spirovski 45), Alioski; Pandev (Jahovic 76), Nestoroski.
Israel: (433) Goresh; Dasa, Tzedek, Tibi■, Davidadze; Golasa (Einbinder 72), Bitton N, Cohen; Zahavi, Hemed (Abed 75), Ben Haim II (Buzaglo 68).

Italy (0) 1 *(De Rossi 82 (pen))*
Spain (0) 1 *(Vitolo 55)* 38,470

Italy: (352) Buffon; Barzagli, Bonucci, Romagnoli, Florenzi, De Rossi, Montolivo (Bonaventura 30), Parolo (Belotti 76), De Sciglio; Eder, Pelle (Immobile 59).
Spain: (433) de Gea; Jordi Alba (Nacho 22), Sergio Ramos, Pique, Carvajal; Iniesta, Busquets, Koke; Silva, Costa (Morata 66), Vitolo (Thiago 83).

Liechtenstein (0) 0
Albania (1) 2 *(Jehle 12 (og), Balaj 71)* 5684

Liechtenstein: (433) Jehle; Oehri, Polverino (Rechsteiner 45), Kaufmann, Goppel; Hasler, Wieser, Marcel Buchel; Burgmeier, Gubser (Frick 59), Salanovic (Kuhne 72).
Albania: (433) Berisha; Hysaj, Djimsiti, Mavraj, Aliji, Kukeli (Basha 44), Hyka, Abrashi (Lila 45); Roshi, Balaj, Llullaku (Cikalleshi 69).

Sunday, 9 October 2016

Albania (0) 0
Spain (0) 2 *(Costa 55, Nolito 63)* 15,245

Albania: (433) Berisha; Hysaj, Djimsiti, Mavraj, Agolli; Lila, Xhaka (Hyka 75), Memushaj (Basha 67); Roshi, Balaj, Lenjani (Aliji 45).
Spain: (4411) de Gea; Koke, Sergio Ramos (Martinez 80), Pique, Monreal; Vitolo (Nolito 59), Iniesta (Isco 77), Busquets, Silva; Thiago; Costa.

FYR Macedonia (0) 2 *(Nestoroski 57, Hasani 59)*
Italy (1) 3 *(Belotti 24, Immobile 75, 90)* 19,195

FYR Macedonia: (532) Bogatinov; Ristovski, Mojsov, Sikov, Ristevski, Zuta (Ibraimi 45); Hasani (Trajcevski 83), Spirovski, Alioski; Pandev, Nestoroski (Petrovic 67).
Italy: (532) Buffon; Candreva, Barzagli, Bonucci, Romagnoli, De Sciglio; Bernardeschi (Sansone 64), Verratti, Bonaventura (Parolo 64); Belotti (Eder 83), Immobile.

Israel (2) 2 *(Hemed 3, 16)*
Liechtenstein (0) 1 *(Goppel 49)* 9000

Israel: (442) Goresh; Dasa, Tzedek, Gershon, Ben Haroush; Ben Haim II (Dabour 81), Cohen, Golasa, Buzaglo (Atzily 63); Zahavi, Hemed (Kahat 76).
Liechtenstein: (3412) Jehle; Rechsteiner, Kaufmann, Goppel; Marcel Buchel (Salanovic 88), Martin Buchel, Wieser, Burgmeier (Kuhne 81); Hasler; Christen, Gubser (Frick 75).

Saturday, 12 November 2016

Albania (0) 0
Israel (1) 3 *(Zahavi 18 (pen), Einbinder 66, Atar 83)* 7600

Albania: (433) Berisha■; Hysaj (Cani 79), Djimsiti■, Mavraj, Agolli; Xhaka (Manaj 82), Kukeli, Memushaj; Roshi, Balaj, Llullaku (Hoxha 57).
Israel: (433) Goresh; Dasa, Tzedek, Tibi, Gershon; Einbinder (Hemed 70), Natcho, Cohen; Sahar (Buzaglo 64), Zahavi, Ben Haim II (Atar 75).

Liechtenstein (0) 0
Italy (4) 4 *(Belotti 11, 44, Immobile 12, Candreva 32)* 5864

Liechtenstein: (451) Jehle; Rechsteiner, Polverino, Kaufmann, Oehri; Christen, Martin Buchel, Wieser, Marcel Buchel, Burgmeier; Salanovic.
Italy: (424) Buffon; Zappacosta, Bonucci, Romagnoli, De Sciglio; De Rossi, Verratti; Candreva (Eder 74), Belotti, Immobile (Zaza 81), Bonaventura (Insigne 67).

Spain (1) 4 *(Velkoski 34 (og), Vitolo 63, Monreal 84, Aduriz 85)*
FYR Macedonia (0) 0 16,622

Spain: (451) de Gea; Carvajal, Bartra, Nacho, Monreal; Vitolo (Callejon 87), Koke (Isco 72), Busquets, Thiago; Silva; Morata (Aduriz 60).
FYR Macedonia: (352) Aleksovski; Velkoski, Mojsov, Ristevski; Ristovski, Hasani (Gjorgjev 87), Bardi, Spirovski (Zuta 60), Alioski; Pandev, Nestoroski (Ibraimi 82).

Friday, 24 March 2017

Italy (1) 2 *(De Rossi 12 (pen), Immobile 72)*
Albania (0) 0 33,136

Italy: (442) Buffon; Zappacosta, Barzagli, Bonucci, De Sciglio; Candreva, De Rossi, Verratti, Insigne; Immobile, Belotti.
Albania: (433) Strakosha; Hysaj, Veseli, Ajeti, Agolli; Basha (Latifi 89), Kukeli, Memushaj; Lila (Sadiku 69), Cikalleshi, Roshi (Grezda 80).

Liechtenstein (0) 0
FYR Macedonia (1) 3 *(Nikolov 43, Nestoroski 68, 72)*
4517

Liechtenstein: (4141) Jehle; Rechsteiner (Wolfinger 78), Gubser, Malin, Goppel; Martin Buchel (Sele A 83); Burgmeier, Hasler, Marcel Buchel, Salanovic (Brandle 87); Frick.
FYR Macedonia: (442) Dimitrievski; Ristovski, Velkoski, Sikov, Ristevski; Trickovski (Babunski 77), Nikolov, Spirovski (Gjorgjev 85); Ibraimi (Trajkovski 64); Pandev, Nestoroski.

Spain (2) 4 *(Silva 13, Vitolo 45, Costa 51, Isco 88)*
Israel (0) 1 *(Rafaelov 77)*   20,321
Spain: (433) de Gea; Carvajal, Sergio Ramos, Pique, Jordi Alba; Busquets, Iniesta (Isco 70), Thiago (Koke 63); Vitolo (Aspas 83), Costa, Silva.
Israel: (433) Marciano; Dasa, Tzedek, Tibi (Tawatha 18), Gershon; Cohen, Natcho, Einbinder (Keltjens 60); Ben Haim II (Hemed 63), Zahavi, Rafaelov.

Sunday, 11 June 2017

FYR Macedonia (0) 1 *(Ristovski 66)*
Spain (2) 2 *(Silva 15, Costa 27)*   20,675
FYR Macedonia: (442) Dimitrievski; Tosevski (Trajkovski 74), Sikov, Mojsov (Trickovski 85), Ristevski; Ristovski, Stjepanovic (Elmas 45), Spirovski, Alioski; Nestoroski, Pandev.
Spain: (433) de Gea; Carvajal, Sergio Ramos, Pique, Jordi Alba; Iniesta (Saul 90), Busquets, Silva (Pedro 68); Isco, Costa, Thiago (Koke 73).

Israel (0) 0
Albania (2) 3 *(Sadiku 22, 44, Memushaj 71)*   15,150
Israel: (442) Goresh; Dasa, Tibi, Tzedek, Tawatha; Natcho, Golasa (Shechter 53), Cohen, Rafaelov (Vered 57); Sahar (Benayoun 67), Zahavi.
Albania: (532) Strakosha; Hysaj, Xhimshiti, Kukeli (Veseli 82), Mavraj, Aliji; Hyka, Memushaj, Roshi (Lila 53); Sadiku (Cikalleshi 69), Abrashi.

Italy (1) 5 *(Insigne 35, Belotti 52, Eder 74, Bernarderschi 82, Gabbiadini 90)*
Liechtenstein (0) 0   20,514
Italy: (442) Buffon; Darmian, Barzagli, Chiellini, Spinazzola; Candreva (Bernarderschi 60), Pellegrini, De Rossi, Insigne; Belotti (Gabbiadini 75), Immobile (Eder 66).
Liechtenstein: (451) Jehle; Rechsteiner, Malin, Gubser, Goppel; Salanovic (Brandle 59), Hasler, Polverino (Quintans 87), Martin Buchel, Burgmeier (Wolfinger 68); Frick.

Saturday, 2 September 2017

Albania (0) 2 *(Roshi 54, Agolli 78)*
Liechtenstein (0) 0   5500
Albania: (442) Berisha; Hysaj, Agolli, Basha, Memushaj (Kukeli 77); Llullaku, Mavraj, Grezda (Ahmedi 86), Ajeti; Roshi, Abrashi (Hyka 83).
Liechtenstein: (442) Jehle; Goppel, Kaufmann, Quintans (Yildiz 79), Malin; Wieser, Burgmeier (Brandle 80), Martin Buchel, Hasler; Salanovic, Frick (Erne 65).

Israel (0) 0
FYR Macedonia (0) 1 *(Pandev 73)*   11,350
Israel: (433) Glazer; Bitton B (Keltjens 70), Ben Haim I, Tzedek, Davidadze; Kabha, Ohana (Hemed 45), Cohen; Melikson, Zahavi, Ben Haim II (Einbinder 53).
FYR Macedonia: (4231) Dimitrievski; Ristovski, Musliu, Velkovski, Ristevski; Spirovski, Bardhi (Zajkov 89); Nikolov (Elmas 63), Pandev, Alioski; Nestorovski (Radeski 86).

Spain (2) 3 *(Isco 13, 40, Morata 77)*
Italy (0) 0   73,628
Spain: (4231) de Gea; Carvajal, Sergio Ramos, Pique, Jordi Alba; Busquets, Koke; Silva, Iniesta (Morata 72), Asensio (Saul 78); Isco (Villa 89).
Italy: (3412) Buffon; Barzagli, Bonucci, Darmian; Candreva (Bernardeschi 70), De Rossi, Verratti, Spinazzola; Insigne; Belotti (Eder 70), Immobile (Gabbiadini 79).

Tuesday, 5 September 2017

FYR Macedonia (0) 1 *(Trajkovski 78 (pen))*
Albania (0) 1 *(Roshi 53)*   3493
FYR Macedonia: (4231) Dimitrievski; Ristovski, Musliu, Velkovski, Ristevski (Trickovski 87); Spirovski (Radeski 87), Bardhi; Nikolov (Trajkovski 58), Pandev, Alioski; Nestorovski.
Albania: (352) Berisha; Hysaj, Ajeti, Mavraj; Roshi, Lila, Kukeli (Basha 45), Agolli (Memolla 73), Llullaku (Memushaj 45); Hyka, Sadiku.

Italy (0) 1 *(Immobile 53)*
Israel (0) 0   15,507
Italy: (442) Buffon; Conti (Zappacosta 49), Barzagli, Astori, Darmian; Candreva (Bernardeschi 87), De Rossi, Verratti (Montolivo 90), Insigne; Immobile, Belotti.
Israel: (451) Harush; Davidadze, Tzedek, Ben Haim I, Keltjens; Melikson (Ben Haim II 62), Cohen (Einbinder 77), Natcho, Kabha, Rafaelov; Shechter (Benayoun 69).

Liechtenstein (0) 0

Spain (4) 8 *(Sergio Ramos 3, Morata 15, 54, Isco 16, Silva 39, Aspas 51, 62, Goppel 89 (og))*   5864
Liechtenstein: (3331) Jehle; Quintans (Yildiz 60), Kaufmann, Malin; Martin Buchel, Polverino (Sele A 78), Wieser; Salanovic, Goppel, Burgmeier (Wolfinger 82); Hasler.
Spain: (433) de Gea; Pedro, Pique, Sergio Ramos (Nacho 45), Monreal; Thiago, Busquets, Iniesta; Isco (Deulofeu 55), Morata, Silva (Aspas 45).

Friday, 6 October 2017

Italy (1) 1 *(Chiellini 40)*
FYR Macedonia (0) 1 *(Trajkovski 77)*   22,603
Italy: (343) Buffon; Barzagli (Rugani 46), Bonucci, Chiellini; Parolo, Gagliardini (Cristante 75), Zappacosta, Darmian; Verdi (Bernardeschi 64), Immobile, Insigne.
FYR Macedonia: (343) Dimitrievski; Ristovski, Musliu, Velkovski (Zajkov 75); Spirovski, Bardhi, Radeski, Alioski; Pandev (Trickovski 80), Nestorovski, Hasani (Trajkovski 64).

Liechtenstein (0) 0
Israel (1) 1 *(Tibi 21)*   3498
Liechtenstein: (4141) Jehle; Wolfinger, Malin (Ospelt 88), Kaufmann (Brandle 51), Goppel; Martin Buchel; Hasler, Polverino, Marcel Buchel, Burgmeier; Erne (Yildiz 72).
Israel: (433) Harush; Keltjens, Tibi, Ben Haim I, Davidadze; Kabha, Melikson (Benayoun 78), Natcho; Rafaelov (Einbinder 63), Hemed, Atar (Ben Haim II 69).

Spain (3) 3 *(Rodrigo 17, Isco 24, Thiago 28)*
Albania (0) 0   25,397
Spain: (343) de Gea; Sergio Ramos, Pique (Nacho 59), Jordi Alba; Odriozola, Thiago, Koke, Saul; Isco, Silva (Asensio 73), Rodrigo (Aduriz 82).
Albania: (433) Berisha; Hysaj, Veseli, Ajeti, Memolla (Agolli 46); Kace, Memushaj, Grezda (Latifi 66); Xhaka, Llullaku, Balliu (Sadiku 46).

Monday, 9 October 2017

Albania (0) 0
Italy (0) 1 *(Candreva 73)*   14,718
Albania: (4231) Berisha; Hysaj, Veseli, Mavraj, Agolli; Basha (Lila 68), Kace; Roshi (Ahmedi 89), Memushaj (Latifi 76), Grezda; Sadiku.
Italy: (442) Buffon; Darmian (Zappacosta 61), Bonucci, Chiellini, Spinazzola; Candreva, Parolo, Gagliardini, Insigne (El Shaarawy 90); Immobile, Eder (Gabbiadini 88).

FYR Macedonia (2) 4 *(Zajkov 36, Trajkovski 38, Bardhi 67, Ademi 69)*
Liechtenstein (0) 0   4518
FYR Macedonia: (442) Dimitrievski; Ristovski, Musliu, Zajkov, Ristevski; Alioski, Bardhi (Doriev 77), Hasani (Elmas 46), Trajkovski; Pandev (Ademi 64), Nestorovski.
Liechtenstein: (4141) Jehle; Quintans, Malin, Kaufmann, Goppel; Polverino; Sele A, Wolfinger (Yildiz 66), Martin Buchel (Sele M 80), Wieser; Brandle (Erne 73).

Israel (0) 0
Spain (0) 1 *(Illarramendi 76)*   28,700
Israel: (433) Harush; Keltjens, Tibi, Ben Haim I, Davidadze; Natcho, Cohen, Kabha (Bitton N 67); Atar (Benayoun 74), Hemed, Melikson (Ben Haim II 54).
Spain: (433) Reina; Azpilicueta, Nacho, Sergio Ramos (Aspas 45), Monreal; Illarramendi, Asensio, Busquets; Viera, Aduriz (Isco 65), Pedro (Callejon 75).

Group G Table	P	W	D	L	F	A	GD	Pts
Spain	10	9	1	0	36	3	33	28
Italy	10	7	2	1	21	8	13	23
Albania	10	4	1	5	10	13	-3	13
Israel	10	4	0	6	10	15	-5	12
FYR Macedonia	10	3	2	5	15	15	0	11
Liechtenstein	10	0	0	10	1	39	-38	0

GROUP H

Tuesday, 6 September 2016

Bosnia-Herzegovina (2) 5 *(Spahic 7, 90, Dzeko 23 (pen), Medunjanin 71, Ibisevic 83)*
Estonia (0) 0 8820

Bosnia-Herzegovina: (442) Begovic; Vranjes (Bicakcic 62), Zukanovic, Spahic, Kolasinac; Visca (Milicevic 75), Pjanic, Medunjanin, Lulic; Ibisevic, Dzeko (Djuric 81).
Estonia: (4411) Aksalu; Teniste, Baranov, Klavan, Pikk; Kams (Kruglov 45), Mets, Antonov (Sappinen 86), Kallaste; Vassiljev; Zenjov (Anier 71).

Cyprus (0) 0
Belgium (1) 3 *(Lukaku R 13, 61, Carrasco 81)* 12,029

Cyprus: (4411) Panagi; Demetriou, Junior, Laifis, Alexandrou; Kastanos (Makris 78), Charis Kyriakou, Laban (Artymatas 70), Efrem; Charalambidis; Sotiriou (Mitidis 69).
Belgium: (451) Courtois; Meunier, Alderweireld, Vermaelen, Vertonghen; Carrasco, Fellaini (Nainggolan 84), Witsel, De Bruyne, Hazard E; Lukaku R (Batshuayi 73).

Gibraltar (1) 1 *(Walker 26)*
Greece (4) 4 *(Mitroglou 10, Wiseman 44 (og), Fortounis 45, Torosidis 45)* 300

Gibraltar: (3331) Perez; Wiseman, Chipolina R, Casciaro R; Garcia, Bosio (Casciaro K 71), Chipolina J; Hernandez, Coombes (Yome 85), Casciaro L; Walker.
Greece: (433) Karnezis; Tzavelas, Papastathopoulos, Manolas, Torosidis; Samaris, Maniatis (Tziolis 71), Fortounis; Mantalos (Gianniotas 62), Bakasetas, Mitroglou (Vellios 73).

Friday, 7 October 2016

Belgium (2) 4 *(Spahic 26 (og), Hazard E 28, Alderweireld 60, Lukaku R 79)*
Bosnia-Herzegovina (0) 0 42,653

Belgium: (433) Courtois; Meunier, Alderweireld, Vertonghen, Lukaku J (Ciman 21); Mertens, Fellaini, Witsel; Hazard E (Mirallas 87), Carrasco, Lukaku R (Benteke 82).
Bosnia-Herzegovina: (4321) Begovic; Bicakcic, Spahic, Zukanovic, Kolasinac; Lulic, Jajalo (Visca 73), Medunjanin; Pjanic (Cimirot 81), Dzeko; Ibisevic (Djuric 64).

Estonia (0) 4 *(Kait 47, 70, Vassiljev 52, Mosnikov 88)*
Gibraltar (0) 0 4678

Estonia: (4231) Aksalu; Teniste, Baranov, Klavan, Kruglov; Kait (Lepistu 80), Mets; Zenjov (Ojamaa 65), Vassiljev (Mosnikov 61), Luts; Anier.
Gibraltar: (442) Perez; Garcia, Casciaro R, Chipolina R, Chipolina J (Casciaro K 90); Bardon, Bosio (Payas 58), Walker, Olivero; Priestley (Coombes 65), Casciaro L.

Greece (2) 2 *(Mitroglou 12, Mantalos 42)*
Cyprus (0) 0 16,512

Greece: (4411) Karnezis; Torosidis, Papastathopoulos, Manolas, Tzavelas (Karelis 87); Mantalos, Maniatis, Stafylidis (Papadopoulos 70); Bakasetas (Holebas 77); Fortounis; Mitroglou.
Cyprus: (433) Panagi; Demetriou, Junior, Laifis, Charalambous; Artymatas (Charalambos Kyriakou 78), Laban, Kastanos; Charalambidis (Christofi 66), Mitidis (Makris 83), Efrem.

Monday, 10 October 2016

Bosnia-Herzegovina (0) 2 *(Dzeko 70, 81)*
Cyprus (0) 0 8900

Bosnia-Herzegovina: (442) Begovic; Vranjes, Sunjic, Spahic, Kolasinac (Hajrovic 64); Visca (Susic 78), Pjanic, Medunjanin, Lulic; Djuric (Ibisevic 83), Dzeko.

Cyprus: (433) Panagi; Demetriou, Junior, Laifis, Alexandrou; Artymatas (Mitidis 85), Kastanos, Laban; Christofi (Charalambidis 77), Sotiriou, Makris (Efrem 72).

Estonia (0) 0
Greece (1) 2 *(Torosidis 2, Stafylidis 61)* 4467

Estonia: (4411) Aksalu; Teniste (Kams 31), Baranov, Klavan, Kallaste; Marin, Aleksandr Dmitrijev (Mosnikov 79), Mets, Luts (Purje 69); Vassiljev; Zenjov.
Greece: (4411) Karnezis; Torosidis (Oikonomou 18), Papastathopoulos (Tachtsidis 6), Manolas, Stafylidis; Bakasetas, Maniatis (Tziolis 86), Papadopoulos, Karelis; Mantalos; Mitroglou.

Gibraltar (0) 0
Belgium (3) 6 *(Benteke 1, 43, 56, Witsel 19, Mertens 51, Hazard E 79)* 1959

Gibraltar: (442) Ibrahim; Wiseman, Casciaro R, Chipolina R, Chipolina J; Garcia, Bosio (Payas 46), Walker (Bardon 81), Olivero; Casciaro K (Yome 86), Casciaro L.
Belgium: (343) Courtois; Alderweireld, Ciman, Vertonghen; Meunier, Witsel, Defour, Carrasco (Chadli 53); Mertens (Mirallas 64), Benteke (Batshuayi 81), Hazard E.

Sunday, 13 November 2016

Belgium (3) 8 *(Meunier 8, Mertens 16, 68, Hazard E 25, Carrasco 62, Klavan 65 (og), Lukaku R 83, 88)*
Estonia (1) 1 *(Anier 29)* 37,128

Belgium: (343) Courtois; Dendoncker, Ciman, Vertonghen; Meunier, De Bruyne, Witsel (Simons 87), Carrasco; Mertens (Tielemans 78), Lukaku R, Hazard E (Mirallas 73).
Estonia: (4411) Aksalu; Teniste, Baranov, Klavan, Kallaste; Mosnikov (Kams 63), Aleksandr Dmitrijev, Mets, Luts (Marin 84); Vassiljev; Anier (Ojamaa 85).

Cyprus (1) 3 *(Laifis 29, Sotiriou 65, Sielis 87)*
Gibraltar (0) 1 *(Casciaro L 51)* 3151

Cyprus: (433) Panagi; Charalambous, Laifis, Sielis, Demetriou; Artymatas, Kastanos, Charalambos Kyriakou (Nicolaou 90); Efrem (Charalambidis 73), Sotiriou (Mitidis 86), Christofi.
Gibraltar: (451) Ibrahim; Garcia, Barnett, Casciaro R, Olivero[*]; Casciaro K (Garro 74), Walker, Casciaro L, Bardon (Hernandez 68), Chipolina J; Cabrera (Priestley 85).

Greece (0) 1 *(Tzavelas 90)*
Bosnia-Herzegovina (1) 1 *(Karnezis 33 (og))* 20,075

Greece: (4231) Karnezis; Torosidis, Papadopoulos[*], Papastathopoulos, Tzavelas; Maniatis (Gianniotas 61), Samaris; Mantalos (Karelis 86), Fortounis, Stafylidis; Mitroglou.
Bosnia-Herzegovina: (4312) Begovic; Vranjes, Spahic (Sunjic 70), Zukanovic, Kolasinac; Hajrovic (Bicakcic 87), Jajalo, Lulic; Pjanic; Ibisevic (Djuric 84), Dzeko[*].

Saturday, 25 March 2017

Belgium (0) 1 *(Lukaku R 90)*
Greece (0) 1 *(Mitroglou 47)* 42,281

Belgium: (3331) Courtois; Alderweireld, Ciman (Mirallas 84), Vertonghen; Fellaini (Dembele 65), Witsel, Nainggolan; Chadli, Mertens, Carrasco; Lukaku R.
Greece: (4411) Kapino; Torosidis, Manolas, Papastathopoulos, Tzavelas[*]; Mantalos (Zeca 84), Tachtsidis[*], Samaris, Stafylidis; Fortounis (Tziolis 68); Mitroglou (Vellios 90).

Bosnia-Herzegovina (2) 5 *(Ibisevic 4, 43, Vrsajevic 52, Visca 56, Bicakcic 90)*
Gibraltar (0) 0 8285

Bosnia-Herzegovina: (442) Begovic; Bicakcic, Cocalic, Zukanovic, Kolasinac (Pavlovic 45); Vrsajevic (Bajic 75), Pjanic (Vrancic 57), Cimirot, Visca; Hodzic, Ibisevic.
Gibraltar: (442) Ibrahim; Chipolina K (Pusey 53), Payas, Chipolina J, Chipolina R; Garcia, Hernandez, Walker, Gulling (Bardon 75); Casciaro K (Duarte 87), Casciaro L.

Cyprus (0) 0

Estonia (0) 0   3864

Cyprus: (4231) Panagi; Stylianou (Avraam 71), Merkis, Laifis, Charalambous; Artymatas, Laban (Roushias 81); Christofi, Charalambos Kyriakou, Kastanos; Mitidis (Makris 88).
Estonia: (4411) Aksalu; Teniste, Baranov, Klavan, Kruglov; Aleksandr Dmitrijev, Mets, Kait, Vassiljev (Anier 90); Ojamaa (Luts 64); Zenjov (Toomet 78).

Friday, 9 June 2017

Bosnia-Herzegovina (0) 0

Greece (0) 0   11,000

Bosnia-Herzegovina: (4231) Begovic; Bicakcic, Vranjes, Sunjic (Dumic 69), Zukanovic; Pjanic, Jajalo; Visca, Ibisevic, Lulic (Kodro 21 (Besic 77)); Dzeko.
Greece: (4231) Karnezis; Torosidis, Manolas, Papastathopoulos, Stafylidis; Tziolis, Zeca; Mantalos (Kourmpelis 90), Fortounis (Maniatis 90), Bakasetas (Donis 50); Mitroglou.

Estonia (0) 0

Belgium (1) 2 *(Mertens 31, Chadli 86)*   10,176

Estonia: (442) Aksalu; Teniste, Baranov, Klavan, Pikk; Kait (Anier 86), Mets, Artjom Dmitrijev[■], Zenjov (Ojamaa 79); Vassiljev, Luts (Kallaste 74).
Belgium: (3421) Courtois; Alderweireld, Vertonghen, Kompany; Fellaini, Witsel, Chadli, Mertens (Batshuayi 81); De Bruyne, Carrasco; Lukaku R.

Gibraltar (1) 1 *(Hernandez 30)*

Cyprus (1) 2 *(Chipolina R 10 (og), Sotiriou 87)*   488

Gibraltar: (433) Ibrahim; Garcia, Chipolina R, Casciaro R (Coombes 81), Chipolina J; Bardon (Casciaro K 90), Barnett, Olivero; Hernandez, Casciaro L, Walker.
Cyprus: (4231) Panagi; Demetriou, Makris, Laifis, Ioannou; Artymatas (Mitidis 81), Charalambos Kyriakou; Christofi (Merkis 73), Charalambidis, Margaca (Alexandrou 61); Sotiriou.

Thursday, 31 August 2017

Belgium (6) 9 *(Mertens 15, Meunier 18, 60, 67,*
Lukaku R 21, 38, 84 (pen), Witsel 27, Hazard E 45)

Gibraltar (0) 0   24,050

Belgium: (3142) Courtois; Alderweireld, Kompany, Vertonghen; Witsel[■]; Meunier, Hazard E (Hazard T 77), De Bruyne (Tielemans 84), Carrasco; Mertens (Dembele 45), Lukaku R.
Gibraltar: (442) Ibrahim; Garcia, Chipolina R, Barnett[■], Chipolina J; Bosio (Pusey 45), Walker, Casciaro R (Gulling 73), Olivero; Hernandez (Pons 61), Casciaro L.

Cyprus (0) 3 *(Christofi 65, Laban 67, Sotiriou 76)*

Bosnia-Herzegovina (2) 2 *(Sunjic 33, Visca 44)*   4143

Cyprus: (4231) Panagi; Demetriou, Katelaris, Merkis, Margaca (Kastanos 71); Artymatas, Laban; Christofi (Alexandrou 80), Charalambos Kyriakou, Charalambidis (Avraam 47); Sotiriou.
Bosnia-Herzegovina: (4231) Begovic; Bicakcic (Hodzic 81), Sunjic, Vranjes, Kolasinac; Pjanic, Lulic; Visca (Milicevic 64), Ibisevic, Cimirot (Jajalo 76); Dzeko.

Greece (0) 0

Estonia (0) 0   12,379

Greece: (433) Karnezis; Retsos, Papadopoulos (Stafylidis 65), Manolas, Tzavelas; Tziolis, Zeca, Mantalos (Bakasetas 80); Fortounis, Donis, Vellios (Diamantakos 70).
Estonia: (343) Aksalu; Baranov, Jaager, Klavan; Teniste, Kait, Aleksandr Dmitrijev (Antonov 81), Kallaste (Miller 89); Zenjov, Kruglov, Anier (Tamm 90).

Sunday, 3 September 2017

Estonia (0) 1 *(Kait 90)*

Cyprus (0) 0   5491

Estonia: (343) Aksalu; Baranov, Jaager, Mets; Teniste, Antonov, Kait, Pikk; Purje (Tamm 87), Anier (Vassiljev 82), Zenjov (Miller 78).
Cyprus: (4231) Panagi; Demetriou, Laifis, Katelaris, Margaca; Charalambos Kyriakou, Laban; Christofi (Charalambidis 87), Artymatas, Avraam (Kastanos 66); Sotiriou.

Gibraltar (0) 0

Bosnia-Herzegovina (1) 4 *(Dzeko 35, 85, Kodro 65,*
Lulic 83)   805

Gibraltar: (4321) Ibrahim; Garcia, Chipolina R, Olivero, Chipolina J; Pons (Pusey 67), Walker, Green (Duarte 80); Bardon, Hernandez; Casciaro L (Coombes 86).
Bosnia-Herzegovina: (4231) Begovic; Vranjes, Cocalic (Dumic 86), Zukanovic, Kolasinac; Hadzic (Milicevic 66), Jajalo; Visca, Kodro (Bajic 80), Lulic; Dzeko.

Greece (0) 1 *(Zeca 73)*

Belgium (0) 2 *(Vertonghen 70, Lukaku R 74)*   29,465

Greece: (4411) Karnezis; Maniatis (Bakasetas 85), Manolas, Papastathopoulos, Tzavelas; Zeca, Tziolis, Samaris, Stafylidis (Lykogiannis 68); Fortounis (Vellios 89); Donis.
Belgium: (343) Courtois; Alderweireld, Vermaelen, Vertonghen; Meunier, Fellaini (Dendoncker 89), Dembele (Hazard E 74), Carrasco (Chadli 79); De Bruyne, Lukaku R, Mertens.

Saturday, 7 October 2017

Bosnia-Herzegovina (2) 3 *(Medunjanin 30, Visca 39,*
Dumic 81)

Belgium (1) 4 *(Meunier 4, Batshuayi 59, Vertonghen 68,*
Carrasco 84)   9657

Bosnia-Herzegovina: (4231) Begovic; Vranjes, Dumic, Sunjic, Kolasinac; Besic (Jajalo 62), Lulic; Visca (Hajrovic 70), Medunjanin (Ibisevic 74), Duljevic; Dzeko.
Belgium: (3421) Courtois; Alderweireld, Vermaelen, Vertonghen; Meunier, De Bruyne, Fellaini (Dendoncker 29), Carrasco (Chadli 86); Mertens (Tielemans 46); Hazard E; Batshuayi.

Cyprus (1) 1 *(Sotiriou 18)*

Greece (2) 2 *(Mitroglou 25, Tziolis 26)*   7222

Cyprus: (4231) Panagi; Demetriou, Katelaris, Laifis, Antoniades (Alexandrou 60); Artymatas, Laban; Charalambos Kyriakou, Kastanos (Economides 80), Margaca (Mitidis 86); Sotiriou.
Greece: (442) Karnezis; Torosidis (Retsos 69), Manolas, Papastathopoulos, Tzavelas; Mantalos, Zeca, Tziolis, Stafylidis; Fortounis (Donis 75), Mitroglou (Samaris 89).

Gibraltar (0) 0

Estonia (3) 6 *(Luts 10, Kait 30, Zenjov 38,*
Tamm 52, 66, 77)   750

Gibraltar: (4411) Ibrahim; Garcia, Chipolina R, Pusey, Barnett; Walker, Olivero, Bardon, Hernandez; Bosio (Lopez 45); Coombes (Yome 73).
Estonia: (343) Aksalu; Jaager, Mets, Klavan; Teniste, Kait, Vassiljev (Antonov 20), Pikk; Zenjov (Anier 58), Tamm, Luts (Mosnikov 66).

Tuesday, 10 October 2017

Belgium (1) 4 *(Hazard E 12, 63 (pen), Hazard T 52,*
Lukaku R 78)

Cyprus (0) 0   37,765

Belgium: (343) Courtois; Alderweireld, Ciman, Vertonghen; Meunier (Lukaku R 66), Tielemans, Witsel, Chadli; Hazard T, Batshuayi (Mertens 56), Hazard E (De Bruyne 77).
Cyprus: (4141) Panagi; Demetriou, Katelaris, Laifis, Margaca; Merkis; Charalambos Kyriakou (Charalambidis 63), Artymatas (Nikolaou 90), Laban, Alexandrou (Kastanos 45); Sotiriou.

Estonia (0) 1 *(Antonov 75)*

Bosnia-Herzegovina (0) 2 *(Hajrovic 48, 84)*   4967

Estonia: (343) Aksalu; Baranov, Mets, Klavan; Teniste, Kait, Antonov, Pikk; Zenjov (Tamm 69), Anier (Jaager 77), Luts.
Bosnia-Herzegovina: (433) Begovic; Susic, Cocalic, Zukanovic, Kolasinac (Dumic 46); Krunic, Cimirot, Hajrovic; Ibisevic (Dzeko 65), Medunjanin, Kodro (Duljevic 74).

Greece (1) 4 *(Torosidis 32, Mitroglou 61, 63, Gianniotas 78)*
Gibraltar (0) 0 12,739
Greece: (4231) Karnezis; Torosidis (Maniatis 68), Papastathopoulos (Tziolis 68), Papadopoulos, Stafylidis; Zeca, Tachtsidis; Christodoulopoulos (Gianniotas 74), Fortounis, Mantalos; Mitroglou.
Gibraltar: (442) Ibrahim; Garcia, Chipolina R, Barnett, Olivero; Hernandez, Walker, Bardon, Pons (Gulling 72); Coombes (Ruiz 88), Lopez (Yome 62).

Group H Table	P	W	D	L	F	A	GD	Pts
Belgium	10	9	1	0	43	6	37	28
Greece	10	5	4	1	17	6	11	19
Bosnia-Herzegovina	10	5	2	3	24	13	11	17
Estonia	10	3	2	5	13	19	–6	11
Cyprus	10	3	1	6	9	18	–9	10
Gibraltar	10	0	0	10	3	47	–44	0

GROUP I
Monday, 5 September 2016
Croatia (1) 1 *(Rakitic 44 (pen))*
Turkey (1) 1 *(Calhanoglu 45)* 0
Croatia: (4231) Kalinic L; Vrsaljko, Corluka, Vida, Strinic; Pjaca (Kalinic N 79), Badelj, Modric, Perisic, Rakitic (Brozovic 64); Mandzukic (Kramaric 84).
Turkey: (451) Babacan; Ozbayrakli, Aziz, Topal, Koybasi; Ozan Tufan, Yokuslu, Ayhan (Yilmaz Calik 53), Mor (Sen 84), Calhanoglu; Tosun (Sahan 71).
Behind closed doors.

Finland (1) 1 *(Arajuuri 18)*
Kosovo (0) 1 *(Berisha V 60 (pen))* 7571
Finland: (352) Hradecky; Lam (Ring 65), Arajuuri, Moisander; Raitala, Lod (Schuller 88), Halsti, Eremenko, Uronen; Pukki (Hamalainen 73), Pohjanpalo.
Kosovo: (451) Ujkani; Perdedaj, Rrahmani, Pnishi, Paqarada; Rashica, Berisha V (Meha 90), Kryeziu, Alushi, Bernard Berisha (Halimi 81); Bunjaku (Celina 65).

Ukraine (1) 1 *(Yarmolenko 41)*
Iceland (1) 1 *(Finnbogason 6)* 0
Ukraine: (442) Pyatov; Butko, Rakitskiy, Kucher, Sobol; Yarmolenko, Sydorchuk (Zozulya 63), Stepanenko, Konoplyanka; Kovalenko, Zinchenko (Shakhov 90).
Iceland: (442) Halldorsson; Saevarsson, Arnason, Sigurdsson R, Skulason A (Magnusson 40); Gudmundsson J (Hallfredsson 84), Gunnarsson, Sigurdsson G, Bjarnason B (Traustason 75); Finnbogason, Bodvarsson.
Behind closed doors.

Thursday, 6 October 2016
Iceland (1) 3 *(Arnason 37, Finnbogason 90, Sigurdsson R 90)*
Finland (2) 2 *(Pukki 21, Lod 39)* 9548
Iceland: (442) Kristinsson; Saevarsson (Bjarnason T 89), Arnason, Sigurdsson R, Skulason A; Bjarnason B, Gunnarsson, Sigurdsson G, Gudmundsson J; Sigurdarson (Kjartansson 75), Finnbogason.
Finland: (442) Hradecky; Vaisanen, Halsti, Arajuuri, Moisander; Hetemaj P, Ring (Schuller 90), Arkivuo, Lod; Hamalainen (Markkanen 55 (Raitala 85)), Pukki.

Kosovo (0) 0
Croatia (3) 6 *(Mandzukic 6, 24, 35, Mitrovic 68, Perisic 83, Kalinic N 90)* 14,612
Kosovo: (4231) Ujkani; Perdedaj, Pnishi, Pepa, Paqarada; Kryeziu, Berisha V; Rashica, Zeneli (Shala 77), Bernard Berisha (Halimi 58); Celina (Bunjaku 70).
Croatia: (442) Subasic; Vrsaljko, Corluka (Mitrovic 45), Vida, Pivaric; Brozovic, Kovacic, Badelj, Perisic; Kramaric (Rog 71), Mandzukic (Kalinic N 59).

Turkey (1) 2 *(Ozan Tufan 45, Calhanoglu 81 (pen))*
Ukraine (2) 2 *(Yarmolenko 25 (pen), Kravets 27)* 36,714
Turkey: (442) Babacan; Ozbayrakli, Toprak, Balta (Ayhan 45), Erkin; Ozan Tufan (Sen 77), Topal, Mor, Calhanoglu; Unal (Cigerci 45), Tosun.
Ukraine: (4141) Pyatov; Butko, Kucher, Ordets, Sobol; Stepanenko; Yarmolenko, Zinchenko (Sydorchuk 46), Kovalenko, Konoplyanka (Petryak 81); Kravets (Zozulya 73).

Sunday, 9 October 2016
Finland (0) 0
Croatia (1) 1 *(Mandzukic 18)* 15,567
Finland: (4321) Hradecky; Raitala, Ojala, Arajuuri, Vaisanen (Riski 86); Arkivuo (Schuller 45), Moisander, Saksela; Ring (Lam 67), Lod; Pukki.
Croatia: (442) Subasic; Vrsaljko, Mitrovic, Vida, Pivaric; Brozovic (Cop 71), Badelj, Kovacic, Perisic; Kramaric (Rog 81), Mandzukic (Kalinic N 87).

Iceland (2) 2 *(Toprak 42 (og), Finnbogason 45)*
Turkey (0) 0 9775
Iceland: (442) Halldorsson; Saevarsson, Arnason, Sigurdsson R, Skulason A; Bjarnason T (Magnusson 86), Sigurdsson G, Bjarnason B, Gudmundsson J; Finnbogason (Kjartansson 68), Bodvarsson (Sigurdarson 62).
Turkey: (433) Babacan; Ozbayrakli, Toprak, Topal, Erkin; Ozan Tufan (Cigerci 44), Ayhan, Calhanoglu; Oztekin (Tosun 59), Mor, Sen (Erdinc 67).

Ukraine (1) 3 *(Kravets 30, Yarmolenko 81, Rotan 87)*
Kosovo (0) 0 999
Ukraine: (442) Pyatov; Butko, Ordets, Kucher, Sobol; Yarmolenko, Kovalenko, Stepanenko, Konoplyanka (Kryvtsov 78); Zinchenko (Rotan 63), Kravets (Zozulya 84).
Kosovo: (4231) Ujkani; Perdedaj (Sulejmani 77), Rrahmani, Pnishi, Paqarada; Kryeziu, Meha (Bernard Berisha 54); Rashica (Zeneli 66), Shala, Berisha V; Muriqi.

Saturday, 12 November 2016
Croatia (1) 2 *(Brozovic 15, 90)*
Iceland (0) 0 0
Croatia: (4231) Subasic; Vrsaljko, Corluka, Vida, Pivaric; Kovacic (Modric 45), Badelj; Brozovic, Rakitic (Kramaric 85), Perisic; Mandzukic (Cop 90).
Iceland: (442) Halldorsson; Saevarsson, Sigurdsson R, Arnason, Magnusson; Gudmundsson, Sigurdsson G, Gunnarsson, Bjarnason T (Traustason 75); Bjarnason B, Bodvarsson (Kjartansson 75).
Behind closed doors.

Turkey (0) 2 *(Yilmaz 51, Sen 56)*
Kosovo (0) 0 26,555
Turkey: (451) Babacan; Gonul, Yilmaz Calik, Topal, Kaldirim; Sen (Under 77), Ozyakup (Malli 47), Inan, Calhanoglu, Turan; Yilmaz (Tosun 87).
Kosovo: (4141) Ujkani; Perdedaj, Rrahmani, Pnishi, Kololli; Alushi; Rashica, Shala, Berisha V, Zeneli; Muriqi.

Ukraine (1) 1 *(Kravets 25)*
Finland (0) 0 26,482
Ukraine: (4141) Pyatov; Butko, Kucher, Rakitskiy, Sobol; Stepanenko; Yarmolenko, Zinchenko (Rotan 67), Kovalenko (Shakhov 89), Konoplyanka (Tsyhankov 83); Kravets.
Finland: (523) Hradecky; Arkivuo, Vaisanen (Saksela 83), Arajuuri, Toivio, Raitala; Mattila, Halsti (Lam 63); Ring (Markkanen 46), Lod, Pukki.

Friday, 24 March 2017
Croatia (1) 1 *(Kalinic N 38)*
Ukraine (0) 0 33,000
Croatia: (433) Subasic; Jedvaj, Mitrovic, Vida, Pivaric; Modric, Rakitic (Kovacic 80), Badelj; Brozovic (Rog 90), Kalinic N (Kramaric 88), Mandzukic.
Ukraine: (4411) Pyatov; Butko, Ordets, Kucher, Matviyenko; Yarmolenko, Rotan (Sydorchuk 77), Stepanenko, Konoplyanka; Kovalenko (Besyedin 86); Kravets (Seleznyov 59).

Kosovo (0) 1 *(Nuhiu 53)*
Iceland (2) 2 *(Sigurdarson 25, Sigurdsson G 35 (pen))* 6832
Kosovo: (4411) Ujkani; Perdedaj (Avdijaj 74), Kololli, Pnishi, Shala; Rashica (Celina 64), Besart Berisha (Bernard Berisha 83), Rrahmani, Berisha V; Kryeziu; Nuhiu.
Iceland: (442) Halldorsson; Saevarsson, Sigurdsson R, Kjartansson (Bodvarsson 69), Sigurdsson G; Arnason, Gunnarsson, Hallfredsson, Traustason (Gislason 72); Sigurdarson (Skulason O 86), Skulason A.

Turkey (2) 2 *(Tosun 9, 13)*
Finland (0) 0   28,990
Turkey: (442) Babacan; Koybasi, Toprak, Gonul, Inan;
Tosun (Unal 83), Turan, Sahan (Mor 72), Topal; Malli
(Yokuslu 62), Sen.
Finland: (442) Hradecky; Arajuuri, Moisander, Ring
(Forsell 84), Lod; Hetemaj P, Pukki, Arkivuo, Mattila
(Yaghoubi 67); Uronen, Pohjanpalo (Markkanen 72).

Sunday, 11 June 2017
Finland (0) 1 *(Pohjanpalo 72)*
Ukraine (0) 2 *(Konoplyanka 52, Besyedin 75)*   8723
Finland: (4411) Hradecky; Raitala, Moisander, Ojala,
Arkivuo; Uronen (Markkanen 84), Yaghoubi, Lam, Lod
(Jensen 68); Hamalainen; Pukki (Pohjanpalo 68).
Ukraine: (4411) Pyatov; Matviyenko, Rakitskiy, Ordets,
Butko; Konoplyanka (Sobol 86), Malinovsky,
Stepanenko, Yarmolenko; Kovalenko (Shepelyev 76);
Seleznyov (Besyedin 64).

Iceland (0) 1 *(Magnusson 90)*
Croatia (0) 0   9800
Iceland: (442) Halldorsson; Saevarsson, Arnason,
Sigurdsson R (Ingason 90), Magnusson; Gudmundsson J,
Gunnarsson, Hallfredsson, Bjarnason B (Gislason 80);
Sigurdsson G, Finnbogason (Sigurdarson 76).
Croatia: (433) Kalinic L; Jedvaj, Lovren, Vida, Pivaric;
Modric, Kovacic, Badelj; Perisic, Kalinic N (Brozovic 63),
Mandzukic (Santini 88).

Kosovo (1) 1 *(Rrahmani 22)*
Turkey (2) 4 *(Sen 7, Under 31, Yilmaz 61,
Ozan Tufan 83)*   6000
Kosovo: (541) Ujkani (Nurkovic 52); Vojvoda,
Rrahmani, Alushi, Pnishi, Aliti; Zeneli (Bernard Berisha■
53), Berisha V, Kryeziu, Avdijaj (Rashica 74); Nuhiu.
Turkey: (433) Babacan; Gonul, Topal, Soyuncu, Ali
Kaldirim (Koybasi 85); Ozan Tufan, Inan, Ozyakup
(Yazici 74); Under, Yilmaz, Sen (Mor 81).

Saturday, 2 September 2017
Finland (1) 1 *(Ring 8)*
Iceland (0) 0   15,835
Finland: (4411) Hradecky; Toivio (Granlund 70),
Arajuuri, Ojala (Vaisanen 33), Uronen; Lod, Ring,
Sparv, Hetemaj M (Lam 83); Hamalainen; Markkanen.
Iceland: (4411) Halldorsson; Saevarsson (Gislason■ 59),
Arnason, Sigurdsson R, Magnusson; Bjarnason B,
Hallfredsson   (Sigurdarson   59);   Gunnarsson,
Gudmundsson   J;   Sigurdsson   G;   Finnbogason
(Bodvarsson 88).

Ukraine (2) 2 *(Yarmolenko 18, 42)*
Turkey (0) 0   36,796
Ukraine: (352) Pyatov; Butko, Khacheridi, Kryvtsov;
Malyshev, Stepanenko, Yarmolenko, Konoplyanka
(Zinchenko 89), Kravets (Besyedin 70); Rotan
(Malinovsky 78), Kovalenko.
Turkey: (361) Babacan; Ozbayrakli, Koybasi, Aziz
(Soyuncu 73); Belozoglu, Tufan (Ozyakup 59), Cigerci,
Calhanoglu (Turan 67), Topal, Under; Tosun.

Sunday, 3 September 2017
Croatia (0) 1 *(Vida 74)*
Kosovo (0) 0   6839
Croatia: (4231) Subasic; Vrsaljko, Lovren, Vida, Pivaric;
Kovacic (Badelj 55), Modric; Brozovic (Kalinic N 72),
Rakitic (Kramaric 54), Perisic; Mandzukic.
Kosovo: (4141) Ujkani; Vojvoda, Rrahmani, Jashanica,
Kololli (Paqarada 71); Alushi; Rashica, Berisha V,
Kryeziu, Zeneli (Nuhiu 79); Muriqi (Fejzullahu 67).

Tuesday, 5 September 2017
Iceland (0) 2 *(Sigurdsson G 47, 66)*
Ukraine (0) 0   9769
Iceland: (4231) Halldorsson; Saevarsson, Ingason,
Sigurdsson R, Magnusson; Hallfredsson (Skulason O 89),
Gunnarsson;   Gudmundsson   J,   Sigurdsson   G
(Finnbogason   90),   Bjarnason   B;   Bodvarsson
(Sigurdarson 67).

Ukraine: (442) Pyatov; Butko, Khacheridi, Rakitskiy,
Matviyenko; Yarmolenko, Malinovsky (Zinchenko 71),
Stepanenko (Rotan 76), Konoplyanka; Besyedin
(Kravets 71), Kovalenko.

Kosovo (0) 0
Finland (0) 1 *(Pukki 84)*   2446
Kosovo: (451) Ujkani; Vojvoda, Jashanica, Rrahmani,
Paqarada (Muriqi 84); Rashica (Halimi 62), Kryeziu,
Alushi, Berisha V, Bernard Berisha (Zeneli 70); Nuhiu.
Finland: (4411) Hradecky; Granlund, Arajuuri, Vaisanen,
Arkivuo (Pirinen 65); Hamalainen, Lam, Sparv, Lod
(Tuominen 90); Jensen (Skrabb 54); Pukki:

Turkey (0) 1 *(Tosun 76)*
Croatia (0) 0   28,600
Turkey: (442) Babacan; Ayhan, Topal, Soyuncu, Erkin;
Calhanoglu, Sahin (Yokuslu 87), Ozyakup, Turan (Mor
71); Yilmaz (Tufan 82), Tosun.
Croatia: (442) Subasic; Vrsaljko (Cop 85), Lovren, Vida,
Pivaric; Brozovic, Modric, Badelj, Perisic; Kovacic
(Kramaric 71), Kalinic N (Mandzukic 62).

Friday, 6 October 2017
Croatia (0) 1 *(Mandzukic 57)*
Finland (0) 1 *(Soiri 90)*   7578
Croatia: (4231) Subasic; Vrsaljko, Mitrovic, Vida, Pivaric;
Modric, Rakitic; Brozovic (Rog 54), Kramaric (Cop 80),
Perisic; Mandzukic (Pasalic 86).
Finland: (3412) Hradecky; Arajuuri, Moisander, Ojala;
Granlund, Schuller (Pukki 68), Sparv, Hetemaj P (Soiri
80); Hamalainen; Pohjanpalo, Skrabb.

Kosovo (0) 0
Ukraine (0) 2 *(Paqarada 61 (og), Yarmolenko 88)*   1261
Kosovo: (4231) Ujkani; Vojvoda, Rrahmani, Jashanica,
Paqarada; Musolli (Kastrati F 84), Kryeziu (Rashani 54);
Rashica, Halimi, Celina; Muriqi (Nuhiu 72).
Ukraine: (4231) Pyatov; Karavayev, Khacheridi, Ordets,
Matviyenko; Rotan (Stepanenko 63), Sydorchuk;
Yarmolenko, Konoplyanka (Buyalsky 89), Harmash;
Kravets (Marlos 46).

Turkey (0) 0
Iceland (2) 3 *(Gudmundsson J 32, Bjarnason B 39,
Arnason 50)*   30,390
Turkey: (4231) Babacan; Ayhan, Topal, Soyuncu, Erkin;
Sahin (Tufan 45), Belozoglu (Malli 78); Tosun, Ozyakup,
Turan (Mor 60); Yilmaz.
Iceland: (442) Halldorsson; Saevarsson, Arnason,
Sigurdsson R, Magnusson; Gudmundsson J (Skulason A
82), Gunnarsson (Ingason 65), Sigurdsson G, Bjarnason
B; Bodvarsson, Finnbogason (Skulason O 78).

Monday, 9 October 2017
Finland (0) 2 *(Arajuuri 76, Pohjanpalo 88)*
Turkey (0) 2 *(Tosun 57, 83)*   6612
Finland: (442) Hradecky; Pirinen, Arajuuri, Vaisanen,
Moisander; Lod, Lam (Markkanen 85), Schuller,
Hetemaj P (Hamalainen 60); Pukki (Soiri 82),
Pohjanpalo.
Turkey: (4411) Babacan; Tufan, Toprak, Soyuncu,
Koybasi; Yazici (Mor 76), Inan (Topal 85), Yokuslu,
Calhanoglu; Ozyakup; Tosun.

Iceland (1) 2 *(Sigurdsson G 40, Gudmundsson 68)*
Kosovo (0) 0   9775
Iceland: (451) Halldorsson; Saevarsson, Sigurdsson R,
Arnason, Magnusson; Gudmundsson J, Hallfredsson
(Sigurjonsson 88), Gunnarsson (Ingason 78), Bjarnason
B, Sigurdsson G; Bodvarsson (Finnbogason 61).
Kosovo: (451) Ujkani; Vojvoda, Jashanica, Rrahmani,
Paqarada; Rashica, Pnishi (Bernard Berisha 53), Halimi
(Kastrati L 78), Berisha V, Celina; Nuhiu (Muriqi 54).

Ukraine (0) 0
Croatia (0) 2 *(Kramaric 62, 70)*   60,200
Ukraine: (4411) Pyatov; Karavayev, Rakitskiy,
Khacheridi, Matviyenko; Yarmolenko, Rotan
(Sydorchuk 68), Stepanenko, Konoplyanka; Marlos
(Besyedin 78); Harmash (Kovalenko 66).
Croatia: (442) Subasic; Vida, Lovren, Mitrovic, Vrsaljko
(Pivaric 86); Kramaric (Pasalic 88), Rakitic, Badelj,
Perisic; Modric, Mandzukic (Rog 90).

Group I Table	P	W	D	L	F	A	GD	Pts
Iceland	10	7	1	2	16	7	9	22
Croatia	10	6	2	2	15	4	11	20
Ukraine	10	5	2	3	13	9	4	17
Turkey	10	4	3	3	14	13	1	15
Finland	10	2	3	5	9	13	–4	9
Kosovo	10	0	1	9	3	24	–21	1

*Russia (hosts), France, Portugal, Germany, Serbia,
Poland, England, Spain, Belgium and Iceland qualify for
the World Cup 2018.*

PLAY-OFFS FIRST LEG

Thursday, 9 November 2017
Croatia (3) 4 *(Modric 13 (pen), Kalinic N 19, Perisic 34,
Kramaric 49)*
Greece (1) 1 *(Papastathopoulos 30)*   30,013
Croatia: (4231) Subasic; Vrsaljko, Lovren, Vida, Strinic;
Rakitic, Brozovic; Kramaric (Vlasic 82), Modric (Pasalic
89), Perisic; Kalinic N (Rebic 75).
Greece: (4231) Karnezis; Maniatis (Retsos 46),
Papadopoulos, Papastathopoulos, Tzavelas; Samaris
(Tachtsidis 62), Tziolis; Zeca, Fortounis, Stafylidis
(Bakasetas 71); Mitroglou.

Northern Ireland (0) 0
Switzerland (0) 1 *(Rodriguez 58 (pen))*   18,269
Northern Ireland: (433) McGovern; McLaughlin C,
McAuley, Evans J, Brunt; Evans C (Saville 66),
Norwood, Davis; Magennis, Lafferty K (Washington 77),
Dallas (Ward 52).
Switzerland: (4231) Sommer; Lichtsteiner, Schar, Akanji,
Rodriguez; Zakaria, Xhaka; Shaqiri, Dzemaili (Frei 83),
Zuber (Mehmedi 87); Seferovic (Embolo 77).

Friday, 10 November 2017
Sweden (0) 1 *(Johansson 61)*
Italy (0) 0   49,193
Sweden: (442) Olsen; Krafth (Svensson 83), Lindelof,
Granqvist, Augustinsson; Claesson, Larsson, Ekdal
(Johansson 57), Forsberg; Toivonen, Berg (Thelin 74).
Italy: (352) Buffon; Barzagli, Bonucci, Chiellini;
Candreva, De Rossi, Parolo, Verratti (Insigne 76),
Darmian; Immobile, Belotti (Eder 65).

Saturday, 11 November 2017
Denmark (0) 0
Republic of Ireland (0) 0   36,189
Denmark: (433) Schmeichel; Ankersen, Kjaer, Bjelland,
Larsen; Delaney, Kvist, Eriksen; Cornelius (Poulsen 64),
Jorgensen N, Sisto (Bendtner 72).
Republic of Ireland: (4411) Randolph; Christie, Duffy,
Clark, Ward; O'Dowda, Hendrick (Hourihane 90), Arter
(Whelan 88), McClean; Brady; Murphy (Long S 73).

PLAY-OFFS SECOND LEG

Sunday, 12 November 2017
Greece (0) 0
Croatia (0) 0   18,667
Greece: (4411) Karnezis; Torosidis, Papastathopoulos,
Manolas, Retsos; Zeca, Tziolis, Tachtsidis,
Christodoulopoulos (Fortounis 59); Bakasetas
(Gianniotas 59); Mitroglou (Pelkas 78).
Croatia: (4231) Subasic; Vrsaljko, Lovren, Vida, Strinic;
Rakitic, Brozovic; Mandzukic, Modric (Mitrovic 90),
Perisic (Rebic 85); Kalinic N (Kramaric 78).
Croatia won 4-1 on aggregate.

Switzerland (0) 0
Northern Ireland (0) 0   36,000
Switzerland: (4411) Sommer; Lichtsteiner, Schar, Akanji,
Rodriguez; Shaqiri (Freuler 80), Zakaria, Xhaka, Zuber;
Dzemaili (Mehmedi 61); Seferovic (Embolo 86).
Northern Ireland: (451) McGovern; Hughes, Evans J,
McAuley, Brunt; Ward (Jones 74), Davis, Norwood
(Magennis 75), Saville, Dallas; Washington (McNair 82).
Switzerland won 1-0 on aggregate.

Monday, 13 November 2017
Italy (0) 0
Sweden (0) 0   72,696
Italy: (352) Buffon; Barzagli, Bonucci, Chiellini;
Candreva (Bernardeschi 76), Florenzi, Jorginho, Parolo,
Darmian (El Shaarawy 63); Gabbiadini (Belotti 63),
Immobile.
Sweden: (442) Olsen; Lustig, Lindelof, Granqvist,
Augustinsson; Claesson (Rohden 71), Johansson
(Svensson 19), Larsson, Forsberg; Toivonen (Thelin 54),
Berg.
Sweden won 1-0 on aggregate.

Tuesday, 14 November 2017
Republic of Ireland (1) 1 *(Duffy 6)*
Denmark (2) 5 *(Christie 29 (og), Eriksen 32, 63, 73,
Bendtner 90 (pen))*   50,000
Republic of Ireland: (451) Randolph; Christie, Duffy,
Clark (Long S 71), Ward; Hendrick, Arter (McGeady
46), Meyler (Hoolahan 46), Brady, McClean; Murphy.
Denmark: (343) Schmeichel; Kjaer, Christensen,
Bjelland; Poulsen (Cornelius 70), Delaney, Kvist, Larsen
(Ankersen 54); Jorgensen N (Bendtner 84), Eriksen,
Sisto.
Denmark won 5-1 on aggregate.

*Croatia, Switzerland, Sweden and Denmark qualify for
the World Cup 2018.*

FIFA WORLD CUP 2018 QUALIFYING COMPETITION – REST OF THE WORLD

SOUTH AMERICA (CONMEBOL)

After extra time.

ROUND ONE

Bolivia v Uruguay	0-2
Colombia v Peru	2-0
Venezuela v Paraguay	0-1
Chile v Brazil	2-0
Argentina v Ecuador	0-2
Ecuador v Bolivia	2-0
Uruguay v Colombia	3-0
Paraguay v Argentina	0-0
Brazil v Venezuela	3-1
Peru v Chile	3-4
Bolivia v Venezuela	4-2
Ecuador v Uruguay	2-1
Chile v Colombia	1-1
Argentina v Brazil	1-1
Peru v Paraguay	1-0
Colombia v Argentina	0-1
Venezuela v Ecuador	1-3
Paraguay v Bolivia	2-1
Uruguay v Chile	3-0
Brazil v Peru	3-0
Bolivia v Colombia	2-3
Ecuador v Paraguay	2-2
Chile v Argentina	1-2
Peru v Venezuela	2-2
Brazil v Uruguay	2-2
Colombia v Ecuador	3-1
Uruguay v Peru	1-0
Venezuela v Chile	1-4
Argentina v Bolivia	2-0
Paraguay v Brazil	2-2
Bolivia v Peru	0-3

Match awarded 3-0 to Peru after Bolivia fielded an ineligible player, original match Bolivia won 2-0.

Colombia v Venezuela	2-0
Ecuador v Brazil	0-3
Argentina v Uruguay	1-0
Paraguay v Chile	2-1
Uruguay v Paraguay	4-0
Chile v Bolivia	3-0

Match awarded 3-0 to Chile after Bolivia fielded an ineligible player, original match drawn 0-0.

Venezuela v Argentina	2-2
Brazil v Colombia	2-1
Peru v Ecuador	2-1
Ecuador v Chile	3-0
Uruguay v Venezuela	3-0
Paraguay v Colombia	0-1
Brazil v Bolivia	5-0
Peru v Argentina	2-2
Bolivia v Ecuador	2-2
Colombia v Uruguay	2-2
Argentina v Paraguay	0-1
Chile v Peru	2-1
Venezuela v Brazil	0-2

Colombia v Chile	0-0
Uruguay v Ecuador	2-1
Paraguay v Peru	1-4
Brazil v Argentina	3-0
Venezuela v Bolivia	5-0
Bolivia v Paraguay	1-0
Ecuador v Venezuela	3-0
Argentina v Colombia	3-0
Chile v Uruguay	3-1
Peru v Brazil	0-2
Colombia v Bolivia	1-0
Paraguay v Ecuador	2-1
Uruguay v Brazil	1-4
Argentina v Chile	1-0
Venezuela v Peru	2-2
Bolivia v Argentina	2-0
Ecuador v Colombia	0-2
Chile v Venezuela	3-1
Brazil v Paraguay	3-0
Peru v Uruguay	2-1
Venezuela v Colombia	0-0
Chile v Paraguay	0-3
Uruguay v Argentina	0-0
Brazil v Ecuador	2-0
Peru v Bolivia	2-1
Bolivia v Chile	1-0
Colombia v Brazil	1-1
Ecuador v Peru	1-2
Argentina v Venezuela	1-1
Paraguay v Uruguay	1-2
Bolivia v Brazil	0-0
Venezuela v Uruguay	0-0
Argentina v Peru	0-0
Chile v Ecuador	2-1
Colombia v Paraguay	1-2
Brazil v Chile	3-0
Ecuador v Argentina	1-3
Paraguay v Venezuela	0-1
Peru v Colombia	1-1
Uruguay v Bolivia	4-2

South America Table

Team	P	W	D	L	F	A	GD	Pts
Brazil	18	12	5	1	41	11	+30	41
Uruguay	18	9	4	5	32	20	+12	31
Argentina	18	7	7	4	19	16	+3	28
Colombia	18	7	6	5	21	19	+2	27
Peru	18	7	5	6	27	26	+1	26
Chile	18	8	2	8	26	27	−1	26
Paraguay	18	7	3	8	19	25	−6	24
Ecuador	18	6	2	10	26	29	−3	20
Bolivia	18	4	2	12	16	38	−22	14
Venezuela	18	2	6	10	19	35	−16	12

Brazil, Uruguay, Argentina and Colombia qualify for the World Cup 2018; Peru qualify for OFC–CONMEBOL inter-confederation play-off.

AFRICA (CAF)

FIRST ROUND FIRST LEG

Somalia v Niger	0-2
South Sudan v Mauritania	1-1
Gambia v Namibia	1-1
Sao Tome & Principe v Ethiopia	1-0
Chad v Sierra Leone	1-0
Comoros v Lesotho	0-0
Djibouti v Swaziland	0-6
Eritrea v Botswana	0-2
Seychelles v Burundi	0-1
Liberia v Guinea-Bissau	1-1
Central African Republic v Madagascar	0-3
Mauritius v Kenya	2-5
Tanzania v Malawi	2-0

FIRST ROUND SECOND LEG (agg)

Niger v Somalia	4-0	6-0
Mauritania v South Sudan	4-0	5-1
Namibia v Gambia	2-1	3-2
Ethiopia v Sao Tome & Principe	3-0	3-1
Sierra Leone v Chad	2-1	2-2

Chad won on away goals.

Lesotho v Comoros	1-1	1-1

Comoros won on away goals

Swaziland v Djibouti	2-1	8-1
Botswana v Eritrea	3-1	5-1
Burundi v Seychelles	2-0	3-0
Guinea-Bissau v Liberia	1-3	2-4
Madagascar v Central African Republic	2-2	5-2
Kenya v Mauritius	0-0	5-2
Malawi v Tanzania	1-0	1-2

SECOND ROUND FIRST LEG

Niger v Cameroon	0-3
Mauritania v Tunisia	1-2
Namibia v Guinea	0-1
Ethiopia v Congo	3-4
Chad v Egypt	1-0
Comoros v Ghana	0-0
Swaziland v Nigeria	0-0
Botswana v Mali	2-1
Burundi v DR Congo	2-3
Liberia v Ivory Coast	0-1
Madagascar v Senegal	2-2
Kenya v Cape Verde Islands	1-0
Tanzania v Algeria	2-2
Sudan v Zambia	0-1
Libya v Rwanda	1-0
Morocco v Equatorial Guinea	2-0
Mozambique v Gabon	1-0
Benin v Burkina Faso	2-1
Togo v Uganda	0-1
Angola v South Africa	1-3

SECOND ROUND SECOND LEG

		(agg)
Cameroon v Niger	0-0	3-0
Tunisia v Mauritania	2-1	4-2
Guinea v Namibia	2-0	3-0
Congo v Ethiopia	2-1	6-4
Egypt v Chad	4-0	4-1
Ghana v Comoros	2-0	2-0
Nigeria v Swaziland	2-0	2-0
Mali v Botswana	2-0	3-2
DR Congo v Burundi	3-0	6-2

Match awarded 3-0 to DR Congo after Burundi fielded an ineligible player, original match drawn 2-2.

Ivory Coast v Liberia	3-0	4-0
Senegal v Madagascar	3-0	5-2
Cape Verde Islands v Kenya	2-0	2-1
Algeria v Tanzania	7-0	9-2
Zambia v Sudan	2-0	3-0
Rwanda v Libya	1-3	1-4
Equatorial Guinea v Morocco	1-0	1-2
Gabon v Mozambique	1-0*	1-1

Gabon won 4-3 on penalties.

Burkina Faso v Benin	2-0	3-2
Uganda v Togo	3-0	4-0
South Africa v Angola	1-0	4-1

THIRD ROUND

GROUP A

DR Congo v Libya	4-0
Tunisia v Guinea	2-0
Libya v Tunisia	0-1
Guinea v DR Congo	1-2
Guinea v Libya	3-2
Tunisia v DR Congo	2-1
Libya v Guinea	1-0
DR Congo v Tunisia	2-2
Guinea v Tunisia	1-4
Libya v DR Congo	1-2
Tunisia v Libya	0-0
DR Congo v Guinea	3-1

Group A Table	P	W	D	L	F	A	GD	Pts
Tunisia	6	4	2	0	11	4	7	14
DR Congo	6	4	1	1	14	7	7	13
Libya	6	1	1	4	4	10	–6	4
Guinea	6	1	0	5	6	14	–8	3

GROUP B

Zambia v Nigeria	1-2
Algeria v Cameroon	1-1
Cameroon v Zambia	1-1
Nigeria v Algeria	3-1
Nigeria v Cameroon	4-0
Zambia v Algeria	3-1
Cameroon v Nigeria	1-1
Algeria v Zambia	0-1

Nigeria v Zambia	1-0
Cameroon v Algeria	2-0
Algeria v Nigeria	3-0

Match awarded 3-0 to Algeria after Nigeria fielded an ineligible player, original match drawn 1-1.

Zambia v Cameroon	2-2

Group B Table	P	W	D	L	F	A	GD	Pts
Nigeria	6	4	1	1	11	6	5	13
Zambia	6	2	2	2	8	7	1	8
Cameroon	6	1	4	1	7	9	–2	7
Algeria	6	1	1	4	6	10	–4	4

GROUP C

Gabon v Morocco	0-0
Ivory Coast v Mali	3-1
Mali v Gabon	0-0
Morocco v Ivory Coast	0-0
Morocco v Mali	6-0
Gabon v Ivory Coast	0-3
Ivory Coast v Gabon	1-2
Mali v Morocco	0-0
Mali v Ivory Coast	0-0
Morocco v Gabon	3-0
Gabon v Mali	0-0
Ivory Coast v Morocco	0-2

Group C Table	P	W	D	L	F	A	GD	Pts
Morocco	6	3	3	0	11	0	11	12
Ivory Coast	6	2	2	2	7	5	2	8
Gabon	6	1	3	2	2	7	–5	6
Mali	6	0	4	2	1	9	–8	4

GROUP D

Burkina Faso v South Africa	1-1
Senegal v Cape Verde Islands	2-0
South Africa v Senegal	0-2

FIFA ordered a replay of the original match after CAS upheld the lifetime ban of the match referee Joseph Lamptey. South Africa won the original match 2-0.

Cape Verde Islands v Burkina Faso	0-2
Cape Verde Islands v South Africa	2-1
Senegal v Burkina Faso	0-0
South Africa v Cape Verde Islands	1-2
Burkina Faso v Senegal	2-2
South Africa v Burkina Faso	3-1
Cape Verde Islands v Senegal	0-2
Burkina Faso v Cape Verde Islands	4-0
Senegal v South Africa	2-1

Group D Table	P	W	D	L	F	A	GD	Pts
Senegal	6	4	2	0	10	3	7	14
Burkina Faso	6	2	3	1	10	6	4	9
Cape Verde Islands	6	2	0	4	4	12	–8	6
South Africa	6	1	1	4	7	10	–3	4

GROUP E

Ghana v Uganda	0-0
Congo v Egypt	1-2
Uganda v Congo	1-0
Egypt v Ghana	2-0
Uganda v Egypt	1-0
Ghana v Congo	1-1
Congo v Ghana	1-5
Egypt v Uganda	1-0
Uganda v Ghana	0-0
Egypt v Congo	2-1
Congo v Uganda	1-1
Ghana v Egypt	1-1

Group E Table	P	W	D	L	F	A	GD	Pts
Egypt	6	4	1	1	8	4	4	13
Uganda	6	2	3	1	3	2	1	9
Ghana	6	1	4	1	7	5	2	7
Congo	6	0	2	4	5	12	–7	2

Tunisia, Nigeria, Morrocco, Senegal and Egypt qualify for the World Cup 2018.

ASIA (AFC)

FIRST ROUND FIRST LEG

India v Nepal	2-0
Yemen v Pakistan	3-1
Timor-Leste v Mongolia	4-1
Cambodia v Macao	3-0
Chinese Taipei v Brunei	0-1
Sri Lanka v Bhutan	0-1

FIRST ROUND SECOND LEG

		(agg)
Nepal v India	0-0	0-2
Pakistan v Yemen	0-0	1-3
Mongolia v Timor-Leste	6-0	

Tie awarded 6-0 (3-0 each leg) to Mongolia after Timor-Leste fielded a number of ineligible players. This ruling was made after the second round, Timor-Leste played in the second round and Mongolia were not re-instated.

Macao v Cambodia	1-1	1-4
Brunei v Chinese Taipei	0-2	1-2
Bhutan v Sri Lanka	2-1	3-1

SECOND ROUND

GROUP A

Malaysia v Timor-Leste*	3-0
Saudi Arabia v Palestine	3-2
Timor-Leste* v United Arab Emirates	0-3
Malaysia v Palestine	0-6
United Arab Emirates v Malaysia	10-0
Saudi Arabia v Timor-Leste*	7-0
Malaysia v Saudi Arabia	0-3

Match abandoned at 2-1 to South Arabia after crowd trouble, and awarded 3-0.

Palestine v United Arab Emirates	0-0
Timor-Leste* v Palestine	0-3
Saudi Arabia v United Arab Emirates	2-1
Timor-Leste* v Malaysia	0-3
Palestine v Saudi Arabia	0-0
Palestine v Malaysia	6-0
United Arab Emirates v Timor-Leste	8-0
Timor-Leste v Saudi Arabia	0-10
Malaysia v United Arab Emirates	1-2
United Arab Emirates v Palestine	2-0
Saudi Arabia v Malaysia	2-0
Palestine v Timor-Leste	7-0
United Arab Emirates v Saudi Arabia	1-1

* Timor-Leste forfeited 5 group matches after fielding a number of ineligible players.

Group A Table	P	W	D	L	F	A	GD	Pts
Saudi Arabia	8	6	2	0	28	4	24	20
United Arab Emirates	8	5	2	1	27	4	23	17
Palestine	8	4	2	2	24	5	19	14
Malaysia	8	2	0	6	7	29	–22	6
Timor-Leste	8	0	0	8	0	44	–44	0

GROUP B

Bangladesh v Kyrgyzstan	1-3
Tajikistan v Jordan	1-3
Bangladesh v Tajikistan	1-1
Kyrgyzstan v Australia	1-2
Australia v Bangladesh	5-0
Jordan v Kyrgyzstan	0-0
Bangladesh v Jordan	0-4
Tajikistan v Australia	0-3
Jordan v Australia	2-0
Kyrgyzstan v Tajikistan	2-2
Kyrgyzstan v Bangladesh	2-0
Jordan v Tajikistan	3-0
Australia v Kyrgyzstan	3-0
Tajikistan v Bangladesh	5-0
Bangladesh v Australia	0-4
Kyrgyzstan v Jordan	1-0
Australia v Tajikistan	7-0
Jordan v Bangladesh	8-0
Australia v Jordan	5-1
Tajikistan v Kyrgyzstan	0-1

Group B Table	P	W	D	L	F	A	GD	Pts
Australia	8	7	0	1	29	4	25	21
Jordan	8	5	1	2	21	7	14	16
Kyrgyzstan	8	4	2	2	10	8	2	14
Tajikistan	8	1	2	5	9	20	–11	5
Bangladesh	8	0	1	7	2	32	–30	1

GROUP C

Hong Kong v Bhutan	7-0
Maldives v Qatar	0-1
Bhutan v China PR	0-6
Hong Kong v Maldives	2-0
China PR v Hong Kong	0-0
Qatar v Bhutan	15-0
Maldives v China PR	0-3
Hong Kong v Qatar	2-3
Bhutan v Maldives	3-4
Qatar v China PR	1-0
Bhutan v Hong Kong	0-1
Qatar v Maldives	4-0
Maldives v Hong Kong	0-1
China PR v Bhutan	12-0
Bhutan v Qatar	0-3
Hong Kong v China PR	0-0
China PR v Maldives	4-0
Qatar v Hong Kong	2-0
China PR v Qatar	2-0
Maldives v Bhutan	4-2

Group C Table	P	W	D	L	F	A	GD	Pts
Qatar	8	7	0	1	29	4	25	21
China PR	8	5	2	1	27	1	26	17
Hong Kong	8	4	2	2	13	5	8	14
Maldives	8	2	0	6	8	20	–12	6
Bhutan	8	0	0	8	5	52	–47	0

GROUP D

Guam v Turkmenistan	1-0
India v Oman	1-2
Guam v India	2-1
Turkmenistan v Iran	1-1
Iran v Guam	6-0
Oman v Turkmenistan	3-1
Guam v Oman	0-0
India v Iran	0-3

Match awarded 3-0 to Iran after India fielded an ineligible player, original match Iran won 3-0.

Turkmenistan v India	2-1
Oman v Iran	1-1
Turkmenistan v Guam	1-0
Oman v India	3-0
Iran v Turkmenistan	3-1
India v Guam	1-0
Guam v Iran	0-6
Turkmenistan v Oman	2-1
Iran v India	4-0
Oman v Guam	1-0
India v Turkmenistan	1-2
Iran v Oman	2-0

Group D Table	P	W	D	L	F	A	GD	Pts
Iran	8	6	2	0	26	3	23	20
Oman	8	4	2	2	11	7	4	14
Turkmenistan	8	4	1	3	10	11	–1	13
Guam	8	2	1	5	3	16	–13	7
India	8	1	0	7	5	18	–13	3

GROUP E

Cambodia v Singapore	0-4
Afghanistan v Syria	0-6
Japan v Singapore	0-0
Cambodia v Afghanistan	0-1
Japan v Cambodia	3-0
Syria v Singapore	1-0
Cambodia v Syria	0-6
Afghanistan v Japan	0-6
Singapore v Afghanistan	1-0
Syria v Japan	0-3
Singapore v Cambodia	2-1
Syria v Afghanistan	5-2
Singapore v Japan	0-3
Afghanistan v Cambodia	3-0
Cambodia v Japan	0-2
Japan v Afghanistan	5-0
Syria v Cambodia	6-0
Afghanistan v Singapore	2-1
Japan v Syria	5-0

Group E Table	P	W	D	L	F	A	GD	Pts
Japan	8	7	1	0	27	0	27	22
Syria	8	6	0	2	26	11	15	18
Singapore	8	3	1	4	9	9	0	10
Afghanistan	8	3	0	5	8	24	–16	9
Cambodia	8	0	0	8	1	27	–26	0

GROUP F

Thailand v Vietnam	1-0
Chinese Taipei v Thailand	0-2
Iraq v Chinese Taipei	5-1
Chinese Taipei v Vietnam	1-2
Thailand v Iraq	2-2
Vietnam v Iraq	1-1
Vietnam v Thailand	0-3
Thailand v Chinese Taipei	4-2
Chinese Taipei v Iraq	0-2
Vietnam v Chinese Taipei	4-1
Iraq v Thailand	2-2
Iraq v Vietnam	1-0

Indonesia suspended, all matches cancelled.

Group F Table	P	W	D	L	F	A	GD	Pts
Thailand	6	4	2	0	14	6	8	14
Iraq	6	3	3	0	13	6	7	12
Vietnam	6	2	1	3	7	8	–1	7
Chinese Taipei	6	0	0	6	5	19	–14	0
Indonesia	0	0	0	0	0	0	0	0

GROUP G

Laos v Myanmar	2-2
Lebanon v Kuwait	0-1
Myanmar v Korea Republic	0-2
Laos v Lebanon	0-2
Korea Republic v Laos	8-0
Kuwait v Myanmar	9-0
Laos v Kuwait	0-2
Lebanon v Korea Republic	0-3
Myanmar v Lebanon	0-2
Kuwait v Korea Republic	0-1
Myanmar v Laos	3-1
Kuwait v Lebanon	0-0
Korea Republic v Myanmar	4-0
Lebanon v Laos	7-0
Laos v Korea Republic	0-5
Myanmar* v Kuwait	3-0
Korea Republic v Lebanon	1-0
Kuwait* v Laos	0-3
Lebanon v Myanmar	1-1
Korea Republic* v Kuwait	3-0

Kuwait suspended on 16 October 2015. All subsequent matches awarded to opposition 3-0 and games not played.

Group G Table	P	W	D	L	F	A	GD	Pts
Korea Republic	8	8	0	0	27	0	27	24
Lebanon	8	3	2	3	12	6	6	11
Kuwait	8	3	1	4	12	10	2	10
Myanmar	8	2	2	4	9	21	–12	8
Laos	8	1	1	6	6	29	–23	4

GROUP H

Philippines v Bahrain	2-1
Yemen v Korea DPR	0-3

Match awarded 3-0 to Korea DPR after Yemen fielded an ineligible player, original match Korea DPR won 1-0.

Korea DPR v Uzbekistan	4-2
Yemen v Philippines	0-2
Uzbekistan v Yemen	1-0
Bahrain v Korea DPR	0-1
Philippines v Uzbekistan	1-5
Yemen v Bahrain	0-4
Korea DPR v Philippines	0-0
Bahrain v Uzbekistan	0-4
Korea DPR v Yemen	1-0
Bahrain v Philippines	2-0
Philippines v Yemen	0-1
Uzbekistan v Korea DPR	3-1
Korea DPR v Bahrain	2-0
Yemen v Uzbekistan	1-3
Uzbekistan v Philippines	1-0
Bahrain v Yemen	3-0
Philippines v Korea DPR	3-2
Uzbekistan v Bahrain	1-0

Group H Table	P	W	D	L	F	A	GD	Pts
Uzbekistan	8	7	0	1	20	7	13	21
Korea DPR	8	5	1	2	14	8	6	16
Philippines	8	3	1	4	8	12	–4	10
Bahrain	8	3	0	5	10	10	0	9
Yemen	8	1	0	7	2	17	–15	3

THIRD ROUND

GROUP A

Korea Republic v China PR	3-2
Uzbekistan v Syria	1-0
Iran v Qatar	2-0
China PR v Iran	0-0
Syria v Korea Republic	0-0
Qatar v Uzbekistan	0-1
Korea Republic v Qatar	3-2
China PR v Syria	0-1
Uzbekistan v Iran	0-1
Uzbekistan v China PR	2-0
Iran v Korea Republic	1-0
Qatar v Syria	1-0
Korea Republic v Uzbekistan	2-1
China PR v Qatar	0-0
Syria v Iran	0-0
China PR v Korea Republic	1-0
Syria v Uzbekistan	1-0
Qatar v Iran	0-1
Korea Republic v Syria	1-0
Iran v China PR	1-0
Uzbekistan v Qatar	1-0
Iran v Uzbekistan	2-0
Syria v China PR	2-2
Qatar v Korea Republic	3-2
China PR v Uzbekistan	1-0
Korea Republic v Iran	0-0
Syria v Qatar	3-1
Qatar v China PR	1-2
Iran v Syria	2-2
Uzbekistan v Korea Republic	0-0

Group A Table	P	W	D	L	F	A	GD	Pts
Iran	10	6	4	0	10	2	8	22
Korea Republic	10	4	3	3	11	10	1	15
Syria	10	3	4	3	9	8	1	13
Uzbekistan	10	4	1	5	6	7	–1	13
China PR	10	3	3	4	8	10	–2	12
Qatar	10	2	1	7	8	15	–7	7

GROUP B

Australia v Iraq	2-0
Japan v United Arab Emirates	1-2
Saudi Arabia v Thailand	1-0
Iraq v Saudi Arabia	1-2
Thailand v Japan	0-2
United Arab Emirates v Australia	0-1
Japan v Iraq	2-1
United Arab Emirates v Thailand	3-1
Saudi Arabia v Australia	2-2
Australia v Japan	1-1
Iraq v Thailand	4-0
Saudi Arabia v United Arab Emirates	3-0
Japan v Saudi Arabia	2-1
Thailand v Australia	2-2
United Arab Emirates v Iraq	2-0
Iraq v Australia	1-1
Thailand v Saudi Arabia	0-3
United Arab Emirates v Japan	0-2
Australia v United Arab Emirates	2-0
Japan v Thailand	4-0
Saudi Arabia v Iraq	1-0
Australia v Saudi Arabia	3-2
Thailand v United Arab Emirates	1-1
Iraq v Japan	1-1
United Arab Emirates v Saudi Arabia	2-1
Japan v Australia	2-0
Thailand v Iraq	1-2
Australia v Thailand	2-1
Iraq v United Arab Emirates	1-0
Saudi Arabia v Japan	1-0

Group B Table	P	W	D	L	F	A	GD	Pts
Japan	10	6	2	2	17	7	10	20
Saudi Arabia	10	6	1	3	17	10	7	19
Australia	10	5	4	1	16	11	5	19
United Arab Emirates	10	4	1	5	10	13	–3	13
Iraq	10	3	2	5	11	12	–1	11
Thailand	10	0	2	8	6	24	–18	2

Iran, Korea Republic, Japan and Saudi Arabia qualify for the World Cup 2108. Syria and Australia play each other in fourth round play-off.

FOURTH ROUND FIRST LEG

Syria v Australia	1-1

FOURTH ROUND SECOND LEG

Australia v Syria	2-1*

Australia qualify for CONCACAF–AFC inter-contfederation play-off.

NORTH, CENTRAL AMERICA AND CARIBBEAN (CONCACAF)

ROUND FIRST LEG

Bahamas v Bermuda	0-5
British Virgin Islands v Dominica	2-3
Barbados v US Virgin Islands	0-1
St Kitts & Nevis v Turks & Caicos Islands	6-2
Nicaragua v Anguilla	5-0
Belize v Cayman Islands	0-0
Curacao v Montserrat	2-1

FIRST ROUND SECOND LEG

		(agg)
Bermuda v Bahamas	3-0	8-0
Dominica v British Virgin Islands	0-0	3-2
US Virgin Islands v Barbados	0-4	1-4
Turks & Caicos Islands v St Kitts & Nevis	2-6	4-12
Anguilla v Nicaragua	0-3	0-8
Cayman Islands v Belize	1-1	1-1
Belize won on away goals.		
Montserrat v Curacao	2-2	3-4

SECOND ROUND FIRST LEG

St Vincent & Grenadines v Guyana	2-2
Antigua & Barbuda v Saint Lucia	1-3
Puerto Rico v Grenada	1-0
Dominica v Canada	0-2
Dominican Republic v Belize	1-2
Guatemala v Bermuda	0-0
Aruba v Barbados	0-2
St Kitts & Nevis v El Salvador	2-2
Curacao v Cuba	0-0
Nicaragua v Suriname	1-0

SECOND ROUND SECOND LEG

		(agg)
Guyana v St Vincent & Grenadines	4-4	6-6
St Vincent & Grenadines won on away goals.		
Saint Lucia v Antigua & Barbuda	1-4	4-5
Grenada v Puerto Rico	2-0	2-1
Canada v Dominica	4-0	6-0
Belize v Dominican Republic	3-0	5-1
Bermuda v Guatemala	0-1	0-1
Barbados v Aruba	0-3	2-3
Match awarded 3-0 to Aruba after Barbados fielded an		
ineligible player, original match Barbados won 1-0.		
El Salvador v St Kitts & Nevis	4-1	6-3
Cuba v Curacao	1-1	1-1
Curacao won on away goals.		
Suriname v Nicaragua	1-3	1-4

THIRD ROUND FIRST LEG

Curacao v El Salvador	0-1
Canada v Belize	3-0
Grenada v Haiti	1-3
Jamaica v Nicaragua	2-3
St Vincent & Grenadines v Aruba	2-0
Antigua & Barbuda v Guatemala	1-0

THIRD ROUND SECOND LEG

		(agg)
El Salvador v Curacao	1-0	2-0
Belize v Canada	1-1	1-4
Haiti v Grenada	3-0	6-1
Nicaragua v Jamaica	0-2	3-4
Aruba v St Vincent & Grenadines	2-1	2-3
Guatemala v Antigua & Barbuda	2-0	2-1

FOURTH ROUND

GROUP A

Mexico v El Salvador	3-0
Canada v Honduras	1-0
Honduras v Mexico	0-2
El Salvador v Canada	0-0
El Salvador v Honduras	2-2
Canada v Mexico	0-3
Honduras v El Salvador	2-0
Mexico v Canada	2-0
Honduras v Canada	2-1
El Salvador v Mexico	1-3
Mexico v Honduras	0-0
Canada v El Salvador	3-1

Group A Table	P	W	D	L	F	A	GD	Pts
Mexico	6	5	1	0	13	1	12	16
Honduras	6	2	2	2	6	6	0	8
Canada	6	2	1	3	5	8	-3	7
El Salvador	6	0	2	4	4	13	-9	2

GROUP B

Costa Rica v Haiti	1-0
Jamaica v Panama	0-2
Haiti v Jamaica	0-1
Panama v Costa Rica	1-2
Jamaica v Costa Rica	1-1
Haiti v Panama	0-0
Panama v Haiti	1-0
Costa Rica v Jamaica	3-0
Haiti v Costa Rica	0-1
Panama v Jamaica	2-0
Jamaica v Haiti	0-2
Costa Rica v Panama	3-1

Group B Table	P	W	D	L	F	A	GD	Pts
Costa Rica	6	5	1	0	11	3	8	16
Panama	6	3	1	2	7	5	2	10
Haiti	6	1	1	4	2	4	-2	4
Jamaica	6	1	1	4	2	10	-8	4

GROUP C

USA v St Vincent & Grenadines	6-1
Guatemala v Trinidad & Tobago	1-2
St Vincent & Grenadines v Guatemala	0-4
Trinidad & Tobago v USA	0-0
St Vincent & Grenadines v Trinidad & Tobago	2-3
Guatemala v USA	2-0
Trinidad & Tobago v St Vincent & Grenadines	6-0
USA v Guatemala	4-0
St Vincent & Grenadines v USA	0-6
Trinidad & Tobago v Guatemala	2-2
USA v Trinidad & Tobago	4-0
Guatemala v St Vincent & Grenadines	9-3

Group C Table	P	W	D	L	F	A	GD	Pts
USA	6	4	1	1	20	3	17	13
Trinidad & Tobago	6	3	2	1	13	9	4	11
Guatemala	6	3	1	2	18	11	7	10
St Vincent & Grenadines	6	0	0	6	6	34	-28	0

FIFTH ROUND

Honduras v Panama	0-1
Trinidad & Tobago v Costa Rica	0-2
USA v Mexico	1-2
Honduras v Trinidad & Tobago	3-1
Costa Rica v USA	4-0
Panama v Mexico	0-0
Trinidad & Tobago v Panama	1-0
Mexico v Costa Rica	2-0
USA v Honduras	6-0
Honduras v Costa Rica	1-1
Trinidad & Tobago v Mexico	0-1
Panama v USA	1-1
USA v Trinidad & Tobago	2-0
Costa Rica v Panama	0-0
Mexico v Honduras	3-0
Mexico v USA	1-1
Panama v Honduras	2-2
Costa Rica v Trinidad & Tobago	2-1
USA v Costa Rica	0-2
Trinidad & Tobago v Honduras	1-2
Mexico v Panama	1-0
Honduras v USA	1-1
Costa Rica v Mexico	1-1
Panama v Trinidad & Tobago	3-0
USA v Panama	4-0
Mexico v Trinidad & Tobago	3-1
Costa Rica v Honduras	1-1
Honduras v Mexico	3-2
Panama v Costa Rica	2-1
Trinidad & Tobago v USA	2-1

Fifth Round Table	P	W	D	L	F	A	GD	Pts
Mexico	10	6	3	1	16	7	9	21
Costa Rica	10	4	4	2	14	8	6	16
Panama	10	3	4	3	9	10	-1	13
Honduras	10	3	4	3	13	19	-6	13
USA	10	3	3	4	17	13	4	12
Trinidad & Tobago	10	2	0	8	7	19	-12	6

Mexico, Costa Rica and Panama qualify for the World Cup 2018. Honduras qualify for CONCACAF–AFC inter-confederation play-off.

OCEANIA (OFC)

FIRST ROUND (TONGA)

GROUP A

Tonga v Cook Islands	0-3
Samoa v American Samoa	3-2
Cook Islands v Samoa	1-0
Tonga v American Samoa	1-2
Tonga v Samoa	0-3
American Samoa v Cook Islands	2-0

Group A Table	P	W	D	L	F	A	GD	Pts
Samoa	3	2	0	1	6	3	3	6
American Samoa	3	2	0	1	6	4	2	6
Cook Islands	3	2	0	1	4	2	2	6
Tonga	3	0	0	3	1	8	-7	0

SECOND ROUND (PAPUA NEW GUINEA)

GROUP A

Papua New Guinea v New Caledonia	1-1
Tahiti v Samoa	4-0
Papua New Guinea v Tahiti	2-2
New Caledonia v Samoa	7-0
Papua New Guinea v Samoa	8-0
Tahiti v New Caledonia	1-1

Group A Table	P	W	D	L	F	A	GD	Pts
Papua New Guinea	3	1	2	0	11	3	8	5
New Caledonia	3	1	2	0	9	2	7	5
Tahiti	3	1	2	0	7	3	4	5
Samoa	3	0	0	3	0	19	-19	0

GROUP B

New Zealand v Fiji	3-1
Vanuatu v Solomon Islands	0-1
Vanuatu v New Zealand	0-5
Solomon Islands v Fiji	0-1
Fiji v Vanuatu	2-3
New Zealand v Solomon Islands	1-0

Group B Table	P	W	D	L	F	A	GD	Pts
New Zealand	3	3	0	0	9	1	8	9
Solomon Islands	3	1	0	2	1	2	-1	3
Fiji	3	1	0	2	4	6	-2	3
Vanuatu	3	1	0	2	3	8	-5	3

SECOND ROUND KNOCKOUT STAGE

SEMI-FINALS

New Zealand v New Caledonia	1-0
Papua New Guinea v Solomon Islands	2-1

FINAL

New Zealand v Papua New Guinea	0-0*

New Zealand won 4-2 on penalties.

THIRD ROUND

GROUP A

New Zealand v New Caledonia	2-0
New Caledonia v New Zealand	0-0
Fiji v New Zealand	0-2
New Zealand v Fiji	2-0
Fiji v New Caledonia	2-2
New Caledonia v Fiji	2-1

Group A Table	P	W	D	L	F	A	GD	Pts
New Zealand	4	3	1	0	6	0	6	10
New Caledonia	4	1	2	1	4	5	-1	5
Fiji	4	0	1	3	3	8	-5	1

GROUP B

Tahiti v Solomon Islands	3-0

Match awarded 3-0 to Tahiti after Solomon Islands fielded an ineligible player, original match Tahiti won 1-0.

Solomon Islands v Tahiti	1-0
Papua New Guinea v Tahiti	1-3
Tahiti v Papua New Guinea	1-2
Solomon Islands v Papua New Guinea	3-2
Papua New Guinea v Solomon Islands	1-2

Group B Table	P	W	D	L	F	A	GD	Pts
Solomon Islands	4	3	0	1	6	6	0	9
Tahiti	4	2	0	2	7	4	3	6
Papua New Guinea	4	1	0	3	6	9	-3	3

THIRD ROUND FINAL FIRST LEG

New Zealand v Solomon Islands	6-1

THIRD ROUND FINAL SECOND LEG

Solomon Islands v New Zealand	2-2

New Zealand won 8-3 on aggregate and qualify for OFC–CONMEBOL inter-continental play-off.

INTER-CONFEDERATION PLAY-OFFS

OFC–CONMEBOL PLAY-OFF FIRST LEG

New Zealand v Peru	0-0

OFC–CONMEBOL PLAY-OFF SECOND LEG

Peru v New Zealand	2-0

Peru won 2-0 on aggregate and qualify for the World Cup 2018.

CONCACAF–AFC PLAY-OFF FIRST LEG

Honduras v Australia	0-0

CONCACAF–AFC PLAY-OFF SECOND LEG

Australia v Honduras	3-1

Australia won 3-1 on aggregate and qualify for the World Cup 2018.

FIFA WORLD CUP 2018

FINALS IN RUSSIA

■ *Denotes player sent off.*

GROUP A

Thursday, 14 June 2018

Russia (2) 5 *(Gazinsky 12, Cheryshev 43, 90, Dzyuba 71, Golovin 90)*

Saudi Arabia (0) 0   78,011

Russia: (4231) Akinfeev; Fernandes, Kutepov, Ignashevich, Zhirkov; Zobnin, Gazinsky; Golovin, Samedov (Kuzyaev 64), Smolov (Dzyuba 70); Dzagoev (Cheryshev 24).
Saudi Arabia: (4141) Al-Muaiouf; Al-Breik, Osama Hawsawi, Omar Hawsawi, Al-Shahrani; Al-Jassam; Otayf (Al-Muwallad 64), Al Dawsari, Al-Shehri (Bahbir 74), Al-Faraj; Al-Sahlawi (Asiri 84).
Referee: Nestor Pitana.

Friday, 15 June 2018

Egypt (0) 0

Uruguay (0) 1 *(Gimenez 89)*   27,015

Egypt: (451) El Shenawy; Fathi, Gabr, Hegazi, Abdel-Shafy; Warda (Sobhi 82), Hamed (Morsy 50), Elneny, Trezeguet, Said; Mohsen (Kahraba 63).
Uruguay: (442) Muslera; Varela, Gimenez, Godin, Caceres; Nandez (Sanchez 58), Vecino (Torreira 87), Bentancur, De Arrascaeta (Rodriguez 58); Suarez, Cavani.
Referee: Bjorn Kuipers.

Tuesday, 19 June 2018

Russia (0) 3 *(Fathi 47 (og), Cheryshev 59, Dzyuba 62)*

Egypt (0) 1 *(Salah 73 (pen))*   64,468

Russia: (4231) Akinfeev; Fernandes, Kutepov, Ignashevich, Zhirkov (Kudryashov 86); Zobnin, Gazinsky; Samedov, Golovin, Cheryshev (Kuzyaev 74); Dzyuba (Smolov 79).
Egypt: (4231) El Shenawy; Fathi, Gabr, Hegazi, Abdel-Shafy; Hamed, Elneny (Warda 64); Salah, Said, Trezeguet (Sobhi 68); Mohsen (Kahraba 82).
Referee: Enrique Caceres.

Wednesday, 20 June 2018

Uruguay (1) 1 *(Suarez 23)*

Saudi Arabia (0) 0   42,678

Uruguay: (442) Muslera; Varela, Gimenez, Godin, Caceres; Sanchez (Nandez 82), Vecino (Torreira 59), Bentancur, Rodriguez (Laxalt 59); Suarez, Cavani.
Saudi Arabia: (451) Al-Owais; Al-Breik, Osama Hawsawi, Al Bulaihi, Al-Shahrani; Bahbir (Kanno 75), Al-Faraj, Otayf, Al-Jassam (Al-Moqahwi 44), Al Dawsari; Al-Muwallad (Al-Sahlawi 78).
Referee: Clement Turpin.

Monday, 25 June 2018

Saudi Arabia (1) 2 *(Al-Faraj 45 (pen), Al Dawsari 90)*

Egypt (1) 1 *(Salah 22)*   36,823

Saudi Arabia: (451) Al-Mosailem; Al-Breik, Osama Hawsawi, Hawsawi M, Al-Shahrani; Al-Faraj, Otayf, Al-Moqahwi, Al Dawsari; Al-Muwallad (Al-Shehri 79).
Egypt: (4231) El Hadary; Fathi, Gabr, Hegazi, Abdel-Shafy; Elneny, Hamed; Salah, Said (Warda 45), Trezeguet (Kahraba 81); Mohsen (Sobhi 64).
Referee: Wilmar Roldan Perez.

Uruguay (2) 3 *(Suarez 10, Cheryshev 23 (og), Cavani 90)*

Russia (0) 0   41,970

Uruguay: (352) Muslera; Caceres, Godin, Coates; Nandez (Rodriguez 73), Bentancur (De Arrascaeta 63), Torreira, Vecino, Laxalt; Suarez, Cavani (Gomez 90).
Russia: (4231) Akinfeev; Smolnikov■, Kutepov, Ignashevich, Kudryashov; Zobnin, Gazinsky (Kuzyaev 46); Samedov, Cheryshev (Fernandes 38), Miranchuk (Smolov 60); Dzyuba.
Referee: Malang Diedhiou.

Group A Table

	P	W	D	L	F	A	GD	Pts
Uruguay	3	3	0	0	5	0	5	9
Russia	3	2	0	1	8	4	4	6
Saudi Arabia	3	1	0	2	2	7	–5	3
Egypt	3	0	0	3	2	6	–4	0

GROUP B

Friday, 15 June 2018

Morocco (0) 0

Iran (0) 1 *(Bouhaddouz 90 (og))*   62,548

Morocco: (343) Mohamedi; Hakimi, Benatia, Saiss; Boussoufa, Ziyech, El Ahmadi, Harit (da Costa 82); Amrabat N (Amrabat S 76), El Kaabi (Bouhaddouz 77), Belhanda.
Iran: (343) Beiranvand; Rezaeian, Cheshmi, Pouraliganji; Ansarifard, Ebrahimi (Hosseini 79), Hajsafi, Shojaei (Taremi 67); Jahanbakhsh (Ghoddos 84), Azmoun, Amiri.
Referee: Cuneyt Cakir.

Portugal (2) 3 *(Ronaldo 4 (pen), 44, 88)*

Spain (1) 3 *(Costa 24, 55, Nacho 58)*   43,866

Portugal: (4231) Rui Patricio; Cedric, Pepe, Fonte, Guerreiro; William Carvalho, Joao Moutinho; Bernardo Silva (Quaresma 69), Goncalo Guedes (Andre Silva 80), Bruno Fernandes (Joao Mario 67); Ronaldo.
Spain: (4231) de Gea; Nacho, Pique, Sergio Ramos, Jordi Alba; Busquets, Koke; Silva (Lucas 86), Isco, Iniesta (Thiago 69); Costa (Aspas 77).
Referee: Gianluca Rocchi.

Wednesday, 20 June 2018

Iran (0) 0

Spain (0) 1 *(Costa 54)*   42,718

Iran: (4231) Beiranvand; Rezaeian, Hosseini, Pouraliganji, Hajsafi (Mohammadi 69); Ebrahimi, Ezatolahi; Ansarifard (Jahanbakhsh 74), Taremi, Amiri (Ghoddos 86); Azmoun.
Spain: (4231) de Gea; Carvajal, Pique, Sergio Ramos, Jordi Alba; Busquets, Iniesta (Koke 71); Silva, Isco, Lucas (Asensio 79); Costa (Rodrigo 89).
Referee: Andres Cunha.

Portugal (1) 1 *(Ronaldo 4)*

Morocco (0) 0   78,011

Portugal: (442) Rui Patricio; Cedric, Pepe, Fonte, Guerreiro; Bernardo Silva (Gelson Martins 59), William Carvalho, Joao Moutinho (Adrien Silva 88), Joao Mario (Bruno Fernandes 69); Goncalo Guedes, Ronaldo.
Morocco: (451) Mohamedi; Dirar, Benatia, da Costa, Hakimi; Amrabat N, El Ahmadi (Fajr 86), Belhanda (Carcela-Gonzalez 75), Boussoufa, Ziyech; Boutaib (El Kaabi 69).
Referee: Mark Geiger.

Monday, 25 June 2018

Iran (0) 1 *(Ansarifard 90 (pen))*

Portugal (1) 1 *(Quaresma 45)*   41,685

Iran: (451) Beiranvand; Rezaeian, Hosseini, Pouraliganji, Hajsafi (Mohammadi 56); Taremi, Jahanbakhsh (Ghoddos 76), Ezatolahi (Ansarifard 76), Ebrahimi, Amiri; Azmoun.
Portugal: (4231) Rui Patricio; Cedric, Pepe, Fonte, Guerreiro; Quaresma (Bernardo Silva 69), William Carvalho, Adrien Silva, Joao Mario (Joao Moutinho 84); Andre Silva (Goncalo Guedes 90), Ronaldo.
Referee: Enrique Caceres.

Spain (1) 2 *(Isco 19, Aspas 90)*

Morocco (1) 2 *(Boutaib 14, En-Nesyri 81)*   33,973

Spain: (4231) de Gea; Carvajal, Pique, Sergio Ramos, Jordi Alba; Busquets, Thiago (Asensio 74); Silva (Rodrigo 84), Isco, Iniesta; Costa (Aspas 74).

Morocco: (4231) Mohamedi; Dirar, da Costa, Saiss, Hakimi; El Ahmadi, Boussoufa; Amrabat N, Belhanda (Fajr 63), Ziyech (Bouhaddouz 85); Boutaib (En-Nesyri 72).
Referee: Ravshan Irmatov.

Group B Table	P	W	D	L	F	A	GD	Pts
Spain	3	1	2	0	6	5	1	5
Portugal	3	1	2	0	5	4	1	5
Iran	3	1	1	1	2	2	0	4
Morocco	3	0	1	2	2	4	-2	1

GROUP C

Saturday, 16 June 2018

France (0) 2 *(Griezmann 58 (pen), Behich 81 (og))*
Australia (0) 1 *(Jedinak 62 (pen))*　　　　41,279
France: (433) Lloris; Pavard, Varane, Umtiti, Lucas; Tolisso (Matuidi 78), Kante, Pogba; Dembele (Fekir 70), Mbappe, Griezmann (Giroud 70).
Australia: (451) Ryan; Risdon, Milligan, Sainsbury, Behich; Leckie, Jedinak, Rogic (Irvine 71), Mooy, Kruse (Arzani 84); Nabbout (Juric 64).
Referee: Andres Cunha.

Peru (0) 0
Denmark (0) 1 *(Poulsen 59)*　　　　40,502
Peru: (4231) Gallese; Advincula, Rodriguez, Ramos, Trauco; Tapia (Aquino 87), Yotun; Carrillo, Cueva, Flores (Guerrero 63); Farfan (Ruidiaz 85).
Denmark: (433) Schmeichel; Dalsgaard, Kjaer, Christensen (Jorgensen M 81), Larsen; Kvist (Schone 35), Eriksen, Delaney; Poulsen, Jorgensen N, Sisto (Braithwaite 67).
Referee: Bakary Gassama.

Thursday, 21 June 2018
Denmark (1) 1 *(Eriksen 7)*
Australia (1) 1 *(Jedinak 38 (pen))*　　　　40,727
Denmark: (4231) Schmeichel; Larsen, Christensen, Kjaer, Dalsgaard; Delaney, Schone; Sisto, Eriksen, Poulsen (Braithwaite 59); Jorgensen N (Cornelius 68).
Australia: (433) Ryan; Sainsbury, Risdon, Behich, Milligan; Rogic (Irvine 82), Jedinak, Mooy; Nabbout (Juric 75), Kruse (Arzani 68), Leckie.
Referee: Antonio Miguel Mateu Lahoz.

France (1) 1 *(Mbappe 34)*
Peru (0) 0　　　　32,789
France: (4231) Lloris; Pavard, Varane, Umtiti, Lucas; Pogba (Nzonzi 89), Kante; Mbappe (Dembele 75), Griezmann (Fekir 80), Matuidi; Giroud.
Peru: (4231) Gallese; Advincula, Ramos, Rodriguez (Santamaria 46), Trauco; Aquino, Yotun (Farfan 46); Carrillo, Cueva (Ruidiaz 82), Flores; Guerrero.
Referee: Mohammed Abdulla Hassan.

Tuesday, 26 June 2018
Australia (0) 0
Peru (1) 2 *(Carrillo 18, Guerrero 50)*　　　　44,073
Australia: (4231) Ryan; Risdon, Sainsbury, Milligan, Behich; Jedinak, Mooy; Leckie, Rogic (Irvine 72), Kruse (Arzani 58); Juric (Cahill 53).
Peru: (4231) Gallese; Advincula, Ramos, Santamaria, Trauco; Tapia (Hurtado 63), Yotun (Aquino 46); Carrillo (Cartagena 79), Cueva, Flores; Guerrero.
Referee: Sergei Karasev.

Denmark (0) 0
France (0) 0　　　　78,011
Denmark: (433) Schmeichel; Dalsgaard, Kjaer, Christensen, Larsen; Delaney (Lerager 90), Jorgensen M, Eriksen; Sisto (Fischer 60), Cornelius (Dolberg 75), Braithwaite.
France: (433) Mandanda; Sidibe, Varane, Kimpembe, Lucas (Mendy 50); Kante, Nzonzi, Lemar; Griezmann (Fekir 69), Dembele (Mbappe 78), Giroud.
Referee: Sandro Ricci.

Group C Table	P	W	D	L	F	A	GD	Pts
France	3	2	1	0	3	1	2	7
Denmark	3	1	2	0	2	1	1	5
Peru	3	1	0	2	2	2	0	3
Australia	3	0	1	2	2	5	-3	1

GROUP D

Saturday, 16 June 2018

Argentina (1) 1 *(Aguero 19)*
Iceland (1) 1 *(Finnbogason 23)*　　　　44,190
Argentina: (451) Caballero; Salvio, Otamendi, Rojo, Tagliafico; Meza (Higuain 84), Mascherano, Messi, Biglia (Banega 54), Di Maria (Pavon 75); Aguero.
Iceland: (442) Halldorsson; Saevarsson, Arnason, Sigurdsson R, Magnusson; Gudmundsson J (Gislason 63), Gunnarsson B (Skulason A 76), Sigurdsson G, Hallfredsson; Bjarnason, Finnbogason (Sigurdarson 88).
Referee: Szymon Marciniak.

Croatia (1) 2 *(Etebo 32 (og), Modric 71 (pen))*
Nigeria (0) 0　　　　31,136
Croatia: (4231) Subasic; Vrsaljko, Lovren, Vida, Strinic; Rakitic, Modric, Rebic (Kovacic 78), Kramaric (Brozovic 60), Perisic; Mandzukic (Pjaca 85).
Nigeria: (4231) Uzoho; Abdullahi, Troost-Ekong, Balogun, Idowu; Ndidi, Etebo; Moses, Mikel (Simy 88), Iwobi (Musa 62); Ighalo (Iheanacho 73).
Referee: Sandro Ricci.

Thursday, 21 June 2018
Argentina (0) 0
Croatia (0) 3 *(Rebic 53, Modric 80, Rakitic 90)*　　　　43,319
Argentina: (343) Caballero; Mercado, Otamendi, Tagliafico; Salvio (Pavon 56), Mascherano, Perez (Dybala 68), Acuna; Messi, Aguero (Higuain 55), Meza.
Croatia: (4231) Subasic; Vrsaljko, Lovren, Vida, Strinic; Rakitic, Brozovic; Rebic (Kramaric 57), Modric, Perisic (Kovacic 82); Mandzukic (Corluka 90).
Referee: Ravshan Irmatov.

Friday, 22 June 2018
Nigeria (0) 2 *(Musa 49, 75)*
Iceland (0) 0　　　　40,904
Nigeria: (352) Uzoho; Omeruo, Troost-Ekong, Balogun; Moses, Etebo (Iwobi 90), Mikel, Ndidi, Idowu (Ebuehi 46); Musa, Iheanacho (Ighalo 85).
Iceland: (442) Halldorsson; Saevarsson, Arnason, Sigurdsson R (Ingason 64), Magnusson; Gislason, Gunnarsson (Skulason A 87), Sigurdsson G, Bjarnason B; Bodvarsson (Sigurdarson 71), Finnbogason.
Referee: Matthew Conger.

Tuesday, 26 June 2018
Iceland (0) 1 *(Sigurdsson G 76 (pen))*
Croatia (0) 2 *(Badelj 53, Perisic 90)*　　　　43,472
Iceland: (4231) Halldorsson; Saevarsson, Ingason, Sigurdsson R (Sigurdarson 71), Magnusson; Gunnarsson, Hallfredsson; Gudmundsson J, Sigurdsson G, Bjarnason B (Traustason 90); Finnbogason (Gudmundsson A 85).
Croatia: (4231) Kalinic; Jedvaj, Corluka, Caleta-Car, Pivaric; Modric (Bradaric 65), Badelj; Pjaca (Lovren 70), Kovacic (Rakitic 82), Perisic; Kramaric.
Referee: Antonio Miguel Mateu Lahoz.

Nigeria (0) 1 *(Moses 51 (pen))*
Argentina (1) 2 *(Messi 14, Rojo 86)*　　　　64,468
Nigeria: (352) Uzoho; Balogun, Troost-Ekong, Omeruo (Iwobi 90); Moses, Etebo, Mikel, Ndidi, Idowu; Musa (Simy 90), Iheanacho (Ighalo 46).
Argentina: (442) Armani; Mercado, Otamendi, Rojo, Tagliafico (Aguero 90); Perez (Pavon 60), Mascherano, Banega, Di Maria (Meza 72); Messi, Higuain.
Referee: Cuneyt Cakir.

Group D Table	P	W	D	L	F	A	GD	Pts
Croatia	3	3	0	0	7	1	6	9
Argentina	3	1	1	1	3	5	-2	4
Nigeria	3	1	0	2	3	4	-1	3
Iceland	3	0	1	2	2	5	-3	1

GROUP E

Sunday, 17 June 2018

Brazil (1) 1 *(Coutinho 20)*
Switzerland (0) 1 *(Zuber 50)*　　　　43,109
Brazil: (4231) Alisson; Danilo, Thiago Silva, Miranda, Marcelo; Casemiro (Fernandinho 60), Paulinho (Renato Augusto 67); Willian, Coutinho, Neymar; Gabriel Jesus (Firmino 79).

Switzerland: (4231) Sommer; Lichtsteiner (Lang 87), Schar, Akanji, Rodriguez; Behrami (Zakaria 71), Xhaka; Shaqiri, Dzemaili, Zuber; Seferovic (Embolo 80).
Referee: Cesar Arturo Ramos Palazuelos.

Costa Rica (0) 0

Serbia (0) 1 *(Kolarov 56)*   41,432
Costa Rica: (541) Navas; Gamboa, Acosta, Gonzalez, Duarte, Calvo; Venegas (Bolanos 60), Guzman (Colindres 73), Borges, Ruiz B; Urena (Campbell 67).
Serbia: (4231) Stojkovic; Ivanovic, Milenkovic, Tosic, Kolarov; Matic, Milivojevic; Tadic (Rukavina 82), Milinkovic-Savic, Ljajic (Kostic 70); Mitrovic (Prijovic 89).
Referee: Malang Diedhiou.

Friday, 22 June 2018

Brazil (0) 2 *(Coutinho 90, Neymar 90)*

Costa Rica (0) 0   64,468
Brazil: (4231) Alisson; Fagner, Thiago Silva, Miranda, Marcelo; Casemiro, Paulinho (Firmino 68); Willian (Douglas Costa 46), Coutinho, Neymar; Gabriel Jesus (Fernandinho 90).
Costa Rica: (541) Navas; Gamboa (Calvo 75), Acosta, Duarte, Oviedo; Venegas, Guzman (Tejeda 83), Borges, Ruiz B; Urena (Bolanos 54).
Referee: Bjorn Kuipers.

Serbia (1) 1 *(Mitrovic 5)*

Switzerland (0) 2 *(Xhaka 52, Shaqiri 90)*   33,167
Serbia: (4231) Stojkovic; Ivanovic, Milenkovic, Tosic, Kolarov; Matic, Milivojevic (Radonjic 81); Tadic, Milinkovic-Savic, Kostic (Ljajic 64); Mitrovic.
Switzerland: (4231) Sommer; Lichtsteiner, Schar, Akanji, Rodriguez; Behrami, Xhaka; Shaqiri, Dzemaili (Embolo 73), Zuber (Drmic 90); Seferovic (Gavranovic 46).
Referee: Felix Brych.

Wednesday, 27 June 2018

Serbia (0) 0

Brazil (1) 2 *(Paulinho 36, Thiago Silva 68)* 44,190
Serbia: (4231) Stojkovic; Rukavina, Milenkovic, Veljkovic, Kolarov; Matic, Milinkovic-Savic; Tadic, Ljajic (Zivkovic 75), Kostic (Radonjic 82); Mitrovic (Jovic 89).
Brazil: (4231) Alisson; Fagner, Thiago Silva, Miranda, Marcelo (Filipe Luis 10); Paulinho (Fernandinho 66), Casemiro; Willian, Coutinho (Renato Augusto 80), Neymar; Gabriel Jesus.
Referee: Alireza Faghani.

Switzerland (1) 2 *(Dzemaili 31, Drmic 88)*

Costa Rica (0) 2 *(Waston 56, Sommer 90 (og))* 43,319
Switzerland: (4231) Sommer; Rodriguez, Akanji, Schar, Lichtsteiner; Xhaka, Behrami (Zakaria 60); Embolo, Dzemaili, Shaqiri (Lang 81); Gavranovic (Drmic 69).
Costa Rica: (541) Navas; Gamboa (Smith 90), Acosta, Gonzalez, Waston, Oviedo; Colindres (Wallace 81), Borges, Azofeifa 90), Ruiz B; Campbell.
Referee: Clement Turpin.

Group E Table	P	W	D	L	F	A	GD	Pts
Brazil	3	2	1	0	5	1	4	7
Switzerland	3	1	2	0	5	4	1	5
Serbia	3	1	0	2	2	4	–2	3
Costa Rica	3	0	1	2	2	5	–3	1

GROUP F

Sunday, 17 June 2018

Germany (0) 0

Mexico (1) 1 *(Lozano 35)*   78,011
Germany: (4231) Neuer; Kimmich, Boateng, Hummels, Plattenhardt (Gomez 79); Kroos, Khedira (Reus 60); Muller, Ozil, Draxler (Werner 86).
Mexico: (4231) Ochoa; Salcedo, Ayala, Moreno, Gallardo; Herrera, Guardado (Marquez 73); Layun, Vela (Alvarez 58), Lozano (Jimenez 66); Hernandez.
Referee: Faghani Alireza.

Monday, 18 June 2018

Sweden (0) 1 *(Granqvist 65 (pen))*

Korea Republic (0) 0   42,300
Sweden: (442) Olsen; Augustinsson, Granqvist, Jansson, Lustig; Claesson, Larsson (Svensson 81), Ekdal (Hiljemark 71), Forsberg; Berg, Toivonen (Thelin 76).
Korea Republic: (433) Cho; Lee Y, Jang, Kim Y, Park (Kim M 28); Lee J, Ki, Koo (Lee S 72); Hwang, Kim S (Jung 67), Son.
Referee: Joel Aguilar.

Saturday, 23 June 2018

Germany (0) 2 *(Reus 48, Kroos 90)*

Sweden (1) 1 *(Toivonen 32)*   44,287
Germany: (4231) Neuer; Kimmich, Rudiger, Boateng∎, Hector (Brandt 87); Rudy (Gundogan 31), Kroos; Muller, Draxler (Gomez 46), Reus; Werner.
Sweden: (442) Olsen; Lustig, Lindelof, Granqvist, Augustinsson; Claesson (Durmaz 74), Larsson, Ekdal, Forsberg; Berg (Thelin 90), Toivonen (Guidetti 78).
Referee: Szymon Marciniak.

Korea Republic (0) 1 *(Son 90)*

Mexico (1) 2 *(Vela 26 (pen), Hernandez 66)*   43,472
Korea Republic: (442) Cho; Lee Y, Jang, Kim Y, Kim M (Hong 84); Moon (Jung 77), Ju (Lee S 63), Ki, Hwang; Lee J, Son.
Mexico: (433) Ochoa; Alvarez, Salcedo, Moreno, Gallardo; Layun, Herrera, Guardado (Marquez 68); Vela (Giovani 77), Hernandez, Lozano (Corona 71).
Referee: Milorad Mazic.

Wednesday, 27 June 2018

Mexico (0) 0

Sweden (0) 3 *(Augustinsson 50, Granqvist 62 (pen), Alvarez 74 (og))*   33,061
Mexico: (4231) Ochoa; Alvarez, Salcedo, Moreno, Gallardo (Edson 65); Layun (Peralta 88), Guardado (Corona 76); Herrera, Vela, Lozano; Hernandez.
Sweden: (4312) Olsen; Lustig, Lindelof, Granqvist, Augustinsson; Claesson, Larsson (Svensson 75), Ekdal (Hiljemark 80); Forsberg; Berg (Thelin 67), Toivonen.
Referee: Nestor Pitana.

Korea Republic (0) 2 *(Kim Y 90, Son 90)*

Germany (0) 0   41,835
Korea Republic: (442) Cho; Lee Y, Yun, Kim Y, Hong; Lee J, Jung, Jang, Moon (Ju 69); Koo (Hwang 56 (Go 79)), Son.
Germany: (4231) Neuer; Kimmich, Hummels, Sule, Hector (Brandt 78); Khedira (Gomez 58), Kroos; Goretzka (Muller 63), Ozil, Reus; Werner.
Referee: Mark Geiger.

Group F Table	P	W	D	L	F	A	GD	Pts
Sweden	3	2	0	1	5	2	3	6
Mexico	3	2	0	1	3	4	–1	6
Korea Republic	3	1	0	2	3	3	0	3
Germany	3	1	0	2	2	4	–2	3

GROUP G

Monday, 18 June 2018

Belgium (0) 3 *(Mertens 47, Lukaku R 69, 75)*

Panama (0) 0   43,247
Belgium: (3421) Courtois; Alderweireld, Boyata, Vertonghen; Meunier, De Bruyne, Witsel (Chadli 90), Carrasco (Dembele 74); Mertens (Hazard T 83), Hazard E; Lukaku R.
Panama: (451) Penedo; Murillo, Torres R, Escobar, Davis; Barcenas (Torres G 63), Cooper, Gomez, Godoy, Rodriguez (Diaz 63); Perez (Tejada 73).
Referee: Janny Sikazwe.

Tunisia (1) 1 *(Sassi 35 (pen))*

England (1) 2 *(Kane 11, 90)*   41,064
Tunisia: (433) Hassen (Ben Mustapha 16); Meriah, Ben Youssef S, Bronn, Maaloul; Skhiri, Badri, Sassi; Ben Youssef F, Khazri (Khalifa 85), Sliti (Ben Amor 73).

England: (352) Pickford; Walker, Stones, Maguire; Trippier, Alli (Loftus-Cheek 80), Henderson, Lingard (Dier 90), Young; Sterling (Rashford 68), Kane.
Referee: Wilmar Roldan Perez.

Saturday, 23 June 2018

Belgium (3) 5 *(Hazard E 6 (pen), 51, Lukaku R 16, 45, Batshuayi 90)*

Tunisia (1) 2 *(Bronn 18, Khazri 90)*   44,190

Belgium: (3421) Courtois; Alderweireld, Boyata, Vertonghen; Meunier, De Bruyne, Witsel, Carrasco; Mertens (Tielemans 86), Lukaku R (Fellaini 58); Hazard E (Batshuayi 68).
Tunisia: (433) Ben Mustapha; Bronn (Nagguez 24), Ben Youssef S (Benalouane 41), Meriah, Maaloul; Khaoui, Skhiri, Sassi (Sliti 59); Ben Youssef F, Khazri, Badri.
Referee: Jair Marrufo.

Sunday, 24 June 2018

England (5) 6 *(Stones 8, 40, Kane 22 (pen), 45 (pen), 62, Lingard 36)*

Panama (0) 1 *(Baloy 78)*   43,319

England: (352) Pickford; Walker, Stones, Maguire; Trippier (Rose 70), Loftus-Cheek, Henderson, Lingard (Delph 64), Young; Sterling, Kane (Vardy 63).
Panama: (451) Penedo; Murillo, Torres R, Escobar, Davis; Barcenas (Arroyo 69), Cooper, Gomez (Baloy 69), Godoy (Avila 64), Rodriguez; Perez.
Referee: Gehad Grisha.

Thursday, 28 June 2018

England (0) 0

Belgium (0) 1 *(Januzaj 51)*   33,973

England: (352) Pickford; Jones, Stones (Maguire 46), Cahill; Alexander-Arnold (Welbeck 78), Loftus-Cheek, Dier, Delph, Rose; Rashford, Vardy.
Belgium: (343) Courtois; Dendoncker, Boyata, Vermaelen (Kompany 75); Chadli, Fellaini, Dembele, Hazard T; Januzaj (Mertens 86), Batshuayi, Tielemans.
Referee: Damir Skomina.

Panama (0) 1 *(Meriah 33 (og))*

Tunisia (0) 2 *(Ben Youssef F 51, Khazri 66)*   37,168

Panama: (451) Penedo; Machado, Torres R (Tejada 56), Escobar, Ovalle; Barcenas, Godoy, Gomez, Avila (Arroyo 81), Rodriguez; Torres G (Cummings 46).
Tunisia: (433) Mathlouthi; Nagguez, Bedoui, Meriah, Haddadi; Sassi (Badri 46), Skhiri, Chaalali; Ben Youssef F, Khazri (Srarfi 89), Sliti (Khalil 76).
Referee: Nawaf Shukralla.

Group G Table	P	W	D	L	F	A	GD	Pts
Belgium	3	3	0	0	9	2	7	9
England	3	2	0	1	8	3	5	6
Tunisia	3	1	0	2	5	8	–3	3
Panama	3	0	0	3	2	11	–9	0

GROUP H

Tuesday, 19 June 2018

Colombia (1) 1 *(Quintero 39)*

Japan (1) 2 *(Kagawa 6 (pen), Osako 73)*   40,842

Colombia: (4231) Ospina; Arias, Sanchez D, Murillo, Mojica; Cuadrado (Barrios 31), Sanchez C*; Lerma, Izquierdo (Bacca 70), Quintero (Rodriguez 58); Falcao.
Japan: (4231) Kawashima; Sakai H, Yoshida, Shoji, Nagatomo; Haraguchi, Hasebe; Shibasaki (Yamaguchi 80), Inui, Kagawa (Honda 70); Osako (Okazaki 85).
Referee: Damir Skomina.

Poland (0) 1 *(Krychowiak 86)*

Senegal (1) 2 *(Cionek 37 (og), Niang 60)*   44,190

Poland: (4231) Szczesny; Piszczek (Bereszynski 83), Pazdan, Cionek, Rybus; Krychowiak, Zielinski; Blaszczykowski (Bednarek 46), Milik (Kownacki 73), Grosicki; Lewandowski.
Senegal: (4231) N'Diaye K; Wague, Sane, Koulibaly, Sabaly; Sarr, N'Diaye A (Kouyate 87); Gueye, Niang (Konate 75); Mane, Diouf (N'Doye 62).
Referee: Nawaf Shukralla.

Sunday, 24 June 2018

Japan (1) 2 *(Inui 34, Honda 78)*

Senegal (1) 2 *(Mane 11, Wague 71)*   32,572

Japan: (4231) Kawashima; Sakai H, Yoshida, Shoji, Nagatomo; Haraguchi (Okazaki 75), Hasebe; Shibasaki, Inui (Usami 87), Kagawa (Honda 72); Osako.
Senegal: (433) N'Diaye K; Sabaly, Koulibaly, Sane, Wague; Ndiaye (N'Doye 81), N'Diaye A (Kouyate 65), Gueye; Sarr, Niang (Diouf 86), Mane.
Referee: Gianluca Rocchi.

Poland (0) 0

Colombia (1) 3 *(Mina 40, Falcao 70, Cuadrado 75)* 42,873

Poland: (343) Szczesny; Piszczek, Bednarek, Pazdan (Glik 80); Bereszynski (Teodorczyk 72), Krychowiak, Goralski, Rybus; Zielinski, Lewandowski, Kownacki (Grosicki 57).
Colombia: (4231) Ospina; Arias, Sanchez D, Mina, Mojica; Aguilar (Uribe 32), Barrios; Cuadrado, Quintero (Lerma 73), Rodriguez; Falcao (Bacca 78).
Referee: Cesar Arturo Ramos Palazuelos.

Thursday, 28 June 2018

Japan (0) 0

Poland (0) 1 *(Bednarek 59)*   42,189

Japan: (4231) Kawashima; Sakai H, Yoshida, Makino, Nagatomo; Yamaguchi, Shibasaki, Sakai G, Okazaki (Osako 47); Usami (Inui 65); Muto (Hasebe 82).
Poland: (343) Fabianski; Bereszynski, Glik, Bednarek; Kurzawa (Peszko 79), Krychowiak, Goralski, Jedrzejczyk; Zielinski (Teodorczyk 79), Lewandowski, Grosicki.
Referee: Janny Sikazwe.

Senegal (0) 0

Colombia (0) 1 *(Mina 74)*   41,970

Senegal: (442) N'Diaye K; Gassama, Sane, Koulibaly, Sabaly (Wague 74); Sarr, Kouyate, Gueye, Mane; Balde (Konate 80), Niang (Sakho 86).
Colombia: (4231) Ospina; Arias, Sanchez D, Mina, Mojica; Uribe (Lerma 83), Sanchez C; Cuadrado, Quintero, Rodriguez (Muriel 31); Falcao (Borja 89).
Referee: Milorad Mazic.

Group H Table	P	W	D	L	F	A	GD	Pts
Colombia	3	2	0	1	5	2	3	6
Japan	3	1	1	1	4	4	0	4
Senegal	3	1	1	1	4	4	0	4
Poland	3	1	0	2	2	5	–3	3

ROUND OF 16

Penalty shout-out (s) = scored; (m) = missed or saved.

Saturday, 30 June 2018

France (1) 4 *(Griezmann 13 (pen), Pavard 57, Mbappe 64, 68)*

Argentina (1) 3 *(Di Maria 41, Mercado 48, Aguero 90)*   42,873

France: (4231) Lloris; Pavard, Varane, Umtiti, Lucas; Kante, Pogba; Mbappe (Thauvin 88), Griezmann (Fekir 83), Matuidi (Tolisso 75); Giroud.
Argentina: (433) Armani; Mercado, Otamendi, Rojo (Fazio 46), Tagliafico; Perez (Aguero 66), Mascherano, Banega; Pavon (Meza 75), Messi, Di Maria.
Referee: Alireza Faghani.

Uruguay (1) 2 *(Cavani 7, 62)*

Portugal (0) 1 *(Pepe 55)*   44,873

Uruguay: (442) Muslera; Caceres, Gimenez, Godin, Laxalt; Nandez (Sanchez 80), Torreira, Vecino, Bentancur (Rodriguez 63); Suarez, Cavani (Stuani 74).
Portugal: (442) Rui Patricio; Ricardo Pereira, Pepe, Fonte, Guerreiro; Bernardo Silva, William Carvalho, Adrien Silva (Quaresma 65), Joao Mario (Fernandes 85); Goncalo Guedes (Andre Silva 73); Ronaldo.
Referee: Cesar Arturo Ramos Palazuelos.

Sunday, 1 July 2018

Croatia (1) 1 *(Mandzukic 4)*

Denmark (1) 1 *(Jorgensen M 1)*   40,851

Croatia: (4231) Subasic; Vrsaljko, Lovren, Vida, Strinic (Pivaric 81); Rakitic, Brozovic (Kovacic 71); Rebic, Modric, Perisic (Kramaric 97); Mandzukic (Badelj 108).
Denmark: (433) Schmeichel; Knudsen, Kjaer, Jorgensen M, Dalsgaard; Christensen (Schone 46), Delaney (Krohn-Dehli 98), Eriksen; Poulsen, Cornelius (Jorgensen N 66), Braithwaite (Sisto 106).
aet; Croatia won 3-2 on penalties.
Penalties – Denmark first: Eriksen (m) 0-0, Badelj (m) 0-0, Kjaer (s) 1-0, Kramaric (s) 1-1, Krohn-Dehli (s) 2-1, Modric (s) 2-2, Schone (m) 2-2, Pivaric (m) 2-2, Jorgensen N (m) 2-2, Rakatic (s) 3-2.
Referee: Nestor Pitana.

Spain (1) 1 *(Ignashevich 11 (og))*

Russia (1) 1 *(Dzyuba 41 (pen))*   78,011

Spain: (4231) de Gea; Nacho (Carvajal 70), Pique, Sergio Ramos, Jordi Alba; Koke, Busquets; Silva (Iniesta 67), Isco, Asensio (Rodrigo 104); Costa (Aspas 80).
Russia: (532) Akinfeev; Fernandes, Kutepov, Ignashevich, Kudryashov, Zhirkov (Granat 46); Samedov (Cheryshev 61), Zobnin, Kuzyaev (Erokhin 97); Dzyuba (Smolov 65), Golovin.
aet; Russia won 4-3 on penalties.
Penalties – Spain first: Iniesta (s) 1-0, Smolov (s) 1-1, Pique (s) 2-1, Ignashevich (s) 2-2, Koke (m) 2-2, Golovin (s) 2-3, Ramos (s) 3-3, Cheryshev (s) 3-4, Aspas (m) 3-4.
Referee: Bjorn Kuipers.

Monday, 2 July 2018

Belgium (0) 3 *(Vertonghen 69, Fellaini 74, Chadli 90)*

Japan (0) 2 *(Haraguchi 48, Inui 52)*   41,466

Belgium: (343) Courtois; Alderweireld, Kompany, Vertonghen; Meunier, De Bruyne, Witsel, Carrasco (Chadli 65); Mertens (Fellaini 65), Lukaku R, Hazard E.
Japan: (4231) Kawashima; Sakai H, Yoshida, Shoji, Nagatomo; Hasebe, Shibasaki (Yamaguchi 81); Haraguchi (Honda 81), Kagawa, Inui; Osako.
Referee: Malang Diedhiou.

Brazil (0) 2 *(Neymar 51, Firmino 88)*

Mexico (0) 0   41,970

Brazil: (4231) Alisson; Fagner, Thiago Silva, Miranda, Filipe Luis; Paulinho (Fernandinho 80), Casemiro; Willian (Marquinhos 90), Coutinho (Firmino 86), Neymar; Gabriel Jesus.
Mexico: (433) Ochoa; Alvarez (Jonathan 55), Ayala, Salcedo, Gallardo; Herrera, Marquez (Layun 46), Guardado; Vela, Hernandez (Jimenez 60), Lozano.
Referee: Gianluca Rocchi.

Tuesday, 3 July 2018

Colombia (0) 1 *(Mina 90)*

England (0) 1 *(Kane 57 (pen))*   44,190

Colombia: (4321) Ospina; Arias (Zapata 116), Mina, Sanchez D, Mojica; Barrios, Sanchez C (Uribe 79), Lerma (Bacca 61); Cuadrado, Quintero (Muriel 88); Falcao.
England: (352) Pickford; Walker (Rashford 113), Stones, Maguire; Trippier, Alli (Dier 81), Henderson, Lingard, Young (Rose 102); Sterling (Vardy 88), Kane.
aet; England won 4-3 on penalties.
Penalties – Colombia first: Falcao (s) 1-0, Kane (s) 1-1, Cuadrado (s) 2-1, Rashford (s) 2-2, Muriel (s) 3-2, Henderson (m) 3-2, Uribe (m) 3-2, Trippier (s) 3-3, Bacca (m) 3-3, Dier (s) 3-4.
Referee: Mark Geiger.

Sweden (0) 1 *(Forsberg 66)*

Switzerland (0) 0   64,042

Sweden: (442) Olsen; Lustig (Krafth 82), Lindelof, Granqvist, Augustinsson; Claesson, Svensson, Ekdal, Forsberg (Olsson 81); Berg (Thelin 90), Toivonen.
Switzerland: (4231) Sommer; Lang■, Djourou, Akanji, Rodriguez; Behrami, Xhaka; Shaqiri, Dzemaili (Seferovic 73), Zuber (Embolo 73); Drmic.
Referee: Damir Skomina.

QUARTER-FINALS

Friday, 6 July 2018

Brazil (0) 1 *(Renato Augusto 76)*

Belgium (2) 2 *(Fernandinho 13 (og), De Bruyne 31)*   42,873

Brazil: (4231) Alisson; Fagner, Thiago Silva, Miranda, Marcelo; Paulinho (Renato Augusto 73), Fernandinho; Willian (Firmino 46), Coutinho, Neymar; Gabriel Jesus (Douglas Costa 58).
Belgium: (343) Courtois; Alderweireld, Kompany, Vertonghen; Meunier, Fellaini, Witsel, Chadli (Vermaelen 83); De Bruyne, Lukaku R (Tielemans 87), Hazard E.
Referee: Milorad Mazic.

Uruguay (0) 0

France (1) 2 *(Varane 40, Griezmann 61)*   43,319

Uruguay: (442) Muslera; Caceres, Gimenez, Godin, Laxalt; Nandez (Urreta 73), Torreira, Vecino, Bentancur (Rodriguez 59); Suarez, Stuani (Gomez 59).
France: (4231) Lloris; Pavard, Varane, Umtiti, Lucas; Pogba, Kante; Mbappe (Dembele 87), Griezmann (Fekir 90), Tolisso (Nzonzi 79); Giroud.
Referee: Nestor Pitana.

Saturday, 7 July 2018

Russia (1) 2 *(Cheryshev 31, Fernandes 115)*

Croatia (1) 2 *(Kramaric 39, Vida 101)*   44,287

Russia: (4231) Akinfeev; Kudryashov, Ignashevich, Kutepov, Fernandes; Kuzyaev, Zobnin; Cheryshev (Smolov 67), Golovin (Dzagoev 102), Samedov (Erokhin 54); Dzyuba (Gazinsky 80).
Croatia: (4231) Subasic; Vrsaljko (Corluka 97), Lovren, Vida, Strinic (Pivaric 74); Rakitic, Modric; Rebic, Kramaric (Kovacic 88), Perisic (Brozovic 63); Mandzukic.
aet; Croatia won 4-3 on penalties.
Penalties – Russia first: Smolov (m) 0-0, Brozovic (s) 0-1, Dzagoev (s) 1-1, Kovacic (m) 1-1, Fernandes (m) 1-1, Modric (s) 1-2, Ignashevich (s) 2-2, Vida (s) 2-3, Kuzyayev (s) 3-3, Rakatic (s) 3-4.
Referee: Sandro Ricci.

Sweden (0) 0

England (1) 2 *(Maguire 30, Alli 58)*   39,991

Sweden: (442) Olsen; Krafth (Jansson 85), Lindelof, Granqvist, Augustinsson; Claesson, Larsson, Ekdal, Forsberg (Olsson 65); Berg, Toivonen (Guidetti 65).
England: (352) Pickford; Walker, Stones, Maguire; Trippier, Alli (Delph 76), Henderson (Dier 85), Lingard, Young; Sterling (Rashford 90), Kane.
Referee: Bjorn Kuipers.

SEMI-FINALS

Tuesday, 10 July 2018

France (0) 1 *(Umtiti 51)*

Belgium (0) 0   64,286

France: (4231) Lloris; Pavard, Varane, Umtiti, Lucas; Pogba, Kante; Mbappe, Griezmann, Matuidi (Tolisso 86); Giroud (Nzonzi 85).
Belgium: (352) Courtois; Alderweireld, Kompany, Vertonghen; Chadli (Batshuayi 90), Dembele (Mertens 60), Witsel, Fellaini (Carrasco 80), De Bruyne; Lukaku R, Hazard E.
Referee: Andres Cunha.

Wednesday, 11 July 2018

Croatia (0) 2 *(Perisic 68, Mandzukic 109)*

England (1) 1 *(Trippier 5)*   78,011

Croatia: (4231) Subasic; Vrsaljko, Lovren, Vida, Strinic (Pivaric 95); Rakitic, Brozovic, Rebic (Kramaric 101), Modric (Badelj 118), Perisic; Mandzukic (Corluka 115).
England: (352) Pickford; Walker (Vardy 112), Stones, Maguire; Trippier, Alli, Henderson (Dier 97), Lingard, Young (Rose 91); Sterling (Rashford 74), Kane.
aet.
Referee: Cuneyt Cakir.

THIRD PLACE PLAY-OFF

Saturday, 14 July 2018

(at St Petersburg, attendance 64,406)

Belgium (1) 2   England (0) 0

Belgium: (343) Courtois; Alderweireld, Kompany, Vertonghen; Meunier, Tielemans (Dembele 78), Witsel, Chadli (Vermaelen 39); De Bruyne, Lukaku R (Mertens 61), Hazard E.
Scorers: Meunier 4, Hazard E 82.

England: (352) Pickford; Jones, Stones, Maguire; Trippier, Loftus-Cheek (Alli 84), Dier, Delph, Rose (Lingard 46); Sterling (Rashford 46), Kane.

Referee: Alireza Faghani.

WORLD CUP FINAL 2018

Sunday 15 July 2018

(at Moscow, attendance 78,011)

France (2) 4   Croatia (1) 2

France: (4411) Lloris; Pavard, Varane, Umtiti, Lucas; Mbappe, Pogba, Kante (Nzonzi 54), Matuidi (Tolisso 73); Griezmann; Giroud (Fekir 81).
Scorers: Mandzukic 18 (og), Griezmann 38 (pen), Pogba 59, Mbappe 65.

Croatia: (4411) Subasic; Vrsaljko, Lovren, Vida, Strinic (Pjaca 81); Rebic (Kramaric 71), Rakitic, Brozovic, Perisic; Modric; Mandzukic.
Scorers: Perisic 28, Mandzukic 69.

Referee: Nestor Pitana.

FIFA WORLD CUP 2018 – STATISTICS

- The Golden Ball for the best player at the FIFA World Cup 2018 was awarded to Luka Modric of Croatia for his outstanding displays in Russia.
- The Golden Boot for the top scorer at the FIFA World Cup 2018 was awarded to Harry Kane of England. He scored six goals in helping England reach the semi-finals for the first time since Italy 1990.
- The Golden Glove for the tournament's most outstanding goalkeeper was awarded to Belgium's Thibaut Courtois.
- The Young Player Award was awarded to Kylian Mbappe of France.
- The Fair Play Award for the team with the best disciplinary record went to Spain. Only teams reaching the knockout phase were eligible.
- Didier Deschamps become only the third person to win the World Cup as a player and as a manager. The others were Brazil's Mario Zagallo and Germany's Franz Beckenbauer.
- Mbappe (19 years 207 days) is the youngest player to score in a World Cup final since Pele for Brazil in Sweden 1958 (17 years 249 days).
- It was the fourth World Cup in succession won by a European team – the first time a single confederation has won four in a row.
- The final had the most goals in regulation time since Sweden 1958 (Brazil 5 Sweden 2).
- Belgium's rally to defeat Japan 3-2 was the first match for 48 years in which a team has overcome a two-goal deficit. The last time was West Germany defeating England by the same score in Mexico 1970.
- A record number of 29 penalties were awarded in the tournament. 22 were scored and VAR contributed to 11 decisions, including the one in the final.
- England scored 9 goals stemming from set-pieces, which is the highest goal tally for any team at a World Cup tournament.
- There was also a record 12 own goals, double the previous record from France 1998.
- The total number of goals scored at Russia 2018 was 169, just behind the record of 171 (Brazil 2014 and France 1998).

THE WORLD CUP 1930–2018

Year	Winners v Runners-up		Venue	Attendance	Referee
1930	Uruguay v Argentina	4-2	Montevideo	68,346	J. Langenus (Belgium)
	Winning Coach: Alberto Suppici				
1934	Italy v Czechoslovakia	2-1*	Rome	55,000	I. Eklind (Sweden)
	Winning Coach: Vittorio Pozzo				
1938	Italy v Hungary	4-2	Paris	45,000	G. Capdeville (France)
	Winning Coach: Vittorio Pozzo				
1950	Uruguay v Brazil	2-1	Rio de Janeiro	173,850	G. Reader (England)
	Winning Coach: Juan Lopez				
1954	West Germany v Hungary	3-2	Berne	62,500	W. Ling (England)
	Winning Coach: Sepp Herberger				
1958	Brazil v Sweden	5-2	Stockholm	49,737	M. Guigue (France)
	Winning Coach: Vicente Feola				
1962	Brazil v Czechoslovakia	3-1	Santiago	68,679	N. Latychev (USSR)
	Winning Coach: Aymore Moreira				
1966	England v West Germany	4-2*	Wembley	96,924	G. Dienst (Sweden)
	Winning Coach: Alf Ramsey				
1970	Brazil v Italy	4-1	Mexico City	107,412	R. Glockner (East Germany)
	Winning Coach: Mario Zagallo				
1974	West Germany v Netherlands	2-1	Munich	78,200	J. Taylor (England)
	Winning Coach: Helmut Schon				
1978	Argentina v Netherlands	3-1*	Buenos Aires	71,483	S. Gonella (Italy)
	Winning Coach: Cesar Luis Menotti				
1982	Italy v West Germany	3-1	Madrid	90,000	A. C. Coelho (Brazil)
	Winning Coach: Enzo Bearzot				
1986	Argentina v West Germany	3-2	Mexico City	114,600	R. A. Filho (Brazil)
	Winning Coach: Carlos Bilardo				
1990	West Germany v Argentina	1-0	Rome	73,603	E. C. Mendez (Mexico)
	Winning Coach: Franz Beckenbauer				
1994	Brazil v Italy	0-0*	Los Angeles	94,194	S. Puhl (Hungary)
	Brazil won 3-2 on penalties.				
	Winning Coach: Carlos Alberto Parreira				
1998	France v Brazil	3-0	Paris	80,000	S. Belqola (Morocco)
	Winning Coach: Aime Jacquet				
2002	Brazil v Germany	2-0	Yokohama	69,029	P. Collina (Italy)
	Winning Coach: Luiz Felipe Scolari				
2006	Italy v France	1-1*	Berlin	69,000	H. Elizondo (Argentina)
	Italy won 5-3 on penalties.				
	Winning Coach: Marcello Lippi				
2010	Spain v Netherlands	1-0	Johannesburg	84,490	H. Webb (England)
	Winning Coach: Vicente del Bosque				
2014	Germany v Argentina	1-0*	Rio de Janeiro	74,738	N. Rizzoli (Italy)
	Winning Coach: Joachim Low				
2018	France v Croatia	4-2	Moscow	78,011	N. Pitana (Argentina)
	Winning Coach: Didier Deschamps				

(*After extra time)

GOALSCORING AND ATTENDANCES IN WORLD CUP FINAL ROUNDS

Year	Venue	Games	Goals (av)	Attendance (av)
1930	Uruguay	18	70 (3.9)	590,549 (32,808)
1934	Italy	17	70 (4.1)	363,000 (21,352)
1938	France	18	84 (4.7)	375,700 (20,872)
1950	Brazil	22	88 (4.0)	1,045,246 (47,511)
1954	Switzerland	26	140 (5.4)	768,607 (29,562)
1958	Sweden	35	126 (3.6)	819,810 (23,423)
1962	Chile	32	89 (2.8)	893,172 (27,912)
1966	England	32	89 (2.8)	1,563,135 (48,848)
1970	Mexico	32	95 (3.0)	1,603,975 (50,124)
1974	West Germany	38	97 (2.6)	1,865,753 (49,098)
1978	Argentina	38	102 (2.7)	1,545,791 (40,678)
1982	Spain	52	146 (2.8)	2,109,723 (40,571)
1986	Mexico	52	132 (2.5)	2,394,031 (46,039)
1990	Italy	52	115 (2.2)	2,516,215 (48,388)
1994	USA	52	141 (2.7)	3,587,538 (68,991)
1998	France	64	171 (2.7)	2,785,100 (43,517)
2002	Japan/S. Korea	64	161 (2.5)	2,705,197 (42,268)
2006	Germany	64	147 (2.3)	3,359,439 (52,491)
2010	South Africa	64	145 (2.3)	3,178,856 (49,669)
2014	Brazil	64	171 (2.7)	3,367,727 (52,621)
2018	Russia	64	169 (2.6)	3,031,768 (47,371)
Total		900	2548 (2.8)	40,470,332 (44,967)

LEADING GOALSCORERS

Year	Player	Goals
1930	Guillermo Stabile (Argentina)	8
1934	Oldrich Nejedly (Czechoslovakia)	5
1938	Leonidas da Silva (Brazil)	7
1950	Ademir (Brazil)	8
1954	Sandor Kocsis (Hungary)	11
1958	Just Fontaine (France)	13
1962	Valentin Ivanov (USSR), Leonel Sanchez (Chile), Garrincha (Brazil), Vava (Brazil), Florian Albert (Hungary), Drazen Jerkovic (Yugoslavia)	4
1966	Eusebio (Portugal)	9
1970	Gerd Muller (West Germany)	10
1974	Grzegorz Lato (Poland)	7
1978	Mario Kempes (Argentina)	6
1982	Paolo Rossi (Italy)	6
1986	Gary Lineker (England)	6
1990	Salvatore Schillaci (Italy)	6
1994	Oleg Salenko (Russia), Hristo Stoichkov (Bulgaria)	6
1998	Davor Suker (Croatia)	6
2002	Ronaldo (Brazil)	8
2006	Miroslav Klose (Germany)	5
2010	Thomas Muller (Germany), David Villa (Spain), Wesley Sneijder (Netherlands), Diego Forlan (Uruguay)	5
2014	James Rodriguez (Colombia)	6
2018	Harry Kane (England)	6

EUROPEAN FOOTBALL CHAMPIONSHIP
1960–2016
(formerly EUROPEAN NATIONS' CUP)

Year	Winners v Runners-up		Venue	Attendance	Referee
1960	USSR v Yugoslavia	2-1*	Paris	17,966	A. E. Ellis (England)
	Winning Coach: Gavriil Kachalin				
1964	Spain v USSR	2-1	Madrid	79,115	A. E. Ellis (England)
	Winning Coach: Jose Villalonga				
1968	Italy v Yugoslavia	1-1	Rome	68,817	G. Dienst (Switzerland)
Replay	Italy v Yugoslavia	2-0	Rome	32,866	J. M. O. de Mendibil (Spain)
	Winning Coach: Ferruccio Valcareggi				
1972	West Germany v USSR	3-0	Brussels	43,066	F. Marschall (Austria)
	Winning Coach: Helmut Schon				
1976	Czechoslovakia v West Germany	2-2	Belgrade	30,790	S. Gonella (Italy)
	Czechoslovakia won 5-3 on penalties.				
	Winning Coach: Vaclav Jezek				
1980	West Germany v Belgium	2-1	Rome	47,860	N. Rainea (Romania)
	Winning Coach: Jupp Derwall				
1984	France v Spain	2-0	Paris	47,368	V. Christov (Slovakia)
	Winning Coach: Michel Hidalgo				
1988	Netherlands v USSR	2-0	Munich	62,770	M. Vautrot (France)
	Winning Coach: Rinus Michels				
1992	Denmark v Germany	2-0	Gothenburg	37,800	B. Galler (Switzerland)
	Winning Coach: Richard Moller Nielsen				
1996	Germany v Czech Republic	2-1*	Wembley	73,611	P. Pairetto (Italy)
	Germany won on sudden death 'golden goal'.				
	Winning Coach: Berti Vogts				
2000	France v Italy	2-1*	Rotterdam	48,200	A. Frisk (Sweden)
	France won on sudden death 'golden goal'.				
	Winning Coach: Roger Lemerre				
2004	Greece v Portugal	1-0	Lisbon	62,865	M. Merk (Germany)
	Winning Coach: Otto Rehhagel				
2008	Spain v Germany	1-0	Vienna	51,428	R. Rosetti (Italy)
	Winning Coach: Luis Aragones				
2012	Spain v Italy	4-0	Kiev	63,170	P. Proenca (Portugal)
	Winning Coach: Vicente del Bosque				
2016	Portugal v France	1-0*	Paris	75,868	M. Clattenburg (England)
	Winning Coach: Fernando Santos				

*(*After extra time)*

OLYMPIC FOOTBALL PAST MEDALLISTS
1896–2016

* No official tournament. ** No official tournament but gold medal later awarded by IOC.

1896 Athens*
1 Denmark
2 Greece

1900 Paris*
1 Great Britain
2 France

1904 St Louis**
1 Canada
2 USA

1908 London
1 Great Britain
2 Denmark
3 Netherlands

1912 Stockholm
1 England
2 Denmark
3 Netherlands

1920 Antwerp
1 Belgium
2 Spain
3 Netherlands

1924 Paris
1 Uruguay
2 Switzerland
3 Sweden

1928 Amsterdam
1 Uruguay
2 Argentina
3 Italy

1932 Los Angeles
no tournament

1936 Berlin
1 Italy
2 Austria
3 Norway

1948 London
1 Sweden
2 Yugoslavia
3 Denmark

1952 Helsinki
1 Hungary
2 Yugoslavia
3 Sweden

1956 Melbourne
1 USSR
2 Yugoslavia
3 Bulgaria

1960 Rome
1 Yugoslavia
2 Denmark
3 Hungary

1964 Tokyo
1 Hungary
2 Czechoslovakia
3 East Germany

1968 Mexico City
1 Hungary
2 Bulgaria
3 Japan

1972 Munich
1 Poland
2 Hungary
3 E Germany/USSR

1976 Montreal
1 East Germany
2 Poland
3 USSR

1980 Moscow
1 Czechoslovakia
2 East Germany
3 USSR

1984 Los Angeles
1 France
2 Brazil
3 Yugoslavia

1988 Seoul
1 USSR
2 Brazil
3 West Germany

1992 Barcelona
1 Spain
2 Poland
3 Ghana

1996 Atlanta
1 Nigeria
2 Argentina
3 Brazil

2000 Sydney
1 Cameroon
2 Spain
3 Chile

2004 Athens
1 Argentina
2 Paraguay
3 Italy

2008 Beijing
1 Argentina
2 Nigeria
3 Brazil

2012 London
1 Mexico
2 Brazil
3 South Korea

2016 Rio
1 Brazil
2 Germany
3 Nigeria

BRITISH AND IRISH INTERNATIONAL RESULTS 1872–2018

Note: In the results that follow, wc=World Cup, ec=European Championship, ui=Umbro International Trophy. tf = Tournoi de France. nc = Nations Cup. Northern Ireland played as Ireland before 1921. *After extra time.

Bold type indicates matches played in season 2017–18.

ENGLAND v SCOTLAND

Played: 114; England won 48, Scotland won 41, Drawn 25. Goals: England 203, Scotland 174.

Year	Date	Venue	E	S	Year	Date	Venue	E	S
1872	30 Nov	Glasgow	0	0	1934	14 Apr	Wembley	3	0
1873	8 Mar	Kennington Oval	4	2	1935	6 Apr	Glasgow	0	2
1874	7 Mar	Glasgow	1	2	1936	4 Apr	Wembley	1	1
1875	6 Mar	Kennington Oval	2	2	1937	17 Apr	Glasgow	1	3
1876	4 Mar	Glasgow	0	3	1938	9 Apr	Wembley	0	1
1877	3 Mar	Kennington Oval	1	3	1939	15 Apr	Glasgow	2	1
1878	2 Mar	Glasgow	2	7	1947	12 Apr	Wembley	1	1
1879	5 Apr	Kennington Oval	5	4	1948	10 Apr	Glasgow	2	0
1880	13 Mar	Glasgow	4	5	1949	9 Apr	Wembley	1	3
1881	12 Mar	Kennington Oval	1	6	wc1950	15 Apr	Glasgow	1	0
1882	11 Mar	Glasgow	1	5	1951	14 Apr	Wembley	2	3
1883	10 Mar	Sheffield	2	3	1952	5 Apr	Glasgow	2	1
1884	15 Mar	Glasgow	0	1	1953	18 Apr	Wembley	2	2
1885	21 Mar	Kennington Oval	1	1	wc1954	3 Apr	Glasgow	4	2
1886	31 Mar	Glasgow	1	1	1955	2 Apr	Wembley	7	2
1887	19 Mar	Blackburn	2	3	1956	14 Apr	Glasgow	1	1
1888	17 Mar	Glasgow	5	0	1957	6 Apr	Wembley	2	1
1889	13 Apr	Kennington Oval	2	3	1958	19 Apr	Glasgow	4	0
1890	5 Apr	Glasgow	1	1	1959	11 Apr	Wembley	1	0
1891	6 Apr	Blackburn	2	1	1960	9 Apr	Glasgow	1	1
1892	2 Apr	Glasgow	4	1	1961	15 Apr	Wembley	9	3
1893	1 Apr	Richmond	5	2	1962	14 Apr	Glasgow	0	2
1894	7 Apr	Glasgow	2	2	1963	6 Apr	Wembley	1	2
1895	6 Apr	Everton	3	0	1964	11 Apr	Glasgow	0	1
1896	4 Apr	Glasgow	1	2	1965	10 Apr	Wembley	2	2
1897	3 Apr	Crystal Palace	1	2	1966	2 Apr	Glasgow	4	3
1898	2 Apr	Glasgow	3	1	ec1967	15 Apr	Wembley	2	3
1899	8 Apr	Aston Villa	2	1	ec1968	24 Jan	Glasgow	1	1
1900	7 Apr	Glasgow	1	4	1969	10 May	Wembley	4	1
1901	30 Mar	Crystal Palace	2	2	1970	25 Apr	Glasgow	0	0
1902	3 Mar	Aston Villa	2	2	1971	22 May	Wembley	3	1
1903	4 Apr	Sheffield	1	2	1972	27 May	Glasgow	1	0
1904	9 Apr	Glasgow	1	0	1973	14 Feb	Glasgow	5	0
1905	1 Apr	Crystal Palace	1	0	1973	19 May	Wembley	1	0
1906	7 Apr	Glasgow	1	2	1974	18 May	Glasgow	0	2
1907	6 Apr	Newcastle	1	1	1975	24 May	Wembley	5	1
1908	4 Apr	Glasgow	1	1	1976	15 May	Glasgow	1	2
1909	3 Apr	Crystal Palace	2	0	1977	4 June	Wembley	1	2
1910	2 Apr	Glasgow	0	2	1978	20 May	Glasgow	1	0
1911	1 Apr	Everton	1	1	1979	26 May	Wembley	3	1
1912	23 Mar	Glasgow	1	1	1980	24 May	Glasgow	2	0
1913	5 Apr	Chelsea	1	0	1981	23 May	Wembley	0	1
1914	14 Apr	Glasgow	1	3	1982	29 May	Glasgow	1	0
1920	10 Apr	Sheffield	5	4	1983	1 June	Wembley	2	0
1921	9 Apr	Glasgow	0	3	1984	26 May	Glasgow	1	1
1922	8 Apr	Aston Villa	0	1	1985	25 May	Glasgow	0	1
1923	14 Apr	Glasgow	2	2	1986	23 Apr	Wembley	2	1
1924	12 Apr	Wembley	1	1	1987	23 May	Glasgow	0	0
1925	4 Apr	Glasgow	0	2	1988	21 May	Wembley	1	0
1926	17 Apr	Manchester	0	1	1989	27 May	Glasgow	2	0
1927	2 Apr	Glasgow	2	1	ec1996	15 June	Wembley	2	0
1928	31 Mar	Wembley	1	5	ec1999	13 Nov	Glasgow	2	0
1929	13 Apr	Glasgow	0	1	ec1999	17 Nov	Wembley	0	1
1930	5 Apr	Wembley	5	2	2013	14 Aug	Wembley	3	2
1931	28 Mar	Glasgow	0	2	2014	18 Nov	Hampden	3	1
1932	9 Apr	Wembley	3	0	wc2016	11 Nov	Wembley	3	0
1933	1 Apr	Glasgow	1	2	wc2017	10 June	Hampden	2	2

ENGLAND v WALES

Played: 102; England won 67, Wales won 14, Drawn 21. Goals: England 247, Wales 91.

Year	Date	Venue	E	W	Year	Date	Venue	E	W
1879	18 Jan	Kennington Oval	2	1	1887	26 Feb	Kennington Oval	4	0
1880	15 Mar	Wrexham	3	2	1888	4 Feb	Crewe	5	1
1881	26 Feb	Blackburn	0	1	1889	23 Feb	Stoke	4	1
1882	13 Mar	Wrexham	3	5	1890	15 Mar	Wrexham	3	1
1883	3 Feb	Kennington Oval	5	0	1891	7 May	Sunderland	4	1
1884	17 Mar	Wrexham	4	0	1892	5 Mar	Wrexham	2	0
1885	14 Mar	Blackburn	1	1	1893	13 Mar	Stoke	6	0
1886	29 Mar	Wrexham	3	1	1894	12 Mar	Wrexham	5	1

Year	Date	Venue	E	W
1895	18 Mar	Queen's Club, Kensington	1	1
1896	16 Mar	Cardiff	9	1
1897	29 Mar	Sheffield	4	0
1898	28 Mar	Wrexham	3	0
1899	20 Mar	Bristol	4	0
1900	26 Mar	Cardiff	1	1
1901	18 Mar	Newcastle	6	0
1902	3 Mar	Wrexham	0	0
1903	2 Mar	Portsmouth	2	1
1904	29 Feb	Wrexham	2	2
1905	27 Mar	Liverpool	3	1
1906	19 Mar	Cardiff	1	0
1907	18 Mar	Fulham	1	1
1908	16 Mar	Wrexham	7	1
1909	15 Mar	Nottingham	2	0
1910	14 Mar	Cardiff	1	0
1911	13 Mar	Millwall	3	0
1912	11 Mar	Wrexham	2	0
1913	17 Mar	Bristol	4	3
1914	16 Mar	Cardiff	2	0
1920	15 Mar	Highbury	1	2
1921	14 Mar	Cardiff	0	0
1922	13 Mar	Liverpool	1	0
1923	5 Mar	Cardiff	2	2
1924	3 Mar	Blackburn	1	2
1925	28 Feb	Swansea	2	1
1926	1 Mar	Crystal Palace	1	3
1927	12 Feb	Wrexham	3	3
1927	28 Nov	Burnley	1	2
1928	17 Nov	Swansea	3	2
1929	20 Nov	Chelsea	6	0
1930	22 Nov	Wrexham	4	0
1931	18 Nov	Liverpool	3	1
1932	16 Nov	Wrexham	0	0
1933	15 Nov	Newcastle	1	2
1934	29 Sept	Cardiff	4	0
1936	5 Feb	Wolverhampton	1	2
1936	17 Oct	Cardiff	1	2
1937	17 Nov	Middlesbrough	2	1
1938	22 Oct	Cardiff	2	4
1946	13 Nov	Manchester	3	0
1947	18 Oct	Cardiff	3	0
1948	10 Nov	Aston Villa	1	0
wc1949	15 Oct	Cardiff	4	1
1950	15 Nov	Sunderland	4	2
1951	20 Oct	Cardiff	1	1
1952	12 Nov	Wembley	5	2
wc1953	10 Oct	Cardiff	4	1
1954	10 Nov	Wembley	3	2
1955	27 Oct	Cardiff	1	2
1956	14 Nov	Wembley	3	1
1957	19 Oct	Cardiff	4	0
1958	26 Nov	Aston Villa	2	2
1959	17 Oct	Cardiff	1	1
1960	23 Nov	Wembley	5	1
1961	14 Oct	Cardiff	1	1
1962	21 Oct	Wembley	4	0
1963	12 Oct	Cardiff	4	0
1964	18 Nov	Wembley	2	1
1965	2 Oct	Cardiff	0	0
EC1966	16 Nov	Wembley	5	1
EC1967	21 Oct	Cardiff	3	0
1969	7 May	Wembley	2	1
1970	18 Apr	Cardiff	1	1
1971	19 May	Wembley	0	0
1972	20 May	Cardiff	3	0
wc1972	15 Nov	Cardiff	1	0
wc1973	24 Jan	Wembley	1	1
1973	15 May	Wembley	3	0
1974	11 May	Cardiff	2	0
1975	21 May	Wembley	2	2
1976	24 Mar	Wrexham	2	1
1976	8 May	Cardiff	1	0
1977	31 May	Wembley	0	1
1978	3 May	Cardiff	3	1
1979	23 May	Wembley	0	0
1980	17 May	Wrexham	1	4
1981	20 May	Wembley	0	0
1982	27 Apr	Cardiff	1	0
1983	23 Feb	Wembley	2	1
1984	2 May	Wrexham	0	1
wc2004	9 Oct	Old Trafford	2	0
wc2005	3 Sept	Cardiff	1	0
EC2011	26 Mar	Cardiff	2	0
EC2011	6 Sept	Wembley	1	0
EC2016	16 June	Lens	2	1

ENGLAND v NORTHERN IRELAND

Played: 98; England won 75, Northern Ireland won 7, Drawn 16. Goals: England 323, Northern Ireland 81.

Year	Date	Venue	E	NI
1882	18 Feb	Belfast	13	0
1883	24 Feb	Liverpool	7	0
1884	23 Feb	Belfast	8	1
1885	28 Feb	Manchester	4	0
1886	13 Mar	Belfast	6	1
1887	5 Feb	Sheffield	7	0
1888	31 Mar	Belfast	5	1
1889	2 Mar	Everton	6	1
1890	15 Mar	Belfast	9	1
1891	7 Mar	Wolverhampton	6	1
1892	5 Mar	Belfast	2	0
1893	25 Feb	Birmingham	6	1
1894	3 Mar	Belfast	2	2
1895	9 Mar	Derby	9	0
1896	7 Mar	Belfast	2	0
1897	20 Feb	Nottingham	6	0
1898	5 Mar	Belfast	3	2
1899	18 Feb	Sunderland	13	2
1900	17 Mar	Dublin	2	0
1901	9 Mar	Southampton	3	0
1902	22 Mar	Belfast	1	0
1903	14 Feb	Wolverhampton	4	0
1904	12 Mar	Belfast	3	1
1905	25 Feb	Middlesbrough	1	1
1906	17 Feb	Belfast	5	0
1907	16 Feb	Everton	1	0
1908	15 Feb	Belfast	3	1
1909	13 Feb	Bradford	4	0
1910	12 Feb	Belfast	1	1
1911	11 Feb	Derby	2	1
1912	10 Feb	Dublin	6	1
1913	15 Feb	Belfast	1	2
1914	14 Feb	Middlesbrough	0	3
1919	25 Oct	Belfast	1	1
1920	23 Oct	Sunderland	2	0
1921	22 Oct	Belfast	1	1
1922	21 Oct	West Bromwich	2	0
1923	20 Oct	Belfast	1	2
1924	22 Oct	Everton	3	1
1925	24 Oct	Belfast	0	0
1926	20 Oct	Liverpool	3	3
1927	22 Oct	Belfast	0	2
1928	22 Oct	Everton	2	1
1929	19 Oct	Belfast	3	0
1930	20 Oct	Sheffield	5	1
1931	17 Oct	Belfast	6	2
1932	17 Oct	Blackpool	1	0
1933	14 Oct	Belfast	3	0
1935	6 Feb	Everton	2	1
1935	19 Oct	Belfast	3	1
1936	18 Nov	Stoke	3	1
1937	23 Oct	Belfast	5	1
1938	16 Nov	Manchester	7	0
1946	28 Sept	Belfast	7	2
1947	5 Nov	Everton	2	2
1948	9 Oct	Belfast	6	2
wc1949	16 Nov	Manchester	9	2
1950	7 Oct	Belfast	4	1
1951	14 Nov	Aston Villa	2	0
1952	4 Oct	Belfast	2	2
wc1953	11 Nov	Everton	3	1
1954	2 Oct	Belfast	2	0
1955	2 Nov	Wembley	3	0
1956	10 Oct	Belfast	1	1

			E	NI					E	NI
1957	6 Nov	Wembley	2	3		1975	17 May	Belfast	0	0
1958	4 Oct	Belfast	3	3		1976	11 May	Wembley	4	0
1959	18 Nov	Wembley	2	1		1977	28 May	Belfast	2	1
1960	8 Oct	Belfast	5	2		1978	16 May	Wembley	1	0
1961	22 Nov	Wembley	1	1		EC1979	7 Feb	Wembley	4	0
1962	20 Oct	Belfast	3	1		1979	19 May	Belfast	2	0
1963	20 Nov	Wembley	8	3		EC1979	17 Oct	Belfast	5	1
1964	3 Oct	Belfast	4	3		1980	20 May	Wembley	1	1
1965	10 Nov	Wembley	2	1		1982	23 Feb	Wembley	4	0
EC1966	20 Oct	Belfast	2	0		1983	28 May	Belfast	0	0
EC1967	22 Nov	Wembley	2	0		1984	24 Apr	Wembley	1	0
1969	3 May	Belfast	3	1		wc1985	27 Feb	Belfast	1	0
1970	21 Apr	Wembley	3	1		wc1985	13 Nov	Wembley	0	0
1971	15 May	Belfast	1	0		EC1986	15 Oct	Wembley	3	0
1972	23 May	Wembley	0	1		EC1987	1 Apr	Belfast	2	0
1973	12 May	Everton	2	1		wc2005	26 Mar	Old Trafford	4	0
1974	15 May	Wembley	1	0		wc2005	7 Sept	Belfast	0	1

SCOTLAND v WALES

Played: 107; Scotland won 61, Wales won 23, Drawn 23. Goals: Scotland 243, Wales 124.

			S	W					S	W
1876	25 Mar	Glasgow	4	0		1934	21 Nov	Aberdeen	3	2
1877	5 Mar	Wrexham	2	0		1935	5 Oct	Cardiff	1	1
1878	23 Mar	Glasgow	9	0		1936	2 Dec	Dundee	1	2
1879	7 Apr	Wrexham	3	0		1937	30 Oct	Cardiff	1	2
1880	3 Apr	Glasgow	5	1		1938	9 Nov	Tynecastle	3	2
1881	14 Mar	Wrexham	5	1		1946	19 Oct	Wrexham	1	3
1882	25 Mar	Glasgow	5	0		1947	12 Nov	Glasgow	1	2
1883	12 Mar	Wrexham	3	0		1948	23 Oct	Cardiff	3	1
1884	29 Mar	Glasgow	4	1		wc1949	9 Nov	Glasgow	2	0
1885	23 Mar	Wrexham	8	1		1950	21 Oct	Cardiff	3	1
1886	10 Apr	Glasgow	4	1		1951	14 Nov	Glasgow	0	1
1887	21 Mar	Wrexham	2	0		1952	18 Oct	Cardiff	2	1
1888	10 Mar	Easter Road	5	1		wc1953	4 Nov	Glasgow	3	3
1889	15 Apr	Wrexham	0	0		1954	16 Oct	Cardiff	1	0
1890	22 Mar	Paisley	5	0		1955	9 Nov	Glasgow	2	0
1891	21 Mar	Wrexham	4	3		1956	20 Oct	Cardiff	2	2
1892	26 Mar	Tynecastle	6	1		1957	13 Nov	Glasgow	1	1
1893	18 Mar	Wrexham	8	0		1958	18 Oct	Cardiff	3	0
1894	24 Mar	Kilmarnock	5	2		1959	4 Nov	Glasgow	1	1
1895	23 Mar	Wrexham	2	2		1960	20 Oct	Cardiff	0	2
1896	21 Mar	Dundee	4	0		1961	8 Nov	Glasgow	2	0
1897	20 Mar	Wrexham	2	2		1962	20 Oct	Cardiff	3	2
1898	19 Mar	Motherwell	5	2		1963	20 Nov	Glasgow	2	1
1899	18 Mar	Wrexham	6	0		1964	3 Oct	Cardiff	2	3
1900	3 Feb	Aberdeen	5	2		EC1965	24 Nov	Glasgow	4	1
1901	2 Mar	Wrexham	1	1		EC1966	22 Oct	Cardiff	1	1
1902	15 Mar	Greenock	5	1		1967	22 Nov	Glasgow	3	2
1903	9 Mar	Cardiff	1	0		1969	3 May	Wrexham	5	3
1904	12 Mar	Dundee	1	1		1970	22 Apr	Glasgow	0	0
1905	6 Mar	Wrexham	1	3		1971	15 May	Cardiff	0	0
1906	3 Mar	Tynecastle	0	2		1972	24 May	Glasgow	1	0
1907	4 Mar	Wrexham	0	1		1973	12 May	Wrexham	2	0
1908	7 Mar	Dundee	2	1		1974	14 May	Glasgow	2	0
1909	1 Mar	Wrexham	2	3		1975	17 May	Cardiff	2	2
1910	5 Mar	Kilmarnock	1	0		1976	6 May	Glasgow	3	1
1911	6 Mar	Cardiff	2	2		wc1976	17 Nov	Glasgow	1	0
1912	2 Mar	Tynecastle	1	0		1977	28 May	Wrexham	0	0
1913	3 Mar	Wrexham	0	0		wc1977	12 Oct	Liverpool	2	0
1914	28 Feb	Glasgow	0	0		1978	17 May	Glasgow	1	1
1920	26 Feb	Cardiff	1	1		1979	19 May	Cardiff	0	3
1921	12 Feb	Aberdeen	2	1		1980	21 May	Glasgow	1	0
1922	4 Feb	Wrexham	1	2		1981	16 May	Swansea	0	2
1923	17 Mar	Paisley	2	0		1982	24 May	Glasgow	1	0
1924	16 Feb	Cardiff	0	2		1983	28 May	Cardiff	2	0
1925	14 Feb	Tynecastle	3	1		1984	28 Feb	Glasgow	2	1
1925	31 Oct	Cardiff	3	0		wc1985	27 Mar	Glasgow	0	1
1926	30 Oct	Glasgow	3	0		wc1985	10 Sept	Cardiff	1	1
1927	29 Oct	Wrexham	2	2		1997	27 May	Kilmarnock	0	1
1928	27 Oct	Glasgow	4	2		2004	18 Feb	Cardiff	0	4
1929	26 Oct	Cardiff	4	2		2009	14 Nov	Cardiff	0	3
1930	25 Oct	Glasgow	1	1		NC2011	25 May	Dublin	3	1
1931	31 Oct	Wrexham	3	2		wc2012	12 Oct	Cardiff	1	2
1932	26 Oct	Tynecastle	2	5		wc2013	22 Mar	Glasgow	1	2
1933	4 Oct	Cardiff	2	3						

SCOTLAND v NORTHERN IRELAND

Played: 96; Scotland won 64, Northern Ireland won 15, Drawn 17. Goals: Scotland 261, Northern Ireland 81.

Year	Date	Venue	S	NI		Year	Date	Venue	S	NI
1884	26 Jan	Belfast	5	0		1935	13 Nov	Tynecastle	2	1
1885	14 Mar	Glasgow	8	2		1936	31 Oct	Belfast	3	1
1886	20 Mar	Belfast	7	2		1937	10 Nov	Aberdeen	1	1
1887	19 Feb	Glasgow	4	1		1938	8 Oct	Belfast	2	0
1888	24 Mar	Belfast	10	2		1946	27 Nov	Glasgow	0	0
1889	9 Mar	Glasgow	7	0		1947	4 Oct	Belfast	0	2
1890	29 Mar	Belfast	4	1		1948	17 Nov	Glasgow	3	2
1891	28 Mar	Glasgow	2	1		wc1949	1 Oct	Belfast	8	2
1892	19 Mar	Belfast	3	2		1950	1 Nov	Glasgow	6	1
1893	25 Mar	Glasgow	6	1		1951	6 Oct	Belfast	3	0
1894	31 Mar	Belfast	2	1		1952	5 Nov	Glasgow	1	1
1895	30 Mar	Glasgow	3	1		wc1953	3 Oct	Belfast	3	1
1896	28 Mar	Belfast	3	3		1954	3 Nov	Glasgow	2	2
1897	27 Mar	Glasgow	5	1		1955	8 Oct	Belfast	1	2
1898	26 Mar	Belfast	3	0		1956	7 Nov	Glasgow	1	0
1899	25 Mar	Glasgow	9	1		1957	5 Oct	Belfast	1	1
1900	3 Mar	Belfast	3	0		1958	5 Nov	Glasgow	2	2
1901	23 Feb	Glasgow	11	0		1959	3 Oct	Belfast	4	0
1902	1 Mar	Belfast	5	1		1960	9 Nov	Glasgow	5	2
1902	9 Aug	Belfast	3	0		1961	7 Oct	Belfast	6	1
1903	21 Mar	Glasgow	0	2		1962	7 Nov	Glasgow	5	1
1904	26 Mar	Dublin	1	1		1963	12 Oct	Belfast	1	2
1905	18 Mar	Glasgow	4	0		1964	25 Nov	Glasgow	3	2
1906	17 Mar	Dublin	1	0		1965	2 Oct	Belfast	2	3
1907	16 Mar	Glasgow	3	0		1966	16 Nov	Glasgow	2	1
1908	14 Mar	Dublin	5	0		1967	21 Oct	Belfast	0	1
1909	15 Mar	Glasgow	5	0		1969	6 May	Glasgow	1	1
1910	19 Mar	Belfast	0	1		1970	18 Apr	Belfast	1	0
1911	18 Mar	Glasgow	2	0		1971	18 May	Glasgow	0	1
1912	16 Mar	Belfast	4	1		1972	20 May	Glasgow	2	0
1913	15 Mar	Dublin	2	1		1973	16 May	Glasgow	1	2
1914	14 Mar	Belfast	1	1		1974	11 May	Glasgow	0	1
1920	13 Mar	Glasgow	3	0		1975	20 May	Glasgow	3	0
1921	26 Feb	Belfast	2	0		1976	8 May	Glasgow	3	0
1922	4 Mar	Glasgow	2	1		1977	1 June	Glasgow	3	0
1923	3 Mar	Belfast	1	0		1978	13 May	Glasgow	1	1
1924	1 Mar	Glasgow	2	0		1979	22 May	Glasgow	1	0
1925	28 Feb	Belfast	3	0		1980	17 May	Belfast	0	1
1926	27 Feb	Glasgow	4	0		wc1981	25 Mar	Glasgow	1	1
1927	26 Feb	Belfast	2	0		1981	19 May	Glasgow	2	0
1928	25 Feb	Glasgow	0	1		wc1981	14 Oct	Belfast	0	0
1929	23 Feb	Belfast	7	3		1982	28 Apr	Belfast	1	1
1930	22 Feb	Glasgow	3	1		1983	24 May	Glasgow	0	0
1931	21 Feb	Belfast	0	0		1983	13 Dec	Belfast	0	2
1931	19 Sept	Glasgow	3	1		1992	19 Feb	Glasgow	1	0
1932	17 Sept	Belfast	4	0		2008	20 Aug	Glasgow	0	0
1933	16 Sept	Glasgow	1	2		NC2011	9 Feb	Dublin	3	0
1934	20 Oct	Belfast	1	2		2015	25 Mar	Hampden	1	0

WALES v NORTHERN IRELAND

Played: 96; Wales won 45, Northern Ireland won 27, Drawn 24. Goals: Wales 191, Northern Ireland 132.

Year	Date	Venue	W	NI		Year	Date	Venue	W	NI
1882	25 Feb	Wrexham	7	1		1906	2 Apr	Wrexham	4	4
1883	17 Mar	Belfast	1	1		1907	23 Feb	Belfast	3	2
1884	9 Feb	Wrexham	6	0		1908	11 Apr	Aberdare	0	1
1885	11 Apr	Belfast	8	2		1909	20 Mar	Belfast	3	2
1886	27 Feb	Wrexham	5	0		1910	11 Apr	Wrexham	4	1
1887	12 Mar	Belfast	1	4		1911	28 Jan	Belfast	2	1
1888	3 Mar	Wrexham	11	0		1912	13 Apr	Cardiff	2	3
1889	27 Apr	Belfast	3	1		1913	18 Jan	Belfast	1	0
1890	8 Feb	Shrewsbury	5	2		1914	19 Jan	Wrexham	1	2
1891	7 Feb	Belfast	2	7		1920	14 Feb	Belfast	2	2
1892	27 Feb	Bangor	1	1		1921	9 Apr	Swansea	2	1
1893	8 Apr	Belfast	3	4		1922	4 Apr	Belfast	1	1
1894	24 Feb	Swansea	4	1		1923	14 Apr	Wrexham	0	3
1895	16 Mar	Belfast	2	2		1924	15 Mar	Belfast	1	0
1896	29 Feb	Wrexham	6	1		1925	18 Apr	Wrexham	0	0
1897	6 Mar	Belfast	3	4		1926	13 Feb	Belfast	0	3
1898	19 Feb	Llandudno	0	1		1927	9 Apr	Cardiff	2	2
1899	4 Mar	Belfast	0	1		1928	4 Feb	Belfast	2	1
1900	24 Feb	Llandudno	2	0		1929	2 Feb	Wrexham	2	2
1901	23 Mar	Belfast	1	0		1930	1 Feb	Belfast	0	7
1902	22 Mar	Cardiff	0	3		1931	22 Apr	Wrexham	3	2
1903	28 Mar	Belfast	0	2		1931	5 Dec	Belfast	0	4
1904	21 Mar	Bangor	0	1		1932	7 Dec	Wrexham	4	1
1905	18 Apr	Belfast	2	2		1933	4 Nov	Belfast	1	1

Year	Date	Venue	W	NI
1935	27 Mar	Wrexham	3	1
1936	11 Mar	Belfast	2	3
1937	17 Mar	Wrexham	4	1
1938	16 Mar	Belfast	0	1
1939	15 Mar	Wrexham	3	1
1947	16 Apr	Belfast	1	2
1948	10 Mar	Wrexham	2	0
1949	9 Mar	Belfast	2	0
wc1950	8 Mar	Wrexham	0	0
1951	7 Mar	Belfast	2	1
1952	19 Mar	Swansea	3	0
1953	15 Apr	Belfast	3	2
wc1954	31 Mar	Wrexham	1	2
1955	20 Apr	Belfast	3	2
1956	11 Apr	Cardiff	1	1
1957	10 Apr	Belfast	0	0
1958	16 Apr	Cardiff	1	1
1959	22 Apr	Belfast	1	4
1960	6 Apr	Wrexham	3	2
1961	12 Apr	Belfast	5	1
1962	11 Apr	Cardiff	4	0
1963	3 Apr	Belfast	4	1
1964	15 Apr	Swansea	2	3
1965	31 Mar	Belfast	5	0
1966	30 Mar	Cardiff	1	4
EC1967	12 Apr	Belfast	0	0
EC1968	28 Feb	Wrexham	2	0
1969	10 May	Belfast	0	0
1970	25 Apr	Swansea	1	0
1971	22 May	Belfast	0	1
1972	27 May	Wrexham	0	0
1973	19 May	Everton	0	1
1974	18 May	Wrexham	1	0
1975	23 May	Belfast	0	1
1976	14 May	Swansea	1	0
1977	3 June	Belfast	1	1
1978	19 May	Wrexham	1	0
1979	25 May	Belfast	1	1
1980	23 May	Cardiff	0	1
1982	27 May	Wrexham	3	0
1983	31 May	Belfast	1	0
1984	22 May	Swansea	1	1
wc2004	8 Sept	Cardiff	2	2
wc2005	8 Oct	Belfast	3	2
2007	6 Feb	Belfast	0	0
NC2011	27 May	Dublin	2	0
2016	24 Mar	Cardiff	1	1
EC2016	25 June	Paris	1	0

OTHER BRITISH INTERNATIONAL RESULTS 1908–2018
ENGLAND

v ALBANIA

			E	A
wc1989	8 Mar	Tirana	2	0
wc1989	26 Apr	Wembley	5	0
wc2001	28 Mar	Tirana	3	1
wc2001	5 Sept	Newcastle	2	0

v ALGERIA

			E	A
wc2010	18 June	Cape Town	0	0

v ANDORRA

			E	A
EC2006	2 Sept	Old Trafford	5	0
EC2007	28 Mar	Barcelona	3	0
wc2008	6 Sept	Barcelona	2	0
wc2009	10 June	Wembley	6	0

v ARGENTINA

			E	A
1951	9 May	Wembley	2	1
1953	17 May	Buenos Aires	0	0
(abandoned after 21 mins)				
wc1962	2 June	Rancagua	3	1
1964	6 June	Rio de Janeiro	0	1
wc1966	23 July	Wembley	1	0
1974	22 May	Wembley	2	2
1977	12 June	Buenos Aires	1	1
1980	13 May	Wembley	3	1
wc1986	22 June	Mexico City	1	2
1991	25 May	Wembley	2	2
wc1998	30 June	St Etienne	2	2
2000	23 Feb	Wembley	0	0
wc2002	7 June	Sapporo	1	0
2005	12 Nov	Geneva	3	2

v AUSTRALIA

			E	A
1980	31 May	Sydney	2	1
1983	11 June	Sydney	0	0
1983	15 June	Brisbane	1	0
1983	18 June	Melbourne	1	1
1991	1 June	Sydney	1	0
2003	12 Feb	West Ham	1	3
2016	27 May	Sunderland	2	1

v AUSTRIA

			E	A
1908	6 June	Vienna	6	1
1908	8 June	Vienna	11	1
1909	1 June	Vienna	8	1
1930	14 May	Vienna	0	0
1932	7 Dec	Chelsea	4	3
1936	6 May	Vienna	1	2
1951	28 Nov	Wembley	2	2
1952	25 May	Vienna	3	2
wc1958	15 June	Boras	2	2
1961	27 May	Vienna	1	3
1962	4 Apr	Wembley	3	1
1965	20 Oct	Wembley	2	3
1967	27 May	Vienna	1	0
1973	26 Sept	Wembley	7	0
1979	13 June	Vienna	3	4
wc2004	4 Sept	Vienna	2	2
wc2005	8 Oct	Old Trafford	1	0
2007	16 Nov	Vienna	1	0

v AZERBAIJAN

			E	A
wc2004	13 Oct	Baku	1	0
wc2005	30 Mar	Newcastle	2	0

v BELARUS

			E	B
wc2008	15 Oct	Minsk	3	1
wc2009	14 Oct	Wembley	3	0

v BELGIUM

			E	B
1921	21 May	Brussels	2	0
1923	19 Mar	Highbury	6	1
1923	1 Nov	Antwerp	2	2
1924	8 Dec	West Bromwich	4	0
1926	24 May	Antwerp	5	3
1927	11 May	Brussels	9	1
1928	19 May	Antwerp	3	1
1929	11 May	Brussels	5	1
1931	16 May	Brussels	4	1
1936	9 May	Brussels	2	3
1947	21 Sept	Brussels	5	2
1950	18 May	Brussels	4	1
1952	26 Nov	Wembley	5	0
wc1954	17 June	Basle	4	4*
1964	21 Oct	Wembley	2	2
1970	25 Feb	Brussels	3	1
EC1980	12 June	Turin	1	1
wc1990	27 June	Bologna	1	0*
1998	29 May	Casablanca	0	0
1999	10 Oct	Sunderland	2	1
2012	2 June	Wembley	1	0
wc2018	**28 June**	**Kaliningrad**	**0**	**1**
wc2018	**14 July**	**St Petersburg**	**0**	**2**

v BOHEMIA

			E	B
1908	13 June	Prague	4	0

v BRAZIL

			E	B
1956	9 May	Wembley	4	2
wc1958	11 June	Gothenburg	0	0
1959	13 May	Rio de Janeiro	0	2
wc1962	10 June	Vina del Mar	1	3
1963	8 May	Wembley	1	1
1964	30 May	Rio de Janeiro	1	5
1969	12 June	Rio de Janeiro	1	2
wc1970	7 June	Guadalajara	0	1
1976	23 May	Los Angeles	0	1

			E	B
1977	8 June	Rio de Janeiro	0	0
1978	19 Apr	Wembley	1	1
1981	12 May	Wembley	0	1
1984	10 June	Rio de Janeiro	2	0
1987	19 May	Wembley	1	1
1990	28 Mar	Wembley	1	0
1992	17 May	Wembley	1	1
1993	13 June	Washington	1	1
UI1995	11 June	Wembley	1	3
TF1997	10 June	Paris	0	1
2000	27 May	Wembley	1	1
wc2002	21 June	Shizuoka	1	2
2007	1 June	Wembley	1	1
2009	14 Nov	Doha	0	1
2013	6 Feb	Wembley	2	1
2013	2 June	Rio de Janeiro	2	2
2017	**14 Nov**	**Wembley**	**0**	**0**

v BULGARIA

			E	B
wc1962	7 June	Rancagua	0	0
1968	11 Dec	Wembley	1	1
1974	1 June	Sofia	1	0
EC1979	6 June	Sofia	3	0
EC1979	22 Nov	Wembley	2	0
1996	27 Mar	Wembley	1	0
EC1998	10 Oct	Wembley	0	0
EC1999	9 June	Sofia	1	1
EC2010	3 Sept	Wembley	4	0
EC2011	2 Sept	Sofia	3	0

v CAMEROON

			E	C
wc1990	1 July	Naples	3	2*
1991	6 Feb	Wembley	2	0
1997	15 Nov	Wembley	2	0
2002	26 May	Kobe	2	2

v CANADA

			E	C
1986	24 May	Burnaby	1	0

v CHILE

			E	C
wc1950	25 June	Rio de Janeiro	2	0
1953	24 May	Santiago	2	1
1984	17 June	Santiago	0	0
1989	23 May	Wembley	0	0
1998	11 Feb	Wembley	0	2
2013	15 Nov	Wembley	0	2

v CHINA PR

			E	CPR
1996	23 May	Beijing	3	0

v CIS

			E	C
1992	29 Apr	Moscow	2	2

v COLOMBIA

			E	C
1970	20 May	Bogota	4	0
1988	24 May	Wembley	1	1
1995	6 Sept	Wembley	0	0
wc1998	26 June	Lens	2	0
2005	31 May	New Jersey	3	2
wc2018	**3 July**	**Moscow**	**1**	**1**

v COSTA RICA

			E	C
wc2014	26 June	Belo Horizonte	0	0
2018	**7 June**	**Leeds**	**2**	**0**

v CROATIA

			E	C
1996	24 Apr	Wembley	0	0
2003	20 Aug	Ipswich	3	1
EC2004	21 June	Lisbon	4	2
EC2006	11 Oct	Zagreb	0	2
EC2007	21 Nov	Wembley	2	3
wc2008	10 Sept	Zagreb	4	1
wc2009	9 Sept	Wembley	5	1
wc2018	**11 July**	**Moscow**	**1**	**2**

v CYPRUS

			E	C
EC1975	16 Apr	Wembley	5	0
EC1975	11 May	Limassol	1	0

v CZECHOSLOVAKIA

			E	C
1934	16 May	Prague	1	2
1937	1 Dec	Tottenham	5	4
1963	29 May	Bratislava	4	2
1966	2 Nov	Wembley	0	0
wc1970	11 June	Guadalajara	1	0
1973	27 May	Prague	1	1
EC1974	30 Oct	Wembley	3	0
EC1975	30 Oct	Bratislava	1	2
1978	29 Nov	Wembley	1	0

			E	C
wc1982	20 June	Bilbao	2	0
1990	25 Apr	Wembley	4	2
1992	25 Mar	Prague	2	2

v CZECH REPUBLIC

			E	C
1998	18 Nov	Wembley	2	0
2008	20 Aug	Wembley	2	2

v DENMARK

			E	D
1948	26 Sept	Copenhagen	0	0
1955	2 Oct	Copenhagen	5	1
wc1956	5 Dec	Wolverhampton	5	2
wc1957	15 May	Copenhagen	4	1
1966	3 July	Copenhagen	2	0
EC1978	20 Sept	Copenhagen	4	3
EC1979	12 Sept	Wembley	1	0
EC1982	22 Sept	Copenhagen	2	2
EC1983	21 Sept	Wembley	0	1
1988	14 Sept	Wembley	1	0
1989	7 June	Copenhagen	1	1
1990	15 May	Wembley	1	0
EC1992	11 June	Malmo	0	0
1994	9 Mar	Wembley	1	0
wc2002	15 June	Niigata	3	0
2003	16 Nov	Old Trafford	2	3
2005	17 Aug	Copenhagen	1	4
2011	9 Feb	Copenhagen	2	1
2014	5 Mar	Wembley	1	0

v ECUADOR

			E	Ec
1970	24 May	Quito	2	0
wc2006	25 June	Stuttgart	1	0
2014	4 June	Miami	2	2

v EGYPT

			E	Eg
1986	29 Jan	Cairo	4	0
wc1990	21 June	Cagliari	1	0
2010	3 Mar	Wembley	3	1

v ESTONIA

			E	Es
EC2007	6 June	Tallinn	3	0
EC2007	13 Oct	Wembley	3	0
EC2014	12 Oct	Tallinn	1	0
EC2015	9 Oct	Wembley	2	0

v FIFA

			E	FIFA
1938	26 Oct	Highbury	3	0
1953	21 Oct	Wembley	4	4
1963	23 Oct	Wembley	2	1

v FINLAND

			E	F
1937	20 May	Helsinki	8	0
1956	20 May	Helsinki	5	1
1966	26 June	Helsinki	3	0
wc1976	13 June	Helsinki	4	1
wc1976	13 Oct	Wembley	2	1
1982	3 June	Helsinki	4	1
wc1984	17 Oct	Wembley	5	0
wc1985	22 May	Helsinki	1	1
1992	3 June	Helsinki	2	1
wc2000	11 Oct	Helsinki	0	0
wc2001	24 Mar	Liverpool	2	1

v FRANCE

			E	F
1923	10 May	Paris	4	1
1924	17 May	Paris	3	1
1925	21 May	Paris	3	2
1927	26 May	Paris	6	0
1928	17 May	Paris	5	1
1929	9 May	Paris	4	1
1931	14 May	Paris	2	5
1933	6 Dec	Tottenham	4	1
1938	26 May	Paris	4	2
1947	3 May	Highbury	3	0
1949	22 May	Paris	3	1
1951	3 Oct	Highbury	2	2
1955	15 May	Paris	0	1
1957	27 Nov	Wembley	4	0
EC1962	3 Oct	Sheffield	1	1
EC1963	27 Feb	Paris	2	5
wc1966	20 July	Wembley	2	0
1969	12 Mar	Wembley	5	0
wc1982	16 June	Bilbao	3	1
1984	29 Feb	Paris	0	2
1992	19 Feb	Wembley	2	0

			E	F
EC1992	14 June	Malmo	0	0
TF1997	7 June	Montpellier	1	0
1999	10 Feb	Wembley	0	2
2000	2 Sept	Paris	1	1
EC2004	13 June	Lisbon	1	2
2008	26 Mar	Paris	0	1
2010	17 Nov	Wembley	1	2
EC2012	11 June	Donetsk	1	1
2015	17 Nov	Wembley	2	0
2017	13 June	Paris	2	3

v FYR MACEDONIA			E	M
EC2002	16 Oct	Southampton	2	2
EC2003	6 Sept	Skopje	2	1
EC2006	6 Sept	Skopje	1	0

v GEORGIA			E	G
wc1996	9 Nov	Tbilisi	2	0
wc1997	30 Apr	Wembley	2	0

v GERMANY			E	G
1930	10 May	Berlin	3	3
1935	4 Dec	Tottenham	3	0
1938	14 May	Berlin	6	3
1991	11 Sept	Wembley	0	1
1993	19 June	Detroit	1	2
EC1996	26 June	Wembley	1	1*
EC2000	17 June	Charleroi	1	0
wc2000	7 Oct	Wembley	0	1
wc2001	1 Sept	Munich	5	1
2007	22 Aug	Wembley	1	2
2008	19 Nov	Berlin	2	1
wc2010	27 June	Bloemfontein	1	4
2013	19 Nov	Wembley	0	1
2016	26 Mar	Berlin	3	2
2017	22 Mar	Dortmund	0	1
2017	**10 Nov**	**Wembley**	**0**	**0**

v EAST GERMANY			E	EG
1963	2 June	Leipzig	2	1
1970	25 Nov	Wembley	3	1
1974	29 May	Leipzig	1	1
1984	12 Sept	Wembley	1	0

v WEST GERMANY			E	WG
1954	1 Dec	Wembley	3	1
1956	26 May	Berlin	3	1
1965	12 May	Nuremberg	1	0
1966	23 Feb	Wembley	1	0
wc1966	30 July	Wembley	4	2*
1968	1 June	Hanover	0	1
wc1970	14 June	Leon	2	3*
EC1972	29 Apr	Wembley	1	3
EC1972	13 May	Berlin	0	0
1975	12 Mar	Wembley	2	0
1978	22 Feb	Munich	1	2
wc1982	29 June	Madrid	0	0
1982	13 Oct	Wembley	1	2
1985	12 June	Mexico City	3	0
1987	9 Sept	Dusseldorf	1	3
wc1990	4 July	Turin	1	1*

v GHANA			E	G
2011	29 Mar	Wembley	1	1

v GREECE			E	G
EC1971	21 Apr	Wembley	3	0
EC1971	1 Dec	Piraeus	2	0
EC1982	17 Nov	Salonika	3	0
EC1983	30 Mar	Wembley	0	0
1989	8 Feb	Athens	2	1
1994	17 May	Wembley	5	0
wc2001	6 June	Athens	2	0
wc2001	6 Oct	Old Trafford	2	2
2006	16 Aug	Old Trafford	4	0

v HONDURAS			E	H
2014	7 June	Miami	0	0

v HUNGARY			E	H
1908	10 June	Budapest	7	0
1909	29 May	Budapest	4	2
1909	31 May	Budapest	8	2
1934	10 May	Budapest	1	2
1936	2 Dec	Highbury	6	2
1953	25 Nov	Wembley	3	6

			E	H
1954	23 May	Budapest	1	7
1960	22 May	Budapest	0	2
wc1962	31 May	Rancagua	1	2
1965	5 May	Wembley	1	0
1978	24 May	Wembley	4	1
wc1981	6 June	Budapest	3	1
wc1982	18 Nov	Wembley	1	0
EC1983	27 Apr	Wembley	2	0
EC1983	12 Oct	Budapest	3	0
1988	27 Apr	Budapest	0	0
1990	12 Sept	Wembley	1	0
1992	12 May	Budapest	1	0
1996	18 May	Wembley	3	0
1999	28 Apr	Budapest	1	1
2006	30 May	Old Trafford	3	1
2010	11 Aug	Wembley	2	1

v ICELAND			E	I
1982	2 June	Reykjavik	1	1
2004	5 June	City of Manchester	6	1
EC2016	27 June	Nice	1	2

v ISRAEL			E	I
1986	26 Feb	Ramat Gan	2	1
1988	17 Feb	Tel Aviv	0	0
EC2007	24 Mar	Tel Aviv	0	0
EC2007	8 Sept	Wembley	3	0

v ITALY			E	I
1933	13 May	Rome	1	1
1934	14 Nov	Highbury	3	2
1939	13 May	Milan	2	2
1948	16 May	Turin	4	0
1949	30 Nov	Tottenham	2	0
1952	18 May	Florence	1	1
1959	6 May	Wembley	2	2
1961	24 May	Rome	3	2
1973	14 June	Turin	0	2
1973	14 Nov	Wembley	0	1
1976	28 May	New York	3	2
wc1976	17 Nov	Rome	0	2
wc1977	16 Nov	Wembley	2	0
EC1980	15 June	Turin	0	1
1985	6 June	Mexico City	1	2
1989	15 Nov	Wembley	0	0
wc1990	7 July	Bari	1	2
wc1997	12 Feb	Wembley	0	1
TF1997	4 June	Nantes	2	0
wc1997	11 Oct	Rome	0	0
2000	15 Nov	Turin	0	1
2002	27 Mar	Leeds	1	2
EC2012	24 June	Kiev	0	0
2012	15 Aug	Berne	2	1
wc2014	14 June	Manaus	1	2
2015	31 Mar	Turin	1	1
2018	**27 Mar**	**Wembley**	**1**	**1**

v JAMAICA			E	J
2006	3 June	Old Trafford	6	0

v JAPAN			E	J
UI1995	3 June	Wembley	2	1
2004	1 June	City of Manchester	1	1
2010	30 May	Graz	2	1

v KAZAKHSTAN			E	K
wc2008	11 Oct	Wembley	5	1
wc2009	6 June	Almaty	4	0

v KOREA REPUBLIC			E	KR
2002	21 May	Seoguipo	1	1

v KUWAIT			E	K
wc1982	25 June	Bilbao	1	0

v LIECHTENSTEIN			E	L
EC2003	29 Mar	Vaduz	2	0
EC2003	10 Sept	Old Trafford	2	0

v LITHUANIA			E	L
EC2015	27 Mar	Wembley	4	0
EC2015	12 Oct	Vilnius	3	0
wc2017	26 Mar	Wembley	2	0
wc2017	**8 Oct**	**Vilnius**	**1**	**0**

		v LUXEMBOURG	E	L
1927	21 May	Esch-sur-Alzette	5	2
wc1960	19 Oct	Luxembourg	9	0
wc1961	28 Sept	Highbury	4	1
wc1977	30 Mar	Wembley	5	0
wc1977	12 Oct	Luxembourg	2	0
EC1982	15 Dec	Wembley	9	0
EC1983	16 Nov	Luxembourg	4	0
EC1998	14 Oct	Luxembourg	3	0
EC1999	4 Sept	Wembley	6	0
EC2006	7 Oct	Old Trafford	0	0

		v MALAYSIA	E	M
1991	12 June	Kuala Lumpur	4	2

		v MALTA	E	M
EC1971	3 Feb	Valletta	1	0
EC1971	12 May	Wembley	5	0
2000	3 June	Valletta	2	1
wc2016	8 Oct	Wembley	2	0
wc2017	**1 Sept**	**Ta'Qali**	**4**	**0**

		v MEXICO	E	M
1959	24 May	Mexico City	1	2
1961	10 May	Wembley	8	0
wc1966	16 July	Wembley	2	0
1969	1 June	Mexico City	0	0
1985	9 June	Mexico City	0	1
1986	17 May	Los Angeles	3	0
1997	29 Mar	Wembley	2	0
2001	25 May	Derby	4	0
2010	24 May	Wembley	3	1

		v MOLDOVA	E	M
wc1996	1 Sept	Chisinau	3	0
wc1997	10 Sept	Wembley	4	0
wc2012	7 Sept	Chisinau	5	0
wc2013	6 Sept	Wembley	4	0

		v MONTENEGRO	E	M
EC1989	8 Mar	Tirana	2	0
2010	12 Oct	Wembley	0	0
EC2011	7 Oct	Podgorica	2	2
wc2013	26 Mar	Podgorica	1	1
wc2013	11 Oct	Wembley	4	1

		v MOROCCO	E	M
wc1986	6 June	Monterrey	0	0
1998	27 May	Casablanca	1	0

		v NETHERLANDS	E	N
1935	18 May	Amsterdam	1	0
1946	27 Nov	Huddersfield	8	2
1964	9 Dec	Amsterdam	1	1
1969	5 Nov	Amsterdam	1	0
1970	14 June	Wembley	0	0
1977	9 Feb	Wembley	0	2
1982	25 May	Wembley	2	0
1988	23 Mar	Wembley	2	2
EC1988	15 June	Dusseldorf	1	3
wc1990	16 June	Cagliari	0	0
2005	9 Feb	Villa Park	0	0
wc1993	28 Apr	Wembley	2	2
wc1993	13 Oct	Rotterdam	0	2
EC1996	18 June	Wembley	4	1
2001	15 Aug	Tottenham	0	2
2002	13 Feb	Amsterdam	1	1
2006	15 Nov	Amsterdam	1	1
2009	12 Aug	Amsterdam	2	2
2012	29 Feb	Wembley	2	3
2016	29 Mar	Wembley	1	2
2018	**23 Mar**	**Amsterdam**	**1**	**0**

		v NEW ZEALAND	E	NZ
1991	3 June	Auckland	1	0
1991	8 June	Wellington	2	0

		v NIGERIA	E	N
1994	16 Nov	Wembley	1	0
wc2002	12 June	Osaka	0	0
2018	**2 June**	**Wembley**	**2**	**1**

		v NORWAY	E	N
1937	14 May	Oslo	6	0
1938	9 Nov	Newcastle	4	0
1949	18 May	Oslo	4	1
1966	29 June	Oslo	6	1

			E	N
wc1980	10 Sept	Wembley	4	0
wc1981	9 Sept	Oslo	1	2
wc1992	14 Oct	Wembley	1	1
wc1993	2 June	Oslo	0	2
1994	22 May	Wembley	0	0
1995	11 Oct	Oslo	0	0
2012	26 May	Oslo	1	0
2014	3 Sept	Wembley	1	0

		v PANAMA	E	P
wc2018	**24 June**	**Nizhny Novgorod**	**6**	**1**

		v PARAGUAY	E	P
wc1986	18 June	Mexico City	3	0
2002	17 Apr	Liverpool	4	0
wc2006	10 June	Frankfurt	1	0

		v PERU	E	P
1959	17 May	Lima	1	4
1962	20 May	Lima	4	0
2014	30 May	Wembley	3	0

		v POLAND	E	P
1966	5 Jan	Everton	1	1
1966	5 July	Chorzow	1	0
wc1973	6 June	Chorzow	0	2
wc1973	17 Oct	Wembley	1	1
wc1986	11 June	Monterrey	3	0
wc1989	3 June	Wembley	3	0
wc1989	11 Oct	Katowice	0	0
EC1990	17 Oct	Wembley	2	0
EC1991	13 Nov	Poznan	1	1
wc1993	29 May	Katowice	1	1
wc1993	8 Sept	Wembley	3	0
wc1996	9 Oct	Wembley	2	1
wc1997	31 May	Katowice	2	0
EC1999	27 Mar	Wembley	3	1
EC1999	8 Sept	Warsaw	0	0
wc2004	8 Sept	Katowice	2	1
wc2005	12 Oct	Old Trafford	2	1
wc2012	17 Oct	Warsaw	1	1
wc2013	15 Oct	Wembley	2	0

		v PORTUGAL	E	P
1947	25 May	Lisbon	10	0
1950	14 May	Lisbon	5	3
1951	19 May	Everton	5	2
1955	22 May	Oporto	1	3
1958	7 May	Wembley	2	1
wc1961	21 May	Lisbon	1	1
wc1961	25 Oct	Wembley	2	0
1964	17 May	Lisbon	4	3
1964	4 June	São Paulo	1	1
wc1966	26 July	Wembley	2	1
1969	10 Dec	Wembley	1	0
1974	3 Apr	Lisbon	0	0
EC1974	20 Nov	Wembley	0	0
EC1975	19 Nov	Lisbon	1	1
wc1986	3 June	Monterrey	0	1
1995	12 Dec	Wembley	1	1
1998	22 Apr	Wembley	3	0
EC2000	12 June	Eindhoven	2	3
2002	7 Sept	Villa Park	1	1
2004	18 Feb	Faro	1	1
EC2004	24 June	Lisbon	2	2*
wc2006	1 July	Gelsenkirchen	0	0
2016	2 June	Wembley	1	0

		v REPUBLIC OF IRELAND	E	RI
1946	30 Sept	Dublin	1	0
1949	21 Sept	Everton	0	2
wc1957	8 May	Wembley	5	1
wc1957	19 May	Dublin	1	1
1964	24 May	Dublin	3	1
1976	8 Sept	Wembley	1	1
EC1978	25 Oct	Dublin	1	1
EC1980	6 Feb	Wembley	2	0
1985	26 Mar	Wembley	2	1
EC1988	12 June	Stuttgart	0	1
wc1990	11 June	Cagliari	1	1
EC1990	14 Nov	Dublin	1	1
EC1991	27 Mar	Wembley	1	1
1995	15 Feb	Dublin	0	1
		(abandoned after 27 mins)		
2013	29 May	Wembley	1	1
2015	7 June	Dublin	0	0

		v ROMANIA	E	R
1939	24 May	Bucharest	2	0
1968	6 Nov	Bucharest	0	0
1969	15 Jan	Wembley	1	1
wc1970	2 June	Guadalajara	1	0
wc1980	15 Oct	Bucharest	1	2
wc1981	29 April	Wembley	0	0
wc1985	1 May	Bucharest	0	0
wc1985	11 Sept	Wembley	1	1
1994	12 Oct	Wembley	1	1
wc1998	22 June	Toulouse	1	2
EC2000	20 June	Charleroi	2	3

		v RUSSIA	E	R
EC2007	12 Sept	Wembley	3	0
EC2007	17 Oct	Moscow	1	2
EC2016	11 June	Marseille	1	1

		v SAN MARINO	E	SM
wc1992	17 Feb	Wembley	6	0
wc1993	17 Nov	Bologna	7	1
wc2012	12 Oct	Wembley	5	0
wc2013	22 Mar	Serravalle	8	0
EC2014	9 Oct	Wembley	5	0
EC2015	5 Sept	Serravalle	6	0

		v SAUDI ARABIA	E	SA
1988	16 Nov	Riyadh	1	1
1998	23 May	Wembley	0	0

		v SERBIA-MONTENEGRO	E	SM
2003	3 June	Leicester	2	1

		v SLOVAKIA	E	S
EC2002	12 Oct	Bratislava	2	1
EC2003	11 June	Middlesbrough	2	1
2009	28 Mar	Wembley	4	0
EC2016	20 June	Lille	0	0
wc2016	4 Sept	Trnava	1	0
wc2017	**4 Sept**	**Wembley**	**2**	**1**

		v SLOVENIA	E	S
2009	5 Sept	Wembley	2	1
wc2010	23 June	Port Elizabeth	1	0
EC2014	15 Nov	Wembley	3	1
EC2015	14 June	Ljubljana	3	2
wc2016	11 Oct	Ljubljana	0	0
wc2017	**5 Oct**	**Wembley**	**1**	**0**

		v SOUTH AFRICA	E	SA
1997	24 May	Old Trafford	2	1
2003	22 May	Durban	2	1

		v SPAIN	E	S
1929	15 May	Madrid	3	4
1931	9 Dec	Highbury	7	1
wc1950	2 July	Rio de Janeiro	0	1
1955	18 May	Madrid	1	1
1955	30 Nov	Wembley	4	1
1960	15 May	Madrid	0	3
1960	26 Oct	Wembley	4	2
1965	8 Dec	Madrid	2	0
1967	24 May	Wembley	2	0
EC1968	3 Apr	Wembley	1	0
EC1968	8 May	Madrid	2	1
1980	26 Mar	Barcelona	2	0
EC1980	18 June	Naples	2	1
1981	25 Mar	Wembley	1	2
wc1982	5 July	Madrid	0	0
1987	18 Feb	Madrid	4	2
1992	9 Sept	Santander	0	1
EC 1996	22 June	Wembley	0	0
2001	28 Feb	Villa Park	3	0
2004	17 Nov	Madrid	0	1
2007	7 Feb	Old Trafford	0	1
2009	11 Feb	Seville	0	2
2011	12 Nov	Wembley	1	0
2015	13 Nov	Alicante	0	2
2016	15 Nov	Wembley	2	2

		v SWEDEN	E	S
1923	21 May	Stockholm	4	2
1923	24 May	Stockholm	3	1
1937	17 May	Stockholm	4	0
1947	19 Nov	Highbury	4	2
1949	13 May	Stockholm	1	3
1956	16 May	Stockholm	0	0

			E	S
1959	28 Oct	Wembley	2	3
1965	16 May	Gothenburg	2	1
1968	22 May	Wembley	3	1
1979	10 June	Stockholm	0	0
1986	10 Sept	Stockholm	0	1
wc1988	19 Oct	Wembley	0	0
wc1989	6 Sept	Stockholm	0	0
EC1992	17 June	Stockholm	1	2
u1995	8 June	Leeds	3	3
EC1998	5 Sept	Stockholm	1	2
EC1999	5 June	Wembley	0	0
2001	10 Nov	Old Trafford	1	1
wc2002	2 June	Saitama	1	1
2004	31 Mar	Gothenburg	0	1
wc2006	20 June	Cologne	2	2
2011	15 Nov	Wembley	1	0
EC2012	15 June	Kiev	3	2
2012	14 Nov	Stockholm	2	4
wc2018	**7 July**	**Samara**	**2**	**0**

		v SWITZERLAND	E	S
1933	20 May	Berne	4	0
1938	21 May	Zurich	1	2
1947	18 May	Zurich	0	1
1948	2 Dec	Highbury	6	0
1952	28 May	Zurich	3	0
wc1954	20 June	Berne	2	0
1962	9 May	Wembley	3	1
1963	5 June	Basle	8	1
EC1971	13 Oct	Basle	3	2
EC1971	10 Nov	Wembley	1	1
1975	3 Sept	Basle	2	1
1977	7 Sept	Wembley	0	0
wc1980	19 Nov	Wembley	2	1
wc1981	30 May	Basle	1	2
1988	28 May	Lausanne	1	0
1995	15 Nov	Wembley	3	1
EC1996	8 June	Wembley	1	1
1998	25 Mar	Berne	1	1
EC2004	17 June	Coimbra	3	0
2008	6 Feb	Wembley	2	1
EC1989	8 Mar	Tirana	2	0
EC2010	7 Sept	Basle	3	1
EC2011	4 June	Wembley	2	2
EC2014	8 Sept	Basel	2	0
EC2015	8 Sept	Wembley	2	0

		v TRINIDAD & TOBAGO	E	TT
wc2006	15 June	Nuremberg	2	0
2008	2 June	Port of Spain	3	0

		v TUNISIA	E	T
1990	2 June	Tunis	1	1
wc1998	15 June	Marseilles	2	0
wc2018	**18 June**	**Volgograd**	**2**	**1**

		v TURKEY	E	T
wc1984	14 Nov	Istanbul	8	0
wc1985	16 Oct	Wembley	5	0
EC1987	29 Apr	Izmir	0	0
EC1987	14 Oct	Wembley	8	0
EC1991	1 May	Izmir	1	0
EC1991	16 Oct	Wembley	1	0
wc1992	18 Nov	Wembley	4	0
wc1993	31 Mar	Izmir	2	0
EC2003	2 Apr	Sunderland	2	0
EC2003	11 Oct	Istanbul	0	0
2016	22 May	Etihad Stadium	2	1

		v UKRAINE	E	U
2000	31 May	Wembley	2	0
2004	18 Aug	Newcastle	3	0
wc2009	1 Apr	Wembley	2	1
wc2009	10 Oct	Dnepr	0	1
EC2012	19 June	Donetsk	1	0
wc2012	11 Sept	Wembley	1	1
wc2013	10 Sept	Kiev	0	0

		v URUGUAY	E	U
1953	31 May	Montevideo	1	2
wc1954	26 June	Basle	2	4
1964	6 May	Wembley	2	1
wc1966	11 July	Wembley	0	0
1969	8 June	Montevideo	2	1
1977	15 June	Montevideo	0	0

			E	U
1984	13 June	Montevideo	0	2
1990	22 May	Wembley	1	2
1995	29 Mar	Wembley	0	0
2006	1 Mar	Liverpool	2	1
wc2014	19 June	Sao Paulo	1	2

v USA

			E	USA
wc1950	29 June	Belo Horizonte	0	1
1953	8 June	New York	6	3
1959	28 May	Los Angeles	8	1
1964	27 May	New York	10	0
1985	16 June	Los Angeles	5	0
1993	9 June	Foxboro	0	2
1994	7 Sept	Wembley	2	0
2005	28 May	Chicago	2	1
2008	28 May	Wembley	2	0
wc2010	12 June	Rustenburg	1	1

v USSR

			E	USSR
1958	18 May	Moscow	1	1
wc1958	8 June	Gothenburg	2	2
wc1958	17 June	Gothenburg	0	1
1958	22 Oct	Wembley	5	0

			E	USSR
1967	6 Dec	Wembley	2	2
EC1968	8 June	Rome	2	0
1973	10 June	Moscow	2	1
1984	2 June	Wembley	0	2
1986	26 Mar	Tbilisi	1	0
EC1988	18 June	Frankfurt	1	3
1991	21 May	Wembley	3	1

v YUGOSLAVIA

			E	Y
1939	18 May	Belgrade	1	2
1950	22 Nov	Highbury	2	2
1954	16 May	Belgrade	0	1
1956	28 Nov	Wembley	3	0
1958	11 May	Belgrade	0	5
1960	11 May	Wembley	3	3
1965	9 May	Belgrade	1	1
1966	4 May	Wembley	2	0
EC1968	5 June	Florence	0	1
1972	11 Oct	Wembley	1	1
1974	5 June	Belgrade	2	2
EC1986	12 Nov	Wembley	2	0
EC1987	11 Nov	Belgrade	4	1
1989	13 Dec	Wembley	2	1

SCOTLAND

v ARGENTINA

			S	A
1977	18 June	Buenos Aires	1	1
1979	2 June	Glasgow	1	3
1990	28 Mar	Glasgow	1	0
2008	19 Nov	Glasgow	0	1

v AUSTRALIA

			S	A
wc1985	20 Nov	Glasgow	2	0
wc1985	4 Dec	Melbourne	0	0
1996	27 Mar	Glasgow	1	0
2000	15 Nov	Glasgow	0	2
2012	15 Aug	Easter Road	3	1

v AUSTRIA

			S	A
1931	16 May	Vienna	0	5
1933	29 Nov	Glasgow	2	2
1937	9 May	Vienna	1	1
1950	13 Dec	Glasgow	0	1
1951	27 May	Vienna	0	4
wc1954	16 June	Zurich	0	1
1955	19 May	Vienna	4	1
1956	2 May	Glasgow	1	1
1960	29 May	Vienna	1	4
1963	8 May	Glasgow	4	1
(abandoned after 79 mins)				
wc1968	6 Nov	Glasgow	2	1
wc1969	5 Nov	Vienna	0	2
EC1978	20 Sept	Vienna	2	3
EC1979	17 Oct	Vienna	1	1
1994	20 Apr	Vienna	2	1
wc1996	31 Aug	Vienna	0	0
wc1997	2 Apr	Celtic Park	2	0
2003	30 Apr	Glasgow	0	2
2005	17 Aug	Graz	2	2
2007	30 May	Vienna	1	0

v BELARUS

			S	B
wc1997	8 June	Minsk	1	0
wc1997	7 Sept	Aberdeen	4	1
wc2005	8 June	Minsk	0	0
wc2005	8 Oct	Glasgow	0	1

v BELGIUM

			S	B
1946	23 Jan	Glasgow	2	2
1947	18 May	Brussels	1	2
1948	28 Apr	Glasgow	2	0
1951	20 May	Brussels	5	0
EC1971	3 Feb	Liege	0	3
EC1971	10 Nov	Aberdeen	1	0
1974	1 June	Brussels	1	2
EC1979	21 Nov	Brussels	0	2
EC1979	19 Dec	Glasgow	1	3
EC1982	15 Dec	Brussels	2	3
EC1983	12 Oct	Glasgow	1	1
EC1987	1 Apr	Brussels	1	4
EC1987	14 Oct	Glasgow	2	0
wc2001	24 Mar	Glasgow	2	2

			S	B
wc2001	5 Sept	Brussels	0	2
wc2012	16 Oct	Brussels	0	2
wc2013	6 Sept	Glasgow	0	2

v BOSNIA-HERZEGOVINA

			S	BH
EC1999	4 Sept	Sarajevo	2	1
EC1999	5 Oct	Ibrox	1	0

v BRAZIL

			S	B
1966	25 June	Glasgow	1	1
1972	5 July	Rio de Janeiro	0	1
1973	30 June	Glasgow	0	1
wc1974	18 June	Frankfurt	0	0
1977	23 June	Rio de Janeiro	0	2
wc1982	18 June	Seville	1	4
1987	26 May	Glasgow	0	2
wc1990	20 June	Turin	0	1
wc1998	10 June	St Denis	1	2
2011	27 Mar	Emirates	0	2

v BULGARIA

			S	B
1978	22 Feb	Glasgow	2	1
EC1986	10 Sept	Glasgow	0	0
EC1987	11 Nov	Sofia	1	0
EC1990	14 Nov	Sofia	1	1
EC1991	27 Mar	Glasgow	1	1
2006	11 May	Kobe	5	1

v CANADA

			S	C
1983	12 June	Vancouver	2	0
1983	16 June	Edmonton	3	0
1983	20 June	Toronto	2	0
1992	21 May	Toronto	3	1
2002	15 Oct	Easter Road	3	1
2017	22 Mar	Easter Road	1	1

v CHILE

			S	C
1977	15 June	Santiago	4	2
1989	30 May	Glasgow	2	0

v CIS

			S	C
EC1992	18 June	Norrkoping	3	0

v COLOMBIA

			S	C
1988	17 May	Glasgow	0	0
1996	29 May	Miami	0	1
1998	23 May	New York	2	2

v COSTA RICA

			S	CR
wc1990	11 June	Genoa	0	1
2018	**23 Mar**	**Glasgow**	**0**	**1**

v CROATIA

			S	C
wc2000	11 Oct	Zagreb	1	1
wc2001	1 Sept	Glasgow	0	0
2008	26 Mar	Glasgow	1	1
wc2013	7 June	Zagreb	1	0
wc2013	15 Oct	Glasgow	2	0

v CYPRUS			S	C
wc1968	11 Dec	Nicosia	5	0
wc1969	17 May	Glasgow	8	0
wc1989	8 Feb	Limassol	3	2
wc1989	26 Apr	Glasgow	2	1
2011	11 Nov	Larnaca	2	1

v CZECHOSLOVAKIA			S	C
1937	15 May	Prague	3	1
1937	8 Dec	Glasgow	5	0
wc1961	14 May	Bratislava	0	4
wc1961	26 Sept	Glasgow	3	2
wc1961	29 Nov	Brussels	2	4*
1972	2 July	Porto Alegre	0	0
wc1973	26 Sept	Glasgow	2	1
wc1973	17 Oct	Bratislava	0	1
wc1976	13 Oct	Prague	0	2
wc1977	21 Sept	Glasgow	3	1

v CZECH REPUBLIC			S	C
EC1999	31 Mar	Glasgow	1	2
EC1999	9 June	Prague	2	3
2008	30 May	Prague	1	3
2010	3 Mar	Glasgow	1	0
EC2010	8 Oct	Prague	0	1
EC2011	3 Sept	Glasgow	2	2
2016	24 Mar	Prague	1	0

v DENMARK			S	D
1951	12 May	Glasgow	3	1
1952	25 May	Copenhagen	2	1
1968	16 Oct	Copenhagen	1	0
EC1970	11 Nov	Glasgow	1	0
EC1971	9 June	Copenhagen	0	1
wc1972	18 Oct	Copenhagen	4	1
wc1972	15 Nov	Glasgow	2	0
EC1975	3 Sept	Copenhagen	1	0
EC1975	29 Oct	Glasgow	3	1
wc1986	4 June	Nezahualcoyotl	0	1
1996	24 Apr	Copenhagen	0	2
1998	25 Mar	Ibrox	0	1
2002	21 Aug	Glasgow	0	1
2004	28 Apr	Copenhagen	0	1
2011	10 Aug	Glasgow	2	1
2016	29 Mar	Glasgow	1	0

v ECUADOR			S	E
1995	24 May	Toyama	2	1

v EGYPT			S	E
1990	16 May	Aberdeen	1	3

v ESTONIA			S	E
wc1993	19 May	Tallinn	3	0
wc1993	2 June	Aberdeen	3	1
wc1997	11 Feb	Monaco	0	0
wc1997	29 Mar	Kilmarnock	2	0
EC1998	10 Oct	Tynecastle	3	2
EC1999	8 Sept	Tallinn	0	0
2004	27 May	Tallinn	1	0
2013	6 Feb	Aberdeen	1	0

v FAROE ISLANDS			S	F
EC1994	12 Oct	Glasgow	5	1
EC1995	7 June	Toftir	2	0
EC1998	14 Oct	Aberdeen	2	1
EC1999	5 June	Toftir	1	1
EC2002	7 Sept	Toftir	2	2
EC2003	6 Sept	Glasgow	3	1
EC2006	2 Sept	Celtic Park	6	0
EC2007	6 June	Toftir	2	0
2010	16 Nov	Aberdeen	3	0

v FINLAND			S	F
1954	25 May	Helsinki	2	1
wc1964	21 Oct	Glasgow	3	1
wc1965	27 May	Helsinki	2	1
1976	8 Sept	Glasgow	6	0
1992	25 Mar	Glasgow	1	1
EC1994	7 Sept	Helsinki	2	0
EC1995	6 Sept	Glasgow	1	0
1998	22 Apr	Easter Road	1	1

v FRANCE			S	F
1930	18 May	Paris	2	0
1932	8 May	Paris	3	1
1948	23 May	Paris	0	3
1949	27 Apr	Glasgow	2	0
1950	27 May	Paris	1	0
1951	16 May	Glasgow	1	0
wc1958	15 June	Orebro	1	2
1984	1 June	Marseilles	0	2
wc1989	8 Mar	Glasgow	2	0
wc1989	11 Oct	Paris	0	3
1997	12 Nov	St Etienne	1	2
2000	29 Mar	Glasgow	0	2
2002	27 Mar	Paris	0	5
EC2006	7 Oct	Glasgow	1	0
EC2007	12 Sept	Paris	1	0
2016	4 June	Metz	0	3

v FYR MACEDONIA			S	M
wc2008	6 Sept	Skopje	0	1
wc2009	5 Sept	Glasgow	2	0
wc2012	11 Sept	Glasgow	1	1
wc2013	10 Sept	Skopje	2	1

v GEORGIA			S	G
EC2007	24 Mar	Glasgow	2	1
EC2007	17 Oct	Tbilisi	0	2
EC2014	11 Oct	Ibrox	1	0
EC2015	4 Sept	Tblisi	0	1

v GERMANY			S	G
1929	1 June	Berlin	1	1
1936	14 Oct	Glasgow	2	0
EC1992	15 June	Norrkoping	0	2
1993	24 Mar	Glasgow	0	1
1999	28 Apr	Bremen	1	0
EC2003	7 June	Glasgow	1	1
EC2003	10 Sept	Dortmund	1	2
EC2014	7 Sept	Dortmund	1	2
EC2015	7 Sept	Glasgow	2	3

v EAST GERMANY			S	EG
1974	30 Oct	Glasgow	3	0
1977	7 Sept	East Berlin	0	1
EC1982	13 Oct	Glasgow	2	0
EC1983	16 Nov	Halle	1	2
1985	16 Oct	Glasgow	0	0
1990	25 Apr	Glasgow	0	1

v WEST GERMANY			S	WG
1957	22 May	Stuttgart	3	1
1959	6 May	Glasgow	3	2
1964	12 May	Hanover	2	2
wc1969	16 Apr	Glasgow	1	1
wc1969	22 Oct	Hamburg	2	3
1973	14 Nov	Glasgow	1	1
1974	27 Mar	Frankfurt	1	2
wc1986	8 June	Queretaro	1	2

v GIBRALTAR			S	G
EC2015	29 Mar	Hampden	6	1
EC2015	11 Oct	Faro	6	0

v GREECE			S	G
EC1994	18 Dec	Athens	0	1
EC1995	16 Aug	Glasgow	1	0

v HONG KONG XI			S	HK
†2002	23 May	Hong Kong	4	0

†match not recognised by FIFA

v HUNGARY			S	H
1938	7 Dec	Ibrox	3	1
1954	8 Dec	Glasgow	2	4
1955	29 May	Budapest	1	3
1958	7 May	Glasgow	1	1
1960	5 June	Budapest	3	3
1980	31 May	Budapest	1	3
1987	9 Sept	Glasgow	2	0
2004	18 Aug	Glasgow	0	3
2018	**27 Mar**	**Budapest**	**1**	**0**

v ICELAND			S	I
wc1984	17 Oct	Glasgow	3	0
wc1985	28 May	Reykjavik	1	0
EC2002	12 Oct	Reykjavik	2	0
EC2003	29 Mar	Glasgow	2	1
wc2008	10 Sept	Reykjavik	2	1
wc2009	1 Apr	Glasgow	2	1

		v IRAN	S	I
wc1978	7 June	Cordoba	1	1

		v ISRAEL	S	I
wc1981	25 Feb	Tel Aviv	1	0
wc1981	28 Apr	Glasgow	3	1
1986	28 Jan	Tel Aviv	1	0

		v ITALY	S	I
1931	20 May	Rome	0	3
wc1965	9 Nov	Glasgow	1	0
wc1965	7 Dec	Naples	0	3
1988	22 Dec	Perugia	0	2
wc1992	18 Nov	Ibrox	0	0
wc1993	13 Oct	Rome	1	3
wc2005	26 Mar	Milan	0	2
wc2005	3 Sept	Glasgow	1	1
EC2007	28 Mar	Bari	0	2
EC2007	17 Nov	Glasgow	1	2
2016	29 May	Ta'Qali	0	1

		v JAPAN	S	J
1995	21 May	Hiroshima	0	0
2006	13 May	Saitama	0	0
2009	10 Oct	Yokohama	0	2

		v KOREA REPUBLIC	S	KR
2002	16 May	Busan	1	4

		v LATVIA	S	L
wc1996	5 Oct	Riga	2	0
wc1997	11 Oct	Celtic Park	2	0
wc2000	2 Sept	Riga	1	0
wc2001	6 Oct	Glasgow	2	1

		v LIECHTENSTEIN	S	L
EC2010	7 Sept	Glasgow	2	1
EC2011	8 Oct	Vaduz	1	0

		v LITHUANIA	S	L
EC1998	5 Sept	Vilnius	0	0
EC1999	9 Oct	Glasgow	3	0
EC2003	2 Apr	Kaunas	0	1
EC2003	11 Oct	Glasgow	1	0
EC2006	6 Sept	Kaunas	2	1
EC2007	8 Sept	Glasgow	3	1
EC2010	3 Sept	Kaunas	0	0
EC2011	6 Sept	Glasgow	1	0
wc2016	8 Oct	Hampden	1	1
wc2017	**1 Sept**	**Vilnius**	**3**	**0**

		v LUXEMBOURG	S	L
1947	24 May	Luxembourg	6	0
EC1986	12 Nov	Glasgow	3	0
EC1987	2 Dec	Esch	0	0
2012	14 Nov	Luxembourg	2	1

		v MALTA	S	M
1988	22 Mar	Valletta	1	1
1990	28 May	Valletta	2	1
wc1993	17 Feb	Ibrox	3	0
wc1993	17 Nov	Valletta	2	0
1997	1 June	Valletta	3	2
wc2016	4 Sept	Ta'Qali	5	1
wc2017	**4 Sept**	**Glasgow**	**2**	**0**

		v MEXICO	S	M
2018	**3 June**	**Mexico City**	**0**	**1**

		v MOLDOVA	S	M
wc2004	13 Oct	Chisinau	1	1
wc2005	4 June	Glasgow	2	0

		v MOROCCO	S	M
wc1998	23 June	St Etienne	0	3

		v NETHERLANDS	S	N
1929	4 June	Amsterdam	2	0
1938	21 May	Amsterdam	3	1
1959	27 May	Amsterdam	2	1
1966	11 May	Glasgow	0	3
1968	30 May	Amsterdam	0	0
1971	1 Dec	Amsterdam	1	2
wc1978	11 June	Mendoza	3	2
1982	23 Mar	Glasgow	2	1
1986	29 Apr	Eindhoven	0	0
EC1992	12 June	Gothenburg	0	1
1994	23 Mar	Glasgow	0	1
1994	27 May	Utrecht	1	3
EC1996	10 June	Villa Park	0	0
2000	26 Apr	Arnhem	0	0
EC2003	15 Nov	Glasgow	1	0
EC2003	19 Nov	Amsterdam	0	6
wc2009	28 Mar	Amsterdam	0	3
wc2009	9 Sept	Glasgow	0	1
2017	**9 Nov**	**Aberdeen**	**0**	**1**

		v NEW ZEALAND	S	NZ
wc1982	15 June	Malaga	5	2
2003	27 May	Tynecastle	1	1

		v NIGERIA	S	N
2002	17 Apr	Aberdeen	1	2
2014	28 May	Craven Cottage	2	2

		v NORWAY	S	N
1929	26 May	Oslo	7	3
1954	5 May	Glasgow	1	0
1954	19 May	Oslo	1	1
1963	4 June	Bergen	3	4
1963	7 Nov	Glasgow	6	1
1974	6 June	Oslo	2	1
EC1978	25 Oct	Glasgow	3	2
EC1979	7 June	Oslo	4	0
wc1988	14 Sept	Oslo	2	1
wc1989	15 Nov	Glasgow	1	1
1992	3 June	Oslo	0	0
wc1998	16 June	Bordeaux	1	1
2003	20 Aug	Oslo	0	0
wc2004	9 Oct	Glasgow	0	1
wc2005	7 Sept	Oslo	2	1
wc2008	11 Oct	Glasgow	0	0
wc2009	12 Aug	Oslo	0	4
2013	19 Nov	Molde	1	0

		v PARAGUAY	S	P
wc1958	11 June	Norrkoping	2	3

		v PERU	S	P
1972	26 Apr	Glasgow	2	0
wc1978	3 June	Cordoba	1	3
1979	12 Sept	Glasgow	1	1
2018	**30 May**	**Lima**	**0**	**2**

		v POLAND	S	P
1958	1 June	Warsaw	2	1
1960	4 May	Glasgow	2	3
wc1965	23 May	Chorzow	1	1
wc1965	13 Oct	Glasgow	1	2
1980	28 May	Poznan	0	1
1990	19 May	Glasgow	1	1
2001	25 Apr	Bydgoszcz	1	1
2014	5 Mar	Warsaw	1	0
EC2014	14 Oct	Warsaw	2	2
EC2015	8 Oct	Glasgow	2	2

		v PORTUGAL	S	P
1950	21 May	Lisbon	2	2
1955	4 May	Glasgow	3	0
1959	3 June	Lisbon	0	1
1966	18 June	Glasgow	0	1
EC1971	21 Apr	Lisbon	0	2
EC1971	13 Oct	Glasgow	2	1
1975	13 May	Glasgow	1	0
EC1978	29 Nov	Lisbon	0	1
EC1980	26 Mar	Glasgow	4	1
wc1980	15 Oct	Glasgow	0	0
wc1981	18 Nov	Lisbon	1	2
wc1992	14 Oct	Ibrox	0	0
wc1993	28 Apr	Lisbon	0	5
2002	20 Nov	Braga	0	2

		v QATAR	S	Q
2015	5 June	Easter Road	1	0

		v REPUBLIC OF IRELAND	S	RI
wc1961	3 May	Glasgow	4	1
wc1961	7 May	Dublin	3	0
1963	9 June	Dublin	0	1
1969	21 Sept	Dublin	1	1
EC1986	15 Oct	Dublin	0	0
EC1987	18 Feb	Glasgow	0	1
2000	30 May	Dublin	2	1
2003	12 Feb	Glasgow	0	2
NC2011	29 May	Dublin	1	0
EC2014	14 Nov	Hampden	1	0
EC2015	13 June	Dublin	1	1

v ROMANIA

			S	R
EC1975	1 June	Bucharest	1	1
EC1975	17 Dec	Glasgow	1	1
1986	26 Mar	Glasgow	3	0
EC1990	12 Sept	Glasgow	2	1
EC1991	16 Oct	Bucharest	0	1
2004	31 Mar	Glasgow	1	2

v RUSSIA

			S	R
EC1994	16 Nov	Glasgow	1	1
EC1995	29 Mar	Moscow	0	0

v SAN MARINO

			S	SM
EC1991	1 May	Serravalle	2	0
EC1991	13 Nov	Glasgow	4	0
EC1995	26 Apr	Serravalle	2	0
EC1995	15 Nov	Glasgow	5	0
wc2000	7 Oct	Serravalle	2	0
wc2001	28 Mar	Glasgow	4	0

v SAUDI ARABIA

			S	SA
1988	17 Feb	Riyadh	2	2

v SERBIA

			S	Se
wc2012	8 Sept	Glasgow	0	0
wc2013	26 Mar	Novi Sad	0	2

v SLOVAKIA

			S	Sl
wc2016	11 Oct	Trnava	0	3
wc2017	**5 Oct**	**Glasgow**	**1**	**0**

v SLOVENIA

			S	Sl
wc2004	8 Sept	Glasgow	0	0
wc2005	12 Oct	Celje	3	0
2012	29 Feb	Koper	1	1
wc2017	26 Mar	Hampden	1	0
wc2017	**8 Oct**	**Ljubljana**	**2**	**2**

v SOUTH AFRICA

			S	SA
2002	20 May	Hong Kong	0	2
2007	22 Aug	Aberdeen	1	0

v SPAIN

			S	Sp
wc1957	8 May	Glasgow	4	2
wc1957	26 May	Madrid	1	4
1963	13 June	Madrid	6	2
1965	8 May	Glasgow	0	0
EC1974	20 Nov	Glasgow	1	2
EC1975	5 Feb	Valencia	1	1
1982	24 Feb	Valencia	0	3
wc1984	14 Nov	Glasgow	3	1
wc1985	27 Feb	Seville	0	1
1988	27 Apr	Madrid	0	0
2004	3 Sept	Valencia	1	1

Match abandoned after 60 minutes; floodlight failure.

			S	Sp
EC2010	12 Oct	Glasgow	2	3
EC2011	11 Oct	Alicante	1	3

v SWEDEN

			S	Sw
1952	30 May	Stockholm	1	3
1953	6 May	Glasgow	1	2
1975	16 Apr	Gothenburg	1	1
1977	27 Apr	Glasgow	3	1
wc1980	10 Sept	Stockholm	1	0
wc1981	9 Sept	Glasgow	2	0
wc1990	16 June	Genoa	2	1
1995	11 Oct	Stockholm	0	2
wc1996	10 Nov	Ibrox	1	0
wc1997	30 Apr	Gothenburg	1	2
2004	17 Nov	Easter Road	1	4
2010	11 Aug	Stockholm	0	3

v SWITZERLAND

			S	Sw
1931	24 May	Geneva	3	2
1946	15 May	Glasgow	3	1
1948	17 May	Berne	1	2
1950	26 Apr	Glasgow	3	1
wc1957	19 May	Basle	2	1
wc1957	6 Nov	Glasgow	3	2
1973	22 June	Berne	0	1
1976	7 Apr	Glasgow	1	0
EC1982	17 Nov	Berne	0	2
EC1983	30 May	Glasgow	2	2
EC1990	17 Oct	Glasgow	2	1
EC1991	11 Sept	Berne	2	2
wc1992	9 Sept	Berne	1	3
wc1993	8 Sept	Aberdeen	1	1
wc1996	18 June	Villa Park	1	0
2006	1 Mar	Glasgow	1	3

v TRINIDAD & TOBAGO

			S	TT
2004	30 May	Easter Road	4	1

v TURKEY

			S	T
1960	8 June	Ankara	2	4

v UKRAINE

			S	U
EC2006	11 Oct	Kiev	0	2
EC2007	13 Oct	Glasgow	3	1

v URUGUAY

			S	U
wc1954	19 June	Basle	0	7
1962	2 May	Glasgow	2	3
1983	21 Sept	Glasgow	2	0
wc1986	13 June	Nezahualcoyotl	0	0

v USA

			S	USA
1952	30 Apr	Glasgow	6	0
1992	17 May	Denver	1	0
1996	26 May	New Britain	1	2
1998	30 May	Washington	0	0
2005	12 Nov	Glasgow	1	1
2012	26 May	Jacksonville	1	5
2013	15 Nov	Glasgow	0	0

v USSR

			S	USSR
1967	10 May	Glasgow	0	2
1971	14 June	Moscow	0	1
wc1982	22 June	Malaga	2	2
1991	6 Feb	Ibrox	0	1

v YUGOSLAVIA

			S	Y
1955	15 May	Belgrade	2	2
1956	21 Nov	Glasgow	2	0
wc1958	8 June	Vasteras	1	1
1972	29 June	Belo Horizonte	2	2
wc1974	22 June	Frankfurt	1	1
1984	12 Sept	Glasgow	6	1
wc1988	19 Oct	Glasgow	1	1
wc1989	6 Sept	Zagreb	1	3

v ZAIRE

			S	Z
wc1974	14 June	Dortmund	2	0

WALES

v ALBANIA

			W	A
EC1994	7 Sept	Cardiff	2	0
EC1995	15 Nov	Tirana	1	1

v ANDORRA

			W	A
EC2014	9 Sept	La Vella	2	1
EC2015	13 Oct	Cardiff	2	0

v ARGENTINA

			W	A
1992	3 June	Tokyo	0	1
2002	13 Feb	Cardiff	1	1

v ARMENIA

			W	A
wc2001	24 Mar	Erevan	2	2
wc2001	1 Sept	Cardiff	0	0

v AUSTRALIA

			W	A
2011	10 Aug	Cardiff	1	2

v AUSTRIA

			W	A
1954	9 May	Vienna	0	2
1955	23 Nov	Wrexham	1	2
EC1974	4 Sept	Vienna	1	2
1975	19 Nov	Wrexham	1	0
1992	29 Apr	Vienna	1	1
EC2005	26 Mar	Cardiff	0	2
EC2005	30 Mar	Vienna	0	1
2013	6 Feb	Swansea	2	1
wc2016	6 Oct	Vienna	2	2
wc2017	**2 Sept**	**Cardiff**	**1**	**0**

v AZERBAIJAN

			W	A
EC2002	20 Nov	Baku	2	0
EC2003	29 Mar	Cardiff	4	0
wc2004	4 Sept	Baku	1	1

			W	A
wc2005	12 Oct	Cardiff	2	0
wc2008	6 Sept	Cardiff	1	0
wc2009	6 June	Baku	1	0

v BELARUS

			W	B
EC1998	14 Oct	Cardiff	3	2
EC1999	4 Sept	Minsk	2	1
wc2000	2 Sept	Minsk	1	2
wc2001	6 Oct	Cardiff	1	0

v BELGIUM

			W	B
1949	22 May	Liege	1	3
1949	23 Nov	Cardiff	5	1
EC1990	17 Oct	Cardiff	3	1
EC1991	27 Mar	Brussels	1	1
wc1992	18 Nov	Brussels	0	2
wc1993	31 Mar	Cardiff	2	0
wc1997	29 Mar	Cardiff	1	2
wc1997	11 Oct	Brussels	2	3
wc2012	7 Sept	Cardiff	0	2
wc2013	15 Oct	Brussels	1	1
EC2014	16 Nov	Brussels	0	0
EC2015	12 June	Cardiff	1	0
EC2016	1 July	Lille	3	1

v BOSNIA-HERZEGOVINA

			W	BH
2003	12 Feb	Cardiff	2	2
2012	15 Aug	Llanelli	0	2
EC2014	10 Oct	Cardiff	0	0
EC2015	10 Oct	Zenica	0	2

v BRAZIL

			W	B
wc1958	19 June	Gothenburg	0	1
1962	12 May	Rio de Janeiro	1	3
1962	16 May	São Paulo	1	3
1966	14 May	Rio de Janeiro	1	3
1966	18 May	Belo Horizonte	0	1
1983	12 June	Cardiff	1	1
1991	11 Sept	Cardiff	1	0
1997	12 Nov	Brasilia	0	3
2000	23 May	Cardiff	0	3
2006	5 Sept	Cardiff	0	2

v BULGARIA

			W	B
EC1983	27 Apr	Wrexham	1	0
EC1983	16 Nov	Sofia	0	1
EC1994	14 Dec	Cardiff	0	3
EC1995	29 Mar	Sofia	1	3
2006	15 Aug	Swansea	0	0
2007	22 Aug	Burgas	1	0
EC2010	8 Oct	Cardiff	0	1
EC2011	12 Oct	Sofia	1	0

v CANADA

			W	C
1986	10 May	Toronto	0	2
1986	20 May	Vancouver	3	0
2004	30 May	Wrexham	1	0

v CHILE

			W	C
1966	22 May	Santiago	0	2
2014	4 June	Valparaiso	0	2

v CHINA

			W	C
2018	22 Mar	Nanning	6	0

v COSTA RICA

			W	CR
1990	20 May	Cardiff	1	0
2012	29 Feb	Cardiff	0	1

v CROATIA

			W	C
2002	21 Aug	Varazdin	1	1
2010	23 May	Osijek	0	2
wc2012	16 Oct	Osijek	0	2
wc2013	26 Mar	Swansea	1	2

v CYPRUS

			W	C
wc1992	14 Oct	Limassol	1	0
wc1993	13 Oct	Cardiff	2	0
2005	16 Nov	Limassol	0	1
EC2006	11 Oct	Cardiff	3	1
EC2007	13 Oct	Nicosia	1	3
EC2014	13 Oct	Cardiff	2	1
EC2015	3 Sept	Nicosia	1	0

v CZECHOSLOVAKIA

			W	C
wc1957	1 May	Cardiff	1	0
wc1957	26 May	Prague	0	1
EC1971	21 Apr	Swansea	1	3
EC1971	27 Oct	Prague	0	1
wc1977	30 Mar	Wrexham	3	0
wc1977	16 Nov	Prague	0	1
wc1980	19 Nov	Cardiff	1	0
wc1981	9 Sept	Prague	0	2
EC1987	29 Apr	Wrexham	1	1
EC1987	11 Nov	Prague	0	2
wc1993	28 Apr	Ostrava†	1	1
wc1993	8 Sept	Cardiff†	2	2

†*Czechoslovakia played as RCS (Republic of Czechs and Slovaks).*

2008	19 Nov	Brondby	1	0

v ESTONIA

			W	E
1994	23 May	Tallinn	2	1
2009	29 May	Llanelli	1	0

v FAROE ISLANDS

			W	F
wc1992	9 Sept	Cardiff	6	0
wc1993	6 June	Toftir	3	0

v FINLAND

			W	F
EC1971	26 May	Helsinki	1	0
EC1971	13 Oct	Swansea	3	0
EC1987	10 Sept	Helsinki	1	1
EC1987	1 Apr	Wrexham	4	0
wc1988	19 Oct	Swansea	2	2
wc1989	6 Sept	Helsinki	0	1
2000	29 Mar	Cardiff	1	2
EC2002	7 Sept	Helsinki	2	0
EC2003	10 Sept	Cardiff	1	1
wc2009	28 Mar	Cardiff	0	2
wc2009	10 Oct	Helsinki	1	2
2013	16 Nov	Cardiff	1	1

v FRANCE

			W	F
1933	25 May	Paris	1	1
1939	20 May	Paris	1	2
1953	14 May	Paris	1	6
1982	2 June	Toulouse	1	0
2017	**10 Nov**	**Paris**	**0**	**2**

v FYR MACEDONIA

			W	M
wc2013	6 Sept	Skopje	1	2
wc2013	11 Oct	Cardiff	1	0

v GEORGIA

			W	G
EC1994	16 Nov	Tbilisi	0	5
EC1995	7 June	Cardiff	0	1
2008	20 Aug	Swansea	1	2
wc2016	9 Oct	Cardiff	1	1
wc2017	**6 Oct**	**Tbilisi**	**1**	**0**

v GERMANY

			W	G
EC1995	26 Apr	Dusseldorf	1	1
EC1995	11 Oct	Cardiff	1	2
2002	14 May	Cardiff	1	0
EC2007	8 Sept	Cardiff	0	2
EC2007	21 Nov	Frankfurt	0	0
wc2008	15 Oct	Moenchengladbach	0	1
wc2009	1 Apr	Cardiff	0	2

v EAST GERMANY

			W	EG
wc1957	19 May	Leipzig	1	2
wc1957	25 Sept	Cardiff	4	1
wc1969	16 Apr	Dresden	1	2
wc1969	22 Oct	Cardiff	1	3

v WEST GERMANY

			W	WG
1968	8 May	Cardiff	1	1
1969	26 Mar	Frankfurt	1	1
1976	6 Oct	Cardiff	0	2
1977	14 Dec	Dortmund	1	1
EC1979	2 May	Wrexham	0	2
EC1979	17 Oct	Cologne	1	5
wc1989	31 May	Cardiff	0	0
wc1989	15 Nov	Cologne	1	2
EC1991	5 June	Cardiff	1	0
EC1991	16 Oct	Nuremberg	1	4

v GREECE

			W	G
wc1964	9 Dec	Athens	0	2
wc1965	17 Mar	Cardiff	4	1

v HUNGARY			W	H
wc1958	8 June	Sanviken	1	1
wc1958	17 June	Stockholm	2	1
1961	28 May	Budapest	2	3
EC1962	7 Nov	Budapest	1	3
EC1963	20 Mar	Cardiff	1	1
EC1974	30 Oct	Cardiff	2	0
EC1975	16 Apr	Budapest	2	1
1985	16 Oct	Cardiff	0	3
2004	31 Mar	Budapest	2	1
2005	9 Feb	Cardiff	2	0

v ICELAND			W	I
wc1980	2 June	Reykjavik	4	0
wc1981	14 Oct	Swansea	2	2
wc1984	12 Sept	Reykjavik	0	1
wc1984	14 Nov	Cardiff	2	1
1991	1 May	Cardiff	1	0
2008	28 May	Reykjavik	1	0
2014	5 Mar	Cardiff	3	1

v IRAN			W	I
1978	18 Apr	Tehran	1	0

v ISRAEL			W	I
wc1958	15 Jan	Tel Aviv	2	0
wc1958	5 Feb	Cardiff	2	0
1984	10 June	Tel Aviv	0	0
1989	8 Feb	Tel Aviv	3	3
EC2015	28 Mar	Haifa	3	0
EC2015	6 Sept	Cardiff	0	0

v ITALY			W	I
1965	1 May	Florence	1	4
wc1968	23 Oct	Cardiff	0	1
wc1969	4 Nov	Rome	1	4
1988	4 June	Brescia	1	0
1996	24 Jan	Terni	0	3
EC1998	5 Sept	Liverpool	0	2
EC1999	5 June	Bologna	0	4
EC2002	16 Oct	Cardiff	2	1
EC2003	6 Sept	Milan	0	4

v JAMAICA			W	J
1998	25 Mar	Cardiff	0	0

v JAPAN			W	J
1992	7 June	Matsuyama	1	0

v KUWAIT			W	K
1977	6 Sept	Wrexham	0	0
1977	20 Sept	Kuwait	0	0

v LATVIA			W	L
2004	18 Aug	Riga	2	0

v LIECHTENSTEIN			W	L
2006	14 Nov	Swansea	4	0
wc2008	11 Oct	Cardiff	2	0
wc2009	14 Oct	Vaduz	2	0

v LUXEMBOURG			W	L
EC1974	20 Nov	Swansea	5	0
EC1975	1 May	Luxembourg	3	1
EC1990	14 Nov	Luxembourg	1	0
EC1991	13 Nov	Cardiff	1	0
2008	26 Mar	Luxembourg	2	0
2010	11 Aug	Llanelli	5	1

v MALTA			W	M
EC1978	25 Oct	Wrexham	7	0
EC1979	2 June	Valletta	2	0
1988	1 June	Valletta	3	2
1998	3 June	Valletta	3	0

v MEXICO			W	M
wc1958	11 June	Stockholm	1	1
1962	22 May	Mexico City	1	2
2012	27 May	New Jersey	0	2
2018	**29 May**	**Pasadena**	**0**	**0**

v MOLDOVA			W	M
EC1994	12 Oct	Kishinev	2	3
EC1995	6 Sept	Cardiff	1	0
wc2016	5 Sept	Cardiff	4	0
wc2017	**5 Sept**	**Chisinau**	**2**	**0**

v MONTENEGRO			W	M
2009	12 Aug	Podgorica	1	2
EC2010	3 Sept	Podgorica	0	1
EC2011	2 Sept	Cardiff	2	1

v NETHERLANDS			W	N
wc1988	14 Sept	Amsterdam	0	1
wc1989	11 Oct	Wrexham	1	2
1992	30 May	Utrecht	0	4
wc1996	5 Oct	Cardiff	1	3
wc1996	9 Nov	Eindhoven	1	7
2008	1 June	Rotterdam	0	2
2014	4 June	Amsterdam	0	2
2015	13 Nov	Cardiff	2	3

v NEW ZEALAND			W	NZ
2007	26 May	Wrexham	2	2

v NORWAY			W	N
EC1982	22 Sept	Swansea	1	0
EC1983	21 Sept	Oslo	0	0
1984	6 June	Trondheim	0	1
1985	26 Feb	Wrexham	1	1
1985	5 June	Bergen	2	4
1994	9 Mar	Cardiff	1	3
wc2000	7 Oct	Cardiff	1	1
wc2001	5 Sept	Oslo	2	3
2004	27 May	Oslo	0	0
2008	6 Feb	Wrexham	3	0
2011	12 Nov	Cardiff	4	1

v PANAMA			W	P
2017	**14 Nov**	**Cardiff**	**1**	**1**

v PARAGUAY			W	P
2006	1 Mar	Cardiff	0	0

v POLAND			W	P
wc1973	28 Mar	Cardiff	2	0
wc1973	26 Sept	Katowice	0	3
1991	29 May	Radom	0	0
wc2000	11 Oct	Warsaw	0	0
wc2001	2 June	Cardiff	1	2
wc2004	13 Oct	Cardiff	2	3
wc2005	7 Sept	Warsaw	0	1
2009	11 Feb	Vila Real	0	1

v PORTUGAL			W	P
1949	15 May	Lisbon	2	3
1951	12 May	Cardiff	2	1
2000	2 June	Chaves	0	3
EC2016	6 July	Lille	0	2

v QATAR			W	Q
2000	23 Feb	Doha	1	0

v REPUBLIC OF IRELAND			W	RI
1960	28 Sept	Dublin	3	2
1979	11 Sept	Swansea	2	1
1981	24 Feb	Dublin	3	1
1986	26 Mar	Dublin	1	0
1990	28 Mar	Dublin	0	1
1991	6 Feb	Wrexham	0	3
1992	19 Feb	Dublin	1	0
1993	17 Feb	Dublin	1	2
1997	11 Feb	Cardiff	0	0
EC2007	24 Mar	Dublin	0	1
EC2007	17 Nov	Cardiff	2	2
NC2011	8 Feb	Dublin	0	3
2013	14 Aug	Cardiff	0	0
wc2017	24 Mar	Dublin	0	0
wc2017	**9 Oct**	**Cardiff**	**0**	**1**

v ROMANIA			W	R
EC1970	11 Nov	Cardiff	0	0
EC1971	24 Nov	Bucharest	0	2
1983	12 Oct	Wrexham	5	0
wc1992	20 May	Bucharest	1	5
wc1993	17 Nov	Cardiff	1	2

v RUSSIA			W	R
EC2003	15 Nov	Moscow	0	0
EC2003	19 Nov	Cardiff	0	1
wc2008	10 Sept	Moscow	1	2
wc2009	9 Sept	Cardiff	1	3
EC2016	20 June	Toulouse	3	0

v SAN MARINO			W	SM
wc1996	2 June	Serravalle	5	0
wc1996	31 Aug	Cardiff	6	0
EC2007	28 Mar	Cardiff	3	0
EC2007	17 Oct	Serravalle	2	1

v SAUDI ARABIA			W	SA
1986	25 Feb	Dahran	2	1

v SERBIA			W	S
wc2012	11 Sept	Novi Sad	1	6
wc2013	10 Sept	Cardiff	0	3
wc2016	12 Nov	Cardiff	1	1
wc2017	11 June	Belgrade	1	1

v SERBIA-MONTENEGRO			W	SM
EC2003	20 Aug	Belgrade	0	1
EC2003	11 Oct	Cardiff	2	3

v SLOVAKIA			W	S
EC2006	7 Oct	Cardiff	1	5
EC2007	12 Sept	Trnava	5	2
EC2016	11 June	Bordeaux	2	1

v SLOVENIA			W	Sl
2005	17 Aug	Swansea	0	0

v SPAIN			W	S
wc1961	19 Apr	Cardiff	1	2
wc1961	18 May	Madrid	1	1
1982	24 Mar	Valencia	1	1
wc1984	17 Oct	Seville	0	3
wc1985	30 Apr	Wrexham	3	0

v SWEDEN			W	S
wc1958	15 June	Stockholm	0	0
1988	27 Apr	Stockholm	1	4
1989	26 Apr	Wrexham	0	2
1990	25 Apr	Stockholm	2	4
1994	20 Apr	Wrexham	0	2
2010	3 Mar	Swansea	0	1
2016	5 June	Stockholm	0	3

v SWITZERLAND			W	S
1949	26 May	Berne	0	4
1951	16 May	Wrexham	3	2
1996	24 Apr	Lugano	0	2
EC1999	31 Mar	Zurich	0	2
EC1999	9 Oct	Wrexham	0	2

EC2010	12 Oct	Basle	1	4
EC2011	8 Oct	Swansea	2	0

v TRINIDAD & TOBAGO			W	TT
2006	27 May	Graz	2	1

v TUNISIA			W	T
1998	6 June	Tunis	0	4

v TURKEY			W	T
EC1978	29 Nov	Wrexham	1	0
EC1979	21 Nov	Izmir	0	1
wc1980	15 Oct	Cardiff	4	0
wc1981	25 Mar	Ankara	1	0
wc1996	14 Dec	Cardiff	0	0
wc1997	20 Aug	Istanbul	4	6

v UKRAINE			W	U
wc2001	28 Mar	Cardiff	1	1
wc2001	6 June	Kiev	1	1
2016	28 Mar	Kiev	0	1

v REST OF UNITED KINGDOM				
1951	5 Dec	Cardiff	3	2
1969	28 July	Cardiff	0	1

v URUGUAY			W	U
1986	21 Apr	Wrexham	0	0
2018	**26 Mar**	**Nanning**	**0**	**1**

v USA			W	USA
2003	27 May	San Jose	0	2

v USSR			W	USSR
wc1965	30 May	Moscow	1	2
wc1965	27 Oct	Cardiff	2	1
wc1981	30 May	Wrexham	0	0
wc1981	18 Nov	Tbilisi	0	3
1987	18 Feb	Swansea	0	0

v YUGOSLAVIA			W	Y
1953	21 May	Belgrade	2	5
1954	22 Nov	Cardiff	1	3
EC1976	24 Apr	Zagreb	0	2
EC1976	22 May	Cardiff	1	1
EC1982	15 Dec	Titograd	4	4
EC1983	14 Dec	Cardiff	1	1
1988	23 Mar	Swansea	1	2

NORTHERN IRELAND

v ALBANIA			NI	A
wc1965	7 May	Belfast	4	1
wc1965	24 Nov	Tirana	1	1
EC1982	15 Dec	Tirana	0	0
EC1983	27 Apr	Belfast	1	0
wc1992	9 Sept	Belfast	3	0
wc1993	17 Feb	Tirana	2	1
wc1996	14 Dec	Belfast	2	0
wc1997	10 Sept	Zurich	0	1
2010	3 Mar	Tirana	0	1

v ALGERIA			NI	A
wc1986	3 June	Guadalajara	1	1

v ARGENTINA			NI	A
wc1958	11 June	Halmstad	1	3

v ARMENIA			NI	A
wc1996	5 Oct	Belfast	1	1
wc1997	30 Apr	Erevan	0	0
EC2003	29 Mar	Erevan	0	1
EC2003	10 Sept	Belfast	0	1

v AUSTRALIA			NI	A
1980	11 June	Sydney	2	1
1980	15 June	Melbourne	1	1
1980	18 June	Adelaide	2	1

v AUSTRIA			NI	A
wc1982	1 July	Madrid	2	2
EC1982	13 Oct	Vienna	0	2
EC1983	21 Sept	Belfast	3	1
EC1990	14 Nov	Vienna	0	0
EC1991	16 Oct	Belfast	2	1
EC1994	12 Oct	Vienna	2	1
EC1995	15 Nov	Belfast	5	3

wc2004	13 Oct	Belfast	3	3
wc2005	12 Oct	Vienna	0	2

v AZERBAIJAN			NI	A
wc2004	9 Oct	Baku	0	0
wc2005	3 Sept	Belfast	2	0
wc2012	14 Nov	Belfast	1	1
wc2013	11 Oct	Baku	0	2
wc2016	11 Nov	Belfast	4	0
wc2017	10 June	Baku	1	0

v BARBADOS			NI	B
2004	30 May	Waterford	1	1

v BELARUS			NI	B
2016	27 May	Belfast	3	0

v BELGIUM			NI	B
wc1976	10 Nov	Liege	0	2
wc1977	16 Nov	Belfast	3	0
1997	11 Feb	Belfast	3	0

v BRAZIL			NI	B
wc1986	12 June	Guadalajara	0	3

v BULGARIA			NI	B
wc1972	18 Oct	Sofia	0	3
wc1973	26 Sept	Sheffield	0	0
EC1978	29 Nov	Sofia	2	0
EC1979	2 May	Belfast	2	0
wc2001	28 Mar	Sofia	3	4
wc2001	2 June	Belfast	0	1
2008	6 Feb	Belfast	0	1

v CANADA

			NI	C
1995	22 May	Edmonton	0	2
1999	27 Apr	Belfast	1	1
2005	9 Feb	Belfast	0	1

v CHILE

			NI	C
1989	26 May	Belfast	0	1
1995	25 May	Edmonton	1	2
2010	30 May	Chillan	0	1
2014	4 June	Valparaiso	0	2

v COLOMBIA

			NI	C
1994	4 June	Boston	0	2

v COSTA RICA

			NI	CR
2018	**3 June**	**San Jose**	**0**	**3**

v CROATIA

			NI	C
2016	15 Nov	Belfast	0	3

v CYPRUS

			NI	C
EC1971	3 Feb	Nicosia	3	0
EC1971	21 Apr	Belfast	5	0
wc1973	14 Feb	Nicosia	0	1
wc1973	8 May	London	3	0
2002	21 Aug	Belfast	0	0
2014	5 Mar	Nicosia	0	0

v CZECHOSLOVAKIA

			NI	C
wc1958	8 June	Halmstad	1	0
wc1958	17 June	Malmo	2	1*

*After extra time

v CZECH REPUBLIC

			NI	C
wc2001	24 Mar	Belfast	0	1
wc2001	6 June	Teplice	1	3
wc2008	10 Sept	Belfast	0	0
wc2009	14 Oct	Prague	0	0
wc2016	4 Sept	Prague	0	0
wc2017	**4 Sept**	**Belfast**	**2**	**0**

v DENMARK

			NI	D
EC1978	25 Oct	Belfast	2	1
EC1979	6 June	Copenhagen	0	4
1986	26 Mar	Belfast	1	1
EC1990	17 Oct	Belfast	1	1
EC1991	13 Nov	Odense	1	2
wc1992	18 Nov	Belfast	0	1
wc1993	13 Oct	Copenhagen	0	1
wc2000	7 Oct	Belfast	1	1
wc2001	1 Sept	Copenhagen	1	1
EC2006	7 Oct	Copenhagen	0	0
EC2007	17 Nov	Belfast	2	1

v ESTONIA

			NI	E
2004	31 Mar	Tallinn	1	0
2006	1 Mar	Belfast	1	0
EC2011	6 Sept	Tallinn	1	4
EC2011	7 Oct	Belfast	1	2

v FAROE ISLANDS

			NI	F
EC1991	1 May	Belfast	1	1
EC1991	11 Sept	Landskrona	5	0
EC2010	12 Oct	Toftir	1	1
EC2011	10 Aug	Belfast	4	0
EC2014	11 Oct	Belfast	2	0
EC2015	4 Sept	Torshavn	3	1

v FINLAND

			NI	F
wc1984	27 May	Pori	0	1
wc1984	14 Nov	Belfast	2	1
EC1998	10 Oct	Belfast	1	0
EC1998	9 Oct	Helsinki	1	4
2003	12 Feb	Belfast	0	1
2006	16 Aug	Helsinki	2	1
2012	15 Aug	Belfast	3	3
EC2015	29 Mar	Belfast	2	1
EC2015	11 Oct	Helsinki	1	1

v FRANCE

			NI	F
1928	21 Feb	Paris	0	4
1951	12 May	Belfast	2	2
1952	11 Nov	Paris	1	3
wc1958	19 June	Norrkoping	0	4
1982	24 Mar	Paris	0	4
wc1982	4 July	Madrid	1	4
1986	26 Feb	Paris	0	0
1988	27 Apr	Belfast	0	0
1999	18 Aug	Belfast	0	1

v GEORGIA

			NI	G
2008	26 Mar	Belfast	4	1

v GERMANY

			NI	G
1992	2 June	Bremen	1	1
1996	29 May	Belfast	1	1
wc1996	9 Nov	Nuremberg	1	1
wc1997	20 Aug	Belfast	1	3
EC1999	27 Mar	Belfast	0	3
EC1999	8 Sept	Dortmund	0	4
2005	4 June	Belfast	1	4
EC2016	21 June	Paris	0	1
wc2016	11 Oct	Hanover	0	2
wc2017	**5 Oct**	**Belfast**	**1**	**3**

v WEST GERMANY

			NI	WG
wc1958	15 June	Malmo	2	2
wc1960	26 Oct	Belfast	3	4
wc1961	10 May	Hamburg	1	2
1966	7 May	Belfast	0	2
1977	27 Apr	Cologne	0	5
EC1982	17 Nov	Belfast	1	0
EC1983	16 Nov	Hamburg	1	0

v GREECE

			NI	G
wc1961	3 May	Athens	1	2
wc1961	17 Oct	Belfast	2	0
1988	17 Feb	Athens	2	3
EC2003	2 Apr	Belfast	0	2
EC2003	11 Oct	Athens	0	1
EC2014	14 Oct	Piraeus	2	0
EC2015	8 Oct	Belfast	3	1

v HONDURAS

			NI	H
wc1982	21 June	Zaragoza	1	1

v HUNGARY

			NI	H
wc1988	19 Oct	Budapest	0	1
wc1989	6 Sept	Belfast	1	2
2000	26 Apr	Belfast	0	1
2008	19 Nov	Belfast	0	2
EC2014	7 Sept	Budapest	2	1
EC2015	7 Sept	Belfast	1	1

v ICELAND

			NI	I
wc1977	11 June	Reykjavik	0	1
wc1977	21 Sept	Belfast	2	0
wc2000	11 Oct	Reykjavik	0	1
wc2001	5 Sept	Belfast	3	0
EC2006	2 Sept	Belfast	0	3
EC2007	12 Sept	Reykjavik	1	2

v ISRAEL

			NI	I
1968	10 Sept	Jaffa	3	2
1976	3 Mar	Tel Aviv	1	1
wc1980	26 Mar	Tel Aviv	0	0
wc1981	18 Nov	Belfast	1	0
1984	16 Oct	Belfast	3	0
1987	18 Feb	Tel Aviv	1	1
2009	12 Aug	Belfast	1	1
wc2013	26 Mar	Belfast	0	2
wc2013	15 Oct	Tel Aviv	1	1

v ITALY

			NI	I
wc1957	25 Apr	Rome	0	1
1957	4 Dec	Belfast	2	2
wc1958	15 Jan	Belfast	2	1
1961	25 Apr	Bologna	2	3
1997	22 Jan	Palermo	0	2
2003	3 June	Campobasso	0	2
2009	6 June	Pisa	0	3
EC2010	8 Oct	Belfast	0	0
EC2011	11 Oct	Pescara	0	3

v KOREA REPUBLIC

			E	KR
2018	**24 Mar**	**Belfast**	**2**	**1**

v LATVIA

			NI	L
wc1993	2 June	Riga	2	1
wc1993	8 Sept	Belfast	2	0
EC1995	26 Apr	Riga	1	0
EC1995	7 June	Belfast	1	2
EC2006	11 Oct	Belfast	1	0
EC2007	8 Sept	Riga	0	1
2015	13 Nov	Belfast	1	0

v LIECHTENSTEIN

			NI	L
EC1994	20 Apr	Belfast	4	1
EC1995	11 Oct	Eschen	4	0
2002	27 Mar	Vaduz	0	0
EC2007	24 Mar	Vaduz	4	1
EC2007	22 Aug	Belfast	3	1

v LITHUANIA

			NI	L
wc1992	28 Apr	Belfast	2	2
wc1993	25 May	Vilnius	1	0

v LUXEMBOURG

			NI	L
2000	23 Feb	Luxembourg	3	1
wc2012	11 Sept	Belfast	1	1
wc2013	10 Sept	Luxembourg	2	3

v MALTA

			NI	M
wc1988	21 May	Belfast	3	0
wc1989	26 Apr	Valletta	2	0
2000	28 Mar	Valletta	3	0
wc2000	2 Sept	Belfast	1	0
wc2001	6 Oct	Valletta	1	0
2005	17 Aug	Ta'Qali	1	1
2013	6 Feb	Ta'Qali	0	0

v MEXICO

			NI	M
1966	22 June	Belfast	4	1
1994	11 June	Miami	0	3

v MOLDOVA

			NI	M
EC1998	18 Nov	Belfast	2	2
EC1999	31 Mar	Chisinau	0	0

v MONTENEGRO

			NI	M
2010	11 Aug	Podgorica	0	2

v MOROCCO

			NI	M
1986	23 Apr	Belfast	2	1
2010	17 Nov	Belfast	1	1

v NETHERLANDS

			NI	N
1962	9 May	Rotterdam	0	4
wc1965	17 Mar	Belfast	2	1
wc1965	7 Apr	Rotterdam	0	0
wc1976	13 Oct	Rotterdam	2	2
wc1977	12 Oct	Belfast	0	1
2012	2 June	Amsterdam	0	6

v NEW ZEALAND

			NI	N
2017	2 June	Belfast	1	0

v NORWAY

			NI	N
1922	25 May	Bergen	1	2
EC1974	4 Sept	Oslo	1	2
EC1975	29 Oct	Belfast	3	0
1990	27 Mar	Belfast	2	3
1996	27 Mar	Belfast	0	2
2001	28 Feb	Belfast	0	4
2004	18 Feb	Belfast	1	4
2012	29 Feb	Belfast	0	3
wc2017	26 Mar	Belfast	2	0
wc2017	**8 Oct**	**Oslo**	**0**	**1**

v PANAMA

			NI	P
2018	**30 May**	**Panama City**	**0**	**0**

v POLAND

			NI	P
EC1962	10 Oct	Katowice	2	0
EC1962	28 Nov	Belfast	2	0
1988	23 Mar	Belfast	1	1
1991	5 Feb	Belfast	3	1
2002	13 Feb	Limassol	1	4
EC2004	4 Sept	Belfast	0	3
EC2005	30 Mar	Warsaw	0	1
wc2009	28 Mar	Belfast	3	2
wc2009	5 Sept	Chorzow	1	1
EC2016	12 June	Nice	0	1

v PORTUGAL

			NI	P
wc1957	16 Jan	Lisbon	1	1
wc1957	1 May	Belfast	3	0
wc1973	28 Mar	Coventry	1	1
wc1973	14 Nov	Lisbon	1	1
wc1980	19 Nov	Lisbon	0	1
wc1981	29 Apr	Belfast	1	0
EC1994	7 Sept	Belfast	1	2
EC1995	3 Sept	Lisbon	1	1
wc1997	29 Mar	Belfast	0	0
wc1997	11 Oct	Lisbon	0	1

			NI	P
2005	15 Nov	Belfast	1	1
wc2012	16 Oct	Porto	1	1
wc2013	6 Sept	Belfast	2	4

v QATAR

			NI	Q
2015	31 May	Crewe	1	1

v REPUBLIC OF IRELAND

			NI	RI
EC1978	20 Sept	Dublin	0	0
EC1979	21 Nov	Belfast	1	0
wc1988	14 Sept	Belfast	0	0
wc1989	11 Oct	Dublin	0	3
wc1993	31 Mar	Dublin	0	3
wc1993	17 Nov	Belfast	1	1
EC1994	16 Nov	Belfast	0	4
EC1995	29 Mar	Dublin	1	1
1999	29 May	Dublin	1	0
NC2011	24 May	Dublin	0	5

v ROMANIA

			NI	R
wc1984	12 Sept	Belfast	3	2
wc1985	16 Oct	Bucharest	1	0
1994	23 Mar	Belfast	2	0
2006	27 May	Chicago	0	2
EC2014	14 Nov	Bucharest	0	2
EC2015	13 June	Belfast	0	0

v RUSSIA

			NI	R
wc2012	7 Sept	Moscow	0	2
wc2013	14 Aug	Belfast	1	0

v SAN MARINO

			NI	SM
wc2008	15 Oct	Belfast	4	0
wc2009	11 Feb	Serravalle	3	0
wc2016	8 Oct	Belfast	4	0
wc2017	**1 Sept**	**Serravalle**	**3**	**0**

v ST KITTS & NEVIS

			NI	SK
2004	2 June	Basseterre	2	0

v SERBIA

			NI	S
2009	14 Nov	Belfast	0	1
EC2011	25 Mar	Belgrade	1	2
EC2011	2 Sept	Belfast	0	1

v SERBIA-MONTENEGRO

			NI	SM
2004	28 Apr	Belfast	1	1

v SLOVAKIA

			NI	S
1998	25 Mar	Belfast	1	0
wc2008	6 Sept	Bratislava	1	2
wc2009	9 Sept	Belfast	0	2
2016	4 June	Trnava	0	0

v SLOVENIA

			NI	S
wc2008	11 Oct	Maribor	0	2
wc2009	1 Apr	Belfast	1	0
EC2010	3 Sept	Maribor	1	0
EC2011	29 Mar	Belfast	0	0
2016	28 Mar	Belfast	1	0

v SOUTH AFRICA

			NI	SA
1924	24 Sept	Belfast	1	2

v SPAIN

			NI	S
1958	15 Oct	Madrid	2	6
1963	30 May	Bilbao	1	1
1963	30 Oct	Belfast	0	1
EC1970	11 Nov	Seville	0	3
EC1972	16 Feb	Hull	1	1
wc1982	25 June	Valencia	1	0
1985	27 Mar	Palma	0	0
wc1986	7 June	Guadalajara	1	2
wc1988	21 Dec	Seville	0	4
wc1989	8 Feb	Belfast	0	2
wc1992	14 Oct	Belfast	0	0
wc1993	28 Apr	Seville	1	3
1998	2 June	Santander	1	4
2002	17 Apr	Belfast	0	5
EC2002	12 Oct	Albacete	0	3
EC2003	11 June	Belfast	0	0
EC2006	6 Sept	Belfast	3	2
EC2007	21 Nov	Las Palmas	0	1

v SWEDEN

			NI	S
EC1974	30 Oct	Solna	2	0
EC1975	3 Sept	Belfast	1	2
wc1980	15 Oct	Belfast	3	0

			NI	S
wc1981	3 June	Solna	0	1
1996	24 Apr	Belfast	1	2
EC2007	28 Mar	Belfast	2	1
EC2007	17 Oct	Stockholm	1	1

v SWITZERLAND			NI	S
wc1964	14 Oct	Belfast	1	0
wc1964	14 Nov	Lausanne	1	2
1998	22 Apr	Belfast	1	0
2004	18 Aug	Zurich	0	0
wc2017	**9 Nov**	**Belfast**	**0**	**1**
wc2017	**12 Nov**	**Basel**	**0**	**0**

v THAILAND			NI	T
1997	21 May	Bangkok	0	0

v TRINIDAD & TOBAGO			NI	TT
2004	6 June	Bacolet	3	0

v TURKEY			NI	T
wc1968	23 Oct	Belfast	4	1
wc1968	11 Dec	Istanbul	3	0
2013	15 Nov	Adana	0	1
EC1983	30 Mar	Belfast	2	1
EC1983	12 Oct	Ankara	0	1
wc1985	1 May	Belfast	2	0
wc1985	11 Sept	Izmir	0	0
EC1986	12 Nov	Izmir	0	0
EC1987	11 Nov	Belfast	1	0
EC1998	5 Sept	Istanbul	0	3
EC1999	4 Sept	Belfast	0	3

			NI	T
2010	26 May	New Britain	0	2
2013	15 Nov	Adana	0	1

v UKRAINE			NI	U
wc1996	31 Aug	Belfast	0	1
wc1997	2 Apr	Kiev	1	2
EC2002	16 Oct	Belfast	0	0
EC2003	6 Sept	Donetsk	0	0
EC2016	16 June	Lyon	2	0

v URUGUAY			NI	U
1964	29 Apr	Belfast	3	0
1990	18 May	Belfast	1	0
2006	21 May	New Jersey	0	1
2014	30 May	Montevideo	0	1

v USSR			NI	USSR
wc1969	19 Sept	Belfast	0	0
wc1969	22 Oct	Moscow	0	2
EC1971	22 Sept	Moscow	0	1
EC1971	13 Oct	Belfast	1	1

v YUGOSLAVIA			NI	Y
EC1975	16 Mar	Belfast	1	0
EC1975	19 Nov	Belgrade	0	1
wc1982	17 June	Zaragoza	0	0
EC1987	29 Apr	Belfast	1	2
EC1987	14 Oct	Sarajevo	0	3
EC1990	12 Sept	Belfast	0	2
EC1991	27 Mar	Belgrade	1	4
2000	16 Aug	Belfast	1	2

REPUBLIC OF IRELAND

v ALBANIA			RI	A
wc1992	26 May	Dublin	2	0
wc1993	26 May	Tirana	2	1
EC2003	2 Apr	Tirana	0	0
EC2003	7 June	Dublin	2	1

v ALGERIA			RI	A
1982	28 Apr	Algiers	0	2
2010	28 May	Dublin	3	0

v ANDORRA			RI	A
wc2001	28 Mar	Barcelona	3	0
wc2001	25 Apr	Dublin	3	1
EC2010	7 Sept	Dublin	3	1
EC2011	7 Oct	Andorra La Vella	2	0

v ARGENTINA			RI	A
1951	13 May	Dublin	0	1
†1979	29 May	Dublin	0	0
1980	16 May	Dublin	0	1
1998	22 Apr	Dublin	0	2
2010	11 Aug	Dublin	0	1

†*Not considered a full international.*

v ARMENIA			RI	A
EC2010	3 Sept	Erevan	1	0
EC2011	11 Oct	Dublin	2	1

v AUSTRALIA			RI	A
2003	19 Aug	Dublin	2	1
2009	12 Aug	Limerick	0	3

v AUSTRIA			RI	A
1952	7 May	Vienna	0	6
1953	25 Mar	Dublin	4	0
1958	14 Mar	Vienna	1	3
wc2013	10 Sept	Vienna	0	1
1962	8 Apr	Dublin	2	3
EC1963	25 Sept	Dublin	0	0
EC1963	13 Oct	Dublin	3	2
1966	22 May	Vienna	0	1
1968	10 Nov	Dublin	2	2
EC1971	30 May	Dublin	1	4
EC1971	10 Oct	Linz	0	6
EC1995	11 June	Dublin	1	3
EC1995	6 Sept	Vienna	1	3
wc2013	26 Mar	Dublin	2	2
wc2013	10 Sept	Vienna	0	1
wc2016	12 Nov	Vienna	1	0
wc2017	11 June	Dublin	1	1

v BELARUS			RI	B
2016	31 May	Cork	1	2

v BELGIUM			RI	B
1928	12 Feb	Liege	4	2
1929	30 Apr	Dublin	4	0
1930	11 May	Brussels	3	1
wc1934	25 Feb	Dublin	4	4
1949	24 Apr	Dublin	0	2
1950	10 May	Brussels	1	5
1965	24 Mar	Dublin	0	2
1966	25 May	Liege	3	2
wc1980	15 Oct	Dublin	1	1
wc1981	25 Mar	Brussels	0	1
EC1986	10 Sept	Brussels	2	2
EC1987	29 Apr	Dublin	0	0
wc1997	29 Oct	Dublin	1	1
wc1997	16 Nov	Brussels	1	2
EC2016	18 June	Bordeaux	0	3

v BOLIVIA			RI	B
1994	24 May	Dublin	1	0
1996	15 June	New Jersey	3	0
2007	26 May	Boston	1	1

v BOSNIA-HERZEGOVINA			RI	BH
2012	26 May	Dublin	1	0
EC2015	13 Nov	Zenica	1	1
EC2015	16 Nov	Dublin	2	0

v BRAZIL			RI	B
1974	5 May	Rio de Janeiro	1	2
1982	27 May	Uberlandia	0	7
1987	23 May	Dublin	1	0
2004	18 Feb	Dublin	0	0
2008	6 Feb	Dublin	0	1
2010	2 Mar	Emirates	0	2

v BULGARIA			RI	B
wc1977	1 June	Sofia	1	2
wc1977	12 Oct	Dublin	0	0
EC1979	19 May	Sofia	0	1
EC1979	17 Oct	Dublin	3	0
wc1987	1 Apr	Sofia	1	2
wc1987	14 Oct	Dublin	2	0
2004	18 Aug	Dublin	1	1
wc2009	28 Mar	Dublin	1	1
wc2009	6 June	Sofia	1	1

		v CAMEROON	RI	C
wc2002	1 June	Niigata	1	1
		v CANADA	RI	C
2003	18 Nov	Dublin	3	0
		v CHILE	RI	C
1960	30 Mar	Dublin	2	0
1972	21 June	Recife	1	2
1974	12 May	Santiago	2	1
1982	22 May	Santiago	0	1
1991	22 May	Dublin	1	1
2006	24 May	Dublin	0	1
		v CHINA PR	RI	CPR
1984	3 June	Sapporo	1	0
2005	29 Mar	Dublin	1	0
		v COLOMBIA	RI	C
2008	29 May	Fulham	1	0
		v COSTA RICA	RI	C
2014	6 June	Philadephia	1	1
		v CROATIA	RI	C
1996	2 June	Dublin	2	2
EC1998	5 Sept	Dublin	2	0
EC1999	4 Sept	Zagreb	0	1
2001	15 Aug	Dublin	2	2
2004	16 Nov	Dublin	1	0
2011	10 Aug	Dublin	0	0
EC2012	10 June	Poznan	1	3
		v CYPRUS	RI	C
wc1980	26 Mar	Nicosia	3	2
wc1980	19 Nov	Dublin	6	0
wc2001	24 Mar	Nicosia	4	0
wc2001	6 Oct	Dublin	4	0
wc2004	4 Sept	Dublin	3	0
wc2005	8 Oct	Nicosia	1	0
EC2006	7 Oct	Nicosia	2	5
EC2007	17 Oct	Dublin	1	1
2008	15 Oct	Dublin	1	0
wc2009	5 Sept	Nicosia	2	1
		v CZECHOSLOVAKIA	RI	C
1938	18 May	Prague	2	2
EC1959	5 Apr	Dublin	2	0
EC1959	10 May	Bratislava	0	4
wc1961	8 Oct	Dublin	1	3
wc1961	29 Oct	Prague	1	7
EC1967	21 May	Dublin	0	2
EC1967	22 Nov	Prague	2	1
wc1969	4 May	Dublin	1	2
wc1969	7 Oct	Prague	0	3
1979	26 Sept	Prague	1	4
1981	29 Apr	Dublin	3	1
1986	27 May	Reykjavik	1	0
		v CZECH REPUBLIC	RI	C
1994	5 June	Dublin	1	3
1996	24 Apr	Prague	0	2
1998	25 Mar	Olomouc	1	2
2000	23 Feb	Dublin	3	2
2004	31 Mar	Dublin	2	1
EC2006	11 Oct	Dublin	1	1
EC2007	12 Sept	Prague	0	1
2012	29 Feb	Dublin	1	1
		v DENMARK	RI	D
wc1956	3 Oct	Dublin	2	1
wc1957	2 Oct	Copenhagen	2	0
wc1968	4 Dec	Dublin	1	1
		(abandoned after 51 mins)		
wc1969	27 May	Copenhagen	0	2
wc1969	15 Oct	Dublin	1	1
EC1978	24 May	Copenhagen	3	3
EC1979	2 May	Dublin	2	0
wc1984	14 Nov	Copenhagen	0	3
wc1985	13 Nov	Dublin	1	4
wc1992	14 Oct	Copenhagen	0	0
wc1993	28 Apr	Dublin	1	1
2002	27 Mar	Dublin	3	0
2007	22 Aug	Copenhagen	4	0
wc2017	**11 Nov**	**Copenhagen**	**0**	**0**
wc2017	**14 Nov**	**Dublin**	**1**	**5**

		v ECUADOR	RI	E
1972	19 June	Natal	3	2
2007	23 May	New Jersey	1	1
		v EGYPT	RI	E
wc1990	17 June	Palermo	0	0
		v ENGLAND	RI	E
1946	30 Sept	Dublin	0	1
1949	21 Sept	Everton	2	0
wc1957	8 May	Wembley	1	5
wc1957	19 May	Dublin	1	1
1964	24 May	Dublin	1	3
1976	8 Sept	Wembley	1	1
EC1978	25 Oct	Dublin	1	1
EC1980	6 Feb	Wembley	0	2
1985	26 Mar	Wembley	1	2
EC1988	12 June	Stuttgart	1	0
wc1990	11 June	Cagliari	1	1
EC1990	14 Nov	Dublin	1	1
EC1991	27 Mar	Wembley	1	1
1995	15 Feb	Dublin	1	0
		(abandoned after 27 mins)		
2013	29 May	Wembley	1	1
2015	7 June	Dublin	0	0
		v ESTONIA	RI	E
wc2000	11 Oct	Dublin	2	0
wc2001	6 June	Tallinn	2	0
EC2011	11 Nov	Tallinn	4	0
EC2011	15 Nov	Dublin	1	1
		v FAROE ISLANDS	RI	F
EC2004	13 Oct	Dublin	2	0
EC2005	8 June	Toftir	2	0
wc2012	16 Oct	Torshavn	4	1
wc2013	7 June	Dublin	3	0
		v FINLAND	RI	F
wc1949	8 Sept	Dublin	3	0
wc1949	9 Oct	Helsinki	1	1
1990	16 May	Dublin	1	1
2000	15 Nov	Dublin	3	0
2002	21 Aug	Helsinki	3	0
		v FRANCE	RI	F
1937	23 May	Paris	2	0
1952	16 Nov	Dublin	1	1
wc1953	4 Oct	Dublin	3	5
wc1953	25 Nov	Paris	0	1
wc1972	15 Nov	Dublin	2	1
wc1973	19 May	Paris	1	1
wc1976	17 Nov	Paris	0	2
wc1977	30 Mar	Dublin	1	0
wc1980	28 Oct	Paris	0	2
wc1981	14 Oct	Dublin	3	2
1989	7 Feb	Dublin	0	0
wc2004	9 Oct	Paris	0	0
wc2005	7 Sept	Dublin	0	1
wc2009	14 Nov	Dublin	0	1
wc2009	18 Nov	Paris	1	1
EC2016	26 June	Lyon	1	2
2018	**28 May**	**Paris**	**0**	**2**
		v FYR MACEDONIA	RI	M
wc1996	9 Oct	Dublin	3	0
wc1997	2 Apr	Skopje	2	3
EC1999	9 June	Dublin	1	0
EC1999	9 Oct	Skopje	1	1
EC2011	26 Mar	Dublin	2	1
EC2011	4 June	Podgorica	2	0
		v GEORGIA	RI	G
EC2003	29 Mar	Tbilisi	2	1
EC2003	11 June	Dublin	2	0
wc2008	6 Sept	Mainz	2	1
wc2009	11 Feb	Dublin	2	1
2013	2 June	Dublin	3	0
EC2014	7 Sept	Tbilisi	2	1
EC2015	7 Sept	Dublin	1	0
wc2016	6 Oct	Dublin	1	0
wc2017	**2 Sept**	**Tbilisi**	**1**	**1**
		v GERMANY	RI	G
1935	8 May	Dortmund	1	3
1936	17 Oct	Dublin	5	2
1939	23 May	Bremen	1	1

			RI	G
1994	29 May	Hanover	2	0
wc2002	5 June	Ibaraki	1	1
EC2006	2 Sept	Stuttgart	0	1
EC2007	13 Oct	Dublin	0	0
wc2012	12 Oct	Dublin	1	6
wc2013	11 Oct	Cologne	0	3
EC2014	14 Oct	Gelsenkirchen	1	1
EC2015	8 Oct	Dublin	1	0

v WEST GERMANY			RI	WG
1951	17 Oct	Dublin	3	2
1952	4 May	Cologne	0	3
1955	28 May	Hamburg	1	2
1956	25 Nov	Dublin	3	0
1960	11 May	Dusseldorf	1	0
1966	4 May	Dublin	0	4
1970	9 May	Berlin	1	2
1975	1 Mar	Dublin	1	0†
1979	22 May	Dublin	1	3
1981	21 May	Bremen	0	3†
1989	6 Sept	Dublin	1	1

†v West Germany 'B'

v GIBRALTAR			RI	G
EC2014	11 Oct	Dublin	7	0
EC2015	4 Sept	Faro	4	0

v GREECE			RI	G
2000	26 Apr	Dublin	0	1
2002	20 Nov	Athens	0	0
2012	14 Nov	Dublin	0	1

v HUNGARY			RI	H
1934	15 Dec	Dublin	2	4
1936	3 May	Budapest	3	3
1936	6 Dec	Dublin	2	3
1939	19 Mar	Cork	2	2
1939	18 May	Budapest	2	2
wc1969	8 June	Dublin	1	2
wc1969	5 Nov	Budapest	0	4
wc1989	8 Mar	Budapest	0	0
wc1989	4 June	Dublin	2	0
1991	11 Sept	Gyor	2	1
2012	4 June	Budapest	0	0

v ICELAND			RI	I
EC1962	12 Aug	Dublin	4	2
EC1962	2 Sept	Reykjavik	1	1
EC1982	13 Oct	Dublin	2	0
EC1983	21 Sept	Reykjavik	3	0
1986	25 May	Reykjavik	2	1
wc1996	10 Nov	Dublin	0	0
wc1997	6 Sept	Reykjavik	4	2
2017	28 Mar	Dublin	0	1

v IRAN			RI	I
1972	18 June	Recife	2	1
wc2001	10 Nov	Dublin	2	0
wc2001	15 Nov	Tehran	0	1

v ISRAEL			RI	I
1984	4 Apr	Tel Aviv	0	3
1985	27 May	Tel Aviv	0	0
1987	10 Nov	Dublin	5	0
EC2005	26 Mar	Tel Aviv	1	1
EC2005	4 June	Dublin	2	2

v ITALY			RI	I
1926	21 Mar	Turin	0	3
1927	23 Apr	Dublin	1	2
EC1970	8 Dec	Rome	0	3
EC1971	10 May	Dublin	1	2
1985	5 Feb	Dublin	1	2
wc1990	30 June	Rome	0	1
1992	4 June	Foxboro	0	2
wc1994	18 June	New York	1	0
2005	17 Aug	Dublin	1	2
wc2009	1 Apr	Bari	1	1
wc2009	10 Oct	Dublin	2	2
2011	7 June	Liege	2	0
EC2012	18 June	Poznan	0	2
2014	31 May	Craven Cottage	0	0
EC2016	22 June	Lille	1	0

v JAMAICA			RI	J
2004	2 June	Charlton	1	0

v KAZAKHSTAN			RI	K
wc2012	7 Sept	Astana	2	1
wc2013	15 Oct	Dublin	3	1

v LATVIA			RI	L
wc1992	9 Sept	Dublin	4	0
wc1993	2 June	Riga	2	1
EC1994	7 Sept	Riga	3	0
EC1995	11 Oct	Dublin	2	1
2013	15 Nov	Dublin	3	0

v LIECHTENSTEIN			RI	L
EC1994	12 Oct	Dublin	4	0
EC1995	3 June	Eschen	0	0
wc1996	31 Aug	Eschen	5	0
wc1997	21 May	Dublin	5	0

v LITHUANIA			RI	L
wc1993	16 June	Vilnius	1	0
wc1993	8 Sept	Dublin	2	0
wc1997	20 Aug	Dublin	0	0
wc1997	10 Sept	Vilnius	2	1

v LUXEMBOURG			RI	L
1936	9 May	Luxembourg	5	1
wc1953	28 Oct	Dublin	4	0
wc1954	7 Mar	Luxembourg	1	0
EC1987	28 May	Luxembourg	2	0
EC1987	9 Sept	Dublin	2	1

v MALTA			RI	M
EC1983	30 Mar	Valletta	1	0
EC1983	16 Nov	Dublin	8	0
wc1989	28 May	Dublin	2	0
wc1989	15 Nov	Valletta	2	0
1990	2 June	Valletta	3	0
EC1998	14 Oct	Dublin	5	0
EC1999	8 Sept	Valletta	3	2

v MEXICO			RI	M
1984	8 Aug	Dublin	0	0
wc1994	24 June	Orlando	1	2
1996	13 June	New Jersey	2	2
1998	23 May	Dublin	0	0
2000	4 June	Chicago	2	2
2017	2 June	New Jersey	1	3

v MOLDOVA			RI	M
wc2016	9 Oct	Chisinau	3	1
wc2017	**6 Oct**	**Dublin**	**2**	**0**

v MONTENEGRO			RI	M
wc2008	10 Sept	Podgorica	0	0
wc2009	14 Oct	Dublin	0	0

v MOROCCO			RI	M
1990	12 Sept	Dublin	1	0

v NETHERLANDS			RI	N
1932	8 May	Amsterdam	2	0
1934	8 Apr	Amsterdam	2	5
1935	8 Dec	Dublin	3	5
1955	1 May	Dublin	1	0
1956	10 May	Rotterdam	4	1
wc1980	10 Sept	Dublin	2	1
wc1981	9 Sept	Rotterdam	2	2
EC1982	22 Sept	Rotterdam	1	2
EC1983	12 Oct	Dublin	2	3
EC1988	18 June	Gelsenkirchen	0	1
wc1990	21 June	Palermo	1	1
1994	20 Apr	Tilburg	1	0
wc1994	4 July	Orlando	0	2
EC1995	13 Dec	Liverpool	0	2
1996	4 June	Rotterdam	1	3
wc2000	2 Sept	Amsterdam	2	2
wc2001	1 Sept	Dublin	1	0
2004	5 June	Amsterdam	1	0
2006	16 Aug	Dublin	0	4
2016	27 May	Dublin	1	1

v NIGERIA			RI	N
2002	16 May	Dublin	1	2
2004	29 May	Charlton	0	3
2009	29 May	Fulham	1	1

v NORTHERN IRELAND			RI	NI
EC1978	20 Sept	Dublin	0	0
EC1979	21 Nov	Belfast	0	1
wc1988	14 Sept	Belfast	0	0
wc1989	11 Oct	Dublin	3	0
wc1993	31 Mar	Dublin	3	0
wc1993	17 Nov	Belfast	1	1
EC1994	16 Nov	Belfast	4	0
EC1995	29 Mar	Dublin	1	1
1999	29 May	Dublin	0	1
NC2011	24 May	Dublin	5	0

v NORWAY			RI	N
wc1937	10 Oct	Oslo	2	3
wc1937	7 Nov	Dublin	3	3
1950	26 Nov	Dublin	2	2
1951	30 May	Oslo	3	2
1954	8 Nov	Dublin	2	1
1955	25 May	Oslo	3	1
1960	6 Nov	Dublin	3	1
1964	13 May	Oslo	4	1
1973	6 June	Oslo	1	1
1976	24 Mar	Dublin	3	0
1978	21 May	Oslo	0	0
wc1984	17 Oct	Oslo	0	1
wc1985	1 May	Dublin	0	0
1988	1 June	Oslo	0	0
wc1994	28 June	New York	0	0
2003	30 Apr	Dublin	1	0
2008	20 Aug	Oslo	1	1
2010	17 Nov	Dublin	1	2

v OMAN			RI	O
2012	11 Sept	London	4	1
2014	3 Sept	Dublin	2	0
2016	31 Aug	Dublin	4	0

v PARAGUAY			RI	P
1999	10 Feb	Dublin	2	0
2010	25 May	Dublin	2	1

v POLAND			RI	P
1938	22 May	Warsaw	0	6
1938	13 Nov	Dublin	3	2
1958	11 May	Katowice	2	2
1958	5 Oct	Dublin	2	2
1964	10 May	Kracow	1	3
1964	25 Oct	Dublin	3	2
1968	15 May	Dublin	2	2
1968	30 Oct	Katowice	0	1
1970	6 May	Dublin	1	2
1970	23 Sept	Dublin	0	2
1973	16 May	Wroclaw	0	2
1973	21 Oct	Dublin	1	0
1976	26 May	Poznan	2	0
1977	24 Apr	Dublin	0	0
1978	12 Apr	Lodz	0	3
1981	23 May	Bydgoszcz	0	3
1984	23 May	Dublin	0	0
1986	12 Nov	Warsaw	0	1
1988	22 May	Dublin	3	1
EC1991	1 May	Dublin	0	0
EC1991	16 Oct	Poznan	3	3
2004	28 Apr	Bydgoszcz	0	0
2013	19 Nov	Poznan	0	0
2008	19 Nov	Dublin	2	3
2013	6 Feb	Dublin	2	0
2013	19 Nov	Poznan	0	0
EC2015	29 Mar	Dublin	1	1
EC2015	11 Oct	Warsaw	1	2

v PORTUGAL			RI	P
1946	16 June	Lisbon	1	3
1947	4 May	Dublin	0	2
1948	23 May	Lisbon	0	2
1949	22 May	Dublin	1	0
1972	25 June	Recife	1	2
1992	7 June	Boston	2	0
EC1995	26 Apr	Dublin	1	0
EC1995	15 Nov	Lisbon	0	3
1996	29 May	Dublin	0	1
wc2000	7 Oct	Lisbon	1	1
wc2001	2 June	Dublin	1	1
2005	9 Feb	Dublin	1	0
2014	10 June	New Jersey	1	5

v ROMANIA			RI	R
1988	23 Mar	Dublin	2	0
wc1990	25 June	Genoa	0	0*
wc1997	30 Apr	Bucharest	0	1
wc1997	11 Oct	Dublin	1	1
2004	27 May	Dublin	1	0

v RUSSIA			RI	R
1994	23 Mar	Dublin	0	0
1996	27 Mar	Dublin	0	2
2002	13 Feb	Dublin	2	0
EC2002	7 Sept	Moscow	2	4
EC2003	6 Sept	Dublin	1	1
EC2010	8 Oct	Dublin	2	3
EC2011	6 Sept	Moscow	0	0

v SAN MARINO			RI	SM
EC2006	15 Nov	Dublin	5	0
EC2007	7 Feb	Serravalle	2	1

v SAUDI ARABIA			RI	SA
wc2002	11 June	Yokohama	3	0

v SCOTLAND			RI	S
wc1961	3 May	Glasgow	1	4
wc1961	7 May	Dublin	0	3
1963	9 June	Dublin	1	0
1969	21 Sept	Dublin	1	1
EC1986	15 Oct	Dublin	0	0
EC1987	18 Feb	Glasgow	1	0
2000	30 May	Dublin	1	2
2003	12 Feb	Glasgow	2	0
NC2011	29 May	Dublin	1	0
EC2014	14 Nov	Hampden	0	1
EC2015	13 June	Dublin	1	1

v SERBIA			RI	S
2008	24 May	Dublin	1	1
2012	15 Aug	Belgrade	0	0
2014	5 Mar	Dublin	1	2
wc2016	5 Sept	Belgrade	2	2
wc2017	**5 Sept**	**Dublin**	**0**	**1**

v SLOVAKIA			RI	S
EC2007	28 Mar	Dublin	1	0
EC2007	8 Sept	Bratislava	2	2
EC2010	12 Oct	Zilina	1	1
EC2011	2 Sept	Dublin	0	0
2016	29 Mar	Dublin	2	2

v SOUTH AFRICA			RI	SA
2000	11 June	New Jersey	2	1
2009	8 Sept	Limerick	1	0

v SPAIN			RI	S
1931	26 Apr	Barcelona	1	1
1931	13 Dec	Dublin	0	5
1946	23 June	Madrid	1	0
1947	2 Mar	Dublin	3	2
1948	30 May	Barcelona	1	2
1949	12 June	Dublin	1	4
1952	1 June	Madrid	0	6
1955	27 Nov	Dublin	2	2
EC1964	11 Mar	Seville	1	5
EC1964	8 Apr	Dublin	0	2
wc1965	5 May	Dublin	1	0
wc1965	27 Oct	Seville	1	4
wc1965	10 Nov	Paris	0	1
EC1966	23 Oct	Dublin	0	0
EC1966	7 Dec	Valencia	0	2
1977	9 Feb	Dublin	0	1
EC1982	17 Nov	Dublin	3	3
EC1983	27 Apr	Zaragoza	0	2
1985	26 May	Cork	0	0
wc1988	16 Nov	Seville	0	2
wc1989	26 Apr	Dublin	1	0
wc1992	18 Nov	Seville	0	0
wc1993	13 Oct	Dublin	1	3
wc2002	16 June	Suwon	1	1
EC2012	14 June	Gdansk	0	4
2013	11 June	New York	0	2

v SWEDEN			RI	S
wc1949	2 June	Stockholm	1	3
wc1949	13 Nov	Dublin	1	3
1959	1 Nov	Dublin	3	2
1960	18 May	Malmo	1	4

v SWEDEN		RI	S
EC1970 14 Oct	Dublin	1	1
EC1970 28 Oct	Malmo	0	1
1999 28 Apr	Dublin	2	0
2006 1 Mar	Dublin	3	0
wc2013 22 Mar	Stockholm	0	0
wc2013 6 Sept	Dublin	1	2
EC2016 13 June	Paris	1	1

v SWITZERLAND		RI	S
1935 5 May	Basle	0	1
1936 17 Mar	Dublin	1	0
1937 17 May	Berne	1	0
1938 18 Sept	Dublin	4	0
1948 5 Dec	Dublin	0	1
EC1975 11 May	Dublin	2	1
EC1975 21 May	Berne	0	1
1980 30 Apr	Dublin	2	0
wc1985 2 June	Dublin	3	0
wc1985 11 Sept	Berne	0	0
1992 25 Mar	Dublin	2	1
EC2002 16 Oct	Dublin	1	2
EC2003 11 Oct	Basle	0	2
wc2004 8 Sept	Basle	1	1
wc2005 12 Oct	Dublin	0	0
2016 25 Mar	Dublin	1	0

v TRINIDAD & TOBAGO		RI	TT
1982 30 May	Port of Spain	1	2

v TUNISIA		RI	T
1988 19 Oct	Dublin	4	0

v TURKEY		RI	T
EC1966 16 Nov	Dublin	2	1
EC1967 22 Feb	Ankara	1	2
EC1974 20 Nov	Izmir	1	1
EC1975 29 Oct	Dublin	4	0
2014 25 May	Dublin	1	2
1976 13 Oct	Ankara	3	3
1978 5 Apr	Dublin	4	2
1990 26 May	Izmir	0	0
EC1990 17 Oct	Dublin	5	0
EC1991 13 Nov	Istanbul	3	1
EC2000 13 Nov	Dublin	1	1
EC2000 17 Nov	Bursa	0	0
2003 9 Sept	Dublin	2	2
2014 25 May	Dublin	1	2
2018 23 Mar	**Antalya**	**0**	**1**

v URUGUAY		RI	U
1974 8 May	Montevideo	0	2
1986 23 Apr	Dublin	1	1
2011 29 Mar	Dublin	2	3
2017 4 June	Dublin	3	1

v USA		RI	USA
1979 29 Oct	Dublin	3	2
1991 1 June	Boston	1	1
1992 29 Apr	Dublin	4	1
1992 30 May	Washington	1	3
1996 9 June	Boston	1	2
2000 6 June	Boston	1	1
2002 17 Apr	Dublin	2	1
2014 18 Nov	Dublin	4	1
2018 2 June	**Dublin**	**2**	**1**

v USSR		RI	USSR
wc1972 18 Oct	Dublin	1	2
wc1973 13 May	Moscow	0	1
EC1974 30 Oct	Dublin	3	0
EC1975 18 May	Kiev	1	2
wc1984 12 Sept	Dublin	1	0
wc1985 16 Oct	Moscow	0	2
EC1988 15 June	Hanover	1	1
1990 25 Apr	Dublin	1	0

v WALES		RI	W
1960 28 Sept	Dublin	2	3
1979 11 Sept	Swansea	1	2
1981 24 Feb	Dublin	1	3
1986 26 Mar	Dublin	0	1
1990 28 Mar	Dublin	1	0
1991 6 Feb	Wrexham	3	0
1992 19 Feb	Dublin	0	1
1993 17 Feb	Dublin	2	1
1997 11 Feb	Cardiff	0	0
EC2007 24 Mar	Dublin	1	0
EC2007 17 Nov	Cardiff	2	2
NC2011 8 Feb	Dublin	3	0
2013 14 Aug	Cardiff	0	0
wc2017 24 Mar	Dublin	0	0
wc2017 9 Oct	**Cardiff**	**1**	**0**

v YUGOSLAVIA		RI	Y
1955 19 Sept	Dublin	1	4
1988 27 Apr	Dublin	2	0
EC1998 18 Nov	Belgrade	0	1
EC1999 1 Sept	Dublin	2	1

BRITISH AND IRISH INTERNATIONAL MANAGERS

England
Walter Winterbottom 1946–1962 (after period as coach); Alf Ramsey 1963–1974; Joe Mercer (caretaker) 1974; Don Revie 1974–1977; Ron Greenwood 1977–1982; Bobby Robson 1982–1990; Graham Taylor 1990–1993; Terry Venables (coach) 1994–1996; Glenn Hoddle 1996–1999; Kevin Keegan 1999–2000; Sven-Goran Eriksson 2001–2006; Steve McClaren 2006–2007; Fabio Capello 2008–2012; Roy Hodgson 2012–2016; Sam Allardyce 2016 for one match; Gareth Southgate from November 2016.

Northern Ireland
Peter Doherty 1951–1952; Bertie Peacock 1962–1967; Billy Bingham 1967–1971; Terry Neill 1971–1975; Dave Clements (player-manager) 1975–1976; Danny Blanchflower 1976–1979; Billy Bingham 1980–1994; Bryan Hamilton 1994–1998; Lawrie McMenemy 1998–1999; Sammy McIlroy 2000–2003; Lawrie Sanchez 2004–2007; Nigel Worthington 2007–2011; Michael O'Neill from December 2011.

Scotland (since 1967)
Bobby Brown 1967–1971; Tommy Docherty 1971–1972; Willie Ormond 1973–1977; Ally MacLeod 1977–1978; Jock Stein 1978–1985; Alex Ferguson (caretaker) 1985–1986 Andy Roxburgh (coach) 1986–1993; Craig Brown 1993–2001; Berti Vogts 2002–2004; Walter Smith 2004–2007; Alex McLeish 2007; George Burley 2008–2009; Craig Levein 2009–2012; Gordon Strachan 2013–2017; Alex McLeish from February 2018.

Wales (since 1974)
Mike Smith 1974–1979; Mike England 1980–1988; David Williams (caretaker) 1988; Terry Yorath 1988–1993; John Toshack 1994 for one match; Mike Smith 1994–1995; Bobby Gould 1995–1999; Mark Hughes 1999–2004; John Toshack 2004–2010; Gary Speed 2010–2011; Chris Coleman 2012–2017; Ryan Giggs from January 2018.

Republic of Ireland
Liam Tuohy 1971–1972; Johnny Giles 1973–1980 (after period as player-manager); Eoin Hand 1980–1985; Jack Charlton 1986–1996; Mick McCarthy 1996–2002; Brian Kerr 2003–2006; Steve Staunton 2006–2007; Giovanni Trapattoni 2008–2013; Martin O'Neill from November 2013.

OTHER BRITISH AND IRISH INTERNATIONAL MATCHES 2017–18

FRIENDLIES

Denotes player sent off.

ENGLAND

Friday, 10 November 2017
England (0) 0
Germany (0) 0   81,382
England: (343) Pickford; Trippier (Walker 71), Rose (Bertrand 71), Jones (Gomez 25); Stones, Maguire, Livermore (Cork 86), Dier; Loftus-Cheek, Vardy (Lingard 86), Abraham (Rashford 60).
Germany: (3421) ter Stegen; Kimmich, Rudiger, Hummels; Ginter, Gundogan (Rudy 86), Ozil, Halstenberg; Draxler (Can 67), Werner (Wagner 73); Sane (Brandt 87).
Referee: Pawel Raczkowski.

Tuesday, 14 November 2017
England (0) 0
Brazil (0) 0   84,595
England: (532) Hart; Walker, Gomez, Stones, Maguire, Bertrand (Young 80); Loftus-Cheek (Lingard 34), Dier, Livermore (Rose 90); Vardy (Solanke 75), Rashford (Abraham 75).
Brazil: (433) Alisson; Dani Alves, Marquinhos, Miranda, Marcelo; Casemiro, Paulinho, Renato Augusto (Fernandinho 68); Coutinho (Willian 67), Gabriel Jesus (Firmino 75), Neymar.
Referee: Artur Soares.

Friday, 23 March 2018
Netherlands (0) 0
England (0) 1 *(Lingard 59)*   51,500
Netherlands: (343) Zoet; de Ligt, de Vrij (Weghorst 90), van Dijk; Hateboer, Wijnaldum, Strootman (van de Beek 89), Van Aanholt; Promes (Propper 66), Depay, Dost (Babel 66).
England: (523) Pickford; Trippier, Walker, Stones, Gomez (Maguire 10 (Dier 89)), Rose (Young 71); Oxlade-Chamberlain, Henderson; Sterling (Welbeck 68), Rashford (Vardy 67), Lingard (Alli 68).
Referee: Jesus Gil Manzano.

Tuesday, 27 March 2018
England (1) 1 *(Vardy 27)*
Italy (0) 1 *(Insigne 88 (pen))*   82,598
England: (3142) Butland; Walker, Stones (Henderson 73), Tarkowski; Dier; Trippier (Rose 59), Oxlade-Chamberlain (Lallana 59), Lingard (Cook 70), Young; Vardy (Rashford 70), Sterling.
Italy: (433) Donnarumma; Zappacosta, Rugani, Bonucci, De Sciglio; Pellegrini (Gagliardini 79), Jorginho, Parolo; Candreva (Chiesa 56), Immobile (Belotti 64), Insigne.
Referee: Deniz Aytekin.

Saturday, 2 June 2018
England (2) 2 *(Cahill 7, Kane 39)*
Nigeria (0) 1 *(Iwobi 48)*   70,025
England: (3142) Pickford; Trippier, Young (Rose 67), Walker; Stones; Cahill, Lingard (Loftus-Cheek 67), Dier, Kane (Welbeck 73); Sterling (Rashford 72), Alli (Delph 81).
Nigeria: (433) Uzoho; Idowu, Troost-Ekong, Balogun (Omeruo 46), Onazi (Etebo 45); Mikel, Obi (Ogu 45), Abdullahi (Ebuehi 46); Ighalo (Iheanacho 76), Moses (Musa 63), Iwobi.
Referee: Marco Guid.

Thursday, 7 June 2018
England (1) 2 *(Rashford 13, Welbeck 76)*
Costa Rica (0) 0   36,104
England: (352) Butland (Pope 64); Jones, Stones (Cahill 65), Maguire; Alexander-Arnold (Trippier 64), Loftus-Cheek (Lingard 79), Henderson (Alli 64), Delph, Rose; Vardy (Welbeck 61), Rashford.

Costa Rica: (352) Navas; Waston, Gonzalez, Calvo; Gamboa (Smith 71), Guzman (Tejeda 69), Borges, Oviedo (Matarrita 61), Venegas (Bolanos 61); Campbell, Urena.
Referee: Hiroyuki Kimura.

SCOTLAND

Thursday, 9 November 2017
Scotland (0) 0
Netherlands (1) 1 *(Depay 41)*   17,838
Scotland: (433) Gordon; Jack, Robertson, Tierney, Berra (Mulgrew 46); McLean, McGinn, McGregor C (Cummings 87); Forrest (Fraser 71), Christie, Phillips.
Netherlands: (433) Cillessen; Fosu-Mensah (Veltman 71), van Dijk, Rekik, Ake; Wijnaldum, Blind, Strootman; Promes (Berghuis 76), Babel, Depay.
Referee: Ruddy Buquet.

Friday, 23 March 2018
Scotland (0) 0
Costa Rica (1) 1 *(Urena 14)*   20,488
Scotland: (4231) McGregor A; Paterson, Robertson, Hanley (McGinn 82); McKenna, McTominay (Armstrong 58); McDonald, Cairney (McGregor C 58), Ritchie (Murphy 87); McBurnie (Phillips 77).
Costa Rica: (541) Navas; Gamboa (Smith 76), Gonzalez, Acosta, Duarte, Oviedo (Calvo 78); Colindres (Wallace 63), Borges, Guzman (Tejeda 56), Ruiz B; Urena (Ruiz Y 70).
Referee: Tobias Stieler.

Tuesday, 27 March 2018
Hungary (0) 0
Scotland (0) 1 *(Phillips 48)*   9000
Hungary: (442) Gulacsi; Fiola, Otigba, Lovrencsics, Hangya (Szabo 47); Dzsudzsak (Nemeth 58), Pinter (Elek 46), Kleinheisler (Patkai 67), Varga (Nikolic 82); Guzmics, Szalai (Bode 77).
Scotland: (541) McGregor A; Fraser (Paterson 81), Hendry, Mulgrew, McKenna, Robertson (Douglas 66); Armstrong (McLean 69), McGregor C (Cummings 90), McGinn, Forrest (Christie 77); Phillips (McBurnie 83).
Referee: Harald Lechner.

Wednesday, 30 May 2018
Peru (1) 2 *(Cueva 37 (pen), Farfan 47)*
Scotland (0) 0
Peru: (433) Carvallo; Advincula (Corzo 86), Rodriguez, Ramos, Trauco; Tapia (Cartagena 84), Yotun (Ruidiaz 69), Flores; Carrillo (Polo 69), Cueva (Aquino 79), Farfan (Hurtado 80).
Scotland: (451) Archer; O'Donnell, Stevenson, McKenna, Mulgrew; McGeouch (Shinnie 76), McLean (Cadden 87), McGinn (Paterson 46), Phillips (Morgan 72), McTominay; Murphy (McBurnie 63).
Referee: Fernando Guerrero Ramirez.

Sunday, 3 June 2018
Mexico (1) 1 *(Giovani 13)*
Scotland (0) 0   70,993
Mexico: (4231) Ochoa; Salcedo (Marquez 46), Ayala, Gallardo, Layun; Herrera (Fabian 57), Alvarez; Lozano (Jesus Corona 73), Giovani (Jonathan 57), Vela (Aquino 63); Jimenez (Peralta 77).
Scotland: (4231) McLaughlin (Bain 46); O'Donnell, McKenna, Hendry, Shinnie; McLean (Cadden 55), McGeouch, Russell, Paterson (Mulgrew 55), Christie (McGinn 55); McBurnie (Morgan 80).
Referee: Henry Bejerano.

WALES

Friday, 10 November 2017

France (1) 2 *(Griezmann 18, Giroud 71)*

Wales (0) 0 60,000

France: (442) Mandanda; Jallet (Pavard 46), Koscielny, Umtiti, Kurzawa; Mbappe (Thauvin 83), Tolisso (Nzonzi 46), Matuidi, Coman (Martial 73); Griezmann (Fekir 63), Giroud (Lacazette 73).
Wales: (3511) Hennessey; Chester, Williams A, Davies (Woodburn 63); Gunter, Allen, Ledley (Ampadu 63), King (Brooks 63), Taylor; Ramsey; Vokes (Lawrence 83).
Referee: Jorge Sousa.

Tuesday, 14 November 2017

Wales (0) 1 *(Lawrence 75)*

Panama (0) 1 *(Cooper 90)*

Wales: (442) Ward; Gunter, Taylor, Davies (Lockyer 46), Chester; Vokes (Bradshaw 46), Lawrence, Edwards (Evans 62), Ampadu (Crofts 68); Brooks (Watkins 71), Woodburn (Hedges 71).
Panama: (442) Penedo; Murillo, Baloy, Escobar, Ovalle; Vargas M (Buitrago 70), Cooper, Heraldez, Avila (Vargas J 66); Perez (Stevens 87), Torres G (Diaz 64).
Referee: Bart Verteuten.

Thursday, 22 March 2018

China PR (0) 0

Wales (4) 6 *(Bale 2, 21, 62, Vokes 38, 58, Wilson 45)*

China PR: (433) Yan; Wang (Li 46), Hao, Huang (He C 47), Zheng; He G (Liu 46), Feng (Deng 71), Wu; Gao (Yu H 46), Yu D (Zhao 46), Wei.
Wales: (523) Hennessey; Gunter, Chester (Watkins 70), Williams A, Davies (Mepham 70), John; King, Allen (Evans 64); Wilson (Lockyer 72), Vokes (Bradshaw 63), Bale (Woodburn 63).
Referee: Mohd Bin Yaacob.

Monday, 26 March 2018

Wales (0) 0

Uruguay (0) 1 *(Cavani 50)*

Wales: (343) Hennessey; Chester (Lockyer 75), Williams A, Davies (Hedges 89); Gunter (Matthews 79), King, Allen, John (Roberts 59); Bale, Vokes (Bodin 67), Wilson (Evans 72).
Uruguay: (442) Muslera; Varela, Godin, Gimenez (Coates 8), Laxalt; Nandez (Stuani 85), Bentancur (Silva 78), Vecino, Rodriguez (Torreira 70); Suarez, Cavani (Gomez 90).
Referee: S Falahi.

Tuesday, 29 May 2018

Mexico (0) 0

Wales (0) 0 82,345

Mexico: (442) Jose de Jesus Corona; Gallardo, Alanis (Damm 46), Ayala, Alvarez; Molina (Salcedo 46), Gutierrez (Fabian 73), Herrera (Jonathan 60), Aquino; Hernandez (Peralta 59), Jesus Corona (Giovani 69).
Wales: (442) Hennessey; Gunter, Mepham, Williams A (Lockyer 20), Davies; Ledley (Brooks 46), King (Roberts 46), Ramsey, Wilson (Thomas 64); Lawrence (Smith 80), Vokes (John 46).
Referee: Armando Villarreal.

NORTHERN IRELAND

Saturday, 24 March 2018

Northern Ireland (1) 2 *(Min-Jae Kim 21 (og), Smyth 86)*

Korea Republic (1) 1 *(Kwon 7)* 18,103

Northern Ireland: (442) Carson; McAuley, Evans J (Cathcart 68), Hughes (McLaughlin C 18), Lewis; Jones (Smyth 82), Evans C (Washington 62), Saville, Norwood (McNair 71); Ward (Boyce 62), Magennis.
Korea Republic : (442) Seung-Gyu Kim; Min-Jae Kim, Jin-Su Kim (Min-Woo Kim 35), Lee Y, Jang; Ki (Jung 67), Park (Lee C 67), Kwon (Hwang 62), Lee J; Son (Yeom 75), Shin-Wook Kim.
Referee: Bobby Madden.

Wednesday, 30 May 2018

Panama (0) 0

Northern Ireland (0) 0 26,000

Panama: (451) Calderon; Machado, Baloy (Torres R 76), Escobar, Ovalle; Gomez (Pimentel 46), Barcenas, Godoy (Avila 49), Cooper (Camargo 46), Rodriguez (Diaz 60); Tejada (Perez 50).
Northern Ireland: (442) Carson; Ferguson (Smyth 75), Evans J, McAuley, Hughes; Evans C (Thompson 82), McNair, Cathcart, Boyce (McLaughlin C 72); Dallas (Hodson 60), Magennis (Lavery 90).
Referee: Henry Bejerano.

Sunday, 3 June 2018

Costa Rica (1) 3 *(Venegas 30, Campbell 46, Calvo 68)*

Northern Ireland (0) 0 35,100

Costa Rica: (541) Navas (Moreira 34); Gamboa (Smith 63), Acosta, Gonzalez (Waston 73), Duarte (Calvo 47), Oviedo; Colindres, Borges (Tejeda 63), Guzman, Campbell; Venegas (Matarrita 70).
Northern Ireland: (4141) Carson (Hazard 74); Hughes, McAuley, Evans J, Hodson (McLaughlin C 59); McNair; Dallas, Boyce (McCartan 38), Evans C (Thompson 85), Cathcart (McCullough 75); Magennis (McLaughlin R 59).
Referee: Fernando Guerrero Ramirez.

REPUBLIC OF IRELAND

Friday, 23 March 2018

Turkey (0) 1 *(Topal 52)*

Republic of Ireland (0) 0 32,000

Turkey: (442) Babacan; Gonul, Aziz (Ayhan 82), Soyuncu, Ali Kaldirim; Yazici (Potuk 87), Yokuslu, Topal, Calhanoglu (Kahveci 80); Akbaba (Malli 69), Tosun (Unal 65).
Republic of Ireland: (433) Doyle; Coleman (Doherty 63), Duffy, Long K, Rice; Hendrick (Judge 80), Browne (Meyler 68), Hourihane (Clark 71); Maguire (Long S 62), Hogan (Horgan 75), McClean.
Referee: Salvko Vincic.

Monday, 28 May 2018

France (2) 2 *(Giroud 41, Fekir 44)*

Republic of Ireland (0) 0 70,000

France: (433) Mandanda; Sidibe (Pavard 82), Rami, Umtiti (Kimpembe 64), Mendy (Lucas 64); Tolisso (Pogba 77), Nzonzi, Matuidi; Mbappe (Dembele 77), Giroud, Fekir (Griezmann 64).
Republic of Ireland: (433) Doyle; Coleman, Long K (Williams S 79), Duffy, Williams D (Doherty 82); Browne (Arter 60), Rice, O'Dowda (Burke 70); Walters (Meyler 60), Long S (Judge 69), McClean.
Referee: Georgi Kabakov.

Saturday, 2 June 2018

Republic of Ireland (0) 2 *(Burke 57, Judge 90)*

USA (1) 1 *(Wood 45)* 32,300

Republic of Ireland: (442) Doyle; Coleman, Duffy (Stevens 77), O'Shea (Lenihan 34), Long K; Rice, Hendrick (Arter 82), O'Dowda (Judge 88), McClean; Burke (Horgan 58), Walters.
USA: (4141) Hamid; Yedlin (Moore 69), Carter-Vickers (Parker 60), Miazga, Villafana; Trapp; Weah, Adams, McKennie (Corona 81), Rubin (De La Torre 77); Wood (Sargent 70).
Referee: Andrew Dallas.

BRITISH AND IRISH INTERNATIONAL APPEARANCES 1872–2018

This is a list of full international appearances by Englishmen, Irishmen, Scotsmen and Welshmen in matches against the Home Countries and against foreign nations. It does not include unofficial matches against Commonwealth and Empire countries. The year indicated refers to the player's international debut season; i.e. 2018 is the 2017–18 season. **Bold** type indicates players who have made an international appearance in season 2017–18.

As at July 2018.

ENGLAND

Abbott, W. 1902 (Everton)	1
Abraham, K. O. T. (Tammy) 2018 (Chelsea)	**2**
A'Court, A. 1958 (Liverpool)	5
Adams, T. A. 1987 (Arsenal)	66
Adcock, H. 1929 (Leicester C)	5
Agbonlahor, G. 2009 (Aston Villa)	3
Alcock, C. W. 1875 (Wanderers)	1
Alderson, J. T. 1923 (Crystal Palace)	1
Aldridge, A. 1888 (WBA, Walsall Town Swifts)	2
Alexander-Arnold, T. J. 2018 (Liverpool)	**2**
Allen, A. 1888 (Aston Villa)	1
Allen, A. 1960 (Stoke C)	3
Allen, C. 1984 (QPR, Tottenham H)	5
Allen, H. 1888 (Wolverhampton W)	5
Allen, J. P. 1934 (Portsmouth)	2
Allen, R. 1952 (WBA)	5
Alli, B. J. (Dele) 2016 (Tottenham H)	**30**
Alsford, W. J. 1935 (Tottenham H)	1
Amos, A. 1885 (Old Carthusians)	2
Anderson, R. D. 1879 (Old Etonians)	1
Anderson, S. 1962 (Sunderland)	2
Anderson, V. A. 1979 (Nottingham F, Arsenal, Manchester U)	30
Anderton, D. R. 1994 (Tottenham H)	30
Angus, J. 1961 (Burnley)	1
Armfield, J. C. 1959 (Blackpool)	43
Armitage, G. H. 1926 (Charlton Ath)	1
Armstrong, D. 1980 (Middlesbrough, Southampton)	3
Armstrong, K. 1955 (Chelsea)	1
Arnold, J. 1933 (Fulham)	1
Arthur, J. W. H. 1885 (Blackburn R)	7
Ashcroft, J. 1906 (Woolwich Arsenal)	3
Ashmore, G. S. 1926 (WBA)	1
Ashton, C. T. 1926 (Corinthians)	1
Ashton, D. 2008 (West Ham U)	1
Ashurst, W. 1923 (Notts Co)	5
Astall, G. 1956 (Birmingham C)	2
Astle, J. 1969 (WBA)	5
Aston, J. 1949 (Manchester U)	17
Athersmith, W. C. 1892 (Aston Villa)	12
Atyeo, P. J. W. 1956 (Bristol C)	6
Austin, S. W. 1926 (Manchester C)	1
Bach, P. 1899 (Sunderland)	1
Bache, J. W. 1903 (Aston Villa)	7
Baddeley, T. 1903 (Wolverhampton W)	5
Bagshaw, J. J. 1920 (Derby Co)	1
Bailey, G. R. 1985 (Manchester U)	2
Bailey, H. P. 1908 (Leicester Fosse)	5
Bailey, M. A. 1964 (Charlton Ath)	2
Bailey, N. C. 1878 (Clapham R)	19
Baily, E. F. 1950 (Tottenham H)	9
Bain, J. 1877 (Oxford University)	1
Baines, L. J. 2010 (Everton)	30
Baker, A. 1928 (Arsenal)	1
Baker, B. H. 1921 (Everton, Chelsea)	2
Baker, J. H. 1960 (Hibernian, Arsenal)	8
Ball, A. J. 1965 (Blackpool, Everton, Arsenal)	72
Ball, J. 1928 (Bury)	1
Ball, M. J. 2001 (Everton)	1
Balmer, W. 1905 (Everton)	1
Bamber, J. 1921 (Liverpool)	1
Bambridge, A. L. 1881 (Swifts)	3
Bambridge, E. C. 1879 (Swifts)	18
Bambridge, E. H. 1876 (Swifts)	1
Banks, G. 1963 (Leicester C, Stoke C)	73
Banks, H. E. 1901 (Millwall)	1
Banks, T. 1958 (Bolton W)	6
Bannister, W. 1901 (Burnley, Bolton W)	2
Barclay, R. 1932 (Sheffield U)	3

Bardsley, D. J. 1993 (QPR)	2
Barham, M. 1983 (Norwich C)	2
Barkas, S. 1936 (Manchester C)	5
Barker, J. 1935 (Derby Co)	11
Barker, R. 1872 (Herts Rangers)	1
Barker, R. R. 1895 (Casuals)	1
Barkley, R. 2013 (Everton)	22
Barlow, R. J. 1955 (WBA)	1
Barmby, N. J. 1995 (Tottenham H, Middlesbrough, Everton, Liverpool)	23
Barnes, J. 1983 (Watford, Liverpool)	79
Barnes, P. S. 1978 (Manchester C, WBA, Leeds U)	22
Barnet, H. H. 1882 (Royal Engineers)	1
Barrass, M. W. 1952 (Bolton W)	3
Barrett, A. F. 1930 (Fulham)	1
Barrett, E. D. 1991 (Oldham Ath, Aston Villa)	3
Barrett, J. W. 1929 (West Ham U)	1
Barry, G. 2000 (Aston Villa, Manchester C)	53
Barry, L. 1928 (Leicester C)	5
Barson, F. 1920 (Aston Villa)	1
Barton, J. 1890 (Blackburn R)	1
Barton, J. 2007 (Manchester C)	1
Barton, P. H. 1921 (Birmingham)	7
Barton, W. D. 1995 (Wimbledon, Newcastle U)	3
Bassett, W. I. 1888 (WBA)	16
Bastard, S. R. 1880 (Upton Park)	1
Bastin, C. S. 1932 (Arsenal)	21
Batty, D. 1991 (Leeds U, Blackburn R, Newcastle U, Leeds U)	42
Baugh, R. 1886 (Stafford Road, Wolverhampton W)	2
Bayliss, A. E. J. M. 1891 (WBA)	1
Baynham, R. L. 1956 (Luton T)	3
Beardsley, P. A. 1986 (Newcastle U, Liverpool, Newcastle U)	59
Beasant, D. J. 1990 (Chelsea)	2
Beasley, A. 1939 (Huddersfield T)	1
Beats, W. E. 1901 (Wolverhampton W)	2
Beattie, J. S. 2003 (Southampton)	5
Beattie, T. K. 1975 (Ipswich T)	9
Beckham, D. R. J. 1997 (Manchester U, Real Madrid, LA Galaxy)	115
Becton, F. 1895 (Preston NE, Liverpool)	2
Bedford, H. 1923 (Blackpool)	2
Bell, C. 1968 (Manchester C)	48
Bennett, W. 1901 (Sheffield U)	2
Benson, R. W. 1913 (Sheffield U)	1
Bent, D. A. 2006 (Charlton Ath, Tottenham H, Sunderland, Aston Villa)	13
Bentley, D. M. 2008 (Blackburn R, Tottenham H)	7
Bentley, R. T. F. 1949 (Chelsea)	12
Beresford, J. 1934 (Aston Villa)	1
Berry, A. 1909 (Oxford University)	1
Berry, J. J. 1953 (Manchester U)	4
Bertrand, R. 2013 (Chelsea, Southampton)	**19**
Bestall, J. G. 1935 (Grimsby T)	1
Betmead, H. A. 1937 (Grimsby T)	1
Betts, M. P. 1877 (Old Harrovians)	1
Betts, W. 1889 (Sheffield W)	1
Beverley, J. 1884 (Blackburn R)	3
Birkett, R. H. 1879 (Clapham R)	1
Birkett, R. J. E. 1936 (Middlesbrough)	1
Birley, F. H. 1874 (Oxford University, Wanderers)	2
Birtles, G. 1980 (Nottingham F)	3
Bishop, S. M. 1927 (Leicester C)	4
Blackburn, F. 1901 (Blackburn R)	3
Blackburn, G. F. 1924 (Aston Villa)	1
Blenkinsop, E. 1928 (Sheffield W)	26
Bliss, H. 1921 (Tottenham H)	1
Blissett, L. L. 1983 (Watford, AC Milan)	14
Blockley, J. P. 1973 (Arsenal)	1

Bloomer, S. 1895 (Derby Co, Middlesbrough) — 23
Blunstone, F. 1955 (Chelsea) — 5
Bond, R. 1905 (Preston NE, Bradford C) — 8
Bonetti, P. P. 1966 (Chelsea) — 7
Bonsor, A. G. 1873 (Wanderers) — 2
Booth, F. 1905 (Manchester C) — 1
Booth, T. 1898 (Blackburn R, Everton) — 2
Bothroyd, J. 2011 (Cardiff C) — 1
Bould, S. A. 1994 (Arsenal) — 2
Bowden, E. R. 1935 (Arsenal) — 6
Bower, A. G. 1924 (Corinthians) — 5
Bowers, J. W. 1934 (Derby Co) — 3
Bowles, S. 1974 (QPR) — 5
Bowser, S. 1920 (WBA) — 1
Bowyer, L. D. 2003 (Leeds U) — 1
Boyer, P. J. 1976 (Norwich C) — 1
Boyes, W. 1935 (WBA, Everton) — 3
Boyle, T. W. 1913 (Burnley) — 1
Brabrook, P. 1958 (Chelsea) — 3
Bracewell, P. W. 1985 (Everton) — 3
Bradford, G. R. W. 1956 (Bristol R) — 1
Bradford, J. 1924 (Birmingham) — 12
Bradley, W. 1959 (Manchester U) — 3
Bradshaw, F. 1908 (Sheffield W) — 1
Bradshaw, T. H. 1897 (Liverpool) — 1
Bradshaw, W. 1910 (Blackburn R) — 4
Brann, G. 1886 (Swifts) — 3
Brawn, W. F. 1904 (Aston Villa) — 2
Bray, J. 1935 (Manchester C) — 6
Brayshaw, E. 1887 (Sheffield W) — 1
Bridge W. M. 2002 (Southampton, Chelsea, Manchester C) — 36
Bridges, B. J. 1965 (Chelsea) — 4
Bridgett, A. 1905 (Sunderland) — 11
Brindle, T. 1880 (Darwen) — 2
Brittleton, J. T. 1912 (Sheffield W) — 5
Britton, C. S. 1935 (Everton) — 9
Broadbent, P. F. 1958 (Wolverhampton W) — 7
Broadis, I. A. 1952 (Manchester C, Newcastle U) — 14
Brockbank, J. 1872 (Cambridge University) — 1
Brodie, J. B. 1889 (Wolverhampton W) — 3
Bromilow, T. G. 1921 (Liverpool) — 5
Bromley-Davenport, W. E. 1884 (Oxford University) — 2
Brook, E. F. 1930 (Manchester C) — 18
Brooking, T. D. 1974 (West Ham U) — 47
Brooks, J. 1957 (Tottenham H) — 3
Broome, F. H. 1938 (Aston Villa) — 7
Brown, A. 1882 (Aston Villa) — 3
Brown, A. 1971 (WBA) — 1
Brown, A. S. 1904 (Sheffield U) — 2
Brown, G. 1927 (Huddersfield T, Aston Villa) — 9
Brown, J. 1881 (Blackburn R) — 5
Brown, J. H. 1927 (Sheffield W) — 6
Brown, K. 1960 (West Ham U) — 1
Brown, W. 1924 (West Ham U) — 1
Brown, W. M. 1999 (Manchester U) — 23
Bruton, J. 1928 (Burnley) — 3
Bryant, W. I. 1925 (Clapton) — 1
Buchan, C. M. 1913 (Sunderland) — 6
Buchanan, W. S. 1876 (Clapham R) — 1
Buckley, F. C. 1914 (Derby Co) — 1
Bull, S. G. 1989 (Wolverhampton W) — 13
Bullock, F. E. 1921 (Huddersfield T) — 1
Bullock, N. 1923 (Bury) — 3
Burgess, H. 1904 (Manchester C) — 4
Burgess, H. 1931 (Sheffield W) — 4
Burnup, C. J. 1896 (Cambridge University) — 1
Burrows, H. 1934 (Sheffield W) — 3
Burton, F. E. 1889 (Nottingham F) — 1
Bury, L. 1877 (Cambridge University, Old Etonians) — 2
Butcher, T. 1980 (Ipswich T, Rangers) — 77
Butland, J. 2013 (Birmingham C, Stoke C) — **8**
Butler, J. D. 1925 (Arsenal) — 1
Butler, W. 1924 (Bolton W) — 1
Butt, N. 1997 (Manchester U, Newcastle U) — 39
Byrne, G. 1963 (Liverpool) — 2
Byrne, J. J. 1962 (Crystal Palace, West Ham U) — 11
Byrne, R. W. 1954 (Manchester U) — 33

Cahill, G. J. 2011 (Bolton W, Chelsea) — **61**
Callaghan, I. R. 1966 (Liverpool) — 4
Calvey, J. 1902 (Nottingham F) — 1
Campbell, A. F. 1929 (Blackburn R, Huddersfield T) — 8
Campbell, F. L. 2012 (Sunderland) — 1

Campbell, S. 1996 (Tottenham H, Arsenal, Portsmouth) — 73
Camsell, G. H. 1929 (Middlesbrough) — 9
Capes, A. J. 1903 (Stoke) — 1
Carr, J. 1905 (Newcastle U) — 2
Carr, J. 1920 (Middlesbrough) — 2
Carr, W. H. 1875 (Owlerton, Sheffield) — 1
Carragher, J. L. 1999 (Liverpool) — 38
Carrick, M. 2001 (West Ham U, Tottenham H, Manchester U) — 34
Carroll, A. T. 2011 (Newcastle U, Liverpool) — 9
Carson, S. P. 2008 (Liverpool, WBA) — 4
Carter, H. S. 1934 (Sunderland, Derby Co) — 13
Carter, J. H. 1926 (WBA) — 3
Catlin, A. E. 1937 (Sheffield W) — 5
Caulker, S. A. 2013 (Tottenham H) — 1
Chadwick, A. 1900 (Southampton) — 2
Chadwick, E. 1891 (Everton) — 7
Chamberlain, M. 1983 (Stoke C) — 8
Chambers, H. 1921 (Liverpool) — 8
Chambers, C. 2015 (Arsenal) — 3
Channon, M. R. 1973 (Southampton, Manchester C) — 46
Charles, G. A. 1991 (Nottingham F) — 2
Charlton, J. 1965 (Leeds U) — 35
Charlton, R. 1958 (Manchester U) — 106
Charnley, R. O. 1963 (Blackpool) — 1
Charsley, C. C. 1893 (Small Heath) — 1
Chedgzoy, S. 1920 (Everton) — 8
Chenery, C. J. 1872 (Crystal Palace) — 3
Cherry, T. J. 1976 (Leeds U) — 27
Chilton, A. 1951 (Manchester U) — 2
Chippendale, H. 1894 (Blackburn R) — 1
Chivers, M. 1971 (Tottenham H) — 24
Christian, E. 1879 (Old Etonians) — 1
Clamp, E. 1958 (Wolverhampton W) — 4
Clapton, D. R. 1959 (Arsenal) — 1
Clare, T. 1889 (Stoke) — 4
Clarke, A. J. 1970 (Leeds U) — 19
Clarke, H. A. 1954 (Tottenham H) — 1
Clay, T. 1920 (Tottenham H) — 4
Clayton, R. 1956 (Blackburn R) — 35
Clegg, J. C. 1872 (Sheffield W) — 1
Clegg, W. E. 1873 (Sheffield W, Sheffield Alb) — 2
Clemence, R. N. 1973 (Liverpool, Tottenham H) — 61
Clement, D. T. 1976 (QPR) — 5
Cleverley, T. W. 2013 (Manchester U) — 13
Clough, B. H. 1960 (Middlesbrough) — 2
Clough, N. H. 1989 (Nottingham F) — 14
Clyne, N. E. 2015 (Southampton, Liverpool) — 14
Coates, R. 1970 (Burnley, Tottenham H) — 4
Cobbold, W. N. 1883 (Cambridge University, Old Carthusians) — 9
Cock, J. G. 1920 (Huddersfield T, Chelsea) — 2
Cockburn, H. 1947 (Manchester U) — 13
Cohen, G. R. 1964 (Fulham) — 37
Cole, A. 2001 (Arsenal, Chelsea) — 107
Cole, A. A. 1995 (Manchester U) — 15
Cole, C. 2009 (West Ham U) — 7
Cole, J. J. 2001 (West Ham U, Chelsea) — 56
Colclough, H. 1914 (Crystal Palace) — 1
Coleman, E. H. 1921 (Dulwich Hamlet) — 1
Coleman, J. 1907 (Woolwich Arsenal) — 1
Collymore, S. V. 1995 (Nottingham F, Aston Villa) — 3
Common, A. 1904 (Sheffield U, Middlesbrough) — 3
Compton, L. H. 1951 (Arsenal) — 2
Conlin, J. 1906 (Bradford C) — 1
Connelly, J. M. 1960 (Burnley, Manchester U) — 20
Cook, L. J. 2018 (Bournemouth) — **1**
Cook, T. E. R. 1925 (Brighton) — 1
Cooper, C. T. 1995 (Nottingham F) — 2
Cooper, N. C. 1893 (Cambridge University) — 1
Cooper, T. 1928 (Derby Co) — 15
Cooper, T. 1969 (Leeds U) — 20
Coppell, S. J. 1978 (Manchester U) — 42
Copping, W. 1933 (Leeds U, Arsenal, Leeds U) — 20
Corbett, B. O. 1901 (Corinthians) — 1
Corbett, R. 1903 (Old Malvernians) — 1
Corbett, W. S. 1908 (Birmingham) — 3
Cork, J. F. P. 2018 (Burnley) — **1**
Corrigan, J. T. 1976 (Manchester C) — 9
Cottee, A. R. 1987 (West Ham U, Everton) — 7
Cotterill, G. H. 1891 (Cambridge University, Old Brightonians) — 4
Cottle, J. R. 1909 (Bristol C) — 1

Cowan, S. 1926 (Manchester C)	3
Cowans, G. S. 1983 (Aston Villa, Bari, Aston Villa)	10
Cowell, A. 1910 (Blackburn R)	1
Cox, J. 1901 (Liverpool)	3
Cox, J. D. 1892 (Derby Co)	1
Crabtree, J. W. 1894 (Burnley, Aston Villa)	14
Crawford, J. F. 1931 (Chelsea)	1
Crawford, R. 1962 (Ipswich T)	2
Crawshaw, T. H. 1895 (Sheffield W)	10
Crayston, W. J. 1936 (Arsenal)	8
Creek, F. N. S. 1923 (Corinthians)	1
Cresswell, A. W. 2017 (West Ham U)	**3**
Cresswell, W. 1921 (South Shields, Sunderland, Everton)	7
Crompton, R. 1902 (Blackburn R)	41
Crooks, S. D. 1930 (Derby Co)	26
Crouch, P. J. 2005 (Southampton, Liverpool, Portsmouth, Tottenham H)	42
Crowe, C. 1963 (Wolverhampton W)	1
Cuggy, F. 1913 (Sunderland)	2
Cullis, S. 1938 (Wolverhampton W)	12
Cunliffe, A. 1933 (Blackburn R)	2
Cunliffe, D. 1900 (Portsmouth)	1
Cunliffe, J. N. 1936 (Everton)	1
Cunningham, L. 1979 (WBA, Real Madrid)	6
Curle, K. 1992 (Manchester C)	3
Currey, E. S. 1890 (Oxford University)	2
Currie, A. W. 1972 (Sheffield U, Leeds U)	17
Cursham, A. W. 1876 (Notts Co)	6
Cursham, H. A. 1880 (Notts Co)	8
Daft, H. B. 1889 (Notts Co)	5
Daley, A. M. 1992 (Aston Villa)	7
Danks, T. 1885 (Nottingham F)	1
Davenport, P. 1985 (Nottingham F)	1
Davenport, J. K. 1885 (Bolton W)	2
Davies, K. C. 2011 (Bolton W)	1
Davis, G. 1904 (Derby Co)	2
Davis, H. 1903 (Sheffield W)	3
Davison, J. E. 1922 (Sheffield W)	1
Dawson, J. 1922 (Burnley)	2
Dawson, M. R. 2011 (Tottenham H)	4
Day, S. H. 1906 (Old Malvernians)	3
Dean, W. R. 1927 (Everton)	16
Deane, B. C. 1991 (Sheffield U)	3
Deeley, N. V. 1959 (Wolverhampton W)	2
Defoe, J. C. 2004 (Tottenham H, Portsmouth, Tottenham H, Sunderland)	57
Delph, F. 2015 (Aston Villa, Manchester C)	**15**
Devey, J. H. G. 1892 (Aston Villa)	2
Devonshire, A. 1980 (West Ham U)	8
Dewhurst, F. 1886 (Preston NE)	9
Dewhurst, G. P. 1895 (Liverpool Ramblers)	1
Dickinson, J. W. 1949 (Portsmouth)	48
Dier, E. J. E. 2016 (Tottenham H)	**32**
Dimmock, J. H. 1921 (Tottenham H)	3
Ditchburn, E. G. 1949 (Tottenham H)	6
Dix, R. W. 1939 (Derby Co)	1
Dixon, J. A. 1885 (Notts Co)	1
Dixon, K. M. 1985 (Chelsea)	8
Dixon, L. M. 1990 (Arsenal)	22
Dobson, A. T. C. 1882 (Notts Co)	4
Dobson, C. F. 1886 (Notts Co)	1
Dobson, J. M. 1974 (Burnley, Everton)	5
Doggart, A. G. 1924 (Corinthians)	1
Dorigo, A. R. 1990 (Chelsea, Leeds U)	15
Dorrell, A. R. 1925 (Aston Villa)	4
Douglas, B. 1958 (Blackburn R)	36
Downing, S. 2005 (Middlesbrough, Aston Villa, Liverpool, West Ham U)	35
Downs, R. W. 1921 (Everton)	1
Doyle, M. 1976 (Manchester C)	5
Drake, E. J. 1935 (Arsenal)	5
Drinkwater, D. N. 2016 (Leicester C)	3
Dublin, D. 1998 (Coventry C, Aston Villa)	4
Ducat, A. 1910 (Woolwich Arsenal, Aston Villa)	6
Dunn, A. T. B. 1883 (Cambridge University, Old Etonians)	4
Dunn, D. J. I. 2003 (Blackburn R)	1
Duxbury, M. 1984 (Manchester U)	10
Dyer, K. C. 2000 (Newcastle U, West Ham U)	33
Earle, S. G. J. 1924 (Clapton, West Ham U)	2
Eastham, G. 1963 (Arsenal)	19
Eastham, G. R. 1935 (Bolton W)	1

Eckersley, W. 1950 (Blackburn R)	17
Edwards, D. 1955 (Manchester U)	18
Edwards, J. H. 1874 (Shropshire Wanderers)	1
Edwards, W. 1926 (Leeds U)	16
Ehiogu, U. 1996 (Aston Villa, Middlesbrough)	4
Ellerington, W. 1949 (Southampton)	2
Elliott, G. W. 1913 (Middlesbrough)	3
Elliott, W. H. 1952 (Burnley)	5
Evans, R. E. 1911 (Sheffield U)	4
Ewer, F. H. 1924 (Casuals)	2
Fairclough, P. 1878 (Old Foresters)	1
Fairhurst, D. 1934 (Newcastle U)	1
Fantham, J. 1962 (Sheffield W)	1
Fashanu, J. 1989 (Wimbledon)	2
Felton, W. 1925 (Sheffield W)	1
Fenton, M. 1938 (Middlesbrough)	1
Fenwick, T. W. 1984 (QPR, Tottenham H)	20
Ferdinand, L. 1993 (QPR, Newcastle U, Tottenham H)	17
Ferdinand, R. G. 1998 (West Ham U, Leeds U, Manchester U)	81
Field, E. 1876 (Clapham R)	2
Finney, T. 1947 (Preston NE)	76
Flanagan, J. P. 2014 (Liverpool)	1
Fleming, H. J. 1909 (Swindon T)	11
Fletcher, A. 1889 (Wolverhampton W)	2
Flowers, R. 1955 (Wolverhampton W)	49
Flowers, T. D. 1993 (Southampton, Blackburn R)	11
Forman, Frank 1898 (Nottingham F)	9
Forman, F. R. 1899 (Nottingham F)	3
Forrest, J. H. 1884 (Blackburn R)	11
Forster, F. G. 2013 (Celtic, Southampton)	6
Fort, J. 1921 (Millwall)	1
Foster, B. 2007 (Manchester U, Birmingham C, WBA)	8
Foster, R. E. 1900 (Oxford University, Corinthians)	5
Foster, S. 1982 (Brighton & HA)	3
Foulke, W. J. 1897 (Sheffield U)	1
Foulkes, W. A. 1955 (Manchester U)	1
Fowler, R. B. 1996 (Liverpool, Leeds U)	26
Fox, F. S. 1925 (Millwall)	1
Francis, G. C. J. 1975 (QPR)	12
Francis, T. 1977 (Birmingham C, Nottingham F, Manchester C, Sampdoria)	52
Franklin, C. F. 1947 (Stoke C)	27
Freeman, B. C. 1909 (Everton, Burnley)	5
Froggatt, J. 1950 (Portsmouth)	13
Froggatt, R. 1953 (Sheffield W)	4
Fry, C. B. 1901 (Corinthians)	1
Furness, W. I. 1933 (Leeds U)	1
Galley, T. 1937 (Wolverhampton W)	2
Gardner, A. 2004 (Tottenham H)	1
Gardner, T. 1934 (Aston Villa)	2
Garfield, B. 1898 (WBA)	1
Garraty, W. 1903 (Aston Villa)	1
Garrett, T. 1952 (Blackpool)	3
Gascoigne, P. J. 1989 (Tottenham H, Lazio, Rangers, Middlesbrough)	57
Gates, E. 1981 (Ipswich T)	2
Gay, L. H. 1893 (Cambridge University, Old Brightonians)	3
Geary, F. 1890 (Everton)	2
Geaves, R. L. 1875 (Clapham R)	1
Gee, C. W. 1932 (Everton)	3
Geldard, A. 1933 (Everton)	4
George, C. 1977 (Derby Co)	1
George, W. 1902 (Aston Villa)	3
Gerrard, S. G. 2000 (Liverpool)	114
Gibbins, W. V. T. 1924 (Clapton)	2
Gibbs, K. J. R. 2011 (Arsenal)	10
Gidman, J. 1977 (Aston Villa)	1
Gillard, I. T. 1975 (QPR)	3
Gilliat, W. E. 1893 (Old Carthusians)	1
Goddard, P. 1982 (West Ham U)	1
Gomez, J. D. 2018 (Liverpool)	**3**
Goodall, F. R. 1926 (Huddersfield T)	25
Goodall, J. 1888 (Preston NE, Derby Co)	14
Goodhart, H. C. 1883 (Old Etonians)	3
Goodwyn, A. G. 1873 (Royal Engineers)	1
Goodyer, A. C. 1879 (Nottingham F)	1
Gosling, R. C. 1892 (Old Etonians)	5
Gosnell, A. A. 1906 (Newcastle U)	1
Gough, H. C. 1921 (Sheffield U)	1
Goulden, L. A. 1937 (West Ham U)	14

Graham, L. 1925 (Millwall)	2
Graham, T. 1931 (Nottingham F)	2
Grainger, C. 1956 (Sheffield U, Sunderland)	7
Gray, A. A. 1992 (Crystal Palace)	1
Gray, M. 1999 (Sunderland)	3
Greaves, J. 1959 (Chelsea, Tottenham H)	57
Green, F. T. 1876 (Wanderers)	1
Green, G. H. 1925 (Sheffield U)	8
Green, R. P. 2005 (Norwich C, West Ham U)	12
Greenhalgh, E. H. 1872 (Notts Co)	2
Greenhoff, B. 1976 (Manchester U, Leeds U)	18
Greenwood, D. H. 1882 (Blackburn R)	2
Gregory, J. 1983 (QPR)	6
Grimsdell, A. 1920 (Tottenham H)	6
Grosvenor, A. T. 1934 (Birmingham)	3
Gunn, W. 1884 (Notts Co)	2
Guppy, S. 2000 (Leicester C)	1
Gurney, R. 1935 (Sunderland)	1

Hacking, J. 1929 (Oldham Ath)	3
Hadley, H. 1903 (WBA)	1
Hagan, J. 1949 (Sheffield U)	1
Haines, J. T. W. 1949 (WBA)	1
Hall, A. E. 1910 (Aston Villa)	1
Hall, G. W. 1934 (Tottenham H)	10
Hall, J. 1956 (Birmingham C)	17
Halse, H. J. 1909 (Manchester U)	1
Hammond, H. E. D. 1889 (Oxford University)	1
Hampson, J. 1931 (Blackpool)	3
Hampton, H. 1913 (Aston Villa)	4
Hancocks, J. 1949 (Wolverhampton W)	3
Hapgood, E. 1933 (Arsenal)	30
Hardinge, H. T. W. 1910 (Sheffield U)	1
Hardman, H. P. 1905 (Everton)	4
Hardwick, G. F. M. 1947 (Middlesbrough)	13
Hardy, H. 1925 (Stockport Co)	1
Hardy, S. 1907 (Liverpool, Aston Villa)	21
Harford, M. G. 1988 (Luton T)	2
Hargreaves, F. W. 1880 (Blackburn R)	3
Hargreaves, J. 1881 (Blackburn R)	2
Hargreaves, O. 2002 (Bayern Munich, Manchester U)	42
Harper, E. C. 1926 (Blackburn R)	1
Harris, G. 1966 (Burnley)	1
Harris, P. P. 1950 (Portsmouth)	2
Harris, S. S. 1904 (Cambridge University,
    Old Westminsters)	6
Harrison, A. H. 1893 (Old Westminsters)	2
Harrison, G. 1921 (Everton)	2
Harrow, J. H. 1923 (Chelsea)	2
Hart, C. J. J. 2008 (Manchester C)	**75**
Hart, E. 1929 (Leeds U)	8
Hartley, F. 1923 (Oxford C)	1
Harvey, A. 1881 (Wednesbury Strollers)	1
Harvey, J. C. 1971 (Everton)	1
Hassall, H. W. 1951 (Huddersfield T, Bolton W)	5
Hateley, M. 1984 (Portsmouth, AC Milan, Monaco,
    Rangers)	32
Hawkes, R. M. 1907 (Luton T)	5
Haworth, G. 1887 (Accrington)	5
Hawtrey, J. P. 1881 (Old Etonians)	2
Haygarth, E. B. 1875 (Swifts)	1
Haynes, J. N. 1955 (Fulham)	56
Healless, H. 1925 (Blackburn R)	2
Heaton, T. 2016 (Burnley)	3
Hector, K. J. 1974 (Derby Co)	2
Hedley, G. A. 1901 (Sheffield U)	1
Hegan, K. E. 1923 (Corinthians)	4
Hellawell, M. S. 1963 (Birmingham C)	2
Henderson, J. B. 2011 (Sunderland, Liverpool)	**44**
Hendrie, L. A. 1999 (Aston Villa)	1
Henfrey, A. G. 1891 (Cambridge University,
    Corinthians)	5
Henry, R. P. 1963 (Tottenham H)	1
Heron, F. 1876 (Wanderers)	1
Heron, G. H. H. 1873 (Uxbridge, Wanderers)	5
Heskey, E. W. I. 1999 (Leicester C, Liverpool,
    Birmingham C, Wigan Ath, Aston Villa)	62
Hibbert, W. 1910 (Bury)	1
Hibbs, H. E. 1930 (Birmingham)	25
Hill, F. 1963 (Bolton W)	2
Hill, G. A. 1976 (Manchester U)	6
Hill, J. H. 1925 (Burnley, Newcastle U)	11
Hill, R. 1983 (Luton T)	3
Hill, R. H. 1926 (Millwall)	1

Hillman, J. 1899 (Burnley)	1
Hills, A. F. 1879 (Old Harrovians)	1
Hilsdon, G. R. 1907 (Chelsea)	8
Hinchcliffe, A. G. 1997 (Everton, Sheffield W)	7
Hine, E. W. 1929 (Leicester C)	6
Hinton, A. T. 1963 (Wolverhampton W, Nottingham F)	3
Hirst, D. E. 1991 (Sheffield W)	3
Hitchens, G. A. 1961 (Aston Villa, Internazionale)	7
Hobbis, H. H. F. 1936 (Charlton Ath)	2
Hoddle, G. 1980 (Tottenham H, Monaco)	53
Hodge, S. B. 1986 (Aston Villa, Tottenham H,
    Nottingham F)	24
Hodgetts, D. 1888 (Aston Villa)	6
Hodgkinson, A. 1957 (Sheffield U)	5
Hodgson, G. 1931 (Liverpool)	3
Hodkinson, J. 1913 (Blackburn R)	3
Hogg, W. 1902 (Sunderland)	3
Holdcroft, G. H. 1937 (Preston NE)	2
Holden, A. D. 1959 (Bolton W)	5
Holden, G. H. 1881 (Wednesbury OA)	4
Holden-White, C. 1888 (Corinthians)	2
Holford, T. 1903 (Stoke)	1
Holley, G. H. 1909 (Sunderland)	10
Holliday, E. 1960 (Middlesbrough)	3
Hollins, J. W. 1967 (Chelsea)	1
Holmes, R. 1888 (Preston NE)	7
Holt, J. 1890 (Everton, Reading)	10
Hopkinson, E. 1958 (Bolton W)	14
Hossack, A. H. 1892 (Corinthians)	2
Houghton, W. E. 1931 (Aston Villa)	7
Houlker, A. E. 1902 (Blackburn R, Portsmouth,
    Southampton)	5
Howarth, R. H. 1887 (Preston NE, Everton)	5
Howe, D. 1958 (WBA)	23
Howe, J. R. 1948 (Derby Co)	3
Howell, L. S. 1873 (Wanderers)	1
Howell, R. 1895 (Sheffield U, Liverpool)	2
Howey, S. N. 1995 (Newcastle U)	4
Huddlestone, T. A. 2010 (Tottenham H)	4
Hudson, A. A. 1975 (Stoke C)	2
Hudson, J. 1883 (Sheffield)	1
Hudspeth, F. C. 1926 (Newcastle U)	1
Hufton, A. E. 1924 (West Ham U)	6
Hughes, E. W. 1970 (Liverpool, Wolverhampton W)	62
Hughes, L. 1950 (Liverpool)	3
Hulme, J. H. A. 1927 (Arsenal)	9
Humphreys, P. 1903 (Notts Co)	1
Hunt, G. S. 1933 (Tottenham H)	3
Hunt, Rev. K. R. G. 1911 (Leyton)	2
Hunt, R. 1962 (Liverpool)	34
Hunt, S. 1984 (WBA)	2
Hunter, J. 1878 (Sheffield Heeley)	7
Hunter, N. 1966 (Leeds U)	28
Hurst, G. C. 1966 (West Ham U)	49

Ince, P. E. C. 1993 (Manchester U, Internazionale,
    Liverpool, Middlesbrough)	53
Ings, D. 2016 (Liverpool)	1
Iremonger, J. 1901 (Nottingham F)	2

Jack, D. N. B. 1924 (Bolton W, Arsenal)	9
Jackson, E. 1891 (Oxford University)	1
Jagielka, P. N. 2008 (Everton)	40
James, D. B. 1997 (Liverpool, Aston Villa, West Ham U,
    Manchester C, Portsmouth)	53
Jarrett, B. G. 1876 (Cambridge University)	3
Jarvis, M. T. 2011 (Wolverhampton W)	1
Jefferis, F. 1912 (Everton)	2
Jeffers, F. 2003 (Arsenal)	1
Jenas, J. A. 2003 (Newcastle U, Tottenham H)	21
Jenkinson, C. D. 2013 (Arsenal)	1
Jezzard, B. A. G. 1954 (Fulham)	2
Johnson, A. 2005 (Crystal Palace, Everton)	8
Johnson, A. 2010 (Manchester C)	12
Johnson, D. E. 1975 (Ipswich T, Liverpool)	8
Johnson, E. 1880 (Saltley College, Stoke)	2
Johnson, G. M. C. 2004 (Chelsea, Portsmouth,
    Liverpool)	54
Johnson, J. A. 1937 (Stoke C)	5
Johnson, S. A. M. 2001 (Derby Co)	1
Johnson, T. C. F. 1926 (Manchester C, Everton)	5
Johnson, W. H. 1900 (Sheffield U)	6
Johnston, H. 1947 (Blackpool)	10
Jones, A. 1882 (Walsall Swifts, Great Lever)	3

Jones, H. 1923 (Nottingham F) 1
Jones, H. 1927 (Blackburn R) 6
Jones, M. D. 1965 (Sheffield U, Leeds U) 3
Jones, P. A. 2012 (Manchester U) **27**
Jones, R. 1992 (Liverpool) 8
Jones, W. 1901 (Bristol C) 1
Jones, W. H. 1950 (Liverpool) 2
Joy, B. 1936 (Casuals) 1

Kail, E. I. L. 1929 (Dulwich Hamlet) 3
Kane, H. E. 2015 (Tottenham H) **30**
Kay, A. H. 1963 (Everton) 1
Kean, F. W. 1923 (Sheffield W, Bolton W) 9
Keane, M. V. 2017 (Burnley, Everton) **4**
Keegan, J. K. 1973 (Liverpool, SV Hamburg,
  Southampton) 63
Keen, E. R. L. 1933 (Derby Co) 4
Kelly, M. R. 2012 (Liverpool) 1
Kelly, R. 1920 (Burnley, Sunderland, Huddersfield T) 14
Kennedy, A. 1984 (Liverpool) 2
Kennedy, R. 1976 (Liverpool) 17
Kenyon-Slaney, W. S. 1873 (Wanderers) 1
Keown, M. R. 1992 (Everton, Arsenal) 43
Kevan, D. T. 1957 (WBA) 14
Kidd, B. 1970 (Manchester U) 2
King, L. B. 2002 (Tottenham H) 21
King, R. S. 1882 (Oxford University) 1
Kingsford, R. K. 1874 (Wanderers) 1
Kingsley, M. 1901 (Newcastle U) 1
Kinsey, G. 1892 (Wolverhampton W, Derby Co) 4
Kirchen, A. J. 1937 (Arsenal) 3
Kirkland, C. E. 2007 (Liverpool) 1
Kirton, W. J. 1922 (Aston Villa) 1
Knight, A. E. 1920 (Portsmouth) 1
Knight, Z. 2005 (Fulham) 2
Knowles, C. 1968 (Tottenham H) 4
Konchesky, P. M. 2003 (Charlton Ath, West Ham U) 2

Labone, B. L. 1963 (Everton) 26
Lallana, A. D. 2013 (Southampton, Liverpool) **34**
Lambert, R. L. 2013 (Southampton, Liverpool) 11
Lampard, F. J. 2000 (West Ham U, Chelsea) 106
Lampard, F. R. G. 1973 (West Ham U) 2
Langley, E. J. 1958 (Fulham) 3
Langton, R. 1947 (Blackburn R, Preston NE, Bolton W)
  11
Latchford, R. D. 1978 (Everton) 12
Latheron, E. G. 1913 (Blackburn R) 2
Lawler, C. 1971 (Liverpool) 4
Lawton, T. 1939 (Everton, Chelsea, Notts Co) 23
Leach, T. 1931 (Sheffield W) 2
Leake, A. 1904 (Aston Villa) 5
Lee, E. A. 1904 (Southampton) 1
Lee, F. H. 1969 (Manchester C) 27
Lee, J. 1951 (Derby Co) 1
Lee, R. M. 1995 (Newcastle U) 21
Lee, S. 1983 (Liverpool) 14
Leighton, J. E. 1886 (Nottingham F) 1
Lennon, A. J. 2006 (Tottenham H) 21
Lescott, J. P. 2008 (Everton, Manchester C) 26
Le Saux, G. P. 1994 (Blackburn R, Chelsea) 36
Le Tissier, M. P. 1994 (Southampton) 8
Lilley, H. E. 1892 (Sheffield U) 1
Linacre, H. J. 1905 (Nottingham F) 2
Lindley, T. 1886 (Cambridge University, Nottingham F)
  13
Lindsay, A. 1974 (Liverpool) 4
Lindsay, W. 1877 (Wanderers) 1
Lineker, G. 1984 (Leicester C, Everton, Barcelona,
  Tottenham H) 80
Lingard, J. E. 2017 (Manchester U) **18**
Lintott, E. H. 1908 (QPR, Bradford C) 7
Lipsham, H. B. 1902 (Sheffield U) 1
Little, B. 1975 (Aston Villa) 1
Livermore, J. C. 2013 (Tottenham H, WBA) **7**
Lloyd, L. V. 1971 (Liverpool, Nottingham F) 4
Lockett, A. 1903 (Stoke) 1
Lodge, L. V. 1894 (Cambridge University, Corinthians) 5
Lofthouse, J. M. 1885 (Blackburn R, Accrington,
  Blackburn R) 7
Lofthouse, N. 1951 (Bolton W) 33
Loftus-Cheek, R. I. 2018 (Chelsea) **8**
Longworth, E. 1920 (Liverpool) 5
Lowder, A. 1889 (Wolverhampton W) 1

Lowe, E. 1947 (Aston Villa) 3
Lucas, T. 1922 (Liverpool) 3
Luntley, E. 1880 (Nottingham F) 2
Lyttelton, Hon. A. 1877 (Cambridge University) 1
Lyttelton, Hon. E. 1878 (Cambridge University) 1

Mabbutt, G. 1983 (Tottenham H) 16
Macaulay, R. H. 1881 (Cambridge University) 1
Macrae, S. 1883 (Notts Co) 5
Maddison, F. B. 1872 (Oxford University) 1
Madeley, P. E. 1971 (Leeds U) 24
Magee, T. P. 1923 (WBA) 5
Maguire, J. H. 2018 (Leicester C) **12**
Makepeace, H. 1906 (Everton) 4
Male, C. G. 1935 (Arsenal) 19
Mannion, W. J. 1947 (Middlesbrough) 26
Mariner, P. 1977 (Ipswich T, Arsenal) 35
Marsden, J. T. 1891 (Darwen) 1
Marsden, W. 1930 (Sheffield W) 3
Marsh, R. W. 1972 (QPR, Manchester C) 9
Marshall, T. 1880 (Darwen) 2
Martin, A. 1981 (West Ham U) 17
Martin, H. 1914 (Sunderland) 1
Martyn, A. N. 1992 (Crystal Palace, Leeds U) 23
Marwood, B. 1989 (Arsenal) 1
Maskrey, H. M. 1908 (Derby Co) 1
Mason, C. 1887 (Wolverhampton W) 3
Mason, R. G. 2015 (Tottenham H) 1
Matthews, R. D. 1956 (Coventry C) 5
Matthews, S. 1935 (Stoke C, Blackpool) 54
Matthews, V. 1928 (Sheffield U) 2
Maynard, W. J. 1872 (1st Surrey Rifles) 2
McCall, J. 1913 (Preston NE) 5
McCann, G. P. 2001 (Sunderland) 1
McDermott, T. 1978 (Liverpool) 25
McDonald, C. A. 1958 (Burnley) 8
Macdonald, M. 1972 (Newcastle U) 14
McFarland, R. L. 1971 (Derby Co) 28
McGarry, W. H. 1954 (Huddersfield T) 4
McGuinness, W. 1959 (Manchester U) 2
McInroy, A. 1927 (Sunderland) 1
McMahon, S. 1988 (Liverpool) 17
McManaman, S. 1995 (Liverpool, Real Madrid) 37
McNab, R. 1969 (Arsenal) 4
McNeal, R. 1914 (WBA) 2
McNeil, M. 1961 (Middlesbrough) 9
Meadows, J. 1955 (Manchester C) 1
Medley, L. D. 1951 (Tottenham H) 6
Meehan, T. 1924 (Chelsea) 1
Melia, J. 1963 (Liverpool) 2
Mercer, D. W. 1923 (Sheffield U) 2
Mercer, J. 1939 (Everton) 5
Merrick, G. H. 1952 (Birmingham C) 23
Merson, P. C. 1992 (Arsenal, Middlesbrough,
  Aston Villa) 21
Metcalfe, V. 1951 (Huddersfield T) 2
Mew, J. W. 1921 (Manchester U) 1
Middleditch, B. 1897 (Corinthians) 1
Milburn, J. E. T. 1949 (Newcastle U) 13
Miller, B. G. 1961 (Burnley) 1
Miller, H. S. 1923 (Charlton Ath) 1
Mills, D. J. 2001 (Leeds U) 19
Mills, G. R. 1938 (Chelsea) 3
Mills, M. D. 1973 (Ipswich T) 42
Milne, G. 1963 (Liverpool) 14
Milner, J. P. 2010 (Aston Villa, Manchester C,
  Liverpool) 61
Milton, C. A. 1952 (Arsenal) 1
Milward, A. 1891 (Everton) 4
Mitchell, C. 1880 (Upton Park) 5
Mitchell, J. F. 1925 (Manchester C) 1
Moffat, H. 1913 (Oldham Ath) 1
Molyneux, G. 1902 (Southampton) 4
Moon, W. R. 1888 (Old Westminsters) 7
Moore, H. T. 1883 (Notts Co) 2
Moore, J. 1923 (Derby Co) 1
Moore, R. F. 1962 (West Ham U) 108
Moore, W. G. B. 1923 (West Ham U) 1
Mordue, J. 1912 (Sunderland) 2
Morice, C. J. 1872 (Barnes) 1
Morley, A. 1982 (Aston Villa) 6
Morley, H. 1910 (Notts Co) 1
Morren, T. 1898 (Sheffield U) 1
Morris, F. 1920 (WBA) 2

Morris, J. 1949 (Derby Co)   3
Morris, W. W. 1939 (Wolverhampton W)   3
Morse, H. 1879 (Notts Co)   1
Mort, T. 1924 (Aston Villa)   3
Morten, A. 1873 (Crystal Palace)   1
Mortensen, S. H. 1947 (Blackpool)   25
Morton, J. R. 1938 (West Ham U)   1
Mosforth, W. 1877 (Sheffield W, Sheffield Alb,
    Sheffield W)   9
Moss, F. 1922 (Aston Villa)   5
Moss, F. 1934 (Arsenal)   4
Mosscrop, E. 1914 (Burnley)   2
Mozley, B. 1950 (Derby Co)   3
Mullen, J. 1947 (Wolverhampton W)   12
Mullery, A. P. 1965 (Tottenham H)   35
Murphy, D. B. 2002 (Liverpool)   9

Neal, P. G. 1976 (Liverpool)   50
Needham, E. 1894 (Sheffield U)   16
Neville, G. A. 1995 (Manchester U)   85
Neville, P. J. 1996 (Manchester U, Everton)   59
Newton, K. R. 1966 (Blackburn R, Everton)   27
Nicholls, J. 1954 (WBA)   2
Nicholson, W. E. 1951 (Tottenham H)   1
Nish, D. J. 1973 (Derby Co)   5
Norman, M. 1962 (Tottenham H)   23
Nugent, D. J. 2007 (Preston NE)   1
Nuttall, H. 1928 (Bolton W)   3

Oakley, W. J. 1895 (Oxford University, Corinthians)   16
O'Dowd, J. P. 1932 (Chelsea)   3
O'Grady, M. 1963 (Huddersfield T, Leeds U)   2
Ogilvie, R. A. M. M. 1874 (Clapham R)   1
Oliver, L. F. 1929 (Fulham)   1
Olney, B. A. 1928 (Aston Villa)   2
Osborne, F. R. 1923 (Fulham, Tottenham H)   4
Osborne, R. 1928 (Leicester C)   1
Osgood, P. L. 1970 (Chelsea)   4
Osman, L. 2013 (Everton)   2
Osman, R. 1980 (Ipswich T)   11
Ottaway, C. J. 1872 (Oxford University)   2
Owen, J. R. B. 1874 (Sheffield)   1
Owen, M. J. 1998 (Liverpool, Real Madrid, Newcastle U)
        89
Owen, S. W. 1954 (Luton T)   3
Oxlade-Chamberlain, A. M. D. 2012 (Arsenal,
    Liverpool)   **32**

Page, L. A. 1927 (Burnley)   7
Paine, T. L. 1963 (Southampton)   19
Pallister, G. A. 1988 (Middlesbrough, Manchester U)   22
Palmer, C. L. 1992 (Sheffield W)   18
Pantling, H. H. 1924 (Sheffield U)   1
Paravicini, P. J. de 1883 (Cambridge University)   3
Parker, P. A. 1989 (QPR, Manchester U)   19
Parker, S. M. 2004 (Charlton Ath, Chelsea, Newcastle U,
    West Ham U, Tottenham H)   18
Parker, T. R. 1925 (Southampton)   1
Parkes, P. B. 1974 (QPR)   1
Parkinson, J. 1910 (Liverpool)   2
Parlour, R. 1999 (Arsenal)   10
Parr, P. C. 1882 (Oxford University)   1
Parry, E. H. 1879 (Old Carthusians)   3
Parry, R. A. 1960 (Bolton W)   2
Patchitt, B. C. A. 1923 (Corinthians)   2
Pawson, F. W. 1883 (Cambridge University, Swifts)   2
Payne, J. 1937 (Luton T)   1
Peacock, A. 1962 (Middlesbrough, Leeds U)   6
Peacock, J. 1929 (Middlesbrough)   3
Pearce, S. 1987 (Nottingham F, West Ham U)   78
Pearson, H. F. 1932 (WBA)   1
Pearson, J. H. 1892 (Crewe Alex)   1
Pearson, J. S. 1976 (Manchester U)   15
Pearson, S. C. 1948 (Manchester U)   8
Pease, W. H. 1927 (Middlesbrough)   1
Pegg, D. 1957 (Manchester U)   1
Pejic, M. 1974 (Stoke C)   4
Pelly, F. R. 1893 (Old Foresters)   3
Pennington, J. 1907 (WBA)   25
Pentland, F. B. 1909 (Middlesbrough)   5
Perry, C. 1890 (WBA)   3
Perry, T. 1898 (WBA)   1
Perry, W. 1956 (Blackpool)   3
Perryman, S. 1982 (Tottenham H)   1

Peters, M. 1966 (West Ham U, Tottenham H)   67
Phelan, M. C. 1990 (Manchester U)   1
Phillips, K. 1999 (Sunderland)   8
Phillips, L. H. 1952 (Portsmouth)   3
Pickering, F. 1964 (Everton)   3
Pickering, J. 1933 (Sheffield U)   1
Pickering, N. 1983 (Sunderland)   1
Pickford, J. L. 2018 (Everton)   **10**
Pike, T. M. 1886 (Cambridge University)   1
Pilkington, B. 1955 (Burnley)   1
Plant, J. 1900 (Bury)   1
Platt, D. 1990 (Aston Villa, Bari, Juventus, Sampdoria,
    Arsenal)   62
Plum, S. L. 1923 (Charlton Ath)   1
Pointer, R. 1962 (Burnley)   3
Pope, N. D. 2018 (Burnley)   **1**
Porteous, T. S. 1891 (Sunderland)   1
Powell, C. G. 2001 (Charlton Ath)   5
Priest, A. E. 1900 (Sheffield U)   1
Prinsep, J. F. M. 1879 (Clapham R)   1
Puddefoot, S. C. 1926 (Blackburn R)   2
Pye, J. 1950 (Wolverhampton W)   1
Pym, R. H. 1925 (Bolton W)   3

Quantrill, A. 1920 (Derby Co)   4
Quixall, A. 1954 (Sheffield W)   5

Radford, J. 1969 (Arsenal)   2
Raikes, G. B. 1895 (Oxford University)   4
Ramsey, A. E. 1949 (Southampton, Tottenham H)   32
Rashford, M. 2016 (Manchester U)   **25**
Rawlings, A. 1921 (Preston NE)   1
Rawlings, W. E. 1922 (Southampton)   2
Rawlinson, J. F. P. 1882 (Cambridge University)   1
Rawson, H. E. 1875 (Royal Engineers)   1
Rawson, W. S. 1875 (Oxford University)   2
Read, A. 1921 (Tufnell Park)   1
Reader, J. 1894 (WBA)   1
Reaney, P. 1969 (Leeds U)   3
Redknapp, J. F. 1996 (Liverpool)   17
Redmond, N. D. J. 2017 (Southampton)   1
Reeves, K. P. 1980 (Norwich C, Manchester C)   2
Regis, C. 1982 (WBA, Coventry C)   5
Reid, P. 1985 (Everton)   13
Revie, D. G. 1955 (Manchester C)   6
Reynolds, J. 1892 (WBA, Aston Villa)   8
Richards, C. H. 1898 (Nottingham F)   1
Richards, G. H. 1909 (Derby Co)   1
Richards, J. P. 1973 (Wolverhampton W)   1
Richards, M. 2007 (Manchester C)   13
Richardson, J. R. 1933 (Newcastle U)   2
Richardson, K. 1994 (Aston Villa)   1
Richardson, K. E. 2005 (Manchester U)   8
Richardson, W. G. 1935 (WBA)   1
Rickaby, S. 1954 (WBA)   1
Ricketts, M. B. 2002 (Bolton W)   1
Rigby, A. 1927 (Blackburn R)   5
Rimmer, E. J. 1930 (Sheffield W)   4
Rimmer, J. J. 1976 (Arsenal)   1
Ripley, S. E. 1994 (Blackburn R)   2
Rix, G. 1981 (Arsenal)   17
Robb, G. 1954 (Tottenham H)   1
Roberts, C. 1905 (Manchester U)   3
Roberts, F. 1925 (Manchester C)   4
Roberts, G. 1983 (Tottenham H)   6
Roberts, H. 1931 (Arsenal)   1
Roberts, H. 1931 (Millwall)   1
Roberts, R. 1887 (WBA)   3
Roberts, W. T. 1924 (Preston NE)   2
Robinson, J. 1937 (Sheffield W)   4
Robinson, J. W. 1897 (Derby Co, New Brighton Tower,
    Southampton)   11
Robinson, P. W. 2003 (Leeds U, Tottenham H,
    Blackburn R)   41
Robson, B. 1980 (WBA, Manchester U)   90
Robson, R. 1958 (WBA)   20
Rocastle, D. 1989 (Arsenal)   14
Rodriguez, J. E. 2013 (Southampton)   1
Rodwell, J. 2012 (Everton)   3
Rooney, W. M. 2003 (Everton, Manchester U)   119
Rose, D. L. 2016 (Tottenham H)   **23**
Rose, W. C. 1884 (Swifts, Preston NE,
    Wolverhampton W)   5
Rostron, T. 1881 (Darwen)   2

Rowe, A. 1934 (Tottenham H) 1
Rowley, J. F. 1949 (Manchester U) 6
Rowley, W. 1889 (Stoke) 2
Royle, J. 1971 (Everton, Manchester C) 6
Ruddlesdin, H. 1904 (Sheffield W) 3
Ruddock, N. 1995 (Liverpool) 1
Ruddy, J. T. G. 2013 (Norwich C) 1
Ruffell, J. W. 1926 (West Ham U) 6
Russell, B. B. 1883 (Royal Engineers) 1
Rutherford, J. 1904 (Newcastle U) 11

Sadler, D. 1968 (Manchester U) 4
Sagar, C. 1900 (Bury) 2
Sagar, E. 1936 (Everton) 4
Salako, J. A. 1991 (Crystal Palace) 5
Sandford, E. A. 1933 (WBA) 1
Sandilands, R. R. 1892 (Old Westminsters) 5
Sands, J. 1880 (Nottingham F) 1
Sansom, K. G. 1979 (Crystal Palace, Arsenal) 86
Saunders, F. E. 1888 (Swifts) 1
Savage, A. H. 1876 (Crystal Palace) 1
Sayer, J. 1887 (Stoke) 1
Scales, J. R. 1995 (Liverpool) 3
Scattergood, E. 1913 (Derby Co) 1
Schofield, J. 1892 (Stoke) 3
Scholes, P. 1997 (Manchester U) 66
Scott, L. 1947 (Arsenal) 17
Scott, W. R. 1937 (Brentford) 1
Seaman, D. A. 1989 (QPR, Arsenal) 75
Seddon, J. 1923 (Bolton W) 6
Seed, J. M. 1921 (Tottenham H) 5
Settle, J. 1899 (Bury, Everton) 6
Sewell, J. 1952 (Sheffield W) 6
Sewell, W. R. 1924 (Blackburn R) 1
Shackleton, L. F. 1949 (Sunderland) 5
Sharp, J. 1903 (Everton) 2
Sharpe, L. S. 1991 (Manchester U) 8
Shaw, G. E. 1932 (WBA) 1
Shaw, G. L. 1959 (Sheffield U) 1
Shaw, L. P. H. 2014 (Southampton, Manchester U) 7
Shawcross, R. J. 2013 (Stoke C) 1
Shea, D. 1914 (Blackburn R) 2
Shearer, A. 1992 (Southampton, Blackburn R,
  Newcastle U) 63
Shellito, K. J. 1963 (Chelsea) 1
Shelton A. 1889 (Notts Co) 6
Shelton, C. 1888 (Notts Rangers) 1
Shelvey, J. 2013 (Liverpool, Swansea C) 6
Shepherd, A. 1906 (Bolton W, Newcastle U) 2
Sheringham, E. P. 1993 (Tottenham H, Manchester U,
  Tottenham H) 51
Sherwood, T. A. 1999 (Tottenham H) 3
Shilton, P. L. 1971 (Leicester C, Stoke C, Nottingham F,
  Southampton, Derby Co) 125
Shimwell, E. 1949 (Blackpool) 1
Shorey, N. 2007 (Reading) 2
Shutt, G. 1886 (Stoke) 1
Silcock, J. 1921 (Manchester U) 3
Sillett, R. P. 1955 (Chelsea) 3
Simms, E. 1922 (Luton T) 1
Simpson, J. 1911 (Blackburn R) 8
Sinclair, T. 2002 (West Ham U, Manchester C) 12
Sinton, A. 1992 (QPR, Sheffield W) 12
Slater, W. J. 1955 (Wolverhampton W) 12
Smalley, T. 1937 (Wolverhampton W) 1
Smalling, C. L. 2012 (Manchester U) 31
Smart, T. 1921 (Aston Villa) 5
Smith, A. 1891 (Nottingham F) 3
Smith, A. 2001 (Leeds U, Manchester U, Newcastle U) 19
Smith, A. K. 1872 (Oxford University) 1
Smith, A. M. 1989 (Arsenal) 13
Smith, B. 1921 (Tottenham H) 2
Smith, C. E. 1876 (Crystal Palace) 1
Smith, G. O. 1893 (Oxford University, Old Carthusians,
  Corinthians) 20
Smith, H. 1905 (Reading) 4
Smith, J. 1920 (WBA) 2
Smith, Joe 1913 (Bolton W) 5
Smith, J. C. R. 1939 (Millwall) 2
Smith, J. W. 1932 (Portsmouth) 3
Smith, Leslie 1939 (Brentford) 1
Smith, Lionel 1951 (Arsenal) 6
Smith, R. A. 1961 (Tottenham H) 15
Smith, S. 1895 (Aston Villa) 1
Smith, S. C. 1936 (Leicester C) 1

Smith, T. 1960 (Birmingham C) 2
Smith, T. 1971 (Liverpool) 1
Smith, W. H. 1922 (Huddersfield T) 3
Solanke, D. A. 2018 (Liverpool) **1**
Sorby, T. H. 1879 (Thursday Wanderers, Sheffield) 1
Southgate, G. 1996 (Aston Villa, Middlesbrough) 57
Southworth, J. 1889 (Blackburn R) 3
Sparks, F. J. 1879 (Herts Rangers, Clapham R) 3
Spence, J. W. 1926 (Manchester U) 2
Spence, R. 1936 (Chelsea) 2
Spencer, C. W. 1924 (Newcastle U) 2
Spencer, H. 1897 (Aston Villa) 6
Spiksley, F. 1893 (Sheffield W) 7
Spilsbury, B. W. 1885 (Cambridge University) 3
Spink, N. 1983 (Aston Villa) 1
Spouncer, W. A. 1900 (Nottingham F) 1
Springett, R. D. G. 1960 (Sheffield W) 33
Sproston, B. 1937 (Leeds U, Tottenham H,
  Manchester C) 11
Squire, R. T. 1886 (Cambridge University) 3
Stanbrough, M. H. 1895 (Old Carthusians) 1
Staniforth, R. 1954 (Huddersfield T) 8
Starling, R. W. 1933 (Sheffield W, Aston Villa) 2
Statham, D. J. 1983 (WBA) 3
Steele, F. C. 1937 (Stoke C) 6
Stein, B. 1984 (Luton T) 1
Stephenson, C. 1924 (Huddersfield T) 1
Stephenson, G. T. 1928 (Derby Co, Sheffield W) 3
Stephenson, J. E. 1938 (Leeds U) 2
Stepney, A. C. 1968 (Manchester U) 1
Sterland, M. 1989 (Sheffield W) 1
Sterling, R. S. 2013 (Liverpool, Manchester C) **44**
Steven, T. M. 1985 (Everton, Rangers, Marseille) 36
Stevens, G. A. 1985 (Tottenham H) 7
Stevens, M. G. 1985 (Everton, Rangers) 46
Stewart, J. 1907 (Sheffield W, Newcastle U) 3
Stewart, P. A. 1992 (Tottenham H) 3
Stiles, N. P. 1965 (Manchester U) 28
Stoker, J. 1933 (Birmingham) 3
Stone, S. B. 1996 (Nottingham F) 9
Stones, J. 2014 (Everton, Manchester C) **33**
Storer, H. 1924 (Derby Co) 2
Storey, P. E. 1971 (Arsenal) 19
Storey-Moore, I. 1970 (Nottingham F) 1
Strange, A. H. 1930 (Sheffield W) 20
Stratford, A. H. 1874 (Wanderers) 1
Streten, B. 1950 (Luton T) 1
Sturgess, A. 1911 (Sheffield U) 2
Sturridge, D. A. 2012 (Chelsea, Liverpool) **26**
Summerbee, M. G. 1968 (Manchester C) 8
Sunderland, A. 1980 (Arsenal) 1
Sutcliffe, J. W. 1893 (Bolton W, Millwall) 5
Sutton, C. R. 1998 (Blackburn R) 1
Swan, P. 1960 (Sheffield W) 19
Swepstone, H. A. 1880 (Pilgrims) 6
Swift, F. V. 1947 (Manchester C) 19

Tait, G. 1881 (Birmingham Excelsior) 1
Talbot, B. 1977 (Ipswich T, Arsenal) 6
Tambling, R. V. 1963 (Chelsea) 3
Tarkowski, J. A. 2018 (Burnley) **1**
Tate, J. T. 1931 (Aston Villa) 3
Taylor, E. 1954 (Blackpool) 1
Taylor, E. H. 1923 (Huddersfield T) 8
Taylor, J. G. 1951 (Fulham) 2
Taylor, P. H. 1948 (Liverpool) 3
Taylor, P. J. 1976 (Crystal Palace) 4
Taylor, T. 1953 (Manchester U) 19
Temple, D. W. 1965 (Everton) 1
Terry, J. G. 2003 (Chelsea) 78
Thickett, H. 1899 (Sheffield U) 2
Thomas, D. 1975 (QPR) 8
Thomas, D. 1983 (Coventry C) 2
Thomas, G. R. 1991 (Crystal Palace) 9
Thomas, M. L. 1989 (Arsenal) 2
Thompson, A. 2004 (Celtic) 1
Thompson, P. 1964 (Liverpool) 16
Thompson, P. B. 1976 (Liverpool) 42
Thompson T. 1952 (Aston Villa, Preston NE) 2
Thomson, R. A. 1964 (Wolverhampton W) 8
Thornewell, G. 1923 (Derby Co) 4
Thornley, I. 1907 (Manchester C) 1
Tilson, S. F. 1934 (Manchester C) 4
Titmuss, F. 1922 (Southampton) 2
Todd, C. 1972 (Derby Co) 27

Toone, G. 1892 (Notts Co) 2
Topham, A. G. 1894 (Casuals) 1
Topham, R. 1893 (Wolverhampton W, Casuals) 2
Towers, M. A. 1976 (Sunderland) 3
Townley, W. J. 1889 (Blackburn R) 2
Townrow, J. E. 1925 (Clapton Orient) 2
Townsend, A. D. 2013 (Tottenham H, Newcastle U, Crystal Palace) 13
Tremelling, D. R. 1928 (Birmingham) 1
Tresadern, J. 1923 (West Ham U) 2
Trippier, K. J. 2017 (Tottenham H) **13**
Tueart, D. 1975 (Manchester C) 6
Tunstall, F. E. 1923 (Sheffield U) 7
Turnbull, R. J. 1920 (Bradford) 1
Turner, A. 1900 (Southampton) 2
Turner, H. 1931 (Huddersfield T) 2
Turner, J. A. 1893 (Bolton W, Stoke, Derby Co) 3
Tweedy, G. J. 1937 (Grimsby T) 1

Ufton, D. G. 1954 (Charlton Ath) 1
Underwood, A. 1891 (Stoke C) 2
Unsworth, D. G. 1995 (Everton) 1
Upson, M. J. 2003 (Birmingham C, West Ham U) 21
Urwin, T. 1923 (Middlesbrough, Newcastle U) 4
Utley, G. 1913 (Barnsley) 1

Vardy, J. R. 2015 (Leicester C) **26**
Vassell, D. 2002 (Aston Villa) 22
Vaughton, O. H. 1882 (Aston Villa) 5
Veitch, C. C. M. 1906 (Newcastle U) 6
Veitch, J. G. 1894 (Old Westminsters) 1
Venables, T. F. 1965 (Chelsea) 2
Venison, B. 1995 (Newcastle U) 2
Vidal, R. W. S. 1873 (Oxford University) 1
Viljoen, C. 1975 (Ipswich T) 2
Viollet, D. S. 1960 (Manchester U) 2
Von Donop 1873 (Royal Engineers) 2

Wace, H. 1878 (Wanderers) 3
Waddle, C. R. 1985 (Newcastle U, Tottenham H, Marseille) 62
Wadsworth, S. J. 1922 (Huddersfield T) 9
Wainscoat, W. R. 1929 (Leeds U) 1
Waiters, A. K. 1964 (Blackpool) 5
Walcott, T. J. 2006 (Arsenal) 47
Walden, F. I. 1914 (Tottenham H) 2
Walker, D. S. 1989 (Nottingham F, Sampdoria, Sheffield W) 59
Walker, I. M. 1996 (Tottenham H, Leicester C) 4
Walker, K. A. 2012 (Tottenham H, Manchester C) **40**
Walker, W. H. 1921 (Aston Villa) 18
Wall, G. 1907 (Manchester U) 7
Wallace, C. W. 1913 (Aston Villa) 3
Wallace, D. L. 1986 (Southampton) 1
Walsh, P. A. 1983 (Luton T) 5
Walters, A. M. 1885 (Cambridge University, Old Carthusians) 9
Walters, K. M. 1991 (Rangers) 1
Walters, P. M. 1885 (Oxford University, Old Carthusians) 13
Walton, N. 1890 (Blackburn R) 1
Ward, J. T. 1885 (Blackburn Olympic) 1
Ward, P. 1980 (Brighton & HA) 1
Ward, T. V. 1948 (Derby Co) 2
Ward-Prowse, J. M. E. 2017 (Southampton) 1
Waring, T. 1931 (Aston Villa) 5
Warner, C. 1878 (Upton Park) 1
Warnock, S. 2008 (Blackburn R, Aston Villa) 2
Warren, B. 1906 (Derby Co, Chelsea) 22
Waterfield, G. S. 1927 (Burnley) 1
Watson, D. 1984 (Norwich C, Everton) 12
Watson, D. V. 1974 (Sunderland, Manchester C, Werder Bremen, Southampton, Stoke C) 65
Watson, V. M. 1923 (West Ham U) 5
Watson, W. 1913 (Burnley) 3
Watson, W. 1950 (Sunderland) 4
Weaver, S. 1932 (Newcastle U) 3
Webb, G. W. 1911 (West Ham U) 2
Webb, N. J. 1988 (Nottingham F, Manchester U) 26
Webster, M. 1930 (Middlesbrough) 3
Wedlock, W. J. 1907 (Bristol C) 26
Weir, D. 1889 (Bolton W) 2
Welbeck, D. N. T. M. 2011 (Manchester U, Arsenal) **40**
Welch, R. de C. 1872 (Wanderers, Harrow Chequers) 2
Weller, K. 1974 (Leicester C) 4

Welsh, D. 1938 (Charlton Ath) 3
West, G. 1969 (Everton) 3
Westwood, R. W. 1935 (Bolton W) 6
Whateley, O. 1883 (Aston Villa) 2
Wheeler, J. E. 1955 (Bolton W) 1
Wheldon, G. F. 1897 (Aston Villa) 4
White, D. 1993 (Manchester C) 1
White, T. A. 1933 (Everton) 1
Whitehead, J. 1893 (Accrington, Blackburn R) 2
Whitfeld, H. 1879 (Old Etonians) 1
Witham, M. 1892 (Sheffield U) 1
Whitworth, S. 1975 (Leicester C) 7
Whymark, T. J. 1978 (Ipswich T) 1
Widdowson, S. W. 1880 (Nottingham F) 1
Wignall, F. 1965 (Nottingham F) 2
Wilcox, J. M. 1996 (Blackburn R, Leeds U) 3
Wilkes, A. 1901 (Aston Villa) 5
Wilkins, R. C. 1976 (Chelsea, Manchester U, AC Milan) 84
Wilkinson, B. 1904 (Sheffield U) 1
Wilkinson, L. R. 1891 (Oxford University) 1
Williams, B. F. 1949 (Wolverhampton W) 24
Williams, O. 1923 (Clapton Orient) 2
Williams, S. 1983 (Southampton) 6
Williams, W. 1897 (WBA) 6
Williamson, E. C. 1923 (Arsenal) 2
Williamson, R. G. 1905 (Middlesbrough) 7
Willingham, C. K. 1937 (Huddersfield T) 12
Willis, A. 1952 (Tottenham H) 1
Winks, H. B. 2018 (Tottenham H) **1**
Wilshaw, D. J. 1954 (Wolverhampton W) 12
Wilshere, J. A. 2011 (Arsenal) 34
Wilson, C. P. 1884 (Hendon) 2
Wilson, C. W. 1879 (Oxford University) 2
Wilson, G. 1921 (Sheffield W) 12
Wilson, G. P. 1900 (Corinthians) 2
Wilson, R. 1960 (Huddersfield T, Everton) 63
Wilson, T. 1928 (Huddersfield T) 1
Winckworth, W. N. 1892 (Old Westminsters) 2
Windridge, J. E. 1908 (Chelsea) 8
Wingfield-Stratford, C. V. 1877 (Royal Engineers) 1
Winterburn, N. 1990 (Arsenal) 2
Wise, D. F. 1991 (Chelsea) 21
Withe, P. 1981 (Aston Villa) 11
Wollaston, C. H. R. 1874 (Wanderers) 4
Wolstenholme, S. 1904 (Everton, Blackburn R) 3
Wood, H. 1890 (Wolverhampton W) 3
Wood, R. E. 1955 (Manchester U) 3
Woodcock, A. S. 1978 (Nottingham F, Cologne, Arsenal) 42
Woodgate, J. S. 1999 (Leeds U, Newcastle U, Real Madrid, Tottenham H) 8
Woodger, G. 1911 (Oldham Ath) 1
Woodhall, G. 1888 (WBA) 2
Woodley, V. R. 1937 (Chelsea) 19
Woods, C. C. E. 1985 (Norwich C, Rangers, Sheffield W) 43
Woodward, V. J. 1903 (Tottenham H, Chelsea) 23
Woosnam, M. 1922 (Manchester C) 1
Worrall, F. 1935 (Portsmouth) 2
Worthington, F. S. 1974 (Leicester C) 8
Wreford-Brown, C. 1889 (Oxford University, Old Carthusians) 4
Wright, E. G. D. 1906 (Cambridge University) 1
Wright, I. E. 1991 (Crystal Palace, Arsenal, West Ham U) 33
Wright, J. D. 1939 (Newcastle U) 1
Wright, M. 1984 (Southampton, Derby Co, Liverpool) 45
Wright, R. I. 2000 (Ipswich T, Arsenal) 2
Wright, T. J. 1968 (Everton) 11
Wright, W. A. 1947 (Wolverhampton W) 105
Wright-Phillips, S. C. 2005 (Manchester C, Chelsea, Manchester C) 36
Wylie, J. G. 1878 (Wanderers) 1

Yates, J. 1889 (Burnley) 1
York, R. E. 1922 (Aston Villa) 2
Young, A. 1933 (Huddersfield T) 9
Young, A. S. 2008 (Aston Villa, Manchester U) **39**
Young, G. M. 1965 (Sheffield W) 1
Young, L. P. 2005 (Charlton Ath) 7

Zaha, D. W. A. 2013 (Manchester U) 2
Zamora, R. L. 2011 (Fulham) 2

NORTHERN IRELAND

Addis, D. J. 1922 (Cliftonville) 1
Aherne, T. 1947 (Belfast Celtic, Luton T) 4
Alexander, T. E. 1895 (Cliftonville) 1
Allan, C. 1936 (Cliftonville) 1
Allen, J. 1887 (Limavady) 1
Anderson, J. 1925 (Distillery) 1
Anderson, T. 1973 (Manchester U, Swindon T, Peterborough U) 22
Anderson, W. 1898 (Linfield, Cliftonville) 4
Andrews, W. 1908 (Glentoran, Grimsby T) 3
Armstrong, G. J. 1977 (Tottenham H, Watford, Real Mallorca, WBA, Chesterfield) 63

Baird, C. P. 2003 (Southampton, Fulham, Reading, Burnley, WBA, Derby Co) 79
Baird, G. 1896 (Distillery) 3
Baird, H. C. 1939 (Huddersfield T) 1
Balfe, J. 1909 (Shelbourne) 2
Bambrick, J. 1929 (Linfield, Chelsea) 11
Banks, S. J. 1937 (Cliftonville) 1
Barr, H. H. 1962 (Linfield, Coventry C) 3
Barron, J. H. 1894 (Cliftonville) 7
Barry, J. 1888 (Cliftonville) 3
Barry, J. 1900 (Bohemians) 1
Barton, A. J. 2011 (Preston NE) 1
Baxter, R. A. 1887 (Distillery) 1
Baxter, S. N. 1887 (Cliftonville) 1
Bennett, L. V. 1889 (Dublin University) 1
Best, G. 1964 (Manchester U, Fulham) 37
Bingham, W. L. 1951 (Sunderland, Luton T, Everton, Port Vale) 56
Black, K. T. 1988 (Luton T, Nottingham F) 30
Black, T. 1901 (Glentoran) 1
Blair, H. 1928 (Portadown, Swansea T) 4
Blair, J. 1907 (Cliftonville) 5
Blair, R. V. 1975 (Oldham Ath) 5
Blanchflower, J. 1954 (Manchester U) 12
Blanchflower, R. D. 1950 (Barnsley, Aston Villa, Tottenham H) 56
Blayney, A. 2006 (Doncaster R, Linfield) 5
Bookman, L. J. O. 1914 (Bradford C, Luton T) 4
Bothwell, A. W. 1926 (Ards) 5
Bowler, G. C. 1950 (Hull C) 3
Boyce, L. 2011 (Werder Bremen, Ross Co) **13**
Boyle, P. 1901 (Sheffield U) 5
Braithwaite, R. M. 1962 (Linfield, Middlesbrough) 10
Braniff, K. R. 2010 (Portadown) 2
Breen, T. 1935 (Belfast Celtic, Manchester U) 9
Brennan, B. 1912 (Bohemians) 1
Brennan, R. A. 1949 (Luton T, Birmingham C, Fulham) 5
Briggs, W. R. 1962 (Manchester U, Swansea T) 2
Brisby, D. 1891 (Distillery) 1
Brolly, T. H. 1937 (Millwall) 4
Brookes, E. A. 1920 (Shelbourne) 2
Brotherston, N. 1980 (Blackburn R) 27
Brown, J. 1921 (Glenavon, Tranmere R) 5
Brown, J. 1935 (Wolverhampton W, Coventry C, Birmingham C) 10
Brown, N. M. 1887 (Limavady) 1
Brown, W. G. 1926 (Glenavon) 1
Browne, F. 1887 (Cliftonville) 5
Browne, R. J. 1936 (Leeds U) 6
Bruce, A. 1925 (Belfast Celtic) 1
Bruce, A. S. 2013 (Hull C) 2
Bruce, W. 1961 (Glentoran) 2
Brunt, C. 2005 (Sheffield W, WBA) **65**
Bryan, M. A. 2010 (Watford) 2
Buckle, H. R. 1903 (Cliftonville, Sunderland, Bristol R) 3
Buckle, J. 1882 (Cliftonville) 1
Burnett, J. 1894 (Distillery, Glentoran) 5
Burnison, J. 1901 (Distillery) 2
Burnison, S. 1908 (Distillery, Bradford, Distillery) 8
Burns, J. 1923 (Glenavon) 1
Burns, W. 1925 (Glentoran) 1
Butler, M. P. 1939 (Blackpool) 1

Camp, L. M. J. 2011 (Nottingham F) 9
Campbell, A. C. 1963 (Crusaders) 2
Campbell, D. A. 1986 (Nottingham F, Charlton Ath) 10
Campbell, James 1897 (Cliftonville) 14
Campbell, John 1896 (Cliftonville) 1
Campbell, J. P. 1951 (Fulham) 2
Campbell, R. M. 1982 (Bradford C) 2

Campbell, W. G. 1968 (Dundee) 6
Capaldi, A. C. 2004 (Plymouth Arg, Cardiff C) 22
Carey, J. J. 1947 (Manchester U) 7
Carroll, E. 1925 (Glenavon) 1
Carroll, R. E. 1997 (Wigan Ath, Manchester U, West Ham U, Olympiacos, Notts Co, Linfield) 45
Carson, J. G. 2011 (Ipswich T) 4
Carson, S. 2009 (Coleraine) 1
Carson, T. 2018 (Motherwell) **3**
Casement, C. 2009 (Ipswich T) 1
Casey, T. 1955 (Newcastle U, Portsmouth) 12
Caskey, W. 1979 (Derby Co, Tulsa Roughnecks) 8
Cassidy, T. 1971 (Newcastle U, Burnley) 24
Cathcart, C. G. 2011 (Blackpool, Watford) **36**
Caughey, M. 1986 (Linfield) 2
Chambers, R. J. 1921 (Distillery, Bury, Nottingham F) 12
Chatton, H. A. 1925 (Partick Thistle) 3
Christian, J. 1889 (Linfield) 1
Clarke, C. J. 1986 (Bournemouth, Southampton, QPR, Portsmouth) 38
Clarke, R. 1901 (Belfast Celtic) 2
Cleary, J. 1982 (Glentoran) 5
Clements, D. 1965 (Coventry C, Sheffield W, Everton, New York Cosmos) 48
Clingan, S. G. 2006 (Nottingham F, Norwich C, Coventry C, Kilmarnock) 39
Clugston, J. 1888 (Cliftonville) 14
Clyde, M. G. 2005 (Wolverhampton W) 3
Coates, C. 2009 (Crusaders) 6
Cochrane, D. 1939 (Leeds U) 12
Cochrane, G. 1903 (Cliftonville) 1
Cochrane, G. T. 1976 (Coleraine, Burnley, Middlesbrough, Gillingham) 26
Cochrane, M. 1898 (Distillery, Leicester Fosse) 8
Collins, F. 1922 (Celtic) 1
Collins, R. 1922 (Cliftonville) 1
Condy, J. 1882 (Distillery) 3
Connell, T. E. 1978 (Coleraine) 1
Connor, J. 1901 (Glentoran, Belfast Celtic) 13
Connor, M. J. 1903 (Brentford, Fulham) 3
Cook, W. 1933 (Celtic, Everton) 15
Cooke, S. 1889 (Belfast YMCA, Cliftonville) 3
Coote, A. 1999 (Norwich C) 6
Coulter, J. 1934 (Belfast Celtic, Everton, Grimsby T, Chelmsford C) 11
Cowan, J. 1970 (Newcastle U) 1
Cowan, T. S. 1925 (Queen's Island) 1
Coyle, F. 1956 (Coleraine, Nottingham F) 4
Coyle, L. 1989 (Derry C) 1
Coyle, R. I. 1973 (Sheffield W) 5
Craig, A. B. 1908 (Rangers, Morton) 9
Craig, D. J. 1967 (Newcastle U) 25
Craigan, S. J. 2003 (Partick Thistle, Motherwell) 54
Crawford, A. 1889 (Distillery, Cliftonville) 7
Croft, T. 1922 (Queen's Island) 3
Crone, R. 1889 (Distillery) 4
Crone, W. 1882 (Distillery) 12
Crooks, W. J. 1922 (Manchester U) 1
Crossan, E. 1950 (Blackburn R) 3
Crossan, J. A. 1960 (Sparta-Rotterdam, Sunderland, Manchester C, Middlesbrough) 24
Crothers, C. 1907 (Distillery) 1
Cumming, L. 1929 (Huddersfield T, Oldham Ath) 3
Cunningham, W. 1892 (Ulster) 4
Cunningham, W. E. 1951 (St Mirren, Leicester C, Dunfermline Ath) 30
Curran, S. 1926 (Belfast Celtic) 4
Curran, J. J. 1922 (Glenavon, Pontypridd, Glenavon) 5
Cush, W. W. 1951 (Glenavon, Leeds U, Portadown) 26

Dallas, S. A, 2011 (Crusaders, Brentford, Leeds U) **30**
Dalrymple, J. 1922 (Distillery) 1
Dalton, W. 1888 (YMCA, Linfield) 11
D'Arcy, S. D. 1952 (Chelsea, Brentford) 5
Darling, J. 1897 (Linfield) 22
Davey, H. H. 1926 (Reading, Portsmouth) 5
Davis, S. 2005 (Aston Villa, Fulham, Rangers, Southampton) **101**
Davis, T. L. 1937 (Oldham Ath) 1
Davison, A. J. 1996 (Bolton W, Bradford C, Grimsby T) 3
Davison, J. R. 1882 (Cliftonville) 8
Dennison, R. 1988 (Wolverhampton W) 18
Devine, A. O. 1886 (Limavady) 4

Devine, J. 1990 (Glentoran) 1
Dickson, D. 1970 (Coleraine) 4
Dickson, T. A. 1957 (Linfield) 1
Dickson, W. 1951 (Chelsea, Arsenal) 12
Diffin, W. J. 1931 (Belfast Celtic) 1
Dill, A. H. 1882 (Knock, Down Ath, Cliftonville) 9
Doherty, I. 1901 (Belfast Celtic) 1
Doherty, J. 1928 (Portadown) 1
Doherty, J. 1933 (Cliftonville) 2
Doherty, L. 1985 (Linfield) 2
Doherty, M. 1938 (Derry C) 1
Doherty, P. D. 1935 (Blackpool, Manchester C, Derby
 Co, Huddersfield T, Doncaster R) 16
Doherty, T. E. 2003 (Bristol C) 9
Donaghey, B. 1903 (Belfast Celtic) 1
Donaghy, M. M. 1980 (Luton T, Manchester U, Chelsea) 91
Donnelly, L. 1913 (Distillery) 1
Donnelly, L. F. P. 2014 (Fulham) 1
Donnelly, M. 2009 (Crusaders) 1
Doran, J. F. 1921 (Brighton) 3
Dougan, A. D. 1958 (Portsmouth, Blackburn R,
 Aston Villa, Leicester C, Wolverhampton W) 43
Douglas, J. P. 1947 (Belfast Celtic) 1
Dowd, H. O. 1974 (Glenavon, Sheffield W) 3
Dowie, I. 1990 (Luton T, West Ham U, Southampton,
 C Palace, West Ham U, QPR) 59
Duff, M. J. 2002 (Cheltenham T, Burnley) 24
Duggan, H. A. 1930 (Leeds U) 8
Dunlop, G. 1985 (Linfield) 4
Dunne, J. 1928 (Sheffield U) 7

Eames, W. L. E. 1885 (Dublin University) 3
Eglington, T. J. 1947 (Everton) 6
Elder, A. R. 1960 (Burnley, Stoke C) 40
Elleman, A. R. 1889 (Cliftonville) 2
Elliott, S. 2001 (Motherwell, Hull C) 39
Elwood, J. H. 1929 (Bradford) 2
Emerson, W. 1920 (Glentoran, Burnley) 11
English, S. 1933 (Rangers) 2
Enright, J. 1912 (Leeds C) 1
Evans, C. J. 2009 (Manchester U, Hull C, Blackburn R) 47
Evans, J. G. 2007 (Manchester U, WBA) 70

Falloon, J. 1931 (Aberdeen) 2
Farquharson, T. G. 1923 (Cardiff C) 7
Farrell, P. 1901 (Distillery) 2
Farrell, P. 1938 (Hibernian) 7
Farrell, P. D. 1947 (Everton) 7
Feeney, J. M. 1947 (Linfield, Swansea T) 2
Feeney, W. 1976 (Glentoran) 1
Feeney, W. J. 2002 (Bournemouth, Luton T, Cardiff C,
 Oldham Ath, Plymouth Arg) 46
Ferguson, G. 1999 (Linfield) 5
Ferguson, S. K. 2009 (Newcastle U, Millwall) 35
Ferguson, W. 1966 (Linfield) 2
Ferris, J. 1920 (Belfast Celtic, Chelsea, Belfast Celtic) 6
Ferris, R. O. 1950 (Birmingham C) 3
Fettis, A. W. 1992 (Hull C, Nottingham F, Blackburn R)
 25
Finney, T. 1975 (Sunderland, Cambridge U) 14
Fitzpatrick, J. C. 1896 (Bohemians) 2
Flack, H. 1929 (Burnley) 1
Flanagan, T. M. 2017 (Burton Alb) 1
Fleming, J. G. 1987 (Nottingham F, Manchester C,
 Barnsley) 31
Forbes, G. 1888 (Limavady, Distillery) 3
Forde, J. T. 1959 (Ards) 4
Foreman, T. A. 1899 (Cliftonville) 1
Forsythe, J. 1888 (YMCA) 2
Fox, W. T. 1887 (Ulster) 1
Frame, T. 1925 (Linfield) 1
Fulton, R. P. 1928 (Larne, Belfast Celtic) 21

Gaffikin, G. 1890 (Linfield Ath) 15
Galbraith, W. 1890 (Distillery) 1
Gallagher, P. 1920 (Celtic, Falkirk) 11
Gallogly, C. 1951 (Huddersfield T) 2
Gara, A. 1902 (Preston NE) 3
Gardiner, A. 1930 (Cliftonville) 5
Garrett, J. 1925 (Distillery) 1
Garrett, R. 2009 (Linfield) 5
Gaston, R. 1969 (Oxford U) 1
Gaukrodger, G. 1895 (Linfield) 1
Gault, M. 2008 (Linfield) 1
Gaussen, A. D. 1884 (Moyola Park, Magherafelt) 6

Geary, J. 1931 (Glentoran) 2
Gibb, J. T. 1884 (Wellington Park, Cliftonville) 10
Gibb, T. J. 1936 (Cliftonville) 1
Gibson W. D. 1894 (Cliftonville) 14
Gillespie, K. R. 1995 (Manchester U, Newcastle U,
 Blackburn R, Leicester C, Sheffield U) 86
Gillespie, S. 1886 (Hertford) 6
Gillespie, W. 1889 (West Down) 1
Gillespie, W. 1913 (Sheffield U) 25
Goodall, A. L. 1899 (Derby Co, Glossop) 10
Goodbody, M. F. 1889 (Dublin University) 2
Gordon, H. 1895 (Linfield) 3
Gordon R. W. 1891 (Linfield) 7
Gordon, T. 1894 (Linfield) 2
Gorman, R. J. 2010 (Wolverhampton W) 9
Gorman, W. C. 1947 (Brentford) 4
Gough, J. 1925 (Queen's Island) 1
Gowdy, J. 1920 (Glentoran, Queen's Island, Falkirk) 6
Gowdy, W. A. 1932 (Hull C, Sheffield W, Linfield,
 Hibernian) 6
Graham, W. G. L. 1951 (Doncaster R) 14
Gray, P. 1993 (Luton T, Sunderland, Nancy, Luton T,
 Burnley, Oxford U) 26
Greer, W. 1909 (QPR) 3
Gregg, H. 1954 (Doncaster R, Manchester U) 25
Griffin, D. J. 1996 (St Johnstone, Dundee U,
 Stockport Co) 29
Grigg, W. D. 2012 (Walsall, Brentford, Milton Keynes D,
 Wigan Ath) 10

Hall, G. 1897 (Distillery) 1
Halligan, W. 1911 (Derby Co, Wolverhampton W) 2
Hamill, M. 1912 (Manchester U, Belfast Celtic,
 Manchester C) 7
Hamill, R. 1999 (Glentoran) 1
Hamilton, B. 1969 (Linfield, Ipswich T, Everton,
 Millwall, Swindon T) 50
Hamilton, G. 2003 (Portadown) 5
Hamilton, J. 1882 (Knock) 2
Hamilton, R. 1928 (Rangers) 5
Hamilton, W. D. 1885 (Dublin Association) 1
Hamilton, W. J. 1885 (Dublin Association) 1
Hamilton, W. J. 1908 (Distillery) 1
Hamilton, W. R. 1978 (QPR, Burnley, Oxford U) 41
Hampton, H. 1911 (Bradford C) 9
Hanna, J. 1912 (Nottingham F) 2
Hanna, J. D. 1899 (Royal Artillery, Portsmouth) 1
Hannon, D. J. 1908 (Bohemians) 6
Harkin, J. T. 1968 (Southport, Shrewsbury T) 5
Harland, A. I. 1922 (Linfield) 2
Harris, J. 1921 (Cliftonville, Glenavon) 2
Harris, V. 1906 (Shelbourne, Everton) 20
Harvey, M. 1961 (Sunderland) 34
Hastings, J. 1882 (Knock, Ulster) 7
Hatton, S. 1963 (Linfield) 2
Hayes, W. E. 1938 (Huddersfield T) 4
Hazard, C. 2018 (Celtic) 1
Healy, D. J. 2000 (Manchester U, Preston NE, Leeds U,
 Fulham, Sunderland, Rangers, Bury) 95
Healy, P. J. 1982 (Coleraine, Glentoran) 4
Hegan, D. 1970 (WBA, Wolverhampton W) 7
Henderson, J. 1885 (Ulster) 3
Hewison, G. 1885 (Moyola Park) 2
Hill, C. F. 1990 (Sheffield U, Leicester C, Trelleborg,
 Northampton T) 27
Hill, M. J. 1959 (Norwich C, Everton) 7
Hinton, E. 1947 (Fulham, Millwall) 7
**Hodson, L. J. S. 2011 (Watford, Milton Keynes D,
 Rangers) 24**
Holmes, S. P. 2002 (Wrexham) 1
Hopkins, J. 1926 (Brighton) 1
Horlock, K. 1995 (Swindon T, Manchester C) 32
Houston, J. 1912 (Linfield, Everton) 6
Houston, W. 1933 (Linfield) 1
Houston, W. J. 1885 (Moyola Park) 2
**Hughes, A. W. 1998 (Newcastle U, Aston Villa, Fulham,
 QPR, Brighton & HA, Melbourne C, Kerala Blasters,
 Hearts) 112**
Hughes, J. 2006 (Lincoln C) 2
Hughes, M. A. 2006 (Oldham Ath) 2
Hughes, M. E. 1992 (Manchester C, Strasbourg,
 West Ham U, Wimbledon, Crystal Palace) 71
Hughes, P. A. 1987 (Bury) 3
Hughes, W. 1951 (Bolton W) 1

Humphries, W. M. 1962 (Ards, Coventry C, Swansea T)   14
Hunter, A. 1905 (Distillery, Belfast Celtic)   8
Hunter, A. 1970 (Blackburn R, Ipswich T)   53
Hunter, B. V. 1995 (Wrexham, Reading)   15
Hunter, R. J. 1884 (Cliftonville)   3
Hunter, V. 1962 (Coleraine)   2

Ingham, M. G. 2005 (Sunderland, Wrexham)   3
Irvine, R. J. 1962 (Linfield, Stoke C)   8
Irvine, R. W. 1922 (Everton, Portsmouth, Connah's Quay, Derry C)   15
Irvine, W. J. 1963 (Burnley, Preston NE, Brighton & HA)   23
Irving, S. J. 1923 (Dundee, Cardiff C, Chelsea)   18

Jackson, T. A. 1969 (Everton, Nottingham F, Manchester U)   35
Jamison, J. 1976 (Glentoran)   1
Jenkins, I. 1997 (Chester C, Dundee U)   6
Jennings, P. A. 1964 (Watford, Tottenham H, Arsenal, Tottenham H)   119
Johnson, D. M. 1999 (Blackburn R, Birmingham C)   56
Johnston, H. 1927 (Portadown)   1
Johnston, R. S. 1882 (Distillery)   5
Johnston, R. S. 1905 (Distillery)   1
Johnston, S. 1890 (Linfield)   4
Johnston, W. 1885 (Oldpark)   2
Johnston, W. C. 1962 (Glenavon, Oldham Ath)   2
Jones, J. 1930 (Linfield, Hibernian, Glenavon)   23
Jones, J. 1956 (Glenavon)   3
Jones, J. L. 2018 (Kilmarnock)   **2**
Jones, S. 1934 (Distillery, Blackpool)   2
Jones, S. G. 2003 (Crewe Alex, Burnley)   29
Jordan, T. 1895 (Linfield)   2

Kavanagh, P. J. 1930 (Celtic)   1
Keane, T. R. 1949 (Swansea T)   1
Kearns, A. 1900 (Distillery)   6
Kee, P. V. 1990 (Oxford U, Ards)   9
Keith, R. M. 1958 (Newcastle U)   23
Kelly, H. R. 1950 (Fulham, Southampton)   4
Kelly, J. 1896 (Glentoran)   1
Kelly, J. 1932 (Derry C)   11
Kelly, P. J. 1921 (Manchester C)   1
Kelly, P. M. 1950 (Barnsley)   1
Kennedy, A. L. 1923 (Arsenal)   2
Kennedy, P. H. 1999 (Watford, Wigan Ath)   20
Kernaghan, N. 1936 (Belfast Celtic)   3
Kirk, A. R. 2000 (Hearts, Boston U, Northampton T, Dunfermline Ath)   11
Kirkwood, H. 1904 (Cliftonville)   1
Kirwan, J. 1900 (Tottenham H, Chelsea, Clyde)   17

Lacey, W. 1909 (Everton, Liverpool, New Brighton)   23
Lafferty, D. P. 2012 (Burnley)   13
Lafferty, K. 2006 (Burnley, Rangers, FC Sion, Palermo, Norwich C, Hearts)   **67**
Lavery, S. F. 2018 (Everton)   **1**
Lawrie, J. 2009 (Port Vale)   3
Lawther, R. 1888 (Glentoran)   2
Lawther, W. I. 1960 (Sunderland, Blackburn R)   4
Leatham, J. 1939 (Belfast Celtic)   1
Ledwidge, J. J. 1906 (Shelbourne)   2
Lemon, J. 1886 (Glentoran, Belfast YMCA)   3
Lennon, N. F. 1994 (Crewe Alex, Leicester C, Celtic)   40
Leslie, W. 1887 (YMCA)   1
Lewis, J. 1899 (Glentoran, Distillery)   4
Lewis, J. P. 2018 (Norwich C)   **1**
Little, A. 2009 (Rangers)   9
Lockhart, H. 1884 (Rossall School)   1
Lockhart, N. H. 1947 (Linfield, Coventry C, Aston Villa)   8
Lomas, S. M. 1994 (Manchester C, West Ham U)   45
Loyal, I. 1891 (Clarence)   1
Lund, M. C. 2017 (Rochdale)   3
Lutton, J. P. 1970 (Wolverhampton W, West Ham U)   6
Lynas, R. 1925 (Cliftonville)   1
Lyner, D. R. 1920 (Glentoran, Manchester U, Kilmarnock)   6
Lytle, J. 1898 (Glentoran)   1

Madden, O. 1938 (Norwich C)   1
Magee, G. 1885 (Wellington Park)   1
Magennis, J. B. D. 2010 (Cardiff C, Aberdeen, St Mirren, Kilmarnock, Charlton Ath)   **38**

Magill, E. J. 1962 (Arsenal, Brighton & HA)   26
Magilton, J. 1991 (Oxford U, Southampton, Sheffield W, Ipswich T)   52
Maginnis, H. 1900 (Linfield)   8
Mahood, J. 1926 (Belfast Celtic, Ballymena)   9
Mannus, A. 2004 (Linfield, St Johnstone)   9
Manderson, R. 1920 (Rangers)   5
Mansfield, J. 1901 (Dublin Freebooters)   1
Martin, C. 1882 (Cliftonville)   3
Martin, C. 1925 (Bo'ness)   1
Martin, C. J. 1947 (Glentoran, Leeds U, Aston Villa)   6
Martin, D. K. 1934 (Belfast Celtic, Wolverhampton W, Nottingham F)   10
Mathieson, A. 1921 (Luton T)   2
Maxwell, J. 1902 (Linfield, Glentoran, Belfast Celtic)   7
McAdams, W. J. 1954 (Manchester C, Bolton W, Leeds U)   15
McAlery, J. M. 1882 (Cliftonville)   2
McAlinden, J. 1938 (Belfast Celtic, Portsmouth, Southend U)   4
McAllen, J. 1898 (Linfield)   9
McAlpine, S. 1901 (Cliftonville)   1
McArdle, R. A. 2010 (Rochdale, Aberdeen, Bradford C)   7
McArthur, A. 1886 (Distillery)   1
McAuley, G. 2005 (Lincoln C, Leicester C, Ipswich T, WBA)   **79**
McAuley, J. L. 1911 (Huddersfield T)   6
McAuley, P. 1900 (Belfast Celtic)   1
McBride, S. D. 1991 (Glenavon)   4
McCabe, J. J. 1949 (Leeds U)   6
McCabe, W. 1891 (Ulster)   1
McCambridge, J. 1930 (Ballymena, Cardiff C)   4
McCandless, J. 1912 (Bradford)   5
McCandless, W. 1920 (Linfield, Rangers)   9
McCann, G. S. 2002 (West Ham U, Cheltenham T, Barnsley, Scunthorpe U, Peterborough U)   39
McCann, P. 1910 (Belfast Celtic, Glentoran)   7
McCartan, S. V. 2017 (Accrington S, Bradford C)   **2**
McCarthy, J. D. 1996 (Port Vale, Birmingham C)   18
McCartney, A. 1903 (Ulster, Linfield, Everton, Belfast Celtic, Glentoran)   15
McCartney, G. 2002 (Sunderland, West Ham U, Sunderland)   34
McCashin, J. W. 1896 (Cliftonville)   5
McCavana, W. T. 1955 (Coleraine)   3
McCaw, J. H. 1927 (Linfield)   6
McClatchey, J. 1886 (Distillery)   3
McClatchey, T. 1895 (Distillery)   1
McCleary, J. W. 1955 (Cliftonville)   1
McCleery, W. 1922 (Cliftonville, Linfield)   10
McClelland, J. 1980 (Mansfield T, Rangers, Watford, Leeds U)   53
McClelland, J. T. 1961 (Arsenal, Fulham)   6
McCluggage, A. 1922 (Cliftonville, Bradford, Burnley)   13
McClure, G. 1907 (Cliftonville, Distillery)   4
McConnell, E. 1904 (Cliftonville, Glentoran, Sunderland, Sheffield W)   12
McConnell, P. 1928 (Doncaster R, Southport)   2
McConnell, W. G. 1912 (Bohemians)   6
McConnell, W. H. 1925 (Reading)   8
McCourt, F. J. 1952 (Manchester C)   6
McCourt, P. J. 2002 (Rochdale, Celtic, Barnsley, Brighton & HA, Luton T)   18
McCoy, R. K. 1987 (Coleraine)   1
McCoy, S. 1896 (Distillery)   1
McCracken, E. 1928 (Barking)   1
McCracken, R. 1921 (Crystal Palace)   4
McCracken, R. 1922 (Linfield)   1
McCracken, W. R. 1902 (Distillery, Newcastle U, Hull C)   16
McCreery, D. 1976 (Manchester U, QPR, Tulsa Roughnecks, Newcastle U, Hearts)   67
McCrory, S. 1958 (Southend U)   1
McCullough, K. 1935 (Belfast Celtic, Manchester C)   5
McCullough, L. 2014 (Doncaster R)   **6**
McCullough, W. J. 1961 (Arsenal, Millwall)   10
McCurdy, C. 1980 (Linfield)   1
McDonald, A. 1986 (QPR)   52
McDonald, R. 1930 (Rangers)   2
McDonnell, J. 1911 (Bohemians)   4
McElhinney, G. M. A. 1984 (Bolton W)   6
McEvilly, L. R. 2002 (Rochdale)   1
McFaul, W. S. 1967 (Linfield, Newcastle U)   6
McGarry, J. K. 1951 (Cliftonville)   3
McGaughey, M. 1985 (Linfield)   1
McGibbon, P. C. G. 1995 (Manchester U, Wigan Ath)   7

McGinn, N. 2009 (Celtic, Aberdeen, Gwangju)   **52**
McGivern, R. 2009 (Manchester C, Hibernian, Port Vale, Shrewsbury)   24
McGovern, M. 2010 (Ross Co, Hamilton A, Norwich C)   28
McGrath, R. C. 1974 (Tottenham H, Manchester U)   21
McGregor, S. 1921 (Glentoran)   1
McGrillen, J. 1924 (Clyde, Belfast Celtic)   2
McGuire, E. 1907 (Distillery)   1
McGuire, J. 1928 (Linfield)   1
McIlroy, H. 1906 (Cliftonville)   1
McIlroy, J. 1952 (Burnley, Stoke C)   55
McIlroy, S. B. 1972 (Manchester U, Stoke C, Manchester C)   88
McIlvenny, P. 1924 (Distillery)   1
McIlvenny, W. R. 1890 (Distillery, Ulster)   2
McKay, W. R. 2013 (Inverness CT, Wigan Ath)   11
McKeag, W. 1968 (Glentoran)   2
McKeague, T. 1925 (Glentoran)   1
McKee, F. W. 1906 (Cliftonville, Belfast Celtic)   5
McKelvey, H. 1901 (Glentoran)   2
McKenna, J. 1950 (Huddersfield T)   7
McKenzie, H. 1922 (Distillery)   2
McKenzie, R. 1967 (Airdrieonians)   1
McKeown, N. 1892 (Linfield)   7
McKie, H. 1895 (Cliftonville)   3
Mackie, J. A. 1923 (Arsenal, Portsmouth)   3
McKinney, D. 1921 (Hull C, Bradford C)   2
McKinney, V. J. 1966 (Falkirk)   1
McKnight, A. D. 1988 (Celtic, West Ham U)   10
McKnight, J. 1912 (Preston NE, Glentoran)   2
McLaughlin, C. G. 2012 (Preston NE, Fleetwood T, Millwall)   33
McLaughlin, J. C. 1962 (Shrewsbury T, Swansea T)   12
McLaughlin, R. 2014 (Liverpool, Oldham Ath)   5
McLean, B. S. 2006 (Rangers)   1
McLean, T. 1885 (Limavady)   1
McMahon, G. J. 1995 (Tottenham H, Stoke C)   17
McMahon, J. 1934 (Bohemians)   1
McMaster, G. 1897 (Glentoran)   3
McMichael, A. 1950 (Newcastle U)   40
McMillan, G. 1903 (Distillery)   2
McMillan, S. T. 1963 (Manchester U)   2
McMillen, W. S. 1934 (Manchester U, Chesterfield)   7
McMordie, A. S. 1969 (Middlesbrough)   21
McMorran, E. J. 1947 (Belfast Celtic, Barnsley, Doncaster R)   15
McMullan, D. 1926 (Liverpool)   3
McNair, P. J. C. 2015 (Manchester U, Sunderland)   20
McNally, B. A. 1986 (Shrewsbury T)   5
McNinch, J. 1931 (Ballymena)   1
McPake, J. 2012 (Coventry C)   1
McParland, P. J. 1954 (Aston Villa, Wolverhampton W)   34
McQuoid, J. J. B. 2011 (Millwall)   5
McShane, J. 1899 (Cliftonville)   4
McVeigh, P. M. 1999 (Tottenham H, Norwich C)   20
McVicker, J. 1888 (Linfield, Glentoran)   2
McWha, W. B. R. 1882 (Knock, Cliftonville)   7
Meek, H. L. 1925 (Glentoran)   1
Mehaffy, J. A. C. 1922 (Queen's Island)   1
Meldon, P. A. 1899 (Dublin Freebooters)   2
Mercer, H. V. A. 1908 (Linfield)   1
Mercer, J. 1898 (Distillery, Linfield, Distillery, Derby Co)   12
Millar, W. 1932 (Barrow)   2
Miller, J. 1929 (Middlesbrough)   3
Milligan, D. 1939 (Chesterfield)   1
Milne, R. G. 1894 (Linfield)   28
Mitchell, E. J. 1933 (Cliftonville, Glentoran)   2
Mitchell, W. 1932 (Distillery, Chelsea)   15
Molyneux, T. B. 1883 (Ligoniel, Cliftonville)   11
Montgomery, F. J. 1955 (Coleraine)   1
Moore, C. 1949 (Glentoran)   1
Moore, P. 1933 (Aberdeen)   1
Moore, R. 1891 (Linfield Ath)   3
Moore, R. L. 1887 (Ulster)   2
Moore, W. 1923 (Falkirk)   1
Moorhead, F. W. 1885 (Dublin University)   1
Moorhead, G. 1923 (Linfield)   4
Moran, J. 1912 (Leeds U)   1
Moreland, V. 1979 (Derby Co)   6
Morgan, G. F. 1922 (Linfield, Nottingham F)   8
Morgan, S. 1972 (Port Vale, Aston Villa, Brighton & HA, Sparta Rotterdam)   18
Morrison, R. 1891 (Linfield Ath)   2
Morrison, T. 1895 (Glentoran, Burnley)   7

Morrogh, D. 1896 (Bohemians)   1
Morrow, S. J. 1990 (Arsenal, QPR)   39
Morrow, W. J. 1883 (Moyola Park)   3
Muir, R. 1885 (Oldpark)   2
Mulgrew, J. 2010 (Linfield)   2
Mulholland, T. S. 1906 (Belfast Celtic)   2
Mullan, G. 1983 (Glentoran)   4
Mulligan, J. 1921 (Manchester C)   1
Mulryne, P. P. 1997 (Manchester U, Norwich C, Cardiff C)   27
Murdock, C. J. 2000 (Preston NE, Hibernian, Crewe Alex, Rotherham U)   34
Murphy, J. 1910 (Bradford C)   3
Murphy, N. 1905 (QPR)   3
Murray, J. M. 1910 (Motherwell, Sheffield W)   3

Napier, R. J. 1966 (Bolton W)   1
Neill, W. J. T. 1961 (Arsenal, Hull C)   59
Nelis, P. 1923 (Nottingham F)   1
Nelson, S. 1970 (Arsenal, Brighton & HA)   51
Nicholl, C. J. 1975 (Aston Villa, Southampton, Grimsby T)   51
Nicholl, H. 1902 (Belfast Celtic)   3
Nicholl, J. M. 1976 (Manchester U, Toronto Blizzard, Sunderland, Toronto Blizzard, Rangers, Toronto Blizzard, WBA)   73
Nicholson, J. J. 1961 (Manchester U, Huddersfield T)   41
Nixon, R. 1914 (Linfield)   1
Nolan, I. R. 1997 (Sheffield W, Bradford C, Wigan Ath)   18
Nolan-Whelan, J. V. 1901 (Dublin Freebooters)   5
Norwood, O. J. 2011 (Manchester U, Huddersfield T, Reading, Brighton & HA)   53

O'Boyle, G. 1994 (Dunfermline Ath, St Johnstone)   13
O'Brien, M. T. 1921 (QPR, Leicester C, Hull C, Derby Co)   10
O'Connell, P. 1912 (Sheffield W, Hull C)   5
O'Connor, M. J. 2008 (Crewe Alex, Scunthorpe U, Rotherham U)   11
O'Doherty, A. 1970 (Coleraine)   2
O'Driscoll, J. F. 1949 (Swansea T)   3
O'Hagan, C. 1905 (Tottenham H, Aberdeen)   11
O'Hagan, W. 1920 (St Mirren)   2
O'Hehir, J. C. 1910 (Bohemians)   1
O'Kane, W. J. 1970 (Nottingham F)   20
O'Mahoney, M. T. 1939 (Bristol R)   1
O'Neill, C. 1989 (Motherwell)   3
O'Neill, J. 1962 (Sunderland)   1
O'Neill, J. P. 1980 (Leicester C)   39
O'Neill, M. A. M. 1988 (Newcastle U, Dundee U, Hibernian, Coventry C)   31
O'Neill, M. H. M. 1972 (Distillery, Nottingham F, Norwich C, Manchester C, Norwich C, Notts Co)   64
O'Reilly, H. 1901 (Dublin Freebooters)   3
Owens, J. 2011 (Crusaders)   1

Parke, J. 1964 (Linfield, Hibernian, Sunderland)   14
Paterson, M. A. 2008 (Scunthorpe U, Burnley, Huddersfield T)   22
Paton, R. 2014 (Dundee U)   4
Patterson, D. J. 1994 (Crystal Palace, Luton T, Dundee U)   17
Patterson, R. 2010 (Coleraine, Plymouth Arg)   5
Peacock, R. 1952 (Celtic, Coleraine)   31
Peacock-Farrell, B. 2018 (Leeds U)   1
Peden, J. 1887 (Linfield, Distillery)   24
Penney, S. 1985 (Brighton & HA)   17
Percy, C. 1889 (Belfast YMCA)   1
Platt, J. A. 1976 (Middlesbrough, Ballymena U, Coleraine)   23
Pollock, W. 1928 (Belfast Celtic)   1
Ponsonby, J. 1895 (Distillery)   9
Potts, R. M. C. 1883 (Cliftonville)   2
Priestley, T. J. M. 1933 (Coleraine, Chelsea)   2
Pyper, Jas. 1897 (Cliftonville)   7
Pyper, John 1897 (Cliftonville)   9
Pyper, M. 1932 (Linfield)   1

Quinn, J. M. 1985 (Blackburn R, Swindon T, Leicester C, Bradford C, West Ham U, Bournemouth, Reading)   46
Quinn, S. J. 1996 (Blackpool, WBA, Willem II, Sheffield W, Peterborough U, Northampton T)   50

Rafferty, P. 1980 (Linfield)   1

Ramsey, P. C. 1984 (Leicester C)   14
Rankine, J. 1883 (Alexander)   2
Rattray, D. 1882 (Avoniel)   3
Rea, R. 1901 (Glentoran)   1
Reeves, B. N. 2015 (Milton Keynes D)   1
Redmond, R. 1884 (Cliftonville)   1
Reid, G. H. 1923 (Cardiff C)   1
Reid, J. 1883 (Ulster)   6
Reid, S. E. 1934 (Derby Co)   3
Reid, W. 1931 (Hearts)   1
Reilly, M. M. 1900 (Portsmouth)   2
Renneville, W. T. J. 1910 (Leyton, Aston Villa)   4
Reynolds, J. 1890 (Distillery, Ulster)   5
Reynolds, R. 1905 (Bohemians)   1
Rice, P. J. 1969 (Arsenal)   49
Roberts, F. C. 1931 (Glentoran)   1
Robinson, P. 1920 (Distillery, Blackburn R)   1
Robinson, S. 1997 (Bournemouth, Luton T)   7
Rogan, A. 1988 (Celtic, Sunderland, Millwall)   18
Rollo, D. 1912 (Linfield, Blackburn R)   16
Roper, E. O. 1886 (Dublin University)   1
Rosbotham, A. 1887 (Cliftonville)   7
Ross, W. E. 1969 (Newcastle U)   1
Rowland, K. 1994 (West Ham U, QPR)   19
Rowley, R. W. M. 1929 (Southampton, Tottenham H)   6
Rushe, F. 1925 (Distillery)   1
Russell, A. 1947 (Linfield)   1
Russell, S. R. 1930 (Bradford C, Derry C)   3
Ryan, R. A. 1950 (WBA)   1

Sanchez, L. P. 1987 (Wimbledon)   3
Saville, G. A. 2018 (Millwall)   **5**
Scott, E. 1920 (Liverpool, Belfast Celtic)   31
Scott, J. 1958 (Grimsby)   2
Scott, J. E. 1901 (Cliftonville)   1
Scott, L. J. 1895 (Dublin University)   2
Scott, P. W. 1975 (Everton, York C, Aldershot)   10
Scott, T. 1894 (Cliftonville)   13
Scott, W. 1903 (Linfield, Everton, Leeds C)   25
Scraggs, M. J. 1921 (Glentoran)   2
Seymour, H. C. 1914 (Bohemians)   1
Seymour, J. 1907 (Cliftonville)   2
Shanks, T. 1903 (Woolwich Arsenal, Brentford)   3
Sharkey, P. G. 1976 (Ipswich T)   1
Sheehan, Dr G. 1899 (Bohemians)   3
Sheridan, J. 1903 (Everton, Stoke C)   6
Sherrard, J. 1885 (Limavady)   3
Sherrard, W. C. 1895 (Cliftonville)   3
Sherry, J. J. 1906 (Bohemians)   2
Shields, R. J. 1957 (Southampton)   1
Shiels, D. 2006 (Hibernian, Doncaster R, Kilmarnock)   14
Silo, M. 1888 (Belfast YMCA)   1
Simpson, W. J. 1951 (Rangers)   12
Sinclair, J. 1882 (Knock)   2
Slemin, J. C. 1909 (Bohemians)   1
Sloan, A. S. 1925 (London Caledonians)   1
Sloan, D. 1969 (Oxford U)   2
Sloan, H. A. de B. 1903 (Bohemians)   8
Sloan, J. W. 1947 (Arsenal)   1
Sloan, T. 1926 (Cardiff C, Linfield)   11
Sloan, T. 1979 (Manchester U)   3
Small, J. M. 1887 (Clarence, Cliftonville)   4
Smith, A. W. 2003 (Glentoran, Preston NE)   18
Smith, E. E. 1921 (Cardiff C)   4
Smith, J. E. 1901 (Distillery)   1
Smith, M. 2016 (Peterborough U)   1
Smyth, P. 2018 (QPR)   **2**
Smyth, R. H. 1886 (Dublin University)   1
Smyth, S. 1948 (Wolverhampton W, Stoke C)   9
Smyth, W. 1949 (Distillery)   4
Snape, A. 1920 (Airdrieonians)   1
Sonner, D. J. 1998 (Ipswich T, Sheffield W,
Birmingham C, Nottingham F, Peterborough U)   13
Spence, D. W. 1975 (Bury, Blackpool, Southend U)   29
Spencer, S. 1890 (Distillery)   6
Spiller, E. A. 1883 (Cliftonville)   5
Sproule, I. 2006 (Hibernian, Bristol C)   11
Stanfield, O. M. 1887 (Distillery)   30
Steele, A. 1926 (Charlton Ath, Fulham)   4
Steele, J. 2013 (New York Red Bulls)   1
Stevenson, A. E. 1934 (Rangers, Everton)   17
Stewart, A. 1967 (Glentoran, Derby Co)   7
Stewart, D. C. 1978 (Hull C)   1
Stewart, I. 1982 (QPR, Newcastle U)   31
Stewart, R. K. 1890 (St Columb's Court, Cliftonville)   11

Stewart, T. C. 1961 (Linfield)   1
Swan, S. 1899 (Linfield)   1

Taggart, G. P. 1990 (Barnsley, Bolton W, Leicester C)   51
Taggart, J. 1899 (Walsall)   1
Taylor, M. S. 1999 (Fulham, Birmingham C, unattached)   88
Thompson, A. L. 2011 (Watford)   2
Thompson, F. W. 1910 (Cliftonville, Linfield, Bradford
C, Clyde)   12
Thompson, J. 1897 (Distillery)   1
Thompson, J. 2018 (Rangers)   **2**
Thompson, P. 2006 (Linfield, Stockport Co)   8
Thompson, R. 1928 (Queen's Island)   1
Thompson, W. 1889 (Belfast Ath)   1
Thunder, P. J. 1911 (Bohemians)   1
Todd, S. J. 1966 (Burnley, Sheffield W)   11
Toner, C. 2003 (Leyton Orient)   2
Toner, J. 1922 (Arsenal, St Johnstone)   8
Torrans, R. 1893 (Linfield)   1
Torrans, S. 1889 (Linfield)   26
Trainor, D. 1967 (Crusaders)   1
Tuffey, J. 2009 (Partick Thistle, Inverness CT)   8
Tully, C. P. 1949 (Celtic)   10
Turner, A. 1896 (Cliftonville)   1
Turner, E. 1896 (Cliftonville)   1
Turner, W. 1886 (Cliftonville)   3
Twomey, J. F. 1938 (Leeds U)   2

Uprichard, W. N. M. C. 1952 (Swindon T, Portsmouth)   18

Vernon, J. 1947 (Belfast Celtic, WBA)   17

Waddell, T. M. R. 1906 (Cliftonville)   1
Walker, J. 1955 (Doncaster R)   1
Walker, T. 1911 (Bury)   1
Walsh, D. J. 1947 (WBA)   9
Walsh, W. 1948 (Manchester C)   5
Ward, J. J. 2012 (Derby Co, Nottingham F)   **33**
Waring, J. 1899 (Cliftonville)   1
Warren, P. 1913 (Shelbourne)   2
Washington, C. J. 2016 (QPR)   **17**
Watson, J. 1883 (Ulster)   9
Watson, P. 1971 (Distillery)   1
Watson, T. 1926 (Cardiff C)   1
Wattie, J. 1899 (Distillery)   1
Webb, C. G. 1909 (Brighton & HA)   3
Webb, S. M. 2006 (Ross Co)   4
Weir, E. 1939 (Clyde)   1
Welsh, E. 1966 (Carlisle U)   4
Whiteside, N. 1982 (Manchester U, Everton)   38
Whiteside, T. 1891 (Distillery)   1
Whitfield, E. R. 1886 (Dublin University)   1
Whitley, Jeff 1997 (Manchester C, Sunderland, Cardiff C)   20
Whitley, Jim 1998 (Manchester C)   3
Williams, J. R. 1886 (Ulster)   2
Williams, M. S. 1999 (Chesterfield, Watford, Wimbledon,
Stoke C, Wimbledon, Milton Keynes D)   36
Williams, P. A. 1991 (WBA)   1
Williamson, J. 1890 (Cliftonville)   3
Willighan, J. 1933 (Burnley)   2
Willis, G. 1906 (Linfield)   4
Wilson, D. J. 1987 (Brighton & HA, Luton T,
Sheffield W)   24
Wilson, H. 1925 (Linfield)   2
Wilson, K. J. 1987 (Ipswich T, Chelsea, Notts Co,
Walsall)   42
Wilson, M. 1884 (Distillery)   3
Wilson, R. 1888 (Cliftonville)   1
Wilson, S. J. 1962 (Glenavon, Falkirk, Dundee)   12
Wilton, J. M. 1888 (St Columb's Court, Cliftonville, St
Columb's Court)   7
Winchester, C. 2011 (Oldham Ath)   1
Wood, T. J. 1996 (Walsall)   1
Worthington, N. 1984 (Sheffield W, Leeds U, Stoke C)   66
Wright, J. 1906 (Cliftonville)   6
Wright, T. J. 1989 (Newcastle U, Nottingham F,
Manchester C)   31

Young, S. 1907 (Linfield, Airdrieonians, Linfield)   9

SCOTLAND

Adam, C. G. 2007 (Rangers, Blackpool, Liverpool,
Stoke C) 26
Adams, J. 1889 (Hearts) 3
Agnew, W. B. 1907 (Kilmarnock) 3
Aird, J. 1954 (Burnley) 4
Aitken, A. 1901 (Newcastle U, Middlesbrough,
Leicester Fosse) 14
Aitken, G. G. 1949 (East Fife, Sunderland) 8
Aitken, R. 1886 (Dumbarton) 2
Aitken, R. 1980 (Celtic, Newcastle U, St Mirren) 57
Aitkenhead, W. A. C. 1912 (Blackburn R) 1
Albiston, A. 1982 (Manchester U) 14
Alexander, D. 1894 (East Stirlingshire) 2
Alexander, G. 2002 (Preston NE, Burnley) 40
Alexander, N. 2006 (Cardiff C) 3
Allan, D. S. 1885 (Queen's Park) 3
Allan, G. 1897 (Liverpool) 1
Allan, H. 1902 (Hearts) 1
Allan, J. 1887 (Queen's Park) 2
Allan, T. 1974 (Dundee) 2
Ancell, R. F. D. 1937 (Newcastle U) 2
Anderson, A. 1933 (Hearts) 23
Anderson, F. 1874 (Clydesdale) 1
Anderson, G. 1901 (Kilmarnock) 1
Anderson, H. A. 1914 (Raith R) 1
Anderson, J. 1954 (Leicester C) 1
Anderson, K. 1896 (Queen's Park) 3
Anderson, R. 2003 (Aberdeen, Sunderland) 11
Anderson, W. 1882 (Queen's Park) 6
Andrews, P. 1875 (Eastern) 1
Anya, I. 2013 (Watford, Derby Co) 29
Archer, J. G. 2018 (Millwall) 1
Archibald, A. 1921 (Rangers) 8
Archibald, S. 1980 (Aberdeen, Tottenham H, Barcelona)
27
Armstrong, M. W. 1936 (Aberdeen) 3
Armstrong, S. 2017 (Celtic) 6
Arnott, W. 1883 (Queen's Park) 14
Auld, J. R. 1887 (Third Lanark) 3
Auld, R. 1959 (Celtic) 3

Bain, S. 2018 (Celtic) 1
Baird, A. 1892 (Queen's Park) 2
Baird, D. 1890 (Hearts) 3
Baird, H. 1956 (Airdrieonians) 1
Baird, J. C. 1876 (Vale of Leven) 3
Baird, S. 1957 (Rangers) 7
Baird, W. U. 1897 (St Bernard) 1
**Bannan, B. 2011 (Aston Villa, Crystal Palace,
Sheffield W)** 27
Bannon, E. J. 1980 (Dundee U) 11
Barbour, A. 1885 (Renton) 1
Bardsley, P. A. 2011 (Sunderland) 13
Barker, J. B. 1893 (Rangers) 2
Barr, D. 2009 (Falkirk) 1
Barrett, F. 1894 (Dundee) 2
Battles, B. 1901 (Celtic) 3
Battles, B. jun. 1931 (Hearts) 1
Bauld, W. 1950 (Hearts) 3
Baxter, J. C. 1961 (Rangers, Sunderland) 34
Baxter, R. D. 1939 (Middlesbrough) 3
Beattie, A. 1937 (Preston NE) 7
Beattie, C. 2006 (Celtic, WBA) 7
Beattie, R. 1939 (Preston NE) 1
Begbie, I. 1890 (Hearts) 4
Bell, A. 1912 (Manchester U) 1
Bell, C. 2011 (Kilmarnock) 1
Bell, J. 1890 (Dumbarton, Everton, Celtic) 10
Bell, M. 1901 (Hearts) 1
Bell, W. J. 1966 (Leeds U) 2
Bennett, A. 1904 (Celtic, Rangers) 11
Bennie, R. 1925 (Airdrieonians) 3
Bernard, P. R. J. 1995 (Oldham Ath) 2
**Berra, C. D. 2008 (Hearts, Wolverhampton W,
Ipswich T)** 41
Berry, D. 1894 (Queen's Park) 3
Berry, W. H. 1888 (Queen's Park) 4
Bett, J. 1982 (Rangers, Lokeren, Aberdeen) 25
Beveridge, W. W. 1879 (Glasgow University) 3
Black, A. 1938 (Hearts) 3
Black, D. 1889 (Hurlford) 1
Black, E. 1988 (Metz) 2
Black, I. 2013 (Rangers) 1
Black, I. H. 1948 (Southampton) 1

Blackburn, J. E. 1873 (Royal Engineers) 1
Blacklaw, A. S. 1963 (Burnley) 3
Blackley, J. 1974 (Hibernian) 7
Blair, D. 1929 (Clyde, Aston Villa) 8
Blair, J. 1920 (Sheffield W, Cardiff C) 8
Blair, J. 1934 (Motherwell) 1
Blair, J. A. 1947 (Blackpool) 1
Blair, W. 1896 (Third Lanark) 1
Blessington, J. 1894 (Celtic) 4
Blyth, J. A. 1978 (Coventry C) 2
Bone, J. 1972 (Norwich C) 2
Booth, S. 1993 (Aberdeen, Borussia Dortmund, Twente)
21
Bowie, J. 1920 (Rangers) 2
Bowie, W. 1891 (Linthouse) 1
Bowman, D. 1992 (Dundee U) 6
Bowman, G. A. 1892 (Montrose) 1
Boyd, G. I. 2013 (Peterborough U, Hull C) 2
Boyd, J. M. 1934 (Newcastle U) 1
Boyd, K. 2006 (Rangers, Middlesbrough) 18
Boyd, R. 1889 (Mossend Swifts) 2
Boyd, T. 1991 (Motherwell, Chelsea, Celtic) 72
Boyd, W. G. 1931 (Clyde) 2
Bradshaw, T. 1928 (Bury) 1
Brand, R. 1961 (Rangers) 8
Brandon, T. 1896 (Blackburn R) 1
Brazil, A. 1980 (Ipswich T, Tottenham H) 13
Breckenridge, T. 1888 (Hearts) 1
Bremner, D. 1976 (Hibernian) 1
Bremner, W. J. 1965 (Leeds U) 54
Brennan, F. 1947 (Newcastle U) 7
Breslin, B. 1897 (Hibernian) 1
Brewster, G. 1921 (Everton) 1
Bridcutt, L. 2013 (Brighton & HA, Sunderland) 2
Broadfoot, K. 2009 (Rangers) 4
Brogan, J. 1971 (Celtic) 4
Brown, A. 1890 (St Mirren) 2
Brown, A. 1904 (Middlesbrough) 1
Brown, A. D. 1950 (East Fife, Blackpool) 14
Brown, G. C. P. 1931 (Rangers) 19
Brown, H. 1947 (Partick Thistle) 3
Brown, J. B. 1939 (Clyde) 1
Brown, J. G. 1975 (Sheffield U) 1
Brown, R. 1884 (Dumbarton) 2
Brown, R. 1890 (Cambuslang) 1
Brown, R. 1947 (Rangers) 3
Brown, R. jun. 1885 (Dumbarton) 1
Brown, S. 2006 (Hibernian, Celtic) 55
Brown, W. D. F. 1958 (Dundee, Tottenham H) 28
Browning, J. 1914 (Celtic) 1
Brownlie, J. 1909 (Third Lanark) 16
Brownlie, J. 1971 (Hibernian) 7
Bruce, D. 1890 (Vale of Leven) 1
Bruce, R. F. 1934 (Middlesbrough) 1
Bryson, C. 2011 (Kilmarnock, Derby Co) 3
Buchan, M. M. 1972 (Aberdeen, Manchester U) 34
Buchanan, J. 1889 (Cambuslang) 1
Buchanan, J. 1929 (Rangers) 2
Buchanan, P. S. 1938 (Chelsea) 1
Buchanan, R. 1891 (Abercorn) 1
Buckley, P. 1954 (Aberdeen) 3
Buick, A. 1902 (Hearts) 2
Burchill, M. J. 2000 (Celtic) 6
Burke, C. 2006 (Rangers, Birmingham C) 7
Burke O. J. 2016 (Nottingham F, RB Leipzig) 5
Burley, C. W. 1995 (Chelsea, Celtic, Derby Co) 46
Burley, G. E. 1979 (Ipswich T) 11
Burns, F. 1970 (Manchester U) 1
Burns, K. 1974 (Birmingham C, Nottingham F) 20
Burns, T. 1981 (Celtic) 8
Busby, M. W. 1934 (Manchester C) 1

Cadden, C. 2018 (Motherwell) 2
Caddis, P. M. 2016 (Birmingham C) 1
Cairney, T. 2017 (Fulham) 2
Cairns, T. 1920 (Rangers) 8
Calderhead, D. 1889 (Q of S Wanderers) 1
Calderwood, C. 1995 (Tottenham H) 36
Calderwood, R. 1885 (Cartvale) 3
Caldow, E. 1957 (Rangers) 40
Caldwell, G. 2002 (Newcastle U, Hibernian, Celtic,
Wigan Ath) 55
Caldwell, S. 2001 (Newcastle U, Sunderland,
Burnley,Wigan Ath) 12

Callaghan, P. 1900 (Hibernian)	1
Callaghan, W. 1970 (Dunfermline Ath)	2
Cameron, C. 1999 (Hearts, Wolverhampton W)	28
Cameron, J. 1886 (Rangers)	1
Cameron, J. 1896 (Queen's Park)	1
Cameron, J. 1904 (St Mirren, Chelsea)	2
Campbell, C. 1874 (Queen's Park)	13
Campbell, H. 1889 (Renton)	1
Campbell, Jas 1913 (Sheffield W)	1
Campbell, J. 1880 (South Western)	1
Campbell, J. 1891 (Kilmarnock)	2
Campbell, John 1893 (Celtic)	12
Campbell, John 1899 (Rangers)	4
Campbell, K. 1920 (Liverpool, Partick Thistle)	8
Campbell, P. 1878 (Rangers)	2
Campbell, P. 1898 (Morton)	1
Campbell, R. 1947 (Falkirk, Chelsea)	5
Campbell, W. 1947 (Morton)	5
Canero, P. 2004 (Leicester C)	1
Carabine, J. 1938 (Third Lanark)	3
Carr, W. M. 1970 (Coventry C)	6
Cassidy, J. 1921 (Celtic)	4
Chalmers, J. 1965 (Celtic)	5
Chalmers, W. 1885 (Rangers)	1
Chalmers, W. S. 1929 (Queen's Park)	1
Chambers, T. 1894 (Hearts)	1
Chaplin, G. D. 1908 (Dundee)	1
Cheyne, A. G. 1929 (Aberdeen)	5
Christie, A. J. 1898 (Queen's Park)	3
Christie, R. 2018 (Celtic)	**3**
Christie, R. M. 1884 (Queen's Park)	1
Clark, J. 1966 (Celtic)	4
Clark, R. B. 1968 (Aberdeen)	17
Clarke, S. 1988 (Chelsea)	6
Clarkson, D. 2008 (Motherwell)	2
Cleland, J. 1891 (Royal Albert)	1
Clements, R. 1891 (Leith Ath)	1
Clunas, W. L. 1924 (Sunderland)	2
Collier, W. 1922 (Raith R)	1
Collins, J. 1988 (Hibernian, Celtic, Monaco, Everton)	58
Collins, R. Y. 1951 (Celtic, Everton, Leeds U)	31
Collins, T. 1909 (Hearts)	1
Colman, D. 1911 (Aberdeen)	4
Colquhoun, E. P. 1972 (Sheffield U)	9
Colquhoun, J. 1988 (Hearts)	2
Combe, J. R. 1948 (Hibernian)	3
Commons, K. 2009 (Derby Co, Celtic)	12
Conn, A. 1956 (Hearts)	1
Conn, A. 1975 (Tottenham H)	2
Connachan, E. D. 1962 (Dunfermline Ath)	2
Connelly, G. 1974 (Celtic)	2
Connolly, J. 1973 (Everton)	1
Connor, J. 1886 (Airdrieonians)	1
Connor, J. 1930 (Sunderland)	4
Connor, R. 1986 (Dundee, Aberdeen)	4
Conway, C. 2010 (Dundee U, Cardiff C)	7
Cook, W. L. 1934 (Bolton W)	3
Cooke, C. 1966 (Dundee, Chelsea)	16
Cooper, D. 1980 (Rangers, Motherwell)	22
Cormack, P. B. 1966 (Hibernian, Nottingham F)	9
Cowan, J. 1896 (Aston Villa)	3
Cowan, J. 1948 (Morton)	25
Cowan, W, D. 1924 (Newcastle U)	1
Cowie, D. 1953 (Dundee)	20
Cowie, D. M. 2010 (Watford, Cardiff C)	10
Cox, C. J. 1948 (Hearts)	1
Cox, S. 1949 (Rangers)	24
Craig, A. 1929 (Motherwell)	3
Craig, J. 1977 (Celtic)	1
Craig, J. P. 1968 (Celtic)	1
Craig, T. 1927 (Rangers)	8
Craig, T. B. 1976 (Newcastle U)	1
Crainey, S. D. 2002 (Celtic, Southampton, Blackpool)	12
Crapnell, J. 1929 (Airdrieonians)	9
Crawford, D. 1894 (St Mirren, Rangers)	3
Crawford, J. 1932 (Queen's Park)	5
Crawford, S. 1995 (Raith R, Dunfermline Ath, Plymouth Arg)	25
Crerand, P. T. 1961 (Celtic, Manchester U)	16
Cringan, W. 1920 (Celtic)	5
Crosbie, J. A. 1920 (Ayr U, Birmingham)	2
Croal, J. A. 1913 (Falkirk)	3
Cropley, A. J. 1972 (Hibernian)	2
Cross, J. H. 1903 (Third Lanark)	1
Cruickshank, J. 1964 (Hearts)	6
Crum, J. 1936 (Celtic)	2

Cullen, M. J. 1956 (Luton T)	1
Cumming, D. S. 1938 (Middlesbrough)	1
Cumming, J. 1955 (Hearts)	9
Cummings, G. 1935 (Partick Thistle, Aston Villa)	9
Cummings, J. 2018 (Nottingham F)	**1**
Cummings, W. 2002 (Chelsea)	1
Cunningham, A. N. 1920 (Rangers)	12
Cunningham, W. C. 1954 (Preston NE)	8
Curran, H. P. 1970 (Wolverhampton W)	5
Dailly, C. 1997 (Derby Co, Blackburn R, West Ham U, Rangers)	67
Dalglish, K. 1972 (Celtic, Liverpool)	102
Davidson, C. I. 1999 (Blackburn R, Leicester C, Preston NE)	19
Davidson, D. 1878 (Queen's Park)	5
Davidson, J. A. 1954 (Partick Thistle)	8
Davidson, M. 2013 (St Johnstone)	1
Davidson, S. 1921 (Middlesbrough)	1
Dawson, A. 1980 (Rangers)	5
Dawson, J. 1935 (Rangers)	14
Deans, J. 1975 (Celtic)	2
Delaney, J. 1936 (Celtic, Manchester U)	13
Devine, A. 1910 (Falkirk)	1
Devlin, P. J. 2003 (Birmingham C)	10
Dewar, G. 1888 (Dumbarton)	2
Dewar, N. 1932 (Third Lanark)	3
Dick, J. 1959 (West Ham U)	1
Dickie, M. 1897 (Rangers)	3
Dickov, P. 2001 (Manchester C, Leicester C, Blackburn R)	10
Dickson, W. 1888 (Dundee Strathmore)	1
Dickson, W. 1970 (Kilmarnock)	5
Divers, J. 1895 (Celtic)	1
Divers, J. 1939 (Celtic)	1
Dixon, P. A. 2013 (Huddersfield T)	3
Dobie, R. S. 2002 (WBA)	6
Docherty, T. H. 1952 (Preston NE, Arsenal)	25
Dodds, D. 1984 (Dundee U)	2
Dodds, J. 1914 (Celtic)	3
Dodds, W. 1997 (Aberdeen, Dundee U, Rangers)	26
Doig, J. E. 1887 (Arbroath, Sunderland)	5
Donachie, W. 1972 (Manchester C)	35
Donaldson, A. 1914 (Bolton W)	6
Donnachie, J. 1913 (Oldham Ath)	3
Donnelly, S. 1997 (Celtic)	10
Dorrans, G. 2010 (WBA, Norwich C)	12
Dougal, J. 1939 (Preston NE)	1
Dougall, C. 1947 (Birmingham C)	1
Dougan, R. 1950 (Hearts)	1
Douglas, A. 1911 (Chelsea)	1
Douglas, B. 2018 (Wolverhampton W)	**1**
Douglas, J. 1880 (Renfrew)	1
Douglas, R. 2002 (Celtic, Leicester C)	19
Dowds, P. 1892 (Celtic)	1
Downie, R. 1892 (Third Lanark)	1
Doyle, D. 1892 (Celtic)	8
Doyle, J. 1976 (Ayr U)	1
Drummond, J. 1892 (Falkirk, Rangers)	14
Dunbar, M. 1886 (Cartvale)	1
Duncan, A. 1975 (Hibernian)	6
Duncan, D. 1933 (Derby Co)	14
Duncan, D. M. 1948 (East Fife)	3
Duncan, J. 1878 (Alexandra Ath)	2
Duncan, J. 1926 (Leicester C)	1
Duncanson, J. 1947 (Rangers)	1
Dunlop, J. 1890 (St Mirren)	1
Dunlop, W. 1906 (Liverpool)	1
Dunn, J. 1925 (Hibernian, Everton)	6
Durie, G. S. 1988 (Chelsea, Tottenham H, Rangers)	43
Durrant, I. 1988 (Rangers, Kilmarnock)	20
Dykes, J. 1938 (Hearts)	2
Easson, J. F. 1931 (Portsmouth)	3
Elliott, M. S. 1998 (Leicester C)	18
Ellis, J. 1892 (Mossend Swifts)	1
Evans, A. 1982 (Aston Villa)	4
Evans, R. 1949 (Celtic, Chelsea)	48
Ewart, J. 1921 (Bradford C)	1
Ewing, T. 1958 (Partick Thistle)	2
Farm, G. N. 1953 (Blackpool)	10
Ferguson, B. 1999 (Rangers, Blackburn R, Rangers)	45
Ferguson, D. 1988 (Rangers)	2
Ferguson, D. 1992 (Dundee U, Everton)	7

Ferguson, I. 1989 (Rangers)	9
Ferguson, J. 1874 (Vale of Leven)	6
Ferguson, R. 1966 (Kilmarnock)	7
Fernie, W. 1954 (Celtic)	12
Findlay, R. 1898 (Kilmarnock)	1
Fitchie, T. T. 1905 (Woolwich Arsenal, Queen's Park)	4
Flavell, R. 1947 (Airdrieonians)	2
Fleck, R. 1990 (Norwich C)	4
Fleming, C. 1954 (East Fife)	1
Fleming, J. W. 1929 (Rangers)	3
Fleming, R. 1886 (Morton)	1
Fletcher, D. B. 2004 (Manchester U, WBA, Stoke C)	**80**
Fletcher, S. K. 2008 (Hibernian, Burnley,	
Wolverhampton W, Sunderland, Sheffield W)	**31**
Forbes, A. R. 1947 (Sheffield U, Arsenal)	14
Forbes, J. 1884 (Vale of Leven)	5
Ford, D. 1974 (Hearts)	3
Forrest, J. 1958 (Motherwell)	1
Forrest, J. 1966 (Rangers, Aberdeen)	5
Forrest, J. 2011 (Celtic)	**22**
Forsyth, A. 1972 (Partick Thistle, Manchester U)	10
Forsyth, C. 2014 (Derby Co)	4
Forsyth, R. C. 1964 (Kilmarnock)	4
Forsyth, T. 1971 (Motherwell, Rangers)	22
Fox, D. J. 2010 (Burnley, Southampton)	4
Foyers, R. 1893 (St Bernards)	2
Fraser, D. M. 1968 (WBA)	2
Fraser, J. 1891 (Moffat)	1
Fraser, J. 1907 (Dundee)	1
Fraser, M. J. E. 1880 (Queen's Park)	5
Fraser, R. 2017 (Bournemouth)	**3**
Fraser, W. 1955 (Sunderland)	2
Freedman, D. A. 2002 (Crystal Palace)	2
Fulton, W. 1884 (Abercorn)	1
Fyfe, J. H. 1895 (Third Lanark)	1
Gabriel, J. 1961 (Everton)	2
Gallacher, H. K. 1924 (Airdrieonians, Newcastle U,	
Chelsea, Derby Co)	20
Gallacher, K. W. 1988 (Dundee U, Coventry C,	
Blackburn R, Newcastle U)	53
Gallacher, P. 1935 (Sunderland)	1
Gallacher, P. 2002 (Dundee U)	8
Gallagher, P. 2004 (Blackburn R)	1
Galloway, M. 1992 (Celtic)	1
Galt, J. H. 1908 (Rangers)	2
Gardiner, I. 1958 (Motherwell)	1
Gardner, D. R. 1897 (Third Lanark)	1
Gardner, R. 1872 (Queen's Park, Clydesdale)	5
Gemmell, T. 1955 (St Mirren)	2
Gemmell, T. 1966 (Celtic)	18
Gemmill, A. 1971 (Derby Co, Nottingham F,	
Birmingham C)	43
Gemmill, S. 1995 (Nottingham F, Everton)	26
Gibb, W. 1873 (Clydesdale)	1
Gibson, D. W. 1963 (Leicester C)	7
Gibson, J. D. 1926 (Partick Thistle, Aston Villa)	8
Gibson, N. 1895 (Rangers, Partick Thistle)	14
Gilchrist, J. E. 1922 (Celtic)	1
Gilhooley, M. 1922 (Hull C)	1
Gilks, M. 2013 (Blackpool)	3
Gillespie, G. 1880 (Rangers, Queen's Park)	7
Gillespie, G. T. 1988 (Liverpool)	13
Gillespie, Jas 1898 (Third Lanark)	1
Gillespie, John 1896 (Queen's Park)	1
Gillespie, R. 1927 (Queen's Park)	4
Gillick, T. 1937 (Everton)	5
Gilmour, J. 1931 (Dundee)	1
Gilzean, A. J. 1964 (Dundee, Tottenham H)	22
Glass, S. 1999 (Newcastle U)	1
Glavin, R. 1977 (Celtic)	1
Glen, A. 1956 (Aberdeen)	2
Glen, R. 1895 (Renton, Hibernian)	3
Goodwillie, D. 2011 (Dundee U, Blackburn R)	3
Goram, A. L. 1986 (Oldham Ath, Hibernian, Rangers)	43
Gordon, C. A. 2004 (Hearts, Sunderland, Celtic)	**52**
Gordon, J. E. 1912 (Rangers)	10
Gossland, J. 1884 (Rangers)	1
Goudie, J. 1884 (Abercorn)	1
Gough, C. R. 1983 (Dundee U, Tottenham H, Rangers)	61
Gould, J. 2000 (Celtic)	2
Gourlay, J. 1886 (Cambuslang)	2
Govan, J. 1948 (Hibernian)	6
Gow, D. R. 1888 (Rangers)	1
Gow, J. J. 1885 (Queen's Park)	1

Gow, J. R. 1888 (Rangers)	1
Graham, A. 1978 (Leeds U)	11
Graham, G. 1972 (Arsenal, Manchester U)	12
Graham, J. 1884 (Annbank)	1
Graham, J. A. 1921 (Arsenal)	1
Grant, J. 1959 (Hibernian)	2
Grant, P. 1989 (Celtic)	2
Gray, A. 1903 (Hibernian)	1
Gray, A. D. 2003 (Bradford C)	2
Gray, A. M. 1976 (Aston Villa, Wolverhampton W,	
Everton)	20
Gray, D. 1929 (Rangers)	10
Gray, E. 1969 (Leeds U)	12
Gray, F. T. 1976 (Leeds U, Nottingham F, Leeds U)	32
Gray, W. 1886 (Pollokshields Ath)	1
Green, A. 1971 (Blackpool, Newcastle U)	6
Greer, G. 2013 (Brighton & HA)	11
Greig, J. 1964 (Rangers)	44
Griffiths, L. 2013 (Hibernian, Celtic)	**17**
Groves, W. 1888 (Hibernian, Celtic)	3
Gulliland, W. 1891 (Queen's Park)	4
Gunn, B. 1990 (Norwich C)	6
Haddock, H. 1955 (Clyde)	6
Haddow, D. 1894 (Rangers)	1
Haffey, F. 1960 (Celtic)	2
Hamilton, A. 1885 (Queen's Park)	4
Hamilton, A. W. 1962 (Dundee)	24
Hamilton, G. 1906 (Port Glasgow Ath)	1
Hamilton, G. 1947 (Aberdeen)	5
Hamilton, J. 1892 (Queen's Park)	3
Hamilton, J. 1924 (St Mirren)	1
Hamilton, R. C. 1899 (Rangers, Dundee)	11
Hamilton, T. 1891 (Hurlford)	1
Hamilton, T. 1932 (Rangers)	1
Hamilton, W. M. 1965 (Hibernian)	1
Hammell, S. 2005 (Motherwell)	1
Hanley, G. C. 2011 (Blackburn R, Newcastle U,	
Norwich C)	**29**
Hannah, A. B. 1888 (Renton)	1
Hannah, J. 1889 (Third Lanark)	1
Hansen, A. D. 1979 (Liverpool)	26
Hansen, J. 1972 (Partick Thistle)	2
Harkness, J. D. 1927 (Queen's Park, Hearts)	12
Harper, J. M. 1973 (Aberdeen, Hibernian, Aberdeen)	4
Harper, W. 1923 (Hibernian, Arsenal)	11
Harris, J. 1921 (Partick Thistle)	2
Harris, N. 1924 (Newcastle U)	1
Harrower, W. 1882 (Queen's Park)	3
Hartford, R. A. 1972 (WBA, Manchester C, Everton,	
Manchester C)	50
Hartley, P. J. 2005 (Hearts, Celtic, Bristol C)	25
Harvey, D. 1973 (Leeds U)	16
Hastings, A. C. 1936 (Sunderland)	2
Haughney, M. 1954 (Celtic)	1
Hay, D. 1970 (Celtic)	27
Hay, J. 1905 (Celtic, Newcastle U)	11
Hegarty, P. 1979 (Dundee U)	8
Heggie, C. 1886 (Rangers)	1
Henderson, G. H. 1904 (Rangers)	1
Henderson, J. G. 1953 (Portsmouth, Arsenal)	7
Henderson, W. 1963 (Rangers)	29
Hendry, E. C. J. 1993 (Blackburn R, Rangers,	
Coventry C, Bolton W)	51
Hendry, J. 2018 (Celtic)	**2**
Hepburn, J. 1891 (Alloa Ath)	1
Hepburn, R. 1932 (Ayr U)	1
Herd, A. C. 1935 (Hearts)	1
Herd, D. G. 1959 (Arsenal)	5
Herd, G. 1958 (Clyde)	5
Herriot, J. 1969 (Birmingham C)	8
Hewie, J. D. 1956 (Charlton Ath)	19
Higgins, A. 1885 (Kilmarnock)	1
Higgins, A. 1910 (Newcastle U)	4
Highet, T. C. 1875 (Queen's Park)	4
Hill, D. 1881 (Rangers)	3
Hill, D. A. 1906 (Third Lanark)	1
Hill, F. R. 1930 (Aberdeen)	3
Hill, J. 1891 (Hearts)	2
Hogg, G. 1896 (Hearts)	2
Hogg, J. 1922 (Ayr U)	1
Hogg, R. M. 1937 (Celtic)	1
Holm, A. H. 1882 (Queen's Park)	3
Holt, D. D. 1963 (Hearts)	5
Holt, G. J. 2001 (Kilmarnock, Norwich C)	10

Holton, J. A. 1973 (Manchester U) 15
Hope, R. 1968 (WBA) 2
Hopkin, D. 1997 (Crystal Palace, Leeds U) 7
Houliston, W. 1949 (Queen of the South) 3
Houston, S. M. 1976 (Manchester U) 1
Howden, W. 1905 (Partick Thistle) 1
Howe, R. 1929 (Hamilton A) 2
Howie, H. 1949 (Hibernian) 1
Howie, J. 1905 (Newcastle U) 3
Howieson, J. 1927 (St Mirren) 1
Hughes, J. 1965 (Celtic) 8
Hughes, R. D. 2004 (Portsmouth) 5
Hughes, S. R. 2010 (Norwich C) 1
Hughes, W. 1975 (Sunderland) 1
Humphries, W. 1952 (Motherwell) 1
Hunter, A. 1972 (Kilmarnock, Celtic) 4
Hunter, J. 1909 (Dundee) 1
Hunter, J. 1874 (Third Lanark, Eastern, Third Lanark) 4
Hunter, W. 1960 (Motherwell) 3
Hunter, R. 1890 (St Mirren) 1
Husband, J. 1947 (Partick Thistle) 1
Hutchison, D. 1999 (Everton, Sunderland, West Ham U) 26
Hutchison, T. 1974 (Coventry C) 17
Hutton, A. 2007 (Rangers, Tottenham H, Aston Villa) 50
Hutton, J. 1887 (St Bernards) 1
Hutton, J. 1923 (Aberdeen, Blackburn R) 10
Hyslop, T. 1896 (Stoke, Rangers) 2

Imlach, J. J. S. 1958 (Nottingham F) 4
Imrie, W. N. 1929 (St Johnstone) 2
Inglis, J. 1883 (Rangers) 2
Inglis, J. 1884 (Kilmarnock Ath) 1
Irons, J. H. 1900 (Queen's Park) 1
Irvine, B. 1991 (Aberdeen) 9
Iwelumo, C. R. 2009 (Wolverhampton W, Burnley) 4

Jack, R. 2018 (Rangers) **1**
Jackson, A. 1886 (Cambuslang) 2
Jackson, A. 1925 (Aberdeen, Huddersfield T) 17
Jackson, C. 1975 (Rangers) 8
Jackson, D. 1995 (Hibernian, Celtic) 28
Jackson, J. 1931 (Partick Thistle, Chelsea) 8
Jackson, T. A. 1904 (St Mirren) 6
James, A. W. 1926 (Preston NE, Arsenal) 8
Jardine, A. 1971 (Rangers) 38
Jarvie, A. 1971 (Airdrieonians) 3
Jenkinson, T. 1887 (Hearts) 1
Jess, E. 1993 (Aberdeen, Coventry C, Aberdeen) 18
Johnston, A. 1999 (Sunderland, Rangers, Middlesbrough) 18
Johnston, L. H. 1948 (Clyde) 2
Johnston, M. 1984 (Watford, Celtic, Nantes, Rangers) 38
Johnston, R. 1938 (Sunderland) 1
Johnston, W. 1966 (Rangers, WBA) 22
Johnstone, D. 1973 (Rangers) 14
Johnstone, J. 1888 (Abercorn) 1
Johnstone, J. 1965 (Celtic) 23
Johnstone, Jas 1894 (Kilmarnock) 1
Johnstone, J. A. 1930 (Hearts) 3
Johnstone, R. 1951 (Hibernian, Manchester C) 17
Johnstone, W. 1887 (Third Lanark) 3
Jordan, J. 1973 (Leeds U, Manchester U, AC Milan) 52

Kay, J. L. 1880 (Queen's Park) 6
Keillor, A. 1891 (Montrose, Dundee) 6
Keir, L. 1885 (Dumbarton) 5
Kelly, H. T. 1952 (Blackpool) 1
Kelly, J. 1888 (Renton, Celtic) 8
Kelly, J. C. 1949 (Barnsley) 2
Kelly, L. M. 2013 (Kilmarnock) 1
Kelso, R. 1885 (Renton, Dundee) 7
Kelso, T. 1914 (Dundee) 1
Kennaway, J. 1934 (Celtic) 1
Kennedy, A. 1875 (Eastern, Third Lanark) 6
Kennedy, J. 1897 (Hibernian) 1
Kennedy, J. 1964 (Celtic) 6
Kennedy, J. 2004 (Celtic) 1
Kennedy, S. 1905 (Partick Thistle) 5
Kennedy, S. 1975 (Rangers) 5
Kennedy, S. 1978 (Aberdeen) 8
Kenneth, G. 2011 (Dundee U) 1
Ker, G. 1880 (Queen's Park) 5
Ker, W. 1872 (Queen's Park) 2
Kerr, A. 1955 (Partick Thistle) 2
Kerr, B. 2003 (Newcastle U) 3

Kerr, P. 1924 (Hibernian) 1
Key, G. 1902 (Hearts) 1
Key, W. 1907 (Queen's Park) 1
King, A. 1896 (Hearts, Celtic) 6
King, J. 1933 (Hamilton A) 2
King, W. S. 1929 (Queen's Park) 1
Kingsley, S. 2016 (Swansea C) 1
Kinloch, J. D. 1922 (Partick Thistle) 1
Kinnaird, A. F. 1873 (Wanderers) 1
Kinnear, D. 1938 (Rangers) 1
Kyle, K. 2002 (Sunderland, Kilmarnock) 10

Lambert, P. 1995 (Motherwell, Borussia Dortmund, Celtic) 40
Lambie, J. A. 1886 (Queen's Park) 3
Lambie, W. A. 1892 (Queen's Park) 9
Lamont, W. 1885 (Pilgrims) 1
Lang, A. 1880 (Dumbarton) 1
Lang, J. J. 1876 (Clydesdale, Third Lanark) 2
Latta, A. 1888 (Dumbarton) 2
Law, D. 1959 (Huddersfield T, Manchester C, Torino, Manchester U, Manchester C) 55
Law, G. 1910 (Rangers) 3
Law, T. 1928 (Chelsea) 2
Lawrence, J. 1911 (Newcastle U) 1
Lawrence, T. 1963 (Liverpool) 3
Lawson, D. 1923 (St Mirren) 1
Leckie, R. 1872 (Queen's Park) 1
Leggat, G. 1956 (Aberdeen, Fulham) 18
Leighton, J. 1983 (Aberdeen, Manchester U, Hibernian, Aberdeen) 91
Lennie, W. 1908 (Aberdeen) 2
Lennox, R. 1967 (Celtic) 10
Leslie, L. G. 1961 (Airdrieonians) 5
Levein, C. 1990 (Hearts) 16
Liddell, W. 1947 (Liverpool) 28
Liddle, D. 1931 (East Fife) 3
Lindsay, D. 1903 (St Mirren) 1
Lindsay, J. 1880 (Dumbarton) 8
Lindsay, J. 1888 (Renton) 3
Linwood, A. B. 1950 (Clyde) 1
Little, R. J. 1953 (Rangers) 1
Livingstone, G. T. 1906 (Manchester C, Rangers) 2
Lochhead, A. 1889 (Third Lanark) 1
Logan, J. 1891 (Ayr) 1
Logan, T. 1913 (Falkirk) 1
Logie, J. T. 1953 (Arsenal) 1
Loney, W. 1910 (Celtic) 2
Long, H. 1947 (Clyde) 1
Longair, W. 1894 (Dundee) 1
Lorimer, P. 1970 (Leeds U) 21
Love, A. 1931 (Aberdeen) 3
Low, A. 1934 (Falkirk) 1
Low, J. 1891 (Cambuslang) 1
Low, T. P. 1897 (Rangers) 1
Low, W. L. 1911 (Newcastle U) 5
Lowe, J. 1887 (St Bernards) 1
Lundie, J. 1886 (Hibernian) 1
Lyall, J. 1905 (Sheffield W) 1

Macari, L. 1972 (Celtic, Manchester U) 24
Mackay-Steven, G. 2013 (Dundee U) 1
Mackail-Smith, C. 2011 (Peterborough U, Brighton & HA) 7
Mackie, J. C. 2011 (QPR) 9
Madden, J. 1893 (Celtic) 2
Maguire, C. 2011 (Aberdeen) 2
Main, F. R. 1938 (Rangers) 1
Main, J. 1909 (Hibernian) 1
Maley, W. 1893 (Celtic) 2
Maloney, S. R. 2006 (Celtic, Aston Villa, Celtic, Wigan Ath, Chicago Fire, Hull C) 47
Malpas, M. 1984 (Dundee U) 55
Marshall, D. J. 2005 (Celtic, Cardiff C, Hull C) 27
Marshall, G. 1992 (Celtic) 1
Marshall, H. 1899 (Celtic) 2
Marshall, J. 1885 (Third Lanark) 4
Marshall, J. 1921 (Middlesbrough, Llanelly) 7
Marshall, J. 1932 (Rangers) 3
Marshall, R. W. 1892 (Rangers) 2
Martin, B. 1995 (Motherwell) 2
Martin, C. H. 2014 (Derby Co) **17**
Martin, F. 1954 (Aberdeen) 6
Martin, N. 1965 (Hibernian, Sunderland) 3
Martin, R. K. A. 2011 (Norwich C) 29

Martis, J. 1961 (Motherwell)	1
Mason, J. 1949 (Third Lanark)	7
Massie, A. 1932 (Hearts, Aston Villa)	18
Masson, D. S. 1976 (QPR, Derby Co)	17
Mathers, D. 1954 (Partick Thistle)	1
Matteo, D. 2001 (Leeds U)	6
Maxwell, W. S. 1898 (Stoke C)	1
May, J. 1906 (Rangers)	5
May, S. 2015 (Sheffield W)	1
McAllister, J. R. 2004 (Livingston)	1
McAdam, J. 1880 (Third Lanark)	1
McAllister, B. 1997 (Wimbledon)	3
McAllister, G. 1990 (Leicester C, Leeds U, Coventry C)	
	57
McArthur, D. 1895 (Celtic)	3
McArthur, J. 2011 (Wigan Ath, Crystal Palace)	**32**
McAtee, A. 1913 (Celtic)	1
McAulay, J. 1884 (Arthurlie)	1
McAulay, J. D. 1882 (Dumbarton)	9
McAulay, R. 1932 (Rangers)	2
Macauley, A. R. 1947 (Brentford, Arsenal)	7
McAvennie, F. 1986 (West Ham U, Celtic)	5
McBain, E. 1894 (St Mirren)	1
McBain, N. 1922 (Manchester U, Everton)	3
McBride, J. 1967 (Celtic)	2
McBride, P. 1904 (Preston NE)	6
McBurnie, O. R. 2018 (Swansea C)	**4**
McCall, A. 1888 (Renton)	1
McCall, A. S. M. 1990 (Everton, Rangers)	40
McCall, J. 1886 (Renton)	5
McCalliog, J. 1967 (Sheffield W, Wolverhampton W)	5
McCallum, N. 1888 (Renton)	1
McCann, N. 1999 (Hearts, Rangers, Southampton)	26
McCann, R. J. 1959 (Motherwell)	5
McCartney, W. 1902 (Hibernian)	1
McClair, B. 1987 (Celtic, Manchester U)	30
McClory, A. 1927 (Motherwell)	3
McCloy, P. 1924 (Ayr U)	2
McCloy, P. 1973 (Rangers)	4
McCoist, A. 1986 (Rangers, Kilmarnock)	61
McColl, I. M. 1950 (Rangers)	14
McColl, R. S. 1896 (Queen's Park, Newcastle U,	
Queen's Park)	13
McColl, W. 1895 (Renton)	1
McCombie, A. 1903 (Sunderland, Newcastle U)	4
McCorkindale, J. 1891 (Partick Thistle)	1
McCormack, R. 2008 (Motherwell, Cardiff C, Leeds U,	
Fulham)	13
McCormick, R. 1886 (Abercorn)	1
McCrae, D. 1929 (St Mirren)	2
McCreadie, A. 1893 (Rangers)	2
McCreadie, E. G. 1965 (Chelsea)	23
McCulloch, D. 1935 (Hearts, Brentford, Derby Co)	7
McCulloch, L. 2005 (Wigan Ath, Rangers)	18
MacDonald, A. 1976 (Rangers)	1
McDonald, J. 1886 (Edinburgh University)	1
McDonald, J. 1956 (Sunderland)	2
McDonald, K. D. 2018 (Fulham)	**1**
MacDougall, E. J. 1975 (Norwich C)	7
McDougall, J. 1877 (Vale of Leven)	5
McDougall, J. 1926 (Airdrieonians)	1
McDougall, J. 1931 (Liverpool)	2
McEveley, J. 2008 (Derby Co)	3
McFadden, J. 2002 (Motherwell, Everton,	
Birmingham C)	48
McFadyen, W. 1934 (Motherwell)	2
Macfarlane, A. 1904 (Dundee)	5
Macfarlane, W. 1947 (Hearts)	1
McFarlane, R. 1896 (Greenock Morton)	1
McGarr, E. 1970 (Aberdeen)	2
McGarvey, F. P. 1979 (Liverpool, Celtic)	7
McGeoch, A. 1876 (Dumbreck)	4
McGeouch, D. 2018 (Hibernian)	**2**
McGhee, J. 1886 (Hibernian)	1
McGhee, M. 1983 (Aberdeen)	4
McGinn, J. 2016 (Hibernian)	**9**
McGinlay, J. 1994 (Bolton W)	13
McGonagle, W. 1933 (Celtic)	6
McGrain, D. 1973 (Celtic)	62
McGregor, A. J. 2007 (Rangers, Besiktas, Hull C)	**38**
McGregor, C. W. 2018 (Celtic)	**3**
McGregor, J. C. 1877 (Vale of Leven)	4
McGrory, J. 1928 (Celtic)	7
McGrory, J. E. 1965 (Kilmarnock)	3
McGuire, W. 1881 (Beith)	2
McGurk, F. 1934 (Birmingham)	1

McHardy, H. 1885 (Rangers)	1
McInally, A. 1989 (Aston Villa, Bayern Munich)	8
McInally, J. 1987 (Dundee U)	10
McInally, T. B. 1926 (Celtic)	2
McInnes, D. 2003 (WBA)	2
McInnes, T. 1889 (Cowlairs)	1
McIntosh, W. 1905 (Third Lanark)	1
McIntyre, A. 1878 (Vale of Leven)	2
McIntyre, H. 1880 (Rangers)	1
McIntyre, J. 1884 (Rangers)	1
MacKay, D. 1959 (Celtic)	14
Mackay, D. C. 1957 (Hearts, Tottenham H)	22
Mackay, G. 1988 (Hearts)	4
Mackay, M. 2004 (Norwich C)	5
McKay, B. 2016 (Rangers)	1
McKay, J. 1924 (Blackburn R)	1
McKay, R. 1928 (Newcastle U)	1
McKean, R. 1976 (Rangers)	1
McKenna, S. 2018 (Aberdeen)	**4**
McKenzie, D. 1938 (Brentford)	1
Mackenzie, J. A. 1954 (Partick Thistle)	9
McKeown, M. 1889 (Celtic)	2
McKie, J. 1898 (East Stirling)	1
McKillop, T. R. 1938 (Rangers)	1
McKimmie, S. 1989 (Aberdeen)	40
McKinlay, D. 1922 (Liverpool)	2
McKinlay, T. 1996 (Celtic)	22
McKinlay, W. 1994 (Dundee U, Blackburn R)	29
McKinnon, A. 1874 (Queen's Park)	1
McKinnon, A. 1966 (Rangers)	28
McKinnon, R. 1994 (Motherwell)	3
MacKinnon, D. 1883 (Dumbarton)	4
MacKinnon, W. W. 1872 (Queen's Park)	9
McLaren, A. 1929 (St Johnstone)	5
McLaren, A. 1947 (Preston NE)	4
McLaren, A. 1992 (Hearts, Rangers)	24
McLaren, A. 2001 (Kilmarnock)	1
McLaren, J. 1888 (Hibernian, Celtic)	3
McLaughlin, J. P. 2018 (Aberdeen)	**1**
McLean, A. 1926 (Celtic)	4
McLean, D. 1896 (St Bernards)	1
McLean, D. 1912 (Sheffield W)	2
McLean, G. 1968 (Dundee)	1
McLean, K. 2016 (Aberdeen)	**5**
McLean, T. 1969 (Kilmarnock)	6
McLeish, A. 1980 (Aberdeen)	77
McLeod, D. 1905 (Celtic)	4
McLeod, J. 1888 (Dumbarton)	5
MacLeod, J. M. 1961 (Hibernian)	4
MacLeod, M. 1985 (Celtic, Borussia Dortmund,	
Hibernian)	20
McLeod, W. 1886 (Cowlairs)	1
McLintock, A. 1875 (Vale of Leven)	3
McLintock, F. 1963 (Leicester C, Arsenal)	9
McLuckie, J. S. 1934 (Manchester C)	1
McMahon, A. 1892 (Celtic)	6
McManus, S. 2007 (Celtic, Middlesbrough)	26
McMenemy, J. 1905 (Celtic)	12
McMenemy, J. 1934 (Motherwell)	1
McMillan, I. L. 1952 (Airdrieonians, Rangers)	6
McMillan, J. 1897 (St Bernards)	1
McMillan, T. 1887 (Dumbarton)	1
McMullan, J. 1920 (Partick Thistle, Manchester C)	16
McNab, A. 1921 (Morton)	2
McNab, A. 1937 (Sunderland, WBA)	2
McNab, C. D. 1931 (Dundee)	6
McNab, J. S. 1923 (Liverpool)	1
McNair, A. 1906 (Celtic)	15
McNamara, J. 1997 (Celtic, Wolverhampton W)	33
McNamee, D. 2004 (Livingston)	4
McNaught, W. 1951 (Raith R)	5
McNaughton, K. 2002 (Aberdeen, Cardiff C)	4
McNeill, W. 1961 (Celtic)	29
McNiel, H. 1874 (Queen's Park)	10
McNiel, M. 1876 (Rangers)	2
McPhail, J. 1950 (Celtic)	5
McPhail, R. 1927 (Airdrieonians, Rangers)	17
McPherson, D. 1892 (Kilmarnock)	1
McPherson, D. 1989 (Hearts, Rangers)	27
McPherson, J. 1875 (Clydesdale)	1
McPherson, J. 1879 (Vale of Leven)	1
McPherson, J. 1888 (Kilmarnock, Cowlairs, Rangers)	9
McPherson, J. 1891 (Hearts)	1
McPherson, R. 1882 (Arthurlie)	1
McQueen, G. 1974 (Leeds U, Manchester U)	30
McQueen, M. 1890 (Leith Ath)	2

McRorie, D. M. 1931 (Morton) 1
McSpadyen, A. 1939 (Partick Thistle) 2
McStay, P. 1984 (Celtic) 76
McStay, W. 1921 (Celtic) 13
McSwegan, G. 2000 (Hearts) 2
McTavish, J. 1910 (Falkirk) 1
McTominay, S. F. 2018 (Manchester U) 2
McWattie, G. C. 1901 (Queen's Park) 2
McWilliam, P. 1905 (Newcastle U) 8
Meechan, P. 1896 (Celtic) 1
Meiklejohn, D. D. 1922 (Rangers) 15
Menzies, A. 1906 (Hearts) 1
Mercer, R. 1912 (Hearts) 2
Middleton, R. 1930 (Cowdenbeath) 1
Millar, J. 1897 (Rangers) 3
Millar, J. 1963 (Rangers) 2
Miller, A. 1939 (Hearts) 1
Miller, C. 2001 (Dundee U) 1
Miller, J. 1931 (St Mirren) 5
Miller, K. 2001 (Rangers, Wolverhampton W, Celtic,
   Derby Co, Rangers, Bursaspor, Cardiff C, Vancouver
   Whitecaps) 69
Miller, L. 2006 (Dundee U, Aberdeen) 3
Miller, P. 1882 (Dumbarton) 3
Miller, T. 1920 (Liverpool, Manchester U) 3
Miller, W. 1876 (Third Lanark) 1
Miller, W. 1947 (Celtic) 6
Miller, W. 1975 (Aberdeen) 65
Mills, W. 1936 (Aberdeen) 3
Milne, J. V. 1938 (Middlesbrough) 2
Mitchell, D. 1890 (Rangers) 5
Mitchell, J. 1908 (Kilmarnock) 3
Mitchell, R. C. 1951 (Newcastle U) 2
Mochan, N. 1954 (Celtic) 3
Moir, W. 1950 (Bolton W) 1
Moncur, R. 1968 (Newcastle U) 16
Morgan, H. 1898 (St Mirren, Liverpool) 2
Morgan, L. 2018 (St Mirren) 2
Morgan, W. 1968 (Burnley, Manchester U) 21
Morris, D. 1923 (Raith R) 6
Morris, H. 1950 (East Fife) 1
Morrison, J. C. 2008 (WBA) 46
Morrison, T. 1927 (St Mirren) 1
Morton, A. L. 1920 (Queen's Park, Rangers) 31
Morton, H. A. 1929 (Kilmarnock) 2
Mudie, J. K. 1957 (Blackpool) 17
Muir, W. 1907 (Dundee) 1
Muirhead, T. A. 1922 (Rangers) 8
Mulgrew, C. P. 2012 (Celtic, Blackburn R) 36
Mulhall, G. 1960 (Aberdeen, Sunderland) 3
Munro, A. D. 1937 (Hearts, Blackpool) 3
Munro, F. M. 1971 (Wolverhampton W) 9
Munro, I. 1979 (St Mirren) 7
Munro, N. 1888 (Abercorn) 2
Murdoch, J. 1931 (Motherwell) 1
Murdoch, R. 1966 (Celtic) 12
Murphy, F. 1938 (Celtic) 1
Murphy, J. 2018 (Rangers) 2
Murray, I. 2003 (Hibernian, Rangers) 6
Murray, J. 1895 (Renton) 1
Murray, J. 1958 (Hearts) 5
Murray, J. W. 1890 (Vale of Leven) 1
Murray, P. 1896 (Hibernian) 2
Murray, S. 1972 (Aberdeen) 1
Murty, G. S. 2004 (Reading) 4
Mutch, G. 1938 (Preston NE) 1

Naismith, S. J. 2007 (Kilmarnock, Rangers, Everton,
   Norwich C) 45
Napier, C. E. 1932 (Celtic, Derby Co) 5
Narey, D. 1977 (Dundee U) 35
Naysmith, G. A. 2000 (Hearts, Everton, Sheffield U) 46
Neil, R. G. 1896 (Hibernian, Rangers) 2
Neill, R. W. 1876 (Queen's Park) 5
Neilson, R. 2007 (Hearts) 1
Nellies, P. 1913 (Hearts) 2
Nelson, J. 1925 (Cardiff C) 4
Nevin, P. K. F. 1986 (Chelsea, Everton, Tranmere R) 28
Niblo, T. D. 1904 (Aston Villa) 1
Nibloe, J. 1929 (Kilmarnock) 11
Nicholas, C. 1983 (Celtic, Arsenal, Aberdeen) 20
Nicholson, B. 2001 (Dunfermline Ath) 3
Nicol, S. 1985 (Liverpool) 27
Nisbet, J. 1929 (Ayr U) 3
Niven, J. B. 1885 (Moffat) 1

O'Connor, G. 2002 (Hibernian, Lokomotiv Moscow,
   Birmingham C) 16
O'Donnell, F. 1937 (Preston NE, Blackpool) 6
O'Donnell, P. 1994 (Motherwell) 1
O'Donnell, S. G. 2018 (Kilmarnock) 2
Ogilvie, D. H. 1934 (Motherwell) 1
O'Hare, J. 1970 (Derby Co) 13
O'Neil, B. 1996 (Celtic, Wolfsburg, Derby Co,
   Preston NE) 7
O'Neil, J. 2001 (Hibernian) 1
Ormond, W. E. 1954 (Hibernian) 6
O'Rourke, F. 1907 (Airdrieonians) 1
Orr, J. 1892 (Kilmarnock) 1
Orr, R. 1902 (Newcastle U) 2
Orr, T. 1952 (Morton) 2
Orr, W. 1900 (Celtic) 3
Orrock, R. 1913 (Falkirk) 1
Oswald, J. 1889 (Third Lanark, St Bernards, Rangers) 3

Parker, A. H. 1955 (Falkirk, Everton) 15
Parlane, D. 1973 (Rangers) 12
Parlane, R. 1878 (Vale of Leven) 3
Paterson, C. 2016 (Hearts, Cardiff C) 9
Paterson, G. D. 1939 (Celtic) 1
Paterson, J. 1920 (Leicester C) 1
Paterson, J. 1931 (Cowdenbeath) 3
Paton, A. 1952 (Motherwell) 2
Paton, D. 1896 (St Bernards) 1
Paton, M. 1883 (Dumbarton) 5
Paton, R. 1879 (Vale of Leven) 2
Patrick, J. 1897 (St Mirren) 2
Paul, H. McD. 1909 (Queen's Park) 3
Paul, W. 1888 (Partick Thistle) 3
Paul, W. 1891 (Dykebar) 1
Pearson, S. P. 2004 (Motherwell, Celtic, Derby Co) 10
Pearson, T. 1947 (Newcastle U) 2
Penman, A. 1966 (Dundee) 1
Pettigrew, W. 1976 (Motherwell) 5
Phillips, J. 1877 (Queen's Park) 3
Phillips, M. 2012 (Blackpool, QPR) 12
Plenderleith, J. B. 1961 (Manchester C) 1
Porteous, W. 1903 (Hearts) 1
Pressley, S. J. 2000 (Hearts) 32
Pringle, C. 1921 (St Mirren) 1
Provan, D. 1964 (Rangers) 5
Provan, D. 1980 (Celtic) 10
Pursell, P. 1914 (Queen's Park) 1

Quashie, N. F. 2004 (Portsmouth, Southampton, WBA) 14
Quinn, J. 1905 (Celtic) 11
Quinn, P. 1961 (Motherwell) 4

Rae, G. 2001 (Dundee, Rangers, Cardiff C) 14
Rae, J. 1889 (Third Lanark) 2
Raeside, J. S. 1906 (Third Lanark) 1
Raisbeck, A. G. 1900 (Liverpool) 8
Rankin, G. 1890 (Vale of Leven) 2
Rankin, R. 1929 (St Mirren) 3
Redpath, W. 1949 (Motherwell) 9
Reid, J. G. 1914 (Airdrieonians) 3
Reid, R. 1938 (Brentford) 2
Reid, W. 1911 (Rangers) 9
Reilly, L. 1949 (Hibernian) 38
Rennie, H. G. 1900 (Hearts, Hibernian) 13
Renny-Tailyour, H. W. 1873 (Royal Engineers) 1
Rhind, A. 1872 (Queen's Park) 1
Rhodes, J. L. 2012 (Huddersfield T, Blackburn R,
   Sheffield W) 14
Richmond, A. 1906 (Queen's Park) 1
Richmond, J. T. 1877 (Clydesdale, Queen's Park) 3
Ring, T. 1953 (Clyde) 12
Rioch, B. D. 1975 (Derby Co, Everton, Derby Co) 24
Riordan, D. G. 2006 (Hibernian) 3
Ritchie, A. 1891 (East Stirlingshire) 1
Ritchie, H. 1923 (Hibernian) 3
Ritchie, J. 1897 (Queen's Park) 1
Ritchie, M. T. 2015 (Bournemouth, Newcastle U) 16
Ritchie, P. S. 1999 (Hearts, Bolton W, Walsall) 7
Ritchie, W. 1962 (Rangers) 1
Robb, D. T. 1971 (Aberdeen) 5
Robb, W. 1926 (Rangers, Hibernian) 2
Robertson, A. 1955 (Clyde) 5
Robertson, A. 2014 (Dundee U, Hull C, Liverpool) 22
Robertson, D. 1992 (Rangers) 3
Robertson, G. 1910 (Motherwell, Sheffield W) 4

Wallace, W. S. B. 1965 (Hearts, Celtic) 7
Wardhaugh, J. 1955 (Hearts) 2
Wark, J. 1979 (Ipswich T, Liverpool) 28
Watson, A. 1881 (Queen's Park) 3
Watson, J. 1903 (Sunderland, Middlesbrough) 6
Watson, J. 1948 (Motherwell, Huddersfield T) 2
Watson, J. A. K. 1878 (Rangers) 1
Watson, P. R. 1934 (Blackpool) 1
Watson, R. 1971 (Motherwell) 1
Watson, W. 1898 (Falkirk) 1
Watt, A. P. 2016 (Charlton Ath) 1
Watt, F. 1889 (Kilbirnie) 4
Watt, W. W. 1887 (Queen's Park) 1
Waugh, W. 1938 (Hearts) 1
Webster, A. 2003 (Hearts, Dundee U, Hearts) 28
Weir, A. 1959 (Motherwell) 6
Weir, D. G. 1997 (Hearts, Everton, Rangers) 69
Weir, J. 1887 (Third Lanark) 1
Weir, J. B. 1872 (Queen's Park) 4
Weir, P. 1980 (St Mirren, Aberdeen) 6
White, John 1922 (Albion R, Hearts) 2
White, J. A. 1959 (Falkirk, Tottenham H) 22
White, W. 1907 (Bolton W) 2
Whitelaw, A. 1887 (Vale of Leven) 2
Whittaker, S. G. 2010 (Rangers, Norwich C) 31
Whyte, D. 1988 (Celtic, Middlesbrough, Aberdeen) 12
Wilkie, L. 2002 (Dundee) 11
Williams, G. 2002 (Nottingham F) 5
Wilson, A. 1907 (Sheffield W) 6
Wilson, A. 1954 (Portsmouth) 1
Wilson, A. N. 1920 (Dunfermline, Middlesbrough) 12
Wilson, D. 1900 (Queen's Park) 1

Wilson, D. 1913 (Oldham Ath) 1
Wilson, D. 1961 (Rangers) 22
Wilson, D. 2011 (Liverpool) 5
Wilson, G. W. 1904 (Hearts, Everton, Newcastle U) 6
Wilson, Hugh 1890 (Newmilns, Sunderland, Third Lanark) 4
Wilson, I. A. 1987 (Leicester C, Everton) 5
Wilson, J. 1888 (Vale of Leven) 4
Wilson, M. 2011 (Celtic) 1
Wilson, P. 1926 (Celtic) 4
Wilson, P. 1975 (Celtic) 1
Wilson, R. P. 1972 (Arsenal) 1
Winters, R. 1999 (Aberdeen) 2
Wiseman, W. 1927 (Queen's Park) 2
Wood, G. 1979 (Everton, Arsenal) 4
Woodburn, W. A. 1947 (Rangers) 24
Wotherspoon, D. N. 1872 (Queen's Park) 2
Wright, K. 1992 (Hibernian) 1
Wright, S. 1993 (Aberdeen) 2
Wright, T. 1953 (Sunderland) 3
Wylie, T. G. 1890 (Rangers) 1

Yeats, R. 1965 (Liverpool) 2
Yorston, B. C. 1931 (Aberdeen) 1
Yorston, H. 1955 (Aberdeen) 1
Young, A. 1905 (Everton) 2
Young, A. 1960 (Hearts, Everton) 8
Young, G. L. 1947 (Rangers) 53
Young, J. 1906 (Celtic) 1
Younger, T. 1955 (Hibernian, Liverpool) 24

WALES

Adams, H. 1882 (Berwyn R, Druids) 4
Aizlewood, M. 1986 (Charlton Ath, Leeds U, Bradford C, Bristol C, Cardiff C) 39
Allchurch, I. J. 1951 (Swansea T, Newcastle U, Cardiff C, Swansea T) 68
Allchurch, L. 1955 (Swansea T, Sheffield U) 11
Allen, B. W. 1951 (Coventry C) 2
Allen, J. M. 2009 (Swansea C, Liverpool, Stoke C) 42
Allen, M. 1986 (Watford, Norwich C, Millwall, Newcastle U) 14
Ampadu, E. K. C. R. 2018 (Chelsea) 2
Arridge, S. 1892 (Bootle, Everton, New Brighton Tower) 8
Astley, D. J. 1931 (Charlton Ath, Aston Villa, Derby Co, Blackpool) 13
Atherton, R. W. 1899 (Hibernian, Middlesbrough) 9

Bailiff, W. E. 1913 (Llanelly) 4
Baker, C. W. 1958 (Cardiff C) 7
Baker, W. G. 1948 (Cardiff C) 1
Bale, G. F. 2006 (Southampton, Tottenham H, Real Madrid) 70
Bamford, T. 1931 (Wrexham) 5
Barnard, D. S. 1998 (Barnsley, Grimsby T) 22
Barnes, W. 1948 (Arsenal) 22
Bartley, T. 1898 (Glossop NE) 1
Bastock, A. M. 1892 (Shrewsbury T) 1
Beadles, G. H. 1925 (Cardiff C) 2
Bell, W. S. 1881 (Shrewsbury Engineers, Crewe Alex) 5
Bellamy, C. D. 1998 (Norwich C, Coventry C, Newcastle U, Blackburn R, Liverpool, West Ham U, Manchester C, Liverpool, Cardiff C) 78
Bennion, S. R. 1926 (Manchester U) 10
Berry, G. F. 1979 (Wolverhampton W, Stoke C) 5
Blackmore, C. G. 1985 (Manchester U, Middlesbrough) 39
Blake, D. J. 2011 (Cardiff C, Crystal Palace) 14
Blake, N. A. 1994 (Sheffield U, Bolton W, Blackburn R, Wolverhampton W) 29
Blew, H. 1899 (Wrexham) 22
Boden, T. 1880 (Wrexham) 1
Bodin, B. P. 2018 (Preston NE) 1
Bodin, P. J. 1990 (Swindon T, Crystal Palace, Swindon T) 23
Boulter, L. M. 1939 (Brentford) 1
Bowdler, H. E. 1893 (Shrewsbury T) 1
Bowdler, J. C. H. 1890 (Shrewsbury T, Wolverhampton W, Shrewsbury T) 4
Bowen, D. L. 1955 (Arsenal) 19
Bowen, E. 1880 (Druids) 2
Bowen, J. P. 1994 (Swansea C, Birmingham C) 2
Bowen, M. R. 1986 (Tottenham H, Norwich C, West Ham U) 41

Bowsher, S. J. 1929 (Burnley) 1
Boyle, T. 1981 (Crystal Palace) 2
Bradley, M. S. 2010 (Walsall) 1
Bradshaw, T. W. C. 2016 (Walsall, Barnsley) 3
Britten, T. J. 1878 (Parkgrove, Presteigne) 2
Brooks, D. R. 2018 (Sheffield U) 3
Brookes, S. J. 1900 (Llandudno) 2
Brown, A. I. 1926 (Aberdare Ath) 1
Brown, J. R. 2006 (Gillingham, Blackburn R, Aberdeen) 3
Browning, M. T. 1996 (Bristol R, Huddersfield T) 5
Bryan, T. 1886 (Oswestry) 2
Buckland, T. 1899 (Bangor) 1
Burgess, W. A. R. 1947 (Tottenham H) 32
Burke, T. 1883 (Wrexham, Newton Heath) 8
Burnett, T. B. 1877 (Ruabon) 1
Burton, A. D. 1963 (Norwich C, Newcastle U) 9
Butler, J. 1893 (Chirk) 3
Butler, W. T. 1900 (Druids) 2

Cartwright, L. 1974 (Coventry C, Wrexham) 7
Carty, T. See McCarthy (Wrexham).
Challen, J. B. 1887 (Corinthians, Wellingborough GS) 4
Chapman, J. 1894 (Newtown, Manchester C, Grimsby T) 7
Charles, J. M. 1981 (Swansea C, QPR, Oxford U) 19
Charles, M. 1955 (Swansea T, Arsenal, Cardiff C) 31
Charles, W. J. 1950 (Leeds U, Juventus, Leeds U, Cardiff C) 38
Chester, J. G. 2014 (Hull C, WBA, Aston Villa) 31
Church, S. R. 2009 (Reading, Charlton Ath) 38
Clarke, R. J. 1949 (Manchester C) 22
Coleman, C. 1992 (Crystal Palace, Blackburn R, Fulham) 32
Collier, D. J. 1921 (Grimsby T) 1
Collins, D. L. 2005 (Sunderland, Stoke C) 12
Collins, J. M. 2004 (Cardiff C, West Ham U, Aston Villa, West Ham U) 51
Collins, W. S. 1931 (Llanelly) 1
Collison, J. D. 2008 (West Ham U) 16
Conde, C. 1884 (Chirk) 3
Cook, F. C. 1925 (Newport Co, Portsmouth) 8
Cornforth, J. M. 1995 (Swansea C) 2
Cotterill, D. R. G. B. 2006 (Bristol C, Wigan Ath, Sheffield U, Swansea C, Doncaster R, Birmingham C) 24
Coyne, D. 1996 (Tranmere R, Grimsby T, Leicester C, Burnley, Tranmere R) 16
Crofts, A. L. 2016 ((Gillingham, Brighton & HA, Norwich C, Scunthorpe U) 29
Crompton, W. 1931 (Wrexham) 3
Cross, E. A. 1876 (Wrexham) 2

Crosse, K. 1879 (Druids) 3
Crossley, M. G. 1997 (Nottingham F, Middlesbrough, Fulham) 8
Crowe, V. H. 1959 (Aston Villa) 16
Cumner, R. H. 1939 (Arsenal) 3
Curtis, A. T. 1976 (Swansea C, Leeds U, Swansea C, Southampton, Cardiff C) 35
Curtis, E. R. 1928 (Cardiff C, Birmingham) 3

Daniel, R. W. 1951 (Arsenal, Sunderland) 21
Darvell, S. 1897 (Oxford University) 1
Davies, A. 1876 (Wrexham) 2
Davies, A. 1904 (Druids, Middlesbrough) 2
Davies, A. 1983 (Manchester U, Newcastle U, Swansea C, Bradford C) 13
Davies, A. O. 1885 (Barmouth, Swifts, Wrexham, Crewe Alex) 9
Davies, A. R. 2006 (Yeovil T) 1
Davies, A. T. 1891 (Shrewsbury T) 1
Davies, B. T. 2013 (Swansea C, Tottenham H) **39**
Davies, C. 1972 (Charlton Ath) 1
Davies, C. M. 2006 (Oxford U, Verona, Oldham Ath, Barnsley) 7
Davies, D. 1904 (Bolton W) 3
Davies, D. C. 1899 (Brecon, Hereford) 2
Davies, D. W. 1912 (Treharris, Oldham Ath) 2
Davies, E. Lloyd 1904 (Stoke, Northampton T) 16
Davies, E. R. 1953 (Newcastle U) 6
Davies, G. 1980 (Fulham, Manchester C) 16
Davies, Rev. H. 1928 (Wrexham) 1
Davies, Idwal 1923 (Liverpool Marine) 1
Davies, J. E. 1885 (Oswestry) 1
Davies, Jas 1878 (Wrexham) 1
Davies, John 1879 (Wrexham) 1
Davies, Jos 1888 (Newton Heath, Wolverhampton W) 7
Davies, Jos 1889 (Everton, Chirk, Ardwick, Sheffield U, Manchester C, Millwall, Reading) 11
Davies, J. P. 1883 (Druids) 2
Davies, Ll. 1907 (Wrexham, Everton, Wrexham) 13
Davies, L. S. 1922 (Cardiff C) 23
Davies, O. 1890 (Wrexham) 1
Davies, R. 1883 (Wrexham) 3
Davies, R. 1885 (Druids) 1
Davies, R. O. 1892 (Wrexham) 2
Davies, R. T. 1964 (Norwich C, Southampton, Portsmouth) 29
Davies, R. W. 1964 (Bolton W, Newcastle U, Manchester C, Manchester U, Blackpool) 34
Davies, S. 2001 (Tottenham H, Everton, Fulham) 58
Davies, S. I. 1996 (Manchester U) 1
Davies, Stanley 1920 (Preston NE, Everton, WBA, Rotherham U) 18
Davies, T. 1886 (Oswestry) 1
Davies, T. 1903 (Druids) 4
Davies, W. 1884 (Wrexham) 1
Davies, W. 1924 (Swansea T, Cardiff C, Notts Co) 17
Davies, William 1903 (Wrexham, Blackburn R) 11
Davies, W. C. 1908 (Crystal Palace, WBA, Crystal Palace) 4
Davies, W. D. 1975 (Everton, Wrexham, Swansea C) 52
Davies, W. H. 1876 (Oswestry) 4
Davis, G. 1978 (Wrexham) 3
Davis, W. O. 1913 (Millwall Ath) 5
Day, A. 1934 (Tottenham H) 1
Deacy, N. 1977 (PSV Eindhoven, Beringen) 12
Dearson, D. J. 1939 (Birmingham) 3
Delaney, M. A. 2000 (Aston Villa) 36
Derrett, S. C. 1969 (Cardiff C) 4
Dewey, F. T. 1931 (Cardiff Corinthians) 2
Dibble, A. 1986 (Luton T, Manchester C) 3
Dorman, A. 2010 (St Mirren, Crystal Palace) 3
Doughty, J. 1886 (Druids, Newton Heath) 8
Doughty, R. 1888 (Newton Heath) 2
Duffy, R. M. 2006 (Portsmouth) 13
Dummett, P. 2014 (Newcastle U) 2
Durban, A. 1966 (Derby Co) 27
Dwyer, P. J. 1978 (Cardiff C) 10

Eardley, N. 2008 (Oldham Ath, Blackpool) 16
Earnshaw, R. 2002 (Cardiff C, WBA, Norwich C, Derby Co, Nottingham F, Cardiff C) 59
Easter, J. M. 2007 (Wycombe W, Plymouth Arg, Milton Keynes D, Crystal Palace, Millwall) 12
Eastwood, F. 2008 (Wolverhampton W, Coventry C) 11
Edwards, C. 1878 (Wrexham) 1

Edwards, C. N. H. 1996 (Swansea C) 1
Edwards, D. A. 2008 (Luton T, Wolverhampton W, Reading) **43**
Edwards, G. 1947 (Birmingham C, Cardiff C) 12
Edwards, H. 1878 (Wrexham Civil Service, Wrexham) 8
Edwards, J. H. 1876 (Wanderers) 1
Edwards, J. H. 1895 (Oswestry) 3
Edwards, J. H. 1898 (Aberystwyth) 1
Edwards, L. T. 1957 (Charlton Ath) 2
Edwards, R. I. 1978 (Chester, Wrexham) 4
Edwards, R. O. 2003 (Aston Villa, Wolverhampton W) 15
Edwards, R. W. 1998 (Bristol C) 4
Edwards, T. 1932 (Linfield) 1
Egan, W. 1892 (Chirk) 1
Ellis, B. 1932 (Motherwell) 6
Ellis, E. 1931 (Nunhead, Oswestry) 3
Emanuel, W. J. 1973 (Bristol C) 2
England, H. M. 1962 (Blackburn R, Tottenham H) 44
Evans, B. C. 1972 (Swansea C, Hereford U) 7
Evans, C. M. 2008 (Manchester C, Sheffield U) 13
Evans, D. G. 1926 (Reading, Huddersfield T) 4
Evans, H. P. 1922 (Cardiff C) 6
Evans, I. 1976 (Crystal Palace) 13
Evans, J. 1893 (Oswestry) 3
Evans, J. 1912 (Cardiff C) 8
Evans, J. H. 1922 (Southend U) 4
Evans, L. 2018 (Wolverhampton W, Sheffield U) **3**
Evans, Len 1927 (Aberdare Ath, Cardiff C, Birmingham) 4
Evans, M. 1884 (Oswestry) 1
Evans, P. S. 2002 (Brentford, Bradford C) 2
Evans, R. 1902 (Clapton) 1
Evans, R. E. 1906 (Wrexham, Aston Villa, Sheffield U) 10
Evans, R. O. 1902 (Wrexham, Blackburn R, Coventry C) 10
Evans, R. S. 1964 (Swansea T) 1
Evans, S. J. 2007 (Wrexham) 7
Evans, T. J. 1927 (Clapton Orient, Newcastle U) 4
Evans, W. 1933 (Tottenham H) 6
Evans, W. A. W. 1876 (Oxford University) 2
Evans, W. G. 1890 (Bootle, Aston Villa) 3
Evelyn, E. C. 1887 (Crusaders) 1
Eyton-Jones, J. A. 1883 (Wrexham) 4

Farmer, G. 1885 (Oswestry) 2
Felgate, D. 1984 (Lincoln C) 1
Finnigan, R. J. 1930 (Wrexham) 1
Fletcher, C. N. 2004 (Bournemouth, West Ham U, Crystal Palace) 36
Flynn, B. 1975 (Burnley, Leeds U, Burnley) 66
Fon Williams, O. 2016 (Inverness CT) 1
Ford, T. 1947 (Swansea T, Aston Villa, Sunderland, Cardiff C) 38
Foulkes, H. E. 1932 (WBA) 1
Foulkes, W. I. 1952 (Newcastle U) 11
Foulkes, W. T. 1884 (Oswestry) 2
Fowler, J. 1925 (Swansea T) 6
Freestone, R. 2000 (Swansea C) 1

Gabbidon, D. L. 2002 (Cardiff C, West Ham U, QPR, Crystal Palace) 49
Garner, G. 2006 (Leyton Orient) 1
Garner, J. 1896 (Aberystwyth) 1
Giggs, R. J. 1992 (Manchester U) 64
Giles, D. C. 1980 (Swansea C, Crystal Palace) 12
Gillam, S. G. 1889 (Wrexham, Shrewsbury, Clapton) 5
Glascodine, G. 1879 (Wrexham) 1
Glover, E. M. 1932 (Grimsby T) 7
Godding, G. 1923 (Wrexham) 2
Godfrey, B. C. 1964 (Preston NE) 3
Goodwin, U. 1881 (Ruthin) 1
Goss, J. 1991 (Norwich C) 9
Gough, R. T. 1883 (Oswestry White Star) 1
Gray, A. 1924 (Oldham Ath, Manchester C, Manchester Central, Tranmere R, Chester) 24
Green, A. W. 1901 (Aston Villa, Notts Co, Nottingham F) 8
Green, C. R. 1965 (Birmingham C) 15
Green, G. H. 1938 (Charlton Ath) 4
Green, R. M. 1998 (Wolverhampton W) 2
Grey, Dr W. 1876 (Druids) 2
Griffiths, A. T. 1971 (Wrexham) 17
Griffiths, F. J. 1900 (Blackpool) 2
Griffiths, G. 1887 (Chirk) 1
Griffiths, J. H. 1953 (Swansea T) 1
Griffiths, L. 1902 (Wrexham) 1

Griffiths, M. W. 1947 (Leicester C) 11
Griffiths, P. 1884 (Chirk) 6
Griffiths, P. H. 1932 (Everton) 1
Griffiths, T. P. 1927 (Everton, Bolton W, Middlesbrough, Aston Villa) 21
Gunter, C. R. 2007 (Cardiff C, Tottenham H, Nottingham F, Reading) **88**

Hall, G. D. 1988 (Chelsea) 9
Hallam, J. 1889 (Oswestry) 1
Hanford, H. 1934 (Swansea T, Sheffield W) 7
Harrington, A. C. 1956 (Cardiff C) 11
Harris, C. S. 1976 (Leeds U) 24
Harris, W. C. 1954 (Middlesbrough) 6
Harrison, W. C. 1899 (Wrexham) 5
Hartson, J. 1995 (Arsenal, West Ham U, Wimbledon, Coventry C, Celtic) 51
Haworth, S. O. 1997 (Cardiff C, Coventry C) 5
Hayes, A. 1890 (Wrexham) 2
Hedges, R. P. 2018 (Barnsley) **2**
Henley, A. D. 2016 (Blackburn R) 2
Hennessey, W. R. 2007 (Wolverhampton W, Crystal Palace) **76**
Hennessey, W. T. 1962 (Birmingham C, Nottingham F, Derby Co) 39
Hersee, A. M. 1886 (Bangor) 2
Hersee, R. 1886 (Llandudno) 1
Hewitt, R. 1958 (Cardiff C) 5
Hewitt, T. J. 1911 (Wrexham, Chelsea, South Liverpool) 8
Heywood, D. 1879 (Druids) 1
Hibbott, H. 1880 (Newtown Excelsior, Newtown) 3
Higham, G. G. 1878 (Oswestry) 2
Hill, M. R. 1972 (Ipswich T) 2
Hockey, T. 1972 (Sheffield U, Norwich C, Aston Villa) 9
Hoddinott, T. F. 1921 (Watford) 2
Hodges, G. 1984 (Wimbledon, Newcastle U, Watford, Sheffield U) 18
Hodgkinson, A. V. 1908 (Southampton) 1
Holden, A. 1984 (Chester C) 1
Hole, B. G. 1963 (Cardiff C, Blackburn R, Aston Villa, Swansea C) 30
Hole, W. J. 1921 (Swansea T) 9
Hollins, D. M. 1962 (Newcastle U) 11
Hopkins, I. J. 1935 (Brentford) 12
Hopkins, J. 1983 (Fulham, Crystal Palace) 16
Hopkins, M. 1956 (Tottenham H) 34
Horne, B. 1988 (Portsmouth, Southampton, Everton, Birmingham C) 59
Howell, E. G. 1888 (Builth) 3
Howells, R. G. 1954 (Cardiff C) 2
Hugh, A. R. 1930 (Newport Co) 1
Hughes, A. 1894 (Rhos) 2
Hughes, A. 1907 (Chirk) 1
Hughes, C. M. 1992 (Luton T, Wimbledon) 8
Hughes, E. 1899 (Everton, Tottenham H) 14
Hughes, E. 1906 (Wrexham, Nottingham F, Wrexham, Manchester C) 16
Hughes, F. W. 1882 (Northwich Victoria) 6
Hughes, I. 1951 (Luton T) 4
Hughes, J. 1877 (Cambridge University, Aberystwyth) 2
Hughes, J. 1905 (Liverpool) 3
Hughes, J. I. 1935 (Blackburn R) 1
Hughes, L. M. 1984 (Manchester U, Barcelona, Manchester U, Chelsea, Southampton) 72
Hughes, P. W. 1887 (Bangor) 3
Hughes, W. 1891 (Bootle) 3
Hughes, W. A. 1949 (Blackburn R) 5
Hughes, W. M. 1938 (Birmingham) 10
Humphreys, J. V. 1947 (Everton) 1
Humphreys, R. 1888 (Druids) 1
Hunter, A. H. 1887 (FA of Wales Secretary) 1
Huws, E. W. 2014 (Manchester C, Wigan Ath, Cardiff C) 11

Isgrove, L. J. 2016 (Southampton) 1

Jackett, K. 1983 (Watford) 31
Jackson, W. 1899 (St Helens Rec) 1
James, E. 1893 (Chirk) 8
James, E. G. 1966 (Blackpool) 9
James, L. 1972 (Burnley, Derby Co, QPR, Burnley, Swansea C, Sunderland) 54
James, R. M. 1979 (Swansea C, Stoke C, QPR, Leicester C, Swansea C) 47

James, W. 1931 (West Ham U) 2
Jarrett, R. H. 1889 (Ruthin) 2
Jarvis, A. L. 1967 (Hull C) 3
Jenkins, E. 1925 (Lovell's Ath) 1
Jenkins, J. 1924 (Brighton & HA) 8
Jenkins, R. W. 1902 (Rhyl) 1
Jenkins, S. R. 1996 (Swansea C, Huddersfield T) 16
Jenkyns, C. A. L. 1892 (Small Heath, Woolwich Arsenal, Newton Heath, Walsall) 8
Jennings, W. 1914 (Bolton W) 11
John, B. S. 2013 (Cardiff C, Rangers) **5**
John, R. F. 1923 (Arsenal) 15
John, W. R. 1931 (Walsall, Stoke C, Preston NE, Sheffield U, Swansea T) 14
Johnson, A. J. 1999 (Nottingham F, WBA) 15
Johnson, M. G. 1964 (Swansea T) 1
Jones, A. 1987 (Port Vale, Charlton Ath) 6
Jones, A. F. 1877 (Oxford University) 1
Jones, A. T. 1905 (Nottingham F, Notts Co) 2
Jones, Bryn 1935 (Wolverhampton W, Arsenal) 17
Jones, B. S. 1963 (Swansea T, Plymouth Arg, Cardiff C) 15
Jones, Charlie 1926 (Nottingham F, Arsenal) 8
Jones, Cliff 1954 (Swansea T, Tottenham H, Fulham) 59
Jones, C. W. 1935 (Birmingham) 2
Jones, D. 1888 (Chirk, Bolton W, Manchester C) 14
Jones, D. E. 1976 (Norwich C) 8
Jones, D. O. 1934 (Leicester C) 7
Jones, Evan 1910 (Chelsea, Oldham Ath, Bolton W) 7
Jones, F. R. 1885 (Bangor) 3
Jones, F. W. 1893 (Small Heath) 1
Jones, G. P. 1907 (Wrexham) 2
Jones, H. 1902 (Aberaman) 1
Jones, Humphrey 1885 (Bangor, Queen's Park, East Stirlingshire, Queen's Park) 14
Jones, Ivor 1920 (Swansea T, WBA) 10
Jones, Jeffrey 1908 (Llandrindod Wells) 3
Jones, J. 1876 (Druids) 1
Jones, J. 1883 (Berwyn Rangers) 3
Jones, J. 1925 (Wrexham) 1
Jones, J. L. 1895 (Sheffield U, Tottenham H) 21
Jones, J. Love 1906 (Stoke, Middlesbrough) 2
Jones, J. O. 1901 (Bangor) 2
Jones, J. P. 1976 (Liverpool, Wrexham, Chelsea, Huddersfield T) 72
Jones, J. T. 1912 (Stoke, Crystal Palace) 15
Jones, K. 1950 (Aston Villa) 1
Jones, Leslie I. 1933 (Cardiff C, Coventry C, Arsenal) 11
Jones, M. A. 2007 (Wrexham) 2
Jones, M. G. 2000 (Leeds U, Leicester C) 13
Jones, P. L. 1997 (Liverpool, Tranmere R) 2
Jones, P. S. 1997 (Stockport Co, Southampton, Wolverhampton W, QPR) 50
Jones, P. W. 1971 (Bristol R) 1
Jones, R. 1887 (Bangor, Crewe Alex) 3
Jones, R. 1898 (Leicester Fosse) 1
Jones, R. 1899 (Druids) 1
Jones, R. 1900 (Bangor) 2
Jones, R. 1906 (Millwall) 2
Jones, R. A. 1884 (Druids) 4
Jones, R. A. 1994 (Sheffield W) 1
Jones, R. S. 1894 (Everton) 1
Jones, S. 1887 (Wrexham, Chester) 2
Jones, S. 1893 (Wrexham, Burton Swifts, Druids) 6
Jones, T. 1926 (Manchester U) 4
Jones, T. D. 1908 (Aberdare) 1
Jones, T. G. 1938 (Everton) 17
Jones, T. J. 1932 (Sheffield W) 2
Jones, V. P. 1995 (Wimbledon) 9
Jones, W. E. A. 1947 (Swansea T, Tottenham H) 4
Jones, W. J. 1901 (Aberdare, West Ham U) 4
Jones, W. Lot 1905 (Manchester C, Southend U) 20
Jones, W. P. 1889 (Druids, Wynnstay) 4
Jones, W. R. 1897 (Aberystwyth) 1

Keenor, F. C. 1920 (Cardiff C, Crewe Alex) 32
Kelly, F. C. 1899 (Wrexham, Druids) 3
Kelsey, A. J. 1954 (Arsenal) 41
Kenrick, S. L. 1876 (Druids, Oswestry, Shropshire Wanderers) 5
Ketley, C. F. 1882 (Druids) 1
King, A. P. 2009 (Leicester C) **47**
King, J. 1955 (Swansea T) 1
Kinsey, N. 1951 (Norwich C, Birmingham C) 7
Knill, A. R. 1989 (Swansea C) 1

Koumas, J. 2001 (Tranmere R, WBA, Wigan Ath) 34
Krzywicki, R. L. 1970 (WBA, Huddersfield T) 8

Lambert, R. 1947 (Liverpool) 5
Latham, G. 1905 (Liverpool, Southport Central,
  Cardiff C) 10
Law, B. J. 1990 (QPR) 1
Lawrence, E. 1930 (Clapton Orient, Notts Co) 2
Lawrence, S. 1932 (Swansea T) 8
Lawrence, T. M. 2016 (Leicester C, Derby Co) 13
Lea, A. 1889 (Wrexham) 4
Lea, C. 1965 (Ipswich T) 2
Leary, P. 1889 (Bangor) 1
**Ledley, J. C. 2006 (Cardiff C, Celtic, Crystal Palace,
  Derby Co) 77**
Leek, K. 1961 (Leicester C, Newcastle U, Birmingham C,
  Northampton T) 13
Legg, A. 1996 (Birmingham C, Cardiff C) 6
Lever, A. R. 1953 (Leicester C) 1
Lewis, B. 1891 (Chester, Wrexham, Middlesbrough,
  Wrexham) 10
Lewis, D. 1927 (Arsenal) 3
Lewis, D. 1983 (Swansea C) 1
Lewis, D. J. 1933 (Swansea T) 1
Lewis, D. M. 1890 (Bangor) 2
Lewis, J. 1906 (Bristol R) 1
Lewis, J. 1926 (Cardiff C) 1
Lewis, T. 1881 (Wrexham) 2
Lewis, W. 1885 (Bangor, Crewe Alex, Chester,
  Manchester C, Chester) 27
Lewis, W. L. 1927 (Swansea T, Huddersfield T) 6
Llewellyn, C. M. 1998 (Norwich C, Wrexham) 6
Lloyd, B. W. 1976 (Wrexham) 3
Lloyd, J. W. 1879 (Wrexham, Newtown) 2
Lloyd, R. A. 1891 (Ruthin) 2
Lockley, A. 1898 (Chirk) 1
Lockyer, T. A. 2018 (Bristol R) 4
Lovell, S. 1982 (Crystal Palace, Millwall) 6
Lowndes, S. R. 1983 (Newport Co, Millwall, Barnsley) 10
Lowrie, G. 1948 (Coventry C, Newcastle U) 4
Lucas, P. M. 1962 (Leyton Orient) 4
Lucas, W. H. 1949 (Swansea T) 7
Lumberg, A. 1929 (Wrexham, Wolverhampton W) 1
Lynch, J. J. 2013 (Huddersfield T) 1

MacDonald, S. B. 2011 (Swansea C, Bournemouth) 4
Maguire, G. T. 1990 (Portsmouth) 7
Mahoney, J. F. 1968 (Stoke C, Middlesbrough,
  Swansea C) 51
Mardon, P. J. 1996 (WBA) 1
Margetson, M. W. 2004 (Cardiff C) 1
Marriott, A. 1996 (Wrexham) 5
Martin, T. J. 1930 (Newport Co) 1
Marustik, C. 1982 (Swansea C) 6
Mates, J. 1891 (Chirk) 3
Matthews, A. J. 2011 (Cardiff C, Celtic, Sunderland) 14
Matthews, R. W. 1921 (Liverpool, Bristol C, Bradford) 3
Matthews, W. 1905 (Chester) 2
Matthias, J. S. 1896 (Brymbo, Shrewsbury T,
  Wolverhampton W) 5
Matthias, T. J. 1914 (Wrexham) 12
Mays, A. W. 1929 (Wrexham) 1
McCarthy, T. P. 1889 (Wrexham) 1
McMillan, R. 1881 (Shrewsbury Engineers) 2
Medwin, T. C. 1953 (Swansea T, Tottenham H) 30
Melville, A. K. 1990 (Swansea C, Oxford U, Sunderland,
  Fulham, West Ham U) 65
Mepham, C. J. 2018 (Brentford) 2
Meredith, S. 1900 (Chirk, Stoke, Leyton) 8
Meredith, W. H. 1895 (Manchester C, Manchester U) 48
Mielczarek, R. 1971 (Rotherham U) 1
Millership, H. 1920 (Rotherham Co) 6
Millington, A. H. 1963 (WBA, Crystal Palace,
  Peterborough U, Swansea C) 21
Mills, T. J. 1934 (Clapton Orient, Leicester C) 4
Mills-Roberts, R. H. 1885 (St Thomas' Hospital,
  Preston NE, Llanberis) 8
Moore, G. 1960 (Cardiff C, Chelsea, Manchester U,
  Northampton T, Charlton Ath) 21
Morgan, C. 2007 (Milton Keynes D, Peterborough U,
  Preston NE) 23
Morgan, J. R. 1877 (Cambridge University,
  Derby School Staff) 10
Morgan, J. T. 1905 (Wrexham) 1
Morgan-Owen, H. 1902 (Oxford University, Corinthians) 4

Morgan-Owen, M. M. 1897 (Oxford University,
  Corinthians) 13
Morison, S. W. 2011 (Millwall, Norwich C) 20
Morley, E. J. 1925 (Swansea T, Clapton Orient) 4
Morris, A. G. 1896 (Aberystwyth, Swindon T,
  Nottingham F) 21
Morris, C. 1900 (Chirk, Derby Co, Huddersfield T) 27
Morris, E. 1893 (Chirk) 3
Morris, H. 1894 (Sheffield U, Manchester C, Grimsby T) 3
Morris, J. 1887 (Oswestry) 1
Morris, J. 1898 (Chirk) 1
Morris, R. 1900 (Chirk, Shrewsbury T) 6
Morris, R. 1902 (Newtown, Druids, Liverpool, Leeds C,
  Grimsby T, Plymouth Arg) 11
Morris, S. 1937 (Birmingham) 5
Morris, W. 1947 (Burnley) 5
Moulsdale, J. R. B. 1925 (Corinthians) 1
Murphy, J. P. 1933 (WBA) 15
Myhill, G. O. 2008 (Hull C, WBA) 19

Nardiello, D. 1978 (Coventry C) 2
Nardiello, D. A. 2007 (Barnsley, QPR) 3
Neal, J. E. 1931 (Colwyn Bay) 2
Neilson, A. B. 1992 (Newcastle U, Southampton) 5
Newnes, J. 1926 (Nelson) 1
Newton, L. F. 1912 (Cardiff Corinthians) 1
Nicholas, D. S. 1923 (Stoke, Swansea T) 3
Nicholas, P. 1979 (Crystal Palace, Arsenal, Crystal Palace,
  Luton T, Aberdeen, Chelsea, Watford) 73
Nicholls, J. 1924 (Newport Co, Cardiff C) 4
Niedzwiecki, E. A. 1985 (Chelsea) 2
Nock, W. 1897 (Newtown) 1
Nogan, L. M. 1992 (Watford, Reading) 2
Norman, A. J. 1986 (Hull C) 5
Nurse, M. T. G. 1960 (Swansea T, Middlesbrough) 12
Nyatanga, L. J. 2006 (Derby Co, Bristol C) 34

O'Callaghan, E. 1929 (Tottenham H) 11
Oliver, A. 1905 (Bangor, Blackburn R) 2
Oster, J. M. 1998 (Everton, Sunderland) 13
O'Sullivan, P. A. 1973 (Brighton & HA) 3
Owen, D. 1879 (Oswestry) 1
Owen, E. 1884 (Ruthin Grammar School) 3
Owen, G. 1888 (Chirk, Newton Heath, Chirk) 4
Owen, J. 1892 (Newton Heath) 1
Owen, T. 1879 (Oswestry) 1
Owen, Trevor 1899 (Crewe Alex) 2
Owen, W. 1884 (Chirk) 16
Owen, W. P. 1880 (Ruthin) 12
Owens, J. 1902 (Wrexham) 1

Page, M. E. 1971 (Birmingham C) 28
Page, R. J. 1997 (Watford, Sheffield U, Cardiff C,
  Coventry C) 41
Palmer, D. 1957 (Swansea T) 3
Parris, J. E. 1932 (Bradford) 1
Parry, B. J. 1951 (Swansea T) 1
Parry, C. 1891 (Everton, Newtown) 13
Parry, E. 1922 (Liverpool) 5
Parry, M. 1901 (Liverpool) 16
Parry, P. I. 2004 (Cardiff C) 12
Parry, T. D. 1900 (Oswestry) 7
Parry, W. 1895 (Newtown) 1
Partridge, D. W. 2005 (Motherwell, Bristol C) 7
Pascoe, C. 1984 (Swansea C, Sunderland) 10
Paul, R. 1949 (Swansea T, Manchester C) 33
Peake, E. 1908 (Aberystwyth, Liverpool) 11
Peers, E. J. 1914 (Wolverhampton W, Port Vale) 12
Pembridge, M. A. 1992 (Luton T, Derby Co, Sheffield
  W, Benfica, Everton, Fulham) 54
Perry, E. 1938 (Doncaster R) 3
Perry, J. 1994 (Cardiff C) 1
Phennah, E. 1878 (Civil Service) 1
Phillips, C. 1931 (Wolverhampton W, Aston Villa) 13
Phillips, D. 1984 (Plymouth Arg, Manchester C,
  Coventry C, Norwich C, Nottingham F) 62
Phillips, L. 1971 (Cardiff C, Aston Villa, Swansea C,
  Charlton Ath) 58
Phillips, T. J. S. 1973 (Chelsea) 4
Phoenix, H. 1882 (Wrexham) 1
Pipe, D. R. 2003 (Coventry C) 1
Poland, G. 1939 (Wrexham) 2
Pontin, K. 1980 (Cardiff C) 2
Powell, A. 1947 (Leeds U, Everton, Birmingham C) 8

Powell, D. 1968 (Wrexham, Sheffield U) 11
Powell, I. V. 1947 (QPR, Aston Villa) 8
Powell, J. 1878 (Druids, Bolton W, Newton Heath) 15
Powell, Seth 1885 (Oswestry, WBA) 7
Price, H. 1907 (Aston Villa, Burton U, Wrexham) 5
Price, J. 1877 (Wrexham) 12
Price, L. P. 2006 (Ipswich T, Derby Co,
Crystal Palace) 11
Price, P. 1980 (Luton T, Tottenham H) 25
Pring, K. D. 1966 (Rotherham U) 3
Pritchard, H. K. 1985 (Bristol C) 1
Pryce-Jones, A. W. 1895 (Newtown) 1
Pryce-Jones, W. E. 1887 (Cambridge University) 5
Pugh, A. 1889 (Rhostyllen) 1
Pugh, D. H. 1896 (Wrexham, Lincoln C) 7
Pugsley, J. 1930 (Charlton Ath) 1
Pullen, W. J. 1926 (Plymouth Arg) 1

Ramsey, A. J. 2009 (Arsenal) **53**
Rankmore, F. E. J. 1966 (Peterborough U) 1
Ratcliffe, K. 1981 (Everton, Cardiff C) 59
Rea, J. C. 1894 (Aberystwyth) 9
Ready, K. 1997 (QPR) 5
Reece, G. I. 1966 (Sheffield U, Cardiff C) 29
Reed, W. G. 1955 (Ipswich T) 2
Rees, A. 1984 (Birmingham C) 1
Rees, J. M. 1992 (Luton T) 1
Rees, R. R. 1965 (Coventry C, WBA, Nottingham F) 39
Rees, W. 1949 (Cardiff C, Tottenham H) 4
Ribeiro, C. M. 2010 (Bristol C) 2
Richards, A. 1932 (Barnsley) 1
Richards, A. D. J. (Jazz) 2012 (Swansea C, Cardiff C) **13**
Richards, D. 1931 (Wolverhampton W, Brentford,
Birmingham) 21
Richards, G. 1899 (Druids, Oswestry, Shrewsbury T) 6
Richards, R. W. 1920 (Wolverhampton W, West Ham U,
Mold) 9
Richards, S. V. 1947 (Cardiff C) 1
Richards, W. E. 1933 (Fulham) 1
Ricketts, S. D. 2005 (Swansea C, Hull C, Bolton W,
Wolverhampton W) 52
Roach, J. 1885 (Oswestry) 1
Robbins, W. W. 1931 (Cardiff C, WBA) 11
Roberts, A. M. 1993 (QPR) 2
Roberts, C. R. J. 2018 (Swansea C) **2**
Roberts, D. F. 1973 (Oxford U, Hull C) 17
Roberts, G. W. 2000 (Tranmere R) 9
Roberts, I. W. 1990 (Watford, Huddersfield T,
Leicester C, Norwich C) 15
Roberts, Jas 1913 (Wrexham) 2
Roberts, J. 1879 (Corwen, Berwyn R) 7
Roberts, J. 1881 (Ruthin) 2
Roberts, J. 1906 (Bradford C) 2
Roberts, J. G. 1971 (Arsenal, Birmingham C) 22
Roberts, J. H. 1949 (Bolton W) 1
Roberts, N. W. 2000 (Wrexham, Wigan Ath) 4
Roberts, P. S. 1974 (Portsmouth) 4
Roberts, R. 1884 (Druids, Bolton W, Preston NE) 9
Roberts, R. 1886 (Wrexham) 3
Roberts, R. 1891 (Rhos, Crewe Alex) 2
Roberts, R. L. 1890 (Chester) 1
Roberts, S. W. 2005 (Wrexham) 1
Roberts, W. 1879 (Llangollen, Berwyn R) 6
Roberts, W. 1883 (Rhyl) 1
Roberts, W. 1886 (Wrexham) 4
Roberts, W. H. 1882 (Ruthin, Rhyl) 6
Robinson, C. P. 2000 (Wolverhampton W, Portsmouth,
Sunderland, Norwich C, Toronto Lynx) 52
Robinson, J. R. C. 1996 (Charlton Ath) 30
Robson-Kanu, T. H. 2010 (Reading, WBA) **44**
Rodrigues, P. J. 1965 (Cardiff C, Leicester C, Sheffield W) 40
Rogers, J. P. 1896 (Wrexham) 3
Rogers, W. 1931 (Wrexham) 1
Roose, L. R. 1900 (Aberystwyth, London Welsh, Stoke,
Everton, Stoke, Sunderland) 24
Rouse, R. V. 1959 (Crystal Palace) 1
Rowlands, A. C. 1914 (Tranmere R) 1
Rowley, T. 1959 (Tranmere R) 1
Rush, I. 1980 (Liverpool, Juventus, Liverpool) 73
Russell, M. R. 1912 (Merthyr T, Plymouth Arg) 23

Sabine, H. W. 1887 (Oswestry) 1
Saunders, D. 1986 (Brighton & HA, Oxford U,
Derby Co, Liverpool, Aston Villa, Galatasaray,
Nottingham F, Sheffield U, Benfica, Bradford C) 75

Savage, R. W. 1996 (Crewe Alex, Leicester C,
Birmingham C) 39
Savin, G. 1878 (Oswestry) 1
Sayer, P. A. 1977 (Cardiff C) 7
Scrine, F. H. 1950 (Swansea T) 2
Sear, C. R. 1963 (Manchester C) 1
Shaw, E. G. 1882 (Oswestry) 3
Sherwood, A. T. 1947 (Cardiff C, Newport Co) 41
Shone, W. 1879 (Oswestry) 1
Shortt, W. W. 1947 (Plymouth Arg) 12
Showers, D. 1975 (Cardiff C) 2
Sidlow, C. 1947 (Liverpool) 7
Sisson, H. 1885 (Wrexham Olympic) 3
Slatter, N. 1983 (Bristol R, Oxford U) 22
Smallman, D. P. 1974 (Wrexham, Everton) 7
Smith, M. 2018 (Manchester C) **1**
Southall, N. 1982 (Everton) 92
Speed, G. A. 1990 (Leeds U, Everton, Newcastle U,
Bolton W) 85
Sprake, G. 1964 (Leeds U, Birmingham C) 37
Stansfield, F. 1949 (Cardiff C) 1
Stevenson, B. 1978 (Leeds U, Birmingham C) 15
Stevenson, N. 1982 (Swansea C) 4
Stitfall, R. F. 1953 (Cardiff C) 2
Stock, B. B. 2010 (Doncaster R) 3
Sullivan, D. 1953 (Cardiff C) 17
Symons, C. J. 1992 (Portsmouth, Manchester C, Fulham,
Crystal Palace) 37

Tapscott, D. R. 1954 (Arsenal, Cardiff C) 14
Taylor, G. K. 1996 (Crystal Palace, Sheffield U, Burnley,
Nottingham F) 15
Taylor, J. 1898 (Wrexham) 1
Taylor, J. W. T. 2015 (Reading) 1
Taylor, N. J. 2010 (Wrexham, Swansea C, Aston Villa) **41**
Taylor, O. D. S. 1893 (Newtown) 4
Thatcher, B. D. 2004 (Leicester C, Manchester C) 7
Thomas, C. 1899 (Druids) 2
Thomas, D. A. 1957 (Swansea T) 2
Thomas, D. S. 1948 (Fulham) 4
Thomas, E. 1925 (Cardiff Corinthians) 1
Thomas, G. 1885 (Wrexham) 2
Thomas, G. S. 2018 (Leicester C) **1**
Thomas, H. 1927 (Manchester U) 1
Thomas, Martin R. 1987 (Newcastle U) 1
Thomas, Mickey 1977 (Wrexham, Manchester U,
Everton, Brighton & HA, Stoke C, Chelsea, WBA) 51
Thomas, R. J. 1967 (Swindon T, Derby Co, Cardiff C) 50
Thomas, T. 1898 (Bangor) 2
Thomas, W. R. 1931 (Newport Co) 2
Thomson, D. 1876 (Druids) 1
Thomson, G. F. 1876 (Druids) 2
Toshack, J. B. 1969 (Cardiff C, Liverpool, Swansea C) 40
Townsend, W. 1887 (Newtown) 2
Trainer, H. 1895 (Wrexham) 3
Trainer, J. 1887 (Bolton W, Preston NE) 20
Trollope, P. J. 1997 (Derby Co, Fulham, Coventry C,
Northampton T) 9
Tudur-Jones, O. 2008 (Swansea C, Norwich C,
Hibernian) 7
Turner, H. G. 1937 (Charlton Ath) 8
Turner, J. 1892 (Wrexham) 1
Turner, R. E. 1891 (Wrexham) 2
Turner, W. H. 1887 (Wrexham) 5

Van Den Hauwe, P. W. R. 1985 (Everton) 13
Vaughan, D. O. 2003 (Crewe Alex, Real Sociedad,
Blackpool, Sunderland, Nottingham F) 42
Vaughan, Jas 1893 (Druids) 4
Vaughan, John 1879 (Oswestry, Druids, Bolton W) 11
Vaughan, J. O. 1885 (Rhyl) 4
Vaughan, N. 1983 (Newport Co, Cardiff C) 10
Vaughan, T. 1885 (Rhyl) 1
Vearncombe, G. 1958 (Cardiff C) 2
Vernon, T. R. 1957 (Blackburn R, Everton, Stoke C) 32
Villars, A. K. 1974 (Cardiff C) 3
Vizard, E. T. 1911 (Bolton W) 22
**Vokes, S. M. 2008 (Bournemouth, Wolverhampton W,
Burnley)** **59**

Walley, J. T. 1971 (Watford) 1
Walsh, I. P. 1980 (Crystal Palace, Swansea C) 18
Ward, D. 1959 (Bristol R, Cardiff C) 2
Ward, D. 2000 (Notts Co, Nottingham F) 5
Ward, D. 2016 (Liverpool) **4**

Warner, J. 1937 (Swansea T, Manchester U) 2
Warren, F. W. 1929 (Cardiff C, Middlesbrough, Hearts) 6
Watkins, A. E. 1898 (Leicester Fosse, Aston Villa,
  Millwall) 5
Watkins, M. J. 2018 (Norwich C) 2
Watkins, W. M. 1902 (Stoke, Aston Villa, Sunderland,
  Stoke) 10
Webster, C. 1957 (Manchester U) 4
Weston, R. D. 2000 (Arsenal, Cardiff C) 7
Whatley, W. J. 1939 (Tottenham H) 1
White, P. F. 1896 (London Welsh) 1
Wilcock, A. R. 1890 (Oswestry) 1
Wilding, J. 1885 (Wrexham Olympians, Bootle, Wrexham) 9
Williams, A. 1994 (Reading, Wolverhampton W,
  Reading) 13
Williams, A. E. 2008 (Stockport Co, Swansea C,
** Everton)** 79
Williams, A. L. 1931 (Wrexham) 1
Williams, A. P. 1998 (Southampton) 2
Williams, B. 1930 (Bristol C) 1
Williams, B. D. 1928 (Swansea T, Everton) 10
Williams, D. G. 1988 (Derby Co, Ipswich T) 13
Williams, D. M. 1986 (Norwich C) 5
Williams, D. R. 1921 (Merthyr T, Sheffield W,
  Manchester U) 8
Williams, E. 1893 (Crewe Alex) 2
Williams, E. 1901 (Druids) 5
Williams, G. 1893 (Chirk) 6
Williams, G. C. 2014 (Fulham) 7
Williams, G. E. 1960 (WBA) 26
Williams, G. G. 1961 (Swansea T) 5

Williams, G. J. 2006 (West Ham U, Ipswich T) 2
Williams, G. J. 1951 (Cardiff C) 1
Williams, G. O. 1907 (Wrexham) 1
Williams, H. J. 1965 (Swansea T) 3
Williams, H. T. 1949 (Newport Co, Leeds U) 4
Williams, J. H. 1884 (Oswestry) 1
Williams, J. J. 1939 (Wrexham) 1
Williams, J. P. 2013 (Crystal Palace) 17
Williams, J. T. 1925 (Middlesbrough) 1
Williams, J. W. 1912 (Crystal Palace) 2
Williams, R. 1935 (Newcastle U) 2
Williams, R. P. 1886 (Caernarvon) 1
Williams, S. G. 1954 (WBA, Southampton) 43
Williams, W. 1876 (Druids, Oswestry, Druids) 11
Williams, W. 1925 (Northampton T) 1
Wilson, H. 2013 (Liverpool) 4
Wilson, J. S. 2013 (Bristol C) 1
Witcomb, D. F. 1947 (WBA, Sheffield W) 3
Woodburn, B. 2018 (Liverpool) 7
Woosnam, A. P. 1959 (Leyton Orient, West Ham U,
  Aston Villa) 17
Woosnam, G. 1879 (Newtown Excelsior) 1
Worthington, T. 1894 (Newtown) 1
Wynn, G. A. 1909 (Wrexham, Manchester C) 11
Wynn, W. 1903 (Chirk) 1

Yorath, T. C. 1970 (Leeds U, Coventry C, Tottenham H,
  Vancouver Whitecaps) 59
Young, E. 1990 (Wimbledon, Crystal Palace,
  Wolverhampton W) 21

REPUBLIC OF IRELAND

Aherne, T. 1946 (Belfast Celtic, Luton T) 16
Aldridge, J. W. 1986 (Oxford U, Liverpool,
  Real Sociedad, Tranmere R) 69
Ambrose, P. 1955 (Shamrock R) 5
Anderson, J. 1980 (Preston NE, Newcastle U) 16
Andrews, K. J. 2009 (Blackburn R, WBA) 35
Andrews, P. 1936 (Bohemians) 1
Arrigan, T. 1938 (Waterford) 1
Arter, H. N. 2015 (Bournemouth) 13

Babb, P. A. 1994 (Coventry C, Liverpool, Sunderland) 35
Bailham, E. 1964 (Shamrock R) 1
Barber, E. 1966 (Shelbourne, Birmingham C) 2
Barrett, G. 2003 (Arsenal, Coventry C) 6
Barry, P. 1928 (Fordsons) 2
Beglin, J. 1984 (Liverpool) 15
Bennett, A. J. 2007 (Reading) 1
Bermingham, J. 1929 (Bohemians) 1
Bermingham, P. 1935 (St James' Gate) 1
Best, L. J. B. 2009 (Coventry C, Newcastle U) 7
Bonner, P. 1981 (Celtic) 80
Boyle, A. 2017 (Preston NE) 1
Braddish, S. 1978 (Dundalk) 2
Bradshaw, P. 1939 (St James' Gate) 5
Brady, F. 1926 (Fordsons) 2
Brady, R. 2013 (Hull C, Norwich C, Burnley) 39
Brady, T. R. 1964 (QPR) 6
Brady, W. L. 1975 (Arsenal, Juventus, Sampdoria,
  Internazionale, Ascoli, West Ham U) 72
Branagan, K. G. 1997 (Bolton W) 1
Breen, G. 1996 (Birmingham C, Coventry C,
  West Ham U, Sunderland) 63
Breen, T. 1937 (Manchester U, Shamrock R) 5
Brennan, F. 1965 (Drumcondra) 1
Brennan, S. A. 1965 (Manchester U, Waterford) 19
Brown, J. 1937 (Coventry C) 2
Browne, A. J. 2017 (Preston NE) 3
Browne, W. 1964 (Bohemians) 3
Bruce, A. S. 2007 (Ipswich T) 2
Buckley, L. 1984 (Shamrock R, Waregem) 2
Burke, F. 1952 (Cork Ath) 1
Burke, G. D. 2018 (Shamrock R) 2
Burke, J. 1929 (Shamrock R) 1
Burke, J. 1934 (Cork) 1
Butler, P. J. 2000 (Sunderland) 1
Butler, T. 2003 (Sunderland) 2
Byrne, A. B. 1970 (Southampton) 14
Byrne, D. 1929 (Shelbourne, Shamrock R, Coleraine) 3
Byrne, J. 1928 (Bray Unknowns) 1

Byrne, J. 1985 (QPR, Le Havre, Brighton & HA,
  Sunderland, Millwall) 23
Byrne, J. 2004 (Shelbourne) 2
Byrne, P. 1931 (Dolphin, Shelbourne, Drumcondra) 3
Byrne, P. 1984 (Shamrock R) 8
Byrne, S. 1931 (Bohemians) 1

Campbell, A. 1985 (Santander) 3
Campbell, N. 1971 (St Patrick's Ath, Fortuna Cologne) 11
Cannon, H. 1926 (Bohemians) 2
Cantwell, N. 1954 (West Ham U, Manchester U) 36
Carey, B. P. 1992 (Manchester U, Leicester C) 3
Carey, J. J. 1938 (Manchester U) 29
Carolan, J. 1960 (Manchester U) 2
Carr, S. 1999 (Tottenham H, Newcastle U) 44
Carroll, B. 1949 (Shelbourne) 2
Carroll, T. R. 1968 (Ipswich T, Birmingham C) 17
Carsley, L. K. 1998 (Derby Co, Blackburn R, Coventry
  C, Everton) 39
Cascarino, A. G. 1986 (Gillingham, Millwall, Aston
  Villa, Celtic, Chelsea, Marseille, Nancy) 88
Chandler, J. 1980 (Leeds U) 2
Chatton, H. A. 1931 (Shelbourne, Dumbarton, Cork) 3
Christie, C. S. F. 2015 (Derby Co, Middlesbrough) 17
Clark, C. 2011 (Aston Villa, Newcastle U) 31
Clarke, C. R. 2004 (Stoke C) 2
Clarke, J. 1978 (Drogheda U) 1
Clarke, K. 1948 (Drumcondra) 2
Clarke, M. 1950 (Shamrock R) 1
Clinton, T. J. 1951 (Everton) 3
Coad, P. 1947 (Shamrock R) 11
Coffey, T. 1950 (Drumcondra) 1
Coleman, S. 2011 (Everton) 46
Colfer, M. D. 1950 (Shelbourne) 2
Colgan, N. 2002 (Hibernian, Barnsley) 9
Collins, F. 1927 (Jacobs) 1
Conmy, O. M. 1965 (Peterborough U) 5
Connolly, D. J. 1996 (Watford, Feyenoord,
  Wolverhampton W, Excelsior, Feyenoord,
  Wimbledon, West Ham U, Wigan Ath) 41
Connolly, H. 1937 (Cork) 1
Connolly, J. 1926 (Fordsons) 1
Conroy, G. A. 1970 (Stoke C) 27
Conway, J. P. 1967 (Fulham, Manchester C) 20
Corr, P. J. 1949 (Everton) 4
Courtney, E. 1946 (Cork U) 1
Cox, S. R. 2011 (WBA, Nottingham F) 30
Coyle, O. C. 1994 (Bolton W) 1
Coyne, T. 1992 (Celtic, Tranmere R, Motherwell) 22
Crowe, G. 2003 (Bohemians) 2

Cummins, G. P. 1954 (Luton T) 19
Cuneen, T. 1951 (Limerick) 1
Cunningham, G. R. 2010 (Manchester C, Bristol C) 4
Cunningham, K. 1996 (Wimbledon, Birmingham C) 72
Curtis, D. P. 1957 (Shelbourne, Bristol C, Ipswich T, Exeter C) 17
Cusack, S. 1953 (Limerick) 1

Daish, L. S. 1992 (Cambridge U, Coventry C) 5
Daly, G. A. 1973 (Manchester U, Derby Co, Coventry C, Birmingham C, Shrewsbury T) 48
Daly, J. 1932 (Shamrock R) 2
Daly, M. 1978 (Wolverhampton W) 2
Daly, P. 1950 (Shamrock R) 1
Davis, T. L. 1937 (Oldham Ath, Tranmere R) 4
Deacy, E. 1982 (Aston Villa) 4
Delaney, D. F. 2008 (QPR, Ipswich T, Crystal Palace) 9
Delap, R. J. 1998 (Derby Co, Southampton) 11
De Mange, K. J. P. P. 1987 (Liverpool, Hull C) 2
Dempsey, J. T. 1967 (Fulham, Chelsea) 19
Dennehy, J. 1972 (Cork Hibernians, Nottingham F, Walsall) 11
Desmond, P. 1950 (Middlesbrough) 4
Devine, J. 1980 (Arsenal, Norwich C) 13
Doherty, G. M. T. 2000 (Luton T, Tottenham H, Norwich C) 34
Doherty, M. J. 2018 (Woverhampton W) **2**
Donnelly, J. 1935 (Dundalk) 10
Donnelly, T. 1938 (Drumcondra, Shamrock R) 2
Donovan, D. C. 1955 (Everton) 5
Donovan, T. 1980 (Aston Villa) 2
Douglas, J. 2004 (Blackburn R, Leeds U) 8
Dowdall, C. 1928 (Fordsons, Barnsley, Cork) 3
Doyle, C. 1959 (Shelbourne) 1
Doyle, C. A. 2007 (Birmingham C, Bradford C) **4**
Doyle, D. 1926 (Shamrock R) 1
Doyle, K. E. 2006 (Reading, Wolverhampton W, Colorado Rapids) 63
Doyle, L. 1932 (Dolphin) 1
Doyle, M. P. 2004 (Coventry C) 1
Duff, D. A. 1998 (Blackburn R, Chelsea, Newcastle U, Fulham) 100
Duffy, B. 1950 (Shamrock R) 1
Duffy, S. P. M. 2014 (Everton, Blackburn R, Brighton & HA) **20**
Duggan, H. A. 1927 (Leeds U, Newport Co) 5
Dunne, A. P. 1962 (Manchester U, Bolton W) 33
Dunne, J. 1930 (Sheffield U, Arsenal, Southampton, Shamrock R) 15
Dunne, J. C. 1971 (Fulham) 1
Dunne, J. 1935 (Manchester C) 2
Dunne, P. A. J. 1965 (Manchester U) 5
Dunne, R. P. 2000 (Everton, Manchester C, Aston Villa, QPR) 80
Dunne, S. 1953 (Luton T) 15
Dunne, T. 1956 (St Patrick's Ath) 3
Dunning, P. 1971 (Shelbourne) 2
Dunphy, E. M. 1966 (York C, Millwall) 23
Dwyer, N. M. 1960 (West Ham U, Swansea T) 14

Eccles, P. 1986 (Shamrock R) 1
Egan, J. 2017 (Brentford) 2
Egan, R. 1929 (Dundalk) 1
Eglington, T. J. 1946 (Shamrock R, Everton) 24
Elliot, R. 2014 (Newcastle U) 4
Elliott, S. W. 2005 (Sunderland) 9
Ellis, P. 1935 (Bohemians) 7
Evans, M. J. 1998 (Southampton) 1

Fagan, E. 1973 (Shamrock R) 1
Fagan, F. 1955 (Manchester C, Derby Co) 8
Fagan, J. 1926 (Shamrock R) 1
Fahey, K. D. 2010 (Birmingham C) 16
Fairclough, M. 1982 (Dundalk) 2
Fallon, S. 1951 (Celtic) 8
Fallon, W. J. 1935 (Notts Co, Sheffield W) 9
Farquharson, T. G. 1929 (Cardiff C) 4
Farrell, P. 1937 (Hibernian) 2
Farrell, P. D. 1946 (Shamrock R, Everton) 28
Farrelly, G. 1996 (Aston Villa, Everton, Bolton W) 6
Feenan, J. J. 1937 (Sunderland) 2
Finnan, S. 2000 (Fulham, Liverpool, Espanyol) 53
Finucane, A. 1967 (Limerick) 11
Fitzgerald, F. J. 1955 (Waterford) 2

Fitzgerald, P. J. 1961 (Leeds U, Chester) 5
Fitzpatrick, K. 1970 (Limerick) 1
Fitzsimons, A. G. 1950 (Middlesbrough, Lincoln C) 26
Fleming, C. 1996 (Middlesbrough) 10
Flood, J. J. 1926 (Shamrock R) 5
Fogarty, A. 1960 (Sunderland, Hartlepools U) 11
Folan, C. C. 2009 (Hull C) 7
Foley, D. J. 2000 (Watford) 6
Foley, J. 1934 (Cork, Celtic) 7
Foley, K. P. 2009 (Wolverhampton W) 8
Foley, M. 1926 (Shelbourne) 1
Foley, T. C. 1964 (Northampton T) 9
Forde, D. 2011 (Millwall) 24
Foy, T. 1938 (Shamrock R) 2
Fullam, J. 1961 (Preston NE, Shamrock R) 11
Fullam, R. 1926 (Shamrock R) 2

Gallagher, C. 1967 (Celtic) 2
Gallagher, M. 1954 (Hibernian) 1
Gallagher, P. 1932 (Falkirk) 1
Galvin, A. 1983 (Tottenham H, Sheffield W, Swindon T) 29
Gamble, J. 2007 (Cork C) 2
Gannon, E. 1949 (Notts Co, Sheffield W, Shelbourne) 14
Gannon, M. 1972 (Shelbourne) 1
Gaskins, P. 1934 (Shamrock R, St James' Gate) 7
Gavin, J. T. 1950 (Norwich C, Tottenham H, Norwich C) 7
Geoghegan, M. 1937 (St James' Gate) 2
Gibbons, A. 1952 (St Patrick's Ath) 4
Gibson, D. T. D. 2008 (Manchester U, Everton) 27
Gilbert, R. 1966 (Shamrock R) 1
Giles, C. 1951 (Doncaster R) 1
Giles, M. J. 1960 (Manchester U, Leeds U, WBA, Shamrock R) 59
Given, S. J. J. 1996 (Blackburn R, Newcastle U, Manchester C, Aston Villa, Stoke C) 134
Givens, D. J. 1969 (Manchester U, Luton T, QPR, Birmingham C, Neuchatel X) 56
Gleeson, S. M. 2007 (Wolverhampton W, Birmingham C) 4
Glen, W. 1927 (Shamrock R) 8
Glynn, D. 1952 (Drumcondra) 2
Godwin, T. F. 1949 (Shamrock R, Leicester C, Bournemouth) 13
Golding, J. 1928 (Shamrock R) 2
Goodman, J. 1997 (Wimbledon) 4
Goodwin, J. 2003 (Stockport Co) 1
Gorman, W. C. 1936 (Bury, Brentford) 13
Grace, J. 1926 (Drumcondra) 1
Grealish, A. 1976 (Orient, Luton T, Brighton & HA, WBA) 45
Green, P. J. 2010 (Derby Co, Leeds U) 20
Gregg, E. 1978 (Bohemians) 8
Griffith, R. 1935 (Walsall) 1
Grimes, A. A. 1978 (Manchester U, Coventry C, Luton T) 18

Hale, A. 1962 (Aston Villa, Doncaster R, Waterford) 14
Hamilton, T. 1959 (Shamrock R) 2
Hand, E. K. 1969 (Portsmouth) 20
Harrington, W. 1936 (Cork) 5
Harte, I. P. 1996 (Leeds U, Levante) 64
Hartnett, J. B. 1949 (Middlesbrough) 2
Haverty, J. 1956 (Arsenal, Blackburn R, Millwall, Celtic, Bristol R, Shelbourne) 32
Hayes, A. W. P. 1979 (Southampton) 1
Hayes, J. 2016 (Aberdeen) 4
Hayes, W. E. 1947 (Huddersfield T) 2
Hayes, W. J. 1949 (Limerick) 1
Healey, R. 1977 (Cardiff C) 2
Healy, C. 2002 (Celtic, Sunderland) 13
Heighway, S. D. 1971 (Liverpool, Minnesota K) 34
Henderson, B. 1948 (Drumcondra) 2
Henderson, W. C. P. 2006 (Brighton & HA, Preston NE) 6
Hendrick, J. P. 2013 (Derby Co, Burnley) **39**
Hennessy, J. 1965 (Shelbourne, St Patrick's Ath) 5
Herrick, J. 1972 (Cork Hibernians, Shamrock R) 3
Higgins, J. 1951 (Birmingham C) 1
Hogan, S. A. 2018 (Aston Villa) **1**
Holland, M. R. 2000 (Ipswich T, Charlton Ath) 49
Holmes, J. 1971 (Coventry C, Tottenham H, Vancouver Whitecaps) 30

Hoolahan, W. 2008 (Blackpool, Norwich C) 43
Horgan, D. J. 2017 (Preston NE) 4
Horlacher, A. F. 1930 (Bohemians) 7
Houghton, R. J. 1986 (Oxford U, Liverpool, Aston Villa,
Crystal Palace, Reading) 73
Hourihane, C. 2017 (Aston Villa) 5
Howlett, G. 1984 (Brighton & HA) 1
Hoy, M. 1938 (Dundalk) 6
Hughton, C. 1980 (Tottenham H, West Ham U) 53
Hunt, N. 2009 (Reading) 3
Hunt, S. P. 2007 (Reading, Hull C, Wolverhampton W)
39
Hurley, C. J. 1957 (Millwall, Sunderland, Bolton W) 40
Hutchinson, F. 1935 (Drumcondra) 2

Ireland S J. 2006 (Manchester C) 6
Irwin, D. J. 1991 (Manchester U) 56

Jordan, D. 1937 (Wolverhampton W) 2
Jordan, W. 1934 (Bohemians) 2
Judge, A. C. 2016 (Brentford) 4

Kavanagh, G. A. 1998 (Stoke C, Cardiff C, Wigan Ath)
16
Kavanagh, P. J. 1931 (Celtic) 2
Keane, R. D. 1998 (Wolverhampton W, Coventry C,
Internazionale, Leeds U, Tottenham H, Liverpool,
Tottenham H, LA Galaxy) 146
Keane, R. M. 1991 (Nottingham F, Manchester U) 67
Keane, T. R. 1949 (Swansea T) 4
Kearin, M. 1972 (Shamrock R) 1
Kearns, F. T. 1954 (West Ham U) 1
Kearns, M. 1971 (Oxford U, Walsall, Wolverhampton W)
18
Kelly, A. T. 1993 (Sheffield U, Blackburn R) 34
Kelly, D. T. 1988 (Walsall, West Ham U, Leicester C,
Newcastle U, Wolverhampton W, Sunderland,
Tranmere R) 26
Kelly, G. 1994 (Leeds U) 52
Kelly, J. 1932 (Derry C) 4
Kelly, J. A. 1957 (Drumcondra, Preston NE) 47
Kelly, J. P. V. 1961 (Wolverhampton W) 5
Kelly, M. J. 1988 (Portsmouth) 4
Kelly, N. 1954 (Nottingham F) 1
Kelly, S. M. 2006 (Tottenham H, Birmingham C,
Fulham, Reading) 38
Kendrick, J. 1927 (Everton, Dolphin) 4
Kenna, J. J. 1995 (Blackburn R) 27
Kennedy, M. F. 1986 (Portsmouth) 2
Kennedy, M. J. 1996 (Liverpool, Wimbledon,
Manchester C, Wolverhampton W) 34
Kennedy, W. 1932 (St James' Gate) 3
Kenny, P. 2004 (Sheffield U) 7
Keogh, A. D. 2007 (Wolverhampton W, Millwall) 30
Keogh, J. 1966 (Shamrock R) 1
Keogh, R. J. 2013 (Derby Co) 17
Keogh, S. 1959 (Shamrock R) 1
Kernaghan, A. N. 1993 (Middlesbrough, Manchester C)
22
Kiely, D. L. 2000 (Charlton Ath, WBA) 11
Kiernan, F. W. 1951 (Shamrock R, Southampton) 5
Kilbane, K. D. 1998 (WBA, Sunderland, Everton,
Wigan Ath, Hull C) 110
Kinnear, J. P. 1967 (Tottenham H, Brighton & HA) 26
Kinsella, J. 1928 (Shelbourne) 1
Kinsella, M. A. 1998 (Charlton Ath, Aston Villa, WBA)
48
Kinsella, O. 1932 (Shamrock R) 2
Kirkland, A. 1927 (Shamrock R) 1

Lacey, W. 1927 (Shelbourne) 3
Langan, D. 1978 (Derby Co, Birmingham C, Oxford U)
26
Lapira, J. 2007 (Notre Dame) 1
Lawler, J. F. 1953 (Fulham) 8
Lawlor, J. C. 1949 (Drumcondra, Doncaster R) 3
Lawlor, M. 1971 (Shamrock R) 5
Lawrence, L. 2009 (Stoke C, Portsmouth) 15
Lawrenson, M. 1977 (Preston NE, Brighton & HA,
Liverpool) 39
Lee, A. D. 2003 (Rotherham U, Cardiff C, Ipswich T) 10
Leech, M. 1969 (Shamrock R) 8
Lenihan, D. P. 2018 (Blackburn R) 1
Lennon, C. 1935 (St James' Gate) 3

Lennox, G. 1931 (Dolphin) 2
Long, K. F. 2017 (Burnley) 7
Long, S. P. 2007 (Reading, WBA, Hull C, Southampton)
80
Lowry, D. 1962 (St Patrick's Ath) 1
Lunn, R. 1939 (Dundalk) 2
Lynch, J. 1934 (Cork Bohemians) 1

Macken, A. 1977 (Derby Co) 1
Macken J. P. 2005 (Manchester C) 1
Mackey, G. 1957 (Shamrock R) 3
Madden, O. 1936 (Cork) 1
Madden, P. 2013 (Scunthorpe U) 1
Maguire, J. 1929 (Shamrock R) 1
Maguire, S. P. 2018 (Preston NE) 2
Mahon, A. J. 2000 (Tranmere R) 2
Malone, G. 1949 (Shelbourne) 1
Mancini, T. J. 1974 (QPR, Arsenal) 5
Martin, C. 1927 (Bo'ness) 1
Martin, C. J. 1946 (Glentoran, Leeds U,
Aston Villa) 30
Martin, M. P. 1972 (Bohemians, Manchester U,
WBA, Newcastle U) 52
Maybury, A. 1998 (Leeds U, Hearts, Leicester C) 10
McAlinden, J. 1946 (Portsmouth) 2
McAteer, J. W. 1994 (Bolton W, Liverpool, Blackburn
R, Sunderland) 52
McCann, J. 1957 (Shamrock R) 1
McCarthy, J. 1926 (Bohemians) 3
McCarthy, J. 2010 (Wigan Ath, Everton) 41
McCarthy, M. 1932 (Shamrock R) 1
McCarthy, M. 1984 (Manchester C, Celtic, Lyon,
Millwall) 57
McClean, J. J. 2012 (Sunderland, Wigan Ath, WBA) 60
McConville, T. 1972 (Dundalk, Waterford) 6
McDonagh, Jacko 1984 (Shamrock R) 3
McDonagh, J. 1981 (Everton, Bolton W, Notts Co,
Wichita Wings) 25
McEvoy, M. A. 1961 (Blackburn R) 17
**McGeady, A. J. 2004 (Celtic, Spartak Moscow, Everton,
Sunderland)** 93
McGee, P. 1978 (QPR, Preston NE) 15
McGoldrick, D. J. 2015 (Ipswich T) 6
McGoldrick, E. J. 1992 (Crystal Palace, Arsenal) 15
McGowan, D. 1949 (West Ham U) 3
McGowan, J. 1947 (Cork U) 1
McGrath, M. 1958 (Blackburn R, Bradford) 22
McGrath, P. 1985 (Manchester U, Aston Villa,
Derby Co) 83
McGuire, W. 1936 (Bohemians) 1
McKenzie, G. 1938 (Southend U) 9
McLoughlin, A. F. 1990 (Swindon T, Southampton,
Portsmouth) 42
McLoughlin, F. 1930 (Fordsons, Cork) 2
McMillan, W. 1946 (Belfast Celtic) 2
McNally, J. B. 1959 (Luton T) 3
McPhail, S. 2000 (Leeds U) 10
McShane, P. D. 2007 (WBA, Sunderland, Hull C,
Reading) 33
Meagan, M. K. 1961 (Everton, Huddersfield T,
Drogheda) 17
Meehan, P. 1934 (Drumcondra) 1
Meyler, D. J. 2013 (Sunderland, Hull C) 25
Miller, L. W. P. 2004 (Celtic, Manchester U, Sunderland,
Hibernian) 21
Milligan, M. J. 1992 (Oldham Ath) 1
Monahan, P. 1935 (Sligo R) 2
Mooney, J. 1965 (Shamrock R) 2
Moore, A. 1996 (Middlesbrough) 8
Moore, P. 1931 (Shamrock R, Aberdeen, Shamrock R) 9
Moran, K. 1980 (Manchester U, Sporting Gijon,
Blackburn R) 71
Moroney, T. 1948 (West Ham U, Evergreen U) 12
Morris, C. B. 1988 (Celtic, Middlesbrough) 35
Morrison, C. H. 2002 (Crystal Palace, Birmingham C,
Crystal Palace) 36
Moulson, C. 1936 (Lincoln C, Notts Co) 5
Moulson, G. B. 1948 (Lincoln C) 3
Muckian, C. 1978 (Drogheda U) 1
Muldoon, T. 1927 (Aston Villa) 1
Mulligan, P. M. 1969 (Shamrock R, Chelsea,
Crystal Palace, WBA, Shamrock R) 50
Munroe, L. 1954 (Shamrock R) 1
Murphy, A. 1956 (Clyde) 1

Murphy, B. 1986 (Bohemians) 1
Murphy, D. 2007 (Sunderland, Ipswich T, Newcastle U,
 Sheffield W) 32
Murphy, J. 1980 (Crystal Palace) 3
Murphy, J. 2004 (WBA, Scunthorpe U) 2
Murphy, P. M. 2007 (Carlisle U) 1
Murray, T. 1950 (Dundalk) 1

Newman, W. 1969 (Shelbourne) 1
Nolan. E. W. 2009 (Preston NE) 3
Nolan, R. 1957 (Shamrock R) 10

O'Brien, A. 2007 (Newcastle U) 5
O'Brien, A. J. 2001 (Newcastle U, Portsmouth) 26
O'Brien, F. 1980 (Philadelphia F) 3
O'Brien J. M. 2006 (Bolton W, West Ham U) 5
O'Brien, L. 1986 (Shamrock R, Manchester U,
 Newcastle U, Tranmere R) 16
O'Brien, M. T. 1927 (Derby Co, Walsall, Norwich C,
 Watford) 4
O'Brien, R. 1976 (Notts Co) 5
O'Byrne, L. B. 1949 (Shamrock R) 1
O'Callaghan, B. R. 1979 (Stoke C) 6
O'Callaghan, K. 1981 (Ipswich T, Portsmouth) 21
O'Cearuill, J. 2007 (Arsenal) 2
O'Connell, A. 1967 (Dundalk, Bohemians) 2
O'Connor, T. 1950 (Shamrock R) 4
O'Connor, T. 1968 (Fulham, Dundalk, Bohemians) 7
O'Dea, D. 2010 (Celtic, Toronto, Metalurh Donetsk) 20
O'Dowda, C. J. R. 2016 (Oxford U, Bristol C) 10
O'Driscoll, J. F. 1949 (Swansea T) 3
O'Driscoll, S. 1982 (Fulham) 3
O'Farrell, F. 1952 (West Ham U, Preston NE) 9
O'Flanagan, K. P. 1938 (Bohemians, Arsenal) 10
O'Flanagan, M. 1947 (Bohemians) 1
O'Halloran, S. E. 2007 (Aston Villa) 2
O'Hanlon, K. G. 1988 (Rotherham U) 1
O'Kane, E. C. 2016 (Bournemouth, Leeds U) 7
O'Kane, P. 1935 (Bohemians) 3
O'Keefe, E. 1981 (Everton, Port Vale) 5
O'Keefe, T. 1934 (Cork, Waterford) 3
O'Leary, D. 1977 (Arsenal) 68
O'Leary, P. 1980 (Shamrock R) 7
O'Mahoney, M. T. 1938 (Bristol R) 6
O'Neill, F. S. 1962 (Shamrock R) 20
O'Neill, J. 1952 (Everton) 17
O'Neill, J. 1961 (Preston NE) 1
O'Neill, K. P. 1996 (Norwich C, Middlesbrough) 13
O'Neill, W. 1936 (Dundalk) 11
O'Regan, K. 1984 (Brighton & HA) 4
O'Reilly, J. 1932 (Brideville, Aberdeen, Brideville,
 St James' Gate) 20
O'Reilly, J. 1946 (Cork U) 2
O'Shea, J. F. 2002 (Manchester U, Sunderland) 118

Pearce, A. J. 2013 (Reading, Derby Co) 9
Peyton, G. 1977 (Fulham, Bournemouth, Everton) 33
Peyton, N. 1957 (Shamrock R, Leeds U) 6
Phelan, T. 1992 (Wimbledon, Manchester C, Chelsea,
 Everton, Fulham) 42
Pilkington, A. N. J. 2013 (Norwich C, Cardiff C) 9
Potter, D. M. 2007 (Wolverhampton W) 5

Quinn, A. 2003 (Sheffield W, Sheffield U) 8
Quinn, B. S. 2000 (Coventry C) 4
Quinn, N. J. 1986 (Arsenal, Manchester C, Sunderland)
 91
Quinn, S. 2013 (Hull C, Reading) 18

Randolph, D. E. 2013 (Motherwell, West Ham U,
 Middlesbrough) 28
Reid, A. M. 2004 (Nottingham F, Tottenham H,
 Charlton Ath, Sunderland, Nottingham F) 29
Reid, C. 1931 (Brideville) 1
Reid, S. J. 2002 (Millwall, Blackburn R) 23
Rice, D. 2018 (West Ham U) 3
Richardson, D. J. 1972 (Shamrock R, Gillingham) 3

Rigby, A. 1935 (St James' Gate) 3
Ringstead, A. 1951 (Sheffield U) 20
Robinson, J. 1928 (Bohemians, Dolphin) 2
Robinson, M. 1981 (Brighton & HA, Liverpool, QPR) 24
Roche, P. J. 1972 (Shelbourne, Manchester U) 8
Rogers, E. 1968 (Blackburn R, Charlton Ath) 19
Rowlands, M. C. 2004 (QPR) 5
Ryan, G. 1978 (Derby Co, Brighton & HA) 18
Ryan, R. A. 1950 (WBA, Derby Co) 16

Sadlier, R. T. 2002 (Millwall) 1
Sammon, C. 2013 (Derby Co) 9
Savage, D. P. T. 1996 (Millwall) 5
Saward, P. 1954 (Millwall, Aston Villa, Huddersfield T)
 18
Scannell, T. 1954 (Southend U) 1
Scully, P. J. 1989 (Arsenal) 1
Sheedy, K. 1984 (Everton, Newcastle U) 46
Sheridan, C. 2010 (Celtic, CSKA Sofia) 3
Sheridan, J. J. 1988 (Leeds U, Sheffield W) 34
Slaven, B. 1990 (Middlesbrough) 7
Sloan, J. W. 1946 (Arsenal) 2
Smyth, M. 1969 (Shamrock R) 1
Squires, J. 1934 (Shelbourne) 1
Stapleton, F. 1977 (Arsenal, Manchester U, Ajax,
 Le Havre, Blackburn R) 71
Staunton, S. 1989 (Liverpool, Aston Villa, Liverpool,
 Aston Villa) 102
St Ledger-Hall, S. P. 2009 (Preston NE, Leicester C) 37
Stevens, E. J. 2018 (Sheffield U) 1
Stevenson, A. E. 1932 (Dolphin, Everton) 7
Stokes, A. 2007 (Sunderland, Celtic) 9
Strahan, F. 1964 (Shelbourne) 5
Sullivan, J. 1928 (Fordsons) 1
Swan, M. M. G. 1960 (Drumcondra) 1
Synnott, N. 1978 (Shamrock R) 3

Taylor, T. 1959 (Waterford) 1
Thomas, P. 1974 (Waterford) 2
Thompson, J. 2004 (Nottingham F) 1
Townsend, A. D. 1989 (Norwich C, Chelsea, Aston Villa,
 Middlesbrough) 70
Traynor, T. J. 1954 (Southampton) 8
Treacy, K. 2011 (Preston NE, Burnley) 6
Treacy, R. C. P. 1966 (WBA, Charlton Ath, Swindon T,
 Preston NE, WBA, Shamrock R) 42
Tuohy, L. 1956 (Shamrock R, Newcastle U,
 Shamrock R) 8
Turner, C. J. 1936 (Southend U, West Ham U) 10
Turner, P. 1963 (Celtic) 2

Vernon, J. 1946 (Belfast Celtic) 2

Waddock, G. 1980 (QPR, Millwall) 21
Walsh, D. J. 1946 (Linfield, WBA, Aston Villa) 20
Walsh, J. 1982 (Limerick) 1
Walsh, M. 1976 (Blackpool, Everton, QPR, Porto) 21
Walsh, M. 1982 (Everton) 4
Walsh, W. 1947 (Manchester C) 9
Walters, J. R. 2011 (Stoke C) 53
Ward, S. R. 2011 (Wolverhampton W, Burnley) 49
Waters, J. 1977 (Grimsby T) 2
Watters, F. 1926 (Shelbourne) 1
Weir, E. 1939 (Clyde) 3
Westwood, K. 2009 (Coventry C, Sunderland,
 Sheffield W) 21
Whelan, G. D. 2008 (Stoke C, Aston Villa) 84
Whelan, R. 1964 (St Patrick's Ath) 2
Whelan, R. 1981 (Liverpool, Southend U) 53
Whelan, R. 1956 (Manchester U) 4
White, J. J. 1928 (Bohemians) 1
Whittaker, R. 1959 (Chelsea) 1
Williams, D. S. 2018 (Blackburn R) 1
Williams, J. 1938 (Shamrock R) 1
Williams, S. 2018 (Millwall) 1
Wilson, M. D. 2011 (Stoke C, Bournemouth) 25

BRITISH AND IRISH INTERNATIONAL GOALSCORERS 1872–2018

Where two players with the same surname and initials have appeared for the same country, and one or both have scored, they have been distinguished by reference to the club which appears *first* against their name in the international appearances section.

Bold type indicates players who have scored international goals in season 2017–18.

ENGLAND

A'Court, A.	1	Brown, A. S.	1	Elliott, W. H.	3	Jagielka, P. N.	3
Adams, T. A.	5	Brown, G.	5	Evans, R. E.	1	Jeffers, F.	1
Adcock, H.	1	Brown, J.	3			Jenas, J. A.	1
Alcock, C. W.	1	Brown, W.	1	Ferdinand, L.	5	Johnson, A.	2
Allen, A.	3	Brown, W. M.	1	Ferdinand, R. G.	3	Johnson, D. E.	6
Allen, R.	2	Buchan, C. M.	4	Finney, T.	30	Johnson, E.	1
Alli, B. J. (Dele)	**3**	Bull, S. G.	4	Fleming, H. J.	9	Johnson, G. M. C.	1
Amos, A.	1	Bullock, N.	2	Flowers, R.	10	Johnson, J. A.	2
Anderson, V.	2	Burgess, H.	4	Forman, Frank	1	Johnson, T. C. F.	5
Anderton, D. R.	7	Butcher, T.	3	Forman, Fred	3	Johnson, W. H.	1
Astall, G.	1	Byrne, J. J.	8	Foster, R. E.	3		
Athersmith, W. C.	3			Fowler, R. B.	7	Kail, E. I. L.	2
Atyeo, P. J. W.	5	**Cahill, G. J.**	**5**	Francis, G. C. J.	3	**Kane, H. E.**	**19**
		Campbell, S. J.	1	Francis, T.	12	Kay, A. H.	1
Bache, J. W.	4	Camsell, G. H.	18	Freeman, B. C.	3	Keegan, J. K.	21
Bailey, N. C.	2	Carroll, A. T.	2	Froggatt, J.	2	Kelly, R.	8
Baily, E. F.	5	Carter, H. S.	7	Froggatt, R.	2	Kennedy, R.	3
Baines, L. J.	1	Carter, J. H.	4			Kenyon-Slaney, W. S.	2
Baker, J. H.	3	Caulker, S. A.	1	Galley, T.	1	Keown, M. R.	2
Ball, A. J.	8	Chadwick, E.	3	Gascoigne, P. J.	10	Kevan, D. T.	8
Bambridge, A. L.	1	Chamberlain, M.	1	Geary, F.	3	Kidd, B.	1
Bambridge, E. C.	11	Chambers, H.	5	Gerrard, S. G.	21	King, L. B.	2
Barclay, R.	2	Channon, M. R.	21	Gibbins, W. V. T.	3	Kingsford, R. K.	1
Barkley, R.	2	Charlton, J.	6	Gilliatt, W. E.	3	Kirchen, A. J.	2
Barmby, N. J.	4	Charlton, R.	49	Goddard, P.	1	Kirton, W. J.	1
Barnes, J.	11	Chenery, C. J.	1	Goodall, J.	12		
Barnes, P. S.	4	Chivers, M.	13	Goodyer, A. C.	1	Lallana, A. D.	3
Barry, G.	3	Clarke, A. J.	10	Gosling, R. C.	2	Lambert, R. L.	3
Barton, J.	1	Cobbold, W. N.	6	Goulden, L. A.	4	Lampard, F. J.	29
Bassett, W. I.	8	Cock, J. G.	2	Grainger, C.	3	Langton, R.	1
Bastin, C. S.	12	Cole, A.	1	Greaves, J.	44	Latchford, R. D.	5
Beardsley, P. A.	9	Cole, J. J.	10	Grovesnor, A. T.	2	Latheron, E. G.	1
Beasley, A.	1	Common, A.	2	Gunn, W.	1	Lawler, C.	1
Beattie, T. K.	1	Connelly, J. M.	7			Lawton, T.	22
Beckham, D. R. J.	17	Coppell, S. J.	7	Haines, J. T. W.	2	Lee, F.	10
Becton, F.	2	Cotterill, G. H.	2	Hall, G. W.	9	Lee, J.	1
Bedford, H.	1	Cowans, G.	2	Halse, H. J.	2	Lee, R. M.	2
Bell, C.	9	Crawford, R.	1	Hampson, J.	5	Lee, S.	2
Bent, D. A.	4	Crawshaw, T. H.	1	Hampton, H.	2	Lescott, J.	1
Bentley, R. T. F.	9	Crayston, W. J.	1	Hancocks, J.	2	Le Saux, G. P.	1
Bertrand, R.	**1**	Creek, F. N. S.	1	Hardman, H. P.	1	Lindley, T.	14
Bishop, S. M.	1	Crooks, S. D.	7	Harris, S. S.	2	Lineker, G.	48
Blackburn, F.	1	Crouch, P. J.	22	Hassall, H. W.	4	**Lingard, J. E.**	**2**
Blissett, L.	3	Currey, E. S.	2	Hateley, M.	9	Lofthouse, J. M.	3
Bloomer, S.	28	Currie, A. W.	3	Haynes, J. N.	18	Lofthouse, N.	30
Bond, R.	2	Cursham, A. W.	2	Hegan, K. E.	4	Hon. A. Lyttelton	1
Bonsor, A. G.	1	Cursham, H. A.	5	Henfrey, A. G.	2		
Bowden, E. R.	1			Heskey, E. W.	7	Mabbutt, G.	1
Bowers, J. W.	2	Daft, H. B.	3	Hilsdon, G. R.	14	Macdonald, M.	6
Bowles, S.	1	Davenport, J. K.	2	**Hine, E. W.**	**4**	**Maguire, J. H.**	**1**
Bradford, G. R. W.	1	Davis, G.	1	Hinton, A. T.	1	Mannion, W. J.	11
Bradford, J.	7	Davis, H.	1	Hirst, D. E.	1	Mariner, P.	13
Bradley, W.	2	Day, S. H.	2	Hitchens, G. A.	5	Marsh, R. W.	1
Bradshaw, F.	3	Dean, W. R.	18	Hobbis, H. H. F.	1	Matthews, S.	11
Brann, G.	1	Defoe, J. C.	20	Hoddle, G.	8	Matthews, V.	1
Bridge, W. M.	1	Devey, J. H. G.	1	Hodgetts, D.	1	McCall, J.	1
Bridges, B. J.	**1**	Dewhurst, F.	11	Hodgson, G.	1	McDermott, T.	3
Bridgett, A.	3	**Dier, E. J. E.**	**3**	Holley, G. H.	8	McManaman, S.	3
Brindle, T.	1	Dix, W. R.	1	Houghton, W. E.	5	Medley, L. D.	1
Britton, C. S.	1	Dixon, K. M.	4	Howell, R.	1	Melia, J.	1
Broadbent, P. F.	2	Dixon, L. M.	1	Hughes, E. W.	1	Mercer, D. W.	1
Broadis, I. A.	8	Dorrell, A. R.	1	Hulme, J. H. A.	4	Merson, P. C.	3
Brodie, J. B.	1	Douglas, B.	11	Hunt, G. S.	1	Milburn, J. E. T.	10
Bromley-Davenport, W.	2	Drake, E. J.	6	Hunt, R.	18	Miller, H. S.	1
Brook, E. F.	10	Ducat, A.	1	Hunter, N.	2	Mills, G. R.	3
Brooking, T. D.	5	Dunn, A. T. B.	2	Hurst, G. C.	24	Milner, J. P.	1
Brooks, J.	2					Milward, A.	3
Broome, F. H.	3	Eastham, G.	2	Ince, P. E. C.	2	Mitchell, C.	1
Brown, A.	4	Edwards, D.	5			Moore, J.	1
		Ehiogu, U.	1	Jack, D. N. B.	3	Moore, R. F.	2

Milne, R. G.	2
Molyneux, T. B.	1
Moreland, V.	1
Morgan, S.	3
Morrow, S. J.	1
Morrow, W. J.	1
Mulryne, P. P.	3
Murdock, C. J.	1
Murphy, N.	1
Neill, W. J. T.	2
Nelson, S.	1
Nicholl, C. J.	3
Nicholl, J. M.	1
Nicholson, J. J.	6
O'Boyle, G.	1
O'Hagan, C.	1
O'Kane, W. J.	1
O'Neill, J.	2
O'Neill, M. A.	4
O'Neill, M. H.	8
Own goals	10
Paterson, M. A.	3
Paterson, D. J.	1
Paterson, R.	1
Peacock, R.	2
Peden, J.	7
Penney, S.	2
Pyper, James	2
Pyper, John	1
Quinn, J. M.	12
Quinn, S. J.	4
Reynolds, J.	1
Rowland, K.	1
Rowley, R. W. M.	2
Rushe, F.	1
Sheridan, J.	2
Sherrard, J.	1
Sherrard, W. C.	2
Shields, D.	1
Simpson, W. J.	5
Sloan, H. A. de B.	4
Smyth, P.	**1**
Smyth, S.	5
Spence, D. W.	3
Sproule, I.	1
Stanfield, O. M.	11
Stevenson, A. E.	5
Stewart, I.	2
Taggart, G. P.	7
Thompson, F. W.	2
Torrans, S.	1
Tully, C. P.	3
Turner, A.	1
Walker, J.	1
Walsh, D. J.	5
Ward, J. J.	4
Washington, C. J.	3
Welsh, E.	1
Whiteside, N.	9
Whiteside, T.	1
Whitley, Jeff	2
Williams, J. R.	1
Williams, M. S.	1
Williamson, J.	1
Wilson, D. J.	1
Wilson, K. J.	6
Wilson, S. J.	7
Wilton, J. M.	2
Young, S.	1

N.B. In 1914 Young goal should be credited to Gillespie W v Wales

SCOTLAND

Aitken, R. (Celtic)	1
Aitken, R. (Dumbarton)	1
Aitkenhead, W. A. C.	2
Alexander, D.	1
Allan, D. S.	4
Allan, J.	2
Anderson, F.	1
Anderson, W.	4
Andrews, P.	1
Anya, I.	3
Archibald, A.	1
Archibald, S.	4
Armstrong, S.	**1**
Baird, D.	2
Baird, J. C.	2
Baird, S.	2
Bannon, E.	1
Barbour, A.	1
Barker, J. B.	4
Battles, B. Jr	1
Bauld, W.	2
Baxter, J. C.	3
Beattie, C.	1
Bell, J.	5
Bennett, A.	2
Berra, C. D.	**4**
Berry, D.	1
Bett, J.	1
Beveridge, W. W.	1
Black, A.	3
Black, D.	1
Bone, J.	1
Booth, S.	6
Boyd, K	7
Boyd, R.	2
Boyd, T.	1
Boyd, W. G.	1
Brackenridge, T.	1
Brand, R.	8
Brazil, A.	1
Bremner, W. J.	3
Broadfoot, K.	1
Brown, A. D.	6
Brown, S.	4
Buchanan, P. S.	1
Buchanan, R.	1
Buckley, P.	1
Buick, A.	2
Burke, C.	2
Burley, C. W.	3
Burns, K.	1
Cairns, T.	1
Caldwell, G.	2
Calderwood, C.	1
Calderwood, R.	2
Caldow, E.	4
Cameron, C.	2
Campbell, C.	1
Campbell, John (Celtic)	5
Campbell, John (Rangers)	4
Campbell, J. (South Western)	1
Campbell, P.	2
Campbell, R.	1
Cassidy, J.	1
Chalmers, S.	3
Chambers, T.	1
Cheyne, A. G.	4
Christie, A. J.	1
Clarkson, D.	1
Clunas, W. L.	1
Collins, J.	12
Collins, R. Y.	10
Combe, J. R.	1
Commons, K.	2
Conn, A.	1
Cooper, D.	6
Craig, J.	1
Craig, T.	1
Crawford, S.	4
Cunningham, A. N.	5
Curran, H. P.	1
Dailly, C.	6
Dalglish, K.	30
Davidson, D.	1
Davidson, J. A.	1
Delaney, J.	3
Devine, A.	1
Dewar, G.	1
Dewar, N.	4
Dickov, P.	1
Dickson, W.	4
Divers, J.	1
Dobie, R. S.	1
Docherty, T. H.	1
Dodds, D.	1
Dodds, W.	7
Donaldson, A.	1
Donnachie, J.	1
Dougall, J.	1
Drummond, J.	2
Dunbar, M.	1
Duncan, D.	7
Duncan, D. M.	1
Duncan, J.	1
Dunn, J.	2
Durie, G. S.	7
Easson, J. F.	1
Elliott, M. S.	1
Ellis, J.	1
Ferguson, B.	3
Ferguson, J.	6
Fernie, W.	1
Fitchie, T. T.	1
Flavell, R.	2
Fleming, C.	2
Fleming, J. W.	3
Fletcher, D.	5
Fletcher, S. K.	9
Fraser, M. J. E.	3
Freedman, D. A.	1
Gallacher, H. K.	23
Gallacher, K. W.	9
Gallacher, P.	1
Galt, J. H.	1
Gemmell, T. (St Mirren)	1
Gemmell, T. (Celtic)	1
Gemmill, A.	8
Gemmill, S.	1
Gibb, W.	1
Gibson, D. W.	3
Gibson, J. D.	1
Gibson, N.	1
Gillespie, Jas.	3
Gillick, T.	3
Gilzean, A. J.	12
Goodwillie, D.	1
Gossland, J.	1
Goudie, J.	1
Gough, C. R.	6
Gourlay, J.	1
Graham, A.	2
Graham, G.	3
Gray, A.	7
Gray, E.	3
Gray, F.	1
Greig, J.	3
Griffiths, L.	**4**
Groves, W.	4
Hamilton, G.	4
Hamilton, J. (Queen's Park)	3
Hamilton, R. C.	15
Hanley, G. C.	1
Harper, J. M.	2
Hartley, P. J.	1
Harrower, W.	5
Hartford, R. A.	4
Heggie, C. W	4
Henderson, J. G.	1
Henderson, W.	5
Hendry, E. C. J.	3
Herd, D. G.	3
Herd, G.	1
Hewie, J. D.	2
Higgins, A. (Newcastle U)	
Higgins, A. (Kilmarnock)	4
Highet, T. C.	1
Holt, G.J.	1
Holton, J. A.	2
Hopkin, D.	2
Houliston, W.	2
Howie, H.	1
Howie, J.	2
Hughes, J.	1
Hunter, W.	1
Hutchison, D.	6
Hutchison, T.	1
Hutton, J.	1
Hyslop, T.	1
Imrie, W. N.	1
Jackson, A.	8
Jackson, C.	1
Jackson, D.	4
James, A. W.	4
Jardine, A.	1
Jenkinson, T.	1
Jess, E.	2
Johnston, A.	2
Johnston, L. H.	1
Johnston, M.	14
Johnstone, D.	2
Johnstone, J.	4
Johnstone, Jas.	1
Johnstone, R.	10
Johnstone, W.	1
Jordan, J.	11
Kay, J. L.	5
Keillor, A.	3
Kelly, J.	1
Kelso, R.	1
Ker, G.	10
King, A.	1
King, J.	1
Kinnear, D.	1
Kyle, K.	1
Lambert, P.	1
Lambie, J.	1
Lambie, W. A.	5
Lang, J. J.	2
Latta, A.	2
Law, D.	30
Leggat, G.	8
Lennie, W.	1
Lennox, R.	3
Liddell, W.	6
Lindsay, J.	6
Linwood, A. B.	1
Logan, J.	1
Lorimer, P.	4
Love, A.	1
Low, J. (Cambuslang)	1
Lowe, J. (St Bernards)	1
Macari, L.	5
MacDougall, E. J.	3
MacFarlane, A.	1
MacLeod, M.	1
Mackay, D. C.	4

Name	Goals
Mackay, G.	1
MacKenzie, J. A.	1
Mackail-Smith, C.	1
Mackie, J. C.	2
MacKinnon, W. W.	5
Madden, J.	5
Maloney, S. R.	7
Marshall, H.	1
Marshall, J.	1
Martin, C. H.	3
Mason, J.	4
Massie, A.	1
Masson, D. S.	5
McAdam, J.	1
McAllister, G.	5
McArthur, J.	**4**
McAulay, J. D.	1
McAvennie, F.	1
McCall, J.	1
McCall, S. M.	1
McCalliog, J.	1
McCallum, N.	1
McCann, N.	3
McClair, B. J.	2
McCoist, A.	19
McColl, R. S.	13
McCormack, R.	2
McCulloch, D.	3
McCulloch, L.	1
McDougall, J.	4
McFadden, J.*	15
McFadyen, W.	2
McGhee, M.	2
McGinlay, J.	4
McGregor, J.	1
McGrory, J.	6
McGuire, W.	1
McInally, A.	3
McInnes, T.	2
McKie, J.	2
McKimmie, S.	1
McKinlay, W.	4
McKinnon, A.	1
McKinnon, R.	1
McLaren, A.	4
McLaren, J.	1
McLean, A.	1
McLean, T.	1
McLintock, F.	1
McMahon, A.	6
McManus, S.	2
McMenemy, J.	5
McMillan, I. L.	2
McNeill, W.	3
McNiel, H.	5
McPhail, J.	3
McPhail, R.	7
McPherson, J. (Kilmarnock)	7
McPherson, J. (Vale of Leven)	1
McPherson, R.	1
McQueen, G.	5
McStay, P.	9
McSwegan, G.	1
Meiklejohn, D. D.	3
Millar, J.	2
Miller, K.	18
Miller, T.	2
Miller, W.	1
Mitchell, R. C.	1
Morgan, W.	1
Morris, D.	1
Morris, H.	3
Morrison, J. C.	3
Morton, A. L.	5
Mudie, J. K.	9
Mulgrew, C. P.	2
Mulhall, G.	1
Munro, A. D.	1
Munro, N.	2
Murdoch, R.	5
Murphy, F.	1
Murray, J.	1
Napier, C. E.	3
Narey, D.	1
Naismith, S. J.	7
Naysmith, G. A.	1
Neil, R. G.	2
Nevin, P. K. F.	5
Nicholas, C.	5
Nisbet, J.	2
O'Connor, G.	4
O'Donnell, F.	2
O'Hare, J.	5
Ormond, W. E.	2
O'Rourke, F.	1
Orr, R.	1
Orr, T.	1
Oswald, J.	1
Own goals	21
Parlane, D.	1
Paul, H. McD.	2
Paul, W.	2
Pettigrew, W.	2
Phillips, M.	**1**
Provan, D.	1
Quashie, N. F.	1
Quinn, J.	7
Quinn, P.	1
Rankin, G.	2
Rankin, R.	2
Reid, W.	4
Reilly, L.	22
Renny-Tailyour, H. W.	1
Rhodes, J. L.	3
Richmond, J. T.	1
Ring, T.	2
Rioch, B. D.	6
Ritchie, J.	1
Ritchie, M. T.	3
Ritchie, P. S.	1
Robertson, A. (Clyde)	2
Robertson, A.	**2**
Robertson, J.	3
Robertson, J. N.	8
Robertson, J. T.	2
Robertson, T.	1
Robertson, W.	1
Russell, D.	1
Scott, A. S.	5
Sellar, W.	4
Sharp, G.	1
Shaw, F. W.	1
Shearer, D.	2
Simpson, J.	1
Smith, A.	5
Smith, G.	4
Smith, J.	1
Smith, John	13
Snodgrass, R.	**7**
Somerville, G.	1
Souness, G. J.	4
Speedie, F.	2
St John, I.	9
Steel, W.	12
Stein, C.	10
Stevenson, G.	4
Stewart, A.	1
Stewart, R.	1
Stewart, W. E.	1
Strachan, G.	5
Sturrock, P.	3
Taylor, J. D.	1
Templeton, R.	1
Thompson, S.	3
Thomson, A.	1
Thomson, C.	4
Thomson, R.	1
Thomson, W.	1
Thornton, W.	1
Waddell, T. S.	1
Waddell, W.	6
Walker, J.	2
Walker, R.	7
Walker, T.	9
Wallace, I. A.	1
Wark, J.	7
Watson, J. A. K.	1
Watt, F.	2
Watt, W. W.	1
Webster, A.	1
Weir, A.	1
Weir, D.	1
Weir, J. B.	2
White, J. A.	3
Wilkie, L.	1
Wilson, A. (Sheffield W)	2
Wilson, A. N. (Dunfermline Ath)	13
Wilson, D. (Liverpool)	1
Wilson, D. (Queen's Park)	2
Wilson, D. (Rangers)	9
Wilson, H.	1
Wylie, T. G.	1
Young, A.	5

WALES

Name	Goals
Allchurch, I. J.	23
Allen, J. M.	2
Allen, M.	3
Astley, D. J.	12
Atherton, R. W.	2
Bale, G. F.	**29**
Bamford, T.	1
Barnes, W.	1
Bellamy, C. D.	19
Blackmore, C. G.	1
Blake, D.	1
Blake, N. A.	4
Bodin, P. J.	3
Boulter, L. M.	1
Bowdler, J. C. H.	3
Bowen, D. L.	1
Bowen, M.	3
Boyle, T.	1
Bryan, T.	1
Burgess, W. A. R.	1
Burke, T.	1
Butler, W. T.	1
Chapman, T.	2
Charles, J.	1
Charles, M.	6
Charles, W. J.	15
Church, S. R.	3
Clarke, R. J.	5
Coleman, C.	4
Collier, D. J.	1
Collins, J.	3
Cotterill, D. R. G. B.	2
Crosse, K.	1
Cumner, R. H.	1
Curtis, A.	6
Curtis, E. R.	3
Davies, D. W.	1
Davies, E. Lloyd	1
Davies, G.	2
Davies, L. S.	6
Davies, R. T.	9
Davies, R. W.	6
Davies, Simon	6
Davies, Stanley	5
Davies, W.	6
Davies, W. H.	1
Davies, William	5
Davis, W. O.	1
Deacy, N.	4
Doughty, J.	6
Doughty, R.	2
Durban, A.	2
Dwyer, P.	2
Earnshaw, R.	16
Eastwood, F.	4
Edwards, D. A.	3
Edwards, G.	2
Edwards, R. I.	4
England, H. M.	4
Evans, C.	4
Evans, I.	1
Evans, J.	1
Evans, R. E.	2
Evans, W.	1
Eyton-Jones, J. A.	1
Fletcher, C.	1
Flynn, B.	7
Ford, T.	23
Foulkes, W. I.	1
Fowler, J.	3
Giles, D.	2
Giggs, R. J.	12
Glover, E. M.	7
Godfrey, B. C.	2
Green, A. W.	3
Griffiths, A. T.	6
Griffiths, M. W.	2
Griffiths, T. P.	3
Harris, C. S.	1
Hartson, J.	14
Hersee, R.	1
Hewitt, R.	1
Hockey, T.	1
Hodges, G.	2
Hole, W. J.	1
Hopkins, I. J.	2
Horne, B.	2
Howell, E. G.	3
Hughes, L. M.	16
Huws, E. W.	1
James, E.	2
James, L.	10
James, R.	7
Jarrett, R. H.	3
Jenkyns, C. A.	1
Jones, A.	1
Jones, Bryn	6
Jones, B. S.	2
Jones, Cliff	16
Jones, C. W.	1
Jones, D. E.	1
Jones, Evan	1
Jones, H.	1
Jones, I.	1
Jones, J. L.	1
Jones, J. O.	1
Jones, J. P.	1
Jones, Leslie J.	1
Jones, R. A.	2
Jones, W. L.	6

The Scottish FA officially changed Robsons's goal against Iceland on 10 September 2008 to McFadden.

SOUTH AMERICA

COPA SUDAMERICANA 2017

FIRST ROUND – FIRST LEG

Nacional Potosi v Sport Huancayo	3-1
Deportivo Cali v Sportivo Luqueno	1-0
Petrolero v Universidad Catolica	1-3
LDU Quito v Defensor Sporting	2-2
Everton v Patriotas	1-0
Estudiantes de Caracas v Sol de America	2-3
Cerro Porteno v Caracas	1-1
Deportivo Anzoategui v Huracan	3-0
Oriente Petrolero v Deportivo Cuenca	1-1
Corinthians v Universidad de Chile	2-0
Independiente v Alianza Lima	0-0
Ponte Preta v Gimnasia y Esgrima	0-0
Boston River v Comerciantes Unidos	3-1
Juan Aurich v Arsenal	0-2
O'Higgins v Fuerza Amarilla	1-0
Deportes Tolima v Bolivar	2-1
Palestino v Atletico Venezuela	0-1
Sport Recife v Danubio	3-0
Racing v Rionegro Aguilas	1-0
Cruzeiro v Nacional	2-1
Defensa y Justicia v Sao Paulo	0-0
Fluminense v Liverpool	2-0

FIRST ROUND – SECOND LEG

		(agg)
Sport Huancayo v Nacional Potosi	2-1	3-4
Sportivo Luqueno v Deportivo Cali	2-1	2-2
Deportivo Cali won on away goals.		
Universidad Catolica v Petrolero	3-0	6-1
Defensor Sporting v LDU Quito	1-2	3-4
Patriotas v Everton	1-0	1-1
Patriotas won 4-3 on penalties.		
Sol de America v Estudiantes de Caracas	7-1	10-3
Caracas v Cerro Porteno	1-2	2-3
Huracan v Deportivo Anzoategui	4-0	4-3
Deportivo Cuenca v Oriente Petrolero	1-1	2-2
Oriente Petrolero won 8-7 on penalties.		
Universidad de Chile v Corinthians	1-2	1-4
Alianza Lima v Independiente	0-1	0-1
Gimnasia y Esgrima v Ponte Preta	1-1	1-1
Ponte Preta won on away goals.		
Comerciantes Unidos v Boston River	1-1	2-4
Arsenal v Juan Aurich	6-1	8-1
Fuerza Amarilla v O'Higgins	2-0	2-1
Bolivar v Deportes Tolima	1-0	2-2
Bolivar won on away goals.		
Atletico Venezuela v Palestino	0-1	1-1
Palestino won 7-6 on penalties.		
Danubio v Sport Recife	3-0	3-3
Sport Recife won 4-2 on penalties.		
Rionegro Aguilas v Racing	1-1	1-2
Nacional v Cruzeiro	2-1	3-3
Nacional won 3-2 on penalties.		
Sao Paulo v Defensa y Justicia	1-1	1-1
Defensa y Justicia won on away goals.		
Liverpool v Fluminense	1-0	1-2

SECOND ROUND – FIRST LEG

Racing v Independiente Medellín	3-1
Deportivo Cali v Junior	1-1
Palestino v Flamengo	2-5
Nacional Potosi v Estudiantes	0-1
Independiente v Deportes Iquique	4-2
Bolivar v LDU Quito	1-0
Ponte Preta v Sol de America	1-0
Fuerza Amarilla v Santa Fe	1-1
Huracan v Libertad	1-5
Sport Recife v Arsenal	2-0
Fluminense v Universidad Catolica	4-0
Oriente Petrolero v Atletico Tucuman	2-3
Nacional v Olimpia	1-1
Defensa y Justicia v Chapecoense	1-0
Cerro Porteno v Boston River	2-1
Patriotas v Corinthians	1-1

SECOND ROUND – SECOND LEG *(agg)*

Independiente Medellín v Racing	2-3	3-6
Junior v Deportivo Cali	1-1	2-2
Junior won 3-2 on penalties.		
Flamengo v Palestino	5-0	10-2
Estudiantes v Nacional Potosi	2-0	3-0
Deportes Iquique v Independiente	1-2	3-6
LDU Quito v Bolivar	1-0	1-1
LDU Quito won 6-5 on penalties.		
Sol de America v Ponte Preta	1-3	1-4
Santa Fe v Fuerza Amarilla	1-0	2-1
Libertad v Huracan	2-0	7-1
Arsenal v Sport Recife	2-1	2-3
Universidad Catolica v Fluminense	1-2	1-6
Atletico Tucuman v Oriente Petrolero	3-0	6-2
Olimpia v Nacional	2-2	3-3
Nacional won on away goals.		
Chapecoense v Defensa y Justicia	1-0	1-1
Chapecoense won 4-2 on penalties.		
Boston River v Cerro Porteno	1-4	2-6
Corinthians v Patriotas	2-0	3-1

ROUND OF 16 – FIRST LEG

Corinthians v Racing	1-1
Cerro Porteno v Junior	0-0
Chapecoense v Flamengo	0-0
Nacional v Estudiantes	1-0
Atletico Tucuman v Independiente	1-0
Fluminense v LDU Quito	1-0
Sport Recife v Ponte Preta	3-1
Libertad v Santa Fe	1-0

ROUND OF 16 – SECOND LEG *(agg)*

Racing v Corinthians	0-0	1-1
Racing won on away goals.		
Junior v Cerro Porteno	3-1	3-1
Flamengo v Chapecoense	4-0	4-0
Estudiantes v Nacional	0-1	0-2
Independiente v Atletico Tucuman	2-0	2-1
LDU Quito v Fluminense	2-1	2-2
Fluminense won on away goals.		
Ponte Preta v Sport Recife	1-0	2-3
Santa Fe v Libertad	1-1	1-2

QUARTER-FINALS – FIRST LEG

Libertad v Racing	1-0
Sport Recife v Junior	0-2
Fluminense v Flamengo	0-1
Nacional v Independiente	1-4

QUARTER-FINALS – SECOND LEG *(agg)*

Racing v Libertad	0-0	0-1
Junior v Sport Recife	0-0	2-0
Flamengo v Fluminense	3-3	4-3
Independiente v Nacional	2-0	6-1

SEMI-FINALS – FIRST LEG

Libertad v Independiente	1-0
Flamengo v Junior	2-1

SEMI-FINALS – SECOND LEG *(agg)*

Independiente v Libertad	3-1	3-2
Junior v Flamengo	0-2	1-4

FINAL – FIRST LEG

Independiente v Flamengo	2-1

FINAL – SECOND LEG *(agg)*

Flamengo v Independiente	1-1	2-3

RECOPA SUDAMERICANA 2017

FINAL – FIRST LEG

Chapecoense v Atletico Nacional	2-1

FINAL – SECOND LEG *(agg)*

Atletico Nacional v Chapecoense	4-1	5-3

COPA BRIDGESTONE LIBERTADORES 2017

ROUND OF 16 – FIRST LEG

Nacional v Botafogo	0-1
Godoy Cruz v Gremio	0-1
Barcelona v Palmeiras	1-0
Atletico Paranaense v Santos	2-3
Emelec v San Lorenzo	0-1
The Strongest v Lanus	1-1
Jorge Wilstermann v Atletico Mineiro	1-0
Guarani v River Plate	0-2

ROUND OF 16 – SECOND LEG *(agg)*

Botafogo v Nacional	2-0	3-0
Gremio v Godoy Cruz	2-1	3-1
Palmeiras v Barcelona	1-0	1-1*
Barcelona won 5-4 on penalties.		
Santos v Atletico Paranaense	1-0	4-2
San Lorenzo v Emelec	0-1	1-1*
San Lorenzo won 5-4 on penalties.		
Lanus v The Strongest	1-0	2-1
Atletico Mineiro v Jorge Wilstermann	0-0	0-1
River Plate v Guarani	1-1	3-1

QUARTER-FINALS – FIRST LEG

Jorge Wilstermann v River Plate	3-0
Barcelona v Santos	1-1
Botafogo v Gremio	0-0
San Lorenzo v Lanus	2-0

QUARTER-FINALS – SECOND LEG *(agg)*

River Plate v Jorge Wilstermann	8-0	8-3
Santos v Barcelona	0-1	1-2
Gremio v Botafogo	1-0	1-0
Lanus v San Lorenzo	2-0	2-2*
Lanus won 4-3 on penalties.		

SEMI-FINALS – FIRST LEG

River Plate v Lanus	1-0
Barcelona v Gremio	0-3

SEMI-FINALS – SECOND LEG *(agg)*

Lanus v River Plate	2-4	4-3
Gremio v Barcelona	0-1	3-1

FINAL – FIRST LEG

Gremio v Lanus	1-0

FINAL – SECOND LEG *(agg)*

Lanus v Gremio	1-2	1-3

COPA BRIDGESTONE LIBERTADORES 2018

FIRST STAGE – FIRST LEG

Montevideo Wanderers v Olimpia	0-0
Macara v Deportivo Tachira	1-1
Oriente Petrolero v Universitario	2-0

FIRST STAGE – SECOND LEG *(agg)*

Olimpia v Montevideo Wanderers	2-0	2-0
Deportivo Tachira v Macara	0-0	1-1
Deportivo Tachira won on away goals.		
Universitario v Oriente Petrolero	3-1	3-3
Oriente Petrolero won on away goals.		

SECOND STAGE – FIRST LEG

Carabobo v Guarani	1-0
Banfield v Independiente del Valle	1-1
Santiago Wanderers v Melgar	1-1
Chapecoense v Nacional	0-1
Universidad de Concepcion v Vasco da Gama	0-4
Deportivo Tachira v Santa Fe	2-3
Oriente Petrolero v Jorge Wilstermann	1-2
Olimpia v Junior	1-0

SECOND STAGE – SECOND LEG *(agg)*

Guarani v Carabobo	6-0	6-1
Independiente del Valle v Banfield	2-2	3-3
Banfield won on away goals.		
Melgar v Santiago Wanderers	0-1	1-2
Nacional v Chapecoense	1-0	2-0
Vasco da Gama v Universidad de Concepcion	2-0	6-0
Santa Fe v Deportivo Tachira	0-0	3-2
Jorge Wilstermann v Oriente Petrolero	2-2	4-3
Junior v Olimpia	3-1	3-2

THIRD STAGE – FIRST LEG

Santiago Wanderers v Santa Fe	1-2
Banfield v Nacional	2-2
Vasco da Gama v Jorge Wilstermann	4-0
Junior v Guarani	1-0

THIRD STAGE – SECOND LEG *(agg)*

Santa Fe v Santiago Wanderers	3-0	5-1
Nacional v Banfield	1-0	3-2
Jorge Wilstermann v Vasco da Gama	4-0	4-4
Vasco da Gama won 3-2 on penalties.		
Guarani v Junior	0-0	0-1

GROUP A

Defensor Sporting v Gremio 1-1, Monagas v Cerro Porteno 0-2, Cerro Porteno v Defensor Sporting 2-1, Gremio v Monagas 4-0, Defensor Sporting v Monagas 3-1, Cerro Porteno v Gremio 0-0, Monagas v Defensor Sporting 1-0, Gremio v Cerro Porteno 5-0, Defensor Sporting v Cerro Porteno 0-1, Monagas v Gremio 1-2, Cerro Porteno v Monagas 3-2, Gremio v Defensor Sporting 1-0

Group A Table	P	W	D	L	F	A	GD	Pts
Gremio	6	4	2	0	13	2	11	14
Cerro Porteno	6	4	1	1	8	8	0	13
Defensor Sporting	6	1	1	4	5	7	–2	4
Monagas	6	1	0	5	5	14	–9	3

GROUP B

Colo-Colo v Atletico Nacional 0-1, Delfin v Bolivar 1-1, Bolivar v Colo-Colo 1-1, Atletico Nacional v Delfin 4-0, Colo-Colo v Delfin 0-2, Bolivar v Atletico Nacional 1-0, Atletico Nacional v Bolivar 4-1, Delfin v Colo-Colo 1-2, Delfin v Atletico Nacional 1-0, Colo-Colo v Bolivar 2-0, Atletico Nacional v Colo-Colo 0-0, Bolivar v Delfin 2-1

Group B Table	P	W	D	L	F	A	GD	Pts
Atletico Nacional	6	3	1	2	9	3	6	10
Colo-Colo	6	2	2	2	5	5	0	8
Bolivar	6	2	2	2	6	9	–3	8
Delfín	6	2	1	3	6	9	–3	7

GROUP C

Atletico Tucuman v Libertad 0-2, The Strongest v Penarol 1-0, Libertad v The Strongest 3-0, Penarol v Atletico Tucuman 3-1, The Strongest v Atletico Tucuman 1-2, Libertad v Penarol 2-1, Atletico Tucuman v The Strongest 3-0, Penarol v Libertad 2-0, Atletico Tucuman v Penarol 1-0, The Strongest v Libertad 1-3, Penarol v The Strongest 2-0, Libertad v Atletico Tucuman 0-0

Group C Table	P	W	D	L	F	A	GD	Pts
Libertad	6	4	1	1	10	4	6	13
Atletico Tucuman	6	3	1	2	7	6	1	10
Penarol	6	3	0	3	8	5	3	9
The Strongest	6	1	0	5	3	13	–10	3

GROUP D

Flamengo v River Plate 2-2, Santa Fe v Emelec 1-1, Emelec v Flamengo 1-2, River Plate v Santa Fe 0-0, Flamengo v Santa Fe 1-1, Emelec v River Plate 0-1, Santa Fe v Flamengo 0-0, River Plate v Emelec 2-1, Santa Fe v River Plate 0-1, Flamengo v Emelec 2-0, River Plate v Flamengo 0-0, Emelec v Santa Fe 0-3

Group D Table

	P	W	D	L	F	A	GD	Pts
River Plate	6	3	3	0	6	3	3	12
Flamengo	6	2	4	0	7	4	3	10
Santa Fe	6	1	4	1	5	3	2	7
Emelec	6	0	1	5	3	11	–8	1

GROUP E

Racing Club v Cruzeiro 4-2, Vasco da Gama v Universidad de Chile 0-1, Universidad de Chile v Racing Club 1-1, Cruzeiro v Vasco da Gama 0-0, Racing Club v Vasco da Gama 4-0, Universidad de Chile v Cruzeiro 0-0, Cruzeiro v Universidad de Chile 7-0, Vasco da Gama v Racing Club 1-1, Vasco da Gama v Cruzeiro 0-4, Racing Club v Universidad de Chile 1-0, Cruzeiro v Racing Club 2-1, Universidad de Chile v Vasco da Gama 0-2

Group E Table

	P	W	D	L	F	A	GD	Pts
Cruzeiro	6	3	2	1	15	5	10	11
Racing Club	6	3	2	1	12	6	6	11
Vasco da Gama	6	1	2	3	3	10	–7	5
Universidad de Chile	6	1	2	3	2	11	–9	5

GROUP F

Nacional v Estudiantes 0-0, Real Garcilaso v Santos 2-0, Estudiantes v Real Garcilaso 3-0, Santos v Nacional 3-1, Real Garcilaso v Nacional 0-0, Estudiantes v Santos 0-1, Santos v Estudiantes 2-0, Nacional v Real Garcilaso 4-0, Real Garcilaso v Estudiantes 0-0, Nacional v Santos 1-0, Santos v Real Garcilaso 0-0, Estudiantes v Nacional 3-1

Group F Table

	P	W	D	L	F	A	GD	Pts
Santos	6	3	1	2	6	4	2	10
Estudiantes	6	2	2	2	6	4	2	8
Nacional	6	2	2	2	7	6	1	8
Real Garcilaso	6	1	3	2	2	7	–5	6

GROUP G

Millonarios v Corinthians 0-0, Deportivo Lara v Independiente 1-0, Corinthians v Deportivo Lara 2-0, Independiente v Millonarios 1-0, Millonarios v Deportivo Lara 4-0, Independiente v Corinthians 0-1, Deportivo Lara v Millonarios 2-1, Corinthians v Independiente 1-2, Millonarios v Independiente 1-1, Deportivo Lara v Corinthians 2-7, Independiente v Deportivo Lara 2-0, Corinthians v Millonarios 0-1

Group G Table

	P	W	D	L	F	A	GD	Pts
Corinthians	6	3	1	2	11	5	6	10
Independiente	6	3	1	2	6	4	2	10
Millonarios	6	2	2	2	7	4	3	8
Deportivo Lara	6	2	0	4	5	16	–11	6

GROUP H

Junior v Palmeiras 0-3, Alianza Lima v Boca Juniors 0-0, Palmeiras v Alianza Lima 2-0, Boca Juniors v Junior 1-0, Palmeiras v Boca Juniors 1-1, Alianza Lima v Junior 0-2, Boca Juniors v Palmeiras 0-2, Junior v Alianza Lima 1-0, Junior v Boca Juniors 1-1, Alianza Lima v Palmeiras 1-3, Palmeiras v Junior 3-1, Boca Juniors v Alianza Lima 5-0

Group H Table

	P	W	D	L	F	A	GD	Pts
Palmeiras	6	5	1	0	14	3	11	16
Boca Juniors	6	2	3	1	8	4	4	9
Junior	6	2	1	3	5	8	–3	7
Alianza Lima	6	0	1	5	1	13	–12	1

Competition still being played.

NORTH AMERICA – MAJOR LEAGUE SOCCER 2017

EASTERN CONFERENCE

	P	W	D	L	F	A	GD	Pts
Toronto	34	20	9	5	74	37	37	69
New York City	34	16	9	9	56	43	13	57
Chicago Fire	34	16	7	11	62	48	14	55
Atlanta United	34	15	10	9	70	40	30	55
Columbus Crew	34	16	6	12	53	49	4	54
New York Red Bulls	34	14	8	12	53	47	6	50
NE Revolution	34	13	6	15	53	61	–8	45
Philadelphia Union	34	11	9	14	50	47	3	42
Montreal Impact	34	11	6	17	52	58	–6	39
Orlando City	34	10	9	15	39	58	–19	39
DC United	34	9	5	20	31	60	–29	32

WESTERN CONFERENCE

	P	W	D	L	F	A	GD	Pts
Portland Timbers	34	15	8	11	60	50	10	53
Seattle Sounders	34	14	11	9	52	39	13	53
Vancouver Whitecaps	34	15	7	12	50	49	1	52
Houston Dynamo	34	13	11	10	57	45	12	50
Sporting Kansas C	34	12	13	9	40	29	11	49
San Jose Earthquakes	34	13	7	14	39	60	–21	46
FC Dallas	34	11	13	10	48	48	0	46
Real Salt Lake	34	13	6	15	48	56	–8	45
Minnesota United	34	10	6	18	47	70	–23	36
Colorado Rapids	34	9	6	19	31	51	–20	33
LA Galaxy	34	8	8	18	45	67	–22	32

EASTERN KNOCKOUT ROUND

Chicago Fire v New York Red Bulls	0-4
Atlanta United v Columbus Crew	0-0

aet; Columbus Crew won 3-1 on penalties.

WESTERN KNOCKOUT ROUND

Vancouver Whitecaps v San Jose Earthquakes	5-0
Houston Dynamo v Sporting Kansas City	1-0

EASTERN SEMI-FINALS – FIRST LEG

New York Red Bulls v Toronto	1-2
Columbus Crew v New York City	4-1

EASTERN SEMI-FINALS – SECOND LEG *(agg)*

Toronto FC v New York Red Bulls	0-1	2-2

Toronto won on away goals.

New York C v Columbus Crew	2-0	3-4

WESTERN SEMI-FINALS – FIRST LEG

Houston Dynamo v Portland Timbers	0-0
Vancouver Whitecaps v Seattle Sounders	0-0

WESTERN SEMI-FINALS – SECOND LEG *(agg)*

Portland Timbers v Houston Dynamo	1-2	1-2
Seattle Sounders v Vancouver Whitecaps	2-0	2-0

EASTERN CHAMPIONSHIP – FIRST LEG

Columbus Crew v Toronto	0-0

EASTERN CHAMPIONSHIP – SECOND LEG *(agg)*

Toronto v Columbus Crew	1-0	1-0

WESTERN CHAMPIONSHIP – FIRST LEG

Houston Dynamo v Seattle Sounders	0-2

WESTERN CHAMPIONSHIP – SECOND LEG *(agg)*

Seattle Sounders v Houston Dynamo	3-0	5-0

MLS CUP FINAL

Saturday 9 December, 2017

Toronto (0) 2 *(Altidore 67, Vazquez 90)*

Seattle Sounders (0) 0   30,584

Toronto: Bono; Beitashour, Moor, Mavinga, Morrow, Bradley, Delgado (Cheyrou 90), Osorio (Cooper 85), Vazquez, Giovinco, Altidore (Haaglun 86).
Seattle Sounders: Frei; Leerdam, Torres, Marshall, Jones J (Tolo 90), Roldan, Svensson, Lodeiro, Dempsey, Rodriguez (Morris 71), Bruin.
Referee: Allen Chapman.

UEFA UNDER-21 CHAMPIONSHIP 2017–19

QUALIFYING ROUND

GROUP 1

Belarus v San Marino	1-0
San Marino v Moldova	0-2
Moldova v Croatia	0-3
Belarus v Greece	0-2
Greece v Moldova	5-1
Czech Republic v Belarus	1-1
Moldova v Greece	0-2
Croatia v Belarus	2-1
Croatia v Czech Republic	5-1
Belarus v Moldova	3-1
San Marino v Greece	0-5
Croatia v San Marino	5-0
Czech Republic v San Marino	3-1
Greece v Croatia	1-1
Moldova v Czech Republic	1-3
Greece v San Marino	4-0
Czech Republic v Croatia	2-1
San Marino v Belarus	0-2
Greece v Czech Republic	3-0
Croatia v Moldova	4-0

Group 1 Table	P	W	D	L	F	A	GD	Pts
Greece	7	6	1	0	22	2	20	19
Croatia	7	5	1	1	21	5	16	16
Belarus	6	3	1	2	8	6	2	10
Czech Republic	6	3	1	2	10	12	–2	10
Moldova	7	1	0	6	5	20	–15	3
San Marino	7	0	0	7	1	22	–21	0

GROUP 2

Estonia v Northern Ireland	1-2
Albania v Estonia	0-0
Northern Ireland v Albania	1-0
Estonia v Slovakia	1-2
Iceland v Albania	2-3
Estonia v Spain	0-1
Slovakia v Northern Ireland	1-0
Slovakia v Iceland	0-2
Albania v Iceland	0-0
Northern Ireland v Estonia	4-2
Slovakia v Spain	1-4
Spain v Iceland	1-0
Albania v Northern Ireland	1-1
Estonia v Iceland	2-3
Spain v Slovakia	5-1
Northern Ireland v Spain	3-5
Albania v Slovakia	2-3
Northern Ireland v Iceland	0-0
Slovakia v Albania	4-1
Spain v Estonia	3-1

Group 2 Table	P	W	D	L	F	A	GD	Pts
Spain	6	6	0	0	19	6	13	18
Slovakia	7	4	0	3	12	15	–3	12
Northern Ireland	7	3	2	2	11	10	1	11
Iceland	6	2	2	2	7	6	1	8
Albania	7	1	3	3	7	11	–4	6
Estonia	7	0	1	6	7	15	–8	1

GROUP 3

Lithuania v Faroe Islands	3-0
Faroe Islands v Denmark	0-3
Georgia v Poland	0-3
Denmark v Lithuania	6-0
Finland v Faroe Islands	1-1
Poland v Finland	3-3
Denmark v Georgia	5-2
Finland v Denmark	0-5
Lithuania v Poland	0-2
Faroe Islands v Georgia	3-1
Georgia v Finland	2-2
Faroe Islands v Poland	2-2
Georgia v Lithuania	1-0
Poland v Denmark	3-1
Georgia v Faroe Islands	1-0
Lithuania v Denmark	0-2
Georgia v Denmark	2-2
Poland v Lithuania	1-0

Group 3 Table	P	W	D	L	F	A	GD	Pts
Poland	6	4	2	0	14	6	8	14
Denmark	6	4	1	1	22	7	15	13
Georgia	7	2	2	3	9	15	–6	8
Finland	5	1	3	1	8	11	–3	6
Faroe Islands	6	1	2	3	6	11	–5	5
Lithuania	6	1	0	5	3	12	–9	3

GROUP 4

Latvia v Andorra	0-0
Latvia v Ukraine	1-1
Netherlands v England	1-1
Andorra v Ukraine	0-6
Scotland v Netherlands	2-0
England v Latvia	3-0
Netherlands v Latvia	3-0
England v Scotland	3-1
Ukraine v Netherlands	1-1
Latvia v Scotland	0-2
Andorra v England	0-1
Ukraine v England	0-2
Netherlands v Andorra	8-0
Scotland v Latvia	1-1
Scotland v Ukraine	0-2
Andorra v Scotland	1-1
Andorra v Netherlands	0-1
England v Ukraine	2-1

Group 4 Table	P	W	D	L	F	A	GD	Pts
England	6	5	1	0	12	3	9	16
Netherlands	6	3	2	1	14	4	10	11
Scotland	6	2	2	2	7	7	0	8
Ukraine	6	2	2	2	11	6	5	8
Latvia	6	0	3	3	2	10	–8	3
Andorra	6	0	2	4	1	17	–16	2

GROUP 5

Republic of Ireland v Kosovo	1-0
Norway v Kosovo	0-3
Israel v Azerbaijan	3-1
Kosovo v Norway	3-2
Azerbaijan v Republic of Ireland	1-3
Norway v Israel	0-0
Germany v Kosovo	1-0
Republic of Ireland v Norway	0-0
Germany v Azerbaijan	6-1
Republic of Ireland v Israel	4-0
Norway v Germany	3-1
Azerbaijan v Germany	0-7
Kosovo v Israel	0-4
Azerbaijan v Kosovo	0-0
Israel v Germany	2-5
Norway v Republic of Ireland	2-1
Germany v Israel	3-0
Kosovo v Azerbaijan	2-0
Kosovo v Germany	0-0
Israel v Norway	1-3
Republic of Ireland v Azerbaijan	1-0

Group 5 Table	P	W	D	L	F	A	GD	Pts
Germany	7	5	1	1	23	6	17	16
Republic of Ireland	6	4	1	1	10	3	7	13
Kosovo	8	3	2	3	8	8	0	11
Norway	7	3	2	2	10	9	1	11
Israel	7	2	1	4	10	16	–6	7
Azerbaijan	7	0	1	6	3	22	–19	1

GROUP 6

Belgium v Malta	2-1
Cyprus v Malta	2-1
Hungary v Malta	2-1
Sweden v Cyprus	4-1
Belgium v Turkey	0-0
Cyprus v Turkey	2-1
Belgium v Sweden	1-1
Cyprus v Belgium	0-2
Turkey v Hungary	0-0
Sweden v Malta	3-0
Belgium v Cyprus	3-2

Malta v Turkey	0-1
Hungary v Sweden	2-2
Cyprus v Hungary	0-2
Turkey v Belgium	1-2
Hungary v Cyprus	4-0
Turkey v Sweden	0-3
Belgium v Hungary	3-0
Cyprus v Sweden	0-1
Turkey v Malta	4-2

Group 6 Table	P	W	D	L	F	A	GD	Pts
Belgium	7	5	2	0	13	5	8	17
Sweden	6	4	2	0	14	4	10	14
Hungary	6	3	2	1	10	6	4	11
Turkey	7	2	2	3	7	9	–2	8
Cyprus	8	2	0	6	7	18	–11	6
Malta	6	0	0	6	5	14	–9	0

GROUP 7

Austria v Gibraltar	3-0
Gibraltar v Armenia	0-3
Russia v Armenia	0-0
Serbia v Gibraltar	4-0
Armenia v FYR Macedonia	0-3
Russia v Gibraltar	3-0
Armenia v Gibraltar	1-0
Russia v Austria	1-0
FYR Macedonia v Serbia	0-2
Armenia v Austria	0-5
Gibraltar v FYR Macedonia	1-0
Serbia v Russia	3-2
Armenia v Russia	1-2
Austria v Serbia	1-3
Armenia v Serbia	0-1
FYR Macedonia v Austria	0-4
FYR Macedonia v Russia	3-4
Gibraltar v Serbia	0-6
Austria v FYR Macedonia	2-0
Gibraltar v Russia	0-5

Group 7 Table	P	W	D	L	F	A	GD	Pts
Serbia	6	6	0	0	19	3	16	18
Russia	7	5	1	1	17	7	10	16
Austria	6	4	0	2	15	4	11	12
Armenia	7	2	1	4	5	11	–6	7
FYR Macedonia	6	1	0	5	6	13	–7	3
Gibraltar	8	1	0	7	1	25	–24	3

GROUP 8

Bosnia-Herzegovina v Liechtenstein	6-0
Liechtenstein v Romania	0-2
Switzerland v Bosnia-Herzegovina	1-0
Bosnia-Herzegovina v Romania	1-3
Switzerland v Wales	0-3
Romania v Switzerland	1-1
Portugal v Wales	2-0
Liechtenstein v Wales	1-3
Switzerland v Romania	0-2
Bosnia-Herzegovina v Portugal	3-1
Liechtenstein v Switzerland	0-2
Romania v Portugal	1-1
Wales v Bosnia-Herzegovina	0-4
Portugal v Switzerland	2-1
Wales v Romania	0-0
Bosnia-Herzegovina v Wales	1-0
Portugal v Liechtenstein	7-0
Switzerland v Portugal	2-4
Liechtenstein v Bosnia-Herzegovina	0-4

Group 8 Table	P	W	D	L	F	A	GD	Pts
Bosnia-Herzegovina	7	5	0	2	19	5	14	15
Portugal	6	4	1	1	17	7	10	13
Romania	6	3	3	0	9	3	6	12
Switzerland	7	2	1	4	7	12	–5	7
Wales	6	2	1	3	6	8	–2	7
Liechtenstein	6	0	0	6	1	24	–23	0

GROUP 9

Luxembourg v Kazakhstan	1-2

Match awarded 3-0 to Kazakhstan; Luxembourg fielded ineligible player.

Kazakhstan v Montenegro	1-1
Slovenia v Luxembourg	3-1
Bulgaria v Luxembourg	0-1
France v Kazakhstan	4-1
Luxembourg v Slovenia	1-1
France v Montenegro	2-1
Bulgaria v Kazakhstan	2-2
Montenegro v Slovenia	1-3
Luxembourg v France	2-3
Kazakhstan v Bulgaria	1-1
France v Bulgaria	3-0
Slovenia v Montenegro	2-0
Slovenia v France	1-3
Bulgaria v Montenegro	3-1
Kazakhstan v France	0-3
Luxembourg v Montenegro	1-3
Kazakhstan v Luxembourg	3-0
Bulgaria v Slovenia	3-0
Montenegro v France	0-2

Group 9 Table	P	W	D	L	F	A	GD	Pts
France	7	7	0	0	20	5	15	21
Slovenia	6	3	1	2	10	9	1	10
Kazakhstan	7	2	3	2	11	11	0	9
Bulgaria	6	2	2	2	9	8	1	8
Luxembourg	7	1	1	5	6	16	–10	4
Montenegro	7	1	1	5	7	14	–7	4

UEFA YOUTH LEAGUE 2017–18

CHAMPIONS LEAGUE PATH

GROUP A

Benfica v CSKA Moscow	5-1
Manchester U v FC Basel	4-3
CSKA Moscow v Manchester U	1-2
FC Basel v Benfica	2-2
CSKA Moscow v FC Basel	2-3
Benfica v Manchester U	2-2
FC Basel v CSKA Moscow	4-2
Manchester U v Benfica	1-1
CSKA Moscow v Benfica	2-0
FC Basel v Manchester U	2-1
Benfica v FC Basel	0-0
Manchester U v CSKA Moscow	1-0

Group A Table	P	W	D	L	F	A	GD	Pts
FC Basel	6	3	2	1	14	11	3	11
Manchester U	6	3	2	1	11	9	2	11
Benfica	6	1	4	1	10	8	2	7
CSKA Moscow	6	1	0	5	8	15	–7	3

GROUP B

Bayern Munich v Anderlecht	1-0
Celtic v Paris Saint-Germain	2-3
Anderlecht v Celtic	1-2
Paris Saint-Germain v Bayern Munich	1-1
Anderlecht v Paris Saint-Germain	0-2
Bayern Munich v Celtic	6-2
Paris Saint-Germain v Anderlecht	2-3
Celtic v Bayern Munich	1-2
Paris Saint-Germain v Celtic	2-0
Anderlecht v Bayern Munich	1-1
Celtic v Anderlecht	3-1
Bayern Munich v Paris Saint-Germain	3-1

Group B Table	P	W	D	L	F	A	GD	Pts
Bayern Munich	6	4	2	0	14	6	8	14
Paris Saint-Germain	6	3	1	2	11	9	2	10
Celtic	6	2	0	4	10	15	–5	6
Anderlecht	6	1	1	4	6	11	–5	4

GROUP C

Chelsea v Qarabag	5-0
Roma v Atletico Madrid	1-2
Qarabag v Roma	0-3
Atletico Madrid v Chelsea	1-3
Qarabag v Atletico Madrid	1-5
Chelsea v Roma	0-2
Atletico Madrid v Qarabag	0-1
Roma v Chelsea	1-2
Qarabag v Chelsea	1-3
Atletico Madrid v Roma	2-1
Roma v Qarabag	3-0
Chelsea v Atletico Madrid	4-2

Group C Table	P	W	D	L	F	A	GD	Pts
Chelsea	6	5	0	1	17	7	10	15
Atletico Madrid	6	3	0	3	12	11	1	9
Roma	6	3	0	3	11	6	5	9
Qarabag	6	1	0	5	3	19	–16	3

GROUP D

Barcelona v Juventus	1-0
Olympiacos v Sporting Lisbon	2-2
Juventus v Olympiacos	3-1
Sporting Lisbon v Barcelona	0-1
Juventus v Sporting Lisbon	1-4
Barcelona v Olympiacos	5-0
Sporting Lisbon v Juventus	2-0
Olympiacos v Barcelona	0-3
Sporting Lisbon v Olympiacos	1-1
Juventus v Barcelona	0-1
Barcelona v Sporting Lisbon	1-1
Olympiacos v Juventus	2-0

Group D Table	P	W	D	L	F	A	GD	Pts
Barcelona	6	5	1	0	12	1	11	16
Sporting Lisbon	6	2	3	1	10	6	4	9
Olympiacos	6	1	2	3	6	14	–8	5
Juventus	6	1	0	5	4	11	–7	3

GROUP E

Maribor v Spartak Moscow	1-0
Liverpool v Sevilla	4-0
Spartak Moscow v Liverpool	2-1
Sevilla v Maribor	1-0
Spartak Moscow v Sevilla	1-1
Maribor v Liverpool	1-4
Liverpool v Maribor	3-0
Sevilla v Spartak Moscow	3-3
Spartak Moscow v Maribor	5-0
Sevilla v Liverpool	0-4
Maribor v Sevilla	0-1
Liverpool v Spartak Moscow	2-0

Group E Table	P	W	D	L	F	A	GD	Pts
Liverpool	6	5	0	1	18	3	15	15
Spartak Moscow	6	2	2	2	11	8	3	8
Sevilla	6	2	2	2	6	12	–6	8
Maribor	6	1	0	5	2	14	–12	3

GROUP F

Shakhtar Donetsk v Napoli	1-2
Feyenoord v Manchester C	0-2
Napoli v Feyenoord	2-2
Manchester C v Shakhtar Donetsk	3-1
Feyenoord v Shakhtar Donetsk	4-0
Manchester C v Napoli	3-1
Shakhtar Donetsk v Feyenoord	1-1
Napoli v Manchester C	3-5
Napoli v Shakhtar Donetsk	1-2
Manchester C v Feyenoord	0-0
Shakhtar Donetsk v Manchester C	2-1
Feyenoord v Napoli	4-3

Group F Table	P	W	D	L	F	A	GD	Pts
Manchester C	6	4	1	1	14	7	7	13
Feyenoord	6	2	3	1	11	8	3	9
Shakhtar Donetsk	6	2	1	3	7	12	–5	7
Napoli	6	1	1	4	12	17	–5	4

GROUP G

Leipzig v Monaco	1-4
Porto v Besiktas	5-1
Besiktas v Leipzig	1-1
Monaco v Porto	3-2
Leipzig v Porto	0-2
Monaco v Besiktas	3-0
Besiktas v Monaco	3-2
Porto v Leipzig	3-2
Besiktas v Porto	0-1
Monaco v Leipzig	2-2
Leipzig v Besiktas	4-0
Porto v Monaco	2-1

Group G Table	P	W	D	L	F	A	GD	Pts
Porto	6	5	0	1	15	7	8	15
Monaco	6	3	1	2	15	10	5	10
RB Leipzig	6	1	2	3	10	12	–2	5
Besiktas	6	1	1	4	5	16	–11	4

GROUP H

Real Madrid v APOEL	10-0
Tottenham H v Borussia Dortmund	4-0
APOEL v Tottenham H	1-0
Borussia Dortmund v Real Madrid	5-3
APOEL v Borussia Dortmund	0-2
Real Madrid v Tottenham H	1-1
Tottenham H v Real Madrid	3-2
Borussia Dortmund v APOEL	5-0
Borussia Dortmund v Tottenham H	1-3
APOEL v Real Madrid	0-3
Tottenham H v APOEL	4-1
Real Madrid v Borussia Dortmund	2-1

Group H Table	P	W	D	L	F	A	GD	Pts
Tottenham H	6	4	1	1	15	6	9	13
Real Madrid	6	3	1	2	21	10	11	10
Borussia Borussia	6	3	0	3	14	12	2	9
APOEL	6	1	0	5	2	24	–22	3

DOMESTIC CHAMPIONS PATH

FIRST ROUND – FIRST LEG

Internationale v Dynamo Kyiv	2-2
Zimbru Chisinau v Vllaznia Shkoder	3-1
Ludogorets Razgrad v Zeljeznicar	1-1
Dinamo Bucharest v Lokomotiva Zagreb	0-2
KaPa v Esbjerg	1-2
Breidablik v Legia Warsaw	1-3
UCD v Molde	2-1
Hammarby v Ajax	0-4
Bordeaux v Red Bull Salzburg	0-1
Nitra v Shkendija	1-0
F91 Dudelange v Sparta Prague	0-4
Sutjeska Niksic v Honved	2-2
Brodarac v Maccabi Haifa	1-1
Kairat v Krasnodar	2-2
Liepaja v Shakhtyor Soligorsk	2-1
Bursaspor v Saburtalo Tbilisi	0-1

Shkendija v Nitra	1-1	1-2
Sparta Prague v F91 Dudelange	3-1	7-1
Honved v Sutjeska Niksic	1-0	3-2
Maccabi Haifa v Brodarac	0-1	1-2
Krasnodar v Kairat	9-0	11-2
Shakhtyor Soligorsk v Liepaja	3-0	4-2
Saburtalo Tbilisi v Bursaspor	1-1	2-1

SECOND ROUND – FIRST LEG

Zimbru Chisinau v Molde	0-0
Lokomotiva Zagreb v Zeljeznicar	1-1
Internationale v Esbjerg	4-1
Legia Warsaw v Ajax	1-4
Brodarac v Saburtalo Tbilisi	1-1
Shakhtyor Soligorsk v Nitra	2-0
Krasnodar v Honved	8-0
Sparta Prague v Red Bull Salzburg	2-4

FIRST ROUND – SECOND LEG

		(agg)
Dynamo Kyiv v Internationale	0-3	2-5
Vllaznia Shkoder v Zimbru Chisinau	2-4	3-7
Zeljeznicar v Ludogorets Razgrad	3-2	4-3
Lokomotiva Zagreb v Dinamo Bucharest	2-2	4-2
Esbjerg v KaPa	2-1	4-2
Legia Warsaw v Breidablik	0-0	3-1
Molde v UCD	2-1	3-3
Molde won 5-4 on penalties		
Ajax v Hammarby	2-0	6-0
Red Bull Salzburg v Bordeaux	4-0	5-0

SECOND ROUND – SECOND LEG

		(agg)
Molde v Zimbru Chisinau	2-0	2-0
Zeljeznicar v Lokomotiva Zagreb	0-0	1-1
Zeljeznicar won on away goals		
Esbjerg v Internationale	0-6	1-10
Ajax v Legia Warsaw	0-2	4-3
Saburtalo Tbilisi v Brodarac	2-2	3-3
Brodarac won on away goals		
Nitra v Shakhtyor Soligorsk	3-0	3-2
Honved v Krasnodar	1-1	1-9
Red Bull Salzburg v Sparta Prague	2-0	6-2

PLAY-OFFS

Molde v Monaco	2-2
Monaco won 4-3 on penalties	
Internationale v Spartak Moscow	3-3
Internationale won 3-1 on penalties	
Ajax v Paris Saint-Germain	0-0
Paris Saint-German won 4-2 on penalties	

Red Bull Salzburg v Sporting Lisbon	5-2
Brodarac v Manchester U	0-2
Nitra v Feyenoord	2-3
Zeljeznicar v Atletico Madrid	1-3
Krasnodar v Real Madrid	0-0
Real Madrid won 3-0 on penalties	

KNOCKOUT STAGE

ROUND OF 16

Bayern Munich v Real Madrid	2-3
Manchester C v Internationale	1-1
Manchester C won 3-2 on penalties	
Atletico Madrid v Basel	1-0
Porto v Red Bull Salzburg	3-1
Paris Saint-Germain v Barcelona	0-1
Liverpool v Manchester U	2-0
Tottenham H v Monaco	1-1
Tottenham H won 3-1 on penalties	
Chelsea v Feyenoord	5-2

QUARTER-FINALS

Real Madrid v Chelsea	2-4
Manchester C v Liverpool	1-1
Manchester C won 3-2 on penalties	
Barcelona v Atletico Madrid	2-0
Tottenham H v Porto	0-2

SEMI-FINALS

Manchester C v Barcelona	4-5
Chelsea v Porto	2-2
Chelsea won 5-4 on penalties	

UEFA YOUTH LEAGUE FINAL 2017–18

Nyon, Monday 23 April 2018

Barcelona (1) 3 *(Marques 33, 52, Ruiz 90)*   4000

Chelsea (0) 0

Barcelona: Pena; Morey, Mingueza, Brandariz, Miranda, Puig (Garcia 90), Orellan (Mora 74), Collado, Ruiz, Marques (Jaime 80), Perez.
Chelsea: Cumming; James, Sterling, Guehi (McEachran 58), Grant, Familio-Castillo, St Clair, Maddox (Lamptey 73), McCormick, Redan (Brown 67), Hudson-Odoi.
Referee: Andreas Ekberg (Sweden).

UEFA UNDER-19 CHAMPIONSHIP 2016–17

FINALS IN GEORGIA

GROUP A

Sweden v Czech Republic	1-2
Georgia v Portugal	0-1
Georgia v Sweden	2-1
Czech Republic v Portugal	1-2
Czech Republic v Georgia	2-0
Portugal v Sweden	2-2

Group A Table	P	W	D	L	F	A	GD	Pts
Portugal	3	2	1	0	5	3	2	7
Czech Republic	3	2	0	1	5	3	2	6
Georgia	3	1	0	2	2	4	–2	3
Sweden	3	0	1	2	4	6	–2	1

GROUP B

Bulgaria v England	0-2
Germany v Netherlands	1-4
England v Netherlands	1-0
Germany v Bulgaria	3-0
Netherlands v Bulgaria	1-1
England v Germany	4-1

Group A Table	P	W	D	L	F	A	GD	Pts
England	3	3	0	0	7	1	6	9
Netherlands	3	1	1	1	5	3	2	4
Germany	3	1	0	2	5	8	–3	3
Bulgaria	3	0	1	2	1	6	–5	1

SEMI-FINALS

Portugal v Netherlands	1-0
England v Czech Republic	1-0

UEFA UNDER-19 CHAMPIONSHIP FINAL

Gori, Saturday 15 July 2017

Portugal (0) 1 *(Sterling 56 (og))*

England (0) 2 *(Suliman 50, Nmecha 68)* 4100

Portugal: Costa; Dalot, Queiros, Conte (Queta 78), Pires, Filipe (Leao 56), Fernandes, Dju (Luis 75) Pedro, Queiros, Quina.
England: Ramsdale; Sterling, Jay Dasilva, Edun∎, Suliman, Buckley-Ricketts (Edwards 84), Dozzell (Josh Dasilva 77), Mount, Sessegnon, Nmecha (Brereton 72), Johnson.
Referee: Srdjan Jovanovic (Serbia).

UEFA UNDER-19 CHAMPIONSHIP 2017–18

QUALIFYING ROUND

GROUP 1 (CROATIA)

Croatia v San Marino	3-0
Latvia v Denmark	1-2
Denmark v San Marino	4-0
Croatia v Latvia	0-0
Denmark v Croatia	5-2
San Marino v Latvia	0-4

Group 1 Table	P	W	D	L	F	A	GD	Pts
Denmark	3	3	0	0	11	3	8	9
Latvia	3	1	1	1	6	3	3	4
Croatia	3	1	1	1	5	5	0	4
San Marino	3	0	0	3	0	11	–11	0

GROUP 2 (POLAND)

Germany v Belarus	5-1
Northern Ireland v Poland	1-2
Germany v Northern Ireland	7-1
Poland v Belarus	3-0
Poland v Germany	0-2
Belarus v Northern Ireland	0-0

Group 2 Table	P	W	D	L	F	A	GD	Pts
Germany	3	3	0	0	14	2	12	9
Poland	3	2	0	1	5	3	2	6
Northern Ireland	3	0	1	2	2	9	–7	1
Belarus	3	0	1	2	1	8	–7	1

GROUP 3 (LUXEMBOURG)

Czech Republic v Armenia	5-0
Luxembourg v Scotland	1-3
Scotland v Armenia	3-3
Czech Republic v Luxembourg	5-0
Scotland v Czech Republic	0-1
Armenia v Luxembourg	2-2

Group 3 Table	P	W	D	L	F	A	GD	Pts
Czech Republic	3	3	0	0	11	0	11	9
Scotland	3	1	1	1	6	5	1	4
Armenia	3	0	2	1	5	10	–5	2
Luxembourg	3	0	1	2	3	10	–7	1

GROUP 4 (NETHERLANDS)

Netherlands v Malta	3-0
Hungary v Slovenia	2-1
Slovenia v Malta	5-0
Netherlands v Hungary	2-0
Slovenia v Netherlands	2-2
Malta v Hungary	1-5

Group 4 Table	P	W	D	L	F	A	GD	Pts
Netherlands	3	2	1	0	7	2	5	7
Hungary	3	2	0	1	7	4	3	6
Slovenia	3	1	1	1	8	4	4	4
Malta	3	0	0	3	1	13	–12	0

GROUP 5 (FYR MACEDONIA)

Belgium v Liechtenstein	3-0
FYR Macedonia v Switzerland	2-1
Belgium v FYR Macedonia	1-2
Switzerland v Liechtenstein	5-1
Switzerland v Belgium	3-5
Liechtenstein v FYR Macedonia	0-6

Group 5 Table	P	W	D	L	F	A	GD	Pts
FYR Macedonia	3	3	0	0	10	2	8	9
Belgium	3	2	0	1	9	5	4	6
Switzerland	3	1	0	2	9	8	1	3
Liechtenstein	3	0	0	3	1	14	–13	0

GROUP 6 (AUSTRIA)

Austria v Kosovo	1-0
Lithuania v Israel	0-1
Austria v Lithuania	2-0
Israel v Kosovo	1-2
Israel v Austria	0-2
Kosovo v Lithuania	0-0

Group 6 Table	P	W	D	L	F	A	GD	Pts
Austria	3	3	0	0	5	0	5	9
Kosovo	3	2	0	1	5	2	3	6
Israel	3	1	0	2	2	4	–2	3
Lithuania	3	0	0	3	0	6	–6	0

GROUP 7 (REPUBLIC OF IRELAND)

Azerbaijan v Republic of Ireland	0-0
Serbia v Cyprus	1-0
Serbia v Azerbaijan	4-1
Republic of Ireland v Cyprus	5-0
Republic of Ireland v Serbia	2-1
Cyprus v Azerbaijan	2-1

Group 7 Table	P	W	D	L	F	A	GD	Pts
Republic of Ireland	3	2	1	0	7	1	6	7
Serbia	3	2	0	1	6	3	3	6
Cyprus	3	1	0	2	2	7	–5	3
Azerbaijan	3	0	1	2	2	6	–4	1

GROUP 8 (BULGARIA)

Iceland v Bulgaria	1-2
England v Faroe Islands	6-0
Bulgaria v Faroe Islands	2-0
England v Iceland	2-1
Bulgaria v England	0-1
Faroe Islands v Iceland	1-2

Group 8 Table	P	W	D	L	F	A	GD	Pts
England	3	3	0	0	9	1	8	9
Bulgaria	3	2	0	1	4	2	2	6
Iceland	3	1	0	2	4	5	–1	3
Faroe Islands	3	0	0	3	1	10	–9	0

GROUP 9 (SWEDEN)

Italy v Moldova	4-0
Estonia v Sweden	0-4
Italy v Estonia	2-1
Sweden v Moldova	3-0
Sweden v Italy	2-3
Moldova v Estonia	3-0

Group 9 Table	P	W	D	L	F	A	GD	Pts
Italy	3	3	0	0	9	3	6	9
Sweden	3	2	0	1	9	3	6	6
Moldova	3	1	0	2	3	7	-4	3
Estonia	3	0	0	3	1	9	-8	0

GROUP 10 (GREECE)

Russia v Gibraltar	6-0
Romania v Greece	2-1
Russia v Romania	1-2
Greece v Gibraltar	5-0
Greece v Russia	2-1
Gibraltar v Romania	0-8

Group 10 Table	P	W	D	L	F	A	GD	Pts
Romania	3	3	0	0	12	2	10	9
Greece	3	2	0	1	8	3	5	6
Russia	3	1	0	2	8	4	4	3
Gibraltar	3	0	0	3	0	19	-19	0

GROUP 11 (BOSNIA-HERZEGOVINA)

France v Andorra	7-0
Bosnia-Herzegovina v Georgia	1-0
France v Bosnia-Herzegovina	2-1
Georgia v Andorra	1-1
Georgia v France	1-1
Andorra v Bosnia-Herzegovina	1-2

Group 11 Table	P	W	D	L	F	A	GD	Pts
France	3	2	1	0	10	2	8	7
Bosnia-Herzegovina	3	2	0	1	4	3	1	6
Georgia	3	0	2	1	2	3	-1	2
Andorra	3	0	1	2	2	10	-8	1

GROUP 12 (ALBANIA)

Norway v Montenegro	3-0
Ukraine v Albania	1-0
Montenegro v Albania	1-0
Ukraine v Norway	2-1
Montenegro v Ukraine	0-4
Albania v Norway	1-7

Group 12 Table	P	W	D	L	F	A	GD	Pts
Ukraine	3	3	0	0	7	1	6	9
Norway	3	2	0	1	11	3	8	6
Montenegro	3	1	0	2	1	7	-6	3
Albania	3	0	0	3	1	9	-8	0

GROUP 13 (TURKEY)

Wales v Slovakia	1-2
Turkey v Kazakhstan	3-0
Slovakia v Kazakhstan	0-0
Turkey v Wales	2-1
Slovakia v Turkey	3-2
Kazakhstan v Wales	3-2

Group 13 Table	P	W	D	L	F	A	GD	Pts
Slovakia	3	2	1	0	5	3	2	7
Turkey	3	2	0	1	7	4	3	6
Kazakhstan	3	1	1	1	3	5	-2	4
Wales	3	0	0	3	4	7	-3	0

ELITE ROUND

GROUP 1 (GERMANY)

Norway v Netherlands	1-6
Germany v Scotland	3-0
Germany v Norway	2-5
Netherlands v Scotland	0-2
Netherlands v Germany	1-4
Scotland v Norway	4-5

Group 1 Table	P	W	D	L	F	A	GD	Pts
Norway	3	2	0	1	11	12	-1	6
Germany	3	2	0	1	9	6	3	6
Scotland	3	1	0	2	6	8	-2	3
Netherlands	3	1	0	2	7	7	0	3

GROUP 2 (MACEDONIA)

Macedonia v Latvia	1-2
Hungary v England	1-4
Macedonia v Hungary	3-4
England v Latvia	3-0
England v Macedonia	0-2
Latvia v Hungary	3-2

Group 2 Table	P	W	D	L	F	A	GD	Pts
England	3	2	0	1	7	3	4	6
Latvia	3	2	0	1	5	6	-1	6
Hungary	3	1	0	2	7	10	-3	3
Macedonia	3	1	0	2	6	6	0	3

GROUP 3 (ITALY)

Czech Republic v Poland	0-0
Greece v Italy	0-2
Czech Republic v Greece	2-3
Italy v Poland	4-3
Italy v Czech Republic	1-1
Poland v Greece	3-1

Group 3 Table	P	W	D	L	F	A	GD	Pts
Italy	3	2	1	0	7	4	3	7
Poland	3	1	1	1	6	5	1	4
Greece	3	1	0	2	4	7	-3	3
Czech Republic	3	0	2	1	3	4	-1	2

GROUP 4 (ROMANIA)

Sweden v Ukraine	0-0
Romania v Serbia	4-0
Ukraine v Serbia	2-1
Romania v Sweden	2-1
Serbia v Sweden	3-2
Ukraine v Romania	2-1

Group 4 Table	P	W	D	L	F	A	GD	Pts
Ukraine	3	2	1	0	4	2	2	7
Romania	3	2	0	1	7	3	4	6
Serbia	3	1	0	2	4	8	-4	3
Sweden	3	0	1	2	3	5	-2	1

GROUP 5 (PORTUGAL)

Slovakia v Republic of Ireland	1-1
Portugal v Kosovo	5-0
Republic of Ireland v Kosovo	3-0
Portugal v Slovakia	1-0
Republic of Ireland v Portugal	0-4
Kosovo v Slovakia	2-1

Group 5 Table	P	W	D	L	F	A	GD	Pts
Portugal	3	3	0	0	10	0	10	9
Republic of Ireland	3	1	1	1	4	5	-1	4
Kosovo	3	1	0	2	2	9	-7	3
Slovakia	3	0	1	2	2	4	-2	1

GROUP 6 (SPAIN)

Belgium v France	2-3
Spain v Bulgaria	0-0
France v Bulgaria	2-0
Spain v Belgium	3-0
France v Spain	4-2
Bulgaria v Belgium	0-2

Group 6 Table	P	W	D	L	F	A	GD	Pts
France	3	3	0	0	9	4	5	9
Spain	3	1	1	1	5	4	1	4
Belgium	3	1	0	2	4	6	-2	3
Bulgaria	3	0	1	2	0	4	-4	1

GROUP 7 (DENMARK)

Turkey v Austria	2-0
Denmark v Bosnia-Herzegovina	3-2
Austria v Bosnia-Herzegovina	3-0
Denmark v Turkey	1-1
Austria v Denmark	2-2
Bosnia-Herzegovina v Turkey	1-2

Group 7 Table	P	W	D	L	F	A	GD	Pts
Turkey	3	2	1	0	5	2	3	7
Denmark	3	1	2	0	6	5	1	5
Austria	3	1	1	1	5	4	1	4
Bosnia-Herzegovina	3	0	0	3	3	8	-5	0

Final Tournament in Finland 16–29 July 2018.

UEFA UNDER-17 CHAMPIONSHIP 2017-18

QUALIFYING ROUND

GROUP 1 (MALTA)
Belgium v Malta   3-1
Northern Ireland v Switzerland   0-5
Belgium v Northern Ireland   3-0
Switzerland v Malta   1-0
Switzerland v Belgium   0-2
Malta v Northern Ireland   0-1

Group 1 Table	P	W	D	L	F	A	GD	Pts
Belgium	3	3	0	0	8	1	7	9
Switzerland	3	2	0	1	6	2	4	6
Northern Ireland	3	1	0	2	1	8	-7	3
Malta	3	0	0	3	1	5	-4	0

GROUP 2 (ALBANIA)
Spain v Liechtenstein   3-0
Albania v Croatia   0-1
Spain v Albania   1-0
Croatia v Liechtenstein   6-0
Croatia v Spain   1-1
Liechtenstein v Albania   0-5

Group 2 Table	P	W	D	L	F	A	GD	Pts
Croatia	3	2	1	0	8	1	7	7
Spain	3	2	1	0	5	1	4	7
Albania	3	1	0	2	5	2	3	3
Liechtenstein	3	0	0	3	0	14	-14	0

GROUP 3 (CZECH REPUBLIC)
Czech Republic v Armenia   7-0
Israel v Turkey   1-0
Czech Republic v Israel   0-2
Turkey v Armenia   4-0
Turkey v Czech Republic   1-1
Armenia v Israel   0-3

Group 3 Table	P	W	D	L	F	A	GD	Pts
Israel	3	3	0	0	6	0	6	9
Czech Republic	3	1	1	1	8	3	5	4
Turkey	3	1	1	1	5	2	3	4
Armenia	3	0	0	3	0	14	-14	0

GROUP 4 (FINLAND)
Russia v Faroe Islands   3-1
Finland v Iceland   0-0
Iceland v Faroe Islands   2-0
Russia v Finland   0-1
Iceland v Russia   2-0
Faroe Islands v Finland   0-4

Group 4 Table	P	W	D	L	F	A	GD	Pts
Finland	3	2	1	0	5	0	5	7
Iceland	3	2	1	0	4	0	4	7
Russia	3	1	0	2	3	4	-1	3
Faroe Islands	3	0	0	3	1	9	-8	0

GROUP 5 (SERBIA)
Norway v Greece   0-1
Serbia v Gibraltar   7-0
Greece v Gibraltar   6-0
Serbia v Norway   2-1
Greece v Serbia   2-3
Gibraltar v Norway   0-10

Group 5 Table	P	W	D	L	F	A	GD	Pts
Serbia	3	3	0	0	12	3	9	9
Greece	3	2	0	1	9	3	6	6
Norway	3	1	0	2	11	3	8	3
Gibraltar	3	0	0	3	0	23	-23	0

GROUP 6 (BELARUS)
Belarus v Slovenia   0-1
France v Kazakhstan   5-0
France v Belarus   3-1
Slovenia v Kazakhstan   1-0
Slovenia v France   1-2
Kazakhstan v Belarus   1-3

Group 6 Table	P	W	D	L	F	A	GD	Pts
France	3	3	0	0	10	2	8	9
Slovenia	3	2	0	1	3	2	1	6
Belarus	3	1	0	2	4	5	-1	3
Kazakhstan	3	0	0	3	1	9	-8	0

GROUP 7 (ESTONIA)
Scotland v Andorra   2-1
Estonia v Denmark   0-1
Denmark v Andorra   1-0
Scotland v Estonia   3-0
Denmark v Scotland   0-0
Andorra v Estonia   0-0

Group 7 Table	P	W	D	L	F	A	GD	Pts
Scotland	3	2	1	0	5	1	4	7
Denmark	3	2	1	0	2	0	2	7
Andorra	3	0	1	2	1	3	-2	1
Estonia	3	0	1	2	0	4	-4	1

GROUP 8 (FYR MACEDONIA)
Bosnia-Herzegovina v FYR Macedonia   0-0
Moldova v Slovakia   0-2
Bosnia-Herzegovina v Moldova   4-0
Slovakia v FYR Macedonia   0-0
Slovakia v Bosnia-Herzegovina   1-1
FYR Macedonia v Moldova   2-0

Group 8 Table	P	W	D	L	F	A	GD	Pts
Bosnia-Herzegovina	3	1	2	0	5	1	4	5
Slovakia	3	1	2	0	3	1	2	5
FYR Macedonia	3	1	2	0	2	0	2	5
Moldova	3	0	0	3	0	8	-8	0

GROUP 9 (HUNGARY)
Netherlands v Kosovo   3-1
Hungary v Wales   2-1
Netherlands v Hungary   0-1
Wales v Kosovo   2-0
Wales v Netherlands   0-4
Kosovo v Hungary   1-3

Group 9 Table	P	W	D	L	F	A	GD	Pts
Hungary	3	3	0	0	6	2	4	9
Netherlands	3	2	0	1	7	2	5	6
Wales	3	1	0	2	3	6	-3	3
Kosovo	3	0	0	3	2	8	-6	0

GROUP 10 (ROMANIA)
Austria v Luxembourg   2-1
Lithuania v Romania   1-2
Austria v Lithuania   2-0
Romania v Luxembourg   0-0
Romania v Austria   0-1
Luxembourg v Lithuania   1-2

Group 10 Table	P	W	D	L	F	A	GD	Pts
Austria	3	3	0	0	5	1	4	9
Romania	3	1	1	1	2	2	0	4
Lithuania	3	1	0	2	3	5	-2	3
Luxembourg	3	0	1	2	2	4	-2	1

GROUP 11 (BULGARIA)
Republic of Ireland v Azerbaijan   6-0
Bulgaria v Ukraine   0-3
Ukraine v Azerbaijan   6-1
Republic of Ireland v Bulgaria   3-0
Ukraine v Republic of Ireland   1-3
Azerbaijan v Bulgaria   2-1

Group 11 Table	P	W	D	L	F	A	GD	Pts
Republic of Ireland	3	3	0	0	12	1	11	9
Ukraine	3	2	0	1	10	4	6	6
Azerbaijan	3	1	0	2	3	13	-10	3
Bulgaria	3	0	0	3	1	8	-7	0

GROUP 12 (CYPRUS)
Poland v San Marino   8-0
Cyprus v Sweden   1-1
Poland v Cyprus   1-0
Sweden v San Marino   9-0
Sweden v Poland   1-1
San Marino v Cyprus   0-5

Group 12 Table	P	W	D	L	F	A	GD	Pts
Poland	3	2	1	0	10	1	9	7
Sweden	3	1	2	0	11	2	9	5
Cyprus	3	1	1	1	6	2	4	4
San Marino	3	0	0	3	0	22	-22	0

GROUP 13 (GEORGIA)

Italy v Montenegro	3-0
Latvia v Georgia	0-1
Italy v Latvia	1-0
Georgia v Montenegro	2-0
Georgia v Italy	0-2
Montenegro v Latvia	1-1

Group 13 Table	P	W	D	L	F	A	GD	Pts
Italy	3	3	0	0	6	0	6	9
Georgia	3	2	0	1	3	2	1	6
Latvia	3	0	1	2	1	3	-2	1
Montenegro	3	0	1	2	1	6	-5	1

ELITE ROUND

GROUP 1 (CZECH REPUBLIC)

Ukraine v Spain	1-1
Serbia v Czech Republic	2-0
Serbia v Ukraine	3-0

Match finished Serbia 1 Ukraine 2. A default victory (3-0) was awarded to Serbia after disqualified Ukrainian players Mykola Yarosh and Roman Bodnia had played.

Spain v Czech Republic	2-0
Spain v Serbia	1-1
Czech Republic v Ukraine	0-0

Group 1 Table	P	W	D	L	F	A	GD	Pts
Serbia	3	2	1	0	6	1	5	7
Spain	3	1	2	0	4	2	2	5
Ukraine	3	0	2	1	1	4	-3	2
Czech Republic	3	0	1	2	0	4	-4	1

GROUP 2 (CROATIA)

Belgium v Cyprus	1-1
Sweden v Croatia	0-0
Belgium v Sweden	0-1
Croatia v Cyprus	1-1
Croatia v Belgium	1-2
Cyprus v Sweden	0-0

Group 2 Table	P	W	D	L	F	A	GD	Pts
Sweden	3	1	2	0	1	0	1	5
Belgium	3	1	1	1	3	3	0	4
Cyprus	3	0	3	0	2	2	0	3
Croatia	3	0	2	1	2	3	-1	2

GROUP 3 (POLAND)

Republic of Ireland v FYR Macedonia	3-0
Georgia v Poland	2-2
Republic of Ireland v Georgia	2-0
Poland v FYR Macedonia	3-0
Poland v Republic of Ireland	0-1
FYR Macedonia v Georgia	1-6

Group 3 Table	P	W	D	L	F	A	GD	Pts
Republic of Ireland	3	3	0	0	6	0	6	9
Georgia	3	1	1	1	8	5	3	4
Poland	3	1	1	1	5	3	2	4
FYR Macedonia	3	0	0	3	1	12	-11	0

GROUP 4 (PORTUGAL)

Switzerland v Finland	2-1
Portugal v Slovakia	2-1
Finland v Slovakia	2-1
Portugal v Switzerland	1-1
Finland v Portugal	0-2
Slovakia v Switzerland	2-4

Group 4 Table	P	W	D	L	F	A	GD	Pts
Switzerland	3	2	1	0	7	4	3	7
Portugal	3	2	1	0	5	2	3	7
Finland	3	1	0	2	3	5	-2	3
Slovakia	3	0	0	3	4	8	-4	0

FINAL TOURNAMENT (ENGLAND)

GROUP A

Italy v Switzerland	2-0
England v Israel	2-1
Switzerland v Israel	3-0
England v Italy	2-1
Switzerland v England	1-0
Israel v Italy	0-2

Group A Table	P	W	D	L	F	A	GD	Pts
Italy	3	2	0	1	5	2	3	6
England	3	2	0	1	4	3	1	6
Switzerland	3	2	0	1	4	2	2	6
Israel	3	0	0	3	1	7	-6	0

GROUP B

Portugal v Norway	0-0
Slovenia v Sweden	0-2
Norway v Sweden	2-1

GROUP 5 (NETHERLANDS)

Netherlands v Iceland	2-1
Italy v Turkey	2-0
Iceland v Turkey	0-3
Italy v Netherlands	0-2
Iceland v Italy	0-1
Turkey v Netherlands	0-2

Group 5 Table	P	W	D	L	F	A	GD	Pts
Netherlands	3	3	0	0	6	1	5	9
Italy	3	2	0	1	3	2	1	6
Turkey	3	1	0	2	3	4	-1	3
Iceland	3	0	0	3	1	6	-5	0

GROUP 6 (AUSTRIA)

France v Bosnia-Herzegovina	3-0
Denmark v Austria	1-0
France v Denmark	1-2
Austria v Bosnia-Herzegovina	1-3
Austria v France	0-0
Bosnia-Herzegovina v Denmark	1-0

Group 6 Table	P	W	D	L	F	A	GD	Pts
Bosnia-Herzegovina	3	2	0	1	4	4	0	6
Denmark	3	2	0	1	3	2	1	6
France	3	1	1	1	4	2	2	4
Austria	3	0	1	2	1	4	-3	1

GROUP 7 (HUNGARY)

Israel v Romania	5-1
Slovenia v Hungary	1-1
Israel v Slovenia	0-3
Hungary v Romania	2-0
Hungary v Israel	0-1
Romania v Slovenia	1-2

Group 7 Table	P	W	D	L	F	A	GD	Pts
Slovenia	3	2	1	0	6	2	4	7
Israel	3	2	0	1	6	4	2	6
Hungary	3	1	1	1	3	2	1	4
Romania	3	0	0	3	2	9	-7	0

GROUP 8 (GREECE)

Germany v Norway	2-2
Greece v Scotland	1-0
Scotland v Norway	1-2
Germany v Greece	3-0
Scotland v Germany	1-0
Norway v Greece	3-0

Group 8 Table	P	W	D	L	F	A	GD	Pts
Norway	3	2	1	0	7	3	4	7
Germany	3	1	1	1	5	3	2	4
Greece	3	1	0	2	1	6	-5	3
Scotland	3	1	0	2	2	3	-1	3

Slovenia v Portugal	0-4
Norway v Slovenia	2-0
Sweden v Portugal	1-0

Group B Table	P	W	D	L	F	A	GD	Pts
Norway	3	2	1	0	4	1	3	7
Sweden	3	2	0	1	4	2	2	6
Portugal	3	1	1	1	4	1	3	4
Slovenia	3	0	0	3	0	8	-8	0

GROUP C

Denmark v Bosnia-Herzegovina	2-3
Republic of Ireland v Belgium	0-2
Republic of Ireland v Denmark	1-0
Bosnia-Herzegovina v Belgium	0-4
Bosnia-Herzegovina v Republic of Ireland	0-2
Belgium v Denmark	1-0

Group C Table

	P	W	D	L	F	A	GD	Pts
Belgium	3	3	0	0	7	0	7	9
Republic of Ireland	3	2	0	1	3	2	1	6
Bosnia-Herzegovina	3	1	0	2	3	8	–5	3
Denmark	3	0	0	3	2	5	–3	0

GROUP D

Germany v Netherlands	0-3
Serbia v Spain	0-1
Serbia v Germany	0-3
Netherlands v Spain	2-0
Netherlands v Serbia	2-0
Spain v Germany	5-1

Group D Table

	P	W	D	L	F	A	GD	Pts
Netherlands	3	3	0	0	7	0	7	9
Spain	3	2	0	1	6	3	3	6
Germany	3	1	0	2	4	8	–4	3
Serbia	3	0	0	3	0	6	–6	0

QUARTER-FINALS

Italy v Sweden	1-0
Norway v England	0-2

Belgium v Spain	2-1
Netherlands v Republic of Ireland	1-1
Netherlands won 5-4 on penalties	

SEMI-FINALS

Italy v Belgium	2-1
England v Netherlands	0-0
Netherlands won 6-5 on penalties.	

UEFA UNDER-17 CHAMPIONSHIP 2017–18 FINAL

Rotherham, Sunday 20 May 2018

Netherlands (0) 2 *(Ricci 61, Riccardi 63)*

Italy (0) 2 *(Timber 46, Brobbey 74)*   4612

Netherlands: Koorevaar; Maduro J, Van Gelderen, Mamengi, Hendriks, Maduro Q, Gravenberch (Brobbey 74), Burger, Ihattaren, Redan, Tavsan (Summerville 69).

Italy: Russo; Barazzetta, Armini, Gozzi Iweru, Brogni, Gyabuaa, Leone (Fagioli 60), Ricci (Rovella 84), Greco, Vergani, Riccardi.

Netherlands won 4-1 on penalties.

Referee: Halil Umut Meler (Turkey).

FIFA UNDER-17 WORLD CUP 2018

FINALS IN INDIA

*After extra time.

GROUP A

Colombia v Ghana	0-1
India v USA	0-3
Ghana v USA	0-1
India v Colombia	1-2
Ghana v India	4-0
USA v Colombia	1-3

Group A Table

	P	W	D	L	F	A	GD	Pts
Ghana	3	2	0	1	5	1	4	6
Colombia	3	2	0	1	5	3	2	6
USA	3	2	0	1	5	3	2	6
India	3	0	0	3	1	9	–8	0

GROUP B

New Zealand v Turkey	1-1
Paraguay v Mali	3-2
Turkey v Mali	0-3
Paraguay v New Zealand	4-2
Turkey v Paraguay	1-3
Mali v New Zealand	3-1

Group B Table

	P	W	D	L	F	A	GD	Pts
Paraguay	3	3	0	0	10	5	5	9
Mali	3	2	0	1	8	4	4	6
New Zealand	3	0	1	2	4	8	–4	1
Turkey	3	0	1	2	2	7	–5	1

GROUP C

Germany v Costa Rica	2-1
Iran v Guinea	3-1
Costa Rica v Guinea	2-2
Iran v Germany	4-0
Costa Rica v Iran	0-3
Guinea v Germany	1-3

Group C Table

	P	W	D	L	F	A	GD	Pts
Iran	3	3	0	0	10	1	9	9
Germany	3	2	0	1	6	5	–1	6
Guinea	3	0	1	2	4	8	–4	1
Costa Rica	3	0	1	2	3	7	–4	1

GROUP D

Brazil v Spain	2-1
Korea DPR v Niger	0-1
Spain v Niger	4-0
Korea DPR v Brazil	0-2
Spain v Korea DPR	2-0
Niger v Brazil	0-2

Group D Table

	P	W	D	L	F	A	GD	Pts
Brazil	3	3	0	0	6	1	5	9
Spain	3	2	0	1	7	2	5	6
Niger	3	1	0	2	1	6	–5	3
Korea DPR	3	0	0	3	0	5	–5	0

GROUP E

New Caledonia v France	1-7
Honduras v Japan	1-6
France v Japan	2-1
Honduras v New Caledonia	5-0

France v Honduras	5-1
Japan v New Caledonia	1-1

Group E Table

	P	W	D	L	F	A	GD	Pts
France	3	3	0	0	14	3	11	9
Japan	3	1	1	1	8	4	4	4
Honduras	3	1	0	2	7	11	–4	3
New Caledonia	3	0	1	2	2	13	–11	1

GROUP F

Chile v England	0-4
Iraq v Mexico	1-1
England v Mexico	3-2
Iraq v Chile	3-0
England v Iraq	4-0
Mexico v Chile	0-0

Group F Table

	P	W	D	L	F	A	GD	Pts
England	3	3	0	0	11	2	9	9
Iraq	3	1	1	1	4	5	–1	4
Mexico	3	0	2	1	3	4	–1	2
Chile	3	0	1	2	0	7	–7	1

ROUND OF 16

Colombia v Germany	0-4
Paraguay v USA	0-5
Iran v Mexico	2-1
France v Spain	1-2
England v Japan *England won 5–3 on penalties.*	0-0
Mali v Iraq	5-1
Ghana v Niger	2-0
Brazil v Honduras	3-0

QUARTER-FINALS

Mali v Ghana	2-1
USA v England	1-4
Spain v Iran	3-1
Germany v Brazil	1-2

SEMI-FINALS

Brazil v England	1-3
Mali v Spain	1-3

THIRD PLACE PLAY-OFF

Brazil v Mali	2-0

FIFA UNDER-17 WORLD CUP FINAL

Kolkata, Saturday 28 October 2017

England (1) 5 *(Brewster 44, Gibbs-White 58, Foden 69, 88, Guehi 84)*

Spain (2) 2 *(Sergio Gomez 10, 31)*   66,684

England: Anderson; Sessegnon, Latibeaudiere, Guehi, Panzo, Oakley-Boothe (Gomes 90), McEachran (Gallagher 87), Foden, Gibbs-White (Kirby 81), Hudson-Odoi, Brewster.

Spain: Alvaro; Mateu Jaume, Miranda, Guillamon, Chust, Blanco (Beita 81), Ferran, Moha (Nacho Diaz 85), Abel Ruiz, Sergio Gomez, Cesar (Lara 72).

Referee: Enrique Caceres (Paraguay).

ENGLAND UNDER-21 RESULTS 1976–2018

EC *UEFA Competition for Under-21 Teams*

Bold type indicates matches played in season 2017–18.

Year	Date		Venue	Eng	Alb
			v ALBANIA	*Eng*	*Alb*
EC1989	Mar	7	Shkroda	2	1
EC1989	April	25	Ipswich	2	0
EC2001	Mar	27	Tirana	1	0
EC2001	Sept	4	Middlesbrough	5	0
			v ANDORRA	*Eng*	*And*
EC2017	**Oct**	**10**	**Andorra la Vella**	**1**	**0**
			v ANGOLA	*Eng*	*Ang*
1995	June	10	Toulon	1	0
1996	May	28	Toulon	0	2
			v ARGENTINA	*Eng*	*Arg*
1998	May	18	Toulon	0	2
2000	Feb	22	Fulham	1	0
			v AUSTRIA	*Eng*	*Aus*
1994	Oct	11	Kapfenberg	3	1
1995	Nov	14	Middlesbrough	2	1
EC2004	Sept	3	Krems	2	0
EC2005	Oct	7	Leeds	1	2
2013	June	26	Brighton	4	0
			v AZERBAIJAN	*Eng*	*Az*
EC2004	Oct	12	Baku	0	0
EC2005	Mar	29	Middlesbrough	2	0
2009	June	8	Milton Keynes	7	0
EC2011	Sept	1	Watford	6	0
EC2012	Sept	6	Baku	2	0
			v BELARUS	*Eng*	*Bel*
2015	June	11	Barnsley	1	0
			v BELGIUM	*Eng*	*Bel*
1994	June	5	Marseille	2	1
1996	May	24	Toulon	1	0
EC2011	Nov	14	Mons	1	2
EC2012	Feb	29	Middlesbrough	4	0
			v BOSNIA-HERZEGOVINA	*Eng*	*B-H*
EC2015	Nov	12	Sarajevo Canton	0	0
EC2016	Oct	11	Walsall	5	0
			v BRAZIL	*Eng*	*B*
1993	June	11	Toulon	0	0
1995	June	6	Toulon	0	2
1996	June	1	Toulon	1	2
			v BULGARIA	*Eng*	*Bul*
EC1979	June	5	Pernik	3	1
EC1979	Nov	20	Leicester	5	0
1989	June	5	Toulon	2	3
EC1998	Oct	9	West Ham	1	0
EC1999	June	8	Vratsa	1	0
EC2007	Sept	11	Sofia	2	0
EC2007	Nov	16	Milton Keynes	2	0
			v CHINA PR	*Eng*	*CPR*
2018	**May**	**26**	**Toulon**	**2**	**1**
			v CROATIA	*Eng*	*Cro*
1996	Apr	23	Sunderland	0	1
2003	Aug	19	West Ham	0	3
EC2014	Oct	10	Wolverhampton	2	1
EC2014	Oct	14	Vinkovci	2	1
			v CZECHOSLOVAKIA	*Eng*	*Cz*
1990	May	28	Toulon	2	1
1992	May	26	Toulon	1	2
1993	June	9	Toulon	1	1
			v CZECH REPUBLIC	*Eng*	*CzR*
1998	Nov	17	Ipswich	0	1
EC2007	June	11	Arnhem	0	0
2008	Nov	18	Bramall Lane	2	0
EC2011	June	19	Viborg	1	2
2015	Mar	27	Prague	1	0
			v DENMARK	*Eng*	*Den*
EC1978	Sept	19	Hvidovre	2	1
EC1979	Sept	11	Watford	1	0
EC1982	Sept	21	Hvidovre	4	1
EC1983	Sept	20	Norwich	4	1
EC1986	Mar	12	Copenhagen	1	0
EC1986	Mar	26	Manchester	1	1
1988	Sept	13	Watford	0	1
1994	Mar	8	Brentford	1	0
1999	Oct	8	Bradford	4	1
2005	Aug	16	Herning	1	0
2011	Mar	24	Viborg	4	0
2017	Mar	27	Randers	4	0
			v EQUADOR	*Eng*	*E*
2009	Feb	10	Malaga	2	3
			v FINLAND	*Eng*	*Fin*
EC1977	May	26	Helsinki	1	0
EC1977	Oct	12	Hull	8	1
EC1984	Oct	16	Southampton	2	0
EC1985	May	21	Mikkeli	1	3
EC2000	Oct	10	Valkeakoski	2	2
EC2001	Mar	23	Barnsley	4	0
EC2009	June	15	Halmstad	2	1
EC2013	Sept	9	Tampere	1	1
EC2013	Nov	14	Milton Keynes	3	0
			v FRANCE	*Eng*	*Fra*
EC1984	Feb	28	Sheffield	6	1
EC1984	Mar	28	Rouen	1	0
1987	June	11	Toulon	0	2
EC1988	April	13	Besancon	2	4
EC1988	April	27	Highbury	2	2
1988	June	12	Toulon	2	4
1990	May	23	Toulon	7	3
1991	June	3	Toulon	1	0
1992	May	28	Toulon	0	0
1993	June	15	Toulon	1	0
1994	May	31	Aubagne	0	3
1995	June	10	Toulon	0	2
1998	May	14	Toulon	1	1
1999	Feb	9	Derby	2	1
EC2005	Nov	11	Tottenham	1	1
EC2005	Nov	15	Nancy	1	2
2009	Mar	31	Nottingham	0	2
2014	Nov	17	Paris	2	3
2016	May	29	Toulon	2	1
2016	Nov	14	Bondoufle	2	3
			v FYR MACEDONIA	*Eng*	*M*
EC2002	Oct	15	Reading	3	1
EC2003	Sept	5	Skopje	1	1
EC2009	Sept	4	Prilep	2	1
EC2009	Oct	9	Coventry	6	3
			v GEORGIA	*Eng*	*Geo*
EC1996	Nov	8	Batumi	1	0
EC1997	April	29	Charlton	0	0
2000	Aug	31	Middlesbrough	6	1
			v GERMANY	*Eng*	*Ger*
1991	Sept	10	Scunthorpe	2	1
EC2000	Oct	6	Derby	1	1
EC2001	Aug	31	Frieburg	2	1
2005	Mar	25	Hull	2	2
2005	Sept	6	Mainz	1	1
EC2006	Oct	6	Coventry	1	0
EC2006	Oct	10	Leverkusen	2	0
EC2009	June	22	Halmstad	1	1
EC2009	June	29	Malmo	0	4
2010	Nov	16	Wiesbaden	0	2
2015	Mar	30	Middlesbrough	3	2
2017	Mar	24	Wiesbaden	0	1
EC2017	June	27	Tychy	2	2
			v EAST GERMANY	*Eng*	*EG*
EC1980	April	16	Sheffield	1	2
EC1980	April	23	Jena	0	1
			v WEST GERMANY	*Eng*	*WG*
EC1982	Sept	21	Sheffield	3	1
EC1982	Oct	12	Bremen	2	3
1987	Sept	8	Ludenscheid	0	2

v GREECE — Eng Gre

			Eng	Gre
EC1982	Nov	16	Piraeus	0	1
EC1983	Mar	29	Portsmouth	2	1
1989	Feb	7	Patras	0	1
EC1997	Nov	13	Heraklion	0	2
EC1997	Dec	17	Norwich	4	2
EC2001	June	5	Athens	1	3
EC2001	Oct	5	Ewood Park	2	1
EC2009	Sept	8	Tripoli	1	1
EC2010	Mar	3	Doncaster	1	2

v GUINEA

			Eng	Gui
2016	May	23	Toulon	7	1

v HUNGARY

			Eng	Hun
EC1981	June	5	Keszthely	2	1
EC1981	Nov	17	Nottingham	2	0
EC1983	April	26	Newcastle	1	0
EC1983	Oct	11	Nyiregyhaza	2	0
1990	Sept	11	Southampton	3	1
1992	May	12	Budapest	2	2
1999	April	27	Budapest	2	2

v ICELAND

			Eng	Ice
2011	Mar	28	Preston	1	2
EC2011	Oct	6	Reykjavik	3	0
EC2011	Nov	10	Colchester	5	0

v ISRAEL

			Eng	Isr
1985	Feb	27	Tel Aviv	2	1
2011	Sept	5	Barnsley	4	1
EC2013	June	11	Jerusalem	0	1

v ITALY

			Eng	Italy
EC1978	Mar	8	Manchester	2	1
EC1978	April	5	Rome	0	0
EC1984	April	18	Manchester	3	1
EC1984	May	2	Florence	0	1
EC1986	April	9	Pisa	0	2
EC1986	April	23	Swindon	1	1
EC1997	Feb	12	Bristol	1	0
EC1997	Oct	10	Rieti	1	0
EC2000	May	27	Bratislava	0	2
2000	Nov	14	Monza*	0	0
2002	Mar	26	Valley Parade	1	1
EC2002	May	20	Basle	1	2
2003	Feb	11	Pisa	0	1
2007	Mar	24	Wembley	3	3
EC2007	June	14	Arnhem	2	2
2011	Feb	8	Empoli	0	1
EC2013	June	5	Tel Aviv	0	1
EC2015	June	24	Olomouc	1	3

*Abandoned 11 mins; fog.

2016	Nov	10	Southampton	3	2

v JAPAN

			Eng	Jap
2016	May	27	Toulon	1	0

v KAZAKHSTAN

			Eng	
EC2015	Oct	13	Coventry	3	0
EC2016	Oct	6	Aktobe	1	0

v LATVIA

			Eng	Lat
1995	April	25	Riga	1	0
1995	June	7	Burnley	4	0
EC2017	**Sept**	**5**	**Bournemouth**	**3**	**0**

v LITHUANIA

			Eng	Lith
EC2009	Nov	17	Vilnius	0	0
EC2010	Sept	7	Colchester	3	0
EC2013	Oct	15	Ipswich	5	0
EC2014	Sept	5	Zaliakalnis	1	0

v LUXEMBOURG

			Eng	Lux
EC1998	Oct	13	Greven Macher	5	0
EC1999	Sept	3	Reading	5	0

v MALAYSIA

			Eng	Mal
1995	June	8	Toulon	2	0

v MEXICO

			Eng	Mex
1988	June	5	Toulon	2	1
1991	May	29	Toulon	6	0
1992	May	25	Toulon	1	1
2001	May	24	Leicester	3	0
2018	**May**	**29**	**Toulon**	**0**	**0**
2018	**June**	**9**	**Toulon**	**2**	**1**

v MOLDOVA

			Eng	Mol
EC1996	Aug	31	Chisinau	2	0
EC1997	Sept	9	Wycombe	1	0
EC2006	Aug	15	Ipswich	2	2
EC2013	Sept	5	Reading	1	0
EC2014	Sept	9	Tiraspol	3	0

v MONTENEGRO

			Eng	M
EC2007	Sept	7	Podgorica	3	0
EC2007	Oct	12	Leicester	1	0

v MOROCCO

			Eng	Mor
1987	June	7	Toulon	2	0
1988	June	9	Toulon	1	0

v NETHERLANDS

			Eng	N
EC1993	April	27	Portsmouth	3	0
EC1993	Oct	12	Utrecht	1	1
2001	Aug	14	Reading	4	0
EC2001	Nov	9	Utrecht	2	2
EC2001	Nov	13	Derby	1	0
2004	Feb	17	Hull	3	2
2005	Feb	8	Derby	1	2
2006	Nov	14	Alkmaar	1	0
EC2007	June	20	Heerenveen	1	1
2009	Aug	11	Groningen	0	0
EC2017	**Sept**	**1**	**Doetinchem**	**1**	**1**

v NORTHERN IRELAND

			Eng	NI
2012	Nov	13	Blackpool	2	0

v NORWAY

			Eng	Nor
EC1977	June	1	Bergen	2	1
EC1977	Sept	6	Brighton	6	0
1980	Sept	9	Southampton	3	0
1981	Sept	8	Drammen	0	0
EC1992	Oct	13	Peterborough	0	2
EC1993	June	1	Stavanger	1	1
1995	Oct	10	Stavanger	2	2
2006	Feb	28	Reading	3	1
2009	Mar	27	Sandefjord	5	0
2011	June	5	Southampton	2	0
EC2011	Oct	10	Drammen	2	1
EC2012	Sept	10	Chesterfield	1	0
EC2013	June	8	Petah Tikva	1	3
EC2015	Sept	7	Drammen	1	0
EC2016	Sept	6	Colchester	6	1

v PARAGUAY

			Eng	Par
2016	May	25	Toulon	4	0

v POLAND

			Eng	Pol
EC1982	Mar	17	Warsaw	2	1
EC1982	April	7	West Ham	2	2
EC1989	June	2	Plymouth	2	1
EC1989	Oct	10	Jastrzebie	3	1
EC1990	Oct	16	Tottenham	0	1
EC1991	Nov	12	Pila	1	2
EC1993	May	28	Zdroj	4	1
EC1993	Sept	7	Millwall	1	2
EC1996	Oct	8	Wolverhampton	0	0
EC1997	May	30	Katowice	1	1
EC1999	Mar	26	Southampton	5	0
EC1999	Sept	7	Plock	1	3
EC2004	Sept	7	Rybnik	3	1
EC2005	Oct	11	Hillsborough	4	1
2008	Mar	25	Wolverhampton	0	0
EC2017	**June**	**22**	**Kielce**	**3**	**0**

v PORTUGAL

			Eng	Por
1987	June	13	Toulon	0	0
1990	May	21	Toulon	0	1
1993	June	7	Toulon	2	0
1994	June	7	Toulon	2	0
EC1994	Sept	6	Leicester	0	0
1995	Sept	2	Lisbon	0	2
1996	May	30	Toulon	1	3
2000	Apr	16	Stoke	0	1
EC2002	May	22	Zurich	1	3
EC2003	Mar	28	Rio Major	2	4
EC2003	Sept	9	Everton	1	2
EC2008	Nov	20	Agueda	1	1
2008	Sept	5	Wembley	2	0
EC2009	Nov	14	Wembley	1	0
EC2010	Sept	3	Barcelos	1	0
2014	Nov	13	Burnley	3	1
EC2015	June	18	Uherske Hradiste	0	1
2016	May	19	Toulon	1	0

v QATAR

			Eng	Q
2018	**June**	**1**	**Toulon**	**4**	**0**

v REPUBLIC OF IRELAND

			Eng	RoI
1981	Feb	25	Liverpool	1	1
1985	Mar	25	Portsmouth	3	2
1989	June	9	Toulon	0	0
EC1990	Nov	13	Cork	3	0
EC1991	Mar	26	Brentford	3	0
1994	Nov	15	Newcastle	1	0

			Eng	RoI
1995	Mar	27	Dublin	2	0
EC2007	Oct	16	Cork	3	0
EC2008	Feb	5	Southampton	3	0

v ROMANIA			Eng	Rom
EC1980	Oct	14	Ploesti	0	4
EC1981	April	28	Swindon	3	0
EC1985	April	30	Brasov	0	0
EC1985	Sept	10	Ipswich	3	0
2007	Aug	21	Bristol	1	1
EC2010	Oct	8	Norwich	2	1
EC2010	Oct	12	Botosani	0	0
2013	Mar	21	Wycombe	3	0
2018	**Mar**	**24**	**Wolverhampton**	**2**	**1**

v RUSSIA			Eng	Rus
1994	May	30	Bandol	2	0

v SAN MARINO			Eng	SM
EC1993	Feb	16	Luton	6	0
EC1993	Nov	17	San Marino	4	0
EC2013	Oct	10	San Marino	4	0
EC2013	Nov	19	Shrewsbury	9	0

v SCOTLAND			Eng	Sco
1977	April	27	Sheffield	1	0
EC1980	Feb	12	Coventry	2	1
EC1980	Mar	4	Aberdeen	0	0
EC1982	April	19	Glasgow	1	0
EC1982	April	28	Manchester	1	1
EC1988	Feb	16	Aberdeen	1	0
EC1988	Mar	22	Nottingham	1	0
1993	June	13	Toulon	1	0
2013	Aug	13	Sheffield	6	0
EC2017	**Oct**	**6**	**Middlesbrough**	**3**	**1**
2018	**June**	**6**	**Toulon**	**3**	**1**

v SENEGAL			Eng	Sen
1989	June	7	Toulon	6	1
1991	May	27	Toulon	2	1

v SERBIA			Eng	Ser
EC2007	June	17	Nijmegen	2	0
EC2012	Oct	12	Norwich	1	0
EC2012	Oct	16	Krusevac	1	0

v SERBIA-MONTENEGRO			Eng	S-M
2003	June	2	Hull	3	2

v SLOVAKIA			Eng	Slo
EC2002	June	1	Bratislava	0	2
EC2002	Oct	11	Trnava	4	0
EC2003	June	10	Sunderland	2	0
2007	June	5	Norwich	5	0
EC2017	June	19	Kielce	2	1

v SLOVENIA			Eng	Slo
2000	Feb	12	Nova Gorica	1	0
2008	Aug	19	Hull	2	1

v SOUTH AFRICA			Eng	SA
1998	May	16	Toulon	3	1

v SPAIN			Eng	Spa
EC1984	May	17	Seville	1	0
EC1984	May	24	Sheffield	2	0
1987	Feb	18	Burgos	2	1
1992	Sept	8	Burgos	1	0
2001	Feb	27	Birmingham	0	4
2004	Nov	19	Alcala	0	1
2007	Feb	6	Derby	2	2
EC2009	June	18	Gothenburg	2	0
EC2011	June	12	Herning	1	1

v SWEDEN			Eng	Swe
1979	June	9	Vasteras	2	1
1986	Sept	9	Ostersund	1	1

			Eng	Swe
EC1988	Oct	18	Coventry	1	1
EC1989	Sept	5	Uppsala	0	1
EC1998	Sept	4	Sundvall	2	0
EC1999	June	4	Huddersfield	3	0
2004	Mar	30	Kristiansund	2	2
EC2009	June	26	Gothenburg	3	3
2013	Feb	5	Walsall	4	0
EC2015	Jun	21	Olomouc	1	0
EC2017	June	16	Kielce	0	0

v SWITZERLAND			Eng	Swit
EC1980	Nov	18	Ipswich	5	0
EC1981	May	31	Neuenburg	0	0
1988	May	28	Lausanne	1	1
1996	April	1	Swindon	0	0
1998	Mar	24	Brugglifeld	0	2
EC2002	May	17	Zurich	2	1
EC2006	Sept	6	Lucerne	3	2
EC2015	Nov	16	Brighton	3	1
EC2016	Mar	26	Thun	1	1

v TURKEY			Eng	Tur
EC1984	Nov	13	Bursa	0	0
EC1985	Oct	15	Bristol	3	0
EC1987	April	28	Izmir	0	0
EC1987	Oct	13	Sheffield	1	1
EC1991	April	30	Izmir	2	2
1991	Oct	15	Reading	2	0
EC1992	Nov	17	Orient	0	1
EC1993	Mar	30	Izmir	0	0
EC2000	May	29	Bratislava	6	0
EC2003	April	1	Newcastle	1	1
EC2003	Oct	10	Istanbul	0	1

v UKRAINE			Eng	Uk
2004	Aug	17	Middlesbrough	3	1
EC2011	June	15	Herning	0	0
EC2017	**Nov**	**10**	**Kiev**	**2**	**0**
EC2018	**Mar**	**27**	**Sheffield**	**2**	**1**

v USA			Eng	USA
1989	June	11	Toulon	0	2
1994	June	2	Toulon	3	0
2015	Sept	3	Preston	1	0

v USSR			Eng	USSR
1987	June	9	Toulon	0	0
1988	June	7	Toulon	1	0
1990	May	25	Toulon	2	1
1991	May	31	Toulon	2	1

v UZBEKISTAN			Eng	Uzb
2010	Aug	10	Bristol	2	0

v WALES			Eng	Wales
1976	Dec	15	Wolverhampton	0	0
1979	Feb	6	Swansea	1	0
1990	Dec	5	Tranmere	0	0
EC2004	Oct	8	Blackburn	2	0
EC2005	Sept	2	Wrexham	4	0
2008	May	5	Wrexham	2	0
EC2008	Oct	10	Cardiff	3	2
EC2008	Oct	14	Villa Park	2	2
EC2013	Mar	5	Derby	1	0
EC2013	May	19	Swansea	3	1

v YUGOSLAVIA			Eng	Yugo
EC1978	April	19	Novi Sad	1	2
EC1978	May	2	Manchester	1	1
EC1986	Nov	11	Peterborough	1	1
EC1987	Nov	10	Zemun	5	1
EC2000	Mar	29	Barcelona	3	0
2002	Sept	6	Bolton	1	1

ENGLAND C 2017–18

■ *Denotes player sent off.*

INTERNATIONAL CHALLENGE TROPHY FINAL
Ziar Nad Hronom, Wednesday 8 November 2017
Slovakia U21s (1) 4 *(Orsula, Ivan, Fasko, Herc)*
England C (0) 0

England C: Smith (Hall 82); Cartwright■, Ferguson, John, Wynter, Gallagher (Powell 67), Barratt (Johnson 46), Croasdale, Ferrier, Rees (Ward 46), Okenabirhie (Afolayan 76).

FRIENDLY
Barry, Tuesday 20 March 2018
Wales C (1) 2 *(Jones T 63, Venables 80)*
England C (1) 3 *(Okenabirhie 10, 53, 75)*

England C: Smith (Montgomery 81); Ling, Horsfall (Jones J 73), Staunton, Jones D, Ramshaw (Adams 62), Croasdale, Pinnock, Hardy, Maguire (Gilchrist 77), Okenabirhie (Barratt 81).

BRITISH UNDER-21 TEAMS 2017–18

■ *Denotes player sent off.*

ENGLAND

UEFA UNDER-21 CHAMPIONSHIPS 2017–19
Friday, 1 September 2017
Netherlands (1) 1 *(Ramselaar 32)*
England (1) 1 *(Calvert-Lewin 20)*
England: (433) Gunn; Cook, Kenny, Chilwell, Fry; Calvert-Lewin (Abraham 77), Gomez, Onomah; Dowell (Gray 71), Solanke (Palmer 71), Lookman.

Tuesday, 5 September 2017
England (2) 3 *(Gray 13, Abraham 35, Palmer 70)*
Latvia (0) 0
England: (433) Woodman; Alexander-Arnold, Tomori, Gomez, Walker-Peters; Palmer (Solanke 70), Cook, Davies; Gray, Abraham (Calvert-Lewin 68), Ojo (Lookman 58).

Friday, 6 October 2017
England (1) 3 *(Onomah 14, Abraham 50 (pen), Solanke 79)*
Scotland (0) 1 *(Cadden 78)*
England: (433) Gunn; Alexander-Arnold, Gomez, Fry, Walker-Peters; Onomah, Cook, Solanke (Lookman 83); Calvert-Lewin, Abraham (Harrison 88), Gray (Kenny 70). *Scotland:* (433) Fulton; Smith, Souttar, McKenna, Taylor; Cadden, Mallan (Docherty 82), Campbell; Thomas (Williamson 67), Burke (McBurnie 45), Morgan.

Tuesday, 10 October 2017
Andorra (0) 0
England (0) 1 *(Davies 53)*
England: (433) Gunn; Kenny, Tomori, Worrall, Walker-Peters; Lookman, Maitland-Niles (Cook 76), Davies; Harrison (Gray 70), Dowell, Calvert-Lewin (Solanke 79).

Friday, 10 November 2017
Ukraine (0) 0
England (1) 2 *(Solanke 17, Lukyanchuk 62 (og))*
England: (433) Gunn; Kenny, Worrall, Tomori, Walker-Peters; Cook, Maitland-Niles (Tuanzebe 56), Gray; Dowell (Calvert-Lewin 57), Solanke (Maddison 81), Lookman.

Tuesday, 27 March 2018
England (1) 2 *(Calvert-Lewin 41, Solanke 88)*
Ukraine (0) 1 *(Shaparenko 83)*
England: (433) Gunn; Kenny, Worrall, Fry, Chilwell; Davies, Onomah, Maddison (Solanke 76); Sessegnon, Calvert-Lewin (Maitland-Niles 90), Gray (Lookman 73).

FRIENDLY
Saturday, 24 March 2018
England (1) 2 *(Gray 8, Clarke-Salter 72)*
Romania (0) 1 *(Costache 79)*
England: Henderson; Alexander-Arnold, Tomori, Clarke-Salter, Walker-Peters; Ejaria, Maitland-Niles (Onomah 70); Gray (Kenny 59), Dowell (Maddison 84), Lookman; Abraham (Calvert-Lewin 84).

TOULON TOURNAMENT – GROUP A
Saturday, 26 May 2018
England (0) 2 *(Fry 52, Abraham 80)*
China PR (1) 1 *(Yan Dinghao 20)*
England: Woodman; Kenny, Cook, Fry, Tomori (Walker-Peters 46 (Pearce 67)), Dowell, Davies, Abraham, Armstrong, Clarke-Salter, Da Silva (Choudhury 73).

Tuesday, 29 May 2018
Mexico (0) 0
England (0) 0
England: Woodman, Kenny, Cook, Fry, Dowell (Armstrong 61), Da Silva, Konsa, Choudhury, Connolly, Nketiah (Abraham 67), Nmecha.

Friday, 1 June 2018
Qatar (0) 0
England (0) 4 *(Al-Hamawende 38 (og), Vieira 53, Abraham 56, Armstrong 67)*
England: Ramsdale; Kenny, Fry, Davies (Cook 46), Abraham (Connolly 78), Vieira, Armstrong, Clarke-Salter, Pearce (Da Silva 46), Nketiah, Nmecha (Dowell 72).

SEMI-FINAL
Wednesday, 6 June 2018
Scotland (1) 1 *(Johnston 30)*
England (0) 3 *(Connolly 45, Nketiah 50, 68)*
Scotland: Robby McCrorie; Ralston, Taylor, Kerr, Porteous, Burke (Watt 82), Johnston, Wilson (Burt 45), Gilmour, Hornby, Campbell (Middleton 82). *England:* Woodman; Kenny, Fry (Tomori 79), Clarke-Salter, Connolly (Konsa 85), Cook, Vieira (Choudhury 73), Da Silva, Dowell, Armstrong (Abraham 84), Nketiah.

FINAL
Saturday, 9 June 2018
Mexico (1) 1 *(Alvarado 2)*
England (2) 2 *(Fry 32, Dowell 36)*
England: Woodman; Kenny, Fry, Clarke-Salter, Connolly (Tomori 86), Cook, Vieira (Choudhury 56), Da Silva, Dowell, Nketiah (Armstrong 76), Abraham (Nmecha 79).

SCOTLAND

UEFA UNDER-21 CHAMPIONSHIPS 2017–19
Tuesday, 5 September 2017
Scotland (0) 2 *(Burke 62, Mallan 79)*
Netherlands (0) 0
Scotland: (4231) Fulton; Ralston, Souttar, McKenna, Taylor; Mallan (Wright 80), Wilson; Cadden, Thomas (Ross McCrorie 72), Morgan; Burke (Archibald 85).

Friday, 6 October 2017
England (1) 3 *(Onomah 14, Abraham 50 (pen), Solanke 79)*
Scotland (0) 1 *(Cadden 78)*
England: (433) Gunn; Alexander-Arnold, Gomez, Fry, Walker-Peters; Onomah, Cook, Solanke (Lookman 83); Calvert-Lewin, Abraham (Harrison 88), Gray (Kenny 70). *Scotland:* (433) Fulton; Smith, Souttar, McKenna, Taylor; Cadden, Mallan (Docherty 82), Campbell; Thomas (Williamson 67), Burke (McBurnie 45), Morgan.

Tuesday, 10 October 2017
Latvia (0) 0
Scotland (2) 2 *(Burke 16, McBurnie 19)*
Scotland: (433) Fulton; Taylor, McKenna, Souttar, Smith; Thomas (Ross McCrorie 65), Cadden, Campbell; Morgan, Burke (Williamson 80), McBurnie (Hardie 85).

Friday, 10 November 2017
Scotland (0) 1 *(Hardie 90 (pen))*
Latvia (1) 1 *(Uldrikris 45) Stuglis■*
Scotland: (433) Fulton; Smith (Hardie 64), Souttar (Ross McCrorie 69), McKenna, Taylor; Cadden, Campbell, Mallan; Wright (Thomas 87), McBurnie, Morgan.

Tuesday, 14 November 2017
Scotland (0) 0
Ukraine (1) 2 *(Boryachuk 45, Kovalenko 90)*
Scotland: (433) Fulton; Smith (Hardie 71), Ross McCrorie, McKenna, Taylor; Campbell, Mallan, Thomas (Williamson 55); Cadden, McBurnie (Wright 74), Morgan.

Friday, 23 March 2018
Andorra (0) 1 *(Fernandez 77 (pen))*
Scotland (0) 1 *(Morgan 90)*
Scotland: (433) Fulton; Cadden, Kerr, Souttar, Taylor; Campbell, Docherty (Brophy 53), Mallan (Smith 61); Burke (Wright 81), Hardie, Morgan.

TOULON TOURNAMENT 2018 – GROUP A
Sunday, 27 May 2018
Togo (1) 1 *(Wogodo 3)*
Scotland (1) 1 *(Hornby 18)*
Scotland: Doohan; Ralston, Taylor, Kerr, Porteous, Burke (Wighton 69), Johnston (Middleton 82), Hornby (St Clair 80), Wright (Burt 51), Wilson, Campbell.

Wednesday, 30 May 2018
Scotland (1) 1 *(Burke 35)*
France (0) 0
Scotland: Robby McCrorie; Ralston, Taylor, Kerr, Porteous, Johnston (Harvie 67), Campbell, Wilson, Burke (Wighton 63), Gilmour, Hornby (Hamilton 74).

Saturday, 2 June 2018
Korea Republic (0) 1 *(Lee Kang-in 71)*
Scotland (2) 2 *(Gilmour 2, Burke 8)*
Scotland: Doohan; Ralston (Hamilton 40), Taylor, Kerr, Porteous, Burke (St Clair 59), Wilson (Watt 40), Middleton (Harvie 68), Campbell, Gilmour, Hornby.

Wednesday, 6 June 2018
Scotland 1
England 3

THIRD PLACE PLAY-OFF
Saturday, 9 June 2018
Scotland (0) 0
Turkey (0) 0
Scotland: Doohan (Robby McCrorie 46); Hamilton, Taylor, Kerr, Harvie, Wilson, Watt, Burt (Hornby 60), Middleton, St Clair (Burke 71), Wighton (Johnston).
Turkey won 5-3 on penalties.

WALES

UEFA UNDER-21 CHAMPIONSHIPS 2017–19
Friday, 1 September 2017
Switzerland (0) 0
Wales (2) 3 *(Roberts 7, Brooks 27, Thomas 90)*
Wales: (442) Pilling; Coxe, Mepham, Rodon, Abbruzzese; Thomas, Smith, Poole, James (Broadhead 65); Brooks (Evans 90), Roberts (Harris 83).

Tuesday, 5 September 2017
Portugal (2) 2 *(Neves 25 (pen), Goncalo Guedes 41)*
Wales (0) 0
Wales: (442) Pilling; Coxe, Mepham■, Rodon, Abbruzzese; Thomas, Smith (Evans 59), Poole, James (Harris 46); Brooks, Roberts (Broadhead 67).

Thursday, 5 October 2017
Liechtenstein (0) 1 *(Kardesoglu 57)*
Wales (2) 3 *(Thomas 24, 31 (pen), Smith 52)*
Wales: (442) Pilling; Rodon, Coxe, Abbruzzese, Poole; Morrell (Matondo 85), Harries, Smith (Evans 85), Thomas; Broadhead (Harris 74), Roberts.

Friday, 10 November 2017
Wales (0) 0
Bosnia-Herzegovina (1) 4 *(Gojak 26, 51, Cavar 71, Menalo 77)*
Wales: (4141) Pilling; Coxe, Dasilva (Norrington-Davies 46), Poole, Rodon; Mepham; Smith, Wilson, Harris (Broadhead 72), Thomas (Matondo 62); Roberts.

Tuesday, 14 November 2017
Wales (0) 0
Romania (0) 0
Wales: (4411) Pilling; Coxe, Mepham, Harries, Norrington-Davies; Thomas, Poole, Evans (Smith 90), Harris (Matondo 79); Wilson; Roberts.

Friday, 23 March 2018
Bosnia-Herzegovina (0) 1 *(Todorovic 65)*
Wales (0) 0
Wales: Pilling; Lewis, Rodon, Harries, Coxe, Evans J, Poole, Thomas G (Matondo 79), Brooks, Morrell (James 63), Harris.

FRIENDLIES
Sunday, 3 June 2018
Georgia (1) 2 *(Mikeitadze 14, 84 (pen))*
Wales (2) 2 *(Morrell 32 (pen), Harris 38)*
Wales: Evans O; Coxe (Lewis), Norrington-Davies, Poole, Rodon, Harries!, Morrell (Matondo), Harris, James (Cullen), Babos, Christie-Davies (Broadhead).

Wednesday, 6 June 2018
Georgia (0) 1 *(Kokhreidze 90)*
Wales (0) 1 *(Morrell 89 (pen))*
Wales: Pilling; Norrington-Davies, Poole, Rodon, Evans J, Harris (Burton 61), Broadhead, James (Cullen 61), Lewis (Coxe 65), Babos (Christie-Davies 46), Matondo (Morrell 70).

NORTHERN IRELAND

UEFA UNDER-21 CHAMPIONSHIPS 2017–19
Thursday, 31 August 2017
Northern Ireland (0) 1 *(Donnelly 90 (pen))*
Albania (0) 0 Bare■
Northern Ireland: (4141) Mitchell; Dummigan, McDermott, Donnelly, Johnson; Dunwoody (Kennedy 63); Smyth, Gorman, Thompson, Doherty B; Parkhouse (McGonigle 77).

Tuesday, 5 September 2017
Slovakia (0) 1 *(Benes 61)*
Northern Ireland (0) 0
Northern Ireland: (433) Mitchell; Dummigan, Donnelly, Johnson, Doherty B (McDonagh 84); Gorman (Gordon 57), Hall, Thompson; Smyth (Parkhouse 78), Kennedy, Owens.

Tuesday, 10 October 2017
Northern Ireland (2) 4 *(Johnson 2, Gorman 43, Sykes 61, 75)*
Estonia (2) 2 *(Liivak 11, Sappinen 20)*
Northern Ireland: (433) Mitchell; Dummigan, Donnelly, Johnson, Doherty B; Sykes, Gorman (Paul 58), Thompson (Owens 81); Kennedy (Smyth 76), Parkhouse, McDonagh.

Friday, 10 November 2017
Albania (0) 1 *(Ramadani 83)*
Northern Ireland (0) 1 *(Lavery 89)*
Northern Ireland: (442) Mitchell; Dummigan, Donnelly, Johnson, Smyth (Lavery 75); Gorman, Thompson (McGonigle 86), Sykes, Doherty J (Doherty B 67); McDonagh, Parkhouse.

Thursday, 22 March 2018
Northern Ireland (2) 3 *(Donnelly 30 (pen), 45, Lavery 69)*
Spain (2) 5 *(Oyarzabal 15, 44, Borja Mayoral 47, 75, 84)*
Northern Ireland: (352) Mitchell; Hall, Donnelly, Johnson; Dummigan (Paul 45), McDermott, Thompson, Sykes, Whyte (Kennedy 72); Lavery (McDonagh 84), Smyth.

Monday, 26 March 2018
Northern Ireland (0) 0
Iceland (0) 0
Northern Ireland: (433) Peacock-Farrell; McDonagh, Hall, Donnelly, Johnson; Thompson, Kennedy (Sykes 84), Gorman; Whyte, Burns, Lavery.

BRITISH UNDER-21 APPEARANCES 1976–2018

Bold type indicates players who made an international appearance in season 2017–18.

ENGLAND

Ablett, G. 1988 (Liverpool)	1	Blackstock, D. A. 2008 (QPR)	2
Abraham, K. O. T. (Tammy) 2017 (Chelsea)	**19**	Blackwell, D. R. 1991 (Wimbledon)	6
Akpom, C. A. 2015 (Arsenal)	5	Blake, M. A. 1990 (Aston Villa)	8
Adams, N. 1987 (Everton)	1	Blissett, L. L. 1979 (Watford)	4
Adams, T. A. 1985 (Arsenal)	5	Bond, J. H. 2013 (Watford)	5
Addison, M. 2010 (Derby Co)	1	Booth, A. D. 1995 (Huddersfield T)	3
Afobe, B. T. 2012 (Arsenal)	2	Bothroyd, J. 2001 (Coventry C)	1
Agbonlahor, G. 2007 (Aston Villa)	16	Bowyer, L. D. 1996 (Charlton Ath, Leeds U)	13
Albrighton, M. K. 2011 (Aston Villa)	8	Bracewell, P. 1983 (Stoke C)	13
Alexander-Arnold, T. J. 2018 (Liverpool)	**3**	Bradbury, L. M. 1997 (Portsmouth, Manchester C)	3
Alli, B. J. (Dele) 2015 (Tottenham H)	2	Bramble, T. M. 2001 (Ipswich T, Newcastle U)	10
Allen, B. 1992 (QPR)	8	Branch, P. M. 1997 (Everton)	1
Allen, C. 1980 (QPR, Crystal Palace)	3	Bradshaw, P. W. 1977 (Wolverhampton W)	4
Allen, C. A. 1995 (Oxford U)	2	Breacker, T. 1986 (Luton T)	2
Allen, M. 1987 (QPR)	2	Brennan, M. 1987 (Ipswich T)	5
Allen, P. 1985 (West Ham U, Tottenham H)	3	Bridge, W. M. 1999 (Southampton)	8
Allen, R. W. 1998 (Tottenham H)	3	Bridges, M. 1997 (Sunderland, Leeds U)	3
Alnwick, B. R. 2008 (Tottenham H)	1	Briggs, M. 2012 (Fulham)	2
Ambrose, D. P. F. 2003 (Ipswich T, Newcastle U,		Brightwell, I. 1989 (Manchester C)	4
Charlton Ath)	10	Briscoe, L. S. 1996 (Sheffield W)	5
Ameobi, F. 2001 (Newcastle U)	19	Brock, K. 1984 (Oxford U)	4
Ameobi, S. 2012 (Newcastle U)	5	Broomes, M. C. 1997 (Blackburn R)	2
Amos, B. P. 2012 (Manchester U)	3	Brown, M. R. 1996 (Manchester C)	4
Anderson, V. A. 1978 (Nottingham F)	1	Brown, W. M. 1999 (Manchester U)	8
Anderton, D. R. 1993 (Tottenham H)	12	Bull, S. G. 1989 (Wolverhampton W)	5
Andrews, I. 1987 (Leicester C)	1	Bullock, M. J. 1998 (Barnsley)	1
Ardley, N. C. 1993 (Wimbledon)	10	Burrows, D. 1989 (WBA, Liverpool)	7
Armstrong, A. J. 2018 (Newcastle U)	**5**	Butcher, T. I. 1979 (Ipswich T)	7
Ashcroft, L. 1992 (Preston NE)	1	Butland, J. 2012 (Birmingham C, Stoke C)	28
Ashton, D. 2004 (Crewe Alex, Norwich C)	9	Butt, N. 1995 (Manchester U)	7
Atherton, P. 1992 (Coventry C)	1	Butters, G. 1989 (Tottenham H)	3
Atkinson, B. 1991 (Sunderland)	6	Butterworth, I. 1985 (Coventry C, Nottingham F)	8
Awford, A. T. 1993 (Portsmouth)	9	Bywater, S. 2001 (West Ham U)	6
Bailey, G. R. 1979 (Manchester U)	14	Cadamarteri, D. L. 1999 (Everton)	3
Baines, L. J. 2005 (Wigan Ath)	16	Caesar, G. 1987 (Arsenal)	3
Baker, G. E. 1981 (Southampton)	2	Cahill, G. J. 2007 (Aston Villa)	3
Baker, L. R. 2015 (Chelsea)	17	Callaghan, N. 1983 (Watford)	9
Baker, N. L. 2011 (Aston Villa)	3	**Calvert-Lewin, D. N. 2018 (Everton)**	**7**
Ball, M. J. 1999 (Everton)	7	Camp, L. M. J. 2005 (Derby Co)	5
Bamford, P. J. 2013 (Chelsea)	2	Campbell, A. P. 2000 (Middlesbrough)	4
Bannister, G. 1982 (Sheffield W)	1	Campbell, F. L. 2008 (Manchester U)	14
Barker, S. 1985 (Blackburn R)	4	Campbell, K. J. 1991 (Arsenal)	4
Barkley, R. 2012 (Everton)	5	Campbell, S. 1994 (Tottenham)	11
Barmby, N. J. 1994 (Tottenham H, Everton)	4	Carbon, M. P. 1996 (Derby Co)	4
Barnes, J. 1983 (Watford)	2	Carr, C. 1985 (Fulham)	1
Barnes, P. S. 1977 (Manchester C)	9	Carr, F. 1987 (Nottingham F)	9
Barrett, E. D. 1990 (Oldham Ath)	4	Carragher, J. L. 1997 (Liverpool)	27
Barry, G. 1999 (Aston Villa)	27	Carroll, A. T. 2010 (Newcastle U)	5
Barton, J. 2004 (Manchester C)	2	Carroll, T. J. 2013 (Tottenham H)	17
Bart-Williams, C. G. 1993 (Sheffield W)	16	Carlisle, C. J. 2001 (QPR)	3
Batty, D. 1988 (Leeds U)	7	Carrick, M. 2001 (West Ham U)	14
Bazeley, D. S. 1992 (Watford)	1	Carson, S. P. 2004 (Leeds U, Liverpool)	29
Beagrie, P. 1988 (Sheffield U)	2	Casper, C. M. 1995 (Manchester U)	1
Beardsmore, R. 1989 (Manchester U)	5	Caton, T. 1982 (Manchester C)	14
Beattie, J. S. 1999 (Southampton)	5	Cattermole, L. B. 2008 (Middlesbrough, Wigan Ath,	
Beckham, D. R. J. 1995 (Manchester U)	9	Sunderland)	16
Berahino, S. 2013 (WBA)	11	Caulker, S. R. 2011 (Tottenham H)	10
Bennett, J. 2011 (Middlesbrough)	3	Chadwick, L. H. 2000 (Manchester U)	13
Bennett, R. 2012 (Norwich C)	2	Challis, T. M. 1996 (QPR)	2
Bent, D. A. 2003 (Ipswich T, Charlton Ath)	14	Chalobah, N. N. 2012 (Chelsea)	40
Bent, M. N. 1998 (Crystal Palace)	2	Chamberlain, M. 1983 (Stoke C)	4
Bentley, D. M. 2004 (Arsenal, Blackburn R)	8	Chambers, C. 2015 (Arsenal)	22
Beeston C 1988 (Stoke C)	1	Chaplow, R. D. 2004 (Burnley)	1
Benjamin, T. J. 2001 (Leicester C)	1	Chapman, L. 1981 (Stoke C)	1
Bertrand, R. 2009 (Chelsea)	16	Charles, G. A. 1991 (Nottingham F)	4
Bertschin, K. E. 1977 (Birmingham C)	3	Chettle, S. 1988 (Nottingham F)	12
Bettinelli, M. 2015 (Fulham)	1	**Chilwell, B. J. 2016 (Leicester C)**	**9**
Birtles, G. 1980 (Nottingham F)	2	Chopra, R. M. 2004 (Newcastle U)	1
Blackett, T. N. 2014 (Manchester U)	1	**Choudhury, H. D. 2018 (Leicester C)**	**4**

Clark, L. R. 1992 (Newcastle U)	11
Clarke, P. M. 2003 (Everton)	8
Clarke-Salter, J. L. 2018 (Chelsea)	**5**
Christie, M. N. 2001 (Derby Co)	11
Clegg, M. J. 1998 (Manchester U)	2
Clemence, S. N. 1999 (Tottenham H)	1
Cleverley, T. W. 2010 (Manchester U)	16
Clough, N. H. 1986 (Nottingham F)	15
Clyne, N. E. 2012 (Crystal Palace)	8
Cole, A. 2001 (Arsenal)	4
Cole, A. A. 1992 (Arsenal, Bristol C, Newcastle U)	8
Cole, C. 2003 (Chelsea)	19
Cole, J. J. 2000 (West Ham U)	8
Coney, D. 1985 (Fulham)	4
Connolly, C. A. 2018 (Everton)	**4**
Connor, T. 1987 (Brighton & HA)	1
Cook, L. J. 2018 (Bournemouth)	**10**
Cooke, R. 1986 (Tottenham H)	1
Cooke, T. J. 1996 (Manchester U)	4
Cooper, C. T. 1988 (Middlesbrough)	8
Cork, J. F. P. 2009 (Chelsea)	13
Corrigan, J. T. 1978 (Manchester C)	3
Cort, C. E. R. 1999 (Wimbledon)	12
Cottee, A. R. 1985 (West Ham U)	8
Couzens, A. J. 1995 (Leeds U)	3
Cowans, G. S. 1979 (Aston Villa)	5
Cox, N. J. 1993 (Aston Villa)	6
Cranie, M. J. 2008 (Portsmouth)	16
Cranson, I. 1985 (Ipswich T)	5
Cresswell, R. P. W. 1999 (York C, Sheffield W)	4
Croft, G. 1995 (Grimsby T)	4
Crooks, G. 1980 (Stoke C)	4
Crossley, M. G. 1990 (Nottingham F)	3
Crouch, P. J. 2002 (Portsmouth, Aston Villa)	5
Cundy, J. V. 1991 (Chelsea)	3
Cunningham, L. 1977 (WBA)	6
Curbishley, L. C. 1981 (Birmingham C)	1
Curtis, J. C. K. 1998 (Manchester U)	16
Daniel, P. W. 1977 (Hull C)	7
Dann, S. 2008 (Coventry C)	2
Dasilva, J. R. 2018 (Chelsea)	**5**
Davenport, C. R. P. 2005 (Tottenham H)	8
Davies, A. J. 2004 (Middlesbrough)	1
Davies, C. E. 2006 (WBA)	3
Davies, K. C. 1998 (Southampton, Blackburn R, Southampton)	3
Davies, T. 2018 (Everton)	**5**
Davis, K. G. 1995 (Luton T)	3
Davis, P. 1982 (Arsenal)	11
Davis, S. 2001 (Fulham)	11
Dawson, C. 2012 (WBA)	15
Dawson, M. R. 2003 (Nottingham F, Tottenham H)	13
Day, C. N. 1996 (Tottenham H, Crystal Palace)	6
D'Avray, M. 1984 (Ipswich T)	2
Deehan, J. M. 1977 (Aston Villa)	7
Defoe, J. C. 2001 (West Ham U)	23
Delfouneso, N. 2010 (Aston Villa)	17
Delph, F. 2009 (Leeds U, Aston Villa)	4
Dennis, M. E. 1980 (Birmingham C)	3
Derbyshire, M. A. 2007 (Blackburn R)	14
Dichio, D. S. E. 1996 (QPR)	1
Dickens, A. 1985 (West Ham U)	1
Dicks, J. 1988 (West Ham U)	4
Dier, E. J. E. 2013 (Sporting Lisbon, Tottenham H)	9
Digby, F. 1987 (Swindon T)	5
Dillon, K. P. 1981 (Birmingham C)	1
Dixon, K. M. 1985 (Chelsea)	1
Dobson, A. 1989 (Coventry C)	4
Dodd, J. R. 1991 (Southampton)	8
Donowa, L. 1985 (Norwich C)	3
Dorigo, A. R. 1987 (Aston Villa)	11
Dowell, K. O. 2018 (Everton)	**9**
Downing, S. 2004 (Middlesbrough)	8
Dozzell, J. 1987 (Ipswich T)	9
Draper, M. A. 1991 (Notts Co)	3

Driver, A. 2009 (Hearts)	1
Duberry, M. W. 1997 (Chelsea)	5
Dunn, D. J. I. 1999 (Blackburn R)	20
Duxbury, M. 1981 (Manchester U)	7
Dyer, B. A. 1994 (Crystal Palace)	10
Dyer, K. C. 1998 (Ipswich T, Newcastle U)	11
Dyson, P. I. 1981 (Coventry C)	4
Eadie, D. M. 1994 (Norwich C)	7
Ebanks-Blake, S. 2009 (Wolverhampton W)	1
Ebbrell, J. 1989 (Everton)	14
Edghill, R. A. 1994 (Manchester C)	3
Ehiogu, U. 1992 (Aston Villa)	15
Ejaria, O. D. 2018 (Liverpool)	**1**
Elliott, P. 1985 (Luton T)	3
Elliott, R. J. 1996 (Newcastle U)	2
Elliott, S. W. 1998 (Derby Co)	3
Etherington, N, 2002 (Tottenham H)	3
Euell, J. J. 1998 (Wimbledon)	6
Evans, R. 2003 (Chelsea)	2
Fairclough, C. 1985 (Nottingham F, Tottenham H)	7
Fairclough, D. 1977 (Liverpool)	1
Fashanu, J. 1980 (Norwich C, Nottingham F)	11
Fear, P. 1994 (Wimbledon)	3
Fenton, G. A. 1995 (Aston Villa)	1
Fenwick, T. W. 1981 (Crystal Palace, QPR)	11
Ferdinand, A. J. 2005 (West Ham U)	17
Ferdinand, R. G. 1997 (West Ham U)	5
Fereday, W. 1985 (QPR)	5
Fielding, F. D. 2009 (Blackburn R)	12
Flanagan, J. 2012 (Liverpool)	3
Flitcroft, G. W. 1993 (Manchester C)	10
Flowers, T. D. 1987 (Southampton)	3
Ford, M. 1996 (Leeds U)	2
Forster, N. M. 1995 (Brentford)	4
Forsyth, M. 1988 (Derby Co)	1
Forster-Caskey, J. D. 2014 (Brighton & HA)	14
Foster, S. 1980 (Brighton & HA)	1
Fowler, R. B. 1994 (Liverpool)	8
Fox, D. J. 2008 (Coventry C)	1
Froggatt, S. J. 1993 (Aston Villa)	2
Fry, D. J. 2018 (Middlesbrough)	**8**
Futcher, P. 1977 (Luton T, Manchester C)	11
Gabbiadini, M. 1989 (Sunderland)	2
Gale, A. 1982 (Fulham)	1
Gallen, K. A. 1995 (QPR)	4
Galloway, B. J. 2017 (Everton)	3
Garbutt, L. S. 2014 (Everton)	11
Gardner, A. 2002 (Tottenham H)	1
Gardner, C. 2008 (Aston Villa)	14
Gardner, G. 2012 (Aston Villa)	5
Gascoigne, P. J. 1987 (Newcastle U)	13
Gayle, H. 1984 (Birmingham C)	3
Gernon, T. 1983 (Ipswich T)	1
Gerrard, P. W. 1993 (Oldham Ath)	18
Gerrard, S. G. 2000 (Liverpool)	4
Gibbs, K. J. R. 2009 (Arsenal)	15
Gibbs, N. 1987 (Watford)	5
Gibson, B. J. 2014 (Middlesbrough)	10
Gibson, C. 1982 (Aston Villa)	1
Gilbert, W. A. 1979 (Crystal Palace)	11
Goddard, P. 1981 (West Ham U)	8
Gomez, J. D. 2015 (Liverpool)	**7**
Gordon, D. 1987 (Norwich C)	4
Gordon, D. D. 1994 (Crystal Palace)	13
Gosling, D. 2010 (Everton, Newcastle U)	3
Grant, A. J. 1996 (Everton)	1
Grant, L. A. 2003 (Derby Co)	4
Granville, D. P. 1997 (Chelsea)	3
Gray, A. 1988 (Aston Villa)	2
Gray, D. R. 2016 (Leicester C)	**18**
Grealish, J. 2016 (Aston Villa)	7
Greening, J. 1999 (Manchester U, Middlesbrough)	18
Griffin, A. 1999 (Newcastle U)	3

Maguire, J. H. 2012 (Sheffield U) 1
Maitland-Niles, A. C. 2018 (Arsenal) **4**
Makin, C. 1994 (Oldham Ath) 5
Mancienne, M. I. 2008 (Chelsea) 30
March, S. B. 2015 (Brighton & HA) 3
Marney, D. E. 2005 (Tottenham H) 1
Marriott, A. 1992 (Nottingham F) 1
Marsh, S. T. 1998 (Oxford U) 1
Marshall, A. J. 1995 (Norwich C) 4
Marshall, B. 2012 (Leicester C) 2
Marshall, L. K. 1999 (Norwich C) 1
Martin, L. 1989 (Manchester U) 2
Martyn, A. N. 1988 (Bristol R) 11
Matteo, D. 1994 (Liverpool) 4
Mattock, J. W. 2008 (Leicester C) 5
Matthew, D. 1990 (Chelsea) 9
Mawson, A. R. J. 2017 (Swansea C) 6
May, A. 1986 (Manchester C) 1
Mee, B. 2011 (Manchester C) 2
Merson, P. C. 1989 (Arsenal) 4
Middleton, J. 1977 (Nottingham F, Derby Co) 3
Miller, A. 1988 (Arsenal) 4
Mills, D. J. 1999 (Charlton Ath, Leeds U) 14
Mills, G. R. 1981 (Nottingham F) 2
Milner, J. P. 2004 (Leeds U, Newcastle U, Aston Villa) 46
Mimms, R. 1985 (Rotherham U, Everton) 3
Minto, S. C. 1991 (Charlton Ath) 6
Mitchell, J. 2017 (Derby Co) 1
Moore, I. 1996 (Tranmere R, Nottingham F) 7
Moore, L. 2012 (Leicester C) 10
Moore, L. I. 2006 (Aston Villa) 5
Moran, S. 1982 (Southampton) 2
Morgan, S. 1987 (Leicester C) 2
Morris, J. 1997 (Chelsea) 7
Morrison, R. R. 2013 (West Ham U) 4
Mortimer, P. 1989 (Charlton Ath) 2
Moses, A. P. 1997 (Barnsley) 2
Moses, R. M. 1981 (WBA, Manchester U) 8
Moses, V. 2011 (Wigan Ath) 1
Mountfield, D. 1984 (Everton) 1
Muamba, F. N. 2008 (Birmingham C, Bolton W) 33
Muggleton, C. D. 1990 (Leicester C) 1
Mullins, H. I. 1999 (Crystal Palace) 3
Murphy, D. B. 1998 (Liverpool) 4
Murphy, Jacob K. 2017 (Norwich C) 6
Murray, P. 1997 (QPR) 4
Murray, M. W. 2003 (Wolverhampton W) 5
Mutch, A. 1989 (Wolverhampton W) 1
Mutch, J. J. E. S. 2011 (Birmingham C) 1
Myers. A. 1995 (Chelsea) 4

Naughton, K. 2009 (Sheffield U, Tottenham H) 9
Naylor, L. M. 2000 (Wolverhampton W) 3
Nethercott, S. H. 1994 (Tottenham H) 8
Neville, P. J. 1995 (Manchester U) 7
Newell, M. 1986 (Luton T) 4
Newton, A. L. 2001 (West Ham U) 1
Newton, E. J. I. 1993 (Chelsea) 2
Newton, S. O. 1997 (Charlton Ath) 3
Nicholls, A. 1994 (Plymouth Arg) 1
Nketiah, E. K. 2018 (Arsenal) **4**
Nmecha, L. 2018 (Manchester C) **3**
Noble, M. J. 2007 (West Ham U) 20
Nolan, K. A. J. 2003 (Bolton W) 1
Nugent, D. J. 2006 (Preston NE) 14

Oakes, M. C. 1994 (Aston Villa) 6
Oakes, S. J. 1993 (Luton T) 1
Oakley, M. 1997 (Southampton) 4
O'Brien, A. J. 1999 (Bradford C) 1
O'Connor, J. 1996 (Everton) 3
O'Hara, J. D. 2008 (Tottenham H) 7
Ojo, O. B. (Sheyi) 2018 (Liverpool) **1**
Oldfield, D. 1989 (Luton T) 1
Olney, I. A. 1990 (Aston Villa) 10
O'Neil, G. P. 2005 (Portsmouth) 9

Onomah, J. O. P. 2017 (Tottenham H) **5**
Onuoha, C. 2006 (Manchester C) 21
Ord, R. J. 1991 (Sunderland) 3
Osman, R. C. 1979 (Ipswich T) 7
Owen, G. A. 1977 (Manchester C, WBA) 22
Owen, M. J. 1998 (Liverpool) 1
Oxlade-Chamberlain, A. M. D. 2011 (Southampton, Arsenal) 8

Painter, I. 1986 (Stoke C) 1
Palmer, C. L. 1989 (Sheffield W) 4
Palmer, K. R. 2016 (Chelsea) **6**
Parker, G. 1986 (Hull C, Nottingham F) 6
Parker, P. A. 1985 (Fulham) 8
Parker, S. M. 2001 (Charlton Ath) 12
Parkes, P. B. F. 1979 (QPR) 1
Parkin, S. 1987 (Stoke C) 5
Parlour, R. 1992 (Arsenal) 12
Parnaby, S. 2003 (Middlesbrough) 4
Peach, D. S. 1977 (Southampton) 6
Peake, A. 1982 (Leicester C) 1
Pearce, I. A. 1995 (Blackburn R) 3
Pearce, S. 1987 (Nottingham F) 1
Pearce, T. M. 2018 (Leeds U) **2**
Pennant, J. 2001 (Arsenal) 24
Pickering N. 1983 (Sunderland, Coventry C) 15
Pickford, J. L. 2015 (Sunderland) 14
Platt, D. 1988 (Aston Villa) 3
Plummer, C. S. 1996 (QPR) 5
Pollock, J. 1995 (Middlesbrough) 3
Porter, G. 1987 (Watford) 12
Potter, G. S. 1997 (Southampton) 1
Powell, N. E. 2012 (Manchester U) 2
Pressman, K. 1989 (Sheffield W) 1
Pritchard, A. D. 2014 (Tottenham H) 9
Proctor, M. 1981 (Middlesbrough, Nottingham F) 4
Prutton, D. T. 2001 (Nottingham F, Southampton) 25
Purse, D. J. 1998 (Birmingham C) 2

Quashie, N. F. 1997 (QPR) 4
Quinn, W. R. 1998 (Sheffield U) 2

Ramage, C. D. 1991 (Derby Co) 3
Ramsdale, A. C. 2018 (Bournemouth) **1**
Ranson, R. 1980 (Manchester C) 10
Rashford, M. 2017 (Manchester U) 1
Redknapp, J. F. 1993 (Liverpool) 19
Redmond, N. D. J. 2013 (Birmingham C, Norwich C, Southampton) 38
Redmond, S. 1988 (Manchester C) 14
Reeves, K. P. 1978 (Norwich C, Manchester C) 10
Regis, C. 1979 (WBA) 6
Reid, N. S. 1981 (Manchester C) 6
Reid, P. 1977 (Bolton W) 6
Reo-Coker, N. S. A. 2004 (Wimbledon, West Ham U) 23
Richards, D. I. 1995 (Wolverhampton W) 4
Richards, J. P. 1977 (Wolverhampton W) 2
Richards, M. 2007 (Manchester C) 15
Richards, M. L. 2005 (Ipswich T) 1
Richardson, K. E. 2005 (Manchester U) 12
Rideout, P. 1985 (Aston Villa, Bari) 5
Ridgewell, L. M. 2004 (Aston Villa) 8
Riggott, C. M. 2001 (Derby Co) 8
Ripley, S. E. 1988 (Middlesbrough) 8
Ritchie, A. 1982 (Brighton & HA) 1
Rix, G. 1978 (Arsenal) 7
Roberts, A. J. 1996 (Millwall, Crystal Palace) 5
Roberts, B. J. 1997 (Middlesbrough) 1
Robins, M. G. 1990 (Manchester U) 6
Robinson, J. 2012 (Liverpool, QPR) 10
Robinson, P. P. 1999 (Watford) 3
Robinson, P. W. 2000 (Leeds U) 11
Robson, B. 1979 (WBA) 7
Robson, S. 1984 (Arsenal, West Ham U) 8
Rocastle, D. 1987 (Arsenal) 14
Roche, L. P. 2001 (Manchester U) 1

Rodger, G. 1987 (Coventry C) 4
Rodriguez, J. E. 2011 (Burnley) 1
Rodwell, J. 2009 (Everton) 21
Rogers, A. 1998 (Nottingham F) 3
Rosario, R. 1987 (Norwich C) 4
Rose, D. L. 2009 (Tottenham H) 29
Rose, M. 1997 (Arsenal) 2
Rosenior, L. J. 2005 (Fulham) 7
Routledge, W. 2005 (Crystal Palace, Tottenham H) 12
Rowell, G. 1977 (Sunderland) 1
Rudd, D. T. 2013 (Norwich C) 1
Ruddock, N. 1989 (Southampton) 4
Rufus, R. R. 1996 (Charlton Ath) 6
Ryan, J. 1983 (Oldham Ath) 1
Ryder, S. H. 1995 (Walsall) 3

Samuel, J. 2002 (Aston Villa) 7
Samways, V. 1988 (Tottenham H) 5
Sansom, K. G. 1979 (Crystal Palace) 8
Scimeca, R. 1996 (Aston Villa) 9
Scowcroft, J. B. 1997 (Ipswich T) 5
Seaman, D. A. 1985 (Birmingham C) 10
Sears, F. D. 2010 (West Ham U) 3
Sedgley, S. 1987 (Coventry C, Tottenham H) 11
Sellars, S. 1988 (Blackburn R) 3
Selley, I. 1994 (Arsenal) 3
Serrant, C. 1998 (Oldham Ath) 2
Sessegnon, K. R. (Ryan) 2018 (Fulham) 1
Sharpe, L. S. 1989 (Manchester U) 8
Shaw, L. P. H. 2013 (Southampton, Manchester U) 5
Shaw, G. R. 1981 (Aston Villa) 7
Shawcross, R. J. 2008 (Stoke C) 2
Shearer, A. 1991 (Southampton) 11
Shelton, G. 1985 (Sheffield W) 1
Shelvey, J. 2012 (Liverpool, Swansea C) 13
Sheringham, E. P. 1988 (Millwall) 1
Sheron, M. N. 1992 (Manchester C) 16
Sherwood, T. A. 1990 (Norwich C) 4
Shipperley, N. J. 1994 (Chelsea, Southampton) 7
Sidwell, S. J. 2003 (Reading) 5
Simonsen, S. P. A. 1998 (Tranmere R, Everton) 4
Simpson, P. 1986 (Manchester C) 5
Sims, S. 1977 (Leicester C) 10
Sinclair, S. A. 2011 (Swansea C) 7
Sinclair, T. 1994 (QPR, West Ham U) 5
Sinnott, L. 1985 (Watford) 1
Slade, S. A. 1996 (Tottenham H) 4
Slater, S. I. 1990 (West Ham U) 3
Small, B. 1993 (Aston Villa) 12
Smalling, C. L. 2010 (Fulham, Manchester U) 14
Smith, A. 2000 (Leeds U) 10
Smith, A. J. 2012 (Tottenham H) 11
Smith, D. 1988 (Coventry C) 10
Smith, M. 1981 (Sheffield W) 5
Smith, M. 1995 (Sunderland) 1
Smith, T. W. 2001 (Watford) 1
Snodin, I. 1985 (Doncaster R) 4
Soares, T. J. 2006 (Crystal Palace) 4
Solanke, D. A. 2015 (Chelsea, Liverpool) 9
Sordell, M. A. 2012 (Watford, Bolton W) 14
Spence, J. 2011 (West Ham U) 1
Stanislaus, F. J. 2010 (West Ham U) 2
Statham, B. 1988 (Tottenham H) 3
Statham, D. J. 1978 (WBA) 6
Stead, J. G. 2004 (Blackburn R, Sunderland) 11
Stearman, R. J. 2009 (Wolverhampton W) 4
Steele, J. 2011 (Middlesbrough) 7
Stein, B. 1984 (Luton T) 3
Stephens, J. 2015 (Southampton) 8
Sterland, M. 1984 (Sheffield W) 7
Sterling, R. S. 2012 (Liverpool) 8
Steven, T. M. 1985 (Everton) 2
Stevens, G. A. 1983 (Brighton & HA, Tottenham H) 8
Stewart, J. 2003 (Leicester C) 1
Stewart, P. 1988 (Manchester C) 1
Stockdale, R. K. 2001 (Middlesbrough) 1

Stones, J. 2013 (Everton) 12
Stuart, G. C. 1990 (Chelsea) 5
Stuart, J. C. 1996 (Charlton Ath) 4
Sturridge, D. A. 2010 (Chelsea) 15
Suckling, P. 1986 (Coventry C, Manchester C,
    Crystal Palace) 10
Summerbee, N. J. 1993 (Swindon T) 3
Sunderland, A. 1977 (Wolverhampton W) 1
Surman, A. R. E. 2008 (Southampton) 4
Sutch, D. 1992 (Norwich C) 4
Sutton, C. R. 1993 (Norwich C) 13
Swift, J. D. 2015 (Chelsea, Reading) 13
Swindlehurst, D. 1977 (Crystal Palace) 1

Talbot, B. 1977 (Ipswich T) 1
Targett, M. R. 2015 (Southampton) 12
Taylor, A. D. 2007 (Middlesbrough) 13
Taylor, M. 2001 (Blackburn R) 1
Taylor, M. S. 2003 (Portsmouth) 3
Taylor, R. A. 2006 (Wigan Ath) 4
Taylor, S. J. 2002 (Arsenal) 3
Taylor, S. V. 2004 (Newcastle U) 29
Terry, J. G. 2001 (Chelsea) 9
Thatcher, B. D. 1996 (Millwall, Wimbledon) 4
Thelwell, A. A. 2001 (Tottenham H) 1
Thirlwell, P. 2001 (Sunderland) 1
Thomas, D. 1981 (Coventry C, Tottenham H) 7
Thomas, J. W. 2006 (Charlton Ath) 2
Thomas, M. 1986 (Luton T) 3
Thomas, M. L. 1988 (Arsenal) 12
Thomas, R. E. 1990 (Watford) 1
Thompson, A. 1995 (Bolton W) 2
Thompson, D. A. 1997 (Liverpool) 7
Thompson, G. L. 1981 (Coventry C) 6
Thorn, A. 1988 (Wimbledon) 5
Thornley, B. L. 1996 (Manchester U) 3
Thorpe, T. J. 2013 (Manchester U) 1
Tiler, C. 1990 (Barnsley, Nottingham F) 13
Tomkins, J. O. C. 2009 (West Ham U) 10
Tomori, O. O. (Fikayo) 2018 (Chelsea) 7
Tonge, M. W. E. 2004 (Sheffield U) 2
Townsend, A. D. 2012 (Tottenham H) 3
Trippier, K. J. 2011 (Manchester C) 2
Tuanzebe, A. 2018 (Manchester U) 1

Unsworth, D. G. 1995 (Everton) 6
Upson, M. J. 1999 (Arsenal) 11

Vassell, D. 1999 (Aston Villa) 11
Vaughan, J. O. 2007 (Everton) 4
Venison, B. 1983 (Sunderland) 1
Vernazza, P. A. P. 2001 (Arsenal, Watford) 2
Vieira, R. A. 2018 (Leeds U) 3
Vinnicombe, C. 1991 (Rangers) 12

Waddle, C. R. 1985 (Newcastle U) 1
Waghorn, M. T. 2012 (Leicester C) 5
Walcott, T. J. 2007 (Arsenal) 21
Wallace, D. L. 1983 (Southampton) 14
Wallace, Ray 1989 (Southampton) 4
Wallace, Rod 1989 (Southampton) 11
Walker, D. 1985 (Nottingham F) 7
Walker, I. M. 1991 (Tottenham H) 9
Walker, K. 2010 (Tottenham H) 7
Walker-Peters, K. L. 2018 (Tottenham H) 6
Walsh, G. 1988 (Manchester U) 2
Walsh, P. A. 1983 (Luton T) 4
Walters, M. 1984 (Aston Villa) 9
Walton, C. T. 2017 (Brighton & HA) 1
Ward, P. 1978 (Brighton & HA) 2
Ward-Prowse, J. M. E. 2013 (Southampton) 31
Warhurst, P. 1991 (Oldham Ath, Sheffield W) 8
Watmore, D. I. 2015 (Sunderland) 13
Watson, B. 2007 (Crystal Palace) 1
Watson, D. 1984 (Norwich C) 7
Watson, D. N. 1994 (Barnsley) 5

Watson, G. 1991 (Sheffield W) — 2
Watson, S. C. 1993 (Newcastle U) — 12
Weaver, N. J. 2000 (Manchester C) — 10
Webb, N. J. 1985 (Portsmouth, Nottingham F) — 3
Welbeck, D. 2009 (Manchester U) — 14
Welsh, J. J. 2004 (Liverpool, Hull C) — 8
Wheater, D. J. 2008 (Middlesbrough) — 11
Whelan, P. J. 1993 (Ipswich T) — 3
Whelan, N. 1995 (Leeds U) — 2
Whittingham, P. 2004 (Aston Villa, Cardiff C) — 17
White, D. 1988 (Manchester C) — 6
Whyte, C. 1982 (Arsenal) — 4
Wickham, C. N. R. 2011 (Ipswich T, Sunderland) — 17
Wicks, S. 1982 (QPR) — 1
Wilkins, R. C. 1977 (Chelsea) — 1
Wilkinson, P. 1985 (Grimsby T, Everton) — 4
Williams, D. 1998 (Sunderland) — 2
Williams, P. 1989 (Charlton Ath) — 4
Williams, P. D. 1991 (Derby Co) — 6
Williams, S. C. 1977 (Southampton) — 14
Wilshere, J. A. 2010 (Arsenal) — 7
Wilson, C. E. G. 2014 (Bournemouth) — 1
Wilson, J. A. 2015 (Manchester U) — 1
Wilson, M. A. 2001 (Manchester U, Middlesbrough) — 6

Winks, H. 2017 (Tottenham H) — 2
Winterburn, N. 1986 (Wimbledon) — 1
Wisdom, A. 2012 (Liverpool) — 10
Wise, D. F. 1988 (Wimbledon) — 1
Woodcock, A. S. 1978 (Nottingham F) — 2
Woodgate, J. S. 2000 (Leeds U) — 1
Woodhouse, C. 1999 (Sheffield U) — 4
Woodman, F. J. 2017 (Newcastle U) — **6**
Woodrow, C. 2014 (Fulham) — 9
Woods, C. C. E. 1979 (Nottingham F, QPR, Norwich C) — 6
Worrall, J. A. 2018 (Nottingham F) — **3**
Wright, A. G. 1993 (Blackburn R) — 2
Wright, M. 1983 (Southampton) — 4
Wright, R. I. 1997 (Ipswich T) — 15
Wright, S. J. 2001 (Liverpool) — 10
Wright, W. 1979 (Everton) — 6
Wright-Phillips, S. C. 2002 (Manchester C) — 6

Yates, D. 1989 (Notts Co) — 5
Young, A. S. 2007 (Watford, Aston Villa) — 10
Young, L. P. 1999 (Tottenham H, Charlton Ath) — 12

Zaha, D. W. A. 2012 (Crystal Palace, Manchester U) — 13
Zamora, R. L. 2002 (Brighton & HA) — 6

NORTHERN IRELAND

Allen, C. 2009 (Lisburn Distillery) — 1
Armstrong, D. T. 2007 (Hearts) — 1

Bagnall, L. 2011 (Sunderland) — 1
Bailie, N. 1990 (Linfield) — 2
Baird, C. P. 2002 (Southampton) — 6
Ball, D. 2013 (Tottenham H) — 2
Ball, M. 2011 (Norwich C) — 5
Beatty, S. 1990 (Chelsea, Linfield) — 2
Black, J. 2003 (Tottenham H) — 1
Black, K. T. 1990 (Luton T) — 1
Black, R. Z. 2002 (Morecambe) — 1
Blackledge, G. 1978 (Portadown) — 1
Blake, R. G. 2011 (Brentford) — 2
Blayney, A. 2003 (Southampton) — 4
Boyce, L. 2010 (Cliftonville, Werder Bremen) — 8
Boyle, W. S. 1998 (Leeds U) — 7
Braniff, K. R. 2002 (Millwall) — 11
Breeze, J. 2011 (Wigan Ath) — 4
Brennan, C. 2013 (Kilmarnock) — 13
Brobbel, R. 2013 (Middlesbrough) — 9
Brotherston, N. 1978 (Blackburn R) — 1
Browne, G. 2003 (Manchester C) — 5
Brunt, C. 2005 (Sheffield W) — 2
Bryan, M. A. 2010 (Watford) — 4
Buchanan, D. T. H. 2006 (Bury) — 15
Buchanan, W. B. 2002 (Bolton W, Lisburn Distillery) — 5
Burns, A. 2014 (Linfield) — 1
Burns, B. 2018 (Glenavon) — **1**
Burns, L. 1998 (Port Vale) — 13

Callaghan, A. 2006 (Limavady U, Ballymena U, Derry C) — 15
Campbell, S. 2003 (Ballymena U) — 1
Camps, C. 2015 (Rochdale) — 1
Capaldi, A. C. 2002 (Birmingham C, Plymouth Arg) — 14
Carlisle, W. T. 2000 (Crystal Palace) — 9
Carroll, R. E. 1998 (Wigan Ath) — 11
Carson, J. G. 2011 (Ipswich T, York C) — 12
Carson, S. 2000 (Rangers, Dundee U) — 2
Carson, T. 2007 (Sunderland) — 15
Carvill, M. D. 2008 (Wrexham, Linfield) — 8
Casement, C. 2007 (Ipswich T, Dundee) — 18
Cathcart, C. 2007 (Manchester U) — 15
Catney, R. 2007 (Lisburn Distillery) — 1
Chapman, A. 2008 (Sheffield U, Oxford U) — 7
Charles, D. 2017 (Fleetwood T) — 3
Clarke, L. 2003 (Peterborough U) — 4

Clarke, R. 2006 (Newry C) — 7
Clarke, R. D. J. 1999 (Portadown) — 5
Clingan, S. G. 2003 (Wolverhampton W, Nottingham F) — 11
Close, B. 2002 (Middlesbrough) — 10
Clucas, M. S. 2011 (Preston NE, Bristol R) — 11
Clyde, M. G. 2002 (Wolverhampton W) — 5
Colligan, L. 2009 (Ballymena U) — 1
Conlan, L. 2013 (Burnley, Morecambe) — 11
Connell, T. E. 1978 (Coleraine) — 1
Cooper, J. 2015 (Glenavon) — 5
Coote, A. 1998 (Norwich C) — 12
Convery, J. 2000 (Celtic) — 4

Dallas, S. 2012 (Crusaders, Brentford) — 2
Davey, H. 2004 (UCD) — 3
Davis, S. 2004 (Aston Villa) — 3
Devine, D. 1994 (Omagh T) — 1
Devine, D. G. 2011 (Preston NE) — 2
Devine, J. 1990 (Glentoran) — 1
Devlin, C. 2011 (Manchester U, unattached, Cliftonville) — 11
Dickson, H. 2002 (Wigan Ath) — 1
Doherty, B. 2018 (Derry C) — **4**
Doherty, J. E. 2014 (Watford, Leyton O, Crawley T) — **6**
Doherty, M. 2007 (Hearts) — 2
Dolan, J. 2000 (Millwall) — 6
Donaghy, M. M. 1978 (Larne) — 1
Donnelly, L. F. P. 2012 (Fulham, Hartlepool U) — **20**
Donnelly, M. 2007 (Sheffield U, Crusaders) — 5
Donnelly, R. 2013 (Swansea C) — 1
Dowie, I. 1990 (Luton T) — 1
Drummond, W. 2011 (Rangers) — 2
Dudgeon, J. P. 2010 (Manchester U) — 4
Duff, S. 2003 (Cheltenham T) — 1
Duffy, M. 2014 (Derry C, Celtic) — 9
Duffy, S. P. M. 2010 (Everton) — 3
Dummigan, C. 2014 (Burnley, Oldham Ath) — **17**
Dunwoody, J. 2017 (Stoke C) — 1

Elliott, S. 1999 (Glentoran) — 3
Ervin, J. 2005 (Linfield) — 2
Evans, C. J. 2009 (Manchester U) — 10
Evans, J. 2006 (Manchester U) — 3

Feeney, L. 1998 (Linfield, Rangers) — 8
Feeney, W. 2002 (Bournemouth) — 8
Ferguson, M. 2000 (Glentoran) — 2
Ferguson, S. 2009 (Newcastle U) — 11
Fitzgerald, D. 1998 (Rangers) — 4

Flanagan, T. M. 2012 (Milton Keynes D) 1
Flynn, J. J. 2009 (Blackburn R, Ross Co) 11
Fordyce, D. T. 2007 (Portsmouth, Glentoran) 12
Friars, E. C. 2005 (Notts Co) 7
Friars, S. M. 1998 (Liverpool, Ipswich T) 21

Garrett, R. 2007 (Stoke C, Linfield) 14
Gault, M. 2005 (Linfield) 2
Gibb, S. 2009 (Falkirk, Drogheda U) 2
Gilfillan, B. J. 2005 (Gretna, Peterhead) 9
Gillespie, K. R. 1994 (Manchester U) 1
Glendinning, M. 1994 (Bangor) 1
Glendinning, R. 2012 (Linfield) 3
Gordon, S. 2017 (Motherwell) **2**
Gorman, D. A. 2015 (Stevenage) **10**
Gorman, R. J. 2012 (Wolverhampton W, Leyton Orient) 4
Graham, G. L. 1999 (Crystal Palace) 5
Graham, R. S. 1999 (QPR) 15
Gray, J. P. 2012 (Accrington S) 11
Gray, P. 1990 (Luton T) 1
Griffin, D. J. 1998 (St Johnstone) 10
Grigg, W. D. 2011 (Walsall) 10

Hall, B. 2018 (Notts Co) **3**
Hamilton, G. 2000 (Blackburn R, Portadown) 12
Hamilton, W. R. 1978 (Linfield) 1
Hanley, N. 2011 (Linfield) 1
Harkin, M. P. 2000 (Wycombe W) 9
Harney, J. J. 2014 (West Ham U) 1
Harvey, J. 1978 (Arsenal) 1
Hawe, S. 2001 (Blackburn R) 2
Hayes, T. 1978 (Luton T) 1
Hazley, M. 2007 (Stoke C) 3
Healy, D. J. 1999 (Manchester U) 8
Hegarty, C. 2011 (Rangers) 7
Herron, C. J. 2003 (QPR) 2
Higgins, R. 2006 (Derry C) 1
Hodson, L. J. S. 2010 (Watford) 10
Holmes, S. 2000 (Manchester C, Wrexham) 13
Howland, D. 2007 (Birmingham C) 4
Hughes, J. 2006 (Lincoln C) 7
Hughes, M. A. 2003 (Tottenham H, Oldham Ath) 12
Hughes, M. E. 1990 (Manchester U) 1
Hunter, M. 2002 (Glentoran) 1

Ingham, M. G. 2001 (Sunderland) 4

Jarvis, D. 2010 (Aberdeen) 2
Johns, C. 2014 (Southampton) 1
Johnson, D. M. 1998 (Blackburn R) 11
Johnson, R. A. 2015 (Stevenage) **11**
Johnston, B. 1978 (Cliftonville) 1
Julian, A. A. 2005 (Brentford) 1

Kane, A. M. 2008 (Blackburn R) 5
Kane, M. 2012 (Glentoran) 2
Kee, B. R. 2010 (Leicester C, Torquay U, Burton Alb) 10
Kee, P. V. 1990 (Oxford U) 1
Kelly, D. 2000 (Derry C) 11
Kelly, N. 1990 (Oldham Ath) 1
Kennedy, B. J. 2017 (Stevenage) **8**
Kennedy, M. C. P. 2015 (Charlton Ath) 1
Kirk, A. R. 1999 (Hearts) 9
Knowles, J. 2012 (Blackburn R) 2

Lafferty, D. 2009 (Celtic) 6
Lafferty, K. 2006 (Burnley) 2
Lavery, C. 2011 (Ipswich T, Sheffield W) 7
Lavery, S. 2017 (Everton) **5**
Lawrie, J. 2009 (Port Vale, AFC Telford U) 9
Lennon, N. F. 1990 (Manchester C, Crewe Alex) 2
Lester, C. 2013 (Bolton W) 1
Lewis, J. 2017 (Norwich C) 1
Lindsay, K. 2006 (Larne) 1
Little, A. 2009 (Rangers) 6
Lowry, P. 2009 (Institute, Linfield) 6

Lund, M. 2011 (Stoke C) 6
Lyttle, G. 1998 (Celtic, Peterborough U) 8

McAlinden, L. J. 2012 (Wolverhampton W) 3
McAllister, M. 2007 (Dungannon Swifts) 4
McArdle, R. A. 2006 (Sheffield W, Rochdale) 19
McAreavey, P. 2000 (Swindon T) 7
McBride, J. 1994 (Glentoran) 1
McCaffrey, D. 2006 (Hibernian) 8
McCallion, E. 1998 (Coleraine) 1
McCann, G. S. 2000 (West Ham U) 11
McCann, P. 2003 (Portadown) 1
McCann, R. 2002 (Rangers, Linfield) 2
McCartan, S. V. 2013 (Accrington S) 9
McCartney, G. 2001 (Sunderland) 5
McCashin, S. 2011 (Jerez Industrial, unattached) 2
McChrystal, M. 2005 (Derry C) 9
McClean, J. 2010 (Derry C) 3
McClure, M. 2012 (Wycombe W) 1
McCourt, P. J. 2002 (Rochdale, Derry C) 8
McCoy, R. K. 1990 (Coleraine) 1
McCreery, D. 1978 (Manchester U) 1
McCullough, L. 2013 (Doncaster R) 8
McDaid, R. 2015 (Leeds U) 5
McDermott, C. 2017 (Derry C) **4**
McDonagh, J. D. C. 2015 (Sheffield U) **6**
McEleney, S. 2012 (Derry C) 2
McElroy, P. 2013 (Hull C) 1
McEvilly, L. R. 2003 (Rochdale) 9
McFlynn, T. M. 2000 (QPR, Woking, Margate) 19
McGeehan, C. 2013 (Norwich C) 3
McGibbon, P. C. G. 1994 (Manchester U) 1
McGivern, R. 2010 (Manchester C) 6
McGlinchey, B. 1998 (Manchester C, Port Vale, Gillingham) 14
McGonigle, C. J. 2017 (Coleraine) **3**
McGovern, M. 2005 (Celtic) 10
McGowan, M. V. 2006 (Clyde) 2
McGurk, A. 2010 (Aston Villa) 1
McIlroy, T. 1994 (Linfield) 1
McKay, W. 2009 (Leicester C, Northampton T) 7
McKenna, K. 2007 (Tottenham H) 6
McKeown, R. 2012 (Kilmarnock) 12
McKnight, D. 2015 (Shrewsbury T, Stalybridge Celtic) 5
McKnight, P. 1998 (Rangers) 3
McLaughlin, C. G. 2010 (Preston NE, Fleetwood T) 7
McLaughlin, P. 2010 (Newcastle U, York C) 10
McLaughlin, R. 2012 (Liverpool, Oldham Ath) 6
McLean, B. S. 2006 (Rangers) 1
McLean, J. 2009 (Derry C) 4
McLellan, M. 2012 (Preston NE) 1
McMahon, G. J. 2002 (Tottenham H) 1
McMenamin, L. A. 2009 (Sheffield W) 4
McNair, P. J. C. 2014 (Manchester U) 2
McNally, P. 2013 (Celtic) 1
McQuilken, J. 2009 (Tescoma Zlin) 1
McQuoid, J. J. B. 2009 (Bournemouth) 8
McVeigh, A. 2002 (Ayr U) 1
McVeigh, P. M. 1998 (Tottenham H) 11
McVey, K. 2006 (Coleraine) 8
Magee, J. 1994 (Bangor) 1
Magee, J. 2009 (Lisburn Distillery) 1
Magennis, J. B. D. 2010 (Cardiff C, Aberdeen) 16
Magilton, J. 1990 (Liverpool) 1
Magnay, C. 2010 (Chelsea) 1
Maloney, L. 2015 (Middlesbrough) 6
Marshall, R. 2017 (Glenavon) 1
Matthews, N. P. 1990 (Blackpool) 1
Meenan, D. 2007 (Finn Harps, Monaghan U) 3
Melaugh, G. M. 2002 (Aston Villa, Glentoran) 11
Millar, K. S. 2011 (Oldham Ath, Linfield) 11
Millar, W. P. 1990 (Port Vale) 1
Miskelly, D. T. 2000 (Oldham Ath) 10
Mitchell, A. 2012 (Rangers) 3
Mitchell, C. 2017 (Burnley) **10**
Moreland, V. 1978 (Glentoran) 1

Morgan, D. 2012 (Nottingham F) 4
Morgan, M. P. T. 1999 (Preston NE) 1
Morris, E. J. 2002 (WBA, Glentoran) 8
Morrison, O. 2001 (Sheffield W, Sheffield U) 7
Morrow, A. 2001 (Northampton T) 1
Morrow, S. 2005 (Hibernian) 4
Mulgrew, J. 2007 (Linfield) 10
Mulryne, P. P. 1999 (Manchester U, Norwich C) 5
Murray, W. 1978 (Linfield) 1
Murtagh, C. 2005 (Hearts) 1

Nicholl, J. M. 1978 (Manchester U) 1
Nixon, C. 2000 (Glentoran) 1
Nolan, L. J. 2014 (Crewe Alex, Southport) 4
Norwood, O. J. 2010 (Manchester U) 11

O'Connor, M. J. 2008 (Crewe Alex) 3
O'Hara, G. 1994 (Leeds U) 1
O'Kane, E. 2009 (Everton, Torquay U) 4
O'Neill, J. P. 1978 (Leicester C) 1
O'Neill, M. A. M. 1994 (Hibernian) 1
O'Neill, S. 2009 (Ballymena U) 4
Owens, C. 2018 (QPR) **2**

Parkhouse, D. 2017 (Sheffield U) **5**
Paterson, M. A. 2007 (Stoke C) 2
Patterson, D. J. 1994 (Crystal Palace) 1
Paul, C. D. 2017 (QPR) **3**
Peacock-Farrell, B. 2018 (Leeds U) **1**

Quigley, C. 2017 (Dundee) 2
Quinn, S. J. 1994 (Blackpool) 1

Ramsey, C. 2011 (Portadown) 3
Ramsey, K. 2006 (Institute) 1
Reid, J. T. 2013 (Exeter C) 2
Robinson, S. 1994 (Tottenham H) 1
Rooney, L. J. 2017 (Plymouth Arg) 1

Scullion, D. 2006 (Dungannon Swifts) 8
Sendles-White J. 2013 (QPR, Hamilton A) 12

Sharpe, R. 2013 (Derby Co, Notts Co) 6
Shiels, D. 2005 (Hibernian) 6
Shields, S. P. 2013 (Dagenham & R) 2
Shroot, R. 2009 (Harrow B, Birmingham C) 4
Simms, G. 2001 (Hartlepool U) 14
Singleton, J. 2015 (Glenavon) 2
Skates, G. 2000 (Blackburn R) 4
Sloan, T. 1978 (Ballymena U) 1
Smylie, D. 2006 (Newcastle U, Livingston) 6
Smyth, P. 2017 (Linfield, QPR) **9**
Stewart, J. 2015 (Swindon T) 2
Stewart, S. 2009 (Aberdeen) 1
Stewart, T. 2006 (Wolverhampton W, Linfield) 19
Sykes, M. 2017 (Glenavon) **7**

Taylor, J. 2007 (Hearts, Glentoran) 10
Taylor, M. S. 1998 (Fulham) 1
Teggart, N. 2005 (Sunderland) 2
Tempest, G. 2013 (Notts Co) 6
Thompson, A. L. 2011 (Watford) 11
Thompson, J. 2017 (Rangers) **10**
Thompson, P. 2006 (Linfield) 4
Toner, C. 2000 (Tottenham H, Leyton Orient) 17
Tuffey, J. 2007 (Partick Thistle) 13
Turner, C. 2007 (Sligo R, Bohemians) 12

Ward, J. J. 2006 (Aston Villa, Chesterfield) 7
Ward, M. 2006 (Dungannon Swifts) 1
Ward, S. 2005 (Glentoran) 10
Waterman, D. G. 1998 (Portsmouth) 14
Waterworth, A. 2008 (Lisburn Distillery, Hamilton A) 7
Webb, S. M. 2004 (Ross Co, St Johnstone, Ross Co) 6
Weir, R. J. 2009 (Sunderland) 8
Wells, D. P. 1999 (Barry T) 1
Whitley, J. 1998 (Manchester C) 17
Whyte, G. 2013 (Crusaders) **7**
Willis, P. 2006 (Liverpool) 1
Winchester, C. 2011 (Oldham Ath) 13
Winchester, J. 2013 (Kilmarnock) 1

SCOTLAND

Adam, C. G. 2006 (Rangers) 5
Adam, G. 2011 (Rangers) 6
Adams, J. 2007 (Kilmarnock) 1
Aitken, R. 1977 (Celtic) 16
Albiston, A. 1977 (Manchester U) 5
Alexander, N. 1997 (Stenhousemuir, Livingston) 10
Allan, S. 2012 (WBA) 10
Anderson, I. 1997 (Dundee, Toulouse) 15
Anderson, R. 1997 (Aberdeen) 15
Andrews, M. 2011 (East Stirlingshire) 1
Anthony, M. 1997 (Celtic) 3
Archdeacon, O. 1987 (Celtic) 1
Archer, J. G. 2012 (Tottenham H) 14
Archibald, A. 1998 (Partick Thistle) 5
Archibald, S. 1980 (Aberdeen, Tottenham H) 5
Archibald, T. V. 2018 (Brentford) **1**
Arfield, S. 2008 (Falkirk, Huddersfield T) 17
Armstrong, S. 2011 (Dundee U) 20

Bagen, D. 1997 (Kilmarnock) 4
Bain, K. 1993 (Dundee) 4
Baker, M. 1993 (St Mirren) 10
Baltacha, S. S. 2000 (St Mirren) 3
Bannan, B. 2009 (Aston Villa) 10
Bannigan, S. 2013 (Partick Thistle) 3
Bannon, E. J. 1979 (Hearts, Chelsea, Dundee U) 7
Barclay, J. 2011 (Falkirk) 1
Beattie, C. 2004 (Celtic) 7
Beattie, J. 1992 (St Mirren) 4
Beaumont, D. 1985 (Dundee U) 1
Bell, D. 1981 (Aberdeen) 2
Bernard, P. R. J. 1992 (Oldham Ath) 15

Berra, C. 2005 (Hearts) 6
Bett, J. 1981 (Rangers) 7
Black, E. 1983 (Aberdeen) 8
Blair, A. 1980 (Coventry C, Aston Villa) 5
Bollan, G. 1992 (Dundee U, Rangers) 17
Bonar, P. 1997 (Raith R) 4
Booth, C. 2011 (Hibernian) 4
Booth, S. 1991 (Aberdeen) 14
Bowes, M. J. 1992 (Dunfermline Ath) 1
Bowman, D. 1985 (Hearts) 1
Boyack, S. 1997 (Rangers) 1
Boyd, K. 2003 (Kilmarnock) 8
Boyd, T. 1987 (Motherwell) 5
Brazil, A. 1978 (Hibernian) 1
Brazil, A. 1979 (Ipswich T) 8
Brebner, G. I. 1997 (Manchester U, Reading, Hibernian) 18
Brighton, T. 2005 (Rangers, Clyde) 7
Broadfoot, K. 2005 (St Mirren) 5
Brophy, E. 2017 (Hamilton A, Kilmarnock) **2**
Brough, J. 1981 (Hearts) 1
Brown, A. H. 2004 (Hibernian) 1
Brown, S. 2005 (Hibernian) 10
Browne, P. 1997 (Raith R) 1
Bryson, C. 2006 (Clyde) 1
Buchan, J. 1997 (Aberdeen) 13
Burchill, M. J. 1998 (Celtic) 15
Burke, A. 1997 (Kilmarnock) 4
Burke, C. 2004 (Rangers) 3
Burke, O. J. 2018 (WBA) **9**
Burley, C. W. 1992 (Chelsea) 7
Burley, G. E. 1977 (Ipswich T) 5

Burns, H. 1985 (Rangers)	2
Burns, T. 1977 (Celtic)	5
Burt, L. 2017 (Rangers)	**5**
Cadden, C. 2017 (Motherwell)	**8**
Caddis, P. 2008 (Celtic, Dundee U, Celtic, Swindon T)	13
Cairney, T. 2011 (Hull C)	6
Caldwell, G. 2000 (Newcastle U)	19
Caldwell, S. 2001 (Newcastle U)	4
Cameron, G. 2008 (Dundee U)	3
Cameron, K. M. 2017 (Newcastle U)	3
Campbell, A. 2018 (Motherwell)	**9**
Campbell, R. 2008 (Hibernian)	6
Campbell, S. 1989 (Dundee)	3
Campbell, S. P. 1998 (Leicester C)	15
Canero, P. 2000 (Kilmarnock)	17
Cardwell, H. 2014 (Reading)	1
Carey, L. A. 1998 (Bristol C)	1
Carrick, D. 2012 (Hearts)	1
Casey, J. 1978 (Celtic)	1
Chalmers, J. 2014 (Celtic, Motherwell)	2
Christie, M. 1992 (Dundee)	3
Christie, R. 2014 (Inverness CT, Celtic)	9
Clark, R. B. 1977 (Aberdeen)	3
Clarke, S. 1984 (St Mirren)	8
Clarkson, D. 2004 (Motherwell)	13
Cleland, A. 1990 (Dundee U)	11
Cole, D. 2011 (Rangers)	2
Collins, J. 1988 (Hibernian)	8
Collins, N. 2005 (Sunderland)	7
Connolly, P. 1991 (Dundee U)	3
Connor, R. 1981 (Ayr U)	2
Conroy, R. 2007 (Celtic)	4
Considine, A. 2007 (Aberdeen)	5
Cooper, D. 1977 (Clydebank, Rangers)	6
Cooper, N. 1982 (Aberdeen)	13
Coutts, P. A. 2009 (Peterborough U, Preston NE)	7
Crabbe, S. 1990 (Hearts)	2
Craig, M. 1998 (Aberdeen)	2
Craig, T. 1977 (Newcastle U)	1
Crainey, S. D. 2000 (Celtic)	7
Crainie, D. 1983 (Celtic)	1
Crawford, S. 1994 (Raith R)	19
Creaney, G. 1991 (Celtic)	11
Cummings, J. 2015 (Hibernian)	8
Cummings, W. 2000 (Chelsea)	8
Cuthbert, S. 2007 (Celtic, St Mirren)	13
Dailly, C. 1991 (Dundee U)	34
Dalglish, P. 1999 (Newcastle U, Norwich C)	6
Dargo, C. 1998 (Raith R)	10
Davidson, C. I. 1997 (St Johnstone)	2
Davidson, H. N. 2000 (Dundee U)	3
Davidson, M. 2011 (St Johnstone)	1
Dawson, A. 1979 (Rangers)	8
Deas, P. A. 1992 (St Johnstone)	2
Dempster, J. 2004 (Rushden & D)	1
Dennis, S. 1992 (Raith R)	1
Diamond, A. 2004 (Aberdeen)	12
Dickov, P. 1992 (Arsenal)	4
Dixon, P. 2008 (Dundee)	2
Docherty, G. 2017 (Hamilton A)	**4**
Dodds, D. 1978 (Dundee U)	1
Dods, D. 1997 (Hibernian)	5
Doig, C. R. 2000 (Nottingham F)	13
Donald, G. S. 1992 (Hibernian)	3
Donnelly, S. 1994 (Celtic)	11
Doohan, R. 2018 (Celtic)	**3**
Dorrans, G. 2007 (Livingston)	6
Dow, A. 1993 (Dundee, Chelsea)	3
Dowie, A. J. 2003 (Rangers, Partick Thistle)	14
Duff, J. 2009 (Inverness CT)	1
Duff, S. 2003 (Dundee U)	9
Duffie, K. 2011 (Falkirk)	6
Duffy, D. A. 2005 (Falkirk, Hull C)	8

Duffy, J. 1987 (Dundee)	1
Durie, G. S. 1987 (Chelsea)	4
Durrant, I. 1987 (Rangers)	4
Doyle, J. 1981 (Partick Thistle)	2
Easton, B. 2009 (Hamilton A)	3
Easton, C. 1997 (Dundee U)	21
Edwards, M. 2012 (Rochdale)	1
Elliot, B. 1998 (Celtic)	2
Elliot, C. 2006 (Hearts)	9
Esson, R. 2000 (Aberdeen)	7
Fagan, S. M. 2005 (Motherwell)	1
Ferguson, B. 1997 (Rangers)	12
Ferguson, D. 1987 (Rangers)	5
Ferguson, D. 1992 (Dundee U)	7
Ferguson, D. 1992 (Manchester U)	5
Ferguson, I. 1983 (Dundee)	4
Ferguson, I. 1987 (Clyde, St Mirren, Rangers)	6
Ferguson, R. 1977 (Hamilton A)	1
Feruz, I. 2012 (Chelsea)	4
Findlay, S. 2012 (Celtic)	13
Findlay, W. 1991 (Hibernian)	5
Fitzpatrick, A. 1977 (St Mirren)	5
Fitzpatrick, M. 2007 (Motherwell)	4
Flannigan, C. 1993 (Clydebank)	1
Fleck, J. 2009 (Rangers)	4
Fleck, R. 1987 (Rangers, Norwich C)	6
Fleming, G. 2008 (Gretna)	1
Fletcher, D. B. 2003 (Manchester U)	2
Fletcher, S. 2007 (Hibernian)	7
Forrest, A. 2017 (Ayr U)	1
Forrest, J. 2011 (Celtic)	4
Foster, R. M. 2005 (Aberdeen)	5
Fotheringham, M. M. 2004 (Dundee)	3
Fowler, J. 2002 (Kilmarnock)	3
Foy, R. A. 2004 (Liverpool)	5
Fraser, M. 2012 (Celtic)	5
Fraser, R. 2013 (Aberdeen, Bournemouth)	10
Fraser, S. T. 2000 (Luton T)	4
Freedman, D. A. 1995 (Barnet, Crystal Palace)	8
Fridge, L. 1989 (St Mirren)	2
Fullarton, J. 1993 (St Mirren)	17
Fulton, J. 2014 (Swansea C)	2
Fulton, R. 2017 (Liverpool)	**10**
Fulton, M. 1980 (St Mirren)	5
Fulton, S. 1991 (Celtic)	7
Fyvie, F. 2012 (Wigan Ath)	8
Gallacher, K. W. 1987 (Dundee U)	7
Gallacher, P. 1999 (Dundee U)	7
Gallacher, S. 2009 (Rangers)	2
Gallagher, P. 2003 (Blackburn R)	11
Galloway, M. 1989 (Hearts, Celtic)	2
Gardiner, J. 1993 (Hibernian)	1
Gauld, R. 2013 (Dundee U, Sporting Lisbon)	11
Geddes, R. 1982 (Dundee)	5
Gemmill, S. 1992 (Nottingham F)	4
Germaine, G. 1997 (WBA)	1
Gilles, R. 1997 (St Mirren)	7
Gillespie, G. T. 1979 (Coventry C)	8
Gilmour, B. C. 2018 (Chelsea)	**4**
Glass, S. 1995 (Aberdeen)	11
Glover, L. 1988 (Nottingham F)	3
Goodwillie, D. 2009 (Dundee U)	9
Goram, A. L. 1987 (Oldham Ath)	1
Gordon, C. S. 2003 (Hearts)	5
Gough, C. R. 1983 (Dundee U)	5
Graham, D. 1998 (Rangers)	8
Grant, P. 1985 (Celtic)	10
Gray, D. P. 2009 (Manchester U)	2
Gray, S. 1987 (Aberdeen)	1
Gray S. 1995 (Celtic)	7
Griffiths, L. 2010 (Dundee, Wolverhampton W)	11
Grimmer, J. 2014 (Fulham)	1
Gunn, B. 1984 (Aberdeen)	9

Hagen, D. 1992 (Rangers)	8
Hamill, J. 2008 (Kilmarnock)	11
Hamilton, B. 1989 (St Mirren)	4
Hamilton, C. 2018 (Hearts)	**3**
Hamilton, J. 1995 (Dundee, Hearts)	14
Hamilton, J. 2014 (Hearts)	8
Hammell, S. 2001 (Motherwell)	11
Handling, D. 2008 (Hibernian)	3
Handyside, P. 1993 (Grimsby T)	7
Hanley, G. 2011 (Blackburn R)	1
Hanlon, P. 2009 (Hibernian)	23
Hannah, D. 1993 (Dundee U)	16
Hardie, R. 2017 (Rangers)	**8**
Harper, K. 1995 (Hibernian)	7
Hartford, R. A. 1977 (Manchester C)	1
Hartley, P. J. 1997 (Millwall)	1
Harvie, D. 2018 (Aberdeen)	**3**
Hegarty, P. 1987 (Dundee U)	6
Henderson, L. 2015 (Celtic)	9
Hendrie, S. 2014 (West Ham U)	3
Hendry, J. 1992 (Tottenham H)	1
Henly, J. 2014 (Reading)	1
Herron, J. 2012 (Celtic)	2
Hetherston, B. 1997 (St Mirren)	1
Hewitt, J. 1982 (Aberdeen)	6
Hogg, G. 1984 (Manchester U)	4
Holt, J. 2012 (Hearts)	7
Hood, G. 1993 (Ayr U)	3
Horn, R. 1997 (Hearts)	6
Hornby, F. D. I. 2018 (Everton)	**5**
Howie, S. 1993 (Cowdenbeath)	5
Hughes, R. D. 1999 (Bournemouth)	9
Hughes, S. 2002 (Rangers)	12
Hunter, G. 1987 (Hibernian)	3
Hunter, P. 1989 (East Fife)	3
Hutton, A. 2004 (Rangers)	7
Hutton, K. 2011 (Rangers)	1
Hyam, D. J. 2014 (Reading)	5
Iacovitti, A. 2017 (Nottingham F)	4
Inman, B. 2011 (Newcastle U)	2
Irvine, G. 2006 (Celtic)	2
Jack, R. 2012 (Aberdeen)	19
James, K. F. 1997 (Falkirk)	1
Jardine, I. 1979 (Kilmarnock)	1
Jess, E. 1990 (Aberdeen)	14
Johnson, G. I. 1992 (Dundee U)	6
Johnston, A. 1994 (Hearts)	3
Johnston, F. 1993 (Falkirk)	1
Johnston, M. 1984 (Partick Thistle, Watford)	3
Johnston, M. A. 2018 (Celtic)	**4**
Jones, J. C. 2017 (Crewe Alex)	4
Jordan, A. J. 2000 (Bristol C)	3
Jules, Z. K. 2017 (Reading)	3
Jupp, D. A. 1995 (Fulham)	9
Kelly, L. A. 2017 (Reading)	11
Kelly, S. 2014 (St Mirren)	1
Kennedy, J. 2003 (Celtic)	15
Kennedy, M. 2012 (Kilmarnock)	1
Kenneth, G. 2008 (Dundee U)	8
Kerr, B. 2003 (Newcastle U)	14
Kerr, F. 2012 (Birmingham C)	3
Kerr, J. 2018 (St Johnstone)	**6**
Kerr, M. 2001 (Kilmarnock)	1
Kerr, S. 1993 (Celtic)	10
Kettings, C. D. 2012 (Blackpool)	3
King, A. 2014 (Swansea C)	1
King, C. M. 2014 (Norwich C)	1
King, W. 2015 (Hearts)	8
Kingsley, S. 2015 (Swansea C)	6
Kinniburgh, W. D. 2004 (Motherwell)	3
Kirkwood, D. 1990 (Hearts)	1
Kyle, K. 2001 (Sunderland)	12

Lambert, P. 1991 (St Mirren)	11
Langfield, J. 2000 (Dundee)	2
Lappin, S. 2004 (St Mirren)	10
Lauchlan, J. 1998 (Kilmarnock)	11
Lavety, B. 1993 (St Mirren)	9
Lavin, G. 1993 (Watford)	7
Lawson, P. 2004 (Celtic)	10
Leighton, J. 1982 (Aberdeen)	1
Lennon, S. 2008 (Rangers)	6
Levein, C. 1985 (Hearts)	2
Leven, P. 2005 (Kilmarnock)	2
Liddell, A. M. 1994 (Barnsley)	12
Lindsey, J. 1979 (Motherwell)	1
Locke, G. 1994 (Hearts)	10
Love, D. 2015 (Manchester U)	5
Love, G. 1995 (Hibernian)	1
Loy, R. 2009 (Dunfermline Ath, Rangers)	5
Lynch, S. 2003 (Celtic, Preston NE)	13
McAllister, G. 1990 (Leicester C)	1
McAllister, R. 2008 (Inverness CT)	2
McAlpine, H. 1983 (Dundee U)	5
McAnespie, K. 1998 (St Johnstone)	4
McArthur, J. 2008 (Hamilton A)	2
McAuley, S. 1993 (St Johnstone)	1
McAvennie, F. 1982 (St Mirren)	5
McBride, J. 1981 (Everton)	1
McBride, J. P. 1998 (Celtic)	2
McBurnie, O. 2015 (Swansea C)	**12**
McCabe, R. 2012 (Rangers, Sheffield W)	3
McCall, A. S. M. 1988 (Bradford C, Everton)	2
McCann, K. 2008 (Hibernian)	4
McCann, N. 1994 (Dundee)	9
McCart, J. 2017 (Celtic)	1
McClair, B. 1984 (Celtic)	8
McCluskey, G. 1979 (Celtic)	6
McCluskey, S. 1997 (St Johnstone)	14
McCoist, A. 1984 (Rangers)	1
McConnell, I. 1997 (Clyde)	1
McCormack, D. 2008 (Hibernian)	1
McCormack, R. 2006 (Rangers, Motherwell, Cardiff C)	13
McCracken, D. 2002 (Dundee U)	5
McCrorie, Robby 2018 (Rangers)	**3**
McCrorie, Ross 2017 (Rangers)	**5**
McCulloch, A. 1981 (Kilmarnock)	1
McCulloch, I. 1982 (Notts Co)	2
McCulloch, L. 1997 (Motherwell)	14
McCunnie, J. 2001 (Dundee U, Ross Co, Dunfermline Ath)	20
MacDonald, A. 2011 (Burnley)	6
MacDonald, C. 2017 (Derby Co)	2
MacDonald, J. 1980 (Rangers)	8
MacDonald, J. 2007 (Hearts)	11
McDonald, C. 1995 (Falkirk)	5
McDonald, K. 2008 (Dundee, Burnley)	14
McEwan, C. 1997 (Clyde, Raith R)	17
McEwan, D. 2003 (Livingston)	2
McFadden, J. 2003 (Motherwell)	7
McFadzean C. 2015 (Sheffield U)	3
McFarlane, D. 1997 (Hamilton A)	3
McGarry, S. 1997 (St Mirren)	3
McGarvey, F. P. 1977 (St Mirren, Celtic)	3
McGarvey, S. 1982 (Manchester U)	4
McGeough, D. 2012 (Celtic)	10
McGhee, J. 2013 (Hearts)	20
McGhee, M. 1981 (Aberdeen)	1
McGinn, J. 2014 (St Mirren, Hibernian)	9
McGinn, S. 2009 (St Mirren, Watford)	8
McGinnis, G. 1985 (Dundee U)	1
McGlinchey, M. R. 2007 (Celtic)	1
McGregor, A. 2003 (Rangers)	6
McGregor, C. W. 2013 (Celtic)	5
McGrillen, P. 1994 (Motherwell)	2
McGuire, D. 2002 (Aberdeen)	2
McHattie, K. 2012 (Hearts)	6
McInally, J. 1989 (Dundee U)	1

McKay, B. 2012 (Rangers)	4
McKay, B. 2013 (Hearts)	1
McKean, K. 2011 (St Mirren)	1
McKenna, S. 2018 (Aberdeen)	**5**
McKenzie, R. 2013 (Kilmarnock)	4
McKenzie, R. 1997 (Hearts)	2
McKimmie, S. 1985 (Aberdeen)	3
McKinlay, T. 1984 (Dundee)	6
McKinlay, W. 1989 (Dundee U)	6
McKinnon, R. 1991 (Dundee U)	6
McLaren, A. 1989 (Hearts)	11
McLaren, A. 1993 (Dundee U)	4
McLaughlin, B. 1995 (Celtic)	8
McLaughlin, J. 1981 (Morton)	10
McLean, E. 2008 (Dundee U, St Johnstone)	2
McLean, S. 2003 (Rangers)	4
McLeish, A. 1978 (Aberdeen)	6
McLean, K. 2012 (St Mirren)	11
MacLeod, A. 1979 (Hibernian)	3
McLeod, J. 1989 (Dundee U)	2
MacLeod, L. 2012 (Rangers)	8
MacLeod, M. 1979 (Dumbarton, Celtic)	5
McManus, D. J. 2014 (Aberdeen, Fleetwood T)	4
McManus, T. 2001 (Hibernian)	14
McMillan, S. 1997 (Motherwell)	4
McMullan, P. 2017 (Celtic)	1
McNab, N. 1978 (Tottenham H)	1
McNally, M. 1991 (Celtic)	2
McNamara, J. 1994 (Dunfermline Ath, Celtic)	12
McNaughton, K. 2002 (Aberdeen)	1
McNeil, A. 2007 (Hibernian)	1
McNichol, J. 1979 (Brentford)	7
McNiven, D. 1977 (Leeds U)	3
McNiven, S. A. 1996 (Oldham Ath)	1
McParland, A. 2003 (Celtic)	1
McPhee, S. 2002 (Port Vale)	1
McPherson, D. 1984 (Rangers, Hearts)	4
McQuilken, J. 1993 (Celtic)	2
McStay, P. 1983 (Celtic)	5
McWhirter, N. 1991 (St Mirren)	1
Mackay-Steven, G. 2012 (Dundee U)	3
Maguire, C. 2009 (Aberdeen)	12
Main, A. 1988 (Dundee U)	3
Malcolm, R. 2001 (Rangers)	1
Mallan, S. 2017 (St Mirren)	**6**
Maloney, S. 2002 (Celtic)	21
Malpas, M. 1983 (Dundee U)	8
Marr, B. 2011 (Ross Co)	1
Marshall, D. J. 2004 (Celtic)	10
Marshall, S. R. 1995 (Arsenal)	5
Martin, A. 2009 (Leeds U, Ayr U)	12
Mason, G. R. 1999 (Manchester C, Dunfermline Ath)	2
Mathieson, D. 1997 (Queen of the South)	3
May, E. 1989 (Hibernian)	2
May, S. 2013 (St Johnstone, Sheffield W)	8
Meldrum, C. 1996 (Kilmarnock)	6
Melrose, J. 1977 (Partick Thistle)	8
Middleton, G. 2018 (Rangers)	**4**
Millar, M. 2009 (Celtic)	1
Miller, C. 1995 (Rangers)	8
Miller, J. 1987 (Aberdeen, Celtic)	7
Miller, K. 2000 (Hibernian, Rangers)	7
Miller, W. 1991 (Hibernian)	7
Miller, W. F. 1978 (Aberdeen)	2
Milne, K. 2000 (Hearts)	1
Milne, R. 1982 (Dundee U)	3
Mitchell, C. 2008 (Falkirk)	7
Money, I. C. 1987 (St Mirren)	3
Montgomery, N. A. 2003 (Sheffield U)	2
Morgan, L. 2017 (St Mirren)	**7**
Morrison, S. A. 2004 (Aberdeen, Dunfermline Ath)	12
Muir, L. 1977 (Hibernian)	1
Mulgrew, C. P. 2006 (Celtic, Wolverhampton W, Aberdeen)	14
Murphy J. 2009 (Motherwell)	13
Murray, H. 2000 (St Mirren)	3

Murray, I. 2001 (Hibernian)	15
Murray, N. 1993 (Rangers)	16
Murray, R. 1993 (Bournemouth)	1
Murray, S. 2004 (Kilmarnock)	2
Narey, D. 1977 (Dundee U)	4
Naismith, J. 2014 (St Mirren)	1
Naismith, S. J. 2006 (Kilmarnock, Rangers)	15
Naysmith, G. A. 1997 (Hearts)	22
Neilson, R. 2000 (Hearts)	1
Nesbitt, A. 2017 (Celtic)	2
Ness, J. 2011 (Rangers)	2
Nevin, P. 1985 (Chelsea)	5
Nicholas, C. 1981 (Celtic, Arsenal)	6
Nicholson, B. 1999 (Rangers)	7
Nicholson, S. 2015 (Hearts)	8
Nicol, S. 1981 (Ayr U, Liverpool)	14
Nisbet, S. 1989 (Rangers)	5
Noble, D. J. 2003 (West Ham U)	2
Notman, A. M. 1999 (Manchester U)	10
O'Brien, B. 1999 (Blackburn R, Livingston)	6
O'Connor, G. 2003 (Hibernian)	8
O'Donnell, P. 1992 (Motherwell)	8
O'Donnell, S. 2013 (Partick Thistle)	1
O'Halloran, M. 2012 (Bolton W)	2
O'Hara, M. 2015 (Kilmarnock, Dundee)	2
O'Leary, R. 2008 (Kilmarnock)	2
O'Neil, B. 1992 (Celtic)	7
O'Neil, J. 1991 (Dundee U)	1
O'Neill, M. 1995 (Clyde)	6
Orr, N. 1978 (Morton)	7
Palmer, L. J. 2011 (Sheffield W)	8
Park, C. 2012 (Middlesbrough)	1
Parker, K. 2001 (St Johnstone)	1
Parlane, D. 1977 (Rangers)	1
Paterson, C. 1981 (Hibernian)	2
Paterson, C. 2012 (Hearts)	12
Paterson, J. 1997 (Dundee U)	9
Pawlett, P. 2012 (Aberdeen)	7
Payne, G. 1978 (Dundee U)	3
Peacock, L. A. 1997 (Carlisle U)	1
Pearce, A. J. 2008 (Reading)	2
Pearson, S. P. 2003 (Motherwell)	8
Perry, R. 2010 (Rangers, Falkirk, Rangers)	16
Polworth, L. 2016 (Inverness CT)	1
Porteous, R. 2018 (Hibernian)	**4**
Pressley, S. J. 1993 (Rangers, Coventry C, Dundee U)	26
Provan, D. 1977 (Kilmarnock)	1
Prunty, B. 2004 (Aberdeen)	6
Quinn, P. C. 2004 (Motherwell)	3
Quinn, R. 2006 (Celtic)	9
Quitongo, J. 2017 (Hamilton A)	1
Rae, A. 1991 (Millwall)	8
Rae, G. 1999 (Dundee)	6
Ralston, A. 2018 (Celtic)	**5**
Redford, I. 1981 (Rangers)	6
Reid, B. 1991 (Rangers)	4
Reid, C. 1993 (Hibernian)	3
Reid, M. 1982 (Celtic)	2
Reid, R. 1977 (St Mirren)	3
Reilly, A. 2004 (Wycombe W)	1
Renicks, S. 1997 (Hamilton A)	1
Reynolds, M. 2007 (Motherwell)	9
Rhodes, J. L. 2011 (Huddersfield T)	8
Rice, B. 1985 (Hibernian)	1
Richardson, L. 1980 (St Mirren)	2
Ridgers, M. 2012 (Hearts)	5
Riordan, D. G. 2004 (Hibernian)	5
Ritchie, M. 2003 (Morton)	1
Ritchie, P. S. 1996 (Hearts)	7
Robertson, A. 1991 (Rangers)	1
Robertson, A. 2013 (Dundee U, Hull C)	4

Robertson, C. 1977 (Rangers)	1
Robertson, C. 2012 (Aberdeen)	10
Robertson, D. 2007 (Dundee U)	4
Robertson, D. A. 1987 (Aberdeen)	7
Robertson, G. A. 2004 (Nottingham F, Rotherham U)	15
Robertson, H. 1994 (Aberdeen)	2
Robertson, J. 1985 (Hearts)	2
Robertson, L. 1993 (Rangers)	3
Robertson, S. 1998 (St Johnstone)	2
Roddie, A. 1992 (Aberdeen)	5
Ross, G. 2007 (Dunfermline Ath)	1
Ross, N. 2011 (Inverness CT)	2
Ross, T. W. 1977 (Arsenal)	1
Rowson, D. 1997 (Aberdeen)	5
Ruddy, J. 2017 (Wolverhampton W)	1
Russell, J. 2011 (Dundee U)	11
Russell, R. 1978 (Rangers)	3
Salton, D. B. 1992 (Luton T)	6
Sammut, R. A. M. 2017 (Chelsea)	3
Samson, C. I. 2004 (Kilmarnock)	6
Saunders, S. 2011 (Motherwell)	2
Scobbie, T. 2008 (Falkirk)	12
Scott, M. 2006 (Livingston)	1
Scott, P. 1994 (St Johnstone)	4
Scougall, S. 2012 (Livingston, Sheffield U)	2
Scrimgour, D. 1997 (St Mirren)	3
Seaton, A. 1998 (Falkirk)	1
Severin, S. D. 2000 (Hearts)	10
Shankland, L. 2015 (Aberdeen)	4
Shannon, R. 1987 (Dundee)	7
Sharp, G. M. 1982 (Everton)	1
Sharp, R. 1990 (Dunfermline Ath)	4
Sheerin, P. 1996 (Southampton)	1
Sheppard, J. 2017 (Reading)	2
Shields, G. 1997 (Rangers)	2
Shinnie, A. 2009 (Dundee, Rangers)	3
Shinnie, G. 2012 (Inverness CT)	2
Simmons, S. 2003 (Hearts)	1
Simpson, N. 1982 (Aberdeen)	11
Sinclair, G. 1977 (Dumbarton)	1
Skilling, M. 1993 (Kilmarnock)	2
Slater, C. 2014 (Kilmarnock, Colchester U)	9
Smith, B. M. 1992 (Celtic)	5
Smith, C. 2008 (St Mirren)	2
Smith, C. 2015 (Aberdeen)	1
Smith, D. 2012 (Hearts)	4
Smith, D. L. 2006 (Motherwell)	2
Smith, G. 1978 (Rangers)	1
Smith, G. 2004 (Rangers)	8
Smith, H. G. 1987 (Hearts)	2
Smith, L. 2017 (Hearts)	**8**
Smith, S. 2007 (Rangers)	1
Sneddon, A. 1979 (Celtic)	1
Snodgrass, R. 2008 (Livingston)	2
Soutar, D. 2003 (Dundee)	11
Souttar, J. 2016 (Dundee U, Hearts)	**11**
Speedie, D. R. 1985 (Chelsea)	1
Spencer, J. 1991 (Rangers)	3
Stanton, P. 1977 (Hibernian)	1
Stanton, S. 2014 (Hibernian)	1
Stark, W. 1985 (Aberdeen)	1
St Clair, H. 2018 (Chelsea)	**3**
Stephen, R. 1983 (Dundee)	1
Stevens, G. 1977 (Motherwell)	1
Stevenson, L. 2008 (Hibernian)	8
Stewart, C. 2002 (Kilmarnock)	1
Stewart, J. 1978 (Kilmarnock, Middlesbrough)	3
Stewart, M. J. 2000 (Manchester U)	17
Stewart, R. 1979 (Dundee U, West Ham U)	12
Stillie, D. 1995 (Aberdeen)	14
Storie, C. 2017 (Aberdeen)	2
Strachan, G. D. 1998 (Coventry C)	7
Sturrock, P. 1977 (Dundee U)	9
Sweeney, P. H. 2004 (Millwall)	8
Sweeney, S. 1991 (Clydebank)	7
Tapping, C. 2013 (Hearts)	1
Tarrant, N. K. 1999 (Aston Villa)	5
Taylor, G. J. 2017 (Kilmarnock)	**12**
Teale, G. 1997 (Clydebank, Ayr U)	6
Telfer, P. N. 1993 (Luton T)	3
Templeton, D. 2011 (Hearts)	2
Thomas, D. 2017 (Motherwell)	6
Thomas, K. 1993 (Hearts)	8
Thompson, S. 1997 (Dundee U)	12
Thomson, C. 2011 (Hearts)	2
Thomson, J. A. 2017 (Celtic)	1
Thomson, K. 2005 (Hibernian)	6
Thomson, W. 1977 (Partick Thistle, St Mirren)	10
Tolmie, J. 1980 (Morton)	1
Tortolano, J. 1987 (Hibernian)	2
Toshney, L. 2012 (Celtic)	5
Turner, I. 2005 (Everton)	6
Tweed, S. 1993 (Hibernian)	3
Wales, G. 2000 (Hearts)	1
Walker, A. 1988 (Celtic)	1
Walker, J. 2013 (Hearts)	1
Wallace, I. A. 1978 (Coventry C)	1
Wallace, L. 2007 (Hearts)	10
Wallace, M. 2012 (Huddersfield T)	4
Wallace, R. 2004 (Celtic, Sunderland)	4
Walsh, C. 1984 (Nottingham F)	5
Wark, J. 1977 (Ipswich T)	8
Watson, A. 1981 (Aberdeen)	4
Watson, K. 1977 (Rangers)	2
Watt, A. 2012 (Celtic)	9
Watt, E. 2018 (Wolverhampton W)	**3**
Watt, M. 1991 (Aberdeen)	12
Watt, S. M. 2005 (Chelsea)	5
Webster, A. 2003 (Hearts)	2
Whiteford, A. 1997 (St Johnstone)	1
Whittaker, S. G. 2005 (Hibernian)	18
Whyte, D. 1987 (Celtic)	9
Wighton, C. R. 2017 (Dundee)	**6**
Wilkie, L. 2000 (Dundee)	6
Will, J. A. 1992 (Arsenal)	3
Williams, G. 2002 (Nottingham F)	9
Williamson, R. 2018 (Dunfermline)	**3**
Wilson, D. 2011 (Liverpool, Hearts)	13
Wilson, I. 2018 (Kilmarnock)	**6**
Wilson, M. 2004 (Dundee U, Celtic)	19
Wilson, S. 1999 (Rangers)	2
Wilson, T. 1983 (St Mirren)	1
Wilson, T. 1988 (Nottingham F)	4
Winnie, D. 1988 (St Mirren)	1
Woods, M. 2006 (Sunderland)	2
Wotherspoon, D. 2011 (Hibernian)	16
Wright, P. 1989 (Aberdeen, QPR)	3
Wright, Stephen 1991 (Aberdeen)	14
Wright, Scott 2018 (Aberdeen)	**5**
Wright, T. 1987 (Oldham Ath)	1
Wylde, G. 2011 (Rangers)	7
Young, Darren 1997 (Aberdeen)	8
Young, Derek 2000 (Aberdeen)	5

WALES

Abbruzzese, R. 2018 (Cardiff C)	3
Adams, N. W. 2008 (Bury, Leicester C)	5
Alfei, D. M. 2010 (Swansea C)	13
Aizlewood, M. 1979 (Luton T)	2
Allen, J. M. 2008 (Swansea C)	13
Anthony, B. 2005 (Cardiff C)	8
Babos, A. 2018 (Derby Co)	2
Baddeley, L. M. 1996 (Cardiff C)	2
Balcombe, S. 1982 (Leeds U)	1
Bale, G. 2006 (Southampton, Tottenham H)	4
Barnhouse, D. J. 1995 (Swansea C)	3
Basey, G. W. 2009 (Charlton Ath)	1
Bater, P. T. 1977 (Bristol R)	2
Beevers, L. J. 2005 (Boston U, Lincoln C)	7
Bellamy, C. D. 1996 (Norwich C)	8
Bender, T. J. 2011 (Colchester U)	4
Birchall, A. S. 2003 (Arsenal, Mansfield T)	12
Bird, A. 1993 (Cardiff C)	6
Blackmore, C. 1984 (Manchester U)	3
Blake, D. J. 2007 (Cardiff C)	14
Blake, N. A. 1991 (Cardiff C)	5
Blaney, S. D. 1997 (West Ham U)	3
Bloom, J. 2011 (Falkirk)	1
Bodin, B. P. 2010 (Swindon T, Torquay U)	21
Bodin, P. J. 1983 (Cardiff C)	1
Bond, J. H. 2011 (Watford)	1
Bowen, J. P. 1993 (Swansea C)	5
Bowen, M. R. 1983 (Tottenham H)	3
Boyle, T. 1982 (Crystal Palace)	1
Brace, D. P. 1995 (Wrexham)	6
Bradley, M. S. 2007 (Walsall)	17
Bradshaw, T. 2012 (Shrewsbury T)	8
Broadhead, N. 2018 (Everton)	6
Brooks, D. R. 2018 (Sheffield U)	3
Brough, M. 2003 (Notts Co)	3
Brown, J. D. 2008 (Cardiff C)	6
Brown, J. R. 2003 (Gillingham)	7
Brown, T. A. F. 2011 (Ipswich T, Rotherham U, Aldershot T)	10
Burns, W. J. 2013 (Bristol C)	18
Burton, R. 2018 (Arsenal)	1
Byrne, M. T. 2003 (Bolton W)	1
Calliste, R. T. 2005 (Manchester U, Liverpool)	15
Carpenter, R. E. 2005 (Burnley)	1
Cassidy, J. A. 2011 (Wolverhampton W)	8
Cegielski, W. 1977 (Wrexham)	2
Chamberlain, E. C. 2010 (Leicester C)	9
Chapple, S. R. 1992 (Swansea C)	8
Charles, J. D. 2016 (Huddersfield T, Barnsley)	9
Charles, J. M. 1979 (Swansea C)	2
Christie-Davies, I. 2018 (Chelsea)	2
Church, S. R. 2008 (Reading)	15
Clark, J. 1978 (Manchester U, Derby Co)	2
Coates, J. S. 1996 (Swansea C)	5
Coleman, C. 1990 (Swansea C)	3
Collins, J. M. 2003 (Cardiff C)	7
Collins, M. J. 2007 (Fulham, Swansea C)	2
Collison, J. D. 2008 (West Ham U)	7
Cornell, D. J. 2010 (Swansea C)	4
Cotterill, D. R. G. B. 2005 (Bristol C, Wigan Ath)	11
Coyne, D. 1992 (Tranmere R)	7
Coxe, C. T. 2018 (Cardiff C)	8
Craig, N. L. 2009 (Everton)	4
Critchell, K. A. R. 2005 (Southampton)	3
Crofts, A. L. 2005 (Gillingham)	10
Crowe, M. T. T. 2017 (Ipswich T)	1
Crowell, M. T. 2004 (Wrexham)	7
Cullen, L. 2018 (Swansea C)	2
Curtis, A. T. 1977 (Swansea C)	1
Dasilva, C. P. 2018 (Chelsea)	1
Davies, A. 1982 (Manchester U)	6

Davies, A. G. 2006 (Cambridge U)	6
Davies, A. R. 2005 (Southampton, Yeovil T)	14
Davies, C. M. 2005 (Oxford U, Verona, Oldham Ath)	9
Davies, D. 1999 (Barry T)	1
Davies, G. M. 1993 (Hereford U, Crystal Palace)	7
Davies, I. C. 1978 (Norwich C)	1
Davies, L. 2005 (Bangor C)	1
Davies, R. J. 2006 (WBA)	4
Davies, S. 1999 (Peterborough U, Tottenham H)	10
Dawson, C. 2013 (Leeds U)	2
Day, R. 2000 (Manchester C, Mansfield T)	11
Deacy, N. 1977 (PSV Eindhoven)	1
De-Vulgt, L. S. 2002 (Swansea C)	2
Dibble, A. 1983 (Cardiff C)	3
Dibble, C. 2014 (Barnsley)	1
Doble, R. A. 2010 (Southampton)	10
Doughty, M. E. 2012 (QPR)	1
Doyle, S. C. 1979 (Preston NE, Huddersfield T)	2
Duffy, R. M. 2005 (Portsmouth)	7
Dummett, P. 2011 (Newcastle U)	3
Dwyer, P. J. 1979 (Cardiff C)	1
Eardley, N. 2007 (Oldham Ath, Blackpool)	11
Earnshaw, R. 1999 (Cardiff C)	10
Easter, D. J. 2006 (Cardiff C)	1
Ebdon, M. 1990 (Everton)	2
Edwards, C. N. H. 1996 (Swansea C)	7
Edwards, D. A. 2006 (Shrewsbury T, Luton T, Wolverhampton W)	9
Edwards, G. D. R. 2012 (Swansea C)	6
Edwards, R. I. 1977 (Chester)	2
Edwards, R. W. 1991 (Bristol C)	13
Evans, A. 1977 (Bristol R)	1
Evans, C. 2007 (Manchester C, Sheffield U)	13
Evans, J. 2018 (Swansea C)	6
Evans, J. A. J. 2014 (Fulham, Wrexham)	6
Evans, K. 1999 (Leeds U, Cardiff C)	4
Evans, L. 2013 (Wolverhampton W)	13
Evans, O. R. 2018 (Wigan Ath)	1
Evans, P. S. 1996 (Shrewsbury T)	1
Evans, S. J. 2001 (Crystal Palace)	2
Evans, T. 1995 (Cardiff C)	3
Fish, N. 2005 (Cardiff C)	2
Fleetwood, S. 2005 (Cardiff C)	5
Flynn, C. P. 2007 (Crewe Alex)	1
Folland, R. W. 2000 (Oxford U)	1
Foster, M. G. 1993 (Tranmere R)	1
Fowler, L. A. 2003 (Coventry C, Huddersfield T)	9
Fox, M. A. 2013 (Charlton Ath)	6
Freeman, K. 2012 (Nottingham F, Derby Co)	15
Freestone, R. 1990 (Chelsea)	1
Gabbidon, D. L. 1999 (WBA, Cardiff C)	17
Gale, D. 1983 (Swansea C)	2
Gall, K. A. 2002 (Bristol R, Yeovil T)	8
Gibson, N. D. 1999 (Tranmere R, Sheffield W)	11
Giggs, R. J. 1991 (Manchester U)	1
Gilbert, P. 2005 (Plymouth Arg)	12
Giles, D. C. 1977 (Cardiff C, Swansea C, Crystal Palace)	4
Giles, P. 1982 (Cardiff C)	3
Graham, D. 1991 (Manchester U)	1
Green, R. M. 1998 (Wolverhampton W)	16
Griffith, C. 1990 (Cardiff C)	1
Griffiths, C. 1991 (Shrewsbury T)	1
Grubb, D. 2007 (Bristol C)	1
Gunter, C. 2006 (Cardiff C, Tottenham H)	8
Haldane, L. O. 2007 (Bristol R)	1
Hall, G. D. 1990 (Chelsea)	1
Harries, C. W. T. 2018 (Swansea C)	4
Harris, M. 2018 (Cardiff C)	8
Harrison, E. W. 2013 (Bristol R)	14

Hartson, J. 1994 (Luton T, Arsenal) 9
Haworth, S. O. 1997 (Cardiff C, Coventry C, Wigan Ath) 12
Hedges, R. P. 2014 (Swansea C) 11
Henley, A. 2012 (Blackburn R) 3
Hennessey, W. R. 2006 (Wolverhampton W) 6
Hewitt, E. J. 2012 (Macclesfield T, Ipswich T) 10
Hillier, I. M. 2001 (Tottenham H, Luton T) 5
Hodges, G. 1983 (Wimbledon) 5
Holden, A. 1984 (Chester C) 1
Holloway, C. D. 1999 (Exeter C) 2
Hopkins, J. 1982 (Fulham) 5
Hopkins, S. A. 1999 (Wrexham) 1
Howells, J. 2012 (Luton T) 5
Huggins, D. S. 1996 (Bristol C) 1
Hughes, D. 2005 (Kaiserslautern, Regensburg) 2
Hughes, D. R. 1994 (Southampton) 1
Hughes, I. 1992 (Bury) 11
Hughes, L. M. 1983 (Manchester U) 5
Hughes, R. D. 1996 (Aston Villa, Shrewsbury T) 13
Hughes, W. 1977 (WBA) 3
Huws, E. W. 2012 (Manchester C) 6

Isgrove, L. J. 2013 (Southampton) 6

Jackett, K. 1981 (Watford) 2
Jacobson, J. M. 2006 (Cardiff C, Bristol R) 15
James, D. 2017 (Swansea C) **8**
James, L. R. S. 2006 (Southampton) 10
James, R. M. 1977 (Swansea C) 3
Jarman, L. 1996 (Cardiff C) 10
Jeanne, L. C. 1999 (QPR) 8
Jelleyman, G. A. 1999 (Peterborough U) 1
Jenkins, L. D. 1998 (Swansea C) 9
Jenkins, S. R. 1993 (Swansea C) 2
John, D. C. 2014 (Cardiff C) 9
Jones, C. T. 2007 (Swansea C) 1
Jones, E. P. 2000 (Blackpool) 1
Jones, F. 1981 (Wrexham) 1
Jones, G. W. 2014 (Everton) 9
Jones, J. A. 2001 (Swansea C) 3
Jones, L. 1982 (Cardiff C) 3
Jones, M. A. 2004 (Wrexham) 4
Jones, M. G. 1998 (Leeds U) 7
Jones, O. R. 2015 (Swansea C) 1
Jones, P. L. 1992 (Liverpool) 12
Jones, R. 2011 (AFC Wimbledon) 1
Jones, R. A. 1994 (Sheffield W) 3
Jones, S. J. 2005 (Swansea C) 1
Jones, V. 1979 (Bristol R) 2

Kendall, L. M. 2001 (Crystal Palace) 2
Kendall, M. 1978 (Tottenham H) 1
Kenworthy, J. R. 1994 (Tranmere R) 3
King, A. 2008 (Leicester C) 11
Knott, G. R. 1996 (Tottenham H) 1

Law, B. J. 1990 (QPR) 2
Lawless, A. 2006 (Torquay U) 1
Lawrence, T. 2013 (Manchester U) 8
Ledley, J. C. 2005 (Cardiff C) 5
Letheran, G. 1977 (Leeds U) 2
Letheran, K. C. 2006 (Swansea C) 1
Lewis, A. 2018 (Swansea C) **3**
Lewis, D. 1982 (Swansea C) 9
Lewis, J. 1983 (Cardiff C) 1
Llewellyn, C. M. 1998 (Norwich C) 14
Lockyer, T. A. 2015 (Bristol R) 7
Loveridge, J. 1982 (Swansea C) 3
Low, J. D. 1999 (Bristol R, Cardiff C) 1
Lowndes, S. R. 1979 (Newport Co, Millwall) 4
Lucas, L. P. 2011 (Swansea C) 19

MacDonald, S. B. 2006 (Swansea C) 25
McCarthy, A. J. 1994 (QPR) 3
McDonald, C. 2006 (Cardiff C) 3

Mackin, L. 2006 (Wrexham) 1
Maddy, P. 1982 (Cardiff C) 2
Margetson, M. W. 1992 (Manchester C) 7
Martin, A. P. 1999 (Crystal Palace) 1
Martin, D. A. 2006 (Notts Co) 1
Marustik, C. 1982 (Swansea C) 7
Matondo, R. 2018 (Manchester C) **6**
Matthews, A. J. 2010 (Cardiff C) 5
Maxwell, C. 2009 (Wrexham) 16
Maxwell, L. J. 1999 (Liverpool, Cardiff C) 14
Meades, J. 2012 (Cardiff C) 4
Meaker, M. J. 1994 (QPR) 2
Melville, A. K. 1990 (Swansea C, Oxford U) 2
Mepham, C. J. 2018 (Brentford) **4**
Micallef, C. 1982 (Cardiff C) 3
Morgan, A. M. 1995 (Tranmere R) 4
Morgan, A. 2004 (Wrexham, Milton Keynes D) 12
Morrell, J. J. 2018 (Bristol C) **4**
Morris, A. J. 2009 (Cardiff C, Aldershot T) 8
Moss, D. M. 2003 (Shrewsbury T) 6
Mountain, P. D. 1997 (Cardiff C) 2
Mumford, A. O. 2003 (Swansea C) 4

Nardiello, D. 1978 (Coventry C) 1
Neilson, A. B. 1993 (Newcastle U) 7
Nicholas, P. 1978 (Crystal Palace, Arsenal) 3
Nogan, K. 1990 (Luton T) 2
Nogan, L. M. 1991 (Oxford U) 1
Norrington-Davies, R. 2018 (Sheffield U) **4**
Nyatanga, L. J. 2005 (Derby Co) 10

Oakley, A. 2013 (Swindon T) 1
O'Brien, B. T. 2015 (Manchester C) 8
Ogleby, R. 2011 (Hearts, Wrexham) 12
Oster, J. M. 1997 (Grimsby T, Everton) 9
O'Sullivan, T. P. 2013 (Cardiff C) 15
Owen, G. 1991 (Wrexham) 8

Page, R. J. 1995 (Watford) 4
Parslow, D. 2005 (Cardiff C) 4
Partington, J. M. 2009 (Bournemouth) 8
Partridge, D. W. 1997 (West Ham U) 1
Pascoe, C. 1983 (Swansea C) 4
Pearce, S. 2006 (Bristol C) 3
Pejic, S. M. 2003 (Wrexham) 6
Pembridge, M. A. 1991 (Luton T) 1
Peniket, R. 2012 (Fulham) 1
Perry, J. 1990 (Cardiff C) 3
Peters, M. 1992 (Manchester C, Norwich C) 3
Phillips, D. 1984 (Plymouth Arg) 3
Phillips, G. R. 2001 (Swansea C) 3
Phillips, L. 1979 (Swansea C, Charlton Ath) 2
Pilling, L. 2018 (Tranmere R) **7**
Pipe, D. R. 2003 (Coventry C, Notts Co) 12
Pontin, K. 1978 (Cardiff C) 1
Poole, R. L. 2017 (Manchester U) **11**
Powell, L. 1991 (Southampton) 4
Powell, L. 2004 (Leicester C) 3
Powell, R. 2006 (Bolton W) 1
Price, J. J. 1998 (Swansea C) 7
Price, L. P. 2005 (Ipswich T) 10
Price, M. D. 2001 (Everton, Hull C, Scarborough) 13
Price, P. 1981 (Luton T) 1
Pritchard, J. P. 2013 (Fulham) 3
Pritchard, M. O. 2006 (Swansea C) 4
Pugh, D. 1982 (Doncaster R) 2
Pugh, S. 1993 (Wrexham) 2
Pulis, A. J. 2006 (Stoke C) 5

Ramasut, M. W. T. 1997 (Bristol R) 4
Ramsey, A. J. 2008, (Cardiff C, Arsenal) 12
Ratcliffe, K. 1981 (Everton) 2
Ray, G. E. 2013 (Crewe Alex) 5
Ready, K. 1992 (QPR) 5
Rees, A. 1984 (Birmingham C) 1
Rees, J. M. 1990 (Luton T) 3

Rees, M. R. 2003 (Millwall) 4
Reid, B. 2014 (Wolverhampton W) 1
Ribeiro, C. M. 2008 (Bristol C) 8
Richards, A. D. J. 2010 (Swansea C) 16
Richards, E. A. 2012 (Bristol R) 1
Roberts, A. M. 1991 (QPR) 2
Roberts, C. 2013 (Cheltenham T) 6
Roberts, C. J. 1999 (Cardiff C) 1
Roberts, C. R. J. 2016 (Swansea C) 2
Roberts, G. 1983 (Hull C) 1
Roberts, G. W. 1997 (Liverpool, Panionios,
   Tranmere R) 11
Roberts, J. G. 1977 (Wrexham) 1
Roberts, N. W. 1999 (Wrexham) 3
Roberts, P. 1997 (Porthmadog) 1
Roberts, S. I. 1999 (Swansea C) 13
Roberts, S. W. 2000 (Wrexham) 3
Roberts, T. W. 2018 (Leeds U) 5
Robinson, C. P. 1996 (Wolverhampton W) 6
Robinson, J. R. C. 1992 (Brighton & HA, Charlton Ath) 5
Robson-Kanu, K. H. 2010 (Reading) 4
Rodon, J. P. 2017 (Swansea C) 9
Rowlands, A. J. R. 1996 (Manchester C) 5
Rush, I. 1981 (Liverpool) 2

Savage, R. W. 1995 (Crewe Alex) 3
Saunders, C. L. 2015 (Crewe Alex) 1
Sayer, P. A. 1977 (Cardiff C) 2
Searle, D. 1991 (Cardiff C) 6
Sheehan, J. L. 2014 (Swansea C) 12
Shephard, L. 2015 (Swansea C) 2
Slatter, D. 2000 (Chelsea) 6
Slatter, N. 1983 (Bristol R) 6
Smith, D. 2014 (Shrewsbury T) 3
Smith, M. 2018 (Manchester C) 5
Somner, M. J. 2004 (Brentford) 2
Speed, G. A. 1990 (Leeds U) 3
Spender, S. 2005 (Wrexham) 6
Stephens, D. 2011 (Hibernian) 7
Stevenson, N. 1982 (Swansea C) 2
Stevenson, W. B. 1977 (Leeds U) 3
Stock, B. B. 2003 (Bournemouth) 4
Symons, C. J. 1991 (Portsmouth) 2

Tancock, S. 2013 (Swansea C) 6
Taylor, A. J. 2012 (Tranmere R) 3
Taylor, G. K. 1995 (Bristol R) 4
Taylor, J. W. T. 2010 (Reading) 12
Taylor, N. J. 2008 (Wrexham, Swansea C) 13
Taylor, R. F. 2008 (Chelsea) 5
Thomas, C. E. 2010 (Swansea C) 3
Thomas, D. G. 1977 (Leeds U) 3
Thomas, D. J. 1998 (Watford) 2
Thomas, G. S. 2018 (Leicester C) 6
Thomas, J. A. 1996 (Blackburn R) 21

Thomas, Martin R. 1979 (Bristol R) 2
Thomas, Mickey R. 1977 (Wrexham) 2
Thomas, S. 2001 (Wrexham) 5
Thompson, L. C. W. 2015 (Norwich C) 2
Tibbott, L. 1977 (Ipswich T) 2
Tipton, M. J. 1998 (Oldham Ath) 6
Tolley, J. C. 2001 (Shrewsbury T) 12
Tudur-Jones, O. 2006 (Swansea C) 3
Twiddy, C. 1995 (Plymouth Arg) 3

Valentine, R. D. 2001 (Everton, Darlington) 8
Vaughan, D. O. 2003 (Crewe Alex) 8
Vaughan, N. 1982 (Newport Co) 2
Vokes, S. M. 2007 (Bournemouth,
   Wolverhampton W) 14

Walsh, D. 2000 (Wrexham) 8
Walsh, I. P. 1979 (Crystal Palace, Swansea C) 2
Walsh, J. 2012 (Swansea C, Crawley T) 11
Walton, M. 1991 (Norwich C.) 1
Ward, D. 1996 (Notts Co) 2
Ward, D. 2013 (Liverpool) 6
Warlow, O. J. 2007 (Lincoln C) 2
Weeks, D. L. 2014 (Wolverhampton W) 2
Weston, R. D. 2001 (Arsenal, Cardiff C) 4
Wharton, T. J. 2014 (Cardiff C) 1
Whitfield, P. M. 2003 (Wrexham) 1
Wiggins, R. 2006 (Crystal Palace) 9
Williams, A. P. 1998 (Southampton) 9
Williams, A. S. 1996 (Blackburn R) 16
Williams, D. 1983 (Bristol R) 1
Williams, D. I. L. 1998 (Liverpool, Wrexham) 9
Williams, D. T. 2006 (Yeovil T) 1
Williams, E. 1997 (Caernarfon T) 2
Williams, G. 1983 (Bristol R) 2
Williams, G. A. 2003 (Crystal Palace) 5
Williams, G. C. 2014 (Fulham) 3
Williams, J. P. 2011 (Crystal Palace) 8
Williams, M. 2001 (Manchester U) 10
Williams, M. P. 2006 (Wrexham) 14
Williams, M. J. 2014 (Notts Co) 1
Williams, M. R. 2006 (Wrexham) 6
Williams, O. fon 2007 (Crewe Alex, Stockport Co) 11
Williams, R. 2007 (Middlesbrough) 10
Williams, S. J. 1995 (Wrexham) 4
Wilmot, R. 1982 (Arsenal) 6
Wilson, H. 2014 (Liverpool) 10
Wilson, J. S. 2009 (Bristol C) 3
Worgan, L. J. 2005 (Milton Keynes D, Rushden & D) 5
Wright, A. A. 1998 (Oxford U) 3
Wright, J. 2014 (Huddersfield T) 2

Yorwerth, J. 2014 (Cardiff C) 7
Young, S. 1996 (Cardiff C) 5

FA SCHOOLS AND YOUTH GAMES 2017–18

ENGLAND UNDER-16

■ *Denotes player sent off.*

UNDER 16 INTERNATIONAL TOURNAMENT

Heriot-Watt University, Scotland,
Tuesday 25 July 2017

England 2 *(Greenwood, Rogers (pen))*

Uruguay 0

England: Jinadu; Caiger, Cover, Simeu, Wood-Gordon, Madueke, Knight, Hoare, Rogers, Carvalho, Greenwood.
Substitutes: Peart-Harris, Pendlebury, Bondswell, Mighten, Collins, Dorsett, Garcia, McCann, Osorio.

Forthbank Stadium, Thursday 27 July 2017

Scotland (0) 2 *(Collins 67 (og), Ecrepont 75)*

England (0) 0

Scotland: Newman; Ecrepont, Cameron, Logan (Patterson 47), Grigor, Smith, Kettings (Weir 47), Forrest, Sparkes (Miller 23), Dembele (Barron 60), Starrs.
England: Collins; Peart-Harris, Bondswell, Pendlebury, Wood-Gordon, Mighten, Dorsett, Garcia, Madueke, McCann, Osorio.
Substitutes: Jinadu, Simeu, Knight, Hoare, Rogers, Carvalho, Caiger, Cover, Greenwood.

Heriot-Watt University, Scotland,
Saturday 29 July 2017

England 9 *(McCann, Hoare (pen), Garcia 2, Osorio, Carvalho, Knight 2, Rogers)*

Qatar 0

England: Collins; Peart-Harris, Cover, Dorsett, Simeu, Hoare, McCann, Osorio, Knight, Garcia, Carvalho.
Substitutes: Jinadu, Pendlebury, Bondswell, Wood-Gordon, Rogers, Mighten, Caiger, Greenwood, Madueke.

THREE TEAM TOURNAMENT

St George's Park, Tuesday 22 August 2017

England (1) 2 *(Okoflex 22, Brown 56)*

Turkey (0) 1 *(Cicekdal 72)*

England: Moulden; Livramento, Sohna, Hodge, Harwood-Bellis, Sarmiento, Musah, Pennant, Brooking, Thompson, Okoflex.
Substitutes: Wood-Gordon, Palmer, Brown, Dennis, Smith, Wilson-Esbrand, Azeez, Tetek, McAtee.

St George's Park, Saturday 26 August 2017

England 2 *(Sarmiento, McAtee)*

Romania 1

England: Smith; Wilson-Esbrand, Dennis, McAtee, Wood-Gordon, Harwood-Bellis, Sarmiento, Tetek, Carvalho, Azeez, Brown.
Substitutes: Talley, Livramento, Hodge, Pennant, Brooking, Thompson, Okoflex.

NIKE INTERNATIONAL TOURNAMENT

Lakewood Ranch, Florida,
Wednesday 29 November 2017

USA (0) 0

England (0) 1 *(Harwood-Bellis 78)*

England: Moulden; Simeu, Brooking (Robinson 62), Hoare (Musah 15), Harwood-Bellis, Mighten, Carvalho, Bondswell (Dorsett 78), Greenwood (Smales-Braithwaite 74), Hodge, Knight.

Lakewood Ranch, Florida, Friday 1 December 2017

England (1) 1 *(Carvalho 18)*

Brazil U15 (2) 2 *(Giovanni 32, Alejandro 39)*

England: Smith; Livramento, Robinson (Simeu 51), Dorsett (Greenwood 80), Bondswell (Harwood-Bellis 50), Pendlebury, Musah, Carvalho, Palmer (Knight 63), Sarmiento (Mighten 51), Smales-Braithwaite.

Lakewood Ranch, Florida, Sunday 3 December

England (1) 1 *(Knight 10)*

Netherlands (1) 3 *(Ihatteren 28, Salah-Eddine 46, Taabouni 71)*

England: Talley; Livramento, Simeu (Robinson 41), Harwood-Bellis, Bondswell, Pendlebury, Musha (Brooking 51), Carvalho (Palmer 58), Knight, Mighten, Greenwood (Smales-Braithwaite 66).

UEFA DEVELOPMENT TOURNAMENT

St George's Park, Wednesday 14 February 2018

England (1) 2 *(Mighten 11, Hodge 44)*

Denmark (0) 0

England: Trafford; Bondswell, Harwood-Bellis, Mengi, Walcott, Madueke, Hodge, Elliott, Mighten, Okoflex, Sarmiento.
Substitutes: Moulden, Cirkin, Livramento, Simeu, Musah, Knight, Carvalho, Azeez, Gelhardt, Rogers.

St George's Park, Friday 16 February 2018

England (1) 2 *(Knight 24, Rogers 53)*

Spain (0) 0

England: Moulden; Cirkin, Harwood-Bellis, Simeu, Musah, Knight (Okoflex 77), Hodge, Carvalho (Sarmiento 67), Azeez, Gelhardt, Rogers.

St George's Park, Monday 19 February 2018

England (0) 2 *(Gelhardt (pen), Okoflex)*

Scotland (0) 0

England: Trafford; Bondswell, Harwood-Bellis, Walcott, Musah, Knight, Hodge, Carvalho, Azeez, Gelhardt, Rogers.
Substitutes: Moulden, Cirkin, Simeu, Madueke, Elliott, Mighten, Okoflex, Sarmiento.
Scotland: Newman; Patterson, Ecrepont, Morrison, Winter, Smith, Fiorini, Kennedy, Hamilton, Ruth, Weir.
Substitutes: Bradley-Hurst, O'Connor, Cameron, Pitblado, Anderson, Forrest, Sparkes, Ward.

MONTAIGU TOURNAMENT

Tuesday 27 March 2018

England *(Rogers 2)*

Russia 0

England: Jinadu; Livramento, Simeu, Musah (Hodge 41), Harwood-Bellis, Cirkin, Knight (Okoflex 48), Azeez, Gelhardt (Mighten 44), Rogers, Carvalho (Peart-Harris 50).

Thursday 29 March 2018

England 2 *(Mighten, Gelhardt)*

Cameroon 0

England: Sanneh; Walcott, Simeu (Cirkin 41), Mengi, Roberts, Hodge, Peart-Harris, Mighten, Pennant, Knight (Carvalho 60), Okoflex (Gelhardt 60).

Saturday 31 March 2018

England (1) 3 *(Carvalho 22, Gelhardt 50, Knight 60)*

Brazil (0) 3 *(Marinho 53, Kaka 80, Reinier 80)*

England: Jinadu; Livramento (Mengi 41), Simeu, Musah, Harwood-Bellis, Cirkin, Knight (Mighten 65), Azeez (Walcott 80), Gelhardt (Okoflex 59), Rogers, Carvalho (Peart-Harris 65).

Monday 2 April 2018

England (0) 1 *(Azeez 77)*

France (0) 0

England: Sanneh; Walcott, Roberts, Peart-Harris (Musah 50), Harwood-Bellis (Livramento), Mengi, Knight (Rogers 50), Hodge (Azeez 50), Carvalho (Cirkin 74), Mighten (Pennant), Okoflex (Gelhardt).

ENGLAND UNDER-17

UNDER-17 FRIENDLY TOURNAMENT

St George's Park, Friday 18 August 2017

England 3 *(Tulloch 2, Saka)*

Turkey 2

England: Seaden; Mumba, Saka, Binks, Broughton, Johnson, Mola, Whittaker, Appiah, Nolan, Tulloch.
Substitutes: Ashby-Hammond, Kpohomouh, Clarke, Sibley, Crowe, Cashman, Hilton, Doyle, Duncan, Wright-Phillips, Perry.

St George's Park, Sunday 20 August 2017

England 2 *(Duncan, TBC)*

Scotland 1 *(Gilmour 20)*

England: Ashby-Hammond; Kpohomouh, Clarke, Sibley, Crowe, Cashman, Doyle, Hilton, Duncan, Wright-Phillips, Perry.
Substitutes: Seaden, Mumba, Saka, Binks, Broughton, Johnson, Mola, Whittaker, Appiah, Nolan, Tulloch.

Kidderminster, Tuesday 22 August 2017

England (0) 1 *(Appiah 71)*

Italy (1) 2 *(Vergant, Tonin)*

England: Seaden; Saka, Clarke, Binks, Crowe (Mumba 63), Mola (Hilton 49), Doyle, Appiah, Duncan (Perry 64), Nolan (Wright-Phillips 75), Tulloch.

FRIENDLIES

Mumbai, Sunday 1 October 2017

England (1) 3 *(Guehi 20, Brewster 84, 86)*

New Zealand (1) 2 *(Whyte 12, Just 81)*

England: Bursik;.Eyoma, Guehi, Gibson, Panzo, Gallagher, Kirby, Oakley-Boothe, Loader, Hudson-Odoi, Smith-Rowe.
Substitutes: Anderson, Crellin, McEachran, Foden, Brewster, Gomes, Latibeaudiere, Sessegnon, Gibbs-White.

Pinatar, Friday 23 March 2018

England 0

Brazil 1 *(Oliveira)*

England: Ashby-Hammond; Crowe, Mola (Sibley 46), Daly, Dixon-Bonner, Alese, Appiah, Doyle, Duncan (Tulloch 65), Anjorin (Amaechi 61), Jones.

Pinatar, Monday 26 March 2018

England (1) 1 *(John-Jules 29)*

Brazil (1) 1 *(Paulo 32)*

England: Dewhurst; Crowe, Sibley, Daly, Dixon-Bonner, Binks, Amaechi, Doyle, John-Jules, Anjorin, Jones.

FIFA UNDER-17 WORLD CUP – GROUP F

Kolkata, Sunday 8 October 2017

Chile (0) 0

England (1) 4 *(Hudson-Odoi 5, Sancho 51, 60, Gomes 81)*

England: Anderson; Eyoma, Latibeaudiere, Guehi, Panzo, McEachran, Oakley-Boothe (Gibbs-White 77), Foden, Hudson-Odoi (Gomes 67), Sancho (Kirby 77), Brewster.

Kolkata, Wednesday 11 October 2017

England (1) 3 *(Brewster 39, Foden 48, Sancho 55 (pen))*

Mexico (0) 2 *(Latibeaudier 61 (og), Lainez 81)*

England: Anderson; Eyoma, Latibeaudiere, Guehi, Panzo, McEachran, Oakley-Boothe (Gallagher 74), Foden, Hudson-Odoi (Gomes 46), Sancho (Gibbs-White 82), Brewster.

Kolkata, Saturday 14 October 2017

England (1) 4 *(Gomes 11, Smith-Rowe 57, Loader 59, 71)*

Iraq (0) 0

England: Crellin; Sessegnon, Latibeaudiere, Guehi (Foden 72), Gibson, Kirby (Gibbs-White 60), Gallagher, Smith-Rowe, Gomes (Hudson-Odoi 67), Sancho, Loader.

FIFA UNDER-17 WORLD CUP – ROUND OF 16

Kolkata, Tuesday 17 October 2017

England (0) 0

Japan (0) 0

England: Anderson; Sessegnon, Latibeaudiere, Guehi, Panzo, Oakley-Boothe (Gibbs-White 68), McEachran (Kirby 78), Foden, Gomes (Smith-Rowe 64), Hudson-Odoi, Brewster.
England won 5-3 on penalties.

FIFA UNDER-17 WORLD CUP – QUARTER-FINALS

Goa, Saturday 21 October 2017

England (2) 4 *(Brewster 11, 14, 90 (pen), Gibbs-White 64)*

USA (0) 1 *(Sargent 72)*

England: Anderson; Sessegnon, Latibeaudiere, Guehi, Panzo, Oakley-Boothe, McEachran, Foden (Kirby 85), Gibbs-White (Gallagher 78), Hudson-Odoi, Brewster.

FIFA UNDER-17 WORLD CUP – SEMI-FINALS

Kolkata, Wednesday 25 October 2017

England (2) 3 *(Brewster 10, 39, 77)*

Brazil (1) 1 *(Wesley 21)*

England: Anderson; Sessegnon (Eyoma 71), Latibeaudiere, Guehi, Panzo, Oakley-Boothe, McEachran, Foden (Kirby 87), Gibbs-White (Smith-Rowe 68), Hudson-Odoi, Brewster.

FIFA UNDER-7 WORLD CUP – FINAL

Kolkata, Saturday 28 October 2017

England (1) 5 *(Brewster 44, Gibbs-White 58, Foden 69, 88, Guehi 84)*

Spain (2) 2 *(Sergio Gomez 10, 31)*

England: Anderson; Sessegnon, Latibeaudiere, Guehi, Panzo, Oakley-Boothe (Gomes 90), McEachran (Gallagher 87), Foden, Gibbs-White (Kirby 81), Hudson-Odoi, Brewster.

UEFA PREPARATORY FRIENDLY TOURNAMENT

Chesterfield, Wednesday 8 November 2017

England (0) 3 *(Doyle 46, Tavares 54 (og), Duncan 77)*

Portugal (2) 2 *(Ribeiro 19, Fernandez 36)*

England: Seaden; Daley-Campbell, Broughton (Sibley 58), Binks, Laird, Doyle, Garner, Longstaff (Jones 58), Perry (Greenwood 46), Appiah, Tulloch (Duncan 68).

Burton, Saturday 11 November 2017

England (0) 2 *(Mola 49, Greenwood 56)*

Russia (1) 1 *(Kutovoi 2 (pen))*

England: Okwonko; Sibley, Binks (Broughton 46), Shihab, Laird (Daley-Campbell 46), Jones, Greenwood, Dixon-Bonner, Mola, Nolan, Duncan (Tulloch 62).

Rotherham, Tuesday 14 November 2017

England (0) 2 *(Duncan 61, Nolan 75)*

Germany (0) 1 *(Hartmann 71)*

England: Okonkwo; Daley-Campbell, Laird, Binks, Sibley, Doyle, Garner, Jones (Duncan 23), Greenwood, Appiah (Perry 76), Tulloch (Nolan 48).

ALGARVE CUP

Algarve, Friday 9 February 2018

Portugal (2) 4 *(Gomes 24, 40, Embalo 69, Correia 74)*

England (0) 0

England: Okonkwo; Daley-Campbell, Mola, Doyle, Alese, Binks, Amaechi, Anjorin (Daly 59), John-Jules (Duncan 69), Coyle (Greenwood 69), Tulloch (Nolan 69).

Algarve, Sunday 11 February 2018
Germany (0) 1 *(Pohlmann 62)*
England (0) 1 *(Duncan 52)*
England: Ashby-Hammond, Doyle, Binks, Crowe, Saka, Greenwood, Garner, Duncan, Appiah (Coyle 72), Nolan (Amaechi 55), Daly.

Algarve, Tuesday 13 February 2018
England (1) 2 *(Amaechi 30, John-Jules 42)*
Netherlands (0) 0
England: Dewhurst; Daley-Campbell (Crowe 41), Mola (Doyle 41), Alese (Binks 69), Amaechi (Nolan 58), Saka (Sibley 41), Greenwood (Coyle 58), Garner, Duncan (John-Jules 41), Appiah (Tulloch 69), Daly.

UEFA UNDER-17 CHAMPIONSHIPS 2018 (IN ENGLAND)

GROUP A

Chesterfield, Friday 4 May 2018
England (1) 2 *(Doyle 29 (pen), Daly 61)*
Israel (1) 1 *(Lugassy 44 (pen))*
England: Ashby-Hammond; Crowe (Tulloch 58), Ogbeta, Laird, Daley-Campbell, Garner, Doyle, Amaechi, Daly (Dixon-Bonner 78), Saka, John-Jules (Balogun 58).

Walsall, Monday 7 May 2018
England (0) 2 *(Appiah 63, Doyle 69 (pen))*
Italy (1) 1 *(Riccardi 13)*
England: Ashby-Hammond; Daley-Campbell (Crowe 41), Laird, Ogbeta, Saka, Garner, Appiah, Doyle (Tulloch 55), Daly, Amaechi, John-Jules (Duncan 41).

Rotherham, Thursday 10 May 2018
Switzerland (1) 1 *(Mambimbi 40)*
England (0) 0
England: Ashby-Hammond; Crowe, Laird, Alese, Appiah, Anjorin (Daly 57), Garner, Doyle (Dixon-Bonner 13), Amaechi, Saka, Balogun (Duncan 52).

QUARTER-FINALS

Burton, Sunday 13 May 2018
Norway (0) 0
England (1) 2 *(Duncan 14, Amaechi 49)*
England: Ashby-Hammond; Laird, Ogbeta (Tulloch 64), Alese, Daly, Garner, Daley-Campbell, Amaechi, Saka, Appiah (Anjorin 51), Duncan (Balogun 74).

SEMI-FINALS

Chesterfield, Friday 17 May 2018
England (0) 0
Netherlands (0) 0
England: Ashby-Hammond; Daley-Campbell, Alese, Ogbeta, Saka, Garner, Daly, Appiah, Tulloch (Balogun 75), Duncan (John-Jules 69), Anjorin (Dixon-Bonner 65).
Netherlands won 6-5 on penalties.

ENGLAND UNDER-18

FRIENDLIES

Shrewsbury, Friday 1 September 2017
England (0) 0
Brazil (0) 0
England: Anderson; Eyoma, Latibeaudiere, Guehi, Panzo, McEachran, Oakley-Boothe, Foden, Gomes (Smith-Rowe 68), Kirby, Brewster (Loader 76).

Leek Town, Monday 4 September 2017
England (0) 1 *(Foden 90)*
South Africa (1) 2 *(Foster 13, Matthews 76)*
England: Bursik (Crellin 46); Wilson (Eyoma 72), Latibeaudiere (Guehi 46), Gibson, Vokins, Skipp, O'Riley (Oakley-Boothe 72), Smith-Rowe (Foden 49), Kirby (Gomes 46), Barlow (McEachran 62), Loader.

St George's Park, Wednesday 21 March 2018
England (2) 4 *(Walker 11, 29, Poveda-Ocampo 73, 81 (og))*
Qatar (0) 0
England: Bursik; Eyoma, Vokins, Skipp, Latibeaudiere, Sessegnon, Wilson (Poveda-Ocampo 68), Gallagher, Walker, Gibbs-White (Denny 78), Wright.

Manchester City Academy, Friday 23 March 2018
England (0) 2 *(Poveda-Ocampo 52, Perez 78 (og))*
Argentina (1) 1 *(Moroni 36)*
England: Crellin; Sessegnon, Gibson, McEachran, Latibeaudiere, Guehi, Poveda-Ocampo (Eyoma 90), Gibbs-White (Walker 78), Loader, Hudson-Odoi (Vokins 90), Wright (Gallagher 46).

St George's Park, Monday 26 March 2018
England (1) 2 *(Poveda-Ocampo 11, Hudson-Odoi 55)*
Balarus (0) 1 *(Kiryl 71)*
England: Bursik (Crellin 46); Eyoma, Vokins, McEachran (Skipp 80), Guehi, Gibson (Latibeaudiere 63), Poveda-Ocampo (Wright 80), Denny, Loader, Gallagher (Wilson 63), Hudson-Odoi.

THE PANDA CUP 2018 (IN CHINA)

Chengdu, Wednesday 23 May 2018
England (0) 2 *(Kirby 63 (pen), Nmecha)*
Uruguay (1) 2 *(Vecino 15, Schiappacasse 78)*
England: Bursik; Vokins, McEachran (Denney 89), Eyoma, Panzo, Poveda-Ocampo, Gallagher, Nmecha, Kirby (Wilson 84), Loader (Walker 84).

Chengdu, Friday 25 May 2018
China (0) 1 *(Guo Tianyu 79)*
England (0) 0
England: Crellin; Lamptey, Eyoma, Panzo, Vokins, Gallagher, Denney, Poveda-Ocampo, Nmecha, Wright (Kirby 55), Loader (Walker 55).

Chengdu, Sunday 27 May 2018
Hungary (0) 0
England (0) 1 *(Kirby 11)*
England: Crellin (Bursik 46); Lamptey, McEachran, Eyoma, Panzo, Gallagher (Denney 77), Walker, Ferguson, Nmecha (Poveda-Ocampo46), Kirby (Loader 66), Wilson (Vokins 46).

ENGLAND UNDER-19

FRIENDLIES

St George's Park, Friday 1 September 2017

England (7) 7 *(Hirst 6, 25, 27, Nketiah 10, 18, 31, Embleton 15)*

Poland (0) 1 *(Kanach 57)*

England: Balcombe (Turner 46); James, Bennett, Willock (Uwakwe 60), Tanganga, Francis, Kemp (Leko 60), Nydam (McGuane 60), Hirst, Embleton (Mount 67), Nketiah (Nelson 67).

Mansfield, Tuesday 5 September 2017

England (1) 1 *(Nelson 11)*

Germany (2) 3 *(Fein 2, Goller 3, Havertz 90)*

England: Schofield; Sterling, Tymon, McGuane (Willock 76), Francis (Tanganga 59), Brown, Leko (Nketiah 76), Downes (Uwakwe 59), Brereton (Hirst 59), Mount, Nelson (Embleton 90).

Znojmo, Friday 6 October 2017

Czech Republic (0) 1 *(Pfeifer 60)*

England (0) 0

England: Schofield; James (Leko 76), Tymon, Adeniran (Tavernier 76), Feeney, Chalobah, Sterling, Diallo (Embleton 59), Hirst, Mount, Nketiah (Nelson 59).

Senec, Monday 9 October 2017

Slovakia (0) 2 *(Brenkus 49, Filinsky 90)*

England (1) 2 *(Mount 6, Embleton 54)*

England: Balcombe; Sterling, Tymon, Embleton, Chalobah, Tanganga, Kemp (Leko 67), Tavernier (Adeniran 87), Brereton (Hirst 87), Mount (Nketiah 67), Nelson.

EURO U19 CHAMPIONSHIP QUALIFYING GROUP 8

Stara Zagora, Bulgaria, Wednesday 8 November 2017

England (1) 6 *(Nketiah 23, 58, 77 (pen), 90, Embleton 62, Brereton 85)*

Faroe Islands (0) 0

England: Schofield; James, Sessegnon, Downes, Tanganga, Chalobah, Nelson (Mount 79), Willock (Tavernier 71), Nketiah, Embleton, Sancho (Brereton 70).

Stara Zagora, Bulgaria, Saturday 11 November 2017

England (0) 2 *(Mount 70, Nketiah 83)*

Iceland (0) 1 *(Hafsteinsson 82)*

England: Schofield; Sterling, Tanganga, Chalobah, Sessegnon, Tavernier, Downes, Mount, Nelson (Embleton 88), Brereton (Sancho 66), Nketiah.

Stara Zagora, Bulgaria, Tuesday 14 November 2017

Bulgaria (0) 0

England (1) 1 *(Sancho 11)*

England: Balcombe; James, Chalobah, Feeney, Tymon, Sterling, Mount, Embleton (Brereton 59), Tavernier (Adeniran 69), Sancho, Nketiah (Willock 59).

EURO U19 CHAMPIONSHIP ELITE QUALIFYING

Skopje, Wednesday 21 March 2018

Hungary (1) 1 *(Bevardi 39)*

England (0) 4 *(Mount 48, Nelson 54, 86, Sancho 87)*

England: Balcombe; James (Chelsea), Lewis, Downes, Tanganga, Chalobah, Nelson, Willock (McGuane 89), Brereton (Sancho 73), Mount, Nketiah (Hirst 85).

Skopje, Saturday 24 March 2018

England (1) 3 *(Mount 22, 82, Nketiah 52)*

Latvia (0) 0

England: Balcombe; James, Lewis (Francis 74), Downes, Tanganga (Wilmot 84), Chalobah, Nelson (Embleton 71), Willock, Mount, Nketiah, Hirst.

Skopje, Tuesday 27 March 2018

England (0) 0

Macedonia (1) 2 *(Atanasov 3, Mitrovski 90)*

England: Cumming; Chalobah, Mount, Sterling, Sancho (Nketiah 69), Hirst (Brereton 84), Foden, Francis, Embleton, McGuane (Nelson 74), Wilmot.

ENGLAND UNDER-20

UNDER-20 ELITE TOURNAMENT

Telford, Thursday 31 August 2017

England (1) 3 *(Edwards 27, Mavididi 70, Johnson 75)*

Netherlands (0) 0

England: Trott; Duhaney (Justin 74), Johnson, Suliman, Jay Dasilva (Kelly 70), Edun (Vieira 70), Field (Josh Dasilva 62), Buckley-Ricketts (Green 62), Edwards, Willock (Maddox 74), Mavididi (Hinds 70).

Winterthur, Monday 4 September 2017

Switzerland (0) 0

England (0) 0

England: Ramsdale; Justin (Duhaney 62), Kelly, Suliman, Josh Dasilva (Field 75), Vieira (Edun 75), Jay Dasilva, Maddox (Buckley-Ricketts 62), Hinds (Edwards 76), Green (Willock 62), Davis.

Gorgonzola, Thursday 5 October 2017

Italy (1) 1 *(Panico 15)*

England (3) 5 *(Buckley-Ricketts 4, 34, Edwards 21, Suliman 63, Ugbo 67 (pen))*

England: Ramsdale; Brittain, Kelly, Edun (Josh Dasilva 75), Oxford (Konsa 78), Suliman, Buckley-Ricketts, Field, Ugbo, Edwards (Barnes 78), Willock (Mahoney 75).

St George's Park, Tuesday 10 October 2017

England (3) 4 *(Johnson 17, Mavididi 25 (pen), 75, Barnes 36)*

Czech Republic (0) 0

England: Trott; Konsa, Johnson, Oxford (Brittain 60), Josh Dasilva (Field 75), Barnes, Jay Dasilva, Mahoney, Edwards (Edun 60), Willock (Buckley-Ricketts 60), Mavididi.

Zwickau, Tuesday 14 November 2017

Germany (2) 2 *(Eggestein 10, 32)*

England (0) 1 *(Barnes 86)*

England: Ramsdale; Konsa (Brittain 73), Suliman, Oxford (Kelly 81), Josh Dasilva, Edun (Barnes 61), Jay Dasilva, Mahoney (O'Hare 81), Edwards, Willock (Buckley-Ricketts 61), Mavididi (Ugbo 73).

Bielsku-Bialej, Thursday 22 March 2018

Poland (0) 0

England (0) 1 *(Davis 89)*

England: Trott; Wan-Bissaka■, Kelly, Dasilva, Johnson, Suliman, Sims (Buckley-Ricketts 68), Field (Edun 68), Hepburn-Murphy (Davis 61), Edwards (Willock 61), Barnes (Brittain 78).

Manchester City Academy, Tuesday 27 March 2018

England (2) 3 *(Willock 15, Davis 41, Suliman 66)*

Portugal (0) 0

England: Trott; Brittain (Wan-Bissaka 67), Kelly, Edun, Konsa (Johnson 82), Suliman, Buckley-Ricketts, Josh Dasilva (Vieira 82), Davis (Hepburn-Murphy 76), Edwards (Barnes 67), Willock (Sims 76).

SCHOOLS FOOTBALL 2017–18

BOODLES INDEPENDENT SCHOOLS FA CUP 2017–18

After extra time.

PRELIMINARY ROUND

Berkhamsted v Bournemouth Collegiate	5-1
Brooke House v Norwich	6-2
Haberdashers' Aske's v Bedales	4-0
Kingston GS v Sherborne	5-3
Lingfield College v Trinity	4-4*
(Lingfield College won 7-6 on penalties)	
Oswestry v Stockport GS	7-0
Radnor House v Harrodian	0-11
RGS Worcester v Box Hill	0-3
Sevenoaks v ACS Cobham	0-2
Truro v Taunton	4-1
Wellington v Canford	6-1

FIRST ROUND

ACS Cobham v Wolverhampton GS	4-1
ACS Hillingdon v Bury GS	1-1*
(Bury GS won 4-2 on penalties)	
Alleyn's v St John's, Leatherhead	1-0
Bede's v RGS Guildford	11-0
Bolton v Lingfield College	4-0
Box Hill v Lancing	0-5
Bradford v King Edward's, Witley	4-0
Brighton College v Kimbolton	3-2
Brooke House v Berkhamsted	3-0
Charterhouse v King's School, Chester	4-0
City of London v Bedford Modern	5-2
Dulwich v LVS Ascot	6-1
Eton v Hurstpierpoint	11-0
Forest v RGS Newcastle	1-2
Grammar School at Leeds v Chigwell	6-4*
Grange v Royal Russell	0-3
Haberdashers' Aske's v St. Bede's Col.	2-0
Harrodian v Tonbridge	5-0
Harrow v Brentwood	5-2
Highgate v Bristol GS	7-1
Ibstock Place v Ardingly	0-4
John Lyon v Aldenham	1-2*
Manchester GS v Birkdale	4-0
Merchant Taylors (Crosby) v Cheadle Hulme	4-2
Oldham Hulme GS v Kingston GS	1-1*
(Kingston GS won 4-2 on penalties)	
Queen Ethelburga's v Repton	1-2*
Shrewsbury v Winchester	2-1*
Truro v Latymer Upper	1-2*
University College School v Millfield	0-4
Wellington v Oswestry	4-0
Westminster v Hampton	0-3
Whitgift v St. Columba's Col.	5-1

SECOND ROUND

Aldenham v Grammar School at Leeds	0-3
Alleyn's v Royal Russell	1-1*
(Alleyn's won 5-4 on penalties)	
Ardingly v Dulwich	7-0
Bede's v Bolton	6-1
Bradfield v Brighton College	5-0

Brooke House v Repton	0-3
Bury GS v Harrodian	0-3
City of London v ACS Cobham	2-6
Hampton v Charterhouse	4-1
Highgate v Manchester GS	3-1
Kingston GS v Wellington	1-3
Lancing v Whitgift	2-2*
(Whitgift won 3-1 on penalties)	
Latymer Upper v Shrewsbury	8-2
Merchant Taylors (Crosby) v Harrow	0-9
Millfield v Haberdashers' Aske's	7-0
RGS Newcastle v Eton	1-6

THIRD ROUND

Alleyn's v Ardingly	0-1
Eton v Hampton	2-1
Harrow v Harrodian	2-1
Highgate v ACS Cobham	2-1
Latymer Upper v Millfield	1-2*
Repton v Bede's	6-1
Wellington v Bradfield	2-3*
Whitgift v Grammar School at Leeds	4-1

FOURTH ROUND

Ardingly v Eton	0-1
Highgate v Bradfield	2-6
Millfield v Whitgift	3-0
Repton v Harrow	2-0

SEMI-FINALS

Eton v Repton	0-1
Bradfield v Millfield	0-0*
(Bradfield won 5-3 on penalties)	

FINAL (at Milton Keynes Dons FC)

Bradfield 3 *(Yeung, Mulikas, Hodgkinson)*

Repton 1 *(Raine)*

Bradfield: Q. McCallion, M. Arber, J. Valentin, E. Cook, S. Haynes, J. Davis, J. Cheung, T. Mulikas, E. Sideso, E. Yeung, J. Hodgkinson.
Substitutes: W. Bray, J. Whishaw, B. Bolt, F. Lapidus, N. Beuchler.
Repton: M. Stanojevic, M. Bowman, C. Cottis, O. Hickman, O. Williams, M. Ferrinho, L. Tandy, E. Killington, J. Raine, A. Aliev, T. Buffin, J. Pollard.
Substitutes: J. Parton, A. Edwards, E. Sawyers, M. Barnes-Batty.
Referee: Martin Atkinson (Yorkshire).

INVESTEC ISFA U15 CUP FINAL

Whitgift v Lochinver House	8-2
(at Burton Albion FC)	

INVESTEC ISFA U13 CUP FINAL

Aldenham v Cheadle Hulme	4-1
(at Burton Albion FC)	

UNIVERSITY FOOTBALL 2018

134th UNIVERSITY MATCH

(Sunday 25 March, at The Hive, Barnet FC)

Oxford (2) 3 *(Thelen 24, 77, Ackerman 31)*   **Cambridge (0) 0**

Oxford squad: Sam Abernethy, Thomas Achtel, Leo Ackerman, Wulfie Bain, Ollie Cantrill, Callum Cleary, Jake Duxbury, Mohamed Eghleilib, Dylan Evans, Tom Faktor, Sean Gleeson, Sam Hale, Harry Langham, Eddy Mort, Matthew Naylor, Jamie Shaw, Danny Simpson, Dom Thelen, Takahiro Tsunoda, Alex Urwin, Cian Wade, Till Wicker, Jack Witt, Laurence Wroe.

Cambridge squad: George Boughton, Jack Congdon), Joe Gregory, George Herring, Michael Hofstetter, Oscar Melbourne, Ollie Lerway, Stefan Wolf, Henry Alexander, Joe Ellis, Ben Bolderson, Nick Gallagher, Adib Badri, Rufus Saunders, James Campsie, Yusuf Mushtaq.

Oxford have won 55 games (2 on penalties), Cambridge 52 games (3 on penalties) and 27 games have been drawn. Oxford have scored 214 goals, Cambridge 207 goals.

WOMEN'S SUPER LEAGUE 2017–18

FA WOMEN'S SUPER LEAGUE 1 SPRING SERIES TABLE 2017

		Home					Away					Total						
		P	W	D	L	F	A	W	D	L	F	A	W	D	L	F	A	GD	Pts
1	Chelsea	8	2	1	0	15	2	4	0	1	17	1	6	1	1	32	3	29	19
2	Manchester C	8	2	1	1	7	3	4	0	0	10	3	6	1	1	17	6	11	19
3	Arsenal	8	2	1	0	9	6	3	2	0	13	3	5	3	0	22	9	13	18
4	Liverpool	8	2	0	1	9	5	2	2	1	11	13	4	2	2	20	18	2	14
5	Sunderland	8	1	2	2	2	9	1	1	1	2	5	2	3	3	4	14	−10	9
6	Reading	8	0	1	2	3	8	2	1	2	7	7	2	2	4	10	15	−5	8
7	Birmingham C	8	1	2	2	2	4	0	2	1	4	6	1	4	3	6	10	−4	7
8	Bristol C	8	0	1	4	2	16	1	0	2	3	5	1	1	6	5	21	−16	4
9	Yeovil T	8	0	0	5	5	15	0	1	2	1	11	0	1	7	6	26	−20	1

FA WOMEN'S SUPER LEAGUE 2 SPRING SERIES TABLE 2017

		Home					Away					Total						
		P	W	D	L	F	A	W	D	L	F	A	W	D	L	F	A	GD	Pts
1	Everton	9	4	0	0	13	0	3	1	1	12	7	7	1	1	25	7	18	22
2	Doncaster Belles	9	3	1	0	11	6	2	2	1	8	3	5	3	1	19	9	10	18
3	Millwall Lionesses	9	3	1	1	7	4	2	1	1	5	4	5	2	2	12	8	4	17
4	Aston Villa	9	4	1	0	15	10	1	1	2	4	6	5	2	2	19	16	3	17
5	Durham	9	5	0	0	8	1	0	1	3	6	9	5	1	3	14	10	4	16
6	Brighton & HA	9	2	2	0	6	3	0	2	3	2	10	2	4	3	8	13	−5	10
7	London Bees	9	2	1	2	7	9	1	0	3	6	12	3	1	5	13	21	−8	10
8	Watford	9	1	2	2	7	7	1	0	3	5	10	2	2	5	12	17	−5	8
9	Sheffield	9	1	0	3	5	9	1	0	4	4	9	2	0	7	9	18	−9	6
10	Oxford U	9	0	1	3	2	8	0	1	4	5	11	0	2	7	7	19	−12	2

FA WOMEN'S SUPER LEAGUE 1 TABLE 2017–18

		Home					Away					Total						
		P	W	D	L	F	A	W	D	L	F	A	W	D	L	F	A	GD	Pts
1	Chelsea	18	7	2	0	23	6	6	3	0	21	7	13	5	0	44	13	31	44
2	Manchester C	18	7	1	1	29	7	5	1	3	22	10	12	2	4	51	17	34	38
3	Arsenal	18	7	2	0	21	6	4	2	3	17	12	11	4	3	38	18	20	37
4	Reading	18	4	3	2	19	10	5	2	2	21	8	9	5	4	40	18	22	32
5	Birmingham C	18	7	1	1	19	4	2	2	5	11	14	9	3	6	30	18	12	30
6	Liverpool	18	5	1	3	18	11	4	0	5	12	16	9	1	8	30	27	3	28
7	Sunderland	18	2	1	6	8	21	3	0	6	7	19	5	1	12	15	40	−25	16
8	Bristol C	18	2	0	7	6	26	3	1	5	7	21	5	1	12	13	47	−34	16
9	Everton	18	3	0	6	13	16	1	2	6	6	14	4	2	12	19	30	−11	14
10	Yeovil T	18	0	2	7	0	19	0	0	9	2	35	0	2	16	2	54	−52	2

No promotion and relegation due to league restructure.

FA WOMEN'S SUPER LEAGUE LEADING GOALSCORERS 2017–18

Player	Team	Goals	Player	Team	Goals
Ellen White	Birmingham C	15	Jill Scott	Manchester C	7
Nikita Parris	Manchester C	11	Fara Williams	Reading	7
Beth England	Liverpool	10	Eniola Aluko	Chelsea	6
Remi Allen	Reading	9	Ji So-yun	Chelsea	6
Isobel Christiansen	Manchester C	9	Danielle van de Donk	Arsenal	5
Brooke Chaplen	Reading	8	Georgia Stanway	Manchester C	5
Francesca Kirby	Chelsea	8	Courtney Sweetman-Kirk	Everton	5
Beth Mead	Arsenal	8	Danielle Turner	Everton	5
Laren Hemp	Bristol C	7			

FA FA WOMEN'S SUPER LEAGUE 2 TABLE 2017–18

		Home					Away					Total						
		P	W	D	L	F	A	W	D	L	F	A	W	D	L	F	A	GD	Pts
1	Doncaster Belles	18	8	1	0	31	8	7	1	1	21	7	15	2	1	52	15	37	47
2	Brighton & HA	18	8	0	1	21	9	4	1	4	14	17	12	1	5	35	26	9	37
3	Millwall Lionesses	18	7	1	1	20	11	5	2	2	20	12	12	3	3	40	23	17	36
4	Durham	18	6	2	1	20	7	5	0	4	24	19	11	2	5	44	26	18	35
5	Sheffield	18	6	0	3	22	16	3	1	5	18	15	9	1	8	40	31	9	28
6	London Bees	18	4	1	4	14	16	2	4	3	15	16	6	5	7	29	32	−3	23
7	Tottenham H	18	4	2	3	21	15	2	2	5	11	19	6	4	8	32	34	−2	22
8	Oxford U	18	2	2	5	16	20	1	1	7	8	21	3	3	12	24	41	−17	12
9	Aston Villa	18	2	2	5	13	18	1	0	8	8	22	3	2	13	21	40	−19	11
10	Watford	18	0	1	8	2	25	1	0	8	6	32	1	1	16	8	57	−49	4

WOMEN'S SUPER LEAGUE CONTINENTAL TYRES CUP 2017–18

After extra time.

PRELIMINARY ROUND

GROUP STAGE

Group One North Table

	P	W	Pn	L	F	A	GD	Pts
Sunderland	4	2	2	0	5	2	3	10
Liverpool	4	2	1	1	11	2	9	8
Sheffield	4	1	0	1	8	10	−2	5
Aston Villa	4	1	1	2	7	12	−5	5
Durham	4	0	0	2	3	8	−5	2

Group Two North Table

	P	W	Pn	L	F	A	GD	Pts
Manchester C	4	4	0	0	13	3	10	12
Everton	4	3	0	1	9	2	7	9
Birmingham C	4	2	0	2	7	5	2	6
Doncaster R Belles	4	1	0	3	9	10	−1	3
Oxford U	4	0	0	4	1	19	−18	0

Group One South Table

	P	W	Pn	L	F	A	GD	Pts
Reading	4	4	0	0	15	1	14	12
Arsenal	4	3	0	1	19	4	15	9
Watford	4	1	0	2	2	11	−9	4
Millwall Lionesses	4	1	0	3	6	14	−8	3
London Bees	4	0	1	3	4	16	−12	2

Group Two South Table

	P	W	Pn	L	F	A	GD	Pts
Chelsea	4	4	0	0	17	2	15	12
Bristol C	4	2	0	2	6	4	2	6
Brighton & HA	4	2	0	2	8	9	−1	6
Tottenham H	4	2	0	2	6	9	−3	6
Yeovil T	4	0	0	4	3	16	−13	0

Pn = won on penalties to gain 2pts.

KNOCK-OUT ROUNDS

QUARTER-FINALS
Everton v Reading	1-1*
Reading won 4-3 on penalties.	
Arsenal v Sunderland	3-1
Bristol C v Manchester C	0-2
Chelsea v Liverpool	5-1

SEMI-FINALS
Chelsea v Manchester C	0-1
Reading v Arsenal	2-3

WOMEN'S CONTINENTAL TYRES CUP FINAL 2018
Wycombe, Wednesday 14 March 2018

Arsenal (1) 1 *(Miedema 32)*

Manchester C (0) 0 2136

Arsenal: Van Veenendaal; Evans, Williamson, Quinn, Mitchell, Janssen, Van de Donk, Mead (O'Reilly 81), Nobbs, Little (McCabe 89), Miedema (Carter 73).
Manchester C: Roebuck; McManus, Houghton, Beattie, Stokes, Scott (Lawley 81), Walsh, Christiansen (Emslie 61), Parris, Nadim (Ross 45), Stanway.
Referee: Amy Fearn.

Fran Kirby scores Chelsea's final goal in their 3-1 win over Arsenal in the Women's FA Cup Final at Wembley on 5 May. (Reuters/Paul Childs)

FA WOMEN'S PREMIER LEAGUE 2017–18

FA WOMEN'S PREMIER LEAGUE NORTHERN DIVISION 2017–18

			Home				Away					Total						
		P	W	D	L	F	A	W	D	L	F	A	W	D	L	F	A	GD	Pts
1	Blackburn R	22	9	0	2	39	7	9	2	0	29	10	18	2	2	68	17	51	56
2	Leicester C Women	22	5	2	4	28	18	9	2	0	40	14	14	4	4	68	32	36	46
3	Middlesbrough	22	7	0	4	32	21	7	0	4	31	31	14	0	8	63	52	11	42
4	Stoke C	22	6	2	3	25	21	6	2	3	27	17	12	4	6	52	38	14	40
5	Fylde	22	5	4	2	17	21	5	2	4	18	14	10	6	6	35	35	0	36
6	Huddersfield T	22	6	2	3	23	9	4	3	4	22	18	10	5	7	45	27	18	35
7	Derby Co	22	2	4	5	9	17	5	1	5	18	20	7	5	10	27	37	–10	26
8	Bradford C	22	4	2	5	26	23	3	2	6	14	22	7	4	11	40	45	–5	25
9	Nottingham F	22	4	1	6	15	26	1	3	7	8	31	5	4	13	23	57	–34	19
10	Guiseley Vixens	22	3	4	4	22	26	1	1	9	11	30	4	5	13	33	56	–23	17
11	Wolverhampton W	22	2	1	8	17	29	2	4	5	13	27	4	5	13	30	56	–26	17
12	WBA	22	3	1	7	13	27	1	1	9	14	32	4	2	16	27	59	–32	14

FA WOMEN'S PREMIER LEAGUE SOUTHERN DIVISION 2017–18

			Home				Away					Total						
		P	W	D	L	F	A	W	D	L	F	A	W	D	L	F	A	GD	Pts
1	Charlton Ath	22	10	0	1	50	8	10	0	1	48	5	20	0	2	98	13	85	60
2	C & K Basildon	22	11	0	0	26	4	6	1	4	25	20	17	1	4	51	24	27	52
3	Crystal Palace	22	8	2	1	32	6	8	0	3	27	9	16	2	4	59	15	44	50
4	Coventry U	22	8	0	3	33	12	6	2	3	36	8	14	2	6	69	20	49	44
5	Lewes	22	8	2	1	26	5	6	0	5	19	20	14	2	6	45	25	20	44
6	Portsmouth	22	7	1	3	27	16	6	0	6	17	19	12	1	9	44	35	9	37
7	West Ham U	22	5	1	5	30	24	4	1	6	27	18	9	2	11	57	42	15	29
8	Chichester C	22	5	1	5	19	22	3	3	5	24	26	8	4	10	43	48	–5	28
9	Gillingham	22	3	1	7	12	26	2	1	8	12	27	5	2	15	24	53	–29	17
10	Cardiff C	22	2	2	7	21	34	2	2	7	19	35	4	4	14	40	69	–29	16
11	QPR	22	1	1	9	9	49	1	1	9	8	45	2	2	18	17	94	–77	8
12	Swindon T	22	0	0	11	6	60	0	0	11	4	59	0	0	22	10	119	–109	0

PROMOTION PLAY-OFF
Blackburn R v Charlton Ath   1-2

FA WOMEN'S PREMIER LEAGUE NORTHERN DIVISION ONE 2017–18

			Home				Away					Total						
		P	W	D	L	F	A	W	D	L	F	A	W	D	L	F	A	GD	Pts
1	Hull C	22	10	1	0	40	6	7	2	2	26	8	17	3	2	66	14	52	54
2	Brighouse T	22	8	0	3	30	16	8	2	1	30	14	16	2	4	60	30	30	50
3	Liverpool Feds	22	8	2	1	32	6	6	2	3	16	12	14	4	4	48	18	30	46
4	Bolton W	22	6	1	4	21	17	5	0	6	17	21	11	1	10	38	38	0	34
5	Newcastle U	22	6	2	3	29	22	3	1	7	15	25	9	3	10	44	47	–3	30
6	Chorley	22	6	1	4	25	16	3	1	7	16	25	9	2	11	41	41	0	29
7	Morecambe	22	4	1	6	30	33	5	1	5	19	27	9	2	11	49	60	–11	29
8	Crewe Alex	22	4	2	5	17	15	3	3	5	13	18	7	5	10	30	33	–3	26
9	Chester-le-Street	22	6	0	5	19	20	2	1	8	16	29	8	1	13	35	49	–14	25
10	Leeds U	22	3	1	7	12	20	4	1	6	14	23	7	2	13	26	43	–17	23
11	Barnsley	22	1	4	6	12	25	3	1	7	20	39	4	5	13	32	64	–32	17
12	Mossley Hill	22	5	1	5	18	16	0	1	10	10	44	5	2	15	28	60	–32	17

FA WOMEN'S PREMIER LEAGUE MIDLANDS DIVISION ONE 2017–18

			Home				Away					Total						
		P	W	D	L	F	A	W	D	L	F	A	W	D	L	F	A	GD	Pts
1	Loughborough Foxes	22	11	0	0	53	3	10	1	0	38	6	21	1	0	91	9	82	64
2	Burton Alb	22	7	2	2	31	15	8	0	3	23	17	15	2	5	54	32	22	47
3	Sheffield U	22	8	2	1	44	11	5	5	1	35	13	13	7	2	79	24	55	46
4	Radcliffe Olympic	22	7	2	2	25	13	6	0	5	26	18	13	2	7	51	31	20	41
5	The New Saints	22	6	2	3	41	20	6	1	4	35	25	12	3	7	76	45	31	39
6	Long Eaton U	22	4	1	6	16	17	6	0	5	22	22	10	1	11	38	39	–1	31
7	Solihull	22	3	2	6	24	24	6	1	4	31	23	9	3	10	55	47	8	30
8	Sporting Khalsa	22	4	0	7	19	19	4	2	5	21	20	8	2	12	40	39	1	26
9	Birmingham & West Midlands	22	3	1	7	29	27	4	5	5	19	25	7	3	12	48	52	–4	24
10	Steel City W	22	4	1	6	23	34	3	1	7	20	39	7	2	13	43	73	–30	23
11	Rotherham U	22	1	1	9	9	50	1	0	10	6	64	2	1	19	15	114	–99	7
12	Leicester City Ladies	22	0	0	11	5	49	1	1	9	6	47	1	1	20	11	96	–85	4

FA WOMEN'S PREMIER LEAGUE SOUTH EAST DIVISION ONE 2017–18

			Home					Away					Total					
		P	W	D	L	F	A	W	D	L	F	A	W	D	L	F	A	GD	Pts
1	Milton Keynes D	22	9	2	0	41	9	9	1	1	35	9	18	3	1	76	18	58	57
2	AFC Wimbledon	22	9	0	2	42	14	8	1	2	26	11	17	1	4	68	25	43	52
3	Ipswich T	22	8	1	2	34	11	7	2	2	42	15	15	3	4	76	26	50	48
4	Leyton Orient	22	6	1	4	34	21	6	2	3	25	12	12	3	7	59	33	26	39
5	Luton T	22	5	2	4	32	23	6	0	5	34	16	11	2	9	66	39	27	35
6	Stevenage	22	5	2	4	25	18	4	2	5	23	19	9	4	9	48	37	11	31
7	Old Actonians	22	5	1	5	37	16	4	2	5	19	16	9	3	10	56	32	24	30
8	Cambridge U	22	5	3	3	22	13	3	3	5	18	15	8	6	8	40	28	12	30
9	Denham U	22	4	2	5	19	23	1	5	5	19	24	5	7	10	38	47	−9	22
10	Enfield T	22	3	4	4	17	14	2	1	8	14	36	5	5	12	31	50	−19	20
11	Norwich C	22	2	1	8	19	26	2	0	9	20	55	4	1	17	39	81	−42	13
12	Haringey Bor	22	0	0	11	9	93	0	0	11	6	103	0	0	22	15	196	−181	0

FA WOMEN'S PREMIER LEAGUE SOUTH WEST DIVISION ONE 2017–18

			Home					Away					Total					
		P	W	D	L	F	A	W	D	L	F	A	W	D	L	F	A	GD	Pts
1	Plymouth Arg	18	9	0	0	64	6	7	2	0	36	6	16	2	0	100	12	88	50
2	Southampton WFC	18	8	1	0	28	4	7	1	1	40	16	15	2	1	68	20	48	47
3	Keynsham T	18	7	1	1	51	12	6	0	3	31	13	13	1	4	82	25	57	40
4	Southampton Saints	18	6	2	1	21	8	6	0	3	17	12	12	2	4	38	20	18	38
5	Poole T	18	2	1	6	20	27	4	1	4	12	19	6	2	10	32	46	−14	20
6	Brislington	18	2	2	5	12	22	3	1	5	13	29	5	3	10	25	51	−26	18
7	Larkhall Ath	18	3	0	6	13	24	1	2	6	8	26	4	2	12	21	50	−29	14
8	Maidenhead U	18	3	1	5	11	24	1	1	7	6	28	4	2	12	17	52	−35	14
9	Cheltenham T	18	2	0	7	7	22	1	1	7	10	36	3	1	14	17	58	−41	10
10	St Nicholas	18	2	1	6	11	31	1	0	8	7	53	3	1	14	18	84	−66	10

11 Basingstoke. *Basingstoke resigned from the league (February 2018). All records expunged.*

FA WOMEN'S PREMIER LEAGUE CUP 2017–18

After extra time.

DETERMINING ROUND

Blackburn R v Barnsley	3-0
Bradford C v Fylde	3-3*

Bradford C won 3-2 on penalties.

C & K Basildon v Basingstoke T	8-0
Cheltenham T v Actonians	1-2
Chester-le-Street v Hull C	3-2
Chichester C v West Ham U	4-1
Chorley v Leicester C Women	1-5
Coventry U v Haringey Bor	16-1
Crystal Palace v Brislington	10-1
Derby Co v Rotherham U	7-0
Enfield T v Keynsham T	3-2
Gillingham v Stevenage	0-1
Larkhall Ath v Ipswich T	1-8
Leicester City Ladies v Bolton W	0-5
Lewes v Southampton	3-1*
Long Eaton U v WBA	1-2*
Loughborough Foxes v Sporting Khalsa	5-0
Luton T v Leyton Orient	2-4
Maidenhead U v Poole T	0-1*
Middlesbrough v Burton Alb	5-0
Milton Keynes D v AFC Wimbledon	0-1
Morecambe v Stoke C	1-3
Mossley Hill v Brighouse T	0-1
Newcastle U v Huddersfield T	0-3
Norwich C v Cardiff C	0-5
QPR v Portsmouth	0-3
Sheffield U v Birmingham & West Midlands	6-0
Solihull v Guiseley Vixens	1-2*
Southampton v Denham U	4-2
St Nicholas v Cambridge U	0-5
Steel City W v Radcliffe Olympic	5-2*
Swindon T v Charlton Ath	0-11
The New Saints v Crewe Alex	3-3*

The New Saints won 5-4 on penalties.

Wolverhampton W v Liverpool Marshalls Feds	0-2
Nottingham F v Leeds U	7-1

PRELIMINARY ROUND

Liverpool Marshalls Feds v Steel City W	3-1
Poole T v Crystal Palace	0-8
Southampton v Actonians	2-0*
The New Saints v Leicester C Women	2-5

FIRST ROUND

Charlton Ath v AFC Wimbledon	3-2
Crystal Palace v Lewes	1-2
Enfield T v Cambridge U	0-2

Sheffield U v Liverpool Marshalls Feds	1-2
Southampton v Portsmouth	1-3
Stoke C v Blackburn R	2-2*

Blackburn R won 4-3 on penalties.

Nottingham F v WBA	5-0
Derby Co v Bradford C	5-2*
Ipswich T v C & K Basildon	1-0

C & K Basildon awarded the match.

Loughborough Foxes v Middlesbrough	2-0
Stevenage v Coventry U	0-2
Brighouse T v Chester-le-Street	5-1
Cardiff C v Leyton Orient	3-1
Guiseley Vixens v Huddersfield T	3-2
Leicester C Women v Bolton W	3-0
Plymouth Arg v Chichester C	3-1

SECOND ROUND

Cardiff C v Plymouth Arg	1-2
Leicester C Women v Loughborough Foxes	3-1
C & K Basildon v Charlton Ath	1-2*
Lewes v Portsmouth	5-1
Liverpool Marshalls Feds v Blackburn R	1-2
Nottingham F v Guiseley Vixens	5-0
Brighouse T v Derby Co	3-2
Cambridge U v Coventry U	0-5

QUARTER-FINALS

Charlton Ath v Lewes	1-2*
Brighouse T v Blackburn R	1-2
Nottingham F v Leicester C Women	1-1*

Leicester C Women won 5-4 on penalties.

Plymouth Arg v Coventry U	0-3

SEMI-FINALS

Leicester C Women v Lewes	4-2
Blackburn R v Coventry U	2-2*

Blackburn R won 3-2 on penalties.

FA WOMEN'S LEAGUE CUP FINAL

Chesterfield, Sunday 29 April 2018

Blackburn R (1) 3 *(Shepherd 33, Cook 74, Jordon 90)*

Leicester C Women (1) 1 *(Domingo 14)*

Blackburn R: Hill; Pearson, Jukes, Cook, McDonald, Fenton, Shepherd, Holbrook, Cunliffe (Walsh 68), Jordan, Taylor.
Leicester C Women: Clarke; James, Morgan, Greengrass, Acton (Brown 79), Nymeon (May 58), Stewart, Johnson (Crossman 79), Domingo, Dugmore, Axten.
Referee: Amy Fearn (Derbyshire).

THE SSE WOMEN'S FA CUP 2017–18

After extra time.

FIRST QUALIFYING ROUND

Alnwick T Juniors v Washington	3-2
Blyth T Lions v South Shields	0-3
RACA Tynedale v Norton & Stockton Ancients (walkover)	
Penrith v South Park Rangers	4-2
Workington Reds v Redcar T	1-2
Prudhoe T v Chester-le-Street SC	A-A

Match abandoned after 116 minutes due to serious injury to a player, 2-5 – tie awarded to Chester-le-Street

Bishop Auckland v Gateshead Leam Rangers	4-2
Carlisle U v Wallsend Boys Club	3-1
Sheffield Wednesday v Yorkshire Amateur	2-1
Altofts (walkover) v Bradford Park Avenue	
Malet Lambert v Wakefield	4-5*

(4-4 at the end of normal time)

Ossett Alb v Farsley Celtic	0-5
Dronfield T v Harworth Colliery	A-A

Match abandoned after 68 minutes due to serious injury to a player, 0-5 – tie awarded to Harworth

Nelson v Blackpool	0-14
Merseyrail Bootle v Stockport Co	4-2
Wigan Ath v Accrington Girls & Ladies	7-0
FC United of Manchester v Altrincham	13-1
West Didsbury & Chorlton v Warrington Wolverines	3-2
Manchester Stingers v Blackburn Community SC	2-1
Fleetwood T Wrens v Burnley	0-6
Lincoln Moorlands Railway v Cosby U	4-3
Loughborough Students v Mansfield T	4-2
AFC Leicester v Leicester C Development	0-2
Rise Park v Teversal	7-3
Market Warsop v Nettleham	0-5
Eastwood CFC v Arnold T	3-0
Leafield Ath v Knowle	5-1
Leek T v Solihull U	2-1
Wyrley v Lye T	0-3
Redditch U v Stockingford AA Pavilion	2-1
Shrewsbury T v Wolverhampton Sporting Community	4-2
Solihull Sporting v Coventry Sphinx	0-8
Crusaders v Abbey Hulton U	6-2
Shrewsbury Juniors v Brereton T	0-3
Coundon Court v Goldenhill W	2-6
Rugby T v Worcester U	1-4
Sutton Coldfield T v Bedworth U	0-4
Gornal (walkover) v Stone Dominoes	
Newmarket T v Histon	4-2
Kettering T v Woodford U	10-0
Sprowston v Wymondham T	0-4
Roade v St Ives T	0-1
Oadby & Wigston v King's Lynn T	1-3
Peterborough Northern Star (walkover) v Netherton U	
Cambridge C v Moulton	8-2
Riverside v Corby T	2-1
March T U v Peterborough U	0-5
Acle U v Thrapston T	4-1
Colchester U v Bungay T	2-4
Harlow T v Little Thurrock Dynamos	4-0
Brentwood T v Corringham Cosmos	6-0
AFC Sudbury v Writtle	4-3
Billericay T v Chelmsford C	8-0
Milton Keynes C v Bedford	2-4*

(2-2 at the end of normal time)

Sandy v Hemel Hempstead T (walkover)	
AFC Dunstable v Houghton Ath	5-0
Royston T v Watford Development	7-0
Hertford T v Bishop's Stortford	0-1
Garston v Colney Heath	1-4
Brentford v Chesham U	1-7
Headington v Ashford T (Middlesex)	0-17
Ascot U v Newbury	1-1*

Ascot U won 4-3 on on penalties

Benson Lionesses v Wargrave	4-2
Fleet T v Alton	1-8
Oxford C v Woodley U	9-0

Tie awarded to Woodley U – Oxford C removed

Chinnor v New London Lionesses	0-12
Queens Park Rangers Girls v Hampton & Richmond Bor	0-1
Meridian v Fulham Foundation	2-1
Ashford Girls v Aylesford	2-3*

(1-3 at the end of normal time)

Kent Football U v London Kent Football U	0-4
Worthing v Godalming T	1-2
Eastbourne T v Dartford	7-0
Worthing T v Parkwood Rangers	1-7
Victoire v Burgess Hill T	2-2*

Burgess Hill T won 4-2 on penalties

Whyteleafe v Bexhill U	1-0
Abbey Rangers v Eastbourne	1-2
Carshalton Ath v Herne Bay	3-0

Tie awarded to Herne Bay – Carshalton Ath removed

Frampton Rangers v New Milton T	2-3
Buckland Ath v Exeter C	9-2
AEK Boco v Downend Flyers	0-9
FC Chippenham v Team Solent	4-3*

(3-3 at the end of normal time)

Middlezoy R v Marine Academy Plymouth	1-7
Royal Wootton Bassett T v AFC Bournemouth	2-5
Warsash Wasps v Ilminster T	4-0
Winchester C Flyers v Frome T	5-0
Bournemouth Sports v Keynsham T Development	3-1
Eastleigh v Torquay U	0-6

SECOND QUALIFYING ROUND

Alnwick T Juniors v Redcar T	1-0
Cramlington U v Carlisle U	1-7
Bishop Auckland v South Shields	1-6
Chester-le-Street SC v Harworth U	0-9
Norton & Stockton Ancients v Penrith	3-2*

(1-1 at the end of normal time)

Worksop v Farsley Celtic	3-5
Altofts v Sheffield Wednesday	4-3*

(1-1 at the end of normal time)

Wakefield v Harworth Colliery	4-3
Blackpool v West Didsbury & Chorlton	2-2*

West Didsbury & Chorlton won 3-2 on penalties

CMB v Tranmere R	2-1
Burnley v Merseyrail Bootle	4-3
Manchester Stingers v MSB Woolton	0-6
Wigan Ath v FC United of Manchester	1-0
Eastwood CFC v Rise Park	4-0
Loughborough Students v Lincoln Moorlands Railway	6-3
Leicester C Development v Nettleham	2-3*

(2-2 at the end of normal time)

Shrewsbury T v Leek T	5-2
Redditch U v Goldenhill W	5-1
Leafield Ath v Lye T	1-2
Bedworth U v Gornal	2-0*

(0-0 at the end of normal time)

Worcester U v Coventry Sphinx	2-8
Brereton T v Crusaders	2-1
Newmarket T v King's Lynn T	4-3*

(3-3 at the end of normal time)

Acle U (walkover) v Riverside	
Cambridge C v Kettering T	5-2
Peterborough Northern Star v Peterborough U	4-2
Wymondham T v St Ives T	7-1
Frontiers v AFC Sudbury	1-8
Harlow T v Bungay T	3-2
Brentwood T v Billericay T	2-3
Colney Heath v Royston T	0-4
Hemel Hempstead T v Bedford	0-12
AFC Dunstable v Bishop's Stortford	7-1
Benson Lionesses v Ashford T (Middlesex)	1-12
New London Lionesses v Hampton & Richmond Bor	2-0
Ascot U v Chesham U	0-2
Woodley U v Alton	2-1
Eastbourne T v Aylesford	5-2
Godalming T v Eastbourne	3-2*

(2-2 at the end of normal time)

Meridian v London Kent Football U	2-3
Hassocks v Margate	5-1
Herne Bay v Parkwood Rangers	1-3
Whyteleafe v Burgess Hill T	6-0
Marine Academy Plymouth v Buckland Ath (walkover)	
FC Chippenham v Bournemouth Sports	2-1
New Milton T v Downend Flyers	5-4
Pen Mill v Forest Green R	1-4
Torquay U v AFC Bournemouth	1-0
Winchester C Flyers v Warsash Wasps	5-1

THIRD QUALIFYING ROUND

Alnwick T Juniors v Rotherham U	5-0
Farsley Celtic v Hartlepool U	1-3
Burnley v Wigan Ath	4-1
West Didsbury & Chorlton v MSB Woolton	6-3
Brighouse T v Wakefield	6-1
Altofts v Chorley	1-5
Chester-Le-Street T v Barnsley	2-1

Crewe Alexandra v Hull C	1-4
South Shields v Norton & Stockton Ancients	0-3
CMB v Bolton W	2-5
Liverpool Marshalls Feds v Mossley Hill	7-0
Steel City W v Morecambe	2-1
Sheffield U v Leeds U	3-3*
Sheffield U won 3-2 on penalties	
Newcastle U v Carlisle U	9-1
Redditch U v Solihull Moors	5-2
Sporting Khalsa v Lye T	6-1
The New Saints v Shrewsbury T	3-1
Eastwood CFC v Coventry Sphinx	5-3
Long Eaton U v Leicester C	3-1
Bedworth U v Birmingham & West Midlands	2-1
Radcliffe Olympic v Loughborough Foxes (walkover)	
Loughborough Students v Brereton T	3-0
Burton Alb v Nettleham	0-4
Milton Keynes Dons v Actonians	2-0
Cambridge C v Ipswich T	1-5
Maidenhead U v Luton T	0-1
Cambridge U's v Norwich C	4-0
Peterborough Northern Star v Acle U	1-3
Harlow T v Denham U	1-0
Wymondham T v Newmarket T	9-2*
(2-2 at the end of normal time)	
Enfield T v AFC Sudbury	1-0
Godalming T v Haringey Bor	5-0
Ashford T (Middlesex) v London Kent Football U	6-4
AFC Dunstable v Eastbourne T	2-0
New London Lionesses v Parkwood Rangers	3-1*
(1-1 at the end of normal time)	
Leyton Orient v Billericay T	7-0
Hassocks v Stevenage	0-8
Bedford v Royston T	2-3
Chesham U v Whyteleafe	2-1
AFC Wimbledon v Woodley U	14-1
Cheltenham T v Southampton Saints	1-4
FC Chippenham v Basingstoke T	1-6
Poole T v Plymouth Arg	2-5
St Nicholas v Keynsham T	0-1
New Milton T v Buckland Ath	1-4
Winchester C Flyers v Southampton	0-7
Forest Green R v Larkhall Ath	0-3
Brislington v Torquay U	0-0*
Brislington won 4-2 on penalties	

FIRST ROUND

Alnwick T Juniors v Burnley	0-4
Liverpool Marshalls Feds v Bolton W	1-0*
(0-0 at the end of normal time)	
Hull C v Steel City W	4-1
Norton & Stockton Ancients v Chorley	0-4
Farsley Celtic v West Didsbury & Chorlton	6-4*
(4-4 at the end of normal time)	
Newcastle U v Sheffield U	3-0
Brighouse T v Chester-le-Street T	6-1
Bedworth U v The New Saints	0-2
Redditch U v Loughborough Foxes	2-4
Nettleham v Loughborough Students	3-0
Sporting Khalsa v Eastwood CFC	5-1
Cambridge U's v Long Eaton U	0-1
Enfield T v Wymondham T	3-2
Harlow T v Royston T	2-1
Stevenage v Acle U	4-1
Ipswich T v Leyton Orient	4-2*
(2-2 at the end of normal time)	
Ashford T (Middlesex) v Milton Keynes Dons	0-6
Chesham U v New London Lionesses	1-2*
(1-1 at the end of normal time)	
AFC Wimbledon v Godalming T	5-0
AFC Dunstable v Luton T	0-4
Larkhall Ath v Southampton	2-3
Buckland Ath v Brislington	1-4
Plymouth Arg (walkover) v Basingstoke T	
Southampton Saints v Keynsham T	1-3

SECOND ROUND

Middlesbrough v Farsley Celtic	8-1
Sporting Khalsa v The New Saints	2-2*
The New Saints won 4-1 on penalties	
Derby Co v Hull C	1-1*
Derby Co won 3-2 on penalties	
Huddersfield T v West Bromwich Alb	7-0
Nettleham v Liverpool Marshalls Feds	1-3
Nottingham Forest v Newcastle U	0-2
Bradford C v Long Eaton U	5-0
Blackburn R v Loughborough Foxes	4-1
Fylde v Guiseley Vixens	2-0
Stoke C v Burnley	0-0*
Burnley won 4-1 on penalties	
Brighouse T v Wolverhampton W	6-3
Chorley v Leicester C	0-3

Keynsham T v Southampton	2-1
Milton Keynes Dons v Cardiff C	0-1
Lewes v Enfield T	7-0
Charlton Ath v Queens Park Rangers	5-0
Gillingham v Plymouth Arg	1-3*
(1-1 at the end of normal time)	
Brislington v Swindon T	3-2*
(2-2 at the end of normal time)	
AFC Wimbledon v Portsmouth	1-2
New London Lionesses v Crystal Palace	0-3
Luton T v Harlow T	3-2*
(2-2 at the end of normal time)	
Coventry U v West Ham U	6-1
Chichester C v C&K Basildon	4-2*
(2-2 at the end of normal time)	
Stevenage v Ipswich T	1-1*
Ipswich T won 3-0 on penalties	

THIRD ROUND

Cardiff C v Burnley	3-2
Fylde v Plymouth Arg	1-3
Keynsham T v Brislington	8-1
Huddersfield T v Lewes	1-2
Leicester C v Bradford C	2-1
Newcastle U v The New Saints	1-2
Blackburn R v Portsmouth	7-0
Brighouse T v Derby Co	3-1
Ipswich T v Charlton Ath	2-5*
(2-2 at the end of normal time)	
Crystal Palace v Coventry U	1-1*
Coventry U won 3-2 penalties	
Middlesbrough v Liverpool Marshalls Feds	4-3*
(3-3 at the end of normal time)	
Chichester C v Luton T	2-0

FOURTH ROUND

Durham v Sheffield	2-1
Aston Villa v Middlesbrough	4-0
Sunderland v Brighouse T	13-0
Keynsham T v Lewes	0-3
Tottenham Hotspur v Doncaster R Belles	0-3
Liverpool v Watford	5-0
Cardiff C v Oxford U	0-0*
Cardiff C won 5-4 on penalties	
The New Saints v Chichester C	1-1*
Chichester C won 5-4 on kicks penalties	
Millwall Lionesses v Coventry U	4-1
Reading v Birmingham C	0-1
Plymouth Arg v Leicester C	2-3
Brighton & Hove Alb v Manchester C	0-2
Blackburn R v Charlton Ath	2-3*
(2-2 at the end of normal time)	
Yeovil v Arsenal	0-3
London Bees v Chelsea	0-10
Everton v Bristol C's	3-1

FIFTH ROUND

Arsenal v Millwall Lionesses	1-0
Cardiff C v Charlton Ath	1-3
Lewes v Everton	0-6
Sunderland v Aston Villa	3-2
Chichester C v Liverpool	0-3
Birmingham C v Manchester C	1-3*
(1-1 at the end of normal time)	
Chelsea v Doncaster R Belles	6-0
Durham v Leicester C	5-2

SIXTH ROUND

Sunderland v Manchester C	2-4
(2-2 at the end of normal time)	
Liverpool v Chelsea	0-3
Arsenal v Charlton Ath	5-0
Durham v Everton	1-6

SEMI-FINALS

Everton v Arsenal	1-2
Chelsea v Manchester C	2-0

THE SSE WOMEN'S FA CUP FINAL 2018

Wembley, Saturday 5 May 2018

Chelsea (0) 3 *(Bachmann 48, 60, Kirby 76)*

Arsenal (0) 1 *(Miedema 73)*   45,423

Chelsea: Lindahl; Bright, Mjelda, Eriksson, Blundell, So-Yun, Chapman, Andersson, (Thorisdottir 70), Spence (Cuthbert 75), Bachmann (Aluko 85), Kirby.
Arsenal: van Veenendaal; Evans (Carter 85), Williamson, Quinn, Mitchell (McCabe 45), Janssen (O'Reilly 63), Nobbs, van de Donk, Little, Mead, Miedema.
Referee: Lindsey Robinson.

UEFA WOMEN'S CHAMPIONS LEAGUE 2017-18

■*Denotes player sent off.*

QUALIFYING ROUND

GROUP 1 (GEORGIA)

Konak Belediyespor v Martve	5-0
Gintra Universitetas v Partizan Bardejov	4-0
Gintra Universitetas v Martve	6-0
Partizan Bardejov v Konak Belediyespor	1-5
Martve v Partizan Bardejov	0-3
Konak Belediyespor v Gintra Universitetas	1-3

Group 1 Table	P	W	D	L	F	A	GD	Pts
Gintra Universitetas	3	3	0	0	13	1	12	9
Konak Belediyespor	3	2	0	1	11	4	7	6
Partizan Bardejov	3	1	0	2	4	9	–5	3
Martve	3	0	0	3	0	14	–14	0

GROUP 2 (ROMANIA)

Hibernian v Swansea C	5-0
Olimpia Cluj v Kharkiv	1-0
Kharkiv v Hibernian	1-1
Olimpia Cluj v Swansea C	3-0
Swansea C v Kharkiv	0-9
Hibernian v Olimpia Cluj	1-1

Group 2 Table	P	W	D	L	F	A	GD	Pts
Olimpia Cluj	3	2	1	0	5	1	4	7
Hibernian	3	1	2	0	7	2	5	5
Kharkiv	3	1	1	1	10	2	8	4
Swansea C	3	0	0	3	0	17	–17	0

GROUP 3 (ESTONIA)

Ajax v Rigas	6-0
Standard Liege v Parnu	2-0
Standard Liege v Rigas	8-0
Parnu v Ajax	1-2
Rigas v Parnu	0-2
Ajax v Standard Liege	3-0

Group 3 Table	P	W	D	L	F	A	GD	Pts
Ajax	3	3	0	0	11	1	10	9
Standard Liege	3	2	0	1	10	3	7	6
Parnu	3	1	0	2	3	4	–1	3
Rigas	3	0	0	3	0	16	–16	0

GROUP 4 (NORTHERN IRELAND)

Medyk Konin v Shelbourne	0-0
PK-35 Vantaa v Linfield	1-0
Medyk Konin v Linfield	4-1
Shelbourne v PK-35 Vantaa	0-0
Linfield v Shelbourne	1-3
PK-35 Vantaa v Medyk Konin	1-2

Group 4 Table	P	W	D	L	F	A	GD	Pts
Medyk Konin	3	2	1	0	6	2	4	7
Shelbourne	3	1	2	0	3	1	2	5
PK–35 Vantaa	3	1	1	1	2	2	0	4
Linfield	3	0	0	3	2	8	–6	0

GROUP 5 (CYPRUS)

Apollon Limassol v NSA Sofia	4-0
Sturm Graz v Noroc Nimoreni	4-0
NSA Sofia v Sturm Graz	1-3
Apollon Limassol v Noroc Nimoreni	6-0
Noroc Nimoreni v NSA Sofia	0-1
Sturm Graz v Apollon Nicosia	1-4

Group 5 Table	P	W	D	L	F	A	GD	Pts
Apollon Limassol	3	3	0	0	14	1	13	9
Sturm Graz	3	2	0	1	8	5	3	6
NSA Sofia	3	1	0	2	2	7	–5	3
Noroc Nimoreni	3	0	0	3	0	11	–11	0

GROUP 6 (SLOVENIA)

Zurich v Olimpija Ljubljana	2-1
Minsk v Birkirkara	8-0
Zurich v Birkirkara	5-0
Olimpija Ljubljana v Minsk	0-5
Birkirkara v Olimpija Ljubljana	0-1
Minsk v Zurich	0-0

Group 6 Table	P	W	D	L	F	A	GD	Pts
Minsk	3	2	1	0	13	0	13	7
Zurich	3	2	1	0	7	1	6	7
Olimpija Ljubljana	3	1	0	2	2	7	–5	3
Birkirkara	3	0	0	3	0	14	–14	0

GROUP 7 (CROATIA)

Stjarnan v Klaksvikar Itrottarfelag	9-0
Osijek v Istatov	7-0
Stjarnan v Istatov	11-0
Klaksvikar Itrottarfelag v Osijek	0-4
Istatov v Klaksvikar Itrottarfelag	1-6
Osijek v Stjarnan	0-1

Group 7 Table	P	W	D	L	F	A	GD	Pts
Stjarnan	3	3	0	0	21	0	21	9
Osijek	3	2	0	1	11	1	10	6
Klaksvikar Itrottarfelag	3	1	0	2	6	14	–8	3
Istatov	3	0	0	3	1	24	–23	0

GROUP 8 (HUNGARY)

MTK Hungaria v Hajvalia	2-0
BIIK-Kazygurt v Sporting Lisbon	2-1
Sporting Lisbon v MTK Hungaria	2-0
BIIK-Kazygurt v Hajvalia	1-0
Hajvalia v Sporting Lisbon	1-4
MTK Hungaria v BIIK-Kazygurt	0-3

Group 8 Table	P	W	D	L	F	A	GD	Pts
BIIK-Kazygurt	3	3	0	0	6	1	5	9
Sporting Lisbon	3	2	0	1	7	3	4	6
MTK Hungaria	3	1	0	2	2	5	–3	3
Hajvalia	3	0	0	3	1	7	–6	0

GROUP 9 (MONTENEGRO)

Spartak Subotica v Kiryat Gat	7-1
Avaldsnes v Breznica Pljevlja	2-1
Kiryat Gat v Avaldsnes	2-6
Spartak Subotica v Breznica Pljevlja	6-0
Breznica Pljevlja v Kiryat Gat	2-2
Avaldsnes v Spartak Subotica	2-0

Group 9 Table	P	W	D	L	F	A	GD	Pts
Avaldsnes	3	3	0	0	10	3	7	9
Spartak Subotica	3	2	0	1	13	3	10	6
Breznica Pljevlja	3	0	1	2	3	10	–7	1
Kiryat Gat	3	0	1	2	5	15	–10	1

GROUP 10 (BOSNIA-HERZEGOVINA)

PAOK Thessaloniki v Bettembourg	8-0
Sarajevo v Vllaznia	0-1
Sarajevo v Bettembourg	3-0
Vllaznia v PAOK Thessaloniki	0-1
Bettembourg v Vllaznia	0-2
PAOK Thessaloniki v Sarajevo	3-0

Group 10 Table	P	W	D	L	F	A	GD	Pts
PAOK Thessaloniki	3	3	0	0	12	0	12	9
Vllaznia	3	2	0	1	3	1	2	6
Sarajevo	3	1	0	2	3	4	–1	3
Bettembourg	3	0	0	3	0	13	–13	0

ROUND OF 32 FIRST LEG

BIIK-Kazygurt v Glasgow C	3-0
Medyk Konin v Lyon	0-5
PAOK Thessaloniki v Sparta Prague	0-5
Apollon Limassol v Linkoping	0-1
Gintra Universitetas v Zurich	1-1
Minsk v Slavia Prague	1-3
LSK Kvinner v Brondby	0-4
Avaldsnes v Barcelona	0-0
Ajax v Brescia	1-0
Atletico Madrid v Wolfsburg	0-3
Chelsea v Bayern Munich	1-0
St Polten v Manchester C	0-3
Fiorentina v Fortuna Hjorring	2-1
Montpellier v Zvezda 2005	0-1
Olimpia Cluj v Rosengard	0-1
Stjarnan v Rossiyanka	1-1

ROUND OF 32 SECOND LEG *(agg)*

Rossiyanka v Stjarnan	0-4	1-5
Wolfsburg v Atletico Madrid	12-2	15-2

Sparta Prague v PAOK Thessaloniki	3-0	8-0
Brondby v LSK Kvinner	1-3	1-3
Zvezda 2005 v Montpellier	0-2	1-2
Linkoping v Apollon Limassol	3-0	4-0
Barcelona v Avaldsnes	2-0	6-0
Lyon v Medyk Konin	9-0	14-0
Slavia Prague v Minsk	4-3	7-4
Rosengard v Olimpia Cluj	4-0	5-0
Bayern Munich v Chelsea	2-1	2-2

Chelsea won on away goals

Zurich v Gintra Universitetas	1-2	2-3
Fortuna v Fiorentina	0-0	1-2
Brescia v Ajax	2-0	2-1
Manchester C v St Polten	3-0	6-0
Glasgow C v BIIK-Kazygurt	4-1	4-4

BIIK-Kazygurt won on away goals

ROUND OF 16 FIRST LEG

BIIK-Kazygurt v Lyon	0-7
Brescia v Montpellier	2-3
Gintra Universitetas v Barcelona	0-6
Sparta Prague v Linkoping	1-1
Fiorentina v Wolfsburg	0-4
Chelsea v Rosengard	3-0
LSK Kvinner v Manchester C	0-5
Stjarnan v Slavia Prague	1-2

ROUND OF 16 SECOND LEG

		(agg)
Wolfsburg v Fiorentina	3-3	7-3
Linkoping v Sparta Prague	3-0	4-1
Rosengard v Chelsea	0-1	0-4
Barcelona v Gintra Universitetas	3-0	9-0
Lyon v BIIK-Kazygurt	9-0	16-0
Montpellier v Brescia	6-0	9-2
Slavia Prague v Stjarnan	0-0	2-1
Manchester C v LSK Kvinner	2-1	7-1

QUARTER-FINALS FIRST LEG

Manchester C v Linkoping	2-0
Montpellier v Chelsea	0-2
Wolfsburg v Slavia Prague	5-0
Lyon v Barcelona	2-1

QUARTER-FINALS SECOND LEG

		(agg)
Chelsea v Montpellier	3-1	5-1
Slavia Prague v Wolfsburg	1-1	1-6
Linkoping v Manchester C	3-5	3-7
Barcelona v Lyon	0-1	1-3

SEMI-FINALS FIRST LEG

| Chelsea v Wolfsburg | 1-3 |
| Manchester C v Lyon | 0-0 |

SEMI-FINALS SECOND LEG

		(agg)
Wolfsburg v Chelsea	2-0	5-1
Lyon v Manchester C	1-0	1-0

UEFA WOMEN'S CHAMPIONS LEAGUE FINAL

Kiev, Thursday 24 May 2018

Lyon (0) 4 *(Henry 98, Le Sommer 99, Hegerberg 103, Abily 116)*

Wolfsburg (0) 1 *(Harder 93)*   14,237

Lyon: Bouhaddi; Bronze, M'Bock Bathy, Renard, Bacha (Cascarino 64), Kumagai (van de Sanden 95), Henry, Marozsan, Hegerberg, Le Sommer (Abily 114), Majri.
Wolfsburg: Schult; Blasse, Fischer, Goessling, Maritz, Hansen (Wullaert 46), Gunnarsdottir (Wedemeyer 57), Popp*, Dickenmann (Kerschowski 89), Pajor, Harder.
aet.
Referee: Jana Adamkova (Czech Republic).

UEFA WOMEN'S EURO 2017

FINALS IN NETHERLANDS

After extra time.

GROUP STAGE

GROUP A

Netherlands v Norway	1-0
Denmark v Belgium	1-0
Norway v Belgium	0-2
Netherlands v Denmark	1-0
Norway v Denmark	0-1
Belgium v Netherlands	1-2

Group A Table	P	W	D	L	F	A	GD	Pts
Netherlands	3	3	0	0	4	1	3	9
Denmark	3	2	0	1	2	1	1	6
Belgium	3	1	0	2	3	3	0	3
Norway	3	0	0	3	0	4	–4	0

GROUP B

Italy v Russia	1-2
Germany v Sweden	0-0
Sweden v Russia	2-0
Germany v Italy	2-1
Sweden v Italy	2-3
Russia v Germany	0-2

Group B Table	P	W	D	L	F	A	GD	Pts
Germany	3	2	1	0	4	1	3	7
Sweden	3	1	1	1	4	3	1	4
Russia	3	1	0	2	2	5	–3	3
Italy	3	1	0	2	5	6	–1	3

GROUP C

Austria v Switzerland	1-0
France v Iceland	1-0
Iceland v Switzerland	1-2
France v Austria	1-1
Iceland v Austria	0-3
Switzerland v France	1-1

Group C Table	P	W	D	L	F	A	GD	Pts
Austria	3	2	1	0	5	1	4	7
France	3	1	2	0	3	2	1	5
Switzerland	3	1	1	1	3	3	0	4
Iceland	3	0	0	3	1	6	–5	0

GROUP D

Spain v Portugal	2-0
England v Scotland	6-0
Scotland v Portugal	1-2
England v Spain	2-0
Scotland v Spain	1-0
Portugal v England	1-2

Group D Table	P	W	D	L	F	A	GD	Pts
England	3	3	0	0	10	1	9	9
Spain	3	1	0	2	2	3	–1	3
Scotland	3	1	0	2	2	8	–6	3
Portugal	3	1	0	2	3	5	–2	3

QUARTER-FINALS

Netherlands v Sweden	2-0
Germany v Denmark	1-2
Austria v Spain	0-0*

Austria won 5-3 on penalties.

| England v France | 1-0 |

SEMI-FINALS

| Denmark v Austria | 0-0* |

Denmark won 3-0 on penalties.

| Netherlands v England | 3-0 |

UEFA WOMEN'S EURO 2017 FINAL

Enschede, Sunday 6 August 2017

Netherlands (2) 4 *(Miedema 10, 89, Martens 28, Spitse 51)*

Denmark (2) 2 *(Nadim 6 (pen), Harder 33)*   28,182

Netherlands: van Veenendaal; van Lunteren (Janssen 57), van der Gragt, van Es (van den Berg 90), Dekker, van de Sanden (Jansen 90), Spitse, Miedema, van de Donk, Martens.
Denmark: Petersen; Kildemoes (Thogersen 61), Boye-Sorensen (Roddik 77), Troelsgaard, Nielsen, Nadim, Harder, Veje, Larsen, Pedersen (Christiansen 82), Sandvej.
Referee: Esther Staubli (Switzerland).

WOMEN'S FIFA WORLD CUP 2019

QUALIFYING – EUROPE

GROUP 1

Kazakhstan v Wales	0-1
England v Russia	6-0
Kazakhstan v Bosnia-Herzegovina	0-2
Russia v Wales	0-0
Wales v Kazakhstan	1-0
England v Bosnia-Herzegovina	4-0
Bosnia-Herzegovina v Wales	0-1
England v Kazakhstan	5-0
Bosnia-Herzegovina v Russia	1-6
England v Wales	0-0
Kazakhstan v Russia	0-3
Bosnia-Herzegovina v England	0-2
Wales v Bosnia-Herzegovina	1-0
Russia v England	1-3
Bosnia-Herzegovina v Kazakhstan	0-2
Wales v Russia	3-0

Group 1 Table	P	W	D	L	F	A	GD	Pts
Wales	7	5	2	0	7	0	7	17
England	6	5	1	0	20	1	19	16
Russia	6	2	1	3	10	13	–3	7
Kazakhstan	6	1	0	5	2	12	–10	3
Bosnia-Herzegovina	7	1	0	6	3	16	–13	3

GROUP 2

Albania v Switzerland	1-4
Poland v Belarus	4-1
Belarus v Albania	1-0
Switzerland v Poland	2-1
Belarus v Scotland	1-2
Scotland v Albania	5-0
Albania v Poland	1-4
Switzerland v Belarus	3-0
Switzerland v Albania	5-1
Switzerland v Scotland	1-0
Poland v Albania	1-1
Albania v Belarus	1-0
Scotland v Poland	3-0
Scotland v Belarus	2-1
Poland v Scotland	2-3
Belarus v Switzerland	0-5

Group 2 Table	P	W	D	L	F	A	GD	Pts
Switzerland	6	6	0	0	20	3	17	18
Scotland	6	5	0	1	16	5	10	15
Poland	6	2	1	3	12	11	1	7
Albania	7	1	1	5	5	20	–15	4
Belarus	7	1	0	6	4	17	–13	3

GROUP 3

Norway v Northern Ireland	4-1
Norway v Slovakia	6-1
Northern Ireland v Republic of Ireland	0-2
Slovakia v Republic of Ireland	0-2
Netherlands v Norway	1-0
Slovakia v Netherlands	0-5
Slovakia v Northern Ireland	1-3
Netherlands v Republic of Ireland	0-0
Republic of Ireland v Slovakia	2-1
Netherlands v Northern Ireland	7-0
Republic of Ireland v Netherlands	0-2
Northern Ireland v Norway	0-3
Republic of Ireland v Norway	0-2
Northern Ireland v Netherlands	0-5
Norway v Republic of Ireland	1-0
Netherlands v Slovakia	1-0

Group 3 Table	P	W	D	L	F	A	GD	Pts
Netherlands	7	6	1	0	21	0	21	19
Norway	6	5	0	1	16	3	13	15
Republic of Ireland	7	3	1	3	6	6	0	10
Northern Ireland	6	1	0	5	4	22	–18	3
Slovakia	6	0	0	6	3	19	–16	0

GROUP 4

Ukraine v Croatia	1-1
Hungary v Denmark	1-6
Croatia v Sweden	0-2
Hungary v Croatia	2-2
Sweden v Denmark	3-0
Match awarded 3-0 to Sweden after game was cancelled.	
Croatia v Denmark	0-4
Sweden v Hungary	5-0
Hungary v Ukraine	0-1
Croatia v Ukraine	0-3
Hungary v Sweden	1-4
Croatia v Hungary	1-3

Denmark v Ukraine	1-0
Sweden v Croatia	4-0
Ukraine v Denmark	1-5
Denmark v Hungary	5-1
Ukraine v Sweden	1-0

Group 4 Table	P	W	D	L	F	A	GD	Pts
Sweden	6	5	0	1	18	2	16	15
Denmark	6	5	0	1	21	6	15	15
Ukraine	6	3	1	2	7	7	0	10
Hungary	7	1	1	5	8	24	–16	4
Croatia	7	0	2	5	4	19	–15	2

GROUP 5

Faroe Islands v Czech Republic	0-8
Germany v Slovenia	6-0
Iceland v Faroe Islands	8-0
Czech Republic v Germany	0-1
Germany v Iceland	2-3
Slovenia v Czech Republic	0-4
Germany v Faroe Islands	11-0
Czech Republic v Iceland	1-1
Slovenia v Faroe Islands	5-0
Slovenia v Iceland	0-2
Germany v Czech Republic	4-0
Slovenia v Germany	0-4
Faroe Islands v Iceland	0-5
Faroe Islands v Slovenia	0-4
Iceland v Slovenia	2-0
Czech Republic v Faroe Islands	4-1

Group 5 Table	P	W	D	L	F	A	GD	Pts
Iceland	6	5	1	0	21	3	18	16
Germany	6	5	0	1	28	3	25	15
Czech Republic	6	3	1	2	17	7	10	10
Slovenia	7	2	0	5	9	18	–9	6
Faroe Islands	7	0	0	7	1	45	–44	0

GROUP 6

Italy v Moldova	5-0
Romania v Italy	0-1
Belgium v Moldova	12-0
Belgium v Romania	3-2
Italy v Romania	3-0
Portugal v Belgium	0-1
Portugal v Moldova	8-0
Romania v Moldova	3-1
Portugal v Italy	0-1
Moldova v Italy	1-3
Belgium v Portugal	1-1
Italy v Belgium	2-1
Moldova v Romania	0-0
Italy v Portugal	3-0
Moldova v Belgium	0-7
Romania v Portugal	1-1

Group 6 Table	P	W	D	L	F	A	GD	Pts
Italy	7	7	0	0	18	2	16	21
Belgium	6	4	1	1	25	5	20	13
Portugal	6	1	2	3	10	7	3	5
Romania	6	1	2	3	6	9	–3	5
Moldova	7	0	1	6	2	38	–36	1

GROUP 7

Serbia v Austria	0-4
Serbia v Israel	2-0
Finland v Serbia	1-0
Israel v Spain	0-6
Austria v Israel	2-0
Serbia v Spain	1-2
Finland v Israel	4-0
Spain v Austria	4-0
Israel v Finland	0-0
Austria v Serbia	1-1
Finland v Spain	0-2
Israel v Serbia	0-1
Austria v Spain	0-1
Spain v Israel	2-0
Finland v Austria	0-2
Serbia v Finland	0-2
Israel v Austria	0-6

Group 7 Table	P	W	D	L	F	A	GD	Pts
Spain	6	6	0	0	17	1	16	18
Austria	7	4	1	2	15	6	9	13
Finland	6	3	1	2	7	4	3	10
Serbia	7	2	1	4	5	10	–5	7
Israel	8	0	1	7	0	23	–23	1

ENGLAND WOMEN'S INTERNATIONALS 2017–18

■ *Denotes player sent off.*

UEFA WOMEN'S EURO 2017 – GROUP D
Utrecht, Wednesday 19 July 2017
England (3) 6 *(Taylor 10, 26, 53, White 32, Nobbs 87, Duggan 90)*
Scotland (0) 0
England: Bardsley; Bronze, Houghton, Bright, Stokes, Nobbs, Moore, Scott J, White (Carney 74), Kirby (Parris 65), Taylor (Duggan 60).

Breda, Sunday 23 July 2017
England (1) 2 *(Kirby 2, Taylor 85)*
Spain (0) 0
England: Bardsley; Bronze, Houghton, Bright, Stokes, Nobbs, Moore, Scott J, White (Duggan 79), Kirby (Christiansen 69), Taylor (Potter 90).

Tilburg, Thursday 27 July 2017
Portugal (1) 1 *(Mendes 17)*
England (1) 2 *(Duggan 7, Parris 48)*
England: Chamberlain; Scott A, Bassett, Bright (Nobbs 60), Greenwood, Carney, Williams, Potter, Christiansen; Duggan (Stokes 81), Parris.

UEFA WOMEN'S EURO 2017 – QUARTER-FINALS
Deventer, Sunday 30 July 2017
England (0) 1 *(Taylor 60)*
France (0) 0
England: Bardsley (Chamberlain 75); Bronze, Houghton, Bright, Stokes, Nobbs, Moore, Scott J, White, Kirby, Taylor.

UEFA WOMEN'S EURO 2017 – SEMI-FINALS
Enschede, Thursday 4 August 2017
Netherlands (1) 3 *(Miedema 22, van de Donk 62, Bright 90 (og))*
England (0) 0
England: Chamberlain; Bronze, Houghton, Bright, Stokes, Nobbs, Moore (Carney 76), Williams (Duggan 67), White, Kirby, Taylor.

2019 FIFA WORLD CUP QUALIFYING – GROUP 1
Tranmere, Tuesday 19 September 2017
England (4) 6 *(Parris 11, Taylor 13, Nobbs 36, Bronze 44, Duggan 57, 84)*
Russia (0) 0
England: Chamberlain; Bronze, Houghton, Bright, Stokes, Scott J, Williams (Moore 61), Nobbs, Carney (Lawley 61), Taylor (Parris 83), Duggan (Christiansen 83).

Walsall, Friday 24 November 2017
England (1) 4 *(Houghton 19, 54, Parris 46, Kirby 83)*
Bosnia (0) 0
England: Chamberlain; Bronze, Houghton, Bright, Greenwood, Nobbs, Kirby, Christiansen (Potter 73), Parris (Lawley 81), Carter, Duggan.

Colchester, Tuesday 28 November 2017
England (1) 5 *(Lawley 15, Kirby 64 (pen), Parris 68, 75, Christiansen 76)*
Kazakhstan (0) 0
England: Bardsley; Bronze (Carter 76), Houghton, Bonner, Greenwood, Walsh, Williams (Christiansen 62), Scott J, Parris, Taylor (Kirby 62), Lawley.
Southampton, Friday 6 April 2018
England (0) 0
Wales (0) 0   25,603
England: Telford; Bronze, Houghton, McManus, Stokes, Nobbs, Walsh, Kirby, Parris (Lawley 55), Taylor (White 55), Duggan (Mead 80).
Wales: O'Sullivan; Dykes, Ingle, Roberts, Harding, James, Green, Fishlock, Rowe, Ladd, Estcourt.

Zenica, Tuesday 10 April 2018
Bosnia-Herzegovina (0) 0
Spahic■
England (0) 2 *(Duggan 56, Taylor 90 (pen))*
England: Telford; Bronze, Houghton, McManus, Greenwood!, Nobbs, Moore, Christiansen (Daly 80), Lawley (Mead 57), White, Duggan (Taylor 87).

Moscow, Friday 8 June 2018
Russia (1) 1 *(Danilova 31)*
England (3) 3 *(Paris 22, Scott J 27, 36)*
England: Telford; Bronze, McManus, Bright, Daly, Scott J, Walsh (Williamson 84), Parris, Kirby, Duggan (Mead 62), White (Taylor 67).

SHEBELIEVES CUP
Columbus, Thursday 1 March 2018
England (3) 4 *(Duggan 7, Scott J 28, Taylor 39, Kirby 47)*
France (0) 1 *(Bright 52)*
England: Bardsley (Telford 83); Bronze, Asante (McManus 14), Bright, Stokes (Greenwood 87), Scott J, Walsh, Kirby (Christiansen 71), Parris (Lawley 61), Taylor, Duggan (White 71).

New Jersey, Sunday 4 March 2018
England (1) 2 *(White 18, 73)*
Germany (1) 2 *(Kayikci 17, Bright 51 (og))*
England: Chamberlain; Bronze, McManus, Bright, Stokes; Scott J (Christiansen 67), Williams (Walsh 59), Kirby (Taylor 90), Lawley (Daly 85), White, Duggan (Parris 67).

Orlando, Thursday 8 March 2018
USA (0) 1 *(Bardsley 58 (og))*
England (0) 0
England: Bardsley; Bronze, Bright, McManus, Stokes (Blundell 87), Walsh (Scott J 87), Christiansen, Lawley (Duggan 52), Kirby (Daly 75), White, Taylor (Parris 52).

FRIENDLIES
Valenciennes, Friday 20 October 2017
France (0) 1 *(Asseyi)*
England (0) 0
England: Chamberlain; Houghton, Bright, Bronze, Stokes, Duggan, Carney (Lawley 62), Nobbs, Williams, Scott J, Taylor (Parris 84).

ENGLAND WOMEN'S INTERNATIONAL MATCHES 1972–2018

Note: In the results that follow, WC = World Cup; EC = European (UEFA) Championships; M = Mundialito; CC = Cyprus Cup; AC = Algarve Cup. * = After extra time. Games were organised by the Women's Football Association from 1971 to 1992 and the Football Association from 1993 to date. **Bold type** indicates matches played in season 2017–18.

v ARGENTINA

wc2007	17 Sept	Chengdu	6-1

v AUSTRALIA

2003	3 Sept	Burnley	1-0
cc2015	6 Mar	Nicosia	3-0
2015	27 Oct	Yongchuan	1-0

v AUSTRIA

wc2005	1 Sept	Amstetten	4-1
wc2006	20 Apr	Gillingham	4-0
wc2010	25 Mar	Shepherd's Bush	3-0
wc2010	21 Aug	Krems	4-0
2017	10 Apr	Milton Keynes	3-0

v BELARUS

EC2007	27 Oct	Walsall	4-0
EC2008	8 May	Minsk	6-1
wc2013	21 Sept	Bournemouth	6-0
wc2014	14 June	Minsk	3-0

v BELGIUM

1978	31 Oct	Southampton	3-0
1980	1 May	Ostende	1-2
M1984	20 Aug	Jesolo	1-1
M1984	25 Aug	Caorle	2-1
1989	14 May	Epinal	2-0
EC1990	17 Mar	Ypres	3-0
EC1990	7 Apr	Sheffield	1-0
EC1993	6 Nov	Koksijde	3-0
EC1994	13 Mar	Nottingham	6-0
EC2016	8 Apr	Rotherham	1-1
EC2016	20 Sept	Leuven	2-0

v BOSNIA-HERZEGOVINA

EC2015	29 Nov	Bristol	1-0
EC2016	12 Apr	Zenica	1-0
2017	**24 Nov**	**Walsall**	**4-0**
2018	**10 Apr**	**Zenica**	**2-0**

v CANADA

wc1995	6 June	Helsingborg	3-2
2003	19 May	Montreal	0-4
2003	22 May	Ottawa	0-4
cc2009	12 Mar	Nicosia	3-1
cc2010	27 Feb	Nicosia	0-1
cc2011	7 Mar	Nicosia	0-2
cc2013	13 Mar	Nicosia	1-0
2013	7 Apr	Rotherham	1-0
cc2014	10 Mar	Nicosia	2-0
cc2015	11 Mar	Larnaca	1-0
2015	29 May	Hamilton	0-1
wc2015	27 June	Vancouver	2-1

v CHINA PR

AC2005	15 Mar	Guia	0-0*
2007	26 Jan	Guangzhou	0-2
2015	9 Apr	Manchester	2-1
2015	23 Oct	Yongchuan	1-2

v COLOMBIA

wc2015	17 June	Montreal	2-1

v CROATIA

EC1995	19 Nov	Charlton	5-0
EC1996	18 Apr	Osijek	2-0
EC2012	31 Mar	Vrbovec	6-0
EC2012	19 Sept	Walsall	3-0

v CZECH REPUBLIC

2005	26 May	Walsall	4-1
EC2008	20 Mar	Doncaster	0-0
EC2008	28 Sept	Prague	5-1

v DENMARK

1979	19 May	Hvidovre	1-3
1979	13 Sept	Hull	2-2
1981	9 Sept	Tokyo	0-1
EC1984	8 Apr	Crewe	2-1
EC1984	28 Apr	Hjorring	1-0
M1985	19 Aug	Caorle	0-1
EC1987	8 Nov	Blackburn	2-1
EC1988	8 May	Herning	0-2
1991	28 June	Nordby	0-0
1991	30 June	Nordby	3-3
1999	22 Aug	Odense	1-0
2001	23 Aug	Northampton	0-3
2004	19 Feb	Portsmouth	2-0
EC2005	8 June	Blackburn	1-2
2009	22 July	Swindon	1-0
2017	1 July	Copenhagen	2-1

v ESTONIA

2015	21 Sept	Tallinn	8-0
EC2016	15 Sept	Nottingham	5-0

v FINLAND

1979	19 July	Sorrento	3-1
EC1987	25 Oct	Kirkkonummi	2-1
EC1988	4 Sept	Millwall	1-1
EC1989	1 Oct	Brentford	0-0
EC1990	29 Sept	Tampere	0-0
2000	28 Sept	Leyton	2-1
EC2005	5 June	Manchester	3-2
2009	9 Feb	Larnaca	2-2
2009	11 Feb	Larnaca	4-1
EC2009	3 Sept	Turku	3-2
cc2012	28 Feb	Nicosia	3-1
cc2014	7 Mar	Larnaca	3-0
cc2015	4 Mar	Larnaca	3-1

v FRANCE

1973	22 Apr	Brion	3-0
1974	7 Nov	Wimbledon	2-0
1977	26 Feb	Longjumeau	0-0
M1988	22 July	Riva del Garda	1-1
1998	15 Feb	Alencon	2-3
1999	15 Sept	Yeovil	0-1
2000	16 Aug	Marseilles	0-1
wc2002	17 Oct	Crystal Palace	0-1
wc2002	16 Nov	St Etienne	0-1
wc2006	26 Mar	Blackburn	0-0
wc2006	30 Sept	Rennes	1-1
cc2009	7 Mar	Paralimni	2-2
wc2011	9 July	Leverkusen	1-1*
cc2012	4 Mar	Paralimni	0-3
2012	20 Oct	Paris	2-2
EC2013	18 July	Linkoping	0-3
cc2014	12 Mar	Nicosia	0-2
wc2015	9 June	Moncton	0-1
2016	9 Mar	Boca Raton	0-0
2016	21 Oct	Doncaster	0-0
2017	1 Mar	Pennsylvania	1-2
2017	**30 July**	**Deventer**	**1-0**
2017	**20 Oct**	**Valenciennes**	**0-1**
2018	**1 Mar**	**Columbus**	**4-1**

v GERMANY

EC1990	25 Nov	High Wycombe	1-4
EC1990	16 Dec	Bochum	0-2
EC1994	11 Dec	Watford	1-4
EC1995	23 Feb	Bochum	1-2
wc1995	13 June	Vasteras	0-3
1997	27 Feb	Preston	4-6
wc1997	25 Sept	Dessau	0-3
wc1998	8 Mar	Millwall	0-1
EC2001	30 June	Jena	0-3
wc2001	27 Sept	Kassel	1-3
wc2002	19 May	Crystal Palace	0-1

2003	11 Sept	Darmstadt	0-4
2006	25 Oct	Aalen	1-5
2007	30 Jan	Guangzhou	0-0
wc2007	14 Sept	Shanghai	0-0
2008	17 July	Unterhaching	0-3
EC2009	10 Sept	Helsinki	2-6
2014	23 Nov	Wembley	0-3
wc2015	4 July	Vancouver	1-0*
2015	26 Nov	Duisburg	0-0
2016	6 Mar	Nashville	1-2
2017	7 Mar	Washington	0-1
2018	**4 Mar**	**New Jersey**	**2-2**

v HUNGARY

wc2005	27 Oct	Tapolca	13-0
wc2006	11 May	Southampton	2-0

v ICELAND

EC1992	17 May	Yeovil	4-0
EC1992	19 July	Kopavogur	2-1
EC1994	8 Oct	Reykjavik	2-1
EC1994	30 Oct	Brighton	2-1
wc2002	16 Sept	Reykjavik	2-2
wc2002	22 Sept	Birmingham	1-0
2004	14 May	Peterborough	1-0
2006	9 Mar	Norwich	1-0
2007	17 May	Southend	4-0
2009	16 July	Colchester	0-2

v ITALY

1976	2 June	Rome	0-2
1976	4 June	Cesena	1-2
1977	15 Nov	Wimbledon	1-0
1979	25 July	Naples	1-3
1982	11 June	Pescara	0-2
M1984	24 Aug	Jesolo	1-1
M1985	20 Aug	Caorle	1-1
M1985	25 Aug	Caorle	3-2
EC1987	13 June	Drammen	1-2
M1988	30 July	Arco di Trento	2-1
1989	1 Nov	High Wycombe	1-1
1990	18 Aug	Wembley	1-4
EC1992	17 Oct	Solofra	2-3
EC1992	7 Nov	Rotherham	0-3
1995	25 Jan	Florence	1-1
EC1995	1 Nov	Sunderland	1-1
EC1996	16 Mar	Cosenza	1-2
1997	23 Apr	Turin	0-2
1998	21 Apr	West Bromwich	1-2
1999	26 May	Bologna	1-4
2003	25 Feb	Viareggio	0-1
2005	17 Feb	Milton Keynes	4-1
EC2009	25 Aug	Lahti	1-2
cc2010	3 Mar	Nicosia	3-2
cc2011	2 Mar	Larnaca	2-0
cc2012	6 Mar	Paralimni	1-3
cc2013	6 Mar	Nicosia	4-2
EC2014	5 Mar	Larnaca	2-0
2017	7 Apr	Port Vale	1-1

v JAPAN

1981	6 Sept	Kobe	4-0
wc2007	11 Sept	Shanghai	2-2
wc2011	5 July	Augsburg	2-0
2013	26 June	Burton	1-1
wc2015	1 July	Edmonton	1-2

v KAZAKHSTAN

2017	**28 Nov**	**Colchester**	**5-0**

v KOREA REPUBLIC

2010	19 Oct	Suwon	0-0
cc2011	9 Mar	Larnaca	2-0

v MALTA

wc2009	25 Oct	Blackpool	8-0
wc2010	20 May	Ta'Qali	6-0

v MEXICO

AC2005	13 Mar	Lagos	5-0
wc2011	27 June	Wolfsburg	1-1
wc2015	13 June	Moncton	2-1

v MONTENEGRO

wc2014	5 Apr	Brighton	9-0
wc2014	17 Sept	Petrovac	10-0

v NETHERLANDS

1973	9 Nov	Reading	1-0
1974	31 May	Groningen	0-3
1976	2 May	Blackpool	2-0
1978	30 Sept	Vlissingen	1-3
1989	13 May	Epinal	0-0
wc1997	30 Oct	West Ham	1-0
wc1998	23 May	Waalwijk	1-2
wc2001	4 Nov	Grimsby	0-0
wc2002	23 Mar	Den Haag	4-1
2004	18 Sept	Heerhugowaard	2-1
2004	22 Sept	Tuitjenhoorn	1-0
wc2005	17 Nov	Zwolle	1-0
wc2006	31 Aug	Charlton	4-0
2007	14 Mar	Swindon	0-1
EC2009	6 Sept	Tampere	2-1*
EC2011	27 Oct	Zwolle	0-0
EC2012	17 June	Salford	1-0
cc2015	9 Mar	Nicosia	1-1
2016	29 Nov	Tilburg	1-0
2017	**3 Aug**	**Enschede**	**0-3**

v NEW ZEALAND

2010	21 Oct	Suwon	0-0
wc2011	1 July	Dresden	2-1
cc2013	11 Mar	Larnaca	3-1

v NIGERIA

wc1995	10 June	Karlstad	3-2
2002	23 July	Norwich	0-1
2004	22 Apr	Reading	0-3

v NORTHERN IRELAND

1973	7 Sept	Bath	5-1
EC1982	19 Sept	Crewe	7-1
EC1983	14 May	Belfast	4-0
EC1985	25 May	Antrim	8-1
EC1986	16 Mar	Blackburn	10-0
1987	11 Apr	Leeds	6-0
AC2005	9 Mar	Paderne	4-0
EC2007	13 May	Gillingham	4-0
EC2008	6 Mar	Lurgan	2-0

v NORWAY

1981	25 Oct	Cambridge	0-3
EC1988	21 Aug	Kleppe	0-2
EC1988	18 Sept	Blackburn	1-3
EC1990	27 May	Kleppe	0-2
EC1990	2 Sept	Old Trafford	0-0
wc1995	8 June	Karlstad	3-2
1997	8 June	Lillestrom	0-4
wc1998	14 May	Oldham	1-2
wc1998	15 Aug	Lillestrom	0-2
EC2000	7 Mar	Norwich	0-3
EC2000	4 June	Moss	0-8
AC2002	1 Mar	Albufeira	1-3
2005	6 May	Barnsley	1-0
2008	14 Feb	Larnaca	2-1
2009	23 Apr	Shrewsbury	3-0
2014	17 Jan	La Manga	1-1
wc2015	22 June	Ottawa	2-1
2017	22 Jan	La Manga	0-1

v PORTUGAL

EC1996	11 Feb	Benavente	5-0
EC1996	19 May	Brentford	3-0
EC2000	20 Feb	Barnsley	2-0
EC2000	22 Apr	Sacavem	2-2
wc2001	24 Nov	Gafanha da Nazare	1-1
wc2002	24 Feb	Portsmouth	3-0
AC2005	11 Mar	Faro	4-0
2017	**27 July**	**Tilburg**	**2-1**

v REPUBLIC OF IRELAND

1978	2 May	Exeter	6-1
1981	2 May	Dublin	5-0
EC1982	7 Nov	Dublin	1-0
EC1983	11 Sept	Reading	6-0
EC1985	22 Sept	Cork	6-0
EC1986	27 Apr	Reading	4-0
1987	29 Mar	Dublin	1-0

v ROMANIA

EC1998	12 Sept	Campina	4-1
EC1998	11 Oct	High Wycombe	2-1

v RUSSIA

EC2001	24 June	Jena	1-1
2003	21 Oct	Moscow	2-2
2004	19 Aug	Bristol	1-2
2007	8 Mar	Milton Keynes	6-0
EC2009	28 Aug	Helsinki	3-2
EC2013	15 July	Linkoping	1-1
wc2017	**19 Sept**	**Tranmere**	**6-0**
2018	**8 June**	**Moscow**	**3-1**

v SCOTLAND

1972	18 Nov	Greenock	3-2
1973	23 June	Nuneaton	8-0
1976	23 May	Enfield	5-1
1977	29 May	Dundee	1-2
EC1982	3 Oct	Dumbarton	4-0
EC1983	22 May	Leeds	2-0
EC1985	17 Mar	Preston	4-0
EC1986	12 Oct	Kirkcaldy	3-1
1989	30 Apr	Kirkcaldy	3-0
1990	6 May	Paisley	4-0
1990	12 May	Wembley	4-0
1991	20 Apr	High Wycombe	5-0
EC1992	17 Apr	Walsall	1-0
EC1992	23 Aug	Perth	2-0
1997	9 Mar	Sheffield	6-0
1997	23 Aug	Livingston	4-0
2001	27 May	Bolton	1-0
AC2002	7 Mar	Quarteira	4-1
2003	13 Nov	Preston	5-0
2005	21 Apr	Tranmere	2-1
2007	11 Mar	High Wycombe	1-0
cc2009	10 Mar	Larnaca	3-0
cc2011	4 Mar	Nicosia	0-2
cc2013	8 Mar	Larnaca	4-4
EC2017	**19 July**	**Utrecht**	**6-0**

v SERBIA

EC2011	17 Sept	Belgrade	2-2
EC2011	23 Nov	Doncaster	2-0
EC2016	4 June	Wycombe	7-0
EC2016	7 June	Stara Pazova	7-0

v SLOVENIA

EC1993	25 Sept	Ljubljana	10-0
EC1994	17 Apr	Brentford	10-0
EC2011	22 Sept	Swindon	4-0
EC2012	21 June	Velenje	4-0

v SOUTH AFRICA

cc2009	5 Mar	Larnaca	6-0
cc2010	24 Feb	Larnaca	1-0

v SPAIN

EC1993	19 Dec	Osuna	0-0
EC1994	20 Feb	Bradford	0-0
EC1996	8 Sept	Montilla	1-2
EC1996	29 Sept	Tranmere	1-1
2001	22 Mar	Luton	4-2
EC2007	25 Nov	Shrewsbury	1-0
EC2008	2 Oct	Zamora	2-2
wc2010	1 Apr	Millwall	1-0
wc2010	19 June	Aranda de Duero	2-2
EC2013	12 July	Linkoping	2-3
2016	25 Oct	Guadalajara	2-1
EC2017	**23 July**	**Breda**	**2-0**

v SWEDEN

1975	15 June	Gothenborg	0-2
1975	7 Sept	Wimbledon	1-3
1979	27 July	Scafati	0-0*
1980	17 Sept	Leicester	1-1
1982	26 May	Kinna	1-1
1983	30 Oct	Charlton	2-2
EC1984	12 May	Gothenburg	0-1
EC1984	27 May	Luton	1-0
EC1987	11 June	Moss	2-3*
1989	23 May	Wembley	0-2
1995	13 May	Halmstad	0-4
1998	26 July	Dagenham	0-1
EC2001	27 June	Jena	0-4
2002	25 Jan	La Manga	0-5

AC2002	5 Mar	Lagos	3-6
EC2005	11 June	Blackburn	0-1
2006	7 Feb	Larnaca	0-0
2006	9 Feb	Achna	1-1
2008	12 Feb	Larnaca	0-2
EC2009	31 Aug	Turku	1-1
2011	17 May	Oxford	2-0
2013	4 July	Ljungskile	1-4
2014	3 Aug	Hartlepool	4-0
2017	24 Jan	La Manga	0-0

v SWITZERLAND

1975	19 Apr	Basel	3-1
1977	28 Apr	Hull	9-1
1979	23 July	Sorrento	2-0
EC1999	16 Oct	Zofingen	3-0
EC2000	13 May	Bristol	1-0
cc2010	1 Mar	Nicosia	2-2
wc2010	12 Sept	Shrewsbury	2-0
wc2010	16 Sept	Wohlen	3-2
cc2012	1 Mar	Larnaca	1-0
2017	10 June	Biel	4-0

v TURKEY

wc2009	26 Nov	Izmir	3-0
wc2010	29 July	Walsall	3-0
wc2013	26 Sept	Portsmouth	8-0
wc2013	31 Oct	Adana	4-0

v UKRAINE

EC2000	30 Oct	Kiev	2-1
EC2000	28 Nov	Leyton	2-0
wc2014	8 May	Shrewsbury	4-0
wc2014	19 June	Lviv	2-1

v USA

M1985	23 Aug	Caorle	3-1
M1988	27 July	Riva del Garda	2-0
1990	9 Aug	Blaine	0-3
1991	25 May	Hirson	1-3
1997	9 May	San Jose	0-5
1997	11 May	Portland	0-6
AC2002	3 Mar	Ferreiras	0-2
2003	17 May	Birmingham (Alabama)	0-6
2007	28 Jan	Guangzhou	1-1
wc2007	22 Sept	Tianjin	0-3
2011	2 Apr	Leyton	2-1
2015	13 Feb	Milton Keynes	0-1
2016	4 Mar	Tampa	0-1
2017	4 Mar	New Jersey	1-0
2018	**8 Mar**	**Orlando**	**0-1**

v USSR

1990	11 Aug	Blaine	1-1
1991	20 July	Dmitrov	2-1
1991	21 July	Kashira	2-0
1991	7 Sept	Southampton	2-0
1991	8 Sept	Brighton	1-3

v WALES

1974	17 Mar	Slough	5-0
1976	22 May	Bedford	4-0
1976	17 Oct	Ebbw Vale	2-1
1977	18 Sept	Warminster	5-0
1980	1 June	Warminster	6-1
1985	17 Aug	Ramsey (Isle of Man)	6-0
wc2013	26 Oct	Millwall	2-0
wc2014	21 Aug	Cardiff	4-0
2018	**6 Apr**	**Southampton**	**0-0**

v WEST GERMANY

M1984	22 Aug	Jesolo	0-2
1990	5 Aug	Blaine	1-3

OTHER MATCHES

v ITALY B

1984	27 Aug	Monfalcone	3-1
M1988	20 July	Riva del Garda	3-0

v USA B

1990	7 Aug	Blaine	1-0

THE BUILDBASE FA TROPHY 2017–18

After extra time.

PRELIMINARY ROUND

Ossett Alb v Droylsden	1-1, 1-1*
Droylsden won 4-2 on penalties	
Ramsbottom U v Colwyn Bay	3-0
Bamber Bridge v Brighouse T	4-2
Cleethorpes T v Hyde U	2-1
Mossley v Skelmersdale U	3-1
Kendal T v Radcliffe Bor	2-1
Stocksbridge Park Steels v Atherton Colleries	1-4
Scarborough Ath v South Shields	2-5
Tadcaster Alb v Glossop North End	0-2
Ossett T v Goole	3-0
Prescot Cables v Trafford	3-1
Clitheroe v Colne	3-0
Sheffield v Frickley Ath	0-3
Romulus v Corby T	0-2
Newcastle T v Soham T Rangers	3-0
Chasetown v Market Drayton T	2-0
AFC Rushden & Diamonds v Kidsgrove Ath	1-3
Basford U v Peterborough Sports	3-0
Stamford v Loughborough Dynamo	3-0
Belper T v Alvechurch	1-2
Gresley v Bedworth U	0-1
Leek T v Lincoln U	4-1
Thamesmead T v AFC Hornchurch	1-1, 2-1
Greenwich Bor v Hanwell T	0-1
Heybridge Swifts v Carshalton Ath	2-0
Hertford T (walkover) v Guernsey	
Kempston R v Hythe T	0-1
Potters Bar T v Tilbury	4-0
Ashford U v Sittingbourne	0-3
Egham T v Shoreham	7-1
Northwood v Maldon & Tiptree	2-5
AFC Sudbury v Aylesbury T	2-2, 2-1
Waltham Abbey v Faversham T	2-1
Romford v Hastings U	0-1
VCD Ath v Bedford T	0-1
Haringey Bor v Whyteleafe	3-0
Bowers & Pitsea v Dereham T	2-2, 4-1
Cray W v Horsham	8-0
Chipstead v Barking	1-1, 1-2
East Grinstead T v Lewes	2-4
Corinthian Casuals v AFC Dunstable	2-0
Cheshunt v Herne Bay	3-0
Ramsgate v Bury T	3-5
Hayes & Yeading U v Barton R	3-1
Brentwood T v South Park	3-3, 7-2
Walton Casuals v Canvey Island	3-0
Phoenix Sports v Chalfont St Peter	0-3
Ashford T (Middlesex) v Uxbridge	4-1
Grays Ath v Norwich U	4-3
Aylesbury v Molesey	4-3
Marlow v Aveley	0-0, 3-5*
(3-3 at the end of normal time)	
Taunton T v AFC Totton	1-1, 2-1*
(1-1 at the end of normal time)	
Mangotsfield U v Thame U	0-1
Bishop's Cleeve v Larkhall Ath	0-1
Shortwood U v Didcot T	1-0
Fleet T v Yate T	1-1, 1-2
Evesham U v Cirencester T	2-3
North Leigh v Wimborne T	1-3
Moneyfields v Bideford	4-2
Swindon Supermarine v Barnstaple T	1-0
Salisbury v Paulton R	2-3
Slimbridge v Hartley Wintney	0-1
Bristol Manor Farm v Cinderford T	4-1
Kidlington v Winchester C	3-1

FIRST QUALIFYING ROUND

Ashton U v Frickley Ath	4-1
Glossop North End v Matlock T	3-2
Mossley v Lancaster C	0-1
Ossett T v Droylsden	1-3
Altrincham v Clitheroe	3-0
Farsley Celtic v South Shields	1-1, 3-4*
(1-1 at the end of normal time)	
Buxton v Cleethorpes T	1-2
Warrington T v Bamber Bridge	2-1

Shaw Lane v Ramsbottom U	2-2, 1-4*
(1-1 at the end of normal time)	
Whitby T v Marine	1-3
Prescot Cables v Stalybridge Celtic	0-0, 1-5
Kendal T v Atherton Colleries	2-4
Workington v Witton Alb	4-0
Grantham T v Halesowen T	1-0
Rushall Olympic v Nantwich T	2-0
Hednesford T v Mickleover Sports	1-0
Newcastle T v Kidsgrove Ath	2-2, 1-2
Stratford T v Bedworth U	2-1
Chasetown v Spalding U	2-1
Stafford Rangers v St Ives T	6-0
Barwell v Carlton T	1-0
Stamford v Sutton Coldfield T	3-0
St Neots T v Corby T	3-2
Redditch U v Coalville T	0-1
Cambridge C v Alvechurch	0-2
Leek T v Kettering T	3-2
Stourbridge v Basford U	1-0
Hitchin T v Cheshunt	5-0
Dorking W v Ware	5-0
Maldon & Tiptree v Walton Casuals	3-0
Billericay T v Tooting & Mitcham U	3-1
Leatherhead v Hythe T	1-0
Sittingbourne v Merstham	1-1, 2-0
Bishop's Stortford v Hanwell T	4-0
Needham Market v Arlesey T	3-1
King's Lynn T v Mildenhall T	0-1
Hendon v Kings Langley	3-1
Aylesbury v Harlow T	0-0, 2-4
Barking v Beaconsfield T	0-2
Brentwood T v Bedford T	0-0, 4-2
Tonbridge Angels v Heybridge Swifts	3-3, 1-2
Bury T v Chalfont St Peter	1-1, 3-0
Hastings U v Ashford T (Middlesex)	3-4
Metropolitan Police v AFC Sudbury	3-0
Dunstable T v Lewes	1-4
Corinthian Casuals v Hertford T	3-1
Cray W v Grays Ath	2-2, 2-0
Worthing v Lowestoft T	3-0
Staines T v Margate	0-3
Waltham Abbey v Dulwich Hamlet	0-3
Thamesmead T v Brightlingsea Regent	3-1
Royston T v Enfield T	2-0
Potters Bar T v Witham T	3-0
Harrow Bor v Haringey Bor	1-1, 0-1
Leiston v Folkestone Invicta	1-1, 1-1*
Leiston won 6-5 on penalties	
Burgess Hill T v Aveley	2-0
Bowers & Pitsea v Egham T	1-1, 5-3
Tie awarded to Egham T – Bowers & Pitsea removed	
Biggleswade U v Wingate & Finchley	0-5
Kingstonian v Thurrock	3-3, 4-1
Hayes & Yeading U v Chesham U	0-3
Taunton T v Merthyr T	2-1
Dorchester T v Basingstoke T	2-1
Paulton R v Cirencester T	2-2, 4-0
Gosport Bor v Bristol Manor Farm	1-0
Yate T v Moneyfields	0-1
Thame U v Wimborne T	5-0
Larkhall Ath v Farnborough	1-3
Swindon Supermarine v Hartley Wintney	0-3
Hereford v Weymouth	4-1
Tiverton T v Banbury U	2-2, 2-3
Kidlington v Slough T	1-4
Shortwood U v Frome T	2-0

SECOND QUALIFYING ROUND

Lancaster C v Stratford T	3-0
Kidsgrove Ath v Grantham T	0-2
Alvechurch v Coalville T	1-5
Warrington T v Ashton U	1-1, 2-2*
Warrington T won 4-2 on penalties	
Altrincham v Ramsbottom U	4-1
Stalybridge Celtic v Rushall Olympic	3-2
Glossop North End v Leek T	4-3
Stamford v Droylsden	1-2
Chasetown v Workington	1-3
Hednesford T v Cleethorpes T	1-1, 1-2
Atherton Colleries v Marine	1-5
St Neots T v Stourbridge	2-3

Barwell v Mildenhall T	0-1
Stafford Rangers v South Shields	3-1
Chesham U v Hitchin T	3-1
Taunton T v Beaconsfield T	1-1, 1-1*
Taunton T won 7-6 on penalties	
Brentwood T v Needham Market	3-1
Hereford v Potters Bar T	0-0, 2-1
Corinthian Casuals v Wingate & Finchley	1-3
Lewes v Bishop's Stortford	2-0
Dorchester T v Heybridge Swifts	1-2
Harlow T v Dulwich Hamlet	2-1
Hendon v Burgess Hill T	3-0
Ashford T (Middlesex) v Kingstonian	2-2, 0-2
Maldon & Tiptree v Slough T	1-4
Sittingbourne v Haringey Bor	1-1, 0-1
Thamesmead v Metropolitan Police	0-1
Royston T v Leatherhead	3-2
Hartley Wintney v Gosport Bor	3-0
Farnborough v Banbury U	3-3, 3-2*
(2-2 at the end of normal time)	
Thame U v Worthing	1-0
Paulton R v Shortwood U	1-2
Margate v Egham T	2-0
Billericay T v Bury T	6-2
Dorking W v Leiston	4-1
Moneyfields v Cray W	1-1, 1-4

THIRD QUALIFYING ROUND

Brackley T v Salford C	4-0
York C v Coalville T	3-1
Cleethorpes T v Spennymoor T	1-2
Grantham v Chorley	3-4
Tamworth v Warrington T	2-2, 0-3
AFC Telford U v Droylsden	4-2
Darlington v Harrogate T	2-3
Gainsborough Trinity v Stafford Rangers	2-0
Bradford (Park Avenue) v Stourbridge	1-1, 1-2
Boston U v Kidderminster H	2-2, 0-2
Nuneaton T v North Ferriby U	5-1
Stockport Co v Southport	2-2, 3-0
Blyth Spartans v Stalybridge Celtic	2-1
Glossop North End v Workington	0-0, 1-5
Alfreton T v Altrincham	0-2
Leamington v Curzon Ashton	3-1
Lancaster C v Mildenhall T	1-0
Marine v FC United of Manchester	1-0
Lewes v Truro C	1-3
Havant & Waterlooville v Dorking W	3-1
East Thurrock U v Shortwood U	3-1
Taunton T v Concord Rangers	3-2
Hemel Hempstead T v Bognor Regis T	1-1, 0-1
Farnborough v Hartley Wintney	1-2
Oxford C v Hereford	1-2
Hendon v Slough T	1-1, 1-1*
Hendon won 3-0 on penalties	
Braintree T v Cray W	3-0
Welling U v Weston Super Mare	0-1
St Albans C v Poole T	3-1
Metropolitan Police v Wingate & Finchley	0-1
Whitehawk v Chippenham T	2-1
Haringey Bor v Thame U	3-1
Brentwood T v Dartford	1-2
Chesham U v Gloucester C	2-1
Hungerford T v Billericay T	0-2
Hampton & Richmond Bor v Harlow T	0-0, 2-2*
Bath C won 5-4 on penalties	
Wealdstone v Chelmsford C	1-1, 2-1
Eastbourne Bor v Royston T	1-1, 2-2*
Eastbourne Bor won 4-3 on penalties	
Kingstonian v Heybridge Swifts	2-2, 1-5

FIRST ROUND

Solihull Moors v Tranmere R	A-A, 2-0
First match abandoned due to floodlight failure.	
Tranmere R leading 1-0	
Blyth Spartans v AFC Telford U	1-0
Kidderminster H v York C	2-1
Chorley v Marine	1-3
FC Halifax T v Macclesfield T	1-0
Spennymoor T v Gainsborough Trinity	4-4*
Spennymoor T won 5-3 on penalties	
Chester FC v AFC Fylde	2-2*
Chester FC won 5-4 on penalties	
Wrexham v Harrogate T	0-2
Leamington v Stourbridge	0-1

Lancaster C v Stockport Co	1-3
Warrington T v Altrincham	0-0, 2-1
Gateshead v Guiseley	2-1*
(1-1 at the end of normal time)	
Nuneaton T v Barrow	0-1
Workington v Hartlepool U	1-0
Haringey Bor v Leyton Orient	1-2
Dover Ath v Eastbourne Bor	3-0
Wealdstone v Wingate & Finchley	1-0
Billericay T v Havant & Waterlooville	3-1
Chesham U v Weston Super Mare	0-2
Sutton U v Truro C	1-0
Woking v Maidenhead U	0-2
Whitehawk v St Albans C	1-2
East Thurrock U v Aldershot T	4-0
Hendon v Bath C	2-1
Ebbsfleet U v Eastleigh	2-1
Hereford v Dagenham & Redbridge	3-2
Torquay U v Maidstone U	0-4
Hartley Wintney v Bromley	0-2
Braintree T v Brackley T	0-0, 0-2
Taunton T v Bognor Regis T	1-4
Hampton & Richmond Bor v Heybridge Swifts	1-1, 2-3
Dartford v Boreham Wood	1-1, 2-2*
Boreham Wood won 3-1 on penalties	

SECOND ROUND

Ebbsfleet U v Warrington T	1-1, 0-2
Kidderminster H v Stockport Co	2-2, 0-3
East Thurrock U v Chester FC	1-0
Bognor Regis T v Leyton Orient	1-2*
(1-1 at the end of normal time)	
Brackley T v Barrow	0-0, 2-0
Weston Super Mare v Workington	1-1, 1-2
Billericay T v Stourbridge	3-2
FC Halifax T v Maidenhead U	1-4
Maidstone U v Heybridge Swifts	2-1
Dover Ath v Marine	4-3
Gateshead v Boreham Wood	3-3, 2-1
Wealdstone v Hereford	1-0
Sutton U v Hendon	3-0
Blyth Spartans v Bromley	1-4
Spennymoor T v Solihull Moors	2-0
St Albans C v Harrogate T	1-1, 0-5

THIRD ROUND

Harrogate T v Billericay T	2-2, 2-3
Maidstone U v Gateshead	2-2, 0-3
Maidenhead U v Stockport Co	1-1, 2-3*
(2-2 at the end of normal time)	
Wealdstone v Warrington T	2-1
Brackley T v Sutton U	3-1
Dover Ath v Leyton Orient	3-4
Spennymoor T v East Thurrock U	1-1, 5-2
Workington v Bromley	1-1, 1-7

FOURTH ROUND

Stockport Co v Brackley T	1-1, 1-2
Billericay T v Wealdstone	2-5
Leyton Orient v Gateshead	3-3, 2-3
Bromley v Spennymoor T	0-0, 2-1

SEMI-FINALS – FIRST LEG

Brackley T v Wealdstone	1-0
Bromley v Gateshead	3-2

SEMI-FINALS – SECOND LEG

Wealdstone v Brackley T	0-2
Brackley T won 3-0 on aggregate	
Gateshead v Bromley	1-1
Bromley won 4-3 on aggregate	

THE BUILDBASE FA TROPHY FINAL 2018

Wembley, Sunday 20 May 2018

Brackley T (0) 1 *(Dean 90)*

Bromley (1) 1 *(Bugiel 19)*

31,403 (combined with FA Vase)

Brackley T: Lewis; Lowe (Diggin 111), Franklin (Myles 78), Byrne, Gudger, Dean, Walker, Armson, Ndlovu (Brown 53), Williams, Walker.
Bromley: Gregory; Holland, Raymond, Dennis (Hanlon 68), Mekki (Chorley 72), Higgs, Sterling, Porter (Rees 62), Johnson, Sutherland, Bugiel.
aet; Brackley T won 5-4 on penalties.
Referee: Chris Kavanagh.

THE BUILDBASE FA VASE 2017–18

After extra time.

FIRST QUALIFYING ROUND

Stokesley SC v Hebburn T	0-8
Chester-Le-Street T v Silsden	2-3
Sunderland Ryhope CW v Guisborough T	7-1
Seaham Red Star v Alb Sports	2-0
Whickham v Newton Aycliffe	3-1
Padiham v Thackley	5-0

Tie awarded to Thackley – Padiham removed

Garforth T v Holker Old Boys	3-1
Blyth v West Allotment Celtic	2-1
Esh Winning v Penrith	0-2
Heaton Stannington v Carlisle C	1-3
Tow Law T v Crook T	3-2
Brandon U v Bishop Auckland	2-3
Ashington v Easington Colliery	3-0
Northallerton T v Alnwick T	4-2
Marske U v Ryton & Crawcrook Alb	2-0
Barnoldswick T v Dunston UTS	0-1
Darlington Railway Ath v Harrogate Railway Ath	4-6
Eccleshill U v Jarrow Roofing Boldon CA	0-2
Campion v Bedlington Terriers	1-2
Widnes v Glasshoughton Welfare	1-2
Alsager T v New Mills	1-2
Vauxhall Motors v 1874 Northwich	4-5*

(4-4 at the end of normal time)

Maltby Main v Cammell Laird 1907	4-2
Northwich Vic v Stockport T	3-4
Hallam v Abbey Hey	1-1, 1-0
St Helens T v Hemsworth MW	1-2
Selby T v Charnock Richard	1-7
Rossington Main v Cheadle T	4-1
Barnton v Penistone Church	3-1
Maine Road v Pontefract Collieries	1-5
Prestwich Heys v Liversedge	1-2
Atherton LR v Irlam	1-2
Litherland Remyca v Ashton T	1-0*

(0-0 at the end of normal time)

Parkgate v Daisy Hill	4-0
Worsbrough Bridge Ath v Dronfield T	2-3
AFC Liverpool v Athersley Recreation	3-2
AFC Blackpool v West Didsbury & Chorlton	1-6
Squires Gate v Congleton T	2-6
Cadbury Ath v Littleton	2-3
Pegasus Juniors v Droitwich Spa	1-3*

(1-1 at the end of normal time)

Lutterworth Ath v AFC Wulfrunians	2-4
Boldmere St Michaels v Coventry Alvis	6-1
Coventry U v Tipton T	3-1
Bewdley T v Rugby T	1-4
Heather St Johns v Coventry Sphinx	5-4
Barnt Green Spartak v Walsall Wood	0-1
Westfields v Stapenhill	4-2
Wellington Amateurs v Dudley T	0-0, 1-3*

(1-1 at the end of normal time)

Hereford Lads Club v Stone Old Alleynians	2-5
Studley v Long Buckby	3-0
Leicester Road v Racing Club Warwick	1-4
Malvern T v Smethwick	1-4
Chelmsley T v AFC Bridgnorth	4-1
Uttoxeter T v Gornal Ath	4-1
Ellesmere Rangers v Highgate U	0-7
Nuneaton Griff v Rocester	5-8*

(4-4 at the end of normal time)

Ashby Ivanhoe v St Martins	3-1
Paget Rangers v Wolverhampton Casuals	3-0
Hanley T v Lichfield C	5-1
Ellistown & Ibstock U v Eccleshall	3-2
Wolverhampton SC v FC Oswestry T	5-0
Shawbury U v Wellington	2-4
Whitchurch Alport v Pershore T (walkover)	
Cradley T v Bromyard T	7-1
Bilston T v Bolehall Swifts	3-2
Coton Green v Heath Hayes	2-5
Tividale v Brocton	0-2
Long Eaton U v Rainworth MW	2-0
Hall Road Rangers v Gedling MW	2-0
Quorn v Oadby T	2-1
Clifton All Whites v Harrowby U	2-2, 0-4
Friar Lane & Epworth v Lutterworth T	0-3
Kimberley MW v Barrow T	1-2

Tie awarded to Kimberley MW – Barrow T removed

South Normanton v Melton T	2-3
Radcliffe Olympic v Belper U	0-6
Kirby Muxloe v Anstey Nomads	3-2
Ilkeston v Clipstone (walkover)	
Leicester Nirvana v Graham St Prims	5-1
Loughborough University v Winterton Rangers	5-0
Worksop T v Aylestone Park	5-2
Grimsby Bor v Shirebrook T	0-3
Hucknall T v Clay Cross T	2-1
Heanor T v Holbrook Sports	0-2
Collingham v Radford (walkover)	
Bottesford T v West Bridgford	5-1
Birstall U v South Normanton Ath	1-6
Skegness T v Sleaford T	3-0
Westella & Willerby v Arnold T	1-1*

Westella & Willerby won 5-4 on penalties

Blaby & Whetstone Ath v Blidworth Welfare	6-0
Raunds T v Wellingborough T	2-0
Stewarts & Lloyds v Swaffham T	1-6
Fakenham T v Huntingdon T	2-3
Downham T v Biggleswade U	0-2
Histon v Blackstones	5-1
Potton U v Netherton U	1-1, 3-0
Pinchbeck U v Holbeach U	1-5
Bourne T v Harborough T	3-2
March T U v Peterborough Northern Star	2-3
Cogenhoe v Rothwell Corinthians	1-1, 2-1
Stansted v Wodson Park	0-3
Basildon U v St Margaretsbury	1-1, 2-1
Barkingside v Southend Manor	2-1
Framlingham T v Waltham Forest	2-0
Brimsdown v Debenham LC	1-2
FC Clacton v Coggeshall T	0-2*

(0-0 at the end of normal time)

Hadleigh U v Wadham Lodge	2-1
Ilford v Cornard U	2-0
Redbridge v Brantham Ath	6-1
Enfield 1893 v Haverhill Bor	1-0
Norwich CBS v Ipswich W	2-0
Saffron Walden T v Sawbridgeworth T	1-2
Enfield Bor v Canning T	4-2
Tower Hamlets v Hackney Wick	2-1
Woodbridge T v Hoddesdon T	2-0
Stowmarket T v Team Bury	7-0
Long Melford v Halstead T	1-2*

(1-1 at the end of normal time)

Great Yarmouth T v FC Broxbourne Bor	3-1
Haverhill R v Whitton U	1-3
Wivenhoe T v Holland	0-2
Great Wakering R v Sporting Bengal U	6-1
Wootton Blue Cross v London Lions	2-3*

(1-1 at the end of normal time)

Welwyn Garden C v Brackley T Saints	3-1
AFC Hayes v Hatfield T	1-1, 3-0
Hillingdon Bor v Marston Shelton R	2-1
Malmesbury Vic v Chipping Sodbury T	5-3*

(3-3 at the end of normal time)

New College Swindon v Ampthill T	0-10
Baldock T v Buckingham T	1-0
North Greenford U v Harpenden T	3-4
Oxford C Nomads v Woodley U	3-1
Royal Wootton Bassett T v Fairford T	3-1
Clanfield 85 v Holmer Green	2-1
Colney Heath v Harefield U	1-0
Abingdon U v Highmoor Ibis	1-0
Hadley v Milton U	2-0
Edgware T v Risborough Rangers	2-1
Cricklewood W v Stotfold	7-2
Crawley Green v Tuffley R	2-1
Highworth T v Easington Sports	4-0
Leighton T v Brimscombe & Thrupp	3-1
Ardley U v Longlevens	2-4
Lydney T v Winslow U	4-2
Buckingham Ath v Bedford	1-1, 6-1
Broadfields U v Pitshanger Dynamo	3-1
Amersham T v Langford	1-3
Rochester U v Lancing	3-5
Southwick v Broadbridge Heath	2-7
Hollands & Blair (walkover) v Tooting & Mitcham W	
AFC Croydon Ath v Bearsted	2-1
Eastbourne U v Newhaven	1-2*

(1-1 at the end of normal time)

Ringmer v AC London	1-3
Erith & Belvedere v Holmesdale	4-2*
(2-2 at the end of normal time)	
Glebe v Deal T	3-3, 2-7
East Preston v Forest Hill Park	4-4, 0-1
Sheppey U v Loxwood	5-1
Oakwood v Langney W	2-4
FC Elmstead v Whitstable T	1-5
Hailsham T v Abbey Rangers	2-3
Banstead Ath v Fisher	1-2
Westside v Steyning T	0-2
Snodland T v Horsham YMCA	0-3
Chessington & Hook U v Lydd T	2-1
Worthing U v Horley T	2-4
Colliers Wood U v K Sports	0-2
Bridon Ropes v Wick	2-0
FC Deportivo Galicia v Lewisham Bor (Community)	6-3
Walton & Hersham v Little Common	7-1
Spelthorne Sports (walkover) v Sutton Ath	
CB Hounslow U v Peacehaven & Telscombe	2-1
St Francis Rangers v Erith T	1-1, 0-2
Seaford T v Saltdean U	1-3
Mile Oak v Chertsey T	2-1
Arundel v Lordswood	0-4
Canterbury C v Sutton Common R	4-3
Stansfeld v Bedfont & Feltham	4-0
Gravesham Bor v Cobham	1-3
Tooting Bec v Littlehampton T	3-1
AFC Uckfield T v Raynes Park Vale	2-0
Redhill v Chatham T	1-3
Beckenham T v Lingfield	3-2*
(2-2 at the end of normal time)	
Bedfont Sports v Three Bridges	1-2
Tadley Calleva v Andover New Street	3-2
Shaftesbury T v Brockenhurst	4-5*
(4-4 at the end of normal time)	
Horndean v Andover T	4-3*
(2-2 at the end of normal time)	
Windsor v Devizes T	2-1
Hamble Club v Bemerton Heath Harlequins	3-1
Ascot U v Farnham T	1-3
Hamworthy U v AFC Stoneham	5-2
Amesbury T v New Milton T	3-0
East Cowes Vic Ath v Calne T	1-3
AFC Aldermaston v Romsey T	2-3
Petersfield v Corsham T	1-0
Swanage T & Herston v Ash U	4-3*
(2-2 at the end of normal time)	
Cove v Westbury U	0-3
Warminster T v Folland Sports	3-1
Knaphill v Sidlesham	1-0
Pewsey Vale v Chippenham Park	0-2
Newport (IW) v Fleet Spurs	5-2
Guildford C v Lymington T	1-2
United Services Portsmouth v Verwood T	2-1*
(1-1 at the end of normal time)	
Ringwood T v Eversley & California	1-0
Laverstock & Ford v Fawley	1-2
Cowes Sports v Baffins Milton R	1-3
Hythe & Dibden v Bagshot	4-3
Camelford v Helston Ath	3-2
Cullompton Rangers v Torpoint Ath	1-0
Wellington v Wells C	3-1
Cheddar v Radstock T	1-3
Bovey Tracey v Keynsham T	3-1
Witheridge v Cribbs	1-9
Plymouth Parkway v Sherborne T	4-1
Axminster T v Crediton U	2-4
Tavistock v Hallen	2-0
Almondsbury UWE v Clevedon T	1-2
Bitton v Brislington	1-3
Welton R v Willand R	0-1
Bridport v Wincanton T	1-2
AFC St Austell v Bishops Lydeard	9-1
Cadbury Heath v St Blazey	3-1
Roman Glass St George v Elburton Villa	2-0*
(0-0 at the end of normal time)	
Ashton & Backwell U v Godolphin Atlantic	2-1

SECOND QUALIFYING ROUND

Sunderland Ryhope CW v Northallerton T	2-0*
(0-0 at the end of normal time)	
Team Northumbria v Durham C	2-0
Stockton T v Consett	4-3*
(2-2 at the end of normal time)	
Garforth T v Nelson	3-2

Hebburn T v Newcastle Benfield	1-3
Billingham Synthonia v Whitley Bay	2-2, 0-3
Willington v Harrogate Railway Ath	0-1
Tow Law T v Penrith	5-1
Carlisle C v Thornaby	2-3
Marske U v Seaham Red Star	2-0*
(0-0 at the end of normal time)	
Whickham v Blyth	3-2
West Auckland T v Silsden	3-0
Thackley v Ashington	2-3*
(1-1 at the end of normal time)	
Dunston UTS v Washington	5-0
Jarrow Roofing Boldon CA v Knaresborough T	1-2
Bedlington Terriers v Bishop Auckland	2-0
Rossington Main v Hallam	2-2, 2-0
Litherland Remyca v Chadderton	3-2
Irlam v Parkgate	2-1
Winsford U v Pontefract Collieries	1-4
Alsager T v Nostell MW	5-1
1874 Northwich v Congleton T	1-1, 1-0
AFC Liverpool v City of Liverpool	0-2
Sandbach U v AFC Emley	0-2
Ashton Ath v Maltby Main	3-1
Charnock Richard v Bacup Bor	3-0
Burscough v Armthorpe Welfare	6-0
West Didsbury & Chorlton v Stockport T	4-3
Glasshoughton Welfare v AFC Darwen	2-4
Dronfield T v Barnton	4-2*
(2-2 at the end of normal time)	
Hemsworth MW v Liversedge	2-3*
(1-1 at the end of normal time)	
Highgate U v Pershore T	6-2
Bilston T v Haughmond	1-4
Dudley T v Atherstone T	0-4
Wellington v Littleton	2-1
Chelmsley T v AFC Wulfrunians	2-4
Dudley Sports v Brocton	0-6
Shifnal T v Droitwich Spa	3-2*
(2-2 at the end of normal time)	
Cradley T v Walsall Wood	0-2
Ellistown & Ibstock U v Wednesfield	0-5
Heather St Johns v Rocester	3-0
Westfields v Daventry T	6-0
Stourport Swifts v Paget Rangers	5-1
Smethwick v Rugby T	1-4
Stafford T v Ashby Ivanhoe	4-1
Studley v Hanley T	0-2
Boldmere St Michaels v Worcester C	3-4*
(2-2 at the end of normal time)	
Racing Club Warwick v Coventry Copsewood	7-1
Heath Hayes v Wolverhampton SC	0-3
Uttoxeter T v Bardon Hill	0-1
Coventry U v Stone Old Alleynians	2-1
Barton T v Clipstone	1-2
Retford U v Pinxton	1-2
Westella & Willerby v Ollerton T	4-0
Leicester Nirvana v Belper U	4-2
Lutterworth T v Teversal	7-0
Shirebrook T v Long Eaton U	3-1
Hall Road Rangers v Skegness T	4-1
Hucknall T v Eastwood Community	1-4
Holwell Sports v Dunkirk	0-1
Melton T v FC Bolsover	1-4
Holbrook Sports v Quorn	1-2
Blaby & Whetstone Ath v Bottesford T	4-0
Loughborough University v Staveley MW	2-4
Worksop T v Kirby Muxloe	3-0
Boston T v South Normanton Ath	1-2
Sandiacre T v Sherwood Colliery	1-3
Harrowby U v St Andrews	4-1
Radford v Kimberley MW	1-4
Godmanchester R v Raunds T	1-0
Northampton ON Chenecks v Irchester U	2-1
Swaffham T v Rushden & Higham U	4-5*
(3-3 at the end of normal time)	
Biggleswade v Northampton Sileby Rangers	5-3
Histon v Cogenhoe U	0-1
Potton U v Peterborough Northern Star	1-2
Bourne T v Wisbech T	0-5
Eynesbury R v Burton Park W	2-1
Biggleswade U v Thrapston T	2-0
Holbeach U v Huntingdon T	2-1
Thetford T (walkover) v Oakham U	
Wellingborough Whitworths v Wisbech St Mary	1-3
Redbridge v Coggeshall T	2-2, 1-3
Tower Hamlets v Little Oakley	10-1
Enfield Bor v Woodbridge T	6-2

Wroxham v Norwich CBS	0-3
Basildon U v Walsham Le Willows	2-1*
(1-1 at the end of normal time)	
Barkingside v Whitton U	2-3
Halstead T v Stanway R	2-1
West Essex v Great Wakering R	1-2
Diss T v Framlingham T	2-3*
(2-2 at the end of normal time)	
Ilford v Hullbridge Sports	0-3
Kirkley & Pakefield v Burnham Ramblers	2-3
Great Yarmouth T v Debenham LC	1-1, 0-2
(0-0 at the end of normal time)	
Wodson Park v Holland	2-2, 1-4
Stowmarket T v Enfield 1893	4-5*
(4-4 at the end of normal time)	
Hadleigh U v Sawbridgeworth T	1-2*
(1-1 at the end of normal time)	
Buckingham Ath v AFC Hayes	1-0
Ampthill v Clanfield 85	4-0
Highworth T v Burnham	5-1
Abingdon U v Welwyn Garden C	0-2
Broadfields U v Holyport	7-0
Wantage T v Lydney T	2-0
Cricklewood W v Rayners Lane	7-2
Hadley v Colney Heath	5-5, 0-3
Hillingdon Bor v Harpenden T	0-3
Wallingford T v Oxhey Jets	1-2*
(1-1 at the end of normal time)	
Tytherington Rocks v Longlevens	1-8
Oxford C Nomads v Baldock T	1-5
Royal Wootton Bassett T v Codicote	5-0
London Lions v Malmesbury Vic	A-A, 3-1
First match abandoned after 60 minutes due to serious injury to a player. London Lions leading 1-0	
Langford v Crawley Green	3-1
Tie awarded to Crawley Green – Langford removed	
Edgware v Henley T	4-0
Leighton T v Leverstock Green	2-0
Whitstable T v Lancing	6-5*
(4-4 at the end of normal time)	
Cobham v Bexhill U	2-0
AC London v Horley T	0-5
Rushtall v Crawley Down Gatwick	2-1
Hassocks v Spelthorne Sports	0-3
Saltdean U v Stansfeld	3-1
Balham v Forest Hill Park	5-0
Horsham YMCA v Langney W	3-1
Broadbridge Heath v AFC Croydon Ath	3-2*
(1-1 at the end of normal time)	
Billingshurst v Lordswood	1-2
Steyning T v Three Bridges	0-3
Sporting Club Thamesmead v Walton & Hersham	0-8
Meridian VP v FC Deportivo Galicia	0-0*
Meridian VP won 3-1 on penalties	
Beckenham T v Bridon Ropes	1-0
Erith & Belvedere v Chessington & Hook U	4-2*
(2-2 at the end of normal time)	
K Sports v Abbey Rangers	4-2
Chatham T v Kensington Bor	2-4*
(1-1 at the end of normal time)	
Tooting Bec v Fisher	0-3
Newhaven v Hollands & Blair	1-2
Deal T v CB Hounslow U	2-1
Erith T v Mile Oak	1-0
Sheppey U v Tunbridge Wells	2-2, 5-1
Canterbury C v AFC Uckfield T	3-0
Newport (IW) v Alresford T	2-1
Badshot Lea v Frimley Green	2-3
Romsey T v Bournemouth	2-0
AFC Portchester v Tadley Calleva	3-0
Knaphill v Horndean	0-2
Fareham T v Binfield	4-2
Godalming T v Brockenhurst	3-5
Alton T v Amesbury T	7-3
Baffins Milton R v Selsey	1-0
Hamworthy U v Lymington T	2-6
Calne T v Downton	0-1
Sandhurst T v Ringwood T	2-1
Warminster T v Farnham T	0-4
Midhurst & Easebourne v U Services Portsmouth	0-2
Swanage T & Herston v Fawley	3-2
Windsor v Whitchurch U	8-0
Westbury U v Christchurch	5-2*, 0-1
Tie ordered to be replayed after Westbury U used 4 substitutes	
Bashley v Hythe & Dibden	4-0

Chippenham Park v Camberley T	0-2
Hamble Club v Petersfield T	5-0
Willand R v Saltash U	4-1
Odd Down v Oldland Abbotonians	3-1
Radstock T v Roman Glass St George	2-0
Hengrove Ath v Ashton & Backwell U	3-1
Cadbury Heath v Shepton Mallet	3-1
Clevedon T v Wellington	0-1
Bovey Tracey v Bishop Sutton	1-0
AFC St Austell v Bridgwater T	4-5*
(4-4 at the end of normal time)	
Wincanton T v Plymouth Parkway	0-3
Tavistock v Camelford	3-2
Cullompton Rangers v Cribbs	2-1
Portishead T v Bodmin T	1-6
Longwell Green Sports v Ivybridge T	2-3*
(2-2 at the end of normal time)	
Crediton U v Brislington	0-0*
Crediton U won 6-5 on penalties	

FIRST ROUND

Ashton Ath v Liversedge	4-2
West Didsbury & Chorlton v West Auckland T	0-3
Irlam v 1874 Northwich	1-4
Garforth T v Knaresborough T	2-3*
(2-2 at the end of normal time)	
Team Northumbria v Runcorn Linnets	1-1, 2-3
AFC Emley v Thornaby	2-6
Rossington Main v Bootle	3-4*
(2-2 at the end of normal time)	
Sunderland Ryhope CW v Harrogate Railway Ath	10-1
Pickering T v Newcastle Benfield	3-4*
(3-3 at the end of normal time)	
Dunston UTS v Burscough	2-1
Ashington v Hall Road Rangers	1-2
Tow Law T v Bridlington T	2-1
Bedlington Terriers v Charnock Richard	1-0
Whickham v Stockton T	0-2
North Shields v Handsworth Parramore	4-2
AFC Darwen v Marske U	2-3
Alsager T v Runcorn T	5-2
Westella & Willerby v Whitley Bay	1-5
Pontefract Collieries v Litherland Remyca	3-1
City of Liverpool v Dronfield T	7-0
Blaby & Whetstone Ath v Northampton ON Chenecks	3-1
Walsall Wood v Atherstone T	1-0
Lutterworth v Coventry U	2-3
Westfields v Shifnal T	6-0
Brocton v Wednesfield	4-1
Stourport Swifts v Shirebrook T	3-2
Worcester C v Sherwood Colliery	4-3
Wolverhampton SC v Staveley MW	4-2
Rugby T v Harrowby U	2-0*
(0-0 at the end of normal time)	
Pinxton v Heather St Johns	3-1
Hanley T v Godmanchester R	1-3
Racing Club Warwick v Clipstone	2-0
Haughmond v Worksop T	1-2
Wellington v Desborough T	0-2
Eastwood Community v Dunkirk	3-2
Bardon Hill v Quorn	3-4
Stafford T v Kimberley MW	0-1
AFC Wulfrunians v Leicester Nirvana	1-1, 1-4
Rushden & Higham U v Highgate U	0-2
FC Bolsover v Deeping Rangers	1-3
Holbeach U v South Normanton Ath	1-0
Hullbridge Sports v Colney Heath	1-1, 1-0
Holland v Great Wakering R	1-2
Burnham Ramblers v Leighton T	0-1
London Colney v Cogenhoe U	4-4, 0-1
Basildon U v Biggleswade	0-2
Enfield 1893 v Coggeshall T	1-0*
(0-0 at the end of normal time)	
Enfield Bor v Newmarket T	4-2
Framlingham T v Cockfosters	2-0
Wisbech St Mary v Whitton U	2-1
Norwich CBS v Oxhey Jets	1-0
Thetford T v Debenham LC	1-1, 2-0
Welwyn Garden C v Takeley	3-0
Halstead T v Tower Hamlets	2-2*
Tower Hamlets won 6-5 on penalties	
Peterborough Northern Star v Baldock T	1-0
Biggleswade U v Yaxley	0-1
Crawley Green v Harpenden T	3-0
Wisbech T v Felixstowe & Walton U	4-0
FC Romania v Eynesbury R	2-0

Edgware T v Walton & Hersham	1-3
Haywards Heath T v Camberley T	2-0
Cobham v Westfield	0-4
Bracknell T v Buckingham Ath	6-2
Erith & Belvedere v Horley T	2-2, 2-3*
(1-1 at the end of normal time)	
Balham v Deal T	1-3
Thatcham T v Horsham YMCA	2-1
London Lions v Clapton	3-2
Sevenoaks T v Longlevens	2-1
Broadbridge Heath v Kensington Bor	3-0
Beckenham T v Sawbridgeworth T	2-0
Saltdean U v Whitstable T	0-1*
(0-0 at the end of normal time)	
Cray Valley (PM) v Cricklewood W	3-1
Tie awarded to Cricklewood W –	
Cray Valley PM removed	
Rushtall v Epsom & Ewell	2-7
Canterbury C v K Sports	4-3
Royal Wootton Bassett T v Ampthill T	2-1
Spelthorne Sports v Lordswood	0-1
Sheppey U v Fisher	2-1
Erith T v Pagham	4-0
Wembley v Broadfields U	3-0
Hanworth Villa v Three Bridges	3-2
Flackwell Heath v Windsor	2-5
Meridian VP v Hollands & Blair	2-0
Bodmin T v Swanage T & Herston	2-1
Odd Down v Tavistock	1-2
AFC Portchester v Cullompton Rangers	2-3
Wellington v Downton	4-3*
(2-2 at the end of normal time)	
Highworth T v Sholing	1-3
Christchurch v United Services Portsmouth	3-0
Romsey T v Hamble Club	2-3
Portland U v Horndean	0-1
Fareham T v Ivybridge T	4-3
Wantage T v Cadbury Heath	4-3
Baffins Milton R v Radstock T	1-0
Hengrove Ath v Alton T	4-2*
(2-2 at the end of normal time)	
Newport (IW) v Bovey Tracey	7-2
Plymouth Parkway v Sandhurst T	6-1
Brockenhurst v Crediton U	2-1*
(1-1 at the end of normal time)	
Willand R v Street	7-1
Farnham T v Lymington T	2-0
Frimley Green v Blackfield & Langley	0-2
Bashley v Bridgwater T	2-3*
(2-2 at the end of normal time)	

SECOND ROUND

Stockton T v Bootle	4-2*
(2-2 at the end of normal time)	
North Shields v Knaresborough T	2-1
Dunston UTS v Worksop T	0-1
Marske U v Shildon	2-1*
(1-1 at the end of normal time)	
Sunderland Ryhope CW v City of Liverpool	1-2
1874 Northwich v Tow Law T	5-1
Hall Road Rangers v Pontefract Collieries	2-4
West Auckland T v Billingham T	3-2
Runcorn Linnets v Sunderland RCA	1-1, 2-1
Ashton Ath v Morpeth T	1-0
Bedlington Terriers v Newcastle Benfield	0-3
Thornaby v Whitley Bay	2-4*
(2-2 at the end of normal time)	
Wolverhampton SC v Rugby T	2-2, 2-0
Hinckley v AFC Mansfield	2-0
Coleshill T v Blaby & Whetstone Ath	8-1
Godmanchester R v Deeping Rangers	3-4
Brocton v Shepshed Dynamo	3-5
Desborough T v Pinxton	7-4*
(4-4 at the end of normal time)	
Quorn v Coventry U	0-6
Racing Club Warwick v Alsager T	2-1
Leicester Nirvana v Eastwood Community	0-2
Walsall Wood v Holbeach U	5-0
Worcester C v Highgate U	1-2
Kimberley MW v Stourport Swifts	0-2
Sporting Khalsa v Bromsgrove Sporting	0-1
Tring Ath v Ely C	4-1
Welwyn Garden C v Newport Pagnell T	2-1
Thetford T v Wisbech T	1-4
Biggleswade v Crawley Green	2-0
Yaxley v Peterborough Northern Star	3-0

Leighton T v London Lions	1-0
Hullbridge Sports v Wembley	3-2
Sun Sports v Cogenhoe U (walkover)	
Tower Hamlets v Enfield 1893	1-2
Enfield Bor v Berkhamsted	2-4*
(2-2 at the end of normal time)	
Gorleston v Framlingham T	2-1
Wisbech St Mary v Norwich CBS	1-4
Great Wakering R v FC Romania	2-2, 1-0
Erith T v Windsor	1-2
Walton & Hersham v Hanworth Villa	2-1
Haywards Heath T v Sevenoaks T	1-2
Whitstable T v Epsom & Ewell	3-2*
(2-2 at the end of normal time)	
Meridian VP v Horley T	0-3
Sheppey U v Beckenham T	2-3
Westfield v Canterbury C	1-0
Thatcham T v Broadbridge Heath	8-2
Southall v Lordswood	1-2
Crowborough Ath v Croydon	5-0
Bracknell T v Cricklewood W	8-0
Corinthian v Eastbourne T	3-4
Chichester C v Deal T	3-0
Christchurch v Fareham T	3-2
Team Solent v Tavistock	2-0
Exmouth T v Blackfield & Langley	1-3
Sholing v Wellington	2-1
Wantage T v Melksham T	1-4
Newport (IW) v Hengrove Ath	6-2
Baffins Milton R v Cullompton Rangers	3-1
Buckland Ath v Bradford T	1-2
Hamble Club v Brockenhurst	5-4*
(4-4 at the end of normal time)	
Willand R v Westfields	1-2
Farnham T v Bridgwater T	2-3
Plymouth Parkway v Bodmin T	4-2
Horndean v Royal Wootton Bassett T	3-2

THIRD ROUND

1874 Northwich v Ashton Ath	2-0
Stockton T v City of Liverpool	1-0
West Auckland T v Whitley Bay	4-3
Pontefract Collieries v Worksop T	3-0
Newcastle Benfield v North Shields	3-1
Runcorn Linnets v Marske U	2-3
Stourport Swifts v Walsall Wood	3-1
Bromsgrove Sporting v Coventry U	1-1, 3-3*
Bromsgrove Sporting won 4-3 on penalties	
Wolverhampton SC v Shepshed Dynamo	5-0
Desborough T v Eastwood Community	4-1
Highgate U v Coleshill T	1-2
Hinckley v Deeping Rangers	3-1
Racing Club Warwick v Wisbech T	0-2
Gorleston v Leighton T	2-4
Hullbridge Sports v Enfield 1893	3-2
Yaxley v Norwich CBS	2-3
Great Wakering R v Cogenhoe U	0-2
Tring Ath v Berkhamsted	1-0
Welwyn Garden C v Biggleswade	1-2
Lordswood v Bracknell T	0-1
Beckenham T v Eastbourne T	2-3
Horley T v Baffins Milton R	4-1
Walton & Hersham v Windsor	1-2
Crowborough Ath v Westfield	1-0
Whitstable T v Chichester C	0-2
Thatcham T v Sevenoaks T	3-1
Christchurch v Newport (IW)	0-1
Sholing v Blackfield & Langley	0-1
Plymouth Parkway v Westfields	2-3
Hamble Club v Horndean	2-1
Bridgwater T v Melksham T	2-2, 0-2
Bradford T v Team Solent	4-0

FOURTH ROUND

Newcastle Benfield v Coleshill T	1-1, 1-1*
Coleshill T won 4-2 on penalties	
Wisbech T v Bromsgrove Sporting	1-3
Cogenhoe U v Wolverhampton SC	2-3
Marske U v Hinckley	5-0
1874 Northwich v Pontefract Collieries	3-1
Stockton T v West Auckland	2-1*
(1-1 at the end of normal time)	
Desborough T v Stourport Swifts	2-4*
(2-2 at the end of normal time)	
Melksham T v Crowborough Ath	2-1

Westfields v Hamble Club	1-4
Blackfield & Langley v Bracknell T	3-3, 1-2
Leighton T v Norwich CBS	5-2*
(2-2 at the end of normal time)	
Newport (IW) v Bradford T	0-1
Eastbourne T v Windsor	1-3
Horley T v Chichester C	1-2
Tring Ath v Hullbridge Sports	5-1
Thatcham T v Biggleswade	2-1

FIFTH ROUND

Wolverhampton SC v Leighton T	3-4
Thatcham T v Bromsgrove Sporting	2-1
Marske U v Bradford T	2-0
Coleshill T v Bracknell T	2-4*
(1-1 at the end of normal time)	
1874 Northwich v Chichester C	1-0
Stockton T v Stourport Swifts	3-0
Windsor v Hamble Club	2-0
Melksham T v Tring Ath	2-1

SIXTH ROUND

Bracknell T v Marske U	0-3
Melksham T v Thatcham T	0-1
Stockton T v Windsor	2-0
Leighton T v 1874 Northwich	0-1

SEMI-FINAL – FIRST LEG

Marske U v Stockton T	0-2
Thatcham T v 1874 Northwich	1-0

SEMI-FINAL – SECOND LEG

Stockton T v Marske U	1-2
Stockton T won 3-2 on aggregate	
1874 Northwich v Thatcham T	2-3
Thatcham T won 4-2 on aggregate	

THE BUILDBASE FA VASE FINAL 2018

Wembley, Sunday 20 May 2018

Thatcham T (1) 1 *(Cooper-Clark 24 (pen))*

Stockton T (0) 0   31,403 (combined with FA Trophy)

Thatcham T: Rackley; Brownhill, Angell, Melledew (James 83), Jarra, Moran, Bayley, Cooper-Clark (Cook 78), James, Elliott, Brown (Johnson 70).
Stockton T: Arthur; Carter (Garbutt 61), Ward (Nicholson 79), Mulligan N, Mulligan D, Coulthard, Hayes, Woodhouse, Owens, Risborough, Stockton (Coleman 66).
Referee: John Brooks.

THE FA YOUTH CUP 2017–18

After extra time.

PRELIMINARY ROUND

Durham C v Spennymoor T	0-2
Morpeth T v Hebburn T	3-0
Curzon Ashton v Nelson	0-1
Ashton Ath v Witton Alb	1-0
AFC Darwen v Daisy Hill	0-4
Irlam v St Helens T	2-1
West Didsbury & Chorlton v Warrington T (walkover)	
Burscough (walkover) v Lancaster C	
Hyde U v Chorley	2-1
Skelmersdale U v FC United of Manchester (walkover)	
Ashton U (walkover) v Chadderton	
Stockport Co v Stockport T	3-4
Salford C v Mossley	1-0
Radcliffe Bor v Nantwich T	2-5
Bamber Bridge v Altrincham (walkover)	
Ossett T v Harrogate T	1-3*
(1-1 at the end of normal time)	
Staveley MW v Stocksbridge Park Steels	4-0
Silsden (walkover) v Glasshoughton Welfare	
Worksop T v Garforth T	3-1
North Ferriby U v Nostell MW (walkover)	
Worsbrough Bridge Ath v Bottesford U	1-2
Sheffield v Hall Road Rangers	4-3
York C v Tadcaster Alb	4-0
Eastwood Community v Deeping Rangers	5-2
Harborough T v Leicester Road	5-2
Ilkeston v Boston U (walkover)	
Long Eaton U v Anstey Nomads	9-4
Aylestone Park v Grantham T	3-2
West Bridgford v Lincoln U	3-0
Dunkirk v Leicester Nirvana	5-2
Ashby Ivanhoe v Belper T	0-2
Alfreton T v Mickleover Sports	2-1*
(1-1 at the end of normal time)	
Sporting Khalsa v Lichfield C	2-3
Nuneaton Griff v Hereford	2-3
Racing Club Warwick v Walsall Wood	2-3
Sutton Coldfield T (walkover) v Wolverhampton Casuals	
Newcastle T v Wednesfield	2-2*
Newcastle T won 4-2 on penalties	
Bedworth U (walkover) v Kidsgrove Ath	
Stafford T v Worcester C	1-3
Bromsgrove Sporting v Leek T	1-2
Leamington v Stratford T	2-3
Kidderminster H v Alvechurch	3-0
AFC Telford U v Bromyard T	3-2
Bilston T v Coton Green	3-2
Tipton T v Tamworth	A-A
Tie abandoned after 76 mins due to serious injury to a player, 1-5 tie awarded to Tamworth	
Rushall Olympic v Dudley T	2-3

Malvern T v Rugby T	3-1
Highgate U v Boldmere St Michaels	4-5
AFC Rushden & Diamonds v Rushden & Higham U	12-0
Peterborough Northern Star v St Neots T	2-1
Brackley T v Yaxley	5-0
Biggleswade T v Huntingdon T	6-0
Cogenhoe U v Biggleswade U	1-3
Cambridge C v Felixstowe & Walton U	3-2*
(1-1 at the end of normal time)	
Framlingham T v Dereham T	1-3
Wisbech St Mary v Swaffham T	0-9
Histon v Gorleston	0-6
AFC Sudbury v King's Lynn T	8-1
Whitton U v Leiston	0-2
Bury T v Wroxham	0-2
Fakenham T v Haverhill R	1-4
Ipswich W v Newmarket T	4-2
Woodbridge T v Walsham Le Willows	3-1
Basildon U v Witham T (walkover)	
Saffron Walden T v Potters Bar T	3-1
Hoddesdon T v Barkingside	5-2
Hitchin T (walkover) v Little Oakley	
Barking v Ware	3-1
AFC Hornchurch v Takeley	2-0
Hullbridge Sports v Waltham Forest	1-0
Ilford v Cheshunt	0-5
Harlow T v Brightlingsea Regent (walkover)	
Halstead T v Bishop's Stortford	1-5
Brentwood T v Stanway R	2-1
Concord Rangers v Waltham Abbey	3-0
Great Wakering R v Hadley (walkover)	
Royston T v Redbridge	4-1
Heybridge Swifts v Romford	2-5
Tower Hamlets v Grays Ath	5-3
Coggeshall T v Sawbridgeworth T	6-0
Thurrock v Aveley	9-1
Northwood v Haringey Bor	5-1
Kings Langley v Colney Heath	3-2
Hemel Hempstead T v Sun Sports	4-0
Staines T v Harrow Bor	5-3*
(3-3 at the end of normal time)	
Bedfont Sports (walkover) v Winslow U	
Edgware T v Cockfosters	5-3
Buckingham Ath v Oxhey Jets	7-0
Harefield U v Spelthorne Sports	4-0
Hendon v North Greenford U	7-0
Flackwell Heath v Newport Pagnell T	2-1
Wealdstone v Uxbridge	1-2
Wingate & Finchley v Chalfont St Peter	10-0
Leverstock Green v Aylesbury	0-4
Carshalton Ath (walkover) v Eastbourne T	
Erith T v Dulwich Hamlet	2-10
Phoenix Sports v VCD Ath	2-1
Lingfield v Croydon	1-4

Ashford U v Chatham T — 8-2
East Grinstead T v Lewisham Bor (Community) (walkover)
Lordswood (walkover) v Glebe
Corinthian v Eastbourne Bor — 0-3
Sevenoaks T v Dartford — 0-2
Ramsgate v Hollands & Blair — 2-2*
   Hollands & Blair won 4-2 on penalties
Margate v Thamesmead T — 3-0
Hampton & Richmond Bor v Chertsey T — 2-1
Steyning T v Chichester C — 5-1
Camberley T v Raynes Park Vale — 7-3
Whitehawk v Worthing — 4-1
Whyteleafe v Balham — 4-1
Dorking W v Bognor Regis T — 1-5
Ash U v Newhaven — 4-0
Knaphill v Metropolitan Police — 5-4*
   (4-4 at the end of normal time)
Chessington & Hook U v East Preston — 4-1*
   (1-1 at the end of normal time)
Shoreham v Three Bridges — 2-3
Frimley Green v Worthing U — 1-4
Corinthian Casuals v Merstham — 1-1
   Corinthian Casuals won 6-5 on penalties
Guildford C v Hastings U — 0-1
Crowborough Ath v Horley T — 4-0
Walton & Hersham v Westfield — 3-1
Oxford C v Basingstoke T — 6-5
Bracknell T v Highmoor Ibis — 5-1
Ascot U v Marlow — 0-3
Alton T (walkover) v Slough T
Kidlington v Fleet Spurs — 0-2
Poole T v Farnborough — 4-4*
   Farnborough won 5-4 on penalties
Havant & Waterlooville v Salisbury — 0-1
Christchurch v Team Solent — 1-2
Cirencester v Oldland Abbotonians — A-A, 5-2
   First match abandoned after 56 mins due to floodlight
   failure, Cirencester leading 3-0
Gloucester C v Bristol Manor Farm — 3-2
Paulton R v Wellington — 1-2
Ashton & Backwell U v Wells C — 1-6
Welton R (walkover) v Willand R
Keynsham T v Tavistock — 0-2
Weston Super Mare v Portishead T — 4-2
Bridgwater T v Radstock T — 1-3

FIRST QUALIFYING ROUND

Carlisle C v Morpeth T — 2-6
Workington (walkover) v Ryton & Crawcrook Alb
Shildon v Darlington — 4-2
Stockton T v Spennymoor T — 0-2
South Shields v Chester-le-Street T — 10-0
Ashton U v Altrincham (walkover)
Irlam v Prescot Cables — 0-6
Warrington T v Colne — 1-0*
   (0-0 at the end of normal time)
Vauxhall Motors v Ashton Ath — 2-1
Nantwich T v Southport — 3-1
Abbey Hey v Ashton T — 3-1
Marine v Bootle — 2-6
Burscough v FC United of Manchester — 0-6
Stalybridge Celtic v Nelson — 1-5
Hyde U v Stockport T — 3-1
Daisy Hill v Salford C — 1-4
Rossington Main v AFC Emley — 2-0
Harrogate Railway Ath v Nostell MW — 6-1
Farsley Celtic v Handsworth Parramore — 0-12
York C v Harrogate T — 5-0
Bottesford T v Worksop T — 3-1
Ossett Alb v Staveley MW — 6-3
Selby T v Sheffield (walkover)
Maltby Main v Silsden — 4-1
Matlock T v Alfreton T — 0-1
Blaby & Whetstone Ath v Aylestone Park — 0-7
Sandiacre T v Buxton — 4-1
Belper T v Eastwood Community — 3-2
West Bridgford v Long Eaton U — 3-4
Bourne T v Harborough T — 1-7
Basford U v Dunkirk — 0-3
Gresley v Boston U — 0-4
Newcastle T v Boldmere St Michaels — 3-1
Worcester C v Bilston T — 4-4*
   Worcester C won 5-3 on penalties
Nuneaton T v Stratford T — 2-0
Romulus v Walsall Wood — 1-4

Halesowen T v Kidderminster H — 2-1
Tamworth v Leek T — 3-2
AFC Telford U v Lichfield C — 2-1*
   (1-1 at the end of normal time)
Hereford v Stourbridge — 1-2*
   (1-1 at the end of normal time)
Malvern U v Sutton Coldfield T (walkover)
Ellesmere Rangers v Dudley T — 3-4
Bedworth U v Pegasus Juniors — 5-2
Evesham U v Eccleshall — 4-0
Wellingborough T v Kempston R — 2-1
AFC Dunstable v Brackley T — 5-1
AFC Rushden & Diamonds v Rothwell Corinthians — 3-2
Kettering T v St Ives T — 1-3
Biggleswade T v Biggleswade U — 4-0
Peterborough Sports v Corby T — 3-4
Godmanchester R v Peterborough Northern Star — 1-1*
   Peterborough Northern Star won 5-4 on penalties
Brantham Ath v Woodbridge T — 2-4
Ely C v Needham Market — 1-12
Haverhill R v Cornard U — 2-0
Gorleston v Wroxham — 1-0
March Town U v Swaffham T — 4-1
Cambridge C v Hadleigh U — 7-0
Leiston v Mildenhall T — 1-0
Ipswich W v AFC Sudbury — 0-7
Stowmarket T v Dereham T — 3-8
Coggeshall T v St Margaretsbury — 3-0
Barking v Chelmsford C — 6-0
Tilbury v Codicote (walkover)
Royston T v Bishop's Stortford — 0-2
Thurrock v Clapton — 7-2
East Thurrock U v FC Broxbourne Bor — 1-3
Cheshunt v Hullbridge Sports — 5-0
Hadley v Tower Hamlets — 1-3
Romford v Witham T — 1-0
Brentwood T v AFC Hornchurch — 1-3
Braintree T v Hoddesdon T — 1-5
Concord Rangers v Hitchin T — 3-4
Saffron Walden T v Brightlingsea Regent — 1-4
Hendon v Aylesbury — 4-2*
   (2-2 at the end of normal time)
Staines T v Hanwell T — 5-2
Bedfont Sports v St Albans C — 2-3*
   (2-2 at the end of normal time)
Sandhurst T v Kings Langley — 1-7
Wingate & Finchley v Ashford T (Middlesex) — 4-1
Hayes & Yeading U v Brimsdown — 7-1
Enfield T v CB Hounslow U — 5-0
Edgware T v Harefield U — 10-2
Chesham U v Northwood — 4-3*
   (3-3 at the end of normal time)
Buckingham Ath v Flackwell Heath — 3-1
Hemel Hempstead T v Uxbridge — 2-0
Lewisham Bor (Community) v Lordswood — 4-2
Ashford U v Folkestone Invicta — 1-5
Carshalton Ath v Dulwich Hamlet — 3-2*
   (1-1 at the end of normal time)
Eastbourne Bor v Welling U — 0-1
Croydon v AFC Croydon Ath — 3-2
Margate v Hollands & Blair — 3-0
Tooting & Mitcham U v Cray W — 1-3
Tonbridge Angels v Greenwich Bor (walkover)
Phoenix Sports v Dartford — 2-1
Faversham T v Chipstead — 1-6
Kingstonian v Mile Oak — 6-1
Whyteleafe v South Park — 4-2
Burgess Hill T v Haywards Heath T — 2-0
Crowborough Ath v Three Bridges — 1-6
Leatherhead v Wick — 7-0
Arundel v Lewes (walkover)
Knaphill v Ash U — 1-2
Hastings U v Abbey Rangers — 2-1
Walton & Hersham v Hampton & Richmond Bor — 2-4
Worthing U v Bognor Regis T — 1-5
Redhill v Camberley T — 1-4
Corinthian Casuals v Whitehawk — 1-7
Steyning T v Chessington & Hook U — 6-2
Hartley Wintney v Holmer Green — 1-3
Fleet T v Fleet Spurs — 3-1
Andover T v Hungerford T — 2-3
Didcot T v Oxford C — 1-4
Windsor v Alton T — 4-0
Clanfield 85 v Bracknell T — 5-2*
   (2-2 at the end of normal time)
Thame U v Binfield — 5-2

Thatcham T v Marlow	1-3*
(1-1 at the end of normal time)	
Salisbury v Winchester C	3-2
Brockenhurst v AFC Totton	4-6*
(4-4 at the end of normal time)	
Farnborough (walkover) v Fareham T	
Team Solent v Stoneham	4-2
AFC Portchester v Romsey T	1-1*
AFC Portchester won 4-3 on penalties	
Sholing v Wimborne T	3-1
Cirencester T v Chippenham T	2-4
Gloucester C v Bishop's Cleeve	6-0
New College Swindon v Malmesbury Vic	1-3
Tuffley R v Yate T	2-3
Welton R v Wells C	4-7*
(4-4 at the end of normal time)	
Tavistock v Elburton Villa	3-1
Bath C v Radstock T	3-2*
(2-2 at the end of normal time)	
Odd Down v Wellington	4-0
Clevedon T v Weston Super Mare	5-2

SECOND QUALIFYING ROUND

Barrow v Gateshead	1-5
South Shields v Spennymoor T	1-2
Shildon v Workington	3-0
Morpeth T v Hartlepool U	0-3
Nelson v Hyde U	8-0
Nantwich T v Tranmere R	0-1
Prescot Cables v FC United of Manchester	3-1*
(1-1 at the end of normal time)	
Bootle v Altrincham	2-3
AFC Fylde v Chester FC	1-3
Salford C v Warrington T	2-1
Vauxhall Motors v Wrexham	0-4
FC Halifax T v Abbey Hey	4-1
Handsworth Parramore v Ossett Alb	2-1
Rossington Main v Guiseley	0-5
Sheffield v Alfreton T	0-3
York C v Harrogate Railway Ath	3-1
Maltby Main v Bottesford T	1-6
Belper T v Sandiacre T	1-0
Tamworth v Boston U	3-1
Dunkirk v Harborough T	7-1
Long Eaton U v Aylestone Park	2-1
Worcester C v Sutton Coldfield T	0-1
Evesham U v Walsall Wood	4-0
Newcastle T v Bedworth U	1-3
Solihull Moors v Nuneaton T	0-2
Halesowen T v AFC Telford U	0-2
Stourbridge v Dudley T	3-0
Corby T v AFC Rushden & Diamonds	1-2
(1-1 at the end of normal time)	
AFC Dunstable v St Ives T	1-0
Biggleswade T v Wellingborough T	2-0
Haverhill R v Cambridge C	0-2
Woodbridge T v Peterborough Northern Star	6-1
Leiston v Dereham T	1-0
Gorleston v Needham Market	3-2
AFC Sudbury v March Town U	5-0
Tower Hamlets v Leyton Orient	0-3
AFC Hornchurch v FC Broxbourne Bor	4-1
Dagenham & Redbridge v Coggeshall T	6-0
Cheshunt v Romford	4-1
(1-1 at the end of normal time)	
Saffron Walden T v Hitchin T	2-3
Thurrock v Bishop's Stortford	0-2
Barking v Hoddesdon T	0-2
(0-0 at the end of normal time)	
Hampton & Richmond Bor v Codicote	3-2
Edgware T v Wingate & Finchley	1-2
Boreham Wood v Hendon	2-1
Hayes & Yeading U v Enfield T	2-3
Hemel Hempstead T v Chesham U	6-0
Kings Langley v St Albans C	2-8
Staines T v Carshalton Ath	3-2
Ebbsfleet U v Phoenix Sports	0-2
Chipstead v Lewisham Bor (Community)	4-1
Dover Ath v Cray W	1-0
Bromley v Maidstone U	3-1
Folkestone Invicta v Welling U	0-2
Greenwich Bor v Margate	0-4
Whitehawk v Woking	3-1
Camberley T v Three Bridges	4-0
Sutton U v Croydon	2-1
Leatherhead v Lewes	1-2
(1-1 at the end of normal time)	

Bognor Regis T v Hastings U	0-3
Burgess Hill T v Whyteleafe	3-2
Kingstonian v Steyning T	1-2
Windsor v Buckingham Ath	4-7
(3-3 at the end of normal time)	
Marlow v Thame U	2-0
Clanfield 85 v Oxford C	4-2
Holmer Green v Maidenhead U	2-1
(1-1 at the end of normal time)	
Fleet T v AFC Portchester	4-1
Ash U v Farnborough	4-2
Eastleigh v Malmesbury Vic	3-1
Aldershot T v Hungerford T	5-3
Salisbury v AFC Totton	1-4
Team Solent v Sholing	2-2
Sholing won 8-7 on penalties	
Wells C v Yate T	4-3
Chippenham T v Clevedon T	1-2
Odd Down v Bath C	1-2
Tavistock v Gloucester C	1-3

THIRD QUALIFYING ROUND

Gateshead v Wrexham	2-3
Nelson v Prescot Cables	1-2
Altrincham v Chester FC	1-3
York C v Salford C	0-1
Spennymoor T v Tranmere R	0-1
Shildon v Guiseley	1-3
Hartlepool U v FC Halifax T	2-1
Nuneaton T v Long Eaton U	1-2
Belper T v Bottesford T	2-3
Dunkirk v AFC Rushden & Diamonds	2-1
Handsworth Parramore v AFC Telford U	2-1
Evesham U v Bedworth U	2-0
Sutton Coldfield T v Stourbridge	0-2
Tamworth v Alfreton T	2-0
Cambridge C v Leiston	1-0*
(0-0 at the end of normal time)	
Gorleston v Dagenham & Redbridge	1-7
Hitchin T v Hoddesdon T	6-1
Woodbridge T v Bishop's Stortford	0-2
Leyton Orient v AFC Hornchurch	4-0
Cheshunt v AFC Sudbury	5-2
Holmer Green v Marlow	0-0*
Marlow won 5-4 on penalties	
Buckingham Ath v Hampton & Richmond Bor	7-1
St Albans C v Biggleswade T	0-2
Clanfield 85 v Hemel Hempstead T	0-0*
Clanfield 85 won 5-3 on penalties	
Boreham Wood v Enfield T	2-0
Wingate & Finchley v AFC Dunstable	2-0
Phoenix Sports v Whitehawk	3-4
Chipstead v Sutton U	4-2
Hastings U v Bromley	1-2
Margate v Staines T	3-0
Lewes v Steyning T	3-0
Camberley T v Burgess Hill T	3-1
Welling U v Dover Ath	1-1*
Welling U won 2-1 on penalties	
Eastleigh v Wells C	3-0
Bath C v Clevedon T	3-4
Aldershot T v Sholing	2-2*
Sholing won 4-3 on penalties	
Fleet T v Gloucester C	0-2
AFC Totton v Ash U	2-2*
AFC Totton won 5-4 on penalties	

FIRST ROUND

Tranmere R v Blackburn R	0-1
Morecambe v Wigan Ath	0-4
Carlisle U v Prescot Cables	5-1
Bradford C v Blackpool	0-3
Oldham Ath v Bury	0-3
Accrington Stanley v Rochdale	1-0
Hartlepool U v Chester FC	3-1
Guiseley v Fleetwood T	0-0*
Fleetwood T won 4-3 on penalties	
Wrexham v Salford C	2-2*
Wrexham won 5-4 on penalties	
Evesham U v Shrewsbury T	0-3
Tie awarded to Evesham U – Shrewsbury T removed	
Rotherham U v Bottesford T	7-0
Doncaster R v Walsall	4-3
Dunkirk v Tamworth	0-2
Stourbridge v Port Vale	2-3*
(2-2 at the end of normal time)	

Grimsby T v Mansfield T	0-1
Long Eaton U v Scunthorpe U	0-3
Chesterfield v Notts Co	3-1
Lincoln C v Coventry C	1-2
Handsworth Parramore v Crewe Alexandra	0-2
Barnet v Wingate & Finchley	4-0
Colchester U v Cheshunt	5-4
Milton Keynes Dons v Southend U	1-0
Leyton Orient v Biggleswade T	5-0
Peterborough U v Cambridge U	1-2*
(1-1 at the end of normal time)	
Hitchin T v Dagenham & Redbridge	4-6
Buckingham Ath v Northampton T	2-4
Clanfield 85 v Cambridge C	2-1
Luton T v Stevenage	1-2
Bishop's Stortford v Boreham Wood	3-1*
(1-1 at the end of normal time)	
Charlton Ath v Whitehawk	4-1
Bromley v Chipstead	2-0
Marlow v AFC Wimbledon	0-3
Welling U v Margate	3-1
Gillingham v Portsmouth	1-2*
(1-1 at the end of normal time)	
Lewes v Camberley T	4-3
Bristol R v Forest Green R	1-1*
Bristol R won 3-1 on penalties	
Swindon T v Newport Co	6-2
AFC Totton v Cheltenham T	0-9
Plymouth Arg v Eastleigh	7-2
Sholing v Clevedon T	2-0
Gloucester C v Oxford U	1-2*
(1-1 at the end of normal time)	
Yeovil T v Exeter C	0-3

SECOND ROUND

Evesham U v Crewe Alexandra	0-4
Cambridge U v Scunthorpe U	0-1
Chesterfield v Port Vale	2-1
Wigan Ath v Bury	1-3
Blackburn R v Wrexham	3-1
Accrington Stanley v Coventry C	2-3
Carlisle U v Hartlepool U	0-2
Tamworth v Fleetwood T	1-2*
(1-1 at the end of normal time)	
Rotherham U v Mansfield T	0-1
Doncaster R v Blackpool	0-2
Colchester U v Bishop's Stortford	5-0
Swindon T v Northampton T	1-0
Plymouth Arg v AFC Wimbledon	3-2
Exeter C v Charlton Ath	1-2
Cheltenham T v Welling U	2-0*
(0-0 at the end of normal time)	
Oxford U v Bristol R	3-1
Portsmouth v Lewes	3-1
Dagenham & Redbridge v Clanfield 85	7-1
Leyton Orient v Sholing	5-0
Barnet v Milton Keynes Dons	1-3
Bromley v Stevenage	1-4

THIRD ROUND

Sheffield U v Burton Alb	2-0
Queens Park Rangers v Charlton Ath	1-3
Tottenham H v Preston North End	5-0
Mansfield T v Crystal Palace	2-2*
Crystal Palace won 6-5 on penalties	
Burnley v Leeds U	1-0
Cheltenham T v Bury	1-2
Brighton & Hove Alb v Newcastle U	0-5
Oxford U v Dagenham & Redbridge	0-3
Blackburn R v Stoke C	2-1
Fleetwood T v Stevenage	1-5
West Bromwich Alb v Leyton Orient	4-0
Plymouth Arg v Manchester C	0-0*
Plymouth Arg won 6-5 on penalties	
Huddersfield T v Fulham	1-1*
Fulham won 4-3 on penalties	
AFC Bournemouth v Hull C	3-0
Portsmouth v Leicester C	1-2*
(1-1 at the end of normal time)	
Chelsea v Scunthorpe U	4-0
Watford v Sunderland	1-0
Swindon T v Nottingham Forest	1-3
Milton Keynes Dons v Cardiff C	1-0
Swansea C v Chesterfield	2-0
Middlesbrough v Bolton W	2-0
Reading v Millwall	2-1
Derby Co v Manchester Utd	2-2*
Derby Co won 3-1 on penalties	
Norwich C v Barnsley	4-1

Everton v Ipswich T	1-2
Bristol C v Birmingham C	1-2
Colchester U v Crewe Alexandra	2-0
West Ham U v Blackpool	0-1
Southampton v Wolverhampton W	4-1
Arsenal v Sheffield Wednesday	2-1
Aston Villa v Coventry C	2-1
Hartlepool U v Liverpool	1-5

FOURTH ROUND

Liverpool v Arsenal	2-3*
(2-2 at the end of normal time)	
Burnley v Plymouth Arg	0-1
Crystal Palace v Newcastle U	2-3*
(2-2 at the end of normal time)	
Blackpool v Southampton	1-1*
Blackpool won 4-2 on penalties	
Stevenage v Middlesbrough	1-2
Chelsea v West Bromwich Alb	7-0
Ipswich T v Dagenham & Redbridge	2-1
Charlton Ath v Reading	3-4*
(3-3 at the end of normal time)	
Bury v Aston Villa	1-0
Colchester U v Milton Keynes Dons	2-0
Birmingham C v Sheffield U	1-0
Nottingham Forest v Leicester C	1-1*
Nottingham Forest won 5-4 on penalties	
Blackburn R v Watford	2-0
Swansea C v Fulham	0-2
Norwich C v Derby Co	4-2*
(2-2 at the end of normal time)	
AFC Bournemouth v Tottenham H	0-3

FIFTH ROUND

Colchester U v Reading	1-4
Tie awarded to Colchester U – Reading removed	
Plymouth Arg v Fulham	1-3*
(1-1 at the end of normal time)	
Bury v Birmingham C	1-3
Middlesbrough v Arsenal	2-3
Blackburn R v Nottingham Forest	5-1
Norwich C v Newcastle U	4-3*
(3-3 at the end of normal time)	
Tottenham H v Chelsea	0-2
Ipswich T v Blackpool	0-2

SIXTH ROUND

Fulham v Chelsea	0-6
Norwich C v Birmingham C	1-3
Colchester U v Arsenal	1-5
Blackburn R v Blackpool	2-3

SEMI-FINALS – FIRST LEG

Blackpool v Arsenal	2-2
Birmingham C v Chelsea	0-3

SEMI-FINALS – SECOND LEG

Chelsea v Birmingham C	4-0
Chelsea won 7-0 on aggregate	
Arsenal v Blackpool	5-0
Arsenal won 7-2 on aggregate	

FA YOUTH CUP FINAL 2018 FIRST LEG

Friday 27 April 2018

Chelsea (0) 3 *(Redan 67, 86, Guehi 78)*
Arsenal (1) 1 *(Amaechi 36)*　　　　　　　3392

Chelsea: Cumming; Lamptey (Familio-Castillo 85), James, Guehi, Panzo, Gallagher, Gilmour, Uwakwe (Sterling 46), McEachran, Hudson-Odoi, Brown (Redan 61).
Arsenal: Virginia; Daley-Campbell, Thompson, Burton, Ballard, Medley (Olowu 88), Olayinka, Smith (Saka 67), John-Jules, Smith-Rowe (Coyle 62), Amaechi.
Referee: Tim Robinson (Sussex).

FA YOUTH CUP FINAL 2018 SECOND LEG

Monday 30 April 2018

Arsenal (0) 0

Chelsea (1) 4 *(Gilmour 10, Hudson-Odoi 55, 76, Anjorin 67)*　　　　　　　3877

Arsenal: Virginia; Daley-Campbell, Thompson, Burton, Ballard (Medley 76), Olowu, Olayinka, Saka, John-Jules (Coyle 70), Smith-Rowe, Amaechi (Balogun 62).
Chelsea: Cumming; Familio-Castillo, James, Guehi, Panzo, Gallagher (Mola 60), Gilmour, Sterling, McEachran (Anjorin 60), Hudson-Odoi, Redan (Brown 70).
Chelsea won 7-1 on aggregate.
Referee: Tim Robinson (Sussex).

PREMIER LEAGUE 2 2017–18

After extra time.

PROFESSIONAL UNDER-23 DEVELOPMENT LEAGUE
LEAGUE 1

DIVISION 1

		P	W	D	L	F	A	GD	Pts
1	Arsenal	22	13	3	6	48	32	16	42
2	Liverpool	22	13	1	8	43	27	16	40
3	Leicester C	22	11	6	5	36	20	16	39
4	Swansea C	22	11	4	7	40	31	9	37
5	West Ham U	22	9	4	9	30	32	–2	31
6	Manchester C	22	8	6	8	41	31	10	30
7	Everton	22	9	3	10	32	36	–4	30
8	Chelsea	22	8	5	9	34	35	–1	29
9	Tottenham H	22	7	5	10	38	48	–10	26
10	Derby Co	22	7	3	12	32	44	–12	24
11	Sunderland	22	6	4	12	19	39	–20	22
12	Manchester U	22	4	8	10	22	40	–18	20

DIVISION 2

		P	W	D	L	F	A	GD	Pts
1	Blackburn R	22	15	4	3	47	20	27	49
2	Aston Villa	22	14	0	8	51	30	21	42
3	Brighton & HA	22	11	7	4	46	25	21	40
4	Middlesbrough	22	11	4	7	41	36	5	37
5	Reading	22	10	4	8	38	44	–6	34
6	Southampton	22	10	3	9	41	37	46	33
7	Norwich C	22	9	5	8	33	33	0	32
8	Fulham	22	9	3	10	38	37	1	30
9	Wolverhampton W	22	8	4	10	30	41	–11	28
10	Newcastle U	22	6	3	13	29	45	–16	21
11	Stoke C	22	6	2	14	31	46	–15	20
12	WBA	22	2	3	17	21	52	–31	9

PROMOTION PLAY-OFFS – SEMI-FINALS
Aston Villa v Reading   4-3
Brighton & HA v Middlesbrough   3-0

PROMOTION PLAY-OFFS FINAL
Aston Villa v Brighton   0-2

FA PREMIER LEAGUE 2 LEAGUE CUP

After extra time.

GROUP STAGE

GROUP A TABLE

		P	W	D	L	F	A	GD	Pts
1	Derby Co	6	4	0	2	14	8	6	12
2	Middlesbrough	6	3	0	3	9	8	1	9
3	Birmingham C	6	3	0	3	10	14	–4	9
4	Nottingham F	6	2	0	4	7	10	–3	6

GROUP B TABLE

		P	W	D	L	F	A	GD	Pts
1	Blackburn R	6	3	2	1	13	6	7	11
2	Southampton	6	3	1	2	6	3	3	10
3	Cardiff C	6	2	2	2	9	8	1	8
4	Watford	6	1	1	4	4	15	–11	4

GROUP C TABLE

		P	W	D	L	F	A	GD	Pts
1	Wolverhampton W	6	4	1	1	14	12	2	13
2	Bournemouth	6	3	1	2	16	7	9	10
3	Norwich C	6	3	1	2	8	8	0	10
4	Bury	6	0	1	5	4	15	–11	1

GROUP D TABLE

		P	W	D	L	F	A	GD	Pts
1	Newcastle U	6	4	1	1	19	9	10	13
2	Swansea C	6	3	1	2	14	13	1	10
3	Burnley	6	3	0	3	10	11	–1	9
4	Colchester U	6	1	0	5	8	18	–10	3

GROUP E TABLE

		P	W	D	L	F	A	GD	Pts
1	Aston Villa	6	5	0	1	14	3	11	15
2	Sheffield U	6	3	0	3	5	5	0	9
3	Ipswich T	6	3	0	3	7	10	–3	9
4	WBA	6	1	0	5	5	13	–8	3

GROUP F TABLE

		P	W	D	L	F	A	GD	Pts
1	Leicester C	6	4	2	0	15	5	10	14
2	Everton	6	3	1	2	8	5	3	10
3	Portsmouth	6	1	2	3	4	8	–4	5
4	Barnsley	6	1	1	4	4	13	–9	4

PREMIER LEAGUE UNDER-23 DEVELOPMENT
LEAGUE 2

NORTH DIVISION

		P	W	D	L	F	A	GD	Pts
1	Bolton W	30	16	3	11	50	44	6	51
2	Nottingham F	30	13	11	6	65	50	15	50
3	Sheffield W	30	14	8	8	48	39	9	50
4	Sheffield U	30	14	3	13	50	43	7	45
5	Hull C	30	14	3	13	47	57	–10	45
6	Leeds U	30	13	5	12	50	46	4	44
7	Huddersfield T	30	12	5	13	49	53	–4	41
8	Birmingham C	30	10	8	12	47	43	4	38
9	Crewe Alex	30	10	5	15	38	53	–15	35
10	Burnley	30	10	4	16	33	54	–21	34
11	Barnsley	30	9	6	15	49	55	–6	33

SOUTH DIVISION

		P	W	D	L	F	A	GD	Pts
1	Crystal Palace	29	19	3	7	67	31	36	60
2	Charlton Ath	29	14	6	9	51	39	12	48
3	Ipswich T	29	13	5	11	61	49	12	44
4	Watford	29	11	8	10	56	44	12	41
5	Coventry C	29	11	6	12	54	60	–6	39
6	QPR	29	11	5	13	54	59	–5	38
7	Colchester U	29	10	7	12	39	48	–9	37
8	Millwall	29	9	10	10	28	38	–10	37
9	Cardiff C	29	10	5	14	38	51	–13	35
10	Bristol C	29	5	8	16	39	57	–18	23

Teams play each team in their own division twice, and each team in the other division once.

KNOCKOUT STAGE – SEMI-FINALS
Bolton W v Charlton Ath   3-1
Crystal Palace v Nottingham F   0-1*

FINAL
Nottingham F v Bolton W   1-2

GROUP G TABLE

		P	W	D	L	F	A	GD	Pts
1	Bristol C	6	4	1	1	10	12	–2	13
2	Liverpool	6	3	1	2	19	7	12	10
3	Stoke C	6	2	1	3	11	14	–3	7
4	Charlton Ath	6	1	1	4	4	11	–7	4

GROUP H TABLE

		P	W	D	L	F	A	GD	Pts
1	Exeter C	6	3	2	1	11	5	6	11
2	Brighton & HA	6	3	1	2	15	9	6	10
3	Sunderland	6	2	1	3	7	12	–5	7
4	Hull C	6	1	2	3	5	12	–7	5

ROUND OF 16
Newcastle U v Bournemouth   3-2
Aston Villa v Blackburn R   2-0
Southampton v Leicester C   0-4
Brighton & HA v Everton   3-0
Wolverhampton W v Exeter C   1-1*
   Wolverhampton W won 3-1 on penalties.
Middlesbrough v Liverpool   3-1
Sheffield U v Derby Co   2-1*
Swansea C v Bristol C   4-2

QUARTER-FINALS
Sheffield U v Newcastle U   2-1
Swansea C v Brighton & HA   1-1*
   Swansea C won 9-8 on penalties.
Leicester C v Wolverhampton W   2-0
Middlesbrough v Aston Villa   1-2*

SEMI-FINALS
Leicester C v Aston Villa   2-3
Swansea C v Sheffield U   3-0

FINAL
Swansea C v Aston Villa   0-0*
   Aston Villa won 4-1 on penalties.

PREMIER LEAGUE
INTERNATIONAL CUP 2017–18

GROUP A

Newcastle U v Sparta Prague	2-1
Liverpool v Newcastle U	2-1
Liverpool v Sparta Prague	0-1
PSV Eindhoven v Sparta Prague	4-3
Liverpool v PSV Eindhoven	3-0
Newcastle U v PSV Eindhoven	3-1

Group A Table	P	W	D	L	F	A	GD	Pts
Liverpool	3	2	0	1	5	2	3	6
Newcastle U	3	2	0	1	6	4	2	6
Sparta Prague	3	1	0	2	5	6	–1	3
PSV Eindhoven	3	1	0	2	5	9	–4	3

GROUP B

Leicester C v Hertha Berlin	3-0
Sunderland v Hertha Berlin	2-0
Sunderland v Legia Warsaw	1-1
Legia Warsaw v Hertha Berlin	0-2
Leicester C v Legia Warsaw	2-2
Sunderland v Leicester C	2-0

Group B Table	P	W	D	L	F	A	GD	Pts
Sunderland	3	2	1	0	5	1	4	7
Leicester C	3	1	1	1	5	4	1	4
Hertha Berlin	3	1	0	2	2	5	–3	3
Legia Warsaw	3	0	2	1	3	5	–2	2

GROUP C

Everton v Wolfsburg	1-3
Derby Co v Wolfsburg	1-0
Dinamo Zagreb v Wolfsburg	3-2
Derby Co v Everton	0-0
Everton v Dinamo Zagreb	0-0
Derby Co v Dinamo Zagreb	0-1

Group C Table	P	W	D	L	F	A	GD	Pts
Dinamo Zagreb	3	2	1	0	4	2	2	7
Derby Co	3	1	1	1	1	1	0	4
Wolfsburg	3	1	0	2	5	5	0	3
Everton	3	0	2	1	1	3	–2	2

GROUP D

Swansea C v Celtic	6-0
Athletic Bilbao v Celtic	1-2
Manchester U v Swansea C	2-1
Manchester U v Athletic Bilbao	2-1
Manchester U v Celtic	2-0
Swansea C v Athletic Bilbao	0-2

Group D Table	P	W	D	L	F	A	GD	Pts
Manchester U	3	3	0	0	6	2	4	9
Swansea C	3	1	0	2	7	4	3	3
Athletic Bilbao	3	1	0	2	4	4	0	3
Celtic	3	1	0	2	2	9	–7	3

GROUP E

Reading v Porto	0-2
Arsenal v Porto	1-0
Arsenal v Reading	0-0
Reading v Bayern Munich	0-1
Arsenal v Bayern Munich	5-2
Bayern Munich v Porto	0-1

Group E Table	P	W	D	L	F	A	GD	Pts
Arsenal	3	2	1	0	6	2	4	7
Porto	3	2	0	1	3	1	2	6
Bayern Munich	3	1	0	2	3	6	–3	3
Reading	3	0	1	2	0	3	–3	1

GROUP F

Tottenham H v West Ham U	7-2
Villarreal v Benfica	3-2
West Ham U v Villarreal	0-3
Tottenham H v Villarreal	0-2
West Ham U v Benfica	0-2
Tottenham H v Benfica	3-3

Group F Table	P	W	D	L	F	A	GD	Pts
Villarreal	3	3	0	0	8	2	6	9
Tottenham H	3	1	1	1	10	7	3	4
Benfica	3	1	1	1	7	6	1	4
West Ham U	3	0	0	3	2	12	–10	0

QUARTER-FINALS

Arsenal v Dinamo Zagreb	2-1
Manchester U v Villareal	0-2
Liverpool v Porto	1-2
Sunderland v Newcastle U	2-2*

Newcastle U won 11-10 on penalties.

SEMI-FINALS

| Arsenal v Villareal | 2-2* |

Arsenal won 5-4 on penalties.

| Newcastle U v Porto | 0-1 |

PREMIER LEAGUE INTERNATIONAL CUP FINAL 2018

Emirates, Tuesday 8 May 2018

Arsenal (0) 0

Porto (1) 1 *(Madi Queta 10)*

Arsenal: Virginia; Bola, Osei-Tutu, Ballard, Dragomir, Sheaf, Gilmour, Eyoma, Smith-Rowe, Dasilva, Fortune (Olayinka 86).
Porto: Mbaye; Leite, Queiros, Reabciuk, Moreira, Bruno Costa, Cassama (Mata 67), Baro (Chikhaoui 80), Luizao, Yahaya, Madi Queta (Vera 90).
Referee: Thomas Bramall.

UNDER-18 PROFESSIONAL DEVELOPMENT LEAGUE 2017–18

PREMIER LEAGUE UNDER-18 DEVELOPMENT
LEAGUE 1
NORTH DIVISION

		P	W	D	L	F	A	GD	Pts
1	Manchester U	22	15	3	4	65	33	32	48
2	Manchester C	22	13	3	6	58	34	24	42
3	Liverpool	22	11	5	6	50	35	15	38
4	Stoke C	22	11	4	7	49	34	15	37
5	Everton	22	11	4	7	51	41	10	37
6	Derby Co	22	9	6	7	45	38	7	33
7	Sunderland	22	10	2	10	39	44	–5	32
8	WBA	22	7	5	10	49	57	–8	26
9	Middlesbrough	22	6	7	9	37	52	–15	25
10	Newcastle U	22	6	6	10	37	48	–11	24
11	Wolverhampton W	22	5	4	13	31	53	–22	19
12	Blackburn R	22	3	1	18	28	70	–42	10

SOUTH DIVISION

		P	W	D	L	F	A	GD	Pts
1	Chelsea	22	17	3	2	64	21	43	54
2	Arsenal	22	14	3	5	61	33	28	45
3	Southampton	22	13	3	6	38	25	13	42
4	Tottenham H	22	10	4	8	58	39	19	34
5	Leicester C	22	9	6	7	38	33	5	33
6	Swansea C	22	9	4	9	32	44	–12	31
7	Fulham	22	8	6	8	40	33	7	30
8	Brighton & HA	22	6	6	10	36	43	–7	24
9	Aston Villa	22	6	5	11	27	36	–9	23
10	West Ham U	22	6	3	13	27	51	–24	21
11	Reading	22	6	3	13	24	50	–26	21
12	Norwich C	22	3	4	14	22	59	–37	13

FINAL
Manchester U v Chelsea 0-3

FA PREMIER UNDER-18 DEVELOPMENT
LEAGUE 2
NORTH DIVISION

		P	W	D	L	F	A	GD	Pts
1	Leeds U	30	19	3	8	72	39	33	60
2	Bolton W	30	17	7	6	84	53	31	58
3	Sheffield W	30	16	6	8	81	42	39	54
4	Nottingham F	30	15	6	9	75	54	21	51
5	Burnley	30	14	7	9	66	60	6	49
6	Birmingham C	30	13	7	10	72	63	9	46
7	Sheffield U	30	11	5	14	42	62	–20	38
8	Hull C	30	11	5	14	57	78	–21	38
9	Crewe Alex	30	10	7	13	62	58	4	37
10	Huddersfield T	30	9	5	16	49	87	–38	32
11	Barnsley	30	9	4	17	46	63	–17	31

SOUTH DIVISION

		P	W	D	L	F	A	GD	Pts
1	Crystal Palace	29	17	8	4	63	29	34	59
2	Charlton Ath	29	17	4	8	77	55	22	55
3	Cardiff C	29	15	3	11	65	48	17	48
4	Watford	29	15	2	12	65	48	17	47
5	Millwall	29	14	5	10	66	57	9	47
6	QPR	29	13	2	14	65	73	–8	41
7	Bristol C	29	9	4	16	44	54	–10	31
8	Ipswich T	29	7	6	16	42	72	–30	27
9	Colchester U	29	7	1	21	47	92	–45	22
10	Coventry C	29	3	1	25	29	82	–53	10

Teams play each team in their own division twice, and each team in the other division once.

KNOCKOUT STAGE – SEMI-FINALS
Crystal Palace v Bolton W 3-1
Leeds U v Charlton Ath 0-1

FINAL
Charlton Ath v Crystal Palace 2-1

U18 PROFESSIONAL DEVELOPMENT LEAGUE CUP
After extra time.

GROUP A

		P	W	D	L	F	A	GD	Pts
1	Everton	3	2	0	1	3	1	2	6
2	Derby Co	3	1	2	0	3	2	1	5
3	WBA	3	0	2	1	3	4	–1	2
4	Swansea C	3	0	2	1	3	5	–2	2

GROUP B

		P	W	D	L	F	A	GD	Pts
1	Chelsea	3	2	1	0	6	2	4	7
2	Brighton & HA	3	2	0	1	7	7	0	6
3	Newcastle U	3	1	0	2	5	6	–1	3
4	Blackburn R	3	0	1	2	4	7	–3	1

GROUP C

		P	W	D	L	F	A	GD	Pts
1	Norwich C	3	2	1	0	8	3	5	7
2	Reading	3	1	1	1	2	5	–3	4
3	Southampton	3	1	0	2	4	3	1	3
4	Manchester C	3	0	2	1	3	6	–3	2

GROUP D

		P	W	D	L	F	A	GD	Pts
1	Liverpool	3	3	0	0	13	5	8	9
2	Sunderland	3	2	0	1	7	6	1	6
3	Middlesbrough	3	1	0	2	9	8	1	3
4	West Ham U	3	0	0	3	4	14	–10	0

GROUP E

		P	W	D	L	F	A	GD	Pts
1	Fulham	3	2	1	0	7	2	5	7
2	Tottenham H	3	2	0	1	7	4	3	6
3	Leicester C	3	1	1	1	3	3	0	4
4	Aston Villa	3	0	0	3	1	9	–8	0

GROUP F

		P	W	D	L	F	A	GD	Pts
1	Arsenal	3	2	0	1	11	8	3	6
2	Wolverhampton W	3	2	0	1	6	6	0	6
3	Manchester U	3	1	0	2	6	7	–1	3
4	Stoke C	3	1	0	2	3	5	–2	3

QUARTER-FINALS
Tottenham H v Liverpool 4-0
Sunderland v Chelsea 1-2*
Everton v Fulham 2-0
Arsenal v Norwich C 4-4*
  Arsenal won 5-4 on penalties.

SEMI-FINALS
Tottenham H v Arsenal 4-1
Everton v Chelsea 0-1

FINAL
Chelsea v Tottenham H 2-0

CENTRAL LEAGUE 2017–18

NORTH GROUP A	P	W	D	L	F	A	GD	Pts
Port Vale	13	11	1	1	38	12	26	34
Morecambe	13	7	1	5	33	31	2	22
Walsall	13	5	3	5	24	19	5	18
Bradford C	13	5	1	7	17	25	–8	16
Doncaster R	13	2	4	7	19	26	–7	10

NORTH GROUP B	P	W	D	L	F	A	GD	Pts
Mansfield T	13	9	2	2	39	16	23	29
Rotherham U	13	6	2	5	19	22	–3	20
Grimsby T	13	5	1	7	22	23	–1	16
Hartlepool U	13	4	1	8	14	34	–20	13
York C	13	2	2	9	18	35	–17	8

SOUTH EAST	P	W	D	L	F	A	GD	Pts
AFC Wimbledon	11	6	3	2	19	11	8	21
Bournemouth	11	6	1	4	25	17	8	19
Milton Keynes D	11	4	3	4	21	30	–9	15
Southend U	11	4	1	6	24	21	3	13

SOUTH WEST	P	W	D	L	F	A	GD	Pts
Bristol R	12	7	1	4	25	16	9	22
Cheltenham T	12	5	3	4	25	20	5	18
Plymouth Arg	12	6	0	6	24	20	4	18
Swindon T	12	3	2	7	20	32	–12	11
Forest Green R	12	3	2	7	19	35	–16	11

CENTRAL LEAGUE CUP 2017–18

NORTHERN GROUP 1	P	W	D	L	F	A	GD	Pts
Wigan Ath	3	2	0	1	11	5	6	6
Carlisle U	3	2	0	1	6	9	–3	6
Fleetwood T	3	1	0	2	7	7	0	3
Morecambe	3	1	0	2	5	8	–3	3

NORTHERN GROUP 2	P	W	D	L	F	A	GD	Pts
Mansfield T	3	3	0	0	8	0	8	9
Notts Co	3	2	0	1	5	3	2	6
Grimsby T	3	1	0	2	6	4	2	3
Burton Alb	3	0	0	3	0	12	–12	0

NORTHERN GROUP 3	P	W	D	L	F	A	GD	Pts
Port Vale	3	2	1	0	8	0	8	7
Rotherham U	3	2	0	1	6	2	4	6
Doncaster R	3	1	0	2	4	10	–6	3
Walsall R	3	0	1	2	0	6	–6	1

NORTHERN SEMI-FINALS

Rotherham U v Mansfield T	2-3
Wigan Ath v Port Vale	3-1

NORTHERN FINAL

Mansfield T v Wigan Ath	3-0

SOUTHERN GROUP A	P	W	D	L	F	A	GD	Pts
Milton Keynes D	4	2	2	0	17	13	4	8
Southend U	4	2	2	0	8	6	2	8
Barnet	4	1	1	2	10	8	2	4
Peterborough U	3	1	0	2	11	13	–2	3
Colchester U	3	1	2	7	13	–6	1

Peterborough U v Colchester U cancelled.

SOUTHERN GROUP B	P	W	D	L	F	A	GD	Pts
Bristol C	2	2	0	0	5	2	3	6
Bristol R	3	2	0	1	5	4	1	6
AFC Wimbledon	2	0	1	1	2	3	–1	1
Portsmouth	3	0	1	2	1	4	–3	1

AFC Wimbledon v Bristol C cancelled.

SOUTHERN SEMI-FINALS

Bristol R v Southend U	2-2
Southend U won 5-4 on penalties.	
Milton Keynes D v Bristol C	5-1

SOUTHERN FINAL

Milton Keynes D v Southend U	0-2

EFL YOUTH ALLIANCE 2017–18

NORTH EAST	P	W	D	L	F	A	GD	Pts
Mansfield T	24	16	7	1	55	16	39	55
Chesterfield	24	13	2	9	52	42	10	41
Rotherham U	24	11	8	5	35	27	8	41
Notts Co	24	12	4	8	53	34	19	40
Grimsby T	24	13	1	10	46	29	17	40
Doncaster R	24	11	6	7	41	31	10	39
Oldham Ath	24	12	3	9	32	40	–8	39
Burton Alb	24	9	3	12	27	33	–6	30
Lincoln C	24	9	2	13	37	50	–13	29
Bradford C	24	8	3	13	29	41	–12	27
Scunthorpe U	24	6	7	11	26	43	–17	25
York C	24	6	4	14	25	49	–24	22
Hartlepool U	24	2	6	16	28	51	–23	12

NORTH WEST	P	W	D	L	F	A	GD	Pts
Rochdale	26	21	3	2	64	19	45	66
Wigan Ath	26	21	2	3	70	21	49	65
Bury	26	13	2	11	49	45	4	41
Tranmere R	26	10	10	6	32	37	–5	40
Blackpool	26	10	6	10	62	54	8	36
Shrewsbury T	26	10	6	10	43	43	0	36
Walsall	26	11	2	13	43	35	8	35
Preston NE	26	10	5	11	53	46	7	35
Carlisle U	26	9	4	13	40	49	–9	31
Fleetwood T	26	8	6	12	26	43	–17	30
Port Vale	26	8	4	14	41	62	–21	28
Wrexham	26	7	6	13	35	39	–4	27
Accrington S	26	6	7	13	30	59	–29	25
Morecambe	26	5	3	18	30	66	–36	18

SOUTH EAST	P	W	D	L	F	A	GD	Pts
Milton Keynes D	22	14	2	6	40	27	13	44
Southend U	22	13	1	8	44	37	7	40
Cambridge U	22	12	2	8	42	25	17	38
Gillingham	22	11	1	10	43	42	1	34
Stevenage	22	8	6	8	37	34	3	30
Luton T	22	9	3	10	30	28	2	30
AFC Wimbledon	22	9	3	10	35	37	–2	30
Dagenham & R	22	9	3	10	32	39	–7	30
Northampton T	22	8	5	9	32	35	–3	29
Leyton Orient	22	7	4	11	33	39	–6	25
Barnet	22	8	1	13	33	46	–13	25
Peterborough U	22	7	3	12	33	45	–12	24

SOUTH WEST	P	W	D	L	F	A	GD	Pts
Exeter C	20	15	3	2	69	19	50	48
Bournemouth	20	12	5	3	50	21	29	41
Swindon T	20	11	3	6	44	35	9	36
Portsmouth	20	10	4	6	53	36	17	34
Oxford U	20	10	4	6	40	31	9	34
Bristol R	20	9	2	9	38	40	–2	29
Plymouth Arg	20	8	2	10	36	41	–5	26
Yeovil T	20	7	3	10	30	35	–5	24
Newport Co	20	4	5	11	29	50	–21	17
Forest Green R	20	3	3	14	20	62	–42	12
Cheltenham T	20	2	4	14	32	71	–39	10

Top six teams in South East and South West divisions qualify for Merit League 1; the remainder contest Merit League 2.

MERIT LEAGUE 1	P	W	D	L	F	A	GD	Pts
Gillingham	11	7	3	1	25	15	10	24
Exeter C	11	7	2	2	34	10	24	23
Luton T	11	6	1	4	28	17	11	19
Bournemouth	11	5	4	2	25	21	4	19
Southend U	11	5	3	3	22	22	0	18
Swindon T	11	5	2	4	22	25	–3	17
Milton Keynes D	11	5	1	5	21	23	–2	16
Stevenage	11	3	3	5	21	22	–1	12
Portsmouth	11	3	3	5	21	27	–6	12
Bristol R	11	3	1	7	18	26	–8	10
Cambridge U	11	3	0	8	15	29	–14	9
Oxford U	11	1	3	7	10	25	–15	6

MERIT LEAGUE 2	P	W	D	L	F	A	GD	Pts
Leyton Orient	10	7	0	3	21	12	9	21
Dagenham & R	10	6	2	2	25	14	11	20
Northampton T	10	6	2	2	21	13	8	20
Plymouth Arg	10	5	1	4	19	11	8	16
Yeovil T	10	4	3	3	17	10	7	15
Peterborough U	10	5	0	5	16	16	0	15
AFC Wimbledon	10	4	2	4	20	19	1	14
Cheltenham T	10	4	1	5	23	32	–9	13
Barnet	10	3	2	5	16	18	–2	11
Newport Co	10	1	3	6	14	27	–13	6
Forest Green R	10	2	0	8	11	31	–20	6

IMPORTANT ADDRESSES

The Football Association: Wembley Stadium, P.O. Box 1966, London SW1P 9EQ. *0800 169 1863*

Scotland: Hampden Park, Glasgow G42 9AY. *0141 616 6000*

Northern Ireland (Irish FA): Chief Executive, Donegall Avenue, Belfast, Northern Ireland BT12 6LU. *028 9066 9458*

Wales: 11/12 Neptune Court, Vanguard Way, Cardiff CF24 5PJ. *029 2043 5830*

Republic of Ireland: National Sports Campus, Abbotstown, Dublin 15. *00 353 1 8999 500*

International Federation (FIFA): Strasse 20, P.O. Box 8044, Zurich, Switzerland. *00 41 43 222 7777. Fax: 00 41 43 222 7878*

Union of European Football Associations: Secretary, Route de Geneve 46, P.O. Box 1260, Nyon 2, Switzerland. *Fax: 00 41 848 00 2727*

THE LEAGUES

The Premier League: R. Scudamore, 30 Gloucester Place, London W1U 8PL. *0207 864 9000*

The Football League: Shaun Harvey, EFL House, 10–12 West Cuff, Preston PR1 8HU. *01772 325 800. Fax 01772 325 801*

The National League: M. Tattersall, 4th Floor, Wellington House, 20 Waterloo Street, Birmingham B2 5TB. *0121 643 3143*

FA Women's Super League: Wembley Stadium, PO Box 1966, London SW1P 9EQ. *+44 844 980 8200*

Scottish Premier League: Letherby Drive, Glasgow G42 9DE. *0141 620 4140*

The Scottish League: Hampden Park, Glasgow G42 9EB. *0141 620 4160*

Football League of Ireland: D. Crowther, National Sports Campus, Abbotstown, Dublin 15. *00 353 1 8999 500*

Southern League: J. Mills, Suite 3B, Eastgate House, 121–131 Eastgate Street, Gloucester GL1 1PX. *07768 750 590*

Northern Premier League: Ms A. Firth, 23 High Lane, Norton Tower, Halifax, W. Yorkshire HX2 0NW. *01422 410 691*

Isthmian League: Kellie Discipline, PO Box 393, Dartford DA1 9JK. *01322 314 999*

Eastern Counties League: N. Spurling, 16 Thanet Road, Ipswich, Suffolk IP4 5LB. *01473 720 893*

Essex Senior League: Secretary: Ms. M. Darling, 39 Milwards, Harlow, Essex CM19 4SG. *01279 635740*

Hellenic League: John Ostinell, 2 Wynn Grove, Hazlemere HP15 7LY. *07900 081 814*

Midland League: N. Wood, 30 Glaisdale Road, Hall Green, Birmingham B28 8PX. *07967 440 007*

North West Counties League: J. Deal, 24 The Pastures, Crossens, Southport PR9 8RH. *01704 211 955*

Northern Counties East: Matt Jones, 346 Heneage Road, Grimsby DN32 9NJ. *07415 068 996*

Northern League: K. Hewitt, 21 Cherrytree Drive, Langley Park, Durham DH7 9FX. *0191 373 3878*

Spartan South Midlands League: M. Appleby, 15 Aintree Close, Bletchley, Milton Keynes MK3 5LP.

Southern Combination League: T. Dawes, 32 Reynolds Lane, Langney, Eastbourne BN23 7NW. *01323 764 218*

United Counties League: Ms W. Newey, 4 Wulfric Square, Bretton, Peterborough PE3 8RF. *01733 330 056*

Wessex League: J. Gorman, 6 Overton House, London Road, Overton, Hants RG25 3TP. *01256 770 059*

Western League: A. Radford, 19 Longney Place, Patchway, Bristol BS34 5LQ. *07872 818 868*

Combined Counties League: A. Constable, 3 Craigwell Close, Staines, Middlesex TW18 3NP. *01784 440 613*

West Midlands League: N.R. Juggins, 14 Badger Way, Blackwell, Bromsgrove, Worcs B60 1EX. *0121 445 2953*

South West Peninsula League: P. Hiscox, 45a Serge Court, The Quay, Exeter, Devon EX2 4EB. *07788 897 706*

Southern Counties East League: D. Peck, secretary@scefl.com *07710 143 944*

East Midlands Counties League: R. Holmes, 9 Copse Close, Hugglescote, Coalville LE67 2GL. *07826 452 389*

OTHER USEFUL ADDRESSES

Amateur Football Alliance: M. Brown, Unit 3, 7 Wenlock Road, London N1 7SL. *0208 733 2613*

Association of Football Badge Collectors: K. Wilkinson, 18 Hinton St, Fairfield, Liverpool L6 3AR. *0151 260 0554*

British Olympic Association: 60 Charlotte Street, London W1T 2NU. *0207 842 5700*

British Blind Sport (including football): Plato Close, Tachbrook Park, Leamington Spa, Warwickshire CV34 6WE. *01926 424 247*

British Universities and Colleges Sports Association: Karen Rothery, Chief Executive: BUCSA, 20–24 King's Bench Street, London SE1 0QX. *0207 633 5080*

England Supporters Club: Wembley Stadium, PO Box 1966, London SW1P 9EQ. *0800 389 1966*

English Schools FA: 4 Parker Court, Staffordshire Technology Park, Stafford ST18 0WP. *01785 785 970*

Fields In Trust: 2D Woodstock Studios, 36 Woodstock Grove, London W12 8LE. *0207 427 2110*

Football Foundation: Niall Malone, Communications Manager: Whittinghton House, 19–30 Alfred Place, London WC1E 7EA. *0345 345 4555*

Football Postcard Collectors Club: PRO: John Farrelly, 163 Collingwood Road, Hillingdon, Middlesex UB8 3EW. Web: www.hobbyist.co.uk/pfcc

Football Safety Officers Association: John Newsham, FSOA Ltd, Suite 17, Blackburn Rovers Enterprise Centre, Ewood Park, Blackburn BB2 4JF. *01254 841 771.*

Institute of Groundsmanship: 28 Stratford Office Village, Walker Avenue, Wolverton, Milton Keynes MK12 5TW. *01908 312 511*

League Managers Association: St George's Park, Newborough Road, Needwood, Burton on Trent DE13 9PD. *0128 357 6350*

National Football Museum: Urbis Building, Cathedral Gardens, Todd Street, Manchester M4 3BG. *0161 605 8200*

Professional Footballers' Association: G. Taylor, 20 Oxford Court, Bishopsgate, Off Lower Moseley Street, Manchester M2 3WQ. *0161 236 0575*

Programme Monthly & Football Collectable Magazine: R. P. Matz, 11 Tannington Terrace, London N5 1LE. *020 7359 8687*

Programme Promotions: 21 Roughwood Close, Watford WD17 3HN. *01923 861 468*

Web: www.footballprogrammes.com

Referees' Association: A.W.S. Smith, 1A Bagshaw Close, Ryton-on-Dunsmore, Coventry CV8 3EX. *024 7642 0360*

Sir Norman Chester Centre for Football Research: Department of Sociology, University of Leicester, University Road LE1 7RH. *0116 252 2741/5.*

Soccer Nostalgia: G. Wallis, Albion Chambers, 1 Albion Road, Birchington, Kent CT7 9DN. *01303 275 432.*

Sport England: 21 Bloomsbury Street, London WC1B 3HF.

Sports Grounds Safety Authority: East Wing, 3rd Floor, Fleetbank House, 2–6 Salisbury Square, London EC4Y 8JX. *0207 930 6693*

Sports Turf Research Institute: St Ives Estate, Harden, Bingley, West Yorkshire BD16 1AU. *01274 565 131*

The Football Supporters' Federation: 1 Ashmore Terrace, Stockton Road, Sunderland, Tyne and Wear SR2 7DE. *0330 440 0044*

The Ninety-Two Club: Mr M. Kimberley, The Ninety-Two Club, 153 Hayes Lane, Kenley, Surrey CR8 5HP.

UK Programme Collectors Club: PM Publications, 38 Lowther Road, Norwich NR4 6QW. *01603 449 237*

FOOTBALL CLUB CHAPLAINCY

Although Martin was a country boy, he had always followed professional football. He'd been through despair at the occasional relegation suffered by his local club, but these had been more than balanced when his favourites soared to promotion or FA Cup success.

Being a bright and devoted young man, Martin studied at University, then at Theological College before being called to serve in a busy inner-city parish.

However, Martin yearned for the countryside, and for his favourite football club, so that when a vacancy occurred in a rural parish some twenty miles from it, he applied to the Bishop and was soon appointed.

The bonus for Martin was a double one. Not only was he able to drive to the town where his football club was based, but he was swiftly approached concerning his availabilty to serve as honorary chaplain there, and after meetings with the club chairman, manager, physio and club captain, Martin was invited to take the new post.

That all took place more than a decade ago, but Martin served his club superbly, delighting club officials and sponsors, as well as the players with his open, friendly and positive approach to a such a degree, that when he was moved from his rural idyll to a busy urban parish, he was swiftly appointed as honorary chaplain to the local Premier League club.

Who says that prayer doesn't change things?

THE REV

OFFICIAL CHAPLAINS TO FA PREMIERSHIP AND FOOTBALL LEAGUE CLUBS

Aston Villa – Ken Baker and Phillip Nott
Barnsley – Peter Amos
Birmingham C – Kirk McAtear
Birmingham C Academy – Tim Atkins
Blackburn R – Ken Howles
Blackpool – Michael Ward
Bolton W – Phillip Mason
Bournemouth – Adam Parrett
Bradford C – Oliver Evans
Brentford – Stuart Cashman
Bristol C – Derek Cleave
Bristol R – David Jeal
Burnley – Barry Hunter
Burton Alb – Phil Pusey
Bury – David Ottley
Cardiff C Academy – Bryon Castle
Carlisle U – Alun Jones
Charlton Ath – Matt Baker
Charlton Ath Academy – Gareth Morgan
Chelsea – Martin Swan
Cheltenham T – Malcolm Allen
Coventry C – Simon Betteridge
Crawley T – Steve Alliston
Crewe Alex – Phil Howell
Crystal Palace – Chris Roe
Derby Co – Tony Luke
Doncaster R – Barry Miller
Everton – Harry Ross
Everton Academy – Henry Corbett
Fleetwood T – George Ayoma
Fulham – Gary Piper
Gillingham – Chris Gill
Huddersfield T – Dudley Martin
Ipswich T – Kevan McCormack
Leeds U – Dave Niblock
Leicester C – Andrew Hulley
Lincoln C – Canon Andrew Vaughan
Liverpool – Bill Bygroves
Luton T – David Kesterton
Macclesfield T – Chris Whiteley
Manchester C – Pete Horlock

Manchester U – John Boyers
Mansfield T – Kevin Charles
Middlesbrough Academy – Maurice Hepworth
Millwall – Canon Owen Beament
Newport Co – Keith Beardmore
Northampton T – Ken Baker and Haydon Spenceley
Norwich C – Jon Norman
Norwich C Academy – Lewis Blois
Nottingham F – John Parfitt
Notts Co – Liam O'Boyle
Oldham Ath – John Simmons
Peterborough U – Richard Longfoot
Peterborough U Academy – Sid Bridges
Plymouth Arg – Arthur Goode
Port Vale – John Hibberts
Portsmouth – Jonathan Jeffery and Mick Mellows
Preston NE – Chris Nelson
QPR – Cameron Collington and Bob Mayo
Reading – Steve Prince
Reading Academy – James Hollands
Scunthorpe U – Alan Wright
Scunthorpe U Academy – David Eames
Sheffield U – Delroy Hall
Sheffield W Wise Old Owls – David Jeans
Sheffield W Academy – Malcolm Drew
Shrewsbury T – Phil Cansdale
Southampton – Andy Bowerman
Southend U – Stuart Alleway and Mike Lodge
Sunderland – Father Marc Lyden-Smith
Swansea C – Kevin Johns
Swansea C Academy – Eirian Wyn
Swindon T – Simon Stevenette
Walsall – Peter Hart
Watford – Clive Ross
WBA – Steven Harper
West Ham U – Alan Bolding
West Ham U Academy – Philip Wright
Wolverhampton W – David Wright
Wolverhampton W Academy – Steve Davies
Wycombe W – Benedict Mwendwa Musola
Yeovil T – Jim Pearce

WOMEN'S FOOTBALL CLUB CHAPLAINS

Bristol C – Esther Legg-Bagg
Charlton Ath Women – Kathryn Sales
Newcastle U Ladies – Catherine Armstrong

Reading Ladies – Angy King
Swansea C Ladies – Ruth Emanuel

The chaplains hope that those who read this page will see the value and benefit of chaplaincy work in football and will take appropriate steps to spread the word where this is possible. They would also like to thank the editors of the Football Yearbook for their continued support for this specialist and growing area of work.

For further information, please contact: Sports Chaplaincy UK, The Avenue Methodist Church, Wincham Road, Sale, Cheshire M33 4PL. Telephone: 0800 181 4051 or email: admin@sportschaplaincy.org.uk. Website: www.sportschaplaincy.org.uk

OBITUARIES

Clark Allison (Born: Dunfermline, 17 January 1963. Died: October 2017.) Defender Clark Allison had a brief association with Cowdenbeath in the 1981–82 season when he made six senior appearances for them. He later forged a 13-year career in the Juniors with Kelty Hearts.

Barry Ansell (Born: Small Heath, Birmingham, 29 September 1947. Died: 2018.) Full-back Barry Ansell played as an amateur for Aston Villa reserves before turning professional in October 1967, but his only senior appearance came at Cardiff on Boxing Day 1967. He was released on a free transfer at the end of the season and emigrated to South Africa, where he continued his career with Bloemfontein City, Arcadia Shepherds and Berea Park.

Tommy Andrews (Died: 8 March 2018.) Tommy Andrews was a centre-half who was initially an amateur for Portadown. He made two appearances for the Northern Ireland Amateur international team in April 1951, captaining the side against Scotland, before turning professional. Later he had a spell with Coleraine before returning to play for Ports.

Jimmy Armfield, OBE, DL (Born: Denton, Lancashire, 21 September 1935. Died: Bispham, Blackpool, 22 January 2018.) Jimmy Armfield was one of the all-time greatest players in the history of Blackpool FC before going on to successful careers in management and then the media. He signed amateur forms for the Seasiders at the age of 16 and made his first-team debut in December 1954. Once established in the line-up he was a regular for some 16 seasons, creating a club record of 626 senior appearances. An accomplished right-back who was selected as the best in his position at the 1962 World Cup finals, he won 43 full caps for England, captaining the side on 15 occasions. When his playing career was over he had spells as manager of both Bolton Wanderers and Leeds United, winning the Third Division title with Bolton in 1972–73 and achieving a top-ten finish in the First Division with Leeds in each of his four seasons at the club; he also took them to the European Cup final in 1975. He subsequently built a third career in the game working in the media, firstly writing for newspapers and latterly as a commentator for BBC Radio 5 Live.

Brian Bades (Born: Farnworth, Lancashire, 3 July 1939. Died: 13 March 2018.) Brian Bades made two appearances at inside-right for Accrington Stanley in February 1962, shortly before the club resigned from Football League membership. After a brief spell with Horwich RMI he spent the 1962–63 season with Stockport County without breaking into the first team, then joined Chester in the 1963 close season. He added a further 17 senior appearances during his time at Sealand Road before moving back into non-league football with Runcorn.

Mal Bailey (Born: Biddulph, Staffordshire, 14 April 1950. Died: 14 November 2017.) Mal Bailey developed in the youth set-up at Port Vale where he spent three years as a professional, making two first-team appearances at right-half towards the end of the 1968–69 season. He later moved into non-league football, switching to the centre of defence and playing for Northwich Victoria, Runcorn and then Altrincham where he gained success in the FA Trophy (1978) and Alliance Premier League (1979–80, 1980–81).

Ray Barnard (Born: Middlesbrough, 16 April 1933. Died: 7 July 2017.) Ray Barnard was a full-back who won representative honours for Yorkshire and England Schools and made his senior debut for Middlesbrough at the age of 17. After completing his National Service he became a regular for Boro' for the best part of three seasons, making over 100 appearances. He concluded his career with a three-year spell at Lincoln City before switching to non-league football with Grantham.

Dick Bate (Born: Birmingham, 25 June 1946. Died: 25 April 2018.) Dick Bate had a rather undistinguished career as a player, featuring as a part-timer in the Northern Premier League while working as a teacher in Sheffield. He subsequently turned to coaching with considerable success and he was the FA's North West regional coach between 1980 and 1985. A spell as head coach of Notts County led to his appointment as manager of Southend United in June 1987, but he lasted just ten games, only one of which was won. He continued to work in coaching for the rest of his working life, notably with Leeds United and as the technical director of the Malaysia national team (1992–1995) and of the Canada Soccer Association (October 2005 to July 2006). He also had a spell working in the England set-up and in April 1998 was briefly caretaker manager of the England women's team.

Cyril Beavon (Born: Barnsley, 27 September 1937. Died: 22 December 2017.) Cyril Beavon was a full-back who joined the then Headington United in January 1959. After making his club debut in a Southern League Cup tie he missed just one first-team game over the next three-and-a-half seasons during which time the club twice won the Southern League title. He appeared in the club's first Football League game at Barrow in August 1962 and in total he made 464 appearances for the U's in his ten years at the club. He later played for Banbury United before becoming manager of Bicester Town. His son (Stuart Beavon senior) and grandson (also Stuart Beavon) both played senior football.

Oliver Beeby (Born: Whetstone, Leicestershire, 2 October 1934. Died: Aberystwyth, 8 March 2018.) Oliver Beeby was capped by England Youths and signed for Leicester City in May 1953, making his first-team debut two years later. This proved to be his only senior outing for the Foxes, with his career put on hold by National Service. He went on to make 15 appearances for Notts County in the 1959–60 season when they gained promotion from the old Division Four, then played in Southern League football with Oxford United and Burton Albion.

George Bentley (Born: December 1922. Died: 18 December 2017.) George Bentley was an outside-right who made two appearances for Aston Villa in the 1941–42 season when the first team played in the Birmingham League due to issues over the availability of Villa Park.

Roy Bentley (Born: Shirehampton, Bristol, 17 May 1924. Died: 20 April 2018.) Roy Bentley served in the Royal Navy during the war and made over 70 appearances for Bristol City in the emergency competitions but when peacetime football resumed he signed for Newcastle United. He spent 18 months on Tyneside and was a great success, netting two on his debut and at a rate of a goal every other game. However, he never really settled in the north and in January 1948 signed for Chelsea. He spent the best years of his career at Stamford Bridge, winning 12 England caps and captaining the team that won the Football League in 1954–55. After making more than 350 appearances for the Blues he moved on to spells with Fulham and then Queens Park Rangers. Soon after his playing career was over he went into management, firstly with Reading (January 1963 to February 1969) and then Swansea Town (August 1969 to October 1972). In his first season at the Vetch Field he led the Swans to promotion from the old Division Four. At the time of his death he was Chelsea's oldest surviving player and the last surviving member of England's 1950 World Cup squad.

Peter Bircumshaw (Born: Mansfield, 29 August 1938. Died: 24 June 2017.) Peter Bircumshaw was a left-winger who signed professional forms for Notts County as a teenager and went on to make over 70 first-team appearances for the Magpies. In the summer of 1962 he moved on to Bradford City, spending a season at Valley Parade and then six months at Stockport before joining Southern League club Cambridge City.

Eddie Blackburn (Born: Houghton-le-Spring, 18 April 1957. Died: 20 April 2018.) Goalkeeper Eddie Blackburn began his career with Hull City where he was mostly an understudy, firstly to Jeff Wealands and then Tony Norman. Moving to York City in April 1980, he excelled in his first full season when he missed just one match and was voted as the club's player of the season. In December 1982 he signed for Hartlepool United and was mostly a regular in five seasons at the Victoria Ground, making a total of 175 competitive appearances. His career was ended by injury when playing in Sweden with Halmstads BK.

Alan Boswell (Born: West Bromwich, 8 August 1943. Died: 24 August 2017.) Goalkeeper Alan Boswell made his debut for Walsall at the age of 18, and seized his opportunity, never looking back. When the Saddlers were relegated at the end of 1962–63 he moved on to Shrewsbury Town where he enjoyed four seasons as a near ever-present, making over 250 appearances. After an unsuccessful time at Wolverhampton Wanderers, he finished his senior career with a flourish at Bolton Wanderers and Port Vale. He later played for and, briefly, managed Oswestry Town.

Eric Brodie (Born: Circa 1943. Died: 18 April 2018.) Eric Brodie was a left-back who developed with Methil Star and Dundee United and then spent three seasons on the books of East Fife after signing in the summer of 1965. He made a total of 89 senior appearances during his time at Bayview before leaving the senior game.

Stan Brown (Born: Lewes, 15 September 1941. Died: March 2018.) Stan Brown started out as a forward, winning a regular place in the Fulham line-up in the 1962–63 season. He went on to make just short of 400 appearances during his time at Craven Cottage, keeping his place as the team dropped from the First to the Third Division in the mid-1960s. He made a useful contribution to the 1970–71 promotion campaign as Fulham regained their place in Division Two, although by this time he was mostly playing in midfield or defence. After a brief loan spell with Brighton & Hove Albion he finished his career at Colchester United. Stan was one of three brothers who played for Brighton (Alan, Irvin & Stan) while his cousin Gary Brown also played for the club.

David Bumpstead (Born: Rainham, Essex, 6 November 1935. Died: Upminster, Essex, 26 August 2017.) Inside-forward David Bumpstead was a member of the Tooting & Mitcham side that reached the FA Cup second round in 1957–58 and they were well on their way to the Isthmian League title when he joined Millwall towards the end of the 1957–58 campaign. He marked his debut in senior football with a goal in a 3-1 win over Gillingham, and turned professional that summer. David went on to make over 120 appearances for the Lions and Bristol Rovers then had a spell out of the game. Later he managed Southern League clubs Brentford and Chelmsford City. He won a single cap for England Amateurs against France in April 1958.

Dennis Bushby (Born: Poole, 25 December 1933. Died: Poole, 3 October 2017.) Dennis Bushby was a wing-half who developed in local football before joining Bournemouth, initially on amateur forms, before turning professional. All his senior appearances came in the 1957–58 season and he later moved on to play for Peterborough United (then members of the Midland League) and Poole Town.

Peter Butler (Born: Nottingham, 3 October 1942. Died: 10 January 2018.) Goalkeeper Peter Butler signed for Notts County in November 1960, but although he spent six seasons on the books at Meadow Lane he was mostly second choice to George Smith, managing just short of 50 senior appearances. He moved on to Bradford City for the 1966–67 campaign before switching to Midland League football with Worksop Town. He was the brother of John Butler, who played for Notts County and Chester, and the son of Herbert (Dick) Butler who played pre-war for Birmingham City and Crewe Alexandra.

Dave Caldwell (Born: Clydebank, 7 May 1932. Died: Balmedie, Aberdeenshire, 2 August 2017.) Left-back Dave Caldwell joined Aberdeen in the summer of 1953 and was a near ever-present in his first season with the Dons when he was a member of the team defeated by Celtic in the Scottish Cup final. Further honours followed as he won a League Cup winners' medal in 1955–56 but after losing his place in the side he moved south to Rotherham United. He was mainly a reserve during his time at Millmoor, before concluding his senior career north of the border with spells at Morton, Fraserburgh and Keith. He spent the summers between 1962 and 1965 playing for Toronto City of the Eastern Canada Professional League.

Ronnie Cant (Born: Hillhead, Glasgow, 6 October 1953. Died: 8 June 2017.) Goalkeeper Ronnie Cant played most of his football in the Scottish amateurs. His senior career was limited to a couple of appearances for Queen's Park in the 1979–80 season although he later returned to the Hampden club as a goalkeeping coach.

Geoff Carter (Born: Northwich, 14 February 1943. Died: March 2018.) Geoff Carter was an outside-left who joined the groundstaff at West Bromwich Albion in the summer of 1959, going on to sign professional forms shortly after his 17th birthday. He made his first-team debut at home to Arsenal shortly afterwards but in a six-year spell at The Hawthorns he was mostly a reserve, making a total of 15 senior appearances. In August 1967 he signed for Bury but in a season at Gigg Lane and a further six months at Bradford City he made little impact before returning to the West Midlands to play in non-league football.

Albert Collins (Born: Chesterfield, 15 April 1923. Died: Chesterfield, June 2017.) Albert Collins made over 70 appearances during wartime for Chesterfield and a highlight came when he played for the Spireites in the 1944–45 League North Cup semi-final. A winger who could play on either flank, he went on to make over 150 senior appearances in peacetime football, turning out for Halifax Town, Carlisle, Barrow, Bournemouth, Shrewsbury Town and Accrington Stanley. He was Chesterfield's oldest living player at the time of his death.

Mike Conroy (Born: Port Glasgow, 5 August 1932. Died: Bridge of Weir, Renfrewshire, 12 July 2017.) Mike Conroy was a wing-half who joined Celtic from Junior club St Anthony's early in 1953 and spent seven years at Parkhead. However, his career was disrupted by National Service and injuries and he made just eight competitive first-team appearances during his stay. One of his sons, Michael junior, also played for Celtic (1978–1982).

Billy Cook (Born: Galston, Ayrshire, 26 June 1940. Died: Adelaide, Australia, 2 July 2017.) A former Scotland Schools international, defender Billy Cook joined Kilmarnock as a youngster, but he was mostly a reserve during his six years at Rugby Park, unable to dislodge Matt Watson from the left-back slot. In the summer of 1963 he emigrated to Australia where he played with Victoria State League club Slavia-Port Melbourne for a number of years and went on to win six caps for his adopted country.

Neale Cooper (Born: Darjeeling, India, 24 November 1963. Died: Aberdeen, 28 May 2018.) Neale Cooper was a powerful and combative midfield player who made his first-team debut for Aberdeen as a 16-year-old. The Dons were managed by Alex Ferguson at the time and Neale went on to become an integral part of their highly successful team of the early 1980s, winning the European Cup Winners' Cup in 1983 as well as four Scottish Cups, a League Cup and two Scottish League titles. He moved to Aston Villa, but injuries restricted his appearances and it was not until he returned north to play for Dunfermline (following further brief spells with Rangers and Reading) that he returned to success, contributing to their 1995–96 promotion campaign. He later turned to management with Ross County (where he gained back-to-back promotions in 1998–99 and 1999–2000), Hartlepool United (two spells), Gillingham and Peterhead. He won 13 caps for Scotland U21s.

Ron Cooper (Born: Thorney, Peterborough, 28 August 1938. Died: Bourne, Lincolnshire, 13 April 2018.) Ron Cooper was a versatile defender who appeared mostly as a full-back throughout his career. He spent 11 seasons on the books of Peterborough United, making a few appearances in their Midland League days, but was then a reserve until stepping up to make his senior debut in October 1963. He went on to make 150 competitive appearances for Posh before moving on to play for Corby Town in the summer of 1969.

Tommy Cormie (Born: Forfar, 14 September 1935. Died: Forfar, 11 October 2017.) A right-sided forward, Tommy Cormie joined Forfar Athletic from local Junior outfit Forfar Celtic and spent three seasons on the club's books in the late 1950s. It was only in the 1958–59 campaign that he featured regularly for the first team, otherwise being mostly a back-up player.

Bill Coxon (Born: Derby, 28 April 1933. Died: Spondon, Derby, 6 March 2018.) Winger Billy Coxon signed professional forms for Derby County in May 1950 but he was unable to make it to the first team and after a spell in non-league with Ilkeston Town he returned to senior football, signing for Norwich City in May 1952. He scored on his debut for the

Canaries and was a regular in the side from September 1955 before moving on to Lincoln City towards the end of the 1957–58 campaign. He stayed only briefly at Sincil Bank, departing for Bournemouth where he become one of the mainstays of the side, making over 200 first-team appearances before eventually leaving senior football at the end of the 1965–66 season.

Matt Crowe (Born: Bathgate, West Lothian, 4 July 1932. Died: Port Elizabeth, South Africa, 2017.) Matt Crowe was a wing-half who signed for Bradford Park Avenue as a 17-year-old. His professional career was initially restricted by injuries but he re-established himself back in Scotland with Partick Thistle and was a big success when he returned south of the border to join Norwich City. He made over 200 appearances for the Canaries and featured in the team that reached the semi-finals of the FA Cup in 1958–59. He later spent two seasons at Brentford, helping the Bees to the Division Four title in 1962–63, before going to play in South Africa.

Ken Cunningham (Born: Glasgow, 26 October 1941. Died: 31 July 2017.) Ken Cunningham was an inside-forward who scored the winning goal for Kirkintilloch Rob Roy in the 1961 Scottish Junior Cup final at Hampden. He subsequently featured in a couple of games for Falkirk and then moved south of the border to join Hartlepool but stayed for only four months before returning to Scotland to play for Ayr United. He returned to the Juniors and won a second Junior Cup winners' medal with Blantyre Victoria in 1970.

Bill Davies (Born: Middlesbrough, 16 May 1930. Died: Woodley, Berkshire, 2017.) Bill Davies signed professional forms for Hull City in April 1949, but progressed only as far as the reserve team at Boothferry Park. He then had spells at Leeds United and Scarborough before joining Reading midway through the 1952–53 season. Having made the transition from inside-forward to centre-half he broke into the Royals' first team at the end of 1954 and went on to make over 200 appearances during his time at Elm Park.

Eddie Davies (Born: Oswestry, 5 June 1937. Died: 2018.) Eddie Davies was a centre- or inside-forward who developed with Chirk AAA before joining Arsenal in August 1948. Although he didn't make the first team during his time at Highbury he made a single first-team appearance for Queens Park Rangers against Brentford in January 1951, scoring in the 1-1 draw, then had a season at Crewe where he made a handful of appearances. He subsequently played in the Birmingham League, where he scored prolifically for both Oswestry Town (champions in 1952–53) and Nuneaton Borough before injury ended his career in January 1954.

Mike Davock (Born: St Helens, 27 April 1935. Died: 19 February 2018.) Mike Davock was a winger who was on Everton's books as a youngster but it was from St Helens Town that he joined Stockport County in January 1957. In his first three seasons at Edgeley Park he was mostly a reserve but he was a regular from the 1959–60 season, going on to make over 250 senior appearances during his time at the club. In the summer of 1964 he moved on to play for Southern League club Poole Town.

Billy Day (Born: South Bank, 27 December 1936. Died: January 2018.) Billy Day was a winger who made his first-team debut for Middlesbrough as an 18-year-old in October 1955. However, his early career was disrupted by National Service and injury and he was rarely a regular in the Boro' line-up despite making over 100 senior appearances. He moved on to Newcastle United in March 1962 and then concluded his career with spells at Peterborough and Cambridge United, then members of the Southern League.

Alan Deakin (Born: Birmingham, 27 November 1941. Died: 2 January 2018.) Alan Deakin was a wing-half who joined the Aston Villa groundstaff in January 1957, progressing to the professional ranks on reaching the age of 17. He gained a League Cup medal as a member of the Villa team that won the inaugural 1960–61 competition and went on to make over 250 appearances during his time at the club. He was also capped six times by England U23s. Alan moved on to Walsall in October 1969 where he ended his senior career. His elder brother Mike also played in senior football and sadly also appears in these obituaries.

Mike Deakin (Born: Birmingham, 25 October 1933. Died: 15 July 2017.) Centre-forward Mike Deakin joined Crystal Palace from Birmingham League club Bromsgrove Rovers midway through the 1954–55 season. He did well at Selhurst Park, finishing as the club's top scorer in three of his four complete seasons there before moving on to Northampton Town and then Aldershot.

Bob Dennison (Born: Hull, 12 September 1932. Died: Willerby, East Yorkshire, 9 July 2017.) Bob Dennison joined Hull City as an amateur in 1952, turning professional during the summer of 1954, but apart from a lengthy spell in the second half of the 1955–56 season when he featured at right-back he was mostly a reserve during his time at Boothferry Park. After 25 senior appearances he moved on to Scarborough in the summer of 1958.

Dougie Devlin (Born: Glasgow, 17 March 1953. Died: 13 June 2017.) Midfielder Dougie Devlin was an apprentice with Wolverhampton Wanderers and was capped by Scotland at Youth international level but he was unable to graduate to the first team at Molineux. He spent the 1972–73 season at Walsall where he made a number of first-team appearances before following manager John Smith to play for Dundalk.

Ron Dickinson (Born: Coventry, 29 June 1930. Died: 2018.) Ron Dickinson was a centre-half who was spotted playing for RAF Oswestry during National Service, signing as a part-time professional with Shrewsbury Town in May 1953. He made a dozen first-team appearances for the Shrews but then moved on to Coventry City for the 1954–55 season. However, he was unable to break into the first team at Highfield Road and after 12 months moved into non-league football with Bedworth Town.

Charlie Douglas (Born: Govan, Glasgow, 1924. Died: Brechin, 14 October 2017.) Charlie Douglas was a versatile forward who joined Montrose during the 1945–46 season. He was a regular for the remainder of that season, scoring in his first six games and finishing with a tally of 13 goals from 23 appearances. Nevertheless, he began the following season in the Juniors with Arbroath Victoria before returning to Links Park. He scored hat-tricks in his first two games, but suffered a facial injury playing at Dens Park the following March which effectively ended his senior career.

Dermot Drummy (Born: Hackney, 16 January 1961. Died: 27 November 2017.) Dermot Drummy was a midfield player as a youngster and joined Arsenal as an apprentice on leaving school. He went on to make over 100 appearances for the club's reserve and youth teams, graduating to the professional ranks in January 1979. However, his only Football League experience came in a short loan spell with Blackpool during the 1979–80 season. Later, he returned to the game coaching the Arsenal youth team and then with the Chelsea Academy before serving as head coach of Crawley Town from April 2016 to May 2017.

Kieron Durkan (Born: Chester, 1 December 1973. Died: Halton, Cheshire, 28 February 2018.) Kieron Durkan was a wide-right midfield player who developed through the youth set-up at Wrexham. He was transferred to Stockport County in February 1996 and the following season he was a regular in the side that reached the semi-finals of the League Cup and won promotion from the Second Division in 1996–97. He went on to make over 300 senior appearances, also turning out for Macclesfield Town, Rochdale and Swansea City. He was capped three times by the Republic of Ireland U21s.

Alec Eisenträger (Born: Hamburg, Germany, 20 July 1927. Died: August 2017.) Alec Eisenträger came to the UK as a German prisoner of war and made his name as footballer with Western League club Trowbridge Town. He signed for Bristol City in the summer of 1949 and went on to make over 200 appearances during his time at Ashton Gate. A stockily built inside-forward who impressed with his ball play, he later played in the Southern League with Merthyr Tydfil and Chelmsford City. As a youngster he had played with the Hamburger SV youth teams.

Tommy Fairley (Born: Houghton-le-Spring, 12 October 1932. Died: 16 April 2017.) Goalkeeper Tommy Fairley joined Sunderland as a 17-year-old but was mostly a reserve during his time at Roker Park. After completing his National Service he signed for Carlisle United in the summer of 1956 and he was a near ever-present during his first season at Brunton Park. He stayed two more seasons as back-up 'keeper then moved to Southern League club Cambridge City for the 1959–60 campaign.

Tommy Farrer (Born: Hoddesdon, 22 December 1922. Died: Maidstone, 16 November 2017.) Left-back Tommy Farrer was a member of the great Bishop Auckland team of the post-war period, featured in three FA Amateur Cup finals and gained representative honours for the Durham County FA. After eight seasons in the North East he returned south, signing for Walthamstow Avenue in March 1953. He was capped on 20 occasions by England Amateurs and also featured for Great Britain in the 1956 Olympic Games tournament.

John Faulkner (Born: Orpington, 10 March 1948. Died: 28 December 2017.) John Faulkner was on Charlton Athletic's books as a youngster before dropping into non-league football with Sutton United, for whom an FA Cup appearance against Leeds United earned him a move to Elland Road in March 1970. Injury meant his career at Leeds never really took off but a transfer to Luton Town earned him a reputation as something of a cult figure in the centre of defence. He made over 200 appearances in six seasons at Kenilworth Road then played in the NASL with Memphis Rogues and California Surf. Later he worked as a coach with both Luton and Norwich City.

Bobby Ferguson (Born: Dudley, Northumberland, 8 January 1948. Died: 28 March 2018.) As a player Bobby Ferguson was a left-back who developed through the junior and reserve teams for Newcastle United, making just a handful of first-team appearances. A move to Derby County followed, where he developed into a solid and dependable defender, playing in over 100 senior games. He subsequently had a spell with Cardiff City before becoming player-manager of Southern League Barry Town. He took on a similar role for Newport County from July 1969 but after a disastrous start to the 1970–71 season, which saw County without a win after 16 matches, he lost his job. Soon afterwards he linked up with fellow North Easterner Bobby Robson on the coaching staff at Ipswich Town and when Robson left to take charge of the England national team Bobby took over as manager, staying in post from August 1982 to May 1987. He later coached in the Middle East and with Sunderland and Birmingham City.

Rodney Fern (Born: Measham, Leicestershire, 13 December 1948. Died: 16 January 2018.) Rodney Fern signed as a professional for Leicester City shortly after his 18th birthday and went on to win an FA Cup runners-up medal with the Foxes in 1969. The following season he was City's leading scorer and he then helped them win a place back in the top flight in 1970–71. He subsequently moved to Luton Town and then Chesterfield where he switched to a role as a central striker and rediscovered his goalscoring touch. He went on to conclude his career with Rotherham United, where he was a member of the team that won the old Third Division title in 1980–81.

Franny Firth (Born: Dewsbury, 27 May 1956. Died: May 2018.) Franny Firth was a winger who joined Huddersfield Town as an apprentice in the summer of 1972, signing professional forms in November 1973. He was a member of the team that reached the FA Youth Cup final in 1973–74 when they lost out to Tottenham Hotspur over two legs and went on to play a number of first-team games before suffering a broken leg in October 1976. In February 1978 he resurrected his career with a move to Halifax Town and featured regularly during his time at the Shay, making over 150 senior appearances. A high point came with an appearance in the FA Cup third round win over Manchester City in January 1980. He ended his career with a season at Bury before switching to non-league football with Witton Albion.

Arthur Fitzsimons (Born: Dublin, 16 December 1929. Died: Dalkey, Co. Dublin, Ireland, 9 May 2018.) Arthur Fitzsimons was an intelligent and skilful inside-forward who signed for Middlesbrough from League of Ireland club Shelbourne in the summer of 1949. He went on to become an influential figure during his time at Ayresome Park, making over 200 appearances. He left towards the end of the 1958–59 season and following a brief association with Lincoln City he concluded his playing career at Mansfield Town. He later coached the Libya national team and Drogheda and was, for a brief period, manager of Shamrock Rovers.

Ronnie Foster (Born: Islington, 22 November 1938. Died: Reading, 28 July 2017.) Ronnie Foster was a skilful midfield schemer who signed for Leyton Orient from amateurs Clapton towards the end of the 1956–57 season. He went on to appear regularly for the O's in 1961–62 when they won promotion from the old Second Division but rarely featured in their season of top-flight football. He later enjoyed four useful seasons with Grimsby Town then had spells with Reading and in the USA with Dallas Tornado of the NASL, before concluding his senior career with a brief association with Brentford.

Albert Franks (Born: Boldon, County Durham, 13 April 1936. Died: 18 June 2017.) Albert Franks signed professional forms for Newcastle United towards the end of 1953 and spent seven seasons at St James' Park including a couple as a regular first-teamer. Spells in Scotland with Rangers and Morton were largely unsuccessful but he went on to make over 50 appearances for Lincoln City. He subsequently had a brief spell with Queen of the South before becoming player-manager of Scarborough.

Juan Carlos Garcia (Born: Tela, Atlantida, Honduras, 8 March 1988. Died: Tegucigalpa, Honduras, 8 January 2018.) Juan Carlos Garcia was a left-back who developed in Honduran football with the Marathon and Olimpia clubs before signing for Wigan Athletic in the summer of 2013. His only first-team appearance for the Latics was in a League Cup tie against Manchester City in September 2013 and he was due to spend the 2014–15 season on loan with CD Tenerife. He returned early, however, and shortly afterwards was diagnosed with leukaemia, which was the cause of his early death. He won 39 caps for Honduras.

Len Gaynor (Born: Ollerton, Nottinghamshire, 22 September 1925. Died: 26 September 2017.) Len Gaynor was an inside-forward who had a brief trial with Nottingham Forest Colts in the 1943–44 season, later joining Hull City towards the end of 1947–48. In three seasons at Boothferry Park he was mainly a reserve, but fared much better with Bournemouth, making over 50 first-team appearances. In March 1954 he signed for Southampton where he was briefly a regular in the side before concluding his career with spells at Aldershot and Yeovil Town.

Jimmy Gibson (Born: Belfast, 4 September 1940. Died: Racine, Wisconsin, USA, 19 August 2017.) Centre-forward Jimmy Gibson signed for Newcastle in January 1959 but received few opportunities at St James' Park. However, he excelled when dropping into the Southern League with Cambridge United, scoring over 30 goals in each of his first two seasons. He eventually earned a return to the Football League with Luton Town in February 1965, where he mostly featured at wing-half. Jimmy later played in the United States with Chicago Mustangs before turning to coaching. He was admitted to the Wisconsin Soccer Association Hall of Fame in 2000.

Jim Gilmour (Born: Irvine, Ayrshire, 31 October 1949. Died: Kilmarnock, 11 September 2017.) Jim Gilmour was a goalkeeper who appeared for Ayr United and St Mirren, making a total of 21 senior appearances between 1969 and 1973. He then began a lengthy career in Scottish Junior football playing for a number of clubs including Cumnock, Auchinleck Talbot, Hurlford United, Kello Rovers, Whitletts Victoria and Annbank United. He went on to manage Kello and Whitletts.

Ray Gough (Born: Belfast, 8 February 1938. Died: Exeter, 11 March 2018.) Ray Gough was a stylish wing-half who won amateur international honours for Northern Ireland while still in his teens and playing for Crusaders. In April 1957 he turned professional with Linfield and went on to become a member of the all-conquering 'seven trophy' team of 1961–62. although he missed the closing stages of the campaign after suffering a broken leg. In October 1963 he signed for Exeter City but was unable to break into the first team, but on moving to Millwall 12 months later he made 17 senior appearances. He later played in the Southern League with Weymouth and Bath City. Ray won two caps for the Irish League representative side.

Wally Gould (Born: Thrybergh, Yorkshire, 25 September 1938. Died: 9 March 2018.) Wally Gould was a pacy winger who could play on either flank. A product of Yorkshire League club Rawmarsh, he signed for Sheffield United in February 1958 and made a bright start to his career at Bramall Lane, scoring within a minute of his debut for the Central League team. However, it was only after moving on to York City in February 1961 that he experienced regular first-team football. He made over a century of appearances for the Minstermen then signed for Brighton & Hove Albion midway through the 1963–64 campaign. He settled in well at the Goldstone Ground and the following season he was a near ever-present in the team that won the Fourth Division title, netting 21 goals. In 1968 he emigrated to South Africa where he played for a number of clubs including Durban United, Hellenic and East London United. In 1969 he was the Cape Football Writers' Association Footballer of the Year.

Bill Graham (Born: Carlisle, 8 May 1929. Died: 3 May 2018.) Bill Graham was a versatile player who joined Carlisle United from Consett in January 1954. A part-time player he stayed six seasons at Brunton Park although he was mainly a reserve, making 35 senior appearances.

Bill Green (Born: Newcastle upon Tyne, 22 December 1950. Died: 21 August 2017.) Bill Green was a tall, lanky centre-half who made his name with Hartlepool United where he was appointed as team captain at the age of 20. He captained Carlisle in 1973–74 when they won promotion to the old First Division and went on to score their first-ever goal in First Division football when he netted at Chelsea on the opening day of the 1974–75 campaign. Although the Cumbrians were relegated that season, he returned to the top flight with West Ham United in 1976–77. Later he enjoyed a four-year spell at Chesterfield where he took on coaching duties and rarely missed a match. He managed Scunthorpe United (February 1991 to January 1993) and Buxton, and at the time of his death he had been chief scout at Southampton for several years.

John Groves (Born: Langwith, Derbyshire, 16 September 1933. Died: 26 June 2017.) John Groves signed professional forms for Luton Town soon after reaching the age of 17, gaining a regular first-team place in the 1957–58 season. A wing-half, he went on to make over 300 appearances for the Hatters, gaining an FA Cup runners-up medal in 1959 as a member of the team defeated by Nottingham Forest in the Wembley final. He concluded his career with a couple of seasons on the South Coast at Bournemouth.

Colin Harper (Born: Ipswich, 25 July 1946. Died: March 2018.) Colin Harper was a left-back who developed through the youth system at Ipswich Town, making his first-team debut at Plymouth in February 1966. He stayed 13 seasons at Portman Road, but it was only in 1971–72 and 1972–73 that he featured regularly in the side. In total he made over 150 appearances during his time with the club, featuring in the side that defeated Norwich City over two legs to win the Texaco Cup in May 1973, while the following season he was a member of the team that knocked Real Madrid out of the UEFA Cup. He subsequently had short spells with Port Vale, where he was briefly acting manager, and as player-manager of Waterford.

Allan Harris (Born: Northamptonshire, 28 December 1942. Died: 23 November 2017.) Defender Allan Harris was a member of the Chelsea team that won the FA Youth Cup in 1959–60 and 1960–61. He contributed to Chelsea's 1962–63 promotion campaign but then lost his place in the side and moved on to Coventry. He was back at Stamford Bridge at the very end of the 1965–66 season, and went on to make an appearance for the Blues alongside his brother Ron in the 1967 FA Cup final when the team lost out to Tottenham Hotspur. After winding down his career with spells at Queens Park Rangers, Plymouth Argyle and Cambridge United, he turned to coaching. He worked as assistant manager to Terry Venables at Crystal Palace, QPR and Barcelona and went on to coach Al-Ahly (Egypt) and the Malaysia national team (2000 to 2004).

Alan Haspell (Born: Northwich, 23 January 1943. Died: Winsford, 16 February 2018.) Alan Haspell spent five years on the books of Burnley without breaking into the first team before joining Doncaster Rovers for the 1963–64 season. A wing-half or inside-forward, he made two senior appearances during his time at Belle Vue before returning to Cheshire where he played for both Witton Albion and Northwich Victoria.

Dick Hewitt (Born: South Elmsall, Yorkshire, 25 May 1943. Died: 11 October 2017.) Dick Hewitt was a wing-half or inside-forward who made over 200 appearances in senior football. He signed for Huddersfield Town at the age of 18 but although he failed to break into the first team at Leeds Road he gained plenty of first-team action with both Bradford City and Barnsley. His best season, however, was probably in 1970–71 when he featured regularly in the York City team which won promotion from the old Fourth Division. He moved on to Scarborough with whom he won an FA Trophy winners' medal in 1973.

John Higgins (Born: Kilmarnock, 27 January 1930. Died: 21 June 2017.) John Higgins was a right-back who joined Hibernian in December 1952 but was mostly a back-up player during five seasons at Easter Road. He helped create history as a member of the team that won 4–0 away to Rot-Weiss Essen in September 1955 – the first time a British team had competed in the European Cup. He went on to play for St Mirren and Swindon Town before returning north to play for Newton Stewart in the South of Scotland League.

Bert Hill (Born: West Ham, 8 March 1930. Died: 14 July 2017.) Bert Hill was a wing-half who signed for Colchester United after spending a couple of seasons on the books of Chelsea. He made his senior debut towards the end of his first season at Layer Road and went on to make over 100 appearances for the U's before leaving in the summer of 1957. He later played for Dartford, Hastings United and Canterbury City.

Albert Hobson (Born: Glossop, 7 April 1925. Died: December 2017.) Winger Albert Hobson joined Blackpool as an 18-year-old from a Manchester works' team but although he spent nine years at Bloomfield Road he was a rarely a first-team regular, generally being restricted in his first-team outings by the presence of the legendary Stanley Matthews. In the summer of 1954 he moved to Huddersfield Town in exchange for John McKenna, but he managed just a handful of appearances for the Terriers before concluding his senior career with a season at York.

Jimmy Hodge (Born: Perth, 1925. Died: Perth, 13 December 2017.) Jimmy Hodge was a full-back who made his first-team debut for St Johnstone towards the end of the 1948–49 season, having previously played for local juvenile club St Johnstone YM. He spent the next two seasons at Muirton Park, mostly playing in the reserves in the C Division before joining Brechin City in the summer of 1952. He stayed at Glebe Park for several seasons, making over 200 first-team appearances before switching to Highland League football with Clachnacuddin.

Frank Hodgetts (Born: Dudley, 30 September 1924. Died: March 2018.) Frank Hodgetts was a winger who made his wartime debut for West Bromwich Albion in October 1940 at the age of 16 years and 26 days, making him the club's youngest ever player. He made over 100 appearances for the Baggies during the hostilities and remained a regular in the first two post-war seasons. In August 1949 he moved on to Millwall but in four seasons at the Den he made only 37 first-team appearances. At the time of his death he was West Brom's oldest surviving player

Ken Hodgkisson (Born: West Bromwich, 12 March 1933. Died: 10 May 2018.) Ken Hodgkisson was a versatile forward, who spent six seasons on the books of West Bromwich Albion, but his time with the club was disrupted by National Service and he made just 21 first-team appearances. He moved on to Walsall in January 1956 where he was a key figure in the team that won back-to-back promotions as Division Four champions in 1959–60 and runners-up in Division Three the following season. He remained at Fellows Park until the end of the 1965–66 season when he moved on to Worcester City.

Brian Hodgson (Born: Cleethorpes, 29 January 1936. Died: 14 February 2018.) Centre-forward Brian Hodgson scored on his debut for Grimsby Town against West Ham United in October 1956 but he was mostly a reserve during his time at Blundell Park, making only seven first-team appearances. He signed for Workington in October 1959 where he

managed a solitary Football League outing before moving on to play in the Southern League for Boston United in 1960–61. His father, Jack, and uncle, Sam Hodgson, both played senior football for the Mariners.

Eric Hornby (Born: Birkenhead, 31 March 1923. Died: 29 January 2018.) Full-back Eric Hornby developed through Tranmere Rovers' youth set-up during the war, progressing to the first team in 1941–42 and becoming a regular in the line-up after signing professional forms in November 1944. When peacetime football returned he struggled to gain a place in the side, although he featured regularly in 1947–48, before concluding his senior career with a season at Crewe Alexandra.

Rene Houseman (Born: La Banda, Argentina, 19 July 1953. Died: Buenos Aires, 23 March 2018.) Rene Houseman was a skilful winger who won 55 caps for Argentina between 1973 and 1979, scoring 13 goals. He was a member of the squad for the World Cup finals in both 1974 and 1978, on the latter occasion coming off the bench in the closing stages of normal time in the final as Argentina went on to beat Netherlands 3-1 and take the trophy. He played most of his club football in Argentina with CA Huracán.

Cliff Jackson (Born: Swindon, 3 September 1941. Died: May 2018.) Cliff Jackson was an England Schoolboys international who joined the groundstaff at Swindon Town before signing professional forms shortly after his 17th birthday. Initially a winger, he was a regular in the Robins team that won promotion from the Third Division in 1962–63. After a spell at Plymouth Argyle he signed for Crystal Palace in September 1966, linking up with his former manager Bert Head. He was converted to a role as centre-forward and in 1968–69 helped Palace reach the First Division for the first time in their history. He played a season in the top flight before concluding his senior career at Torquay United.

Vic Keeble (Born: Colchester, 25 June 1930. Died: 31 January 2018.) Centre-forward Vic Keeble was at Arsenal as a schoolboy before joining then Southern League club Colchester United in May 1947 and scoring a hat-trick on his debut against Bedford Town. He scored prolifically for the U's in 1951–52, earning a move to Newcastle United where he netted at a rate of a goal every other game. He was the last surviving member of Newcastle United's FA Cup winning teams of the 1950s having played in the 1955 final. He subsequently had a street named after him in Ashington. He retired from football after sustaining a bad back injury playing for West Ham United in October 1959.

Brian Kirkup (Born: Burnham, 16 April 1932. Died: Kempston, Bedfordshire, 22 April 2018.) Brian Kirkup was initially a centre-forward who signed for Reading in August 1955 shortly after completing his National Service. He did well in his first season at Elm Park, netting 16 goals from 38 games, but then found first-team opportunities harder to come by. In the summer of 1958 he moved on to Northampton Town and then Aldershot, where he eventually switched to playing in the half-back line. He made 59 appearances for the Shots and was a member of the team that reached the fourth round of the FA Cup in 1960–61 before going out to Stoke City in a second replay.

John Kurila (Born: Glasgow, 10 April 1941. Died: Northampton, 6 March 2018.) John Kurila was a powerful central defender who made his bow in senior football with Celtic in April 1959. He helped Northampton Town win promotion from the Third Division in 1962–63 and after a brief association with Bristol City returned to the County Ground for a further five-year spell during which time he featured in the top flight. A move to Southend United in July 1968 was successful and he won the Player of the Season award in his first season, before he concluded his career with spells at Colchester United and Lincoln City.

Davie Laing (Born: Strathmiglo, Fife, 20 February 1925. Died: East Kilbride, 15 July 2017.) Wing-half Davie Laing joined Hearts from Bayview Youth Club in 1942 and went on to make over 250 first-team appearances during his time at Tynecastle. He later served Clyde, with whom he won a Scottish Cup winners' medal in 1955, and Hibernian before his daytime job took him south to Kent in the summer of 1957. He enjoyed two seasons as a regular with Gillingham before moving into non-league with Margate, Ramsgate and Canterbury City.

John Lambie (Born: Whitburn, 19 March 1941. Died: 10 April 2018.) John Lambie enjoyed a successful career as a full-back with Falkirk and Whitburn, amassing some 400 appearances in a career that spanned the period from 1960 to 1974. A highlight came when he gained a League Cup runners-up prize as a member of the St Johnstone team defeated by Celtic in the 1969–70 final. He subsequently turned to coaching and then, with some success, management, winning two divisional titles with both Hamilton Academical and Partick Thistle (serving both on more than one occasion) as well as a brief spell in charge of Falkirk.

Tommy Lawrence (Born: Dailly, Ayrshire, 14 May 1940. Died: 10 January 2018.) Tommy Lawrence was big, burly goalkeeper who signed professional forms for Liverpool at the age of 17 and waited five years to break into the first team. However, he quickly established himself as first choice and in a run of six seasons he missed just four league games. During this time the Reds won two Football League titles (1963–64 and 1965–66) as well as the FA Cup in 1964–65. He stayed at Anfield until the end of the 1970–71 season, by which time he had made 390 first-team appearances before concluding his career at Tranmere Rovers. He won three full caps for Scotland.

Malcolm Lawton (Born: Leeds, 7 November 1935. Died: 4 November 2017.) Malcolm Lawton signed professional forms for Leeds United at the age of 17, but was unable to break into the first team at Elland Road. A solid, committed defender, he joined Bradford at the end of the 1956–57 season and went on to make over 100 senior appearances during his stay at Park Avenue before injury ended his career.

Jack Lovering (Born: Nuneaton, 10 December 1922. Died: 21 September 2017.) Jack Lovering was on Coventry City's books as a junior during the war and signed for Birmingham City for the 1945–46 season, turning out for the club's 'A' team in the Birmingham Combination. After being released on a free transfer he returned to Highfield Road, but in two seasons with the club he made just six first-team appearances. He subsequently joined Bedworth Town then went on to play for Atherstone Town and Nuneaton Borough.

Graham Lovett (Born: Sheldon, Birmingham, 5 August 1947. Died: 10 May 2018.) Graham Lovett signed as a professional for West Bromwich Albion in November 1964 and within a few weeks he had made his First Division debut for the Baggies. He mostly featured in a midfield role, but his career was twice interrupted by serious injuries sustained in road traffic accidents, the second of which effectively ended his career. The high point of his career came in May 1968 when he lined up for Albion in the FA Cup final, gaining a winners' medal following their 1-0 win over Everton.

Don McCalman (Born: Greenock, 18 October 1935. Died: 14 September 2017.) Don McCalman was a solid centre-half who developed in Scotland with Hibernian before Bradford Park Avenue signed him up in the summer of 1959. He rarely missed a game during his time with the club. He was an ever-present in the team that won promotion from Division Four in 1960–61 and from March 1960 commenced a run of 156 consecutive appearances, then a club record. After being released he had a short spell with Barrow before a knee injury ended his playing career. He returned to Park Avenue in May 1968 as trainer and was later assistant manager before later serving as caretaker manager.

Bert McCann (Born: Dundee, 15 October 1932. Died: 12 September 2017.) Bert McCann was a wing-half who signed for Dundee United on amateur forms, featuring in the first team in the 1953–54 season. He went on to study at Edinburgh University and after graduating he was employed as a teacher. He subsequently signed for Queen's Park, winning amateur international honours before joining the professional ranks at Motherwell. Bert made over 300 appearances during his stay at Fir Park, featuring in three Scottish Cup semi-finals and winning five full caps for Scotland.

Bill McCarry (Born: Tillicoultry, Clackmannanshire, 4 December 1938. Died: Alloa, 12 May 2018.) Bill McCarry was a powerful, ball-winning wing-half who signed for Falkirk as a teenager and went on to assist them to promotion back to the top flight in the 1960–61 season. Moving on to St Johnstone he became a regular in the side for most of the 1960s, accumulating over 250 competitive appearances and featuring in the 1969–70 League Cup final defeat by Celtic. He concluded at Stirling Albion where he took his career total of senior games beyond the 450 mark.

Mike McCartney (Born: Musselburgh, 28 September 1954. Died: Carlisle, 2 January 2018.) Mike McCartney was a full-back who was capped by Scotland Schools before signing professional terms for West Bromwich Albion. Although he failed to make the first team at The Hawthorns, he went on to make over 300 senior appearances in two separate spells with Carlisle United, initially as a midfielder and later at left-back. In between he spent a season in the top flight with Southampton and also played for Plymouth Argyle. He left Carlisle at the end of the 1986–87 season and later had a spell as manager of Gretna, then playing in the Northern League.

John McCormick (Born: Glasgow, 18 July 1936. Died: 2 July 2017.) John McCormick was a big, powerful centre-half who made his name with Third Lanark where he gained representative honours when he played for Scotland against the Scottish League in a trial for the international team early in 1962. He later spent two seasons at Aberdeen before moving south with Tom White to sign for Crystal Palace. He was ever-present for Palace when they won promotion to the First Division for the first time in 1968–69 and in 1972 he won the club's first Player of the Year award.

Revd Kenny MacDonald (Born: Skinidin, Isle of Skye, 8 January 1935. Died: Bonar Bridge, Sutherland, 21 January 2018.) Kenny MacDonald was an inside-right who was signed by St Johnstone on amateur forms at the start of the 1957–58 season. He made three League Cup appearances for the Perth side, scoring on his debut against Albion Rovers, and later moved south to work as a customs officer at Heathrow Airport. During this time he played for Hounslow Town and went on to win seven amateur international caps for Scotland. In later life he became a minister of the Free Church of Scotland.

Jimmy MacEwan (Born: Dundee, 22 March 1929. Died: Birmingham, 28 November 2017.) Winger Jimmy MacEwan signed for Arbroath in November 1947, moving on to Raith Rovers in the summer of 1951 for a reported fee of £4,000, a record at the time for the Kirkcaldy club. He went on to make over 200 appearances for Raith, topping the scoring charts on three occasions and earning a trial for the full Scotland team. Jimmy was well into his 30th year when he signed for Aston Villa, but scored on his debut at Brighton & Hove Albion and quickly impressed with some dazzling skills on the flank. He helped Villa win the Second Division title in 1959–60 and the following season played in both legs of the inaugural Football League Cup final. He concluded his career at Walsall before joining the backroom staff at Fellows Park where he remained until 1975.

Tommy McGhee (Born: Manchester, 10 May 1929. Died: May 2018.) Full-back Tommy McGhee came to prominence as an amateur with Wealdstone while serving as a Petty Officer in the Royal Navy. He was capped by England Amateurs and after leaving the Navy signed professional forms for Portsmouth in May 1954. He enjoyed five seasons of top-flight football at Fratton Park, making 136 Football League appearances before winding down his senior career with a season at Reading. He later joined Poole Town where he stayed for several years.

John McGlashan (Born: Dundee, 3 June 1967. Died: 10 January 2018.) John McGlashan was a powerful midfield player who developed with Montrose before moving south to sign for Millwall in the summer of 1990. He never quite established himself with the South London club and in January 1993 he was sold to Peterborough United for what was then a club record fee for Posh. He concluded his career south of the border with Rotherham United before returning to Scotland to play for Dundee, Ross County and Arbroath, where he was a regular in the team that won promotion from the Second Division in 2001–02. He was later manager of Arbroath from September 2005 to October 2009.

Ray McGuigan (Born: Bellshill, 30 October 1969. Died: 2018.) Ray McGuigan was a midfield player who was on the books of Hamilton Academical between October 1987 and the end of the 1991–92 season. He made 64 appearances for the club during his stay, many of which were from the substitutes' bench. He had brief spells with Albion Rovers and Ayr United in 1992–93 before joining Highland League club Fort William.

Joe McGurn (Born: Hamilton, Lanarkshire, 2 January 1965. Died: August 2017.) Joe McGurn developed as a tough-tackling centre-half with East Kilbride Youth Club in the early 1980s before stepping up to senior football with St Johnstone. Here he switched to centre midfield where his hard, uncompromising style was very effective. He later had brief spells with Alloa Athletic and Stenhousemuir but the closing stages of his career were marred by injury.

Frank McKenna (Born: Blaydon, 8 January 1933. Died: Leeds, 12 December 2017.) Frank McKenna was a versatile forward who came to prominence with Bishop Auckland, gaining an FA Amateur Cup winners' medal in 1956 and earning representative honours for England Amateurs and the Great Britain Olympic teams. He turned professional with Leeds United in the summer of 1956, but was mostly a reserve during his time at Elland Road. However, he featured regularly in subsequent spells at Carlisle United and Hartlepools United, finishing with career totals of 84 Football League appearances and 20 goals.

Johnny MacKenzie (Born: Dennistoun, Glasgow, 4 September 1925. Died: Tiree, Inner Hebrides, 5 July 2017.) Johnny MacKenzie was a winger who signed for Partick Thistle during the war and stayed for more than a decade, although for the 1947–48 season he turned out for Bournemouth when he was stationed nearby on National Service. He made over 300 appearances for Thistle and played in the League Cup finals for 1953–54, 1956–57 and 1958–59, all of which ended in defeat. He eventually left for two seasons at Dumbarton and then Derry City, with whom he was an Irish Cup winner in 1964. Johnny was a member of the Scotland squad that toured North America in the summer of 1949 and later appeared for his country in the 1954 World Cup finals.

Phil McKnight (Born: Camlachie, Scotland, 15 June 1924. Died: 25 May 2018.) Phil McKnight was a hard-working right-half who had served in the Royal Navy during the war, linking up with Alloa Athletic when peacetime football returned. His performances during the first half of 1946–47 earned him a move to Chelsea, but in seven years at Stamford Bridge he was mostly a reserve, making just 33 first-team appearances. A move to Leyton Orient in July 1954 was more successful and he was a regular in the line-up, helping the O's win the Division Three South title in 1955–56. He made over 150 appearances during his time with the club and also featured for the London FA XI in the Inter Cities Fairs Cup. At the time of his death he was the oldest surviving former Orient player.

Jimmy McMillan (Born County Durham, 16 December 1932. Died: Gateshead, 1 November 2017.) Jimmy McMillan was an outside-left who was a mainstay of the Crook Town team in the 1950s and early '60s. He won four FA Amateur Cup winners medals (1954, 1959, 1962 and 1964) and was awarded a solitary cap for England Amateurs against France in April 1959.

Ian McNeill (Born: Baillieston, Lanarkshire, 24 February 1932. Died: October 2017.) Ian McNeill gained representative honours for Scotland Youths and signed for Aberdeen in August 1949. He impressed by scoring seven goals for the 'A' team in a 15-0 win over East Fife A but his chances of first-team football at Pittodrie were restricted by National Service. He subsequently followed manager David Halliday to Leicester City where his 18 goals contributed to the Foxes' 1956–57 Division Two title success. In later spells at Brighton & Hove Albion and Southend United he adopted a deeper role before taking up an appointment as player-coach with Dover Athletic. He went on to enjoy success as a manager, leading Ross County to the Highland League title in 1966–67 and taking Wigan Athletic into the Football League in 1978. He was later assistant manager of Chelsea (1981–1985) and manager of Shrewsbury Town (1987–1990), then worked with Millwall before taking on various scouting roles.

Ken McPherson (Born: Hartlepool, 25 March 1927. Died: January 2018.) Ken McPherson was only a reserve at Hartlepools but joined Notts County in August 1950 where he understudied England international Tommy Lawton at centre-forward. A spell with Middlesbrough followed, but it was not until he signed for Coventry City midway through the 1955–56 season that he won a regular first-team place. His best seasons were probably with Newport County towards the end of his career, where he finished as top scorer in two out of his three seasons at Somerton Park. He concluded his career with Swindon Town where he switched to playing at centre-half.

Brian Macready (Born: Leicester, 25 March 1942. Died: 2017.) Brian Macready signed amateur forms for West Bromwich Albion at the age of 17, graduating to the professional ranks in February 1960. He was mostly a reserve at The Hawthorns, generally featuring on the right flank. On moving to Mansfield Town in the summer of 1964 he switched to inside-forward and in his first season he was a regular in the line-up as the Stags narrowly missed out on promotion from the old Third Division. In October 1965 he became the first substitute to be used by Mansfield, coming on in the away game at Peterborough United. Injury led to his departure from Field Mill although he later played in the Southern League with Worcester City and Banbury United.

Ron Mailer (Born: Auchterarder, 18 May 1932. Died: Auchterarder, 28 March 2018.) Ron Mailer was a wing-half who joined Dunfermline Athletic from Auchterarder Primrose in March 1951 and went on to stay 13 years, making over 300 senior appearances. During his National Service he also played a number of games for Darlington when he was stationed nearby at Catterick. He captained the Pars team that won the Scottish Cup in 1961 and made his final appearance for the club in April 1964.

George Mansell (Born: Doncaster, 19 January 1943. Died: 4 October 2017.) George Mansell made a single first-team appearance for Doncaster Rovers, featuring at centre-forward in a 5-1 defeat at Darlington in November 1962. He later played for Hinckley Athletic, Retford Town and Matlock Town.

George Meek (Born: Glasgow, 15 February 1934. Died: March 2018.) George Meek was a winger who was introduced to senior football by Hamilton Academical in the 1951–52 season. The following summer he was sold to Leeds United, beginning a lengthy association with the Elland Road club which saw him make exactly 199 first-team appearances. During this time he also had a brief spell at Walsall while on National Service. He spent the 1960–61 season at Leicester City then became Walsall's record signing in July 1961 and added a further century of appearances during his second spell at Fellows Park. He retired from senior football in the summer of 1965.

Andrew 'Minty' Miller (Born: Troon, 1 December 1932. Died: 18 April 2018.) Andrew 'Minty' Millar was capped for Scotland Juniors against Ireland in February 1955 and went on to sign for Rangers although he never progressed further than the 'A' team playing in Division C. In the 1954–55 season he was on the books of Alloa Athletic for whom he made a number of senior appearances before leaving senior football. 'Minty' was also an outstanding golfer, winning the Scottish Boys' Championship in 1950 and later representing Scotland in the Home International Championships in 1954 and 1955. On five occasions he took part in the British Amateur Championship, reaching the quarter-final in 1953.

Liam Miller (Born: Cork, 13 February 1981. Died: Curraheen, Co. Cork, 9 February 2018.) Liam Miller was a tenacious midfield player who developed in the youth set-up at Celtic, going on to win a regular place in the first-team squad in the 2003–04 campaign. The following season he moved to Manchester United, but in two seasons at Old Trafford he was mostly a fringe player and most of his senior experience came in a loan spell with Leeds United. He moved on to Sunderland in August 2006, assisting in their Championship promotion campaign in his first season with the club. There followed a brief association with Queens Park Rangers and two seasons at Hibernian before he moved to Australia where he played for Perth Glory, Brisbane Roar and Melbourne City. There were further spells with Cork Celtic and in the USA with Wilmington Hammerheads before illness led to his retirement. Liam won 21 full caps for the Republic of Ireland. His early death was a result of pancreatic cancer.

Jimmy Milner (Born: Newcastle upon Tyne, 3 February 1933. Died: 2017.) Jimmy Milner signed for Burnley in December 1952 and stayed five years at Turf Moor, but was mostly a reserve, managing a solitary first-team appearance. However, he featured regularly in four seasons at Darlington where he was a member of the team that defeated Chelsea 4-1 in an FA Cup fourth round replay in front of a 15,000 gate at Feethams in January 1958. He played for Accrington Stanley in their final season of existence before winding down his senior career with Tranmere.

John Molyneux (Born: Warrington, 3 February 1931. Died: 7 March 2018.) John Molyneux was capped for England Youths and by the age of 18 he was a regular in the Chester line-up. Apart from a spell of National Service, he retained his place until Liverpool paid a four-figure fee for his services in the summer of 1955. At Anfield he built a reputation as a solid but unspectacular right-back and went on to make over 200 first-team appearances before losing his place in the 1961–62 promotion season. He subsequently returned to Chester where he featured regularly for the next 18 months and when he left senior football at the end of the 1964–65 season he had played more than 500 senior games for his two clubs.

Jackie Mooney (Born: Dublin, 1938. Died: Dublin, 30 December 2017.) Inside-forward Jackie Mooney spent three seasons on the books of Manchester United without breaking into the first team, before returning to Ireland in 1958. After brief spells with Bangor City and Cork Hibs he signed for Shamrock Rovers with whom he was a member of the team that achieved a double of the League of Ireland and the FAI Cup in 1963–64. The following season he won two full caps for the Republic of Ireland. Later he had spells with Athlone Town and Bohemians and he also won representative honours for the League of Ireland XI.

Tony Moore (Born: Scarborough, 4 September 1947. Died: 7 July 2017.) Winger Tony Moore progressed from an apprenticeship with Chesterfield to the professional ranks at the age of 17 and made his senior debut shortly afterwards. He went on to make over 150 appearances for the Spireites, assisting them to the Fourth Division title in 1969–70.

Andrew Morgan (Born: Freuchie, Fife, 18 April 1921. Died: 14 August 2017.) Andrew Morgan was an inside-forward who made a single appearance for Brechin City as a trialist towards the end of the 1938–39 season and later featured for Dundee and Raith Rovers as a guest player during the war during which time he spent 18 months as a prisoner of war after his plane was shot down over France. Post-war he had brief associations with Chelsea and Fulham without adding to his experience of senior football.

John Muir (Born: 4 September 1947. Died: 28 February 2018.) John Muir developed a reputation as a goalscoring forward with Alloa Athletic before signing for St Johnstone in November 1969. His early time at Muirton was affected by injuries and it was not until the 1972–73 campaign that he was able to establish himself in the side. He eventually returned to Alloa where he was a member of the team that won promotion in 1976–77 (the club's first success for almost 40 years). In total he netted over 100 senior goals at a rate of around one every three games.

Bob Murray (Born: Kemnay, Aberdeenshire, 24 April 1932. Died: September 2017.) Bob Murray was a tall, intelligent wing-half who came to prominence with Scottish Junior outfit Inverurie Loco. In November 1951 he signed for Stockport County and he went on to make close on 500 senior appearances during a 12-year stay at Edgeley Park, including a run of 226 consecutive League and Cup appearances between August 1954 and February 1959. On leaving Stockport he had spells with Bangor City and Ashton United.

Terry Murray (Born: Dublin, 22 May 1928. Died: Bedford, 18 October 2017.) Terry Murray started out as a winger and was capped for the Republic of Ireland at Junior international level. He signed for Dundalk in the summer of 1948 where he gained further representative honours, being capped by his country and also appearing for the League of Ireland representative XI. His form earned him a transfer to Hull City shortly after the start of the 1951–52 season and he was converted to inside-forward by the Tigers. However, he never really established himself at Boothferry Park or during a brief spell with Bournemouth before moving into non-league football with King's Lynn, Bedford Town and Rushden Town (where he was player-manager).

Les Mutrie (Born: Newcastle upon Tyne, 1 April 1952. Died: 3 October 2017.) Les Mutrie was a successful non-league striker in Northern League football for Ashington and from there went on to Gateshead United. When that club folded he joined the senior ranks at CarlisleUnited, making his Football League debut at the age of 25. He then returned to non-league football with Blyth Spartans and after some fine performances in a series of FA Cup ties against Hull City

the Tigers were persuaded to purchase him for what was then a record fee for a non-league player in December 1980. In his first full season at Boothferry Park he set a new club record by scoring in nine consecutive Football League games and finished the campaign as leading scorer with 28 goals. Les later played for Colchester United and Hartlepool United before retiring through injury.

Tommy Neilson (Born: Gorebridge, Midlothian, 15 March 1935. Died: Johannesburg, South Africa, 10 February 2018.) Wing-half Tommy Neilson began his career with Heart of Midlothian but failed to make the first team at Tynecastle and in May 1957 he signed for East Fife. He went on to enjoy the best period of his career with Dundee United, signing in October 1959 and remaining for nearly a decade. He made over 300 appearances during his time with the Fifers and captained the team that won promotion to the top flight in 1959–60. He later had a season with Cowdenbeath prior to emigrating to South Africa in 1969.

Peter Newbery (Born: Derby, 4 March 1938. Died: February 2018.) Peter Newbery was a versatile forward who joined Derby County on amateur forms on leaving school, progressing to a professional contract at the age of 17. He mostly featured for the Central League team during his time at the Baseball Ground, making five first-team appearances and scoring two goals. He left the club at the end of the 1960–61 season and subsequently played non-league football for Burton Albion, Lockheed Leamington and Long Eaton United.

Derek Nippard (Born: Poole, Dorset, 1930. Died: Bournemouth, 14 July 2017.) Derek Nippard progressed via the Football Combination to the Football League linesman's list in 1963 and three years later was promoted to the referees' list where he remained until the age of 47. A highlight of his career was taking charge of the 1978 FA Cup final between Ipswich Town and Arsenal.

Cliff Nugent (Born: Islington, 3 March 1929. Died: Weymouth, 17 February 2018.) Cliff Nugent was a winger who featured for Headington United in their early days in the Southern League before joining Cardiff City in January 1951. It took him some time to win a regular place in the Bluebirds' line-up but he went on to make more than 100 appearances for them, mostly in the top flight. In November 1958 he was transferred to Mansfield Town where he played for the next two seasons before dropping down to Southern League football with Weymouth.

John Ogston (Born: Aberdeen, 15 January 1939. Died: Aberdeen, 17 August 2017.) John Ogston was a goalkeeper who signed for Aberdeen after being a member of the Banks O'Dee team which won the Scottish Junior Cup in 1957. He was an ever-present for the Dons between August 1961 and August 1965 – a run of 164 consecutive games. He later spent three seasons at Liverpool for whom he made a single first-team appearance and was then at Doncaster Rovers where he was a regular in the side that won the Fourth Division title in 1968–69. He subsequently returned north and continued to play Highland League football until 1974.

Terry Oldfield (Born: Bristol, 1 April 1939. Died: 28 March 2018.) Terry Oldfield was a tall and powerful wing-half who initially signed for Bristol Rovers as an amateur, switching to professional status in 1960. He spent three seasons as a regular in the Pirates' line-up, making over 150 appearances during his stay. He moved on to Wrexham for the 1966–67 season where he continued to make a useful contribution before suffering an injury playing against Cardiff City in the Welsh Cup final which effectively ended his career. He had a brief spell as trainer for Bradford Park Avenue before leaving the game. He was also a talented cricketer who had played for Somerset Second XI.

Bert Ormond (Born: Falkirk, 12 January 1931. Died: Auckland, New Zealand, 15 November 2017.) Inside-forward Bert Ormond stepped up to the seniors in the summer of 1954 and went on to enjoy a healthy career in the Scottish League, making over 100 senior appearances with Falkirk, Airdrieonians and Dumbarton. In 1961 he emigrated to New Zealand where he continued to play and he captained the New Zealand national team that embarked on a world tour in 1964. Bert was a member of a well-known footballing family. He was the brother of Willie (Hibernian, Falkirk, Scotland and Scottish League XI) and Gibby (Airdrie, Dundee United, Cowdenbeath, Alloa and Scottish League XI). His sons Ian and Duncan represented New Zealand, while his grand-daughter Vicki played for New Zealand women.

Stéphane Paille (Born: Scionzier, France, 27 June 1965. Died: Lyon, France, 27 June 2017.) Stéphane Paille enjoyed the best seasons of his career with Sochaux, notably in 1987–88 when he was a member of the team that won promotion from Division Two and lost out on penalties in the final of the Coupe de France. In 1988 he was a member of the France team that won the UEFA U21 title and later was voted as France Football's Player of the Year. His career subsequently took him across France and also to Portugal and Switzerland but he was unable to achieve the same level of success. A failed drugs test led to a ban from the game before he signed for Heart of Midlothian in the 1996–97 season, gaining a League Cup runners-up medal during his stay. He was released having failed another drugs test in May 1997. He won six full caps for France between 1986 and 1989.

Karoly Palotai (Born: Békéscsaba, Hungary, 11 September 1935. Died: Gyr, Hungary, 3 February 2018.) Karoly Palotai was a member of the Hungary team which won the Gold Medal in the 1964 Olympic Games in Tokyo. He played in all four matches leading up to the final but was an unused substitute in the final. He played his club football for Rába ETO Gyr. He later became a well-known international referee, officiating at the 1974, 1978 and 1982 World Cup finals and taking charge of two European Cup finals (1976 and 1981).

Arthur Peel (Born: Manchester, 1937. Died: July 2017.) Arthur Peel was an outside right who won a single England amateur international cap in April 1958 while a student at Sheffield University. He later played for Whitley Bay, Wealdstone and Hendon before becoming player-coach of Wembley.

Willie Penman (Born: Wemyss, Fife, 7 August 1939. Died: December 2017.) Willie Penman was a member of the St Andrew's United team that won the Scottish Junior Cup in 1960, signing for Rangers shortly afterwards. He had few first-team opportunities at Ibrox and moved on to Newcastle United where he proved to be an effective member of the team that won the Second Division title in 1962–63. He made less of an impact in the top flight and was sold to Swindon Town where he featured from the bench in the 1969 Football League Cup final when the Robins defeated Arsenal in extra time to win the trophy. He went on to conclude his career with spells at Walsall, Dundalk and Seattle Sounders before leaving the game.

Pavel Pergl (Born: Prague, Czechoslvakia, 14 November 1977. Died: Magdeburg, Germany, 1 May 2018.) Pavel Pergl was a central defender who played most of his football in the Czech Republic, notably with Sparta Prague, before spending the second half of the 2006–07 season with Preston North End. He subsequently went on to play in Cyprus for AEK Larnaca and then moved around a string of clubs in Germany, Israel and Switzerland.

John Petrie (Born: July 1927. Died: Dalbeattie, 29 June 2017.) Goalkeeper John Petrie first came to notice with his performances for Glasgow's renowned Queen's Park School and he was on the point of signing for Wolves before joining Third Lanark in June 1944. He made 30 appearances for Thirds in 1945–46, the final season of wartime football, then continued to feature in the early post-war seasons before suffering a broken leg in November 1949. Although he recovered, he spent much of the rest of his playing career with trial periods and short-term contracts.

Ted Phillips (Born: Gromford, Suffolk, 21 August 1933. Died: Ipswich, January 2018.) Ted Phillips signed professional forms for Ipswich Town in December 1953 after completing his National Service and made his first-team debut shortly afterwards. It was not until the 1956–57 season that he fully established himself in the side and that season he set a new club record of 41 League goals as the team won the Division Three South title. He formed a prolific goalscoring partnership with fellow striker Ray Crawford, the two leading Ipswich to success in the Second Division in 1960–61 and the Football League title 12 months later, when they netted some 61 League goals between them. Ted scored a grand total of 179 goals from 293 senior appearances for Town. He later played for Leyton Orient, Luton Town and Colchester United before a spell in Malta as player-manager of Floriana.

Steve Piper (Born: Brighton, 2 November 1953. Died: December 2017.) Steve Piper was a defender who was just 19 years old when he made his first-team debut for Brighton & Hove Albion. He went on to establish himself in the side in the mid-1970s and was an ever-present in the team that won promotion from the old Third Division in 1976–77 when he featured as a midfield enforcer. In February 1978 he moved on to Portsmouth, but he was never a regular in the Pompey line-up and left at the end of the following season.

Johnny Powell (Born: York, 10 March 1936. Died: 25 December 2017.) Johnny Powell was a creative inside-forward or wing-half who signed for York City in September 1956 after developing in local junior football. He spent four seasons on the books at Bootham Crescent but was mostly a back-up player, making a total of 28 senior appearances. He went on to play for Scarborough and Goole Town.

Keith Pring (Born: Newport, 11 March 1943. Died: Southport, 25 January 2018.) Keith Pring was a pacy winger who developed with Newport County before being sold to Rotherham United in October 1964. He enjoyed the best seasons of his career at Millmoor, then playing in the old Division Two, and won his three full caps for Wales during his stay. He moved on following a change in management and later played for Notts County and Southport before a broken leg ended his soccer career, although he later played rugby for Southport RUFC, for whom he established a record points total in 1973–74.

Bob Raine (Born: Chesterfield, 17 November 1927. Died: Dover, 31 January 2018.) Bob Raine was a prolific goalscorer in junior football for Newbould Youth Club, earning him a contract with Chesterfield. However, the switch to Second Division football proved a step too far and he dropped down a few levels to further his career with Kidderminster Harriers. In February 1951 he returned to senior football with Aldershot, with whom he enjoyed a useful career over the next couple of seasons, finishing 1951–52 as the Shots' leading scorer and in total netting 22 goals from 50 senior appearances.

Cyrille Regis, MBE (Born: Mariapousoula, French Guinea, 9 February 1958. Died: 14 January 2018.) Cyrille Regis was a powerful and athletic striker who burst on the scene at West Bromwich Albion by scoring two on his debut in a League Cup game against Rotherham United in August 1977. He quickly became a fixture in the side, earning a reputation for scoring spectacular goals. In seven years at The Hawthorns he netted 111 goals and established himself as one of the club's greatest strikers. In October 1984 he moved on to Coventry City where he was less prolific but nevertheless enjoyed one of the high points of his career as a member of the team that defeated Tottenham Hotspur to win the FA Cup in 1987. In the summer of 1991 he linked up again with his former manager Ron Atkinson at Aston Villa and continued playing until his late 30s, turning out for Wolverhampton Wanderers, Wycombe Wanderers and Chester City. One of the first iconic black players in the domestic game, he won five full caps for England and was PFA Young Player of the Year in 1978–79.

Andy Reid (Born: Urmston, Lancashire, 4 July 1962. Died: October 2017.) Andy Reid was a committed and uncompromising central defender who was on Everton's books as a youngster before dropping into non-league football. A prominent figure with Altrincham after signing in the summer of 1989, he later moved back into senior football for an 18-month spell with Bury. He subsequently returned to Altrincham with whom he was capped for the England Semi Professional team.

Jimmy Reid (Born: Dundee, 14 December 1935. Died: Dundee, 9 October 2017.) Jimmy Reid was a skilful inside-forward who progressed from Dundee St Joseph's to sign for Dundee United in March 1955. His goalscoring exploits at Tannadice earned him a move south to Bury and Stockport County but he never really established himself in England. Jimmy later returned to Scotland to conclude his career with spells at East Fife, Arbroath and Brechin City.

Felix Reilly (Born: Wallyford, East Lothian, 12 September 1933. Died: Comrie, Perthshire, 2 January 2018.) Felix Reilly was signed as a winger by Dunfermline in February 1954 but was quickly converted to inside-forward. He assisted the Pars to promotion from the Second Division in 1954–55 and in February 1957 he was capped for Scotland U23s against England. Spells with Dundee, East Fife and Portsmouth followed before he moved south in March 1960 to sign for Bradford Park Avenue. Bradford won promotion from the Fourth Division in 1960–61 but he left soon afterwards to wind down his senior career with a spell at Crewe Alexandra. He was the younger brother of Terry Reilly (Bradford PA and Dunfermline)

Alex Rennie (Born: Falkirk, 27 September 1948. Died: Denny, Falkirk, 4 March 2018.) Alex Rennie was a defender who joined the senior ranks with Rangers as a 17-year-old. His playing career was slow to develop and he was unable to progress beyond the reserves at Ibrox, while a move to Stirling Albion was brief and unsuccessful, although he did make his debut in senior football. However, after signing for St Johnstone in October 1967 he became a regular first-team player, making over 200 appearances for the Perth club. He was released at the end of the 1974–75 season and signed for Dundee United, where he stayed for three years before an eye injury ended his career. He subsequently turned to coaching and then management with St Johnstone (April 1980 to May 1985) and Stenhousemuir (October 1987 to April 1989). In 1982–83 he won the First Division title (second tier) with St Johnstone.

Brian Riley (Born: Bolton, 14 September 1937. Died: Great Lever, Lancashire, 19 October 2017.) Brian Riley spent almost five years as a professional with Bolton Wanderers in the late 1950s but was restricted to just eight first-team appearances on the left wing. He moved on to non-league football, firstly with Weymouth and then with Buxton where his career was ended by an injury.

Alan Rodgerson (Born: Easington, 19 March 1939. Died: Hereford, 17 May 2018.) Alan Rodgerson was an inside-forward who spent five seasons on the books of Middlesbrough after signing as a professional in May 1956, and scored twice on his first-team debut at Rotherham. However, almost all of his 14 senior appearances came in the 1958–59 season and he subsequently played for several years in the Southern League with Hereford United, Gloucester City and Cheltenham Town. His son Ian played senior football for Hereford United, Cardiff City, Birmingham City and Sunderland.

Andy Rowland (Born: Taunton, 1 October 1965. Died: 20 July 2017.) Andy Rowland gained representative honours for England Schools U18s and after completing his education he played for Exmouth Town before joining Southampton in November 1989. He featured regularly for the Saints' reserves in the Football Combination before signing for Torquay United towards the end of the 1990–91 season and went on to feature as a substitute in the Gulls' Division Four play-off success against Blackpool in May 1991. He stayed another season at Plainmoor and soon after leaving moved to live in the Netherlands. His early death was due to Motor Neurone Disease.

Duncan Russell (Born: London, 12 March 1958. Died: Derby, 18 August 2017.) Duncan Russell was a coach at a number of clubs including Derby County, Walsall, Wolverhampton Wanderers, MK Dons and Blackburn Rovers before being appointed assistant manager to David Holdsworth at Mansfield Town in May 2010. In November 2010 he became caretaker manager following the departure of Holdsworth and the following month was appointed manager until the end of the season. His final match was the FA Trophy final at Wembley when the Stags were defeated by Darlington and he left Field Mill in May 2011. He was later appointed manager of Hucknall Town but left the club after just a few weeks.

Eddie Russell (Born: Cranwell, Lincolnshire, 15 July 1928. Died: Lanivet, Cornwall, 8 November 2017.) Eddie Russell was a tall, constructive wing-half who made his first-team debut for Wolverhampton Wanderers at the age of 20 but although he toured North America with an FA representative squad in the summer of 1950 he struggled to establish himself at Molineux. Towards the end of 1951 he was sold to Middlesbrough where he was appointed as captain of the side. However, from the autumn of 1953 he commenced a training course to qualify as a PE teacher at Loughborough College

and this led to a return to the Midlands as he signed for Leicester City. In his first season at Filbert Street he helped the Foxes win the Division Two title, staying with the club for five seasons before ending his career with Notts County.

Fred Rycraft (Born: Southall, 29 August 1939. Died: 26 September 2017.) Goalkeeper Fred Rycraft played in a pre-season public practice match for Brentford in August 1958, but it was a further 12 months before he signed for the Bees. He was mostly a reserve during his time at Griffin Park, making a total of 38 first-team appearances, all in the 1962–63 and 1963–64 seasons. In the summer of 1962 he had toured South East Asia with a British Army representative side.

Stefano Salvatori (Born: Rome, 29 December 1967. Died: Australia, 31 October 2017.) Stefano Salvatori was a powerful midfield player who developed with AC Milan. However, he was unable to establish himself in the team and after a series of loan spells moved on to Fiorentina in December 1990 and then went on to feature for SPAL and Atalanta. Shortly after the start of the 1996–97 season he signed for Heart of Midlothian where he became an influential figure, assisting them to a 2-1 victory over Rangers in the Scottish Cup final of 1998, the club's first success in the competition since 1956. Stefano wound down his playing career in the lower divisions in Italy, then switched to coaching firstly in Italy and then in Australia.

Jlloyd Samuel (Born: San Fernando, Trinidad & Tobago, 29 March 1981. Died: High Legh, Cheshire, 15 May 2018.) Jlloyd Samuel was a powerful and athletic defender who was best employed at left-back or as a left-wing-back. A product of the East London junior club Senrab, he was attached to Charlton Athletic academy when Aston Villa signed him as a 17-year-old. Within a year he had made his Premier League debut and he went on to play over 150 times for Villa. In the summer of 2007 he moved on to Bolton Wanderers but after a couple of seasons of first-team football he fell out of favour. He subsequently played in Iran with Esteghlal and Paykan before retiring from senior football. Capped at several levels up to U21s by England, he also made two appearances for Trinidad & Tobago. His tragically early death was the result of a road traffic accident.

Derek Saunders (Born: Ware, 6 January 1928. Died: March 2018.) Wing-half Derek Saunders made his name in amateur football, captaining the Walthamstow Avenue team that won the FA Amateur Cup in 1952 and gaining representative honours for England Amateurs and the Great Britain Olympic side. In the summer of 1953 he signed professional forms for Chelsea and was soon a fixture in the line-up. He was an ever-present in 1954–55 when the Blues won the Football League title for the first time and in total made over 200 senior appearances for the club. He also featured for the London FA team in the Inter Cities Fairs Cup.

Hans Schäfer (Born: Cologne, West Germany, 19 October 1927. Died: Cologne , Germany, 7 November 2017.) Hans Schäfer was an outside-left who was one of only two surviving members of the West Germany team that defeated Hungary to win the 1954 World Cup. He went on to feature in both the 1958 and 1962 World Cup finals and captained his country on a number of occasions. He spent his senior career with his home town club 1. FC Köln with whom he won the German championship in 1962 and 1964 and was German Footballer of the Year in 1963.

Dick Scott (Born: Thetford, 26 October 1941. Died: 11 February 2018.) Dick Scott was a wing-half and occasional centre-forward who was still a teenager when he made his debut for Norwich City in April 1961. He went on to appear for the Canaries in the 1961–62 Football League Cup final when they defeated Rochdale over two legs to win the trophy but then lost his place in the side. He was a regular for Cardiff City in 1963–64 and for Scunthorpe the following season before concluding his senior career with Lincoln City.

Joe Scott (Born: Fatfield, County Durham, 9 January 1930. Died: 30 January 2018.) As a youngster Joe Scott was on the books of Newcastle United without making the first team. He dropped into non-league football later, joining Luton Town from Spennymoor United in February 1952. Although he made little impact at Kenilworth Road, he enjoyed three good seasons with Middlesbrough, for whom he scored 30 goals in exactly 99 first-team appearances. He went on to conclude his career in senior football with spells at Hartlepools United and York City, taking his tally of senior games to just short of 200.

Nigel Sims (Born: Coton-in-the Elms, Derbyshire, 9 August 1931. Died: Gorseinon, Swansea, 6 January 2018.) Goalkeeper Nigel Sims was an amateur on the books of Wolverhampton Wanderers, progressing to a professional contract on reaching the age of 17. He spent eight seasons at Wolves as understudy to Bert Williams before signing for local rivals Aston Villa. In his first full season at Villa Park he gained an FA Cup winners' medal, while in 1960–61 he was a near ever-present in the team that won the Second Division title. He went on to make over 300 appearances and in 1958 was the first winner of the club's player of the season award (the Terrace Trophy) before winding down his career with spells at Toronto City and Peterborough United. He made two appearances for the Football League representative XI.

Raymond Smith (Born: Evenwood, County Durham, 14 April 1929. Died: 21 June 2017.) Wing-half Ray Smith had a seven-year spell with Luton Town in the 1950s but was mostly a reserve during his time at Kenilworth Road. After dropping down a couple of divisions to play for Southend United he featured regularly in the 1957–58 season but thereafter was mostly a back-up player. He concluded his career in the Southern League with Hastings United.

Zdeněk Šreiner (Born: Ostrava, 2 June 1954. Died: 28 November 2017.) Zdeněk Šreiner was a midfielder who spent over a decade with Baník Ostrava, winning the Czechoslovakia League title in 1979–80 and 1980–81. He was a member of the Czechoslovakia squad that won the Gold Medal in the 1980 Moscow Olympic Games. He played in both the quarter-finals and semi-finals (when he scored) but was an unused substitute in the final against East Germany. He later concluded his career with spells at AS Beauvais (France) and VSE St Pölten (Austria).

Arthur Stewart (Born: Ballymena, 13 January 1942. Died: 3 March 2018.) Arthur Stewart developed as a wing-half in the Irish League with Ballymena United and Glentoran with whom he won the Irish League title twice and the Irish Cup on one occasion. In December 1967 he joined Brian Clough's Derby County and was a regular in his first season, but thereafter mostly a reserve. He returned to Ballymena in the summer of 1970 and went on to spend five years as the club's player-manager. Arthur won seven full caps for Northern Ireland and also appeared in amateur and youth internationals as well as featuring for the Irish League representative side. He was Ulster Footballer of the Year in 1974.

Ian Stewart (Died: Forfar, 22 July 2017.) Ian Stewart was a wing-half who joined Forfar Athletic from local Junior outfit Forfar Celtic in June 1953 and went on to become a regular in the line-up for a run of four seasons. In total he made over 150 competitive appearances for the Station Park club before concluding his career with a season at Brechin City.

Jimmy Stormont (Born: 2 March 1934. Died: Newcastle, December 2017.) Jimmy Stormont was a versatile attacking player who played in the Juniors with Brechin Victoria and Arbroath Vics before stepping up to senior football in December 1955 when he signed for Arbroath. He made just a handful of first-team appearances during his brief stay with the Red Lichties but went on to enjoy three seasons of regular first-team football with Brechin City, making just short of 100 senior appearances and featuring at right-half in the team that lost to Rangers in the League Cup semi-final in September 1957.

Archie Styles (Born: Smethwick, 29 October 1939. Died: 9 January 2018.) Wing-half Archie Styles broke into the West Bromwich Albion line-up at the age of 18 but this proved to be his only senior appearance for the Baggies. In March 1960 he moved on to Wrexham, where gained further experience of senior football before switching to non-league football with Hereford United for the 1961–62 season. He was later player-coach of Kidderminster Harriers and Stourbridge for several seasons.

Rod Taylor (Born: Corfe Castle, 9 September 1943. Died: Poole, 16 April 2018.) Rod Taylor was a combative wing-half who signed professional forms for Portsmouth at the age of 17, but it was not until he moved to Gillingham in July 1963 that he gained experience of first-team football. He was only a fringe player with the Gills but fared much better after a switch to Bournemouth where he featured regularly in the 1966–67 season before leaving senior football.

Jackie Teasdale (Born: Rossington, 15 March 1929. Died: 2018.) Jackie Teasdale was a hard-tackling wing-half who signed for Doncaster Rovers in October 1949 but it was not until the 1953–54 season that he won a regular place in the line-up. He made over 100 senior appearances during his time with Rovers and toured South Africa with an FA XI in the summer of 1956. However, he suffered a serious knee injury during the tour and this effectively ended his playing career.

Dionatan Teixeira (Born: Londrina, Brazil, 24 July 1992. Died: Londrina, Brazil, 5 November 2017.) Dionatan Teixeira was a central defender who developed in Europe with Slovakian clubs MFK Košice and Dukla Banská Bystrica. In the summer of 2014 he signed for Stoke City, but managed just a couple of appearances from the bench for the Premier League club although he played a number of games on loan for Fleetwood Town in League One during the 2015–16 campaign. He was released by Stoke during the January 2017 transfer window and signed for Moldovan club FC Sheriff Tiraspol, assisting them to the national league title for 2016–17. His early death was a result of suffering a heart attack.

Ken Turner (Born: Great Houghton, Yorkshire, 22 April 1941. Died: Barnsley, 17 August 2017.) Ken Turner was a left-back who signed for Huddersfield Town in October 1958. He received few opportunities at Leeds Road, but featured regularly for both Shrewsbury Town and York City, taking his total of Football League appearances beyond the 150-mark. He subsequently signed for League of Ireland club Sligo Rovers where he became player-manager in 1969 and led the team to the 1970 FAI Cup final.

Bob Turpie (Born: Hampstead, 13 November 1949. Died: Nuneaton, 10 April 2018.) Bob Turpie was an apprentice with Queens Park Rangers, progressing to a full contract at the age of 18. He made two senior appearances during his time at Loftus Road, then spent a couple of seasons with Peterborough United, featuring fairly regularly during 1970–71. He subsequently signed for Nuneaton Borough where he became something of a legendary striker before eventually ending his career with AP Leamington.

Wayne Tutty (Born: Oxford, 18 June 1963. Died: Oxfordshire, 1 October 2017.) Wayne Tutty joined Oxford United a youngster but was released at the end of his apprenticeship and signed for Banbury United. Later he joined Reading, initially on a non-contract basis, where he made 17 senior appearances, mostly in midfield.

Ian Twitchin (Born: Teignmouth, 22 January 1952. Died: 3 December 2017.) Ian Twitchin completed an apprenticeship with Torquay United and signed professional forms for them at the age of 18. The Gulls proved to be his only senior club and he went on to become one of only five players to make more than 400 appearances for them in a career that spanned more than a decade. He made his debut on the right wing towards the end of the 1969–70 season, but eventually settled into the right-back position and was a regular in the line-up for most of the 1970s.

Jim Upton (Born: Coatbridge, 3 June 1940. Died: Cardiff, 24 November 2017.) Jim Upton was a full-back who signed for Celtic from Junior club St Roch in November 1959. He was only a reserve during two seasons at Parkhead and then spent the 1961–62 season with Southern League club Tonbridge. After a spell back in Scotland he signed for Cardiff City and made seven first-team appearances in the first half of 1963–64 before returning to non-league football once more with Bath City.

Arnold Walker (Born: Haltwhistle, Northumberland, 23 December 1932. Died: Grimoldby, Lincolnshire, 25 December 2017.) Wing-half Arnold Walker joined Grimsby Town from Scunthorpe junior football in May 1950 and was on the Mariners' books for eight seasons. He played in a total of 71 senior games but it was only in 1953–54 that he was a regular in the side. He concluded his career with a season at Walsall before signing for Midland League club Gainsborough Trinity.

Ron Walker (Born: Sheffield, 4 February 1932. Died: 29 October 2017.) Ron Walker was on Sunderland's books as an amateur before signing for Doncaster Rovers in the summer of 1950. Featuring mostly on the left wing or at inside-left, he went on to make over 250 appearances for Rovers and rarely missed a match between August 1957 and December 1960. He subsequently moved to Southern League Bath City where he featured regularly in the first half of the 1960s.

Joe Walters (Born: 10 February 1935. Died: 19 July 2017.) Joe Walters was a wing-half recruited by Clyde from Glasgow Perthshire during the 1955–56 season. He helped the Bully Wee win the Second Division title in 1956–57 and 12 months later appeared at right-half as Clyde defeated Hibernian to win the Scottish Cup final. A broken leg suffered playing for the Scottish League representative XI in September 1960 led to a lengthy time out but he returned to assist Clyde to a second Division Two title in 1961–62. He later played for Albion Rovers, Ards and Stenhousemuir before leaving senior football.

Ralph Wetton (Born: Rowlands Gill, County Durham, 6 June 1927. Died: Edmonton, North London, 2 June 2017.) Ralph Wetton was a tall, clever, ball-playing wing-half who signed for Tottenham Hotspur in August 1950. However, in five seasons at White Hart Lane he was mostly a deputy to the likes of Ron Burgess and Bill Nicholson. He featured regularly in the 1955–56 season for Plymouth Argyle but was then out of favour after the club were relegated and he moved on to Aldershot before he concluded his senior career.

Jeff Whalley (Born: Rossendale, 8 February 1952. Died: Blackburn, 23 February 2018.) Jeff Whalley was an apprentice with Blackburn Rovers before signing professional terms at the age of 18. A midfield player he was only ever on the fringes of the first team and made just three senior appearances during his time at Ewood Park. He subsequently played in Australia for South Sydney Croatia and more locally with Accrington Stanley, Great Harwood and Colne.

Jim White (Born: Parkstone, Dorset, 13 June 1942. Died: 24 July 2017.) Jim White became Bournemouth's youngest ever Football League player at the age of 15 when he turned out against Port Vale in April 1958. However he made no further appearances for the Cherries before signing for Portsmouth. It was not until moving on to Gillingham in the summer of 1963 that he experienced regular first-team football before he returned to Dean Court for a second spell. He was a near ever-present over four seasons before joining Cambridge United as player-coach during their first season in the Football League.

Ray Wilkins, MBE (Born: Hillingdon, 14 September 1956. Died: Tooting, 4 April 2018.) Ray Wilkins was one of the finest English players of the last 40 years and enjoyed a glittering career at home and also in Italy and Scotland. An intelligent central midfield player who was adept at maintaining control of the ball when under pressure, he was nicknamed 'The Crab' during his time at Manchester United for his tendency to play the safe option of the square ball. Ray started out as an apprentice with Chelsea and after signing professional forms quickly became a key figure in the side, featuring as an ever-present in the team that won promotion from Division Two in 1976–77. When Chelsea were relegated again at the end of the 1978–79 campaign he was sold to Manchester United for what was a club record fee. However, the only success gained at Old Trafford was an FA Cup winners' medal in 1983. He moved on to Serie A, spending three seasons with AC Milan, then after a brief association with Paris Saint-Germain he signed for Rangers in November 1987, winning two Scottish League titles and a League Cup during his time at Ibrox. A lengthy spell with Queens Park Rangers followed (during which there was the briefest of stays at Crystal Palace) before he concluded his playing career with cameo appearances at Wycombe, Hibernian, Millwall and Leyton Orient. He won 84 caps for England between 1976 and 1986, captaining the side on ten occasions. He later had spells as manager of Queens Park Rangers and Fulham and coached a number of clubs, notably Chelsea. Ray was the son of George and brother of Graham, Dean and Stephen, all of whom played in the Football League.

Ray Wilkins (Born: Church Gresley, 16 August 1928. Died: Derby, 3 March 2018.) Ray Wilkins was a centre-forward who signed as a professional for Derby County in January 1950 after completing a spell of National Service. He scored on his second appearance for the Rams at Molineux and although mostly a back-up player he had a useful scoring record when selected. He moved on to Boston United and in December 1954 was one of six former Derby players who

turned out for the Pilgrims in an FA Cup tie at the Baseball Ground. Boston won 6-1 with Ray scoring twice. He made a brief return to senior football with Wrexham later in the 1950s and then played in non-league football for a number of clubs including Oswestry Town and Macclesfield Town.

Derek Wilkinson (Born: Stalybridge, 4 June 1935. Died: 13 September 2017.) Derek Wilkinson was a pacy winger who signed for Sheffield Wednesday from Stalybridge junior football and went on to make over 200 first-team appearances for the Owls. He established himself in the line-up from November 1957 and was a near ever-present in the team that won the Second Division title in 1958–59, when he also made two appearances for the Football League representative XI.

Barrie Williams (Born: Carmarthen, 6 January 1939. Died: Spain, 23 April 2018.) Barrie Williams was best known as manager of Sutton United, leading the team to FA Cup success in the 1980s. In 1987–88 his team knocked out Aldershot and Peterborough United before going out to Middlesbrough in a third round replay, while the following season they reached the fourth round after eliminating holders Coventry City in a historic victory. He left Sutton in 1989 and after spell out of the game was briefly manager of the England women's team in 1991, later also having a spell as manager of Hendon.

Gordon Wills (Born: West Bromwich, 24 April 1934. Died: 10 January 2018.) Gordon Wills was an outside-left who was on the books of Wolverhampton Wanderers as a youngster but was unable to break into the first team. Moving on to Notts County in the summer of 1953 he established himself in the line-up in the 1954–55 season. He went on to forge a reputation as a versatile forward and in 1956–57 led the scoring charts for County. He continued to feature regularly during a four-year spell at Leicester City although he missed out on a place in the 1961 FA Cup final team after being injured in the semi-final against Sheffield United. He eventually concluded his senior career at Walsall having made exactly 300 Football League appearances.

Billy Wilson (Born: Seaton Delaval, Northumberland, 10 July 1946. Died: 22 February 2018.) Full-back Billy Wilson joined Blackburn Rovers from North East club New Hartley Juniors and became a regular in the line-up from the 1965–66 season. Shortly after Rovers were relegated to the old Third Division he signed for Portsmouth where he remained until retiring from the game. He made over 450 senior appearances during his career and in 2015 was chosen for a place in the Pompey Hall of Fame.

Paul Wilson (Born: Bangalore, India, 23 November 1950. Died: 18 September 2017.) Paul Wilson was born in India but raised in Glasgow and went on to become the only non-white player to appear for the Scotland international team in the twentieth century. He joined Celtic on leaving school and went on to spend a decade at Parkhead making over 200 first-team appearances. His best season was 1974–75 when he played and scored in four cup finals at Hampden (Drybrough, League Cup, Scottish Cup and Glasgow Cup) and also won his only cap for Scotland when he came off the bench for the final 15 minutes of the European Championship qualifying tie against Spain in February 1975. Paul went on to play for Motherwell and Partick then came out of retirement to play for Blantyre Celtic, winning a Scottish Junior cap.

Ray Wilson, MBE (Born: Shirebrook, 17 December 1934. Died: Huddersfield, 15 May 2018.) Ray Wilson was converted from half-back to the left-back position by Huddersfield Town manager Bill Shankly and never looked back in his career. He became a fixture in the Terriers' line-up from the 1957–58 season and in April 1960 he made his debut for England against Scotland at Hampden. Although playing in the Second Division at Leeds Road he was justifiably recognised as the best full-back in the country, offering pace and mobility in the position, both relatively unusual characteristics in the early 1960s. In the summer of 1964 he was sold to Everton and two years later there followed an exceptional summer when he won the FA Cup with the Toffees and was a key member of the England team that lifted the World Cup for the first time in history. There followed a second FA Cup final appearance in 1968, with Everton on the losing side this time, before he wound down his playing career with spells at Oldham Athletic and Bradford City. In total he won 63 full caps for England between 1960 and 1968.

Ken Wimshurst (Born: South Shields, 23 March 1938. Died: Spain, 6 July 2017.) Wing-half Ken Wimshurst was on Newcastle United's books as a youngster before signing for Gateshead for whom he featured in their final season of League football. After an unsuccessful time at Wolverhampton Wanderers he moved on to Southampton where he made over 150 appearances. A player with good passing skills and vision, he contributed to the Saints' success in reaching the top flight in 1965–66 before joining Bristol City where he spent five seasons as a player and remained on the coaching staff until 1981.

Jim Witheford (Born: Ecclesall, Sheffield, 16 April 1930. Died: Launceston, Tasmania, 1 January 2018.) Jim Witheford was a Sheffield PE teacher playing on the wing for Norton Woodseats in the Yorkshire League before joining Chesterfield on amateur forms in December 1953. He made nine Football League appearances for the Spireites and subsequently had a very brief association with Grantham. In 1965 he emigrated to Australia where he appeared for Launceston United and in 1971 had the distinction of scoring 10 goals in a game for the club against Launceston Croatia.

Alan Withers (Born: Bulwell, Nottinghamshire, 20 October 1930. Died: 29 November 2017.) Alan Withers signed for Blackpool in the summer of 1949 and after doing well with the Central League team he stepped up to make a sensational debut at inside-left against Huddersfield Town in November 1950, scoring a hat-trick in the first half of the game. He netted twice more in his next three appearances but rarely featured after that and moved on to Lincoln City in February 1955. He featured on the left wing at Sincil Bank and was a member of the team that won the last six games of the 1957–58 season to avoid relegation from the old Division Two in dramatic style. He later returned to his home town, assisting Notts County to promotion from the Fourth Division in 1959.

Allen Wood (Born: Newport, South Wales, 13 January 1941. Died: 2018.) Allen Wood was a centre-half who won amateur international honours for Wales while playing for Lovell's Athletic. In August 1962 he signed for Bristol Rovers, playing a solitary senior game as an amateur before signing professional forms. He moved to the Southern League with Merthyr Tydfil before making a comeback to the senior game when he signed for Newport County in the summer of 1967. He went on to make over 150 appearances for County and was later involved in coaching at the club as well as serving as chairman of the former players' association.

Wilson Wood (Born: Whitburn, West Lothian, 25 January 1943. Died: 2017.) After a brief spell on the books of Newcastle United, Wilson Wood joined Rangers as an 18-year-old, eventually breaking through to win a regular first-team place at left-half in the 1964–65 season, when he also helped the Ibrox club win the League Cup final. Later he had two seasons as a regular with Dundee United before concluding his career with spells at Heart of Midlothian and Raith Rovers.

John Worsdale (Born: Stoke-on-Trent, 29 October 1948. Died: Stoke-on-Trent, 22 September 2017.) John Worsdale was a pacy winger who captained the Stoke City team that won the 1963 English Schools FA title before joining his local club as an apprentice. He was restricted to just four first-team games before he moved to Lincoln City on a free transfer in May 1971. He spent three seasons at Sincil Bank, making over 70 senior appearances, but was released in the summer of 1974 and finished his playing career with spells at Worksop Town, Gainsboro

Ian Nannestad, Soccer History Magazine
www.soccer-history.co.uk

THE FOOTBALL RECORDS

BRITISH FOOTBALL RECORDS

ALL-TIME PREMIER LEAGUE CHAMPIONSHIP SEASONS ON POINTS AVERAGE

	Team	Season	P	W	D	L	F	A	Pts	Pts Av
1	Manchester C	2017–18	38	32	4	2	106	79	100	2.63
2	Chelsea	2004–05	38	29	8	1	72	15	95	2.50
3	Chelsea	2016–17	38	30	3	5	85	33	93	2.45
4	Manchester U	1999–2000	38	28	7	3	97	45	91	2.39
5	Chelsea	2005–06	38	29	4	5	72	22	91	2.39
6	Arsenal	2003–04	38	26	12	0	73	26	90	2.36
	Manchester U	2008–09	38	28	6	4	68	24	90	2.36
8	Manchester C	2011–12	38	28	5	5	93	29	89	2.34
	Manchester U	2006–07	38	28	5	5	83	27	89	2.34
	Manchester U	2012–13	38	28	5	5	86	43	89	2.34
11	Arsenal	2001–02	38	26	9	3	79	36	87	2.28
	Manchester U	2007–08	38	27	6	5	80	22	87	2.28
	Chelsea	2014–15	38	26	9	3	73	32	87	2.28
14	Chelsea	2009–10	38	27	5	6	103	32	86	2.26
	Manchester C	2013–14	38	27	5	6	102	37	86	2.26
16	Manchester U	1993–94	42	27	11	4	80	38	92	2.19
17	Manchester U	2002–03	38	25	8	5	74	34	83	2.18
18	Manchester U	1995–96	38	25	7	6	73	35	82	2.15
19	Leicester C	2015–16	38	23	12	3	68	36	81	2.13
20	Blackburn R	1994–95	42	27	8	7	80	39	89	2.11
21	Manchester U	2000–01	38	24	8	6	79	31	80	2.10
	Manchester U	2010–11	38	23	11	4	78	37	80	2.10
23	Manchester U	1998–99	38	22	13	3	80	37	79	2.07
24	Arsenal	1997–98	38	23	9	6	68	33	78	2.05
25	Manchester U	1992–93	42	24	12	6	67	31	84	2.00
26	Manchester U	1996–97	38	21	12	5	76	44	75	1.97

PREMIER LEAGUE EVER-PRESENT CLUBS

	P	W	D	L	F	A	Pts
Manchester U	1000	629	215	156	1924	876	2102
Arsenal	1000	544	253	203	1772	963	1885
Chelsea	1000	537	248	215	1707	965	1859
Liverpool	1000	499	255	246	1685	1024	1752
Tottenham H	1000	423	255	322	1480	1267	1524
Everton	1000	362	287	351	1303	1265	1373

TOP TEN PREMIER LEAGUE APPEARANCES

1	Barry, Gareth	653	6	Heskey, Emile	516
2	Giggs, Ryan	632	7	Schwarzer, Mark	514
3	Lampard, Frank	609	8	Carragher, Jamie	508
4	James, David	572	9	Neville, Phil	505
5	Speed, Gary	535	10=	Ferdinand, Rio and Gerrard, Steven	504

TOP TEN PREMIER LEAGUE GOALSCORERS

1	Shearer, Alan	260	6	Fowler, Robbie	163
2	Rooney, Wayne	208	7	Defoe, Jermain	162
3	Cole, Andrew	187	8	Owen, Michael	150
4	Lampard, Frank	177	9	Ferdinand, Les	149
5	Henry, Thierry	175	10	Sheringham, Teddy	146

SCOTTISH PREMIER LEAGUE SINCE 1998–99

	P	W	D	L	F	A	Pts
Celtic	756	556	115	85	1762	576	1783
Rangers	604	404	110	90	1255	512	1312
Aberdeen	756	299	173	284	953	976	1070
Hearts	718	281	181	256	931	866	1009
Motherwell	756	265	164	327	946	1143	959
Kilmarnock	756	245	193	318	900	1103	928
Dundee U	680	214	184	282	842	1021	823
Hibernian	606	209	158	239	805	858	785

Rangers deducted 10 pts in 2011–12; Hearts deducted 15 pts in 2013–14; Dundee U deducted 3 pts in 2015–16.

DOMESTIC LANDMARKS 2017–18

AUGUST 2017

4 Bradley Johnson scored the first league goal of the season in the 11th minute against Sunderland at the Stadium of Light. The black cats equalised in the 42nd minute with a penalty from Lewis Grabban and the match finished 1-1.

15 The Premier League became 25 years old.

21 Everton's Wayne Rooney became only the second player to score 200 goals in the Premier League. He scored the first goal in the 1-1 draw with Manchester City at the Etihad Stadium after 35 minutes. Raheem Sterling equalised with only 11 minutes remaining. The only other player to have reached 200 goals in the Premier League is Alan Shearer (260).

SEPTEMBER 2017

25 Gareth Barry broke the all-time Premier League appearance record in his 633rd game, a 2-0 defeat to Arsenal at the Emirates with two goals from Alexandre Lacazette spoiling the celebrations. He overtook Ryan Giggs' total of 632.

OCTOBER 2017

5 England qualified for the World Cup in Russia. Harry Kane's late strike in the Group F qualifier against Slovenia helped England through. Kane's 94th minute winner was his 11th international goal in 22 appearances.

17 Liverpool broke their record away victory in Europe with a 7-0 victory over Maribor at the Stadion Ljudski in Champions League Group E. Goals from Firmino (2), Salah (2), Coutinho, Oxlade-Chamberlain and Alexander-Arnold surpassed 5-0 wins against Icelandic club Reykjavik in 1964 and Irish club Crusaders in 1975.

NOVEMBER 2017

1 Sergio Aguero became Manchester City's all-time top scorer after netting his 178th goal for the club in the 4-2 away victory over Napoli in the Group F Champions League match. City came from behind to book their place in the knockout stage of the competition.

9 Northern Ireland's Steven Davis won his 100th cap for his county in the 0-1 defeat to Switzerland in the World Cup Qualifying play-off at Windsor Park.

11 Wisbech Town's goalkeeper Paul Bastock overtook Peter Shilton's all-time appearance record. The 47-year-old made his 1,250th appearance playing for away to Thetford Town in the FA Vase second round. His side managed a comfortable 4-1 victory.

DECEMBER 2017

31 Arsene Wenger broke the all-time Premier League record by managing in 811 games. He surpassed Alex Ferguson's total of 810 matches in the 1-1 draw with West Bromwich Albion at the Hawthorns. An own goal by James McClean looked to have given Arsenal the win, but a late Jay Rodriguez penalty brought the Baggies level.

JANUARY 2018

8 The FA Cup third-round tie between Brighton & Hove Albion and Crystal Palace became the first competitive British VAR (video assisted referee) match. Neil Swarbrick was the video referee assisted by Peter Kirkup while Andre Marriner was the match referee. Marriner did not need to call on the VAR until late in the game when Glenn Murray scored for Brighton and after consultation the goal was awarded. Brighton ran out 2-1 winners.

FEBRUARY 2018

3 Brighton & Hove Albion's game against West Ham United was the 10,000th Premier League match to be played. The Seagulls were 3-1 winners.

4 Harry Kane scored his 100th Premier League goal with a penalty in added time against Liverpool. The match finished 2-2. Kane's 100th goal came in his 141st appearance, only Alan Shearer was quicker to the milestone taking 124 appearances.

MARCH 2018

11 Arsenal goalkeeper Petr Cech became the first keeper to reach 200 clean sheets. Cech saved a Troy Deeney penalty in Arsenal's 3-0 victory with the goals coming from Mustafi, Aubameyang and Mkhitaryan.

23 Gareth Bale became the top goalscorer for Wales with a hat-trick against China. Playing in Ryan Giggs' first game as Wales manager, Bale reached 29 goals in 69 appearances breaking the record of Ian Rush who scored 28 in 26 appearances.

MAY 2018

9 Manchester City broke three Premier League records. The record for most points (97) beat the previous record of 95 set by Chelsea; the record for most league wins in a season with 31 which also beat the previous record of 30 held by Chelsea; and the 3-1 victory over Brighton & Hove Albion also set a new record for the most goals scored in a single season at 105, two more than Chelsea's 103. All of this while still one game to play in the season!

13 Promoted clubs Newcastle United, Brighton & Hove Albion and Huddersfield Town avoided relegation – only the third Premier League season this feat has occurred following 2001–02 and 2011–12.

EUROPEAN CUP AND CHAMPIONS LEAGUE RECORDS

MOST WINS BY CLUB

Real Madrid	13	1956, 1957, 1958, 1959, 1960, 1966, 1998, 2000, 2002, 2014, 2016, 2017, 2018.
AC Milan	7	1963, 1969, 1989, 1990, 1994, 2003, 2007.
Bayern Munich	5	1974, 1975, 1976, 2001, 2013.
Liverpool	5	1977, 1978, 1981, 1984, 2005.
Barcelona	5	1992, 2006, 2009, 2011, 2015.

MOST APPEARANCES IN FINAL
Real Madrid 15; AC Milan 11; Bayern Munich 10

MOST FINAL APPEARANCES PER COUNTRY
Spain 29 (18 wins, 11 defeats)
Italy 28 (12 wins, 16 defeats)
England 20 (12 wins, 8 defeats)
Germany 17 (7 wins, 10 defeats)

MOST CHAMPIONS LEAGUE/EUROPEAN CUP APPEARANCES
171 Iker Casillas (Real Madrid, Porto)
157 Xavi (Barcelona)
157 Cristiano Ronaldo (Manchester U, Real Madrid)
151 Ryan Giggs (Manchester U)
144 Raul (Real Madrid, Schalke)
139 Paolo Maldini (AC Milan)
132 Andreas Iniesta (Barcelona)
131 Clarence Seedorf (Ajax, Real Madrid, Internazionale, AC Milan)
130 Paul Scholes (Manchester U)
128 Roberto Carlos (Internazionale, Real Madrid, Fenerbahce)
127 Xabi Alonso (Real Sociedad, Liverpool, Real Madrid, Bayern Munich)
125 Lionel Messi (Barcelona):
Gianluigi Buffon (Parma, Juventus)

MOST WINS WITH DIFFERENT CLUBS
Clarence Seedorf (Ajax) 1995; (Real Madrid) 1998; (AC Milan) 2003, 2007.

MOST WINNERS MEDALS
6 Francisco Gento (Real Madrid) 1956, 1957, 1958, 1959, 1960, 1966.
5 Alfredo Di Stefano (Real Madrid) 1956, 1957, 1958, 1959, 1960.
5 Jose Maria Zarraga (Real Madrid) 1956, 1957, 1958, 1959, 1960.
5 Paolo Maldini (AC Milan) 1989, 1990, 1994, 2003, 2007.
5 Cristiano Ronaldo (Manchester U, Real Madrid) 2008, 2014, 2016, 2017, 2018

CHAMPIONS LEAGUE BIGGEST WINS
HJK Helsinki 10, Bangor C 0 19.7.2011
Liverpool 8 Besiktas 0 6.11.2007
Real Madrid 8 Malmo 0 8.12.2015

MOST SUCCESSIVE CHAMPIONS LEAGUE APPEARANCES
Real Madrid (Spain) 21 1997–98 to 2017–18.
Manchester U (England) 18: 1996–97 to 2013–14.

MOST SUCCESSIVE EUROPEAN CUP APPEARANCES
Real Madrid (Spain) 15: 1955–56 to 1969–70.

MOST SUCCESSIVE WINS IN THE CHAMPIONS LEAGUE
Barcelona (Spain) 11: 2002–03.

LONGEST UNBEATEN RUN IN THE CHAMPIONS LEAGUE
Manchester U (England) 25: 2007–08 to 2009 (Final).

MOST GOALS OVERALL
121 Cristiano Ronaldo (Manchester U, Real Madrid).
100 Lionel Messi (Barcelona).
71 Raul (Real Madrid, Schalke).
60 Ruud van Nistelrooy (PSV Eindhoven, Manchester U, Real Madrid).
58 Andriy Shevchenko (Dynamo Kyiv, AC Milan, Chelsea, Dynamo Kyiv).
56 Karim Benzema (Lyon, Real Madrid).
51 Thierry Henry (Monaco, Arsenal, Barcelona).
50 Filippo Inzaghi (Juventus, AC Milan).
49 Alfredo Di Stefano (Real Madrid).
49 Zlatan Ibrahimovic (Ajax, Juventus, Internazionale, Barcelona, AC Milan, Paris Saint-Germain).
47 Eusebio (Benfica).
45 Robert Lewandowski (Borussia Dortmund, Bayern Munich.).

MOST GOALS IN CHAMPIONS LEAGUE MATCH
5 Lionel Messi, Barcelona v Bayer Leverkusen (25, 42, 49, 58, 84 mins) (7-1), 7.3.2012.
5 Luiz Adriano, Shaktar Donetsk v BATE (28, 36, 40, 44, 82 (0-7), 21.10.2014.

MOST GOALS IN ONE SEASON
17 Cristiano Ronaldo 2013–14
16 Cristiano Ronaldo 2015–16
15 Cristiano Ronaldo 2017–18
14 Jose Altafini 1962–63
14 Ruud van Nistelrooy 2002–03
14 Lionel Messi 2011–12

MOST GOALS SCORED IN FINALS
7 Alfredo Di Stefano (Real Madrid), 1956 (1), 1957 (1 pen), 1958 (1), 1959 (1), 1960 (3).
7 Ferenc Puskas (Real Madrid), 1960 (4), 1962 (3).

HIGHEST SCORE IN A EUROPEAN CUP MATCH
European Cup
14 KR Reykjavik (Iceland) 2 Feyenoord (Netherlands) 12, *(First Round First Leg 1969–70)*
Champions League
12 Borussia Dortmund 8, Legia Warsaw 4 22.11.2016

HIGHEST AGGREGATE IN A EUROPEAN CUP MATCH
Benfica (Portugal) 18, Dudelange (Luxembourg) 0 8-0 (h), 10-0 (a) *(Preliminary Round 1965–66)*

FASTEST GOALS SCORED IN CHAMPIONS LEAGUE

10.12 sec	Roy Makaay for Bayern Munich v Real Madrid, 7.3.2007.
10.96 sec	Jonas for Valencia v Bayer Leverkusen, 1.11.2011.
20.07 sec	Gilberto Silva for Arsenal at PSV Eindhoven, 25.9.2002.
20.12 sec	Alessandro Del Piero for Juventus at Manchester U, 1.10.1997.

YOUNGEST CHAMPIONS LEAGUE GOALSCORER
Peter Ofori-Quaye for Olympiacos v Rosenborg at 17 years 195 days in 1997–98.

FASTEST HAT-TRICK SCORED IN CHAMPIONS LEAGUE
Bafetimbi Gomis, 8 mins for Lyon in Dinamo Zagreb v Lyon (1-7) 7.12.2011

MOST GOALS BY A GOALKEEPER
Hans-Jorg Butt (for three different clubs)
Hamburg 13.9.2000, Bayer Leverkusen 12.5.2002, Bayern Munich 8.12.2009 – all achieved against Juventus.

LANDMARK GOALS CHAMPIONS LEAGUE
1st Daniel Amokachi, Club Brugge v CSKA Moscow 17 minutes 25.11.1992
1,000th Dmitri Khokhlov, PSV Eindhoven v Benfica 41 minutes 9.12.1998
5,000th Luisao, Benfica v Hapoel Tel Aviv 21 minutes 14.9.2010

HIGHEST SCORING DRAW
Hamburg 4, Juventus 4 13.9.2000
Chelsea 4, Liverpool 4 14.4.2009
Bayer Leverkusen 4, Roma 4 20.10.2015

MOST CLEAN SHEETS
10: Arsenal 2005–06 (995 minutes with two goalkeepers Manuel Almunia 347 minutes and Jens Lehmann 648 minutes).

EUROPEAN CUP AND CHAMPIONS LEAGUE RECORDS – continued

CHAMPIONS LEAGUE ATTENDANCES AND GOALS FROM GROUP STAGES ONWARDS

Season	Attendances	Average	Goals	Games
1992–93	873,251	34,930	56	25
1993–94	1,202,289	44,529	71	27
1994–95	2,328,515	38,172	140	61
1995–96	1,874,316	30,726	159	61
1996–97	2,093,228	34,315	161	61
1997–98	2,868,271	33,744	239	85
1998–99	3,608,331	42,451	238	85
1999–2000	5,490,709	34,973	442	157
2000–01	5,773,486	36,774	449	157
2001–02	5,417,716	34,508	393	157
2002–03	6,461,112	41,154	431	157
2003–04	4,611,214	36,890	309	125
2004–05	4,946,820	39,575	331	125
2005–06	5,291,187	42,330	285	125
2006–07	5,591,463	44,732	309	125
2007–08	5,454,718	43,638	330	125
2008–09	5,003,754	40,030	329	125
2009–10	5,295,708	42,366	320	125
2010–11	5,474,654	43,797	355	125
2011–12	5,225,363	41,803	345	125
2012–13	5,773,366	46,187	368	125
2013–14	5,713,049	45,704	362	125
2014–15	5,207,592	42,685	361	125
2015–16	5,116,690	40,934	347	125
2016–17	5,398,851	43,191	380	125
2017–18	5,744,918	45,959	401	125

HIGHEST AVERAGE ATTENDANCE IN ONE EUROPEAN CUP SEASON
1959–60   50,545 from a total attendance of 2,780,000.

GREATEST COMEBACKS
Werder Bremen beat Anderlecht 5-3 after being three goals down in 33 minutes on 8.12.1993. They scored five goals in 23 second-half minutes.

Deportivo La Coruna beat Paris Saint-Germain 4-3 after being three goals down in 55 minutes on 7.3.2001. They scored four goals in 27 second-half minutes.

Liverpool after being three goals down to AC Milan in the first half on 25.5.2005 in the Champions League Final. They scored three goals in five second-half minutes and won the penalty shoot-out after extra time 3-2.

Liverpool three goals down to FC Basel in 29 minutes on 12.11.2002. They scored three second half goals in 24 minutes to draw 3-3.

MOST SUCCESSFUL MANAGER
Bob Paisley 3 wins, 1977, 1978, 1981 (Liverpool);
Carlo Ancelotti 3 wins, 2002–03, 2006–07 (AC Milan), 2013–14 (Real Madrid).
Zinedine Zidane 3 wins, 2015–16, 2016–17, 2017–18 (Real Madrid).

REINSTATED WINNERS EXCLUDED FROM NEXT COMPETITION
1993 Marseille originally stripped of title. This was rescinded but they were not allowed to compete the following season.

EUROPEAN LANDMARKS 2017–18

SEPTEMBER 2017

20 Borussia Dortmund scored their 3000th goal in the Bundesliga. A 79th minute goal from USA international Christian Pulisic in a 3-0 victory over Hamburg took Dortmund to the milestone. Only Bayern Munich and Werder Bremen have scored more goals in the Bundesliga.

OCTOBER 2017

5 Robert Lewandowski became Poland's all-time leading goalscorer, scoring a hat-trick against Armenia in their Group E World Cup qualifier in Armenia. Two first-half goals took his total to 49 to overtake the record that had stood at 48 for Wlodzimierz Lubanski. A second-half strike brought up 50 goals.

Luka Modric made his 100th international appearance for Croatia in the 1-1 draw with Finland in the Group I World Cup qualifier. A 57th minute opener for Croatia from Mario Mandzukic looked to have won the game until Pyry Soiri equalised in the last minute.

Yossi Benayoun made his 100th international appearance for Israel in the 1-0 victory over Liechtenstein in the Group G World Cup qualifier in Vaduz. Eitan Tibi's 21st minute goal proved to be the winner for Israel.

Arda Turan made his 100th international appearance for Turkey in the 3-0 defeat to Iceland in the Group I qualifier in Eskisehir. Johann Berg Gundmundsson, Birkir Bjarnason and Kari Arnason scored the goals for Iceland.

9 Sergio Busquets made his 100th international appearance for Spain in the 1-0 victory over Israel in the Group G World Cup qualifier. Asier Illarramendi scored the 76th minute winner for Spain.

10 Lionel Messi became the all-time top goalscorer in South American World Cup qualifying. His hat-trick in Argentina's 3-1 victory in Ecuador helped his country qualify for the 2018 World Cup in Russia. His total goals in South American qualifying came to 21 surpassing Hernan Crespo and Luiz Suarez.

NOVEMBER 2017

13 Italy failed to qualify for the World Cup for the first time since 1958. The 0-0 draw with Sweden in Milan meant that they lost 0-1 on aggregate. Goalkeeper Gianluigi Buffon retired from international football.

14 Branislav Ivanovic made his 100th international appearance for Serbia in the 1-1 friendly draw with Korea Republic in Ulsan. Adam Ljajic opened the scoring for Serbia in the 59th minute, but Ja-Cheol Koo equalised with a penalty three minutes later.

22 Zlatan Ibrahimovic became the first player to appear for seven different clubs in the Champions League. He came off the bench for Manchester United in their 1-0 defeat to Basel at St Jakob Park. He had previously lined up for Ajax, Juventus, Inter Milan, Barcelona, AC Milan and Paris Saint-Germain.

MAY 2018

26 Zinedine Zidane became the first manager to win the Champions League in three successive seasons. Real Madrid's 3-1 victory over Liverpool meant that they had won the elite European competition three times in a row – the first time since Bayern Munich between 1974 and 1976.

JUNE 2018

2 Jan Vertonghen became the first player to make 100 international appearances for Belgium in the 0-0 friendly draw with Portugal.

TOP TEN PREMIER LEAGUE AVERAGE ATTENDANCES 2017–18

1	Manchester U	74,975
2	Tottenham H	67,952
3	Arsenal	59,320
4	West Ham U	56,884
5	Manchester C	54,070
6	Liverpool	53,047
7	Newcastle U	51,991
8	Chelsea	41,280
9	Everton	38,773
10	Leicester C	31,559

TOP TEN FOOTBALL LEAGUE AVERAGE ATTENDANCES 2017–18

1	Aston Villa	32,097
2	Leeds U	31,521
3	Wolverhampton W	28,298
4	Sunderland	27,635
5	Derby Co	27,175
6	Sheffield U	26,854
7	Sheffield W	25,995
8	Norwich C	25,785
9	Middlesbrough	25,544
10	Nottingham F	24,680

TOP TEN AVERAGE ATTENDANCES

1	Manchester U	2006–07	75,826
2	Manchester U	2007–08	75,691
3	Manchester U	2012–13	75,530
4	Manchester U	2011–12	75,387
5	Manchester U	2014–15	75,335
6	Manchester U	2008–09	75,308
7	Manchester U	2016–17	75,290
8	Manchester U	2015–16	75,279
9	Manchester U	2013–14	75,207
10	Manchester U	2010–11	75,109

TOP TEN AVERAGE WORLD CUP FINALS CROWDS

1	In USA	1994	68,991
2	In Brazil	2014	52,621
3	In Germany	2006	52,491
4	In Mexico	1970	50,124
5	In South Africa	2010	49,669
6	In West Germany	1974	49,098
7	In England	1966	48,847
8	In Italy	1990	48,388
9	In Brazil	1950	47,511
10	In Russia	2018	47,371

TOP TEN ALL-TIME ENGLAND CAPS

1	Peter Shilton	125
2	Wayne Rooney	119
3	David Beckham	115
4	Steven Gerrard	114
5	Bobby Moore	108
6	Ashley Cole	107
7	Bobby Charlton	106
7	Frank Lampard	106
9	Billy Wright	105
10	Bryan Robson	90

TOP TEN ALL-TIME ENGLAND GOALSCORERS

1	Wayne Rooney	53
2	Bobby Charlton	49
3	Gary Lineker	48
4	Jimmy Greaves	44
5	Michael Owen	40
	Tom Finney	30
6	Nat Lofthouse	30
	Alan Shearer	30
	Vivian Woodward	29
9	Frank Lampard	29

GOALKEEPING RECORDS
(without conceding a goal)

FA PREMIER LEAGUE
Edwin van der Sar (Manchester U) in 1,311 minutes during the 2008–09 season.

FOOTBALL LEAGUE
Steve Death (Reading) 1,103 minutes from 24 March to 18 August 1979.

SCOTTISH PREMIER LEAGUE
Fraser Forster (Celtic) in 1,215 minutes from 6 December 2013 to 25 February 2014.

MOST CLEAN SHEETS IN A SEASON

Petr Cech (Chelsea) 24 2004–05

MOST CLEAN SHEETS OVERALL IN PREMIER LEAGUE

Petr Cech (Chelsea and Arsenal) 201 games.

MOST GOALS FOR IN A SEASON

FA PREMIER LEAGUE		*Goals*	*Games*
2017–18	Manchester C	106	38

FOOTBALL LEAGUE			
Division 4			
1960–61	Peterborough U	134	46

SCOTTISH PREMIER LEAGUE			
2016–17	Celtic	106	38

SCOTTISH LEAGUE			
Division 2			
1937–38	Raith R	142	34

MOST GOALS AGAINST IN A SEASON

FA PREMIER LEAGUE		*Goals*	*Games*
1993–94	Swindon T	100	42

FOOTBALL LEAGUE			
Division 2			
1898–99	Darwen	141	34

SCOTTISH PREMIER LEAGUE			
1999–2000	Aberdeen	83	36
2007–08	Gretna	83	38

SCOTTISH LEAGUE			
Division 2			
1931–32	Edinburgh C	146	38

MOST LEAGUE GOALS IN A SEASON

FA PREMIER LEAGUE		*Goals*	*Games*
1993–94	Andy Cole (Newcastle U)	34	40
1994–95	Alan Shearer (Blackburn R)	34	42
2017–18	Mohamed Salah (Liverpool)	32	38

FOOTBALL LEAGUE			
Division 1			
1927–28	Dixie Dean (Everton)	60	39
Division 2			
1926–27	George Camsell (Middlesbrough)	59	37
Division 3(S)			
1936–37	Joe Payne (Luton T)	55	39
Division 3(N)			
1936–37	Ted Harston (Mansfield T)	55	41
Division 3			
1959–60	Derek Reeves (Southampton)	39	46
Division 4			
1960–61	Terry Bly (Peterborough U)	52	46

FA CUP			
1887–88	Jimmy Ross (Preston NE)	20	8

LEAGUE CUP			
1986–87	Clive Allen (Tottenham H)	12	9

SCOTTISH PREMIER LEAGUE			
2000–01	Henrik Larsson (Celtic)	35	37

SCOTTISH LEAGUE			
Division 1			
1931–32	William McFadyen (Motherwell)	52	34
Division 2			
1927–28	Jim Smith (Ayr U)	66	38

MOST FA CUP FINAL GOALS

Ian Rush (Liverpool) 5: 1986(2), 1989(2), 1992(1)

SCORED IN EVERY PREMIERSHIP GAME

Arsenal 2001–02: 38 matches

FEWEST GOALS FOR IN A SEASON

FA PREMIER LEAGUE		*Goals*	*Games*
2007–08	Derby Co	20	38

FOOTBALL LEAGUE			
Division 2			
1899–1900	Loughborough T	18	34

SCOTTISH PREMIER LEAGUE			
2010–11	St Johnstone	23	38

SCOTTISH LEAGUE			
New Division 1			
1980–81	Stirling Alb	18	39

FEWEST GOALS AGAINST IN A SEASON

FA PREMIER LEAGUE		*Goals*	*Games*
2004–05	Chelsea	15	38

FOOTBALL LEAGUE			
Division 1			
1978–79	Liverpool	16	42

SCOTTISH PREMIER LEAGUE			
2001–02	Celtic	18	38

SCOTTISH LEAGUE			
Division 1			
1913–14	Celtic	14	38

MOST LEAGUE GOALS IN A CAREER

FOOTBALL LEAGUE			
Arthur Rowley	*Goals*	*Games*	*Season*
WBA	4	24	1946–48
Fulham	27	56	1948–50
Leicester C	251	303	1950–58
Shrewsbury T	152	236	1958–65
	434	619	

SCOTTISH LEAGUE			
Jimmy McGrory			
Celtic	1	3	1922–23
Clydebank	13	30	1923–24
Celtic	396	375	1924–38
	410	408	

MOST HAT-TRICKS

Career
37: Dixie Dean (Tranmere R, Everton, Notts Co, England)

Division 1 (one season post-war)
6: Jimmy Greaves (Chelsea), 1960–61

Three for one team in one match
West, Spouncer, Hooper, Nottingham F v Leicester Fosse, Division 1, 21 April 1909
Loasby, Smith, Wells, Northampton T v Walsall, Division 3S, 5 Nov 1927
Bowater, Hoyland, Readman, Mansfield T v Rotherham U, Division 3N, 27 Dec 1932
Barnes, Ambler, Davies, Wrexham v Hartlepools U, Division 4, 3 March 1962
Adcock, Stewart, White, Manchester C v Huddersfield T, Division 2, 7 Nov 1987

MOST CUP GOALS IN A CAREER

FA CUP (pre-Second World War)
Henry Cursham 48 (Notts Co)

FA CUP (post-war)
Ian Rush 43 (Chester, Liverpool)

LEAGUE CUP
Geoff Hurst 49 (West Ham U, Stoke C)
Ian Rush 49 (Chester, Liverpool, Newcastle U)

GOALS PER GAME (Football League to 1991–92)

Goals per game	Division 1		Division 2		Division 3		Division 4		Division 3(S)		Division 3(N)	
	Games	Goals	Games	Goals	Games	Goals	Games	Goals	Games	Goals	Games	Goals
0	2465	0	2665	0	1446	0	1438	0	997	0	803	0
1	5606	5606	5836	5836	3225	3225	3106	3106	2073	2073	1914	1914
2	8275	16550	8609	17218	4569	9138	4441	8882	3314	6628	2939	5878
3	7731	23193	7842	23526	3784	11352	4041	12123	2996	8988	2922	8766
4	6229	24920	5897	23588	2837	11348	2784	11136	2445	9780	2410	9640
5	3752	18755	3634	18170	1566	7830	1506	7530	1554	7770	1599	7995
6	2137	12822	2007	12042	769	4614	786	4716	870	5220	930	5580
7	1092	7644	1001	7007	357	2499	336	2352	451	3157	461	3227
8	542	4336	376	3008	135	1080	143	1144	209	1672	221	1768
9	197	1773	164	1476	64	576	35	315	76	684	102	918
10	83	830	68	680	13	130	8	80	33	330	45	450
11	37	407	19	209	2	22	7	77	15	165	15	165
12	12	144	17	204	1	12	0	0	7	84	8	96
13	4	52	4	52	0	0	0	0	2	26	4	52
14	2	28	1	14	0	0	0	0	0	0	0	0
17	0	0	0	0	0	0	0	0	0	0	1	17
	38164	117060	38140	113030	18768	51826	18631	51461	15042	46577	14374	46466

Extensive research by statisticians has unearthed seven results from the early years of the Football League which differ from the original scores. These are 26 January 1889 Wolverhampton W 5 Everton 0 (not 4-0), 16 March 1889 Notts Co 3 Derby Co 5 (not 2-5), 4 January 1896 Arsenal 5 Loughborough 0 (not 6-0), 28 November 1896 Leicester Fosse 4 Walsall 2 (not 4-1), 21 April 1900 Burslem Port Vale 2 Lincoln C 1 (not 2-0), 25 December 1902 Glossop NE 3 Stockport Co 0 (not 3-1), 26 April 1913 Hull C 2 Leicester C 0 (not 2-1).

GOALS PER GAME (from 1992–93)

Goals per game	Premier		Championship/Div 1		League One/Div 2		League Two/Div 3	
	Games	Goals	Games	Goals	Games	Goals	Games	Goals
0	860	0	1180	0	1115	0	1139	0
1	1849	1849	2679	2679	2690	2690	2735	2735
2	2438	4876	3639	7278	3644	7288	3574	7148
3	2137	6411	3107	9321	3148	9444	3088	9264
4	1502	6008	1984	7936	1999	7996	1890	7560
5	750	3750	1061	5305	1066	5330	998	4990
6	356	2136	475	2850	443	2658	409	2454
7	146	1022	161	1127	173	1211	169	1183
8	64	512	49	392	51	408	52	416
9	18	162	9	81	18	162	19	171
10	5	50	6	60	5	50	6	60
11	1	11	2	22	0	0	3	33
	10126	26787	14352	37051	14352	37237	14082	36014

New Overall Totals (since 1992)		Totals (up to 1991–92)		Complete Overall Totals (since 1888–89)	
Games	52912	Games	143119	Games	196031
Goals	137089	Goals	426420	Goals	563509
Goals per game	2.59		2.98		2.87

A CENTURY OF LEAGUE AND CUP GOALS IN CONSECUTIVE SEASONS

George Camsell	League	Cup	Season
Middlesbrough	59	5	1926–27
(101 goals)	33	4	1927–28

(Camsell's cup goals were all scored in the FA Cup.)

Steve Bull			
Wolverhampton W	34	18	1987–88
(102 goals)	37	13	1988–89

(Bull had 12 in the Sherpa Van Trophy, 3 Littlewoods Cup, 3 FA Cup in 1987–88; 11 Sherpa Van Trophy, 2 Littlewoods Cup in 1988–89.)

PENALTIES

Most in a season (individual)

Division 1	Goals	Season
Francis Lee (Manchester C)	13	1971–72

Also scored 1 in League Cup and 2 in FA Cup.

Most awarded in one game
Five   Crystal Palace (1 scored, 3 missed)
        v Brighton & HA (1 scored), Div 2   1988–89

Most saved in a season
Division 1
Paul Cooper (Ipswich T)   8 (of 10)   1979–80

MOST GOALS IN A GAME

FA PREMIER LEAGUE
4 Mar 1995   Andy Cole (Manchester U)
           5 goals v Ipswich T
19 Sept 1999   Alan Shearer (Newcastle U)
           5 goals v Sheffield W
22 Nov 2009   Jermain Defoe (Tottenham H)
           5 goals v Wigan Ath
27 Nov 2010   Dimitar Berbatov (Manchester U)
           5 goals v Blackburn R
3 Oct 2015   Sergio Aguero (Manchester C)
           5 goals v Newcastle U

FOOTBALL LEAGUE
Division 1
14 Dec 1935   Ted Drake (Arsenal) 7 goals v Aston Villa
Division 2
5 Feb 1955   Tommy Briggs (Blackburn R)
           7 goals v Bristol R
23 Feb 1957   Neville Coleman (Stoke C) 7 goals v
           Lincoln C
Division 3(S)
13 Apr 1936   Joe Payne (Luton T) 10 goals v Bristol R
Division 3(N)
26 Dec 1935   Bunny Bell (Tranmere R)
           9 goals v Oldham Ath
Division 3
24 Apr 1965   Barrie Thomas (Scunthorpe U)
           5 goals v Luton T
20 Nov 1965   Keith East (Swindon T)
           5 goals v Mansfield T
16 Sept 1969   Steve Earle (Fulham) 5 goals v Halifax T
2 Oct 1971   Alf Wood (Shrewsbury T)
           5 goals v Blackburn R
10 Sept 1983   Tony Caldwell (Bolton W)
           5 goals v Walsall
4 May 1987   Andy Jones (Port Vale)
           5 goals v Newport Co
3 Apr 1990   Steve Wilkinson (Mansfield T)
           5 goals v Birmingham C
5 Sept 1998   Giuliano Grazioli (Peterborough U)
           5 goals v Barnet
6 Apr 2002   Lee Jones (Wrexham)
           5 goals v Cambridge U
Division 4
26 Dec 1962   Bert Lister (Oldham Ath)
           6 goals v Southport

FA CUP
20 Nov 1971   Ted MacDougall (Bournemouth)
           9 goals v Margate (*1st Round*)

LEAGUE CUP
25 Oct 1989   Frankie Bunn (Oldham Ath)
           6 goals v Scarborough

SCOTTISH LEAGUE
Premier Division
17 Nov 1984   Paul Sturrock (Dundee U)
           5 goals v Morton
Premier League
23 Aug 1996   Marco Negri (Rangers) 5 goals v
           Dundee U
4 Nov 2000   Kenny Miller (Rangers) 5 goals v
           St Mirren
25 Sept 2004   Kris Boyd (Kilmarnock) 5 goals v
           Dundee U
30 Dec 2009   Kris Boyd (Rangers) 5 goals v
           Dundee U
13 May 2012   Gary Hooper (Celtic) 5 goals v Hearts
Division 1
14 Sept 1928   Jimmy McGrory (Celtic)
           8 goals v Dunfermline Ath
Division 2
1 Oct 1927   Owen McNally (Arthurlie)
           8 goals v Armadale
2 Jan 1930   Jim Dyet (King's Park)
           8 goals v Forfar Ath
18 Apr 1936   John Calder (Morton)
           8 goals v Raith R
20 Aug 1937   Norman Hayward (Raith R)
           8 goals v Brechin C

SCOTTISH CUP
12 Sept 1885   John Petrie (Arbroath)
           13 goals v Bon Accord (*1st Round*)

LONGEST SEQUENCE OF CONSECUTIVE DEFEATS

FOOTBALL LEAGUE	Team	Games
Division 2		
1898–99	Darwen	18

LONGEST UNBEATEN SEQUENCE

FA PREMIER LEAGUE	Team	Games
May 2003–Oct 2004	Arsenal	49
FOOTBALL LEAGUE – League 1		
Jan 2011–Nov 2011	Huddersfield T	43

LONGEST UNBEATEN CUP SEQUENCE

Liverpool	25 rounds	League/Milk Cup	1980–84

LONGEST UNBEATEN SEQUENCE IN A SEASON

FA PREMIER LEAGUE	Team	Games
2003–04	Arsenal	38
FOOTBALL LEAGUE – Division 1		
1920–21	Burnley	30
SCOTTISH PREMIERSHIP		
2016–17	Celtic	38

LONGEST UNBEATEN START TO A SEASON

FA PREMIER LEAGUE	Team	Games
2003–04	Arsenal	38
FOOTBALL LEAGUE – Division 1		
1973–74	Leeds U	29
1987–88	Liverpool	29

LONGEST SEQUENCE WITHOUT A WIN IN A SEASON

FA PREMIER LEAGUE	Team	Games
2007–08	Derby Co	32
FOOTBALL LEAGUE	**Team**	**Games**
Division 2		
1983–84	Cambridge U	31

LONGEST SEQUENCE WITHOUT A WIN FROM SEASON'S START

FOOTBALL LEAGUE	Team	Games
Division 4		
1970–71	Newport Co	25

LONGEST SEQUENCE OF CONSECUTIVE SCORING (individual)

FA PREMIER LEAGUE
Jamie Vardy (Leicester C) 13 in 11 games   2015–16
FOOTBALL LEAGUE RECORD
Tom Phillipson
(Wolverhampton W)   23 in 13 games   1926–27

LONGEST WINNING SEQUENCE

FA PREMIER LEAGUE	Team	Games
2001–02 and 2002–03	Arsenal	14
FOOTBALL LEAGUE – Division 2		
1904–05	Manchester U	14
1905–06	Bristol C	14
1950–51	Preston NE	14
FROM SEASON'S START – Division 3		
1985–86	Reading	13
SCOTTISH PREMIER LEAGUE		
2003–04	Celtic	25

HIGHEST WINS

Highest win in a First-Class Match
(Scottish Cup 1st Round)
Arbroath   36 Bon Accord   0 12 Sept 1885

Highest win in an International Match
England   13 Ireland   0 18 Feb 1882

Highest win in an FA Cup Match
Preston NE   26 Hyde U   0 15 Oct 1887
(1st Round)

Highest win in a League Cup Match
West Ham U   10 Bury   0 25 Oct 1983
(2nd Round, 2nd Leg)
Liverpool   10 Fulham   0 23 Sept 1986
(2nd Round, 1st Leg)

Highest win in an FA Premier League Match
Manchester U   9 Ipswich T   0 4 Mar 1995
Tottenham H   9 Wigan Ath   1 22 Nov 2009

Highest win in a Football League Match
Division 2 – highest home win
Newcastle U   13 Newport Co   0 5 Oct 1946
Division 3(N) – highest home win
Stockport Co   13 Halifax T   0 6 Jan 1934
Division 2 – highest away win
Burslem Port Vale 0 Sheffield U   10 10 Dec 1892

Highest wins in a Scottish League Match
Scottish Premier League – highest home win
Celtic   9 Aberdeen   0 6 Nov 2010
Scottish Division 2 – highest home win
Airdrieonians 15 Dundee Wanderers 1   1 Dec 1894
Scottish Premier League – highest away win
Hamilton A   0 Celtic   8 5 Nov 1988

MOST HOME WINS IN A SEASON

Brentford won all 21 games in Division 3(S), 1929–30

RECORD AWAY WINS IN A SEASON

Doncaster R won 18 of 21 games in Division 3(N), 1946–47

CONSECUTIVE AWAY WINS

FA PREMIER LEAGUE
Chelsea 11 games (2007–08 (3), 2008–09 (8)).
Manchester C 11 games (2016–17 (1), 2017–18 (10))

FOOTBALL LEAGUE
Division 1
Tottenham H 10 games (1959–60 (2), 1960–61 (8))

HIGHEST AGGREGATE SCORES

FA PREMIER LEAGUE
Portsmouth   7 Reading   4 29 Sept 2007

Highest Aggregate Score England
Division 3(N)
Tranmere R   13 Oldham Ath   4 26 Dec 1935

Highest Aggregate Score Scotland
Division 2
Airdrieonians   15 Dundee Wanderers 1   1 Dec 1894

MOST WINS IN A SEASON

		Wins	Games
FA PREMIER LEAGUE			
2017–18	Manchester C	32	38
FOOTBALL LEAGUE			
Division 3(N)			
1946–47	Doncaster R	33	42
SCOTTISH PREMIERSHIP			
2016–17	Celtic	34	38
SCOTTISH LEAGUE			
Division 1			
1920–21	Rangers	35	42

FEWEST WINS IN A SEASON

		Wins	Games
FA PREMIER LEAGUE			
2007–08	Derby Co	1	38
FOOTBALL LEAGUE			
Division 2			
1899–1900	Loughborough T	1	34
SCOTTISH PREMIER LEAGUE			
1998–99	Dunfermline Ath	4	36
SCOTTISH LEAGUE			
Division 1			
1891–92	Vale of Leven	0	22

UNDEFEATED AT HOME OVERALL

Liverpool 85 games (63 League, 9 League Cup, 7 European, 6 FA Cup), Jan 1978–Jan 1981

UNDEFEATED AT HOME LEAGUE

Chelsea 86 games, March 2004–October 2008

UNDEFEATED AWAY

Arsenal 19 games, FA Premier League 2001–02 and 2003–04 (only Preston NE with 11 in 1888–89 had previously remained unbeaten away) in the top flight.

MOST POINTS IN A SEASON
(three points for a win)

		Points	Games
FA PREMIER LEAGUE			
2017–18	Manchester C	100	38
FOOTBALL LEAGUE			
Championship			
2005–06	Reading	106	46
SCOTTISH PREMIER LEAGUE			
2001–02	Celtic	103	38
SCOTTISH LEAGUE			
League One			
2013–14	Rangers	102	36

MOST POINTS IN A SEASON
(under old system of two points for a win)

		Points	Games
FOOTBALL LEAGUE			
Division 4			
1975–76	Lincoln C	74	46
SCOTTISH LEAGUE			
Division 1			
1920–21	Rangers	76	42

FEWEST POINTS IN A SEASON

		Points	Games
FA PREMIER LEAGUE			
2007–08	Derby Co	11	38
FOOTBALL LEAGUE			
Division 2			
1904–05	Doncaster R	8	34
1899–1900	Loughborough T	8	34
SCOTTISH PREMIER LEAGUE			
2007–08	Gretna	13	38
SCOTTISH LEAGUE			
Division 1			
1954–55	Stirling Alb	6	30

NO DEFEATS IN A SEASON

FA PREMIER LEAGUE
2003–04 Arsenal won 26, drew 12

FOOTBALL LEAGUE
Division 1
1888–89 Preston NE won 18, drew 4
Division 2
1893–94 Liverpool won 22, drew 6

SCOTTISH LEAGUE
Premiership
2016–17 Celtic won 34, drew 4
Division 1
1898–99 Rangers won 18
League One
2013–14 Rangers won 33, drew 3

ONE DEFEAT IN A SEASON

FA PREMIER LEAGUE	Defeats	Games
2004–05 Chelsea	1	38
FOOTBALL LEAGUE		
Division 1		
1990–91 Arsenal	1	38
SCOTTISH PREMIER LEAGUE		
2001–02 Celtic	1	38
2013–14 Celtic	1	38
SCOTTISH LEAGUE		
Division 1		
1920–21 Rangers	1	42
Division 2		
1956–57 Clyde	1	36
1962–63 Morton	1	36
1967–68 St Mirren	1	36
New Division 1		
2011–12 Ross Co	1	36
New Division 2		
1975–76 Raith R	1	26

MOST DEFEATS IN A SEASON

FA PREMIER LEAGUE	Defeats	Games
1994–95 Ipswich T	29	42
2005–06 Sunderland	29	38
2007–08 Derby Co	29	38
FOOTBALL LEAGUE		
Division 3		
1997–98 Doncaster R	34	46
SCOTTISH PREMIER LEAGUE		
2005–06 Livingston	28	38
SCOTTISH LEAGUE		
New Division 1		
1992–93 Cowdenbeath	34	44

MOST DRAWN GAMES IN A SEASON

FA PREMIER LEAGUE	Draws	Games
1993–94 Manchester C	18	42
1993–94 Sheffield U	18	42
1994–95 Southampton	18	42
FOOTBALL LEAGUE		
Division 1		
1978–79 Norwich C	23	42
Division 3		
1997–98 Cardiff C	23	46
1997–98 Hartlepool U	23	46
Division 4		
1986–87 Exeter C	23	46
SCOTTISH PREMIER LEAGUE		
1998–99 Dunfermline Ath	16	38
SCOTTISH LEAGUE		
Premier Division		
1993–94 Aberdeen	21	44
New Division 1		
1986–87 East Fife	21	44

SENDINGS-OFF

SEASON
451 (League alone) 2003–04
(Before rescinded cards taken into account)

DAY
19 (League) 13 Dec 2003

FA CUP FINAL
Kevin Moran, Manchester U v Everton 1985
Jose Antonio Reyes, Arsenal v Manchester U 2005
Pablo Zabaleta, Manchester C v Wigan Ath 2013
Chris Smalling, Manchester U v Crystal Palace 2016
Victor Moses, Chelsea v Arsenal 2017

QUICKEST
FA Premier League
Andreas Johansson, Wigan Ath v Arsenal (7 May 2006) and Keith Gillespie, Sheffield U v Reading (20 January 2007) both in 10 seconds
Football League
Walter Boyd, Swansea C v Darlington, Div 3 as
substitute in zero seconds 23 Nov 1999

MOST IN ONE GAME
Five: Chesterfield (2) v Plymouth Arg (3) 22 Feb 1997
Five: Wigan Ath (1) v Bristol R (4) 2 Dec 1997
Five: Exeter C (3) v Cambridge U (2) 23 Nov 2002
Five: Bradford C (3) v Crawley T (2)* 27 Mar 2012
All five sent off after final whistle for fighting

MOST IN ONE TEAM
Wigan Ath (1) v Bristol R (4) 2 Dec 1997
Hereford U (4) v Northampton T (0) 6 Sept 1992

MOST SUCCESSFUL MANAGERS

Sir Alex Ferguson CBE
Manchester U
1986–2013, 25 major trophies:
13 Premier League, 5 FA Cup, 4 League Cup,
2 Champions League, 1 Cup-Winners' Cup.

Aberdeen
1976–86, 9 major trophies:
3 League, 4 Scottish Cup, 1 League Cup, 1 Cup-
Winners' Cup.

Bob Paisley – Liverpool
1974–83, 13 major trophies:
6 League, 3 European Cup, 3 League Cup, 1 UEFA Cup.

Bill Struth – Rangers
1920–54, 30 major trophies:
18 League, 10 Scottish Cup, 2 League Cup

LEAGUE CHAMPIONSHIP HAT-TRICKS

Huddersfield T	1923–24 to 1925–26
Arsenal	1932–33 to 1934–35
Liverpool	1981–82 to 1983–84
Manchester U	1998–99 to 2000–01
Manchester U	2006–07 to 2008–09

MOST FA CUP MEDALS

Ashley Cole 7 (Arsenal 2002, 2003, 2005; Chelsea 2007, 2009, 2010, 2012)

MOST LEAGUE MEDALS

Ryan Giggs (Manchester U) 13: 1993, 1994, 1996, 1997, 1999, 2000, 2001, 2003, 2007, 2008, 2009, 2011 and 2013.

MOST SENIOR MATCHES

1,390 Peter Shilton (1,005 League, 86 FA Cup, 102 League Cup, 125 Internationals, 13 Under-23, 4 Football League XI, 20 European Cup, 7 Texaco Cup, 5 Simod Cup, 4 European Super Cup, 4 UEFA Cup, 3 Screen Sport Super Cup, 3 Zenith Data Systems Cup, 2 Autoglass Trophy, 2 Charity Shield, 2 Full Members Cup, 1 Anglo-Italian Cup, 1 Football League play-offs, 1 World Club Championship)

MOST LEAGUE APPEARANCES
(750+ matches)

1,005 Peter Shilton (286 Leicester C, 110 Stoke C, 202 Nottingham F, 188 Southampton, 175 Derby Co, 34 Plymouth Arg, 1 Bolton W, 9 Leyton Orient) 1966–97

931 Tony Ford (355 Grimsby T, 9 Sunderland (loan), 112 Stoke C, 114 WBA, 68 Grimsby T, 5 Bradford C (loan), 76 Scunthorpe U, 103 Mansfield T, 89 Rochdale) 1975–2002

909 Graeme Armstrong (204 Stirling A, 83 Berwick R, 353 Meadowbank Thistle, 268 Stenhousemuir, 1 Alloa Ath) 1975–2001

863 Tommy Hutchison (165 Blackpool, 314 Coventry C, 46 Manchester C, 92 Burnley, 178 Swansea C, 68 Alloa Ath) 1965–91

833 Graham Alexander (159 Scunthorpe U, 150 Luton T, 370 Preston NE, 154 Burnley) 1990–2012

824 Terry Paine (713 Southampton, 111 Hereford U) 1957–77

790 Neil Redfearn (35 Bolton W, 10 Lincoln C (loan), 90 Lincoln C, 46 Doncaster R, 57 Crystal Palace, 24 Watford, 62 Oldham Ath, 292 Barnsley, 30 Charlton Ath, 17 Bradford C, 22 Wigan Ath, 42 Halifax T, 54 Boston U, 9 Rochdale) 1982–2004

788 David James (89 Watford, 214 Liverpool, 67 Aston Villa, 91 West Ham U, 93 Manchester C, 134 Portsmouth, 81 Bristol C, 19 Bournemouth) 1988–2013

782 Robbie James (484 Swansea C, 48 Stoke C, 87 QPR, 23 Leicester C, 89 Bradford C, 51 Cardiff C) 1973–94

777 Alan Oakes (565 Manchester C, 211 Chester C, 1 Port Vale) 1959–84

774 Dave Beasant (340 Wimbledon, 20 Newcastle U, 133 Chelsea, 6 Grimsby T (loan), 4 Wolverhampton W (loan), 88 Southampton, 139 Nottingham F, 27 Portsmouth, 1 Tottenham H (loan), 16 Brighton & HA) 1979–2003

771 John Burridge (27 Workington, 134 Blackpool, 65 Aston Villa, 6 Southend U (loan), 88 Crystal Palace, 39 QPR, 74 Wolverhampton W, 6 Derby Co (loan), 109 Sheffield U, 62 Southampton, 67 Newcastle U, 65 Hibernian, 3 Scarborough, 4 Lincoln C, 3 Aberdeen, 3 Dumbarton, 3 Falkirk, 4 Manchester C, 3 Darlington, 6 Queen of the S) 1968–96

770 John Trollope (all for Swindon T) 1960–80†

764 Jimmy Dickinson (all for Portsmouth) 1946–65

763 Stuart McCall (395 Bradford C, 103 Everton, 194 Rangers, 71 Sheffield U) 1982–2004

761 Roy Sproson (all for Port Vale) 1950–72

760 Mick Tait (64 Oxford U, 106 Carlisle U, 33 Hull C, 240 Portsmouth, 99 Reading, 79 Darlington, 139 Hartlepool U) 1975–97

758 Ray Clemence (48 Scunthorpe U, 470 Liverpool, 240 Tottenham H) 1966–87

758 Billy Bonds (95 Charlton Ath, 663 West Ham U) 1964–88

757 Pat Jennings (48 Watford, 472 Tottenham H, 237 Arsenal) 1963–86

757 Frank Worthington (171 Huddersfield T, 210 Leicester C, 84 Bolton W, 75 Birmingham C, 32 Leeds U, 19 Sunderland, 34 Southampton, 31 Brighton & HA, 59 Tranmere R, 23 Preston NE, 19 Stockport Co) 1966–88

755 Jamie Cureton (98 Norwich C, 5 Bournemouth (loan), 174 Bristol R, 108 Reading, 43 QPR, 30 Swindon T, 52 Colchester U, 8 Barnsley (loan), 12 Shrewsbury (loan), 88 Exeter C, 19 Leyton Orient, 35 Cheltenham T, 83 Dagenham & R) 1992–2016

752 Wayne Allison (84 Halifax T, 7 Watford, 195 Bristol C, 101 Swindon T, 74 Huddersfield T, 103 Tranmere R, 73 Sheffield U, 115 Chesterfield) 1987–2008

† record for one club

CONSECUTIVE
401 Harold Bell (401 Tranmere R; 459 in all games) 1946–55

YOUNGEST PLAYERS

FA Premier League appearance
Matthew Briggs, 16 years 65 days, Fulham v Middlesbrough, 13.5.2007

FA Premier League scorer
James Vaughan, 16 years 271 days, Everton v Crystal Palace 10.4.2005

Football League appearance
Reuben Noble-Lazarus, 15 years 45 days, Barnsley v Ipswich T, FL Championship 30.9.2008

Football League scorer
Ronnie Dix, 15 years 180 days, Bristol Rovers v Norwich C, Division 3S, 3.3.1928

FA Cup appearance (any round)
Andy Awford, 15 years 88 days as substitute Worcester City v Boreham Wood, 3rd Qual. rd, 10.10.1987

FA Cup goalscorer
George Williams, 16 years 66 days, Milton Keynes D v Nantwich T, 12.11.2011

FA Cup appearance (competition rounds)
Luke Freeman, 15 years 233 days, Gillingham v Barnet 10.11.2007

FA Cup Final appearance
Curtis Weston, 17 years 119 days, Millwall v Manchester U, 22.5.2004

FA Cup Final scorer
Norman Whiteside, 18 years 18 days, Manchester United v Brighton & HA, 1983

FA Cup Final captain
David Nish, 21 years 212 days, Leicester C v Manchester C, 1969

League Cup appearance
Connor Wickham, 16 years 133 days, Ipswich T v Shrewsbury T, 11.8.2009

League Cup goalscorer
Connor Wickham, 16 years 133 days, Ipswich T v Shrewsbury T, 11.8.2009

League Cup Final scorer
Norman Whiteside, 17 years 324 days, Manchester U v Liverpool, 1983

League Cup Final captain
Barry Venison, 20 years 7 months 8 days, Sunderland v Norwich C, 1985

Scottish Premier League appearance
Scott Robinson, 16 years 45 days, Hearts v Inverness CT, 26.4.2008

Scottish Football League appearance
Jordan Allan, 14 years 189 days, Airdrie U v Livingston, 26.4.2013

Scottish Premier League scorer
Fraser Fyvie, 16 years 306 days, Aberdeen v Hearts, 27.1.2010

OLDEST PLAYERS

FA Premier League appearance
John Burridge, 43 years 162 days, Manchester C v QPR, 14.5.1995

Football League appearance
Neil McBain, 52 years 4 months, New Brighton v Hartlepools U, Div 3N, 15.3.47 (McBain was New Brighton's manager and had to play in an emergency)

Division 1 appearance
Stanley Matthews, 50 years 5 days, Stoke C v Fulham, 6.2.65

INTERNATIONAL RECORDS

MOST GOALS IN AN INTERNATIONAL

Record/World Cup	Archie Thompson (Australia) 13 goals v American Samoa	11.4.2001
England	Howard Vaughton (Aston Villa) 5 goals v Ireland, at Belfast	18.2.1882
	Steve Bloomer (Derby Co) 5 goals v Wales, at Cardiff	16.3.1896
	Willie Hall (Tottenham H) 5 goals v N. Ireland, at Old Trafford	16.11.1938
	Malcolm Macdonald (Newcastle U) 5 goals v Cyprus, at Wembley	16.4.1975
Northern Ireland	Joe Bambrick (Linfield) 6 goals v Wales, at Belfast	1.2.1930
Wales	John Price (Wrexham) 4 goals v Ireland, at Wrexham	25.2.1882
	John Doughty (Newton Heath) 4 goals v Ireland, at Wrexham	3.3.1888
	Mel Charles (Cardiff C) 4 goals v N. Ireland, at Cardiff	11.4.1962
	Ian Edwards (Chester) 4 goals v Malta, at Wrexham	25.10.1978
Scotland	Alexander Higgins (Kilmarnock) 4 goals v Ireland, at Hampden Park	14.3.1885
	Charles Heggie (Rangers) 4 goals v Ireland, at Belfast	20.3.1886
	William Dickson (Dundee Strathmore) 4 goals v Ireland, at Belfast	24.3.1888
	William Paul (Partick Thistle) 4 goals v Wales, at Paisley	22.3.1890
	Jake Madden (Celtic) 4 goals v Wales, at Wrexham	18.3.1893
	Duke McMahon (Celtic) 4 goals v Ireland, at Celtic Park	23.2.1901
	Bob Hamilton (Rangers) 4 goals v Ireland, at Celtic Park	23.2.1901
	Jimmy Quinn (Celtic) 4 goals v Ireland, at Dublin	14.3.1908
	Hughie Gallacher (Newcastle U) 4 goals v N. Ireland, at Belfast	23.2.1929
	Billy Steel (Dundee) 4 goals v N. Ireland, at Hampden Park	1.11.1950
	Denis Law (Manchester U) 4 goals v N. Ireland, at Hampden Park	7.11.1962
	Denis Law (Manchester U) 4 goals v Norway, at Hampden Park	7.11.1963
	Colin Stein (Rangers) 4 goals v Cyprus, at Hampden Park	17.5.1969

MOST GOALS IN AN INTERNATIONAL CAREER

		Goals	Games
England	Wayne Rooney (Everton, Manchester U)	53	119
Scotland	Denis Law (Huddersfield T, Manchester C, Torino, Manchester U)	30	55
	Kenny Dalglish (Celtic, Liverpool)	30	102
Northern Ireland	David Healy (Manchester U, Preston NE, Leeds U, Fulham, Sunderland, Rangers, Bury)	36	95
Wales	Ian Rush (Liverpool, Juventus)	28	73
Republic of Ireland	Robbie Keane (Wolverhampton W, Coventry C, Internazionale, Leeds U, Tottenham H, Liverpool, Tottenham H, LA Galaxy)	68	146

HIGHEST SCORES

World Cup Match	Australia	31	American Samoa	0	2001
European Championship	San Marino	0	Germany	13	2006
Olympic Games	Denmark	17	France	1	1908
	Germany	16	USSR	0	1912
Olympic Qualifying Tournament	Vanuatu	46	Micronesia	0	2015
Other International Match	Libya	21	Oman	0	1966
	Abandoned after 80 minutes as Oman refused to play on.				
European Cup	KR Reykjavik	2	Feyenoord	12	1969
European Cup-Winners' Cup	Sporting Lisbon	16	Apoel Nicosia	1	1963
Fairs & UEFA Cups	Ajax	14	Red Boys Differdange	0	1984

GOALSCORING RECORDS

World Cup Final	Geoff Hurst (England) 3 goals v West Germany	1966
World Cup Final tournament	Just Fontaine (France) 13 goals	1958
World Cup career	Miroslav Klose (Germany) 16 goals	2002, 2006, 2010, 2014
Career	Artur Friedenreich (Brazil) 1,329 goals	1910–30
	Pele (Brazil) 1,281 goals	*1956–78
	Franz 'Bimbo' Binder (Austria, Germany) 1,006 goals	1930–50
World Cup Finals fastest	Hakan Sukur (Turkey) 10.8 secs v South Korea	2002
Pele subsequently scored two goals in Testimonial matches making his total 1,283.		

MOST CAPPED INTERNATIONALS IN THE BRITISH ISLES

England	Peter Shilton	125 appearances	1970–90
Northern Ireland	Pat Jennings	119 appearances	1964–86
Scotland	Kenny Dalglish	102 appearances	1971–86
Wales	Neville Southall	92 appearances	1982–97
Republic of Ireland	Robbie Keane	146 appearances	1998–2016

THE FA PREMIER LEAGUE AND FOOTBALL LEAGUE FIXTURES 2018–19

All fixtures subject to change.

Community Shield

Sunday, 5 August 2018
Chelsea v Manchester C

Premier League

Saturday, 11 August 2018
Arsenal v Manchester C
Bournemouth v Cardiff C
Fulham v Crystal Palace
Huddersfield T v Chelsea
Liverpool v West Ham U
Manchester U v Leicester C
Newcastle U v Tottenham H
Southampton v Burnley
Watford v Brighton & HA
Wolverhampton W v Everton

Saturday, 18 August 2018
Brighton & HA v Manchester U
Burnley v Watford
Cardiff C v Newcastle U
Chelsea v Arsenal
Crystal Palace v Liverpool
Everton v Southampton
Leicester C v Wolverhampton W
Manchester C v Huddersfield T
Tottenham H v Fulham
West Ham U v Bournemouth

Saturday, 25 August 2018
Arsenal v West Ham U
Bournemouth v Everton
Fulham v Burnley
Huddersfield T v Cardiff C
Liverpool v Brighton & HA
Manchester U v Tottenham H
Newcastle U v Chelsea
Southampton v Leicester C
Watford v Crystal Palace
Wolverhampton W v Manchester C

Saturday, 1 September 2018
Brighton & HA v Fulham
Burnley v Manchester U
Cardiff C v Arsenal
Chelsea v Bournemouth
Crystal Palace v Southampton
Everton v Huddersfield T
Leicester C v Liverpool
Manchester C v Newcastle U
Watford v Tottenham H
West Ham U v Wolverhampton W

Saturday, 15 September 2018
Bournemouth v Leicester C
Chelsea v Cardiff C
Everton v West Ham U
Huddersfield T v Crystal Palace
Manchester U v Fulham
Newcastle U v Arsenal
Southampton v Brighton & HA
Tottenham H v Liverpool
Watford v Manchester U
Wolverhampton W v Burnley

Saturday, 22 September 2018
Arsenal v Everton

Brighton & HA v Tottenham H
Burnley v Bournemouth
Cardiff C v Manchester C
Crystal Palace v Newcastle U
Fulham v Watford
Leicester C v Huddersfield T
Liverpool v Southampton
Manchester U v Wolverhampton W
West Ham U v Chelsea

Saturday, 29 September 2018
Arsenal v Watford
Bournemouth v Crystal Palace
Cardiff C v Burnley
Chelsea v Liverpool
Everton v Fulham
Huddersfield T v Tottenham H
Manchester C v Brighton & HA
Newcastle U v Leicester C
West Ham U v Manchester U
Wolverhampton W v Southampton

Saturday, 6 October 2018
Brighton & HA v West Ham U
Burnley v Huddersfield T
Crystal Palace v Wolverhampton W
Fulham v Arsenal
Leicester C v Everton
Liverpool v Manchester C
Manchester U v Newcastle U
Southampton v Chelsea
Tottenham H v Cardiff C
Watford v Bournemouth

Saturday, 20 October 2018
Arsenal v Leicester C
Bournemouth v Southampton
Cardiff C v Fulham
Chelsea v Manchester U
Everton v Crystal Palace
Huddersfield T v Liverpool
Manchester C v Burnley
Newcastle U v Brighton & HA
West Ham U v Tottenham H
Wolverhampton W v Watford

Saturday, 27 October 2018
Brighton & HA v Wolverhampton W
Burnley v Chelsea
Crystal Palace v Arsenal
Fulham v Bournemouth
Leicester C v West Ham U
Liverpool v Cardiff C
Manchester U v Everton
Southampton v Newcastle U
Tottenham H v Manchester C
Watford v Huddersfield T

Saturday, 3 November 2018
Arsenal v Liverpool
Bournemouth v Manchester U
Cardiff C v Leicester C
Chelsea v Crystal Palace
Everton v Brighton & HA
Huddersfield T v Fulham
Manchester C v Southampton
Newcastle U v Watford
West Ham U v Burnley
Wolverhampton W v Tottenham H

Saturday, 10 November 2018
Arsenal v Wolverhampton W
Cardiff C v Brighton & HA
Chelsea v Everton
Crystal Palace v Tottenham H
Huddersfield T v West Ham U
Leicester C v Burnley
Liverpool v Fulham
Manchester C v Manchester U
Newcastle U v Bournemouth
Southampton v Watford

Saturday, 24 November 2018
Bournemouth v Arsenal
Brighton & HA v Leicester C
Burnley v Newcastle U
Everton v Cardiff C
Fulham v Southampton
Manchester U v Crystal Palace
Tottenham H v Chelsea
Watford v Liverpool
West Ham U v Manchester C
Wolverhampton W v Huddersfield T

Saturday, 1 December 2018
Arsenal v Tottenham H
Cardiff C v Wolverhampton W
Chelsea v Fulham
Crystal Palace v Burnley
Huddersfield T v Brighton & HA
Leicester C v Watford
Liverpool v Everton
Manchester C v Bournemouth
Newcastle U v West Ham U
Southampton v Manchester U

Tuesday, 4 December 2018
Bournemouth v Huddersfield T
Brighton & HA v Crystal Palace
Burnley v Liverpool
Fulham v Leicester C
Watford v Manchester C
West Ham U v Cardiff C
Wolverhampton W v Chelsea
Manchester U v Arsenal

Wednesday, 5 December 2018
Everton v Newcastle U
Tottenham H v Southampton

Saturday, 8 December 2018
Arsenal v Huddersfield T
Bournemouth v Liverpool
Burnley v Brighton & HA
Cardiff C v Southampton
Chelsea v Manchester C
Everton v Watford
Leicester C v Tottenham H
Manchester U v Fulham
Newcastle U v Wolverhampton W
West Ham U v Crystal Palace

Saturday, 15 December 2018
Brighton & HA v Chelsea
Crystal Palace v Leicester C
Fulham v West Ham U
Huddersfield T v Newcastle U
Liverpool v Manchester U
Manchester C v Everton
Southampton v Arsenal
Tottenham H v Burnley

Watford v Cardiff C
Wolverhampton W v Bournemouth

Saturday, 22 December 2018
Arsenal v Burnley
Bournemouth v Brighton & HA
Cardiff C v Manchester U
Chelsea v Leicester C
Everton v Tottenham H
Huddersfield T v Southampton
Manchester C v Crystal Palace
Newcastle U v Fulham
West Ham U v Watford
Wolverhampton W v Liverpool

Wednesday, 26 December 2018
Brighton & HA v Arsenal
Burnley v Everton
Crystal Palace v Cardiff C
Fulham v Wolverhampton W
Leicester C v Manchester C
Liverpool v Newcastle U
Manchester U v Huddersfield T
Southampton v West Ham U
Tottenham H v Bournemouth
Watford v Chelsea

Saturday, 29 December 2018
Brighton & HA v Everton
Burnley v West Ham U
Crystal Palace v Chelsea
Fulham v Huddersfield T
Leicester C v Cardiff C
Liverpool v Arsenal
Manchester U v Bournemouth
Southampton v Manchester C
Tottenham H v Wolverhampton W
Watford v Newcastle U

Tuesday, 1 January 2019
Arsenal v Fulham
Bournemouth v Watford
Cardiff C v Tottenham H
Chelsea v Southampton
Everton v Leicester C
Huddersfield T v Burnley
Manchester C v Liverpool
Newcastle U v Manchester U
West Ham U v Brighton & HA
Wolverhampton W v Crystal Palace

Saturday, 12 January 2019
Brighton & HA v Liverpool
Burnley v Fulham
Cardiff C v Huddersfield T
Chelsea v Newcastle U
Crystal Palace v Watford
Everton v Bournemouth
Leicester C v Southampton
Manchester C v Wolverhampton W
Tottenham H v Manchester U
West Ham U v Arsenal

Saturday, 19 January 2019
Arsenal v Chelsea
Bournemouth v West Ham U
Fulham v Tottenham H
Huddersfield T v Manchester C
Liverpool v Crystal Palace
Manchester U v Brighton & HA
Newcastle U v Cardiff C
Southampton v Everton
Watford v Burnley
Wolverhampton W v Leicester C

Tuesday, 29 January 2019
Arsenal v Cardiff C
Bournemouth v Chelsea
Fulham v Brighton & HA
Huddersfield T v Everton
Wolverhampton W v West Ham U
Manchester U v Burnley

Wednesday, 30 January 2019
Newcastle U v Manchester C
Southampton v Crystal Palace
Liverpool v Leicester C
Tottenham H v Watford

Saturday, 2 February 2019
Brighton & HA v Watford
Burnley v Southampton
Cardiff C v Bournemouth
Chelsea v Huddersfield T
Crystal Palace v Fulham
Everton v Wolverhampton W
Leicester C v Manchester U
Manchester C v Arsenal
Tottenham H v Newcastle U
West Ham U v Liverpool

Saturday, 9 February 2019
Brighton & HA v Burnley
Crystal Palace v West Ham U
Fulham v Manchester U
Huddersfield T v Arsenal
Liverpool v Bournemouth
Manchester C v Chelsea
Southampton v Cardiff C
Tottenham H v Leicester C
Watford v Everton
Wolverhampton W v Newcastle U

Saturday, 23 February 2019
Arsenal v Southampton
Bournemouth v Wolverhampton W
Burnley v Tottenham H
Cardiff C v Watford
Chelsea v Brighton & HA
Everton v Manchester C
Leicester C v Crystal Palace
Manchester U v Liverpool
Newcastle U v Huddersfield T
West Ham U v Fulham

Tuesday, 26 February 2019
Arsenal v Bournemouth
Cardiff C v Everton
Huddersfield T v Wolverhampton W
Leicester C v Brighton & HA
Crystal Palace v Manchester U

Wednesday, 27 February 2019
Chelsea v Tottenham H
Newcastle U v Burnley
Southampton v Fulham
Liverpool v Watford
Manchester C v West Ham U

Saturday, 2 March 2019
Bournemouth v Manchester C
Brighton & HA v Huddersfield T
Burnley v Crystal Palace
Everton v Liverpool
Fulham v Chelsea
Manchester U v Southampton
Tottenham H v Arsenal
Watford v Leicester C
West Ham U v Newcastle U
Wolverhampton W v Cardiff C

Saturday, 9 March 2019
Arsenal v Manchester U
Cardiff C v West Ham U
Chelsea v Wolverhampton W
Crystal Palace v Brighton & HA
Huddersfield T v Bournemouth
Leicester C v Fulham
Liverpool v Burnley
Manchester C v Watford
Newcastle U v Everton
Southampton v Tottenham H

Saturday, 16 March 2019
Bournemouth v Newcastle U
Brighton & HA v Cardiff C

Burnley v Leicester C
Everton v Chelsea
Fulham v Liverpool
Manchester U v Manchester C
Tottenham H v Crystal Palace
Watford v Southampton
West Ham U v Huddersfield T
Wolverhampton W v Arsenal

Saturday, 30 March 2019
Arsenal v Newcastle U
Brighton & HA v Southampton
Burnley v Wolverhampton W
Cardiff C v Chelsea
Crystal Palace v Huddersfield T
Fulham v Manchester C
Leicester C v Bournemouth
Liverpool v Tottenham H
Manchester U v Watford
West Ham U v Everton

Saturday, 6 April 2019
Bournemouth v Burnley
Chelsea v West Ham U
Everton v Arsenal
Huddersfield T v Leicester C
Manchester C v Cardiff C
Newcastle U v Crystal Palace
Southampton v Liverpool
Tottenham H v Brighton & HA
Watford v Fulham
Wolverhampton W v Manchester U

Saturday, 13 April 2019
Brighton & HA v Bournemouth
Burnley v Cardiff C
Crystal Palace v Manchester C
Fulham v Everton
Leicester C v Newcastle U
Liverpool v Chelsea
Manchester U v West Ham U
Southampton v Wolverhampton W
Tottenham H v Huddersfield T
Watford v Arsenal

Saturday, 20 April 2019
Arsenal v Crystal Palace
Bournemouth v Fulham
Cardiff C v Liverpool
Chelsea v Burnley
Everton v Manchester U
Huddersfield T v Watford
Manchester C v Tottenham H
Newcastle U v Southampton
West Ham U v Leicester C
Wolverhampton W v Brighton & HA

Saturday, 27 April 2019
Brighton & HA v Newcastle U
Burnley v Manchester C
Crystal Palace v Everton
Fulham v Cardiff C
Leicester C v Arsenal
Liverpool v Huddersfield T
Manchester U v Chelsea
Southampton v Bournemouth
Tottenham H v West Ham U
Watford v Wolverhampton W

Saturday, 4 May 2019
Arsenal v Brighton & HA
Bournemouth v Tottenham H
Cardiff C v Crystal Palace
Chelsea v Watford
Everton v Burnley
Huddersfield T v Manchester U
Manchester C v Leicester C
Newcastle U v Liverpool
West Ham U v Southampton
Wolverhampton W v Fulham

Sunday, 12 May 2019
Brighton & HA v Manchester C
Burnley v Arsenal
Crystal Palace v Bournemouth
Fulham v Newcastle U
Leicester C v Chelsea
Liverpool v Wolverhampton W
Manchester U v Cardiff C
Southampton v Huddersfield T
Tottenham H v Everton
Watford v West Ham U

EFL Championship

Friday, 3 August 2018
Reading v Derby Co

Saturday, 4 August 2018
Birmingham C v Norwich C
Brentford v Rotherham U
Bristol C v Nottingham F
Ipswich T v Blackburn R
Millwall v Middlesbrough
Preston NE v QPR
Sheffield U v Swansea C
WBA v Bolton W
Wigan Ath v Sheffield W

Sunday, 5 August 2018
Leeds U v Stoke C

Monday, 6 August 2018
Hull C v Aston Villa

Tuesday, 7 August 2018
Nottingham F v WBA

Saturday, 11 August 2018
Aston Villa v Wigan Ath
Blackburn R v Millwall
Bolton W v Bristol C
Derby Co v Leeds U
Middlesbrough v Birmingham C
Norwich C v WBA
Nottingham F v Reading
QPR v Sheffield U
Rotherham U v Ipswich T
Sheffield W v Hull C
Stoke C v Brentford
Swansea C v Preston NE

Saturday, 18 August 2018
Birmingham C v Swansea C
Brentford v Sheffield W
Bristol C v Middlesbrough
Hull C v Blackburn R
Ipswich T v Aston Villa
Leeds U v Rotherham U
Millwall v Derby Co
Preston NE v Stoke C
Reading v Bolton W
Sheffield U v Norwich C
WBA v QPR
Wigan Ath v Nottingham F

Tuesday, 21 August 2018
Aston Villa v Brentford
Derby Co v Ipswich T
Middlesbrough v Sheffield U
QPR v Bristol C
Rotherham U v Hull C
Sheffield W v Millwall

Wednesday, 22 August 2018
Blackburn R v Reading
Bolton W v Birmingham C
Norwich C v Preston NE
Stoke C v Wigan Ath
Swansea C v Leeds U

Saturday, 25 August 2018
Aston Villa v Reading
Blackburn R v Brentford

Bolton W v Sheffield U
Derby Co v Preston NE
Middlesbrough v WBA
Norwich C v Leeds U
Nottingham F v Birmingham C
QPR v Wigan Ath
Rotherham U v Millwall
Sheffield W v Ipswich T
Stoke C v Hull C
Swansea C v Bristol C

Saturday, 1 September 2018
Birmingham C v QPR
Brentford v Nottingham F
Bristol C v Blackburn R
Hull C v Derby Co
Ipswich T v Norwich C
Leeds U v Middlesbrough
Millwall v Swansea C
Preston NE v Bolton W
Reading v Sheffield W
Sheffield U v Aston Villa
WBA v Stoke C
Wigan Ath v Rotherham U

Saturday, 15 September 2018
Birmingham C v WBA
Blackburn R v Aston Villa
Bolton W v QPR
Brentford v Wigan Ath
Bristol C v Sheffield U
Hull C v Ipswich T
Millwall v Leeds U
Norwich C v Middlesbrough
Preston NE v Reading
Rotherham U v Derby Co
Sheffield W v Stoke C
Swansea C v Nottingham F

Tuesday, 18 September 2018
Derby Co v Blackburn R
Leeds U v Preston NE
Stoke C v Swansea C
WBA v Bristol C
Wigan Ath v Hull C

Wednesday, 19 September 2018
Aston Villa v Rotherham U
Ipswich T v Brentford
Middlesbrough v Bolton W
Nottingham F v Sheffield W
QPR v Millwall
Reading v Norwich C
Sheffield U v Birmingham C

Saturday, 22 September 2018
Aston Villa v Sheffield W
Derby Co v Brentford
Ipswich T v Bolton W
Leeds U v Birmingham C
Middlesbrough v Swansea C
Nottingham F v Rotherham U
QPR v Norwich C
Reading v Hull C
Sheffield U v Preston NE
Stoke C v Blackburn R
WBA v Millwall
Wigan Ath v Bristol C

Saturday, 29 September 2018
Birmingham C v Ipswich T
Blackburn R v Nottingham F
Bolton W v Derby Co
Brentford v Reading
Bristol C v Aston Villa
Hull C v Middlesbrough
Millwall v Sheffield U
Norwich C v Wigan Ath
Preston NE v WBA
Rotherham U v Stoke C
Sheffield W v Leeds U
Swansea C v QPR

Tuesday, 2 October 2018
Aston Villa v Preston NE
Brentford v Birmingham C
Ipswich T v Middlesbrough
Reading v QPR
Stoke C v Bolton W
Wigan Ath v Swansea C

Wednesday, 3 October 2018
Blackburn R v Sheffield U
Derby Co v Norwich C
Hull C v Leeds U
Nottingham F v Millwall
Rotherham U v Bristol C
Sheffield W v WBA

Saturday, 6 October 2018
Birmingham C v Rotherham U
Bolton W v Blackburn R
Bristol C v Sheffield W
Leeds U v Brentford
Middlesbrough v Nottingham F
Millwall v Aston Villa
Norwich C v Stoke C
Preston NE v Wigan Ath
QPR v Derby Co
Sheffield U v Hull C
Swansea C v Ipswich T
WBA v Reading

Saturday, 20 October 2018
Aston Villa v Swansea C
Blackburn R v Leeds U
Brentford v Bristol C
Derby Co v Sheffield U
Hull C v Preston NE
Ipswich T v QPR
Nottingham F v Norwich C
Reading v Millwall
Rotherham U v Bolton W
Sheffield W v Middlesbrough
Stoke C v Birmingham C
Wigan Ath v WBA

Tuesday, 23 October 2018
Middlesbrough v Rotherham U
Millwall v Wigan Ath
Norwich C v Aston Villa
QPR v Sheffield W
Sheffield U v Stoke C
Swansea C v Blackburn R

Wednesday, 24 October 2018
Birmingham C v Reading
Bolton W v Nottingham F
Bristol C v Hull C
Leeds U v Ipswich T
Preston NE v Brentford
WBA v Derby Co

Saturday, 27 October 2018
Birmingham C v Sheffield W
Bolton W v Hull C
Bristol C v Stoke C
Leeds U v Nottingham F
Middlesbrough v Derby Co
Millwall v Ipswich T
Norwich C v Brentford
Preston NE v Rotherham U
QPR v Aston Villa
Sheffield U v Wigan Ath
Swansea C v Reading
WBA v Blackburn R

Saturday, 3 November 2018
Aston Villa v Bolton W
Blackburn R v QPR
Brentford v Millwall
Derby Co v Birmingham C
Hull C v WBA
Ipswich T v Preston NE
Nottingham F v Sheffield U
Reading v Bristol C

Rotherham U v Swansea C
Sheffield W v Norwich C
Stoke C v Middlesbrough
Wigan Ath v Leeds U

Saturday, 10 November 2018
Birmingham C v Hull C
Blackburn R v Rotherham U
Bolton W v Swansea C
Bristol C v Preston NE
Derby Co v Aston Villa
Middlesbrough v Wigan Ath
Norwich C v Millwall
Nottingham F v Stoke C
QPR v Brentford
Reading v Ipswich T
Sheffield U v Sheffield W
WBA v Leeds U

Saturday, 24 November 2018
Aston Villa v Birmingham C
Brentford v Middlesbrough
Hull C v Nottingham F
Ipswich T v WBA
Leeds U v Bristol C
Millwall v Bolton W
Preston NE v Blackburn R
Rotherham U v Sheffield U
Sheffield W v Derby Co
Stoke C v QPR
Swansea C v Norwich C
Wigan Ath v Reading

Tuesday, 27 November 2018
Brentford v Sheffield U
Hull C v Norwich C
Leeds U v Reading
Millwall v Birmingham C
Rotherham U v QPR

Wednesday, 28 November 2018
Aston Villa v Nottingham F
Ipswich T v Bristol C
Preston NE v Middlesbrough
Sheffield W v Bolton W
Stoke C v Derby Co
Swansea C v WBA
Wigan Ath v Blackburn R

Saturday, 1 December 2018
Birmingham C v Preston NE
Blackburn R v Sheffield W
Bolton W v Wigan Ath
Bristol C v Millwall
Derby Co v Swansea C
Middlesbrough v Aston Villa
Norwich C v Rotherham U
Nottingham F v Ipswich T
QPR v Hull C
Reading v Stoke C
Sheffield U v Leeds U
WBA v Brentford

Saturday, 8 December 2018
Birmingham C v Bristol C
Brentford v Swansea C
Leeds U v QPR
Middlesbrough v Blackburn R
Millwall v Hull C
Norwich C v Bolton W
Nottingham F v Preston NE
Reading v Sheffield U
Sheffield W v Rotherham U
Stoke C v Ipswich T
WBA v Aston Villa
Wigan Ath v Derby Co

Saturday, 15 December 2018
Aston Villa v Stoke C
Blackburn R v Birmingham C
Bolton W v Leeds U
Bristol C v Norwich C

Derby Co v Nottingham F
Hull C v Brentford
Ipswich T v Wigan Ath
Preston NE v Millwall
QPR v Middlesbrough
Rotherham U v Reading
Sheffield U v WBA
Swansea C v Sheffield W

Saturday, 22 December 2018
Aston Villa v Leeds U
Blackburn R v Norwich C
Brentford v Bolton W
Derby Co v Bristol C
Hull C v Swansea C
Ipswich T v Sheffield U
Nottingham F v QPR
Reading v Middlesbrough
Rotherham U v WBA
Sheffield W v Preston NE
Stoke C v Millwall
Wigan Ath v Birmingham C

Wednesday, 26 December 2018
Birmingham C v Stoke C
Bolton W v Rotherham U
Bristol C v Brentford
Leeds U v Blackburn R
Middlesbrough v Sheffield W
Millwall v Reading
Norwich C v Nottingham F
Preston NE v Hull C
QPR v Ipswich T
Sheffield U v Derby Co
Swansea C v Aston Villa
WBA v Wigan Ath

Saturday, 29 December 2018
Birmingham C v Brentford
Bolton W v Stoke C
Bristol C v Rotherham U
Leeds U v Hull C
Middlesbrough v Ipswich T
Millwall v Nottingham F
Norwich C v Derby Co
Preston NE v Aston Villa
QPR v Reading
Sheffield U v Blackburn R
Swansea C v Wigan Ath
WBA v Sheffield W

Tuesday, 1 January 2019
Aston Villa v QPR
Blackburn R v WBA
Brentford v Norwich C
Derby Co v Middlesbrough
Hull C v Bolton W
Ipswich T v Millwall
Nottingham F v Leeds U
Reading v Swansea C
Rotherham U v Preston NE
Sheffield W v Birmingham C
Stoke C v Bristol C
Wigan Ath v Sheffield U

Saturday, 12 January 2019
Birmingham C v Middlesbrough
Brentford v Stoke C
Bristol C v Bolton W
Hull C v Sheffield W
Ipswich T v Rotherham U
Leeds U v Derby Co
Millwall v Blackburn R
Preston NE v Swansea C
Reading v Nottingham F
Sheffield U v QPR
WBA v Norwich C
Wigan Ath v Aston Villa

Saturday, 19 January 2019
Aston Villa v Hull C
Blackburn R v Ipswich T

Bolton W v WBA
Derby Co v Reading
Middlesbrough v Millwall
Norwich C v Birmingham C
Nottingham F v Bristol C
QPR v Preston NE
Rotherham U v Brentford
Sheffield W v Wigan Ath
Stoke C v Leeds U
Swansea C v Sheffield U

Saturday, 26 January 2019
Aston Villa v Ipswich T
Blackburn R v Hull C
Bolton W v Reading
Derby Co v Millwall
Middlesbrough v Bristol C
Norwich C v Sheffield U
Nottingham F v Wigan Ath
QPR v WBA
Rotherham U v Leeds U
Sheffield W v Brentford
Stoke C v Preston NE
Swansea C v Birmingham C

Saturday, 2 February 2019
Birmingham C v Nottingham F
Brentford v Blackburn R
Bristol C v Swansea C
Hull C v Stoke C
Ipswich T v Sheffield W
Leeds U v Norwich C
Millwall v Rotherham U
Preston NE v Derby Co
Reading v Aston Villa
Sheffield U v Bolton W
WBA v Middlesbrough
Wigan Ath v QPR

Saturday, 9 February 2019
Aston Villa v Sheffield U
Blackburn R v Bristol C
Bolton W v Preston NE
Derby Co v Hull C
Middlesbrough v Leeds U
Norwich C v Ipswich T
Nottingham F v Brentford
QPR v Birmingham C
Rotherham U v Wigan Ath
Sheffield W v Reading
Stoke C v WBA
Swansea C v Millwall

Tuesday, 12 February 2019
Birmingham C v Bolton W
Hull C v Rotherham U
Ipswich T v Derby Co
Preston NE v Norwich C
WBA v Nottingham F

Wednesday, 13 February 2019
Brentford v Aston Villa
Bristol C v QPR
Leeds U v Swansea C
Millwall v Sheffield W
Reading v Blackburn R
Sheffield U v Middlesbrough
Wigan Ath v Stoke C

Saturday, 16 February 2019
Aston Villa v WBA
Blackburn R v Middlesbrough
Bolton W v Norwich C
Bristol C v Birmingham C
Derby Co v Wigan Ath
Hull C v Millwall
Ipswich T v Stoke C
Preston NE v Nottingham F
QPR v Leeds U
Rotherham U v Sheffield W
Sheffield U v Reading
Swansea C v Brentford

Saturday, 23 February 2019
Birmingham C v Blackburn R
Brentford v Hull C
Leeds U v Bolton W
Middlesbrough v QPR
Millwall v Preston NE
Norwich C v Bristol C
Nottingham F v Derby Co
Reading v Rotherham U
Sheffield W v Swansea C
Stoke C v Aston Villa
WBA v Sheffield U
Wigan Ath v Ipswich T

Saturday, 2 March 2019
Aston Villa v Derby Co
Brentford v QPR
Hull C v Birmingham C
Ipswich T v Reading
Leeds U v WBA
Millwall v Norwich C
Preston NE v Bristol C
Rotherham U v Blackburn R
Sheffield W v Sheffield U
Stoke C v Nottingham F
Swansea C v Bolton W
Wigan Ath v Middlesbrough

Saturday, 9 March 2019
Birmingham C v Aston Villa
Blackburn R v Preston NE
Bolton W v Millwall
Bristol C v Leeds U
Derby Co v Sheffield W
Middlesbrough v Brentford
Norwich C v Swansea C
Nottingham F v Hull C
QPR v Stoke C
Reading v Wigan Ath
Sheffield U v Rotherham U
WBA v Ipswich T

Tuesday, 12 March 2019
Birmingham C v Millwall
Blackburn R v Wigan Ath
Bolton W v Sheffield W
Bristol C v Ipswich T
Nottingham F v Aston Villa
Reading v Leeds U
Sheffield U v Brentford

Wednesday, 13 March 2019
Derby Co v Stoke C
Middlesbrough v Preston NE
Norwich C v Hull C
QPR v Rotherham U
WBA v Swansea C

Saturday, 16 March 2019
Aston Villa v Middlesbrough
Brentford v WBA
Hull C v QPR
Ipswich T v Nottingham F
Leeds U v Sheffield U
Millwall v Bristol C
Preston NE v Birmingham C
Rotherham U v Norwich C
Sheffield W v Blackburn R
Stoke C v Reading
Swansea C v Derby Co
Wigan Ath v Bolton W

Saturday, 30 March 2019
Aston Villa v Blackburn R
Derby Co v Rotherham U
Ipswich T v Hull C
Leeds U v Millwall
Middlesbrough v Norwich C
Nottingham F v Swansea C
QPR v Bolton W
Reading v Preston NE
Sheffield U v Bristol C

Stoke C v Sheffield W
WBA v Birmingham C
Wigan Ath v Brentford

Saturday, 6 April 2019
Birmingham C v Leeds U
Blackburn R v Stoke C
Bolton W v Ipswich T
Brentford v Derby Co
Bristol C v Wigan Ath
Hull C v Reading
Millwall v WBA
Norwich C v QPR
Preston NE v Sheffield U
Rotherham U v Nottingham F
Sheffield W v Aston Villa
Swansea C v Middlesbrough

Tuesday, 9 April 2019
Blackburn R v Derby Co
Bolton W v Middlesbrough
Bristol C v WBA
Norwich C v Reading
Preston NE v Leeds U
Sheffield W v Nottingham F
Swansea C v Stoke C

Wednesday, 10 April 2019
Birmingham C v Sheffield U
Brentford v Ipswich T
Hull C v Wigan Ath
Millwall v QPR
Rotherham U v Aston Villa

Saturday, 13 April 2019
Aston Villa v Bristol C
Derby Co v Bolton W
Ipswich T v Birmingham C
Leeds U v Sheffield W
Middlesbrough v Hull C
Nottingham F v Blackburn R
QPR v Swansea C
Reading v Brentford
Sheffield U v Millwall
Stoke C v Rotherham U
WBA v Preston NE
Wigan Ath v Norwich C

Friday, 19 April 2019
Birmingham C v Derby Co
Bolton W v Aston Villa
Bristol C v Reading
Leeds U v Wigan Ath
Middlesbrough v Stoke C
Millwall v Brentford
Norwich C v Sheffield W
Preston NE v Ipswich T
QPR v Blackburn R
Sheffield U v Nottingham F
Swansea C v Rotherham U
WBA v Hull C

Monday, 22 April 2019
Aston Villa v Millwall
Blackburn R v Bolton W
Brentford v Leeds U
Derby Co v QPR
Hull C v Sheffield U
Ipswich T v Swansea C
Nottingham F v Middlesbrough
Reading v WBA
Rotherham U v Birmingham C
Sheffield W v Bristol C
Stoke C v Norwich C
Wigan Ath v Preston NE

Saturday, 27 April 2019
Birmingham C v Wigan Ath
Bolton W v Brentford
Bristol C v Derby Co
Leeds U v Aston Villa
Middlesbrough v Reading

Millwall v Stoke C
Norwich C v Blackburn R
Preston NE v Sheffield W
QPR v Nottingham F
Sheffield U v Ipswich T
Swansea C v Hull C
WBA v Rotherham U

Sunday, 5 May 2019
Aston Villa v Norwich C
Blackburn R v Swansea C
Brentford v Preston NE
Derby Co v WBA
Hull C v Bristol C
Ipswich T v Leeds U
Nottingham F v Bolton W
Reading v Birmingham C
Rotherham U v Middlesbrough
Sheffield W v QPR
Stoke C v Sheffield U
Wigan Ath v Millwall

EFL League One

Saturday, 4 August 2018
Accrington S v Gillingham
Barnsley v Oxford U
Burton Alb v Rochdale
Coventry C v Scunthorpe U
Fleetwood T v AFC Wimbledon
Peterborough U v Bristol R
Portsmouth v Luton T
Shrewsbury T v Bradford C
Southend U v Doncaster R
Sunderland v Charlton Ath
Walsall v Plymouth Arg
Wycombe W v Blackpool

Saturday, 11 August 2018
AFC Wimbledon v Coventry C
Blackpool v Portsmouth
Bradford C v Barnsley
Bristol R v Accrington S
Charlton Ath v Shrewsbury T
Doncaster R v Wycombe W
Gillingham v Burton Alb
Luton T v Sunderland
Oxford U v Fleetwood T
Plymouth Arg v Southend U
Rochdale v Peterborough U
Scunthorpe U v Walsall

Saturday, 18 August 2018
Accrington S v Charlton Ath
Barnsley v AFC Wimbledon
Burton Alb v Doncaster R
Coventry C v Plymouth Arg
Fleetwood T v Rochdale
Peterborough U v Luton T
Portsmouth v Oxford U
Shrewsbury T v Blackpool
Southend U v Bradford C
Sunderland v Scunthorpe U
Walsall v Gillingham
Wycombe W v Bristol R

Tuesday, 21 August 2018
AFC Wimbledon v Walsall
Blackpool v Coventry C
Bradford C v Burton Alb
Bristol R v Portsmouth
Charlton Ath v Peterborough U
Doncaster R v Shrewsbury T
Gillingham v Sunderland
Luton T v Southend U
Oxford U v Accrington S
Plymouth Arg v Wycombe W
Rochdale v Barnsley
Scunthorpe U v Fleetwood T

Saturday, 25 August 2018
AFC Wimbledon v Sunderland
Blackpool v Accrington S
Bradford C v Wycombe W
Bristol R v Southend U
Charlton Ath v Fleetwood T
Doncaster R v Portsmouth
Gillingham v Coventry C
Luton T v Shrewsbury T
Oxford U v Burton Alb
Plymouth Arg v Peterborough U
Rochdale v Walsall
Scunthorpe U v Barnsley

Saturday, 1 September 2018
Accrington S v Scunthorpe U
Barnsley v Gillingham
Burton Alb v AFC Wimbledon
Coventry C v Rochdale
Fleetwood T v Bradford C
Peterborough U v Doncaster R
Portsmouth v Plymouth Arg
Shrewsbury T v Bristol R
Southend U v Charlton Ath
Sunderland v Oxford U
Walsall vs Blackpool
Wycombe W v Luton T

Saturday, 8 September 2018
Accrington S v Burton Alb
Barnsley v Walsall
Blackpool v Bradford C
Bristol R v Plymouth Arg
Charlton Ath v Wycombe W
Doncaster R v Luton T
Gillingham v AFC Wimbledon
Oxford U v Coventry C
Portsmouth v Shrewsbury T
Scunthorpe U v Rochdale
Southend U v Peterborough U
Sunderland v Fleetwood T

Saturday, 15 September 2018
AFC Wimbledon v Scunthorpe U
Bradford C v Charlton Ath
Burton Alb v Sunderland
Coventry C v Barnsley
Fleetwood T v Accrington S
Luton T v Bristol R
Peterborough U v Portsmouth
Plymouth Arg v Blackpool
Rochdale v Gillingham
Shrewsbury T v Southend U
Walsall v Doncaster R
Wycombe W v Oxford U

Saturday, 22 September 2018
Accrington S v AFC Wimbledon
Barnsley v Burton Alb
Blackpool v Luton T
Bristol R v Coventry C
Charlton Ath v Plymouth Arg
Doncaster R v Bradford C
Gillingham v Peterborough U
Oxford U v Walsall
Portsmouth v Wycombe W
Scunthorpe U v Shrewsbury T
Southend U v Fleetwood T
Sunderland v Rochdale

Saturday, 29 September 2018
AFC Wimbledon v Oxford U
Bradford C v Bristol R
Burton Alb v Scunthorpe U
Coventry C v Sunderland
Fleetwood T v Barnsley
Luton T v Charlton Ath
Peterborough U v Blackpool
Plymouth Arg v Doncaster R
Rochdale v Portsmouth
Shrewsbury T v Gillingham
Walsall v Accrington S
Wycombe W v Southend U

Tuesday, 2 October 2018
AFC Wimbledon v Bradford C
Accrington S v Doncaster R
Barnsley v Plymouth Arg
Burton Alb v Southend U
Coventry C v Portsmouth
Fleetwood T v Wycombe W
Gillingham v Blackpool
Oxford U v Luton T
Rochdale v Bristol R
Scunthorpe U v Charlton Ath
Sunderland v Peterborough U
Walsall v Shrewsbury T

Saturday, 6 October 2018
Blackpool v Rochdale
Bradford C v Sunderland
Bristol R v Walsall
Charlton Ath v Coventry C
Doncaster R v Fleetwood T
Luton T v Scunthorpe U
Peterborough U v Barnsley
Plymouth Arg v AFC Wimbledon
Portsmouth v Gillingham
Shrewsbury T v Accrington S
Southend U v Oxford U
Wycombe W v Burton Alb

Saturday, 13 October 2018
AFC Wimbledon v Portsmouth
Accrington S v Bradford C
Barnsley v Luton T
Burton Alb v Bristol R
Coventry C v Wycombe W
Fleetwood T v Shrewsbury T
Gillingham v Southend U
Oxford U v Plymouth Arg
Rochdale v Doncaster R
Scunthorpe U v Peterborough U
Sunderland v Blackpool
Walsall v Charlton Ath

Saturday, 20 October 2018
Blackpool v AFC Wimbledon
Bradford C v Rochdale
Bristol R v Oxford U
Charlton Ath v Barnsley
Doncaster R v Gillingham
Luton T v Walsall
Peterborough U v Accrington S
Plymouth Arg v Burton Alb
Portsmouth v Fleetwood T
Shrewsbury T v Sunderland
Southend U v Coventry C
Wycombe W v Scunthorpe U

Tuesday, 23 October 2018
Blackpool v Scunthorpe U
Bradford C v Coventry C
Bristol R v AFC Wimbledon
Charlton Ath v Oxford U
Doncaster R v Sunderland
Luton T v Accrington S
Peterborough U v Fleetwood T
Plymouth Arg v Gillingham
Portsmouth v Burton Alb
Shrewsbury T v Barnsley
Southend U v Walsall
Wycombe W v Rochdale

Saturday, 27 October 2018
AFC Wimbledon v Luton T
Accrington S v Portsmouth
Barnsley v Bristol R
Burton Alb v Peterborough U
Coventry C v Doncaster R
Fleetwood T v Blackpool
Gillingham v Bradford C
Oxford U v Shrewsbury T
Rochdale v Charlton Ath
Scunthorpe U v Plymouth Arg
Sunderland v Southend U
Walsall v Wycombe W

Saturday, 3 November 2018
AFC Wimbledon v Shrewsbury T
Barnsley v Southend U
Blackpool v Bristol R
Bradford C v Portsmouth
Charlton Ath v Doncaster R
Coventry C v Accrington S
Gillingham v Fleetwood T
Plymouth Arg v Sunderland
Rochdale v Luton T
Scunthorpe U v Oxford U
Walsall v Burton Alb
Wycombe W v Peterborough U

Saturday, 17 November 2018
Accrington S v Barnsley
Bristol R v Scunthorpe U
Burton Alb v Coventry C
Doncaster R v AFC Wimbledon
Fleetwood T v Walsall
Luton T v Plymouth Arg
Oxford U v Gillingham
Peterborough U v Bradford C
Portsmouth v Charlton Ath
Shrewsbury T v Rochdale
Southend U v Blackpool
Sunderland vs Wycombe

Saturday, 24 November 2018
AFC Wimbledon v Southend U
Barnsley v Doncaster R
Blackpool v Burton Alb
Bradford C v Oxford U
Charlton Ath v Bristol R
Coventry C v Peterborough U
Gillingham v Luton T
Plymouth Arg v Fleetwood T
Rochdale v Accrington S
Scunthorpe U v Portsmouth
Walsall v Sunderland
Wycombe W v Shrewsbury T

Tuesday, 27 November 2018
Accrington S v Wycombe W
Bristol R v Gillingham
Burton Alb v Charlton Ath
Doncaster R v Blackpool
Fleetwood T v Coventry C
Luton T v Bradford C
Oxford U v Rochdale
Peterborough U v AFC Wimbledon
Portsmouth v Walsall
Shrewsbury T v Plymouth Arg
Southend U v Scunthorpe U
Sunderland v Barnsley

Saturday, 8 December 2018
AFC Wimbledon v Rochdale
Accrington S v Sunderland
Blackpool v Charlton Ath
Bristol R v Doncaster R
Burton Alb v Shrewsbury T
Luton T v Fleetwood T
Peterborough U v Oxford U
Plymouth Arg v Bradford C
Portsmouth v Southend U
Scunthorpe U v Gillingham
Walsall v Coventry C
Wycombe W v Barnsley

Saturday, 15 December 2018
Barnsley v Portsmouth
Bradford C v Walsall
Charlton Ath v AFC Wimbledon
Coventry C v Luton T
Doncaster R v Scunthorpe U
Fleetwood T v Burton Alb
Gillingham v Wycombe W
Oxford U v Blackpool
Rochdale v Plymouth Arg
Shrewsbury T v Peterborough U
Southend U v Accrington S
Sunderland v Bristol R

Saturday, 22 December 2018
Blackpool v Barnsley
Bradford C v Scunthorpe U
Bristol R v Fleetwood T
Charlton Ath v Gillingham
Doncaster R v Oxford U
Luton T v Burton Alb
Peterborough U v Walsall
Plymouth Arg v Accrington S
Portsmouth v Sunderland
Shrewsbury T v Coventry C
Southend U v Rochdale
Wycombe W v AFC Wimbledon

Wednesday, 26 December 2018
AFC Wimbledon v Plymouth Arg
Accrington S v Shrewsbury T
Barnsley v Peterborough U
Burton Alb v Wycombe W
Coventry C v Charlton Ath
Fleetwood T v Doncaster R
Gillingham v Portsmouth
Oxford U v Southend U
Rochdale v Blackpool
Scunthorpe U v Luton T
Sunderland v Bradford C
Walsall v Bristol R

Saturday, 29 December 2018
AFC Wimbledon v Blackpool
Accrington S v Peterborough U
Barnsley v Charlton Ath
Burton Alb v Plymouth Arg
Coventry C v Southend U
Fleetwood T v Portsmouth
Gillingham v Doncaster R
Oxford U v Bristol R
Rochdale v Bradford C
Scunthorpe U v Wycombe W
Sunderland v Shrewsbury T
Walsall v Luton T

Tuesday, 1 January 2019
Blackpool v Sunderland
Bradford C v Accrington S
Bristol R v Burton Alb
Charlton Ath v Walsall
Doncaster R v Rochdale
Luton T v Barnsley
Peterborough U v Scunthorpe U
Plymouth Arg v Oxford U
Portsmouth v AFC Wimbledon
Shrewsbury T v Fleetwood T
Southend U v Gillingham
Wycombe W v Coventry C

Saturday, 5 January 2019
AFC Wimbledon v Fleetwood T
Blackpool v Wycombe W
Bradford C v Shrewsbury T
Bristol R v Peterborough U
Charlton Ath v Sunderland
Doncaster R v Southend U
Gillingham v Accrington S
Luton T v Portsmouth
Oxford U v Barnsley
Plymouth Arg v Walsall
Rochdale v Burton Alb
Scunthorpe U v Coventry C

Saturday, 12 January 2019
Accrington S v Bristol R
Barnsley v Bradford C
Burton Alb v Gillingham
Coventry C v AFC Wimbledon
Fleetwood T v Oxford U
Peterborough U v Rochdale
Portsmouth v Blackpool
Shrewsbury T v Charlton Ath
Southend U v Plymouth Arg
Sunderland v Luton T
Walsall v Scunthorpe U
Wycombe W v Doncaster R

Saturday, 19 January 2019
AFC Wimbledon v Barnsley
Blackpool v Shrewsbury T
Bradford C v Southend U
Bristol R v Wycombe W
Charlton Ath v Accrington S
Doncaster R v Burton Alb
Gillingham v Walsall
Luton T v Peterborough U
Oxford U v Portsmouth
Plymouth Arg v Coventry C
Rochdale v Fleetwood T
Scunthorpe U v Sunderland

Saturday, 26 January 2019
Accrington S v Oxford U
Barnsley v Rochdale
Burton Alb v Bradford C
Coventry C v Blackpool
Fleetwood T v Scunthorpe U
Peterborough U v Charlton Ath
Portsmouth v Bristol R
Shrewsbury T v Doncaster R
Southend U v Luton T
Sunderland v Gillingham
Walsall v AFC Wimbledon
Wycombe W v Plymouth Arg

Saturday, 2 February 2019
Accrington S v Blackpool
Barnsley v Scunthorpe U
Burton Alb v Oxford U
Coventry C v Gillingham
Fleetwood T v Charlton Ath
Peterborough U v Plymouth Arg
Portsmouth v Doncaster R
Shrewsbury T v Luton T
Southend U v Bristol R
Sunderland v AFC Wimbledon
Walsall v Rochdale
Wycombe W v Bradford C

Saturday, 9 February 2019
AFC Wimbledon v Burton Alb
Blackpool v Walsall
Bradford C v Fleetwood T
Bristol R v Shrewsbury T
Charlton Ath v Southend U
Doncaster R v Peterborough U
Gillingham v Barnsley
Luton T v Wycombe W
Oxford U v Sunderland
Plymouth Arg v Portsmouth
Rochdale v Coventry C
Scunthorpe U v Accrington S

Saturday, 16 February 2019
Barnsley v Wycombe W
Bradford C v Plymouth Arg
Charlton Ath v Blackpool
Coventry C v Walsall
Doncaster R v Bristol R
Fleetwood T v Luton T
Gillingham v Scunthorpe U
Oxford U v Peterborough U
Rochdale v AFC Wimbledon
Shrewsbury T v Burton Alb
Southend U v Portsmouth
Sunderland v Accrington S

Saturday, 23 February 2019
AFC Wimbledon v Charlton Ath
Accrington S v Southend U
Blackpool v Oxford U
Bristol R v Sunderland
Burton Alb v Fleetwood T
Luton T v Coventry C
Peterborough U v Shrewsbury T
Plymouth Arg v Rochdale
Portsmouth v Barnsley
Scunthorpe U v Doncaster R
Walsall v Bradford C
Wycombe W v Gillingham

Saturday, 2 March 2019
Accrington S v Coventry C
Bristol R v Blackpool
Burton Alb v Walsall
Doncaster R v Charlton Ath
Fleetwood T v Gillingham
Luton T v Rochdale
Oxford U v Scunthorpe U
Peterborough U v Wycombe W
Portsmouth v Bradford C
Shrewsbury T v AFC Wimbledon
Southend U v Barnsley
Sunderland v Plymouth Arg

Saturday, 9 March 2019
AFC Wimbledon v Doncaster R
Barnsley v Accrington S
Blackpool v Southend U
Bradford C v Peterborough U
Charlton Ath v Portsmouth
Coventry C v Burton Alb
Gillingham v Oxford U
Plymouth Arg v Luton T
Rochdale v Shrewsbury T
Scunthorpe U v Bristol R
Walsall v Fleetwood T
Wycombe W v Sunderland

Tuesday, 12 March 2019
AFC Wimbledon v Peterborough U
Barnsley v Sunderland
Blackpool v Doncaster R
Bradford C v Luton T
Charlton Ath v Burton Alb
Coventry C v Fleetwood T
Gillingham v Bristol R
Plymouth Arg v Shrewsbury T
Rochdale v Oxford U
Scunthorpe U v Southend U
Walsall v Portsmouth
Wycombe W v Accrington S

Saturday, 16 March 2019
Accrington S v Rochdale
Bristol R v Charlton Ath
Burton Alb v Blackpool
Doncaster R v Barnsley
Fleetwood T v Plymouth Arg
Luton T v Gillingham
Oxford U v Bradford C
Peterborough U v Coventry C
Portsmouth v Scunthorpe U
Shrewsbury T v Wycombe W
Southend U v AFC Wimbledon
Sunderland v Walsall

Saturday, 23 March 2019
AFC Wimbledon v Gillingham
Bradford C v Blackpool
Burton Alb v Accrington S
Coventry C v Oxford U
Fleetwood T v Sunderland
Luton T v Doncaster R
Peterborough U v Southend U
Plymouth Arg v Bristol R
Rochdale v Scunthorpe U
Shrewsbury T v Portsmouth
Walsall v Barnsley
Wycombe W v Charlton Ath

Saturday, 30 March 2019
Accrington S v Fleetwood T
Barnsley v Coventry C
Blackpool v Plymouth Arg
Bristol R v Luton T
Charlton Ath v Bradford C
Doncaster R v Walsall
Gillingham v Rochdale
Oxford U v Wycombe W
Portsmouth v Peterborough U
Scunthorpe U v AFC Wimbledon
Southend U v Shrewsbury T
Sunderland v Burton Alb

Saturday, 6 April 2019
AFC Wimbledon v Accrington S
Bradford C v Doncaster R
Burton Alb v Barnsley
Coventry C v Bristol R
Fleetwood T v Southend U
Luton T v Blackpool
Peterborough U v Gillingham
Plymouth Arg v Charlton Ath
Rochdale v Sunderland
Shrewsbury T v Scunthorpe U
Walsall v Oxford U
Wycombe W v Portsmouth

Saturday, 13 April 2019
Accrington S v Walsall
Barnsley v Fleetwood T
Blackpool v Peterborough U
Bristol R v Bradford C
Charlton Ath v Luton T
Doncaster R v Plymouth Arg
Gillingham v Shrewsbury T
Oxford U v AFC Wimbledon
Portsmouth v Rochdale
Scunthorpe U v Burton Alb
Southend U v Wycombe W
Sunderland v Coventry C

Friday, 19 April 2019
AFC Wimbledon v Bristol R
Accrington S v Luton T
Barnsley v Shrewsbury T
Burton Alb v Portsmouth
Coventry C v Bradford C
Fleetwood T v Peterborough U
Gillingham v Plymouth Arg
Oxford U v Charlton Ath
Rochdale v Wycombe W
Scunthorpe U v Blackpool
Sunderland v Doncaster R
Walsall v Southend U

Monday, 22 April 2019
Blackpool v Fleetwood T
Bradford C v Gillingham
Bristol R v Rochdale
Charlton Ath v Scunthorpe U
Doncaster R v Accrington S
Luton T v AFC Wimbledon
Peterborough U v Sunderland
Plymouth Arg v Barnsley
Portsmouth v Coventry C
Shrewsbury T v Oxford U
Southend U v Burton Alb
Wycombe W v Walsall

Saturday, 27 April 2019
AFC Wimbledon v Wycombe W
Accrington S v Plymouth Arg
Barnsley v Blackpool
Burton Alb v Luton T
Coventry C v Shrewsbury T
Fleetwood T v Bristol R
Gillingham v Charlton Ath
Oxford U v Doncaster R
Rochdale v Southend U
Scunthorpe U v Bradford C
Sunderland v Portsmouth
Walsall v Peterborough U

Saturday, 4 May 2019
Blackpool v Gillingham
Bradford C v AFC Wimbledon
Bristol R v Barnsley
Charlton Ath v Rochdale
Doncaster R v Coventry C
Luton T v Oxford U
Peterborough U v Burton Alb
Plymouth Arg v Scunthorpe U
Portsmouth v Accrington S
Shrewsbury T v Walsall
Southend U v Sunderland
Wycombe W v Fleetwood T

EFL League Two

Saturday, 4 August 2018
Bury v Yeovil T
Cheltenham T v Crawley T
Crewe Alex v Morecambe
Exeter C v Carlisle U
Grimsby T v Forest Green R
Mansfield T v Newport Co
Northampton T v Lincoln C
Notts Co v Colchester U
Oldham Ath v Milton Keynes D
Port Vale v Cambridge U
Stevenage v Tranmere R
Swindon T v Macclesfield T

Saturday, 11 August 2018
Cambridge U v Notts Co
Carlisle U v Northampton T
Colchester U v Port Vale
Crawley T v Stevenage
Forest Green R v Oldham Ath
Lincoln C v Swindon T
Macclesfield T v Grimsby T
Milton Keynes D v Bury
Morecambe v Exeter C
Newport Co v Crewe Alex
Tranmere R v Cheltenham T
Yeovil T v Mansfield T

Saturday, 18 August 2018
Bury v Forest Green R
Cheltenham T v Carlisle U
Crewe Alex v Milton Keynes D
Exeter C v Newport Co
Grimsby T v Lincoln C
Mansfield T v Colchester U
Northampton T v Cambridge U
Notts Co v Yeovil T
Oldham Ath v Macclesfield T
Port Vale v Crawley T
Stevenage v Morecambe
Swindon T v Tranmere R

Tuesday, 21 August 2018
Cambridge U v Exeter C
Carlisle U v Port Vale
Colchester U v Crewe Alex
Crawley T v Swindon T
Forest Green R v Stevenage
Lincoln C v Bury
Macclesfield T v Cheltenham T
Milton Keynes D v Grimsby T
Morecambe v Northampton T
Newport Co v Notts Co
Tranmere R v Mansfield T
Yeovil T v Oldham Ath

Saturday, 25 August 2018
Cambridge U v Cheltenham T
Carlisle U v Crewe Alex
Colchester U v Northampton T
Crawley T v Bury
Forest Green R v Swindon T
Lincoln C v Notts Co
Macclesfield T v Mansfield T
Milton Keynes D v Exeter C
Morecambe v Oldham Ath
Newport Co v Grimsby T
Tranmere R v Port Vale
Yeovil T v Stevenage

Saturday, 1 September 2018
Bury v Morecambe
Cheltenham T v Colchester U
Crewe Alex v Macclesfield T
Exeter C v Lincoln C
Grimsby T v Yeovil T
Mansfield T v Carlisle U
Northampton T v Tranmere R

Notts Co v Forest Green R
Oldham Ath v Crawley T
Port Vale v Newport Co
Stevenage v Cambridge U
Swindon T v Milton Keynes D

Saturday, 8 September 2018
Bury v Grimsby T
Cambridge U v Carlisle U
Crewe Alex v Mansfield T
Exeter C v Notts Co
Forest Green R v Port Vale
Lincoln C v Crawley T
Morecambe v Swindon T
Northampton T v Cheltenham T
Oldham Ath v Newport Co
Stevenage v Macclesfield T
Tranmere R v Colchester U
Yeovil T v Milton Keynes D

Saturday, 15 September 2018
Carlisle U v Tranmere R
Cheltenham T v Crewe Alex
Colchester U v Cambridge U
Crawley T v Morecambe
Grimsby T v Oldham Ath
Macclesfield T v Lincoln C
Mansfield T v Exeter C
Milton Keynes D v Forest Green R
Newport Co v Yeovil T
Notts Co v Stevenage
Port Vale v Northampton T
Swindon T v Bury

Saturday, 22 September 2018
Bury v Carlisle U
Cambridge U v Mansfield T
Crewe Alex v Port Vale
Exeter C v Cheltenham T
Forest Green R v Crawley T
Lincoln C v Milton Keynes D
Morecambe v Macclesfield T
Northampton T v Notts Co
Oldham Ath v Colchester U
Stevenage v Grimsby T
Tranmere R v Newport Co
Yeovil T v Swindon T

Saturday, 29 September 2018
Carlisle U v Stevenage
Cheltenham T v Lincoln C
Colchester U v Bury
Crawley T v Yeovil T
Grimsby T v Morecambe
Macclesfield T v Forest Green R
Mansfield T v Northampton T
Milton Keynes D v Tranmere R
Newport Co v Cambridge U
Notts Co v Crewe Alex
Port Vale v Exeter C
Swindon T v Oldham Ath

Tuesday, 2 October 2018
Cambridge U v Forest Green R
Carlisle U v Grimsby T
Cheltenham T v Morecambe
Colchester U v Yeovil T
Crewe Alex v Swindon T
Exeter C v Stevenage
Mansfield T v Oldham Ath
Newport Co v Macclesfield T
Northampton T v Bury
Notts Co v Crawley T
Port Vale v Milton Keynes D
Tranmere R v Lincoln C

Saturday, 6 October 2018
Bury v Mansfield T
Crawley T v Cambridge U
Forest Green R v Newport Co
Grimsby T v Port Vale
Lincoln C v Crewe Alex

Macclesfield T v Notts Co
Milton Keynes D v Cheltenham T
Morecambe v Tranmere R
Oldham Ath v Carlisle U
Stevenage v Colchester U
Swindon T v Northampton T
Yeovil T v Exeter C

Saturday, 13 October 2018
Cambridge U v Milton Keynes D
Carlisle U v Morecambe
Cheltenham T v Yeovil T
Colchester U v Crawley T
Crewe Alex v Bury
Exeter C v Swindon T
Mansfield T v Grimsby T
Newport Co v Stevenage
Northampton T v Forest Green R
Notts Co v Oldham Ath
Port Vale v Lincoln C
Tranmere R v Macclesfield T

Saturday, 20 October 2018
Bury v Notts Co
Crawley T v Newport Co
Forest Green R v Cheltenham T
Grimsby T v Exeter C
Lincoln C v Cambridge U
Macclesfield T v Carlisle U
Milton Keynes D v Northampton T
Morecambe v Colchester U
Oldham Ath v Port Vale
Stevenage v Crewe Alex
Swindon T v Mansfield T
Yeovil T v Tranmere R

Tuesday, 23 October 2018
Bury v Newport Co
Crawley T v Exeter C
Forest Green R v Tranmere R
Grimsby T v Colchester U
Lincoln C v Carlisle U
Macclesfield T v Northampton T
Milton Keynes D v Notts Co
Morecambe v Mansfield T
Oldham Ath v Cheltenham T
Stevenage v Port Vale
Swindon T v Cambridge U
Yeovil T v Crewe Alex

Saturday, 27 October 2018
Cambridge U v Macclesfield T
Carlisle U v Yeovil T
Cheltenham T v Stevenage
Colchester U v Lincoln C
Crewe Alex v Grimsby T
Exeter C v Forest Green R
Mansfield T v Milton Keynes D
Newport Co v Morecambe
Northampton T v Oldham Ath
Notts Co v Swindon T
Port Vale v Bury
Tranmere R v Crawley T

Saturday, 3 November 2018
Cambridge U v Grimsby T
Carlisle U v Newport Co
Cheltenham T v Mansfield T
Colchester U v Swindon T
Crawley T v Milton Keynes D
Lincoln C v Forest Green R
Macclesfield T v Bury
Morecambe v Yeovil T
Northampton T v Crewe Alex
Port Vale v Notts Co
Stevenage v Oldham Ath
Tranmere R v Exeter C

Saturday, 17 November 2018
Bury v Stevenage
Crewe Alex v Tranmere R
Exeter C v Northampton T
Forest Green R v Morecambe

Grimsby T v Crawley T
Mansfield T v Port Vale
Milton Keynes D v Macclesfield T
Newport Co v Colchester U
Notts Co v Cheltenham T
Oldham Ath v Cambridge U
Swindon T v Carlisle U
Yeovil T v Lincoln C

Saturday, 24 November 2018
Cambridge U v Bury
Carlisle U v Forest Green R
Cheltenham T v Newport Co
Colchester U v Exeter C
Crawley T v Crewe Alex
Lincoln C v Mansfield T
Macclesfield T v Yeovil T
Morecambe v Notts Co
Northampton T v Grimsby T
Port Vale v Swindon T
Stevenage v Milton Keynes D
Tranmere R v Oldham Ath

Tuesday, 27 November 2018
Bury v Cheltenham T
Crewe Alex v Cambridge U
Exeter C v Macclesfield T
Forest Green R v Colchester U
Grimsby T v Tranmere R
Mansfield T v Crawley T
Milton Keynes D v Morecambe
Newport Co v Northampton T
Notts Co v Carlisle U
Oldham Ath v Lincoln C
Swindon T v Stevenage
Yeovil T v Port Vale

Saturday, 8 December 2018
Bury v Exeter C
Cheltenham T v Grimsby T
Colchester U v Macclesfield T
Crawley T v Northampton T
Crewe Alex v Oldham Ath
Mansfield T v Notts Co
Milton Keynes D v Carlisle U
Morecambe v Port Vale
Stevenage v Lincoln C
Swindon T v Newport Co
Tranmere R v Cambridge U
Yeovil T v Forest Green R

Saturday, 15 December 2018
Cambridge U v Yeovil T
Carlisle U v Colchester U
Exeter C v Crewe Alex
Forest Green R v Mansfield T
Grimsby T v Swindon T
Lincoln C v Morecambe
Macclesfield T v Crawley T
Newport Co v Milton Keynes D
Northampton T v Stevenage
Notts Co v Tranmere R
Oldham Ath v Bury
Port Vale v Cheltenham T

Saturday, 22 December 2018
Bury v Tranmere R
Crawley T v Carlisle U
Forest Green R v Crewe Alex
Grimsby T v Notts Co
Lincoln C v Newport Co
Macclesfield T v Port Vale
Milton Keynes D v Colchester U
Morecambe v Cambridge U
Oldham Ath v Exeter C
Stevenage v Mansfield T
Swindon T v Cheltenham T
Yeovil T v Northampton T

Wednesday, 26 December 2018
Cambridge U v Crawley T
Carlisle U v Oldham Ath
Cheltenham T v Milton Keynes D

Colchester U v Stevenage
Crewe Alex v Lincoln C
Exeter C v Yeovil T
Mansfield T v Bury
Newport Co v Forest Green R
Northampton T v Swindon T
Notts Co v Macclesfield T
Port Vale v Grimsby T
Tranmere R v Morecambe

Saturday, 29 December 2018
Cambridge U v Lincoln C
Carlisle U v Macclesfield T
Cheltenham T v Forest Green R
Colchester U v Morecambe
Crewe Alex v Stevenage
Exeter C v Grimsby T
Mansfield T v Swindon T
Newport Co v Crawley T
Northampton T v Milton Keynes D
Notts Co v Bury
Port Vale v Oldham Ath
Tranmere R v Yeovil T

Tuesday, 1 January 2019
Bury v Crewe Alex
Crawley T v Colchester U
Forest Green R v Northampton T
Grimsby T v Mansfield T
Lincoln C v Port Vale
Macclesfield T v Tranmere R
Milton Keynes D v Cambridge U
Morecambe v Carlisle U
Oldham Ath v Notts Co
Stevenage v Newport Co
Swindon T v Exeter C
Yeovil T v Cheltenham T

Saturday, 5 January 2019
Cambridge U v Stevenage
Carlisle U v Mansfield T
Colchester U v Notts Co
Crawley T v Cheltenham T
Forest Green R v Grimsby T
Lincoln C v Exeter C
Macclesfield T v Swindon T
Milton Keynes D v Oldham Ath
Morecambe v Crewe Alex
Newport Co v Port Vale
Tranmere R v Northampton T
Yeovil T v Bury

Saturday, 12 January 2019
Bury v Milton Keynes D
Cheltenham T v Tranmere R
Crewe Alex v Newport Co
Exeter C v Morecambe
Grimsby T v Macclesfield T
Mansfield T v Yeovil T
Northampton T v Carlisle U
Notts Co v Cambridge U
Oldham Ath v Forest Green R
Port Vale v Colchester U
Stevenage v Crawley T
Swindon T v Lincoln C

Saturday, 19 January 2019
Cambridge U v Northampton T
Carlisle U v Cheltenham T
Colchester U v Mansfield T
Crawley T v Port Vale
Forest Green R v Bury
Lincoln C v Grimsby T
Macclesfield T v Oldham Ath
Milton Keynes D v Crewe Alex
Morecambe v Stevenage
Newport Co v Exeter C
Tranmere R v Swindon T
Yeovil T v Notts Co

Saturday, 26 January 2019
Bury v Lincoln C
Cheltenham T v Macclesfield T

Crewe Alex v Colchester U
Exeter C v Cambridge U
Grimsby T v Milton Keynes D
Mansfield T v Tranmere R
Northampton T v Morecambe
Notts Co v Newport Co
Oldham Ath v Yeovil T
Port Vale v Carlisle U
Stevenage v Forest Green R
Swindon T v Crawley T

Saturday, 2 February 2019
Bury v Crawley T
Cheltenham T v Cambridge U
Crewe Alex v Carlisle U
Exeter C v Milton Keynes D
Grimsby T v Newport Co
Mansfield T v Macclesfield T
Northampton T v Colchester U
Notts Co v Lincoln C
Oldham Ath v Morecambe
Port Vale v Tranmere R
Stevenage v Yeovil T
Swindon T v Forest Green R

Saturday, 9 February 2019
Cambridge U v Port Vale
Carlisle U v Exeter C
Colchester U v Cheltenham T
Crawley T v Oldham Ath
Forest Green R v Notts Co
Lincoln C v Northampton T
Macclesfield T v Crewe Alex
Milton Keynes D v Swindon T
Morecambe v Bury
Newport Co v Mansfield T
Tranmere R v Stevenage
Yeovil T v Grimsby T

Saturday, 16 February 2019
Cambridge U v Tranmere R
Carlisle U v Milton Keynes D
Exeter C v Bury
Forest Green R v Yeovil T
Grimsby T v Cheltenham T
Lincoln C v Stevenage
Macclesfield T v Colchester U
Newport Co v Swindon T
Northampton T v Crawley T
Notts Co v Mansfield T
Oldham Ath v Crewe Alex
Port Vale v Morecambe

Saturday, 23 February 2019
Bury v Oldham Ath
Cheltenham T v Port Vale
Colchester U v Carlisle U
Crawley T v Macclesfield T
Crewe Alex v Exeter C
Mansfield T v Forest Green R
Milton Keynes D v Newport Co
Morecambe v Lincoln C
Stevenage v Northampton T
Swindon T v Grimsby T
Tranmere R v Notts Co
Yeovil T v Cambridge U

Saturday, 2 March 2019
Bury v Macclesfield T
Crewe Alex v Northampton T
Exeter C v Tranmere R
Forest Green R v Lincoln C
Grimsby T v Cambridge U
Mansfield T v Cheltenham T
Milton Keynes D v Crawley T
Newport Co v Carlisle U
Notts Co v Port Vale
Oldham Ath v Stevenage

Swindon T v Colchester U
Yeovil T v Morecambe

Tuesday, 5 March 2019
Cheltenham T v Bury

Saturday, 9 March 2019
Cambridge U v Oldham Ath
Carlisle U v Swindon T
Cheltenham T v Notts Co
Colchester U v Newport Co
Crawley T v Grimsby T
Lincoln C v Yeovil T
Macclesfield T v Milton Keynes D
Morecambe v Forest Green R
Northampton T v Exeter C
Port Vale v Mansfield T
Stevenage v Bury
Tranmere R v Crewe Alex

Tuesday, 12 March 2019
Cambridge U v Crewe Alex
Carlisle U v Notts Co
Colchester U v Forest Green R
Crawley T v Mansfield T
Lincoln C v Oldham Ath
Macclesfield T v Exeter C
Morecambe v Milton Keynes D
Northampton T v Newport Co
Port Vale v Yeovil T
Stevenage v Swindon T
Tranmere R v Grimsby T

Saturday, 16 March 2019
Bury v Cambridge U
Crewe Alex v Crawley T
Exeter C v Colchester U
Forest Green R v Carlisle U
Grimsby T v Northampton T
Mansfield T v Lincoln C
Milton Keynes D v Stevenage
Newport Co v Cheltenham T
Notts Co v Morecambe
Oldham Ath v Tranmere R
Swindon T v Port Vale
Yeovil T v Macclesfield T

Saturday, 23 March 2019
Carlisle U v Cambridge U
Cheltenham T v Northampton T
Colchester U v Tranmere R
Crawley T v Lincoln C
Grimsby T v Bury
Macclesfield T v Stevenage
Mansfield T v Crewe Alex
Milton Keynes D v Yeovil T
Newport Co v Oldham Ath
Notts Co v Exeter C
Port Vale v Forest Green R
Swindon T v Morecambe

Saturday, 30 March 2019
Bury v Swindon T
Cambridge U v Colchester U
Crewe Alex v Cheltenham T
Exeter C v Mansfield T
Forest Green R v Milton Keynes D
Lincoln C v Macclesfield T
Morecambe v Crawley T
Northampton T v Port Vale
Oldham Ath v Grimsby T
Stevenage v Notts Co
Tranmere R v Carlisle U
Yeovil T v Newport Co

Saturday, 6 April 2019
Carlisle U v Bury
Cheltenham T v Exeter C
Colchester U v Oldham Ath
Crawley T v Forest Green R

Grimsby T v Stevenage
Macclesfield T v Morecambe
Mansfield T v Cambridge U
Milton Keynes D v Lincoln C
Newport Co v Tranmere R
Notts Co v Northampton T
Port Vale v Crewe Alex
Swindon T v Yeovil T

Saturday, 13 April 2019
Bury v Colchester U
Cambridge U v Newport Co
Crewe Alex v Notts Co
Exeter C v Port Vale
Forest Green R v Macclesfield T
Lincoln C v Cheltenham T
Morecambe v Grimsby T
Northampton T v Mansfield T
Oldham Ath v Swindon T
Stevenage v Carlisle U
Tranmere R v Milton Keynes D
Yeovil T v Crawley T

Friday, 19 April 2019
Cambridge U v Swindon T
Carlisle U v Lincoln C
Cheltenham T v Oldham Ath
Colchester U v Grimsby T
Crewe Alex v Yeovil T
Exeter C v Crawley T
Mansfield T v Morecambe
Newport Co v Bury
Northampton T v Macclesfield T
Notts Co v Milton Keynes D
Port Vale v Stevenage
Tranmere R v Forest Green R

Monday, 22 April 2019
Bury v Northampton T
Crawley T v Notts Co
Forest Green R v Cambridge U
Grimsby T v Carlisle U
Lincoln C v Tranmere R
Macclesfield T v Newport Co
Milton Keynes D v Port Vale
Morecambe v Cheltenham T
Oldham Ath v Mansfield T
Stevenage v Exeter C
Swindon T v Crewe Alex
Yeovil T v Colchester U

Saturday, 27 April 2019
Cambridge U v Morecambe
Carlisle U v Crawley T
Cheltenham T v Swindon T
Colchester U v Milton Keynes D
Crewe Alex v Forest Green R
Exeter C v Oldham Ath
Mansfield T v Stevenage
Newport Co v Lincoln C
Northampton T v Yeovil T
Notts Co v Grimsby T
Port Vale v Macclesfield T
Tranmere R v Bury

Saturday, 4 May 2019
Bury v Port Vale
Crawley T v Tranmere R
Forest Green R v Exeter C
Grimsby T v Crewe Alex
Lincoln C v Colchester U
Macclesfield T v Cambridge U
Milton Keynes D v Mansfield T
Morecambe v Newport Co
Oldham Ath v Northampton T
Stevenage v Cheltenham T
Swindon T v Notts Co
Yeovil T v Carlisle U

NATIONAL LEAGUE
FIXTURES 2018–19

†*BT Sport   All fixtures subject to change.*

Saturday, 4 August 2018
AFC Fylde v Bromley
Aldershot T v Barnet
Barrow v Havant & W'ville
Boreham Wood v Dagenham & R
Braintree T v FC Halifax T
Dover Ath v Wrexham
Dover Ath v Solihull Moors
Ebbsfleet U v Chesterfield
Harrogate T v Sutton U
Maidenhead U v Gateshead
Maidstone U v Hartlepool U
Salford C v Leyton Orient

Tuesday, 7 August 2018
Barnet v Braintree T
Bromley v Dover Ath
Chesterfield v Aldershot T
Dagenham & R v Maidstone U
FC Halifax T v Barrow
Gateshead v Salford C
Hartlepool U v Harrogate T
Havant & W'ville v Boreham Wood
Leyton Orient v Ebbsfleet U
Solihull Moors v Maidenhead U
Sutton U v Dover Ath
Wrexham v AFC Fylde

Saturday, 11 August 2018
Barnet v Dover Ath
Bromley v Harrogate T
Chesterfield v Braintree T
Dagenham & R v Maidenhead U
FC Halifax T v Maidstone U
Gateshead v Dover Ath
Hartlepool U v Ebbsfleet U
Havant & W'ville v AFC Fylde
Leyton Orient v Barrow
Solihull Moors v Aldershot T
Sutton U v Salford C
Wrexham v Boreham Wood

Tuesday, 14 August 2018
AFC Fylde v Solihull Moors
Aldershot T v Dagenham & R
Barrow v Chesterfield
Boreham Wood v Gateshead
Braintree T v Hartlepool U
Dover Ath v Havant & W'ville
Dover Ath v Bromley
Ebbsfleet U v Sutton U
Harrogate T v Barnet
Maidenhead U v Wrexham
Maidstone U v Leyton Orient
Salford C v FC Halifax T

Saturday, 18 August 2018
AFC Fylde v Dover Ath
Aldershot T v Harrogate T
Barnet v Ebbsfleet U
Braintree T v Havant & W'ville
Bromley v Gateshead
Dover Ath v Wrexham
FC Halifax T v Dagenham & R
Hartlepool U v Maidenhead U
Leyton Orient v Boreham Wood
Maidstone U v Barrow
Salford C v Chesterfield
Solihull Moors v Sutton U

Saturday, 25 August 2018
Barrow v Braintree T
Boreham Wood v FC Halifax T
Chesterfield v Barnet
Dagenham & R v Hartlepool U
Dover Ath v Dover Ath
Ebbsfleet U v Aldershot T
Gateshead v Leyton Orient
Harrogate T v Solihull Moors
Havant & W'ville v Salford C
Maidenhead U v Maidstone U
Sutton U v AFC Fylde
Wrexham v Bromley

Monday, 27 August 2018
AFC Fylde v Harrogate T
Aldershot T v Sutton U
Barnet v Dagenham & R
Braintree T v Maidenhead U
Bromley v Havant & W'ville
Dover Ath v Ebbsfleet U
FC Halifax T v Gateshead
Hartlepool U v Chesterfield
Leyton Orient v Dover Ath
Maidstone U v Boreham Wood
Salford C v Barrow
Solihull Moors v Wrexham

Saturday, 1 September 2018
Barrow v Solihull Moors
Boreham Wood v Braintree T
Chesterfield v Leyton Orient
Dagenham & R v Salford C
Dover Ath v Barnet
Ebbsfleet U v AFC Fylde
Gateshead v Maidstone U
Harrogate T v Dover Ath
Havant & W'ville v Hartlepool U
Maidenhead U v Bromley
Sutton U v FC Halifax T
Wrexham v Aldershot T

Tuesday, 4 September 2018
AFC Fylde v Salford C
Boreham Wood v Chesterfield
Bromley v Barnet
Dagenham & R v Braintree T
Dover Ath v Ebbsfleet U
Gateshead v Harrogate T
Hartlepool U v Barrow
Havant & W'ville v Aldershot T
Leyton Orient v Solihull Moors
Maidenhead U v Dover Ath
Maidstone U v Sutton U
Wrexham v FC Halifax T

Saturday, 8 September 2018
Aldershot T v Bromley
Barnet v Maidenhead U
Barrow v Dagenham & R
Braintree T v Wrexham
Chesterfield v Dover Ath
Dover Ath v AFC Fylde
Ebbsfleet U v Gateshead
FC Halifax T v Leyton Orient
Harrogate T v Havant & W'ville
Salford C v Maidstone U
Solihull Moors v Hartlepool U
Sutton U v Boreham Wood

Saturday, 15 September 2018
AFC Fylde v Aldershot T
Boreham Wood v Barrow
Bromley v Salford C
Dagenham & R v Chesterfield
Dover Ath v Solihull Moors
Gateshead v Braintree T
Hartlepool U v Dover Ath
Havant & W v Sutton U
Leyton Orient v Barnet
Maidenhead U v FC Halifax T
Maidstone U v Harrogate T
Wrexham v Ebbsfleet U

Saturday, 22 September 2018
Aldershot T v Dover Ath
Barnet v AFC Fylde
Barrow v Maidenhead U
Braintree T v Maidstone U
Chesterfield v Gateshead
Dover Ath v Dagenham & R
Ebbsfleet U v Havant & W'ville
FC Halifax T v Hartlepool U
Harrogate T v Leyton Orient
Salford C v Boreham Wood
Solihull Moors v Bromley
Sutton U v Wrexham

Tuesday, 25 September 2018
Aldershot T v Maidstone U
Barnet v Havant & W'ville
Barrow v Gateshead
Braintree T v Leyton Orient
Chesterfield v Maidenhead U
Dover Ath v Boreham Wood
Ebbsfleet U v Bromley
FC Halifax T v AFC Fylde
Harrogate T v Wrexham
Salford C v Hartlepool U
Solihull Moors v Dagenham & R
Sutton U v Dover Ath

Saturday, 29 September 2018
AFC Fylde v Braintree T
Boreham Wood v Harrogate T
Bromley v FC Halifax T
Dagenham & R v Ebbsfleet U
Dover Ath v Barrow
Gateshead v Dover Ath
Hartlepool U v Aldershot T
Havant & W'ville v Solihull Moors
Leyton Orient v Sutton U
Maidenhead U v Salford C
Maidstone U v Chesterfield
Wrexham v Barnet

Saturday, 6 October 2018
Aldershot T v FC Halifax T
Barnet v Solihull Moors
Barrow v Sutton U
Braintree T v Dover Ath
Chesterfield v AFC Fylde
Dover Ath v Salford C
Ebbsfleet U v Harrogate T
Gateshead v Dagenham & R
Hartlepool U v Boreham Wood
Maidenhead U v Leyton Orient
Maidstone U v Bromley
Wrexham v Havant & W'ville

Saturday, 13 October 2018
AFC Fylde v Maidstone U
Boreham Wood v Maidenhead U
Bromley v Barrow
Dagenham & R v Wrexham
Dover Ath v Aldershot T
FC Halifax T v Chesterfield
Harrogate T v Dover Ath
Havant & W'ville v Gateshead
Leyton Orient v Hartlepool U
Salford C v Braintree T
Solihull Moors v Ebbsfleet U
Sutton U v Barnet

Saturday, 27 October 2018
Barrow v Barnet
Boreham Wood v Bromley
Braintree T v Dover Ath
Chesterfield v Wrexham
Dagenham & R v Harrogate T
FC Halifax T v Dover Ath
Gateshead v Aldershot T
Hartlepool U v Sutton U
Leyton Orient v
    Havant & W'ville
Maidenhead U v AFC Fylde
Maidstone U v Solihull Moors
Salford C v Ebbsfleet U

Tuesday, 30 October 2018
AFC Fylde v Gateshead
Aldershot T v Boreham Wood
Barnet v Salford C
Bromley v Braintree T
Dover Ath v Dagenham & R
Dover Ath v Leyton Orient
Ebbsfleet U v Maidstone U
Harrogate T v Barrow
Havant & W'ville v Maidenhead U
Solihull Moors v FC Halifax T
Sutton U v Chesterfield
Wrexham v Hartlepool U

Saturday, 3 November 2018
AFC Fylde v Leyton Orient
Aldershot T v Braintree T
Barnet v Maidstone U
Bromley v Hartlepool U
Dover Ath v Maidenhead U
Dover Ath v Salford C
Ebbsfleet U v Barrow
Harrogate T v Chesterfield
Havant & W'ville v
    FC Halifax T
Solihull Moors v Boreham Wood
Sutton U v Dagenham & R
Wrexham v Gateshead

Saturday, 17 November 2018
Barrow v Dover Ath
Boreham Wood v Ebbsfleet U
Braintree T v Solihull Moors
Chesterfield v Havant & W'ville
Dagenham & R v AFC Fylde
FC Halifax T v Dover Ath
Gateshead v Sutton U
Hartlepool U v Barnet
Leyton Orient v Bromley
Maidenhead U v Harrogate T
Maidstone U v Wrexham
Salford C v Aldershot T

Saturday, 24 November 2018
AFC Fylde v Boreham Wood
Aldershot T v Barrow
Barnet v Gateshead
Bromley v Dagenham & R
Dover Ath v Hartlepool U
Dover Ath v Chesterfield

Ebbsfleet U v FC Halifax T
Harrogate T v Braintree T
Havant & W'ville v Maidstone U
Solihull Moors v Salford C
Sutton U v Maidenhead U
Wrexham v Leyton Orient

Tuesday, 27 November 2018
Barrow v Wrexham
Boreham Wood v Dover Ath
Braintree T v Sutton U
Chesterfield v Bromley
Dagenham & R v Havant & W'ville
FC Halifax T v Barnet
Gateshead v Solihull Moors
Hartlepool U v AFC Fylde
Leyton Orient v Aldershot T
Maidenhead U v Ebbsfleet U
Maidstone U v Dover Ath
Salford C v Harrogate T

Saturday, 1 December 2018
AFC Fylde v Sutton U
Aldershot T v Ebbsfleet U
Barnet v Chesterfield
Braintree T v Barrow
Bromley v Wrexham
Dover Ath v Dover Ath
FC Halifax T v Boreham Wood
Hartlepool U v Dagenham & R
Leyton Orient v Gateshead
Maidstone U v Maidenhead U
Salford C v Havant & W'ville
Solihull Moors v Harrogate T

Saturday, 8 December 2018
Barrow v Maidstone U
Boreham Wood v Leyton Orient
Chesterfield v Salford C
Dagenham & R v FC Halifax T
Dover Ath v AFC Fylde
Ebbsfleet U v Barnet
Gateshead v Bromley
Harrogate T v Aldershot T
Havant & W'ville v Braintree T
Maidenhead U v Hartlepool U
Sutton U v Solihull Moors
Wrexham v Dover Ath

Saturday, 22 December 2018
AFC Fylde v Ebbsfleet U
Aldershot T v Wrexham
Barnet v Dover Ath
Braintree T v Boreham Wood
Bromley v Maidenhead U
Dover Ath v Harrogate T
FC Halifax T v Sutton U
Hartlepool U v Havant & W'ville
Leyton Orient v Chesterfield
Maidstone U v Gateshead
Salford C v Dagenham & R
Solihull Moors v Barrow

Wednesday, 26 December 2018
Barrow v AFC Fylde
Boreham Wood v Barnet
Chesterfield v Solihull Moors
Dagenham & R v Leyton Orient
Dover Ath v Maidstone U
Ebbsfleet U v Braintree T
Gateshead v Hartlepool U
Harrogate T v FC Halifax T
Havant & W'ville v Dover Ath
Maidenhead U v Aldershot T
Sutton U v Bromley
Wrexham v Salford C

Saturday, 29 December 2018
Barrow v Salford C
Boreham Wood v Maidstone U
Chesterfield v Hartlepool U
Dagenham & R v Barnet
Dover Ath v Leyton Orient
Ebbsfleet U v Dover Ath
Gateshead v FC Halifax T
Harrogate T v AFC Fylde
Havant & W'ville v Bromley
Maidenhead U v Braintree T
Sutton U v Aldershot T
Wrexham v Solihull Moors

Tuesday, 1 January 2019
AFC Fylde v Barrow
Aldershot T v Maidenhead U
Barnet v Boreham Wood
Braintree T v Ebbsfleet U
Bromley v Sutton U
Dover Ath v Havant & W'ville
FC Halifax T v Harrogate T
Hartlepool U v Gateshead
Leyton Orient v Dagenham & R
Maidstone U v Dover Ath
Salford C v Wrexham
Solihull Moors v Chesterfield

Saturday, 5 January 2019
Barnet v Aldershot T
Bromley v AFC Fylde
Chesterfield v Ebbsfleet U
Dagenham & R v Boreham Wood
FC Halifax T v Braintree T
Gateshead v Maidenhead U
Hartlepool U v Maidstone U
Havant & W'ville v Barrow
Leyton Orient v Salford C
Solihull Moors v Dover Ath
Sutton U v Harrogate T
Wrexham v Dover Ath

Saturday, 19 January 2019
AFC Fylde v Wrexham
Aldershot T v Chesterfield
Barrow v FC Halifax T
Boreham Wood v Havant & W'ville
Braintree T v Barnet
Dover Ath v Bromley
Dover Ath v Sutton U
Ebbsfleet U v Leyton Orient
Harrogate T v Hartlepool U
Maidenhead U v Solihull Moors
Maidstone U v Dagenham & R
Salford C v Gateshead

Saturday, 26 January 2019
Barnet v Harrogate T
Bromley v Dover Ath
Chesterfield v Barrow
Dagenham & R v Aldershot T
FC Halifax T v Salford C
Gateshead v Boreham Wood
Hartlepool U v Braintree T
Havant & W'ville v Dover Ath
Leyton Orient v Maidstone U
Solihull Moors v AFC Fylde
Sutton U v Ebbsfleet U
Wrexham v Maidenhead U

Saturday, 2 February 2019
AFC Fylde v Havant & W'ville
Aldershot T v Solihull Moors
Barrow v Leyton Orient
Boreham Wood v Wrexham
Braintree T v Chesterfield
Dover Ath v Gateshead
Dover Ath v Barnet
Ebbsfleet U v Hartlepool U

Harrogate T v Bromley
Maidenhead U v Dagenham & R
Maidstone U v FC Halifax T
Salford C v Sutton U

Saturday, 9 February 2019
Aldershot T v Dover Ath
Barnet v Sutton U
Barrow v Bromley
Braintree T v Salford C
Chesterfield v FC Halifax T
Dover Ath v Harrogate T
Ebbsfleet U v Solihull Moors
Gateshead v Havant & W'ville
Hartlepool U v Leyton Orient
Maidenhead U v Boreham Wood
Maidstone U v AFC Fylde
Wrexham v Dagenham & R

Saturday, 16 February 2019
AFC Fylde v Chesterfield
Boreham Wood v Hartlepool U
Bromley v Maidstone U
Dagenham & R v Gateshead
Dover Ath v Braintree T
FC Halifax T v Aldershot T
Harrogate T v Ebbsfleet U
Havant & W'ville v Wrexham
Leyton Orient v Maidenhead U
Salford C v Dover Ath
Solihull Moors v Barnet
Sutton U v Barrow

Saturday, 23 February 2019
Barrow v Ebbsfleet U
Boreham Wood v Solihull Moors
Braintree T v Aldershot T
Chesterfield v Harrogate T
Dagenham & R v Sutton U
FC Halifax T v Havant & W'ville
Gateshead v Wrexham
Hartlepool U v Bromley
Leyton Orient v AFC Fylde
Maidenhead U v Dover Ath
Maidstone U v Barnet
Salford C v Dover Ath

Saturday, 2 March 2019
AFC Fylde v Maidenhead U
Aldershot T v Gateshead
Barnet v Barrow
Bromley v Boreham Wood
Dover Ath v Braintree T
Dover Ath v FC Halifax T
Ebbsfleet U v Salford C
Harrogate T v Dagenham & R
Havant & W'ville v Leyton Orient
Solihull Moors v Maidstone U
Sutton U v Hartlepool U
Wrexham v Chesterfield

Saturday, 9 March 2019
Barrow v Aldershot T
Boreham Wood v AFC Fylde
Braintree T v Harrogate T
Chesterfield v Dover Ath
Dagenham & R v Bromley

FC Halifax T v Ebbsfleet U
Gateshead v Barnet
Hartlepool U v Dover Ath
Leyton Orient v Wrexham
Maidenhead U v Sutton U
Maidstone U v Havant & W'ville
Salford C v Solihull Moors

Tuesday, 12 March 2019
AFC Fylde v Hartlepool U
Aldershot T v Leyton Orient
Barnet v FC Halifax T
Bromley v Chesterfield
Dover Ath v Boreham Wood
Dover Ath v Maidstone U
Ebbsfleet U v Maidenhead U
Harrogate T v Salford C
Havant & W'ville v Dagenham & R
Solihull Moors v Gateshead
Sutton U v Braintree T
Wrexham v Barrow

Saturday, 16 March 2019
AFC Fylde v Dagenham & R
Aldershot T v Salford C
Barnet v Hartlepool U
Bromley v Leyton Orient
Dover Ath v FC Halifax T
Dover Ath v Barrow
Ebbsfleet U v Boreham Wood
Harrogate T v Maidenhead U
Havant & W'ville v Chesterfield
Solihull Moors v Braintree T
Sutton U v Gateshead
Wrexham v Maidstone U

Saturday, 23 March 2019
Barrow v Harrogate T
Boreham Wood v Aldershot T
Braintree T v Bromley
Chesterfield v Sutton U
Dagenham & R v Dover Ath
FC Halifax T v Solihull Moors
Gateshead v AFC Fylde
Hartlepool U v Wrexham
Leyton Orient v Dover Ath
Maidenhead U v Havant & W'ville
Maidstone U v Ebbsfleet U
Salford C v Barnet

Saturday, 30 March 2019
Aldershot T v AFC Fylde
Barnet v Leyton Orient
Barrow v Boreham Wood
Braintree T v Gateshead
Chesterfield v Dagenham & R
Dover Ath v Hartlepool U
Ebbsfleet U v Wrexham
FC Halifax T v Maidenhead U
Harrogate T v Maidstone U
Salford C v Bromley
Solihull Moors v Dover Ath
Sutton U v Havant & W'ville

Saturday, 6 April 2019
AFC Fylde v Dover Ath
Boreham Wood v Sutton U

Bromley v Aldershot T
Dagenham & R v Barrow
Dover Ath v Chesterfield
Gateshead v Ebbsfleet U
Hartlepool U v Solihull Moors
Havant & W'ville v Harrogate T
Leyton Orient v FC Halifax T
Maidenhead U v Barnet
Maidstone U v Salford C
Wrexham v Braintree T

Saturday, 13 April 2019
Aldershot T v Hartlepool U
Barnet v Wrexham
Barrow v Dover Ath
Braintree T v AFC Fylde
Chesterfield v Maidstone U
Dover Ath v Gateshead
Ebbsfleet U v Dagenham & R
FC Halifax T v Bromley
Harrogate T v Boreham Wood
Salford C v Maidenhead U
Solihull Moors v Havant & W'ville
Sutton U v Leyton Orient

Friday, 19 April 2019
AFC Fylde v Barnet
Boreham Wood v Salford C
Bromley v Solihull Moors
Dagenham & R v Dover Ath
Dover Ath v Aldershot T
Gateshead v Chesterfield
Hartlepool U v FC Halifax T
Havant & W'ville v Ebbsfleet U
Leyton Orient v Harrogate T
Maidenhead U v Barrow
Maidstone U v Braintree T
Wrexham v Sutton U

Monday, 22 April 2019
Aldershot T v Havant & W'ville
Barnet v Bromley
Barrow v Hartlepool U
Braintree T v Dagenham & R
Chesterfield v Boreham Wood
Dover Ath v Maidenhead U
Ebbsfleet U v Dover Ath
FC Halifax T v Wrexham
Harrogate T v Gateshead
Salford C v AFC Fylde
Solihull Moors v Leyton Orient
Sutton U v Maidstone U

Saturday, 27 April 2019
AFC Fylde v FC Halifax T
Boreham Wood v Dover Ath
Bromley v Ebbsfleet U
Dagenham & R v Solihull Moors
Dover Ath v Sutton U
Gateshead v Barrow
Hartlepool U v Salford C
Havant & W'ville v Barnet
Leyton Orient v Braintree T
Maidenhead U v Chesterfield
Maidstone U v Aldershot T
Wrexham v Harrogate T

THE SCOTTISH PREMIER LEAGUE AND SCOTTISH LEAGUE FIXTURES 2018–19

All fixtures subject to change.

SPFL Premiership

Saturday, 4 August 2018
Celtic v Livingston
Hamilton A v Hearts
Hibernian v Motherwell
Kilmarnock v St Johnstone
St Mirren v Dundee

Sunday, 5 August 2018
Aberdeen v Rangers

Saturday, 11 August 2018
Dundee v Aberdeen
Hearts v Celtic
Livingston v Kilmarnock
Motherwell v Hamilton A
Rangers v St Mirren
St Johnstone v Hibernian

Saturday, 25 August 2018
Celtic v Hamilton A
Hibernian v Aberdeen
Kilmarnock v Hearts
Motherwell v Rangers
St Johnstone v Dundee
St Mirren v Livingston

Saturday, 1 September 2018
Aberdeen v Kilmarnock
Celtic v Rangers
Dundee v Motherwell
Hamilton A v St Johnstone
Hearts v St Mirren
Livingston v Hibernian

Saturday, 15 September 2018
Hibernian v Kilmarnock
Livingston v Hamilton A
Motherwell v Hearts
Rangers v Dundee
St Johnstone v Aberdeen
St Mirren v Celtic

Saturday, 22 September 2018
Aberdeen v Motherwell
Dundee v Hibernian
Hamilton A v St Mirren
Hearts v Livingston
Kilmarnock v Celtic
Rangers v St Johnstone

Saturday, 29 September 2018
Celtic v Aberdeen
Hamilton A v Dundee
Hearts v St Johnstone
Kilmarnock v Motherwell
Livingston v Rangers
St Mirren v Hibernian

Saturday, 6 October 2018
Aberdeen v St Mirren
Dundee v Kilmarnock
Hibernian v Hamilton A
Motherwell v Livingston

Rangers v Hearts
St Johnstone v Celtic

Saturday, 20 October 2018
Celtic v Hibernian
Hamilton A v Rangers
Hearts v Aberdeen
Livingston v Dundee
Motherwell v St Johnstone
St Mirren v Kilmarnock

Saturday, 27 October 2018
Aberdeen v Livingston
Celtic v Motherwell
Dundee v Hearts
Hibernian v Rangers
Kilmarnock v Hamilton A
St Johnstone v St Mirren

Wednesday, 31 October 2018
Aberdeen v Hamilton A
Dundee v Celtic
Hearts v Hibernian
Livingston v St Johnstone
Rangers v Kilmarnock
St Mirren v Motherwell

Saturday, 3 November 2018
Celtic v Hearts
Hamilton A v Livingston
Hibernian v St Johnstone
Kilmarnock v Aberdeen
Motherwell v Dundee
St Mirren v Rangers

Saturday, 10 November 2018
Aberdeen v Hibernian
Dundee v St Mirren
Hearts v Kilmarnock
Livingston v Celtic
Rangers v Motherwell
St Johnstone v Hamilton A

Saturday, 24 November 2018
Hamilton A v Celtic
Hibernian v Dundee
Motherwell v Aberdeen
Rangers v Livingston
St Johnstone v Kilmarnock
St Mirren v Hearts

Saturday, 1 December 2018
Aberdeen v Dundee
Celtic v St Johnstone
Hearts v Rangers
Kilmarnock v Hibernian
Livingston v Motherwell
St Mirren v Hamilton A

Wednesday, 5 December 2018
Dundee v Hamilton A
Hibernian v St Mirren
Kilmarnock v Livingston
Motherwell v Celtic
Rangers v Aberdeen
St Johnstone v Hearts

Saturday, 8 December 2018
Aberdeen v St Johnstone
Celtic v Kilmarnock
Dundee v Rangers
Hamilton A v Hibernian
Hearts v Motherwell
Livingston v St Mirren

Saturday, 15 December 2018
Hibernian v Celtic
Kilmarnock v Dundee
Livingston v Hearts
Rangers v Hamilton A
St Johnstone v Motherwell
St Mirren v Aberdeen

Saturday, 22 December 2018
Aberdeen v Hearts
Celtic v Dundee
Hamilton A v Kilmarnock
Hibernian v Livingston
Motherwell v St Mirren
St Johnstone v Rangers

Wednesday, 26 December 2018
Aberdeen v Celtic
Dundee v Livingston
Hearts v Hamilton A
Motherwell v Kilmarnock
Rangers v Hibernian
St Mirren v St Johnstone

Saturday, 29 December 2018
Dundee v St Johnstone
Hamilton A v Motherwell
Hibernian v Hearts
Kilmarnock v St Mirren
Livingston v Aberdeen
Rangers v Celtic

Wednesday, 23 January 2019
Celtic v St Mirren
Hamilton A v Aberdeen
Hearts v Dundee
Kilmarnock v Rangers
Motherwell v Hibernian
St Johnstone v Livingston

Saturday, 26 January 2019
Aberdeen v Kilmarnock
Celtic v Hamilton A
Dundee v Motherwell
Hearts v St Johnstone
Livingston v Rangers
St Mirren v Hibernian

Saturday, 2 February 2019
Hamilton A v Dundee
Hibernian v Aberdeen
Kilmarnock v Hearts
Motherwell v Livingston
Rangers v St Mirren
St Johnstone v Celtic

Wednesday, 6 February 2019
Aberdeen v Rangers

Celtic v Hibernian
Dundee v Kilmarnock
Hamilton A v St Johnstone
Hearts v Livingston
St Mirren v Motherwell

Saturday, 16 February 2019
Aberdeen v St Mirren
Hibernian v Hamilton A
Kilmarnock v Celtic
Livingston v Dundee
Motherwell v Hearts
Rangers v St Johnstone

Saturday, 23 February 2019
Celtic v Motherwell
Dundee v Hibernian
Hamilton A v Rangers
Hearts v St Mirren
Livingston v Kilmarnock
St Johnstone v Aberdeen

Wednesday, 27 February 2019
Aberdeen v Hamilton A
Hearts v Celtic
Kilmarnock v Motherwell
Rangers v Dundee
St Johnstone v Hibernian
St Mirren v Livingston

Saturday, 9 March 2019
Celtic v Aberdeen
Dundee v Hearts
Hibernian v Rangers
Livingston v St Johnstone
Motherwell v Hamilton A
St Mirren v Kilmarnock

Saturday, 16 March 2019
Aberdeen v Livingston
Dundee v Celtic
Hamilton A v Hearts
Hibernian v Motherwell
Rangers v Kilmarnock
St Johnstone v St Mirren

Saturday, 30 March 2019
Celtic v Rangers
Hearts v Aberdeen
Kilmarnock v Hamilton A
Livingston v Hibernian
Motherwell v St Johnstone
St Mirren v Dundee

Wednesday, 3 April 2019
Aberdeen v Motherwell
Hibernian v Kilmarnock
Livingston v Hamilton A
Rangers v Hearts
St Johnstone v Dundee
St Mirren v Celtic

Saturday, 6 April 2019
Celtic v Livingston
Dundee v Aberdeen
Hamilton A v St Mirren
Hearts v Hibernian
Kilmarnock v St Johnstone
Motherwell v Rangers

SPFL Championship

Saturday 4 August 2018
Ayr U v Partick Thistle
Dundee U v Dunfermline
Falkirk v Inverness CT
Greenock Morton v
    Queen of the South
Ross Co v Alloa Ath

Saturday, 11 August 2018
Alloa Ath v Greenock Morton
Dunfermline v Ross Co
Inverness CT v Ayr U
Partick Thistle v Falkirk
Queen of the South v Dundee U

Saturday, 25 August 2018
Ayr U v Dunfermline
Dundee U v Partick Thistle
Falkirk v Queen of the South
Inverness CT v Alloa Ath
Greenock Morton v Ross Co

Saturday, 1 September 2018
Alloa Ath v Dundee U
Dunfermline v Inverness CT
Partick Thistle v Greenock Morton
Queen of the South v Ayr U
Ross Co v Falkirk

Saturday, 15 September 2018
Ayr U v Falkirk
Dundee U v Greenock Morton
Dunfermline v Alloa Ath
Inverness CT v Partick Thistle
Queen of the South v Ross Co

Saturday, 22 September 2018
Alloa Ath v Ayr U
Falkirk v Dundee U
Greenock Morton v Dunfermline
Partick Thistle v Queen of the South
Ross Co v Inverness CT

Saturday, 29 September 2018
Alloa Ath v Falkirk
Dundee U v Ross Co
Dunfermline v Partick Thistle
Inverness CT v Queen of the South
Greenock Morton v Ayr U

Saturday, 6 October 2018
Ayr U v Dundee U
Falkirk v Dunfermline
Inverness CT v Greenock Morton
Partick Thistle v Ross Co
Queen of the South v Alloa Ath

Saturday, 20 October 2018
Alloa Ath v Partick Thistle
Dundee U v Inverness CT
Dunfermline v Queen of the South
Greenock Morton v Falkirk
Ross Co v Ayr U

Saturday, 27 October 2018
Alloa Ath v Inverness CT
Dunfermline v Dundee U
Partick Thistle v Ayr U
Queen of the South v Falkirk
Ross Co v Greenock Morton

Tuesday, 30 October 2018
Ayr U v Alloa Ath
Falkirk v Ross Co
Inverness CT v Dunfermline
Partick Thistle v Dundee U
Queen of the South v Greenock
    Morton

Saturday, 3 November 2018
Alloa Ath v Dunfermline
Dundee U v Queen of the South
Falkirk v Ayr U
Inverness CT v Ross Co
Greenock Morton v Partick Thistle

Saturday, 10 November 2018
Ayr U v Queen of the South
Dunfermline v Falkirk
Greenock Morton v Alloa Ath
Partick Thistle v Inverness CT
Ross Co v Dundee U

Saturday, 17 November 2018
Ayr U v Greenock Morton
Dundee U v Alloa Ath
Falkirk v Partick Thistle
Queen of the South v Inverness CT
Ross Co v Dunfermline

Saturday, 1 December 2018
Alloa Ath v Ross Co
Dundee U v Ayr U
Dunfermline v Greenock Morton
Inverness CT v Falkirk
Queen of the South v Partick Thistle

Saturday, 8 December 2018
Ayr U v Inverness CT
Falkirk v Alloa Ath
Greenock Morton v Dundee U
Partick Thistle v Dunfermline
Ross Co v Queen of the South

Saturday, 15 December 2018
Ayr U v Ross Co
Falkirk v Greenock Morton
Inverness CT v Dundee U
Partick Thistle v Alloa Ath
Queen of the South v Dunfermline

Saturday, 22 December 2018
Alloa Ath v Queen of the South
Dundee U v Falkirk
Dunfermline v Ayr U
Greenock Morton v Inverness CT
Ross Co v Partick Thistle

Saturday, 29 December 2018
Alloa Ath v Dundee U
Falkirk v Dunfermline
Partick Thistle v Greenock Morton
Queen of the South v Ayr U
Ross Co v Inverness CT

Saturday, 5 January 2019
Ayr U v Falkirk
Dundee U v Partick Thistle
Dunfermline v Alloa Ath
Inverness CT v Queen of the South
Greenock Morton v Ross Co

Saturday, 12 January 2019
Alloa Ath v Greenock Morton
Dundee U v Dunfermline

Inverness CT v Ayr U
Partick Thistle v Falkirk
Queen of the South v Ross Co

Saturday, 26 January 2019
Ayr U v Dundee U
Falkirk v Inverness CT
Greenock Morton v Dunfermline
Partick Thistle v Queen of the South
Ross Co v Alloa Ath

Saturday, 2 February 2019
Alloa Ath v Ayr U
Dundee U v Greenock Morton
Dunfermline v Ross Co
Falkirk v Queen of the South
Inverness CT v Partick Thistle

Saturday, 16 February 2019
Alloa Ath v Partick Thistle
Dunfermline v Inverness CT
Greenock Morton v Ayr U
Queen of the South v Dundee U
Ross Co v Falkirk

Saturday, 23 February 2019
Ayr U v Dunfermline
Falkirk v Dundee U
Inverness CT v Greenock Morton
Partick Thistle v Ross Co
Queen of the South v Alloa Ath

Tuesday, 26 February 2019
Alloa Ath v Falkirk
Dundee U v Inverness CT
Dunfermline v Partick Thistle
Greenock Morton v Queen of the South
Ross Co v Ayr U

Saturday, 2 March 2019
Ayr U v Partick Thistle
Dundee U v Ross Co
Dunfermline v Queen of the South
Inverness CT v Alloa Ath
Greenock Morton v Falkirk

Saturday, 9 March 2019
Alloa Ath v Dunfermline
Falkirk v Ayr U
Partick Thistle v Dundee U
Queen of the South v Inverness CT
Ross Co v Greenock Morton

Saturday, 16 March 2019
Ayr U v Queen of the South
Dunfermline v Dundee U
Falkirk v Partick Thistle
Inverness CT v Ross Co
Greenock Morton v Alloa Ath

Saturday, 23 March 2019
Ayr U v Greenock Morton
Dundee U v Alloa Ath
Partick Thistle v Inverness CT
Queen of the South v Falkirk
Ross Co v Dunfermline

Saturday, 30 March 2019
Alloa Ath v Ross Co
Dundee U v Queen of the South
Dunfermline v Ayr U
Inverness CT v Falkirk
Greenock Morton v Partick Thistle

Saturday, 6 April 2019
Ayr U v Inverness CT
Falkirk v Alloa Ath
Partick Thistle v Dunfermline
Queen of the South v
  Greenock Morton
Ross Co v Dundee U

Saturday, 13 April 2019
Alloa Ath v Queen of the South
Dundee U v Ayr U
Dunfermline v Falkirk
Greenock Morton v Inverness CT
Ross Co v Partick Thistle

Saturday, 20 April 2019
Ayr U v Ross Co
Falkirk v Greenock Morton
Inverness CT v Dundee U
Partick Thistle v Alloa Ath
Queen of the South v Dunfermline

Saturday, 27 April 2019
Alloa Ath v Inverness CT
Dundee U v Falkirk
Dunfermline v Greenock Morton
Partick Thistle v Ayr U
Ross Co v Queen of the South

Saturday, 4 May 2019
Ayr U v Alloa Ath
Falkirk v Ross Co
Inverness CT v Dunfermline
Greenock Morton v Dundee U
Queen of the South v Partick Thistle

SPFL League One

Saturday, 4 August 2018
East Fife v Dumbarton
Forfar Ath v Airdrieonians
Montrose v Arbroath
Stenhousemuir v Brechin C
Stranraer v Raith R

Saturday, 11 August 2018
Airdrieonians v Montrose
Arbroath v Stranraer
Brechin C v East Fife
Dumbarton v Forfar Ath
Raith R v Stenhousemuir

Saturday, 18 August 2018
Dumbarton v Arbroath
Forfar Ath v Stranraer
Montrose v Brechin C
Raith R v East Fife
Stenhousemuir v Airdrieonians

Saturday, 25 August 2018
Airdrieonians v Raith R
Brechin C v Dumbarton
East Fife v Arbroath
Forfar Ath v Stenhousemuir
Stranraer v Montrose

Saturday, 1 September 2018
Airdrieonians v Stranraer
Arbroath v Brechin C
Montrose v East Fife
Raith R v Forfar Ath
Stenhousemuir v Dumbarton

Saturday, 15 September 2018
Arbroath v Forfar Ath
Brechin C v Raith R
Dumbarton v Montrose
East Fife v Airdrieonians
Stranraer v Stenhousemuir

Saturday, 22 September 2018
Airdrieonians v Dumbarton
Forfar Ath v Brechin C
Raith R v Montrose
Stenhousemuir v Arbroath
Stranraer v East Fife

Saturday, 29 September 2018
Arbroath v Airdrieonians
Brechin C v Stranraer
Dumbarton v Raith R
East Fife v Stenhousemuir
Montrose v Forfar Ath

Saturday, 6 October 2018
Airdrieonians v Brechin C
Forfar Ath v East Fife
Raith R v Arbroath
Stenhousemuir v Montrose
Stranraer v Dumbarton

Saturday, 20 October 2018
Arbroath v Dumbarton
East Fife v Brechin C
Montrose v Airdrieonians
Raith R v Stranraer
Stenhousemuir v Forfar Ath

Saturday, 27 October 2018
Airdrieonians v Stenhousemuir
Brechin C v Montrose
Dumbarton v East Fife
Forfar Ath v Raith R
Stranraer v Arbroath

Saturday, 3 November 2018
Airdrieonians v Forfar Ath
Arbroath v East Fife
Montrose v Dumbarton
Raith R v Brechin C
Stenhousemuir v Stranraer

Saturday, 10 November 2018
Arbroath v Montrose
Brechin C v Forfar Ath
Dumbarton v Stenhousemuir
East Fife v Raith R
Stranraer v Airdrieonians

Saturday, 17 November 2018
Airdrieonians v East Fife
Brechin C v Arbroath
Forfar Ath v Dumbarton
Montrose v Stranraer
Stenhousemuir v Raith R

Saturday, 1 December 2018
Arbroath v Stenhousemuir
Dumbarton v Brechin C
East Fife v Montrose
Raith R v Airdrieonians
Stranraer v Forfar Ath

Saturday, 8 December 2018
Brechin C v Stenhousemuir
Dumbarton v Airdrieonians
East Fife v Stranraer

Forfar Ath v Arbroath
Montrose v Raith R

Saturday, 15 December 2018
Airdrieonians v Arbroath
Forfar Ath v Montrose
Raith R v Dumbarton
Stenhousemuir v East Fife
Stranraer v Brechin C

Saturday, 22 December 2018
Arbroath v Raith R
Brechin C v Airdrieonians
Dumbarton v Stranraer
East Fife v Forfar Ath
Montrose v Stenhousemuir

Saturday, 29 December 2018
Airdrieonians v Stranraer
Forfar Ath v Brechin C
Montrose v Arbroath
Raith R v East Fife
Stenhousemuir v Dumbarton

Saturday, 5 January 2019
Arbroath v Brechin C
Dumbarton v Forfar Ath
East Fife v Airdrieonians
Raith R v Stenhousemuir
Stranraer v Montrose

Saturday, 12 January 2019
Airdrieonians v Raith R
Brechin C v Dumbarton
Forfar Ath v Stranraer
Montrose v East Fife
Stenhousemuir v Arbroath

Saturday, 26 January 2019
Arbroath v Forfar Ath
Brechin C v Raith R
Dumbarton v Montrose
Stenhousemuir v Airdrieonians
Stranraer v East Fife

Saturday, 2 February 2019
Airdrieonians v Dumbarton
East Fife v Arbroath
Montrose v Brechin C
Raith R v Forfar Ath
Stranraer v Stenhousemuir

Saturday, 9 February 2019
Arbroath v Stranraer
Brechin C v East Fife
Dumbarton v Raith R
Forfar Ath v Airdrieonians
Stenhousemuir v Montrose

Saturday, 16 February 2019
Airdrieonians v Brechin C
East Fife v Stenhousemuir
Montrose v Forfar Ath
Raith R v Arbroath
Stranraer v Dumbarton

Saturday, 23 February 2019
Arbroath v Airdrieonians
Brechin C v Stranraer
East Fife v Dumbarton
Forfar Ath v Stenhousemuir
Raith R v Montrose

Saturday, 2 March 2019
Airdrieonians v Montrose

Dumbarton v Arbroath
Forfar Ath v East Fife
Stenhousemuir v Brechin C
Stranraer v Raith R

Saturday, 9 March 2019
Arbroath v Stenhousemuir
Brechin C v Forfar Ath
East Fife v Stranraer
Montrose v Dumbarton
Raith R v Airdrieonians

Saturday, 16 March 2019
Arbroath v East Fife
Brechin C v Montrose
Dumbarton v Airdrieonians
Forfar Ath v Raith R
Stenhousemuir v Stranraer

Saturday, 23 March 2019
Airdrieonians v Forfar Ath
East Fife v Brechin C
Montrose v Stenhousemuir
Raith R v Dumbarton
Stranraer v Arbroath

Saturday, 30 March 2019
Brechin C v Airdrieonians
Dumbarton v Stenhousemuir
East Fife v Raith R
Forfar Ath v Arbroath
Montrose v Stranraer

Saturday, 6 April 2019
Airdrieonians v East Fife
Arbroath v Montrose
Dumbarton v Brechin C
Stenhousemuir v Raith R
Stranraer v Forfar Ath

Saturday, 13 April 2019
Airdrieonians v Stenhousemuir
Brechin C v Arbroath
East Fife v Montrose
Forfar Ath v Dumbarton
Raith R v Stranraer

Saturday, 20 April 2019
Arbroath v Raith R
Dumbarton v East Fife
Montrose v Airdrieonians
Stenhousemuir v Forfar Ath
Stranraer v Brechin C

Saturday, 27 April 2019
Airdrieonians v Arbroath
Dumbarton v Stranraer
Forfar Ath v Montrose
Raith R v Brechin C
Stenhousemuir v East Fife

Saturday, 4 May 2019
Arbroath v Dumbarton
Brechin C v Stenhousemuir
East Fife v Forfar Ath
Montrose v Raith R
Stranraer v Airdrieonians

SPFL League Two

Saturday, 4 August 2018
Annan Ath v Elgin C
Berwick R v Stirling Alb

Clyde v Cowdenbeath
Edinburgh C v Albion R
Peterhead v Queen's Park

Saturday, 11 August 2018
Albion R v Peterhead
Cowdenbeath v Annan Ath
Elgin C v Edinburgh C
Queen's Park v Berwick R
Stirling Alb v Clyde

Saturday, 18 August 2018
Albion R v Elgin C
Annan Ath v Queen's Park
Cowdenbeath v Berwick R
Edinburgh C v Stirling Alb
Peterhead v Clyde

Saturday, 25 August 2018
Berwick R v Annan Ath
Clyde v Edinburgh C
Elgin C v Cowdenbeath
Queen's Park v Albion R
Stirling Alb v Peterhead

Saturday, 1 September 2018
Albion R v Berwick R
Annan Ath v Clyde
Elgin C v Stirling Alb
Peterhead v Edinburgh C
Queen's Park v Cowdenbeath

Saturday, 15 September 2018
Berwick R v Elgin C
Clyde v Albion R
Cowdenbeath v Peterhead
Edinburgh C v Annan Ath
Stirling Alb v Queen's Park

Saturday, 22 September 2018
Clyde v Elgin C
Cowdenbeath v Albion R
Peterhead v Berwick R
Queen's Park v Edinburgh C
Stirling Alb v Annan Ath

Saturday, 29 September 2018
Albion R v Stirling Alb
Annan Ath v Peterhead
Berwick R v Clyde
Edinburgh C v Cowdenbeath
Elgin C v Queen's Park

Saturday, 6 October 2018
Annan Ath v Albion R
Cowdenbeath v Stirling Alb
Edinburgh C v Berwick R
Peterhead v Elgin C
Queen's Park v Clyde

Saturday, 27 October 2018
Albion R v Queen's Park
Berwick R v Cowdenbeath
Clyde v Peterhead
Elgin C v Annan Ath
Stirling Alb v Edinburgh C

Saturday, 3 November 2018
Cowdenbeath v Elgin C
Edinburgh C v Clyde
Peterhead v Albion R
Queen's Park v Annan Ath
Stirling Alb v Berwick R

Saturday, 10 November 2018
Albion R v Edinburgh C
Annan Ath v Cowdenbeath
Clyde v Stirling Alb
Elgin C v Berwick R
Queen's Park v Peterhead

Saturday, 17 November 2018
Annan Ath v Stirling Alb
Berwick R v Albion R
Cowdenbeath v Queen's Park
Edinburgh C v Peterhead
Elgin C v Clyde

Saturday, 1 December 2018
Albion R v Cowdenbeath
Clyde v Berwick R
Edinburgh C v Queen's Park
Peterhead v Annan Ath
Stirling Alb v Elgin C

Saturday, 8 December 2018
Annan Ath v Edinburgh C
Berwick R v Peterhead
Cowdenbeath v Clyde
Elgin C v Albion R
Queen's Park v Stirling Alb

Saturday, 15 December 2018
Berwick R v Queen's Park
Clyde v Annan Ath
Edinburgh C v Elgin C
Peterhead v Cowdenbeath
Stirling Alb v Albion R

Saturday, 22 December 2018
Albion R v Clyde
Annan Ath v Berwick R
Cowdenbeath v Edinburgh C
Peterhead v Stirling Alb
Queen's Park v Elgin C

Saturday, 29 December 2018
Albion R v Annan Ath
Berwick R v Edinburgh C
Clyde v Queen's Park
Elgin C v Peterhead
Stirling Alb v Cowdenbeath

Saturday, 5 January 2019
Annan Ath v Elgin C
Cowdenbeath v Berwick R
Edinburgh C v Stirling Alb
Peterhead v Clyde
Queen's Park v Albion R

Saturday, 12 January 2019
Albion R v Peterhead
Berwick R v Clyde

Elgin C v Cowdenbeath
Queen's Park v Edinburgh C
Stirling Alb v Annan Ath

Saturday, 19 January 2019
Clyde v Elgin C
Cowdenbeath v Albion R
Edinburgh C v Annan Ath
Peterhead v Berwick R
Stirling Alb v Queen's Park

Saturday, 26 January 2019
Albion R v Stirling Alb
Annan Ath v Peterhead
Clyde v Cowdenbeath
Elgin C v Edinburgh C
Queen's Park v Berwick R

Saturday, 2 February 2019
Berwick R v Annan Ath
Cowdenbeath v Peterhead
Edinburgh C v Albion R
Elgin C v Queen's Park
Stirling Alb v Clyde

Saturday, 9 February 2019
Albion R v Elgin C
Annan Ath v Clyde
Berwick R v Stirling Alb
Peterhead v Edinburgh C
Queen's Park v Cowdenbeath

Saturday, 16 February 2019
Clyde v Albion R
Cowdenbeath v Annan Ath
Edinburgh C v Berwick R
Elgin C v Stirling Alb
Peterhead v Queen's Park

Saturday, 23 February 2019
Annan Ath v Albion R
Berwick R v Elgin C
Edinburgh C v Cowdenbeath
Queen's Park v Clyde
Stirling Alb v Peterhead

Saturday, 2 March 2019
Albion R v Berwick R
Annan Ath v Queen's Park
Clyde v Edinburgh C
Cowdenbeath v Stirling Alb
Peterhead v Elgin C

Saturday, 9 March 2019
Berwick R v Cowdenbeath
Edinburgh C v Queen's Park
Elgin C v Clyde
Peterhead v Annan Ath
Stirling Alb v Albion R

Saturday, 16 March 2019
Albion R v Cowdenbeath
Annan Ath v Edinburgh C
Berwick R v Peterhead
Clyde v Stirling Alb
Queen's Park v Elgin C

Saturday, 23 March 2019
Clyde v Annan Ath
Cowdenbeath v Queen's Park
Edinburgh C v Peterhead
Elgin C v Albion R
Stirling Alb v Berwick R

Saturday, 30 March 2019
Albion R v Clyde
Berwick R v Edinburgh C
Elgin C v Annan Ath
Peterhead v Cowdenbeath
Queen's Park v Stirling Alb

Saturday, 6 April 2019
Albion R v Queen's Park
Annan Ath v Berwick R
Clyde v Peterhead
Cowdenbeath v Edinburgh C
Stirling Alb v Elgin C

Saturday, 13 April 2019
Annan Ath v Stirling Alb
Berwick R v Queen's Park
Cowdenbeath v Elgin C
Edinburgh C v Clyde
Peterhead v Albion R

Saturday, 20 April 2019
Albion R v Edinburgh C
Clyde v Berwick R
Elgin C v Peterhead
Queen's Park v Annan Ath
Stirling Alb v Cowdenbeath

Saturday, 27 April 2019
Annan Ath v Cowdenbeath
Berwick R v Albion R
Clyde v Queen's Park
Edinburgh C v Elgin C
Peterhead v Stirling Alb

Saturday, 4 May 2019
Albion R v Annan Ath
Cowdenbeath v Clyde
Elgin C v Berwick R
Queen's Park v Peterhead
Stirling Alb v Edinburgh C

FOOTBALL ASSOCIATION FIXTURES 2018–19

JULY 2018

10 Tuesday	UEFA Champions League 1Q(1)
11 Wednesday	UEFA Champions League 1Q(1)
12 Thursday	UEFA Europa League 1Q(1)
17 Tuesday	UEFA Champions League 1Q(2)
18 Wednesday	UEFA Champions League 1Q(2)
19 Thursday	UEFA Europa League 1Q(2)
24 Tuesday	UEFA Champions League 2Q(1)
25 Wednesday	UEFA Champions League 2Q(1)
26 Thursday	UEFA Europa League 2Q(1)
31 Tuesday	UEFA Champions League 2Q(2)

AUGUST 2018

1 Wednesday	UEFA Champions League 2Q(2)
2 Thursday	UEFA Europa League 2Q(2)
4 Saturday	EFL Commences
	National League Commences
5 Sunday	FA Community Shield
7 Tuesday	UEFA Champions League 3Q(1)
8 Wednesday	UEFA Champions League 3Q(1)
9 Thursday	UEFA Europa League 3Q(1)
11 Saturday	Premier League Commences
	The Emirates FA Cup EP
14 Tuesday	UEFA Champions League 3Q(2)
15 Wednesday	UEFA Champions League 3Q(2)
	UEFA Super Cup
	Carabao Cup 1
16 Thursday	UEFA Europa League 3Q(2)
21 Tuesday	UEFA Champions League Qualifying Play-Off (1)
22 Wednesday	UEFA Champions League Qualifying Play-Off (1)
23 Thursday	UEFA Europa League Qualifying Play-Off (1)
25 Saturday	The Emirates FA Cup P
27 Monday	Bank Holiday
28 Tuesday	UEFA Champions League Qualifying Play-Off (2)
29 Wednesday	UEFA Champions League Qualifying Play-Off (2)
	Carabao Cup 2
30 Thursday	UEFA Europa League Qualifying Play-Off (2)

SEPTEMBER 2018

1 Saturday	The Buildbase FA Vase 1Q
2 Sunday	The SSE Women's FA Cup 1Q
3 Monday	The FA Youth Cup P+
5 Wednesday	Checkatrade Trophy MD1
8 Saturday	England v Spain – UEFA Nations League
	The Emirates FA Cup 1Q
11 Tuesday	England v Switzerland – International Friendly
15 Saturday	The Buildbase FA Vase 2Q
17 Monday	The FA Youth Cup 1Q+
18 Tuesday	UEFA Champions League MD1
19 Wednesday	UEFA Champions League MD1
20 Thursday	UEFA Europa League MD1
22 Saturday	The Emirates FA Cup 2Q

23 Sunday	The SSE Women's FA Cup 2Q
26 Wednesday	Carabao Cup 3
29 Saturday	The Buildbase FA Trophy EP

OCTOBER 2018

1 Monday	The FA Youth Cup 2Q+
2 Tuesday	UEFA Champions League MD2
3 Wednesday	UEFA Champions League MD2
4 Thursday	UEFA Europa League MD2
6 Saturday	The Emirates FA Cup 3Q
	The FA County Youth Cup 1*
7 Sunday	The SSE Women's FA Cup 3Q
	The FA Sunday Cup 1
10 Wednesday	Checkatrade Trophy MD2
12 Friday	Croatia v England – UEFA Nations League
13 Saturday	The Buildbase FA Trophy P
	The Buildbase FA Vase 1P
15 Monday	Spain v England – UEFA Nations League
	The FA Youth Cup 3Q+
20 Saturday	The Emirates FA Cup 4Q
23 Tuesday	UEFA Champions League MD3
24 Wednesday	UEFA Champions League MD3
25 Thursday	UEFA Europa League MD3
27 Saturday	The Buildbase FA Trophy 1Q
31 Wednesday	Carabao Cup 4

NOVEMBER 2018

3 Saturday	The Buildbase FA Vase 2P
	The FA Youth Cup 1P*
	The FA County Youth Cup 2*
6 Tuesday	UEFA Champions League MD4
7 Wednesday	UEFA Champions League MD4
8 Thursday	UEFA Europa League MD4
10 Saturday	The Emirates FA Cup 1P
	The Buildbase FA Trophy 2Q
11 Sunday	The SSE Women's FA Cup 1P
	The FA Sunday Cup 2
14 Wednesday	Checkatrade Trophy MD3
15 Thursday	England v USA – International Friendly
17 Saturday	The FA Youth Cup 2P*
18 Sunday	England v Croatia – UEFA Nations League
24 Saturday	The Buildbase FA Trophy 3Q
27 Tuesday	UEFA Champions League MD5
28 Wednesday	UEFA Champions League MD5
29 Thursday	UEFA Europa League MD5

DECEMBER 2018

1 Saturday	The Emirates FA Cup 2P
	The Buildbase FA Vase 3P
2 Sunday	The SSE Women's FA Cup 2P
5 Wednesday	Checkatrade Trophy 32
8 Saturday	The FA County Youth Cup 3*
9 Sunday	The FA Sunday Cup 3
11 Tuesday	UEFA Champions League MD6
12 Wednesday	UEFA Champions League MD6
13 Thursday	UEFA Europa League MD6
15 Saturday	The Buildbase FA Trophy 1P
	The FA Youth Cup 3P*

19 Wednesday	Carabao Cup 5
25 Tuesday	Christmas Day
26 Wednesday	Boxing Day

JANUARY 2019

1 Tuesday	New Year's Day
5 Saturday	The Emirates FA Cup 3P
	The Buildbase FA Vase 4P
6 Sunday	The SSE Women's FA Cup 3P
9 Wednesday	Carabao Cup SF (1)
	Checkatrade Trophy 16
12 Saturday	The Buildbase FA Trophy 2P
19 Saturday	The FA Youth Cup 4P*
	The FA County Youth Cup 4*
20 Sunday	The FA Sunday Cup 4
23 Wednesday	Carabao Cup SF (2)
	Checkatrade Trophy QF
26 Saturday	The Emirates FA Cup 4P

FEBRUARY 2019

2 Saturday	The Buildbase FA Trophy 3P
	The Buildbase FA Vase 5P
3 Sunday	The SSE Women's FA Cup 4P
9 Saturday	The FA Youth Cup 5P*
12 Tuesday	UEFA Champions League 16(1)
13 Wednesday	UEFA Champions League 16(1)
14 Thursday	UEFA Europa League 32(1)
16 Saturday	The Emirates FA Cup 5P
17 Sunday	The SSE Women's FA Cup 5P
	The FA Sunday Cup 5
19 Tuesday	UEFA Champions League 16(1)
20 Wednesday	UEFA Champions League 16(1)
21 Thursday	UEFA Europa League 32(2)
23 Saturday	The Buildbase FA Trophy 4P
	The Buildbase FA Vase 6P
	The FA County Youth Cup SF*
24 Sunday	Carabao Cup Final
27 Wednesday	Checkatrade Trophy SF

MARCH 2019

2 Saturday	The FA Youth Cup 6P*
5 Tuesday	UEFA Champions League 16(2)
6 Wednesday	UEFA Champions League 16(2)
7 Thursday	UEFA Europa League 16(1)
12 Tuesday	UEFA Champions League 16(2)
13 Wednesday	UEFA Champions League 16(2)
14 Thursday	UEFA Europa League 16(2)
16 Saturday	The Emirates FA Cup QF
	The Buildbase FA Trophy SF(1)
	The Buildbase FA Vase SF(1)
17 Sunday	The SSE Women's FA Cup QF
23 Saturday	UEFA Euro 2020 Qualifier
	The Buildbase FA Trophy SF(2)
	The Buildbase FA Vase SF(2)
	The FA Youth Cup SF*
26 Tuesday	UEFA Euro 2020 Qualifier
31 Sunday	Checkatrade Trophy Final
	The FA Sunday Cup SF

APRIL 2019

6 Saturday	The Emirates FA Cup Semi Final
7 Sunday	The Emirates FA Cup Semi Final
9 Tuesday	UEFA Champions League QF(1)
10 Wednesday	UEFA Champions League QF(1)
11 Thursday	UEFA Europa League QF(1)
13 Saturday	The FA County Youth Cup Final (prov)
14 Sunday	The SSE Women's FA Cup SF
16 Tuesday	UEFA Champions League QF(2)
17 Wednesday	UEFA Champions League QF(2)
18 Thursday	UEFA Europa League QF(2)
19 Friday	Good Friday
22 Monday	Easter Monday
27 Saturday	National League Ends
28 Sunday	The FA Sunday Cup Final (prov)
30 Tuesday	UEFA Champions League SF(1)

MAY 2019

1 Wednesday	UEFA Champions League SF(1)
2 Thursday	UEFA Europa League SF(1)
4 Saturday	The SSE Women's FA Cup Final
	EFL Ends
7 Tuesday	UEFA Champions League SF(2)
8 Wednesday	UEFA Champions League SF(2)
9 Thursday	UEFA Europa League SF(2)
11 Saturday	National League Promotion Final
12 Sunday	Premier League Ends
18 Saturday	The Emirates FA Cup Final
19 Sunday	The Buildbase FA Trophy Final
	The Buildbase FA Vase Final
25 Saturday	EFL League Two Play-off Final
26 Sunday	EFL League One Play-off Final
27 Monday	EFL Championship Play-off Final
29 Wednesday	UEFA Europa League Final

JUNE 2019

1 Saturday	UEFA Champions League Final
8 Saturday	UEFA Euro 2020 Qualifier
11 Tuesday	UEFA Euro 2020 Qualifier

The FA Youth Cup Final – date to be confirmed
EFL Play-Off Semi Finals – dates to be confirmed
*closing date of round
+week commencing

STOP PRESS

England reach semi-final of World Cup but are defeated 2-1 by Croatia after extra time ... France defeat Croatia 4-2 in Moscow final to win World Cup ... Harry Kane wins World Cup Golden Boot ... Ronaldo leaves Real Madrid and joins Juventus ... Manchester City break their transfer record to sign Riyad Mahrez from Leicester City ... West Ham's rejuvenation under Manuel Pellegrini continues with record signing of Filipe Anderson from Lazio ... England Under-19s begin their defence of the European Championship with a 3-2 win over Turkey ... Chelsea sack Antonio Conte and appoint Maurizio Sarri – the new manager faces a stiff test as Hazard, Kante, Courtois and Willian are pursued after fine World Cup performances ... A goalkeeper merry-go-round may erupt after Liverpool agree a world record fee for Roma's Allison ... Celtic progress in Champions League qualifying, but Crusaders and New Saints fall ... Rangers and Hibernian progress in Europa League ... Burnley's first European tie in 51 years will be an England v Scotland clash against Aberdeen.

SUMMER TRANSFER DIARY 2018

Reported fees only, otherwise Free or Undisclosed.

June 1: Benik Afobe Bournemouth to Wolverhampton W – £10m; Willy Boly Porto to Wolverhampton W – £10m; Tahvon Campbell WBA to Forest Green R; Ben Hamer Leicester C to Huddersfield T; Kane Hemmings Oxford U to Notts Co; Konstantin Kerschbaumer Brentford to FC Ingolstadt; Manny Oyeleke Aldershot T to Port Vale; Andrew Shinnie Birmingham C to Luton T; Tom Smith Swindon T to Cheltenham T.

June 4: Matt Godden Stevenage to Peterborough U; Craig MacGillivray Shrewsbury T to Portsmouth; Byron Moore Bristol R to Bury; Will Patching Manchester C to Notts Co; Louis Robles San Roque De Lepe to Grimsby T.

June 5: Santi Cazorla Arsenal to Villarreal; Leo Da Silva Lopes Peterborough U to Wigan Ath; Chris Forrester Peterborough U to Aberdeen; George Francomb AFC Wimbledon to Crawley T; Ryan Fredericks Fulham to West Ham U; Mark Gillespie Walsall to Motherwell; Josh Ginnelly Burnley to Walsall; Stephan Lichtsteiner Juventus to Arsenal; David Meyler Hull C to Reading.

June 6: Neal Bishop Scunthorpe U to Mansfield T; Junior Brown Shrewsbury T to Coventry C; Michael Crowe Ipswich T to Preston NE; Diogo Dalot Porto to Manchester U – £19m; Sam Matthews Bournemouth to Bristol R; John O'Shea Sunderland to Reading; Alex Penney Peterborough U to Hamilton A.

June 7: Fabio Borini Sunderland to AC Milan; Harry Davis St Mirren to Grimsby T; Conor Grant Everton to Plymouth Arg; Jeremain Lens Sunderland to Besiktas; Ethan Ross WBA to Colchester U; Miles Welch-Hayes Bath to Macclesfield T.

June 8: Emi Buendia Getafe to Norwich C; Niall Canavan Rochdale to Plymouth Arg; Jonny Evans WBA to Leicester C – £3.5m; Vicente Guaita Getafe to Crystal Palace; Terence Kongolo Monaco to Huddersfield T; Jason Lowe Birmingham C to Bolton W; Joseph Mills Perth Glory to Forest Green R; Tom Naylor Burton Alb to Portsmouth; Frank Nouble Newport Co to Colchester U.

June 9: Freddie Ladapo Southend U to Plymouth Arg.

June 10: Pierluigi Gollini Aston Villa to Atalanta; Kieran Kennedy Macclesfield T to Shrewsbury T; Fejiri Okenabirhie Dagenham & R to Shrewsbury T; Joe Riley Shrewsbury T to Plymouth Arg.

June 11: Lee Brown Bristol R to Portsmouth; Gerard Deulofeu Barcelona to Watford – £11.5m; Callum Dyson Everton to Plymouth Arg; Oghenekaro Etebo Feirense to Stoke C – £6.35m; Madger Gomes Leeds U to Sochaux; Seb Larsson Hull C to AIK Solna; Ashley Nathaniel-George Hendon to Crawley; Michael Timlin Southend U to Stevenage; Harry Toffolo Millwall to Lincoln C.

June 12: Sonny Bradley Plymouth Arg to Luton T; Paul Farman Lincoln C to Stevenage; Thomas Isherwood Bayern Munich to Bradford C; Nikola Katic Slaven Belupo to Rangers; Ezri Konsa Charlton Ath to Brentford; Josh Murphy Norwich C to Cardiff C; Jason Naismith Ross Co to Peterborough U; John O'Sullivan Carlisle U to Blackpool; Josh Rees Bromley to Gillingham; Ramadan Sobhi Stoke C to Huddersfield T – £5.7m; Jordan Storey Exeter C to Preston NE; Harry Toffolo Millwall to Lincoln C; George Williams Fulham to Forest Green R.

June 13: Graham Burke Shamrock R to Preston NE; Jonson Clarke-Harris Rotherham U to Coventry C; Greg Cunningham Preston NE to Cardiff C; Connor Goldson Brighton & HA to Rangers; Erhun Oztumer Walsall to Bolton W; Emmanuel Sonupe Kidderminster H to Stevenage; Chris Taylor Bolton W to Blackpool.

June 14: Joao Carvalho Benfica to Nottingham F – £13.2m; Anthony O'Connor Aberdeen to Bradford C; Jordan Thompson Rangers to Blackpool; Jordan Williams Liverpool to Rochdale.

June 15: Darius Charles AFC Wimbledon to Wycombe W; Tom Hopper Scunthorpe U to Southend U; Christoph Knasmullner Barnsley to Rapid Vienna; Marc Navarro Espanyol to Watford; Mitch Pinnock Dover Ath to AFC Wimbledon; Marley Watkins Norwich C to Bristol C – £1m; Elliott Whitehouse Lincoln C to Grimsby T.

June 17: Michael O'Halloran Rangers to Melbourne C.

June 18: Nathan Blissett Plymouth Arg to Macclesfield T; Fraser Franks Stevenage to Newport Co; Jermaine McGlashan Southend U to Swindon T; Rui Patricio Sporting Lisbon to Wolverhampton W.

June 19: Ryan Allsop Bournemouth to Wycombe W; Chris Dagnall Crewe Alex to Bury; Issa Diop Toulouse to West Ham U – £22m; Chris Dunn Wrexham to Walsall; Stephen Gleeson Ipswich T to Aberdeen; Bernd Leno Bayer Leverkusen to Arsenal – £19.3m; Jordan Moore-Taylor Exeter C to Milton Keynes D; Craig Morgan Wigan Ath to Fleetwood T; Louis Reed Sheffield U to Peterborough U; Felix Wiedwald Leeds U to Eintracht Frankfurt.

June 20: Juninho Bacuna Groningen to Huddersfield T; Lukasz Fabianski Swansea C to West Ham U – £7m; Macaulay Gillespey Newcastle U to Carlisle U; James Maddison Norwich C to Leicester C; Hordur Magnusson Bristol C to CSKA Moscow; Gary Miller Plymouth Arg to Carlisle U; Michael O'Connor Notts Co to Lincoln C; Murray Wallace Scunthorpe U to Millwall; Ryan Watson Barnet to Milton Keynes D.

June 21: Fred Shakhtar Donetsk to Manchester U – £47m; Will Aimson Blackpool to Bury; Joel Byrom Mansfield T to Stevenage; Emre Can Liverpool to Juventus; Carl Dickinson Notts Co to Yeovil T; Jon Flanagan Liverpool to Rangers; Ramiro Funes Mori Everton to Villarreal; George Glendon Fleetwood T to Carlisle U; Mitch Hancox Macclesfield T to Milton Keynes D; Andrew Hughes Peterborough U to Preston NE; Zak Mills Grimsby T to Morecambe; Rhys Oates Hartlepool to Morecambe; Alim Ozturk Boluspor to Sunderland; Connor Wood Leicester C to Bradford C.

June 22: Max Clark Hull C to Vitesse Arnhem; Jordan Cook Luton T to Grimsby T; Siriki Dembele Grimsby T to Peterborough U; Jamie Grimes Cheltenham T to Macclesfield T; Jeff King Bolton W to St Mirren; Harry Lennon Charlton Ath to Southend U; Eric Lichaj Nottingham F to Hull C; Sam Mantom Scunthorpe U to Southend U; Ricky Miller Peterborough U to Port Vale; Joe Rothwell Oxford U to Blackburn R; Ben Stephens Stratford to Macclesfield T.

June 25: **Max Gradel** Bournemouth to Toulouse; **Jake Hessenthaler** Gillingham to Grimsby T; **Chris Maguire** Bury to Sunderland; **Jon McLaughlin** Hearts to Sunderland; **Paul Mullin** Swindon T to Tranmere R; **Kristian Pedersen** Union Berlin to Birmingham C; **Grant Smith** Boreham Wood to Lincoln C; **Robert Tesche** Birmingham C to Bochum; **John Welsh** Preston NE to Grimsby T; **Aaron Wilbraham** Bolton W to Rochdale.

June 26: **Stuart Armstrong** Celtic to Southampton – £7m; **Clayton Donaldson** Sheffield U to Bolton W; **Jonathan Forte** Notts Co to Exeter C; **James Hanson** Sheffield U to AFC Wimbledon; **Johnny Hunt** Mansfield T to Stevenage; **Zeli Ismail** Bury to Walsall; **Moritz Leitner** Augsburg to Norwich C; **Sean Long** Lincoln C to Cheltenham T; **Paddy McNair** Sunderland to Middlesbrough £5m; **Abu Ogogo** Shrewsbury T to Coventry C; **Matty Pearson** Barnsley to Luton T; **Ashley Smith-Brown** Manchester C to Plymouth Arg.

June 27: **Aden Flint** Bristol C to Middlesbrough – £7m; **Peter Grant** Falkirk to Plymouth Arg; **Piero Mingoia** Cambridge U to Accrington S; **Marc Muniesa** Stoke C to Girona; **Luke Norris** Swindon T to Colchester U; **Richard O'Donnell** Northampton T to Bradford C; **Jason Oswell** Stockport Co to Morecambe; **Ollie Palmer** Lincoln C to Crawley T; **Dusan Tadic** Southampton to Ajax – £10m; **Lyle Taylor** AFC Wimbledon to Charlton Ath; **Scott Wootton** Milton Keynes D to Plymouth Arg.

June 28: **Jake Caprice** Leyton Orient to Tranmere R; **Tom Flanagan** Burton Alb to Sunderland; **Brian Galach** Aldershot T to Crawley T; **Reggie Lambe** Carlisle U to Cambridge U; **Tony McMahon** Bradford C to Oxford U; **Isaac Pearce** Fulham to Forest Green R; **Bobby Reid** Bristol C to Cardiff – £10m; **Jordan Roberts** Crawley T to Ipswich T; **Liam Shephard** Peterborough U to Forest Green R; **Alex Smithies** QPR to Cardiff C – £3.5m; **Theo Vassel** Gateshead to Port Vale; **Gary Warren** Inverness CT to Yeovil T; **Adam Webster** Ipswich T to Bristol C.

June 29: **Andy Dales** Mickleover Sports to Scunthorpe U; **Craig Davies** Oldham Ath to Mansfield T; **Timothee Dieng** Bradford C to Southend U; **Mohamed Elyounoussi** Basel to Southampton – £16m; **Gustav Engvall** Bristol C to KV Mechelen; **Otis Khan** Yeovil T to Mansfield T; **Clark Robertson** Blackpool to Rotherham C; **Hillal Soudani** Dinamo Zagreb to Nottingham F; **Ki Sung-yeung** Swansea C to Newcastle U; **Andrew Tutte** Bury to Morecambe; **Kyle Vassell** Blackpool to Rotherham U.

June 30: **Ben Marshall** Wolverhampton W to Norwich C; **Teemu Pukki** Brondby to Norwich C; **Jack Robinson** QPR to Nottingham F.

July 1: **David Brooks** Sheffield U to Bournemouth; **Joe Felix** Fulham to QPR; **Toni Leistner** Union Berlin to QPR.

July 2: **Hakeeb Adelakun** Scunthorpe U to Bristol C; **Jacob Davenport** Manchester C to Blackburn R; **Barry Fuller** AFC Wimbledon to Gillingham; **Brandon Hanlan** Charlton Ath to Gillingham; **Luke Hyam** Ipswich T to Southend U; **Reece James** Wigan Ath to Sunderland; **Nicky Law** Bradford C to Exeter C; **Adam Masina** Bologna to Watford; **Dylan McGeouch** Hibernian to Sunderland; **Sokratis Papastathopoulos** Borussia Dortmund to Arsenal; **Alex Rodman** Shrewsbury T to Bristol R; **Theo Widdrington** Portsmouth to Bristol R; **Morgan Williams** Mickleover Sports to Coventry C.

July 3: **Johan Branger** FC Dieppe to Oldham Ath; **Jordan Cranston** Cheltenham T to Morecambe; **Adam Federici** Bournemouth to Stoke C; **Lee Grant** Stoke C to Manchester U; **Sam Johnstone** Manchester U to WBA – £6.5m; **Costel Pantilimon** Watford to Nottingham F; **Gavin Reilly** St Mirren to Bristol R; **Callum Reilly** Bury to Gillingham; **Andreas Weimann** Derby Co to Bristol C.

July 4: **Hope Akpan** Burton Alb to Bradford C; **Enzo Boldewijn** Crawley T to Notts Co; **Adam Collin** Notts Co to Carlisle U; **Brad Inman** Peterborough U to Rochdale; **Lloyd James** Exeter C to Forest Green R; **Harry Smith** Millwall to Macclesfield T.

July 5: **Bernardo** RB Leipzig to Brighton & HA – £9m; **Ben Foster** WBA to Watford; **Scott Fraser** Dundee U to Burton Alb; **Mark Howard** Bolton W to Blackpool; **Dominic Poleon** Bradford C to Crawley C; **Ken Sema** Ostersund to Watford; **David Templeton** Hamilton A to Burton Alb.

July 6: **John Akinde** Barnet to Lincoln C; **Said Benrahma** Nice to Brentford; **Lewis Grabban** Bournemouth to Nottingham F; **Jordan Houghton** Chelsea to Milton Keynes D; **Jack Hunt** Sheffield W to Bristol C; **Stevie Mallan** Barnsley to Hibernian; **Brandon Mason** Watford to Coventry C; **Marc McNulty** Coventry C to Reading; **Tom Miller** Carlisle U to Bury; **Alex Nicholls** Barnet to Crewe Alex; **David Vaughan** Nottingham F to Notts Co; **Josh Yorwerth** Crawley T to Peterborough U.

July 9: **Mark Halstead** Southport to Morecambe; **Ryan Harley** Exeter C to Milton Keynes D; **David Milinkovic** Genoa to Hull C; **Hakeem Odoffin** Wolverhampton W to Northampton T; **Robbie Simpson** Exeter C to Milton Keyes D; **Jack Wilshere** Arsenal to West Ham U.

July 10: **Reece Burke** West Ham U to Hull C; **Ali Crawford** Hamilton A to Doncaster R; **Jonathan Flatt** Wolverhampton W to Scunthorpe U; **Alex Gilliead** Newcastle U to Shrewsbury T; **Angus Gunn** Manchester C to Southampton – £13.5m; **Riyad Mahrez** Leicester C to Manchester C – £60m; **Pawel Olkowski** Cologne to Bolton W; **Steven Taylor** Peterborough U to Wellington Phoenix; **Lucas Torreira** Sampdoria to Arsenal – £26m; **Fernando Torres** Atletico Madrid to Sagan Tosu.

July 11: **Jordy de Wijs** PSV to Hull C; **Matteo Guendouzi** Lorient to Arsenal; **Scott Wagstaff** Gillingham to Wimbledon; **Andriy Yarmolenko** Borussia Dortmund to West Ham U.

July 12: **Jordan Archer** Chester FC to Bury; **Maxime le Marchand** Nice to Fulham; **Prince Oniangue** Wolverhampton W to Caen; **Jean Michael Seri** Nice to Fulham; **Anthony Wordsworth** Southend U to AFC Wimbledon.

July 13: **Aaron Amadi-Holloway** Oldham Ath to Shrewsbury T; **Sessi D'Almeida** Blackpool to Yeovil T; **Erik Durm** Borussia Dortmund to Huddersfield T; **Christopher Missilou** Unattached to Oldham Ath; **Junior Morias** Peterborough U to Northampton T; **Gold Omotayo** Unattached to Bury; **Xherdan Shaqiri** Stoke C to Liverpool £13m; **Jannik Vestergaard** Borussia Monchengladbach to Southampton; **Gavin Whyte** Crusaders to Oxford U.

July 14: **Joel Asoro** Sunderland to Swansea C; **Fabian Balbuena** Corinthians to West Ham U; **Jorginho** Napoli to Chelsea; **Curtis Thompson** Unattached to Wycombe W.

July 15: **Felipe Anderson** Lazio to West Ham U £33.5m rising to £42.

July 16: **Kyle Bartley** Swansea C to WBA; **Jonathan Bond** Reading to WBA; **David Button** Fulham to Brighton & HA; **Chris Stokes** Coventry C to Bury; **Terell Thomas** Wigan Ath to AFC Wimbledon; **Thomas Verheydt** Crawley T to Go Ahead Eagles.

July 17: **Yves Bissouma** Lille to Brighton & HA; **Daley Blind** Manchester U to Ajax £14m; **Marc Bola** Arsenal to Blackpool; **Isaac Buckley-Ricketts** Manchester C to Peterborough U; **Gwion Edwards** Peterborough U to Ipswich T; **James Horsfield** NAC Breda to Scunthorpe U; **Wahbi Khazri** Sunderland to Saint Etienne; **Jak McCourt** Chesterfield to Swindon T; **Ryan McLaughlin** Fleetwood T to Blackpool; **Darren Sidoel** Ajax to Reading.

Compiler's pick: Finley Davies, Ashton Boys U12 – Players' player of the season and Coaches player of the season 2017–18.

Now you can buy any of these other football titles from your
normal retailer or *direct from the publisher.*

FREE P&P AND UK DELIVERY
(Overseas and Ireland £3.50 per book)

Old Too Soon, Smart Too Late	Kieron Dyer and Oliver Holt	£20
Football: My Life, My Passion	Graeme Souness	£9.99
The Beast: My Story	Adebayo Akinfenwa	£9,99
Fearless	Jonathan Northcroft	£9.99
The Artist: Being Iniesta	Andrés Iniesta	£10.99
Football Clichés	Adam Hurrey	£9.99
I Believe in Miracles	Daniel Taylor	£8.99
Big Sam: My Autobiography	Sam Allardyce	£10.99
Crossing the Line	Luis Suarez	£9.99
Bend it Like Bullard	Jimmy Bullard	£10.99
The Gaffer	Neil Warnock	£10.99
Jeffanory	Jeff Stelling	£10.99
The Didi Man	Dietmar Hamann	£9.99

TO ORDER SIMPLY CALL THIS NUMBER

01235 400 414

or visit our website:
www.headline.co.uk

Prices and availability subject to change without notice.